Ref
PE
1625
.087
1989
Vol. 20
The Oxford
English dictionary
REFERENCE
29022
D0435164
The Oxford English dictionary.
Ref PE1625.087 1 63079
SOUTH PUGET SOUND COMM. COLLEG

THE OXFORD ENGLISH DICTIONARY

SECOND EDITION

THE OXFORD ENGLISH DICTIONARY

First Edited by

JAMES A. H. MURRAY, HENRY BRADLEY, W. A. CRAIGIE
and C. T. ONIONS

COMBINED WITH

A SUPPLEMENT TO THE OXFORD ENGLISH DICTIONARY

Edited by

R. W. BURCHFIELD

AND RESET WITH CORRECTIONS, REVISIONS
AND ADDITIONAL VOCABULARY

THE OXFORD ENGLISH DICTIONARY

SECOND EDITION

Prepared by

J. A. SIMPSON *and* E. S. C. WEINER

VOLUME XX

Wave–Zyxt

BIBLIOGRAPHY

CLARENDON PRESS · OXFORD
1989

Oxford University Press, Walton Street, Oxford OX2 6DP
Oxford New York Toronto
Delhi Bombay Calcutta Madras Karachi
Petaling Jaya Singapore Hong Kong Tokyo
Nairobi Dar es Salaam Cape Town
Melbourne Auckland
and associated companies in
Berlin Ibadan

Oxford is a trade mark of Oxford University Press

British Library Cataloguing in Publication Data
Oxford English dictionary.—2nd ed.
1. English language-Dictionaries
I. Simpson, J. A. (John Andrew), 1953-
II. Weiner, Edmund S. C., 1950-
423
ISBN 0-19-861232-X (vol. XX)
ISBN 0-19-861186-2 (set)

Library of Congress Cataloging-in-Publication Data
The Oxford English dictionary.—2nd ed.
prepared by J. A. Simpson and E. S. C. Weiner
Bibliography: p.
ISBN 0-19-861232-X (vol. XX)
ISBN 0-19-861186-2 (set)
1. English language—Dictionaries. I. Simpson, J. A.
II. Weiner, E. S. C. III. Oxford University Press.
PE1625.087 1989
423—dc19 88-5330

Data capture by ICC, Fort Washington, Pa.
Text-processing by Oxford University Press
Typesetting by Filmtype Services Ltd., Scarborough, N. Yorks.
Manufactured in the United States of America by
Rand McNally & Company, Taunton, Mass.

KEY TO THE PRONUNCIATION

THE pronunciations given are those in use in the educated speech of southern England (the so-called 'Received Standard'), and the keywords given are to be understood as pronounced in such speech.

I. *Consonants*

b, d, f, k, l, m, n, p, t, v, z *have their usual English values*

g as in *go* (gəʊ)
h ... *ho!* (həʊ)
r ... *run* (rʌn), te*rr*ier ('tɛrɪə(r))
(r) ... he*r* (hɜː(r))
s ... *see* (siː), *success* (sək'sɛs)
w ... *wear* (wɛə(r))
hw ... *wh*en (hwɛn)
j ... *yes* (jɛs)

θ as in *th*in (θɪn), ba*th* (bɑːθ)
ð ... *th*en (ðɛn), ba*the* (beɪð)
ʃ ... *sh*op (ʃɒp), di*sh* (dɪʃ)
tʃ ... *ch*op (tʃɒp), di*tch* (dɪtʃ)
ʒ ... vi*si*on ('vɪʒən), dé*j*euner (deʒøne)
dʒ ... *j*u*dg*e (dʒʌdʒ)
ŋ ... si*ng*i*ng* ('sɪŋɪŋ), thi*n*k (θiŋk)
ŋg ... fi*ng*er ('fɪŋgə(r))

(FOREIGN AND NON-SOUTHERN)

ʎ as in It. serra*gl*io (ser'raʎo)
ɲ ... Fr. co*gn*ac (kɔɲak)
x ... Ger. a*ch* (ax), Sc. lo*ch* (lɒx), Sp. fri*j*oles (fri'xoles)
ç ... Ger. i*ch* (ɪç), Sc. ni*ch*t (nɪçt)
ɣ ... North Ger. sa*g*en ('zaːɣən)
c ... Afrikaans baardmanne*tj*ie ('baːrtmanəci)
ɥ ... Fr. c*u*isine (kɥizin)

Symbols in parentheses are used to denote elements that may be omitted either by individual speakers or in particular phonetic contexts: e.g. *bottle* ('bɒt(ə)l), *Mercian* ('mɜːʃ(ɪ)ən), *suit* (s(j)uːt), *impromptu* (ɪm'prɒm(p)tjuː), *father* ('fɑːðə(r)).

II. *Vowels and Diphthongs*

SHORT

ɪ as in p*i*t (pɪt), -n*e*ss, (-nɪs)
ɛ ... p*e*t (pɛt), Fr. *sept* (sɛt)
æ ... p*a*t (pæt)
ʌ ... p*u*tt (pʌt)
ɒ ... p*o*t (pɒt)
ʊ ... p*u*t (pʊt)
ə ... *a*noth*er* (ə'nʌðə(r))
(ə) ... beat*e*n ('biːt(ə)n)
i ... Fr. s*i* (si)
e ... Fr. b*é*b*é* (bebe)
a ... Fr. m*a*ri (mari)
ɑ ... Fr. b*â*timent (bɑtimɑ̃)
ɔ ... Fr. h*o*mme (ɔm)
o ... Fr. *eau* (o)
ø ... Fr. p*eu* (pø)
œ ... Fr. b*oeu*f (bœf) c*oeu*r (kœr)
u ... Fr. d*ou*ce (dus)
ʏ ... Ger. M*ü*ller ('mʏlər)
y ... Fr. d*u* (dy)

LONG

iː as in b*ea*n (biːn)
ɑː ... b*ar*n (bɑːn)
ɔː ... b*or*n (bɔːn)
uː ... b*oo*n (buːn)
ɜː ... b*ur*n (bɜːn)
eː ... Ger. Schn*ee* (ʃneː)
ɛː ... Ger. F*ä*hre ('fɛːrə)
aː ... Ger. T*a*g (taːk)
oː ... Ger. S*oh*n (zoːn)
øː ... Ger. G*oe*the ('gøːtə)
yː ... Ger. gr*ü*n (gryːn)

NASAL

ɛ̃, æ̃ as in Fr. f*in* (fɛ̃, fæ̃)
ɑ̃ ... Fr. fr*an*c (frɑ̃)
ɔ̃ ... Fr. b*on* (bɔ̃)
œ̃ ... Fr. *un* (œ̃)

DIPHTHONGS, etc.

eɪ as in b*ay* (beɪ)
aɪ ... b*uy* (baɪ)
ɔɪ ... b*oy* (bɔɪ)
əʊ ... n*o* (nəʊ)
aʊ ... n*ow* (naʊ)
ɪə ... p*eer* (pɪə(r))
ɛə ... p*air* (pɛə(r))
ʊə ... t*our* (tʊə(r))
ɔə ... b*oar* (bɔə(r))

aɪə as in f*ie*ry ('faɪərɪ)
aʊə ... s*our* (saʊə(r))

The incidence of main stress is shown by a superior stress mark (') preceding the stressed syllable, and a secondary stress by an inferior stress mark (ˌ), e.g. *pronunciation* (prəˌnʌnsɪ'eɪʃ(ə)n).

For further explanation of the transcription used, see *General Explanations*, Volume I.

LIST OF ABBREVIATIONS, SIGNS, ETC.

Some abbreviations listed here in italics are also in certain cases printed in roman type, and vice versa.

a. (in Etym.)	adoption of, adopted from
a (as *a* 1850)	*ante*, 'before', 'not later than'
a.	adjective
abbrev.	abbreviation (of)
abl.	ablative
absol.	absolute, -ly
Abstr.	(in titles) *Abstract, -s*
acc.	accusative
Acct.	(in titles) *Account*
A.D.	*Anno Domini*
ad. (in Etym.)	adaptation of
Add.	Addenda
adj.	adjective
Adv.	(in titles) *Advance, -d, -s*
adv.	adverb
advb.	adverbial, -ly
Advt.	advertisement
Aeronaut.	(as label) in Aeronautics; (in titles) *Aeronautic, -al, -s*
AF., AFr.	Anglo-French
Afr.	Africa, -n
Agric.	(as label) in Agriculture; (in titles) *Agriculture, -al*
Alb.	Albanian
Amer.	American
Amer. Ind.	American Indian
Anat.	(as label) in Anatomy; (in titles) *Anatomy, -ical*
Anc.	(in titles) *Ancient*
Anglo-Ind.	Anglo-Indian
Anglo-Ir.	Anglo-Irish
Ann.	Annals
Anthrop., *Anthropol.*	(as label) in Anthropology; (in titles) *Anthropology, -ical*
Antiq.	(as label) in Antiquities; (in titles) *Antiquity*
aphet.	aphetic, aphetized
app.	apparently
Appl.	(in titles) *Applied*
Applic.	(in titles) *Application, -s*
appos.	appositive, -ly
Arab.	Arabic
Aram.	Aramaic
Arch.	in Architecture
arch.	archaic
Archæol.	in Archæology
Archit.	(as label) in Architecture; (in titles) *Architecture, -al*
Arm.	Armenian
assoc.	association
Astr.	in Astronomy
Astrol.	in Astrology
Astron.	(in titles) *Astronomy, -ical*
Astronaut.	(in titles) *Astronautic, -s*
attrib.	attributive, -ly
Austral.	Australian
Autobiogr.	(in titles) *Autobiography, -ical*
A.V.	Authorized Version
B.C.	Before Christ
B.C.	(in titles) British Columbia
bef.	before
Bibliogr.	(as label) in Bibliography; (in titles) *Bibliography, -ical*
Biochem.	(as label) in Biochemistry; (in titles) *Biochemistry, -ical*
Biol.	(as label) in Biology; (in titles) *Biology, -ical*
Bk.	*Book*
Bot.	(as label) in Botany; (in titles) *Botany, -ical*
Bp.	Bishop
Brit.	(in titles) *Britain, British*
Bulg.	Bulgarian
Bull.	(in titles) *Bulletin*
c (as *c* 1700)	*circa*, 'about'
c. (as 19th c.)	century
Cal.	(in titles) *Calendar*
Cambr.	(in titles) *Cambridge*
Canad.	Canadian
Cat.	Catalan
catachr.	catachrestically
Catal.	(in titles) *Catalogue*
Celt.	Celtic
Cent.	(in titles) *Century, Central*
Cent. Dict.	*Century Dictionary*
Cf., cf.	*confer*, 'compare'
Ch.	Church
Chem.	(as label) in Chemistry; (in titles) *Chemistry, -ical*
Chr.	(in titles) *Christian*
Chron.	(in titles) *Chronicle*
Chronol.	(in titles) *Chronology, -ical*
Cinemat., *Cinematogr.*	in Cinematography
Clin.	(in titles) *Clinical*
cl. L.	classical Latin
cogn. w.	cognate with
Col.	(in titles) *Colonel, Colony*
Coll.	(in titles) *Collection*
collect.	collective, -ly
colloq.	colloquial, -ly
comb.	combined, -ing
Comb.	Combinations
Comm.	in Commercial usage
Communic.	in Communications
comp.	compound, composition
Compan.	(in titles) *Companion*
compar.	comparative
compl.	complement
Compl.	(in titles) *Complete*
Conc.	(in titles) *Concise*
Conch.	in Conchology
concr.	concrete, -ly
Conf.	(in titles) *Conference*
Congr.	(in titles) *Congress*
conj.	conjunction
cons.	consonant
const.	construction, construed with
contr.	contrast (with)
Contrib.	(in titles) *Contribution*
Corr.	(in titles) *Correspondence*
corresp.	corresponding (to)
Cotgr.	R. Cotgrave, *Dictionarie of the French and English Tongues*
cpd.	compound
Crit.	(in titles) *Criticism, Critical*
Cryst.	in Crystallography
Cycl.	(in titles) *Cyclopædia, -ic*
Cytol.	(in titles) *Cytology, -ical*
Da.	Danish
D.A.	*Dictionary of Americanisms*
D.A.E.	*Dictionary of American English*
dat.	dative
D.C.	District of Columbia
Deb.	(in titles) *Debate, -s*
def.	definite, -ition
dem.	demonstrative
deriv.	derivative, -ation
derog.	derogatory
Descr.	(in titles) *Description, -tive*
Devel.	(in titles) *Development, -al*
Diagn.	(in titles) *Diagnosis, Diagnostic*
dial.	dialect, -al
Dict.	Dictionary; *spec.*, the *Oxford English Dictionary*
dim.	diminutive
Dis.	(in titles) *Disease*
Diss.	(in titles) *Dissertation*
D.O.S.T.	*Dictionary of the Older Scottish Tongue*
Du.	Dutch
E.	East
Eccl.	(as label) in Ecclesiastical usage; (in titles) *Ecclesiastical*
Ecol.	in Ecology
Econ.	(as label) in Economics; (in titles) *Economy, -ics*
ed.	edition
E.D.D.	*English Dialect Dictionary*
Edin.	(in titles) *Edinburgh*
Educ.	(as label) in Education; (in titles) *Education, -al*
EE.	Early English
e.g.	*exempli gratia*, 'for example'
Electr.	(as label) in Electricity; (in titles) *Electricity, -ical*
Electron.	(in titles) *Electronic, -s*
Elem.	(in titles) *Element, -ary*
ellipt.	elliptical, -ly
Embryol.	in Embryology
e.midl.	east midland (dialect)
Encycl.	(in titles) *Encyclopædia, -ic*
Eng.	England, English
Engin.	in Engineering
Ent.	in Entomology
Entomol.	(in titles) *Entomology, -logical*
erron.	erroneous, -ly
esp.	especially
Ess.	(in titles) *Essay, -s*
et al.	*et alii*, 'and others'
etc.	et cetera
Ethnol.	in Ethnology
etym.	etymology
euphem.	euphemistically
Exam.	(in titles) *Examination*
exc.	except
Exerc.	(in titles) *Exercise, -s*
Exper.	(in titles) *Experiment, -al*
Explor.	(in titles) *Exploration, -s*
f.	feminine
f. (in Etym.)	formed on
f. (in subordinate entries)	form of
F.	French
fem. (*rarely* f.)	feminine
fig.	figurative, -ly
Finn.	Finnish
fl.	*floruit*, 'flourished'
Found.	(in titles) *Foundation, -s*
Fr.	French
freq.	frequent, -ly
Fris.	Frisian
Fund.	(in titles) *Fundamental, -s*
Funk or *Funk's Stand. Dict.*	*Funk and Wagnalls Standard Dictionary*
G.	German
Gael.	Gaelic
Gaz.	(in titles) *Gazette*
gen.	genitive
gen.	general, -ly
Geogr.	(as label) in Geography; (in titles) *Geography, -ical*

Geol.	(as label) in Geology; (in titles) *Geology, -ical*
Geom.	in Geometry
Geomorphol.	in Geomorphology
Ger.	German
Gloss.	Glossary
Gmc.	Germanic
Godef.	F. Godefroy, *Dictionnaire de l'ancienne langue française*
Goth.	Gothic
Govt.	(in titles) *Government*
Gr.	Greek
Gram.	(as label) in Grammar; (in titles) *Grammar, -tical*
Gt.	Great
Heb.	Hebrew
Her.	in Heraldry
Herb.	among herbalists
Hind.	Hindustani
Hist.	(as label) in History; (in titles) *History, -ical*
hist.	historical
Histol.	(in titles) *Histology, -ical*
Hort.	in Horticulture
Househ.	(in titles) *Household*
Housek.	(in titles) *Housekeeping*
Ibid.	*Ibidem*, 'in the same book or passage'
Icel.	Icelandic
Ichthyol.	in Ichthyology
id.	*idem*, 'the same'
i.e.	*id est*, 'that is'
IE.	Indo-European
Illustr.	(in titles) *Illustration, -ted*
imit.	imitative
Immunol.	in Immunology
imp.	imperative
impers.	impersonal
impf.	imperfect
ind.	indicative
indef.	indefinite
Industr.	(in titles) *Industry, -ial*
inf.	infinitive
infl.	influenced
Inorg.	(in titles) *Inorganic*
Ins.	(in titles) *Insurance*
Inst.	(in titles) *Institute, -tion*
int.	interjection
intr.	intransitive
Introd.	(in titles) *Introduction*
Ir.	Irish
irreg.	irregular, -ly
It.	Italian
J., (J.)	(quoted from) Johnson's *Dictionary*
(Jam.)	Jamieson, *Scottish Dict.*
Jap.	Japanese
joc.	jocular, -ly
Jrnl.	(in titles) *Journal*
Jun.	(in titles) *Junior*
Knowl.	(in titles) *Knowledge*
l.	line
L.	Latin
lang.	language
Lect.	(in titles) *Lecture, -s*
Less.	(in titles) *Lesson, -s*
Let., Lett.	letter, letters
LG.	Low German
lit.	literal, -ly
Lit.	Literary
Lith.	Lithuanian
LXX	Septuagint
m.	masculine
Mag.	(in titles) *Magazine*
Magn.	(in titles) *Magnetic, -ism*
Mal.	Malay, Malayan
Man.	(in titles) *Manual*
Managem.	(in titles) *Management*
Manch.	(in titles) *Manchester*
Manuf.	in Manufacture, -ing
Mar.	(in titles) *Marine*
masc. (*rarely* m.)	masculine
Math.	(as label) in Mathematics; (in titles) *Mathematics, -al*
MDu.	Middle Dutch
ME.	Middle English
Mech.	(as label) in Mechanics; (in titles) *Mechanics, -al*
Med.	(as label) in Medicine; (in titles) *Medicine, -ical*
med.L.	medieval Latin
Mem.	(in titles) *Memoir, -s*
Metaph.	in Metaphysics
Meteorol.	(as label) in Meteorology; (in titles) *Meteorology, -ical*
MHG.	Middle High German
midl.	midland (dialect)
Mil.	in military usage
Min.	(as label) in Mineralogy; (in titles) *Ministry*
Mineral.	(in titles) *Mineralogy, -ical*
MLG.	Middle Low German
Misc.	(in titles) *Miscellany, -eous*
mod.	modern
mod.L	modern Latin
(Morris),	(quoted from) E. E. Morris's *Austral English*
Mus.	(as label) in Music; (in titles) *Music, -al; Museum*
Myst.	(in titles) *Mystery*
Mythol.	in Mythology
N.	North
n.	neuter
N. Amer.	North America, -n
N. & Q.	*Notes and Queries*
Narr.	(in titles) *Narrative*
Nat.	(in titles) *Natural*
Nat. Hist.	in Natural History
Naut.	in nautical language
N.E.	North East
N.E.D.	*New English Dictionary*, original title of the *Oxford English Dictionary* (first edition)
Neurol.	in Neurology
neut. (*rarely* n.)	neuter
NF., NFr.	Northern French
No.	Number
nom.	nominative
north.	northern (dialect)
Norw.	Norwegian
n.q.	no quotations
N.T.	New Testament
Nucl.	Nuclear
Numism.	in Numismatics
N.W.	North West
N.Z.	New Zealand
obj.	object
obl.	oblique
Obs., obs.	obsolete
Obstetr.	(in titles) *Obstetrics*
occas.	occasionally
OE.	Old English (= Anglo-Saxon)
OF., OFr.	Old French
OFris.	Old Frisian
OHG.	Old High German
OIr.	Old Irish
ON.	Old Norse
ONF.	Old Northern French
Ophthalm.	in Ophthalmology
opp.	opposed (to), the opposite (of)
Opt.	in Optics
Org.	(in titles) *Organic*
orig.	origin, -al, -ally
Ornith.	(as label) in Ornithology; (in titles) *Ornithology, -ical*
OS.	Old Saxon
OSl.	Old (Church) Slavonic
O.T.	Old Testament
Outl.	(in titles) *Outline*
Oxf.	(in titles) *Oxford*
p.	page
Palæogr.	in Palæography
Palæont.	(as label) in Palæontology; (in titles) *Palæontology, -ical*
pa. pple.	passive participle, past participle
(Partridge),	(quoted from) E. Partridge's *Dictionary of Slang and Unconventional English*
pass.	passive, -ly
pa.t.	past tense
Path.	(as label) in Pathology; (in titles) *Pathology, -ical*
perh.	perhaps
Pers.	Persian
pers.	person, -al
Petrogr.	in Petrography
Petrol.	(as label) in Petrology; (in titles) *Petrology, -ical*
(Pettman),	(quoted from) C. Pettman's *Africanderisms*
pf.	perfect
Pg.	Portuguese
Pharm.	in Pharmacology
Philol.	(as label) in Philology; (in titles) *Philology, -ical*
Philos.	(as label) in Philosophy; (in titles) *Philosophy, -ic*
phonet.	phonetic, -ally
Photogr.	(as label) in Photography; (in titles) *Photography, -ical*
phr.	phrase
Phys.	physical; (*rarely*) in Physiology
Physiol.	(as label) in Physiology; (in titles) *Physiology, -ical*
Pict.	(in titles) *Picture, Pictorial*
pl., plur.	plural
poet.	poetic, -al
Pol.	Polish
Pol.	(as label) in Politics; (in titles) *Politics, -al*
Pol. Econ.	in Political Economy
Polit.	(in titles) *Politics, -al*
pop.	popular, -ly
Porc.	(in titles) *Porcelain*
poss.	possessive
Pott.	(in titles) *Pottery*
ppl. a., pple. adj.	participial adjective
pple.	participle
Pr.	Provençal
pr.	present
Pract.	(in titles) *Practice, -al*
prec.	preceding (word or article)
pred.	predicative
pref.	prefix
pref., Pref.	preface
prep.	preposition
pres.	present
Princ.	(in titles) *Principle, -s*
priv.	privative
prob.	probably
Probl.	(in titles) *Problem*
Proc.	(in titles) *Proceedings*
pron.	pronoun
pronunc.	pronunciation
prop.	properly
Pros.	in Prosody
Prov.	Provençal
pr. pple.	present participle
Psych.	in Psychology
Psychol.	(as label) in Psychology; (in titles) *Psychology, -ical*
Publ.	(in titles) *Publications*
Q.	(in titles) *Quarterly*
quot(s).	quotation(s)
q.v.	*quod vide*, 'which see'
R.	(in titles) *Royal*
Radiol.	in Radiology
R.C.Ch.	Roman Catholic Church
Rec.	(in titles) *Record*
redupl.	reduplicating
Ref.	(in titles) *Reference*
refash.	refashioned, -ing
refl.	reflexive
Reg.	(in titles) *Register*

reg.	regular
rel.	related to
Reminisc.	(in titles) *Reminiscence, -s*
Rep.	(in titles) *Report, -s*
repr.	representative, representing
Res.	(in titles) *Research*
Rev.	(in titles) *Review*
rev.	revised
Rhet.	in Rhetoric
Rom.	Roman, -ce, -ic
Rum.	Rumanian
Russ.	Russian
S.	South
S.Afr.	South Africa, -n
sb.	substantive
sc.	*scilicet*, 'understand' or 'supply'
Sc., Scot.	Scottish
Scand.	(in titles) *Scandinavia, -n*
Sch.	(in titles) *School*
Sc. Nat. Dict.	*Scottish National Dictionary*
Scotl.	(in titles) *Scotland*
Sel.	(in titles) *Selection, -s*
Ser.	Series
sing.	singular
Sk.	(in titles) *Sketch*
Skr.	Sanskrit
Slav.	Slavonic
S.N.D.	*Scottish National Dictionary*
Soc.	(in titles) *Society*
Sociol.	(as label) in Sociology; (in titles) *Sociology, -ical*
Sp.	Spanish
Sp.	(in titles) *Speech, -es*
sp.	spelling
spec.	specifically
Spec.	(in titles) *Specimen*
St.	Saint
Stand.	(in titles) *Standard*
Stanf.	(quoted from) *Stanford Dictionary of Anglicised Words & Phrases*
str.	strong
Struct.	(in titles) *Structure, -al*
Stud.	(in titles) *Studies*
subj.	subject
subord. cl.	subordinate clause
subseq.	subsequent, -ly
subst.	substantively
suff.	suffix
superl.	superlative
Suppl.	Supplement
Surg.	(as label) in Surgery; (in titles) *Surgery, Surgical*
s.v.	*sub voce*, 'under the word'
Sw.	Swedish
s.w.	south-western (dialect)
Syd. Soc. Lex.	Sydenham Society, *Lexicon of Medicine & Allied Sciences*
syll.	syllable
Syr.	Syrian
Syst.	(in titles) *System, -atic*
Taxon.	(in titles) *Taxonomy, -ical*
techn.	technical, -ly
Technol.	(in titles) *Technology, -ical*
Telegr.	in Telegraphy
Teleph.	in Telephony
(Th.),	(quoted from) Thornton's *American Glossary*
Theatr.	in the Theatre, theatrical
Theol.	(as label) in Theology; (in titles) *Theology, -ical*
Theoret.	(in titles) *Theoretical*
Tokh.	Tokharian
tr., transl.	translated, translation
Trans.	(in titles) *Transactions*
trans.	transitive
transf.	transferred sense
Trav.	(in titles) *Travel(s)*
Treas.	(in titles) *Treasury*
Treat.	(in titles) *Treatise*
Treatm.	(in titles) *Treatment*
Trig.	in Trigonometry
Trop.	(in titles) *Tropical*
Turk.	Turkish
Typog., Typogr.	in Typography
ult.	ultimately
Univ.	(in titles) *University*
unkn.	unknown
U.S.	United States
U.S.S.R.	Union of Soviet Socialist Republics
usu.	usually
v., vb.	verb
var(r)., vars.	variant(s) of
vbl. sb.	verbal substantive
Vertebr.	(in titles) *Vertebrate, -s*
Vet.	(as label) in Veterinary Science; (in titles) *Veterinary*
Vet. Sci.	in Veterinary Science
viz.	*videlicet*, 'namely'
Voy.	(in titles) *Voyage, -s*
v.str.	strong verb
vulg.	vulgar
v.w.	weak verb
W.	Welsh; West
wd.	word
Webster	*Webster's (New International) Dictionary*
Westm.	(in titles) *Westminster*
WGmc.	West Germanic
Wks.	(in titles) *Works*
w.midl.	west midland (dialect)
WS.	West Saxon
(Y.),	(quoted from) Yule & Burnell's *Hobson-Jobson*
Yrs.	(in titles) *Years*
Zoogeogr.	in Zoogeography
Zool.	(as label) in Zoology; (in titles) *Zoology, -ical*

Signs and Other Conventions

Before a word or sense

† = obsolete
‖ = not naturalized, alien
¶ = catachrestic and erroneous uses

In the listing of Forms

1 = before 1100
2 = 12th c. (1100 to 1200)
3 = 13th c. (1200 to 1300), etc.
5-7 = 15th to 17th century
20 = 20th century

In the etymologies

* indicates a word or form not actually found, but of which the existence is inferred
:— = normal development of

The printing of a word in SMALL CAPITALS indicates that further information will be found under the word so referred to.

.. indicates an omitted part of a quotation.

- (in a quotation) indicates a hyphen doubtfully present in the original; (in other text) indicates a hyphen inserted only for the sake of a line-break.

PROPRIETARY NAMES

THIS Dictionary includes some words which are or are asserted to be proprietary names or trade marks. Their inclusion does not imply that they have acquired for legal purposes a non-proprietary or general significance nor any other judgement concerning their legal status. In cases where the editorial staff have established in the records of the Patent Offices of the United Kingdom and of the United States that a word is registered as a proprietary name or trade mark this is indicated, but no judgement concerning the legal status of such words is made or implied thereby.

wave (weɪv), *sb.* (Also 6 **whave**, 8 **weave.**) [f. WAVE *v.*

In sense 1, which appears early in the 16th c., it seems to have been substituted by popular etymology for the older WAW *sb.*, which it rapidly superseded in use. In branch II it is a new formation on the verb.]

I. 1. a. A movement in the sea or other collection of water, by which a portion of the water rises above the normal level and then subsides, at the same time travelling a greater or smaller distance over the surface; a moving ridge or swell of water between two depressions or 'troughs'; one of the long ridges or rollers which, in the shallower parts of the sea, follow each other at regular intervals, assuming an arched form, and successively break on the shore. Sometimes the word is applied to the ridge and the accompanying trough taken together, and occasionally to the concave curve of the surface between the crest of one ridge and that of the next.

1526 TINDALE *Jas.* i. 6 For he that douteth is lyke the waues [**1539** *Cranmer*, **1557** *Geneva*, **1611** *Authorized*, a waue; **1535** *Coverdale*, the wawes] of the see. **1530** PALSGR. 287/1 Wave of the see, *uague*. **1551** ROBINSON tr. *More's Utopia* II. i. (1895) 116 A large and wyde sea, which..is not rough nor mountith not with great waues. **1565** STAPLETON tr. *Bede's Hist. Ch. Eng.* 91 The tempest encreased, the whaues multiplied so faste..that nothing but present death was looked for. **1585** HIGINS *Junius' Nomencl.* 400/1 *Vnda sequax*,..waue vpon waue: one waue following vpon anothers necke. **1593** SHAKS. *3 Hen. VI*, II. vi. 36 As doth a Saile, fill'd with a fretting Gust Command an Argosie to stemme the Waues. **1603** HOLLAND *Plutarch's Mor.* 255 As in a setled calme, without winde, weather and wave. **1671** MILTON *P.R.* IV. 18 As..surging waves against a solid rock, Though all to shivers dash't, the assault renew. **1697** DRYDEN *Virg. Georg.* IV. 767 Proteus..in the Billows plung'd his hoary Head; And where he leap'd, the Waves in Circles widely spread. **1781** COWPER *Expost.* 272 What ails thee, restless as the waves that roar, And fling their foam against thy chalky shore? **1810** SCOTT *Lady of L.* VI. xviii, Like wave with crest of sparkling foam, Right onward did Clan-Alpine come. **1855** TENNYSON *Maud* I. xviii. 8 Is that enchanted moan only the swell Of the long waves that roll in yonder bay? **1860** —— *Islet* 16 Waves on a diamond shingle dash. **1877** W. H. WHITE *Naval Archit.* xi. 443 The main bow wave may also be followed by a train of waves, successive waves in a series having diminished heights. **1877** HUXLEY *Physiogr.* 171 It is merely the form of the wave, and not the actual water that travels.

b. = *tidal* or *tide wave*: see TIDAL 1 b, TIDE 16 b.

1812–16 PLAYFAIR *Nat. Phil.* I. 329 The great Wave which, in this manner, constitutes the tide, is to be considered as an undulation..of the ocean, in which [etc.].

c. *Poet.* Used in collective sing. for 'water', 'sea'. The plural is also similarly used (*poet.* and *rhetorically*), but without quite losing the primary meaning.

1588 SHAKS. *L.L.L.* v. i. 61 Now by the salt waue of the mediteranium, a sweet tutch. **1590** SPENSER *F.Q.* II. vii. 57 He..looking downe, saw many damned wights, In those sad waues [of Cocytus]. **1616** CHAPMAN tr. *Musæus* F 1, Virgin, for thy Loue, I will swim a waue That Ships denies. **1667** MILTON *P.L.* I. 193 Thus Satan talking to his neerest Mate With Head up-lift above the wave. **1742** GRAY *Eton* 26 Say, Father Thames,..Who foremost now delight to cleave With pliant arm thy glassy wave? **1784** COWPER *Task* v. 835 When he sees afar His country's weather-bleach'd and batter'd rocks, From the green wave emerging. **1820** BYRON *Mar. Fal.* II. i, The calm wave Favours the gondolier's light skimming oar. **1825** SCOTT *Talism.* i, Where the waves of the Jordan pour themselves into an inland sea. **1844** HOOD *Bridge of Sighs* 11 Whilst the wave constantly Drips from her clothing. **1860** PATMORE *Faithf. for Ever* I. viii, Perhaps ..They wander whispering by the wave. **1864** TENNYSON *Voy.* v, We came to warmer waves, and deep Across the boundless east we drove.

2. *transf.* **a.** An undulatory movement, or one of an intermittent series of movements, of something passing over or on a surface or through the air.

1810 SCOTT *Lady of L.* I. xi, The western waves of ebbing day Roll'd o'er the glen their level way. **1827** KEBLE *Chr. Y., Christm. Day*, In waves of light it thrills along. **1833** TENNYSON *Dream Fair Wom.* xlviii, The holy organ rolling waves Of sound on roof and floor. **1850** —— *In Mem.* xci, The thousand waves of wheat, That ripple round the lonely grange. **1899** *Allbutt's Syst. Med.* VIII. 86 Thus..there are the waves of goose-skin passing over the body. **1903** K. C. THURSTON *Circle* iii. 23 It was like a wave of sun through a chill room.

b. = *pulse-wave*: see PULSE *sb.*[1] 6.

1838 *Penny Cycl.* XII. 81/1 The dilatation of the arteries produced by the wave which is propagated along the column of blood contained in them. **1850** TENNYSON *In Mem.* cxxii. Till all my blood, a fuller wave, Be quicken'd with a livelier breath.

c. A forward movement of a large body of persons (chiefly invaders or immigrants overrunning a country, or soldiers advancing to an attack), or of military vehicles or aircraft, which either recedes and returns after an interval, or is followed after a time by another body repeating the same movement.

1852 T. WRIGHT *Celt, Roman & Saxon* I. 1 Europe was peopled by several successive migrations, or, as they have been technically named, waves of population, all flowing from one point in the east. **1862** STANLEY *Jew. Ch.* (1877) I. ix. 176 The Israelite conquest of Palestine..is in itself but one amongst a succession of waves which have swept over the country. **1875** STUBBS *Const. Hist.* I. ii. 16 The populations..which..were still affected by the great migratory wave. **1879** GREEN *Readings fr. Eng. Hist.* xix. 98 Turned back wave after wave of the enemy. **1893** O. M. EDWARDS in Traill *Soc. Eng.* i. 1 The first wave of immigrants that reached Britain..was a wave of men of short stature and swarthy countenance. **1915** *Times* 3 Feb. 9/1 They send forward wave after wave of men, regardless of the punishment. **1943** R. V. JONES *Most Secret War* (1978) xli. 382 Longer raids will always be liable to attacks on their last waves whenever fighters can fly. **1951** O. BERTHOUD tr. *Clostermann's Big. Show* I. 38 The airfield at Triqueville.. was going to be bombed in force by two waves of 72 Marauders. **1982** *Daily Tel.* 12 Oct. 17/8 The fly past will take place in two waves—a slow one consisting of five formations of helicopters.., then the fixed-wing aircraft, again in five formations.

d. A long convex strip of land between two long broad hollows; one of a series of such strips; also occas. a rounded ridge of sand or snow formed by the action of the wind.

1788 A. YOUNG in *J. Baxter's Libr. Pract. Agric.* (ed. 4) II. p. viii, The Downs are..nearly flat, or only in gentle waves at the top. **1789** J. WILLIAMS *Min. Kingd.* I. 108 The variation of the dip and rise there generally consists of gentle easy swelling waves. **1796** W. H. MARSHALL *W. Eng.* II. 212 A fine Vale District: rich waves of grass land. **1819** S. ROGERS *Human Life* 682 A hollow wave Of burning sand their everlasting grave. **1886** RUSKIN *Præterita* I. viii. 248 The field fences buried under crested waves of snow. **1887** RIDER HAGGARD *Allan Quaterm.* xx, The crest of a great green wave of land, that rolled down a gentle slope to the banks of a little stream.

e. A wave-like effect produced in a grandstand or stadium by successive sections of the crowd of spectators standing up, raising their arms, and sitting down again. Usu. as ***human***, ***Mexican***, or ***Mexico wave***. orig. *U.S.*

This form of crowd participation was publicized through its popularity among spectators at the World Cup football competition held in Mexico City in 1986.

1984 *N.Y. Times* 6 Oct. I. 21/1 This undulating human wave..apparently became popular at University of Washington football games a few years ago. **1986** *Financial Times* 2 June 1/8 The huge Azteca amphitheatre was roaring and rolling, as the crowd performed the jump-up-and-down body 'wave'. **1986** *Times* 21 June 40/2 As if India were not already finding batting hard enough, the crowd started during this final session to behave as they have seen others doing in Mexico, and performing what is apparently called the 'human wave'. **1986** *Today* 29 June, 100,000 fans had turned up at the Aztec stadium and performed the wave for two hours..on a day when there was no match. **1986** *Sunday Times* (Colour Suppl.) 27 July 27/3 There was the uncertainty among us media people about whether to stand when the congregation did. Half of us would rise, a third sit confusedly down again, then a fifth struggle to their feet. The Queen must have thought we were trying out a Mexico Wave. **1986** *Guardian* 18 Aug. 23/2 An occasion and result that satisfied the partisan bulk of the 88,000 crowd. We even saw a passable Mexican Wave.

3. *fig.* and in figurative context. **a.** chiefly *pl.*, rough, stormy, or fluctuating conditions (of life, care, passion, etc.).

a **1548** HALL *Chron., 14 Hen. VII* (1550) 49 One fierce & strong waue..swalowed both their lyues not long asonder. **1563** B. GOOGE *Eglogs* IV. 93 A Creature, cause of all my Care,..A woman Waue of Wretchednes. **1590** SPENSER *F.Q.* I. x. 34 That he should neuer fall In his wayes through this wide worldes waue. *Ibid.* III. viii. 20 That cruell Queene ..Did heape on her new waues of weary wretchednesse. **1606** S. GARDINER *Bk. Angling* 12 Waues of tribulation, tempests of tentations. **1781** COWPER *Truth* 1 Man, on the dubious waves of error toss'd, His ship half founder'd, and his compass lost. **1846** MRS. A. MARSH *Father Darcy* II. iii. 75 Alas! was there no one..to bid the waves of passion be still? **1847** TENNYSON *Princess* III. 224 And thus your pains May only make that footprint upon sand Which oft-recurring waves of prejudice Resmooth to nothing. **1856** GEO. ELIOT *Scenes Cler. Life, Amos Barton* v, An unfecundated egg, which the waves of time wash away into nonentity.

b. chiefly *sing.* A swelling, onward movement and subsidence (of feeling, thought, opinion, a custom, condition, etc.); a movement (of common sentiment, opinion, excitement) sweeping over a community, and not easily resisted. Also, a sharp increase in the extent or degree *of* some phenomenon; cf. *crime wave* s.v. CRIME *sb.* 4.

1851 G. BRIMLEY *Ess.* (1858) 112 Its last vestiges were fast disappearing before the wave of democratic equality. **1855** BAIN *Senses & Int.* II. iv. §18 (1864) 285 All the muscles of the body may be thrown into agitation under a wave of strong feeling. **1859** DICKENS etc. *Haunted Ho.* ii. 10/1 What floods of thought came, wave upon wave, across my mind! **1870** DK. ARGYLL *Iona* i. 29 Certain waves of opinion which at successive periods were propelled from the ancient centres of Christendom. **1903** MYERS *Hum. Personal.* 7 The highest wave of materialism which has ever swept over these shores. **1910** *Sat. Even. Post* 29 Oct. 46/2 A good many 'waves of crime' occur in the imagination of newspapers. **1915** *Contemp. Rev.* May 615 A wave of militarism sweeps through the nation. **1920** *Times* 21 Jan. 12/1 The probability of a 'wave' of crime after the war has been foreseen and foretold by students of social problems. **1927** *New Republic* 21 Sept. 109/2 The Metropolitan Life Insurance Company, commenting on the alleged suicide wave among young people, reports..that the suicide rate for the population as a whole is decreasing. **1958** W. S. CHURCHILL *Hist. Eng.-Speaking Peoples* IV. x. i. 10 Throughout the country a fresh wave of demonstrations followed. **1971** *Daily Tel.* 13 Apr. 6 The pace of dismissals is accelerating as companies strive to restore profits after the massive wave of inflation in costs and wages.

c. ***the wave of the future***: the inevitable future fashion or trend; the coming thing.

1940 A. M. LINDBERGH (*title*) The wave of the future, a confession of faith. **1959** *Daily Tel.* 8 July 10/3 Mr. Khruschev, in the eyes of these critics, feels that he is riding the 'wave of the future'. **1969** M. PUZO *Godfather* I. xi. 150 The business I am in is the coming thing, the wave of the future. **1971** *Sci. Amer.* Sept. 5/2 (Advt.), Fan jets are the wave of the future. You'll find them on all the 747's. **1976** L. BERNSTEIN *Unanswered Question* v. 266 They were all, including Mahler, swept along by the mighty 'wave of the future' that Wagner, in his hyper-romantic egomania, had predicted and initiated.

d. Phr. ***to make waves***: to stir up trouble, make things worse, make a fuss. orig. and chiefly *U.S.*

In quot. 1925 used in the literal sense.

[**1925** 'KIMBO' *Tropical Tales* 10 Back at the foul stinking bog Potts heard himself hailed by the well-known voice of his late father. 'Hello, sonny,..slip in gently...for the Lord's sake don't make any waves.'] **1962** A. LURIE *Love & Friendship* xiv. 277, I think it will be best if she tells him herself... After I've left. We don't want to make waves. **1972** *Publishers' Weekly* 10 Apr. 58/2 Dr. Wilkins..had just been fired from Willowbrook for allegedly making waves about conditions. **1983** *Times* 19 Feb. 11/5 He is..a solid dependable Scotsman who runs a company at a profit in an orderly fashion and doesn't make waves.

4. a. An undulating conformation; each of the undulations of such a conformation; *spec.* one in the hair; also, a set that leaves the hair in waves.

1547 in Feuillerat *Revels Edw. VI* (1914) 9 Clothe of Syluer in waues. **1547** *Ibid.* 12 The nether skyrtes or Basse of blewe clothe of golde playne leyd on with waves of clothe of Syluer. **1664** EVELYN *Sylva* xxx. 95 That [is] the Grain which runs in waves, and makes the divers and beautiful chamfers which some woods abound in. **1667** MILTON *P.L.* IX. 496 [The Serpent] toward Eve Addres'd his way, not with indented wave, Prone on the ground, as since, but on his reare. **1678** MOXON *Mech. Exerc.* vi. 104 It hath its under flat cut into those fashioned waves you intend your work shall have. **1702** PETIVER *Gazophyl.* I. v, *Concha Veneris* ..[is] easily distinguish'd from all others, by its peculiar Waves and spotted Belly. **1721** W. GIBSON *Diet. Horses* i. 13 The Mane..is always the more graceful with a natural Weave from the Roots. **1795** SOUTHEY *Joan of Arc* x. (1853) 126 The pennons rolling their long waves Before the gale. **1864** DICKENS *Mut. Fr.* (1865) I. I. iv. 31 Bella..employed both her hands in giving her hair an additional wave. **1866** MRS. WHITNEY *Leslie Goldthwaite* iv, Freedom's northern wind will take all the wave out of your hair. **1884** R. F. BURTON *Bk. Sword* vii. 137 Often the waves [of sabre-blades] are broken into saw-teeth. **1895** M. HEWLETT *Earthwork Tuscany* 75 A bush of yellow hair falling over his forehead in a wave. **1895**, etc. [see MARCEL *sb.*]. **1922** JOYCE *Ulysses* 343 Gerty's crowning glory was her wealth of wonderful hair. It was dark brown with a natural wave in it. **1925** F. SCOTT FITZGERALD *Great Gatsby* ii. 44 All the things I've got to get. A massage and a wave, and a collar for the dog. **1938** E. AMBLER *Cause for Alarm* v. 79 Prolonged steaming operations take the wave out of my hair. **1959** *Chambers's Encycl.* VI. 691/2 There are three main denominations of heat waving: the 'machine wave'..the 'machineless' wave..and the 'wireless' wave. **1973** [see KIRBY-GRIP].

b. An undulating line or streak of colour.

1662 MERRETT tr. *Neri's Art of Glass* xlii, It will shew some waves, and divers colours. **1704** NEWTON *Optics* I. (1721) 34 If the Glass of the Prisms be..without those numberless Waves, or Curles which usually arise from Sand-holes. **1856** R. KNOX tr. *Edwards' Man. Zool.* §414 It [the cat] is of a brown colour, somewhat greyish, with deeper coloured transverse waves. **1891** *Hardwicke's Sci.-Gossip* XXVII. 15 The waves written by the syphon above the central line corresponding to the dots of the Morse Code.

c. *Arch.* An undulated moulding; a cyma or ogee moulding.

1663 GERBIER *Counsel* 70 The wave with Lace under it at one peny *per* foot. *Ibid.* 71 The upper Wave cut with Leaves at six pence *per* foot. **1825** RICKMAN *Archit.* (ed. 3) 46 These mouldings are generally much ornamented, and the wave or zigzag ornament..is almost universal.

d. A wavy or zigzag pattern; something made in this pattern: see quots.

1845 G. DODD *Brit. Manuf.* Ser. v. 176 There are several descriptions of [straw-] plait made in England—such as.. the 'wave', the 'diamond', &c. **1888** C. P. BROWN *Cotton Manuf.* 168 *Waves*, zigzag twill pattern.

5. Modern scientific uses.

a. *Physics.* Each of those rhythmic alternations of disturbance and recovery of configuration in successively contiguous portions of a fluid or solid mass, by which a state of motion travels in some direction without corresponding progressive movement of the particles successively affected. Examples are the waves in the surface of water (sense 1), the waves of the air which convey sound, and the (hypothetical) waves of the ether which are concerned in the transmission of light, heat, and electricity.

Hertzian waves: radio waves (discovered by the German physicist Heinrich Hertz in 1888).

1832 BREWSTER *Nat. Magic* viii. (1833) 195 They will produce each equal waves of sound. **1833** [see *wave-surface, -theory*]. **1839** G. BIRD *Nat. Philos.* 292 The waves of light, like those of sound, are transmitted in every direction. **1846** GREENER *Sci. Gunnery* 50 It is necessary so to prolong the explosion, that the wave of vibration has time to travel throughout the whole of the mass acted upon. **1860** TYNDALL *Glac.* II. i. 227 An aërial wave of sound travels at about the rate of 1100 feet in a second. **1863** —— *Heat* viii. 257 The condensation and rarefaction [of the air] constitute what is called a sonorous pulse or wave. **1889** ROWLAND in *Amer. Jrnl. Math.* XI. 378 Starting with very good conductors and very long waves, the electric current will be uniformly distributed throughout the section of the conductors. **1902** KIPLING *Wireless* in *Scribner's Mag.* Aug. 136/2 Hertzian waves which vibrate, say, two hundred and thirty million times a second. **1920** *Discovery* Apr. 115/2 These wireless waves are often called Hertzian waves.

b. *Meteorol.* A change of atmospheric pressure or temperature, consisting of gradual rise and fall or fall and rise, taking place successively at successive points in some particular line of direction on the earth's surface. In popular language, a 'heatwave' or a 'cold wave' denotes a spell of abnormal heat or cold, which is assumed to be travelling over the country in a particular direction.

1843 SIR J. F. W. HERSCHEL in *Rep. Brit. Assoc.* 61 If this minimum represent..the trough of a barometric wave which at 3 A.M. was vertically over Brussels, and at 11 A.M. over London, the wave must have been travelling westwards. **1846** W. R. BIRT in *Rep. Brit. Assoc.* I. 147 Now a wave generated in any way and approaching the continent of Europe from the north-west would most probably impinge on it with a high..crest... Again a negative wave, with a deep trough..would present large fluctuations as it impinged on the land. **1901** *Scotsman* 4 Oct. 5/1 When a cold wave strikes Northern Minnesota, there is no knowing where the thermometer may go.

c. *Seismol.* A seismic disturbance of a portion of the crust or surface of the earth, travelling continuously for a certain distance.

1760 *Phil. Trans. R. Soc.* LI. 601 A large quantity of vapour may be conceived to raise the earth in a wave, as it passes along between the strata. **1848** *Trans. R. Irish Acad.* XXI. 58 The only motion that will fulfil these conditions, is the transit of a wave of elastic compression, or of a succession of these,..through the solid substance and surface of the disturbed country. **1862** R. MALLET *First Princ. Observ. Seismol.* I. iv. 33 If an isolated wall..be subjected to the transit of an earth wave..the resulting fractures will vary with the direction of the wave-path. **1877** F. W. RUDLER *Earthquake* in *Encycl. Brit.* VII. 609/2 From the seismic centre waves are propagated in all directions through the solid materials of the earth's crust. **1886** J. MILNE *Earthquakes* iii. 55 Hitherto we have chiefly considered earthquake vibrations; now we will say a few words about earthquake waves.

d. Phys. ***wave of contraction***, the onward contraction of a muscle from the point where the stimulus is applied. ***wave of stimulation***, the (hypothetical) impulse of molecular vibration travelling along a nerve from the point at which it is stimulated.

1851 CARPENTER *Man. Phys.* (ed. 2) 214 Successive contractions and relaxations may be produced..by a single prick with a scalpel; a sort of wave of contraction being transmitted in the direction of its length. **1885** ROMANES *Jelly Fish* etc. i. 25 A stimulus applied to a nerveless muscle ..giving rise to a visible wave of contraction, which spreads in all directions. *Ibid.*, I shall always speak of muscle-fibres as conveying a visible wave of contraction, and of nerve-fibres as conveying an invisible, or molecular, wave of stimulation.

e. *Physics.* A de Broglie wave (see DE BROGLIE).

1924 L. DE BROGLIE in *Phil. Mag.* XLVII. 450 We are then inclined to admit that any moving body may be accompanied by a wave and that it is impossible to disjoin motion of body and propagation of wave. **1930**, etc. [see *matter wave* s.v. MATTER *sb.*[1] 26]. **1942**, **1956** [see *probability wave* s.v. PROBABILITY 4]. **1978** D. A. DAVIES *Waves, Atoms & Solids* i. 21 In order to represent the electron by a wave, or group of waves, we require to be able to state whether the wave will show dispersion.

6. A book-name of certain geometrid moths.

1819 SAMOUELLE *Entomol. Compend.* 423 Geometra inornata. The plain Wave. **1832** J. RENNIE *Consp. Butterfl. & Moths* 139 The Small White Wave (Emmelesia candidata, Stephens). *Ibid.* 140 The Small Fan-footed Wave (Ptychopoda dilutaria, Stephens). *Ibid.* 141 The Dwarf Cream Wave (Acidalia osseata, Stephens). *Ibid.* 143 The Subangled Wave (Timandra variegata, Stephens). **1882** *Cassell's Nat. Hist.* VI. 67 The *Acidalidæ* or 'Waves,' comprise a large number of small species.

II. An act of waving.

7. A motion to and fro of the hand or of something held in the hand, used as a signal or as an expressive sign.

1688 HOLME *Armoury* III. xix. (Roxb.) 155/2 Termes used about the displaying or florishing of an ensigne... A Wave, or plaine wave, is A Turne or florish. **1840** DICKENS *Old C. Shop* xv, And so, with many waves of the hand, and cheering nods,..they parted company. **1854** SURTEES *Handley Cr.* i. (1901) I. 8 With a wave of his hat [he] brought the pack forward. **1883** D. C. MURRAY *Hearts* iii. (1885) 20 With a charming smile and a reassuring wave of the right hand. **1898** KIPLING *Fleet in Being* i. 4 The man-of-war..must also be ready to drop three or four knots at the wave of a flag.

8. A swaying to and fro.

1648 HERRICK *Hesper., Delight in Disorder* 9 A winning wave (deserving Note) In the tempestuous petticote. **1825** SCOTT *Talism.* x, The point at which he had seen the last slight wave of the Templar's mantle. **1849** M. ARNOLD *Obermann* xlii, Where with clear-rustling wave The scented pines of Switzerland Stand dark round thy green grave.

III. *attrib.* and *Comb.*

9. a. simple attrib., as ***wave-beat***, ***-crest***, ***energy***, ***-head***, ***-noise***, ***-ridge***, ***-top***, ***-wail***, ***-water***; (sense 2d) ***wave-region***; (sense 5a) ***wave-problem***, ***-transmission***, ***-velocity***; (sense 7) ***wave gesture***.

1979 *East Anglian Mag.* Aug. 532/2 Four wild swans came high overhead, the chanting *wave-beats of their wings making a windy threnody in the great silence of the Fen sky. **1823** SCOTT *Peveril* xxvii. *Motto*, The restless foam Of the wild *wave-crest. **1976** *Jrnl. R. Soc. Arts* CXXIV. 729/1 The seasonal distribution of *wave energy fits nicely into the pattern of energy demand, that is, more in the winter than in the summer. **1922** JOYCE *Ulysses* 512 He invokes grace from on high with large *wave gestures. **1849** CUPPLES *Green Hand* ii. (1856) 16 The *wave-heads..were crested here and there with light. **1922** JOYCE *Ulysses* 47 At the lacefringe of the tide he halted... His snout lifted barked at the *wavenoise. **1910** S. P. THOMPSON *Ld. Kelvin* II. xxi. 862 Sir William read four papers bearing on *wave-problems. **1856** OLMSTED *Slave States* 397 For an hour or two we got above the sandy zone, and into the..'*wave' region of the State. The surface here was extremely undulating. **1849** C. BRONTE *Shirley* xiii, She rises high, and glides all revealed, on the dark *wave-ridge. **1893** CONAN DOYLE *Refugees* III. xxv. 30 For hours a glimpse could be caught of the boat, dwindling away on the *wave tops. **1907** V. CORNISH in *Geogr. Jrnl.* Jan. 23 The effect of this *wave-transmission is to diminish the initial inequality of slope. **1906** HARDY *Dynasts* II. IV. viii. 185 Weary *wave-wails from the clammy shore. **1889** WELCH *Text Bk. Naval Archit.* iii. 59 The amount of the buoyancy in *wave-water is also constantly varying.

b. objective, as ***wave-breaker***, ***wave-drawing***; (sense 4a) ***wave-curler***, ***-setter***; also ***wave-compelling***, ***-setting***, ***-subjected*** adjs.; ***wave-making*** sb. and adj.

1764 GOLDSM. *Trav.* 297 The wave-subjected soil [of Holland] Impels the native to repeated toil. **1881** BROADHOUSE *Mus. Acoustics* 59 Constant practice in wave-drawing..will soon familiarize the student [etc.]. **1885** L. F. VERNON-HARCOURT *Harbours & Docks* I. 93 The open jetty does not act as a wave-breaker. **1890** G. NEILSON *Trial by Combat* ix. 27 The remark presents the great Dane in a light somewhat different from that suggested by his wave-compelling attitude on the wild sea shore. **1915** R. LANKESTER *Diversions of Naturalist* 61 Specially powerful wave-compelling winds. **1931** *Lady* 26 Feb. 300/1 Fix your wave-setting combs in place. **1932** *Mod. Woman* Feb. 72/1 A perfectly easy method of keeping your hair permanently waved, set and curled at home... Wave curlers 1/- pair. **1932** *Even. Standard* 1 July 9 (Advt.), A..wavesetter in your bag is almost as good as taking your hairdresser on holiday with you. **1942** Wave-making [see SONIC *a.* 1b]. **1961** *Guardian* 29 Apr. 1/5 Mr. Hardy sprayed on a sweet-smelling wave-setting lotion. **1979** *United States 1980/81* (Penguin Travel Guides) 235 A resort-style motel with a lake and wave-making swimming pool.

c. similative, as ***wave-green***, ***-white***; also with the sense 'having a waved form or markings', as ***wave-blade***, ***-bladed***, ***-breasted***, ***-edged***, ***-haired***, ***-leaved***, etc.

1877 LANE-FOX *Catal. Anthrop. Coll. Bethnal Green Branch S. Kens.* 183 Malay Krisses, with *wave blades. **1866** W. J. FITZPATRICK *Sham Squire* 115 He..with a *wave-bladed dagger..made some stabs at the intruder. **1811** SHAW *Gen. Zool.* VIII. 405 *Wave-breasted Parrakeet. *Psittacus versicolor.* **1884** R. F. BURTON *Bk. Sword* vii. 137 The *wave-edged form [of blade] is well shown in an iron dagger. **1621** G. SANDYS *Ovid's Met.* IX. (1626) 175, I..let my *waue-greene Mantle sink. **1866** CHRISTINA ROSSETTI *Prince's Progr.* x, A *wave-haired milkmaid. **1816–20** T. GREEN *Univ. Herbal* II. 828 *Xysmalobium Undulatum*; *Wave-leaved Xysmalobium. **1922** JOYCE *Ulysses* 11 *Wavewhite wedded words shimmering on the dim tide.

d. locative, as ***wave-bowered***, ***-reflected***.

1812 BYRON *Ch. Har.* II. xxiv, Thus bending o'er the vessel's laving side, To gaze on Dian's wave-reflected sphere. **1820** SHELLEY *Prometh. Unb.* III. ii. 32 Tracking their path..by the light Of wave-reflected flowers. **1881** ROSSETTI *Ballads & Sonn., House of Life* lvi, The wave-bowered pearl.

e. instrumental, as ***wave-beat***, ***-beaten***, ***-buffeted***, ***-circled***, ***-cut***, ***-dashed***, ***-encircled***, ***-eroded***, ***-hollowed***, ***-kissed***, ***-lashed***, ***-moist***, ***-rusted***, ***-shattered***, ***-swept***, ***-tossed***, ***-walled***, ***-washed***, ***-wet***, ***-whitened***, ***-worn***, etc. Also ***wave-free***, ***-weary***; ***wave erosion***.

a **1593** MARLOWE *Ovid's Eleg.* I. xiv. 34 Such were they [her locks] as Diana painted stands All naked holding in her waue-moist hands. **1610** SHAKS. *Temp.* II. i. 120 He..oared Himselfe..To th' shore; that ore his waue-worne basis bowed As stooping to releeue him. **1741** BOYSE *Patience* 200 On the sea-weed spray,..the wave-toss'd body lay. **1777** POTTER *Æschylus* 51 The tort'ring sting Thence drove thee wand'ring o'er the wave-wash'd strand. **1810** SCOTT *Lady of L.* I. xiii, The shaggy mounds..wave-encircled, seem'd to float. **1819** BYRON *Juan* II. cxcviii, Amidst the barren sand and rocks so rude She and her wave-worn love had made their bower. **1843** J. R. LOWELL in *Pioneer* Jan. 40 Stands a maiden..Musing by the wave-beat strand. **1848** LYTTON *K. Arthur* II cvii, Wave-hollow'd caves. **1854** F. W. FABER *Oratory Hymns* 67 Angelic songs are swelling O'er earth's green fields, and ocean's wave-beat shore. **1856** LEVER *Martins of Cro' M.* xxiii, The dark cliffs and rugged crags, the wave-beaten rocks. **1857** DICKENS *Dorrit* II. xx, Every wave-dashed, storm-beaten object. **1857** DUFFERIN *Lett. High Lat.* (ed. 3) 225 A..channel, between two wave-lashed ridges of drift ice. **1861** M. ARNOLD in A. A. Procter *Victoria Regina* 181 The wave-kiss'd marble stair. **1876** MORRIS *Sigurd* II. 92 So Sigurd turned to the river and stood by the wave-wet strand. **1878** O. WILDE *Ravenna* 14, I have wandered far From the wave-circled islands of my home. **1881** —— *Poems* 131 Be not afraid To leave this wan and wave-kissed shore. *Ibid.* 161 Some wave-shattered steep. **1885** G. K. GILBERT in *5th Ann. Rep. U.S. Geol. Survey* 84 The submerged plateau whose area records the landward progress of littoral erosion, becomes a terrace after the formative has disappeared, and, as such, requires a distinctive name. It will be called the wave-cut terrace. **1889** W. B. YEATS *Wanderings of Oison* II. 73 And she with a wave-rusted chain was tied To two old eagles. **1892** —— *Countess Kathleen* 126 When her own people ruled in wave-worn Eri. **1894** *Outing* XXIV. 92/1 The long, wave-swept margin was left to the solitude of primeval nature. **1901**, etc. Wave-cut [see PLATFORM *sb.* 6c(i)]. **1906** HARDY *Dynasts* II. I. vi. 38 The Universal-empire plot Demands the rule of that wave-walled spot. **1919** D. W. JOHNSON *Shore Processes & Shoreline Devel.* iv. 161 The wave-erosion features associated with the coast, shore, shoreface, and offshore, are three in number. **1924** E. SITWELL *Sleeping Beauty* xiv. 47 Pan, with his satyrs on the rocks Feeding their wave-weary flocks. **1929** W. B. YEATS in *New Republic* 2 Oct. 173/2 A bone wave-whitened and dried in the wind. **1939** W. H. TWENHOFEL *Princ. Sedimentation* ii. 30 As sea level before the rise is assumed to have been stationary, a wave-eroded surface may be expected to have developed in places. **1952** C. DAY LEWIS tr. *Virgil's Aeneid* III. 72 Over against wave-worn Plemyrium there's an island Athwart the gulf of Syracuse. **1968** R. W. FAIRBRIDGE *Encycl. Geomorphol.* 133/1 Coasts made irregular by wave erosion are less common. **1974** C. TAYLOR *Fieldwork in Medieval Archaeol.* iv. 60 On the valley sides above the dam is ridge and furrow which ends just above the slight wave-cut platform which still marks the former edge of the water in the lake. **1979** *United States 1980/81* (Penguin Travel Guides) 611 Cruising on these wave-free waterways is relaxing.

10. Special comb.: **wave-action**, (*a*) *Geol.*, the action of water flowing in waves; (*b*) *Gunnery*, 'abnormally high pressure in a gun from very large charges' (*Cent. Dict.* 1891); **wave analyser**, any instrument for analysing a wave motion into its Fourier components; **waveband**, a range of (esp. radio) wavelengths or frequencies between specified limits; **wave base** *Physical Geogr.*, the greatest depth at which sediment can be disturbed by surface waves; **wave change** *Radio*, used *attrib.* to designate a switch for changing the wavelength to which a transmitter or receiver is tuned; also **wave changer**; **wave cloud** *Meteorol.*, an elongated cloud that is one of a parallel series formed at the crests of atmospheric waves in the lee of high ground and remaining stationary in relation to the ground; **wave-detector**, an instrument designed to detect very feeble electric waves in wireless telegraphy; **wave-disk**, a metal disk with a waved edge, used in the *wave-siren*; **wave drag** *Aerodynamics*, the drag experienced by a body at supersonic speeds as a result of the formation of a shock wave; **wave equation** *Physics*, an equation that represents wave motion, esp. (*a*) the differential equation $\partial^2 U/\partial t^2 = c^2\nabla^2 U$; (*b*) Schrödinger's equation (see SCHRÖDINGER); **wave filter** *Electr. Engin.* = FILTER *sb.* 3e; **wave-front** *Physics*, the continuous line or surface including all the waves or radiatory emissions which are in the same phase; **wave function** *Physics*, a function that satisfies a wave equation; *esp.* a Schrödinger wave function (see SCHRÖDINGER); **wave group**, a short group of waves, not necessarily of uniform wavelength or amplitude; **wave-hop** *v. intr. colloq.* [after *hedge-hop* vb. s.v. HEDGE *sb.* 9], to fly low over the sea; hence **wave-hopper**; **wave-horse** = SEA-HORSE 5; **wave machine**, an apparatus for producing waves in water; **wave-making**, the production of waves by the movement of a floating body on the surface of the water; also *attrib.*; **wave-mark**, (*a*) *Geol.* (see quot. 1863); (*b*) a wavy marking, stain, or blemish; so also **wave-marked** *a.*, **wave-marking** *Geol.*; **wave-meter** *Electr.* a device for measuring the wavelength or frequency of radiofrequency waves; **wave-motion**, motion in curves alternately concave and convex; **wave-motor**, a machine or apparatus designed to utilize the energy in the waves of water as a motive power; also *attrib.*; **wave number** *Physics* and *Chem.*, the number of waves per unit length, used esp. as a spectroscopic unit to represent the frequency of electromagnetic radiation and usu. expressed in reciprocal centimetres, $cm.^{-1}$ (see KAYSER); the reciprocal of wavelength, or this multiplied by 2π; symbol *k*; **wave packet** *Physics*, a group of superposed waves which together form a travelling localized disturbance; *esp.* one described by the Schrödinger equation and regarded as representing a particle; cf. PACKET *sb.* 1h; **wave-particle** *Physics*, used *attrib.* to designate the two-fold description of matter and energy in terms of two seemingly incompatible concepts, waves and particles; **wave-path** *Seismol.* (see quot. 1886); **wave pattern** = *Vitruvian scroll* s.v. VITRUVIAN *a.* b; **wave period** *Physics*, the period between the arrival at a given point of successive maxima of a travelling wave; **wave picture** *Physics*, the conception of sub-atomic particles as waves, in accordance with wave theory; **wave-power**, power derived from the action of water waves; **wave-rainbow**, a rainbow formed on the spray of sea-waves; **wave-rate** *Acoustics*, the rate of vibration of a sounding body in a given time; **wave resistance**, the retarding force of the action of waves of water; **waverider** *Aeronaut.*, a wing that derives lift from a shock wave close to its under-surface; an aeroplane having such wings; **wave screen**

(see quot.); **waveshape** = WAVEFORM; **wave-shell** *Physics*, each of the imaginary concentric spherical layers in any medium traversed by a wave, such that the vibration of the particles of the layer is always in the same phase; **wave-siren**, a form of the SIREN (*sb.* 7) in which a current of air is driven through a narrow slit against an undulatory curve on the periphery of a cylinder or disk; **wave-slope**, the angle of inclination of the surface of a wave to the horizontal; **wave-surface** *Physics*, a geometrical surface which is the locus of all points reached at one instant by an undulatory agitation propagated from any centre; **wave-system** *Ship-building*, see quot. and WAVE-LINE 1; **wave theory** = (*a*) *undulatory theory* (see UNDULATORY 1 c); more widely in *Physics*, any theory treating of something as waves, esp. such a theory of sub-atomic particles; (*b*) *Philol.* = WELLENTHEORIE; **wave-train** *Physics* (see quot.); **wave trap**, (*a*) (see quots.); (*b*) *Radio* = TRAP *sb.* 8 d; **wave vector** *Physics*, a vector whose direction is the direction of propagation of a wave and whose magnitude is its wave number; **wave velocity** *Physics* = *phase velocity* s.v. PHASE *sb.* 5; **wave winding**, a kind of armature winding in which the coils are wound between commutator bars just over 180° apart so that there are two routes in parallel between the positive and the negative brush; †**wave work**, watered work (see quot.). Also WAVE-LIKE *a.* and *adv.*, WAVE-LINE.

1880 Dana *Man. Geol.* (ed. 3) 910 Index, *Wave-action on coral reefs. **1886** A. Winchell *Walks Geol. Field* 63 Here the torrential action was less turbulent: it was perhaps wave-action along a beach. **1931** H. A. Brown *Radio-Frequency Electr. Measurements* ix. 314 (*caption*) Balanced modulator used in *wave analyzer. **1946** *Nature* 7 Sept. 329/2 A wave-analyser was developed..in 1944 in order to analyse ocean waves and swell and ship movement. **1975** G. J. King *Audio Handbk.* v. 112 Harmonic distortion. For this test an audio wave analyser is required. **1923** *Daily Mail* 28 Apr. 5 A receiver which will function efficiently over a *waveband stretching from 300 metres to 20,000 metres. **1935** *Discovery* Sept. 278/1 Recent developments..have made possible..room within this waveband (30 to 75 million cycles) to accommodate several independent high-definition sound and picture channels. **1958** *Observer* 17 Aug. 8/3 By international agreement, four wavebands are available for television. **1971** I. G. Gass et al. *Understanding Earth* x. 144/2 Ultraviolet light (primarily in the wave-band 1500 to 2100 angstroms). **1899** F. P. Gulliver in *Proc. Amer. Acad. Arts & Sci.* XXXIV. 177 The term *wave-base is here introduced as a comparable term to river baselevel or hard stratum baselevel. It is another local baselevel, which ought to be distinguished from the grand baselevel of the sea. **1968** R. W. Fairbridge *Encycl. Geomorphol.* 1226/1 Historically, there has been much confusion about the lower limit of wave base and marine abrasion. **1930** *Telegraph & Telephone Jrnl.* XVI. 86/1 It is necessary to have a split battery at the distant end to provide the momentary impulse for the *wave change relay. **1957** *Practical Wireless* XXXIII. 520/1 The front panel carries the wave-change switch. **1924** S. R. Roget *Dict. Electr. Terms* 289/1 **Wave changer*, a switching arrangement enabling connections to be altered rapidly in a wireless transmitting apparatus to cause waves of a different wave length to be transmitted. **1929** Duncan & Drew *Radio Telegr. & Telephony* xxi. 673 A five position wave-changer switch changes the wavelength of the closed oscillatory circuit..simultaneously with the open radiative circuit. **1959** R. E. Huschke *Gloss. Meteorol.* 620 *Wave cloud. **1977** *Sci. Amer.* July 40/2 (*caption*) Wave clouds in the lee of a Martian crater were photographed by *Mariner 9*. **1905** *Athenæum* 18 Mar. 339/2 The centre of interest in wireless telegraphy seems to be shifting from the *wave-detector or coherer to the means of producing the energy required to act upon it. **1890** S. P. Thompson in *Nature* (1891) 8 Jan. 226/2 Two such *wave-disks, looking rather like circular saws with irregular teeth. **1948** *Sci. News* VII. 30 To attain very high velocities in a practicable aircraft it is obvious that *wave drag must be reduced to a minimum. **1951** [see *form drag* s.v. FORM *sb.* 22]. **1981** C. E. Dole *Flight Theory & Aerodynamics* vii. 217 The heat rise behind the shock wave is either radiated to the atmosphere or absorbed by the wing surface,..and this lost energy must be continuously supplied by the engines. This energy loss represents a type of drag known as wave drag. **1926** E. Schrödinger in *Physical Rev.* XXVIII. 1049 (*heading*) The *wave equation and its application to the hydrogen atom. **1927**, etc. [see Schrödinger]. **1936** P. M. Morse *Vibration & Sound* vi. 188 Plane waves of sound, longitudinal waves, obey the same wave equation as do the transverse waves on a string. **1982** W. H. Hayward *Introd. Radio Frequency Design* iv. 114 A complete solution of the voltage wave equation..is the sum of positive and negative moving voltage waves. **1908** *Phil. Mag.* XVI. 481 This machine has been used with a *wave filter, consisting of series inductances of low effective resistance and parallel capacities. **1947** R. Lee *Electronic Transformers & Circuits* vi. 150 Many wave filters are composed of several sections which simulate transmission lines. **1973** S. K. Mitra et al. in Temes & Mitra *Mod. Filter Theory & Design* i. 1 The theory of filters owes its origin to Wagner and Campbell, who in 1915 advanced the concept of passive electric wave filters. **1867** Tait *Quaternions* xi. 289 The planes of polarizaton of the two rays whose *wave-fronts are parallel, bisect the angles [etc.]. **1888** Rutley *Rock-Forming Min.* 57 The plane wave-surfaces or wave-fronts of the two rays will respectively be represented by the tangent planes. **1925** *Proc. R. Soc.* A. CVII. 43 (*heading*) Spheroidal *wave-functions. **1926** E. Schrödinger in *Physical Rev.* XXVIII. 1049 The wave-function physically means and determines a continuous distribution of electricity in space, the fluctuations of which determine the radiation by the laws of..electrodynamics. **1935**, etc. [see PROPER *a.* 3* b]. **1961** Powell & Crasemann *Quantum Mech.* ii. 59 Until suitable boundary conditions and requirements concerning the continuity of solutions are imposed, the properties of the wave function are not completely described by the Schrödinger equation. **1979** *Sci. Amer.* Nov. 128/1 In quantum mechanics an elementary particle such as an electron is represented by the mathematical expression called a wave function, which often describes the electron as if it were smeared out over a large region of space. [**1877** *Nature* 23 Aug. 343/1 (*heading*) On the rate of progression of groups of waves.] **1923** H. Moore *Textbk. Intermediate Physics* xxxii. 317 A noise consists of a single wave or of a very short *wave-group, while a musical note consists of a regular succession of similar waves constituting a regular wave-train. **1952** R. W. Ditchburn *Light* iv. 95 In a dispersive medium, the components of a wave group move with different speeds, and the phase relations between the components are altered. **1978** I. G. Main *Vibrations & Waves in Physics* xii. 210 Any isolated wave group may be viewed as a superposition of many sinusoidal waves. **1943** *Times* 21 Dec. 2/3 Sneak-raiding FW 190s which *wave-hopped across the Channel and North Sea to surprise seaside towns were a daytime menace. **1952** C. Day Lewis tr. *Virgil's Aeneid* IV. 80 Like a bird which along the shore and around the promontories Goes fishing, flying low, wave-hopping over the water. **1984** J. Savarin *Wolfrun* xiii. 175 'What I can do with a chopper will surprise you.' They'd be wave-hopping all the way across [the Channel]. **1957** R. Watson-Watt *Three Steps* xxxviii. 218 Our fears about the *wave-hopper. **1888** Rider Haggard *Mr. Meeson's Will* xi. (1897) 140 They..looked out across the troubled ocean. There was nothing in sight..but the white *wave-horses. **1968** *Surfer Mag.* Jan. 46/1 They constructed a *wave machine that could be a forerunner of a fantastic era of artificial surfing. **1979** *Listener* 1 Mar. 315/3 A swimming-pool..a place to bring the family..and enjoy the wave-machine. **1877** W. H. White *Naval Archit.* xi. 447 Mr. Scott Russell first drew attention to the importance of *wave-making resistance. **1878** D. Kemp *Man. Yacht Sailing* vi. 41 There are only two principal sources of resistance, and they are consequent upon surface friction and wave-making. **1863** Dana *Man. Geol.* (ed. 3) 94 **Wave-marks.*—Faint outlinings, of curved form, on a sandstone layer, like the outline left by a wave along the limit where it dies out upon a beach. **1902** *Westm. Gaz.* 14 Apr. 4/2 When the novice finds a few pinholes in his negatives, or wave marks on parts of the image. *Ibid.*, The wave-marks were the result of careless development. **1903** *Amer. Geol.* June 356 The top of the Lorraine is formed by a *wavemarked layer of lime-stone. *Ibid.*, Numerous other instances of *wavemarking at this horizon might be given. **1904** *Electrician* 1 Jan. 408/2 (*caption*) General view of *wave meter. **1905** *Athenæum* 27 May 662/2 Prof. Fleming's direct-reading cymometer or wave-meter, for measuring the length of the waves used in wireless telegraphy. **1945** *Electronic Engin.* XVII. 720/1 The absorption wavemeter can be greatly improved by the addition of a valve which will provide the necessary energy to maintain the tuned circuit in continuous oscillation. **1979** P. Hawker *Guide to Amat. Radio* iv. 63/2 A convenient method of calibrating the wavemeter is to use a communication receiver. **1846** W. R. Birt in *Rep. Brit. Assoc.* I. 135 In contemplating the transference of the barometric maxima and minima, we regard only the *wave-motion—but very different must be the air-motion. **1882** P. G. Tait *Light* in *Encycl. Brit.* XIV. 603 The essential characteristic of wave-motion is that a disturbance of some kind is handed on from one portion of a solid or fluid mass to another. **1898** *Daily News* 9 June 7/2 The Linden *wave-motor boat. **1899** *Ibid.* 15 Apr. 8/6 A wave motor, which may be seen working off Dover. **1873** *Rep. Brit. Assoc. Adv. Sci. 1872* 53 The term **wave-numbers* appears preferable to the equivalent term 'inverse wavelengths' which has been hitherto used. **1936** *Physical Rev.* L. 59/2 The vector **k** is called 'the reduced wave number vector'. **1973** *Physics Bull.* July 419/2 These devices are characterized by a relatively small tuning range (a few wave-numbers). **1979** *Nature* 20–27 Dec. 887/2 It is confusing to find both the chemists' wavenumber ($1/\lambda$) and physicists' wavenumber ($2\pi/\lambda$) used in different parts of the text. **1928** *Proc. R. Soc.* A. CXVII. 276 Schrödinger has shown that for a harmonic oscillator a *wave packet can be constructed which, though it spreads in the intermediate states, always returns to its original form at each end of the swing. **1955** Friedman & Weisskopf in W. Pauli *Niels Bohr* 153 More insight into this equation is provided by examining the time behaviour of a neutron wave packet. **1968** G. Ludwig *Wave Mech.* I. iv. 47 A wave packet is not to be regarded as an approximation to a corpuscle, so that the corpuscles are *in fact* more or less extended *waves*, but the 4-wave determines only the probability..of the position of the corpuscles. **1979** *Nature* 22 Mar. 312/1 Observations in Massachusetts Bay of high-frequency internal wave packets indicate that they are caused by lee waves generated outside a submarine bank at the Bay's seaward margin during ebb tide. **1938** R. C. Tolman *Princ. Statistical Mech.* vii. 231 The foregoing considerations are sufficient to give an idea of the quantum mechanical treatment of *wave-particle duality in the cases of entities which were customarily regarded solely from the particle point of view. **1968** M. S. Livingston *Particle Physics* iii. 47 The growing understanding of the wave-particle dualism in the properties of light led Louis de Broglie in 1925 to propound the hypothesis that a material particle should also have a wave property associated with it. **1862** R. Mallet *First Princ. Observ. Seismol.* I. iv. 35 The line of transit, or *wave-path. **1886** J. Milne *Earthquakes* i. 9 The radial lines along which an earthquake may be propagated from the centrum are called 'wave-paths'. **1905** G. W. Rhead *Princ. Design* 116 Another motive in Egyptian borders..is a kind of spiral or *wave pattern, starting from a series of small circles. **1956** G. Taylor *Silver* ix. 192 All kinds of classical motifs, such as anthemion, key..and wave patterns. **1909** *Proc. R. Soc. Edin.* XXIX. 446 The energy propagated in one *wave-period across a plane at right angles to the direction of the wave-motion is equal to the energy contained in one wave-length of the group multiplied by the ratio of group-velocity to wave-velocity. **1946** *Nature* 7 Sept. 330/2 These peaks are equivalent to wave-periods of submultiples of 3 × 20 or 60 sec. **1975** *BP Shield Internat.* May 13/3 Wave heights and wave periods..are the crucial statistics that spell work or no work on the crane barges. **1955** W. Heisenberg in W. Pauli *Neils Bohr* 15 The complete equivalence of the particle and *wave pictures in the quantum theory was thus demonstrated for the first time. **1974** G. Reece tr. *Hund's Hist. Quantum Theory* xi. 142 Quantum and wave pictures combine to give $\Delta p = uh/l$. **1973** *Bull. Amer. Assoc. Petroleum Geologists* LVII. 1835/1 *Wave-power gradient studies along the mainland [of the Florida coast]..indicate that the dominant wave approach direction, responsible for littoral drift towards the south-southeast, is from the west. **1974** *Times* 7 Oct. 1/3 A significant part of Britain's future energy requirements could come from cheap, pollution-free wave power. **1980** D. Bloodworth *Trapdoor* xiii. 75 There are studies for deriving solar energy from seaweed, wind-power from the trades, wave-power from the surf. **1984** *Times* 8 Nov. 16/1 The pilot wave-power plant at Toftestallen, about 50 miles west of Bergen, is expected to be operational next year. **1848** Tennyson in Ld. Tennyson *Mem.* (1897) I. 275 Sat watching *wave-rainbows [at the Lizard]. **1903** G. M. Stratton *Exper. Psychol.* v. 83 Musical notes whose *wave-rates do not differ at least a fifth of a vibration a second. **1889** Welch *Text Bk. Naval Archit.* iii. 56 *Wave resistance is by far the most powerful agent in extinguishing the oscillations. **1964** *Times* 29 May 12/3 The R.A.E. had designed a new type of delta wing known as a '*waverider' which has a convex upper surface and is supported by the pressure generated by the shock wave trapped under the concave lower surface. **1978** D. Küchemann *Aerodynamic Design of Aircraft* iii. 77 In general terms, waveriders are a type of aircraft where the means for providing volume, lift, and propulsion are so closely integrated that their effects cannot readily be separated from one another. **1883** *Fisheries Exhib. Catal.* 48 *Wave Screen, or Breakwater, for breaking the force of the sea, at entrance of bar..or elsewhere. **1940** *Chambers's Techn. Dict.* 902/2 Wave-form, *wave-shape. **1947** R. Lee *Electronic Transformers & Circuits* ix. 234 It is sometimes convenient to know whether a transformer, whose frequency response is known, can deliver a given wave shape. **1965** *Wireless World* July 364/1 The use of cameras to make a permanent photographic record of a waveshape on an oscilloscope screen is now commonplace. **1984** *Sounds* 1 Dec. 59/5 Vibrato is offered with four waveshapes to choose from, and may be programmed. **1877** F. W. Rudler *Earthquake* in *Encycl. Brit.* VII. 610/1 The points at which a *wave-shell reaches the surface form a curve which is conveniently called a coseismal line. **1881** *Nature* 18 Aug. 359/2 Helmholtz..has constructed a new instrument, the *wave-siren. **1890** S. P. Thompson in *Nature* 15 Jan. 250/2 Dr. Kœnig had recourse to the wave-siren, an earlier invention of his own. **1877** W. H. White *Naval Archit.* vi. 212 In considering the sufficiency of the range of the curve of stability for any vessel, it is desirable to regard it as abridged by this 8 or 10 degrees, in order to allow for the *wave slope. **1833** MacCullagh *Collected Wks.* (1880) 34 In this theory, the surface of waves, or the *wave surface, is a geometrical surface used to determine the directions and velocities of refracted or reflected rays, being the surface of a sphere in a singly refracting medium; a double surface, [etc.]. **1860** Cayley *Math. Papers* (1891) IV. 420 Some very beautiful results in relation to the Wave Surface have been recently obtained by Herr Zech. **1910** S. P. Thompson *Ld. Kelvin* II. xx. 820 Stokes has found by minute experiment that the Huygens wave-surface is most accurately obeyed by light. **1886** *Encycl. Brit.* XXI. 66/2 His [J. Scott Russell's] observations led him to propose and experiment on a new system of shaping vessels, which is known as the *wave system. **1833** MacCullagh *Collected Wks.* (1880) 34 On the *Wave Theory of Light. **1873** Cooke *Chem.* 22, I cannot agree with those who regard the wave-theory of light as an established principle of science. **1926** Wave theory [see *emission theory* s.v. EMISSION 7]. **1932** *Discovery* Apr. 109/1 This new physics was soon to be revolutionized further by De Broglie and Schrödinger, with their enthusiasm for the new wave theory of matter. **1933** L. Bloomfield *Language* xviii. 318 The presentation of these factors became known as the wave-theory, in contradistinction to the older family-tree theory of linguistic relationship. **1966** C. R. Tottle *Sci. Engin. Materials* i. 8 The adaptation of classical mechanics to wave theory dates back only some forty years, so that modern concepts of the structure of atoms are very new. **1971** [see STAMMBAUM]. **1974** G. Reece tr. *Hund's Hist. Quantum Theory* xi. 150 Schroedinger regarded this equation as the basis of the wave theory of particles. **1897** E. L. Nichols & Franklin *Elem. Physics* III. 12 A periodic disturbance sends out what is called a *train of waves*, each one of which is exactly like its forerunner... Graphic representation of *wave trains. **1875** Knight *Dict. Mech.*, **Wave-trap* (Hydraulic Engineering), a widening inwards of the sides of piers, to afford space for storm-waves which roll in at the entrance to spread and extend themselves. **1923** *Mod. Wireless* I. 247/2 The second frame aerial..is stated..to act as a 'wave-trap'. **1968** *Radio Communication Handbk.* (ed. 4) xvi. 3/1 If the generator whine remains pronounced, a fully screened tuned wave trap may be inserted in series with the output from the generator. **1955** L. Rosenfeld in W. Pauli *Niels Bohr* 88 The Fourier components of *wave vector *k*. **1978** H. M. Rosenberg *Solid State* (ed. 2) ii. 21 However, in the mathematical treatment of waves it is much more convenient to use the wave vector **k** instead of the wavelength λ. **1887**, etc. *Wave velocity [see *group velocity* s.v. GROUP *sb.* 6]. **1909** [see *wave period* above]. **1910** S. P. Thompson *Ld. Kelvin* II. xxi. 861 The proposition that the wave-velocity is double [that] of the group-velocity. **1969** R. H. Webb *Elementary Wave Optics* v. 61 It is the wave velocity rather than the group velocity which is measured by refraction. **1892**, etc. *Wave-winding [see *lap winding* s.v. LAP *sb.*[3] 6]. **1893** Sloane *Electr. Dict.*, **Wave Winding*, a method of winding disc and drum armatures. **1980** Slemon & Straughen *Electric Machines* iv. 272 If the paths of the current through the wave winding from a positive to a negative brush are traced, only two parallel paths from the positive to the negative armature terminal will be found. **1601** Holland *Pliny* VIII. xlviii. I. 228 The very roiall robe..made..after the manner of water-chamlot in *wave worke [L. *togam undulatam*].

†ˈ**wavé**, *a. Her. Obs.* [Hybrid f. WAVE *sb.* + AF. suffix *-é*, after *undé*.] = WAVY. Cf. UNDEE, UNDÉ.

1513, **1688** [see UNDEE]. **1572** Bossewell *Armorie* 26 Crosse taue, checkey, waue. **1646** Sir T. Browne *Pseud. Ep.* v. x. 249 Three Barres wave. **1680** Sir G. Mackenzie *Sci. Her.* vii. 26 The Drummonds bear three faces *undé* or *wavé*.

1684 *Lond. Gaz.* No. 1980/4 Two pair of Gold Buckles.. dented and wave.

wave (weɪv), *v.* Inflected **waved, waving.** Also ? 4 *Sc.* **vaf, wayve.** [OE. *wafian* (twice, in sense 6), corresp. formally to MHG. (and rare mod.G.) *waben* (see Grimm s.v. *wabben*) to wave, undulate; the Teut. root **wab-* is found in ON. *vafe* wk. masc. doubt, uncertainty, and in WAVER vb. and the cognates there mentioned; the ablaut-variants **wĕb-*, **wǣb-* occur in G. *weben* to wave, move about (cf. WEAVE *v.*², WEVE *v.*), which, however, is believed to be partly a dial. form of MHG. *wêwen* (mod.G. *wehen*) to wave, flutter, etc.; and in ON. *váfa* to swing, vibrate.

It is not always possible to distinguish between this vb. and the obsolete WAIVE *v.*²; the two approximate or coincide in some of their senses, and in some dialects and periods were identical in sound.]

I. To move to and fro or up and down.

* Of involuntary movement.

1. a. *intr.* Of a thing having a free end: To move to and fro, shake or sway in the air by the action of the wind or breeze.

1375 BARBOUR *Bruce* IX. 245 The discurrouris saw thame cumande With baneris to the vynd vafand [*v.rr.* wawand, waiuand]. **1508** DUNBAR *Poems* iv. 14 As with the wynd wavis the wickir, [So] wavis [*v.rr.* wannis, waveris] this warldis vanite. **1523** BERNERS *Froiss.* I. ciii. 50 b/2 Whanne those fotemen.. sawe the baners and standerdes waue with the wynde. **1577** KENDALL *Flowers Epigr.* 73 His crisped locks wavde all behinde. **1593** SHAKS. *3 Hen. VI*, II. ii. 173 Sound Trumpets, let our bloody Colours waue, And either Victorie, or else a Graue. **1671** MILTON *Samson* 718 Like a stately Ship.. With all her bravery on, and tackle trim, Sails fill'd, and streamers waving. **1713** POPE *Windsor For.* 350 High in the midst..(His sea-green mantle waving with the wind), The god appear'd. **1810** SCOTT *Lady of L.* III. xxv, No banner waved on Cardross gate. **1837** DICKENS *Pickw.* xxxv, Dresses rustled, feathers waved,..and jewels sparkled. **1846** RUSKIN *Mod. Paint.* II. III. I. xii. §5 The bending trunk, waving to and fro in the wind above the waterfall. **1846** MCCULLOCH *Acc. Brit. Empire* (1854) II. 7 It was then that the flag of England began to wave over every sea. **1884** BIBLE (R.V.) *Judges* ix. 9 But the olive tree said unto them, Should I leave my fatness.. and go to wave to and fro over the trees?

fig. **1648** HERRICK *Hesper.*, *Mrs. Eliz. Wheeler* Poet. Wks. (1915) 107 In bloome of Peach, and Roses bud, There waves the Streamer of her blood.

†**b.** *to wave in the wind*: to be hanged. (Cf. WAG *v.* 3 d.) *Obs.*

a **1533** BERNERS *Huon* xvi. 43 Or it be nyght, I shall cause thee to waue in the wynde.

c. Of long hair: To hang down loose. *poet.*

1671 MILTON *Samson* 1493 And view him sitting in the house,.. And on his shoulders waving down those locks. **1767** M. BRUCE *Last Day* Poems (1796) 129 His golden hair Wav'd on his shoulders.

d. *trans.* Of the wind, etc.: To cause (a thing) to sway or move to and fro.

1602 KYD *Span. Trag.* III. xii A, Behold a man hanging, and tottering, and tottering, as you know the winde will waue a man. **1817** SHELLEY *Rev. Islam* VIII. xxx, Beneath a bright acacia's shadowy hair, Waved by the wind amid the sunny noon. **1828** LYTTON *Pelham* x, The wind waved my long curls. **1829** SCOTT *Anne of G.* xi, No sound was heard save that of the night wind, when it.. waved the tattered banners which were the tapestry of the feudal hall.

†**2. a.** *intr.* To move to and fro restlessly or uncertainly; to waver. *Obs.*

1406 HOCCLEVE *La Male Regle* 399 And whil my breeth may in my body waue, To recorde it vnnethe I may souffyse. **1500–20** DUNBAR *Poems* xxi. 59 [This world] Quhair fortoun evir, as so, dissavis With freyndly smylingis of ane hure, Quhais fals behechtis as wind hyne wavis. **1508** [see I above]. **1628** [see WAVING *ppl. a.* 2]. **1665** [see WAVING *vbl. sb.* I].

†**b.** To move to and fro unsteadily on its base or (of a person) on the feet; to totter. *Obs.*

1538 ELYOT *Dict.*, *Vacillo*, to moue inconstantly, to wagge or waue, to be vnstable, or vnsure. **1605** SYLVESTER *Du Bartas* II. iii. IV. 645 As an Infant which the Nurse lets go To goe alone, waves weakly to and fro. **1608** A. WILLET *Hexapla in Exod.* xx. 18. 445 [Vatablus renders the verb by] *vacillabant*, they waued. **1609** LD. BROOKE *Mustapha* IV. iv. Chorus iv, Thus reeles our present State, And her foundation waues.

†**c.** Of a floating body: To move restlessly by the impulse of the air or water. Also, To hover about in the air. *Obs.*

1606 G. W[OODCOCKE] *Hist. Ivstine* XXVI. 94 b, The Ghoasts of them whose liues they had rauished from their bodies, wauing before their eyes. **1632** MILTON *Penseroso* 148 And let som strange mysterious dream, Wave at his Wings in Airy stream. *c* **1639** *Roxb. Ball.* (1887) VI. 429 They waving up and down the Seas, upon the Ocean Main. *c* **1645** HOWELL *Lett.* (1650) II. xix. 32 Those, that have their heads lightly ballasted.. are like buys [buoys] in a barrd Port, waving perpetually up and down. **1728** POPE *Dunc.* IV. 538 Int'rest that waves on Party-colour'd wings.

†**d.** *to wave oneself*: ? to give oneself up to the motion of the water. In quot. *fig. Obs.*

1628 FELTHAM *Resolves* I. i. 1 When a Rich Crowne ha's newly kiss'd the Temples of a gladded King, where he finds all things in a golden swimme,.. hee carelesly waues himselfe in the swelling plenty.

†**3.** Of a person: To be restless in mind; to alternate between different opinions or courses of action; to vacillate, waver. Said also of the mind, will, etc. *Obs.*

1387–8 T. USK *Test. Love* I. ii. (Skeat) 167 'Ye wete wel, lady, eke', quod I, 'that I have not.. with the wethercocke waved.' **1566** DRANT *Horace, Sat.* I. i. A v, Thy mynde it waues and wagges, And wisheth after greater things. **1582** T. WATSON *Pass. Cent. Love* v. Poems (Arb.) 41, I waue in doubt what helpe I shall require, In Sommer freeze, in winter burne like fire. **1597** HOOKER *Eccl. Pol.* v. xliii. §5 The truth is they waue in and out, no way sufficiently grounded, no way resolued what to thinke, speake or write. **1607** SHAKS. *Cor.* II. ii. 19 If he did not care whether he had their loue, or no, hee waued indifferently, 'twixt doing them neyther good, nor harme. **1611** [see WAVING *ppl. a.* 2]. **1628** FELTHAM *Resolves* II. xvi. 46 Variety, in any thing, distracteth the minde; and leaues it waving in a dubious trouble. **1642** H. MORE *Song of Soul* II. iii. I. ii, Thus waves the mind in things of greatest weight. **1796** MORSE *Amer. Geog.* II. 62 The court waved between these two factions.

4. a. Of water, the sea: To move in waves, undulate.

1530 PALSGR. 772/2, I wave, as the see dothe. *Je vague.* After a storme the see waveth. **1552** HULOET, Waue as water doth in tempest, *fluctuo.* **1571** [see WAVING *vbl. sb.* 2]. *c* **1797–1804** W. BLAKE *Poet. Wks.* (1913) 366 Wave freshly, clear waters, flowing around the tender grass. **1820** [see WAVING *vbl. sb.* 2]. **1865** TYLOR *Early Hist. Man.* iv. 63 Water is that which waves, undulates.

b. *transf.* Of a crowd: To move to and fro restlessly in a body.

1579–80 NORTH *Plutarch, Pompeius* (1595) 708 Pompey.. perceiuing.. that his owne battell on the other side waued vp and downe disorderly, as men vnskilfull in warres. **1591** SAVILE *Tacitus, Hist.* I. xl. 23 Galba was driuen to and fro with the crowde of the companie, as it waued up and downe [L. *vario turbæ fluctuantis impulsu*]. **1646** SIR J. TEMPLE *Ir. Rebellion* 25 The people.. continued waving up and down the streets. **1860** FROUDE *Hist. Eng.* V. 387 He was still speaking, when the crowd began suddenly to wave and shift.

c. Of a field of corn, etc.; To undulate like the waves of the sea.

1667 MILTON *P.L.* IV. 981 As when a field Of Ceres ripe for harvest waving bends Her bearded Grove of ears. **1720** POPE *Iliad* XX. 78 The forests wave, the mountains nod around. **1725** —— *Odyss.* IX. 124 With wheat and barley wave the golden fields. **1775** JOHNSON *Tax. no Tyr.* 20 Regions smiling with pleasure and waving with fertility. **1784** COWPER *Task* IV. 313 The lands, where lately wav'd The golden harvest. *a* **1830** H. COCKBURN *Memor.* (1856) 171 The whole place waved with wood, and was diversified by undulations of surface. **1834** RUSKIN *Months* iii, Rejoice! ye fields, rejoice! and wave with gold. **1851** J. H. GURNEY *Hymn*, Fair waved the golden corn In Canaan's pleasant land.

†**5. a.** *intr.* To turn aside. Also *trans.* To move (a person) aside. ***to wave one's way***: ? to take a divergent route. [But this may belong to WAIVE *v.*¹]

a **1548** HALL *Chron., Hen. VIII* 206 b, The kynges train waued on the lefte hande, to geue the Frenche kyng and his train the right hande. **1642** WOTTON *Buckingham* in *Reliq. W.* (1651) 109 Notwithstanding all which importunity, he resolved not [ed. 1642 *omits* not] to wave his way upon this reason;.. that if.. he should but once by such a diversion make his Enemy believe he were afraid of danger, he should never live without. **1646** SIR T. BROWNE *Pseud. Ep.* VII. xviii. 381 Æschilus.. was brained by a Tortoise which an Eagle let fall upon it... Some men.. would perhaps from hence confute the opinion of Copernicus, never conceiving how the motion of the earth below should not wave him from a knock perpendicularly directed from a body in the ayre above.

†**b.** Of the sun: To decline. *Obs. rare.*

1615 KYD *Span. Trag.* I. ii. 83 Till, Phoebus wauing to the western deepe, Our Trumpeters were chargde to sound retreat.

** Of voluntary movements.

†**6.** *intr.* To make a movement to and fro (with the hands). Only *OE.*

c **1000** ÆLFRIC *Saints' Lives* xxvii. 151 þeah þe man wafiȝe wundorlice mid handa ne bið hit þeah bletsung buta he wyrce tacn þære halȝan rode. *c* **1000** *Sax. Leechd.* II. 318 Ymbfo hine [a dung beetle] mid twam handum.. wafa mid þinum handum swiþe & cweð þriwa Remedium facio [etc.].

†**7. a.** To make motions (with the uplifted hands or with something held in the hands) by way of signal. Chiefly *Naut.* (Cf. WEAVE *v.*²) *Obs.*

Cf. the OE. sense 6, which may possibly have survived unrecorded to the 16 c.

1513 ECHYNGHAM in *Lett. & Papers War France* (1897) 148 He sayth he see my lord Admirall wayvyng with his handes and cryeng to the galeye: 'Comme aborde agayne!' *c* **1595** CAPT. WYATT *Dudley's Voy.* (Hakl. Soc.) 30 Wee might discrie.. two or three with a flagg of truce, wavinge unto us that it might be lawfull to com and speake with us. **1611** SHAKS. *Cymb.* I. iii. 12 He did keepe The Decke, with Gloue, or Hat, or Handkerchife, Still wauing. **1611** B. JONSON *Catiline* I. i. C 1 b, A Bloody arme it is, that holds a pine Lighted, aboue the Capitoll: And, now, It waues vnto vs. **1644** MANWAYRING *Sea-mans Dict.* 114 *Waving* is making a signe for a ship, or boate, to come towards them, or else to goe from them, as the signe is made, either towards or from-wards the ship.

†**b.** *trans.* To signal to (a person). Chiefly *Naut.* (Cf. WEAVE *v.*²) *Obs.*

1555 W. TOWRSON in *Hakluyt* (1599) II. II. 33 We mistrusted some knauery, and being waued by them to come a shoare, yet we would not. *Ibid.*, Certaine Negroes.. waued vs with a white flagge, but we.. would not stay. *Ibid.* 34 A great sort came downe to the water side, and waued vs on shoare with a white flagge. *c* **1595** CAPT. WYATT *Dudley's Voy.* (Hakl. Soc.) 4 Our Generall commaunded to wave them, and halinge them.. made them know their dwtie unto our English collers by vailinge theire topsailes. **1602** SHAKS. *Ham.* I. iv. 61 Looke with what courteous action It wafts [Qos. 1603–4 waues] you to a more remoued ground. *Ibid.* 68 It waues me forth againe; Ile follow it. **1616** CAPT. J. SMITH *Descr. New Eng.* (Arb.) 225 We were haled by two West Indy men: but when they saw vs waue them for the King of France, they gaue vs their broad sides. **1627** —— *Sea Gram.* xiii. 60 He waues vs to to lee-ward with his drawne sword.

†**8.** To move to and fro or up and down regularly or rhythmically.

a. *intr.* To move the wings up and down in or as in flight. Said also of the wings. Also *trans.*, to actuate or flap (the wings) in or as in flight. *Obs.*

1526 *Pilgr. Perf.* (W. de W. 1531) 202 b, Than with her wynges she fanneth & waveth vnto she haue kyndled in them fyre. **1584–7** GREENE *Carde of Fancie* Wks. (Grosart) IV. 165 The Bird[s].. being young, seeing the olde ones through age growen so weake, as they are not able to waue their wings, carrie them.. on their backs. **1657** [see WAVING *vbl. sb.* 5]. **1667** MILTON *P.L.* VII. 476 Those wav'd thir limber fans For wings. **1712–14** POPE *Rape Lock* II. 68 Colours that change whene'er they wave their wings. **1728** —— *Dunc.* IV. 422 Of all th' enamell'd race, whose silv'ry wing Waves to the tepid Zephyrs of the spring. **1808** W. BLAKE *Poet. Wks.* (1913) 145 Before her throne my wings I wave.

†**b.** *intr.* To move the body from side to side. Also *refl.* (Cf. WEAVE *v.*²) *Obs.*

1608 TOPSELL *Serpents* 138 As fast as the bayte was to the rope and hooke, so fast is he also ensnared and tyed vnto it, which while hee waueth and strayneth to vnloose and breake, he wearieth himselfe in vaine. **1697** DRYDEN *Virg. Georg.* III. 649 A Snake.. With curling Crest, and with advancing Head: Waving he rolls, and makes a winding Track. *a* **1700** EVELYN *Diary* 15 Jan. 1645 All the company fell a singing an Hebrew hymn.. waving themselves to and fro.

†**c.** *transf.* To move (the head *up and down*) with a significant gesture; to incline (the head). *Obs.*

1602 SHAKS. *Ham.* II. i. 93 At last, a little shaking of mine Arme: And thrice his head thus wauing vp and downe, He rais'd a sigh. **1607** —— *Cor.* III. ii. 77 Goe to them, with this Bonnet in thy Hand,.. Thy Knee bussing the stones:.. wauing thy head. **1768** STERNE *Sent. Journ.*, *Passport* (*Versailles*), I see the injured spirit wave her head, and turn off silent from the author of her miseries.

9. a. *trans.* To move through the air with a sweeping gesture (the uplifted or extended arm or hand, or something held in the hand by one extremity, e.g. a wand, a hat, or something that flutters in the breeze, as a flag, a handkerchief), often as a sign of greeting or farewell, or as an expression of exultation; usually implying repeated movements to and fro or up and down.

1607 SHAKS. *Cor.* II. iii. 175 And with his Hat, thus wauing it in scorne, I would be Consull, sayes he. **1611** —— *Cymb.* I. iii. 6 *Pisa.* It [i.e. his last speech] was his Queene, his Queene. *Imo.* Then wau'd his Handkerchiefe. **1634, 1667, 1794** [see WAND *sb.* 10]. **1697** DRYDEN *Virg. Georg.* IV. 513 At once she wav'd her Hand on either side, At once the Ranks of swelling Streams divide. **1712–14** POPE *Rape Lock* V. 7 Then grave Clarissa graceful wav'd her fan; Silence ensu'd. **1784** COWPER *Task* VI. 699 Maidens wave Their 'kerchiefs, and old women weep for joy. **1794** MRS. RADCLIFFE *Myst. Udolpho* xix, [He] waved his hand for him to leave the room. **1814** SCOTT *Wav.* xx, Many sprung up and waved their arms in ecstasy. **1847** TENNYSON *Princess* IV. 501 She, ending, waved her hands: Thereat the crowd Muttering, dissolved. **1849** MACAULAY *Hist. Eng.* viii. II. 385 Halifax sprang up and waved his hat. At that signal, benches and galleries raised a shout. **1859** H. KINGSLEY *G. Hamlyn* xli, Sam only waved his hand in good-bye, and sped on across the plain. **1896** CONAN DOYLE *Rodney Stone* vi, He waved his white hands as if to brush aside all opposition.

b. of impersonal things personified; chiefly *poet.*

1667 MILTON *P.L.* V. 193 And wave your tops, ye Pines, With every Plant, in sign of Worship wave. **1749** SMOLLETT *Regicide* I. vi, Ye spreading boughs, that wave Your blossoms o'er the stream! **1783** CRABBE *Village* I. 74 Above the slender sheaf, The slimy mallow waves her silky leaf. **1804** W. L. BOWLES *Spir. Discov.* II. 271 Dark Lebanon Waved all his pines for thee. **1820** SHELLEY *Orpheus* 106 And cypresses that seldom wave their boughs. **1886** J. G. WOOD *Man & Handiwork* iii. 31 Where the corn waves its yellow ears.

c. To brandish (a weapon).

1601 SHAKS. *Jul. C.* III. i. 109 And wauing our red Weapons o're our heads, Let's all cry Peace, Freedome, and Liberty. **1606** —— *Tr. & Cr.* V. v. 9 Bastard Margarelon Hath Doreus prisoner, And stands Calossus-wise wauing his beame. **1718** POPE *Iliad* XIII. 728 King Helenus wav'd high the Thracian blade. **1799** CAMPBELL *Pleas. Hope* I. 363 By that dread name we wave the sword on high, And swear for her to live! **1825** SCOTT *Talism.* xxviii, The sabre of Saladin left its sheath as lightning leaves the cloud. It was waved in the air,—and the head of the Grand Master rolled to the extremity of the tent. **1869** W. S. GILBERT '*Bab*' *Ballads, Ben Allah Achmet* 56 'My rival!' shrieked the invalid, And drew a mighty sword and waved it. **1911** G. M. TREVELYAN *Garibaldi* viii. 184 Men and women waved swords which they would never wield in earnest.

absol. **1607** SHAKS. *Cor.* I. vi. 74 Let him alone: Or so many so minded, Waue thus to expresse his disposition, And follow Martius. *They all shout and waue their swords.*

d. *intr.* (for *pass.*) To be moved to and fro. Of a weapon: To be brandished. †Also *trans.*, to pass over (something) with a brandishing movement.

1605 *First Pt. Jeronimo* III. ii. 105 See, a reuengfull sword Waues ore my head. **1667** MILTON *P.L.* VI. 304 Now wav'd thir fierie Swords, and in the Aire Made horrid Circles. *Ibid.* XII. 643 They looking back, all th' Eastern side beheld Of Paradise,.. Wav'd over by that flaming Brand. **1671** T. HUNT *Abeced. Scholast.* 90 Give a child as long as he will crave, and a dog as long as his tail will wave. **1828** LYTTON *Pelham* xvii, The lady's handkerchief waved in token of encouragement and triumph. **1896** CONAN DOYLE *Rodney Stone* vi, I see, too, the figures at the garden gate: my mother, with her face turned away, and her handkerchief waving.

†**e.** *trans.* In the Levitical law: To elevate and move from side to side (an oblation or *wave-offering*) before the altar. *Obs.*

First in Tindale, following Luther, who renders the verb by *weben*, and also has the compounds *webebrot, webebrust, webeopfer* = wave-loaf, -breast, -offering (see 13).

1530 TINDALE *Exod.* xxix. 24 And put all apon the handes of Aaron and on the handes of his sonnes: and waue them in and out a waueoffrynge vnto the Lorde. —— *Lev.* xiv. 21 Let him bringe one lambe for a trespaceoffrynge to waue it. [So **1535** COVERDALE; and all later versions.]

f. Occasional uses. Of a dog: To wag (its tail). Of a fish: To flap (a fin).

1677 GILPIN *Demonol.* III. v. 31 The Devil.. stands like a Fawning Dog scratching and waving his Tail. **1883** E. W. GOSSE in *Longm. Mag.* I. 559 Beneath the granite gray The sulky ferox lay And waved a fin.

10. a. To signify (something) by a wave of the hand or arm. Also with dative of person.

1810 SCOTT *Lady of L.* II. v, Perchance the maiden smiled to see Yon parting lingerer wave adieu. **1847** TENNYSON *Princess* II. 84 She spoke, and bowing waved Dismissal. **1874** *Sankey's Sacred Songs* (1878) 3 'Hold the Fort, for I am coming', Jesus signals still; Wave the answer back to heaven, 'By thy grace we will.' **1878** BROWNING *La Saisiaz* 16 From no far mound Waved salute a tall white figure. **1888** BESANT *Inner House* iii, The women wept and laughed at the same time, and waved them welcome.

b. To motion (a person, etc.) *aside, away, back, in, off* by a movement of the hand, etc.; also with preps. *from, over, to*, etc. Also *fig.*

1840 DICKENS *Old C. Shop* lxxi, Waving them off with his hand, and calling softly to her as he went, he stole into the room. **1841** C. WHITEHEAD *R. Savage* I. xi. 322 He waved me from him. **1854** SURTEES *Handley Cr.* (1901) I. i. 6 Michael took off his broad-brimmed, low-crowned hat, and waving in the pack, cheered them to the echo. *Ibid.* 7 He presently had the old hounds at his heels, and hat in hand he waved them over the wall. **1864** MRS. H. WOOD *Ld. Oakburn's Dau.* xxxvii, An attendant opened the door to see if anything might be wanted, but was waved away again. **1883** D. C. MURRAY *Hearts* ix, 'There is a fire in the sitting-room', he said, closing the outer door and waving her along the hall. **1894** MRS. H. WARD *Marcella* II. 100 Marcella waved him aside and ran on. **1914** H. JAMES in *Q. Rev.* Apr. 338 If we put ourselves questions we yet wave away doubts. **1916** W. SANDAY *In View of End* 89 Hitherto the pacifist writings have been waved aside simply on the ground that they were pacifist.

(*b*) *to wave down* [cf. *flag down* s.v. FLAG *v.*[4] 2 a], to wave at (a driver of a vehicle) as a signal to stop; also with the vehicle as object.

1955 J. P. DONLEAVY *Ginger Man* xxx. 343 A taxi roaring by. Wave it down. To the Red Lion Square. Fast. **1967** J. WEATHERHEAD *Sacred Shaft* ii. 15 There was a man.. waving her down on the fast stretch near Oxted. **1972** T. LILLEY '*K' Section* xl. 176 A man on a motor-bike.. stopped when Carter waved him down. **1981** M. C. SMITH *Gorky Park* I. xvii. 253 It took him twenty minutes to wave down a taxi.

c. *intr.* To make a sign by a wave of the hand.

1803 *Edwin* I. xiii. 205, I waved to the door, and in silence proceeded to the tyrant. **1847** C. BRONTE *Jane Eyre* xii, I retained my station when he waved to me to go, and announced:—'I cannot think of leaving you, sir.' **1855** TENNYSON *Maud* I. ix. 8 Rapidly riding far away, She waved to me with her hand. **1905** MABEL BARNES-GRUNDY *Vacill. Hazel* xvi. 219 He looks very miserable and cold and pinched. Poor old Sammy! I must wave to him.

d. *trans.* To mark (musical measures) by waving something.

1851 MRS. BROWNING *Casa Guidi Wind.* I. 804 All, to please The donna waving measures with her fan.

II. (From WAVE *sb.*)

11. To ornament with an undulating design; to make (something) wavy in outline.

1547 in Feuillerat *Revels Edw. VI* (1914) 9, vj Couering of Bardes of clothe of golde wherof three ar waved with clothe of golde. *c* **1611** CHAPMAN *Iliad* xxiii. 482 Arms.. forged of brass, and waved about with tin. **1652** CULPEPER *Eng. Physit.* (1656) 137 Leavs..a little unevenly waved sometimes about the edges. **1667** MILTON *P.L.* IV. 306 Shee ..Her unadorned golden tresses wore Dissheveld, but in wanton ringlets wav'd As the Vine curles her tendrils. **1678** MOXON *Mech. Exerc.* vi. 104 When one end of the Riglet you wave, is with the Vice Screwed to the plain side of the Rack. *Ibid.* 105 The Riglet will on its upper side receive the form of the several waves on the under side of the Rack, and also the form or Molding that is on the edge of the bottom of the Iron and so at once the Riglet will be both Molded and waved. **1686** tr. *Chardin's Trav. Persia* 394 The lower part of which Chappel is cover'd with large Tiles of Porphiry wav'd, and painted with Flowers. **1706** PHILLIPS (ed. Kersey), To *Wave*, to fashion, or make like the waves of the Sea; as watered Silks or Stuffs are. **1733** *School of Miniature* 39 Finish.. by fine thin Strokes,.. waving and curling them according to the turn of the Hair. **1815** J. SMITH *Panorama Sci. & Art* II. 763 Strokes following the same direction, but gently waved. **1875** SWINBURNE *Ess. & Studies* 319 A head-dress of eastern fashion,.. raised and waved and rounded in the likeness of a sea-shell. **1888** SWEET *Hist. Eng. Sounds* §221 Earlier in the [11th] century they began to wave and lengthen the top tags of *i, n, h*, etc. **1909** *Daily Chron.* 1 Oct. 7/4 Hair that has been waved by hot irons till it is broken and irregular.

12. *intr.* To undulate in form or outline.

1789 J. WILLIAMS *Min. Kingd.* I. 108 The horizontal coals ..are found to wave considerably in several places. **1795** ANDERSON *Narr. Embassy China* 73 Its [*sc.* the river's] course waves in the finest meanders. **1796** W. H. MARSHALL *W. Eng.* II. 84 A slip or coomb, of water formed land, waving with the stream. **1859** RUSKIN *Two Paths* iv. §121 From this, and in subordination to this, waved the arch and sprang the pinnacle. **1883** MISS BROUGHTON *Belinda* II. ix, Now and then the type waves up and down before her like the furrows of a ploughed field; but she reads on.

III. 13. The verb-stem in combination, in the names of the several offerings which, according to the Levitical law, were 'waved' (see 9 e) by the priest when presented in sacrifice, as **wavebreast, -loaf, -offering, -sheaf**; also **wave-bread**, a mod. synonym of *wave-loaf.*

1530 TINDALE *Lev.* vii. 30 Euen the fatt apon the brest he shall bringe with the brest to waue it a waueoffrynge before the Lorde. *Ibid.* 34 For the wauebrest and the heueshulder I haue taken of the childern of Israel. *Ibid.* xxiii. 17 And ye shall brynge out of youre habitacions two waueloaues. **1535** COVERDALE *Lev.* xxiii. 15 From the nexte daye after the Sabbath, whan ye brought y[e] Waueshefe [1530 TINDALE, the sheffe of the waueoffrynge]. **1625** T. GODWIN *Moses & Aaron* VI. ii. 268 These two words, Thenuphoth, and Therumoth; both signifie shake-offrings, heaue-offrings, or waue-offrings. **1879** FARRAR *St. Paul* II. 297 Which with the wave-bread and the heave-shoulders the priest afterwards took as his own perquisites.

14. wave-off *Aeronaut.*, a signal or instruction to an approaching aircraft that it is not to land.

1951 *Jrnl. R. Aeronaut. Soc.* LV. 526/2 To avoid embarrassment to the pilot, the sudden increase of power on the wave-off signal should not be accompanied by violent changes of trim. **1973** *Black Panther* 20 Oct. 10/2 When a tower calls 'missed approach' to an aircraft, they are obliged to obey and accept the tower's 'wave-off'.

wave, obs. form of WAIF *sb.*[1], WAIVE *v.*[1], *v.*[2]

wave, obs. pa. t. of WEAVE *v.*[1]

waved (weɪvd), *ppl. a.* [f. WAVE *v.* + -ED[1].]

1. Having the form of waves, presenting a wavy outline or appearance, undulating, undulated.

a. *gen.*

1599 HAKLUYT *Voy.* II. II. 86 In the hole is laied good store of wood, whereon is raised gallantly a waued roofe. **1605** SYLVESTER *Du Bartas* II. iii. IV. *Captains* 114 A large Cave,.. Whose waved Seeling,.. The Nymphs.. rarely had imbost With Pearls and Rubies. **1768** BOSWELL *Corsica* i. (ed. 2) 25 A rich waved country.. reaches along the east and south coasts to Bonifaccio. **1808** ELEANOR SLEATH *Bristol Heiress* I. 61 This surface.. is gently waved, rising with a varied swell from a small hollow, or valley. **1863** *Illustr. Lond. News* 1 Aug. 116/4 Advt., Crinoline.—The Patent Ondina, or Waved Jupon, does away with the unsightly results of the ordinary hoops. **1875** KNIGHT *Dict. Mech.*, *Waved Wheel.* The edge of the wheel is waved or convoluted so that as it revolves it imparts a lateral oscillation to an arm, pitman, or what not. **1890** HESSELS *Corpus Gloss.* Introd. p. xi, [The letter] l, with a waved stroke through it, indicates uel.

b. of hair, etc.

1863 'HOLME LEE' *A. Warleigh* III. 58 Her hat in her lap, and her waved brown hair uncovered. **1884** M[c]LAREN *Spinning* (ed. 2) 6 Take some hairs and some fibres of South Down wool and hold them together. The hair will hang straight and smooth, the wool will be curly, something like a corkscrew, and will have a waved appearance. **1913** *Play Pictorial* No. 138, p. vi/2 The waved hair is drawn smoothly back from the forehead.

c. *Her.* = UNDEE, WAVÉ, WAVY.

1610 GUILLIM *Heraldry* II. iii. 44 Of these [Lines] some are.. Waued. **1680** SIR G. MACKENZIE *Sci. Her.* 26 Waved is so call'd, from the waves of the Sea, which it represents, and is therefore called *undê*, and is used for signifying that the Bearer got his Arms for service done at sea. *Ibid.* 44 A cross waved. *Crux undosa.* **1704** J. HARRIS *Lex. Techn.* I, Waved or Wavy.

d. Of a sword, dagger, etc.: Having the edge undulated. Also in *Her.*

1688 HOLME *Armoury* III. xviii. (Roxb.) 126/1 He beareth Azure, a waved sword, or a sword waved, or wavey. **1780** EDMONDSON *Heraldry* II. Gloss., *Waved Sword*, by some erroneously called a flaming sword. **1855** tr. *Labarte's Arts Mid. Ages* p. xxxv, Malay knife.., blade waved.

2. Having undulated markings. Of silk, etc. = WATERED. Also in comb. †*waved-wise* adv.

1547 in Feuillerat *Revels Edw. VI* (1914) 14 Gardyd abowtes with clothe of golde wavyd wyse. **1601** HOLLAND *Pliny* VIII. xlviii. I. 228 The waved water chamelot was from the beginning esteemed the richest and bravest wearing. **1667** MILTON *P.L.* VII. 406 Fish.. through Groves Of Coral stray, or sporting with quick glance Show to the Sun thir wav'd coats dropt with Gold. **1711** *Fr. Bk. Rates* 378 Camblets, watered and not watered, waved, and not waved.

3. *Bot., Zool.*, and *Min.* Undulate; having a wavy form or texture; having wavy markings.

1664 POWER *Exp. Philos.* I. 6 The Gray, or Horse-Fly. Her eye is.. of a semisphæroidal figure; black and waved. **1776** J. LEE *Introd. Bot.* Expl. Terms 379 *Flexuosus*, waved, bent backwards and forwards from Bud to Bud. **1796** WITHERING *Brit. Plants* (ed. 3) III. 673 Leaves.. waved at the edge. **1822** J. PARKINSON *Outl. Oryctol.* 187 The hinge ..without tooth, waved and rather sinuous and unequal. **1841** *Florist's Jrnl.* (1846) II. 277 The sepals and petals are very linear and waved. **1843** HUMBLE *Dict. Geol.* etc. (ed. 2), *Waved*,.. In botany, applied to the margins of leaves, when bordered alternately with numerous minute segments of circles and angles. In entomology, applied to insects when the margin of the body is marked with a succession of arched incisions. **1845** A. GRAY *Bot. Text-bk.* (ed. 2) 112 A slightly waved or sinuous margin is said to be *repand.* **1870** HOOKER *Stud. Flora* 276 Lobes of lower lip subequal, waved and toothed.

b. In specific names of animals, plants, etc.

1668 CHARLETON *Onomast.* 130 *Raia Vndulata*.. the waved Scate. **1681** GREW *Musæum* I. §vi. ii. 147 The Great Waved-Muscle.. is commonly found in the Red-Sea. **1822** *Hortus Anglicus* II. 397 Aster Undulatus. *Waved Star Wort.* **1824** R. K. GREVILLE *Flora Edin.* 20 *Aira flexuosa*.. Waved Hair-grass. **1832** RENNIE *Consp. Butterfl. & Moths* 139 The Waved Carpet (*Emmelesia sylvata*, Stephens).

Comb. **1796** MARSHALL *Planting* II. 66 The Curled Cistus, or Waved-leaved Rock Rose.

4. Moved in waves.

1820 SHELLEY *Prometh. Unb.* IV. 187 'Tis the deep music of the rolling world Kindling within the strings of the waved air Æolian modulations.

5. Held aloft and moved to and fro.

1883 MISS BROUGHTON *Belinda* I. iii, A burly middle-aged figure gesticulating with raised arms and waved umbrella in mid-road. **1891** F. TENNYSON *Daphne* 3 Beeches swung their heads Before the waved banners of the winds. **1916** BAYFIELD tr. *Ovid's Met.* XI. in *19th Cent.* May 1013 She.. was the first to see Her lord.. Who with waved hand made signal, and her own She waved in answer.

ˈ**waveform.** Also **wave form, wave-form.** [f. WAVE *sb.* + FORM *sb.*] The shape of a wave at any moment, or that of the graphical representation of a (usu. periodically) varying physical quantity; a wave regarded as characterized by a particular shape or manner of variation, esp. a varying voltage.

1845 *Rep. Brit. Assoc. Adv. Sci. 1844* I. 340 The wave of the first order has a definite form and magnitude... This wave-form has its surface wholly raised above the level of repose of the fluid. **1846** W. R. BIRT in *Rep. Brit. Assoc.* I. 138 Should the rarefying process cease,.. not only will the wave-form be continued, but also the wave-motion. **1889** WELCH *Text. Bk. Naval Archit.* iii. 58 It is only the wave form which advances, and not the water composing that wave. **1903** *Whittaker's Electr. Engineer's Pocket-Bk.* 104 The effects produced by the various wave forms may be calculated by summing the effects produced by each component having this peculiar form. *Ibid.* 108 The wave form of an alternating E.M.F. **1923** *Proc. R. Soc.* A. CIII. 84 The term 'wave-form' is used throughout as a convenient abbreviation for the 'temporal variation of the electric field'. **1947** CROWTHER & WHIDDINGTON *Science at War* 15 A cathode ray tube would be suitable for finding the wave-form of the atmospheric. **1958** *Engineering* 31 Jan. 160/1 Electrical waveforms can be generated electronically and fed to the speaker which transforms them into 'artificial' sounds. **1968** *Brit. Med. Bull.* XXIV. 251/2 They established that the breathing waveforms contain at least four significant components, having approximate frequencies of 0.27, 0.12, 0.07, and 0.03 cycles per breath. **1977** *Rolling Stone* 24 Mar. (Advt.), These new speakers come with a test record that lets you pinpoint the output level where your particular amplifier begins to clip the peaks of the musical waveform.

wave guide. Also **wave-guide, waveguide.** [f. WAVE *sb.* + GUIDE *sb.*] A device which constrains or guides electromagnetic waves along a path defined by its physical structure and conducts them with minimum energy loss; *spec.* a metal tube, usu. of rectangular cross-section, doing this in the hollow space along its length. Also *transf.* Cf. *transmission line* s.v. TRANSMISSION e.

1936 *Bell Syst. Techn. Jrnl.* XV. 284 A novel form of electrical propagation by means of which extremely high-frequency waves may be transmitted from one point to another, through specially constructed wave guides. The guide.. may be a hollow copper pipe. **1960** M. REDWOOD *Mech. Waveguides* 1 In much of the research work in which mechanical waveguides are found the waveguide itself is of only subsidiary interest. **1969** *Guardian* 7 Nov. 13/4 Experimental lengths of a kind of special pipe called a 'wave-guide'.. are expected to be the very high capacity trunk telecommunications cables of the future. **1976** *Jrnl. R. Soc. Arts* CXXIV. 591/2 The electron beam is fired into a 'wave guide' carrying a very intense flow of radar waves. **1979** *Sci. Amer.* Oct. 71/3 Some whistlers have proved to be signals generated by a lightning stroke in one hemisphere of the earth and conducted to the opposite hemisphere through a natural waveguide formed by the lines of force of the earth's magnetic field. **1984** *Which?* Dec. 542/1 Microwaves.. are directed into the oven by a wave guide.

wavel (wevl), *v. Sc.* Also 7 **waivle, weavle**, 9 **wavle.** [Freq. of WAVE *v.*: see -EL.]

†**1.** *intr.* 'To move backwards and forwards, to wave' (Jam. 1808). *Obs.*

a **1689** W. CLELAND *Poems* (1697) 107 He making Hands, and Gown, and sleives wavel, Half Singing vents this Reavel Ravel.

†**b.** *trans.* To twist (the mouth). *Obs.*

1654 SIR A. JOHNSTON (Ld. Wariston) *Diary* (S.H.S.) II. 277 Folks observing in the kirk.. my wagging my head and weavling my mouth in the singing.

2. To stagger.

[**1638**: cf. *ppl. a.* below.] **1896** J. J. H. BURGESS *Lowra Biglan* 56 (E.D.D.) So up he waavles to da door.

3. ? To embroider with a wavy pattern.

a **1844** W. MILLER in A. Whitelaw *Scot. Song* 536 His coat's o' glowin' ruddy brown, and wavilet wi' gold.

Hence ˈ**wavelled** *ppl. a.* ? twisted; ˈ**wavelling** *ppl. a.*

1638 SIR A. JOHNSTON (Ld. Wariston) *Diary* (S.H.S.) I. 383 Using al and only his auin means, without waivling steps to byrods and bypayths, they may find that sprit within telling them realy and sensibly This is not the way, walk not in it. **1886** J. J. H. BURGESS *Shetland Sk.* 30 He's sic a wavlit ill-vyndid lookin' objec', nae manly wy wi him ava.

ˈ**wavelength.** Also **wave length, wave-length.** [f. WAVE *sb.* + LENGTH *sb.*] **1. a.** The distance between successive peaks or maxima of a wave; *esp.* this as a distinctive feature of the radio

waves used to carry a particular programme service.
1850 *Rep. Brit. Assoc. Adv. Sci. 1849* II. 11 It was well known..that Fraunhofer had most accurately measured the wave lengths of seven of the principal fixed lines in the solar spectrum. **1871** SCHELLEN *Spectrum Anal.* §18. 59 The rays of shortest wave-length, namely the violet. **1881** BROADHOUSE *Mus. Acoustics* 66 The fork..condenses..a bulk of air equal in length to the wave-length of its own pitch. **1907** V. CORNISH in *Geogr. Jrnl.* Jan. 25 The water may commonly be seen to..grow in the space of a few yards to a uniform wave-length of about 2 feet. **1925** *Scribner's Mag.* July 47/2 He swung the dials round to where he could receive the commercial wave lengths. **1950** *Engineering* 24 Mar. 337/3 The reasons for changes in the wavelengths of European broadcasting stations..are explained. **1971** *Daily Tel.* 18 Jan. 7/4 His experts have also juggled wavelengths to make air space for both Radio 1 and the commercial network. **1977** P. B. & J. S. MEDAWAR *Life Sci.* i. 20 Ordinary light microscopy has the disadvantage that nothing can be seen that is smaller than the wavelength of visible light.

b. Electromagnetic waves of the wavelength described.
1915 R. A. HOUSTON *Treat. Light* xxv. 449 He assumes the existence of an enclosure containing a great number of Hertzian oscillators all radiating and absorbing the same wave-length. **1937** JENKINS & WHITE *Fund. Physical Optics* xii. 277 Substances are said to show selective reflection when certain wave-lengths are reflected much more strongly than others. **1982** *Sci. Amer.* Aug. 52/1 Most ultraviolet wavelengths..cannot penetrate the earth's atmosphere.

c. The distance between adjacent heights or hollows in a body with a wave-like surface.
1958 *Spectator* 31 Jan. 133/3 The wavelength of the corrugations [on Persian roads] is considerably larger than the pace of a sheep or goat. **1977** *Sci. Amer.* Apr. 30/1 Nearly constant winds blow across the basin with such force that they pile up sand dunes as much as 150 kilometres long with wavelengths of three to five kilometres, clearly visible in satellite pictures.

2. *fig.* with allusion to radio reception, implying (esp. mutual) understanding; esp. in phr. ***to be on the same wavelength*** (as someone else), to understand each other.
1927 *Amer. Speech* II. 276/2 *Have one's wave length*, know one's sentiments. **1929** A. E. HOUSMAN *Let.* 16 Feb. (1971) I. 276 Only the archangel Raphael could recite my poetry properly, but..you would do it quite nicely, and I shall try not to set up interfering wave-lengths. *a* **1936** KIPLING *Let.* in C. Carrington *Rudyard Kipling* (1955) xx. 509 Every man has to work out his creed according to his own wave-length, and the hope is that the Great Receiving Station is tuned to take *all* wave-lengths. **1938** *Times Lit. Suppl.* 24 Sept. 617/3 She finally comes to believe that she is the only person in Riverville who was 'born civilized' and that nobody else there is of her own 'wavelength'. **1947** T. S. ELIOT *Milton* 12 It is only in the period that the wave-length of Milton's verse is to be found. **1959** *Economist* 6 June 919/2 Editors and publishers..have to..find the wave-length of their.. readers. **1964** H. WALDOCK in *Barcelona Traction, Light & Power Co. Case* (Internat. Court of Justice) II. 112, I do not think that it would assist the Court if I were to deal with every contention advanced by our opponents in their Observations and Conclusions; for on some points we are really not on the same wave-length. **1976** LD. HOME *Way Wind Blows* ii. 27 In September A. W. Whitworth took over, and I like to think we were soon on each other's wave-length. **1983** D. DUNNETT *Dolly & Bird of Paradise* xiii. 168 We weren't on the same wavelength really... He was clever. And my thoughts are easy to read.

3. Special Comb.: **wavelength constant** = *propagation constant* s.v. PROPAGATION 8.
1940 *Chambers's Techn. Dict.* 902/2 Wavelength constant. **1963** [see *propagation constant* s.v. PROPAGATION 8].

waveless ('weɪvlɪs), *a.* [f. WAVE *sb.* + -LESS.] Having no waves or undulation; not agitated or disturbed by waves. Also *fig.*
? *a* **1597** PEELE *David & Bethsabe* (1599) Bj b, Thy body smoother then this wauelesse spring. **1799** CAMPBELL *Pleas. Hope* II. 127 In the waveless mirror of his mind. **1804** GRAHAME *Sabbath* 212 A waveless lake, In which the wintry stars all bright appear. **1818** SHELLEY *Eugan. Hills* 91 Beneath is spread like a green sea The waveless plain of Lombardy. **1842** BARHAM *Ingol. Leg., Fragm. Westm. Abbey* 12 Above each knightly stall Unmoved, the banner'd blazonry hung waveless as a pall. **1872** M. COLLINS *Two Plunges for Pearl* III. 166 Lotos-islands in a waveless bay. **1887** G. W. CABLE *Grande Pointe* v. in *Century Mag.* Mar. 668/1 Their delicately penciled brows, their dark, waveless hair. **1890** 'R. BOLDREWOOD' *Col. Reformer* xii, Waveless uniformity, not to say monotony, of existence.

Hence **'wavelessly** *adv.*
1819 *Blackw. Mag.* VI. 136 Wavelessly the river spread Its silver mirror. **1845** JANE ROBINSON *Whitehall* iii, So placidly and wavelessly the winds of passion or guilt glide past the waters of time.

wavelet ('weɪvlɪt). [f. WAVE *sb.* + -LET.] A little wave, a ripple.
1813 SHELLEY *Q. Mab* viii. 24 Like the vague sighings of a wind at even, That wakes the wavelets of the slumbering sea. **1856** GEO. ELIOT *Scenes Cler. Life, Amos Barton* ii, The head, with its thin wavelets of brown hair, indents the little pillow. **1873** BLACK *Pr. Thule* v. 77 The white wavelets that were breaking on the beach.

b. *transf.* and *fig.*
c **1810** COLERIDGE in *Lit. Rem.* (1838) III. 360 You only hide it by foam and bubbles, by wavelets and steam-clouds, of ebullient rhetoric. **1874** H. R. REYNOLDS *John Baptist* i. 3 The transcendent Intelligence which presides over the law and measure of every wavelet of the universal energy. **1879** MACDONALD *P. Faber* I. vi. 61 Slowly she rose through a sky freckled with wavelets of cloud.

'wave-like, *a.* and *adv.* [f. WAVE *sb.* + -LIKE.]

A. *adj.* Resembling a wave, or what pertains to a wave.
1685 BOYLE *Effects of Motion* iii. (1690) 18, I see no necessity of having recourse to any thing but the wave-like motion of the Air for the production of our Phænomenon. **1830** LYELL *Princ. Geol.* I. 468 The wave like motion of the ground during earthquakes. **1887** T. STEVENS *Around World on Bicycle* I. 3 The wave-like macadam abruptly terminates, and I find myself on a common dirt road. **1889** *Hardwicke's Sci.-Gossip* XXV. 124 Every now and then a wave-like movement is seen to traverse through them.

B. *adv.* After the manner of a wave or waves.
1872 *Routledge's Every Boy's Ann.* 215 The dark solid wall of the enemy's infantry rolled, wave-like against this position. **1884** J. PAYN *Lit. Recoll.* 33 When I think of that inimitable scene, the humour of it sweeps wavelike over all.

'wave-line.

1. *Ship-building.* An outline recommended by some naval architects for the hull of a vessel as facilitating movement through the waves.
1846 *Mechanic's Mag.* 24 Oct. 391 What is the wave line? According to its ingenious author, Mr. J. Scott Russell, it differs from an ordinary ship's bow..in this, that it is 'gently hollower than such a bow towards the cutwater, and a little rounder towards the greatest breadth'. **1883** *Harper's Mag.* Aug. 441/2 The wave-line theories..had been adopted.

2. *Physics.* The path of a wave of light, sound, etc.; also, the graphic representation of the path.
1888 RUTLEY *Rock-forming Min.* 30 They are thrown into a wave line through the successive vibration of the other particles from the line of rest. *Ibid.* 31 The wave-line..is just half a wave-length.

3. Each of the lines or furrows produced by the action of the waves on a sandy beach.
1891 *Century Dict.*

wavellite ('weɪvəlaɪt). *Min.* [Named 1805 after Dr. W. *Wavel* its discoverer: see -ITE.] Hydrous phosphate of aluminium, found in globular aggregates with a radiated structure.
1805 *Phil. Trans.* XCV. 162. **1822** G. YOUNG *Geol. Surv. Coast Yorks.* (1828) 129 Silky crystals, resembling wavellite. **1885** *Encycl. Brit.* XVIII. 818/1.

wave me'chanics. *Physics.* Also wave-mechanics (with hyphen). [f. WAVE *sb.* + MECHANICS.] A form of non-relativistic quantum mechanics introduced by E. Schrödinger in which particles are regarded as having some of the properties of waves, the waves being described by the wave functions produced as solutions of the Schrödinger wave equation.
1926 *Physical Rev.* XXVIII. 726 Schroedinger's presentation is based on his wave-mechanics, while this is based on the matrix-mechanics. **1942** J. D. STRANATHAN *'Particles' Mod. Physics* vi. 228 On wave mechanics the electron is not regarded as a localized particle. **1953** *Sci. News* XXX. 13 When wave mechanics is applied to any problem, the first step is to write down an expression for the energy of the system. **1974** *Encycl. Brit. Macropædia* XI. 796/1 The revolutionary development of quantum mechanics (of which wave mechanics and matrix mechanics are specialized partial formulations) occurred with breath-taking rapidity in the years 1925–30.

Hence **wave-me'chanical** *a.*, **-me'chanically** *adv.*
1928 E. SCHRÖDINGER *Four Lect. Wave Mech.* 6 In replacing the ordinary mechanical description by a wave-mechanical description our object is to obtain a theory. **1951** C. N. HINSHELWOOD *Struct. Physical Chem.* vi. 129 The number of solutions of the ψ equation, which correspond to a given value of the permitted energy value *E*, is the expression for the statistical weight in the wave-mechanical formulation. **1971** *Physics Bull.* Jan. 16/2 A molecule is harder to deal with wave-mechanically than either an atom or an atomic crystal.

† **'wavenger.** *Sc.* and *north. Obs.* Forms: 5–6 **vau-,** 6 **wauengeour,** 9 **waff-, whiffinger, waifinger.** [App. f. WAIF *sb.* after *messenger, passenger, scavenger*, etc.]

1. *Sc.* A vagabond. Also *attrib.*
1493 *Sc. Acts Jas. IV* (1814) II. 235/1 To causs idill men vauengeouris to laubour for þair leuing. **1513** DOUGLAS *Æneis* IV. xi. 17 [Shall it be] lefull till a wauengeour strangeir Me and my realm betrump on this maneir. *Ibid.* XII. v. 99 Follow me Quham now ȝon vauengeour, ȝon ilk stranger, Affrays so.

2. *dial.* A stray animal, estray.
1825 BROCKETT *N.C. Gloss, Waifinger*, an estray. *a* **1864** R. B. PEACOCK *Lonsdale Gloss., Waifinger*, stray cattle.

waver ('weɪvə(r)), *sb.*[1] Also 6 **wayver, weaver,** 6–8 **waiver.** [Of obscure origin: the early forms do not favour derivation from WAVE *v.* Possibly f. WAIVE *v.*[1], in the sense 'to leave untouched'.] A young tree left standing when the surrounding wood is felled.
1555 *Anc. Deed C 7700* (P.R.O.), The said Luke shall leave..standynge..all suche wayuers of oke and asshe that be vnder the compace of twelue ynches in thycknesse. **1590** W. WEST *Symbol.* §267 (§406) Except the land and soile of the same woodes and vnderwoodes, and also wayuers called standers of &c. **1595** *Holmesfield Court Rolls* in *Sheffield Gloss.* s.v., That no persone or persons within this manor shall cutt vpp or carry away any of the lorde's woodes..vpon payne of every burden of greene wood vj d. and every weaver xij d. and every burden of dry wood being hedgwood iiij d. **1597** *Ibid.*, Every weaver or poole. **1664** EVELYN *Sylva* xxvii. 71 It is a very ordinary Copse which will not afford three or four Firsts, that is, Bests; fourteen Seconds; twelve Thirds; eight Wavers, &c. according to which proportions the sizes of young Trees in Copsing are to succeed one another. **1768** Waiver [see TILLER *sb.*[3] 2]. **1800** J. TUKE *Agric. N. Riding Yorks.* 186 Leaving at certain distances, when the timber and under-wood are cut down, the thriving young trees, which so left, are very properly called *wavers*, from their being agitated by every breeze. **1888** *Sheffield Gloss.*

waver ('weɪvə(r)), *sb.*[2] [f. WAVE *v.* + -ER[1].]

† **1.** One who vacillates. *Obs.*
1667 WATERHOUS *Fire Lond.* 189 No waver in Judgment, have I, through Gods mercy, ever been.

2. One who waves, or causes to undulate, swing, or flutter.
1835 T. MITCHELL *Aristoph. Acharn.* 1059 *note*, Groupes of tumblers, jugglers, ball-players, and wavers of the torch. **1860** W. G. CLARK in Galton *Vac. Tour.* (1861) 46 The wavers of flags, and the brandishers of daggers. **1869** 'MARK TWAIN' *Innoc. Abr.* xiii. (1872) 91 The..house-tops..burst into a snow storm of waving handkerchiefs, and the wavers of the same mingled their cheers with those of the masses below.

† **3.** A name for the star Fomalhaut in the constellation Piscis Australis. *Obs.*
1556 RECORDE *Cast. Knowl.* IV. 267 [*marg.*] The Wauer.

4. *Printing.* See quots. Also ***waver roller.***
1882 SOUTHWARD *Pract. Print.* 471 Next set in their places the wavers and the inkers. **1888** *Encycl. Brit.* XXIII. 706/1 As the carriage returns, this strip of ink is distributed on the inking table by rollers placed diagonally across the machine. The diagonal position gives them a waving motion; hence they are called *wavers*. **1888** JACOBI *Printers' Vocab.*, *Waver rollers*, rollers which distribute ink on the ink table in a diagonal direction. *Wavers*, short term for 'waver rollers'.

5. An implement for making the hair wavy.
1895 *Army & Navy Stores List* 15 Sept. 180/2 Hair Wavers..Price per box, containing 5 wavers, 0/8½. **1909** *Daily Chron.* 1 Oct. 7/4 These wavers may be left in the slightly dampened hair for an hour or two, and the result will be a soft, natural-looking wave.

waver ('weɪvə(r)), *sb.*[3] [f. WAVER *v.*] The act or condition of wavering.

a. In physical sense, a flutter or trembling.
1826 J. WILSON in *Blackw. Mag.* XX. 90 No a bit butter-flee on its silent waver, meeting the murmur of the straight-forward bee. **1886** GUILLEMARD *Cruise of Marchesa* I. 137 Here and there a little gap revealed a Hobbema-like scene of sunny distance, whose clearness was unbroken by the waver of a single leaf. **1891** 'R. BOLDREWOOD' *Sydney-side Sax.* xii, Sitting square, without the slightest waver or tremble in her saddle. **1918** MERRICK *When Love flies* iv. 44 She sat watching the waver of the candles in the draught.

b. A condition of vacillation or faltering. † ***in a waver*** (*obs.*), ***on*** or ***upon the waver,*** in uncertainty or unsteadiness; inclining now this way, now that.
1519 HORMAN *Vulgaria* 57b, I stande in doubte or in a wauer. *Anceps sum concilii.* **1806** HENRY SIDDONS *Maid, Wife, & Widow* III. 64 His reason was on the waver. *a* **1809** J. PALMER *Like Master* (1811) I. xii. 167 His regret to leave the coppers he touch'd in his present service, and his inclination to embrace the brazier's offer, kept him upon the waver, like an ass between two bundles of hay. **1864** SHERMAN *Let.* 31 Dec. (1894) 241 Not a waver, doubt, or hesitation when I order, and men march to certain death without a murmur if I call on them. **1865** MRS. H. WOOD *Mildred Arkell* xlviii, 'Does she mean to accept him?' asked Travice. 'Well, she's on the waver. She does not dislike him, and she does not particularly like him.'

waver ('weɪvə(r)), *v.* Also 4 **wever,** 4–5 *Sc.* **wayver, wafer,** 4–6 *Sc.* **vaver,** 4–7 *Sc.* **wawer,** 5 **wavere, wavur, wafyr,** 6 **wavor,** *Sc.* **vaifer,** 7 **wavour.** [ME. *waver, wever* = MHG. *waberên*, mod.G. (now dial.) *wabern, webern* to move about, ON. *vafra* to move unsteadily, flicker (cf. *vafrloge* flickering flame), Norw. *vavra* to go to and fro, stagger; a frequentative f. Teut. root **wab-*: see WAVE *v.*
Shoreham's *weverinde* (*c* 1315, sense 5) shows that the word in the south at least is native English (cf. OE. *wæfre* unsteady, also nimble); it is possible that in the north the word may partly represent an adoption of ON. *vafra*, but the supposition is not necessary.]

I. Intransitive.

1. a. To go about or travel at random or without fixed destination; to wander, rove. Also with adv., as *about*.
1375 BARBOUR *Bruce* VII. 41 The sleuth-hund maid stynting thar, And vaueryt [*v.r.* waweryt] lang tyme to and fra. *c* **1375** *Sc. Leg. Saints* xxv. (*Julian*) 287 Waferand fra place to place. *c* **1440** *Alphabet of Tales* 490 þai waxed so pure at þai wavurd aboute here & þer. *c* **1470** HENRY *Wallace* IV. 283 He saw mony rout Off wyld bestis wauerand in wode and playne. **1483** *Cath. Angl.* 411/1 To Wavere Aboute (*v.r.* Wafyr Abowt), *vagari*. **1513** DOUGLAS *Æneis* VI. v. 70 Quha ar vnbereit a hundreth ȝeir man byde, Wauerand and wandrand by this bankis syde. **1599** NASHE *Lenten Stuffe* C 1, There were two Channels..where through the fishermen did wander and wauer vp to Norwitch and diuers parts of Suffolke and Norfolke. **1924** GALSWORTHY *White Monkey* I. viii. 63 Michael watched him down the corridor, saw him waver into the dusky street. **1977** D. FRANCIS *Risk* ii. 20 One of them [*sc.* the two horses in front] wavered up the straight at a widening angle. The other seemed to be stopping second by second... Tapestry scorched past both of them..and won the Gold Cup.

† **b.** To stray *from. Obs.*
1456 SIR G. HAYE *Bk. Knighthood* Wks. (S.T.S.) II. 6 He slepit apon his palfray, and waverit fra his folk out of the hye way. **1599** *Extracts Aberd. Reg.* (1848) II. 204 The said Thomas hes bene accusit of..wavering oftentymes fra his wyff, bairnis, and famelie. **1609** SKENE *Reg. Maj., Quon.*

Attach. x. 78 Gif.. he.. sall sweare that, that beast did waver away from him.

2. To sway to and fro, as if in danger of falling; to reel, stagger, totter. Now *rare* (cf. 5 d, 7).

c **1400** *Destr. Troy* 8266 All in wer for to walt, wayueronde he sote. *c* **1440** *Promp. Parv.* 447/2 Schoggyn, schakyn or waveryn, *vacillo.* **1500–20** DUNBAR *Poems* liii. 10 Bot ay his ane futt did wawer, He stackerit lyk ane strummall awer. **1531** ELYOT *Gov.* I. xi. (1883) I. 95 Oza, for puttyng his hande to the holy shryne that was called *Archa federis*,.. though it were wauerynge and in daunger to fall, yet was he stryken of god. **1691** RAY *Creation* I. (1692) 142 When they [sc. the Fins] are cut off, it [*sc.* the Body of the Fish] wavers to and fro. **1852** MRS. STOWE *Uncle Tom's C.* xxxiii. 298 She was evidently in a condition of great suffering, and Tom often heard her praying, as she wavered and trembled, and seemed about to fall down.

3. a. To swing or wave in the air; to float or flutter.

c **1440** *Promp. Parv.* 518/2 Wawyn, or waueryn, yn a myry totyr, *oscillo.* *c* **1514** BARCLAY *Eclogue* iii, Sometime must thou stoupe unto a rude vilayne Calling him master,.. Although thou would see him waver in a bande. **1548** UDALL *Erasm. Par. Matt.* viii. 18–22 The byrdes fleyng and wauoring in the ayer. **1574** T. HILL *Art Garden.*, *Weather* viii. 72 The kytes playing and wauering about in the aire. **1610** GUILLIM *Heraldry* III. xv. 136 Two Lions came running with their shaggy lockes wauering about their shoulders. **1726–30** THOMSON *Winter* 230 Thro' the hush'd air the whitening shower descends, At first thin-wavering. **1818** SCOTT *Hrt. Midl.* vii, He could discern a figure wavering and struggling as it hung suspended above the heads of the multitude. **1847** TENNYSON *Princess* VI. 64 On their curls From the high tree the blossom wavering fell. **1864** SKEAT *Uhland's Poems* 252 Lo! down waver clustering ringlets Round a soft and gentle face! **1883** *Chamb. Jrnl.* 689 Huge butterflies wavered about the cactus plants.

b. Phr. *to waver with* or *in the wind.* ? *Obs.*

c **1500** *Nut-brown Maid* 74 in Arnolde *Chron.* (1811) 200 Wythout pytee, hanged to bee, and wauer w[t] the wynde. **1523** BERNERS *Froiss.* I. cccxxxiii. 522 With baners and penons waueryng with the wynde. **1526** TINDALE *Matt.* xi. 7 A rede waueringe with the wynde. **1582** N. LICHEFIELD tr. *Castanheda's Conq. E. Ind.* I. lxxviii. 158 After this, hee went up and downe, wauering in the winde, tarryeng for the rest of the shippes. **1725** POPE *Odyss.* XXII. 508 Soon fled the soul impure, and left behind The empty corse to waver with the wind. **1818** SCOTT *Hrt. Midl.* xl, Here many an outlaw.. had wavered in the wind during the wars. **1828** MISS MITFORD *Village, Country Barber* III. 165 A lank, long, stooping figure, which seemed wavering in the wind like a powder-puff.

c. *transf.*

1860 HAWTHORNE *Transform.* xxix, Now tumbling down, down, down, with a long shriek wavering after him, all the way. **1876** MORRIS *Sigurd* II. 141 The wind in his raiment wavered.

†**4.** Of water, waves: To surge. *Obs. rare.*

c **1425** WYNTOUN *Cron.* IV. 1963 As rewaris reythe for rayn wil rysse And wauer mare wiþe wawis woide þan wil a kyndly standande flude.

5. a. Of persons, their sentiments, etc.: To exhibit doubt or indecision; to change or vary; to fluctuate or vacillate (*between*); to falter in resolution or allegiance; to show signs of giving way.

c **1315** SHOREHAM *Poems* I. 424 And þi bi-leaue of ihesu crist His nou al weuerinde. **1375** BARBOUR *Bruce* XII. 185 Mony ane hert sal vaverand [*v.r.* wawerand] be That semyt ere of gret bounte. *c* **1407** LYDG. *Reson & Sens.* 2901 And thus I stood al in a rage With look cast fix in hir visage, Wavering as in a were. *c* **1425** WYNTOUN *Cron.* v. 4318 He was curyousse in his stille,.. Mad in metyr meit his dyte, Litil or noucht neuir þe lesse Wauerande fra þe suythtfastnes. *c* **1440** *Promp. Parv.* 18/2 Waueron yn hert for vnstabylnesse, *muto.* *c* **1440** *Gesta Rom.* xxv. 97 þat he sette fully his hope in god, and not be dul in the feithe, ne wauere in the comavndementes of god. **1526** TINDALE *Jas.* i. 6 But let hym axe in faythe and waver not [**1611** nothing wauering]. **1526** *Pilgr. Perf.* (W. de W. 1531) 223 b, That we his yongest chylden.. sholde not.. wauer in our fayth. **1548** UDALL *Erasm. Par. Matt.* i. 20, 21 Why art thou vexed? why doest thou wauer in & out? **1579** SHAKS. *Lover's Compl.* 97 And nice affections wavering stood in doubt If best were as it was, or best without. **1610** HOLLAND *Camden's Brit.* (1637) 43 They that wavered betweene warre and peace. **1641** MILTON *Ch. Govt.* I. vii. 28 Vertue that wavers is not vertue. **1714** ADDISON *Spect.* No. 585 ¶8 Her Mind continued wavering about twenty Years longer between Shalum and Mishpach. **1849** MACAULAY *Hist. Eng.* v. I. 603 While he was thus wavering between projects equally hopeless. **1856** FROUDE *Hist. Eng.* (1858) I. iv. 355 The allegiance even of the bishops and the secular clergy to Rome had begun to waver. **1874** GREEN *Short Hist.* iv. §2. 172 Only on one occasion.. did the burgesses waver from their general support of the Crown. **1883** FROUDE *Short Stud.* IV. I. xi. 131 Many people had begun to waver in their allegiance. **1884** M. CREIGHTON *Hist. Ess.* viii. (1902) 239 For a time opinions wavered which boundary to choose.

†**b.** Phr. *to waver as, like, with the wind.* Cf. 3 b.

c **1480** HENRYSON *Fox, Wolf & Cadger* 218 (Harl.) With that þe cadger, wauering as the wind, Come rydand on the laid. *a* **1548** HALL *Chron., Edw. V* 13 Not common people onely, which wauer with the wynde, but wyse menne also. **1565** B. GOOGE tr. *Palingenius' Zodiac* VII. A a vj b, And so corrupt the mindes Of rude vnskilfull common sort, that wauer lyke the wyndes. *a* **1825** *Child Noryce* i. in Child *Ballads* II. 266 Child Noryce is a clever young man, He wavers wi the wind.

†**c.** To hesitate *to* (do something). *Obs. rare.*

1644 MILTON *Divorce* II. xv. 61, I shall not much waver to affirm, that [etc.].

d. Of a combatant, body of troops, line of battle: To become unsteady, flinch, give way.

1831 JAMES *Phil. Augustus* xlii, He wavered not a step; but, still striding over the body of the king,.. maintained his ground. **1860** FROUDE *Hist. Eng.* V. xxvi. 213 The sustained fire of the Lanzknechts threw their dense and unorganized masses into rapid confusion. As they wavered, Warwick's horse were in the midst of them. **1915** J. BUCHAN *Hist. War* IV. xxvi. 75 The line wavered and broke.

6. Of things (or a person as an unconscious agent): To change, vary, fluctuate.

1490 CAXTON *Eneydos* 2 We englysshe men ben borne vnder the domynacyon of the mone, whiche is neuer stedfaste, but euer wauerynge. *a* **1548** HALL *Chron., Hen. VI* 116 Thus the Englishe affaires.. within the realme began to wauer, and waxe variable. **1560** DAUS tr. *Sleidane's Comm.* 91 b, To suffer this gere to hange waueringe [L. *ut rem ita fluctuare sinat*]. **1565** COOPER *Thesaurus* s.v. *Nuto*, Victorie wauereth or flitteth betweene both vncertaynly. **1837** DICKENS *Pickw.* xxxviii, During the whole space of time just mentioned, Mr. Benjamin Allen had been wavering between intoxication partial and intoxication complete. **1859** DICKENS etc. *Haunted Ho.* iii. 14/1 He had.. a waistcoat that wavered in hue between a sunny buff and a stony drab. **1922** *19th Cent.* Apr. 681 Among all Arabs succession is hereditary, but it wavers between the eldest son and the eldest male member of the family.

7. Of the voice, the eye, etc. (or a person with reference to these): To become unsteady; to shake, tremble, falter (through emotion or bodily weakness). †Of the wits: To become confused, reel.

1621 FLETCHER *Pilgr.* III. iii, Keep my wits Heaven, I feel 'em wavering, O God my head. **1840** DICKENS *Old C. Shop* xlv, 'No,' replied the old man, wavering in his voice, no less than in his manner. **1850** SUSAN WARNER *Wide World* xv, Miss Fortune's conscience must have troubled her a little, for her eye wavered uneasily. **1876** MISS BROUGHTON *Joan* I. ix, Her voice wavers and breaks. The tears well up into her eyes. **1883** A. K. GREEN *X. Y. Z.* iv. 65 His eye did not waver from its steady solemn look toward the door. **1886** KIPLING *Departm. Ditties* etc. (1888) 45 The white hands wavered —the bright head drooped.

8. Of light, shade, objects seen unsteadily or through a haze: To flicker, quiver.

1664 BOYLE *Exper. Colours* III. xiv. 227, I took.. two Triangular Glasses, and one of them being kept fixt in the same Posture, that the Iris it projected on the Floor might not Waver. **1842** TENNYSON *Gardener's Dau.* 129 The shadow of the flowers.. wavering Lovingly lower, trembled on her waist.. and still went wavering down. **1842** —— *Will Water-proof* 38 The gas-light wavers dimmer. **1849** CUPPLES *Green Hand* xvii. (1856) 173 Tall palms and cocoas —their stems wavering in the thin haze. **1914** *Blackw. Mag.* Oct. 491/2 A little gleam wavered ahead on my right.

fig. **1837** WHEWELL *Hist. Induct. Sci.* IV. i. I. 247 It may serve to illustrate.. the extent to which, under the Roman empire, men's notions of mechanical relations became faint, wavered, and disappeared, if we observe the change which took place in architecture.

II. Transitive.

†**9.** *causal.* To cause to waver; to wave to and fro; to set in waving or fluttering motion; to render unsteady or unsteadfast. *Obs.*

c **1425** WYNTOUN *Cron.* III. 798 þus in seige a sote to se, Or do a dowde in dignyte, Sal ger standande statis stauer, And wil bathe wit and worschep wauer. *c* **1440** *Promp. Parv.* 518/2 Waueron, or mevyn or steryn, *agito.* **1456** SIR G. HAYE *Law of Arms* (S.T.S.) 227 Nocht gaynstandand that he be wauerit [*printed* wanerit] in his wit. **1561** in Tytler *Hist. Scot.* (1864) III. 148 Seeing he.. showed himself so constant in religion, that neither the fear of his soueireign's indignation could wauer him, nor great promises win him. **1583** in Hakluyt *Voy.* (1589) 683 Item, if the Admirall shall happen to hull in the night: then to make a wauering light ouer his other light, wauering the light vpon a pole. **1594** NASHE *Unfort. Trav.* E 2 b, A third wauerd and wagled his head, like a proud horse playing with his bridle. **1812** *Courier* in *Examiner* 24 Aug. 540/1 Shot, shells, grape,.. could not.. waver the line of the.. infantry.

†**10.** To vacillate under, falter in resistance to. *Obs. rare*[−1].

1596 DRAYTON *Mortimer.* B 4 b, Th'vnconstant Barrons, wauering euery houre, The fierce encounter of this raging tyde.

waver, var. WAIVER.

waverer ('weɪvərə(r)). [f. WAVER *v.* + -ER[1].] One who wavers; one who is undecided or vacillates in opinion or choice; one who falters in allegiance or hesitates to embrace a particular party or cause.

1592 SHAKS. *Rom. & Jul.* II. iii. 89 But come young wauerer, come goe with me. **1640** tr. *Verdere's Rom. of Rom.* I. xxviii. 134, I went to Cloria, unto whom I discovered the desires of my waverer [orig. (1626) 744 *les desseins de cet inconstant*]. **1850** GROTE *Greece* II. lx. (1862) V. 259 The waverers thought it time to declare themselves. **1855** MACAULAY *Hist. Eng.* xiii. III. 271 More than one waverer was kept steady by being assured in confident terms that a speedy restoration was inevitable. **1885** *Manch. Guard.* 20 July 5/5 A section of waverers who have inclined lately to the Tory side.

b. *Hist.* The name given to a section of Peers who were willing to make terms with the Reform government of 1832 rather than wreck the Upper House.

1832 GREVILLE *Mem.* 27 Mar. (1874) II. 273, I have no doubt that all the ultras will be deeply mortified at the moderation of Lord Grey and of the Duke of Wellington, and at the success *so far* of 'the Waverers'. **1886** KEBBEL *Hist. Toryism* iv. 210 The second reading of the Bill had been carried in the Lords.., with the help of the well-known 'Waverers', led by Lords Harrowby and Wharncliffe.

wavering ('weɪvərɪŋ), *vbl. sb.* [-ING[1].] The action of the verb WAVER, in various senses.

1375 BARBOUR *Bruce* VI. 584 The hund alwais followit the kyng, And changit nocht for na parting, Bot ay followit the kyngis tras, But vaueryng, as he passit was. ? *a* **1400** *Morte Arth.* 2224, I watte be thi wauerynge, thow willnez aftyre sorowe. **1548** UDALL *Erasm. Par. Luke* vi. 12–16 Whan the people wer in a waueryng and mammeryng what he was. **1593** NASHE *Christ's T.* E 3 b, Had you rested them on the true Rocke, they had beene ruine-proofe; but now the raine wil rough-enter through the crannies of theyr wauering. **1605** BACON *Adv. Learn.* II. §8. 13 Massiue bodies.. haue certaine trepidations and wauerings before they fixe and settle. *a* **1768** SECKER *Serm.* (1770) IV. 2 Why this perpetual Wavering and Fluctuation, about the first thing, that you ought to fix. **1816** JANE AUSTEN *Emma* xxii, Had there been no pain to her friend, or reproach to herself, in the waverings of Harriet's mind, Emma would have been amused by its variations. **1828–41** TYTLER *Hist. Scot.* (1864) I. 120 The wavering of the English lines was now discernible by the Scottish soldiers. **1831** ALFORD in *Life* (1873) 68 Quick waverings about of bands of light such as take place in the Polar Auroras. **1868** E. EDWARDS *Ralegh* I. xx. 443 The King's wavering between a course of clemency and one of rigour.

'**wavering**, *ppl. a.* [f. WAVER *v.* + -ING[2].]

†**1.** Wandering, vagrant. *Obs.*

1375 BARBOUR *Bruce* VII. 112 Thai saw on syde thre men cumand, Lik to licht men and vauerand. **1607** *N. Riding Rec., Q. Sess. Rec.* (1884) I. 91 Tho. Best of Wath, a wavering person, [presented] for three assaults on the Constable of Melmerby.

2. Tottering, shaking, faltering, reeling.

c **1400** *Destr. Troy* 13546 And wayuerand, weike, [I] wan to the lond. **1569** ROEST tr. *J. van der Noot's Theat. Worldlings* 76 Theyr proude titles haue no sure foundation, but are buylded only vppon the waueryng sandes of doubtefulnesse and falshode. **1816** BYRON *Siege of Corinth* xxix, The portal wavering grows, and weak! **1839** KINNEAR *Cairo, Petra & Damascus* iii. (1841) 95 A dim shadowy figure on a dromedary appeared, moving at a wavering and uncertain pace through the sand drift. **1845–7** LONGF. *Ev.* I. v. 127 And like the day of doom it seemed to her wavering senses. **1896** H. G. WELLS *Wheels of Chance* i, The nervous clutch of the wavering rider.

3. Fluttering, floating, waving, surging.

c **1425** WYNTOUN *Cron.* v. 845 Wauerande [*v.r.* welterand] wawis. *c* **1470** *Golagros & Gaw.* 290 As leif of the lynd.. That welteris doun with the wynd, sa wauerand it is. **1534** BERNERS *Gold Bk. M. Aurel.* (1546) P viii b, Their waueryng boughes ar aduentured in the wynde. **1660** BOYLE *New Exper. Spring of Air* xxiv. 193 These bubbles.. ascended with a wavering or wrigling motion. **1662** DRYDEN *Astræa Redux* 225 The wavering Streamers, Flags, and Standart out. **1703** POPE *Thebais* I. 266 As when two winds with rival force contend, This way and that, the wav'ring sails they bend. **1884** W. C. SMITH *Kildrostan* I. i. 42 Broken prismic lights are woven On the thin veils of wavering cloud.

4. Vacillating, undecided, inconstant; faltering in resolution or allegiance.

c **1315** [see WAVER *v.* 5]. **1375** BARBOUR *Bruce* XII. 185 Mony ane hert sall vaverand be That semyt ere of gret bounte. *c* **1440** *Alphabet of Tales* 244 He went vnto his prayers, & stude with a waveryng ee and a waveryng mynde. *a* **1548** HALL *Chron., Hen. IV* (1550) 16 b, This realm.. inuaded and infested with the frantike waueryng Welshemen. **1591** SHAKS. *1 Hen. VI*, IV. i. 138 Remember where we are, In France, amongst a fickle wauering Nation. **1598** R. BERNARD tr. *Terence, Andria* I. v. (1607) 27 Hee is as wauering as a wether-cocke. **1642** J. TAYLOR (Water P.) *Henry Walker* A 3 b, To Allienate or estrange the hearts of wavering Subjects from their allegiance. *c* **1660** in *Verney Mem.* (1907) II. 227 His mind is so wavouring that I think hee will setill to nothing. **1743** LD. HARDWICKE in G. Harris *Life* (1847) II. 37 If our allies are timorous and wavering, it is necessary to encourage them by vigorous measures. **1862** SIR C. DILKE *Let.* 7 Nov. *Life* (1917) I. 32 How wavering and shortsighted the policy of England in Turco-Grecian matters has been of late! *a* **1886** STUBBS *Germany in E. Middle Ages* (1908) 167 The wavering princes returned to their allegiance.

b. *absol.* (with *the*).

1603 KNOLLES *Hist. Turks* (1638) 380 Carambey.. incouraged the wauering, and restored the battel. **1780** *Mirror* No. 94 That I might be able.. to alarm the inconsiderate, to confirm the wavering. **1891** FARRAR *Darkn. & Dawn* lv, The most wavering could not but be confirmed by his calm wisdom.

c. *Comb.*

1526 TINDALE *Jas.* i. 8 A waveryng mynded man is vnstable in all his wayes. **1658** J. SPENCER *Things New & Old* 179 How to prevent wavering-mindedness.

5. Of fortune, affairs, etc.: Variable, mutable. †Of a person: Having a doubtful or uncertain title.

c **1425** WYNTOUN *Cron.* lxv. 1838 (Wemyss) Few personis lynealye, Sum vther few collateralye, As cours maid and qualite Airis waverand for to be. **1500–20** DUNBAR *Poems* lxvi. 1 This waverand warldis wretchidness. *a* **1548** HALL *Chron., Hen. VI* 148 b, Suche is worldly vnstablenes, and so waueryng is false flatteryng fortune. **1660** MILTON *Free Commw.* Wks. 1851 V. 438 In this wavering condition of our Affairs.

6. Changing in intensity, now strong, now faint; flickering, fitful, intermittent; tremulous, unsteady; tending to fade or become dim.

c **1470** HENRY *Wallace* IV. 340 Now wauerand wind, now weit. **1513** DOUGLAS *Æneis* II. xii. 64 Or mast liklie a waverand sweving or dreyme [L. *volucrique simillima somno*]. *c* **1622** ROWLEY *Birth of Merlin* III. vi. 17 The incertain Changes of a wavering Skie. **1688** HOLME *Armoury* III. xvi. (Roxb.) 62/2 It is a kind of wavering fluteing sound. **1815** SCOTT *Guy M.* xlviii, The fire.. now rose high into the air, a wavering column of brilliant light. **1842** J. WILSON *Chr. North* (1857) I. 152 His sight is dim and wavering. **1866** MISS BRADDON *Lady's Mile* i, Making a little spot of crimson amongst the wavering shadows of the trees. **1868** MORRIS *Earthly Par.* I. I. 393 Till these things shall seem The wavering memory of a lovely dream. **1890** *Retrospect Med.* CII. 370 It is heard as a wavering or tremolo note.

Hence '**waveringly** *adv.*, '**waveringness**.

c1400 *Sc. Trojan War* II. 1547 He has chapit, & so long past Throw þe wyld sees waverandly [*v.r.* wauerandly]. **1549** COVERDALE etc. *Erasm. Par. 1 Pet.* v. 6–14 Loke not waueringly about you, haue no distrust, be not afrayed. *a***1603** T. CARTWRIGHT *Confut. Rhem. N.T.* (1618) 27 How doubtfully and waueringly Augustine iudged of this case. **1614** J. ROBINSON *Relig. Commun.* 124 Men become perfit, and growen past that childish waveringnes. **1698** ATTERBURY *Serm.* (1734) II. 311 The Uncertainty and Waveringness of this [belief]. **1820** *Blackw. Mag.* VII. 176 The candles glimmer somewhat waveringly. **1863** GEO. ELIOT *Romola* xxi, His hearers more or less waveringly believed, that he had a mission like that of the Hebrew prophets. **1885** BRIDGES *Nero* II. ii, Speak nothing waveringly.

wavery ('weɪvərɪ), *a.* [f. WAVER *v.* or *sb.* + -Y[1].] Characterized by wavering or fluttering; tremulous, unsteady.

1820 *Blackw. Mag.* VI. 679 Across the silence seem to go With dream-like motion, wavery, slow,.. The friends we loved long long ago! **1883** MRS. R. T. RITCHIE *Bk. Sibyls* i. 2 Some old letters covered with a wavery writing. **1897** F. THOMPSON *New Poems* 184 All her wavering hair..Lapsing like music, wavery as water, Slid to her waist. **1913** MRS. STRATTON-PORTER *Laddie* iv. (1917) 79 Making his voice all wavery and tremulous he began reciting from 'Lochiel's Warning' in tones of agonized pleading.

Waves (weɪvz), *sb. pl. U.S.* [See quot. 1972.] The women's section of the United States Naval Reserve, established in 1942. In *sing.*, a member of this Reserve, or, since 1948, a woman serving in the U.S. Navy. Cf. WREN[2].

1942 *Chicago Tribune* 9 Aug. I. 6/1 The navy's new women's reserve corps—the Waves—will learn to drill, salute, wear the regular insignia of the service..and they will receive..detailed instructions in navy customs. **1943** N. W. ROSS *Waves* 1 The initials of the WAVES stand for the words 'Women Accepted for Voluntary Emergency Service'. *Ibid.* 150 Orders tell the WAVE where she is to go next. **1972** J. B. HANCOCK *Lady in Navy* 61 In 1942, when the planning for the Women's Reserve began, the question of a short and catchy name was posed... Miss [Elizabeth] Reynard addressed herself to the problem... 'I realized that there were two letters which had to be in it: W for women and V for volunteer... So I played with those two letters and the idea of the sea and finally came up with "Women Appointed for Volunteer Emergency Service"—WAVES.' (Later, when it was realized that *Appointed* applied only to officers, *Accepted* was the word substituted.) **1977** *Time* 10 Jan. 43/3 Mainbocher's creations graced Wallis Warfield Simpson at her marriage to the Duke of Windsor, as well as millions of WAVES and Girl Scouts, whose uniforms he fashioned.

†'**wavesch**, *v. Obs. rare.* [Extended form of WAIVE *v.*[1]: see -ISH[2].] *trans.* To put aside.

*a***1400–50** *Wars Alex.* (Dubl.) 822 Then fyndes he philip ..Had weddit hym ane oþer wife & wauesched [*Ashm.* wayfid] hys moder.

waveson ('weɪvsən). *Maritime Law.* [App. formed after AF. *floteson* FLOTSAM: perh. originally f. WAIVE *v.*[1], but associated with WAVE *sb.*] (See quot. 1701.) Also *fig.*

1526 in Kennett *Cowel's Interpr.* (1701) s.v., Waveson, Flotteson, Lagason & Wrecks & Regalia videl. Magnas pisces captas, &c. **1701** KENNETT *ibid.*, *Waveson*, such Goods as after Shipwreck do appear swimming on the waves. [Whence **1706** in PHILLIPS: and in later Dicts.] **1894** E. P. EVANS in *Pop. Sci. Monthly* XLIV. 299 Persons of unknown origin were treated as waifs (*épaves*), the mere flotson and waveson on the drifting tide of humanity.

wavey ('weɪvɪ), *Pl.* **waveys, wavies.** [See WAWA.] A northern (American) goose of the genus *Chen*, esp. the common wavey, *C. hyperboreus*. Blue wavey, *C. cærulescens*. Horned wavey, *C. rossi*.

1795 S. HEARNE *Journ. North. Ocean* 329 The laughing goose, wavey, (or white goose,) gulls, [etc.]. *Ibid.* 442 Horned Wavey. *Ibid.*, I have seen them in as large flocks as the Common Wavey, or Snow Goose. **1831** SWAINSON & RICHARDSON *Fauna Bor.-Amer.* II. 467 Anser hyperboreus. .. Snow Goose... Wavey. Hudson's Bay Residents. **1892** W. PIKE *Barren Ground N. Canada* 161 Here the snow geese, or white 'wavies' were resting in thousands.

wavey, obs. variant of WAVY *a.*

wavicle ('weɪvɪk(ə)l). *Physics.* [Blend of WAVE *sb.* and PARTICLE *sb.*] An entity having characteristic properties of both waves and particles.

1928 A. S. EDDINGTON *Nature Physical World* x. 201 We can scarcely describe such an entity as a wave or as a particle; perhaps as a compromise we had better call it a 'wavicle.' **1934** *Times Lit. Suppl.* 11 Jan. 20/3 It [*sc.* X-ray diffraction] has revolutionized conceptions of the electron, which has had to be looked upon as something intermediate between a corpuscle and a packet of waves—a 'wavicle' in fact. **1962** J. NEEDHAM *Sci. & Civilisation in China* IV. I. 135 Old Chinese philosophers..thought of *chhi* as something between what we should call matter in a rarefied gaseous state on one hand, and radiant energy on the other. Though all our assured knowledge gained by experiment makes us infinitely richer than they, is the concept of 'wavicles' in modern physical theory so much more penetrating? **1976** *New Scientist* 26 Aug. 461/4 To think that a particle or wavicle or whatever, is small for us, therefore it is small for the Universe, is to be biased or homo-centred.

wavily, waviness: see WAVY *a.*

waving ('weɪvɪŋ), *vbl. sb.* [f. WAVE *v.* + -ING[1].] The action of the verb.

†**1.** The action of changing capriciously; vacillation, wavering, *Obs.*

*a***1628** F. GREVILLE *Life of Sidney* (1652) 223 She preserved her Religion without waving. **1665** E. HOPKINS *Serm. Vanity* (1685) 88 Such is the waving and fluctuation of all things here below.

2. a. Movement (of water, the sea) in waves; undulatory surface-movement (of a forest, crop, etc.).

1571 GOLDING *Calvin on Ps.* lxii. 6. 235 Like as if a soft gale stir yᵉ sea, so as the waves ryse not with great rage, and yit there is some waving. **1714** ADDISON *Spect.* No. 585 ¶2, What tho' I am delighted with the Wavings of thy Forests. **1820** SOUTHEY *Wesley* I. 80 Neither the waving of the sea, nor the motion of the ship, could take away the refreshing sleep which God gave them. **1853** DICKENS *Bleak Ho.* xviii, The waving of the corn.

†**b.** Undulating play of colour. *Obs.*

1662 MERRETT tr. *Neri's Art of Glass* II. xxxvii. 61 Hardly would you believe the beauty, the toyes and wavings of divers colours.

3. Undulation in form.

1789 J. WILLIAMS *Min. Kingd.* I. 103 This is what I call the waving of the strata.

4. Motion to and fro (of something having a free end).

1751 J. HARRIS *Hermes* III. iii. (1765) 336 Sound and Motion..such as the Murmurs and Wavings of a Tree during a storm. **1828–41** TYTLER *Hist. Scot.* (1864) I. 151 The gleam of arms, and the waving of the pennons of an encamped army. **1883** ABP. BENSON in A. C. Benson *Life* (1899) II. i. 15 Beech trees and cedars standing as still as possible in it [*sc.* the soft rain] with such gentle slow wavings as to make the most of it.

5. a. The action or an act of moving (the hand or something held in the hand, the wings, etc.) to and fro.

1611 BIBLE *Lev.* xiv. 21 Hee shall take one lambe for a trespasse offring to be waued [*marg.* for a wauing.] **1612** PARKES *Curtain-Drawer* 47 Each Play-house aduanceth his flagge in the aire, whither quickly at the waving thereof, are summoned whole troopes of men, women and children. **1657** J. TRAPP *Comm., Ps.* lxxx. 7 As the bird by much waving gathereth wind under the wing, and mounteth higher. **1711** ADDISON *Spect.* No. 159 ¶3 He beckoned to me, and by the waving of his Hand directed me to approach the Place where he sat. **1784** tr. *Beckfords Vathek* 88 The waving of fans was heard. **1837** DICKENS *Pickw.* xxxiii, The waving of handkerchiefs was renewed. **1859** TENNYSON *Guinevere* 579 She..in the darkness o'er her fallen head, Perceived the waving of his hands that blest.

b. A signal or direction given by waving the hand, a flag, or the like. *Obs.*

1563 P. WHITEHORNE *Onosandro Platon.* 87 The commaundements, wauinges, and signes, ought likewyse first to be geuen to the heads and leaders of men.

6. Comb.: **waving-base**, an observation terrace at an airport from which members of the public may watch the aircraft and wave to the travellers; †**waving-engine**, a machine for cutting waved indentations on wood.

1678 MOXON *Mech. Exerc.* vi. 103 Of the Waving Engine. **1688** HOLME *Armoury* III. 354/2 The Waving Engine..is a thing wherewith Waved Work is generally made upon small Frames for Pictures and Looking Glasses. **1954** *Archit. Rev.* CXV. 24 Opening off this is a roof-garden 'waving-base' from which passengers' friends can watch the departure of aircraft. **1958** [see *jet age* s.v. JET *sb.*[3] 11]. **1965** *New Statesman* 20 Aug. 261/2 Even at dreary old Heathrow you can get out on to one of the waving-bases..for free.

waving ('weɪvɪŋ), *ppl. a.* [f. WAVE *v.* + -ING[2].] That waves.

1. Of water, the sea: That rises in waves; full of waves, billowy. Also of the shore (see quot. 1591).

1552 HULOET, Wauynge lyke water, *fluctuosus.* *a***1586** SIDNEY *Arcadia* III. xi. §8 (1912) 416 As when the Sunne shines upon a waving water. **1591** SYLVESTER *Du Bartas* I. ii. 230 The subtill race Of roving Polypes; who (to rob more) Transform them hourly on the waving shore [Fr. *l'ondeux rivage*]. **1717** ADDISON tr. *Ovid's Met.* II. *Phaeton* 9 A waving sea th' inferiour earth embrac'd. **1835** R. NICOLL *Poems* (1842) 81 Noo Scotland's cliffs sae dear to me Aneath the wavin' waters fa'.

b. *transf.* of things, esp. of a crop, forest, etc.: Agitated or ruffled on the surface like the waves of the sea.

1585 HIGINS *Junius' Nomencl.* 156/2 *Vestis vndans*,..a wauing garment that ruffleth in going, specially when the bodye is moued or shaken. **1676** DRYDEN *Aurengz.* I. 4 The Vale an Iron-Harvest seems to yield Of thick-sprung Lances in a waving Field. **1798** W. L. BOWLES *Poems. St. Michael's Mt.* 43 Mountain, no pomp of waving woods hast thou. **1846** DICKENS *Battle of Life* i. 1 The waving grass was green. **1872** BLACK *Adv. Phaeton* xxxi, A country rich with waving fields of grain.

†**2.** Vacillating, wavering. *Obs.*

1611 SPEED *Hist. Gt. Brit.* IX. viii. §29. 493/1 Their might ..depends of the wauing humors, and wils of those inferiour vassels, of whom they thinke themselues vnresistable Commaunders. *a***1625** LD. BROOKE *Let. to Hon. Lady* iv. Wks. (1633) 282 His hollow, and wauing minde.

3. That moves to and fro at its free end by the impulse of the wind or breeze.

1591 SHAKS. *1 Hen. VI*, I. vi. 1 Aduance our wauing Colours on the Walls. **1596** —— *Tam. Shr.* Induct. ii. 55 Euen as the wauing sedges play with winde. **1676** DRYDEN *Aurengz.* v. 78 The waving Arms of Aureng-Zebe appear'd, Display'd with your Morat's. **1697** —— *Æneis* VII. 869 With Joy they view the waving Ensigns fly. **1767** SIR W. JONES *Seven Fountains* Poems (1777) 33 The crimson streamer's waving pride. **1829** MRS. HEMANS *Casabianca* 22 Upon his brow he felt their breath, And in his waving hair. **1842** DICKENS *Amer. Notes* v, A forest of ships' masts, cheery with flapping sails and waving flags.

4. Undulating in form or outline.

1604 E. G[RIMSTONE] *D'Acosta's Hist. Indies* v. ix. 352 An azured staffe, cutte in fashion of a waving snake. **1753** HOGARTH *Anal. Beauty* vii. 38 The waving line, which is a line more productive of beauty than any of the former. **1810** SOUTHEY *Kehama* I. ii, The fragrant smoke..hangeth visible on high, A dark and waving canopy. **1848** THACKERAY *Van. Fair* xliv, He was a fine open-faced boy, with blue eyes and waving flaxen hair. **1870** HOOKER *Stud. Flora* 462 Asplenium Filix-fœmina..Frond 1–5 ft., bright green, flaccid, waving. **1899** *Allbutt's Syst. Med.* VIII. 553 A single waving or cyclical line results.

5. Of sound: Undulating in tone.

1876 HILES *Catech. Organ* ix. (1878) 62 *Unda Maris*..a stop with two pipes, one of which is tuned a little higher than the other, producing a waving kind of tone.

b. quasi-*sb.* (See quot.)

1876 HILES *Catech. Organ* iii. (1878) 21 *Waving*, is a lighter species of tremulant, for the more delicate stops.

6. Of wings: Moving rhythmically in flight.

1735 SOMERVILLE *Chase* I. 236 Th' industrious Beagle twists his waving Tail. **1795** W. BLAKE *Song of Los* II. 34 And his shudd'ring waving wings Went enormous above the red flames. **1820** SHELLEY *Prometh. Unb.* III. iii. 145 And it circles round, Like the soft waving wings of noonday dreams. **1896** CONAN DOYLE *Rodney Stone* viii, I..saw the gliding lines of windows with staring faces and waving handkerchiefs.

Hence '**wavingly** *adv.*

1750 G. HUGHES *Barbados* 108 The extremities of the higher branches bend wavingly downwards. **1843** *Blackw. Mag.* LIII. 573 The sea below gleams wavingly. **1882** W. JAMES in *Amer. Ann. Deaf & Dumb* (1883) 108 Moving the hand wavingly across the forehead.

†'**wavous,** *a. Obs. rare*[−1]. [f. WAVE *sb.* + -OUS.] Full of waves.

1581 T. NEWTON *Seneca's Thebais* I. 43 b, Where is the surging wauous Sea?

†'**wavure.** *Obs.* Erroneous var. WAIVER.

1847–64 WEBSTER (citing *R. Peel*), *Wavure*, the act of waving or putting off.

wavy ('weɪvɪ), *a.* (and *sb.*) Also 8 *Sc.* **wavey.** [f. WAVE *sb.* or *v.* + -Y.] **A.** *adj.*

1. a. Full of waves, abounding in waves, billowy.

1593 NASHE *Christ's T.* H 3 b, The waters..putting all theyr wauy shoulders together, bare the whole shole of them [*sc.* the dead carcases] before them. **1685** DRYDEN tr. *Lucretius* I. 10 For thee the Ocean smiles, and smooths her wavy breast. **1712** BROOME *Iliad* xv. III. 208 They.. Travers'd the Mountains, and the Wavy Main. **1816** J. N. BREWER *Beauties Eng. & Wales* X. IV. 28 *note*, In this fine and bold reach the waters of the Thames are more subject to wavy roughness, than in any other part west of the ancient bridge of London. **1887** MORRIS *Odyss.* XI. 253 Then under the wavy deep he dived adown once more.

b. *poet.* Pertaining to waves of the sea.

1725 POPE *Odyss.* XII. 256 Strain ev'ry nerve, and bid the vessel fly. If from yon justling rocks and wavy war Jove safety grants; he grants it to your care.

2. *transf.* **a.** Said of the air, clouds, etc.

c**1586** C'TESS PEMBROKE *Ps.* LXVIII. iv, [The dove] That glides with feathered oare through wavy sky. **1619** BP. J. WILLIAMS *Serm. Apparell* (1620) 5 The wavie Curtaines of the Ayre about us. **1794–6** COLERIDGE *Relig. Musings* 245 Then o'er the wild and wavy chaos rush And tame the outrageous mass. **1844** KINGLAKE *Eothen* xvii, The fair, wavy cloud that fled in the morning.

b. *Path.* ***wavy breathing, respiration***: respiration in which the inspiratory, and sometimes the expiratory, sounds are not continuous but broken into two or more separate parts.

1898 *Allbutt's Syst. Med.* V. 203 Jerky, interrupted, or wavy breathing. **1913** DORLAND *Med. Dict.* (ed. 7) s.v. *Respiration, Wavy respiration.*

3. *fig.* Fluctuating, wavering, changing.

1795 COLERIDGE *Friend* I. xvi. (1863) II. 20 When the public feelings are wavy and tumultuous, artful demagogues may create this opinion. c**1825** BEDDOES *Poems, Sacrif. self-compensated*, Weighing well man's frail and perilous tenure Of all good in the restless wavy world.

4. a. Moving to and fro or up and down with a sinuous, wave-like motion.

1700 PRIOR *Carmen Sec.* xxvi, Let her glad Vallies smile with wavy Corn. **1708** J. PHILIPS *Cyder* I. 61 Where full-ear'd Sheaves of Rye Grow wavy on the Tilth. **1816** KEATS *'I stood Tip-toe'* 73 Where swarms of minnows show their little heads, Staying their wavy bodies 'gainst the streams. **1830** TENNYSON *Dying Swan* 38 The wavy swell of the soughing reeds. **1884** *Manch. Exam.* 30 Sept. 5/7 This rolling sea of wavy grass.

b. Of movements: Taking place in undulating curves, sinuous.

1836 *Blackw. Mag.* XXXIX. 439 [She] spread out her white canvass to the freshening breeze, while winging her wavy way over the blue Atlantic. **1856** KANE *Arctic Expl.* I. xxxi. 421 An active wavy movement [of the Aurora], dissipating itself into barely-perceptible cirrhus. **1859** JEPHSON *Brittany* xii. 201 Representing the serpent's teeth, or his wavy motion, or his circular figure.

5. Of ground, the surface of the country: Rising and falling gently in a succession of rounded heights and hollows.

1774 GOLDSM. *Nat. Hist.* I. 143 The lofty mountains of the other class have a very different aspect. At a distance their tops are seen, in wavy ridges, of the very colour of the clouds. **1789** J. WILLIAMS *Min. Kingd.* I. 114 A wavy country, which gently swells into broad ridges. **1891** HUXLEY in L. Huxley *Life & Lett.* (1900) II. 285 A fine wavy chalk down with 'cwms' and soft turfy ridges.

6. a. Forming an undulating line or a series of wave-like curves. Also, having an undulating margin.

a **1701** MAUNDRELL *Journ. Jerus.* (1707) 6 The sides of this Fissure are firm and solid Rock, perpendicular and smooth, only seeming to lie in a wavy form all down, as it were to comply with the motion of the Water. **1725** POPE *Odyss.* IV. 202 Such wavy ringlets o'er his shoulders flow. **1726** LEONI *Alberti's Archit.* I. 47 The Wall..must be..exactly even.., so as not in any part to swell out or sink in, or to be wavy. **1738** LOGAN in Rigaud *Corr. Sci. Men* (1841) I. 339 A straight rod or line, viewed at some little distance through the wavy glass of a window. **1839** URE *Dict. Arts* etc. 385 If these [Damascus bars] be drawn in length, the veins will be longitudinal;..if they be made wavy in the two directions, undulated veins will be produced like those in the oriental damascus. **1846** LANDOR *Imag. Conv.*, *Landor, Engl. Visitor, & Florentine* Wks. I. 340/2 Byron dealt chiefly in felt and furbelow, wavy Damascus daggers, and pocket pistols studded with paste. **1858** G. MACDONALD *Phantastes* i. (1878) 10 Her dark hair flowed behind, wavy but uncurled. **1882** CAULFEILD & SAWARD *Dict. Needlework* 195 *Wavy Stitch*, a raised Couching. **1888** JACOBI *Printers' Vocab.*, *Wavy rule*, brass rule made with an undulating face.

b. *Bot.* and *Zool.* Of marks, margins, etc.: Undulate, sinuate; having undulate or sinuate markings.

1832 G. RENNIE *Consp. Butterfl. & Moths* 147 Between these streaks and the hinder margin a third streak wavy, brown, terminated by a paler colour. **1857** A. GRAY *1st Less. Bot.* (1866) 62 Leaves are said to be..*Repand, undulate*, or *wavy*, when the margin of the leaf forms a wavy line, bending slightly inwards and outwards in succession. **1859** ANNE PRATT *Brit. Grasses* 74 *Aira flexuosa* (Wavy Hair-grass). *Ibid.* 92 *Poa laxa* (Wavy Meadow-grass). **1866** *Treas. Bot.*

c. *Her.* = UNDEE. ***barry wavy***, of the field: Divided into waving bands of generally horizontal direction.

1562 LEGH *Armory* 134 b, He beareth party per crosse wauey Sable, and Argent. **1610** GUILLIM *Heraldry* II. v. (1632) 69 He beareth, Argent, a Bend, Wauey, Sable... This is termed *wauey*, or *waued*, in respect it beareth a Representation of the Swelling Waue or Billowe of the Sea. **1722** A. NISBET *Syst. Her.* I. vi. 22 *Wavey* or *Waved*, is said of a Line or Lines that are formed after the Waves of the Sea, as parted *per Fess Wavey* in the Arms of Drummond of Concraig, and the Lines which form the *Barrs waved* in the Arms of the Earl of Perth, which signifies, that the Bearer got his Arms for Services done at Sea. **1864** BOUTELL *Her. Hist. & Pop.* xxi. (ed. 3) 266 Per fesse arg. and barry wavy az. **1890** CONAN DOYLE *White Company* xviii, 'How read you this..?' 'Argent and azure, a barry wavy of six.'

d. Of a dog (short for *wavy-coated*): Having the coat in waves, not curly.

1884 *Live Stock Jrnl.* 28 Nov. 512/2 The Retrievers were good,..the curly Doctor having to give place to the wavy Harvester in Dogs. **1887** *Field* 1 Oct. Advt. p. xvi/2 Champion Zelstone (Wavy Retriever).

7. *Comb.*, as ***wavy-coated***, ***-edged***, ***-haired***, ***-handled***, ***-leaved***; **Wavy Navy** *colloq.*, the Royal Naval Volunteer Reserve, so nicknamed from the wavy braid worn by officers on their sleeves prior to 1956; †**wavy-ways** *adv.*, after the manner of waves.

1867 'STONEHENGE' *Dogs Brit. Isl.* 43 Windham..is a good example of the *wavy-coated dog. **1865** DICKENS *Mut. Fr.* I. ii, Veneering; forty, *wavy-haired, dark. **1927** PEAKE & FLEURE *Peasants & Potters* 72 The *wavy-handled pots. **1928** V. G. CHILDE *Most Anc. East* iv. 94 The wavy-handled jars..have been connected by Petrie, Frankfort, and Scharff with Palestine and Syria. **1816–20** T. GREEN *Univ. Herbal* II. 828 *Xyris Flexifolia*; *Wavy-leaved Xyris. **1855** ANNE PRATT *Flower. Pl.* V. 78 *Salix undulata*..is..sometimes called the Wavy-leaved Willow. **1918** W. OWEN *Let.* 21 Mar. (1967) 541 Her son, a Lieut. in the '*Wavy Navy' was at home. **1944** A. JACOB *Traveller's War* iii. 40 The ship's doctor and the paymaster-lieutenant, both 'Wavy Navy' men..have been in the service only a few months and know next to nothing of the sea. **1960** D. FEARON *Murder-on-Thames* xiv. 115, I remember him when he was a Sub. He was Wavy Navy then. **1671** *Phil. Trans.* VI. 2103 When the Load dips almost perpendicularly for many fathoms together, and may rise again in the next Hill (*wavie-ways).

B. *sb.* A wavy-coated retriever.

1884 *Live Stock Jrnl.* 5 Sept. 227/3 Retrievers: first and second both wavys. **1884** *Ibid.* 24 Dec. 612/2 Such a Kennel of wavies as is not equalled in any part of the world.

Hence **'wavily** *adv.*, **'waviness**.

1790 J. WEDGWOOD (*title*) An attempt to discover the causes of cords and waviness in Flint Glass and the most probable means of removing them. **1816** KEATS *Epist. Bro. George* 59 The coy moon, when in the waviness Of whitest clouds she does her beauty dress. **1860** GEO. ELIOT *Mill on Fl.* I. ix, Mr. Rappit, the hair-dresser, with his well-anointed coronal locks tending wavily upward. **1877** WATERHOUSE in *Abney's Photogr.* (1881) 190 A fine, even, glossy surface, perfectly free from the streaks and waviness so common when working with thick films. **1886** J. J. QUELCH *Coral-Reefs* in *Challenger Rep.* XVI. III. 136 The waviness and plications of the margins of the septa.

wavys, obs. pl. of WAIF *sb.*[1]

†**waw**, *sb.*[1] *Obs.* Forms: 3–4 **waȝe**, 4–6 **wawe**, 3 **wau**, (4 **quawe**), 4–5 **waghe**, (5 **whaghe**, **wawghe**), 6 **wawhe**, *Sc.* **wa**, 4–6, 9 *arch.* **waw**. [ME. *waȝe*, related to OE. *waᵹian* WAW *v.*[1]

There may have been an OE. **waᵹu* str. fem. or **waᵹe* wk. fem., corresponding to MHG., MLG. *wage*, MDu. *waege* movement, agitation. In ME. the word took the place of the OE. *wǣᵹ* masc. = OS., OHG. *wâg* (MHG. *wâc*, *wâg*- masc., mod.G. *woge* fem.), ON. *vág-r*, Goth, *wêg-s*:—OTeut. **wǣᵹo-z* flood, wave, and in the 16th c. was superseded by WAVE *sb.* In northern ME. dialects the present word would coincide in form with a possible adoption of ON. *vág-r*.]

A wave.

c **1275** LAY. 11977 Waȝes [*c* **1205** vðen] þar arne. *c* **1290** *St. Brendan* 530 in *S. Eng. Leg.* 234 Þe wawes of þe se beoten also bi-fore and bi-hynde. *a* **1300** *Cursor M.* 1844 On þe streme þat arche can ride, þe wauus [**13..** *Gott.* wawis, *c* **1375** *Fairf.* waghes] beft on ilk side. *c* **1325** *Metr. Hom.* 135 This schippe..That Crist rad in and his felawes, Imang dintes of gret quawes. *c* **1330** R. BRUNNE *Chron. Wace* (Rolls) 2973 Þe se gan fighte, þe wawes ros. ?*a* **1366** CHAUCER *Rom. Rose* 1561 The water is ever fresh and newe That welmeth up with wawes brighte [Fr. *a grans ondes*]. *c* **1400** *Destr. Troy* 1992 So wode were the waghes & þe wilde ythes. *Ibid.* 12310 Tho shippes to shilde o þe shyre whaghes. *c* **1400** *Emaré* 322 She was so dryuen fro wawe to wawe, She hyd her hede and lay fulle lawe. *c* **1440** *Generydes* 91 Full wekydly he and his vj felawes In to the see were cast among the wawis. *c* **1460** *Towneley Myst.* iii. 426 Thise wawghes ar so wode. *a* **1513** FABYAN *Chron.* VII. (1811) 373 The water of yᵉ ryuer..was so troublous of wawe, that the brydge therwith was all to shaken. **1518** *Ortus Vocab.* (ed. 3), *Flustrum*,..sterynge of the see or a wawhe. *a* **1533** BERNERS *Huon* xlvi. 156 The wawes..semyd so greate and hye as mounteyns. **1535** COVERDALE *Jas.* i. 6 He that douteth, is lyke the wawes [1526 TINDALE waues] of the see. **1549** THOMAS *Hist. Italie* 172 The little vessel..whiche the wawes of the sea by little and little draue towardes the lande. **1571** SIR. J. MAITLAND *Admon. to Regent* 31 Bewar thairfoir wᵗ wadder, waw, and wind. **1590** SPENSER *F.Q.* II. xii. 4 They on this rock are rent, and sunck in helplesse wawes. **1600** J. MELVILL *Diary* (Wodrow Soc.) 169 A tempestous schoure and drow..with sic a how wa and spenedrift, that.. he lukit for grait danger. [**1821** SCOTT *Pirate* xxix, As I would pilot a boat betwixt Swona and Stroma, through all the waws, wells, and swelchies of the Pentland Firth.]

†**waw**, *sb.*[2] *Sc.* and *north. dial. Obs.* Forms: 4 **wagh**, **waugh**, **wawe**, 5–6 **waw**, **wall**, 5 **wal**. [a. MLG. and MDu. *wage* (Du. *waag*), corresp. to OE. *wǣᵹ*: see WEY *sb.*] A measure of weight, usually equal to twelve stone.

1316 *Durham Acc. Rolls* (Surtees) 11 In 3 Wawes plumbi emp., 11*s.* 3*d.* **1399** *Acc. Exch. K.R.* 473/11 m. 3, Pro batellagio ix. Waugh[es] plumbi. **14..** *Assisa de Toll.* vii. in *Sc. Acts* (1844) I. 669 And of wax at þe entre nathyng bot of ilk waw at þe oute passyng aucht peniis gif it be weyit be wawys. **1484** *Acta Auditorum* I. (1839) 138*/2, xiij wall and five stane of hollande cheisis. **1499** HALYBURTON *Ledger* (1867) 225 Ane [sack of wool] weyand vj wall xxv naill, and tother vj wal xv naill. **1501** *Acc. Ld. High Treas. Scot.* II. 82, viij waw v stane of irne,..ilk waw xxv s. **1541–2** *Ibid.* VIII. 122, xv wall thre stane xiiij pund Spanze irne.

waw (wɔː), *sb.*[3] *Sc.* and *north. dial.* Also 8 **weaw**, 9 **wauw**. [f. WAW *v.*[2]] The cry of a cat.

c **1746** J. COLLIER (Tim Bobbin) *View Lancs. Dial.* Gloss., Wks. (1862) 108 *Weaw.* **1825** *Newcastle Mag.* Sept. 393/2 O, ye of little faith!..to be frightened by the cry of an owl or the wauw of a cat. **1835** CARRICK etc. *Laird of Logan* (1841) 163 Its a wee weak i' the wauw, like Barr's cat, that ale o' yours. **1859** A. WHITEHEAD *Leg. Westmld.* 35 (E.D.D.) They ofttimes saw a cat,..Unearthly was its waw.

‖**waw**, *sb.*[4], **wau**, the name of the 6th letter in Hebrew (see VAU, VAV) and the corresponding letter in the Arabic and other Semitic alphabets. **waw consecutive** *Heb. Gram.* = *vau conversive* s.v. CONVERSIVE *a.*[1] 2 b.

1832 S. LEE *Grammar Heb. Lang.* (ed. 2) 3 Vaw, or Waw. **1880** E. C. MITCHELL tr. *Gesenius' Heb. Gram.* II. ii. 125 (*heading*) The perfect and the imperfect with Wāw consecutive. **1880** *Encycl. Brit.* XI. 596/2 Among the points in which Hebrew differs both from Arabic and Aramaic may be mentioned..the use of Waw consecutive. **1889** J. KENNEDY *Introd. Biblical Heb.* 117 Ewald and other modern Grammarians prefer to call it *Waw Consecutive*. **1906** *Expositor* May 428 John xii. 15 follows the Hebrew of Zechariah ix. 9, the waw being epexegetic. **1914** J. E. McFADYEN *Davidson's Introd. Heb. Gram.* (ed. 19) xxiii. 84 Waw consecutive with the imperf. is pointed exactly like the Article. **1916** M. ROBERTS in *Folk-Lore* XXVII. 222 As there is no Arabic character to represent the *v* sound the Turks use the *wau* for this purpose. **1957** *Encycl. Brit.* XI. 362/1 Further relief was provided by '*wāw*-consecutive', a construction almost confined to Biblical Hebrew.

†**waw**, *v.*[1] *Obs.* Forms: 1 **waᵹian** (**weaᵹian**), 3 **waȝien**, **wawi(e**, 3–5 **waw(e**. [OE. *waᵹian* = MLG. *wagen*, MDu. *waghen* (mod.WFlem. *wagen*), OHG. *wagôn* (MHG., mod.G. *wagen*), ON. *vaga*:—OTeut. **waᵹōjan*, f. **waᵹō* agitation: see WAW *sb.*[1] Cf. WAG *v.*]

1. *intr.* To shake, totter, move loosely; to be ready to fall. Only *OE.*

c **725** *Corpus Gloss.* (Hessels) L 81 *Labat*, weaᵹat. *a* **1000** *Riddles* iv. 8 (Gr.) Hornsalu waᵹiað, wera wicstede. *c* **1000** ÆLFRIC *Deut.* xxxiv. 7 His eaᵹan ne mistodon ne his teð ne waᵹodon [Vulg. *nec dentes illius moti sunt*].

2. To sway to and fro on a base; to wave in the wind. Cf. WAG *v.* 3. Also *fig.*

c **888** ÆLFRED *Boeth.* xxxv. §7 Ða ongon mon secgan be ðam hearpere þæt he meahte hearpian þæt se wudu waᵹode & þa stanas hi styredon. *c* **1380** WYCLIF *Sel. Wks.* I. 72 Sawe ȝe a reede wawinge wiþ þe wynde? **1387** TREVISA *Higden* (Rolls) VI. 425 It was i-made sotilliche by gravynge craft þat it semed verrailiche þat corn growynge þerynne wawed hider and þider, as longe corn dooþ in feeldes. **14..** LYDG. *Test.* 653 Min. Poems (1911) 353 [I] Wawed with eche wynd, as doth a reedspere.

b. Of the beard, tongue: = WAG *v.* 4.

13.. *K. Alis.* 1164 Swithe mury hit is in halle, When the burdes wawen [*Laud MS.* waweþ] alle! *c* **1400** *Laud Troy Bk.* 6765 Afftir that strok his tonge neuere wawed.

c. Of a person: To swing.

c **1440** *Promp. Parv.* 518/2 Wawyn, or waueryn, yn a myry totyr, *oscillo.*

3. Of water, the wind: To move restlessly or uncertainly (*about*). Also *transf.* and *fig.*

c **1200** *Trin. Coll. Hom.* 175 Ðe se is eure waȝiende and þere fore unstedefast. **1496** *Dives & Pauper* (W. de W.) IX. 352/1 His worde & his loue & his fayth wawen about as the wynde. **1538** ELYOT *Dict.*, *Vndans*, wawyng or mouing like to wawes.

4. Of a person, animal: To move, stir; to go; also with *away*. Also *refl.*

c **1205** LAY. 26941 Hit agon diaȝen and deor gunnen waȝeȝen [*c* 1275 pleoye]. *c* **1290** *Beket* 2148 in *S. Eng. Leg.* 168 He nas nouȝt þe man þat he wolde is heued enes withdrawe Ne fondi for-to fleo heore strokes, ne enes a-weiward wawe. *c* **1425** *Cast. Persev.* 210 in *Macro Plays* 83 Wretthe, þis wrecche, with me schal wawe.

5. *trans.* To cause to move or stir.

c **1290** *St. Lucy* 114 in *S. Eng. Leg.* 104 A þousend men with al heore main on hire gonne drawe: Ac euere heo lai stille a-ȝein, huy ne miȝhten hire enes wawe. **1297** R. GLOUC. *Chron.* (Rolls) 4220 þis geant..bigan is mace adrawe þat tueye stalwarde men ne ssolde noȝt enes wawe. **13..** *K. Alis.* 2634 A spere..Yn the ground y-stikit fast,.. Ac non of his myghte up-drawe, No forth in eorthe hit wawe. **1382** WYCLIF *Matt.* xi. 7 A reede wawid with wynd [Vulg. *arundinem vento agitatam*].

b. To move (a limb).

c **1290** *Marie Egiptiace* 192 in *S. Eng. Leg.* 266 Heo ne wawede leome non bote hire lippene vnneþe. **13..** *Sir Beues* 2177 Hit [the horse] ne wawede no fot, Til Beues hadde þe stirop. *a* **1400** *Festiv. Ch.* 330 in *Leg. Rood* App. 221 Þe Egle is frikest fowle in flye, Ouer all fowles to wawe hys wenge.

c. Of wind: To agitate (water).

c **1380** WYCLIF *Serm.* Sel. Wks. I. 70 And wyndis of pryde wawen þes floodis, so þat it is perilous to shippis for to wandre.

Hence †**'wawing** *vbl. sb.*

c **1305** *Pop. Treat. Sci.* 386 This soule deieth in a man.. whan he leveth his breth and his wawinge also. **1500** *Ortus Vocab.*, *Cellinium*, the wawynge of the water.

waw (wɔː), *v.*[2] *Sc.* and *north. dial.* Also 6 **wawe**, 8 **weawgh**. [Echoic: cf. WAUL *v.*] *intr.* To cry as a cat or utter a similar sound. Hence **'wawing** *vbl. sb.*

1570 LEVINS *Manip.* 45/40 To Wawe as a cat, *lallare*. **1576** [see MOONER]. **1664** ETHEREGE *Com. Revenge* IV. iii, Well said Widow, i' faith; I will get upon thy body A generation of wild Cats, children that shall Waw, waw, scratch their Nurses, and be drunk With their sucking-bottles. *c* **1746** J. COLLIER (Tim Bobbin) *View Lancs. Dial.* Wks. (1862) 47 Three little tyney Bandyhewits..coom Weawghing os if th' little Rott'ns wou'd ha worrit meh. *c* **1817** HOGG *Tales, Mary Montgomery* (1865) 590/2 He was a' covered wi' blood, an' had a bit bloody bairn wawin' on afore him. **1876** J. RICHARDSON *Cummerland Talk* Ser. II. 147 Oor Betty's allus wawin', wawin'..Nowt in this warld, o' that I's sarten, Wad keep her fra her wawin' lang! **1887** [G. G. GREEN] *Gordonhaven* v. 54 Ah thocht Ah heard a kin' o' a wawin' or something o' that sort oot o' the sea.

waw, variant of WOUGH, wall.

‖**wawa** ('weɪwə). Also 8 **way-way**. [Cree *wehwew* goose (Lacombe *Dict. Lang. des Cris*); Odjibwa *wêwe* goose, *wabwêwe* white goose (Baraga *Otchipwe Gram.*). The current Eng. form of the word is WAVEY.] An American-Indian name for the wild goose.

1768 *Phil. Trans.* LX. 126 There are various sorts of the geese, as the grey-goose, the way-way, the brant, the dunter. **1855** LONGF. *Hiaw.* II. 162 When the Wawa has departed, When the wild-goose has gone southward.

wa-wa, wa-wah, var. forms of WOW-WOW.

wa-wa, var. WAH-WAH[2].

wawag, obs. Sc. form of VOYAGE.

waward(e, -art, obs. Sc. forms of VAWARD.

wawaskeesh (wɑːwə'skiːʃ). *N. Amer.* Also 8 **wewashkish**. [repr. Odjibwa *wawaskeshi* (Baraga *Otchipwe Dict.*, 1880) = Cree *wawaskāsew* (Watkins *Cree Dict.*, 1865).] = WAPITI.

1796 S. HEARNE *Journ. North. Ocean* 360 The wewashkish ..is quite a different animal from the moose. **1896** J. MACLEAN *Canad. Savage Folk* 620 The Wapiti, known amongst the Cree Indians as Wawaskish.

wawcer, obs. form of VOUSSOIR.

wawd, obs. form of *would*: see WILL *v.*

wawe, obs. form of WOE.

wawhte, variant of WOTHE.

wawil-eyed, obs. form of WALL-EYED.

wawill, obs. Sc. form of WAUL *v.*

†**'wawish**, *a. Obs. rare*[−1]. [f. WAW *sb.*[1] + -ISH[1].] Of the sea: Turbulent.

c **1450** *Mirour Saluacioun* (Roxb.) 21 Amanges the wawes tempestuouses ledere and help singulere With out wham we may noght this wawishe see ouerpasse.

wawk, obs. form of WAKE *v.*, WALK *v.*[2]

wawl: see WAUL *v.*

wawl(e, obs. forms of WALL *sb.*[1], *v.*[4]

wawlme, wawme, var. ff. WALM *sb.*[1]

wawou, var. form of WOW-WOW.

wawsper (ˈwɑspər). *Sc.* Also 5, 9 **wasper**, 9 **wausper**. [The first element is obscure; the second element is SPEAR *sb.*] A fishing-spear. Cf. WASTER *sb.*[3]

1472 *Munim. de Melros* (Bannatyne Club) 591 That nane ..presume..till..fisch thare Wateris with Wasperis nettis or any vthir Instrumentis. **1547** *Extracts Aberd. Reg.* (1844) I. 246 For keiping of thair watteris and fischingis of Done and Dee..in raid tyme fra all maner of nettis, cobillis, wawsperis, heryvalteris, and all wther instrumentis. **1887** JAMIESON *Suppl.*, and *Add.*

wawt, obs. Sc. form of WELT *v.*

waw-waw (ˈwɔːwɔː). A West Indian climbing shrub (see quot.).

1864 GRISEBACH *Flora W. Ind. Isl.* 788 Waw-waw, *Rajania pleioneura*.

†**ˈwawy**, *a. Obs.* [f. WAW *sb.*[1] + -Y.] Full of waves, billowy; = WAVY *a.* 1.

1412-20 LYDG. *Chron. Troy* I. 3938 Þe see is calme and blaundisching From trouble of wynde and wawy boilyng. **1426** —— *De Guil. Pilgr.* 19244 Alle pylgrymes..That swymmen in the wawy see. *a* **1500** *Chaucer's Dreme* 697 Ten thousand shipes at a sight, I saw come ouer the wawy flood. **1503** HAWES *Examp. Virt.* x. 181 This stormy troublous and wawy water.

wax (wæks), *sb.*[1] Forms: 1 **wæx, wex**, 1, 2 **weax**, 3-6, 9 *dial.* **wex**, 4-6 **wexe** (5 **vexe**), 4-7 **waxe**, (4 **waxche**, *Sc.* **vax**, 5 **whax**), 5-7 *Sc.* **walx**, (6 *Sc.* **valx, waux, waks**), 3- **wax**. [Com. Teut. (not recorded in Goth.): OE. *weax* neut. = OFris. *wax*, OS. *wahs* (LG., Du. *was*), OHG., MHG. *wahs* (mod.G. *wachs*), ON. *vax* (Sw. *vax*, Da. *vox*):—OTeut. **waχso-m*.

Outside Teut. the word occurs as Lith. *wäškas*, OSl. *voskŭ* (Russ. *vosk*, Pol. *wosk*, Czech *vosk*), but prob. adopted from Teut. The root may be identical with Teut. **waχs-* to grow (WAX *v.*[1]); it seems not impossible that the etymological sense may have been 'that which grows (in the honeycomb)'. The view now most in favour refers the word to the Indogermanic root **weg-* to weave, found in OIrish *figim* I weave, L. *vēlum* veil, sail (believed to be from prehistoric **veg-slom*), and in certain Teut. words (see WICK *sb.*[1]); the advocates of this etymology appeal to the apparent semasiological parallel of G. *wabe*, honeycomb, presumed to be from the root of *weben* WEAVE *v.*[1] Some other hypotheses have been proposed, but they are all unsatisfactory with regard either to form or meaning.]

1. a. A substance (also distinctively called BEESWAX) produced by bees, and used by them as the material of the honeycomb. It is a secretion of special glands in the abdomen, mixed with the secretion of the salivary glands in the process of mastication; when slightly warmed it is readily moulded into any shape, and when heated to about 150° melts into a liquid; in its natural state it is of a bright yellow colour. ***butter of wax***: see BUTTER *sb.*[1] 3. Cf. *wax-butter* in 13.

Chemically beeswax is a combination of palmitic, cerotic, and melissic acids with myricil alcohol.

805-1375 [see 2]. *c* **1386** CHAUCER *Cant. T.*, Prol. 675 This Pardoner hadde heer as yelow as wex. **1398** TREVISA *Barth. De P.R.* XIX. lxi. (1495) 897 Wexe is the drastes of hony. *c* **1440** *Pallad. on Husb.* I. 1023 Of tyme is wex and hony maad swettest. **1526** *Pilgr. Perf.* (W. de W. 1531) 165 b, Lyke as yᵉ hony is closed within the come of waxe. *c* **1560** A. SCOTT *Poems* i. 105 As beis takkis walx and honye of þe floure. **1601** SHAKS. *All's Well* I. ii. 65 Since I not wax nor honie can bring home. *a* **1679** SIR J. MOORE *England's Interest* (1703) 137 Break the Combs..into three parts. The first Honey and Wax, the 2d. Honey and Wax with Sandarack, the 3d. dry Wax without Honey. **1792** J. HUNTER in *Phil. Trans.* LXXXII. 145 The wax is formed by the bees themselves; it may be called an external secretion of oil, and I have found that it is formed between each scale of the under side of the belly. **1834** MᶜMURTRIE *Cuvier's Anim. Kingd.* 433 Wax, according to the experiments of the same naturalists, is nothing more than elaborated honey. **1871** STAVELEY *Brit. Insects* 248 The substances or materials collected or produced by Bees are four in number—honey, bee-bread, wax, and propolis.

¶ **b. *rough wax***: a term formerly applied to the pollen adhering to the legs of bees, which was erroneously supposed to be the crude substance from which the wax was elaborated. *Obs.*

1744 tr. *Bazin's Nat. Hist. Bees* 43 This dust then, which falls upon these stamina of flowers, is the sole matter, of which wax is made, which I shall call rough wax. **1792** J. HUNTER in *Phil. Trans.* LXXXII. 144 The substance brought in on their legs, which is the farina of the flowers of plants, is, in common, I believe, imagined to be the materials of which the wax is made, for it is called by most the wax.

2. a. Beeswax as melted down, bleached, or otherwise prepared for some special purpose in the arts, in medicine, or in manufactures.

The more prominent uses are: as material for candles and tapers, as a plastic material for modelling, as a component of plasters, as a vehicle for encaustic painting, and as a protective coating to exclude the air.

805-10 in Birch *Cartul. Sax.* (1885) I. 459 Mon ðaet weax agæfe to ciricean. **971** *Blickl. Hom.* 129 Swa swa eles ȝecynd bið þæt he beorhtor scineþ þonne wex on sceafte. *c* **1200** *Trin. Coll. Hom.* 47 Alse wex on þe candele sene, þe wueke wiðinnen unsene. *c* **1205** LAY. 2370 Muchel win, muchel wex, muchel wunsum þing. **1340-70** *Alex. & Dind.* 236 While þe weke & þe waxe vn-wasteþ lasteþ. **1375** BARBOUR *Bruce* XI. 119 Vyne and vax, schot and vittale. **1402** in *E.E. Wills* 11, ij torchis of wax. **1406** HOCCLEVE *La Male Regle* 254 Alle eres of men of his compaignie, With wex he stoppe leet, for þat they noght Hir song sholde heere. *a* **1425** tr. *Arderne's Treat. Fistula* etc. 81 If þou wilt make it in maner of one emplastre, putte þer-to wax and blak pich. **1597** JAS. VI *Dæmonol.* II. v. 44 To some others at these times hee teacheth, how to make Pictures of waxe or clay: That by the rosting thereof, the persones that they beare the name of, may be continuallie melted or dryed awaie by continuall sicknesse. **1601** HOLLAND *Pliny* XXXV. xi. II. 546 As touching the feat of setting colours with wax, and enamelling with fire, who first began and devised the same, it is not known. **1612** *Sc. Bk. Rates* in *Halyburton's Ledger* (1867) 293 Candles of walx the pound weght thairof, iiii s. **1638** JUNIUS *Paint. Ancients* 133 There should be made three images of wax, in the place of three men that were to be offered unto Juno. **1676** WISEMAN *Surg.* I. vi. 40 A Cerote of Wax and Oyl over the Leg. **1702** in Ashton *Soc. Life Reign Q. Anne* (1882) I. 283 Effigies..Curiously done in Wax to the Life. **1707-21** MORTIMER *Husb.* II. 255 Cleft Grafting. .. Cover the Head of the Stock with temper'd Clay, or with soft Wax. **1768** W. LEWIS *Mat. Med.* (ed. 2) 202 The chief medicinal use of wax is in plasters, unguents, and other like external applications. **1787** *Trans. Soc. Arts* V. 104 The Art of Painting in Wax as described in the following letter and account. **1789** MRS. PIOZZI *Journ. France & Italy* II. 227 They..I think excel Mrs. Wright's finest figures in wax. **1803** *Nicholson's Jrnl. Nat. Philos.* (8°) IV. 176 A stream of wax has just overflowed the cup of the wax candle by which I have been reading. **1815** S. PARKES *Chem. Ess.* II. 148 In some particular styles of work the operation of certain colours is resisted by means of stopping out with wax. **1832** CARLYLE *Ess., Death Goethe* (1840) IV. 118 The true Sovereign of the world, who moulds the world like soft wax, according to his pleasure. **1840** DICKENS *Old C. Shop* xxviii, Children, who..were fully impressed with the belief that her grandfather was a cunning device in wax. **1875** KNIGHT *Dict. Mech.* 2312/2 Cover the inside of the [plaster] sections with a shell of wax.

b. As used for the coating of writing tablets.

1533 BELLENDEN *Livy* (S.T.S.) I. 55 Als richtuislie as þai ar here Ingravin in þir tabillis or walx. **1565** COOPER *Thesaurus* s.v. *Cera*, *Ceræ credere aliquid*, Plaut. To wryte in tables of waxe. **1854** FAIRHOLT *Dict. Terms Art* s.v. *Encaustic*, The artists of antiquity..used the stylus and wax for tablet-pictures and architectural decorations.

c. A particular variety of wax. Usually with qualifying adj., as ***bleached, white, yellow wax***. See also VIRGIN WAX.

1545 RAYNALDE *Byrth Mankynde* 118 If the child be in great heate annoynte hym with the oyle of violettes, or with oyle olyfe, tempered with a lyttell whyte wexe. **1601** HOLLAND *Pliny* XXI. xiv. II. 96 The best wax is that which is called Punica,..and is white. The next, in goodnesse is the yellowest,..such commeth from the countrey of Pontus. **1630** in *Abridgm. Specif. Patents, Oils* etc. (1873) 2 To make yellow wax white verie speedily. **1768** W. LEWIS *Mat. Med.* (ed. 2) 201 *Cera alba*..White wax: the yellow wax artificially bleached. *Ibid.*, *Cera flava*..Yellow wax; in the state wherein it is obtained from the combs. **1811** A. T. THOMSON *Lond. Disp.* (1818) 112 Unbleached Wax... Yellow wax is prepared immediately from the honeycomb. **1843** R. J. GRAVES *Syst. Clin. Med.* xxix. 390 The applications in use were yellow wax ointment and nitrate of silver.

†**d. *man of wax***: a waxen image of a man. *Obs.*

Cf. **1439** *E.E. Wills* 118 Allso I woll the great Image of wex that is at London be offred to our lady of Worcestre.

1500 *Will of Rigawell* (Somerset Ho., Blamyr 23 b), I wille that my seid executors..shalle offre for me a man a [*sic*] of wax..at our lady of Walsyngham..also at the rode of Berkles a man of waxe.

†**e.** *pl.* Pieces of wax. *nonce-use*.

1550 CRANMER *Def. Sacram.* III. 81 As two waxes, that be molten & put togither, they close so in one, that euery part of the one, is ioyned to euery parte of the other.

f. An object made of wax. (*a*) A wax candle. (*b*) A figure or model in wax.

(*a*) **1844** HEWLETT *Parsons & W.* xlix, A resplendent October moon..seemed to impose upon us the notion that it would be a sacrilege against Diana if we were to shut out her rays, and substitute a pair of waxes for her clear beams. **1871** BESANT & RICE *Ready-money Mort.* iii, Don't waste the light, Dick. You're burning one of your poor aunt's waxes. (*b*) **1865** TYLOR *Early Hist. Man.* vi. 125 A mediæval sermon speaks of baptizing a 'wax' to bewitch with. **1906** *Westm. Gaz.* 9 May 8/2 The original 'waxes' of Flaxman, Angelino, Pacetti, and other famous designers, from which the moulds for the familiar classical decorations were made.

3. a. In figurative and similative uses, referring to the easy fusibility of wax, its softness and readiness to receive impressions, its adhesiveness, etc. ***nose of wax***: see NOSE *sb.* 4.

c **825** *Vesp. Psalter* xxi. 15 Ȝeworden wes heorte min swe swe wæx ȝemaeltende in midle wombe minre. *c* **1000** *Ags. Ps.* (Th.) lvii. 7 Swa weax melteþ, ȝif hit byð wearmum neah fyre ȝefæstnad. *c* **1375** *Sc. Leg. Saints* iv. (*James*) 266 Þe stane..wex nesch as it wax war. **1471** RIPLEY *Comp. Alch.* I. vi. in Ashmole (1652) 130 Fluxyble as Wex. **1546** J. HEYWOOD *Prov.* II. vi. (1867) 61 At my wil I wend she should haue wrought, like wax. **1592** SHAKS. *Rom. & Jul.* III. iii. 126 Thy Noble shape is but a forme of waxe, Digressing from the Valour of a man. **1598** E. GUILPIN *Skial.* (1878) 58 He hath a wit of waxe, fresh as a rose. **1608** DEKKER *2nd Pt. Honest Wh.* I. (1630) B 3, *Hip.* I'm glad you are wax, not marble: you are made Of mans best temper. **1612** BEAUM. & FL. *Coxcomb* II. ii, I'll work her as I go, I know shee's wax, now. *a* **1700** B. E. *Dict. Canting Crew*, *Pliant*,..Wax to every Thumb. **1717** POPE *Hor. Ep.* II. ii. 9 He's your slave, for twenty pound a year, Mere wax as yet, you fashion him with ease. **1748** RICHARDSON *Clarissa* (1768) VII. 365 When my mind is made such wax, as to be fit to take what impression she pleases to give it. **1817** BYRON *Beppo* xxxiv, His heart was one of those which most enamour us, Wax to receive, and marble to retain. **1875** STUBBS *Const. Hist.* II. xiv. 99 John's heart was of millstone, Henry's of wax.

b. Phrases: ***close, tight, neat as wax; to stick*** (to one) ***like wax; to fit like wax***.

1772 CUMBERLAND *Fashionable Lover* III. 35 But you mun be as close as wax, d'ye see. **1809** BYRON *Lines to Mr. Hodgson* 30 All are wrangling, Stuck together close as wax. **1850** SUSAN WARNER *Wide Wide World* xvi, The furniture was common, but neat as wax. **1859** LYTTON *What will he do* IV. xiv, 'Cabined, cribbed, confined', in a coat that fits him like wax. **1865** DICKENS *Mut. Fr.* IV. vi, Bella and John Rokesmith followed; Gruff and Glum stuck to them like wax. **1898** N. GOULD *Landed at Last* v. 52 Not much chance of drawing Sim Sharples when he's alone. He's as close as wax, and so is Sam Rogers. **1902** [see TIGHT *a.* 5].

c. *man, lad of wax*: used as a term of emphatic commendation. Now *arch.* and *dial.* (see *Eng. Dial. Dict*).

The origin of this expression is not clear. It may have meant 'as faultless as if modelled in wax' (cf. 2 d.). Some would refer it to WAX *sb.*[2]

1592 SHAKS. *Rom. & Jul.* I. iii. 76 Why hee's a man of waxe. **1607** DEKKER & WEBSTER *West-w. Hoe* II. i, Hees a Knight made out of waxe. **1611** BEAUM. & FL. *Philaster* I. i, Oh! 'tis a Prince of wax. **1612** FIELD *Woman is Weathercock* I. B 4 b, By Ioue it is a little man of wax. **1821** W. T. MONCRIEFF *Tom & Jerry* III. iii, A glass of good max.. Wou'd have made them, like us, lads of wax. **1840** *Peter Parley's Ann.* I. 131 The shoemaker..surveyed the Prince from top to bottom. 'No tailor could do that,' said he; 'he must be a lad of wax.' **1858** TROLLOPE *Dr. Thorne* iv, All right, my lad of wax. **1880** BLACKMORE *Mary Anerley* xxiii, Could any lad of wax put up with this, least of all a daring mariner?

4. a. In early use, beeswax (or a mixture of this with other substances) as employed to receive the impression of a seal; in later use, a compound, chiefly consisting of lac, serving the same purpose: = SEALING-WAX.

971 *Blickl. Hom.* 205 Þa fotlastas wæron swutole & ȝesyne on þæm stane, swa hie on wexe wæron aðyde. *a* **1300** *Cursor M.* 557 Als prient of seel in wax es thrist þer in he has his lic[nes] fest. *a* **1340** HAMPOLE *Psalter* iv. 7 Þe prynt we bere of þᵉ light as þe wax does of þe sele. **1398** TREVISA *Barth. De P.R.* XIX. lxi. (1495) 898 Preuyte is hydde vnder wexe: and pryueleges be confermyd with wexe. *c* **1450** *Cov. Myst.* (1841) 341 Loo! here is wax fful redy dyght, Sett on ȝour sele anon ful ryght. **1511-2** *Act 3 Hen. VIII* c. 6 § 1 The Alnager ..shall..not put to eny suche clothes eny seales of wexe in any wise. **1535** W. STEWART *Cron. Scot.* (Rolls) III. 464 Brekand promit to him befoir he maid In writ and walx, wnder thair seillis braid. **1560** DAUS tr. *Sleidane's Comm.* 119 For al the sorte of them occupie waxe..in sealyng their letters. **1588** SHAKS. *L.L.L.* IV. i. 59 We will reade it, I sweare. Breake the necke of the Waxe, and euery one giue eare. **1593** —— *Lucr.* 1245 No more then waxe shall be accounted euill, Wherein is stampt the semblance of a Deuill. **1607** MIDDLETON *Michaelmas Term* IV. i, Hee will neuer trust his land in Waxe and Parchment as many Gentlemen haue done before him. **1609** SKENE *Reg. Maj.*, *Forme of Proces* 120 The deposition..sould be stampit and sealit be the Lords examinatours, with seale and walx, and sould not be opened at the secund or thrid examination. **1622** J. TAYLOR (Water P.) *Farew. Tower Bottles* A 3, Bound fast in Bonds in Parchment and with waxe. **1676** WYCHERLEY *Pl. Dealer* IV. i, O do not squeeze Wax, Son; rather go to Ordinaries, and Baudy-houses, than squeeze Wax. **1717** PRIOR *To Harley* 1 Pen, ink, and wax, and paper send. **1761** COLMAN *Jealous Wife* I. 14 *Maj.* A Letter!—Hum—A suspicious Circumstance to be sure!—What, and the Seal a True-Lover's Knot now, hey!..or possibly the Wax bore the industrious Impression of a Thimble. **1818** CRUISE *Digest* (ed. 2) IV. 32 One piece of wax may serve for all the grantors, &c...if every one of them put his seal upon the same piece of wax. **1818** BYRON *Juan* I. cxcviii, The seal a sun-flower,..The wax was superfine, its hue vermilion.

b. With designation of colour. See also GREEN WAX.

1485 *Nottingham Rec.* III. 230 For rede wax to seale þe endentures. **1496** *Acta Dom. Conc.* II. 19 Ane decrete of the Lordis under the quhite walx. **1532** *Acc. Ld. High Treas. Scot.* (1905) VI. 50 For rede waks and quhite to sele the citationis. **1641** 'SMECTYMNUUS' *Vind. Answ. Humb. Rem.* § 16. 218 The Greene Wax and Red Wax of the Bishops. **1653** in *Verney Mem.* (1907) I. 525 Stone Bottles with White Wine. They are all sealed with Black Wax. **1712** STEELE *Spect.* No. 431 ¶ 3, I then nibbled all the red Wax of our last Ball-Tickets, and three Weeks after the black Wax from the Burying-Tickets of the old Gentleman.

†**c. *hard wax*** = SEALING-WAX. *Obs.*

1603 R. JOHNSON *Kingd. & Commw.* 35 The Ilands affoorde plenty of hides, cotten,..hand wax and pearles. **1616** B. JONSON *Devil an Ass* V. i, My purse, my seales, My hard-wax, and my table-bookes. **1660** F. BROOKE tr. *Le Blanc's Trav.* ix. 26 Laca d'Alaca..Of this is likewise made Spanish hard wax. *a* **1674** CLARENDON *Hist. Reb.* XIV. § 139 A clean piece of paper sealed with three impressions of an antique head in hard wax.

5. Applied to artificial compounds having the properties of wax, and substituted for it in various applications.

1763 W. LEWIS *Commerc. Phil.-Techn.* 78 The gilding wax is composed of bees-wax, red ochre or ruddle, verdegris, vitriol or alum, and sometimes other additions.

6. Any of a class of substances, found in nature in greater or less purity, including beeswax and other compounds resembling it in general properties and (more or less) in chemical composition. In *Chem.* properly restricted to those 'waxes' of animal and vegetable origin which, like beeswax, are composed of fatty acids and alcohols. The mineral 'waxes' are hydrocarbons.

a. A vegetable product obtained from various trees and plants.

1799 *Med. Jrnl.* I. 268 The matter of wax, as forming an ingredient in many vegetables, is discoverable, partly from their shining surface, partly from a certain flexibility in such bodies. **1803** *Nicholson's Jrnl. Nat. Philos.* (8°) IV. 187 The light matter which is called the down of fruits, which silvers the surface of prunes and other fruits, is wax. **1813** SIR H. DAVY *Agric. Chem.* iii. (1814) 96 Wax is found in a number of vegetables, it is procured in abundance from the berries of the wax myrtle, it may likewise be obtained from the leaves of many trees. **1839** URE *Dict. Arts*, etc. *s.v.*, Wax exists also as a vegetable product, and may, in this point of view, be regarded as a concrete fixed oil. It forms a part of the green fecula of many plants, particularly of the cabbage; it may be extracted from the pollen of most flowers; as also from the skins of plums, and many stone fruits. It constitutes a varnish upon the upper surface of the leaves of many trees, and it has been observed in the juice of the cow-tree. The berries of the *Myrica angustifolia*, *latifolia*, as well as the *cerifera*, afford abundance of wax. **1880** ALCOCK in *Encycl. Brit.* XIII. 590/2 The *Urushi* tree growing in Japan (the fruit of which yields the vegetable wax). **1887** MOLONEY *Forestry W. Africa* 461 Gums and Resins, Vegetable Waxes.

b. A substance resembling beeswax secreted or produced by various species of scale-insects. Sometimes called ***Chinese wax***. Also, 'the product of some other homopterous insects' (*Cent. Dict.*).

1802 BINGLEY *Anim. Biog.* (1805) III. 290 To their [the larvæ of the cicada] labours the Chinese are indebted for the fine white wax that is so much esteemed in the East-Indies. They form a sort of white grease which attaches to the branches of trees, hardens there, and becomes wax. **1815** KIRBY & SP. *Entomol.* x. (1818) I. 328 In China wax is also produced by another insect, which..seems to be a species of *Coccus*. *Ibid.* 331 Early in the spring vast numbers of these caterpillars [of *Phalæna ceraria*] collect on the branches of the *Chila*, where they form their cells of a kind of soft white wax or resin... This wax, which is at first very white, but by degrees becomes yellow and finally brown, is collected in autumn by the inhabitants, who boil it in water, and make it up into little cakes for market. **1852** W. GREGORY *Handbk. Org. Chem.* (ed. 3) 247 Chinese Wax. **1876** WESTWOOD in *Trans. Entom. Soc. Lond.* 521 Now this 'cottony' covering was doubtless formed of the wax secreted by the *Fulgora*. **1899** D. SHARP *Insects* II. 575 A great many [of the *Fulgoridæ*] have the curious power of excreting large quantities of a white flocculent wax. *Ibid.* 597 *Ceroplastes ceriferus*, a Lecaniid, produces white wax in India... The white wax of China is understood to be produced by another Lecaniid, *Ericerus pela*.

c. A mineral product somewhat resembling bees-wax. ***fossil*** or ***mineral wax*** = OZOCERITE. ***paraffin wax***: see PARAFFIN *sb.* 4.

1838 T. THOMSON *Chem. Org. Bodies* 448 Fossil wax of Moldavia. **1842** FRANCIS *Dict. Arts*, etc., *Wax, Mineral*, a bituminous substance, found at the foot of the Carpathian mountains, near Slarick. **1868** WATTS *Dict. Chem.* (1877) V. 1037 *Wax, Fossil.* Syn. with *Ozocerite*.

d. *gen.*

1866 WATTS *Dict. Chem.* (1877) IV. 322 Ozocerite..is like a resinous wax in consistence and translucency. **1868** *Ibid.* V. 1037 Japan-wax..is not a true wax, but a glyceride.

e. (See quots.) Cf. *paraffin wax* s.v. PARAFFIN *sb.* 4.

1924 *Ski Terms* in *Tourist* (Winter Sports No.) 12/2 *Wax*, a paraffin preparation to prevent the snow balling under the ski. **1962** *Austral. Women's Weekly* 24 Oct. (Suppl.) 3/4 *Wax*, paraffin wax, rubbed on a [surf]board to prevent slipping.

f. ***lost wax***: see LOST *ppl. a.* 6.

7. = EAR-WAX.

[**1398–1614**: see EAR-WAX]. **1706** PHILLIPS (ed. Kersey), *Cerumen*, the filth or Wax of the Ear, which serves to hinder Dust, Motes, or any little Creatures from getting into it. **1889** L. HUMPHRY *Man. Nursing* (1892) 216 When there is hard wax blocking up the canal [of the ear].

8. A thick resinous composition used by shoemakers for rubbing their thread. More fully ***cobblers'***, ***shoemakers' wax***: see COBBLER, SHOEMAKER.

1622 MASSINGER & DEKKER *Virg. Martyr* III. iii, Long I cannot last, for all sowterly waxe of comfort melting away, and misery taking the length of my foote, it bootes not me to sue for life. **1837** KIRKBRIDE *North. Angler* 11 The amateur ..must..be provided with..shoe-maker's wax. I prepare my own wax,..by boiling a little pitch and rosin together,.. and tempering it with a very little tallow. **1885** LENO *Boot & Shoemaking* 222 Wax that will work up into the pure bronze colour so much liked by shoemakers may be made of 4 lbs. resin, 1 lb. pitch, 4 ounces beeswax, 3 ounces tallow.

9. *U.S.* A thick syrup produced by boiling down the sap of the sugar-maple tree, cooling on ice, etc. (*Cent. Dict.*)

1845 S. JUDD *Margaret* II. i, [Making maple sugar] The 'wax' is freely distributed to be cooled on lumps of snow or the axe-head.

10. *Mining.* (See quot.)

1883 GRESLEY *Gloss. Coal-mining*, *Wax* (Leicester.) soft or puddled clay used for *dams* or *stoppings*, and in which the colliers stick and carry about their candles in the mine.

11. *U.S. slang.* A gramophone record; ***to put on wax***, to make a gramophone record of, to record. [From the 'wax' discs in which the recording stylus cuts its groove.]

1932 *New Yorker* 11 June 56/2 An extraordinarily competent bit of manufacture is the latest wax by Miss Jeanette MacDonald (Victor 24103). **1940** J. O'HARA *Pal Joey* (1952) 107, I am going to play the tune and cut a wax of it. **1941** *Jazz Information* Nov. 28/1 Some of the most beautiful piano playing Jelly Roll ever put on wax. **1941** W. C. HANDY *Father of Blues* xvi. 219 Recording companies.. made them available on wax. **1968** P. OLIVER *Screening Blues* 4 The more sophisticated types of vaudeville entertainment were to be heard on wax before the Southern rural blues. **1979** *Early Music* Oct. 469/1 Scarlatti, Rameau, Couperin, Handel and, of course, Bach were committed to wax during the 1930s, as well.

12. *attrib.* and *Comb.* **a.** Attrib. (quasi-adj.) with the sense 'composed of wax'. (See also WAX TAPER.)

1585 HIGINS *Junius' Nomencl.* 474/2 *Ceroplastes*,..a maker of wax images. **1685** G. SINCLAIR *Satans Invis. World* 3 This woman..had formed an Wax-Picture, with pins in the side. **1811** A. T. THOMSON *Lond. Disp.* (1818) 714 Wax Plaster. **1825** in R. W. Goulding *Louth Old Corpor. Rec.* (1891) 185 By Cash of Madame Tussaud for 5 weeks use of the Mansion House for her Exhibitⁿ of Wax Figures, 9 19 6. **1840** DICKENS *Master Humphrey's Clock* I. 101 A young hairdresser..opened a wery smart little shop with four wax dummies in the winder. **1846** DICKENS *Pict. Italy*, Lyons, etc., There was a wax saint, in a little box..with a glass front to it. **1847** *Ann. Reg.* 20 A little box of about a dozen wax lucifer matches. **1849** CHRISTMAS *Cradle of Twin Giants* II. iv. I. 271 An empty bier, surrounded by an hundred wax-torches. **1853** C. C. FELTON *Fam. Lett.* viii. (1865) 61 The oddest thing of all is a wax figure of Frederic the Great. **1854** *Poultry Chron.* II. 105 Some freak of wax-fruit modelling. **1858** SIMMONDS *Dict. Trade*, *Vesta*, a kind of wax match. **1870** BOWEN *Logic* xi. 353 It may be only a wax counterfeit. **1892** *Photogr. Ann.* II. 45 A wax vesta which is lit and the head knocked off. **1914** 'IAN HAY' *Knt. on Wheels* xx, His wife kept wax fruit under a glass case in her parlour window. **1969** Y. CARTER *Mr Campion's Farthing* xix. 188 A wax dummy displaying a garment for sale. **1978** J. ANDERSON *Angel of Death* xii. 139 Her body as motionless, her face as impassive as a wax dummy.

b. simple attrib., 'of or pertaining to wax', as ***wax-chip***, ***-solution***, ***-spot***.

1859 *Habits of Gd. Society* xiii. 336 After the Tuileries' balls, we often returned with complete epaulettes of wax-spots on our shoulders, if in moments of carelessness we had stood under the chandeliers. **1889** *Anthony's Photogr. Bull.* II. 241 A wax solution or wax chips melted by a hot iron.

c. objective, as ***wax-bearer***, ***-bleacher***, ***-manufacturer***, ***-modeller***, †***-nibbler***, ***producer***, ***-refiner***; ***wax-modelling*** vbl. sb.; ***wax-bearing***, ***-forming***, ***-producing***, ***-secreting*** ppl. adjs. Also WAX-MAKER, -MAKING.

1577 tr. *Bullinger's Decades* V. iii. (1592) 884 The Acoluthes say they are *waxe-bearers, because they carrie waxe-candles. **1796** MARSHALL *Planting* II. 232 The Candleberry Myrtle, or *Wax-bearing Myrick. **1881** *Instructions to Census Clerks* (1885) 77 *Wax, beeswax—bleacher, refiner [etc.]. **1908** *Westm. Gaz.* 29 Apr. 1/3 He.. became a wax-bleacher at Hoxton. **1802** BINGLEY *Anim. Biog.* (1805) III. 289 The *Wax-forming Cicada. **1858** SIMMONDS *Dict. Trade*, *Wax-manufacturer. *Ibid.*, *Wax-modeller. **1850** OGILVIE, *Wax-modelling. **1712** STEELE *Spect.* No. 431 ⁋3 Chalk-lickers, *Wax-nibblers, Coal-scranchers, [etc.]. **1889** *Hardwicke's Sci.-Gossip* XXV. 131 Insects..highly prized as *wax-producers. **1861** HULME tr. *Moquin-Tandon* II. iii. 206 Bees are the principal *wax-producing animals. **1881** *Wax-refiner [see *wax-bleacher* above]. **1881** *Globe Encycl.* VI. 484 The *wax-secreting glands [in the bee].

d. instrumental, as ***wax-coated***, ***-composed***, ***-daubed***, ***-erected***, ***-jointed***, ***-lighted***, ***-polished***, ***-rubbed***, ***-tipped***, ***-topped*** adjs.

1875 KNIGHT *Dict. Mech.* 2748/2 A machine for preparing *wax-coated matches for dipping. *a* **1642** SIR F. KYNASTON *Leoline & Sydanis* 1874 His *wax-composed wings unfeathered were. **1942** W. FAULKNER *Go down, Moses* 305 The tawny *wax-daubed shapeless lump. *a* **1718** PARNELL *Hesiod* 131 Thus in a thousand *wax-erected forts A loitering race the painful bee supports. **1846** PROWETT *Prometh. Bound* 27 While murmurs ever and anon From his *wax-jointed reed the same low sleepy drone. **1839** HOOD *Lines to Friend at Cobham* 17 You'll sometimes have *wax-lighted rooms. **1866** J. B. ROSE tr. *Ovid's Met.* 245 Chestnut bowls, *wax-polished was their wood. **1598** E. GUILPIN *Skial.* (1878) 26 Like a *wax-rubd Citty roome. **1898** CONAN DOYLE *Trag. Korosko* i, He had..a small *wax-tipped moustache. **1822** W. IRVING *Bracebridge Hall* (1823) I. 113 The Stout Gentleman and his *wax-topped boots.

e. similative, as ***wax finish***; with adjs. denoting colour, as ***wax-blond***, ***-brown***, ***-pale***, ***-red***, ***-white***, ***-yellow***; also ***wax-like*** adj.

1925 E. SITWELL *Troy Park* 92 Oh, *wax-blond orange-blossoms' calice Of their hair. **1887** W. PHILLIPS *Brit. Discomyc.* 70 Cup medium size,..pale *wax-brown. **1897** C. T. DAVIS *Manuf. Leather* (ed. 2) 464 The making of a *wax finish on chrome-tanned horse hide butts. **1748** RICHARDSON *Clarissa* (1768) III. 27 Her *wax-like flesh.. answers for the soundness of her health. **1816** COLERIDGE *Statesman's Man.* 4 We..need not be surprised at the fact, that a jealous priesthood should have ventured to represent the applicability of the Bible to all the wants and occasions of men as a wax-like pliability to all their fancies and prepossessions. **1862** MILLER *Elem. Chem.*, *Org.* (ed. 2) 474 If its chloride be mixed with a solution of bichloride of platinum it yields a wax-like mass. **1885** *Cornhill Mag.* Mar. 284 A lovely..plant with masses of waxlike lilac blossom. **1899** J. HUTCHINSON in *Archives Surg.* X. Descr. Pl. xvii, The greater part of the hand is of wax-like pallor. **1942** E. SITWELL *Street Songs* 31 Dark-leaved arbutus blooms with *wax-pale bells. **1592** SHAKS. *Ven. & Ad.* 516 Which purchase if thou make, for feare of slips, Set thy seale manuell, on my *wax-red lips. **1883** 'MARK TWAIN' *Life on Miss.* xxxi. 338 All of them with *wax-white, rigid faces. **1890** KIPLING *Life's Handicap*, *Incarn. Krishna Mulvaney* 29 My face was wax-white, an' at the worst I must ha' looked like a ghost. **1805** T. WEAVER *Werner's Ext. Charact. Fossils* 58 *Wax-yellow [G. *wachsgelb*] is a light honey-yellow, mixed with a little light ashes-grey.

f. in parasynthetic formations, as ***wax-featured***, ***-headed***, †***-hearted*** adjs.

1612 T. TAYLOR *Comm. Titus* i. 11. (1619) 227 How many who haue seemed waxe-hearted Christians, soft and pliable. **1913** MRS. E. WHARTON *Custom of Country* II. xii. 156 A showy Parisianized figure, with a small wax-featured husband. **1914** *Glasgow News* 22 Dec. 4 The map was bristling with wax-headed pins of great variety in size and colour. They represented army units.

13. Special comb.: **wax bath**, an application of warm liquid wax which is allowed to solidify to a part of the body, for cosmetic or medical purposes; also, an immersion in liquid wax; **wax bean** *U.S.* = *wax-pod bean* below; † **wax boot**, a boot made of waxed leather, for walking in marshy ground; **wax-bush**, the plant *Cuphea viscosissima*; **wax-butter** = *butter of wax* (see quot.); **wax-cloth**, cloth coated with wax as a protection from wet; also, oil-cloth for covering floors or tables; **wax-cluster** *Austral.*, the plant *Gualtheria hispida*; **wax-colour**, (*a*) a pigment ground with wax for encaustic painting; (*b*) the yellow colour of wax; hence **wax-coloured** *a.*; † **wax-comb**, a honeycomb; **wax-creeper** *S. African*, a name of two plants with wax-like flowers, *Hoya carnosa* and *Microloma tenuifolium*; **wax-cup**, the hollow at the top of a burning wax candle; **wax-end**, thread coated with cobblers' wax, used by shoemakers; hence **wax-ended** *a.*, bound with wax-ends; **wax-eye** *Austral.* and *N.Z.* = *silver-eye* s.v. SILVER *sb.* and *a.* 21 c; cf. ZOSTEROPS; † **wax-farthing**, a farthing paid by parishioners at Easter to provide wax candles for use in church; **wax-gland**, a gland (in certain insects) secreting wax; **wax-hair**, one of the long hairs occurring on the bodies of the young of *Psyllidæ* or flea-lice; † **wax-house**, a building in a monastery where wax candles were made; **wax-insect**, an insect producing wax; also *attrib.*; **wax jack**, a contrivance designed for holding a coiled taper with its end ready for lighting, to provide a flame for melting sealing wax; **wax lathe** *Watchmaking*, a lathe in which the object to be turned is fastened with shellac or sealing-wax; **wax-leather**, leather 'waxed' or finished on the 'flesh' side; also *attrib.*; † **wax-man**, the officer of a trade guild who collected the contributions of the members for the wax candles to be used in the processions; **wax-moth**, a moth whose larva preys on the honeycomb; **wax-mould**, †(*a*) a mould for running melted wax into; (*b*) a mould made of wax; **wax museum**, a waxworks; also *fig.*; **wax-myrtle** = WAX-BERRY a; **wax-nose**, a 'nose of wax' (see NOSE *sb.* 4); hence **wax-nosed** *a.*; **wax-oil** *Chem.* (see quot.); † **wax-opal** (see quot.); **wax-painting**, encaustic painting; **wax-palm**, a name for two S. American wax-yielding palms, *Ceroxylon andicola* and *Corypha* or *Copernica cerifera*; **wax-paper** (see quot.); **wax pear**, a variety of pear of a wax-like colour; **wax pigment**, a pigment prepared with wax; **wax-pine**, **wax-pink** (see quots.); **wax-pocket** *Ent.*, each of the sacs on the abdomen of the bee, for receiving the wax secreted by the wax-glands; **wax-pod bean**, a dwarf French bean belonging to any of several varieties having yellow, stringless pods; a butter-bean; **wax print**, cloth patterned by a batik process; **wax rose**, a variety of rose whose petals have a waxy appearance; † **wax shoe**, a shoe made of waxed leather (cf. *wax boot*); † **wax-silver**, money paid by parishioners at Easter for wax candles to be used in the church; **wax tablet**, a board coated with wax, to be written upon with a stylus; **wax-weed** = *wax-bush*; **wax-worm**, the larva of the wax-moth.

1916 *Chambers's Jrnl.* Oct. 701/1 The *wax-bath has not been found beneficial in chronic rheumatoid arthritis. **1975** *Harpers & Queen* June 168/1 Sauna, steam cabinet baths, wax baths. [**1900** L. H. BAILEY *Cycl. Amer. Hort.* I. 136/2 The Wax or Yellow-podded sorts need a richer soil.] **1905** *Outing* July 502/2 White bush *wax-beans are best for very early, but the pole varieties are better for late. **1967** R. M. CARLETON *Vegetables for To-day's Gardens* ii. 14 No one has produced a wax bean with better flavour than Pencil Rod Black Wax. **1676** SHADWELL *Virtuoso* II. 29 'Twill be as common to buy a pair of Wings to fly to the World in the Moon, as to buy a pair of *Wax Boots to ride into Sussex with. **1845–50** MRS. LINCOLN *Lect. Bot.* II. 96 *Cuphea viscosissima* (*wax-bush). **1868** WATTS *Dict. Chem.* (1877) V. 1036 Beeswax is decomposed by dry distillation, giving off a product which forms, on cooling, a white buttery mass, called *wax-butter, or *Butyrum ceræ*. **1816** SCOTT *Bl. Dwarf* i, The first..having a hat covered with *wax-cloth,..and dreadnought overalls. **1834** CARLYLE *Let. to Mrs. Austin* (Thorpe's Catal. 1913) Some sort of wax-cloth for a lobby. **1868** *Chamb. Encycl.* X. 111/2 *Wax-cloth*, a name sometimes given, but very erroneously, to *Floor-cloth* (q.v.). **1834** J. ROSS *Van Diemen's Land Ann.* 133 *Gaultheria hispida*. The *wax cluster, abundant in the middle region of Mount Wellington. **1854** FAIRHOLT *Dict. Terms Art* s.v. *Wax Painting*, In Encaustic Painting, the *wax colours were burnt into the ground by means of a hot iron. **1901** *Macm. Mag.* Apr. 439/2 His sun-burned face turned wax-colour. **1842** LOUDON *Suburban Hort.* 581 Varieties of cornel..with *wax-coloured fruit. **1375** BARBOUR *Bruce* XI. 368 Thai mycht liknyt be Till ane *vax-cayme that beis mais. **1890** ANNIE MARTIN *Home Life Ostrich Farm* 20 The little '*wax-creeper,' than which tiny as it is, I do not think a more perfect flower could be imagined. **1800** HERSCHEL in *Phil. Trans.* XC. 463 That the *wax-cup of the candle be kept clean, and never suffered to run over. **1825** Brockett *N.C. Gloss.*, **Wax-end*, the waxed thread used by cordwainers. **1838** Dickens *O. Twist* vii, 'I will not, sir,' replied the beadle, adjusting the wax-end which was twisted round the bottom of his cane for purposes of parochial flagellation. **1888** Fenn *Dick o' the Fens* 68, I could mend all this in less than an hour with some wax-ends and a brad-awl. **1838** Dickens *Nickleby* xiii, A fearful instrument of flagellation, strong, supple, *wax-ended, and new. **1874** A. Bathgate *Colonial Experiences* xvii. 239 While some species are seemingly dying out, others, such as the moko-moko and the *wax-eye.. appear to be increasing. **1957** J. Frame *Owls do Cry* ix. 39 The wax-eyes hungry for honey, will make their green and yellow cloud to follow her. *c* **1588** in *Rel. Ant.* I. 255 Every house payd at Easter..j farthynge called a *waxfarthinge. **1899** D. Sharp *Insects* II. 589 Certain gall-dwelling Aphidae..possess numerous *wax glands. *Ibid.* 580 In these earlier stages the body [of various Psyllidae] bears long hairs called *wax-hairs. **1385–6** *Durham Acc. Rolls* (Surtees) 391 In factura unius camini in le *Waxhous. **1472–3** *Ibid.* 413 Cum emendacione unius patelle de le wax-house, 14d. **1815** Kirby & Sp. *Entomol.* x. (1818) I. 329 This account is in the main confirmed by Geomelli Careri, except that he calls the *wax-insect a worm which bores to the pith of certain trees. **1857** Fortune *Resid. among Chinese* 147 The wax-insect tree is no doubt a species of ash (fraxinus). **1881** *Globe Encycl.* VI. 484/1 The Hemipterous family *Coccidæ* includes the chief wax insects, familiarly known as bark lice. **1937** *Times Lit. Suppl.* 13 Mar. 189/2 Such diversities as a coach model, a silver *wax-jack and devices of human hair. **1956** G. Taylor *Silver* v. 114 The wax jack..is a simple framework supporting a horizontal reel which revolves to feed a length of taper up through a central nozzle. **1980** *Halcyon Days Catal.* 16/1 A bougie box or wax jack (designed to encase a flexible wax taper). South Staffordshire, c. 1770..£520. **1884** F. J. Britten *Watch & Clockm.* 139 For many operations required in watch jobbing Mr. Ganney recommends the *wax or cement lathe. **1711** Steele *Spect.* No. 48 ¶4, I am mounted in high-heel'd Shoes with a glased *Wax-leather Instep. **1852** Morfit *Tanning & Currying* (1853) 152 Wax leather is blackened in the flesh. **1885** *Harper's Mag.* Jan. 278/1 Wax leather, the serviceable leather for the upper parts of men's boots. **1766** *Complete Farmer* s.v. *Bee*, A small caterpillar, termed the wax-worm, or *wax-moth, because of the havock it makes on wax. **1815** Kirby & Sp. *Entomol.* xii. (1818) I. 390 The wax-moth larva (*Galleria Cereana*) will for want of wax eat paper, wafers, wool, etc. **1877** J. G. Wood *Nature's Teach.* 151 The Wax-moth, or Galleria-moth (*Galleria alvearia*)..is in its larval state extremely injurious to beehives. *a* **1679** Sir J. Moore *England's Interest* (1703) 137 First provide necessary Instruments, as..Honey-Pots, *Wax-Molds. **1849** G. W. Francis *Art of Modelling Waxen Flowers* 16 Wax moulds for plaster casting, or the electro-type, should have [etc.]. **1963** V. Nabokov *Gift* i. 35 A Russian foodshop, which was a kind of wax museum of the old country's cuisine. **1981** J. Valin *Dead Letter* viii. 68 There was something a little scarey about this artificial paradise... The place had the shallow charm of a wax museum. **1813** Sir H. Davy *Agric. Chem.* iii. (1814) 96 Wax..is procured in abundance from the berries of the *wax-myrtle. **1884** Sargent *Rep. Forests N. America* (10th Census IX) 136 *Myrica cerifera*..Bayberry. Wax Myrtle. *a* **1843** Southey *Commonpl. Bk.* (1851) IV. 11 It is fitter for the dotage dreams of Sir William Jones, than the visions of the poet. Let the *wax-nose be tweaked by Volney on one side and Maurice on the other! *c* **1615** Sylvester *Mem. Mortal.* II. xciv, Let's leave out I, and No, in Conversation: Words now transposed, and *wax-nosed, Both. **1852** J. M. Honigberger *Thirty-five Yrs. in East* I. 69, I kept the wound open for several days, and ordered the swollen parts to be embrocated with *wax-oil. **1868** Watts *Dict. Chem.* (1877) V. 1036 [Beeswax gives off wax-butter, and] afterwards a more and more liquid oil, called wax-oil, still retaining a small quantity of solid matter. **1896** Chester *Dict. Names Min.*, **Wax-opal*, an early name for yellow opal with a waxy lustre. **1854** Fairholt *Dict. Terms Art*, **Wax Painting*. This art practised by the ancients under the name of Encaustic, has lately been revived in several countries. **1859** Gullick & Timbs *Painting* 75 Various attempts have been made to re-introduce wax-painting; but the art of *pencillum-encaustic*, as practised by the ancients, seems to be lost. **1830** Lindley *Nat. Syst. Bot.* 282 The Ceroxylon andicola, or *Wax Palm of Humboldt, has its trunk covered by a coating of wax, which exudes from the spaces between the insertion of the leaves. **1882** J. Smith *Dict. Pop. Names Plants* 436 *Wax Palm.* There are two so called: 1. *Copernicia cerifera*, a fan palm native of Brazil... 2. *Ceroxylon andicola*, a tall wing-leaved palm, native of the elevated regions of New Grenada. **1844** Hoblyn *Dict. Med.*, *Wax-paper. *Charta cerata.* Melt, in a water-bath, 48 parts each of white wax and fine turpentine, and 32 parts of spermaceti, and spread on paper. **1600** Surflet *Country Farm* III. xlix. 537 The best..perrie is made of little yellow *waxe peares. **1854** Fairholt *Dict. Terms Art* s.v., This medium is employed in making the cakes of *wax-pigments for water-colours. **1891** *Century Dict.*, **Wax-pine*, the general name for the species of *Agathis* (*Dammara*), coniferous trees producing a large amount of resin. *Ibid.*, **Wax-pink*, a name for garden species of *Portulaca*: so called from their wax-like leaves and showy flowers. **1815** Kirby & Sp. *Entomol.* xv. (1818) I. 492 The apparatus in which the wax is secreted consists of four pair of membranous bags or *wax-pockets. [**1913** L. C. Corbett *Garden Farming* ix. 136 A different variety..may have either green or wax pods.] **1921** *Culture of Vegetables & Flowers* (Sutton & Sons) (ed. 16) 24 Many visitors to the Continent have learned to appreciate the fine qualities of the *Waxpod Beans. **1951** [see butter-bean]. **1962** *Amateur Gardening* 5 May 19 The golden waxpod beans have always attracted a good deal of attention. **1969** *Times* 24 Nov. (Congo Suppl.) p. iv/3 English Calico is planning a factory to manufacture 20m. yards of '*wax prints' a year. **1979** *Guardian* 8 June 17/3 Accra's famous market mammies have their stalls..broken into..and their contents—waxprint cloth, provisions,..taken away. **1837** Rivers *Rose Amateur's G.* 18 Duchess d'Angoulême, or the *wax rose, is an old but deservedly favourite variety. **1664** Wood *Life* (O.H.S.) II. 20 For a pair of *wax shoes [cf. below 1666, waxt shoes], 4s. 4d. **1692** Sir J. Foulis *Acc. Bk.* (S.H.S.) 144 For 2 pair wax shoes. **1432** in Glasscock *Rec. St. Michael's, Bp.'s Stortford* (1882) 3 Et in *waxsilver collecto in ecclesia in die Paschali, vijs. viijd. **1496** *Cov. Leet Bk.* 574 Item, that no maister make no brother to þe Craft yf he haue be prentes in þe Cite no lesse þen xiij s. iiij d. & his wax siluer. **1807** Douce *Illustr. Shaks.* II. 228 The Roman practice of writing on *wax tablets with a stile was continued also during the middle ages. **1905** J. B. Bury *Life St. Patrick* iii. 40 Honoratus sent a messenger across in a boat with a letter on a wax tablet. **1884** W. Miller *Plant-n.* I. 144 *Wax-weed, Blue, *Cuphea viscosissima.* **1766** *Wax-worm [see *wax-moth*].

wax (wæks), *sb.*² Now *rare* exc. *dial.* [f. wax *v.*¹ Cf. G. *wachs.*]

1. The process of waxing; growth.

a **1300** *Cursor M.* 1430 Euer stod þai [*sc.* þe wandes] still in an, Wit-outen wax, wit-outen wain. *Ibid.* 8244 A-boute þat tre, A siluer cercle son naild he, þat was þe stouen for to strength, And knau þe wax o gret and length. **1892** *Athenæum* 30 Jan. 146/2 'On the Wane' (which should strictly be called 'On the Wane, on the Wax, and on the Wane Again').

2. Stature; size (of something growing).

c **1460** *Towneley Myst.* xxx. 245 Thou art best on thi wax that euer was clekyt, or knawen. **1618** W. Lawson *New Orch. & Garden* (1626) 35 The boale will be first, and best serued and fed, because he is next the root, and of greatest waxe and substance. **1868** Atkinson *Cleveland Gloss.*, and **1876–89** in Yorks. and Lincs. glossaries.

wax (wæks), *sb.*³ *colloq.* or *slang.* [Of doubtful origin; possibly evolved from some phrase like *to wax angry* (arch.), *to wax warm* (now *dial.*): see wax *v.*¹ 9 a (*b*).] Angry feeling; a fit of anger; chiefly ***to be in a wax.***

1854 'C. Bede' *Verdant Green* II. vii, I used to rush out in a frightful state of wax, and show a leg. **1865** H. Kingsley *Hillyars & Burtons* xxxv, Can't you get into a wax, old girl? **1874** H. Belcher *Cramleigh Coll.* I. 181 It ain't my fault if you've been bohooin'; so don't be in a wax with me. **1880** 'Ouida' *Moths* I. 112 What a wax you're in, Dolly.

wax (wæks), *v.*¹ Pa. t. and pa. pple. **waxed** (wækst); also pa. pple. **waxen.** Forms: *Inf.* (and Pres. stem). 1 **weaxan, weacsan, weahsan, weahxan, wexan, wehsan,** 2–3 **wecsen,** 2–4, 6–7 *arch.* **wexen,** 3 **uexen, wexi,** 4–5 **wix(e,** 5 **vexe, wexyn, vix(e, vyx(e,** 3–6 **wexe,** 4–7 (9 *arch.*) **wex;** 2–4 **wacse(n,** 3 *Orm.* **waxenn, waxxenn,** 3–6 **waxen,** 5 **waxyn,** 4–6 *Sc.* **vax,** 6 **weaxe,** *Sc.* **walx,** 3–7 **waxe,** 3– **wax.** *Contracted 2 sing.* 1 **wyxt,** 4 **wext;** 3 *sing.* 1 **weaxt, wexþ, wixt,** etc., 3 **west,** 3–4 **wexþ,** 4 **wext.** *Pa. t. sing.* 1 **wéox, wéocs, wéohs,** *Northumb.* **-wóx,** 2 **weax, weacs,** 2–3 **wæx,** 3 **weox,** 2–5 **wex,** 4–5 **wexe, weex,** *north.* **wix, wyx,** 4 *north.* **vex;** 2 **wacxs,** 3–6 **wax,** 4–5 **waxe,** 4 **waux;** 3–6 (7, 9 *arch.*) **wox,** 4–6 (9 *arch.*) **woxe,** 4–6 *Sc.* **vox,** 5 **woxse,** 4–5 *Sc.* **woux,** 6 *Sc.* **woix, wolx.** *Plur.* 1 **wéoxon, wéohson, wéoxson,** *Northumb.* **wóxon,** *Mercian* **wéxon,** 2 **weoxan,** 3 **weoxen,** 3–5 **wexe(n;** 3 **wuxen,** 4 **wuxe,** 3–5 **woxe(n,** 4 **waxen.** *weak.* 4 **wast,** 4–5 **wex-, waxide, -ede,** *pl.* **wexiden, -eden,** 5 **wexedde, wexid, wexte, waxet, waxte, waxhid,** *pl.* **waxiden,** 5–6 **waxt,** 5–7 **wext, wexed,** 6 **weaxed,** 5– **waxed.** *Pa. pple.* 1 **weaxen,** 2 (**ȝe**)**wexon,** 3 (**i**)**wexan,** 3–6 **wexen,** 3–5 **wexe,** 4–5 **wex, wexun,** 5 **-in, -yn, wixen;** 3–7 (8–9 *arch.*) **waxen,** 3–6 **waxin,** 4–5 **-yn, wax(e,** 4 **ywax,** 5 **waxun, waxson,** 6 *Sc.* **walxin;** 3–7 **woxen,** 3–4 **i-, ywoxe,** 3–5 **woxe, woxin,** 3 (**i**)**wox,** 4, 6 **wox,** 4 **woxyn, woxsen,** 4–5 **woxun.** *weak.* 4 **wexid,** 5 **y-wexed,** 5–7 **wext,** 6 **waxt, weaxed,** *Sc.* **vaxit,** 6–7 **wexed,** 6– **waxed.** [A Common Teut. strong verb (which became weak in late ME.): OE. *weaxan* (pa. t. *wéox*, Northumb. *wóx*; pa. pple. *weaxen*) corresp. to OFris. *waxa* (W.Fris. *waechsje, wachse*, N.Fris. *wāks*), OS. *wahsan*, (M)Du. *wassen*, OHG. *wahsan* (MHG., mod.G. *wachsen*), ON. *vaxa* (Sw. *växa*, Da. *vokse*), Goth. *wahsjan* (with *ja-* suffix in the pres.-stem; pa. t. *wōhs*, pa. pple. *wahsan-s*):—OTeut. **waχs-*:—pre-Teut. **woks-*, an ablaut variant of Indogermanic **aweks-*, **auks-*, **uks-* (Gr. ἀέξειν, αὔξειν, αὐξάνειν to increase, Skr. *ukš* to grow, perf. *va- vakša*, causative *vakšayati*), an extended form of **aweg-* **aug-*, **ug-* (L. *augēre* to increase, Sk. *ōjas* neut., strength, Lith. *augu* I grow, OTeut. **auk-* in Goth. *aukan*, OHG. *ouhhôn*, OE. *éacian* to grow, increase: see eke *v.*)

The OTeut. conjugation of the verb is retained in Goth., OHG., OS., and ON.; in OE. it is confined to the Northumbrian dialect (pa. t. *wóx*); the WS. pa. t. *wéox* and the Du. *wies* are due to the analogy of the reduplicating verbs.

The strong pa. t. became rare after the 14th c., and is now wholly obsolete; the one or two examples in the poetry of the 18–19th c. are deliberately archaistic. For the pa. pple. the Bible of 1611 has *waxed* four times and *waxen* eight times; in recent use *waxen* is not unfrequent when the verb is conjugated with *to be*, but is otherwise very rare.]

Originally a more frequent synonym of grow *v.*, which has now superseded it in general colloquial use, exc. with reference to the moon (see 6). With this exception, the senses below which are not marked as obsolete are confined to literary use, and have, in varying degrees, a somewhat archaic flavour; some of those under branch I survive only in the traditional antithesis with wane *v.* The verb is said still to be current in certain dialects: see *Eng. Dial. Dict.*

I. To grow, increase. (Opposed to *wane*, †*wanze.*)

1. *intr.* Of a plant or its parts: To increase gradually in size and vigour; to develop, sprout (*up*). *Obs.* exc. *dial.* †Also, to grow in a specified habitat or situation (*obs.*).

c **897** Ælfred *Gregory's Past. C.* xl. 293 Sumu twiȝu he lehte mid wætere, ðonne hie to hwon weoxson, ðæt hie ðy suiður weaxan sceolden. *c* **1000** Ælfric *Hom.* II. 402 Rixe weaxst ȝewunelice on wæteriȝum stowum. *c* **1200** *Trin. Coll. Hom.* 161 Hie wenden þe eorðe, and wurpen god sad þaronne, and hit wacxs and wel þeagh. **1297** R. Glouc. (Rolls) 494 Corn & frut hom wax inouȝ. *c* **1381** Chaucer *Parl. Foules* 206 There wex ek euery holsum spice & gres. **1382** Wyclif *Matt.* xiii. 7 The thornis wexen vp. *a* **1400–50** *Wars Alex.* 4772 Lo, þis was a wondirfull werk..þat þai [trees] suld wax soo & wane within a wale time. **14..** in *Rel. Ant.* I. 54 Tak everferne that waxes on the ake. **1577** B. Googe *Heresbach's Husb.* I. 40b, When the Corne is ripe..you must then haue it in, that it may rather waxe in the Barne then in the Feelde. **1612** Drayton *Poly-olb.* v. 51 The Stem shall strongly wax, as still the Trunk doth wither. **1886** *S.W. Linc. Gloss.* s.v., The plums are waxing nicedly.

†**b.** Of a mineral: To be native, be found, in a specified place; = grow *v.* 2b. *Obs.*

c **1000** Ælfric *Gen.* ii. 11 þæt land þe ys ȝehaten Euilað, þær þær gold wext [Vulg. *ubi nascitur aurum*]. **1362** Langl. *P. Pl.* A. XI. 12 Al þe presciouse Peerles þat in paradys waxen.

2. Of human beings and animals: To increase gradually in size and strength of body and limb. *arch.* and *dial.*

c **1000** *Ags. Gosp.* Luke ii. 40 Soðlice þæt cild weox. *c* **1200** Ormin 3182 & swiþe wel he wex & þraf. *c* **1205** Lay. 30073 þa children wuxen and wel iðoȝen. *a* **1300** *Havelok* 791 Ich am wel waxen. *a* **1300** *Cursor M.* 10613 Als sco wex on hir licame, Sua wex hir loueword and hir fame. **13..** *Coer de L.* 2836 For fourty pound men sold an oxe, Though it were but lytyl woxe. *c* **1400** *Destr. Troy* 12449 Thies [two sons] were gyuen to the gouernaunce of a gay kyng,..Till þai waxen were of wit & of wight dedis. **1471** Caxton *Recuyell* (Sommer) 247 In this nourysshing he waxe and grewe in all beawte, strengthe, and prudence. *a* **1547** Surrey *Æneid* IV. 353 Ascanius yet that waxeth fast behold. **1575** Turberv. *Faulconrie* 358 You must beware that you take them not before they are somewhat woxen. **1677** in *Ray's Corresp.* (1848) 127, I think they [salmon] wax for five or six years. **1875** F. J. Scudamore *Day Dreams* 83 For a time he grows and waxes in his stye. **1887** Morris *Odyss.* XI. 311–2 And when nine years they were waxen, nine cubits length outright Was the measure of their bigness. **1889** *N.W. Linc. Gloss.* s.v., Thy bairn waxes fast, she's taller ivery time I see her.

†**b.** of a part of the body, the hair, etc. *Obs.*

a **1000** Ælfric *Hom.* II. 434 His feax weox swa swa wimmanna. *a* **1300** *Cursor M.* 7257 Wexen was sumdel his hare. **1303** R. Brunne *Handl. Synne* 9224 Here cloþes ne roted, ne nayles grewe, Ne heere ne wax. *c* **1374** Chaucer *Boeth.* IV. met. iii. (1886) 95 þat oother is chaunged in to a lyoun..and hise nayles and hise teth wexen. **1548–77** Vicary *Anat.* ii. (1888) 24 The Nayles..are alwayes waxing in the extremitie of the fyngers and toes.

†**c.** Of a morbid growth or disease: To arise and develop on or in the body. *Obs.*

c **1000** *Sax. Leechd.* I. 118 Gif nebcorn on wifmannes nebbe wexen. *a* **1225** *Ancr. R.* 288 þeonne..þer waxeð wunde & deopeð into þe soule. *a* **1400–50** *Stockh. Med. MS.* 117 For angenayll þat waxin in feet. *c* **1400** *Lanfranc's Cirurg.* 100 A surgian muste þanne be bisy in al þat he myȝte, þat a crampe ne wexe not in þe wounde.

†**3.** Of a company, host, people: To increase in numbers. *Obs.*

c **897** Ælfred *Gregory's Past. C.* xvii. 109 Dryhten cuæð to Noe & to his bearnum: Weahsað ȝe & moniȝfaldiað & ȝefyllað eorðan. *a* **1122** *O.E. Chron.* (Laud MS.) an. 999 And a hi leton heora feonda wærod wexan. *c* **1200** Ormin 3947 þatt heoffness here mihhte swa þurrh hallȝhe sawless waxenn. **1297** R. Glouc. (Rolls) 3259 Wexinge euere beþ vre fon, bi water & bi londe. **13..** *K. Alis.* 6023 (Laud MS.), Now gynneþ his Oost fast to wexe. *c* **1330** R. Brunne *Chron. Wace* (Rolls) 1255 þey wil waxe & we schal wanye; When we ben fewe, þey schol be manye. *c* **1380** *Sir Ferumb.* 1485 Cryst of heuene ȝow alle saue my messagers alle sixe! & ȝut þe vij schulle ȝe haue ȝour felaschip to make wixe. **1581** Mulcaster *Positions* xxxvii. (1887) 148 Will ye haue the multitude waxe, where the maintenance waines? **1612** Drayton *Poly-olb.* xiii. 26 Her people wexing still, and wanting where to build. *a* **1656** Ussher *Ann.* (1658) 1 Then blessing them, he bade them wex and multiply.

4. Of a person, nation, institution: To advance in power, importance, prosperity, etc. Const. *in*, †*on*.

a **1122** *O.E. Chron.* (Laud MS.) an. 1052 þa wæx hit [*sc.* the minster] swiðe on land & on gold & on seolfer. *c* **1200** Ormin 10868 Iwhillc mann..Birrþ..þrifenn aȝȝ & waxenn aȝȝ Inn alle gode þinge. *Ibid.* 17967 Ned iss..þatt he nu forrþwarrd waxe, & ec iss ned & god off me, þatt I nu forrþwarrd wannse. **1340** *Ayenb.* 26 Al-huet þanne þet hi byþ uol wexe and heȝe ycliue ine dyngnetes. *c* **1380** *Sir Ferumb.* 1666 Al-so mot y waxe. **1449** Pecock *Repr.* III. viii. 322 Sithen the chirche wexid in dignitees, he decrecid in vertues. **1567–9** Jewel *Def. Apol.* (1611) 32 *Mali proficiunt: Boni deficiunt*: The wicked wax: the godly wane. **1597** Bp. Hall *Sat.* III. i. 44 Now man, that earst Haile-fellow was with beast, Woxe on to weene himself a God at least. **1607** Shaks. *Cor.* II. ii. 103 His Pupill age Man-entred thus, he waxed like a Sea. **1624** J. Taylor (Water P.) *Praise Clean Linen* Ded., Hee is a firme and stable man, and waxeth much oftner then hee wanes. **1690** Child *Disc. Trade* Pref. (B 2b), Land and Trade, which are Twins, and have always, and ever will wax and wane together. **1864** Tennyson *Boädicea* 40 Thou shalt wax and he shall dwindle. **1873** Burton *Hist. Scot.* VI. lxviii. 112 A democratic party equally hostile to them was waxing in size and strength. **1875** Jowett *Plato* (ed. 2) V. 54 The nation waxed in freedom and friendship and communion of soul. **1876** Morris *Sigurd* II. 85 Now waxeth the son of Sigmund in might and goodliness. **1914** H. H. Henson *War-time Serm.* xix. 244 Elmham waned as Norwich waxed.

5. Of inanimate things: To increase in size, quantity, volume, intensity, etc. Of water, the sea: To rise, swell; to flow *out* in a flood. Of day or daylight, night: To grow longer.

971 *Blickl. Hom.* 245 þæt wæter weox oþ mannes swuran. **1122** *O.E. Chron.* (Laud MS.), Hi sægon norðeast fir micel & brad wið þone eorðe, & weax on lengþe up on an to þam wolcne. *c* **1200** Ormin 1901 Marrchess nahhtess wannsenn aȝȝ, & Marrchess daȝhess waxenn. *Ibid.* 1918 O þatt daȝȝs biginneþþ uss þe daȝȝess lihht to waxenn. *Ibid.* 2472 Hire wambe siþþenn toc To waxenn alls itt birrde. *a* **1225** *Ancr. R.* 124 þer ase muchel fur is, kundeliche hit waxeð mid winde. *c* **1250** *Gen. & Ex.* 599 Dunes wexen, ðe flod wiðdroȝ. *c* **1290** *St. James* 136 in *S. Eng. Leg.* 38 þe ston bi-gan to wexe a-brod and holuȝ bi-cam a-midde. **1297** R. Glouc. (Rolls) 6562 þe se flode..bigan to wexi uaste ase it deþ atte tide. *a* **1300** *Cursor M.* 1775 þe water wex oute ouer þe plains. *c* **1325** *Spec. Gy Warw.* 1001 þi mele ne shal wante noht, And þin oyle shal waxen. *c* **1425** Wyntoun *Cron.* I. vii. 398 The watters wox as thai war wod. *c* **1430** *Chev. Assigne* 158 It [the chain] wexeth in hys honde & multyplyethe swyde. *a* **1500** *Chaucer's Dreme* 1550 Wexing the se, comming the flode. **1820** Scott *Monast.* v, Whereby I may be obliged to take the river, which I observed to be somewhat waxen. **1869** A. McLaren *Serm.* Ser. II. xi. 201 Energy which wanes as the years wax. **1884** *Spectator* 2 Aug. 1009/2 Glaciers..wax and wane in some mysterious manner. **1888** F. Hume *Mme. Midas* I. iv, Whereon the sacred fire should be kept constantly burning, waxing and waning with the seasons.

6. Of the moon: To undergo the periodical increase in the extent of its visible illuminated portion, characteristic of the first half of the lunation.

971 *Blickl. Hom.* 17 þonne he [the moon] wexeþ, he bið ȝelic þæm godum men þe ahopað to þæm ecean leohte. *c* **1000** Ælfric *Hom.* I. 154 Se mona deð æȝðer ȝe wycxð ȝe wanað: healfum monðe he bið weaxende, healfum he bið waniȝende. *a* **1225**, *c* **1386**, *c* **1440** [see wane *v.* 2]. **1591** Sylvester *Du Bartas* I. iv. 760 Tho wexing us-ward, heav'n-ward thou dost wane. **1781** Cowper *Expost.* 324 States thrive or wither, as moons wax and wane. **1859** Jephson *Brittany* viii. 110 Twelve moons had waxed and waned. **1865** Tylor *Early Hist. Man.* vi. 133 Grafts are to be set while the moon is waxing. **1914** *Blackw. Mag.* Aug. 177/1 The moon was now waxing fast.

7. Of a quality, state of things, activity, wealth, etc.: To become gradually greater or more striking; to increase in potency or intensity.

Beowulf 1741 Oð þæt him on innan oferhyȝda dæl weaxeð ond wridað. *c* **897** Ælfred *Gregory's Past. C.* xxxiii. 217 Æȝhwelces lareowes lar wihxð [*Cott.* wihst] ðurh his ȝeðylde. *c* **1200** Ormin 3949 þurrh whatt biforenn Drihhtin Godd Wurrþshipe waxenn shollde. *a* **1250** *Owl & Night.* 689 Wit west among his sore An for his sore hit is þe more. *c* **1250** *Gen. & Ex.* 1268 Abimalech saȝ abraham, Hu welðe him wex and migte cam. *a* **1300** *Cursor M.* 19399 Godds word wex fast and greu. *c* **1350** *Will. Palerne* 737 His langure gan wex. **1581** A. Hall *Iliad* I. 17 When so his furie woxe, from skies he did me thro Down by the foote. **1598** Sylvester *Du Bartas* II. i. IV. *Handie-Crafts* 560 His Art, still wexing, sweetly marrieth His quavering fingers to his warbling breath. **1624** Quarles *Job Militant* i. 13 As did his Name, his Wealth did daily wex. **1627** Drayton *Agincourt* cxcii, Now wexed horror to the very height. **1855** Motley *Dutch Rep.* IV. iv. III. 65 Moreover, the discord among the Reformers themselves waxed daily.

b. in contrast with *wane* or †*wanze*.

13.. *Pol. Rel. & L. Poems* (1903) 263 Worldes catel passet sone, þat wacset & wansit rit as te mone. **1377** Langl. *P. Pl.* B. xv. 3 And so my witte wex and wanyed til I a fole were. **1601** *2nd Pt. Return fr. Parnass.* v. iv. 2203 My fortunes cannot wax but they may waine. **1711** Pope *Temple Fame* 486 Some [lies] to remain, and some to perish soon; Or wane and wax alternate like the moon. **1809–10** Coleridge *Friend* xiv. (1865) 63 Its impulses wax as its motives wane. **1826** Wordsw. '*Once I could hail*' 42 In that domain Where joys are perfect—neither wax nor wane. **1899** E. J. Chapman *Drama Two Lives* 9 All life's poor glamours wax and wane.

†**8. a.** Of a quality, activity, event, etc.: To come into being, spring up, begin, arise, occur. Also with *up*. Of the day: To appear, dawn. *Obs.*

c **888** Ælfred *Boeth.* v. § 3 Of ðam ðonne onginnað weaxan þa mistas ðe þæt mod ȝedrefað. **1154** *O.E. Chron.* (Laud MS.) an. 1140, þer efter wæx suythe micel uuerre betuyx þe king & Randolf eorl of Cæstre. *c* **1230** *Hali Meid.* 3 Hu muche god mihte of inker streon waxen. *c* **1250** *Gen. & Ex.* 273 An wid ðat pride him wex a nyð. **1297** R. Glouc. (Rolls) 1713 Bituene þe romeins & þis lond þer wax þo striuing. *c* **1300** *K. Horn* 1452 (Laud) þe day by gan to wexe. *c* **1320** *Sir Tristr.* 3327 þer wex a kene crie. *a* **1340** Hampole *Psalter* xxvi. 6 If..temptacyons wax ageynes me. *c* **1374** Chaucer *Boeth.* I. pr. vi. (1886) 18 Of which false opynions the dirkenesse of perturba[ciouns] wexit [Addit. MS. wexeþ] vp. *c* **1425** *Engl. Conq. Ireland* xi. 26 In thys whyle, wax a grett wreth & a grete stryfe betwyx þe kyng of Connaght, & donoll Obreyn.

†**b.** *to wax forth*, to be born or created. *Obs.*

1362 Langl. *P. Pl.* A. x. 33 For wiþ word þat he warp woxen forþ Beestes.

II. With complement: To change by growth or increase, to become. (Cf. grow *v.* 12.)

9. a. With adj. complement: (*a*) With more or less of the idea of growth or increase: To become gradually, grow.

c **1200** Ormin 2479 þatt ȝho wass waxenn summ del græt & tatt ȝho wass wiþþ childe. *a* **1300** *Leg. Rood* ii. 133 So þat wiþþinne þritti ȝer þis tre wox wel heie. **13..** *E.E. Allit. P.* A 538 þe sunne was doun & hit wex late. **1387** Trevisa *Higden* VIII. 287 þe Scottes wex [*v.r.* wuxe] strenger and strenger. *a* **1400** *Octouian* 670 Florent ys x. yere old and fyyf, And heghe y-woxe. **1422** Yonge tr. *Secreta Secret.* 243 The medys wixen grene. *c* **1460** *Towneley Myst.* i. 163 Bryng ye furth and wax ye mo. **1542** Udall *Erasm. Apoph.* 241 b, Signifiyng..the dayes to haue weaxed longer. **1560** Bible (Geneva) *Deut.* xxxii. 15 But he that shulde haue bene vpright, when he waxed fat, spurned with his hele [**1611** Jesurun waxed fat, and kicked]. **1562** A. Brooke *Romeus & Jul.* 209 This sodain kindled fyre in time is wox so great. **1590** Spenser *F.Q.* II. x. 32 Till that her sisters children, woxen strong Through proud ambition, against her rebeld. **1651** R. Child in *Hartlib's Legacy* (1655) 64 According as your plants are waxen strong. **1764** H. Walpole *Otranto* v, Manfred..pushed on the feast until it waxed late. **1836–7** Sir W. Hamilton *Metaph.* xxxvii. (1870) II. 335 By degrees, our conception waxes fuller. **1874** Green *Short Hist.* viii. §6. 525 The panic waxed greater when it was found they claimed to be acting by the King's commission. **1881** Besant & Rice Chapl. Fleet I. 15 Even the foxes and their cubs..had of late waxed fat and lazy.

(*b*) Without the idea of growth or increase: To become, turn. (Sometimes used with reference to a sudden or immediate change.)

c **1220** *Bestiary* 151 If he [the adder] cloðed man se, Cof he waxeð. *a* **1300** *Cursor M.* 3563 His blode þan wexus dri and cald. **13..** *K. Horn* 302 (Harl.) Vpon Athulf childe rymenild con waxe wilde. **1382** Wyclif *Matt.* xxiv. 12 The charite of manye schal wexe coold. **1390** Gower *Conf.* I. 34 Whan he wax seke, thei woxen seke. **1422** Yonge tr. *Secreta Secret.* 213 Yf the messager wix dronke. *c* **1489** Caxton *Blanchardyn* xx. 64 þe proude lady..wexed red as a rose. **1513** Douglas *Æneis* II. viii. 78 The wyde hallis wolx patent [*L. atria longa patescunt*]. **1542** Udall *Erasm. Apoph.* 344 Ye people..whished & weaxed dumme. **1545** Raynalde *Byrth Mankynde* 127 Take fyne meale, and bake..tyll it waxe browne. **1593** Shaks. *2 Hen. VI*, III. ii. 76 What? Art thou like the Adder waxen deafe? **1610** Holland *Camden's Brit.* (1637) 183 Cornwall..waxeth smaller and smaller in manner of an horne. **1627** Drayton *Agincourt* cxliii, Nor aske of God the victory to gaine, Vpon the English wext so poore and fewe. **1632** Lithgow *Trav.* I. 29 Deuotion waxed scant amongst the Christians. **1712** Steele *Spect.* No. 276 ¶4 My Daughter Tabitha beginneth to wax wanton. *a* **1770** Jortin *Serm.* (1774) I. ii. 30 When..the inward light waxes dim, the faith is gone. **1815** Byron *Vis. Belshazzar* iii, All bloodless wax'd his look. **1820** Keats *Hyperion* I. 326 Pale wox I, and in vapours hid my face. **1831** Macaulay *Ess.*, *Byron* ¶11 The howl of contumely..gradually waxed fainter. **1840** Dickens *Old C. Shop* xxxviii, Mr. Chuckster waxed wroth at this answer. **1865** Trollope *Belton Est.* xxiv. 283 Captain Aylmer saw that the man was waxing angry. **1880** W. Watson *Prince's Quest* (1892) 61 Whereat the eyes of heaven wox thundrous-dim.

†**b.** with sb. as complement. *Obs.*

c **1300** *Havelok* 281 þe kinges douther bigan þriue, And wex þe fayrest woman on liue. *c* **1350** *Will. Palerne* 2931 þe white beres þat waxen seþþe hertes. *c* **1374** Chaucer *Troylus* v. 1014 Whan it was woxen eeue. *c* **1449** Pecock *Repr.* II. xvi. 243 Summe othere..weren quycker in natural witt and waxiden better philsophiris. **1477** Earl Rivers (Caxton) *Dictes* 22 He sawe a peyntour that was waxe a physicien. **1530** Palsgr. 793 Whan any preposycion waxeth an adverbe. **1542** Udall *Erasm. Apoph.* 334 He weaxed a woondreous buisie medler in all causes. *a* **1550** *A pore helpe* 269 in Hazl. *E.P.P.* III. 262, I feare me he be wext A popistant stout. **1593** Nashe *Christs T.* M 3, In three Tearmes, of a banqrout he wexeth a great landed man. **1622** Mabbe tr. *Aleman's Guzman d'Alf.* I. 21 It beginning now to waxe night, they gaue off play. **1869** Thirlwall *Serm.* Rem. 1878 III. 390 When the grain of mustard seed has waxed a great tree.

c. with complement an adv. or a prepositional phr.

a **1300** *Cursor M.* 19451 þan wex þaa wreches vte of wite. *c* **1350** *Will. Palerne* 140 He wex to a werwolf. **1377** Langl. *P. Pl.* B. XI. 111 In a were gan I waxe and with myself to dispute. **1388** Wyclif *Mark* iv. 32 It waxith in to a tre. *c* **1400** *Destr. Troy* 10824 Oft in wanton werkes wex þai with childe. *c* **1420** *Chron. Vilod.* 4551 þe meyst..woxse in to so fayre and so bryȝt a day. **1530** Palsgr. 773/1, I dare eate no crabbes, for my tethe wyll waxe and edge than. **1591** Spenser *M. Hubberd* 1103 Whereby the Ape in wondrous stomack woxe. **1831** James *Phil. Augustus* xxvii, It was now waxing towards morning. **1864** Burton *Scot Abr.* II. i. 78 A dangerous position, apt to wax from pleasant warmth into deadly heat. **1870** M. D. Conway *Earthward Pilgr.* i. 21 As time waxed on, I perceived that [etc.]. **1888** Stevenson *Across the Plains* x. (1892) 276 A small taste..waxes with indulgence into an exclusive passion. **1914** S. Phillips in *Contemp. Rev.* Oct. 552 Must that wistful dawn ne'er wax to noon?

†**d.** *to wax in age* or *eld*, to advance in years. Similarly, *to wax to man's estate*. *Obs.*

1340–70 *Alex. & Dind.* 943 A weih woxen on elde. *c* **1385** Chaucer *L.G.W.* 727 That, as they wex in age, wex here loue. *a* **1400** *St. Alexius* (Laud 622) 136 þe more he wex in elde & lengþe, To seruen god he dude his strengþe. **1588** Greene *Pandosto* (1607) D i b, As it [*sc.* the child] waxed in age, so it increased in beautie. **1590** Spenser *F.Q.* II. x. 20 When her sonne to mans estate did wex. **1916** G. W. Robinson *Willibald's Life St. Boniface* ii. 31 After he waxed in age..and the glory of boyhood came.

†**e.** Of fire. *to wax out*: to burn out, be extinguished for want of fuel. *Obs.*

c **1400** *Melayne* 463 The fire wexe owte at þe laste. **1579** L. Tomson *Calvin's Serm. Tim.* 686/2 If a fire that hath but little woode, wax out, wee put the brandes together, and blowe it, that it may burne.

†**10.** With complement a numeral: To amount to (a specified number). *Obs.*

c **1330** R. Brunne *Chron. Wace* 13327 A legion ys of folk þat wex Sex þousand, sex hundred sexti & sex. *Ibid.* 13937.

wax (wæks), *v.*[2] Also 4–5 **wexe**, pa. pple. **wexed, -yd, ywexede.** [f. wax *sb.*[1]

The ME. form *wexe* may be an umlaut derivative (= ON. *vexa*, OHG. *wahsen*, MHG. *wihsen* mod.G. *wächsen*, *wichsen*); but this is not certain, because *wex* was a frequent form of wax *sb.*[1]]

1. a. *trans.* To cover with a layer of wax; to dress with wax; to polish or stiffen with a dressing of wax. Also with *over*.

a **1380** [see waxed *ppl. a.*]. *c* **1391** Chaucer *Astrol.* II. §40 Tho tok I & wexede my label in Maner of a peyre tables. **1398** Trevisa *Barth. De P.R.* xix. lxi. (1495) 898 Tables ben wexed and dressid wyth wexe and ben planyd. *Ibid.*, For diuers vse lynnen clothes ben wexyd. *c* **1400** *Master of Game* (MS. Digby 182) xxi, þai one manere [of horn] is waxed with grene wex and gretter of sowne. *Ibid.*, A good hunters horne shuld..be wele ywexede, þikker or þinner, after at þe hunter þinketh þat it woll best sowne. **1580** Hollyband *Treas. Fr. Tong*, *Cirer*, to waxe. **1615** tr. *De Monfart's Surv. E. Indies* 40 As a Shoemaker waxeth his thread. **1659** H. Turbervil *Walk Knaves Walk* 8 You are to take notice..next of the manner, how to wax your winter boots. **1661** [T. Powell] *Hum. Industry* 56 Smal boards or tables of wood waxed over, were in frequent use among the later Romans to write in. **1825** J. Nicholson *Oper. Mech.* 745 Many cabinet-makers are contented with waxing common furniture. **1833** [S. Smith] *Lett. J. Downing* xxii. (1835) 131 With that I wax'd a thread, and got a new button. **1848** Dickens *Dombey* liv, The floors were waxed and polished. **1863** Miss Braddon *Aurora Floyd* iii, The elegant ignoramus whose sole accomplishments consist in parting his hair, waxing his moustaches, and smoking a meerschaum. **1886** J. H. Keene *Fishing Tackle* 160 Waxing your silk afresh, fasten it with two loops.

†**b.** *Photogr.* To saturate (paper) with wax. *Obs.*

1853 *Le Gray's Waxed Paper Process* 5 The paper..after the development of the image..does not require to be again waxed to obtain a positive picture. **1856** *Orr's Circ. Sci., Pract. Chem.* 146 Mode of Waxing the Negatives.

c. To remove unwanted hair from (legs, etc.) by applying hot wax and then peeling off wax and hairs together.

1953 W. P. McGivern *Big Heat* x. 134 When the boys talk business I go out and get my legs waxed. **1971** *Sunday Express* (Johannesburg) 28 Mar. (Home Jrnl.) 12/2, I would also like my legs waxed. **1977** J. Didion *Bk. Common Prayer* v. ix. 232 Carmen Arrellano had been having her legs waxed in the Caribe beauty shop.

†**2.** To stop (an aperture) with or as with wax. Also with *up*. *Obs.*

1377 Langl. *P. Pl.* B. v. 351 Alle þat herde þat horne..wissheden it had be wexed with a wispe of firses. **1697** Dampier *Voy.* I. 231 Some of them that had not waxt up their Cartrage or Catouche Boxes, wet all their Powder. **1709** T. Robinson *Vind. Mosaick Syst.* 91 They..fill their little Cells with Honey, and then do so wax it up, that it may not melt and run out.

†**3.** To join with wax. *Obs. rare.*

1693 Dryden *Ovid's Met.* I. *Transform. Syrinx* 36 He form'd the Reeds, proportion'd as they are: Unequal in their length, and wax'd with care.

4. *Leather-manuf.* To dress (a skin) with a mixture of lamp-black, oil, etc.

1885 A. Watt *Leather Manuf.* 348 Bruise on the flesh and grain up, then wax them [*sc.* the skins].

5. To make a gramophone record of (music, etc.); to record. Cf. wax *sb.*[1] 11. *slang* (chiefly *U.S.*).

1935 *Melody Maker* 12 Oct. 11/4 Mario..took his harp to the Columbia Studios, and there he well and truly waxed a couple of the classics of jazz. **1946** [see Dixie[2] 1 c]. **1954** *Cleveland Press* 7 Aug. (Home Mag.) 31 Gertrude Berg has waxed a comedy duet with Red Buttons for Columbia records. **1976** *Daily Times* (Lagos) 13 Aug. 18/2 (Advt.), Another new LP Record waxed by the Celestial Church of Christ Choir.

wax (wæks), *v.*[3] *dial.* [f. wax *sb.*[3]] *intr.* *to wax up*, to burst into anger, 'flare' up.

1859 Dickens *Haunted House* vii. 33/2 Nay, wench, dunna wax up so; whatten's done, 's done.

wax (wæks), *v.*[4] *U.S. colloq.* *trans.* 'To beat thoroughly, gain a decisive victory over' (Funk).

1884 A. A. Putnam *Ten Years Police Judge* xxii. 199 Mr. Bungle..would in nine [out of twelve cases] be waxed but for the commiseration and the magnanimity of [etc.]. **1909** *Century Dict.*, Suppl., *Wax*, to beat, thrash.

'**wax-,berry.** A name given to the fruit of certain plants and also to the plants themselves. **a.** The genus *Myrica*, esp. *M. cerifera* of North America (bayberry 2) and *M. cordifolia*, native to South Africa. **b.** = snow-berry 2 (Webster 1911).

1835 Moodie *Ten Yrs. S. Afr.* II. 197, I occasionally employed my people at spare times in gathering wax-berries, that..yield a substance partaking of the nature of wax and tallow, which is mixed with common tallow, and used by the colonists for making candles. **1855** W. A. Newman *Biogr. Mem. J. Montagu* vii. 169 Parts of the reclaimed soil..were not found suitable for the waxberry-bush. **1892** Stevenson *In South Seas* IV. vi. (1900) 328 Tamaiti..returned with coco tinder, dry leaves, and a spray of waxberry. **1897** E. Glanville *Tales fr. Veld* xiii. 100, I..found him peacefully employed boiling down wax berries for the manufacture of candles. **1953** [see kankerbos, kankerbossie].

'**wax-bill.** **a.** *sb.* Any one of numerous small birds of the *Ploceidæ* or Weaver-bird family, whose bills have a waxy appearance; *esp.* one of the genus *Estrelda*, the best-known species being *E. astrild* of South Africa.

1751 G. Edwards *Nat. Hist. Birds* IV. 179 The Wax Bill. .. The Bill is of..a fine red Colour, like Sealing-Wax, which I suppose gave the Bird its Name. **1769** Lady Mary Coke *Jrnl.* 19 Aug. (1892) III. 137 The two little birds the East India Capt. gave me..seem to be the same as some of the Duchess of Montagu's and I think she calls them wax bills. **1851–61** MAYHEW *Lond. Labour* II. 72 In St. Helena birds, known also as wax-bills and red-backs, there is a trade to the same extent. **1875–84** A. H. LAYARD *Birds S. Africa* 470. **1909** *Westm. Gaz.* 17 July 14/3 The name waxbill is another of those misleading trade names that cover many species of small birds of different genera which have brightly coloured bills resembling sealing-wax.

b. *attrib.* or *adj.* = next.

1776 P. BROWN *Illustr. Zool.* 72 White-tailed Wax-bill Finch. **1783** LATHAM *Gen. Synopsis Birds* II. I. 152 Wax-bill Grosbeak.

wax-billed, *a.* In names of certain birds: Having a bill resembling sealing-wax.

1776 P. BROWN *Illustr. Zool.* 70 The Red-rumped Wax-billed Finch. **1782** LATHAM *Gen. Synopsis Birds* I. II. 507 Wax-billed Barbet.

†**wax-bred.** *Obs.* [f. WAX *sb.*[1] + BRED *sb.*] A wax tablet. Also *transf.* a 'table', list.

In quots. *c* 1000 and *a* 1175 misapplied to the stone 'tables' of the Decalogue.

c **960** *Bened. Rule* (Schröer) lv. 92 Weaxbreda [L. *tabulæ*]. *c* **1000** ÆLFRIC *Hom.* II. 196 Þa awrat se Ælmihtiᵹa God him twa stænene wexbredu mid his aᵹenum fingre. *c* **1055** *Byrhtferth's Handboc* in *Anglia* VIII. 332 Swa us her æfter ᵹelustfullaþ to amearkianne on þissum æfterfyliᵹendum wexbredum, þe se arwurða beda ᵹesette. *a* **1175** *Cott. Hom.* 235 Þer efter arerde god þas laᵹe þurh moysen..and wrate his him self in stanene waxbredene. [**1853** ROCK *Ch. of Fathers* III. II. 128 Long after paper became known, the use of such tablets, which we may call the wax-brede, was kept on.]

wax candle. A candle made of wax.

c **725** *Corpus Gloss.* (Hessels) F419 *Funalia, cerei*, waexcondel. *a* **1000** *Ags. Gloss.* in Wr.-Wülcker 202/28 *Cereus*, wexcandel. **1398** TREVISA *Barth. De P.R.* XIX. lxi. (1495) 898 They that serue in chyrches of wexe candyls ben callyd Ceroferarii. *c* **1450** *Mirk's Festial* 295/2 Þan is þer anoþer cros of a wax-candul leyde on hys breste. *a* **1586** SIDNEY *Arcadia* II. v. §1 Sitting in a chaire,..& looking upon a wax-candle which burnt before her. **1605** ERONDELLE *Fr. Gard.* O 7 b, Make readie the Siluer-candlestickes with the waxe candles. **1753** HANWAY *Trav.* II. xxxiii. I. 224 In the middle of the room..was one large wax-candle. **1840** MRS. A. MARSH *Father Darcy* II. xviii. 300 Blazing wax candles. **1892** LADY F. VERNEY *Verney Mem.* I. 22 Two great wax candles of 12 lbs. weight, to be burnt before the high altar of the church.

attrib. **1663** *Cup of Coffee* in D'Israeli *Cur. Lit.* (1866) 296/1 Should any of your grandsires' ghosts appear In your wax-candle circles.

ˈ**wax-ˌchandler.** [See CHANDLER[1] 2.] One whose trade is to make or sell wax candles.

1418 *E.E. Wills* (1882) 34 Iohn Baldok,..Waxchaundeler of London. **1466** *Paston Lett.* II. 270 To John Orford, wax chandeler, for xii. torches and one candell of i. *lb.*, lvs. iid. *ob.* **1503** *Privy Purse Exp. Eliz. York* (1830) 103 To John Hynsted of London wexchaundeler for iij rolles of white wex [etc.]. **1543** tr. *Act 11 Hen. VI*, c. 12 The waxchaundelers in dyuers parties of England. **1633** *Stow's Surv. Lond.* 625 The Company of Wax-Chandlers, having beene a Brotherhood of very ancient standing,..became yet to be incorporated in Anno, 1484. **1706** *Lond. Gaz.* No. 4287/4 William Rack, late of St. Saviour's.., Waxchandler. **1861** T. A. TROLLOPE *La Beata* I. viii. 197 The old wax-chandler was a widower of many years' standing.

†**wax-chandlery, -chandry.** *Obs.* The department of a royal household concerned with the provision and storage of wax candles.

1398 *Acc. Exch. K.R.* 470/17 m. 2 Et eidem pro ij ceruris emptis pro ij ostiis in le Wexchaundelerye. **1602** in Jeaffreson *Midsx. County Rec.* (1886) I. 282 The Waxe Chandrie.

wax doll.

1. A doll with head and bust (often also the limbs) of wax.

1786 J. WOODFORDE *Diary* 16 Mar. (1926) II. 231 It was a wax Doll, a female Figure, dressed with a Trumpet in her Mouth. **1816** JANE AUSTEN *Let.* 21 Apr. (1952) 455 It might do for a quilt for your little wax doll. **1828** MISS MITFORD *Village, Country Barber* III. 165 A certain huge wax-doll, called Sophy, who died the usual death of wax-dolls, by falling out of the nursery-window. **1834** DICKENS *Sk. Boz, Boarding-ho.* i, Mrs. Tibbs..looked like a wax doll on a sunny day.

attrib. **1847** THACKERAY *Van. Fair* (1848) xii. 97 That silly insignificant simpering Miss Thompson, who has nothing but her wax-doll face to recommend her. **1852** MRS. CARLYLE *New Lett.* (1903) II. 50 Her wax-doll face took the fancy of Boys at that period.

2. *pl.* = FUMITORY.

1855 ANNE PRATT *Flower. Pl.* I. 81 The flowers [of *Fumaria officinalis*]..are rose-coloured, and tipped with purple and children, in many parts of Kent, call them wax dolls. **1886** BRITTEN & HOLLAND *Plant-n.*

waxed (wækst), *ppl. a.* [f. WAX *v.*[2] + -ED[1].] In the senses of the verb; esp., coated with a layer of wax; polished or stiffened with wax; dressed or saturated with wax, e.g. for water-proofing.

a **1380** *St. Augustine* 387 in Horstm. *Altengl. Leg.* (1878) 68 In a waxed table He wrot. **1586** WHITNEY *Choice Emblems* 28 His [Icarus's] waxed winges, the sonne did make so softe, They melted straighte. **1597** A. M. tr. *Guillemeau's Fr. Chirurg.* 15/1 This suture is done with a waxed threde. **1633** J. LAW in *Scotsman* (1907) 7 Sept., [He paid 16 shillings] for soleing walxt boots. **1651** T. BARKER *Art of Angling* (1653) 13 You must work al these grounds upon a waxed silk. *c* **1790** IMISON *Sch. Arts* II. 46 When you take off the paper you will find every line which you drew with the black lead pencil upon the waxed plate. **1846** BRITTAN *Oper. Surg.* 347 The piercer is withdrawn, and a double waxed thread passed through its canula. **1857** DICKENS *Dorrit* II. xx, Waxed floor very slippery. **1883** D. C. MURRAY *Hearts* xxi, Tapping his visitor's hand with the waxed end of his long pipe. **1900** *Westm. Gaz.* 22 Oct. 2/2 A waxed moustache.

b. *Leather-manuf.* Of a skin: Dressed on the flesh side with a mixture of lamp-black and oil.

1851–3 *C. Tomlinson's Cycl. Useful Arts* (1866) II. 36/1 The skin of leather now curried is called black on the flesh, or waxed, in contradistinction to leather which is curried on the hair or grain side. **1883** SIMMONDS *Dict. Useful Anim.*, *Waxed Fleshes*, a trade name for certain leathers, prepared of the inner side of a split skins. **1885** A. WATT *Leather Manuf.* 341 Waxed Leather. *Ibid.* 350 Waxed Calf-skins.

c. *Photogr.* Of paper, a paper negative: Saturated with wax.

1853 *LeGray's Waxed Paper Process* 8 Method of rendering the iodised waxed paper sensitive. *Ibid.* 16 Renovating the transparency of the waxed negative. **1857** W. CROOKES *Hand Bk. Waxed Paper Process in Photogr.* 25 When this has taken place the waxed sheets must be separated one from the other.

d. waxed-end = *wax-end* (WAX *sb.*[1] 13).

1914 *Daily News* 30 June 4 It is entirely due to the awl and the waxed-end.

waxen (ˈwæksən), *a.* Also 7 *Sc.* **wexin.** [f. WAX *sb.*[1] + -EN[4].

OE. had *wexen*, **wiexen* = (M)Du., (M)LG. *wassen*, OHG. *wahsîn* (MHG. *wähsîn*, *wehsîn*, mod.G. *wächsen*):—OTeut. **waχsino-*.]

1. Made of wax.

c **1000** *Sax. Leechd.* III. 210 Hlaf wexenne [L. *cerarium*, error for *cencrium* 'of millet'] niman freo[n]dscipas niwe ᵹefeᵹð. **13..** *Gaw. & Gr. Knt.* 1650 Waxen torches Seggez sette..in sale. *a* **1513** FABYAN *Chron.* VI. (1811) 170 The whiche ordre he kepte duely by waxen tapers kepte by certayne persones. **1590** SPENSER *F.Q.* III. i. 58 Eftsoones long waxen torches weren light, Vnto their bowres to guiden euery guest. **1591** SHAKS. *Two Gent.* II. iv. 201 For now my loue is thaw'd, Which like a waxen Image 'gainst a fire Beares no impression of the thing it was. **1611** CORYAT *Crudities* 36 By the light of a waxen candle. **1643** ALEX. ROSS *Mel Heliconium* 40 In that we do injoy our lives, In that our wexin kingdom thrives. **1646** CRASHAW *Steps Delights Muses* 115 The working Bees soft melting Gold, That which their waxen Mines enfold. **1667** MILTON *P.L.* VII. 491 The Femal Bee that..builds her waxen Cells With Honey stor'd. **1706** Z. CRADOCK *Serm. Charity* (1740) 21 They are but the.. artificial Counterfeit of Virtue, Trees laden with waxen Fruit. **1782** V. KNOX *Ess.* cxxvi. (1819) III. 40 A resemblance scarcely less exact than that of the bust to its mould, or the waxen seal to the sculptured gem. **1825** SCOTT *Talism.* iii, Two waxen torches, which the hermit lighted, gave a cheerful air to the place. **1855** MACAULAY *Hist. Eng.* xvi. III. 677 A waxen figure..was dragged about Westminster in a chariot. **1860** *Family Economist* 3 Mar. 142/1 Waxen Flowers and Fruit. **1887** *Harper's Mag.* July 185/2 The metal (or glass) plate is covered with a waxen composition.

b. *waxen image*: spec. an effigy in wax representing a person whom it was desired to injure by witchcraft.

The victim was believed to waste away as the wax melted at the fire, and to suffer pain from stabs or the like inflicted on the effigy. Cf. quot. 1591 above.

1685 G. SINCLAIR *Satans Invis. World* 101 The Waxen-Image being found and broken..the King did..recover. **1697** DRYDEN *Virg. Past.* VIII. 101 Around his waxen Image first I wind Three woollen Fillets. **1821** LAMB *Elia*, *Witches* ¶1 That maidens pined away, wasting inwardly as their waxen images consumed before a fire. **1837** BARHAM *Ingol. Leg.* Ser. I. *Leech Folkest.*, Fixed against [the doors]..was a waxen image—of himself! **1870** ROSSETTI *Sister Helen* 1 Why did you melt your waxen man, Sister Helen?

2. *trans.* and *fig.* As if made of wax. **a.** With reference to the softness, impressibility, or fusibility of wax. Chiefly of immaterial things (often with opposition to *steel* or *marble*).

1591 SYLVESTER *Du Bartas* I. ii. 211 The World's owne Matter is a waxen Lump, Which, un-self-changing, takes all kind of stamp. **1593** SHAKS. *Rich. II*, I. iii. 75 Oh thou the earthy author of my blood..with thy blessings steele my Lances point, That it may enter Mowbrayes waxen Coate. **1593** —— *Lucr.* 1240 For men haue marble, women waxen mindes. **1653** MARVELL *Corr.* (Grosart) II. 4 Truly he is of a gentle and waxen disposition. **1767** G. CANNING *Poems* 28 Watch o'er my son, inform his waxen youth. **1794** GOUV. MORRIS in Sparks *Life & Writ.* (1832) II. 424 Those who remain are of that waxen substance called the men of property. **1849** LYTTON *K. Arthur* III. l, But men are waxen when the Fates are steel'd. **1850** TENNYSON *In Mem.* xxi, This fellow would make weakness weak, And melt the waxen hearts of men.

b. With reference to the smooth and lustrous surface of things modelled in wax. Said, e.g., of fruits, flowers, youthful limbs. Also applied to the pallor of a corpse or a sick person.

a **1700** SEDLEY *Virg. Past.* ii. Wks. 1722 I. 268 And waxen Plumbs [L. *cerea pruna*]. **1743** FRANCIS tr. *Hor.*, *Odes* I. xiii. 2 His rosy neck, and waxen arms [L. *cerea bracchia*]. **1853** DICKENS *Bleak Ho.* viii, But the small waxen form [*sc.* the dead baby]..had been composed afresh. **1853** KANE *Grinnel Exp.* xxxi. (1856) 266 It makes a man feel badly to see the faces around him bleaching into waxen paleness. **1894** CROCKETT *Raiders* xii, I saw..a few waxen lobes of bell-heath, perfectly white.

¶**c.** ? As if written on wax; soon effaced. *nonce-use.*

1599 SHAKS. *Hen. V*, I. ii. 233 Or else our graue Like Turkish mute, shall haue a tonguelesse mouth, Not worshipt with a waxen Epitaph.

3. Covered or coated with wax, loaded with wax.

waxen wings: often in allusions to the story of Icarus: see ICARIAN *a.*[1]

1590 SHAKS. *Mids. N.* III. i. 172 The honie-bags steale from the humble Bees, And for night-tapers crop their waxen thighes. *c* **1590** MARLOWE *Faustus* (1604) Chorus 21 Till swolne with cunning, of a selfe conceit, His waxen wings did mount aboue his reach, And melting heauens conspirde his ouerthrow. **1605** BACON *Adv. Learn.* I. i. §3 Hence it is true..that diuers great learned men haue beene hereticall, whilest they haue sought to flye vp to the secrets of the Deitie by the waxen winges of the Sences. **1695** LD. PRESTON *Boeth.* v. 232 As heretofore with a swift Stile Men us'd on waxen Tables smooth Letters and Figures to ingrave. **1781** COWPER *Anti-Thelyphth.* 54 She tutor'd some in Dædalus's art, And promis'd they should..On waxen pinions soar without a fall. **1789–96** MORSE *Amer. Geog.* II. 27 The old..manner of writing, before the use of paper of any kind, and waxen tables, was known.

4. Special collocations: **waxen chatterer**, the Bohemian waxwing, *Ampelis garrulus*; †**waxen vein** *Min.*, argilliferous marlite.

1797 BEWICK *Brit. Birds* I. 83 Silk Tail, or *Waxen Chatterer. (*Ampelis Garrulus*, Lin.) **1862** JOHNS *Brit. Birds* 625 Waxen Chatterer or Waxwing. **1681** GREW *Musæum* III. §i. v. 311 The *Waxen Vein. *Ludus Helmontii.* A Stone composed of two distinct Bodies. **1705** S. DALE *Pharmacol.* Suppl. 29 Ludus Paracelsi..Waxen Vein. **1740** *Phil. Trans.* XLI. 836 Masses of the Waxen-vein or Ludus Helmontii, which is also found in great Plenty on the Sea-shore near the Spaw at Scarborough.

5. Comb., as ***waxen-faced, -hued, -like, -winged*** adjs.

1856 KANE *Arct. Expl.* I. xv. 170 Three stools, and as many *waxen-faced men. **1916** *Chamb. Jrnl.* Feb. 116/2 A sorrow-laden, *waxen-hued face. **1845** HIRST *Coming of Mammoth*, etc. 34 How *waxen-like his hands! **1909** *Essex Rev.* XVIII. 75 Waxen-like flowers of pale pink. **1645** QUARLES *Sol. Recant.* VII. 9 Since *waxen-winged Honour is not void Of danger.

†ˈ**waxen**, *ppl. a. Obs.* [Strong pa. pple. of WAX *v.*[1]] Grown up, full-grown, adult. *little waxen*, young.

c **1250** *Gen. & Ex.* 2060 Me drempte, ic stod at a win-tre, ðat adde waxen buᵹes ðre. **1338** R. BRUNNE *Chron.* (1810) 252 Himself in ille likyng, & had no waxen heyre, þat mot kepe þe coroune, if he of lond went. **1382** WYCLIF *Gen.* iv. 23 A litle waxen man [Vulg. *adolescentulum*]. **1422** YONGE tr. *Secreta Secret.* 161 When hit is a wixen tree, and hundrid oxyn vnneth hit may bowe. *a* **1425** tr. *Arderne's Treat. Fistula* etc. 21 In ȝong men..or waxen men, I hafe seene few [*sc.* fistulas] euer be cured. **1555** RIDLEY *Confer.* in Foxe *A. & M.* (1583) 1722/2 The Lordes supper is, and ought to be geuen to them that are waxen. **1599** *Return fr. Parnass.* II. i. 812 Fonde they to thinke that this child's waxen daye Will be well spente when maister beares no swaye. **1632** LITHGOW *Trav.* IX. 415 Such a man can neither seduce his [pupil's] minority with ill examples, nor marre his waxen age with a false impression.

†ˈ**waxen**, *v.*[1] *Obs.* Also **wexen, weaxen.**

In several writers of the 16th c. (chiefly poetical) the forms *waxen, wexen* occur for WAX *v.*[1], but only in those parts of the verb (inf. and 3rd pers. pl. present) in which these were in ME. the normal inflected forms of *wax*. This may sometimes be due to intentional grammatical archaism; but when these forms are used by writers whose grammar is in all other respects normal, it seems probable that the inflexional *waxen* in quotations from older writers was mistaken for a verb synonymous but not identical with *wax*. It has been thought desirable to give here all the examples in our material, in order that their individual significance may be judged of by comparison. The 17th c. quots. from H. More, which are added for completeness, are of course intentionally archaistic.

1540 CRANMER *Bible* Prol. ✠ jb, Anone..theyr consciences bene admonished, and they waxen sory & ashamed of the facte. **1542** UDALL *Erasm. Apoph.* 4 And contrariewise, what thynges been moste honest the same weaxen also moste pleasaunt, yf a man haue been accustomed vnto theim. **1562** A. BROOKE *Romeus & Jul.* 1039 The courage of the Mountagewes, by Romeus sight doth growe, The townes men waxen strong, the prince doth send his force. **1565** GOLDING *Ovid's Met.* III. 852 This Licabs chappes did waxen wide, his nose-thrils waxed flat. **1567** *Ibid.* XIV. 327, I felt a hooked groyne Too wexen hard vppon my mouth. **1584** PEELE *Arraign. Paris* v. i, Then first gan Cupids eysight wexen dim. **1590** SHAKS. *Mids. N.* II. i. 56 And then the whole quire hold their hips, and loffe, And waxen in their mirth. **1590** VALLANS *Tale Two Swans* (1744) p. ix, As these Swannes began to waxen old. **1594** BARNFIELD *Sheph. Content* (Arb.) 30 When their fleeces gin to waxen rough. **1642** H. MORE *Song of Soul* I. i. 3 What man ..Would woxen [**1647** wexen] wroth. **1647** —— *Cupids Confl.* lxxv, This is the measure of mans industry To wexen some body and getten grace To's outward presence.

†ˈ**waxen**, *v.*[2] *Obs. rare.* [f. WAX *sb.*[1] + -EN[5].] *trans.* To cover or dress with wax.

1552 HULOET, Waxen, *cæro, cero.* **1641** J. JACKSON *True Evang. T.* I. 24 Others [Nero] staked through..and waxened over their bodies, and so set them lighted up, as torches.

waxen-kernel. *dial.* [Of uncertain formation; the second element is KERNEL *sb.*[1]

Variants are *waxen-churnel, -crindle, -crundle, -curl, waxing-kernel, -churnel, -curl, waxy-kernel*: see *Eng. Dial. Dict.* It is doubtful whether the first element was originally WAXEN *a.*, WAXEN *ppl. a.*, or WAXING *vbl. sb.* or *ppl. a.*]

= WAX-KERNEL.

1500 STANBRIDGE *Vocabula* (1510) A iij b, In plurali he glandille, for waxen kyrnels. **1825** JAMIESON, *Waxen-kernel.* **1866** S. THOMSON *Dict. Dom. Med.* 8/1 Popularly, these enlarged glands go by the name of 'waxen kernels'.

waxer (ˈwæksə(r)). [f. WAX *v.*[2] + -ER[1].] One who or something that waxes. **a.** One who waxes leather in currying. **b.** (See quot. 1875.)

1875 KNIGHT *Dict. Mech.*, *Waxer*, an attachment to a leather sewing-machine to wax the thread as it runs from the spool to the needle. **1885** A. WATT *Leather Manuf.* 343 The waxer rubs the size into the coloured side of the leather.

c. *gen.*
1890 O. Wilde in *19th Cent.* July 127 The waxers and gilders of images. **1930** in C. S. Johnson *Negro in Amer. Civilization* I. vii. 100 Gas pipe layer, car washers, floor waxer. **1978** *Detroit Free Press* 16 Apr. F5/3 (Advt.), Dental technician. Experienced waxer for crown and bridge lab.

waxey, variant of WAXY *a.*[1]

wax flower, 'wax-flower.
1. An imitation flower made of wax.
1843 A. McLaren in E. T. McLaren *Mem.* (1911) 26 Mary, the wax flowers arrived in safety. **1844** Mintorn (*title*) The Hand-book for modelling Wax Flowers. **1858** Geo. Eliot *Scenes Cler. Life, Janet's Repent.* iii, Wax-flowers presuppose delicate fingers and robust patience.
Comb. **1858** Simmonds *Dict. Trade*, Wax-flower maker.
2. A name given to certain plants: **a.** the genus *Hoya*, esp. *H. carnosa*; **b.** *Clusia insignis* of Guyana (Ogilvie 1883); **c.** *Stephanotis floribunda* (*Cent. Dict.*).
1848 Schomburgk *Hist. Barbados* 611 *Hoya carnosa*... Fleshy-leaved Hoya. Wax Flower. **1884** W. Miller *Plant-n.* I. 144 Wax-flower. The genus *Hoya*.

waxily, -ness: see after WAXY *a.*[1]

'waxing ('wæksɪŋ), *vbl. sb.*[1] [f. WAX *v.*[1] + -ING[1].] The action of WAX *v.*[1]; growth; increase.
c **1055** *Byrhtferth's Handboc* in *Anglia* VIII. 323 Þonne se mona beo tyn nihta eald, and na þænne his leoht beo ærest on weaxunge. **1297** R. Glouc. (Rolls) 6572 [Cnut addressing the tide] Þeruore ich hote þe, þin wexing þat þou lete. **13..** *Cursor M.* 1430 (Gött.) Euer stod þai still in ane, widuten waxing [*Cott.* wax] or wane. **13..** *Amis & Amil.* 89 So like thei were both of syght, And of on wexing ryght. *c* **1449** Pecock *Repr.* III. x. 339 Thilk wexing in possessiouns was cause or occasioun of thilk decrecing in vertues. **1589** *Pappe w. Hatchet* (1844) 36 Yet the emptie caske sounds lowder than when it was ful; and protests more in his waining, than he could performe in his waxing. **1652** Urquhart *Jewel* 134 The Moon, which was then but in the first week of his waxing. **1863** *Possibilities of Creation* 100 The waxings and wanings of light in these variable objects. **1870** *Eng. Mech.* 11 Mar. 630/2 The waxing of the light of the Satellite arises from its gradual passage out of the shadow.

'waxing, *vbl. sb.*[2] [f. WAX *v.*[2] + -ING[1].]
1. a. The process of covering or dressing with wax.
c **1440** *Promp. Parv.* 519/1 Waxynge, wythe wax, *ceracio*. **1538** Elyot *Dict.*, *Cæratura*, the waxinge. **1659** H. Turbervil *Walk Knaves Walk* 8 Lastly, you must observe the waxing of the boot. **1818** *Art Preserv. Feet* 137 The waxing of the thread is..for the purpose of preventing it from slipping. **1857** Miller *Elem. Chem.*, *Org.* xi. §2. 673 Previous to sale,..another process [of currying leather], technically termed waxing, is performed. **1890** *Anthony's Photogr. Bull.* III. 344 Refusal to strip, is..due to..touching the waxed surface with the fingers after waxing.
b. (See quot. 1858.)
1815 S. Parkes *Chem. Ess.* II. 148 *note*, In printing those silk handkerchiefs called Bandanas, a process called waxing is still followed. **1858** Simmonds *Dict. Trade*, *Waxing*, the process of stopping out colours in calico-printing.
†**c.** A method of cheating at dice. *Obs.*
1726 [see TOPPING *vbl. sb.*[1] 1 c].
d. Depilation by means of wax (see WAX *v.*[2] 1 c).
1974 *Times* 27 Aug. 9/2 Services..include waxing, manicure, pedicure. **1977** *Evening Post* (Nottingham) 27 Jan. 6/1 (Advt.), Get rid of unfeminine hair with the entirely new and painless method. No needle, no scarring, no waxing. **1982** *Oxford Times* 5 Nov. 13/5 (Advt.), Beauty Therapy, facials, manicure, pedicure, waxing.
2. a. *concr.* Wax as a polish on furniture.
1825 J. Nicholson *Oper. Mech.* 745 Waxing.., like varnish,..is attended with inconveniences as well as advantages.
b. *U.S. slang.* A gramophone record or phonograph cylinder.
1936 *Metronome* Feb. 21/4 *Waxing*, phonograph record. **1941** *Jazz Information* Nov. 26/1 I'll stick to the Victor-Bluebird waxings, for they are the best. **1965** [see FRUG]. **1981** *Listener* 1 Jan. 30/1 Buddy Bolden..is said to have recorded a phonograph cylinder, somewhere around 1902. .. The rumoured waxing has never been discovered.

'waxing, *ppl. a.* [f. WAX *v.*[1] + -ING[2].] That waxes, grows, or increases.
1297 R. Glouc. (Rolls) 7228 A grene wexinge tre þat is fram þe more Ismite adoun. *c* **1330** R. Brunne *Chron. Wace* (Rolls) 7328 So waxynge [*Petyt MS.* waxand] folk in al þys werde, Ne so gendryng, ne so plentyue.. Als we arn of oure kynde, In no lond scholde men fynde. **1387-8** T. Usk *Test. Love* III. v. (Skeat) l. 5 Blosmes of waxing frute. *c* **1440** *Promp. Parv.* 471/1 Sprynygynge, of a welle or oþer waxynge watyr, *scaturacio*. **1588** Shaks. *Tit. A.* III. i. 95, I stand as one vpon a Rocke.. Who markes the waxing tide grow waue by waue. **1666** Dryden *Ann. Mirab.* iv, Each wexing Moon supplied her watry store, To swell those Tides. **1820** Wiffen *Aonian Hours* (ed. 2) 36 The mutable moon Stamps all the changes of her wexing phase. **1883** M. Creighton *Let.* in *Life* (1904) I. 263, I am sorry that you think me a waxing Conservative. **1910** Rosebery *Chatham* xxi. 456 The Duke..was at war with the waxing power of Leicester House.
†**b.** Of flesh: Excrescent. *Obs.*
c **1400** *Master of Game* (MS. Digby 182) xii, Sometyme commeth to þe houndes sekenes in her eyenn, for þer commeth a webbe vpon hem and waxynge flesshe, þe which commeth into þe one syde of þe eye and is cleped an nayle.
†**c.** *waxing kernel* = WAX-KERNEL, WAXEN-KERNEL. *Obs.*
?*c* **1460** *Medulla* (MS. St. John's, Cambr.) in *Cath. Angl.* 411 note 2 *Glandula, nodus sub cute*, a waxynge curnelle. **1530** Palsgr. 287/1 Waxyng kyrnels *glandes, glanders*. **1538** Elyot *Dict.*, *Tolles*, a waxynge kernell. **1684** J. S. *Profit & Pleas. United* 206 Waxing-Kernel, Struma, Choaking, or the Strangles.
†**d.** absol. *in the waxand*, in the waxing (phase). Cf. WANIAND.
a **1300** *Cursor M.* 22496 Þe mone þat es sa scene, quen it es in þe waxand sene.
Hence †**'waxingly** *adv.*, increasingly.
1483 *Cath. Angl.* 411/2 Waxingly, *auctim*.

wax-kernel. Now *dial.* (see Eng. Dial. Dict.) [Prob. f. WAX *sb.*[2], either with the sense of 'a growth', or with reference to the growing-time of children (cf. *wax-pain* dial. = growing-pain); but associated with WAX *sb.*[1]] A hard glandular swelling in the neck or armpit or under the jaw. Also called WAXEN-KERNEL, WAXING-KERNEL.
14.. *Nom.* in Wr.-Wülcker 707/29 *Hoc glandulum*, a wax-kyrnylle. **1569** E. Fenton *Secr. Nature* 38 b, As knots in wood, waxkernels in men, or seede in herbes. **1576** Newton *Lemnie's Complex.* II. iii. 110 b, Wherupon happen..sometime behinde the eares Impostumes, botches and wexe-kernelles. **1825** Jamieson, *Wax-kernel*. **1889** Wagstaffe *Mayne's Med. Voc.* (ed. 6), *Wax-kernels*, popular name for irritated submaxillary glands.

†**'waxless**, *a. Obs.* [f. WAX *v.*[1] or *sb.*[2] + -LESS.] Not liable to wax or increase.
a **1618** [see WANELESS].

'wax-light. A candle, taper, or night-light made of wax.
1600 M. Hoby *Diary* 18 Sept. (1930) 145, I reed, praied, was busie about waxe lightes, and then I dined. *a* **1700** Evelyn *Diary* 16 Aug. 1654, [Doncaster] a large faire towne, famous for greate wax-lights and good stockings. *a* **1715** Burnet *Own Time* II. (1823) II. 154 There were many drops of white wax-lights on his breeches. **1798** Sophia Lee *Canterb. T.*, *Young Lady's T.* II. 134 Shades over the wax-lights softened the glare. **1828** Scott *Jrnl.* 12 Apr. (1891) 572 Tom S...said in a whisper, 'I advise you to secure a wax-light to go to bed with,' shewing him..a morsel which he had stolen from a sconce. **1855** Macaulay *Hist. Eng.* xx. IV. 535 Within the Abbey, nave, choir, and transept were in a blaze with innumerable waxlights. **1864** Kingsley *Roman & T.* v. (1875) 129 The Emperor coming out to meet him with processions and wax-lights. **1870** *Chamb. Jrnl.* 16 Apr. 241/1 Visions of private sitting-rooms, wax-lights, bad wines,..at once rise before his experienced eyes.

†**waxloke.** *Obs.*[−1] (Unexplained.)
13.. *E.E. Allit. P.* B. 1037 And þer waltez of þat water in waxlokes grete, þe spumande aspaltoun þat spyserez sellen.

'wax-,maker.
1. A maker of wax or of wax candles. ? *Obs.*
14.. *Nom.* in Wr.-Wülcker 688/22 *Hic cerarius*,..whax-maker. **1483** *Cath. Angl.* 411/2 A Wax maker, *cerarius*. **1515** *Guild Bk. St. Mary, Boston* (MS.) fol. 15 In stipendio Willielmi Pynnell Waxmaker. **1543** *Star Chamber Cases* (Selden Soc.) II. 271 Maister Anthony Payne wex-maker.
2. A worker-bee that makes wax.
Translating Huber's term (*abeille*) *cirière*.
1815 Kirby & Sp. *Entomol.* xv. (1818) I. 493 When wax is not wanted in the hive, the wax-makers disgorge their honey into the cells. **1816** *Ibid.* xix. II. 128 There are two sorts of workers, the wax-makers and nurses. **1835** *Partington's Brit. Cycl. Nat. Hist.* I. 354/1.
So **'wax-,making** *vbl. sb.* and *ppl. a.*
1543 *Star Chamber Cases* (Selden Soc.) II. 271 Costes and Paymentes of the wex makynges. **1815** Kirby & Sp. *Entomol.* xv. (1818) I. 492 The stomach..in the wax-making bees is much larger than in the nurse-bees.

'wax-plant. A name given to various plants either yielding a vegetable wax or having a waxy appearance; *esp.* **a.** the candleberry myrtle, *Myrica cerifera*; **b.** any species of *Hoya*, esp. *H. carnosa*; **c.** the corpse-plant, *Monotropa uniflora*.
1801 J. Barrow *Trav. S. Afr.* I. 19 In most of the sandy flats are found..two varieties of the *Myrica cerifera*, or wax plant. **1865** Mrs. H. Wood *Mildred Arkell* xxxv, Mamma made me bring this down at once for your conservatory... It is a wax plant, and a very beautiful one. **1875** Melliss *St. Helena* 311 Hoya carnosa,..Wax plant... *Hab.* China. **1877** Sir C. Warren *On Veldt in Seventies* (1902) 379 On the window there hung a 'wax plant,' which has beautiful waxen-looking flowers. **1879** Webster Suppl., *Wax-plant*, a white fleshy plant (*Monotropa uniflora*).

wax-scot: see next.

wax-shot. *Obs.* exc. *Hist.* [WAX *sb.*[1] + SHOT *sb.*[1] OE. had *weaxȝescot* (Wulfstan): whence the form *wax-scot* in 18-19th cent. Dicts.] A customary payment made for the maintenance of lights in churches.
15.. *Eng. Gilds* (1870) 190 *marg.*, To paye for the mayntenyng off the wax and lights, iiij. d. [*marg.*, in later hand, 'Waxshote']. **15..** in *Proc. Soc. Antiq.* Ser. II. XIV. 232 Every householder payeth..for Wax-shot and Gardens two pence. **1664** [see MAINPORT]. **1706** Phillips (ed. Kersey), *Waxshot* or *Wax-scot*. **1829** [J. Chambers] *Gen. Hist. Norfolk* II. 968 *note*, Ceragium, or waxshot, was the term used for money expended in church lights.

wax taper.
1. A taper made of wax.
1398 Trevisa *Barth. De P.R.* XIX. lxii. (1495) 898 A wexe tapre hyght Cereus of cera wexe for it is made of wexe. **1408-17** in *Rec. St. Mary at Hill* Introd. p. xcvi, And .xij. wex tapers to be set vpon euery crosse. **1676** A. Marvell *Gen. Councils* Wks. (Grosart) IV. 97 Demetrius had no more reason in law against them, than a chandler might have had, if by Paul's preaching, wax-tapers..had grown out of fashion. **1765** J. Brown *Chr. Jrnl.*, *Harvest Day* 226 Such is the death of the wicked: but may I like a wax-taper, leave a sweet and edifying savour of Christ behind me. **1907** J. A. Hodges *Elem. Photogr.* (ed. 6) 148 Ignited by means of a long wax taper.
†**2.** A cone-shell (see quot.).
1815 S. Brookes *Introd. Conchol.* 157 Wax Taper, *Conus Virgo*.

'wax-tree. A name given to various trees, of different localities, yielding vegetable or insect wax; *esp.* **a.** the candleberry myrtle, *Myrica cerifera*, of North America; **b.** the privet, *Ligustrum lucidum*, of China; **c.** the genus *Vismia* of South America; **d.** the varnish-tree of South America, *Elæagia utilis*; **e.** the Japanese shrub *Rhus succedanea*.
1791 W. Bartram *Trav.* 405 A species of Myrica (Myrica inodora)..which the French inhabitants call the Wax tree. **179.** Curtis *Bot. Mag.* 2565 Ligustrum lucidum. Chinese Privet, or Wax-tree. **1803** *Nicholson's Jrnl. Nat. Philos.* (8°) IV. 188 The *myrica cerifera*, or wax tree. **1843** *Penny Cycl.* XXVII. 152/1 *Wax-tree*, the common name of the plants belonging to the genus *Vismia*. **1866** *Treas. Bot.* 442/2 The natives [S. America] speak of the tree producing this resin, *Elæagia utilis*, as the Wax tree or Varnish tree. *Ibid.* 1229/2 Wax-tree,..Japan, *Rhus succedaneum*. **1890** Hosie *West China* 197 The tree is known to the Chinese as the *Pai-la shu*, or 'white wax tree'.

waxwing ('wækswɪŋ). A passerine bird of the genus *Ampelis* (*Bombycilla*), esp. *A. garrulus*, the Bohemian waxwing.
1817 J. F. Stephens *Shaw's Gen. Zool.* X. II. 420 The Wax-wings, which have been detached from the Chatterers by Monsieur Vieillot, have a most remarkable and peculiar appendage on the tips of some of the quills, which has very much the appearance of red sealing-wax. *Ibid.* 421 Bohemian Waxwing. *Ibid.* 422 Carolina Waxwing. **1876** Smiles *Sc. Nat.* xi. 214 Among the rarer birds found in this district, were the Bohemian Waxwing or Chatterer (*Bombycilla garrula*). **1884** *Harper's Mag.* Mar. 616/1 The Carolina Wax-wing, alias cedar or cherry bird. **1888** Lees & Clutterbuck *B.C.* *1887* (1892) 348 A large flock of waxwings..was well worth seeing.

waxwork ('wækswɜːk).
1. Work executed in wax.
1723 Blackmore *Alfred* II. 67 Th' industrious Tenants of the narrow Hive..fetch Home Spoils their Wax-works to renew.
2. a. *esp.* Modelling in wax; an object or objects modelled in wax; usually applied to life-size effigies of persons, with head, hands, and bust of wax, coloured and clothed to look like life.
1697 *Post Boy* 20-23 Nov. 2/2 At the Golden Salmon in St. Martins, near Aldersgate, is to be seen, in Wax-work, about Fifty Figures, all big as the Life. **1701** in *Cath. Rec. Soc. Publ.* VII. 103 Ye Procession which began before 7 with 12 Pageants of History in large Wax Work. *a* **1704** T. Brown *Walk Lond. & Westm.* Wks. 1719 III. 316 Here stood Edward III as they told us, which was a broken Piece of Waxwork, a batter'd Head, and a Straw-stuff'd Body. **1774** Wesley *Jrnl.* 24 Jan., I was desired by Mrs. Wright, of New-York, to let her take my effigy in wax-work. **1840** Dickens *Old C. Shop* xxvii, I've seen wax-work quite like life. **1865** —— *Mut. Fr.* I. ix, 'It's no good my being kept here like Wax-Work, is it now?' 'People have to pay to see Wax-Work, my dear,' returned her husband.
fig. **1858** Gladstone *Homer* III. 512 Homer gives us figures that breathe and move. Virgil usually treats us to waxwork.
b. *pl.*
1774 Goldsm. *Nat. Hist.* II. 267 Of Mummies, Wax-Works, &c. **1896** S. Butler *Life & Lett. Dr. S. Butler* I. 228 This can only be surpassed..by Dr. Arnold's taking the terracotta figures of the Varese chapels for waxworks.
3. An exhibition of wax figures representing celebrated or notorious characters; also, the place of exhibition. Now *pl.*
1763 Boswell *Jrnl.* 4 July in *London Jrnl.* (1950) 289, I went and saw Mrs. Salmon's famous wax-work in Fleet Street. **1773** Duchess of Northumberland *Diary* (1926) 207 The Tower, the Venetian Lady, Westminster Abbey, Salmon's Waxworks. **1796** T. Morton *Way to get Married* v. i, You must show me the sights—The lions at the Tower, ..the parliament-house, and the wax-work. **1806** J. Beresford *Miseries Hum. Life* vii. §67 Escorting two or three coaches full of country-cousins..to the Lions, the Wax-work, the Monument, &c. **1831** *Cruchley's Pict. Lond.* 112 Wax Works. Fleet Street. **1837** Thackeray *Ravenswing* ii, He looked like a figure out of a wax-work. **1895** Sir H. Irving in *Daily News* 17 June 6/4 'You didn't go [to the Lyceum]! Why not?' 'Well, sir, you see there's the missus, and she preferred the wax-works.'
4. *U.S.* The climbing bitter-sweet, *Celastrus scandens*; so called from the waxy scarlet aril of the fruit.
1818 W. P. C. Barton *Compendium Floræ Philadelphicæ* I. 128 Wax Work. A climbing plant frequently reaching the tops of trees. **1856** A. Gray *Man. Bot.* (1860) 81 *Celastrus scandens* (Wax-work. Climbing Bitter-sweet).
5. *attrib.* and *Comb.*, as ***waxwork-figure***, ***-show***; **waxwork-man**, the proprietor of a waxworks.
1827 Syd. Smith *Wks.* (1859) II. 131/1 There is a wax-work Pope, and a wax-work Court of Rome. **1836** Dickens *Sk. Boz, Gt. Winglebury Duel*, Whenever a juggler, or wax-work man, or concert-giver, takes Great Winglebury in his circuit. **1840** —— *Old C. Shop* xxvii, Mrs. Jarley's wax-work show. *Ibid.* xxix, She slept..in the room where the waxwork figures were. **1889** R. Buchanan in *Contemp. Rev.* Dec. 912 The highway is strewn with the corpses of dead poets who never lived,..with loud inglorious Cowleys, with waxwork Popes. **1898** Watts-Dunton *Aylwin* VIII. i, The

House of Commons has become a bear-garden, and t'other House a wax-work show.

'wax-'worker. A worker in wax: **a.** a bee that makes wax; **b.** a maker of waxwork (Worcester 1860).

1821 tr. *Huber's New Observ. Nat. Hist. Bees* (ed. 3) 336 When hives are full of combs, the wax workers disgorge their honey into the ordinary magazines, making no wax.

So **'wax-'working** *a.* (of a bee) making wax. **1827** E. BEVAN *Honey-Bee* 367 The power of producing wax is common both to the nursing- and wax-working bees.

waxy ('wæksɪ), *a.*¹ Also 7 **waxey.** [f. WAX *sb.*¹ + -Y¹.]

†**1.** Made of wax, waxen. *Obs.*

1552 HULOET, Waxie or of waxe, *cæreus.* **1615** *Montgomerie's Cherrie & Slae* v. in Ramsay *Evergreen* (1875) II. 101 And sum [bees] the waxie Veschells wrocht, Thair Purchase to preserve. **1625** K. LONG tr. *Barclay's Argenis* v. i. 330 The Bees so sudden joyes Their waxie-houses fill with buzzing noyse.

2. a. Having the nature or distinctive properties of wax.

1799 G. SMITH *Laboratory* I. 434 Boil a quantity of honey in order to get all the waxy part out of it. **1866** *Treas. Bot.* s.v. *Elæagia,* These trees are remarkable for the quantity of green resinous or waxy matter which is secreted by the stipules. **1884** BOWER & SCOTT *De Bary's Phaner.* 82 In company with the cuticular bodies there are usually found compounds of a waxy nature.

b. *fig.* Of a person, his heart, mind: Soft, plastic, impressionable like wax.

1596 WILLOBIE *Avisa* (1880) 88 If you had had a waxye hart That would haue melt at hot desyre. **1608** BP. HALL *Char.* II. 111 The Vnconstant... He is seruile in imitation, waxey to persuasions. **1632** T. GOFF *Courageous Turk* II. v, Thinke you my minde is waxie, to be wrought, By any fashion. *a* **1660** HAMMOND *19 Serm.* xvii. Wks. 1684 IV. 679 Now..that the softer waxy part of you, may receive some impression from this Discourse, let us close all with an Application. **1843** DICKENS *Let.* 13 Nov. *Lett.* (1880) I. 93 If you will impress this on the waxy mind of —— I shall be truly and unaffectedly obliged to you.

3. a. Resembling wax in colour or consistence; (of a quality) like that of wax. Often said of boiled potatoes that have not become 'mealy'.

1835–6 *Todd's Cycl. Anat.* I. 428/1 The..waxy appearance which those who are the subjects of this disease [i.e. chlorosis] generally exhibit. **1841** HOOD *Tale of Trumpet* 209 Great Philosophers talking like Platos,..And your ears as dull as waxy potatoes! **1845** *Florist's Jrnl.* (1846) VI. 6 Ground colour a clear primrose, edging a bright purple, petals very waxy. **1868** 'HOLME LEE' *B. Godfrey* xxviii, There are two daughters, pretty little waxy girls they were. **1875** BUCKLAND *Log-Bk.* 140 The general colour of the scorpion is a horrid-looking waxy brown. **1890** *Lancet* 16 Aug. 333/1 The fat is abnormally waxy and soft. **1905** R. BAGOT *Passport* xxv. 268 The waxy whiteness of the rest of the face [in an old picture].

b. *Med.* Affected with amyloid degeneration.

1845 BUDD *Dis. Liver* 243 These characters are well expressed by the epithet 'waxy,' which has been applied to livers in this state by Dr. Home and Rokitansky. **1866** A. FLINT *Princ. Med.* (1880) 57 The waxy material is exceptionally deposited in large nodules, constituting the waxy tumors. **1876** BRISTOWE *Th. & Pract. Med.* 800 Gall-stones..sometimes consist..of a nearly homogeneous waxy mass. **1881** W. H. DAY *Dis. Childr.* 256 The lardaceous or waxy kidney. **1897** *Allbutt's Syst. Med.* IV. 537 The diffuse, waxy spleen.

4. Soiled or covered with wax. In quots. as a derisive epithet for a cobbler.

1851 MAYHEW *Lond. Labour* (1861) III. 75/2 Your child ..called me cobbler waxy, waxy, waxy. **1914** A. MACDONALD *Story & Song fr. Loch Ness-side* xiii. 223 They got there [into the fairy mound], and immediately observed the 'waxy cobbler' still dancing.

5. *Comb.*, as ***waxy-faced, -looking, -skinned, -white.***

1846 DICKENS *Cricket on Hearth* i, The little waxy-faced Dutch clock in the corner. **1927** *Scots Observer* 1 Jan. 3/1 Barefoot women..some with waxy-faced infants in their arms. **1859** D. BUNCE *Trav. with Dr. Leichhardt* vi. 44 A race of plants having waxy-looking berries. **1871** T. H. GREEN *Introd. Pathol.* 65 The cut-surface is..translucent, and waxy-looking. **1964** S. DUKE-ELDER *Parsons' Dis. Eye* (ed. 14) xxii. 328 Oedema is usually not marked, but all over the posterior pole there tend to gather hard, white or yellow, waxy-looking patches of exudates. **1930** J. DOS PASSOS *42nd Parallel* I. 34 He was a sharpnosed waxyskinned young man. **1929** W. FAULKNER *Sanctuary* xxiii. 261 His nostrils were waxy white with rage. **1954** A. G. L. HELLYER *Encycl. Garden Work* 452 *Kindingeri,* waxy-white, reddish at base.

Hence **'waxily** *adv.*, **'waxiness.**

1855 HYDE CLARKE, Waxiness. **1880** *Jrnl. Linn. Soc.* XV. 98 Shell..not thin, but waxily translucent. **1890** *Sat. Rev.* 22 Nov. 588/2 [He] was originally a sculptor, and now paints rather waxily, as if he were modelling in oil-colour.

waxy ('wæksɪ), *a.*² *colloq.* or *slang.* [f. WAX *sb.*³ + -Y¹.] Angry, 'in a wax'.

A supposed example of 1648 in the *Hamilton Papers* (Camden) 229 is an editorial misreading of *wary.*

1853 DICKENS *Bleak Ho.* xxiv, It would cheer him up more than anything, if I could make him a little waxy with me. **1866** BROGDEN *Lincolnsh. Gloss., Waxey,* peevish, cross, irritable. *Ex.* You need-na be so waxey. **1872** *Punch* 1 June 222/1 It's no good being waxy about it.

way (weɪ), *sb.*¹ Forms: 1 **weȝ,** *North.* **woeȝ,** 2–3 **weiȝ,** 2–6 **wei,** 4–6 **weie, weye,** 3 **wæi, wæiȝ, waiȝ, weȝ,** *Ormin* **weȝȝe,** 4–5 **weiȝe,** 3–6 **wai, wey,** 4 **veie, wa, weieȝe, wie, wye,** 4–5 **veye,** 4, 6 **vay(e,** 4–7 **waie,** 4–8 **waye,** 5 **whay, weij,** 4–6 **wy,** 9 *Sc.* **wye,** 3– **way.** *Pl.* 4 **waiis,** 5 **weyse, waiez, waiss, wayse, weyys.** [Com. Teut.: OE. *weȝ* str. masc. = OFris. *wei, wi* (WFr. *wei,* NFr. *wāi*), OS. *weg* (MLG. *wech*), (M)Du. *weg,* OHG. *weg* (MHG. *wec, weg-,* Mod.G. *weg*), ON. *veg-r* (Sw. *väg,* Da. *vei*), Goth. *wig-s*:—OTeut. **weȝo-z,* f. **weȝ-* (:**waȝ-*: **wǣȝ-*) to move, journey, carry (see WEIGH *v.*, WAIN, WAW *sb.*¹ and *v.*¹, WEY):—Indogermanic **wegh-* (:**wogh-*), found in L. *vehĕre* to carry, Gr. ὄχος (:—**wogho-s*) vehicle, Skr. *vah* to journey, carry. The L. *via,* way, formerly regarded as cognate, is now generally referred to a different root. The sense-development of the Eng. word, however, has been to some extent influenced by L. *via* and its descendant F. *voie* (see also VOYE, WOYE), of both which it has always been the normal translation. Many of the uses are of Biblical origin: the Heb. *dérek,* and the Gr. ὁδός in Hellenistic use (Vulg. *via,* all Eng. versions *way*) have a very wide range of meaning.]

I. Road, path.

* *for passage of persons, animals, vehicles.*

1. a. *gen.* A track prepared or available for travelling along; a road, street, lane, or path. Now esp. in phrases like ***beside, over, across the way, the other side*** (***of***) ***the way, to cross the way,*** etc.

c **950** *Lindisf. Gosp.* Matt. xx. 30 And heonu tuoeȝe blindo sittende æt weȝ [*c* **975** *Rushw.* bi ðæm weȝe; *c* **1000** *Ags. Gosp.* wiþ ðone weȝ; **1382** WYCLIF besidis the weye; Vulg. *secus viam*]. *c* **1055** *Byrhtferth's Handboc* in *Anglia* VIII. 303 Forðon we sittað ymb þam weȝe wædliende mid timeus sunu. *c* **1205** LAY. 524 He ferde..to þan ilke weie þe he.. wuste þat þe king mid his ferde forð sculde iwenden. *Ibid.* 5511 Heo þohten heom beon on fest þer þe hulles weore mest & senden heom arewen i þon weie narewe. *a* **1300** *K. Horn* 1304 (Camb. MS.) þe kniȝt him aslepe lay Al biside þe way. *c* **1330** *Arth. & Merl.* 7404 þer was a launde of noblay Where come to gider seuen way. *c* **1350** *Will. Palerne* 1732 Abide ȝou in a brod weie bi a large mile. *c* **1475** *Rauf Coilȝear* 394 Tak thy hors and thy harnes in the morning, For to watche weill the wayis. **1579** BURGHLEY in Nicolas *Sir C. Hatton* (1847) 126 Approaching to the house, being led by a large, long, straight fair way, I found [etc.]. **1585** HIGINS *Junius' Nomencl.* 389/1 *Compitum,*..a waye where manye wayes doe meete. **1585** T. WASHINGTON tr. *Nicholay's Voy.* I. xii, A bridge..vnder the which is a waye to an old ruined Church. **1632** LITHGOW *Trav.* x. 433, I saw..women trauayling the way, or toyling at home, carry their Infants about their neckes. **1700** T. BROWN *Amusem. Ser. & Com.* 127, I cross'd the way to a Book-sellers. **1831** JAMES *Phil. Augustus* ii, Instead of attempting to continue the way along the side of the hill..a single arch had been thrown over the narrow ravine, and the road carried on..on the other side. **1834** DICKENS *Sk. Boz, Boarding-ho.* ii, He called out to a gentleman on the opposite side of the way. **1835** *Ibid., Streets—Morning,* Mr. Todd's young man just steps over the way. **1886** C. E. PASCOE *Lond. To-day* xxxi. (ed. 3) 287 The War Office is altogether out of keeping with the clubs upon the same side of the way. **1887** J. ASHBY-STERRY *Cucumber Chron.* 5 The village is..one long street. On either side of the way are picturesque little cottages. **1887** RUSKIN *Præterita* II. v. 155 For the most part, no English creature ever *does* see farther than over the way. **1904** H. BELLOC *Old Road* 96 A sunken way of great antiquity leads directly from St. Catherine's Hill down to the river. **1910** D. G. HOGARTH in *Encycl. Brit.* I. 248/1 The latest type of tomb is a flatly vaulted chamber approached by a horizontal or slightly inclined way, whose sides converge above.

transf. **1594** HOOKER *Eccl. Pol.* I. iii. §2 If the Moone should wander from her beaten way.

b. In figurative context, with reference to a metaphorical walking or travelling. ***parting of the ways***: see PARTING *vbl. sb.* 2 b.

†***way of indulgence***: said of the Virgin Mary as the medium or channel of access to divine mercy. (Cf. Christ's words in John xiv. 6, 'I am the Way..; no man cometh to the Father but by me'.)

c **825** *Vesp. Psalter* xxvi. 12 Fot..min stod in weȝe ðæm rehtan. *c* **950** *Lindisf. Gosp.* Matt. iii. 3 ȝearuas woeȝ drihtnes [Vulg. *parate viam Domini*]. *Ibid.* vii. 13 Rum-welle weȝ ðiu lædas to lose. *c* **1200** *Vices & Virtues* 21 Ðar ðe wei is slider and we lihtliche to fællen. *c* **1400** *Pety Job* 268 in *26 Pol. Poems* xxv. 129 All the pathes thow hast mette That euer I yede in wey or walle. *c* **1420** HOCCLEVE *Mother of God* 8 Modir of mercy, wey of indulgence. **1471** CAXTON *Recuyell* (Sommer) 213 Thou haste passid the strayte waye and passage of Infortune fro whens thou art yssued cler as the sonne. **1602** SHAKS. *Ham.* II. ii. 277 But in the beaten way of friendship, What make you at Elsonower? **1605** BACON *Adv. Learn.* II. xi. §1. 45 The trauaile therein taken, seemeth to haue ben rather in a Maze, than in a way. **1738** WESLEY *Hymns* 'Join all the glorious Names' v, O let my Feet ne'er ..rove, nor seek the crooked Way. **1898** M. PEMBERTON *Phantom Army* I. vii, The way before him was no longer hidden in darkness. He saw that it lay straight—the road to the prison or the scaffold.

c. A main road connecting different parts of a country. Now *rare* except in names of Roman roads, as the rendering of L. *via.* Cf. HIGHWAY.

†***the king's way***: = the king's HIGHWAY.

a **900** *O.E. Martyrol.* 28 Aug. 156 On þæm weȝe þe æt Rome is nemned Salaria. *c* **1000** ÆLFRIC *Num.* xxi. 22 Swa swa se weȝ lið we farað [Vulg. *via regia gradiemur*]. **1297** R. GLOUC. (Rolls) 169 Veire weies manion þer beþ in englonde, Ac voure mest of alle..þoru þe olde kinges imad. **1313** *Newminster Cartul.* (Surtees) 51 De Sticeleydike per Heddeley wai usque en le Spenstrete. *c* **1450** *Godstow Reg.* 541, ij. acris of arable lond..strecche them-self fro the north toward the sowthe beside the kyngis wey. **1482** *Cov. Leet Bk.* 510 þe grounde..in brede fro London weye stretchyng vnto a Corner of a Close of þe Trinite Gildes. *c* **1489** CAXTON *Sonnes of Aymon* ix. 227 There was a waye crossed in four, the one waye was towarde Fraunce. **1533** BELLENDEN *Livy* v. 227 Ane tempil was commandit to be maid in þe new way quhare þe voce was herde. **1535** COVERDALE *Judges* v. 6 In the tyme of Iael the wayes fayled. **1685** STILLINGFL. *Orig. Brit.* ii. 63 Whereever the Romans inhabited, they may be traced by their Ways, by their Buildings [etc.]. **1688** HOLME *Armoury* III. 198/2 The Overseers of the Ways are Men chosen yearly for to see, and..put in repair all decayed Highways..within the Bounds of the Parish. **1805** SCOTT *Last Minstr.* I. xxvi, Broad on the left before him lay, For many a mile, the Roman way. **1840** ARNOLD *Hist. Rome* xxxii. II. 288 Nor will the mightiest works of modern engineers ever rival the fame of the Appian Way.

d. *transf.* In MILKY WAY and various synonyms.

c **725** *Corpus Gloss.* (Hessels) U 174 *Uia secta,* iringes uueȝ. **1384** [see MILKY WAY]. **1555** Mylke way [see MILK *sb.* 10]. **1555** Mylke whyte way [see MILK-WHITE *a.* b.]. **1563** FULKE *Meteors* (1571) 38 The mylke waye called of some the waye to saint Iames, and Watlyng streate. **1594** BLUNDEVIL *Exerc., Cosmogr.* I. xxi. (1597) 158 The milke-white impression in heauen, like vnto a white way, called..of the common people our Ladies Way. **1775** *Blomefield's Hist. Norf.* V. 839 They believed..the Milky Way was appointed by Providence to point out the particular place and residence of the virgin, beyond all other places, and was, on that account, generally in that age, called Walsingham-Way; and I have heard old people of this country, so to call and distinguish it some years past. **1844** M. A. RICHARDSON *Local Hist. Table Bk.* Leg. Div. II. 86 The Via lactea, or 'milky way,' which the peasantry of the North frequently designate 'the way'.

e. A road considered with reference to the condition of its surface or to difficulties or dangers of transit.

a **900** *O.E. Martyrol.* 18 Apr. 58 Ðæt ða wildan hors scealden iornan [on] hearde weȝas in westenne & him þa limo all [to] brecan. **1418** in *E.E. Wills* 31, I be-quethe to the mendyng of the feble & foule weye beside Portmannes Crosse..xl s. **1577** *Knaresb. Wills* (Surtees) I. 126 To amend a pece of evill waie betwene my house and Hampistwhaite, xij d. **1588** SHAKS. *L.L.L.* v. ii. 926 When blood is nipt, and waies be fowle. **1632** LITHGOW *Trav.* I. 10, I bequeathed my proceedings to God,..and my feete to the hard brusing way. **1663** PATRICK *Parab. Pilgr.* ii. (1687) 5 The weather was cold, the ways dirty and dangerous. *c* **1710** CELIA FIENNES *Diary* (1888) 135 To Litchfield is 5 mile more all very good way mostly Gravel. **1712** ARBUTHNOT *John Bull* III. ix, I hope thou wilt not come too heavy laden, to spoil my Ways. **1789** DURNFORD & EAST *Cases K.B.* (1790) III. 263 If the way be founderous and out of repair, the public have a right to go on the adjoining land. **1846** MRS. A. MARSH *Father Darcy* xxviii, 'How are the ways?' 'Deep and difficult enough, please your honour.' **1849** MACAULAY *Hist. Eng.* I. iii. 379 In winter, when the ways were bad and the nights long. **1871** M. LEGRAND *Cambr. Freshm.* 301 A heap of smaller stones, placed there at the expense of the parish, for the purpose of mending the way.

f. A place of passage, e.g. an opening made through a crowd, a door or gate, etc. Also ***way in, way out.*** Hence ***Way Out sign.*** Cf. ARCHWAY, DOORWAY, GATEWAY. Also *fig.*

c **1250** *Gen. & Ex.* 3244 On twel doles delt ist ðe se, xii. weiȝes ðer-in ben faiȝer and fre. *c* **1400** *Destr. Troy* 5932 In the brest of the batell,..He ffrusshet so felly freikes to ground; Made wayes full wide þe weghis among. *Ibid.* 6513. *c* **1400** MANDEV. (E.E.T.S.) viii. 36 And men seyn þat the wlcanes ben weyes of helle. *a* **1400–50** *Wars Alex.* 1324 Quare althire-thickest was þe thrange þurȝe þaim he rynnes, And makis a wai wyde enoȝe waynes to mete. **1851** MRS. BROWNING *Casa Guidi Wind.* II. 217 Here fortitude can never cut a way Between the Austrian muskets, out of thrall. **1892** C. TAYLOR *Witness of Hermas* 126 The gate is the Son of God. This is the one way-in [εἴσοδος] to the Lord. **1898** G. B. SHAW *Plays* II. *You never can tell* II. *stage direct.,* Near the parapet there lurks a way to the kitchen. masked by a little trellis porch. **1914** S. LOW in *Edin. Rev.* Oct. 261 To a Prussian statesman it seems more natural to 'hack a way' through the territory of an unoffending neighbour than it would be to public men else-where. *a* **1926** *Mod.* The words 'Way out' are painted on the door. **1972** L. MEYNELL *Death by Arrangement* xiii. 178 Hooky was forced to follow him along an uncomfortably empty platform towards the 'Way Out' sign. **1982** J. O'FAOLAIN *Obedient Wife* iii. 59 Just follow the Way Out signs.

g. Applied to a path in a wood or through the fields. See also GREEN *a.* 2 b.

13.. *K. Alis.* 6055 (Laud MS.), Hij hadden..Calk trappes made ynowe In wayes & vnder wood bowe. **1484** CAXTON *Fables of Auian* xxii, The snowe had couerd al the wayes [in the forest]. **1530** PALSGR. 286/1 Way in a woode syde, *sente.*

h. *Fortification.* A passage left between walls or buildings. ***covered*** (†***covert***) ***way*** (= F. *chemin couvert*), a passage running along the top of the counterscarp, protected from the enemy's fire by a parapet. (See COVERED *ppl. a.* 6, COVERT *a.* 1 b.) †***way of the rounds*** (= F. *chemin des rondes*): see quot. 1704.

1481 CAXTON *Godeffroy* clxxiii. 257 They..dyde do make engyns,..castellys, chattes, and wayes couerd, moche grete plente. **1704** J. HARRIS *Lex. Techn.* I, *Way of the Rounds*.. is a space left for the Passage of the Rounds between the Rampart and the Wall of a Fortify'd Town.

i. *Railways.* ***line of way,*** a track formed by a pair of rails. See also PERMANENT *way,* SIX-FOOT *way,* WAGON-WAY.

** *for passage of things.*

†**2.** *Phys.* A duct or channel of any kind in the body of man or other animal. *Obs.*

[tr. mod.L. *via*; cf. *primæ viæ* (lit. 'first ways') the alimentary canal.]

c **1425** tr. *Arderne's Treat. Fistula,* etc. 21 þat may be known by..feblynez of þe pacient and if it haue perced þe waiez of þe vryne. **1541** COPLAND *Guydon's Quest.* I. iv, The bladder..receyueth the superfluyte vrynall by two longe wayes that descende fro the kydnees. **1615** CROOKE *Body of Man* 281 Wee must therefore enquire further for the cause of this sterility or barrennesse and not impute it to the interception of the wayes.

3. *pl.* **a.** *Naut.* (See quot. 1867.)

1639 in Foster *Crt. Min. E. Ind. Comp.* (1907) 332 [The use of one of the..docks with its] shores and waies [to fit and prepare the *Cæsar*]. *a* **1647** PETTE in *Archaeologia* XII. 258 The smaller [ship]..was so ill struck upon the launching ways, that she could by no means be put off, which did somewhat discontent his majesty. **1748** *Anson's Voy.* III. iii. 325 A dry dock was dug for the bark, and ways laid from thence quite into the sea, to facilitate the bringing her up. **1864** MISS S. P. FOX *Kingsbridge Estuary* xiii. 163 When once the boat is close on the shore, the dogs are on the look out for the pieces of wood, technically called *ways*, which are placed underneath the boats to draw them up on the beach. It is very rarely that a single *way* is lost. **1867** SMYTH *Sailor's Word-bk.*, *Ways*, balks laid down for rolling weights along. *Launching ways*, two parallel platforms of solid timber, one on each side of the keel of a vessel while building, and on which her cradle slides on launching.

transf. **1840** R. H. DANA *Bef. Mast* xxix, Smooth strips of wood, well oiled, called 'ways' were placed above and below, to cause the book [*sc.* a packet of hides] to slide in easily.

b. Parallel wooden rails or planks, forming an inclined plane for heavy loads to slide down upon.

1868 B. J. LOSSING *The Hudson* 264 The ice, cut in blocks from the lake above..is sent down upon wooden 'ways', that wind through the forest.

c. *Mech.* Parallel sills forming a track for the slides of the uprights of a planing machine, the carriage of a lathe, or the like.

1869 RANKINE *Cycl. Mach. & Hand-tools* Plate I 5, Improved Planing Machine... These uprights are so arranged as to slide in ways..provided for the purpose in the sides of the stationary platform.

II. Course of travel or movement.

4. a. A line or course of travel or progression (whether direct or circuitous) by which a place may be reached, or along which a person or thing may pass. Const. *to*, *into*, *out of* (hence with *in*, *out* advs.). ***to go a person's way***, to go along with him.

c **1000** *Ags. Gosp.* Matt. ii. 12 Hi on oðerne weȝ [Vulg. *per aliam viam*] in hyra rice ferdon. *c* **1205** LAY. 26915 Heom ladden twelue of þan leod-folke þa..þa weiȝes [*c* **1275** weyes] cuðen. *c* **1250** *Gen. & Ex.* 3255 Biforen hem fleȝ an skiȝe briȝt ðat night hem made ðe weiȝe liȝt. *a* **1300** *Cursor M.* 11736 We wil þe wai ga bi þe se. *c* **1300** *Havelok* 772 Ful we[l] he couþe þe rithe wei To lincolne. **1362** LANGL. *P. Pl.* A. VI. 24 Const þou wissen vs þe wey wher þat he dwelleþ? **1420** J. STOKES in Ellis *Orig. Lett.* Ser. III. I. 68 He hadde sent forth Mayster Jon Lobaim vn to zow by the nexte wey. *c* **1440** *Generydes* 5923 With hym ther went Sygrem to be his gide, Costyng the contre many dyuers way, And so came he in to perse the redy waye. **1470–85** MALORY *Arthur* I. xi. 51 He had the hoost Northward the pryuyest wey that coude be thoughte vnto the foreist of Bedegrayne. **1585** T. WASHINGTON tr. *Nicholay's Voy.* II. vi, An vniversall flood, which by croked wayes finally issueth into the Sea. **1604** E. G[RIMSTONE] *D'Acosta's Hist. Indies* III. iii. 127 The waies at Sea are not as at Land, to returne the same way they passe. **1676** COTTON *Angler* II. ii. 12, I hope our way does not lye over any of these [hills]; for I dread a precipice. **1682** WHELER *Journ. Greece* VI. 475, I return'd by the same way. **1732** LEDIARD *Sethos* II. IX. 293 There the way was stopp'd by mountains. **1818** SCOTT *Hrt. Midl.* xiii, Is the Cowgate Port a nearer way to Liberton..than Bristo Port? **1820** KEATS *Eve St. Agnes* xl, Down the wide stairs a darkling way they found. **1849** MACAULAY *Hist. Eng.* I. iii. 371 If he asked his way to St. James's, his informants sent him to Mile End. **1856** G. W. CURTIS *Prue & I* iii. (1892) 113 Mr. Bourne.. hospitably asked if I were going his way. His way was towards the southern end of the island. **1865** MRS. NEWBY *Comm. Sense* li. III. 15 Are you coming my way, father?

Proverbs. **1562** J. HEYWOOD *Prov. & Epigr.* (1867) 77 There be mo waies to the wood than one. **1635** QUARLES *Embl.* IV. Epig. 2 The next way Home's the farthest way about. **1661** BOYLE *Style Script.* (1675) 56 The Longest way about is the nearest Way Home. **1669** STURMY *Mariner's Mag.* VII. xvii. 27 There is several ways to the Wood besides one.

b. *fig.* with conscious reference to literal travelling. † ***to take the way of death***: to die.

a **1225** *Leg. Kath.* 1752 þer me unwreah me þe wei, þet leadeð to liue. **1297** R. GLOUC. (Rolls) 5320 þe king aldred sone þo þen wey of deþe nom. *c* **1380** WYCLIF *Sel. Wks.* III. 106 By þese wytty wordes of oure Lord Jesus Christ, mowe malicious men..knowe þat þey beþ in þe weye to helleward. **1605** SHAKS. *Macb.* II. iii. 21 That go the Primrose way to th' euerlasting Bonfire. **1646** GATAKER *Mistake Removed* 38 There is no new way to Heaven now, but the same that ever was. *a* **1729** J. ROGERS *Nineteen Serm.* v. (1735) 97 Every Path before us appears beset with Snares and Dangers, Ways in which we must walk with Fear and Trembling. *a* **1832** MACKINTOSH *Revol. 1688* i. (1834) 11 Having found a way to court through some of those who ministered to the pleasures of the King,..he made his value known by [etc.]. **1864** NEWMAN *Apol.* iv. §2 (1913) 296 There are but two alternatives, the way to Rome, and the way to Atheism. **1890** W. BOOTH (*title*) In darkest England and the way out.

c. Phrases. ***to hold, keep*** (a certain) ***way***: to follow it without deviation. ***to know one's way around*** (or ***about***): to know how to get from place to place in a neighbourhood; *fig.* to know how to act in any emergency; to have shrewdness born of experience. ***to light*** (***a person***) ***the way***: to hold out a light to enable a person to direct his course. † ***there lies your way***: please to go away. † ***here lies our, your way***: it is time to go. ***everything coming*** (or ***going***) ***one's way***: everything happening in one's favour. ***to go separate ways***: to cease to work or operate together and follow different paths.

For *to ask, find, lose, miss the way, one's way, to feel* (†*out*) *one's way, to clear, lead, show, stop the way*, see those verbs.

c **1200** *Trin. Coll. Hom.* 161 Ðan þe safarinde men seð þe sa stere, hie wuten sone wuderward hie sullen weie holden. *c* **1386** CHAUCER *Man of Law's T.* 709 This Messager on morwe whan he wook Vn to the Castel halt the nexte way. **1420** J. STOKES in Ellis *Orig. Lett.* Ser. III. I. 68 To declar vn to zow the tyme of hys comyng, and the weyes also the qwych he wele holde. **1548** HALL *Chron.*, *Hen. VI*, 173 b, Knowyng by his espials whiche waie therle kept. **1565** [see LIGHT *v.*² 4]. **1596** SHAKS. *Tam. Shr.* III. ii. 212 The dore is open sir, there lies your way. **1601** —— *Twel. N.* I. v. 216 Will you hoyst sayle sir, heere lies your way. **1606** —— *Tr. & Cr.* IV. i. 79 Here lyes our way. **1616** T. DRAXE *Bibl. Scholast.* 29 Contempt. Heere is the doore, and there is the way. **1815** SCOTT *Guy M.* xi, 'Certainly, sir,' said Mrs. MacCandlish, and hastened to light the way. **1867** *All Year Round* 13 July 56/2 In this case the tramp who 'knows his way about' knows what to do. **1903** G. B. SHAW *Maxims for Revolutionists* in *Man & Superman* 242 In moments of progress the noble succeed, because things are going their way. **1903** *Red Bk.* June 167/2 Everything was coming his way. **1921** GALSWORTHY *To Let* I. v. 52 'That's a young woman who knows her way about,' he said. **1932** KIPLING *Limits & Renewals* 385 They must be enjoying themselves now at a theatre. Everything's coming their way. [**1935** N. L. MCCLUNG *Clearing in West* xix. 152 Jack knew his way around, having been here many times the winter before... He drove straight down to Pacific Street to the Farmer's Home.] **1938** *Times* 1 Jan. 10/4 Much was certainly lost when the original directorate decided to go separate ways, as from the separation both parties seem to have suffered. **1943** O. HAMMERSTEIN *Oklahoma!* (1947) 18, I got a beautiful feelin' Ev'rythin's goin' my way. **1957** 'R. WEST' *Fountain Overflows* xi. 241 And whatever you could say about my Ma, you couldn't say she didn't know her way about. **1968** H. R. F. KEATING *Inspector Ghote hunts Peacock* vii. 95 That girl was a pretty slick chick..She knew her way around. **1973** G. JENKINS *Cleft of Stars* v. 60, I cursed that old rifle for letting me down at the moment when everything was going my way.

†**d.** ? Guidance, direction. *Obs.*

c **1380** WYCLIF *Sel. Wks.* III. 340 þe þridde part of þe Chirche fiȝtiþ here aftir Crist, and takiþ ensaumple and weie of him to come to hevene as he cam. **1450–1530** *Myrr. Our Ladye* III. 307 Lyghte to the blynde, way to the croked.

e. ***to go the wrong way***: of food or drink, to go into the windpipe instead of the gullet when being swallowed.

1764 *Phil. Trans.* LV. 42 An acquaintance..was killed by a piece of chesnut, which went the wrong way, as we commonly express it. **1860** HUGHES *Tom Brown Oxf.* iv, In a constant sort of mild epileptic fit, from laughter, and wine going the wrong way. **1860** O. W. HOLMES *Elsie Venner* vii. (1887) 94 He's swallered somethin' the wrong way.

f. Mode of transport.

1708 *Caldwell Papers* (Maitl. Club) I. 214, I have inquired what way my goods may safeliest be sent, and am told that by Holstein ships.

g. ***Way of the Cross*** (= eccl.L. *Via Crucis*): a series of images or pictures representing the 'Stations of the Cross' (see STATION *sb.* 23), ranged round the interior of a church, or on the road to a church or shrine; also, the series of devotions prescribed to be used at these stations in succession.

1868 WALCOTT *Sacred Archæol.* 554 The stations of the way of the cross..are—(1) the condemnation of our Lord; (2) Christ bearing His cross; (3) [etc.].

5. a. Course or line of actual movement.

1382 WYCLIF *Prov.* xxx. 19 The weie of an egle in heuene, the weie of the shadewe eddere on a ston, the weie of a ship in the myd se. **1632** LITHGOW *Trav.* VII. 327 Our way is Serpent like. **1665–6** *Phil. Trans.* I. 6 At what Angle the Way of the Comet cuts the Æquator. **1683** HOOKE in Birch *Hist. Roy. Soc.* (1757) IV. 231, I shewed an instrument..by which the way of a ship through the sea might be exactly measured. **1715** DESAGULIERS *Fires Impr.* 146 The winding Lines..shew the way of the Air in different Constructions of Chimneys. **1735** SOMERVILLE *Chase* IV. 431 See there he dives along! Th' ascending Bubbles mark his gloomy Way. **1868** LOCKYER *Elem. Astron.* vii. (1879) 261 The direction of the Earth's motion in its orbit, called the Earth's Way.

†**b.** The wake of a vessel. *Obs.*

c **1565** J. SPARKE *Sir J. Hawkins' 2nd Voy.* in *Hakluyt* (1589) 535 [The alligator] plunged into the water, making a streame like the way of a boate. *c* **1635** CAPT. N. BOTELER *Dial. Sea Services* (1685) 300 In speaking of the Wake of a Ship..You said that it was also called the Way. **1706** PHILLIPS (ed. Kersey), *Way of a Ship*, the smooth Water that she makes a-stern when under Sail.

c. *Engraving.* (See quot. 1891.)

1874 WILLSHIRE *Anc. Prints* iii. 96 This operation.. consists in rocking the cradle to and fro in certain directions or 'ways', determined by a plan or scale that enables the engraver to pass over the plate in very many directions without any one of them being repeated. **1891** *Adeline's Art Dict.*, *Way* (Engrav.) the series of parallel paths hewn out by the rocker on a mezzotint is technically termed a *way*.

6. a. In generalized use: Opportunity for passage or advance; absence of obstruction to forward movement; hence *fig.* freedom of action, scope, opportunity. In various phrases, as ***give way*** (see GIVE *v.* 49), ***have way*** (see 24), ***make way*** (see 25); also ellipt. ***way!*** (= 'make way').

a **1400–50** *Bk. Curtasye* 277 In *Babees Bk.*, 3if þou go with a-noþer at þo gate, And ȝe be bothe of on astate, Be curtasye and let hym haue þe way. **1634** SIR T. HERBERT *Trav.* 188 If any vulgar fellow meet them, they presently shake and vibrate their Swords..and so obtaine the way without opposition. **1714** in *Jrnl. Friends Hist. Soc.* (1918) 29 Having seen the comfort of our labours I found my way opened for a Return [*sc.* home]. **1850** TENNYSON *In Mem.* cii, Poor rivals in a losing game, That will not yield each other way. **1898** A. BALFOUR *To Arms* v, Once or twice I saw a courier flying north,..and clearing the road with a loud shout of 'Way, way!'

b. in legal documents sometimes equivalent to RIGHT OF WAY.

1766 BLACKSTONE *Comm.* II. iii. 35 A fourth species of incorporeal hereditaments is that of ways; or the right of going over another man's ground. **1790** DURNFORD & EAST *Cases K.B.* III. 766 The plaintiff..by reason of his possession thereof was entitled to a certain way from the said messuage unto into through and over a certain close of the defendant &c. unto and into the king's common highway &c. and so back again &c. **1803** C. BARTON *Elem. Convey.* (1821) III. 180 If a copyholder has had time out of mind, a way over another's copyhold. **1832** *Act 2 & 3 Will IV*, c. 71 §2 No Claim which may be lawfully made at the Common Law, by Custom, Prescription, or Grant, to any Way or other Easement, [etc.].

7. a. Travel or motion along a particular route or in a particular direction. ***to take*** (a place, etc.) ***in one's way***: to visit in the course of one's journey.

c **1000** *Sax. Leechd.* II. 16 Læcedom ȝif mon on langum weȝe teoriȝe. *a* **1400** *Minor Poems fr. Vernon Ms.* xlvii. 121 Ȝif þou haue eny wey to wende, I rede þou here a masse.. In þe Morennynge. **14..** *Tundale's Vis.* (Cott. MS.) 42 But Tundale hadde a harde warnynge, For as he yn a transynge lay Hys sowle was in a dredefull way, There as hit sawe mony a hydwysse payne Ere hit come to þe body agayne. *c* **1430** *Chev. Assigne* 220 The grypte eyþur a staffe in here honde & on here wey strawȝte. **1568** GRAFTON *Chron.* II. 262 They were well onward on their way toward Gascoyn. **1590** SHAKS. *Com. Err.* IV. iii. 92 Belike his wife acquainted with his fits, On purpose shut the doores against his way. **1600** E. BLOUNT tr. *Conestaggio* 230 The ioints thereof [*sc.* of the boats] were so shaken and open with the waie. **1617** J. TAYLOR (Water P.) *Three Weeks Observ.* B 1, We past the way away by telling tales by turnes. **1697** DRYDEN *Æneis* III. 714 Our way we bend To Pallas. **1735** JOHNSON *Lobo's Abyssinia, Descr.* xi. 111, I left the place of my Abode, and took in my way four Fathers,..so that the Company..was five. **1741** C'TESS POMFRET in *C'tess Hartford's Corr.* (1805) III. 166 Here we left the shore, but continued our way on very good roads, till [etc.]. **1777** EARL CARLISLE in Jesse *Selwyn & Contemp.* (1844) III. 228 As to our motions,..We may take Chatsworth in our way. **1779** STORER *Ibid.* IV. 242, I shall look in upon you at Matson in my way. **1818** SCOTT *Hrt. Midl.* xl. The attendants on the execution began to pass the stationary vehicle in their way back to Carlisle. **1827** —— *Highl. Widow* i, There was some originality in the man's habits of thinking and expressing himself..which made his conversation amuse the way well enough. *a* **1863** FABER *Hymn*, '*I was wandering*', As He came along His way.

b. Qualified by poss. pron., the word often occurs as object or as adverbial accusative to the verb *go* (see GO *v.* 21 b) and its synonyms, †*fare*, †*fere* (see FARE *v.* 1, FERE *v.*), *wend*, etc. From an early period *my*, *his* (etc.) *way* in these collocations were often nearly equivalent to 'away', and with this weakened sense they were formerly used with other verbs of motion, as *flee* (see FLEE *v.* 1 d), *run* (see RUN *v.* 34), *come*, *pass*, *ride*. In present literary use *to go*, *wend one's way* survive as archaisms; mod. dialects have only the imperatives *go*, *come your* (*thy*) *way* (or *ways*: see 23 b).

c **1205** [see FLEE *v.* 1 d]. *c* **1205** LAY. 25954 Ich wulle faren minne wæi. *a* **1250** *Owl & Night.* 308 þe hauec folȝeþ gode rede & fliȝt his wei & lat him grede. *c* **1250** *Gen. & Ex.* 1429 Eliezer is went his wei. *a* **1325** *Prose Psalter* xviii. 6 He ioyed as a giaunt to erne his waye. **1390** GOWER *Conf.* I. 94 'Ryd thanne forth thi wey', quod sche. *a* **1400–50** *Wars Alex.* 133 Furþe on his fete withouten fole he passis his way. *a* **1450** *Knt. de la Tour* x. 14 Yef ye fare rudely and be cruell with hym [the hawk], he will fle his way and neuer come atte you. **1487** *Cely Papers* (Camden) 167 The Kynge..muste flee hys weye owte of the contrey. **1678** BUNYAN *Pilgr.* I. 90 Then she railed on me, and I went my way. **1772** CUMBERLAND *Fashionable Lover* II. 23 Go your way for a simpleton, and say no more about the matter. **1837** DICKENS *Pickw.* xviii, As he wended his way to the Peacock. *Ibid.* xxvi, Mr. Weller went his way back to the George and Vulture.

c. In the Bible phrase ***to go the way of all the earth*** (Josh. xxiii. 14, 1 Kings ii. 2) meaning 'to die'. Also in erroneous forms (due to confusion with other Bible passages), ***the way of all flesh***, ***of all living***. (*The way of all flesh* has sometimes been used to mean the experience common to all men in their passage through life.)

A passage (dated 900) in Birch's *Cartul. Sax.* II. 241 'Quando Ælfred rex..viam vniverse carnis adiit', shows that the substitution of 'of all flesh' (*universæ carnis*) for 'of all the earth' (*universæ terræ*) was current in med. Latin. The reading of the Douay Bible (quot. 1609) suggests that the substitution must have found its way into some printed copies of the Vulgate; also, the Plantin Concordance (1642) reads *carnis* s.vv. *Caro* and *Ingredior*, though elsewhere the two passages are cited with the reading *terræ*.

1597 SHAKS. *2 Hen. IV*, v. ii. 4 Hee's walk'd the way of Nature, And to our purposes, he liues no more. **1609** BIBLE (Douay) *1 Kings* ii. 2, I enter into the way of all flesh [Vulg. *universæ terræ*]. *Ibid.*, *Josh.* xxiii. 14. **1611** HEYWOOD *Golden Age* III. i. F 4 b, If I go by land, and mis-carry, then I go the way of all flesh. If I go by sea and mis-carry, then I go the way of all fish. **1809** MALKIN *Gil Blas* I. v. ¶ 10, I heard that Don Rodrigo had gone the way of all flesh. **1835** DICKENS *Sk. Boz, Mr. Watkins Tottle* i, He pardoned us off-hand, and allowed us something to live on till he went the way of all flesh. **1887** *Murray's Mag.* Sept. 422 His former retainer, Phil Judd, had long gone the way of all flesh, however seasoned.

jocularly. **1607** DEKKER & WEBSTER *West-w. Hoe* II. ii, I saw him euen now going the way of all flesh (thats to say) towardes the Kitchin.

d. In verbal phrases with the sense 'to effect a forward movement by the action denoted by the verb', e.g. in ***to force, push, squeeze one's way***; also occas. with the sense 'to accompany one's advance by the specified action'.

1694 ATTERBURY *Serm., Isa.* lx. 22 (1726) I. 101 In this manner the Prophet of the East hew'd out his way by the power of the Sword. **1697** DRYDEN *Virg. Georg.* III. 843 The slow creeping Evil eats his way, Consumes the parching Limbs, and makes the Life his Prey. **1748** RICHARDSON *Clarissa* (1768) VIII. 137 McDonald, being surrounded, attempted to fight his way thro', and wounded his man. **1750** GRAY *Elegy* 3 The plowman homeward plods his weary way. **1770** GOLDSM. *Des. Vill.* 42 No more thy glassy brook reflects the day, But, choked with sedges, works its weedy way. **1833** [see ELBOW *v.* 4]. **1836** DICKENS *Sk. Boz, Hosp. Patient*, We..entered the office, in company with..as many dirty-faced spectators as could squeeze their way in. —— *Ibid., Streets—Night*, The muffin-boy rings his way down the little street. **1859** —— *T. Two Cities* II. iii, The virtuous servant, Roger Cly, swore his way through the case at a great rate. **1883** WHITELAW *Sophocles, Oed. Col.* 717 The oar-blade wings its wondrous way, Sped by stout arms. **1892** LADY F. VERNEY *Verney Mem.* I. 3 If enemies forced their way into the house. **1897** J. L. ALLEN *Choir Invisible* ii, He failed to urge his way through the throng as speedily as he may have expected.

†**e.** A journey, voyage; a pilgrimage. *lit.* and *fig.* Also = EYRE. *Obs.*

With quot. *c* 1325 cf. OF. 'faire une voie a Saint Jacques' quoted by Du Cange (s.v. *Via*) with date 1368.

a **1225** *Ancr. R.* 350 þauh heo beon ine worldliche weie, as ich seide er, of pilegrimes, auh habbeð hore heorte euer toward heouene. *c* **1325** *Metr. Hom.* 53 It was a man..That til sain Jamis hit [= *hight*, promised] the way. **1382** WYCLIF *Gen.* xxiv. 21 Wilnyng to wite whether the Lord had maad his weye welsom [Vulg. *utrum prosperum iter suum fecisset Dominus*], or noon. ? *a* **1400** *Morte Arth.* 553 He wylle wyghtlye in a qwhyle on his wayes hye. *c* **1400** *Three Kings Cologne* (1886) 56 Whan þey had spoke togedir and euerych of hem had tolde his purpos and þe cause of his weye. *a* **1500** in *Arnolde's Chron.* (1502) Bij b, That the citezens may recorde ther libarteis afore the kingis Justicis and mynystres what so euer notwythstandyng Statutis of the Wey or domes in the contrey made or shewyd oute. *Ibid.* C vj, And that the forsayd Citezens in the weys of Justice to the tour of London fro hensforward goyng, that they bee not lad by the lawes by which they were ledde in the Weys holden in the tymes of John and herry Somtyme kynge of englande.

†**f.** ***the way's end***: lit. the end of the journey; *fig.* the completion of a process. *Obs.*

1526 in *Househ. Ord.* (1790) 219 It shall be lawfull for the purveyour..to take..such Poultry stuff..paying unto them such prices..as the said purveyor..should have paid therefore at the wayes end. **1528** TINDALE *Obed. Chr. Man* 141 b, Thou must therfore goo alonge by the scripture as by a lyne, vntyll thou come at Christ, which is the wayes ende and restynge place. **1662** PETTY *Taxes* 84 The one [stuff] wanting nothing but tacking up, to be at its ways end; and the other tayloring..and several other particulars.

g. ***to hold, keep one's way*** (cf. 4 c): to travel without interruption; *fig.* to continue one's course of action, to 'keep going'. †***to hold, keep way***: to keep pace (const. *with* or dative).

c **1375** *Sc. Leg. Saints* xi. (*Simon & Jude*) 326 Syne to þe eddris can þai sa; 've commawnd ȝow to hald ȝour va'. **1598** SHAKS. *Merry W.* III. ii. 1 Nay keepe your way (little Gallant) you were wont to be a follower, but now you are a Leader. **1599** —— *Much Ado* I. i. 144, I would my horse had the speed of your tongue..but keepe your way a Gods name, I haue done. **1605** BACON *Adv. Learn.* II. vii. §2. 25 It seemeth best to keepe way with Antiquities, *vsque ad aras.* **1625** —— *Ess., Fortune* (Arb.) 377 When there be not Stonds, nor Restiuenesse in a Mans Nature. But that the wheeles of his Minde keepe way with the wheeles of his Fortune. **1640** YORKE *Union Hon., Battles* 63 She..had her fore mast broken off, which so hindred her sayle, that shee was unable to keepe way with the Fleete. **1706** E. WARD *Wooden World Diss.* (1708) 1 It flies so far, that no bird..but a Woodcock, can hold way with it. **1708** *Constit. Watermen's Co.* 82 All plying to keep Way, on forfeiture of 00. 00. 06. **1726** SHELVOCKE *Voy. round World* 2, I did not doubt but that I should be able to hold him away. **1818** *Tuckey's Narr. Exped. R. Zaire* Introd. p. xxvii, In running..from the Nore to the North Foreland,..she kept way with the transport. **1827** SCOTT *Surg. Dan.* xiii, The..reeds of the jungle were moving like the ripple of the ocean, when distorted by the course of a shark holding its way near the surface. **1848** DICKENS *Dombey* x, People who have enough to do to hold their own way..had better be content with their own obligations and difficulties.

†**h.** ***by the way of my soul*** (as an oath): by my soul's salvation. *Obs.*

1460 *Paston Lett.* I. 522 For be the weye of my sowle, this lond wer uttirly on done.

i. *Naut.* Progress (of a ship or boat) through the water; rate of progress, velocity; impetus gained by a vessel in motion. ***to freshen way***: see FRESHEN *v.* 3.

Cf. *under way* (38), from which this sense was perh. evolved.

1663 DAVENANT *2nd Pt. Siege of Rhodes* II. i, Those who withstand The Tide of Flood..Fall back when they in vain would onward row: We strength and way preserve by lying still. **1669** STURMY *Mariner's Mag.* IV. vi. 160 If you sail against a Current, if it be swifter than the Ship's way, you fall a Stern. **1744** M. BISHOP *Life* 15 She stood away for Brest, and we..fired a Chace Gun, but we fired too soon, for we lost Way and she gained. **1757** *Phil. Trans.* L. 34 The sea was rough, and the yacht had great way. **1764** J. BYRON in Hawkesw. *Voy.* (1773) I. 23 On the 7th, I found myself much farther to the northward than I expected, and therefore supposed the ship's way had been influenced by a current. **1860** HUGHES *Tom Brown Oxf.* xiii, Now mind, boys, don't quicken,..four short strokes to get way on her, and then steady. **1885** *Law Rep. 10 P.D.* 101 She ran into the *Nio* before her way could be stopped. **1889** JEROME *Three Men in Boat* ix, We can't steer, if you keep stopping. You must keep some way on the boat. **1899** F. T. BULLEN *Log of Sea-waif* 27 By the time our way was exhausted, about ninety fathoms had been paid out on the first anchor.

transf. **1857** DICKENS *Dorrit* I. xiii, A..short dark man came into the room with so much way upon him, that he was within a foot of Clennam before he could stop. **1911** *Times* 22 Aug. 8/2 He shut off his engine and by so doing took the 'way' off the biplane. **1914** *Contemp. Rev.* Nov. 680 The train gathered way.

j. *Colloq. phr.* ***on the*** (or ***one's***) ***way out*** (or ***down***): going down in status, position, estimation, or favour; similarly with ***in*** or ***up***, expressing the opposite sense.

1937 *Time* 25 Jan. 12/3 Every time one of them has called on the President and emerged smiling, rumor has whispered throughout Washington that the other was 'on his way out'. **1938** *Sat. Rev.* (U.S.) 17 Sept. 17/1 The thrill of being on the way up, of being prominent, being envied. **1938** H. L. ICKES *Diary* 5 Nov. (1955) II. 497 France is but little better than a third-rate power and is on the way down. **1955** A. L. ROWSE *Expansion Eliz. Eng.* i. 27 The Scottish king could well afford to make the concession: she was on her way out, he was on his way in. **1960** *Guardian* 9 Dec. 8/5 Sunrise yellows and pinks are definitely on the way in. **1962** in R. Jarrell *Sad Heart at Supermarket* 92 Poetry is on the way out! **1975** D. BAGLEY *Snow Tiger* xx. 163 This is the last job I'll hold as chief engineer. If I lose it I'll be on the way down—I'll be assistant to some smart young guy who is on his way up. **1980** A. SCHOLEFIELD *Berlin Blind* I. 5 Calland was a good-looking young man on the way up.

8. a. Distance travelled or to be travelled along a particular route. Hence (with adjs. *long, short, good, great, little*), a distance between places or to a place; often as advb. accusative. Also with *off.* Cf. HALFWAY.

a little goes a long way and varr.: see GO *v.* 43 c, LITTLE *sb.* 4. †*a mile of way*: = 'a mile away' (*obs. rare*).

c **900** tr. *Bæda's Hist.* I. xxiii, Hiȝ..sumne dæl ðæs weȝes ȝefaren hæfdon. *c* **1000** *Ep. Alexandri* in Cockayne *Narratiunculæ* (1861) 25 Ða ondswarodon hie mec & sægdon þ nære mara weȝ þonne meahte on tyn daȝum ȝeferan. *c* **1400** MAUNDEV. (Roxb.) viii. 32 It es a grete way betwene þam. **1535** COVERDALE *1 Kings* xix. 7 Stonde vp, and eate, for thou hast a greate waye to go. **1551** T. WILSON *Logic* II. I vii b, It is no good argument, if I se a tree a good way from me, to say, it is a tree, therefore it is an Apple tree. **1585** T. WASHINGTON tr. *Nicholay's Voy.* III. viii. 82 b, Trauailing both day and night..[they] do dispatch more way then the best horse..coulde doe. **1588** SHAKS. *L.L.L.* III. 57 The way is but short, away. **1590** SPENSER *F.Q.* I. i. 28 Long way he traveiled before he heard of ought. **1632** LITHGOW *Trav.* v. 176 There came a man, and two women swimming to vs, more then a mile of way. **1662** J. DAVIES tr. *Olearius' Voy. Ambass.* 36 The Sand-banks..reach out a good way into the Sea. **1667** SPRAT *Hist. Royal-Soc.* 250 A Chariot-way-wiser, measuring exactly the length of the way of the Chariot or Coach to which it is apply'd. **1697** *C'tess D'Aunoy's Trav.* (1706) 44 They commit these Villanies hard by a Sanctuary, so have the less way to an Altar. **1711** BUDGELL *Spect.* No. 77 ¶ 1, I saw him squirr away his Watch a considerable way into the Thames. **1818** SCOTT *Hrt. Midl.* xxxvi, I must ask the favour of your company a little way. **1835** DICKENS *Sk. Boz, Pawnbroker's Shop*, It is a low,..dusty shop, the door of which stands always doubtfully, a little way open. **1844** BROUGHAM *Alb. Lunel* I. ii. 39 The Marchioness's walk seldom lasted less than an hour, so that she must have some way to go. **1856** F. O. MORRIS *Brit. Birds* V. 8 Ventriloquism..making the sound at one moment appear close to the listener, and the next a long way off. **1882** BESANT *All Sorts* xxi, But the village of Davenant is not a great way off. **1898** FLOR. MONTGOMERY *Tony* 18 She stood a little way from the door.

fig. **1744** HARRIS *Three Treat.* I. (1765) 18 And now then, continued he, as we have gone thus far, and have settled between us what we believe Art to be; shall we go a little farther, or is your Patience at an end? Oh! no, replied I, not if any thing be left. We have walked so leisurely, that much remains of our Way.

†**b.** For ***a mile way, a furlong way***, meaning the time which it takes to go that distance, see MILEWAY, FURLONG b. *Obs.*

c. In advb. phrases used figuratively. (***by***) ***a long way***: qualifying a comparative, = 'far' (better, etc.). ***at the least way***(***s***: see LEASTWAYS. †***a great way***: to a great extent. †***a foul way out***: miserably far from success. ***some way***: for some distance (in time). ***to go a long*** or ***great way***: (*a*) see GO *v.* 43 c, d; (*b*) to be in agreement ***with*** someone. ***all the way***: completely; cf. senses 8 e, f below.

1601 SHAKS. *All's Well* I. i. 112, I loue him for his sake, And yet I..Thinke him a great way foole. **1601** —— *Jul. C.* II. i. 107 Heere, as I point my Sword, the Sunne arises, Which is a great way growing on the South. **1601** —— *Twel. N.* II. iii. 201 If I cannot recouer your Neece, I am a foule way out. **1699** BENTLEY *Phal.* 484 Why, forsooth, so much ado, why such a vast way about, to obtain a few Verses? **1850** LADY LYTTELTON *Let.* 12 June (1912) 401, I cannot *quite* enter into his politics... But a very great way I go along with him. **1859** DARWIN *Let.* Nov. (1887) II. vi. 224 Also from Quatrefages, who is inclined to go a long way with us. **1859** T. HUGHES *Tom Brown at Oxf.* iv, in *Macmillan's Mag.* Dec. 102/1 He is more of a gentleman by a long way than most. **1874** SWEET in *Trans. Philol. Soc.* 1873–4, 516 The most characteristic features of Middle English, as, for instance, *ii* and *uu*, were preserved some way into the sixteenth century. **1890** W. E. NORRIS *Misadventure* xiv, Bligh, who was his junior by a long way. **1973** 'N. CARTER' *Spanish Connection* x. 112 I'm saying I can't buy your story all the way, Corelli.

d. ***all the way from*——*to*——**: (*a*) throughout the specified interval, at every point in it; (*b*) *U.S.*, (estimated, etc.) at any amount between the specified quantities.

(*a*) **1791** R. MYLNE *2nd Rep. Thames Navig.* 10 There is the finest navigable Water, all the Way from Mr. Tovey's Meadows to Clieve Lock. **1966** *Listener* 5 May 643/2 The peak age [for crime] is during the last year at school... The rate is fairly high all the way from twelve to twenty.

(*b*) **1878** J. H. BEADLE *Western Wilds* xxxi. 493 The value of the booty taken has been estimated all the way from $150,000 to $300,000. **1931** G. T. CLARK *Leland Stanford* xi. 365 The amount said to have been wagered..has been variously stated all the way from $5,000 to $50,000.

e. ***to go all the way, the whole way***: (*a*) to continue a course of action to its conclusion; *spec.* (*slang*), to engage in sexual intercourse (*with* someone), as opposed just to fondling; (*b*) to agree completely ***with*** someone.

1915 J. C. POWYS *Visions & Revisions* 12 If you lack the courage, or the variability, to *go all the way* with very different masters, and to let your constructive consistency take care of itself, you may become, perhaps, an admirable moralist; you will never by a clairvoyant critic. **1922** H. J. LASKI in *Holmes-Laski Lett.* (1953) I. 412, I can't go all the way with it, for if it was as a business man that the tyrant found the path to power I should have thought there would have been mention of it in Aristotle. **1924** P. MARKS *Plastic Age* xiv. 151 'Wonder if Janet would have gone the whole way,' flitted across his mind. **1927** H. T. LOWE-PORTER tr. *Mann's Magic Mountain* I. iii. 78 'Am I right?' 'You certainly are, I can go all the way with you there.' **1961** L. P. HARTLEY *Two for River* 49 I'd sooner go the whole way with somebody than natter with them at a tea-table. **1970** W. J. BURLEY *To kill Cat* x. 186 The things we found in her room! I mean it was obvious she was going all the way and her not fifteen! **1975** *Listener* 30 Oct. 574/4, I am not sure that I go all the way with Mr Miller in some of his analysis. **1979** R. JAFFE *Class Reunion* (1980) I. i. 24 She would go to medical school... She didn't know if she would have the guts to go all the way: intern, resident, actually practice medicine. *Ibid.* vi. 86 They would do as much as they could without either removing the rest of her clothes or going all the way.

f. ***to come*** or ***go a long way*** (with personal subj.: for impersonal subj. see GO *v.* 43 c, d): to achieve much, to make much progress; ***to have a long way to go***, etc., to be far short of some accomplishment; so ***a long way from***, far short of, much inferior to.

1917 H. J. LASKI in *Holmes-Laski Lett.* (1953) I. 121 Your bretheren [*sic*]..have still a long way to go before they understand the meaning of a certain dissent in *Adair* v. *U.S.* **1922** W. S. MAUGHAM in *Pearson's Mag.* Oct. 320/2 He had come a long way since then. **1925** *New Yorker* 5 Sept. 11/3 Which is another way of saying that he will go a very long way. **1933** F. BALDWIN *Innocent Bystander* viii. 150 Sherry had a long way to travel before she would be a Fontanne or a Cornell. **1935** H. L. MENCKEN *Let.* 4 Jan. (1961) 386 You must yet go a long way, of course, before you are eligible to it. **1940** *Chatelaine* July 37/2 Pat and Rosemary have come a long way; they started their careers with Fred Waring's Pennsylvanians and ended up stars in one of the largest motion picture studios in the world. **1957** *Practical Wireless* XXXIII. 684/2 The system is a very long way from Hi-Fi, but is sufficient for the transmission of speech. **1966** *Seventeen* July 140/3 Society seems to have come a long way since the days of the Puritans, and now we're up to topless bathing suits. **1977** P. BAELZ *Ethics & Belief* vii. 79 Man has still a long way to go before he exercises his freedom responsibly and responsively.

9. a. Direction of motion, relative position, or aspect. Chiefly in advb. phrases, as ***this way*** (= hitherwards), ***my way*** (= towards me, into my neighbourhood), ***that way, which way, all ways***, etc.

In early use *way* often followed a local name or a sb. preceded by *to* with the force of the suffix *-ward*. In mod. colloquial and esp. rustic speech expressions like (*down*) *Essex way* (i.e. in Essex or its neighbourhood) are common.

For *the right way, the wrong way*, in uses belonging to this sense, see those adjs.

a **1300** *Cursor M.* 22573 þe fixses þat þar-in er stade,..Til erth wai [*Gött.* Till erdward] þan sal þai fle. **1573–80** TUSSER *Husb.* (1878) 103 In Cambridge shire forward to Lincolne shire way, the champion maketh his fallow in May. **1591** SHAKS. *1 Hen VI*, III. iii. 52 Oh turne thy edged Sword another way. **1605** —— *Macb.* IV. i. 45 By the pricking of my Thumbes, Something wicked this way comes. **1607** —— *Cor.* I. iii. 8 When youth with comelinesse pluck'd all gaze his way. **1632** LITHGOW *Trav.* VI. 276 From whence we saw ..to the Westward, in the way of Egypt, the Castle of.. Elisha. *a* **1654** SELDEN *Table-T.* (Arb.) 67 As take a straw and throw it up into the Air, you shall see by that which way the Wind is. **1680** MOXON *Mech. Exerc.* xiv. 235 The Work must run always one way. **1697** DRYDEN *Æneis* XI 1123 This way and that his winding Course he bends. **1744** M. BISHOP *Life* 190 Our advantageous Ground was the Destruction of a great many Thousands of the French, for we had them all Ways, Front, and Rear, and Flank. **1800** LATHOM *Dash of Day* I. iii, I seldom come your way now. **1821** SCOTT *Kenilw.* xxiii, Janet..ventured to ask her lady, which way she proposed to direct her flight. **1841** THACKERAY *Gt. Hoggarty Diamond* ii, As it was a very fine night, [we] strolled out for a walk West End way. **1846** JAMES *Stepmother* xxxviii. II. 106 The instant he entered—though the servant said, 'this way, sir,' and walked on towards the opposite door—Mr. Morton's visitor stopped, bowed to the ladies, [etc.]. **1850** NEWMAN *Difficulties Anglicans* I. ii. (1891) I. 55 Drive a stake into a river's bed, and you will at once ascertain which way it is running. **1853** LYTTON *My Novel* VI. xix, The first time you come my way you shall have two glasses of brandy-and-water. **1873** RUSKIN *Fors Clav.* xxxiii. 2 When last I was up Huntly Burn way, there was no burn there. **1878** TRELAWNY *Rec. Shelley* etc. I. 167 A vehement exclamation..from one of the trio of ladies, drew all eyes her way. **1891** 'R. BOLDREWOOD' *Sydneyside Sax.* vi, At last I made out a whirlwind coming our way. **1896** GRATIANA CHANTER *Witch of Withyford* xv. 185 Joan she married Farmer Blake as lives over Molton way. **1902** 'VIOLET JACOB' *Sheep-Stealers* viii, 'Where are you going to now?'.. 'Down Crishowell way'. **1904** P. LANDON in *Times* 24 Sept. 8/2 We took care not to offend..by deviating from the orthodox left-to-right course... The 'way of the wine' is a custom which would need no explanation to a Buddhist. **1912** S. H. WARREN in *Jrnl. R. Anthrop. Inst.* XLII. 115 The shaft-hole is bored through the thinnest way of the [stone] blade, so that the cutting-edge comes at right angles to the shaft.

b. *fig.* in non-spatial applications. ***that way***: in the direction indicated contextually; *spec.* (*a*) homosexual; (*b*) (const. *about*) in love or infatuated; also (in general sense) ***that way inclined***, ***to get that way***.

In colloquial use sometimes in predicative phrases, as (***a little***) ***that way***, approximating to that condition; (***all, quite very much***) ***the other way***.

1598 SHAKS. *Merry W.* III. ii. 79 My consent goes not that way. **1603** [see INCLINED *ppl. a.* 3a]. **1605** —— *Lear* III. iv. 21 O that way madnesse lies, let me shun that. *a* **1647** FLETCHER *Lovers' Progr.* I. i, You are Poetical. *Mal.* Something given that way. **1652** HOWELL *Giraffi's Rev. Naples* II. 90 Three Brothers were detected to have a Design that way. **1707** ATTERBURY *Vind. Doctr. Funeral Serm. Bennet* 32 As to the words themselves, there is nothing in them that sounds that way. **1711** ADDISON *Spect.* No. 108 ¶7 Finding his Genius did not lie that Way. **1794** J. H. MOORE *Pract. Navig.* (1828) 179 Suppose the sun's true azimuth S. 17° 45′ E. and the magnetic azimuth S. 5° 48′ W., required the variation, and which way? **1837** DICKENS *Pickw.* li, 'I'm afraid you're wet.'.. 'Yes, I am a little that way.' **1858** TROLLOPE *Three Clerks* xxvi, You must not compare me with them,..They are patterns of excellence. I am all the other way. **1859** T. HUGHES *Tom Brown at Oxf.* (1861) I. x. 163 Both 'smalls' and 'greats' are sufficiently distant to be altogether ignored, if we are that way inclined. **1882** J. H. BLUNT *Ref. Ch. Eng.* II. 126 Foxe, whose evidence is often one way and his assertions the other. **1885** *Law Times* LXXIX. 161/2 The evidence on the point had in his view been all one way. **1916** A. BENNETT *These Twain* xx. 518 'He simply hates doing a thing straight off.' 'Yes, he is rather that way inclined.' **1922** C. SANDBURG *Slabs of Sunburnt West* 6 How do you get that way? *a* **1960** E. M. FORSTER *Maurice* (1971) vii. 42 The Greeks, or most of them, were that way inclined, and to omit it is to omit the mainstay of Athenian society. *Ibid.* xii. 62 In his second year he met Risley, himself 'that way'. **1960** WENTWORTH & FLEXNER *Dict. Amer. Slang* 540/2 *That way*, in love. Usu. in 'They are that way about each other.' c. 1940. **1961** V. SACKVILLE-WEST *No Signposts in Sea* 82 If I were that way inclined, which I am *not*, I can imagine falling in love with him myself. **1965** J. P. CARSTAIRS *Concrete Kimono* xxiii. 207 Sharon. Be reasonable. I thought you were 'that way' about Roderick. **1966** 'J. HACKSTON' *Father clears Out* 91 It got that way in the end that I used to look forward to seeing Nolan and his team come lumbering down from the north. *a* **1967** J. R. ACKERLEY *My Father & Myself* (1968) xvi. 185, I divined that he was homosexual, or as we put it, 'one of us,' 'that way', 'so', or 'queer'.

c. Prov. ***to look nine ways***, ***to look two ways for Sunday***: to squint excessively. ***to go, look nine ways*** (***at once, at thrice***): expressing the indecision produced by terror or eagerness.

1542 [see NINE A. 3b]. *a* **1617** BAYNE *On Ephes.* (1643) 253 Some, if a thing come into the head, turne them forth-with to it, as busily as if they would goe nine waies at once. **1649** [see NINE A 3b]. **1869** A. MACDONALD *Love, Law & Theol.* xxi. 451 He has..a bad squint, so that..he seemed to be looking two ways for Sunday.

d. ***the other way about***, ***round***: conversely, vice versa; also ***the other way***, ***the other way around***.

1834 *Edin. Rev.* Oct. 83 The fault, in the present instance, is the other way. **1879** R. L. STEVENSON in *Cornh. Mag.* Oct. 412 He [*sc.* Burns] was 'constantly the victim of some fair enslaver'—at least, when it was not the other way about. **1894** 'M. RUTHERFORD' *Cath. Furze* vi, She..never could recollect whether the verb was conjugated, and the noun declined, or whether it was the other way round, to use one of her favourite expressions. **1914** *Q. Rev.* Apr. 382 Whilst with Hegel the Logic is the *a priori* framework of the whole philosophy, with Eucken it is secondary, adjusting itself to the life-process and not the other way about. **1925** *New Yorker* 28 Mar. 25/2 It is just as good the other way around. **1963** *Christian Century* 9 Jan. 49/1 But the Augustinian, and biblical, position addresses man the other way around: Find God and you will find yourself.

e. ***one way or*** (***the***) ***other***, ***either way*** (advb. phr.): in one direction or the other; in the direction of excess or defect, of assent or denial, of confirmation or disproof, etc.

1560 B. HAMPTON in T. Wright *Q. Eliz.* (1838) I. 36 As sone as th'ende thereof, either one waye or other, shall be knowne, I will not fayle to move the Quene's Majestie that the same may be [etc.]. **1732** BERKELEY *Alciphr.* VI. §5, I should..be glad to be convinced one way or other. **1860** DICKENS *Uncomm. Trav.* vii, The housekeeper who saw it all ..seemed to have no opinion about it, one way or other. *a* **1878** B. TAYLOR *Germ. Lit.* 105 There are but a few years' difference between them, either way. **1884** *Law Times Rep.* L. 29/2 The Summary Jurisdiction Act 1879 has no real bearing one way or the other on the question.

f. ***to have it both ways*** and varr.: to have advantages from two opposed or contradictory standpoints; to make use of alternatives or contradictions as it suits one.

1914 G. B. SHAW *Fanny's First Play* II. 191 Then I suppose what I did was not evil; or else I was set free for evil as well as good. As father says, you cant have anything both ways at once. **1926** F. M. FORD *Man could stand Up* I. ii. 33 An oafish thing to do! To take a school-girl..just past the age of consent, out all night in a dog-cart... You'd think any man who *was* a man would have avoided that! Most men knew enough to know that the Woman Pays.., the school-girl too! But they get it both ways. **1964** C. HODDER-WILLIAMS *Main Experiment* vii. 73 'It was only folklore.'.. 'Yes, but you can't have it both ways. If it frightens you it must mean something.' **1967** *Listener* 13 Apr. 489/2 So our dual terminology helps us to have it both ways.

†**10.** *Naut.* The run or rake of a ship. (Cf. RAKE *sb.*[4] 1, RUN *sb.* 25b.) *Obs.*

1627 CAPT. J. SMITH *Sea Gram.* ii. 10 The meane is the best if her after way be answerable. **1691** T. H[ALE] *Acc. New Invent.* 122 The proportion between the way of the Ship cut off at its greatest transverse section, and the way of the same shaped from the same section forward in the usual manner.

III. Course of life or action, means, manner.

11. a. A path or course of life; the activities and fortunes of a person.

The use is mainly of Heb. origin, and is extremely frequent in all English versions of the Bible.

c **897** ÆLFRED *Gregory's Past. C.* xlii, 306 Hie etað ðone wæsðm hiera æȝnes weȝes [L. *comedent fructus viæ suæ* (Prov. i. 31)]. **971** *Blickl. Hom.* 21 Oþon leohte is fulfremednesse weȝ þe we on feran sceolan, þæt is se rihta ȝeleafa. *c* **1200** ORMIN 18068 Forr all þe Laferrd Cristess lif & all hiss hallȝhe lare, & all hiss weȝȝe, & all hiss werrc, [etc.]. **1375** *Cursor M.* 8590 (Fairf.) Of mister was þer wimmen twyn atte led þaire life in way of syn [*Cott.* wit sike and sin; *other texts* in sake and sine (synne)]. **1382** WYCLIF *Prov.* xxi. 2 Eche weie of a man riȝt to hym semeth. **1653** HANE *Jrnl.* (1906) 1 By the Lord's providence who disposeth of all the wayes and actions of man. **1667** MILTON *P.L.* IV. 620 Man hath his daily work..Appointed, which declares his Dignitie, And the regard of Heav'n on all his waies; While other Animals unactive range And of thir doings God takes no account. **1709** PRIOR *Henry & Emma* 395 One Destiny our Life shall guide; Nor Wild, nor Deep our common Way divide. **1750** GRAY *Elegy* 76 They kept the noiseless tenor of their way.

b. *pl.* Habits of life, esp. with regard to moral conduct.

c **825** *Vesp. Psalter* xxxviii. (xxxix.) 1 Ic cweð ic haldu weȝas mine ðet ic ne agylte in tungan minre. [Similarly in all later versions.] **1513** MORE *Rich. III* Wks. 39/1 So that euer at length euil driftes dreue to nought, & good plain wayes prosper. **1567** *Gude & Godlie B.* (S.T.S.) 95 Thow sall not follow wickit mennis wayis. **1599** SHAKS. etc. *Pass. Pilgr.* 323 And to her will frame all thy waies. **1675** OWEN *Indwelling Sin* xvii. (1732) 235 His Companions in Sin not finding him in his old Ways, begin to laugh at him. **1832** HT. MARTINEAU *Manch. Strike* i. 8 Those who knew his ways could easily guess at which of his haunts he might be expected when missing from home. **1852** MRS. STOWE *Uncle Tom's C.* xxxvii, I wish, friend, thee would leave off cursing and swearing, and think upon thy ways. **1857** HUGHES *Tom Brown* I. i, I shall here shut up for the present, and consider my ways. **1887** M. CREIGHTON in Mrs. Creighton *Life* (1904) I. 375 Your letter will give me much food for meditation, and may in time lead to an amendment of my ways.

c. ***the way*** or ***ways of God***: the course of God's providence; very common in Bible use.

c **825** *Vesp. Psalter* xliv. 17 Rehtwis dryhten in allum weȝum his. **1382** WYCLIF *Prov.* viii. 22 The Lord weldide me [*sc.* Wisdom] in the begynnyng of his weies [so 1535 *Coverdale*; **1611** way]. **1667** MILTON *P.L.* VIII. 413 To attaine The highth and depth of thy Eternal wayes All human thoughts come short, supream of things. **1738** C'TESS HARTFORD *Corr.* (1805) I. 28 It tells us..that a day will come when the ways of Providence will be cleared up.

d. A prescribed course of life or conduct; the law or commandments (of God); also in *pl.*

a **1000** *Andreas* 170 Leode [he] lærde on lifes weȝ. *a* **1300** *Cursor M.* 6858, I..sal hald yow lel mi hight, To-quils yee folu mi wais right. **1382** WYCLIF *Job* xxi. 14 The which seiden to God, Go awei fro vs; the kunnyng of thi weies we wiln not. **1786** S. TOLD *Acc. Life* 166, I walked closely in the ways of God. **1879** R. K. DOUGLAS *Confucianism* iii. 72 The Sage..maintains a perfect uprightness and pursues the heavenly way without the slightest deflection.

e. ***the Way***: in the Acts of the Apostles, a name for the Christian religion (ἡ ὁδός, Vulg. *via*).

In Acts ix. 2, xix. 9, 23, xxiv. 14, 22, the Greek has 'the way'; the only English translation that has the literal rendering in all the passages is the Revised Version of 1881 ('the Way', with capital). In ix. 2 Wyclif, following an error in some MSS. of the Vulgate, has 'this life'; later versions down to 1611 have 'this way'. In xix. 9 and 23 Wyclif, after some MSS. of the Vulgate, has 'the way of the Lord' (so, in verse 9, Tindale 1526 and Geneva 1557); later versions of verse 23 down to 1611 'that way'. In xxiv. 14 Wyclif has 'the sect' (after Vulg. *sectam*), Tindale and Geneva 'that way', Cranmer and 1611 'the way'. In xxiv. 22 Wyclif has 'the way', Geneva 'this sect', and other versions down to 1611 'that way'. In Acts xxii. 4 the Greek has 'this way', which all the English translators render literally.

12. a. A course of action. Often with the phraseology of sense 4, as ***to go the right***, ***wrong***, ***nearest way***.

a **1300** *Cursor M.* 29222 For-þi to weind þe seker wai I rede we be in penance ai. **1390** GOWER *Conf.* I. 2, I wolde go the middel weie And wryte a bok betwen the tweie, Somwhat of lust, somewhat of lore. *c* **1500** MEDWALL *Nature* (Brandl) I. 342 Yf thou se hym not take hys owne way, Call me cut, when thou metest me a nother day. **1526** *Pilgr. Perf.* (W. de W. 1531) 9 In this we may knowe, what waye to take, & what waye to leue. *c* **1530** BERNERS *Arth. Lyt. Brit.* 352, I thinke this is a better waye than all to fyght at ones. **1539** in W. A. J. Archbold *Somerset Relig. Houses* (1892) 75 Albeyt we have vsed as many wayes with her as our poore wittes cowde atteyne, yet in the ende we cowde not..bring her to any conformytie. **1560** DAUS tr. *Sleidane's Comm.* 216 Theyr Archebysshop Herman hathe gon a new waye to worke [L. *iniisse novam rationem*]. *a* **1586** SIDNEY *Arcadia* II. xxii. §8 (1912) 293 He durst not take open way against them: and as harde it was to take a secrete. **1610** SHAKS. *Temp.* II. ii. 39 My best way is to creepe vnder his Gaberdine. **1616** DRAXE *Bibl. Scholast.* 2 He goeth the wrong way to worke, or to the wood. **1656** COWLEY *Davideis* I. Note 37 There is so much to be said of this subject, that the best way is to say nothing of it. **1693** LOCKE *Educ.* §39 The sooner this Way is begun with Children, the easier it will be for them, and their Governors too. **1748** SMOLLETT *R. Random* lxii, He told me that I went the wrong way to work.

†**b.** (One's) best or most advisable course. *Obs.*

1590 SHAKS. *Com. Err.* IV. iii. 93 My way is now to hie home to his house, And tell his wife, that [etc.]. **1594** —— *Rich. III*, I. i. 78, I thinke it is our way, If we will keepe in fauour with the King, To be her men, and weare her Liuery. **1603** —— *Meas. for M.* v. 280, I will goe darkely to worke with her. That's the way: for women are light at midnight. **1604** —— *Oth.* II. iii. 393 And bring him iumpe, when he may Cassio finde Soliciting his wife: I that's the way.

c. ***to have*** (***get***, etc.) ***one's*** (***own***) ***way***: to be allowed to follow or to enforce on others the course of action on which one is resolved; hence ***to love, be fond of one's own way***. Cf. 14i.

1593 SHAKS. *3 Hen. VI*, III. ii. 139 Like one that..chides the Sea, that sunders him from thence, Saying hee 'le lade it dry, to haue his way. **1611** B. JONSON *Catitine* IV. iii, Had I had my way, He' had mew'd in flames, at home, not i' the Senate. **1622** BACON *Hen. VII* 238 Hee was of an High Mind, and loued his owne Will, and his owne Way. **1748** RICHARDSON *Clarissa* (1768) I. 147 Obstinate, perverse, undutiful Clarissa!..then take your own way, and go up! **1849** MACAULAY *Hist. Eng.* viii. II. 298 Every child knew that his majesty loved to have his own way and could not bear to be thwarted. **1859** TENNYSON *Marr. Geraint* 466, I myself sometimes despise myself; For I have let men be, and have their way. **1859** —— *Grandmother* xviii, Kind, like a man, was he; like a man, too, would have his way. **1866** MRS. WHITNEY *Leslie Goldthwaite* xi, I'll..thank you unutterably, if you'll only let me have my way in this. It will do me so much good, mamma! **1873** MRS. OLIPHANT *Innocent* III. 310 You are..silly, pig-headed, unreasonable, and more fond of your own way than of anything else in the world. **1885** *Manch. Exam.* 8 June 4/7 If they do not get their own way they will resign. **1893** *Law Times* XCIV. 559/1 If I had had my way, I would have fought every one of these actions.

(*b*) *spec.* in phr. ***to have one's way***, to have sexual intercourse *with* (used chiefly of a man).

1915 CONRAD *Victory* IV. xii. 399 If I had taken you by the throat this morning and had my way with you, I should never have known what you are. **1939** *Ottawa Jrnl.* 23 Aug. 15/2 He might destroy Phil..to have his way with Joan. **1961** W. BROWN *Bedeviled* 113 Although she struggled, she was no match for him and he had 'had his way with her'. **1980** E. JONG *Fanny* III. xiii. 440 Thus could Anne Bonny defend herself when she did not fancy a Man, but when she fancied one, she also had her Way with him.

†**d.** ***take better way with you***: take a more reasonable course. *Obs.*

a **1553** UDALL *Royster D.* IV. iii. (Arb.) 65 Let me now treate peace, For bloudshed will there be in case this strife increace. Ah good dame Custance, take better way with you.

13. a. A course of action, a device, expedient method, or means, by which some end may be attained or some danger escaped. Const. *to* with inf. or sb., *of* with gerund.

Proverb, ***where there's a will there's a way***.

c **1175** *Lamb. Hom.* 49 Þet we maȝen mid ure muðe bringen us ut of þisse putte..and þet þurh þreo herde weies þe þus beoð ihaten: *Cordis contritione*, *Oris confessione*, *Operis satisfactione*. *c* **1400** *26 Pol. Poems* iv. 36 By al way make hym þi frende. *c* **1400** *Pety Job* 382 ibid. 133, I may nat from thy respeccioun By no way, lorde, hyde now me. *c* **1470** *Stonor Papers* (Camden) I. 109 As for the nexte corte they hathe founde a wey þat ther schull no thyng be do, yn so myche as ye be absent. *a* **1548** HALL *Chron., Hen. VII*, 50 For after yt tyme there were an hundred wayes practised and invented how at one time or another, to deliver or convey them out of pryson. **1550** CROWLEY *Last Trumpet* 699 Why should not I..Haue benefices two or thre? Sens thou hast taught me the wei how I may kepe them and blamelesse be. **1606** SHAKS. *Ant. & Cl.* I. iii. 10 Thou teachest like a foole: the way to lose him. **1624** DONNE *Devot.* x. (ed. 2) 217 Those are the greatest mischiefes, which are least discerned; the most insensible in their *waies* come to be the most sensible in their *ends*. *a* **1633** G. HERBERT *Outlandish Prov.* (1640) 730 To him that will, waies are not wanting. **1668** R. STEELE *Husbandm. Calling* v. (1672) 96 The way to have full barns, is to have free hands. **1685** F. CHENEAU (*title*) French Grammar enriched with a compendious and short way to learn the French tongue in a very short time..; and a very rare way to find out all the articles, nouns, pronouns [etc.]. **1720** DE FOE *Capt. Singleton* ii. (1840) 25 They took ways.. to satisfy us. **1753** RICHARDSON *Grandison* I. ii. 5 And tho' he finds a way, by his sister..to let Miss Byron know his passion. **1844** BROUGHAM *Alb. Lunel* xvi. II. 176 Against England he is implacable and the only way to ruffle his temper is to praise her. **1849** MACAULAY *Hist. Eng.* x. II. 554 He now saw that there was only one way of averting general confusion. **1882** BESANT *All Sorts* xxi, 'Is there no way,' she asked, 'in which he can earn money?' **1892** *Speaker* 3 Sept. 292/2 Mr. Huxley..can see but one way of arriving at truth; which he calls experience. **1918** *Cornhill Mag.* June 634 Radicals who preached Colonial Self-government as the way and the only way to Imperial Unity.

b. Coupled with the synonymous MEAN *sb.*: see WAYS AND MEANS. Also †***mean way*** (see MEAN *a.*[2] 4), †***way moyen*** (see MOYEN *a.*). Also †***ways and grounds***.

c **1400** *Rom. Rose* 4844 Wher they ne may Finde non other mene wey [Fr. *ou nus ne set le moien querre*]. **1430–1** *Rolls of Parlt.* IV. 375/2 Upon grete subtilite.., and colored menes and weyes. **1440** in *Wars Eng. in France* (Rolls) II. 444 For elles youre partie adverse and the saide duc might not godely have founden the moyens and the weyes to have communed to geder to conclude thaire confedracy. **1455** *Rolls of Parlt.* V. 287/2 So the weyes and groundes may be founde and hadde for paiement. **1470** *Stonor Papers* (Camden) I. 115 Our Traitours..which daily labour þe weyes moyens at þeir power of our final destruccion. **1560** DAUS tr. *Sleidane's Comm.* 82 This is the onely meane and waye, that is euermore certayne and sure. **1561** T. HOBY tr. *Castiglione's Courtyer* II. (1577) N 1b, Ech honest louer..vseth so manye meanes and wayes to please the woman whome hee loueth.

†**c.** ***to have the way(s***: to know how *to* do something. *Obs.*

1542 UDALL *Erasm. Apoph.* 163 O the right philosophicall herte of this prince, who had the waye, euen of his enemies, also to take vtilitee and profite. *Ibid.* 200 Oh what an horse these folkes dooe marre, while through defaulte of skylle.. thei haue not the wayes to handle hym [L. *dum illo per imperitiam..uti nesciunt*].

d. ***way out of***: a means of escape from (a difficulty). Cf. sense 4.

1875 JOWETT *Plato* (ed. 2) V. 430 Let us..ask ourselves.. whether we have discovered a way out of the difficulty.

14. a. Manner in which something is done or takes place; method of performing an action or operation.

c **725** *Corpus Gloss.* (Hessels) Q 74 *Quocumque modo*, ȝehwelci weȝa. *c* **1350** *Will. Palerne* 5526 He wold haue do beter, ȝif is witte in eny weiȝes wold him haue serued. **1450–1530** *Myrr. Our Ladye* I. v. 17 Lyghtnynge hys soule ..with the spiritual vnderstondyng of hys wordes & that in tow wayes. **1563** T. GALE *Antidot.* Pref. 2 The methode and way of composition of suche medicines. **1577** B. GOOGE *Heresbach's Husb.* II. 72 But are there more wayes then one of plantyng and setting? **1603** SHAKS. *Meas. for M.* III. ii. 112 They say this Angelo was not made by Man and Woman, after this downe-right way of Creation. **1617** MORYSON *Itin.* I. 67 After dinner we rode in like way two miles, to the City Lowen. **1638** JUNIUS *Paint. Ancients* 227 As for the things an Artificer shall judge to be worth his pains, he shall not onely invent them after the best way, but also after the easiest way. **1651** BAXTER *Inf. Bapt.* 23 There is more ways of teaching then by preaching in a Pulpit. **1669** STURMY *Mariner's Mag.* IV. xvii. 202 A perfect Method and Way of keeping Account. **1687** A. LOVELL tr. *Thevenot's Trav.* I. 34, I have said enough of the Turks way of Eating, Drinking and Sleeping. **1711** ADDISON *Spect.* No. 124 ¶4, I may pronounce their Characters from their Way of Writing. **1743** BULKELEY & CUMMINS *Voy. S. Seas* 66 We have found out a new way of managing the Haugh. **1747** MRS. GLASSE *Cookery* i. 4 There are several Ways of making Sauce for a Pig. **1798** SOPHIA LEE *Canterb. T., Yng. Lady's T.* II. 341 She exacted, in consideration of this concession, that he should allow her to do it in her own way. **1827** FARADAY *Chem. Manip.* xxiii. (1842) 586 In many other situations a bad conductor is of service in a similar way. **1860** GEO. ELIOT *Mill on Floss* II. III. vii. 107 I'm not a-defending him, in no way, for being so hot about th' erigation. **1878** HARDY *Ret. Native* II. ii. (1890) 113 Yet why, aunt, does everybody keep on making me think that I do, by the way they behave towards me? **1895** *Law Times* XCIX. 546/1 Any practical suggestions pointing out in what way assistance may be rendered to students generally. **1897** J. W. CLARK *Barnwell* Introd. 9 A few words on the way in which I was led to undertake the work. **1952** M. R. RINEHART *Pool* (1953) xx. 170 It's no way to talk about a sister, but I've had about all I can take.

†**b.** Literary style or method. *Obs.*

1632 J. HAYWARD tr. *Biondi's Eromena* To Rdr. A iv, The Authours peculiar way of imbellishing it..gained so much on the Italian humour, as it induced divers of that Nobility to procure him to second it..with another Tome. *a* **1639** WOTTON *Surv. Educ.* Reliq. (1651) 334 And this is enough for the disclosing of a good Capacity in the popular way; which I have followed, because the Subject is generall. **1671** DRYDEN *Even. Love* Pref. a 1 b, I admire and applaud him where I ought: those who do more, do but value themselves in their admiration of him: and, by telling you they extoll Ben. Johnson's way, would insinuate to you that they can practice it. **1691** WOOD *Ath. Oxon.* II. 641 Five Sermons in five several stiles or waies of preaching. The first in Bishop Andrews way... The second in B. Halls way.

c. In Chemistry and Assaying. ***the humid***, ***moist***, or ***wet way***, ***the dry way*** (= F. *voie humide*, *voie sèche*), processes distinguished by the presence or absence of liquid.

1796 [see DRY *a.* 11 e]. **1800** tr. *Lagrange's Chem.* I. 398, I am not yet able to give an account..of the results of this analysis by the wet way. **1838** [see HUMID *a.* c]. **1839** [see MOIST *a.* 5].

d. Adverbial phrases without prep. See also ANYWAY, SOMEWAY.

Now somewhat *rare*, the form with *in* being commonly preferred. For *no way* see NOWAY *adv.*

a **1300** *Cursor M.* 12623 Leue sun,..þi fader and i has mani wais Soght þe abute this thre dais. *c* **1380** WYCLIF *Sel. Wks.* III. 348 Freris..spuylen þe puple many weies by ipocrisie and oþer leesingis. **1526** TINDALE *Heb.* i. 1 God in tyme past diversly and many wayes [Gr. πολυτρόπως] spake vnto the fathers by prophetes. **1553** T. WILSON *Rhet.* III. 90 b, When by deuersity of inuention, a sentence is manye wayes spoken. **1560** DAUS tr. *Sleidane's Comm.* 286 He declareth..how many wayes they have rebelled [L. *quam multis modis rebellarint ostendit*]. **1589** HAKLUYT *Voy.* Ep. Ded. ¶5 It hath passed..the censure of the learned phisitian M. Doctor Iames, a man many wayes very notably qualified. **1599** SHAKS. *Much Ado* II. i. 198 What fashion will you weare the Garland off?.. You must weare it one way, for the Prince hath got your Hero. *c* **1600** —— *Sonn.* xvi. 1 But wherefore do not you a mightier waie Make warre vppon this bloudie tirant time? **1612** PEACHAM *Gentl. Exerc.* III. 167 The Lion..is borne these waies, Rampant, Passant, Saliant, Seisant or couchant. **1651** HOBBES *Leviath.* II. xxxi. 187 God declareth his Lawes three wayes. **1653** WALTON *Angler* x. 187 Some say, they [*sc.* eels] breed..out of the putrifaction of the earth, and divers other waies. **1659** *Nicholas Papers* (Camden) IV. 122 There Fleetewood, Desborow, with the greatest officers seeke God for councell and act theire owne way. **1682** DRYDEN *Mac Flecknoe* 208 There thou maist..torture one poor word Ten thousand ways. **1695** W. J. tr. *Bossu's Treat. Epick Poem* II. vii. 72 An Action may be entire and compleat two ways. **1780** JOHNSON *Let. to Mrs. Thrale* 4 July, I..hope she will not be too rigorous with the young ones, but allow them to be happy their own way.

e. Coupled with *manner*. Also in advb. phrases, ***all manner of ways***, ***any manner of way*** (†*ways*). Now *rare*.

1430 *Reg. Mag. Sig. Scot.* 38/2 The fermys and the frottis in the menc tyme tane in the principale some of na maner of waye to be contyt. ? **1474** *Stonor Papers* (Camden) I. 141 The grace of Jhesu, hom I mekely beseche..to preserve your fadyrhod yn alle maner of weyys. **1508** *Reg. Privy Seal Scot.* I. 253/1 Alienatioun thairof in heretage, lyferent, or lang takis forthir than thre ȝeris, onymaner of way. **1533** GAU *Richt Vay* (S.T.S.) 26 Ane man ma trow ii maner of wais of god. **1654** DOROTHY OSBORNE *Lett.* (1888) 225 My Lady Ruthin..has put a tune to them that I may hear them all manner of ways. **1705** in W. S. Perry *Hist. Coll. Amer. Col. Ch.* I. 162 Signed; but without the Privity..of Govr Nicholson or his being any manner of ways connected in it. **1718** in *Nairne Peerage Evid.* (1874) 33 In such way and manner as to his Majesty should seem meet. **1720** A. PETRIE *Rules Good Deportm.* (1877) 20 It is rude in Company to break Wind any Manner of Way, tho amongst Inferiors. **1815** SCOTT *Guy M.* xii, O ay, sir, there's nae doubt o' that, though there are mony idle clashes about the way and manner.

f. ***in his*** (***her, its, their***) ***way***: appended to expressions of praise, with the implication that the praise given is to be understood in a limited sense appropriate to the object. ***in a way*** (colloq. ***in a sort of way***): appended to a statement to intimate that it might be taken to imply more than it is meant to do.

1711 STEELE *Spect.* No. 43 ¶3 We are all Grave, Serious, Designing Men, in our Way. **1742** RICHARDSON *Pamela* III. 255 You are two beloved Creatures: Both excellent in your way. **1749** in *10th Rep. Hist. MSS. Comm.* App. I. 303, I have received from Cairo the Egyptian figures one of which in their way I do not think bad. **1829** SCOTT *Rob Roy* Introd. 1st half, All whom I have conversed with, and I have in my youth seen some who knew Rob Roy personally, gave him the character of a benevolent and humane man 'in his way.' **1835** DICKENS *Sk. Boz, Parl. Sk.*, Jane is as great a character as Nicholas, in her way. **1855** PRESCOTT *Philip II*, I. viii. (1857) 149 The letter of plenipotentiaries..is a model in its way. **1865** MRS. WHITNEY *Gayworthys* xxix, Of all the looks I ever see in a human face, his was the grievedest then..; and yet, in a kind of way, it was the grandest. **1878** BROWNING *Poets Croisic* xlviii, Latin verses, lovely in their way. **1885** 'MRS. ALEXANDER' *Valerie's Fate* iii, He is handsome in a way—not elegant and soigné like Captain Grey, but there is something about him [etc.]. **1905** R. BAGOT *Passport* iii. 16 Its apartments, though stately in their way, were neither historic nor [etc.].

g. ***way of thinking***: now usually, a set of opinions or principles characteristic of a party or sect. In earlier use with other senses, e.g. a purpose or intention, a (high or low) level of moral principle.

1709 STEELE *Tatler* No. 66 ¶1 Lysander, who is something particular in his Way of Thinking and Speaking, told us, a Man could not be Eloquent without Action. **1737** *Gentl. Mag.* VII. 81 The Thing..was, at the best, but a very mean Action, and argued a low Way of Thinking. **1744** M. BISHOP *Life* 3, I hope he will turn your Heart from this Way of thinking [*sc.* wanting to go to sea]. **1841** HELPS *Ess., Transaction of Business* (1842) 93 It is often worth while to bestow much pains in gaining over foolish people to your way of thinking. **1891** KIPLING *Light That Failed* xi, More than you will be of that way of thinking, young woman.

h. ***way of living*** or ***life***: habits (of an individual or a community) with regard to food, habitation, intercourse, etc. Now also in weakened use: a principle or activity that governs all one's actions; a dominating interest or occupation.

1605 SHAKS. *Macbeth* v. iii. 24 My way of life Is falne into the Seare, the yellow Leafe. **1681** RYCAUT tr. *Gracian's Critick* To Rdr. A 8 b, Their Customs and way of living are different to other Nations of Europe. **1729** T. INNES *Crit. Ess.* (1879) 238 The same author..tells us that in his time the Britains were, as to their manners and way of living, partly like to the inhabitants of the Gauls. **1741** C'TESS POMFRET in *C'tess Hartford's Corr.* (1805) III. 369, I have got into as regular a way of life here as I could be in at my own house. **1774** GOLDSM. *Nat. Hist.* VIII. 184 If we examine their way of living, we shall find these insects chiefly subsisting upon others, much less than themselves. **1777** SIR W. JONES *Ess.* i. 180 Since their way of life gives them leisure to pursue those arts. **1898** M. PEMBERTON *Phantom Army* I. vi, That the hour would come when he must lay down the sword..and turn with shame from the old way of life. **1917** H. J. LASKI in *Holmes-Laski Lett.* (1953) I. 104 Education is a way of life and not the collection of information. **1938** *Amer. Jrnl. Sociol.* XLIV. 1 (*heading*) Urbanism as a way of life. **1957** *Times Lit. Suppl.* 1 Nov. 650/5 Democracy has not yet been accepted as a way of life in Germany. **1970** *Daily Tel.* 4 Sept. 5/2 The investigation ..is expected to ask searching questions into the safety of supertankers, which have now become a 'way of life'. **1974** *Times* 8 Mar. 23/5 (*heading*) Hong-kong... Where a quick profit is a way of life. **1981** Q. CRISP *How to become a Virgin* 188 Giving talks to American universities could easily be converted into a way of life.

i. ***to have everything one's own way***, ***to have it all one's own way***: to have one's wishes carried out; to meet with no resistance or opposition. Cf. 12 c.

1709 STEELE *Tatler* No. 66 ¶2 Therefore he would have it his Way, and our Friend is to drink till he is carbuncled and Tun-bellied. **1744** M. BISHOP *Life* 107 Never deny him any Thing, for he loves to have every Thing his own Way. **1847** HELPS *Friends in C.* I. viii. 154 That easiness of mind, which is easy because it is tolerant, because it does not look to have everything its own way. **1853** LYTTON *My Novel* IV. vii, That literature admits no controversialists, and the writer has it all his own way. **1858** SEARS *Athan.* xvi. 133 What sort of a world would you make for yourself, if you could have everything your own way?

j. In various phrases. †***there is no way but one***: death (or ruin) is certain. ***no two ways about it*** or ***that*** (? orig. *U.S. colloq.*): there can be no doubt of the fact. ***it is always the way with*** (***him***): (he) always acts so. ***by*** (or ***with***) ***his way of it*** (*Sc.*): according to his account of it. ***there is no way*** (with dependent clause) (*colloq.*): there is no possibility that; cf. NOWAY *adv.*

1570 ? TARLTON in *Old Ballads* (Percy Soc. 1840) 82 No horse nor man could passe Of busines small or post, For issue none there was, No way but to be lost. **1586** MARLOWE *1st Pt. Tamburl.* v. ii. 1982 The Souldan and the Arabian king together Martch on vs with such eager violence, As if there were no way but one with vs. **1599** SHAKS. *Hen. V*, II. iii. 16 After I saw him fumble with the Sheets..[etc.], I knew there was but one way. **1678** DRYDEN *All for Love* Pref. b 4, For if he heard the malicious Trumpetter proclaiming his name before his betters, he knew there was but one way with him. **1796–7** JANE AUSTEN *Pride & Prej.* xliii, 'And this is always the way with him,' she added. 'Whatever can give his sister any pleasure, is sure to be done in a moment.' **1818** FEARON *Sk. America* 320 (Thornton s.v. *No*) You and I have got to dovetail, and no two ways about it. **1834** J. HALL *Kentucky* I. 145 'This has been a powerful hot day.'.. 'No two ways about that,' said the hunter. **1842** DICKENS *Amer. Notes* vi, Well, they're [i.e. the cells are] pretty nigh full, and that's a fact, and no two ways about it. **1852** H. ROGERS *Ecl. Faith* (1853) 221 It is too much the way with you objectors to say [etc.]. **1867** MRS. OLIPHANT *Madonna Mary* I. viii. 119 But then that is often the way with those well-off people. **1889** STEVENSON *Master of Ballantrae* ii, Onyway he was a great hand by his way of it, and he up and rebuked the Master for some of his on-goings. **1975** *New Yorker* 1 Dec. 55/2 There is no way a losing candidate can pick himself up and pretend nothing has happened to him. **1977** *Daily Tel.* 10 Oct. 12/8 We are operating an emergency service and there is no way we would strike and let the old folk down. **1978** S. BRILL *Teamsters* x. 380 There was no way he would support the President's reelection. **1978** G. A. SHEEHAN *Running & Being* xiii. 188 He had recognized the bald head and there was no way I was going to beat him.

k. ***in this way***: in colloquial lang. sometimes used vaguely for 'thus' or 'so', when not the manner of an action but the action itself is in question.

1837 DICKENS *Pickw.* xxviii, I can't let you cut an old friend in this way.

l. (***in***) ***one way or*** (or ***and***) ***another***: by any of various methods, for any of various reasons, in any of various respects. Cf. sense 9 e.

1861 T. HUGHES *Tom Brown at Oxf.* I. iii. 40 Being a good whist and billiard player, and not a bad jockey, he managed in one way or another to make his young friends pay well for the honour of his acquaintance. **1923** R. MACAULAY *Told by Idiot* I. v. 23 One way and another, what with papa's friends and mamma's and the children's, a good deal of life flowed into the..house. **1955** L. P. HARTLEY *Perfect Woman* viii. 79 What, after all, had he to tell Alec that mattered so much, one way or another? **1965** M. ALLINGHAM *Mind Readers* xix. 211 We're in for a very busy time, my lad, one way and another. **1973** *Listener* 15 Nov. 661/3, I was quite well educated, one way and another. **1979** A. PRICE *Tomorrow's Ghost* xii. 216 Captain Fitzgibbon wouldn't come back from that last Ulster tour, one way or another.

m. ***way of looking at it*** or ***things***: the (personal) perspective from which one views a situation or event, esp. as regards attitudes brought to it or implications seen in it; a point of view.

[**1845**: see LOOK *v.* 3 a. **1861** T. HUGHES *Tom Brown at Oxf.* III. v. 95 Mary's habits, and thoughts, and ways of looking at and judging of people and things, were much changed.] **1881** H. JAMES *Portrait of Lady* I. xvii. 218, I can't make out that what he tells me about the royal family is much to their credit; but he says that's only my peculiar way of looking at it. **1893** 'L. CARROLL' *Sylvie & Bruno Concluded* ii. 27 It's a new way of looking at it—to me..but it seems a *true* way, also. **1905** E. G. WHITE *Ministry of Healing* 483 We differ so widely in disposition, habits, education, that our ways of looking at things vary. **1911** D. H. LAWRENCE *White Peacock* II. i. 202 It's one way of looking at things. **1963** D. LESSING *Man & Two Women* 141, I mean to say, you've got to take the rough with the smooth, and there's no other way of looking at it.

n. ***the way***: so that, with the result that. *Ir.*

1899 SOMERVILLE & 'ROSS' *Some Experiences Irish R.M.* v. 118 A couple o' dhraws o' th' ash plant across the butt o' the tail, the way I wouldn't blind her. **1912** J. STEPHENS *Crock of Gold* xiv. 225 Be sure and hold him tight..the way we can have a good look at him. **1924** R. MACAULAY *Orphan Island* i. 16 We must see about fermenting some of this fruit-juice, the way we'll get something fit to drink.

o. ***it's this way***: a colloq. formula introducing an oral explanation.

1905 'O. HENRY' *Strictly Business* (1910) But it's this way: Suppose you're a Fifth Avenue millionaire, soaring high. **1938** T. CALDWELL *Dynasty of Death* (1939) I. 385 Well, it's this way, Paul: you see, a number of us must stay at home to make the guns..for our soldiers to use. **1961** *East Anglian Mag.* July 505 'It's this way,' he expounded to his cronies in the know. **1970** [see LOSE *v.*[1] 9 b].

15. In advb. phrases like (***in***) ***all ways***, (***in***) ***any way***, (***in***) ***one way***, (***in***) ***more ways than one***, etc., the sense of 'manner' (see 14) passes into that of: An aspect, feature, or respect; a point or particular of comparison.

1598 SHAKS. *Merry W.* I. iv. 15 His worst fault is that he is giuen to prayer; hee is something peeuish that way. *a* **1600** HOOKER *Wks.* (1836) III. 796 That justice exacteth punishment for offending, even after their offences be forgiven them, there is, as it seemeth, proof sufficient more ways than one. *a* **1626** BACON *New Atl.* (1900) 38/13 Also we make them differ in Colour, Shape, Activity, many wayes. **1630** B. JONSON *New Inn* IV. iii, The office of a man Thats truly valiant, is considerable Three ways: the first in respect of matter..; in respect of forme..; And in the end [etc.]. **1816** *Edin. Rev.* Dec. 464 The foreign Commissioners had not yet reached St Helena, whose presence in the island may justly have alarmed Sir Hudson, in more ways than one, for the safety of his prisoner. **1885** 'MRS. ALEXANDER' *Valerie's*

Fate v, May you find a companion better in all ways than I could have been! **1893** LE GALLIENNE *Retrosp. Rev.* (1896) II. 21 A teetotaler, however admirable in other ways, is not the fit person to edit Burns. **1895** HARDY *Jude* v. viii. 398 Her loss was a loss to me in more ways than one! **1952** M. R. RINEHART *Swimming Pool* xiv. 129 It's a dead end, in more ways than one.

16. a. A condition regarded as hopeful or the contrary. Chiefly with qualifying adj.: ***in a good, bad, forward*** (etc.) ***way***. † ***to stand in good way***: to be likely to prosper. † ***to be in way with***: to be in treaty with (a person) *for* something. † ***to put*** (a business) ***in a way***: to put in train. (***to put***) ***in the*** (or ***a, that***) ***way***: (to make) pregnant; cf. *in the family way* s.v. FAMILY 10 b.

Also *to be in a fair way* (*to do* something): see FAIR *a.* 14.

1467 *Paston Lett.* Suppl. 113 Wer by, I undy[r]stand,.. all thyng standyth in good way. **1480** *Cely Papers* (Camden) 49, I am in whay w^t^ Iyshbryght van whennysbarge for an ij of yowr sarplers. I hope I shall go thorow w^t^ hym. *c* **1500** in *Joseph Arimath.* (E.E.T.S.) 32 He..set his realme & his housholde in good waye..& toke his Iourney. **1624** in *Eng. Hist. Rev.* (1913) Jan. 129 When he hath put the business in a way, then he [the Secretary] is to go back and take his own place. **1648** GAGE *West Ind.* 210, I am in a good way for salvation. **1691** T. H[ALE] *Acc. New Invent.* p. xviii, Timber sufficient for the use of the Navy Royal had now been in a forward way to its sufficient growth. **1698** J. COLLIER *Immor. Stage* 211 When ever you see a thorough Libertine, you may almost swear he is in a rising way, and that the Poet intends to make him a great Man. **1726** SHELVOCKE *Voy. round World* 347 People in such a forlorn way are apt to form innumerable apprehensions. **1742** RICHARDSON *Pamela* III. 228 [She] told me..that the Way I was in [*sc.* 'in the family way'], made her love me better and better. *Ibid.* 354 So having congratulated their hopeful Way, and wished them to take care of themselves [etc.]. **1809** WINDHAM *Let.* 23 July in *Sp.* (1812) I. 109 But one of the poor men who were hurt at the fire is dead, and another of them is, I fear, in a bad way. **1817** JANE AUSTEN *Let.* 23 Mar. (1952) 488 Mrs Clement too is in that way again. I am quite tired of so many Children. **1828** CARR *Craven Gloss.* s.v., 'To be in a hinging way,' neither well nor ill. **1831** MRS. ARBUTHNOT *Let.* 18 Feb. in C. Arbuthnot *Corr.* (1941) 140 Young Ly. C. is *not in a way*; the old housekeeper wrote to her something about it, & she wrote back word, 'God's will be done.' **1838** DICKENS *Nickleby* xxiii, There was Mrs. Lenville, in a very limp bonnet and veil, decidedly in that way in which she would wish to be if she truly loved Mr. Lenville. **1867** QUEEN VICTORIA *Let.* 25 Oct. in R. Fulford *Your Dear Letter* (1971) 155 Dearest child, why did you not tell me, your own mother, when you first began being in that way? **1871** SMILES *Charac.* i. 26 The nation that has no higher god than pleasure, or even dollars or calico, must needs be in a poor way. **1960** *Pick of Today's Short Stories* XI. 215 They'd both eloped... 'I'll bet he put her in the way'. **1980** J. ROSE *Elizabeth Fry* iii. 44 She suspected herself of being pregnant, 'in the way' as she called it.

b. ***to be in a way*** (with or without specifying adj.): to be in a state of mental distress or anxiety. *dial.* Cf. STATE *sb.* 2 c.

1855 *Mag. for Young* XIV. 131 She keeps on crying out for her mamma..and she is in such a way as I never saw. **1869** A. MACDONALD *Love, Law & Theol.* xvi. 313 But they say she's in a dreedfu' wey..She's never yet heerd frae her man [etc.]. *Ibid.* xviii. 354 She'll gae clean distrackit—a hear she's in a sair wey aboot it. **1873** SPILLING *M. Miggs* 81 (E.D.D.) Well, there, I was in a way. **1883** FRANCES M. PEARD *Contrad.* xxvi, Mother's in a way. **1896** GRATIANA CHANTER *Witch of Withyford* iv. 45, I suppose her was in a proper way about it and fell to crying.

17. Kind, sort, description. Now only in certain phrases. ***in the way of***: of the nature of, belonging to the class of, 'in the shape of'. Also, with similar sense, and more frequently, ***in the —— way***, where *way* is qualified by an attributive sb. or an adj. So occas. ***in this way*** = 'of this kind'.

1647 CLARENDON *Hist. Reb.* III. §140 He averred that 'in that way of bill [*sc.* a bill of attainder] private satisfaction to each man's conscience was sufficient, although no evidence had been given in at all'. **1736** BUTLER *Anal.* Introd., Wks. 1874 I. 4 Though so little in this way has been attempted by those who have treated of our intellectual powers. **1757** FOOTE *Author* I. Wks. 1799 I. 134 You have nothing in the compiling or index way, that you wou'd intrust to the care of another? *Ibid.* 136 In the year forty-five, when I was in the treasonable way. **1770** LANGHORNE *Plutarch's Lives, Philopœmen* ¶4 From a child he was fond of everything in the military way. **1791** SMEATON *Edystone L.* §94, I could have every thing here, that I could desire in the freestone way. **1797** MRS. A. M. BENNETT *Beggar Girl* (1813) I. 214 In the afternoon tea-way, her bar exhibited the genteel thing. **1809** MALKIN *Gil Blas* I. xii. ¶4, I should want for nothing in the bread and water way! **1823** J. BADCOCK *Dom. Amusem.* 170 Sheet lead, which comes to us in the way of lining round tea-chests. **1835** DICKENS *Sk. Boz, Making a Night of it*, It was his ambition to do something in the celebrated 'kiddy' or stage-coach way. **1837** —— *Pickw.* lv, Mr. Solomon Pell, finding that nothing more was going forward, either in the eating or drinking way, took a friendly leave. **1875** FREEMAN *Norm. Conq.* (ed. 2) III. xiii. 305 He did a good deal in the way of ravaging. **1875** E. WHITE *Life in Christ* IV. xxvii. (1878) 442 More certainty is attainable respecting some things which Divine Goodness will *not* do, than as to what it *will* do in the way of positive benefaction.

18. a. Kind of occupation, work, or business. Now only more explicitly ***way of business***. Formerly also † ***way of life*** = 'walk of life'.

1690 NORRIS *Beatitudes* (1694) 81 If God would not accept an House of Prayer from a Man of a Military Way and Character, much less will he accept [etc.]. **1711** ADDISON *Spect.* No. 21 ¶8 To place their Sons in a way of Life where an honest Industry cannot but thrive. **1721** *Lond. Gaz.* No. 6020/4 Diapers, Damasks, Huckabacks, and all sorts of.. Linnens in a Linnen-Draper's Way. **1727** GAY *Begg. Op.* I. ix, The Lawyers are bitter enemies to those in our way. **1752** *Lond. Even.-Post* 28–30 May 4/1 We hear that there hath been lately an Order made in some of the Royal Hospitals, that no Governor should serve them in his Way of Business. **1782** MISS BURNEY *Cecilia* IX. vi, Her mother, she was sure, would never be at rest till he got into some higher way of life. **1787** T. JEFFERSON *Writ.* (1859) II. 90 The best workmen in this way, acknowledge that his is like a new art. **1791** SMEATON *Edystone L.* §293 This day the plumber completed every thing in *his* way about the balcony. **1920** *Act 10 & 11 Geo. V* c. 13 §2 (3) In the case of a seller who was in the same way of business before the war.

b. Preceded by an attributive sb. denoting the kind of commodity dealt in.

1760 DERRICK *Lett.* (1767) I. 45 The different manufactures of this town, more particularly in the cutlery and toy way. **1766** ENTICK *London* IV. 114 There are several ..wholesale traders in the haberdashery way. **1786** *Phil. Trans.* LXXVI. 27 *note*, [He] had some years past the honour to work in the instrument way under the direction of the late Dr Demainbray. **1788** *Ann. Reg., Projects* 93 A gentleman of ability in the steel way. **1838** DICKENS *Nickleby* iv, I am in the oil and colour way. **1841** THACKERAY *Gt. Hoggarty Diamond* ii, It was a new house, but did a tremendous business in the fig and sponge way.

c. ***in my*** (***his,*** etc.) ***way***: = in my (etc.) line; suited to my (etc.) capacity, tastes, or requirements. Chiefly in negative context. Cf. 37 d.

1806 J. BERESFORD *Miseries Hum. Life* i. Introd., Quoting from a dead language looks a little like skulking, and that's not at all in my way, as you know. **1863** DICKENS *Uncomm. Trav.* xvii, One..is made angry by my modestly suggesting the possibility of Paris time being more in their way. *a* **1865** MRS. GASKELL *Wives & Dau.* xiv, I knew it [*sc.* an agricultural meeting] wasn't much in his way. **1887** BIRRELL *Obiter Dicta* Ser. II. 64 Research was not in his way.

19. a. ***in a great, small way***: (living) on a large or small scale of income and expenditure. Also with reference to the magnitude of a business establishment.

c **1750** J. NELSON *Jrnl.* (1836) 9 We..lived in a good way (as the world calls it), that is, in peace and plenty, and love to each other. **1779** *Mirror* No. 17, I was married, about five years ago, to a young man in a good way of business as a grocer. **1815** JANE AUSTEN *Emma* ii, Having brothers already established in a good way in London. *Ibid.* xxii, The elder sister..was very well married, to a gentleman in a great way, near Bristol, who kept two carriages! **1833** CARLYLE in *Fraser's Mag.* July 27/1 Next, however, as another more lasting resource, he forges; at first in a small way. **1849** THACKERAY *Pendennis* viii, It was very right that he should take lodgings in his aunt's house, who lived in a very small way. **1864** *Law Times' Rep.* N.S.X. 719/1 The defendants.. were contractors and builders in a large way of business. **1885** *Field* 26 Sept. 476/1 Young men..go headlong into some big scheme they take into their heads..instead of starting cautiously and in a small way.

b. ***in a big way***: on a large scale, intensively; (*colloq.*) with great enthusiasm or display; very much, very well. orig. *U.S.*

[**1903** *Dialect Notes* II. 306 *Big way* (to get in a), *v. phr.*, to become excited. 'The preacher got in a *big way* and you could hear him a mile.'] **1927** F. HARRIS *My Life & Loves* III. v. 69, I meant to take up the whole problem of journalism in a big way when I came back. **1932** *N.Y. Times Bk. Rev.* 10 Jan. 17/3 A gangster who calls himself Napoleon and who goes in for crime in a big way. **1936** H. L. ICKES *Diary* 30 June (1955) I. 626 The speech went over in a big way. **1943** J. S. HUXLEY *TVA* vii. 51 Over half a million acres..of fishable water..are already being taken advantage of in a big way. **1950** C. MACINNES *To Victors* II. 211, I could go for her in a big way. **1955** A. HUXLEY *Let.* 18 Mar. (1969) 738 Amanita muscaria..he thinks will open the doors of ESP in a big way. **1958** *Times Rev. Industry* Dec. 57/2 Users of traditional materials are looking to the..use of..plastics in a big way. **1980** A. MARS-JONES *Lantern Lect. & Other Stories* (1981) 10 The Trust people played hard-to-get until he started bequeathing the property..to the Welsh nationalists. *Then* they sat up and took notice In A Big Way.

†20. In the 17–18th c. often used for: A particular form of church government or polity. *Obs.*

a **1647** [see CONGREGATIONAL 3]. **1648** J. COTTON *Way of Congreg. Ch.* I. iii. 1 Nor is Independency a fit name of the way of our Churches. **1651** BAXTER *Inf. Bapt.* 145 The Episcopall Party are far more confirmed in their way by it. **1737** WATERLAND *Eucharist* 449 From our own Divines I may next proceed to some learned Foreigners, of the *Lutheran* way. **1750** [see PRESBYTERIAN *a.* 1].

21. a. The customary or usual manner of acting or behaving.

1613 SHAKS. *Hen. VIII*, III. i. 157 Why shold we (good Lady) Vpon what cause wrong you? Alas, our Places, The way of our Profession is against it. **1700** CONGREVE *Way of World* v. xiii, Even so Sir, 'tis the way of the World, Sir. **1729** LAW *Serious C.* i. 13 Here you see, that one person has Religion enough, according to the way of the world, to be reckon'd a pious Christian. **1830** tr. *Caillié's Trav. Timbuctoo* I. 94, I tried in vain to discover the origin of this whimsical custom; the only answer I could obtain was, 'It is our way'. **1839** THACKERAY *Fatal Boots* Jan., Living with dukes and peeresses, and writing my recollections of them, as the way now is. **1850** —— *Pendennis* lvi, Almost every person [in this story], according to his nature,..and according to the way of the world as it seems to us, is occupied about Number One.

b. *pl.* Customary modes of behaviour; usages, customs.

1742 FIELDING *J. Andrews* I. iii, He..was..as entirely ignorant of the ways of this world as an infant just entered into it could possibly be. **1893** F. T. RICHARDS in Traill *Soc. Eng.* i. 10 Contending parties among the barbarians looked for Roman support, courted it by assuming Roman ways, and invited Roman interference. **1884** W. C. SMITH *Kildrostan* 46 We judge a stranger by our home-bred ways, Who, maybe, walks by other rule of right.

22. a. A habitual or characteristic manner of action, behaviour, expression, or the like. Often in collective plural.

it is (*only*) *his way*: often said of some perverse or annoying habit of behaviour which the friends of the person guilty of it are accustomed to regard with toleration. So proverbially, *Pretty Fanny's way* (after quot. *a* 1718). † *after my way*: in accordance with my custom.

1709 STEELE *Tatler* No. 6 ¶1 Now upon any Occasion, they only cry, 'Tis her Way, and That's so like her. **1709** —— *Ibid.* No. 45 ¶6 As it is my Way to write down all the good Things I have heard in the last Conversation to furnish my Paper, I can from this only tell you my Sufferings and my Pangs. **1711** ADDISON *Spect.* No. 90 ¶7, I was, after my Way, in Love with both of them. *a* **1718** PARNELL *Elegy to Old Beauty* 34 And all that's madly wild, or oddly gay, We call it only pretty Fanny's way. **1748** RICHARDSON *Clarissa* (1768) III. 103 The free dislike I expressed to his ways, his manners, and his contrivances. **1779** *Mirror* No. 25, I was about to be angry; but on such occasions it is not my way to say much. **1779** *Ibid.* No. 47 ¶4 He often indulges in jokes ..which could not be heard without a blush from any other person; but from Tom, for his way is known, they are heard without offence. **1800** MRS. HERVEY *Mourtray Fam.* II. 269 Henry gone! without our knowing any thing about the letter; and all by your slow ways! **1824** SCOTT *St. Ronan's* i, The exuberant frolics of Meg's temper, which were to them only 'pretty Fanny's way'. **1857** G. A. LAWRENCE *Guy Livingstone* vi, She had the ways of a child petted all its life through. **1865** DICKENS *Mut. Fr.* I. vi, I ought to have begun with a word of explanation: but it's my way to make short cuts at things. **1871** LOWELL *Pope* Writ. 1890 IV. 15 Dryden, in his rough-and-ready way, has hinted at this in his verses to Congreve. **1884** W. C. SMITH *Kildrostan* 79 He settled near us In the next glen, and lived a sumptuous life, Costly, luxurious, though his ways were coarse. **1899** *Allbutt's Syst. Med.* VIII. 217 The teacher may observe slow action, wandering eyes, twitchings, awkward ways, or stooping.

b. *pl.* Habits, usual modes of acting (of an animal); †(of a horse) acquired habits, accomplishments.

1706 *Lond. Gaz.* No. 4285/8 Stolen or strayed.., a roan Mare.., all her Ways, except Pacing. **1899** W. T. GREENE *Cage-Birds* 68 The Red-sided Tit is nearly akin to the Liothrix, which it resembles in many of its ways.

c. *transf.* Occas. with reference to a thing: A tendency or liability to some particular kind of action.

1883 *Manch. Guard.* 3 Oct. 7/2 A policy has a way of becoming unrecognisable when it is administered by a man who does not believe in it. **1918** *Times Lit. Suppl.* 14 Mar. 122/3 Each of our nerves has a nature of its own and ways of its own.

d. ***to have a way with one***: to have a persuasive manner. Also in plural (usually with qualifying word) applied to ingratiating tricks of manner.

1711 R. MARTIN in E. H. Burton *Life Bp. Challoner* (1909) I. iii. 33 Saying yt he'd make a most excellent missioner; he had such an honest way with him. **1840** DICKENS *Old C. Shop* iv, Quilp has such a way with him when he likes, that the best-looking woman here couldn't refuse him if..he chose to make love to her. **1872** LEVER *Ld. Kilgobbin* lxxviii, All your little beguiling ways and insinuating tricks. **1877** PATMORE *Unkn. Eros, Departure* 1 It was not like your great and gracious ways! **1901** *Athenæum* 27 July 120/2 Sticking through thick and thin to the fascinating good-for-nothing who has a way with him.

IV. 23. Uses of *ways* as a singular.

a. The genitive *ways* (OE. *wezes*) occurs in many advb. phrases in which it is combined with a preceding pronominal adj. Most of these phrases came to be written as single words, and are treated as such in this Dict.: see ANYWAYS, NOWAYS, OTHERWAYS (OE. *óðres wezes*) and -WAYS *suffix*. Other similar collocations, now *Obs.* or *dial.*, are ***each ways, this ways, that ways, which ways, the same ways***, synonymous with 'each way', 'this way', etc. (see 9 a, 9 b, 14 d).

†Occas. also with a prep., as *in each ways, by this ways*.

11.. *O.E. Chron.* an. 1016, [Hi] wendon him suðweard oðres wezes. *c* **1205** LAY. 18702 Ælches weies [*c* **1275** weyes] him wes wa. *Ibid.* 25428 Neoren hit noht cnihtes no þes wæies idihte. *a* **1225** *Leg. Kath.* 1984 þis pinfule gin wes o swuch wise iginet, þet te twa turnden eiðer wiðward oðer; & anes weis baðe: þe oðer twa turnden anes weis alswa. *a* **1225** *Juliana* 42 Sei me ȝet witerluker, quod ha, hwuches weis ȝe wurcheð ant bicherreð godes children. *c* **1230** *Hali Meid.* (Bodl. MS.) 112 Hit is þah i wedlac summes weies to þolien. **1338** R. BRUNNE *Chron.* (1725) 123 Roberd þe Marmion þe same wayes did he, He robbed þorgh treson þe kirke of Couentre. *c* **1420** *Contin. Brut* ccxli. (E.E.T.S.) 352 þe tokyn ij smale tewellys.., and caste þe tewellys aboute þe Dukis nek..; and þan þei drowen her towellis eche wayez. **1530** *Palsgr.* 421/1 He hath altered his stayre another wayes, *il a coutourne ses degrez tout aultrement.* **1585–6** EARL LEYCESTER *Corr.* (Camden) 463 Before which tyme, the winde beinge as it was, the fleete wolde be gonne over landes end, and passe that waies to the seas. **1590** PAYNE *Brief. Descr. Irel.* (1841) 9 Let the slope side of your ditch be towardes your marraine, and that wayes throw vp all your earth. **1597** BEARD *Theatre God's Judgem.* (1612) 20 He could not tell which wayes to turn himselfe. **1598** SHAKS. *Merry W.* II. ii. 50, i pray your worship come a little neerer this waies. **1622** CALLIS *Stat. Sewers* (1647) 127 Doctor Bonhams Case, fol. 119 in the same Report, wherein the principal Case there put sways the same ways. **1896** GRATIANA CHANTER *Witch of Withyford* xiv. 170 Going..up over the track that ways to Witches' Combe.

b. Similarly *to go, come one's ways* (also † *on one's ways*), synonymous with *to go, come one's way* (see 7 b), and parallel to the G. *er ging seines* *weges*. In the later period a loose use of the plural may have coalesced with the use of the advb. genitive.

Now only *dial.* and *vulgar*, and chiefly in the imperative; in rustic use *come thy ways* is often addressed playfully to children and animals.

c **893** ÆLFRED *Oros.* 21 þonne rideð ælc hys weȝes mid ðan feo. **13..** *Cursor M.* 22063 (Edinb.), [Satan shall be] laisid at te laste.. to walc his waiis forþe [*Cott.* his forth; *other texts* his way] fra þat quile. **1450–1530** *Myrr. Our Ladye* I. xxii. 57 He anon lefte there the stynkeynge body that he appered in, & wente hys wayes. *c* **1460** *Macro Plays, Wisdom* 878 Turne þi weys! þou gost a-myse. **1576** GASCOIGNE *Kenelworth Castle* Wks. 1910 II. 101 And death.. will end my dayes, As soone as you shall.. wish to go your wayes. **1581** RICH *Farew.* Bb ij, To conueigh her.. a sute of mannes apparell: wherin the next daie in the after noone,.. she should shift herself, and so come her waies vnknowne of any, to suche a place. *Ibid.* Bb iij, Alberto, seyng matters so throughlie concluded, tooke his leaue of theim bothe, and goyng his waies home, he caused all his daughters apparell to be looked together. **1600** SHAKS. *A.Y.L.* I. ii. 221 You meane to mocke me after: you should not haue mockt me before: but come your waies. **1610** —— *Temp.* II. ii. 85 Come on your wayes: open your mouth. **1701** FARQUHAR *Sir H. Wildair* V. vi, Go thy ways for a true Pattern of the Vanity, Impertinence, Subtlety, and Ostentation of thy Country. **1768** GOLDSM. *Goodn. Man* I. i, Well, go thy ways, Sir William Honeywood. **1815** SCOTT *Guy M.* viii, 'Ride your ways,' said the gipsy, 'ride your ways, Laird of Ellangowan'. **1840** DICKENS *Old C. Shop* lxxii, Go thy ways with him, sir,.. and Heaven be with ye both! **1884** *Chesh. Gloss., Come thy ways*, a coaxing way of calling an animal; or even of addressing children.

c. In *a good, great, little, long ways*, the origin of the use of *ways* for *way* is obscure. Also without qualifying adj. Now only *dial* and *U.S.*

It might possibly have arisen from the analogy of phrases containing the advb. genitive (see a and b). There is no known instance in OE. of such a construction as **lýtel weȝes* (= 'paululum viæ'), which might possibly account for it.

1588 PARKE tr. *Mendoza's Hist. China* 289 They.. came vnto the gates of the cittie, after they had gon a good wayes in the suburbs. **1594** R. ASHLEY tr. *Loys Le Roy* 105 b, Selim Ottoman.. assailed him with a mightie armie, a good waies within his owne kingdome. **1749** FIELDING *Tom Jones* XII. iii, Not that I hope.. to live to any such Age as that neither —But if it be only to eighty or ninety: Heaven be praised, that is a great Ways off yet. **1809** BYRON *To Mr. Hodgson* 25 June, Falmouth.. is no great ways from the sea. **1841** CATLIN *N. Amer. Ind.* xli. II. 62 The beautiful Arabian.. must.. be a great ways further South than this. **1845** S. JUDD *Margaret* I. xiv. 113 'It is only a little ways,' replied she, 'and I went clear down to the village to-day alone.' **1890** BICKLEY *Surrey Hills* III. 206 Maybe 'ee's lost his ways. **1895** S. CRANE *Red Badge* v, His mouth was still a little ways open. **1907** J. H. MCCARTHY *Needles & Pins* xiii, The man staggered a little ways across the hall and fell in a heap. **1927** W. FAULKNER *Mosquitoes* 202 I'll carry you a ways, until we get somewhere. **1933** BLOOMFIELD *Language* ii. 40 A speaker can be heard only a short ways and only for an instant or two. **1938** T. WILDER *Our Town* I. 52 Can I walk along a ways with you? **1976** *New Yorker* 15 Mar. 67/1 As it passed over the ridge to land on the other side it hit a tree quite a ways up. **1979** N. MAILER *Executioner's Song* (1980) I. xxix. 445 Though I suppose at some point in the future.. he may be eligible for parole, that's a long long ways away.

V. Idiomatic phrases.

* *with governing verb.*

For *clear the way, fetch way* (Naut.), *gather way* (Naut.), *give way, pave the way*, see the verbs.

24. have way. (See 6 above.)

†**a.** To be allowed liberty of action. *Obs.*

1603 SHAKS. *Meas. for M.* v. 238 Let me haue way, my Lord, To finde this practise out.

b. Of feelings or their manifestation: To find vent.

1846 JAMES *Step-mother* xxxii, He evidently strove to speak calmly, but the father's apprehensions would have way, and his voice trembled, and his lip quivered. **1883** D. C. MURRAY *Hearts* xix, Tom dropped his face into his hands, and a scalding tear or two had way in spite of him.

25. make way.

a. To open a passage, remove obstacles to progress, to facilitate passage or entrance. (See 6 above.) Const. *for*, †*to*, or †dative.

c **1200** *Trin. Coll. Hom.* 91 Ðo þe þe weie makeden biforen him bien folkes lorþeawes. *c* **1330** R. BRUNNE *Chron. Wace* (Rolls) 1555 þorow þe host he made hem [? *read* hym] weye. On ilk a side he dide þem deye. *a* **1400–50** *Bk. Curtasye* 533 in *Babees Bk.*, Byfore þe cours þo stuarde comes þen, þe seruer hit next of alle kyn men Mays way and stondes by syde, Tyl alle be serued at þat tyde. *c* **1450** *Merlin* xxxii. 655 Gawein com thourgh the presse makinge wey with the trenchaunt suerde. **1567** MAPLET *Gr. Forest* 68 b, And the fift or odde Crane in maner of a persiue sterne, to make the other way in the Ayre, flieth all alone before. **1588** PARKE tr. *Mendoza's Hist. China* 184 They were carried in little chayres vpon mens backes, and the Captaine.. before them making way. **1593** SHAKS. *2 Hen. VI*, IV. viii. 62 My sword make way for me, for heere is no staying. **1616** R. C. *Times' Whistle* (1871) 81 Wher gold makes way Ther is no interruption. **1638** R. BAKER tr. *Balzac's Lett.* (vol. II) 107 Hee seemes to thinke.. that vertue had neede of delight, to make way for her into the soule. **1693** LOCKE *Educ.* §140 All the World forwardly joyn to oppose and defeat them: whilst the open, fair, wise Man has every Body to make way for him, and goes directly to his Business.

†**b.** Of ground: To allow of passage. *Obs.*

c **1300** *K. Horn* 1489 (Laud MS.) þe sond by gan to drye And hyt hym makede weye.

c. To move from one's place so as to allow a person to pass.

c **1400** MAUNDEV. (Roxb.) xxv. 120 He commaundez þe lordes þat rydez nere him to make way þat þe men of religioun may comme to him. **1593** SHAKS. *Rich. II*, v. ii. 110 Make way, vnruly Woman. **1842** BORROW *Bible in Spain* vii, A Portuguese or Spaniard will seldom make way for a stranger, till called upon or pushed aside. **1911** GOULDSBURY & SHEANE *Gt. Plateau N. Rhodesia* 259 If a young man sees his mother-in-law coming along the path, he must retreat into the bush and make way for her.

d. To leave a place vacant *for* a successor or substitute.

1760–72 H. BROOKE *Fool of Qual.* (1809) III. 122 When my family.. were thus turned out of doors, an old follower made way for them in his own cottage, and retired.. to a cow-house hard by. *a* **1828** H. NEELE *Lit. Rem.* (1829) 33 The tragedies of Shakspeare were driven from the stage to make way for those of Addison and Rowe. **1853** KINGSLEY *Hypatia* xxx, If they [the philosophers] had no better Gospel than that to preach, they must make way for those who had. **1869** FREEMAN *Norm. Conq.* III. xii. 151 His castle .. has been wantonly destroyed to make way for one of the barbarous official buildings of modern France. **1896** *Law Times* C. 407/2 At Durham.. [Sir Charles] refused to stand, and his refusal made way for the present Lord Herschell.

e. To make progress on a journey or voyage. Often with qualifying word, as *to make good, much, little way*. (Cf. 7 above.)

(*a*) *Naut.* (see 7 i).

1490 CAXTON *Eneydos* xxvii, 97 Castyng her sight ferder towarde the see, she sawe the saylles, wyth the flote of the shippes that made good waye. **1556** TOWESON in Hakluyt *Voy.* (1589) 98 The windes and seas were high, yet we made some way. *a* **1626** BACON *New Atl.* 1 The Winde.. setled in the West for many dayes, so as we could make little or no way. **1624** CAPT. J. SMITH *Virginia* III. vi. 60 We seeing them prepare to assault vs, left our Oares and made way with our sayle to incounter them. **1626** —— *Accid. Yng. Seamen* 29 Fetch the log-line to try what way shee makes. **1744** M. BISHOP *Life* 49 We lost our Main top Mast, so that after the Storm was over we could not make any Way. **1791** SMEATON *Edystone L.* §155 Our vessels.. made better Way in a rough sea. **1837** MARRYAT *Dog-Fiend* xlii, He stood up on the choak to ascertain what way she was making through the water. **1882** DE WINDT *Equator* 75 The river, however, widened to nearly a mile in breadth.. and we made better way.

(*b*) *gen.* Also *fig.*

1588 SHAKS. *Tit. A.* II. ii. 24 And I haue horse will follow where the game Makes way. **1590** SPENSER *F.Q.* I. i. 39 He making speedy way through spersed ayre. *a* **1593** MARLOWE & NASHE *Dido* 221 Æneas is my name.. With twise twelue Phrigian ships I plowed the deepe, And made that way my mother Venus led. **1596** SHAKS. *Tam. Shr.* I. i. 239 Waite you on him,.. While I make way from hence to saue my life. **1820** SCOTT *Monast.* Introd. Ep., So great is the difference betwixt reading a thing one's self, making toilsome way through all the difficulties of manuscript, and, as the man says in the play, 'having the same read to you'. **1845** MCCULLOCH *Taxation* III. ii. (1852) 446 Should the system [of life annuities] not make any greater way than it has done, it may not.. be worth objecting to. **1860** MOZLEY *Univ. Serm.* vii. (1876) 182 See.. how little way they have made in truly spiritual, unselfish affections and inclinations. **1882** BESANT *All Sorts* xviii, And he made no more way with his wooing. That was stopped, apparently, altogether. **1883** FRANCES M. PEARD *Contrad.* i, His companion.. was making rapid way towards the point. **1888** BRYCE *Amer. Commw.* xxxix. II. 71 There are some signs the view is making way.

†**f.** To make a hole *in, through*. *Obs.*

1581 A. HALL *Iliad* IV. 73 That of the staffe the steeled point made in his forehead way. **1596** SHAKS. *Tam. Shr.* II. 155 With that word she stroke me on the head, And through the instrument my pate made way. **1611** COTGR., *Faire jour à*, to make way vnto.

†**g.** Of an event or action: To lead *to*, afford facilities *for* something; to render it possible *to* do something. *Obs.*

1646 H. LAWRENCE *Commun. & War with Angels* 14 And this will not be unusefull to consider since it makes way to shew to what end they appeare and what they.. can doe for us. **1677** TEMPLE *Moxa* Miscell. (1680) 194 About which time [the age of forty] the natural heat beginning to decay, makes way for those distempers. *a* **1715** BURNET *Own Time* III. viii. (1900) II. 143 This made way to more desperate undertakings.

†**h.** *to make way to*: to approach (a person) with a view to establishing relations with him.

1671 MILTON *Samson* 481, I already have made way To some Philistian Lords, with whom to treat About thy ransom.

26. make one's (its) way. (Cf. 7 above.)

a. To travel or proceed in an intended direction or to a certain place. *to make the best of one's way* (also, † *to make one's best way*): to go as quickly as one can; †to decamp.

c **1400** MAUNDEV. (Roxb.) xxxiv. 156, I made my way.. vnto Rome. **1582** N. LICHEFIELD tr. *Castanheda's Conq. E. Ind.* I. iii. 7 b, The rest then departed,.. making their waye into the Sea, with a South southwest winde. **1668** CLARENDON *Contempl. Ps.* Tracts (1727) 473 Those who.. make their way through a sea of blood and rapine to grasp an authority which belonged not to them. **1697** DRYDEN *Virg. Georg.* III. 395 He makes his way o're Mountains, and contemns Unruly Torrents, and unfoorded Streams. **1705** ADDISON *Italy* Monaco, etc. 4 The next Day we again set Sail, and made the best of our way 'till we were forc'd, by contrary Winds, into St. Remo. **1742** FIELDING *J. Andrews* I. xvi, The Thief.. without any Ceremony, stepped into the Street, and made the best of his Way. **1836** THIRLWALL *Greece* xxii. III. 215 A very small number made their way to Ambracia. **1840** DICKENS *Old C. Shop* xxiii, With that they parted; Mr. Swiveller to make the best of his way home and sleep himself sober; and Quilp [etc.]. **1844** DISRAELI *Coningsby* VII. iv, Coningsby bade his friend farewell till the morrow, and made his best way to the Castle. **1849** MACAULAY *Hist. Eng.* iii. I. 366 Hardly any gentleman had any difficulty in making his way to the royal presence. **1864** TROLLOPE *Small Ho. Allington* xxi, Johnny made his way on to the road by a stile that led out of the copse. *Ibid.*, Then we'll make the best of our way home, and have a glass of wine there. **1874** GREEN *Short Hist*, vi. §4. 300 It was in despair of reaching Italy that the young scholar [Erasmus] made his way to Oxford.

†**b.** To effect a passage by force, force one's way. *Obs.*

1647 CLARENDON *Hist. Reb.* VI. §157 But if they compelled him to make his way, and enter the town by force, it would not be in his power to keep his soldiers from taking that which they should win with their blood.

c. To make progress in one's career; to advance in wealth, station, reputation, etc. by one's own efforts.

1605 SHAKS. *Lear* v. iii. 29 If thou do'st As this instructs thee, thou dost make thy way To Noble Fortunes. **1711** ADDISON *Spect.* No. 123 ¶4 He was to make his Way in the World by his own Industry. **1771** SMOLLETT *Humphry Cl.* 18 July II. (1815) 261, I am not at all surprised that these Scots make their way in every quarter of the globe. **1853** LYTTON *My Novel* II. vi, A young man who has his own way to make in life had better avoid all intimacy with those of his own age who have no kindred objects.

†**d.** To find means *to do* something. *Obs.*

a **1300** *Cursor M.* 23179 Quat he war wijs þat moght Stedfast hald þis dai in thoght!.. For þan mund he her make his wai Fra wrak to were him on þat dai.

†**e.** (Also † *to make one's ways*.) To gain favour, establish relations *with* a person. *Obs.*

1618 RALEGH *Apol.* Wks. 1751 II. 250 It was bruited.. that.. being once at Liberty,.. having made my Way with some foreign Prince, I would turn Pirate. *a* **1660** *Contemp. Hist. Irel.* (Ir. Archæol. Soc.) II. 37 He made his waies with Colonell Monke, Governor of Dundalke, for the Parliament, and bought of him worth £1500 of amunition.

f. Of a thing. *to make its way*: to travel, make progress; (of an opinion, custom, etc.) to gain acceptance.

1656 COWLEY *To Sir W. Davenant* 35 Thy Fancy like a Flame its way does make, And leave bright Tracks for following Pens to take. **1711** ADDISON *Spect.* No. 119 ¶6 This infamous Piece of Good-breeding, which reigns among the Coxcombs of the Town, has not yet made its way into the Country. **1861** M. PATTISON *Ess.* (1889) I. 48 It might have been anticipated that Luther's doctrines would have made their way early among this little colony of his countrymen. **1874** MICKLETHWAITE *Mod. Par. Churches* 80 Brass instruments have already begun to make their way.

27. pay one's way. †**a.** To defray one's expenses on a journey. *Obs.*

a **1825** *Willie Wallace* vi. in Child *Ballads* III. 271/2 Take ye that, ye belted knight, 'T will pay your way till ye come down.

b. To succeed in paying one's expenses as they arise, without incurring debts. Of a business undertaking, *to pay its way*: To be carried on at least without loss, to be self-supporting.

1803 G. COLMAN *John Bull* II. iii. 22, I earned my fair profits; I paid my fair way. **1823** BYRON *Age of Bronze* xiv, But bread was high, the farmer paid his way. **1858** TROLLOPE *Three Clerks* iii, Mrs. Woodward.. had there maintained a good repute, paying her way from month to month as widows with limited incomes should do. **1885** *Times* (weekly ed.) 2 Oct. 15/3 The pier has never come near paying its way. **1892** *Law Times' Rep.* LXVII. 139/1 It seems to me a most reasonable thing for a person applying for shares to look for a guarantee of interest until the concern can pay its own way. **1899** LADY M. VERNEY *Verney Mem.* IV. 155 By great economy John has just paid his way.

28. see one's way. a. In literal sense, to have a view of the portion of the road or route immediately before one, so as to be able to avoid wandering or stumbling. **b.** *fig.* in obvious metaphorical uses; now often, to know that some object is attainable (const. *to*); also (chiefly in negative contexts) to feel justified in deciding *to do* something.

1774 BURKE *Let. to Marq. Rockingham* 25 Sept., I must see my way much more clearly before me, before I take any other step in that business. **1775** —— *Sp. Concil. Amer.* 22 Mar. 56, I do not absolutely assert the impracticability of such representation [of the Colonies]. But I do not see my way to it. **1823** KEBLE *Serm.* iii. (1848) 64 To see his way safely, if not clearly or comfortably, through all the snares of error and disputation. **1861** M. PATTISON *Ess.* (1889) I. 33 Simple fighting John Bull can understand, but in a negotiation he can't see his way. **1865** MRS. NEWBY *Comm. Sense* lv. III. 44, I feel that I know my business pretty well already, and that I begin to see my way. *Ibid.* lvi. III. 55, I wish I could do more.. but I think I see a way. **1870** NEWMAN *Gram. Assent* II. ix. 353 Laud said that he did not see his way to come to terms with the Holy See, till Rome was 'other than she is'. **1875** HELPS *Soc. Press.* ii. 24 The neighbours do not see their way to altering it. **1885** *Law Times* LXXIX. 342/1 He did not see his way clear to allow their names to remain upon the register. **1886** *Manch. Exam.* 16 Jan. 5/4 Lord Salisbury has at last seen his way to the final choice of a bishop for Manchester.

29. a. take the way. (Cf. sense 4 and TAKE *v.* 25 b.) To enter on and follow the route leading to a specified place. In early use sometimes without mention of destination; †To set out, travel.

c **1300** *Harrowing of Hell* (Harl. MS.) 38 In godned toke he þen way þat to helle gates lay. **13..** *Guy Warw.* (A.) 1708 Gij him spedde niȝt & day; Into Inglond he toke þe way. **1375** BARBOUR *Bruce* II. 146 All him alane the way he tais Towart the towne off Louchmabane. *c* **1386** CHAUCER *Man of Law's T.* 556 The Constable and his wyf also And Custance han ytake the righte way Toward the see. *c* **1420** ? LYDG. *Assembly of Gods* 551 Wherfore Cerberus tooke the next way. *c* **1485** *Digby Myst., Christ's Burial & Resurr.* 983 Then let us tak þe way furth strayte. *a* **1533** BERNERS *Huon* lxii. 215 They departyd & tooke the way towardes Rome. **1801** SCOTT *Eve of St. John* 86 O fear not the priest,.. For to Dryburgh the way he has ta'en. **1831** —— *Ct. Robt.* xxxiv, Count Robert subjected himself to necessity,.. and.. took the way to Europe by sea. **1831** JAMES *Phil. Augustus* xx, Here the anchorite bade God speed him, and, turning his steps back again, took the way to his hut.

†**b.** To go about *to do* something. Also, to take its course without interference. *Obs.*

1605 BACON *Adv. Learn.* II. xvii. §9. 64 That opinion.. hath beene of ill desert, towardes Learning, as that which taketh the way, to reduce Learning to certaine emptie and barren Generalities. *a* **1700** DRYDEN *Theod. & Hon.* 138 Give me leave to seize my destin'd Prey, And let eternal Justice take the way.

30. to take one's way. To set out on a journey; to journey, travel.

a **1300** *Cursor M.* 11382 Þis kinges thre þar wai þai tok A tuelmoth ar þe natiuite. **1338** R. BRUNNE *Chron.* (1810) 327 After þe enterment þe kyng tok his way. To þe south he went þorgh Lyndesay. **1375** BARBOUR *Bruce* XVIII. 114 For the laiff has thair vayis tane Till the Erische kyngis. *c* **1386** CHAUCER *Melib.* ⁋2996 And right anon they tooken hire wey to the Court of Melibee. *c* **1450** *St. Cuthbert* (Surtees) 7456 His way barfote þan he toke. **1484** CAXTON *Fables of Poge* vii, Sayinge these wordes [the foxe] toke his waye & ranne as fast as he myght. **1498** *Cov. Leet Bk.* 588 And they came forth at þe south durre in þe Mynstere & toke their wey thurgh the newe bildyng downe þe Bailly-lane. *c* **1600** SHAKS. *Sonn.* xlviii. 1 How carefull was I, when I tooke my way, Each trifle vnder truest barres to thrust. **1642–4** VICARS *God in Mount* 149 Lord Paulet..took his way toward Myncard. **1667** MILTON *P.L.* XII. 649 They hand in hand with wandring steps and slow, Through Eden took thir solitarie way. **1697** DRYDEN *Virg. Georg.* III. 405 Alone, by Night, his watry Way he took; About him, and above, the Billows broke. **1761** GRAY *Odin* 13 Onward still his way he takes. **1893** ASHBY-STERRY *Naughty Girl* xviii. 157 As she took her way sadly and slowly down the pier.

** *with prepositions.*

31. by the way. a. Along or near the road by which one travels; by the road-side. In early use also † *by way*.

971 *Blickl. Hom.* 15 Þa sæt þær sum blind þearfa be ðon weȝe. *c* **1205** LAY. 26612 Whaðer heo liue weoren, þa heo bi wæie læien. *a* **1300** *Cursor M.* 8055 A riche man was þar bi wai Was seke, to him þan turnd þai. **1550** CROWLEY *Epigr.* 227 Than, by the waye syde, hym chaunced to se A pore manne that craued of hym for charitie. Whye (quod thys Marchaunt)..Do ye begge by the waye. **1879** JEFFERIES *Wild Life in S. Co.* ii. (1889) 17, I passed flocks of dying sheep: in the hollows by the way their skeletons were here and there to be seen.

b. While going along, in the course of one's walk or journey. In early use † *by way*.

c **1000** *Ags. Gosp.* Luke x. 4 Ne bere ȝe sacc..ne nanne man be weȝe [Vulg. *per viam*] ne gretað. *a* **1122** *O.E. Chron.* (Laud MS.) an. 1096, Ac þes folces þe be Hungrie for, fela þusenda þær & be wæȝe earmlice forforan. *c* **1290** *Beket* 1208 in *S. Eng. Leg.* 141 Þov hauest selde i-seiȝe þene Erchebischop of caunterburi wende in swuche manere bi weie. *a* **1300** *K. Horn* 759 He fond bi þe weie Kynges sones tweie. **1387** TREVISA *Higden* III. 115 Þe kyng..wente homwarde, and was i-slawe by þe weie. **1550** CROWLEY *Last Trumpet* 31 The rauens fed him [*sc.* Elias] by the way. **1590** SHAKS. *Mids. N.* IV. i. 204 Lets follow him, and by the way let vs recount our dreames. **1617** MORYSON *Itin.* I. 204 By the way, in this mornings journey, we did see Weyssenburg, a free but not imperiall City. **1719** DE FOE *Crusoe* I. (Globe) 156 Nor is it possible to describe..what strange unaccountable Whimsies came into my Thoughts by the Way. **1760** [see BY *prep.* 12]. **1898** M. PEMBERTON *Phantom Army* I. vii, It had been in his mind when he rode out of Zaragoza that he would find an early opportunity by the way to question the gipsy.

fig. **1603** SHAKS. *Meas. for M.* v. 458 His Act did not ore-take his bad intent, And must be buried but as an intent That perish'd by the way.

c. *fig.* with reference to the tenor of discourse: Incidentally, in passing, as a side-topic.

1556 ROBINSON tr. *More's Utopia* I. (Arb.) 38 *margin*, Land-lordes by the wai checked for Rent-raisyng. **1581** J. BELL *Haddon's Answ. Osor.* 45 Whiche I thought meete to touch briefly by the way. **1598** SHAKS. *Merry W.* I. iv. 150 Shee is pretty, and honest, and gentle, and one that is your friend, I can tell you that by the way. **1620** T. GRANGER *Div. Logike* 100 They are inferred often by the way for illustration sake. **1632** LITHGOW *Trav.* v. 228 And now by the way I recall the aforesayd Turke. **1731** *Art of Drawing & Paint.* 32 But we must take this by the Way, that in the refining of it, two Ounces will not produce above 40 Grains of good Colour. **1847** H. GOODWIN *Serm.* Ser. I. viii. 131, I would hint to you by the way, that we are perhaps not fair judges of our own actions.

d. used parenthetically to apologize for introducing a new topic, a casual remark, or the like.

a **1614** DONNE *Biathanatos* (1644) 99 Though, by the way, this may not passe so generally, but that it must admit the exception, which the Rule of Law upon which it is grounded, carries with it. **1668** DRYDEN *Ess. Dram. Poesy* 46, I mean besides the Chorus, or the Monologues, which by the way, show'd Ben. no enemy to this way of writing. *c* **1730** BURT *Lett. N. Scot.* (1754) II. 97 By the Way, altho' the Weather was not warm, he was without Shoes, Stockings, or Breeches. **1836** DICKENS *Sk. Boz, Sentiment*, This, by the way, was another bit of diplomacy. **1840** THACKERAY *Barber Cox* Feb., When we lost sight of him, and of his little account, too, by the way. **1884** RIDER HAGGARD *Dawn* xxvii, By the way, talking of letters, there was one came for you this morning in your Cousin Philip's handwriting.

e. in predicative or complemental use.

1564 T. DORMAN *Proofe Cert. Art. Relig.* 95 b, This is yow saie but by the waie, before yow entre into the matter. **1652** NEDHAM tr. *Selden's Mare Cl.* 46 Also, a word by the way, touching the Mediterranean Sea in possession of the Romanes. **1653** RAMESEY *Astrol. Restored* 5 But this by the way, let us now proceed. **1719** DE FOE *Crusoe* I. (Globe) 245 However, I allow'd Liberty of Conscience throughout my Dominions: But this is by the Way. **1904** BURNAND *Records & Remin.* II. 285 But this by the way.

f. As a by-work; as a subordinate piece of work.

1611 COTGR. s.v. *Passant, En passant*, sleightly, lightly, cursarily, accidentally, by the way. *a* **1708** BEVERIDGE *Thes. Theol.* (1711) III. 265 It is not to be done by the way, but with all our might. **1881** JOWETT *Thucyd.* I. 91 Maritime skill is..not a thing to be cultivated by the way [ἐκ παρέργου] or at chance times.

†**g.** Indirectly, by a side channel of information.

1605 SHAKS. *Macb.* III. iv. 130 *Macb.* How say'st thou that Macduff denies his person At our great bidding. *La.* Did you send to him Sir? *Macb.* I heare it by the way: But I will send.

h. *attrib.* as adj. phr.: Incidental, casual, haphazard.

1869 MRS. WHITNEY *We Girls* ii, At parting, she..said.. in an off-hand, by-the-way fashion—'Ruth' [etc.]. **1881** F. HUEFFER *Wagner* 32 The introduction in a by-the-way manner of the two great religious principles appears not particularly happy. **1881** SAINTSBURY *Dryden* i. 21 The ordinary prose style of the day..indulged..in every *détour* and involution of second thoughts and by-the-way qualifications.

32. by way of ——. A prepositional phrase used in various senses. Also † *by the way of*. (The governed sb. is usually without article.)

†**a.** By means of; through the medium of; by the method of. *Obs.*

1390 GOWER *Conf.* I. 69 This lord..spak so that be weie of schrifte He drowh hem [*sc.* the priests] unto his covine. **1439** in *Fenland N. & Q.* (1905) July 222 And yat..ye wole at yis tyme in yis oure grete necessite putte youre handes and ese us by wey of lone of ye somme of C marc. *a* **1450** MARG. ANJOU *Let. to Dame J. Carew* (Camden) 97 Burneby.. desireth with all his hert to do yow worship by wey of marriage. **1495** *Rolls of Parlt.* VI. 493/2 That noo persone.. be not empeached nor chargeable.., by wey of accion or otherwise. **1526** *Pilgr. Perf.* (W. de W. 1531) 2, I requyre you..that..ye neuer by way of curiosite be besy to attempte ony persone therin. **1530** PALSGR. 898 Diuerse comunications by way of dialoges. **1577–87** HOLINSHED *Chron.* III. 1149/2 To indamage some of his countries by waie of inuasion. **1598** GRENEWEY *Tacitus, Ann.* II. xvi. (1622) 56 Flaccus..by way of great promises [*per ingentia promissa*], perswaded him..to enter into the Romane garrison. **1613** SHAKS. *Hen. VIII*, III. i. 54 We come not by the way of Accusation, To taint that honour euery good Tongue blesses. **1663** GERBIER *Counsel* 5 Master-work-men may receive Instructions by way of Draughts, Models, Frames, &c. **1675** J. OWEN *Indwelling Sin* viii. (1732) 96 At least spiritual Sense is not radically in them, but only by way of Communication.

†**b.** By the action of (a person or persons). *Obs.*

1447 in *Reg. Mag. Sig. Scot.* *1450*, 70/2 Gif it happnis the said landis to be distroublit or vexit be way of Inglismen it sal be alowit to the said Alex. of the malis.

†**c.** *Law.* ***by way of feat*** [= AF. *par voye de fait*]: see FEAT *sb.* 1 b. Also (*Sc.*), ***by way of deed***.

1535 STEWART *Cron. Scot.* III. 141 The tother part with haill power and mycht, Without ressone agane he wald persew, Be way of deid his richtis till reskew. **1564** *Reg. Privy Council Scot.* I. 275 In caise ather of the saidis partiis.., sall happin to be hurt, harmit, invadit, or persewit be utheris be way of deid. **1582–8** *Hist. James VI* (1864) 62 That na injure be done to ony subiect be way of deid.

d. As an instance or a mode of; in the capacity or with the function of; as something equivalent to.

[Cf. AF. 'par voye de charite', 1321 in *Rolls Parlt.* I. 393.]

13.. *E.E. Allit. P.* A. 580 By þe way of ryȝt to aske dome. *c* **1380** WYCLIF *Wks.* (1880) 59 He were a cruel fadir þat myȝtte not ȝeue his owene childre bred..& ȝit wolde not suffre anoþer man to helpe þes children bi weie of mercy. *c* **1389** in *Eng. Gilds* (1870) 38 Also þese bretherin han ordeyned, be weye of charite, þat [etc.]. *a* **1400** MAUNDEV. (1839) xviii. 199 The Kyng of that Contree, ones every ȝeer, ȝevethe leve to pore men to gon in to the Lake, to gadre hem precyous Stones and Perles, be weye of Alemesse. **1429** *Rolls of Parlt.* IV. 349/1 Bi weie of hongyng or keveryng. **1551** SIR J. WILLIAMS *Accompte* (Abbotsf. Club) 99 To be gevin vnto straungers by waie of his maiesties reward, v^{ml} li. **1589** PUTTENHAM *Eng. Poesie* III. xviii. (Arb.) 203 We be allowed now and then to ouer-reach a little by way of comparison. **1672** VILLIERS (Dk. Buckhm.) *Rehearsal* I. i. (Arb.) 31 My next Rule is the Rule of Record, and by way of Table-book. **1674** *Essex Papers* (Camden) I. 168 There ought to be a distinction made in Letters of that nature, betweene passing a thing over by way of Connivance and giving a Publick Liberty. **1711** STEELE *Spect.* No. 78 ⁋4 Nothing was wanting but some one to sit in the Elbow Chair, by way of President. **1712** ADDISON *Ibid.* No. 267 ⁋2 Virgil makes his Heroe relate it by way of Episode. **1744** M. BISHOP *Life* 260 Most of them were very industrious in selling one Thing or other by Way of turning the Peny to a good Use. **1749** FIELDING *Tom Jones* III. vii, I ask pardon for this short appearance, by way of chorus, on the stage. **1806** J. BERESFORD *Miseries Hum. Life* ii. §22 Attempting to spring carelessly..over a five-barred gate, by way of shewing your activity to a party of ladies. **1820** BYRON *Juan* v. liii. *note*, In Turkey nothing is more common than for the Mussulmans to take several glasses of strong spirits by way of appetizer. **1842** DICKENS *Amer. Notes* xiv, The drapers always having hung up at their door, by way of sign, a piece of bright red cloth. **1843** PRESCOTT *Mexico* I. ii. I. 31 The sovereign.. holding a golden arrow, by way of sceptre, in his left hand. **1856** RUSKIN *King of Golden River* i. 4 He used to clean..the plates, occasionally getting what was left on them, by way of encouragement. **1868** J. BRUCE *Digby's Voy. Mediterr.* (Camden) Pref. p. x, Dr. Richard Farrar composed some lines upon him by way of epitaph. **1868** LOUISA M. ALCOTT *Little Women* vi, 'You'll have to go and thank him,' said Jo, by way of a joke. **1892** *Bookseller* 17/1 The summary [of the Act] given by way of introduction is concise and clear.

†**e.** ***by way of excellency*** (or ***eminence***): = 'par excellence.' *Obs.*

1621–31 [see EMINENCE 8 c]. **1643** [see EMINENCY 8]. **1694** LOCKE *Advers. Theol.* in King *Life* (1858) 343 There is one Spirit manifestly distinguished from God, i.e. one created Spirit by way of excellency; i.e. the Holy Spirit. **1699** tr. *Dupin's Hist. Canon O. & N. Test.* I. 2 They are likewise styl'd the Scriptures by Way of Eminence. **1703** [see EMINENCY 8]. *a* **1704** [see EXCELLENCE 1 b]. **1711** SHAFTESB. *Charac.* Misc. v. ii. III. 278 Have you writ..a Play, a Song, an Essay, or a Paper, as by way of Eminence, the current Pieces of our Weekly Wits are generally stil'd.

f. Followed by gerund, forming predicative phrases with the sense: In the habit of (doing something); also, more usually, making a profession of, or having a reputation for (being or doing so-and-so). *colloq.*

1824 MISS FERRIER *Inher.* xxxii, The Colonel was by way of introducing him into the fashionable circles. **1852** C. B. MANSFIELD *Paraguay*, etc. (1856) 182 A wiseacre passenger, who is by way of knowing the river well, says they are called *capinchos* in these parts. **1862** H. KINGSLEY *Ravenshoe* xlvii, Mary was 'by way of' helping Lady Hainault's maid, but she was very clumsy about it. **1877** LADY M. A. BROOME *Yr.'s Housekeeping S. Africa* iv. 61 'Charlie,' our groom, who is by way of being a very fine gentleman,..only condescends to work until he can purchase a wife. **1881** MALLOCK *Rom. 19th Cent.* III. v. II. 34, I am by way, here, of doing the same thing. **1891** *Sat. Rev.* 18 July 77/1 Mr. Brander Matthews finds fault with the phrase 'by way of being', and says an American can hardly understand it... 'By way of being' is endeavouring or purporting to be, holding oneself out in a certain character, or being so reputed; and this with an implied disclaimer of precise knowledge or warranty on the speaker's part. **1897** DU MAURIER *Martian* v. 236 The Gibsons were by way of spoiling me. *Ibid.* IX. 379 Nor did he..come across them at any house he was by way of frequenting. **1906** *Lit. World* 15 Nov. 515/1 The character of this woman, who is by way of being the female villain of the story, is drawn with skill.

g. By the route which passes through or over (a specified place): = VIA *prep.* Also † ***by the way of***.

Formerly with omission of *of*, the place-name being prefixed to *way*. Cf. sense 9.

11.. *O.E. Chron.* (MS. F.) an. 888, Heo forðferde be Rome weȝe [L. *in itinere Rome*]. **1460** *Paston Lett.* I. 515 He schall send his man hom be Newmarket wey. **1701** W. WOTTON *Hist. Rome* 481 He went by the way of Illyricum. **1771** SMOLLETT *Humph. Cl.* To Sir W. Phillips 21 Sept., We set out from Glasgow by the way of Lanark. **1865** *Cornh. Mag.* XI. 595 It invaded France by way of Avignon. **1901** ALLDRIDGE *Sherbro* xxvi. 291 From Bafodia we were diverging from the main road to Freetown which is by way of the Bumban hills.

†**h.** Through the medium of (a person). *Obs.*

1560 SIR N. THROGMORTON in Wright *Q. Eliz.* (1838) I. 49 The 29th of October last, I wrote to you from Paris by the waye of Monsieur de Chantonet.

†**33. from the way**: Out of the way, in a secluded place. *Obs.*

1593 SHAKS. *Lucr.* 1144 Some darke deepe desert seated from the way,..Will wee find out.

34. in the (etc.) **way.** (See also senses 16 a, 17–19.)

†**a.** As one proceeds or goes along; in the course of one's journey (*to* a place). Also ***in one's way***; in early use, ***in way***. Cf. *to take in one's way* (sense 7). *Obs.*

to do (a person, etc.) ***in the way***: to send out (*refl.* to set forth) on a journey or expedition.

1297 R. GLOUC. 3765 He..greiþede is noble ost & dude him in þe weye. *a* **1300** *K. Horn* 1007 Horn dude him in þe weie On a god Galeie. **13..** *K. Alis.* 3392 (Laud MS.), Þine Olifauntz & þine beest Do alle ordeyne on hast And do hem done in þe waye þat hij weren in feld contreye. **13..** *Guy Warw.* 259 At Felice he tok his leue þo, and in his way he goþ apliȝt. **1377** LANGL. *P. Pl.* B. XVII. 47 As we wenten þus in þe weye wordyng togyderes. **1382** WYCLIF *Gen.* xlv. 24 Ne wraththe ȝe in the weye. *c* **1450** *Mirk's Festial* 9 He stervet yn þe way. **1629** HOBBES *Thucyd.* II. 127 But they of Stratus, aware of this, whilest they were yet in their way..placed diuers Ambushes not farre from the Citie. *c* **1643** LD. HERBERT *Autobiog.* (1886) 140 Going from St. Julian's to Abergavenny, in the way to Montgomery Castle. **1712** BUDGELL *Spect.* No. 277 ⁋11 If you please to call at my House in your Way to the City. **1748** RICHARDSON *Clarissa* (1811) VII. 143 In the afternoon [she] was at Islington church, in her way home. **1791** SMEATON *Edystone L.* §264 The master of the floating light saw the buoy in his way to Plymouth. **1822** [MARY A. KELTY] *Osmond* I. 186 A heavy foreboding made her linger in her way to her own apartment.

b. In Biblical use, ***to be*** or ***walk in the way with*** (†***mid***) = to accompany a person on a journey; *fig.* to associate with.

c **950** *Lindisf. Gosp.* Matt. v. 25 Uæs ðu ȝeðafsum wiðer-bracæ ðinum hraðe miððy bist in uoeȝ mið him [Vulg. *dum es in via cum eo*]. **1611** BIBLE *Prov.* i. 15 My sonne, walke not thou in the way with them.

c. (Chiefly ***in one's way***.) On or along the road by which one travels; so as to be met, encountered, or observed.

c **1205** LAY. 26770 Wo wæs heom iboren þa iþan weie heom weoren biuoren. *Ibid.* 26793 In his wæiȝe þat he funde al he hit aqualde. *a* **1591** H. SMITH *Caveat Chr.* Serm. (1601) 498 Sinne is not long in comming: nor quickly gone, vnlesse God stop vs, as hee met Balaam in his way. **1592** SHAKS. *Ven. & Ad.* 879 Like one that spies an adder, Wreath'd vp in fatall folds iust in his way. **1610** —— *Temp.* II. ii. 11 Like Hedg-hogs, which Lye tumbling in my bare-foote way. **1721** E. WARD *Merry Trav.* I. (1729) 35 Resolving to..moisten well our dusty Clay, At the next Alehouse in our Way. **1726** SWIFT *Gulliver* IV. i, I had not got far when I met one of these Creatures full in my way, and coming up directly to me. **1840** DICKENS *Old C. Shop* xlii, She had gained a little wooden bridge, which..led into a meadow in her way.

d. *fig.* in phrases like ***to come, fall, lie in*** (one's) ***way***, to be met with in one's experience, to come within (one's) range of possible observation, utilization, or attainment. Similarly *to lay, put, throw in* (a person's) *way*. Also predicatively, in phrases like *it will be* (a certain sum of money, etc.) *in my way* = I shall gain (so much) in the specified contingency.

1596 SPENSER *State Irel.* (Globe) 631/2 Under it [*sc.* his mantle] he can cleanly convay any fitt pillage that cometh handsomely in his way. **1596** SHAKS. *1 Hen. IV*, v. i. 28 Rebellion lay in his way, and he found it. **1605** [see FALL *v.* 34]. **1617** J. CHAMBERLAIN in *Crt. & Times Jas. I* (1848) II. 43 It [*sc.* his having a son] may be a hundred thousand pounds in his way, if his father keep his word. *a* **1662** DUPPA *Rules & Helps Devot.* I. (1675) 72 The Imagination..casting thoughts in our way, and forcing the Understanding to reflect upon them. **1677** TEMPLE *Moxa* Miscell. (1680) 193 The General Officers of Armies,..the publick Ministers..(that have fallen in my way) being generally subject to it [*sc.* the Gout] in one degree or other. **1691** T. H[ALE] *Acc. New Invent.* p. xii, It comes in my way here to retaliate to him. **1722** WOLLASTON *Relig. Nat.* v. 107 When one man alters the opinion of another by throwing a book, proper for that purpose, in his way. **1743** BULKELEY & CUMMINS *Voy. S. Seas* 154 We have now nothing to live on but Seal, and what Providence throws in our Way. **1744** M. BISHOP *Life* 46 Though it might have been Thousands in my Way had I continued my Business. **1763** COWPER in Southey *Life & Wks.* (1835) I. 163 My friends must excuse me, if I write to none but those who lay it fairly in my way to do so. **1789** WOLCOT (P. Pindar) *Subj. Painters* i. (*note*), Which will be a benefit ticket in Sir William's way. **1797** JANE AUSTEN *Pride & Prej.* xliii, It might seem as if she had purposely thrown herself in his way again. **1828** SCOTT *Tales Grandf.* Ser. I. xxiv, A warrant empowering them to take all Portuguese vessels which should come in their way. **1841** S. WARREN *Ten Thou.* II. vii. 189 They say he has a cousin who is one of the officers to the Sheriff of Middlesex, and puts a good many little things in his way! **1882** BESANT *All Sorts* xxxi, These things he knew nothing of; they had not come in his way. **1888** MCCARTHY & PRAED *Ladies' Gall.* II. ii. 19 Every actor whom it had come in my way to know..was a poor devil.

e. In such a position, or of such a nature, as to obstruct, impede, or be an annoyance. Chiefly in phr. *to be* or *stand in* (one's) *way*, or *in the way of* (a person or thing); also *to put, throw in* (one's) *way*.

1500–20 DUNBAR *Poems* xii. 14 Welth, warldly gloir, and riche array Ar all bot thornis laid in thy way. **1564** *Brief Exam.* B iij, Ye must..take heede, lest ye stande in your owne way. *a* **1700** EVELYN *Diary* 27 Aug. 1667, He thwarted some of them and stood in their way. *a* **1750** LD. DARTMOUTH in Burnet *Own Time* (1900) II. 251 *note*, King Charles gave him [Godolphin] a short character when he was page,..of being never *in* the way, nor *out* of the way. **1773** FOOTE *Bankrupt* I. Wks. 1799 II. 99 To throw some confounded rub in the way. **1787** 'G. GAMBADO' *Acad. Horsem.* 41 Thus, then, you go off with eclat, provided nothing is in your horse's way; and if there is,..he will probably leap over it. **1796** MME. D'ARBLAY *Camilla* II. iii. I. 183 [His] egotism..sacrificed his best friends and first duties, if they stood in its way. **1836** DICKENS *Sk. Boz, Sentiment*, The smaller girls managed to be in everybody's way, and were pushed about accordingly. **1866** LE FANU *All in Dark* xxxv, He would have been in the way—unutterably *de trop*. **1867** TROLLOPE *Last Chron. Barset* II. lix. 159 She considers herself to have a claim upon [him]..and that I stand in her way. **1868** FREEMAN *Norm. Conq.* II. vii. 132 At such a moment as this, when one would have thought that horses were distinctly in the way. **1885** *Manch. Exam.* 11 June 4/7 The Liberal party will be bound in honour to throw no factious obstacles in their way. **1887** BARING-GOULD *Gaverocks* II. xxiii. 17 His pride stood in the way of success.

f. Within reach or call, at hand, get-at-able; in a place where things are going on or where one can be found readily. ? Now *rare* or *Obs.*

1598 R. BERNARD *Terence, Eun.* v. ix. (1607) 188 Whether you be in the way, or out of the way [*te praesente absente*]. **1687** MIÈGE *Gt. Fr. Dict.* II. s.v., To be in the way, or in a readiness, *se tenir prêt, ne pas s' écarter*. **1729** SWIFT *Direct. Serv.* Gen. ¶1 When your Master or Lady call a Servant by Name, if that Servant be not in the Way, none of you are to answer. *c* **1760** CHALLONER in E. Burton *Life* (1909) II. xxiv. 28 We will spend our evenings..at our own lodgings, so that we may..be in the way for such as shall come for Instructions. **1814** JANE AUSTEN *Mansf. Park* xviii, I came here to-day intending to rehearse it with Edmund..but he is not in the way. **1840** DICKENS *Old C. Shop* viii, In order that..he might take care to be in the way at the time. **1859** H. KINGSLEY *G. Hamlyn* xxxix, I'm glad, too, to see you here. One feels safer when you're in the way. **1897** R. N. BAIN tr. *Jókai's Pretty Michal* xxx. 229 He himself, however, had not been in the way when beauty was being served out.

g. In the humour or mood (for what is going on). *Obs.* exc. *dial.*

1703 *Rules of Civility* 114 A sort of People never in the way, never pleas'd with any thing. **1856** J. BALLANTINE *Poems* 108 He is aye in the way for a crack.

†**h.** (*to be*) *in one's way*: in the right course of action, within one's rights. *Obs.*

1689 *Andros Tracts* I. 111 Answer was made by the Deponent, that if we [the Watch] should kill them [suspicious persons resisting arrest], we were in our way, then Mr. Randolph..said, you are in the way to be hanged.

i. *once in a way*: on a single (exceptional) occasion; as a solitary or rare instance; rarely, exceptionally; quasi-*adj.*, of rare occurrence, exceptional. Also *for once in a way*.

This phrase would seem to be a corruption of the earlier *once and away*, which may have meant originally 'once and then go away', 'once and no more', though all the instances quoted under ONCE *adv.* 8 c admit of being interpreted in the sense above explained. Cf. *once in a while* (see ONCE 8 c).

1842 NEWMAN *Ch. Fathers* 302, I must beg indulgence once in a way, to engage myself in a dry and somewhat tedious discussion. **1853** [see ONCE B. 9 b]. **1858** TROLLOPE *Dr. Thorne* xix, Now I like this kind of thing once in a way. **1860** READE *Cloister & H.* liii, They agreed to take a holiday for once in a way. **1913** *Sat. Rev.* 21 June 762/2 The case of Ulster..really offers him this luxury for once in a way.

35. in the way of ——. (Or equivalent construction.) (See also sense 17.)

†**a.** As a mode, instance, or manifestation of; as tantamount to or supplying the place of. Also *in way of*. Cf. *by way of* (32 d). *Obs.*

c **1450** *Godstow Reg.* 97 The Abbesse and the Couente..graunted..that, in the wey of charite, that they wold fynde for ever a prest conuenient þat shold do a prestis service every day, namely for the sowles of the forsaid peple. *a* **1513** FABYAN *Chron.* cxxvii. (1533) 62 Dagobert..bete his mayster, & after in way of dyspyte caused the berd of his tutour to be shauen of. **1534** *Star Chamber Cases* (Selden Soc.) II. 310 Onlesse your said highenes be good and gracious lord vnto hym in weye of right and justice. **1565** COOPER *Thesaurus* s.v. *Abijcio, Abiicere se alteri ad pedes*..to prostrate him self at ones feete in way of intreatie. **1568** GRAFTON *Chron.* II. 23 King William should geue him yerely in the way of a fee .xij. Markes of Golde. **1606** SHAKS. *Tr. & Cr.* III. iii. 13, I doe beseech you, as in way of taste To giue me now a little benefit. **1621** J. CHAMBERLAIN in *Crt. & Times Jas. I* (1848) II. 273 He concluded with a wish..for the felicity..of that..happy couple; and, in a way of amen, caused the Bishop of London..to give them a benediction. **1633** BP. HALL *Hard Texts* Amos ii. 1 Moab..burnt the very bones of the King of Edoms sonne to ashes, in way of sacrifice to his gods. *c* **1643** LD. HERBERT *Autob.* (1886) 176 Which I then bestowed upon some servants of the Prince, in way of retribution for my welcome thither. **1817** JAS. MILL *Brit. India* II. v. i. 327 In way of compensation, he was allowed a pension.

b. By means of, by adopting the method of. Now *rare*. Also †*in way of*.

The first quot. may perhaps belong to sense 17.

1607 SHAKS. *Cor.* III. ii. 137 Ile returne Consull, Or neuer trust to what my Tongue can do I' th way of Flattery further. **1771** SMOLLETT *Humph. Cl.* To Sir W. Phillips 18 July, He attempted to open her eyes in the way of exhortation, and, finding it produced no effect, had recourse to prayer. **1823** SCOTT *Quentin D.* xxx, That in the way of treaty more permanent advantages could be obtained..than by an action which would stain her with a breach of faith and hospitality. **1849** MACAULAY *Hist. Eng.* I. ii. 220 The attack was made, not in the way of storm, but by slow and scientific approaches.

†**c.** With a view to; as a means of attaining or performing; so as to effect or produce. Also *in way of, in a way of*. *Obs.*

1588 SHAKS. *L.L.L.* IV. ii. 14 A kinde of insinuation, as it were *in via*, in way of explication. *c* **1643** LD. HERBERT *Autobiog.* (1886) 138 He commanded me..not to send any more to Sir John Ayres, nor to receive any message from him, in the way of fighting. **1655** FULLER *Ch. Hist.* IX. 190 And yet in way of recovering health by changing of Aire, of study for a time in the University,..or of being imployed in publick Affairs, they [licences to clergy for non-residence] cannot be wholy abrogated. **1662** H. MORE *Antid. Atheism* Ep. Ded., Which was done in way of Divine Honour to the Wisdom of the Deity. —— *Philos. Writ.* (1712) Pref. Gen. p. xxi, The ancient Divines and Prophets..witness that the Soul is join'd to this earthly body in a way of punishment. **1760–72** H. BROOKE *Fool of Qual.* (1809) III. 17 Coming closer.., in the way, as it were, of claiming acquaintance with him.

d. In the course or routine of.

1639 S. DU VERGER tr. *Camus' Admir. Events* 58 Providing that it were done in the way of publicke justice. **1693** CONGREVE *Old Bach.* IV. iii, In the way of Trade, we still suspect the smoothest Dealers of the deepest designs. **1765** FOOTE *Commissary* I. 3 Not at all given to lying, but like other tradesfolks, in the way of her business. **1863** KINGSLEY *Water-Bab.* i. 6 Remembering that he had come in the way of business, and was, as it were, under a flag of truce.

†**e.** When one is concerned with. *Obs.*

1596 SHAKS. *1 Hen. IV*, III. i. 139 But in the way of Bargaine,..Ile cauill on the ninth part of a hayre. **1606** —— *Tr. & Cr.* II. ii. 189 Hect... Hectors opinion Is this in way of truth: yet nere the lesse [etc.].

†**f.** *in the way of honesty*: under honourable conditions; so far as honour allows. *Obs.*

1595 SHAKS. *John* I. i. 181 For thou wast got i' th way of honesty. **1598** —— *Merry W.* II. ii. 75, I defie all Angels..but in the way of honesty. **1606** —— *Ant. & Cl.* v. ii. 253. **1639** J. CLARKE *Parœm.* 25 Yours to command in the way of honesty.

g. *to be in the way of*: to be likely to do or obtain (something), to have a good chance of (doing or attaining something); formerly also †*in way of*, †*in a way of*. *to put* (a person) *in the* or *a way of*, †*in way for*: to put him in a position to obtain or achieve (something). Also with *to* and inf. instead of *of*.

See also FAIR *a.* 14.

1303 R. BRUNNE *Handl. Synne* 1212 For ȝyf þou mayst, & wylt noght, þou art yn weye to peyne be broght. **1477** EARL RIVERS (Caxton) *Dictes* 32 The whiche ypocras seeyng the crafte of physike in weye of perdicion because alle his felawes were dede. **1542** *Lament. & Piteous Treat.* Ep. Ded., I purpose, as sone as my dysease is paste, to put me in waye with all dylygence to se you ryght soone. **1625** BACON *Ess., Friendship* (Arb.) 179 A Physician, that..is vnacquainted with your body.., may put you in way for a present Cure, but ouerthroweth your Health in some other kinde. **1677** in *12th Rep. Hist. MSS. Comm.* App. v. 36 Lord Mohun is now in a way of recovery. **1689** [see 34 h]. **1719** DE FOE *Crusoe* II. (Globe) 410 Being very ingenious at such Work, when they were once put in the Way of it. *Ibid.* 423 Seeing Things..in so fine a way of thriving upon my Island. **1729** LAW *Serious C.* viii. 112 She has educated several poor children,..and put them in a way of an honest employment. **1779** WARNER in Jesse *Selwyn & Contemp.* (1844) IV. 259 You cannot expect a Dyer's letter from me, as your nephew Charles is so much more in the way of having authentic information. **1823** SCOTT *Quentin D.* iv, Why did you not tarry at Brussels, then, with the Duke of Burgundy? He would put you in the way to have your bones broken every day. **1827** —— *Surg. Dau.* Pref., Mr. Croftangry is in the way of doing a foolish thing. **1844** BROUGHAM *A. Lunel* xii, I soon was put in a way of earning a moderate weekly payment as a translator from the English and Italian. **1847** MRS. CARLYLE *Lett.* II. 4 Now I am in the way of getting well again. **1860** DICKENS *Uncomm. Trav.* vi, Even then they might sometimes put themselves in the way of being blown into the Regent's Canal. **1883** D. C. MURRAY *Hearts* xiv, I am getting on a little in the world, and am in the way to earn a little money. **1885** *L'pool Daily Post* 7 July 4/4 Diplomatic difficulties, which he hoped were in the way of solution.

†**h.** *to be in way of marriage*: to have a prospect of being married. Also, *in* (*the*) *way of marriage, in way to marriage*, with a view to matrimony. *Obs.*

1482 *Cely Papers* (Camden) 102 He askyd me hefe I wher in any whay of maryayge. **1579** Q. ELIZ. in Nicolas *Sir C. Hatton* (1847) 106 Such Princes as in former time have sought us in way of marriage. **1583** RICH *Phylotus* (1835) 11 But Phylotus in the ende desired Emelia of her father in the waie of Mariage. **1596** SHAKS. *Merch. V.* II. i. 42 Neuer to speake to Ladie afterward In way of marriage. **1598** —— *Merry W.* I. iv. 89 To speake a good word to Mistris Anne Page for my Master in the way of Marriage. **1642** FULLER *Holy & Prof. St.* IV. xiii. 301 As if their sex in reference to men were not capable of any other kind of familiar friendship but in way to marriage.

†**i.** *in a way of*: in the habit of (doing something). *Obs.*

c **1704** *Buccleuch MSS.* (Hist. MSS. Comm.) I. 353 The House of Lords are in a way of having hours very uncertain.

j. *in way of* (*Naut.*): = *in wake of* s.v. WAKE *sb.*[2] 4 b (*a*).

1950 L. BAKER *Design Marine Water-Tube Boilers* ix. 144 *Arboring*, a term applied to the removal of tube plate material in way of tube ends to reduce the unsupported length of tube inside the drum. **1957** *Shipping World* 21 Aug. 153/2 Longitudinal centre-line bulkheads are provided in all the main and tweendeck holds,..and in way of the hatch openings there are steel supports for removable wooden longitudinal bulkheads. **1960** *Fishing Gaz.* (N.Y.) 15 Mar. 18/1 The propeller shaft has 5/8" thick centrifugally cast liners or wearing sleeves shrunk on in way of the stern bearing and stuffing box.

36. a. on (or **upon**) **the,** or **one's, way,** on, or in the course of, a journey. *to be well on one's way*: to have fairly started, or to have made some progress. Also *fig.*, in progress towards completion or accomplishment.

In OE. *on weȝe*: see also AWAY *adv.*

c **1000** *Ags. Gosp.* Matt. v. 25 Beo þu onbuȝende þinum wiðerwinnan hraðe þa hwile þe ðu eart on weȝe mid him. —— Mark ix. 34 Witodlice hi on weȝe [Vulg. *in via*] smeadon hwylc hyra yldost wære. *a* **1122** *O.E. Chron.* (Laud MS.) an. 1086, þæt þa godan men..gan on ðone weȝ þe us lett to heofonan rice. *c* **1205** LAY. 1348 Brutus..ferde riht on his wei. *c* **1300** *Cursor M.* 8054 Fand þai noþer fra þat sith Man ne beist þat þai wit met, þat on þair wai þam moght do lett. *c* **1400** *Ywaine & Gaw.* 549 He thoght to be wele on hys way Or it war passed the thryd day. *c* **1420** *Anturs of Arth.* 315, I mot walke one my wey, þorgh þis wilde wood. **1470–85** MALORY *Arthur* I. i. 36 Ryde on your wey, for I wille not be long behynde. **1523** SURREY in Ellis *Orig. Lett.* Ser. I. I. 227 Trusting that the gonners be well on the waye hiderwards. **1526** TINDALE *Acts* viii. 39 He went on his waye reioysynge. **1596** DANETT tr. *Comines* (1614) 41 He sent a trumpeter to them, who met with the hostages vpon the way. **1597** SHAKS. *2 Hen. IV*, II. i. 73 You should haue bene well on your way to Yorke. **1653** HOLCROFT *Procopius* I. x. 16 Overtaking him upon the way. **1697** DRYDEN *Virg. Georg.* IV. 576, I will my self conduct thee on thy Way. **1812** BYRON *Ch. Har.* I. xiv, And Cintra's mountain greets them on their way. **1840** DICKENS *Old C. Shop* lxx, Day broke, and found them still upon their way. *Ibid.* lxxii, The boy had led him to his own dwelling..on their way back. **1860** TYNDALL *Glac.* I. iii. 23 On the following morning I was on my way towards this valley. **1861** MILL *Utilit.* ii. 35 To inform a traveller respecting the place of his ultimate destination, is not to forbid the use of land-marks and direction-posts on the way. **1885** *Law Rep.* 15 *Q.B.D.* 329 The debtor was on his way to the office of the official receiver.

on the way (this form only): *spec.* (*colloq.*) (*a*) pregnant; (*b*) (of a child) conceived but not yet born.

(*a*) **1588** SHAKS. *L.L.L.* v. ii. 679 She is two moneths on her way [*sc.* with child]. **1865** A. MACDONALD *Let.* Apr. in A. W. Baldwin *Macdonald Sisters* (1960) vi. 100 Poor Mrs Hughes..is 'on the way again, blest if she ain't'. **1941** E. WELTY *Curtain of Green* (1943) 39, I bet you another Jax that lady's three months on the way.

(*b*) [**1858**: cf. sense 38 b.] **1896** KIPLING *Day's Work* (1898) 271 I'm a married man, an' my fourth's on the ways [*sic*] now, she says. **1919** V. WOOLF *Night & Day* ix. 121 He has two children, and another on the way. **1961** G. GREENE *Burnt-Out Case* VI. i. 183, I think I have a baby on the way... He doesn't want one. **1983** R. RENDELL *Speaker of Mandarin* v. 69 We've..four simply adorable grandchildren with another on the way.

b. imp. (*be*) *on your way*: go away, get going; also (*U.S.*), 'get away' (GET *v.* 61 b). *colloq.* (orig. *U.S.*).

1903 'O. HENRY' *Trimmed Lamp* (1907) 236 Be on your way, Freddie. **1929** WODEHOUSE *Gentleman of Leisure* xi. 86 'We're going down with him to the country today, Spike, so be ready.' 'On your way, boss. What's dat?' **1974** 'P. B. YUILL' *Bornless Keeper* xii. 113 Toddle off back to Victoria. .. On your way, amigo.

c. (*I am*) *on my way*: a formula used to express the speaker's intention of hurrying or of making an immediate departure.

1919 in N. I. White *Amer. Negro Folk-Songs* ii. 124 Lord I'm on my way... Lord I'm on my way. **1948** G. VIDAL *City & Pillar* ii. 35 'I'm on my way,' said Jim. **1971** 'L. EGAN' *Malicious Mischief* (1972) ix. 158 'Call just in..—they had a prowler over on Jackson... He was armed.'.. 'I'm on my way!' snapped Varallo. **1972** J. PHILIPS *Vanishing Senator* I. iv. 37 'Step on it, will you?' 'On my way,' Peter said. **1978** A. PRICE *'44 Vintage* xii. 152 If it's all the same to you, m'sieur, we'll be on our way.

37. out of the way. (See also OUT-OF-THE-WAY *adj. phr.*)

a. Away from the road by which one is travelling; off the track or proper route. Also in *fig.* context.

1483 *Cath. Angl.* 405/2 Oute of Way, *devius, delirus.* **1565** COOPER *Thesaurus* s.v. *Deflecto, Ex itinere ad visendum aliquem deflectere*, to turne out of the way to see one. **1610** SHAKS. *Temp.* II. ii. 7 Nor lead me like a fire-brand, in the darke Out of my way. **1653** W. RAMESEY *Astrol. Restored* 161 Let us then..step a little out of our way, and say somewhat of the Critical days. *a* **1704** LOCKE *Cond. Und.* §34 They are more in danger to go out of the way, who are marching under the Conduct of a Guide, that 'tis an hundred to one will mislead them, than he that has not yet taken a Step, and is likelier to be prevail'd on to enquire after the right Way. **1719** DE FOE *Crusoe* II. (Globe) 323 It being a Month's Sail out of his Way. **1890** BICKLEY *Surrey Hills* III. 214 It was a good mile out of his way, but he felt he must see it again. **1913** J. G. FRAZER *Psyche's Task* iv. (ed. 2) 80 If the two meet on a path they carefully avoid each other; he will step out of the way and she will hurry on.

b. *fig.*, with the notion of going astray or being off the right path. †(*to be*) ***out of the way***: in error, mistaken; also, ? missing the point (*obs.*).

a **1225** *Juliana* 42 (Royal MS.) Hwen he sent us to wrenchen eni rihtwise ut of þe weie. **1487** *Cely Papers* (Camden) 159 He sayth yee schall be to far owte of the weye w[t] owte yee gree & bergeyne togeder. **1530** PALSGR. 715/1 He hath set me out of the waye with his teachynge: *par son enseignement il ma desuoyé.* **1561** T. HOBY tr. *Castiglione's Courtyer* IV. (1577) Xiij, Perhappes M. Morrello is not altogither out of the waye in saying that beauty is not alwayes good. **1603** HOLLAND *Plutarch's Mor.* 3 Know he, that he is much deceived, and to say more truely, quite out of the way. **1608** TOPSELL *Serpents* 102 They are cleane out of the way, who when they wold vse them for any inward cause, doe cast away their winges and feete. **1694** ATTERBURY *Serm.* (1726) I. v. 181 Thus it is in all Matters of Speculation or Practice; He that knows but a little of them ..is more out of the way of true Knowledge than if he knew nothing at all. **1728** GAY *Begg. Op.* I. v, Never was a man more out of the way in an argument than my husband. **1742** RICHARDSON *Pamela* III. 173 Our Governors cannot always be in the wrong; and he therefore who never gives them a Vote, must probably be as often out of the Way as they.

c. With *of* or possessive: Away from the path in which a person or thing is moving; in a position where one does not meet or impede another; at a distance from, clear of, a person's or thing's activities; out of reach of, not in danger from.

For *out of harm's way* see HARM *sb.* 1 c.

1550 CROWLEY *Epigr.* 832 If Abner had knowne what was in Ioabs harte, I do not doubt but he would haue out of his waye sterte. **1650** JER. TAYLOR *Holy Living* ii. §5 Men stand upon their guard against them [*sc.* inquisitions], as they secure their meat against harpies and cats, laying all their counsels and secrets out of their way. *a* **1701** MAUNDRELL *Journ. Jerus.* (1707) 56 The embroylments and factions that were then amongst the Arabs..made us desirous to keep as far as possible out of their way. **1744** M. BISHOP *Life* 28 They sent us a great many Bombs,..there came one swift as Lightning. I had much ado to get out of it's Way. **1858** TROLLOPE *Dr. Thorne* xvi, The fellow kept out of my way, and I couldn't see him. **1886** RUSKIN *Præterita* I. xii. 423 Always glad to have me out of her way.

d. (*to be*) ***out of*** (a person's) ***way***: not in his line, not in accordance with his present purpose or taste, outside his scope, beyond his abilities. (Cf. 18 c.) ? *Obs.*

1562 J. HEYWOOD *Prov. & Epigr.* (1867) 167 It is out of my way, so it lyghtly may, To all good thyngis thy way is out of the way. **1687** MIÉGE *Gt. Fr. Dict.* II. s.v., This is a Thing out of my Way, not proper to me, *cela n'est pas mon Affaire.* **1707** FREIND *Peterboro's Cond. Sp.* 165 What other Negotiations his Lordship carried on..is out of my way to relate. **1722-7** BOYER *Dict. Angl.-Fr.* s.v., This is a thing out of my Way (it is not in my Power). **1763** FOOTE *Mayor of G.* II. Wks. 1799 I. 186, I don't much care for your poppers and sharps, because why, they are out of my way. **1780** MRS. COWLEY *Belle's Stratagem* III. i, Now, I beg, Mr. Hardy, you won't interfere in this business; it is a little out of your way. **1841** S. WARREN *Ten Thou.* II. vii. 188 I'd give a trifle to know how..such people ever came to be concerned in such a case. 'Tis quite out of their way—which is in the criminal line of business!

e. ***to go out of one's way to*** (do something): to do something which the circumstances do not call for or invite.

1748 RICHARDSON *Clarissa* III. 321 The culpable freedoms of persons, who, in what they went out of their way to say, must either be guilty of absurdity, meaning *nothing*; or, meaning *something*, of rudeness. **1867** FREEMAN *Norm. Conq.* (1877) I. App. 729 One hardly sees why any one should go out of his way to invent the tale.

f. ***to put*** (a person) ***out of his,*** or ***the, way***: to disturb, inconvenience, trouble; †to disappoint, foil; †to vex, 'put out'. Often *refl.*, to submit to inconvenience or bother for the sake of others; const. *for* (another), *to* (do something).

† ***to be out of the way***: to be out of temper or vexed (*with* a person). *rare.*

1692 LOCKE *Educ.* §11 (1693) 10 They should be afraid to put Nature out of her Way in fashioning the Parts [of the body]. **1741** RICHARDSON *Pamela* I. 57 By what Mr. Jonathan tells me just now, he was quite out of the way with you. **1748** —— *Clarissa* (1768) VII. 183 If, indeed, I am out of the way a little, I always take care to reward the varlets for patiently bearing my displeasure. **1796** *Plain Sense* (ed. 2) III. 173 Though, at present, we are put something out of our way, we hope still to find some sacred spot of earth. **1818** HAZLITT *Table Talk* xxv. (1869) 346 They cannot put themselves out of their way on any account. **1838** DICKENS *O. Twist* xxxi, Anything [to drink] that's handy, miss; don't put yourself out of the way, on our accounts. **1858** THACKERAY *Virgin.* ii, Why should Lady Castlewood put herself out of the way to welcome the young stranger?.. Was a great lady called upon to put herself out of the way for such a youth? **1873** MRS. OLIPHANT *Innocent* III. xi. 177 The maids not caring to put themselves out of the way for such guests.

g. Away from the resort or society of other persons; away from the place where one would be looked for or wanted; in a position remote or inconvenient to get at.

c **1350** *Will. Palerne* 1019 Sche trowed trewly..were sche out of þe weye þat william wold fonde for to pleie in þat place þe priue loue game. **1554** SIR J. MASON in Tytler *Edw. VI* II. 452, I had for answer, that I should not be out of the way in the afternoon, for that he intended to signify unto me his pleasure for answer to my request. **1560** DAUS tr. *Sleidane's Comm.* 33 b, Duke Fridericke appointed certein..to conveighe Luther out of the way, in to some secrete place. **1604** SHAKS. *Oth.* III. i. 40 Ile deuise a meane to draw the Moore Out of the way. **1662** J. DAVIES tr. *Olearius' Voy. Ambass.* 84 They seeing..that it was impossible to save the Prince, kept out of the way. **1697** DAMPIER *Voy.* I. 389 This seemed to us then to be a place out of the way, where we might lye snug for a while. **1739** H. BARNES *Pract. Cases C.P.* (1772) 320 'Tis plain he kept out of the Way to prevent being arrested. **1745** POCOCKE *Descr. East* II. II. 71 In order to make people resort to a place which was so much out of the way. *a* **1750** [see 34 e]. **1812** J. H. VAUX *Flash Dict.*, *Out of the way*, a thief who knows that he is sought after by the traps on some information and consequently goes out of town or otherwise conceals himself is said by his palls to be out of the way for so and so. **1843** DICKENS *Martin Chuz.* xxxviii, He had speculated too much and was keeping out of the way. **1853** LYTTON *My Novel* I. xii, The Leslies don't mix with the county; and Rood lies very much out of the way. **1873** MISS BRADDON *Str. & Pilgr.* III. x. 332 Fancy his coming area-sneaking here while his Ludship's out of the way!

h. Away from an obstructive position.

1535 COVERDALE *Isa.* lvii. 14 Take vp what ye can out of the waye, that ledeth to my people [**1611** take vp the stumbling blocke out of the way of my people]. **1919** K. PEARSON in C. Goring *Eng. Convict* Introd. 12 [Goring] clears out of the way for ever the tangled and luxuriant growths of the Lombrosian School.

i. ***to put*** (†***bring,*** †***take,*** †***rid,*** etc.) ***out of the way***: to make away with, kill. Also, † ***to hang,*** † ***shoot out of the way.*** (*to be*) ***out of the way***: no longer alive.

c **1535** SIR F. BYGOD *Treat. conc. Impropriations* Cj, As moche as lyeth in you, both god and all preachynge, and all other holy thynges ben clene extyncte..and specyally this holy ordynaunce [*sc.* preaching] put out of the waye. *a* **1548** HALL *Chron., Edw. V* 17 b, When..these other lordes & knightes were thus beheaded and ryd out of the waye. *Ibid., Hen. VIII* 93 He doubted lest he might be brought out of the waie, as other dukes of Albany before had serued the heires of Scotlande. **1560** DAUS tr. *Sleidane's Comm.* 138 b, Of Luther and the rest, there is no hope unlesse they be dispatched out of the way [*nisi opprimantur*]. **1563-83** FOXE *A. & M.* 2097/1 The said wicked Gardiner..bent all hys deuises, to bring this our happy and deare soueraigne out of the way. **1607** TOPSELL *Four-f. Beasts* 187 If this do not cure him [the dog] within seuen daies, then let him be knocked on the head, or hanged out of the way. **1632** MASSINGER *Maid of Hon.* III. iii, I am halfe Hang'd out of the way already. **1679** *Trials of Green*, etc. *for Murder of Sir E. Godfrey* 30 He told me there was a Gentleman that was to be put out of the Way; that was the Phrase he used, he did not really say *Murther* him. **1757** in *10th Rep. Hist. MSS. Comm.* App. I. 313 Old Admiral Holbourn, who curst and swore..because Byng was not Shot out of the Way. **1867** FROUDE *Short Stud.* (ed. 2) 114 The Earl of Moray..was put out of the Way by an assassin. **1879** M. J. GUEST *Lect. Hist. Eng.* xxxviii. 388 Though he [Richard] had a wife already, he determined to put her out of the way, and marry his own niece Elizabeth sooner than let Henry Tudor win her. **1881** JOWETT *Thucyd.* I. 123 The living have their rivals and detractors, but when a man is out of the way, the honour and good-will which he receives is unalloyed.

†**j.** ***to be out of the way***: (of a thing) to be lost or missing. *Obs.*

1604 SHAKS. *Oth.* III. iv. 80 Is 't lost? Is 't gon? Speak, is 't out o' th' way? **1687** MIÉGE *Gt. Fr. Dict.* II. s.v., To be out of the Way or out of its proper Place, *être dispersé, égaré.*

†**k.** ***it is out of*** (my, his, etc.) ***way***: it amounts to or entails a loss of (a specified sum). *Obs.*

1616 J. CHAMBERLAIN in *Crt. & Times Jas. I* (1848) I. 405 He did the lady a great piece of service to get her out of the Tower, where, if she had been at this time, it might chance been out of her way fifty or three score thousand pounds, at least. **1633** SHIRLEY *Gamester* III. (1637) F 3, A curse upon these reeling Dice, that last in and in Was out of my way ten peeces. *c* **1645** HOWELL *Lett.* (1650) I. III. xxix. 84 It is like to be out of my way 3000 l. **1687** MIÉGE *Gt. Fr. Dict.* II. s.v., 'Tis much out of my Way, or to my Loss, *cela m'a fait grand tort, ou j'y ai beaucoup perdu.* *c* **1750** J. NELSON *Jrnl.* (1836) 23 Though it may be ten pounds out of my way to be turned out of my work at this time of the year.

†**l.** Beside the mark, amiss; oddly, extraordinarily.

c **1374** CHAUCER *Anel. & Arc.* 318 (Harl. 7333) Have I ought saide oughte of þe waye [*Fairf.* seyd oght amys I prey]. **1577** *F. de L'isle's Legendarie* I. vij b, Of him therefore did not a gentleman of Caux speake much out of the waye, when [etc.]. **1782** MISS BURNEY *Cecilia* v. xii, It's surprizeable to me, Mr. Hobson, you can behave so out of the way!

m. Predicatively (with the substantive vb. expressed or understood) as adj.: Beside the mark, out of place, inappropriate; odd, bizarre; †not in vogue, unfashionable; †erroneous, incorrect; extraordinary, unusual, remarkable. Cf. OUT-OF-THE-WAY.

1568 HACKET tr. *Thevet's New found World* xvi. 25 Also it shal not be out of the way [orig. *hors de propos*], to say that [etc.]. **1604** SHAKS. *Oth.* I. iii. 366 A pox of drowning thy selfe, it is cleane out of the way. **1676** PHILLIPS *Purchasers Pattern* 106 This rule of reckoning..will not be much out of the way, if you reckon the money by the Tables of rebate. **1681** W. ROBERTSON *Phraseol. Gen.* 1299/1, I think it not out of the way, *non alienum puto.* *a* **1699** TEMPLE *Health & Long Life* Wks. 1720 I. 273 Mine [*sc.* my three wishes] were Health, Peace, and fair Weather; which, though out of the way among young Men, yet perhaps might pass well enough among old. **1765** *Museum Rust.* IV. 99 The writers of them fell entirely in [with] my opinions, odd, unaccountable, and out of the way as they may appear to many. **1873** MRS. OLIPHANT *Innocent* III. xx. 331 If anything out of the way turns up, nobody will remember that such a thing ever happened. **1885** HOWELLS *Silas Lapham* xxvi. 476 Did you ever know me to do anything out of the way? **1892** *Nation* (N.Y.) LIV. 232/3 Therefore much that still passes current as opinion about him is pitifully out of the way.

38. a. under way. *Naut.* [ad. Du. *onderweg* (also *-wegen*) on the way, under way, f. *onder* under, in the course of, etc. + *weg* (dat. pl. *wegen*) way.] Of a vessel: Having begun to move through the water; cf. sense 7 i; often spelt *under weigh*: see WEIGH *sb.*[2] Now freq. as one word: see UNDERWAY *adv.*

1743 BULKELEY & CUMMINS *Voy. S. Seas* 98 To prevent which, we do agree, that when Under-way they shall not separate. **1751** PALTOCK *P. Wilkins* viii. (1884) I. 78 We drew up the two boats, and set all hands at work to put the ship under way. **1788** CHARLOTTE SMITH *Emmeline* (1816) IV. 75 It was near ten o'clock before the vessel got under way. **1836** MARRYAT *Midsh. Easy* xxiv, He has proposed to me that he shall go on board, and get the brig under way. **1836** W. IRVING *Astoria* xi, Mr. M'Kay urged the captain to clear the ship and get under way. **1863** A. YOUNG *Naut. Dict.* (ed. 2) 431 *Under way*, this expression, often used instead of under weigh, seems to be a convenient one for denoting that a ship or boat is making progress through the water, whether by sails or other motive power. **1867** SMYTH *Sailor's Word-bk.* 706 *Under way*, a ship beginning to move under her canvas after her anchor is started. Some have written this *under weigh*, but improperly. A ship is under weigh when she has weighed her anchor... As soon as she gathers way she is under way. **1883** *Stubbs' Mercantile Circular* 8 Nov. 982/2 Of the collisions on or near our shores, most were between steam and sailing vessels when under way. **1885** *Law Times' Rep.* LIII. 61/2 Trawlers..are bound to show the same lights as a vessel under way.

b. *transf.* and *fig.*

1822 BYRON *Vis. Judgem.* xci, Ere he could get a word Of all his founder'd verses under way. **1837** CARLYLE *Fr. Rev.* I. v. viii, A courier is, this night, getting under way for Necker. **1858** —— *Fredk. Gt.* x. iii. (1873) III. 240 The little Wife has already brought him one child, a Daughter; and has (as Friedrich notices) another under way. **1856** *Chamb. Jrnl.* 2 Feb. 80/1, I took the honest waiter home with me in my cab, and under-way we had a good laugh at the spy. *a* **1874** L. STEPHEN *Hours in Libr.* Ser. I. 309 They are restlessly anxious to get their stories well under way.

VI. Combinations.

39. Obvious combinations. **a.** simple attrib., as ***way-book***, ***-end***, ***-pane*** (PANE *sb.*[1] 9), ***-signal***; **b.** objective, as ***way-taking***, ***-traveller***, ***-wanderer***; ***way-beguiling***, ***-stopping*** adjs.; **c.** instrumental, as ***way-bewildered***, ***-sore***, ***-spent***, ***-wearied***, ***-weary*** adjs.

1645 QUARLES *Sol. Recant.* IX. 6 Short miles, and *way-beguiling Company. **1796** *Way-bewildered [see THOUGHT[1] 7 c]. **1895** *Westm. Gaz.* 11 Mar. 1/2 A complete *way-book of the journey from Cherbourg to Nice has been printed. **1869** W. BARNES *Early England & Saxon-English* 106 When the railway was taken into the hands of more learned men, we had..the *terminus* instead of the rail-end, or *way-end, or outending. **1886** J. BARROWMAN *Sc. Mining Terms* 72 *Way-end*, the inner extremity of the wooden railways formerly used in mines. **1805** R. W. DICKSON *Pract. Agric.* II. 923 *Way-Pane.—The strip of land left for cartage along the side of the main [*i.e.* principal ditch]. **1883** *Century Mag.* Oct. 807/1 Each palm, orange tree, and vineyard left on the old mission sites was a *way signal to the new people. **1871** PALGRAVE *Lyr. Poems* 125 *Way-sore feet. **1777** POTTER *Æschylus, Choeph.* 355 The *way-spent traveller. **1623** J. TAYLOR (Water P.) *World runs on Wheels* Wks. (1630) II. 238/2 It cleered the Streetes of these *way-stopping Whirligigges! **1471** *Hist. Arrival Edw. IV* (Camden) 27 They thowght..to have gotten into theyr companye, by that *way-takynge, great nombar of men of Lancashire and Chesshere. **1872** HOWELLS *Wedd. Journ.* (1892) 101 Loquacious, acquaintance-making *way-travellers. **1795** SOUTHEY *Soldier's Wife* 1 Weary *way-wanderer, languid and sick at heart. **1796** COLERIDGE *Destiny of Nations* 149 And minister refreshment to the tired Way-wanderer. **1758** J. G. COOPER *Epist. Aristippus* iv. 28 Life's *way-wearied travellers. **1916** BLUNDEN *Harbingers* 60 *Wayweary traveller, with your broad bright eyes. **1926** T. E. LAWRENCE *Seven Pillars* (1935) 5 Love, the way-weary, groped to your body.

40. a. Special comb.: **way-baggage** *U.S.*, the baggage or luggage of a way-passenger; **way-beam**, a beam used in the construction of a form of longitudinal railway sleeper; † **way-beaten** *a.*, exhausted by travel; † **way-beater**, ? one who frequents the highway for felonious purposes; **way-chain**, a brake for the wheel of a vehicle; in quot. *fig.*; † **way-door**, a door opening on the street; **way-fare** *U.S.*, a fare charged for travelling between intermediate stations on a railway; cf. *way-passenger*, *-station*; † **way-fere** [FERE *sb.*[1]], a companion in travel; † **way-flax** (meaning obscure); † **wayfood**, provision for a journey; **way-freight** *N. Amer.*, goods that are picked up or set down at intermediate stopping places on a railway or shipping route; also, a train carrying such freight; **way-gang, -go** *Sc.* = WAYGATE[2]; † **waygoer**, a traveller by road, a wayfarer; † **wayhire** *local*, payment made for the concession of way-leave; † **way-lead** *v. trans.*, to guide, conduct; † **way-leader**, one who conducts a traveller; **way letter** (see quot.; cf. *by-letter*, BY- 4 and *by-way letter*, BY-WAY 3); † **way-mate**, a fellow-traveller; **way passenger** *U.S.*, a passenger picked up or set down at a stage on a coaching route or station on a railway line intermediate between the main stopping-places; **way-place** *U.S.*, a stopping place on a road or railway; a wayside hostelry or an intermediate station; **way-point** orig. *U.S.*, a stopping-place on a journey; also, (on an air journey) the computer-checked coordinates of each stage of a long flight; **way-port**, a port which normally serves as a port of call rather than as an ultimate destination; **way-post** = GUIDE-POST; **way-rate** *north.*, a rate levied by a local authority for the upkeep of the roads; † **way-reeve**, † **-serjeant**, officers appointed to supervise the repair of the roads; † **way-shide**, ? one of the planks used to form gangways; **way-stop**, chiefly *U.S.*, an intermediate stopping place on a journey; also *fig.*; **way-ticket** = WAY-BILL 4; also *attrib.*; **way train** *U.S.*, a train which stops at intermediate stations on a railway; a stopping train; † **way-walking** *a.*, vagrant; † **way-went**, ? a turn of the road; **way-wise** *a. dial.* and *U.S.*, of a horse, familiar with the roads he is required to travel; also *fig.* of a person, experienced, trained; † **way-witere** (*ME.*), one who shows the way, a guide; † **waywoodware**, timber to be used in the construction of roads.

1847 WEBSTER, **Way-baggage*. **1860** in WORCESTER; and in later Dicts. **1883** *Specif. Alnwick & Cornhill Rlwy.* 46 Within the troughs [*sc.* trough-girders] are to be laid ..*way-beams,..packed between the gussets with stemming pieces. **1742** JARVIS *Quixote* II. IV. vii. 311 The *way-beaten couple, master and man, sat them down. *a* **1586** SIDNEY *Arcadia* II. xxii. §9 This we learned chiefly, by the chiefe of those *way-beaters. **1694** MOTTEUX *Rabelais* V. xxvi. 122 A sort of People whom they call'd High-way-men, Way-beaters [Fr. *Batteurs de pavez*], and makers of Inroads in Roads. **1882** LD. SALISBURY in T. Williams *Polit. Wit & Humour* (1889) 67, I will take the Duke of Wellington's simile. He said it [the House of Lords] was a *way-chain, or, as in these days we should say, a vacuum-brake. **1597** BP. HALL *Sat.* III. iv. 7 But hee must needes his Posts with blood embrew, And on his *way-doore fixe the horned head. **1863** DICEY *Federal St.* I. 55 You can go from New York to Chicago..for four pounds; but the *way-fares are three-halfpence a mile. *c* **1450** PECOCK *Donet* (1921) 89 Jesus..oure *weifere, oure techer. *c* **1610** *Cry in Sturbridge Fair* in Gutch *Coll. Cur.* II. 16 Also that no man shall regrate of the aforesaid things, as..*Way-flax,..Rosin, Yarn, Pitch, Tar-Cloth, or other thing of Grocery ware. **1382** WYCLIF *Deut.* xv. 14 But thow shalt ȝyue *weyfode [Vulg. *viaticum*] of the flockis. **1833** *Niles' Reg.* XLIV. 260/2 The hatch..was open to get out a lot of *way-freight. **1875** 'MARK TWAIN' in *Atlantic Monthly* Aug. 191 No way-freights and no way-passengers were allowed, for the racers would stop only at the largest towns. **1898** H. E. HAMBLEN *Gen. Manager's Story* 37 The way freight..had crossed over to load some freight. **1977** *Islander* (Victoria, B.C.) 8 May 2/3 The discharging of cargo and the loading of way-freight. **1744** in Kames *Decis. Crt. Sess. 1730–52* (1799) 81 To cause the water restagnate upon the *way-gang of the pursuer's mill. **1700** SIR A. BALFOUR *Lett.* 130 They use to stop the *way-goe of the Water, sometimes in the Summer, and lett the Place overflow with Water. **1382** WYCLIF *Gen.* xxxvii. 25 And sittynge for to eet breed, thei seen Ysmaelites *weiegoers [Vulg. *viatores*] to comen fro Galaad. **1482** CAXTON *Trevisa's Higden* V. xii. 145 b, Also for refresshyng of weygoers there as clere welles were by hye weyes, the same kyng made arere postes and to honge theron shelles or cuppes of bras. **1577–87** HOLINSHED *Chron.* I. *Hist. Eng.* 181/1 Such tolles and tallages as were demanded of way-goers at bridges. **1747–8** in *N. Riding Record Soc.* (1890) VIII. 267 To save the country the several rates pay'd by the Riding for *wayhires..when the said road is overflowed with water. **1470–85** MALORY *Arthur* VII. xiii. 232 Whether ward ar ye *way ledyng this knyghte. *a* **1586** SIDNEY *Arcadia* III. xiv. §6 Let the Gods dispose of me as shall please them; but sure it shall be no such way, nor *way-leader, by which I will come to libertie. **1598** BARRET *Theor. Warres* IV. i. 99 They are to procure faithful and trusty guides, and skilful way leaders. **1773** H. FINLAY *Jrnl.* 11 Nov. (1867) 38 *Way letters he makes his own perquisite. **1851** E. BOWEN *U.S. Post-Office Guide* 47 On the letters brought by a mail carrier to be mailed, called way-letters, one cent. is to be charged in addition to the usual postage. **1893** H. JOYCE *Hist. Post Office* x. 147 For purposes of illustration..A bye or way letter would be a letter passing between any two towns on the Bath road and stopping short of London. **1638** BRATHWAIT *Barnabees Jrnl.* (1818) 183 Thee, pleasing *way-mates titled have their patron. **1799** *Mass. Mercury* 12 Feb. (Thornton) The fare is 4*d* per mile for *way passengers. **1834** in McClure *Early Life Abr. Lincoln* (1886) 174 Fare through..nine dollars: way passengers six and a fourth cents per mile. **1835** C. F. HOFFMAN *Winter in West* I. 102 At Huron, where the boat put in to land way-passengers. **1849** H. MELVILLE *Jrnl. Visit to London* (1948) 67 In a fit of the nightmare was going to stop at a *way-place, taking it for the place of my destination. **1883** 'MARK TWAIN' *Life on Mississippi* lii. 512 She got out of the cars at a way-place. **1880** *Harper's Mag.* Dec. 53 The Ohio is plied by a line of Cincinnati and Pittsburgh packets, and by smaller craft earning a precarious existence between '*way' points. **1899** J. LONDON *Let.* 12 Sept. (1966) 54 And to-morrow I start out on that postponed trip of mine to Stanford University and Mt. Hamilton, to say nothing of way points. **1902** O. WISTER *Virginian* xxiv. 276 The letter..had gone by private hand at the outset, taken the stage-coach at a way point [etc.]. **1971** *Flying* Apr. 29/1 (Advt.), Computer and waypoint selector lets you fly direct to a destination hundreds of miles away..forget about airways dog-legs. **1983** *Times* 6 Sept. 26/2 They plot course by typing..a series of 'way-points' into the computer. Such way-points occur every four hundred miles, so even if one were wrong, the next should put aircraft back on course. **1984** *Sunday Times* 20 May 34/2 The co-ordinates of the different 'waypoints', or intermediate stages along the flight..were checked and found correct. **1897** 'MARK TWAIN' *Following Equator* xxxii. 303 A good many of us got ashore at the first *way-port to seek another ship. **1901** *Daily Colonist* (Victoria, B.C.) 11 Oct. 3/2 The steamer Princess Louise.. has been tied up for repairs, and there will be no steamer leaving for the canneries and way ports of the north until Monday at least. **1927** *Blackw. Mag.* Mar. 330/2 'A way-port!' he sighed, after ordering coffee. 'It's turned out to be a terminus for a good many fellows like me.' **1773** BERRIDGE *Wks.* (1864) 184 They were like *wayposts, which shew a road but cannot help a cripple forwards. *a* **1845** BARHAM *Ingol. Leg.* Ser. III. *Blasph. Warn.* 338 And you came to a place where three cross-roads divide, Without any way-post, stuck up by the side Of the road to direct you and act as a guide. **1813** *Examiner* 8 Feb. 91/2, I was..appointed Way-warden for the parish; and was dragged from my business to collect the *way-rate. **1788** W. H. MARSHALL *Yorks.* I. 189 Every township ought to employ a roadman or working-*way-reave..for the same excellent purpose [of road-mending]. **1334** *Rolls of Parlt.* II. 84/2 En eyde de lour ferme de *Wey-serjauntz qe soleyent estre en foreyn boys pur le Cheminage, laquele Cheminage & Weywodewares sount ore defete par reson de la Porale. **1535** *Act 27 Hen. VIII* c. 18 Conveyeng awaye of *wayshydes shores pyles.. from the said bankes and walles [of the Thames]. **1961** WEBSTER, *Way-stop. **1969** *Islander* (Victoria, B.C.) 17 Aug. 12/3 She [*sc.* a steamboat] makes various way-stops on each trip and as Skipper McMinn says—'We stop for anyone who jumps up and down on the shore and gives us a holler.' **1981** *Southern Horticulture* (N.Z.) Spring 13 A town that's now making it. Martinborough was once just a way stop on the road to Pirinoa. **1983** C. G. HART *Rich die Young* iv. 45 Pat was using the Academy as a way-stop while he tried to break into the movies. **1893** *Times* 28 Sept. 3/5, I agree with your correspondent..that the *way-ticket system is a good one. **1906** *Westm. Gaz.* 27 Feb. 4/1 Men really in search of work would be given 'way tickets' for definite routes... Holders would be entitled to lodging, supper, and breakfast at the casual ward. **1873** 'MARK TWAIN' & WARNER *Gilded Age* xxix. 269 Next morning..he descended, sleepy and sore, from a *way-train. **1920** S. LEWIS *Main Street* 22 The hordes of the way-trains were not altogether new to Carol. **1534** MORE *Comf. agst. Trib.* III. xix. (1553) R v, Whether euery *waye walking beggre be by this reason out of prieson or no, we shall considre. *c* **1425** *Macro Plays, Cast. Persev.* 158 Worthy wytis, in al þis werd wyde, Be wylde wode wonys, & euery *weye-went. **1775** ASH, **Waywise*, expert in choosing the road. **1840** HALIBURTON *Clockm.* Ser. III. ix. 122 If they [*sc.* women as wives] are too old they are apt to be headstrong from havin' had their head so long; and, if they are too young, they are hardly way-wise enough to be pleasant. **1901** *Munsey's Mag.* XXV. 740/2 When a colt can be safely driven around the home grounds, he is considered 'farm broke,' or way wise. **1918** F. HACKETT *Ireland* xi. 309 Flung into the medley of American life, he was compelled.. to become way-wise in the factory, [etc.]. *c* **1205** LAY. 12860 þa cleopeden þe æorl Costantin & bad þa *wæi-witere [*c* **1275** wei-wittie] for-ærnen þa wateres. **1334** *Weywode-wares [see *wayserjeant* above].

b. In the names of plants found growing by the wayside and in stony places, as † **way-barley, -bennet, -bent**, *Hordeum murinum*; † **way-cress** = SCIATICA *cress*; **way-grass** (see quot. 1887); **way-thistle**, *Carduus arvensis*. Also WAYBREAD, WAYWORT.

1597 GERARDE *Herbal* I. xlvi. 67 This kinde of wilde Barly ..is called..in English Wall Barly, *Way Barly, or after old English writers, Way Bennet. **1578** LYTE *Dodoens* IV. xlv. 504 Wall Barley, or *Way Bennet. **1665** LOVELL *Herball* (ed. 2) 464. **1763** [see *wall barley*, WALL *sb.*[1] 25 c]. **1538** TURNER *Libellus, Phenix*,..*waybent. **1548** —— *Names of Herbes* (1881) 43 Phenix Dioscoridis semeth to be the herbe which is called in Cambrigshire Way bent. **1562** —— *Herbal* II. 20 b, [Iberis] may be called in Englishe *way-cresses. **1565** COOPER *Thesaurus, Calligonon*... *Waygrasse: knotgrasse. **1887** *Kentish Gloss.*, *Way-grass*, a weed; knot-grass. *Polygonum aviculare*. **1597** GERARDE *Herbal* II. ccccl xxiv. 1012 The *way Thistles grow euery where by high way sides and common paths, in great plenty. **1796** W. PITT *Agric. Stafford* 78 The common, cursed, or way thistle.

† **way**, *sb.*[2] *Obs. rare.* [? var. of WEY.] A certain quantity of glass.

1545 *Rates of Custom Ho.* C iij, Glasses Reinish the way or web containing lx. bunches. **1550–1600** *Customs Duties* MS. Addit. 25097 lf. 7 b, Glasse the waye or wabe. **1656** *Act Commw.* c. 20 Rates (1658) 468 Glass for Windows called.. Rhenish, the Way or Web.

† **way**, *v. Obs.* [f. WAY *sb.*[1]]

1. *intr.* To go, journey, proceed.

1596 SPENSER *F.Q.* IV. ii. 12 On a time as they together way'd, He made him open chalenge, and thus boldly sayd. **1708** *Yorkshire Racers* 10 They..Way'd to the course, and gallop'd true and well.

2. *trans.* (See quot. 1706.) Also erron. *weigh*, *waigh*.

1639 T. DE GREY *Compl. Horsem.* I. v. (1656) 43 Untill such time as he hath been..made gentle,..content to be shod, to be Back'd, Broken, Ridden, Wayed, Mouthed. *a* **1652** A. WILSON in Peck *Desid. Curiosa* (1735) II. XII. 25 My spotted Nag..being younge & not well waigh'd, run away with mee. *a* **1654** SELDEN *Table-T.* (Arb.) 39 He that hath a Scrupulous Conscience, is like a Horse that is not well weigh'd, he starts at every Bird that flies out of the Hedge. **1706** PHILLIPS (ed. Kersey), To *Way a Horse*, is to teach him to travel in the Ways. **1708** *Lond. Gaz.* No. 4490/4 Lost.., a young black Gelding, comes 4, not thorough weigh'd.

3. To set (a waggon) on the made way or track on which it runs.

1763 in *London Mag.* (1764) 145/2 When a waggon happens to be off the waggon-way, if laden, it will take two or three horses to way the waggon again.

† **4.** *intr.* To construct a way. In quot. *indirect passive*. *Obs.*

1640 SOMNER *Antiq. Canterb.* 195 It was a Free-Schoole for the City..anciently wayed unto, and having a passage to it from some part of Burgate-street.

Hence † **wayed** *ppl. a.*

? **1640** SUCKLING *Let.* Fragm. Aur. (1658) 77 A well-wayed horse will safely convey thee to thy journeys end. **1727** BAILEY vol. II, *Way'd Horse* [with Horsemen] is one who is already backed, suppled, and broken, and shews a Disposition to the Manage.

way (weɪ), *adv.* [Aphetic f. AWAY. Cf. G. *weg* similarly used.]

1. = AWAY *adv.* in various senses. † *do way*: see DO *v.* 53. Now only *Sc.*, *north.*, and *U.S.*

c **1205** LAY. 15933 Let alæten þis wæter & wei weorpen [*c* **1275** awey werpe]. *a* **1300–1578** Do way [see DO *v.* 53]. **1460** *Paston Lett.* I. 525 As for tythyngs here, the Kyng is way at Eltham. **1533** MORE *2nd Pt. Confut. Tindale* IV. Wks. 593/2 Which great occasyons Godde suffred to fal vpon him and carye hym waye. [*Tindale's words are*: to carye him clene oute of the waye.] **1818** SCOTT *Hrt. Midl.* xxvi, Gae wa', gae wa'. **1871** W. ALEXANDER *Johnny Gibb* iii, Gae 'wa', ye haveril. **1908** *Collier's Mag.* Oct., '*Travelling for the Presidency*' (Thornton s.v. *Lunch-counter*) Mr. Bryan has, during the past twelve years, eaten or otherwise made way with over 1,700 meals at railroad lunch-counters.

2. *esp.* At or to a (great) distance, far. **a.** with preps.

1849 W. S. MAYO *Kaloolah* v. (1850) 44 You see it was way towards Tupper's Lake. **1888** MRS. CUSTER *Tenting on Plains* viii. (1893) 151 He sat 'way under the mantel, to let the tobacco-smoke go up the chimney. **1891** *Anthony's Photogr. Bull.* IV. 29, I would have sold at a very low price, way below cost. **1927** BARONESS ORCZY *Sir Percy hits Back* v. 35 The three men had become mere specks, 'way down the road. **1959** *Times Lit. Suppl.* 16 Oct. 589/3 You are feet deep in snow and the temperature is way below zero. **1972** *Guardian* 17 Nov. 1/6 The census figures confirm..that unemployment is way above the official figure. **1979** R. PERRY *Bishop's Pawn* v. 76 You're way off course... It's back on Unter den Linden.

b. With advs., as *down*, *over*, *through*. Now only *Sc.*, *north.*, and *U.S.* For *way back*, *in*, *off*, *out*, *up* see main entries below.

1908 S. E. WHITE *Riverman* ix, Until you got sick of it *way through. **1851** E. S. WORTLEY *Trav. in U.S.* xxiii. 138 The trading and wealthy cities of far off Alabama and Louisiana, 'way down south'. **1854** SEBA SMITH (*title*) Way down East. **1866** *Atlantic Monthly* May 640 Nor these ain't metters thet with pol'tics swings, But goes 'way down amongst the roots o' things. **1850** L. H. GARRARD *Wah-to-Yah* xvii. 222 Calyforny! way over yonder!

c. *fig.* Much, far. *U.S.*

1941 L. I. WILDER *Little Town on Prairie* v. 34 'I wonder how much it costs,' said Ma. ''Way too much for ordinary folks,' said Pa. **1957** *New Yorker* 2 Nov. 105/2 Go by plane, train or ship. Arrive way sooner—relaxed! **1977** *Rolling Stone* 24 Mar., He was a country & western singer and he drank way too much.

3. *Comb.* (Chiefly *Sc.*)

a. with a pa. pple. or verb, as *way-gone*; † **way-put** *v. Sc.*, to put away: (*a*) to effect the escape of (a fugitive from justice); (*b*) = PUT *v.* 39 d.

1831 *Sutherland Farm Rep.* 81 in *Libr. Usef. Knowl., Husb.* III, They are sorted into their wedder herdings to replace the *waygone lot of the last year's ewe hogs. **1538** in Pitcairn *Crim. Trials* (Bannatyne Club) I. *205 [John Tuedy, in Lyntoun, convicted of art and part of the treasonable assistance given to James Douglas..: And for art and part of] *way-putting [him]. **1540** *Extracts Aberd. Reg.* (1844) I. 170 That nane of thaim way put nor dispone vpon the necessaris requirit to the said schip as ane schip of weir.

b. with vbl. sbs. (or other nouns of action), chiefly *Sc.*, as *waycoming*, *-fleeing*, *-passing*, *-sending*, *-sliding*; **way-ganging** = WAY-GOING; † **wei-sith**, departure, death; **way-taking**, the action or an act of taking (something) away, removal. Also WAY-GOING.

1651 SIR A. JOHNSTON (Ld. Wariston) *Diary* (S.T.S.) II. 95 Heard of the Scots airmy coming to Dumfermling after hir *waycoming. **1513** DOUGLAS *Æneis* IV. vi. 93 Tofoir thi *wayfleing, Had I ane child consavit of thi ofspring. **1456** SIR G. HAYE *Law Arms* (S.T.S.) 176 Gif a man..assuris ane othir frely to cum, and spekis nocht of his *way ganging. *a* **1605** *R. Bannatyne's Jrnl.* (1806) 490 It was ewin, at the way ganging of the day light. **1898** LD. E. HAMILTON *Mawkin of Flow* xi. 125 I'd be laith to get an ill name at the very outset of our way-ganging. **1479** *Acta Dom. Concil.* (1839) 45/1 þat þe persouns þ[t] past fra þe eleccioun of þe said Alexander be summond..to ansuer..for þair *way passing. *a* **1578** LINDESAY (Pitscottie) *Chron. Scot.* (S.T.S.) II. 11 [They] brunt the toun at thair way passing. *a* **1572** KNOX *Hist. Ref.* Wks. 1846 I. 420 Sche farther willit, to offer the *way-sending of the men of weir. *c* **1205** LAY. 25846 [She] weop for hire *wei-sið. *Ibid.* 28199 Scullen alle mine feond wæi-sið makeȝe. **1818** SCOTT *Hrt. Midl.* xviii, Avoiding right-hand snares and extremes, and left-hand *way-slidings. **1479** *Acta Audit.* (1839) 93/1 Befor þe lordis comperit Dauid Wemys summond..anent þe *wataking of thre oxin furth of þe landis of myrecarny. *a* **1572** KNOX *Hist. Ref.* Wks. 1846 I. 56 And so did Jesus Christ, the onlye trew Light, schyne unto many, for the way-tackin of one. **1625** in *Spalding Club Misc.* V. 218 The gryt trubill and discord betuin the laird and his tenantis anent the waytaking of doris at thair removing.

way (weɪ), *int.* Also **whay**. [Cf. WO *int.*] A call to a horse to stop.

1836 DICKENS *Sk. Boz, Tuggs's at Ramsgate*, Away went the donkey..'Way-way! Wo-o-o-o-!' cried Mr. Cymon Tuggs. **1846** —— *Cricket on Hearth* ii, 'Way!' This monosyllable was addressed to the Horse, who didn't mind it at all. 'Oh *do* Way, John!' said Mrs. Peerybingle. 'Please!' **1856** MISS YONGE *Daisy Chain* I. xv, Whay! Stop. There's an old woman in here.

way, obs. form of WEIGH *v.*, WEY, WHEY, WOE.

-way (weɪ), as a terminal element of advs., is identical with WAY *sb.*[1]

1. Phrases consisting of the sb. qualified by an adj. are often used adverbially (see WAY *sb.*[1] 8, 14 d, etc.), and some of the combinations of adj. and sb. thus used have come to be apprehended as single words, and so pronounced and written; the second element, losing its separate stress, has assumed in some degree the aspect of an adverbial suffix. The only early example of this process is the OE. *ealne weȝ*, an adverbial accusative, which after the disappearance (in the 14th c.) of adjectival flexion became ALWAY (q.v. for the development of meaning). *Anyway, everyway, noway, someway*, written as single words, are not found before the 16th c. The only advs. in *-way* f. descriptive adjs. are *broadway* (16th c.), *crossway* (early 17th c.), *straightway* (as two words in 15th c.; as one word from 1530). Most of the above-mentioned advs. have parallel and synonymous forms in -WAYS.

2. The few advs. f. sb. + *-way* do not originate from phrases, but are genuine compounds; they all have parallel forms in -WAYS. †*Needway* 'necessarily' occurs in Barbour *c* 1375 (*needways* in *Cursor M. a* 1300). *Edgeway, endway, sideway, sunway*, which denote direction of movement, are, like the corresponding forms in -WAYS, not older than the 16th century.

3. *Crossway* and *sideway* are frequently used as adjs.; the other advs. in *-way* expressing spatial direction would perhaps admit of a similar use, but it is not evidenced in our quotations.

wayag(e, obs. Sc. forms of VOYAGE.

wayang ('wɑːjæŋ). [a. Javanese *wajang, wayang.*]

1. In Indonesia and Malaysia, a theatrical performance employing puppets or human dancers; *spec.* a type of Javanese shadow puppet play.

1808 *Asiatick Res.* X. iii. 181 Scenic exhibitions termed 'Wayang-wayang', were till lately, very common in the peninsula of Malayu [*sic*]. **1853** *Jrnl. Indian Archipelago* VII. 271 A very large collection of Wayang figures, cut out of hide. **1881** *Encycl. Brit.* XIII. 604/2 The wayangs or puppet plays, in which grotesque figures of gilded leather are moved by the performer, who recites the appropriate speeches, and as occasion demands plays the part of chorus. **1910** [see *shadow-play* s.v. SHADOW *sb.* 16]. **1934** H. W. PONDER *Java Pageant* iv. 49 The stories have been immortalized..by the 'Wayang', or native theatre, which for countless generations has been so much a part of Javanese life. **1965** L. PALMIER *Indonesia* xi. 171 The wayang performance has always had a magic and religious significance. **1973** D. MAY *Laughter in Djakarta* iv. 71 Tonight he was going..to see a *wayang*, an old Hindu-Javanese story acted and danced by a famous company from central Java. **1978** N. FREELING *Night Lords* xvi. 72 The wayang dollies depended..upon the skill and suppleness of the manipulator's fingers.

2. With qualifying term (see quot. 1969), as **wayang kulit** [Javanese *kulit* skin, leather], the Javanese shadow puppet play.

1893 W. B. WORSFOLD *Visit to Java* x. 178, I had an opportunity of witnessing..the wayang *klitik*, in which the puppets are exhibited themselves to the audience instead of being made to project shadows. **1894** J. D. VAUGHAN in N. B. Dennys *Descr. Dict. Brit. Malaya* 324 In a puppet show the figures are seen and in this their shadows are. The show is called *wayang kulit*, or leather puppets. **1936** G. B. GARDNER *Keris* i. 21 The figures are usually grotesque, of the *wayang kulit* type. **1965** *Economist* 13 Mar. 1149/3 The traditional Indonesian *wayang purwa* puppet theatre show, usually performed at night, in which the vague shadows of leather puppets are fuzzily silhouetted on a screen. **1966** D. FORBES *Heart of Malaya* viii. 100 Figures that moved across the frame of the doorway looked like silhouettes in the *wayang kulit*, the shadow play. **1969** A. R. PHILPOTT *Dict. Puppetry* 277 The precise nature of the performance is distinguished by a qualifying term—e.g. wayang purwa, wayang gedog,..wayang wong—the last being a performance by human actors... The qualifying term may indicate type of puppet or the type of plays. **1976** *Times* 31 Aug. (Malaysia Suppl.) p. iv/4, Both farmers and fishermen are largely confined to their houses during the monsoon season, when some of them cut silhouette puppets from cowhide for the traditional Wayang Kulit shadow play—a long procession of characters, based on the Indian epic *The Ramayana.*

'way-back, *adv.*, *a.*, and *sb. colloq.* (chiefly *U.S.*, *Austral.*, and *N.Z.*). Forms: see below. [f. WAY *adv.* + BACK *adv.*] **A.** *adv.* Usu. written **way back**. **1.** Far away; in or *from* a remote rural area.

1855 *Merry's Museum* XXIX. 58, I did not know that there was such a fine Magazine,..for I live 'way back in the woods'. **1884** *Boston Globe* Oct., His unkempt hair, gawky appearance, and homespun suit..all bespoke the citizen from wayback. **1889** KIPLING *From Sea to Sea* (1899) II. xxvi. 28 'You'll see the salmon-wheels 'fore long,' said a man who lived 'way back on the Washoogle'. **1916** G. THORNTON *Wowser* 85 The condition of those living 'wayback'. **1930** M. R. E. BLAIR *By Pacific Waters* ii. 12 I'm sure they are getting a storm way-back. **1936** 'F. GERALD' *Millionaire in Memories* iii. 106 Blackall was much the same as any other township 'way back'. **1976** *National Observer* (U.S.) 6 Nov., 'We needed something to let people know that there was a church there,' says Rector Mart Gayland Pool. 'We sat way back on a slope near a golf course, and out facility looked more like a bowling alley or a Kinney shoe store.'

2. A long time ago; ***from way back***, since a long time ago; hence, through and through.

1887 *Lantern* (New Orleans) 30 July 3/3 Nick is a walker from way back. **1889** 'MARK TWAIN' *Yankee at Crt. Arthur* xxxi, He *thinks* he's a Sheol of a farmer; thinks he's old Grayback from Wayback. **1889** KIPLING *From Sea to Sea* (1899) I. xxii. 432, I am an American by birth—an American from way back. **1892** 'MARK TWAIN' *Amer. Claimant* 167, I tell you, he's an artist from way back! **1907** *Daily Chron.* 2 Sept. 2/7 The Whitmans were American 'from way-back'. **1923** J. H. COOK 50 *Yrs. Old Frontier* III. 227 This occurred 'way back', when the Indians had no horses. **1939** *Country Life* 11 Feb. p. xxxvi/1 The 'Rule for Anchoresses', written way back in the thirteenth century. **1948** *Sporting Mirror* 19 Nov. 6/2 Way back in September I said that Norwich City have got what it takes and would be a power this season. **1969** J. D. A. WIDDOWSON in Halpert & Story *Christmas Mumming in Newfoundland* 218 The real mummers we used to have way back. **1970** J. LENNON in J. Wenner *Lennon Remembered* (1972) 144 He not only knew my work, and the lyrics that I had written but he also understood them, and from *way* back. **1978** R. HILL *Pinch of Snuff* ix. 87 'You know Burkill, sir?' he asked. 'From way back.'

B. *adj.* Usu. written **way-back, wayback**.

1. Of long ago.

1885 *Santa Fé Weekly New Mexican* 10 Sept. 1/2 A writer in giving a description of the plains of Kansas in the 'way back' time, speaks of it as a 'wilderness of grasses'. **1962** *Observer* 17 June 3/6 [U.S. writer] He had an ancestor cult. There was a painting of a way-back ancestor wearing a woollen waistcoat.

2. Hailing from, or located in, a remote rural area.

1887 *New York Ev. Post* 4 Oct., The way-back delegates, those from the farms and the small villages. **1918** *Blackw. Mag.* May 608/2 There was a *fundi*..who used to let on that the pictures on some vases..were done from wayback Masai. **1933** *Bulletin* (Sydney) 24 May 21/2 Mrs. Smallbeer sold her very wayback pub. **1950** K. S. PRICHARD *Winged Seeds* xv. 165 Sally understood that this visit to a way-back station was an experience for them. **1951** *Landfall* V. 278 Miss Dane..imagined herself a pioneer of progress in a wayback community. **1973** M. CARNEGIE *Friday Mount* 218 No wonder some of the way-back towns had that look.

C. *sb.* Form as for the adj. **1.** A person inhabiting or coming from a remote district.

1890 E. CUSTER *Following Guidon* xvii. 261 We were, in Western terms, 'waybacks from wayback'. **1912** R. S. TAIT *Scotty Mac, Shearer* 125 At a group in front of him a thimble-rigger was expending much eloquence to induce a party of waybacks to relieve him of his surplus cash. **1924** *Contemp. Rev.* Aug. 236 The well-known resourcefulness and sense of location of the present-day way-backs of Australia..are due..to lessons taught the pioneers by the natives.

2. Remote rural areas; *spec.* the Australian outback.

1890 [see prec. sense]. **1901** F. J. GILLEN *Diary* 5 Oct. (1968) 277 The station is built on a stony rise on the western bank of the Newcastle and like most stock stations in the 'wayback' there has been no attempt made to improve the appearance of the surroundings. **1925** H. H. COOK *Far Flung* v. 39 Some 50 miles in the 'way-back'. **1933** *Bulletin* (Sydney) 27 Sept. 20/4 Waltzing Matilda in the waybacks of S.A. I came upon a well-found homestead.

'way-bill.

1. A list of passengers booked for seats in a stagecoach or other public vehicle for places on the road. Also a detailed statement of goods entrusted to a public carrier for delivery at stated destinations.

1791 BOSWELL *Johnson* 3 June 1784, The Oxford post-coach took us up in the morning at Bolt-Court... I found from the way-bill, that Dr. Johnson had made our names be put down. **1821** *Massachusetts Spy* 23 May (Thornton), Packages of the larger kind, belonging to any passenger, were always entered on the way-bill. **1824** BARNEWALL & CRESSWELL *Rep. K.B.* II. 718 He did not see any Norwich way-bill [in the waggon]. **1849** DE QUINCEY *Eng. Mail Coach* Wks. 1862 IV. 297 Ucalegon, as it happened, was not in the way-bill and therefore could not have been booked. **1864** T. S. WILLIAMS & SIMMONDS *Engl. Commerc. Corresp.* 91 You will also be kind enough to repay him the carriage according to the bills of lading or the waybills he will show you. **1897** BRAM STOKER *Dracula* xvii. (1912) 244 The official..sending also..the way-bill and all the papers connected with the delivery of the boxes at Carfax.

2. A list of places to be visited on a journey.

1851 W. KELLY *Excursion to California* I. x. 172 According to our way-bill, and comparing it with our computed travel, we could not be far off the next crossing of the Platte. **1866** *Daily Tel.* 16 Jan. 7/4 All of which places.. are set down for visit in my way-bill. **1879** TOURGEE *Fool's Errand* xxxv. 242 He had been traveling on what is known in that country as a 'way-bill', or a description of a route received from another.

transf. **1823** MOORE *Rhymes on Road* Introd. 89, I've got into the easy mode, You see, of rhyming on the road—Making a way-bill of my pages, Counting the stanzas by my stages.

3. *U.S.* A label attached to an article in transit to indicate its destination, mode of transport, etc.

1887 GUNTER *Mr. Barnes* xx. 145 The old and dilapidated little dirty trunk covered with numerous way-bills.

4. A kind of pass by producing which a man 'on the road' can obtain relief at certain stages of his journey. So ***way-bill system***.

1893 *Times* 20 Sept. 3/6 This system, which became known as the 'waybill' system, was worked in this way. When a destitute wayfarer left a casual ward in the morning, he could, on application, obtain a waybill or passport, on which were recorded..the day and hour at which the bearer left it, and the route on which he was travelling, [etc.]. **1897** *Church Times* 20 Aug. 187/1 Any poor traveller..will be.. fed, lodged, and passed on, the following morning, with a stamped way-bill, to the next lodging-house on the route.

Hence **way-bill** *v. U.S. trans.*, to enter (goods) on a way-bill.

1877 W. H. BURROUGHS *Taxation* 140 Freight being way-billed through. **1890** *Railways Amer.* 412 He..must count, seal, superscribe, and way-bill money packages and handle oyster-kegs..at a moment's notice.

†'way-bit. *north. Obs.* Forms: 6 **waybitte, wye byt**, 6–7 **wey-**, 7 **wea-**, 7–8 **wee-**, (9 **wai-**), 7– **way-bit.** [First element uncertain, but prob. representing northern dialectal variants of WEE *sb.*[1] and *a.* + BIT *sb.*[2]] A short distance.

As shown by the quotations, the source of the word was the alleged habit of Northern rustics, on being asked the distance to a place, of giving it as 'a mile (etc.) and a way-bit', which the inquiring traveller found practically to mean two or three miles.

1589 *Almond for Parrat* 2 If..my full points seeme as tedious to thy puritane perusers, as the Northren mans mile, and a waybitte to the weary passenger. **1600** *Wisd. Dr. Dodypoll* IV. i. in Bullen *O. Pl.* III. 139 How far am I from Court? Some two myles and a wye byt, sir. **1603** T. M. *True Narr. Entert. H.M.* C3b, The miles according to the Northren phrase, are a wey-bit longer then they be here in the South. *c* **1645** HOWELL *Lett.* (1655) IV. xxviii. 67 In the North parts where there is a wea bit to evry mile. **1651** J. C[LEVELAND] *Poems, Dial. Two Zealots* 52 A York-shire Wea-bit, longer then a mile. *a* **1661** FULLER *Worthies, Yorks.* (1662) 190 Ask a Country-man here on the high-way, how far it is to such a Town, and they commonly return, So many miles and a way-bit... It is not Way-bit, though generally so pronounced, but Wee-bit is a pure Yorkshirisme, which is a small bit in the Northern Language. *Ibid.* 225 Generall Leslie with his Scottish ran away more then an York-shire mile, and a Wee-bit. **1775** J. WATSON *Hist. Halifax* 548 *Way-bit.* As a mile and a way-bit. Meaning a wee, or little bit. **1834** MEDWIN *Angler in Wales* I. 255 You shall have his description of it, preface and all—which is like the mile and the wai bit, in Sussex, the one twice the length of the other.

fig. a **1670** HACKET *Abp. Williams* I. (1692) 59, I have heard him prefer divers, and very seriously, before himself, who came short a Mile and a way-bit. **1692** *Poems in Burlesque* 15 From Sleep to Death, there's but a way-bit.

b. *transf.* of time.

1687 SETTLE *Refl. Dryden's Plays* 51 In his *anno ætatis*, thirty and a Way-bit. **1732** LADY B. GERMAIN *Let. to Swift* 13 May, You will find forty years and a wee bit have done no more good to my head than it has to my face.

'way-board. *Mining.* Also **weigh-**. [app. f. WAY *sb.*[1] + BOARD *sb.* (cf. sense 16).] (See quot. 1859.)

α. **1747** HOOSON *Miner's Dict.* L3, These Leaps never happen but at some Way-board, or large Bed-joynt. **1818** W. PHILLIPS *Geol.* 137 The limestone strata contain thin beds of clay, termed by the miner way-boards. **1859** PAGE *Handbk. Geol. Terms, Wayboards*, a mining term, now pretty generally employed by geologists to designate any thin layers or bands that separate or define the boundaries of thicker strata.

β. **1802** J. MAWE *Mineral. Derbysh.* Gloss. (E.D.S.), *Weighboard*, clay intersecting the vein. **1860** WORCESTER. **1864** WEBSTER. (And in later Dicts.)

waybread, waybred ('weɪbrɛd). Forms: *α.* 1 **weȝbrádae, -bræ̂de**, (2 **weibreode**, 3 **wei-**, 5 **weybrode**), 4–6 **weybrede** (6 **-bred**), 5–6 **waybrede**, 6–7 **waybreed**, 6, 9 **waybread**, (7 **whaybred**, 8 **way-broad**), 5– **waybred** (6 **wabred**, 6, 9 **wabret**, 9 **waybret**, **wabert**). *β.* 7 **wayburne**, 9 **-burn**; 7 **waburne**, 9 **wabran, -bron, waveren.** [Com. WGer.: OE. *weȝbráde, weȝbræ̂de* wk. fem., corresponds to OS. *wegabreda, wegbrede* (MLG., M.Du. *wegebrede*, Du. *weegbree*; WFris. *weibré*), OHG. *wegabreita* fem. (MHG. *wegebreite*, mod.G. *wegebreite, wegbreite* fem., *weg(e)breit* masc.); Da. has *vejbred* from LG. The word means 'broad-leaved plant growing beside the ways'; f. WAY *sb.*[1] (the early continental forms have genit. pl.) + OTeut. type **braidjōn-* broad object (cf. OHG. *wintbreita* 'ventilabrum', *breite* flat cake). In the *β*-forms, occurring only with *-leaf*, the *d* of the stem has disappeared before the *-n* of the OE. genitive sing. in *weȝbrǣdan léaf* (Leechd. I. 84, 86).] = PLANTAIN[1] 1. Also ***water waybread*** = water plantain: see PLANTAIN[1] 2.

c **700** *Epinal Gloss.* 65 *Arniglosa*,..uueȝbradae. *c* **1000** *Sax. Leechd.* II. 292 Ꝥenim..þa ruwan weȝbrædan [etc.]. **11..** *Voc.* in Wr.-Wülcker 544/38 *Plantago*, weibreode. *c* **1265** *Voc. Plants* ibid. 558/22 Weibrode. **1398** TREVISA *Barth. De P.R.* XVII. cxxix. (1495) 687 Weybrede chewed easyth and clensyth swellynge gomes. *c* **1450** *Alphita*

(Anecd. Oxon.) 14 Arnoglossa, .. plantago maior idem... Anglice weybrode. *c* **1500** *Gloss.* 69 in *Makculloch MS.* (S.T.S.) 28 Hec plantago, a wabred. **1538** TURNER *Libellus, Alisma dioscoridæ*, .. water plantane or water waybrede. **1562** —— *Herbal* II. 94 There ar two kyndes of plantayn or Waybrede, the lesse and the greater. **1601** HOLLAND *Pliny* xxv. viii. II. 223 Themison .. set forth a whole booke of the hearbe Waibread or Plantain, wherein he highly praiseth it. **1657** W. COLES *Adam in Eden* lxxvi, The generall English name is Plantaine; but that which the Greeks call *Eptaneuron*, we call Way-bred, because it commonly breeds by the wayside. **1705** tr. *Cowley's Plants* Wks. (1711) III. 303 Next Waybred rose .. Her Nature is astringent, which great Hate Of her among Blood-letters does create. **1861** MRS. LANKESTER *Wild Flowers* 109 The common name of Plantago Major is undoubtedly Way-bred (not Way-bread, as it is usually spelt), from its frequency by the way-side, seeming as if bred on the road. **1866** *Treas. Bot.*, Waybread.

b. *Comb.*: **waybread-leaf** (also *Sc.* **wayburn-leaf**), sometimes used as the name of the plant.

α. **1599** T. CUTWODE *Caltha Poet.* (Roxb.) cxvii, And with a Wabret leafe he made a wallet. **1614** G. MARKHAM *Cheap & Gd. Husb.* Table hard words, *Plantayne* .. is called Whaybred leafe. **1803** LEYDEN *Scenes of Infancy* I. 101 The wabret leaf, that by the pathway grew.

β. **1609** in T. Craig-Brown *Hist. Selkirksh.* (1886) I. 180 Being demandit if she gave drinks, she answered she gave nane bot off Waburne leavis for the hart-axes. **1623** *Sel. Rec. Presbyt. Lanark* (Abbotsford Club) 1 She appoyntit thame the wayburne leaf to be eattin nyne morningis. **1808** JAMIESON, *Wabran leaves*, Great Plantain or Waybread. **1820** *Blackw. Mag.* Nov. 202, I thought the grey whin was gaun frae below me—it shook like a wabron-leaf. **1831** W. PATRICK *Plants Lanark.* 94 Greater Plantain... The leaves (vulgarly called the Wayburn-leaf) are spread on the ground. **1914** J. S. ANGUS *Shetland Gloss.* 154 *Waveren leaf*, plantain (*Plantago major*).

waycett, obs. form of WATCHET.

waycht, Sc. var. *wicht*: see WIGHT *a.*

† **waycoriant.** *Obs. rare.* The three obscure terms in the quot. (as also *wagron* on the prec. page: see quot. s.v. GHEEREAGUAR) seem to be arbitrary formations, pretended names of pigments.

1658 W. SANDERSON *Graphice* 69 For an Amethyst, the same Gheereaguar mixed with Waycoriant and waywick.

† **wayed,** *ppl. a. Obs. rare.* [f. WAY *sb.*1 + -ED2.] Having a way. Also in *three-wayed* = THREE-WAY *a.*

1382 WYCLIF *Isa.* xv. 3 In his thre weied places thei ben gird with a sac. —— *Ezek.* xix. 13 Now it is plauntid ouere in deseert, in loond not wayed [Vulg. *invia*].

wayer(e: see WARE *sb.*3, WAYOUR *Obs.*, WEIGHER.

† **'wayfarage.** *Feudal Law. Obs.* [f. WAYFARE *sb.* or *v.* + -AGE.] = CHIMINAGE.

1594 CROMPTON *Jurisd.* 189 Chimynage, that is toll for wayfearage. **1607** COWELL *Interpr.*, Chiminage .. signifieth a toll for wayfarage through the forest. **1679** BLOUNT *Ant. Tenures* 91 They ought to have .. Toll for wayfarage through the whole Farm aforesaid.

wayfare ('weɪfɛə(r)), *sb. arch.* [f. WAY *sb.*1 + FARE *sb.*, after WAYFARING *a.*]

1. Wayfaring, travelling. Also *fig.*

?*a* **1400** *Morte Arth.* 1797 He .. Wroghte wayes fulle wyde, and wounded knyghttez; Wyrkez his in wayfare fulle werkand sydez, And hewes of þe hardieste halsez in sondyre. **1601** HOLLAND *Pliny* XI. xxx. I. 328 Their [*sc.* ants'] waifare is so ordinarie and continuall, that wee may see the very hard flint and pebble stones worne with their passage too and fro. **1614** SYLVESTER *Little Bartas* 714 The heavy load Of Cares and Crosses (in a thousand things) Which this our wretched, sad, short, Way-fare brings. **1850** S. DOBELL *Crazed* 24, I .. entered on my wayfare when I saw Gold on the ground and glory in the trees. **1886** BURTON *Arab. Nts.* (abr. ed.) I. 4 On the fourth day he made ready for wayfare. **1887** MORRIS *Odyss.* x. 501 O Circe, and what helmsman for my wayfare shall I get?

b. Guidance in travel. *rare*−1.

1875 MORRIS *Æneids* VIII. 336 Me .. my mother's word well worshipped hither drave, The nymph Carmentis; and a god, Apollo, wayfare gave.

†**2.** Provision for a journey, travelling expenses. [tr. L. *viaticum*]. *Obs.*

1600 HOLLAND *Livy* XXII. lii. 464 A noble Lady .. named Busa, relieved them with some victuall, apparrell, yea and mony also in their purses for their wayfare. **1609** BIBLE (Douay) *Deut.* xv. 14 Thou shalt in no case suffer him to depart emptie: but geve him his wayfare of thy flockes, and of thy barne floore, and thy presse.

wayfare ('weɪfɛə(r)), *v.* Now *rare* and *arch.* [Back-formation from WAYFARING *sb.*] *intr.* To journey or travel, esp. on foot. Also *to wayfare it.*

1547 *Act 1 Edw. VI*, c. 3 §3 Divers wemen and men goeth on begging wayefaring. **1587** GOLDING *De Mornay* xxiv. (1617) 411 Abraham, Isaac and Iacob wayfared from place to place vpon the earth. **1596** SPENSER *F.Q.* v. xi. 37 There as he traueld by the way, he met An aged wight, wayfaring all alone. **1603** HOLLAND *Plutarch's Mor.* 474 A certaine Laconian as he way-fared, came unto a place where there dwelt an olde friend and host of his. **1818** KEATS *Lett.* Wks. 1889 III. 142, I hope soon to be writing you about the things of the north, purposing to wayfare all over those parts. **1850** *Fraser's Mag.* XLII. 446 Shoals of people .. wayfared it up the Rhine. **1898** HARDY *Wessex Poems* 135 Along through the Stour-bordered Forum, Where Legions had wayfared.

b. *fig.* and in fig. context.

1535 *Goodly Primer, Commendations* Ps. cxix. Zaïn, Whilst I here wayfared a stranger. **1578** *Bk. Chr. Prayers* 12 Most louing Father, .. harken to the prayers of thy seruants, yet wayfaring here on earth. **1674** N. FAIRFAX *Bulk & Selv.* 141 Not jading it in the great road of bare motion, which other stirr'd bodies are wayfaring in. **1875** MANNING *Mission Holy Ghost* i. 23 That he is but a stranger wayfaring upon earth.

wayfarer ('weɪfɛərə(r)). [f. WAY *sb.*1 + FARER. Cf. WAYFERER.] A traveller by road, esp. one who journeys on foot.

c **1440** *Promp. Parv.* 520/1 Weyfarere, *viator, viatrix.* **1514** BARCLAY *Eglog* iii. (1570) B vj b, Iugglers and pipers, and scuruy wayfarers. **1551** T. WILSON *Logic* 43 The way-fairer shall not (or very hardly) come to his iourneies ende, except he haue some money in his purse. **1602** CAREW *Cornwall* I. 66 But in stead of remedy, they receyued in answere, that neither such an outcorner was frequented with many wayfarers, nor by hanging out signes .. did they inuite any. **1836** DICKENS *Sk. Boz, Streets—Night*, Savoury steams of hot dinners salute the nostrils of the hungry wayfarer, as he plods wearily by the area railings. **1858** CHR. G. ROSSETTI *Poems, Up-hill* 9 Shall I meet other wayfarers at night? Those who have gone before. **1896** CONAN DOYLE *Exploits of Gerard* vi. 217 There were few wayfarers between there and Greiz.

b. *wayfarer's-tree*, the hobble-bush. *U.S.*

1858 [see HOBBLE-BUSH].

wayfaring ('weɪfɛərɪŋ), *vbl. sb.* Somewhat *arch.* [f. WAY *sb.*1 + FARING *vbl. sb.*, after WAYFARING *a.*] Journeying, travelling; an instance of this. Also *fig.*

1536 *Primer Eng. & Lat., Commend.* (Rouen) 149 b, Thy iustifications were to me songes in ye place of my wayfaring. **1540** PALSGR. *Acolastus* II. iii. L iv, Wherfore comest thou a wayfarynge into this countrey .. ? **1548** UDALL *Erasm. Par. Acts* ii. 22–28 He him selfe went on wayfarynge frome place to place. **1561** T. NORTON *Calvin's Inst.* III. xxv. (1634) 484 To us the onely and perfect felicitie is knowne even in this earthly waifaring. *a* **1677** BARROW *Wks.* (1686) III. Serm. xv. 178 The Scripture aptly resembles our life to a wayfaring, a condition of travel and pilgrimage. **1818** KEATS *Endym.* I. 132 That I may dare, in wayfaring, To stammer where old Chaucer used to sing. **1832** W. IRVING *Alhambra* (1851) 122 To hear a mass and put up a prayer for a prosperous wayfaring across the Sierra. **1840** DICKENS *Old C. Shop* xlii, Gipsy camps they had passed in their wayfaring. **1881** O'SHAUGHNESSY *Songs of a Worker* 42 A certain traveller, sad and .. worn With wayfaring.

b. *Comb.*, as *wayfaring-journey, -life, -sketch*; † **wayfaring-book**, an itinerary; † **wayfaring-shrub** = WAYFARING-TREE.

1549 in Strype *Eccl. Mem.* (1721) III. App. lxxxiii. 289 Give us Grace to forget this Way-faring Journey, and to remember our proper and true Country. **1610** HOLLAND *Camden's Brit.* I. 204 No farther this way did Antonine specifie any place in his way-faring book. **1614** LITHGOW *Trav.* B 4 Some notable illusions .. which I found in my wayfaring iourney. **1731** MILLER *Gard. Dict.* s.v. *Viscum*, The Bark of our Lantone or Way-faring Shrub. **1847** MISS F. SKENE (*title*) Wayfaring Sketches among the Greeks and Turks. **1889** LUCY TOULMIN SMITH (*title*) English Wayfaring Life in the Middle Ages [tr. J. J. Jusserand *La Vie nomade*].

wayfaring ('weɪfɛərɪŋ), *ppl. a. arch.* Forms: 1 **weȝfarende**, 4 **weyfarende, -faringe, -varyng,** (5 **-fareng**), 4–6 **wayfarynge, -inge,** 6 **wayefa(y)rynge, waifaring,** 7 **way-fairing,** 6– **wayfaring.** [OE. *weȝfarende*, f. *weȝ* WAY *sb.*1 + pres. pple. of *faran* FARE *v.*1 Cf. Icel. (14th c.) *vegfarandi*, MSw. *vägh-*, Sw. *vägfarande*, Da. *veifarende.* Cf. the cognate WAYFERING.] Travelling or journeying by road. Usually *wayfaring man*, a traveller by road. Also *fig.*

c **1000** ÆLFRIC *Saints' Lives* xxvi. 204 Sum weȝfarende man ferde wið þone feld. *c* **1330** R. BRUNNE *Chron. Wace* 3659 We ar .. Weyfarende men þat wolde haue gryþ. **1387** TREVISA *Higden* V. 449 For refresshynge and socour of way farynge [MS. γ weyvaryng] men. **1502** ATKYNSON tr. *De Imitatione* III. xxiii. (1893) 216 O iesu, .. the solace & conforte of wayfarynge soules. **1545** ASCHAM *Toxoph.* II. (Arb.) 157 The waye beyng sumwhat trodden afore, by waye fayrynge men. **1597** HOOKER *Eccl. Pol.* v. lxxviii. §11. 241 The necessities of trauailers waifaring men and such like. **1611** BIBLE *Isa.* xxxv. 8 The wayfaringmen, though fooles, shall not erre therein. **1678** BUNYAN *Pilgr.* I. 155 When the Shepherds perceived that they were way-fairing men, they also put questions to them, .. as, Whence came you? **1897** 'EDNA LYALL' (*title*) Wayfaring Men.

† **b.** *wayfaring man's tree*, the fuller form of WAYFARING-TREE.

Both are found in Gerarde for the first time, but only the latter survived.

1597 GERARDE *Herbal* III. cxv. 1305 The Wayfaring mans tree groweth vp to the height of an hedge tree, of a meane bignesse.

Hence **wayfaringly** *adv. rare.*

1552 HULOET, Wayfayryngly, *peregrine, uiatice.*

wayfaring-tree. [Short for *wayfaring man's tree* (see above); cf. *traveller's joy.*]

1. The tall shrub *Viburnum Lantana*, with broad leaves downy underneath, white flowers in dense cymes, and green berries turning first red then black. It grows wild in hedges and underwood.

1597 GERARDE *Herbal* III. cxv. 1305 Of the Wayfaring tree. **1670** EVELYN *Sylva* xxi. §19. (ed. 2) 101 The *Viburnum*, or Way-faring tree, .. makes the most plyant and best bands to Fagot with. **1671–96** PHILLIPS, *Weafering-tree.* **1731** MILLER *Gard. Dict.*, *Viburnum*; The Wayfaring or Pliant Mealy Tree. **1785** MARTYN *Lett. Bot.* xvii. (1794) 239. **1830** HOWITT *Bk. Seasons* (1837) 117 Wayfaring tree! what ancient claim Hast thou to that right pleasant name? **1859** W. S. COLEMAN *Woodlands* (1866) 121 The Wayfaring Tree, belonging to the same genus as the Guelder Rose, bears a considerable resemblance to that shrub, both in its flowers and berries; but in the leaves differs entirely.

2. *U.S.* The hobble-bush (*V. lantanoides*).

1814 PURSH *Flora Amer. Septentr.* 711. **1856** A. GRAY *Man. Bot. U.S.* (1860) 168.

wayfe: see WAIF *sb.*1, WAIVE *v.*2

† **wayferer.** *Obs.* [f. WAY *sb.*1 + FERE *v.*1 + -ER1.] = WAYFARER.

1388–9 in *1st Rep. Hist. MSS. Comm.* 80/1 De xvi *d.* solutis uni weyferer eodem tempore. *c* **1450** MYRC. *Par. Pr.* 1364 Hast þou in herte rowþe I-had, Of hem þat were nede be-stad, To seke & sore and prisonerus, I-herberet alle weyfer[er]us?

† **wayfering,** *ppl. a. Obs.* Forms: 1 **weȝférende,** 3 **weiverinde,** 4 **wayverinde, -ferande, way-, weyferyng(e.** [OE. *weȝférende*, f. *weȝ* WAY *sb.*1 + pres. pple. of *féran* FERE *v.*1] = WAYFARING *ppl. a.*

c **890** WÆRFERTH tr. *Gregory's Dial.* 128 þa cwæð se weȝferenda to þam æwfæstan mæn. *c* **1000** ÆLFRIC *Hom.* I. 164 Dysiȝ bið se weȝferenda man seðe nimð þone smeðan weȝ þe hine mislæt. *a* **1225** *Ancr. R.* 350 Heo iuindeð, iwis, Sein Julianes in, þet weiuerinde men ȝeorne secheð. **1303** R. BRUNNE *Handl. Synne* 10510 Be a man yn sykenes, or yn prysoun, Weyferyng, or yn temptacyun. **1340** *Ayenb.* 39 Robberes and kueade herberȝeres þet berobbeþ þe pilgrimes an þe marchons and þe oþre wayuerindemen. **13..** *E.E. Allit. P.* B. 79 þe wayferande frekez, on fote & on hors, .. Laþez hem alle luflyly to lenge at my fest. *c* **1374** CHAUCER *Boeth.* II. pr. v. (1886) 34 (Cambr. MS.) Yif thow haddyst entred in the paath of this lyf a voyde wayferynge [*Addit. MS.* way-faryng] man. *c* **1380** WYCLIF *Sel. Wks.* II. 348 In þis epistle techiþ Poul how wey-ferynge men þat lyven here shulden go þe streiȝt wey þat lediþ men to þe blisse of hevene.

wayff(e, wayft: see WAIF *sb.*1, WEFT *sb.*2

wayfire, obs. f. WAFER.

way-gang. *Sc.* [GANG *sb.*1] = WAY-GOING.

1737 RAMSAY *Sc. Prov.* 27 Frost and fawshood have baith a dirty waygang. **1894** LATTO *Tam. Bodkin* xxxi. 315 Their wa' gang [*sc.* the death of her parents] brak the hindmost link that bund her affections to Breeriebuss.

† **'waygate**1. *Obs.* Also 6 **-gait.** [f. WAY *adv.* + GATE *sb.*2] The act of going away, departure.

1575–6 *Durham Depos.* (Surtees) 269 This examinate at his waygait bad the said Thomas fairwell. **1598** R. BERNARD tr. *Terence, Heautontim.* III. i. (1607) 221 Least that old wonted austeritie of yours bee worse then it was at his way-gate. **1600** HEYWOOD *2nd Pt. Edw. IV* (1613) Q 4 b, So God respect the waygate of my soule, as I know nothing. **1641** BEST *Farm. Bks.* (Surtees) 77 It is an usuall course (amongst shepheards) att the way-gate of a snowe .. to keepe theire sheepe .. on some swarth-grownd.

waygate2. *Sc.* and *north.* [f. WAY *sb.*1 + GATE *sb.*2 Cf. *way-gang, -go* s.v. WAY *sb.*1 40.]

1. A passage-way.

For various special uses see *Eng. Dial. Dict.*

a **1800** in Hogg *Jacobite Relics* (1819) I. 24 He's awa to sail, Wi' water in his waygate, An' wind in his tail. **1866** CARLYLE *E. Irving* in Froude *Remin.* (1881) I. 101 'Upon all these [books] you have will and waygate', an expressive Annandale phrase of the completest welcome.

2. Speed, progress, headway. *Sc.* and *north.*

1825–82 JAMIESON. **1894** *Northumbld. Gloss.*

waygh, obs. form of WEIGH *v.*

way-going ('weɪgəʊɪŋ). *Sc.* and *north.* Also 9 *Sc.* **-ga'en, -gaun.** [f. WAY *adv.*] The action or fact of going away, departure (on a journey, from life); the act of leaving (a habitation, employment).

1633 SIR A. JOHNSTON (Ld. Wariston) *Diary* (S.H.S.) I. 98 Coming hoome .. my saule blissed God .. for his goodnes to me in this comunion conforme to my voue befor my way-going. **1649** J. CARSTAIRES *Lett.* (1846) 58 Fearing much the [letter] bearer's way-going, I dare say no more; but let [etc.]. **1702** H. GUTHRY *Mem.* 56 They press'd that the prorogation might be with the consent of the Estates, and upon his refusal they oppos'd his way-going. **1819** ALEX. BALFOUR *Campbell* I. xviii. 326 It was a wae wa-ga'en to mae nor me at that time. **1825–82** JAMIESON, *Way-gaun, Wa'-gaun, Way-going, adj.*, removing from a farm or habitation. **1896** 'G. SETOUN' *Robert Urquhart* xxiii. 248 He may ha'e so putten the words in my mouth just to ease the wa-gaun o' a faithfu' servant. **1899** CROCKETT *Kit Kennedy* ii. 13 Christopher Kennedy had lost his position .. for drunkenness, and even at that very moment with his companions he was celebrating his way-going.

b. *attrib.*, as *way-going premium*; **way-going crop** (see quots.).

1773 *Harpham Inclos. Act* 8 Such farmer .. shall .. have a *way going crop or crops following him. **1797** J. BAILEY & G. CULLEY *Agric. Northumbld.* ii. 25 Where the tenant quits on the 12th of May, he is allowed to have a crop of corn from off two-thirds of the arable lands; this is called the way-going crop. **1855** H. BROOM *Comm. Common Law* (1856) 13 A custom that a tenant shall have the waygoing crop after the expiration of his term is reasonable and good. **1920** *Act 10 & 11 Geo. V*, c. 76 §10 (7) (f) The tenant shall, along with the last or waygoing crop, sow permanent grass seeds. **1881** *Times* 17 Mar. 4/5 They [*sc.* Irish tenants] care not to realize five years' rent for the *way-going premium which at any time they might receive.

Similarly **way-going** *a.*, departing, outgoing. *Sc.*

1812 Sir J. Sinclair *Syst. Husb. Scot.* II. 62 Much depends on the conditions obligatory on the way-going tenant. **1845** R. Hunter *Law Landl. & Tenant* Index, Waygoing tenant's right to value of fallow land.

waygoose. Now *dial.* or *Obs.* [Of obscure etymology; there is no evidence that the second element is to be identified with GOOSE *sb.*] (See quots. and cf. WAYZGOOSE.)

1683 Moxon *Mech. Exerc., Printing* 361 It is also customary for all the Journey-men to make every Year new Paper Windows..; Because that day they make them, the Master Printer gives them a Way-goose; that is, he makes them a good Feast, and not only entertains them at his own House, but besides, gives them Money to spend at the Ale-house or Tavern at Night. These Way-gooses, are always kept about Bartholomew-tide. And till the Master-Printer have given this Way-goose, the Journey-men do not use to Work by Candle Light. **1833** Timperley *Songs of the Press* 23 Song, Composed for a Printers' Way Goose. **1847** Halliwell, *Way-goose*, an entertainment given by an apprentice to his fellow-workmen. *West.* **1857** Wright *Dict. Obs. & Prov. Engl., Way-goose*, an annual feast among printers. It appears to have been formerly a practice peculiar to Coventry, where it was usual in the large manufactories of ribbons and watches, as well as amongst the silk dyers, at the season of the year when they commenced the use of candles, to have what was called a *way-goose*, when all the persons of the establishment were accustomed to go a short distance into the country and partake of an entertainment provided for the occasion at the charge of their employers: and this practice uniformly preceded the working by candle-light. **1865** J. Brown *J. Leech*, etc. (1882) 13 *note*, Once a year they attend the annual dinner of the firm, at which compositors, readers, printers, machinemen, clerks, etc. dine. This dinner is called the 'Way Goose', and is often referred to in *Punch.* **1886** *Cheshire Gloss., Waygoose* or *wayzgoose*, an entertainment given to journeymen workmen.

'way-in, *a. slang.* [f. WAY *adv.* + IN *adv.*, after WAY OUT *a.*] Conventional; fashionable, sophisticated.

1960 *N.Y. Times Mag.* 12 June 19/1 A famous lady columnist with a way-out taste in millinery but a way-in taste in film fare. *Ibid.* 78/4 Many artists..have sought refuge in..way-in or way-out religious conversions. **1967** *Punch* 29 Nov. 817/2 There's a real way-in guy looking like how a guy on *The Times Saturday Review* ought to look like.

waying ('weɪɪŋ), *vbl. sb. poet. nonce-wd.* [f. WAY *v.* + -ING[1].] A going away; departure.

1922 Hardy *Late Lyrics & Earlier* 120 So, with this saying, 'Good-bye, good-bye,' We speed their waying.

wayk(e, wayken: see WEAK, WEAKEN.

wayl, obs. form of VAIL *v.*[1], WALE *v.*[1]

waylaway, obs. form of WELLAWAY.

waylay (weɪ'leɪ, 'weɪleɪ), *v.* Pa. t. and pa. pple. **waylaid** (weɪ'leɪd, 'weɪleɪd). Also 6-7 **way-laye,** 6-9 **way-lay.** [f. WAY *sb.*[1] + LAY *v.*[1] (where see senses 18 b, c.), after MLG., MDu. *wegelâgen* (= MHG. and early mod.G. *wegelagen, weglagen*, superseded in later German by *wegelagern*), f. *wegelage*:—OS., OHG. **wega lâga* besetting of ways (*wega* genit. pl. of *weg* way + *lâge* besetting, ambush, related to LAY *v.*[1]).]

1. *trans.* To lie in wait for (a person or thing) with evil or hostile intent; to seize or attack in the way.

1513 in G. P. Scrope *Castle Combe* (1852) 292 The saynd [*sic*] Robert Bruer, Richard Pollen, John Lewis cam and wayelaynd [*sic*] my kepers man, and so hert hyem. **1596** Shaks. *1 Hen. IV*, I. ii. 183 [They] shall robbe those men that wee haue already way-layde. **1601** —— *Twel. N.* III. iv. 176, I will way-lay thee going home, where if it be thy chance to kill me [etc.]. **1666** Dryden *Ann. Mirab.* ccii, Now on their Coasts our conquering Navy rides, Way-lays their Merchants, and their Land besets. **1674** Milton *P.R.* I. 184 How thou lurk'st..In Valley or Green Meadow to way-lay Some beauty rare. **1759** Johnson *Idler* No. 73 ¶3 The rich are neither way-laid by robbers, nor watched by informers. **1779** Forrest *Voy. N. Guinea* 144 Then we should be way-laid by armed corocoros. **1813** Scott *Rokeby* III. xii, Thou art a wanderer, it is said; For Mortham's death, thy steps way-laid. **1861** *Sat. Rev.* 7 Dec. 578 A screw-steamer of war ..waylaid the English Royal West India Mail steamer in the Bahama Channel..and brought her to by firing a round shot across her bows. **1883** *Manch. Guardian* 18 Oct. 4/7 A ruffian..waylaid her in the street and assaulted her in the most brutal manner.

b. *fig.*

a **1616** Beaum. & Fl. *Little Fr. Lawyer* II. iii, Dost thou way-lay me with ladies? **1635** Quarles *Embl.* III. Epig. ix, Thy soule's way-laid by sea; by Hell; by earth. **1680** C. Nesse *Church Hist.* 495 That Word of God *There must be ten horns* way-lays them. **1750** Johnson *Rambler* No. 69 ¶3 All the other Miseries, which way-lay our Passage through the World, Wisdom may escape, and Fortitude may conquer. **1760** Sterne *Tr. Shandy* III. vi, The accidents which unavoidably way-lay them.

c. To intercept and seize (a thing in transit). Also *fig.* to seize (an opportunity).

1599 B. Jonson *Ev. Man out of Hum.* Dram. Pers. (1600) A iij, He way laies the reports of seruices, & cons them without booke, [etc.]. **1639** Mayne *City Match* II. iii, Use stratagems To get her silver whistle, and way-lay Her pewter knots or bodkin. **1672** *Essex Papers* (Camden) I. 37, I..resolve to waylay all opportunityes for ye future. **1851** Helps *Comp. Solit.* iv. (1874) 43 The fond wife used to waylay and open large packets. **1856** Kane *Arct. Expl.* II. vii. 84 Hans has not returned. I give him two days more before I fall in with the opinion..that Godfrey has waylaid or seized upon his sledge.

2. *transf.* (without implication of hostility). To wait for (a person) in the way and accost; to stop (a person) in order to converse with him.

1612-15 Bp. Hall *Contempl., O.T.* XIX. i. (1625) 1355 The Prophet..way-layes the King of Israel, and sadly complaines of himselfe in a reall parable. *a* **1625** Fletcher *Chances* IV. i, Our loves shall now way-lay ye; welcome, Gentlemen. **1728** Sir R. Walpole *Let.* 8 Oct. in *10th Rep. Hist. MSS. Comm.* App. I. 241 Our scheme about the Duke of Riperda must be alter'd unlesse you can way-lay this Evening or to-morrow morning, & prevail wth him to alter his course. **1804** Wordsw. '*She was a Phantom*' 10 A dancing Shape, an Image gay, To haunt, to startle, and way-lay. **1807** Miss Mitford in L'Estrange *Life* (1870) I. iii. 62 The driver of the Reading coach is quite accustomed to be waylaid by our carriage. **1840** Dickens *Old C. Shop* xlviii, Being directed to the chapel [he] betook himself there, in order to waylay her, at the conclusion of the service. **1886** Ruskin *Præterita* II. 60, I have held it a first principle of manners not to way-lay other people. **1914** *Blackw. Mag.* Nov. 577 The canal lock-keepers waylay me for the latest information.

†**3.** To impede or intercept (a person) in his progress; to block the path of. Also, to impede or obstruct (an activity). *Obs.*

1625 Bacon *Ess., Usury* (Arb.) 543 For the Employment of Money, is chiefly, either Merchandizing, or Purchasing; And Vsury Way-layes both. **1649** Milton *Eikon.* viii. 68 Using a strange iniquity to require justice upon him whom he then waylayd and debarr'd from his appearance. **1660** Ingelo *Bentiv. & Ur.* I. (1682) 156 By this means we endeavour to way-lay an inconvenience which others accelerate by Excess in meats and drinks. **1681** Flavel *Right Man's Ref.* 170 'Tis our wisdom to way-lay our troubles. **1688** Bunyan *Jerus. Sinner Saved* (1886) 121 Art thou crossed, disappointed, and way-laid, and overthrown in all thy foolish ways and doings?

4. To beset or blockade (a road, position, district) with an armed force or the like. ? *Obs.*

1609 [Bp. W. Barlow] *Answ. Nameless Cath.* 292 The Pope caused them to bee staied from that meeting, way-laying the Coastes of Verona and Millan. **1618** J. Taylor (Water P.) *Pennyles Pilgr.* F 1 b, Then all the valley on each side being way-laid with a hundred couple of strong Irish Grey-hounds, they are let loose as occasion serues vpon the heard of Deere. **1757** Washington *Lett.* Writ. 1889 I. 498, I..ordered the passes of the mountains to be waylaid by commands from other places. **1784** Belknap *Tour to White Mts.* (1876) 19 The next morning they waylaid the road and killed these men. **1813** Scott *Rokeby* II. xiii, Is our path way-laid? **1828** W. Irving *Columbus* VIII. iii. II. 237 He spread his army through the adjacent forests; and waylaid every pass.

Hence **waylaid** *ppl. a.* **waylayer,** one who waylays. **waylaying** *vbl. sb.* and *ppl. a.* (Stress variable, as in the vb.)

1626 Breton *Fantasticks* C 4, The quarter Sessions take order with the way-layers. **1666** Dryden *Ann. Mirab.* xxv, Like hunted Castors, conscious of their Store, Their way-laid wealth to Norways coasts they bring. **1674** N. Fairfax *Bulk & Selv.* 71 Something..as powerful to check or bind motion, as the way-laying of a gross unweildy body. **1694** Motteux *Rabelais* V. xxvi. 125 As we went back to our Ships, we saw three Way-Layers [Fr. *trois guetteurs de chemins*], who having been taken in Ambuscado, were going to be broken on the Wheel. **1759** Dilworth *Life of Pope* 149 A lurking way-laying coward. **1828** Smeeton *Doings in London* 222 That fellow..is one of the way-layers, a contemptible class of thieves, who attend the waggon and coach-yards, pretending to be porters; they watch the country people, and offer their services to carry their parcels. **1855** Landor *Imag. Conv., Asin. Pollio & Licin. Calvus* i. Wks. 1876 II. 437 Wherever there are rich wayfarers there also are sly and alert waylayers. **1870** Morris *Earthly Par.* II. III. 501 Without a will for aught, did Bodli stand, Nor once cast eyes on the waylayer's band. **1872** Greg *Enigm. Life* v. 190 It [*sc.* death] continues the most *waylaying* thought of the thoughtful man, till he silences its importunity by listening to all it has to say, and reasoning it back into the tomb. **1897** 'O. Rhoscomyl' *White Rose Arno* 224 Ned ran rapidly over the history of the waylaying of Ithel.

wayle, obs. form of VAIL *v.*[2]

1601 W. Percy *Cuckqueanes & Cuckolds Errants* IV. i. (Roxb.) 48 Cause your Friggats Bonnets to wayle.

wayle: see WAIL *sb.*, *v.*, WALE *sb.*[1], *a.* (*a. absol.*).

†**waylead.** *Sc. Obs.* Forms: 6 **wayleid, -laud, walaid, waled.** [f. WAY *sb.*[1] + LEAD *sb.*[2]] An artificial watercourse leading to a mill; a mill-lead or mill-leat.

1547 *Reg. Mag. Sig. Scot.* 33/1 Cum molendino..cum.. aqueductu et cursu ac *le walaid* ejusdem. *Ibid.* 39/1 Lie waylaud. **1565** *Ibid.* 1583, 173/2 Cum *lie wayleid* pro deservitione dicti molendini. **1588** *Ibid.* 1591, 656/2 Molendinum..cum sequelis..*lie dam, waled et wattergait.*

'way-leave, 'wayleave. In 5 waylefe, -leve. [f. WAY *sb.*[1] + LEAVE *sb.*[1]] Permission to make and use a way for conveying coal from the pit-head across a person's land; the rent or royalty paid for such permission; the way or road constructed for the purpose. Also, permission to carry telephone wires over or along buildings, or to lay water-pipes or drains across private land, and the charge or rent payable therefor. More widely, a right of way granted by the owner of land to a particular body and for a particular purpose, often in return for payment; also, a document conferring the right.

1427-8 *Durham Acc. Rolls* (Surtees) 709 Elemosinario pro waylefe, 6*s.* 8*d.* **1431-2** *Ibid.* 711 Wayleve. **1661** in *N. & Q.* Ser. XII. XI. 391/2 (Lease of a coalmine) Vna cum bona et sufficienti wayleave et stayleave in per et trans territorium de Casterton Fell..pro omnibus..carriagiis. **1725** *Portland Papers* (Hist. MSS. Comm.) VI. 104 These way leaves are an artificial road made for the conveyance of coal from the Pit to the Steaths on the riverside. *a* **1734** North *Life Ld. Keeper Guilford* (1742) 136 Another thing, that is remarkable, is their Wayleaves; for, when Men have Pieces of Ground between the Colliery and the River, they sell Leave to lead Coals over their Ground. **1739** *Enq. Price Coals* 14 For leave of way he must pay a consideration, called a way-leave. **1879** *Cases Crt. Session* Ser. IV. VI. 929 His property is advantageously situated for enabling him to demand wayleave. **1884** *Standard* 26 Sept. 4/2 The Telephone Companies are now permitted..to make their own arrangement for way-leaves. **1892** *Times* 23 Mar. 8/3 The Royal Commission on Mining Royalties and Way-leaves. *Ibid.* 9/4 As between towns the Post Office usually has way-leaves enough to accommodate trunk telephones. **1893** Neasham *North-country Sk.* 28 By agreement with Mr. Tempest who let them both wayleave and staithroom they were limited to an annual vend of 12000 chaldrons. **1928** H. G. Wells *Way World is Going* xi. 127 The exploitation of the air, as a means of..available travel, is hopeless without..secure wayleaves over Europe. **1930** *Times* 22 Mar. 19/2 We have also practically completed the Scottish overhead 'Grid' system for the Central Electricity Board... Owing to the difficulty of securing permission for wayleaves our work was necessarily interfered with. **1960** *Farmer & Stockbreeder* 1 Mar. 91/1 The Central Electricity Generating Board has no legal right of entry on your land without your permission or until such time as you have signed a wayleave. **1963** *Times* 24 May 16/6 A wayleave for a future subway linking the triangle with the Radcliffe Infirmary and passing under the Banbury and the Woodstock roads.

attrib. **1830** *Edin. Rev.* LI. 179 Those whose collieries are in that situation, have to pay way-leave rents. **1960** *Times Rev. Industry* Feb. 75/1 There is no way-leave payment. **1971** P. Gresswell *Environment* 215 Landowners are in a strong position to influence power line proposals through granting or refusing wayleave consent.

†**way-leet.** *Obs.* Forms: 3 **weienlæte, weynleate,** 4 **weonlete, weielot;** 4 **weilot,** 5 **weylate, -lete,** 6 **waileete,** 6-7 **wayleet(e.** [Partly repr. OE. *weȝȝelǽte*, partly *weȝa, weȝena ȝelǽte*: see WAY *sb.*[1] and LEET *sb.*[3]

The forms with *-lot, -late* show obscuration of vowel in the second syllable due to absence of stress.]

A place where two or more roads meet.

For *two-, three-, four-way-leet* see LEET *sb.*[3]

c **1000** *O.E. Glosses* (Napier) I. 4716 *Competalia*, weȝȝelæte. *c* **1205** Lay. 15509 Summe heo wenden to þan wude, summe to weien-læten [*c* **1275** weynleates]. **13..** in *Minor Poems fr. Vernon MS.* 341 Ren a-boute bi þe strete, Bi wey and bi weonlete. **1388** Wyclif *Gen.* xxxviii. 14 Sche sat in the weilot [Vulg. *in bivio itineris*] that ledith to Tampna. —— *2 Sam.* i. 20 Nether telle ȝe in the weilottis of Ascolon [Vulg. *in compitis Ascalonis*]. *c* **1430** *Pilgr. Lyf Manhode* III. xlviii. (1869) 161 A verrey dunghep in a weylate, ther eche at his time may come to make filthe. **1450** Myrc *Par. Pr.* 748 (ed. 1868) Al þat leyen her childeren at eny wey-letes or at eny church dores or at eny other comyn weyes and leveth hem.

wayless ('weɪlɪs), *a.* Also 4 **weyles,** 4, 7 **wayles,** 6-7 **wai-, waylesse, way-less,** 7 **waieless.** [OE. *weȝléas*: see WAY *sb.*[1] and -LESS. Cf. Icel. *vegalauss* out of the way, lost in the woods, MHG. *wegelôs*, mod.G. *weg(e)los.*] Having no way or road. Chiefly of a country, region, etc.: Trackless, pathless.

c **1100** *Voc.* in Wr.-Wülcker 149/20 *Auiaria*, weȝlæsa beara, *secreta nemora. Ibid.* 177/17 *Inuium*, unȝefere, *uel* weȝleas pæð. **1387** Trevisa *Higden* II. 219 Man..fel.. out of hous in to maskynge and wayles contray [L. *de domo ad devium*]. **1398** —— *Barth. De P.R.* XIV. lii. (Tollemache MS.) A weyles wildirnesse [L. *invia solitudo*]. **1591** Sylvester *Du Bartas* I. v. 389 If without wings we fly.. Through hundred sundry way-less wayes addrest. **1612** Drayton *Poly-olb.* ii. 164 As though the peopled townes had way-less deserts been. **1630** Drumm. of Hawth. *Flowres of Sion, Hymne Fairest Faire* 162 With wonders new my Spirits range possest, And wandring waylesse in a maze them rest. **1690** C. Nesse *O. & N. Test.* I. 462 He was also their courteous companion in all their wayless ways. **1821** R. S. Hawker *Cornish Ballads*, etc. (1904) 258 Joys such as these, Visions of wayless fancy, were the fire That burnt within me. **1901** 'Zack' *Tales Dunstable Weir* 151 The bush which from his account was wide-spreading and wayless.

Hence **'waylessness.**

1871-4 Hort *The Way*, etc. i. (1894) 37 The delightfulness of the opening world depends in no small measure on its semblance of waylessness.

wayll, obs. Sc. form of WELL *adv.*

waylle, variant of VAIL *sb.*[1] (advantage, profit).

a **1550** *Vox Populi* iv. 115 in *Skelton's Wks.* (1843) II. 405 Lett marchantmen goe sayle For that ys ther trwe waylle.

waylle, var. VAIL *v.*[1]; obs. f. WALE *sb.*[2]

waylor(e, obs. forms of VALOR.

a **1483** in *Eng. Gilds* (1870) 313 Every person..that ys of the waylore of xx. *li.* of goodes, and aboffe. *Ibid.* 314 Euery seruant..that takyt wagys to the waylor of xx. *s.* and a-boffe.

†**way-maker.** *Obs.*

1. One who makes or mends roads.

1483 *Cath. Angl.* 405/2 A Way maker or mender, *portitor.* **1609** in F. Devon *Issues Exch., Jas. I* (1836) 95 To Thomas Norton, his Majesty's way-maker, appointed to oversee the performance of the mending of the highways..£29. 10s.

2. A person or thing that prepares the way for another; a forerunner, precursor; a prelude (*to*).

1574 T. Newton *Health Mag.* T j b, Sleepe at noone..is a foremessanger or way-maker to Feuers, Apostumations, and Abscesses. *c* **1614** SIR C. CORNWALLIS in Gutch *Coll. Cur.* I. 139 Which match, I conceived, had been a preparation, and a way-maker to this other. **1634** BP. HALL *Contempl., N.T.* IV. iv. 117 What was his [John Baptist's] errand, but to be the way-maker unto Christ? **1640** BASTWICK *Ld. Bishops* viii. I j, Now the spirit of Prelacie was the very beginning of the Apostacie, which was Antichrists way-maker.

ˈway-man. [WAY *sb.*[1]]

† **1.** A waywarden. *Obs.*

1570 in Toulmin Smith *Parish* vii. (1857) 509 Jhon Stone, Jhon Margorn, Waymen of West Ashton do give up their Accounts. **1630** in G. P. Scrope *Hist. Castle Combe* (1852) 336 That every housekeeper within the parish which hath noe ploughe, doe com or send one to dige or picke stones one day before the aforesayd day, being warned by the way-men.

† **2.** A traveller, wayfarer. *Obs.*

1638 BRATHWAIT *Barnabees Jrnl.* III. (1818) 83 Shew thy selfe a famous way-man. **1876** *Whitby Gloss., Wayman*, a journier.

3. A workman employed on the permanent way of a railway; a plate-layer.

1840 F. WHISHAW *Railw. Gt. Brit. & Irel.* 252 Waymen, who are paid by the contractors for keeping the permanent way in repair. **1885** *Pall Mall Gaz.* 7 Oct. 7/2 A party of waymen found that a wood and iron bridge.. had been.. destroyed by fire.

ˈwaymark, ˈway-mark, *sb.* An object, whether natural feature or artificial structure, which serves as a guide to the traveller. Also *fig.*

1611 BIBLE *Jer.* xxxi. 21 Set thee vp way-markes. *a* **1656** BP. HALL *Rem. Wks.* (1660) 2 Wherein it seems there was continual fire kept for the way-mark of travellers. **1703** THORESBY *Diary* (1830) I. 424 Now it is so naked that there is not so much as one [tree] left for a way-mark. **1780** COWPER *Progr. Error* 117 Is this the path of sanctity? Is this To stand a way-mark in the road to bliss? **1871** TYLOR *Prim. Cult.* I. 19 Survival in Culture, placing all along the course of advancing civilization way-marks full of meaning to those who can decipher their signs. **1882** PUSEY *Paroch. & Cathedr. Serm.* xv. 211 The brilliant way-marks in the corners of our else dark streets are the palaces for the drunken. **1899** BARING-GOULD *Bk. West* II. viii. 131 High towers.. serve as waymarks over land that was all formerly waste.

ˈwaymark, *v.* [f. the sb.] *trans.* To provide or identify (a path) with waymarks. Hence **ˈwaymarked** *ppl. a.*, **ˈwaymarking** *vbl. sb.*

1960 *Guardian* 5 Nov. 6/3 The Ramblers' Association.. is cleft.. over the question of 'waymarking' paths and routes by means of blobs of coloured paint. *Ibid.* 9 Nov. 8/3 The plan to provide 'waymarking' on some popular British fells. **1973** *Village* Autumn 51 Walkers on the Continent or in America find themselves well supplied with long-distance trails and with waymarked paths in tourist areas. **1982** *Walker's Britain* 328/2 There are still several stretches where the waymarking is incomplete because public rights of way have not been obtained. **1983** *Out of Town* July 72/2 Much effort and imagination has gone into waymarking the walks.

waymb, wayme, obs. forms of WAME.

† **wayˈment,** *sb. Obs.* Also 4 **weyment.** [a. OF. *waiment, weyment, guaiment,* f. *waimenter*: see next.] Lamentation.

c **1400** *Laud Troy Bk.* 4435 A gret wayment and hideous cry Might men here then witterly, That the Troyens made y-wys For the wounde of Philomenys. **1590** SPENSER *F.Q.* III. iv. 35 She made so piteous mone and deare wayment, That [etc.]. **1647** H. MORE *Song of Soul* II. i. III. ix, All things did augment My heavie plight, that fouly I blam'd the hest Of stubborn destiny cause of this wayment.

† **wayˈment,** *v. Obs.* Also 4–5 **waymente, weyment(e,** 4–5, 7 **wament,** 5–6 *Sc.* **woment, wement,** 6–7 **waiment.** [a. OF. *waimenter, weymenter, guaimenter,* f. *wai, guai* int., wo, alas; prob. after *lamenter* to lament.]

1. *intr.* To lament, wail; to sorrow bitterly.

1375 *Cant. Creat.* 177 in Horstm. *Altengl. Leg.* (1878) 126/2 þus seuentene dayes and more Alle þe fisches sorweden þore And waymentide wiþ Adam. *c* **1386** CHAUCER *Pars. T.* ¶230 Thilke science, as seith seint Augustyn, maketh a man to waymenten in his herte. *c* **1450** *Mirour Saluacioun* (Roxb.) 94 The whilk for hire two sons waymentid doelfully. **1530** PALSGR. 779/2, I wement, I make mone... It dyd my hert yll to here the poore boye wement whan his mother was gone. **1590** SPENSER *F.Q.* II. i. 16 For what bootes it to weepe and to wayment, When ill is chaunst? **1595** *Locrine* II. ii. 89 And therefore well may I wayment. **1678** LITTLETON *Eng.-Lat. Dict.*, To wament, *lamento.* **1814** CARY *Dante, Purg.* XXVI. 135 Sorely waymenting for my folly past. **1861** K. H. DIGBY *Chapel St. John* (1863) 182 The profane laity chuckling or waymenting when conferring professionally with one another on their.. gains, or losses.

refl. c **1450** *Merlin* xvi. 262 Whan he hadde thus hym longe waymented.

2. *trans.* To bewail, lament for.

c **1475** *Partenay* 3324 He thaim complained And waymented sore. **1566** GASCOIGNE *Jocasta* II. i. 57 And mee thy wretched dame,.. waymenting still Th' vnworthie exile thy brother to thee gaue. **1593** G. HARVEY *New Let. Notable Cont.* Wks. (Grosart) I. 296 Magnifique Mindes.. In grisly weedes His Obsequies waiment.

Hence † **wayˈmenting** *vbl. sb.* and *ppl. a.*

a **1340** HAMPOLE *Psalter* xxxiii. 21 The ded of synfulmen .. is werst.., thof it be endid in riches and honurs and waymentynge of men. *c* **1386** CHAUCER *Knt.'s T.* 137 The grete clamour and the waymentynge That the ladyes made at the brennynge Of the bodies. *c* **1470** HENRY *Wallace* II. 161 The pittows wementyng [*ed.* **1570** womenting], The wofull wepyng that was for his takyng. **1513** DOUGLAS *Æneis* IV. viii. 2 How mony sobbis gaif thow and womentingis? **1566** GASCOIGNE *Jocasta* v. v. 116, I will.. washe thy wounds with my waymenting teares. **1603** FLORIO *Montaigne* III. iv. 504 For their lost husbands they entreate their waymentings by repetition of the good and gracefull partes they were endowed with. **1621** MOLLE *Camerar. Liv. Libr.* II. xviii. 130 The.. pittifull waymenting of the people. **1883** R. W. DIXON *Mano* I. xvi. 53 How waymenting Came in joy's place.

† **waymenˈtation.** *Obs.* [f. WAYMENT *v.* + -ATION.] Lamentation.

c **1403** LYDG. *Temple of Glas* 949 Of him I had so gret compassiuon, Forto reherse his weymentacioun, That.. I want connyng, his peynes to discryue. *c* **1425** *St. Eliz. Spalbeck* in *Anglia* VIII. 113/43 She schewith in weymentacyouns and turmentz hir owne compassyone. *c* **1450** *Merlin* xx. 347 Thus wente kynge Rion, makynge grete sorowe and weymentacion in-to his contrey.

waymot, var. WEMOD *a. Obs.*, wrathful.

wayn(e: see VAIN *a.*, VEIN *sb.*, WAIN *sb.*[1], *sb.*[2], *sb.*[3], *v.*, WANE *sb.*[1], *sb.*[2], *v.*, WEAN *v.*

waynd, Sc. variant of WONDE *v. Obs.*

wayneschot, -scot, etc.: see WAINSCOT.

waynge, obs. f. WANG[1].

† **waynoun.** *Obs. rare.* [a. OF. *waignon*, north-eastern var. of *gaignon* dog, cur, scoundrel.] A worthless person, scoundrel.

a **1310** in Wright *Lyric P.* xv. 47 Ther me calleth me fulle flet, ant waynoun wayte-glede.

† **waynpain.** *Obs.* Forms: 4 **waynepayne, weine pain,** 4–5 **waynpain, -payn,** 5 **-pane, wanpayn, -pan.** [a. OF. *wagnepan*, north-eastern form of *gaignepain*: see GAINPAIN.]

1. A sort of gauntlet; = GAINPAIN I.

c **1300** *Wills & Invent. N.C.* (Surtees) I. 16, ij galeæ xiij[s]. iij[d]. j par de Waynpayns & ij brasers vj[s]. viij[d].

2. A servant or scullion.

Freq. in the *Durham Acc. Rolls*, both as an appellative and as a proper name.

13.. *Sir Beues* (A.) 926, I will þe douȝter ȝeue To a weine pain. **1364** *Durham Acc. Rolls* (Surtees) 44 Le Waynpain, 2*d.* **1438–9** *Ibid.* 71 Cuidam famulo coquine vocato Waynpayn.

waynscot(e, -skot(e, etc.: see WAINSCOT.

waynt, waynte: see QUAINT *a.*, WANTY.

way off, *adv.* and *a.* orig. *U.S.* [f. WAY *adv.* + OFF *adv.*] **A.** *adv.* Far away.

1853 G. C. HILL *Dovecote* 29, I found her 'way off in them woods yonder! **1897** S. CRANE *Third Violet* xxxiii. 215, I am going somewhere; but I don't know where. 'Way off, anyhow. **1897** KIPLING *Captains Courageous* iii. 60 'Way off yander's the *Day's Eye.* **1929** D. H. LAWRENCE *Pansies* 72 Out of the soul's middle to the middle-most sun, way-off, or in every atom. **1952** *Manch. Guardian Weekly* 22 May 7/2 Way off to the right was a beery Irishman.

2. Far from the intended target; greatly mistaken, quite wrong.

1892 *Harper's Mag.* Feb. 438/2 The papers are generally 'way off in some things. **1906** A. H. LEWIS *Confessions of Detective* I. i. 10 'You're dead wrong, Doc!' broke in Mugsey... 'You're 'way off.' **1962** J. GLENN in *Into Orbit* 209 My attitude indications on the instrument panel are way off. **1973** 'H. HOWARD' *Highway to Murder* x. 118 Seemed first impressions could be 'way off. **1977** H. KAPLAN *Damascus Cover* (1978) iv. 33 On the pistol range Ari discovered.. that his aim was way off.

B. *adj.* **1.** Usu. **ˈway-off.** Distant.

1870 A. D. WHITNEY *We Girls* (1871) xi. 229 General and Mrs. Ingleside.. had come from their way-off, beautiful Wisconsin home. **1928** D. H. LAWRENCE *Woman rode Away* 93 The way-off things like the sun.

† **wayour.** *Obs.* Forms: 4 **waier, wayer(e, wayh(o)ur,** 4–5 **wayour,** 5 **wayor, -owre, wayȝowr, wayir, wayr,** 5–6 **wayre.** [a. AF. *wayour* (Britton) = OF. *gayoir*, f. *waer, gaer* (mod.F. *guéer*) to bathe (a horse) in a pond or stream.] A horse-pond.

1310 *Bridgwater Corp. MSS.* No. 833 Sicut itur versus le West Wayhur. *c* **1330** R. BRUNNE *Chron. Wace* 11186 Siþen in wayers to watre & wasche, Sythen to wype, & to mangers teye [their steeds]. **1374** *Bridgwater Corp. MSS.* No. 488 Iacentem in le longheyys eiusdem ville versus le Wayere. *c* **1440** *Promp. Parv.* 513/2 Wayowre, stondynge watyr [wayowr, or wayȝowr, water *P.*], *piscina.* *c* **1450** BURGH *Secrees* 1877 Slepyng wayours, watrys incertayn, Salt, bittir, and fumous. *c* **1475** *Pict. Voc.* in Wr.-Wülcker 800/15 *Hec pissina*, a wayir. **1488** *Maldon* (Essex) *Liber B* fol. 39 They come to the townes ende at the wayour. **1530** PALSGR. 286/1 Wayre where water is holde, *gort.*

way out, *adv.*, *a.*, and *sb.* orig. *U.S.* [f. WAY *adv.* + OUT *adv.*] **A.** *adv.* Far out, far away. *colloq.*

1868 G. A. CUSTER *Let.* 20 Feb. in E. Custer *Following Guidon* (1890) 53 They had braved the perils.. in order to bring us, 'way out here, news from our loved ones. **1882** *Congress. Rec.* 9 Mar. 1758/1 Instead of that they go way out to Peoria, Illinois. **1933** L. I. WILDER *Farmer Boy* xvi. 119 This country.. goes 'way out beyond Kansas.. down to the Pacific Ocean. **1944** M. LASKI *Love on Supertax* xi. 102 After a.. journey by 'bus, Clarissa alighted way out on the North Circular Road. **1977** *Chicago Tribune* 2 Oct. v. 2/2 There is more clout in the Senate, you see, than way out west away from the mainstream.

B. *adj.* Also **way-ˈout.** **1.** Far removed from reality or from convention; extreme; progressive, avant-garde, advanced. *slang.*

1958 G. LEA *Somewhere there's Music* xix. 164, I turn on [*sc.* smoke marijuana] a little and I get way out. **1959** *Encounter* June 42/2 The ego-ideal of the Beatnik is the 'cool hipster'—..the man who is 'way out'. **1959** N. MAILER *Advts. for Myself* (1961) 296 Mine [*sc.* my hypothesis] is interesting, mine is way out (on the avenue of the mystery along the road to 'It') but still I am just one cat in a world of cool cats. **1961** *Life* (Internat. ed.) 8 May 44 The way-out world of micro-electronics. **1964** J. DUNBAR in Hamblett & Deverson *Generation X* 179 One thing I like about Cambridge, people don't try to be too way out. At places like Oxford, or Reading, I've seen blokes going around barefoot and wearing ear-rings. **1967** *Times* 13 Apr. 23 The 'way out' field of nuclear fusion. **1972** J. PHILIPS *Vanishing Senator* III. iii. 162 Vardon thought up a way-out scheme to commit a murder. **1979** *Dædalus* Spring 141 These [*sc.* Radio Città in Bologna and Radio Alice] were 'way-out' examples of local radio. **1982** BARR & YORK *Official Sloane Ranger Handbk.* 38/1 She would not wear Art Nouveau jewels (too way out).

2. Greatly mistaken. *slang.*

1959 M. SUMMERTON *Small Wilderness* viii. 112 You're way out, Puss. If anybody has got a perfect alibi.. it's Cliff. **1965** *New Statesman* 7 May 721/3, I would not presume to argue with Edward Hyams on matters botanical, but he is way out on snakes.

C. *sb.* A person who holds extreme or unconventional views.

1968 *Manch. Guardian Weekly* 17 Oct. 19 The drop-outs have copped out, the redskins have bitten the dust, the way-outs have faced the nitty-gritty (truth). **1970** *Encycl. Sci. Suppl.* (Grolier) 158 Two years ago we were considered way-outs. Nobody knew what conservation meant.

Hence **way-ˈoutness** *slang*, unconventionality.

1965 *Tablet* 27 Nov. 1327/1 Some way-outness prevents him from acquiescing in the wisdom of acceptance. **1968** R. V. BESTE *Repeat Instructions* i. 10 That's the kind of way-outness that should have made Security suspicious. **1979** S. SMITH *Survivor* xvii. 185 Young people of all degrees of 'way-outness'.

wayr(e: see VAIR, WARE, WEAR *v.*[1], WEIR.

† **way-rope,** altered form of WARROPE.

1641 S. SMITH *Herring Buss Trade* 8 To every Seizon belongs a Buye, which is fastned to the Way-rope.

wayryngle, variant of WARIANGLE *Obs.*

-ways, the terminal element of certain advs., was originally a use of the genitive of WAY *sb.*[1]

1. Many phrases consisting of the genitive of *way* (in various senses) qualified by an adj., were formerly used adverbially (see WAY *sb.*[1] 23 a). The earliest known examples are in the Peterborough Chronicle (first hand, A.D. 1124) which twice has *óðres weȝes* in the sense 'by another route'; in this phrase the adj. appears uninflected before the end of the 12th c. (see OTHERWAYS). Similarly *alles weis, nanes* (*nones*) *weis* occur early in the 13th c., becoming *always, noways* in the 14th c. On the analogy of these words were subsequently formed †*everyways* (1398), *anyways*, †*likeways* (16th c.), and (from descriptive adjs.) *crossways, longways, straightways* (16th c.), *broadways* (18th c.).

2. A solitary instance of an adv. f. sb. + *-ways* before the 16th c. is †*needways* 'necessarily', occurring in the *Cursor M.* (*a* 1300) and in Barbour. In the later formations the general sense is 'in a specified direction'; so *endways, lengthways, sideways* (16th c.), *edgeways, breadthways* (17th c.), *sternways* (19th c.), *sunways*.

3. As there is no perceptible difference of function between the adverbial genitive and the adverbial accusative, most of the advs. in *-ways* have synonyms in *-way*. Further, most of the advs. in *-ways* are synonymous with actual or possible parallel formations in -WISE; and the similarity of sound of the two suffixes has given rise to the notion that they are mere alternative forms of one and the same ending. Johnson's erroneous statement (s.v. *Way*) that '*way* and *ways* are often used corruptly for *-wise*' has probably led many to prefer *-wise* to *-ways* or *-way* on the ground of supposed correctness. Cf. *alway, always*, †*alwise*; *anyway, anyways, anywise*; *breadthways, -wise*; *broadway, -ways, -wise*; *crossway, -ways, -wise*; *edgeway, -ways, -wise*; *endway, -ways*; *everyway*, †*-ways*; *lengthways, -wise*; †*likeways* (obs.), *likewise*; *longways, -wise*; *noway, -ways, -wise*; *otherways, -wise*; *sideway, -ways, -wise*; *straightway, -ways*, †*-wise*; *sunway, -ways, -wise*.

4. The combinations of *-ways* are, unlike those of *-way*, hardly ever used as adjs., with the exception of SIDEWAYS.

waysande, obs. form of WEASAND.

ways and means.

Formerly also *means and ways*, *moyens and ways*, *ways and grounds*: see WAY *sb.*^{1} 13 b. Cf. F. *voies et moyens* (? after Eng. Parliamentary use).

1. a. The methods and resources which are at a person's disposal for effecting some object.

1433 *Rolls of Parlt.* IV. 449/2 All the weys and menes by the whiche yei mowe enhaunce ye prises of her Merchandises. **1483** in *Lett. Rich. III & Hen. VII* (Rolls) I. 48 His grace is wele content that his said commissioners finde suche weyes and meanes as the said Sir Rauff shalle move frely without enpechement or trouble. **1561** T. HOBY tr. *Castiglione's Courtyer* III. (1577) O viij, After he had long attempted by all wayes and meanes to compasse hir. **1583** WHITGIFT *Serm.* (1589) C 5 b, Gregorie.. sought also waies and means secretly to murther him. **1699** G. HARVEY *Van. Philos. & Physick* v. 40 To preserve Health.. no better ways and means can be used, than applying at certain intervals, to those cleansers or abstersives here before mentioned. **1710** STEELE *Tatler* No. 195 ¶6, I send with this, my Discourse of Ways and Means for encouraging Marriage. *a* **1737** M. GREEN *Seeker* 30 Dominion and wealth are the aim of all three, Tho' about ways and means they may disagree. **1775** BURKE *Sp. Concil. Amer.* 22 Mar. 56 Fortunately I am not obliged for the ways and means of this substitute to tax my own unproductive invention. **1848** DICKENS *Dombey* liii, He has been devising ways and means all the way here of explaining himself, and has been satisfied with none. **1882** 'EDNA LYALL' *Donovan* xv, It was true that there were ways and means of raising money. **1905** P. LANDON *Lhasa* II. 136 In Tibet there are ways and means unknown to western nations.

†**b.** rarely in sing. ***way and mean***. *Obs.*

c **1400** *Apol. Loll.* 83 In þe þrid maner is a þing seid better þan an oþer, in þis, as it helpiþ better by sum wey and mene to þe ȝend of a þing, þan an oþer doþ. **1500–20** DUNBAR *Poems* lxxvii. 70 The for to pleis thay socht all way and mein. [**1530** PALSGR. 287/2 Wey or meane, *acheison*.]

2. a. *spec.* In *Legislation*: Methods of procuring funds or supplies for the current expenditure of the state. Also *attrib.*

Committee of Way and Means. (*a*) A committee of the whole House of Commons, which sits to receive the annual financial statement from the Chancellor of the Exchequer, and to consider the means of procuring the necessary annual supply. (*b*) *U.S.* A standing committee of the House of Representatives, to which are referred bills dealing with revenue, tariff, etc.

1644 *Jrnl. Ho. Comm.* III. 509/1 This Committee, or any Four of them, is to consider of all Ways and Means for raising of Monies.. and to make Report to the House. **1685** *Ibid.* IX. 759/1 The House then.. resolved into a Committee of the whole House, to consider of the Ways and Means to raise his Majesty's Supply. **1695–6** LUTTRELL *Brief Rel.* IV. 16 The commons were yesterday in a committee of the whole house upon wayes and means for raising two millions. **1695** (*title*) An Essay upon ways and means of supplying the war. [By C. Davenant.] **1737** *Gentl. Mag.* VII. 654/1 When we take this Affair into our Consideration in the Committee of Ways and Means. **1738** JOHNSON *London* 245 Ye Senatorian Band, Whose *Ways and Means* support the sinking Land. **1767** STERNE *Tr. Shandy* IX. xi, The first Lord of the Treasury thinking of *ways and means*, could not have returned home, with a more embarrassed look. **1785** *Rolliad, Prob. Odes* xi. 92 Rapt in St. Stephen's future scenes, I sit perpetual Chairman of the Ways and Means. **1798** T. JEFFERSON *Let. to J. Madison* 26 Apr., Writ. 1854 IV. 237 The Committee of Ways and Means have voted a land tax. **1824** MACAULAY *Prophetic Acct. Epic Poem* Misc. Writ. 1860 I. 149 His Lordship.. advises him [Mr. Vansittart] to look after the ways and means, and leave questions of peace and war to his betters.

attrib. **1867** *Oregon State Jrnl.* 5 Jan. 2/2 The Ways and Means Committee decided to postpone an action on Mr. Boutwell's bill. **1919** *Lit. Digest* 22 Mar. 21/2 Mr. Fordney, of Michigan,.. will probably be.. Chairman of the Ways and Means Committee. **1973** B. J. SIMS *Suppl. to Sergeant on Stamp Duties* (ed. 6) A55 This section and the associated Ways and Means Resolution provides powers whereby changes in stamp duty may be given effect to by means of a Budget Resolution. **1977** *Time* 12 Dec. 34/2 Al Ullman, the House Ways and Means chairman, has been pleading with Carter for a 'minimalist' rather than a 'maximalist' tax bill.

fig. **1699** GARTH *Dispensary* VI. 108 No Ways and Means their Cabinet employ, But their dark Hours they waste in barren Joy.

b. Pecuniary resources in general.

† ***to be upon ways and means***, to be trying to raise money.

1738 *Gentl. Mag.* VIII. 41/2 So have I known a buxom lad.. taught by kind mamma at home; Who gives him many a well try'd rule, With ways and means—to act a fool. **1760** FOOTE *Minor* II. Wks. 1799 I. 250 People that are upon ways and means, must not be nice. **1791** SMEATON *Edystone L.* §313 And whenever it shall appear to be necessary to renew it [*sc.* the gilding], I doubt not but ways and means will be found. **1869** A. MACDONALD *Love, Law & Theol.* x. 159 The party then adjourned to McGroggy's large room, and.. resolved themselves into a committee of ways and means. **1872** GEO. ELIOT *Middlem.* lviii, She had not yet had any anxiety about ways and means. **1879** 'EDNA LYALL' *Won by Waiting* xxi, She.. went to the nursery, to discuss ways and means with Bella's nurse.

wayse, obs. form of OOZE *sb.*^{3} and of WASE.

c **1475** *Cath. Angl.* 409/2 (Addit. MS.) Wayse, *alga*.

'wayside. a. The side of a road or path, the land bordering either side of the way. Phr. ***to fall by the wayside*** [after Luke viii. 5: see quot. 1526], to fail to stay the course, to drop out.

? *a* **1400** *Morte Arth.* 1713 They are enbuschede one blonkkes, with baners displayede, In ȝone bechene wode appone the waye sydes. **1526** TINDALE *Luke* viii. 5 As he sowed some fell by the waye syde. **1550** CROWLEY *Epigr.* 221 By the waye syde, hym chaunced to se A pore manne that craued of hym for charitie. **1673** RAY *Journ. Low C.* 19 Among the Corn by the way-sides as we went. **1752** J. HILL *Hist. Anim.* 498 This species is very frequent with us especially on heaths and by way-sides. *a* **1784** JOHNSON in Mrs. Piozzi *Anecd.* (1786) 5 A stone he saw standing by the way-side, set up.. in honour of a man who had leaped a certain leap thereabouts. **1850** ANNE PRATT *Comm. Things of Sea-side* iii. 171 The wild-flowers, which grace every way-side. **1878** SWINBURNE *Poems & B.* Ser. II. *Before Sunset* 6 Lighted shade and shadowy light In the wayside and the way. **1893** MAX PEMBERTON *Iron Pirate* i, A crucifix that stood on the wayside by the hill-foot yonder. **1894** J. DAVIDSON *Ballads & Songs* 121 All the waysides now are flowerless. **1965** *New Statesman* 7 May 719/1 Responding to persuasion, young wives go back into teaching... Some toughen and survive, others fall by the wayside. **1973** *Times* 24 May 10/1 She went to San Diego for a world junior tournament last year and fell by the wayside only because of a marker's error. **1977** L. T. MILIC in Bond & McLeod *Newslett. to Newspapers* I. 41 As society changes, so must the tone of a publication or it falls by the wayside.

b. *attrib.* passing into *adj.* Of or pertaining to the wayside; situated on, lying near, occurring, growing or living by the wayside. ***wayside pulpit***, a board, usu. placed outside a place of worship, displaying a religious text or maxim.

1807 J. RUICKBIE (*title*) The Way-side Cottager; consisting of Pieces in Prose and Verse. **1845** J. SAUNDERS *Cab. Pict. Engl. Life, Chaucer* 17 The little wayside chapels, erected for the accommodation of travellers. **1861** MISS JANE M. CAMPBELL *Hymn*, '*We plough the fields*' He paints the wayside flower. **1878** B. TAYLOR *Deukalion* III. vi. 132 Free as the wayside brook to whoso thirsts. **1883** S. C. HALL *Retrospect* II. 388 The coach stopped to change horses at a way-side inn. **1906** PETRIE *Relig. Anc. Egypt* xiii. 85 Such were the places for wayside devotions and passing prayers. **1925** *Advertising World* Dec. 302/2 (*heading*) How the 'wayside pulpit' scheme was organized. **1932** Q. D. LEAVIS *Fiction & Reading Public* II. iv. 193 An inspection of the slogans displayed on Wayside Pulpits.. reveals that they are largely devoted to denunciation of an attitude described as pessimistic. **1976** *Church Times* 20 Feb. 11/1 'My greed is another's need' and 'Live simply that others may simply live' have become familiar slogans on wayside pulpits and in parish magazines. **1981** F. INGLIS *Promise of Happiness* iii. 93 We most of us *know* when we are lying. My wayside pulpit-point is that we no longer care very much.

wayst, wayster: see WASTE, WASTER.

way station. *U.S.* Also **way-station.**

a. An intermediate station on a railway route, a way-side station. Also *transf.*

1850 *Ann. Rep. Railroad Corp. Massachusetts 1849* 21 Way stations for express trains. **1854** *Harper's Mag.* VIII. 566/2 The boats touched at most of the prominent towns on the river, to land such passengers as might desire to disembark at 'way-stations'. **1855** [see LOCK *v.*^{1} 7 d]. **1856** OLMSTED *Slave States* 53 Twenty minutes spent at way-stations. **1881** R. G. WHITE *Eng. Without & Within* ii. 44 If it is at a way-station, the passengers give up their tickets as they pass out through the station. **1891** C. ROBERTS *Adrift Amer.* 67 This was only what is called a way station. There was nothing but a section house and a long siding, besides the usual offices. **1912** F. J. HASKIN *Amer. Govt.* 210 Cities which are to-day mere way stations on the international routes of trade will grow into rich world centers. **1914** *Sat. Even. Post* 4 Apr. 52/2 At ten o'clock that night at a way-station the kid was ditched. **1934** A. WOOLLCOTT *While Rome Burns* 258 To fly by way of Ottawa, Point Barrow, and other way-stations. **1944** *Daily Progress* (Charlottesville, Va.) 21 July 1/8 The island [*sc.* Guam].. formerly served as a way-station on the trans-Pacific airroute to the East. **1976** N. THORNBURG *Cutter & Bone* vi. 134 It was.. a way station carefully restored and preserved to offer at least a semblance of its original state. **1984** *New Yorker* 9 July 43/2 The United States may.. use Moroccan facilities.. as way stations for combat troops destined for service in, say, the Middle East.

b. *fig.*, or in fig. context.

1892 *Congress. Rec.* 23 Mar. 2462/2 'Will the gentleman allow me to ask him a question?'.. 'The gentleman will excuse me. On a fast schedule I can not stop at way stations.' **1926** [see TECTAL *a.*]. **1948** MENJOU & MUSSELMAN *It took Nine Tailors* 10 She thought a theater was just a way station on the road to perdition. **1960** BRUNER & KLEIN in Kaplan & Wapner *Perspectives in Psychol. Theory* 65 There are corticofugal impulses that go down through the reticular formation to program selectivity of intake by way stations in the sensory system. **1973** *Sci. Amer.* July 52/1 Lymphocytes are found in high concentrations in the lymph nodes, way stations along the lymphatic vessels. **1978** W. GARNER *Möbius Trip* (1979) i. 12 The Belgravia apartment was not a home... It was a way station. **1982** H. KISSINGER *Yrs. of Upheaval* viii. 302 The cease-fire was merely a tactic, a way station toward their objective of taking over the whole of Indochina by force.

wayt(e, obs. ff. WAIT *sb.*, *v.*^{1}, *v.*^{2}, WEIGHT.

wayte, obs. Sc. f. WITE *sb.*; obs. f. WOT *v.*

wayth, variant of WAITH *sb.*^{1}, WOTHE *Obs.*

way-tree. *dial.* [? f. WAY *sb.*^{1} or WEIGH *v.*] (See quot.)

1854 ANNE E. BAKER *Northampt. Gloss.* s.v. *Batticle*, Sway-tree, Swingel-tree, and Way-tree, are synonymous in different parts of the county. **1856** J. C. MORTON *Cycl. Agric.* II. 726 *Way-tree*, (Lincolns.), the largest tree of the three 'swingle-trees'.

way up, *adv.* and *a.* orig. *U.S.* [f. WAY *adv.* + UP *adv.*] **A.** *adv.* Far up.

1851 'E. WETHERELL' *Wide, Wide World* I. xii. 150 Do you live 'way up there? **1862** O. W. NORTON *Army Lett.* 100 A minister of the gospel who was so wonderfully.. war-like way up in Erie. **1901** LEE BACON *Houseboat on Nile* 51 The Howadji.. was 'way up in that painter's paradise where [etc.]. **1946** K. TENNANT *Lost Haven* (1947) vii. 95 If you owned a bath, it put you 'way, 'way up in the world. **1956** H. KURNITZ *Invasion of Privacy* xiv. 92 She came down the stairs and I thought that was funny because they live way up top. **1972** *National Observer* (N.Y.) 27 May 14/1 Way up in the high-level social circles are those who are so rich they never, ever talk about money.

B. *adj.* Usu. **'way-up.** Excellent, first-class; of high social standing. *slang* (chiefly *U.S.*).

1887 F. FRANCIS *Saddle & Mocassin* 81 A real way-up cook, who could make chile-con-carne, tamales, and all the best Mexican dishes. **1902** KIPLING *Traffics & Discoveries* (1904) 17 He's a way-up barrister when he's at home. **1909** 'O. HENRY' *Roads of Destiny* xviii. 299, I want to be manager of something way up—like a railroad or a diamond trust or an automobile factory.

way-up (weɪ'ʌp), *sb. Geol.* [f. phr. (*which, this, the right*, etc.) *way up* (WAY *sb.*^{1} 9 a, UP *adv.*^{2} 9 a).] Orientation as regards which part is uppermost or was deposited last.

1958 *Q. Jrnl. Geol. Soc.* CXIII. 364 Way-up has been determined from graded bedding. **1969** BENNISON & WRIGHT *Geol. Hist. Brit. Isles* ii. 34 Certain characters, such as.. the way-up of shells, provide evidence of bottom conditions and the strength of currents. **1982** COLLINSON & THOMPSON *Sedimentary Structures* vi. 97/1 Aeolian structures could help to establish way-up in highly dipping sequences.

wayve, obs. form of WAIVE *v.*^{1} and *v.*^{2} *Obs.*

wayward ('weɪwəd), *a.* Not now in colloquial use. Also 4 **waiwerd, weiward,** 4–5 **weyward** (4 **-werd,** 6 **-warde**), 4, 6 **waywarde,** 6–7 **waiward** (6 **-warde**), (7 **waward**). [Aphetic f. AWAYWARD. Cf. *froward*.

The word has prob. often been apprehended as a derivative of WAY *sb.*^{1}, with the literal sense 'bent on going one's own way'; this notion seems to have influenced the development of meaning.]

1. Disposed to go counter to the wishes or advice of others, or to what is reasonable; wrongheaded, intractable, self-willed; froward, perverse. Of children: Disobedient, refractory.

In recent use the sense is somewhat milder, and perhaps always with some mixture of 2. If applied to conduct deserving severe moral reprobation it would now be apprehended as euphemistic.

c **1380** WYCLIF *Wks.* (1880) 376 As waiwerd clerkis wolden in seynt Austyns time haue done owte.. þis worde of þe gospelle. **1382** —— *Matt.* xvii. 16 A! thou generacioun vnbyleeful and weiward [Vulg. *perversa*]. *c* **1425** *Eng. Conq. Irel.* 142 Folk so weyward & so vnredy. *c* **1475** *Lament. Mary Magd.* 237 Wherfore ye lyke tyrantes wode & waywarde Now haue him thus slayne for his rewarde. **1526** *Pilgr. Perf.* (W. de W. 1531) 20 Than he waxeth testy and weywarde, and for every tryfell is impacyent and angry. **1557** NORTH *Gueuara's Diall Pr.* Gen. Prol. A ij, Many sorowes endureth the woman in nouryshyng a waywerde chylde. **1583** STUBBES *Anat. Abus.* II. 102 [They] shewe them selues either wilfull, waiwarde, or maliciouslye blinde. **1583** WHITGIFT *Serm.* (1589) C 6 b, The third kinde is of those that are conceited and wayward, who onely obey when they list, wherein they list, and so long as they list. **1590** SHAKS. *Com. Err.* IV. iv. 4 My wife is in a wayward moode to day. **1651** FEATLY *Abel Rediv., Reinolds* 486 A waward Patient maketh a froward Physitian. **1830** D'ISRAELI *Chas. I.* III. 97 Charles.. used the wayward genius with all a brother's tenderness. **1833** TENNYSON *New Year's Eve* 25, I have been wild and wayward, but you'll forgive me now. **1840** DICKENS *Old C. Shop* lxix, The wayward boy soon spurned the shelter of his roof, and sought associates more congenial to his tastes. **1894** LADY M. VERNEY *Verney Mem.* III. 326 Sir Ralph treated the wayward girl with a courtesy to which her mother never condescended.

absol. **1581** J. BELL *Haddon's Answ. Osor.* 63 b, Here our old peevish wayward, piketh a new quarell agaynst me. **1582** N. T. (Rhem.) *1 Pet.* ii. 18 Not only the good and modest, but also the waiward [Vulg. *dyscolis*]. **1912** *Spectator* 27 July 135/2 The two together supply the unwise and the wayward with the necessary instructions.

†**b.** Of things personified. Also of conditions, natural agencies, etc.: Untoward. *Obs.*

1567 TURBERV. *Epit.*, etc. 80 b, When waywarde Winter spits his gall. *a* **1586** SIDNEY *Arcadia* III. xxix. §1 What spiteful God.. hath brought me to such a waywarde case, that neither thy death can be a reuenge, nor thy ouerthrow a victorie. **1608** SHAKS. *Pericles* IV. iv. 10 Pericles Is now againe thwarting thy wayward seas. **1718** PRIOR *Solomon* II. 803 My Coward Soul shall bear it's wayward Fate. **1792** MME. D'ARBLAY *Diary* Apr., This wayward month opened upon me with none of its smiles. **1821** JOANNA BAILLIE *Metr. Leg., Ghost of Fadon* vii, We war with wayward fate.

†**c.** Of judgement: Perverse, wrong, unjust. Also of the eye: Perverted. *Obs.*

1382 WYCLIF *Matt.* vi. 23 ȝif thyn eiȝe be weyward [Vulg. *nequam*]. —— *Hab.* i. 4 Weywerd dom [Vulg. *judicium perversum*]. **1551** ROBINSON tr. *More's Utopia* (1895) 40 Suche prowde, lewde, ouerthwarte, and waywarde iudgementes [L. *superba, absurda ac morosa iudicia*]. **1668** DRYDEN *Dram. Poesy* 51 The wayward authority of an old man in his own house.

†**d.** Of words, actions, countenance: Indicating or manifesting obstinate self-will. *Obs.*

c **1450–1530** *Myrr. Our Ladye* 44 An other he [the Evil One] sturreth to make som weywarde token. **1599** SANDYS *Europæ Spec.* (1632) 94 If a man should heap together all the cholerike speeches, all the way-ward actions, that ever scaped from him in his life. **1630** *Pathomachia* I. iv. 8 From wayward words they passed on to bloody blowes. **1818** SCOTT *Rob Roy* xii, I shall never forget the diabolical sneer which writhed Rashleigh's wayward features.

†**e.** Of a disease, etc.: Not yielding readily to treatment, obstinate. *Obs.*

1541 R. COPLAND *Galyen's Terap.* 2 F iv, By the occasyon of them the vlcere is waywarde and rebel to be healed.

2. Capriciously wilful; conforming to no fixed rule or principle of conduct; erratic.

a **1533** BERNERS *Golden Bk. M. Aurel.* Let. iv. (1537) 118 b, Our lyfe is so doubtefull, and fortune so waywarde, that she dothe not alway threate in strykynge, nor striketh in thretnynge. **1604** DEKKER *Honest Wh.* I. B 1, My longings are not wanton, but wayward. **1750** GRAY *Elegy* 106 Hard by yon wood.. Mutt'ring his wayward fancies he would rove. **1832** WORDSW. *Loving & Liking* 44 Instinct is neither wayward nor blind. **1881** JOWETT *Thucyd.* I. 88 The movement of events is often as wayward and incomprehensible as the course of human thought.

b. *transf.* and *fig.* (of things).

1786 BURNS *Brigs of Ayr* 51 He left his bed and took his wayward rout, And down by Simpsons wheel'd the left about. **1799** WORDSW. *Poems Imag.* x. 28 In many a secret place Where rivulets dance their wayward round. **1817** SCOTT *Harold* II. xv, Thus muttering, to the door she bent Her wayward steps. **18..** SMITHSON *Usef. Bk. Farmers* 32 (Cassell) Send its rough wayward roots in all directions. **1905** *C.T.C. Gaz.* June 254/1 The wayward hoop is a fruitful cause of those accidents for which no one except the victim gets punished.

†'**wayward**, *v.* *Obs.* *rare*$^{-1}$. [f. prec. adj.] In passive: To be perversely prejudiced.

1586 STANIHURST *Ded.* in *Holinshed* II. 81 If anie be ouerthwartlie waiwarded, as he will sooner long for that I haue omitted, than he will be contented with that I haue chronicled.

[**wayward, -wards.** In the 17–18th c. the suffix *-ward(s* was often appended to phrases like *this way*, *that way*, *our way*, etc., preceded or not by *to* or *from*. (See -WARD 4, -WARDS 2, 5.) In printed books it was common to join the suffix to the word *way* (either with or without hyphen), but to leave the preceding words of the phrase without hyphen, so that *way-ward(s* or *wayward(s* has a fallacious appearance of being a word.

1599 *Warn. Faire Women* II. 548 To creep that way-ward whilst I live ile trye. **1662** PEPYS *Diary* 7 May, He left the Queene and fleete in the Bay of Biscay, coming this way-ward. **1682** WHELER *Journ. Greece* IV. 317 Turning back to our way-ward, we had the view of the highest Part of Parnassus. *Ibid.* VI. 474 Not very far from hence we cross'd a stream that ran from this Way-wards thither. **1686** F. SPENCE tr. *Varilla's Ho. Medicis* 169 He invited their children to a match of hunting that way-wards where he was to embarque. **1770** H. WALPOLE *Let. to G. Montagu* 31 Mar., I depend upon seeing you whenever you return this wayward.]

wayward(e, variant forms of VAWARD.

c **1530** BERNERS *Arth. Lyt. Brit.* civ. (1814) 497 The baner of Britaine sholde be in the way ward. *Ibid.* cv. 500 The King of Orqueney.. was put to the wayward with xxx. M. hawberts.

waywarden ('weɪwɔːd(ə)n). [f. WAY *sb.*^{1} + WARDEN *sb.*^{1}] A person (later, one of a board) elected to supervise the highways of a parish or district.

1776 G. WHITE *Selborne, To Barrington* 8 Jan., As to that [shrew-ash] on the Plestor, 'The late vicar stubb'd and burnt it,' when he was way-warden. **1829** in *Archaeologia* (1831) XXIII. 398 Mr. George Charman, the way-warden ..had frequently observed that the cattle resorted to a particular spot to rest. **1862** *Act 25 & 26 Vict.* c. 61 §9 The Highway Board shall consist of the Waywardens elected in the several Places within the District. **1863** TROLLOPE *Rachel Ray* I. 274 He was poor-law guardian and way-warden. **1872–4** JEFFERIES *Toilers of Field* (1892) 238 This man.. was enabled to do a quantity of hauling, flint-carting for the way-wardens, [etc.].

waywardly ('weɪwədlɪ), *adv.* [f. WAYWARD *a.* + -LY^2.] In a wayward manner.

1388 WYCLIF *Ecclus.* xxvii. 26 At the last he schal turne weiwerdli his mouth [Vulg. *pervertet os suum*]. **1395** PURVEY *Remonstr.* (1851) 45 These principlis vndirstonden weiwardli, and applied blasfemeli to a synful man. **1545** ELYOT *Dict.*, *Morosè*, waywardely. **1549** COVERDALE etc. *Erasm. Par. 1 John* ii. 7–11 He loued his enemies, yea those that turned waywardly from him and that were worthy of euyll. *a* **1586** SIDNEY *Arcadia* II. xxii. §2 Waiwardly proud; and therefore bold, because extreamely faultie. **1825** J. NEAL *Bro. Jonathan* III. 331 Thou art still a creature of.. courage and power. But why went such power so waywardly? **1880** *Academy* 23 Oct. 299/2 Taste changes so waywardly.

waywardness ('weɪwədnɪs). [f. WAYWARD *a.* + -NESS.] The quality of being wayward (see the various senses of the adj.).

1382 WYCLIF *Rom.* i. 29 Fulfillid with al wickidnesse,.. couetyse, weywardnesse [Vulg. *nequitia*]. *c* **1450–1530** *Myrr. Our Ladye* 152 Wretched were that persone that for eny waywardenes of harte wolde be vnreconcyled.. at that tyme. **1577** tr. *Bullinger's Decades* II. vi. 165 Our faulte and not the waywardnesse of God [*non Dei morositatem*] is the cause. **1676** HALE *Contempl.* II. *Lord's Prayer* 116 Therefore in great condescension to the waywardness of our Natures, he is often pleased to keep the Treasury of outward Blessings in his own hands [etc.]. **1796** MME. D'ARBLAY *Camilla* V. 528 The barbarous waywardness that could deprive me.. of the exquisite felicity of my lot! **1823** LAMB *Elia*, *Poor Relations*, The waywardness of his fate broke out against him with a second and worse malignity. **1853** DICKENS *Bleak Ho.* xviii, For all his waywardness, he took great credit to himself as being determined to be in earnest 'this time'. **1863** KINGLAKE *Crimea* (ed. 4) II. vi. 137 There was a waywardness in the course of the disease.. for which it is difficult to account. **1872** TENNYSON *Gareth & Lynette* 1150 He, who lets His heart be stirr'd with any foolish heat At any gentle damsel's waywardness. **1919** *19th Century* May 897 Parliament.. has rallied the people from the waywardness of rebellion.

¶ In lists of 'Proper Terms' mentioned as the typical attribute of haywards.

1486 *Bk. St. Albans* f vij, A waywardnes of haywardis.

†**waywards**, aphetic form of AWAYWARDS.

a **1400** *Pistill of Susan* 55 Heore wittes wel wai-wordus þei wrethen awai.

way-way, obs. form of WAWA.

way-wiser ('weɪwaɪzə(r)). Now *Hist.* Also 8–9 **-wizer.** [Formed after G. *wegweiser* (= Du. *wegwijzer*, Sw. *vägvisare*, Da. *vejviser*), f. *weg* WAY *sb.*^{1} + *weiser*, agent-n. f. *weisen* to show.

The Eng. sense is not found in the other Teut. langs. In German the word has, besides its primary sense 'one who or something which shows the way', several other meanings, the most common being 'guide-post', which is also current in Du., Da., and Sw.]

1. An instrument for measuring and indicating a distance travelled by road.

Of various forms, usually operated either by the step of the pedestrian or by the revolution of the wheels of the vehicle.

1651 R. CHILD in *Hartlib's Legacy* (1655) 70, I say twenty Ingenuities have been found even in our days, as Watches, Clocks, Way-wisers, [etc.]. **1654** EVELYN *Diary* 13 July, He [Dr. Wilkins] had above in his lodgings and gallery variety of shadows, dyals,.. a way-wiser, [etc.]. **1657** *Ibid.* 6 Aug., I went to see Colonel Blount, who showed me the application of the Way-wiser to a coach, exactly measuring the miles, and showing them by an index as we went on. *a* **1679** J. WARD *Diary* (1839) 160 An instrument calld a waywiser, by the motion whereof a man may see how many steps he takes in a-day. **1683** HOOKE in Birch *Hist. Roy. Soc.* (1757) IV. 231 It was one part of a way-wiser for the sea.. designed to keep a true account, not only of the length of the run of the ship through the water, but the true rumb or leeward way [etc.]. **1701** MOXON *Math. Instr.* 21 *Waywiser*, for the pocket; a movement, like a Watch to Number or count your steps or paces, in Order to find how far you walk in a day. *a* **1734** R. NORTH *Life Sir D. North* (1744) 202, I contrived a Way-wiser, and we both wrought upon it hard till it came to Perfection, and was fixed upon a Calash we used. **1886** *Cheshire Gloss.*, *Way-wizer*, a pedometer. [**1891** *N. & Q.* Ser. VII. XI. 195/2 The waywiser [of *c* 1800].. registers only up to twelve miles, after which distance the index must be again adjusted.]

fig. **1801** *Monthly Mag.* XII. 98 It is with the spying-glass of conjecture, not with the way-wiser of record, that the bearing of their sources must be made out.

¶ **2.** [In the German sense.] A guide-post, finger-post. *rare*$^{-1}$.

1855 W. WHITE *To Switz. & Back* x. 127 Why should one side of the mountains have all the crosses, and the other all the way-wisers?

waywode ('weɪwəʊd). Now *Hist.* Forms: 7–9 **waywode, -wood, weywode,** (7 **weiwode,** 8 **weyvode, -wod**), 8–9 **waiwode,** (8 **waivod, woewood**). [Var. of VAIVODE, repr. an early Magyar form of a common Slavonic title of office. Cf. mod.L. *wayvoda*.] = VOIVODE.

1661 *Mercurius Caled.* in *Sir A. Boswell's Poet. Wks.* (1871) 64 There is a considerable number of horses to carry on the work of the day; among others, a Waywood of Polonia hath a Tartarian horse. **1662** J. DAVIES tr. *Olearius' Voy. Ambass.* 7 The Weywode or Governour of Novogorod. **1739** ELTON in *Hanway's Trav.* (1762) I. I. iv. 11 We arrived at the city of Saratoff, and waited on the Weyvode. **1812** BYRON *Ch. Har.* II. xii. *Note*, Lusieri has laid his complaint before the Waywode. **1837** ALISON *Hist. Europe* xvii. (1848) V. 13 Their waywodes or military chieftains [in Poland]. **1905** *Sat. Rev.* 21 Oct. 522/2 There were hospodars in Wallachia and waywodes in Moldavia.

¶ **b.** = WAYWODESHIP.

1837 ALISON *Hist. Europe* xvii. (1848) V. 11 The waywodes and palatinates into which every province was divided [in Poland].. became divided against each other.

Hence '**waywodeship** [-SHIP], the province or district ruled by a waywode.

1684 *Scanderbeg Rediv.* iv. 62 [He] returned his thanks to the several Waywodeships. **1704** *Lond. Gaz.* No. 3988/1 General Reinschild.. is marching towards the Weywoodship of Cracow. **1908** *Contemp. Rev.* Aug. 226 The Servians desired to transform the territory inhabited by them into a Servian waywodeship.

way-worn, *a.* Worn or wearied by travel.

1777 POTTER *Æschylus, Choeph.* 350, I, like a stranger, harness'd in this coarse And way-worn garb. **1788** CROWE *Levesdon Hill* 14 By soft gradations of ascent to lead The labouring and way-worn feet along. **1824** MISS L. M. HAWKINS *Annaline* II. 24 [He had a] wayworn look and meagre aspect. **1836** W. IRVING *Astoria* II. 141 The wayworn and hungry travellers. **1866** LE FANU *All in Dark* xxi, The horses.. emerged from the inn-yard gate.. to replace the way-worn team.

fig. **1848** THACKERAY *Van. Fair* liii, That night.. she prayed humbly for that poor wayworn sinner.

waywort ('weɪwɜːt). Also 3 **waiwurt,** 5 **weyewourth,** 6 **weywort.** [f. WAY *sb.*^{1} + WORT. Cf. early mod.G. *weg(e)wurz*, synonym of G. *weg(e)wart(e* endive.] A name for †**a.** the saxifrage (*obs. rare*$^{-1}$); **b.** the pimpernel.

c **1265** *Voc. Plants* in Wr.-Wülcker 556/25 *Saxifragium*,.. waiwurt. *a* **1400–50** *Stockh. Med. MS.* p. 194 Pympernol or selfhol or weyewourth or morecrop: *ipia maior.* **1597** GERARDE *Herbal* Suppl., Waywort is Pimpernell. *Ibid.*, Weywort is *Ipia maior.* **1886** BRITTEN & HOLLAND *Plant-n.*, Way-wort. *Anagallis arvensis.*

wayzgoose ('weɪzguːs). [Alteration of WAYGOOSE, under which the earlier evidence for the word is given.

The eccentrically spelt form *wayzgoose*, which, although established in recent use, has not been found, exc. in Bailey's Dictionary, earlier than 1875, is prob. a figment invented in the interest of an etymological conjecture (see quot. 1731). Bailey's assertion that the word had the sense of 'stubble-goose' is unsupported, and is very unlikely; this allegation, and the accompanying fantastic misspelling of WASE, may have been suggested by the idea that the obscure word *waygoose* could be explained on the assumption that it had lost a *z*. (The *Eng. Dial. Dict.* refers to Cope's *Hampshire Glossary* for '*waze-goose*, a stubble-goose', but Cope's authority for this is a MS. word-list which, he says, 'contained many words that had certainly no relation to the dialect of the county'.) It seems clear that the genuine traditional form among printers was *waygoose*, and that the form *wayzgoose*, now prevailing, is a supposed correction following the authority of Bailey. The statement that goose was 'the principal dish' (or even that it was eaten at all) at the 'waygoose' dinner is destitute of evidence. It is possible that *waygoose* may be a corruption by popular etymology of some earlier word, but no satisfactory explanation has been found either in English or in any foreign language.]

Originally, an entertainment given by a master-printer to his workmen 'about Bartholomew-tide' (24 August), marking the beginning of the season of working by candle-light. In later use, an annual festivity held in summer by the employees of a printing establishment, consisting of a dinner and (usually) an excursion into the country.

1731 BAILEY (ed. 5), *Wayz*, a Bundle of Straw. *Wayz-goose*, a Stubble-Goose, an Entertainment given to Journey-men at the beginning of Winter. [**1833** TEMPERLEY *Songs of the Press* 23 *note*, Way Goose.— The derivation of this term is not generally known. It is from the old English word *wayz*, stubble. A wayz Goose was the head dish at the annual feast of the forefathers of our fraternity. '*Wayz Goose*, a stubble Goose, an entertainment given to journeymen at the beginning of Winter.'—Bailey.]

1875 SOUTHWARD *Dict. Typogr.* 137 The wayzgoose generally consists of a trip into the country, open air amusements, a good dinner, and speeches and toasts afterwards. **1895** *Surrey Mirror* 23 Aug. 2/7 The members of the typographical staffs of the *Surrey Advertiser* (Guildford) and the *Surrey Mirror* (Redhill) had their wayzgoose on Saturday last, when they journeyed to Brighton.

b. *attrib.*

a **1880** F. T. BUCKLAND *Notes & Jottings* (1882) 39 London printers generally have a 'wayzgoose' dinner in the autumn. **1897** F. T. BULLEN *Cruise of 'Cachalot'* 372 Carriages were chartered, an enormous quantity of eatables and drinkables provided, and away we went, a regular wayzgoose or bean-feast party.

‖**wazir**^{1} (wə'zɪə(r)). Also 9 **wezeer, wuzeer.** [Arab. *wazīr*, whence the Turkish *vezīr*: see VIZIER.] = VIZIER 1.

1715 J. STEVENS *Hist. Persia* 191 Kobad.. accordingly gave Orders to his Wazirs or Viziers. **1807** E. S. WARING *Tour Sheeraz* 27 We.. reached a Surae, built by a son of the late Wuzeer. **1839** LANE *Arab. Nts.* I. 2 King Shahriyár.. ordered his Wezeer to repair to him. **1902** E. G. BROWNE *Lit. Hist. Persia* vii. 256 The office of Wazír, for all the power and dignity which it carried with it, was a perilous one.

So **wazirate** (wə'zɪərət) = VIZIERATE 1, 2; **wa'zirship** = VIZIERSHIP 1.

1715 J. STEVENS *Hist. Persia* 163 Dividing them [*sc.* his dominions] all into four wazir, or Vizierships, that is, Governments. **1886** BURTON *Arab. Nts.* (abr. ed.) I. 173 After which time they entered upon the Wazirate, and the power passed into their hands as it had been in the hands of their father [the Wazir]. **1902** E. G. BROWNE *Lit. Hist. Persia* vii. 256 When the 'Abbásids came to the throne, the laws of the Wazirate were fixed. **1919** SIR S. LOW in *Edin. Rev.* Apr. 399 The country was annexed to the Wazirate.

Wazir^2 (wə'zɪə(r)). Also Waziri; 9 Vazírí, Vizeeree, Wuzeerá, etc. A member of a Pathan people of north-west Pakistan; also, this people collectively. Also *attrib.* or as *adj.*

1815 M. ELPHINSTONE *Caubul* III. iii. 385 The Vizeerees are said to be tall and muscular. **1838** in *Parl. Papers 1839* XL. 29 The Vezeree territory. **1842** C. MASSON *Journeys* I. vii. 100 A few Vazírí huts. **1847** H. B. EDWARDES *Diary* 3 Dec. (1911) 156 A very extensive triangular *Thull*, or sand, occupied by the Vizeeree tribes. **1851** R. G. LATHAM *Ethnol. Brit. Colonies* iv. 182 The mountaineers around them—the *Vizeri*—are a pure branch. **1873**, etc. [see MAHSUD]. **1924** LD. RONALDSHAY *India* vii. 76 Our dealings with the Mahsud Waziris. **1957** B. J. GOULD *Jewel in Lotus* x. 134 The 'girls' were Wazir tribesmen and the welcome they received was a salvo of rapid fire. **1977** J. CLEARY *High Road to China* v. 163 The Mahsuds and Wazirs have.. shot down several of our machines. *Ibid.* 175 The four Waziri.. remained behind.

wch, wch., abbrev. of WHICH *pron.*

1739 T. CORAM *Let.* 15 Sept. in R. McClure *Coram's Children* (1981) iii. 31 The Attorny & Solicitor Generals Fees.. wch they had for Examining the Proposals. **1793** C. BURNEY *Let.* 10 July in F. Burney *Jrnls. & Lett.* (1972) II. 171, I dread the evils into wch their sudden union w^d involve them. **1811** SHELLEY *Let.* 6 Jan. (1964) I. 37 Ignorant of the refinements in Love, wch. can only be attained by solitary reflexion.

wd, wd., abbrev. of *would* s.v. WILL *v.*^{1}

1793 [see WCH, WCH.]. **1800** [see WHOLESALE *v.*]. **1811** SHELLEY *Let.* 12 Jan. (1964) I. 44 Wd. that I cd. believe them to be as [they] are represented. **1888** H. O. D. DAVIDSON *Let.* 12 July in R. S. Churchill *Winston S. Churchill* (1967) I. Compan. I. v. 169, I thought it wd do him good to spend a day with you. **1910** [see *week-endize* vb. s.v. WEEK-END]. **1930** E. POUND *XXX Cantos* vi. 24 They wd. have given him poison But for the shape of his sword-hilt. **1981** J. STUBBS *Ironmaster* xiv. 188 There w^d be an Outcry if the wedding was to fall in the month of May.

wder, var. *uder*, Sc. f. OTHER.

1531 *Abstr. Protocols Town Clerks Glasgow* (1897) IV. 44 Wderis commissionaris of Dwmbertane protestit for rameyd.

we (wiː, wɪ), *pron.* Forms: 1 **we, wé**, *Northumb.* **woe**, 2 **weo, hwe**, 4–5 **whe**, 5 **whee**, 4–7 **wee**, *Sc.* **ve**, 2– **we**. Also 7 *rarely* **w'** (before a vowel or *h*). [Com. Teut.: OE. *wē̆* corresponds to OFris. *wî* (WFris. *wi, wy*, NFris. *wi, we, wü*), OS. *wî, wê*, MDu. *wî* (mod. Du. *wij*), OHG. *wir, wêr, wier* (MHG., mod.G. *wir*), ON. *vér, vær* (Sw., Da. *vi*), Goth. *weis*.

These forms seem to go back to more than one OTeut. type. The Gothic form represents OTeut. **wīz*:—pre-Teut. **weis*, an extension (with nominative suffix *-s*) of Indogermanic **wei* found in Skr. *vayám*, Avestic *vaēm*, we. With regard to the OE., ON., and some other forms, there is difference of opinion, some scholars referring them to an ablaut-variant (either **wĕ-z* or **wē-z*) of **wī-z*, and others to a pre-Teut. **wē̆* of which **wei* is supposed to be an extension by the addition of a demonstrative particle.]

1. a. The pronoun of the first person plural nominative, denoting the speaker and one or more other persons whom he associates with himself as the subject of the sentence.

For the obsolete dual see WIT *pron.* For emphasized compounds see OURSELF 2, OURSELVES 2.

Beowulf 260 We synt gumcynnes Ʒeata leode. *c* **1000** *Ags. Gosp.* Luke xxii. 71 And hiȝ cwædon: hwi ȝyrne we ȝyt ȝewitnesse? sylfe we ȝehyrdon of hys muðe. *a* **1250** *Owl & Night.* 1690–1 Ah hit was unker uoreward þo we come hiderward þat we þarto holde scholde þar riht dom us ȝiue wolde. *a* **1300** *Cursor M.* 4820 'Childer,' he said, 'weþen are yee?' 'Sir, wee are o farr cuntre.' **1382** WYCLIF *2 Thess.* i. 4 So that we silf glorien in ȝou. *c* **1420** WYNTOUN *Cron.* VIII. xxxiii. 5785 Ȝhe se þat þai ar ma þan we. *c* **1460** *Oseney Reg.* 174 Vppon the texte whee sware, both I and my wiffe. **1640** J. GOWER *Ovid's Festiv.* I. 8 Gold-temples please us, though the old w' approve. **1673** HICKERINGILL *Greg. F. Greybeard* 142 Hold, w' have sprung a mast. **1697** DRYDEN *Æneis* XI. 392 We; (for myself I speak, and all the Name Of Grecians, who to Troy's Destruction came). **1847** HELPS *Friends in C.* I. vii. 103 A thorough perception of the simple fact, that they are not we. **1879** MISS BRADDON *Cloven Foot* xx, 'We must have everything ready for him.' 'So we will, ma'am, spick and span,' answered Mrs. Trimmer.

b. following, as subject, a verb in the subjunctive mood; = let us (do something). Now only *rhet.* or *poet.*

971 *Blickl. Hom.* 11 Arweorþian we Crist on binne asetene. *a* **1250** *Owl & Night.* 177 (Cott.), Ac lete we awei þos cheste. *a* **1300** *K. Horn* 1527 Make we vs glade eure among. **13..** *Guy Warw.* 5060 'Lordinges,' he seyd, 'ginneþ ȝou armi, & gin whe hem to asaily.' *c* **1325** *Metr. Hom.* 53 Forthi I red we it forsak, And hald we us in rihtwisnes. **1470–85** MALORY *Arthur* VII. xv. 235 Noo leue we the knyghte and the dwerf, and speke we of Beaumayns. **1540** PALSGR. *Acolastus* I. iv. G iv, Go we in adores. **1593** SHAKS. *Rich. II*, I. ii. 6 Put we our quarrell to the will of heauen. **1657–83** EVELYN *Hist. Relig.* (1850) I. 33 Consider we, first, the structure of his body. **1814** WORDSW. *Excurs.* VIII. 391 Turn we then To Britons born and bred within the pale Of civil polity.

c. defined or made precise by some qualifying word or phrase.

a **900** CYNEWULF *Crist* 746 Swa we men sculon heortan ȝehyȝdum hlypum styllan. **1582** STANYHURST *Æneis* I. (Arb.) 35 Wee caytiefe Troians. *a* **1596** *Sir T. More* I. i. 121 And if you men durst not vndertake it, before God, we women would. **1605** SHAKS. *Macb.* I. i. 1 When shall we three meet againe? **1612** R. CH. *Olde Thrift newly revived* 39, I must confesse that we poore Farmers..doe exclaime against Inclosures. **1631** CHAPMAN *Cæsar & Pompey* I. B 3 b, *Met.*..We will haue the army Of Pompey entred. *Cato.* We? which we intend you? Haue you already bought the peoples voices? **1702** DE FOE *Shortest Way w. Dissenters* 23 We of the Church of England. **1751** F. COVENTRY *Pompey the Little* I. iii. 27 We Girls are under so many Restraints. **1848** DICKENS *Dombey* xlii, 'We in the City know you better,' replied Carker. **1865** MRS. WHITNEY *Gayworthys* xl, Mother, we two must make our wills. **1883** J. W. SHERER *At Home & in India* 99 She must have been what we westerns should call a child. **1918** *Act 8 Geo. V*, c. 1 We, Your Majesty's most dutiful and loyal subjects, the Commons of the United Kingdom..in Parliament assembled.

d. qualified by a prefixed adj. *poet.*

[**1607, 1635**: see 3.] **1646** CRASHAW *Steps to Temple* 27 (Ps. 137) While unhappy captiv'd wee Lovely Sion thought on thee. **1697** DRYDEN *Æneis* V. 810 O wretched we, whom not the Grecian Pow'r, Nor Flames destroy'd, in Troy's unhappy hour!

e. used confidentially or playfully to mean the person addressed, with whose interests the speaker thus identifies himself; esp. by a doctor in friendly or cheering address to a patient.

1702 VANBRUGH *False Friend* I. i. C 3, Well, old Acquaintance, we are going to be Married then? **1834** DICKENS *Sk. Boz, Boarding-ho.* ii, 'Well, my dear ma'am, and how are we?' inquired [Doctor] Wosky, in a soothing tone. **1884** *Harper's Mag.* Dec. 172/2 Well, Jane, and how are we this morning?

f. used indefinitely in general statements in which the speaker or writer includes those whom he addresses, his contemporaries, his fellow-countrymen, or the like.

c **1000** ÆLFRIC *Hom.* II. 442 On ðisum wræcfullum life we sceolon earmra manna helpan. *a* **1300** *Cursor M.* 247–8 Giue we ilkan þare langage, Me think we do þam non outrage. *c* **1386** CHAUCER *Knt.'s T.* 408–10 We seken faste after felicitee, But we goon wrong ful often trewely. Thus may we seyn alle and namely I. *a* **1450** *Le Morte Arth.* 2363 Launcelot hyr brydelle ledde, In the romans as we rede. *a* **1500** *Hist. K. Boccus & Sydracke* (? 1510) P ij, And yf they [*sc.* fishes] felt the ayre also As we or foules or beastes do. **1612** in *Eng. Hist. Rev.* (1914) XXIX. 251 Yf we should have any difference with Spaine (as happely wee may have before wee looke for yt). **1712** ADDISON *Spect.* No. 512 ⁋1 There is nothing which we receive with so much Reluctance as Advice. **1752** J. HILL *Hist. Anim.* 263 The Swedes and Danes call it Fjarsing;..the French, Viver; and we, the Weever. **1845** CARLYLE *Cromwell* (1871) II. 7 Of Sheriff Morgan..we have no farther notice whatever. **1865** RUSKIN *Sesame* i, I say first we have despised literature. What do we, as a nation, care about books? **1875** JEVONS *Money* (1878) 25 In ordinary life we use a great many words with a total disregard of logical precision. **1876** STEDMAN *Victorian Poets* vi. 183 He is well broken, as we say of a thoroughbred.

g. used in conjunction with *they* to allude to the tension between two mutually exclusive groups or categories of people, or their opposing interests. Cf. *them and us* s.v. THEM *pers. pron.* 1 e.

[**1884** F. MAURICE *F. D. Maurice* II. xvii. 531 That division of all men into the two classes of 'we' and 'the rest', ..which we most of us adopt.] **1926** KIPLING *Debits & Credits* 327 Would you believe it?—They look upon We As only a sort of They! **1942** H. HAYCRAFT *Murder for Pleasure* xv. 316 The..fundamental contradiction between the We and They in government. **1948** R. H. TAWNEY in F. A. Iremonger *William Temple* v. 88 The 'We and They' complex..could not survive continuous co-operation with colleagues..whose experience of life was quite different from his own. **1965** *Observer* (Colour Suppl.) 25 Apr. 13/1 The children have a chance of learning to deal with adults, without the we-they feeling. **1973** *Guardian* 30 Mar. 14/2 Anything which emphasises the 'we' and 'they' of the situation will drive men..towards the extremes of politics.

2. Used by a single person to denote himself: **a.** by a sovereign or ruler. Often defined by the name or title added.

Beowulf 958 Beowulf maþelode..: We þæt ellenweorc.. feohtan fremedon. *c* **1425** *Eng. Conq. Irel.* (1896) 6 We, dermot, prince of leynester. **1436** HEN. VI in *Rep. Hist. MSS. Comm.* Var. Coll. IV. 199 We forse alle the gret discoragyng and discomfort that mygte growe to oure trewe sugectis. **1482** in *Eng. Hist. Rev.* (1910) XXV. 122 We Elizabeth abbas of þe Monastere of Syon..wylle and ordeyne that [etc.]. **1603** JAS. I in Rymer *Fœdera* (1705) XVI. 538 Wee, Myndinge of our Royall and absolute Power to Us commytted, to visitt [etc.]. **1613** SHAKS. *Hen. VIII*, II. iv. 71 Sir, I am about to weepe; but thinking that We are a Queene [etc.]. **1642** CHAS. I in Clarendon *Hist. Reb.* v. §20 In plain English, it is to take away the freedom of our vote; which were we but a subject were high injustice; but being your king, we leave all the world to judge what it is. **1835** LYTTON *Rienzi* IV. vii, Noticed you the *we*— the style royal? **1850** WISEMAN *Pastoral* 7 Oct., In that same Consistory we were enabled ourselves to ask for the Archiepiscopal Pallium, for our new See of Westminster. **1872** TENNYSON *Gareth & Lynette* 362 But Arthur, 'We sit King, to help the wrong'd Thro' all our realm'.

b. by a speaker or writer, in order to secure an impersonal style and tone, or to avoid the obtrusive repetition of 'I'.

Regularly so used in editorial and unsigned articles in newspapers and other periodicals, where the writer is understood to be supported in his opinions and statements by the editorial staff collectively.

c **893** ÆLFRED *Oros.* I. i. §11 Nu hæbbe we scortlice ȝesæd ymbe Asia londȝemæro. *c* **1000** ÆLFRIC *Hom.* I. 556 We mihton ðas halȝan rædinge menigfealdlicor trahtnian. *a* **1300** *Cursor M.* 265 Now o þis prolog wil we blin. **1513** BRADSHAW *St. Werburge* I. 295 The second sone of Penda, we meane kynge Wulfere. **1589** PUTTENHAM *Eng. Poesie* I. xix. (Arb.) 56 We our selues who compiled this treatise. **1610** HEALEY *St. Aug. Citie of God* III. xviii. 133 Should we particularize, wee should become a direct Historiographer. **1807** COPLESTON *Advice to Yng. Reviewer* 1 There is a mysterious authority in the plural *we*, which no single name, whatever may be its reputation, can acquire. **1836** DICKENS *Sk. Boz, Criminal Courts*, We shall never forget the mingled feelings of awe and respect with which we used to gaze on the exterior of Newgate in our schoolboy days. **1860** *Leader* 11 Feb., The volume that we have now before us. **1879** T. P. O'CONNOR *Beaconsfield* xiv. 577 In this official report [of a speech] the vain-glorious and significant 'I' is toned down to the softer and less candid 'we'.

c. Hence jocularly as quasi-*sb.*: The editor of a periodical, or a contributor who uses this style; the periodical itself.

1853 R. S. SURTEES *Sponge's Sp. Tour* ix, It reached the ears of the great Mr. Seedeyman, the mighty *we* of the country, as he sat in his den penning his 'stunners' for his market-day *Mercury*. **1866** *Chamb. Jrnl.* 15 Dec. 788/2 Not only was I myself overwhelmed by these accounts of foreign travel, when I was a We, but I noticed [etc.]. **1902** *Monthly Rev.* Aug. 124 Yet the two great 'Wes' of the eighteenth century, the 'Monthly' and the 'Critical' played no unimportant part in the literary education of our great-grandparents.

3. Used for the accus. *us* (now only by the uneducated). Cf. LET *v.*[1] 14 b.

c **1500** *Melusine* xix. 106 Lete we send for the two knightes. **1553** *Respublica* III. iii. 682 *People*..He fliereth on youe & beareth vs faire in hande And therewhile robbeth bothe youe & we of oure Lande. **1607** SHAKS. *Cor.* V. iii. 103 And to poore we Thine enmities most capitall. **1635** R. CAREW in *Lismore Papers* (1888) Ser. II. III. 222 Those.. fauours..vouthsafed vnto poore immeritinge we. **1782** COWPER *John Gilpin* 16 So you must ride On horseback after we. **1883** D. C. MURRAY *Hearts* xxxii, Not as ever you was proud to folks like we. **1890** BICKLEY *Surrey Hills* III. 207 He a' never disappinted we afore, why should 'un now? *Ibid.* 209 Maister Fenton ain't here yet, so let we have another hymn.

†**we**, *int. Obs.* Also 5 **whe**. An exclamation app. used for emphasis, or to demand attention. Cf. WI *int.*

13.. *Sir Orfeo* 176 (Sisam) O we, quaþ he, allas allas. **13..** *Gosp. Nicod.* 28 (MS. Harl.) We, whatkyn godes er þire? **13..** *Gaw. & Gr. Knt.* 2185 We, lorde, quoth þe gentyle knyȝt, Wheþer þis be þe grene chapelle. *c* **1440** *York Myst.* xi. 139 We! lord, þai wil noght to me trayste. *Ibid.* xv. 46 Whe! hudde! be-halde into the heste! *c* **1460** *Towneley Myst.* ii. 147 We! ryn on, in the dwills nayme Before!

we: see WEE *sb.*[1] and *a.*, WOE, WY (man).

wea-bit, var. WAY-BIT *Obs.*

weach, weack: see WITCH (*tree*), WICK.

weade, obs. form of WEED *v.*[1]

weaden, obs. pl. of WEED *sb.*[2]

weafe, ? etymologizing var. WOOF.

1657 C. BECK *Universal Char.* M 2 b, The weafe or woof of cloth.

weage, obs. Sc. form of VOYAGE.

weak (wiːk), *a.* and *sb.* Forms: α. 3–5, 4–9 *Sc.*, 9 *dial.* **waik**, (6 *Sc.* **waek**), 4–6 **waike, wayk(e**, (4 *Sc.* **vayk**, 5–6 *Sc.* **vaik, vaike**), 3–6 **weik(e, weyk(e**, (6 *Sc.* **vaeik, veik**). β. 4, 6 **wek**, 4 **weck**, 6 **wecke**; 5–6 **weke**, 4–7 **weeke**, 6–7 **weake**, 6– **weak.** [a. ON. *veik-r*, corresponding to OE. *wác*: see WOKE *a.*

The earliest known examples are in the *Cursor Mundi* (*a* 1300, but MSS. 14th c.); the word gradually took the place of the corresponding native adj. (OE. *wác*, ME. WOKE) which did not survive beyond the 15th c. There seems to have been some difference of meaning between OE. *wác* and ON. *veikr*; in OE. the primary Teut. sense 'yielding, not rigid or firm, pliant' was still prominent, while in ON. it had developed into the sense 'not strong'.

The β-forms show the same development of Scand. *ei* to *ē* which is found in BLEAK *a.* (earlier *bleyke*, ON. *bleik-r*), STEAK *sb.* (ME. *steke, steyke*, ON. *steik*; still pron. dialectally with *ī*), and REAN, var. of RAIN *sb.*[2] (ON. *rein*).

In mod. dialect literature the word is often written *waik* or *wake*. Graphically, these forms belong to the α group; but in certain areas it may be doubtful whether the shade of pronunciation denoted by the spelling descends from ME. *ē* or from ME. *ei*. As the normal Sc. representative of OE. *wác* is *wake*, which in late Scottish might have been written *waik*, it is possible that some of the Sc. examples given below belong etymologically to WOKE *a.* rather than to the present word.]

A. *adj.*

†**1.** Of a material thing: Pliant, flexible, readily bending. (Usually with implication of want of strength.) = WOKE *a.* 1. *Obs.*

The recognition of this sense by Johnson (who has been followed by later Dicts.) is remarkable; his authority has not been identified.

? *a* **1366** CHAUCER *Rom. Rose* 225 A mantel heng hir faste by, Upon a perche weyke and smalle [Fr. *A une perche moult greslete*]. *c* **1440** *Promp. Parv.* 520/1 Weyke, or lethy, *lentus*. **14..** *Sir Beues* 647 (MS. M) All to lethy [*MS. O* weyke] the spere was wrought. *c* **1480** HENRYSON *Age & Youth* 13, I.. saw ane catyf [Age]..cumand,..walowit & wane, waik as ane wand. **1500–20** DUNBAR *Poems* lv. 22 Sum, thocht tham selffis stark, lyk gyandis, Ar now maid waek lyk willing wandis. **1755** JOHNSON, *Weak*, 3. Soft; pliant; not stiff. [Whence in later Dicts.]

2. a. Wanting in moral strength for endurance or resistance; lacking fortitude or courage, strength of purpose or will; unsteadfast, wavering.

1375 BARBOUR *Bruce* VIII. 340 [Thai] dang on thame so hardely That in schort tyme men mycht se by At erd ane hundreth weill, and mar; The remanand the vaykar war. *a* **1425** tr. *Arderne's Treat. Fistula*, etc. 7 He, forsoþ, þat is wayke of hert is noȝt in way of curacion. *c* **1450** CAPGRAVE *St. Augustine* xxv. 34 The man was weyk and dred mech þe knyf. **1456** SIR G. HAYE *Law Arms* (S.T.S.) 170 Peple villain and wayke in the faith. **1526** TINDALE *Matt.* xxvi. 41 The spirite ys willynge but the flesshe is weeke. *c* **1540** R. MORICE in *Lett. Lit. Men* (Camden) 24 [He] being very moche combered with the concupisscence of the fleshe, and stryvyng gretely to suppresse the same, felt himself to wek to overcom it. **1593** SHAKS. *3 Hen. VI*, IV. i. 12 Which are so weake of courage..That they'le take no offence at our abuse. **1667** MILTON *P.L.* VIII. 532 Here onely weake Against the charm of Beauties powerful glance. *a* **1716** SOUTH *Serm.* (1727) VI. xi. 385 It is the just Shame..of the Frailty of our Condition to consider..how weak we are to intend, and how much weaker to perform. **1774** GOLDSM. *Nat. Hist.* V. 180 But though so furious among themselves, they [turkeys] are weak and cowardly against other animals, though far less powerful than they. **1779** COWPER *Human Frailty* 1 Weak and irresolute is man. —— *Olney Hymns* xxix. 12 And Satan trembles, when he sees The weakest saint upon his knees. **1889** W. ARMSTRONG *Wrestling* (Badm. Libr.) 224 Outsiders often clamour loudly over these falls, and a weak judge is liable to be influenced.

absol. **1667** MILTON *P.L.* VI. 909 But list'n not to his Temptations, warne Thy weaker. **1784** COWPER *Task* II. 343 He 'stablishes the strong, restores the weak. **1902** W. ADAMSON *Joseph Parker* xxiii. 299 Faith leads to the Rock higher than self, on which the weak can rest in safety.

b. In the translations of the Bible from Tindale onward, used to render Gr. ἀσθενής, ἀσθενῶν, applied by St. Paul (esp. in Rom. xiv and 1 Cor. viii) to believers whose scruples, though unsound, should be treated with tenderness, lest they should be led by the example of the more enlightened into acts condemned by their conscience. Hence allusively in ***weaker brethren*** (often supposed to be a scriptural phrase), applied to the more timorous members of a party, who are in danger of being shocked by extreme statements of principle or policy; ***weak sister*** (*colloq.*, orig. *U.S.*), an ineffectual or unreliable person (of either sex); a person of weak character; also *transf.*

In the Wycliffite and other early versions the rendering is 'sick' (Vulg. *infirmus*).

1526 Tindale *1 Cor.* viii. 11 But take hede that youre libertie cause nott the weake to faule. *Ibid.*, And so thorow thy knowledge shall the weake brother perisshe for whom christ dyed. **1573** T. C[artwright] *Reply to Answ. Whitgift* A iij b, That the setters forwarde of thys cause..giue occasion to the papists of slaundering the religion, and to the weake of offence. **1674** B. Parry *Duppa's Rules & Helps Devot.* I. To Rdr., If Noise and Clamour might pass for Inspiration, the Apostles must go for Weak-Brethren, and mere Novices, compared with our New Lights. **1779** [R. Richardson] *Epist.* Ded. to Bp. Lond. p. xvii, But recollecting the many Christian Injunctions in Favour of weak Brethren, you thus proceeded with your Charge. **1857** *Call* (San Francisco) 3 May 1/1 G. W. Swerzy..is a 'weak sister' and a rather 'bad egg'. **1866** Geo. Eliot *Felix Holt* I. iv. 95 'I lack grace to deal with these weak sisters,' said the minister. **1882** Besant *All Sorts* viii, I do as little as I can..on Sunday, because of the weaker brethren. The Sunday we [*sc.* Seventh Day Independents] keep as a holiday. **1949** R. B. West *Rocky Mt. Cities* 311 The morning *Rocky Mountain News*..dawdled along as one of the weakest sisters in the Scripps-Howard string [of newspapers]. **1955** E. Berckman *Beckoning Dream* (1956) xix. 135 Luanna was a softie.., a weak sister. She's the one you'd expect to go all to pieces, and she did. **1976** 'J. Ross' *I know what it's like to Die* xvii. 116 Birdsell was a weak sister... He was..known to be greedy and a physical coward.

c. of actions, attributes, etc.

1667 Milton *P.L.* ix. 1186 And left to her self, if evil thence ensue, Shee first his weak indulgence will accuse. **1671** Marvell *Corr.* Wks. (Grosart) II. 391 The Lord Lucas made a fervent bold speech against our prodigality in giving, and the weak looseness of the government. **1800** Coleridge *Piccolom.* v. v. 78 Because he had a weak hour and forgot himself. **1819** Shelley *Cenci* v. iii. 22 They must have told some weak and wicked lie To flatter their tormentors. **1878** Lucy *Diary Two Parl.* (1885) I. 365 Disraeli, in a weak moment, offered him office again.

d. Of features, expression of countenance, etc.: Indicating weakness of character or intention.

1877 W. S. Gilbert *Foggerty's Fairy* (1890) 30 The nurse smiled a weak smile, as who should say, 'Master's joke is always so amusingly chosen'. **1882** Besant *All Sorts* xxix, His forehead, when the original thatch was thick, must have been rather low and weak. **1897** Kipling *Capt. Cour.* x. 227 'What have you two men been doing now?' she said, with a weak little smile.

e. Deficient in power to control emotion; unduly swayed by grief, compassion, or affection. Of tears: Indicating weakness.

1768 Sterne *Sent. Journ.*, *Snuff-Box*, But I am as weak as a woman; and I beg the world not to smile, but pity me. **1794** Mrs. Radcliffe *Myst. Udolpho* xlv, 'They are weak tears, for they are useless ones,' replied the count, drying them. **1848** Dickens *Dombey* i, It's very weak and silly of me, I know, to be so trembly and shaky from head to foot. **1886** 'Mrs. Alexander' *By Woman's Wit* ii, You must have a weak spot in your heart for him, or you would never stand it.

3. a. Wanting in strength and skill as a combatant; relatively deficient in fighting power as shown by the result of the contest.

c **1330** R. Brunne *Chron. Wace* (Rolls) 1814 Þer was turn ageynes turn; þat waykest [of the wrestlers] was, byhoued spurn. *c* **1471** *Pol. Poems* (Rolls) II. 276 Fayne was the waykyer away for to flee. **1481** Caxton *Reynard* (Arb.) 102 Yet thought the foxe I haue good auauntage, the clawes of his for feet ben of, and his feet ben yet sore therof..he shal be somwhat the weyker. **1593** Shaks. *Rich. II*, III. ii. 62 Then if Angels fight, Weake men must fall. **1602** —— *Ham.* v. ii. 273 Your Grace hath laide the oddes a' th' weaker side.

b. Deficient as a fighting power in numbers, resources, etc. †Also const. *of*.

c **1470** Henry *Wallace* iv. 162 With waik power thai durst him nocht persew. *c* **1489** Caxton *Sonnes of Aymon* i. 55 The folke of the duke were weke and almoste gon. For, of the two hundred that he hadde broughte, he hadde noo moo wyth hym but fourthi. **1574** *Southampton Court Leet Rec.* (1905) I. 102 The watche of this towne ys neither good nor sufficient but very weak and vnmeet for the preservacon of thys towne. **1592** *Soliman & Pers.* III. i. 48 Their fleete is weake; Their horse, I deeme them fiftie thousand strong. **1593** Shaks. *3 Hen. VI*, IV. v. 7 And often but attended with weake guard. **1611** W. Adams *Let.* in Rundall *Mem. Japon* (Hakl. Soc.) 22 The king's ships were out seeking vs,..vnderstanding that wee were weake of men. **1614** Ralegh *Hist. World* v. iii. §21. 578 He was indeede farre too weake for the Enemie in Horse, both in number and in goodnesse. **1670** Dryden *1st Pt. Conq. Granada* v. (1672) 53 We are not provided for a siege... The foe is strong without, we weak within. **1749** Fielding *Tom Jones* v. xi, Having concluded, from seeing three men engaged, that two of them must be on one side, he..espoused the cause of the weaker party. **1784** Cowper *Task* II. 273 Sham'd as we have been..and in our own sea prov'd Too weak for those decisive blows that once Ensur'd us mast'ry there. **1871** Freeman *Norm. Conq.* IV. xvii. 54 Each detachment of William's great army of occupation was weak and isolated. **1912** *Eng. Hist. Rev.* Oct. 662 The French..were much weaker in large vessels.

†c. *transf.* ***weak of friends***: having few influential friends. *Obs.*

1586 T. Morgan in *Eng. Hist. Rev.* (1913) Jan. 56 *note*, Burghley..was weak of friends in the Privy Council.

d. Of a position: Poorly garrisoned.

1650 J. Nicoll *Diary* (Bannatyne Club) 25 The Englische Generall, taking this very grevouslie, that such a waik hous sould hald out aganes him, [etc.].

e. *Chess-playing.* Of a man: Insufficiently protected against capture.

1860 Löwenthal *Morphy's Games Chess* 57 The K. Kt's P. and K's P. are now both of them weak and the cause of much subsequent embarrassment. *Ibid.* 59 The Pawn..would have been left isolated and weak.

f. Wanting in skill as a performer in a game, sport, athletic exercise, contest, etc. Of play, a move, stroke: Exhibiting want of skill. So, ***weak place, spot*** (in a person's play).

1827 in W. Denison *Sk. Players* (1846) 57 In other points England was weak: her fielding was not near so good, her bowling was not equal, [etc.]. **1860** Löwenthal *Morphy's Games Chess* 62 On principle it is weak play, as it leaves a Pawn behind unsupported. *Ibid.* 98 A weak move. **1862** *Baily's Mag.* Sept. 142 But the Surrey bowling was weak, and the men of The North scored 266 in their first innings. **1872** *Ibid.* Aug. 168 Mr. Grace..gave..a chance at his one weak place, short leg. **1891** Grace *Cricket* ix. 248 (Bowling.) And that brings me to my last point—seek for the weak spot in the batsman's defence. **1901** Jessop in *Badminton Mag.* Apr. 371 We [Gloucestershire] shall be even a weaker side than usual in the first two months.

4. a. Of a person, the body, limbs: Deficient in bodily or muscular strength; esp. of a child or woman, inferior in respect of physical strength.

a **1300** *Cursor M.* 15033 Þe childer þat war waike To ga þat pres a-mang. *Ibid.* 23624 Þir [the good] sal be selcut strang and wight, þai [the wicked] sal be weck [*MS. Gött.* waike] wit-vten might. *c* **1300** *Havelok* 1012 Þider komen bothe stronge and wayke. *a* **1340** Hampole *Psalter* xii. 5, I..sett noght by þane stirynge, na mare þan a geaunte dos at þe puttynge of a waik man. *c* **1386** Chaucer *Man of Law's T.* 834 How may this wayke womman han this strengthe Hire to defende agayn this renegat. **1393** Langl. *P. Pl.* C. vi. 23 Certes, ich seyde..Ich am to waik to worche with sykel oþer with sythe. **1470–85** Malory *Arthur* iv. xx. 144, I am the yongest and moost weykest of yow bothe. **1596** Shaks. *Tam. Shr.* v. ii. 165 Why are our bodies soft, and weake, and smooth, Vnapt to toyle? **1628** Milton *Vacation Exerc.* 1 Hail native Language, that by sinews weak Didst move my first endeavouring tongue to speak. **1646** Sir T. Browne *Pseud. Ep.* iv. v. 190 Divers continue all their life..left-handed, and have but weak and imperfect use of the right. **1697** Dryden *Æneis* xi. 1044 It shall be seen, weak Woman, what you can, When Foot to Foot, you combat with a Man. **1709** Pope *Ess. Crit.* 197 That on weak wings, from far, pursues your flights. **1757** Foote *Author* Prol., But as the sluggish animal was weak, They fear'd, if both should mount, his back would break. **1776** A. Smith *W.N.* v. i. II. 315 He is a very strong man who by mere strength of body can force two weak ones to obey him. **1821** Shelley *Adonais* xxvii, O gentle child..Why didst thou..with weak hands though mighty heart Dare the unpastured dragon in his den?

b. *absol.* (Cf. 10 b.)

a **1300** *Cursor M.* 832 Þe strang [bigan] þe weker for to sla. **1456** Sir G. Haye *Law Arms* (S.T.S.) 257 Oft tymes the starkare..puttis the waykar to the wer. For it is agayne nature that the waykare wan the starkare. *a* **1500** *Coventry Corpus Chr. Pl.* ii. 447 But the weykist gothe eyuer to the walle. **1535–** [see wall *sb.*[1] 13]. **1546** J. Heywood *Prov.* II. v. (1867) 56 And where the small with the great, can not agree, The weaker goeth to the potte, we all daie see. **1565** Stapleton tr. *Bede's Hist. Ch. Eng.* 95 Thinking it a light matter to iniury, beguile or vse violence toward our wekers and inferiours. **1579** Kendall *Flowers Epigr.*, *Trifles* 5 The weake may stand the strong in sted: a dog may haue a day. **1768** Ross *Helenore* II. 85 The weak wins ay the warr.

c. ***the weaker vessel*** [cf. vessel *sb.*[1] 3], in 1 Pet. iii. 7 said of the wife as compared with the husband; hence occas. used jocularly for 'the wife' or female partner. ***the weaker sex***: see sex *sb.* 1 c.

1526 Tindale *1 Pet.* iii. 7 Gevynge honoure vnto the wyfe as vnto the weaker vessel [Gr. ὡς ἀσθενεστέρῳ σκεύει]. **1588** Shaks. *L.L.L.* I. i. 276 Iaquenetta (so is the weaker vessell called) which I apprehended with the aforesaid Swaine. **1668** St. Serfe *Tarugo's Wiles* III. 23 B[aker's] *Wife.* O! you are a fine man indeed! to leave the Government of the Oven now..to me that's the weaker vessel.

d. of physical effort.

1783 Crabbe *Village* I. 197 Alternate masters now their slave command, Urge the weak efforts of his feeble hand.

5. a. Deficient in bodily vigour through age, sickness, privation, etc.; wanting in strength of the vital functions of the body; debilitated.

1340 Hampole *Pr. Consc.* 767 Bot als tyte als a man waxes alde, þan waxes his kynde wayke and calde. *Ibid.* 6157 Seke I was and in ful wayke state. **1399** Langl. *Rich. Redeles* II. 64 Ȝoure owen lymmes..so ffeble and wayke wexe in þe hammes. **1470–85** Malory *Arthur* xxi. xi. 857 Thyder they came within two dayes for they were wayke & feble to goo. **1519** *Knaresb. Wills* (Surtees) I. 8, I, John Gill, hole in mynde and wake in stomak, &c., to be buried in Pannall Chyrchyerd. **1524** *Reg. Privy Seal Scot.* I. 501/1 Patrik..is now of grete aige, febill and waik in his persoun. *a* **1548** Hall *Chron.*, *Hen. VIII* 20 Thei hired shippes and putte the lorde Marques in one, which was so weake that he asked where he was. **1599** Dallam in *Early Voy. Levant* (Hakl. Soc.) 81, I was verrie wayke, not able to goo on foute one myle in a daye. **1651** Hobbes *Leviath.* II. xxix. 173 Till (if Nature be strong enough) it break at last the contumacy of the parts obstructed.., or (if Nature be too weak) the Patient dyeth. **1687** Miège *Gt. Fr. Dict.* I, *Tendre*, tender, ..of a weak constitution. **1780** Selwyn in Jesse *S. & Contemp.* (1844) IV. 363, I am at present in a weaker state of health from a present disorder than I ever was. **1840** Dickens *Old C. Shop* lxiv, You're too weak to stand, indeed. **1889** 'J. S. Winter' *Mrs. Bob* xx, And, as is generally the case after hysteria, she is now very weak and prostrate. **1891** Farrar *Darkn. & Dawn* lix, Pomponia sat by the bedside, holding the weak hand.

Similative phrases. **1840** [see rat *sb.*[1] 2 c]. **1902** C. N. & A. M. Williamson *Lightning Conductor* 327 Poor Lady B. was as weak as a rag, but..Pa kept her up on a raw egg in wine.

b. Feeble through exhaustion; faint. ? Now chiefly *dial.*

a **1707** Prior *Dk. Ormond's Pict.* 10 'Till weak with Wounds,..He faints. **1849** Lever *Con Cregan* i, I am getting wake; just touch my lips again with the jug. **1880** *Antrim & Down Gloss.*, *Weak turn*, fainting fit. **1905** *Brit. Med. Jrnl.* 1 July 23 He took a 'weak turn' and died the following day. **1918** *Pall Mall Gaz.* 29 June 8/1 A wound over the eye, which caused the Welshman to go so weak that the referee stopped the contest.

6. a. Constitutionally feeble; not vigorous or robust in health.

1523–34 Fitzherb. *Husb.* liii. 50 Of euery sort of shepe, it may fortune there be some, that like not and be weike. *a* **1548** Hall *Chron.*, *Edw. IV* (1550) 36 The French kyng had no heire male, but one weake boy. **1602** Shaks. *Ham.* III. iv. 114 Conceit in weakest bodies, strongest workes. **1772** Priestley *Inst. Relig.* (1782) I. 218 Laws to prevent the education of weak children. **1774** Goldsm. *Nat. Hist.* II. 201 Fontenelle..was naturally of a very weak and delicate habit of body. **1780** Bentham *Introd. Morals & Legisl.* vi. (1789) 43 A man may be weak all his life long, without experiencing any disease.

b. of a tree, plant, fruit, etc.

1596 Shaks. *Merch. V.* iv. i. 115 The weakest kinde of fruite Drops earliest to the ground, and so let me. **1696** W. W. *New Help to Discourse* (ed. 4) 224 Stake and bind up the weakest Plants, against the Winds. **1754** Justice *Scots Gard. Director* 173 If your Artichokes are weak in the Spring, hill them up with rich Earth, and they will recover. **1768** [J. Gibson] *Fruit-Gardener* 208 Early pruning is commonly recommended for weak trees. **1892** *Speaker* 3 Sept. 290/1 The roses..will deteriorate year after year,..getting too weak to open leafy buds.

7. Of bodily organs or their functions: Deficient in functional strength (either naturally or by impairment).

The usual collocations are: ***weak eyes, sight***; ***weak stomach, digestion***; ***weak chest, lungs, heart***; also (later) ***weak nerves***, which has commonly the loose sense of 'nervousness', liability to be easily agitated.

c **1480** Henryson *Swallow & other Birds* 19 Hir ene ar waik, the sone scho may nocht se. **1597** Shaks. *Lover's Compl.* 214 The deepe greene Emrald in whose fresh regard, Weake sights their sickly radience do amend. **1599** —— *Hen. V*, III. ii. 56 Their Villany goes against my weake stomacke, and therefore I must cast it vp. **1655** Fuller *Ch. Hist.* vi. 299 My weak and squeazie stomack will hardly digest the wing of a small rabbet. **1661** Boyle *Style of Script.* (1675) 27 Batts ..are only pleased with (what is alone proportioned to their weak sight) a Twilight. **1732** Berkeley *Alciphr.* vi. §7, I have naturally weak eyes, and know that there are many things that I cannot see. **1760** Sterne *Tr. Shandy* III. xx. Author's Pref., With such weak nerves and spirits, and in the condition I am in at present. **1781** Cowper *Truth* 98 Fancy shall apply To your weak sight her telescopic eye. **1822–9** *Good's Study Med.* (ed. 3) I. 210 Shell-fishes do not always agree with weak stomachs. **1825** J. Denniston *Leg. Galloway* 95 His amiable lady being a woman of weak nerves. **187.** *Cassell's Nat. Hist.* I. 184 One of the large Monkeys in the Zoological Gardens had weak teeth, and he used to break open the nuts with a stone.

8. a. Of the mind or mental faculties: Deficient in power.

c **1374** Chaucer *Anel. & Arc.* 341 But me to rede out of this drede or guye Ne may my wit, so weyke is hit, not streche. *c* **1400** tr. *Secreta Secret.*, *Gov. Lordsh.* 80 But of wyn þat ys takyn abundanly..it makys wayk þe vertuz of þe sawle. *c* **1480** Henryson *Swallow & other Birds* 24 Mannis saule is febill and ouer small, Of vnderstanding waik and imperfite. **1562** Winȝet *Cert. Tractatis* Wks. (S.T.S.) I. 27 It apperis to my waik iugement that to attempt sic proude misordour sall [etc.]. **1593** Shaks. *Lucr.* 460 Such shadowes are the weake-brains forgeries. *Ibid.* 1825 Such childish humor from weake minds proceeds. **1597** —— *2 Hen. IV*, II. iv. 273 And such other Gamboll Faculties hee hath, that shew a weake Minde, and an able Body. **1642** J. Taylor (Water P.) *Walker the Ironmonger* A 2, This hath past without controlement to..the raysing of strifes..in many people of weake capacities and judgements. **1671** Milton *P.R.* II. 221 For Beauty stands In the admiration only of weak minds Led captive. **1690** Locke *Hum. Und.* II. xxiii. §12. 140 We are furnished with Faculties (dull and weak as they are) to discover enough in the Creatures, to lead us to the Knowledge of the Creator. **1751** Smollett *Per. Pic.* xcviii, Lord A——m..was a man of weak intellects. **1781** Cowper *Truth* 366 Earth gives too little, giving only bread, To nourish pride, or turn the weakest head. **1798** Ferriar *Illustr. Sterne*, etc. 8 Persons of weak understanding. **1857** Buckle *Civiliz.* I. vii. 446 No where are the weakest parts of the human mind more clearly seen than in the history of legislation. **1865** H. Kingsley *Hillyars & Burtons* lxi, Her suspicions..were only the product of a weak brain in a morbid state. **1908** [Miss E. Fowler] *Betw. Trent & Ancholme* 317 A boy of weak intellect, a Natural.

b. Lacking force of intellect or strength of mind; easily deceived, credulous.

1423 Jas. I *Kingis Q.* xiv, Thou (sely) ȝouth, of nature Indegest,..of wit wayke and vnstable. **1660** Jer. Taylor *Ductor* III. iv. 290 And that Priest were..a weak person who should chuse to wear gray, because there is no religion in the colour. **1665** Glanvill *Def. Van. Dogm.* 52 If any are so weak to affirm nothing can be demonstrated, against which any thing is or can be objected [etc.]. **1736** Butler *Anal.* II. viii. Wks. 1874 I. 293 By these means weak men are often deceived by others. **1759** Robertson *Hist. Scot.* III. Wks. 1851 I. 217 Though Elizabeth was as much inferior to Mary in beauty and gracefulness of person as she excelled her in political abilities..., she was weak enough to compare herself with the Scottish queen. **1781** Cowper *Convers.* 225 Credulous infancy, or age as weak, Are fittest auditors for such to seek. **1842** Newman *Eccl. Miracles* (1843) 127 It can mean nothing else but that St. Gregory did no miracles, and that it is weak, nay, even heathenish, to believe he did. **1849** Macaulay *Hist. Eng.* viii. II. 295 He..was everywhere received with outward signs of joy and respect, which he was weak enough to consider as proofs that the discontent.. had subsided. **1885** 'Mrs. Alexander' *Valerie's Fate* ii, Do you think I should be so weak and stupid as to fall in love with a man.. I know nothing about?

absol. **1784** Cowper *Task* II. 566 The weak perhaps are mov'd, but are not taught, While prejudice in men of stronger minds Takes deeper root.

c. Feeble (*in* one's intellect, the brain, head, etc.).

*a***1661** Fuller *Worthies, Warwicksh.* (1662) 119 Hence was it that the Earl was kept in so strict Restraint, which made him very weak in his Intellectuals. **1831** Scott *Cast. Dang.* ii, Shrewd and wise men wax weak in the brain in these troublous times. **1853** Dickens *Bleak Ho.* xxi, Until Mr. Smallweed's grandmother, now living, became weak in her intellect.

9. Inefficient, ill-qualified. **a.** Of a person's abilities, productions, qualities, etc. (Often used in modesty or self-disparagement.)

*c***1386** Chaucer *Prioress' T.* 29 My konnyng is so wayk, o blisful queene, For to declare thy grete worthynesse That [etc.]. *c***1450** Holland *Houlate* 37 And I haue mekle matir in metir to gloss.. And waike is my eloquence. *c***1590** J. Stewart *Poems* (S.T.S.) II. 6 My vaeik and friuole versis. **1594** Shaks. *Rich. III*, III. i. 37 *Card.* My Lord of Buckingham, if my weak Oratorie Can from his Mother winne the Duke of Yorke, Anon expect him here.

b. Of a person: Wanting in ability, ill-qualified, unskilled or inefficient *in*, *of* or *to* do (something).

1423 Jas. I *Kingis Q.* cxlix, And, sone, of wit or lore Sen thou art wayke and feble. **1564** Becon *Wks.* I. Pref. ☛ C iv, When such as are yet weake in knowledge of Christ and of his holy Gospel heare y^t [etc.]. *Marg.*, Weakeynges. **1590** Spenser *F.Q.* I. Introd. ii, Helpe then, O holy Virgin chiefe of nine, Thy weaker Nouice to performe thy will. **1653** W. Ramesey *Astrol. Restored* 28 One of the silliest and weakest Students in Astrologie was chosen out of all the other to confute the Doctor. **1780** Cowper *Progr. Err.* 15 Weak to perform, though mighty to pretend. **1781** —— *Charity* 633 But if, unhappily deceiv'd, I dream, And prove too weak for so divine a theme. **1818** Keats *Endym.* III. 938 O 'tis a very sin For one so weak to venture his poor verse In such a place as this. **1831** Sir J. Sinclair *Corr.* II. 257 Some weak politicians would startle at the expense it might occasion. **1885** *Leeds Mercury* 24 June 4/4 The new Government will be so lamentably weak in debating power.

transf. **1821** Shelley *Adonais* lii, Rome's azure sky, Flowers, ruins, statues, music, words, are weak The glory they transfuse with fitting truth to speak.

c. Of literary work or composition: Showing little evidence of ability.

1713 Steele *Englishm.* No. 20. 132 It is the weakest Part of a very weak Book. **1733** Pope *Hor. Sat.* II. i. 5 The lines are weak, another's pleas'd to say.

10. a. Wanting in power or authority over others.

1423 Jas. I *Kingis Q.* cxlviii, And quhare a persone has tofore knawing Off It that is to fallen purposely, Lo, fortune is bot wayke in suich a thing. **1538** Starkey *England* I. iii. 84 Our cuntrey ys now weke, and no thyng so strong as hyt hath byn in old tyme. **1550** Crowley *Way to Wealth* 265 If the gentlemen and rulars of thy countreie shoulde be to weake for the, he would bring in strainge nations to subdue the. **1651** Hobbes *Leviath.* II. xxx. 182 It is a weak Soveraign, that has weak Subjects; and a weak People, whose Soveraign wanteth Power to rule them at his will. ?**1761** Goldsm. *Misc. Wks.* (1837) I. 472 England, therefore, grew weaker, or, what amounts to the same thing, saw her neighbours grow stronger. **1855** Macaulay *Hist. Eng.* xx. IV. 437 Sometimes.. no set of men who can be brought together possesses the full confidence and steady support of a majority of the House of Commons. When this is the case, there must be a weak Ministry.

b. *absol.* (Cf. 4 b.)

1601 Shaks. *Jul. C.* I. iii. 91 Therein, yee Gods, you make the weake most strong; Therein, yee Gods, you Tyrants doe defeat. **1697** [see strong *a.* 5 b]. **1733** Pope *Ess. Man* III. 49 Grant that the pow'rful still the weak controul. **1844** Disraeli *Coningsby* IV. iv, The idea of restraining the powerful by the weak is an absurdity.

c. of power, strength, authority, etc.

*c***1386** Chaucer *Pars. T.* ⁋311 And moore-ouer contricion destroyeth the prison of helle and maketh wayk and fieble alle the strengthes of the deueles. **1533** Bellenden *Livy* (S.T.S.) II. 38 The strenth of every office & power begynnys to be febil and waik in þe lattir parte of þe ȝere. **1570** *Satir. Poems Reform.* xviii. 47 Thay thocht his deith wald mak thy power waik. **1593** Shaks. *Rich. II*, II. iii. 154, I cannot mend it, I must needes confesse, Because my power is weake. *a***1656** [see strong *a.* 5 d].

11. a. *Card-playing.* Of a game, hand, suit: Not of a commanding nature or value. Of a player: Ill-provided with commanding cards (*in* a specified suit).

1680 Cotton *Gamester* (ed. 2) 75 [L'Ombre] If the Players have but a weak Game, they are to imitate cunning Beast-players in dividing the Tricks. **1742** Hoyle *Whist* 28 Your Adversary on your Right-hand begins with playing the Ace of your weak Suit. **1746** *Ibid.* (ed. 6) 62 When ought you to make Tricks early? *Ans.* When you are weak in Trumps. **1864** [see strong *a.* 24].

b. *Money-market.* Of money or stock: Insufficient to meet a demand or to carry on operations. Similarly of a holder of stock.

1875 *Economist* 23 Jan. 95/1 The Bank reserve will continue too weak for the probable demands upon it in the spring. *Ibid.* 6 Mar. 289/2 Several of the weaker holders have been forced to dispose of their stocks at a considerable reduction on former rates.

12. Not strong or energetic in action; lacking in force or power. **a.** of natural agents, etc.

*c***1400** tr. *Secreta Secret., Gov. Lordsh.* 68 For þat stomake ys lykned to a wayk & feble feer, þat vnnethes may to-brenne rosels and smal chippys. **1585** Higins *Junius' Nomencl.* 226/1 *Siparum*,.. a saile wherewith the course or voyage of a ship is holpen, when the wind is weake and faileth. **1597** Shaks. *2 Hen. IV*, IV. v. 100 For my Cloud of Dignitie Is held from falling, with so weake a winde, That it will quickly drop. **1604** E. G[rimstone] tr. *Acosta's Hist. Indies* II. vii. 97 If the sunnebeames be weake, they draw vp no fogge from the rivers. *a***1626** [see strong *a.* 13 c]. **1660** F. Brooke tr. *Le Blanc's Trav.* 45 'Tis to be noted that the tides are weakest at the full of the Moon. **1815** J. Smith *Panorama Sci. & Art* II. 175 A combination of weak magnets.. will communicate magnetism in proportion to their accumulated power. **1899** *Allbutt's Syst. Med.* VIII. 515 The above list gives them [i.e. external astringents] in order of their efficacy—from the weakest to the strongest. **1907** J. A. Hodges *Elem. Photogr.* (ed. 6) 112 Weak sunlight will be found to give the best lighting.

†**b.** Of food: Not highly nourishing. *Obs.*

1382 *Pol. Poems* (Rolls) I. 264 Men may se by thair contynaunce.. that thair sustynaunce Simple is and wayke. **1615** Sandys *Trav.* 118 Of these [Moors] it is strange to see such a number of broken persons: so being by reason of their strong labour and weake foode.

c. Of the voice: Feeble in enunciation.

*a***1300** *Cursor M.* 24314 Þir martirs tuin.., quen þai herd crists voice Sa waik þat vnethes most þai here, Come neuer care þair hert sa nere. *a***1568** Ascham *Scholem.* I. (Arb.) 39 A voice, not softe, weake, piping, womannishe, but audible, stronge, and manlike. **1697** Dryden *Æneis* VI. 666 They rais'd a feeble Cry, with trembling Notes: But the weak Voice deceiv'd their gasping Throats. **1810** Crabbe *Borough* xxii. 324 And 'Come,' they said, with weak, sad voices, 'come.' **1873** March. Dufferin *Canad. Jrnl.* (1891) 81 The voices of the singers were thin and weak. **1878** Hardy *Ret. Native* V. v, 'Are you not ashamed of me'.. she asked in a weak whisper.

d. Of the pulse: Having little force.

1700 Dryden *Pal. & Arc.* I. 154 Weak was the Pulse, and hardly heav'd the Heart. **1707** Floyer *Physic. Pulse-Watch* 403 A weak Pulse, languid, profund, subtile, slow, indicates a cold Disease. **1876** [see strong *a.* 13 b].

e. Of faith, conviction, affection, passions: Wanting in strength, not intense.

1530 Tindale *Answ. More* Wks. (1573) 267 The fayth that dependeth of an other mans mouth is weake. *c***1600** Shaks. *Sonn.* cii. 1 My loue is strengthned, though more weake in seeming. **1732** Pope *Ess. Man* II. 130 Hence diff'rent Passions more or less inflame, As strong or weak, the organs of the frame. **1768** Cowper *Olney Hymns* xviii. 22 Lord, it is my chief complaint That my love is weak and faint.

f. (*a*) Of words or expressions: Wanting in force, inadequate; implying relatively little fullness of meaning.

1771 *Junius Lett.* lxiv. (1772) II. 327 If these terms are weak, or ambiguous, in what language can Junius express himself? **1861** Paley *Æschylus* (ed. 2) *Choeph.* 913 *note*, 'To waft fate' is, however, a much weaker term than the other.

(*b*) *Math.* Of a mathematical entity or concept: implying less than others of its kind; defined by fewer conditions.

1950 W. Feller *Introd. Probability Theory* I. viii. 157 The strong law of large numbers was first formulated by Cantelli (1917)... Like the weak law, it is only a very special case of a general theorem on random variables. **1964** A. P. & W. Robertson *Topological Vector Spaces* p. vii, It often clarifies results in the theory of normed spaces, especially those concerned with the weak topology, to regard them as particular cases of more general results about topological vector spaces. **1971** G. Higman in Powell & Higman *Finite Simple Groups* vi. 211 We then define E_n to be the weakest equivalence relation on Ω_n satisfying the following three conditions. **1979** *Proc. London Math. Soc.* XXXVIII. 439 Let L be the collection of minimal edge-sets of paths which join *s* to *s'* or *t* to *t'*. Then L has the weak MFMC property (but.. in general, not the strong).

g. Of a dose of medicine: Less in quantity (and hence in power) than the normal dose.

1899 *Allbutt's Syst. Med.* VIII. 588 Weak doses of thymol, tar, or subacetate of lead.

†**h.** Of slumber: Light, not deep or heavy. *Obs.*

1663 Patrick *Parab. Pilgr.* x. (1687) 56 A weak slumber.. chaining up his reason, left only his imagination at liberty to rove about.

i. Of a chance: Slight, slender, small in degree.

1853 Dickens *Bleak Ho.* x, Shall I call him down? But it's a weak chance if he'd come, sir!

j. Of an attack of disease: Not severe or acute.

1899 *Allbutt's Syst. Med.* VIII. 586 It [i.e. 'red gum'] is more probably urticarial or a weak form of prurigo.

k. *Physics.* Applied to one of the four known kinds of force between particles, which is effective only at distances less than about 10^{-15} cm., is very much weaker than the electromagnetic and the strong interactions, and conserves neither strangeness, parity, nor isospin.

[**1953** M. Gell-Mann in *Physical Rev.* XCII. 833/2 Let us suppose that both 'ordinary particles' (nucleons and pions) and 'new unstable particles'.. have interactions of three kinds:..(iii) Other charge-dependent interactions, which we take to be very weak.] **1954** [see strong *a.* 10 e]. **1968** M. S. Livingston *Particle Physics* vii. 139 Parity conservation is violated in this weak interaction. **1972** G. L. Wick *Elementary Particles* iii. 43 Typical weak interactions are nuclear beta decay and the slow decays of elementary particles. **1976** *Sci. Amer.* Jan. 45/1 The weak force affects every particle but one, the exception being the photon. **1982** *Ann. Reg. 1981* 385 Theorists had already inferred that electromagnetism and the weak force were two extremes of the same thing.

13. a. Wanting in effectiveness.

1591 Shaks. *1 Hen. VI*, V. iii. 27 My ancient Incantations are too weake. **1600** —— *Sonn.* xxxiv. 11 Th' offenders sorrow lends but weake releife To him that beares the strong offenses crosse. **1667** Milton *P.L.* XII. 291 When they see Law can discover sin, but not remove, Save by those shadowie expiations weak, The bloud of Bulls and Goats. *a***1718** Prior *Engraven on Column* 14 Yet Spires and Towers in Dust shall lye, The weak Efforts of Human Pains. **1721** Pope *Epitaph Hon. S. Harcourt*, How vain is Reason, Eloquence how weak! If Pope must tell what Harcourt cannot speak. **1741** C'tess Pomfret in *C'tess Hartford's Corr.* (1805) III. 52 Knowing with what goodness you receive my weak endeavours to amuse you. **1822** Shelley *Chas. I*, ii. 292 *Strafford.* Be these the expedients until time and wisdom Shall frame a settled state of government. *Laud.* And weak expedients they.

b. Of evidence, argument, etc.: Not convincing. Of a case, title, etc.: Not having strong evidence.

1538 Starkey *England* I. ii. 27 That where as my resonys schal appere to you sklender and weke, wyth your dylygence you may them supply. **1542** Elyot *Dict.*, *Caussa inferior*, the lesse right, or weker title. **1560** Daus tr. *Sleidane's Comm.* 18 b, Which is a light and verye weake reason. **1593** Shaks. *3 Hen. VI*, I. i. 134 *Henry.* I know not what to say, my Titles weake. **1594** Hooker *Eccl. Pol.* II. v. §5, I wonder that a cause so weak and feeble hath bene so much persisted in. *c***1600** Montgomerie *Cherrie & Slae* 1112 Ȝour warrand is but waik. **1630** Milton *On Shaks.* 6 Dear son of memory, great heir of Fame, What need'st thou such weak witnes of thy name? **1662** Stillingfl. *Orig. Sacræ* III. i. §8 Hee admits them upon far weaker grounds than wee do attribute them to God. **1686** Tillotson *Serm. at White-Hall, 1 Cor. iii. 15*, 18 [An argument] so intolerably weak and sophistical that any considerate man ought to be asham'd to be catch'd by it. **1707** Atterbury *Vind. Doctr. Funeral Serm. Bennet* 4 Pretending to shew, how weak and improper the Proofs are, which their Asserters employ in the defence of them. **1781** Cowper *Convers.* 722 Will they believe, though credulous enough To swallow much upon much weaker proof. **1863** Twistleton in *W. Smith's Dict. Bible* III. s.v. *Zidon*, Justin, however, is such a weak authority for any disputed historical fact. **1871** Freeman *Norm. Conq.* IV. xviii. 188 But the direct evidence for a siege of Oxford is so weak that the tale cannot be relied on. **1904** H. Belloc *Old Road* 119 The first evidence afforded us was weak enough. We saw [etc.].

†**14.** Of a thing: Of little account or worth, inconsiderable. *Obs.*

1590 Shaks. *Mids. N.* V. i. 434 And this weake and idle theame, No more yeelding but a dreame, Gentles, doe not reprehend. **1604** —— *Oth.* III. iii. 443 O that the Slaue had forty thousand liues; One is too poore, too weake for my reuenge. **1822** Shelley *Chas. I*, ii. 207 *Strafford.* How weak, how short, is life to pay— *King.* Peace, peace. Thou ow'st me nothing yet.

15. a. Having less than the full or proper amount of a specific ingredient. Of an infusion: Over-diluted.

1597 Shaks. *2 Hen. IV*, II. ii. 10 Doth it not shew vildely in me, to desire small Beere? *Poin.* Why, a Prince should not be so loosely studied, as to remember so weake a Composition. **1676** J. Smith *Art of Painting* vii. 38 You must give it such a quantity of your fat Oyl, that it may not be so weak as to run when you have laid it on, nor so stiff, that it may not work well. **1755** Johnson, *Weak*... 6. Not much impregnated with any ingredient: as a weak tincture, weak beer. **1769** J. Skeat *Art of Cookery* Expl. Terms, *Cooley*; is a white broth or weak gravy. **1791** W. Hamilton *Berthollet's Dyeing* I. 5 By means of a very weak acid. **1815** J. Smith *Panorama Sci. & Art* II. 837 To a weak solution of galls, add a few drops of weak solution of sulphate of iron. **1840** Dickens *Old C. Shop* lxiv, A great basin of weak tea. **1891** 'J. S. Winter' *Lumley* xv, A little brandy and water, not too weak.

b. *spec.* of iron.

1841 Greener *Sci. Gunnery* 120 An iron which is technically termed 'Weak,' can never be made a strong bodied iron. **1868** Joynson *Metals* 58 What is called 'weak' pig-iron, which contains a high percentage of phosphorus and sulphur.

c. Of corn: ? Having a small proportion of grain to the chaff.

1842 J. Aiton *Domest. Econ.* (1857) 205 Let the cows get.. a little clover hay, mixed with weak oats, the refuse of what is sent to the mill. *Ibid.* 252 The horse gets about the fourth part of a peck of oats, with some weak and refuse corn for supper daily.

d. Of flour: Made from soft wheat, so that it contains relatively less gluten and more starch, rises less with yeast, and is less cohesive. Of wheat: Soft.

1889 J. Blandy *Bakers' Guide* (ed. 2) 65 It is very important that young bakers should know how to buy, and blend flour for bread-making; and we.. direct them to use a hard dry flour in the sponge, with an eighth part of soft weak flour.. to feed the yeast. **1914** *Times* 8 June 16/5 Some flours, among which that from English wheat may be taken as a familiar example, produce small flat close-textured and 'runny' loaves. These are called weak flours. **1924** J. Stewart *Bread & Bread Baking* ii. 15 Weak flours are.. important in pastry baking and confectionery. **1951** *Good Housek. Home Encycl.* 466/2 'Soft' or 'weak' wheats contain less gluten and more starch. **1962** *Listener* 22 Mar. 510/1 As a general rule, 'strong' flour contains more nitrogen than 'weak' flour.

e. Of the mixture in an internal-combustion engine: = lean *a.* 4 f.

1918 V. W. Pagé *Aviation Engines* iii. 114 A rich mixture ignites much quicker than a weak mixture. **1948** 'N. Shute' *No Highway* ix. 217 Mr. Honey's estimate of the time to tailplane failure, under normal weak mixture cruising conditions, was 1,440 hours. **1981** R. Bacon *Two-Strike Tuning* ix. 63 All two-stroke engines are sensitive to mixture strength. Too rich and the power and acceleration suffer, while if too weak the result can be a seized or holed piston.

16. a. Wanting in material strength, unsound, insecure.

*c***1400** *Contin. Brut* ccxxxii. 315 Oþer strong werkes.. were so yshake þerewith, þat þey.. shol be euermore, the febelere & weyker while þey stonde. **1535–6** in *Trans.*

Shropsh. Archæol. Soc. (1880) III. 256 This yeare was a maltman slayne in grope lone in Shrewsburie with the fall of a wecke chymney in an old howse there. **1545** ASCHAM *Toxoph.* II. (Arb.) 121 Freates begynne many tymes in a pin, for there the good woode is corrupted, that it muste nedes be weke, and bycause it is weake, therfore it freates. **1612** R. CH. *Olde Thrift newly revived* 69 Where that many fences bee weake..[to] bee strengthened. **1622** J. TAYLOR (Water P.) *Shilling* B 5, And by misfortune if the Caske be weake, Three or foure Gallons in the ground may leake. **1855** TENNYSON *Brook* 84 The gate, Half-parted from a weak and scolding hinge, Stuck. **1856** J. C. MORTON *Cycl. Agric.* I. 840/1 This causes inequality of growth, weak and deficient places in the hedge.

b. *fig.* and in fig. context. Freq. in ***weak link***: the weakest or least dependable of a number of interdependent items; also in *Proverb.* Cf. *weak point (a)*, sense 16 e.

1581 N. BURNE *Disput.* xxv. 111 b, Thairfoir all that quhilk ye grounde vpone this vaik fundament, man fall altogidder. **1595** SHAKS. *John* v. vii. 78 Returne with me againe To push destruction, and perpetuall shame Out of the weake doore of our fainting Land. **1692** PRIOR *Ode Imit. Hor.* vii, Your mould'ring Monuments in vain ye raise On the weak Basis of the Tyrant's Praise. **1868** *Cornh. Mag.* XVII. 295 A chain is no stronger than its weakest link. **1885** E. P. HOOD *World of Proverb* 131 The strength of the chain is in the weakest link. **1926** H. CRANE *Let.* 12 Aug. (1965) 272 Mrs. Simpson was enormously pleased at your postcard; and I with your praise of the Dedication. You generally do pick the weakest link; that verse has bothered me. **1942** I. S. SHRIBER *Body for Bill* (1947) xiv. 183 'Stansfield was a pretty weak individual... He was threatening to give the whole thing away.'.. 'A chain is no stronger than its weakest link, remember?' **1965** M. FRAYN *Tin Men* xv. 88 An unreliable man, Haugh, a weak link in the team. **1975** R. LEWIS *Double Take* iv. 138 All right, he lifted the heart drug, but we..picked out the weak link in Ward too. **1984** *Bookseller* 8 Sept. 1049/2, I sometimes seek comfort in the old adage that a chain is only as strong as its weakest link.

c. Of a fortified place: Not possessed of sound defence (esp. in some part or on a particular side). Also †***weak-breach*** (in quot. *fig.*).

c **1400** MAUNDEV. (Roxb.) x. 40 Ynentes þe kirk of þe Sepulchre es þe citee maste wayke, for þe grete playne þat es betwene þe citee and þe kirke. *a* **1586** SIDNEY *Arcadia* III. xiii. §7 The glittering of the armour, and sounding of the trumpets giving such an assault to the weake-breache of his false senses. **1604** JAS. I *Counterbl. Tobacco* (Arb.) 107 He makes his breach and entrie, at some..parts thereof, which hee hath tried and found to bee weakest and least able to resist. **1652** H. COGAN tr. *Scudery's Ibrahim* Pref., in *Villiers' Rehearsal* (Arb.) 30 It is of works of this nature, as of a place of war, where notwithstanding all the care the Engineer hath brought to fortifie it, there is alwayes some weak part found. **1673** TEMPLE *Observ. Netherl.* viii. 251 Those Out-works which are either weak of themselves, or not well defensible for want of men. **1849** MACAULAY *Hist. Eng.* v. I. 597 Bristol had fortifications which, on the north of the Avon..were weak.

quasi-*adv.* **1720** OZELL tr. *Vertot's Rom. Rep.* II. XIV. 418 Hirtius found out a Place weaker guarded than the rest, which he carried Sword in hand.

d. ***weak side*** [cf. F. *côté faible*]. *(a)* Of a fortified place: A side defectively fortified or unsound in its defences. *(b) fig.*

(a) **1667** DRYDEN *Secret Love* 1st Prol. iv, Plays are like Towns, which, howe're fortifi'd By Engineers, have still some weaker side, By the o'reseen Defendant unespy'd.

(b) **1671** TEMPLE *Surv. Const. Empire, Sueden* etc., Miscell. (1680) 13 Their Application..to trade, has much increast their Shipping and Seamen (which they found to be their weak-side in their last attempts). **1692** L'ESTRANGE *Fables* I. cccxxx. 288 This Dog here would perhaps have Fought for his Master in any Other Case..: But the Love of Mutton was his Weak side. **1713** ADDISON *Cato* I. i, To quell the tyrant Love, and guard thy heart On this weak side, where most our nature fails. **1730** T. BOSTON *Mem.* vii. (1899) 140 Satan soon after got in upon my weak side. **1780** *Mirror* No. 92 My friend..is a little inclined to take things on their weak side. **1809** MALKIN *Gil Blas* XI. v. ¶1 He spared you the trouble of finding out the weak side of that prelate and his principal officers, by discovering their different characters to you.

e. ***weak point.*** *(a)* Of a thing: The point or feature where it is defective or unsound. *(b)* (A person's) ***weak point***, a failing or weakness (moral or intellectual).

(a) **1865** MILL *Auguste Comte* 126 M. Littré..is a disciple only of the Cours de Philosophie Positive, and can see the weak points even in that. **1868** S. NEIL *Publ. Meetings* 81 In it [*sc.* the peroration] the strong points should be enforced, and the weak should be slipped airily over. **1869** TOZER *Highl. Turkey* II. 21 A magnificent view indeed it was... The weak point in it was that the country on one side was.. excluded from view. **1875** [see WEAR *v.* 15]. **1883** A. SIDGWICK *Fallacies* 218 To use it as a rough guide in finding the weak point of an argument. **1908** *Animal Management* (War Office) 180 Every weak point in the fit of a saddle in a squadron should be known. **1920** *Times Lit. Suppl.* 29 Apr. 263/3 The weak point of modern capitalism is the opportunity it gives of bad spending.

(b) **1827** HARE *Guesses* I. 183 Do you want to find out a person's weak points? Observe the failings he has the quickest eye for in others. **1849** C. BRONTË *Shirley* xxv, Other people betrayed consciousness of, and annoyance at her weak points.

17. Wanting in solidity or firmness; slight; of a texture easily broken, fragile, frail.

1581 [1582] T. NORTON in Nicolas *Sir C. Hatton* (1847) 235, I desire not to undertake any such work, but do shun it as storms in a broad sea for a weak vessel. **1601** SHAKS. *Jul. C.* I. iii. 108 Those that with haste will make a mightie fire, Begin it with weake Strawes. **1680** J. COLLINS *Plea Irish Cattell*, etc. 26 The Hurds,..or Tow, of Flax and Hemp, will serve to make a weaker, or a worser sort of Linnen. **1705** tr. *Bosman's Guinea* 260 Their Eggs are..covered..with a thick Flesh which is pliable and weak. **1756** R. ROGERS *Jrnls.* (1769) 11 We then attempted to cross the lake, but found the ice too weak. **1817** SHELLEY *To William Shelley* 2 The billows on the beach are leaping around it, The bark is weak and frail. **1897** PR. RANJITSINHJI *Jubilee Bk. Cricket* iv. 148 A weak, springy [bat] handle is a mistake. A handle should bend like the butt-end of a good fly-rod and not like an aspen stick.

fig. **1592** SHAKS. *Ven. & Ad.* Ded., I know not..how the worlde will censure mee for choosing so strong a proppe to support so weake a burthen. **1781** COWPER *Expost.* 629 What web too weak to catch a modern brain? **1784** —— *Tiroc.* 169 How weak the barrier of mere nature proves, Oppos'd against the pleasures nature loves!

18. Not strongly marked. **a.** Of colours, markings: Not vivid.

1585 HIGINS *Junius' Nomencl.* 177/2 *Buxeus*,..a weake or vnperfect yellow, like box. **1591** SHAKS. *Two Gent.* III. ii. 6 This weake impresse of Loue, is as a figure Trenched in ice, which with an houres heate Dissolues to water, and doth loose his forme. **1831** BREWSTER *Optics* x. 87 In the spectrum of Pollux there were many weak but fixed lines. **1876** ABNEY *Instr. Photogr.* (ed. 3) 100 For a negative of the weak type the bromide may be omitted. **1878** —— *Treat. Photogr.* xii. 85 Defects in negatives... A weak image may be due—1, to an unsuitable collodion [etc.].

b. *Mining* and *Geol.* (See quot. 1884.)

1833 T. SOPWITH *Mining Distr. Alston Moor* 107 Old Carr's Cross Vein, in Alston Moor, in mining language, is weakest at the north end. **1884** J. A. PHILLIPS *Ore Deposits* 185 In the Alston-Moor district a vein is said to be weak when the strata on either side are but slightly displaced.

c. Of an animal's scent: Faint.

1854 SURTEES *Handley Cr.* xxxvii. (1901) II. 6 Pigg lifted his 'ounds, the scent being weak from the water.

19. *Comm.* Of market prices, the market: Having a downward tendency, not firm. Hence of commodities with regard to their prices.

1856 in Tooke & Newmarch *Hist. Prices* (1857) V. 657 In January ('56) the market opened with much firmness at 75*s*...; subsequently the tone became weaker. **1882** *Daily News* 23 Aug. 2/7 Prices for wheat, however, were decidedly weaker. **1900** *Ibid.* 17 Sept. 2/5 Hematite continues to be weak, as was the case at Tuesday's market. **1903** S. S. PRATT *Work of Wall St.* 100 If there are more offers than bids the market is weak and the price declines.

20. *Phonetics* and *Prosody.* Of a sound: Pronounced with less force than the adjacent sound or sounds. Of accent, stress: Having relatively little force. Of a syllable, the ending of a verse: Unstressed or without metrical ictus. Of the caesura: Falling after a short syllable. Of a variant pronunciation: usual in contexts where the word is unstressed.

weak ending, the occurrence of an unstressed or proclitic monosyllable (a preposition or conjunction) in the normally stressed place at the end of an iambic line. Sometimes distinguished from *light ending* (e.g. a relative pronoun or auxiliary verb), on which the voice can dwell slightly.

a **1637** B. JONSON *Engl. Gram.* iv. (1640) 43 Before *e.* and *i.* it [C] hath a weake sound, and hisseth like *s.* **1662** HOWELL *New Engl. Gram.* 28 This letter *n*..hath three degrees of sounds, full in the beginning, weak in the middle, and flat at the end of a word. **1765** J. ELPHINSTON *Princ. Engl. Lang.* II. 329 Combinations of two syllables. Iamb, a short and a long, or a weak and a strong. **1774** [W. MITFORD] *Ess. Harmony Lang.* 100 Besides these, feet often occur with the strong accent on both syllables; and frequently one foot, sometimes two in a verse, have the weaker accent only. **1824** T. MARTIN *Philol. Eng. Gram.* 117 When two consonants fall together and will not combine, the weaker is sometimes silent. **1838** E. GUEST *Engl. Rhythms* I. 86 The primary accent of the adjective ought always, when not emphatic, to be weaker than that of the substantive. **1852** *Proc. Philol. Soc.* V. 153 A foot catalectic on the weak syllable. **1857** C. BATHURST *Shaks. Versif.* 38 There are several instances of the weak endings. **1871** J. HADLEY *Ess.* (1873) 273 The effect of a weak *r* on the preceding short vowel. **1874** B. H. KENNEDY *Publ. Sch. Lat. Gram.* §260 (ed. 2) 529 A weak trochaic caesura, after the trochee or second syllable of the dactyl. **1874** J. K. INGRAM in *Trans. New Shaks. Soc.* II. 447 The former may with convenience be called 'light endings', whilst to the latter may be appropriated the name (hitherto vaguely given to both groups jointly) of 'weak endings'. **1886** J. B. MAYOR *Engl. Metre* 103 Some have maintained that the basis of the metre is a double trochee with a weaker stress on the first syllable and stronger on the third. **1890** H. SWEET *Primer Spoken Eng.* 13 Words that occur very frequently with weak stress often develope a *weak* form by the side of the original *strong* one. **1917** D. JONES *Eng. Pronouncing Dict.* p. xix, Circumstances exist in which strong forms occur unstressed, but in no case does a weak form occur stressed. **1982** J. C. WELLS *Accents of Eng.* I. iii. 227 In many accents the pronoun *you* has a weak form /jə/ (conventionally spellable *ya* in the United States, but *yer* in non-rhotic-oriented England).

21. *Philol.* In various applications, opposed to *strong* (see STRONG *a.* 22). **a.** Of Teut. nouns and adjs.: Belonging to any of the declensions in which the stem in OTeut. ended in *-n*. **b.** Of Teut. verbs: Forming the preterite by the addition of a suffix. **c.** In Greek grammar, sometimes applied to the sigmatic or 'first' aorist, in contradistinction to the 'second' or 'strong' aorist. **d.** In Sanskrit grammar, the designation of the reduced stems of nouns, and of the cases in which the reduced stem occurs. **e.** In Hebrew and Syriac grammar applied to certain consonants (otherwise called 'feeble') and to verbs which have one or more of these in the root. **f.** The designation of the ablaut-grade which results from absence of stress.

a. **1841** [see STRONG *a.* 22 a]. **1885** J. BYRNE *Struct. Lang.* II. 194 There is also in all the Teutonic languages a weak declension, as Grimm has called it, which has arisen from the insertion of *n* or *an* between the stem and the element of case or number.

b. **1833** *Philol. Museum* II. 385 No weak verb ever in process of time became strong, while strong verbs do become weak. **1841** LATHAM *Eng. Lang.* xviii. 198 Weak Tenses. The Præterite Tense of the Weak Verbs is formed by the addition of *d* or *t*... The Verbs of the Weak Conjugation fall into Three Classes. **1845** *Proc. Philol. Soc.* II. 50 In the weak perfects of the Teutonic languages..no such difficulty presents itself. **1886** KINGTON OLIPHANT *New Engl.* I. 228 There is a curious confusion of the Strong and Weak verb in *metal moltynnyd*.

c. **1875** E. ABBOTT *Curtius' Elucid. Student's Grk. Gram.* 104 The sibilant common to both naturally leads from the future to the weak aorist. **1876** PAPILLON *Man. Comp. Philol.* 196 The Weak or Compound Aorist (1 aor.).

d. **1863** BENFEY *Sansk. Gram.* §220. 176 There are some nouns which have a strong and a weak form. *Ibid.* §238. 198 In the Veda the distinction between the strong and weak cases is less regularly observed than in the later Sanskrit.

e. **1874** A. B. DAVIDSON *Hebr. Gram.* 69 A weak verb is a verb which has one or more of its three stem letters a weak letter. The weak letters are the gutturals, the quiescents, and *nun*. **1904** J. A. CRICHTON *Nöldeke's Syriac Gram.* 42 Weak roots vary a good deal in their weak letters. *Ibid.* 106 A few verbs *primae n* also take *e*, as well as a few weak verbs.

f. **1888** SWEET *Hist. Engl. Sounds* §249 The result was a variety of vowel-series, each with the three stages, strong, medium, and weak. **1891** A. L. MAYHEW *O.E. Phonol.* §645 Weak (i.e. Zero) Grades. **1908** WRIGHT *O.E. Gram.* §472 In the athematic verbs the personal endings were added to the bare root, which had the strong grade form of ablaut in the singular, but the weak grade in the dual and plural.

22. Similative phrases in which *weak* may have any of various meanings. (See also sense 5 a.)

1535 BIBLE (Coverdale) *Ezek.* vii. 17 All knees shalbe weake as the water [**1611** (A.V.) weake as water]. **1874** TROLLOPE *Phineas Redux* II. xxx. 244 She would not sin... Having so resolved, she became weak as water. **1926** J. BUCHAN *Dancing Floor* I. ii. 54 We were as weak as kittens, but..extraordinarily happy. **1980** A. PRICE *Hour of Donkey* ix. 123 He must have been as weak as a kitten, with all the blood he'd lost. **1983** J. WAINWRIGHT *Their Evil Ways* v. 154, I think you're mad... Mad and as weak as water.

23. Comb. **a.** In parasynthetic adjs., as ***weak-backed***, ***-brained***, ***-chined***, ***-fleshed***, ***-limned***, ***-principled***, ***-skinned***, ***-stressed***, etc. See also WEAK-HANDED, -HEADED, -HEARTED, -KNEED, -MINDED, -SIGHTED.

1535 COVERDALE *Isa.* xxviii. 7 They are..*weake braned thorow stronge drynke. **1841** DICKENS *Barn. Rudge* xxxiv, It is a foolish fancy on the part of this weak-brained man. *a* **1663** KILLIGREW *Parson's Wedd.* I. i. (1664) 75 The *weak-chin'd slave hir'd me once to say, I was with Child by him. **1657** J. SERGEANT *Schism Dispach't* 94 This *weak-conscienc'd man. **1645** WALLER *To Mistris Braughton* 8 So in those Nations which the Sun adore Some modest Persian, or some *weak-ey'd Moore, No higher dares advance his dazled sight. **1746** COLLINS *Ode to Evening* iii, Save where the weak-eyed bat With short shrill shriek flits by on leathern wing. **1822** SHELLEY *Chas. I*, ii. 127 And banish weak-eyed Mercy to the weak. **1967** *Weak-fleshed [see *raw-jawed* adj. s.v. RAW *a.* 9]. **1611** SHAKS. *Wint. T.* II. iii. 119 Not able to produce more accusation Then your owne *weake-hindg'd Fancy. **1853** DICKENS *Bleak Ho.* liii, You're not one of the *weak-legged ones. **1852** THACKERAY *Esmond* I. xii, My Lord Firebrace was but a feeble-minded and *weak-limbed young nobleman. *a* **1918** W. OWEN *Poems* (1963) 90 The *weak-limned hour when sick men's sighs are drained. **1802** 'AN ENGLISH TRAVELLER' *Sk. Paris* II. lx. 293 These *weak-nerved females, who would have fainted at the sight of a spider mangling a fly. **1835** DICKENS *Sk. Boz, Parlour Orator*, *Weak-pated dolts they are. **1913** D. H. LAWRENCE *Sons & Lovers* ix. 246 It was the nose and eyes of her own mother's people—good-looking, *weak-principled folk. **1933** DYLAN THOMAS *Lett.* (1966) 72 And unless you want to regard the man [*sc.* D. H. Lawrence] as a vain, *weak-skinned, egocentric, domineering little charlatan, *don't* borrow the book. **1796** W. H. MARSHALL *W. Eng.* II. 207 A *weaksoiled arable District. **1508** FISHER *Wks.* (1876) 253 Those the whiche be basshefull and *weyke spyryted. **1898** H. SWEET *New Eng. Gram.* II. 32 If three strong-stressed words come together—especially in immediate succession, but also with intervening *weak-stressed words—the stress of the middle word is often reduced. **1966** *English Studies* XLVII. 83 In languages that use interrogatives as indefinites, such as Dutch, the latter are always weak-stressed. **1896** *Allbutt's Syst. Med.* I. 229 A *weak-walled heart..is much more easily influenced by digitalis than a healthy one. **1885** *Graphic* 21 Feb. 174/2 *Weak-willed folk. **1909** G. M. TREVELYAN *Garibaldi & Thousand* iv. 73 The doubtful and weak-willed guide of Europe's destiny. **1649** G. DANIEL *Trinarch., Hen. IV*, ccxxiv, Soe cutting through a Swarme Of Gnatts, an Eagle scoureing after Prey, Beats downe the *weak-wing'd vermin in her way. **1865** SWINBURNE *Chastelard* IV. i. 159 These men be *weaker-witted than mere fools When they fall mad once.

b. as adv. with pa. pples., ***weak-built***, ***-made***; with pres. pples., ***weak-growing***, ***-shivering***.

1593 SHAKS. *Lucr.* 130 Yet euer to obtaine his will resoluing. Though *weake-built hopes perswade him to abstaining. **1656** COWLEY *Pindar. Odes, Life and Fame* i, Oh Life.. Vain weak-built Isthmus, which dost proudly rise Up betwixt two Eternities. **1842** LOUDON *Suburban Hort.* 705 In *weak-growing sorts, apt to fruit, they should be encouraged with manure. **1593** SHAKS. *Lucr.* 1260 Those proud Lords to blame, Make *weak-made women tenants to their shame. **1727–46** THOMSON *Summer* 1260 Nor, when cold Winter keens the brightening flood, Would I *weak-shivering linger on the brink.

c. †**weak-back**, †**-wit**, one who is weak in the back, in mind; †**weak-heart** *a.*, = WEAK-HEARTED.

a **1425** tr. *Arderne's Treat. Fistula*, etc. 8 All þinges ar hard to a waik hert man, for þai trow euermore yuellez to be nyȝe to þam. **1656** Earl Monm. tr. *Boccalini's Advts. fr. Parnass.* i. ix. (1674) 11 [Greek] proves hard of digestion to the squeasie stomacks of modern weak-wits. **1659** Cleveland *Vit. Uxoris* xviii, By thee 'tis likely shee'l have none. Whilst thou for weak-back go.

†**B.** *sb.* = feeble *sb.* 4, foible 2. In quot. 1683 *fig. Obs.*

1683 D. A. *Art of Converse* 87 And so [we] lose a considerable advantage over our Adversary by not reflecting where the weak of his discourse lies; we think only on't when the stroke is past. **1692** Sir W. Hope *Fencing Master* 28 Thrust with the Fort of your Sword upon the weak of his.

†**weak,** *v. Obs.* Forms: 5–6 **weke, weyk, weik, wayk,** *Sc.* **waik,** (6 **vaik**), 6 **week,** 6–9 **weak.** [f. weak *a.*]

1. *trans.* To make weak or weaker, to weaken or enfeeble. Also *fig.*

c **1400** *Rom. Rose* 4737 A strengthe, weyked to stonde vp-right [Fr. *force enfermé*], And feblenesse, ful of might. **1459** *Paston Lett.* I. 444 He.. is ryte lowe browt, and sore weykid and feblyd. **1502** *Ord. Crysten Men* (W. de W.) iii. iii. (1506) 156 In weykynge them and dyscouragynge, be it by theyr euyll example or otherwyse. **1513** Douglas *Æneis* ix. x. 50 Nor ȝit the slaw nor febill onwieldy age May waik our spreit, nor mynys our curage. *a* **1536** Tindale *Brief Decl. Sacram.* (*c* 1550) B v b, All that comme to the sacrament.. with the medytacyon to weak the flesh and strenght the Spyrite agaynst her. *c* **1560** A. Scott *Poems* (S.T.S.) xxxiv. 14 Ane fowsum appetyte, That strenth of persoun waikis. *a* **1635** Randolph *Poems* (1638) 50 It weaks the Braine; it spoiles the memory. **1642–7** H. More *Song of Soul* i. ii. lxxx, Which will empair the flesh and weak the knee. **1856** J. Ballantine *Poems* 190 Time hasna dimmed my goshawk ee, Nor weak'd my hand.

absol. **1568** Skeyne *Pest* (Bannatyne Club) 25 Fasting mundifeis.. bot vaikis thair with.

b. To soak in water, to macerate. Cf. woke *v.* [? After Du. *weeken*, LG. *wêken*.]

1559 Morwyng *Evonymus* 10 This herbe.. if it be dried and weikte or stiept in wyne a few dayes, then destilled in Balneo Mariæ. *Ibid.* 72 Newe herbes nede the lesse time, when they are stiept or weekt in wine or other liquor.

2. *intr.* To become weaker or less severe, be mitigated.

c **1374** Chaucer *Troylus* iv. 1144 (Campsall MS.) Somwhat to wayken [*Harl. MS.* woken] gan þe peyne.

Hence †'**weaking** *vbl. sb.*

1559 Morwyng *Evonymus* 67 Maceration, yt is steping or weking, or els infusion, a watring & moistening. **1581** W. S. *Exam. Compl.* i. 6 Albeit we labour not much with our bodies.. yet yee know we labour with our mindes, more to ye weaking of ye same, then by any other bodily exercise we should do. *Ibid.* ii. 18 b, It may come to ye great desolation and weaking of the strenght of this realme.

weak, obs. form of wick.

weake, obs. form of week.

weaken ('wiːk(ə)n), *v.* Also 6 **wayken, weyken,** *Sc.* **waken.** *Pa. t.* and *pple.* 4 **waykned,** 6–8 **weakned,** 7 *Sc.* **waikned.** [f. weak *a.* + -en[5].

In the following early instance the word may be a direct adoption from Scand.; cf. Norw. dial. *veikna*, MSw. and Sw. *vekna*, to become weak.

13.. *E.E. Allit. P.* B. 1422 So faste þay weȝed to him wyne, hit.. breyþed vppe in to his brayn & blemyst his mynde, & al waykned his wyt, & wel neȝe he foles.]

I. *trans.* To make weak or weaker.

†**1.** To soften. **a.** To steep (salt meat) in water, so as to remove the salt (cf. woke *v.*). **b.** To dissolve in acid. *Obs.*

1530 Palsgr. 770/1, I wayken salte meates, I lay them in water. *Je attrempe en leaue.* **1540** —— *Acolastus* ii. i. H iv b, Clodius Esopus his sonne dyd at a banket eate a perle, weakened in stronge vyneyger.

2. To lessen the physical strength or vigour of (an animal or plant, its parts or organs); to lessen the functional vigour of (an organ or an organic power).

1568 Grafton *Chron.* II. 707 At the laste battayle the very strengthe of his chiefe souldiours was weakened. **1577** B. Googe *Heresbach's Husb.* iii. 149 b, Swyne.. Afore they goe to pasture, they must be medicined, least the grasse skarre [*sic*] them to much, by which they wylbe greatly weakened. **1588** Greene *Pandosto* (1607) G 1 b, Who gazeth at the Sunne, weakeneth his sight. **1643** Baker *Chron., Hen. II* (1653) 87 So strong a Corrosive is grief of mind, when it meetes with a body weakened before with sicknesse. **1764** *Museum Rust.* IV. 30 Such running to seed will weaken the plants much more than several cuttings. **1810** Crabbe *Borough* xxii. 331 Through the water came A hollow groan, that weaken'd all my frame. **1831–3** E. Burton *Eccles. Hist.* xii. (1845) 282 The venerable Apostle was so weakened by age, that his disciples were obliged to carry him to the religious meetings. **1845** Budd *Dis. Liver* 130 Such measures.. weaken the patient, at a time when his assimilating powers can scarcely maintain his actual condition. **1864** Tennyson *En. Arden* 821 A languor came Upon him, gentle sickness, gradually Weakening the man, till he could do no more, But kept the house, his chair, and last his bed.

b. In Bible phrase, ***to weaken the hands of***: *fig.* to reduce the effectiveness of (a person or body of persons), to hinder, discourage. Cf. strengthen *v.* 2 b.

1560 Bible (Geneva) *Jer.* xxxviii. 4, *Neh.* vi. 9. **1864** Pusey *Lect. Daniel* (1876) 135 The people of the land weakened the hands of the people of Judah.

3. To enfeeble or decrease the vigour of (the mind, etc.).

1536 *Primer Eng. & Lat., Dirige* (Rouen) 133 My spyryte god wotte is wekenyd wonders sore. **1683** Burnet tr. *More's Utopia* 88 Unless Age has weakned his Understanding. **1748** Richardson *Clarissa* (1768) VI. 217 When peoples minds are weakened by a sense of their own infirmities. **1840** Dickens *Old C. Shop* xii, His consciousness came back; but the mind was weakened and its functions were impaired.

4. To lessen (authority, influence, power, credit), †to lower the value of (something); †to impoverish (an estate).

1530 Palsgr. 770/1 Their power is waykenned: *leur pouuoyr est affoyblié* or *infermé*. **1560** Daus tr. *Sleidane's Comm.* 155 There can no greater plage inuade a commen wealth, than what time thauthoritie of lawes is weakened and disolued. **1612** *Two Noble K.* v. iv, A Steed.. a black one, owing Not a hayr worth of white, which some will say Weakens his price. **1618–20** *Essex Archd. Bk. Depositions* (MS.) 21 b, He.. nowe found his estate much weakned and impaired sithence the makinge of the said will. **1639** Du Verger tr. *Camus' Admir. Events* 6 Her Father Venon.. had much weakned his estate in drawing his deare friend out of prison. **1667** Milton *P.L.* ii. 1002 Weakning the Scepter of old Night. **1673** Temple *Observ. United Prov.* viii. 251 Because the loss of every small Outwork does not only weaken the Number, but sink the Courage of the Garrison within. **1706** E. Ward *Wooden World Diss.* (1708) 7 Such a Prostitution of his Presence, he thinks, weakens his Authority. *a* **1715** Burnet *Own Time* (1766) II. 71 While the witnesses were weakening their own credit. **1748** Richardson *Clarissa* (1768) VIII. 215 Which must weaken the influences of their good works. **1776** Adam Smith *W.N.* iii. ii. I. 467 That the power, and consequently the security of the monarchy, may not be weakened by division, it must descend entire to one of the children. **1847** G. Harris *Ld. Chanc. Hardwicke* I. iii. 245 The witness may also be made to weaken his own credit, by the account which he admits of himself, or of his character. **1885** 'Mrs. Alexander' *Valerie's Fate* iii, The slight difference of age between herself and those she taught somewhat weakened her authority.

5. To reduce the strength of (a body of men) in numbers or fighting power; to render (a position) less secure.

1560 Daus tr. *Sleidane's Comm.* 129 b, What tyme the one parte was thus weakened, the Anabaptistes doe chouse newe senatours, all of their owne faction. **1600** Hakluyt *Voy.* III. 228 Considering how in number we were diminished, and in strength greatly weakned, both by reason of our sicknesse and also of the number that were dead. **1617** Moryson *Itin.* ii. 111 Imagining that Tyrone.. would not have.. any minde to.. hinder his retreate when he should have weakened his forces by that Plantation [of a garrison]. **1698** J. Collier *Immor. Stage* i. 5 Such Licentious Discourse tends.. to weaken the Defences of Virtue. **1760** *Cautions & Advices to Officers of Army* 171 If you should be sent on a Party, observe this Precaution yourself; but let them not be *too* strong, lest you weaken your main Body. **1860** Löwenthal *Morphy's Games Chess* 114 This move, however, weakens the K. B's P., which immediately becomes the focus of Black's attack. **1875** Gossip *Chess-player's Man.* 846 Black would gain a move, but weaken his position.

6. To render weaker in resources, authority, political or military power, or the like.

1568 Bible (Bishops') *Isa.* xiv. 12 O Lucifer.. Howe hast thou gotten a fall euen to the grounde, which didst weaken the nations? **1597** Hooker *Eccl. Pol.* v. lxxvi. §6 As long as their amitie with God continued,.. nothing could weaken them but Apostasie. **1651** Hobbes *Leviath.* ii. xvii. (1904) 116 So now do Cities and Kingdomes.. endeavour as much as they can, to subdue, or weaken their neighbours. **1673** Temple *Observ. United Prov.* i. 17 Both Philip and his Son.. found themselves a Match for France, then much weakned, as well by the late wars of England, as the Factions of their Princes. **1713** Addison *Cato* ii. iii, Let us not weaken still the weaker side, By our divisions. **1727** De Foe *Engl. Tradesm.* (1732) I. vi. 67 As they [*sc.* those adventures] very rarely add to his credit, so if they lessen the man's stock, they weaken him in the main, and he must at last faint under it. **1853** Newman *Hist. Sk.* (1873) II. i. vi. 137 They took every means to weaken and annoy the very men whom they had invited. **1864** Bryce *Holy Rom. Emp.* viii. (1875) 129 He [Otto] is commonly said to have wished to weaken the aristocracy by raising up rivals to them in the hierarchy. **1887** *Field* 3 Dec. 862/1 The Old Harrovians were now greatly weakened by the enforced retirement of Rendall. **1915** J. W. Headlam *Hist. Twelve Days* iii. 83 Serbia would certainly have been humbled and weakened.

7. To render less efficacious.

1639 Saltmarshe *Policy* 301 Perseverance preserves and advances that grace which relapses weaken and loose. **1712** Addison *Spect.* No. 309 ¶16 An ordinary Poet would indeed have spun out so many Circumstances to a great Length, and by that means have weakned, instead of illustrated, the principal Fable. **1823** Scott *Quentin D.* xxxiii, I.. swore.. upon another fragment of the true cross which I got from the Grand Seignior, weakened in virtue, doubtless, by sojourning with infidels. **1877** Tennyson *Harold* v. i, Let not my strong prayer Be weaken'd in thy sight.

b. To lessen or destroy the strength of (an argument, a case, etc.); to render (a probability) less likely.

1606 Shaks. *Tr. & Cr.* i. iii. 195 Aiax.. sets Thersites A slaue,.. To match vs in comparisons with durt, To weaken and discredit our exposure. **1644** J. Maxwell *Sacro-sancta Reg. Maj.* 46 This weakeneth no wayes our argument. **1796** H. Hunter tr. *St.-Pierre's Stud. Nat.* (1799) I. 166 This concession no more weakens the probability of the hydraulic cause, which I apply to it, than that of the principle of the attraction of the heavenly bodies, which [etc.]. **1855** Macaulay *Hist. Eng.* xx. IV. 527 They well knew that an inquiry could not strengthen their case, and might weaken it. **1886** J. B. Mayor *Engl. Metre* 76 This would very much weaken, if not entirely destroy, the evidence in favour of such feet.

c. To render (faith, resolve, conviction) weaker.

1848 Mrs. Gaskell *Mary Barton* xii, Don't let my being an unbelieving Thomas weaken your faith.

8. To render (a material thing) less strong or more liable to fracture.

1827 Faraday *Chem. Manip.* ix. (1842) 242 A hole.. will appear before the filter is finished; or if not, it will be so weakened as to be unable to bear a quantity of fluid without breaking. **1857** Dempsey *Archit. Pract.* 51 Closers must never be allowed except in the quoins; where they necessarily must occur, in order not to weaken the work by cutting those bricks which show on both faces. **1910** J. Bartlett in *Encycl. Brit.* V. 387/1 The timbers are held together with a spike. In this way they are not weakened. **1914** M. Barrett *Footpr. Anc. Scot. Ch.* i. 36 This weakened the central tower, which fell with a crash in 1688.

9. To reduce the intensity of (a colour, sound, fire).

1683 Salmon *Doron Med.* ii. 378 Then weaken the fire, and draw off a strong cinnamon water. **1733** *School of Miniature* 34 In working thereon with Green, it constantly weakens the Red which had first been laid on. **1791** W. Hamilton *Berthollet's Dyeing* II. 143 This weakens the colour of the madder. **1805** *Nicholson's Jrnl. Nat. Philos.* (8°) XI. 129 Both sounds grew weaker in proportion as I retired from the striking point; but that transmitted by the stone was weakened much more rapidly than that transmitted through the air. **1815** J. Smith *Panorama Sci. & Art* II. 531 The oxygen.. acts upon the colouring particles; it combines with them, and weakens their colour. **1876** Tait *Rec. Adv. Phys. Sci.* ix. 220 The atmosphere might merely have weakened the various kinds of sunlight.

b. *Phonetics.* To reduce in force of utterance.

1863 Benfey *Sansk. Gram.* §187. 153 Many verbs.. are weakened.. by rejecting final or penultimate nasals. **1869** J. Peile *Grk. & Lat. Etymol.* 124 As for example when *a* in Greek is weakened to *ι*. **1874** A. J. Ellis *E.E. Pronunc.* iv. 1282 In the first case the vowel is strengthened, in the latter weakened. **1877** Sweet *Primer Phonetics* §273 (1902) 95 There is a distinct tendency to weaken the stress of the last syllable of a syllable-group. **1888** —— *Hist. Engl. Sounds* 186 In *drawen* the *w* was probably soon weakened into an *u*. **1908** —— *Sounds of English* 51 The falling diphthongs weaken their second elements, so that they are no longer full *i, u*.

10. *Card-games.* To lessen the strength of (one's hand, etc.).

1742 Hoyle *Whist* (1746) 25 Whereas if you had trumped one of your Adversaries best Cards, you had so weakened your Hand, as probably not to make more than five Tricks without your Partner's Help. **1862** 'Cavendish' *Whist* (1864) 47 You weaken a suit by discarding from it, and lessen the number of long cards you might otherwise establish.

11. To render (market prices, a market) less firm.

1875 *Economist* 2 Jan. 20/1 Stocks being quite small, the increased receipts do not have much effect as yet in weakening prices. **1883** *Manch. Exam.* 26 Nov. 4/2 Advices from Manchester have tended to weaken the cotton market.

II. *intr.* **12.** To grow or become weak or weaker.

1541 R. Copland *Guydon's Quest. Chirurg.* O j, It shuld be daunger of to moche resolucyon and that the strength shuld weyken. **1594** R. Ashley tr. *Loys le Roy* 81 b, By transporting the principal forces, and riches, from Rome to Bizantium, diuiding of the Empire into the East and West; they weakned much. **1605** Shaks. *Lear* i. iv. 248 His Notion weakens. **1607** Rowlands *Guy Warw.* 32 The Emperor.. with new forces gave a new assault, Knowing the City could not be relieved, And then their strength would weaken by default. **1733** *School of Miniature* 34 With the same Mixture form all the Shades, adding White as they weaken. **1821** Clare *Vill. Minstr.* etc. II. 202 While o'er the meadow's little fluttering rill The twittering sunbeam weakens cool and dim. **1855** Browning *Old Pict. Florence* vi, Wherever an outline weakens and wanes. **1876** J. Ellis *Caesar in Egypt* 151 The body weakens, but the soul is strong. **1884** Howells in *Harper's Mag.* Dec. 123/2 These hydraulic elevators weaken sometimes, and can't go any further. **1886** Hardy *Mayor Casterbr.* I. xviii. 224 Mrs. Henchard was weakening visibly [in health]. **1920** *Times Lit. Suppl.* 23 Sept. 621/4 The plot weakens a little towards the end.

b. (orig. *U.S.*) To take a less firm attitude, to recede from a standpoint, to give way.

1876 'Mark Twain' *Tom Sawyer* xxvii, Don't you ever weaken, Huck, and I won't. **1882** Bret Harte *Flip* ii, 'Go 'long. Dad, you're talking silly!' The old man weakened. **1890** *Boston* (Mass.) *Jrnl.* 13 Sept. 73 A man whom he took for an accomplice weakened when the first child was to be taken and exposed the scheme. **1899** *Westm. Gaz.* 2 Dec. 2/2 The Church will indeed suffer an immense loss of moral prestige if she now weakens on this subject.

Hence '**weakened** *ppl. a.*

1548 *Elyot's Dict.*, *Attenuatus*,.. appayred, weakened, diminished. **1577** Grange *Golden Aphrod.* G iv b, The fountayne Granus giueth strength vnto the weakened bone. **1594** *Selimus* 157 My sonnes.. May take occasion of my weakned age, And rise in rebell armes against my state. **1694** Atterbury *Serm., Isa.* lx. 22 (1726) I. 130 When a Warlike and Savage Race of Men.. set upon a dissolute, divided, and weakned Enemy. **1797** Jane Austen *Sense & Sensib.* xxix, An aching head, a weakened stomach, and a general nervous faintness. **1869** J. Peile *Grk. & Lat. Etymol.* 159 The French *u* is a similar example of weakened articulation. **1870** Jevons *Elem. Logic* xvi. 140 They are said to have a weakened conclusion because the conclusion is particular. **1874** A. J. Ellis *E.E. Pronunc.* iv. 1284 In point of fact this (ə) is a 'weakened' (u) reduced to (o). **1893** Liddon *Life Pusey* I. xiii. 305 The proposed change, in Pusey's eyes, involves at least a weakened recognition of that duty [of propagating religious truth].

weakener ('wiːk(ə)nə(r)). Also 6–8 **weakner.** [f. weaken *v.* + -er[1].] One who or something which weakens.

1589 L. Andrewes *Serm., Lent* i. (1629) 268 If this Ego, be not Saul, but David. David, which giveth strength vnto the Pillers; and not Saul, an empairer or weakner of them. **1694** [S. Bethel] *Provid. God* (ed. 2) 94 There being no such Traitors to the Strength of a Land, Underminers and

Weakners thereof, as are unreformed Provocations. *a* **1716** South *Serm.* (1727) VI. xi. 397 Fastings and Mortifications ..which..rightly managed, are..great weakners of Sin. **1817** Coleridge *Biog. Lit.* (1907) I. iii. 35 Averrhoes' catalogue of Anti-Mnemonics, or weakeners of the memory. **1870** Emerson *Soc. & Sol.* viii. (1883) 161 The crowds and centuries of books are only..echoes and weakeners of these few great voices of Time.

weakening (ˈwiːk(ə)nɪŋ), *vbl. sb.* [-ING¹.]

1. The action of the vb. WEAKEN in various senses; an instance of this.

1548 *Elyot's Dict., Debilitatio*, a weakenyng, or makyng faynte. *c* **1550** W. S. *Disc. Comm. Weal Eng.* (1893) 21 Yet youe knowe we labour with oure myndes, more to the weaknynge of the same then by anie other bodyly exercise we can doe. *a* **1568** Ascham *Scholem.* II. (Arb.) 135 To the great weakening euen at this day of Christes Church in England. **1651** Hobbes *Leviath.* I. xii. 59 All which causes of the weakening of mens faith, do manifestly appear in the Examples following. **1674** R. Godfrey *Inj. & Ab. Physick* 72 What with the weakennings of this fit, twice bleeding an Issue, often vomitting, and oftner purging; I was every year as duly as autumn came, laid up with a continual Fever. **1748** *Anson's Voy.* I. x. 100 The diminishing and weakening of our crew by deaths and sickness. **1869** J. Peile *Grk. & Lat. Etymol.* 124 Here we have cases of pure weakening—the substitution of a weaker for a stronger sound. **1874** A. J. Ellis *E.E. Pronunc.* IV. 1270 Weakening consists, according to Grimm, in 'an unaccountable diminishing of vowel content'. **1876** Tait *Rec. Adv. in Phys. Sci.* iv. 86 The efficiency of the engine is directly proportional to the weakening of the current. **1886** Jago *Chem. Wheat* etc. 315 The rate at which weakening goes on during panification. **1901** *Brit. Med. Jrnl.* 2 Feb. 263/1 The opening can be enlarged and then resutured without causing any weakening in the lower part of the abdominal wall.

2. Something that weakens; a cause or source of weakness. Now *rare* or *Obs.*

1545 Visct. Lisle in Hooker *Life Sir P. Carew* (1857) 130 Which wilbe a great weakening to the navye, yf any thing in the meane tyme shall happen. **1663** Gerbier *Counsel* 18 If Doores and Windowes..were as wide as they are high; it must through necessity be a weakening to a Building. **1703** R. Neve *City & C. Purchaser* 7 All Openings are Weaknings. **1744** M. Bishop *Life* 208 This was a great weakening to us,..for we were environed round on all sides by our Enemies, [etc.].

weakening (ˈwiːk(ə)nɪŋ), *ppl. a.* [-ING².] That weakens, in various senses of the vb.

a **1586** Sidney *Arcadia* III. ix. (1912) I. 397 You see we both doo feele The weakning worke of Times for ever-whirling wheele. **1694** tr. *Milton's Lett. of State* 240 To our great grief we have beheld the Protestant Princes..more and more at weakning variance among themselves. **1746** Francis tr. *Horace, Art of Poetry* 558 The weakening Joys of Wine and Love. **1797** Jane Austen *Sense & Sensib.* xlvi, Marianne's illness, though weakening in its kind, had not been long enough to make her recovery slow. **1843** R. J. Graves *Syst. Clin. Med.* xx. 230 All weakening measures were therefore contra-indicated. **1866** Max Müller *Skr. Gram.* 290 Changed..before weakening terminations beginning with consonants. **1899** *Allbutt's Syst. Med.* VII. 595 A diagnosis easily explained by the weakening influence of influenza.

weakfish (ˈwiːkfɪʃ). *U.S.* [ad. obs. Du. *weekvisch, -vis*, f. *week* soft + *visch* fish. Cf. G. *weichfisch*, a gadoid fish.] A marine sciænoid food-fish of the genus *Cynoscion*, esp. *C. regalis*, the squeteague or sea-trout of the Atlantic. Other varieties are the spotted weakfish, *C. nebulosus*, and the white or bastard weakfish, *C. nothus*.

The Dutch name (in the form *weekvis*) occurs in a poem in praise of 'New Netherland' by Jacob Steendam (1661), cited in Goode *American Fishes* (1888) 110.

1791 J. Baxter *Jrnl.* 21 June in *Amer. Speech* (1965) XL. 200 Went a fishing..had 350 weekfish. *c* **1838** *Encycl. Metrop.* (1845) XXIV. 365/2 This species..is known to the Anglo-Americans by the name of *Weak-fish*, because considered by some as a debilitating food, and by others from it pulling but slightly on the line with which it is caught. **1844** *Amer. Jrnl. Sci.* XLVII. 61 Otolithus regalis, Cuv., Weak Fish, Yellow-fin. **1873** T. Gill *Catal. Fishes E. Coast N. Amer.* 26 Cynoscion regalis..Squeteague or squit ..weak-fish (New York).

Hence **ˈweakfishing**, fishing for weakfish.

1888 Goode *Amer. Fishes* 125 Much the same rig as is used in weakfishing.

ˈweak-ˈhanded, *a.*

1. Having weak hands; *fig.* not capable of effective exertion.

1539 Bible (Great) *2 Sam.* xvii. 2 And I wyll come vpon hym, whyle he is werye and weake handed. **1868** Miss Yonge *Cameos* I. iv. 27 Crimes were committed which he had no power to restrain, and, weak-handed and bewildered, he seems to have acted in great matters [etc.].

2. = SHORT-HANDED *a.*² 2.

1817 J. Bradbury *Trav.* 292 This mode is called girdling, and is only resorted to by those who, to use their own phrase, are weak-handed. **1836** Marryat *Pirate* xvi, We certainly may defend the schooner from the shore as well as on board; but we are weak-handed.

ˈweak-ˈheaded, *a.*

1. Lacking strength of mind or purpose.

1654 [see SISTERNITY]. **1705** De Foe *Consolidator* Wks. 1840 IX. 387 A weak-headed prince, who neither had a right to give his crown, nor a brain to know what he was doing. **1889** Labouchere in *Daily News* 20 Feb. 3/2 A more weak-kneed, weak-headed lot of men could not be conceived. **1908** Jacobs *Salthaven* xiii, That weak-headed Cecilia Willett believes him.

2. Easily overcome by strong liquor.

Hence **ˈweak-ˈheadedness**.

1894 Ld. Dufferin in *Lady Dufferin's Poems & Verses* 15 *footnote*, In contrast to Sheridan's weak-headedness, I may cite the instance of my paternal grandfather... He would occasionally begin a convivial evening with what he called a 'clearer', *i.e.*, a bottle of port [etc.].

ˈweak-ˈhearted, *a.* **a.** Lacking fortitude, faint-hearted. **b.** Tender-hearted, soft-hearted.

a. 1549 *Bk. Com. Prayer, Letany* 123 To comfort and helpe the weake hearted. **1613** Shaks. *Hen. VIII*, III. ii. 390 My Weake-hearted Enemies.

b. 1841 *Lost Brooch* II. xvi. 114 Those soft weak-hearted persons, who think that religion consists in nothing but what they call kindness and forgiveness.

weakish (ˈwiːkɪʃ), *a.* [f. WEAK *a.* + -ISH.] Somewhat weak.

1594 Lady Bacon *Let.* in *Lambeth MSS.* 650, fol. 223, I wold fayn have gon to London for phisick next weeke, but I perceive I cannot being weakish to Ryd so farr. **1809** *Med. Jrnl.* XXI. 386 If the pulse be felt, it will be found to be quick and weakish. **1865** Dickens *Mut. Fr.* IV. iv, An innocent young waiter..with weakish legs. **1890** Abp. Benson in A. C. Benson *Life* (1899) II. 305 Spoke at Oxford House to about 400 men... They were attentive—and afterwards they asked weakish questions.

Hence **ˈweakishness**. *rare*⁻⁰.

1864 Webster.

ˈweak-ˈkneed, *a.* Having weak knees; chiefly *fig.* wanting in resolution or determination.

1863 *Rio Abajo Press* (Albuquerque, N.M.) 24 Feb. 2 But we must forego these comforts and conveniences, because our legislators are too weak-kneed to enact a tax law. **1870** *Daily News* 16 Nov., The Prefects of the Republic..know how to keep down the malcontents and to enliven the weak-kneed. **1875** *N. Amer. Rev.* CXX. 208 Kitty Ellison and her weak-kneed lover, we find, are still objects of current allusion. **1891** Kipling *Light that Failed* xiv. (1900) 235 Suicide..would be..a weak-kneed confession of fear.

Hence **ˈweak-ˈkneedness**.

1882 *Standard* 19 Sept. 5/1 The peculiar awkward running gait of women..is due to a weak-kneedness characteristic of the sex. **1887** *Sat. Rev.* 10 Sept. 340 The weak-kneedness of the Irish landlords has had much to do with the triumph of anarchy.

ˈweakliness. [-NESS.] Weakly quality.

1826 Galt *Last of Lairds* iii. 28 Does na everybody ken I'm a seven-months bairn, the which is the cause of my weakliness. **1865** Kingsley *Herew.* Prel. 1 The weakliest and the silliest..transmit to their offspring their own weakliness or silliness. **1897** *Allbutt's Syst. Med.* IV. 258 This has been attributed to the weakliness of hospital infants.

weakling (ˈwiːklɪŋ). Also 6 **weak(e)lyng, weikling**, *Sc.* **waykling**, 6-7 **weakeling**. [f. WEAK *a.* + -LING¹. Cf. G. *weichling* effeminate man.]

†**1.** An effeminate or unmanly person. *Obs.*

1526 Tindale *1 Cor.* vi. 9 Nether fornicators,..nether whor-mongers, nether weaklinges [μαλακοί; Luther, *weichlinge*]. **1600** Holland *Livy* XXXIII. xxviii. 840 Men were much deceived to thinke, that so horrible and straunge a murder was committed by such weaklings and persons as they were [*qui tam atrocem caedem pertinere ad illos semiviros crederent*].

2. A person or animal that lacks physical strength, or is weak in health or constitution.

1576 Fleming *Panopl. Epist.* 358 Will you lay a heauie and weightie burthen, vppon the..shoulders of a young beginner, of a weakling, of an infant, which is able to make Demosthenes sincke vnder it, and falter to the grounde? **1579–80** North *Plutarch, Hannibal* (1595) 1143 There it was that Annibals souldiers..became then of valiant men, rancke cowardes: of strong menne weakelings. **1593** Shaks. *Lucr.* 584 Thy selfe art mightie,..My selfe a weakling, do not then insnare me. **1609** Holland *Amm. Marcell.* 133 Hewen in pieces they were pell-mell one with another, armed souldiors and unarmed weaklings, and no regard of sex was made. **1641** Milton *Animadv.* 31 Like a carved Gyant terribly menacing to children, and weaklings. **1684** J. S. *Profit & Pleasure united* 2 It will..cause her [the Cow] to produce weaklings, or unhealthy Calves. **1697** J. Puckle *New Dial.* 33 Of pitiful Weaklings at Land, they come to be hardy, stout, and healthfull Persons. **1822** Lamb *Elia, Roast Pig*, The strong man may batten on him [the pig], and the weakling refuseth not his mild juices. **1850** Kingsley *Alton Locke* iv, Shakspeare was lame; Alfred, a rickety weakling. **1881** Besant & Rice *Chapl. of Fleet* II. viii, I say nothing for that poor weakling, that hot-house plant, [etc.]. **1889** *Spectator* 27 Apr. 571/2 The caravans must have dropped many dead weaklings, men and beasts alike, in every hundred miles.

fig. **1648** Jenkyn *Blind Guide* i. 14 So poor a weakling, and so mishapen a monster it [*sc.* a book] is, that..none will doubt it for his.

3. One who is weak in character or intellect.

1577–87 Holinshed *Chron.* III. 1121/2 Those honest men that had beene of Throckmortons quest..submitted them-selues, and said they had offended like weakelings. **1616** Hayward *Sanct. Troub. Soul* I. xiv. (1620) 290 What then shall I doe, wretched weakeling? Shall I speake? or shall I be silent? I must not bee silent, and I cannot speake. *a* **1656** Hales *Serm.* Golden Rem. I. (1673) 47 Weaklings are able to begin a quarrel, but the prosecution and finishing is a work for stronger men. **1844** Thirlwall *Greece* lxvi. VIII. 448 If they were men they would be in no want of allies, nor, if weaklings, of masters. **1884** Browning *Ferishtah's Fancies* i. 28 Should he play The helpless weakling, or the helpful strength That captures prey and saves the perishing? **1896** W. Watson *Purple East* 36 Only the witling's sneer, the worldling's smile, The weakling's tremors, fail him not who fain Would rouse to noble deed.

b. One who is a tiro or unskilled *in* (a subject).

1575 Fleming *Virg. Bucol.* Ep. Ded. Aiij, Leauing nothing vnsifted which might appertaine to the vttermost exposition of these Bucolikes, that weakelinges in Poetrie myght rather be supported then suppressed.

4. One who is weak in the faith or in spiritual attainments.

Common in 16–17th centuries.

1548 Udall *Erasm. Par. Mark* i. 9–11 A ministre..muste ..eschew all thinges wherwith the weakelinges may be offended. **1577** Hanmer *Socr. Schol. Eccl. Hist.* III. vii. 304 Eusebius..confirmed like a cunning Phisicion such as were weakelings in the faith. **1657** Owen *Commun. with God* II. iii. Digress. ii. 123 We that can doe nothing in our selves, we are such weaklings, can doe all things in Jesus Christ, as Giants. **1865** C. Stanford *Symb. Christ* vii. 201 Many a weakling has thought himself strong.

5. *appositive* or as *adj.* Weak, feeble.

1557 Grimald in *Tottel's Misc.* (Arb.) 102 Hee shall, for man, a weaklyng woman prooue. **1821** Lamb *Elia, Mackery End*, In the days of weakling infancy I was her tender charge. **1848** Kingsley *Saint's Trag.* II. v, But now to wash Christ's feet were dangerous honour For weakling grace. **1906** *Times Lit. Suppl.* 13 July 246/1 The author does not spare himself, and he does not spare the weakling reader.

weakly (ˈwiːklɪ), *a.* [f. WEAK *a.* + -LY¹.]

1. Weak in constitution, not strong or robust, delicate.

1577 tr. *Bullinger's Decades* II. viii. 203 Not to suppresse such a fellowe as this, is to put a sword in a madde mans hand, to kill vnwise and weakelie men. **1582** T. Watson *Centurie of Love* xcii, Little of stature, and in apparence weakelie. **1678** W. Mountagu in *Buccleuch MSS.* (Hist. MSS. Comm.) I. 329 Anne Coke is brought to bed of a son, ..a very weakly one. **1684** Bunyan *Pilgr.* II. (1900) 248 Neither objected he against my weakly Looks, nor against my Feeble Mind. **1753** Miss Collier *Art Torment.* II. iv. (1811) 171 Hermia is far from being of a weakly constitution. **1832** Ht. Martineau *Manch. Strike* ix. 103 The more weakly of the labourers lie down and die. **1843** R. J. Graves *Syst. Clin. Med.* xii. 133 From the weakly habit of the patient,..he thought it advisable to let her have some weak chicken broth and light negus. **1877** Conder *Basis of Faith* v. 225 The swiftest hare may be run down by the dogs, weaklier ones meanwhile lurking in safe covert. **1899** *Allbutt's Syst. Med.* VII. 857 In weakly children the syrup of the phosphate of iron..is of advantage.

absol. **1621** T. Granger *Expos. Eccles.* I. 3. 6 The sicke and weakly, thinketh the strong and healthfull happy. **1848** Mrs. Gaskell *Mary Barton* viii, She, the weakly, was left behind, while the strong man was taken. **1865** Kingsley *Herew.* Prel. 1 In the civilised state..the weakliest and the silliest..have their chance likewise.

b. of a plant, tree, etc.

1775 J. Tait *Land of Liberty* II. xxxv. 47 She cuts him off like some poor weakly flow'r. **1842** Loudon *Suburban Hort.* 364 It would be ridiculous to lay the same quantity of wood into a weakly tree as into a tree in full vigour. **1887** *Field* 15 Oct. 603/2 A weakly grower [*sc.* a rose-tree].

2. Characterized by moral weakness.

1890 'R. Boldrewood' *Col. Reformer* xxiv, Of no avail are weakly condolences or mild assenting pity. **1900** *Month* Aug. 135 A sort of cruel kindness and weakly indulgence.

3. Of a laugh: Feeble, faint, half-hearted.

1883 Miss Broughton *Belinda* III. iii, 'Are they?' she says, with a weakly laugh.

weakly (ˈwiːklɪ), *adv.* [f. WEAK *a.* + -LY².] In a weak manner.

1. a. With little energy, force, or strength; †with gentle action, softly (*obs.*).

1398 Trevisa *Barth. De P.R.* XII. xxvii. (1495) 429 A kite is weke in flyghte and in strengthe and is callyd Miluus as it were weekely fleenge [L. *molliter volans*]. ? *a* **1400** *Morte Arth.* 697 Waynour waykly wepande hym kyssiz. **1526** *Pilgr. Perf.* (W. de W. 1531) 155 b, By more easy meanes commeth to perfeccyon, whiche they slowly & weykly or fayntly desyre. **1600** Surflet *Country Farm* III. ix. 441 For the yong plant which can attract & draw but weakly, & at hand any substance for it selfe, will hardly [etc.]. *a* **1626** Bacon *Sylva* §33 It is very probable that the Motion of Grauitie worketh weakly, both farre from the Earth, and also within the Earth. **1641** Symonds *Serm. bef. Ho. of Comm.* B iiij b, An arrow weakly shot, will fall short of the mark. **1657** Baxter *Present Th.* 12 Grace may act weaklier than it did before. **1715** Desaguliers *Fires Impr.* 11 Upon account of their distance from the Fire, they are but very weakly reflected. **1876** Papillon *Man. Comp. Philol.* 69 Final *m* [in Latin]..must have been weakly pronounced.

b. In a weak or enfeebled condition. Also *transf.*

c **1400** *Destr. Troy* 10151 Philmen..the gome hit,..gert hym to stoupe, þat he wauerit þerwith, & weikly he sete. **1470–85** Malory *Arthur* XIX. xii. 794 Thenne the wounded knyghte syr Vrre sette hym vp weykely. **1509** Hawes *Past. Pleas.* xl. (Percy Soc.) 202 In his hand he hadde A croked staffe; he wente full wekely. **1590** Spenser *F.Q.* II. i. 45 As one out of a deadly dreame affright, She weakely started, yet she nothing drad. **1606** Sir E. Coke in *True & Perf. Relat.* T 3 b, This paper of his Retractation, which hee had weakely and dyingly subscribed. **1844** Mrs. Browning *Lost Bower* lxix, By this couch I weakly lie on, While I count my memories.

†**2. a.** Insecurely, unsubstantially. *Obs.*

1522 Bp. Foxe in Ellis *Orig. Lett.* Ser. II. II. 8 Also my Lord, I have not soo sklenderly buylded my selve, nor soo weykly established my house in thies parties, that I can honestely or conveniently so sodenly depart hens. **1665** Sir T. Herbert *Trav.* (1677) 123 That supposition is but weakly founded, at least in my apprehension. **1784** *Cook's 3rd Voy.* I. Introd. 12 The visits were..so transient, that it was scarcely possible to build upon a foundation, so weakly laid, any information that could even gratify idle curiosity.

b. With weakness of constitution.

1613 Shaks. *Hen. VIII*, II. iii. 40 *Old Lady.* Haue you limbs To beare that load of Title? *Anne Bullen.* No in truth. *Old Lady.* Then you are weakly made.

3. With slight defensive strength.

1582 Stanyhurst *Æneis* II. (Arb.) 60 Our state eke and persons may not thus weaklye be shielded. **1591** Shaks. *1*

Hen. VI, II. i. 74 'Tis sure they found some place, But weakely guarded, where the breach was made. **1593** —— *Lucr.* 28 Honour and Beautie in the owners armes, Are weaklie fortrest from a world of harmes. **1680** Cotton *Gamester* (ed. 2) 52 When you find your adversaries King any way weakly guarded. **1705** Addison *Italy, Pesaro* 145 Some have wonder'd that the Turk never attacks this Treasury, since it..is so weakly guarded. **1921** *Times Lit. Suppl.* 3 Feb. 67/3 Haig..was quite right to hold the southern end of his line..more weakly than the rest.

4. a. With deficiency of numbers or amount; sparsely, meagrely. ? *Obs.*

1605 Bacon *Adv. Learn.* II. xiii. §7. 52 If a shooemaker should haue no shooes in his shoppe, but onely worke, as hee is bespoken, hee should bee weakely customed. *a* **1649** Winthrop *Hist. N. Eng.* (1853) II. 232 Here came a pinnace ..for procuring powder..but we were weakly provided ourselves. **1748** *Anson's Voy.* II. i. 112 The capstan was so weakly manned, that it was near four hours before we hove the cable right up and down.

b. In a slight degree; to a small extent or amount.

1775 *Phil. Trans.* LXVI. 204 A battery so weakly electrified that its shock will not pass through a chain. **1789–96** Morse *Amer. Geog.* I. 617 The waters weakly mineralized. **1805** W. Saunders *Min. Waters* 557 The ochre ..is, when dry, weakly magnetic. **1805** T. Weaver *Werner's Ext. Charact. Fossils* 191 Solid fossils that stain..either strongly or weakly. **1827** Faraday *Chem. Manip.* xvii. (1842) 450 This may be done..by bringing the body, if weakly electrified, into contact with the cap.

5. With weakness of mind or character; with lack of mental grasp or firmness of will.

1610 Shaks. *Temp.* II. i. 188, I will not aduenture my discretion so weakly. **1662** Stillingfl. *Orig. Sacræ* III. iv. §1 The meaning is not that all mankind was made of the same uniform matter, as the authour of the Præ-Adamites weakly imagined. **1671** Milton *Samson* 50 Who this high gift of strength committed to me,..Under the Seal of silence could not keep, But weakly to a woman must reveal it. **1705** S. Clarke *Disc. Nat. Relig.* vi. Wks. 1738 II. 661 Plato, after having delivered very noble..Truths concerning the Nature and Attributes of the Supreme God, weakly advises Men to worship likewise Inferiour Gods. **1864** Mrs. Carlyle *Lett.* III. 208 What may strike you as weakly fanciful in my desire. **1885** 'Mrs. Alexander' *At Bay* vii, He was weakly credulous. **1892** Lady F. Verney *Verney Mem.* I. 267 She was not at all inclined to be weakly indulgent.

6. With little vigour of action, inefficiently.

1663 Jer. Taylor *Serm. Funeral Abp. Armagh* 1 The Condition of Man in this World is so limited..that the best things he does he does weakly. **1751** Johnson *Rambler* No. 162 ¶4 We please our pride with the effects of our influence thus weakly exerted. **1853** Dickens *Bleak Ho.* xiii, Mr. Boythorn, who interested himself strongly in the subject —though I need not say that, for he could do nothing weakly. **1905** Ld. E. Fitzmaurice *Ld. Granville* I. xv. 430 Mr. Lowe considered that he had been but weakly defended by some of his colleagues in the House of Commons.

7. With little force of argument; unconvincingly.

1662 Stillingfl. *Orig. Sacræ* III. i. §7 Now I appeal to the reason of any Person..Whether either of these two Hypotheses..be not far more weakly proved, then the existence of a Deity is. **1855** Pusey *Doctr. Real Presence in Fathers* Note F 73 He is blamed by others, as exposing the doctrine which he defends weakly. **1870** Emerson *Soc. & Solit.* i. 9 He spoke weakly, and from the point, like a flighty girl.

8. *Math.* In a way that implies less or that satisfies fewer conditions (cf. weak *a.* 12 f (*b*)).

1955 M. Loève *Probability Theory* ix. 443 If all sequences $T_n X$ are weakly compact, then it is easily proved that sup $\|T_n\| < \infty$. **1972** R. J. Wilson *Introd. Graph Theory* vii. 102 A digraph *D* is said to be connected (or weakly-connected) if it cannot be expressed as the union of two disjoint digraphs.

'weak-'minded, *a.*

1. Having a weak mind; lacking strength of purpose. Of actions, opinions, etc.: Indicating weakness of mind.

1716 T. Cave *Let.* 5 Aug. in M. M. Verney *Verney Lett.* (1930) II. xxii. 43 We all continue in perfect sanity of body but very weak-minded this hott weather, as you'l judg by this Scrawll. **1782** Miss Burney *Cecilia* v. xiii, 'Oh fie,' cried he, 'to suffer *your* understanding to be lulled asleep, because the weak-minded Mr. Arnott's could not be kept awake!' **1842** Abdy *Water Cure* 57 Nor will any one, who wilfully prejudices the weak-minded and uninstructed against this method,..stand guiltless. **1863** Miss Braddon *Eleanor's Vict.* III. xv. 227 It is my misfortune to be weak-minded. I can't say 'no' to people. **1878** J. Gairdner *Rich. III*, i. 7 The Duke of York..fruitlessly endeavoured to bind a weak-minded king by pledges. **1890** H. James *Tragic Muse* xxxv, If he should go abroad his mother might think he had some weak-minded view of joining Julia Dallow.

2. Mentally deficient; half-witted.

1883 *Encycl. Brit.* XV. 797/1 The care of the weak-minded and the insane. **1899** *Allbutt's Syst. Med.* VII. 744 The educative and disciplinary influences resorted to in the treatment of weak-minded children. **1899** *Daily News* 28 Sept. 7/3 This woman had two sisters weak-minded, who were in the lunatic asylum.

Hence **'weak-'mindedness**.

1854 Mill *Diary* 4 Feb., in *Lett.* (1910) II. 367 It might well be that even good men..thought that to be scrupulous about means was weakmindedness. **1888** *Fortn. Rev.* 1 Oct. 449 Murderous attacks may result from..Insanity of primary weak-mindedness. **1897** Mary Kingsley *W. Africa* 400 How long ago this happened it is impossible to say, owing to..the weak-mindedness of the African regarding time.

weakness ('wi:knis). [f. weak *a.* + -ness.]

1. The quality or condition of being weak, in any sense of the adj.; deficiency of strength, power, or force.

a **1300** *Cursor M.* 27054 Botes thre, Quar-wit þat we mai strenghed be. Þe first for waikenes of vr fa þat qua-sum will mai were him fra. *Ibid.* 28932 [Of alms-giving] 'Weiknes' sal þou lok for mede, For þou man agh all helpe in nede, þe waikest and þe mast vn-fere. **1340** Hampole *Pr. C.* 9026 Alle þe strenthe of Sampson þat was pereles, War noght tald þare bot wayknes. *c* **1400** *Destr. Troy* 3323 Syn weikenes of wemen may not wele stryve, Ne haue no myght tawardes men maistries to fend. *c* **1440** *Promp. Parv.* 520/2 Weykenesse, of hert, *vecordia, pusillanimitas.* **1525** *Grete Herbal* clxxiii. (1529) Lj, Agaynst vomyte caused of weykenesse of the vertue retentyfe, take [etc.]. **1538** Starkey *England* 43 Wych thyng [*sc.* retirement from the world] surely ys not amys downe of them wych perceyue theyr owne imbecyllyte and wekenes. **1595** Shaks. *John* v. iii. 17 To my litter straight, Weaknesse possesseth me, and I am faint. **1601** —— *Jul. C.* IV. iii. 276, I thinke it is the weakenesse of mine eyes That shapes this monstrous Apparition. **1651** Hobbes *Leviath.* III. xxxvii. 236 And so make the weaknesse of his voice seem to proceed..from distance of place. **1678** Lady Chaworth in *12th Rep. Hist. MSS. Comm.* App. v. 45 Lady Portsmouth [is] going to Bourbon as soone as her weaknesse will permitt. **1686** Tillotson *Serm. at White-Hall* (1 Cor. iii. 15) 19, I shall shew the weakness of the principle upon which this argument relies. **1707** *Curios. Husb. & Gard.* 259 The weakness of the Sun in that Season. **1748** Richardson *Clarissa* (1768) VII. 33 They depend upon the indulgent weakness of their Parents tempers. **1769** *Junius Lett.* xvi. 69 The man who is conscious of the weakness of his cause is interested in concealing it. **1774** [W. Mitford] *Ess. Harmony Lang.* 153 The expression of the 829 line is much heightened by the extreme weakness of the accent in the first foot [etc.]. **1781** Burns *Let. W. Burnes* 27 Dec., The weakness of my nerves. **1782** *Jrnl. Yng. Lady of Virginia* (1871) 22 Nancy was much better... Weakness is her only complaint. **1818** Cruise *Digest* (ed. 2) VI. 162 Where..a testator..was incapable of disposing of his lands from any weakness of mind. **1821** Lamb *Elia, Witches* Wks. 1908 I. 554 Credulity is the man's weakness, but the child's strength. **1838** Prescott *Ferd. & Is.* II. xxiii. III. 425 The independence of Navarre had hitherto been maintained less through its own strength than the weakness of its neighbours. **1856** Kane *Arctic Expl.* I. xxiii. 301 He was startled by the growing weakness of the ice. **1861** M. Pattison *Ess.* (1889) I. 33 The weakness of Henry III would not suffer him to commit himself heartily to a Ghibelline policy. **1869** Tanner *Clin. Med.* (ed. 2) 20 Dementia... This form of insanity is often seen in those who in early life exhibit weakness of will, or of moral self-control. **1875** *Economist* 23 Jan. 95/2 The special causes of weakness affecting the markets have..been greatly influential here. **1884** *Law Times Rep.* L. 118/2 Rule 15..is a rule meant to make a litigant expose the weakness of his case. **1920** *Conquest* Nov. 7/2 The mountains..are lines of weakness caused by the crumpling of the earth's crust.

2. In particularized uses. **a.** A weak point, a circumstance of disadvantage.

1597 Bacon *Ess., Of Negotiating* (Arb.) 92 If you would worke any man, you must either know his nature, and fashions and so leade him,..or his weakenesses or disaduantages, and so awe him. **1627** Donne *Serm.* lxxxi. (1649) II. 9 Here, it is a faire portion of that Angelicall happinesse, if you be alwaies ready to support, and supply one another in any such occasionall weaknesses. **1914** 'Ian Hay' *Knt. on Wheels* xix, The brakes of the Britannia cars have always been their weakness. **1920** *Discovery* Apr. 114/1 Any weakness there was in our pre-war small house design was a tendency to fussiness.

b. An infirmity of character, a failing.

c **1645** Howell *Lett.* (1650) I. v. xii. 148, I shall heartily thank you..if you tell me of my weaknesses. **1671** Milton *Samson* 773 *Dalila.* First granting, as I do, it was a weakness In me, but incident to all our sex, Curiosity. **1711** Addison *Spect.* No. 255 ¶10 This very Thirst after Fame..is it self looked upon as a Weakness in the greatest Characters. **1748** Chesterf. *Let. to Son* 29 Oct., Not to seem to perceive the little weaknesses, and the idle but innocent affectations of the company. **1776** Gibbon *Decl. & F.* xiv. (1782) I. 525 The laws of Constantine against rapes were dictated with very little indulgence for the most amiable weaknesses of human nature. **1797** Jane Austen *Sense & Sensib.* xlix, His heart was now open to Elinor, all its weaknesses, all its errors confessed. *a* **1859** Macaulay *Hist. Eng.* xxv. V. 256 Many who could not help smiling at Burnet's weaknesses did justice to his abilities and virtues.

†**c.** A weakened condition of body; an attack of faintness. *Obs.*

1602 Shaks. *Ham.* II. ii. 148 He..Fell into a Sadnesse,.. thence into a Weaknesse. **1617** Moryson *Itin.* I. 236, I was all the day troubled with a weaknesse of bodie. **1749** Hartley *Observ. Man* I. i. §1. 51 The Numbness, and paralytic Weaknesses, which frequently succeed after Opiates. **1756** Mrs. Calderwood in *Coltness Collect.* (Maitl. Club) 203 And ever since, I am given to violent passions and weaknesses in my head.

3. An unreasonable or self-indulgent liking or inclination *for* (a person or thing).

1712 Steele *Spect.* No. 442 ¶1, I must own my Weakness for Glory is such, that if I consulted that only, I might [etc.]. **1746** Chesterf. *Let. to Son* 4 Oct., I have no womanish weakness for your person. **1852** Thackeray *Esmond* III. xi, He hath every great and generous quality, with perhaps a weakness for the sex which belongs to his family. **1869** A. Macdonald *Love, Law & Theol.* x. 172, I think she would like to have Porter, but he doesn't seem to see that she has a weakness for him. **1895** H. A. Kennedy in *19th Cent.* Aug. 330, I own to a weakness for a play that, without any flourish of pretence, does very distinctly amuse me. **1913** *Jrnl. Friends' Hist. Soc.* Jan. 4 He had a weakness for getting on his feet several times in the course of one First-day morning.

b. quasi-*concr.* Something for which one has an unreasonable liking.

1822 Byron *Vis. Judgm.* xxxix, Nor wine nor lust Were of his weaknesses. **1840** Dickens *Old C. Shop* iv, You have been exciting yourself too much—talking perhaps, for it is your weakness. **1853** —— *Bleak Ho.* xx, It's the fashionable way; and fashion and whiskers have been my weaknesses, and I don't care who knows it.

'weak-'sighted, *a.* Having weak sight; also *fig.*

a **1591** H. Smith *Sinner's Convers.* (1613) A5b, If our faith be so weake sighted that we cannot see Christ. **1606** Marston *Parasit.* III. F1, Las we are now growne old, weake sighted, alas anyone fooles vs. *a* **1652** Brome *City Wit* II. ii, My Mayd is very thick of hearing, and exceeding weake sighted. **1768–74** Tucker *Lt. Nat.* (1834) I. 596 The weak-sighted cannot sustain thy piercing look. *Ibid.* 623 Nor are the views of God so narrow as to want those helps..which are necessary to weak-sighted mortals. **1833** T. Hook *Parson's Dau.* I. ii, Luckily it was getting dark, and Lovell, moreover, was somewhat weak-sighted.

Hence **'weak-'sightedness**.

1632 Brome *Northern Lass* II. iii, I hope you will pardon my weake sightednes... Could not your worship make your selfe knowen sooner? **1860** Mayne *Expos. Lex.*, Weak-sightedness,..*Asthenopia.*

weaky ('wi:kɪ), *a. north. dial.* [f. weak *a.* + -y[1]. Cf. dial. *woky* moist, sappy, f. woke *a.*] Moist, damp; juicy.

1641 [implied in weakiness: see below]. **1691** Ray *N.C. Words* 80 Weaky, moist. **1703** Thoresby *Let. to Ray, Weiky*, moist. **1788** Marshall *Rur. Econ. Yorks.* II. 364 *Weaky*; juicy; opposed to 'hask'. **1876** *Whitby Gloss.* s.v., 'Weaky weather', rainy. 'Don't make the paste too weaky', don't make the dough with over much water.

Hence **'weakiness**, moisture. *dial.*

1641 Best *Farm. Bks.* (Surtees) 75 On the day time wee putte them into one close or other, and lette them eate snowe, and gette the weekinesse on the grownde. **1878** *Cumberld. Gloss.*, *Weekiness*, moisture.

weal (wi:l), *sb.*[1] Forms: 1–2 wela; 1 weola (3 weolla), 3–4 weole (2 wole); 1 weala (3 wale); 2–6 wele (3–4 wel, well), 5–6 weel(e (5 weell), 5 weyle; *Sc.* 5–6 weile (6 weille), 5–7 weill, weil (6 veill, veil), 6 weyll, 8 weel; 6–7 weale, 6– weal. [OE. *wela* (*weola, weala*) wk. masc. = OS. *welo*, OHG. *wolo*:—OTeut. *welon-, f. root *wel-: see well *adv.*

The 14th cent. northern form *wel* (*well*) is merely a variant spelling, and the length of the vowel is proved by rhymes; but from the 15th cent. in midland and southern texts a real confusion between *wēle* and *wĕl* appears, owing to the currency of double forms of the adverb 'well'. In consequence of this the noun is sometimes written *wel, well*, or *welle*, and in this form is latterly identified in pronunciation with the adv. (For examples see well *sb.*[2]) On the other hand the adv. in the form *wele* or *weele* has influenced the meaning of the noun in sense 4 below, and probably contributed to its use in sense 3 (and in weal-public) as an equivalent of L. *bonum* and F. *bien.*]

†**1.** Wealth, riches, possessions. *Obs.* (as distinct from 2).

Often *world-, world's, worldly weal.*

c **888** Ælfred *Boeth.* xi. §1 Ac for bearnleste eallne þone welan þe hi ȝegaderiȝað hi lætað fræmdum to brucanne. **971** *Blickl. Hom.* 197 Se man ahte mycelne welan. *c* **1205** Lay. 7732 For eowre muchele wurðscipe weole ȝe scullen habben. *a* **1225** *Ancr. R.* 196 Ant te world bit mon ȝiscen worldes weole, & wunne, & wurschipe. *a* **1250** *Prov. Ælfred* 120 Wyþ-vte wysdome is weole wel vnwurþ. **1340–70** *Alex. & Dind.* 32 For what richesse, rink, vs miȝht þou bireue, Whan no wordliche wele is wiþ us founde? *c* **1400** *26 Pol. Poems* viii. 68 Beter is litel ryȝtwys wonne..þan..Wiþouten desert take pore mennys wele. **1531** Elyot *Governor* I. i, In our olde vulgare, profite is called weale. **1594** Greene & Lodge *Looking Gl.* III. ii. 1057 (Collins) Behold with ruthfull eyes Thy parents robd of all their worldly weale By subtle meanes of vsurie and guile. **1838** Prescott *Ferd. & Is.* I. i. i. 119 He paid the usual penalty of such indifference to worldly weal, by seeing himself eventually stripped of his lordly possessions.

†**b.** *pl. Obs.*

c **900** *Bæda's Hist.* IV. xi. (1890) 294 Ond he sundorliif & munucliif wæs forebeorende allum þam weolum & arum þæs eorðlecan riices. *c* **1000** *Ags. Gosp.* Luke viii. 14 Þæt synd þa ðe..of welum [Vulg. *divitiis*] & of lustum þyses lifes synd forþrysmode. *c* **1175** *Lamb. Hom.* 111 Ðu gederast mare and mare..and þine welan forrotiað beforan þine ehȝan. *a* **1300** *Cursor M.* 4503 Man þat weltres in his welis And, thoru his welth, na fautes felis. **1543** Recorde *Gr. Artes* B iij b, How many waies also Arithmetike is conducible for al priuat weales of Lordes and all possessioners. **1628** Pemble *Salomon's Recant.* 24 Dislike and Hatred of all his magnificent workes, weales, possessions and pleasures.

†**c.** Pomp, splendour, rich array. *Obs.*

c **1290** *S. Eng. Leg.* 264/123 For no Monuk ne scholde gon out þar-of, þe worldes weole to seo. *c* **1386** Chaucer *Knt.'s T.* 37 This duc..Whan he was come almoost vn to the toun In al his wele and in his mooste pride.

†**d.** Stores, supplies. *Obs.*

13.. *Coer de L.* 4786 Agaynes hem comen her naveye, Cogges, and dromoundes, many galeye,..That were chargyd with al weel, With armour and with other vytayle. *c* **1400** *Emare* 824 He lette ordeyne shypus fele, And fylled hem fulle of wordes wele, Hys men mery wyth to make.

2. Welfare, well-being, happiness, prosperity.

a **1000** *Cædmon's Gen.* 431 Siððan bið him se wela onwended & wyrð him wite ȝeȝearwod. *a* **1122** *O.E. Chron.* (Laud MS.) an. 1086, Eala hu leas & hu unwrest is þysses middaneardes wela. *c* **1205** Lay. 10394 He heom wolden mucle wele & wurðscipe itæchen. *a* **1225** *Ancr. R.* 192 Þeo ilke uondunges..wendeð efterward to weole and to eche blisse. *c* **1250** *Gen. & Ex.* 809 Abram let loth in welðe and wale. **13..** *Guy Warw.* 822 Wele is him þat it winne may. *c* **1386** Chaucer *Knt.'s T.* 2243 For now is Palamon in alle wele. *c* **1477** Caxton *Jason* 50b, I am right ioyous of thy wele and worship. **1491** *Act 7 Hen. VII* c. 12 Preamble, Dedis of charite..to be doon for him..for the wele of his soule. **1549** Coverdale etc. *Erasm. Par. Rom.* vi. 15 Ye nowe are become Christes seruauntes, whose seruice is all weale and blisse. **1612** BACON *Ess., Goodness* (Arb.) 198, I take goodnesse in this sence, the affecting of the Weale of men, which is that the Græcians call *Philanthropia*. **1642** D. ROGERS *Naaman* 165 To read Masse or Dirigies for the weale of his soule after his decease. **1805** SCOTT *Last Minstr.* VI. xxvii. And monks should sing, and bells should toll, All for the weal of Michael's soul. **1822** GOOD *Study Med.* (1829) I. 396 The flux..becomes a conditional of the corporeal weal. **1859** TENNYSON *Enid* 799, I doubted whether daughter's tenderness, Or easy nature, might not let itself Be moulded by your wishes for her weal.

b. freq. in contrast with *woe* (†*wowe*).

a **1000** *Cædmon's Gen.* 466 þæt þær yldo bearn moste onceosan godes & yfeles, gumena æȝhwilc welan & wawan. *c* **1200** *Vices & Virtues* 29 Ne on wele ne on wauȝhe. *a* **1250** *Prov. Ælfred* 142 For God may yeue, þenne he wule, god after vuele, weole after wowe. *a* **1300** *Cursor M.* 4054 His waa, his well, yee sal here bath. *c* **1300** *Havelok* 2777 For wel ne for wo. **1393** LANGL. *P. Pl.* B. XVIII. 202-4. *c* **1400** *Pride of Life* 376 in *Non-Cycle Myst. Plays* 100 þer is dred & sorow & wo wytoutin wel. **1470-85** MALORY *Arthur* I. xii. 51 How they sware that for wele nor woo they shold not leue other. **1590** SPENSER *F.Q.* I. viii. 43 But welcome now my Lord, in wele or woe. **1667** MILTON *P.L.* VIII. 638 Thine and of all thy Sons The weal or woe in thee is plac't. **1771** BEATTIE *Minstr.* I. xxix, All human weal and wo learn thou to make thine own. **1814** SCOTT *Lord of Isles* IV. v, 'Come weal, come woe, by Bruce's side,' Replied the Chief, 'will Ronald bide.' **1850** TENNYSON *In Mem.* cxxix. 2 Dear friend, far off, my lost desire, So far, so near in woe and weal. **1863** MISS BRADDON *Aurora Floyd* xv, Impulsive and impetuous, she had always taken her own course, whether for weal or woe. **1897** Q. VICTORIA in *Daily News* 17 July 5/4 In weal and woe I have ever had the true sympathy of all my people.

†**c.** *pl. Obs.*

13.. *E.E. Allit. P.* A. 154 & euer me þoȝt I schulde not wonde For wo, þer welez so wynne wore. **1483** CAXTON *Golden Leg.* 260/2 Thou arte begynnynge myddell and ende of alle weles and goodes. *c* **1500** *Three Kings' Sons* 24 He [God] hath gyuen me more of weles than y haue or can deserue. **1544** *Late Exped. Scot.* (1798) 13 To proue whether the Scottes had yet learned, by theyr importable losses lately chaunced to them, to tendyr theyr own weales, by true and reasonable vnytynge & adioynyng them selues to the Kynges Maiesties louyng liege people. **1568** GRAFTON *Chron.* II. 156 Nor regardyng..their awne weales and states, neyther the weales of their householdes, as their wives, children, or friendes.

†**d.** applied to a person, as a source of felicity, or an object of delight. *Obs.*

a **1225** *St. Marher.* 8 þu art iweddedes weole ant widewene warant. *a* **1240** *Ureisun* in *O.E. Hom.* I. 183 Ihesu mi weole, mi wunne. *c* **1375** *Sc. Leg. Saints* xxx. (*Theodera*) 363 þu art my welth & wele. **1390** GOWER *Conf.* I. 288 O thou my wele, o thou my wo. *c* **1489** CAXTON *Sonnes of Aymon* xii. 290 He is our lord and our wele, and therfore I praye you, fayr bredern, that ye wyll obeye hym. **1490** —— *Eneydos* vi. 28 Sith that he hath..taken awaye hym whiche was alle my wele.

3. *contextually.* The welfare of a country or community; the general good. Often with defining word, as *common, general, public, universal.* See also COMMON WEAL I, PUBLIC *a.* 2 a, WEAL-PUBLIC I. Now *arch.*

†Phr. *the weal of peace* = OF. *le bien de paix.*

1444 *Rolls of Parlt.* V. 121/1 Where afore this tyme for the wele of Peas, Tranquillite and gode Governance, bitwene the Baillifs and Cominalte of the Toun of Shroesbury, divers composicions were made bitwene hem. **1483** *Eng. Gilds* 335 To..the wele of the kyng our soueraygn lordez people. **1531** ELYOT *Governor* Proheme, Your graces moste beneuolent inclination towarde the vniuersall weale of your subiectes. **1568** GRAFTON *Chron.* II. 146 It was agreed by the king..for his more suretie, and for the weale of the lande. **1643** in Clarendon *Hist. Reb.* VII. §342 As enemies to the weal of both kingdoms. **1697** DE LA PRYME *Diary* 16 Sept. (Surtees) 150 Who vallues the weal politic above the ecclesiastic. **1726-30** THOMSON *Winter* 35 For thy country's weal. **1820** BYRON *Mar. Fal.* IV. i, This needful violence is for thy safety, No less than for the general weal. **1826** *Pennsylv. Hist. Soc. Mem.* I. 132 He appears in them as a watchful guardian of the domestic weal. **1838** PRESCOTT *Ferd. & Is.* II. xxiii. III. 430 This enterprise, undertaken for the weal of the church. **1870** BRYANT *Iliad* IX. 122 Thou.. shouldst follow willingly Another's judgment when it best promotes The general weal.

b. Hence, a state, community; = COMMON WEAL 2. ? *Obs.*

1513 DOUGLAS *Æneis* XI. vii. 92 Avys heiron amangis ȝou for the best, And help to bring our feble weill to rest. **1560** DAUS tr. *Sleidane's Comm.* 304 For the universall Christen weale [L. *pro republica Christiana*]. **1591** SHAKS. *1 Hen. VI*, III. i. 66 The speciall Watch-men of our English Weale. **1597** BP. HALL *Sat.* II. iii. 15 Wo to the weale where many lawiers bee. **1603** R. JOHNSON *Kingd. & Commw.* 102 We ought not to meruaile, if this weale haue florished now these 250. yeares in great reputation of armes and valor. **1605** SHAKS. *Macb.* V. ii. 27 Meet we the Med'cine of the sickly Weale. **1608** HEYWOOD *Rape of Lucrece* B4b, Tarquins abilitie will in the weale, Beget a weake vnable impotence. **1727** GAY *Fables* I. xvii. 27 (Shepherd's Dog & Wolf) If mindful of the bleating weal, Thy bosom burn with real zeal. **1763** CHURCHILL *Epist. Hogarth* 42 To enlarge the mind, Purge the sick weal, and humanize mankind.

†**4. a.** Goodness, virtuous behaviour. *Obs.*

c **1500** *Three Kings' Sons* 33 She wist wele that without grete nurture..he might not knowe the weelis and honoures that he coude. *Ibid.* 36 In his company, wheryn men may lerne bothe wele and honour. *c* **1500** *Melusine* 11 Yf that ye think th̄eron but wele & honour.

†**b.** Good or honourable report. *Obs.*

c **1500** *Three King's Sons* 133 For the grete weeles that euery man rehersed of you.

weal (wiːl), *sb.*[2] [A mod. variant of WALE *sb.*[1], by confusion with WHEAL *sb.*[1], a pustule: see WHEAL *sb.*[2]] The mark or ridge raised on the flesh by the blow of a rod, lash, etc.; = WALE *sb.*[1] 2, WHEAL *sb.*[2]

1821 CLARE *Vill. Minstr.* etc. II. 68 Who, soon as mounted, with his switching weals, Puts Dob's best swiftness in his heavy heels. **1842** LOVER *Handy Andy* iv, From shoulder to flank, sir, I am one mass of welts and weals. **1845** DARWIN *Voy. Nat.* vi. (1852) 111 He told us that his legs were marked by great weals, where the thong had wound round as if he had been flogged with a whip. **1872** TENNYSON *Last Tourn.* 58 His visage ribb'd From ear to ear with dogwhip-weals. **1900** CONAN DOYLE *Green Flag* etc. 185 Black and bitter were the thoughts of Frenchmen when they saw this weal of dishonour slashed across the fair face of their country.

†**weal**, *v.*[1] Var. WHEAL *v.*[1] *Obs.*

1664 in Pepys *Diary* 31 Dec. (1879) III. 96 [Charm against a thorn] Jesus..Was pricked both with nail and thorn; It neither wealed, nor belled, rankled, nor boned.

weal (wiːl), *v.*[2] [var. of WALE *v.*[2], by confusion with WHEAL *v.*[1]] *trans.* To mark (the flesh) with weals; = WALE *v.*[2] I.

1722 DE FOE *Col. Jack* i, I saw him afterwards, with his back all wealed with the lashes. **1820** CLARE *Rural Life* (ed. 3) 100 The lash that weal'd poor Dobbin's hide. **1825** SCOTT *Talism.* xviii, His bare arm..wealed with the blows of the discipline. **1886** FENN *Master Cerem.* xxx, Were you ever beaten—cut—and wealed with your own whip?

b. *absol.*

1908 *Times* 17 Jan. 4/6 The school authorities allowed only four strokes, two on each hand, as a maximum punishment, and they must not weal. **1922** *Blackw. Mag.* Mar. 355 The knotted ropes that weal and flay.

Hence **wealed** *ppl. a.*, **'wealing** *vbl. sb.*

1841 TUPPER *Twins* xvii. (1844) 131 His wealed body, full of pains and aches and bruises. **1902** *Westm. Gaz.* 20 Nov. 7/2 The governess and upper housemaid examined the child afterwards and found severe wealing of the back and stomach, besides bruises.

weal, var. WEEL; obs. Sc. f. WELL *a.*, *adv.*

wealaway, obs. form of WELLAWAY.

weald (wiːld). Forms: 1 weald, 3-4, 6 welde, 5 weeld, 5-6, 8 weld; 6-9 wild(e, wyld(e, 7 wile; 6 weylde, 6-7 weild(e, 7 wield, 6- **weald**. [OE. *weald* 'forest' (the WS. equivalent of Anglian *wald*: see WOLD), normally developing into southern ME. *wēld(e, weeld*; the modern spelling, which is due to Lambarde, is a re-adoption of the OE. form. The form *wild(e*, which occurs early in the 16th c., is probably parallel to Kentish and Sussex dial. *fild* for *field*, but in later use was apparently assimilated in pronunciation to the more intelligible WILD *sb.*, which had an appropriately descriptive meaning.

The OE. *weald* is applied in the Chronicle (see below) to the forest of Andred, which included at least part of the present 'Weald'.]

1. (Now usu. with capital initial.) The name of the tract of country, formerly wooded, including the portions of Sussex, Kent, and Surrey which lie between the North and South Downs. Chiefly with *the.*

(*a*) *O.E. Chron.* an. 893, Se [Limene] muþa is on easteweardre Cent, æt þæs miclan wuda eastende þe we Andred hatað;..seo ea..lið ut of þæm wealda; on þa ea hi tuȝon up hiora scipu oþ þone weald. [**1018** *Charter of Cnut* (Ord. Surv. Facs. III. No. xxxix) Quoddam siluulae nemus concedo famosa in silua Andredesweald e.] *c* **1290** *St. Kenelm* 52 in *S. Eng. Leg.* 346 Sethþe hadde þe kyng of westsex southsex also, þe welde and al þe bischopriche of Cicestre þerto. [**1357** in *Cal. Pat. Rolls, 31 Edw. III* m. 17 (1909) X. 578 Towns and places within La Welde, co. Kent.] **1471** CAXTON *Recuyell* Pref. (Sommer) 4, I..was born & lerned myn englissh in kente in the weeld where I doubte not is spoken as brode and rude englissh as in ony place of englond. **1483** DK. NORFOLK in *Paston Lett.* III. 308 The Kentysshmen be up in the weld, and sey they wol come and robbe the cite. **1523** *Act 14 & 15 Hen. VIII*, c. 6 The hundred of Cranebroke, in the wilde of your county of Kent. **1543-4** *Act 35 Hen. VIII*, c. 17 §11 Townes parishes or places..within the weldes of the counties of Kent, Surrey and Sussex. **1558-9** *Act 1 Eliz.* c. 15 §2 The Weilde of Kent. *Ibid.*, In the Weylde of the Countye of Surreye. **1580** LYLY *Euphues* (Arb.) 268, I was borne in the wylde of Kent. **1596** SHAKS. *1 Hen. IV*, II. i. 60. **1619** DALTON *Country Justice* xxvi. (1630) 72 In the highways within the Wields of Sussex Surrey or Kent. **1642** HOWELL *For. Trav.* v. 61 The Wiles of Kent. **1662** *Act 14 Chas. II*, c. 6 §17 Any Owner Farmer or Lessee of any Iron worke..within the Wildes of the Counties of Surrey Sussex or Kent. **1697** DE FOE *Ess. Projects* 109 That unpassable County of Sussex, which especially in some parts in the Wild, as they very properly call it,..hardly admits the Countrey People to Travel to Markets in Winter, [etc.]. **1778** *England's Gazetteer* (ed. 2) s.v. *Newdigate, Surry*, The Wyld hereabouts is observed to bear excellent oats. **1801** W. HUNTINGTON *God Guardian of Poor* 66 Being a native of the Wild of Kent, which is none of the most polite parts of the world.

(*b*) **1570** LAMBARDE *Peramb. Kent* (1576) 167 Nowe then we are come to the Weald of Kent, which (after the common opinion of men of our time) is conteined within very streight and narrowe limits, notwithstanding that in times paste, it was reputed of suche exceeding bignesse, that it was thought to extende into Sussex, Surrey, and Hamshyre. **1625** MARKHAM *Inrichment Weald Kent* 1 The Weald of Kent is the lower part of that Shire, lying on the South side thereof, and adioyneth to the Weald of Sussex, towards the West. **1787** *Phil. Trans.* LXXVII. 190 The right hand stations occupy..the heights which extend across the Wealds. **1822** W. D. CONYBEARE & PHILLIPS *Outl. Geol.* 144 The Weald. This district may be generally described as stretching along the coast of the channel from Folkstone to Beachy Head, and thence extending westwards into the interior as far as the confines of Sussex and Hampshire. **1846** MCCULLOCH *Acc. Brit. Empire* (1854) I. 196 There is a great deal of valuable timber and coppice-wood in Surrey, particularly in the weald... Turnpike roads good; but cross-roads, particularly in the weald, very indifferent. **1863** HERSCHEL *Fam. Lect. Sci. Subj.* I. §4 What has become of all that great bed of chalk which once covered all the weald of Kent? **1903** KIPLING *Five Nations, Sussex* 24 And through the gaps revealed Belt upon belt, the wooded, dim Blue goodness of the Weald.

2. A wooded district or an open country; a wold. Now only *poet.*

1544 BALE *Chron. Oldcastell* 47 Manye fledde..into the welde of Scotlande, Walys, and Irelande. **1603** S. DANIEL *To Lady Marg. C'tess Cumberland* 8 What a faire seate hath he, from whence he may The boundlesse wastes, & weilds of man suruay. **1851** MEREDITH *Sunrise* 18 Poet. Wks. (1912) 78 Glimmering fields, And wakening wealds. **1855** BAILEY *Mystic* etc. 83 Forest and upland frith, and the wide weald Hercynian, where the demon shadow stalks. **1859** TENNYSON *Guinevere* 127 But she to Almesbury Fled all night long by glimmering waste and weald.

3. *attrib.* and *Comb.*, chiefly 'of or pertaining to the Weald'. **weald clay**, the upper stratum of the Wealden formation immediately above the 'Hastings sand'; also *pl.* with reference to the various subdivisions of this stratum. **weald saurian** = HYLÆOSAURUS. **wealdsman**, an inhabitant of the Weald.

1822 W. D. CONYBEARE & PHILLIPS *Outl. Geol.* 145 A second valley..occupied by the argillaceous beds which we have called the *Weald clay. **1878** *Chamb. Encycl.* X. 114 The Hastings beds contain more sandstone and less clay than those of the upper Weald Clays. **1828** P. I. MARTIN *Geol. Mem. W. Sussex* Advt. p. vi, The space thus comprised, has otherwise, in geological language, got the name of the '*Weald Denudation'. *Ibid.* 40 *Weald Formation, or Wealden. **1869** J. TIMBS *Ancestral Stories* 164 The forest or *Weald Saurian (*Hylæosaurus*). **1928** *Daily Tel.* 29 May 8/5 The flares signalled her triumph to the *wealdsmen of Sussex. **1828** P. I. MARTIN *Geol. Mem. W. Sussex* 54 Although any considerable segment of the circle of the *weald valley may be taken as a specimen of the whole.

weald, obs. form of WIELD.

Wealden ('wiːldən), *a.* and *sb.* [f. WEALD + -EN[4].

The suffix is here employed arbitrarily in a sense remote from its ordinary use. As the formation of the word was app. suggested by the adjs. in *-en*, it may be presumed that the inventor regarded the adjectival use as primary, and the substantival use as elliptical for 'wealden formation'; but Martin's own use of the term affords no evidence of this.]

A. *adj.*

1. Of or pertaining to the geological formation known as the Wealden (see B). ***Wealden lizard*** = HYLÆOSAURUS.

1828 P. I. MARTIN *Geol. Mem. W. Sussex* 42 This bed of wealden sand. **1829** W. BUCKLAND in *Trans. Geol. Soc.* (1835) Ser. II. III. 425 On the discovery of Fossil Bones of the Iguanodon, in the Iron Sand of the Wealden Formation in the Isle of Wight. **1833** MANTELL *Geol. S.E. Eng.* 181 The Wealden strata may be separated into three principal divisions; namely, the Weald clay; the Hastings beds, including the strata of Tilgate Forest; and the Ashburnham or inferior limestones and shales. *Ibid.* 328 *note*, The Wealden Lizard, or Fossil Lizard of Tilgate Forest. **1846** MCCULLOCH *Acc. Brit. Empire* (1854) I. 65 *Wealden series*, a name given to a series of clays, sands, and limestones, from being well developed in the weald of Sussex, and which is remarkable for containing the remains of terrestrial, freshwater, and æstuary animals. **1863** A. C. RAMSAY *Phys. Geog.* 125 It [Weald Clay] was left in its native state, and formed those broad forests which once covered the Wealden area.

2. a. Of or pertaining to the Weald.

1870 LOWER *Hist. Sussex* I. 137 This ancient Wealden parish is about five miles in length, [etc.]. **1896** A. AUSTIN *England's Darling* IV. ii, And wealden wolves will batten on the rest. **1907** *Sat. Rev.* 14 Sept. 327/1 An epitaph in a wealden churchyard.

b. Applied to a style of timber house built in the Weald in the late medieval and Tudor periods (see quots. 1961, 1963).

1956 *Archaeol. Jrnl.* CXII. 93 In Kent the aisled hall was replaced by the type of building often called the 'Wealden' house, though it has a wider distribution than that. **1961** M. W. BARLEY *Eng. Farmhouse & Cottage* I. ii. 27 The Wealden house has a central hall open to the roof with a storeyed wing at one end or both. The whole is under a continuous roof, but the storeyed wing is jettied out, to overhang the ground floor by a foot or more. **1963** S. E. RIGOLD in Foster & Alcock *Culture & Environment* xiii. 351 The characteristic hall-house of Kent and Sussex has a unitary hipped roof.. covering both the hall and the two-storeyed ends... When the upper stories are jettied laterally, the façade of the hall between them is relatively recessed, and the lateral wall-plate of the jettied ends is carried right across..in front of the wall-plate of the hall... This is the so-called 'Wealden house'. **1974** *Country Life* 14 Feb. 312/4 A yeoman farmer's house of the Wealden type that existed in the mid 15th century.

B. *sb. Geol.* The name of a formation or series of estuarine and freshwater deposits of Lower Cretaceous age, extensively developed in the Weald.

1828 P. I. MARTIN *Geol. Mem. W. Sussex* 9 To avoid the inconvenience of the periphrasis of weald sands and clays, it is proposed, as any compound from weald must have a Saxon termination, to call the whole formation the *Wealden*. *Ibid.* 48 Fossils of the Wealden. The fossil shells most frequent in this district of the weald, (and they are common to the whole Wealden,) are of the genera Vivipara, [etc.]. **1842** H. MILLER *O.R. Sandst.* i. (ed. 2) 39 From the

Grauwacke of the Lammermuirs, to the Wealden of Moray. **1876** D. Page *Adv. Text-bk. Geol.* xvii. 308 Regarding the Lias, Oolite and Wealden as portions of one great system.

wealdend(e, wealdent: see WALDEND.

†**'Wealding.** *Obs. rare*$^{-1}$. [f. WEALD + -ING^{3}.] An inhabitant of the Weald.

1767 S. Paterson *Another Trav.* I. 297 Ye Essex hundreds, and ye Kentish wealdings, rejoice!

†**'Wealdish,** *a. Obs.* Also 6 weldish(e. [f. WEALD + -ISH^{1}.]

1. Of or pertaining to the Weald.

[**1317** *Kent Fines* in *Archæol. Cant.* (1882) XIV. 241 Agnes, dau. of Simon le Wealdissh'. **1318** *Ibid.* 250 William, son of Robert de Weldysh'.]

1554 J. Proctor *Wyat's Rebell.* (1555) 28 Sir Henrie Isleye, the two Kneuettes and certayne other with .v. C. weldishe menne were at Seuenocke. **1625** Markham *Inrichment Weald Kent* 6, I will open the nature and conditions of this wealdish ground, comparing it with the Soyle of the Shire at large. *a* **1661** Fuller *Worthies, Kent* (1662) 56 A considerable part of this County is called the Wealde, that is, a Wood-land ground, the Inhabitants whereof are called the Wealdish-men.

2. Having the character of uncultivated land.

1598 Norden *Spec. Brit., Herts.* 1 The disposition of this part of the countrie to forrest and weldish groundes, fitte for the fostering of such kinde of wild beastes.

†**'Wealdy,** *a. Obs. rare*$^{-1}$. [f. WEALD + -Y^{1}.] Of or pertaining to the Weald.

1570 Lambarde *Peramb. Kent* (1576) 169 But when they come to the Tenauntes inhabiting within the Wealdy countrey, then the stile and Intituling, is first, *Redditus de Walda*, Then [etc.].

weale, obs. form of WALE *sb.*^{1}, WEEL.

weale away, obs. form of WELLAWAY.

†**'wealful,** *a. Obs.* Forms: 3 weole-, 3–5 wele-, 4–5 welful, 4 wellful, *Sc.* velfull, 5 welfull, 6 weelful, 6–7 weal(e)full. [f. WEAL *sb.*^{1} + -FUL.] Happy, prosperous, fortunate, blessed, gladsome.

c **1230** *Hali Meid.* (MS. Titus) 31 For, beo hit nu, þat te beo richedom riue, ant tine wide wahes wlonke & welefulle. *a* **1240** *Sawles Warde* in *O.E. Hom.* I. 259 Hire wlite se weoleful þat euch eorðlich liht is þeoster þer oȝeines. **1352** Minot *Poems* viii. 17 Weleful men war ȝe, i-wis. *c* **1374** Chaucer *Boeth.* I. met. i. (1868) 4 Þilke deeþ of men is welful þat ne comeþ not in ȝeres þat ben swete. *c* **1386** —— *Man of Law's T.* 353 O cleere, o welful Auter, hooly croys. **1406** Hoccleve *La Male Regle* 402 O god!..Weleful lord. **1426** Lydg. *De Guil. Pilgr.* 16999 And wel-full and blyssed be the betynges and skowrynges, that compellyn a chylde to declyne ffrom his trespacys and his Errours. **1556** Grimalde *Cicero De Offic.* Pref. to Rdr. ¶vj, If it bee well, and wisely, and conueniently done: we shall be wealfull, and in a blessed case. **1609** J. Davies (Heref.) *Holy Rood* D 3, To tell the Ierkes with ioy, that ioy do bring, Is both a wealefull, and a wofull thing.

Hence †**'wealfully** *adv.*, †**'wealfulness** *Obs.*

c **1374** Chaucer *Boeth.* II. pr. iii. (1868) 37 It deliteþ me to comen now to þe singuler vphepyng of þi welefulnesse. *c* **1375** *Sc. Leg. Saints* iii. (*Andrew*) 663 Alhale, þu blissit croice, þat is hallowit welfully of Ihesu cryste in þe body. *Ibid.* 785 A matrone þat wellfully quhile maryt wes with a senatour of þe place. **1387–8** T. Usk *Test. Love* I. vi. 24 If a man be riche and fulfild with worldly welfulnesse, some commenden it. **1388** Wyclif 3 *John* 2 Of alle thingis Y make preyer, that thou entre and fare weelfulli, as thi soule doith welefuli. **1412–20** Lydg. *Chron. Troy* IV. 274 Þat euery þing miȝt in welfulnes To ȝoure encres perseueren and contvne.

wealked, variant of WELKED, WHELKED.

we-all ('wiːɔːl), *pron. U.S. dial.* [f. WE *pron.* + ALL *a.*] Used in place of WE *pron.*

1875 'Mark Twain' *Let.* 23 Nov. (1917) I. xv. 268 We-all send love to you-all. **1905** A. V. Culbertson *Banjo Talks* 25 Ter do lak we-all in de pas'. **1926** E. M. Roberts *Time of Man* vii. 266 His wife was young..and we-all made a jolly set. **1949** *Chicago Tribune* 27 Feb. VII. 6/6 Did we-all see Smokey hold? **1964** *N.Y. Times Mag.* 23 Aug. 62/2 *Soul brother*, Negro; also referred to as..*we-all*,..*the people.*

So '**we-all's**, our; ours.

1887 *Scribner's Mag.* Oct. 475/1 O Lawd, 'lighten we-all's unnerstandin's. **1893** H. A. Shands *Some Peculiarities of Speech in Mississippi* 67 'That house is we all's' means that the house belongs to all of us. **1905** A. V. Culbertson *Banjo Talks* 160 Bin settin' yer..lak dis, So I be sut'n dat I doan' miss De train dat teck me back ter we-all's place.

weall, obs. form of WALE *v.*^{1}, WELL *adv.*

weallinde, variant of WALLING *ppl. a.*^{1}

a **1225** *Ancr. R.* 216 Gif þe gulchecuppe weallinde bres to drincken.

†**weal-public.** *Obs.* Also *pl.* 6–7 **weale publiques.** [WEAL *sb.*^{1} + PUBLIC *a.* 2 a, after F. *le bien publique* and L. *bonum publicum.*]

1. The general good of the community; public welfare or interest. Hence, the state or body politic.

1495 *Act 11 Hen. VII* c. 34 Preamble, The reformacion of the weale publique..in the seid parties of Southwales. **1540–1** Elyot *Image Gov.* 16 b, The sondry dignities and offices in the weale publik were aptly distributed. *a* **1586** Sidney *Arcadia* III. iv. ¶2 Therefore, the weale-publicke was more to be regarded, then any person or magistrate that therevnto was ordeined. **1602** F. Hering *Anatomyes* 19 The Weale-publike Prudently and Religiously prouided for. **1641** Milton *Reform.* II. 46 What is all this either here, or there to the temporal regiment of Wealpublick, whether it be Popular, Princely, or Monarchical? **1671** F. Philipps *Reg. Necess.* 338 Private mens Actions and Suits must be suspended for a convenient time, where it is *pro bono publico*, the Weal-publick. **1710** Steele & Addison *Tatler* No. 253 ¶6 The Advantages that may arise to the Weal-Publick from this Institution. **1731** Peyton *Divine Catastrophe Ho. Stuarts* 62 To..keep and defend the Weal-publick in Health and Prosperity.

2. A state, community, or commonwealth.

1540–1 Elyot *Image Gov.* 83 b, Truely god gyueth wysedome, but fauour and aucthoritie mooste chiefely sheweth it in a weale publyke. **1551** Robinson tr. *More's Utopia* I. (1895) 30 They found townys and cytyes, and weale publyques, full of people, gouerned by good and holsom lawes. **1610** Healey *St. Aug. Citie of God* I. xxix. 45 When Carthage was raized downe, and the greatest curber and terror of the Romaine weale-publike vtterly extinguished and brought to nothing. **1622** [E. Misselden] *Free Trade* 33 This is our case in this Weale-publike; no Kingdome hath better Lawes. **1627** Hakewill *Apol.* (1630) 107 Whatsoever the force of the starres be, upon the persons of private men, or the states of weale-publiques.

†'**wealsman.** *Obs. rare*$^{-1}$. [f. *weal's* genitive of WEAL *sb.*^{1} + MAN *sb.*^{1}] One devoted to the public weal; a commonwealth's-man.

1607 Shaks. *Cor.* II. i. 59 Meeting two such Weales men as you are (I cannot call you Licurgusses).

†'**wealsome,** *a. Obs.* Forms: 4 **welsom, -sum, weelsom,** 5 **weylsum, welsumme.** [f. WEAL *sb.*^{1} + -SOME^{1}.] Happy, prosperous; fraught with happiness.

1382 Wyclif *Gen.* xxiv. 21 Wilnyng to wite whether the Lord hath maad his weye welsom [L. *prosperum*] or noon. —— *Eccles.* iv. 3, I preisede more the deade than the liuende; and I demede hym welsumere [L. *feliciorem*] than either, that ȝit is not born. *c* **1425** *Found. St. Bartholomew's* (1886) p. xcix, O ye happy and weylsum ȝe, and most weylsum religious men.

Hence †'**wealsomely** *adv. Obs.*

1382 Wyclif *Gen.* xxxix. 2 He was a man in alle thingis welsumly [L. *prospere*] doynge. —— 3 *John* 2 Of alle thingis I make preyer, thee for to entre, and fare welsumly, as thi soule doth welsumly.

wealth (wɛlθ). Forms: 3 **welðe, welðhe,** 3–5 **welþe,** (4 **weolthe, -þe**), 3–7 **welth,** (3 **weltht,** 5 **welt**), 4–5 **welþ,** 4–6 *Sc.* **velth,** 6 *Sc.* **veltht,** 4–6 **welthe,** (6 **wellthe**), 6 **wealthe,** (7 **waelth**), 5– **wealth.** [ME. *welþe*, f. WELL *adv.* or WEAL *sb.*^{1} + -TH^{1}, on the analogy of *health.* Parallel formations are MDu. *weelde, welde* (mod.Du. *weelde*), MLG. *welede* (mod.LG. *welde*), OHG. *welida.*]

†**1.** The condition of being happy and prosperous; well-being. *Obs.* (exc. *arch.*). **a.** of a person.

c **1250** *Gen. & Ex.* 1550 And bad him [Esau] of his kindes louerd ben, In welðe and miȝt wurðinge ðen. *a* **1300** *Cursor M.* 755 Adam ȝode walkand in þat welth. *c* **1340** Hampole *Pr. Consc.* 1288, 1290 And in welthe men wald ay be; Bot parfit men, þat þair lif right ledes, Welthe of þe worlde ay flese and dredes. *Ibid.* 1293 Worldly welthe. **1398** Trevisa *Barth. De P.R.* VI. xiii. (1495) 197 Noo man hath more welth [L. *nullus est felicior*] than he that hath a gode woman to his wyfe. *c* **1450** *Merlin* xxxiii. 680 The grete love that I haue to you hath made me forsake alle other.., for with-oute yow haue I neither ioye ne welthe. **1470–85** Malory *Arthur* IX. xxxvii. 400 But whanne sekenes toucheth a prysoners body thenne may a prysoner say al welthe is hym berafte. **1523** Berners *Froiss.* I. Pref., Aboue all thynges, wherby mans welthe ryseth, speciall laude and cause ought to be gyuen to historie. **1526** Tindale *1 Cor.* x. 24 Lett no man seke his awne prophet: but lett every man seke his neghbours welthe. **1548–9** (Mar.) *Bk. Com. Prayer* 122 To preserue thy people ..in wealth, peace, and Godlynes. *Ibid.* 122 b, In all tyme of our tribulacion, in all tyme of our wealth. **1559** —— *Prayer for Queen* 12 Graunt her in health and wealthe longe to liue. **1592** *Soliman & Pers.* V. i. 24 Vpon great affaires, Importuning health and wealth of Soliman, His highnes by me intreateth you. **1596** Shaks. *Merch. V.* V. i. 249, I once did lend my bodie for thy wealth. **1596** Fitz-Geffrey *Drake* (1881) 104 And o long may wee have them, and enioy These worthies to our wealth, and thine annoy.

b. Contrasted with *woe, wandreth, care.*

a **1300** *Cursor M.* 23981 Wede o welth wil i namar, Clething wil i me tak o care. *c* **1330** R. Brunne *Chron. Wace* (Rolls) 2462 Welþe a-wey to wo þou [Fortune] strykes. **1357** *Lay Folks' Catech.* (T.) 433 Euenly to sofir the wele and the wa, Welthe or wandreth, whethir so betides. *a* **1529** Skelton *Agst. Garnesche* iv. 124 Wherfore in welthe beware of woo. *a* **1542** Wyatt *Epigr.* xxiv. (1908) 51, I trust somtyme my harme may be my helth, Syns euery wo is ioynid to some welth. *a* **1566** R. Edwards *Damon & Pithias* (1571) H iij b, In wealth a double ioye, in woe a present stay, A sweete compagnion in eche state true Friend-ship is alway.

c. Of the world, a country, town, community, its people or members; hence (the common or public) welfare. Cf. COMMONWEALTH 1, PUBLIC *a.* 2 a.

1390 Gower *Conf.* Prol. 95 The world stod thanne in al his welthe: Tho was the lif of man in helthe, Tho was plente, tho was richesse. **1456** *Cov. Leet Bk.* 290 Your own soueraign lorde & kynge..Whome God..preserve in good helthe..to this landys welthe! *c* **1470** Henry *Wallace* VIII. 1610 Was neuir befor..Sic welth and pes at anys in the land. **1490** *Little Red Bk. Bristol* (1900) II. 126 In divers matiers concernyng the welth of the same Town. **1521** *Cov. Leet Bk.* 672 For the worship of the Cyte or the welthe of the Craft. *c* **1530** L. Cox *Rhet.* (1899) 46 That the maker of the lawe apply his hole studye to the welth of his subiectes. **1550** J. Coke *Eng. & Fr. Heralds* §153 (1877) 101 You enpeche the welth of marchaundise, pyllyng and robbyng the christen people. **1551** Robinson tr. *More's Utopia* II. vi. (1895) 218 The inuentyon of feates, helpynge annye thynge to the aduantage and wealthe of lyffe. **1552** Huloet, Wealthe of a comminaltye, *bonum publicum, respublica.* **1557** North *Gueuara's Diall Pr.* 454 He alwaies studied the wealth of his people. **1607** in M. H. Peacock *Hist. Wakefield Grammar Sch.* iv. (1892) 56 And when I shall knowe any thinge..that ..toucheth the welth or good order of this schole, I will call my fellowe governours together.

d. An instance or kind of prosperity; a felicity, blessing. Chiefly *pl.*

The pl. is also used as in 3 b.

a **1300** *Cursor M.* 23432 O welthes mar mai na man tell, þan haf to will o welth þe well. **1340** Hampole *Pr. Consc.* 1319 For angres mans lyf clenses, and proves, And welthes his lif trobles and droves. *c* **1430** *Hymns Virg.* (1867) 86 Whi is þis world biloued þat fals is & veyn, Siþen þat hise welþis ben so unserteyn? **1523** Berners *Froiss.* I. clxxxii. 88 b/2 They sayd howe the noble men of the realme of Fraunce, knyghtes and squyers shamed the realme, and that it shulde be a great welth to dystroy them all. **1548** Patten *Exped. Scot.* Pref. d j b, Whyche shoulde be greatly for the wealthes of vs bothe. **1560** *Irish Act 2 Eliz.* c. 5 §1 That it hath pleased God..to preserue and keepe for vs and our wealths your royall Maiestie..to raigne ouer vs. *a* **1652** Brome *Queen & C.* III. ii, And show The Elder sort how to improve Their Wealths by Neighbour-hood and Love.

†**e.** Used for: State, government (of a nation): = WEAL *sb.*^{1} 3 b. *Obs. rare.*

a **1682** Sir T. Browne *Misc. Tracts* x. (1683) 160 Julius Cæsar..was once in mind to translate the Roman wealth unto it [Troy].

†**2.** Spiritual well-being. Often in the testamentary phrase *for the wealth of* (one's) *soul. Obs.*

c **1400** *Lay-Folks Mass-Bk.* 30 (MS. F) And alle that hit hereth to here soules helthe, Thu [Lord] help hem with thi grace and thi welthe. *c* **1450** *Godstow Reg.* 652 For the helthe of her owne sowle and the welthe of her husbond. **1463** in *Somerset Med. Wills* (1901) 201 And where as there can nott be soo hasty recompense as nedid for the welth of my soule therefore [etc.]. **1483** *Act 1 Rich. III* c. 2 §1 Such memorialles as they had ordeigned to be done for the welth of their soules. **1526** *Pilgr. Perf.* (W. de W. 1531) 18 It is all thynges that necessaryly is requyred to the welthe and helthe of mannes soule. **1537** *Instit. Christen Man* A 7, I Beleue..that this Christe..liued..and..suffred..for our sakes, and for our welthe. **1540** Hyrde tr. *Vives' Instr. Chr. Wom.* (1541) 76 b, She..procured both suche as was for the welthe of his soule, and prepared holsome meates for his body. **1553** *Primer, Prayer Adversity* V iij, As shal be moste metest and agreable to thyne honor and glory & to my moste perfecte wealth and euerlastynge saluacion.

3. a. Prosperity consisting in abundance of possessions; 'worldly goods', valuable possessions, esp. in great abundance: riches, affluence.

In mod. use *wealth* tends to be felt as a stronger term than *riches.*

c **1250** *Gen. & Ex.* 796 God gaf him ðor siluer and gold, And hird, and orf, and srud, and sat, Vn-achteled welðe he ðor bi-gat. *Ibid.* 2374 Of alle egiptes welðhe best Gaf he is breðere. *a* **1275** *Prov. Ælfred* 382 Werldes welðe to wurmes shal wurþien. **1352** Minot *Poems* vii. 153 For here es welth inogh to win, To make vs riche for euermore. *a* **1400–50** *Wars Alex.* 3582 Oure boundis ere barrayne and bare and þine full of welth. **1447** Bokenham *Seyntys, St. Faith* 303 Alle these profers hye Of wurshyp welt or of dygnyte Wych dacyan hym hycht he set not a stye. **1508** Dunbar *Tua Mariit Wemen* 394 Quhen he had warit all on me his welth, et his substance Me thoght his wit wes all went away with the laif. **1567** *Gude & Godlie B.* (S.T.S.) 51 For all this warldis welth and gude, Can na thing ryche thy celsitude. **1570** Levins *Manip.* 59/6 Welth, *abundantia rerum.* **1590** Spenser *F.Q.* II. vii. 7 What art thou man..That..these rich heapes of wealth doest hide apart From the worldes eye? **1591** Shaks. *Two Gent.* I. ii. 13 *Julia.* What think'st thou of the rich Mercatio? *Lucetta.* Well of his wealth; but of himselfe, so, so. **1639** J. Clarke *Parœm.* 99 Wealth makes worship. **1667** Milton *P.L.* I. 722 When Ægypt with Assyria strove In wealth and luxurie. **1701** De Foe *Trueborn Eng.* I. (1703) 13 Wealth, howsoever got, in England makes Lords of Mechanicks, Gentlemen of Rakes. **1746** Francis tr. *Hor. Epist.* II. ii. 45 He..sack'd a royal Fort, Replete with various Wealth. **1749** Fielding *Tom Jones* VIII. xi, My female companion..at first remonstrated against it: but upon producing my wealth, she immediately consented. **1770** Goldsm. *Des. Vill.* 62 His best companions, innocence and health; And his best riches, ignorance of wealth. **1796** H. Hunter tr. *St. Pierre's Study Nat.* (1799) II. 577 There the man of wealth would be instructed really to practise virtue. **1809** Campbell *Gertrude* II. xxiv, More than all the wealth that loads the breeze, When Coromandel's ships return from Indian seas. **1833** Tennyson *Lady Clara* 61 In glowing health, with boundless wealth. **1840** Dickens *Old C. Shop* vii, Sole inheritor of the wealth of this rich old hunks. **1861** M. Pattison *Ess.* (1889) I. 47 All this material wealth and splendour was of course in official connexion with the Church.

personified. **1712** Budgell *Spect.* No. 506 ¶2, I have somewhere met with a Fable that made Wealth the Father of Love. **1813** Byron *Giaour* 344 Alike must Wealth and Poverty Pass heedless and unheeded by.

†**b.** in *plural*, with reference to more than one possessor. *Obs.*

c **1530** Berners *Golden Bk. M. Aurel.* (1536) 157 b, Many leaue dyuers welthes that they haue in straunge landes, and lyue straitly, for to lyue in their owne land. **1574** *Mirr. Mag., Albanact* lxiii, To late you shall repent the act When all my realme, and all your wealthes are sackt. **1650** Stapylton *Strada's Low C. Wars* II. 48 He would be supported by the counsels and wealths of forrein Princes.

†**c.** *pl.* Things in which material riches consist; rich and costly goods or possessions; luxuries. *Obs.*

1352 Minot *Poems* x. 11 In holl þan þai hided grete welthes,..Of gold and of siluer, of skarlet and grene. **1377** Langl. *P. Pl.* B. x. 83 Þe more he wynneth and welt welthes & ricchesse. *c* **1400** *Sege Melayne* 801 The Bischoppe..

pyghte Pauylyons with mekill pryde, With wyne & welthes at will. *c* **1450** HOLLAND *Howlat* 847 All thus thir hathillis in hall heirly remanit, With all welthis at wiss, and worschipe to vale. **1551** ROBINSON tr. *More's Utopia* I. (1895) 106 Lawes, wherby all men shoulde haue and enioye equall portions of welthes and commodities.

d. Abundance of possessions or of valuable products, as characteristic of a people, country, or region; the collective riches of a people or country.

The phrase ***the wealth of nations*** had some currency before it was adopted by Adam Smith in the title of his famous work; but its early history is obscure.

1666 DRYDEN *Ann. Mirab.*, *To Duchess of York* 20 The Winds were hush'd, the Waves in ranks were cast..: Those, yet uncertain on whose Sails to blow, These, where the wealth of Nations ought to flow. **1667** MILTON *P.L.* II. 2 High on a Throne of Royal State, which far Outshon the wealth of Ormus and of Ind. *a* **1687** PETTY *Pol. Anat.* (1691) 35 'Tis suppos'd that the Wealth of Ireland is about the ⅛ or $\frac{1}{10}$ of that of England. **1737** POPE *Hor. Epist.* I. i. 126 Their Country's wealth our mightier Misers drain. **1739** C'TESS HARTFORD *Corr.* (1805) I. 152 He declared that he would rather live upon his small annuity all his days, than marry a woman he did not previously love, though she possessed the wealth of the Indies. **1752** JOHNSON *Rambler* No. 202 ¶6 To be poor, in the epic language, is only not to command the wealth of nations. **1757** [BURKE] *Europ. Settlem. Amer.* VII. xxviii. 274 Our American colonies..pour in upon us a wealth of another kind..from their fisheries. **1776** A. SMITH (*title*), An Inquiry into the Nature and Causes of the Wealth of Nations. **1778** JOHNSON 17 Apr. in *Boswell*, As the Spanish proverb says, 'He, who would bring home the wealth of the Indies, must carry the wealth of the Indies with him.' **1820** BYRON *Mar. Fal.* v. i. 14 A city which has open'd India's wealth To Europe. **1858** A. TROLLOPE *Dr. Thorne* xxv, Not for all the wealth of India would he have given up his lamb to that young wolf.

e. said of a specific commodity as the chief source of a country's riches. Also with defining word, indicating a particular source.

1645 SIR R. WESTON *Husb. Brabant* (1652) 7 That Land is natural to bear Flax, which is called the Wealth of Flanders. **1854** J. D. WHITNEY (*title*), The Metallic Wealth of the United States Described and Compared with that of other Countries.

f. *fig.*

1596 SHAKS. *Merch. V.* III. ii. 257, I freely told you all the wealth I had Ran in my vaines; I was a Gentleman. *Ibid.* III. v. 61 Yet more quarrelling with occasion, wilt thou shew the whole wealth of thy wit in an instant. *a* **1627** MIDDLETON *Witch* II. i, O honestie's a rare wealth in a woman, It knowes no want. **1635–56** COWLEY *Davideis* IV. 488 To Help seems all his Power, his Wealth to Give; To do much Good his sole Prerogative. **1667** MILTON *P.L.* IV. 207 Beneath him..he views..To all delight of human sense expos'd..Nature's whole wealth. **1675** DRYDEN *Aurengz.* III. (1676) 47 Whom Heav'n would bless, from Pomp it will remove, And make their wealth in privacy and Love. **1697** COLLIER *Ess. Mor. Subj.* II. 158 Those who come last [in the Roll of Time], seem to enter with Advantage. They are born to the Wealth of Antiquity. *a* **1771** GRAY *Death Hoel* 9 He ask'd no heaps of hoarded gold; Alone in Nature's wealth array'd, He ask'd and had the lovely maid. **1820** HAZLITT *Lect. Dram. Lit.* 12 There is no time more..prolific of intellectual wealth. **1868** T. T. LYNCH *Rivulet* CXLIX. iii. (ed. 3), Then darkening heavens disclose Their starry wealth.

†**g.** Condition with regard to riches or poverty; degree of wealthiness. *Obs.*

1607 DEKKER & WEBSTER *Northw. Hoe* I. ii, It shall then bee giuen out, that I'me a Gentlewoman of such a birth, such a wealth,..and so foorth. **1662** PETTY *Taxes & Contrib.* 16 Ignorance of the Number, Trade, and Wealth of the people, is often the reason why the said people are needlesly troubled.

4. *Economics.* A collective term for those things the abundant possession of which (by a person or a community) constitutes riches, or 'wealth' in the popular sense.

There has been much controversy among economists as to the precise extent of meaning in which the term should be used. The definition that has been most widely accepted is that of Mill (quot. 1848 below).

1821 TORRENS *Ess. Product. Wealth* i. 3 When we say, a man of wealth, the term implies quantity, and signifies an abundance of the comforts and luxuries of life. But when we say, agriculture is a source of wealth, the accessory idea of quantity is not implied, and the term comprises the products of agriculture, whether they be raised from one acre or from a million; whether they are capable of subsisting an individual, or a nation. **1825** BENTHAM *Ration. Reward* 237 All wealth is either the spontaneous production of the earth, or the result of labour, employed in the cultivation of the earth or upon the materials which it yields. **1832** HT. MARTINEAU *Life in Wilds* ii. 23 Whatever lives, or grows, or can be produced, that is necessary or useful, or agreeable to mankind, is wealth. **1848** MILL *Pol. Econ.* I. Prel. Rem. 8 Money, being the instrument of an important public and private purpose, is rightly regarded as wealth; but everything else which serves any human purpose, and which nature does not afford gratuitously, is wealth also. *Ibid.* 9 To an individual, anything is wealth, which, though useless in itself, enables him to claim from others a part of their stock of things useful or pleasant. Take for instance, a mortgage of a thousand pounds on a landed estate. This is wealth to the person to whom it brings in a revenue... But it is not wealth to the country; if the engagement were annulled, the country would be neither poorer nor richer. *Ibid.* 10 Wealth, then, may be defined, all useful or agreeable things which possess exchangeable value; or in other words, all useful or agreeable things except those which can be obtained, in the quantity desired, without labour or sacrifice. **1856** FROUDE *Hist. Eng.* (1858) I. i. 87 An attempt..was made to bring the production and distribution of wealth under the moral rule of right and wrong. **1883** H. SIDGWICK *Pol. Econ.* I. iii. 71 The wealth of any individual is considered to include all useful things—whether material things, as food, clothes, houses, &c., or immaterial things as debts, patents, copyrights, &c.—which..admit of being sold at a certain price. This aggregate is suitably measured by its exchange value; the common standard of value, money, being taken for convenience' sake. **1891** SCRIVENER *Fields & Cities* xx. 194 The Companies Acts..have not, and will not, create wealth; it is not the function of law to create wealth,—only to regulate its distribution. Wealth is created..by labour. **1920** A. W. KIRKALDY *Wealth* 15 If this definition [Mill's] be accepted, the importance of abundance disappears. Wealth may be a very small as well as a very big thing. A single pin..has exchange value, it is useful, and is therefore wealth... So is a motor-car or a fine yacht or an Atlantic liner.

5. Plenty, abundance, profusion (*of* what is specified). Also, the condition of abounding *in* something valuable.

1596 DALRYMPLE tr. *Leslie's Hist. Scot.* (S.T.S.) I. 42 The firth..quhair gret welth of Salmonte. **1816** SCOTT *Old Mort.* xxxiii, And they hae walth o' beef, that's ae thing certain, for here's a raw hide that has been about the hurdies o' a stot not half an hour syne. **1850** TENNYSON *In Mem.* Concl. xxvi, Again the feast, the speech,..the wealth Of words and wit. **1858** HAWTHORNE *Fr. & It. Note-bks.* (1872) I. 48 This wealth of silver, gold, and gems, that adorned the shrines of the saints. **1874** SAYCE *Compar. Philol.* vi. 217 The manifold wealth of articulate speech. **1882** RHYS *Celtic Brit.* i. 21 There is no reason, however, to suppose that the great wealth of the country in iron ore had been discovered by Cæsar's time. **1894** CONAN DOYLE *Mem. Sherlock Holmes* 218 With..dark Italian eyes, and a wealth of deep black hair.

6. *attrib.* and *Comb.* (chiefly objective and obj. gen.), as ***wealth-acquiring***, ***-bearing***, ***-centre***, ***-creating***, ***-creation***, ***-creator***, ***-despising***, ***-getting***, ***-holder***, ***-maker***, ***-making***, ***-monger***, ***-owner***, ***-producing***, ***-store***, ***-worship***, ***-yield***, ***-yielding***; ***wealth-fantasy***; instrumental, as ***wealth-elated***, ***-encumbered***, ***-fraught***; † **wealth boastingly** *adv.*, in a way that shows pride in wealth; **wealth tax**, a tax levied on the basis of a person's capital or financial assets.

1879 GEO. ELIOT *Theo. Such* xviii. 346 The predominance of *wealth-acquiring immigrants. **1865** J. MACGREGOR *Rob Roy on Baltic* (1867) 269 The mighty, *wealth-bearing Thames. **1593** NASHE *Christ's T.* T 3, Nothing about them but is *wealth-boastingly & elaborately beautified. **1890** O. CRAWFURD *Round Calend. Portugal* 19 The first stronghold and *wealth-centre of this ancient kingdom. **1964** M. MCLUHAN *Understanding Media* (1967) x. 110 In the Roman world the army was the work force of a mechanized *wealth-creating process. **1892** F. W. BAIN (*title*), On the Principle of *Wealth-creation. **1740** J. DYER *Ruins of Rome* 330 Th' humble roof..Of good Evander, *wealth-despising king. **1801** MRS. ROBINSON *Sylphid* II. 149 (Jod.) The report..awakened the jealousy of the *wealth-elated baronet. **1844** LD. LEIGH *Walks in Country* 79 A *wealth-encumber'd Peer. **1940** 'G. ORWELL' in *Horizon* Mar. 181 This kind of thing is a perfectly deliberate incitement to *wealth-fantasy. **1798** B. JOHNSON *Orig. Poems* 30 *Wealth-fraught keels in safety cut the seas. **1904** R. T. ELY & WICKER *Elem. Princ. Economics* 3 Those social phenomena that are due to the *wealth-getting and wealth-using activities of man. **1957** A. C. L. DAY *Outl. Monetary Econ.* ii. 19 Similar considerations will influence many other *wealth-holders. **1980** *TWA Ambassador* Oct. 14/1 Much of the growth in the number of wealthholders in the United States has been among the affluent, but clearly non-wealthy middle-class and upper-middle-class households. **1899** *Daily Tel.* 11 Oct. 8/7 The *wealth-makers whom he always hated. **1964** M. MCLUHAN *Understanding Media* (1967) x. 111 The Roman Army as a mobile, industrial *wealth-making force. **1654** WHITLOCK *Zootomia* 396 These are sawcy Truths to obtrude on the Power-mongers, *Wealth-mongers, and Pleasure-mongers of the World. *a* **1665** J. GOODWIN *Being filled with the Spirit* xvii. (1670) 476 If the Question should be put to all rich Wealth-mongers and Honour-mongers. **1896** *Daily Tel.* 3 Feb. 4/7 The vast *wealth-producing industries of the Rand. **1891** MEREDITH *Invect. Achilles* Poet. Wks. (1912) 554 Thou mayest gather here plunder and *wealth-store. **1963** *Daily Tel.* 22 Feb. 26/6 (*heading*) *Wealth tax statement next week. **1974** *Guardian* 23 Mar. 12/1 The Labour Party..suggested an annual wealth tax starting at 1 per cent on £50,000, and running up to 5 per cent on £400,000 and more. **1976** *Jrnl. R. Soc. Arts* Mar. 200/1 Until the final form of wealth tax has been decided it is not possible to decide whether it will be fiscally neutral as regards private woodlands. **1850** GROTE *Greece* II. lxvii. VIII. 540 Plato was not the man to preach king-worship, or *wealth-worship, as social or political remedies. **1877** GLADSTONE *Glean.* (1879) I. 168 The wealth-worship which marks and deforms our time. **1917** *19th Cent.* Dec. 1237 Its [*sc.* the ocean's] *wealth-yield appears to be beyond words bounteous. **1888** CLODD *Creation* iv. 30 Rich as are igneous rocks in *wealth-yielding mineral veins and ores, they are..destitute of fossils.

wealthful ('wɛlθfʊl), *a.* Now *rare.* [f. WEALTH + -FUL.] Abounding in wealth; †happy (*obs.*), rich, prosperous; conducive to wealth. † *wealthful of*, abounding in.

13.. *Cursor M.* 641 (Gött.) Þis is a stede of welthful wone. **1398** TREVISA *Barth. De P.R.* xv. lviii. (1495) 509 Though Flaundres be lityll in space yet it is welthfull of many specyall thynges and good. *Ibid.* XVII. clvi. 707 In good and fatte grounde growyth good eere in grete quantytee and welthfull of greynes. **1447** BOKENAM *Seyntys, Christina* 4 A cyte..Weldful and ful off werldly solas. *c* **1470** HENRY *Wallace* XI. 211 This man..at ye sa welthfull mak. **1513** MORE *Rich. III*, Wks. 38/1 All is..quiete, and likelie righte wel to prosper in wealthful peace under youre coseyns. **1534** —— *Comf. agst. Trib.* III. Wks. 1235/2 God hauynge manye mancions, and al wonderfull wealthfull in his fathers house. **1577–87** HOLINSHED *Chron.* I. 20/2 All things necessarie for the wealthfull state of man. **1776** MICKLE tr. *Camoens' Lusiad* 464 Malacca's castled harbour here survey, The wealthful seat foredoom'd of Lusian sway. **1883** MISS BROUGHTON *Belinda* III. vi, It is a lovely rain,..healthful, wealthful, beneficent.

Hence † **'wealthfully** *adv.*, † **'wealthfulness.**

c **1450** tr. *Boeth. de Consol.* I. met. vii., MS. Bodl. Auct. F. 3. 5, lf. 220 b, Gladnes in hauynge of worldely welthefulnes. **1535** STEWART *Cron. Scot.* (Rolls) III. 206 To leve ay in welthfulnes. **1540** HYRDE tr. *Vives' Instr. Chr. Wom.* II. ii. (1592) N 8, To lead thy life wealthfully.

wealthily ('wɛlθɪlɪ), *adv.* Now *rare.* Also 6–7 **wealthely.** [-LY².] In a wealthy manner.

1534 WHITINTON *Tullyes Offices* II. (1540) 75 That pertayne and avayle a man to lyue well and welthyly. **1551** ROBINSON tr. *More's Utopia* I. (1895) 105 All thynges be so well and wealthelye ordered, that vertue is had in pryce and estimatyon. **1567** J. SANFORD *Epictetus* Epist. A ij b, That we should be in felicitie and leade our life both well and wealthilie. **1596** SHAKS. *Tam. Shr.* I. ii. 75, I come to wiue it wealthily in Padua. **1614** S. DANIEL *Hymen's Tri.* II. i, And thus they all vnhappy by that meanes Which they accompt would bring all happinesse; Most wealthely are plagu'd, with rich distresse. **1658** *Whole Duty Man* xiv. §25 When out of an eagerness of bestowing them wealthily, they force them to marry utterly against their own inclinations. **1755** JOHNSON, *Richly*, adv.,..with riches; wealthily. *c* **1885** E. DICKINSON *Poems* (1955) III. 1123 Ill it becometh me to dwell so wealthily When at my very Door are those possessing more, In abject poverty.

wealthiness ('wɛlθɪnɪs). Now *rare.* [f. WEALTHY *a.* + -NESS.] Wealthy quality or condition; wealth.

a **1513** FABYAN *Chron.* III. lvi. (1533) 20 This in tracte of tyme made hym welthy. And by meane of this welthynes ensued pryde. **1535** COVERDALE *Job* xxi. 13 They spend their dayes in welthynesse: but sodenly they go downe to hell. **1536** *Primer Eng. & Lat.* (Rouen) 144 b, Verely I sayde in my welthynes I shall neuermore be mouyd. **1567** *Trial Treasure* D iv b, You shall wante no kinde of welthines. **1596** DALRYMPLE tr. *Leslie's Hist. Scot.* (S.T.S.) I. 7 *marg.*, The Welthines of fische in Scotland. **1747** SHENSTONE *Let. to Graves* 21 Sept., I almost hate the idea of wealthiness as much as the word.

wealthless ('wɛlθlɪs), *a. rare.* [f. WEALTH + -LESS.] Without wealth, having no money. In quot. 1605 *absol.*

1605 A. WARREN *Poor Man's Pass.* B 2 b, In vaine the wealthlesse doe their wants repeat. **1799** CAMPBELL *Pleas. Hope* II. 42 Barr'd from delight by Fate's untimely hand, By wealthless lot, or pitiless command. **1886** A. WEIR *Hist. Basis Mod. Europe* (1889) 220 Wealthless maidens..cut off their..locks in order to get a mite for the national cause.

† **'wealthling.** *Obs. rare.* [f. WEALTH + -LING¹.] A wealthy wight.

1581 MULCASTER *Positions* xxxvii. (1887) 147 Be there not as vntoward poorelinges, as there be wanton wealthlinges? **1605** A. WARREN *Poor Man's Pass.* etc. G 4, Wealthlings suppose their parting peale they heare.

† **'wealthly,** *a. Obs. rare*⁻¹. [f. WEALTH + -LY¹.] Happy, delightful.

c **1460** *Towneley Myst.* i. 185 It is not good to be alone, to walk here in this worthely wone, In all this welthly wyn.

wealthy ('wɛlθɪ), *a.* [f. WEALTH + -Y¹.]

†**1. a.** Possessing well-being, happy, prosperous. Of conditions of life: Comfortable, luxurious. *Obs.*

c **1375** *Sc. Leg. Saints* xxxi. (*Eugenia*) 222 Quhen hyre chawmir wast saw he, quhare welthi wes scho wont to be. **1540** HYRDE tr. *Vives' Instr. Chr. Wom.* (1592) X 2, If the wife have skil to rule an house..then shal al the mariage be more wealthy and fortunate. **1551** ROBINSON tr. *More's Utopia* II. ix. (1895) 301 A pleasaunt and a welthy lyuynge [*lautam ac splendidam vitam*]. *Ibid.*, [They] lyue so wretched and miserable a lyfe, that the state and condition of the labouring beastes maye seme muche better and welthier. **1563** WIN3ET *Bk. Quest.* Wks. (S.T.S.) I. 128 In our days the samin wes abusit amang mony in idilnes and welthy lyfe.

†**b.** Of the body: Thriving (in phr. ***healthy and wealthy***). *Obs.*

1538 STARKEY *England* 179 You schal see veray few of sobur and temperat dyat, but they haue helthy and welthy bodys.

c. *dial.* Of cattle: Well-fed.

1829 BROCKETT *N.C. Gloss.* (ed. 2). Hence in recent Dicts.

2. Of persons: Having wealth or abundant means at command; rich, opulent.

a **1430** *Hymns Virg.* (1867) 115 Charite dooþ neuere wickidli.. Ne blowen is with pride thou3 sche be welþi. **1560** DAUS tr. *Sleidane's Comm.* 118 Ryche and welthy marchauntes. **1596** SHAKS. *Tam. Shr.* IV. ii. 37, I wil be married to a wealthy Widdow, Ere three dayes passe. **1703** DAMPIER *Voy.* III. 58 Besides Merchants and others that Trade by Sea from this Port, here are other pretty Wealthy Men. **1781** COWPER *Expost.* 419 The flocks and herds of wealthy Lot. **1807** CRABBE *Par. Reg.* III. 786 Come, surly John, thy wealthy kinsman view. **1820** SCOTT *Monast.* i, The donations of land with which the King endowed these wealthy fraternities. **1825** MᶜCULLOCH *Pol. Econ.* I. 7 He is said to be wealthy, according to the degree in which he can afford to command those necessaries, conveniences and luxuries, which are not the gifts of nature, but the products of human industry. **1848** MILL *Pol. Econ.* I. Prel. Rem. 8 To be wealthy is to have a large stock of useful articles, or the means of purchasing them. **1860** RUSKIN *Unto this Last* iv. (1862) 126 Many of the persons commonly considered wealthy, are in reality no more wealthy than the locks of their own strong boxes are. **1881** 'RITA' *My Lady Coquette* i, The Mervyns are by no means a wealthy family.

Prov. **1639** J. CLARKE *Parœm.* 91 Earely to bed and earely to rise, makes a man healthy, wealthy, and wise.

absol. *c* **1380** *Antecrist* in Todd *Three Treat. Wyclif* (1851) 131 Crist fedde þe needy pore; & þei þe riche & welþi. *c* **1412** HOCCLEVE *De Reg. Princ.* 1288 He sparith hem that vnwelthy heer ben, And to þe velthy dooth as þat ye seen. **1682** DRYDEN *Medal* 183 The wise and wealthy love the surest way. **1784** COWPER *Task* IV. 426 Meanwhile ye shall not want..what a wealthier than ourselves may send. **1890** R. H. WRIGHTSON *Sancta Respublica Romana* 12 The wealthy fled with their moveables.

3. Of a country, community, period, etc.: Prosperous, flourishing, thriving; commanding riches.

c **1460** FORTESCUE *Abs. & Lim. Mon.* xvi. (1885) 149 Yff the kyng haue such a Counsell..his lande shall..be ryche and welthy. **1538** STARKEY *England* 88 Thys reame hath byn callyd euer rych, and of al Chrystundome one of the most welthys. **1539** BIBLE (Great) *Ps.* lxvi. 12 Thou broughtest vs out in to a welthy place. **1596** DALRYMPLE tr. *Leslie's Hist. Scot.* I. 38 A citie maist welthie to name Inverlouth. **1610** HOLLAND *Camden's Brit.* (1637) 700 The wealthy Abbay of Fountaines. **1653** MILTON *Hirelings* (1659) 12 Thus we see that not only the excess of hire in wealthiest times, but also [etc.]. **1827** SOUTHEY *Penins. War* II. xvi. 26 The southern provinces, the most fertile and wealthiest of the kingdom.

4. In extended use: Rich *in* some possession or advantage; plentifully furnished with something; abundant, copious.

1601 SHAKS. *All's Well* II. iii. 72, I am a simple Maide, and therein wealthiest That I protest, I simply am a Maide. **1607** —— *Timon* II. ii. 193, I am wealthie in my Friends. **1608** B. JONSON *Masque Ld. Haddington's Marr.* Wks. (1616) 943 Loues wealthy croppe of kisses. *a* **1616** —— *Epigr.* lxxxi. To Proule, I will not show A line vnto thee, till ..I' haue by two good sufficient men, To be the wealthy witnesse of my pen [after L. *testis locuples*]. **1635–56** COWLEY *Davideis* I. 77 The mighty Oceans wealthy Caves. *c* **1645** HOWELL *Lett.* I. v. xxvii, Upon Dr. Davies Brittish Grammer. Twas a tough task believe it, thus to tame A wilde and wealthy language. **1746** FRANCIS tr. *Horace, Epist.* II. i. 184 And with glad Harvests crown the wealthy Year. **1830** TENNYSON *Madeline* 11 Revealings deep and clear are thine Of wealthy smiles. **1859** HT. MARTINEAU *Biog. Sk.* IV. ii. (1869) 283 The 'Kosmos' of Humboldt..is wealthy in its facts, and splendid in its generalizations. **1869** BLACKMORE *Lorna D.* iii, By her side was a little girl..with a wealthy softness on her, as if she must have her own way. **1887** *Athenæum* 31 Dec. 900/1 Mr. Foster..has rendered the wealthy coloration and tonality of Walker with great judgment. **1905** HOLMAN HUNT *Pre-Raphael.* I. 145 The language of the painter [Rossetti] was wealthy and polished.

†**5.** Of great worth or value, valuable. *Obs.*

1565 COOPER *Thesaurus* s.v. *Copiosus*, A great and wealthy heritage. **1589** GREENE *Menaphon* (Arb.) 47 My food the pleasant Plaines of Arcadie and the wealthie riches of Flora. **1593** MARLOWE & NASHE *Dido* II. i. 360 Queene Dido..for Troyes sake, hath entertaind vs all, And clad vs in these wealthie robes we weare. **1611** CHAPMAN *Iliad* XVIII. 313 Then they washt, and fild the mortall wound With wealthy oyle, of nine yeares old. **1612** in *Eng. Hist. Rev.* (1914) Apr. 251 An assured trade that way..will.. proove more wealthy and beneficiall for this state then any other. **1652–62** HEYLYN *Cosmogr.* II. (1682) 160 A wealthy race of sheep, which bring forth young twice a year, and are shorn four times. **1660** F. BROOKE tr. *Le Blanc's Trav.* 382 In divers Islands they finde most wealthy Mines. **1715** POPE *Iliad* I. 217 Thine in each Conquest is the wealthy Prey. **1746** FRANCIS tr. *Hor., Sat.* II. iii. 335 An actor's son dissolv'd a wealthy pearl..In vinegar.

6. (With capital initial.) Name of a N. American variety of late-ripening, red-skinned cooking or dessert apple. Freq. *absol.*

1869 C. DOWNING *Fruits & Fruit Trees Amer.* (ed. 2) ix. 398 Wealthy. A new variety originated by Peter M. Gideon, near St. Paul, Minn., from seed gathered in Maine about 1860... Fruit medium, oblate or roundish oblate, whitish yellow ground, shaded with deep rich crimson. **1921** *Daily Colonist* (Victoria, B.C.) 7 Oct. 7/4 Seal of Quality Groceries. No. 1 Wealthy Apples, excellent, sound stock, in boxes containing about 40 lbs. **1944** *Chicago Daily News* 25 Sept. 13/3 Right now Wealthies or Maiden's Blush are the choice varieties for cooking or pie. **1975** *New Yorker* 11 Aug. 39/1 The five apples so suddenly swept from the general market were the Baldwin, the Wealthy, the Golden Grimes, the Ben Davis, and the Black Twig.

†'**wealy**, *a.*[1] *Obs.* Forms: 1 **weliȝ, -eȝ, wæliȝ, weoliȝ,** 2–4 **weli,** 3 **weoli, -eȝ,** 4–5 **wely,** 6 *Sc.* **velie.** [OE. *weliȝ* = OS. *welag* (MLG. and MDu. *welich*, LG. and Du. *welig* luxuriant, rank, wanton), OHG. *welac*:—WGer. **welaȝo-*, f. **wela-* WEAL *sb.*[1]: see -Y[1].]

1. Wealthy, prosperous, happy.

Beowulf 2607 Ðemunde ða ða are, þe he him ær forȝeaf, wicstede weliȝne Wæȝmundinga. *c* **893** ÆLFRED *Oros.* IV. v. (1883) 166 Sum weliȝ mon..se wæs haten Hanna. **11..** *Gloss.* in Wr.-Wülcker 540/6 *Diues*, weli. *c* **1205** LAY. 427 þa weoleȝen & þa weaðlen. *Ibid.* 13904 þe þridde hæhte Woden þæt is an weoli godd. *a* **1300** *Cursor M.* 7879 Bot oft þe weliest o win Riue-liest þai fal in sin. *Ibid.* 9958 þan was þar never suilk a hald, Ne nan welier in werld to wald. *c* **1380** in *Polit. Poems* (Rolls) I. 267 Suche annuels has made thes frers, so wely and so gay, That ther may no possessioners mayntene thair array.

2. In good condition, healthy.

13.. *E.E. Allit. P.* B. 1244 þo þat byden wer so biten with þe bale hunger, þat on wyf hade ben worþe þe welgest fourre. *c* **1440** *Pallad. on Husb.* III. 266 The clawes drie & scabbid, old, vnsely, Kitte al away, & kepe up that is wely.

3. Luxurious, self-indulgent.

1545 JOYE *Expos. Dan.* iv. 50b, The peple of Israell as oft as thei wexed wealy and fatte as saith the song of Moses. *Ibid.* v. 71 Let siche sewer wealy rulers beware of a soden fall. *c* **1590** J. STEWART *Poems* (S.T.S.) II. 216 Sum velie var, Sum vickit, And Sum vaine.

Hence †'**wealiness**, luxuriousness. *Obs.*

1545 JOYE *Expos. Dan.* xi. 181 Therfore of pryde and wealynes [he] gaue himselfe vp vnto his owne lustis. **1571** GOLDING *Calvin on Ps.* xxx. 7. 109 Hereuppon groweth wealynesse of the flesh [*hinc carnis lascivia*], that they licentiously folow theyr owne lusts.

†'**wealy**[2], '**weely**, *a. Obs.* Also 7 **wealie, weally.** [Of obscure origin; common in P. Holland.] Of land: Unproductive, marshy, poor.

1601 HOLLAND *Pliny* XVII. viii. I. 506 If the ground be cold, moist, and weely. **1610** —— *Camden's Brit.* 203 This river [Ex] hath his head and springeth first in a weely and barren ground named Exmore. *Ibid.* 364 Flockes of sheepe long necked and square of bulke and bone, by reason (as it is commonly thought) of the weally and hilly situation of their pasturage. **1610** FOLKINGHAM *Feudigr.* I. x. 33 Sandy Marle serues (for want of other) chiefely in cold moist and weely grounds.

weam(b: see WAME.

weame, obs. form of WAME, WEM.

†'**weamish**, *a. Obs.* [? Variant of QUEIMISH *a.*] Squeamish.

1571 T. FORTESCUE *Mexia's Foreste* 46b, Wee in this Age are colde and drie, of complexion none other or better then Melancoly, angrye, weamishe [Fr. *ennuyeuse*], harde to please and enuious. **1777** *Horæ Subsecivæ* (MS.) 462 (*Eng. Dial. Dict.*) *Weamish*, squeamish.

wean (win, wen), *sb. Sc.* and *dial.* Also 9 **ween, wain, wane.** [A contraction of *wee ane*: (see WEE *a.* and ONE), the full form still appearing in the first group of quotations. In the north-eastern Sc. counties the equivalent *little ane* has similarly given *littlan, littlen.*] A young child.

α. **1692** [see WEE *a.*]. **1721** RAMSAY *Poems* I. Gloss. 397 *Wean*, or *wee ane*, a Child. **1755** JOHNSON s.v. *Wee*, In Scotland it denotes small or little; as *wee* ane, a little one, or child. **1768** ROSS *Helenore* 6 The name the wean [**1789** weeane] gat, was Helenore. *a* **1774** FERGUSSON *Hallow-Fair* viii, Than there's sic yellowchin and din, Wi' wives and weeanes gablin.

β. **1725** RAMSAY *Gentle Sheph.* II. iii, When Bessy Freetock's chuffy-cheeked We'an To a Fairy turn'd. **1728** —— *Anacreontic on Love* 8 A poor young Wean. **1786** BURNS *Inventory* 52 Wi' weans I'm mair than weel contented, Heav'n sent me ane mae than I wanted! **1789** —— *To Dr. Blacklock* 52 To make a happy fire-side clime To weans and wife, That's the true pathos and sublime Of human life. **1818** SCOTT *Hrt. Midl.* iv, There was my daughter's wean, little Eppie Daidle. **1822** GALT *Provost* xxiv, The major part were sailors' wives and weans. **1825** BROCKETT *N.C. Gloss.*, *Weens*, children. Little ones. 'How are the weens?' **1826** J. WILSON *Noctes Ambr.* Wks. 1855 I. 175 Returnin back hame, the wife and weans were a' at the door. **1841** BARHAM *Ingol. Leg.*, *Nell Cook* end, So bless the Queen and her Royal Weans. **1856** MRS. BROWNING *Aur. Leigh* III. 927, I being but a yearling wean. **1887** P. M'NEILL *Blawearie* 85 Here comes that great grumpus crying like a wane once more. **1900** *Century Mag.* Feb. 601/2 But poor Shamus he had a wife an' a congregation of wains on his han's.

wean (wiːn), *v.* Forms: 1 **wenian,** 4–6 **wene,** 4–7 **wain(e, wane,** 5–7 **wayn(e, weyn(e,** 6 **ween,** 6–7 **wein(e, weane,** 6– **wean.** [OE. *węnian* to accustom (once only, to wean), corresponding to OFris. *wennia*, OS. *wennian* (MLG., MDu., mod.Du. *wennen*), OHG. *wennen* (MHG. *wenen*, mod.G. *-wöhnen*), ON. *venja* (Sw. *vänja*, Da. *vænne*):—OTeut. **wanjan*, f. **wano-* accustomed (ON. *van-r*); cognate with ON. *vane* wk. masc., custom, habit. For the Teut. root **wan-*: **wun-*, to be accustomed, to dwell, see WANE *sb.*[2], WONE *sb.*[2], WONT.

The OE. *węnian* occurs very frequently in the sense 'to accustom', but this use is not illustrated here, as it did not survive into ME. The sense 'to wean (a child)' was ordinarily expressed in OE. by *áwęnian* (cf. G. *entwöhnen*), and occasionally by *ȝewęnian*.]

1. *trans.* To accustom (a child or young animal) to the loss of its mother's milk; to cause to cease to be suckled. **a.** with obj. a child.

c **960** ÆTHELWOLD *Bened. Rule* vii. 22 Aȝyld þu me, drihten, mid biternesse lean, swa swa moder deþ hyre bearne, þonne hio hit fram hire breosta ȝesoce weneþ. **13..** HAMPOLE *Psalter* cxxx. 4 As a childe þat has nede to be on his modur kne and fostird with hur mylke, perisch if he be wenyd [*earlier MS.* spaned] & takyn fro mylke. **1382** WYCLIF *Hos.* i. 8 And she wenyde hir [Vulg. *et ablactavit eam*] that was With outen mercye. **1398** TREVISA *Barth. De P.R.* VI. vi. (Tollem. MS.), The childe is propirly clepid 'puer', when he is wained from milke and departid from þe breste. *c* **1425** *Cursor M.* 3018 (Trin.) Whenne he was wened [*earlier texts* spaned] fro þe pappe. *c* **1440** *Jacob's Well* 231 Whan þe modyr wanyth here child, sche wetyth here tetys wyth sum byttere thyng. *c* **1440** *Promp. Parv.* 522/1 Wene chylder fro sokynge, *ablacto, elacto.* *c* **1450** *Mirk's Festial* 16 Then aftyr, when scho was wened, þay broght hur to þe tempull. **1530** PALSGR. 770/2, I wayne a chylde from soukyng, *Je seure.* **1563–87** FOXE *A. & M.* (1596) 106/1 Before the child that is borne be waned. **1592** SHAKS. *Rom. & Jul.* I. iii. 24 'Tis since the Earth-quake now eleuen yeares, And she was wean'd. **1634** T. JOHNSON *Parey's Chirurg.* XXIV. xxiv. (1678) 554 If the child be weak, sickly, or feeble, he ought not to be weaned. *a* **1641** BP. MOUNTAGU *Acts & Mon.* (1642) 526 Untill shee be wayned, which must be at three yeers end, shee shall remaine with you in her fathers house. **1652** CULPEPPER *Eng. Phys.* 178 It is much used to dry up the Milk in Womens breasts when they have weyned their children. **1789** BUCHAN *Dom. Med.* (1790) 187 As soon as they perceive their strength and appetite begin to fail, they ought immediately to wean the child. **1888** MISS BRADDON *Fatal Three* I. iii, His wife would return to him as soon as Lady Castle-Connell's daughter was weaned.

absol. **1823** BYRON *Juan* XII. xxi, Unless a man can calculate his means Of feeding brats the moment his wife weans.

b. with obj. a young animal.

1481 CAXTON *Reynard* (Arb.) 34 Reynart..said thus.. Neuertheles yet was I vnto the tyme that I was wened fro the tete, one [etc.]. **1485** in *Descr. Catal. Anc. Deeds* (1890) I. 359 William and Agnes to have the calves of them and thei to be weynyd at the age of x. wekes. **1523–34** FITZHERB. *Husb.* §39 It is tyme to wayne theyr lambes, whanne they be .xvi. wekes old. *Ibid.* §66 If thou waine thy calues with hey it wyl make them haue great belyes. **1575** FLEMING *Virg. Bucol.* I. 2 Our Lambs new weined from yͤ dam. **1588** SHAKS. *L.L.L.* V. ii. 250. **1600** SURFLET *Country Farm* I. v. 23 Adding to the end of these great houses a little one, to keepe calues in of both kindes, which you haue wained. **1759** R. BROWN *Compleat Farmer* 22 The best time for weaning calves is from January to May. **1846** *Baxter's Libr. Pract. Agric.* II. 193 The meal or flour mixed with milk..is excellent food for weaning calves. **1908** WEYMAN *Wild Geese* xviii. 282 The low of a cow whose calf was being weaned.

c. in figurative context.

1571 CAMPION *Hist. Irel.* II. x. (1633) 134 No doubt the name and reputation thereof would have bin a spurre to these erections, as nurses for babes to suck in, till they might repaire thither [*sc.* to the University] to be wained. **1584** LYLY *Campaspe* III. iv. 121 Reason [must] weane what appetite noursed. **1592** tr. *Junius on Rev.* xii. 1 Vntil that time wherin this Church were as it were weyned & taken away from the breast or milk of her mother. **1866** KINGSLEY *Herew.* xiv, I put my love out to nurse, instead of weaning it.

d. *transf.*

1615 J. STEPHENS *Satyr. Ess.* iv. 53 As Wormewood, rubbed upon the nipple of a Nurses Teate, weanes the childe. **1618** W. LAWSON *New Orch. & Gard.* xii. (1623) 41 The Tree ouer-loden with fruit, and wanting sap to feed all she hath brought forth, will waine all she cannot feed, like a woman bringing forth moe children at once then she hath teats. *Ibid.* xv. 51.

2. *fig.* To detach or alienate (a person, his desires or affections) *from* some accustomed object of pursuit or enjoyment; to reconcile by degrees to the privation of something.

1526 *Pilgr. Perf.* (W. de W. 1531) 81b, By obedyence they were wayned from this worlde. **1581** PETTIE tr. *Guazzo's Civ. Conv.* (1586) III. 157 If they thinke them fit to enter into religion, the mother, who ought to haue cheefe charge of them, must seeke to waine them from all worldlie vanities. **1596** DRAYTON *Legends, Cromwell* 187 When first the wealthy Netherlands me trayn'd, In wise Commerce..And from my Countrie carefully me wayn'd. **1607** WALKINGTON *Optic Glass* B7b, Hee must wisely defeate, and waine his appetite of all such dainty morsels. **1608** *Merry Devil Edmonton* II. iii. 22 You are enioynd to waine your friendship from mee. **1616** B. JONSON *Every Man in H.* I. i, How happie, yet, should I esteeme my selfe, Could I (by any practise) weane the boy From one vaine course of studie, he affects. **1670** T. BROOKS *London's Lament.* 192 Luther was a man weaned from the world; and therefore when honours, preferments, and riches were offered to him, he despised them. **1741** BERKELEY *Let.* Wks. 1871 IV. 266 A long continuance of ill health has weaned me from the world. **1751** SMOLLETT *Per. Pickle* lxxxvi, He endeavoured to wean his eyes from the fatal object. **1836** DICKENS *Sk. Boz, Sentiment*, I trust the plan I have devised will be effectual in weaning my daughter from this absurd idea. **1837** WHEWELL *Hist. Induct. Sci.* (1857) I. 226 Mankind cannot be weaned from the opinion. **1856** MERIVALE *Rom. Emp.* xxxiii. (1865) IV. 64 Already men's minds were becoming weaned from positive belief in the concrete divinities of Olympus. **1876** BRIDGES *Growth of Love* xxxv, Few there be are wean'd from earthly love. **1907** C. S. PARKER *Sir J. Graham* I. i. 4 He..strove with some success to wean his tenantry from thriftless habits.

absol. **1850** ROBERTSON *Serm.* Ser. III. viii. 108 The consequences of sin are meant to wean from sin.

b. with *away.*

1891 F. H. WILLIAMS *Âtman* v. 270, I deliberately planned to wean you away from Margaret. **1913** WOODROW WILSON *New Freedom* ix. 203 If they refuse to be weaned away from their independence they cannot continue to enjoy the benefits extended to them.

c. *refl.*

1593 SHAKS. *3 Hen. VI*, IV. iv. 17 And I the rather waine me from dispaire For loue of Edwards Off-spring in my wombe. *c* **1645** HOWELL *Lett.* I. §1. xlii, Before I wean my self from Italy, a word or two touching the genius of the Nation. **1711** STEELE *Spect.* No. 27 ¶2 Let us not stand upon a Formal taking of Leave, but wean our selves from them [*sc.* the allurements of the world], while we are in the midst of them. **1725** BOLINGBR. *Let. to Swift* 24 July, If your heart tells you nothing, say nothing, that I may take the hint, and wean myself from you by degrees. **1874** GREEN *Short Hist.* iii. §4. 131 A love of secular learning from which Edmund [Rich] found it hard to wean himself.

d. *intr.* for *refl.*

c **1665** MRS. HUTCHINSON *Mem. Col. Hutchinson* (1885) I. 93 While she was weaning from the friends and places she had so long conversed in. **1827** HOOD *Hero & L.* vi, Leander, weaning from sweet Hero's side, Must leave a widow where he found a bride.

†**3.** To dissuade (whether successfully or not).

1607 *Scholast. Disc. agst. Antichrist* I. iii. 139 They wayned the people from this hipocrisie by these reproofes in vaine. **1621** BURTON *Anat. Mel.* Democr. to Rdr. 38 Tell an Epicure..of his irregular course, weine him from it a little.

4. To remove or abate gradually (a desire, affection). *rare.*

1706 E. WARD *Wooden World Diss.* (1708) 35 He weans by Degrees his Longings after the Flesh-pots of Sodom. **1842** SARAH, LADY LYTTELTON *Corr.* (1912) 327 The [baby] Princess has exactly..the same 'morbid' love of one nursery-maid, as Meriel has for you. That is to be weaned, I think, by a little less fondling her yourself.

†**5.** To train, accustom *to* (good habits). *Obs.*

[Not a survival of the OE. sense (see the etymology); the use seems to have been developed from the notion of 'weaning' from the contrary evil.]

1579 LODGE *Def. Plays* 8 Weane thy selfe to wisedome, and vse thy tallant in zeale not for enuie. **1579** LYLY *Euphues* (Arb.) 149 When the Father weaneth [*later edd.* warneth] them to continencie, the flatterer allureth them to lust. **1597** HOOKER *Eccl. Pol.* v. lxxi, The Iewes by reason of their long aboade in a place of continuall seruile toyle could not suddainely be wained and drawne vnto contrarie offices without some strong impression of terror.

weanable (ˈwiːnəb(ə)l), *a.* [f. WEAN *v.* + -ABLE.] Capable of being weaned.
1570 LEVINS *Manip.* 2/28 Weanable, *ablactabilis.* **1811** *Ann. Reg., Chron.* 94 The lambs are weanable when they can thrive on the same food that the dam subsists on.

†**wean-calf.** *Obs.* [f. WEAN *v.*] A calf newly weaned.
1618 *Depos. Bk. Archd. Essex & Colchester* 66 b, There was..a custome within the parish of Elmsted..for therbage of weane calues..that the partie who weaned the said calues should paie no tithe therof.

weane, variant of WANE *sb.*[3]

weaned (wiːnd), *ppl. a.* [f. WEAN *v.* + -ED[1].] In senses of the verb, *lit.* and *fig.*
c **1440** *Promp. Parv.* 522/1 Wenyd, as chylder fro sokynge, *ablactatus.* **1535** COVERDALE *Ps.* cxxxi. 2 My soule is euen as a weened childe. **1620** BRINSLEY *Virg. Ecl.* iii. (1633) 35 The wained kids. **1670** T. BROOKS *London's Lament.* 215 With what a weaned heart and cold affections do men look upon all the pomp, state, bravery and glory of the world, when [etc.]. **1836** C. BRADLEY *Pract. Serm.* 360 A weaned heart is absolutely needful for you. **1837** YOUATT *Sheep* xv. 517 Many farmers are very fanciful as to the provision for the weaned lambs.
Hence ˈ**weanedness,** spiritual detachment.
a **1617** BAYNE *Eph.* (1643) 278 Adorning this their age in Christ, with graces correspondent, viz. experience, wisdome, weanednesse, all kinde of mortification. **1689** MANTON *Serm.* III. I. *Life of Faith* 28 The Spiritual life..begets a holy weanedness in us. **1702** C. MATHER *Magn. Christi* I. iii. 13/2 An Example of..Weanedness from the things of this World. **1858** J. S. C. ABBOTT *Heroines Fr. Revol.* 215 Her weanedness from the world. **1885** SPURGEON *Treas. Dav.* Ps. cxxxi. 2 Such weanedness from self springs from the gentle humility declared in the former verse.

weanel (ˈwiːnəl), **wennel** (ˈwɛn(ə)l). Now *dial.* Forms: 5 **weynelle,** 6 **weanell, weannel, wennell,** 6, 8–9 **wennel,** 7– **weanel.** [f. WEAN *v.* + -EL[2].] An animal newly weaned, a weanling.
1488–9 in *Rep. MSS. Ld. Middleton* (Hist. MSS. Comm. 1911) 472, xv. weynelles, le pece ij s. viij d. **1557** TUSSER *100 Points Husb.* lxxvii, Pinch weannels at no time of water nor meate. **1573–80** —— *Husb.* (1878) 61 Yoong colts with thy wennels together go serue. **1579** SPENSER *Sheph. Cal.* Sept. 198 A Lambe, or a Kidde, or a weanell wast. **1669** WORLIDGE *Syst. Agric.*, Dict. Rust., *Weanel*, a young Beast newly weaned. **1787** GROSE *Prov. Gloss.*, Wennel. **1879** *Hertford Mercury* Dec., Advt., 26 Home-bred Steers and Sturks,..4 Weanels, 2 Down Calving Cows.
appositive. **1588** *Theocritus' Idillia* viii. A ij b, Ile pawne a calfe, a wennell lambe laie thou to it.

weaner (ˈwiːnə(r)). [f. WEAN *v.* + -ER[1].]
†**1.** One who takes care of a young person. *Obs.*
1579 LYLY *Euphues* (Arb.) 131 Plato..admonished all nursses and weaners of youth, that they should [etc.].
2. A calf or lamb weaned during the current year; also, a pig or any other animal weaned during the current year. Also *attrib.* Cf. WEANYER. orig. *Austral.* and *N.Z.*
1865 R. HENNING *Let.* 19 Aug. (1966) 208 He takes the heaviest flock of all, 2,200 weaners. **1881** MRS. C. PRAED *Policy & P.* I. 137 These are the weaners to be looked after. **1890** 'R. BOLDREWOOD' *Col. Reformer* xi, Wether, hogget, ewe, weaner. *Ibid.*, You won't have that weaner flock drafted before breakfast. **1928** *Daily Express* 3 Feb. 5/2 Instruction is given in..the rearing of calves for stock, for market as 'weaners', and for sale as veal. **1950** *N.Z. Jrnl. Agric.* Jan. 63/1 Pigs sold as weaners through saleyards. **1958** *Times* 29 Sept. 2/7 Though weaner prices fell..during 1957/58, high prices for fat pigs are still reflected in the store market. **1969** T. WEST in R. Blythe *Akenfield* xi. 179, I want to produce weaner-pigs... Are you interested? **1981–2** *Deer Farmer* (N.Z.) Summer 10/3 The trial of disbudding of 80 to 100 weaner bucks will start in March next year. *Ibid.* 16/2 A herd of 300 New Zealand wapiti and wapiti-red hybrid females, is run at Criffel, along with 200 bulls, and 30 male and 30 female New Zealand wapiti weaners. **1984** *N.Z. Farmer* 12 Apr. 12/1 The cattle policy is to winter all weaners.

weangeance, obs. Sc. form of VENGEANCE.

weanie, weany (ˈwiːniː), *dial.* [dim. of WEAN *sb.*: see -IE, -Y[6].] A very young child.
1785 BURNS *Scotch Drink* xii, When skirlin weanies see the light, Thou maks the gossips clatter bright. **1864** BLACKMORE *Clara Vaughan* xxiv, The two weanies (big baby and little baby) only attending for the sake of example. **1894** A. REID *Songs Heatherland* 103 Davie..Mindit neebors' crawlin' weanies.

weaning (ˈwiːnɪŋ), *vbl. sb.* [-ING[1].] The action of the vb. WEAN; an instance of this.
1382 WYCLIF *Gen.* xxi. 8 Abraham made a greet feest in the day of the wanyng of hym. *c* **1460** *Oseney Reg.* 91 Mylke of þere kyne fro þe tyme of þe wenyng of þe calues. **1610** FLETCHER *Faithf. Sheph.* I, Whose Lambs are ever last And dye before their waining. **1697** DRYDEN *Virg. Georg.* III. 295 This from his Weaning, let him [the horse] well be taught. **1784** COWPER *Tiroc.* 557 This second weaning, needless as it is, How does it lac'rate both your heart and his! **1848** DICKENS *Dombey* viii, A waiter's wife,..from within a day or two of Paul's sharp weaning, had been engaged as his nurse. **1895** MEREDITH *Amazing Marr.* xxix, The time for the weaning of the babe approached.

b. *Comb.* as *weaning-feast, -time*; with sense 'in process of weaning', as *weaning calf, child, colt, lamb*; **weaning-brash** (see quot.).
1844 DUNGLISON *Med. Lex.* (ed. 4), Brash, *Weaning,..A severe form of diarrhœa, which supervenes at times on weaning. **1598** in *Lancs. & Chesh. Wills* (Chetham Soc. 1897) III. 8 To the children of John Holcrofte my best *weaning calf. **1778** *Reading Merc. & Oxf. Gaz.* 30 Nov., A weaning Bull Calf. **1844** MARRYAT *Settlers in Canada* xxviii, He also took six weaning calves to bring up. **1820** CLARE *Rural Life* (ed. 3) 110 Like *weaning child that's lost its rattle. **1913** E. NESBIT in *New Witness* 23 Jan. 369 The limbs of our weaning children You crushed in your mills of power. **1523–34** FITZHERB. *Husb.* §135 If there be moche grasse..than put in calues newly wained..and also *waynynge coltes. **1896** JESSOPP & JAMES *Life St. William of Norwich* p. lxv, The miracle which happened on his *weaning-feast. **1697** DRYDEN *Virg. Past.* VII. 21 To house, and feed by hand my *weaning Lambs. **1577** B. GOOGE *Heresbach's Husb.* III. 139 b, The Lambes..must be well cherished in their *weaning time with good pasture.

weanling (ˈwiːnlɪŋ), *sb.* and *a.* Also 6 **wayne-, weyn-, wenling,** 6–7 **wain(e)ling.** [f. WEAN *v.* + -LING[1].] **A.** *sb.* A young child or animal newly weaned.
1532–3 *Act 24 Hen. VIII* c. 9 §1 Diuers persons..haue vsed..to kille yonge beastes, called waynelinges, steres, bullockes, and hesters, of one or two yeres old. **1536** *Primer, Compline* (Ps. cxxxi. 2) K vij, I am a weanlynge in very dede. **1550** *S'hampton Crt. Leet Rec.* (1905) 5 Yf any of them have two kyne or wenlings. **1589** A. F. *Virg. Bucol.* I. 2 The tender weanlings of our sheepe. **1614** ROWLANDS *Fooles Bolt* D 2 b, Mens Children went not then to write and read As euery weaneling now a dayes must do. **1655** MOUFET & BENNET *Health's Improv.* viii. 58 Calves are either Sucklings or Wainlings. **1710** HILMAN *Tusser Rediv.* Dec. (1744) 145 By this Stanza it seems as though he recommended the Housing of Weanlings. **1883** O. W. HOLMES in *Atlantic Monthly* Sept. 322 Is it a weanling's weakness for the past That..Still keeps our gray old chapel's name of 'King's'? **1916** K. J. SAUNDERS *Adv. Chr. Soul* 24 Akbar..shut up a score of weanlings away from all contact with adults.
fig. **1594** O. B. *Quest. Profit. Concern.* L 4 b, The other starre here meant, is called Luciferum, Venus her owne starre, to whom bawdes are wont to complaine, when they were deceiued or robbed of any of their sequestred weanlings.
B. *adj.* Recently weaned.
1637 MILTON *Lycidas* 46 As killing as the Canker to the Rose, Or Taint-worm to the weanling Herds that graze. *a* **1722** LISLE *Husb.* (1757) 214, I doubted some weanling-calves I had wanted water. **1726** POPE *Odyss.* XIX. 469 Hermes,..Whose shrine with weanling lambs he wont to load. **1869** BLACKMORE *Lorna D.* lxxv, Into the old farmhouse I tottered, like a weanling child.
fig. **1859** MEREDITH *R. Feverel* xxxix, That part of his pastoral duty he wisely leaves to weanling laymen. **1871** SWINBURNE *Songs bef. Sunrise, Eve Revol.* 57 Breasts that bare Our fathers' generations, whereat lay The weanling peoples and the tribes that were.

weanscot, -scott, obs. forms of WAINSCOT.

weany, variant of WEANIE, WEENY.

weanyer (ˈwiːnjə(r)), *dial.* Also 6 **wanyer, wayner, wenyer.** [f. WEAN *v.* + -YER, -IER I.] A weanling. Cf. WEANER 2. Also *attrib.*
1524 *Inv.* in *Surrey Archæol. Collect.* (1880) VII. 235 Itm vii Wanyers price xxxiiij[s]. **1544** R. BROKER *Will* (Brit. Mus. Addit. MS. 24,925 lf. 21 b), A heffer and ij wenyers of this yere. **1884** *W. Sussex Gaz.* 25 Sept., Advt., Two weanyers. **1902** *Oxf. Times* 28 June 2/3 Advt., A Weanyer Calf.

weap(e, obs. ff. WEEP *v.*

weapon (ˈwɛp(ə)n), *sb.* Forms: α. 1 **wǽpen, wœ́p(e)n, wépen, wǽmn,** 1–2 **wǣpn,** 2–3 *Orm.* **wæpenn,** 3–7 **wepen,** 4 **wepene, -in,** 4–5 **wepne,** 4–6 **weppen,** 5–6 **wepun, wep(p)yn,** 5–7 **wepon,** 5 **weppon, weppun, (vepen),** 6 **weapen,** 6– **weapon;** β. 3 *E. Anglian* **wopen;** *north.* and *Sc.* 3–7 **wapen,** 4 **wappen, vap(p)yn,** 4–7 **wapin,** 5–6 **wappin, wap(p)yn,** 5 **vappin,** 5, 7 **wappon,** 6 **wapon, vapon, vapin, vaupyn, waippin, waipone, wapoune,** 7 **wapone.** [Com. Teut.: OE. *wǽpen* neut. = OFris. *wêpin*, OS. *wâpan* (MLG. *wâpen*, whence MHG. *wâpen, wâppen*, mod.G. *wappen* only in the sense of armorial bearings), OHG. *wâfan* (MHG. *wâfen* neut., mod.G. *waffe* fem.), ON. *vápn* neut. (Sw. *vapen*, Da. *vaaben*), Goth. **wēpn* (pl. *wēpna*):—OTeut. **wǣpno-m*:—pre-Teut. **wēbno-m.* A parallel type **wǣbno-m* (:—pre-Teut. **wēpnó-m*) is supposed by some scholars to be implied by certain rare forms in various Teut. langs.: OHG. or OS. (*Hildebrandslied*) *wâbnum* dat. pl., OE. *wǽmn*, ON. *vámn.* Outside Teut. no probable cognates have been found.
The northern ME. *wāpen* (later *wappen*) and the rare (E. Anglian) *wopen* represent the ON. *vápn*: cf. WAPENTAKE, WAPPENSHAW. The shortening of the long stressed vowel in the first syllable is normal; Ormin has still the OE. quantity.
The pl. in OE. was normally identical in form with the sing., but in the 10th and 11th c. forms with final *-u* occur. In Layamon *c* 1205 the plural is usually *wepnen*, though there are also examples of *wepne* and *wapen.* From the beginning of the 14th c. the plural has in ordinary use been formed with the suffix *-(e)s*; with regard to the occasional uninflected plural see 1 b below.]
1. a. An instrument of any kind used in warfare or in combat to attack and overcome an enemy.
α. *Beowulf* 1509 Swa he ne mihte no..wæpna ʒewealdan. *Ibid.* 1573 He..wæpen hafenade heard be hiltum. *c* **930** *O.E. Chron.* an. 917, & a-hreddon eall þæt hie ʒe-numen hæfdon, & eac hira horsa & hira wæpna micelne dæl. *c* **1205** LAY. 6424 Morpidus..seouen hundred of-sloh and swemde mið wepnen. *a* **1225** *Ancr. R.* 240 Þe þet his wepnen worpeð awei, him luste beon iwunded. *c* **1330** R. BRUNNE *Chron. Wace* (Rolls) 15518 When þey were waxen on elde, Armes to bere, & wepne to welde. **1377** LANGL. *P. Pl.* B. III. 304 Alle þat bereth baslarde, brode swerde or launce, Axe other hachet or eny wepne ellis. *c* **1386** CHAUCER *Monk's T.* 34 With-outen wepene saue his handes tweyne He slow and al torente the leon. **1415** HOCCLEVE *To Sir J. Oldcastle* 471 A clod Of eerthe, at your heedes to slynge or caste, Were wepne ynow. *c* **1511** *1st Eng. Bk. Amer.* (Arb.) Introd. 28/1 There wepyns is lange pykes and stones ther they caste myghtly with. **1559** *Mirr. Mag., Dk. Suffolk* xxi, And sum with weapons would have layed on lode. **1610** SHAKS. *Temp.* II. i. 322 'Tis best we stand vpon our guard..: let's draw our weapons. **1614** RALEGH *Hist. World* V. iii. §21. 579 The Battels of foote..drew neere together..till they were almost within a weapons cast. **1636** MASSINGER *Bashf. Lover* I. ii, In a cause like this, The Husbandman would change his ploughing-irons To weapons of defence. **1697** DRYDEN *Æneis* v. 668 Fix'd in the Mast the feather'd Weapon stands. **1750** GRAY *Long Story* 39 They hid their armour And veil'd their weapons bright and keen. **1821** BYRON *Sardanap.* II. i, My sword! O fool, I wear no sword: here, fellow, Give me thy weapon. **1859** DICKENS *T. Two Cities* I. v, Nothing was represented in a flourishing condition, save tools and weapons. **1870** EMERSON *Soc. & Solit., Eloquence* (end), The Arabian warrior of fame, who wore seventeen weapons in his belt. **1880** *Encycl. Brit.* XI. 278 The term 'small arms' includes sporting and military weapons carried by the shooter. **1902** A. S. HURD *How Navy is run* 81 There is a roar and a crash as the great 25-ton weapon speaks.
β. *c* **1250** *Gen. & Ex.* 469 Wopen of wiʒte and tol of grið. *a* **1300** *Cursor M.* 15722 Sper and suerd and mace þai bring, And wapens oþer maa. **1375** BARBOUR *Bruce* IX. 711 Thair fayis thaim met vith vapnys bar. *c* **1470** HENRY *Wallace* I. 193 Wapynnys he bur, outhir gud suerd or knyff. *c* **1470** *Gol. & Gaw.* 461 With alkin wappyns..that wes for were wroght. **1549** *Compl. Scot.* XI. 96 Al the vaupynis and armour of scotland to be delyuerit to the inglismen. *a* **1578** LINDESAY (Pitscottie) *Chron. Scot.* (S.T.S.) I. 194 All the arteilzerrie..with all maner of vaponis. **1650** J. NICOLL *Diary* (Bann. Club) 28 Our Scottis army being all drowsie..and many of thame thair horsses and wapines to seik.
†*Proverb. a* **1575** PILKINGTON *Expos. Neh.* iv. (1585) 64 b, A weapon boods peace, as the common saying is.
transf. (*humorously*) **1712–14** POPE *Rape Lock* III. 128 Just then, Clarissa drew with tempting grace A two-edg'd weapon from her shining case. **1853** DICKENS *Bleak Ho.* xix, For Chadband..can wield such weapons of the flesh as a knife and fork, remarkably well. **1873** TRISTRAM *Moab* v. 95 Those, to him, novel weapons, a knife and fork.
†**b.** Down to the end of the 16th c., the plural, when used in the collective sense = 'arms', was often identical in form with the sing. *Obs.*
c **825** *Vesp. Psalter* xlv. 10 Boȝan forþreste[ð] & ȝebriceð wepen [Vulg. *arma*]. *c* **1200** ORMIN 8187 & hise cnihhtess alle imæn Forþ ȝedenn wiþþ þe bære, Wiþþ heore wæpenn alle bun, Swa summ þeȝȝ sholldenn fihhtenn. *c* **1205** LAY. 499 Al þæt wapmon-cun þa mihte beren wapen. *c* **1250** *Gen. & Ex.* 3283 Wepen, and srud, siluer, and gold. *a* **1300** *Cursor M.* 7572 Þat all mai wit þat godd o might Sauues noght man in wapen bright. *c* **1425** *Eng. Conq. Irel.* xxi. 54 Out of wepne [*v.r.* wepyn], he was as redy to otheres byddynge as other to hys. *c* **1450** in Kingsford *Chron. Lond.* (1905) 137 And then the erll of Arondell sett gouernance in that contre and tokyn all wepyn from hem. *c* **1520** BARCLAY *Salust's Jugurth* xl. 56 b, Their ennemies..lette them to go to the castell of the towne where their armoure and wepyn was. **1550** HARINGTON tr. *Cicero's Bk. Friendship* (1562) 26 As if Coriolanus hadde anye freendes, whether they oughte to haue borne weapon with hym agaynste their countrey. **1561** T. HOBY tr. *Castiglione's Courtyer* I. (1900) 89 He was forced to arise from bankettes and runne to weapon. **1585–6** EARL LEYCESTER *Corr.* (Camden) 426 They doe make reckoning of all ther vyttell, of ther armour, and wepon. **1596** DALRYMPLE tr. *Leslie's Hist. Scot.* (S.T.S.) II. 363 Thair myndes war sa in ydleset, and close fra weir and wapoune.
c. *fig.*
c **888** ÆLFRED *Boeth.* iii. §1 Ic [Wisdom] wat þæt þu hæfst þara wæpna to hraðe forgiten þe ic þe ær sealde. *a* **1000** *Guthlac* 148 (Gr.) Syrede hine ʒeorne mid gæstlicum wæpnum. *c* **1175** *Lamb. Hom.* 69 [God] ȝeue us wepne for to boren Mid gode werkes for us to weren. *a* **1200** *Moral Ode* 336 in *O.E. Hom.* I, Mid fasten and almesse..Mid þo wepnen þe god haued ȝiuen alle mancunne. *c* **1200** ORMIN 12485 Þe deofell comm to wundenn Crist þurrh gluterrnessess wæpenn. *a* **1225** *Ancr. R.* 366 Þe wepnen þet slowen him, þet weren ure sunnen. **1398** TREVISA *Barth. De P.R.* II. v. (1495) 32 Angels ben callyd Smythes for they araye for vs ghostly wepyn. **1561** T. NORTON *Calvin's Inst.* III. (1634) 405 That they..should dedicate themselves to God,..and their members, weapons of righteousness to God. **1593** SHAKS. *2 Hen. VI*, I. iii. 61 His Champions, are the Prophets and Apostles, His Weapons, holy Sawes of sacred Writ. **1605** —— *Lear* II. iv. 280 And let not womens weapons, water drops, Staine my mans cheekes. **1718** POPE *Iliad* xx. 297 So voluble a weapon is the tongue. **1832** HT. MARTINEAU *Manch. Strike* iv. 53 The first man who deserts the work..puts the weapon of the law into the hands of our opponents. **1849** MACAULAY *Hist. Eng.* vi. II. 151 A consummate master of all the weapons of controversy. **1864** BRYCE *Holy Rom. Emp.* xv. (1875) 253 The charge of heresy was one of the weapons used with most effect against Frederick II. **1871** FREEMAN *Norm. Conq.* IV. xviii. 188 William was not slow to follow with other weapons. His course was..to seize the towns.
d. *transf.* Any part of the body (esp. of a bird or beast) which is or may be used as a means of attack or defence, as a claw, horn, tusk, or the like; in pl., the spurs of a game cock or hen.
(Cf. ARM *sb.*[2] 11, ARMATURE 5.)
1635 MARKHAM *Pleas. Princes* 43 Your [Game] Henne..must be..well tufted on the crowne, which shewes courage: if shee have weapons she is better. **1749** FIELDING *Tom Jones*

II. iv, Those weapons which she wore at the ends of her fingers. **1823** 'JON BEE' *Dict. Turf*, *Weapons*, in cocking, the spurs appearing on hens or young cocks. **1914** A. S. WOODWARD *Guide Fossil Rem. Man, Brit. Mus. Nat. Hist.* (1915) 5 Typical modern monkeys, with the canine teeth enlarged into weapons.

†**e.** A soldier of a class distinguished by the weapon he uses. *Obs. rare*$^{-1}$.

1590 SIR J. SMYTH *Disc. Weapons* 12 Whilest the Piquers and other weapons doo reduce themselues into forme vnder their Ensignes.

f. Used for: One skilled in the use of a weapon. *rare*$^{-1}$. (? quasi-*arch.*)

1852 THACKERAY *Esmond* II. viii, Blandford knows which of us two is the best weapon. At small-sword, or back-sword,.. I can beat him.

2. Phrases.

†**a.** ***to take weapon in hand***: to take up arms.

1538 STARKEY *England* 79 In tyme of warr, hyt ys necessary for our plowmen and laburarys of the cuntrey to take wepun in hand. **1630** *R. Johnson's Kingd. & Commw.* 573 Amurath never tooke weapon in hand against this people, before he understood .. that all Persia was in uprore.

b. ***at all, any weapons***: with weapons of any kind. † ***at the weapons of*** ——: with the weapons used by ——. † ***to play one's prize***(***s at all, at several, in all weapons***: *fig.* to use every or several means to win one's contest (cf. PRIZE *sb.*^{2} b).

1620, *a* **1670** [see PRIZE *sb.*^{2} b]. *a* **1656** BP. HALL *Soliloquies* lxxv. Wks. 1662 III. 461 If the question be concerning some scrupulous act to be done or omitted, now self-respect plays its prizes at all weapons. **1760–72** H. BROOKE *Fool of Qual.* (1809) III. 97 At any weapons, against any odds I will prove him a traitor. **1781** C. JOHNSTON *Hist. J. Juniper* II. 139 [He] said he was not a porter to fight with his fists; but would give him .. satisfaction .. at the weapons of a gentleman. **1831** JAMES *Phil. Augustus* vi, He was .. expert at all weapons.

c. (To challenge, fight, beat, etc. an adversary) ***at*** (***with***) ***his own weapon*** or ***weapons***, i.e. with such as he is expert in. Chiefly *fig.*

1610 MARCELLINI *Triumphs Jas. I* 83 To deale and cope with the envious and perfidious malignity of these calumniators, even at their owne weapons. **1618** BOLTON *Florus* III. i. (1636) 163 Metellus, .. fayning flight when he meant nothing lesse, matcht him at his own weapons. **1622** MABBE tr. *Aleman's Guzman d'Alf.* II. 145 That he should put a full stoccado vpon me, and go brag when he had done, that he had beaten a master of defence at his owne weapon. **1678** CUDWORTH *Intell. Syst.* 12 We insist so much upon this philosophy here, .. because, without the perfect knowledge of it, we cannot deal with the atheists at their own weapon. **1760** FOOTE *Minor* I. (1767) 11 You cockneys now beat us suburbians at our own weapons. **1781** C. JOHNSTON *Hist. J. Juniper* I. 51 This was truly foiling the Devil, at his own weapons. **1781** JOHNSON *Lives of Poets*: *Congreve* 17 He is very angry, and, hoping to conquer Collier with his own weapons, allows himself in the use of every term of contumely and contempt. *c* **1810** COLERIDGE *Lit. Rem.* (1838) III. 239 Their undue predilection for Patristic learning and authority .. originated in the wish to baffle the Papists at their own weapons. **1850** C. KINGSLEY *Alton Locke* II. xvi. 259 Try no more to meet Mammon with his own weapons, but commit your cause to Him who judges righteously. **1897** B. STOKER *Dracula* xxii. 306 He has chosen this earth because it has been holy. Thus we defeat him with his own weapon, for we make it more holy still.

3. The penis. *coarse slang.*

a **1000** *Ags. Gloss.* in Wr.-Wülcker 265/33 *Calamus*, teors, þæt wæpen, *uel* lim. **1377** LANGL. *P. Pl.* B. IX. 180 Whiles þow art ȝonge and þi wepne kene, Wreke þe with wyuynge. **1762** T. BRIDGES *Homer Travestie* IV. 189 She guides his weapon where she lists: Nay more, a touch of her soft hand, If fallen down, will make him stand. **1922** JOYCE *Ulysses* 529 Well for you, you muff, if you had that weapon with knobs and lumps and warts all over it. **1972** H. & R. GREENWALD *Sex-Life Lett.* (1974) 279 This sexual thrill still comes over me whenever I see a horse flashing his weapon, and although I feel guilty and try to look away, I usually look as long as decently possible.

4. attrib. and Comb.: simple attrib., as ***weapon-clang***, ***-crash***, ***-hoard***, ***-pit***, ***-point***, ***-power***, ***-stroke***; ***weapon-like***, ***-proof*** adjs.; objective, as ***weapon-delivery*** (also *attrib.*), ***-maker***, ***-whetter***; ***weapon-making*** vbl. sb.; also †**weapon-bearer** = ARMOUR-BEARER; †**weapon-love**, love as a WEAPON-SALVE; †**weapon-man**, one skilled in the use of weapons; **weapon(s)-carrier**, a vehicle or aircraft specially designed for carrying weapons; **weapons-grade** *a.*, applied to fissile material of suitable quality for making nuclear weapons; **weapon-smith** *Hist.*, a forger or maker of weapons; **weapon(s) system** orig. *U.S.*, a military weapon together with all the equipment required to make use of it, such as detection and control apparatus, a launcher, and a delivery vehicle; **weapon-tool**, a tool which could also be used as a weapon; **weapon-training** *vbl. sb.*, training in the use of weapons. Also WEAPON-SALVE.

1535 COVERDALE *I Sam.* xiv. 1 Ionathas sayde vnto his lad which was his *wapen-bearer: Come, let vs go ouer to the Philistynes watch. ? **1547** —— *Confut. Standish* To Rdr., So am I ready to do the same agaynst .. greate Goliath of Rome and his weapen-bearer. **1938** *19th Cent.* Feb. 195 The possibilities of the new *weapon-carrier in the air. **1947** *Horizon* Sept. 207 A weapons-carrier flew by loaded with G.I.s. **1810** SCOTT *Lady of Lake* III. xviii, Then *weapon-clang, and martial call, Resounded through the funeral hall. **1813** —— *Rokeby* V. xxxi, And *weapon-crash and maddening cry, Of those who kill, and those who die! **1963** *Daily Tel.* 10 Oct. 15/8 TSR 2, the RAF's tactical and strategical bomber, .. has the most secret and sophisticated all-weather *weapons delivery system in the world. **1977** *R.A.F. News* 22 June–5 July 2/5 Live ammunition, bombs and missiles were, in general, carried only by aircraft flying sorties which would culminate in weapon delivery at one of the recognised ranges. **1961** *Ann. Reg. 1960* 152 Both countries .. should each set aside 30,000 kilograms of *weapons-grade uranium 235, as a first step in their transfer to peaceful uses. **1977** N. FREELING *Gadget* I. 11 It won't make a bomb... It's nowhere near weapons grade. **1955** J. R. R. TOLKIEN *Return of King* 50 There are no great *weapon-hoards here, lord. **1922** D. H. LAWRENCE *England, my England* (1924) 36 Not what we would call love, but a *weapon-like kinship. *a* **1711** KEN *Hymns Evang.* Poet. Wks. 1721 I. 168 Thou when the Sword went through her tender Heart, With *Weapon-love didst then anoint the Blade. **1915** MARY JOHNSTON *Fortunes of Garin* XV. 239 Armourers and *weapon-makers. **1936** AUDEN *Look, Stranger!* 67 Built by the conscience-stricken, the *weapon-making, By us. **1635** J. HAYWARD tr. *Biondi's Banish'd Virg.* II. 90 Practising my selfe in .. imitating whatsoever I had seene done by any judicious *weapon-man. *a* **1944** K. DOUGLAS *Alamein to Zem Zem* (1946) 29 Looking down .. at a *weapon-pit beside us, I saw a Libyan soldier reclining there. **1958** M. K. JOSEPH *I'll soldier no More* ix. 161 The neat row of weapon-pits so convenient for sleeping. **1814** SCOTT *Lord of Isles* VI. xxi, Each *weapon-point is downward sent, Each warrior to the ground is bent. **1937** L. HART *Europe in Arms* xvii. 238 At night .. an increase of man-power in proportion to *weapon-power is desirable. **1870** BRYANT *Iliad* XXI. 699, I cannot think That he is *weapon-proof. **1849** KEMBLE *Saxons in Eng.* II. vii. II. 306 The heroical *weapon-smith on the one hand, and on the other the poor professors of such rude arts as the homestead cannot do without. **1908** *Expositor* Sept. 265 The settled weapon-smiths of ancient Egypt .. were quite a different class from the nomad clans of tinsmiths and coppersmiths. **1870** BRYANT *Iliad* XI. 471 Lightly falls the *weapon-stroke Of an unwarlike weakling. **1956** W. A. HEFLIN *U.S. Air Force Dict.* 564/2 *Weapon system. *Also* weapons system. **1958** *Engineering* 11 Apr. 450/1 The 'weapon system concept'—that is, a unified integration of airframe, weapon-firing control, and enemy identification. **1977** M. EDELMAN *Polit. Lang.* viii. 147 Americans and Russians are constantly told that the other is ahead in this or that weapons system. **1980** R. L. DUNCAN *Brimstone* x. 244 There were always 10,000 diverse elements which were required to come together at precisely the right instant, the total testing of a weapons system and a defense against that system. **1861** W. R. WILDE *Catal. Antiq. Anim. Materials R. Ir. Acad.* 360 Weapons and *Weapon Tools. **1945** E. WAUGH *Brideshead Revisited* 9 Had I put in the names of two corporals for the *weapon-training course? **1979** R. PERRY *Bishop's Pawn* vi. 106 Their weapon training had been sadly neglected... In killing Moss, they'd used sufficient ammunition to decimate a small army. **1585** HIGINS *Junius' Nomencl.* 519/2 *Samiarii*, .. *weapon whetters.

weapon ('wɛp(ə)n), *v.* Now *rare* exc. in pa. pple.: see WEAPONED. Forms: *α.* 1 **wǽpnian, wǽmnian,** 3 **wepne-n, wepnie-n, wepni,** 5 **weppen, wepen,** 6 **wepon,** 6– **weapon;** *β. E. Anglian* 3 **wop(e)nen;** *north.* 4 **wapne.** [OE. *wǽpnian*, f. *wǽpen* WEAPON *sb.*; cf. OHG. *wâffanen*, *-ôn* (MHG. *wafenen*, *wæfenen*, mod.G. *waffnen*), also MHG. *wapenen* (mod.G. *wappnen*, to clothe in armour), ON. *vápna*.] *trans.* To furnish with weapons or a weapon; to arm.

c **1000** ÆLFRIC *Gram.* xix. (Z.) 122 *Armor* ic eom ȝewæpnod, *armo te* ic wæpniȝe ðe. *c* **1205** LAY. 8644 He seide forð rihtes: wepneð eow cnihtes. *Ibid.* 8655 He wepnede his cnihtes and ȝarewede heom to fehten. *c* **1425** *Eng. Conq. Ireland* v. 16 Ne shamefully ne didde hym to flight, bot euer mor he was I-lich redy to weppen and to defend hym-self. **1535** COVERDALE *I Macc.* xiv. 32 Then Symon withstode them, and .. weapened the valeaunt men of his people. **1591** SIR J. SMITH *Instruct.* (1595) 217 All sortes of souldiours may presentlie .. arme and weapon themselues in warrelike manner.

b. *fig.*

c **1000** ÆLFRIC *Hom.* I. 72 He mid rodetacne his muð and ealne his lichaman ȝewæpnode. *a* **1225** *Juliana* 43 Hwer se we eauer iseoð mon oðer wummon eani god biginnen; we wepnið us aȝein ham. **1593** NASHE *Christ's T.* D 3, A great many more allegations hath hee to thys end, which heere to recite were to weapon presumption.

Hence '**weaponing** *vbl. sb.*

1590 SIR J. SMYTH *Disc. Weapons* 3 b, And as they doo mistake the conuenient arming of horsemen and footmen, so they also mistake the weaponing of them.

weaponed ('wɛpənd), *pa. pple.* and *ppl. a.* [f. WEAPON *v.* and *sb.* + -ED^{1,2}.

OE. had *wǽpned* male (cf. WEAPON *sb.* 3).]

Furnished with weapons or a weapon; armed.

(*a*) *c* **1000** ÆLFRIC *N.T.* (Gr.) 18/19 He com þa ȝewæmnod. *a* **1122** *O.E. Chron.* (Laud MS.) an. 992, Hi .. þæt scip ȝenamon eall ȝewæpnod & ȝewædod. *c* **1250** *Gen. & Ex.* 3373 Wopened he ben a-gen israel. **1352** MINOT *Poems* iv. 39 He broght folk .. þat ful wele wapnid were. **1387** TREVISA *Higden* VII. 359, I and þow be here allone, iliche wel i-horsed and i-wepened. *c* **1450** in Kingsford *Chron. Lond.* (1905) 136 And all this tyme chorlys of Normandy weren wepond, and born harnes. **1600** *Looke about You* C 4, You see I am weapned .. Ile stab them come there twenty. *a* **1652** BROME *Queenes Exch.* II. iii, They are three sturdy knaves and strongly weapon'd. **1813** SCOTT *Rokeby* V. xxxii, For they were weaponed, and prepared Their mistress on her way to guard. *a* **1861** T. WINTHROP *Life in Open Air* i. (1863) 8, I was weaponed with a staff, should brute or biped uncourteous dispute our way. **1907** MᶜCARTHY *Needles & Pins* xx, You shall be well clad, well weaponed, well horsed.

(*b*) *c* **1200** ORMIN 10225 Þe cnihhtess wærenn wæpnedd follc. *c* **1250** *Gen. & Ex.* 2479 Wel wopnede men. *c* **1425** *Eng. Conq. Ireland* 10 Robert .. sette the bowmen for to wer the fight of the kernels, and turned the wepned men to fill þe diches. **1535** COVERDALE *Prov.* vi. 11 Necessite [shall come to us] like a wapened man. **1603** T. WALE in *Lismore Papers* Ser. II. (1887) I. 65 There should be two hundreth weaponed men put into armes by the cyttie. **1680** C. NESSE *Church Hist.* 372 In the sight and despight of sixty weaponed witnesses. **1798** W. TAYLOR in Robberds *Mem.* (1843) I. 219 The weapon'd slaves of tyranny. **1898** MEREDITH *Odes Fr. Hist.* 76 Her weaponed children's moan Of stifled rage invoking vengeance.

b. quasi-*Her.*

1685 H. MORE *Illustr. Daniel* etc. 344 He alone is said to ride weaponed, *viz.* with a Sword coming out of his mouth. **1762** tr. *Busching's Syst. Geog.* V. 413 A griffin gules, crowned Or and weaponed, in a field azure.

c. *fig.*

c **1200** ORMIN 677 Whas itt iss þatt wæpnedd iss Wiþþ fulle trowwþe o Criste. **1548** UDALL etc. *Erasm. Par. Luke* xxi. 5–11 Great pestilences .. shal .. consume a mightie great noumbre of people in sort as though the aire were armed & weaponed to doe vengeaunce vpon the euil sort. **1563** SHUTE *Archit.* 3 b, Yf a man myght be parfaict in al these sciences as were Aristarchus, .. Architas, [etc.] .. (for all these were strongely weaponed with al these sciences before rehersed). **1616** J. HAYWARD *Sanct. Troub. Soul* I. iii. (1620) 10, I was come to a greater staiednesse, .. I was warned, I was weaponed; I was instructed, I was encouraged. **1839** J. STERLING *Poems* 156 The scathed and haggard face of will, And look so strong with weaponed thought. **1844** EMERSON *Ess.* xx. Wks. (Bohn) I. 249 We are amphibious creatures, weaponed for two elements, having two sets of faculties, the particular and the catholic. **1860** —— *Cond. Life* vi. ibid. II. 408 In all the encounters that have yet chanced, I have not been weaponed for that particular occasion, and have been historically beaten. **1916** *Edin. Rev.* July 15 'Responsible Government' .. may also be found incompatible with that kind of weaponed and sentinelled peace that will follow the conflict.

d. *transf.* (Cf. WEAPON *sb.* 1 d, 3.)

1577 B. GOOGE *Heresbach's Husb.* III. 126 It [the ass] is a woonderful Coltishe beast, & vnreasonably weapned [L. *animal mire salax, & pro corporis portione membrosius*]. **1643** MILTON *Divorce* 2 Yet they shall, so they be but found suitably weapon'd to the lest possibilitie of sensuall enjoyment, be made, spight of antipathy, to fadge together. **1810** SOUTHEY *Kehama* XVI. xiii, His mouth, from ear to ear, Weapon'd with triple teeth, extended wide.

weaponeer (wɛpə'nɪə(r)). *U.S.* [f. WEAPON *sb.* + -EER.] **a.** One who has charge of a weapon of war prior to its deployment.

Orig. used *spec.* of nuclear weapons.

1945 in *Amer. Speech* (1947) XXII. 149/2 Here are the names of the Superfortress crew which carried the atomic bomb to Japan... Naval observer and 'weaponeer', Capt. William S. Parsons. **1952** *Word Study* Feb. 4/1 United States atomic weaponeers probably will set off the world's greatest explosion within the next few days.

b. An expert or specialist in the development of weapons of war.

1979 *New Yorker* 13 Aug. 67/1 Robert Wilson .. head of experimental physics at Los Alamos; Philip Morrison, who had gone .. to take care of the bombs ..; Richard Feynman, who had been in charge of one of the computing sections... I fitted in with this bunch of weaponeers. **1982** *Christian Sci. Monitor* 22 June 22/1 Probably the most interesting to the weaponeers of the great powers was the testing of US vs. Soviet fighter planes.

So **weapo'neering** *vbl. sb.*, the development and production of weapons of war.

1955 *Bull. Atomic Sci.* Sept. 239/3 Nearly half of our expenditure for research and development each year goes to weaponeering. **1960** *N.Y. Times Mag.* 29 May 20 You must .. make those essential advances in the state of the weaponeering art which will most intercept any possible aggression by any potential enemy. **1976** *Aviation Week* 19 Jan. 54/1 It's easier to conceptualize bombs, weaponeering and 'hard kill' missiles than the wizardry of electronic detection and countermeasures equipment.

weaponization (wɛpənaɪ'zeɪʃən). *U.S.* [f. as prec. + -IZATION.] The process of equipping with weapons of war, or adapting something for use as a weapon. So '**weaponized** *ppl. a.*

1969 *U.S. Dept. Defense Appropriation Bill 1970* (91st Congress 1 Sess., House Rep. 698) 72 Aircraft Weaponization (advanced and exploratory development) was reduced. **1973** *Black Panther* 7 Apr. 10/2 Observers worry that the fledgling crime protection industry may follow a similar line, with huge profits made in this industry supporting a new domestic lobby for more weaponized solutions to the anger of the ghetto, the barrio and the poor white hollow. **1976** *Aviation Week* 1 Nov. 19/2 He said the Navy plans to build a 3,000-ton 'weaponized' surface-effect ship. **1982** *N.Y. Times* 23 Mar. A-14/2 Chemical warfare agents were .. weaponized with Soviet assistance in Laos, Vietnam and Kampuchea. **1983** *Aviation Week* 17 Jan. 27/2 He cited an alarming trend toward the weaponization of space as the reason for his new emphasis on the civilian uses of space.

weaponless ('wɛpənlɪs), *a.* [f. WEAPON *sb.* + -LESS.] **a.** Without weapons or a weapon; unarmed.

a **1000** in Napier *OE. Glosses* i. 724 *Inermes quosque*, .i. *sine armis*, .i. *uniuersos*, ȝehwylce wæpenlease. *c* **1000** ÆLFRIC *Saints' Lives* xxix. 175 Wundor-lic godes gifu þæt þam wæpenleasan menn ne mihton þa wælhreowan mid wæpnum wið-standan. **1390** GOWER *Conf.* III. 181 He sette a lawe for the pes, That non, but he be wepneles, Schal come into the conseil hous. *c* **1430** *Lybeaus Disc.* 366 Hyt wer greet vylanye To do a knyght to deye Wepeneles yn place. **1548** UDALL etc. *Erasm. Par. Mark* vi. 6–9 He sent them out weaponlesse, leste that mans aydes shoulde chalenge any thing in this heauenly busynesse. **1596** SPENSER *F.Q.* V. v. 14 Soone as the knight she there by her did spy, Standing with emptie hands all weaponlesse. **1641** EARL MONM. tr. *Biondi's Civil Wars* V. 140 The defendants being suffered to depart away weaponlesse. **1671** MILTON *Samson* 130 [He] Ran on embattelld Armies clad in Iron, And weaponless himself, Made Arms ridiculous. **1795** SOUTHEY *Joan of Arc* II. 100 Here the poor captives, weaponless and bound, Saw their stern victors draw again the sword. **1820** BYRON *Mar. Fal.* III. ii. 95 A lone, unguarded, weaponless old man. **1870** MORRIS *Earthly Par.* II. III. 399 Take my sword, and leave me weaponless. **1895** SCULLY *Kafir Stories* 96 Naked and weaponless fugitives from the Tonga and other tribes.

fig. **1629** RUTHERFORD *Let. to Mar. M'Naught* 17 Nov., Lett. (1891) 45 My Captain, Christ, hath said, I must fight and overcome the world, and with a weak, spoiled, weaponless devil. **1680** C. NESSE *Church Hist.* 32 God will not war with a weaponless devil.

b. *transf.* Of an animal: Without natural means of attack or defence.

1537 COVERDALE *Expos. Ps. xxii* A viij b, Loke how lytle a naturall shepe can kepe, gyde, rule, saue or defende it selfe agaynst daunger and mysfortune (for it is a feble and wapenlesse beast). **1644** J. STRICKLAND *Immanuel* 6 Dennes or burroughes where weaponlesse creatures find shelter when they are hunted. **1666** J. SMITH *Old Age* 58 That audacious Carper at the works of God (who complained that other Creatures had naturally a defence given, and man only left weaponless).

c. Not containing a weapon.

1863 THORNBURY *True as Steel* III. 327 'What a poor soldier am I' said the Ritter..looking down to his weaponless belt.

weaponry (ˈwɛpənrɪ). [f. WEAPON *sb.* + -RY.] Weapons collectively. Now esp. weapons of war.

1844 *N. Brit. Rev.* I. 143 The armour of our ancient halls, the weaponry, the device. **1875** TALMAGE *Old Wells* 269 Look over the weaponry of olden times—javelins, battle-axes [etc.]. **1956** C. W. MILLS *Power Elite* viii. 184 The new weaponry has been developed as a 'first line of defense'. **1959** *Times Lit. Suppl.* 16 Jan. 27/2 War has become inevitable because of the weaponry which both sides are amassing. **1961** *New Left Rev.* Jan.-Feb. 49/1 Modern weaponry advances faster than any other branch of technology. **1972** *Daily Tel.* 27 May 1/1 The Russians have deployed 64 defensive Galesh missiles around Moscow since 1969, but the Americans are more advanced in this weaponry. **1977** *Irish Times* 8 June 5/2 The US should put aside hopes of outstripping the Soviet Union in doomsday weaponry.

fig. **1966** *New Statesman* 23 Dec. 942/1 Its weaponry of surprises..allows Miss Smith free movement in areas where the clichés lie thick.

†**weapon-salve.** *Obs.* [Cf. G. *waffensalbe.*] An ointment superstitiously believed to heal a wound by sympathetic agency when applied to the weapon by which the wound was made.

1631 W. FOSTER (*title*), Hoplocrisma-Spongus; or, A Sponge to wipe away the Weapon-Salve..wherein is proved, that the Cure late-taken up amongst us, by applying the Salve to the Weapon, is Magicall and unlawfull. **1633** HART *Diet of Diseased* III. xxx. 373 Cures..supposed to have been performed by the weapon-salve. *a* **1646** J. GREGORY *Posthuma, Serm.* etc. (1649) 63 The Principal Ingredient of the weapon-Salv, is the Moss of a dead Man's-skul. **1670** DRYDEN *Tempest* v. i, Anoint the Sword which pierc'd him with this Weapon-Salve, and wrap it close from air till I have time to visit him again. **1830** SCOTT *Demonol.* vi. 191 The effects of healing by the weapon-salve.

fig. **1659** STILLINGFL. (*title*), Irenicum. A Weapon-salve for the Churches Wounds. **1679** ALSOP *Melius Inq.* Pref., The Title raised me on tip-toes to see..that famous Weapon-salve which might consolidate the Churches bleeding wounds.

weapon-s(c)haw, -shawing, -showing: see WAPPENS(C)HAW, -S(C)HAWING.

weapontack, -tage, obs. ff. WAPENTAKE.

wear (wɛə(r)), *sb.* Also 5 **were**, 6–7 **weare**, 7–8 **ware**. [f. WEAR *v.*[1]]

I. 1. a. The action of wearing or carrying on the person (an article of clothing, an ornament, a watch, sword, or the like); the condition or fact of being worn or carried upon the person.

1464 *Rolls of Parlt.* V. 567/2 The best and lightest Tymbre to make of Patyns and Clogges, and moost esiest for the were of all estate. **16..** *Bell my Wiffe* 26 in *Percy Fol. MS.* II. 323 My cloake itt was a verry good cloake, it hath beene alwayes good to the weare. **1713** STEELE *Guardian* No. 170 ¶16 'Tis a Demonstration, that they have more [Woollen Goods] than is sufficient for their own Wear. **1716** J. PERRY *State Russia* 74 The wear of Furs is a great Fashion in China. **1757** [BURKE] *Europ. Settlem. Amer.* VII. v. II. 161, I have seen cloths made there, which..were..as far as I could judge, superior for the ordinary wear of country people, to any thing we make in England. **1818** *Min. Evid. Committee Ribbon Weavers* 178 Every one who visits France brings over some [articles of manufactured silk] for their own wear. **1903** R. BARR *Over Border* I. vi. 66 His costume ..hung, loosely unfitting, about a frame that had become gaunt since its wear began. **1912** *Daily Graphic* 31 Dec. 13/2 A charming coat for restaurant wear.

b. ***the worse for wear***: deteriorated through wearing (cf. WEARING *vbl. sb.*[1] 3); drunk. See also WORSE *a.* 4 c.

1782 COWPER *Gilpin* 183 A hat not much the worse for wear. **1840** 'OUIDA' *Moths* I. ii. 32 The statuette..never seemed the worse for wear. **1857** C. M. YONGE *Dynevor Terrace* II. xvii. 270 His boots were less polished..and he looked somewhat the worse for wear. **1936** J. BUCHAN *Island of Sheep* iii. 44 When I came across him in Persia..he was rather the worse for wear. **1966** D. FRANCIS *Flying Finish* x. 127 You'll be kicking your heels about the airport for a few hours. Don't let any of them get . . . er . . . the worse for wear. **1977** M. ALLEN *Spence in Petal Park* xix. 87 The blonde girl left about ten, looking distinctly the worse for wear. **1982** T. BERGER *Reinhart's Women* iii. 46 The vehicles in view were routine automobiles, two of them the worse for wear, with dents and rust and jagged antenna-stems.

†**c.** Use, the using or making use (of a utensil). *Obs.*

1571 *Aldeburgh Rec.* in *N. & Q.* 12th Ser. VII. 185/1 For ye wear of a kettil and a trevet xii[d].

2. Phr. ***to be in wear.*** **a.** Of an article of clothing, an ornament, etc.: To be actually on the person of the wearer; also, to be (still) habitually worn by a person, not to have been discarded. Similarly (of a person), ***to have in wear.*** **b.** Of a kind or style of garment, etc.: To be worn by people generally; to be in vogue or fashion. Similarly, ***to come into wear.***

1786 MRS. A. M. BENNETT *Juvenile Indiscr.* III. 106 Sophia, do you know patches are coming into wear again? **1799** WASHINGTON *Lett.* Writ. 1893 XIV. 150 If there are any handsome cockades (but not whimsically foolish) in wear,..I should be glad if they were sent with the eagles fixed thereon. **1809** W. IRVING *Knickerb.* II. ii. (1849) 92 Several gigantic knee-buckles of massy silver are still in wear, that made gallant display in the days of the patriarchs of Communipaw. **1851-61** MAYHEW *Lond. Labour* II. 33/1 If there be any part of silk in a dress not suitable for any of these purposes it is wasted, or what is accounted wasted, although it may have been in wear for years. **1855** DICKENS *Holly-Tree* i, The lesser roadside Inns of Italy; where all the dirty clothes in the house (not in wear) are always lying in your anteroom.

fig. **1704** SWIFT *Mech. Operat. Spir.* Misc. (1711) 274 Now, Sir, to proceed after the Method in present Wear. **1853** DICKENS *Bleak Ho.* xix, Assuredly that shield and buckler of Britannia are not in present wear.

3. a. What one wears or should wear; the thing or things worn or proper to be worn at a particular time or in certain circumstances.

1570 LAMBARDE *Peramb. Kent* (1576) 12 Makers of coloured woollen clothes..from whome is drawne.. sufficient stoare to furnishe the weare of the best sort of our owne nation. **1581** A. HALL *Iliad* x. 180 And without crest or plume at all his morian on [he] doth pull, Of bullish hyde, a yong mans weare, men do it call a scul. **1599** B. JONSON *Cynthia's Rev.* I. iv, *Amo.* Your ribband too do's most gracefully, in troth. *Aso.* Tis the most gentile, and receiu'd weare now, sir. **1600** SHAKS. *A.Y.L.* II. vii. 34 Motley's the onely weare. **1611** —— *Wint. T.* IV. iv. 327 Will you buy.. Any Silke, any Thred, any Toyes for your head Of the news't and fins't, fins't weare-a. **1619** FLETCHER *Knt. Malta* II. i, What's in that pack there? 1 *Sold.* 'Tis English Cloth. *Nor.* That's a good wear indeed, Both strong, and rich. **16..** CLEVELAND *News fr. Newcastle* 130 Wks. (1687) 290 Our Wear's plain Out-side, but is richly lin'd. **1688** HOLME *Armoury* III. 257/2 It is a wear amongst little Children with us to this day. **1796** MORSE *Amer. Geog.* II. 166 A particular kind of flowered and striped lawns, which are a cheap and fashionable wear. **1812** W. TAYLOR in *Monthly Mag.* XXXIII. 229 It has occasionally been questioned whether hats or turbans were the prevailing wear. **1860** THACKERAY *Round. Papers, Ribbons* (1876) 18 The Great Duke's theory was..that for common people your plain coat without stars and ribbons, was the most sensible wear. **1865** in G. Hill *Hist. Dress* (1893) II. 261 Little insects of all kinds, especially flies, are good wear in bonnets. **1885** *Manch. Exam.* 5 June 5/6 Their cotton gowns are much cooler wear in the broiling weather of the present week than the warm Welsh woollens. **1902** *Times* 29 July 11/3 The makers..are fairly well supplied with orders, men's wear excepted.

b. *transf.* and *fig.*

1603 SHAKS. *Meas. for M.* III. ii. 78 *Clo.* I hope Sir, your good Worship wil be my baile? *Luc.* No indeed wil I not Pompey, it is not the wear. **1742** YOUNG *Nt. Th.* v. 829 Hence burly corpulence Is his familiar wear, and sleek disguise. **1847** L. HUNT *Men, Women, & B.* I. xiv. 232 Meeting one day with a lovely face that had flaxen locks about it, we thought for a good while after, that flaxen was your only wear. **1876** C. L. SMITH *Tasso's Jerus. Delivered* III. vii, Each from his head removes the bauble there Of silk or gold,..Each doffs too from his heart its haughty wear.

4. a. Capacity for being worn or for further advantageous use.

1699 BOYER *Royal Dict., Eng.-Fr.* s.v., A Stuff of good Wear, *une Etoffe d'un bon usé.* **1881** *Punch* 26 Feb. 94/1 The shoe that has still wear in it. **1901** ALLDRIDGE *Sherbro* xxviii. 339 The native-made cloths..of never-ending wear.

b. Advantage of continued wearing.

1836 [HOOTON] *Bilberry Thurland* ii. I. 35, I've had more wear out of this one waistcoat, than any hafe dozen agen.

II. 5. a. The process or condition of being worn or gradually reduced in bulk or impaired in quality by continued use, friction, attrition, exposure to atmospheric or other natural destructive agencies; loss or diminution of substance or deterioration of quality due to these causes.

1729 [T. PRIOR] *Observ. Coin* (1856) 305 This Scarcity will be farther increased by the Wear of Silver Coins, which has lessened their Weights considerably. **1730** CONDUITT *Observ. Coins* (1774) 51 The telling money on wood, especially with a mixture of sand, very much encreases the wear. **1791** SMEATON *Edystone L.* §321, I then saw the coast was in a state of wear. **1797** *Monthly Mag.* III. 546 The foundation should be covered to the depth that is necessary to sustain the wear to which the road is subject. **1869** F. KOHN *Iron & Steel Manuf.* 90 The saw, not being constantly in use, is driven by an independent engine to save the wear of its bearings. **1891** FLOWER *Horse* iii. 115 The shape of the table alters as the wear of the tooth proceeds. **1894** A. M. BELL in *Jrnl. Anthrop. Inst.* XXIII. 273 So also with surface finds; if they possess definite characteristics of form, of wear, of weather,..of position when found, each of which places them in a class by themselves.

b. *transf.* and *fig.*

1882 SPURGEON *Treas. Dav.* Ps. cxix. 20. VI. 51 They [*sc.* desires for holiness] cause a wear of heart, a straining of the mind. **1899** *Allbutt's Syst. Med.* VIII. 311 Those who..are already showing signs of wear in their nervous systems.

6. a. wear and tear, wearing or damage due to ordinary usage; deterioration in the condition of a thing through constant use or service. Also (less usual) ***tear and wear***: see TEAR *sb.*[2] 1.

1666 PEPYS *Diary* 29 Sept., The wages, victuals, wear and tear, cast by the medium of the men, will come to above £3,000,000. **1691** T. H[ALE] *Acc. New Invent.* 119 Wear and tear of Ground-Tackle. **1699** LUTTRELL *Brief Rel.* IV. 595 Allowing 4*l.* a man per mensem for ware and tear, charge of the ordnance included. **1702** SAVERY *Miner's Friend* 64 A Work..that cost forty-two shillings per diem..besides Ware and Tare of Engines. **1776** ADAM SMITH *W.N.* IV. ix. (1869) II. 249 The wear and tear of the implements of husbandry. **1835** MARRYAT *J. Faithful* i, A pair of shoes may have lasted her for five years, for the wear and tear that she took out of them. **1839** STONEHOUSE *Axholme* 46 It is difficult to calculate the daily wear and tear of four horses, straining through the thick mud, breaking the gears, and almost pulling the waggon to pieces. **1867** SMYTH *Sailor's Wordbk.*, *Wear and Tear*, the decay and deterioration of the hull, spars, sails, ropes, and other stores of a ship in the course of a voyage. **1868** STANLEY *Westm. Abb.* (ed. 2) 508 The wear-and-tear of four centuries..had rendered this venerable building quite unfit for its purpose. **1902** *Act 2 Edw. VII* c. 42 §7 (d), Such damage as the local authority consider to be due to fair wear and tear in the use of any room in the school house.

b. *transf.* and *fig.*

1678 BUTLER *Hud.* III. i. 1182 That in return would pay th'expence, The Wear-and-tear of Conscience. **1775** JOHNSON in *Boswell* (1791) I. 515 You are not to wonder at that; no man's face has had more wear and tear. **1806** J. BERESFORD *Miseries Hum. Life* ii. §31 There is not a whit less wear and tear to the nerves. **1828** MACAULAY *Ess., Hallam* (1897) 89 Mr. Hallam..scarcely makes a sufficient allowance for the wear and tear which honesty almost necessarily sustains in the friction of political life. **1848** DICKENS *Dombey* xxv, Unequal to the wear and tear of daily life, as he had often professed himself to be. **1881** M. ARNOLD *Ess. Crit.* Ser. II. vi. (1888) 166 Nay, I doubt whether his [Shelley's] delightful Essays and Letters..will not resist the wear and tear of time better..than his poetry.

c. ***wear-and tear-pigment*** (Biochem.) [tr. G. *abnutzungspigment*]: a pigment that accumulates in cells as they age.

1928 *Amer. Jrnl. Path.* IV. 236 This pigment (lipofuscin) was recognized by Lubarsch who classified it along with melanin as 'wear-and-tear' pigment (*Abnutzungspigmente*). **1943** *Jrnl. Compar. Neurol.* LXXVIII. 45 It would be better to abandon the attempt to group all these substances [from different tissues] under the common term 'wear-and-tear' pigment. **1968** [see *lipofuscin* s.v. LIPO-].

7. *Pugilism.* (See quots.)

1819 *Sporting Mag.* N.S. III. 231 It was who should stay upon the wear-out game in the rain the longest. **1832** *P. Egan's Bk. Sports* 45/1 Bravo, Neal—he must win it—he has too much wear-and-tear for Gaynor.

III. 8. The anterior surface of the lower part of the mouth of a carpenter's plane.

185. *Tomlinson's Cycl. Useful Arts* II. 318/2 The narrow opening between the face of the iron and the line *m w'* is termed the *mouth* of the plane; the line *m w'* is called the *wear*: the angle between the mouth and the wear should be as small as possible, so that as the sole wears away,..the mouth may not be too much enlarged.

IV. 9. *attrib.* and *Comb.*, as ***wear-resistance, -resisting***; ***wear-proof, -resistant, -resisting*** adjs.; **wear-dated** *a.* (see quot. 1968).

1897 *Sears, Roebuck Catal.* 183/2 This suit..is regular wear-resisting goods. **1921** *Daily Colonist* (Victoria, B.C.) 9 Apr. 7/1 Wearproof Suits for Boys. Specially selected materials and extra care in the making of these suits enable them to give every wearing satisfaction. **1943** *U.S. Patents Q.* LVI. 494/2 Wear-resisting, anti-fatigue, and shock-absorbing properties are relative and not absolute terms. **1946** *Nature* 5 Oct. 476/2 The advantage of these new processes is that the weight and wear-resistance of the fabrics are increased. **1960** *Farmer & Stockbreeder* 29 Mar. (Suppl.) 4/1 A wear-resistant outer lining. **1968** J. IRONSIDE *Fashion Alphabet* 102 *Wear-dated*, officially recognised guaranteeing the length of normal wear of garments. **1978** *Detroit Free Press* 16 Apr. (Detroit Suppl.) 14 (Advt.), Choice of covers includes lush acrylic velvet by Monsanto with two-year wear-dated guarantee.

wear (wɛə(r)), *v.*[1] Pa. t. **wore** (wɔə(r)); pa. pple. **worn** (wɔːn). Forms: 1 **werian**, 3–4 **werie, werye**, 3–5 *north.* **wer**, 3–7 **were**, 4 **weri**, 4–6 **wher(e**, 5 **weyr(e, wheer**, 5–6 **weer(e**, 5–8 (chiefly *Sc.*) **weir**, 6 **wayre**, *Sc.* **weire, veir, veyr**, 6–7 **weare, waire**, 7 **ware**, (8 **wair**), 6– **wear**. *Pa. t.* *α.* 1–5 **werede**, 3 **weorede**, 4–5 **wered, -id, werd(e**, 5 **weryd(e, werryde, -id, veryd**, *Sc.* **werit, -yt, weiret**, 6 **weard**, 8 **weared**. *β.* 4–6 **were**, 4–5 **wer, weyr**, *Sc.* **war, wour**, 5–6 *Sc.* **woir**, 5–7 **ware**, 6 **weer, weare, wayre, waare, warre, woore**, *Sc.* **wair, woure**, 6–7 **woare**, 6– **wore**. *Pa. pple.* *α.* 1–5 **wered**, 4 **(y)werd**, 5 **werid, -yd**, *Sc.* **-it, werde, werede**. *β.* 5 **woryn**, 5–8 **worne**, 6 **woren**, *Sc.* **vorne**, 6–8, 9 *dial.* **wore**, 5– **worn**. [A Com. Teut. weak vb. (wanting in Frisian, LG., Du., Sw., Da., and mod.Norw.): OE. *wẹrian* corresponds to OHG. *werjan, werjen* to clothe, ON. *verja* to clothe, also to invest, lay out (money: see WARE *v.*[2]), Goth. *wasjan* to clothe (also in comb. *gawasjan* to clothe, *andwasjan* to unclothe, strip):—OTeut. **wazjan* (? and **wasjan*), f. Teut. root **was-*, whence Goth. *wasti* fem., garment, MHG. *wester* fem., christening robe; ablaut variant of OTeut. and Indogermanic **wes-*, whence ON. *vesl* neut., cloak, L. *vestis* garment, Gr. ἐννύναι (:—*wesnu-) to clothe, ϝεσθής, ἐσθής raiment, Skr. *vas* to clothe, *vasman* neut., a cover, garment, *vasana* neut., *vastra* neut., clothing.

The change from the weak to the strong conjugation, due to the analogy of verbs like *swear, bear, tear*, seems to have begun in the 14th c., but is rare before the 16th. In OE. the pa. pple. *forworen* occurs once, along with the regular *forwered*, as a gloss to *decrepita* (Napier *OE. Gl.* i. 2109), and in *The Ruined City* 7 we should probably read *forworene ȝelorene* for the *forweorone ȝeleorene* of the MS.]

I. 'To carry appendant to the body' (J.).

1. a. *trans.* To carry or bear on one's body or on some member of it, for covering, warmth, ornament, etc.; to be dressed in; to be covered or decked with; to have on.

c **893** ÆLFRED *Oros.* IV. ix. (1883) 190 þæt nan oþer ne moste gyldenne hring werian, buton he æþeles cynnes wære. *c* **1205** LAY. 17695 He weorede ane burne. *c* **1290** *St. Patrick* 506 in *S.E. Leg.* 214 Ech werede cloþes of þe en-taile þat heo wereden on eorþe here. **13..** *Gaw. & Gr. Knt.* 1928 He were a bleaunt of blwe, þat bradde to þe erþe. *c* **1386** CHAUCER *Squire's T.* 139 If hire lust it [*sc.* this ring] for to were Vp on hir thombe or in hir purs it bere. *c* **1450** *Mirk's Festial* 197 He..werd þe her next to hys flesch. *c* **1470** HENRY *Wallace* III. 84 Gude souir weide dayly on him he wour. **1526** *Pilgr. Perf.* (W. de W. 1531) 72 Though he ware the habit of religyon, yet his herte was in the worlde. **1535** COVERDALE *1 Macc.* xi. 58 To weare a colar of golde. **1590** *Tarlton's Newes Purgatorie* 35 A crewe of men that weare Baye garlands on their heads. **1601, 1696** [see TRUSS *sb.* 4]. **1657** HOWELL *Londinop.* 319 These [Irons] he [*sc.* a prisoner] ware from Thursday till Sunday. **1707** J. STEVENS tr. *Quevedo's Com. Wks.* (1709) 355 Wearing Watches in their Pockets. **1721** BERKELEY *Pres. Ruin Gt. Brit.* Wks. III. 199 More fine linen is wore in Great Britain than in any other country. **1857** W. A. BUTLER *Nothing to wear* 19 Miss McFlimsey.. The last time we met, was in utter despair, Because she had nothing whatever to wear! **1879** HARLAN *Eyesight* vi. 78 In Germany..it has long been impossible to fill the ranks of the army without allowing soldiers to wear glasses. **1902** J. BUCHAN *Watcher by Threshold* 289 He wears the same clothes for years. **1913** M. ROBERTS *Salt of Sea* ix. 215 His ears had been pierced for earrings, though he wore none.

fig. **1697** DRYDEN *Virg. Past.* iv. 30 Each common Bush shall Syrian Roses wear. **1859** FITZGERALD *Omar* xviii, Every Hyacinth the Garden wears.

b. To dress oneself habitually or at a particular season in (a material, garment) of a particular sort or fashion. Also in *passive*, of the material or garment.

a **1225** *Ancr. R.* 418 Nexst fleshe ne schal mon werien no linene cloð. *c* **1250** *Doomsday* 28 in *O.E. Misc.* 164 Moni of þisse riche þat wereden foh and grei. *a* **1300** *Cursor M.* 11112 He..wered noþer wol ne line. **13..** *Sir Orfeo* 241 (Sisam) He þat hadde ywerd þe fowe and griis. *c* **1449** PECOCK *Repr.* v. xii. 543 The habitis, whiche..ben assigned to be worn of the religiose persoones. **1516** *Life of St. Bridget* in *Myrr. our Ladye* lii, She weer euer rough & sharpe wolen cloth. **1535** COVERDALE *2 Sam.* xiii. 18 Soch garmentes wayre ye kynges doughters whyle they were virgins. **1597** HOOKER *Eccl. Pol.* v. lxxv. §1 The Church..suffereth mourning apparell to bee worne. **1785** GEO. A. BELLAMY *Apol.* III. 50 Brown rateen, which at that time was much wore. **1848** THACKERAY *Van. Fair* lii, When the Court went into mourning, she always wore black. **1860** O. W. HOLMES *Prof. Breakf.-t.* vii. 136 She wears her trains very long, as the great ladies do in Europe. *a* **1891** R. W. BARBOUR *Thoughts* (1900) 66 Wearing scarlet is a badge of being in the Queen's service.

fig. **1896** A. E. HOUSMAN *Shropshire Lad* ii, Loveliest of trees, the cherry now..stands about the woodland ride Wearing white for Eastertide.

†**c.** with *on* or *upon* adv. (= on one's person; cf. *have on, put on*). *Obs.*

? *a* **1366** CHAUCER *Rom. Rose* 564 A chapelet, so semly oon Ne werede neuer mayde vpon. *c* **1386** —— *Wife's Prol.* 559, I..wered vpon my gaye scarlet gytes. **1387** TREVISA *Higden* I. 239 þis victor hym self schulde were on Iupiter his cote. **1567** HARMAN *Caveat* 62 A lytle whystell of syluer that his mother dyd vse customablye to weare on. **1570** LEVINS *Manip.* 209/43 To Weare on, *ferre*. **1579–80** NORTH *Plutarch, Aristides* (1595) 364 He weareth on a purple coloured coate.

d. said of an animal.

1486 *Bk. St. Albans, Hawking* d iii, The bellis that yowre hawke shall wheer looke in any wise that thay be not to heuy ouer hir power to weyr. **1579** W. WILKINSON *Confut. Fam. Love* 13 b, A ring of gold..ceaseth not to be a ryng of gold though a swine weare it.

†**e.** *absol.* To dress, be clad (in a specified fashion). *Obs. rare.*

a **1225** *Ancr. R.* 4 þet techeð al hu me schal beren him wiðuten, hu eten, drincken, werien, liggen, slepen, wakien. **1597** J. PAYNE *Royal Exch.* 28 They walkinge and wearinge in that common place agreable to there caullinge and state.

f. *intr.* (for *passive*) = to be worn; to be the fashion.

1601 SHAKS. *All's Well* I. i. 172 Virginitie like an olde Courtier, weares her cap out of fashion,..iust like the brooch and the toothpick, which were not now. **1888** QUILLER-COUCH in *Echoes fr. Oxf. Mag.* (1890) 105 Are 'hems' wearing?

2. a. *trans.* To bear or carry (arms, also a stick or cane). †Hence, to display (a heraldic charge) on one's shield.

c **1000** *Canons of Ælfric* xxx, Ne preost..wæpna ne werige. **1375** BARBOUR *Bruce* I. 355 The byschop..gert him wer His knyvys, forouch him to scher. ? *a* **1400** *Morte Arth.* 3872 He was the sterynneste in stoure that euer stele werryde. **1456** SIR G. HAYE *Law of Armys* (S.T.S.) 276 Than will he declare the armes that all princis and nobleis and othir gentillis aw to were, and of thair colouris and discripciouns. **1463** *Bury Wills* (Camden) 15 To Davn Willm Boxforde my knyves that I veryd my selfe. **1535** COVERDALE *1 Chron.* vi. 18 Soch as were fightinge men, which wayre shylde & swerde, and coulde bende the bowe. **1585** T. WASHINGTON tr. *Nicholay's Voy.* I. xvii. 19 b, [They had] sworne, at no time after to wear armes against the Turkish nation. **1596** DALRYMPLE tr. *Leslie's Hist. Scot.* (S.T.S.) I. 131 *marg. note*, The ryd lyon he weires in his armes. **1604** SHAKS. *Oth.* v. i. 2 Weare thy good Rapier bare, and put it home. **1690** in *Nairne Peerage Evid.* (1874) 26 The said Lord William Murray is..to..bear and wear the armes and cognizance of the house and family of Nairne. **1749** CHESTERF. *Lett. to Son* 27 Sept., His cane (if unfortunately he wears one) is at perpetual war with every cup of tea or coffee he drinks. **1775** SHERIDAN *Duenna* III. vii, You shall know that I have a brother who wears a sword. **1819** D. B. WARDEN *Acc. U.S.* III. 219 Both sexes..wear an umbrella in all seasons. **1847** MRS. A. KERR tr. *Ranke's Hist. Servia* 270 Their small arms, which they had formerly been permitted to wear.

†**b.** To use, employ, handle. *Obs.*

a **1400** *Nominale* (Skeat) 138 F[emme] vse nase et criuere. W[oman] weruth seue and riddell. *c* **1440** *Alphabet of Tales* 367 He offerd vnto hym..a grete porcion of syluer vessell, & bad hym were þaim for his sake.

3. To allow (one's hair, beard) to grow in a specified fashion, or as opposed to shaving or to the use of a wig.

c **1100** *O.E. Chron.* (MS. C) an. 1056 Leofgar..se werede his kenepas on his preosthade oððæt he wæs biscop. *c* **1449** PECOCK *Repr.* I. xx. 124 Noone wommen weriden thanne eny lynnen or silken keuercheefis, but weriden her open heer. **1560** DAUS tr. *Sleidane's Comm.* 55 Speake seldome, and weare a long beard. **1596** SHAKS. *Merch. V.* v. i. 158 The Clearke wil nere weare haire on's face that had it. **1624** CAPT. J. SMITH *Virginia* 3 The women weare their haire long on both sides. **1697** DAMPIER *Voy.* I. 407 Many of them have abandoned their Country to preserve their liberty of wearing their Hair. **1766** GOLDSM. *Vicar W.* xxx, Be so good as to inform me, if the fellow wore his own red hair. **1802** WORDSW. *Resol. & Independ.* viii, The oldest man he seem'd that ever wore grey hairs. **1841** DICKENS *Barn. Rudge* i, He wore his own dark hair. **1862** *Queen's Regul. Naval Service* 336 The Officers, Petty Officers, and Seamen of the Fleet are not to wear moustaches or beards. **1905** H. G. WELLS *Kipps* II. ii. §1 She wore her hair in a knob behind.

4. Phrases (*lit.* and *fig.*).

a. ***to wear a crown, diadem, mitre, palm, the purple***, etc.: to hold the dignity or office of which the ornament is a symbol.

c **893** ÆLFRED *Oros.* VI. xxx. (1883) 280 þæt hie woldon þa onwaldas forlætan, & þa purpuran alecgan þa hie weredon. **1382** WYCLIF *1 Esdras* iii. 2 King Darie made a gret soper.. to alle that wereden [*v.r.* werden] purper. *c* **1393** CHAUCER *Gentilesse* 7 Al were he mytre, croune or dyademe. *c* **1470** *Three Fifteenth-C. Chron.* (Camden) 4 He was the fyrst kynge þat ever wered crowne of golde in this londe. **1588** SHAKS. *Tit. A.* I. i. 6 The last That wore the Imperiall Diadem of Rome. **1597** —— *2 Hen. IV*, III. i. 31 Vneasie lyes the Head, that weares a Crowne. **1797** BURKE *Regic. Peace* iii. Wks. VIII. 274 It is the power of winning that palm which ensures our wearing it. **1849** MACAULAY *Hist. Eng.* I. ii. 205 Degrading that crown which it was probable that he would himself one day wear. **1895** 'H. S. MERRIMAN' *Sowers* i, He [the Emperor] is a gentleman, although he has the misfortune to wear the purple.

†**b.** ***to wear the horn(s***: to be a cuckold. *Obs.*

c **1530** *Hyckescorner* 706 And, knyght of the halter, my fader ware an horne. **1600** SHAKS. *A.Y.L.* IV. ii. 14 Take thou no scorne to weare the horne. **1632** SIR T. HAWKINS *Mathieu's Unhappy Prosperitie* 98 By reason he was old, and without children,..his wife should doe well to make him weare the horne. **1639** J. CLARKE *Paræm.* 328 The good wife weares the breeches, the good man the hornes.

†**c.** ***to wear papers***: (of an offender) To have a note of one's offence fastened on one's back or head. *Obs.*

a **1529–1588**: see PAPER *sb.* 7 b.
a **1548** HALL *Chron., Hen. VIII* 1 Sone after were apprehended diuerse called promoters..of the whiche, the moste part ware papers, and stoode on the Pillorie. **1552** HULOET, Weare a paper for some infamye or offence, *contamidio* [read *catomidio*]. **1560–1** MACHYN *Diary* (Camden) 250 They ware paper a-pon ther hedes for pergure. **1616** BRETON *Good & Bad* 14 Least when the Law indeede laies them open, in steade of carrying papers in their hands, they weare not papers on their heads.

d. ***to wear one's arm in a scarf*** or ***sling***: to support it thus when injured. ***to wear one's heart upon one's sleeve***: see HEART *sb.* 54 f.

1597, 1600 [see SCARF *sb.*[1] 4]. **1660** F. BROOKE tr. *Le Blanc's Trav.* 27 My companion was so bruised, that he wore his arm in a scarf for two months after. **1727** BOYER *Dict. Royal* II. s.v. *Sling*, To wear one's Arm in a Sling, *Porter le bras en écharpe*. **1794** [see SLING *sb.*[2] 3 c].

e. ***to wear the breeches***: see BREECH *sb.* 2. ***to wear yellow hose*** (or ***breeches***): see YELLOW *a.* 2. ***to wear the willow***: see WILLOW. ***to wear the trousers***: see TROUSERS *sb. pl.* 2 c.

†**f.** *slang.* (See quots.) *Obs.*

1812 J. H. VAUX *Flash Dict.* s.v. *Bands*, To wear the bands, is to be hungry, or short of food for any length of time. *Ibid.* s.v. *Wear it*, to wear it upon a person, (meaning to wear a nose, or a conk,) is synonymous with nosing, conking, splitting, or coming it.

5. Of a ship (or its commander): To fly (a flag, colours).

†Formerly also, to carry (a mast).

1558 in W. G. Perrin *Brit. Flags* (1922) 88 Mr. Broke, Captaine of the reed Gallie, who is apointed to ware the flagge of vize Admyrall for this present Jorney. **1575** FLEMING *Virg. Bucol.* IV. 12 No shyp that weares a maste, Shal make exchaunge of wares. **1627** J. SMITH *Sea Gram.* xiii. 62 Any ship..where he..resideth.., is to weare his flag in the maine top. **1666** *Lond. Gaz.* No. 82/1 Thirteen French Gallies, wearing Swedes Colors. **1715** *Lond. Gaz.* No. 5359/1 The Czar on board his Ship wears the Distinction of Vice-Admiral of the Blue. **1803** in Nicolas *Disp. Nelson* (1845) V. 287 *note*, Saint George's Ensigns are to be worn by every Ship in Action. **1862** *Queen's Regul. Naval Service* 17 The Admiral of the Fleet, and the Admirals of the Red, White, and Blue, shall wear their proper Flag. **1881** MACGEORGE *Flags* 73 The other [pendant] is worn at the mast-head of all armed vessels in the employ of the government of a British colony.

6. *transf.* To bear or possess as a member or part of the body.

1513 DOUGLAS *Æneis* VIII. Prol. 156 Quhy the corn hes the caff, And kow weris clufe. **1591** G. FLETCHER *Russe Commw.* iii. 10 b, The fish that weareth it [the 'fishe tooth'] is called a Morse. **1596** SHAKS. *Tam. Shr.* II. i. 214 Who knowes not where a Waspe does weare his sting? In his taile. **1600** —— *A.Y.L.* II. i. 14 Sweet are the vses of aduersitie Which like the toad, ougly and venemous, Weares yet a precious Iewell in his head. **1614** RALEGH *Hist. World* Pref. D 2, Euery man weares but his owne skin. **1621** BURTON *Anat. Mel.* Democr. to Rdr. 34 To see a man to weare his braines in his belly, his guts in his head. **1697** DRYDEN *Virg. Georg.* IV. 531 Two Golden Horns on his large Front he wears. *a* **1721** PRIOR *Turtle & Sparrow* 132 All that wear Feathers first or last, Must one Day perch on Charon's Mast. **1794** GODWIN *Caleb Williams* 47, I will not put my estate to nurse to you, nor to the best he that wears a head. **1847** H. MILLER *First Impr. Eng.* xvii. (1861) 215 Fish that wear an armature of bone outside. **1848** THACKERAY *Van. Fair* liii, Steyne wore the scar to his dying day.

7. To exhibit or present (a particular look, expression, appearance, etc.).

1611 SHAKS. *Wint. T.* I. ii. 344 With a countenance as cleare As Friendship weares at Feasts. **1669** DRYDEN *Tyrannic Love* I. i, When an action does two faces wear. **1749** FIELDING *Tom Jones* XI. vii, He now assumed a carriage to me so very different from what he had lately worn. **1766** GOLDSM. *Vicar W.* iii, The world now began to wear a different aspect. **1840** R. H. DANA *Bef. Mast* xviii. 48 There everything wore the appearance of a holiday. **1841** THACKERAY *Gt. Hoggarty Diam.* xi, Both wore very long faces. **1870** DISRAELI *Lothair* xli. 211 The countenance of Lord St. Aldegonde wore a rueful expression.

8. a. In various *fig.* uses: To carry about with one in one's heart, mind, or memory; to have as a quality or attribute; to bear (a name, title).

a **1586** SIDNEY *Apol. Poetrie* (Arb.) 47 Let Aeneas be worne in the tablet of your memory. **1599** SHAKS. *Much Ado* I. i. 75 He weares his faith but as the fashion of his hat, it euer changes with ye next block. **1602** —— *Ham.* III. ii. 77 Giue me that man, That is not Passions Slaue, and I will weare him In my hearts Core. **1605** —— *Macb.* II. ii. 65 My Hands are of your colour: but I shame To weare a Heart so white. **1655** FULLER *Ch. Hist.* IX. 191 Suffragan of Nottingham, (the last I beleeve who wore that title). **1668** DAVENANT *Man's the Master* v. i, He did wear your Brother in his bosome as his dearest Friend. **1777** THICKNESSE *Journ. France* (1789) I. 348 'Roach; an unfortunate name!' said he; —'but, as it is my name, I will wear it.' **1827** in Scott *Chron. Canongate* Introd. App., He was vain of the cognomen which he had now worn for eight years. **1848** *Classical Museum* V. 382 The dithyramb wore the same character as Pindar's ἆθλα. **1884** *Christian Commw.* 21 Feb. 439/1 Those who wear His name.

b. To possess and enjoy as one's own. Chiefly in phr. ***to win and wear*** (a lady as one's wife).

The lit. reference may have been to a favour won in the tilt, or to a king's crown (cf. Shaks. *2 Hen. IV*, IV. v. 222).

1573 G. HARVEY *Letter Bk.* (Camden) 114 Thou hast woone her—weare her. **1588** GREENE *Pandosto* (1607) G j, Meliagrus is a Knight that hath wonne me by loue, and none but he shall weare me. **1599** SHAKS. *Much Ado* v. i. 82 Win me and weare me, let him answere me. **1611** —— *Cymb.* I. iv. 96 You may weare her in title yours. **1621** FLETCHER *Wild-goose Chase* II. i, Win 'em, and wear 'em, I give up my interest. **1748** RICHARDSON *Clarissa* III. 350, I, who have won the gold, am only fit to wear it. **1847** MARRYAT *Childr. N. Forest* xxvii, As for his daughter..you have yet to 'win her and wear her', as the saying is.

c. To tolerate, accept, or agree to (a proposal, etc.). Usu. in negative with *it* as obj.

1925 FRASER & GIBBONS *Soldier & Sailor Words* 301 *To wear*, to put up with, *e.g.*, 'I won't wear it', I won't stand it. **1945** C. H. WARD-JACKSON *It's a Piece of Cake!* (ed. 2) 61 *Wear it. Agree to it, accept it.* Thus, 'I've asked the old man for permission to keep the bar open an hour later, but he won't wear it.' **1950** C. MACINNES *To Victors the Spoils* I. 70 'The new Captain would never wear it.' 'Then it's up to you to put it to him the right way.' **1961** E. WAUGH *Unconditional Surrender* III. i. 203 Presently the Lieutenant came across to them bearing a cigar-case. 'I can't wear them myself,' he said. **1970** P. H. JOHNSON *Honours Board* 61 The mother said this was very kind but that Peter would never —she was given to girlish slang—'wear it'. **1981** S. JACKMAN *Game of Soldiers* I. 53 No.. Watson wouldn't wear it... Nor will I.

II. To waste, damage, or destroy by use.

9. a. To waste and impair (a material) gradually by use or attrition. ? Primarily with clothes as obj. = to damage them by ordinary wearing.

Perh. originally short for FORWEAR, which is found earlier.

1382 WYCLIF *Josh.* ix. 13 Clothis and shoon..for the length of lenger weye ben to troden, and almeest wered. **1398** TREVISA *Barth. De P.R.* XIV. iii. (1495) 469 Waters dygge and weer the nesshe partes of the erthe. *c* **1400** *Master of Game* (MS. Digby 182) xxiv (end), Whan his tuskes aboue beth..ywered of þe neyther tuskes. *c* **1440** *Promp. Parv.* 522/2 Weryn, or vson, as clothys and other thyngys, *vetero*. **1539** *Test. Ebor.* (Surtees) VI. 89 If any of the said housholde stuf be worne or gone, then she to be resonablie recompensed. **1542** UDALL *Erasm. Apoph.* 45 How it chaunced, that the philosophiers did frette and weare the threshholdes of riche mennes houses. **1579** SPENSER *Sheph. Cal.* Oct. 8, I haue pyped erst so long with payne, That all mine Oten reedes bene rent and wore. **1610** HOLLAND *Camden's Brit.* (1637) 752 All the letters beside..are so worne and gone, that they could not be read. **1611** BIBLE *Ecclus.* vi. 36 Let thy foote weare [ἐκτριβέτω] the steps of his doore. **1717** POPE *Eloisa* 19 Ye rugged rocks, which holy knees have worn! **1764** J. FERGUSON *Lect.* 47 When the stone is considerably wore, and become light, the mill must be fed slowly. **1849** M. ARNOLD *Forsaken Merman* 74 We climb'd on the graves, on the stones worn with rains. **1855** BOHN *Ray's Prov.* etc. 339 Constant dropping wears the stone. **1872** L. P. MEREDITH *Teeth* 112 When the teeth are crowded too closely together, they..wear one another. **1898** 'H. S. MERRIMAN' *Roden's Corner* iv. 33 The house..is of dark red brick with facings of stone, long since worn by wind and weather.

absol. **1478** *Rental Bk. Cupar-Angus* (1879) I. 212 He sal defend the watyr at it were na ferrar in, eftir vale and quantyte of his land.

b. with intensifying adv., as *away, down, off, out.*

1538 ELYOT *Dict.* Addit., *Contero*, to weare out with occupienge. **1561** in *Inuentaires de la Royne Descosse* (Bannatyne Club) 33 Ane auld cannabie of grene serge worne away and brokin. **1590** SPENSER *F.Q.* II. iv. 4 Her lockes..Grew all afore,..But all behind was bald, and worne away. **1600** FAIRFAX *Tasso* XVIII. xxi, Downe fell the bridge, swelled the streame, and weard The worke away. **1647** in *Verney Mem.* (1907) I. 373 All the linnen is quite worne out. **1674** BOYLE *Corpusc. Philos.* 28 Such an attrition, as wears off the edges and points. **1676** J. SMITH *Art of Painting* xvii. 75 Too frequent operations in this kind must needs wear off a little of the Colours. **1782** MISS BURNEY *Cecilia* v. viii, Never sweep a room out of use; only wears out brooms for nothing. **1835** T. MITCHELL *Acharn. of Aristoph.* 620 *note*, The metaphor is derived from a flute, the mouth-piece of which is worn out. **1852** LYELL *Elem. Geol.* (ed. 4) iii. 25 These flinty cases and spiculæ..are..admirably adapted, when rubbed, for wearing down into a fine powder fit for polishing the surface of metals. **1885** *Law Rep.* 15 *Q.B.D.* 316 The catch on the pin..was worn away. **1922** C. ALINGTON *Strained Relations* xiv. 222 If you can't get into Parliament without my wearing out your old suits.

c. with pred. extension, as ***to wear threadbare, smooth, blunt***; ***to wear to rags*** or ***tatters, to the stumps.*** (Also in fig. context.)

c **1520** SKELTON *Magnyf.* 223 Welth and Wyt, I say, be so threde bare worne, That all is without Measure. *a* **1555–1732** [see STUMP *sb.* 3 b]. **1575** GASCOIGNE *Weedes, Compl. greene Knt.* 180 She did but weare Cosmanes cloutes, which she in spite had torne: And yet betwene them both they waare the threeds so neere [etc.]. **1639** J. TAYLOR (Water P.) *Part Summers Trav.* 48 My Pen is worn blunt. **1661** BOYLE *Style Script.* (1675) 232 All his too frequent kisses have worn it to tatters. **1756** AMORY *Buncle* (1770) II. 69 There was no water dropping from the roof of this cave; but in a thousand places..it crept through the sides, and formed streams that ran softly over the ground and weared it smooth. **1765** FOOTE *Commissary* I. 7 He'll stick to his honour too, till his cassock is wore to a rag. **1808** SCOTT *Marmion* I. v, His forehead, by his casque worn bare. **1852** THACKERAY *Esmond* I. vii, She would wear a gown to rags, because he had once liked it.

10. a. To sap the strength or energy of (a person, his faculties, etc.) by toil, age, etc.; to fatigue, weary; †to exhaust (a soil).

1508 DUNBAR *Tua Mariit Wemen* 127 He is waistit and worne fra Venus werkis. **1523–34** FITZHERB. *Husb.* §14 All these maner of otes weare the grounde very sore. **1585** HIGINS *Junius' Nomencl.* 384/1 *Ager effœtus*,..a ground that by continuall fruitfulnes is quite spent, worne, and out of occupyeng. **1591–5** C'TESS PEMBROKE *Lay of Clorinda* 95 Thus do we weep and waile, and wear our eies. **1601** SHAKS. *All's Well* v. i. 4 Since you haue made the daies and nights as one, To weare your gentle limbes in my affayres. **1694** DRYDEN *To Congreve* 66 Already I am worn with Cares and Age. **1825** SCOTT *Talism.* iii, Both warriors, worn by toil and travel, were soon fast asleep. **1833** HT. MARTINEAU *Loom & Lugger* II. i. 7 He had brought me up to an occupation that wears the spirits. **1865** M. ARNOLD *Ess. Crit.*, *M. de Guérin* (1875) 121 Still the yoke wore him deeply, and he had moments of bitter revolt. **1870** BRYANT *Iliad* IV. 402 Age, the common fate of all, has worn Thy frame.

b. with adv., as *away, out, down, †up.* Also with advb. phr., as *to wear to death.*

c **1524** in Ellis *Orig. Lett.* Ser. I. I. 193 Ells they [the Irish] shall never be woren out, but increas more and more. **1577** WOLTON *Cast. Christians* F ij b, Peruerse affections, which doo euen weare awaye, and consume vs. **1603** SHAKS. *Meas. for M.* I. ii. 109 You that haue worne your eyes almost out in the seruice, you will bee considered. **1607** NORDEN *Surv. Dial.* v. 241 A weed that groweth commonly upon grounds ouertilled, and worne out of heart. **1672** W. WALKER *Parœm.* 56 They win by wearing their enemies out. **1691** SIR T. P. BLOUNT *Ess.* 165 In most of these Places the old Inhabitants, or their Breed, are quite wore away. **1701** COLLIER *M. Anton.* (1726) 8 That she may not live too fast, wear up her constitution, and destroy the capacities of enjoyment. **1729** LAW *Ser. Call* xi. 169 She tells you that her patience is quite wore out. **1735** JOHNSON *Lobo's Abyssinia, Voy.* viii. 42 The concern they shew'd at seeing us worn away with Hunger, Labour, and Weariness. **1783** —— *Let. to Mrs. Thrale* 23 July, Do not let your mind wear out your body. **1803** BEDDOES *Hygëia* IX. 105 At the close of the season in London women appear worn down, haggard and spent. **1840** ARNOLD *Hist. Rome* II. 344 With these missiles [they] endeavoured to wear down the mass of their enemies. **1840** DICKENS *Old C. Shop* lxiv, This poor little Marchioness has been wearing herself to death! **1847** W. E. FORSTER in Reid *Life* (1888) I. vi. 190 Found my father..pretty well, but worn up and worn down. **1848** THACKERAY *Van. Fair* xiv, And still you go hanging on to my sister, who'll fling you off like an old shoe, when she's wore you out. **1872** DASENT *Three to One* x, He always looks well when he doesn't wear himself down dancing all night. **1881** JOWETT *Thucyd.* I. 230 They carried on uninterrupted war against the new settlers until they completely wore them out. **1886** 'SARAH TYTLER' *Buried Diamonds* xviii, To-night, when one is worn off one's feet already, with this miserable ball. **1904** M. HEWLETT *Queen's Quair* III. xi. 500 She wore herself to thread, padding up and down the room. **1912** *World* 7 May 700/1 As the soil..becomes worn out the farmers have to buy more artificial manure.

c. With *on* or *upon*. Of a circumstance: to affect (a person) adversely; to fatigue or debilitate. Cf. WEIGH *v.*[1] 22 a.

1864 O. W. NORTON *Army Lett.* (1903) 245, I did not suppose these things were serious enough to wear upon your health. **1901** 'L. MALET' *Hist. Sir R. Calmady* v. ii. 389, I have had a detestable winter... It wore upon me. It demoralised me. **1915** D. H. LAWRENCE *Let.* ? 29 Apr. (1962) 335 You can't imagine how it wears on one, having at every moment to resist this established world.

11. a. *fig.* With object a quality, condition, activity, disease, etc.: To cause to weaken, diminish, or disappear gradually. Chiefly with adv. or advb. phr. (as above). ***to wear out***: to efface, destroy, exhaust, abolish, by gradual loss or the lapse of time.

1390 GOWER *Conf.* I. 33 The world..welnyh is wered oute. ? *a* **1400** *Morte Arth.* 2930 Oure wages are werede owte, and thi werre endide. **1586** A. DAY *Eng. Secretorie* I. vi. (1595) 18 But that custome..is long since worne out. **1657** in *Verney Mem.* (1907) II. 59 That acquaintance with you which time and far distance hath worne something out of our memories. **1663** BUTLER *Hud.* I. i. 47 We grant, although he had much wit, H' was very shie of using it, As being loath to wear it out. **1697** DRYDEN *Virg. Georg.* III. 6 All other Themes that careless Minds invite, Are worn with Use, unworthy me to write. **1705** ADDISON *Italy, Venice* 100 By the Pompousness of the whole Phrase to wear off any Littleness that appears in the particular Parts that compose it. **1711** —— *Spect.* No. 39 ¶1 Diversions of this kind wear out of our Thoughts every thing that is mean and little. **1751** F. COVENTRY *Pompey the Little* I. x. 91 When he had a little wore off the Relish of Pleasure. **1831** JAMES *Phil. Augustus* xxii, As the fire wore away the strength of the wood. **1857** B. TAYLOR *Northern Trav.* xii. (1858) 124 When the novelty of the thing is worn off. **1865** DICKENS *Mut. Fr.* IV. xvi, As if Time alone could quite wear her injury out. **1871** FREEMAN *Norm. Conq.* (1876) IV. xviii. 145 He did not strike a blow till all the powers of diplomacy had been thoroughly worn out between himself and his rival. **1899** *Allbutt's Syst. Med.* VIII. 846 Repeated operations with the idea of 'wearing out' the disease.

b. ***to wear down***: to blunt the force of and overcome by steady resistance or counter-attack. Also, to get gradually ahead of (a competitor in a race) by superior endurance.

1843 R. J. GRAVES *Syst. Clin. Med.* xix. 221 These medicines..remove the aguish fits..gradually, and as it were, by wearing down the paroxysms. **1851** DIXON *W. Penn* viii. (1872) 66 The young Quaker..strove to wear down malice by his patient and forgiving mood. **1889** RIDER HAGGARD *Allan's Wife* 20 Be a man, and wear it down. **1895** *Daily News* 27 Sept. 3/2 Macbriar..gradually wearing down Balm of Gilead, won by three-quarters of a length.

†**c.** ***to wear out***: to forget, lose mental hold of, through disuse or lapse of time. *Obs.*

a **1676** HALE *Prim. Orig. Man.* To Rdr., My application to another Study and Profession, rendred my skill in that Language of little use to me, and so I wore it out by degrees. **1708** SWIFT *Sent. Ch.-of-Eng. Man* §2 Misc. (1711) 131 When these Doctrines began to be Preached among us, the Kingdom had not quite worn out the Memory of that unhappy Rebellion.

12. To form or produce by attrition.

1597 DRAYTON *Heroic. Ep., Chas. Brandon* 17 That Nectar-stayned way, The restlesse sunne by trauailing doth weare. **1697** DRYDEN *Æneis* IX. 520 Few Paths of Humane Feet, or Tracks of Beasts, were worn. **1726** LEONI *Alberti's Archit.* I. 74/1 Ants, with constant passing up and down, will wear traces even in flints. **1782** MISS BURNEY *Cecilia* IV. vii, Wish I had not come now; wore a hole in my shoe. **1834** PRINGLE *Afr. Sk.* vi. 203 A steep and rugged path, worn by the boors' cattle.

III. *intr.* To suffer waste or decay by use or by lapse of time.

13. a. Of persons or living things, activities, qualities, etc.: To lose strength, vitality, keenness, sharpness, or intensity, by the decay of time; to waste, diminish, or fade by gradual loss.

c **1275** *Serving Christ* 68 in *O.E. Misc.* 92 Þer wereþ vre wlite in wurmene won. **1530** PALSGR. 780/1 All thyng weareth save the grace of God. **1589** R. ROBINSON *Gold. Mirr.* (1851) 28 Tyme is my name, young once I was, Though now, I weare and wast alas. **1595** DANIEL *Civ. Wars* IV. viii. [v. vii], How blessed they that gaine what neuer weares. *a* **1600** MONTGOMERIE *Misc. P.* xii. 10 (Laing MS.) My eyes with tereis dois weir. **1605** BACON *Adv. Learn.* I. II. §5 It..refresheth their reputation, which otherwise would weare. **1840** DICKENS *Old C. Shop* liv, The deaf old man..muttered to himself..that the sexton was wearing fast. **1864** BROWNING *Jas. Lee's Wife* IV. vii, Yet this turns now to a fault..That I..wait too well, and weary and wear.

b. most commonly with adv., as *away, off, out,* or advb. phr.

1377 in *Polit. Poems* (Rolls) I. 215 Alle thing weres and wasteth away. **1390** GOWER *Conf.* I. 16 Bot whan god wole, it [the schism] schal were oute, For trowthe mot stonde ate laste. *c* **1480** HENRYSON *Test. Cress.* 467 All Welth in Eird away as Wind it weiris. **1547** BOORDE *Brev. Health* ccclxxix. (1557) 121 b, Were before the eyes a pece of blacke sarcenet ..and it ['a blast in the eye'] wyll were awaye. **1574** tr. *Marlorat's Apoc.* 28 To the intent these things myght neuer weare out of minde. **1611** BIBLE *Exod.* xviii. 18 Thou wilt surely weare away..: for this thing is too heauy for thee. **1697** DAMPIER *Voy.* I. 282, I found that my strength increased, and my Dropsy wore off. **1719** DE FOE *Crusoe* I. (Globe) 247 In a little Time, however, no more Canoes appearing, the Fear of their Coming wore off. **1720** S. PAYNE *Bp. R. Cumberland's Sanchon.* Pref. p. xiv, His usual Reply was, A Man had better wear out than rust out. **1742** KAMES *Decis. Court Sess.* 1730–52 (1799) 49 Hence the strict way of interpreting such clauses..wore by degrees out of use. **1759** R. BROWN *Compl. Farmer* 111 If clover is apt to wear out of your ground. **1789–96** MORSE *Amer. Geog.* I. 398 Many persons conjecture that the Cape [Cod] is gradually wearing away. **1798** [see LAND *sb.*[1] 3 c]. **1821** BYRON *Sardanap.* I. ii. 112 Till summer heats wear down. **1842** DICKENS *Amer. Notes* ii, When its novelty had long worn off. **1843** R. J. GRAVES *Syst. Clin. Med.* xxviii. 362 He..seldom got any relief until the attacks were wearing off. **1859** H. KINGSLEY *G. Hamlyn* xx, Her anger, so far from wearing out, grew on what fed it. **1872** BLACK *Adv. Phaeton* ix, The chill of driving through the fogs of the plain had worn off. **1889** S. WALPOLE *Ld. John Russell* xxi. II. 98 The strange distrust which had so frequently separated Sir Robert Peel and Lord John began visibly to wear away.

c. with predicative adj. *rare.*

1837 CARLYLE *Fr. Rev.* III. IV. viii, The chorus is wearing weak; the chorus is worn *out*. **1875** SWINBURNE *Ess. & Stud.* 334 An old man of great strength now wearing weak.

†**d.** ***to wear out, forth,*** of something which holds good for a limited time: To determine, expire. *Obs.*

1412–20 LYDG. *Chron. Troy* IV. 2420 Whan þe trews þat þei had take Wer werid oute. *c* **1420** WYNTOUN *Cron.* VIII. 1682 Neuirþeles he was in dowt, Or his condyte was worne out. **1472** *Paston Lett.* III. 73, I gat a lycence of hym for a yere, and it is nyghe woryn ought. **1525** in *Reg. Mag. Sig. Scot.* 1527 97/2 Gif ony feman of the said craft pass furth of the toun or his band of his service be worne furth. **1530** PALSGR. 780/1, I weare out, as thynges do after their tyme prefyxed is passed, *je me faulx*... The pardons shall weare out within these thre dayes.

14. a. Of clothing and other material things: To suffer gradual destruction, loss, or decay from attrition or use.

1402 *Jack Upland* 45 Maketh youre habit you men of religion, or no? If it do, than, ever as it weareth, your religion weareth; and, after that the habit is better, is your religion better. **1414** BRAMPTON *Penit. Ps.* (Percy Soc.) 38 As clothys doth were with wedyr and wynde. *c* **1440** *Promp. Parv.* 522/2 Weryn or wax olde and febyl [by] vse, *veterasco*. **1530** PALSGR. 780/1, I weare, as a garment or any other thyng weareth and consumeth with the tyme, *je me use*. **1582** N. T. (Rheims) *Luke* xii. 33 Make to you purses that weare not [Vulg. *qui non veterascunt*]. **1587** TURBERV. *Trag. Tales* 33 By lingring loue she made his monie mealte, As waxe doth weare against the flaming fire. **1836** *Penny Cycl.* VI. 380/1 These milk-teeth..gradually wear and fall out, and are replaced by the second and permanent teeth.

b. with intensifying adv. or advb. phr., as *away, down, off, out,* †*on* or *to the thread.*

1414 BRAMPTON *Penit. Ps.* (Percy Soc.) 38 Alle erthely thynges schul were owte; Castellys and towrys schul bende and breste. **1530** PALSGR. 780/1, I weare awaye, as a scrypture, or thyng made for remembraunce weareth awaye with the weather or with the tyme, *je me oblitere*. **1566** A. EDWARDS in Hakluyt *Voy.* (1599) I. 358 When it [cloth] commeth to weare on the threed, it renteth like paper. **1601** *Offic. Papers Sir N. Bacon* (Camden) 117 Jettyes and pyles ..to defend theis mershes and bankes from wearing awaye by the rage of the sea. **1643** CARYL *Expos. Job* I. 104 Our flesh wears off quickly in the grave. **1687** MIEGE *Gt. Fr. Dict.* II, My Suit begins to wear out. **1793** [EARL DUNDONALD] *Descr. Estate of Culross* 22 Many of the old established Collieries in the Firth are wearing fast out. **1836** wear off [see c]. **1860** W. W. READE *Liberty Hall* II. 38 The gilt beginning to wear off. **1882** [see THREAD *sb.* 2 b]. **1886** *Manch. Exam.* 22 Feb. 6/1 When their carts wear out they need the services of the wheelwright. **1886** BESANT *Childr. Gibeon* II. xxiii, Her scanty wardrobe would wear out.

c. with predicative adj., as *wide, flat, thin.*

1641 BEST *Farm. Bks.* (Surtees) 7 Teeth blacke, wearinge wide. **1836** *Penny Cycl.* VI. 380/1 After six years old the edges of the teeth begin to wear flat, and as they wear off the root of the tooth is pushed up in the socket. **1896** HOUSMAN *Shropshire Lad* xxxiv, Where the standing line wears thinner and the dropping dead lie thick. **1931** J. VAN DRUTEN *London Wall* II. i. 69 You must have known yourself it's [*sc.* a love affair] been wearing thin. **1942** J. S. HUXLEY in *Polit. Q.* XIII. 384 The inter-war disputation between the 'have' and the 'have-not' powers is wearing a bit thin. **1982** G. M. FRASER *Flashman & Redskins* 52, I knew Susie's first good opinion of Spring had worn thin.

IV. 15. *intr.* To last or hold out in use or with the lapse of time; to resist (well or ill) the attrition or waste of use and age; also, to stand the test of experience, criticism, etc.

a **1568** *Satir. Poems Reform.* xlviii. 19, I haif Quhyt off grit delyt,..Weill wearand Reid, quhill ȝe be deid. **1687** MIEGE *Gt. Fr. Dict.* II, This Stuff wears very well. **1710** STEELE *Tatler* No. 208 ¶1 The Flattery with which he began, in telling me how well I wore, was not disagreeable. **1766** GOLDSM. *Vicar W.* i, I..chose my wife, as she did her wedding-gown, not for a fine glossy surface, but such qualities as would wear well. **1771** *Junius Lett.* liv. 286 These praises..will wear well, for they have been dearly earned. **1788** *Monthly Mag.* Mar. 183 The natives [of New York]..do not appear to wear so well as the English. **1816** BYRON *Siege Cor.* xiv, Tyrant and slave are swept away, Less form'd to wear before the ray. **1833** DICKENS *Sk. Boz, Mr. Minns*, How are you, Minns? 'Pon my soul you wear capitally! **1875** H. JAMES *R. Hudson* i, Rowland examined the statuette at his leisure... He discovered its weak points, but it wore well. **1905** MRS. BARNES-GRUNDY *Vacill. Hazel* 96, I am tired of old-fashioned, made-to-wear-for-ever clothes.

†**16.** trans. ***to wear out***: to come safe through, 'weather' (a storm, an attack of sickness). *Obs.*

1617 in *Buccleuch MSS.* (Hist. MSS. Comm.) I. 252 She has fallen into it [the ague] again..but..I hope she may wear it out. **1645** BP. HALL *Rem. Discontent.* 63 The poor man..when hee foresees a storm to threaten him, puts into the next Creek; and wears out in a quiet security that Tempest, wherein he sees prouder Vessels..fatally wracked.

V. In reference to time, change, endurance, etc.

17. In *pa. pple.*, of time, a period of time, a season: Past, spent, passed away. Also with adv., as *out*, †*by*, †*forth*. Now chiefly *poet.*

This use is found earlier than senses 18 and 19, and the vb. may here be regarded as either *trans.* or *intr.*

c **1400** *Beryn* 1090 Fawnus lyvid wyfles [till] thre yeer wer werid. *c* **1420** WYNTOUN *Cron.* II. 1301 Qwhen hir tyme was werit [*Wemyss* worne] out. *c* **1470** HENRY *Wallace* IX. 659 Off tym that is by worn. **1472** in *Reg. Mag. Sig. Scot. 1476*, 258/1 Eftir the termes of 5 yeris are worne furth and bipassit. *a* **1547** SURREY '*The soote season*' 12 in *Tottel's Misc.* (Arb.) 4 Winter is worne that was the flowers bale. *a* **1548** HALL *Chron., Edw. IV* 221 b, Mornyng in continuall sorowe, not so much for her selfe and her husbande, whose ages were almost consumed and worne, but for the losse of prince Edward her sonne. **1557** TUSSER *100 Points Husb.* §83 Share not thy lammes, till mid July be worne. **1587** TURBERV. *Trag. T.* 55 And there he staied vntill such time as all his yere was worne. **1590** SHAKS. *Mids. N.* IV. i. 187 And for the morning now is something worne, Our purpos'd hunting shall be set aside. **1842** TENNYSON *Love & Duty* 69 Till now the dark was worn, and overhead The lights of sunset and of sunrise mix'd In that brief night. **1890** HALL CAINE *Bondman* II. vii, The year was far worn towards winter.

18. a. *trans.* To spend, pass (one's time, a period of time). Chiefly *poet.* Cf. WARE *v.*² b.

1567 FENTON *Trag. Disc.* xii. 263 b, She weard her youth in dule in steade of ioye. **1590** SPENSER *F.Q.* I. i. 31 To shew the place, In which that wicked wight his dayes doth weare. *c* **1750** SHENSTONE *Elegy* i. 45 Where with Œnone thou hast worn the day. *a* **1777** T. WARTON *Suicide* v. 26 He wore his endless noons alone, Amid th' autumnal wood. **1809** CAMPBELL *Gert. Wyom.* II. ix, A deep untrodden grot Where oft the reading hours sweet Gertrude wore. **1821** CLARE *Vill. Minstrel* I. 18 Spinning long stories, wearing half the day. **1875** MORRIS *Æneids* XII. 398 He..speeding of a silent craft, inglorious life would wear.

b. with adv., as *away*, *out*, †*by*, †*forth*.

1535 COVERDALE *Job* xxxvi. 11 They shall weere out their dayes in prosperite. *a* **1586** SIDNEY *Arcadia* I. end (1598) 95 She, perceiuing the song had alreadie worne out much time. **1625** DONNE *Serm.* lxvi. (1640) 665 Let me wither and weare out mine age in a discomfortable..prison. **1669** in Sturmy *Mariner's Mag.* a 4 b, No novel Romance, nor no paultry Plays, To wear out Time with, and mis-spend our Days. **1769** E. BANCROFT *Guiana* 384 They..thus wear out a life of solitude. **1773** *Life N. Frowde* 150 In this Manner we wore away near seven Months. **1809** MALKIN *Gil Blas* VII. vii. (Rtldg.) 25 We wore away a good part of the night in laughing and drinking. **1821** CLARE *Vill. Minstrel* I. 174 There they their games..pursue, With chuck and marbles wearing Sunday through. **1842** MANNING *Serm.* xxi. (1848) I. 315 They wore out with patience the years of this toilsome life. **1852** M. ARNOLD *A Farewell* xiii, And though we wear out life, alas!..In seeking what we shall not find.

c. To enable (a person) to last or hold out *through* a given period. *Sc.*

1815 SCOTT *Guy M.* xxiv, She should have a pint bottle o' brandy and a pound o' tobacco to wear her through the winter.

19. a. *intr.* Of time, a period of time: To pass on or advance gradually to its conclusion; to pass away. Also, *to wear late*, † *short*.

1597 E. S. *Discov. Knts. Poste* B 4 The day weares, and I haue farre to go. **1598** SHAKS. *Merry W.* V. i. 8 Away I say, time weares. **1637** RUTHERFORD *Lett.* (1664) 197 Your afternoon will wear short, and your sun fall low and goe down. **1763** FOOTE *Mayor of G.* II. i, Well said, Master Mug; but come, time wears. **1826** SCOTT *Woodstock* I. iii. 98 It wears late, and gets dark. **1837** J. E. MURRAY *Summer in Pyrenees* II. 213 It was now wearing late in the day. **1842** LEVER *J. Hinton* xix, As the evening wore late, the noise and uproar grew louder. **1865** DICKENS *Mut. Fr.* I. xiii, Without that aid they would have known how the night wore, by the falling of the tide. **1870** MORRIS *Earthly Par.* III. II. 376 But time went on, and still the days did wear With little seeming change.

b. with adv., as *away*, *on*, *out*, *through*.

1526 TINDALE *Luke* ix. 12 The daye began to weare awaye [so **1611**, **1882**; Gr. κλίνειν]. **1600** E. BLOUNT tr. *Conestaggio* 183 The short season for galleies to liue in that sea began to weare away. *a* **1764** LLOYD *Milk-maid* 14 How slowly wears the time away! **1834** DICKENS *Sk. Boz, Steam Excurs.*, The time wore on; half-past eight o'clock arrived. **1853** KINGSLEY *Hypatia* xxii, And so the week wore out, in dull and stupified despair. **1865** H. PHILLIPS *Amer. Paper Curr.* II. 89 Three years had now worn away in the unequal conflict. **1872** BLACK *Adv. Phaeton* ix, The afternoon is wearing on apace. **1879** MEREDITH *Egoist* xlix, The night wore through.

c. *to wear on*, of an action or activity: To be prolonged or continued.

1886 R. C. TEMPLE in *Folk-Lore Jrnl.* IV. 193 What follows is meant to be merely the expression of my ideas for the time being, subject to modification as the discussion wears on.

20. a. To pass gradually *into* (a condition, etc.).

1555 WATREMAN *Fardle Facions* I. v. 68 Estiemed but a villaine, vntill with his forwardnes and wel doyng, he could weare into estimacion again. **1805** FOSTER *Ess.* II. vi. 205 The mind should not be allowed, if I may so express it, to wear into a conclusion, by a slow imperceptible inclination.

b. *trans.* To bring (a person) gradually *into* (a habit or disposition). Also to instil (a view or opinion) gradually *into* the mind.

1690 LOCKE *Hum. Und.* II. xxi. §69 Trials..by Repetitions wear us into a liking of what possibly, in the first Essay, displeas'd us. **1712** ADDISON *Spect.* No. 409 ⁋8 A Man who has any Relish for fine Writing..naturally wears himself into the same manner of Speaking and Thinking. **1871** MORLEY *Crit. Misc., Carlyle* 225 Mr. Carlyle has done much to wear this just and austere view into the minds of his generation.

VI. With reference to movement in space.

21. a. *intr.* To go, proceed, advance; with adv. or advb. phr. indicating the direction. Usually of a slow or gradual movement. Chiefly *Sc.*

c **1470** HENRY *Wallace* x. 355 Byschop Beik com with sic force and slycht, The worthy Scottis weryt fer on bak. **1581** A. HALL *Iliad* I. 7 Pallas away she weares, She leaues the Greekes, to Gods aloft in Heauen she repaires. **1768** ROSS *Helenore* 70, I think I see't my sell, we'll wear in by, Gin we get there. **1821** CLARE *Vill. Minstrel* I. 210 [The bee] wearing home on heavy wing. **1821** JOANNA BAILLIE *Metr. Leg., Wallace* xxxiv, And mazy waters, slyly seen, Glancing thro' shades of Alder green, Wore eastward from the sight to distance grey. *Ibid., Malcolm's Heir* xxix, Faint, doleful music struck his ear, As if waked from the hollow ground. And loud and louder still it grew, And upward still it wore. **1876** BLACK *Madcap Violet* xxi, The sun was wearing round to the west.

b. quasi-*trans.* To move over (a space or distance). *poet.*

1596 SPENSER *F.Q.* IV. ix. 19 Thus many miles they two together wore. **1623** J. TAYLOR (Water P.) *Discov. by Sea* A 8 b, Thus we our weary Pilgrimage did weare.

†**22.** *trans.* To cause to fly or flutter *out*. *Sc. Obs.*

c **1480** HENRYSON *Test. Cress.* 165 His widderit weid fra him the wind out woir.

23. *Sc.* To conduct (sheep or cattle) gradually to the fold or other inclosure. Also with *in*, *up*.

a **1724** *The Ew-Bughts, Marion* 2 in Ramsay *Tea-t. Misc.*, Will ye gae to the ew-bughts, Marion, And wear in the sheip wi' mee? **1725** RAMSAY *Gentle Sheph.* I. i, [She] bade me hound my dog, To wear up three waff ewes stray'd on the bog. **1767** in R. S. Craig & A. Laing *Hawick Tradition* (1898) 246 He..thereby wore in the sheep and nolt..so that they could not get to the Common. *Ibid.* 247 Weiring his sheep and nolt from the Common. **1790** A. WILSON *Poems, Sheph. Dream*, She..wore them homewards to the fold. **1827** *Ann. Reg., Chron.* 48/1 Some [shepherds] perished in wearing their flocks from the weather-side of the hills. **1828** W. McDOWALL *Poems* 23 An' my auld dog's nae worth a doit He winna wear the sheep. **1912** A. MCCORMICK *Words fr. Wild-wood* iii. 47 Or it may be the bark of a dog or the voice of a shepherd as they 'wear' the sheep down the mountain sides to the rees for the clipping.

wear (wɛə(r)), *v.*² *Naut.* Pa. t. and pa. pple. **wore** (wɔə(r)). Forms: 7 **weare, warre, wayer, werr, 7–9 ware, 7– wear.** *Pa. t.* 8–9 **wared, 7– wore.** *Pa. pple.* 9 **weared, 8–9 wore.** [Of obscure origin; in sense it coincides with VEER *v.*² 2, but the early forms seem to forbid the supposition of connexion with that verb unless they are due to association with WEAR *v.*¹]

1. *intr.* Of a ship: To come round on the other tack by turning the head away from the wind. Often with *round.* Opposed to *tack.*

1614 GORGES *Lucan* v. 200 To guide the helme the maister dreads: To port, to weare, or serue the seas, The labouring ship he cannot ease. **1626** CAPT. J. SMITH *Accid. Yng. Seamen* 28 The ship will not wayer. **1627** —— *Sea Gram.* ix. 37 Touch the wind, and warre no more. **1669** STURMY *Mariner's Mag.* I. ii. 18 Werr no more. **1697** *Lond. Gaz.* No. 3318/3 They both wore round and Attackt us on the Starboard-side. **1761** *Brit. Mag.* II. 535 The Bellona was made to ware round by means of her studding-sails. **1795** NELSON in Nicolas *Disp.* (1845) II. 14, I saw the Sans Culotte, who had before wore with many of the Enemy's Ships, under our lee bow. **1840** R. H. DANA *Bef. Mast* xi. 25 We wore round and stood off again. **1865** W. G. PALGRAVE *Arabia* II. 203 Wearing slowly up with a side wind we anchored a little after sunset. **1880** *Times* 25 Dec. 7/4 The ship sails well,..stays quickly and surely; also wears well.

2. *trans.* To put (a ship) about, bringing her stern to windward.

1719 DE FOE *Crusoe* II. (Globe) 519 We..war'd the Ship again, and brought our Quarter to bear upon them. **1726** SHELVOCKE *Voy. round World* 261 They..wore ship, and hauled close on a wind to the westward. **1797** NELSON in Duncan *Life* (1806) 40, I ordered the ship to be wore. **1820** SCORESBY *Acc. Arctic Regions* II. 374 The ship was instantly 'weared'. *Ibid.* 440 When we attempted to ware the ship.. she refused to turn round. **1840** R. H. DANA *Bef. Mast* x. 23 When the watch came up, we wore ship, and stood on the other tack. **1904** *Times* 22 Mar. 9/5 The Mona continued to run before the wind, her crew having seemingly been unable to wear her.

†**wear**, *v.*³ *north. dial. Obs.* [Of uncertain origin.] *trans.* To cool.

1674 RAY *N.C. Words*, To Wear the pot, to cool it. *a* **1743** JOSIAH RELPH *Misc. Poems* (1747) 1 Thur callar blasts may wear the boilen sweat: But my het bluid, my heart aw' in a bruil, Nor callar blasts can wear, nor drops can cuil.

wear: see WEIR. Also obs. f. WARE *sb.*¹, *a.*, *v.*²

weara'bility. [f. WEARABLE *a.* + -ITY.] The capability of being worn or of enduring wear; suitability for wear; durability.

1927 *Daily Express* 5 Sept. 5/2 A series of distinctive models to demonstrate individuality with wearability. **1958** *Vogue* Dec. 108 This is the sweater you must have this autumn for its soft lines, its beautiful wearability. **1966** *Chem. & Engin. News* 19 Dec. 13/2 Corfam sells in the U.K. for about the same as top-quality shoe leather, with which Du Pont compares its product for wearability under flexing and for 'breathability'. **1981** *Observer* (Colour Suppl.) 12 Apr. 75 (Advt.), A 100% cotton shirt with all the comfort and wearability men associate with cotton.

wearable ('wɛərəb(ə)l), *a.* and *sb.* [f. WEAR *v.*¹ + -ABLE.]

A. *adj.* Capable of being worn; fit or suitable to be worn.

1590 SIR J. SMYTHE *Disc. Weapons* 14 He..did encrease his numbers of Mosquettiers, the blowes of the bullets of which, no armours wearable can resist. **1650** HOWELL *Giraffi's Rev. Naples* I. 15 Oil, Cheese, Silk, and all other either edible, or wearable commodities. **1801** LADY SARAH LENNOX *Lett.* (1901) II. 151, I assure you a poplin is not weareable in these days. **1842** R. OASTLER *Fleet Papers* II. 26 It..will not weave into wearable cloths. **1853** G. J. CAYLEY *Las Alforjas* I. 105 By the time I had made and smoked a cigarette, the powerful sun of January had dried the sock to a wearable state. **1882** MISS BRADDON *Mt. Royal* II. ix. 180 The only shop in London at which wearable gloves could be bought. **1896** J. L. ALLEN *Summer in Arcady* iii. 11 The thousand..things, eatable, wearable, or otherwise usable that may be sent to and fro between friendly households.

B. *sb.* A wearable commodity, an article of clothing. Chiefly in *plural.*

1711 *Lond. Gaz.* No. 4817/7 Gloves, Buttons, Wearables. *c* **1720** *Lett. fr. Mist's Jrnl.* (1722) I. 215, I had..provided her handsome Lodgings..and, for her Wearables, rich Sattins, Gold Watch, and a hundred other Trinkets. **1726** BERKELEY *Let.* Wks. 1871 IV. 137 Whether a minor be not chargeable for eatables and wearables supplied on the credit of another. **1818** SCOTT *Hrt. Midl.* xli, He..moved off with Mrs. Dutton's wearables and deposited the trunk containing them safely in the boat. **1849** C. BRONTE *Shirley* xxiv, Let a woman ask me to give her an edible or a wearable ..I can, at least, understand the demand. **1859** LEVER *Dav. Dunn* xlvi, Drawers were crammed with his wearables.

weard, obs. form of WEIRD *sb.*

weare, obs. form of WAR, WEIR.

wearer ('wɛərə(r)). [f. WEAR *v.*¹ + -ER¹.]

1. One who wears or carries on his person (a garment, ornament, etc.). Also *transf.* and *fig.*

1402 *Pol. Poems* (Rolls) II. 69 But if my cloth be over presciouse, Jakke, blame the werer. *c* **1449** PECOCK *Repr.* I. xvi. 88 Wereers of pilious. *c* **1460** *Towneley Myst.* xxviii. 333 Mi gyrdill gay and purs of sylk..whils I am werere of swylke, the longere mercy may I call. **1495** *Act 11 Hen. VII*, c. 27 To the great damage losse and disceite of the Kingis true subgettis biers and werers of such fustian. **1596** SHAKS. *Merch. V.* II. ix. 43 O..that cleare honour Were purchast by the merrit of the wearer. **1606** —— *Ant. & Cl.* II. ii. 7 By Iupiter, Were I the wearer of Anthonio's Beard, I would not shaue't to day. *a* **1633** G. HERBERT *Outlandish Prov.* (1640) 491 The wearer knowes, where the shoe wrings. **1667** MILTON *P.L.* III. 490 Then might ye see Cowles, Hoods and Habits with thir wearers tost And flutterd into Raggs. **1725** POPE *Odyss.* VIII. 440 This sword..Whose ivory sheath inwrought with curious pride, Adds graceful terror to the wearer's side. **1815** W. H. IRELAND *Scribbleomania* 104 Half of the wearers of buskin and sock. **1849** C. BRONTE *Shirley* vi, Her style of dress announced taste in the wearer. **1860** TROLLOPE *Castle Richmond* xiii, There are great red swollen noses, very disagreeable both to the wearer and his acquaintances. **1869** TOZER *Highl. Turkey* II. 264 Caps, cloaks, and rings, which render the wearer invisible. **1878** J. DAVIDSON *Inverurie* i. 14 What wearers of flesh and blood dwelt then in the sheltered dell?

b. said of a lower animal.

1876 E. PARFITT in *Rep. & Trans. Devonsh. Assoc.* VIII. 247 This brilliancy of colouring [of some birds] would seem ..to compensate the wearers for the melodious voice..of their more sober-painted relatives.

2. That which wears away, consumes or diminishes by attrition.

1773 JOHNSON (ed. 4). (But his example belongs to sense 1.) Hence in later Dicts.

weariable ('wɪərɪəb(ə)l), *a.* [f. WEARY *v.* + -ABLE.] Capable of being wearied.

1775 ASH, *Unweariable*, not weariable. **1856** RUSKIN *Mod. Paint.* III. IV. x. §14 The imagination is eminently a weariable faculty, eminently delicate, and incapable of bearing fatigue. **1904** *Contemp. Rev.* Oct. 546 Lord Leighton..could judge..with the minimum of æsthetic strain; while most critics..have to depend..on weariable taste.

Hence **'weariableness.**

1904 *Contemp. Rev.* Oct. 540 The sensitiveness, the weariableness of the æsthetic faculties..causes, in the Art-world, the demand for novelty to outrun the legitimate supply.

wearie, obs. form of WORRY *v.*

wearied ('wɪərɪd), *ppl. a.* [f. WEARY *v.* + -ED¹.] (Excessively) fatigued; tired out. Also with *out.* Of a look, sigh: Expressive of or indicating weariness.

1538 ELYOT *Dict.*, *Exercitus*, exercised, vsed in labour, weried, hardned. **1560** DAUS tr. *Sleidane's Comm.* 419 b, Being so faint and weried with traveling. **1577** GRANGE *Golden Aphrod.* D iij, Whilest he thought to haue rested his weried limmes in a bedde of securitye. **1594** SHAKS. *Rich. III*, IV. iv. 112 Now thy proud Necke, beares halfe my burthen'd yoke, From which, euen heere I slip my wearied head. **1628** MAY *Virg. Georg.* II. 63 And time it is to ease our wearyed horse. *a* **1646** Z. BOYD in *Zion's Flowers* (1855) App. 17 My wearied soul he doth restore. **1667** MILTON *P.L.* I. 320 Or have ye chos'n this place After the toyl of Battel to repose Your wearied vertue. **1746** FRANCIS tr. *Hor., Sat.* I. v. 28 Till wearied passenger retires to rest. **1820** SCOTT *Monast.* xvii, Why art thou so well pleased that the morning should call thee up to daily toil, and the evening again lay thee down a wearied-out wretch? **1823** —— *Quentin D.* xxxvi, The wearied and wounded..were calling in vain for shelter and refreshment. **1840** DICKENS *Old C. Shop* xlviii, Wearing the depressed and wearied look of one who [etc.]. **1841** S. WARREN *Ten Thou.* I. viii, He stretches his wearied limbs to their uttermost. **1872** TENNYSON *Gareth & Lyn.* 1234 Yet not less I felt Thy manhood thro' that wearied lance of thine. **1888** BLACK *In Far Lochaber* xxiii, She turned away with a wearied sigh.

Comb. **1849** C. BRONTE *Shirley* xi, She came back..pale and wearied-looking.

Hence **'weariedly** *adv.*, **'weariedness.**

a **1617** BAYNE *Lect.* (1634) 308 The more wearied nesse we feele, the more we may be bold this way. **1681** RYCAUT tr. *Gracian's Critick* 81 Having..weariedly travelled over much ground, they met no Man. *Ibid.* 161 When the other Sences weariedly retire to their repose,..these careful Centinels of the Soul, attend their guards. **1688** SANDILANDS *Salut. Endeared Love* 30 Which brings a weariedness, faintness, and benummedness over them. **1815** SCOTT *Guy*

M. xlvi, The poor Dominie..weariedly plodded his way towards Woodbourne. **1865** Mrs. Newby *Comm. Sense* xlvi. II. 247 ‘What a mother!’ exclaimed Mrs. Sowerby, weariedly. **1872** Tennyson *Last Tourn.* 156 Sighing weariedly. **1886** *Daily News* 12 Oct. 3/1 Weariedly trudging home.

wearier (ˈwɪərɪə(r)). *rare*. [f. weary *v.* + -er^{1}.] One who wearies or fatigues.

1765 J. Brown *Chr. Jrnl., Winter Day* 253 To be..a wearier of God with iniquity, a blasphemer [etc.].

weariful (ˈwɪərɪfʊl), *a.* [f. weary *v.* + -ful.]

1. That causes weariness; that tires one's endurance or patience.

c **1454** Pecock *Folewer* 15 Maters..which ellis schulde haue be to hem ouyr hard and ouer weriful to be vndirstonde. **1482** *Monk of Evesham* (Arb.) 82 Yef y schulde ..declare synglerly the peynys and tormentys of euery syngler cryme..hit wulde be ouer teduse and weriful to the redder therof. **1591** R. Turnbull *St. James* 51 That we.. with inuincible fortitude and pacience, may finish our wearifull pilgrimage in his feare, religion and seruice. *a* **1825** Forby *Voc. E. Anglia*, *Weariful*, tiresome; giving exercise to patience. Ex. ‘I have had a weariful bout of it.’ **1826** Galt *Last of Lairds* i. 8 O that wearyfu' jaunt to Embro' to see the King! **1846** G. S. Faber *Lett. Tractar. Secess.* 194 So proceeds the Professor through ten weariful pages. **1849** C. Bronte *Shirley* vi, This foreign style of darning..was done stitch by stitch, so as exactly to imitate the fabric of the stocking itself; a wearifu' process. **1886** Symonds *Renaiss. It., Cath. React.* (1898) VII. xiii. 210 Visions of dreary wanderings through weariful saloons. **1912** W. S. Blunt *Land War in Ireland* ix. 339 Twenty weariful Irish miles.

b. of a person. *Sc.*

a **1700** *Gaberlunzie-Man* vii, The weirifou' Gaberlunzie-man. **1882** Stevenson *Fam. Stud.* (1888) 299 She was a religious hypochondriac, a very weariful woman.

c. of the weather. Chiefly *Sc.*

1872 J. Payne *Songs of Life & Death* 224 Wearyful winter is gone at last. **1874** R. Tyrwhitt *Sketch. Club* 223 Spite of gray winter and weariful weather. **1894** A. Reid *Sangs o' the Heatherland* 48 The wearifu' snaw, O, the wearifu' snaw!

2. Full of weariness; utterly fatigued. Of a person: Languid or affecting languor. Of a look, sigh, smile: Exhibiting or expressing weariness.

1862 Matilda B. Edwards *John & I* xxiv. (1876) 323 He lay still for some time with a weariful smile upon his lips. **1880** G. Macdonald *Diary Old Soul* Feb. 25, And the thought-spirit, weariful and wan,..Sinks moveless. **1880** Jefferies *Greene Ferne Farm* 209 The wearyful women came homeward from the gleaning. **1885** Jean Ingelow *Sleep of Sigismund* 8 His weird is on him to grope in the dark with endless Weariful feet for a goal that shifteth still. **1891** Meredith *One of our Conq.* xxviii, Colney cast a weariful look backward. **1899** Crockett *Kit Kennedy* 9 Lilias sighed the long, weariful sigh of hope deferred.

Hence ˈ**wearifully** *adv.*, ˈ**wearifulness**.

1838 *Lett. fr. Madras* (1843) 226, I quite dread to hear the subject mentioned, for fear of a quarrel, besides the wearifulness. **1885** Meredith *Diana* iv, There was a strange interjection, as to the wearifulness of constantly wandering. **1888** Black *In Far Lochaber* xxiii, The long night passed, slowly and wearifully. **1907** C. G. Harper *Rural Nooks* 14 The blurred lights of the streets and shops going weirdly and wearifully by.

ˈ**wearihood.** *nonce-wd.* [-hood.] The condition of being weary.

1883 *Academy* 27 Oct. 278/1 After years of doubt and deception and the wearihood of waiting, the Wanderer at last returns.

weariless (ˈwɪərɪlɪs), *a.* [f. weary *v.* + -less.] That does not weary or become weary.

c **1430** Lydg. *Min. Poems* (Percy Soc.) 75 Weryles I walke ay in trouble and travaile, Ever travilyng witheout werynes. **1608** Hieron *Defence* ii. 184 Will ever any man but a wearylesse wrangler..affirme and stand to it, that wisdome is taken diversely here. **1799** Sheridan *Pizarro* i. i, With weariless remonstrance he sued to win me from my purpose. **1813** Hogg *Queen's Wake* i. (1814) 51 How came yon white doves from the window to fly, And hover on weariless wing to the sky? **1879** Lowell *Mem. Poems, To W. L. Garrison* 42 O small beginnings, ye are great and strong, Based on a faithful heart and weariless brain! **1886** Blackmore *Springhaven* ix, The weariless tide came up and lifted the bedded keel. **1906** *Times Lit. Suppl.* 30 Nov. 402/2 A sturdy Dissenter, a weariless promoter of Godliness.

Hence ˈ**wearilessly** *adv.*

1791 Collinson *Hist. Somerset* 610 A headland..where a huge disjointed rock..is wearilessly combated by the waves. **1893** F. Adams *New Egypt* 192 He opposed openly and wearilessly the ruinous policy of his master.

wearily (ˈwɪərɪlɪ), *adv.* [f. weary *a.* + -ly^{2}.] In a weary manner; with weariness.

1481 Caxton *Godfrey* clxxxv. 271 Theyr enemyes wexed wery and weryly and slowly defended them. **1523** Berners *Froiss.* clxxxvi. (1812) I. 221 And so they went weryly by heapes. **1568** Grafton *Chron.* II. 298 They perceaued a flocke of men of armes comming together right werily. **1610** Shaks. *Temp.* iii. i. 32 *Mir.* You looke wearily. **18..** Moore ‘*Merrily every Bosom*’ ii, Wearily every bosom pineth. **1859** Tennyson *Marr. Geraint* 254 [He] down the long street riding wearily, Found every hostel full. **1866** Geo. Eliot *Felix Holt* i, A heavy moth floated by, and, when it settled, seemed to fall wearily. **1891** Farrar *Darkn. & Dawn* lix, ‘What is heaven?’ asked Poppæa, wearily.

weariness (ˈwɪərɪnɪs). [f. weary *a.* + -ness.]

1. Weary condition; extreme tiredness or fatigue resulting from exertion, continued endurance of pain, or want of sleep.

c **900** *Bæda's Hist.* iii. ix. (1890) 178 [þæt hors] þy ȝewunelican þeawe horsa æfter weriȝnesse ongon wealwian. *c* **1200** *Trin. Coll. Hom.* 35 [Adam] ne þurte naure þolen hunger ne þurst,..ne werinesse, ne elde, ne unhelðe, ne deð. **1297** R. Glouc. (Rolls) 4920 +34 He lay muchedel of þe nyȝt in wo & in sorwe,..So þat aslep atte laste vor werynysse hym nome. *c* **1380** Wyclif *Sel. Wks.* III. 35 Upberynge us in oure werynes. *c* **1450** *Merlin* ii. 39 Than the white [dragon] leide hym down to reste for werynesse. **1500–20** Dunbar *Poems* xxxv. 9 For weirines on me ane slummer soft Come with ane dremyng. **1584** Cogan *Haven Health* i. 11 First I shall declare what remedie is to be vsed against wearinesse which commeth by immoderate labour. **1611** Shaks. *Cymb.* iii. vi. 33 Wearinesse Can snore vpon the Flint, when restie Sloth Findes the Downe-pillow hard. **1649** J. Taylor (Water P.) *Wandering to see West* 8 At last, wearinesse and watching, began to inforce sleep upon me. **1707** Floyer *Physic. Pulse-Watch* 86 If the Exercise be Immoderate with great Weariness, the Spirits and Heat are very much evaporated. **1797** Coleridge *Christabel* i. 74, I scarce can speak for weariness. **1856** Sir B. Brodie *Psychol. Inq.* I. iv. 136 The muscles..may be for a long time in a state of involuntary contraction..without weariness being induced.

2. Tedium or distaste induced by monotonous or uncongenial conditions or occupations; tiredness *of* a course of action, a state of things, a person or thing. †Also *rarely* const. *to* with inf.

1526 *Pilgr. Perf.* (W. de W. 1531) 129 b, Therof foloweth ..tedyousnes in all goostly exercyse, & werynes of holy company. **1560** Daus tr. *Sleidane's Comm.* 376 A certeyne wearynes, and impacience of long imprisonment. **1625** Bacon *Ess., Death* (Arb.) 387 A man would die, though he were neither valiant, nor miserable, only vpon a wearinesse to doe the same thing, so oft ouer and ouer. **1643** R. Baker *Chron.* (1653) 9 Osred, whose wife Cutburga, out of a loathing wearinesse of wedlock, sued out a divorce from her husband. **1853** Dickens *Bleak Ho.* xii, Weariness of soul lies before her, as it lies behind. **1858** Froude *Hist. Eng.* IV. xviii. 37 The struggle..terminated, through weariness of enduring and inflicting suffering. **1885** *Manch. Exam.* 15 May 5/6 Sheer weariness of things which are to them common and familiar.

3. Something that wearies.

1560 Bible (Geneva) *Eccl.* xii. 12 There is none end in making manie bokes: and muche reading is a wearines of the flesh. **1845** Froude *Nemesis of Faith* (1849) 109 Long devotions are a weariness to healthy children. **1856** Miss Yonge *Daisy Chain* ii. x, The children were dull, and she began to believe she was doing no good—it was all a weariness. **1905** R. Bagot *Passport* x. 90 To be compelled by fashion to sit down to a meal at the pleasantest hour in all the twenty-four is a weariness to the flesh and a vexation to the spirit.

wearing (ˈwɛərɪŋ), *vbl. sb.*^{1} [f. wear *v.*^{1} + -ing^{1}.]

†**1.** The fact or habit of being clothed in a particular way; kind or style of clothing; also *concr.* what a person wears or might wear. *Obs.*

a **1225** *Ancr. R.* 8 Gif heo hit ne bihat nout heo hit mai don þauh, & leten hwon heo wel wule, alse of mete & of drunch, fleschs forgon oþer visch,..of weriunge, of liggunge, of vres, of beoden. *Ibid.* 368 Mid festen, mid wechchen, mid disciplines, mid herd weriunge. **1340** Hampole *Pr. Consc.* 1521 Of bathe þer worldes gret outrage we se..In worldis havyng and beryng, In vayn apparail and in weryng. *c* **1400** *Brut* ccxx. (1906) 261 [He] disgisede him wiþ wonder ryche cloþes oute of al maner resoun boþe of shaping and of wering. **1526** *Pilgr. Perf.* (W. de W. 1531) 137 Pamperyng or ouer-moche cherysshyng of our bodyes by soft lyenge, soft weryng, or moche fedyng. **1600** Holland *Pliny* viii. xlviii. I. 228 The waved water chamelot, was from the beginning esteemed the richest and bravest wearing. **1605** Shaks. *Oth.* iv. iii. 16 Giue me my nightly wearing, and adieu. *a* **1613** Overbury *Wife, Characters, Milkmaid* (1618) I 4 b, For though she be not arraied in the spoile of the Silke-worme, she is deckt in innocence, a far better wearing. **1621** Lady M. Wroth *Urania* 510 Hee perswaded his companion to put on his Wast-coate, and night-wearing, and walk into the garden. **1629** Gaule *Holy Madn.* 134 Another shape out, and another trim up their wearings. **1654** Gayton *Pleas. Notes* ii. iv. 48 He shifted his Velvet Truncks, which was his customary wearing. **1690** Locke *Govt.* i. i, Chains are but an ill wearing, how much Care soever hath been taken to file and polish them.

b. *pl.* (See quot.)

1837 *Patent* 27 Nov. in *Civil Engin. & Arch. Jrnl.* I. 54/2 Certain Improvements for producing Ornamental Lace or Wearings.

2. The action of carrying on the body (an article of dress, an ornament, or the like). †*of one's wearing*: forming part of one's wardrobe (*obs.*). Also *fig.*

13.. *E.E. Allit. P.* B. 1123 For ho schynes so schyr þat is of schap rounde,..& wax euer in þe worlde in weryng so olde, ȝet þe perle payres not whyle ho in pyese lasttes. **1426** *E.E. Wills* (1882) 71, I woll þat..my preest haue..a gowne of my weryng. *a* **1450** *Knt. de la Tour* xxvii. 39 Seint Bernarde,..for his holy lyuing, and of weringe of the heyre, ..was chose to be abbot of that place. **1482** *Cely Papers* (Camden) 103 My mother has gewyn to Myhellz wyfe a cremsyn goune of hyr wheryng. **1581** Pettie *Guazzo's Civ. Conv.* i. (1586) A 3 b, Such rare iewels are well worth the wearing. **1607** Shaks. *Timon* v. i. 146 Speciall Dignities, which vacant lye For thy best vse and wearing. **1704** Swift *T. Tub* ii. 54 With good wearing, they will last you fresh and sound as long as you live. **1711** Steele *Spect.* No. 43 ⁋10 But a Fool of a colder Constitution would have..made Buff of his Skin, for the Wearing of the Conqueror. **1719** De Foe *Crusoe* ii. (Globe) 421, I desir'd that they might all take an equal Quantity of the Goods that were for wearing. **1818** Scott *Br. Lamm.* xxx, He rushed into the room with a willow branch in his hand, which he told her had arrived that instant from Germany for her special wearing. **1849** Macaulay *Hist. Eng.* vii. II. 182 The opposition, it seemed, wished..to make the crown of England not worth the wearing.

b. *attrib.* in **wearing apparel, wearing gear** (*arch.*), articles of clothing collectively. †Formerly also in many other collocations with the senses ‘suitable or intended for wearing’, as ***wearing clothes, garments, gown, jewels, linen, rapier***.

Also † **wearing plate**, plate in actual household use (cf. wear *v.*^{1} 2 b).

1418 *E. E. Wills* (1882) 32 Myne owne werynge clothes. **1498** in *Somerset Med. Wills* (1901) 365 All my weryng kercheff evenly to be departed betwene her and..Agnes Huyssh. **1542** Udall *Erasm. Apoph.* 204 He would of a custome diligently serche his robes, and al his wearyng geare, & saie [etc.]. **1575** Fleming *Virg. Bucol.* viii. 26 These wearing geere somtimes to me that faithles fellowe lefte. **1576** —— *Panopl. Epist.* 354 The sheepe..yeeldeth her woll, which is wouen and wrought to make vs wearing garmentes. **1593** Shaks. *2 Hen. VI*, i. iii. 88 The very trayne of her worst wearing Gowne, Was better worth then all my Fathers Lands. **1616** *MS. Liber Depos. Archd. Colcestr.* 94 His wife's wearing lynnen. **1617** in W. F. Shaw *Mem. Eastry* (1870) 227 Item all her weareinge apparell, xvij^{li}. **1620** *Inv.* in *Essex Rev.* (1907) XVI. 206 His purs and waringe parell, ij^{li}. **1661** in W. M. Sargent *Maine Wills* (1887) 3, I giue vnto Anthony Littlefejld all my weareing Cloaths. **1683** in *J. Hull's Diaries* (1857) 260 The s^{d} Judith Hull [the widow] shall have and enjoy out of the personal estate..one halfe part of all the wearing plate. **1685** in *Verney Mem.* (1907) II. 421 Bring along with you..yr Best Waring Things. **1688** Holme *Armoury* iv. xii. (Roxb.) 487/1 His owne weareing rapier carried by his servant. **1721** De Foe *Mem. Cavalier* (1840) 72 Some wearing linen. **1740** C'tess Hartford *Corr.* (1805) II. 29 Her wearing jewels are the finest and most various of any sovereign's now living. **1835** Dickens *Sk. Boz, Pawnbroker's Shop*, Wearing apparel of every description. **1900** H. Sutcliffe *Shameless Wayne* xiv, With blood on his wearing-gear and sorrow on his face.

3. The condition or process of being continuously in wear or use. Chiefly in phrases with prep., as ***in* (†*the*) *wearing*, (*the*) *worse for* (†*the*) *wearing***.

1546 J. Heywood *Prov.* (1867) 44 All thyng is the woors for the wearyng. **1581** Pettie *Guazzo's Civ. Conv.* i. (1586) 11 That the..Boote was made of such leather as would shrinke in the wearing. **1613** J. May *Decl. Estate of Cloth* 38 After a moneths wearing, it will looke like a souldiers coat which hath line sixe moneths out of garrison. **1697** Collier *Ess. Mor. Subj.* ii. (1703) 69 Friendship is one of those few things which are the better for the wearing. **1706** E. Ward *Wooden World Diss.* (1708) 74 His hardest Tools are the worse for Wearing. **1711** *Dissenting Teachers Addr. agst. Bill for building 50 New Churches* 18 A Pulpit little worse for wearing to dispose off. **1724** Ramsay *Widow* 10 The Widow she's youthfu', and never ae Hair The war of the wearing.

4. The action of wasting, damaging, or exhausting, or the process of being wasted, by continuous use or exposure. Also with *away*, *down*, *out*.

1473 *Rental Bk. Cupar-Angus* (1879) I. 177 For the defens of the said land for the weryng awa of watter als far as thar bundys rekys. **1500–20** Dunbar *Poems* lxiii. 31 Haill in everie circumstance, In forme, in mater, and substance, But wering, or consumptioun. **1523** *Act 14 & 15 Hen. VIII* c. 6 §2 Many other Comon wayes..be so depe and noyous by wearyng and Course of Water and other occasions, that [etc.]. **1542** Udall *Erasm. Apoph.* 17 b, To liuing a single lif is annexed..vtter decaiyng and wearyng out of the name. **1597** Shaks. *2 Hen. IV*, v. i. 89, I will deuise matter enough out of this Shallow, to keepe Prince Harry in continuall Laughter, the wearing out of sixe Fashions (which is foure Tearmes). **1711** Addison *Spect.* No. 10 ⁋3 Such Writings as tend to the wearing out of Ignorance, Passion, and Prejudice. **1802** Playfair *Illustr. Huttonian Theory* 294 The thinnest part of that rock..has been perfectly defended by them from every sort of wearing and decay. **1853** Mrs. Gaskell *Ruth* xxix, The final and unmendable wearing-out of the parlour carpet, which there was no spare money to replace. **1855** W. H. Barlow in *Phil. Trans.* CXLV. 226 This arose from a slight wearing of the working parts of the measuring instrument. **1877** Huxley *Physiogr.* ix. 149 The great wearing down of land which must be effected by rain and rivers. **1883** *Science* II. 75/2 The wearing-away of the falls would injure navigation above. **1908** *Animal Managem.* (War Office) 183 This wearing out of a tired horse by a tired man.

b. *concr.* in *pl.* Worn places, marks of wear.

1885 Lock *Workshop Rec.* Ser. iv. 313/1 If the pallets are worn, the wearings must be filed out.

c. Wasting from disease: in quot. with *away*. (? *Obs.*) Hence *dial.* a wasting illness, consumption.

1654 Sir A. Johnston (Ld. Wariston) *Diary* (S.H.S.) II. 240 Hearing of my Lord Craighall his fayling and wearyng away, I went to him. **1824** Carr *Craven Gloss.*, *Wearing*, consumption. **1876** *Mr. Gray & his Neighbours* I. 116, I do believe one on 'em is going into a wearin'.

d. Wearying or exhausting effect.

1845 Mrs. S. C. Hall *Whiteboy* I. ix. 140 The woe and wearing of weeks [of sickness] sobered and softened her.

†**5.** Manner in which a cloth, etc. wears (well or badly); degree of resistance to the effects of wear. Also *fig.*, degree in which a person continues to merit approval; also, degree of resistance to the effects of time. *Obs. rare.*

1549 Latimer *2nd Serm. bef. Edw. VI* (Arb.) 59 Salomon sayed to hym [*sc.* Adonias]: Gette the into thy house, bilyke he meante to warde, and ther to se hys wearynge, as if he shoulde saye, shewe thyselfe wythoute gall of ambition, to be a quiet subiecte, and I wyll pardon the for thys tyme. But I wyll se the wearynge of the. **1566** A. Edwards in Hakluyt *Voy.* (1599) I. 358 They talke much of London clothes, and they that know the wearing, are desirous of them before the cloth of the womens making, for they find it nothing durable. **1740** Cibber *Apol.* 177 In the Wearing of her Person, she was particularly fortunate; her Figure was always improving, to her Thirty-sixth Year.

6. Passing, elapsing (of a period of time). *rare.*

1876 Morris *Sigurd* i. 30 Now again in a half month's wearing goes Signy into the wild. **1895** *Funk's Stand. Dict.*,

Wearing..3. Diminution or passing away; as, the wearing of the season. **1905** A. T. Sheppard *Red Cravat* iii. ii. 238 Before the wearing of a moon, [he] was back again.

'wearing, *vbl. sb.*^{2} *Naut.* [f. WEAR *v.*^{2} + -ING^{1}.] The action of turning a vessel's stern to windward: opposed to *tacking*. Also *attrib.*

1769 Falconer *Dict. Marine* (1780), *Wearing*. See the article *Veering*. **1840** R. H. Dana *Bef. Mast* xxiii, A regular tacking and wearing bill was made out.

wearing ('wɛərɪŋ), *ppl. a.* [f. WEAR *v.*^{1} + -ING^{2}.]

1. Exhausting, tiring; enfeebling by continued strain or irritation. Also ***wearing-out***.

1811 Lady Granville *Lett.* (1894) I. 20, I have been prevented writing by most wearing nervous headaches. **1815** Chalmers in Hanna *Life* (1851) II. 18 A heartless, hard driving, distracting, and wearing out life among the bustle of unministerial work. **1824** Susan Ferrier *Inher.* xl, She..remarked, what a wearing-out thing it [reading aloud] was for the reader. **1837** Carlyle *New Lett.* (1904) I. 55 My toil is great; but it is not a wearing toil, as that of writing is. **1859** J. Bright *Sp. India* 1 Aug. (1876) 50 This wearing exasperating question of how money is to be got. **1865** Dickens *Mut. Fr.* iii. xvi, You see the occupations of the day are sometimes a little wearing. **1876** Hardy *Ethelberta* xx, She began to know how wearing were miserable days, and how much more wearing were miserable nights. **1887** *Murray's Mag.* Aug. 267 It was in many respects a wearing life.

2. That gradually destroys, diminishes, or impairs by continued use or attrition.

1859 R. Hunt *Guide Mus. Pract. Geol.* (ed. 2) 292 The specimens exhibited show the wearing and grinding force of the modern glaciers. **1876** Geo. Eliot *Deronda* xxxv, This cloister was built of harder stone than the church, and had been in greater safety from the wearing weather. **1903** W. Chrystal *Kingd. Kippen* 146 All the lower ground is covered with sheets of boulder clay, the material resulting from the wearing action of the ice.

3. That is undergoing wear, diminution, or impairment by continued use or attrition. ***wearing course*** (Highway Engin.) (see quot. 1940).

1908 *Animal Managem.* (War Office) 36 The surface [of the tooth] which bites on the food or its fellow in the opposite jaw is the *table*, or *wearing surface*. **1940** *Gloss. Highway Engin. Terms* (*B.S.I.*) 28 *Wearing course*, the layer of material applied to form the carriage-way. **1977** *Bitumen* (Shell Internat. Petroleum Co.) 2/4 The traffic load is carried mainly by the base layer, while the wearing course provides a waterproof non-skid cover which resists traffic wear.

Hence **'wearingly** *adv.*

1870 *Public Opinion* 6 Aug. 170 It is the trivial, every-day suffering..that is most wearingly, if not most keenly, felt.

wearish ('wɪərɪʃ), *a. Obs.* exc. *dial.* Forms: 4 **werische**, 5–6 **werysshe**, **weris(s)he**, **-ysh(e**, **wearysh(e**, **wear-**, **weerishe**, **weerysh**, 6–7 **werish**, **weerish**, 9 *dial.* **warish**, **werrish**, 6– **wearish**. [Late ME. *werische*; of obscure origin. Cf. WERSH *a.* which is prob. a contracted form of this.

There is some resemblance in form and sense to the early mod.Du. *wers*, *wars*, *warsch*, 'contrarius, adversus, malus' (Kilian), mod.Du. *wars*, disgusted, averse, weary of, Du. dial. *warsig*, Fris. *wêrzich* disgusting; but etymological connexion seems improbable.]

1. Destitute of savour, sickly-flavoured, tasteless, insipid; unsalted. Cf. WERSH *a.* 1.

1398 Trevisa *Barth. De P.R.* iv. ix. (Tollem. MS.) Flemme is an humouris kyndely colde and moyste, werische and unsauoury [L. *insipidus*]. *c* **1425** *St. Mary of Oignies* ii. ii. in *Anglia* VIII. 154 As any man..amonge many manere deynte metes wolde forsake an vnsauory and werysshe mete. **1477** Norton *Ordin. Alch.* v. in Ashm. (1652) 74 Also is Weerish tast called Unsavoury. **1530** Palsgr. 328/2 Werysshe as meate is that is nat well tastye, *mal sauouré*. **1531** Tindale *Expos. 1 John* Prol. (1538) 7 b, As the tayste of the sycke maketh wholsome and well seasoned meate bytter, weerysh, and unsauery. **1533** More *Debell. Salem* iv. Wks. 938/1 If the salt waxe ones freshe & werish, wherin shal ani thing be wel seasoned? **1538** Elyot *Dict.*, *Inconditus*..weryshe. **1607** *Barley-Breake* (1877) 28 When Hyems shall vpon them shake his lockes, Their grazing feast will haue a wearish tatch. **1828** Carr *Craven Gloss.*, *Warish*, unsavoury. **1881** *Leic. Gloss.*, *Werrish*,..as applied to drinks, 'small', weak, sickly, insipid.

b. *fig.* Void of relish, insipid, savourless; flat, futile, ineffectual.

1532 Tindale *Expos. Matt.* v–vii. (? 1550) 23 b, All werysh and vnsauerye ceremonies whyche haue lost theyr significations. **1542** Udall *Erasm. Apoph.* Erasm. Pref. *vij b, In expressyng and vttreyng suche saiynges Xenophon seemeth to me somewhat weeryshe [*mihi dilutior uidetur*]. **1548** —— *Erasm. Par. Matt.* v. 10–12 Beeyng ouerwhelmed with weryshe opinions and vayne desyres. *Ibid.* vii. 28, 29 They vsed to brynge furth certaine weryshe constitutions, of wasshyng their handes before meate, [etc.]. *Ibid. Luke* Pref. (∴) iiij b, So werishe and vneffectual was ye vertue of the medicine of Physicke whiche thei brought [*adeo Pharmacum quod adferebant uim habebat dilutam & inefficacem*]. **1549** Coverdale, etc. *Erasm. Par. 1 Cor.* i. 9–20 The rude and wearysh preaching [*sermo rudis et inconditus*]. **1603** Florio *Montaigne* iii. v. 523 Yeelding hir pleasures weerish, and hir amours tastelesse. **1650** H. Brooke *Conserv. Health* 4 A sickly, wearish, and momentany Delight.

2. Of persons and animals, their limbs, etc.: Sickly, feeble, delicate; lean, wizened, shrivelled. Also, of a countenance: Sickly-looking. Cf. WERSH *a.* 2.

1513 More *Rich. III* Wks. (1557) 54/1 Therw^{t} he plucked vp hys doublet sleue to his elbow,..where he shewed a werish withered arme and small. **1566** Drant *Horace, Sat.* ii. v. H iij b, If thou canst spye a wealthie man, that hath a wearyshe chylde, There, shewe thy selfe officious. *a* **1568** Ascham *Scholem.* i. (Arb.) 39 A countenance, not werishe and crabbed, but faire and cumlie. **1569** V. Skinner tr. *Montanus Inquis.* 20 b, A full weake & wearish body [L. *corpore infirmo ac caduco*]. **1577** B. Googe *Heresbach's Husb.* iii. 116 b, If they [the stallions] be to yong, they get but weake and wearish Coltes. *Ibid.* 137 b, A small and a weerysh Sheepe. **1579** Lodge *Def. Plays* 5 That they like good Phisitions should so frame their potions, that they might be appliable to the quesie stomaks of their werish patients. **1594** Nashe *Unfort. Trav.* I 4 b, They haue hid a little weerish leane face vnder a broad French hat. **1596** Spenser *F.Q.* iv. v. 34 A wretched wearish elfe, With hollow eyes and rawbone cheekes forspent. **1600** Surflet *Country Farm* vi. xxii. 784 The deepe red wine which is harsh and rough,..is profitable to comfort the loose & wearish stomacke. **1624** Burton *Anat. Mel.* (ed. 2) Democr. to Rdr. 2 Democritus..was a little wearish [**1621** wearyish] old man, very melancholy by nature. **1633** Ford *Love's Sacr.* v. i, A crooked leg,..a wearish hand, A bloodlesse lip. **1685** Burnet *Life Bp. Bedell* 257 It might often have been easily done, especially upon such a weakly and wearish Body. **1881** *Leic. Gloss.*, *Werrish*, feeble; deficient in stamina; of a delicate constitution. **1888** Doughty *Trav. Arab. Des.* I. v. 148 All the date-eaters are of a certain wearish visage.

b. Comb.: ***wearish-coloured***, sickly-hued, pale.

1548 Thomas *Ital. Gram.*, *Dict.* (1567), *Pallida*, pale, or wearishe coloured.

c. Lacking energy, languid.

1650 H. Brooke *Conserv. Health* 163 A wearish and impotent giving up of the spirits. *a* **1656** Ussher *Ann.* vi. (1658) 328 At the first setting out they seemed to run exceeding well, but after a while, to grow somewhat wearish.

3. Dull-witted, stupid.

1519 Horman *Vulg.* 52 A werisshe [L. *insulsus*] felowe made al this besynes. **1537** in Ellis *Orig. Lett.* Ser. iii. III. 103 My thyncke yt ys butt a weryshe persson to have any such lernyng of prophessye.

4. ? Peevish, cross-grained, crabbed.

a **1586** Sidney *Arcadia* ii. xxvi. §4 (1912) 317 Have any of you children, that be not sometimes cumbersome? Have any of you fathers, that be not sometime weerish? What, shall we ..hate our children, or disobey our fathers?

Hence **'wearishly** *adv.*, languidly, without energy; **'wearishness**, lack of savour.

1398 Trevisa *Barth. De P.R.* xix. lii. (1495) 893 The nynthe sauour hyght werysshenesse and vnsauerynesse. **1542** Udall *Erasm. Apoph.* 106 *marg.*, Beetes is an herbe.. of whose excedyng weryshenesse and vnsauerynesse [etc.]. **1633** Ames *Fresh Suit agst. Ceremonies* Pref. p. xvii, How wearishly & unwillingly goe they to the worke?

wearisome ('wɪərɪsəm), *a.* Forms: 5 **werysom**, 6 **weerysom**, **werisum**, **wearisom**, 7 **wearysome**, 6– **wearisome**. [f. WEARY *v.* and *a.* + -SOME.]

†**1.** Weary; showing signs of weariness. *Obs.*

c **1460** J. Russell *Bk. Nurture* 751 The sotelte a man with sikelle in his hande, In a ryvere of watur stande wrapped in wedes in a werysom wyse. *c* **1475** *Partenay* 4406 Hyt declare and tell shall my wer[y]som gost. **1561** T. Hoby tr. *Castiglione's Courtyer* ii. (1577) K iv b, At banckettes they refreshed their weerysome mindes, in those high discourses and diuine imaginations of theirs. **1632** Lithgow *Trav.* ii. 49 The wearisome creatures of the world declining to their rest. *a* **1656** Ussher *Ann.* vi. (1658) 190 They came, and saw no attendance about him, onely a decrepit and wearisom old man, lying along upon the beach.

2. Causing weariness through monotony, or the continuance of uncongenial circumstances; tedious.

1450–1530 *Myrr. Our Ladye* 55 The remedy hereof [undevotion] ys..to abyde vpon the tretable sayng of theyre seruice, be yt neuer so werysom. **1590** Spenser *F.Q.* ii. xii. 32 This is..The worlds sweet In, from paine and wearisome turmoyle. **1596** Ralegh *Discov. Guiana* 97 It is nowe time to returne towardes the North, and we founde it a wearisome way backe. *a* **1653** Binning *Sinner's Sanct.* xxix. Wks. (1735) 316/2 What is your Life, but a tedious and wearisome Repetition of such brutish Actions which only terminate on the Body? *a* **1699** Temple *Health & Long Life* Wks. 1720 I. 288 All will allow..the several Conditions of Fortune to be all wearysome, dull or disagreeable without good Humour. **1782** Miss Burney *Cecilia* vii. vi, Simplicity uninformed, becomes wearisome. **1822** Lamb *Elia* Ser. ii. *Conf. Drunkard*, A forecast of the wearisome day that lies before me. **1825** Scott *Betrothed* xxii, It was impossible for life to glide away in more wearisome monotony that at the castle of the Garde Doloureuse. **1883** 'Ouida' *Wanda* I. 218 The ceremonies of a court are wearisome to me. **1891** *Speaker* 2 May 533/2 The author might do much better if he would give up this wearisome murder-mongering, and take a fresh subject. **1902** *Spectator* 11 Oct. 520/1 At almost wearisome length we have endeavoured to set forth the..case.

b. of a speaker or writer.

1573 G. Harvey *Letter-bk.* (Camden) 35, I persaiv how werisum and tœdius I have bene unto your wurship. **1634** W. Tirwhyt tr. *Balzac's Lett.* I. 43 Were it not that I feare to be wearisome unto you, I should never make an end of my newes. **1841–44** Emerson *Ess.*, *Intellect* Wks. (Bohn) I. 141 How wearisome the..political or religious fanatic..whose balance is lost by the exaggeration of a single topic.

3. Causing weariness from bodily or mental exertion or protracted pain; fatiguing, exhausting. Now somewhat *rare*.

1594 Hooker *Eccl. Pol.* i. vii. §7 The roote hereof, diuine malediction; whereby the instruments being weakned wherewithall the soule (especially in reasoning) doth worke, it preferreth rest in ignorance before wearisome labour to knowe. **1691** Ray *Creation* ii. (1692) 4 The Head..would have been very painful and wearisome to carry, if the Neck had lain parallel or inclining to the Horizon. **1703** M. Warwick in Baynard *Cold Bathing* ii. 297 A weak and wearisom Pain, together with a soreness upon the Part. **1750** Johnson *Idler* No. 6 ⁋2 There was once a time when Wreaths of Bays or Oak were considered as recompences equal to the more wearisome labours. **1751** Labelye *Westm. Br.* 66 Their great Trouble, Care, and wearisome Attendance. **1883** Josephine E. Butler *Autob.* xii. (1909) 177, I climbed up the wearisome gallery stairs. **1916** *Lancet* 8 Jan. 73/2 The hand-bellows is of such a size that it fills the hand comfortably, and continuous pumping is not wearisome.

'wearisomely, *adv.* [-LY^{2}.] In a wearisome manner. **a.** So as to cause weariness.

c **1735** Secker *Lect. Catech.* xxxviii. (1769) II. 276 In the whole of this Work, we must be careful, neither to hurry over any Part thoughtlessly, nor lengthen it wearisomely. **1828** *Harrovian* 155 Although wearisomely fond of description, L. E. L. is deficient in giving the shades of character, and variety of illustration. **1865** Lowell *Study Wind.*, *Thoreau* (1871) 156 If he botanise somewhat wearisomely, he gives us now and then superb outlooks from some jutting crag. **1884** *Manch. Exam.* 14 July 5/5 The comedy drags somewhat wearisomely towards the end. **1885** *Spectator* 8 Aug. 1048/1 The wearisomely abundant current literature concerning actors and acting.

b. In a state of weariness or ennui. *rare*.

1831 Carlyle *Sartor Res.* ii. vii, As he wanders wearisomely through this world. **1858** —— *Fredk. Gt.* iii. iii. I. 214 What struggles and inextricable armed-litigations there were for it, readers of Brandenburg-History too wearisomely know.

'wearisomeness. [-NESS.]

†**1.** The condition of being wearied; liability to become wearied. **a.** Fatigue, exhaustion from effort or pain; liability to be easily fatigued. **b.** Tedium, ennui; weariness *of* something uncongenial or uninteresting. *Obs.*

a. **1560** tr. *J. Fisher's Godly Treat. Benef. Prayer* G 4, Excepte eyther the great weerysomenes of our bodyes, or some other lyke necessitie inforce vs. **1600** Surflet *Country Farm* iv. x. 643 The fresh leaues..being put vnder the naked soles of the feete, they greatly take awaie their wearisomnes, which by far walking haue wearied themselues. *a* **1653** Gouge *Comm. Heb.* ii. 17. (1655) 240 Sundry infirmities of body, as hunger, thirst, cold, wearisomnesse. **1672** T. Venn *Milit. Observ.* 184 But if the wind blow stiff, or there is a weakness or wearisomness in the Ensign-bearer, then he may set the butt end against his waste and not otherwise. *a* **1768** Secker *Serm.* (1770) III. 270 For in his Turn, every one must expect to be in a State of Wearisomeness and Pain, of Weakness and Danger. **1780** *Ann. Reg.* 1 A kind of languor and wearisomeness. **1882** E. W. Hamilton *Diary* 25 Nov. (1972) I. 364 R. G. evidently wants to get out of harness also, partly from a feeling of wearisomeness and partly from bad health.

b. **1557** Phaer *Æneid* v. L 4 b, *Argt.*, The Troiane wyues, at the instigation of the Raynbow, and for wearysomnesse of theyr longe trauayle: cast fier amonge the fleet. *a* **1568** Ascham *Scholem.* i. (Arb.) 37 Such a witte, as is..diligent in painfull thinges without werisomnes. **1586** A. Day *Engl. Secretorie* ii. (1625) 109 Scanderbeg declaring his wearisomenes of captivitie..desired to visit his kingdome. **1631** Gouge *God's Arrows* iii. §46. 266 That wearisomnesse which is taxed in the Iewes that said, when will the New-Moones and Sabbaths be gone? **1643** Milton *Divorce* Pref. 2 Yet they shall..be made, spight of antipathy to fadge together, and combine as they may to their unspeakable wearisomnes & despaire of all sociable delight in the ordinance which [etc.]. **1822** [Mary A. Kelty] *Osmond* I. 289 Their wearisomeness of Osmond's stupidity. **1824** Dibdin *Libr. Comp.* II. 119 Where there is no variety, and where wearisomeness as naturally follows. **1840** Pusey in Liddon *Life* (1893) II. xxiv. 156, I should have been afraid of the casting lots, lest it should arise from a wearisomeness of indecision, instead of waiting patiently for the time when He would enable one to decide according to His will.

2. The quality or fact of causing weariness; tendency to weary. **a.** Aptness to cause fatigue. **b.** Tediousness.

a. **1576** Fleming *Panopl. Epist.* 254 The commoditie is answearable in proportion and measure, to the wearisomnesse of the labour. **1671** Woodhead *St. Teresa* ii. 261 Amidst the joltings of the Waggon, the trouble and wearisomness of the journey, they kept their Prayer, as in the Quire. **1843** Poe *Tales*, *Pit & Pendulum*, As if those who bore me..had paused from the wearisomeness of their toil.

b. **1579** Twyne *Petrarch's Phisicke agst. Fortune* i. 109 b, *Ioy.* The ayre is very cleere, I would it might not be changed. *Reason.* Thou knowest not how soone this cleerenes wil bring weerisomnesse: There is nothing so pleasant which continuall frequentyng the same maketh not loathsome. **1662** J. Davies tr. *Olearius' Voy. Ambass.* 5 The Ambassadours endeavour'd to abate the wearisomenesse of our stay there, by banquets, hunting matches, and walking. **1879** Hingston *Austral. Abr.* vii. 71 A great sameness about it was soon, however, observable, producing even the usual effect of monotony—wearisomeness. **1886** *Manch. Exam.* 27 Jan. 3/2 A second article..which has, notwithstanding these good qualities, just a suspicion of wearisomeness.

†**3.** Loathing (for food). *Obs.*$^{-1}$

1642 D. Rogers *Naaman* 346 Evell which causeth such a fulsomeneße and wearisomenesse in Gods stomacke.

wearne, obs. f. WARN *v.*^{1}; var. WARN *v.*^{2} *Obs.*

'wear-out. *rare*. Also wearout. [f. vbl. phr. *to wear out*: see WEAR *v.*^{1} 9, 14.] Wearing out; destruction or damage from use.

1897 C. T. Davis *Manuf. Leather* (ed. 2) 270 There is absolutely no wear-out to any of the working parts of the bed. **1979** *Arizona Daily Star* 5 Aug. C 4/1 (Advt.), They are ..protected against premature wearout during the warranty period.

wearry, obs. form of WORRY *v.*

weary ('wɪərɪ), *a.* Forms: 1 **wériȝ**, (**uoeriȝ**), **wériȝ**; 2–4 **weri**, (3 **wæri**), 3–6 **werie**, **-y**, (4 **wiry**, 5 **wyry**), 4, 6 *Sc.* **very**, (5 **were**, **werre**), 5–6 **werye**, 6 **weery**, **wiery**, 6–9 *Sc.* **wearie**, 6– **weary**. [OE. *wériȝ*, corresponding to OS. (*sîð-*) *wôrig* weary (with a journey), OHG. *wuarag* drunk:—W.Ger. **wōrizo-*, *-azo-*. The root **wōr-* seems to be identical with that in OE. *wórian* to wander, go astray, and in ON. *órar* fits of madness, *ǿr-r* mad, insane; the primary sense was perhaps 'bewildered', 'stupefied'.]

I. 1. a. Having the feeling of loss of strength, languor, and need for rest, produced by continued exertion (physical or mental), endurance of severe pain, or wakefulness; tired, fatigued. Now with stronger sense: Intensely tired, worn out with fatigue.

The strong emotional emphasis which the word has acquired in modern times tends to exclude it from colloquial use and from unimpassioned prose.

c **825** *Vesp. Psalter*, Hymn xii, *Mentes fessas*, mod woeriȝu. *a* **900** *Elene* 357 (Gr.) þa wereȝan neat, þe man.. drifeð & þirsceð. *c* **900** *Bæda's Hist.* III. ix. (1890) 180 þa heo þa on þære stowe ȝeseted wæs, ða wæs heo weriȝ. *c* **940** *Brunanburh in O.E. Chron.* an. 937 þær læȝ secg mæniȝ, garum aȝeted,.. ofer scild scoten,.. weriȝ, wiȝes sæd. *a* **1200** *Moral Ode* 240 (Lamb. MS.) Ho [*sc.* souls in hell] walkeð weri up and dun, se water deð mid winde. *c* **1290** *Katerine* 24 in *S.E. Leg.* 92 Of sonne and Mone and steorrene also, fram þe este to þe weste þat trauaillieth and neuere werie ne beoth. *c* **1290** *Beket* 1158 ibid. 139 Swiþe weri was þe holi man, onneþe he bar up is fet. *c* **1350** *Will. Palerne* 2518 Meliors was so wery þat sche ne walk miȝt. **1375** BARBOUR *Bruce* XII. 143 His men als that wer very Hynt of thair basnetis. *c* **1400** MAUNDEV. (Roxb.) xvi. 75 He was so wery þat he myȝt na ferther. **1557** N. T. (Genev.) *Matt.* xi. 28 Come vnto me all ye that are wearie and laden. **1567** MAPLET *Gr. Forest* 68b, The fift or odde Crane.. flieth all alone before, till he be wearie so doing. **1684** J. S. *Profit & Pleasure united* 159 To know when the Stag is weary, is easily done by his Slavering, froathing at the Mouth, [etc.]. **1837** W. IRVING *Capt. Bonneville* xliv. III. 188 After an absence of twenty days, they returned weary and discouraged. **1856** MRS. BROWNING *Aur. Leigh* I. 465 Producing what? A pair of slippers, sir, To put on when you're weary. **1865** SWINBURNE *Chastelard* I. ii. 30, I am tired too soon; I could have danced down hours Two years gone hence and felt no wearier.

absol. **1382** WYCLIF *Job* iii. 17 There resteden the wery in strengthe [**1611** There the wearie be at rest]. **1382** —— *Isa.* xl. 29 The Lord.. ȝyueth to the weri vertue. **1568** GRAFTON *Chron.* II. 627 The Duke of Yorke sent euer fresh men, to succor the werie, and put new men in places of the hurt persons. **1760–72** H. BROOKE *Fool of Qual.* (1809) II. 160 Death may bring rest to the weary and overladen. **1804** CAMPBELL *Soldier's Dream* 4 Thousands had sunk on the ground overpowered, The weary to sleep, and the wounded to die. **1848** DICKENS *Dombey* lviii, The eternal book for all the weary and the heavy-laden. **1887** I. R. *Lady's Ranche Life Montana* 105 In a few minutes we were sleeping the sleep of the weary.

b. said of the body, its limbs or organs.

c **1205** LAY. 16592 To lechinien þa wunden of leofenen his cnihten & baðien on burȝe heore wærie ban. **1573** GASCOIGNE *Posies, Hearbes* Wks. 1907 I. 354 If thou sitte at ease to rest thy wearie bones. **1590** SPENSER *F.Q.* I. ii. 29 There they alight, in hope.. to.. rest their weary limbs a tide. **1697** DRYDEN *Virg. Georg.* IV. 264 Late at Night, with weary Pinions come The lab'ring Youth, and heavy laden home. **1792** ROGERS *Pleas. Mem.* I. 73 (1810) 12 How oft.. We.. Welcom'd the wild-bee home on weary wing. **1841** LONGF. *Excelsior* v, 'O stay,' the maiden said, 'and rest Thy weary head upon this breast!'

c. with the source of weariness indicated. Const. *with*, formerly also †*of* (now only in sense 2), †*for*, or †genitive.

Beowulf 579 Siþes weriȝ. *a* **1000** *Riddles* liv [lv]. 10 Weriȝ þæs weorces. *c* **1205** LAY. 18406 Heo beoð swiðe werie iboren heore wepnen. *c* **1220** *Bestiary* 635 Ðanne he is of walke weri. **1362** LANGL. *P. Pl.* A. Prol. 7, I was weori of wandringe [B. wery forwandred]. ?*a* **1366** CHAUCER *Rom. Rose* 440 Ne certis she was fatt no thing But semed wery for fasting. **1382** WYCLIF *John* iv. 6 Jhesu maad wery, or feynt, of the iurney, sat thus on the welle. *c* **1400** MAUNDEV. (Roxb.) x. 40 When he was wery of bering of þe crosse. **1489** CAXTON *Faytes of A.* II. xxxvii. 157 They fonde the watchemen sore wery of longe watche. **1584** POWEL *Lloyd's Cambria* 93 Both armies being werie with fighting. **1596** SPENSER *F.Q.* VI. vii. 19 Weary of trauell in his former fight, He there in shade himselfe had laid to rest. **1610** SHAKS. *Temp.* IV. 134 You Sun-burn'd Sicklemen of August weary. **1617** MORYSON *Itin.* I. 179 My horse weary of this long journey without so much as a daies rest, beganne to faint. **1697** DRYDEN *Virg. Georg.* IV. 581 Weary with his Toyl, and scorch'd with Heat. **1805** SCOTT *Last Minstrel* I. ii, The stag-hounds, weary with the chase, Lay stretch'd upon the rushy floor.

d. Of pace, tread, voice, etc.: Showing signs of fatigue.

a **1000** *Cynewulf's Christ* 993 Beornas gretað.. werȝum stefnum. **1638** QUARLES *Hierogl.* i. 8 When at length His weary steps have reach'd the top. **1697** DRYDEN *Æneis* XI. 803 His Foes in sight, he mends his weary pace. **1784** BURNS *Man was made* 6, I spy'd a man, whose aged step Seem'd weary, worn with care. **1820** SHELLEY *Sensit. Pl.* III. 9 The weary sound and the heavy breath, And the silent motions of passing death. **1821** —— *Epipsych.* 155 The beaten road Which those poor slaves with weary footsteps tread. **1840** DICKENS *Old C. Shop* xv, Accordingly, towards this spot, they directed their weary steps.

†**e.** quasi-*sb.* in *for weary*: see FOR- *prefix* 10.

c **1350**, *c* **1400** [see FOR- *prefix* 10]. *c* **1400** *Laud Troy Bk.* 5574 Then were the Troyens wel weri, Thei myght not for weri hem steri. *c* **1420** *Avow. Arth.* xvii, For werre slidus he on slepe, No lengur myȝte he wake. **14..** *Sir Beues* (O.) 2449 What for wery and what for faynt, Syr Beuys was nerehande attaynt. *a* **1450** *Mirk's Festial* 180 But on þe morow, what for wach, what for wery, he fylle on slepe. *c* **1460** *Towneley Myst.* xxx. 226 Vnethes may I wag, man, for wery in youre stabill Whils I set my stag, man.

f. *Weary Willie*: see *Tired Tim* s.v. TIRED *ppl. a.*[1] 1 c.

1896 *Illustr. Chips* 16 May 1/3 *Lazy Larry*: 'Watcher doin', Willie?' *Weary Willie*: 'Oh, jest wipin out a little debt I owe.' **1901** *Munsey's Mag.* Sept. 884/2 Dan had not been gone a day when the first Weary Willy appeared and demanded pie, with a horrid leer. **1906** E. DYSON *Fact'ry 'Ands* vii. 76 'Garn,' he said, 'no airs. Yer Weary Willie's brother Sam, *halias* Ther Frequent Sleeper, [etc.].' **1909** *Punch* 20 Jan. 46 (*caption to picture of two tramps*) *Weary Willie*: I'd sooner walk up 'ill than I would down, any day—it do throw yer into yer boots so. **1927**, etc. [see TIRED *ppl. a.*[1] 1 c]. **1929** *Amer. Speech* IV. 345 *Weary Willie*, a tramp who usually hikes it and is too tired to work. **1972** [see TIRED *ppl. a.*[1] 1 c].

2. a. Discontented at the continuance or continued recurrence of something, and desiring its cessation; having one's patience, tolerance, zeal, or energy exhausted; 'sick and tired' *of* something. Also with *in*, and *to* with inf.

c **1205** LAY. 1328 Ne bið na man weri heora songes to heræn. **1377** LANGL. *P. Pl.* B. xv. 181 Whan he is wery of þat werke þanne wil he some tyme Labory in a lauendrye. *c* **1386** CHAUCER *Parson's T.* 1042 It [*sc.* the Paternoster] is schort.. for a man schulde be þe lasse wery to say it. *c* **1400** *Rom. Rose* 6298, I wol no more of this thing seyn, If I may passen me herby; I mighte maken you wery. **1470–85** MALORY *Arthur* XVI. i. 664, I am nyghe wery of this quest. **1526** TINDALE *2 Thess.* iii. 13 Brethren be not weary in well doynge. [So all later versions exc. Rheims.] **1534** —— *Gal.* vi. 9 Let vs not be wery of well doynge [**1611** in well doing]. **1535** COVERDALE *Ps.* vi. 6, I am weery of gronynge. **1551** ROBINSON *More's Utopia* II. vi. (1895) 212 In the exercyse and studdye of the mynde they be neuer werye. *c* **1590** *Fair Em* IV. i. 28, I am growen werie of his companie. **1605** SHAKS. *Lear* I. iv. 218 He that keepes not crust, nor crum, Weary of all, shall want some. **1647** CLARENDON *Hist. Reb.* IV. §42 By this time the King was as weary of Scotland as he had been impatient to go thither. **1670** DRYDEN *1st. Pt. Conq. Granada* I. i, 'Tis just some joyes on weary Kings should waite. **1711** in *10th Rep. Hist. MSS. Comm.* App. I. 143 He cannot be ignorant how weary we are of the war. **1726** SWIFT *Gulliver* I. i, The last of these voyages not proving very fortunate, I grew weary of the sea. **1790** BURNS *The Taylor fell* 13 There's somebody weary wi' lying her lane. **1817** SHELLEY *Rev. Islam* Ded. 33 For I grow weary to behold The selfish and the strong still tyrannize Without reproach or check. **1855** TENNYSON *Maud* I. xxii. 4 She is weary of dance and play. **1864** —— *Islet* 29 His compass is but of a single note, That it makes one weary to hear. **1875** JOWETT *Plato* (ed. 2) V. 122 Plato is never weary of speaking of the honour of the soul.

b. Tired *of*, anxious to be rid *of* (a person). *rare.*

?*c* **1472** *Stonor Papers* (Camden) I. 123 Me thynk þay sshuld nat be so wery of yow, þat dyd so gret labour & diligence to have yow. **1602** W. S. *Thomas Ld. Cromwell* IV. ii. 6 All parts abroade where euer I haue beene Growes wearie of me, and denies me succour. *a* **1653** R. BROME *City Wit* IV. i, I will suddenly take occasion to break with the Foole Wolsie; of whom I am heartily weary. **1859** TENNYSON *Vivien* 687, I am weary of her.

3. Depressed and dispirited through trouble, anxiety, disappointment, etc.; sick at heart.

c **888** ÆLFRED *Boeth.* xxxi. §1 Eala Wisdom, þu ðe eart sio hehste frofer ealra weriȝra moda. *c* **1000** *Wanderer* 15 Ne mæȝ weriȝ mod wyrde wiðstondan. *c* **1205** LAY. 28081 þa wes ich al wet & weri of sorȝen and seoc. *a* **1300** *Cursor M.* 15875 Mate and weri war þai þan. **1535** COVERDALE *2 Esdr.* xii. 5 Yet am I weery in my minde. **1538** STARKEY *England* II. i. 150 Many febul and wery soulys, wych haue byn oppressyd wyth wordly vanyte. **1605** SHAKS. *Macb.* III. i. 112, *1 Murth.* So wearie with Disasters, tugg'd with Fortune. **17..** *Slighted Nansy* in Ramsay *Tea-t. Misc.* (1733) I. 23 Far ben the house I rin; And a weary wight am I. **1792** BURNS *Banks of Doon* (later version) 4 How can ye chant, ye little birds, And I sae weary fu' o' care! **1892** L. JOHNSON in *1st Bk. Rhymers' Club* 6 Our wearier spirit faints, Vexed in the world's employ.

4. Of persons: Having little strength, feeble, sickly. *Sc.* and *dial.*

c **1375** *Sc. Leg. Saints* xviii. (Egipciane) 240 þocht he auld & very vas. **1533** BELLENDEN *Livy* III. iii. (S.T.S.) I. 250 Than was Ebucius, ane of þe consullis, dede in þe ciete, and his colleig seruilius sa wery þat he mycht skarsly draw his aynd. **1808** JAMIESON s.v., A weary bairn, a child that is declining, S. *a* **1825** FORBY *Voc. E. Anglia* s.v., It is a poor weary child. **1879** *Good Words* 405/1 The minister had christened Nicky Macdonald's bairn in the house, since it was far too weary a thing to be brought to the kirk.

fig. **1533** BELLENDEN *Livy* III. vii. (S.T.S.) I. 273 þe ciete was nocht sa wery [L. *aegram*] þat It mycht be dantit with sic remedis as It was wont to be.

II. Causing weariness.

5. Fatiguing, toilsome, exhausting. (Sometimes blending indistinguishably with sense 6.)

c **1315** SHOREHAM II. 84 To bere hyt [*sc.* the cross] to caluary, I-wys, hyt was wel wery. *c* **1386** CHAUCER *Miller's T.* 457 The dede slepe for wery bisynesse ffil on this Carpenter. **1560** DAUS tr. *Sleidane's Comm.* 219b, They wente a werye and a paynefull Jorney [L. *difficili et molesto itinere*]. **1560** BIBLE (Geneva) *Isa.* xxxii. 2 As the shadowe of a great rocke in a wearie land. [Literal from the Heb.] **1575** FLEMING *Virg. Bucol.* ix. 29 Let's synging passe our weary waye, lesse trouble wyll be oures. **1719** DE FOE *Crusoe* I. (Globe) 129 Many a weary Stroke it [*sc.* the boat] had cost, you may be sure; and there remained nothing but to get it into the Water. **1764** GOLDSM. *Trav.* 423 Vain, very vain, my weary search to find That bliss which only centres in the mind. **1783** BURNS *Despondency* 5 O Life! Thou art a galling load, Along a rough, a weary road, To wretches such as I. **1832** HT. MARTINEAU *Life in Wilds* vi. 76 It was weary work with any tool but the hatchet. **1833** TENNYSON *Lotos-Eaters* 41 Evermore Most weary seem'd the sea, weary the oar. **1849** AYTOUN *Lays Scott. Cavaliers* (ed. 2) 72 And aye we sail'd, and aye we sail'd Across the weary sea. **1894** J. A. STEUART *In Day of Battle* iv, India.. is far away. Many a weary mile lies between us and it.

6. a. Irksome, wearisome, tedious; in graver sense, burdensome to the spirit.

1465 *Paston Lett.* II. 188 Thys ys to wyry a lyffe to a byde for you and all youre. **1603** SHAKS. *Meas. for M.* III. i. 129 The weariest, and most loathed worldly life That Age, Ache, periury, and imprisonment Can lay on nature. **1798** WORDSW. *Lines Tintern Abbey* 39 In which the heavy and the weary weight Of all this unintelligible world, Is lightened. **1813** SCOTT *Rokeby* v. iii, In the rude guard-room, where of yore Their weary hours the warders wore. **1850** KINGSLEY *Alton Locke* xli, Like the clear sunshine after weary rain. **1884** TENNYSON *Cup* I. ii. 26, I have had a weary day in watching you. Yours must have been a wearier.

†**b.** Of discourse, a speaker or writer: Tedious, wearisome. *Obs.*

1549 COVERDALE etc. *Erasm. Par. 1 Tim.* i. 1–7 Wherto should a man labour for saluacion by meanes of so many wiery obseruacions [*per tot molestas obseruatiunculas ad salutem contendere*]. **1571** T. FORTESCUE *Mexia's Foreste* vii. 15b, Sundry are the considerations, of whiche Lactantius Firmianus.. as also somme others, haue written, large, & wery volumes. **1603** SHAKS. *Meas. for M.* I. iv. 25 Your Brother kindly greets you: Not to be weary with you; he's in prison.

7. *Sc.* and *north. dial.* **a.** Sad, sorrowful, hard to endure.

a **1785** W. FORBES *Dominie* in R. Forbes *Poems Buchan Dial.* II. 35 With blubber'd cheeks and watry nose, Her weary story she did close. **1813** SCOTT *Rokeby* III. xxviii. Song, A weary lot is thine, fair maid. *a* **1893** in R. Ford *Harp Perths.* 24 This weary, waefu' tale o' mine.

b. As an expression of irritation: Tiresome, vexatious, 'wretched', 'confounded'.

a **1785** W. FORBES *Dominie* in R. Forbes *Poems Buchan Dial.* II. 27 Wae worth that weary sup of drink He lik'd so well! **1802** SIBBALD *Chron. Sc. Poetry* IV. Gloss., *Weary*, wretched, cursed; as the weary or weariful fox. **1845** MRS. S. C. HALL *Whiteboy* x. 85, I went hunting everywhere for the weary cat and her kittens. **1864** LATTO *Tam. Bodkin* xiv. 131 Ye weary, weirdless, ne'er-do-weel vagabond. **1893** 'L. KEITH' *'Lisbeth* ii, 'Lisbeth, mind these weary steps. Your aunt's very infirm in the feet.

c. quasi-*adv.* as an intensive: Grievously, 'sadly'.

1790 SHIRREFS *Poems Sc. Dial.* 262 Poor Scota now is daz'd and auld, Her childrens blood rins weary cauld, To see her Palace like a fauld For haddin' sheep! **1860** J. P. KAY-SHUTTLEWORTH *Scarsdale* II. 155 Hoo'll be weary pottert (disturbed) wi' a letter fro' onybody bur mysel'.

8. *Sc.* in certain phrases, perh. influenced by WARY *v.*, to curse: ***weary fa' (fall)***, ***weary on***, ***weary set*** (a person or thing), a curse on (him, etc.).

1788 BURNS *Duncan Gray* 1 Weary fa' you, Duncan Gray. **1816** SCOTT *Old Mort.* xxxix, O, weary on the wars! mony's the comely face they destroy. **1816** —— *Bl. Dwarf* iii, O weary fa' thae evil days! **1828** W. MCDOWALL *Poems* 21 There's Brawnie, weary on her, Hear how she roars an' rowts. **1875** W. ALEXANDER *Sk. Life Ain Folk* 149 Weary set that chiel',.. he has seerly nae taste ava. **1893** STEVENSON *Catriona* ii, The French recruiting, weary fall it! **1896** A. LILBURN *Borderer* xxix. 221 Eh, weary on us! There seems no end to our misfortunes.

III. 9. *Comb.*, as ***weary-brained***, ***-eyed***, ***-laden***, ***-looking***, ***-winged***, ***-worn*** adjs.; † **weary-foot** *a.*, having weary feet, tired with walking.

1898 G. B. SHAW *Let.* 1 May (1972) II. 38, I finish the book at a sitting, as I don't want to be *weary-brained when Charlotte comes. **1930** J. MASEFIELD *Wanderer of Liverpool* 24 *Weary-eyed men came on deck. **1798** O'KEEFFE *Wild Oats* II. i, The hungry and *weary-foot traveller. **1784** BURNS *Man was made to mourn* end, A blest relief to those That *weary-laden mourn! **1885** LD. R. GOWER *Old Diaries* (1902) 21 A worn *weary-looking man of middle age. **1833** SCARGILL *Puritan's Grave* (1846) 63 The occasional cawing of the *weary-winged rooks. **1795–6** WORDSW. *Borderers* I. 420 If you knew.. how sleep will master The *weary-worn. **1819** KEATS *Otho* II. ii. 117 For I am sick and faint with many wrongs, Tir'd out and weary-worn with contumelies.

Hence † **'werihede** [-HEAD], weariness.

1340 *Ayenb.* 33 Efterward comþ werihede þet makeþ þane man weri and worsi uram daye to daye.

weary ('wɪərɪ), *v.* Pa. t. and pa. pple. **wearied** ('wɪərɪd). Forms: 1 (ȝe)wériȝian, (ȝe)wérȝian, wérian, 3 werȝe, 4–6 wery(e, werie, 6 weerie, 6–7 wearie, 6– weary. [OE. *wér(i)ȝian*, *-ȝean* intr., and *ȝewérȝian* trans., f. *wériȝ* WEARY *a.*]

I. *intr.* To grow weary.

1. To become tired; to suffer fatigue. Now *rare.*

c **890** WÆRFERTH *Gregory's Dial.* 204 þæt ilce mod æȝþer ȝe mid healicum mæȝnum weaxeð & stranȝað & eac of his aȝenre untrymnysse werȝað & teorað. *c* **900** *Bæda's Hist.* I. xxvii. (1890) 78 Forðon hyngran, þyrstan, hatian, calan, wæriȝian, al þæt is of untrymnesse þæs ȝecyndes. *Ibid.* III. ix. 178 þa ongon his hors semninga werȝian & ȝestondan. *a* **1225** *Ancr. R.* 252, & ȝif þet heo werȝeð, eurichon wreoðeð him bi oðer. **1577** GRANGE *Golden Aphrod.* etc. Rjb, My hande with long holdyng werieth. **1686** P. GORDON *Diary* (Spalding Club 1859) 126, I had not ridden four miles when one of the horses wearyed. *a* **1776** *Lizae Baillie* xi. in Child *Ballads* IV. 269 She was nae ten miles frae the town When she began to weary. **1850** TENNYSON *In Mem.* xxv. 9 Nor could I weary, heart or limb, When [etc.].

b. Of the heart, mind, patience, etc.: To become tired or exhausted. Also of a person, to grow dispirited or sick at heart.

1434 MISYN *Mending of Life* xi. 124 Stedfastly he bidys in body & werus not in hart. **1600** in Harington *Nugæ Antiq.* (1779) II. 257 Thus I will lay down my quill, which seldom wearys in a friendly tale. **1650** J. CARSTAIRES *Lett.* (1846) 74,

I hope he [God] keeps you from wearieing in reference to the delay of our libertie. **1769** Eliz. Carter *Lett.* (1809) III. xlvii. 379 The spirit wearies with perpetual dissipation. **1829** Herschel *Ess.* (1857) 514 That diligence which never wearies,..goes on adding grain by grain to the mass of results. **1891** E. Peacock *N. Brendon* II. 76 His poetic mind never wearied.

c. To become affected with tedium or ennui.

1798 *Monthly Mag.* Dec. 436 ['Improper expressions used in Edinburgh'] I *weary* when I am alone; I become weary. **1853** G. J. Cayley *Las Alforjas* II. 288 There is one kind and sympathising spirit which does not weary over my dilated gossip.

2. With various constructions. **a.** To grow tired *of* (something, doing something); *to* do (= of doing) or *to* be (= of being) (*arch.* or *poet.*); also with pres. pple.

a **1225** *Juliana* 22 For ne werȝeð he neauer to wurchen ow al þat wandreðe world a buten ende. *c* **1400** *Destr. Troy* 12997 Thai werit of þere werke þe wallis to kepe. *c* **1475** *Wisdom* 847 in *Macro Plays* 63 Þat of hys lyff he xall wery, & qwak for very fere. *c* **1480** Henryson *Swallow & other Birds* 1891 Quhilk day and nicht weryis not for to ga Sawand poysoun..In mannis Saull. **1627** Bp. P. Forbes *Eubulus* 15 Whence anie, who in singlenesse seeketh Resolution will not wearie to search it. **1782** Miss Burney *Cecilia* II. iv, She now wearied of passing all her time by herself, and sighed for the comfort of society. **1829** Carlyle in *Foreign Rev.* IV. 120 Into the ocean of air he gazed incessantly; and never wearied contemplating its clearness. *a* **1834** Coleridge *Lit. Rem.* II. 376 How the mind wearies of, and shrinks from, the more than painful interest, the μισητόν, of utter depravity. **1846** G. Warburton *Hochelaga* I. 217 The eye does not weary to see, but the hand aches, in even writing the one word—beauty. **1859** Tennyson *Elaine* 628 He..had ridd'n a random round To seek him, and had wearied of the search. *Ibid.* 894 As a little helpless innocent bird..Will sing the simple passage o'er and o'er.., till the ear Wearies to hear it. **1876** L. Stephen *Eng. Th. 18th C.* I. 356 It is not wonderful that a man pursuing so vast a plan..should have wearied of his task before it was completed.

b. To suffer weariness from long waiting or deferred hope; to wait wearily *for* or *to* do (something), or *through* (a period of time); to long or languish *for* something. Chiefly *Sc.*

1809 Syd. Smith *Serm.* II. 131 Why may it not..induce him to carry on the load of life who pants, and wearies for the grave. **1818** Hogg *Brownie of Bodsbeck* II. iii. 42, I hae wearied to see them. *a* **1830** H. Cockburn *Memor.* (1856) 155 The Lord Advocate..generally leaves his representatives..to endure the summing up, and to weary for the verdict. **1830** Galt *Lawrie T.* III. vi, [They were] watching the corpse and wearying for my return. **1856** Whewell in *Life* (1881) 480, I was beginning to weary for a letter from you. **1866** 'Annie Thomas' *Played Out* I. ix. 153 A congregation of women assembled immediately after a dinner, wearying through the hour before the men rejoin them. **1876** *Whitby Gloss.* s.v., They keep me wearying for dinner. **1885** 'Mrs. Alexander' *At Bay* viii, I have just been wearying to see you. **1888** R. Buchanan *Heir of Linne* iii, I was wearying to speak with you. **1894** G. Moore *Esther Waters* 39 She wearied for a companion.

3. quasi-*trans.* with *out*: To go wearily through to the end of.

1594–5 *Merchant's Daughter of Bristow* I. vi. in *Roxb. Ball.* (1872) II. I. 87 There will I waste and wearie out my dayes in woe. **1648** Gage *West Ind.* xvii. 114 After I had here wearied out the wearinesse, which I brought in my bones from the Cuchumatlanes. **1889** *Boy's Own Paper* 17 Aug. 730/2, I soon forgot to be sorry for Sister Mary, left to weary out the holidays in vacant loneliness.

II. *trans.* To make weary.

4. To exhaust the strength or endurance of (a person, his limbs, etc.); to fatigue or tire with toil, sickness, watching, sustained mental effort, etc.

Beowulf 2852 He ȝewerȝad sæt. *c* **897** Ælfred *Gregory's Past. C.* xxxv. 239 He..ȝewerȝað ðonne his heortan suiðe hearde mid ðy ȝesuince. *c* **1000** Ælfric *Saints' Lives* (1900) I. 192 Þurh godes fore-stihtunge ne hors ne he sylf ȝewerȝod wæs. ? *a* **1400** *Morte Arth.* 796 He hade weryede the worme [*sc.* dragon] by wyghtnesse of strenghte, Ne ware it fore the wylde fyre that he hyme wyth defendez. *c* **1440** *Promp. Parv.* 522/2 Weryyn, or make wery,..*fatigo, lasso.* **1530** Palsgr. 779/1, I werye by over moche labour or travayle, *je lasse*... This horse trotteth so harde that he hath weryed me more than I was a gret whyle. **1563** Golding *Cæsar* I. (1565) 18 b, Many hauing a long time wearied their armes, chose rather to cast their targets out of their hands. **1597** Hooker *Eccl. Pol.* v. lxxxi. §10 They in the practise of their religion wearied chiefly their knees and hands, we especially our eares & tongues. **1610** Shaks. *Temp.* III. i. 19 Pray set it downe, and rest you: when this [log] burnes 'Twill weepe for hauing wearied you. **1657** Earl Monm. tr. *Paruta's Pol. Disc.* 186 By drawing out the War in length, they might think to weary and disorder the Enemy. **1675** J. Owen *Indwelling Sin* ix. (1732) 107 They brought their Offerings or Sacrifices on their Shoulders, which they pretended wearyed them, and they panted and blowed as Men ready to faint under them. **1759** Johnson *Rasselas* iv, Resolving to weary by perseverance, him whom he could not surpass in speed. **1825** Scott *Talism.* vi, A mighty curtal axe, which would have wearied the arm of any other than Cœur de Lion. **1825** —— *Betrothed* xi, She wearied her memory with vain efforts to recollect..his features. **1859** Tennyson *Elaine* 827 'Alas,' he said, 'your ride hath wearied you.'

b. *transf.* and *fig.*

1573–80 Baret *Alv.* P 496 If the vine be wearied with plentifull bearing. **1593** Shaks. *Lucr.* 1363 So woe hath wearied woe, mone tired mone. *Ibid.* 1570 Thus ebs and flowes the currant of her sorrow, And time doth wearie time with her complayning. **1604** Jas. I *Counterbl. to Tobacco* (Arb.) 108 So being euer and continually vsed, it [medicine] doth but weaken, wearie and weare nature. **1697** Dryden *Virg. Georg.* IV. 638 Then roaring Beasts, and running Streams he tryes, And wearies all his Miracles of Lies.

c. With adv. or advb. phr.; esp. ***to weary out***, to fatigue completely, so as to render incapable of further exertion.

1647 Cowley *Mistress, Thraldom* v, Like an Egyptian Tyrant, some Thou weariest out, in building but a Tomb. **1670** Dryden *1st Pt. Conq. Granada* IV. (1672) 35 In walls we meanly must our hopes inclose, To wait our friends, and weary out our foes. **1829** Landor *Imag. Conv. Greeks & Rom.* (1853) 352 Whose movements would have irritated, distracted, and wearied down the elephants. **1848** Dickens *Dombey* lv, He was stupefied, and he was wearied to death. **1859** Tennyson *Vivien* 586 Then he found a door..; And wearied out made for the couch and slept.

5. To tire the patience of; to affect with tedium or ennui; to satiate (*with*). Also with *out*.

1340 *Ayenb.* 99 He wolde þet hit were ssort uor þet non ne ssolde him werye hit uor to lyerny. *c* **1386** Chaucer *Can. Yeom. Prol. & T.* 751 It weerieth me to telle of his falsnesse. *c* **1460** Sir R. Ros *La Belle Dame* 62 It werieth me this mater for to trete. *c* **1489** Caxton *Sonnes of Aymon* x. 271 How am I shamed for four glotons! certes this weryes me sore! **1553** T. Wilson *Rhet.* 115 b, But nowe because I haue halfe weried the reader with a tedious matter, I will harten him agayne wyth a merye tale. **1600** Shaks. *A.Y.L.* v. ii. 56, I will wearie you then no longer with idle talking. **1667** Milton *P.L.* XII. 107 Till God at last Wearied with their iniquities, withdraw His presence from among them. **1675** E. Wilson *Spadacr. Dunelm.* Pref., And now, good Reader, I have even wearied thee out. **1797** Mrs. Radcliffe *Italian* xvi, Our patience is wearied already. **1798** Sophia Lee *Canterb. T., Young Lady's T.* II. 384 Wearied out at last by the tender importunity..she reluctantly took solemn charge of the child. **1830** Tennyson *Lilian* iii, Gaiety without eclipse Wearieth me. **1855** Macaulay *Hist. Eng.* xvi. III. 649 He was..doing his best to weary out his benefactor's patience and good breeding. **1877** Mrs. Oliphant *Makers Flor.* v. 138 Oddly enough, however, this excessive applause wearied the simple-minded artist. **1883** 'Ouida' *Wanda* I. 206 He had a sensitive fear of wearying with his presence ladies to whom he owed so much.

b. To trouble by importunity (heaven, the gods, etc.).

1633 Ford *'Tis Pity* I. iii, I have even wearied heaven with pray'rs. *a* **1718** Prior *Henry & Emma* 411 Watchful I'll guard Thee, and with Midnight Pray'r Weary the Gods to keep Thee in their Care. **1831** Scott *Quentin D.* Introd., He ..wearied Heaven and every saint with prayers..for the prolongation of his life. **1846** H. G. Robinson *Odes of Hor.* II. xviii, I weary not The Gods to mend my present lot. **1879** Froude *Cæsar* xv. 227 There, for sixteen months, to weary Heaven and his friends with his lamentations.

c. *absol.* To cause weariness or ennui.

1815 Sir R. Peel in *Croker Papers* (1884) I. III. 76 Which would have been ludicrous enough for half an hour, but, like other good things, wearied by constant repetition. **1849** Lever *Con Cregan* xx, There was so much novelty to me in all around, that the monotonous character of the scene never wearied.

Hence '**wearying** *vbl. sb.*

a **1225** *Ancr. R.* 252 Vondunge is sliddrunge: & þuruh werȝunge beoð bitocned þeo unðeauwes under slouhðe þet beoð inemned þer uppe. **1621** Bp. Hall *Heaven upon Earth* §4 Hence are those vaine wearyings of places and companies together with our selues.

weary, obs. form of worry *v.*

wearying ('wɪərɪɪŋ), *ppl. a.* [-ing^2.]

1. That causes weariness, fatigue, or lassitude.

1798 Bloomfield *Farmer's Boy, Spring* 62 When Giles with wearying strides From ridge to ridge the ponderous harrow guides. **1834** Southey *Lett.* (1856) IV. 369 A day in London is more wearying to me than a walk up Scawfell. **1864** Disraeli in G. E. Buckle *Life* (1916) IV. xii. 405 Lord P., after the division, scrambled up a wearying staircase to the ladies' gallery. **1862** Wraxall tr. *Hugo's Les Misérables* I. iii. 7 The two old females generally accompanied him, but when the journey was too wearying for them he went alone. **1898** E. Glanville *Kloof Bride* viii, They took up their position and began a wearying watch.

2. That causes tedium or ennui.

1796 Mme. D'Arblay *Camilla* V. 216 Cutting short.. all the wearying round of explanation. **1840** Marryat *Poor Jack* xxv, He was never wearying, and often..amusing. **1857** Livingstone *Trav.* ix. 185 Nothing is so wearying to the spirit as talking to those who agree with everything advanced. **1911** Petrie *Revol. Civilisation* iii. 59 Roman copies of Greek work, of wearying banality.

Hence '**wearyingly** *adv.*

1829 *Examiner* 325/1 The piece..was wearyingly long. **1902** Elinor Glyn *Refl. Ambrosine* 287 You said you were not wearyingly faithful.

† '**wearyish**, *a. Obs. rare.* [f. weary *a.* + -ish.] Done or passed in weariness.

1615 Jackson *Creed* IV. I. viii. 83 If wee deferred this suruey til old age come vpon vs, in which life it self becomes a burthen, our returne of thanks for fruition of it, and the vnpleasant appertinences, would be but wearyish. *a* **1618** [see remissal]. **1702** C. Mather *Magn. Chr.* III. I. App. (1852) 340, I have drawn forth many wearyish hours.

weasand ('wiːzənd). Now chiefly *dial.* Forms: α. 1 **wásend**, 4 **wosen**, 7 **wozen**. β. 4–8 **wesand**, 5 *Sc.* **vassand**, 5 **waysande**, 5–6 **wesande**, **weysand(e**, 6 **wessande**, **wezzand**, 7 **wezand**, **weazond**, 7–9 **weazand**, 9 **weezand**, 6– **weasand**; 4–6 **wesaunt**, 5–6 **-aunnt**, **-awnt**, **-ant**, 6 **-ante**, **weasaunte**, 6–7 **weasant**; 6 **weasan**, 6–7 **-en**, 7 **wezon**, **-en**, **weeson**, **-zon**, 7–8 **weazon**, 7–9 **weason**; 5 **wesing**, **-yng**, 7 **weasin**. γ. (*Sc.* and *north.*) 8–9 **wyson**, **wizen**, 8 **wyzen**, (**whizzen**), 9 **wizzen**, **-on**, **wezzon**. (See also *Eng. Dial. Dict.*) [OE. *wásend* masc. (? and fem.) corresp. to OFris. *wâsande*, *-ende*, throat, OS. *wâsend* ruminant stomach, OHG. *weisant*, *-ont*, *-unt*, throat, windpipe, gullet (MHG. *weisen*, early mod.G. *waisen*, *waise*, mod. dial. *wäs* etc.). The word has the form of a pres. pple. or ppl. agent-noun (for the formation cf. ON. *vélindi* neut., gullet). The etymology has not been determined; for various conjectures see K. v. Bahder in Grimm s.v. *Waisen.* A parallel synonymous formation from the same root with different suffix appears in weezle (= G. dial. *waisel*).

The forms *wosen* (14th c.), *wozen* (17th c.), and the mod. dial. *oosen*, *hoosen*, are normal descendants of the OE. *wásend*; and possibly the Sc. form *vassand* comes from *wásend* with shortening of the vowel. The remaining ME. and mod.E. forms (including *weasand*) are anomalous; etymologists have generally attempted to account for them by the assumption of an OE. parallel form **wǽsend.* This is not impossible, but Sweet (*Ags. Dict.*) appears to be in error in giving *wǽsend* as an actually recorded variant of *wásend.*]

1. The œsophagus or gullet.

a **1000** in Napier *O.E. Glosses* i. 2447 *Ingluuie*, ȝyfernesse, wasende. *c* **1000** *Sax. Leechd.* II. 44 Læcedomas..wið ȝealhswile & þrotan & wasende. *c* **1050** *Gloss.* in Wr.-Wülcker 264/19 *Rumen*, wasend. *c* **1050** *Voc.*, *Ibid.* 421/37 *Ingluuiem*, in þane wasend. **13..** *Gaw. & Gr. Knt.* 1336 Þay gryped to þe gargulun, & grayþely departed þe wesaunt fro þe wynt-hole. **1375** [see thropple]. *c* **1400** *Lanfranc's Cirurg.* 148 And betwene þe necke & gula wiþinneforþ þere is ordeyned mary [see meri^1], that is to seie þe wesant. **14..** *Nom.* in Wr.-Wülcker 676/24 *Hic ysophagus*, a wesande. *c* **1440** *Promp. Parv.* 523/1 Wesaunnt, of a beestys throte, *ysofagus.* *c* **1450** *Two Cookery-bks.* 80 Pulle him [a snipe], late his necke be hole, save the wesing. **1548–77** Vicary *Anat.* v. (1888) 44 Also in the mouth is ended the vppermoste extremitie of the Wesande, which is called Myre or Isofagus. **1578** Lyte *Dodoens* II. ccii. 305 It will cause the Horseleaches..to fall of, which happen to cleaue fast in the throote or wesande of any man. **1593** Nashe *Christs Teares* H 4, Their watry wesands were like to leape out of theyr mouthes for meate. **1601** Holland *Pliny* XI. xxxvii. I. 339 The other is more inward, called properly the Gullet, or the Wezand, by which we swallow downe both meat and drinke. **1634** Bp. Hall *Contempl., N.T.* IV. *Loaves & Fishes* 123 As if the soules of these men lay in their weasand, in their gutt. **1669** *Phil. Trans.* IV. 1021 Its Wind-pipe; which..together with the Oesophagus or Weasand.. reaches down to the Sternum. **1715** Ramsay *Christ's Kirk Gr.* III. 83 Now what the Friends wad fain been at,..Was e'en to get their Wysons wat. **1785** Burns *Scotch Drink* xiv, But monie daily weet their weason Wi' liquors nice. **1819** Scott *Ivanhoe* xlii, By Heaven,..better food hath not passed my weasand for three livelong days. **1915** G. Sinclair *Poems* 58 May their wysons never want A drop o' dew tae weet them.

2. The trachea or windpipe: = artery 1.

1398 Trevisa *Barth. De P.R.* v. xxiii. (Bodl. MS.), And somme of þese fonge the voice as þe lunges with þe receptacles wosen and pipes þereof. *a* **1529** Skelton *Col. Cloute* 1156 Herke, howe the losell prates, With a wyde wesaunt! **1541** R. Copland *Guydon's Quest. Chirurg.* F ij b, The wesaunt..is a cartylagynous grystled partycle created and fourmed for to be instrument of ye voyce. **1547** Boorde *Brev. Health* 80 *Trachea arteria*... In Englyshe it is named the wesande, or the throte bol. **1609** J. Davies (Heref.) *Hum. Heaven on Earth* I. cxx, His wozen whez'd when his breath it did fill. **1646** Sir T. Browne *Pseud. Ep.* IV. viii. 198 The weazon, rough artery, or winde-pipe. **1672** Wiseman *Wounds* I. viii. 68 The Aspera Arteria or Weazond. **1697** Dryden *Æneis* IX. 592 Th' unerring Steel descended while he spoke; Pierc'd his wide Mouth, and thro' his Weazon broke. **1798** Eliz. Inchbald *Lovers' Vows* III. ii, They.. held so strongly by his throat, They almost stopt his whizzen.

¶ **b.** Erroneously used for artery 2.

1398 Trevisa *Barth. De P.R.* III. xii. (1495) 55 Of the herte spryngyth the wosen, as the veynes sprynge out of the lyuer. *Ibid.* III. xii. (Tollemache MS.), The vertu þat hat vitalis, þe vertu of lyf, haþ meuynge by þe wosen and smale weyis [L. *per arterias*].

3. The throat generally.

c **1450** *Mankind* 803 in *Macro Plays* 30 A-lasse, my wesant! ȝe wer sumwhat to nere [the rope]. **1550** Latimer *Last Serm. bef. Edw. VI* (1562) 121 Should I haue named hym? nay they should as sone haue this wesaunt of mine. **1570** Foxe *A. & M.* (ed. 2) II. 1405/1 But God of his mercye so directed his wicked purpose, that the backe of his knife was towarde hys wesand. **1610** Shaks. *Temp.* III. ii. 99 There thou maist braine him,..Or cut his wezand with thy knife. **1630** J. Taylor (Water P.) *Epigr.* xxxviii. Wks. II. 266/1 See'st thou a villaine hang vp by the weason? **1668** Dryden *Even. Love* v. i, Give me a Razor there, that I may scrape his weeson, that the bristles may not hinder me when I come to cut it. **1684** J. S. *Profit & Pleas. United* 162 A perfect Greyhound..a long Neck..with a loos hanging wezand. **1720** Ramsay *Rise & Fall of Stocks* 77 The Miser ..Syne shores to grip him by the Wyson. **1724** Swift *Verses upright Judge* Misc. 1735 V. 147 The Church I hate, and have good Reason: For there my Grandsire cut his Weazon. **1819** Scott *Leg. Montrose* xiii, Clap your hand thus on the weasand of this high and mighty prince, under his ruff. **1833** M. Scott *Tom Cringle* xviii, He..drew his knife across the Leopard's weasand. **1837** Carlyle *Fr. Rev.* I. VII. ii, They are parted and no weasands slit. **1841** Borrow *Zincali* II. 47 I'd straight unsheath my dudgeon knife And cut his weasand through.

4. *Comb.*, as ***weasand muscle***; ***weasand-stopping*** adj.; **weasand-pipe** = senses 1–3 above.

c **1720** W. Gibson *Farrier's Guide* I. v. (1722) 60 The.. Bronchium, or the *Weasand Muscles. **1544** Phaer *Regim. Lyfe* (1560) S viij b, Somtyme it lyeth..upon the *wesaunt pype, and than..it stoppeth the breath & strangleth the pacient anone. **1596** Spenser *F.Q.* IV. iii. 12 His weasand pipe it through his gorget cleft. **1620** I. C. *Two Merry Milk-maids* IV. i. L 1 b, *Ray.* Cut my throate! *Fre.* I, your Weason pipe, your Gullet. *a* **1656** R. Cox *Actæon & Diana* 31 He will come armed with nothing but a Razor, with which if he does slit your wezand-pipe, it will not be amiss to take it patiently. **1872** O. W. HOLMES *Poet Breakf.-t.* viii. 267 Poor, yelling, scalping Indians, . . *weasand-stopping Thugs.

wease-alley, corrupt form of WEESE-ALLAN.

weasel (ˈwiːz(ə)l), *sb.* Forms: 1 ueoesule, uuesulae, wesle, 4 wesill, 4–5 wesel(e, 4–6 wesell, -il, 5 wesyl(le, wees-, wessylle, weysyl, wezel, whesille, *Sc.* quhasill, 6 wesyll, weysell, 6–7 weazell, -ill, weesell, we(e)sill, 6–9 weesel, 7 weasell, -il, weassel, weesle, we(e)zill, weezle, wheezle, *Sc.* waesel, 7–8 weezel, *Sc.* whessell, 8–9 weasle, 9 *dial.* wizzel, 7– weasel. [OE. *wesule, wesle* wk. fem. = NFris. *wisel* (WFris. *wezel-, weezling*), (M)Du. *wezel*, OHG. *wisula, -ala* (MHG. *wisele, wisel*, mod.G. *wiesel* fem.):—OTeut. **wisulōn-*, of obscure origin.

From German dialects come the Icel. (*hreysi*)*visla*, '(cairn-) weasel', Sw. *vesla, vessla*, Da. *væsel*.]

1. a. A carnivorous animal (*Putorius nivalis*), the smallest European species of the genus (of the order *Mustelidæ*) which includes the polecat, stoat, etc. It is remarkable for its slender body, and for its ferocity and bloodthirstiness.

c **725** *Corpus Gloss.* M 337 *Mustela*, ueoesule. *c* **1000** ÆLFRIC *Gram.* vi. (Z.) 19 *Mustela*, wesle. **11..** *Conf. Ecgbert* xxxix. in Thorpe *Ags. Laws* II. 164 Ʒif on hwylcne mycelne wætan mus oððe wesle onbefealle . . sprenge mid haliʒ wætere. *c* **1325** *Gloss. W. de Bibbesw.* in Wright *Voc.* 166 Ceste belette, a wesele. *a* **1340** HAMPOLE *Psalter* xc. 13 Þe wesill ouercumys him [*sc.* the basilisk] & slas him. **1398** TREVISA *Barth. De P.R.* XVIII. lxxiv. (1495) 829 The wesell hathe a red and a whyte wombe and chaungeth colour. *c* **1440** *Pallad. on Husb.* I. 540 The wesil shal for this doon hem noon harm. *c* **1480** HENRYSON *Mor. Fab.* v. (*Parl. Beasts*) xvii, The quhirand quhitret with the quhasill went. **1577** B. GOOGE *Heresbach's Husb.* III. 156b, I would . . counsell you to destroy your Rattes and Mise with . . Weesels. **1579** LYLY *Euphues* (Arb.) 272 If thou be [be]witched with eyes, weare the eie of a wesill in a ring, which is an enchauntment against such charmes. **1606** N. B[AXTER] *Sydney's Ourania* G 1, The Pole-catte, and wilde-catte, the Weezle, & Stoate. **1624** CAPT. J. SMITH *Virginia* II. 35 Of Weesels and other Vermines skins a good many. **1726** LEONI *Alberti's Archit.* I. 97/2 Pole-cats, Weezels, . . or the like Vermin. **1832** L. HUNT *Sir R. Esher* (1850) 336 Staring like a weasel. **1844** JESSE *Scenes Country Life* 357 Keepers have informed me that Weazles will sometimes kill and feed on Snakes. **1883** SIMMONDS *Dict. Useful Anim.* s.v., The long-tailed weasel (*Mustela longicauda*). **1919** *Contemp. Rev.* Aug. 183, I came across a bloodthirsty weasel, dragging a large buck rabbit after it.

transf. and *fig.* **1599** SHAKS. *Hen. V*, I. ii. 170 For once the Eagle (England) being in prey, To her vnguarded Nest, the Weazell (Scot) Comes sneaking, and so sucks her Princely Egges. **1632** CHAPMAN & SHIRLEY *Ball* I. (1639) A 4, *Co.* Dee not know him, tis the Court dancing Weesill. *Ma.* A Dancer, and so gay. **1633** B. JONSON *Tale Tub* I. vi, Wherefore did I, Sir, bid him Be call'd, you Weazell, Vermin of a Huisher? **1638** FORD *Fancies* II. ii, Whoreson, lecherous weazle! **1790** WOLCOT (P. Pindar) *Advice to Future Laureat* II. 39 Brudenell, thou stinkest! weasel, polecat, fly! **1886** P. ROBINSON *Teetotum Trees* 39 A thin little weasel of a Bengalee Baboo.

b. In proverbial sayings. † *to be bit by a barn weasel*: to be drunk.

1673 R. HEAD *Canting Acad.* 171 He is bit by a barn Weesel. **1825** J. NEAL *Bro. Jonathan* III. 269 'On with your story, will you; and if you are caught another time—' 'Caught! me!— . . catch a weasel asleep!' **1840** DICKENS *Old C. Shop* xxiii, I'm . . as sharp as a ferret, and as cunning as a weazel.

¶**c.** Erroneously spoken of as a corn-eating animal.

c **1600** *Distr. Emperor* III. i. in Bullen *Old Pl.* (1884) III. 208 True, daughter; love is like the weassel that went into the meale-chamber; . . it growes plumpe and full of humor; it asks a crannye as bygg as a conye borrowe to gett out agayne. *a* **1744** POPE *Imit. Hor.* Ep. I. vii. 51 A Weasel once made shift to slink In at a Corn-loft thro' a Chink. [Hence **1755** JOHNSON, *Weasel*, a small animal that eats corn and kills mice.]

d. In some parts of England and Ireland confused with the STOAT, which is sometimes called *ermine weasel* or (when wearing its winter coat) *white weasel*.

1607 TOPSELL *Four-f. Beasts* 726 The white Weasel is called *Minever*. **1676** COTTON *Angler* II. viii. 75 A Flie called the Owl-Flie; the dubbing of a white Weesel's tail. **1774** GOLDSM. *Nat. Hist.* III. 358 This animal [*sc.* the ermine] is sometimes found white in Great Britain, and is then called a white weasel. **1891** *Fishing Gaz.* 3 Jan. 7/2 The stoat, or ermine weasel (*Mustela erminea*) . . in many parts of England is called a weasel. **1916** *Field* 22 Apr. 661/3 The stoat . . in many parts [of Ireland] is known as 'weasel'.

2. Applied with qualifying words to various animals belonging to the family *Mustelidæ*, or having some marked resemblance to the weasel, as *fisher w.* (see FISHER¹ 2 b); *four-toed w.* = SURICATE; *Malacca w.* = RASSE; *Mexican w.* = KINKAJOU; *water-w.* (see WATER *sb.* 30).

1771 PENNANT *Syn. Quadr.* 228 Four-toed Weesel. **1781** —— *Hist. Quadr.* II. 328 Fisher Weesel. *Ibid.* 338 Mexican Weesel. **1800** SHAW *Gen. Zool.* I. II. 406 Malacca Weesel.

†**3.** [transl. L. *mustela* (*marina*).] A fish, taken to be the lamprey. (Cf. *weasel-fish, -ling* in 8 b, and Fr. *belette*.) *Obs.*

1601 HOLLAND *Pliny* XXXII. ix. II. 445 The liver also of the fish named the Sea-cat or Weazill, is given in like case.

†**4.** The SMEW. Cf. *weasel coot, duck* in 8 b.

a **1682** SIR T. BROWNE *Norf. Birds* Wks. 1835 IV. 317 The . . *mustela variegata*, . . the variegated or party-coloured weasel, so called from the resemblance it beareth unto a weasel in the head.

5. *U.S.* A nickname for a native of S. Carolina.

1845 in C. Cist *Cincinnati Misc.* I. 240 The inhabitants of . . S. Carolina [are called] Weasels. **1875** *Chamb. Jrnl.* 13 Mar. 171/2 South Carolina is Palmetto State, and the natives are Weasels.

6. A tracked vehicle capable of travelling over difficult terrain; *spec.* (*a*) a light cargo and personnel carrier (*U.S. Mil.*); (*b*) a snow tractor (see quot. 1958).

1944 *Yank* 4 Aug. 17/2 Cargo carrier M29, nicknamed the Weasel, is now in full production. **1949** [see *snow-buggy* s.v. SNOW *sb.*¹ 8 b]. **1958** *Times* 11 Nov. 6/7 The Weasel—one of the snow vehicles used by Sir Vivian Fuchs on his trans-Antarctic journey—was invented by a civilian, the late Mr. Geoffrey Pyke. **1964** 'J. H. ROBERTS' *Q Document* (1965) ix. 206 The hotels operated what the student referred to as 'wesaru'—which . . was the Japanese way of pronouncing 'weasel', a cross between a jeep and an army tank—to carry the guests. **1980** *Globe & Laurel* July/Aug. 227/2 We in fact lost two vehicles doing this, one being my own command vehicle which was a cargo LVT with a weasel in the back.

7. An equivocal statement or claim, esp. one used in an intentionally misleading advertisement. See *weasel word*, sense 8 b below.

1959 T. GRIFFITH *Waist-High Culture* (1960) 83 The answer may have to be a 'weasel', the phrasing that avoids or begs the question. **1963** D. OGILVY *Confessions Advert. Man* xi. 155, I plead guilty to one act of *suggestio falsi*—what Madison Avenue calls a 'weasel'. **1975** *Idle Moments* (Austral.) Dec. 26/2 The 'weasels' are so cleverly written, so subtle, you hardly notice them at all.

8. a. *attrib.* and *Comb.*, as *weasel family, kind, tribe* (designations for the order *Mustelidæ*); *weasel-colour, -mind, -run, -skin, -whelp*; similative, as *weasel-†becked* (= beaked), *-eyed, -faced, -headed, -like* adjs.

1587 HARRISON *England* II. vii. 172/1 in *Holinshed*, If a man . . be *wesell becked then much heare left on the cheekes will make the owner looke big like a bowdled hen. **1585** HIGINS *Junius' Nomencl.* 177/2 *Fuluus*, . . fox or *weazill colour. **1922** *Weasel-eyed [see *peanut-brained* adj. s.v. PEANUT 3 a]. **1985** C. FITZGIBBON *Love lies a Loss* v. 59 The weasel-eyed creditors lined the dock. **1596** NASHE *Saffron-Walden* X 1 b, Mounsieur Fregeuile Gautius, that prating *weazell fac'd vermin, is one of the Pipers in this consort. **1807–8** W. IRVING *Salmagundi* (1824) 148 A little meagre, weazel-faced Frenchman. **1877** *Cassell's Nat. Hist.* II. 182 The *Weasel Family. **1681** GREW *Musæum* I. §ii. i. 19 The *Weesle-Headed Armadillo, *Tatu Mustelinus*. **1768** PENNANT *Brit. Zool.* I. 82 This species is the least of the *weesel kind. **1899** F. V. KIRBY *Sport E.C. Africa* 322 Their . . *weasel-like slenderness of body. **1923** *Chambers's Jrnl.* Feb. 88/1 Simon would have dallied by the way, his *weasel-mind alert to draw news of the hindering from this Heseltine. **1901** 'LINESMAN' *Words by Eyewitness* 153 Setting his traps in a *weasel run. **1583** *Rates Custome ho.* F ij b, *Wesel skinnes the dosen, iiij. d. **1800** SHAW *Gen. Zool.* I. II. 378 The *Weesel tribe. **1398** TREVISA *Barth. De P.R.* XVIII. lxxiii. (Bodl. MS.), Ʒif þe *wesel whelpes falleþ bi ony happe in chynnes . . þe wesel heleþ ham wiþ a certeyne herbe.

b. Special comb.: **weasel-coot, -duck**, the female or young male of the smew; † **weasel-fish**, a rockling (cf. WHISTLE-*fish*); **weasel-lemur**, a small short-tailed lemur (*Lepilemur mustelinus*); † **weasel-ling**, a kind of rockling; † **weasel-monger**, one who hunts rats, etc., with weasels; **weasel-snout**, the yellow dead-nettle or archangel (*Lamium Galeobdolon*), from the shape of the corolla; **weasel word** orig. *U.S.*, an equivocating or ambiguous word which takes away the force or meaning of the concept being expressed; hence **weasel-worded** *a.*

1804 BEWICK *Brit. Birds* II. 266 Red-headed Smew, or *Weasel Coot. **1885** SWAINSON *Prov. Names Birds* 165 *Weasel ducks or Weasel coots. **1773** *Gentl. Mag.* XLIII. 220 The Bladder Fish, and the *Weasel Fish. **1877** *Cassell's Nat. Hist.* I. 223 This *Weasel Lemur . . has fair-sized ears, and its colours are of all sorts of shades of red, grey, white, and yellow. *a* **1682** SIR T. BROWNE *Norf. Fishes* Wks. 1835 IV. 328 *Mustela Marina*; called by some a *weazel ling, which, salted and dried, becomes a good Lenten dish. **1591** ? PEELE *Sp. to Q. Eliz. at Theobalds, Gard. Sp.*, This *weasel-monger [*i.e.* a mole-catcher]. **1796** WITHERING *Brit. Plants* (ed. 3) III. 530 Yellow Archangel. Yellow Dead Nettle, or *Weasel snout. **1900** S. CHAPLIN in *Century Mag.* June 306/2 'The public should be protected—' 'Duly protected,' said Gamage, 'That's always a good *weasel word.' **1916** *N.Y. Times* 1 June 1/2 Colonel Roosevelt began the day's speechmaking by opening his guns upon President Wilson. . . He accused Mr. Wilson of using 'weaselwords' in advocating universal military training, but 'only the compulsion of the spirit of America'. A weasel, the Colonel explained, would suck all the meat out of an egg and leave it an empty shell. **1939** *Florida* (Federal Writers' Project) I. 125 There were no 'weasel word' qualifications, such as 'it is alleged'. **1952** G. SARTON *Hist. Sci.* I. xvi. 404 It is perhaps a little ambiguous to call them idealists. [*Note*] The weasel word idealist is sometimes understood as the opposite of realist. **1977** P. JOHNSON *Enemies of Society* viii. 108 Whereas in the spheres of advertising, education and economics the use of weasel words tends to be towards gross overstatement, in the field of killing and mass destruction, the tendency is to understate and minimize. **1923** LD. CHARNWOOD *Theodore Roosevelt* x. 215 It is even comically reminiscent of the writer's own criticisms later of Mr. Wilson's '*weasel-worded' phrases. **1981** *N.Y. Times* 29 Mar. 4/1 The facts it contained did not support what one official termed the agency's 'weasel-worded' conclusion.

c. *attrib.* or as *adj.*, after *weasel word*, above. Of a statement, etc.: equivocating, ambiguous, quibbling.

1912 T. ROOSEVELT in *Outlook* 27 July 662/2 The weasel sentence about States' rights could well have been suggested by the astuteness of Mr. Bryan's fellow-Democrat Mr. Ryan. **1965** M. NAYLOR *Your Money* x. 59 If . . other things remain equal . . , the price will rise. . . It is now time to deal with that weasel qualification, 'other things being equal'. **1974** R. M. PIRSIG *Zen & Art of Motorcycle Maintenance* (1976) IV. xxviii. 337 The whole business seemed to many of them merely a new and pretentious jargon of weasel concepts. **1979** *Financial Rev.* (Melbourne) 27 Apr. 2 The probability is that the commission will deliver another of its weasel judgements, recognising merit on all sides.

ˈweasel, *v. colloq.* (orig. *U.S.*). [f. the sb.]

1. a. *trans.* To render (a word, phrase, etc.) ambiguous or equivocal; to remove or detract from (its meaning) intentionally.

1900 *Century Mag.* June 305/2 I've seen him take his pen, and go through a proposed plank or resolution, and weasel every flat-footed word in it. **1919** T. ROOSEVELT in *Maine, my State* (Maine Writers Research Club) 20 'His words weasel the meaning of the words in front of them,' said David, 'just like a weasel when he sucks the meat out of an egg and leaves nothing but the shell'.

b. *intr.* To equivocate or prevaricate, to use weasel words.

1956 [see DIRT *sb.* 6 e]. **1963** D. OGILVY *Confessions Advert. Man* v. 99 If you tell lies, weasel, you do your client a disservice. **1972** C. WESTON *Poor, Poor Ophelia* xxv. 151 He listened to the younger detective weaseling at the other end.

2. a. To extricate oneself from or get *out of* a place in the manner of a weasel. Also with *in* (with movement in the opposite direction).

1925 J. BONE *London Perambulator* 162 How to weasel out of London, north, south, east and west, with the fewest possible obstructions. **1963** T. PYNCHON *V.* vii. 171, I was always weaseling in, you know, on some show where you wouldn't expect to find naval personnel. **1968** P. DICKINSON *Skin Deep* ix. 176 Pibble weaseled out of the car and ran across the road.

b. To escape from or extricate oneself *out* (*of* a situation, obligation, etc.), esp. dishonourably; to welsh *on*. Also with *one's way*.

1956 *Washington Post* 7 Aug., For this country to weasel on its obligation would be both to fracture the Atlantic alliance and to engage in the most offensive and immoral sort of appeasement. **1962** N. MAXWELL *Witch-Doctor's Apprentice* ii. 10, I wanted to commit myself publicly to it so that it would be hard to weasel out after only a day or two. **1973** *New Yorker* 3 Mar. 85/1 Canterbury is one of the 'decadent' communities that gradually weaseled out of the Shaker strictures against ornament and luxury. **1978** M. PUZO *Fools Die* xxi. 239 A real fucking claim agent weaseling out of his obligations. **1980** *Logophile* IV. I. 46/1 It required weaseling his way into the confidence of his bank-manager. **1981** *Spectator* 6 June 16/2 Jilly Cooper was too kind-hearted to name those who weaseled out of the exercise.

3. *trans.* To obtain or extract (something) *out of* another, esp. by cunning.

1975 L. DEIGHTON *Yesterday's Spy* xii. 99 He . . 'weaseled' luggage for the boat-train passengers and was not above stealing the occasional camera. **1975** *Observer* 30 Nov. 22/4 My sole achievement was weaselling a medical certificate out of my G.P.

Hence **ˈweaselling** *ppl. a.* and *vbl. sb.*

1956 H. KURNITZ *Invasion of Privacy* xii. 81 Never could get along with lawyers. . . Bunch of weaseling doubletalkers. **1969** *Listener* 31 July 132/2 'Legitimate puffery' is often plain lying. At best, it encourages 'weaselling'—the use of meaningless and unverifiable formulae like 'Bloggo is better'; at worst, it is demonstrably fraudulent. **1978** *N.Y. Times* 30 Mar. D 18/1 Arum says there has been heavy pressure for a return bout from all over the world. He offers this as justification for his weaseling out of a commitment to match Spinks with Ken Norton.

weaselish (ˈwiːz(ə)lɪʃ), *a. rare.* [f. WEASEL *sb.* + -ISH¹.] = WEASELLY *a.*

1923 D. H. LAWRENCE *Captain's Doll* xiv, in *Ladybird* 225 The driver, who was thin and weaselish.

†**ˈweaselled**, *a. Obs.* [f. WEASEL *sb.* + -ED² (irregularly used).] = next. Only in Comb. *weaselled-coloured, -faced* adjs.

1607 TOPSELL *Four-f. Beasts* 714 The colour of them was like a Weaseled coloured horse. *a* **1692** SHADWELL *Volunteers* IV. i. (1693) 36, I never saw so weasell'd-faced a Puppy.

weaselly (ˈwiːz(ə)lɪ), *a.* Also **weas(e)ly**. [WEASEL *sb.* + -Y¹.] Weasel-like. Also *weaselly-looking*.

1838 *Bentley's Misc.* III. 582 He was a weaselly-looking little man. **1857** BORROW *Romany Rye* II. App. xi. 359 An individual . . of middle stature, a thin and weaselly figure, a sallow complexion. **1900** 'ANTHONY HOPE' *Quisanté* i. 10 He was a little weaselly perhaps. **1973** M. AMIS *Rachel Papers* 128 He was wearing a fashionable black polo-neck jersey (fashionable, that is, among the weasly middle-aged) whose sleeves he was rolling down. **1982** BARR & YORK *Official Sloane Ranger Handbk.* 17/2 What a funny little weasely face he has!

weaselship (ˈwiːz(ə)lʃɪp). [f. WEASEL *sb.* + -SHIP.] †**a.** A mock title for a weasel. **b.** The condition or qualities of a weasel. In quot. *fig.*

1702 YALDEN *Æsop at Crt.* vii. 23 A Fox . . ask'd him . . why his Weazleship would keep In durance vile. **1861** *Macm. Mag.* IV. 311/1 Such a representation . . as would . . exhibit his weaselship in the most striking light.

weasen, obs. form of WEASAND.

weaseny, variant of WEAZENY.

weasill, variant of WEEZLE *Obs.*

weason, variant of WEASAND.

weast, obs. form of WEST.

wea-swa, obs. form of WHOSO.

[**weasy**, spurious word in Dicts., is based on a misreading of WEALY in *Joye's Expos. Dan.* 1545. So **weasiness** (Joye *wealynes*).]

weat(e, obs. forms of WAIT *v.*[1], WET.

1557 N. T. (Geneva) *2 Thess.* iii. 5 The Lord guyde your hearts to the loue of God, and the weating for of Christe.

weather ('wɛðə(r)), *sb.* Forms: 1 **weder**, 2 **wæder**, 2–5 **weder**, 4 *Sc.* **vedir**, **weddire**, **wedyre**, 4–5 **wedir(e**, **wedre**, **wedur**, **wedyr**, **whedir**, 5 *Sc.* **weddre**, **-ir**, **-yr**, **wedere**, **wedyer**, **wheder**, **whed(d)yr**, 6 **weddur**, **wedor**, *Sc.* **wadder**, (**veddir**), **wodder**, **-ir**, **woder**, (**vodder**); 5 **wethyr**, 5–7 **wether**, 5–6 **whether**, 6, 9 *Sc.* **wathir**, (6 **vedthir**), 6– **weather**. [Com. Teut. (not recorded in Gothic): OE. *weder* neut., OFris. *weder*, *wether* (NFris. *wedder*, WFris. *waer*, *war*), OS. *wedar* weather, storm, Du. *weder*, *weer*, OHG. *wetar* (MHG. *weter*, mod.G. *wetter*), ON. *veðr* (Sw. *väder*, Da. *vejr*):—OTeut. **wedro-m.* It is uncertain whether the pre-Teut. form was **wedhro-m* (= OSl. *vedro*, Russian *vedro* good weather, *vedrŭ* adj., fair, said of weather; cogn. w. Lith. *vidras*, *vydra*, storm, *áudra* storm, flood) or **wetró-m* (ablaut-var. of Lith. *vė́tra* storm, OSl. *větrŭ* air, wind); on either alternative the word is prob. f. the Indogermanic root **wē* to blow (see WIND *sb.*[1]) + suffix *dhro-* or *tro-*.

The spelling with *th* instead of the earlier *d* first occurs in the 15th c. (though the pronunciation which it indicates may well be much older); before the end of the 16th c. it had become universal. In several dialects, chiefly *Sc.* and n.w., the pronunciation with (d) still survives. See TH 6, and the note s.v. FATHER *sb.*

The nautical use = wind, direction of the wind (see senses 3, 8) is probably derived from ON. *veðr*.]

I. 1. a. The condition of the atmosphere (at a given place and time) with respect to heat or cold, quantity of sunshine, presence or absence of rain, hail, snow, thunder, fog, etc., violence or gentleness of the winds. Also, the condition of the atmosphere regarded as subject to vicissitudes.

For *wind and weather* (rarely † *weather and wind*) see WIND *sb.*

c **725** *Corpus Gloss.* (Hessels) T 121 *Temperiem*, uueder. *a* **1000** *Azarias* 62 Wedere onlicust, þonne on sumeres tid sended weorþeð dropena dreorung. *a* **1100** *Gerefa* in *Anglia* IX. 259 þæt he friðige & forðige ælce [tilþe] be ðam. ðe hine weder wisað. *c* **1205** LAY. 12042 þe wind gond aliðen & þat weder leoðede. **1297** R. GLOUC. (Rolls) 2441, & vor weder & oþer þing on erþe after hom [*sc.* the planets] moche is, þis misbileuede men hom clupede godes. *c* **1374** CHAUCER *Troylus* III. 670 And if ye liggen wel to-night, com ofte, And careth not what weder is on-lofte. *c* **1400** T. CHESTRE *Launfal* 223 And for hete of the wedere Hys mantell he feld togydere And sette hym doun to reste. *c* **1403** LYDG. *Temple of Glas* 395 And oft also, aftir a dropping mone, The weddir clereþ. *c* **1450** *St. Cuthbert* (Surtees) 627 But sodanly þe wedir chaunged. *c* **1520** SKELTON *Garl. Laurel* 1442 How men were wonte for to discerne By candelmes day what wedder shuld holde. **1545** ASCHAM *Toxoph.* II. (Arb.) 161 The lengthe or shortnesse of the marke is alwayes vnder the rule of the wether. **1545** RAYNALDE *Byrth Mankynde* 88 Item the intemperancie & mutation of the ayre, & whether, may be cause of aborcement. **1528** LYNDESAY *Dreme* 774 Surmountyng the myd Regioun of the air, Quhare no maner of perturbatioun Off wodder may ascend so hie as thair. **1609** *Pimlyco, or Runne Red-Cap* D 2, To know what Wether was to come By 'th Almanacke. **1667** SPRAT *Hist. Royal-Soc.* 247 A Wheel-Barometer, and other Instruments for finding the pressure of the Air, and serving to predict the changes of the Weather. **1678** LADY CHAWORTH in *12th Rep. Hist. MSS. Comm.* App. v. 45 Lady Portsmouth..goes to Bourbon as soone as the weather opens to allow travelling. **1779** *Mirror* No. 35 The conversation began about the weather, my aunt observing, that the seasons were wonderfully altered in her memory. **1853** MRS. GASKELL *Ruth* xxv, It was weather for open doors and windows. **1859** H. KINGSLEY *G. Hamlyn* viii, However, I am sincerely glad you are come, I knew no weather would stop you. **1890** C. DIXON *Ann. Bird Life* 309 They are birds which have no regular winter home...they wander to and fro, south and north, just as the exigency of the weather drives them.

¶ In advb. phrases sometimes with omission of *in*.

1738 C'TESS POMFRET in *C'tess Hartford's Corr.* (1805) I. 10 On your left hand is the fire (no bad thing this weather), and on your right a window. **1896** HOUSMAN *Shropshire Lad* xxv, Fred keeps the house all kinds of weather.

b. With descriptive adj., e.g., *good, bad; hot, cold, warm; bright, dull; fine, fair, foul; dry, wet, rainy; clear, thick; rough, windy, still, calm.*

c **893** ÆLFRED *Oros.* VI. xxxii, þa het he betan þærinne micel fyr, for þon hit wæs ceald weder. *c* **1000** *Ags. Gosp.* Matt. xvi. 2 To-morȝen hyt byð smylte weder, þes heofen ys read. *c* **1220** *Bestiary* 236 Ðe mire is maȝti, Mikel ȝe swinkeð In sumer and in softe weder. *c* **1290** *S.E. Leg.* 198 þat weder þat was so cler and fair. **1340** *Ayenb.* 129 Ase uayr weder went in-to rene. **1340** HAMPOLE *Pr. Consc.* 1442 Nowes the wedir bright and shynand, And now waxes it alle domland. *c* **1350** *Will. Palerne* 2440 What of here hard heiȝing & of þe hote weder, Meliors was al mat. **1362** LANGL. *P. Pl.* A. VII. 310 þorw Flodes and foul weder Fruites schul fayle. *c* **1394** *P. Pl. Crede* 300 Nou han þei..hosen in harde weder. *c* **1440** *Promp. Parv.* 146/1 Fayre, mery wedur or tyme, *amenus.* **1470–85** MALORY *Arthur* XIV. ix. 653 And at that tyme the wheder was hote. **1490** CAXTON *Eneydos* xv. 56 The reyny wedre therto propyce and conuenable. **1578** LYTE *Dodoens* II. xlvi. 204 Sometimes they flower againe in Autumne when the whether is milde and pleasant. **1600** SHAKS. *A. Y. L.* v. iv. 142 You and you, are sure together, As the Winter to fowle Weather. **1631** PELLHAM *Gods Power* 4 But the next day,.. the weather falling out something thicke, and much yce in the Offing [etc.]. **1653** WALTON *Angler* ii. 41 The gloves of an Otter are the best fortification for your hands against wet weather that can be thought of. **1774** M. MACKENZIE *Marit. Surv.* 95 In moderate Weather, anchor a Vessel at the Shoal. **1782** MISS BURNEY *Cecilia* VIII. ix, To go out in all weather to work. *Ibid.* IX. v, The weather being good on the morning he called. **1842** DICKENS *Amer. Notes* ii, The vessel being pretty deep in the water,..and the weather being calm and quiet, there was but little motion. **1853** —— *Bleak Ho.* xv, There was no fire, though the weather was cold. **1919** H. L. WILSON *Ma Pettengill* 165 Will you look at that mess of clouds? I bet it's falling weather over in Surprise Valley.

c. *fig.* and in figurative context; *spec.* (*Lit.*), applied to an intellectual climate, state of mind, etc.

1603 R. JOHNSON *Kingd. & Commw.* 65 Iustinian restored it [the Empire] somewhat to a better state, driuing the Vandals out of Africke, and the Gothes out of Italy by his captaines; but this faire weather lasted not long. **1630** BP. HALL *Occas. Medit.* §73 O God..Let mee haue no Weather but Sunne-shine from thee. **1751** SMOLLETT *Per. Pickle* xcvi, Pipes, who..knew the contents of the piece [a pistol], asked..if it must be foul weather through the whole voyage. **1818** SCOTT *Hrt. Midl.* xlvii, Certain polemical skirmishes betwixt her father and her husband, which..often threatened unpleasant weather between them. **1862** THACKERAY *Philip* xxviii, We hadn't much besides our pay, had we? we rubbed on through bad weather and good, managing as best we could. **1878** E. W. BENSON in *Life* (1899) I. xiii. 463 But we have foul weather coming. We have to do the Church's work without sacrificing those party men, [etc.]. **1901** *N. Amer. Rev.* Feb. 266 A barometer is thus formed by which the financial weather of the country is forecast. **1909** H. JAMES *Roderick Hudson* (rev. ed.) vii. 147 He supposed that these changes of intellectual weather.. were the lot of every poet. **1922** G. SANTAYANA *Soliloquies in England* 30 What governs the Englishman is his inner atmosphere, the weather in his soul. **1927** T. WILDER *Bridge of San Luis Rey* 17 Such authors live always in the noble weather of their own minds. **1962** K. ALLOTT *Penguin Bk. Contemp. Verse* 18 A short introduction giving explicit attention to the poetic 'weather' of each of the last four decades.

†d. With indef. article: A kind of weather; a spell of a particular kind of weather. *Obs.*

c **1205** LAY. 4573 Æst aras a ladlich weder. *Ibid.* 7398 þeo com heom a wedere wunderliche feire. *c* **1374** CHAUCER *Troylus* III. 657 Lord, this is an huge rayn! This were a weder for to slepen inne. *c* **1400** *Laud Troy Bk.* 12914 It made tho a lothely wedur, Hit raynes faste, thondres, & blowes. **1546** *Gassar's Prognost.* A viij b, Not long before the Sonne shall set, we may looke for a trobelous wether, & perchaunce snow. **1548** *Elyot's Dict.*, *Apricitas*,..a fayre clere wether. **1618** ROWLANDS *Sacred Mem.* 25 Their storme was chang'd into a fayre calme weather.

e. *pl.* Kinds of weather: sometimes equivalent to *sing.* Now *rare* exc. in phr. (*in*) ***all weathers***.

Beowulf 546 Wedera cealdost, nipende niht ond norþan wind, heaðogrim ondhwearf. *a* **900** *Andreas* 1256 Weder coledon heardum hæȝelscurum. *c* **1000** *Sax. Leechd.* II. 244 Swa bið eac on wintra, for cyle & for þara wedra missenlicnesse, þæt se milte wyrð ȝelefed. *c* **1175** *Lamb. Hom.* 13 Westmes þorð uuele wederas oft and ilome scal forwurðan. *c* **1325** *Poem temp. Edw. II* (Percy) xxxv, Catel cometh and goth As wederis don in lyde. **1340** HAMPOLE *Pr. Consc.* 1424 Sere variaunce, for certayn skille, Of þe tyms and wedirs and sesons. *c* **1350** *Will. Palerne* 5216 For wind & gode wederes hade þei at wille. **1377** LANGL. *P. Pl.* B. xv. 349 For þorw werre and wykked werkes and wederes vnresonable Wederwise shipmen..Han no believe to þe lifte ne to þe lore of philosofres. *c* **1449** PECOCK *Repr.* II. ii. 146 God is such oon, that he nedith not to haue housis ouer him for to couere him fro reyne and fro othir sturne wedris. *a* **1450** *Le Morte Arth.* 2470 Wederes had they feyre and good. **1526** in Willis & Clark *Cambridge* (1886) I. 618 Dowble bandes of leade for defence of great wyndes and other outragious wethers. **1639** J. TAYLOR (Water P.) *Pt. Summers Trav.* 44 Every Sunday, be it Winter or Summer, all manner of weathers. **1697** T. SMITH in *Lett. Lit. Men* (Camden) 247, I was forced..to go downe to Westminster ..in all weathers. **1706** E. WARD *Wooden World Diss.* (1708) 21 He's..not so stiff as to carry Sail against all Weathers. **1717** LADY M. W. MONTAGU *Let. to Abbé Conti* 17 May, It is covered on the top with boards to keep out the rain, that merchants may meet conveniently in all weathers. **1849** C. BRONTE *Shirley* xi, She took walks in all weathers—long walks in solitary directions. **1862** H. KINGSLEY *Ravenshoe* xix, It was impossible to pass round the promontory on horseback in the best of weathers; now doubly so. **1865** DICKENS *Mut. Fr.* I. v, All weathers saw the man at the post.

fig. **1611** SHAKS. *Wint. T.* v. i. 195 Camillo ha's betray'd me; Whose honor, and whose honestie till now, Endur'd all Weathers.

†f. With implied favourable qualification: Weather suitable for some purpose. *Obs.*

c **1375** *Sc. Leg. Saints* xxvii. (*Machar*) 1486 þar-to weddire had þai þane, þat þai wane froyt of land & se thru his prayere in gret pleynte. **1393** LANGL. *P. Pl.* C. VII. 113 Bote ich hadde wedir at my wil ich wited god þe cause. *c* **1400** *Laud Troy Bk.* 3280 Thei..passed the see, when thei hadde wedur, To Thenedoun. **1469** *Plumpton Corr.* (Camden) 21 Whether is so latesum in this cuntrey, that men can neither well gett corne nor hay.

g. With unfavourable implication: Adverse, unpleasant, hurtful, or destructive condition of the atmosphere; rain, frost, wind-driven waves, etc. as destructive agents. ***stress of weather***: see STRESS *sb.* 3.

a **1122** *O.E. Chron.* (Laud) an. 1097, He þohte his hired on Winceastre to healdenne, ac he wearð þurh weder ȝelet. *Ibid.* an. 1114, Ac wæder him lætte. **1340–70** *Alex. & Dind.* 443 Swich housinge we han to holde out þe wedures. *c* **1400** *Sowdone Bab.* 76 A drift of wedir vs droffe to Rome. **1425** *Paston Lett.* Suppl. (1901) 5 Whether it wille chippe or chynne or affraye with frost or weder or water. *a* **1548** HALL *Chron., Edw. IV* 233 b, Which bridge was made and covered with bordes, onely to kepe of the wether. **1557** TUSSER *100 Points Husb.* xxxv, Thinges sowne, set or graft, in good memory haue: from beast, birde and weather to cherishe and saue. **1606** G. W[OODCOCKE] *Hist. Ivstine* II. 7 Before the vse of garments was found out against weathers iniury. **1616** T. SCOT *Philomythie* H 6 b, His [the weathercock's] taile was too too weake, when euery feather Was bent with storms, and broken with the weather. **1638** M. CASAUBON *Use & Custom* 77 It hath beene observed of some free stones, that ..if they bee laid in that proper posture, which they had naturally in their quarries, they grow very hard and durable against both time and weather. **1665** in *10th Rep. Hist. MSS. Comm.* App. v. 4 The stones..being of a soft.. condition and not able to endure the sunn and weather. **1693** MOXON *Mech. Exerc.* (1703) 251 Chords, which should be well Pitched to preserve them from the Weather, and rotting. **1814** SCOTT *Ld. of Isles* IV. xxii, Weather and war their rougher trace Have left on that majestic face. **1853** DICKENS *Bleak Ho.* lvii, 'Are you well wrapped up?'.. I told him I cared for no weather, and was warmly clothed. **1872** SHIPLEY *Gloss. Eccl. Terms* s.v. *Louvre Boards*, Boards..to keep out the weather.

fig. **1663** CHARLETON *Chorea Gigant.* 18 An Invention.. not so firmly founded, as to be impregnable; nor so closely compacted in all its parts, as to keep out all weather of Contradiction.

h. Violent wind accompanied by heavy rain or agitation of the waves. Now *dial.* and *Naut.* †Also, a storm, tempest; often pleonastically, ***storm, tempest of weather(s***. *Obs.*

c **888** ÆLFRED *Boeth.* xxxviii. §1 Ða ȝestod hine heah weder & stormsæ. *c* **1205** LAY. 102 Mid wolcnen & mid wedere heo poleden wensiðes. *c* **1250** *Gen. & Ex.* 3055 Moyses, do ðis weder charen, And ȝu sal [ic] leten ut-faren. *a* **1300** *Cursor M.* 6018 þe seuend on-sand [*sc.* of the plagues of Egypt] Was a weder ful selcut snell. **13..** *K. Alis.* 5794 (Laud MS.), þe wederes stronge & tempestes..hem duden grete molestes. *c* **1381** CHAUCER *Parl. Foules* v. 681 Now welcom somer, with thy sonne softe, That hast this wintres weders over-shake. **1387–8** T. USK *Test. Love* I. iii. 63 And so by mokel duresse of weders and of stormes..I was driven to an yle. *c* **1400** MAUNDEV. (Roxb.) xxxii. 144 þer es neuermare..nowþer thunner ne leuenyng, haile ne snawe, ne oþer tempestez of ill weders. **1402** *Pol. Poems* (Rolls) II. 44 To were us from wederes of wynteres stormes. *c* **1420** WYNTOUN *Cron.* VII. x. 3278 And þar be a tempest fel Off gret wedderis scharpe and snel. **1450–1530** *Myrr. Our Ladye* III. 303 There are gendered tempastes of weder and hayle. **1490** CAXTON *Eneydos* xxx. 114 Whan thenne they had ronne & saylled so moche that they were in the highe see a stronge weddre arose. **1523** BERNERS *Froiss.* (1812) I. cccxxiv. 506 This rayne and wether endured tyll the sonne rose. **1526** TINDALE *Heb.* xii. 18 Ye are not come..to myst and darcknes and tempest of wedder [Gr. θυέλλῃ]. **1531** *Test. Ebor.* (Surtees) VI. 26 Tempestes of wedder or stormes. **1553** T. WILSON *Rhet.* 106 b, Diogenes beeyng vpon the Sea emong a number of naughtie packes in a greate storme of wether, when diuerse of these wicked felowes cried out for feare of drownyng, [etc.]. **1598** in *Rec. Convent. Burghs Scot.* (1870) II. 27 [They] alegeit thai war impeidit be storme of wedder. **1703** DAMPIER *Voy.* III. I. 10 Upon these Signs Ships either get up their Anchors, or slip their Cables and put to Sea, and ply off and on till the Weather is over. **1718** HEARNE *Collect.* (O.H.S.) VI. 212 The Master and the other Servant, running through the Weather towards the Houses, were both struck dead. **1894** HALL CAINE *Manxman* III. v, 'Then don't be late,' said he, 'there's weather coming.' **1898** *Morn. Post* 11 Nov. 5/2 Wasn't it a beautifully disciplined Mess, though? I wish you could see 'em at sea in weather.

†i. What falls from the clouds; rain, snow, etc. Also in fig. context. *Obs.*

1382 WYCLIF *Deut.* xxxii. 2 Flowe as dewe my speche, as wedre [Vulg. *imber*] vpon erbe. *Ibid. Job* xxiv. 8, *Eccl.* xi. 3, *Isa.* v. 6, *Jer.* xiv. 22. *c* **1400** *Rom. Rose* 4336 But er he it in sheves shere, May falle a weder that shal it dere. *c* **1475** *Rauf Coilyear* 74 The wedderis ar sa fell, that fallis on the feild. *a* **1533** BERNERS *Golden Bk. M. Aurel.* xxxiv. (1535) 59 The labourer whan it reyneth not, coureth his house, thinkinge that an other tyme the wethers or raynes wyll fall theron and trouble hym. **1595** SHAKS. *John* IV. ii. 109 A fearefull eye thou hast!.. So foule a skie cleeres not without a storme: Poure downe thy weather! how goes all in France? **1825** JAMIESON, *Weather*, a fall of rain or snow accompanied with boisterous wind. Roxb. When the wind comes singly.., [people say] 'It 'ill be no weather the day, but wind'.

†j. In contexts relating to clouds or fog, the word sometimes assumes the sense of: Air, sky. *Obs.*

c **1375** *Cursor M.* 24414 (Fairf.) þe wedder [*earlier texts* air, aier] be-gan to derkin & blake. *c* **1475** *Pict. Voc.* in Wr.-Wülcker 801/1–4 *Hic aier*, *Hec aera*, *Hic ether*, *Hec ethera*, the wethyr. *a* **1500** *Coventry Corpus Chr. Plays* i. 209 These wedurs ar darke and dym of lyght. **1530** PALSGR. 648/1, I overcast, as the weather dothe wan it is close or darke and lykely to rayne.. We shall have a rayne a none, the weather is sore overcaste sodaynly... I overcast, as the cloudes do the weather. *c* **1605** DRAYTON *Ballad Agincourt* 76 Arrowes ..that like to serpents stoong, pearcing the Wether.

2. Phrases.

†a. ***the weather rains, thunders***, etc. = 'it rains', etc. *Obs.*

1390 GOWER *Conf.* I. 140 The weder schal upon thee reine. **1590** SIR J. SMYTHE *Disc. Weapons* 19 b, If in the tyme of anie battle..the weather doth happen to raine, haile, or snow. **1634** SIR T. HERBERT *Trav.* 24 The weather thundring and storming exceedingly.

†b. ***to make*** (rarely ***bear***) ***fair weather***: to be conciliatory, make a show of friendliness (*to* or *with* a person); also, to make a specious show of goodness, etc. ***to make fair weather of*** (a state of things): to gloss over, represent as better than it is. *Obs.*

c **1400** *Laud Troy Bk.* 8289 At here comyng thei made fair wedur, And spak of many thynges to-gedur. **1537** Cromwell in Merriman *Life & Lett.* (1902) II. 93 Thother parte declare him in wordes towardes his Maieste to make only faire wether, and in his harte..to doo all that he canne to his graces dishonour. **1547** Cheke in Harington *Nugæ Ant.* (1804) I. 20 And if anye suche shall be, that shall of all things make fair weather, and, whatsoever they shall see to the contrarye, shall tell you all is well. **1560** Daus tr. *Sleidane's Comm.* 369b, Duke Moris..to make fayre weather [L. *pacificationis causa*] sendeth his ambassadors to the Counsell. **1583** Golding *Calvin on Deut.* cxix. 732 And that is the cause why wee see so fewe holde out in weldoing. Many make faire wether for a time, so as yee woulde thinke them to bee maruellous good men: but in the turning of a hande all is marde. **1589** R. Payne *Brief Descr. Irel.* 7 Al the better sort doe deadly hate yᵉ Spaniardes, & yet I thinke they beare them fayre weather, for that they are the popes champions. **1593** Shaks. *2 Hen. VI*, v. i. 30 But I must make faire weather yet a while, Till Henry be more weake, and I more strong. **1596** *Edw. III*, I. ii. 23 Returne and say, That we with England will not enter parlie, Nor neuer make faire wether, or take truce. **1598** Marston *Pygmal., Sat.* i. 31 Ixion makes faire weather vnto Ioue. **1622** Bacon *Hen. VII*, 49 To which message, although the French King gaue no full credit, yet he made faire weather with the King, and seemed satisfied. **1673** Kirkman *Unlucky Cit.* 163 My Mother-in-law made very fair weather to me, and gave me many good words.

c. *Naut.* Of a ship, ***to make good, bad,*** etc. ***weather of it***: to behave well or ill in a storm.

1669 Sturmy *Mariner's Mag.* I. ii. 17 We make foul weather. **1781** *Naval Chron.* XI. 287 The Ship makes a very good weather of it. **1860** *Merc. Marine Mag.* VII. 86 The ship making very bad weather and shipping large quantities of water. **1867** Smyth *Sailor's Word-bk.*, *Make bad weather, To.* A ship rolling, pitching, or leaking violently in a gale. **1881** *Daily Tel.* 28 Jan., The sea was..not so heavy but that in my judgment a twenty-ton yacht would have made excellent weather of it.

fig. **1915** 'Ian Hay' *1st Hund. Thou.* I. xiii. §2 The feckless and muddle-headed, making heavy weather of the simplest tasks.

d. ***in the weather***: in an exposed situation, unprotected from rain, cold, and wind; in the open air (usually with implication of severe weather). Similarly ***to go into, through the weather.***

a **1513** Fabyan *Chron.* v. lxxxiii. (1516) 32 The kynges Herdemen passyd by, And seynge this Bysshop with his company syttyng in the weder, desyred hym to his howse to take there such poore lodgynge as he had. **1669** Sturmy *Mariner's Mag.* II. 102 The Tree roots best, that in the Weather stands. **1693** Moxon *Mech. Exerc.* (1703) 241 The out side of Buildings that lies in the Weather. **1842** Dickens *Amer. Notes* ii, The captain..turns up his coat collar..and goes laughing out into the weather as merrily as to a birthday party. **1865** Mrs. H. Wood *Mildred Arkell* xlvi, They started together through the weather to the house of William Arkell. **1880** Howells *Undisc. Country* xiii. 190 Her longing to be in the weather [after an illness].

† **e.** ***down the weather***: in adversity. ***to go down the weather***: to become bankrupt. *Obs.*

1611 Cotgr., s.v. *Aller*, *Aller au saffran*, to fall to decay, to grow bankrupt in estate, to goe downe the weather. **1641** J. Shute *Sarah & Hagar* (1649) 63 We see how Job was despised when he was down the weather, yea even by those, whom, when he prospered, he would scarce have set with the dogs of his flock.

f. ***under the weather*** (orig. *U.S.*): indisposed, not quite well.

1827 *Austin Papers* (1924) I. 1622 The fredonians is all here rather under the wether. **1850** D. G. Mitchell *Lorgnette* (1852) I. 50 As for the Frenchman, though now, between the valorous Poussin and the long-faced Bonaparte, a little under the weather [etc.]. **1882** Miss Braddon *Mt. Royal* II. iv. 59 'What, old lady, are you under the weather?' he asked, turning to survey his mother with a critical air. **1887** F. R. Stockton *Borrowed Month* 68 They had been very well as a general thing, although now and then they might have been under the weather for a day or two.

g. ***weather permitting***: often appended to an announcement (e.g. of the sailing of a vessel) to indicate that it is conditional on the weather being favourable.

1712 *Lond. Gaz.* No. 4953/4 The Edgley Gally will be ready to Sail.., Wind and Weather permitting. **1842** Dickens *Amer. Notes* i, There was a beautiful port-hole which could be kept open all day (weather permitting). **1883** *Black's Guide Devon.* (ed. 11) 164 The steamers from Portishead to Ilfracombe call, going and returning, weather permitting.

h. ***clerk of the weather***: see CLERK *sb.* 3.

1829 P. Egan *Boxiana* 2nd Ser. II. 302 Asking of no favours from the clerk of the weather to keep off 'the pitiless pelting storm', as their greasy jackets were proof against all watery attacks. **1835** C. F. Hoffman *Winter in West* I. 38, I could not, if I had made my own private arrangements with the clerk of the weather, have fixed it upon the whole more to my satisfaction.

i. ***to stretch wing to weather***: to fly.

1825 Scott *Betrothed* xxiii, If they be not carefully trained..I would rather have a gosshawk on my perch than the fairest falcon that ever stretched wing to weather.

j. ***above*** (or ***over***) ***the weather*** (Aeronaut.), above the range of weather conditions acting at ground-level; above the clouds.

1944 *Aviation* Feb. 497/1 The plane climbs..to fly 'over the weather'. **1958** *Listener* 16 Oct. 593/1 It was said that they [*sc.* accidents] had destroyed all prospect of carrying passengers at speeds not far short of the speed of sound, far above the weather, at heights of 35,000 feet.

3. *Naut.* The direction in which the wind is blowing. 'Applied to anything lying to windward of a particular situation' (Adm. Smyth). In various phrases: ***to luff nigh the weather***: to sail near the wind; in quot. *fig.* ***to drive with the weather***: to drift with the wind and waves. ***to have the weather of***: to be to windward of (another ship); similarly ***in, into, on, to, upon (the) weather of***. Also, ***in, into the weather***; ***up to weather***: to windward. Cf. A-WEATHER.

1390 Gower *Conf.* II. 370 Or elles thei take ate leste Out of hir hand or ring or glove, So nyh the weder thei wol love. **1526** Tindale *Acts* xxvii. 15 We lett her goo, and drave with the wedder [ἐφερόμεθα]. **1557** Towrson in Hakluyt *Voy.* (1589) 113 Wee had sight of three sailes of shippes..which were in the weather of vs. *Ibid.*, When we met, they had the weather of vs. ? **1565** J. Sparke *Ibid.* 524 His pinnesse.. being in the weather of him. **1588** in *St. Papers Defeat Sp. Armada* (Navy Rec. Soc. 1894) II. 107 After this we cast about our ship, and kept ourselves close by the Spaniard until midnight, sometime hearing a voice in Spanish calling us; but the wind being very great and we in the weather, the voice was carried away. *c* **1595** Capt. Wyatt *Dudley's Voy. W. Ind.* (Hakl. Soc.) 18 [Hee] gave commaundement that the carvell shoulde plie up into the weather. *Ibid.*, The French admerall, who laie aloofe of some six leagues to weather. **1692** *J. Smith's Sea-mans Gram.* I. xvi. 78 *Weather Gage*, is when one Ship has the Wind (or is to weather) of another. **1842** Browning *Waring* iii. 12 Then the boat.. from the lee, Into the weather, cut somehow Her sparkling path beneath our bow. **1868** *Field* 25 July 83/2 The Mabella [yacht] too, was much closer on her weather than was pleasant. **1903** *Times* 21 Aug. 4/3 Reliance, though astern, was well up to weather. *Ibid.*, Reliance by now had unmistakably got upon the challenger's weather.

4. The angle which the sails of a windmill make with the perpendicular to the axis. More fully, ***angle of weather***.

1759 Smeaton in *Phil. Trans.* LI. 141 *note*, The angle of the sails is accounted from the plain of their motion; that is, when they stand at right angles to the axis, their angle is denoted 0°, this notation being agreeable to the language of practitioners, who call the angle so denoted, the weather of the sail. **1825** J. Nicholson *Oper. Mech.* 138 In the mill-wright's terms, the greatest angle of weather was 30 degrees, and the least varied from 12 to 6 degrees, as the inclination of the windshaft varied from 8 to 15 degrees.

5. = WEATHERING *vbl. sb.* 3. *rare.*

1894 A. M. Bell in *Jrnl. Anthrop. Inst.* XXIII. 272 Beyond doubt they [two flints] were chipped at the same time..yet one is weathered, and the other is unaltered. So from an isolated example of weather I am in no haste to draw a conclusion. *Ibid.* 273 So also with surface finds; if they possess definite characteristics of form, of wear, of weather, ..then these are certainly local accidents.

II. *attrib.* and *Comb.*

6. a. Simple *attrib.*, as ***weather bulletin***, ***-cast***, ***-change***, ***-chart***, ***-forecast***, ***-journal***, ***-lore***, ***-lorist***, ***-map***, ***-mark***, ***prediction***, ***-report***, ***-saw***, ***-screen***, ***-wear***, †***-wrack***.

1926 R. Macaulay *Crewe Train* II. viii. 157 She asked Arnold..to tell her when the *weather bulletin came on; that was normally the only part of the programme to which she cared to listen. **1980** P. Moyes *Angel Death* xv. 198 The weather bulletin..advised guests that Hurricane Beatrice was..moving at a brisk fourteen knots. **1866** Steinmetz *Weathercasts* 142 *Weathercasts by the Barometer. **1878** R. Strachan in *Mod. Meteorology* (1879) 84 A system of storm-warnings and weather-casts. **1980** *Time* 17 Mar. 37/1 A native American art form, the television weathercast. **1876** Geo. Eliot *Deronda* lii, Something as dim as the sense of approaching *weather-change. **1901** *Westm. Gaz.* 26 Oct. 5/2 The *weather-chart...showed that there were several small atmospheric disturbances in the neighbourhood of the British Isles. **1883** *Encycl. Brit.* XVI. 158/1 *Weather Forecasts and Storm Warnings. **1868** G. M. Hopkins *Jrnls. & Papers* (1959) 189 Henceforth I keep no regular *weather-journal but only notes. **1875** *Chamb. Jrnl.* 2 Jan. 7/2 We shall thereby add every year to our *weather-lore of the various oceans and seas. **1905** *Westm. Gaz.* 21 Aug. 10/1 A remarkable dearth of acorns..which, according to the *weather lorists, is a favourable augury for the coming weather. **1877** *Weather map [see FACSIMILE 3]. **1883** *Encycl. Brit.* XVI. 157/1 The International Monthly Weather Maps issued by the United States Signal Service. **1693** *Humours Town* 15 Bringing Old Age and *Weather marks on you before you have run half your Course. **1909** *Weather prediction [see GAFFE]. **1951** M. McLuhan *Mech. Bride* (1967) 75/1 The comment is given in the style of stock-market operations or weather predictions. **1863** R. Fitzroy *Weather Bk.* 349 Local changes should be indicated to observers..by due attention to the published *Weather Reports. **1939** T. S. Eliot *Family Reunion* II. i. 97 And now it is nearly time for the news We must listen to the weather report. **1980** A. E. Fisher *Midnight Men* vii. 78 He could do without unfavourable weather reports. **1871** G. M. Hopkins 6 Aug. *Jrnls. & Papers* (1959) 213 The common *weather-saw about the rainbow. **1914** 'Bartimeus' *Naval Occasions* xx. 181 The men on the bridge ducked their heads as..a shower of spray drifted over the *weather-screens. **1977** P. Smalley *Trove* ii. 84 The triple-panel weather screen was fitted with heavy duty wipers. **1824** Mactaggart *Gallovid. Encycl.* 191 Owre moor and dale for mony a year, May Davie's famous dykes appear, Ne'er bilged out wi' *wather-wear, But just the same. **1875** Brash *Eccl. Archit. Irel.* 96 In truth, I have seldom seen a better executed piece of masonry, despite the weather-wear of over seven hundred years. *a* **1616** Beaum. & Fl. *Wit at Sev. Weapons* II. i, Well, well, you have built a nest That will stand all stormes, you need not mistrust A *weather-wrack.

b. objective, as ***weather-caster*** (so ***-casting***), ***-forecaster***, †***-wielder***; ***weather-braving***, ***-withstanding*** ppl. adjs.

1800 Hurdis *Fav. Village* 4 How long upon the hill has stood Thy weather-braving tower. *c* **1904** *Encycl. Dict. Suppl.*, Weather-caster. **1965** *Punch* 5 May 660/2 His great ambition in life is to be a TV weathercaster. **1980** *Time* 17 Mar. 37 TV weather-casters have been much mocked for their polyester jocularity. *Ibid.* (*heading*) The wonderful art of weather-casting. **1900** *Nature* 29 Nov. 110/2 Disappointing..from the viewpoint of the weather forecaster. **1981** *Times* 9 Dec. 1 The weather forecasters were criticized..for not giving enough warning..of the snowfall. *c* **1611** Chapman *Iliad* VII. 3 As the weather-wielder sends, to Sea-men prosperous gales. **1818** Scott *Hrt. Midl.* xliii, Those prudent and resolved and weather-withstanding professors, wha hae kend what it was to lurk.. in bogs and in caverns.

c. instrumental, as ***weather-bleached***, ***-blown***, ***-borne***, ***-bronzed***, ***-eaten***, ***-hardened***, ***-roughened***, ***-scarred***, ***-stayed***, ***-tanned***, ***-tinted***, †***-waft***, ***-wasted***, ***-worn*** ppl. adjs. Also WEATHER-BEATEN, etc.

1784 Cowper *Task* v. 834 His country's *weather-bleach'd and batter'd rocks. *c* **1611** Chapman *Iliad* II. 532 Strong Enispe, that for height, is euer *weather-blowne. **1867** Smyth *Sailor's Word-bk.*, **Weather-borne*, pressed by wind and sea. **1837** W. Irving *Capt. Bonneville* xv, Their ..*weather-bronzed complexions. **1814** Coleridge *Lett.* (1895) 640 [A Janus face] all *weather eaten. **1834** Southey *Doctor* ix. I. 111 A countenance which, *weather-hardened as it was, might have given the painter a model for a Patriarch. **1897** W. B. Yeats *Secret Rose* 187 Her dark, *weather-roughened skin. **1876** Miss Broughton *Joan* I. i, The *weather-scarred gray walls. **1854** Mrs. C. L. Balfour *Working Women* (1868) 395 Whenever he had a guest belated or *weather-staid in that lonely region. **1853** Dickens *Bleak Ho.* lii, A *weather-tanned..woman with a basket. **1814** Scott *Wav.* v (verses), The *weather-tinted rock and tower. **1647** Ward *Simple Cobler* 20 Men.., that are *weather-waft up and down with every eddy-wind of every new doctrine. **1822** Scott *Pirate* xix, These haggard and *weather-wasted features. **1609** Healey *Discov. New World* I. v. 13 We beheld a tombe, which as far as I could guesse by the *weather-worne inscription conteined the bones of the Romane Apicius. **1827** Carlyle *Germ. Lit. Misc.* 1857 I. 48 The weather-worn sculptures of the Parthenon. **1862** Ansted *Channel Isl.* I. i. (ed. 2) 8 Sark, somewhat the loftiest of the islands, is also the most weather-worn.

d. with adjectives expressing imperviousness or power of resistance (to the weather), as ***weather-free***, ***-resistant***, ***-resisting***, ***-tight***, ***-tough***. Also ***weather-resistance***; WEATHER-PROOF.

1648 G. Daniel *Eclog* ii. 6 Lambs, sooner wise then wee, Have got the Hedge, and now stand Weather-free. **1819** Byron *Juan* II. xi, The dashing spray Flies in one's face, and makes it weather-tough. **1832** Ht. Martineau *Ella of Garv.* i. 10 If your honour would order the place down below to be made weather-tight for us. **1855** *Poultry Chron.* III. 388 Place a hen, with her brood, under a good weather-tight coop. **1894** Weather-resisting [see ROOFING (*vbl.*) *sb.* 1 b]. **1902** A. Austin *Haunts Anc. Peace* 20 The cottages..looked solid, sturdy, and weather-tight. **1934** *Archit. Rev.* LXXVI. 16/1 Many years of use have proved the method satisfactory, both as a weather-resistant and as insulation. **1942** *E. African Ann. 1941–2* 98 (Advt.), Anti-rust paint.. durable, elastic, weather-resisting. **1967** M. Chandler *Ceramics in Mod. World* iv. 117 Another property that makes both porcelain and glass insulators particularly suitable for high-voltage insulators is their weather-resistance. **1970** *New Yorker* 3 Oct. 27/2 You can bolt on anything from redwood to weather-resistant aluminum.

7. Special comb.: **weather balloon**, a balloon sent up to provide meteorological information, either by the course it takes or by means of instruments it carries; †**weather-basket**, a wickerwork screen or covering to protect a plant; **weather-box** = *weather-house*; **weather-brained** *a.* = WEATHER-HEADED; **weather bureau** *U.S.*, an agency (*spec.* one established by the Government) which observes and reports on weather conditions; †**weather-caster**, a weather-prophet; **weather centre**, an office which provides weather information and analysis; *spec.* in U.K., part of the Meteorological Office; **weather clerk** = *clerk of the weather* s.v. CLERK *sb.* 6c; **weather-cloth** *Naut.*, a covering of canvas or tarpaulin used to protect boats, hammocks, etc., or to shelter persons from wind and spray; **weathercoat**, a weather-proof coat, a raincoat; **weather-cord**, a cord used as a hygrometer; **weather-cottage** = *weather-house*; **weather cycle**, a recurring pattern of weather or of some tendency in the weather; **weather-dog** *dial.* [DOG *sb.* 10] = WEATHER-GALL; **weather-door**, (*a*) a louver-hole in a church steeple (cf. LOUVER 4, quot. 1858); (*b*) *Mining* (see quot.); †**weather-fan**, a punkah; **weather-fane** = FANE *sb.*[1] 2; **weather-fast** *a.*, secure against the weather; **weather-fence** *v. trans.* = WEATHER-FEND; **weather-fish** = *thunder-fish* b (s.v. THUNDER *sb.* 6); †**weather-flag**, a vane; **weather-gleam**, **-glim** *Sc.* and *north. dial.*, clear sky near a dark horizon; also, the horizon; **weather-god**, a god who presides over the weather; **weather-guard** *v. trans.*, to guard against bad weather; **weather-head** *dial.*, a secondary rainbow; **weather-hen** *jocular*, a female weathercock; an inconstant woman; **weather-house**, a toy hygroscope in the form of a small house with figures of a man and woman standing in two porches; by the varying torsion of a string the man comes out of his porch in wet weather and the woman out of hers in dry; **weather-line**, the surface of an embedded timber just above the ground; **weather-maker**, a weather-prophet; also **weather-making** *vbl. sb.*; **weather-man**, (*a*) one who observes the weather; now also *spec.* one who presents a weather forecast on radio, television, etc.; (*b*) (freq. with capital initial and in *pl.*) (a member of) a violent revolutionary group in the U.S. (see quot. 1970); cf. *Weather Underground* below; **weather modification**, the deliberate alteration of the weather in an area; **weather-monger**, a weather-prophet; **weather-moulding** *Arch.*, a dripstone; **weather plane**, an aeroplane designed to collect data on weather conditions at high altitudes; † **weather-plate**, a plate marked with a scale for indicating the height of the mercury in a barometer; † **weather-prophecy** *Obs.*, the foretelling of the weather; **weather-prophet**, one who foretells the weather; one who is weather-wise; also *fig.*; **weather radar**, radar used for meteorological investigations (e.g. of rain); † **weather-rope** (see quot.); **weather satellite**, a satellite especially equipped to observe weather conditions and to provide meteorological information; **weather-sharp** *U.S. colloq.*, a weather-prophet; an official meteorologist (*Cent. Dict.* Suppl. 1909); **weather ship**, a ship serving as a weather station; **weather-sick** *a.*, sick of, suffering from, the weather; **weather-sign**, a phenomenon that indicates change of weather; also *fig.*; † **weather-skirt** *U.S.* = SAFEGUARD *sb.* 8; **weather-slated, -slating** (cf. *weather-tiled, -tiling*); † **weather-spar** = WEATHERBOARD 2; † **weather-spy**, a weather-prophet; **weather station**, a meteorological observation post; † **weather-stone**, a kind of stone classed according to its imperviousness to weather; **weather-strip** orig. *U.S.*, a strip of wood or rubber applied to a crevice in order to exclude rain and cold (Webster 1864); hence as *vb. trans.*, to apply a weather-strip to (*Cent. Dict.* 1891); hence **weather-stripped** *ppl. a.*; **weather-stripping** *vbl. sb.*, material used to weather-strip a door, window, etc.; the process of applying this; **weather-table** *Arch.* = WATER-TABLE 1 b; **weather-tile**, a kind of tile used instead of weather-board to cover a wall; **weather-tiled** *ppl. a.*, covered with overlapping tiles; **weather-tiling** *vbl. sb.*, the process or result of covering a wall with tiles; **weather-tree**, the white poplar, *Populus alba*; **Weather Underground**, the revolutionary organization formed by the Weathermen (see above); **weather-vane** = VANE 1; also *fig.*; **weather-wall**, a wall serving as a shield from the weather; **weather-warning** (see quot.); **weather window** *Oil Industry*, a brief interval in the year when the weather is calm enough to allow construction, loading, etc., operations to be carried out at sea; **weather-wiseacre** *nonce-wd.*, one who professes to be weather-wise; † **weather-wizard**, a weather-prophet; **weather woman**, (*a*) (with capital initial) a female member of the revolutionary Weatherman organization; (*b*) a woman who presents a weather forecast on radio or television; † **weather-works**, devices to protect a ship from rough weather.

1940 *War Illustr.* 19 Jan. 614/3 (*caption*) Finnish soldiers are investigating weather conditions by sending up a *weather balloon. **1979** J. Gribbin *Weather Force* vii. 160 (*caption*) Russian scientists..prepare to launch a flock of weather balloons, which will radio back information about conditions in the atmosphere's lower levels. **1699** Meager *New Art Garden.* 28 When they are Grafted they must be fenced, either with a *weather-basket, or some earthen Vessel. **1848** Thackeray *Van. Fair* x, The elder and younger son of the house of Crawley were, like the gentleman and lady in the *weather-box, never at home together. **1826** Scott *Woodst.* vii, But art thou not an inconsiderate *weather-brained fellow, to set forth as thou wert about to do, without any thing to bear thy charges..? **1854** H. Miller *Sch. & Schm.* i. (1858) 10 There was a weather-brained tailor in the neighbourhood, who used to do very odd things, especially, it was said, when the moon was at the full. **1871** *Harper's Mag.* Aug. 401/1 In the year 1857 Lieutenant M. F. Maury..appealed to the public and Congress, through the press, urging the establishment of a storm and *weather bureau. **1890** *U.S. Statutes* XXVI. 653 The civilian duties now performed by the Signal Corps of the Army shall hereafter devolve upon a bureau to be known as the Weather Bureau. **1950** *Los Angeles Times* 12 Feb. 1/4 Weather Bureau figures show that ·34 inch fell during the rainstorm. **1978** S. Sheldon *Bloodline* iv. 71 July turned out to be the rainiest month in the history of the French weather bureau. **1607** Dekker *Knt.'s Conjur.* (1842) 9 The storme beeing at rest, what buying vp of almanacks was there to see if the *weather-casters had playd the doctors to a haire. [**1959** *Times* 19 Aug. 8/7 The Air Ministry Meteorological Office is to open a 'weather shop' where the public may call in person at the new home of the London forecasting office at Princes House, Kingsway.]. **1961** *A.A. Handbk.* 17 '*Weather Centres' staffed by the Meteorological Office are open in London, in Glasgow, and in Manchester. **1973** C. Bonington *Next Horizon* xiii. 185, I..went through the daily ritual of getting the weather forecast. This entailed 'phoning..the weather centre in London. **1877** 'Mark Twain' *New England Weather* in *Index* (Boston) 11 Jan. 16/2 It must be raw apprentices in the *weather-clerk's factory who experiment and learn how in New England.., and then are promoted to make weather for countries that require a good article. **1898** H. S. Canfield *Maid of Frontier* 111, I wouldn't have a weather clerk inside of me for any thing. **1856** Kane *Arct. Expl.* I. xxiv. 315 A sort of *weather-cloth, which..would certainly make her more comfortable in heavy weather. **1897** *Outing* XXIX. 547/1 A coil of rope for head-rest, a discarded sail for weather cloth. **1897** J. L. Allen *Choir Invisible* x. 132 He got up at last and wrapped his *weather-coat about him. **1930** *Daily Express* 6 Oct. 13/5 (*caption*), Real Harris tweed weathercoat. **1978** *Sunday Times* 21 May 1/6 (Advt.), A pure silk wrap-around weathercoat..to protect you from summer showers..£165. **1746** *Phil. Trans.* XLIV. 169 The *Weather-Cord is an Hygrometer of a very ancient Invention. **1906** E. V. Lucas *Wanderer in Lond.* 170 One of the old *weather-cottages, with a little man and a little woman to swing in and out and foretell rain and shine. **1930** *Engineering* 31 Jan. 148/2 Based upon a *weather cycle or period of almost fourteen years. **1758** Borlase *Nat. Hist. Cornw.* 17 There appeared in the North-East the frustum of a large rainbow... They call it here in Cornwall a *weather dog,..and pronounce it a certain sign of hard rain. **1865** R. Hunt *Pop. Rom. W. Eng.* (1881) 434 'Weather dogs'..are regarded as certain prognostications of showery or stormy weather. **1753** F. Price *Observ. Cathedral-Ch. Salisbury* 40 The upper part of the Spire..just below the *weather Door. **1881** Raymond *Mining Gloss.*, *Weather-door*, a door in a level to regulate the ventilating current. **1611** Cotgr., *Poille*,..also, an Vmbrello, or great *weather-fanne. **1773** *Phil. Trans.* LXIV. 140 The *weather-fane which terminates the conductor. **1910** J. Farnol *Broad Highway* I. xxiv, It was somewhat roughly put together, but still very strong, and seemed, save for the roof, *weather-fast. *a* **1850** W. L. Bowles *Poems, Sylph of Summer* 466 Yon eastern downs, That *weather-fence the blossoms of the vale. **1886** H. G. Seeley *Freshw. Fishes Europe* 248 In Germany and Austria it [*Misgurnus fossilis*] is regarded as a weather prophet, and sometimes is called the *Weather-fish, because it usually comes to the surface about twenty-four hours before bad weather, and moves about with unusual energy. **1611** Cotgr., *Girouette*, a fane, or *weather-flag. **1802** Sibbald *Chron. S.P.* Gloss., **Weddir-glim*, clear sky, near the horizon; spoken of objects seen in the twilight or dusk; as 'between him and the wedder-glim'. **1817** *Blackw. Mag.* Oct. 84/1 While..the weather-gleam of the eastern hills began to be tinged with the brightening dawn. **1819** W. Tennant *Papistry Storm'd* (1827) 185 Nae cloud owr-head the lift did dim, But i' the wastern weddir-glim A black up-castin'. **1905** E. Clodd *Animism* § 11. 58 Indra, the old Vedic *weather-god, has been completely elbowed out as an object of worship by special rain-gods. **1885** *Buck's Handbk. Med. Sci.* I. 338/2 The pioneers attend to this work, trenching the ground, *weather-guarding the shelters. *a* **1825** Forby *Voc. E. Anglia*, **Weather-head*, the secondary rainbow. **1904** Edith Rickert *Reaper* 318 The old folk watched for weatherheads and talked of storms. **1632** Heywood *2nd Pt. Iron Age* I. i. C 2, And now faire Troian *Weather-hen adew, And when thou next louest, thinke to be more true. **1899** B. Thomas & Granv. Barker (*title*), The Weather-Hen. **1726** *Post-Man* 1–3 Sept. 2/2 Advt., The Gentlemen, Ladies and Farmers famous new invented *Weather Houses. **1784** Cowper *Task* I. 211 Peace to the artist, whose ingenious thought Devis'd the weather-house, that useful toy! **1800** Lathom *Dash of Day* I. i, He is always in bed when I am up, and I am always at rest, when he is stirring; our movements put me in mind of the man and woman in the Dutch weather-house. **1915** 'Q' (Quiller-Couch) *Nicky-Nan* xiii. 156 A man has no business to stand grimacing in his own doorway..like a figure in a weather-house. **1830** R. Mudie *Pop. Guide Observ. Nature* 302 As little was the injury done at the '*weather-line', just by the surface of the earth, where the durability of timber is put to the severest test. **1888** Emily Gerard *Land beyond Forest* II. 30 *note*, Instances of *weather-makers are also common in Germany. **1891** *Pall Mall Gaz.* 13 Oct. 7/2 A weather-maker for an almanack got into conversation with a shepherd. **1883** Stallybrass tr. *Grimm's Teut. Mythol.* III. 1152 The gift of prophecy and the art of *weather-making. **1545** Ascham *Toxoph.* II. (Arb.) 152 Therefore in shootynge there is as muche difference betwixt an archer that is a good *wether man, and an other that knoweth and marketh nothynge, as is betwixte a blynde man and he that can se. **1901** Weather man [see *hot wave* s.v. HOT *a.* 12]. **1944** *Sun* (Baltimore) 15 Nov. 11/2 Nobody ever gets anywhere telling the weatherman how to behave. **1952** W. Stevens *Let.* 26 June (1967) 757 It did not go below 85° in N.Y. last night according to the weather man. **1970** *Guardian* 28 Oct. 13/3 The Weathermen have been in existence for just over a year, since the SDS [*sc.* Students for a Democratic Society] split of June, 1969... The Weathermen got their name from a line in a Bob Dylan song: 'You don't need a weatherman to know which way the wind blows.' **1971** *Times* 15 Jan. 12/6 Could this country have acquired an Anglicized offshoot of the American Weatherman—or Weathermen as these violent urban guerillas are less accurately but probably more widely known? **1979** R. Perry *Bishop's Pawn* i. 23 The West was agreed that the IRA, the Weathermen, the Red Army Faction..were composed of criminals, terrorists and murderers. **1983** *Listener* 14 July 17/3 We asked the weatherman, Jack Scott, to demonstrate some of those extraordinary regional variations for us. **1951** *U.S. Congr. Senate Committee Interior Hearings* Apr. 152 *Weather modification on a small scale, such as protection against frost ..is known to be possible. **1968** *Times* 1 Nov. 6/6 Russian research on methods of reducing damage to crops by hailstorms is being examined seriously in the United States, according to a National Science Foundation report on last year's activities in weather modification. **1977** *Time* 7 Mar. 55/1 The Governors also agreed to create a task force that could channel such requests for aid and coordinate weather-modification (cloud seeding) programs. **1656** *2nd Ed. New Alamanack* 3 If the *weather-mongers rule hold true. **1911** J. G. Frazer *Golden Bough: Magic Art* (ed. 3) I. iv. 227 Wizards, doctors, weather-mongers, prophets. **1841** *Few Words to Churchwardens* I. (Camb. Camden Soc.) 10 You may see what is called the *weather-moulding of the old roof remaining. *a* **1878** Sir G. Scott *Lect. Archit.* I. 165 A hollow projecting moulding containing the foliage, capped by a weather moulding. **1962** *Listener* 18 Oct. 632/2 The 'Coliseum of cloud' that a *weatherplane captured for us. **1976** *Evening Post* (Nottingham) 13 Dec. 7/2 Experts.. identified it as a crashed weather plane which sends wind and temperature conditions from a height of 90,000 feet. **1698** Derham in *Phil. Trans.* XX. 4 The *Weather-plates are to be put upon the Frame [of a portable barometer], by setting them to the same height, at which the Mercury stands in a common Barometer. **1843** Mill *Logic* I. III. iv. 389 The reliance on astrology, or on the *weather-prophecies in almanacs. **1866** Steinmetz *Weathercasts* 7 The most successful *weather-prophet of modern times,.. the late lamented Admiral Fitzroy. **1884** S. E. Dawson *Handbk. Dom. Canada* 4 The metaphors of political weather-prophets. **1946** *1st Technical Rep. Weather Radar Research* (Mass. Inst. Technol. Dept. Meteorol.) (AD 54113) 3 (*heading*) *Weather-radar observations at M.I.T.'s Radiation Laboratory. **1979** *Atmosphere-Ocean* XVII. 78 The radar data were obtained from the McGill Weather Radar located just outside Montreal. **1867** Smyth *Sailor's Word-bk.*, **Weather-ropes*, an early term for those which were tarred. **1960** *Aeroplane* XCIX. 90/2 After taking 22,952 photographs of the Earth's cloud cover, Tiros I, the World's first *weather satellite, has ended its useful life.. after the satellite's electronics had suffered a failure. **1976** L. Deighton *Twinkle, twinkle, Little Spy* xi. 115 His factories make complicated junk for communications satellites... And there are weather satellites too. **1884** *Graphic* 13 Dec. 610/3 The New York '*weathersharps', who have to their westward some three thousand miles of land studded with signal stations. **1946** *Shell Aviation News* No. 100. 6/3 A proposal by the Search and Rescue Committee that *weather ships should be maintained in the North Atlantic for meteorological observations. **1978** *Nature* 1 June 407/1 Following the withdrawal of US weatherships in 1973, it is the only regularly reporting deep ocean (3,000 m) station in the North Atlantic north of the tropics and south of 50° N. **1757** Dyer in J. Duncombe *Lett.* (1773) III. 62, I think I never was so *weather-sick; the deep snows forbid me air and exercise. **1892** Meredith *Ode to Comic Spirit* Poems 1898 II. 222 A statue losing feature, weather-sick. **1856** Mrs. Browning *Aur. Leigh* II. 691, I can tell The *weather-signs of love: you love this man. **1915** *19th Cent.* Jan. 190 His prophecies [about India] are perpetual, and he read the weather-signs at a glance. **1903** Alice M. Earle *Two Cent. Costume Amer.* II. 617 Another name for a safeguard was a *weather-skirt. **1870** *Lond. Society* Sept. 266 A..house, *weather-slated from top to bottom. **1859** Jephson *Brittany* xvi. 269 Buildings of lath and plaster, covered on the most exposed parts with *weather-slating. **1632–3** in Willis & Clark *Cambridge* (1886) II. 698 The Windowes in ye Roofe, to be of good Oake Timber, with *Wether sparrs handsomely wrought. *c* **1595** Donne *Sat.* i. 59 And sooner may a gulling *weather Spie By drawing forth heavens Scheme tell certainly [etc.]. **1895** *Funk's Stand. Dict.*, *Weather station. **1953** *Encounter* Nov. 7/1 Japan gets its weather from China, but no weather reports—at least not until the Japanese experts again manage to break the code of the Chinese weather-stations. **1981** 'E. Lathen' *Going for Gold* vii. 87, I was on to the weather station... The forecasters are talking about the blizzard of the century. **1686** Plot *Staffordsh.* 168 It being all of it good *weather-stone, but not enduring the fire. **1847** *Rep. Comm. Patents 1846* (U.S.) 94 One patent has been granted for improvement in fences, and another for a *weather strip for doors. **1921** *Daily Colonist* (Victoria, B.C.) 25 Oct. 6/6 (Advt.), Weather Strip—'Stormproof', 24 feet in box. **1970** K. Ball *Fiat 600, 600D Autobook* xii. 143/2 The front windscreen and rear window are secured in place by a special weatherstrip. **1985** *Times* 19 July 13/4 In windy winter conditions the windloading presses the door up against the weatherstrip. **1908** I. N. Stevens *Liberators* 8 The wind that shook the windows, *weather-stripped as they were, crept into the room. **1945** Nelson & Wright *Tomorrow's House* xiii. 147/2 A heavy flush door, weather-stripped,..would..reduce the direct transmission of sound. **1942** *Archit. Rev.* XCI. 99/3 The windows are pine with aluminium *weatherstripping. **1959** 'S. Ransome' *I'll die for You* xii. 144 A part of the weather stripping was loose, and in a heavy rain it leaked. **1975** *Globe & Mail* (Toronto) 14 Nov. 2/5 As for weather-stripping, Mrs. Macdonald said their house doesn't need it because of extra insulation and double windows. **1839** *Civil Engin. & Arch. Jrnl.* II. 361/2 A weather fillet, or *weather table, which projects half an inch from the general face of the window. **1906** *Antiquary* Jan. 7/2 A weather-table on the north wall. **1875** Knight *Dict. Mech.* 2568/2 Siding-tiles are sometimes called *weather-tiles. **1887** Hissey *Holiday on Road* 230 A somewhat quaint little inn, having a *weather-tiled upper story. **1904** A. C. Benson *House of Quiet* iv, One wing is weather-tiled. **1703** [R. Neve] *City & C. Purchaser* 286 *Weather-tyling..Is the Tyling, (or Covering with Tyles) the upright Sides of Houses. **1833** Loudon *Encycl. Archit.* §438 The weather-boarding may be covered..with what is called weather-tiling. **1847** C. A. Johns *Forest Trees* I. 357 *note*, I think there will be rain,..for the *weather tree is shewing its white lining. **1972** *National Observer* (U.S.) 27 May 10/2 The..'*Weather Underground', which boasts that it is responsible for so many of these bombings, is down to only 15 or 20 members now, according to sources in the House Internal Security Committee. **1982** H. Kissinger *Years of Upheaval* iv. 89 The terrorism of the Weather Underground. **1721** Bailey, **Weather-vane*. **1866** Le Fanu *All in Dark* x, The pointed gables, with stone cornices and glittering weather-vane on the summit. **1896** *Tablet* 1 Feb. 167 *The Pall Mall Gazette* even prefers to regard him as a Royal weather-vane. **1838** *Civil Engin. & Arch. Jrnl.* I. 235/1 A *weather wall in the centre will run the whole length [of the pier]. **1867** Smyth *Sailor's Word-bk.*, **Weather-warning*, the telegraphic cautionary warning given by hoisting the storm-drum on receiving the forecast. **1974** *Petroleum Rev.* XXVIII. 787/1 The *weather-window is normally reckoned to last into September. **1983** *Sunday Times* 6 Mar. 69/4 It's been said that Esso's development of artificial islands has not merely opened the weather window further but ripped it off its hinges. **1807** W. Irving

Salmagundi (1824) 122 This is the universal remark among the..*weather-wiseacres of the day. 1596 NASHE *Saffron Walden* Ep. Ded. B 3 b, False Prophets, *Weather-wizards, Fortune-tellers. 1652 GAULE *Magastrom.* 23 Weather-wizzards, planet-prognosticators, and fortune-spellers! 1971 *Times* 15 Jan. 12/7 Only one unconnected *Weatherwoman has since been traced. 1973 *Daily Tel.* 14 Dec. 3/3 BBC Television is to have its first weather woman. She is Miss Barbara Edwards,..who at present reads weather forecasts on radio. 1982 *Times* 28 May 9/3 Diana Arp..was from a very wealthy family and became a Weather woman, making bombs. 1776 COOK *3rd Voy.* I. iii. (1784) I. 34 The caulkers were set to work..to caulk the decks and inside *weather-works of the ship.

8. *Naut.* Used attrib. or as adj. with the sense: Situated on the side which is turned towards the wind; having a direction towards the wind; windward; opposed to *lee*, *leeward* adjs.; as ***weather-anchor***, ***-beam*** (BEAM *sb.*[1] 17), ***-bowline***, ***-brace***, ***-division***, ***-earing***, ***-gangway***, ***-gun***, ***-leech***, ***-lift***, ***-lurch***, ***-port***, ***-quarter***, ***-rail***, ***-roll***, ***-sheet***, ***-shore***, ***-shrowd***, ***-spoke***, ***-tack***, ***-tide***, ***-topping-lift***, ***-wheel***; **weather-bow**, the bow that is turned towards the wind; hence as *v. trans.*, to turn the weather-bow to; **weather-deck**, a deck exposed to the weather [cf. G. *wetterdeck*]; the uppermost unprotected deck, other than the forecastle, bridge and poop; **weather-dodger** *slang*, a screen on the bridge of a ship, affording protection from the weather; **weather-gage**, **-gauge** (see GAUGE *sb.* 5); hence as *v. trans.*, to keep the weather-gage of; **weather-helm**, a tendency in a ship under sail to come too near the wind, requiring the tiller to be kept constantly a little to windward; **weather-mark** *Sailing*, a mark on a racing course towards which boats sail into the wind. Also (*to the*) *weatherward* adv.

1867 SMYTH *Sailor's Word-bk.*, **Weather-anchor*, that lying to windward, by which a ship rides when moored. 1790 BEATSON *Nav. & Mil. Mem.* II. 140 Two sail..gave us chase and..kept on our *weather-beams till morning. 1867 SMYTH *Sailor's Word-bk.*, *Weather-beam*, a direction at right angles with the keel, on the weather side of the ship. 1626 CAPT. J. SMITH *Accid. Yng. Seamen* 18 On the *weather bow. 1851 H. MELVILLE *Whale* xvi. 80 Take a peep over the weather-bow..and tell me what ye see there. 1840 R. H. DANA *Bef. Mast* xxxvi, We made but little by *weather-bowing the tide. 1669 STURMY *Mariner's Mag.* I. 18 Set in the Lee-Braces, and hawl forward by the *Weather Bowlines. *Ibid.* 17 Let go the..Lee-Braces;..set in your *Weather Braces. 1762–9 FALCONER *Shipwr.* ii. 308 The sheet and weather-brace they now stand by. 1836 MARRYAT *Midsh. Easy* xxv[i], 'A small pull of that weather main-top-gallant brace—that will do,' said the master. 1850 *Rep. Committee* in G. Moorsom *Admeas. Tonnage* (1853) 167 The Depth in Midships from the Underside of the *Weather Deck to the Ceiling at the Limber Strake. 1906 ATTWOOD *War-ships* 46 Wood is now only used for weather decks [etc.]. 1908 PAASCH *From Keel to Truck* (ed. 4) 75 *Weather-deck*, Term given to an upper deck on account of its exposure to the sun, rain and wind. 1973 H. GRUPPE *Truxton Cipher* (1974) xiii. 135 Tolley..disappeared down the weather-deck ladder. 1920 *Discovery* Nov. 329/2 Nelson had intended his *weather division to be in line ahead. 1924 R. CLEMENTS *Gipsy of Horn* v. 84 One was..in comparative comfort under the lee of the *weather-dodger. 1840 R. H. DANA *Bef. Mast* iv, The first [sailor] on the yard goes to the *weather earing, the second to the lee, and the next two to the 'dog's ears'. 1834 MARRYAT *P. Simple* xiii, Walk this boy up and down the *weather gangway. 1892 *Field* 2 July 30/3 Daffodil..was sufficiently far to windward to *weather-gauge her. 1759 *Ann. Reg.* 120 We..run our *weather-guns out. 1691 T. H[ALE] *Acc. New Invent.* 126 *Weather, or Leeward Helm..may be fitted to promote or hinder the Sailing upon occasion. 1882 NARES *Seamanship* (ed. 6) 190 A screw ship carries more weather helm than a sailing ship. 1836 MARRYAT *Midsh. Easy* xxv[i], The Aurora dashed through at the rate of eight miles an hour, with her *weather leeches lifting. 1899 F. T. BULLEN *Log of Sea-waif* 279 The weather-leech of the lower stun' sails began to flap. 1867 SMYTH *Sailor's Word-bk.*, **Weather-lurch*, a heavy roll to windward. 1894 *Outing* XXIV. 36/2 The 'Una' turned the *weather-mark with a lead of nearly half an hour. 1963 *Times* 8 June 5/1 By the weather mark Andromeda was in front. 1809 *Sporting Mag.* XXXIII. 127 A great sea poured through one of the *weather-ports. 1626 CAPT. J. SMITH *Accid. Yng. Seamen* 19 Boord him on his *weather quarter. 1743 BULKELEY & CUMMINS *Voy. S. Seas* 9 The Commodore being on the Weather-Quarter, bore down under our Lee, and spoke with us. 1834 M. SCOTT *Cruise of Midge* i. (1836) 16 The felucca was now within long pistol-shot of our weather-quarter. 1888 E. J. MATHER *Nor'ard of Dogger* 352 We had to hang on the *weather-rail, the seas rolling along like mountains. 1815 *Falconer's Dict. Marine* (ed. Burney), **Weather-Rolls*, those inclinations which a ship makes to windward in a heavy sea. *a* 1625 MANWAYRING *Sea-mans Dict.* (1644) 76 If the *weather-sheate be as farre as the Bulk-head. 1851 H. MELVILLE *Whale* xiii. 67 The tremendous strain upon the main-sheet had parted the weather-sheet. 1626 CAPT. J. SMITH *Accid. Yng. Seamen* 30 Come to an Anchor vnder the Ley of the *weather shore. 1697 J. PUCKLE *New Dial.* 16 A North-West Wind..makes Holland a Lee and England a Weather Shore. *a* 1625 MANWAYRING *Sea-mans Dict.* (1644) 32 Then cutting the *weather shrowdes, the mast will instantly and without danger fall over boord. 1849 CUPPLES *Green Hand* vi. (1856) 59, I looked to the wheel..as he coolly gave her half a *weather-spoke more. 1883 *Man. Seamanship Boys* 56 Haul on the *weather-tack and lee-sheet. 1815 *Falconer's Dict. Marine* (ed. Burney), **Weather-Tide*, denotes that which, by setting against a ship's lee-side, while under sail, forces her up to windward. 1883 *Man. Seamanship Boys* 163 The fiddle-block is hooked to the *weather-topping lift. 1557 TOWRSON in Hakluyt *Voy.* (1589) 127 At night the Minion, and the pinnesse came vp to vs, but could not fetch so farre to the *weatherward as we, and therefore they ankered about a league a wether the castle. 1600 (25 Dec.) *Adm. Ct. Exam.* 34 (P.R.O.) [A ship] to the weatherward about a league. 1904 DOWDEN *R. Browning* 73 The boat veers weatherward. 1867 SMYTH *Sailor's Word-bk.*, **Weather-wheel*, the position of the man who steers a large ship, from his standing on the weather-side of the wheel.

weather ('wɛðə(r)), *v.* Forms: 5 **wederyn**, 5–7 **wether**, 6– **weather**. [f. WEATHER *sb.*

OE. had *wedrian*, *widrian*, *wuderian*, *ȝewiderian*, to be (good or bad) weather = ON. *viðra*: see WEATHERING *vbl. sb.* 1. Cf. MHG. *weteren* (mod.G. *wettern*), to subject to wind and sun (= sense 1 below), *witeren* (mod.G. *wittern*) to storm, etc.; also WITHER *v.*]

1. *trans.* To subject to the beneficial action of the wind and sun; to air. **a.** *Hawking* (see quot. 1856). Also *refl.* and *intr.* in passive sense.

14.. in Harting *Perf. Bk. Kepinge Sparhawkes* (1886) Introd. p. ix, For wetheringe yo[r] hauke offer yo[r] hauke water. 1575 TURBERV. *Faulconrie* 134 When you haue kept hir two houres vpon the fist, then set hir in the Sunne to weather hir half an houre. *c* 1575 *Perf. Bk. Kepinge Sparhawkes* (1886) 11 Set her to wether fastinge a longe tyme. *Ibid.* 14 In myste they will neuer wether, nor flye well. 1615 MARKHAM *Country Contentm.* I. vii. 88 Then he shall bee sure to weather his Hawke abroad euery euening except on her bathing daies. 1773 J. CAMPBELL *Mod. Faulconry* 191 Of Bathing and Weathering Hawks. 1856 'STONEHENGE' *Brit. Sports* I. IV. §5. 223/2 Hawks must also be weathered; that is to say, they should be put out on perches..in the open air, and then left..for many hours a-day, but not in the rain.

transf. 1590 SPENSER *Muiopotmos* 184 And then he [the butterfly] pearcheth on some braunch thereby, To weather him, and his moyst wings to dry. 1596 —— *F.Q.* v. iv. 42.

b. To air (linen, etc.); to dry thoroughly (a harvested crop).

c 1440 *Promp. Parv.* 519/2 Wederyn, or leyn or hangyn yn the wedyr, *auro.* 1530 PALSGR. 780/2, I wether a thyng, I lay it abrode in open ayre. *Je ayre...* It shall be well done to weather your garmentes in Marche for feare of mothes. *a* 1569 KYNGESMILL *Man's Est.* xii. (1574) F vj b, They may not flourish long: Euen as herbes that growe in the shadowe, neuer well weathered with the warme sunne. 1580 TUSSER *Husb.* (1878) 129 Maides, mustard seede gather, for being too ripe, and weather it well. 1844 *Jrnl. R. Agric. Soc.* V. I. 269 After reaping..the produce of the several plots was well weathered, and then thrashed. 1847 HALLIWELL, *Weather*, to dry clothes in the open air. 1892 P. H. EMERSON *Son of Fens* xvii. 173 'Well, the stuff [cut reeds] is rather heava, ain't it?' 'It want to be weathered, bor.'

c. To expose (land, clay for brick- or tile-making) to the pulverizing action of the elements.

1548 [see WEATHERING *vbl. sb.* 3 b]. 1865 *Daily Tel.* 3 Nov. 5/4 The clay bank, where the raw material is stored and 'weathered'.

2. To change by exposure to the weather. **a.** *trans.* To wear away, disintegrate, or discolour by atmospheric action. Const. *into*, *to* a specified form or condition. Chiefly in *passive*. Also with *away*. Also, to produce as an incrustation *on* a surface by the action of the weather. Spec. in *Geol.*

1757 tr. *J. F. Henckel's Pyritol.* v. 61 This leady clay..derived from a lead-ore, weathered and reduced to earth. *Ibid.* 87 On this sinter..we find glitter, iron and copper pyrites, not conveyed by streams of water, nor agglutinated, but weathered thereon, or produced by weather or damps. 1789 [see WEATHERED *ppl. a.* 1]. 1833 LYELL *Princ. Geol.* III. 210 The face of the limestone is hollowed out and weathered into such forms as are seen in the calcareous cliffs of the adjoining coast. 1867 H. MACMILLAN *Bible Teach.* xiii. (1870) 267 The rain-cloud hangs low..overhead; the smoke hovers around; and they weather the finest sculptured surface. 1878 ANSTED *Water & Water Supply* 89 It [*sc.* percolation] acts also very powerfully in weathering the rocks through which the water passes. 1918 H. BALFOUR in *Man* XVIII. 147 The nose either was not represented or has been weathered away.

b. *intr.* To become worn, disintegrated, or discoloured under atmospheric influences. Const. *into*, *to* a specified condition. ***to weather out***: to become prominent or isolated by the decay or disintegration of the surrounding rock.

1789 J. WILLIAMS *Min. Kingd.* II. 20 The grey granite begins to weather or decompose. 1839 MURCHISON *Silur. Syst.* I. xxxiii. 441 The lower shale is here clearly seen beneath the limestone, and weathers to the same light ashen colour as in Salop. 1862 ANSTED *Channel Isl.* I. i. 7 Hard crystalline rock, decomposing or weathering by the constant action of the sea and weather. 1883 RUSKIN *Fors Clav.* xcii. 207 The dark rock weathers easily into surface soil. 1885 SIR J. W. DAWSON *Egypt & Syria* v. 112 The pillar-like masses of salt that weather out of the salt cliff of Jebel Usdum. 1914 MOIR in *Man* XIV. 179 Those fragments of flint would in time, by thermal effects, 'weather out' and leave a clean-cut groove behind.

c. In *pass.*, esp. of a crop: To be deteriorated by too long exposure to bad weather.

1821 CLARE *Vill. Minstr.* I. 74 With feet nigh shoeless.. And napless beaver, weather'd brown. 1875 *Ure's Dict. Arts* III. 185 All barleys that have been weathered in the field.. should be rigidly rejected [for malting].

d. *intr.* To wear (well or ill) under atmospheric influences.

1883 R. HALDANE *Workshop Rec.* Ser. II. 436/2 For outside work, boiled oil is used, because it weathers better than raw oil.

3. *Naut.* **a.** *trans.* To sail to the windward of (a point or headland, another ship, etc.).

c 1595 CAPT. WYATT *Dudley's Voy. W. Ind.* (Hakl. Soc.) 18 Our carvell plyinge up into the winde weathered the saile which came from the shore. 1608 W. HAWKINS in *Hawkins' Voy.* (Hakl. Soc.) 383 We lay close E.S.E. with a S.W. wynd, seeking to wether Socotora but could not. 1627 CAPT. J. SMITH *Sea Gram.* xii. 57 You cannot boord him except you weather him. 1660 INGELO *Bentiv. & Ur.* I. (1682) 170 When they have weather'd the Cape of Good-Hope. 1694 LUTTRELL *Brief Rel.* (1857) III. 323 Not being able to weather the Lizard Point because of the strong south west wind. 1703 BURCHETT *Mem. Trans. at Sea* 141 Our Blue Squadron..by a shift of Wind had weather'd the French. 1801 NELSON in *Nicolas's Disp.* (1845) IV. 314 The Agamemnon could not weather the shoal of the middle, and was obliged to anchor. 1820 SCORESBY *Arctic Regions* II. 476 An impervious mass of ice..which..we could neither weather, nor discover a passage through. 1878 DIXON KEMP *Yacht & Boat Sailing* 378/1 To weather is to pass on the windward side of an object. In cross tacking the vessel 'weathers' another that crosses ahead of her.

b. *fig.* To get safely round; to get the better of.

1626 DONNE *Serm.* xxi. (1640) 210 That soule which is but neare destruction, may weather that mischiefe. 1654 WHITELOCKE *Swed. Ambassy* (1772) I. 449 Butt, through mercy, he weathered this point also. 1708 ADDISON *Pres. St. War* 15 We have been tugging a great while against the Stream, and have almost weather'd our point. 1833 MARRYAT *P. Simple* xxxvii, Peter, read me about Jacob, and his weathering Esau with a mess of pottage.

†**c.** To aim wide of (the mark) on the windward side. *Obs. rare*$^{-1}$.

1588 LUCAR *Tartaglia's Colloq.*, *Lucar Appendix* 4 Euery Gunner ought to weather the marke according to the hardnes of the winde, and the distance.

d. intr. ***to weather on*** or ***upon***: to gain upon in a windward direction; also *fig.*, to get the advantage of, take liberties with.

c 1595 CAPT. WYATT *Dudley's Voy. W. Ind.* (Hakl. Soc.) 16 Some fowre leagues of, wee sawe a saile to weather on us. 1706 E. WARD *Wooden World Diss.* (1708) 35 How well soever he can weather upon others, he is never able to fore-reach upon his Commander. 1748 *Anson's Voy.* II. iv. 163 We had both weathered and fore-reached upon her considerably. 1829 MARRYAT *F. Mildmay* xvii, How do you think the scoundrels weathered on me at last? 1836 *Fraser's Mag.* XIV. 475, I weathered upon my duty without discredit, my leisure without care, my liquor without quarrelling. 1863 READE *Hard Cash* I. ix. 252 The other [pirate]..came up to weather on him and hang on his quarters, pirate fashion. 1881 *Daily News* 9 June 5/4 There is a triumph, too, which only a genuine yachtsman can feel when inch by inch a dreaded rival is weathered on.

4. *trans.* **a.** *Naut.* To withstand and come safely through (a storm). Often with *out* (also *absol.*).

1673 TEMPLE *Observ. United Prov.* viii. 255 Such old Seamen in so strong a Ship that had weathered so many storms without loss. 1681 H. NEVILE *Plato Rediv.* 22 [No more than] the Pilot and Marriners [are answerable] for not weathering out a Storm, when the Ship hath sprung a planck. 1748 *Anson's Voy.* I. vi. 62 Had they [the masts] weathered the preceding storm, it would have been impossible..to have stood against those..tempests we afterwards encountered. 1790 COWPER *On Receipt of Mother's Pict.* 89 As a gallant bark..(The storms all weather'd and the ocean cross'd) Shoots into port. 1819 BYRON *Juan* II. xli, But the ship labour'd so, they scarce could hope To weather out much longer. *a* 1859 MACAULAY *Hist. Eng.* xxiv. V. 204 In the port lay fleets of great ships which had weathered the storms of the Euxine and the Atlantic. 1864 TENNYSON *Enoch Arden* 135 To sell the boat —and yet he loved her well—How many a rough sea had he weather'd in her! 1866 R. M. BALLANTYNE *Shifting Winds* ii, She had sailed from the antipodes, had weathered many a gale.

b. *fig.* or in fig. context. To come safely through (a period of trouble, adversity, affliction, etc.); to sustain without disaster.

1655 FULLER *Ch. Hist.* IX. xvi. 192 He Weathered out the Raign of Queen Mary. 1671 CARYL *Sir Salomon* IV. 66 My designs of Revenge are vain, and unjust. I must pull down my Sailes to weather out this storme. 1674 BOYLE *Excell. Theol.* I. iii. 95 Afflictions slight and short may well be weather'd out by these Philosophical Avocations. 1706 E. WARD *Wooden World Diss.* (1708) 78 They value no such Puffs, if they can but weather a Beating. 1772 MACKENZIE *Man of World* II. xx, After having weathered so many disasters, I at last arrived near the place of my nativity. 1775 JEFFERSON *Let.* 4 July in H. S. Randall *Life* (1858) III. 568 If we can weather out this campaign, I hope that we shall be able to have a plenty [of gunpowder] made for another. 1787 BURNS *Let. Earl Glencairn* Dec., My brother's farm is but a wretched lease, but I think he will probably weather out the remaining seven years of it. 1834 CREEVEY in *C. Papers* (1904) II. xii. 296 The Government..could not have weathered the session. 1849 MACAULAY *Hist. Eng.* x. II. 623 They were..thrown into the shade by two younger Whigs, ..who weathered together the fiercest storms of faction. 1853 DICKENS *Bleak Ho.* xiv, Pa told me, only yesterday morning,..that he couldn't weather the storm. 1865 —— *Lett.* (1880) II. 242, I rather doubt..their being able to weather it out. 1885 *Contemp. Rev.* June 906 Their proprietors are less indebted and weather a crisis better. 1900 G. C. BRODRICK *Mem. & Impr.* 143 The other weathered a serious illness and lived on for two or three years.

c. *gen.* To pass through and survive (severe weather).

1680 OTWAY *Orphan* IV. i, The Beasts that under the Warm Hedges slept, And weather'd out the cold bleak Night, are up. 1742 T. WOODROOFE in Hanway *Acc. Brit. Trade Caspian Sea* (1753) I. I. xvii. 113 We had weathered out the inclement season with as good spirits as could be expected in so bad a neighbourhood. 1785 COWPER *Let. Lady Hesketh* 9 Nov., Wks. 1835 I. 171, I began..to fear I should never be able to weather out the winter in so lonely a dwelling. 1795–6 WORDSW. *Borderers* I. 513 My husband, Sir, Was of Kirkoswald—many a snowy winter We've weathered out together. 1805 —— *Waggoner* III. 80 Among these hills, from first to last, We've weathered many a furious blast. 1854 THOREAU *Walden* xiv. (1863) 275, I weathered some merry snow storms.

†**d.** To take shelter from (a storm). *Obs.*

1742 FIELDING *J. Andrews* II. iii, They said there was a violent shower of rain coming on, which they intended to weather there [i.e. at an alehouse]. **1749** —— *Tom Jones* XII. viii, Partridge, with much earnest Entreaty, prevailed with Jones to enter, and weather the Storm. **1798** BLOOMFIELD *Farmer's Boy, Winter* 296 Beneath whose trunk I've weather'd many a show'r.

5. *intr.* ***to weather along***, † ***to weather it on***: to sail or make headway in spite of wind and weather. Also ***to weather her way***.

1599 NASHE *Lenten Stuffe* D 3, [All] that euer Yarmouth vnshelled or ingendred to weather it on till they lost the North-starre. **1836** W. IRVING *Life & Lett.* (1866) III. 91, I have ever since made my calculations to 'weather along', as the sailors say, for some time to come, without any of the funds I have invested. **1881** J. K. SCOTT *Galloway Glean.* 14 See the 'Press Home' steerin' strecht for lan', Will she weather her way to the shore?

6. *trans.* To set (the sails of a windmill) at the proper angle to obtain the maximum effect of the wind-force. Cf. WEATHER *sb.* 4.

1745 *Phil. Trans.* XLIV. 1 All which Sails [of a water-wheel] are weathered in the same Manner as those designed for Windmills. **1759** SMEATON *Ibid.* LI. 144 Plain sails weather'd according to the common practice. **1825** J. NICHOLSON *Oper. Mech.* 138 From which it appears that sails weathered in the Dutch manner produced nearly a maximum effect.

7. *Arch.* To slope or bevel (a surface) so as to throw off the rain; to furnish (a wall, buttress) with a weathering or water-table.

1833 LOUDON *Encycl. Archit.* §860, 13 feet 6 inches oak wrought, framed, and weathered (beveled to throw off the wet). **1878** MACVITTIE *Ch. Ch. Cathedral, Dublin* 66 A plinth which is weathered in the depth of the buttresses by nine courses of Water-tables. **1879** *Cassell's Techn. Educ.* II. 294/1 Fig. 391 shows the manner in which the sill is sloped off, or 'weathered'.

weather, obs. f. WETHER, WITHER *sb.*

'weatherable, *a.* [f. WEATHER *v.* + -ABLE.] Capable of withstanding the effects of the weather. Also **,weathera'bility**.

1961 WEBSTER, Weatherability. **1963** H. R. CLAUSER *Encycl. Engin. Materials & Processes* 662/1 The poor weatherability of some of the man-made fibers can be overcome by the use of special finishing and/or coating treatments. **1972** J. G. CRUICKSHANK *Soil Geogr.* ii. 52 Even where the parent material is rock in place, the weatherable minerals—or what has survived complete chemical weathering—are of continuing importance for soil profile development. **1979** *New Scientist* 17 May 547 Silicones in paint prevent colour fading, and give better long-term weatherability and heat resistance.

'weather-beaten, *pa. pple.* and *ppl. a.*

1. Beaten or buffeted by wind and rain; that has been exposed to severe weather.

c **1560** T. MOWNTAYNE in *Narratives Reform.* (Camden) 210 Thence to Colchester, and there toke shypynge, thynkynge to have gone ynto Seland,..but we were so whether-beatyn that of force we were glad to returne bake agayn. **1563** GOLDING *Cæsar* IV. (1565) 102 b, Most of our shyps were thus broosed and weatherbeaten. **1589** GREENE *Menaphon* (Arb.) 32 To rest our wearie and weather-beaten bones. **1632** J. HAYWARD tr. *Biondi's Eromena* 16 The galleys of Sardegna being (by a great tempest) wether-beaten and driven to that shore. **1647** CLARENDON *Hist. Reb.* VI. §137 The King's harassed, weatherbeaten, and half-starved troops. **1722** CROXALL *Fables Æsop* xli. 76 The Sun ..darted his warm sultry Beams upon the Head of the poor weather-beaten Traveller. **1830** J. G. STRUTT *Sylva Brit.* 141 It becomes harder and tougher in proportion as it is weather-beaten. **1882** 'OUIDA' *Bimbi* 98 The tall old houses are weatherbeaten into the most delicious hues. **1904** *Daily Chron.* 16 July 9/2 Another weather-beaten pigeon sought rest on the brigantine Jantyre.

fig. or in *fig.* context. **1621** T. WILLIAMSON tr. *Goulart's Wise Vieillard* 22 At that time when Saint Cyprian liued, the whole world was iudged to be very much weather-beaten. **1639** FULLER *Holy War* II. xxxvii. 94 Mean time Jerusalem was a poore weather-beaten kingdome. **1668** BP. E. HOPKINS *Van. World* Wks. (1710) 19 If honourable, we are but raised above others to be the more weather-beaten.

2. As adj., expressing the result.

a. Of things: Worn, defaced, or damaged by exposure to the weather.

1547 SURREY *Eccles.* iii. 12 Auncient walls to race,..and of their wether beten stones, to buylde some new deuyse. **1593** NORDEN *Spec. Brit., Midsx.* 38 Pancras Church standeth all alone..old and wetherbeaten. **1608** MACHIN *Dumb Knt.* I. B 3, Orators wiues shortly will bee knowne like images on water staires, euer in one wetherbeaten suite. *a* **1618** RALEGH *Royal Navy* 27 They make their Ocum..of old seere and weather-beaten ropes. **1697** *Lond. Gaz.* No. 3260/4 Wearing a Weather-beaten Periwig. **1848** THACKERAY *Van. Fair* i, A very small and weather-beaten old cow's-skin trunk. **1860** WHYTE MELVILLE *Mkt. Harb.* xii, Under the weather-beaten winkers and shabby harness of a four-horse waggon.

b. Of persons, their countenances, etc.: Bronzed, coarsened, toughened, hardened by exposure to all kinds of weather.

1530 PALSGR. 844/1 Weather beaten, as men be that have lyen in the felde or see. **1577–87** HOLINSHED *Chron.* I. 175/1 Harold answered, that they were not priests, but wether-beaten and hardie souldiers. **1607** DEKKER *Knt.'s Conjur.* ii. D 1 b, Neither they, nor the weather-beatenst Cosmographicall Starre-catcher of em all. **1662** HIBBERT *Syntagma Theol.* II. 144 Such was his undoubted resolution, that neither their great words, nor their high looks could daunt him, Weather-beaten-souldier (as I may so speak) in Christianity. **1769** FALCONER *Dict. Marine* (1780) A aa 2, s.v. *Emmariné, Matelot emmariné*, a case-hardened or weather-beaten tar; a veteran sailor. **1771** SMOLLETT *Humph. Cl.* 5 May (1815) 63 An old man, with a wooden leg and a weather-beaten face. **1853** KINGSLEY *Hypatia* xviii. 209 The scarred and weatherbeaten features of the old warrior. **1855** MACAULAY *Hist. Eng.* xv. III. 613 Two weatherbeaten old seamen who had risen from being cabin boys to be Admirals.

Similarly †**'weather-beat** (*dial.* **-bet**) *ppl. a.* Also †**'weather-beat** *v. trans. rare*$^{-0}$. †**'weather-beating** *vbl. sb.*

1586 [? J. CASE] *Praise Mus.* vi. 75 Alas what pleasure could they take at the whippe and ploughtaile in so often and vncessant labours, such bitter weatherbeatings. **1598** FLORIO, *Sbattere*,..to thrash, to wetherbeate. **1615** CHAPMAN *Odyss.* VI. 193 [Ulysses] So wet, so weather-beate. **1621** T. GRANGER *Expos. Eccles.* xii. 3. 319 The teeth.. standing like weather-beate stakes,..falling out one after another. **1719** D'URFEY *Pills* IV. 198 The Devil he was so Weather-beat, He was forc'd to take to a Tree. **1886** *S.W. Lincs. Gloss.*, *Weather-bet*, weather-beaten.

†**'weather-bit, -bitten**, *ppl. a. Obs. rare.* [Cf. Da. *veirbidt*, Norw. *vederbiten*, Sw. *väderbiten*.] Nipped, gnawed, or worn by the weather.

1611 SHAKS. *Wint. T.* v. ii. 60 Now he thanks the old Shepheard (which stands by, like a Weather-bitten Conduit, of many Kings Reignes). **1624** HEYWOOD *Captives* II. i. in Bullen *O. Pl.* IV, What are you poore soules Thus wett and wether-bitt?

'weatherbitt, -bit, *sb. Naut.* [See BITT.] An extra turn of the cable about the bitts in bad weather. Also *v. trans.*, to give this extra turn to (the cable).

1769 FALCONER *Dict. Marine* (1780), *Weather-bit*, a turn of the cable of a ship about the end of the windlass, without the knight-heads. It is used to check the cable, in order to slacken it gradually out of the ship, in tempestuous weather, or when the ship rides in a strong current. **1840** R. H. DANA *Bef. Mast* xxiv, Weather-bit your chain and loose the topsails! **1867** SMYTH *Sailor's Word-bk.*, *Weather-bitt*, is that which holds the weather-cable when the ship is moored. **1883** *Man. Seamanship for Boys* 191 To weather bitt a cable is to take another turn round the bitt end. **1900** *Century Mag.* Feb. 600/2, I now moor ship, weather-bitt cables, and leave the sloop *Spray*..safe in port.

weather-blate, -blade, -bleat. *Anglo-Irish.* [Etymologizing perversion (after WEATHER *sb.*) of OE. *hæferblǽte*: see HEATHER-BLEAT.] The snipe.

1802 G. V. SAMPSON *Statist. Surv. Londonderry* 459 The weather-blate, or snipe, flying high in a calm night, is a good sign. **1890** D. A. SIMMONS *Words Armagh & S. Donegal* (E.D.D.), *Weather-blade*, a snipe which utters a sound like a goat. **1908** *Westm. Gaz.* 29 Sept. 2/3 The black water-hen and the sad weather-bleat.

'weatherboard.

1. a. One of a series of boards nailed horizontally, with overlapping edges, as an outside covering for walls. Also *collect. sing.*

1539–40 in Swayne *Churchw. Acc. Sarum* (1896) 268, C fowt of whether borde to whetherborde the howes end. **1759** *Phil. Trans.* LI. 287 Some of the weather-boards were thrown outwards to the bottom of the garden. **1802** *Barrington's Hist. N.S. Wales* x. 420 The stores were of brick, and the guard-house of weather-boards. **1845** J. O. BALFOUR *Sk. N.S. Wales* 87 Settlers..have, according to their means, built of free-stone, brick, or weather-boards, cottages and houses. **1883** SLADEN *Austral. Lyrics* 25 The other, sore-dinted, scarcely crawled to the sheltering weatherboards. **1890** 'R. BOLDREWOOD' *Miner's Right* vi. 61 The more ambitious buildings are of weather-board, sawn pine or hardwood boards, roofed with large sheets of galvanized iron.

attrib. **1894** A. ROBERTSON *Nuggets*, etc. 173 The weather-board walls creaked and groaned like a ship's timbers in a gale.

b. A board laid over builders' work or material as a protection.

1851 *B'ham & Midl. Gardeners' Mag.* Apr. 30 Every heap [*sc.* of quick lime] being covered by mats or weatherboards. **1879** *Cassell's Techn. Educ.* I. 195 Unfinished walls should be covered with straw, on which boards, called weather-boards, should be laid.

c. A weatherboarded dwelling or other building. *Austral.*

1925 'H. H. RICHARDSON' *Way Home* II. i. 123 Jerry and his bride had made ready their tiny weatherboard. **1935** L. MANN *Human Drift* xxxvi. 238 Magnificently the two stories of Geelong weatherboards, new that year, overlooked on the ridge. **1975** D. MALOUF *Johnno* ii. 28 But our one-storeyed weatherboard wasn't the only one to be fortified. The whole city had taken on the aspect of an armed camp.

2. a. A board placed sloping over a window or other opening to throw off or keep out rain; †*pl.* louver-boards; also, a board used to carry off water.

1568 *Ludlow Churchw. Acc.* (Camden) 128, ij bordes to make wether bordes for the windowes in the steple. **1569** *Ibid.* 138, iij bordes..ffor wetherbordes in the steple windowes. **1585** HIGINS *Junius' Nomencl.* 210/2 *Deliquiæ*,.. water boords, or weather bordes; gutters whereinto the house eaues doe drop. **1598** HAKLUYT *Voy.* I. 577 The Cathedrall Church of Holen hauing..also beames and weather-bourdes, and the rest of the roofe proportionally answering to this lower building. **1741** *Phil. Trans.* XLII. 498 A great Number of large Holes, regularly placed,..with Weather-boards placed over each Range of Holes, so as to hang over them obliquely downwards. **1818** MOORE *Fudge Fam. Paris* iii. 80 Such hats!—fit for monkeys—I'd back Mrs. Draper To cut neater weather-boards out of brown paper. **1833** T. HOOK *Love & Pride, Marquess* xii, Rattle went all the windows—*slap* went the weather boards [of an omnibus]. **1892** *Dict. Arch.* (Archit. Publ. Soc.), *Weather board*, a board fixed..at the bottom of a door or window, to keep out driving rain.

b. *Naut.* (See quots.)

1760–72 tr. *Juan & Ulloa's Voy.* (ed. 3) II. 304 On the 30th we took down our weather-boards. **1815** *Falconer's Dict. Marine* (ed. Burney), *Weather-Boards* are pieces of plank placed in the ports of a ship, when laid up in ordinary; they are fixed in an inclined position, so as to turn off the rain without preventing the circulation of the air. **1867** SMYTH *Sailor's Word-bk.* **1908** PAASCH *From Keel to Truck* (ed. 4) 546 *Weather-boards*,..boards fitted closely together..in front or on the sides of a bridge, poop or raised quarter-deck.

3. *Naut.* [See WEATHER *sb.* 8 and BOARD *sb.* 12. Cf. Icel. *veðr-borð*.] The windward side of a ship.

a **1625** MANWAYRING *Sea-mans Dict.* (1644) 12 The weather-boord, that is as much as to say, to windward. **1706** PHILLIPS (ed. Kersey). **1867** SMYTH *Sailor's Word-bk.*

Hence **'weatherboard** *v. trans.*, to nail weatherboards upon (a wall or roof); also *absol.* **'weatherboarded** *ppl. a.* **'weatherboarding** *vbl. sb.*, the work of covering a building with weatherboards; also *concr.*, weatherboards collectively.

1515 in *Compotus Rolls Obedientiaries St. Swithun's, Winch.* (1892) 461 Et in solutis duobus carpentariis conductis ad wetherbordandum finem coquinæ. **1535–6** *Rec. St. Mary at Hill* 370 Paid ffor viij c di. of borde ffor to wederborde the sowth syde of wolston wynnys howse. **1613** *S'hampton Crt. Leet Rec.* (1905) 464 The Towne howse now in the tenure of Thomas beare..would requier to be weather-boorded. **1632** in E. B. Jupp *Carpenters' Co.* (1887) 300 The boarding and weatherboarding of howses shedds and hovells. **1703** [R. NEVE] *City & C. Purchaser* 285 Weather-boarding..is us'd to signifie the Boards themselves, when nail'd up. **1737** W. SALMON *Country Builder's Estimator* (ed. 2) 16 To build a Barn with all new Oak-Timber, to thatch, underpin, and weather-board with Feather-edged Deals. **1796** W. H. MARSHALL *W. Eng.* II. 211 Farm houses..with weatherboarded barns. **1805** R. W. DICKSON *Pract. Agric.* I. 48 The outside covered over with strong weather-boarding. **1847** J. D. LANG *Phillipsland* 283 A neat, comfortable, weather-boarded cottage. **1885** *Harper's Mag.* Mar. 606/1 Narrow strips of weather-boarding.

'weather-bound, *ppl. a.* Detained by bad weather; prevented by stress of weather from sailing, travelling, or other outdoor activity.

1590 R. FERRIS *Dang. Adventure* B 1, There we were wether bound, and constrained to stay full seuenteene dayes. *a* **1641** BP. MOUNTAGU *Acts & Mon.* (1642) 334 The messenger who carried those Letters, being weather bound and sea-beaten, could not come so soone. **1667** *Lond. Gaz.* No. 193/4 The Fleet of Colliers that lay here weather-bound, are now under sail for the Thames. **1726** R. GALE in *Mem. Stukeley* (Surtees) I. 187, I lye weatherbound here by a deep snow. **1887** T. A. TROLLOPE *What I remember* I. xvii. 346 Two young Americans..were in the house, equally weather-bound with ourselves.

fig. **1779** JOHNSON *L.P.*, *Milton*, This dependence of the soul upon the seasons..may, I suppose, justly be derided as the fumes of vain imagination... The author that thinks himself weather-bound will find, with a little help from hellebore, that he is only idle or exhausted.

weather-breeder. A day of exceptionally sunny and calm weather, popularly supposed to be a presage of a coming storm. Also *fig.*

1655 H. L'ESTRANGE *Chas. I* (1655) 160 The King had intentions of being present at the General Assembly; but this lucid interval proved but a weather-breeder. **1659** J. ARROWSMITH *Chain Princ.* 391 Look at a very fair day, as that which may prove a weather-breeder, and usher in storms. **1780** T. SMITH *Jrnl.* (1849) 281 A most delightful day; a weather breeder. **1828** CARR *Craven Gloss.*, s.v., A cloudless sky, after a succession of rainy weather, denotes rain, and is said to be a *weather-breeder*. **1879** J. BURROUGHS *Locusts* 98 Weather-breeders..are usually the finest days in the calendar, all sun and sky. **1903** *Daily Chron.* 10 Feb. 5/2 Isolated fine days in February are known in Surrey as 'weather-breeders'.

So **weather-breeding** *a.*

1899 R. M. GILCHRIST *Nicholas* 23 The last se'nnight of March had been dull and weather-breeding.

'weathercock, *sb.* Forms: see WEATHER *sb.* and COCK *sb.* [Cf. Du. *weerhaan*, G. *wetterhahn*, Sw. *väder-*, Da. *veirhane*.]

1. A vane in the form of a cock, which turns with its head to the wind. Also used *gen.* for a vane of any form. Often mentioned as a symbol of mutability or fickleness.

a **1300** *Neckam de Utensil.* in Wright *Vocab.* 115 *Ventilogium*, veder-coc. **1340** *Ayenb.* 180 þeruore hi byeþ ase þe wedercoc þet is ope þe steple, þet him went mid eche wynde. *a* **1400** CHAUCER *Agst. Woman Unconstant* 12 As a wedercok, that turneth his face With every wind. *c* **1480** HENRYSON *Test. Cress.* 567 Thairfoir, I reid ȝe tak thame as ȝe find, For thay ar sad as Widdercock in Wind. **1546** *Inv. Ch. Goods York* etc. (Surtees) 86 The said Steple havyng a whether cokke theruppon all gylt. **1683** D. A. *Art of Converse* 21 Some are as changeable as weather-cocks in their humours. **1790** COWPER *Let. Lady Hesketh* 22 Mar., I have as many opinions about it as there are whims in a weathercock. **1833** L. RITCHIE *Wand. Loire* 37 The Duc de Choiseul..consoled himself by setting up the head of Voltaire as a weathercock. **1867** H. LATHAM *Black & White* 100 The most conspicuous weather-cock in the town is a golden trumpet on the spire of one of the churches.

2. *fig.* **a.** of things (in various obvious allusions). † ***upon the weathercock***, inclined to turn and vary.

1589 GREENE *Menaphon* (Arb.) 48 No doubt your mother was made of a Weathercocke, that brought foorth such a wauering companion. **1661** GODOLPHIN *View Adm. Jurisd.* Introd. [a], He that vents his own Notions, or sails by the weather-cock of his own Brain. **1687** DRYDEN *Hind & P.* I. 465 The Word's a weathercock for ev'ry wind. **1702**

VANBRUGH *False Fr.* I. B 2, As much upon the Weather-cock as the Ladies are, there are some the Wind must blow hard to fetch 'em about. **1888** BRYCE *Amer. Commw.* III. lxxix. 35 Newspapers are powerful in three ways, as narrators, as advocates, and as weathercocks.

b. of persons; esp. one who is changeable or inconstant.

1588 SHAKS. *L.L.L.* IV. i. 97 What plume of feathers is hee that indited this Letter? What veine? What Wether-cocke? **1598** —— *Merry W.* III. ii. 18 Where had you this pretty weather-cocke? **1607** MIDDLETON *Fam. Love* II. (1608) C 2, I thinke we loose part of our happinesse when we make these weathercocks our equalls. **1670** DRYDEN *1st Pt. Conq. Granada* III. (1672) 21 The word which I have giv'n shall stand like Fate; Not like the King's, that weathercock of State. **1799** NELSON 6 Apr. in Nicolas *Disp.* III. 316 The last are weathercocks, and will always be on the side of the conqueror. *a* **1850** CALHOUN *Wks.* (1874) II. 178, I ask the advocates of this doctrine, in what do they differ in their actions from the mere trimmer, the political weather-cock? **1870** R. BROUGH *Marston Lynch* xiv. 118 He was..a terrible weathercock in the matter of opinion.

3. a. *attrib.* and *appos.*, passing into *adj.* = changeable, inconstant.

a **1680** CHARNOCK *Attrib. God* (1834) I. 558 The wavering and weathercock resolutions of men. **1710** in Hearne *Collect.* 7 Mar. (O.H.S.) II. 356 Not weather-Cock Kennett such turning can show. **1801** *Marvellous Love-Story* II. 316 Miss Harrison was one of those every-day sort of weather-cock characters who veer about with every varying gust of prejudice, folly, or envy. **1818** COLERIDGE *Friend* (1865) 216 Their political opinions depend with weathercock uncertainty on the winds of rumour that blow from France. **1881** MISS BRADDON *Asphodel* II. 162 In affairs of the heart, Mr. Turchill belonged to the weathercock species.

b. *Comb.*: ***weathercock-like*** adj., ***-wise*** adv.

1663 GERBIER *Counsel* 2 Inslaved by Weather-cok-like-spirits to make their Buildings according unto things *a la mode.* **1874** LISLE CARR *Jud. Gwynne* II. vii. 192 It was not in his steadfast nature to veer about, weather-cock-wise.

c. *Aeronaut.* Used *attrib.* and as *adj.* with reference to the tendency of an aircraft to turn away from the set compass direction into the relative wind.

1898 *Aeronaut. Jrnl.* Jan. 6/2 The little vertical rudder has a little bit of a weather-cock action. If the wind suddenly shifts, it swings the machine round to head the wind. **1916** G. C. LOENING *Military Aeroplanes* xii. 166 Some tendency to head into the relative wind is necessary. This is obtained by having enough rudder or fin surface aft to bring the directional center back of the c.g. and is called 'weathercock' stability. **1928** N. MACMILLAN *Art of Flying* vii. 74 A seaplane is usually directionally stable to the wind on the water with engine stopped, a quality which is described as being 'weathercock'... If the seaplane is weathercock, she will ride head to wind and drift backward. **1935** C. G. BURGE *Compl. Bk. Aviation* 616 Weathercock instability. **1945** *Jrnl. R. Aeronaut. Soc.* XL. 461/2 Weathercock stability should be reasonably high, to cut down the magnitude of the inadvertent skid. **1970** T. HACKER *Flight Stability & Control* vii. 160 The variation of the vertical tail area will influence the weathercock stability.

Hence **'weathercockish, -cocky** *adjs.*, fickle, changeable. **'weathercockism**, changeableness.

1843 *Fraser's Mag.* XXVII. 301 Thiers will always be regarded as the very condensed essence of weathercockism. **1886** 'OUIDA' *House Party* ix. (1887) 198 She is what her husband characterises as 'weathercocky'. **1887** *Sat. Rev.* 12 Feb. 213/2 To do these Radicals justice, there is a great deal of consistency in their weathercockism.

'weathercock, *v.* [f. prec. sb.]

†**1.** intr. ***to weathercock it***: to veer or vary like a weathercock. *Obs.*

1654 J. P. *Tyrants & Protectors* 39 Men that will be of the Kings Religion, be he of what Religion he will, and are clamorous against all that cannot weather-cock it like themselves. **1824** *Blackw. Edin. Mag.* June 703/2 No change of times can ever change that feeling in me. Let others weather-cock it to and fro as they please.

2. *trans.* To provide with a weathercock; to serve as a weathercock for.

1658 *S. Austin's Naps upon Parnassus* B 4, But that's a work onely befits the Gods, To Weather-cock their Eyes with fishing-rods. **1864** TENNYSON *Aylmer's Field* 17 Whose blazing wyvern weathercock'd the spire. **1883** *Harper's Mag.* Apr. 698/2 Elaborately adorned gables,..scrolled, and weather-cocked.

3. To send (a person) up to the weathercock. *jocular nonce-use.*

a **1845** [see MASTHEAD *v.* 1].

4. *intr.* **a.** *Naut.* Of a ship: to (tend to) head into the wind.

1952 SMITH & VIOLET *Wind calls Tune* i. 19 She would weathercock head to seas and, under mizzen and foresail, she would sail well without anybody at the tiller. **1974** *Tel.* (Brisbane) 4 June 8/5 In these conditions the boats had a strong tendency to weathercock, making it exceptionally difficult to pick up buoys.

b. *intr.* (See quot. 1956.) Also *trans.*, to cause to weathercock.

1956 W. A. HEFLIN *U.S. Air Force Dict.* 565/2 *Weathercock.* Of an airplane, rocket, or similar body: to align, or attempt to align, its longitudinal axis with the direction of the wind. **1976** 'M. ALBRAND' *Taste of Terror* v. 38 That terrible cross-wind caught the plane's high vertical stabilizer and began to weathercock it into the wind.

Hence **'weathercocking** *vbl. sb.*

1952 SMITH & VIOLET *Wind calls Tune* vi. 59 We had to get the mizzen as flat as possible to make it more efficient as a 'weather cocking' influence. **1985** *Flight* 4 May 23/3 The butterfly tail..actually eliminates weathercocking in crosswinds.

weather-coil, *v. Naut.* ? *Obs.* [See WEATHER *sb.* 3 and COIL *v.*[4]] *intr.* Of a ship (see quots.). Also **weather-coiling** *vbl. sb.*

a **1625** MANWAYRING *Sea-mans Dict.* (1644) 115 *Weather-coile* is when a ship is a hull, to lay her head the other way, without looseing any saile; which is only done, by bearing up the helme. It is an excellent condition in a ship; for most ships will not weather-coile. **1626** CAPT. J. SMITH *Accid. Yng. Seamen* 29 Weather coyle. **1627** —— *Sea Gram.* ix. 40 If shee will weather coile, and lay her head the other way without loosing a saile, that must bee done by bearing vp the Helme. *c* **1635** CAPT. N. BOTELER *Dial. Sea Serv.* (1685) 222 The Weather-coiling of a Ship, is, when being a Hull [etc.]. **1753** *Chambers' Cycl.* Suppl., *Weather-Quoil*, or *Coile.* **1867** SMYTH *Sailor's Word-bk.*, *Weather-coil*, when a ship has her head brought about, so as to lie that way which her stern did before, as by the veering of the wind; or the motion of the helm, the sails remaining trimmed. *Weather-coiling*, a ship resuming her course after being taken aback; rounding off by a stern-board, and coming up to it again.

†**'weather-driven**, *pa. pple.* and *ppl. a. Obs.* [See WEATHER *sb.* 6 c. Cf. Sw. *väderdrifven.*] Driven by stormy weather.

a **1513** FABYAN *Chron.* VI. ccxiii. (1811) 230 He, in his course of saylyng, was weder dryuen, and by tempest, into ye countre or prouynce of Pontife. **1530** PALSGR. 844/1 Weather driuen, as a shyppe is that is let go at all aduentures, *abandonner* [sic]. **1539** CROMWELL in Merriman *Life & Lett.* (1902) II. 193 A certain frenshe ship laden with Scotishe goodes wetherdryven at South schelis. **1602** CAREW *Cornwall* II. 151 Philip..during his voyage..towards Spayne..was weather-driuen into Weymouth. **1659** O. WALKER *Oratory* 16 Like a weather-driven ship destitute of her Pilot.

weathered ('wɛðəd), *ppl. a.* [f. WEATHER *v.* + -ED[1].]

1. Worn, stained, or seasoned by the weather or by atmospheric influences. Also ***weathered out.*** Chiefly *Geol.* (See WEATHER *v.* 2 a, b.)

1789 J. WILLIAMS *Min. Kingd.* I. 420 This weathered or dissolved copper is found in many places in the state of an ochre or of a loose powder. **1820** *Edin. Philos. Jrnl.* III. 185 The weathered surface of several specimens of calcareous sandstone. **1827** CARLYLE *Germ. Rom.* IV. 212 The weathered aspect of the towers. **1843** RUSKIN *Mod. Paint.* I. II. I. vii. §26, I have never yet seen any restoration or cleaned portion of a building whose effect was not inferior to the weathered parts. **1854** HOOKER *Himal. Jrnls.* I. xi. 254 The weathered surface of each block was black. **1860** TYNDALL *Glac.* I. vii. 54 The weathered ice of the surface..could be cloven with great facility. **1879** *Encycl. Brit.* X. 230/1 Practice enables a geologist to discriminate some rocks by the feel of their weathered or fresh surfaces. **1906** *Cornish N. & Q.* Ser. I. 235 A collection of weathered-out crystals of felspar. **1914** MOIR in *Man* XIV. 180 What we have regarded as deep striæ caused by immense pressure are in all probability simply weathered out shattered scratches.

2. Of a crop of grain or hay: Deteriorated by too long exposure to the elements.

1875 *Ure's Dict. Arts* III. 185 Weathered barley has a dull and often a dirty appearance. **1879** MISS JACKSON *Shropsh. Word-bk.*, *Weathered*, damaged, but not spoilt, by too long exposure to weather—wet and bad harvesting weather: said of hay or corn. **1892** *Daily Chron.* 6 Sept. 3/5 Barley is particularly liable to become 'weathered' and unfit for malting.

3. *Arch.* Made sloping, so as to prevent the lodgement of water; furnished with a weathering or water-table.

1840 *Civil Engin. & Arch. Jrnl.* III. 2/1 Two octagonal turrets..strengthened by massive double buttresses in three stages, the lower part terminating in weathered canopies, the middle having weathered offsets. **1879** *Cassell's Techn. Educ.* II. 294/1 Copings are worked with..an inclined or 'weathered' upper surface.

'weather-eye. [? a jocular use of the *Naut.* sense, WEATHER *sb.* 8; or perh. = the eye which is specially used for observing the weather. Cf. ON. *veðr-eygr*, ? keen-eyed.] Used in fig. phrases, such as ***to keep one's weather-eye open***, to be watchful and alert, keep one's wits about one.

1829 P. EGAN *Boxiana* 2nd Ser. II. 505 Lads of the Fancy, who always keep their 'weather eye' up towards business, *i.e.* looking after the blunt. **1839** HOOD *Storm at Hastings* 189 Howbeit his weather eye the seaman aim'd Across the calm, and hinted by his speech A gale next morning. **1846** DICKENS *Dombey* x. 89 Joe is awake, Ma'am... Josh has his weather-eye open, Sir. **1851** H. MELVILLE *Moby Dick* I. xxxiv. 253 All whale-ships' standing orders, 'Keep your weather eye open, and sing out every time'. **1865** DICKENS *Mut. Fr.* II. v, You look out. Keep your weather eye awake. **1887** RIDER HAGGARD *She* vii. 88 Job returned in a great state of nervousness, and keeping his weather eye fixed upon every woman who came near him. **1916** 'TAFFRAIL' *Pincher Martin* iv. 53 Even the captain and the navigator..did not seem to be taking things very seriously, though in reality they both had their weather-eyes very much lifting. **1959** B. WOOTTON *Soc. Sci.* 10, I have tried to keep a weather eye open to what is going on elsewhere: references to work in other areas..will be found scattered through these pages. **1981** *Times* 7 Apr. 6/7 The Russians..are keeping a weathereye on other nations.

'weather-fend, *v. trans.* [f. WEATHER *sb.*] To defend from the weather; to shelter. Also *fig.* Hence **'weather-fending** *ppl. a.*

A Shakespearian word echoed by later writers.

1610 SHAKS. *Temp.* V. i. 10 In the Line-groue which weather-fends your Cell. **1788** CROWE *Levesdon Hill* 4 This friendly mount, that weather-fends My reed-roof'd cottage. **1800** COLERIDGE *Pitt & Buonaparte* in Hazlitt *Pol. Ess.* (1819) 396 A young man,..sheltered and weather-fended from all the elements of experience. **1814** WORDSW. *Excurs.* II. 420 A penthouse, framed..To weather-fend a little turf-built seat. **1858** EMERSON *Adirondacs* 35 We..Barked the white spruce to weatherfend the roof. **1873** RUSKIN *Crown of Wild Olive* App. 191 Finding its work prosper, the little medicinal and weather-fending company took vows on itself.

weather-gall. Also 6, 9 *Sc.* **-gaw**, 9 **-go.** [f. WEATHER *sb.* + GALL *sb.*[2] Cf. G. *wettergalle*, Du. *weergal*; also WATERGALL 2 and WINDGALL.] An imperfect rainbow, believed to be a presage of storm: = WATERGALL 2. Sometimes applied to other appearances in the sky to which the same significance is attributed.

1613–35 MARKHAM *Eng. Husb.* I. I. iii. 12 If you shall see one or more Weather-galls which are like Raine-bowes, onely they arise from the Horison but a small way upward. **1621** BRATHWAIT *Time's Curtain drawn* L 7, He..taukes of Starres, and clipses of the Sun,..Of wether-gaws and many sike as these. **1694** tr. *Marten's Voy. Spitzbergen* in *Acc. Sev. Late Voy.* II. 50 These Lights are called Weather-galls by the Sea-men. **1808** JAMIESON, *Weddir-gaw.* **1822** SCOTT *Pirate* iv, See how much heavier the clouds fall every moment, and see these weather-gaws that streak the lead-coloured mass with partial gleams of faded red and purple. **1823** W. SCORESBY *Jrnl. Whale Fish.* 23 A little before sun-set, a weather-gall (or the limb of a rain-bow), of extraordinary brilliancy, appeared. **1824** CARR *Craven Gloss.*, *Weather-gall*, a secondary rain-bow. **1867** SMYTH *Sailor's Word-bk.* s.v., A weather-gall at morn, Fine weather all gone. *Ibid.*, *Weather-go*, the end of a rainbow, as seen in the morning in showery weather. **1878** J. VEITCH *Hist. Scot. Border* xiv. 515 They eyed carefully the weather-gaw, or broken bit of rainbow above the horizon.

'weather-glass. [Cf. Du. *weerglas*, Da. *veirglas*, Sw. *väderglas*, G. *wetterglas.*]

†**1.** A kind of thermometer, used to ascertain the temperature of the air, and also to prognosticate changes in the weather. *Obs.*

It consisted in its simplest form of an upright tube filled with water, terminating at the top in a bulb containing rarefied air. The water sank or rose in the tube as the air in the bulb expanded or contracted.

1626 BACON *Sylva* §27 Cold..doth manifestly Condense; As wee see in the Contracting of the Aire in the Weather-Glasse. **1634** J. B[ATE] *Myst. Nat. & Art* 28 A Weather-glasse is a structure of, at the least, two glasses, sometimes of three, foure, or more, as occasion serueth, inclosing a quantity of water, and a portion of ayre proportionable, by whose condensation or rarifaction the included water is subject unto a continuall motion, either upward or downward; by which motion of the water is commonly foreshewn the state, change, and alteration of the weather. *a* **1643** SUCKLING *Brennoralt* II. i, His colour..sanke down As water in a weather-glasse Prest by a warme hand. **1669** WORLIDGE *Syst. Agric.* 257 For the true discovery of the nature and temper of the Air, as to its density or rarity, we have not met with a more certain or compleat invention than the Weather-glass. *Ibid.* 259 The Weather-glass or Thermoscope. **1670** DRYDEN *1st Pt. Conq. Granada* IV. ii. (1672) 36 As in some wether-glass my Love I hold; Which falls or rises with the heat or cold. **1694** *Phil. Trans.* XVIII. 205 A tender Weather-Glass or Thermometer. **1720** *Ibid.* XXXI. 117 Two Thermometers, the one the common seal'd Weather-glass, having no Communication with the outward Air, wherein the temper as to Heat and Cold was shewn by the swelling or shrinking of the included Spirit.

2. A barometer.

1695 *Lond. Gaz.* No. 3103/4 A Portable Barometer, or Weather-Glass. **1710** ADDISON *Tatler* No. 220 ¶3 Toricellius, the Inventor of the common Weather Glass. **1758** JOHNSON *Idler* No. 33 ¶2 Weather rainy. Consulted my weather-glass. **1848** CLOUGH *Bothie* II. 17 The weather-glass, say they, is rising. **1885** *New Bk. Sports* 23 There is no trusting the weather-glass among the Highland hills.

3. *fig.*

1654 WHITLOCK *Zootomia* 276, I shall onely refer you to the Polititians Weather-glasse, whereby he not onely foreseeth (but discerneth aright when fallen) the unseasonable weather of his respective Place he liveth in. **1681** D'URFEY *Progr. Honesty* xiv. 32 His Bone's his Weather-Glass, and his Back Is his perpetual Almanack. **1742** H. WALPOLE *Let. to Mann* 24 June, My uncle, who is my political weather-glass, and whose quicksilver rises and falls with the least variation of parliamentary weather. **1748** RICHARDSON *Clarissa* (1768) VIII. 180 When the weather-glass of my pride got up again, I found I had gone too far to recede. **1864** G. A. LAWRENCE *Maurice Dering* II. 80 Besides, I'm not at all sure that he *was* losing heavily: his own face is a bad weather-glass.

4. ***poor man's***, or ***shepherd's, weather-glass***: a name for the scarlet pimpernel, *Anagallis arvensis*, from its closing its flowers before rain.

1827, **1872** [see SHEPHERD *sb.* 8 d]. **1836** J. T. MACKAY *Flora Hibern.* I. 194 Common Pimpernel, or Poor Man's Weatherglass.

†**'weather-headed**, *ppl. a. Obs.* [Prob. f. WETHER (cf. *sheep-headed*), but admitting of association with WEATHER (expressing the notion of instability).] Light-headed, foolish.

a **1652** BROME *Queen & Concub.* IV. iii. 86 Here come more of our weather-headed wise neighbours. **1695** CONGREVE *Love for Love* II. vii. 36 For that old Weather-headed Fool, I know how to laugh at him. **1822** SCOTT *Peveril* vii, You deserved to be ducked for it..for a weather-headed puppy.

weathering ('wɛðərɪŋ), *vbl. sb.* Forms: 1 **wæderung**, 2 **widerung**, 4 **wedring**, **weduring**, **-ynge**, **widdringe**, 4–6 **wederyng(e**, 5 **wedryng(e**, **weddrynge**, **wedyrryng**, 5–6 **wethering(e**, **-yng(e**, 6 **wedering**, 7 **wethring**, 6– **weathering.** [In sense 1, repr. OE. *wederung*, f. *wed(e)rian* (see

WEATHER *v.*); in later uses f. WEATHER *v.* + -ING[1].]

†**1. a.** Weather conditions; (good or bad) weather; in nautical use chiefly with reference to the direction and force of the winds. *Obs.*

a **1122** *O.E. Chron.* (Laud MS.) an. 1085, & þæs ilcan ȝeares wæs swiðe hefelic ȝear..& swa mycel unȝelimp on wæderunge swa man naht æðelice ȝeþencean ne mæȝ swa stor þunring & læȝt wes. *c* **1175** *Lamb. Hom.* 13 Gif ȝe mine bibode healded þenne sende ic eou rihte widerunge. *c* **1325** *Poem temp. Edw. II* lxxvi, God hath..send wederyng on erthe Cold & unkynde. **1387–8** T. USK *Test. Love* III. vii. 74 After suche stormes [in budding-time], how hard is it to avoyde, til efte wedring and yeres han maked her circute cours al about, er any frute be able to be tasted! **1425** *Rolls of Parlt.* IV. 290/1 Grett rayne, and longe abydyng upon the water, be fortune of wederyng or otherwise. *c* **1440** *Promp. Parv.* 519/2 Wederynge, of þe eyre, *temperies*. *a* **1450** *Mirk's Festial* 284 ȝe prayen to God forto haue kynde wedryng to all maner of sedys þat ben cast yn þe erthe. *c* **1489** CAXTON *Sonnes of Aymon* xxiv. 524 And wyte it, that by fortune of wedryng, they were well eyght monethes vpon the see. *c* **1500** *Melusine* xxvi. 206 That no raynne or other fowll wedryng myght lette þeire entree within the tounne. *a* **1513** FABYAN *Chron.* VII. (1811) 314 By reason of the vnreasonable wederynge, as in yᵉ laste yere fell, yᵉ whete was solde for xv.s. a quarter. **1528** R. COPLAND tr. *Rutter of Sea* (*c* 1550) D viij b, The maister and his mariners trimmeth not their sayle as it should be, and ill wethering taketh them in the sea. *c* **1565** SPARKE in Hakluyt *Voy.* (1589) 537 He did consider what time he should spend ere he could get so farre to windeward againe, which would haue bene with the weathering which we had 10 or 12 dayes worke.

†**b.** Propitious or suitable weather. *Obs.*

1340–70 *Alex. & Dind.* 1 Whan þis weith at his wil weduring hadde, Ful raþe rommede he rydinge þedirre. **1389** in *Eng. Gilds* (1870) 23 We shul preyen..for alle trewe shipmen,..yᵗ godd for his grace yeue hem wederyng and passage. *c* **1400** in *York Manual* (Surtees) 221* ȝe schulleþ also bidde þat god..suche widdringes vs sende on erþe þat þe fruyt þat is þer inne thriue. *c* **1440** *Jacob's Well* 261 So þou synfull man..excusyst þe, & seyst, I may noȝt kepe þe halyday, for god wil sende no wederyng on þe werkeday. **1532** TINDALE *Expos. Matt.* v.–vii. 59 Where the prieste oughte to praye in the mother tounge..for wedering and frutes [etc.]. **1553** BECON *Reliques of Rome* (1563) 236 b, Ye shal pray for al manner of frutes..yᵗ almightye God..maye sende suche wederynges, yᵗ they maye come to the sustenaunce of man.

†**c.** Stormy weather; also, a storm. So ***great, strong weathering*** [cf. F. *gros temps*]. *Obs.*

c **1450** *Contin. Brut* 482 þere was such wedryng of thonder, lightnyng, hayll and rayne, þat the peple were sore adredde. *c* **1450** LOVELICH *Grail* II. 68 So thanne Cam þere bothe wynd & wedrynge, and fer Into the See it gan hem brynge. **1455** *Rolls of Parlt.* V. 335 Atte all tymes that any Carrik or Galey arryveth by force of Wederynge..in the Portes. **1490** CAXTON *Eneydos* xv. 52 The duke Eneas and Dydo fleynge the wedrynge, shalle rendre hemself bothe togydre alle alone. *Ibid.* 55 Vnto the tyme that the sayde cloudes were well thyk gadred with the stronge wedrynge that surprised them all atones. *a* **1513** FABYAN *Chron.* v. cii. (1811) 76 Both hoostes were so greuously betyn with the sayd tempest and wederynge. *Ibid.* VII. ccxxiii. 249 In..the .v. daye of October, passynge tempeste of wederynge fell in sondry places of Englonde. **1526** in Willis & Clark *Cambridge* (1886) I. 616 For defense of great wyndes and outragious wetheringes. **1605** STOW *Ann.* 633 On Candlemas euen..was great weathering of wind, hayle, snow, rayne.

2. The action of exposing a hawk to the action of the weather. (Cf. WEATHER *v.* 1 a.) Also ***weathering ground***.

1575 TURBERV. *Faulconrie* 76 He muste remember euery euening to tye out his hawke a weathering. **1677** N. COX *Gentl. Recr.* II. (ed. 2) 168 *Weathering*, is when you air your Hawk in Frost, Sun, or by the Fire-side. **1773** J. CAMPBELL *Mod. Faulconry* 264 *Weathering*, the setting out of a hawk to take the air. **1855** SALVIN & BRODERICK *Falconry in Brit. Isles* iii. 44 In the morning..they may be..placed upon blocks in the open air, without their hoods; this is called 'weathering'.

attrib. **1635** QUARLES *Embl.* v. ix. 5 Ev'n like the Hawlk, (whose keepers wary hands Have made a prisner to her wethring stock). [See STOCK *sb.*[1] 19.] **1960** M. WOODFORD *Man. Falconry* ii. 9 The weathering ground should be a level, well-drained area of short grass protected from the prevailing winds. **1978** *Country Life* 27 July 215/3 Hawking enthusiasts will be delighted to find a well-stocked weathering ground at Kinmount.

3. a. The action of the atmospheric agencies or elements on substances exposed to its influence; the discoloration, disintegration, etc. resulting from this action.

1665 J. WEBB *Stone-Heng* (1725) 88 The weathering of so many Centuries of Years. **1757** tr. *J. F. Henckel's Pyritol.* v. 87 The ore on sinter is a plain and easy proof in behalf of a weathering, or a production by damps, rather than by way of streaming. **1774** *Phil. Trans.* LXIV. 489 The miners have called this decaying of the sulphurous ores of copper, iron, and other metals and semi-metals, the weathering of these ores. **1830** LYELL *Princ. Geol.* I. 211 It is snow-white, a description which is very applicable to the newer part of the deposit at San Filippo, where it has not become darkened by weathering. **1845** J. PHILLIPS *Geol.* in *Encycl. Metrop.* VI. 702/2 The weathering of the surfaces of buildings by the fluctuations of heat and moisture is partly dependent on the structure and composition of the stone. **1856** RUSKIN *Mod. Paint.* IV. v. xvii. §2 Now this sculpture by streams, or by gradual weathering, is the finishing work by which Nature brings her mountain forms into the state in which she intends us..to..love them. **1878** *A. K. Johnston's Africa* viii. 94 Hills of red sand formed from the weathering of a ferruginous sandstone of which the plain..is composed. **1888** RUTLEY *Rock-Forming Min.* 122 Through weathering, the iron..becomes converted into sesquioxide. **1914** MOIR in *Man* XIV. 179 The second part of my paper..deals with the 'weathering out' of scratches upon flint.

b. The action of the elements (on land, clay, etc.) as a beneficial agency; the state of being pulverized and rendered workable by this action.

1548 LATIMER *Ploughers* (1562) 16 And I feare me this land is not yet rype to be plowed. For as the saying is: It lacketh wetheryng: This geare lacketh wethering, at least waye it is not for me to plough.

c. *Philol.* Phonetic decay. *rare.*

1870 F. A. MARCH *Gram. Anglo-Sax.* §102 Weathering of Case-endings. *Ibid.* §226 Weathering of Inflexion Endings.

d. Exposure (of the face or skin) to all kinds of weather.

1887 STEVENSON *Mem. & Portr.* vi. 96 His face..was ruddy and stiff with weathering.

4. *Naut.* The action of passing (an object) on the windward side. Also *attrib.*

1878 DIXON KEMP *Yacht & Boat Sailing* 378/2 *Weathering.*—A relative term used in sailing to define the action of one vessel that is eating to windward of another. **1894** *Times* 30 July 7/3 Britannia had stood far enough out into the English Channel to get weathering distance.

5. *Arch.* A projecting course on the face of a wall, serving as a 'drip' to throw off rain-water; a sloped 'set off' of a wall or buttress; the inclination or slope given to a surface in order to prevent the lodgement of water.

1739 LABELYE *Piers Westm. Bridge* 69 The Sally, or Projection of a Cordon or rustic Cornish..serves also as a Weathering to the Stone-work. **1825** J. NICHOLSON *Oper. Mech.* 545 The measurer takes a line or tape and begins..at the plinth, then stretching the line to the top, bends it into the offset, or weathering. **1833** LOUDON *Encycl. Archit.* §1882 The massive buttress, with its deep weatherings, or water-tables between each graduation or stage of the height. **1850** PARKER *Gloss. Archit.*, *Weathering*, a slight inclination given to horizontal surfaces, especially in masonry, to prevent water from lodging on them. **1875** BRASH *Eccl. Archit. Irel.* 98 The weatherings..were contrived with skill and judgment.

attrib. **1886** *Cheshire Gloss.*, *Weathering course*, bricks set out from the wall round the bottom of a chimney, to protect the thatch where it joins the chimney.

weathering (ˈwɛðərɪŋ), *ppl. a.* [f. WEATHER *v.* + -ING[2].] That wears away or disintegrates through the action of the weather.

1855 KINGSLEY *Glaucus* 21 Syenite usually does so in our damp climate, from the 'weathering' effect of frost and rain. **1860** TYNDALL *Glac.* I. xxi. 148 The cliffs of the Breithorn are much exposed to weathering action. **1892** in A. E. Lee *Hist. Columbus* (Ohio) I. 676 The uses of the clays derived from the weathering shale are only in their infancy as yet. **1912** *Hibbert Jrnl.* Oct. 106 What we call changing physical objects—weathering hills or ageing suns.

ˈweatherize, *v. U.S.* [f. WEATHER *sb.* + -IZE.] *trans.* To make weatherproof; *spec.* to render (a building) impervious to the effects of weather, by insulation, double-glazing, etc. Also **ˈweatherized** *ppl. a.*; **ˈweatherizing** *vbl. sb.*; **ˌweatheriˈzation**.

1946 *Woman's Home Compan.* Mar. 117/3 (Advt.), Weather-Bird Shoes for boys and girls are weatherized. **1946** *Collier's* 9 Nov. 92 (Advt.), A brand-new portable [radio] with new weatherized case. **1976** *Laurel* (Montana) *Outlook* 9 June 3/2 A project which could provide insulation and other weatherization materials... A coordinator for the Weatherizing program. **1977** *Time* 4 Apr. 52/2 Plants and office buildings will have to be weatherized to prevent energy loss. **1980** *New Age* (U.S.) Oct. 38/1 In Fitchburg, Massachusetts, people were so scared of freezing last winter that they dreamed up a program of door-to-door citizen action which was supposed to weatherize half their houses in five weeks. **1983** *Hyde Park* (Chicago) *Herald* 6 July 21 The city's weatherization program makes it worthwhile.

weatherliness (ˈwɛðəlɪnɪs). [f. WEATHERLY *a.* + -NESS.] Weatherly quality (of a ship).

1883 DIXON KEMP in *Fortn. Rev.* 1 Sept. 324 The Mosquito..carried her ballast much lower than any existing yacht. This..was a principal cause of her weatherliness. **1893** MAHAN *Infl. Sea Power* I. 223 The superior speed and weatherliness of the Spanish ships might have enabled them seriously to molest the British.

†**ˈweatherling.** *Obs.*[−1] [-LING.] A student of the weather.

1656 S. PARTRIDGE *Synopsis* B 3, Many more the like rules [for Prediction of the Weather]..I might here have added; but in this little Booke, let the Weatherling be satisfied with these.

weatherly (ˈwɛðəlɪ), *a.* (and *adv.*).

†**1.** Of or pertaining to the weather. *Obs. rare*[−1].

1652 GAULE *Magastrom.* 61 Any proposition or prognostication (as well touching weatherly events as arbitrary contingents).

2. *Naut.* Of a sailing vessel: Able to sail close to the wind without drifting to leeward. Also used loosely (see quot. 1904).

1729 *Phil. Trans.* XXXVI. 57, I proposed to make a Ship work far better to Windward, than it is possible for the most Weatherly one to do at present. **1833** M. SCOTT *Tom Cringle* viii, Notwithstanding her weatherly qualities, the heavy cross sea, as she drove into it, headed her off bodily. **1846** G. WARBURTON *Hochelaga* I. 19 Those stout weatherly boats crowding up to the wharves, have just now returned from fishing for cod. **1867** SMYTH *Sailor's Word-bk.*, *Weatherly*, said of a well-trimmed ship with a clean bottom, when she holds a good wind, and presents such lateral resistance to the water, that she makes but little lee-way while sailing close-hauled. **1886** R. C. LESLIE *Sea Painter's Log* 226 For downright weatherly qualities, lead and leverage will beat beam without depth. **1904** *Dixon Kemp's Yacht & Boat Sailing* 649/2 *Weatherly*, the quality of hanging to windward well or holding a good wind. This term is often improperly used to denote good behaviour in a sea way or in bad weather.

†**3.** *adv.* To the windward. *Obs. rare*[−1].

1708 *Lond. Gaz.* No. 4422/7 Three of their Ships being almost as far Weatherly as we were.

weathermost (ˈwɛðəməʊst), *a.* *Naut.* [f. WEATHER *sb.* (8) + -MOST.] Furthest to windward.

1557 TOWRSON in Hakluyt *Voy.* (1589) 125 The Christopher being the headmost & the weathermost man. **1622** SIR R. HAWKINS *Voy. S. Sea* lix. 140 But in equitie and reason, the le-ward shippe ought euer to giue way to the weather most. **1726** G. ROBERTS *Voy.* 292 Having got the Length of the Weathermost of the little Islands, I bore away afore the Wind for the Fuurno. **1761** COLMAN *Jealous Wife* III. 43 One of Them made use of small Arms, which carried off the weathermost Corner of Ned Gage's Hat. **1834** MARRYAT *P. Simple* xlvi, The brig rounded up on the wind, shooting up under the sterns of the two weathermost schooners.

weatherology (ˌwɛðəˈrɒlədʒɪ). [f. WEATHER *sb.* + -OLOGY.] The science and study of the weather and its phenomena.

1823 BYRON *Juan* XIII. xliii, Whatever other blunders lie Upon my shoulders, here I must aver My Muse a glass of weatherology. **1860** *Chamb. Encycl.* I. 563/1 But the poverty of Australian hydrography is aggravated by the singularities of the so-styled 'weatherology'. **1881** S. T. S. LECKY *Wrinkles Pract. Navig.* I. xv. 114 Weatherology.

Weather-ometer (wɛðəˈrɒmɪtə(r)). Also **Weatherometer, weatherometer.** [f. WEATHER *sb.* + -OMETER.] A proprietary name for a device which subjects substances to simulated weather conditions in order to determine their weather-resistance.

1929 *Official Gaz.* (U.S. Patent Office) 11 June 308/2 Atlas Electric Devices Company, Chicago, Ill... Weather-ometer. For Apparatus for Testing the Effect of Weather Upon the Surfaces of Objects. Claims use since Dec. 3, 1926. **1937** *Nature* 28 Aug. 353/1 For accelerated weathering tests on various paints the weatherometer..has been used. **1951** [see FADE-OMETER]. **1965** *New Scientist* 1 July 25/3 A cyclic weatherometer developed as a screening test for new types of timber preservatives and water repellants.

ˈweatherproof, *a.* and *sb.* [See PROOF *a.* 1 b.]

A. *adj.* Impervious to the weather.

c **1620** Z. BOYD *Zion's Flowers* (1855) 16 Our Bark's not weather proof. **1647** HERRICK *Noble Numb.*, *Thanksgiving to God* 4 A little house, whose humble Roof Is weather-proof. **1665** J. WEBB *Stone-Heng* (1725) 45 Some are hard and Weather Proof; some soft, and subject to Decay. **1778** MISS BURNEY *Evelina* (1791) I. xvi. 66 'O never mind the old Beldame,' cried the Captain; 'she's weather-proof, I'll answer for her.' **1848** DICKENS *Dombey* lix, The house stands, large and weather-proof, in the long dull street. **1914** *Illustr. Lond. News* 3 Jan. 32/3 Weather-proof overcoats, suits, and costumes.

B. *sb.* Weatherproof material. Also, a weatherproof coat; a raincoat.

1876 SMILES *Sc. Nat.* x. 186 Nothing but the stiffest weather-proof can keep the water out. **1925** *Studio* (Art & Publicity Special Autumn No.) (Advt. suppl.) p. ix, Aquascutum pure wool weatherproofs come in one quality only—the best. **1935** *Times* 21 Feb. 14/2 [The Queen] saw the colour first in a crêpe de Chine weatherproof made with a cape. **1962** *N.Y. Times* 16 Nov. 3 A & F presents a selection of Burberry topcoats, overcoats and weatherproofs.

Hence as *v. trans.*, to make weatherproof or impervious to weather; **ˈweatherproofed** *ppl. a.*; **ˈweatherproofness**.

1926 T. E. LAWRENCE *Seven Pillars* (1935) VI. lxxix. 435 The Indians weather-proofed their own north-west rooms. **1929** *Punch* 17 Apr. p. xxii/2 Weatherproofed by Burberrys, their value as overcoats is enhanced in every way. **1933** *Times Lit. Suppl.* 7 Dec. 874/3 There is something animal —..in their strength, endurance, weather-proofness and capacity to live rough. **1963** *N.Y. Times* 1 Dec. 12 The 'Stormster'..all-climate coat... Weather-proofed cotton-poplin..lined. **1969** *Jane's Freight Containers 1968–69* 9/2 It is recommended that the test for weatherproofness (Test No. 9) be made last. **1976** *West Lancs. Evening Gaz.* 8 Dec. 11/9 The revolutionary roof coating system designed to protect, insulate and weatherproof your home.

weather side.

1. *Naut.* The windward side (of a vessel, etc.).

1399 LANGL. *Rich. Redeles* IV. 77 þan lay þe lordis a-lee with laste and with charge,..And warned him wisely of þe wedir-side. *a* **1548** HALL *Chron.*, *Hen. VIII* 21 b, The Caricke was on the wetherside and the Regent on the lye side. **1769** FALCONER *Dict. Marine* (1780) s.v. *Weather*, When a ship under sail presents either of her sides to the wind, it is then called the weather-side. **1840** R. H. DANA *Bef. Mast* ii, I stood in the waist on the weather side. **1883** *Man. Seamanship for Boys* 3 Salutes on Board Ship. The starboard side in harbour, and the weather side at sea, is the officers' side.

2. The side (e.g. of a building, a tree) that is most exposed to injury from weather.

1827 STEUART *Planter's G.* (1828) 136 Most Trees are unequally balanced, and show what is called a 'weather-side', usually to the west and south-west, in this island. **1827** *Ann. Reg.*, *Chron.* 48/1 Many shepherds..had hair-breadth escapes, and some perished in wearing their flocks from the weather-side of the hills. **1838** *Civil Engin. & Arch. Jrnl.* I. 338/2 On the occasion of repairing the weather side of the tower of the Lady Church, at Munich. **1860** MAURY *Phys.*

Geog. Sea 96 The weather side of all such mountains as the Andes is the wet side, and the lee side the dry.
fig. **1816** 'QUIZ' *Grand Master* I. 11, I now am present, Sir, you see, So leave the weather side to me.

'weather-stain. A stain or discoloration caused by the weather. Also *fig.*
1815 SCOTT *Guy M.* iii, The grey old towers..bearing the rusty weather-stains of ages. **1817** T. L. PEACOCK *Melincourt* vii, Though I have endeavoured to leave them as much mould, mildew and weather-stain as possible. **1847** EMERSON *Poems*, '*Butler, fetch the ruby wine*' 43 Give me wine to wash me clean Of the weather-stains of cares. **1858** HAWTHORNE *Fr. & It. Note-bks.* (1871) II. 54 A marble statue, grey with ancient weather-stains.
Also **'weather-stained** *ppl. a.*, **'weather-staining** *vbl. sb.*
1849 THOREAU *Week Concord Riv.* 57 Town records, old, tattered, time-worn, weather-stained chronicles. **1851** H. MELVILLE *Whale* xvi, She was a ship of the old school,..Long-seasoned and weather-stained in the typhoons and calms of all four oceans. **1868** BOYD *Less. Middle Age* 16 The lowly dwelling..with its weather-stained walls. **1884** *Daily News* 4 Sept. 3/1 The only detriment time has wrought in the monument is the weather-staining of the marble statues.

weather-wisdom. The traditional lore of weather prognostics.
1822 *Lights & Shades* II. 53 That science of guesses commonly called weather-wisdom. **1837** WHEWELL *Hist. Induct. Sci.* I. 29 Another reason, founded apparently upon some limited empirical maxim of weather-wisdom taken from the climate of Greece. **1866** STEINMETZ *Weathercasts* 7 'Weather-wisdom' is very far from being a mere superstition.

weather-wise ('wɛðəwaɪz), *a.* (*sb.*) [f. WEATHER *sb.* + WISE *a.*] **a.** Skilled in prognostics of the weather. Also *absol.* as *sb.*
1377 LANGL. *P. Pl.* B. xv. 350 Wederwise shipmen. **1556** S. BURROUGH in Hakluyt *Voy.* (1589) 319, I maruelled why he departed so suddenly, and went ouer the shoales... But after I perceiued them to be weather wise. **1637** J. TAYLOR (Water P.) *Drinke & Welcome* C 3 b, Some by their cornes are wondrous Weather-wise. **1735** B. FRANKLIN *Poor Richard* (1890) 50 Some are weatherwise, some are otherwise. **1802** COLERIDGE *Dejection* 1 If the Bard was weather-wise, who made The grand old ballad of Sir Patrick Spence. **1849** JAMES *Woodman* vi, Auguring rain to the minds of the weather-wise. **1866** STEINMETZ *Weathercasts* 35 A certain weather-wise nobleman, Lord Portarlington, predicted the intensely hot summer of last year. **1895** MEREDITH *Amazing Marr.* I. xv. 167 Are you weather-wise?—able to tell when the clouds will hold off or pelt? **1922** JOYCE *Ulysses* 390 Biggish swollen clouds to be seen as the night increased and the weatherwise poring up at them.
b. *fig.*
1581 W. STAFFORD *Exam. Compl.* i. (1876) 27 Some weather-wise fellowes, that coulde chaunge their opinions as the more and stronger part did chaunge theirs. **1917** GWYNN & TUCKWELL *Sir C. Dilke* li. II. 313 He was weatherwise in the assembly, and knew the conditions which might lead to unforeseen disturbance.

'weatherwise, *adv.* orig. *U.S.* [f. WEATHER *sb.* + WISE *sb.*[1] II.] As regards the weather.
1963 [see *personnel-wise* advb. s.v. PERSONNEL 3]. **1971** *Country Life* 21 Oct. 1084/1 October is usually a very good month weatherwise. **1975** *Budget* (Sugarcreek, Ohio) 20 Mar. 15/6 Weatherwise the last week has been real nice.

†weather-wiser. *Obs.* [ad. Du. *wederwijzer*, *weerwijzer*, f. *weder*, *weer* WEATHER *sb.* + *wijzer*, agent-n. f. *wijzen* to show; cf. WAY-WISER.] An instrument serving to foretell the weather.
1667 SPRAT *Hist. Royal-Soc.* 255 Several Discourses about Thermometers, Hygroscopes, Baroscopes, and other Weather-wisers. **1676** GLANVILL *Ess.* III. 40 He hath there given an account of the defectiveness of common Weather-Glasses,..and Ascent of Water by Cold in the ordinary Weather-wisers. **1708** R. NEVE *Baroscop.* 4 By which means it is now become an excellent Weather-wiser, to predict dry and moist Weather. **1787** BEST *Angling* (ed. 2) 152 The flowers of pimpernel; the opening and shutting of which..are the countryman's weather-wiser, whereby he tells the weather of the following day.

weathery ('wɛðərɪ), *a. rare.* [f. WEATHER *sb.* + -Y[1].] Fitful, changing like the weather.
1563 *Mirr. Mag., Ld. Hastings* xiv, As nought may last, so Fortunes weathery cheare With powtyng lookes gan lower on my Syre. **1880** BLACKMORE *Mary Anerley* II. vi. 82 The flitting fancy of boy and girl, who pop upon one another, and skip through zig-zag vernal ecstasy, like the weathery dalliance of gnats.

Weatings ('wiːtɪŋz), *sb. pl.* Also **w(h)eatings.** [f. respelling of WHEAT *sb.* + *-ings*, as in *middlings* s.v. MIDDLING *sb.* 3 c.] A proprietary name for the residue of the milling of wheat (the sharps: see SHARP *sb.* 9), used as food for farm animals.
1931 *Trade Marks Jrnl.* 30 Sept. 1329/1 Weatings... Fine wheat offals (for food). The M.M.A., Limited,..London E.C. 3. **1937** C. FORMAN *Pig Breeding & Feeding* vii. 79 These wheatings are advertised as not more than 5 per cent fibre. **1937** E. M. RICKARD-BELL *Handbk. Mod. Pig Farming* vii. 81 For the weatings we can substitute up to 10 per cent. with coconut cake. **1960** *Farmer & Stockbreeder* 8 Mar. 5/1 Weatings and bran both quoted at £25 per ton ex mill. **1976** G. JOHNSON *Profitable Pig Farming* (ed. 5) viii. 124 Sharps, weatings or middlings have not been included in any of the above selection of suitable rations.

weavable ('wiːvəb(ə)l), *a. rare.* [f. WEAVE *v.*[1] + -ABLE.] That may be woven.
1483 *Cath. Angl.* 412/1 Weffabylle, *texibilis.* **1856** RUSKIN *Mod. Paint.* III. IV. xvii. §37 The world..got weavable fibres out of the mosses, and made clothes for itself.

weave (wiːv), *sb.* [f. WEAVE *v.*[1]]
†1. Something that has been woven, a woven fabric. *Obs.*
1581 A. HALL *Iliad* IX. 171 A couerlet fine aloft, Of woollen weaue. **1597** MIDDLETON *Wisd. Solomon* iv. 11 So righteous are allurde by sins deceit, And oft inticed into sinners weave. **1646** SIR T. BROWNE *Pseud. Ep.* v. xv. 257 This habit of Iohn, was..rather some finer weave of Camelot.
2. A particular method or pattern of weaving.
1888 C. P. BROOKS *Cotton Manuf.* 132 This weave is not confined to the making of fabrics with an unbroken pile surface. **1888** R. BEAUMONT *Woollen Manuf.* x. 279 It may..be useful to consider how, from a plain weave warped and woven one thread black and one thread white, the solid lines of these colours..have been formed. **1901** *Scotsman* 1 Apr. 11/1 With reference to linens there has been a larger demand for weaves of this kind.

weave (wiːv), *v.*[1] Pa. t. **wove** (wəʊv); pa. pple. **woven** ('wəʊv(ə)n). Forms: *Inf. and pres. stem* 1 **wefan** (2 *sing.* **wyfst,** 3 *sing.* **wefð, wifeð, wyfð**), **weofan,** 3–6 **weve,** 4–5 **wewe, wef(e,** 5–6 **weyve,** *Sc.* **weif(f, weff,** 6 **weeve, wayve, wyeve,** *Sc.* **weive, weiwe, wif(f, wyf, wywe,** 6–9 *Sc.* **wyve,** 6– **weave.** *Pa. t. sing.* 1 **wæf, wef,** 4 **wof, woof,** 4–5 **waf, wafe, wave,** 6– **wove;** *weak forms* 4 **wevede,** 7 **weavde,** 6–9 **weaved.** *Pa. t. pl.* 1 **wǽfon,** 4 **weven, woven.** *Pa. pple.* 1 **wefen, ȝewefen, ȝiwefen,** *North.* **ȝeuoefen,** 3 **iweove, iweven,** 4 **iweve, wovun, ywoven, (i)wovyn,** 5–6 *Sc.* **weif,** 6 *Sc.* **weffin, wiffin, woifen, wowein, wolvin,** 7–9 **wove,** 4– **woven;** *weak forms* 4–6 **weved,** 4 **weft, woved,** 5 **weuyd,** 7 **weevd, weavd,** 6–9 **weaved.** [A Common Teut. strong verb (not recorded in Gothic): OE. *wefan*, pa. t. *wæf*, pl. *wǽfon*, pa. pple. *wefen*, corresponds to OFris. **weva* (NFris. *weewen*, WFris. *weve*, *weevje*), (M)LG., (M)Du. *weven*, OHG. *weban*, *wepan* (MHG., mod.G. *weben*), ON. *vefa* (MSw. *väva*, Sw. *väfva*, Da. *væve*):—OTeut. **weƀ-* (:**waƀ-*: **wǣƀ-*):—Indogermanic **webh-* (:**wēbh-* :**ubh-*), represented in Skr. *ūrṇavā́bhi* spider (lit. 'wool-weaver'), Gr. *ὑφή*, *ὕφος*, web, *ὑφαίνειν* to weave. The same root occurs in *web* (and *abb*), *weft*, *woof*.
In the 14th and 15th c. the form of the pa. pple. became assimilated to that of the pa. pples. of strong verbs with root ending in a liquid (e.g. *steal*, *stolen*), and, as in most verbs of that class, the *o* of the pa. pple. was extended to the pa. t. both sing. and pl. The weak inflexion has been occasionally used in all periods from the 14th c. onwards, but has never become general.]
1. *trans.* To form or fabricate (a stuff or material) by interlacing yarns or other filaments of a particular substance in a continuous web; to manufacture in a loom by crossing the threads or yarns called respectively the warp and the weft. Also with obj. the web itself, a garment made up of such a stuff or material. † *to weave out*: to complete the weaving of.
† *to weave in a stool*: see STOOL *sb.* 3.
c **900** *Bæda's Hist.* IV. xxv. (1890) 354 Hio smælo hræȝel weofaþ & wyrcaþ. *c* **1050** *Voc.* in Wr.-Wülcker 504/2 *Ordiretur*, wefen wæs. *c* **1200** *Virtues & Vices* 39 Al swa nan webb ne mai bien iweuen wið-uten twa beames. *c* **1290** *St. Edmund Conf.* 167 in *S. Eng. Leg.* 436 Heo [a hair shirt] nas i-sponne ne i-weoue, ake i-broide strengus longue. *c* **1300** *Assump. Virg.* 668 This ilke webbe here self woof. **1390** GOWER *Conf.* III. 237 Thei tawhten him a Las to breide, And weve a Pours. *c* **1450** *Mirk's Festial* 246 Scho occupiet hir craft of weuyng cloþes and ornamentes to þe auter. **1483** *Cath. Angl.* 412/1 To Wefe, *texere.* **1513** DOUGLAS *Æneis* XIII. viii. 86 The precyus wedis, Wrocht craftely, and weif of goldin thredis Quhilum be fair Andromachais hand. **1528** MORE *Dyaloge* III. x. O vb/2 Yt were as sone done to weue a new web of clothe as to sowe vppe euery hole in a net. **1530** PALSGR. 779/1 The weyver sayeth he can nat wayve my clothe tyll he have more yarne. **1535** COVERDALE *Job* vii. 6 My dayes passe ouer more spedely, then a weeuer can weeue out his webbe. **1538** ELYOT *Dict.*, *Textrina*.., the place where thinges be weaued or wounden. **1539** BIBLE (Great) *2 Kings* xxiii. 7 Where the wemen woue hanginges for the groue. *a* **1548** HALL *Chron.*, *Hen. VIII*, 73 b, For all the copes and Vestementes wer but of one pece, so wouen for the purpose. **1584** *Shuttleworths' Acc.* (Chetham Soc.) 13 For weavinge forescore yerdes and four of canuise, vs. **1632** LITHGOW *Trav.* VI. 250 He weau'd these Napkins. **1670** SIR S. CROW in *12th Rep. Hist. MSS. Comm.* App. v. 15 The silke..beeing ill woven will shrink and pucker. **1697** DRYDEN *Æneis* VII. 340 These Purple Vests were weav'd by Dardan Dames. *Ibid.* IX. 651 The Mantle..which I wove with Care. **1725** POPE *Odyss.* XV. 139 Accept, dear youth, this monument of love, Long since, in better days, by Helen wove. **1789–96** MORSE *Amer. Geog.* I. 541 Woollen stockings..of excellent quality are wove by the Germans, especially in Germantown. **1856** G. ROBERTS *Soc. Hist.* 376 Our lace was not wove. It had neither warp nor woof. **1872** YEATS *Techn. Hist. Comm.* 69 The shawls and the textile furniture used in the rites of religion were frequently woven in the temples.
b. in figurative context.
In many langs. the equivalent vb. is used in metaphorical expressions relating to the contriving of plots or deception: so Gr. *ὑφαίνειν*, L. *texere*, *ordiri*, Fr. *ourdir*. Cf. 1 f.
1382 WYCLIF *Isa.* xxx. 1 Wo!.. seith the Lord, that ȝee schulden do counseil, and not of me; and wefen a web [Vulg. *ordiremini telam*], and not bi my spirit. **1606** *Sir G. Goosecappe* v. i. in Bullen *Old Pl.* (1884) III. 85 All the wiles Weeud in the loomes of greatnes, and of state. *c* **1620** MORYSON *Itin.* Suppl. (1903) 191 If..each Deputy should giue in writing to the State in England a full relation of his gouernment and the State of that kingdome [Ireland], so as his successour might weaue the same webb he had begunn, and not make a newe frame of his owne. *a* **1662** HEYLIN *Cypr. Angl.* 64 For much they feared that Abbot would unravel all the Web which Bancroft with such pains had weaved. **1796** ELIZA HAMILTON *Lett. Hindoo Rajah* (1811) II. 220 The robes of the seasons, wove in the changeful looms of nature. **1808** SCOTT *Marm.* VI. xvii, O what a tangled web we weave, When first we practise to deceive! **1842** LYTTON *Zanoni* I. i, All this helped silently to weave charmed webs over Viola's imagination. **1893** F. THOMPSON *Poems* 59 Better thou wov'st thy woof of life than thou didst weave thy woof of song.
c. said of the loom.
1804 W. L. BOWLES *Spir. Discov.* II. 275 Thy mariners.. furled th' embroidered sails, That looms of Egypt wove.
d. To depict in tapestry.
c **1385** CHAUCER *L.G.W.* 2360 She hadde I-wouyn In a stamyn large How she was brought from Athenys in a Barge. *Ibid.* 2364 And al the thyng that Tereus hath wrought She waf it wel & wrot the storye a-boue. **1513** DOUGLAS *Æneis* v. v. 15 Quhairon wes weif in subtell goldin threidis King Troyus son [etc.]. *a* **1683** OLDHAM *Rem.* (1684) 114, I have seen a handsomer Mortal carv'd in Monumental Ginger-bread, and woven in Hangings at Mortlock.
fig. **1802** SCOTT *T. Rhymer* III. xvi, Their loves, their woes, the gifted bard In fairy tissue wove.
e. *fig.* To contrive, fabricate, or construct (a mental product) with elaborate care. Also with *out*, *up*.
c **1420** *Wyclif Bible* I. 71/1 Of whom the first [Isaiah] is not seyn to me to weuen prophecie, but euangelie. *a* **1586** SIDNEY *Arcadia* III. (1598) 351 Your wise, but very darke speeches..are wouen vp in so intricate a maner, as I know not how to proportion mine answere vnto them. *a* **1600** HOOKER *Eccl. Pol.* VI. vi. 6 For answer whereunto Acesius weaveth out a long History of things that hapned in the persecution under Decius. **1656** EARL MONM. tr. *Boccalini's Advts. fr. Parnass.* I. xxxv. (1674) 44 The Author's subtilty in weaving of his Poem. **1799** CAMPBELL *Pleas. Hope* I. 165 Then weave in rapid verse the deeds they tell. **1819** W. S. ROSE *Lett. N. Italy* I. 24, I had already woven a little romance for him in my imagination. **1824** LAMB *Elia*, *Blakesmoor*, Contemplations on the great and good..weave for us illusions. **1849** MISS MULOCK *Ogilvies* ii, Katherine had already woven the whole romance of the stranger's life. **1861** GEO. ELIOT *Silas M.* I. i, *You* stole the money, and you have woven a plot to lay the sin at my door. **1862** SPENCER *First Princ.* I. iii. §21 (1875) 66 The original materials out of which all thought is woven. **1874** M. CREIGHTON *Hist. Ess.* i. (1902) 42 The..desire for reality that made him [Dante] weave his poem around himself. **1876** THOMPSON *Chron. A. de Usk* 186 The evil arts of brewing charms and weaving spells. **1885–94** BRIDGES *Eros & Psyche* May 15 Pathetic strains and passionate they wove, Urgent in ecstasies of heavenly sense. **1913** W. K. FLEMING *Mysticism Chr.* 108 In his writings, his weakness lay in his proneness..to weave endless allegories out of the Old Testament writings.
f. To form (e.g. a basket, a wreath) by interlacing rods or twigs, flowers, etc.
1398 TREVISA *Barth. De P.R.* XVII. clii. (1495) 704 Stakes be pyghte in the grounde and there abowte ben wrethes wouen and wounden of thornes. **1599** T. CUTWODE *Caltha Poet.* (Roxb.) cxxiv, And others very busie do begin: To weaue their litle baskets..to put their hearbs and all their flowers in. **1667** MILTON *P.L.* IX. 839 Adam the while..had wove Of choicest Flours a Garland to adorne Her Tresses. **1757** DYER *Fleece* I. 375 Hurdles to weave, and chearly shelters raise, Thy vacant hours require. **1813** SCOTT *Rokeby* v. xiii, But, Lady, weave no wreath for me, Or weave it of the cypress-tree! **1839** FR. A. KEMBLE *Resid. Georgia* (1863) 21 Among the Brobdignagian sedges..the nightshade..weaves a perfect matting of its poisonous garlands. **1839** EMERSON *Poems, The Problem* 25 Know'st thou what wove yon woodbird's nest Of leaves, and feathers from her breast? **1842** MACAULAY *Horatius* lxix, When the girls are weaving baskets, And the lads are shaping bows. **1902** S. E. WHITE *Blazed Trail* viii, With the skill of ghastly practice some of them wove a litter on which the body was placed.
fig. **1893** LIDDON *Life Pusey* I. App. A. 451 Legend has woven a wreath round the early history of the family.
g. *Sc.* To knit. Also *dial.* to plait (hair).
1695 *Rec. Old. Aberd.* (New Spalding Club) I. 160 Privat schooles..wherein children ar taught to sew or wyve. **1785** BURNS *Epist. to J. Lapraik* 1 Apr. ii, On Fasteneen we had a rockin, To ca' the crack and weave our stockin. **1825** JAMIESON, To *Weave* v. a. and n. To knit, applied to stockings, &c.; pron. Wyve. Aberd. **1884** J. C. EGERTON *Sussex Folk* 132 He..used to go regularly twice a week to the house of one of his principal customers, 'to weave his cue', or, in less professional language, to plait his pigtail.
¶h. In figurative use app. sometimes confusedly: To spin, twine (a cord, thread).
1426 LYDG. *De Guil. Pilgr.* 24413 The cordeler that waf the corde Of pes, vnyte, and concorde,..Hyr name was called 'Charyte'. **1648** GAGE *West. Ind.* 19 The Indians uproar had weaved for us a thred of long discourse. **1856** KANE *Arctic Expl.* II. xxv. 249 The men weave their long yarns with peals of rattling hearty laughter between.
2. *absol.* or *intr.* To practise weaving; to work with a loom.
c **1000** ÆLFRIC *Gram.* xv. (Z.) 104 *Tui ancilla texit* Ðin wyln wefð. **1390** GOWER *Conf.* II. 170 Hire moder..Bad that sche scholde..lerne forto weve and spinne. *c* **1450** CAPGRAVE *St. Gilbert* l. 129 A conuerse of þat same ordre.. sat stille in his craft weuyng. **1585** E. D. *Prayse of Nothing* A ij b, For equity would not..that Arachne weaue in the frames of Minerua. **1608** SHAKS. *Per.* IV. vi. 194, I can sing, weaue, sow, and dance, with other vertues. **1781** COWPER *Truth* 317 Yon cottager who weaves at her own door, Pillow and bobbins all her little store. **1818** *Min. Evid. Committee Ribbon Weavers* 112 My father is a silk weaver; it is about twenty years since I first began to weave. **1828** CARLYLE *Heyne* Ess. 1840 II. 41 The poor cottage, where his father had weaved. **1917** T. R. GLOVER *From Pericles to Philip* i.

17 [In Egypt] Women go to market and men stay at home and weave, and they weave down where others weave up. *fig.* **1622** FLETCHER *Sp. Curate* II. i, They that pretend to wonders must weave cunningly.

3. *trans.* Of a spider, insect: To spin (a web, a cocoon). Also *absol.*

c **1220** *Bestiary* 468 Ðe spinnere..werpeð ðus hire web and weueð on hire wise. **1382** WYCLIF *Isa.* lix. 5 The webbis of an attercop thei wouen [*v.r.* weueden]. **1398** TREVISA *Barth. De P.R.* XVIII. xi. (Bodl. MS.) Þe female leieþ egges and þereof comeþ smal spiþeres and þe modre setteþ hem to weue as sone as þei beþ yheiȝt. **1426** LYDG. *De Guil. Pilgr.* 19269 As an yreyne wewyth a calle, To make fflyes there-in to ffalle. *a* **1548** HALL *Chron., Hen. VII* 30 She..beganne to devyse & spynne a new webbe, lyke a spyder that dayly weveth when hys calle is torne. **1604** DRAYTON *Owle* E 2 b, The spyders woue their webbs euen in his wings. **1617** MORYSON *Itin.* III. 111 Silke-wormes..infold themselues in a piece of silk they weaue of an ouall forme and yellow color. **1784** COWPER *Tiroc.* 595 While ev'ry worm industriously weaves And winds his web about the rivell'd leaves.

fig. **1593** SHAKS. *2 Hen. VI*, III. i. 340 My Brayne, more busie then the laboring Spider, Weaues tedious Snares to trap mine Enemies. **1663** BUTLER *Hud.* I. i. 159 He..Could twist as tough a Rope of Sand, And weave fine Cobwebs, fit for Skull That's empty when the Moon is full. **1850** TENNYSON *In Mem.* l, Men the flies of latter spring, That lay their eggs, and sting and sing And weave their petty cells and die.

4. To form a texture with (threads, filaments, strips of some material); to interlace or intertwine so as to form a fabric.

1538 ELYOT *Dict.*, *Licia*, be thredes, whiche sylke women do weaue in lyncelles or stooles. **1601** SHAKS. *Twel. N.* II. iv. 46 The Spinsters and the Knitters in the Sun, And the free maides that weaue their thred with bones. **1608** —— *Per.* IV. Gower 21 When they weaude the sleded silke, With fingers long, small, white as milke. **1638** H. PEACHAM *Valley of Varietie* 131 There remains fine hairie threds, like unto Flax, which are woven into cloth. **1697** DRYDEN *Virg. Past.* x. 103 This while I sung, my Sorrows I deceiv'd, And bending Osiers into Baskets weav'd. **1789** *Massachusetts Spy* 27 Aug. 3/2 A young lady of Milton lately spun 70 skeins of thread out of a pound of Cotton—which another young lady wove. **1808** FORSYTH *Beauties Scot.* V. 272 To send cotton yarn from the mills..into the remote glens of the Highlands, for the purpose of being weaved. **1877–80** *Gt. Industr. Gt. Brit.* III. 212 Milligan..wove-in the silk white, and dyed the flowers their natural colour in the piece. *a* **1908** C. BIGG *Orig. Chr.* (1909) 459 The art of weaving flax had been introduced from Babylon.

b. To entwine or wreathe together.

1578 [see INTERTEX *v.*]. **1617** MORYSON *Itin.* III. 167 Citizens daughters..weare nothing vpon their heads but their haire wouen with laces, and so gathered on the forepart of the head. **1697** DRYDEN *Virg. Past.* ix. 57 The Grottoes cool, with shady Poplars crown'd, And creeping Vines on Arbours weav'd around. **1727** [DORRINGTON] *Philip Quarll* (1816) 42 He bent the branches..and weaved them across one another. **1850** TENNYSON *In Mem.* lxxviii, Again at Christmas did we weave The holly round the Christmas hearth.

c. *fig.* To intermingle or unite closely or intimately as if by weaving; to work up *into* an elaborate and connected whole. Also with *in.*

1545 GARDINER in Abp. Parker *Corr.* (Parker Soc.) 27 In the tragedy untruth is so maliciously weaved with truth [etc.]. **1605** SHAKS. *Lear* II. i. 17 This weaves it selfe perforce into my businesse. **1637** RUTHERFORD *Let. to Lady Kilconquhair* 8 Aug., Is not this hell and heaven woven thorow other? **1638** SIR T. HERBERT (*title*), Some Yeares Travels..Describing especially the two famous Empires, the Persian, and great Mogull: weaved with the History of these later Times. **1690** LOCKE *Hum. Und.* I. ii. §25 Can they receive and assent to adventitious Notions, and be ignorant of those, which are supposed woven into the very Principles of their Being..? **1711** ADDISON *Spect.* No. 40 ¶2 An Author might as well think of weaving the Adventures of Æneas and Hudibras into one Poem. *a* **1719** —— *Evid. Chr. Relig.* v. (1733) 42 When religion was woven into the civil government, and flourished under the protection of the Emperors. **1816** BYRON *Ch. Har.* III. cxii, And for these words, thus woven into song, It may be that they are a harmless wile. **1862** J. MARTINEAU *Ess.* (1866) I. 203 Science weaves phenomena into unity. **1875** OUSELEY *Mus. Form* ix. 49 Put the melody in the bass, or in an inner part, and weave in a new melody with it in the upper part. *c* **1904** BRIDGES *Voltaire* Poems (1912) 381 Grave Dante weaving well His dark-eyed thought into a song divine.

d. *intr.* for *refl.* To become woven or interwoven. Also *fig. rare.*

1613–16 W. BROWNE *Brit. Past.* I. ii. 30 The amorous Vine which in the Elme still weaues. **1849** LYTTON *K. Arthur* II. lxxi, Tears weave with smiles to form the bridge to heaven!

e. *intr.* With quasi-passive sense: To admit of being woven.

1842 R. OASTLER *Fleet Papers* II. 26 It will not spin into good yarn, nor weave into wearable cloths.

†**f.** intr. *to weave out*: to become unwoven. *nonce-use* (suggested by the context). *Obs.*

1641 MILTON *Reform.* II. 78 The government of Episcopacy, is now so weav'd into the common Law In Gods name let it weave out againe.

5. *trans.* To enmesh or entangle, to wrap up, as in a net, etc. In quots. *fig.*

1620 [? G. BRYDGES] *Horæ Subs.* 394 And thus being wouen in their [Roman] nets, they be in a manner destitute of all possibility of recouery. **1869** LOWELL *Study Wind.*, *Condescension in Foreigners* (1871) 43 The mind can weave itself warmly in the cocoon of its own thoughts.

6. To cause to move in a devious course; to direct (one's steps) in a devious or intricate course, as in dancing.

1650 HEATH *Clarastella* 11 Her steps with such an evenness she wove, As shee could hardly be perceiv'd to move. **1839** DE QUINCEY *Mem. Grasmere* Wks. 1890 XIII. 132 Sarah was going about the crowd, and weaving her person in and out. **1893** KATE D. WIGGIN *Cathedral Courtship* 136 To weave that donkey and that Bath 'cheer' through the narrow streets..is a task for a Jehu.

b. To go through the intricate movements of (a dance).

1792 ROGERS *Pleas. Mem.* II. 36 Weave the light dance and swell the choral song. **1862** NEALE *Hymns East. Ch.* 46 They ..to that eternal Pascha Wove the dance and raised the strain.

Hence **weaved** *ppl. a.* = WOVEN *ppl. a.* Also ***weaved-up.***

1552 HULOET, Weued, *textus.* **1561** B. GOOGE tr. *Palingenius' Zodiac* VI. R vj, Lyke as the flye that smallest is in weued Cobweb hye. **1593** SHAKS. *Rich. II*, IV. i. 229 (Qo. 1608) And must I rauell out My weaud vp Folly?

weave, *v.*[2] Also 6 wheave, 7 weive. [Continuation of ME. WEVE.]

1. a. *intr.* To move repeatedly from side to side; †to toss *to and fro*; to sway the body alternately to one side and the other; to pursue a devious course, thread one's way amid obstructions.

1596 SPENSER *F.Q.* v. iv. 10 Whilest thus amidst the billowes beating of her Twixt life and death, long to and fro she weaued [*rhymes* bereaued, deceaued]. **1615** G. SANDYS *Trav.* 146 Their fantasticall gestures exceed all barbarisme, continually weauing with their bodies, and often iumping vp-right (as is the manner in dauncing). **1682** T. FLATMAN *Heraclitus Ridens* No. 72/4 By and by I saw him weaving from one side of the Pulpit to t'other. **1805** WORDSW. *Prelude* VII. 700 Him who grinds The hurdy-gurdy, at the fiddle weaves, Rattles the salt-box [etc.]. **1854** MISS A. E. BAKER *Northampt. Gloss.*, *Weaving*, moving backward and forward in a chair when uneasy or in trouble. 'You're weaving your web of sorrow,' is often said to any one so doing. A metaphor from the loom. **1884** 'MARK TWAIN' *Huck. Finn* xx, The preacher..begun in earnest too; and went weaving first to one side of the platform and then the other. **1897** BARRÈRE & LELAND *Dict. Slang*, *Weave* (American), to work along from one side to the other... A drunken man 'weaves along'. **1898** CROCKETT *Standard Bearer* ii. 14 Twenty or thirty dragoons were urging their horses forward in pursuit, weaving this way and that among the soft lairy places.

b. *spec.* of a horse or a wild animal in captivity: To move the head, neck, and body restlessly from side to side of the stall.

1831 YOUATT *Horse* xix. 345. **1869** FITZWYGRAM *Horses & Stables* §194. 121 As a general rule, horses do not weave, unless they are tied up. **1934** [implied in WEAVING *vbl. sb.*[2] 2]. **1973** G. DURRELL *Beasts in my Belfry* vii. 140, I could only presume that he [*sc.* a buffalo doing a sort of waltz] put on this performance for the same reason that a lion paces up and down its cage or a polar bear or an elephant will weave from side to side—a soothing and interesting habit to pass the time till the next meal.

c. *R.A.F.* Of an aircraft or its pilot: to fly a devious course, usu. in attempting to avoid enemy planes or anti-aircraft fire. Also *transf.* (in this use *slang*).

1941 *Battle of Britain August–October 1940* (Min. of Information) 13 Enemy bomber formations were..protected by a box of fighters, some of which flew slightly above to a flank or in rear,..and..others weaving in and out between the sub-formations of the bombers. **1942** *R.A.F. Jrnl.* 3 Oct. 22, I took my Edgar Wallace from the billet and weaved out to the Nissen hut. **1943** P. BRENNAN et al. *Spitfires over Malta* 26 The remaining four 110's at once broke, and began weaving, each steering a different course home. **1952** [see PREDICT *v.* 4]. **1973** N. MONSARRAT *Kappillan of Malta* 38 The sky above him seemed full of planes, weaving and circling like the flies in the wine-shop.

d. *to get weaving*, to apply oneself briskly to something; to 'get a move on'. Cf. *to get cracking* s.v. CRACK *v.* 22 b. *colloq.* (orig. *R.A.F.*).

1942 *R.A.F. Jrnl.* 30 May 19 We'll knock that..place off the map. Get weaving. **1942** T. RATTIGAN *Flare Path* III. 83 We'd better get weaving, or we'll find this chemist feller has gone to lunch. **1948** A. BARON *From City, from Plough* v. 36 There won' 'alf be a queue at the NAAFI... Let's get weaving. **1959** M. PUGH *Chancer* 49 When he gets weaving, the dashboard ashtray does three thousand revs. **1964** R. BRADDON *Year of Angry Rabbit* i. 8 And this call's costing me a ruddy fortune so how's about you hang up and get weaving, eh? **1971** B. W. ALDISS *Soldier Erect* 185 Pack your night things in a small pack and get weaving, while I lay on transport.

2. *trans.* To move (the hand or something held by it) *to and fro, up and down.*

1607 TOPSELL *Four-f. Beasts* 404 Make the ointment to sinke wel into the flesh, by holding a hot broad barre ouer the place annointed, weauing your hand too and fro, vntil the ointment be entred into the skin. *Ibid.* 417 Hauing annointed all the raw places with this ointment, make it to sinke into the flesh, by holding and weauing vp and downe ouer it, a hot broad barre of yron.

3. To make a signal to (a ship or its occupants) by waving a flag or something used as a substitute. Also *intr.* with *for.*

1593 P. NICHOLS *Sir F. Drake Revived* (1628) 27 He wheaued vs with his hat, and his long hanging sleeues to come a shoare. **1599** DALLAM in *Early Voy. Levant* (Hakl. Soc.) 41 The nexte daye..he came to the sea sid, and weaved for a boate. **1600** HAKLUYT *Voy.* III. 566 Then shaking a pike of fire in defiance of the enemie, and weauing them amaine, we bad them come aboord: and an Englishman in the gallie made answer, that they would come aboord presently. **1622** in Foster *Eng. Factories Ind.* (1908) II. 33 Which when they perceaved, they weived us with naked swords. **1628** DIGBY *Voy. Mediterr.* (Camden) 59 Although I shott towardes them and weaued them to follow me.

4. *Pugilism.* (*trans.* and *intr.*) To creep close into (one's opponent) before delivering one's blow; to step in feinting and try to approach close to one's opponent in order to administer punishment. Also (? *Obs.*), to get (the adversary's head) 'in chancery'.

1818 *Sporting Mag.* (N.S.) II. 23 Spring held his opponent's hand..to prevent being weaved. *Ibid.*, Painter ..endeavoured to weave his antagonist. *Ibid.* III. 133 Neither were expert hands at weaving, and Martin was thrown. **1820** *P. Egan's Boxiana* (1829) III. 397 The strength and skill of Belasco enabled him to hold up his opponent, and weave on, till he got Sampson down on both his knees. **1832** *P. Egan's Bk. Sports* 26/2 In closing, Curtis captured his opponent's 'knowledge-box', and was endeavouring to weave it under his arms, but [etc.]. **1921** *Times* 29 June 10/6 Defensively he [*sc.* Dempsey] is a much better boxer than one might easily suppose... His body sways as he weaves in and out, making him a very elusive target and very difficult to land on with a hard punch.

weavel(l, obs. ff. WEEVIL.

weaver[1] ('wiːvə(r)). Forms: 4 **wefere,** 4–5 **wevere,** 5 **wevyr, wewar(e, weiver, weyver,** 5–6 **weffer(e,** 5–7 **wever,** 6 **wevar, wayver,** 6–7 *Sc.* **wiver,** 6, 9 *Sc.* **weyver,** 7 *Sc.* **weifer,** 8 **weever,** 9 *Sc.* **wyver,** 6– **weaver.** [f. WEAVE *v.*[1] + -ER[1].]

1. a. One who weaves textile fabrics; a workman or workwoman whose occupation is weaving.

1362 LANGL. *P. Pl.* A. Prol. 99 Wollene websteris and weueris of lynen. **1382** WYCLIF *Job* vii. 6 My daȝes swiftliere passiden than of the weuere the web is kut of. *c* **1450** CAPGRAVE *St. Gilbert* I. 31 Þe apostell, which was a weuer of cloth. **1531** ELYOT *Gov.* I. i, A wayuer or fuller shulde be an unmete capitaine of an armie. **1596** SHAKS. *1 Hen. IV*, II. iv. 146, I would I were a Weauer, I could sing all manner of songs. **1638** *Burgh Rec. Glasgow* (1876) 388 The wiveris friemen within this burgh feirit that [etc.]. **1675** in *10th Rep. Hist. MSS. Comm.* App. I. 80 Last week there was ane uproar in London occationed by the weavers. **1765** H. WALPOLE *Let. to Mann* 25 May, Many thousand Weavers rose, on a bill for their relief being thrown out of the House of Lords. **1768** *True Copy Poll City Oxf.* 16 Mitchel, James, Wytham, Weaver. *c* **1778** *Life Capt. Socivizca* 28 Every Wallachian Man is his own Cartwright, and every Woman a Weaver for her own Family. **1851–5** *Tomlinson's Cycl. Usef. Arts* (1867) II. 857/2 The weaver..pressing with one foot on one of the treadles,..lowers one of the healds, [etc.]. **1871** C. GIBBON *Lack of Gold* v, The weavers obtained employment principally from the manufacturers of Kingshaven. **1892** *Labour Commission* Gloss., *Weavers*, women employed in the manufacture of cloth.

b. One who plaits. Also *Sc.*, one who knits.

1783 *European Mag.* Sept. 176 Betty got the hair wove into a tail at the..wig-makers..assuring the nimble-fingered weaver, it was for herself. **1825** JAMIESON, *Weaver, wyver*,..a knitter of stockings, Aberd.

2. *fig.* One who weaves, in metaphorical senses of the vb.; one who contrives, constructs, etc. (something specified).

In the first quot. the word may be misread for *wenere* WEENER.

c **1430** *Hymns Virg.* (1867) 77 Þanne comeþ forþ good hope; To saue man he wolde fonde: 'Þou wronge weuere ouerhope! I make him free, þou woldist make him bonde.' **1587** M. GROVE *Pelops & Hipp.* (1878) 73 Yet say not naythelesse that I..am the weauer of your woe. **1781** COWPER *Conversat.* 207 Sedentary weavers of long tales Give me the fidgets. **1885** CLODD *Myths* I. iii. 20 The savage is not a conscious weaver of allegories. **1905** J. B. FIRTH *Highways Derbysh.* xvi. 245 A weaver of rhymes.

3. *Sc.* A spider.

1825 JAMIESON, *Wyver*, a spider, Aberd. **1882** *Ibid.*, *Wyvers'-wobs*, cobwebs.

4. One of numerous Asiatic or African tropical birds of the family *Ploceidae*, so called from the elaborately interwoven nests that many of them build. Also more fully *weaver-bird* (see 7).

1828 STARK *Elem. Nat. Hist.* I. 240 *Ploceus Philippinus*, Tem... Philippine Weaver... *P. Abyssinicus*... Abyssinian Weaver. **1844** LADY G. FULLERTON *Ellen Middleton* (1854) II. xiv. 149 The weavers with their endless tails. **1894–5** *Lydekker's Roy. Nat. Hist.* III. 363 The red-billed black weaver (*Textor niger*) is found in the Transvaal. **1909** *African Monthly* VI. 270 A colony of Spotted-backed Weavers.

5. A water-beetle of the family *Gyrinidae.* = WHIRLIGIG *sb.* 4.

1864 WEBSTER.

6. *Basket-making.* Any cane which is woven between the stakes of a basket.

1897 A. FIRTH *Cane Basket Work* ii. 17 *Weavers*, the canes which are placed alternately behind and before the spokes. **1960** E. LEGG *Country Baskets* 27 If you will just bear in mind the names of the parts—sticks or stakes, and weavers —..you will never forget the different grades required... The stakes must be stouter or stronger than the weavers.

7. a. *attrib.* and *Comb.*, as ***weaver-body, -boy,*** †***-craft, -girl, -leg,*** †***-trindle***; also in the names of certain birds, as ***weaver-bird*** (see sense 4), ***-bunting, -finch, -oriole.*** **weaver ant,** a tropical ant, esp. one of the genus *Oecophylla*, which builds nests of leaves fastened together by the silk of its own larvæ.

1913 *Ann. Rep. Smithsonian Inst. 1912* 456 The highly interesting *weaver ants..use their larvæ as weaver's shuttles. **1977** *Sci. Amer.* Dec. 146/1 Weaver ants are extremely abundant, aggressive and territorial. **1826** J. F. STEPHENS *Shaw's Gen. Zool.* XIV. 34 Ploceus, Cuvier. *Weaver-bird. **1879** LUBBOCK *Sci. Lect.* ii. 38 The pendulous nests of the weaver-bird are a protection from snakes and other enemies. **1818** SCOTT *Rob Roy* xxvi, Ye are willing to be guided by the Glasgow *weaver-body's advice.

1817 Cobbett *Pol. Reg.* XXXII. 98 The appellation of '*Weaver Boys' was..bestowed on the speakers at the numerous meeting, held at Manchester in November last. **1783** Latham *Gen. Syn. Birds* III. 193 *Weaver Bunting. **1515** *Sel. Cases Star Chamber* (Selden Soc.) II. 87 Robert Rossell being freman of the *wever Crafte sworne saith [etc.]. **1876** A. R. Wallace *Distrib. Anim.* II. 286 The Ploceidæ, or *Weaver-finches, are especially characteristic of the Ethiopian region. **1849** C. Bronte *Shirley* i, The *weaver-girls in their flowers and ribbons. **1875** G. Macdonald *Malcolm* II. 44 He wad..rin as fest as his wee *weyver (*spider*) legs cud wag. **1782** Latham *Gen. Syn. Birds* I. 435 *Weever Oriole. **1483** *Cath. Angl.* 412/2 A *Weffer tryndylle, *jnsubulus*.

b. Possessive combinations, as ***weaver's beam***, † ***brush***, ***-craft***, ***-glue***, † ***hand-roll***, † ***-jack***, ***-loom***, † ***-weight***, ***-winder***; † **weaver's beef of Colchester**, a name given to sprats; **weaver's bottom, weavers' cramp** (see quots.); **weaver's knot**, a sheet-bend or single bend, used for joining threads in weaving; † **weaver's larum**, an alarum made of a candle, a weight, and string; **weaver's lights** (see quot.: cf. *weaver's windows*); **weaver's shuttle**, (*a*) the shuttle used by weavers: (*b*) a shell *Radius* (*Ovulum*) *volva*; **weaver's windows** (see quot.: cf. *weaver's lights*).

1539 Bible (Great) *1 Sam.* xvii. 7 Yᵉ shafte of his spere was like a *weuers beame. **1598** Shaks. *Merry W.* v. i. 24. *a* **1679** J. Ward *Diary* (1839) 112 Sprats are proverbially called *Weaver's beef of Colchester. **1865** W. White *East. Eng.* I. 145 She had never heard sprats described as weaver's beef, as they are (or were) at Colchester. **1899** *Syd. Soc. Lex.*, **Weaver's bottom*, term for chronic inflammation of the bursa over the ischial tuberosity from pressure. **1583** *Rates Custome ho.* A vij, Brusshes called *weuers brusshes of heare, the dosen, ij.s. vj.d. **1462** in C. A. Markham *Northampton Bor. Rec.* (1898) I. 298 Euery persone that shall occupie and set vp the seide *Weyverescrafte within the ffraunchese of this town. **1881** W. Rivington in *Brain* IV. 257 The patient, who had been a weaver, suffered from what we may call '*weavers' cramp', by which is meant a condition analogous to 'writers' cramp'. **1872** C. W. Heaton *Experim. Chem.* iii. 308 When cotton thread or cotton fabrics are bleached, it is merely in order to remove the oily, sweaty, and mealy substances (**weaver's glue*, &c.) which have become attached to them during spinning and weaving. **1688** Holme *Armoury* III. xxi. (Roxb.) 251/1 A *weavers hand Roll. *Ibid.*, A *Weavers Jack. **1532** [G. Walker] *Dice Play* B iij b, To turne his pricke vpward, and cast a *weauers knot on both his thumbs behind him. **1678** Wanley *Wonders Little World* I. x. 16 With the flexure of her Tongue only she could readily tye that fast Knot, which we call the Weaver's Knot. **1745** *Phil. Trans.* XLIII. 555 This little Apparatus goes commonly by the Name of the *Weaver's Larum, from its being chiefly or originally made use of by Persons employed in that Trade. **1866** *Morn. Star* 14 Aug. 4/5 Broad windows extending the breadth of the house, and known as '*weavers' lights'. **1535** Coverdale *1 Sam.* xvii. 7 The shaft of his speare was like a *weuers lome. **1538** Elyot *Dict.*, *Radius*,..a *wayuers shyttell, wherwith he throweth the yern in to the webbe. **1560** Bible (Geneva) *Job* vii. 6 My dayes are swifter then a weauers shittle. **1815** S. Brookes *Introd. Conchol.* 157 Weaver's Shuttle, *Bulla Volva*. **1576** Gascoigne *Steele Gl.* (Arb.) 80 When *weauers weight is found in huswiues web. **1867** H. Latham *Black & White* 19 The trades taught are those of the..weaver, *weaver's winder, carpenter, and blacksmith. **1896** K. Snowden *Web of Weaver* xii. 152 The house had what we used to call *weavers' windows—three or four narrow lights together.

'weaver². [f. weave *v.*² + -er¹.] **a.** A horse that 'weaves' or rolls the neck and body from side to side.

1847 T. Brown *Modern Farriery* 387 Animals of an impatient, irritable temper,..will sometimes keep moving their head, neck, and body to and fro, like the motion of a weaver's shuttle: these have been called weavers. **1863** Mrs. Gaskell *Sylvia's L.* xi, T' horse was a weaver, if iver one was. **1880** W. Day *Racehorse in Training* i. 6 If a horse is a weaver put him into a box, for in it he is more contented and often forgets his tricks.

b. *Boxing.* A boxer who weaves from side to side as a tactical move. Cf. weave *v.*² 4.

1829 P. Egan *Boxiana* 2nd Ser. II. 165 They again became weavers, till they measured their lengths upon the ground, Warren again undermost. **1950** J. Dempsey *Championship Fighting* xi. 54 'Bobbers and weavers'—chaps who come in bobbing low and weaving from side to side.

c. *R.A.F. slang.* A pilot (or aircraft) pursuing a devious course. Cf. weave *v.*² 1 c.

1942 in Forbes & Allen *Ten Fighter Boys* 47, I called up the C.O. and said I would like to take up position as a 'weaver'. **1956** J. E. Johnson *Wing Leader* iv. 53 Some of our squadrons provided two weavers in an attempt to guard themselves from the bounce. The weavers flew above the squadron and continually weaved and criss-crossed.

d. A driver of a motor vehicle who moves continuously from lane to lane, esp. in order to pass other vehicles. *colloq.*

1960 *Amer. Speech* XXXV. 312 For a long time we have heard of the *weaver*, the driver who shifts from lane to lane in driving. **1973** *Telegraph* (Brisbane) 13 Sept. 30/1 Then we have the weaver, who careers from lane to lane, passing other cars right and left.

weaver, obs. f. waver *sb.*¹; var. weever.

weaveress ('wiːvərɪs). [f. weaver¹ + -ess.] A female weaver.

1723 *Lond. Gaz.* No. 6194/7 Mary Griffin,..Weaveress. **1877** J. H. Blunt *Dursley* 222 He found two looms alone remaining at work in the hands of an ancient weaver and weaveress. **1890** *Tablet* 4 Jan. 25 An old weaveress, a widow 72 years of age.

† **'weavering**, *vbl. sb. Obs. rare.* [f. weaver¹.] Weaver's work.

1719 D'Urfey *Pills* VI. 92 In Weavering and in Fulling, I have..Skill; And underneath my Weavering-Beam, There stands a Fulling-Mill.

† **'weaverly**, *a. Obs. rare*⁻¹. [f. weaver *sb.* + -ly¹.] As a depreciatory epithet: Like a weaver.

1643 J. White *First Cent. Scandalous Malignant Priests* 47 [He] calls his parishioners..Plow joggers, Bawling doggs, Weaverly Iacks, and Church-Robbers.

weavill, obs. form of weevil.

weaving ('wiːvɪŋ), *vbl. sb.*¹ [f. weave *v.*¹ + -ing¹.]

1. The action of the *vb.* weave; *esp.* the operation of forming cloth or other stuff by the interlacing of yarn or other filaments in a loom.

1377 Langl. *P. Pl.* B. xv. 444 Cloth þat cometh fro þe weuyng is nouȝt comly to were. **1398** Trevisa *Barth. De P.R.* xviii. xi. (Bodl. MS.), þe female [spider] is more of bodie þan þe male and haþ lengre feete and more pliaunte and more able to meuynge and to weuynge. *c* **1475** *Pol. Poems* (Rolls) II. 284 As myche for gardyng, spynnyng, and wevyng. **1511–12** *Act 3 Hen. VIII*, c. 6 §1 The Wever whiche shall have the wevyng of eny wollen yerne to be webbed into cloth. **1601** Holland *Pliny* vii. lvi. I. 188 Weauing was the invention of the Ægyptians. **1774** Bryant *Mythol.* (1775) II. 525 Erech; in which place likewise the weaving of linen, and making of nets was first found out. **1843** J. S. Knowles *Secretary* iii. i. 25 His grace the duke Is in a net of his own weaving caught. **1872** Yeats *Techn. Hist. Comm.* 45 Weaving was an art in which the Egyptians excelled.

† **b.** *concr.* A tissue, plexus. *Obs.*

1758 J. S. tr. *Le Dran's Observ. Surg.* (1771) Dict. Dd 3, *Varicosum Corpus*, that Weaving of Blood-Vessels, which enters into the Testicles.

2. *slang.* (See quot. 1865.)

1803 *Sporting Mag.* XXI. 326 Weaving—Is securing one or more cards upon the knee, under the table played at. **1865** *Hotten's Slang Dict.*, *Weaving*, a notorious card-sharping trick, done by keeping certain cards on the knee, or between the knee and the underside of the table, and using them when required by changing them for the cards held in the hand.

3. *attrib.*, as ***weaving-factory***, ***-frame***, † ***-house***, ***-loom***, ***-mill***, ***-room***, ***-shed***, † ***-shop***, † ***-work***.

1845 G. Dodd *Brit. Manuf.* Ser. iv. 95 Some being 'spinning-factories', some '*weaving-factories', and some both conjoined. **1530** Palsgr. 288/1 *Wevyng frame, *mestier*. *c* **1440** *Promp. Parv.* 523/2 *Wevynge howse, *textrinum*. **1772** [see spinning-house 1]. **1496** in Weaver *Somerset Med. Wills* (1901) 343 A *weving lome wᵗ his apparell and portenances. **1675** in Jeaffreson *Midsx. County Rec.* (1892) IV. 63 Wooden frames of weaveing Loomes. **1835** Ure *Philos. Manuf.* 380 A *weaving-mill near Manchester. **1844** Disraeli *Coningsby* iv. ii, Nor should the *weaving-room be forgotten. **1867** Morris *Jason* ii. 455 Whom soon they found, within the weaving-room, Bent earnestly above the rattling loom. **1844** *Penny Mag.* Jan. Suppl. 38 We next descend to the '*weaving-shed',..Here we find eight hundred and forty power-looms in one room. **1897** *Q. Rev.* Oct. 432 The men from the..imperial weaving-sheds. **1564** *Inv.* in Noakes *Worcs. Relics* (1877) 13 In the *weaving shoppe ij loomes, v geares [etc.]. ? **14..** in *Hampole's Wks.* (1895) I. 159 Fro vndern to none sche occupied hir in *weving werke. **1535** Coverdale *Tobit* ii. 11 Anna..wente daylie to the weeuynge worke.

'weaving, *vbl. sb.*² [f. weave *v.*² + -ing¹.]

1. *Pugilism.* (See weave *v.*² 4.)

1820 *P. Egan's Boxiana* (1829) III. 465 In closing, after a struggle, they broke away from each other. Neither of them seemed to have any idea of the weaving system. **1827** De Quincey *Murder* i. in *Blackw. Mag.* Feb. 210/2 In the course of this round we tried the weaving system, in which I had greatly the advantage, and hit him repeatedly on the conk. **1897** R. G. Allanson-Winn *Boxing* 261, I was obliged to retreat, and did so, as slowly as possible, using the weaving guards with both arms and completely escaping punishment.

2. The side-to-side movement by an animal of its head and neck.

1934 Miller & Robertson *Pract. Animal Husbandry* 59 Weaving is a nervous habit acquired by many wild animals in captivity (especially bears), and occasionally by horses. **1973** G. Durrell *Beasts in my Belfry* iv. 70 Sam had a habit—not uncommon in bears—which is called weaving.

weaving ('wiːvɪŋ), *ppl. a.* [f. weave *v.*¹ + -ing².] That weaves, in senses of the verb. Hence **'weavingly** *adv.*

c **1000** *Song Hezekiah* in *Lambeth Ps.* (Lindelöf) 236 Forcorfen is swylce fram wefendum wife [L. *uelut a texente*] lif min. **1590** Shaks. *Mids. N.* ii. ii. 20 Weauing Spiders come not heere. **1809** Shaw *Gen. Zool.* VII. 429 Weaving Oriole. **1815** Kirby & Sp. *Entomol.* xiii. (1818) I. 411 The weaving spider..presses her spinners against one of the walls, and thus glues to it one end of her thread. **1945** L. MacNeice in *Horizon* Nov. 295 Loom of wind Weavingly laughingly leavingly weepingly. **1959** C. Ogburn *Marauders* (1960) vi. 183 Overby ran erect, like a halfback, ..carrying his rifle weavingly before him as if it were a football.

weavle, obs. f. wavel *v. Sc.*

† **weavy**, *a. Obs. rare*⁻¹. [f. weave *v.*¹ + -y.] Suitable for weaving.

16.. Chalkhill *Thealma & Cl.* (1683) 44 Others fell'd Wood, and some dye weavy Yarn, The Women Spun.

weazand, weazell: see weasand, weezle.

weazen ('wiːz(ə)n), *a.* Also 8 **weezen**, 9 **weasen**. Altered form of wizen *a.*

1765 Foote *Commissary* i. 10 His little weezen face as sharp as a razor. **1793** Charlotte Smith *Old Manor House* I. iii. (ed. 2) 53 However she may set her weazen face against it..she likes at the bottom of her heart a young fellow of spirit. **1820** W. Irving *Sketch Bk.*, *Inn Kitchen* I. 317 A little swarthy Frenchman, with a dry weazen face. **1839** Dickens *Nickleby* lxii, A little, weazen, hump-backed man. **1877** W. S. Gilbert *Foggerty's Fairy* (1892) 76 A weazen little body, with over ladylike manners.

fig. **1901** *Blackw. Mag.* Oct. 577 Their policy was not weazen and anæmic.

b. *Comb.*: **weazen-face, -faced** *adjs.*

1794 Godwin *Caleb Williams* 37 He is but a poor, weazen-face chicken of a gentleman. **1824** W. Irving *T. Trav.*, *Bold Dragoon* (1848) 30 A pale, weazen-faced fellow. **1841** Thackeray *Gt. Hoggarty Diamond* ii, A little weazen-faced old lady. **1844** Dickens *Mart. Chuz.* xi, A little blear-eyed, weazen-faced, ancient man came creeping out.

weazen ('wiːz(ə)n), *v.* Also 9 **weezen**. [Altered form of wizen *v.*] *intr.* To shrink, shrivel. Also *trans.* (? *nonce-use*) to cause to shrink.

1821 *Lonsdale Mag.* II. 409, I put those three shillings..into a hole, and I found them weezened every time I went to look at them... I have just found it out that Dick has weezend them. **1850** *Jrnl. R. Agric. Soc.* XI. ii. 605 Nothing retards their [*sc.* pigs'] feeding so much as allowing them to be pining and weazening for their anticipated regular meal.

weazened ('wiːz(ə)nd), *ppl. a.* = wizened *ppl. a.*

1842 Thackeray *Sultan Stork* Wks. 1900 V. 739 The old woman blushed as far as her weazened old face could blush. **1862** Sala *Seven Sons* III. iv. 65 Jockeys..dwindled from strong men into little weazened brats of children. **1879** J. Payn *Under One Roof* i, A small grey man, frail of limb, somewhat weazened as to face. **1883** *Chamb. Jrnl.* 12 May 289/2 Weazened black and tan terriers.

transf. **1854** Thackeray *Newcomes* I. xi. 115 Old and weazened as that piano is. **1882** Constance F. Woolson *Anne* i. 22 The small face showed the most profound, almost weazened, solicitude.

weazeny ('wiːzənɪ), *a.* [f. weazen *a.* + -y¹.] Somewhat weazen.

1854 Lowell *Fireside Trav.*, *Roman Mosaic* (1909) 202 A half-dozen of weazeny baked pears. **1865** Mrs. H. Wood *Mildred Arkell* xxviii, A thin, weaseny sort of man.

weazon, weazond, obs. ff. weasand.

web (wɛb), *sb.* Forms: 1 web, 1–2 webb, 3 weob, 3–8 webb, 4–5 veb(b, 4–7 webbe, 5–7 webe, 6 wabe, 3– web. Also *Sc.* and *north.* 6 vob, wobb(e, 6–9 wob, 7 woob, 8– 9 wab. [OE. *web(b* neut., corresp. to OFris. *web*, *wob* (WFris. *web*, *webbe*, NFris. *wêb*, *wäb*), OS. *webbi* (MLG. and LG. *webbe*), MDu. and Du. *webbe*, *web*, OHG. *wappi*, *weppi*, *webbi* (MHG. *weppe*, *webbe*) neut., ON. *vef-r* masc. (genit. *vefjar*; Da. *væv*, Sw. *väf*):—OTeut. **wabjo-m*, *-z*, f. **wab-* ablaut-var. of **web-*: see weave *v.*¹]

I. 1. a. A woven fabric; *spec.* a whole piece of cloth in process of being woven or after it comes from the loom. Also *collect.*, woven stuff. Often as cognate obj. to *weave*.

Regularly used to translate L. *tela*.

c **725** *Corpus Gloss.* (Hessels) T 89, 90 *Telum*, web. *Textrinum*, webb. *a* **1050** *Liber Scintill.* (1889) 216 *Tela consummatur filis*, webb byþ ȝefylled mid þrædum. *c* **1200** *Vices & Virtues* 39 Al swa nan webb ne mai bien iweuen wið-uten twa beames. *a* **1225** *Ancr. R.* 322 Wule a weob beon, et one cherre, mid one watere wel ibleched? *c* **1325** *Gloss. W. de Bibbesw.* in Wright *Voc.* 157 A webe to wewen. *a* **1340** Hampole *Psalter* 496 þe wefand þat sheris down þe web are it be fulfild. **1362** Langl. *P. Pl.* A. v. 92 þenne I wussche hit [a new coat] weore myn, and al þe web aftur. **1382** Wyclif *Job* vii. 6 My daȝes swiftliere passiden than of the weuere the web is kut of. **1514** *Act 6 Hen. VIII* c, 9 §2 The Weaver..to restore..the Surplus of the same Yarn, if any shall be left not put into the same Web. **1546** *Extracts Aberd. Reg.* (1844) I. 236 Ane vob of tartane, contenand x ellis. **1577** B. Googe *Heresbach's Husb.* i. 38 b, Flaxe..being beaten to a softnesse, serueth for webbes of Linnen. **1629** *Orkney Witch Trial* in *County Folk-Lore* (1903) III. 78 Christane Reid in Clett cam in ane mraid errand, seiking woft to ane wob. **1697** Dryden *Æneis* ix. 633 Her Hand the Web forsakes. **1789** Burns *Robin shure in hairst*, I gaed up to Dunse, To warp a wab o' plaiden. **1797** *Encycl. Brit.* (ed. 3) XVIII. 835/2 The breast-bar, a smooth square beam in which there is an opening to let the web through as it is wove. **1815** J. Smith *Panorama Sci. & Art* I. 81 A whole web or piece of calico is printed by them in three minutes. **1849** M. Arnold *Sick King in Bokhara* 8 Ye shall pay Each fortieth web of cloth to me, As the law is. **1854** Surtees *Handley Cr.* (1901) I. i. 5 Peter was dressed like his master —coat, waistcoat, and breeches of the same web. **1909** R. Law *Tests of Life* xv. 312 The pattern of the cloth is more clearly displayed in the web than in the patch.

in figurative context. **1576** Fleming *Panopl. Epist.* 114 Should I..recant now in mine aged years,..and as it were begin a new webbe? **1579** Spenser *Sheph. Cal.* Oct. 102 Vnwisely weaues, that takes two webbes in hand. **1587** Greene (*title*), Penelope's Web. **1771** Wesley *Jrnl.* 6 Sept., How long shall we be constrained to weave Penelope's web?

† **b.** ? A breadth of woven material. So med.L. *tela*, OF. *toile* (Du Cange).

c **1460** *Invent. Sir J. Fastolfe* in *Archæologia* XXI. 263, ij fustian Blanketts, every of hem vj webbys. **1465** *Paston Lett.* III. 435, ij. payr shytes of iij. webbys, ij. hedshytes of ij. webbys, vj. payre shytes of ij. webbys.

c. *transf.* and *fig.* Something likened to a woven fabric; something of complicated structure or workmanship. Also, the texture of such a fabric.

1599 ALEX. HUME *Hymns* i. 10 Skarse nature yet my face about, Hir virile wob had spun. **1601** SHAKS. *All's Well* IV. iii. 83 The webbe of our life is of a mingled yarne, good and ill together. **1610** HOLLAND *Camden's Brit.* (1637) To Rdr., Some there be who may object to the silly web of my stile. **1663** CHARLETON *Chorea Gigant.* 28 Having thus, thread after thread, unravell'd Mr Jones his long Web of Reasons, which he thought so closely and artificially woven, as to be strong enough to bind his Readers to a belief of his Opinion, that Stone-heng was a Roman Structure. **1820** W. IRVING *Sketch Bk., A Royal Poet* I. 171 That passionate and fanciful amour, which has woven into the web of his story the magical hues of poetry and fiction. **1822** HAZLITT *Table-t.* Ser. II. v. (1869) 122 The web and texture of the universe.. is a mystery to them. **1860** MOTLEY *Netherl.* I. i. 24 The web of diplomatic negotiation and court-intrigue which had been slowly spreading over the leading states of Christendom. **1894** LADY M. VERNEY *Verney Mem.* III. 108 Sir Ralph.. is soon trying to disentangle the complicated web of John Denton's debts. **1917** O. WILDRIDGE *Captains & Co.* xx. 235 His cheeks had a web of criss-cross wrinkles.

d. Used for WARP. *lit.* and *fig.*

1538 ELYOT *Dict., Liciatorium*, a weauers shyttel, or a sylke womans tauell, wheron sylke or threde beinge wounden, is shot through the web or lome. *a* **1644** QUARLES *Sol. Recant.* x. 51 How mungrell nature weaves Wisdome and Folly in the self-same Loome, Like webbe and woof. **1781** COWPER *Expost.* 331 He.. Strikes the rough thread of error right athwart The web of ev'ry scheme they have at heart. **1862** GOULBURN *Pers. Relig.* I. iv. (1873) 38 Service and prayer are the web and woof of the Christian life. **1883** OGILVIE, *Web*, locally, the warp in a loom.

2. a. An article made of woven stuff (e.g. a garment, tapestry, a winding-sheet). Also *collect.* woven stuff of a particular material or pattern. Now chiefly literary or *arch.*

In quot. *c* 1205 *gode webbe* app. represents OE. *godweb, godeweb*, 'fine linen', etc., the first element being perh. interpreted as = 'good'.

Beowulf 995 Goldfag scinon web æfter wagum. *c* **1205** LAY. 19947 Iscrud mid gode webbe. *c* **1275** *Ibid.* 22584 þe king.. caste on his rugge swiþe riche webbes. *a* **1400–50** *Wars Alex.* 1523 All þe wawis withoute in webis of ynde. **1560** ROLLAND *Seven Sages* 19 The riche Badkins, the coistlie veluot wobbis. *c* **1590** GREENE *Fr. Bacon* III. i. 992 If Phœbus tired in Latonas webs Came courting. **1757** DYER *Fleece* II. 540 What nation did not seek, Of thy new-modell'd wool, the curious webs? *Ibid.* III. 59 A diff'rent spinning ev'ry diff'rent web Asks from your glowing fingers. **1791** HAMILTON *Berthollet's Dyeing* I. 133 Common woollen stocking web. **1813** J. THOMSON *Inflammation* 283 Linen cloth is the web on which the plaster is commonly spread. **1852** THACKERAY *Esmond* III. ix, Kneeling down at the bedside and kissing the sheets out of respect for the web that was to hold the sacred person of a King. **1867** MORRIS *Jason* VI. 477 With richest webs the marble walls were hung. **1871** ROSSETTI *Staff & Scrip* xxx, Fair flew my web [a banner]. **1883** MISS BROUGHTON *Belinda* II. vii, Costly fabrics and dainty webs.

†**b.** ? A kind of net for catching fish. *Obs.*

1533–4 *Act 25 Hen. VIII*, c. 7 To take or distroye in or by meanes of any wele.. lepe hyve crele rawe webbe lister syer ..the yonge frye.. of any kynde of Salmon.

†**c.** A bandana or large handkerchief. *Obs.*

1843 CARLYLE *Past & Pr.* IV. iv. 369 The waste cotton-shrub,.. have ye not.. made it into beautiful bandana webs? **1850** 'SYLVANUS' *Bye-lanes & Downs* iv. 53 The inimitable web of cambric carefully folded. *Ibid.* vi. 74 The flash, reared up fellow, in the light blue pantaloons and huge web of satin round his neck!

†**d.** *pl.* Stockinet pantaloons. ? *nonce-use.*

1825 T. HOOK *Sayings* Ser. II. *Sutherl.* (Colburn) 27 Our tall friend in the webs.

3. a. A band of material woven strongly without pile. Also *collect.* = WEBBING. Cf. GIRTH-WEB.

1337–8 [see WAME-TOW]. **1395** [see WAME-TOW *attrib.*]. **1794** in *Jrnl. Friends' Hist. Soc.* (1918) 7 The Coffin was.. lowered down with Ropes and Webb. **1823** J. BADCOCK *Dom. Amusem.* 115 Procure two yards, more or less, of web, of broad tape, or cloth listing. **1862** *Catal. Internat. Exhib., Brit.* II. No. 3841, Elastic gusset webs. *Ibid.* No. 4962 The elastic web is so placed as to allow the free rising of the instep. **1875** KNIGHT *Dict. Mech., Web* 5. (*Vehicle*) Stout bands of textile fabric, used as straps to limit the extension of the hood.

b. *attrib.* (and *Comb.*). Made of webbing.

1844 *Queen's Regul. Army* 351 A web-headed halter with two reins. **1890** 'R. BOLDREWOOD' *Col. Reformer* x, Have you no.. breaking-bit, or web surcingle? **1915** 'IAN HAY' *1st Hund. Thou.* viii, Sam Browne belts have been wisely discarded by the officers in favour of web-equipment. **1915** P. MACGILL *Amateur Army* 100 Web-belts were cleaned, and every speck of mud and grease removed.

4. a. A cobweb. Also applied to the filmy textures spun by some caterpillars. Also *collect. sing.*

So L. *tela*, F. *toile*.

c **1220** *Bestiary* 468 Ðe spinnere.. werpeð ðus hire web. *a* **1340** HAMPOLE *Psalter* lxxxix. 10 As þe erayn makes vayn webbes forto take fleghis with gile. *c* **1391** CHAUCER *Astrol.* I. §3 Thi Riet shapen in manere of a net or of a webbe of a loppe. *a* **1400** *Nominale* (Skeat) 625 *Vn teile de filaundre*, A web of gossomer. **1426** LYDG. *De Guil. Pilgr.* 23576 The place is not.. Clenly kept with reuerence; For beforn, and ek behynde, Yraynes and webbes men may fynde. **14..** in *W. of Henley's Husb.* (1890) 55 Yeff ye se at morowe a dewe vpon þe grounde that is callid webe off arayne hongynge vpon þe grasse. **1555** EDEN *Decades* (Arb.) 219 Her bodye was.. full of that laune wherof they make their webbes. **1606** N. B[AXTER] *Sydney's Ourania* G 3 b, Th' admirable Silke-worme Whose daintie webbe doth cloath potentates. **1718** *Poor Robin* Feb. A 5 b, Cut Caterpillars Webbs from Tops Of Twigs. **1774** GOLDSM. *Nat. Hist.* VIII. 22 Some [caterpillars] spin themselves a cone or web, in which they lie secure till they have arrived at maturity. **1823** BYRON *Juan* x. lxxxiv, With a soft besom will I sweep your halls, And brush a web or two from off the walls. **1859** TENNYSON *Vivien* 108 A gilded summer fly Caught in a great old tyrant spider's web. **1869** J. J. WEIR in *Trans. Entom. Soc.* I. 21 Larvæ which spin webs.. are eaten by birds, but not with avidity; they appear very much to dislike the web sticking to their beaks. **1879** JEFFERIES *Wild Life in S. Co.* xvii. 317 At the end of September.. acres of furze may be seen covered with web in the morning.

b. A single thread or line spun by a spider, used in optical instruments; = COBWEB *sb.* 1 b.

1877 LD. LINDSAY & D. GILL in *Dun Echt Observ. Publ.* II. 11 The webs *a, b, c, d,* and *f* are all attached to the frame which is moved by the micrometer screw. **1883** *Encycl. Brit.* XVI. 248/1 A spider.. is caught.. and placed on a wire fork. The insect immediately attaches a web to the wire.. This web is wound up on the fork till ten or twelve turns.. have been secured.

c. *fig.*; esp. (*a*) a subtly-woven snare or entanglement; (*b*) something flimsy and unsubstantial; fanciful reasoning or the like. Cf. COBWEB *sb.* 3.

When the spider is not indicated in the context, it is often difficult to decide whether the quot. belongs here or to 1 c.

1574 *Mirr. Mag., Q. Elstride* xxvi, O wretched wight bewrapt in webbes of woe. **1577** tr. *Bullinger's Decades* I. i. 5 They taught that man.. by his owne faulte,.. brought into the worlde death and damnation, together with a webbe of miseries, out of whiche it can not ridde it selfe. **1604** SHAKS. *Oth.* II. i. 169 With as little a web as this, will I ensnare as great a Fly as Cassio. **1605** BACON *Adv. Learn.* I. iv. §5. 19 The Schoole-men.. did out of no great quantitie of matter, and infinite agitation of wit, spin out vnto vs those laborious webbes of Learning which are extant in their Bookes. **1672** DRYDEN *2nd Pt. Conq. Granada* I. ii (end), I.. Silk-worm-like, so long within have wrought, That I am lost in my own Webb of thought. **1838** PRESCOTT *Ferd. & Is.* I. Introd. 88 The law seemed only the web to ensnare the weak. **1841** DICKENS *Barn. Rudge* xxiii, He.. felt that accident and artifice had spun a web about him. **1859** H. KINGSLEY *G. Hamlyn* vi, He is entangled in a web of crime and guilt from which there is no escape. **1864** TENNYSON *Aylmer's Field* 780 Who wove coarse webs to snare her purity, Grossly contriving their dear daughter's good.

5. *Paper-making*, etc. **a.** An endless wire-cloth working on rollers and carrying the pulp. **b.** A large sheet or roll of paper made in this way. **c.** A continuously moving plastic sheet or film.

1825 J. NICHOLSON *Oper. Mech.* 369 A horizontal frame, .. furnished with a roller or cylinder at each end, over which is stretched an endless web of brass wire, of the requisite texture or fineness for the paper about to be manufactured. .. The web proceeds slowly forward with a tremulous motion, which arranges and disperses the pulp regularly over the whole surface of the web. **1854** C. TOMLINSON *Obj. Art-Manuf., Paper* 30 A continuous or endless web of wire cloth, stretched over two or more revolving rollers. **1854** *Tomlinson's Cycl. Usef. Arts* II. 263/1 An endless wire-cloth, over which the web of paper is formed. **1855** HERRING *Paper & Paper Making* 76 The web, as it is termed by the paper-maker, being thus severed longitudinally. **1867** *Tomlinson's Cycl. Usef. Arts* III. 514/2 White paper, supplied by the paper-maker in large rolls of web, about 18 inches in diameter. **1958** E. G. FISHER *Extrusion of Plastics* vii. 96 The sheet passes through one or two pairs of nip rolls which draw the web through the take-off. **1974** J. H. BRISTON *Plastics Films* xv. 191 The web of material is controlled at all stages of the wrapping operation and cut-off only takes place when the product has been fully enclosed.

II. 6. a. A tissue or membrane in an animal body or in a plant. Also applied to similar pathological formations.

c **1290** *St. Michael* 720 in *S. Eng. Leg.* 320 A smal weob it [the fœtus] biluppez al aboute, to holden it togadere faste. **1398** TREVISA *Barth. De P.R.* v. i. (Tollemache MS.) Sumtyme an ey haþ twey ȝolkes, þat ben distingued a tuo by on webbe and call [*una tela*]. **1541** COPLAND *Guydon's Quest. Cyrurg.* E iij b, The sayde webbe or tunycle called Rethina. **1728** CHAMBERS *Cycl.* s.v. *Ear*, A delicate Web, that lines the *Vestibulum, Cochlea*, &c. **1807** J. E. SMITH *Phys. Bot.* 324 The five filaments of the *Celosia*, Cock's-comb, are connected at their lower part by a membranous web. *a* **1827** GOOD *Study Med.* (1829) III. 511 When these sinuosities are first formed or scooped out, their walls are soft, irritable, and of the common cellular web. **1899** *Syd. Soc. Lex., Web*, in *Anat.*, any membrane-like, semi-transparent structure. **1897** *Allbutt's Syst. Med.* IV. 812 Chronic stenosis of the larynx,.. due to.. the formation of membranous webs.

attrib. **1876** tr. *E. Wagner's Gen. Pathol.* 167 The circulation in the web-membrane is retarded after closure of the femoral artery. **1897** *Allbutt's Syst. Med.* IV. 812 Cicatricial web formations [in the larynx] should be divided by cutting dilators.

b. The omentum or caul of cattle.

1808 JAMIESON, *Web*, the covering of the entrails, the cawl, or omentum, apparently denominated from its resemblance to something that is woven. *a* **1825** FORBY *Voc. E. Anglia* s.v., 'The web of the body'; the omentum. **1842** J. AITON *Domest. Econ.* (1857) 212 Meal is understood to darken the flesh, web, and lights of the animal [a calf].

†**7. a.** A thin white film or opacity growing over the eye; a kind of cataract, albugo, leucoma, or pterygium. Also ***pin and web***: see PIN *sb.*[1] 11. Also *fig. Obs.*

1387 T. USK *Test. Love* I. ii. 180 That hath caused my cominge in-to this prison, to voyde the webbes of thyne eyen, to make thee clerely to see the errours thou hast ben in. **1388** WYCLIF *Tobit* vi. 9 To anoynte iȝen, in whiche is a web. **1398** TREVISA *Barth. De P.R.* VII. xvi. (1495) 234 Another euyll of the eyen we calle a webbe and Constantin calleth it Albugo and Pannus. *c* **1400** *Master of Game* (MS. Digby 182) xii, Sometyme commeth to þe houndes sekenes in hir eyenn, for þer commeth a webbe vpon hem and waxynge flesshe. **1464** *Mann. & Househ. Exp.* (Roxb.) 280 For a webbe and a pynne in yhe. **1538** ELYOT *Dict., Suffusio*, a webbe in the eye. *c* **1575** *Perf. Bk. Kepinge Sparhawkes* (1886) 31 Pyn or Web or other dymnes by strokes &c. must be spedely loked unto. **1607** TOPSELL *Four-f. Beasts* 28 If a horsse haue a web in his eye. **1622** BANISTER *Treat. Eyes* VI. iii. H 8, Of the webbe or cataract, called in Greeke, *hypochyma*, in Latin, *suffusio, gutta, aqua, imaginatio. a* **1638** MEDE *Wks.* (1672) 645 Lord! that the whole strain of Scripture.. should not cure this web, and take this filme from the eyes of men! **1747** WESLEY *Prim. Physick* (1762) 67 Drop a drop or two at a time into the Eye, and it takes away all.. Spots, Webs, or any other Disorder whatever. *a* **1827** GOOD *Study Med.* (1829) IV. 220 This opacity [caligo], as well as the pterygium, was denominated a 'web of the eye', from its giving the idea of a film spreading across the sight.

†**b.** *gen.* A crust or film. *Obs.*

1594 PLAT *Jewell Ho.* I. 61 [The candle] alwayes supporting it selfe aboue the water, by a thin crust or webbe, which it worketh about the flame in the nature of Camphire.

8. a. The membrane or fold of skin which connects the digits of an animal; esp. that which connects the toes of an aquatic bird or beast, forming a palmate foot.

1576 TURBERV. *Venerie* lxxiii. 201 They [*sc.* otters] are footed like a Goose: I meane they haue a webbe betweene theyr clawes. **1768** PENNANT *Brit. Zool.* (1776) II. 533 The lower part of the toes and webs black. *Ibid.* 548 Mr. Ray calls this a cloven-footed gull; as the webs are depressed in the middle, and form a crescent. **1774** GOLDSM. *Nat. Hist.* IV. 150 Each foot [of the otter] is furnished with five toes, connected by strong broad webs like those of water fowl. **1813** J. THOMSON *Inflammation* 77 The capillary vessels in the web of the foot of the frog. **1842** TENNYSON *Morte d'Arthur* 269 Like some full-breasted swan That.. takes the flood With swarthy webs. **1894** CROCKETT *Raiders* xxvi. 226 My hands pricked at the thin fine skin between the fingers that we call the webs. **1899** *Allbutt's Syst. Med.* VIII. 865 The burrows [of the itch insect] will generally be found in the webs between the fingers and toes.

b. *Path.* An extension of the normal fold which occurs as a congenital malformation in the human hand or foot.

1866 BARWELL in *Med. Press* 25 Apr. 416 On examining the fingers I found them connected together, not merely by a thin web, but by a thick layer of tissue covered.. by skin from corresponding parts of the fingers. **1876** T. BRYANT *Pract. Surg.* (ed. 2) II. 300 When the fingers are well formed, the Surgeon should, if possible, divide the web.

9. The series of barbs on each side of the shaft of a bird's feather; the vane or vexillum.

1713 DERHAM *Phys.-Theol.* VII. i. 375 *note*, The Mechanism of the Vanes, or Webs of the Feathers. **1768** PENNANT *Brit. Zool.* (1776) II. 590 The greater quil feathers are black; the exterior webs of the next are a fine green. **1828** STARK *Elem. Nat. Hist.* I. 216 First feather of the tail white, with a black square spot on the interior web. **1837** GOULD *Birds Europe* V. Pl. 372 The shaft and the narrow inner web white; the outer web broad and deep bluish black. **1893** GADOW in Newton *Dict. Birds* 239 The rami, radii, and cilia compose the inner and outer web, vane, or *vexillum* of the feather.

III. 10. a. A sheet of lead, such as is used for roofing and for coffins. ? *Obs.*

Cf. med.L. *tela plumbi*: **1312** *Acc. Exch. K.R.* 492/18 m. 2 (P.R.O.).

1470–85 MALORY *Arthur* XXI. xi. 857 After she was put in a webbe of leed & than in a coffyn of marbyl. **1489** in Peck *Desid. Curiosa* (1735) II. VII. 10 For the Balmynge, Fencyng and Scowering of the Corse, with the Webbe of Led and Chest. **1555** *Inv. Ch. Goods York* etc. (Surtees 97) 152 Leade. In the covering upon the same colledge MlDxiiij square yerdes of webbe. **1577** in *Assoc. Archit. Soc. Rep.* (1866) VIII. 301 One webb of Lead liynge in the gutter within the said battlement cont. in lenght iijxx. yardes and in bredth one yarde. **1600** FAIRFAX *Tasso* X. xxvi, And there with stately pompe by heapes they wend, And Christians slaine rolle vp in webs of lead. **1601** HOLLAND *Pliny* XXXI. vi. II. 411 Those pipes be called properly in Latin Denariæ, the web or sheet whereof beareth ten fingers in breadth. **1660** *Churchw. Acc. Pittington* etc. (Surtees) 197 For taking upp the high roofe of the leades and laying the webbs againe. **1852** R. BURN *Naval & Mil. Dict.* II. s.v., Web of lead, *feuille de plomb.*

†**b.** A quantity of glass. Cf. WAY *sb.*[2] *Obs.*

1545–1656 [see WAY *sb.*[2]].

11. The piece of bent iron which forms a horseshoe.

1587 MASCALL *Cattle, Horses* (1596) 156 Make your shooes with a broade webbe. **1639** T. DE GREY *Compl. Horsem.* 111 That no gravell be remaining betwixt the web of the shoo and the sole. **1725** *Bradley's Family Dict.* s.v. *Shoeing*, The Shoe must be made of Spanish Iron, with a broad Web, fitting it to the Hoof. **1831** YOUATT *Horse* xvii. 312 The inside part of the web is bevelled off, or rendered concave, that it may not press upon the sole. **1908** *Animal Managem.* (War Office) 227 The whole of the substance of the shoe is called the 'web'.

12. †**a.** The blade of a sword or of a carpenter's plane; the iron head of an axe or hatchet. *Obs.*

1600 FAIRFAX *Tasso* II. xciii, A sword, whereof the web was steele. *Ibid.* VII. xciv, The brittle web of that rich sword. **1676** *Depos. Cast. York* (Surtees) 223 This informant got hold of the head or web of the ax. **1747** HOOSON *Miner's Dict.* R 3 b, This [Rudder] we use to let in the ends of Sliders, or Headtrees, where the Web of the Hack is too short for the purpose. **1812** P. NICHOLSON *Mech. Exerc., Joinery* 204 Web of an Iron, is the broad part of it which comes to the sole of the plane, the upper edge or end of the web has generally one shoulder, and sometimes two, where it joins the tang.

b. (See quot.)

1784 J. SMALL *Ploughs* 13 The web may be three inches broad at the broadest, and taper from a foot down all the way to the point. **1819** REES *Cycl., Web of a Coulter*,.. that part of it which is drawn out thin and sharp, in order to cut and separate the ground... In the sock, too, any thin sharp part has the name of web or wing.

c. The detachable long narrow blade of a frame-saw or fret-saw. Cf. *web-saw*.

1831 J. HOLLAND *Manuf. Metal* I. 330 It [the Grecian saw] consists of a square frame, having in the middle a blade or web, the teeth of which stand perpendicular to the plane of the frame. **1846** HOLTZAPFFEL *Turning*, etc. II. 725 The mill-saw webs [are used] for cutting deals into thin boards. **1866** *Chambers's Encycl.* VIII. 508/1 The Ribbon-saw.. consists of a very long band—or web, as it is called—of steel, usually very narrow, and with finely-cut teeth.

13. The bit of a key; also, each of the 'steps' or incisions in this.

1773 W. EMERSON *Princ. Mech.* (ed. 3) 284 *Web*, the thin broad part of an instrument, as the web of a key. **1800** *Trans. Soc. Arts* XVIII. 241 So that the webs or bits of the Key may clear the Tumblers in the lock. **1856** *Jrnl. Brit. Archæol. Assoc.* XII. 125 This key has a solid or blank web. **1862** *Catal. Internat. Exhib., Brit.* II. No. 6105, The 'bits' or steps on the 'web' of the key, that act on the levers inside the lock.

14. a. The vertical plate (or its equivalent) which connects the upper and lower laterally-extending plates in a beam or girder. Also applied to each of these lateral plates or flanges. Also, a longitudinal vertical member joining the upper and lower components of a wooden rib, spar, or beam in an aircraft.

1851 DEMPSEY *Builder's Guide* 144 The two [flanges of the girder] are united by a vertical rib or web of just sufficient thickness to connect the flanges properly. **1856** *Min. Proc. Inst. Civ. Engin.* XV. 155 On the Relative Proportions of the Top, Bottom, and Middle Webs of Iron Girders and Tubes. **1862** SMILES *Engineers* III. 409 Cast-iron girders, with their lower webs considerably larger than their upper, were ordinarily employed where the span was moderate. **1870** B. BAKER *Strengths of Beams* etc. 290 The experiments on the model tube for the Britannia bridge indicated clearly that diagonal strains, both compressive and tensile, occurred in the webs of the tube. **1877** W. H. WHITE *Nav. Archit.* ix. 333 So long as the beam is in one piece, or so long as the pieces forming its web are well connected together edgewise, there is no difficulty in meeting this racking strain. **1892** *Dict. Arch.* (Arch. Publ. Soc.), *Web*. The iron plate, fixed vertically, in a single web girder; or two plates in a tubular girder. **1909** *Flight* 11 Sept. 553/2 The rib for a double-surfaced deck [*sc.* wing] is more elaborate in construction, and is itself stiffened with 'webs'. **1918** *Ibid.* 25 July 830/2 Each of the spars is built up of spruce flanges, connected on front and rear faces by three-ply webs, the whole forming a box. **1919** PIPPARD & PRITCHARD *Aeroplane Struct.* xvii. 199 The load is transmitted by shear across the web portion of the rib, and so this portion must be very strongly attached to the web of the spar. **1962** *Flight Handbk.* (ed. 6) iii. 45 Platz's wing employed box spars with plywood sides (webs) and heavier wooden tops and bottoms (booms).

b. The upright portion between the tread and the bottom flange of a rail. †Formerly applied to the tread and the bottom flange (***upper, lower web***); also to the upright ridge of an edge-rail.

1838 *Civil Engin. & Arch. Jrnl.* I. 169/1 The lower web is, in some examples, not so wide as the upper web by nearly half an inch. **1840** H. S. TANNER *Canals & Rail Roads U.S.* 156 Which lip extends upwards and laps over the lower web of the rails on that side. *Ibid.* 264 *Web*, the outer projection of a rail, intended to prevent the wheels of carriages from running off the track. **1886** *Encycl. Brit.* XX. 225/1 There was a waste of metal in these early rails..owing to the excessive thickness of the vertical web.

c. The arm of a crank, connecting the shaft and the wrist.

1875 KNIGHT *Dict. Mech.* **1884** *Manch. Exam.* 27 Aug. 4/7 Cranks having the additional strength provided by an increase of metal in the webs of the crank itself. **1889** HASLUCK *Model Engin. Handybk.* 79 It is best to turn the shaft and outsides of the crank webs first; the insides and the pin can be turned after.

d. The thinner part of an anvil, between the head and the base.

1874 KNIGHT *Dict. Mech.* I. 120/2 Body or web of the anvil.

e. (See quot.)

1908 PAASCH *Dict. Naval Terms* (ed. 4) 770 *Web*,..that part of a boat-oar, between the blade and the loom.

f. In a sheave (see quot.).

1794 *Rigging & Seamanship* I. 153 *Web*, the thin partition on the inside of the rim, and between the spokes of an iron sheave.

g. A solid disc connecting the centre and the rim of a wheel, instead of spokes.

1875 KNIGHT *Dict. Mech., Web* 3. That portion of a car-wheel which extends between the hub and the rim. *Ibid.* s.v. *Web-wheel*, Clock and watch wheels are cast or stamped with webs and then *crossed out*.

h. *pl.* Snow-shoes. *N. Amer.*

1923 *Beaver* Jan. 145 It is said they still enjoy an occasional zestful tramp on the 'webs' over leagues of new Manitoba snow. **1939** K. PINKERTON *Wilderness Wife* ix. 103 After breakfast we went out to slip on our webs. **1966** M. E. & O. MURIE *Wapiti Wilderness* xviii. 223 Snowshoes, or 'webs' as the Jackson Hole people call them, were the tried and true aids.

15. The basketwork of a gabion.

1852 R. BURN *Naval & Mil. Dict.* II. s.v., Web of a gabion, hurdle, &c., *clayonnage*. **1859** F. A. GRIFFITHS *Artil. Man.* (1862) 255 Gabions are..2 feet 9 inches high, in the web.

16. *Mining.* (See quots.)

1883 GRESLEY *Gloss. Coal-mining, Web*, the face or wall of a long-wall stall in course of being holed and broken down for removal. The web varies in thickness (according to the height of the seam) from 2 or 3 to 7 feet. Fig. 135 shows a cross-section of a long-wall with a web of coals after drawing the timber. **1886** J. BARROWMAN *Sc. Mining Terms* 51 *Plane*, a working room driven at right angles to or facing the plane joints. *Ibid.* 72 *Web*, the plane.

17. *Math.* A tangential net.

1911 WEBSTER s.v. *Net*, But if [represented] in line co-ordinates, the net is tangential or a web.

IV. 18. *Comb.*, as ***web-like*** adj.; objective, as ***web-spinning*** adj.; similative, as ***websoft*** adj.; **web-fed** *a. Printing* = *reel-fed* adj. s.v. REEL *sb.*[1] 6; **web-fingered** *a.*, having the fingers united for a considerable part of their length by a fold of skin; also, applied to a fish, *Prionotus carolinus* or *palmipes*; **web-frame**, (*a*) the frame to which the spider-threads are attached in a filar micrometer; (*b*) in iron ship-building (see quot.); †**web-garn** [GARN *sb.*], weaver's yarn; †**web-lace** (see quot.); **web-lead**, sheet-lead; †**web-loom**, a weaver's loom; **web-machine**, a printing machine which is automatically supplied with paper from a roll or web (see 5); **web-nest**, a filmy tissue enclosing a group of certain caterpillars or web-spinners (sense b); cf. *web-worm*; **web offset**, offset lithographic printing on a continuous reel of paper (cf. sense 5 b); freq. *attrib.*; **web-(perfecting) press** = *web-machine*; **web-plate** (see quot. 1908); **web-printing**, printing on a web-press; **web-saw**, a frame-saw; **web-spinner**, (*a*) a web-spinning spider; (*b*) a brownish gregarious insect of the order Embioptera, the females of which are wingless; †**web-stand**, a folding tray-stand with a top composed of strips of webbing; **web-toed** *a.*, web-footed; **web-weaver**, in quots. applied to a spider; **web-wheel** (see quot. and 14 g); **web-work**, a tissue like that of a woven fabric; also *fig.*; **web-worked** *a.*, worked with cobweb; **web-worker**, a spider that spins a web; **web-worm** *U.S.*, a name for various lepidopterous larvæ which are more or less gregarious and spin large webs in which they feed or rest. Also WEB-BEAM, -FOOT, -FOOTED.

1949 MELCHER & LARRICK *Printing & Promotion Handbk.* 358/1 Newspapers are printed on *web-fed rotary presses. **1965** ZIGROSSER & GAEHDE *Guide Coll. Orig. Prints* iv. 73 In the rotogravure process the plate is in the form of a copperplated cylinder, functioning in a web-fed rotary press for long and speedy runs of printing. **1781** BLAND in *Phil. Trans.* LXXI. 362 Of these [children] 1 was *web-fingered. **1844** *Amer. Jrnl. Sci.* XLVII. 59 Prionotus Carolinus, Cuv., Web-fingered Grunter. **1851** MAYHEW *Lond. Labour* (1861) II. 137/1 He was, it is said, web-footed, naturally, and partially web-fingered. **1873** T. GILL *Catal. Fishes E. Coast N. Amer.* 21 Prionotus carolinus..Web-fingered sea-robin; Carolina robin. **1883** *Encycl. Brit.* XVI. 248/2 As the *web-frame is generally thicker than the fork, the web will now be stretched across the former, with a certain amount of tension. **1898** KIPLING *Day's Work* 81 A huge web-frame by the main cargo-hatch. **1908** PAASCH *Dict. Naval Terms* (ed. 4) 81 Web-frames consist of strong plates fitted transversally to the frames to which they are riveted... They serve for extra strength or in lieu of hold-beams, etc. **1440** *York Memo. Bk.* (Surtees) I. 78 That noon of the said craft shal make no capez of *webb garn nother blew ne meld nor noon other collour. **1801** FELTON *Carriages* (ed. 2) II. Gloss., *Webb Lace*, a thick coarse kind of lace, mostly used for footman holders. **1894** *Athenæum* 14 Apr. 482/3 The casting of *web lead for roofs. **1768–74** TUCKER *Lt. Nat.* (1834) I. 390 This *web-like expansion of the ethereal strings. **1815** KIRBY & SP. *Entomol.* ii. (1818) I. 31 The web-like nests [of the larva of *Bombyx chrysorrhœa*] which so often deform our fruit trees. **1902** *Westm. Gaz.* 29 Dec. 3/3 The silk Chantilly laces..are..very pretty and weblike. **1316** in Rock *Text. Fabr.* (1870) 96 Pro *weblomes emptis, xxs. **1404** *Rec. Borough Nottingham* 27 Aug. II. 22 Appretiatores unius wollyn weblome cum uno cam et j. slay. **1884** *West. Daily Press* 16 Sept. 5/6 The splendid *web machines now in use. **1888** JACOBI *Printers' Vocab., Web machines*, cylindrical printing machines in which the paper is laid on by tapes. **1895** W. SCHLICH *Man. Forestry* IV. 279 The caterpillars, enclosed in the common *web-nest, first gnaw the upper side of the leaves. **1903** *Biol. Bull.* IV. 100 They [*sc.* Embiidæ] still spin their web-nests. **1959** *Times Lit. Suppl.* 15 May 296/3 America, the land of newspapers on the giant scale,..is making great strides..with *web-offset colour on newsprint. **1967** E. CHAMBERS *Photolitho-Offset* xv. 238 Web offset can be defined as a method of lithographic printing in..one or more colours on one or both sides of a web of paper in a single operation. **1981** *Printing World* 28 Jan. 13/1 It was printed on a new Timson T32 web offset press. **1875** KNIGHT *Dict. Mech.*, s.v. *Web Printing-machine*, A *web perfecting-press. **1887** *Harper's Mag.* July 176/1 The web perfecting press, containing two printing cylinders, printing both sides of the paper. **1878** *Schiller's Technol. Dict.* III, *Web*, **Web-plate* (Iron ship-b.). **1908** PAASCH *Dict. Naval Terms* (ed. 4) 103 *Web-plate*. Term given to a plate of great breadth and thickness, as for instance to one forming a shifting-beam in a hatchway. **1875** KNIGHT *Dict. Mech.*, s.v. *Web Printing-machine*, The *web-press is a late improvement. **1890** W. J. GORDON *Foundry* 198 Printing from continuous paper is known as '*web-printing', 'roll-printing' or 'reel-printing'. **1875** KNIGHT *Dict. Mech.*, *Web-saw. **1889** *Century Mag.* Jan. 418/2 The web-saw, the glue-pot, the plane, and the hammer are the principal tools used. *a* **1915** JOYCE *Giacomo Joyce* (1968) 7, I hold the *websoft edges of her gown. **1923** *Jrnl. & Proc. R. Soc. Western Australia* IX. 1. 61 The Order Embioptera, or *Web-spinners, is a small but very distinct and isolated group of insects. **1941** J. S. HUXLEY *Uniqueness of Man* ix. 193 In the spiders, we find a very interesting difference between the hunters and the web-spinners. **1944** *Proc. U.S. Nat. Mus.* XCIV. 401 (*title*) A revision of the Embioptera, or web-spinners, of the New World. **1972** SWAN & PAPP *Common Insects N. Amer.* vi. 85 Embiids or Webspinners.. occur mostly in the tropics and sub-tropics. **1904** W. H. HUDSON *Green Mansions* v. 57 This was no *web-spinning, sedentary spider. **1946** *Nature* 2 Nov. 630/2 The web-spinning Tineid caterpillar..is usually an inhabitant of hawthorn bushes. **1837** *Fraser's Mag.* XV. 435 A large tray of glasses..stood in the room on a *web stand. **1872** MIVART *Anat.* 236 In some cases these folds extend far along, binding the digits together, and causing the person so affected to be what is called 'web-fingered' or '*web-toed'. **1884** COUES *Key N. Amer. Birds* (ed. 2) 622 *Macrorhamphus*. Web-toed Snipe. **1550** BALE *Apol.* 15 b, It hath bene so handeled and tosed amonge the spyders *webbe weuers of Babylon..that it is become moche larger both in length and bredthe than afore. **1826** KIRBY & SP. *Entomol.* IV. xxxvii. 31 The instinct of a crippled spider so completely changed, that from a sedentary web-weaver it became a hunter. **1875** KNIGHT *Dict. Mech.*, **Web-wheel*, a wheel in which the hub and rim are connected by a web or plate, which is sometimes intact and sometimes perforated... The term is applied in contradistinction to one with spokes. **1790** R. MERRY *Laurel of Liberty* (ed. 2) 10 A *web-work of despair, a mass of woes. **1812** [see VENOMED *ppl. a.* 2 c]. **1862** LYTTON *Str. Story* II. 199 The tyro who dissects the webwork of tissues and nerves in the dead. **1874** J. T. MOGGRIDGE *Suppl. to Harvesting Ants* 200 A glutinized, *web-worked purse, about three inches long. **1658** ROWLAND *Moufet's Theat. Ins.* 1071 All Net-workers, and *Web-workers amongst Spiders. **1841** T. W. HARRIS *Insects Inj. Vegetation* (1862) 357 The little caterpillars known by the name of fall *web-worms, whose large webs..may be seen on our native elms, and also on apple and other fruit trees, in the latter part of summer. **1885** *Manch. Exam.* 14 July 4/5 The webworm..did considerable damage to the stands. **1896** LODEMAN *Spraying of Plants* 256 Fall Web-worm (*Hyphantria cunea*). *Ibid.* 325 Web-worm (*Depressaria heraclina*). *Ibid.* 352 Privet Web-worm (*Margarodes quadristigmalis*).

web (wɛb), *v.* [OE. *webbian*, f. WEB *sb.* All the senses after 1 are new derivatives from the sb.]

1. *trans.* To weave (a fabric) in the loom. ? *Obs.*

In OE. only in fig. phr. *wroht webbian*, to devise a (false) accusation.

c **1440** *Promp. Parv.* 519/1 Webbon, or webbe clothe of lynnyne, *linifico*. **1449** in Hudson & Tingey *Rec. Norwich* (1910) II. 285 Providinge alwey that the cloþinge be webbed be the avyse of the said wardeyns. **1511–12** *Act 3 Hen. VIII* c. 6 §1 The Wever whiche shall have the wevyng of eny wollen yerne to be webbed into cloth. **1530** PALSGR. 778/2, I webbe a clothe, *Je ourdis*. I have nat yerne ynough to webbe my clothe with all. **1809** J. BARLOW *Columb.* II. 513 Her sprightly mind A vesture white had for the prince design'd; And here she seeks the wool to web the fleece. **1892** *Labour Commission* Gloss., *Web*, to weave.

†**2.** *intr.* Of a spider: To spin its web. *nonce-use. Obs.*

a **1604** HANMER *Chron. Irel.* (1809) 195 The roofe of Westminster Hall, where no English Spider webbeth or breedeth to this day.

3. *trans.* To cover with (spider's or caterpillar's) web; to weave a web upon.

1853 *Zoologist* XI. 4044 The canker-worm..forms itself a house by webbing the corner of a leaf.

b. *transf.* To cover with a web or fine network.

1895 *Forum* (N.Y.) Jan., Continents were being ribbed with railways, the atmosphere was being webbed with telegraph wires. **1905** P. LANDON *Lhasa* I. 361 An exquisite head-dress in which the high aureole..was barely recognisable under the strings and riggings of pearls which webbed the whole thing.

c. To stretch threads of spider's web across (a micrometer, etc.).

1883 *Encycl. Brit.* XVI. 248/1 Method of Webbing the Filar Micrometer. The webbing of a micrometer is a process that should be familiar to all practical astronomers. **1890** W. F. STANLEY *Surv. & Levelling Instrum.* 50 It is a somewhat delicate process to web a diaphragm... The webs are taken from a rather small or young garden spider. *Ibid.* 100 The diaphragm of the telescope of the Y-level is generally webbed with plain cross webs.

4. To entangle or envelop in, or as in, a (spider's) web. Also with *round*.

1864 WEBSTER *Web* v.t., to unite or surround with a web, or as if with a web; to envelop; to entangle. **1901** *Fun* 20 Apr. 189/2 A peasant kills a giant spider who has webbed a fly. **1907** *Black Cat* June 26 The girl was ready when again they [*sc.* wolves] webbed her round, each trumpet-mouthed with his own hunting cry. She lashed out.

5. To connect (fingers, toes, etc.) with a web or membrane. Also with *together*.

1774 GOLDSM. *Nat. Hist.* VI. 45 Nature..by broad skins, has webbed their toes together. **1890** W. P. BALL *Effects of Use & Disuse* 147 Use-inheritance..aids in webbing the feet of water-dogs, but fails to web the feet of the water-hen.

b. To imprint with the marks of web-feet. *nonce-use.*

1866 HOWELLS *Venetian Life* xiv. 203 The ground was webbed with the feet of geese.

‖**webb, webbe.** *Amer. Indian. Obs.* [perh. obs. Algonkin.] (See quots.)

1634 W. WOOD *New Englands Prospect* Nomencl. O 3 b, *Web*, a wife. **1672** JOSSELYN *New Eng. Rarities* 20 The Indian Webbes make use of the broad Teeth of the Fawns to hang about their Childrens Neck when they are breeding of their Teeth. *Ibid.* 62 One Christopher Luxe..was healed again by an Indian Webb, or Wife, (for so they call those Women that have Husbands). **1676** I. MATHER *War with Indians* 28 A party of English came in a Warlike posture upon some of their Webbs (as they call them) *i.e.* Women, as they were gathering corn.

†**webbe.** *Obs.* Also 5 web. [ME. *webbe* represents (1) OE. *webba* masc.; (2) OE. *webbe* fem. (only in *freoðuwebbe* peace-weaver, woman); OTeut. types **wabjon-, -ōn-*, f. **wab-*:

*web-: see WEAVE v. The word survives in the surnames *Webb*, *Webbe*.]

1. A male weaver.

c **1100** in Wr.-Wülcker 188/10 *Textor*, webba. *a* **1327** *Pol. Songs* (Camden) 188 The webbes ant the fullaris assembleden hem alle. *c* **1386** CHAUCER *Prol.* 362 A Webbe, a Dyere, and a Tapycer. **1389** in *Eng. Gilds* (1870) 12 Johanni de Bokkynge, webbe, ciui Londonie. **1393** LANGL. *P. Pl.* C. x. 204 These eremytes.. Whilom were workmen, webbes and taillours. *c* **1400** tr. *Secreta Secret., Gov. Lordsh.* 99 Some þat assemblyd yn a toune, & herberd hem yn a webbe hous, to whom þat nyght a child was born. **1403** *Will of John Oxstret* (Somerset Ho.), Johanni Anketell Webbe de Sarum.

b. In gen. sing. or plur. (OE. *webban, webbena*), with *light* and *loom*.

1346 *Little Red Bk. Bristol* (1900) II. 3 Si aliquod instrumentum textoris, videlicet Webanlam [*sic*] de nouo fiat. *Ibid.* 4. **1403** *Will of Ralph Stylle* (Somerset Ho.), Lego ad lumen beate marie vocatum Webben lyȝt xl d.

2. A female weaver, a webster.

1377 LANGL. *P. Pl.* B. v. 215 My wyf was a webbe and wollen cloth made. *a* **1425** *Cursor M.* 1525 (Trin.) She was þe formast web [*Cott.* webster] in kynde þat men of þat crafte dud fynde.

web-beam. [Cf. OHG. *weppi-*, *weppe-*, *webboum*, mod.G. *webebaum*.] The roller in a loom on which the web is wound as it is woven.

c **1100** in Wr.-Wülcker 187/11 *Liciatorium*, lorh, *uel* web-beam. *Ibid.* 188/4 *Insubula*, webbeamas. **14..** *Ibid.* 696/19 *Hoc laciatorium* [sic], a webbeme. **1797** *Encycl. Brit.* XVIII. 835/2 From this opening the web passes to the knee-roll or web-beam, round which it is rolled by means of the spokes.

webbed (wɛbd), *ppl. a.* [f. WEB *sb.* + -ED[2].]

1. Furnished with a web or connecting membrane; *esp.* of the feet of certain birds.

1664 POWER *Exp. Philos.* I. 5 The Common Fly..her wings look like a Sea-fan with black thick ribs or fibers, dispers'd and branch'd through them, which are webb'd between with a thin membrane or film, like a slice of Muscovy-glasse. **1678** RAY *Willughby's Ornith.* III. III. 322 Such [birds] as have all four toes webb'd together. **1773** PENNANT *Genera of Birds* p. xi, The toes of birds that swim are either plain,..or pinnated,..or entirely webbed or palmated. **1816** TUCKEY *Narr. Exped. R. Zaire* ii. (1818) 47 Three toes full webbed, the fourth toe..quite free. **1851** WOODWARD *Mollusca* 71 Arms (except the ventral pair), webbed high up. **1859** DARWIN *Orig. Spec.* vi. (1873) 142 What can be plainer than that the webbed feet of ducks and geese are formed for swimming?

b. *Path.* Having a 'web' as a congenital malformation. See WEB *sb.* 8 b.

1862 E. J. CHANCE *Bodily Deform.* I. 86 The Fingers or Toes may be more or less webbed together. **1876** T. BRYANT *Pract. Surg.* (ed. 2) II. 300 Webbed fingers and toes are another common deformity. **1913** DORLAND *Med. Dict.* (ed. 7) s.v. *Penis*, *Webbed penis*, a penis that is inclosed by the skin of the scrotum.

c. *Machinery.* In various uses: see WEB *sb.* 14.

1794 *Rigging & Seamanship* I. 154 Sheaves..are made.. of iron, with a brass coak, either open or webbed. **1913** J. B. BISHOP *Panama Gateway* v. iii. 365 Each [lock gate] is a huge webbed steel box, the girders of which are covered with a steel sheathing.

2. Covered with, or as with, cobweb. In *Bot.* = COBWEBBED 2.

1810 *Splendid Follies* I. 110 The tender blades of trefoil were still webbed in silvery gossamer. **1862** THORNBURY *Turner* I. 360 There were skies of an orange purple, skies webbed with grey showers. **1870** HOOKER *Stud. Flora* 191 Carduus crispus..involucre webbed. **1905** E. T. THURSTON *Traffic* II. ii, Only the gaunt, gray forms of the stunted poplars stood out, webbed, against the leaden colour of the sky.

† **'webber.** *Obs.* Also 5 webbare. [f. WEB *v.* + -ER[1].] A weaver.

c **1440** *Promp. Parv.* 312/1 Loome of webbarys crafte (*v.r.* of webstare), *telarium*. *Ibid.* 519/1 Webbare of lynnyne clothe, *linifex*. *c* **1515** *Cocke Lorelles B.* (Percy Soc.) 9 Gyrdelers, forborers, and webbers.

webbing ('wɛbɪŋ), *vbl. sb.* [f. WEB *v.* + -ING[1].]

1. The action or process of weaving. ? *Obs.*

c **1440** *Promp. Parv.* 519/1 Webbynge, of wullyne clothe, *lanificium*... Webbynge, of lynnyne, *linificium*. **1463-4** *Rolls of Parlt.* V. 501/2 Withoute dyversite in webbyng, fullyng, knottyng and burlyng. **1483** *Vulgaria abs Terentio* 3 Wyth woll and webbynge wemen were wont to gete their lyuynge. **1558** in *Eng. Hist. Rev.* (1897) XII. 439 Which yerely fee ferme was paid so long as webbyng in the said citie was used. **1562** PHAER *Æneid* IX. E e ij, In webbing wasting tyme to eas thereby myne aged care [*tela curas solabar anilis*]. **1657** J. WATTS *Scribe* etc. Author's Epist. b 2, Woman, get you home, and follow your own businesses of spinning and webbing.

2. *concr.* A woven material.

1754 POCOCKE *Trav.* (Camden) II. 15 Welch Webbings.. a thick sort of flannel, of which the Soldiers' clothing is chiefly made. **1883** *Daily News* 10 Sept. 2/6 In elastic webbings there is no improvement in the trade for gussets [of boots]. **1884** *Health Exhib. Catal.* 84/1 Webbing made of reed and used in substitution of fir-lathing.

b. Woven material in the form of a strong wide band, used by upholsterers and others. Also *attrib.* in ***webbing belt, tape***.

1794 Girth-webbing [see GIRTH-WEB]. **1796** *Repert. Arts & Manuf.* VI. 76 A chain, webbing, strap or line, is applied on the ledge on the face of the wheel. **1833** LOUDON *Encycl. Archit.* §634 A box footstool... The top is formed of an outside frame, on which is stretched strong webbing, for the purpose of supporting the stuffing above. **1858** SIMMONDS *Dict. Trade*, *Webbing tape*, a kind of broad tape. **1885** *Manch. Exam.* 5 May 5/2 A broad band of Turcoman webbing of extremely fine texture. **1888** JACOBI *Printers' Vocab.*, *Webbing*, a term for the wider tapes of a printing machine; also applied to the girthing used for running in and out the carriage of hand-presses. **1916** *Blackw. Mag.* Apr. 548/2 Trench coat, rifle, bayonet, webbing belts [etc.].

3. Material for a (spider's) web. ? *nonce-use*.

1883 G. MACDONALD *Princess & Curdie* xxvii, A huge spider,..which, having made an excellent supper, was full of webbing.

4. = PALMATION 2. Also *Path.*, a webbed state of the fingers or toes.

1872 ERICHSEN *Surg.* (ed. 6) II. 298 Webbing of the Fingers is occasionally met with. **1888** *Med. Press* 18 July 59/2 In the feet..the webbing is less thick and complete than in the hands, the terminal phalanges being separate from each other. **1894** *Century Mag.* Jan. 353/2 As the palmation, or webbing [of the larger moose's antlers], is not so wide as in the first variety, the points are longer.

webby ('wɛbɪ), *a.* [f. WEB *sb.* + -Y.]

1. Consisting of web; resembling web or a web.

1661 LOVELL *Hist. Anim. & Min.* 289 The Cæruleous [Spider] causeth a paine of heart, deep sleep and vomiting of a webby matter. **1768-74** TUCKER *Lt. Nat.* (1834) I. 596 They delight to..entangle the feeble in their webby filaments. **1854** LADY LYTTON *Behind the Scenes* I. I. iv. 124 His gloves were..of some webby elastic texture. **1904** E. NESBIT *Phœnix & Carpet* x. 185 The big darn in the middle of the carpet was all open and webby like a fishing-net.

2. Of the digits: Furnished with a web, palmated. Also *fig.* of a person.

1807 CRABBE *Par. Reg.* I. 381 Bats on their webby wings in darkness move. **1861** G. H. K[INGSLEY] in F. Galton *Vacation Tourists* iv. 165, I am of so fishy and webby a nature, that I take to the water at once. **1895** *Westm. Gaz.* 14 Sept. 2/1 If I have not pointed ears or webby fingers, [etc.].

weber[1] ('veɪbə(r), 'wiːbə(r)). *Electr.* Also † **veber**. [After the German physicist Wilhelm *Weber* (1804-91).] **a.** A name (now disused) for the unit of electrical quantity (now COULOMB) and the unit of electrical current (now AMPÈRE).

1872 *Telegr. Jrnl.* I. 11/1 The current through *a b* will then be equal to one British Association unit of current, or one veber per second. **1874** [see FARAD 2]. **1876** PREECE & SIVEWRIGHT *Telegraphy* 3 The unit quantity of electricity in general use has been called a *weber*. **1879** G. PRESCOTT *Sp. Telephone* 469 In the veber current and the electro-motive force, we have the data for comparing the work of these machines. **1881** *Rep. Brit. Assoc.* 425 The current produced by a Volt acting through an Ohm..is called a Weber. **1881** S. P. THOMPSON in *Jrnl. Soc. Arts* XXX. 32/2 To tear away a single gramme of hydrogen from the oxygen with which it is combined requires no less than 95,050 webers ('coulombs') to flow through. **1883** J. SWINBURNE *Pract. Electr. Units* 28 The coulomb has taken the place of the weber as unit of quantity, and the ampère is used instead of the weber-per-second as unit of current.

† **b.** A unit of magnetic pole strength, equal to the pole strength that produces a field of 1 oersted ('gauss') at 1 centimetre. *Obs.*

1882 R. CLAUSIUS in *Phil. Mag.* XIII. 394, I would take leave to propose that for it [*sc.* the unit of magnetism] the name 'weber' be introduced. **1892** G. F. BARKER *Physics* IV. iii. 645 The unit pole just now defined..is called a weber and the unit field which it produces at unit distance is called a gauss.

c. The M.K.S. unit of magnetic flux (now incorporated in the International System of Units), equal to 100 million maxwells; one volt-second. Symbol Wb.

1891 *Trans. Amer. Inst. Electr. Engineers* VIII. 542 We can start by defining 10^8 lines of force as the unit of induction and call it, say, a weber. **1895** *Rep. Brit. Assoc. Adv. Sci.* 196 The Committee..recommend for tentative adoption the following terminology: —— 1. That as a unit for magnetic field, a hundred million 'c.g.s. lines' be called a weber. **1935** *Proc. Nat. Acad. Sci.* XXI. 579 Various International Electrical Congresses..and since then, the I.E.C., have adopted, by successive steps, the well-known series of nine practical electromagnetic units (ohm, volt, ampere, farad, coulomb, joule, watt, henry and weber). **1963** G. TROUP *Masers & Lasers* (ed. 2) v. 67 For magnetic dipole transitions, $|p_{mn}|$ is of the order of a Bohr magneton ($1{\cdot}2 \times 10^{-29}$ weber metre). **1971** I. G. GASS et al. *Understanding Earth* iv. 71/2 The [magnetic] field varies over the Earth from 7×10^{-5} to $2{\cdot}5 \times 10^{-5}$ weber metre^{-2} (Wb m^{-2}).

Weber[2] ('veɪbə(r)). *Physiol.* [The name of Ernst H. *Weber* (1795-1878), German physiologist and anatomist.] **1.** ***Weber's law***: the observation made by Weber that the increase in a stimulus that is just noticeable is a constant proportion (the ***Weber fraction*** or ***ratio***) of the initial stimulus, for any one sense.

1872 [see PSYCHOPHYSICAL *a.*]. **1890** W. JAMES *Princ. Psychol.* I. xiii. 537 So much for a general account of what Fechner calls Weber's law. **1935** *Brit. Jrnl. Psychol.* XXVI. 226 The obvious fact that Weber's Law is disobeyed both for very high and for very low light intensities leads to the clearly apparent result that..the various greys at either end of Dr. Ostwald's scale are never even approximately equidistant. **1938** STEVENS & DAVIS *Hearing* iv. 149 We are not here concerned with the constancy of the Weber fraction $\Delta I/I$, which was *another* of Fechner's assumptions, but only with..the ability of an added just-noticeable difference to contribute always the same increment to the total subjective effect. **1952** I. J. HIRSH *Measurement of Hearing* vii. 194 We conclude that Weber's Law holds (for white noise) from about 20 to 100 db Sensation Level. **1970** *Jrnl. Gen. Psychol.* LXXXII. 38 The results of the present experiment suggest that the use of contrasting St[andard] and Co[mparison] vibrotactile stimuli will result in relatively small Weber ratios.

2. ***Weber-Fechner law*** [FECHNER] = *Weber's law* above; also, the related statement that the strength of a sensation is proportional to the logarithm of the stimulus causing it.

1891 A. D. WALLER *Introd. Human Physiol.* xv. 536 (*heading*) The Weber-Fechner law. **1968** PASSMORE & ROBSON *Compan. Med. Stud.* I. xxiv. 30/2 To increase the loudness by steps that seem equal to the listener the intensity of sound must be multiplied by approximately the same factor for each step (Weber-Fechner relation).

Weberian (wɪ'bɪərɪən), *a.*[1] [f. name of E. H. *Weber* (see WEBER[2]) + -IAN.] ***Weberian corpuscle*** or ***organ***, a tubular vesicle in the prostatic portion of the urethra. ***Weberian ossicles***, a chain of small bones between the ear and the air-bladder in certain fishes; ***Weberian apparatus***, the set of structures, including the ossicles, which connect the air-bladder with the ear.

1849-52 *Todd's Cycl. Anat.* IV. II. 1415/2 The Weberian organ or corpuscle. **1889** *Amer. Naturalist* May 427 Hypophthalmus possesses an air-bladder connected with the auditory organ by intervention of a Weberian apparatus, formed of parts of the anterior vertebræ. **1889** *Proc. Roy. Soc.* 20 June 309 The Air-bladder and Weberian Ossicles in the Siluridæ.

Weberian (veɪ'bɪərɪən), *a.*[2] [f. the name of Carl Maria von *Weber* (1786-1826), German composer + -IAN.] Of, pertaining to, or characteristic of Weber or his music.

1958 *Listener* 28 Aug. 321/3 Many of the typically Weberian passages in dotted notes. **1978** *Gramophone* June 56/2, I hope I have not led you to underestimate the quality of so much of the music—the Weberian horns at the start of No. 1.

Weberian (veɪ'bɪərɪən), *a.*[3] [f. the name of Max *Weber* (1864-1920), German sociologist and political economist + -IAN.] Of, pertaining to, or characteristic of Weber, his philosophy, or his writings.

1959 G. D. MITCHELL *Sociol.* 114 The importance of this Weberian analysis is that a system of stratification is seen to depend upon the economic character of society, the way prestige is distributed, and the kind of legal and political institutions it possesses. **1969** P. A. ROBINSON *Freudian Left* 6, I consider the Weberian ideal of a *wertfreien* science misguided. **1975** *Times Lit. Suppl.* 1 Aug. 880/5 This account of the transformation of Wolof war-leaders into bureaucrats, bringing Weberian theory to bear, is a new departure. **1979** L. LERNER *Love & Marriage* vi. 231, I shall use 'sublimation' essentially in its Weberian meaning.

Webernesque (veɪbə'nɛsk), *a.* [f. the name of Anton von *Webern* (1883-1945), Austrian composer + -ESQUE.] Characteristic of the music of Webern. So **'Webernish** *a.*, somewhat resembling the music of Webern.

1959 *Listener* 28 May 960/3 The ejaculatory, disjointed, Webernish texture. **1961** *Times* 13 Oct. 18/5 The instrumentation is carried out in characteristically Webernesque fashion. **1976** *Gramophone* Sept. 437/3 The surface is..rather Webernesque.

Weber number ('veɪbə(r), 'wɛbə(r)). *Physics.* Also **Weber's number.** [tr. G. *webersche zahl* (F. Eisner 1932, in Wien & Harms *Handb. d. Experimentalphysik* IV. IV. 225), f. the name of Moritz *Weber* (1871-1951), German naval engineer, who first formulated it in 1919.] A dimensionless quantity used in the study of surface tension, bubbles, and waves, usu. expressed as $\rho l v^2/\gamma$ or the reciprocal of this, where γ is the surface tension of the fluid, ρ its density, l the characteristic length, and v the velocity of the fluid or of waves in the fluid; also, the square root of either quantity.

1937 O'BRIEN & HICKOX *Appl. Fluid Mech.* v. 149 Generalized Representation of Weir Coefficients... The first three terms [in the coefficient of discharge] merely represent the geometrical similarity including the roughness. The other two are Weber's number and Reynolds' number. **1946** H. ROUSE *Elem. Mech. of Fluids* x. 322 The radical form of this ratio $W = V/\sqrt{(\sigma/\rho L)}$ is known as the Weber number. **1977** R. A. DUCKWORTH *Mech. of Fluids* vii. 149 In ship testing, the influence of surface tension forces, for which the Weber number, $(\sigma/\rho V^2 l)$, provides the criterion for dynamic stability, may be ignored because..such forces are negligible compared with the viscous and gravitational forces. **1979** A. L. LYDERSEN *Fluid Flow & Heat Transfer* ii. 39 Examples of force ratios are.. inertia forces/surface forces = ..$\rho LV^2/\gamma$ = We = Weber number. **1979** *Sci. Amer.* Aug. 170/3 When the beaker is made to create water sheets in the middle range of Weber numbers, the ridge sends out curved waves.

'web-foot. [See WEB *sb.* 8.]

1. A foot with webbed toes. Also, the condition of being web-footed.

1765 *Museum Rust.* IV. lxxv. 325 *note*, It was common to say a fenman was an amphibious creature; and that their children were born with web-feet. **1777** PENNANT *Brit. Zool.* IV. 5 This is among the species taken notice of by Aristotle on account of the broad feet, which, he says, assist them in swimming: as web-feet do the water-fowl. **1884** J. TAIT *Mind in Matter* (1892) 64 If it dive, it will generally have a hull-shaped body, short legs, and web-feet.

2. A bird or other animal having web-feet.
1895 *Funk's Stand. Dict.* **1911** WEBSTER.
3. a. A nickname for a dweller in the Fens. ?*Obs.* **b.** A native of the State of Oregon. So called on account of the moist climate.
1765 *Museum Rust.* IV. lxxv. 325, I would fain rouse up the spirits of some of my brother webfeet. [*Note.*] This is a contemptuous term given to fenmen. **1845** W. WHITMAN in *Amer. Speech* (1961) XXXVI. 297 Oregonese [are called] *Webfoots.* **1873** J. H. BEADLE *Undeveloped West* xxxv. 759 Everybody and everything we saw had the unmistakable 'Oregon look'. We were among the 'Web-feet' at last, and a comely race they are. **1875** *Chamb. Jrnl.* 13 Mar. 171/2 The inhabitants of Alabama are Lizards;..Oregon, Hard-cases or Web-feet.
c. An infantryman. *U.S. slang.*
1867 B. W. DUKE *Hist. Morgan's Cavalry* xiv. 400 When the 'webfeet' called us 'buttermilk rangers', we did not get angry with them. **1917** J. MORGAN *Recoll. Rebel Reefer* 210, I was only a poor 'webfoot'.

'web-ˌfooted, *a.* Having web-feet. Also *fig.* (in quots. 1945 and 1980, *Mil.*).
1681 GREW *Musæum* I. §iv. iii. 69 Web-footed Fowl or Palmipede's. **1745** P. THOMAS *Voy. S. Seas* 337 Flamingoes... The Legs are..Web-footed like a Goose. **1774** GOLDSM. *Nat. Hist.* III. 191 It [the capibara] is in a manner web-footed. **1818** KEATS *Endym.* IV. 245 Web-footed alligators. **1851** MAYHEW *Lond. Labour* (1861) II. 137/1 One of these men..was, it is said, web-footed, naturally, and partially web-fingered. **1910** *Encycl. Brit.* XI. 352/1 Platypus..is of aquatic habits, being web-footed.
fig. **1945** *Tee Emm* (Air Ministry) V. 49 We feel that the web-footed boys [i.e. Coastal Command] are not the only ones who may fall into the water out East. **1980** *Globe & Laurel* July/Aug. 226/1 The Small Raids Wing of the newly established Amphibious School based at Fort Cumberland and RMB Eastney, which also absorbed former web-footed units like RM Det 385.
Hence **'web-ˌfootedness** (*Cent. Dict.* 1891).

webless ('wɛblɪs), *a. rare.* [f. WEB *sb.* + -LESS.] Not furnished with a web.
1848 KINGSLEY *Saint's Trag.* II. v. [iv.], O'er still and webless looms The listless craftsmen through their elf-locks scowled.

Webley ('wɛblɪ). The proprietary name of various types of revolver and other small arms, etc., originally made by the firm of P. Webley and Son. Also *absol.*
1889 *Field* 4 May 618/1 After an exhaustive trial..the new Webley revolver..has been adopted by the English Government. **1897** *Sears, Roebuck Catal.* 586/2, 44 caliber, center fire, Webley cartridge. **1911** *Encycl. Brit.* XXI. 656/1 In the Webley the bolt is upon the standing breech and grips the extremity of the hinged barrel. **1920** *Trade Marks Jrnl.* 24 Mar. 567 Webley... Small-arms. Webley & Scott, Limited,..Birmingham; small arms manufacturers. **1923** *Official Gaz.* (U.S. Patent Office) 16 Jan. 502/2 Revolvers, automatic pistols, and other small arms. Webley & Scott Limited, Birmingham, England. **1937** S. SMITH *Good Time was had by All* 53 A Webley, service pattern, is a useful weapon. **1979** P. COSGRAVE *Three Colonels* vi. 137 Haddad was wearing a heavy Webley ostentatiously on his hip.

webster[1] ('wɛbstə(r)). *Obs.* exc. *Hist.* Forms: 2 **webbestre,** 4 **web(b)ester, webister,** 4–5 **webstere,** 5 **webstar,** 6 **wyebster,** 3– **webster;** *Sc.* 5–6 **wobstar,** 6–7 **wobster,** 6– **wabster.** [OE. *webbestre*, fem. of *webba* weaver, WEBBE: see -STER.] A weaver: **a.** as the designation of a woman.
c **1100** *Gloss.* in Wr.-Wülcker 188/11 *Textrix*, webbestre. *a* **1300** *Cursor M.* 1525 Scho was þe formest webster þat man findes o þat mister. **1375** *Durham Acc. Rolls* (Surtees) 330 Anota Milner, Webster. *c* **1475** *Pict. Voc.* in Wr.-Wülcker 795/8 *Hec textrix*, a webster.
b. extended, or applied *spec.*, to a male weaver.
1362 LANGL. *P. Pl.* A. Prol. 99 Wollene websteris [**1377** B. Prol. 219 Wollewebsteres, **1393** C. I. 222 Webbesters] and weueris of lynen. **1379** *Poll-tax W. Riding* in *Yorks. Archæol. Jrnl.* V. 14 Thomas Webester..Webester vj *d.* *Ibid.* 15 Johannes Clerke.., Webester vj *d.* **1382** WYCLIF *1 Sam.* xvii. 7 The shaft of his speer was as the beem of websters. *c* **1400** *Destr. Troy* 1587 Wrightes, websters, walkers of clothe. *c* **1440** *Promp. Parv.* 519/1 Webstar (or weware), *textor, textrix.* **1467** *Ord. Worcester* §17 in *Eng. Gilds* 383 Spynners, websters, dyers, shermen, and other laborers or artificers apperteynynge to the same [i.e. cloth-making]. **1525** in *Reg. Mag. Sig. Scot.* 1530–1, 219/2 The best and worthiest of the haile craft of the wobstaris within the burgh. **1535** LYNDESAY *Satyre* 4106 Find me ane Wobster that is leill, Or ane Walker that will nocht steill. **1573–80** TUSSER *Husb.* (1878) 32 Sell webster thy wull. **1607** TOPSELL *Four-f. Beasts* 626 The wooll of Istria and Liburnia, which if it were not for the spinning in Portugall, and the web-sters Art thereupon, it were no better then haire. *a* **1733** *Shetland Acts* 16 in *Proc. Soc. Ant. Scot.* (1892) XXVI. 199 That the webster's ell be 3 feet 4 inches, or 40 inches long, on which only unscoured cloth is measured. **1792** BURNS '*Willie Wastle dwelt on Tweed*' i, Willie was a wabster gude, Cou'd stown a clew wi' ony bodie. **1841** GEN. P. THOMPSON *Exerc.* (1842) VI. 12 Is it likely that it is only because the websters and hosiers do not set about it themselves? **1847** H. S. RIDDELL *Poems* 194 The wabsters weary at their looms, Maun still at them be thruming. **1892** STEVENSON *Catriona* xv, Tod was a wabster to his trade.
c. *attrib.*, as ***webster beam, loom.***
1334–5 *Leicester Borough Rec.* (1901) II. 17 Webstere bem. **1599** *Lanc. & Cheshire Wills* (Chetham Soc.) 152 Webster Lomes.
d. *appositive.*
a **1568** *Satir. Poems Reform.* xlviii. 43 A weid..Weill wrocht in the lwmis with wobster gwmis [see GOME[1]]. **1721** RAMSAY *Elegy on Patie Birnie* xii, A crishy Webster Loun. **1785** BURNS *Holy Fair* ix, An' there, a batch o' wabster lads, Blackguarding frae Kilmarnock. **1818** SCOTT *Rob Roy* xxvi. A puir wabster body. **1888** DOUGHTY *Arabia Deserta* I. 225 Good webster-wives weave in white borders made of their sheep's wool.

Webster[2] ('wɛbstə(r)). The name of Noah *Webster* (1758–1843), the American lexicographer, used *absol.* to designate his Dictionary (first published in 1828), and any of its later revisions and abridgements (now published by G. and C. Merriam Co., Springfield, Mass.).
1843 *Quincy* (Illinois) *Herald* 17 Mar. 4/1 (*heading*) Definitions not found in Webster. **1928** *Amer. Speech* IV. 90 We use *Webster* (in America) colloquially as synonymous with *dictionary.* **1950** [see OXFORD 2]. **1978** *Amer. Speech* LIII. 70 Many 'Websters' later, came the controversial dictionary edited by Philip B. Gove and published in 1961 by the G. and C. Merriam Company of Springfield, Massachusetts, to whom Webster's heirs had sold the rights to the dictionary in 1843.

Websterian (wɛb'stɪərɪən), *a.*[1] [f. the name of Noah *Webster* (see prec.) + -IAN.] Of, pertaining to, or characteristic of Webster's Dictionary (see prec.) or any of its later versions or abridgements.
1874 B. F. TAYLOR *World on Wheels* 28 Websterian 'probabilities' says that is not the derivation of 'scale' at all. **1897** *Bookman* Nov. 201 We are quite sure that if the English were to adopt the Websterian spelling, Professor Matthews would very, very soon experience a conservative reaction. **1935** A. C. BAUGH *Hist. Eng. Lang.* xi. 442 James Fenimore Cooper..was pronouncing..*beard* as *berd* or *baird* (another Websterian pronunciation). **1962** *New Yorker* 10 Mar. 156/2 Nearly all the books that come off the press..are edited and printed in accordance with Websterian usage. **1979** *Amer. Speech* LIV. 13 Thus was the battle joined between the traditional grammarians and those who might well be called the Websterian grammarians.

Web'sterian, *a.*[2] [f. the name of the English dramatist John *Webster* (1580–1625) + -IAN.] Of, pertaining to, or characteristic of Webster or his plays.
1928 *Observer* 12 Feb. 4 With the great Websterian passages there is mingled a great deal of melodramatic fustian. **1940** M. LOWRY *Let.* 27 July (1967) 32 It is 'original' if you fear for past Websterian, not to say Miltonian, minor lacks of ethics on my part. **1950** *Scrutiny* XVII. 152 The other (*The Insatiate Countess*) a rather Websterian account of a promiscuous noblewoman's destruction. **1971** *Guardian* 19 Jan. 8/5 The true Websterian frisson is achieved on an empty stage.

websterite[1] ('wɛbstəraɪt). *Min.* [Named in 1822 after T. *Webster*, who discovered it: see -ITE.] A synonym of ALUMINITE.
1823 H. J. BROOKE *Crystallogr.* 452. **1837** DANA *Min.* 450. **1855** J. PHILLIPS *Man. Geol.* 386.

websterite[2] ('wɛbstəraɪt). *Petrogr.* [f. *Webster*, name of a village in N. Carolina + -ITE[1].] An ultramafic intrusive igneous rock composed essentially of orthorhombic and monoclinic pyroxenes.
1890 G. H. WILLIAMS in *Amer. Geologist* VI. 44 The specimens obtained by Mr. Merrill from Webster are such admirable representatives of the bronzite-diopside rocks that the name Websterite is suggested..for them; and there seems to be no impropriety in extending this term over all the massive intrusives which are composed entirely of monoclinic and orthorhombic pyroxene. **1978** S. R. NOCKOLDS in S. R. Nockolds et al. *Petrol. for Students* xiii. 148 Pyroxenite with both ortho- and clino-pyroxene ('websterite') is the commonest variety, found both in connection with some great layered igneous bodies..and in small intrusions.

†**'webstery.** *Obs. rare.* [f. WEBSTER[1] + -Y.] Goods made by a webster; woven materials.
1588 PARKE tr. *Mendoza's Hist. China* 7 They do sell none of their silkes there by the yard, neither any other kinde of websterie,..but by the waight. *Ibid.* 368 There is also great store of flaxe, cotton, and other kinde of webstrie.

†**wecche,** *v. Obs.* Forms: 1 **weccan,** 3 **wecche,** 4 **wechche.** *Pa. t.* 3 **wæht(e, wehte,** 3–4 **weiȝt(t)e,** 4 **wight.** [OE. *weccan* = OHG. *wecchen* (mod.G. *wecken*), ON. *vekja*, Goth. (*us-*) *wakjan*, f. root **wak-*: see WAKE *v.*]
1. *trans.* To rouse from sleep. (Cf. AWECCHE *v.* 1.)
c **897** ÆLFRED *Gregory's Past. C.* lxiv. 461 Se kok ..ærðæmðe he crawan wille, hefð up his fiðru, & wecð hine selfne. *a* **900** *Crist* 889 (Gr.) Englas ælbeorhte on efen blawað byman on brehtme,..weccað of deaðe dryhtgumena bearn. *c* **1205** LAY. 798 Ohtliche heom slæð on & weccheð heom of slepa. *c* **1300** *St. Brandan* 446 That hi ne weiȝte noȝt the [sleeping] fisches, leste hi here schip breke. **13..** *K. Alis.* 2925 We weore aslepe, Darie us wight. **13..** *Seuyn Sag.* (W.) 1628 Thous [he] the king bigan to wechche, And saide, 'Sire, vp! vp! hit is dai!'
2. To stir up, excite (e.g. wind, fire, passion, strife). (Cf. AWECCHE *v.* 2.)
Beowulf 2046 Onginneð ȝeomormod ȝeongum cempan.. wiȝbealu weccean. *c* **900** *Bæda's Hist.* IV. iii. (1890) 268 Forþon Drihten lyfte ontyneð, windas weceð. *c* **1200** *Trin. Coll. Hom.* 137 Ne beo þu noht..wilful to wecchen lust þar to. *Ibid.* 161 [The devil] weccheð among hem flite and win. *c* **1205** LAY. 16216 þe wind wæht [*c* **1275** wehte] þat fur þæt hit wunderliche born.

wech(e, obs. ff. WATCH, WHICH, WITCH, WYCH.

wechesafe, obs. form of VOUCHSAFE.

Wechsler ('wɛkslə(r)). *Psychol.* The name of David *Wechsler* (b. 1896), American psychologist, used *attrib.* or as *adj.* in connection with various intelligence tests devised by him (and in use since 1939), esp. the ***Wechsler-Bellevue Intelligence Scale,*** the ***Wechsler Intelligence Scale for Children*** (WISC), and the ***Wechsler Adult Intelligence Scale*** (WAIS). Also *absol.*
1942 *Amer. Jrnl. Psychol.* LV. 608 The Wechsler-Bellevue Intelligence Scale, an individual scale adapted to ages 10–60 and consisting of 5 verbal and 5 performance-tests, with vocabulary-test as alternate. **1954** A. ANASTASI *Psychol. Testing* xii. 306 Two scales for measuring 'general intelligence', namely, the Wechsler-Bellevue Intelligence Scale and the Wechsler Intelligence Scale for Children. *Ibid.*, One of the primary objectives of the Wechsler-Bellevue is to provide an intelligence test suitable for adults. **1961** *New Scientist* 16 Mar. 665/3 Special psychological tests, including the well-known Wechsler Memory Scale, were employed to assess memory. **1970** *Jrnl. Gen. Psychol.* July 69 The tasks of the Wechsler..are not composed of stimuli all of the same degree of structuredness either. **1981** D. STATT *Dict. Human Behav.* 129 *Wechsler Adult Intelligence Scale*, one of the most widely used intelligence tests for adults, combining performance and verbal ability testing.

wecht, wechty, Sc. ff. WEIGHT, WEIGHTY.

weck, obs. form of WEAK *a.*, WICK.

weckid, -it, obs. forms of WICKED.

wed (wɛd), *sb. Obs.* exc. *dial.* Also 1, 4 **wedd,** 3–6 **wedde,** (5 **wede, weed**); 5–9 *Sc.* **wad,** (5 **vad**), 9 *Sc.* and *dial.* **wadd;** 7 **wade.** [Com. Teut.: OE. *wed(d* neut. = OFris. *wed* neut., pledge, covenant, OS. *weddi* neut., pledge (MLG. *wedde* pledge, wager, etc.), (M)Du. *wedde* fem., wages, OHG. *wetti* neut. (MHG. *wette, wet* neut., fem., pledge, wager, etc., mod.G. *wette* fem., wager), ON. *veð* neut., pledge (MSw. *väþ* neut., pledge, wager, Sw. *väd* neut., wager), Goth. *wadi* neut., earnest-money, pledge :— OTeut. **wadjo-m*, cogn. w. L. *vadem* (*vas*) masc., surety (whence *vadimōnium* bail), Lith. *wadúoti* to redeem a pledge. The OTeut. word was adopted in the Rom. langs.: see GAGE *sb.*[1], WAGE *sb.*]
1. A pledge, something deposited as security for a payment or the fulfilment of an obligation; sometimes of a person, a hostage.
a **1122** *O.E. Chron.* (Laud MS.) an. 1016, & heora freondscipe þær ȝefæstnodon, ȝe mid wedde ȝe mid aþe. *a* **1225** *Ancr. R.* 394 Ne telleð me him god feolawe þet leið his wed ine Giwerie uorto acwiten ut his fere? *a* **1300** *Cursor M.* 6798 If þat þou..O pur man tas wedd o clath Yeil[d] again þat clath..Ar sun ga dun þat ilk dai. *a* **1310** in Wright *Lyric P.* xxxix. 110 He hath hewe sum wher a burthen of brere, tharefore sum hay-ward hath taken ys wed. **1377** LANGL. *P. Pl.* B. v. 244, I lerned amonge Lumbardes and Iewes a lessoun..to legge a wedde and lese it. **1382** WYCLIF *Ezek.* xviii. 7 He shal ȝeelde the wed [Vulg. *pignus*] to the dettour. *c* **1389** *Eng. Gilds* (1870) 91 And qwo-so come after prime be smeten, he shal pay *jd*, or leye a wed. **1436** *E.E. Wills* (1882) 107 Item I wolle that the prioresse & the house of Chesthunt haue freely theire Weddys ayen withouten any mony payenge. *c* **1440** *Promp. Parv.* 519/1 Wedde, or thynge leyyd yn plegge, *vadium, pignus.* *c* **1450** *Godstow Reg.* 155 And he nother his heires shold never take wedde of the forsaide Anneys or of her assignes. **1458** *Forman's Monumt. Christ's Hosp., Abingdon* 70 For now is Culham hithe i com to an ende,..Few folke there were coude that wey wende, But they waged a wed or payed of her purse. *a* **1500** in *Arnolde's Chron.* (1811) 18 Yf any man of our landis..take any tolle or custume of the citezens of London other wyse than they shulde the Sherefs of London shall take wed of hem at London. **1560** ROLLAND *Seven Sages* Prol. iii, My buke to borrow greitlie scho did Inquyre, Ane wed thairfoir scho said scho wald doun lay. **1609** SKENE *Reg. Maj.* 49 Some things are borrowed and lent, be giving and receaving of ane wad. *Ibid., Stat. Alex. II*, 18 And gif he may not giue wades ..he sall remaine as wade: aye and quhill he enter the pledges, quhilkis he promised. **1776** *Herd's Sc. Songs* II. Gloss., *Wad* or *wed*, pledge, wager, pawn. **1818** SCOTT *Rob Roy* xxxiv, I thought the chield Morris looked devilish queer when I determined he should remain a wad, or hostage, for my safe back-coming.
b. *fig.*, or in reference to staking one's life (cf. 2 c, 4).
1340 *Ayenb.* 102 þis adopcion is ase weddes ase zayþ saynte paul huerby we byþ zikere þet we ssolle habbe þe eritage of oure uader. [Cf. Vulgate *pignus*, Eph. i. 14.] **1362** LANGL. *P. Pl.* A. III. 195 Hedde I be Marchal of his Men.. I durste haue I-leid my lyf, and no lasse wed, He hedde beo lord of þat lond. *c* **1375** *Sc. Leg. Saints* xviii. (*Egipciane*) 624 For oure sawete one quhilk [tree] vas he put, & his blud schede, & for ws put nane vthir wed. **1399** LANGL. *Rich. Redeles* III. 309 And ho so grucche or grone, aȝeins her grette willes, May lese her lyff lyghtly, and no lesse weddis. *c* **1400** *Beryn* 2984 No les wed þen lyvis! *c* **1530** *Pol. Rel. & L. Poems* (1903) 59 He that lawith at a mynstrels worde, gevith to hym a wedde.
†**c.** A nuptial pledge or promise. *Obs.*
c **1375** *Sc. Leg. Saints* xli. (*Agnes*) 400 Here-of in vitnesyng remanis ay þe forsad ryng one þe fyngire of þat ymag of vad of weding in-to vag. **1390** GOWER *Conf.* I. 94 Bot ferst, er thou be sped, Thou schalt me leve such a wedd,

That I wol have thi trowthe in honde That thou schalt be myn housebonde.

†**2.** In various phrases the sb. assumes the contextual sense: The condition of being pawned, mortgaged, given up as a hostage, etc. (Cf. PLEDGE *sb.* 6.) *Obs.*

a. *to, in wed*: as a pledge or hostage. *in wed of*: as security for (a payment, etc.).

For *dead wed* (= MORTGAGE) see DEAD *a.*

Beowulf 2998 Ond þa Iofore forȝeaf anȝan dohtor, hamweorðunge, hyldo to wedde. *c* **1250** *Gen. & Ex.* 2198 Ðis symeon bi-lef ðor in bond, To wedde under Iosepes hond. *c* **1440** *Gesta Rom.* xxiv. 88 But if þou pay now, I shal holde thi wif to wed, tyll tyme þat I be paied fully my salary. **1460** *Extracts Aberd. Reg.* (1844) I. 405 That na induellande of this burgh..tak in wed ony gudis that Wat Cutlaris wife bryngis for ony penyworthis oythir than dry siluer. **1488** *Acc. Ld. High Treas. Scot.* I. 98 [13*l.* 10*s.*] quhilk he had gevin away at the Kingis command, and had the Thesauraris signet in wed tharof. **1530** *Burgh Rec. Edin.* (1871) II. 28 Item, that na maner of parsonis man nor woman tak ony claith in wedd fra vtheris. **1561** *Burgh Rec. Stirling* (1887) 79 Ane chenyie of gold..quhilk the Lady Caterene..deliverit him in wed of the sowme of ane hundreth and tuenty merkis. **1596** DALRYMPLE tr. *Leslie's Hist. Scot.* (S.T.S.) I. 333 The Scotis sulde gyue Cumbirland,..in wedd of payment of the hail soume.

†**b.** *to set, put, lay to* or *in wed, to betake on wed*: to pawn, pledge (valuables), to deposit (money) as security; to mortgage (land); to give up (a person) as a hostage. *to take out of wed*: to redeem (something pledged). *Obs.*

?*a* **900** *Ælfred's Dooms* xxxvi, Ȝif mon..hræȝl..to wedde selle. *c* **1205** LAY. 25172 Mi lond ich wulle sette to wedde for seoluere. **1297** R. GLOUC. (Rolls) 8083 He..leide willam is broþer to wedde normandye & borowede þer uppe of him an hondred þousend marc. **1382** WYCLIF *Amos* ii. 8 And on clothis leyde to wedde thei eeten bysidis eche auter. **1387** TREVISA *Higden* V. 31 Hym was levere legge to wedde [L. *distrahere*] his vessel of silver and of gold..þan greve provinces and londes and þe senatoures. *c* **1412** HOCCLEVE *De Reg. Princ.* 4904 And yf he stire you and meeve Your jewels ley in wedde, certein he Lovethe your estate and prosperitee. **1430** *Reg. Mag. Sig. Scot.* 38/2 Wyt yhe me in my strenyeand myster til haf put in wede til my lowyt..frend Andro Osteler..al the landis of [etc.]. **1450** *Rolls of Parlt.* V. 205/2 His plate and other goodes sold, and in wed layed. *c* **1450** *Merchant & Son* 162 in Hazl. *E.P.P.* I. 143 Fadur, y schall do my parte to helpe yow owt of peyne, Yf y schulde leye my selfe to wedd, or that ye come ageyne. **1462** in *Spalding Club Misc.* V. 22 His tua sponys..at wer laid in wede to the said Thome. **1483** *Cath. Angl.* 412/1 To take owt of Wedde, *depignerare*. *c* **1500** *Lyt. Geste Robyn Hode* 212 My londes bethe sette to wedde..To a ryche abbot..Of saynt Mary abbay. **1536** BELLENDEN *Cron. Scot.* (1821) I. p. lvii, He that sald his swerd, or laid it to wed, was degradit of auctorite, and banist, as unworthy creature, out of thair cumpany. **1567** in *6th Rep. Hist. MSS. Comm.* 643/2 Layd in wed to Maister Robert Rychartson..in pledge of fywe thousand pundis thir jowellis after following. **1573** in *Inventaires de la Royne Descosse* (Bannatyne Club) Pref. p. cliii, All that was lefte of the juelles unlayde to wed. **1597** J. S. *Cert. MS. Poems, Way to Thrift* F 6, And lay to wed both pot and panne When the fire clean is blowne out. **17..** *Druken Wife o' Gallowa* v. in Herd *Sc. Songs* (1776) II. 39 My Sunday's coat she has laid it a wad.

†**c.** *fig.* Often, *to lay one's life, head, to wed*, used to confirm or guarantee an assertion or an undertaking (cf. 4). *Obs.*

971 *Blickl. Hom.* 131 Þæs Halȝan Gastes, se wæs of heofenum onsended..to wedde þæs heofonlican eþles. *a* **1300** *Cursor M.* 16670 þare he gaf his suete flesche for ur ranscun in wedd. **1338** R. BRUNNE *Chron.* (1725) 246 Sir Adam of Stretton fulle hard was he led, Nouht without encheson, I lay my gloue to wed. **1377** LANGL. *P. Pl.* B. XVIII. 31 Lyf seyth þat he likth and leyth his lif to wedde, þat [etc.]. *c* **1380** WYCLIF *Sel. Wks.* III. 423 Herby þei myght bye mennis synnes, and laye hor soules in wedde, þat oþer mennis soules shulde be saved. **1390** GOWER *Conf.* I. 95 And thus his trowthe he leith to wedde. *c* **1400** MAUNDEV. (1839) xv. 167 Thei..profreden here hedes to wedde, but ȝif it wolde falle as thei seyden. *c* **1400** *Gosp. Nicodemus* (Galba) 100 þaire carping þare no thing þou knew, We lay oure heuiddes in wed. **1430–40** LYDG. *Bochas* VIII. xxiv. (1554) 194 b, The sweord of Arthur he durst not abide, Lest he should lay his lyfe to wed. *c* **1460** *Towneley Myst.* xxviii. 56, I dar lay my heede to wed, Or that we go vntill oure bed That we shall here anothere. *c* **1470** HENRY *Wallace* IV. 633 3it felle Sothron left the lyff to wed. *Ibid.* IX. 1209 My hed to wed, Lochlewyn he past to se. *a* **1500** in *Pol. Rel. & L. Poems* (1903) 247 A leche hath layd hys hed to wed To make a plaster that wolde me please. *c* **1530** *Hickscorner* C j, I warraunt you she wyll neuer saye you naye My lyfe I dare laye to wedde.

†**d.** *to lie* or *be to* or *in wed*: to be in pawn. *lit.* and *fig. Obs.*

c **1386** CHAUCER *Knt.'s T.* 360 Lat hym be war, his nekke lith to wedde. **1464** *Paston Lett.* II. 146 For in London lyth to wedde many ryche jowells of ouris. **1497** *Acc. Ld. High Treas. Scot.* I. 345 Item..giffin to the Prothonotar, to quit out the Duke of Yorkis broune hors that lay in wed in the toune, xiiij lib. *c* **1518** SKELTON *Magnyf.* 2168 He may rynse a pycher, for his plate is to wed. **1556–7** *Rec. Inverness* (New Spalding Club) I. 5 The forsaid pece of land wes lyand to hyme in wed of ten pundis.

†**3.** Something taken or left that serves as evidence. *Obs.*

a **1300** *Cursor M.* 4402 Bot for mi cri ful suith he [Joseph] fled And left wit me a taken wedd [*Gött.* a tokin in wedd]; His mantel es bi-left wit me, þat ilk man þee sothe mai see. *Ibid.* 7706 Fra þe kings aun bedd þus he [*sc.* David] broght a priue wedd.

4. A stake in a game or wager. Also *fig.* †*to lay wed*: to wager (cf. 2 c).

c **1320** *Sir Tristr.* 320 Now boþe her wedde lys, And play þai biginne. *c* **1375** *Sc. Leg. Saints* i. (*Petrus*) 488 Lat Symone one fer stand fra þe bede, And ȝe sal se, I lay wede, þe fendis craft sone onhyde. **1540** *St. Papers Hen. VIII* (1836) V. 178 He harde the Kynge say..that He trestyd to gett that proffett that never Kynge of Scottes had, and He shulde other have yt, or yt shulde coste Hym the best wed He had to leysse. **1665** BRATHWAIT *Comm. Two Tales* 166 It is a dear wade, when your Life lies upon last Stake. **1670** BLOUNT *Glossogr.* (ed. 3), *Wed*, a gage or pawn; a word still retained in the Country sport, called *Pray my Lord a course in your park*. **1721** J. KELLY *Sc. Prov.* 19 A Wad is a Fool's Argument. Spoken when, after hot disputing, we offer to lay a Wager that we are in the Right. **1802** SIBBALD *Chron. Sc. P.* IV. Gloss., *Wadds*, a youthful amusement, wherein much use is made of pledges. **1808** JAMIESON, *Wadds*... In this game, the players being equally divided..each lays down one or more *wads* or pledges at that extremity where the party, to which he belongs, chuse their station. A boundary being fixed at an equal distance from the extremities, the object is to carry off the *wads* from the one of these to the other.

†**5.** A gage of battle. *Obs.*

c **1330** R. BRUNNE *Chron. Wace* (Rolls) 8404 Tak ȝe non hede of þeyr grete host, ffor wel ȝe wot þei ar bot bost,..ffor þem our wed schal nought be leued. *c* **1435** in Kingsford *Chron. London* (1905) 54 'This shull I preve with my body, and se here my wedde': and threwe fforth his hode.

†**6.** *Comb.* (all *Obs.*): **wed-bed**, the marriage bed; **wedbedrip** *Law*, some kind of BEDRIP (the force of *wed-* is uncertain); **wed-breach**, breach of covenant (*OE.*), adultery; **wed-break** [as if OE. **wedbreca*], an adulterer; **wed-brother** [cf. ON. *veðbróðir*], a sworn brother; **wed-fee**, a wager, the prize in a contest; **wed-fere**, a spouse; **wed-keeper**, a stakeholder; **wedman**, a married man; *pl.* married people; **wed-shooting** (Sc. *wad-*), shooting for a prize; **wed-spite** *nonce-wd.* = SPITE-WED.

In the later instances referring to marriage prob. directly associated with WED *v.*

a **1650** *Old Robin* 9 in *Percy Fol. MS.* I. 235 They had not in their *wed bed laid, scarcely were both on sleepe, but vpp shee rose. **1798** W. TAYLOR in *Monthly Mag.* V. 367 Those priests the wed-bed who renounce. *c* **1325** in Kennett *Par. Antiq.* (1818) I. 575 Et debet unam *Wedbedrip pro voluntate dominæ. *c* **1020** WULFSTAN *Hom.* xxxiii. (1883) 164 Eac syndan wide..þurh aðbrycas and ðurh *wed-brycas and ðurh mistlice leasunga forloren and forloȝen. **1638** W. LISLE *Heliodorus* II. 29 This crime of wed-breach. *a* **1300** *E.E. Psalter* xlix. 18 If..with *wedbrek [Vulg. *cum adulteris*] þi dele þou sete. *c* **1100** *O.E. Chron.* (MS. D) an. 1016, Coman beȝen þa cyningas to gædre..& wurdon feolaȝan & *wed broðra. *c* **1205** LAY. 14469 Send after mine sune Octa & æfter..Ebissa his wed-broðer. *c* **1300** *K. Horn* (Laud MS.) 295 He tok wit him anoþer þat was hornes wed broþer. *c* **1330** *Florice & Bl.* (Abbotsf. Club) 163 We beth wed brethren and trewthe iplight. *c* **1400** *Brut* (1906) 120 O þow false traitoure! haste þow my trewe wed-broþer slayn for cause of me? *c* **1420** *Avow. Arth.* x, Butte carpe we now of ther othir thre, How thay preuyd hor *wedde-fee. **1504–5** *Acc. Ld. High Treas. Scot.* III. 128 Item, to Dande Doule, that the King tynt on ane wedfee, xiiij s. *a* **1600** MONTGOMERIE *Devot. Poems* iii. 7 Sleep na mair in sleuth and sin, Bot..richtly rin That hevinly wedfie for to win Vhilk he prepairs for his. **1620** in A. Maxwell *Hist. Old Dundee* (1884) 408 [He] put in the hands of Thomas Scot..twa double-angels of gold upon ane woodfie betwix himself and Alexander Hering. **1637** RUTHERFORD *Let. to Alex. Gordon* 16 June, It is folly then for men to say, this is not Christ's plea, he will lose the wed-fee, men are like to beguile him: that were indeed a strange play. **13..** *Sir Beues* (A) 3168, I trowe, he is nouȝt now here, þat schel be me *wedde-fere! **1591** R. BRUCE *Serm. Edin.* C 4 b, For as to this conscience, it is a faithfull *wed-keeper: the gages that it receiveth, it randeris. *c* **1460** *Towneley Myst.* iii. 400 Me thynk my hert ryfis,..To se sich stryfis *wedmen emong. *Ibid.* xiii. 65 We sely wedmen dre mekyll wo. *c* **1475** *Pict. Voc.* in Wr.-Wülcker 806/22 *Hic sponsus*, a wedman. **1792** *Statist. Acc. Scot.* II. 509 Many amuse themselves..with shooting for prizes, called here *wad-shooting. *c* **1560** SIR T. SMITH in Strype *Life* (1698) App. 24 You may well be called Mr. Agamus or Misogamus, Surnamed in right English, *Wedspite, or Spitewed. For I never heard Man speak so despitefully against Wedding and Marriage of the Queens Majesty in my Life.

wed (wɛd), *v.* Inflected **wedded** (also **wed**), **wedding**. Forms: 1 **weddian**, 2–3 **weddenn**, 3–4 **wedden**, **weddi**, **-y**, 3–5 **wedd**, (4 **weed**, 5 **weede**, **wid**, **weddon**), 3–6 **wedde**, 8–9 *Sc.* **wad**, 4– **wed**. [Com. Teut.: OE. *weddian* corresponds to OFris. *weddia*, MLG. *wedden*, OHG. *wettôn* (MHG., mod.G. *wetten*), to pledge, wager, ON. *veðja* to pledge, Goth. *ga-wadjōn* to espouse (ἁρμόζεσθαι):—OTeut. **wadjōjan*, f. **wadjo-m* WED *sb.*

The form *wed* in the pa. t. is now only dialectal; in the pa. pple. it is common *dial.* but otherwise rare exc. in poetry.]

†**1.** *intr.* To engage, covenant (to do something). Only OE. (Const. *genitive* or *to* with gerundial inf.)

a **1000** *Laws Æthelstan* §23 (Liebermann) Ȝif hwa ordales weddiȝe, ðonne cume he [etc.]. *c* **1000** *Ags. Gosp.* Luke xxii. 5 And hiȝ..him weddedon feoh to syllenne.

2. *trans.* To wager, stake (e.g. money, one's life, one's head). *Obs.* exc. *Sc.* and *north.*

1362 LANGL. *P. Pl.* A. IV. 129 And ȝif þou worchest hit in wit Ich wedde boþe myn Eres, þat lawe schal ben a laborer. **1393** *Ibid.* C. III. 36 My lyf ich dar wedde, He shal lese for hure loue a lappe of trewe charite. *c* **1430** *Chev. Assigne* 27 & þat dare I my hedde wedde. **1560** *Peebles Burgh Rec.* (1872) 262 Stene Robesone weddit ten merkis of money aganes the said tar barrell that scho suld nocht mary the said king of Swane. *c* **1600** MONTGOMERIE *Sonn.* xlvi. 8 Shute on; lat sie vho first my wedfie wins; For I will wed ane apple and a nute. **1786** BURNS *Earnest Cry & Prayer* xv, Or faith! I'll wad my new pleugh-pettle, Ye'll see't or lang. **1818** SCOTT *Hrt. Midl.* xxxvi, I'll wad ye a plack, as we say in the north, that you get the pardon from the king. **1843** in T. Doubleday *Coquet-Dale Fishing Songs* (1852) 110 I'se wad a pund, when night comes round, That, creel for creel, we bang them a'! **1876** *Whitby Gloss.*, *Wad*, to pledge; to bet. **1894** A. REID *Sangs o' the Heatherland* 54 I'll wad that sune our neebors' heids Will doors and windocks thrang.

3. To marry. (Common in dialects; otherwise only *literary*.) **a.** *trans.* Originally, to make (a woman) one's wife by the giving of a pledge or earnest. More fully, †*to wed* (a woman) *to wife, to* or *unto his wife*. Hence, of a person of either sex: To take in marriage; to become the husband or wife of (a person) by participating in a prescribed ceremony or formal act.

a **1000** *Laws Edmund, Be wifmannes beweddunge* §1 (Liebermann) Ȝif man mædan oððe wif weddian wille, & hit swa hire & freondan ȝeliciȝe, [etc.]. *Ibid.* §6 Ȝif hy þonne ælces þinges sammæle beon, ðonne fon maȝas to & weddian heora maȝan to wife. *c* **1205** LAY. 22243 þis maiden he gon wedde and nom heo to his bedde. *c* **1250** *Gen. & Ex.* 1090 Two ðor werren quam him ðoȝte ear To wedden his two doȝtres ðear; Loth hem warnede. *c* **1275** LAY. 4500 A king of Britayne hadde hire i-wedded [*c* 1205 biwedded]. **13..** *E.E. Allit. P.* A. 772 Quat-kyn þyng may be þat lambe, þat þe wolde wedde vnto hys vyf? *c* **1380** *Sir Ferumb.* 1422 Wolde he be my worldly make & weddy me to wyue. *Ibid.* 2012, & she hym wedede after þan þat was hure fader fo. *c* **1400** MAUNDEV. (Roxb.) xv. 70 þe lady had mykill sorow þat scho had wedded him. *c* **1475** *Rauf Coilȝear* 925 Wed ane worthie to wyfe. **1485** *Plumpton Corr.* (Camden) 48 My lord Schanchler publyshed in the Parlament house the same day, that the Kings gud grace shall weede my lady Elizabeth. *a* **1533** BERNERS *Huon* lxii. 216, I wyll wed her to my wyfe. **1548–9** *Bk. Com. Prayer, Matrimony* 14 With thys ring I thee wed. **1552** HULOET, Wedde, *denubo*, for the woman; *desponso*, for the man. **1599** SHAKS. *Much Ado* III. ii. 118 If you loue her, then to morrow wed her. *a* **1663** KILLIGREW *Parson's Wedd.* IV. i. (1664) 124 *Pars.* If she be my wife Sir? I have wedded her and Bedded her, what other Ceremonies would you have? **1794** BURNS *Weary Pund o' Tow* iv, And 'or I wad anither jad, I'll wallop in a tow. **1816** J. WILSON *City of Plague* I. iv. 248 The husband, now no longer tied May wed a new and blushing bride. **1856** AYTOUN *Bothwell* I. xxiv, I wed A trembling, sickly, shrewish dame, And put her from my bed. **1873** BLACK *Pr. Thule* ix. 133 To think that your aunt would forbid your wedding a King's daughter!

fig. *c* **1380** WYCLIF *Sel. Wks.* III. 339 Cristis Chirche is his Spouse... And for he it fro Cristene men to graunte þat Crist haþ weddid þe fend. *c* **1450** *Godstow Reg.* 15 O true valeyntyne is oure lord to me... With his blode, Seynt dauid! he did me wedde. **1593** SHAKS. *Rich. II*, v. i. 94 Come, come, in wooing Sorrow let's be briefe, Since wedding it, there is such length in Griefe. **1667** MILTON *P.L.* v. 216 They led the Vine To wed her Elm. **1670** DRYDEN *2nd Pt. Conq. Granada* III. (1672) 113 In gaining him, I gain that Fortune too Which he has Wedded, and which I but Wooe. **1781** COWPER *Retirem.* 229 As woodbine weds the plant within her reach.

†**b.** Phrase. *to wed* (*a*) *wife*: to get married.

1297 R. GLOUC. (Rolls) 6798 Me sede þe king þat he moste nede wede wif. *a* **1300** *Cursor M.* 3216 Abraham wald in his lijf þat ysaac had wedded a wijf. *c* **1325** *Lai le Freine* 248 Than was ther..A riche knight..yong, and jolie; And had nought yete y-wedded wiue. **1377** LANGL. *P. Pl.* B. x. 149 He hath wedded a wyf with-inne this syx monethes. **1460** CAPGRAVE *Chron.* (Rolls) 139 The fader of Gefrey Plauntgenet wedded a wyf only for beute. **1542** UDALL *Erasm. Apoph.* 124 b, To one demaundyng when best season wer to wedde a wife.

4. To bind (the contracting parties) in wedlock; to conduct the marriage ceremony for (a man and woman); also *absol.*

1... *Rule of Chrodegang* (Napier) 81 Brydguman & bryde mid ȝebedum & mid ofringum mæssepreost sceal bletsian & weddian hi & betæcan hi be laȝum. *c* **1440** *Jacob's Well* 21 We schewyn acursyd..alle preestys þat..weddyn ony oþere but here owyn parysschenys wyth-oute leve, or weddyn wythoute þe banys askyd. *c* **1450** *Godstow Reg.* 1 Alle men of religion þat howselith, or weddith, or anelith any man or woman, with-out leve. *c* **1450** *Contin. Brut* 425 The Erchebisshop of Caunturburi..weddid hem togederis there by ordynaunce of God and holy chirche. *c* **1533** BERNERS *Huon* lxii. 214 How Huon..went to Rome to the pope, who weddyd togyther Huon and the fayr Esclaramonde. **1546** *Yorks. Chantry Surv.* (Surtees) 228 The sayd incumbent shuld..burye, wedde, and christen wythin the sayd chappell. **1876** MISS BROUGHTON *Joan* I. xxxii, The *Helmsley Courier* devotes three columns to the describing of ..how they were clad, who wed them, [etc.].

b. To give (a woman) in marriage; to cause to be married.

c **1374** CHAUCER *Troylus* v. 863 And whi here fader tarieth so longe To wedden here vn-to som worthi wight. *c* **1375** *Sc. Leg. Saints* vi. (*Thomas*) 47 þe kinge of þat cunctre of nev his douchtir vedit had. **1843** J. S. KNOWLES *Secretary* II. i. 21 My father cannot wed me 'gainst my will.

5. *pass.* To be joined in wedlock; to be married †*with*, †*unto*, *to* (a husband or wife); also, to be joined together as husband and wife.

c **1200** ORMIN 1942 & ȝuw birrþ witenn þatt ȝho wass Weddedd þurrh Godess wille Wiþþ an weppmann off hire kinn. *Ibid.* 1990 & forrþi wass ȝho till Josæp Wiþþ Godess laȝhe weddedd. *a* **1225** *Ancr. R.* 394 Auh þauh heo were iwedded him heo muhte i-wurðen so unwrest, [etc.]. *c* **1300** *Havelok* 1127 To-mo[r]we ȝe sholen ben weddeth, And, maugre þin, to-gidere beddeth. **138.** WYCLIF *Serm.* Sel. Wks. I. 334 She lyvede sevene ȝeer wiþ hir hosebonde þat was weddid wiþ hir fro her maidenhod. *a* **1450** *Knt. de la Tour* xlvii–xlix. 66 After the knight was wedded to another wiff, and he and the secounde wiff leued togedre .v. yere. **1529** FRITH *Antithesis* 96 b, The Pope sayeth.., my prestes also shall not be wedded. **1590** SHAKS. *Com. Err.* I. i. 37 In Siracusa was I borne, and wedde Vnto a woman, happy but for me. **1610** HOLLAND *Camden's Brit.* 231 Cecilie..was wedded to Thomas Greie. **1667** MILTON *P.L.* IX. 828 And Adam, wedded to another Eve, Shall live with her enjoying,

I extinct. **1673** J. W[ADE] *Vinegar & Mustard* (1873) 21 Before that ever we were wed. **1819** SCOTT *Ivanhoe* xxiv, When I returned..I found her wedded to a Gascon squire. **1874** GREEN *Short Hist.* iv. §1. 162 Eleanor the daughter of Simon of Montfort..was wedded to him [Llewelyn] at the English court.

fig. c **1374** CHAUCER *Anel. & Arc.* 131 Hir hart was to him weddid with a Ringe. *a* **1400** *Minor Poems fr. Vernon MS.* xl. 253 Ihesu, my soule is weddet to þe.

6. *intr.* (†also *refl.*). To enter into the matrimonial state; to take a wife or husband; to contract matrimony. Const. †*to*, *with*.

a **1225** *Ancr. R.* 368 Nolde him liken betere þen þauh me seide him þet heo gleowede & gomede, & wedde mid oðer men, & liuede in delices? *c* **1393** CHAUCER *Marriage* 18 Bet ys to wedde than brenne in worse wise. **1483** CAXTON *Golden Leg.* 170/1 Aurelyan..came to domycelle for to wedde and accomplissh the maryage by force ageynst hir wyll. **1530** PALSGR. 778/2 There be seasons forbydden to wedde in. **1562** J. HEYWOOD *Prov. & Epigr.* (1867) 132 Who wedth ere he be wise, shall die ere he thriue. **1592** KYD *Murther. I. Brewen* Wks. (1901) 292 'But if I were so minded' (quoth he), 'I would be twice aduised how I did wed with such a strumpet as thy selfe'. **1596** SHAKS. *Tam. Shrew* III. ii. 17 Hee'll wooe a thousand,..Yet neuer meanes to wed where he hath woo'd. **1619** J. DYKE *Counterpoyson* (1620) 21 And yet how many sticke not to wed to Canaanites! **1721** *Lett. fr. Mist's Jrnl.* (1722) II. 248 A Country Fellow had the Misfortune to wed with one of the Godly. **1781** COWPER *Table-T.* 554 As if the poet, purposing to wed, Should carve himself a wife in gingerbread. **1807** CRABBE *Par. Reg.* I. 434 Yet..there were times of joy, (The day they wed, the christening of the boy). *a* **1834** COLERIDGE in *Lit. Rem.* (1839) IV. 59 Alas! alas! this is the misery of it, that so many wed and so few are Christianly married! **1859** TENNYSON *Marr. Geraint* 227 And may you..live to wed with her whom first you love. **1884** H. SPENCER in *Contemp. Rev.* Feb. 155 Dissenters..were made free to wed by a purely civil rite.

fig. a **1225** *Leg. Kath.* 1517 He haueð iweddet him to mi meiðhad mit te ring of rihte bileaue. **1621** HEYLIN *Microcosmus* 243 [The Thames] flieth through Berks, Buck: Middlesex, Surrey, Kent, and Essex; and so weddeth himself with the Kentish Medway.

7. *trans.* To unite as in marriage. **a.** To attach (a person, his thoughts, etc.) indissolubly by affection *to* something. Chiefly in *passive*, to be obstinately attached *to* (an opinion, one's own will, a habit, a faction, etc.). Also (rarely) *refl.*, to addict or devote oneself *to* a party.

c **1397** CHAUCER *Lack Stedf.* 28 (MS. Cotton) O prince.. Drede god..And wed thi folk ayen to stedfastnesse. **1421** 26 *Pol. Poems* xviii. 6 Swete þouȝt in deuocion, Is weddid to chastite. **1542** UDALL *Erasm. Apoph.* 279 b, This Pompeius ..wedded hymselfe wholly to the faccion of Sylla. *a* **1548** HALL *Chron., Hen. VIII* 181 b, The kyng perceived & knewe well, that the quene was wedded to her awne opinion. **1562** J. HEYWOOD *Prov. & Epigr.* L ij b, I was wedded vnto my wyll. **1575** FLEMING *Virg. Bucol.* To Indifferent Rdr., The Bucolikes of Virgil..I haue translated into the Englishe tongue, wedding my selfe (as it were) to yᵉ vulgar and common phrase of speach. **1614** RALEGH *Hist. World* III. i. §5. 9 It highly commends his diligence and iudgement, that he was not so wedded to any author, as affected with the loue of truth. **1669** STURMY *Mariner's Mag.* VII. xxxi. 47 They are so wedded to superstition, that some adore the Devil. **1703** R. NEVE *City & C. Purchaser* 45 Nations..are very apt to be wedded to their own Ways and Methods. **1707** *Curios. in Husb. & Gard.* 20 The frivolous Cares that wed you to the Town. **1712** ARBUTHNOT *John Bull* IV. vi, Your Honour has it in your power to wed me still closer to your interest! *c* **1750** SHENSTONE *Love & Hon.* 88 The love That weds each bosom to its native soil. **1800** CAMPBELL *On leaving a Scene in Bavaria* xvii, Then wed thee to an exile's lot. **1866** TROLLOPE *Claverings* iii, He was not wedded to the joys of his college hall, or the college common room. **1887** COLVIN *Keats* ii. 34 Ready to entertain..any set of ideas.., he could never wed himself to any as representing ultimate truth. **1889** MRS. E. KENNARD *Landing a Prize* viii, You have been wedded to your comforts all your life. **1913** WOODROW WILSON *New Freedom* vi. 119 There are those, of course, who are wedded to the old ways.

†**b.** To unite by liking or custom *with*. *Obs.*

c **1380** WYCLIF *Sel. Wks.* III. 364 And errour in weiyng of þis love makiþ many fals weddingis; as men ben weddid wiþ þer habitis, and þer custumes, and þer singular maners, as ȝif þei weren Cristis comaundementis.

†**c.** To commit or pledge (a person) irrevocably *to* a course of action. *Obs.*

1578 H. WOTTON *Courtlie Controv.* 251 Hauing maried a woman which did but dishonour the countrey, and had wedded him vnto a war so daungerous, as [etc.].

d. To join or couple (a thing) intimately *with* or *to* something else; to associate closely *together*.

1818 KEATS *Endym.* II. 408 Above his head, Four lily stalks did their white honours wed To make a coronal. **1839** HOOD *Storm at Hastings* x, Whilst we were panting with the sultry weather, And hardly cared to wed two words together. **1851** WESTCOTT *Introd. Study Gospels* i. (1860) 78 The LXX. wedded Greek language to Hebrew thought. **1887** SAINTSBURY *Hist. Elizab. Lit.* ii. (1890) 46 The *Ecclesiastical Polity* remains a book in which matter and manner are wedded as in few other books of the same kind. **1891** *Lindley's New Holidays in Essex* 38 There is an excellent thing locally wedded with Blackwater boating. It is sausages.

†**8.** To espouse, adopt (a cause, a course of conduct, a custom, etc.). *Obs.*

1626 T. H[AWKINS] tr. *Caussin's Holy Crt.* 4 Men, who willingly wed the manners, and affections of those on whom they see theyr fortunes depend. **1647** CLARENDON *Hist. Reb.* I. §49 And though..most of the principal men of the House of Commons were again elected to serve in this Parliament, yet they were far from wedding the war. *Ibid.* II. §57 Most of the King's Privy Council..now as frankly wedded that interest as any of the leaders. **1742** YOUNG *Nt. Th.* I. 51 O lead my mind,..and fix my firm resolve Wisdom to wed. **1837** CARLYLE *Fr. Rev.* II. I. ii, Or, in milder language, They have *wedded* their delusions: fire nor steel, nor any sharpness of Experience, shall sever the bond.

wed (wɛd), *ppl. a. rare.* [pa. pple. of WED *v.*] = WEDDED.

? *a* **1400** *Morte Arth.* 700 This werre..That warnes me wyrchippe of my wedde lorde. *a* **1400** *Relig. Pieces fr. Thornton MS.* 5 The sexte commandement forbeddes vs.. to foly fleschely with any womane owþer..wedde or unwedde. *c* **1440** *Alphabet of Tales* xxxv. 25 He was a wed man. **1823** BYRON *Juan* XI. xlvi, A rib's a thorn in a wed gallant's side, Requires decorum.

wed(d, obs. forms of WEED *sb.*[1], *sb.*[2], *v.*[1]

wedaw, obs. form of WIDOW.

Wedda, variant of VEDDA.

†'**weddable**, *a. Obs.*$^{-0}$ [f. WED *v.* + -ABLE.] That may be wedded.

1611 COTGR., *Mariable*..Mariable, weddable, mariageable.

wedde, obs. form of WIDDY *Sc.*

wedded ('wɛdɪd), *ppl. a.* [f. WED *v.* + -ED[1].]

1. Joined in wedlock; living in the married state.

? *a* **800** *Conf. Abp. Ecgbert* xx. in Thorpe *Laws* (1840) II. 146 Ða ȝeweddodan fæmnan [L. *puellam desponsatam*] hire yldran hi ne moton syllan oðrum men. *c* **1175** *Lamb. Hom.* 143 Þe weddede wiues. *c* **1200** ORMIN 4604 Weddedd were & weddedd wif. **13..** *Cursor M.* 10458 (Gött.) Quar-of suld i haue ioy or bliss, Quen i mi weddid lauerd miss? *c* **1381** CHAUCER *Parl. Foules* 355 The wedded turtil with hire herte trewe. *c* **1412** HOCCLEVE *De Reg. Princ.* 1623 And many wedded couples haue I knowe. **1548–9** *Bk. Com. Prayer, Matrimony* 13 b, N. wilte thou haue this woman to thy wedded wife. **1607** SHAKS. *Per.* III. iv. 9 My wedded Lord, I nere shall see againe. **1667** MILTON *P.L.* VIII. 605 Harmonie to behold in wedded pair More grateful then harmonious sound to the eare. **1717** POPE *Eloïsa* 77 Let wealth, let honour, wait the wedded dame. **1740** RICHARDSON *Pamela* (1824) I. 205, I have been a close observer of the behaviour of wedded folks. **1798** T. MORTON *Speed the Plough* V. i, She is my wife... My lawful, wedded wife. **1848** MRS. GASKELL *Mary Barton* xxxiii, If she lives, she shall be my wedded wife. **1908** G. TYRRELL in M. D. Petre *Life* (1912) II. 380, I thought that Utrecht would faint at the idea of a wedded bishop.

b. *absol. rare.*

c **1230** *Hali Meid.* 5 Þat bihald as of heh alle widewen under hire & weddede baðe. **1450–1530** *Myrr. Our Ladye* II. 149 She fayled not..the chastyte of vyrgyns ne the plenteousnesse of wedded. *a* **1849** MANGAN *Poems* (1859) 62 Who pleads for thee thus, thy wedded shall be.

2. Of or pertaining to marriage or to married persons.

1592 SHAKS. *Rom. & Jul.* I. v. 137 (Fo.) Go aske his name: if he be married, My graue is like to be my wedded bed [*Qq.* wedding bed]. **1667** MILTON *P.L.* IV. 750 Haile wedded Love, mysterious Law, true sourse Of human ofspring. **1709** STEELE *Tatler* No. 184 ⁋2 As soon as she took upon her the wedded Condition. **1823** SCOTT *Quentin D.* xxxi, I care not myself for the wedded state. **1830** COLERIDGE *Table-t.* 27 Sept., Luther has sketched the most beautiful picture of the nature, and ends, and duties of the wedded life I ever read. **1866** NEALE *Sequences & Hymns* 130 And wedded troth remains as firm, and wedded love as pure. **1888** BURGON *Lives 12 Gd. Men* II. v. 8 The sun of his wedded happiness set in this same year.

3. Obstinately attached (to an indulgence, a habit, opinion, party, etc.).

1579 LYLY *Euphues* (Arb.) 117 If thou be either so wicked that thou wilt not, or so wedded that thou canst not abstein from their glaunces. **1721** MORTIMER *Husb.* I. 1 The wedded Opinions of the Generality to the Custom and Practice of their Neighbours. **1854** C. E. NORTON *Lett.* (1913) I. 106 New Hampshire,..the most wedded of all the Northern States to the Democratic party.

4. Of things: Coupled or joined together.

1842 TENNYSON *Godiva* 43 Then fled she to her inmost bower and there Unclasp'd the wedded eagles of her belt. **1916** *Blackw. Mag.* Nov. 572/1 The country-side [Italy].. with its wedded vines and elms.

†**5.** ***wedded brother*** = *wed-brother* (see WED *sb.* 6). *Obs. rare.*

c **1350** *Athelston* ii. (Zupitza), For loue of here metyng þare þey swoor hem weddyd breþeryn for euer mare, In trewþe trewely dede hem bynde. *Ibid.* xiv, Þy weddid broþir.

Hence †'**weddedhood** [-HOOD], '**weddedness** [-NESS], wedded state or condition.

a **1450** MYRC *Par. Pr.* 212 Dedly synne hyt ys forthe broght, Saue in here wedhode [*v.r.* wedeedhood] That ys feyre to-fore gode. **1891** *Harper's Mag.* July 181/1 His weddedness. **1903** LD. R. GOWER *Rec. & Remin.* 538 He and his wife appear exceedingly fond of one another, a rare and refreshing state of weddedness nowadays.

Weddell ('wɛdəl). The name of James *Weddell* (1787–1834), Scottish navigator, used *attrib.* or in the possessive as **Weddell('s) seal**, to designate a large brown Antarctic seal, *Leptonychotes weddellii*, first recorded by him and named in his honour in 1826. Cf. *sea-leopard* s.v. SEA *sb.* 23 b. Also *absol.*

1902 G. E. H. BARRETT-HAMILTON in *Rep. Coll. Nat. Hist. Voy. 'Southern Cross'* i. 19 Weddell's seal is probably of wide distribution. **1923** F. WILD *Shackleton's Last Voy.* vi. 118 Near by a fat Weddell seal lay asleep. **1938** [see CRABEATER 3]. **1971** R. SALE *Man who raised Hell* I. i. 14 He was trying to tag a Weddell mother seal... Weddells are big animals, going to twelve feet. **1979** *Nature* 11 Jan. 87/3 The Weddell seal has adapted to fill a specialised niche—the inshore fast ice zone—where it winters under the ice, keeping breathing holes open with its teeth.

weddellite ('wɛdəlaɪt). *Min.* [f. the name of the *Weddell* Sea, Antarctica, where it was first found + -ITE[1].] A hydrated calcium oxalate, $CaC_2O_4.2H_2O$, which occurs as colourless tetragonal crystals and is common in calculi.

1942 FRONDEL & PRIEN in *Science* 24 Apr. 431/1 Stones [formed in the body] composed wholly of carbonate-apatite are relatively rare. Whewellite ($CaC_2O_4{\cdot}H_2O$), weddellite ($CaC_2O_4{\cdot}2H_2O$) and especially struvite..are ordinarily present. **1961** *Lancet* 26 Aug. 452/1 (*caption*) The large crystals in the centre of the field were of calcium oxalate dihydrate (weddellite). **1976** *Chem. Abstr.* 20 Sept. 190/1 (*heading*) Whewellite ($CaC_2O_4{\cdot}H_2O$) and weddellite ($CaC_2O_4{\cdot}2H_2O$) from the Upper Cretaceous limestone near Zminj in Istria (Croatia, Yugoslavia).

wedder ('wɛdə(r)). [f. WED *v.* + -ER[1].] One who weds. ***penny wedder*** (? cf. PENNY-*wedding*).

1866 *Morning Star* 15 Sept. 2/5 The sounds of hobnailed feet and giggling was heard in the church porch, denoting the arrival of the first batch of penny wedders. **1891** in *Century Dict.*

wedder, obs. and dial. f. WEATHER, WETHER.

weddesette, obs. form of WADSET *v.*

weddewede, obs. form of WIDOWHOOD.

wedding ('wɛdɪŋ), *vbl. sb.* Forms: 1 **weddung**, 3 **weddingue**, 4 **weddin**, 5 **-yn**, 4–5 **weding**, **-yng**, 4–6 **weddyng(e**, **-inge**, 6 *Sc.* **vedding**, 3– **wedding**. [f. WED *v.* + -ING[1].]

1. The action of marrying; marriage, espousal. Chiefly *gerundial*. †Also, the married state, wedlock, matrimony (*obs.*).

c **1000** *Gosp. Nicod.* vii. 3 in Thwaites *Hept.* (1698), Seo weddung wæs beweddod, eal swa eowre aȝene ðeoda secgaþ. *c* **1250** *Gen. & Ex.* 1428 Siðen men hauen holden skil, first to freinen ðe wimmanes wil, Or or men hire to louerd giue, for wedding or for morgen-giwe. *c* **1290** *St. Edmund Conf.* 97 in *S. Eng. Leg.* 434 Wel he huld is treuþe setþe and his weddingue also, And trewe spouse was inovȝ. *a* **1300** *K. Horn* 423 Hit nere no fair wedding Bitwexe a þral & a king. **1362** LANGL. *P. Pl.* A. x. 178 Summe..For Couetise of Catel vnkuyndeliche beoþ maried, And Careful Concepcion comeþ of such weddyng. **1375** BARBOUR *Bruce* I. 267 Wedding is the hardest band That ony man may tak on hand. *a* **1400** CHAUCER *Envoy to Bukton* 24 So may happe That the were leuer to be take in Frise Than eft falle of weddynge in the trappe. *c* **1460** *Towneley Myst.* xiii. 92 Be well war of wedyng. **1483** *Cath. Angl.* 412/1 Ye secund Weddynge, *bigamia*, *deutrogamia*. **1490** CAXTON *Eneydos* xiv. 52 My sone hyemen, whiche is named the god of weddynge. **1564** *Brief Exam.* *****iij, Who vsed the ring fyrst in weddyng? the Heathen. **1599** SHAKS. *Much Ado* II. i. 76 Wooing, wedding, and repenting, is as a Scotch ijgge, a measure, and a cinque-pace.

Prov. **1562** J. HEYWOOD *Prov. & Epigr.* (1867) 129 Weddyng and hangyng are desteny.

2. a. The performance of the marriage-rite; the ceremony of a marriage, with its attendant festivities.

This is the word in general use for this sense.

c **1300** *K. Horn* 1295 (Laud) He rongen þe bellen þe wedding [*Cambr.* wedlak] for to fullen. *c* **1386** CHAUCER *Knt's T.* 25 The feste that was at hir weddynge. **1490** CAXTON *Eneydos* lxiii. 163 Moche Ioye was there made atte theyr weddynge. **1526** TINDALE *Matt.* xxii. 10 The weddinge was furnysshed with gestes. **1530** PALSGR. 287/2 Weddyng, *nopces*. **1602** SHAKS. *Ham.* I. ii. 178, I thinke it was to see my Mothers Wedding. **1663** KILLIGREW *Pars. Wedd.* V. ii, I'll run and invite them to the Wedding. **1754** RICHARDSON *Grandison* V. lv. 347 Every woman's heart leaps..when a wedding is described. **1797** SIR F. M. EDEN *St. Poor* I. 598 The custom of a general feasting at weddings and christenings. **1848** DICKENS *Dombey* v, The very wedding looked dismal as they passed in front of the altar. **1885** 'MRS. ALEXANDER' *At Bay* x, Are you to be at the Milton wedding next week? **1897** STOPF. BROOKE in Jacks *Life & Lett.* (1917) II. 532, I am told the wedding went off well.

fig. a **1901** F. W. H. MYERS *Hum. Personality* (1903) II. 295 Since that great wedding between Reason and Experience, which immortalises the name of Galileo.

b. Phr. ***penny wedding***: see PENNY 12 c. ***silver wedding*** [G. *silberhochzeit*, *silberne hochzeit*], the 25th anniversary of a wedding (see SILVER *sb.* 20). ***golden wedding***, the 50th anniversary. ***diamond wedding***, the 60th or 75th anniversary (see DIAMOND *sb.* 12).

1850 J. VON TAUTPHŒUS *Initials* I. v. 121 'Perhaps you have no golden or silver wedding in England?' 'I confess I never heard of any thing of the kind,' said Hamilton... 'To be fifty years married and to have a golden wedding, is a sort of event in a family.' **1860** *Illustr. Lond. News* 24 Nov. 485/3 The celebration of the fiftieth anniversary of the marriage of Prince William of Hesse and the Princess Charlotte... This 'golden wedding', as such an event is called [etc.]. **1874** LONGF. *Hanging of Crane* vii, It is the Golden Wedding day.

†**3.** Occas. found in other senses of the verb: Close union or association; the action of pledging or wagering. *Obs.*

c **1380** WYCLIF *Sel. Wks.* III. 364 [see WED *v.* 7 b]. *Ibid.* 431 But Lord! wheþer weddyng wiþ siche signes helpiþ to holde religioun of Crist, and love hym of hert? — *Wks.* (1880) 448 Wedding wiþ þes newe bilawis, passinge þe wedding wiþ goddis lawe, makiþ þes newe rotun sectis. **1503** *Acc. Ld. High Treas. Scot.* II. 401 Item, the xj day of October, to the King quhilk he tynt on wedding with the Abbot of Cambuskinneth, xiiij s.

4. a. *attrib.*, as ***wedding-anniversary***, ***-appearance***, ***-banquet***, ***-bed***, ***-bell***, ***-chamber***, †***-cheer***, ***-clothes***, ***-coat***, ***-dinner***, ***-dower***, ***-dress***, ***-feast***, ***festival***, ***-gown***, ***-guest***, ***-journey***, ***-mass***, ***-night***, ***-peal***, ***photo***, ***photograph***, ***-present***, ***-robe***, ***-sermon***, † ***smock***, ***-song***, ***-suit***, ***-supper***, ***-table***, ***-torch***, ***tour***, † ***trim***, ***trip***, ***visit***.

a **1700** EVELYN *Diary* 13 Aug. 1673, It being his *wedding anniversarie. **1971** 'D. HALLIDAY' *Dolly & Doctor Bird* iii. 33 It's our wedding anniversary. **1748** RICHARDSON *Clarissa* (1768) IV. 257 How bravely shall we enter a court, .. dressed out each man, as if to his *wedding-appearance. **1855** LONGF. *Hiaw.* xii. 372 Thus the *wedding-banquet ended. **1592** SHAKS. *Rom. & Jul.* I. v. 137 (Qo. 1599) If he be married, My graue is like to be my *wedding bed. **1685** ? DRYDEN *Daphnis* 64 in *Sylvæ* 118, I bargain for a wedding Bed at least. *a* **1849** POE *The Bells* ii, Hear the mellow *wedding bells. **1552** HULOET, *Weddynge chamber, *thalamus.* **1611** BIBLE *2 Esdras* x. 1 When my sonne was entred into his wedding chamber, he fell downe and died. **1592** SHAKS. *Rom. & Jul.* IV. v. 87 Our *wedding cheare [turns] to a sad buriall Feast. **1678** BUTLER *Hud.* III. i. 737 The Bride, That with her *Wedding-cloaths undresses Her Complaisance and Gentilesses. **1824** MISS MITFORD *Village* I. 288 Betsy .. prepared her wedding-clothes, and looked hourly for the bridegroom. **1838** M. R. WALKER *Let.* 27 July in C. M. Drury *Elkanah & Mary Walker* (1940) iii. 92, I was glad indeed to see him safe & sound with his cloths sadly rent having lost his coat his **wedding coat.* **1857** DICKENS *Lett.* (1880) II. 26 A pair of common nankeen tights, .. and blue wedding-coat. **1633** ROWLEY *Match at Midn.* II. i. D 2 b, One *wedding dinner must serve both marriages. **1835** DICKENS *Sk. Boz, Mistaken Milliner*, Miss Amelia Martin was invited .. to honour the wedding-dinner with her presence. **1591** SHAKS. *Two Gent.* III. i. 78 Then let her beauty be her *wedding dowre. **1801** M. EDGEWORTH *Belinda* II. xxxi. 357 Something must be left to the imagination. Positively I will not describe *wedding dresses. **1863** KINGSLEY *Water-Bab.* ii, They helped her on with her wedding-dress. **1633** FORD *'Tis Pity* III. v, They that now dreame of a *wedding-feast, May chance to mourne the lusty Bridegromes ruine. **1855** LONGF. *Hiaw.* xi (*heading*), Hiawatha's Wedding-feast. **1795–6** WORDSW. *Borderers* I. 331 The villagers Are flocking in—a *wedding festival. **1439** *E.E. Wills* (1882) 118 My *weddynggown and all my clothis of gold. **1767** MURPHY *School for Guard.* IV. iv. 66, I have brought your young lady's wedding-gown. **1798** COLERIDGE *Anc. Mar.* I. 31 The *Wedding-Guest here beat his breast, For he heard the loud bassoon. **1841** THACKERAY *Gt. Hoggarty Diamond* in *Fraser's Mag.* Nov. 598/1 She lent us her chariot for the *wedding journey. **1881** HOWELLS (*title*), Their Wedding Journey. **1612** WEBSTER *White Devil* II. I. 190 Accursed be the priest That sang the *wedding masse. **1661** PEPYS *Diary* 10 Oct., So home, and intended to be merry, it being my sixth *wedding night. **1682** OTWAY *Venice Preserved* I. 7 The very bed, which on thy wedding night Receiv'd thee to the Arms of Belvidera. **1835** DICKENS *Sk. Boz, Watkins Tottle* i, I spent my wedding-night in a back-kitchen chimney. **1808** SKURRAY *Bidcombe Hill* 25 *note*, In the village of Horningsham .. it is customary, when a young person dies unmarried, to ring the *wedding peal on muffled bells, immediately on the interment of the corpse. **1966** P. WILLMOTT *Adolescent Boys* iii. 46 They showed us different *wedding photos. **1956** *Focal Encycl. Photogr.* 1273/2 A good set of *wedding photographs calls for a surprising amount of planning and organization. **1972** C. FREMLIN *Appointment with Yesterday* x. 76 Cora should have received the wedding photograph. **1854** C. SCHREIBER *Jrnl.* 27 May (1952) 35 My *wedding present to Felicia, a white and gold bookcase. **1898** G. B. SHAW *Plays* II. *Candida* 81 A travelling clock in a leather case (the inevitable wedding present). **1450–1530** *Myrr. Our Ladye* II. 238 Thys noble yonge lorde ys clad in a new *weddynge robe. **1694** T. BROWN *Lottery for Ladies & G.* Wks. 1711 IV. 169 Dr. B——s shall preach the *Wedding Sermon. *c* **1610** BEAUM. & FL. *Scornf. Lady* I. i, If my *Wedding smock were on. **1648** HERRICK *Hesper.*, *'Come sit we under yonder Tree'* 22 Next we will .. talke of Brides; and who shall make That wedding-smock, this Bridal-Cake. **1598** R. BERNARD *Terence, Adelphi* V. vii. (1607) 327 They which sing the *wedding song. **1594** *Taming of a Shrew* (1844) 22 For this I sweare shall be my *wedding sute. **1728** CIBBER *Provoked Husb.* III. i. 53 The Wedding-suit of a first Dutchess. **1807** Wedding suit [see *family tree* s.v. FAMILY *sb.* 11]. **1959** W. FAULKNER *Mansion* xiii. 296 Maybe he picked it up along with that-ere white wedding suit. **1695** CONGREVE *Love for L.* IV. xv, Ha, ha, ha! That a Man shou'd have a Stomach to a *Wedding Supper, when the Pidgeons ought rather to be laid to his feet. **1961** NEW ENG. BIBLE *Rev.* xix. 9 Happy are those who are invited to the wedding-supper of the Lamb! **1722** RAMSAY *Three Bonnets* IV. 53 To tell how meikle cakes and ale .. Was serv'd upon the *wedding-table. **1591** SHAKS. *1 Hen. VI*, III. ii. 26 Behold, this is the happy *Wedding Torch, That ioyneth Roan vnto her Countreymen. **1847** C. M. YONGE *Scenes & Characters* xxxi. 340 The wedding had been hurried on, and the *wedding-tour was shortened. **1955** C. CARRINGTON *Rudyard Kipling* ix. 201 It will not be necessary to retrace Rudyard's steps throughout his wedding tour. *a* **1729** TICKELL *Colin & Lucy* 43 He in his *wedding-trim so gay, I in my winding-sheet! **1855** DICKENS *Dorrit* (1857) I. ii. 17 A clerical English husband .. on a *wedding trip with his young wife. **1925** F. SCOTT FITZGERALD *Great Gatsby* viii. 183 Tom and Daisy were still on their wedding trip. **1974** *News & Reporter* (Chester, S. Carolina) 22 Apr. 4-A/8 After a wedding trip to Charlottesville, Virginia the couple will reside on Morreene Road, Durham. **1794** J. WOODFORDE *Diary* 7 Apr. (1929) IV. 103 Mr. & Mrs. Carbould are gone out for a few days to make a *wedding visit to Mrs. Carbould's Brother at Castor near Yarmouth. **1872** GEO. ELIOT *Middlem.* II. III. xxviii. 89 Through the next weeks there would be wedding visits received and given.

b. wedding band *U.S.* = *wedding-ring*; **wedding-breakfast**, the entertainment given at the bride's house etc. after the marriage-ceremony and before the departure for the honeymoon; cf. BREAKFAST *sb.* 2 b; **wedding-bush**, a shrub of the genus *Ricinocarpos*, of the family Euphorbiaceæ, esp. *R. pinifolius*, which is native to eastern Australia and bears clusters of fragrant white flowers; **wedding-cake**, a large rich cake, covered with icing and decorated with sugar ornaments, cut and distributed to the guests at the wedding-feast and sent in small portions to absent friends; also *attrib.*; also *fig.*, esp. applied *attrib.* (often somewhat dismissively) to a sumptuously ornate style of architecture, and (also *absol.*) to buildings in this style; **wedding canopy** *Judaism* = CHUPPAH; **wedding-cards**, cards, bearing the names of the two parties, sent out to friends as an announcement of the wedding; also in *sing.*; **wedding-chest**, an ornamental chest made to contain a bride's clothes, etc.; † **wedding church door** = *wedding door*; **wedding-coffer** = *wedding-chest*; **wedding-day**, the day on which a marriage is performed, or which is fixed for the marriage; also, an anniversary of this day; also *attrib.*; † **wedding door**, the church-door, or porch, at which couples were married; **wedding-favour**, a knot of white ribbon, or a white rosette, sometimes worn by guests at a wedding; **wedding-finger** = RING-FINGER; **wedding-flower**, (*a*) *Moræa* (*Iris*) *robinsoniana*, of Lord Howe's Island, N.S.W.; (*b*) *Dombeya natalensis*, of S. Africa; **wedding-garment**, a garment appropriate to, or customarily worn at, a wedding; also *fig.* (with ref. to Matt. xxii. 11–12); † **wedding-garter**, a garter worn as a wedding-favour; **wedding group**, (a photograph of) a wedding party; † **wedding-house** = BRIDEHOUSE; † **wedding kirk door** = *wedding door*; † **wedding-knives**, ? a pair of knives worn at the girdle by a bride; **wedding-knot**, (*a*) *fig.* the bond of matrimony; (*b*) *Naut.*, a tie for uniting the looped ends of two ropes (Knight *Dict. Mech.* 1875); **wedding list**, a list of acceptable wedding gifts for guests to consult and act upon; **wedding-march**, a march (Mendelssohn's, if not otherwise specified) composed for performance at a wedding; † **wedding-monger**, one who is busied about a wedding; **wedding party**, the assemblage of persons at a wedding; **wedding reception**, a party at which the wedding guests are formally greeted and entertained after the marriage ceremony; cf. RECEPTION 2 d; **wedding-ring**, a ring, usually of plain gold, placed by the bridegroom on the third finger of the bride's left hand as part of the ceremony, and worn by her ever after; a ring similarly presented by the bride to the bridegroom, and worn afterwards by him; also *attrib.* and *fig.*; **wedding-sheet**, a sheet laid on the bridal bed and sometimes kept to form a shroud for the bride at her death.

1946 R. LYLE *Mademoiselle's Handbk. Bridal Consultants* vi. 79 *Wedding bands have in centuries past been made of iron as well as gold. **1977** 'E. MCBAIN' *Long Time no See* i. 16 On the third finger of his left hand, there was a wedding band. **1850** THACKERAY *Pendennis* II. xv. 144 There is a *wedding breakfast. **1853** DICKENS *Bleak Ho.* xxx, To make the furnished lodging decent for the wedding-breakfst. **1859** *Habits Gd. Society* xv. 372 It must be borne in mind that the wedding-breakfast is not a *dinner*. **1962** *Sunday Times* 11 Nov. 25/4 They married in church, and had a wedding breakfast but no honeymoon. **1923** *Census of Plants of Victoria* (Field Naturalists' Club of Victoria) 41 *Wedding Bush. **1961** Wedding-bush [see MANNA[1] 9]. **1648** HERRICK *Hesper.*, *Bride-Cake*, This day my Julia thou must make for Mistresse Bride, the *wedding cake. **1798** COLERIDGE *Three Graves* 60 The wedding-cake with her own hand The ruthless mother brought. **1879** MRS. F. D. BRIDGES *Jrnl. Lady's Trav.* iii. (1883) 43 The Palace, somewhat of the wedding-cake style of architecture, all over stucco ornaments and whitewash. **1925** F. SCOTT FITZGERALD *Great Gatsby* i. 8 A breeze .. blew curtains, .. twisting them up toward the frosted wedding-cake of the ceiling. **1949** H. G. ALSBERG *Amer. Guide* 105 *Kennebunk* .. Among numerous old mansions are .. Wedding Cake H. (c. 1825), with most unusual Vict. trimmings. **1968** *N.Y. City* (Michelin Tire Corp.) 16 Others [*sc.* skyscrapers], sometimes known as *wedding cakes*, were covered with ornate sculpture in the 1900 '*Gigi style*'. **1971** J. WILLETT in A. Bullock *20th Cent.* 242/1 A massive piece of wedding-cake architecture (.. fortunately never built) for the projected Palace of Soviets in Moscow. **1892** I. ZANGWILL *Childr. Ghetto* I. 37 The hope was expressed that Mr. and Mrs. Belcovitch would like .. to see their daughters' daughters under the *Chuppah*, or *wedding canopy. **1978** I. B. SINGER *Shosha* iv. 74 You should lead your daughter to a black wedding canopy! **1847** C. M. YONGE *Scenes & Characters* ii. 9 She was putting her sister's *wedding cards into their shining envelopes. **1867** AUGUSTA WILSON *Vashti* xxix, I .. noticed a basket containing some of the wedding cards. **1888** A. K. GREEN *Behind Closed Doors* ii, My daughter's wedding-cards are out. **1953** DYLAN THOMAS *Let.* 31 Mar. (1966) 401 Had your wedding card. Congratulations. **1874** J. H. POLLEN *Anc. & Mod. Furniture S. Kens. Mus.* 127 Coffer .. The figures of angels .. on the ends and the front panel are uninjured. It has been a *wedding chest. **1560** *Ludlow Churchw. Acc.* (Camden) 97 Paid .. for mendynge .. the window over the *wedinge churche dore. **1904** *Studio* Sept. 303/2 *Wedding-coffers, or 'cassones,' as they are sometimes called. *a* **1553** UDALL *Royster D.* I. iv. (Arb.) 26 What weepe on the *weddyng day? be merrie woman. **1592** SHAKS. *Rom. & Jul.* IV. v. 35 O Sonne, the night before thy wedding day, Hath death laine with thy wife. *a* **1700** EVELYN *Diary* 18 Nov. 1659, Sir John Evelyn invited us to the 41st wedding-day feast. **1782** COWPER *Gilpin* 9 Though wedded we have been These twice ten tedious years, yet we No holiday have seen. Tomorrow is our wedding-day. **1847** C. BRONTE *Jane Eyre* xxxvii, The third day from this must be our wedding-day, Jane. **1470–3** *Rec. Andover* 11 Paid vnto John helyer for reperacon don at the *weddyndor, vid. **1636** in Swayne *Churchw. Acc. Sarum* (1896) 205 A gallerie over the Wedding doare in the Church. **1681** W. ROBERTSON *Phraseol. Gen.* 592/1 A *wedding favour, *Lemniscus nuptialis.* **1882** BESANT *Revolt of Man* xi. (1883) 263 The church was crammed with the guests in wedding-favours. **1542** RECORDE *Gr. Artes* P ij, The *weddyng fynger (whiche is the nexte to the little fynger). **1548** PATTEN *Exped. Scot.* H iv, Hurt vppon the weddyng fynger of hys righte hande. **1888** 'J. S. WINTER' *Bootle's Childr.* xiii, She slipped it on to her wedding-finger. **1869** in *Gardeners' Chron.* (1872) 23 Mar. 393/3 A large Iridaceous plant, termed the '*Wedding Flower'. **1526** TINDALE *Matt.* xxii. 11 The kynge .. spyed there a man which had not on a *weddinge garment. *c* **1540** COVERDALE *Fruitful Less.* To Rdr. (1593) A 4 b, The old Adam ought we to lay aside .. and to put on Christ the Lord, as the new wedding garment. **1596** SHAKS. *Tam. Shr.* IV. i. 51 Is supper ready, the house trim'd, .. and every officer his wedding-garment on? **1663** BUTLER *Hud.* I. ii. 524 Are these the fruits o' th' Protestation, .. Which all the Saints, and some, since Martyrs, Wore in their Hats, like *Wedding-Garters. **1861** GEO. ELIOT *Silas Marner* 361 The *wedding group had passed on .. to the humbler part of the village. **1930** R. LEHMANN *Note in Music* v. 190 The texts, the wedding group, and the photograph of a grave on the wall. **1979** J. ADAM SMITH *John Buchan* 51 People in Scotland, she said, might like to have wedding groups, but she doubted if it was ever done in London. *c* **1440** *Promp. Parv.* 519/2 *Weddynge (howus *K.*, hous *P.*), *idem quod* Brydale howse, *supra.* **1483** *Cath. Angl.* 412/1 A Weddyng howse, *nuptorium.* **1684** D'URFEY *Pills* (1719) II. 31 Willy was late at a Wedding house, Where Lords and Ladies danc'd all arow. **1530** *Extracts Aberd. Reg.* (1844) I. 137 He was found in the *vedding kirk dur with his bonat on his heid. **1596** *Edw. III*, II. ii. 173 Here by my side doth hang my *wedding knifes. *c* **1620** DEKKER *Match me in London* v. (1631) 70 See at my Girdle hang my wedding kniues. **1902** 'ROMA WHITE' *Backsheesh* iii. 33 Of course, from the British Public point of view the Moslem *wedding knot is not altogether respectable. **1981** *Times* 7 Mar. (Bride & Home Suppl.) p. vi/1 Today's brides .. confine romance to their wedding dress and .. Roneo their less personal requirements... The stores still keeping *wedding lists do provide a valuable service. **1850** J. BENEDICT *Sk. Life Mendelssohn* 42 The gorgeous *Wedding-march. **1903** J. L. ALLEN *Mettle of Pasture* ii. 33 The loud crash of the wedding march closed their separate pasts with a single melody. **1671** CARYL *Sir Salomon* II. 29 By that time the Lawyers, the Taylers, the Semstresses, and riming Poets, with the rest of the *Wedding-Mongers, will have all things in readiness. **1873** C. M. YONGE *Pillars of House* IV. xlvii. 340 The blow was known to all that sad *wedding party. **1877** W. S. GILBERT *Engaged* (? 1883) II. 31, I have ordered four flys for the wedding party. **1979** J. GARDNER *Nostradamus Traitor* xxxv. 165 Another alert. This time the wedding party had to take shelter. **1871** A. J. MUNBY *Diary* 4 Nov. in D. Hudson *Munby* (1972) 299 We, Council and Students .. offered this evening a *wedding reception to Litchfield and his bride. **1965** [see STUNG *ppl. a.* 2]. **1978** S. SHELDON *Bloodline* xlv. 374 After the ceremony there was a wedding reception at the Baur-au-Lac. *c* **1386** CHAUCER *Clerk's T.* 812 And heere agayn my clothyng I restoore, And eek my *weddyng ryng. *c* **1540** COVERDALE *Fruitful Less.* (1593) Kk 2 b, The same holie Ghost, who is .. the earnest pennie of saluation, the wedding ring of grace. **1590** SHAKS. *Com. Err.* II. ii. 139 Wouldst thou not .. from my false hand cut the wedding ring? **1630** *R. Johnson's Kingd. & Commw.* 41 The sand about us seemes to be our wedding Ring, and the riches of the Sea our Dowrie. **1704** PRIOR *To Yng. Gent. in Love* 70 The Moral of the Tale I sing (A Posy for a Wedding Ring). **1853** DICKENS *Bleak Ho.* xxvii, The only article of ornament of which she stands possessed appears to be her wedding-ring. **1953** DYLAN THOMAS *Under Milk Wood* (1954) 74 His mother .. with her wedding-ring waist and bust like a black-clothed dining-table suffers in her stays. **1980** *Quilt World* Sept./Oct. 23/1 Sheri's mother feels that it is a single wedding ring quilt because when four blocks are pieced together a ring is formed. **1604** SHAKS. *Oth.* IV. ii. 105 Prythee to night, Lay on my bed my *wedding sheetes, remember. **1823** LOCKHART *Reg. Dalton* I. viii. (1842) 46 Her wedding-sheet, which, according to the primitive fashion of the district, had been carefully laid by for that purpose, was formed into the shroud which enveloped her remains.

¶ For alternative forms of many of these collocations see BRIDAL 2, BRIDE *sb.*[1] 5 a, 6, MARRIAGE 8, NUPTIAL *a.* 1. The adjectival force of *wedding* is recognized in the following quot.:

1530 PALSGR. 329/1 ('The Table of Adjectyves') Weddyng, belongyng to maryage, *nuptial.*

weddinger (ˈwɛdɪŋə(r)). *dial.* [f. WEDDING + -ER[1].] A wedding-guest; *pl.* the whole wedding-party, including bride and bridegroom.

1802 G. V. SAMPSON *Statist. Surv. Londonderry* 458 After a few days' carousal among the groom's friends, the weddingers move towards the bride's country. **1811** *Ora & Juliet* IV. 185 But wont you have some cake, ladies, before the weddingers come to church? **1887** HALL CAINE *Son of Hagar* II. xv, 'Good luck to the weddiners!' they said. **1891** ATKINSON *Moorland Par.* (ed. 2) 205 The weddingers passed down the little slope leading to the churchyard gate.

weddir(e, obs. ff. WEATHER, WETHER.

weddow(e, obs. forms of WIDOW.

weddre, -ur, -yr, obs. forms of WEATHER.

† **wede**, *v.* *Obs.* Forms: 1 **wédan** (3 *sing. pres.* **wét(t)**, 3 **weden, -enn**, 3–5 **wede**, (3 **weede**, 4 **wed, wedde**, 3–4 **wide**), 5 *Sc.* **weide, weid, weyd**. [OE.

wédan = OS. *wôdian*, OHG. *wuoten* (MHG. *wueton*, mod.G. *wüten*), ON. *œ́ða*:—OTeut. **wōdjan*, f. **wōdo-* mad: see WOOD *a.*]

1. *intr.* To be or become mad. Cf. AWEDE.

c **900** *Bæda's Hist.* v. xiii. (1890) 438 Cwæð he; Ne wede ic [L. *non insanio*]. *c* **1000** *Ags. Gosp.* John x. 20 Deofol is on him & he wet. *a* **1225** *Leg. Kath.* 1264 Þes keiser..as mon þet bigon to weden & to wurðen ut of his ahne witte, wodeliche ȝeide [etc.]. *a* **1300** *Cursor M.* 3749 Me es sua waa, almast i weede. *c* **1350** *Will. Palerne* 1509 He..went hom aȝeine, Weping as he wold wide for wo & for sorwe. **13..** *E.E. Allit. P.* B 1585 So was þe wyȝe wytles, he wed wel ner. *a* **1400–50** *Wars Alex.* 539, I am all in aunter, sa akis me þe wame, Of werke well ne I wede. *c* **1400** *Rowland & Otuel* 936 He..ferde als he wolde wede. *a* **1413** *Anturs of Arth.* 558 (Ireland MS.) Neȝtehond Syr Wauan wold wede, So wepputte he fulle sore.

b. Phrase. ***to wede (out) of, but wit.***

13.. *Cursor M.* 13975 Of þis womman þe grete fairede Did mani man of witt to wede. *c* **1425** WYNTOUN *Cron.* v. x. 1903 Bot ay withe roris reythe he [rerde], Wedande but wit as a wode man. *a* **1450** *Le Morte Arth.* 651 Nighe of witte she wold wede. *c* **1470** HENRY *Wallace* II. 205 Thocht I for wo all out off witt suld weid!

2. To be wild with anger or desire; to rage. Const. *again*; *to* (do something).

c **1000** ÆLFRIC *Saints' Lives* xvi. 225 He [the Devil] wet nu swiðe and wynð on ða cristenan. *c* **1200** ORMIN 14140 Fra þatt gredįȝnesse þatt doþ þe mann to wedenn rihht To winnenn erþlic ahhte. *a* **1225** *Ancr. R.* 264 Hwon mon loggeð him bi ure Louerde, þeonne on erest biginneð þe deoflen to weden. *a* **1300** *Cursor M.* 2408 Quen þai þe see, for þi fairhede To reue me þe þan sal þai wede. *c* **1425** WYNTOUN *Cron.* v. vi. 1179 Fra þine he cessit for to weide Agayne þe cristyn men in deide. *Ibid.* v. xiii. 4624 In ire as he was wedande þen. *c* **1460** *Towneley Myst.* xv. 47 No wonder if I wede, I that may do no dede; how shuld I theder wyn ffor eld? *a* **1500** *Ratis Raving* 2480 Wedand in a rage.

b. Of waves, pestilence: To rage, be furious.

c **900** *Bæda's Hist.* III. xv. (1890) 200 Þa yða weollon & weddon þæs sæs. *c* **1425** WYNTOUN *Cron.* IX. iii. 230 In Scotlande þat ȝhere in wiolence [Was] wedande þe thride pestilence.

Hence †'**weding** (Sc. *wedand*) *ppl. a.*, raging, raving.

c **725** *Corpus Gloss.* L 198 *Limphaticus*, woedendi. *c* **888** ÆLFRED *Boeth.* vii. §4 Hwa mæȝ þæm wedendan ȝietsere ȝenoh forȝifan? *c* **1375** *Sc. Leg. Saints* xliii. (*Cecilia*) 572 Almacius cane til hire say: þat wedand wodnes do away, & sacryfy oure godis til. *c* **1425** WYNTOUN *Cron.* VIII. xi. 1776 Al brym he belyt in to brethe, And wrythit al in wedand wrethe. *a* **1500** *Ratis Raving* 1644 Fore wedand Joy beand in vages Lattis al suthfast gud knawleges.

wede, obs. form of WEED.

‖**wedeln** ('veːdəln), *sb. Skiing.* Also **wedel**. [a. G. *wedeln* (in same sense).] A skiing technique using a swaying movement of the hips to make short parallel turns (see PARALLEL *a.* 1 b). Also *attrib.*

1957 J. CEELY tr. *Joubet & Vuarnet's Ski ABC* ii. 106 The skier effects a real wedeln when he is able to minimize the second step of the above progression. *Ibid.* iii. 130 In linked turns or wedeln, planting the pole adds favorable *rhythm* to the movements. **1958** *Times* 1 Mar. 7/6 The reverse shoulder technique of *wedeln*..or *godille* as the French call it, has become so universal among first-class racers of all nations that no one using the classical rotation can hope to be placed in a serious race. **1963** *New Yorker* 2 Feb. 37 Down he goes, anyway, his wedeln so crisp he never seems to care at all for the configuration of the snow. **1963** *Amer. Speech* XXXVIII. 208 Other attributive uses are *wedel track* and *wedel turn*. **1973** R. HAYES *Hungarian Game* xxxii. 195 We had skied nearly to the base of the mountain and Mary Louise shot over a drop... I did a quick wedeln series and looked for her. **1974** H. EVANS et al. *We learned to Ski* 44 Those who can do the long radius parallel turn learn to make shorter linked parallel turns—the wedel. **1975** *Oxf. Compan. Sports & Games* 965/2 Between 1956 and 1958, the Austrian, *Sailer*, won seven out of eight world titles,..and he introduced the *wedeln* style to a wide public.

‖**wedeln** ('veːdəln), *v. Skiing.* Also (app. more commonly) **wedel**. [a. G. *wedeln* (in same sense), lit. to wag (the tail).] *intr.* To use the wedeln technique in skiing. Also *transf.* in *Skate-boarding*.

1961 *Times* 7 Jan. 7/7 Sign-posted high roads which shepherd each carload of uninspired humanity down from the heights..wedelning as best they can. **1963** *Amer. Speech* XXXVIII. 208 *Wedel*; *wedeln*, *v.* to execute a special kind of short parallel turns close to the fall line in quick succession. **1968** *Time* 15 Nov. 49 They wedeled down the 1,200-ft. slope or slammed through the slalom course. **1973** P. A. WHITNEY *Snowfire* iii. 36, I don't care..whether my skis are expertly parallel. I've never been able to wedel. **1977** *Skateboard Special* Sept. 3/1 Special slalom decks have a raised centre to make it easier to 'pump' or 'wedel'.

Hence '**wedel(l)ing** *vbl. sb.*

1977 *Skateboard Special* Sept. 2/2 *Wedeling*, a sophisticated method of reducing speed while zig-zagging down steep hills. *Ibid.* 5/1 Slalom decks..are often slightly raised in the middle to make pumping and wedeling easier. **1979** N. SLATER *Falcon* ix. 161 His *wedelling* turns between each traverse were smothered in a flurry of snow.

Wedenisdai, obs. form of WEDNESDAY.

†**wedenonfa'**. *Sc. Obs.* Forms: 6 **wedonynpha** (vedumfa), 8 **wytenon-fa**, 9 **weidinonfa**. [f. OE. *wéden-* (in *wéden-heort*, *-séoc*) mad + *onfa*', ONFALL. Cf. WIDDENDREAM.] Ague (in later use *spec.* puerperal ague, WEED *sb.*³), or a fit of this.

c **1500** *Rowlis Cursing* 57 in *Bannatyne MS.* (Hunter. Club) 300 The worme, the wareit wedonynpha [*Maitl. MS.* vedumfa], Rumbursin, ripplis, or bellythra[w]. **1597** in Pitcairn *Crim. Trials* (Bannatyne Club) II. 27 Item, for hailling of women of the Wedonynpha [by sorcery]. **1755** R. FORBES *Ajax.* etc. *Jrnl. to Portsmouth* 33, I wis fley'd that she had taen the wytenon-fa,..far she shuddered a' like a klippert in a cauld day. **1808** JAMIESON, *Wedonypha*... This [see quot. 1755] is rendered 'trembling, chattering'. But it is the term generally used in the North, to express that disease peculiar to women, commonly called a *weid*; *weidinonfa*. Ang[us].

weder(e: see WEATHER, WETHER, WHITHER.

‖**Wederdoper.** *rare*⁻¹. [Du. *wederdooper*, f. *weder* again + *dooper* baptizer: see DOPPER².] (See quot.)

1647 N. WARD *Simp. Cobler* 16 The Crowds of foraigne Wederdopers, that is Anabaptists.

wederlyng, corrupt f. *querdlyng*, CODLING².

a **1400** *Pistill of Susan* 102 Þe wince and þe wederlyng.

wedester. *Obs.*⁻¹ (Meaning uncertain.)

1346 *Little Red Bk. Bristol* (1900) II. 12 [Ordinaciones pro fullonibus.] Item ordynee est qe nul mestre paye a nule femme quest appelee Wedestere..synoun *jd.* le iour.

wedeu, -ew(e, wedewer: see WIDOW, -ER.

wedge (wɛdʒ), *sb.* Forms: 1 **waecg, wecg, wegge,** (4 **weeg**), 4–7 **wegge,** (5 **vegge, weegge, wegghe**), 5–6 **weg(e,** 5–7 **wagge,** 6 **wadge, wegg,** 7 **wedg,** 3– **wedge.** Pl. 6 **wedgies,** *Sc.* **vagis, wagis.** [Com. Teut. (not found in Gothic): OE. *węcg* masc. corresponds to OS. *weggi* wedge (MLG. *wegge*, *wigge*, LG. *wegge* wedge, wedge-shaped cake), MDu. *wegge*, *wigge* (mod.Du. *wegge* fem., wedge-shaped cake, *wig* fem., wedge), OHG. *weggi*, *wecki*, wedge (MHG. *wegge*, *wecke*, wedge, wedge-shaped cake; mod.G. dial. *weck*, *wecken* masc., wedge, wedge-shaped cake), ON. *vegg-r* wedge (Norw. *vegg*, Da. *vægge*, MSw. *vägge*, *vigge*, Sw. *vigg*, *vigge*):—OTeut. **waȝjo-z*.

The affinities of the word are somewhat uncertain. Some scholars regard it as cognate with OHG. *waganso* (see *wagense* in Grimm *D. Wb.*), ON., Norw. *vangne*, Gr. ὀφνίς (Hesychius) ploughshare, OPrussian *wagni-s* coulter, Lith. *vágis* pin, plug, f. Indogermanic root **woghʷ-* (Teut. **waȝ-*); cf. Skr. *vāh-* ? to force.

The LG. and Du. form with *i* for *e* (whence perh. the Sw. form and the Eng. WIG *sb.*¹, a kind of cake) is not easy to account for. It may be due to a special sound-change in some local dialect; the hypothesis that it represents an ablaut-variant (OTeut. **weȝjo-z*) is inadmissible.]

1. a. A piece of wood, metal, or other hard material, thick at one end and tapering to a thin edge at the other; chiefly used as a tool operated by percussion (or, less frequently, pressure) applied to the thick end, for splitting wood, stone, etc., forcing apart contiguous objects, dilating a fissure or cavity, tightening or securing some part of a structure, raising a heavy body, and other similar purposes. Hence, in *Mechanics*, the type of simple machine of which the wedge proper is an example, and which includes also knives, chisels, and cutting and piercing instruments in general; formerly reckoned separately among the 'mechanical powers', but now regarded as a variety of the inclined plane.

c **725** *Corpus Gloss.* (Hessels) C 970 *Cuneus*, waecg. *a* **1050** *Liber Scintill.* xxvii. (1889) 103 Yfele treowes on oste yfel næȝel oððe wecg on to fæstniȝenne ys. *a* **1250** *J. de Garlande* in Wright *Voc.* (1857) 137 Et cum cuneis [*glossed* wedgys] et cavillis. **1357** in *Pipe Roll 32 Edw. III* m. 34/2 ij. Wegges ferri. *c* **1391** CHAUCER *Astrol.* I. xiv. 4 Thorw wich pyn ther goth a litel wegge which þat is cleped the hors, þat streyneth alle thise parties to hepe. *c* **1440** *York Myst.* xxxv. 235 Goode wegges schall we take þis tyde, and feste þe foote [of the cross]. *Ibid.* 242 Gyffe me þis wegge, I schall it in dryue. *c* **1440** *Promp. Parv.* 81/2 Clyte, or clote, or vegge, *cuneus*. ? **1474** *Stonor Papers* (Camden) I. 147, j weegge of yron. **1523–34** FITZHERB. *Husb.* §3 The plough-fote is a lyttell pece of wodde, with a croked ende set before in a morteys in the ploughe-beame, sette fast with wedges, to dryue vppe and downe. **1542** *Extracts Aberd. Reg.* (1844) I. 184 To..reforme and mend the artillery, and to mak carttis, boolis, vagis, and all vder necessaris belangand thairto. **1555** EDEN *Decades* (Arb.) 369 The marble stone..they breake and cleaue with wedgies of iren. **1569** SPENSER *Theat., Sonets* v, I heard the tronke to grone vnder the wedge. **1613** in *Trans. Exeter Dioc. Archit. Soc.* Ser. II. (1867) I. 395 For 5 peire of iron wegges to make faste the brasses, xij d. **1648** WILKINS *Math. Magic* I. viii. 52 The fift Mechanicall faculty is the Wedge, which is a known instrument, commonly used in the Cleaving of wood. **1697** DRYDEN *Æneis* VII. 711 Tyrrheus.. left his Wedge within the cloven Oak. **1711** *Milit. & Sea Dict.* II. (ed. 4), *Wedges* are us'd to make fast the Mast in the Partners. They also put a Wedge into the Heels of the Top-Masts, to bear them upon the Tressel-Trees. **1728** CHAMBERS *Cycl.*, *Wedge*, *Cuneus*, in Mechanicks, the last of the five Powers or simple Machines... To the Wedge may be refer'd all Edge-Tools, and Instruments which have a sharp Point, in order to cut, cleave, slit, chop, pierce, bore, or the like; as Knives, Hatchets, Swords, Bodkins, &c. **1773** W. EMERSON *Princ. Mech.* (ed. 3) 44 The sharper the wedge, or the more acute its angle, the easier it will divide any thing or overcome any resistance. **1784** COWPER *Task* v. 43 Forth goes the woodman..To wield the axe And drive the wedge in yonder forest drear. *a* **1790** W. NEWTON tr. *Vitruvius* x. xviii. (1791) 266 The distended ropes..are then confined at the holes with wedges, that they may not slip. **1842** *Min. Proc. Inst. Civil Engin.* II. 73 The wedges employed to secure the rails in the chairs are similarly compressed. **1858** SIMMONDS *Dict. Trade*, *Wedge*,..a small fastening for a door or window. **1867** SMYTH *Sailor's Wordbk.*, *Setting-up*, raising a ship from her blocks, shores, &c. by wedges driven between the heels of the shore and the dock foundation. **1888** W. E. NICHOLSON *Gloss. Terms Coal Trade* (E.D.D.), *Wedge*, a sharp or flat pointed iron or steel, used for splitting and breaking coal or stone. **1923** *My Magazine* Jan. 22 Wedge. A small piece of wood placed under the heel of a living model for support. It is seen in statues.

b. *Grafting.* (*a*) A peg to keep the cleft open. (*b*) The tongue or tapered end of a scion or stock.

1523–34 FITZHERB. *Husb.* §136 Thou muste haue..a mallet, to dryue the knyfe and thy wedge in-to the tree. **1653** AUSTEN *Fruit-Trees* 48 Being cloven with the knife, and a wedge of Box, or other hard wood knockt in, to keep it open, then prepare the Graft [etc.]. **1832** *Planting* 30 in *Libr. Usef. Knowl.*, *Husb.* III, The upper division of the scion made by the slit, termed the tongue or wedge, is then inserted into the cleft of the stock.

c. The movable slip of wood, tapered on one side, by means of which the blade of a carpenter's plane is adjusted and fastened in the stock.

1678 MOXON *Mech. Exerc.* iv. 64 This knocking on the Britch [of a plane] raises the Iron, so it also raises and loosens the wedge: therefore..whenever you knock upon the Britch, you must also knock upon the wedge, to fasten the Iron again.

d. *Arch.* A voussoir.

1726 LEONI *Alberti's Archit.* I. 73 b, The last wedge, which is called the key-stone, shou'd be cut according to the lines of the other wedges, but left a small matter bigger at the top, so that it may..drive the lower wedges closer together. *a* **1790** W. NEWTON tr. *Vitruvius* VI. xi. (1791) 147 In edifices which are built with piers and arches of wedges with the joints tending to their centers, the extreme piers are to be made of a greater breadth, that they may resist the force when the wedges, pressed by the weight of the walls, and impelling toward the center, thrust against the abutments. **1849** FREEMAN *Archit.* 20 We might conceive an arch whose voussoirs should be wedges, not of stone..but of wood.

2. a. *fig.* and in fig. context.

1581 J. BELL *Haddon's Answ. Osor.* 278 Take an other unvanquishable argument such as all yᵉ Heretiques wedges with all their Beatelles and malles cannot beat abroad. *c* **1620** A. HUME *Brit. Tongue* (1865) 13 Now I am cum to a knot that I have noe wedg to cleave. **1645** FULLER *Good Th. in Bad Times* II. vi, The same wedge wil serve to cleave the former difficulty. **1704** F. FULLER *Med. Gymn.* (1711) 78, I hope these Reflections will not be misinterpreted..as a Wedge to make way for any Design of mine. **1841** CALHOUN *Sp.* Wks. 1861 IV. 11 This bill is the entering wedge for all the measures of the session. **1857** G. A. LAWRENCE *Guy Liv.* xxvii. 267 Just as he had fixed on the astute question which was to drive the first wedge into the mystery, Guy turned.. and met him full. **1909** G. A. T. MIDDLETON *Eng. Ch. Archit.* i. 17 England became a wedge of paganism driven in as it were between the Christianity of the Continent..and the Christianity of Ireland. **1913** R. LUCAS *Ld. North* xiv. II. 168 Shelburne..perceived that there was room for a wedge to be driven in between the French and the Americans.

b. Phr. ***the thin*** (***little*** or ***small***) ***end of the wedge***, a small beginning which it is hoped or feared may lead to something greater. Also *attrib.*

1856 C. FOX *Jrnl.* 8 Nov. in *Memories Old Friends* (1882) xxii. 308 Beware, Englishmen, of the tendencies to hierarchy in your country when the thin end of the wedge is introduced: it will work its way on to all this. **1858** TROLLOPE *Dr. Thorne* xxxi, (Chapter-heading) The Small End of the Wedge. *Ibid.*, We have all heard of the little end of the wedge... That pill had been the little end of Lady Arabella's wedge. Up to that period she had been struggling in vain to make a severance between her husband and her enemy [the doctor]. **1867** *Hansard Commons* 27 June 615 The thin end of the wedge. **1868** FREEMAN *Norm. Conq.* (1877) II. x. 460 The rule [of Chrodegang] was but the small end of the wedge. **1884** *Graphic* 20 Dec. 639/3 Cremation advocates have managed to get in the thin end of the wedge in France.

attrib. **1896** *Daily News* 21 Feb. 5/1 How many reforms have the Tories resisted with the thin-end-of-the-wedge argument.

3. a. An ingot of gold, silver, etc. ? *Obs.*

Presumably so called because the ordinary form of an ingot was that of a wedge; cf. Heb. *lāšōn*, lit. 'tongue', used in the same sense; but in the Eng. use of the word there appears to be no evidence of any reference to shape. The OE. *wecg* is in translations of Matt. xvii. 27 used for 'piece of money' (rendering L. *stater*).

c **900** *Bæda's Hist.* I. i. (1890) 26 Berende on wecga orum ares & isernes, leades & seolfres. *c* **1000** ÆLFRIC *Hom.* I. 60 Hi behwyrfdon heora are..on sumum ȝyldenum wecge, and ðone on sæ awurpan. *c* **1100** *Gloss.* in Wr.-Wülcker 141/34 *Metallum*, ælces kynnes wecg vel ora oððe clyna. *c* **1380** WYCLIF *Wks.* (1880) 49 Þei wilen not touche an halpeny or ferþing wiþ þe coyn..of the kyng,..a weeg of siluer or a cuppe of gold þei wolen handil faste. **1436** *Libel Eng. Policy* in *Pol. Poems* (Rolls) II. 171 Also Pruse mene make here aventure Of plate of sylvere, of wegges gode and sure In grete plente. *c* **1450** CAPGRAVE *St. Aug.* (1910) 48 He..made þe vesseles of syluyr whech longed on-to þe cherch to be molten, and þe weggis þerof be sold and departed to þor men. **1535** COVERDALE *Job* xxviii. 16 No wedges of gold of Ophir. **1560** BIBLE (Geneva) *Josh.* vii. 21 Two hundreth shekels of siluer and a wedge of golde of fyftie shekels weight. [So **1611** (*margin*, Heb. tunge)]. **1585** HIGINS *Junius' Nomencl.* 403/1 *Aurum purum, infectum*,..gold vnwrought, and in the wedge. **1613** [see INGOT 1]. **1634** SIR T. HERBERT *Trav.* 140 Fifty thousand Talents of vncoyned Gold, besides siluer wedges. **1694** BRAGGE *Disc. Parables* v. 194 'Tis like a child's slighting a wedge of gold, and rather pursuing an empty bubble because it shines and glitters. **1719** DE FOE *Crusoe* I. (Globe) 196, I found there..some small Bars or Wedges of Gold.

b. *Cant.* Silver, whether money or plate.

1725 *New Cant. Dict.*, *Wedge*, Plate, or Silver or Gold Moveables and Trinkets: Also Money. **1812** *Sporting Mag.* XXXIX. 209 A convenient fencing repository, from the lady's tyke to the nobleman's wedge. **1821** *Life D. Haggart* (ed. 2) 98, I had some wedge planked in a garret in North Leith... I was anxious to convert it into blunt. **1896** *Westm. Gaz.* 29 May 2/1 Between two and three I turns over a pawnbroker's shop, and gets safe away with a lot of wedge—that's silver plate.

attrib. **1812** J. H. VAUX *Flash Dict.* s.v. *Wedge*, A wedge-feeder, a silver-spoon. **1839** AINSWORTH *Jack Sheppard* II. xiv, A wedge-lobb, otherwise known as a silver snuff-box.

4. A lump or cake of any solid substance.

1577 B. GOOGE *Heresbach's Husb.* III. 146b, The Creame ..is..put into a vessell..wherin with often beating and mouing up and downe, they so shake the milke, as they seuer the thinnest part of from the thicke, which at the fyrst gather together in little crombles, and after with the continuance of the violent moouing commeth to a whole wedge, or cake [L. *in massam cogatur*]. **1728** E. S[MITH] *Compleat Housew.* (ed. 2) 57 When you have churned, wash your Butter..and beat it well..; let it stand in a Wedge..till the next morning. **1833** HT. MARTINEAU *Berkeley* I. iv. 74 Different kinds of rude money..; skins in one country, shells in another, and wedges of salt in a third.

5. *transf.* **a.** A formation of troops tapering to the front or van, in order to cleave a way through an opposing force. (Orig. after L. *cuneus*; cf. *wedge-battle* in 10.) Now more widely of a body of people.

1614 RALEGH *Hist. World* III. xii. §7. 152 Taking a choise Companie of the most able men, whom he cast into the forme of a Wedge, or Diamond. **1615** H. PEACHAM *Relat. Affairs Cleve & Gulick* C 2b, The Horse..were showne in the field in order of fight: their manner was in forme of a Pile or wedge, called of the old Romans, *Cuneus*. **1674** MILTON *P.R.* III. 309 See how in warlike muster they appear, In Rhombs and wedges, and half moons, and wings. **1697** DRYDEN *Æneis* XII. 842 One Soul inspiring all, Form'd in a Wedge, the Foot approach the Wall. **1802** C. JAMES *Milit. Dict.* s.v. **1821** SHELLEY *Hellas* 377 Thrice their keen wedge of battle pierced our lines. **1887** *Times* (weekly ed.) 21 Oct. 2/1 A wedge of 15 or 18 policemen were endeavouring to be driven into that meeting. **1900** M. HEWLETT *Richard Yea-and-Nay* II. ix, The wedge held firm; red work for axe and swords while it lasted. **1913** J. H. MORRISON *On Trail Pioneers* 1 Every entrance is blocked, and down every gangway a long wedge of standing people has been driven deep into the heart of the house.

b. The **V**-shaped formation adopted by a number of geese or other wildfowl when flying.

[**1725** WATTS *Logic* II. ii. §1 The wild Geese flew over the Thames in the Form of a Wedge.] **1869** BLACKMORE *Lorna Doone* xxix, So like half a wedge of wildfowl, to and fro we swept the field. **1889** *Daily News* 11 Jan. 5/3 There drifts over the moor a wedge of clangorous geese, making for the Channel.

c. *gen.* Something in the form of a wedge; a wedge-shaped part or piece of anything.

1821 SHELLEY *Adonais* l, One keen pyramid with wedge sublime, Pavilioning the dust of him who planned This refuge for his memory. **1835** DICKENS *Sk. Boz, Making a Night of it*, A pot of the real draught stout, and..cushions of bread, and wedges of cheese. **1860** TYNDALL *Glac.* I. xii. 89 The glacier here..was cut up into thin wedges. **1889** H. SAUNDERS *Man. Brit. Birds* 660 The three outer primaries are of a dusky-black which becomes paler towards the edges of the inner webs, though there is no grey 'wedge'. **1897** *Allbutt's Syst. Med.* IV. 430 It is better, instead of removing such a kidney, to treat each focus independently by scraping or by the excision of a wedge.

d. A strip of land narrowing to a point.

[**1678** PHILLIPS (ed. 4), *Wedge*, a Sand so called, being broad at the West end, and sharp at the East end, and lies on the North side of the Marget Sands.] **1867** MURCHISON *Siluria* xvii. (ed. 4) 412 The Coal-field..thins out..so much that to the west of Béthune it has merely become a narrow wedge. **1918** *Blackw. Mag.* June 771/2 The white wedge of Kildin Island is now on our port bow.

e. In an organ (see quot.).

1852 SEIDEL *Organ* 78 The wedge of the mouth..is the interval between the under lip and the language.

f. *Meteorol.* A narrow wedge-shaped area of high pressure between two adjacent cyclonic systems; also the representation of this on a weather-chart.

1887 R. ABERCROMBY *Weather* ii. 26 Between the two cyclones the isobar of 29·9 ins. projects upwards, like a wedge or an inverted letter V., but this time encloses high pressure; this shape of lines is called a 'wedge'.

g. The wedge-shaped stroke in cuneiform characters. Also *attrib.*

1821 RICH *Babylon & P.* (1839) 249 The wedges in the third [kind of inscription] cross each other. **1883** G. EVANS *Ess. Assyriol.* 6 The kind of writing in the copies, with the wedge as its fundamental element, was to them perfectly new.

1881 TYLOR *Anthrop.* i. 11 Deciphered from the wedge-characters of Nineveh. **1915** PINCHES in *Proc. Soc. Bibl. Archæ ol.* XXXVII. 90 We have a direct testimony to the practice outside the wedge-inscriptions.

h. Short for *wedge-shell* (see 10).

1815 S. BROOKES *Introd. Conchol.* 157 Wedge, *Donax*.

i. A v-shaped sign used in various musical and other notations (see quots.).

1893 E. M. THOMPSON *Handbk. Greek & Latin Palæogr.* v. 68 The paragraph-mark was not..uniformly the horizontal stroke; the wedge >..and similar forms were employed. **1970** *Language* XLVI. 78 Wedges printed after vowel symbols, e.g. [aˇaˇaˇaˇ], indicate raising, backing, lowering, and fronting. **1980** *Early Music* July 401/1 The most fascinating [signs] are the wedges indicating *crescendo*, *diminuendo* and *messa da voce* on single long notes: ◀, ▶, ◆, and a passage with second-position fingerings.

j. *Golf.* A golf club with a wedge-shaped head, used for lofting the ball at approach shots, or (= *sand wedge* s.v. SAND *sb.*[2] 10a) out of a bunker, etc. Also, a shot made with a wedge.

[**1924** J. WHITE *Easier Golf* iv. 100 What I attempt to do is to use this heel [of a club]..as a wedge, and by driving this into the sand behind the ball I create sufficient disturbance to force the ball out of any lie.] **1937** [see *sand wedge* s.v. SAND *sb.*[2] 10a]. **1952** *Chambers's Jrnl.* May 300/1 Basil walked moodily off the tee, and after five minutes' search found his ball embedded in a patch of the foulest rough on the course, hacked it out with his wedge, and, playing two odd to the green, lost the hole. **1961** *Times* 1 July 4/1 He..played an overcautious wedge at the Royal. **1975** *Daily Tel.* (Colour Suppl.) 12 Sept. 9/4 Putting is out; most golfers carry just a driver, a four-wood, mid-iron and wedge.

k. A wedge heel; a wedge-soled shoe. See sense 9b below. *colloq.*

1959 *Chambers's 20th Cent. Dict.* Add. **1965** R. HARDWICK *Plotters* (1966) xi. 102 Stretch pants, wedges, and a leghorn hat. **1968** J. IRONSIDE *Fashion Alphabet* 137 *Wedge*, a solid heel joined to the sole in one solid piece. **1976** *Washington Post* 19 Apr. A12/3 (Advt.), Casual style wedges in Oxford and slip-on styles. **1983** *Times* 14 July 11/3 Gladiator straps on stacked wooden wedge..£44.50.

l. A hair style in which the ends of the hair are slightly graduated so that they form a series of wedges. orig. *U.S.*

1976 *Time* 19 Apr. 69 There are many variations on the new wedge. Stylists at the Paul McGregor shops in New York and Los Angeles have shaped the back of the cut into three inverted pyramids. **1977** *Daily News* (Perth, Austral.) 19 Jan. 6/4 After she became a headliner, Dorothy's hairdo, called the wedge, sent girls rushing off to hairdressers to duplicate the look. **1985** *Hair* Summer 78 (*caption*), Short, sculptured sweeping version of the wedge has classy clout in the form of a pink flash.

6. *Geom.* **a.** A triangular prism. **b.** A simple solid formed by cutting a triangular prism by any two planes.

1710 J. CLARKE tr. *Rohault's Nat. Philos.* (1729) I. 87 Let ABC represent a Wedge; and let CG be perpendicular to AB. **1829** *Nat. Philos., Mech.* II. x. 43 (U.K.S.) A Wedge is a solid figure, which is called in geometry a triangular prism. **1883** *Encycl. Brit.* XVI. 24/2 The wedge being merely the frustum of a triangular prism, we have at once [etc.]. **1895** A. LODGE *Mensuration* 7 If from a triangular prism of indefinite length, a piece is cut off by two transverse planes which are not parallel, this piece is called a wedge.

7. *Her.* A charge consisting of an isosceles triangle with a very acute angle at its vertex.

1716 S. KENT *Gramm. Her., Proctor of Norfolk*; He beareth Or, three Wedges Sable. **1780** EDMONDSON *Her.* II. *Alph. Arms*, *Isam* or *Isham*. Vert, three wedges ar. **1847** W. S. EVANS *Gramm. Her.* 151 The Nail (sometimes called the Passion-nail)..must not be confounded with the Wedge, which is of course wider at the top, and in shape something like a pile.

8. Cambridge University. ***the (wooden) wedge***: the student last in the classical tripos list.

This counterpart to the older 'wooden spoon' (see WOODEN *a.*), designating the last man in the mathematical tripos, was suggested by the fact that in the first classical tripos (1824) the last man was Wedgwood of Christ's College, afterwards famous as an English etymologist.

1852 BRISTED *Five Yrs. Eng. Univ.* (ed. 2) 253 Of the remainder, five were Wranglers, four of these Double men, and a fifth a favorite for the Wedge... The last man is called the Wedge, corresponding to the Spoon in Mathematics.

9. a. Combinations, chiefly similative, as ***wedge-blade***, ***-block***, ***-bolt***, ***-fashion***, ***-form***, ***-head***, ***-shape***, ***-stone***, ***-wad***; ***wedge-balancing***, ***-billed***, ***-sided*** adjs.

1921 D. H. LAWRENCE *Tortoises* 19 Four rowing limbs, and one *wedge-balancing head. **1836** E. STANLEY *Fam. Hist. Birds* xiii. (1848) 289 Tribe 1. Cuneirostral (*Wedge-Billed). **1917** D. H. LAWRENCE *Look! We have come Through!* 113 The fine, fine wind... Like a fine, an exquisite chisel, a *wedge-blade inserted. **1868** *Rep. to Govt. U.S. Munitions of War* 55 The breech is opened and closed by a *wedge-block worked by a hinged lever. **1892** GREENER *Breech-Loader* 22 A round steel *wedge-bolt. **1665** J. WEBB *Stone-Heng* 190 These [stones] also were either of a *Wedge fashion, or wedged under the Great One. **1802** PLAYFAIR *Illustr. Hutton. Theory* 295 This *wedge-form of the whinstone masses. **1899** *Westm. Gaz.* 7 June 4/2 A disc on which black and white wedge-forms alternated. **1880** *Encycl. Brit.* XIII. 343/1 These [bars of steel] are welded together by forging to *wedge-heads, tying together with wire [etc.]. **1812** SIR J. SINCLAIR *Syst. Husb. Scot.* I. 43 The white thorn [hedge]..when properly trained, and occasionally cut over, or dressed in the *wedge-shape,..will last for ages. **1895** HOFFMAN *Begin. Writing* 141 The end of the stick would be sharpened into a wedge-shape. **1852** *Mechanics' Mag.* 10 July 23 When taper or '*wedge-sided' type is employed, the cylinder need not be more in circumference than the size of the sheet of paper. **1854** CT. E. DE WARREN tr. *De Saulcy's Round Dead Sea* II. 113 The voussoir, or early *wedge-stone. **1879** *Man. Artill. Exerc.* 53 *Wedge wads..consist of two wooden wedges connected by a piece of cane... These wads are to be rammed home separately after the projectiles.

b. Designating a wedge-shaped heel extended under the instep of a woman's shoe (also, the sole which includes this), or a shoe having such a heel. Freq. as ***wedge-heel***, ***shoe***, ***sole***; ***wedge-heeled***, ***-soled*** adjs. Cf. sense 5k above.

1939 M. B. PICKEN *Lang. Fashion* 164/3 *Wedge-soled*, having a wedge-shaped piece making a solid sole, flat on the ground from heel to toe. **1940** GRAVES & HODGE *Long Week-End* xxi. 375 A high-heeled fancy shoe..and a wedge-heeled streamlined type. **1940** *Manch. Guardian Weekly* 11 Oct. 259 Today's displays of courts..and wedge-heel, and all other of the creations of the fashion-designer, give no indication..of what was really a welcome weeding out. **1940** O. NASH in *New Yorker* 23 Nov. 18/2 Let us give thanks that women's wedge shoes weren't invented until they were. **1942** in C. W. Cunnington *Eng. Women's Clothing in Present Cent.* (1952) viii. 271 Practical [shoes], with flatter heels, square toed and wedge-soled. **1951** [see CREEPER 1 d]. **1957** R. HOGGART *Uses of Literacy* iv. 102 Mail-order firms advertise fancy wedge-shoes. **1975** D. BEATY *Electric Train* 153 Painted faces clumping up..on six-inch wedge shoes. **1983** P. DEVLIN *All of us Here* x. 112 Her daughter, in a new permanently pleated skirt, wedge-heeled shoes.

10. Special comb.: † **wedge-battle** = sense 5a; **wedge-bill**, a bird with a wedge-shaped bill, as (*a*) the Australian *Sphenostoma cristatum*; (*b*) a S. American humming-bird of the genus *Schistes*; **wedge-bone**, † (*a*) the sphenoid bone; (*b*) a small bone sometimes occurring in lizards on the undersurface of the spinal column at the junction of a pair of vertebræ; **wedge-coral** (see quot.); **wedge-draining**, a mode of draining land, somewhat similar to *plug-draining*; **wedge-fern**, a fossil fern of the genus *Sphenopteris*; **wedge-fid** *Naut.* (see quot.); **wedge-form**, **-formed** *adjs.* = WEDGE-SHAPED; **wedge-grafting** (see quots.); **wedge-gun**, a field-gun in which a wedge is used in closing the breech; **wedge-leaf fern** = *wedge-fern*; **wedge-micrometer**, a graduated wedge-shaped piece of metal or glass, to be thrust between two fixed points to determine their distance apart; **wedge-photometer** *Astr.*, an instrument consisting of a wedge of glass, used for measuring the comparative brightness of stars; **wedge-press**, a press used for extracting oil from seeds; **wedge-shell**, a marine bivalve, belonging to *Donax* or allied genera; **wedge-tail** *Austral.*, the wedge-tailed eagle (see *wedge-tailed* adj.); = EAGLE-HAWK 2; **wedge-tailed** *a.*, having a wedge-shaped tail; used *spec.* in the names of birds, as the wedge-tailed eagle (*Uroaetus audax*) of Australia, and the wedge-tailed gull, *Rhodostethia rosea*; **wedge tent** = A TENT.

1598 BARRET *Theor. Warres* 78 Out of a square of men hath bin reduced a triangle or *wedge battell in perfect order to fight. **1603** KNOLLES *Hist. Turks* (1638) 273 The wedge battell of the Christians could not of the Turks be broken. **1848** GOULD *Birds of Australia* III. Pl. 17 Crested *Wedge-bill. **1861** —— *Trochil.* IV. Pl. 219 *Schistes personatus*,.. Masked Wedge-bill. *Ibid.* Pl. 220 White-throated Wedge-bill. **1615** CROOKE *Body of Man* 442 *Sphenoides* or the *Wedge-bone. **1871** HUXLEY *Anat. Vert.* v. 217 Such a..sub-vertebral wedge-bone is commonly developed beneath and between the odontoid bone and the body of the second vertebra. **1860** GOSSE *Actinol. Brit.* 324 The Smooth-ribbed *Wedge-coral. *Sphenotrochus Macandrewanus*. *Ibid.* 326 The Knotted Wedge-coral. *Sphenotrochus Wrightii*. **1830** *Cumb. Farm Rep.* 67 in *Libr. Usef. Knowl., Husb.* III, The *wedge or brick draining..is certainly not so well known among practical farmers as its merits deserve. **1867** W. W. SMYTH *Coal & Coal-mining* 36 Sphenopteris (*wedge-fern). **1867** SMYTH *Sailor's Word-bk.*, **Wedge-fids*, for top and top-gallant masts; in two parts, lifting by shores and sett-wedges. **1822** J. PARKINSON *Outl. Oryctol.* 221 Ovatedly *wedge-form. **1843** HOLTZAPFFEL *Turning* I. 15 In many plants the wedge-form plates..appear as an irregular cellular tissue. **1822** J. PARKINSON *Outl. Oryctol.* 188 A longitudinal, *wedge-formed, equivalved bivalve. **1861** DARWIN in *Life & Lett.* (1887) III. 265 These packets cohere into many wedge-formed masses in Orchis. **1838** W. BARRON in *Gardener's Mag.* XIV. 80 The grafting of the *Cedrus Deodara* on the Cedar of Lebanon..is accomplished by what I call *wedge-grafting. **1842** LOUDON *Suburban Hort.* §657 Wedge-grafting..is a modification of side-grafting. *Ibid.* §664 Herbaceous wedge-grafting is effected by paring the scion into a wedge shape, and inserting it into a corresponding slit in the stock. **1876** VOYLE & STEVENSON *Milit. Dict.* (ed. 3), *Wedge Gun. **1851** MANTELL *Petrif.* 32 The other characteristic Wealden plant is the Sphenopteris (*S. Mantelli*), or *wedge-leaf fern. **1891** *Century Dict.* s.v. *Micrometer*, *Wedge-micrometer. **1883** C. PRITCHARD in *Mem. R. Astron. Soc.* XLVII. 394 The question, then, arises as to the applicability of the *wedge-photometer to the measurement of the magnitude..of such stars. **1844** *Penny Mag.* Sept. 381 The triturated seeds were put into woollen bags which were wrapped up in hair-cloths, and then submitted to the *wedge-press. **1820** WODARCH *Introd. Conchol.* 23 Donax.—*Wedge-shell. **1935** A. C. CHISHOLM *Bird Wonders Austral.* x. 102 The *Wedge-tail is a formidable foe for any native mammal. **1965** [see EAGLE-HAWK 2]. **1974** D. STUART *Prince of my Country* ii. 9 Watching the long effortless circling of the wedgetail high in the air. **1977** *Times Lit. Suppl.* 21 Jan. 76/2 Australia is the only place in the whole world where the wedgetail eagle is known. **1848** GOULD *Birds of Australia* I. Pl. 1 *Wedge-tailed Eagle. **1872** COUES *Key N. Amer. Birds* 316 Wedge-tailed, or Ross' Rosy Gull. **1898** 'R. BOLDREWOOD' *Canvas Town Rom.* 73 The great wedge-tailed Eagle soaring above them. **1862** O. W. NORTON *Army Lett.* (1903) 49 We used to sleep on the ground or on pine boughs when we had the small *wedge tents. **1940** G. W. MARTIN *Mod. Camping Guide* v. 86 The wedge tent, known also as the A tent, is a popular model with explorers and other outdoorsmen who want something a little larger than a tiny crawl-in tent. **1980** D. T. ROSCOE *Your Bk. Camping* ('Your Bk.' Ser.) ii. 22 Wedge tents..are designed to save weight and bulk and to withstand wind better when the smaller end is pitched directly into it.

wedge (wɛdʒ), *v.*[1] Also 5–6 wegge. [f. WEDGE *sb.*]

1. a. *trans.* To tighten, fasten tight by driving in a wedge or wedges. Also with *in*, *on*, *up*.

c **1440** *Promp. Parv.* 520/1 Wedge, wythe a wedge [*Winch.* Wegge with a wegge], *cuneo*. **1523–34** FITZHERB. *Husb.* §24

Than maye he.. tothe the rakes.. and driue the tethe vpwarde faste and harde, and than wedge them aboue with drye woode of oke. **1667** BOYLE in *Phil. Trans.* II. 590 A piece of Shining Wood, wedged in with a piece of Cork. **1678** MOXON *Mech. Exerc.* iv. 66 The Iron [of the Plane] being then well wedg'd up. **1722** A. PHILIPS *Briton* III. v. 32 My Chariot straight; another, for the Prince. Store them with Spears; wedge on the keenest Scythes. *a* **1790** W. NEWTON tr. *Vitruvius* VI. xi. (1791) 146 When posts are placed under them, and wedged, the beams cannot settle or be damaged. **1816** JANE AUSTEN *Emma* xxviii, I have been assisting Miss Fairfax in trying to make her instrument stand steadily... You see we have been wedging one leg with paper. **1826** GWILT tr. *Vitruvius* VI. xi. (1860) 148 When posts are introduced and wedged up under them, the beams are prevented from sagging. **1840** H. S. TANNER *Canals & Rail Roads U.S.* 151 The wooden key used in wedging fast the upper string piece. **1842** *Min. Proc. Inst. Civil Engin.* II. 78 Compressed trenails.. would hold tighter than the trenails now used, which require to have the points split and wedged up. **1875** *Carpentry & Joinery* 55 The simple but useful operation of wedging tenon and mortice joints.

†**b.** *transf.* and *fig.* To fasten firmly or attach to. *Obs.*

1629 MAXWELL tr. *Herodian* IV. 191 Both the Emperours .. seeking to win and wedge men to their seuerall Factions, by faire Promises. **1670** G. H. *Hist. Cardinals* I. II. 46 They find the Prelates and Popes themselves, so wedg'd and link'd to Secular advantages, they have not time to think upon God.

†**c.** To render (a gun) useless by the insertion of a wedge. *Obs.*

1680 *Exact Jrnl. Siege Tangier* 8 Leaving the Guns double shotted, spiked and wedged with steel. *Ibid.* 11 The Men of Charles Fort having Spiked and Wedged their great Guns.

d. *to wedge up*: to raise a ship before launching, by means of slivers or wedges driven between the false keel and the bilgeways.

1879 'H. COLLINGWOOD' *Secret of Sands* xix, Four months .. saw her caulked, her seams paid, her hull painted, and, in short, everything ready, even to wedging up, for launching.

2. a. To cleave or split by driving in a wedge.

1530 PALSGR. 778/2, I wedge a blocke, I put in a wedge to cleave it, *je coigne*... Wedge this blocke, it wyll ryve the soner. **1606** SHAKS. *Tr. & Cr.* I. i. 35 My heart, As wedged with a sigh, would riue in twaine. **1678** [see WEDGING *vbl. sb.* 1].

b. To split *off*, to force *apart*, *asunder*, or *open*, by driving in a wedge. Also *fig.*

1853 KANE *Grinnell Exp.* xlvi. (1856) 423 And even now great ledges are wedged off from the hillsides by the ice. **1865** CARLYLE *Fredk. Gt.* XIX. vi. (1873) VIII. 201 Friedrich and he are wedged asunder by that dike of Russians and Austrians. **1873** MOGGRIDGE *Harv. Ants* I. 33 Having contrived to wedge off several large flakes of the rock. **1894** *Advance* (Chicago) Oct. 4 It is not commonly the big things but the little ones which wedge pastor and people apart. **1914** H. BALFOUR in *Jrnl. R. Anthrop. Inst.* XLIV. 33 A billet of lime wood, split at one end and wedged open with a stone.

3. a. *transf.* To drive, push, or squeeze (an object) into something where it is held fast; to fix firmly by driving in, or by pressing tight. Const. *into*, *in*, *under*, *between*. Also with adv., as *in*, *up*, *down*.

1513 DOUGLAS *Æneis* XI. xv. 85 Quhill that the lance.. wedgyt deip within hir cost stude. **1607** DEKKER *Whore of Babylon* L 1, Fall thunder, And wedge me into earth, stiffe as I am. **1613** SHAKS. *Hen. VIII*, IV. i. 58 Among the crow'd i' th' abbey, where a finger Could not be wedg'd in more. **1665** J. WEBB *Stone-Heng* 190 These [stones] also were either of a Wedge fashion, or wedged under the Great One. **1697** DAMPIER *Voy.* I. vii. 195 Besides what Gold and Sand they take up together, they often find great lumps, wedg'd between the Rocks. **1697** DRYDEN *Æneis* v. 285 Sergestus in the Centaur soon he pass'd, Wedg'd in the Rocky Sholes, and sticking fast. **1726** SWIFT *Gulliver* II. iii, Squeezing my legs together, [he] wedged them into the marrow-bone above my waist. **1764** FOOTE *Patron* III. Wks. 1799 I. 353, I was wedged so close in the pit, that I could scarcely get out. **1806** A. DUNCAN *Life of Nelson* 12 They became.. fast wedged in the ice. **1849** MACAULAY *Hist. Eng.* iii. I. 336 If a coach or a cart entered those alleys, there was danger that it would be wedged between the houses. **1852** MRS. STOWE *Uncle Tom's C.* vii. 43 The boy.. tried to wedge some of his cake into her mouth. **1869** DICKENS *Mut. Fr.* I. xiv, Driven into that nook, and wedged as he had described, was Gaffer's boat. **1870** *Spectator* 19 Nov. 1370/1 If they are permitted to go on, they will wedge themselves in between the Germans, and be able to enfilade the corps on each side. **1890** *Hardwicke's Sci.-Gossip* XXVI. 239 In its persevering search for the snails, it had got its head tightly wedged some distance into the wall. **1908** H. WALES *Old Allegiance* i. 14 He.. sat with.. his pipe firmly wedged in the corner of his mouth.

b. *fig.*

1607 SHAKS. *Cor.* II. iii. 30 Nay your wit will not so soone out as another mans will, 'tis strongly wedg'd vp in a blocke head. *a* **1659** BP. BROWNRIG *Serm.* (1674) I. xxvi. 340 He wedges in the other Prayer for a competency of temporal things. **1730** *Portland Papers* (Hist. MSS. Comm.) VI. 29 Having been wedged down in this detestible place [the Fleet prison] by an incurable and painful malady, poverty and tatters.

4. To pack or crowd (a number of persons or animals) in close formation, or in a limited space. Also with *together*.

1720 POPE *Iliad* XVII. 846 While Greece a heavy, thick Retreat maintains, Wedg'd in one Body like a Flight of Cranes. **1776** GIBBON *Decl. & F.* i. (1782) I. 16 The strength of the phalanx depended on sixteen ranks of long pikes, wedged together in the closest array. **1807** J. BARLOW *Columb.* III. 766 Here Zamor ranged his ax-men deep and wide, Wedged like a wall and thus the king defied. **1844** MARIA T. ASMAR *Mem. Babylonian Princ.* II. 68 The crowd was prodigious. Men, women, and even children were wedged in one dense mass. **1856** STANLEY *Sinai & Pal.* xiv. (1858) 465 A dense mass of pilgrims who sit or stand wedged round it. **1871** CARLYLE in *Mrs. Carlyle's Lett.* (1883) I. 8 The 2,000 human figures, wedged in the huge room into one dark mass, were singular to look down upon.

5. *intr.* **a.** To become fixed or jammed tight by (or as by) the operation of a wedge.

1726 LEONI *Alberti's Archit.* I. 55 Which all wedge together and intersect one another both with equal and unequal Angles. **1893** *Atlantic Monthly* Feb. 197/2 The men started carefully, holding the saw quite true that later it might not wedge.

b. To force one's way *in*. *rare.*

1616 B. JONSON *Devil an Ass* III. iii. 26 This comes of.. haunting The *Globes*, and *Mermaides*! wedging in with Lords, Still at the table!

c. *to wedge their way*, to fly in a wedge-shaped formation, tapering to the front or van. *poet.*

1667 MILTON *P.L.* VII. 426 Part loosly wing the Region, part more wise In common, rang'd in figure wedge thir way.

6. *to wedge out* (Geol.): = *thin out* s.v. THIN *v.*[1] 2 a; = *lens out* s.v. LENS *v.*

1819 [implied in *wedging out* s.v. WEDGING *vbl. sb.* 4]. **1839** R. I. MURCHISON *Silurian Syst.* 140 Limestone.. can be traced tapering away from a central mass to thin extremities, which really wedge out between the coal grits and the older deposits. **1945** *Bull. Amer. Assoc. Petroleum Geologists* XXIX. 1563 The distinction from the Permeability Trap Reservoirs is made by restricting the Pinch-Out Trap Reservoirs to types located in such stratigraphic intervals or zones which actually wedge out. **1966** *Earth-Sci. Rev.* I. 163 Ignimbrites tend to wedge out against or thin over topographic highs. **1979** *Nature* 27 Sept. 267/1 These nappes wedge out and converge to the west and seem to represent a telescoping of Lower Palæozoic Facies.

wedge (wɛdʒ), *v.*[2] In 7 wage. [Of obscure origin; the modern form is prob. less correct than the earlier *wage*, but cf. WEDGE *sb.* 4.] *trans.* To cut (wet clay) into masses and work them by kneading and throwing down, in order to expel air-bubbles. Hence **'wedging** *vbl. sb.*

1686 PLOT *Staffordsh.* 123 [Potter's clay] is brought to the wageing board, where it is slit into flat thin pieces..: This being done, they wage it, i.e. knead or mould it like bread. **1825** J. NICHOLSON *Oper. Mech.* 461 Wedging the clay is a similar process [to that of slapping]... The presser cuts off, with a thin brass wire, a piece of clay from the mass, which he slaps forcibly between the palms of his hands, and then with great violence throws it on the board. **1839** URE *Dict. Arts* 1011 The first of which is called the potter's *sloping* [ed. 5, 1860 *slapping*] or *wedging*. **1860** W. WHITE *Wrekin* xxvii. 297 The [pug-]mill, however, continued to work, and in time convinced the men of their stupidity; and now, if a man were ordered to 'wedge' his own clay, his answer would be 'Aw'll stroike first'. *Ibid.*, The clay.. is.. thrown into the 'pug-mill', or 'wedging-mill', a large upright cylinder, in which it is forced or screwed gradually downwards, and extruded at the bottom in a continuous cubical mass.

wedge, obs. var. WAGE *sb.* and *v.*

1530 PALSGR. 287/2 Wedge a pledge, *gaige*, *pleige*. *Ibid.* 778/2, I wedge, I lay in pledge, *je gaige*. I wedge my heed it is nat so.

wedged (wɛdʒd), *ppl. a.*[1] [f. WEDGE *sb.* and *v.*[1] + -ED.] Shaped like a wedge.

1552 HULOET, Wedged, *cuneatus*. **1722** A. PHILIPS *Briton* I. i. 2 In Chariots, fang'd with Scythes, they scour the Field: Drive through our wedged Batalions with a Whirl. **1730** A. GORDON *Maffei's Amphith.* 307 The Key-Stone in the middle is wedged, and, as we say, Swallow-tail'd. **1809** CAMPBELL *Gert. Wyom.* III. xxv, With.. arrowy frize, and wedged ravelin. *a* **1813** A. WILSON *Foresters* Wks. (Belfast 1846) 250 Above, around, in numerous flocks are seen Long lines of ducks o'er this their fav'rite scene; Some to the lake in wedged divisions bend. **1827** *Encycl. Lond.* XXII. 806/2 Two fore-teeth, of which the upper are wedged, the lower are acute. **1867** EMERSON *Poems, May-day* 29 Or hark, Where yon wedged line the Nestor leads, Steering north with raucous cry Through tracts and provinces of sky. **1874** THEARLE *Naval Archit.* 336 The cover being secured by wedged buttons worked with a spanner. **1891** *Century Dict.*, *Wedged*, in *zool.*, wedge-shaped; cuneiform or cuneate: as, a wedged bone; the wedged tail of a bird.

wedged (wɛdʒd), *ppl. a.*[2] [f. WEDGE *v.*[2] + -ED[1].] Of wet clay: that has been wedged to expel air-bubbles before it is worked.

1903 in J. Burnett *Useful Toil* (1974) III. 298 From balls of wedged or refined clay he made the pancake-like shapes of clay which he had to use in making the next set of plates. **1967** M. CHANDLER *Ceramics in Mod. World* ii. 63 However well pugged or well *wedged* (hand worked to eliminate air) his clay may be, the ceramic sculptor cannot be certain that it contains no *blebs*.

wedge-like ('wɛdʒlaɪk), *a.* [f. WEDGE *sb.* + -LIKE.] Like or resembling a wedge.

1594 T. B. *La Primaud. Fr. Acad.* II. 48 There are commonly sixe bones, which compasse the braine on eche side, besides that which is called the wedge-like bone, which is vnder the pallat of the mouth. **1610** HOLLAND *Camden's Brit.* I. 456 The Wedge-like-forme of the country. **1652** BENLOWES *Theophila* X. xci, But still thy knotty Brain with wedg-like Anguish cleave. **1774** GOLDSM. *Nat. Hist.* VI. 239 Of these [teeth] there are six rows,.. sharp-pointed, and of a wedge-like figure. **1840** *Civil Engin. & Arch. Jrnl.* III. 125/1 They are farther secured by a wedgelike pin driven into their centres. **1899** *Allbutt's Syst. Med.* VIII. 598 Diminished by degrees into mere wedge-like streaks.

wedger ('wɛdʒə(r)). [f. WEDGE *v.*[2] + -ER[1].] A workman who wedges clay to expel air-bubbles from it.

1881 *Harper's Mag.* Feb. 361/2 The 'wedger' takes a lump of.. twenty pounds, lays it on the kneading block before him, [etc.]. **1921** *Dict. Occup. Terms* (1927) §104 *Wedger*, *clay wedger*, cuts lump of clay into pieces or wedges with wire cutter, and beats one piece of clay vigorously against another to make it homogeneous and free of air bubbles, for use in manufacture of highest class ware.

wedge-shaped ('wɛdʒʃeɪpt), *a.* Shaped like a wedge, cuneiform; *Bot.* and *Zool.* = CUNEATE.

1788 J. WHITE *Jrnl. Voy. N.S. Wales* (1790) 143 The tail [of this bird] is long and wedge-shaped. **1796** WITHERING *Brit. Plants* (ed. 3) III. 843 Leaves wedge-shaped. **1837** *Civil Engin. & Arch. Jrnl.* I. 24/2 The rafters to be of wood .. and the section to be wedge-shaped. **1845** LINDLEY *Sch. Bot.* i. (1858) 10 If very much wider at the point than at any other part, they [leaves] are *cuneate* or *wedge-shaped*. **1867** SCHELE DE VERE *Studies in English* 10 The wedge-shaped inscriptions of Cyrus, Darius, and Xerxes. **1893** TUCKEY tr. *Hatschek's Amphioxus* 90 Changing to high and sharply pointed wedge-shaped cells.

wedgewise ('wɛdʒwaɪz), *adv.* [f. WEDGE *sb.* + -WISE.] After the manner, in the form, of a wedge.

1548 *Elyot's Dict.*, *Cuneatim*, wedgewyse, by lyttell bandes or companies, imbattayled wedgewise. **1600** HOLLAND *Livy* II. l. 79 They.. with a pointed battaile wedgewise pierced through and made themselves passage. **1610** —— *Camden's Brit.* I. 456 It lieth Wedg-wise upon the sea. **1657** R. CARPENTER *Astrol.* 28 That these words may be understood to the bottom, and withstand all Objections; and that no opposition may wedge-wise enter upon them. **1703** NEVE *City & C. Purchaser* 10 Bricks moulded.. Wedge-wise, broader above, than they are below. **1852** DE MORGAN in Graves *Life Sir W. R. Hamilton* (1889) III. 415 Nothing but two sheets of thin pasteboard.. with three bits of book-covering cloth.. pasted on, so as to open out wedgewise. **1900** M. HEWLETT *Richard Yea-and-Nay* II. ix, Inside the town gate they took up close order, wedgewise, linked and riveted.

wedgie ('wɛdʒɪ). *colloq.* Also **wedgy.** [f. WEDGE *sb.* + -Y[6].] A wedge-heeled shoe (see WEDGE *sb.* 9 b); more recently, also *spec.* one with a built-up or 'stacked' sole. Usu. in *pl.*

1940 *Women's Wear Daily* 15 Mar. 18/1 New streamlined wedgies that make the foot look smaller. **1943** *Consumers' Res. Bull.* (U.S.) Dec. 20/2 Brown leather 'wedgie' with bottom-sole of thin leather. **1950** [see *sling-back* s.v. SLING *sb.*[2] 7]. **1962** A. HUXLEY *Island* ix. 133 Soft Platform Wedgies in Wide Widths. **1974** E. BRAWLEY *Rap* (1975) I. v. 83 She always wore those white wedgies, old Marie-Claude, claimed they eased her feet on the job.

wedging ('wɛdʒɪŋ), *vbl. sb.* [f. WEDGE *v.*[1] and *sb.* + -ING[1].]

1. a. The action of driving in a wedge or wedges, or of fixing or cleaving by this means; the condition of being thus fixed.

1678 MOXON *Mech. Exerc.* v. 98 They drive a Wedge so far in the kerf as they dare.. and so provide the Saw a freer and easier passage through the Stuff: This Wedging they continue so oft as they find occasion. **1825**, **1842** Foxtail wedging [see FOXTAIL 4]. **1893** TUCKEY tr. *Hatschek's Amphioxus* 140 We saw the oval notochord transverse section still wedged in between the cells of the mesenteron. .. In the region of the later segments we still find the former condition of the wedging.

b. *concr.* A wedge-shaped piece or pieces of some hard material driven in for tightening or securing.

1825 J. NICHOLSON *Oper. Mech.* 337 The wheels are fixed on the shaft by means of a wedging of hard wood, driven in all round.

2. *Geol.* The flaking *off* (of rock, etc.), as if by the operation of a wedge.

1882 A. GEIKIE *Text-bk. Geol.* VII. 928 Their naked precipices are kept bare and steep by the wedging off of successive slices of rock along lines of joint.

3. *Sport.* (See quot.)

1897 *Encycl. Sport* I. 583 *Spraint*, the excrement of the otter; also called *wedging*.

4. *Geol.* With *out*: the narrowing of a stratum or the like to the point of extinction. Cf. WEDGE *v.*[1] 6.

1819 J. FORBES *Geol. Land's-End District* (1822) 21 At one point of this natural section, an instructive example of what is called by geologists the *wedging out* of a bed, is observable. **1883** W. S. GRESLEY *Gloss. Coal-Mining* 283 *Wedging out*, cropping or thinning out.

5. *attrib.*, as ***wedging joint***; **wedging crib, curb** *Mining* (see CRIB *sb.* 12 and CURB *sb.* 10).

1839 URE *Dict. Art* 972 Three kinds of cribs are employed; called wedging, spiking, and main cribs. *Ibid.* 973 The flange for the wedging joint is best turned inwards. **1881** RAYMOND *Mining Gloss.*, *Wedging-curb* or *Wedging-crib*, Eng.

Wedgwood ('wɛdʒwʊd). Also incorrectly **Wedgewood.** [A proper name: see below.]

1. a. Used *attrib.* to designate the pottery made by Josiah Wedgwood (1730–95) and his successors at Etruria, Staffs. The best-known kinds are vases, plaques, medallions, etc., of fine clay lightly glazed, with classical designs in white relief on a blue or black ground.

Sometimes spelt with lower-case initial. Now a proprietary name both in the U.K. (since 1876) and the U.S. (since 1906).

1787 COLMAN *Inkle & Yarico* III. i, She's.. quite dark; but very elegant; like a Wedgwood tea-pot. **1798** *Phil. Trans.* LXXXVIII. 568 A piece of black Wedgwood-pottery. *Ibid.*, Wedgwood-ware. **1819** CHILDREN *Chem. Anal.* 374 A still simpler.. method is to place the filters in a wedgewood basin on the sand bath. **1861** J. GARDNER *Househ. Med.* 410 Two Wedgwood-ware mortars.. and pestles to match. **1862** *Catal. Internat. Exhib., Brit.* II. No. 6897, Solid jasper, that is the material now exclusively called Old Wedgwood Ware. **1873** Sir J. D. Hooker in L. Huxley *Life* (1918) II. 133, I sent Gladstone a Wedgwood medallion of my Father. **1876** *Trade Marks Jrnl.* 2 Aug. 325 Wedgwood. Godfrey Wedgwood . . trading under the Firm of Josiah Wedgwood and Sons . . Pottery Manufacturers. . . Pots. 2823. 28th Feb. 1876. **1906** *Official Gaz.* (U.S. Patent Office) 4 Dec. 1671/1 Wedgwood. Particular description of goods.—Porcelain, stoneware, and earthenware, including Jasper.

b. Used *attrib.* and *absol.* to designate the blue colour which is characteristic of Wedgwood ware.

1900 *Bladud* (Bath) 28 Mar. 6/3 You will recollect how many of the Christmas cards were wedgewood blue last year. *Ibid.* 7/1 The wedgewood frock I have described. **1909** *Daily Graphic* 20 Oct. 13/2 Touches of cherry colour or Wedgwood blue insets of velvet. **1923** *Daily Mail* 19 Feb. 1 (Advt.), Coloured Jap silks (36 inches wide)... In pink, coral, wedgwood, helio, [etc.]. **1974** P. Dickinson *Poison Oracle* ii. 41 Her angry Wedgwood eyes held his.

c. *sb.* = Wedgwood pottery or ware. Also, with *pl.*, a piece or specimen of this.

1863 Sir J. D. Hooker in L. Huxley *Life* (1918) II. 78 Wedgwoods are an unspeakable relief to me. I look over them every Sunday morning, and poke into all the little second-hand shops I pass in London, seeking medallions. **1890** *Pall Mall Gaz.* 12 Mar. 3/1 Mr. Cornelius Cox's unique collection of wedgwood. **1892** *Ibid.* 25 Mar. 6/3 The very choice collection of old Wedgwood belonging to the late Mr. W. D. Holt, of Liverpool.

2. Designating the scale of temperature used in the pyrometer invented by Josiah Wedgwood for testing the heat of kilns. The zero corresponds to 1077° F.

1807 T. Thomson *Chem.* (ed. 3) II. 510 Flint-glass melts at the temperature of 19° Wedgewood.

wedgy (ˈwɛdʒɪ), *a. rare.* [f. wedge *sb.* + -y^{1}.] Resembling a wedge; shaped like a wedge.

1799 W. Taylor in *Monthly Rev.* XXVIII. 525 An attraction of cohesion . . which is darting its wedgy crystals in every direction, and severing, with resistless interstitial force, the comparatively loose and feeble organization of every contiguous state. **1846** Landor *Imag. Conv., Lucian & Timotheus* Wks. II. 31/2 He . . pushed his wedgy snout far within the straw subjacent. **1888** J. Inglis *Tent Life in Tigerland* 296 She shoots from aloft and cleaves the water with her wedgy beak.

†ˈ**wedhood.** *Obs. rare*$^{-1}$. [f. wed *ppl. a.* + -hood.] The married state.

a **1450** [see weddedhood].

wedir, weðer, obs. forms of whether.

wedir(e, obs. forms of weather.

wedirwyn(e, variants of witherwin.

wedlock (ˈwɛdlɒk), *sb.* Forms: 1 **wedlác,** 2–3 **wedlac,** (*Ormin* **weddlac**), 3–4 **wedlak(e, wedlayk,** 4 **weddelak, wedlek,** (5 **vedlak**), 6 **wedlaike;** 4–7 **wedlok,** 4–6 **wedloke,** 5–7 **wedlocke,** 7– **wedlock.** [OE. *wedlác*, f. *wed* pledge, wed *sb.* + *-lác* suffix forming nouns of action: see -lock.

In two vocabularies of the 11th c. *wedlác* renders L. *arrabo* earnest-money; but the sense, if it existed, did not survive into ME.]

†**1.** The marriage vow or obligation. Chiefly in phrases, ***to hold, keep wedlock***, to be faithful in marriage; ***to break*** (*one's*) ***wedlock***, to commit adultery. *Obs.*

a **1100** *Aldhelm Gloss.* in *Zeitschr. f. deutsches Alterthum* IX. 498/2 *Pacta sponsalia refutans*, wedlac wiðsacende. *c* **1200** Ormin 2499 And tohh wass heh & soþ weddlac Haldenn onn eȝȝþerr hallfe. *c* **1230** *Hali Meid.* 19 Ȝif ha hare wedlac laheliche halden. *c* **1275** *XI Pains of Hell* 105 in *O.E. Misc.* 150 Heo þat her wedlac brekeþ To heore muþe þe flod takeþ. *c* **1385** Chaucer *L.G.W.* 295 For alle kepid they here maydynhed Or ellis wedlek. **1426** Audelay *Poems* 3 Kepe ȝoure wedloke. **1450–1530** *Myrr. Our Ladye* II. 207 How wedlocke betwyxte man and woman shulde be kepte after the lawe of god. *c* **1511** *1st Eng. Bk. Amer.* (Arb.) Introd. 35/2 There is . . noman so hardy that dare breke his wedloke. **1523** Berners *Froiss.* (1812) I. xxi. 30 Howe be it she kept but euyll the sacrament of matrimony, but brake her wedloke. **1526** Tindale *Matt.* v. 32 And whosoever maryeth her that is divorsed, breketh wedlocke. **1553** T. Wilson *Rhet.* Pref. Aiii, None remembred the true obseruation of wedlocke. **1579** Rice *Invect. Vices* Eiv, Christe aunswered, . . Thou shalte not breake wedlocke: Thou shalte not kill. **1604** Shaks. *Oth.* v. ii. 142 *Æmil.* That she was false to Wedlocke? *Oth.* I, with Cassio. **1611** —— *Wint. T.* v. i. 124 Your Mother was most true to Wedlock.

2. The condition of being married; marriage as a state of life or as an institution; matrimonial relationship. Now only in literary or legal use.

a **1225** *Ancr. R.* 206 Uor hwuso hit euer is idon, . . bute one ine wedlake, hit is deadlich sunne. *c* **1230** *Hali Meid.* (Titus MS.) 13 Hit [*sc.* coition] is tah in wedlac summes weis to þolien. *Ibid.* 33 Wedlac haueð hire frut þritti fald in heuene; widewehad, sixti fald. **1303** R. Brunne *Handl. Synne* 11201 For many come neuer yn wedlak But for þe fyrst cunnaunt þat men spak. *c* **1362** Langl. *P. Pl.* A. x. 202 (MS. T.) Siþ þe lawe haþ y-grauntid þat iche man haue a make in maner of wedlak. *c* **1386** Chaucer *Merch. T.* 20 Noon oother lyf, seyde he, is worth a bene, For wedlok is so esy and so clene That in this world it is a Paradys. **1387** Trevisa *Higden* IV. 353 In a nyȝt whan þei hadde i-payde dette of wedlok eyþer to oþer. *c* **1440** *York Myst.* xiii. 261 In lele wedlak þou lede þe. *a* **1450** *Mirk's Festial* 108 Yf scho had conceyuet out of wedlocke, þe Iewes wold haue sayde scho had ben a lechore. **1490** Caxton *Eneydos* xiii. 46 Iuno, the goddesse of wedlocke. **1548–9** *Bk. Com. Prayer, Marriage* 14b, Forasmuche as N. and N. haue consented together in holye wedlocke. **1576** Fleming *Panopl. Epist.* 287 They put away their wyues, and enter againe into wedlocke. **1582** Stanyhurst *Æneis* II. (Arb.) 68 Of Venus in wedlock thee daughter [*Veneris nurus*]. **1595** Shaks. *John* I. i. 117 Your brother is Legittimate, Your fathers wife did after wedlocke beare him. **1597** Hooker *Eccl. Pol.* v. lxxiii. §2 That kind of loue which is the perfectest ground of wedlocke is seldome able to yeeld any reason of it selfe. **1634** Sir T. Herbert *Trav.* 39 [The Banians] so extreamely honour Wedlocke, that they seldome are vnmarried at seuen yeares of age. **1671** Milton *Samson* 353, I pray'd for Children, and thought barrenness In wedlock a reproach. **1765** Foote *Commissary* I. 9, I look upon wedlock to be a kind of lottery. **1797** S. James *Narr. Voy.* 170 He offered Haswell his sister in wedlock. **1807** Crabbe *Par. Reg.* II. 362 Children from wedlock we by laws restrain. **1829** Lytton *Devereux* I. i, Sir Arthur had two children by wedlock. **1854** Milman *Lat. Christ.* VI. iii. (1864) III. 441 Heribert himself, the great Archbishop, was a married man; his wedlock had neither diminished his power nor barred his canonisation. **1879** Dixon *Windsor* I. iv. 34 In her early days of wedlock, he neglected her.

fig. *c* **1400** *26 Pol. Poems* xxii. 25 To god, thi wedlok wiþ loue holde. *c* **1530** Tindale *Jonah* Prol. (1863) Bijb, This euell . . nacion (which breake ye wedlocke of faith wherwith they be maried vn to God).

transf. **1697** Dryden *Virg. Georg.* III. 203 Instructed thus, produce him [the stallion] to the Fair; And join in Wedlock to the longing Mare.

b. ***born in*** (or †***under***), ***out of wedlock***: said distinctively of legitimate or illegitimate offspring. Now the most frequent use of the sb.

c **1205** Lay. 395 Assaracus heuede enne broþer þe wes under wedlac iboren. **1340** Hampole *Pr. Consc.* 8261 Som þat er in lele wedlayk born. *c* **1400** *Gosp. Nicodemus* (G.) 252 In wedlayk [*v.rr.* wedlake, wedloyke] was he born. **1470–85** Malory *Arthur* x. xxiii. 451 Sire Aglouale was his fyrste sone begoten in wedlok. **1547** *Test. Ebor.* (Surtees) VI. 262 His bretheren and susters gotten in wedlaike. **1634** Canne *Necess. Separ.* v. 219 Those children . . which are born under wedlock. **1675** *Charac. Town-Gallant* 2 He is so bitter an Enemy to Marriage, that one would suspect him born out of Lawful Wedlock. **1765** Blackstone *Comm.* I. 434 A legitimate child is he that is born in lawful wedlock. **1824** W. Irving *T. Trav.* II. II. 25, I forgave the fellow . . his two heinous crimes, of having been born in wedlock, and inheriting my estate. **1891** E. Peacock *N. Brendon* II. 97 He did not believe that little Bessy was born in wedlock. **1911** *Encycl. Brit.* XVI. 379/2 The question remains, how far, if at all, English law recognizes the legitimacy of a person born out of wedlock.

c. In particularized sense: A matrimonial union; a married life.

1377 Langl. *P. Pl.* B. IX. 152 And þus þourw cursed caym cam care vppon erthe; And al for þei wrouȝt wedlokes aȝein goddis wille. **1450–1520** *Myrr. Our Ladye* II. 206 Thys lesson tellyth . . how holy a wedlocke was betwyxte Ioachym and Anne. *Ibid.* 207 Whyle he [God] behelde all the rightwys and honeste wedlockes that shulde be from the fyrste makeynge of man vnto the laste day. **1581** Studley *Seneca's Herc. Œtæus* II. 197 O woefull wight, it pitieth vs to see Thy wedlock in this tickle state to bee. **1624** Fletcher *Rule a Wife* v. (1640) 64 Tis sacriledge to violate a wedlock. **1825** Scott *Betrothed* xii, It was then your mother . . of whose unhappy wedlock you have spoken? **1846** Jerrold *St. Giles* xxxiv, And Snipeton, his wife in her winding-sheet, might so have solemnised a second wedlock.

†**d.** A marriage ceremony, wedding. *Obs.*

a **1300** *K. Horn* (Camb. MS.) 1254 Hi Runge þe belle þe wedlak for to felle.

†**3.** A wife. *Obs.*

1561 Nuce *Seneca's Octavia* IV. i. Fiij, Cæsars wedlock are you. **1567** Turberv. *Ovid's Epist.* 149b, [Ulysses says] But I, not forcing of their giftes, did loue my wedlock best. **1567** Golding *Ovid's Met.* IX. (1593) 213 He heard his wedlocke shreeking out, and did her calling knowe. **1601** B. Jonson *Poetaster* IV. iii, Which of these is thy wedlocke, Menelavs? thy Hellen? **1605** Chapman *All Fooles* I. ii. 118 Valerio, here's a simple meane for you To lye at racke and manger with your wedlocke. **1606** Marston *Parasitaster* II. i. C3, But to lie with ones brothers wedlocke, O my deere Herod, tis vile and vncommon lust. **1611** Middleton & Dekker *Roaring Girl* I. i. E4b, He watches For quarrelling wedlockes, and poore shifting sisters. **1617** Fletcher *Valentinian* v. vi, The most true constant lover of his wedlock. **1690** Dryden *Don Sebast.* II. ii, For his Wedlock for all her haughtiness, I find her coming.

4. *Comb.* **a.** Simple attrib. (now *rare* or *Obs.*) as in ***wedlock-band, -bed, -debt, -knot***, etc.

1422 Yonge tr. *Secreta Secret.* 194 To pay wedlak dette hit is of no syn. **1557** *Will J. Amcottes* (Somerset Ho.), In the choyse of their wedlockmates. **1586** T. B. *La Primaud. Fr. Acad.* I. 457 By wedlocke copulation we came into the world. **1593** Shaks. *3 Hen. VI*, III. iii. 243 Ile ioyne mine eldest daughter . . To him forthwith, in holy Wedlocke bands. **1596** —— *Merch. V.* v. i. 32 She kneeles and prayes For happy wedlocke houres. **1600** —— *A.Y.L.* v. iv. 150 Whiles a Wedlocke Hymne we sing. **16..** Middleton, etc. *Old Law* v. i, Will it please you to taste of the wedlock courtesie? **1624** Davenport *City Night-cap* II. (1661) 17 Since our marriage, I have perform'd So fairly all judicial wedlock-offices, That [etc.]. **1635** J. Taylor (Water P.) *Old Old Man* B3b, She dead, he ten yeares did a Widdower stay; Then once more ventred in the Wedlock way. **1671** Milton *Samson* 986 Who to save Her countrey from a fierce destroyer chose Above the faith of wedlock-bands. *Ibid.* 1009 Love-quarrels oft in pleasing concord end, Not wedlock-trechery endangering life. **1819** Scott *Noble Moringer* i, It was the noble Moringer in wedlock bed he lay. **1824** Symmons tr. *Æschylus' Agamemnon* 64 To Ilion came the wedlock-woe.

†**b. wedlock-bound** *a.*, bound in marriage; **wedlock-breaker**, an adulterer; so **wedlock-breaking** *sb.* and *a.* *Obs.*

? *a* **1400** in Horstm. *Altengl. Leg.* (1881) 370 Werne euery man . . Off wedloke-brekynge wer to be. *c* **1500** *Mayd Emlyn* in *Anc. Poet. Tracts* (Percy Soc.) 23 All wedlocke brekers. *c* **1530** Tindale *Jonah* Prol. (1863) Bijb, This euell & wedlocke breakinge nacion . . seke a signe. **1552** Latimer *Serm. Lincs.* i. (1562) 67 Thou shalt not be a wedlock breaker. **1608** Topsell *Serpents* 267 Wedlocke breakers, & Cockold-makers. **1667** Milton *P.L.* x. 905 Alreadie linkt and Wedlock-bound To a fell Adversarie.

Hence †ˈ**wedlock** *v. trans.*, to unite in marriage (in quots. *passive*); also (nonce-use), ***to wedlock it***, to get married. †ˈ**wedlockable** *a.*, marriageable. †ˈ**wedlockhood**, the married state.

c **1230** *Hali Meid.* (Titus MS.) 33 Of þeos þre had, meidenhad & widewehad, & te þridde, wedlachad [*Bodley MS.* wedlac]. **1557** Phaer *Æneid* VII. (1558) Siij, One doughter did remayne . . Now husbandripe, now wedlockable full, of laufull yeres. **1644** Milton *Divorce* II. xv. (ed. 2) 60 Is it not most likely that God in his Law had more pitty towards man thus wedlockt, then towards the woman that was created for another. **1674** N. Fairfax *Bulk & Selv.* Ep. Ded., That man . . will never feel himself less at ease for being wedlockt but to one. **1737** Ozell *Rabelais* III. ix. 50 A single Person is never seen to reap the Joy and Solace that is found among those that are Wedlockt. Wedlock it then in the Name of God, quoth Pantagruel.

wedmell, -mole, -moll, obs. ff. wadmal.

Wednesday (ˈwɛnzdeɪ, -dɪ). Forms: α. 1 **Wódnes dæȝ** (**dœ́ȝ**), **dei,** 3 **Wodnesdei,** 3–4 **-day,** (3 *pl.* **-dawes**), 3–5 **Wodenes-,** 4 **Wodenis-,** 5–6 **Wodens-, Wodinsday.** β. 3 **Wednes-, Weodnes-, Wendesdei,** 3–4 **Wednesdai,** 4 **Wendes-,** 4–5 **Wedenis-, Wedenys-, Wedenes-, Wedonesday, -dai,** 4–7 **Wedins-,** 5 **Wyndenesse day,** *Sc.* **Wedynnisda,** 5–6 **Wed(d)ens-, Wed(d)yns-, Wednys-,** 6 **Weddynnis-, Wednis-, Wedns-,** *Sc.* **Veddynis-,** 6–7 **Weddins-,** 3– **Wednesday.** γ. **Wannesdai,** 5 **Wan(n)ys-, Wones-, Won(n)ysday;** 5 **Wenness-, W(h)enysday, Wenstay,** 5–6 **Wennysday, Wensdaie,** 6 **Wenes-,** 4–7 **Wensday(e.** [OE. *Wódnes dæȝ* = OFris. *wôns-, woenis-, wern(i)s-, wernes-, wers-, wer(ren)dei, wênsdei* (mod. WFris. *woansdei, wansdei, wensdei, wernsdei*, NFris. *winjsdei, wadensdei*), MLG. *Wôdenesdach, Gudensdag*, MDu. *Woensdach* (mod.Du. *-dag*), ON. *Óðensdagr* (Sw., Da. *Onsdag*), 'the day of (the god) *Woden*', a translation of late L. *Mercurii dies*, whence the name of the day in the Rom. langs. (F. *Mercredi*, Sp. *Miercoles*, It. *Mercoledì*). In High German the day appears always to have been called 'mid-week' (mod.G. *Mittwoch*), although for the other days (exc. Saturday) the translated Roman (planetary) names were adopted as in the other WGer. langs. and ON.

The name of Woden (OE. *Wóden*, OS. *Wôden*, OHG. *Wuotan*, ON. *Óðenn*:—OTeut. **Wōđono-z*) is referred to the Teut. root **wōđ-*, found in OTeut. **wōđo-* mad, furious (see wood *a.*), ON. *óð-r* (:—**wōđo-z*) poetic frenzy, inspiration; cognate with L. *vātēs*, Irish *fáith*, prophet. The identification of Woden, the highest god of the Teutonic pantheon, with Mercury, appears already in Tacitus ('Deorum maxime Mercurium colunt', *Germ.* ix); it was probably chiefly suggested by Woden's character as the god of eloquence; another feature common to the German and the Roman deity is their swiftness and wide range of travel.

As representing the OE. *Wódnes dæȝ*, the β forms are anomalous. The same irregularity appears in some of the Frisian forms above quoted, and in the English place-names Wednesbury and Wednesfield, Staffordshire, and Wensley, Derbyshire (1086 Domesday *Wodneslei*, *c* 1200 *Wednesle*). Some scholars have proposed to account for the change of vowel by the assumption that an unrecorded form **Wēden* (:—**Wōđino-z*, with suffix-ablaut) existed in OE. and OFris. beside the form without umlaut; but the supposition involves some difficulties.

The uncontracted pronunciation (ˈwɛd(ə)nzdeɪ), though not recognized in the dictionaries (Webster 1911 gives it as 'in British use, esp. in the north'), is not unfrequently heard from speakers belonging to the northern and north midland counties. The contracted pronunciation now prevailing goes back to the 15th c.; the earlier metathetic form *wendesdei* (*c* 1275) is noteworthy.]

The fourth day of the week.

c **950** *Lindisf. Gosp.* Mark *Introd.* p. 5 *Feria .iiii.* wodnes doeȝe. *c* **1000** *Ags. Gosp.* Matt. iii. (*heading*), On Wodnesdæȝ. *c* **1123** *O.E. Chron.* an. 1123 (Laud MS.) On an Wodnes dei. *a* **1225** *Leg. Kath.* 2215 Þet wes on Wodnesdei [*v.rr.* Wednesdei, Weodnesdei] þet ha þus wende. *a* **1225** *Ancr. R.* 70 Iðen Aduent, & iðe Umbridawes, wodnesdawes, & fridawes. *c* **1275** Lay. 13925 Tydea we ȝefue tisdei Woden we ȝefue wendesdei. **1297** R. Glouc. (Rolls) 2432 In oure tonge ycluped in honour of him is wodnes day [*v.rr. 14–15th c.* Wednesday, Wodenesday, Wedonesday, Wensdaye]. *a* **1300** *Cursor M.* 270 + 1 *Luna* Monenday *Mars* Tisday *Mercurius* Wednesday. **1377** Langl. *P. Pl.* B. XIII. 154 In a signe of the Saterday that sette firste the kalendare, And al the witte of the Wednesday of the nexte wyke after. *c* **1385** Fordun *Chron. Gentis Scot.* v. lii. (1871) 253 Quartam [feriam] suo nomini dedicantes, diem Woden vocabant, quæ consuetudo per Anglos etiam hodie servatur, vocant enim eundem diem Wodenisday. *c* **1400** *Rule St. Benet* xli. 29 Al þe wukis in þe summir, sal ye faste . . þe wedenisdai and te fryday. *Ibid.* 1708 Wedinsday. *c* **1425** in *Rep. MSS. Ld. Middleton* (Hist. MSS. Comm.) 107 Other men or wymmen that have non peyse of their owen growyng, lett hem gedur hem twyse in the weke on Wennessday and on Friday. *a* **1450** *Mirk's Festial* 40 Yche Wenysday and Fryday, he made hys confessour bete hym wyth a ȝarde apon þe backe al bare. *c* **1450** *St. Cuthbert* (Surtees) 3411 On a wedensday he fell seke. *c* **1450** *Godstow Reg.* (1911) 206 The wonysday Afore wytsonday. **1457** *Paston Lett.* I. 414 At Norwich hastly, the Wenstay in Ester weke. *c* **1470** Henry *Wallace* XI. 1280 Now thai him kep to martyr in London toun On Wednysday, befor King and commoun. *c* **1485** *Digby Myst.* (1882) III. 1505 On þe weddysday, ower lord..made..fysche In flod. **1490** *Acc. Ld. High Treas. Scot.* I. 131 On Wedynnisda the xxiiij da of Marche. **1529** Cromwell in Merriman *Life & Lett.* (1902) I. 324 To morow at nyght or wenesday by none at the Ferthest. *a* **1533** Berners *Huon* lxviii. 235 On a wednysday they came to Parys. **1534** More *Treat. Passion* Wks. 1299/2 The day before his maundy, that is to wyt the wedynsday before hys passyon. **1536** Wriothesley *Chron.* (Camden) I. 39 The 17th day of May, beinge Weddensday. **1537** Cromwell in Merriman *Life & Lett.* (1902) II. 59 At the Wodensday next after pentecost. **1544** in Rymer *Foedera* (1719) XV. 54 The thirtieth of July (beinge Wensdaye). *Ibid.*, Wednsdaye (the sixth of August). **1544** in *Sel. Cases Crt. Requests* (Selden Soc.) 98 By the Wennysday in the Wytsonweke. **1552** Huloet, Wensdaye, *mercurij dies.* **1556** in Lodge *Illustr. Brit. Hist.* (1791) I. 214 And upon Wedynsday..she..departed. **1558** in T. Wright *Q. Eliz.* (1838) I. 4 Mr. Teylle wil be with you apon Wensdaye week. **1562–3** *Act 5 Eliz.* c. 5 §11 Every Wednesdaye..which heretofore hathe not by the Lawes or Customes of this Realme bene used and observed as a Fishe Daye..shalbe hereafter observed and kepte as the Saterdays in every Weeke bee or ought to be. **1563** Winȝet *Bk. Quest.* Wks. (S.T.S.) I. 126 The Kirk of God heirfor, obseruing.. abstinence..on Wodinsday generalie in the orient Kirk. **1574** [? Whittingham] *Brieff Discours* 40 The next daie beinge wensdaie. **1579** Fulke *Heskins's Parl.* 456 On Sunday and Wednesday,..and on other dayes. **1607** Shaks. *Cor.* I. iii. 64, I look'd vpon him a Wensday halfe an houre together. **1639** Sir T. Hope *Diary* (Bannatyne Club) 100 On 3 July, Weddinsday, wes the tumult of women in Edinburgh. **1715** Gay *Trivia* II. 419 Wednesdays and Fridays you'll observe from hence, Days, when our sires were doom'd to abstinence. **1808** Jamieson, *Wensday*, Wednesday. **1822** Downes *Lett. fr. Mecklenburg* 173 The evening of Wednesday was a gloomy one. **1905** 'G. Thorne' *Lost Cause* ii, Wait till you see my leader in Wednesday's issue.

b. In names of certain days of the ecclesiastical calendar, as Ash-Wednesday [= med.L. *dies cinerum*, Fr. *jour* or *mercredi des cendres*, It. *dì delle ceneri*, G. *aschermittwoch*, Du. *aschdag*, ON. *ǫskudagr*, *ǫsku-óðensdagr*, Da. *askeonsdag*, Sw. *askonsdag*], the first day of Lent, also called †pulver-*Wednesday* [from the words 'pulvis es et in pulverem reverteris', used in the service]. Also ***Good W.***, ***Holy W.***, ***Spy W.*** (*Anglo-Irish*: see spy *sb.* 5), the Wednesday before Easter.

1297, **1387** [see Ash-Wednesday]. *c* **1450** *Mirk's Festial* 82 Ȝe schull begyn your fast at Aske-Wanysday. *c* **1454** [see pulver *sb.* b]. **1471** *Acta Auditorum* (1839) 16/1 Onne gude Wednisday in passioun woulk. **1842** [see spy *sb.* 5]. **1845** *Dublin Rev.* June 425 On Holy Wednesday at the words in the Passion, 'et velum templi scissum est', it [the veil] is torn open in two parts. **1894** *Northumb. Gloss.*, Good Wednesday.

c. *attrib.*

138. Wyclif *Sel. Wks.* II. 423 Bigynnynge first at þe Wednesdai gospel in þe firste woke of Advent bifore Cristemasse. **1650** in *Rep. Hist. MSS. Comm.* Var. Coll. (1907) IV. 241 The defrayinge of the chardge for the Wensdaye lecture. **1672** Marvell *Rehearsal transpros'd* I. 246 You say that the Clause 5° Eliz. of the Wednesday-Fast has been the original of all the Puritan-Disorders. **1673** *S'too him Bayes* 100 To your long business about the Clause to the Wednesday Act, and its binding the Conscience or no, I answer, [etc.]. **1819** Lady Morgan *Autobiog.* (1859) 304 Several of my liberal Wednesday-evening guests have been made peers. **1848** Dickens *Dombey* liii, My Wednesday nights came regularly round. **1883** D. C. Murray *Hearts* vii, They're going to play my 'Dream of Venice' at Hoffmann's Wednesday Concerts.

Similarly †**Wodnes-niȝt**, Wednesday night.

c **1000** *Ecgb. Pœnit.* II. §21 in Thorpe *Laws* II. 190 Æfre Sunnan-nihte & Wodnes-nihte. *c* **1000** *Wulfstan's Hom.* lviii. (1883) 305 Sunnannihtum..ne Wodnesnihtum. *c* **1297** *Beket* 1125 in *S. Eng. Leg.* 138 His wei wodnes-niȝt out of þe toune he nam.

wedo, obs. form of widow.

wedonynpha, var. obs. Sc. wedenonfa'.

wedou(e, -ow(e, obs. forms of widow.

wedre, -ur, obs. forms of weather.

wedred, obs. form of withered *ppl. a.*

wedset(t, -sette, obs. forms of wadset.

wedue, wedw(e, obs. forms of widow.

wedy, obs. variant of widdy.

wedyr, obs. f. weather, wether, whether.

wee (wiː), *sb.*[1] and *a.* orig. *Sc.* Forms: 4 **wei, wey(e**, 4–6 **we**, 6–9 **wie**, 7 **wea**, 8 **wi**, 6– **wee**. [Northern ME. *wei*, repr. earlier Anglian *wéȝ*, *wéȝe* = WS. *wǽȝ*, *wǽȝe* (see weigh *sb.*); the later *we*, *wee* shows the normal loss of the final palatal spirant which is still indicated in all the rhymes of the earliest texts.

In the sb. the original sense of 'quantity', 'amount', is very slightly recorded, the word being mainly used (almost always with *little*) as a measure of time or space. In adjectival use, however, the idea of quantity or size has been retained; this use evidently originated in the Sc. idiom exemplified by bit *sb.*[2] 9 (*a bit thing* = 'a bit of a thing', 'a little thing'); cf. *wee bit* in B. c below. It is however remarkable that, although found as early as the 15th c., the adj. is rare in Sc. writers before 1721, though our quots. from Shakespeare and Heywood show that it had become known to Englishmen early in the 17th c. The word (both *sb.* and *adj.*) is current in the dialects of some English counties (see *Eng. Dial. Dict.*), but there is no evidence to show that it was commonly used in England before the 19th c.; see however way-bit.]

A. *sb.* In early use almost always ***a little wee***, later also ***a wee***: = 'a little', 'a (little) bit'; in various applications (chiefly as adverbial accusative).

†**1. a.** A little or young thing; a child. *Obs.*

a **1300** *Cursor M.* 8419 He ne es yitt bot a littel wei, þow do him for to foster slei.

b. A small quantity.

c **1375** *Sc. Leg. Saints* xix. (*Christopher*) 605 þe kinge tuk þan a lytil we of þe fresche blude, & vet his ee.

c. To a small extent, in a small degree.

1513 Douglas *Æneis* I. ix. 61 The quene Dido, astonist a litle wie [**1710**, we] At the first sycht. **1720** Ramsay *Rise & Fall of Stocks* 85 It lulls a wee my Mullygrubs, To think upon these bitten Scrubs. **1793** *Regal Rambler or Devil in London* 69 Dinna be angry,..I have been drinking a wi, and I believe the Devil was in me.

d. Qualifying an adj. or adv.: Somewhat, rather.

1816 Scott *Old Mort.* xxxvii, His brain was a wee ajee, but he was a braw preacher for a' that. **1818** —— *Br. Lamm.* xxv, I thought it right to look a wee strange upon it at first. **1818** —— *Hrt. Midl.* li, 'Are you sure you know the way?' ..'I maybe kend it a wee better fifteen years syne.'

2. A short time.

a **1300** *Cursor M.* 11665 Quen sco had sitten þar a wei [*Gött.* wey] Sco bihild a tre was hei. *Ibid.* 12531 [James, stung by an adder] Bolnand in a litel wei, þat al-mast bigan he to dei. *c* **1375** *Sc. Leg. Saints* xvi. (*Magdalene*) 449 Quhene he..wist þat in a lytil we for falt of met þe barne suld de. **1375** Barbour *Bruce* VII. 182 The Kyng than vynkit a litill we. *c* **1500** *Priests of Peblis* 817 Ane lytill wie befoir the feist of Ȝule. **1535** Stewart *Cron. Scot.* (Rolls) I. 183 Now will I leif of this ane lytill we. *Ibid.* II. 139 So at the last the cloude ane lytill we Discouerit wes, that tha micht better se. *c* **1560** Rolland *Seven Sages* 154 Scho was wyteles a lytill we. **1592** Montgomerie *Misc. Poems* lvi. 2 Stay, passinger, thy mynd, thy futt, thy ee: Vouchsaif, a we, his epitaph to vieu, Quha [etc.]. *a* **1700** *Gaberlunzie-Man* iv, They raise a wee befor the cock. *a* **1728** Ramsay *Ode Birth of Drumlanrig* 47 Ye hardy Heroes..Forsake a wee th' Elysian Plains. **1818** Scott *Rob Roy* xiv, Bide a wee—bide a wee; you southrons are aye in sic a hurry. **1869** A. Macdonald *Love, Law & Theol.* vii. 120 In a wee they baith felt their wames leavin' them, an' they maist lost their senses.

3. A short distance; a little way.

1375 Barbour *Bruce* XIII. 217 Arrowes that felly Mony gret voundis can thame ma, And slew fast of thair hors alsua, That thai vayndist a litell we. *Ibid.* XVII. 677 Behynd hir a litill we It fell. *c* **1420** Wyntoun *Cron.* VIII. xxxiii. 5788 We sal fenȝhe ws as we walde fle, And wiþe draw ws a litil we.

B. *adj.* **a.** Extremely small, tiny. (In Sc. use with weaker sense, as a synonym of *little*.) Often more emphatically ***wee wee***, ***little wee***, ***wee little***.

The Shaks. example is not found in the quarto of 1602; as this has 'a whay-coloured beard' in the corresponding sentence, it has been conjectured that the 'wee-face' of the Folio may be a mistake for *whey-face* (cf. *Macb.* v. iii. 17). However, the reading of the Folio may be taken as evidence that the adj. was known in 1623. In this and in quot. 1617 the adj. is hyphened to the following sb., and preceded by *little*.

c **1450** Holland *Houlate* 649 The litill we Wran, That wretchit dorche was. ? **1598** Shaks. *Merry W.* (1623) I. iv. 32 He hath but a little wee-face, with a little yellow beard. **1617** Heywood *Fair Maid of West* II. i, Hee was nothing so tall as I, but a little wee-man, and somewhat huckt backt. **1638** in W. N. Clarke *Coll. Lett.* (1848) 173 Her ministers gangand in guid auld little short cloakes, with wea blacke velvet neckes. *Ibid.* 180 Upon his weake wea nagg. **1692** [? Calder] *Sc. Presbyt. Eloq.* 104 The very wie-ones [*marg.* Little Children] were then so serious that [etc.]. **1721** Kelly *Sc. Prov.* A 178 A wie [*Foot-note*: little] Mouse will creep under a mickle Corn-stack. *Ibid.* B 35 Better a wie Fire to warm us, than a mickle Fire to burn us. **1721** Ramsay *Poems* Gloss. 397 *Wee*, Little; as, A wanton wee Thing. **1726** *Fleming's Fulfilling Script.* (ed. 5) Table Scots Phr., *Wie*, little or small. **1786** Burns *Inventory* 37 Wee Davock hauds the nowt in fother. **1792** —— *Song*, She is a winsome wee thing. **1818** Scott *Hrt. Midl.* v, It wad aye serve to keep the puir thing's heart up for a wee while. **1819** J. R. Drake *Culprit Fay* xv, He banned the water-goblins' spite,—For he saw.. Their little wee faces above the brine. **1827** Darley *Sylvia* 31 Neater, I ween, though not much ampler, Than wee miss works upon her sampler. **1832** Motherwell *Poems, Oh Wae be* 6 The wee wee fifes piped loud and shrill. **1846** H. Coleridge *Poems* II. 23 Like a wee bird struggling in the nest. *a* **1856** in Strang *Glasgow & Clubs* 574 You have only to raise the window, haud up your wee finger, and, [etc.]. **1884** Q. Victoria *More Leaves* 204 We met little Alix on her wee pony. **1889** 'J. S. Winter' *Mrs. Bob* iii, She would be free..to hie herself to London-town and take a dear wee little flat.

b. in *superlative*.

1728 Ramsay *Reasons Hackney Scribblers* 22 To wiest Insects even'd and painted. *a* **1856** in Strang *Glasgow & Clubs* 572 They're a' awa, fra the wee'st to the biggest o' them. **1863** 'Holme Lee' *A. Warleigh* II. 271 Strangers.. who wore such amplitude of petticoat that in passing between the ranks of infants..they literally swept the wee-est over. **1878** A. J. C. Hare *Story of Life* (1896) I. 206 Tell me all about the wedding—every smallest, weeest thing. **1883** Black *Shandon Bells* v, The boat the wee-est black speck on the silver of the water.

c. ***a wee bit***: = 'a wee' (see A. *sb.*). Often quasi-*adj.* (cf. bit *sb.*[2]) and quasi-*adv.* (qualifying an adj.).

a **1661** [see way-bit]. **1721** Kelly *Sc. Prov.* A 183 A wie House well fill'd, a wie bit Land well till'd, and a wie Wife well will'd will make a happy Man. **1785** Burns *Cottar's Sat. Night* 23 His wee-bit ingle, blinkan bonilie. **1823** Moor *Suffolk Words* 474 'A wee bit of a thing'—applied to a child, and to almost every little thing. **1828** Scott *F.M. Perth* xxvii, A boat will wait for you..at a wee bit creek about half a mile westward from the head of the Tay. **1901** W. R. H. Trowbridge *Lett. her Mother to Eliz.* xxviii. 140 The champagne..that I had this morning has given me just a wee bit of a *migraine*.

d. ***the wee folk***: the fairies.

1819 W. S. Mason *Stat. Acc. Irel.* III. 27 The curate has heard a man swear most solemnly, that he has seen some hundreds of the 'wee folk' dancing round these trees. **1854** Allingham *Fairies* 5 Wee folk, guid folk, Trooping all together; Green jacket, red cap, And grey-cock's feather. **1894** K. Grahame *Pagan Papers* 162 The quotation suggested a fairy story,..But the Wee Folk were under a cloud: sceptical hints had embittered the chalice.

e. ***the Wee Free Kirk***: a nickname given to the minority of the Free Church of Scotland which stood apart when the main body amalgamated with the United Presbyterian Church to form the United Free Church in 1900. Hence ***Wee Frees***, ***Wee Kirkers***, the members of the 'Wee Free' church. Also *transf.*

1904 *Monthly Rev.* Oct. 5 The Free Kirk and the 'Wee' Kirk. **1904** *Times* 31 Dec. 8/1 The funds must be handed over to the remnant of the old Free Church—the 'Wee Frees', as Scotland nicknames them. **1905** P. W. Wilson *Why we believe* v. 61 Scotland is convulsed because the property of the United Free Church has been handed over by a court of law to a remnant of Wee Kirkers. **1953** Earl Winterton *Orders of Day* viii. 92 In 1919..both the Labour and Liberal Oppositions were small and ineffective. The latter, facetiously known as the 'Wee Frees'..split into two halves led by Sir Donald Maclean and Mr. George Lambert respectively. **1966** *Punch* 20 July 123/3 His account of the way in which the Wahabis—the Calvinistic 'wee frees' of Islam—are surrendering to the worst of Western culture is a lively moral tale in itself. **1979** H. Wilson *Final Term* i. 10 The smell of power..was in their nostrils, for the first time since the 'Wee Frees', the Samuelite Liberals, had left the 1931 Coalition Government.

f. ***the wee (small) hours*** = *small hours* s.v. hour 3 b. *colloq.*

[**1787** Burns *Death & Dr. Hornbook* in *Poems & Songs* (1968) I. 84 The auld kirk-hammer strak the bell Some wee, short hour ayont the *twal*.] **1849** C. Brontë *Shirley* II. ii. 73 She followed the steps of the night, on its pathway of stars, far into the 'wee sma' hours ayont the twal.' **1859** [see hour 3 b]. *a* **1891** H. Melville *To Major John Gention* in *Compl. Wks.* (1924) XIII. 366 In the wee hours..how affluent hast thou been on that theme. **1932** 'L. G. Gibbon' *Sunset Song* 232 They'd another long dram, and they argued far into the wee, small hours. **1949** P. Michaels *This Perverse Generation* v. 44 No one has a persistent inner compulsion to ..talk about silly things in crowded, stuffy, little night-club rooms at wee hours of the morning. **1966** 'H. MacDiarmid' *Company I've Kept* viii. 193 We walked back..in the 'wee sma' 'oors' of the following morning. **1979** *United States 1980/81* (Penguin Travel Guides) 278 Several acts keep the place hopping from dinner time until the wee hours.

wee (wiː), *sb.*[2] *colloq.* [See wee *v.*] = wee-wee *sb.* 1.

1968 R. Clapperton *No News on Monday* vi. 61 Wanda is downstairs having a wee. **1971** P. Purser *Holy Father's Navy* ii. 12 Hurry up, I want to do a wee. **1973** *Punch* 1 Aug. 139/1 Thought I saw someone comin' in de gate, but it only a dog havin' a wee on de magnolia.

wee (wiː), *v. colloq.* [Echoic: see wee-wee *v.*] *intr.* To urinate. Also *refl.* = wet *v.* 5 d.

1934 Dylan Thomas *Let.* 11 May (1966) 128 Wee on the sun that he bloody well shines not. **1970** *Guardian* 13 July 9/2 Ladies always have to walk a mile and they'll wee themselves if they don't find something soon. **1976** *West Lancs. Evening Gaz.* 15 Dec., She hit her daughter because she kept on 'weeing' all the time. **1983** *Daily Mail* 30 May 17/5 Our headmaster told us that any boy caught short should if absolutely necessary wee into an empty milk bottle.

wee (wiː), *int.* Imitation of the squeal of a pig.

a **1842** in Halliwell *Nursery Rhymes* 119 This little pig said Wee, wee, wee! **1860** *Hist. Five little Pigs* 31 Poor Piggy ran off crying out in great pain, '*Wee! wee!! wee!!!*' all the way home.

†**wee**, = *wi'ye*, with you. *Obs.*

1611 Chapman *May-Day* IV. 67 And yet I speake no hurt of them neither. *Inno.* No Captaine, thus farre, I goe wee.

wee, obs. f. we, why, woe; var. wy *Obs.*, man.

wee-bit: see way-bit.

weeble, obs. or dial. form of weevil.

weech, obs. variant of wych.

weed (wiːd), *sb.*[1] Forms: 1 **wéod, wíod**, 3 **wied, (wod)**, 3–4 **wed, weod**, (4 *pl.* **weoden**), 4–6 **wede**, 4 **wyed**, (5 ? **wade**), 5–6 *Sc.* **weid**, 6 **wyde**, *Sc.* **weyd**, 6–7 **wide**, 5–7 **weede**, 5– **weed**. [OE. *wéod* neut. = OS. *wiod* neut., mod.LG. *wêd*, Flem. dial. *wied*, EFris. *wiud*; the ulterior etymology is unknown.]

1. a. A herbaceous plant not valued for use or beauty, growing wild and rank, and regarded as cumbering the ground or hindering the growth of superior vegetation.

c **888** ÆLFRED *Boeth.* xxiii, Swa hwa swa wille sawan westmbære land, atio ærest of.. ealle þa weod þe he ȝesio þæt þam æcerum deriȝen. *c* **1200** *Trin. Coll. Hom.* 129 For þi is þis westren forgrouwen mid brimbles and mid þornes and mid iuele wiedes. *c* **1290** *St. Mary of Egypt* 108 in *S. Eng. Leg.* 264 Heo ne et no mannische mete bote weodes and wilde more. **1393** LANGL. *P. Pl.* C. XIII. 224 On fat londe and ful of donge foulest wedes groweth. *c* **1440** *Promp. Parv.* 519/2 Weed, or wyyld herbe, *aborigo.* **1480** *Coventry Leet Bk.* 445 [They] stoppen the dyches with þe wedes of their gardeyns & other swepyng of their houses. **1532** HERVET *Xenoph. Househ.* 49 b, The grounde must be clene kept and deliuered from wides. **1592** SHAKS. *Ven. & Ad.* 946 They bid thee crop a weed, thou pluckst a flower. *a* **1660** *Contemp. Hist. Irel.* (Ir. Archæol. Soc.) I. 128 To keep a field from over growinge with wides. **1669** WORLIDGE *Syst. Agric.* 87 Whilest they [*sc.* Hedges] are yet young, they are to be constantly weeded, least the Weeds prevent the thick spreading of the Hedge at the bottom. **1726** J. LAURENCE *New Syst. Agric.* 451 Couch-Grass is a pernicious Weed, keeping the Land hollow and loose. **1781** COWPER *Expost.* 214 But grace abus'd brings forth the foulest deeds, As richest soil the most luxuriant weeds. **1815** WORDSW. *White Doe* vii. 1896 Plate of monumental brass, Dim-gleaming among weeds and grass. **1840** DICKENS *Old C. Shop* xxii, In the garden there was not a weed to be seen. **1885** MISS BRADDON *Wyllard's Weird* I. i. 32 The soil teemed with flowers. There was no room left for a weed.

b. A plant that grows wild in fresh or salt water. Cf ORE-WEED, PONDWEED, RIVER-WEED, SEAWEED, WATER-WEED.

1538 ELYOT *Dict.*, *Alga*, reyte, or wedes of the see. **1607** SHAKS. *Cor.* II. ii. 109 As Weeds before A Vessell vnder sayle, so men obey'd, And fell below his Stem. **1617** MORYSON *Itin.* III. 146 Both Ilands [Jersey and Guernesey] burne a weede of the Sea or Sea coales brought out of England. **1653** WALTON *Angler* ix. 177 This fish.. loves.. to live.. in standing waters, where mud and the worst of weeds abound. **1669** WORLIDGE *Syst. Agric.* 65 *marg.*, Of Sea-weeds, and Weeds in Rivers. **1774** GOLDSM. *Nat. Hist.* VIII. 177 They are bred from eggs, which are laid upon the weeds along the sea-shore. **1825** SIR H. DAVY in *Phil. Trans.* CXV. 329 Weeds and shell fish. **1886** STEVENSON *Kidnapped* vi, The weeds were new to me—some green, some brown and long, and some with little bladders that crackled between my fingers.

c. *collect. sing.*

c **1220** *Bestiary* 245 [The ant] gaddreð ilkines sed boðen of wude and of wed. *a* **1250** *Owl & Night.* 593 Among þe wede [*Cott.* wode], among þe netle. *a* **1300** *Cursor M.* 1140 Insted o þin oþer sede, Ne sal þe groue bot thorne and wede. **1434** *Maldon* (Essex) *Court Rolls* Bundle 20. no. 1 Ricardus Kynge jactat le weede gardini sui in Skykkis lane. **1523–34** FITZHERB. *Husb.* §54 The grasse that groweth vppon falowes is not good for shepe; for there is moche of it wede. **1596** SPENSER *F.Q.* IV. vii. 4 When suddenly behind her backe she heard One rushing forth out of the thickest weed. **1791–3** SMEATON *Edystone L.* §252 The coat of weed, which was likely to fix upon it during the winter. **1832** TENNYSON *Œnone* 197 A wild and wanton pard.. Crouch'd fawning in the weed. **1865** MRS. L. L. CLARKE *Common Seaweeds* i. 18 They [needles] will be extremely useful in laying out the weed.

d. Prov. †*the weed overgroweth the corn. ill weeds grow apace.*

1470–85 MALORY *Arthur* VII. viii. 224 To see suche a ladde to matche suche a knyghte as the wede ouer grewe the corne. **1546** J. HEYWOOD *Prov.* I. x. (1867) 22 Ill weede growth fast .. wherby the corne is lorne. For surely the weede ouergrowth the corne. **1594** SHAKS. *Rich. III*, II. iv. 13 Small Herbes haue grace, great Weeds do grow apace. **1616** DRAXE *Bibl. Scholast.* 216 An ill weede growth apace. *a* **1692** POLLEXFEN *Disc. Trade* (1697) 100 As ill Weeds grow apace, so these Manufactured Goods from India. **1721** J. KELLY *Sc. Prov.* 319 The Weeds o'er grow the Corn, the bad are the most numerous.

e. Used, with defining word, to form the names of wild plants, as BINDWEED, COTTONWEED, CUDWEED, DUCKWEED, DYER'S WEED, GREENWEED, HOGWEED, *hungerweed* (HUNGER *sb.* 4 e), IRONWEED, KNAPWEED, KNOTWEED, *matweed* (MAT *sb.*[1] 8), MILKWEED, MUGWEED, NECKWEED, RAGWEED, *yellow-weed* (YELLOW C. 1).

2. a. *gen.* Any herb or small plant. Chiefly *poet.*

c **1000** *Ags. Gosp.* Matt. vi. 30 Ȝif æceres weod [Vulg. *fænum agri*].. God swa scryt,.. þam mycle ma he scryt eow. **13..** *K. Alis.* 796 Mury time is the wood to sere [*Laud MS.* is wede sere]; The corn riputh in the ere. **1590** SPENSER *F.Q.* II. i. 52 And then with words, and weedes, of wondrous might, On them she workes her will to vses bad. **1614** SYLVESTER *Bethulia's Rescue* 56 The Sun-burnt Reaper had yet scarcely rid The ridged Acres of their richest Weed. **1807–8** W. IRVING *Salmag.* (1824) 365 These evils have all come upon you through tea! Cursed weed. **1859** TENNYSON *Vivien* 321, I once was looking for a magic weed.

b. Applied to a shrub or tree; *esp.* to a large tree, on account of its abundance in a district.

1697 DAMPIER *Voy.* I. 165 Cotton-trees.. are the biggest Trees, or perhaps Weeds rather, in the West Indies. **1707** MORTIMER *Husb.* 604 The Rasberry Tree.. is rather a Weed than a Tree, never living two Years together above ground. **1860** W. WHITE *Wrekin* xi. 99 There is no lack of wood or of 'Herefordshire weeds', as oaks are called. **1885** MOZLEY *Remin.* II. 206 The ash is the weed of the county [Northants]. **1890** W. J. GORDON *Foundry* 127 The elm, which from its abundance in the country, is still known as the 'Warwickshire weed.'

3. *spec.* **a.** Tobacco.

1606 WARNER *Alb. Eng.* XIV. xci. (1612) 369 An Indian weede, That feum'd away more wealth than would a many thousands feed. **1609** DEKKER *Guls Horne-bk.* iv. 19 Where, if you cannot reade, exercise your smoake, and inquire who has writ against this diuine weede. **1687** MONTAGUE & PRIOR *Hind & Panth. Transv.* 17 Your Pipe's so foul, that I disdain to smoak; And the Weed worse than e're Tom. I----s took. **1781** COWPER *Conversat.* 251 Pernicious weed! whose scent the fair annoys. **1797** *Sporting Mag.* X. 58 And chaunt the song, and puff the weed. **1841** LYTTON *Nt. & Morn.* I. vi, He knocked the weed from his pipe. **1899** *Allbutt's Syst. Med.* VIII. 153 Tobacco vertigo and the other nervous consequences of the weed resemble those of neurasthenia.

b. A cigar or cheroot. *colloq.*

1847 ALB. SMITH *Chr. Tadpole* Introd. (1879) 9 Pulling a melancholy looking weed from the lining of his hat. **1848** THACKERAY *Bk. Snobs* xli, We.. kept up with brandy and soda-water and weeds till four. **1885** C. LOWE *Bismarck* I. 388 *note*, The strategist carefully selected the best weed in the Chancellor's case.

c. Marijuana; a marijuana cigarette. *slang* (orig. *U.S.*).

1929 *Amer. Speech* IV. 345 *Weed*, marijuana cigarette. (A Mexican drug.) **1932**, **1933** [see REEFER[1] 3]. **1939** C. R. COOPER *Designs in Scarlet* viii. 145 There are certain centers in which marihuana offers more of a menace... The peddling of the weed is dependent upon persons.. content with small profits. **1949** R. CHANDLER *Little Sister* xxiv. 173 They were looking for.. a suitcase full of weed. **1955** J. KEROUAC in *Paris Rev.* Winter 14 You could smell tea, weed, I mean marijuana, floating in the air. **1965** W. SOYINKA *Road* 24 Say Tokyo reaches out a stick of weed to him which he accepts behind his back. **1978** R. HILL *Pinch of Snuff* iii. 28 She *might* be on the game. Or she might have a bit of weed about the place. Or anything.

4. *fig.* An unprofitable, troublesome, or noxious growth. (Formerly often applied to persons.)

? *a* **1400** *Morte Arth.* 4322 Latt no wykkyde wede waxe, ne wrythe one this erthe. **1422** YONGE tr. *Secreta Secret.* 164 So rysyth of the roote of an.. appert traytoure, othyre rebellis, many wickid wedis sone growynge, that al trewe men in londe Sore greuyth. **1568** GRAFTON *Chron.* II. 349 And if.. any persons.. entended the contrary, there must also be deuised howe such euill wedes may be destroyed. **1598** BARRET *Theor. Warres* 7 Justices, to disburden their shire of corrupt weeds, as they tearme it, do picke out the scumme of their countrie for the warres. **1604** SHAKS. *Oth.* IV. ii. 67 Oh thou weed: Who art so louely faire, and smell'st so sweete, That the Sense akes at thee, Would thou had'st neuer bin borne. **1647** CLARENDON *Hist. Reb.* I. §72 An immoderate ambition.. is a weed (if it be a weed) apt to grow in the best soils. **1750** JOHNSON *Rambler* No. 183 ¶11 Envy is, indeed, a stubborn weed of the mind, and seldom yields to the culture of philosophy. **1850** GROTE *Greece* II. lxviii. (1862) VI. 156 Intolerance is the natural weed of the human bosom, though its growth or development may be counteracted by liberalizing causes. **1915** F. S. OLIVER *Ordeal by Battle* II. v. 146 Militarism is a tough weed to kill.

5. *slang.* (Cf. WEEDY *a.*[1] 4.) **a.** A poor, leggy, loosely-built horse.

In Shaks. *Meas. for M.* I. iii. 20 the word has been explained to mean 'an ill-conditioned horse'. Theobald's correction, 'steeds', may be right.

1845 STOCQUELER *Handbk. Brit. India* (1854) 181 The necessity.. for constant renewal of the blood.. without which the breed degenerates into weeds. **1859** LEVER *Davenport Dunn* ii, He bore the same relation to a man of fashion as a 'weed' does to a 'winner of the Derby'. **1861** *Farmer's Mag.* LV. 1/2 A leggy weed that can go the fastest for half a mile or so over the flat. **1890** 'R. BOLDREWOOD' *Squatter's Dream* iii. 28 Here she pointed to her steed, a small violent weed.

b. A lank delicate person without muscle or stamina. Hence, a small, feeble, or contemptible person; a 'weedy' type (see WEEDY *a.*[1] 4 b). *slang.*

1869 A. L. SMITH in Morgan *Univ. Oars* (1873) 231, I know men who, from being weeds, have grown into strong and healthy men on the river. **1953** WILLANS & SEARLE *Down with Skool!* (1954) 12 There are a grate number of other weeds and wets about the place. **1959** I. & P. OPIE *Lore & Lang. Schoolch.* ix. 170 *Little 'uns*.. Tiny Tim, Tom Thumb, tot, and, very common, weed. **1960** M. SPARK *Bachelors* x. 179 She's mad in love with that little weed Patrick Seton. **1970** *Times* 4 Mar. 13/5 A girl torn between a brainy weed and a moronic body-builder. **1982** BARR & YORK *Official Sloane Ranger Handbk.* 71/1 Don't try too hard: swots are weeds.

†**6.** *Mining.* (See quot 1710.) *Obs.*

1671 *Phil. Trans.* VI. 2102 (Tin), So [we] continue sinking from cast to cast.. till we find either the Load to grow small, or degenerate into some sort of weed.. as Mundick, or Maxy .. Daze,.. Iremould. *Ibid.* 2105 The Load is usually in an hard.. Countrey, made up of metal, spars and other weeds. **1710** J. HARRIS *Lex. Techn.* II, *Weed*, in the Miners Language is the Degeneracy of a Load or Vein of fine Metal, into an useless Marchasite.

7. *attrib.* and *Comb.* **a.** simple attrib., as ***weed-bed***, ***-bush***, ***-case***, ***control***, ***-drift***, ***-field***, ***-fish***, ***-growth***, ***-life***, ***-nosegay***, ***-root***, ***-seed***. Also WEED-HOOK.

1664 *Phil. Trans.* I. 13 They went into the Weed-beds of the Gulf of Florida. *a* **1682** SIR T. BROWNE *Norf. Fishes* Wks. 1835 IV. 330 A weed-fish, somewhat like a haddock. **1782** MRS. DELANY *Autob.* (1861) I. 368 My amusement was running after butterflies and gathering weed nosegays. **1791** W. H. MARSHALL *W. Eng.* (1796) II. 279 The weed seeds having spent themselves.. the dressing will be turned in. **1844** H. STEPHENS *Bk. Farm* III. 993 The weeds and weed-roots will then be seen upon the surface. **1848** ALB. SMITH *Chr. Tadpole* xlv. 395 Metal weed-cases. **1851** KINGSLEY *Yeast* x, Even if marriage was but one weed-field of temptations, as these miserable pedants say. **1899** *Contemp. Rev.* Dec. 884 One of those curious round weed-bushes known as 'tumble weeds'. **1915** *Blackw. Mag.* Aug. 199/1 He would make the rod bend like a bow and quiver as he ran out the line, always making for the weed-bed at the bottom. **1923** KIPLING *Irish Guards in Great War* I. 222 They broke and disappeared in the rank weed-growth. **1934** A. HUXLEY *Beyond Mexique Bay* 249 Lawrence wrote eloquently of Oaxaca and Lake Chapala,.. of the merits of that rank weed-life of the natural man. **1948** S. B. WHITEHEAD *Reclaiming your Garden* ii. 17 Chemicals.. have a selective action in weed control. **1951** *Sport* 7–13 Jan. 8/1 It had the drawback of increasing weed-growth. ? **1953** DYLAN THOMAS *Sel. Lett.* (1966) 416 In the slimy squid-rows of the sea there's such a weed-drift and clamour of old plankton drinkers. **1966** *Listener* 1 Sept. 304/1 The improvement of cultivation techniques to make weed control possible.

b. instrumental, as ***weed-choked***, ***-clogged***, ***-covered***, ***-entwined***, ***-fringed***, ***-grown***, ***-hidden***, ***-hung***, ***-laden***, ***-mantled***, ***-ridden***, ***-sodden***, ***woven*** adjs.

1799 CAMPBELL *Pleas. Hope* II. 201 O'er each Runic altar, weed-entwined. **1818** KEATS *Endym.* I. 65 Weed-hidden roots. **1856** LEVER *Martins of Cro' M.* i, Weed-grown walks. **1857** GOSSE *Omphalos* viii. 216 This weed-fringed tide-pool. **1870** H. MACMILLAN *True Vine* v. (1872) 188 The idleness of another is seen in the meagre, weed-choked produce of his neglected fields. **1897** KIPLING *Capt. Cour.* iii. 57 The weed-hung flukes of the little anchor. **1898** O. WILDE *Ballad Reading Gaol* 12 Every day Crawled like a weed-clogged wave. **1910** W. DE LA MARE *Three Mulla-Mulgars* xxiii. 305 Nod's raft swam last across this weed-mantled lagoon. **1922** JOYCE *Ulysses* 699 In loose allwool garments.. trundling a weedladen wheelbarrow without excessive fatigue at sunset amid the scent of newmown hay. **1938** W. DE LA MARE *Memory* 29 Roofless and eyeless, weed-sodden, dank, old, cold. **1944** BLUNDEN *Shells by Stream* 15 Weed-woven the shallowing pool. **1953** L. KUPER *Living in Towns* 300 Waste land and weed-covered pit banks. **1968** E. A. MCCOURT *Saskatchewan* xvii. 195 The inscriptions on the wooden crosses in the weed-ridden settlement graveyard. **1972** R. ADAMS *Watership Down* xxxii. 245 The rough, weed-covered ground of the combe sloped away below them.

c. objective, as ***weed-cutter***, ***-grubber***; ***weed-cutting*** vbl. sb.; ***weed-waving***, ***-winding*** adjs.; also ***weed-free***, ***-like*** adjs.

a **1693** *Urquhart's Rabelais* III. ii. 32, I save the Expence of the Weed-grubbers. **1729** SAVAGE *Wanderer* II. 415 Upsprung, such weed-like Coarseness it betrays, Flocks on th' abandon'd Blade permissive graze. **1850** *Rep. Comm. Patents 1849* (U.S.) I. 297, I likewise claim the combination of the adjustive weed cutter and leveler F. **1863** HAWTHORNE *Old Home, Consular Exp.* I. 16 The weedlike decay and growth of our localities. **1879** G. M. HOPKINS *Poems* (1967) 78 On meadow and river and wind-wandering weed-winding bank. **1899** *Westm. Gaz.* 12 May 3/2 An endeavour is being made on the Test to have all weed-cutting completed by the middle of May. **1903** *Ibid.* 2 Oct. 2/1 Patent weed-cutters, worked by machinery. **1940** J. BETJEMAN *Old Lights for New Chancels* 33 The light skiff is push'd from the weed-waving shore. **1960** *Farmer & Stockbreeder* 22 Mar. 56/3 It is the modern alternative.. to secure weed-free cropping. **1981** M. SELLERS *From Eternity to Here* i. 7 A well-planned and weed-free vegetable garden.

d. † **weed-ash**, ? soda-ash (which is made from sea-weed); **weedhead** *slang* (chiefly *U.S.*), one who is addicted to marijuana; a marijuana smoker (see HEAD *sb.*[1] 7 e); **weed inspector**, an official in charge of controlling the growth of noxious weeds; **weed-killer**, something that kills weeds, *spec.* any of various chemical preparations used for killing weeds; liquid, powder, etc., of this kind; also *fig.*

1753 HANWAY *Trav.* (1762) I. VII. lxxxviii. 407 Also pot-ash, weed-ash, and pearl-ash. **1952** *Amer. Speech* XXVII. 30 *Weedhead*,.. marijuana smoker. **1966** C. HIMES *Heat is On* xx. 157 Weedheads jabbered and gesticulated. **1973** R. PARKES *Guardians* x. 178 The students that spat and jeered at authority, the weed-heads that threw acid in a vicar's eyes. **1909** *Chambers's Jrnl.* Nov. 702/2 The writer, in his capacity as weed-inspector, has had.. to direct the settlers to plough under entire fields of growing grain in order to eradicate such weeds. **1974** D. SEARS *Lark in Clear Air* iv. 48 The one in overalls was Brad-Awl Callum, weed inspector, pound-keeper, truant officer and County Constable all rolled into one. **1745** W. ELLIS *Agric. Improv'd* in *Mod. Husbandman* July xi. 88 Such Wheat commonly runs up into such rank Stalks, as to become great Weed-killers. **1890** *Daily News* 6 Sept. 2/7 In mistake [he] took up a bottle of weed killer, some of which he drank. **1901** M. FRANKLIN *My Brilliant Career* xxi. 179 Every one would be wanting to engage me as the great noxious weed-killer and poisonous insect exterminator if I made away with you. **1929** WODEHOUSE *Mr. Mulliner Speaking* i. 23 What this woman needed was a fluid ounce of weed-killer. **1967** B. PATTEN *Little Johnny's Confession* 46 Who poured weedkiller over your innocence? *a* **1974** R. CROSSMAN *Diaries* (1976) II. 291 She only talked to Anne and myself about a new weedkiller called Paraquat, pointing out of the window to a field where it was being used.

weed (wiːd), *sb.*[2] *arch.* exc. in sense 6 b. Forms: 1 **wǣd, wǣde,** *North.* **wéde, wœ́de,** 3 *Orm.* **wæde,** *pl.* **weaden,** 3–6 **wede,** 3–4 *pl.* **weden,** 4 *north.* and *Sc.* **wed, veid, ved,** (5 *pl.* **vedis**), 4–7 *Sc.* **weid(e,** 5–6 *Sc.* **weyd,** 6–7 **wide,** 4–7 **weede,** 5– **weed.** [ME. *wēde*, repr. two formations: (1) OE. *wǣd* fem. = OS. *wâd* (MLG. *wât*), OHG., MHG. *wât* (early mod.G. *wat*), also in comb. *lînwât* fem., linen (= Du. *lijnwaad* neut.; mod.G. in perverted form *leinwand*), ON. *váð*, *vóð* fem. (Norw. *vaad*, Sw. *våd*):—OTeut. **wǣði-z*; (2) OE. *wǣde* str. neut. = OS. *wâdi* (MLG. *wêde*), prob. shortened from the collective formation OE. *ȝewǣde* (ME. I-WEDE), OS. *giwâdi*, Du. *gewaad*, OHG. *giwâti*:—OTeut. type **gawǣdjo-m*.

It is disputed whether the Teut. **wǣði-* descends from a pre-Teut. **wēti-*, root **wē-* to weave (= Skr. *vā*), or from **wēdhi-*, root **wēdh-* (= Zend *vad* to clothe oneself; the Goth. *ga-widan* (OHG. *wetan*), to join together, is by some regarded as cognate).]

1. An article of apparel; a garment.

c **888** ÆLFRED *Boeth.* xxviii, Ðeah nu se unrihtwisa cynig Neron hine ʒescyrpte mid eallum þam wliteʒestum wædum. *c* **1000** ÆLFRIC *Hom.* II. 500 Martinus me bewæfde efne mid ðyssere wæde. *a* **1225** *Ancr. R.* 314 Uorði þet heo hefde ileaned one wummone to one wake on of hore weaden. *c* **1250** *Gen. & Ex.* 1972 He..boden him sen If his childes wede it miȝte ben. *c* **1350** *Will. Palerne* 2563 ȝif we walken in þes wedes..what man so vs metes may vs sone knowe. **13..** *Gaw. & Gr. Knt.* 2358 Hit is my wede þat þou werez, þat ilke wouen girdel. *c* **1430** *Chev. Assigne* 119 Of sadde leues of þe wode wrowȝte he hem wedes. **1542** UDALL *Erasm. Apoph.* 289 b, By & by dooyng on hym a wede aunswerable vnto his presente fortune, he fled awaye secretely. **1569** J. SANFORD tr. *Agrippa's Van. Artes* xxv. 36 There was an obstinate strife..concerning the habite, or apparrel of S. Augustine, that is to saie, whether he did weare a blacke weede vpon a white Coate, or a white weede vpon a blacke Coate. **1614** CAMDEN *Rem., Apparel* 233 They ..began to wanton it in a new round curtall weede which they called a Cloake. **1621** FLETCHER *Pilgr.* v. vi, To my house now, and suite you to your worths; Off with these weeds, and appeare glorious. *a* **1706** in *Watson's Collect. Sc. Poems* I. 35 On Sabbath days his Cap was fedder'd, A seemly Weid. **1725** POPE *Odyss.* xvi. 293 An aged mendicant in tatter'd weeds. **1764** H. WALPOLE *Otranto* v, One in a long, woolen weed. **1805** WORDSW. *Prelude* III. 457 Spare diet, patient labour, and plain weeds. **1808** SCOTT *Marm.* v. vi, The Baron dons his peaceful weeds. **1846** KEBLE *Lyra Innoc.* (1873) 168 Her innocent vesture, the pure Chrisom weed. **1850** TENNYSON *In Mem.* v. 9 In words, like weeds, I'll wrap me o'er, Like coarsest clothes against the cold.

2. *collect. sing.* Clothing, raiment, dress, apparel.

a **1000** *Daniel* 103 þæt þam ʒengum þrym gad ne wære wiste ne wæde. *c* **1290** *St. Mary of Egypt* 160 in *S. Eng. Leg.* 265 Ne wilne þou nouȝt þat ich þe abide, for ich am withoute wede. *a* **1300** *K. Horn* 1052 We schulle chaungi wede: Haue her cloþes myne, & tak me þi sclauyne. **1393** LANGL. *P. Pl.* C. XXIII. 211 Lacke shal þe neuere Wede ne worldlich mete. *c* **1450** *Mirk's Festial* 9, I stale forþe yn pore wede. **1551** CROWLEY *Pleas. & Payne* 140 Wyllynge that eche should at his nede, Haue breade and broth, harbour and wede. **1576** HANMER *Anc. Eccl. Hist., Socr. Schol.* II. xxxiii. 292 A little before he had bene deposed..for apparelling himselfe in such weede as was not decent for the dignity and order of priesthood. **1595** SPENSER *Colin Clout* 713 For each mans worth is measured by his weed. **1616** CHAPMAN tr. *Musæus* F 6, This sayd, his faire Limbes of his weede, he strip't. **1788** BURNS *Written in Friars-Carse Hermitage* 2 Be thou clad in russet weed. **1868–70** MORRIS *Earthly Par.* I. I. 250 In face, in figure, and in weed, She wholly changed before his wondering eyes. *Ibid.* 325 Who robbed me, and with blows Stripped off my weed and left me on the shore.

†**b.** In the expletive phrase *in* or *under weed*, usually appended to an adj., as *worth(l)y*, *wight*, *wise*. Cf. *under gore*, GORE *sb.*[2] 2. *Obs.*

c **1330** *Amis & Amil.* 30 Twoo ladyes..That worthi were in wede. *c* **1350** *Will. Palerne* 585 Of lumbardie a dukes douȝter ful derworþ in wede. *a* **1352** MINOT *Poems* ix. 37 Iohn of Coupland, a wight man in wede. *c* **1400** *Emare* 250 Then sayde þat wordy vnþur wede. *a* **1435** *Torr. Portugal* 2397 One of the ffeyrest knyghtis That slepith on somer nyghtes Or walkyd in wede. *a* **1440** *Sir Degrev.* 392 Many bold mene and wyght, Wyse undere wede. *c* **1460** *Towneley Myst.* xviii. 230 Yond worthy wyghtys in wede. *a* **1580** *Murning Maiden* 55 in *Maitl. Fol. MS.* 361 Than wepit scho lustie in weyd.

3. *transf.* and *fig.* (e.g. our 'garment' of flesh).

c **1320** *Cast. Love* 657 God..þat from heuene dude alihte, And vnder vre wede vre kynde nom. *c* **1374** CHAUCER *Troylus* III. 1431 O blake nyght..That shapen art by god þis world to hide At certeyn tymes with þi derke wede. **1390** GOWER *Conf.* II. 335 Sche fliħ before his yhe a Crowe..To kepe hire maidenhede whit Under the wede of fethers blake. **14..** LYDG. *Ballad of Deceitful Women* 26 Hir galle is hid under a sugred wede. **1557** GRIMALD in *Tottel's Misc.* (Arb.) 96 As morning bright, with scarlet sky, doth passe the euenings weed. **1567** JEWEL *Def. Apol.* II. 221 Therefore the Greekes calle Baptisme, ἀφθαρσίας ἔνδυμα, That is, the Weede of immortalitie. **1590** SHAKS. *Mids. N.* II. i. 256 And there the snake throwes her enammel'd skinne, Weed wide enough to rap a Fairy in. **1613–16** BROWNE *Brit. Past.* I. i. 11 That heart..That neuer wore dissimulations weed. *a* **1618** RALEGH *Rem.* (1644) 116 Being stripped out of this mortall weed. *a* **1639** CAREW *Comparison* 20 Thy skin's a heavenly and immortall weede. **1785** BURNS *Scotch Drink* vii, Aft, clad in massy, siller weed, Wi' Gentles thou erects thy head. **1793** —— *By Allan Stream* 20 How cheery through her shortening day Is Autumn, in her weeds o' yellow. **1805–6** CARY *Dante, Inf.* xxxiii. 60 Father,..thou gavest These weeds of miserable flesh we wear; And do thou strip them off from us again.

4. Used contextually for: Defensive covering, armour, mail. *collect. sing.* or *pl.* Also *iron*, *steel weed*.

c **1205** LAY. 23773 Þe king mid his weden [*c* **1275** wede] leop on his stede. *c* **1350** *Will. Palerne* 3535 Was non so stif stelen wede þat withstod his wepen. **1375** BARBOUR *Bruce* XVI. 580 A chemeyr, for till heill his weid, Aboue his armyng had he then. *c* **1400** *Laud Troy Bk.* 3994 Thei..drow out horses and stedes And here strong Iren wedes. *c* **1470** HENRY *Wallace* II. 112 The thrid he straik throuch his pissand of maile, The crag in twa; no weidis mycht him waill. **1480** *Robt. Devyll* 910 in Hazl. *E.P.P.* I. 254 Greate horses stamped in yron wedes. **1515** *Scottish Field* 537 in *Chetham Misc.* II, They will sticke with their standarts in their stele weedes. **1611** W. AUSTIN in *Coryat's Crudities* Panegyr. Verses g 5 b, His garments..Which heretofore like weedes of proofe Serued him to keepe the colde aloofe. **1813** SCOTT *Trierm.* III. xx, Oh for his arms! Of martial weed Had never mortal Knight such need!

5. A garment, or garb, distinctive of a person's sex, profession, state of life. **a.** *sing.* (collect. or particular).

1297 R. GLOUC. (Rolls) 4918 Sire bissop wu ne ȝifstus of þine wite brede þat þou est þi sulf at þi masse in þine vayre wede. *a* **1300** *Cursor M.* 23981 Wede o welth wil i namar, Clething wil i me tak o care. **13..** *Guy Warw.* 1721 Gij seye a man of rewly ble Go in pilgrims wede. **1303** R. BRUNNE *Handl. Synne* 2343 Seþyn toke þe knyȝt palmers wede. *c* **1450** *St. Cuthbert* (Surtees) 6548 þat day þat cuthbert toke bischop wede. **1470–85** MALORY *Arthur* XVII. ix. 702 They ..sawe the good man in a relygyous wede. **1581** J. BELL *Haddon's Answ. Osor.* 276 b, Such as are buryed in the cowle & weede of a Franciscane Fryer. **1587** FLEMING *Contn. Holinshed* III. 1280/1 Wherin also is buried John Yoong.. in his doctors weed. **1605** ERONDELLE *Fr. Gard.* G 3 b, It is not the weed yt maketh the monke. *a* **1670** SPALDING *Troub. Chas. I* (Bannatyne Club) I. 16 This was the ordinary weid of thir his majestie's foot guards. **1684** BUNYAN *Pilgr.* II. 153 They neither have the Pilgrim's Weed nor the Pilgrim's Courage. **1859** TENNYSON *Enid* 1528 This poor gown, This silken rag, this beggar-woman's weed.

b. *pl.*

1362 LANGL. *P. Pl.* A. VI. 7 Apparayled as a Palmere In pilgrimes wedes. *c* **1450** in Kingsford *Chron. Lond.* (1905) 129 Sche eschapede thens in a mannys weeds. **1570** GOOGE *Popish Kingd.* III. 39 b, Who can declare the massing weedes? **1590** SPENSER *F.Q.* I. Introd. i, Whose Muse whilome did maske..in lowly Shepheards weeds. **1650** HOWELL *Giraffi's Rev. Naples* I. 89, I wold never have shaken off my mariners weeds. **1667** MILTON *P.L.* III. 479 They who to be sure of Paradise Dying put on the weeds of Dominic. **1673** HICKERINGILL *Greg. Father Greyb.* 74 A Conformist Minister with all his Aaronical weeds on. **1763** C. JOHNSTON *Reverie* II. 104 Though he was habited in the humble weeds of a slave. **1781** COWPER *Truth* 81 In shirt of hair and weeds of canvass dress'd. **1838** PRESCOTT *Ferd. & Is.* II. xxi. III. 372 The spirit of the soldier burned strong and bright under his monastic weeds.

c. Sometimes without specifying word = a palmer's dress, the religious habit, etc. (as indicated by the context).

c **1400** *Rule St. Benet* (verse) 1338 If ane so for wikkid dede Leue hir abbay & hir wede. *c* **1489** CAXTON *Sonnes of Aymon* xxi. 459 He shet the dore of his chapell, and toke his wede & his staffe. **1561** T. HOBY tr. *Castiglione's Courtyer* II. Z i j, The frier..beesought me to lett him goe downe, and not to showe suche shame to the weede. **1706** [see 6 b]. **1760–72** H. BROOKE *Fool of Qual.* (1809) I. 147, I gave her two-pence, re-assumed my former garb, and left my weeds in her custody.

6. With defining word, esp. *mourning*: A black garment worn in token of bereavement; mourning apparel. Also, a scarf or band of crape worn by a mourner.

1536 BELLENDEN *Cron. Scot.* (1821) II. 165 This other sall pas in dolorus weid, on ane blak hors. **1546** in Strype *Eccl. Mem.* (1721) II. App. A. 4 Commandment was given..to.. put on them every man his mourning weeds. **1592** KYD *Sp. Trag.* I. iii. 20 Let Fortune doe her worst, She will not rob me of this sable weed. **1603** H. PETOWE *Eliza's Funeral* A 4, Then weepe no more, Your sighing weedes put off. **1656** EARL MONM. tr. *Boccalini's Advts. fr. Parnass.* 289 Being clad in a long mourning weed, he appeared in the Colledge of the Litterati. **1787** BURNS *On Death Sir J. Hunter Blair* 15 A stately Form In weeds of woe. **1852** MRS. STOWE *Uncle Tom's C.* xxvii, People who saw him in the street..knew of his loss only by the weed on his hat. *Ibid.* xxviii, A long strip of black crape, torn from the funeral weeds. **1905** *Eng. Dial. Dict., Weed*, a band of cloth or crêpe for a man's hat in time of mourning. W. Yks.

b. *spec.* The deep mourning worn by a widow, including a crape veil, 'weepers,' etc. Now always *pl.*; with or without *widow's* prefixed. (The sing. seems to have been used formerly to mean the veil.)

The only use of the word now generally known; quite *colloq.* while the custom of wearing deep mourning was still widespread.

1595 *Locrine* v. i. 24 Let her there prouide her mourning weeds And mourn for euer her owne widdow-hood. **1706** MRS. CENTLIVRE *Platonick Lady* I. iii. 14 The disconsolate Wife having borrowed a Weed of her Neighbour, is consulting her Glass to see how it becomes her. **1706** PHILLIPS (ed. Kersey), *Weed* or *Wede*, a Garment or Suit of Cloaths; whence it is still us'd for a Frier's Habit, a Widow's Vail, &c. **1711** ADDISON *Spect.* No. 44 ¶4 An afflicted Widow in her Mourning-Weeds. **1715** —— *Drummer* II. i, The Taylor had made her Widow's weeds. **1748** RICHARDSON *Clarissa* (1768) VII. 117 What a charming widow would she have made! How would she have adorned the weeds! **1749** FIELDING *Tom Jones* III. i, As this [her habit] changed from weeds to black, from black to grey, from grey to white. **1836** DICKENS *Sk. Boz, Parish* vii, The mother wore a widow's weeds. **1849** THACKERAY *Pendennis* iii, There were no entertainments..during the year of her weeds. **1887** *Poor Nellie* (1888) 428 He had heard the cook remark..that his mother would now wear weeds.

†**7.** A cloth, covering, hanging, or the like. Also *collect. sing. Obs.*

c **1200** ORMIN 8171 All þatt wæde þatt tær wass Uppo þe bære fundenn, All wass itt off þe bettste pall. *c* **1400** *Destr. Troy* 372 And þan sylen to sitte vppon silke wedis. *c* **1440** *Pallad. on Husb.* I. 830 Eek as for hail a russet weede is To kest vpon the querne [L. *Panno roseo mola cooperitur*]. **1582** STANYHURST *Æneis* III. (Arb.) 72 With black weede the altar is hanged.

weed (wiːd), *sb.*[3] *Sc.* and *Anglo-Irish.* Also weid. [The first syllable of *weeden-* WEDENONFA', wrongly analysed as *weed an' onfa'* (see quot. *c* 1830).] A sudden febrile attack; esp. a kind of puerperal fever.

1790 A. DUNCAN *Med. Comm.* Dec. II. V. 300 It may be difficult, therefore, in the beginning, to distinguish puerperal fever from accumulations of fæces in the alimentary canal, especially if joined to an Ephemera, or Weed. **1818** SCOTT *Br. Lamm.* xii, Dinna ye hear the bairn greet? I'se warrant it's that dreary weid has come ower't again. **1819** *Edin. Mag.* Mar. 220 There to appearance she still lay, very sick of a fever, incident to women in her situation, and here termed *a weed.* **1830** CARLETON *Traits Irish Peas.* (1843) I. 308 Besides, I'm a bit bothered on both sides of my head, ever since I had that weary *weid.* *c* **1830** in *Proc. Berwick. Nat. Club* (1916) 86 Ephemeral colds, vulgarly called weeds and onfas. **1902** *Brit. Med. Jrnl.* 19 July 209 A touch of the 'weed' (or weid), which means a sudden febrile attack.

b. A feverish disease in cattle.

1811 J. TROTTER *Agr. Surv. W. Lothian* 168 Milch cows, however, are not unfrequently subject to what is here called a weed, which is a kind of feverish affection. **1851** *Jrnl. R. Agric. Soc.* XII. II. 523 Irritation and inflammation of the absorbent vessels and glands..constituting the disease termed *weed* [in horses].

weed (wiːd), *v.* *Pa. t.* and *pa. pple.* weeded. Forms: 1 wéodian, 4–6 wede, (4 wed), 4–7 weede, (5 wedy, 6 weade, 7 weydde), 6 *Sc.* weid, 6– weed; *pa. t.* and *pa. pple.* occasionally 5–9 wed, 8 wedd, 9 *Sc.* wede. [OE. *wéodian* = OS. *wiodôn* (LG. *weden*), (M)Du. *wieden*, (M)LG. *wedon*, WFris. *wjudde*, f. OE. *wéod*, OS. *wiod*, WEED *sb.*[1]]

1. *intr.* (or *absol.*) To clear the ground of weeds; to pull up weeds.

a **1100** *Gerefa* in *Anglia* IX. 261 Me [*read* Mon] mæiȝ..on sumera fealȝian..tymbrian, wudian, weodian, faldian. **1393** LANGL. *P. Pl.* C. IX. 66 And alle þat helpen me to erye oþer elles to weden, Shal haue leue, by our lorde to go and glene after. *Ibid.* 186. **1523–34** FITZHERB. *Husb.* §21 The chyefe instrument to wede with is a paire of tonges made of wode. **1593** HYLL *Art Garden.* 74 If any by ignorance doth weede about the plantes without gloues on their handes. **1600** *Shuttleworths' Acc.* (Chetham Soc.) 128 A woman that helped to weydde in the garthinge iij days, iijd. **1732** BERKELEY *Alciphr.* v. §21 Whoever hath a mind to weed will never want work. **1733** W. ELLIS *Chiltern & Vale Farm.* 221 The Sheep can't weed amongst them [Beans and Peas], and eat up the wild Oat and Curlock. **1782** MISS BURNEY *Cecilia* VIII. v, To the garden then they all went, and saw him upon the ground, weeding. **1847** F. W. ROBERTSON *Human Race* vii. (1881) 73 When once the farmer has sown, he can do little more except weed. **1860** W. WHITE *Wrekin* xxix. 342 The gardens adjoin the inclosure, and there I saw boys digging, hoeing and weeding amid plentiful crops of cabbage and beans.

2. a. *trans.* To free (land, a crop, plant) from weeds.

c **1325** *Gloss. W. de Bibbesw.* in Wright *Voc.* 156 Vostre lyn en tens sarchet [*glossed*] wed thi flax. **1398** TREVISA *Barth. De P.R.* XVII. lxv. (1495) 642 It nedyth that corne be clene wedyd and clensyd of..euyll wedys. *c* **1440** *Pallad. on Husb.* II. 289 And wattre hem..Ek delue hem al aboute, and wede hem clene. *c* **1440** *Alphabet of Tales* 359 A man went to wede hys vynys. **1523–34** FITZHERB. *Husb.* §21 How to wede corne. **1534** *MS. Acc. St. John's Hosp., Canterb.*, For a woman wedyng bens ij days, iiij d. **1553** BRENDE *Q. Curtius* IV. 34 They..came into his gardein..and found him weding of his ground. **1562** TURNER *Herbal* II. 52 When it is an inche long, it must be diligently wedede wt handes & not wt a weding yron. **1646–47** in Willis & Clark *Cambridge* (1886) II. 94 To the gardener for weeding ye garden and the walkes. **1693** EVELYN *De la Quint. Compl. Gard.* I. I. iii. 5 Your small Plants, as Strawberries, Lettice, Succory, &c. require to be often Weeded, the better to perform their Duty. *c* **1710** CELIA FIENNES *Diary* (1888) 301 One Garden wth Grass plotts and Earth walks Cut and wedd. **1766** *Complete Farmer* s.v. *Turnep* 7 Q b/1, I hand-hoed them once, and wed them twice. **1816** J. SMITH *Panorama Sci. & Art* II. 685 Weed the beds of onions, lettuces, carrots, and leeks. **1824** LOUDON *Encycl. Gard.* (ed. 2) §1352 Garden-pincers. .. Their chief use is to weed ponds. **1858** SLIGHT & BURN *Bk. Farm Implements* 328 The hand draw-hoe is used for weeding corn sown in rows. **1859** TENNYSON *Geraint & Enid* 942 As now Men weed the white horse on the Berkshire hills To keep him bright and clean as heretofore. *a* **1894** STEVENSON *In South Seas* II. ii. (1900) 152 The alleys where we walked were smoothed and weeded like a boulevard.

b. *fig.*

1377 LANGL. *P. Pl.* B. XVI. 17 Herte hatte þe herber þat it [the tree of Patience] in groweth, And *liberum arbitrium* hath þe londe to ferme, Vnder Piers þe plowman to pyken it and to weden it. *a* **1400** *Hymns Virg.* (1867) 77 God! sowe þi merci amonge my seede, Þanne schal it growe þouȝ y sowe late, And Repentaunce my corne schal weede. **1545** BRINKLOW *Compl.* 46 b, The kyngs grace began wel to wede the garden of Ingland. **1579** BP. ELY in W. Wilkinson *Confut. Fam. Love* Back of title-p., That our Church of England might be well weeded from to to grosse errors. **1600** SHAKS. *A. Y. L.* II. vii. 45 Prouided that you weed your better iudgements Of all opinion that growes ranke in them. **1648** EARL WESTMORLAND *Otia Sacra* (1879) 41 So let our Hearts be throughly wed of Sin, And then They'll prove good ground agen. **1662** EVELYN *Sculptura* i. 10 It is not to shew how diligently we have weeded the Calepines, and Lexicons..but the result of much diligent collection. **1735** SWIFT *Gulliver, Introd. Let. fr. Capt. Gulliver*, I desired you would let me know..when..courts and levees of great ministers [were] thoroughly weeded and swept. **1818** KEATS *Endym.* II. 106 Could I weed Thy soul of care. **1847** TENNYSON *Princess* v. 454 A lusty brace Of twins may weed her of her folly. **1879** FROUDE *Cæsar* x. 110 The Senate was at once weeded of many of its disreputable members. **1897** *Bookman* Jan. 129/1 The story would be better from a literary point of view if weeded of some of its clevernesses.

3. a. To remove (weeds) from land, esp. from cultivated land or from a crop. Also with *out*, *up*.

c **1430** LYDG. *Min. Poems* (Percy Soc.) 173 Heretykys have lefte there frowardnes, Wedyde the cokkelle frome the puryd corne. **1523–34** FITZHERB. *Husb.* §21 Dogfenell, goldes, mathes, and kedlokes are yll to wede after this maner. **1557** TUSSER *100 Points Husb.* (1878) 231 In June get thy wede-hoke,..and wede out such wede, as the corne doth not loue. **1611** A. STANDISH *Commons Compl.* 44 Weede the grasse cleane vp from about the rootes. **1628** FOLKINGHAM *Panala Med.* 77 Like a discreet Damsell, which preserues wholesome Herbes, and weeds-vp hurtfull Weeds. **1656** EARL MONM. tr. *Boccalini's Advts. fr. Parnass.* I. xvi. (1674) 18 So great abundance of Weeds grew up..[they could not] undergo the charges they were at in weeding them out. **1710** HILMAN *Tusser Rediv.* Mar. (1744) 32 Wild Oats..are not easily weeded when in the Blade. **1765** *Ann. Reg.* II. 146 The natural grass is to be considered as a weed, which, if not at first wed out of the ground, will soon destroy .. the artificial grass. **1902** W. W. JACOBS *At Sunwich Port* ii. 13 Mr. Wilks .. weeded two pieces of grass from the path, and carefully removed a dead branch from a laurel.

†**b.** *transf.* To remove (vermin, noxious animals). *Obs.*

1583 MELBANCKE *Philotimus* T ij b, The Kite canne weede the worme, can kill the Moulewarpe. **1593** SHAKS. *Rich. II*, II. iii. 167 Bushie, Bagot, and their Complices, The Caterpillers of the Commonwealth, Which I haue sworne to weed, and plucke away.

c. *fig.* To eradicate (errors, faults, sins, etc.); to remove (things or persons) as noxious or useless. Also with *away*, *out*.

1526 *Pilgr. Perf.* (W. de W. 1531) 30 By holy exercyse of the same plucketh out by the rotes & wedeth away all þe euill customes of synne. **1536** TINDALE *N.T.* To Chr. Rdr., Thou hast here .. the newe Testament .. Which I haue loked ouer agayne .. with all dilygence, .. & haue weded out of it many fautes. **1546** *Supplic. Poore Commons* (E.E.T.S.) 62 Your Hyghnes .. hath .. supplanted, and, as it were, weeded out, a great numbre of valiaunt and sturdye monckes, fryers, [etc.]. *a* **1568** ASCHAM *Scholem.* I. (Arb.) 56 If wise fathers, be not as well ware in weeding from their Children ill thinges. **1588** SHAKS. *L.L.L.* v. ii. 857 To weed this Wormewood from your fruitfull braine. **1603** —— *Meas. for M.* III. ii. 284 Twice trebble shame on Angelo, To weede my vice, and let his grow. **1615** *John Flodder* in Rollins *Pepysian Garl.* (1922) 58 And weed away from euery place and Cittie, Such idle Drones, you cherish with your pittie. **1643** PRYNNE *Sov. Power Parl.* I. (ed. 2) 24 That they were assembled for the good of the King and kingdome, and to weed from about him, such Traytours as he continually held with him. **1662** J. DAVIES tr. *Olearius' Voy. Ambass.* 43 These customs savour of their antient Idolatry. The Ministers do all they can to weed it out of them by little and little. **1690** LOCKE *Educ.* §147 Where you may .. gently correct and weed out any Bad Inclinations, and settle in him good Habits. **1736** BERKELEY *Disc.* Wks. 1871 III. 415 Those who are so active to weed out the prejudices of education. **1817** BYRON *Lament. Tasso* iv, I weed all bitterness from out my breast. **1870** LOWELL *Study Wind., Chaucer* (1871) 170 Sir Harris Nicolas, with the help of original records, weeded away the fictions by which the few facts were choked and overshadowed.

4. a. To clear *away* (plants, not necessarily noxious or useless); to take *out* (plants or trees) to prevent overcrowding; to thin (a crop).

1543– [see WEEDING *vbl. sb.* 2]. **1791** W. GILPIN *Rem. Forest Scenery* I. 85 If you want to shelter a nursery of young trees, plant Scotch firs: and the phrase is, you may afterwards *weed them out*, as you please. **1825** JAMIESON, To *Weed*, to thin growing plants by taking out the smaller ones; as, 'to weed firs', S.

¶**b.** The refrain of Jean Elliot's song (quot. *c* 1760) has often been quoted in the form 'The flowers of the forest are a' wede away'. In allusion to this, Scottish writers have sometimes used *wede away* (app. without associating it with the verb *weed*) in the vague sense 'carried off by death'; sometimes it has been interpreted as 'withered, faded'. Similarly *to wede away* used intr. for 'to die off', trans. for 'to carry off by death'.

c **1760** JEAN ELLIOT in F. Elliot *Trustworthiness of Border Ballads* (1906) 166 The Flowers of the Forest are weeded away. **1808** SCOTT *Marmion* VI. xxxvi, One of those flowers, whom plaintive lay In Scotland mourns as 'wede away'. **1824** —— 4 Apr. in *Fam. Lett.* (1894) II. xx. 198 How sad it is to see those whom we love gradually weeded away from the world in which we are left. **1824** MACTAGGART *Gallovid. Encycl.* 28 Ava my gude auld native parish, the Browns and the Sproats are a weedin awa. **1851** A. MACLAGAN *Sk. Nature* 225 If sad Fate before me should Wede him away.

c. *transf.* To remove (inferior or superfluous individuals) from a company, herd, etc.; also with *out*.

1863 E. FARMER *Scrap Bk.* (ed. 3) 27 The hounds have been 'weeded', some sold and some hung. **1869** WHYTE-MELVILLE *Songs & Verses* 87 Faster and faster comes grief and disaster, All but the good ones are weeded at last. **1889** 'J. S. WINTER' *Mrs. Bob* i, She had her house, as heretofore, all her old society (excepting such as she had judiciously weeded out). **1893** FORBES-MITCHELL *Great Mutiny* 3 Those unfit for foreign service were carefully weeded from the service companies. **1901** *Essex Weekly News* 15 Mar. 5/7 If a herd is to be made profitable, about one fourth of the cows must be weeded-out every year.

d. *intr.* Of a company: To become thinned *down*.

1887 SIR R. H. ROBERTS *In the Shires* v. 90 The field has weeded down to the select few.

e. *trans.* To perform a process of selecting from (a collection of documents, a file, etc.), rejecting those items which are unimportant or not worth retaining; to select (papers, etc.) in this manner. Also, to select (papers, etc.) in order to withhold them from general inspection. Also with *out*.

1874 H. TAYLOR *Let.* 30 Sept. in J. Brown *Lett.* (1912) 412, I am not sure that when I admired his poetry most, I did not admire his letters more, but like almost every collection of letters they should be weeded. **1946** A. E. PORTER *Let.* 26 Aug. in P. Moon *Transfer of Power* (1979) VIII. 309 Dick Tottenham, who compiled most of the files and is now on leave preparatory to retirement, would be singularly well qualified to weed them out and present you with those which are in fact worth keeping. **1977** *Times* 31 Aug. 4/1 The Ministry of Defence has begun a review of the way classified papers are written, filed, preserved (or 'weeded').

f. *to weed down*, to reduce (a list of candidates, etc.) to a short-list.

1942 *R.A.F. Jrnl.* 18 Apr. 6 Those who pass are further weeded down by a ballot. **1962** J. GLENN in *Into Orbit* 17 NASA asked us to take a series of tests which would help weed us down further.

5. *slang.* (See quots.)

1812 J. H. VAUX *Flash Dict.*, *Weed*, to pilfer or purloin a small portion from a large quantity of anything; .. an apprentice or shopman will *weed* his master's *lob*, that is take small sums out of the till... To *weed the swag* is to embezzle part of the booty, unknown to your *palls* before a division takes place. **1823** 'JON BEE' *Dict. Turf*, To *weed*, to steal part only. **1894** J. G. LITTLECHILD *Remin.* xv. (ed. 2) 158 Thus, in the case of a famous American bank robbery, he is suspected of having 'weeded the swag' to the amount of nearly £10,000.

6. *Angling.* Of a trout: to bury itself in weeds when hooked (*refl.* and *intr.*). Also, to entangle (the fish) in weeds (const. in *pass.*).

1889 F. M. HALFORD *Dry-Fly Fishing* ix. 211 Do not be afraid of weedy places. Trout .. seldom weed at night, probably because they do not see the angler. *Ibid.* 224 When a fish is once weeded, the following tactics are what I suggest. **1960** *Times* 2 July 11/2 The risk of allowing a fish to weed itself is much reduced .. if the weedbed lies upstream. *Ibid.*, More good trout have been lost in attempts to prevent them reaching weedbeds than have been lost in efforts to get them out once they have become weeded.

weed, obs. form of WED *v.*

weedable ('wiːdəb(ə)l), *a.* [f. WEED *v.* + -ABLE.] That may be weeded.

1611 COTGR., *Sarcable*, weedable, fit to be weeded.

weedage ('wiːdɪdʒ). [f. WEED *sb.*[1] + -AGE.] Weeds collectively. Also *fig.*

1855 LYNCH *Rivulet* CIX. vii, When [wilt Thou] with last desolations Earth's weedage consume. **1866** REDGRAVE *Cent. Painters* II. 112 The weedage, leafage, and flowers have been painted white, or approaching to it.

†**weedbind.** *Obs.* = BINDWEED I.

1551 TURNER *Herbal* I. L vj b, The properties of byndweed. The iuice of weedbynde, purgeth the belly.

weede, obs. form of WED *v.*, WIDE.

weeded ('wiːdɪd), (*ppl.*) *a.*[1] [f. WEED *sb.*[1] and *v.*[1] + -ED.]

1. Covered with weeds. Of a crop: Abounding in or choked with weeds; weedy.

1818 KEATS *Endym.* III. 193 Upon a weeded rock this old man sat. **1822** *Blackw. Mag.* XII. 785 [It] sent up only weeded, raggy, and mixed crops. **1830** TENNYSON *Mariana* i, Unlifted was the clinking latch; Weeded and worn the ancient thatch Upon the lonely moated grange.

2. Freed from weeds. Also *fig.*

1766 *Sp. agst. Suspending & Dispensing Prerogative* in *Parl. Hist.* (1813) XVI. 310 It was the rump of a well weeded parliament that abolished the monarchy. **1846** MRS. A. MARSH *Father Darcy* II. i. 5 The fields are covered with fine well-weeded turf.

3. Of a crop: Thinned out; sparse.

1831 T. MACQUEEN *Gloaming Amusem.* 65, O! white, white was his weedit hair.

weeded ('wiːdɪd), *a.*[2] *arch.* [f. WEED *sb.*[2] + -ED[2].] Dressed in widow's weeds.

1895 HARDY *Jude* v. vii. 369 Having ascertained thus much the immensely weeded widow retraced her steps. **1971** 'A. BURGESS' *MF* i. 18 An untrustworthy young man in black spoke to the frail weeded widow.

†**'weeden**, *a. Obs. rare.* [f. WEED *sb.*[1] + -EN[4].] Composed of weeds.

1599 DALLAM in *Early Voy. Levant* (Hakl. Soc.) 54 We that had our weeden pillowes.

weeder ('wiːdə(r)). [f. WEED *v.* + -ER[1].]

1. An implement used to eradicate weeds.

c **1440** *Promp. Parv.* 519/2 Wedare, *runco*. **1688** HOLME *Armoury* III. xx. (Roxb.) 246/1 The Fift is a long staffe, with a Broad Hooke of three teeth turning vp made fast on the end of it... This is termed a weeder. **1862** ANSTED *Channel Isl.* IV. xx. 478 Weeding is commonly done by hand with a small weeder. **1875** J. GRANT *One of 'Six Hundred'* ii, Occupied with a weeder, which he always carried, and with which the ends of all his walking-sticks were furnished.

2. A person employed to remove weeds from a crop, land, etc.

1534 *MS. Acc. St. John's Hosp., Canterb.*, For mett & drynk for ij weders ij days, ij d. **1538** ELYOT *Dict.*, *Sarritor*, *& sartor*, a weder of corne. *Ibid.*, *Stirpices*, wieders in gardeynes. **1577** B. GOOGE *Heresbach's Husb.* II. 52 b, The beddes and the borders must be so cast, as the weeders hands may reach to the middest of them. **1645** WITHER *Vox Pacif.* 74 Some Weeds, and Corne, are in the blade so like, That many Weeders have deceived bin. **1691** SIR J. FOULIS *Acc. Bk.* (S.H.S.) 136 To y[e] weiders in y[e] yard to drink, 0 4 0. *a* **1722** LISLE *Husb.* (1757) 385 My wheat was putting out into ear when I sent weeders to weed it. **1760** STERNE *Tr. Shandy* III. xxxiv, Whilst I am worth one [*sc.* shilling] to pay a weeder—thy path from thy door to thy bowling-green shall never be grown up. **1794** J. BOYS *Agric. Kent* 25 Women weeders, per day .. *os.* 8*d.* **1827** CLARE *Sheph. Cal.* 47 Each morning now, the weeders meet To cut the thistle from the wheat. **1835** *App. Munic. Corpor. Rep.* III. 1699 [Among Officers of Richmond, Yorks., corporation] Weeder of Foot-paths. **1870** *Inquiry, Yorksh. Deaf & Dumb* 20 He is employed as weeder in the garden at Wighill Park.

fig. **1607** [see WATERER I]. **1801** W. TAYLOR in *Monthly Mag.* XI. 648 Novels, Poems, Plays, and Periodical Trash, without end, press upon us for notice—it must be left to the weeders.

3. a. An extirpator (of weeds). Chiefly *fig.* Also with *out*.

1594 SHAKS. *Rich. III*, I. iii. 123, I was a packe-horse in his great affaires: A weeder out of his proud Aduersaries. **1598** YONG *Diana* 228 Thou art a weeder out Of vices, from the place of vertues graine. **1611** COTGR., *Eschardonneur*, a weeder of thistles.

b. *spec.* A person employed by a government department to weed documents, letters, etc. (WEED *v.* 4 e).

In quots. 1976 and 1984 the process is one of selecting papers in order to withhold or suppress them rather than to discard them.

1976 SUMMERS & MANGOLD *File on Tsar* v. xx. 254 Before papers get anywhere near the Public Record Office the weeders, for that is what they are called in government circles, have first bite; beavering away in Whitehall basements, they plough through the documents accumulated by all government ministries, deciding what should be suppressed. **1983** W. GARNER *Think Big, Think Dirty* vii. 101 The weeders worked in Central Registry, thinning down documentation as it grew bulky, repetitive or outdated. **1984** *Times* 23 May 10/3 Highly secret work, so secret that the weeders will see that it is not disclosed, even after 30 years.

4. *attrib.*, as ***weeder woman***; **weeder-clips** *Sc.* = *weeding shears* (see WEEDING *vbl. sb.* 3).

1748 LADY M. W. MONTAGU *Let. to C'tess of Bute* 10 July, I generally rise at six, and as soon as I have breakfasted, put myself at the head of my weeder women and work with them till nine. **1787** Weeder-clips [see WEEDING-HOOK].

weedery ('wiːdərɪ), *sb.*[1] [f. WEED *sb.*[1] + -ERY.] Weeds collectively; also, a place where weeds abound.

1642 H. MORE *Song of Soul, Psychozoia* II. lxxii, Hard by there was a place, all covered o're With stinging nettles and such weedery. **1814** SOUTHEY *Roderick* VI. 46 The weedery which through The interstices of those neglected courts Uncheck'd had flourish'd long, and seeded there. **1837** *Tait's Mag.* IV. 629 Two poplars at the end of a strip of weedery. *a* **1890** MARIANNE NORTH *Recoll. Happy Life* (1892) I. i. 29 Our garden was much of a weedery in those days at Hastings.

weedery ('wiːdərɪ), *sb.*[2] *poet. nonce-wd.* [f. WEED *sb.*[2] + -ERY.] Mourning garments.

1908 HARDY *Dynasts* III. VI. ii. 459 Even as he For whom thou wear'st that filial weedery Was waylaid by my tipstaff nine years since.

weedful ('wiːdfʊl), *a. rare.* [f. WEED *sb.*[1] + -FUL.] Abounding in weeds. *lit.* and *fig.*

1614 SYLVESTER *2nd Sess. Parl. Vertues Royall* Ded., Need-full in this Weed-full Time. **1849** MANGAN *Poems, To Jos. Brenan* 14 Unheedful Of the thorns and tares, that choked the weedful Garden of my mind!

'weed-hook. In 1 wéodhóc, 4 wyed hoc, 5 weod hook, wedhoc, -hoke, -huke, 4–6 wedehoke. [f. WEED *sb.*[1] + HOOK *sb.*[1]] A hook for cutting away weeds. Also in fig. contexts.

c **725** *Corpus Gloss.* S 20 *Sarculum*, ueodhoc. **1340** *Ayenb.* 121 þe yefþe of drede .. is þe wyed hoc of þe gardine þet uordeþ al þet kueade gers. *c* **1340** *Nominale* (Skeat) 527 *Sarcle* .. Wedehoke. **1408** *Wyclif's Bible* Isa. vii. 25 (2nd text, MS. K.) A sarpe, *id est*, a weod hook. *c* **1420** ? LYDG. *Assembly of Gods* 1361 Then Reson & Sadnesse toke wede hokes tweyn, and all wylde wantones out of the fylde gan wede. **1557** TUSSER *100 Points Husb.* lxxix, In June get thy wedehoke, thy knife and thy gloue. **1561** T. NORTON *Calvin's Inst.* IV. xi. § 11 (1562) 72 Learne that thou hast nede of a wedehoke, not of a scepter, that thou mayste doo the worke of a Prophete. **1610** J. ROBINSON *Justif. Separat.* 117 How dare the Prelates .. take this forbidden weedhook into their hands, & vse it against any tare amongst them? **1631** MABBE *Celestina* i. 21 To root it out streight with the weed-hooke of good workes. **1710** HILMAN *Tusser Rediv.* Mar. (1744) 32 These [thistles] may .. be weeded off with a Weed-hook, or Stabbing-knife. **1844** H. STEPHENS *Bk. Farm* III. 941 The only implements used in weeding corn are the hand draw-hoe .. and the weed-hook. **1858** SLIGHT & BURN *Bk. Farm Implements* 328 The Weed-Hook .. consists of an acute hook of iron, flattened, .. with the two inner edges as far set asunder as to embrace the stem of succulent herbaceous plants, and made as sharp as easily to cut through them.

weedicide ('wiːdɪsaɪd). [f. WEED *sb.*[1] + -I- + -CIDE.] A chemical preparation designed as a weed-killer; weed-killer.

1934 *Jrnl. Dept. Agric. W. Austral.* XI. 521 Sodium arsenite has been employed extensively .. as a weedicide, and .. proved the most successful weed killer. **1951** *Chambers's Jrnl.* Aug. 457/1 Agricultural scientists .. have set themselves the task of finding efficient straight weedicides. **1975** *N.Z. Jrnl. Agric.* Sept. 21/1 Maize farmers .. spend a great deal of time and money on ground preparation, seed, fertilisers and weedicide. **1979** *Indian Express* 10 Apr. 10/4 As preparatory cultivations are carried out to control weeds only, efforts should be made to use weedicides for it whenever necessary.

weeding ('wiːdɪŋ), *vbl. sb.* [f. WEED *v.* + -ING[1].]

1. a. The action or process of freeing (land, a crop, etc.) from weeds.

c **1100** *Gloss.* in Wr.-Wülcker 105/3 *Runcatio*, weodung. *c* **1440** *Promp. Parv.* 519/2 Weddynge, *runcacio*. **1468–9** *Stonor Papers* (Camden) I. 102 For wedyng in the whete, iij s. j d. **1523–34** FITZHERB. *Husb.* § 21 After a shoure of raine it is beste wedynge. *Ibid.*, But as for terre, there wyll noo wedynge serue. **1583** *Shuttleworths' Acc.* (Chetham Soc.) 10 John Hewode for the dresing, wyedinge and kypinge of the gardenes .. foure and tynty shillynges. **1641** MILTON *Animadv.* 52 The weeding and worming of every bed both in that, and all other Gardens thereabout. **1707** MORTIMER *Husb.* 126 The common price of weeding of it [*sc.* woad] is about eight pence an Acre. **1846** *J. Baxter's Libr. Pract. Agric.* (ed. 4) I. 381 When draining is properly attended to, there will be little occasion for weeding. **1921** *Times Lit.*

Suppl. 8 Sept. 574/3 The subsequent weeding of the young crop [of teak] until it can hold its own against the rapid growth of weeds and useless trees.

b. The eradication (of weeds); also with *out*. Also *fig*.

1560 Daus tr. *Sleidane's Comm.* 68 b, The wedyng out of Heretikes. **1656** Earl Monm. tr. *Boccalini's Advts. fr. Parnass.* I. xvi. 28 It was..ridiculous to compare the purging of the world from seditious spirits, with the weeding of noysome hearbs out of a Garden. **1901** *Scotsman* 13 Mar. 9/4 One who..was all for the weeding out of incapacity and the selection of the fittest officers.

c. That which is weeded out.

1588 Shaks. *L.L.L.* I. i. 96 Hee weedes the corne, and still lets grow the weeding.

2. a. The action of thinning out plants, trees, etc. Also *concr.* (*pl.*) the plants removed in the process.

1543 *Act 35 Hen. VIII* c. 17 §5 Persons..which have.. Woods or Coppice..shall, at the felling or weeding thereof, leave standing..twelve Trees of Oak. *a* **1715** Burnet *Own Time* (1734) II. 274 They charged him [Ld. Halifax] for another Grant..to the waste of the Timber... [He replied] His Grant in the Forest of Dean was only of the Weedings. **1799** J. Robertson *Agric. Perth* 254 At a second weeding, when it appears necessary, another third of the original number may be cut down. *Ibid.* 255 Ditto number of weedings, taken out before 20 years, and valued at one half-penny each. **1825** Jamieson, *Weedins*, what is pulled up, or cut out, in thinning trees, &c. **1844** H. Stephens *Bk. Farm* III. 1098 To erect a pyramid of 3 small trees or weedings of larch or Scots fir.

b. *transf.* and *fig.* Also with *out*.

1844 Disraeli *Coningsby* II. i, The accession of Mr. Canning to the cabinet..soon led to a further weeding of the Mediocrities. **1853** Surtees *Sponge's Sp. Tour* lx. 342 It seemed agreed on all hands that their party rather wanted weeding than increasing. **1870** *Daily News* 11 Nov., The feeling..is so strong, that a great weeding of the judicial bench is probable if the Republic lasts. **1884** *Athenæum* 20 Dec. 800/3 Its value would have been greater if the two volumes had been reduced to one by the judicious weeding of the articles dealing with the controversy with Mill. **1916** *Kinematograph Year Bk.* 36 (*heading*) The weeding-out process. **1932** *New Yorker* 14 May 56/2, I should like to hear some of the manuscripts that the weeding-out committee considered inferior to the final five. **1953** J. S. Huxley *Evolution in Action* ii. 42 This weeding-out process. **1968** *North Amer. Rev.* CVII. 589 In one case, and in one case only, could this weeding [of a library's collection] be properly made. **1977** *Times* 31 Aug. 4/1 Valuable material may have been destroyed during 'weeding'. **1981** D. Francis *Twice Shy* xii. 139 He disagreed strongly with my weeding-out policy, even though I'd..discussed every dud [horse] to be discarded.

3. *attrib.* and *Comb.*, as ***weeding season***, ***time***; in the names of many tools used in removing weeds, as ***weeding chisel***, †***dog***, ***forceps***, ***fork***, †***iron***, †***knife*** (lit. and fig.), ***pincers***, ***shears***, †***tongs*** (lit. and fig.), ***tool***, also WEEDING-HOOK; **weeding dues** *slang* (see quot. and WEED *v.* 4 e); **weeding shim** *dial.* (see quot.); **weeding-woman** (cf. *weeder woman*, WEEDER 4).

1819 Rees *Cycl.*, **Weeding-chisel*, an useful tool with a divided chisel point, for cutting the roots of large weeds within the ground. **1688** Holme *Armoury* III. 392/2 In the Base is..a Gardiners *Weeding Dog. It is made with a Taper Fork, and a Cross bar of Iron, some six or eight Inches above, [etc.]. **1812** J. H. Vaux *Flash Dict.* s.v., Speaking of any person, place, or property, that has been weeded, it is said *weeding dues have been concerned. **1819** Rees *Cycl.*, **Weeding-Forceps*, or *Tongs*, the tool of the nipper kind which is made use of for taking up some sorts of plants in weeding corn and other crops. **1611** Cotgr., *Serfoët*, a weeding hooke, or *weeding forke. **1828–32** Webster, *Weeding-Fork*, a strong three-pronged fork, used in cleaning ground of weeds. **1921** *Blackw. Mag.* June 769/2, I was summoned into the house..and leaving my weeding-fork and basket, was absent..perhaps an hour. **1562** *Weding yron [see WEED *v.*^{1} 2]. **1683** J. Reid *Scots Gard.* (1907) 149 Pull up the roots cleanly, taking the help of the weeding-iron where needful. **1728** Swift *Pastoral Dial.* xi. Misc. 1732 III. II. 38 Him on my Lap you never more should see; Or may I lose my *Weeding-knife—and Thee. **1751** Earl Orrery *Remarks Swift* (1752) 183 The scythe of time, or the weeding-knife of a judicious editor, will cut down the docks and thistles. **1842** Loudon *Suburban Hort.* 381 When large weeds only are to be pulled out of shrubberies, this may sometimes be done with *weeding pincers. *a* **1722** Lisle *Husb.* (1757) 385 The latter end of the *weeding-season. **1906** Alice Werner *Natives Brit. Central Africa* vi. 137 In the planting and weeding seasons, people set out for the gardens before daylight. **1688** Holme *Armoury* III. xx. (Roxb.) 246/1 He beareth Gules, a paire of Weeding Tonges Or, else a paire of *Weeding Sheares, erected and open. **1850** Ogilvie, *Weeding-shears*, shears used for cutting weeds. **1819** Rees *Cycl.*, **Weeding-Shim*, an implement..made with a frame somewhat like that of the common wheel-barrow... It is a very useful and convenient tool for the purpose of tearing up weeds. **1523–34** Fitzherb. *Husb.* §16 The whiche shal be great hurte to the corne, whan it shall be sowen, and specially in the *weding-tyme of the same. **1733** W. Ellis *Chiltern & Vale Farm.* 298, I was obliged several Years after, to cut them up in Weeding-time. *a* **1555** Bradford in Coverdale *Lett. Martyrs* (1564) 462 Yf god..perchaunce beginne..to poure hys showers vpon you: to nippe you with his *weeding tonges, &c. **1688** [see *weeding shears*]. **1850** Ogilvie, **Weeding tool*, an implement for pulling up, digging up, or cutting weeds. **1710** Addison *Tatler* No. 221 He gave me positive Orders to turn off an old *Weeding-Woman. **1908** [Miss E. Fowler] *Betw. Trent & Ancholme* 40 Two old weeding-women, cheek by cheek, taking up daisies.

weeding-hook. = WEED-HOOK.

1378 *Acc. Roll Doune, Wandsworth, Surrey* (Westm. Chapter Munim.), iij Wedynghokes. *c* **1440** *Promp. Parv.* 519/2 Wedynge hooke, *runco*. **1523–34** Fitzherb. *Husb.* §21 And if it be drye wether, than muste ye haue a wedynge-hoke. *a* **1661** Holyday *Juvenal* (1673) 270 When weeding-hooks and rakes The first Smiths made. **1763** Mills *Syst Pract. Husb.* III. 22 The common weeding-hook will not go deep enough to take out the whole of the long slender tap root of this plant. **1787** Burns *Answ. Gudewife of Wauchope-House* ii, The rough burr-thistle, spreading wide Amang the bearded bear—I turn'd my weeding heuk [*Ibid.* Wks. 1800 III. 378 weeder-clips] aside, An' spar'd the symbol dear! **1842** Loudon *Suburban Hort.* 135 The weeding-hook, which is a narrow strap of iron forked at the lower extremity, and a wooden handle at the other, is also used for raising weeds.

fig. **1641** Milton *Ch. Govt.* I. v, He little dreamt then that the weeding-hook of reformation would after two ages pluck up his glorious poppy from insulting over the good corne.

weedless ('wi:dlɪs), *a.* [f. WEED *sb.*^{1} + -LESS.] Free from weeds. *lit.* and *fig.*

1611 Donne *Anat. World, 1st Anniv.* 82 For all assum'd vnto this dignitee, So many weedlesse paradises bee. **1659** W. Chamberlayne *Pharon.* III. i. 95 Whose weedless banks no pining winter knew. **1670** Dryden *1st Pt. Conq. Granada* IV. (1672) 35 When troubled most, it does the bottom show, 'Tis weedless all above; and rockless all below. **1841** Catlin *N. Amer. Ind.* (1844) II. 164 The thousand treeless, bushless, weedless hills of grass. **1874** W. Cory *Lett. & Jrnls.* (1897) 371 A clear, weedless, rocky pool. **1908** H. Wales *Old Allegiance* viii. 137 Straight shaded walks and weedless lawns.

weedling ('wi:dlɪŋ). [f. WEED *sb.*^{1} + -LING.]

1. A small weed.

1820 Clare *Rural Life* (ed. 3) 62 And though thou seem'st a weedling wild, Wild and neglected like to me. **1881** R. Buchanan *God & the Man* III. i. 17 Beyond this moss there seemed no other sign of vegetation;..not even the weedlings of the rock.

2. A slight, weakly person.

1890 *Universal Rev.* 15 July 410 What is pathetic is the maternal anxiety shown by the weedy lady for her weedier child... Her whole care is that the weedling's days shall be long [etc.]. **1911** *Times* 9 Aug. 6/1 The strong, able-bodied ones go off to the Colonies and only the weedlings remain.

†**weedwind.** *Obs.* [ad. MDu. *wedewinde* = G. *wehdwinde* (see WITHWIND), with assimilation of the first element to WEED *sb.*] **a.** Black Bindweed, *Polygonum Convolvulus*. **b.** Wild Convolvulus, *Convolvulus arvensis*.

1578 Lyte *Dodoens* III. liii. 394 Of blacke Withiwinde, or Bindeweede..This kinde of Bindeweede is called..in shoppes *Volubilis media*, that is to say, The meane Bindeweede..in English Weedewinde, and Windweede, or Iuybindweede. **1597** Gerarde *Herbal* Table Engl. Names, Weedwind, that is withywind. **1601** R. Chester *Love's Mart.* (1878) 82 Sweete Trefoile, Weedwind, the wholesome Wormewood. **1665** Lovell *Herball* (ed. 2) 465 Weed wind, see Withy wind.

weedy ('wi:dɪ), *a.*^{1} [f. WEED *sb.*^{1} + -Y^1.]

1. Full of, abounding or overgrown with, weeds.

c **1420** *Pallad. on Husb.* Tab. 219 Lond, weet, wodi, wedi, or stony, to remedie. **1596** Spenser *F.Q.* IV. x. 55 But I.. Like warie Hynd within the weedie soyle, For no intreatie would forgoe so glorious spoyle. **1611** Bible *Jer.* xlix. 21 The noise thereof was heard in the Red [*marg.* weedy] Sea. *a* **1631** Donne *Lett. to Persons of Honour* (1651) 50 A sullen weedy lake, where I could not have so much as exercise for my swimming. **1707** Mortimer *Husb.* 100 If Wheat is weedy it must lie upon the Gravel. **1767** A. Young *Farmer's Lett. to People* 261 Dividing the field in such a manner as to give each method a fair proportion of the weedy and clean parts. **1828** Davy *Salmonia* 47 The fish here are large, and the river weedy, so you must take care of your fish and your tackle. **1852** Mrs. Stowe *Uncle Tom's C.* xxxii, The waggon rolled up a weedy gravel-walk. **1914** 'Ian Hay' *Knt. on Wheels* xiv, The garden was weedy and the lawn unshaven.

fig. **1579** Spenser *Sheph. Cal.* Dec. 122, I haue Nought reaped but a weedye crop of care. **1628** Prynne *Brief Surv. Cozens* 15 The infallibilitie of the Church of Rome, from whose weedie Garden, this Garland of Deuotion hath beene gathered. **1859** Meredith *R. Feverel* xiii[x], A sad downfall if we forget what human nature, in its green weedy Spring, is composed of. **1892** *Daily Tel.* 31 Aug. 5/4 [The library] of the Church House is still scrappy, weedy and incomplete.

2. Of the nature of or resembling a weed; made or consisting of weeds.

1602 Shaks. *Ham.* IV. vii. 175 When downe the weedy Trophies, and her selfe, Fell in the weeping Brooke. **1610** G. Fletcher *Christ's Tri.* I. l, Let..nettles, kixe, and all the weedie nation, With emptie elders grow, sad signes of desolation. **1733** W. Ellis *Chiltern & Vale Farm.* 349 The Sheep..in quest of their weedy Food. **1753** Dodsley *Publ. Virtue* I. ii. 94 His new machine; form'd to exterminate The weedy race. **1881** Grant Allen *Evolutionist at large* 44 Thus the crowfoot, too, cannot blossom to any purpose below the water;..only those lucky individuals whose chance lot it was to grow a little taller and weedier than the rest, and so overtop the stream, have handed down their race to our time. **1885** *L'pool Daily Post* 30 June 4/6 Grasping in their tired little hands the weedy spoils of the hedgerow.

fig. **1819** H. Busk *Vestriad* II. 84 The brawny Tritons, with their weedy hair. **1835** Waterworth *Exam. Distinctive Princ. Protestantism* 9 These weedy prejudices never will be torn up. **1874** Burnand *My Time* xxvi. 238 A long-legged gentleman with weedy whiskers. **1888** D. C. Murray *Weaker Vessel* xiv, Some of them are clever in a way; rooted fools by nature, who bear a weedy little blossom of wit, and suppose themselves to flower all over.

3. Having a taste or tang of weeds.

1867 *Trans. Illinois Agric. Soc.* VI. 638 *Weedy*, flour made from wheat that has come in contact with a noxious weed imparting an unpleasant smell. **1892** J. M. Walsh *Tea* 107 The liquor [of Neilgherry] is thin, muddy and rank or 'weedy' in flavour.

4. *colloq.* (Cf. WEED *sb.*^{1} 5.)

a. Of animals, esp. horses and hounds: Lean, leggy, loose-bodied, and lacking in strength and mettle.

1800 *Sporting Mag.* XV. 107 The poor, slight, weedy, spindle-shanked stock of brood mares. **1854** Surtees *Handley Cr.* xxxviii. (1901) II. 15 He rode a weedy chestnut. **1865** Morley *Mod. Characteristics* 11 A very shabby old brougham drawn by a pair of very weedy horses. **1877** Stables *Pract. Kennel Guide* 37 *Weedy* a very expressive word, as applied to a dog who looks leggy, thin, badly-bred, and apparently going to seed. **1888** 'R. Boldrewood' *Robbery under Arms* xi, We drafted out all the worst and weediest of the cattle.

b. Of persons: Unhealthily tall and thin; lanky and wanting physical vigour; also, weakly, of poor physique. Also without reference to physical qualities: feeble, half-hearted, weak; lacking firmness or strength.

1852 Surtees *Sponge's Sp. Tour* xxi, 'Nice size, too,' continued he,..'plenty of substance..(puff)... Hate a weedy woman—fifteen two and a half—that's to say, five feet four, 's plenty of height for a woman'. *a* **1865** Mrs. Gaskell *Wives & Dau.* viii, Grace..is looking rather pale and weedy. **1892** *Nation* 21 Apr. 295/3 In order to fill the ranks large numbers of weedy men have been enlisted. **1922** E. M. Forster *Life to Come* (1975) 73 The chief had developed into an affable and rather weedy Christian with a good knowledge of English. **1971** *Petticoat* 24 July 4/3 I'm just too weedy, I don't threaten to expose them. **1982** Barr & York *Official Sloane Ranger Handbk.* 122/1 At whatever grade, they are fearless ('Be weedy in front of the wops?').

c. Of things.

1950 *Chambers's Jrnl.* Mar. 131/1 He must have conveyed this to her in one way or another, because soon afterwards she sent back his presents, and the weedy friendship which might have blossomed into a beautiful love was nipped in the bud.

5. *Comb.*, as ***weedy-brown***, ***-haired***, ***-looking*** adjs.; ***weedy-slow*** adv.

1958 J. Betjeman *Coll. Poems* 263 A mounting arch of water weedy-brown. **1819** Keats *Lines to Fanny* 36 That monstrous region, whose dull rivers pour, Ever from their sordid urns unto the shore, Unown'd of any weedy-haired gods. **1854** Whyte Melville *Gen. Bounce* vii, His fastidious taste cannot but admit that there are 'some weedy-looking ones among 'em'. **1861** Hughes *Tom Brown at Oxf.* xxxiii, Tom thought them weedy-looking animals. **1866** *Treas. Bot.* 139/2 Various genera of coarse weedy-looking plants. **1923** E. Sitwell *Bucolic Comedies* 38 In the Castles drownèd long ago Where the empty years pass weedy-slow.

Hence '**weediness**, the quality or state of being 'weedy'; lack of physical presence; feebleness.

1924 Wodehouse *Bill the Conqueror* v. 103 He had a certain weediness, a lack of thews and sinews. **1925** W. Deeping *Sorrell & Son* viii. 80 He realized that in spite of the other man's weediness he was a competitor who was to be respected.

weedy ('wi:dɪ), *a.*^{2} [f. WEED *sb.*^{2} + Y^1.] Of a woman: Wearing widow's 'weeds', clad in mourning.

1848 Longf. *Life* (1891) II. 133 A weedy woman came sweeping up to us, and introduced herself as an admirer. **1850** Dickens *David Copp.* xvii, She still wore weeds. I think there was some compromise in the cap; but otherwise she was as weedy as in the early days of her mourning. **1887** Jessopp *Arcady* 155 Think of the blank despair that would take hold of the weedy widows and desolate orphans when they applied for their share of the surplus.

weef (wi:f). Also **wef.** [? Var. of WEETH, dial. f. WITHE *sb.*] (See quot.)

1832 *Planting* 90 in *Husb.* (L.U.K.) III, *Bavins.* House-faggots, bound with two withers or weefs. *Ibid.*, The tops of hedge-stakes, coopers' ware, &c., bound with one wither or wef. *Ibid.*, *Withers* or *weefs*. The pliant shoots of hazel, ash, willow, &c., for binding the spray and prunings of trees into faggots, brooms, &c.

weef, weeft: see WEFFE, WEFT.

weegle, Sc. var. WAGGLE *v.*

weehee: see WEHEE.

week (wi:k), *sb.* Forms: α. 1 **wice** (*rare*), **wicu** (inflected **wican, wiecan**), 3–5 **wike**, 3–6 **wyke**, 5 **wyeke**, 6 **wieke**; 4 **wycke**, 6–7, 9 *dial.* **wick**; β. 3–6 **weke**, 6 **weeke**, **weicke**, **weake**, 6– **week**; γ. 1 **wucu**, 2–3 **wuke**, 3–5 **wouke**, 4–5 **woke**, 4–6 **wok**, 5 **wooke**, **wouyk**, **wowke** (**wokk**), 5–6 **wolk(e**; δ. *Sc.* 4–8 **ouk**, **owk(e**, 5–8 **oulk**, **owlk**, **ulk**, **olk**, 6 **wke**, 9 **ook**. [Com. Teut.: OE. *wice* wk. fem. corresponds to OFris. *wike* (WFris. *wike*, NFris. *week*, *wik*), OS. *-wika* in *crûcewika* Passion Week (MLG., LG. *weke*), MDu. *weke* (Du. *week*), OHG. *wehha*, *wohha* (MHG., mod.G. *woche*), ON. *vika* (Norw. *vika*, Sw. *vecka*, Da. *uge*), ? Goth. *wikō* (once only, rendering τάξις 'order' in Luke i. 8):—OTeut. **wikōn-*.

As there is no reason to suppose that the Germanic peoples used a reckoning by weeks before they came in contact with the Romans, it is probable that the OTeut. **wikōn-* had originally some meaning wider than that of 'period of seven days', which the word has in WGer. and Scandinavian; perh. it meant 'succession, series,' and this may have been the sense of Goth. *wikō* in the only recorded example. The root **wik-* is found in ON. *víkja* to turn, move, OHG. *wehsal* (mod.G. *wechsel*) change.

The remarkable diversity of forms in the Eng. word is due to the different effect, in different dialects, of the initial (w) on the following vowel. The original form with *wi-* appears rarely in OE. literature (exc. in combinations, where it was general); the β type represented by the standard English form descends from this. The form *wucu* (inflected *wucan*) is the ancestor of the γ type (ME. *woke*, *wouke*, etc.), whence the δ type was developed in the North by the loss of the initial (w) before the labial vowel. (The written *l* in many of the Sc. forms, *wolk*, *oulk*, etc., was never pronounced.)]

1. a. The cycle of seven days, recognized in the calendar of the Jews and thence adopted in the calendars of Christian, Muslim, and various other peoples; a single period of this cycle, i.e. a space of seven successive days beginning with the day traditionally fixed as the first day of the week.

The Jewish week began with the day after the Sabbath, and this beginning was adopted by the Christian church. The days of the Jewish week, except the seventh (the Sabbath) were not named, but distinguished only by number; in early Christian use the name Sabbath was retained for the seventh day, and the first was called the Lord's day (ἡ κυριακὴ ἡμέρα, *dies dominicus*), the other days being numbered only. The English names, Sunday, Monday, etc., belong to an astrological week which, quite independently of the Jewish-Christian week, arose from the practice of assigning the successive hours to the seven planets in the order of their distance, and then naming each whole day (of 24 hours) from the planet supposed to rule its first hour. The planetary names, *Dies Solis*, *Dies Lunæ*, *Dies Martis*, etc., came into common use in the Roman empire, and were adopted in translated form by the English (before they came to Britain) and other Teut. peoples; the names Mars, Mercurius, etc., being apprehended as names of Roman gods, were rendered by the names of the Teutonic deities supposed to correspond to these: for details see the articles TUESDAY, WEDNESDAY, etc.

α. **a900** *O.E. Chron.* an. 878 (Parker MS.) On þære seofoðan wiecan ofer Eastron. **c900** *Bæda's Hist.* V. ii. (Miller) 388 Mid ðy hit ða án wiice ðæs fæstnes ȝefylled wæs. **c950** *Lindisf. Gosp.* Luke xviii. 12 Ic fæsto tuiȝo in wico [**c975** *Rushworth* wica]. **c1175** *Lamb. Hom.* 139 Alle oðer daȝes of þe wike beoð to þreldome to þis dei [sunnen dei]. **c1205** LAY. 13927 Þene feorðe dæi i þere wike heo ȝifuen him [Woden] to wurðscipe. **a1225** *Ancr. R.* 70 Euerich urideie of ðe yer holdeð silence, bute ȝif hit beo duble feste; & teonne holdeð hit sum oðer dai iðe wike. **c1290** *S. Eng. Leg.* 312/438 Þe seoue Dawes in þe wyke. **c1374** CHAUCER *Troylus* II. 430, I shal nomore com here þis wyke. **c1394** *P. Pl. Crede* 13 Þe Lengþe of a Lenten, flech moot y leue..And Wedenes-day iche wyke wiþouten flech-mete. **c1400** *Ywaine & Gaw.* 3058 Ilkone of us, withouten lesyng, Might win ilk wike fourty shilling. **a1450** *Mirk's Festial* 172 [A Saracen said to a Christian] Þis is þe wyke þat ȝoure gret profete deyt in. **1450–1530** *Myrr. Our Ladye* I. i. 4 The seconde parte ys of youre seuen storyes, accordynge to the seuen dayes of the wyeke. **1456** *Paston Lett.* Suppl. (1901) 57 My lord of Norwich shal the next wyke visite the hous of Hykelyng. **1590** in P. H. Hore *Hist. Wexford* (1900) I. 271 James..went to St. James' faire to Bristowe the last wick.

β. **c1275** [see 2. **c1205**]. **c1380** WYCLIF *Sel. Wks.* II. 1 Þe Wednesdai in þe firste weke of Advent. **1390** GOWER *Conf.* III. 116 He..Of sevene daies made a weke. **c1400** MAUNDEV. (Roxb.) xiv. 61 On þe Seterday it rynnes fast, and all þe weke elles it standes still. **1529** MORE *Let. to Wife* 3 Sept., Wks. 1419/2, I shal (I think)..get leaue this next weke to come home and se you. **1556–7** *Cal. Anc. Rec. Dublin* (1889) 458 The said [Recorder] shall thre daies every weicke gyve attendaunce. **1560** DAUS tr. *Sleidane's Comm.* 231 That thre daies in the weke they tame theyr body with fastynge. **a1633** G. HERBERT *Outlandish Prov.* (1640) 587 [*Proverb*] Thursday come, and the week's gone. **1740** C'TESS POMFRET in *C'tess Hartford's Corr.* (1805) I. 208 As this is a week of great devotion and retirement with all good catholics, so it is a week of great idleness and equal retirement with us protestants. **1748** *Anson's Voy.* II. viii. 222 At Cheripe,..there is a constant store of provisions prepared for the vessels who go thither every week from Panama. **1837** WHEWELL *Hist. Induct. Sci.* (1857) I. 111 We may probably consider the Week, with Laplace as 'the most ancient monument of astronomical knowledge'. **1837** DICKENS *Pickw.* xliv, You couldn't make it convenient to lend me half a crown till the latter end of next week, could you? **1849** C. BRONTE *Shirley* i, The present week is yet but at Thursday, and on Monday [etc.]. **1867** E. A. FREEMAN in Stephens *Life* (1895) I. 391 Last week I have been working at the early life of Lanfranc.

γ. **c1000** *Rule St. Benet* (1888) 51 Þæt beon an ælcere wucan saltere..ȝesungenne. **a1122** *O.E. Chron.* an. 1118, On þison ȝeare on þære wucon Theophanie wæs anes æfenes swyðe mycel lihtinge. **c1200** ORMIN 4173 Itt iss aȝȝ heh messedaȝȝ Att here wukess ende. **c1200** *Trin. Coll. Hom.* 3 And hit [*sc.* Advent] lasteð þre wuke fulle and sum del more. **1297** R. GLOUC. (Rolls) 2431 Vr eldore him [*sc.* Woden] bitoc of þe wouke þen verþe day. **a1325** *MS. Rawl. B.* 520 lf. 32 Ant te baillifs..eche woke oþer eche forteniȝt ate leste sullen maken enquestes of men herburgers. **c1380** WYCLIF *Wks.* (1880) 454 Þus þe persoun þat al þe wouke disposiþ hym to preche to his sheep or [etc.]. **c1400** *Rule St. Benet* xli. 29 Al þe wukis in þe summir, sal ye faste ilke wuke tua dais. **c1400** MAUNDEV. (1839) xxv. 261 For thei schryven hem and howsele hem evermore ones or twyes in the Woke. **1425–6** in *Acta Dom. Conc.* II. Introd. 13 The secunde terme begynande the Monunday of the first hail wolke of lenteryn with lik continuacion of termes. **c1440** *Promp. Parv.* 532/1 Woke (*v.rr.* wok, wooke), *ebdomada*, *septimana*. **c1450** *Godstow Reg.* 231 To gefe to þe power nedy parysshens of bloxham euery woke & euery ȝere halfe a quarter of corne menglyd. **1456** SIR G. HAYE *Law Arms* (S.T.S.) 303 The peple desyris..the mare to se him na he rade every day, or every wolk or moneth. **1552** ABP. HAMILTON *Catech.* (1884) 51 Als well on the Satterday as ony other day of the wouke.

δ. **c1470** *Gol. & Gaw.* 1343 With reualing and reuay all the oulk hale. **1526** *Cartul. S. Nicholai Aberd.* (New Spald. Club) I. 154 With ane trentell of messis in ye ouik [? *read* oulk] yat ye said obit sall happin in. **1565** *Reg. Privy Council Scot.* I. 332 That na sellaris be oppynnit bot thryis in the oulk for selling of thair geir. **1566** in Hay Fleming *Mary Q. of Scots* (1897) 495 Nocht onlie the twa Sondayis bot also the hole rest of the olk. **1584** J. MELVILL *Autob. & Diary* (Wodrow Soc.) 181 Ther shalbe four Sermones in the ouk; twa on the Sunday, and twa on the ouk-dayes. **1608** *Rec. Innerwick* in A. I. Ritchie *Ch. St. Baldred* (1880) 114 The examination to begin ye nixt olk..for that purpose. **1728** RAMSAY *Robt., Richy, & Sandy* 31 Last ouk I dream'd my tup..brak his leg. **1807** TANNAHILL *Soldier's Return* II. iii, Wife—fetch my bonnet that I caft last owk. **1868** G. MACDONALD *R. Falconer* I. xi. 137, I'll think aboot it whan ance I'm throu wi' this job. That'll be neist ook or thereabouts, or aiblins two days efter.

b. With prefixed word, denoting some particular week of the year. Also, a week during which some event takes place, either annually or on one occasion only; a week during which attention is focused on a particular topic for promotional, charitable, etc., purposes.

The weeks of the ecclesiastical calendar commonly thus referred to are *Easter week*, *the ember weeks* (EMBER[2]), PASSION-WEEK, HOLY WEEK (also called GREAT *week*), ROGATION *week* (also called GANG-WEEK, GRASS-*week*, PROCESSION-*week*), WHIT-*week* (also called WHITSUN-*week*, † WHITSUN DAY-*week*, †*Pentecost-week*).

a950 *Guthlac* (Prose) xx. 161 On þære eastorwucan. **c1450** *Brut* II. 437 In Cristemesse wike. **1450–1530** *Myrr. Our Ladye* II. 278 In Penthecoste weke... In trynyte wyke. **1482** *Cely Papers* (Camden) 94, I perposed to a byn with yow in the esterne weke. **c1500** *Cartul. S. Nicholai Aberd.* (New Spald. Club) I. 259 One Wedinsday in ye penthicost owk nixt eftir ye synod. **1622** LAUD *Diary* 23 Apr., Wks. 1853 III. 138 Being the Tuesday in Easter week. **1692** PEPYS *Let. to Evelyn* Easter Monday, The last being Confession, this in all good conscience should be Restitution Week. **1761** G. COLMAN *Jealous Wife* II. 21 How unlucky it is, that this damn'd Accident shou'd happen in the Newmarket Week! **c1810** W. HICKEY *Mem.* (1960) xx. 326 We had previously enjoyed private lodgings at Epsom..for the race week. **1890** W. BOOTH *In Darkest Eng.* II. vi. 231 Self-denial..[which] the Soldiers of the Salvation Army practice every year in Self Denial Week. **1917** *Wells Fargo Messenger* V. 133/2 (*caption*) Native sons of the Golden West begin 'Prune Week' ceremonies. **1965** 'E. MCBAIN' *He who Hesitates* iii. 34 'How come everybody's so eager to join me this morning?' Roger asked. 'Who knows?... Maybe it's national brotherhood week.' **1977** *Lancashire Life* Mar. 99/1 He won a prize for the best money-raising poster during Warships Week.

¶c. Sometimes applied *transf.* to other artificial cycles of a few days that have been employed by various peoples, e.g. the eight days' 'week' of the Romans (see NUNDINE), the five days' 'week' believed to have been used by the ancient Germans, etc.

1604 E. G[RIMSTONE] *D'Acosta's Hist. Indies* VI. ii. 435 They accompted their weekes by thirteene dayes, marking the dayes with a Zero or cipher.

2. a. A space of seven days, irrespective of the time from which it is reckoned. † ***all a week***: for a whole week.

†***forty weeks***: often used for the length of the period of gestation.

c1055 *Byrhtferth's Handboc* in *Anglia* VIII. 288 On þam beoð twa & fifti wucena. **c1205** LAY. 22931 To feouwer wikene [**c1275** wekene] uirste þat wrec [*read* werc] wes iuorðed. **c1250** *Gen. & Ex.* 2473 So woren forð .x. wukes gon, get adde Iacob birigeles non. **c1290** *S. Eng. Leg.* 66 And two ȝer and al-mest þreo wyke. **1297** R. GLOUC. (Rolls) 7942 Þis ost..bisegede þen castel, six wuke wel vaste. **a1300** *Cursor M.* 18587 He..Was tua and thritti winturs ald, And monet sex and wyckes tua. **c1315** SHOREHAM V. 110 In þyssere ioye we scholde by-louken Al hyre ioyen of uourti woken þe wylest he ȝede wyþ chylde. **c1330** R. BRUNNE *Chron. Wace* (Rolls) 9353 Al a wyke þe kyng þer lay, He spilte his tyme. **1375** BARBOUR *Bruce* IX. 359 He gert his menȝe busk ilkane, Quhen sex owkis of the sege ves gane. **1377** LANGL. *P. Pl.* B. XVI. 100 And in þe wombe of þat wenche was he fourty wokes. **1398** TREVISA *Barth. De P.R.* IX. ix. (1495) 354 A monthe conteynyth foure wekes and a weke seuen naturall dayes. **c1400** *Beryn* 1047 For foure wookis full, or he did hir entere, She lay in lede within his house. **c1420** WYNTOUN *Cron.* IV. xxv. 2375 Þat about þe hundrethe day, Wouyk, monethe or moment [etc.]. **c1420** *Chron. Vilod.* 1662 He regnede not foure ȝere here, By sixe wykeus as yche vnderstonde, þat he was martrid. **1466** *Paston Lett.* Suppl. 108, I thynke of every day a wyke tyl ye be content. **c1470** HENRY *Wallace* II. 273 Hyr dochtir had of xij wokkis ald a knayff. **a1520** SKELTON *Magnyf.* 1003, I haue not kept her yet thre wokys. **1534** *Star Chamber Cases* (Selden Soc.) II. 214 Whiche catall hath ben..Impoundyd by the tyme and space of ten wykes at the leste. **1553** *Edin. Burgh Rec.* (1871) II. 278 The expensis of the ulk precedand the xxvj day of Marche. **1593** SHAKS. *3 Hen. VI*, II. v. 36 So many Dayes, my Ewes haue bene with yong: So many weekes, ere the poore Fooles will Eane. **1596** DALRYMPLE tr. *Leslie's Hist. Scot.* II. 248 Efter mony oulkes quhen mekle tha had wrocht and mekle had swat, tha [etc.]. **1615** R. COCKS *Diary* (Hakl. Soc.) I. 9 He hath byn in this place a wick, and never came into the English howse till now. **1734** POPE *Hor. Sat.* II. ii. 93 A Buck was then a week's repast, And 'twas their point, I ween, to make it last. **1736** BUTLER *Anal.* I. i. Wks. 1874 I. 24 A man determines..that he will walk to such a place with a staff a week hence. **1744** M. BISHOP *Life* 114 Thinking every Day a Week, and Week a Month. **1751** F. COVENTRY *Pompey the Little* II. xii. 236 As he had expected a Parcel from London by the Coach for a Week before, he naturally concluded this to be the same. **1787** HOY *Let.* 31 Oct. in *Burns' Wks.* (1809) II. 110, I should give him nought but Stra'bogie castocks to chew for sax ouks, or ay until he [etc.]. **1856** MISS YONGE *Daisy Chain* I. ix, She was within six weeks of seventeen, and surely she need not be sent down again to the schoolroom. **1865** MRS. WHITNEY *Gayworthys* xlii, Then there came a week of rain.

b. Seven days as a term for periodical payments (of wages, rent, or the like), or as a unit of reckoning for time of work or service.

1426–7 *Rec. St. Mary at Hill* (1904) 66 Also payd to Thomas Seviere and his felawe to set vndir þe clerkis chamber dore þe o mason a hole woke iiij s. iij d. **1492** *Acc. Ld. High Treas. Scot.* I. 205 And for alimos, gevin woulkly, of xxiiij wokkis, xlviij li. **1527** *St. Papers Hen. VIII*, IV. 473 After the rate of 18d by the wooke. **1552–3** *Burgh Rec. Edin.* (1871) II. 342 Item to Andro Mansioun for half ane ulk's wage. **1557–8** *Rec. St. Mary at Hill* 409 Payde to wyllyam Elssame for j quarter and vj wyekes the soms of xix s. vj d. **1580** *Fermor Acc.* in *Archæol. Jrnl.* (1851) VIII. 181 Pd for xii weickes bord for Mr. Richard Farmor and his man, at viis the weicke iiijli iiijs. **1784** *Morn. Chron.* 26 May 4/1 Advt., The above premises may be taken by the week, and entered upon immediately. **1842** DICKENS *Amer. Notes* iii. (end), The house is full of boarders,..many of whom..contract by the week for their board and lodging. **1882** BESANT *All Sorts* xxi, Eighteen shillings a week would buy him outright until his engagements begin again. *Ibid.* xxii, And in two days more the week's rent would be due. **1886** C. E. PASCOE *Lond. To-day* ii. (ed. 3) 39 A week's notice is the general rule before vacating rooms. **1914** 'IAN HAY' *Knt. on Wheels* xviii, I have two thousand a year... I don't know how much that is a week, but I'll work it out some day in shillings and see.

†c. Followed by *day* used pleonastically. (See DAY *sb.* 11.)

c1440 *Partonope* 6634 This lyfe they ladde vj. wekes day. **c1670** [see DAY *sb.* 11].

d. Used vaguely for an indefinite time, as in ***a week or two***, implying a moderate space of time; ***weeks***, referring to a duration which is felt as long.

c1386 CHAUCER *Frankl. T.* 567 But thurgh his magik for a wyke or tweye It semed that alle the Rokkes were aweye. **c1422** HOCCLEVE *Min. Poems* 174 My freend, aftir, I trowe, a wike or two That this tale endid was, hoom to me cam, And seide [etc.]. **15..** LYNDESAY *Play* 1048 in *Bannatyne MS.* (Hunter. Club) 505 Than scho deit to, within ane olk or two. **1550** CROWLEY *Way to Wealth* 195 How often hast thou gone whole dayes togither, whole weakes, yea whole yeres, and neuer thought once to loue hym aryght? **1597** in *J. Melvill's Autob. & Diary* (Wodrow Soc.) 424 Alas! the mounths, alas! the wkes and dayes, That I consum'd in foolishe sports and plays. **1797** JANE AUSTEN *Sense & Sensib.* xxix, He *did* feel the same, Elinor—for weeks and weeks he felt it. I know he did. **1891** 'J. S. WINTER' *Lumley* vi, 'Oh, Vere is not going for weeks—weeks,' declared Mrs. Jock with great decision. **1918** *Times Lit. Suppl.* 18 Apr. 183/2 The unbounded hospitality of a time when a few letters of introduction gave weeks of princely entertainment.

e. feast of weeks *Heb. Antiq.* [tr. Heb. *ḥag šābūᵉōth*] = PENTECOST 1.

1382 WYCLIF *Exod.* xxxiv. 22 The solempnyte of weekis. **1535** COVERDALE *ibid.*, The feast of wekes. [So the later versions.]

3. The six working days, as opposed to the Sunday; the period from Monday to Saturday inclusive. Cf. WEEKDAY. Now also meaning five working days, from Monday to Friday inclusive, as opposed to the weekend; ***three-day week***: see THREE III. 2.

c1000 *Sax. Leechd.* III. 244 Ȝif se terminus ȝescyt on sumon dæȝe þære wucan þonne byð se sunnan dæȝ þær æfter easter dæȝ. **1340** *Ayenb.* 212 Þeruore me let of bodiliche workes of þe woke uor betere to onderstonde to bidde god. **1362** LANGL. *P. Pl.* A. VII. 243 For summe of my seruauns beoþ seke oþer-while, Of alle þe wike [*v.rr.* wyke, weke, wowke] heo worcheþ not so heor wombe akeþ. **1602** SHAKS. *Ham.* I. i. 76 Why such impresse of Ship-wrights, whose sore Taske Do 's not diuide the Sunday from the weeke. **1882** BESANT *All Sorts* xxix, On this Sunday morning, when the old man looked as if the cares of the week were off his mind.

4. a. ***week of years***: used in Lev. xxv. 8 by Wyclif, Tindale, and in the Douay Bible (after the Vulgate) for 'a period of seven years' (Coverdale has 'yeare sabbathes', and the other versions 'sabbaths of years', following the Heb.). Also used by commentators in explanation of the 'weeks' mentioned in Dan. ix. 24–27, where periods of seven years are meant.

1382 WYCLIF *Levit.* xxv. 8 And thow shalt noumbre to thee seuen wekes [**1388** woukis] of ȝeerys. **a1591** H. SMITH *God's Arrow* ii. (1593) D 1 b, This worde *Hebdomada* ..is sometimes taken for a weeke of daies, that is, seauen daies. .. But at other times it signifieth the space of seauen yeares, and then is it called *Hebdomada Annorum*, A weeke of yeares. **1621** T. WILLIAMSON tr. *Goulart's Wise Vieillard* 147 Doe wee not obserue how in three weeks of yeares three are dead? **1650** SCLATER *Expos. Rom.* iv. Ep. Ded. A 2, Having now, (by the space of full three weeks of years, and more)..had a strong dispute with my thoughts, whether [etc.]. **c1680** R. FLEMING *Fulfilling Script.* II. iii. (1726) 278 They know Daniel's seventy weeks..clearly takes in his [the Messiah's] coming, and though it were taken either for weeks of days, or of years, it must long since be expired, but if they should mean weeks of ages, then for many thousand years his coming could not be yet expected.

b. ***week of days***: used by Bible commentators (following a mistranslation of Dan. x. 2) to denote a literal week as opposed to the 'week of years': see quots. in 4 a.

It is not clear whether Scott's use for 'a whole week' is an echo of this, or whether it was a current phrase.

1560 BIBLE (Geneva) *Dan.* x. 2 At the same time, I Daniel was in heauines for thre weekes of daies. *Ibid.* 3 Til thre weekes of daies were fulfilled. **1611** *Ibid.*, Three full weekes [*margin*, Heb. weeks of dayes]. **1818** SCOTT *Br. Lamm.* x, They dared not keep me a week of days in durance.

5. In various idioms. **a.** ***a week*** [see A *adj.* 2, 4, *prep.*[1]], every week, weekly, per week. (See also 2 b.)

a1225 *Ancr. R.* 344 Of alle swuche þinges schriue hire enes a wike ette leste. **1387** TREVISA *Higden* V. 415 He usede twyes a wooke to sitte al day to fore þe chirche dore. **a1450** *Knt. de la Tour* 12 A good woman..that fasted .iij. tymes a woke. **1861** BROUGHAM *Brit. Const.* ix. 118 It is repeated seven times a-week.

b. In expressions serving to fix a date. ***this day, tomorrow, Monday,*** etc. ***week***: seven days before or after the day specified. Similarly ***this***

day, etc. (so many) *weeks*. *yesterday, Monday*, etc. *was a week* (dial.), seven days before the day mentioned. †Formerly also *four* (etc.) *weeks day*, exactly four weeks (cf. 2 c).

1398 *Munim. de Melros* (Bannatyne Club) 490 [Gif] defaut be of þir paymentis.. ovre runnene ande ganeby sex wowkis daye eftir þe lymite terme. **1454** *Cal. Anc. Rec. Dublin* (1889) 281 That al maner of men of Iryshe blode.. avoyde [*i.e.* quit Dublin] by this day iiii. wekys. And gyff eny of this Iryssh blode.. may be founde within the said cite or frauncheis after the said iiii. wekys day, they shall.. be put in prisone. **1531** *Star Chamber Cases* (Selden Soc.) II. 187 The same Court so adiorned to be kepte ther that day thre wekes next ensuyng. **1582** SIR J. POPHAM in H. Hall *Soc. Eliz. Age* (1886) 262, I mene if God please to be at Salisburie the wekes-daie at night before Easterdaie. **1700** in *Jrnl. Friends' Hist. Soc.* (1914) Oct. 181 Wee heard.. of her being ther last 4th day was a weeke. **1810** *Sporting Mag.* XXXVI. 160 The whole of the money must be made good that night week. **1815** SCOTT *Guy M.* v, Allow me to recommend some of the kipper—it was John Hay that catch it, Saturday was three weeks. **1831** *Lincoln Herald* 23 Sept. 4/4 Early on Monday morning week, an attempt was made [etc.]. **1853** DICKENS *Bleak Ho.* xliv, Send Charley to me this night week—'for the letter'. **1857** HUGHES *Tom Brown* II. vi, The crisis came on Saturday, the day week that Thompson had died. **1863** MISS BRADDON *Aurora Floyd* xx, Last Saturday was a week I touched at Liverpool with a cargo of furs [etc.]. *Ibid.*, When I came back last Saturday week. **1883** D. C. MURRAY *Hearts* xiii, Can you make it convenient to be there this day week? **1889** 'J. S. WINTER' *Mrs. Bob* i, Let us say Thursday week, dear—This is Saturday, so it is quite enough notice to give.

c. *week and week about*: in alternate weeks.

1891 KIPLING *Light that Failed* vi. 94 The girls were supposed to market week and week about.

d. *week in, week out*: see IN *adv.* 2.

e. *week-to-week* (attrib. phr.), continuing or recurring in successive weeks; continual. Cf. TO *prep.* 6 c.

1959 *New Statesman* 24 Jan. 92/2 The lightning flashed above Sinai, and in its glare, the starry-eyed observer, remote from the week-to-week grind of party work, saw a great machine, whirring smoothly to life. **1981** J. SUTHERLAND *Bestsellers* i. 15 The bestseller lists... Their week-to-week attention singles out sensational books of the moment.

6. Proverbial phrases. †**a.** *to be in by the week*: to be ensnared, caught; *fig.* to be deeply in love. *to go to it by the week*: to commit oneself thoroughly.

1546 J. HEYWOOD *Prov.* (1867) 69 This prouerbe shewth the in by the weeke. *a* **1553** UDALL *Royster D.* I. ii. 4 He is in by the weke, we shall haue sport anon. **1586** A. DAY *Eng. Secretorie* II. (1595) 47 Yet now we be in, let vs go to it by the week. **1588** SHAKS. *L.L.L.* v. ii. 61 O that I knew he were but in by th' weeke. **1598** R. BERNARD *Terence, Andria* I. i. (1607) 12 He is in the snare; he is in for a bird, hee is in by the weeke. **1612** WEBSTER *White Devil* E 1, Enter Flamineo and Marcello guarded, and a Lawyer. *Law.* What are you in by the weeke.

b. *too late a week*: a jocular understatement for 'far too late'. Now only as echo of Shaks.

1600 SHAKS. *A.Y.L.* II. iii. 74 At seauenteene yeeres, many their fortunes seeke But at fourescore, it is too late a weeke. **1826** SCOTT *Jrnl.* (1890) I. 105 If she had her youthful activity, and could manage things, it.. would amuse her. But I fear it is too late a week. **1829** *Ibid.* II. 220.

c. † *the week of the four Fridays*: an imaginary date that will never arrive (*obs.*). *a week of Sundays*: seven Sundays or weeks as representing a long time. † *a week of Saturdays*, an indefinite period, a long period. Cf. *month of Sundays* s.v. MONTH[1] 3 f.

1760–72 H. BROOKE *Fool of Qual.* (1809) I. Ded. p. x, At the period that the hogs shall.. feed along with the herrings; .. or on the week of the four Fridays, so long looked for by astrologians. **1831** *Constellation* 8 Jan. 57/3 No, you couldn't gess a week of Saturdays and so I'll tell you—cause it is *unginteel*. **1898** 'C. HARE' *Broken Arcs* I. ii. 13 Tes wark .. never done, an' nar' a bit o' play for I,.. no, not in a week o' Sundays. **1901** D. SLADEN *My Son Richard* iv, He.. got to know her more intimately in that five minutes than he might otherwise have done in a week of Sundays.

d. *to knock* (a person) *into the middle of next week*: to give (him) a decisive blow, to punish severely; to astound, flabbergast. *slang* (orig. *Pugilistic*).

1821 MONCRIEFF *Tom & Jerry* II. iv, They knock'd me into the middle of next week—besides tipping me this here black eye—only see how red it is! **1833** [S. SMITH] *Lett. J. Downing* xv. (1835) 95 The first clip I made was at Amos, —but he dodged it, and I hit one of the Editors of the Globe, and knocked him about into the middle of next week. **1846** W. T. PORTER *Quarter Race Kentucky* 105 The next moment he was knocked into the middle of the next three weeks! **1859** GEO. ELIOT *Adam Bede* xvi, I believe you would knock me into next week if I were to have a battle with you. **1883** *Harper's Mag.* Oct. 720/2 It would not be comfortable to be knocked by his heels into the middle of next week.

7. Combinations: † **week-boy**, a boy hired by the week, as distinguished from an apprentice; **week-long**, continuing for a week; **week-night**, a night in the week other than Sunday night; also *attrib.*; **week-old** *a.*, that has lived or lasted a week; † **week-silver**, some kind of feudal dues (prob. in commutation of WEEK-WORK).

1662 *Act 14 Chas. II* c. 5 §17 No Master Weaver.. shall.. sett on worke above two Apprentices or any *weeke-Boy to weave in a Lombe in the said Trade in worsted weaving. **1683** [see DEVIL *sb.* 5 a]. **1898** *Daily News* 15 Sept. 6/4 The ladies, true to their *week-long enthusiasm,.. made the University College Theatre look very bright. **1847** LD. LINDSAY *Chr. Art* I. p. clxviii, I lay at the feet of Jesus,.. yoking down my struggling flesh with week-long fastings. **1859** H. KINGSLEY *G. Hamlyn* xl, Both he and Ellen thought it strange that their mother should insist on that book on a *week-night; they never usually read it [the bible], save on Sunday evenings. **1877** SPURGEON *Serm.* XXIII. 120 Week-night services. **1892** *Lichfield Mercury* 25 Mar. 8/5 If we obstinately shut our eyes and keep company with the hapless *week-old kittens. **1903** KIPLING *Five Nations* 115 Out of the darkness we reach For a handful of week-old papers And a mouthful of human speech. **1430** in *N. & Q.* 13th Ser. I. 449/1 Exceptis redditibus, seruiciis,.. et xvij. s. annuis vocatis *Weikseluer.

Hence † **wukemalum** *adv.* [-MEAL], by weeks.

c **1200** ORMIN 536 Drihhtin Godd To þewwtenn wukemalumm. *Ibid.* 554.

week (wiːk), *int.* Also 8 weeck, 9 weke. [Cf. WHEAK *v.* and *sb.*, WHICK *v.*, WEE *int.*] Imitation of the squeak of a pig or mouse.

1588 SHAKS. *Tit. A.* IV. ii. 146 Weeke, weeke, so cries a Pigge prepared to th' spit. *a* **1719** D'URFEY *Pills* II. 87 Weeck, Weeck, Weeck, squeak'd the Pig. **1855** BROWNING *Fra Lippo Lippi* 11 Harry out.. Whatever rat, there, haps on his wrong hole, And nip each softling of a wee white mouse, *Weke, weke*, that's crept to keep him company!

week(e, obs. forms of WEAK, WICK.

weekday ('wiːkdeɪ). Forms: see WEEK *sb.* and DAY *sb.* [OE. *wicdæȝ*, f. *wic(u)* WEEK. Cf. OHG. *wehhatag*, ON. *vikudagr*.]

† **1.** A day of the week. (In quot. *c* 1200 a literal as opposed to a metaphorical day.) *Obs.*

c **900** tr. *Bæda's Hist.* III. v, þæt hi þy feorðan wicdæȝe & þy syxtan fæstan to nones. *c* **1200** ORMIN 13182 Alls itt off þiss werrldess daȝȝ Rihht onnfasst efenn wære, Forrþi þatt ure wukedaȝȝ Bi twellfe timess erneþþ [etc.]. *a* **1300** *Cursor M.* 2857 Sir loth wijf.. in a salt stan men seis hir stand þat bestes likes o þat land, þat anes o þe wok day, þan es sco liked al a-way. **1456** SIR G. HAYE *Law Arms* (S.T.S.) 166 [They] do mare the Sonday or the haly day na othir wolk dayes.

†**2.** A day of the week other than market-day or Sunday. *Obs.*

1477 in *Charters* etc. *Edin.* (1871) 141 The nolt merket .. [to be held] about the Trone,.. and nocht on the wolk day. **1588** in G. P. Scrope *Castle Combe* (1852) 332 That none shall bye any grayne or other vittell on our markett-daye before nyne of the clocke in the fore-none, nor in the wicke-dayes more then shall serve their owne howsolde.

3. a. A day of the week other than Saturday or Sunday (formerly, other than Sunday).

c **1546** COVERDALE *Calvin's Treat. Sacram.* etc. F j b, In lyk maner as thou seist this blessed sacrament ministred on the sonday, euen so wyth lyke reuerence do they vse it at the same houre on those wyke dayes, that the congregacyon.. hath appointed to that vse. **1563** *Homilies, Of Place & Time of Prayer* I. II. 139 For although they wyll not trauayle nor labour on the Sunday, as they do on the weeke day, yet they wyll not rest in holynes. **1593** in *Maitl. Club Misc.* I. 57 That .. wpone the oulk dayes thai begin at viij houris and end preciselie at ix houris. **1633** G. HERBERT *Temple, Sunday* ix, Thou art a day of mirth! And where the week-dayes trail on ground, Thy flight is higher. **1654** J. AUDLAND in *Jrnl. Friends' Hist. Soc.* (1919) XVI. 135, I have been in Bristoll severall first dayes.. and I have gone into the Countrey, in the Weekdayes. **1732** SWIFT etc. *What passed in London* Misc. III. 263 My Wife and I went to Church (where we had not been for many Years on a Week-day). **1835** DICKENS *Sk. Boz, Seven-Dials*, Pass through St. Giles's in the evening of a week-day, there they are in their fustian dresses. **1860** *Sat. Rev.* 3 Mar. 277/2 His [*sc.* Spurgeon's] father was a hard-working man on week-days, and a preacher on Sundays. **1976** P. R. WHITE *Planning for Public Transport* ii. 32 On weekdays (Mondays to Fridays), to which many urban surveys are confined, many trips are made within a confined time budget.

b. *attrib.*

[**1595** in *Maitl. Club Misc.* I. 72 In the oulk dayes preiching in Glasgw it is desyrit that the ministeris keip preciselie the hour.] **1693** O. HEYWOOD *Diaries* (1885) IV. 147 That house where the week-day lecture had been kept. **1732** POPE *Ep. Bathurst* 345 One solid dish his week-day meal affords, An added pudding solemniz'd the Lord's. **1762** SECKER *2nd Charge Dioc. Canterb.* (1771) 253 Diligence .. in bringing your People to the holy Communion, and where it can be, to Week-Day Prayers. **1802** WORDSW. *Sonn. 'I grieved for Buonaparté'*, The talk Man holds with week-day man in the hourly walk Of the mind's business. **1859** GEO. ELIOT *Adam Bede* lii, He knew nothing of week-day services, and thought none the worse of the Sunday sermon if it allowed him to sleep from the text to the blessing. **1877** A. MACLAREN (*title*), Week-day Evening Addresses.

week-end. 1. a. (with *a* and *pl.*). The end of a week; the holiday period at the end of a week's work, usually extending from Saturday noon or Friday night to Monday; esp., this holiday when spent away from home. *long week-end*: see LONG *a.*[1] 18.

1638 in *Victoria County Hist. Yorkshire* (1912) II. 415/2 The greatest weight of the said exaction will fall upon very poor people.. who making every week a coarse kersey and being compelled to sell the same at the week end.. are nevertheless constrained to yield one half penny apiece. **1793** W. B. STEVENS *Jrnl.* 27 Feb. (1965) I. 70 Wrote to Dewe that I would put on my seven league boots next weekend and stretch my course to Appleby. **1870** *Food Jrnl.* 1 Mar. 97 'Week-end', that is from Saturday until Monday, —it may be a later day in the week if the money and credit hold out,—is the season of dissipation. **1879** *N. & Q.* Ser. v. XII. 428/2 In Staffordshire, if a person leaves home at the end of his week's work on the Saturday afternoon to spend the evening of Saturday and the following Sunday with friends at a distance, he is said to be spending his *week-end* at So-and-so. **1889** MISS BRADDON *Day will Come* xxiv, Theodore and his friend betook themselves to Cheriton Chase on the following Friday, for that kind of visit which north country people describe as 'a week end'. **1892** *Times* 18 Mar. 8/2 They had evidently taken the house for week-ends. **1899** S. R. GARDINER *O. Cromwell* vi. 192 Oliver.. may be regarded as the inventor of that modified form of enjoyment to which hard-worked citizens have, in our day, given the name of the 'week-end'. **1905** *Spectator* 26 Aug. 289/1 What a 'week-end' it must have been for the host, whatever it may have been for the guest.

b. The period from Saturday to Monday during which business is suspended and shops are closed.

1878 J. ALMOND *Bunch of Water-cresses* 4 If I get my 'bacco now, I can manage to see th' week-end o'er very well. **1913** *Times* 13 Sept. 17/3 The Money Market was steady with a fair demand for advances over the week-end at about previous rates.

c. The end (i.e. the last day) of the week; Saturday. *dial.*

1880 C. H. POOLE *Staffs. Gloss.*, *Week-end*, Saturday.

2. *attrib.* **a.** For use at week-ends, as ***week-end** bag, case, cottage*, etc.; occurring at or for the duration of a week-end, as ***week-end** course, leave, school, war*, etc.

1887 *Advt. of G.W.R.* (in Lancs.), Week-end tickets. **1896** *Hetton-le-Hole* (Durham) *Gloss.* s.v., 'Week-end trips' are now advertised on most of the [railway] lines. **1911** 'SAKI' in *Bystander* 12 Apr. 70/2 I've seen a week-end cottage near Dorking that I should rather like to buy. **1924** KIPLING *Debits & Credits* (1926) 316 You live like a home defence Brigadier, besides week-end leaf [sic]. **1934** WEBSTER, Weekend case. **1944** J. S. HUXLEY *On Living in Revolution* 117 Short weekend courses and longer 'study workshops' for teachers. **1946** C. MCCULLERS *Member of Wedding* I. 10 At dark John Henry came to the back door with a little week-end bag. **1952** 'M. COST' *Hour Awaits* 136 She carried a small, smart week-end case of crocodile. **1958** O. CAROE *Pathans* xxv. 418 Roos-Keppel did indeed start his tour of office with two small operations the scale of which is sufficiently shown by the fact that one of them was called the week-end war. **1962** J. BRAINE *Life at Top* x. 136, I came to each and every week-end school here. **1967** R. V. BESTE *Repeat Instructions* (1968) xiv. 148, I haven't a week-end cottage. **1973** *Guardian* 22 Jan. 1/1 Lieutenant Mark Phillips, on weekend leave from Germany, went hunting on Saturday with Princess Anne. **1982** J. O'FAOLAIN *Obedient Wife* ii. 42 A weekend bag packed with scent, toothbrush and so forth.

b. Carrying out a specified activity or fulfilling a specified role only at week-ends or for pleasure (sometimes with the implication 'casual, amateur'); e.g. ***week-end** Air Force, athlete, father, gardener, motorist, sailor, soldier, writer*. Cf. SUNDAY *sb.* 3.

1935 *Discovery* Oct. 314/1 The publisher suggests that *English Earth* will interest equally the farmer and the week-end motorist. **1941** *Time* 30 June 31/1 Week-end athletes should be careful. **1943** C. H. WARD-JACKSON *Piece of Cake* 62 *Week-end Air Force, The*, the Auxiliary Air Force. It was formed in 1925, its officers and men being citizens who gave week-ends and other part-time to their duties. **1959** *Listener* 12 Mar. 461/1 None of your present week-end, or decade-end writers realize that the present agitators are the sons of a former day, of which these writers presumably know nothing. **1962** *Jrnl. Family Law* Fall 104 The law is, in fact, uncertain as to the rights of the ex-spouse. Consequently, it seems even more uncertain about the privileges which the law should extend to the children with 'week-end fathers'. **1970** *New Yorker* 3 Oct. 40/3 Will you look at them weekend soldiers. **1974** *Harper's & Queen* Sept. 117 Humphrey Brooke was only a weekend gardener until.. he decided to retire. **1976** 'D. HALLIDAY' *Dolly & Nanny Bird* ix. 120 The boat was.. full of tanned, husky weekend sailors.

Hence **week-end** *v. intr.*, to spend a week-end holiday; **week-ending** *vbl. sb.*; also as *ppl. a.*, (in the habit of) spending the week-end away from home. **week-endize** *v. intr.*, to spend a week-end away from home (*nonce-wd.*). **week-endy** *a.*, suggestive of the week-end.

1901 *Daily Chron.* 31 July 7/2 Where shall we week end? **1906** B. VAUGHAN *Sins of Society* 66 You see 'week-endings' have become part of the British Constitution, and nowadays everybody who is anybody has to be out of town in the season, say from Saturday to Tuesday. **1910** R. BRIDGES *Let.* 21 June in Bridges & Bradley *Corr.* (1940) 77, I was glad to get your note saying that you wd week-endize. **1913** W. J. LOCKE *Stella Maris* xv. 201 Where have you been week-ending? **1914** A. N. LYONS *Simple Simon* I. iii. 42 He week-ends at Paris-Plage. **1930** J. B. PRIESTLEY *Angel Pavement* xi. 567 She spent the next few minutes getting from the bus to the station, which was very crowded and week-endy. **1934** WEBSTER, Weekending *adj.* **1947** J. HAYWARD *Prose Lit. since 1939* 36 *The Long Week-end*—an ironical title which only the 'week-ending' Englishman will appreciate. **1973** A. GREY *Some put their Trust in Chariots* xiii. 72 Weekending French families setting out in their saloons for the countryside. **1976** G. EWART *No Fool* II. 61 Contrariwise, would you admire what's trendy (you were a fashion once yourself) or see virtue in what's suburban or weekendy?

week'ender.

1. One who spends the week-ends away from home.

1880 *N. & Q.* Ser. VI. I. 42 Lodging-house keepers and tradesmen in Llandudno, Rhyl, and other holiday resorts in n. Wales, employ the derivative form 'week-enders'.. when they speak of.. visitors who come on Saturday and go on Monday. **1901** C. G. HARPER *Gt. North Road* I. 144 Three bedrooms for the use of the week-enders. **1905** *Sat. Rev.* 14 Oct. 490/1 Saturday morning is quite time enough for the week-enders to get away.

2. a. A week-end cottage (see WEEK-END 2 a). *colloq.*

1941 BAKER *Dict. Austral. Slang* 81 *Weekender*, a week-end holiday cottage or shack. **1967** E. HUNT *Danger Game* iii. 59 He had a week-ender at Palm Beach and a lovely car. **1976** *Billings* (Montana) *Gaz.* 16 June 10-c/5 (Advt.), Small, clean..home in Red Lodge. Perfect weekender any season. **1983** *Austral. Women's Weekly* Aug. 21/2 There is, says Pauline, constant confusion over..shacks and holiday homes. 'A shack in NSW is a tumbledown wreck. In NSW you have a weekender.'

b. A bag large enough to carry everything needed for a week-end away from home; a week-end bag. *U.S. colloq.*

1961 *Harper's Bazaar* June 24/2 A capacious week-ender in pale coffee-bean hide. **1980** *TWA Ambassador* Oct. 99/1 You'll use the Kluge Bag like a week-ender too, because it's just as easy to carry on and a whole lot better.

† **weekfish.** *Obs.* [ad. Du. *weekvisch*, f. *week* soft + *visch* fish. Cf. WEAKFISH.] A fish of the Dutch East Indies, the size of a whiting, esteemed a delicacy.

1686 RAY *Willughby's Hist. Pisc.* App. 6 Pisces Indiæ Orientalis a Joanne Nieuhofs Descripti... Wit fish or Week fish.

weekly ('wi:klɪ), *a.* and *sb.* [f. WEEK *sb.* + -LY[1].]

A. *adj.*

† **1.** Of or pertaining to the week (either as a seven-days period or as opposed to Sunday). *Obs.*

1563 *Homilies, Of Place & Time of Prayer* I. II. 138 That vpon the Sabboth day..they shoulde ceasse from all weekely and workeday labour. **1612** DRAYTON *Poly-olb.* xi. 178 Hengists noble heyres; their Idols that to raise Heere put their German names vpon our weekly daies.

2. a. That occurs, is done, made, given, etc. once a week.

weekly bill: see BILL *sb.*[3] 10. *weekly boat*: a coaster on which the crew is paid by the week. Cf. *monthly boat* s.v. MONTHLY *a.* 4. *weekly tenancy*: one determinable at the end of any week.

1489 *Reg. Mag. Sig. Scot.* 1528, 120/1 In the delivering of thir oulkly penny to God and to Sanct Jhonne. **1525** *Reg. Mag. Sig. Scot.* 1527, 97 The forsaid wolklie penny and halpeny salbe payit ilk Setterday. **1576–77** *Reg. Privy Council Scot.* II. 582 His releif of the said owlklie wageis as accordis. **1597** HOOKER *Eccl. Pol.* v. xix. §1 The Iewes haue alwaies had their weekely readings of the law of Moses. **1621** (*title*) Corante: or weekely newes from Italy, Germany, [etc.]. **1681** in *Nairne Peerage Evid.* (1874) 16 With a weekly markett and two free faires yearly. **1699** G. HARVEY *Van. Philos. & Physick* vi. 46 The daily, weekly, or frequent use of Opiates. **1711** STEELE *Spect.* No. 79 ¶9 The Indiscretion of the Books themselves, whose very Titles of Weekly Preparations..lead People of ordinary Capacities into great Errors. **1712** ADDISON *Spect.* No. 289 ¶2 The Use I make of the above-mentioned Weekly Paper. **1732** POPE *Ep. Bathurst* 264 The Man of Ross divides the weekly bread. *a* **1806** HORSLEY *Serm.* (1812) II. xxiii. 227 A public weekly assertion of the two first articles in our Creed. **1842** DICKENS *Amer. Notes* iv, The weekly charge in this establishment for each female patient is three dollars. **1849** MACAULAY *Hist. Eng.* I. iii. 390 In this way he gathered materials for weekly epistles destined to enlighten some county town. **1899** S. R. GARDINER *O. Cromwell* vi. 192 He found repose in a weekly visit to Hampton Court. **1920** *Act 10 & 11 Geo. V* c. 30 §2 Entitled..to receive payments..at weekly or other prescribed intervals. **1927** F. H. SHAW *Knocking Around* 4 She was a weekly boat, where the crew provided their own food. **1946** J. BATTEN *Dirty Little Collier* 12 These weekly boat men are quite used to slipping home for a few hours.

b. With a personal designation: Performing some action, or employed in some capacity, once a week; that has a contract by the week.

weekly boarder: a school pupil who boards at the school during the week and returns home at week-ends. *weekly man* Austral., an extra hand taken on for one or more weeks. *weekly tenant*, 'one paying rent by the week, and liable to removal on a week's notice' (Simmonds *Dict. Trade*, 1858).

1712 PRIOR *Extempore Invit.* 1 Our Weekly Friends To-morrow meet At Matthew's Palace. **1737** POPE *Hor. Ep.* I. i. 155 They change their weekly Barber. **1841** DICKENS *Let.* 6 Mar. (1969) II. 225, I will send [him] as a weekly boarder to the best school I can find in the place... I say weekly boarder, because I should wish the boy..to be at home from Saturday night to Monday Morning. **1890** 'R. BOLDREWOOD' *Col. Reformer* xx, Filling up the station with a lot of weekly men. **1973** J. MANN *Only Security* i. 9 It had a school where Clovis might be a weekly boarder.

† **c.** slang. *weekly-accompts* pl., a name given to the small square white patches on each side of a midshipman's collar.

1819 VAUX *Mem.* I. 69 The midshipmen proceeded to cut off the weekly accompts from the coat I had on.

B. *sb.* A newspaper or review published once in each week.

1833 [see MONTHLY *sb.* 2]. **1845** DICKENS *Let.* 26 July (1977) IV. 337 A notion..has occurred to me in connection with our abandoned little weekly. **1846** C. MITCHELL *Newsp. Press Directory* 81 Not any of the newspapers published at the close of the week display more activity or success than this [the *Observer*] in the acquisition of news, which, after the preceding six days, has been swept and exhausted by the immense resources of the *dailys*; and this is the great difficulty in a *weekly*. **1858** *Times* 29 Nov. 6/3 Clever weeklies and less clever dailies. **1863** *Morn. Star* 3 Jan., To-day a new literary Weekly of high pretensions begins its existence. **1914** in *Civil Service Year Bk.* (1916) 294 They take 6 penny daily papers and 3 halfpenny ones; 3 weeklies costing 3*d.* each and 5 weeklies costing 6*d.* each.

weekly ('wi:klɪ), *adv.* [f. WEEK *sb.* + -LY[2].] In each or every week, week by week. Usually, once in seven days.

1465 in *Paston Lett.* II. 193 He payth for hys borde wykely xx[d]. **1474** *Burgh Rec. Edin.* (1869) I. 29 It is statut..that the said penny be rasit wolkly on the Monundaye. **1522** *Galway Arch.* in *10th Rep. Hist. MSS. Comm.* App. v. 400 No man shalbe made fre unlesse he can specke the Englishe tonge and shave his upper lipe wicklye. **1540** *Sc. Acts Jas. V* (1814) II. 378/1 That þair be wokly thre market dais for selling of breid within the said toune. *a* **1548** HALL *Chron., Hen. VIII* 182 The Legates sat wekely, & euery daie were argumentes on bothe partes and nothyng els doen. **1604** E. G[RIMSTONE] *D'Acosta's Hist. Indies* v. xxx. 427 There was one Priest alone resident continually, the which they changed weekely. **1670** in *12th Rep. Hist. MSS. Comm.* App. v. 15 Our daughter..tells me she gives your Ladyship weekely an account of her selfe. *a* **1700** EVELYN *Diary* 7 Sept. 1665, There perishing neere 10,000 poore creatures weekly. **1726** AYLIFFE *Parergon* 140 As these Persons are oblig'd to perform the Communion Service..in their turns Weekly, they are sometimes called Hebdomadal Canons. **1842** BORROW *Bible in Spain* xxxvi, An acute Gallegan..who gave me weekly a faithful account of the copies sold. **1905** R. BAGOT *Passport* xv. 142 You had arranged for her [a governess] to come here two or three days weekly.

weeksite ('wi:ksaɪt). *Min.* [f. the name of Alice M. D. *Weeks* (b. 1909), U.S. geologist + -ITE[1].] A hydrated silicate and oxide of uranium and potassium, $K_2(UO_2)_2(Si_2O_5)_3{\cdot}4H_2O$, found as soft, yellow orthorhombic crystals.

1960 W. F. OUTERBRIDGE et al. in *Amer. Mineralogist* XLV. 43 Weeksite at the Autunite No. 8 claim occurs as small spherulites of yellow radiating crystals. **1978** *Mineral. Abstr.* XXIX. 232/1 Weeksite..is described for the first time from France in the uranium deposit of Les Bois Noirs.

weeksman ('wi:ksmən). [f. *week's*, genitive of WEEK. Cf. *month's-man*, MONTH *sb.*[1] 6 b.] A functionary whose term of office is a week; *spec.* (see quot.).

1855 HARE *Cases Chancery* X. 298 Until..1850 (when the Defendants..were appointed day oyster meters), all monies received in respect of such compensation were divided equally among them. A list was kept, and each of the eighteen meters in rotation took upon himself the duties of 'weeksman,' whose office it was to allot the boats to each of the meters in his turn.

weekwam, obs. form of WIGWAM.

week-work. *Hist.* [OE. *wic-*, *wiceweorc*, f. *wic(u)* WEEK + *weorc* WORK *sb.* Cf. OS. *wekewerk*.] In Old English Law, work done for the lord by the tenant so many days a week. Also *attrib.* in † *weekwork-silver* (cf. *week-silver*, WEEK *sb.* 7).

c **1000** *Rectitudines* in Thorpe *Laws* I. 434 On sumen lande is þæt he [sc. the *ʒebúr*] sceal wyrcan to wicweorce .ii. daʒas swilc weorc swilc him man tæcð ofer ʒeares fyrst ælcre wucan, and on hærfest .iii. daʒas to wicweorce [etc.]. ? **1050** in Kemble *Cod. Dipl.* No. 461. III. 450 Consuetudines in Dyddanhamme.. Se ʒebur sceal his riht don; he sceal erian healfne æcer to wiceweorce. **1355** *MS. Rental of Winchcombe Abbey, Glos.*, Toto homagio pro Wikewerkselver xi s. xi d. **1883** SEEBOHM *Engl. Village Comm.* ii. 78 Week-work—i.e. work for the lord for so many days a week, mostly three days. **1916** *Edin. Rev.* July 73 A feature which reminds us of the week-works of the villein under our own manorial system.

weel[1] (wi:l). *Sc.* and *north.* Forms: 1 wǽl, 3 wel, 4, 6 wele (4–5 welle), 6 vele, 6–7 weill, 7 weell, 8–9 wiel, weil, wheel, 9 weal, 4, 7–9 weel. [OE. *wǽl* masc. and neut. = WFris. *wiel*, OLow Frankish *wâl* (pl. *wâlâ*), 'abyssus', MDu. *wael* (Flem. *weele*), MLG. *wêl* (LG. *weel*, *weele*, whence mod.G. *wehl* masc., *wehle* fem.).] A deep pool; a deep place in a river or the sea; a whirlpool or eddy.

c **897** ÆLFRED *Gregory's Past. C.* Envoy 469 Ac se wæl wunað on weres breostum..diop & stille. *c* **1000** ÆLFRIC *Gram.* ix. (Z.) 52 *Hic gurges* þis wæl, þæt is, deop wæter. *c* **1200** ORMIN 19690 Godd..þatt mihhte hemm alle..Inn helle wel bisennkenn. *c* **1275** *XI Pains of Hell* 89 in *O.E. Misc.* 149 Of vych a wrm þat atter bereþ..Ifulled is þat fule pool... Hwenne þe feondes heom [lost souls] forleteþ, Snaken and neddren heom imeteþ, And dreyeð heom in-to a wel þer heo þolyeþ al vnsel. *a* **1300** *Cursor M.* 2903 Bituixand þai sink in þat wele þar neuer man sank þat was o sele. *a* **1300** *E.E. Psalter* xxxv. 9 And with welle [*Harl.* weel] of þi liking ai Sal tou drinke þam [Vulg. *torrente voluptatis tuae potabis eos*]. **1483** *Cath. Angl.* 413/1 A Welle, *gurges.* **1513** DOUGLAS *Æneis* VII. ii. 13 Tybir flowand soft and esely, Wyth swirland welis [L. *verticibus rapidis*] and mekle ʒallow sand. **1536** BELLENDEN *Cron. Scot.* (1821) I. p. xlviii, The gretest vele heirof is namit Corbrek; for it will othir sink, or ellis draw ane schip to it, howbeit it be distant thairfra ane mile. **1553** *Rec. Burgh Lanark* (1893) 26 Sir Jhone Cunygam ..settis the tan half of his bait gangand apone Sant Katrynis weill in Clydisholm to Wylyam Pumfra. **1599** ALEX. HUME *Hymnes* iii. 211 The bels and circles on the weills, Throw lowpping of the trouts. **1674** RAY *N.C. Words*, *Weel*, Lanca. a whirlpool. **1683** in *Nairne Peerage Evid.* (1874) 18 From the said foord of Gellie to the weell of Buckmenem. **1786** BURNS *Halloween* xxv, Whyles owre a linn the burnie plays, ..Whyles in a wiel it dimpl't. *a* **1800** *Rare Willie* viii. in Child *Ballads* IV. 182/2 In the deepest weil in a' the burn, Oh, there she fand her Willie! **1817** SCOTT *Rob Roy* xxxvi, The deep waters and weils o' the Avondow. **1818** W. PHILLIPS *Geol.* 113 The pool of still water or wheel, above the falls. **1834** HOGG *Dom. Manners Scott* (1909) 59 In a few minutes we reached Gleddie's Weal, the deepest pool in all that part of Tweed. **1909** *Jedburgh Gaz.* 28 May 3/7 A large, deep pool known as the 'Old Weal'.

b. *attrib.*

1703 THORESBY *Let. to Ray*, A *Wheel-pit*, whirl-pool. *a* **1800** *Young Hunting* xvii. in Child *Ballads* II. 153/1 They douked in at ae weil-heid, And out aye at the other.

weel[2] (wi:l). Forms: α. 3–5 wyle, 6 wyele, 7 wile; 6 wyll(e, whyll. β. 5 wele (5–6 welle), 5–7 weele (6 weyle, weale), 7– weel, (6 *Sc.* weill, 7 well, 9 weal); 6–9 wheel (7 wheele). [OE. *wile-* (in *wilewise*), a reduced form of *wiliʒe*, *wilie* basket: see WILLY. The form *wele*, *weel* is a normal development from this.]

1. A wicker trap for catching fish, esp. eels.

1256 *Northumb. Assize Roll* (Surtees) 103 Fit destructio [in the Tyne] salminiculorum per wyles et per minuta retia. **1369–70** *Acc. Obedientiars Abingdon Abbey* (Camden) 19 In wylys et pottus, iij s. **1426** LYDG. *De Guil. Pilgr.* 18057 Lyke a wyle in a ryver, to cache the fysche bothe fer and nere; the entre large, the comynge out is so strayt, it stant in dout. **1450–1** *Acc. Obedientiars Abingdon Abbey* (Camden) 130 Et in welez emptis pro piscibus capiendis in fossato Conuentus, iiij s. x d. **1483** *Cath. Angl.* 413/1 A Welle, *nassa.* **1510** STANBRIDGE *Vocabula* (W. de W.) C vj b, *Nassula*, a wyll, or a leepe. **1519** HORMAN *Vulg.* Z i b, One hath robbed my wyele, *predo nassam diripuit.* **1573–80** TUSSER *Husb.* (1878) 87 Watch ponds, go looke to weeles and hooke. **1649** E. REYNOLDS *Hosea* iii. 26 We are like Fishermens wheels, wide at that end which lets in the Fish, but narrow at the other end, so that they cannot get out againe. **1725** *Bradley's Family Dict.*, Weel,..made of Osier-twigs, which are supported by Circles or Hoops, that go round, and are ever diminishing;..Its Mouth is somewhat Broad, but the other end terminates in a Point: It's so contrived, that when the Fishes are got in, they cannot come out of it again, because of the Osier Twigs, which advance on the inside, to the Place where the Hoops are, and which stop the Passage, leaving but a small opening there. **1769** PENNANT *Brit. Zool.* III. 163 It does not often take a bait, but is generally caught in weels. **1873** *Act 36 & 37 Vict.* c. 71 §15 Any basket, trap, or device for taking fish, except wheels or leaps for taking lamperns. **1883** *Fisheries Exhib. Catal.* (ed. 4) 125 Weels used on the apron of Weirs for taking Lamperns. **1902** CORNISH *Naturalist Thames* 163 The movable eel-trap or 'grig-wheel', like a crayfish basket, only larger.

b. in fig. context.

1639 MAYNE *City Match* III. iv, 'Slight who would think your Father should lay weeles To catch you thus? **1688** HOLME *Armoury* III. xvi. (Roxb.) 80/1 A weele with two ends, or holes: for fish to get in at; which when in, there is no getting out againe, from whence came the proverbe, I catched him with a weele: that is I got him in so, that he could not get out. **1694** MOTTEUX *Rabelais* v. xiv, When did you ever hear that..any body ever got out of this Weel without leaving something of his behind him.

c. *Her.* A conventional representation of such a fish-trap, borne as a charge.

1688 HOLME *Armoury* III. xvi. (Roxb.) 80/1 He beareth Azure, a Weele with its hoope vpward, Or. **1780** EDMONDSON *Her.* II. Gloss., *Weel*, for catching of fish, is always drawn in armory, as in Plate VIII. Fig. 39. *c* **1828** BERRY *Encycl. Her.* I. Gloss.

d. *attrib.*, in † *weel-net.*

1603 HOLLAND *Plutarch's Mor.* 218 Weaving them close together in a round and large forme, after the maner of a fishers leape or weele net.

2. A basket, *esp.* one in which fish are kept.

1432–50 tr. *Higden* (Rolls) II. 319 Moyses..was putte in a weele made of rishes [L. *in fiscella scirpea*] dressede with picche, and caste in to the water. *Ibid.* IV. 353 The fader and mother abhorrenge to sle theire owne son..putte hym in a wele in to the see. **1530** PALSGR. 287/2 Welle or lepe for fysshe, *bouticle.* **1651** T. BARKER *Art of Angling* (1659) 44 Providing a little weele made of wicker to carry their fish. **1659** TORRIANO, *Cavágna*..a fisher's-weel, or haske. **1678** LITTLETON *Dict., Lat.-Eng., Fiscella*,..a wile wherein fishes are kept. **1883** *Fisheries Exhib. Catal.* (ed. 4) 125 Hard Weels [are] large baskets in which eels and lamperns are kept alive until sold.

wee'l, obs. contr. form of *we will.*

1652 COTTERELL *Cassandra* v. (1676) 543 Wee'l set our selves up again.

weel(e, obs. forms of WEAL *sb.*[1], WELL.

weeld, obs. form of WEALD.

weeld(e, obs. forms of WIELD.

weele, wee'll, obs. contr. forms of *we will.*

1591 SHAKS. *Two Gent.* II. ii. 6 Why then wee'll make exchange. **1598** CHAPMAN *Blinde Begger Alexandria* B 3 b, Weele strike vp a drumme. **1606** MARSTON *Parasit.* IV. G 2, Stay foole weele follow thee. **1620** T. MAY *Heir* I. (1633) B 4 b, Lay it [the child] to him, weele out face him tis his.

weelful, -som, var. ff. WEALFUL, -SOME.

weely, var. WEALY *a.*[2] *Obs.*

weem (wi:m). [a. early Gael. *uaim* (now *uaimh*) cavern.] The name applied in Scotland to a cave or underground dwelling-place used by early inhabitants of the country.

1792 *Statist. Acc. Scot.* IV. 101 An artificial cave or subterraneous passage, such as is sometimes called by the country people a weem. **1851** D. WILSON *Preh. Ann.* I. iv. (1863) 107 The general name applied in Scotland to these subterranean habitations is Weems, from the Gaelic word *uamha* a cave. **1865** C. W. KETT in *Q. Jrnl. Sci.* Apr. 247 We find in Scotland underground dwelling-places formed of large unhewn stones without cement of any kind; these are called *weems.* **1892** D. MACRITCHIE *Underground Life* 47 It would be an easy matter for proprietors to fence in and otherwise protect existing 'weems'.

weem, var. WAME.

weemen, obs. pl. of WOMAN.

† **ween**, *sb. Obs.* Forms: 1–2, 3–4 wen, 3–6 wene, (3 wæne), 4–5 weene; *Sc.* and *north.* 4–5 weyne, 4 vene, veyn, 5 weyn. [OE. *wén* fem. (rarely masc. or neut.) corresp. to OFris. *wên* opinion, OS. *wân* masc., hope, OHG., MHG. *wân* masc., opinion, hope, etc. (mod.G. *wahn* fem.,

delusion), ON. *ván* fem., hope, Goth. *wēn-s* hope:—OTeut. **wǣni-z*, f. Teut. and Indogermanic root **wen-* to love.]

1. Opinion, belief. (Cf. Wone *sb.*)

c **888** Ælfred *Boeth.* xl. §3 Ne bið lof na ðy læsse, ac is wen þæt hit sie þy mare. *a* **1250** *Ancr. R.* 390 *note*, Efter monnes wene. *c* **1250** *Gen. & Ex.* 73 Ðis ik wort in ebrisse wen, He witen ðe soðe ðat is sen. *Ibid.* 3271 Egipcienes woren in twired wen queðer he sulden folȝen or flen. *a* **1275** *Prov. Ælfred* 215 in *O.E. Misc.* 115, & ich her ȝu wille leren wenes mine, wit & wisdome.

2. Expectation, hope. (Cf. Wone *sb.*)

Beowulf 383 (Gr.) þæs ic wen hæbbe. *c* **1205** Lay. 28141 Of þine kume nis na wene for no weneð heo nauere to soðe þat þu cumen aȝin from Rome. *a* **1300** *Floriz & Bl.* 651 Camb. MS.) To hire was mi meste wene, For to habbe to mi quene. **1390** Gower *Conf.* II. 88 It were betre be refused Than forto worchen upon weene.

3. Probability, supposition; doubt.

Beowulf 1845 (Gr.) Wen ic taliᵹe.. þæt þe Sæ-ᵹeatas selran næbben to ᵹeceosenne cyning æniᵹne. *c* **1205** Lay. 13503 Hit bið a muchele wæne whær ȝe i-seon me auere mare. *Ibid.* 18752 Þa ȝet hit weore a wene whar þu heo mihtes aȝe. *c* **1300** *Cursor M.* 1104 Bituixand þei þe southe had sene O thing þai wist noght bot a wene.

4. Phrases. **a.** ***wen is, is wen***: the probability is (*that* . . .), it is probable (*that* . . .).

c **897** Ælfred *Gregory's Past. C.* xi. 72 Forðæm hit is wen ðæt se ne mæᵹe oðerra monna scylde ofaðwean [etc.]. **971** *Blickl. Hom.* 235 Wen is þæt ic ᵹefyrenode. *Ibid.* 239 Cum nu mid us.. þy læs wen is þæt hi us eft ᵹenimon. *c* **1000** *Ags. Gosp.* John viii. 19 ᵹyf ᵹe me cuþon, wen is þæt ᵹe cuþon minne fæder. *c* **1200** Ormin 7152, & wen iss þatt he wass forrdredd & serrhfull in hiss herrte.

b. ***without(en (any) ween, but ween*** (Sc.), ***forout(en ween*** (Sc.): without doubt.

c **1200** Ormin 4326 Þu findesst wiss wiþþutenn wen Rihhte ehhte siþe an hunndredd. *c* **1205** Lay. 6311 To soðen wihuten wene þe laȝe hehte Marciane. *a* **1300** *Cursor M.* 468 In þat curt þat is so clene, May na filth in dwell wituten wene. ?*a* **1366** Chaucer *Rom. Rose* 574 Withouten wene, Wel semyde by hir apparayle She was not wont to gret trauayle. *c* **1374** —— *Troylus* iv. 1593 Er Phebus suster lucyna the shene, The leon passe out of þis ariete, I wol ben here with-outen ony wene. **1375** Barbour *Bruce* vi. 162 Thai presit hym so fast, That, had he nocht the bettir beyn, He had beyn ded forouten veyn. *Ibid.* xix. 292 The erll sperit giff he had seyne The Inglis host; 'ȝa, schir, but weyne'. *c* **1440** *York Myst.* xi. 104, I will go witte with-owten wene. *c* **1450** Holland *Houlate* 382 Of Scotland the wer wall, wit ȝe but wene, Our fais force to defend. *c* **1500** *Lancelot* 2880 The thrid.. was o manly knycht, but weyne. *c* **1550** Rolland *Crt. Venus* iii. 51 Twentie and fiue, quhen thay war red but wene.

†**ween**, *a.* *Obs. rare.* [a. ON. *vǽnn*:—OTeut. type **wǣnjo-*, f. **wǣni-* Ween *sb.*] Beautiful.

13.. *Gaw. & Gr. Knt.* 945 Ho watz þe fayrest in felle.., & wener þen Wenore [Guenever], as þe wyȝe þoȝt.

ween (wiːn), *v.* *Obs.* exc. *arch.* Pa. t. and pa. pple. **weened** (wiːnd). Forms: 1 **wénan, wǽnan,** 2–4 **wenen,** 3 **weone,** 3–5 **wen,** 3–6 **wene,** 4–5 **whene,** *Sc.* **ven(e, vein,** 4–6 *Sc.* and *north.* **weyn(e,** 5 **veyn,** 6 **wean,** 6–7 *Sc.* **wein(e,** 4–7 **weene,** 5– **ween;** 3–4, 6 **win(n, wyn(n.** *Pa. t.* 1 **wénde,** 3–6 **wende,** 3 **wænde,** 3–6 **wend,** 4 *Sc.* **whende, vend,** 5–6 *Sc.* **weind, weynd;** 3–6 **went(e,** 4 *north.* **weint,** 5 **wentt, whente,** (6 *Sc.* **wont, wount, wint).** *Pa. pple.* 4–6 **wend(e, went,** 5 **whent.** [A Common Teut. weak verb: OE. *wénan* corresp. to OFris. *wêna* to think, OS. *wânian* (MLG. *wênen, wânen*, LG. *wanen*), OLow Frankish *wânan* (MDu., Du. *wanen* to fancy, think), OHG. *wânnen, wânen* (MHG. *wænen*, mod.G. *wähnen* to suppose wrongly, imagine), ON. *vǽna* to hope, Goth. *wēnjan* to hope:—OTeut. **wǣnjan*, f. **wǣni-* Ween *sb.*

The word seems to have gone out of general use in the 17th c. It has survived as an archaism, esp. in the parenthetic formula illustrated in 1 h.]

1. *trans.* In regard to what is present or past: To think, surmise, suppose, conceive, believe, consider. In ME. often with *well.*

a. *Const.* object-clause, with or without *that.*

971 *Blickl. Hom.* 55 Þa word þe he wenþ þæt him leofoste syn to ᵹehyrenne. **1154** *O.E. Chron.* (Laud MS.) an. 1137 Al þe tunscipe fluᵹæn for heom, wenden ðæt hi wæron ræueres. *c* **1200** Ormin 11585 Forr þatt te deofell shollde Wel wenenn þatt he wære mann. *c* **1250** *Gen. & Ex.* 1543 Ysaac wende it were esau. *a* **1300** *Cursor M.* 7557 Quat! wyns þou i am a hund? **1303** R. Brunne *Handl. Synne* 10596 He went he had be hys brother. **1471** Caxton *Recuyell* (Sommer) 148 Whan they sawe Iupiter, they had went he had ben half man and half hors. **1530** Palsgr. 756/2 The castell which men wente had ben inprennable, is throwen downe nowe. **1532** More *Confut. Tindale* Wks. 455/1 If they had but tolde the myracles that Christ did, the countries to whom they were sent, woulde haue went that they had lyed. **1580** Fulke *Martiall Confuted* iv. 169 Let him looke in his lexicon, where I weene al his Greeke is. **1600** Holland *Livy* v. xxxix. 205 The Romanes.. weening that there was none left alive. **1614** Camden *Rem., Prov.* 313 They that be in hell wene there is no other heauen. **1721** *Colin's Mistakes* iv. 3 Well I ween, That.. Dan Spenser makes the fav'rite Goddess known. **1805** Scott *Last Minstr.* iii. xxxi, Some said that there were thousands ten; And others ween'd that it was nought But Leven clans, or Tynedale men. **1838** Mrs. Browning *Deserted Garden* xii, Though never a dream the roses sent Of science or love's compliment, I ween they smelt as sweet. **1848** Lytton *Harold* vi. i, But well I ween that Gryffyth will never keep troth with the English.

†**b.** *Const.* infin. ***to ween to be*** or ***do*** = to think that one is or does. *Obs.*

c **1200** *Vices & Virtues* 9 Sume weneð bien sacleas of ðessere senne [of swearing], for ðan ðe me nett hem to ðan aðe. *c* **1205** Lay. 24535 Ælc wende to beon betere þene oðer. *a* **1300** *Cursor M.* 12119 Þof þou wen make-less to be, þat nan in lare sal teche þe. *c* **1374** Chaucer *Anel. & Arc.* 96 So that she wende haue al his hert yknowe. **1390** Gower *Conf.* I. 15 Betwen tuo Stoles lyth the fal, Whan that men wenen best to sitte. *c* **1450** *Knt. de la Tour* cxi. 151 After this sorw, that she went to haue loste her sone, she hadde another. **1513** Douglas *Æneis* i. Prol. 131 Quhen we best wene To haue Virgill red, understand, and sene, The richt sentence perchance is fer to seik. **1638** Junius *Paint. Ancients* 150 The parret.. weening to see another parret in the glasse.

†**c.** *Const.* obj. and compl. (sb. or adj.). *Obs.*

c **1230** *Hali Meid.* (1922) 10 Al is þet tu wendest golt, iwurðe to meastling. **1380** Wyclif *Sel. Wks.* III. 40 Weenynge his liif glorios þat is vicious. *c* **1385** Chaucer *L.G.W.* 12 Men schal nat wenyn euery thyng a lye For that he say it nat of ȝore ago. *c* **1430** *Pilgr. Lyf Manhode* ii. lxvi. (1869) 100 Gretli j am abasht þat þou þat j wende a nice man answerest me so wel. **1533** More *Answ. poysoned Bk.* Wks. 1036/1 They.. should shortlye perceiue in euery place where they wene themselfe many, how very few they be. **1582** Stanyhurst *Æneis* ii. (Arb.) 44 Weene you.. thee Greekish nauye returned? **1596** Spenser *F.Q.* vii. vi. 11 Shee her selfe more worthy thereof wend.

†**d.** *Const.* obj. and infin. *Obs.*

1340–70 *Alex. & Dind.* 534 So wis wenst þou þe be. **1390** Gower *Conf.* I. 96, I wot thou wolt nothing forbere Of that thou wenest be thi beste. **1456** Sir G. Haye *Law Arms* (S.T.S.) 265 That thai may be kend wenand thame self till have rychtwis caus. **1528** in Pocock *Rec. Reform.* I. 85 We wening the same to have been our way. **1570** Dee *Math. Pref.* 19 While the eye weeneth a round Globe.. to be a flat and plaine Circle. **1606** Holland *Sueton.* 43 Kenning a farre of Pompeis gallies.. and weening them to be his owne.

†**e.** With simple object (usually a neut. pronoun): To think, believe, credit (something). Also, to surmise or suspect to exist. *Obs.*

c **888** Ælfred *Boeth.* xlii, Nis þæt ðeah no licumlice to wenanne, ac gastlice. *c* **1000** Ælfric *Hom.* I. 440 Þeah.. us ᵹedafenað þæt we hit wenon swiðor þonne we unrædlice hit ᵹeseþan. *c* **1230** *Hali Meid.* (1922) 11 Hwen þus is of þe riche, hwat wenes tu of the poure. **1340** Hampole *Pr. Consc.* 2154 Na man ille dede shuld wene þar, whar gude lyf byfor has bene. **13..** *E.E. Allit. P.* C. 244 Hit were a wonder to wene. *c* **1374** Chaucer *Troylus* i. 1031 But herke, Pandare, o word, for I nolde That thow in me wendest so gret folye. *c* **1375** *Sc. Leg. Saints* xxvii. (*Machor*) 78 Þis quhen þe king had herd & sen, þe Ioy he had wald na man wen. *c* **1400** *Rom. Rose* 5672 Is no man wrecched, but he it wene. **1560** Daus tr. *Sleidane's Comm.* 239 Neither must we here consyder, what the greatest multitude weneth, but what the trewthe is. **1570** *Satir. Poems Reform.* xx. 117 Quhat sall we wene of tratours kene. *c* **1570** *Pride & Lowl.* (1841) 65 These matters.. So straunge, and so incredible to weene.

†**f.** coupled or contrasted with *wit* (*wot*, etc.).

c **1290** *Holy Cross* 11 in *S. Eng. Leg.* 1 Ich wene þat ich wot ȝwat þis somunce amounti schal. **13..** *E.E. Allit. P.* A. 47 Þer wonys þat worþyly I wot & wene. **1375** Barbour *Bruce* iv. 771 But quhethir scho.. Wenit, or vist it vitterly, It fell eftir all halely As scho said. *c* **1435** *Torr. Portugal* 1559 Wot ye well and not wene, Whan eyther of hem had other sene, Smertely rerid her dede. **1721** J. Kelly *Sc. Prov.* 69 Before I ween'd, but now I wat.

g. *ellipt.* or *absol.* Usually with adv. or conj. (*as, than, when,* etc.).

c **888** Ælfred *Boeth.* xl. §2 Uton healdan unc þæt wit ne wenen swa swa þis folc wenð. *c* **1200** Ormin 9826 Annd tatt wass mikell wherrfeddleȝȝc þatt dide hemm swa to wenenn. *a* **1225** *Ancr. R.* 222 Moni þet ne weneð nout bredeð in hire breoste sum liunes hweolp. *c* **1350** *Will. Palerne* 706 Ich am a mad man.. Forto wene in þis wise. *c* **1375** *Sc. Leg. Saints* xv. (*Barnabas*) 3 Bot þai wene wrang. **1377** Langl. *P. Pl.* B. xv. 470 Riȝt so rude men.. Louen and by-leuen by lettred mennes doynges, And by here wordes and werkes wenen and trowen. *c* **1400** *Rule St. Benet* 1019, I am wastid wor þan I wend. *c* **1450** *Merlin* i. 19 Thow art not so wyse as thow weneste. **1470–85** Malory *Arthur* vi. v. 189, I know you better than ye wene. *a* **1568** Ascham *Scholem.* i. (Arb.) 45 Which is an opinion not so trewe, as some men weene. **1601** *Song of Mary* in Farr *S.P. Eliz.* (1845) 432 Farre more they be than we can weene. **1615** Bp. Andrewes *Serm.* Nativ. x. (1629) 90 And sure, the way is not readie to hit;.. It is but a foolish imagination, so to ween of it. **1746** Francis tr. *Hor., Sat.* ii. viii. 26 If haply right I ween. **1808** Scott *Marm.* i. xxi, Even our good chaplain, as I ween, Since our last siege we have not seen. **1850** Mrs. Browning *House of Clouds* viii, Named as Fancy weeneth.

h. used parenthetically (esp. in ***I ween***) rather than as governing the sentence. In verse often a mere tag.

c **1175** *Lamb. Hom.* I. 157 Eiðer of þisse teres schedde þe apostel leste ich wene [L. *fudit fortasse apostolus*] þa þe he seide [etc.]. *a* **1225** *Ancr. R.* 210 Nis, ich wene, no mon þet [etc.]. *c* **1300** *Havelok* 655 Þre dayes þer-biforn, i wene, Et he no mete. *c* **1420** ? Lydg. *Assembly of Gods* 278 Of royall rychesse wantyd she noone I wene. *c* **1500** *Nut-Brown Maid* xxviii, Ye shape some wyle, me to begyle, and stele fro me I wene. **1564** Anne Lady Bacon tr. *Jewel's Apol.* (1859) 47 And do all they themselves, ween you, agree well together? **1667** Milton *P.L.* iv. 741 Nor turnd I weene Adam from his fair Spouse. **1764** H. Walpole *Otranto* iv, He, I ween, is no sacred personage. **1787** Burns *Humble Petit. Bruar Water* iii, A panegyric rhyme, I ween, Even as I was he shor'd me. **1819** Scott *Ivanhoe* iii, See what tidings that horn tells us of—to announce, I ween, some hership and robbery. **1835** Lytton *Rienzi* i. v, And never, I ween well, had she greater need of true friends than now. **1842** Barham *Ingol. Leg.* Ser. ii. *Ingol. Penance* 2 A stalwart knight, I ween, was he. *a* **1873** Deutsch *Lit. Rem.* (1874) 251 There will be a greater harvest still, we ween.

2. In regard to what is future or contingent: To expect, anticipate, count on; to surmise, suspect; to think possible or likely. *Const.* object-clause, with or without *that*, etc.

c **1000** *Ags. Gosp.* Matt. xx. 10 Þa þe þær ærest comon wendon þæt hiᵹ sceoldon mare onfon. *a* **1225** *Ancr. R.* 178 Ne wene non of heie liue þet heo ne beo itempted. *c* **1290** *Beket* 2045 in *S. Eng. Leg.* 165 Wenst þou þat ichulle fleo? *c* **1374** Chaucer *Troylus* iv. 384 Who wolde haue wend þat yn so lytel a þrowe Fortune oure Ioye wolde han ouerþrowe. **1375** Barbour *Bruce* iv. 210 My lif wend I thair suld be gane. **1456** Sir G. Haye *Law Arms* (S.T.S.) 182 [He] gafe the sauf condyt, wenand it wald be obeyde. **15..** *Freiris of Berwik* 246 Quha wenit that ȝe sa lait wald haif cum hame? **1535** *Goodly Primer* P ij, I had wente that I shulde haue gone to my graue in my beste dayes.

†**b.** with direct object (sb. or neut. pronoun).

In OE. the object is in the genitive. So (rarely) in early ME.

971 *Blickl. Hom.* 51 ᵹif we ane hwile beoþ on hwylcum earfoþum þær we ures feores ne wenaþ. *a* **1240** *Ureisun* in *Lamb. Hom.* 187 Nai soþes nai. Ne wene hit neuer no mon. *a* **1250** *Prov. Alfred* 161 in *O.E. Misc.* 112 Monymon weneþ þat he wene ne þarf, longes lyues. *a* **1275** *Prov. Alfred* (2nd version) 650 Ac þanne þu hid lest wenest þe luþere þe biswiket. *a* **1300** *Cursor M.* 10128 Prophecies com al to end, Quen Iues alþerlest it wend. **1338** R. Brunne *Chron.* (1810) 317 Whan William was comen, & wende no tresoun, Sone was he nomen, & don in prisoun. **1390** Gower *Conf.* I. 81 Thei that wende pees Tho myhten finde no reles Of thilke swerd which al devoureth. *a* **1450** *Le Morte Arth.* 1973 So nere hys herte the sorowe sought All-moste hys lyffe wolde no man wene. **1513** Douglas *Æneis* vi. ii. 38 Ȝour first reskew.. Furth of a Gregioun cetie sall be schaw, Quhilk thow lest wenis [L. *quod minime reris*].

Prov. *c* **1386** Chaucer *Reeve's T.* 400 Hym thar nat wene wel that yuele dooth. **1670** Ray *Prov.* 227 (Scottish Proverbs) He that evil does, never good weines.

c. With inf., present or perfect, with or without *to* (†*for to*, †*till*): To expect, hope, wish; to purpose, intend, be minded.

Beowulf 933 Ðæt wæs unᵹeara, þæt ic æniᵹra me weana ne wende.. bote ᵹebidan. **1154** *O.E. Chron.* an. 1140, Eustace .. wende to biᵹæton Normandi þær þurh. *c* **1205** Lay. 1848 Þa heo best wende to fleonne, þa weoren heo faie. *c* **1250** *Owl & Night.* 814 He [the fox] weneþ eche hunde at wrenche. *a* **1300** *Cursor M.* 6853 Your faas þat yow winnes [*v.r.* wenis] witstand Sal haue na might o fote and hand. *c* **1330** R. Brunne *Chron. Wace* (Rolls) 5298 In-to Egipte þen schiped he, ffor wel wend he þer siker haue be. **1375** Barbour *Bruce* xviii. 50, I wend neuir till here that of the! **1470–85** Malory *Arthur* ii. vi. 83, I lytel wende to haue met with yow at this sodayne auenture. **1561** Hollybush *Hom. Apoth.* 17 b, A colde sweat brake out, so that he wened to dye straght waye. **1590** Spenser *F.Q.* i. iii. 41 And ramping on his shield, did weene the same Haue reft away with his sharpe rending clawes. **1591** Shaks. *1 Hen. VI*, ii. v. 88 Thy Father.. Leuied an Army, weening to redeeme, And haue install'd me in the Diademe. **1611** Bible *2 Macc.* v. 21 Weening in his pride to make the land nauigable. **1667** Milton *P.L.* vi. 86 They weend That self same day by fight, or by surprize To win the Mount of God. **1805** Scott *Last Minstr.* ii. xxix, Ye ween to hear a melting tale, Of two true lovers in a dale. **1854** J. S. Blackie in *Blackw. Mag.* LXXVI. 266 Beyond the bounds of earth to fly Impious he weened.

d. ellipt. with adv. (e.g. *least*), or conj. (*ere, sooner, than,* etc.), instead of inf. or object-clause.

c **888** Ælfred *Boeth.* vii. §1 Þonne hy læst wenað. *c* **1000** *Ags. Gosp.* Matt. xxiv. 50 Þonne cymþ ðæs weles hlaford on þam dæᵹe ðe he na ne wenþ. *a* **1225** *Ancr. R.* 222 Ich chulle .. worpen hire oðere half, & breden uerliche adun er he lest wene. *c* **1330** R. Brunne *Chron. Wace* (Rolls) 9471 As he stod, er he lest wende, He was schot to deþe. **1340** Hampole *Pr. Consc.* 1376 That may fal soner than som wenes. **1375** Barbour *Bruce* xi. 23 And wis menis etling cumis nocht Till sic end as thai weyn alwayis. *c* **1440** *Pallad. on Husb.* v. 211 And heer an ende, er then y wende, y fynde. *c* **1450** tr. *De Imitatione* i. xxiii. 31 What houre we wene not þe sonne of man shal come. *a* **1600** Montgomerie *Misc. Poems* iii. 62 Quhen ȝe leist wein, ȝour baks may to the wall. **1814** Cary *Dante, Par.* xxxi. 53 Round I turned With purpose of my lady to inquire.. But answer found from other than I weened.

†**3.** With neut. adj. or adv. and prep.: To think (much or highly) *of*; to feel or be affected *towards*; to trust *in*. Also without const. (cf. *overween*). *Obs.*

1340 *Ayenb.* 21 Þanne þe man wenþ more of him-zelue þanne he ssolde. **1390** Gower *Conf.* I. 109 Whan he most in his strengthe wende. *Ibid.* 222 Bot wolde god that grace sende, That toward me my lady wende As I towardes hire wene! **1593** G. Harvey *Pierces Super.* Wks. (Grosart) II. 125 He winneth not most abroad that weeneth most at-home.

†**4.** *intr.* with *of, for*: To dream of, look for, expect. *Obs.*

1589 *Martins Months Minde* E 1 b, Howbeit, it was not that so well, as they do ween for, (being perhappes reserued for his two sonnes hereafter). **1613** Shaks. *Hen. VIII*, v. i. 136 Weene you of better lucke, I meane in periur'd Witnesse, then your Master, Whose Minister you are..?

5. In renderings of certain Latin words.

†**a.** *trans.* To esteem, respect; to reckon or esteem equal *to.*

c **1000** *Lamb. Psalter* lxxxvii. 5 *Aestimatus sum cum descendentibus in lacum*, ᵹewened ic eom mid nyþerastiᵹendum to seaðe. *a* **1300** *E.E. Psalter* lxxxvii. 5, I am wened in ilka land To þas þat ere in flosche falland. *Ibid.* cxliii. 3 Lauerd, whilk es.. sone of man, for þou wenest him [Vulg. *quia reputas eum*]?

†**b.** To impute (an offence) *to* (a person). *Obs.*

a **1300** *E.E. Psalter* xxxi. 2 Seli man to wham noght wenes lauerd sinne [Vulg. *cui non imputavit Dominus peccatum*].

†**6.** In impersonal use. Only in the absol. pres. pple. *weening* = it seeming, as (because, since) it seemed (*to* some one). *Const.* clause (usually with *that*) or inf. *Obs.*

c **1450** Capgrave *Life St. Aug.* xxxiii. 42 For þat same had he do or þis tyme had not Valery sent him owt of þe weye, wenyng to many men þat he schuld not sone come a-geyn. c **1470** GREGORY *Chron.* in *Hist. Coll. Cit. Lond.* (Camden) 234 Wenyng unto the thevys that the boxys hadde ben sylvyr ovyr gylt, but was but copyr. **1485** CAXTON *Chas. Gt.* 92 Wherof they were sore aferde.., wenyng to them that it had be the deuyl. **1523** BERNERS *Froiss.* (1812) I. cclxv. 391 They came..to a village called Puiernon, and toke their lodgynge, wenyng to them to be in surety. *Ibid.* ccclxxxv. 652 Y^e duke and his went to Berwyk, wenyng to the duke to haue entred into the towne;..but the capitane of the towne ..refused to him the entre, and closed the gates agaynst hym and his. **1542** UDALL *Erasm. Apoph.* 233 Aiax..in his madnesse..slewe a greate noumbre of theim, weenyng to hym that he had slain Ulysses and his coumpaignie. **1568** GRAFTON *Chron.* II. 276 The common of Roane and of Beuioys..sodainely met with the Englishe Marshalles, wenyng to them they had bene Frenchmen.

weend(e, obs. forms of WEND *v.*, to go.

† **'weener.** *nonce-wd.* [f. WEEN *v.* + -ER[1].] One who weens; ***easy weener***, a credulous person.

For an earlier doubtful instance see quot. c 1430 s.v. WEAVER[1] 2.

1604 EDMONDS *Observ. Cæsar's Comm.* VI. v. 13 The inconuenience of ouer light credulitie, leading such easie weeners to a disappointment of their hopes.

'weeness. *rare.* [f. WEE *sb.*[1] and *a.*] Smallness.

1882 *Jamieson's Sc. Dict.* s.v.

weening ('wiːnɪŋ), *vbl. sb. Obs.* or *arch.* [f. WEEN *v.* + -ING[1]. Cf. OHG. *anawânunga* 'existimatio', *piwânunga* 'deliberatio', MHG. *wænunge*, *wenung(e*, G. *wähnung*.]

1. The action of thinking, supposing, expecting, etc. In ME. often = mere opinion, surmise or suspicion (as opposed to certain knowledge).

c **900** *Bæda's Hist.* IV. xix. (MS. Ca.) þæt heo ða wenunge æt nyhstan ðurhteah. c **1330** R. BRUNNE *Chron. Wace* (Rolls) 7423 Þer wenyng þat day þey tynt. **1340** *Ayenb.* 113 Hit is ope substance, þet is, uirtuous and substanciel aboue onderstondingge and wenynge. **1377** LANGL. *P. Pl.* B. xx. 33 Wenynge is no wysdome ne wyse ymagynacioun. **1397** *Rolls of Parlt.* III. 379/2 It was my menyng and my wenyng for to have do the best. c **1400** *Rom. Rose* 2601 Hit is but foly and wrong wenyng To aske so outrageous a thyng. c **1420** *Prose Life Alex.* 36 Ȝe wende hafe done till vs as ȝour eldirs didde sumtyme till kynge ȝerses, bot ȝour wenyng dessayued ȝow. **1477** NORTON *Ord. Alch.* i. in Ashm. (1652) 22 An old Proverbe, In a Bushell of weeninge, Is not found one handfull of Cunninge. **1570** DEE *Math. Pref.* 2 Surmountyng the imperfection of coniecture, weenyng and opinion. **1625** GILL *Sacr. Philos.* I. 96 These upstart weenings are so witlesse, as they are false. a **1633** G. HERBERT *Outlandish Prov.* 811 Weening is not measure. **1652** H. BELL *Luther's Colloq. Mensalia* 225 A Preacher.. should..not build upon a weening,..but must bee sure of the Caus. a **1761** LAW *Behmen's Myst. Magn.* xl. (1765) 231 It lies not in any Mans own willing, weening, running, or going to will.

† **b.** Phrases. ***to be at*** or ***in weening***: to be in a state of uncertainty or expectation. ***to (one's) weening***: to the best of one's belief. ***to put in weening***: to make (a person) think or believe. *Obs.*

c **1275** *Passion of our Lord* 595 in *O.E. Misc.* 54 As heo stode and speken and weren at wenynge Of vre louerdes aryste and fele oþer þinge. **1375** BARBOUR *Bruce* IV. 765 Sen thai ar in sic venyng, Forouten certane vitting. c **1375** *Sc. Leg. Saints* xlvi. (*Anastace*) 184 As he wend he had done til his wenyng Inuch. c **1430** *Pilgr. Lyf Manhode* I. cviii. (1869) 57 Vn yrened j took it thee, for to my weenynge thou shuldest bere it the bettere. c **1440** *Partonope* 8588 Ye haue chose some new thinge, And wolde put me in wenyng That it were for good Partonope. **1481** CAXTON *Reynard* xvii. (Arb.) 42 Nay I shal brynge you out of wenyng and shewe it you by good wytnes.

† **2.** Arrogant opinion, self-conceit. *Obs.* Cf. *overweening*.

1575 FENTON *Gold. Epist.* (1582) 88 Temporall riches bring with them pride and wening to him that hath them. **1603** HOLLAND *Plutarch's Mor.* 1016 Yong gentlemen.. filled with a great weening and opinion of themselves.

† **'weening,** *ppl. a. Obs.* [-ING[2].]

1. That weens or thinks; cogitative.

c **1391** CHAUCER *Boeth.* III. pr. x. (1886) 71 Yif so be þat this good be in hym by nature, but that it is diuers fro hym by wenynge resoun [*sed ratione diversum*].

2. Self-conceited, arrogant, overweening.

1579 FENTON *Guicciard.* IX. 465 The Swizzers being of nature proude and weening, became more raysed and lifted vp in minde by the estimation that others had of them.

weenong ('wiːnɒŋ). [Jav. *winong.*] The Javanese name for the tree *Tetrameles nudiflora*.

a **1838** HORSFIELD in J. J. Bennett *Pl. Javan. Rariores* 80 Weenong of the Javanese. It is a large tree. I found it in full flower..in 1815. **1866** *Treas. Bot.* s.v. *Tetrameles*, This tree is the Jungle-bendy of India, and the Weenong of Java.

weent, var. WENT *sb. Obs.*

weeny ('wiːnɪ), *a. dial.* and *colloq.* Also 8 **weny**, 9 **weany**. [f. WEE, with ending imitated from TINY, TEENY *a.*[2]]

1. Very small, tiny. Also ***teeny-weeny*** (see TEENY *a.*[2]).

1790 GROSE *Prov. Gloss.* (ed. 2), *Wee and weny*, very small. North. **1833** *Christmas Improvement* iii. (1841) 40 Such a little tiny weeny pill can never cure such a great big headache as I have got. **1876** *Mr. Gray & Neighbours* II. 140 You have to keep her head the tinyest, weanyest bit in the world to the nor-east. **1911** C. BEADLE *City of Shadows* vii, The cupid bow of a mouth opened just the weeniest bit. **1922** W. J. LOCKE *Tale of Triona* ii. 23 They're little tiny weeny shells.

2. Special collocation: **weeny-bopper** *colloq.* [after *teeny-bopper*], a very young (esp. female) pop fan (sometimes notionally of a younger age group than a teeny-bopper, but the two terms are freq. interchangeable).

1972 *Daily Express* 2 Nov. 16 Britain's 'weeny-boppers' are in danger of dancing their way to incurable deafness. **1975** *Evening News* 5 July 16/5 Being a weeny-bopper can be a problem when it comes to clothes... Our model, Karen, nearly 13, got her mum to take her round the stores. **1976** M. BUTTERWORTH *Festival!* viii. 133 A couple of weenie-boppers at a pop concert.

weeny ('wiːnɪ), *sb.*[1] Also **weenie**. [f. the adj.]

1. *colloq.* A very young child.

1844 C. RIDLEY *Let.* Oct. (1958) xv. 180, I must tell you now about the chicks [i.e. children]. Little weeny is growing visibly. **1973** 'D. HALLIDAY' *Dolly & Starry Bird* vi. 82 Not Mr. Paladrini who was so nice to the weenies? **1977** *Ottawa Citizen* 29 June 7/1 Our five-year-old granddaughter keeps asking when the trip is going to begin. Travelling with weenies is something that Mama and I have done for most of our lives.

2. *U.S. slang.* **a.** A girl; an effeminate man. **b.** An objectionable person.

1929 [see PHOOEY *int.* (*sb.*)]. **1963** *Amer. Speech* XXXVIII. 171 Some of the less frequent..phrases [for an effeminate young man] are: *dink*..and *weenie*. **1964** *Ibid.* XXXIX. 118 Free variation..is also established in the interchangeability of the names of smaller animals for socially unacceptable persons: *toad*, *squirrel*, and *shrimp* all serve for the zoologically unsound but all-inclusive *weenie*.

weeny ('wiːnɪ), *sb.*[2] *U.S. slang.* Also **weeney**, **weenie**. Var. WIENIE. Cf. WINNY.

1906 *Dialect Notes* III. 163 *Weenie*..Wiener Wurst, sausage. 'Hot *Weenies*.' **1935** *Amer. Speech* X. 159 'Weinies', 'Wienies', and 'Weenies' are also for sale. **1960** C. HAMBLETT in *Pick of Today's Short Stories* 136 The simplest basics... Marilyn Monroe, hot dogs, weenies. **1981** P. THEROUX *Mosquito Coast* viii. 72 Father said, '..I've got other weenies to roast.' And he went back to his maps.

weep (wiːp), *sb.* Also 3 **woep**, **weop**, 3, 4 **wep**, 3–6 **wepe**, 6 **weepe**. [f. WEEP *v.* Cf. WOP.]

† **1. a.** Weeping, lamentation. ***to burst a-weep***: to burst out weeping. *Obs.*

c **1205** LAY. 11991 þe iherde þesne weop [cf. *wop* ibid. 5970, 15066]. c **1250** *Gen. & Ex.* 2328 He..broȝte hem bi-for iosep Wid reweli lote, and sorwe, and wep. a **1300** in *Anecd. Lit.* (1844) 90 Al the blisse of thisse live Thou shalt, mon, henden in woep. **1303** R. BRUNNE *Handl. Synne* 5721 For comunlych aftyr wepe, Fal men sone on slepe. **13..** *K. Alis.* 7871 (Laud MS.), Michel weep, mychel waylying. c **1374** CHAUCER *Troylus* II. 408 She bygan to brest a wep a-noon. a **1425** *Cursor M.* 10496 (Trin.) Whil she mened þus hir mone Wiþ wepe [*other texts* weping] & sorwes mony one. **1512** *Helyas* in Thoms *Pr. Rom.* (1828) III. 116 The which in weepe piteously bewayled her good spouse. **1545** *Hen. VIII's Primer, Lauds* C iij b, Deuout prayer, meynt with wepe, Suffreth not the hart to slepe.

b. A fit or bout of weeping. Also ***the weeps***: a fit of weeping or melancholy. Also *transf.*

Also in 'Hence these weeps', a burlesque alteration of 'Hence these tears'.

1836 C. SHAW *Mem.* etc. (1837) II. 574, I had nothing else for it, but in the middle of the night to go aside and have a very hearty weep by myself. **1876** J. P. STRUTHERS in *Life & Lett.* iv. (1918) 49 But those days are gone. Hence these weeps. **1886** KIPLING *Departm. Ditties, Mare's Nest* 43 There was a scene—a weep or two—With many kisses. **1922** JOYCE *Ulysses* 297 And Bob Doran starts doing the weeps about Paddy Dignam. **1937** 'G. ORWELL' *Let.* 31 July in *Coll. Ess.* (1968) I. 280, I heard from Murry who seemed in the weeps about something. **1982** *Medico-Legal Jrnl.* L. 10 Leaving his Counsel to do what we call 'The weeps', i.e. to plead in mitigation of sentence.

2. An exudation, percolation, or sweating of moisture.

1838 *Civil Engin. & Arch. Jrnl.* I. 213/2 Weeps which in iron would speedily be stopped by the natural operation of rust, go on in copper indefinitely, working their way like worms in wood. **1891** *Century Dict.*, *Weep*, exudation, sweat, as of a gum-tree. **1901** *Oxf. Times* 2 Mar. 3/4 The water..did not come by any jets or spouts..but by simple oozes or weeps or whatever term they used to describe what took place.

3. Comb.: † **weep-drop**, a drop of moisture like a tear; **weep-hole**, an opening through which water percolates or drips.

1509 FISHER 7 *Penit. Ps.* li. Wks. (1876) 120 A mannes brethynge whan it toucheth ony thynge that is colde as yren or glasse, anone it is resolued in to wepe droppes of water. **1851** *Colon. Mag.* July 8 The water..filters through the red sand, running through 'weep holes' made of brick, into a reservoir.

weep (wiːp), *v.* Pa. t. and pa. pple. **wept** (wɛpt). Forms: *Inf.* 1 **wépan**, **wêpan**, 2–3 **wepen**, (*Orm.* **-enn**), 3 **weopen**, 3–6 **wepe**, (3 **weape**), 4 **wipe**, **weope**, 3–4 **wep**, (5 **wepyn**, **wape**), 5–8 *Sc.* **weip**, 6 *Sc.* **veip**, **vepe**, 6–7 **weepe**, (7 **weap**), 7– **weep**. *Pa. t.* 1 **wéop**, 2–4 **weop**, 3 **weap**, **wiep**, 3–4 **wep**, **wop**, 3–5 **wepe**, (4 **weep**, **wip**, 5 **wippe**); 3 **wepude**, 4 **wepped**, 4–5 **weped**, (4 **wepid**, **wepet**), 4–6 **wepit**, (4 **weppit**, 5 **wepput**, 6 *Sc.* **weipit**, **vepit**), 6–9 **weeped**, 4– **wept**. *Pa. pple.* 1 **wópen**, 4 **wopen**, **i-wope**, 4 **wepen**; 4 **wepid**, 8 **weeped**; 4 **ywept**, **wepte**, 7 **weept**, 4– **wept**. [A Com. Teut. vb., prob. originally weak, but in WGer. assimilated to the reduplicating conjugation: OE. *wépan* (pa. t. *wéop*) corresponds to OFris. *wêpa* to cry aloud (str. pa. pple. *wêpin*, *-en*), OS. *wôpian* to bewail (pa. t. *weop*), OHG. *wuofan* to bewail, pa. t. *wiof* (MHG. *wuofen*, pa. t. *wief*), also OHG. *wuoffen*, pa. t. *wuofita* (MHG. *wüefen*, pa. t. *wüefte*), ON. *œpa* (pa. t. *œpta*) to scream, shout (whence ME. EPE *v.*), Goth. *wōpjan* to cry aloud, call; f. the OTeut. **wōpo-* represented in OE. *wóp* masc., weeping (see WOP), OS. *wôp* masc., lamentation, OHG., MHG. *wuof* masc., lamentation, ON. *óp* neut., cry. Outside Teut. no certain cognates are known.

The weak inflexion first appears in the 13th c., and became prevalent in the 14th.]

I. *intr.*

1. a. To manifest the combination of bodily symptoms (instinctive cries or moans, sobs, and shedding of tears) which is the natural, audible, and visible expression of painful (and sometimes of intensely pleasurable) emotion; also, and in mod. use chiefly, to shed tears (more or less silently).

In mod.English somewhat rare in non-literary use, being superseded by *cry*; recently a sense of the inappropriateness of that verb as applied to silent manifestations seems to have in some degree revived the colloquial currency of *weep* in the sense 'to shed tears'.

c **900** *Bæda's Hist.* III. xiv. (1890) 198 He ongon wepan hluttrum tearum. c **1000** *Ags. Gosp.* Matt. xxvi. 75 And he eode ut & weop [Vulg. *ploravit*] bityrlice. c **1175** *Lamb. Hom.* 43 Nu bi-gon paul to wepen wunderliche, and mihhal heh engel þer weop forð mid him. c **1205** LAY. 6650 Þer Elidur þe king weop [c **1275** wep] mid his eȝenen. *Ibid.* 18895 þæ æremite gon to weopen. **1297** R. GLOUC. 6924 Þe quene wepinde [*v.r.* wepude] wel sore, þe king ansuerede þis. a **1300** *Cursor M.* 14023 Þis womman [Mary Magdalene] wepand on his fete. **1340** *Ayenb.* 93 Ne þet ne is naȝt lyf of man ac of child þet nou wepþ nou lheȝþ. **138.** WYCLIF *Serm.* Sel. Wks. II. 249 Þei shulden..wipe wiþ men þat wepen here. c **1386** CHAUCER *Prol.* 144 She was..so pitous She wolde wepe if that she saugh a Mous Kaught in a trappe, if it were deed or bledde. c **1425** *Seven Sag.* (P.) 570 Scho wippe and hir hondis wronge. c **1450** *Merlin* ii. 30 And a-noon this othir [child] began to crye and wape. **1570** *Satir. Poems Reform.* xiii. 150 The tyme sall cum that he sall weip and murne. **1604** SHAKS. *Oth.* IV. i. 143 She..So hangs, and lolls, and weepes vpon me. **1610** —— *Temp.* III. i. 74, I am a foole To weepe at what I am glad of. **1667** MILTON *P.L.* XI. 495 Sight so deform what heart of Rock could long Drie-ey'd behold? Adam could not, but wept. **1700** DRYDEN *Sigism. & G.* 578 Away, with Women weep, and leave me here, Fix'd, like a Man to die, without a Tear. **1782** MISS BURNEY *Cecilia* IV. i, Mrs. Harrel..had shut herself up in her own room to weep and lament. **1850** TENNYSON *In Mem.* XXX. v, 'They rest', we said,..And silence follow'd, and we wept. **1860** TYNDALL *Glac.* I. xxv. 191, I could have wept like a child.

b. said of animals.

c **1400** MAUNDEV. (1919) xxxii. 192 Þeise serpentes [*sc.* crocodiles] slen men & þei eten hem wepynge. **1602** SHAKS. *Ham.* III. ii. 282 Let the strucken Deere go weepe. **1612** WEBSTER *White Divel* D 3, Here is a Stag my Lord hath shed his hornes, And for the losse of them the poore beast weepes. **1872** DARWIN *Emotions* vi. 167 The Indian elephant is known sometimes to weep. **1875** JOWETT *Plato* (ed. 2) V. 361 Man..is..affected with the inclination to weep more than any other animal.

c. Const. *for*, *over*, †*on* (a person or thing regretted or commiserated).

a **900** *O.E. Martyrol.* 30 July 132 Þa weop eall Romana dugoð for þære dæde. c **950** *Lindisf. Gosp.* Luke xxiii. 28 Nallað ȝie woepa ofer mec [Vulg. *super me*] ah ofer iuh seolfo woepað. c **1175** *Lamb. Hom.* 157 He iseh Martham and Mariam Magdalene þe sustren wepe for hore broðer deð. a **1225** *Ancr. R.* 312 He weop oðe rode, & o Lazre, & o Jerusalem. c **1250** *Gen. & Ex.* 4149, .xxx. daiȝes wep israel for his dead. a **1300** *Cursor M.* 1799 For þar misdedes wepe þai þan. c **1374** CHAUCER *Boeth.* II. pr. ii. (1868) 35 Paulus.. whan he hadde take þe kyng of perciens weep pitously for þe captiuitee of þe self kyng. **1382** WYCLIF *Luke* xix. 41 He seynge the citee, wepte on it [Vulg. *flevit super illam*]. a **1450** *Mirk's Festial* 32 Þen for Ion segh mony wepe for hyr, Ion sayde to hyr: Drusyan, ryse vp. **1549** *Compl. Scot.* ii. 25 The prophet hieremye vepit for the stait of the public veil of babillone. **1593** SHAKS. *Rich. II*, V. i. 87 Weepe thou for me in France; I, for thee heere. **1601** —— *All's Well* I. i. 3 And I in going Madam, weep ore my fathers death anew. **1623** COCKERAM III. s.v. *Crocodile*, Hauing eaten the body of a man, it [*sc.* a crocodile] will weepe ouer the head, but in fine eate the head also. **1711** ADDISON *Spect.* No. 70 ¶8 Instead of weeping over the Wound she had received, as one might have expected from a Warrior of her Sex. **1803** M. G. LEWIS *Sir Agilthorne* iv, They who can weep for others' woes, Should ne'er have cause to weep their own. **1827** CARLYLE *Ess., Richter* (1840) I. 29 Like him we have long laughed at them or wept for them. **1833** TENNYSON *Two Voices* 149 In some good cause..To perish, wept for, honour'd, known. **1855** —— *Maud* I. VIII, An angel watching an urn Wept over her, carved in stone. **1853** DICKENS *Bleak Ho.* lv, I knew by that time..how you had mourned for me, and wept for me.

d. Const. *for* (the emotion that prompts weeping). Similarly with *to* and inf., or a *that*-clause.

1297 R. GLOUC. (Rolls) 6954 Þe bissopes þat hir ladde vor ioye wepe al so. a **1352** MINOT *Poems* xi. 12 For wo will he wepe. **1375** BARBOUR *Bruce* xx. 237 Thar wes nane in that Cumpany That thai ne wepit for pite. c **1420** *Anturs of Arthur* 560 (Douce MS.) Thus wepus for wo Wowayne þe wighte. **1591** SHAKS. *Two Gent.* II. iii. 12 A Iew would haue wept to haue seene our parting. **1593** —— *2 Hen. VI*, III. ii. 121 Henry weepes, that thou dost liue so long. **1593** —— *Rich. II*, III. ii. 4, I weepe for ioy To stand vpon my Kingdome once againe. **1648** HERRICK *Hesper.*, *To Daffadills* 1 Faire Daffadills, we weep to see You haste away so soone. 1667 MILTON *P.L.* IX. 991 So saying, she embrac'd him, and for joy Tenderly wept. 1784 COWPER *Task* VI. 700 Maidens wave Their 'kerchiefs, and old women weep for joy. *a*1806 H. K. WHITE *Solitude* vi, I start, and when the vision's flown, I weep that I am all alone. 1865 SWINBURNE *Chastelard* III. i. 104, I have wept for wrath Sometimes and for mere pain, but for love's pity I cannot weep at all.

e. To call †*on*, cry or pray *to* with weeping. *rare*.

1297 R. GLOUC. (Rolls) 7822 He wep on god vaste ynou & criede him milce & ore. *c*1460 *Merita Missæ* 105 in *Lay Folks Mass Bk.* 151 And how he dide for the weop To his fader on olywete. 1560 BIBLE (Geneva) *Num.* xi. 13 For they wepe vnto me, saying, Giue vs flesh that we may eat. 1845 MRS. NORTON *Child of Islands* (1846) 43 Then sweet St. Mary stands in her recess, Worshipped and wept to, as a thing divine.

f. Phr. *to weep one's fill* or *bellyful*.

*a*1290 *S. Eustace* 193 in Horstm. *Altengl. Leg.* (1881) 215 Ich habbe I-wopen al mine fille. 1548 UDALL, etc. *Erasm. Par. John* xi. 28–31 They folowed hir: suspectyng that..she woulde haue gooen to the graue, and there to wepe hir belly full. 1593 SHAKS. *3 Hen. VI*, II. v. 113 Ile beare thee hence, where I may weepe my fill.

g. Proverbial expressions.

1546 J. HEYWOOD *Prov.* I. xi. (1867) 28 Naie good childe, better children weepe then olde men. 1616 T. DRAKE *Bibl. Scholast.* 23 It is better that children weepe, then old men. [1603 SHAKS. *Meas. for M.* II. ii. 122 But man..Plaies such phantastique tricks before high heauen, As makes the Angels weepe.] 1859 H. KINGSLEY *G. Hamlyn* xliii, To see a young fellow like that..only ripe for the gallows at five-and-twenty, is enough to make the angels weep. 1889 'J. S. WINTER' *Mrs. Bob* xii, Ye Gods! it is a sight to make the angels weep.

2. Phrases. †*to weep Irish*: to weep unfeelingly, as a professional mourner weeps at an Irish wake. *to weep with* (or *over*) *an onion*: fig. to weep with feigned grief.

1586 STANYHURST *Descr. Irel.* viii. 44/2 in *Holinshed*, They follow the dead corpse to the graue with howling and barbarous outcries, pitifull in apparance: whereof grew, as I suppose, the prouerbe: To weepe Irish [orig. *Hibernice lacrimari*]. 1589 *Pappe w. Hatchet* D iv b, Ile make thee to forget Bishops English, and weep Irish. 1650 FULLER *Pisgah* II. xii. §15. 247 Surely the Egyptians did not weep-Irish with faigned and mercenary teares. 1681 W. ROBERTSON *Phraseol. Gen.* (1693) 1305 To weep Irish, or to feign sorrow.

[1601 SHAKS. *All's Well* v. iii. 321 Mine eyes smell Onions, I shall weepe anon.] 1616 *Withals' Dict.* 557 *Flere ad nouercæ tumulum*, to weepe with an Onion. 1882 T. G. BOWLES *Flotsam & Jetsam* 144 Here again is..the Vicomte weeping ruefully over the strongest onion that ever man sliced.

3. a. Of the eyes: To shed tears.

1567 *Gude & Godlie B.* (S.T.S.) 16 And wowis vaine, quhilk thay did neuer keip, Sall gar thame gnasche thair teith, & eyis weip. 1588 SHAKS. *Tit. A.* III. i. 59 (Qo. 1600) Titus, prepare thy aged eyes to weepe. 1780 COWPER *Boadicea* iii, Princess! if our aged eyes Weep upon thy matchless wrongs, 'Tis because [etc.]. 1810 SCOTT *Lady of L.* II. xxii, 'Twas an hero's eye that weep'd. 1848 THACKERAY *Van. Fair* viii, Her eyes are always weeping for the loss of her beauty. 1871 R. ELLIS tr. *Catullus* lxi. 85 Her innocent Eyes do weep to be going.

b. *fig.* of the heart. (Cf. 6 b.)

13.. *Adam Davy's Five Dreams* 64 Myne herte wop for grete drede. 1550 CROWLEY *Epigr.* 163 The other sorte..Do make my harte wepe whan they come to my mind. 1613 SHAKS. *Hen. VIII*, III. ii. 335 My heart weepes to see him So little, of his great Selfe. 1796 *Let. to Cowper* in *Jrnl. Friends Hist. Soc.* (1918) 32 My heart wept for thee..with the tenderest solicitude for thy welfare.

4. *transf.* **a.** Of things: To shed water or moisture in drops; to exude drops of water. Also, to waste *away* in drops.

1387 TREVISA *Higden* IV. 3 The preost.. seide þat þere come nevere reyn..; but the trees hadde i-wope in þe eclipses of þe sonne and of þe moone. *c*1400 MAUNDEV. (1839) vii. 78 And there besyde ben 4 Pileres of Ston, that alle weys droppen Watre: and sum men seyn, that thei wepen for our Lordes Dethe. *c*1440 *Pallad. on Husb.* IX. 75 Clayes wepe Vncerteynly, whos teres beth right swete. 1570 *Satir. Poems Reform.* xv. 1 ȝe Montaines, murne; ȝe valayis, vepe. 1603 G. OWEN *Pembrokesh.* (1891) 78 In these buildinges you shall finde..all the walles of the house to be all weapinge and covered with streames of water. 1607 SHAKS. *Timon* II. ii. 168 When all our Offices haue beene opprest With riotous Feeders, when our Vaults haue wept With drunken spilth of Wine. 1698 FRYER *Acc. E. India & P.* 126, I saw..Women..waiting the distilling of Water from its [the tank's] dewy sides; which they catch in Jarrs, and..carrying it away, leave it only weeping. *a*1722 LISLE *Husb.* (1757) 23 If you lay dung on a sandy or rocky ground ..it will be weeping away. 1732 P. MILLER *Gard. Kalendar* (1762) 280 Where..resinous trees..require some of their branches to be cut off, this is the best season..for now they are not so subject to weep. 1810 SCOTT *Lady of L.* I. xxxv, The birch-trees wept in fragrant balm. 1854 J. S. C. ABBOTT *Napoleon* (1855) II. xxvii. 501 The sky ceased to weep, and the vail of clouds was withdrawn. 1909 *Engl. Rev.* Mar. 617 Within the forest nought weeps save the rain.

b. To issue in drops; to trickle or fall as tears. Also with *out*.

1596 SHAKS. *2 Hen. IV*, IV. iv. 58 The blood weepes from my heart, when I doe shape [etc.]. 1739 [S. BERINGTON] *G. De Lucca's Mem.* (1738) 173 Gold..comes oftentimes in great lumps from the Mineral Rocks, as if it wept out from between the joints. 1828 SPEARMAN *Brit. Gunner* 340 The water will continue to weep or run from the holes. 1884 *Manch. Exam.* 3 May 5/3 There would evidently have been some difficulty in keeping the tunnel clear of water, which 'wept' into the heading at the rate of 447 gallons a minute. *fig.* 1847 TENNYSON *Princess* VI. 251 Down thro' her limbs a drooping languor wept. 1872 —— *Gareth & Lynette* 213 Barefoot..The Lady of the Lake stood: all her dress Wept from her sides as water flowing away.

c. Of a boiler, etc.: To allow small drops of water to percolate or trickle through; to leak in drops from a joint or rivet.

1869 SIR E. REED *Shipbuild.* i. 11 Every rivet being tested not one of them was found to weep. 1869 *Daily News* 21 Aug., Nearly all new boilers 'weep' for the first few weeks. 1886 R. C. LESLIE *Sea Painter's Log* 31 He will admit, 'she veeps a trifle in her garboards'.

d. Of a sore, etc.: To exude a serous fluid.

1882 *W. Worc. Gloss., Weep*, to run as a sore does. 1899 *Allbutt's Syst. Med.* VII. 243 The fluid escapes just as any raw surface weeps. *Ibid.* VIII. 559 It [i.e. psoriasis] never weeps.

e. Of certain explosives: to exude liquid (indicative of a dangerous condition).

1972 *Guardian* 9 Feb. 6/8 The freighter Autolycus..was ordered to leave the harbour..after her cargo of nitro-glycerine was found to be 'weeping'. 1978 C. EGLETON *Mills Bomb* ix. 91 Gelignite... Dangerous? Only if they were handling jelly that was beginning to weep. 1982 *Times* 6 Jan. 7/7 Stirring the loyalists up was like..playing with jelly that had been weeping for two years.

5. To hang limply; to droop. Of a tree: To droop its branches. Cf. WEEPING *ppl. a.* 6.

1764 CHURCHILL *Gotham* I. 285 The Willow weeping o'er the fatal wave, Where many a Lover finds a watry grave. 1830 TENNYSON *Dying Swan* ii, One willow over the river wept. 1872 OLIVER *Elem. Bot.* II. 207 Young plants, raised from seeds of the Weeping Ash.., had a tendency to 'weep' in their first branching.

II. *trans.*

6. To shed tears over; to lament with tears.

*c*897 ÆLFRED *Gregory's Past. C.* x. 61 Ðæt ðætte oðre menn unaliefedes dot he sceal wepan sua sua his agne scylde. *c*1000 ÆLFRIC *Gen.* xxxvii. 34 He..weop his sunu lange tide. *a*1122 *O.E. Chron.* (Laud MS.) an. 1086 Oððe hwa is swa heard heort þæt ne mæg swylces unȝelimpes? *a*1300 *Cursor M.* 1357 Þi fader sin now wepes he. *c*1330 R. BRUNNE *Chron. Wace* (Rolls) 2928 Sche wepede weddyng, ..ffor scheo had loued longe byfore þe kyng of Denmark. 1387 TREVISA *Higden* VIII. 95 Þe monkes come unneþe at þe laste, whan þey had longe i-wope [*v.r.* ywept] þe wrong of her violent out puttynge. 1450–1530 *Myrr. Our Ladye* I. xii. 32 Many..by swetenes of the songe, ar styrred to wayle and to wepe theyr synnes. 1593 SHAKS. *2 Hen. VI*, III. i. 221 His fortunes I will weepe. 1603 B. JONSON *Sejanus* v. N 2, Now they 'gin to weepe The mischiefe they haue done. 1697 DRYDEN *Æneis* IX. 648 Nor was I near to close his dying Eyes, To wash his Wounds, to weep his Obsequies. *c*1726 SAVAGE *Epist. to Dyer* 54 My sympathizing breast his grief can feel, And my eye weep the wound I cannot heal. 1790 COWPER *Castaway* ix, No poet wept him: but the page Of narrative sincere..Is wet with Anson's tear. 1808 SCOTT *Marm.* v. xvi, A child will weep a bramble's smart. 1825 —— *Talism.* xvii, Edith, for whom he dies, will know how to weep his memory. 1847 TENNYSON *Princess* IV. 50 Nor is it Wiser to weep a true occasion lost. 1860 C. READE *Cloister & Hearth* lxxii. (1896) 209 The princess went barefoot to Loretto, weeping her crime and washing the feet of base born men.

fig. 1633 G. HERBERT *Temple, Vertue* i, Sweet day,..The dew shall weep thy fall to night, For thou must die.

7. a. To let fall from the eyes, to shed (tears).

The object is freq. expressed by a synonym, as *water, drop, brine*, or a hyperbolic term, as *flood, sea, rain*, etc. *to weep crocodile tears*: to feign grief (see CROCODILE *sb.* 2).

*c*1200 *Trin. Coll. Hom.* 65 Þat þridde þing..is wop þe we for ure synnes wepeð. *Ibid.* 149 Swiche teares wiep þe holie spuse uppen hire spus. 1362 LANGL. *P. Pl.* A. v. 44 Þenne Ron Repentaunce and Rehersed þis teeme, And made William to weope watur with his eȝen. *c*1374 CHAUCER *Troylus* I. 941 Sithen þat þow hast wopen [*v.r.* wepen] many a drope. 1588 SHAKS. *L.L.L.* IV. iii. 33 Thou shin'st in euery teare that I doe weepe. 1606 —— *Tr. & Cr.* III. ii. 84 When we vowe to weepe seas. 1612 *Two Noble K.* I. iii. 25 Women That have sod their Infants in..The brine, they wept at killing 'em. 1631 MILTON *Epit. March. Winchester* 56 Here be tears of perfect moan Weept for thee in Helicon. 1667 —— *P.L.* I. 620 Tears such as Angels weep, burst forth. 1781 COWPER *Hope* 519 The wretch..Has wept a silent flood, revers'd his ways, Is sober, [etc.]. 1819 KEATS *Lamia* II. 66 She..wept a rain Of sorrows at his words. 1853 MRS. GASKELL *Ruth* xxv, All tears had been wept out of her long ago. 1891 FARRAR *Darkn. & Dawn* xxix, The eyes of Nero had to weep crocodile tears.

b. *fig.* Of the heart, or a wound: *to weep (tears of) blood.*

1592 SHAKS. *Ven. & Ad.* 1054 His soft flanke, whose wonted lillie white With purple tears that his wound wept, was drencht. 1605 B. JONSON *Volpone* III. ii. (1607) F 4 b, My heart Weepes bloud, in anguish. 1613–16 W. BROWNE *Brit. Past.* I. iii. 49 His wound (yet sore) That grieu'd, it could weepe blood for him no more. ?*a*1634 ?CHAPMAN *Rev. for Hon.* IV. i. (1659) 48 My heart weeps tears of blood, to see thy age thus like a lofty pine fall. 1718 POPE *Iliad* XIII. 160 My heart weeps blood to see your glory lost!

†**c.** *to weep millstones*: cf. MILLSTONE 2 b.

1594 SHAKS. *Rich. III*, I. iv. 245 *Clarence.* Bid Glouster thinke on this, and he will weepe. *1st Murderer.* I Milstones, as he lessoned vs to weepe. [Cf. *Ibid.* I. iii. 354 Your eyes drop Mill-stones, when Fooles eyes fall Teares.]

d. To declare, express, utter with lamentation. Also with *forth*. *rare* (chiefly *poet.*).

1599 MARSTON *Ant. & Mel.* v. (1602) H 3, Ile weepe my passion to the senselesse trees. 1611 SHAKS. *Wint. T.* IV. iv. 559 Leontes opening his free Armes, and weeping His Welcomes forth. 1621 LADY M. WROTH *Urania* 347 Both chain'd togeather..complaining and weeping their sorrowes to those walles. 1782 MISS BURNEY *Cecilia* III. ii, The poor woman wept her thanks. 1790 COWPER *On Receipt Mother's Picture* 31, I..drew A long, long sigh, and wept a last adieu! 1847 TENNYSON *Princess* III. 14 'My fault' she wept 'my fault! and yet not mine'.

8. quasi-*trans.* with adv. or compl. **a.** in phrases expressing excessive or prolonged weeping; esp. *to weep out one's eyes* or *heart.*

*c*1290 *St. Lawrence* 40 in *S. Eng. Leg.* 341 That hadde so much i-wope That he weop out both is eiyene. 1601 SHAKS. *Jul. C.* IV. iii. 99 O I could weepe My Spirit from mine eyes. 1630 *Pathomachia* v. iv. 44, I haue wept out mine Eyes for Griefe, I cannot read. 1688 PRIOR *Ode Exod. iii. 14* viii, Weep out thy Reason's, and thy Body's Eyes. 1887 F. M. CRAWFORD *Saracinesca* vi, It seemed unspeakably pathetic to hear her weeping her heart out.

b. To bring (oneself, another, etc., into a specified state or condition) by weeping. Const. *into, to*, or with adj. complement.

1591 SHAKS. *Two Gent.* II. iii. 14 Why my Grandam hauing no eyes, looke you, wept her selfe blinde at my parting. 1605 —— *Macb.* IV. iii. 2 Let vs seeke out some desolate shade, and there Weepe our sad bosomes empty. 1643 TRAPP *Comm. Gen.* l. 1 'And Joseph fell upon his fathers face' as willing to have wept him alive again, if possible. 1647 R. STAPYLTON *Juvenal* 108 Weeping her selfe into a stone fountaine. 1818 SHELLEY *Rosalind & Helen* 363 But now—'twas the season fair and mild When April has wept itself into May. 1847 TENNYSON *Princess* IV. 116 She wept her true eyes blind for such a one. 1891 *Temple Bar* Dec. 600 Phil wept herself to sleep in her sister's arms.

c. with advs. *to weep* (a thing) *back*: to recover it by weeping. *to weep out*: to remove, put out, extinguish, by weeping; also, to expend (one's life) in weeping. *to weep down*: to weep until the setting of (the sun).

1593 SHAKS. *Rich. II*, v. i. 48 The sencelesse Brands will sympathize The heauie accent of thy mouing Tongue, And in compassion weepe the fire out. 1595 —— *John* IV. iii. 105, I lou'd him, and will weepe My date of life out, for his sweete liues losse. 1606 —— *Ant. & Cl.* II. vi. 111 *Men.* Pompey doth this day laugh away his Fortune. *Enob.* If he do, sure he cannot weep't backe againe. 1606 CHAPMAN *Mons. D'Olive* I. i, He like a mortified hermit clad, Sits weeping out his life. 1681 FLAVEL *Meth. Grace* xxvi. 453 As it is with the eye when any thing offends it, it cannot leave twinkling and watering till it have wept it out. 1726 POPE *Odyss.* XXI. 240 Thus had their joy wept down the setting Sun.

d. esp. *to weep away*: (*a*) to spend, consume in tears and lamentation; (*b*) to remove or wash *away* with tears of commiseration. (Said also of the tears.)

(*a*) 1590 SHAKS. *Com. Err.* II. i. 115 Since that my beautie cannot please his eie, Ile weepe (what's left away) and weeping die. 1599 MARSTON *Antonio's Rev.* v. vi, Ile weepe away my braine In true affections teares. 1705 ADDISON *Italy* 2 Mary Magdalene..is said to have wept away the rest of her Life among these solitary Rocks. 1859 TENNYSON *Vivien* 734 Nothing left But into some low cave to crawl, and there..weep my life away.

(*b*) 1762 STERNE *Tr. Shandy* v. iii, My father managed his affliction otherwise;..he neither wept it away, as the Hebrews and the Romans—or slept it off. 1823 PRAED *Australasia* 262 And the mild Charity which day by day Weeps every wound and every stain away.

9. To shed (moisture or water) in drops; to exude (a liquid, etc.). Also *to weep forth*.

1634 SIR T. HERBERT *Trav.* 47 Ormus Iland, has no fresh water, saue what the fruitfull Cloudes weepe ouer her, in sorrow of her desolation. 1651 BIGGS *New Disp.* ⁋79 Celandin weepeth a golden juice. 1667 MILTON *P.L.* IV. 248 Groves whose rich Trees wept odorous Gumms and Balme. *Ibid.* IX. 1003 Skie lowr'd, and muttering Thunder, som sad drops Wept at compleating of the mortal Sin. 1669 W. SIMPSON *Hydrol. Chym.* 328 Cut a vine in January..you shall find it weep forth a deal of insipid water. 1697 DRYDEN *Virg. Past.* IV. 35 The Knotted Oaks shall show'rs of Honey weep. 1705 POPE *Spring* 62 And trees weep amber on the banks of Po. 1810 SCOTT *Lady of L.* III. ix, Forgetful that its branches grew Where weep the heavens their holiest dew On Alpine's dwelling low. 1860 TENNYSON *Tithonus* 2 The vapours weep their burthen to the ground. 1870 *Edinb. Med. Jrnl.* Dec. 514 The surface of the..integument had been weeping a bloody sanies for three days.

weep, obs. var. WYPE *dial.*, lapwing.

†**'weepable**, *a. Obs. rare.* [f. WEEP *v.* + -ABLE.] Deplorable, lamentable.

*c*1449 PECOCK *Repr.* I. xvi. 86 Bi this now seid cause bifille the rewful and wepeable destruccion of the worthi citee and vniuersite of Prage. *c*1456 —— *Bk. Faith* Prol. (1909) 110 For which so bireweable and wepeable perel whiche the clergie may se in the lay party, which ouȝte [etc.].

weepe, obs. form of WIPE *v.*

weepentack, obs. f. WAPENTAKE.

1676 in *Trans. Cumb. & Westmorld. Antiq. Soc.* (N.S.) XX. 247.

weeper ('wiːpə(r)). [f. WEEP *v.* + -ER[1].]

1. a. One who weeps or sheds tears, *esp.* one who is constantly weeping; also one who has tears at command.

*c*1380 *Antecrist* in Todd *Three Treat. Wyclif* (1851) 142 Crist chese to him wepers; & þei chesen to hem myrye syngers. 1382 WYCLIF *Judg.* ii. 5 The name of that place [Bochim] is clepid, of wepers, or of terys. [Similarly in 1611 *marg.*] *a*1400 *Prymer* (1891) 46 Seynte marie..do fauour to weperes. 1597 SHAKS. *Lover's Compl.* 124 To make the weeper laugh, the laugher weepe. 1646 CRASHAW *Steps to Temple* 1 The Weeper. 1693 DRYDEN *Juvenal* x. 46 Laughter is easie; but the Wonder lies, What stores of Brine supplyd the Weepers Eyes. 1735 CRAIG tr. *Veda's Past.* i. (1736) 167 Thus, while he sigh'd and dropt a tender Tear, The Hiefers..Nor Crystal Brooks, nor sprouting Grass regard, So much they in the Weeper's Sorrow shar'd. 1825 T. HOOK *Sayings* Ser. II. *Passion & Princ.* xi. III. 230 My first wife was a weeper, Ma'am; and I *did* hope to have escaped a second. However, it seems you are come of a crying family. 1842 C. WHITEHEAD *R. Savage* xii, Had I been at any time of my life a weeper and wailer. 1874 L. STEPHEN *Hours in Libr.* (1892) II. vii. 212 Cowper's tears..

never..suggest that the weeper is proud of his excessive tenderness.

b. *spec.* A hired mourner at a death-bed or funeral.

1412–20 LYDG. *Troy Bk.* IV. 3062 It neded hem no wepers for to here,—þei hadde I-nowe of her owne stoor. *c* **1485** *Digby Myst.* III. 835 With wepers to þe erth yow hym bryng. **1634** W. TIRWHYT tr. *Balzac's Lett.* I. 386 At funerals in Paris, weepers are usually hired for money. **1714** SWIFT *Poems, In Sickness* 23 Ye formal Weepers for the Sick. **1824** MORIER *Adv. Hajji Baba* xxv, Leilah, who is a professed weeper at burials. **1895** PETRIE *Egypt. Tales* Ser. I. 115 The weepers crouching at the door of thy tomb shall cry aloud the prayers for offerings.

c. One of a number of little images in niches on a funeral monument, representing mourners.

1656 DUGDALE *Antiq. Warw.* 354, xiv Images embossed, of Lords and Ladyes in divers vestures, called Weepers, to stand in housings made about the Tombe. **1790** PENNANT *Lond.* 64 The sides [of the tombs] are..embellished..with figures of mourners, *pleureurs*, or weepers, frequently in monastic habits. **1864** BOUTELL *Her. Hist. & Pop.* xxiii. (ed. 3) 388 Eight compartments, each of them having a canopied effigy or 'weeper'. **1912** J. S. M. WARD *Brasses* 85 A magnificent canopy with figures either of saints or of 'weepers' in niches.

d. *Ch. Hist.* One of the lowest class of penitents (προσκλαίοντες, *flentes*) in the early Eastern Church.

1841 *Gentl. Mag.* Aug. 152/2 That abject class of penitents, mentioned in ancient ecclesiastical canons as mourners, kneelers, and weepers,..who, covered with sackcloth and ashes, were enjoined to perform penance in the open air. **1885** *Encycl. Brit.* XVIII. 486/1.

2. The Capuchin monkey (*Cebus capucinus*) of South America. Also ***weeper sai, capuchin, monkey***. Cf. F. *singe pleureur* and BEWAILER 2.

1781 SMELLIE *Buffon's Nat. Hist.* (1791) VIII. 174 The sai, which some travellers have called the weeper, is somewhat larger than the sajou. **1781** PENNANT *Hist. Quad.* I. 204 Weeper monkey. **1821** HELEN M. WILLIAMS tr. *Humboldts Trav.* V. 532 Those bearded monkeys called *capuchins*, which must not be confounded with the weeper or sai. **1841** *Penny Cycl.* XX. 417/1 One of the most common species is the Weeper (*Cebus Apella*). **1894** H. O. FORBES *Handbk. Primates* I. 216 When sleeping the Weeper Çai curls itself up, covering its face with its arms and tail.

3. A conventional badge of mourning. Usually *pl.* **a.** A strip of white linen or muslin formerly worn on the cuff of a man's sleeve. Cf. F. *pleureuse*.

1724 *Lond. Gaz.* No. 6255/2 All..being enjoyned to appear..in long black Cloaks, Cambrick Bands, Chamoy Shoes, Weepers, &c. **1746** H. WALPOLE *Let. to Mann* 1 Aug., I..was assisted by the sight of the Marquis of Lothian in weepers for his son who fell at Culloden. **1760–2** GOLDSM. *Cit. W.* xcvi, Our merry mourners clap bits of muslin on their sleeves, and these are called *weepers*. **1827** HOOD *True Story* 115 There comes some unexpected stroke And hangs a weeper on the cuff. **1892** D. FRASER *Autob.* ii. 4 Our cuffs were covered with white linen 'weepers'.

b. A broad white cuff worn by widows.

1755 in W. Macgill *Old Ross-sh.* (1909) 148 Making 6 shirts..6 suit double mobs—6 lawn hoods—6 pair weepers. **1786** BURNS *On a Scotch Bard* 25 Auld, cantie Kyle may weepers wear, An' stain them wi' the saut, saut tear. **1811** *Sporting Mag.* XXXVIII. 47 With weepers she has tipped her sleeve The while she's laughing in it. **1843** THACKERAY *Bluebeard's Ghost* in *Fraser's Mag.* Oct. 413/1 She [the widow] had her beautiful hair confined in crimped caps, and her weepers came over her elbows. **1889** 'J. S. WINTER' *Mrs. Bob* xix, Mrs. Antrobus..wore very deep and very wide weepers.

c. A long black hat-band formerly worn by men.

1832 STANDISH *Maid of Jaen* 40 The plumes broad floating in the air, And weepers which the followers bear. **1834** MARRYAT *P. Simple* xli, My father..tore off the crape weepers, and then threw them on the floor as he walked away. **1898** BESANT *Orange Girl* I. vi, The undertaker..was ..tying the weepers on the hats.

d. The long black crape veil of a widow.

1860 GEO. ELIOT *Mill on Fl.* I. xii, He might cherish the mean project of heightening her grief at his death by leaving her poorly off, in which case she was firmly resolved that she would have scarcely any weeper on her bonnet. **1872** —— *Middlem.* lxxx, If anybody was to marry me, flattering himself as I should wear those hijeous weepers..for him.

e. *transf.* A streamer of moss hanging from a tree.

1857 B. TAYLOR *Northern Trav.* xiv. (1858) 144 The firs were hung with weepers of black-green moss.

4. Usually *pl.* Long flowing side-whiskers as worn by 'Lord Dundreary' (E. A. Sothern) in the play 'Our American Cousin'. So ***Dundreary*** (or ***Piccadilly***) ***weepers***.

1894 DU MAURIER *Trilby* I. (1912) 4 He wore an immense pair of drooping auburn whiskers, of the kind that used to be called Piccadilly weepers. **1903** *Athenæum* 13 June 760/3 A mid-Victorian Englishman with 'Dundreary weepers'. **1908** *Sat. Rev.* 20 June 775/2 Sir James Day was..adorned with the 'weeper'—a form of whisker..at one time a popular forensic compromise between the bare face and the full beard.

5. A hole or pipe in a wall for the escape of dripping water. (Cf. *weep-hole* in WEEP *sb.* 3.)

1890 *N.Y. Tribune* 2 Feb. (Cent.) The eyes with which it [*sc.* the aqueduct tunnel] weeps are rightly called weepers, being small rectangular openings in the side walls, through which all the water collected and collecting on the outside of the masonry pours into the inside. **1893** G. D. LESLIE *Lett. Marco* xxxvii. 255 A drain-pipe, or what builders term a weeper... The weepers in it are to allow the water from the bank behind it to escape.

6. = WEEPIE. *colloq.*

1934 'N. BELL' *Winding Road* xvii. 445 A few hot-eared scribes have written weepers about such things and kidded themselves they'd done the trick. **1949** M. LASKI in *Sketch* 21 Dec. 551/2 Every magazine..reckons to print at least one weeper every Christmas. **1977** *New Yorker* 8 Aug. 10/1 Irene Dunn does the suffering in this version of the Fannie Hurst classic weeper about a woman who loves a selfish married man. **1984** *Miami Herald* 30 Mar. 7D/4 We have been hearing that romance is making a comeback in the movies, and here it is: the old-fashioned, meet-ya-when-this-war-is-over weeper.

Hence **'weepered** *a.*, furnished with weepers.

1908 EDITH SOMERVILLE & 'ROSS' *Further Exp. Irish R.M.* ii. 54 John Cullinane, very dusty, and waving a crushed and weepered hat.

† **'weepful,** *a. Obs. rare.* [f. WEEP *sb.* + -FUL.] Full of weeping, mournful.

1382 WYCLIF *Wisd.* xviii. 10 And wepful weiling [L. *flebilis planctus*] of bewepte ȝunge childer was herd. [**1860** in WORCESTER (citing *Wickliffe*), and in later Dicts.]

weepie ('wi:pɪ). *colloq.* Also **weepy.** [f. WEEP *v.* + -IE; cf. TALKIE, etc.] A sentimental film, story, play, etc.; a 'tear-jerker'.

1928 *Sunday Dispatch* 23 Dec. 12/2 There are undoubtedly times when a film calculated to raise buckets of tears has its appeal. Someone recently christened this type of picture..a 'weepie'. **1948** *Sunday Pictorial* 18 July 11/4 'If Winter Comes' (Empire) is a re-make of the famous weepie novel. **1958** *Spectator* 18 July 85/3 *Chicken Soup with Barley*..is an East End Jewish weepie. **1962** *Times* 14 May 14/1 An all-out weepy is the only possible description for *Girl in a Birdcage*. **1977** D. FRANCIS *Risk* xvi. 207 How much easier if the miscreant would confess..a sentimental solution..which happened only in weepie films. **1984** *Listener* 5 July 35/1 'Weepies' come in all shapes and sizes. Ostensibly they are women's pictures, because only women cry at them, right?

weeping ('wi:pɪŋ), *vbl. sb.* [f. WEEP *v.* + -ING[1].] The action of the verb in the various senses; an instance of this.

1. The expression or manifestation of sorrow, pain, etc. by shedding tears.

c **1200** *Trin. Coll. Hom.* 53 We muȝen michel eðere forðen wepinge þene song. *c* **1275** LAY. 5970 Mochel was þar wepinge. *c* **1369** CHAUCER *Dethe Blaunche* 600 My sorowe is turned to playnyng And al my laughter to wepyng. *c* **1450** *Mirour Saluacioun* (Roxb.) 158 Flodes..of trewest sorow and wepyng. **1561** HOBY tr. *Castiglione's Courtier* I. Dij, The great Alexander, hearing a certayne Philosophers oppinion to be that there were infinite worldes, fell in weping. **1573** BEDINGFIELD tr. *Cardanus' Conf.* II. (1576) 16 b, The wepyng of yᵉ heire is the weepynge of one that laugheth vnder a vizar. **1633** P. FLETCHER *Ps.* cxxxvii. 5 There we laid asteeping Our eyes in endlesse weeping For Sions fall. **1651** HOBBES *Leviath.* I. vi. 27 Sudden Dejection is the passion that causeth Weeping. **1711** STEELE *Spect.* No. 95 ¶3 There is nothing, on these Occasions, so much in their Favour as immoderate Weeping. **1808** SCOTT *Marm.* v. xxxii, Weeping and wailing loud arose. **1881** BESANT & RICE *Chapl. Fleet* I. i, So must this book begin with tears and weeping. **1896** H. G. WELLS *Wheels of Chance* xix, Such weeping as he had seen before had been so much a matter of damp white faces, red noses, and hair coming out of curl.

b. With *a* and *pl.*

1297 R. GLOUC. (Rolls) 4180 He hurde..Of a womman a deoluol cry & a pitos wepinge. *c* **1374** CHAUCER *Boeth.* I. pr. ii. (1868) 9 And wiþ þe lappe of hir garment..she driede myn eyen þat were ful of þe wawes of my wepynges. *c* **1420** *Prymer* (1895) 52 [Ps. cxvi. 8] He haþ delyuerid..myn iȝen fro wepingis. **1523** BERNERS *Froiss.* (1812) I. ccexxvi. 683 Euery day encreased the complayntes, wepynges, and cryes, made to Phylyp Dartuell. **1630** MILTON *Passion* 51 Should I..Take up a weeping on the Mountains wilde. **1777** THICKNESSE *Journ. France* (1789) II. 51 You seem to hear the groans, weepings, and bewailings, from the dying. **1889** 'J. S. WINTER' *Mrs. Bob* xx, And then what a weeping and a wailing there was!

2. The exudation or dripping of moisture generally; the flow or discharge of humours from the body, of gum, etc. from a tree; also the liquid so falling. Also *fig.* the produce (of the vine).

a **1655** G. S. in Hartlib *Ref. Commw. Bees* 29 The Bees gather out of the weepings of Pine..Trees..abundance, both of Honey and Wax. **1699** W. SALMON *Pharm. Bateana* (1713) 654 They are good against a Gonorrhæa, Whites, Gleets, Weepings, &c. **1730** *Phil. Trans.* XXXVI. 453 The mucous Particles and Steams arising from the Lungs, made a constant weeping of a thin slavery Liquor from the Mouth of the Pipe. **1744** BERKELEY *Siris* §28 The weepings of the lentiscus and cypress. **1817** MOORE *Lalla Rookh, Veiled Prophet* 499 Vases, filled with Kishmee's golden wine, And the red weepings of the Shiraz vine. **1877** A. W. BENNETT tr. *Thomé's Bot.* 48 A process on which depends, for example, the 'weeping' of wounded grape-vines. **1889** WELCH *Naval Archit.* x. 118 Any weeping of the rivets or caulking which results, is rectified.

3. The drooping or downward sweep (of hair).

1869 BLACKMORE *Lorna D.* viii, The dark soft weeping of her hair.

4. *attrib.* and *Comb.*, as ***weeping-match, -scene***; † **weeping-dale** = 'vale of tears' (VALE *sb.*[1] 2 b); **weeping-hole**, an opening through which moisture percolates; **weeping-ripe** *a.*, ready to weep; † **weeping-room**, opportunity for weeping; † **weeping-spot**, a spot or stain where a tear has fallen; **weeping-time, -while**, a time when one weeps or may weep.

c **1400** *Pety Job* 410 in *26 Pol. Poems* 134 In thys wofull *wepyng dale, I byde alwey. **1866** *Chamb. Encycl.* VIII. 217/2 Holes are left through the wall called '*weeping-holes'. **1903** C. BALD *Indian Tea* vii. (1917) 97 It is imperatively necessary to have weeping holes, to carry off any water which may get behind the building. **1856** KANE *Arctic Expl.* II. xi. 117 They often assemble by concert for a general *weeping-match. **1548** *Elyot's Dict.*, *Lachrymabundus*,..*weepyng rype. **1588** SHAKS. *L.L.L.* v. ii. 274 The King was weeping ripe for a good word. **1593** —— *3 Hen. VI*, I. iv. 172. *a* **1614** FLETCHER *Valentinian* I. iii, Then as Souldiers..they tell their wounds Even weeping ripe they were no more nor deeper. **1648** HERRICK *Hesper.*, *Pastorall to King* 7 Behold him weeping ripe. **1611** CHAPMAN *Iliad* XXIV. 554 Ilion Shall finde thee *weeping roomes enow. **1809** A. HENRY *Trav.* 285 Had I not previously been witness to a *weeping-scene of this description, I should certainly have been apprehensive of some disastrous catastrophe. *c* **1430** *Syr Gener.* (Roxb.) 2370 The *weping spottes in no wise Thei coude with noo craft gete a-way While thei had wesh it so many a day. *c* **1400** LOVE *Bonavent. Mirr.* (1907) 191 And of thise three *wepynge tymes spekeþ holy writte. **1893** F. THOMPSON *Poems* 71 Smile, sweet baby, smile, For you will have *weeping-while.

† **b.** *Anat.*, as ***weeping corner*** (of the eye); ***weeping-flesh***, the lachrymal caruncle; ***weeping vein***, the ophthalmic vein. *Obs.*

to ope the weeping vein: to cause weeping. *poet.*

1543 TRAHERON *Vigo's Chirurg.* II. IV. 257 b, In the weping corners of the eyes, there groweth a fistula [etc.]. **1616** CHAPMAN *Odyss.* x. 519, I granted, went, and op't the weeping veine In all my men. **1639** T. DE GREY *Compl. Horsem.* II. i. (1656) 65 The *Veines* which we do usuallie open, are; First the two *Temple-Veines*... Secondlie, we open the two *Eye* or *weeping-Veines*. *Ibid.* II. xv. 494 First let him bloud in the neck and weeping veines. **1656** J. SMITH *Pract. Physick* 120 A Haw in the Eye..is discerned from the weeping flesh, because the roots of the Nail ever inclineth most to whitenesse. *Ibid.* 345 An Ulcer of the weeping flesh, namely an Ægylops.

weeping ('wi:pɪŋ), *ppl. a.* [f. WEEP *v.* + -ING[2].]

1. a. That weeps. Said of persons, also of the eyes.

c **1000** ÆLFRIC *Josh.* vi. 21 Hi ofslogon..ða wepende cild. **1297** R. GLOUC. (Rolls) 6938 þe quene was þo vorþ ilad mid moni a wepinde eye Of bissopes & of heyemen. *c* **1425** *Cursor M.* 14023 (Trin.) Were þis mon prophete so good þis wepynge wommon [*Earlier texts* þis womman wepand] on him wood He auȝte to witen what she were. **1450–1530** *Myrr. Our Ladye* II. 233 The gretnes of godhed was mekely hyd in the lytel body of a weping chylde. **1554** *Bury Wills* (Camden) 145, I bequeath to my nece Mary Gifford..my ringe with the wepinge eie. **1575** GASCOIGNE *Flowers, Mask Mountacute* 164 That so he might be shewed..Unto us all, whose weeping eyes dyd much abhorre the sight. **1596** SHAKS. *Merch. V.* I. ii. 53, I feare hee will proue the weeping Phylosopher when he growes old, being so full of vnmannerly sadnesse in his youth. **1617** R. WHITE *Cupid's Banishm.* in Nichols *Progr. Jas. I* (1828) III. 293 The Weeping Drunkard next. **1667** DRYDEN *Ind. Emp.* IV. iv, *Cyd.* More cruel than the Tyger o're his spoil; And falser than the Weeping Crocodile. **1697** —— *Æneis* v. 797 Turning to the Sea their weeping Eyes. **1706** ROWE *Ulysses* IV. i, Sadly attentive to the weeping Queen. **1711** STEELE *Spect.* No. 252 ¶3 There is something so moving in the very Image of weeping Beauty. **1748** RICHARDSON *Clarissa* (1768) IV. 146 A weeping eye indicates a gentle heart. **1754** GRAY *Progr. Poesy* 44 Disease, and Sorrow's weeping train. **1848** DICKENS *Dombey* xxxv, Edith looked down upon the weeping girl, and once kissed her. **1848** THACKERAY *Van. Fair* xxxii, He had taken leave of his weeping sweetheart. **1884** J. PARKER *Apost. Life* III. 124 When men speak of Jeremiah, they think of him as the weeping prophet.

† **b.** *absol.* Persons weeping. *Obs.*

c **1482** *Monk of Evesham* (Arb.) 24 He..fulbitterly beganne to wepe and with rennyng terys sorofully sobbyd as wepyng doth [L. *ut plorantes solent*].

c. ***weeping monkey***: a name applied to the sapajous. Cf. WEEPER 2.

1834 McMURTRIE *Cuvier's Anim. Kingd.* 48 Their name of *Weeping Monkeys* is derived from their plaintive voice.

2. Of the voice, the countenance: Tearful, lachrymose. Of utterances: Accompanied with weeping, tearful. Of emotion: Expressed by weeping.

c **900** *Bæda's Hist.* I. xii, Ða..onsendon hi ærendwrecan to Rome mid ȝewritum & wepindre bene [L. *lacrimosis precibus*]. *c* **1000** *Ags. Ps.* (Thorpe) vi. 7 Forðam þe Drihten hyrde mine wependan stefne [Vulg. *vocem fletus mei*]. *a* **1300** *Cursor M.* 17947 Wiþ wepynge preyere. **1382** WYCLIF *Dan.* vi. 20 With a wepynge voice [Vulg. *voce lacrimabili*]. *c* **1400** *26 Pol. Poems* xi. 46 Repentaunce makeþ wepyng mon [= moan]. **1561** HOBY tr. *Castiglione's Courtier* II. (1900) 161 For undoubtedlye it is not meete for a Gentle manne to make weeping and laughing faces. **1593** SHAKS. *2 Hen. VI*, I. i. 34 Her words yclad with wisedomes Maiesty, Makes me from Wondring, fall to Weeping ioyes, Such is the Fulnesse of my hearts content. **1632** LITHGOW *Trav.* x. 457 Leauing me with a weeping good-night. **1760–72** H. BROOKE *Fool of Qual.* (1809) II. 154 Having taken a weeping leave of all the family. *Ibid.* IV. 17 We behold him with weeping gratitude. **1827** POLLOK *Course T.* IX. 1156 Bards..bewailed them much, With doleful instruments of weeping song.

3. † **a.** ***weeping tears***, abundant weeping. Rarely in *sing.* *Obs.*

a **1470** HARDING *Chron.* cxl. x, He shroue hym then vnto abbots three With great sobbyng and hye contricion, And wepyng teares. **1471** CAXTON *Recuyell* (Sommer) 644 The troians toke the body of parys with wepyng teres and bare hit vnto the cyte. **1513** DOUGLAS *Æneis* XIII. iv. 40 Wyth sik plente of bittir wepand teris. **1560** tr. *J. Fisher's Godly Treat. Benef. Prayer* H i, With many sighes and aboundaunce of weepyng teares. **1593** SHAKS. *Lucr.* 1375 Many a dry drop seem'd a weeping teare, Shed for the slaughtred husband by the wife. **1652** C. B. STAPYLTON *Herodian* i. 7 This Message was receiv'd with weeping teares. *a* **1700** *Tri. Patience* in Halliw. *Yorks. Anthol.* (1851) 359 With weeping tears she did reply, My heart is overwhelm'd with grief. *a* **1825** FORBY *Voc. E. Anglia*, *Weeping-tears*, A very odd pleonasm, but in very common use for excessive sorrow.

b. Falling or issuing in drops like tears. Now *rare* or *Obs.*

1686 PLOT *Staffordsh.* 79 The Springs on, or near the tops of hills, if weak and weeping, may proceed from rains. **1704** POPE *Windsor For.* 30 Let India boast her plants, nor envy we The weeping amber or the balmy tree. **1735** J. PRICE *Stone-br. Thames* 6 To empty out the weeping Water and Springs. **1766** *Complete Farmer* s.v. *Lucern*, Except it be obstructed by a stratum of rock, or chilled at root by weeping springs. **1827** POLLOK *Course T.* v. 98 Though poets..talked and sang Of brooks, and crystal founts, and weeping dews. **1831** WORDSW. *Sonnet Depart. Sir W. Scott* I A trouble, not of clouds, or weeping rain..Engendered.

4. Exuding moisture: **a.** Of soil: Oozing, swampy.

1577 B. GOOGE *Heresbach's Husb.* I. 17 b, Yf it be wette or weepyng ground, or subiect vnto other inconueniences. **1597** SHAKS. *Lover's Compl.* 39 A riuer..Vpon whose weeping margent she was set. **1625** MARKHAM *Inrichment Weald Kent* 9 The Haisell ground being dry, and not subiect to Winter-springs, or teares of water (for which some call such, A whining or weeping ground) is to be handled thus. *Ibid.* 19 A sandy and grauelly ground that is wet and weeping. **1644** G. PLATTES in *Hartlib's Legacy* (1655) 216 The last Experiment, shewing how weeping land may be drained where there is no level. *a* **1700** EVELYN *Diary* 2 June 1676, The soil a cold weeping clay, not answering the expence. **1707** MORTIMER *Husb.* 33 Ray-Grass..is reckoned to grow on any Land, but chiefly in Cold sour Clays, and weeping Grounds. **1801** *Farmer's Mag.* Nov. 409 Upon poor, weak, weeping clays, where..the dung is locked up,..the application of lime is equally salutary. **1813** VANCOUVER *Agric. Devon* 40 The shaley rock, covered with a grey loam of a moderate staple, and producing a very wet and weeping surface. **1816** *Trial Berkeley Poachers* 30 There I could see, for there was a wet or weeping place, the tracks of sixteen men.

b. *Path.* Of the eyes: Running, watering. Also of diseased tissues or structures from which moisture exudes. ***weeping eczema***, a variety of eczema characterized by abundant exudation.

1580 BLUNDEVIL *Curing Horses Dis.* xxviii. 15 Of weeping or watering eies. **1810** *Sporting Mag.* XXXV. 140 It appeared that at the time of sale the horse had weeping eyes. **1899** *Allbutt's Syst. Med.* VIII. 503 A general raw, red, weeping surface is produced. *Ibid.* 608 Squamous or weeping eczema. *Ibid.* 749 The epidermis is exfoliated..leaving the skin underneath red and tender but never moist or weeping as in eczema.

c. In general use.

1550 BALE *Acts Engl. Votaries* II. O vj, I coulde here shewe ye wonders of wepinge Roodes, and sweating ladies. **1697** DRYDEN *Virg. Georg.* I. 647 The yawning Earth disclos'd th' Abyss of Hell: The weeping Statues did the Wars foretel. **1710** HILMAN *Tusser Rediv.* Apr. (1744) 45 His Bark clean without fungi or Toad-stools, no weeping Holes or decayed Boughs upon him. **1805** R. W. DICKSON *Pract. Agric.* I. 283 Oozing springs,..weeping rocks. **1903** E. CHILDERS *Riddle of Sands* ix. 92, I returned, with a shock, to the present, to the weeping walls, the discoloured deal table, the ghastly breakfast litter.

d. †***weeping bower***, the name given in Barbados to a tree that exudes a gum of some kind. ***weeping gum***, the name of two species of Eucalyptus, *E. pauciflora* and *E. viminalis* (Morris *Austral Engl.* s.v. *Gum*).

1696 PLUKENET *Almagestum* Wks. 1769 II. 43 Arbor.. Scenam topiariam efformans Lachrymifera, fortè Stacteflua, *s.* Myrrham liquidam fundens... Nostratibus Colonis Weeping Bower nuncupata.

5. Of climate, weather, skies, etc.: Dripping, rainy.

1597 SHAKS. *2 Hen. IV*, I. iii. 61 A naked subiect to the Weeping Clouds. *a* **1668** DENHAM *To Sir John Mennis* I All on a weeping Monday,..Little Admiral John To Bologne is gone. **1771** SMOLLETT *Humphry Cl.* 6 Sept., This country would be a perfect paradise, if it was not, like Wales, cursed with a weeping climate. **1819** KEATS *Otho* V. v. 39 Gauzes of silver mist, Loop'd up with cords of twisted wreathed light, And tassell'd round with weeping meteors! **1821** SCOTT *Pirate* iv, The inconveniences arising from a cold soil and a weeping climate. **1844** H. STEPHENS *Bk. Farm* III. 981 In a weeping season, the hay on one property was effectually saved by the use of the tedding-machine. **1846** MRS. A. MARSH *Father Darcy* xxxviii, It was a weeping day—a cold, cloudy day, at the very beginning of September. **1884** ANNIE S. SWAN *Carlowrie* ii. 30 The rain still falling desolately from weeping skies. **1896** KIPLING *Seven Seas, Three Sealers*, The weeping fog rolled fold on fold the wrath of man to cloak.

transf. **1615** CHAPMAN *Odyss.* XIX. 646 Ioy and griefe together Her brest inuaded: and of weeping weather Her eyes stood full.

6. Used to designate trees (less frequently other plants) the branches of which arch over and hang down drooping. Chiefly in the distinctive names of particular species or varieties. [So F. *pleureur* in *saule pleureur* weeping willow, *frêne pleureur* weeping ash.]

weeping oak, the Californian white oak, *Quercus lobata*; also, a cultivated variety of the English oak, *Quercus Robur*. The ***weeping ash***, ***beech***, ***birch***, ***elm***, etc. are varieties of certain species of those trees; in botanical works they are designated by the addition of *pendula* after the specific name. See also WEEPING WILLOW.

1606 N. B[AXTER] *Sydney's Ourania* F 4 b, The weeping Elme, the Beech, the Byrch. **1791** W. GILPIN *Forest Scenery* I. 41 There is another variety also of this tree, called the weeping elm. *Ibid.* 66 Of the white birch there is a..variety, sometimes called the lady-birch, or the weeping-birch. **1807** J. E. SMITH *Phys. Bot.* 61 The weeping variety of the Common Ash. **1824** 'A. SINGLETON' *Lett. from South & West* 62 The weeping-cherry..bears blossoms when a part of the fruit is ripe. **1838** LOUDON *Arboretum* II. 1214 *Fraxinus pendula*... The pendulous, or weeping Ash. *Ibid.* III. 1691 *Betula pendula*..the weeping Birch. *Ibid.* 1732 *Quercus pendula*..the Weeping Oak. *Ibid.* 1952 *Fagus pendula*..the weeping Beech. **1849** *Florist* 273 Among weeping trees, we found the weeping purple Beech, the weeping Holly, the new weeping Elm,..the weeping Yew, the weeping Oak, weeping silver Fir, and weeping red Cedar. **1859** D. BUNCE *Trav. Dr. Leichhardt* 91 Many species of *Acacia* made their appearance, including the celebrated Weeping Myall. **1865** GOSSE *Land & Sea* (1874) 343 The..rhizome of Goniophlebium dissimile..allows to droop on every side its long, weeping fronds. **1868** *Rep. U.S. Commissioner Agric.* (1869) 202 Weeping and drooping trees. **1869** S. R. HOLE *Bk. about Roses* viii. 124 They may soon be trained into Weeping Roses. **1882** *Proc. Berw. Nat. Club* IX. No. iii. 436 At the upper end stands..a purple beech, and a weeping elm, there being weeping ashes elsewhere. **1889** Weeping myall [see BOREE[2]]. **1895** CORNISH *Wild Eng.* 92 On the shaded bank, a line of weeping-birches dips into the pool. **1898** MORRIS *Austral Engl.* 171 Rice Grass, Meadow, *Microtæna stipoides.* Called also *Weeping Grass. Ibid.* 506 *Weeping-Myall*, an Australian tree, *Acacia pendula.* Cunn. **1951** *Dict. Gardening* (R. Hort. Soc.) IV. 1825/2 Newly planted bush and standard (not weeping) roses should be pruned back. **1969** *Better Homes & Gardens* (U.S.) Apr. 83 *Weeping cherry*, bright pink blossoms are artistically spaced along the gracefully hanging branches.

Weeping Cross.

1. A place-name occurring in several English counties, presumably indicating the site of a stone cross (now destroyed) formerly known by this designation.

Recent Ordnance Maps have shown places so named (1) about 2 miles S.E. of Shrewsbury; (2) about 2 miles S.E. of Stafford; (3) about 2 miles S.E. of Banbury; (4) near Bury St. Edmunds (see quot. *a* 1500); (5) near Ludlow. See also quot. 1893. All the places seem to be at cross-roads. It is said that the remains of the 'weeping cross' near Banbury were removed in 1803 (Beesley *Hist. Banbury*, 1841); with reference to that near Ludlow cf. quot. 1826. It is usually assumed that the name indicates that acts of devotion at these crosses were enjoined upon penitents, but there appears to be no evidence of this. Pennant's explanation (quot. 1782) seems to be merely a conjecture; another conjecture (Beesley *Hist. Banbury*) is that the cross marked the place at which bodies carried to interment were set down for the bearers to rest.

[*a* **1500** in *East Anglian* (1887–8) II. 226 [Bury St. Edmunds.] Falda incipit juxta riperam apud Wlnothes, et procedit ita ulterius ascendendo versus Austrum usque ad Crucem Lacrymantem.] **1675** OGILBY *Britannia* (1698) 39 At 21'3 come to Weeping-Cross a noted Place, where 4 Ways meet;..and at 22'7 enter Banbury. **1782** PENNANT *Journ. from Chester* 78 After leaving the town [Stafford] I crossed the Wolverhampton Navigation at Radford Bridge... A little further is Weeping Cross; so stiled from its vicinity to the antient place of execution. **1826** T. WRIGHT *Hist. Ludlow* (ed. 2) 175 Passing along the road which leaves the town at the bottom of Holgate Fee, we come to a small tump of earth and stones which marks the boundary of the parish. The name of the 'Weeping Cross', yet retained by this land mark serves to preserve the traditionary record of a Cross. **1893** *Dublin Rev.* July 557 There is a road outside Salisbury named 'King John's Lane,' leading from Clarendon to Old Sarum; it is crossed by another road, and at this point there is a clump of elm-trees. These trees are known as 'the weeping cross trees.'

2. Used allusively, esp. in the proverbial phrase *to come home by* ***Weeping Cross***, to suffer grievous disappointment or failure.

Cf. the occasional variants 'to come home by broken cross' (1662 Howell *New Engl. Gramm., Peramb. Spain* 68) and 'to make our prayers at whining cross' (1602: see WHINING *vbl. sb.* b).

1579 GOSSON *Sch. Abuse* (Arb.) 46 They.. pull the house on their owne heds, returne home by weeping Crosse, and fewe of them come to an honest ende. **1580** LYLY *Euphues* (Arb.) 243 The tyme will come when comming home by weeping crosse, thou shalt confesse [etc.]. **1592** GREENE *Upst. Courtier* D 2, Heerein I hold the Tailor for a necessary member to teach proud nouices the way to weeping crosse. **1612** WITHER *Pr. Henries Obseq.* Ded. A 3, For here I mourne, for your-our publike losse; And doe my pennance, at the Weeping Crosse. **1625** FLETCHER & SHIRLEY *Nt. Walker* I. i, One is a kind of weeping cross, Jack, A gentle Purgatory. **1643** TRAPP *Gen.* iv. 16 God fetcht Jonas home again by weeping-cross. **1665** J. DAVIES tr. *Scarron's Novels* II. iv. 125 And so the poor Boy was forc'd to get back again to Madrid with a weeping-cross. **1741** OZELL tr. *Brantome's Sp. Rhodom.* (1744) 56 Making an Irruption into Provence, he came home by Weeping-Cross. **1884** W. MORRIS *Archit. & Hist.* (1900) 16 How different that [*sc.* artistic finish] is from mechanical or trade finish, some of us, at least, have learned, maybe, by the way of Weeping Cross.

†**'weepingly**, *a. Obs. rare*[−1]. [f. WEEPING *ppl. a.* + -LY[1].] Tearful.

c **1440** *Gesta Rom.* lxi. (1878) 259 The Emperoure gothe into swiche a chaumbr glad I-nowe, but when he comythe oute, al his visage is wepingly [*tota facies eius est lacrimosa*].

weepingly ('wiːpɪŋlɪ), *adv.* [f. WEEPING *ppl. a.* + -LY[2].] In a weeping manner.

1340 *Ayenb.* 192 Huet yefþe is þet..þet þe on nimþ gled liche and þe oþer hit lyest wepindeliche? *c* **1450** LOVELICH *Merlin* 7205 Ful tendirly the teres he dide down lete, and so wepyngly he torned ageyn. **1565** COOPER *Thesaurus, Lachrymose*,..weepyngly: as though one wepte. **1597** SHAKS. *Lover's Compl.* 207 Their kind acceptance wepingly beseecht. **1621** LADY M. WROTH *Urania* 76 Thy sap doth weepingly bewray thy paine. *a* **1700** B. E. *Dict. Cant. Crew, Mawdlin*, weepingly Drunk. **1876** MISS BROUGHTON *Joan* I. xxx, It is four months..since Wolferstan went—since, weepingly, his love said to him, 'God keep you, Anthony!' **1890** W. C. RUSSELL *Ocean Trag.* II. xxv. 259 My mind revolving..blackly and weepingly.

weeping willow. [See WEEPING *ppl. a.* 6. Cf. F. *saule pleureur*, G. *trauer-, thränenweide.*]

1. A species of willow, *Salix babylonica*, a large tree, native of Eastern Asia, having long and slender pendulous branches, cultivated in Europe as an ornamental tree and regarded as symbolical of mourning.

1731 MILLER *Gard. Dict.*, *Salix*; *orientalis*,..The Weeping Willow. **1755** YOUNG *Centaur* iii. Wks. 1757 IV. 171 Their wretched joys flourish, like dismal weeping willows watered by a ditch. **1810** SCOTT *Lady of L.* I. xvii, Eddying..The weeping willow twig to lave. **1898** 'MERRIMAN' *Roden's Corner* xxi. 224 A weeping-willow, trimly trained in the accurate Dutch fashion.

2. Rhyming slang for 'pillow'. Now *rare* or *Obs.*

1880 D. W. BARRETT *Life & Work among Navvies* (ed. 2) II. ii. 43, I have been told..that often when a man is ready to retire to rest, he will inform his mates, 'That he's done his lot for the day, and is goin' to lay his pen'oth o' bread (head) on the weeping-willow (pillow).' **1944** N. STREATFEILD *Curtain Up* x. 123 Time young Holly was in bed... Hannah wants your head on your weeping willow, pillow to you.

†**'weeply**, *a. Obs. rare.* [f. WEEP *sb.* or *v.* + -LY[1].] Lamentable, tearful.

c **1374** CHAUCER *Boeth.* I. pr. i. (1868) 5 My wepli compleynte [*querimoniam lacrimabilem*]. *Ibid.* III. met. xii. 106 By hys wepely [*v.r.* wepply] songes [*flebilibus modis*].

weepy ('wiːpɪ), *a.* [f. WEEP *v.* + -Y[1].]

†**1.** Weeping, mournful. *Obs.*

1602 DAVISON *Poet. Rapsody* C 2, And when I weep, And sigh full deep, A weepy sighing Voice againe thou lendest.

2. Inclined to weep or shed tears, tearful.

1863 'HOLME LEE' *A. Warleigh* II. 95 She appeared with ..her watery eyes more weepy than ever. **1894** DU MAURIER *Trilby* IV. (1912) 166 The bold dragoon sang..'My Sister Dear',..with such pathos,..that his audience felt almost weepy in the midst of their jollification. **1897** BRAM STOKER *Dracula* xix. (1912) 276, I shall put a bold face on, and if I do feel weepy, he shall never see it.

3. *dial.* Exuding moisture, damp, oozy.

1825 JENNINGS *Observ. Dial. W. Eng.*, *Weepy*, abounding with springs; moist. **1879** MISS JACKSON *Shropsh. Word-bk.* s.v., One o' the fat cheeses is weepy. **1886** *W. Somerset Word-bk.* s.v., Terr'ble weepy field o' ground. **1906** KIPLING *Puck of Pook's Hill* 196 An old marlpit full of black water, where weepy, hairy moss hangs round the stumps of the willows and elders.

'weequashing, *vbl. sb. U.S.* Also **wigwassing**. [f. Algonkin *wigwas* birch-bark (canoe) + -ING[1].] The spearing of eels or fish from a canoe by torchlight.

1888 GOODE *Amer. Fishes* 436 Vast quantities [of suckers] are taken..by spearing by torchlight or 'weequashing'. **1902** A. F. CHAMBERLAIN in *Jrnl. Amer. Folk-lore* Oct. 267 The word *weequashing*, or *wigwassing*, would seem to be derived ..from *wigwas*, a widespread Algonkian..term for 'birch bark', the immediate source of the word being Passamaquoddy or Micmac.

weer, obs. form of WEIR, and var. WERE *Obs.*

weer, obs. pa. t. of WEAR *v.*, BE *v.*

c **1400** *Beryn* 2617 And therfor wisdom weer..Nevir to dele with hem. *Ibid.* 3049 And wher weer þow Ibore?

weerd, obs. form of WEIRD.

weere, var. VERE, spring; obs. form of WEIR.

weerie, obs. form of WEARY *v.*

weerish, var. WEARISH *a.*

weerne, var. WARN *v.*[2] *Obs.*

weerock, var. WIRROCK.

wees, obs. form of *was*: see BE *v.*

weesand, obs. form of WEASAND.

weese, weeze (wiːz), *v. Obs.* exc. *dial.* Forms: 1 wésan, 5 wese, 6–7 wheeze, 8–9 *dial.* **weeze**, 6– weese. [OE. *wésan* (:—**wōsjan*), f. *wós* OOZE *sb.*[1]] *intr.* To ooze, drip or distil gently.

c **1000** *Sax. Leechd.* II. 44 þonne ærest onȝinne se healsȝund wesan. **14..** *Seven Deadly Sins* 58 in *Pol. Rel. & L. Poems* (1903) 246 He toke me 'carytas', and put it in a clout, And bade me bame me well aboute, when hit wolde other water or wese. *a* **1555** BRADFORD *Writ.* (Parker Soc.) I. 303, I will not speak of the often weesing out. **1591** SYLVESTER *Du Bartas* I. ii. 79 At his knots his Water wheezes forth. *c* **1620** Z. BOYD *Zion's Flowers* (1855) 11 It seemes I heare the water wheesing in. **1790** D. MORISON *Poems* 105 Yon greetin' cheese, Frae which the tears profusely weeze. **18..** in var. dial.: see *Eng. Dial. Dict.* s.v. *Weeze*.

weese, var. WASE.

weese allan (also **wease alley**), an alleged local name of the skua (cf. SCOUTY-AULIN).

1849 *Zoologist* VII. 2393 The common skua is a 'wease-alley'. **1885** SWAINSON *Prov. Names Birds* 210 Richardson's Skua (*Stercorarius crepidatus*)... Weese allan (Orkney Isles).

weesel(l: see WEASEL *sb.*, WEEZLE.

weeshy ('wiːʃɪ), *a. Anglo-Irish.* [Of obscure origin. Cf. WEE *sb.*[1] and *a.*] Very small, tiny.

1825 [see DEESHY *a.*]. **1830** CARLETON *Traits Ir. Peasantry* (1843) I. 141 The first man he met was the weeshy fraction of a tailor, as nimble as a hare. **1842** LOVER *Handy Andy* iii, And what weeshee little balls thim is, sir. **1894** McNULTY *Misther O'Ryan* v. 48, I had larned.. as a weeshy lad, to repate some 'Spaches from the Dock'.

weesil(l, var. ff. WEASEL *sb.*, WEEZLE *Obs.*

†'**weesle**, *v. Obs. rare*⁻¹. [dim. of WEESE *v.*] *intr.* To ooze.

a **1555** BRADFORD *Writ.* (Parker Soc.) I. 304 For a time the streams of our affections may be stopped..; howbeit so yet they will weesel out now and then.

weesle, obs. form of WEASEL *sb.*

weeson, obs. form of WEASAND.

weesp, Sc. form of WISP *sb.*

weesshe, ? obs. form of WISH *v.*

wee'st heart, var. of the northern dial. phrase *wae's t'heart*: see WOE *sb.*

1695 CONGREVE *Love for L.* II. ii, Nurse, where's your young Mistress? *Nurse.* Wee'st heart, I know not, they're none of 'em come home yet.

weet (wiːt), *v.*¹ *arch.* Also 6 wete, 6–7 weete. [repr. ME. *wēte(n*, var. ff. *wite(n* inf. and pl. pres. ind. and subj., and *wite* imperative and sing. pres. subj., of WIT *v.* (for the other parts of the verb see WOT *v.*, WIST *v.*). From the middle of the 16th c., if not earlier, the form *weet* seems to be obsolete in ordinary speech, but down to the second decade of the 17th c. it was frequent as a literary archaism (chiefly *poet.*), as attributed in the drama to rustic speakers, and as a variant of *wit* in the phrases *to do* or *give* (a person) *to wit*, (*that is*) *to wit*. The archaistic use in the 16th and early 17th c. was confined to the inf., the plural present, and the present participle; but the poets of the 18th c. and later, who have used the word in imitation of Spenser, have often treated it as a regular verb, with 1 sing. pres. *I weet*, and inflexions *weets*, *weeted*.

For the examples of *wete* before 1550, and of the phrases above-mentioned in which *to weet* = 'to wit', see WIT *v.*]

a. *trans.* To know (a fact, the answer to a question); also with clause as obj. **b.** *intr.* To know of something.

In Shaks. only once: see quot. 1606.

a **1547** SURREY *Æneis* II. 144 Then we in dout to Phebus temple sent Euripilus, to wete the prophesye. **1560** PILKINGTON *Aggeus* D j, Thy money.. shal waste away, thou not weetynge how nor when. **1561** T. HOBY tr. *Castiglione's Courtyer* III. (1577) O vj b, The innocent children, that could not only be in no fault, but not so much as weetting of their fathers yll dooings. **1575** *Gamm. Gurton* II. iii, Tush, man, is Gammers neele found? That chould gladly weete! **1584** R. SCOT *Discov. Witchcr.* XV. xxvi. (1886) 443 Then would I wéet of our witchmongers the reason why. **1590** SPENSER *F.Q.* I. v. 3 Forth he comes into the commune hall, Where.. waite him many a gazing eye, To weet what end to straunger knights may fall. *Ibid.* I. xii. 3 That aged Sire.. looked forth, to weet, if true indeede Those tydings were. **1594** CAREW *Huarte's Exam. Wits* Author's Pref., Curious parents may haue an art and maner to discouer the wit of their children, and may weet how to set each of them in hand with that science wherein he shall principally profit. **1599** T. M[OUFET] *Silkwormes* 53 Others diuine that they themselues did weete No other tree could yeelde their silken threede. **1603** G. OWEN *Pembrokesh.* (1891) 103 When Percellye weareth a hatte All Pembrokeshire shall weete of that. **1606** SHAKS. *Ant. & Cl.* I. i. 39 In which I binde One paine of punishment, the world to weete We stand vp Peerelesse. **1706** PRIOR *Ode to Queen* iv, Me all too mean for such a Task I weet. **1717** —— *Alma* II. 289 Well I weet, thy cruel Wrong Adorns a nobler Poet's Song. *a* **1721** —— *Wandering Pilgr.* 5 The gracious Knight full well does weet, Ten farthings ne'er will do, To keep a man each day in meat. **1742** SHENSTONE *Schoolm.* 251 Nor weeting how the Muse should soar on high Wisheth, poor starviling elf! his paper kite may fly. **1747** [G. RIDLEY] *Psyche* x. in *Museum* III. 83 Thou weetest not what Med'cines in them are. **1751** MENDEZ *Seasons* xi. in Pearch *Collect. Poems* (1768) II. 238 And while the lambs in fainter voices bleat, Their mothers hang their head, in doleful plight I weet. **1817** SHELLEY *Rev. Islam* IV. xiv, But, when one meets Another at the shrine, he inly weets, Though he says nothing, that the truth is known. *a* **1846** LUNDIE *Mission. Life Samoa* iii. 17 Ah! little weet those who dwell at ease among their own people, what the missionary endures! **1861** PATMORE *Angel in Ho.* II. II. xv, Nature's infinite ostent Of lovely flowers.. That weet not whether any heed. **1865** SWINBURNE *Poems & Ballads*, *St. Dorothy* 302 That is a noble scripture, well I weet, That likens women to an empty can. **1886** R. F. BURTON *Arab. Nts.* (abr. ed.) I. 111 Well weeting that Fortune is fair and constant to no man.

weet (wiːt), *int.* and *v.*² [Echoic. Cf. WEET-WEET and TWEET.] **a.** *int.* An imitation of the cry of certain small birds. **b.** *v. intr.* Of a bird: To chirp or twitter. Hence '**weeting** *ppl. a.* Also '**weet-bird**, the wryneck.

1852 *Zoologist* X. 3649, I was completely surrounded by curious, restless weeting little willow-wrens. **1863** WISE *New Forest* 186 The wry-neck.. is in the Forest known as the 'weet-bird', from its peculiar cry of 'weet', which it will repeat at short intervals for an hour together. *a* **1897** LADY C. GURDON *Suffolk Tales* etc. 160 A robin weeting or chirping at the window foretells a death in the house.

weet(e, obs. and Sc. forms of WET.

Weetabix ('wiːtəbɪks). The proprietary name of a breakfast cereal in the form of thick crumbly biscuits made from wheat.

1936 *Official Gaz.* (U.S. Patent Office) 3 Mar. 31/1 Olive Cross, Washington, D.C. Filed Jan. 11, 1936. *Weetabix* for crushed wheat breakfast food biscuits. **1938** *Trade Marks Jrnl.* 17 Aug. 1009/2 *Weetabix*... Wholemeal biscuits. Weetabix Limited,.. Kettering, Northamptonshire; manufacturers. **1974** R. RENDELL *Face of Trespass* i. 14 He .. poured milk over a couple of Weetabix and sat down to eat his breakfast. **1981** F. INGLIS *Promise of Happiness* ii. 47, I changed loyalties.. from cornflakes to Weetabix.

weete, obs. form of WHEAT.

1464 *Stonor Papers* (Camden) I. 68 The chirchemen of Dudcote wer in bargenyng off a ryke of weete for the welfare and help off the church.

weetingly, obs. var. WITTINGLY *adv.* (Cf. WEET *v.*¹ and next.)

1542 UDALL *Erasm. Apoph.* 23 b, That a manne should weetyngly & willingly come in the presence.. of theim. **1570** LEVINS *Manip.* 100/45 Weetingly, *sciens & prudens*. **1596** SPENSER *F.Q.* VI. iii. 11 This ill state,.. To which she for his sake had weetingly Now brought her selfe. **1642** H. MORE *Song Soul* II. i. III. xv, That man is wood That weetingly hastes on the thing he hates.

weetless ('wiːtlɪs), *a. arch.* [f. WEET *v.*¹ + -LESS. App. coined by Spenser; distinct from *witless*.] Unknowing, unconscious. †Also (quot. 1579), meaningless.

1579 SPENSER *Sheph. Cal.* July 35 Syker, thous but a laesie loord, and rekes much of thy swinck, That with fond termes, and weetlesse words to blere myne eyes doest thinke. [E. K. *Glosse*, Weetlesse, not vnderstoode.] **1590** —— *F.Q.* III. ii. 26 But the false Archer, which that arrow shot So slyly, that she did not feele the wound, Did smyle full smoothly at her weetlesse wofull stound. **1596** *Ibid.* VI. viii. 47 And now all weetlesse of the wretched stormes In which his loue was lost, he slept full fast. **1747** [J. UPTON] *New Canto F.Q.* xix. 13 Nathless the Soul, from her true heavenly Way, Caught by some Semblance fair, too weetless wends astray. [*Footn.*, *Weetless*, thoughtless, careless, unknowing: too thoughtless goes astray.]. **1751** MENDEZ *Seasons* xxx. in Pearch *Collect. Poems* (1768) II. 246 Or how the way-ward mother to chastise When from her vetchy nest the weetless vagrant hies. **1767** MICKLE *Concub.* I. xx, Bashfully the weetlesse Boy did look. **1802** LEYDEN *Cout of Keeldar* xxxviii, 'Twas here for Mangerton's brave lord A bloody feast was set, Who weetless, at the festal board, The bull's broad frontlet met. **1814** CARY *Dante, Parad.* x. 31 And I was with him, weetless of ascent, But as a man, that weets him come, ere thinking. **1829** G. DARLEY *Wedding Wake, Anniv.* 73 Look how the weetless, reckless air Moves its dead tresses now! *a* **1849** MANGAN *Poems* (1859) 256 Mother dear, thy happy heart is weetless of my dolour.

weet-weet, *int.* and *sb.*¹ [Echoic.]

1. *int.* ('wiːt'wiːt). An imitation of the cry of certain birds, esp. the sandpiper and chaffinch. Also *sb.* as the name for this cry.

1808–13 A. WILSON *Amer. Ornith.* (1831) III. 170, I could still hear their low note of *weet weet*, as they approached near to the vessel below me. **1831** HOWITT *Seasons* (1837) 106 The weet-weet and pink-pink of the chaffinch. **1843** *Zoologist* I. 221 The 'weet weet' of the sandpiper.

2. *sb.* ('wiːtwiːt). Used as a name for the sandpiper.

1852 MACGILLIVRAY *Brit. Birds* IV. 350 *Actitis*. Weet-weet. *Ibid.*, The Weet-weets are small migratory birds, which frequent the sandy and muddy margins of lakes, rivers, and estuaries. *Ibid.* 351 *Actitis Hypoleucos*. The White-breasted Weet-weet. *Ibid.* 356 *Actitis macularia*. The Spotted Weet-weet. **1862** JOHNS *Brit. Birds* 625 Weet-weet, the Common Sandpiper.

‖**weet-weet** ('wiːtwiːt), *sb.*² [Native Australian: see quot. 1878.] An Australian toy (see quot. 1878), contrived to be capable of being thrown to a great distance.

1878 R. B. SMYTH *Aborigines of Victoria* I. 352 The plaything (Fig. 170) called by the natives of the Yarra *Wi-tch-wi-tch*, *We-a-witcht*, *Weet-weet*, or *Wa-voit*, is one of the most extraordinary instruments used by savages... The head—in shape like two cones placed base to base—is about four inches and a half in length and one inch in diameter; and the stem, not quite two-tenths of an inch in diameter, is about twenty-one inches in length. **1886** *Daily News* 20 Dec. 5/3 The Australian toy called the *weet-weet* which can be thrown for several hundred yards, bounding off the ground at frequent intervals all the way. **1910** T. A. JOYCE *Handbk. Ethnogr. Coll. Brit. Mus.* 117 A peculiar toy is the weet-weet or 'kangaroo-rat', which the practised player can throw to enormous distances.

weet-weet, *v.* [f. WEET-WEET *int.*] *intr.* To cry 'weet, weet'.

1845 S. JUDD *Margaret* I. ii. (1871) 7 A sand-piper glided weet weeting along the shore.

weety ('wiːtɪ), *a. Sc.* Also 7 **weytie**, 9 **weetie**. [f. *weet*, Sc. f. WET *a.* + -Y¹.] Rainy, wet.

1658 J. NICOLL *Diary* (Bannatyne Club) 222 The crop wes verie pure, be ressoun of the spring tyme, quhilk wes verie cold and weytie by the space of many weekis. *a* **1774** FERGUSSON *Mutual Compl.* 23 In sunshine, and in weety weather. **1887** SERVICE *Duguid* 241 Noo the spring time.. was weety and cauld. **1915** SIR J. WILSON *Lowland Scotch* 169 [Written Eng.] a wet day. [Spoken Sc.] a weetee day.

weeve, obs. form of WEAVE *v.*

weever ('wiːvə(r)). Also 7 **wiver**, 7–9 **weaver**. [Prob. originally *wīver*, a. OF. (north-eastern) *wivre* the weever (13th c.), a transferred use of *wivre* serpent, dragon (see WYVER, WYVERN), = Central OF. *guivre* (mod. heraldic F. *guivre*, *givre*), repr. L. *vīpera* VIPER; the more normal OF. descendant of L. *vīpera* is *vivre*, the weever (whence VIVER², QUAVIVER), mod.F. *vive*. The fish was called 'viper' from its venomous spines: see quot. 1622.] A fish of the genus *Trachinus* or family *Trachinidae*, common on the coasts of Europe; esp. *T. draco*, the Greater, and *T. vipera*, the Lesser Weever. They have sharp dorsal and opercular spines with which they can inflict painful wounds.

1622 DRAYTON *Poly-olb.* xxv. 167 The Weauer, which although his prickles venom bee, By Fishers cut away, which Buyers seldom see. **1666** MERRETT *Pinax* 187 Araneus, a Weaver, or Wiver. **1747** MRS. GLASSE *Cookery* ix. 88 To Broil Weavers. **1752** J. HILL *Hist. Anim.* 263 Trachinus.. The Weever. **1766** SMOLLETT *Trav.* I. xviii. 292 Here too are found the *vyvre*, or, as we call it, weaver; remarkable for its long, sharp spines, so dangerous to the fingers of the fishermen. **1832** *Proc. Berw. Nat. Club* I. 7 These are, the greater weaver.. and the tadpole fish. **1848** JOHNS *Week at Lizard* 171 It was the Lesser Weever.

Comb. **1867** J. G. WOOD *Routledge's Pop. Nat. Hist.* III. 97 The Great Weaver, or Weever Fish.

weevil ('wiːv(ə)l, 'wiːvɪl). Forms: α. 1 **wibl**, **wibil**, **wifel**, 5 **wyvyl**, **-oll**, 6 **wyvel(l(e**, 6–7 **wivel(l**; 5 **wevel**, **-yl**, 6 **wevell** (**wew-**), **-yll**, 6–7 **wevill**, 6–8 **wevil**; 6 **weavill** (7 **-il**), 6–7, 9 **weavel** (7 **-ell**); 6 **weevell**, 6– **weevil** (6–7 **-ill**). β. *dial.* 7 **wibel**, **-ill**, 9 **wibble**; 8–9 **weeble**, 9 **weabel**. γ. *dial.* 7 **whule**, 8–9 **whool**, 9 **wheul**, **whewl**, **wule**, **weuel**, **yule**. [OE. *wifel* masc., beetle, corresp. to OS. (*gold-*)*wivil* glowworm, MLG. *wevel*, OHG. *wibil*, *wipil* beetle, chafer, ON. *vifill* in *tordyfill* dung-beetle (MSw. pl. *torddöffla*, Sw. *tordyfvel*, Norw. *tordivel*; cf. OE. *tordwifel*):—OTeut. **webilo-z*, f. **web-* to move about briskly (see WAVE *v.*) or **web-* to WEAVE, 'from the filaments spun for the larva-case' (Skeat). From the same root is the synonymous OE. *wibba* (:—**webjon-*) beetle, glowworm.

For the special phonology in English cf. *beetle* repr. OE. *bitela*; the OE. *i* when lengthened in an open syllable became *ē* in ME. The β and γ forms illustrate normal dialectal alterations of the *v*.

In the 16th and 17th c. some writers app. confused the name of the weevil with that of the weasel, using *wesell*, *weezel*, for the insect; see the quotations under WEEZEL.]

1. In OE., a beetle of any kind; in later use, any beetle classed under the group *Rhyncophora*, the larvæ of which, and sometimes the beetles themselves, are destructive by boring into grain, fruit, nuts, the bark of trees, etc.; esp. a beetle belonging to any of the numerous species of the family *Curculionidæ*, the true weevils; also one belonging to the families *Brenthidæ* and *Bruchidæ*.

The best known are the corn-weevil, *Calandra granaria*, a small red beetle that does much damage in granaries by boring into the grains of corn in order to deposit its eggs, and the NUT-WEEVIL. For *clover-*, *grain-*, *palm-*, *pea-*, *rice-weevil* see those words.

c **725** *Corpus Gloss.* (Hessels) C 151 *Cantarus*, wibil. *Ibid.* P 110 *Panpila*, wibl. *a* **1000** *Riddles* xli. 73 (Gr.) Is þæs gores sunu gonge hrædra þone we wifel wordum nemnað. *c* **1440** *Promp. Parv.* 523/2 Wevyl, or malte boode (Winch. MS. *gurgulio*). **1455** *Rolls of Parlt.* V. 324/2 Whether ye Malt be bad or good, all is cast togeder in soo grete a multitude, that noo man can kepe it from Wormes called Wevels. **1469** in *Plumpton Corr.* (Camden) 21 Also that you gar the malt be windowd, or it be laid in any garners, for ells there will brede wyvolls in it. **1528** *Star Chamber Cases* (Selden Soc.) II. 174 The wyche malte was etten with wewells. **1587** GOLDING *De Mornay* xvi. (1617) 284 The Husbandman createth not the wiuell in the Corne. **1623** T. SCOT *Highw. God* 78 Mothes are no worse in cloth, rust in yron, nor whules in Mault, then these in the Commonwealth. **1626** BACON *Sylva* §696 A Worm called a Wevill.. that feedeth upon Roots. **1628** MAY *Virg. Georg.* I. 10 There little Weeuills heapes of corne destroy. **1741** *Compl. Fam.-Piece* I. vi. 284 Your Malt.. not having had Time to contract.. Weebles, (an Insect that eats out the Heart of Malt). **1750** W. ELLIS *Country Housew. Fam. Compan.* 7 Whools, or Wevils, or Maggots, may be screened and sifted from the Flower. **1760** R. BROWN *Compl. Farmer* II. 95 Pease.. are very apt to breed worms, wevils, and mites. **1817** KIRBY & SP. *Entomol.* II. xxiii. 322 The whole tribe of weevils (*Curculionidæ*). **1834** *J. Ross's Van Diemen's Land Ann.* 70 The wheat of New South Wales is seldom six months old before it is affected with the weavel. **1863** J. G. WOOD *Illustr. Nat. Hist.* III. 474 We now arrive at a vast group of beetles, embracing several thousand species, which are popularly classed under the name of Weevils. **1883** STEVENSON *Treas. Isl.* v, If you had the pluck of a weevil in a biscuit you would catch them still.

b. *collect. sing.*

1866 *Standard* 16 July 5 The plaintiff stated that he found the malt contained 'weevil,' a very destructive insect. **1908** *Animal Managem.* (War Office) 99 Beans should be hard and dry.. and free from weevil.

c. *fig.* and in fig. context.

1598 E. GUILPIN *Skial.*, Sat. VI. E 3, If that some weeuil, mault-worme, barly-cap, Hearing my lines halfe-snorting ore his kanne, Sweares them for good. **1793** WOLCOT (P. Pindar) *Epist. Pope* 179 The French are.. downright devils; In heavenly wheat, accurs'd destructive weevils!

2. Applied to other insects or their larvæ.

1789 T. WRIGHT *Meth. Watering Meadows* (1790) 41 One of the ewes was kill'd, and..its liver was putrid, and replete with the insect called the Fluke or Weevil.

3. *attrib.* and *Comb.*, as ***weevil-beetle, tribe***; ***weevil-damaged*** adj.; †**weevil malt**, malt infested with weevils.

1720 STRYPE *Stow's Surv.* II. v. xi. 202 In the End of the Year they commonly brewed with Wyvel Malt. **1817** KIRBY & SP. *Entomol.* xxi. II. 235 The weevil tribe. **1871** DARWIN *Desc. Man* II. viii. (1890) 208 In some weevil-beetles..there is a great difference between the male and female in the length of the rostrum or snout. **1890** *Kapunda Herald* 26 July 2/4 Sheepskins.—..Broken and weevil-damaged skins bring from 1⅞d. to 3½d. per lb.

weeviled (ˈwiːv(ə)ld), *a.* [f. WEEVIL + -ED.] Infested with weevils.

1901 *Contemp. Rev.* Mar. 409 The system which flogged the men and fed them on weeviled biscuit.

weevily (ˈwiːvɪlɪ), *a.* Also 8 **weavely**, 9 **weevilly**. [f. WEEVIL + -Y[1].] Infested with weevils.

1757 W. THOMPSON *R.N. Advoc.* 21 Rotten, musty, weavely Flour. **1803** NELSON in Nicolas *Disp.* (1845) V. 280, I sincerely hope no weevily bread will be sent. **1859** SALA *Tw. Round Clock* (1861) 365 Men who are sometimes brought to live when on shipboard upon weevily biscuit that breaks the teeth. **1889** MRS. C. PRAED *Romance of Station* 45, I threw out [to the hens] a handful of weevily rice. **1891** C. ROBERTS *Adrift Amer.* 6 Some old salt who has forgotten the tough salt horse and weevily biscuit.

weevle, *v. rare*$^{-1}$. [? f. WEEVIL *sb.*] *refl.* To wriggle (oneself) *out*.

1889 A. T. PASK *Eyes of Thames* 254 The small boy weevles himself out from the boxes.

wee-wee, var. WI-WI[2].

wee-wee (ˈwiːwiː), *v. colloq.* [Echoic: freq. as a child's word.] *intr.* To urinate.

1930 C. BEATON *Diary* Dec. in *Wandering Years* (1961) IX. 192 Young men..hurried into the garden to wee-wee. **1944** D. WELCH *In Youth is Pleasure* vi. 113 Orvil hated Guy... He was glad that the dog had wee-weed on Guy's expensive jacket. **1954** D. ABSE *Ash on Young Man's Sleeve* 167, I suddenly rushed into the sea..and wee-weed in the water for a joke. **1960** L. PINCUS *Marriage* ii. 110 Mrs. Robinson felt disgusted at the thought of 'the tail' touching her, 'because it wee-wee'd'. **1975** 'J. LYMINGTON' *Spider in Bath* ii. 40 Show us the way to the bar and the lady would probably like to wee-wee.

wee-wee (ˈwiːwiː), *sb. colloq.* [f. as prec.: cf. PEE-PEE[2].] **1.** Urine; an act of urination; ***to do*** (***have***, etc.) ***a wee-wee***, ***to go*** (***make***) ***wee-wee***, to urinate. Cf. WATER *sb.* 18 a.

1937 PARTRIDGE *Dict. Slang* 943/1 *Wee-wee*, a urination; esp. *do a wee-wee*..late C. 19–20. **1938** *Life & Health* Sept. 19/2 If he wants to urinate, it's, 'Mommie, wee, wee, duty.' **1948** A. N. KEITH *Three came Home* x. 184 Our barrack..smelled of kids, pots, and wee-wee. **1955** J. P. DONLEAVY *Ginger Man* xvi. 175 If you'll excuse me a moment, I must make wee wee. **1961** J. STROUD *Touch & Go* xiii. 138 He made his voice deliberately offensive: 'He's gone to do a wee-wee.' **1969** M. BRAITHWAITE *Never sleep Three in Bed* xvii. 76 Hub and I had to go wee wee, and when advised by Mother that we were to go upstairs instead of in the back yard we took the stairs two at a time to see if such a thing could be true. **1982** J. SCOTT *Uprush of Mayhem* vi. 67 When he needed a wee-wee he did it in a corner of the hut.

2. A penis.

1964 W. & J. BREEDLOVE *Swap Clubs* xv. 233 Our grandmothers, wielding butcher knives, threatened to cut off our fathers' wee-wees if they didn't stop playing with them. **1972** *Screw* 12 June 16/3 [The] self-righteous defender of what he thought to be his threatened wee wee, could not contain his machismo.

weeze: see WEESE.

†**weezel** (also 6 **wesell**), erron. var. of WEEVIL.

*a***1533** BERNERS *Golden Bk. M. Aurel.* (1535) 101 Nor the darnell amonge the corne, nor the wesell amonge the grayn, ..dothe so muche domage. **1697** DRYDEN *Virg. Georg.* I. 268 The Corn devouring Weezel [L. *curculio*] here abides, And the wise Ant her wintry Store provides.

†ˈ**weezle**. *Obs.* Forms: 6 **weesel**, **-zill**, 6–7 **wesell**, **-ill**, **-yll**, **weesell**, **-sil(l**, **weasill**, **wezill**, 7 **weazell**, **wizzel(l**, 8 **weezle**. [First recorded in the 16th c., but perh. repr. an OE. **wǣsel*, corresponding to G. dial. *waisel*:—WGer. **waisilo-*, from the same root as WEASAND. Substitution of *-el* for *-en* is however possible.]

1. The trachea or windpipe: = WEASAND 2.

1538 ELYOT *Dict.*, *Curculio*,..the wesyll of the throte of a man, wherby he drawyth wynde. **1579–80** NORTH *Plutarch*, *Demosthenes* (1595) 908 But wise men laughing at his fine excuse, tolde him it was no sinanche that had stopped his wesill that night, as he would make them beleeue. ?*a***1597** PEELE *David & Bethsabe* (1599) B iv, The mastiues of our land, shall werry ye, And pull the weesels from your greedy throtes. **1626** BACON *Sylva* §174 The Weasill or Wind-pipe. **1639** MAYNE *City Match* III. iv, Death you Pander, Forbid the banes or I will cut your wizzell.

b. *Comb.*

1632 tr. *Bruel's Praxis Med.* 198 Blood..if it doe come from the throate, or weazell-pipe..it is voyded by hemming. **1647** LILLY *Chr. Astrol.* xliv. 269 The Weesell-pipe of a man's Throat or Lung-pipe. **1726** LEONI *Alberti's Archit.* III. 34 From the Weezle-pipe to the Joynt of the Neck.

2. The epiglottis.

1594 T. B. *La Primaud. Fr. Acad.* II. 86 The wesell of the throte, which is a litle fleshy and spongie bodie, in figure like to a pine-apple, hanging at the end of the palat. **1598** FLORIO, *Epiglotti*, the couer or wesill of the throte. **1601** HOLLAND *Pliny* XX. ix. II. 51 The ashes of the root being burnt, cure the Vvula or swelling of the wezill in the throat. **1671** H. M. tr. *Erasm. Colloq.* 292 He [a cock] wants..such a tongue as we have, nor has he a weesil [L. *nec* (*adest*) *epiglottis*].

weezon, obs. form of WEASAND.

wef, obs. form of WEAVE *v.*; var. WEEF, WEFFE.

wefde, wefed, var. forms of WEVED, altar.

wefe, var. of WEVE *v. Obs.*

wefere, obs. form of WEAVER[1].

weff, obs. Sc. form of WEAVE *v.*

†**weffe**[1]. *Obs.* Forms: 3–4 **wef**, 4–5 **weef(e**, 4–6 **weffe**. [Of obscure etymology; represented later by *weft* WAFT *sb.*[1] 1.]

1. A (foul or unsavoury) scent or odour: = WAFT *sb.*[1] 1 b. Cf. WHIFF *sb.*[1] 3.

*a***1300** *Body & Soul* (Laud MS.) in *Map's Poems* (Camden) 335 And nouȝ so lodly thouȝ list grenne, fro the comeþ a wikke wef. **13..** *Ibid.* (Vernon MS.) 342 A wikked weef. **13..** *Metr. Hom.* (Vernon MS.) in *Archiv Stud. neu. Sprach.* LVII. 288 Wondur him þouȝt þat of þat bodi [= corpse] wef hedde he nouȝt. *c***1440** *Promp. Parv.* 520/1 (MS. K.) Weffe, *vapor*.

2. Flavour, taste; ill-savour: = WAFT *sb.*[1] 1 a. Cf. WHIFF *sb.*[1] 3 b.

*c***1440** *Promp. Parv.* 520/1 Weef [*Winch. MS.* Weefe], or summe what semynge to badnesse, *inclinacio ad malum*. **1530** PALSGR. 287/2 Weffe tast, *goust*. *Ibid.* 475/1, I can nat awaye with this ale, it hath a weffe: ..*elle est de mauluays goust*.

†**weffe**[2]. *Obs.*$^{-1}$ [? f. WEVE *v.*] A blow or cut. (Cf. WAFF *sb.* 3.)

13.. *Coer de L.* 5291 He took to hys mace off bras,..And gaff hym a sory weffe, That hys helme al to-cleff.

†**weffe**[3], earlier form of *weft* WAFT *sb.*[1] 6 (a small flag waved as a signal).

1562 BULLEIN *Bulwarke, Dial. Health & Sicknes* 76 b, Then Ariadne rente from her, her womanly apparell, making a weffe thereof upon the ende of a pole.

weffer, obs. form of WAFER, WEAVER.

weffin, obs. Sc. pa. pple. of WEAVE *v.*

weffler, var. WHIFFLER[1].

wefforne, obs. form of WYVERN.

weft (wɛft), *sb.*[1] Forms: 1 **wefta**, **weft**, **wift**, 4 **wyft**, **weeft**, 4–6 **wefte**, 4– **weft**; 6 **woft(e**, 7–9 *Sc.* **woft**, **waft**. [OE. *wefta* wk. masc., *weft* str. masc., ? *wift* fem., corresp. to ON. *veptr* masc., *vipta* fem., weft, MHG. *wift* masc., fine thread; repr. OTeut. types **wefton-*, **wefto-z*, **wefti-z*, f. **web-* to WEAVE.]

1. *Weaving.* The threads that cross from side to side of a web, at right angles to the warp threads with which they are interlaced: = WOOF 1.

*c***725** *Corpus Gloss.* (Hessels) D 57 *Deponile* wefta. *a***1100** *Gerefa* in *Anglia* IX. 263 He sceal fela tola to tune tilian & fela andlomena to husan habban... Fela towtola: flexlinan, spinle, reol, ȝearnwindan, wifte, wefle, wulcamb, [etc.]. *c***1100** *Gloss.* in Wr.-Wülcker 187/32 *Deponile*, wefta, *uel* weft. **1382** WYCLIF *Gen.* xiv. 23 A threed of the weeft. *Ibid.* *Exod.* xxxix. 3 He made hem into thredes, that thei myȝten be plattid with the weft of the rather colours. **1398** TREVISA *Barth. De P.R.* XVIII. xi. (Bodl. MS.), ȝif þe wefte is ibroke þei begynneþ to amende it. **14..** *Nom.* in Wr.-Wülcker 696/21 *Hec trama*, a wefte. **1570** LEVINS *Manip.* 52 Wefte, wofte, *stamen*. *Ibid.* 157 Yᵉ Woft of a web, *subtegmen*. **1615** MARKHAM *Eng. Housew.* II. iii. 89 The one they call warpe, the other weft, or els Wooffe. **1629** *Orkney Witch Trial* in *County Folk-Lore* (1903) III. 78 Christane Reid in Clett cam in ane maid errand, seiking woft to ane wob. **1664** POWER *Exp. Philos.* I. 46 In the Silk Ribbans, you might plainly see the Contexture, how the Warp and the Weft cross one another at right Angles. **1767** STERNE *Tr. Shandy* IX. xxi, She..wets it—dries it—then takes her teeth to both warp and weft of it. **1788** PICKEN *Poems Scot. Dial.* 248 Gloss., *Waft*, woof. **1822** SCOTT *Pirate* xxxii, And we have many of foreign knacks Of finer waft than woo' or flax. **1832** HT. MARTINEAU *Manch. Strike* ix. 106 My father used to..set my mother to card and spin the raw cotton for the weft. **1860** SMILES *Self Help* ii. 34 'Blackburn Greys,' consisting of linen weft and cotton warp. **1867** MORRIS *Jason* xv. 360 And Eradne left The carding of the fine wool for the weft. **1876** ROCK *Text. Fabr.* v. 41 Bagdad or Baldak silks, with a weft of gold, known among us as 'baudekins'.

fig. **1563** *Mirr. Mag., Richard Dk. Glouc.* xx, Of ambicion behold the worke [? *read* warpe] and weft, Prouoking me to do this haynous treason. *a***1693** *Urquhart's Rabelais* III. xxviii. 237 Wouldst thou..untwist all the Threads of the warp and the waft of the weer'd Sister Parques?

b. The strips of cane, palm-leaf, straw, etc. used as the filling, in weaving baskets, mats, etc. Also, the woven fabric.

1845 *Jrnl. R. Agric. Soc.* VI. I. 212 Many workmen thoughtlessly force their feet between the weft or horizontal branches of the hurdle. **1859** C. WILLIAMS *Narr. & Adv. Trav. Africa* xvii. 189 Flags, reeds, and bulrushes..are woven..into mats..and so close is their weft that neither light, nor wind..can penetrate it. **1859** *Abridgm. Specif. Patents, Weaving* (1861) 1015 For these purposes wires..may be used as the warps of the fabric, and straw or rushes or other materials being the weft. **1875** KNIGHT *Dict. Mech.*, *Straw-fabric Loom.* A loom for making goods the weft of which is straw.

2. Yarn to be used for the weft-threads.

1795 AIKIN *Country Round Manchester* 233 Employed in spinning cotton wefts for check-makers. **1802** *Bancks's Manch. & Salford Directory* 29 Brown, Richard and Co. dealers in twist, weft, &c. **1846** MᶜCULLOCH *Acc. Brit. Empire* (1854) I. 677 All sorts of wefts, from the lowest to the highest numbers, are now spun by means of this machine. **1898** *Daily News* 16 May 8/5 Tow wefts..have been dealt in to a larger extent than for weeks back. **1902** *Times* 29 July 11/3 Doubled wefts are offered at easy prices; single wefts are dull.

3. That which is spun or woven.

1398 TREVISA *Barth De P.R.* XIX. lv. (1495) 896 Certen smalle wormes as it were attercoppes..done spynne and weue and make webbes and weftes abowte the hony combes. **1570** LEVINS *Manip.* 52/45 Wefte, wofte, *stamen*. **1697** DRYDEN *Virg. Georg.* I. 381 Then Weavers stretch your Stays upon the Weft. **1706** PHILLIPS (ed. Kersey), *Weft*, a thing woven; as *A Weft of Hair*. **1799** H. GURNEY *Cupid & Psyche* xx. 44 See those crones that on the left Weave the many-colour'd weft. **1851** MRS. BROWNING *Casa Guidi Wind.* II. 122 Let thy weft Be of one woof and warp. **1883** WHITELAW *Sophocles, Trachin.* 675 The investiture O' the robe, a weft of wool, fleecy and white.

b. *fig.* and in figurative context.

*c***1400** *26 Pol. Poems* xxi. 64 In helle is shewed euell-sponnen wyft. *c***1460** *Towneley Myst.* ii. 435 Yey, ill spon weft ay comes foule out. **1719** HAMILTON *Ep. to Ramsay* 24 July v, I'm unco iri, and dirt feart I mak' wrang waft. **1864** SWINBURNE *Atalanta* 738 The weft of the world was untorn That is woven of the day on the night. **1891** 'R. BOLDREWOOD' *Sydney-side Sax.* ii, I cannot unravel the weft of it. I've made and helped to make a sight of victual in my day, and now [etc.].

4. Transferred uses. †**a.** A film formed over the eye. *Obs.*

1661 LOVELL *Hist. Anim. & Min.* 29 The ashes of the head of a black Cat..put into the eye..helpe the haw, weft, and web in the eye. *Ibid.* 105 The gall [of the Rock-goat] cureth the weft in the eye.

b. A layer of closely interwoven hyphæ produced in certain fungi; also a 'mat' of hairs on the stem or leaf of a plant.

1875 COOKE *Fungi* ii. 26 Certain filaments of the weft of the fungus. **1879** *Academy* 11 Jan. 33/1 The access of..injurious insects to the flower is prevented..by the dense weft of woolly hairs which covers the stem and leaves. **1887** tr. *De Bary's Fungi* v. 217 The peripheral portion of the delicate hyphal weft..takes an active part in the further growth.

c. (See quot.)

1847 HALLIWELL, *Weft*,..(5) The ground of a wig.

5. A streak of cloud; a thin layer of smoke or mist. Cf. WAFT *sb.*[1] 2 d, WAIF *sb.*[3]

*a***1822** SHELLEY *Queen of My Heart* ii, And thy beauty more bright Than the stars' soft light, Shall seem as a weft from the sky. **1883** SYMONDS *Ital. Byways* 97 Exceedingly soft and grey, with rose-tinted weft of steam upon its summit, stood Vesuvius above us in the twilight. **1897** MARY KINGSLEY *W. Africa* 187 The mountains..opposite were just enough illumined to let one see the wefts and floating veils of blue-white mist upon them.

6. *attrib.* and *Comb.*, as ***weft cop*** (COP *sb.*[2] 3), ***dealer, thread, warehouse, winding, yarn***; **weft-finger** (*Knitting*), the forefinger; **weft fork**, (*a*) a pronged *weft stopper*; (*b*) (see quot. 1875); **weft-hook** (see quot.); **weft line**, flax (see LINE *sb.*[1] 1 b) for the manufacture of weft-thread; **weft (stop) motion, stopper**, a device that automatically causes a stoppage of the loom when the weft-thread breaks or fails; **weft-way** (see quot.).

1881 *Weft cop [see TWIST *sb.*[1] 23]. **1892** *Daily News* 16 July 7/1 There is only a very small demand for twist and weft cops for the home trade. **1802** *Bancks's Manch. & Salford Directory* 34 *Weft and twist dealer. **1880** [MRS. FLOYER] *Plain Hints Needlework* 37 The..fore, or '*weft', finger; the thumb, or 'rest:' the second, or 'position' finger. **1851** in *Abridgm. Specif. Patents, Weaving* (1861) 329 Improvements in the manufacture of *weft forks..for looms. **1875** KNIGHT *Dict. Mech.*, *Weft-fork*, one used in certain kinds of looms where the filling is laid in, one piece at a time. **1898** *Daily News* 7 Mar. 2/1 As soon as either thread breaks the machine is stopped immediately by the weft forks. **1875** KNIGHT *Dict. Mech.*, **Weft-hook*, one for drawing in the filling in the case of slat-weaving looms and some forms of narrow-ware and ribbon looms. **1896** *Daily News* 5 Dec. 9/4 The range of *weft lines continues unchanged at 3*s.* 1½*d.* **1863** in *Abridgm. Specif. Patents Weaving* II. (1871) 410 That part of the loom known as the '*weft motion' for stopping the loom when the weft breaks. **1878** A. BARLOW *Hist. Weaving* xxiv. 261 The fork and grid *weft stop motion. **1853** in *Abridgm. Specif. Patents Weaving* (1861) 408 An improved *weft stopper for two or more shuttles. **1843** *Penny Cycl.* XXVII. 177/1 Into this shed..he throws the shuttle containing the *weft-thread. **1802** *Bancks's Manch. & Salford Directory* p. iv, Twist, *weft and calico warehouse. **1888** C. P. BROOKS *Cotton Manuf.* 168 **Weft-way*, yarn twisted over to the right in spinning. Weft may be either twist-way or weft-way. **1863** B. WOODCROFT *Brief Biogr.* 44 A *weft-winding engine. **1835** URE *Philos. Manuf.* 330 It must be spun into warp-yarn and *weft yarn, each of peculiar grist.

†**weft**, *sb.*[2] *Obs.* Also 6 **waift**, **wayft**, 7–8 **waft**. Variant or perversion of WAIF *sb.*[1]

1579 *Acts Privy Counc.* (1895) XI. 196 Claiming the ship and goodes as a weft dewe to the lordes of the soile. *Ibid.* 247. **1590** SPENSER *F.Q.* III. x. 36 The gentle Lady..did..wander wide At wilde aduenture, like a forlorne weft. **1596** *Ibid.* IV. ii. 4. *Ibid.* IV. xii. 31 For that a waift [i.e. Florimell], the which by fortune came Vpon your seas, he claym'd as propertie. **1591** *Art. conc. Admiralty* 21 July §46 Those, which vpon the high Seas, haue found any..Boates forsaken, or wayfts, driuing, or floating, without any creature in the same. **1599** B. JONSON *Ev. Man out of Hum.* I. ii, The Lord of the soile ha's al wefts and straies here? *a* **1625** FLETCHER *Elder Brother* IV. iv, You are Lord o' the soile Sir, Lilly is a Weft, a Straie, shee's yours, to use Sir. **1678** DRYDEN *Limberham* V. i, Do you know that I am Lady of the Mannour: and that all Wefts and Strays belong to me? *a* **1680** BUTLER *Characters* (1908) 127 His Belly is provided for,..his Back..takes other Courses to maintain itself by weft and stray Silver Spoons, stragling Hoods and Scarfs, [etc.]. *c* **1680** BEVERIDGE *Serm.* (1729) I. 532 It is as a waft or stray, that belongs only to the head landlord of the world, to whom therefore you must restore it. **1708** J. CHAMBERLAYNE *St. Gt. Brit.* II. II. xii. 498 The Causes competent to the Admiralty Court of Scotland, are these among others... Wafts, and Strays, and Deodands, and Wrecks. **1838** SOUTHEY *Lett.* (1856) IV. 560 Farther corrections I shall make..for a posthumous edition, in which also I shall embody some wefts and strays.

weft (wɛft), *v. rare.* Also *Sc.* waft. [f. WEFT *sb.*[1]] *intr.* To form a weft or web; to interlace the weft with the warp. Hence **'wefting** *vbl. sb.*

1785 BURNS *2nd Ep. J. Lapraik* viii, Ne'er mind how Fortune waft an' warp. **1897** *Westm. Gaz.* 19 Jan. 8/1 The warping, wefting, milling and finishing occupied 3h. 15 min.

weft, Sc., dial., and Naut. form of WAFT *sb.*[1]

weft, obs. pa. pple. of WEAVE *v.*

†**'weftage**[1]. *Obs. rare*⁻¹. [f. *weft* var. WAFT *v.*[1] + -AGE.] Conveyance: = WAFTAGE.

1615 CROOKE *Body of Man* 175 The naturall faculty needeth no vehicle or weftage, because it is inbred in euery part.

weftage[2] ('wɛftɪdʒ). [f. WEFT *sb.*[1] + -AGE.] The arrangement of the threads of a woven fabric. Chiefly *transf.*

1681 GREW *Musæum* I. §i. 3 Whereby also the weftage of the fibers..of the Muscules might more easily..be observed. **1746** G. ADAMS *Microgr.* xxxvii. §4. (1747) 203 The Weftage of the Fibres [of wood]. **1901** F. E. TAYLOR *Folk-Sp. S. Lanc.* (E.D.D.), *Weftage*, the texture of woven cloth.

wefted ('wɛftɪd), *a.* [f. WEFT *sb.*[1] + -ED.] Composed of interwoven hyphæ.

1902 *Encycl. Brit.* XXVIII. 554/1 The thallus..is..composed of..cell-filaments, with apical growth (hyphæ), or of more or less complex wefted sheets or tissue-like masses of such (mycelium).

wefty ('wɛftɪ), *a. rare.* [f. WEFT *sb.*[1] + -Y[1].] Of the nature of a weft (of thread, filament, vapour).

1867 W. BARNES *J. Poole's Gloss. Eng. Colony Forth & Bargy, Wexford*, s.v., *Wefty*, webby, cobwebby. **1876** J. W. MARSTON *Dram. & Poet. Wks.* II. 379 There stood a gaunt form pale But regal... His brow Was circled by a wefty coronet.

Wegener[1] ('veɪgənə(r)). *Geol.* The name of Alfred *Wegener* (1880–1930), German geophysicist, used in the possessive with reference to the theory of continental drift which he first published in 1912.

1922 *Living Age* 10 June 657 Professor F. E. Weiss..writes in the Manchester Guardian that Professor Wegener's theory 'constitutes a good working hypothesis, and the striking simplicity with which it allows many phenomena to be explained will greatly stimulate further enquiry'. **1926** [see *continental drift* s.v. CONTINENTAL *a.* 1 d]. **1963** *Sci. Amer.* Apr. 90/1 Between 1920 and 1922 Wegener's hypothesis excited great controversy. **1982** *Nature* 23/30 Dec. 681/2 Jeffreys refers with regret to the defection of Sir Arthur Holmes to 'Wegener's theory'.

Hence **Wege'nerian** *a.*

1960 *Bull. Amer. Assoc. Petroleum Geologists* XLIV. 245 (*caption*) Early tertiary paleography and trans-Atlantic migration route for shelf benthos according to Wegenerian hypothesis of continental drift. **1967** *Oceanogr. & Marine Biol.* V. 340 Some zoologists are inclined to accept the Wegenerian idea that the Atlantic Ocean is indeed young, and of no greater antiquity than the Cretaceous. **1980** *Guardian* 20 Nov. 13/8 Pangea..probably existed for a few hundred million years before it..began to break up to generate Wegenerian drift.

Wegener[2] ('veɪgənə(r)). *Path.* [The name of F. *Wegener*, 20th-century German physician.] ***Wegener's granulomatosis***: an often fatal disease characterized by granulomatosis of the respiratory tract and necrotizing blood-vessels.

1948 *Acta Path. & Microbiol. Scandinav.* XXV. 582 Clinically, this case agreed well with the previously described cases of Wegener's granulomatosis. **1957** *Thorax* XII. 57/1 The syndrome has been known as Wegener's granulomatosis since his detailed description of three cases in 1936 and 1939. **1977** *Daily Colonist* (Victoria, B.C.) 4 Dec. 27/6 An autopsy showed that my grandmother died of a very rare disease called Wegener's granulomatosis.

wegg(e, obs. forms of WEDGE.

weggebobble ('wɛdʒɪbɒb(ə)l). *nonce-wd.* Humorous alteration of VEGETABLE *sb.*

1922 JOYCE *Ulysses* 163 Coming from the vegetarian. Only weggebobbles and fruit.

wegh, var. WYE *Obs.*, a man; obs. f. WEY.

weghe, obs. form of WEIGH *v.*

weght, obs. form of WEIGHT *sb.*[1] and *sb.*[2]

wegion, -yon, obs. ff. WIDGEON.

wegotism ('wiːgətɪz(ə)m). [A jocular formation on WE and EGOTISM.] An obtrusive and too frequent use of the first person plural by a speaker or writer.

1797 *Brit. Critic* IX. 424 A more trifling matter of objection is the use of the plural form [we] throughout in speaking of himself... In an individual preacher..it seems a strange desertion of propriety: and if used to avoid egotism, leads to that which..if we did not too much respect etymology, we might jocularly style *Wegotism*. **1811** MISS L. M. HAWKINS *C'tess & Gertr.* I. Introd., We may have blended *wegotism* and *egotism*; but Cæsar writes 'dixeram' and 'scripsimus'. **1881** H. J. JENNINGS *Curios. Crit.* 156 What has been called the 'wegotism' of the press.

wehee (wiːˈhiː), *int.* and *sb. Obs.* exc. *dial.* Forms: α. 4, 6 wehe (4 wey), 4 wehee, 6–7 weehee, 7 wehie, weahae; 9 *Sc.* wehaw. β. 4 whi (? wihi), 6 wyhie, wigh-hie, 6–7 wihy, 7 wihee (whhi-hhee), 7–9 *dial.* wighee. [Echoic.]

A. *int.* A conventional representation of the sound uttered by horses.

1362 LANGL. *P. Pl.* A. VIII. 75 (MS. T.) As wilde bestis wiþ wehe worþ vp togedere. *c* **1386** CHAUCER *Reeve's T.* 146 Whan the hors was laus, he gynneth gon Toward the fen, ther wilde Mares renne Forth with wehee [*v.r.* wehe]. *c* **1520** SKELTON *Magnyf.* 477 And Annot wolde be nyce, and laughes, 'tehe, wehe'. **1567** *Triall of Treasure* E iij, We, he, he, he, he, ware the horse heles I saye. **1594** LYLY *Mother Bombie* IV. ii. 194 Hee neither would cry wyhie, nor wag the taile. **1603** DEKKER *Patient Grissill* 567 So they can crie wighee and hollow, kicking iade. **1606** CHAPMAN *Gentl. Usher* I. i. 30 One cannot crie 'wehie', but straight shee [your Barbarie mare] cries 'tihi'. **1654** [see TEE-HEE *int.*]. *c* **1690** *Roxb. Ballads* (1890) VII. 56 The Tapster bid them welcome then, and wea-hae did cry.

b. Used to a horse.

1821 MACTAGGART *Gallov. Encycl.* 472 *Wehaw!* a cry which displeases horses. **1847** HALLIWELL, *Wighee*, an exclamation to horses.

B. *sb.* An utterance of this sound; a whinny or neigh.

1362 LANGL. *P. Pl.* A. IV. 21 ȝit wol he make moni a whi [*v.rr.* many (a) wehe, wey] er he come þere. *c* **1589** *Whip for Ape* 26 in *Lyly's Wks.* (1902) III. 418 Such hahaes, teehees, weehees, wild colts play. **1592** *Def. Conny-Catching* in *Greene's Wks.* (Grosart) XI. 59 The olde Churle comming an hower before Supper time,..for an amorous wehe or two, as olde Jades wynnie when they cannot wagge the tayle. **1599** B. JONSON *Ev. Man out of Hum.* II. i, There's ne're a Gentleman i' the countrey has the like humors for the Hobby-horse as I haue? I haue the Methode for the threeding of the needle,..and the wigh-hie, and the daggers in the Nose,..all the Humors incident to the qualitie. **1618** FLETCHER *Women pleas'd* IV. i, His [the hobby-horse's] lewd wihies. **1654** GAYTON *Pleas. Notes* To Rdr., Rosinante looks for your Tih-hee, and you shall have his Whhi-hhee. **1673** *Char. Coffee-House* 6 To..make an Oration to Caligula's Horse, whence you can only expect a weehee or Jadish spurn.

†**wehee**, *v. Obs.* Forms: 6–7 wighy, 7 wighie, wihy, wyhee, weyhey. [f. prec.] *intr.* To neigh or whinny, as a horse does.

1599 MARSTON *Ant. & Mel.* III. (1602) F 2, Tis an old horse can neither wighy, nor wagge his taile. **1606** —— *Parasit.* IV. G 1 b, Al that can wyhee or wag the taile, are vpon grievous paines of their backe summond to be assistant in that Session of loue. **1615** [HOBY] *Curry-Combe for Coxe-Combe* iv. 156 'Tis an ill Horse that can neyther wey-hey, nor wagge his taile. **1618** BRETON *Courtier & Countryman* (Grosart) 8/2 The young Colts wighie at their parting with their Fillies. **1668** DAVENANT *Rivals* III. 36 Tho' lightly on the hobby-horse and dancers, He learns to Wighy, and the rest to prance—Sirs. **1847** HALLIWELL, Wehee, Wihie.

wehl, obs. form of WAIL *v.*[1]

‖**Wehmut** ('veːmuːt). [Ger.] Sadness, melancholy, wistfulness, nostalgia.

1907 M. A. VON ARNIM *Fräulein Schmidt & Mr. Anstruther* xlii. 130 What I feel when I listen to music is chiefly *Wehmut*, and I don't think much of *Wehmut*... It is a forlorn thing, made up mostly of vague ingredients—vague yearnings, vague regrets, vague dissatisfactions. **1920** D. H. LAWRENCE *Let.* in C. Mackenzie *My Life & Times* (1966) V. 170, I get a sort of Wehmut. Quoi faire! **1933** J. HILTON *Lost Horizon* 20 A sort of universal sadness,..something remote or impersonal, a *Wehmut* or *Weltschmerz*, or whatever the Germans call it.

wehrgeld, -gelt: see WERGELD.

wehrlite ('veəlaɪt, 'wɜːlaɪt). [f. the name of Adolf *Wehrle* (1795–1835), Austrian Councillor of Mines: see -ITE[1].] **1.** *Petrogr.* [ad. G. *wehrlit* (F. von Kobell *Grundzüge d. Mineral.* (1838) iii. 313).] A peridotite mainly consisting of olivine and monoclinic pyroxene with common accessory opaque oxides.

1861 H. W. BRISTOW *Gloss. Mineral.* 404/1 *Wehrlite*, the name given by von Kobell to a massive granular mineral, which is probably a variety of Lievrite. **1913** J. P. IDDINGS *Igneous Rocks* II. I. vi. 316 Wehrlite is closely associated with olivine-gabbro, into which it grades with increasing feldspar. **1979** *Nature* 7 June 489/2 The cumulate peridotites are recognised in thin sections which show serpentinised wehrlite with 50% clinopyroxene.

2. *Min.* [a. F. *wehrlite* (J. J. N. Huot *Nouveau Man. complet de Minéral.* (1841) I. 188).] A native rhombohedral alloy of bismuth and tellurium occurring as tin-white to steel-grey foliated masses.

1874 *Amer. Jrnl. Sci.* CVIII. 259 The following minerals are positive (+), or negative (−), in contact with copper:.. Wehrlite $Bi_2(TeS)_4$ +. **1931** *Chem. Abstr.* XXV. 1762 Eleven Te minerals are found in Hungary... Tetradymite, ..wehrlite..and stützite are described. **1972** *Doklady Earth Sci.* CC. 167/1 Wehrlite is a sulfur-free bismuth telluride whose composition and position in the classification of minerals are interpreted differently by various authors. Wehrlite was first described at the Deutsch Pilsen deposit, Hungary.

‖**Wehrmacht** ('veːrmaxt). Now *Hist.* [Ger., lit. 'defence force'.] The name used for the German armed forces between 1921 and 1945. Also *attrib.*

1935 in *Documents on German Foreign Policy* (1959) III. 1008 Ranks and badges of rank of the members of the Reich Air Ministry..will assume a military character and resemble those of the Wehrmacht. **1945** *Daily Mirror* 8 May 3/2 The Wehrmacht commander announced that he did not recognise what he described as the 'armistice'. **1945** 'G. ORWELL' in *Tribune* 9 Nov. 10/3 He..attempted to pass himself off as an ordinary soldier of the Wehrmacht. **1959** M. CROSLAND tr. *J. Rovan's Germany* 176 Young Germans ..begin travelling around the country armed with a stewpan and an old Wehrmacht kitbag. **1965** *English Studies* XLVI. 226 The Wehrmacht mentality is plain, the terrible joyous uplift in the fact of killing, the terrible satisfaction to be extracted from a sense of the irresistible. **1978** L. HEREN *Growing up on The Times* vii. 257 Of all the armies which fought in the second world war, the *Wehrmacht* was undoubtedly the best, perhaps the best in history.

wehrwolf: see WERWOLF.

wehte, pa. t. of WECCHE *v. Obs.*

wehy, var. WYE *Obs.*, a man.

Wei (weɪ). The name of a Chinese dynasty, esp. one of the partial dynasties ruling (in the north of China) from the mid-4th to the mid-6th cent. A.D. Also used *attrib.* and *absol.* to designate works of art, esp. sculpture and pottery, produced in the period.

1894 G. N. CURZON *Probl. Far East* viii. 276 The Inner Wall is attributed to the Wei dynasty in A.D. 542. **1913** R. FRY *Let.* 31 May (1972) II. 368 I've just seen a show in Paris full of the most amazing things; among them the finest Wei Dynasty statues from somewhere away in the west of China. **1952** WATSON-GANDY & GORDON tr. *Grousset's Rise & Splendour Chinese Empire* xv. 111 Their dynasty was called Wei (often referred to as T'o-pa Wei to distinguish it from the Three Kingdoms Wei). *Ibid.* 114 Wei sculpture has been called the Far Eastern equivalent of the Romanesque and Gothic sculptures which developed six and eight centuries later in Europe. **1960** C. WINICK *Dict. Anthropol.* 556/1 *Wei*,..unglazed pottery often decorated with pigment and tomb figures of the Wei dynasty in China, A.D. 368–557. **1982** M. YOUNG *Elmhirsts of Dartington* viii. 196 Ancient Chinese pots of the Han, Wei, Tang and Sung dynasties.

wei, obs. f. WAY, WEIGH, WEY, WHEY, WOE.

weibullite ('vaɪbʊlaɪt). *Min.* [ad. Sw. *weibullit* (G. Flink 1910, in *Ark. f. Kemi, Mineral. och Geol.* III. xxxv. 4), f. the name of K. O. M. *Weibull* (1856–1923), Swedish mineralogist: see -ITE[1].] A mineral containing lead, bismuth, selenium, and sulphur and occurring as grey crystals at Falun, Sweden; now regarded as an orthorhombic species but for long of uncertain status.

1913 *Mineral. Mag.* XVI. 375 Weibullite... This mineral, from Falun, Sweden, was described by M. Weibull in 1885 as a seleniferous variety of galenobismutite. **1980** *Amer. Mineralogist* LXV. 789 Studies of specimens from Falun, Sweden, reported to contain the two minerals weibullite and wittite have established at least *three* selenium-rich bismuth-lead sulphosalts of similar chemistry. A nomenclature is proposed in which two of the minerals retain the old names weibullite and wittite, while the third is given the new name nordströmite.

‖**wei ch'i** (weɪ tʃiː). Also **wei chi**. [Chinese *wéiqí*, f. *wei* to surround + *qí* chess.] A traditional Chinese board game of territorial possession, equivalent to GO *sb.*[2]

1871 *Jrnl. North-China Branch R. Asiatic Soc.* VI. 107 The chessman of the *wei ch'i*..are generally *not* made of ivory, but of stone or a glassy substance. **1892** *Ibid.* XXVI. 80 *Wei-ch'i* is considered *par excellence* the game of the literary class, while Chess is the favourite diversion of military men. **1911** H. F. CHESHIRE *Handbk. Goh or Wei Chi* 148 To the cultured classes..'Wei Chi',..was, and is an almost essential part of their life. **1917** *Encycl. Sinica* 594/1 *Wei ch'i, surrounding chess*, often called chess by foreigners. .. The square board on which it is played is divided by eighteen lines each way, making 324 squares. The play..is at the points where the lines cut or meet. **1969** R. C. BELL *Board & Table Games* II. iii. 59 The eighteenth-century Chinese painting on glass reproduced as the frontispiece, shows two ladies playing Wei-ch'i on an antique form of board of 13 × 11 squares. **1976** *New Yorker* 26 Jan. 23/2 The pattern recalls the Chinese game of wei-ch'i (known here by its Japanese name, *go*), in which a player captures his opponent's counters by surrounding them with his own.

Weichsel ('vaɪksəl). *Geol.* The German form of the name of the river Vistula in Poland, used *attrib.* and *absol.* to designate the fourth and final Pleistocene glaciation in northern Europe, corresponding to the Würm glaciation of the Alps. Hence **Weich'selian** *a.* (also *absol.*).

1934 R. A. DALY *Changing World of Ice Age* i. 29 Recently four Glacial stages have been traced in Germany. Figure 19 shows the nested moraines of three, named in order of decreasing age, Elster, Saale, and Weichsel. **1968** EMBLETON & KING *Glacial & Periglacial Geomorphol.* 10 The links with North America, apart from the correlation of the Wisconsinan with the Würm/Weichselian, are more tenuous. **1969** BENNISON & WRIGHT *Geol. Hist. Brit. Isles* xvi. 361 After the early Weichselian glaciation the climate varied considerably. **1974** *Encycl. Brit. Micropædia* X. 598/3 The Weichsel Glacial Stage has been divided into at least two main cold phases,..separated from each other by a period of more moderate climatic conditions, an interstadial. **1979** *Jrnl. Arid Environments* II. 293 Five successive units of time, respectively the Palaeozoic, the Mesozoic, the Tertiary, the Quaternary, and the late Weichselian and Flandrian.

weid(e: see WEED *sb.*[1], *sb.*[2], *v.*[1], WEDE *v.*, WIDE *adv.*

weidenagemoot, obs. form of WITENAGEMOT.

weido, obs. Sc. form of WIDOW.

weie, obs. form of WAY, WEIGH, *v.*, WEY, WYE.

Weierstrassian (ˌvaɪəˈstrɑːsɪən), *a. Math.* [f. name of Karl W. *Weierstrass* (1815–97), an eminent German mathematician + -(I)AN.] Pertaining to or invented by Weierstrass, esp. *Weierstrassian function.*

1878 CAYLEY *Math. Papers* (1896) X. 434 We have thus in all 21 equations which exhibit the form of the Weierstrassian functions al $(u, v, w)_{12}, \ldots$, al $(u, v, w)_{67}$. **1884** DANIELS in *Amer. Jrnl. Math.* VI. 256 The Weierstrassian proof of this ..is as follows. **1901** OSGOOD in *Ann. Math.* Ser. II. II. 122 The Weierstrassian function 𝔈.

weiete, obs. form of WET *a.*

weif(f, obs. Sc. forms of WEAVE *v.*[1]

weife, obs. form of WIFE.

‖**Weigela, Weigelia** (waɪˈdʒiːlə, -ˈdʒiːlɪə). *Bot.* [mod.L., f. name of C. E. *Weigel*, a German physician (1748–1831).] A genus of caprifoliaceous shrubs from China and Japan cultivated for its flowers, now commonly merged in *Diervilla*; a plant of this genus.

1846 *Jrnl. Horticultural Soc.* I. 66 A Weigela..from the North of China. **1851** GLENNY *Handbk. Fl. Garden* (1855) 401 Weigela. Very handsome hardy deciduous shrubs, adapted for planting against ornamental walls. **1875** W. CORY *Lett. & Jrnls.* (1897) 384 Weigelia is out in glory. **1882** *Garden* 18 Mar. 184/2 All the Weigelas delight in a good, free soil.

†**Wei'gelian**, *sb.* and *a. Obs.* [f. the proper name *Weigel* (see below) + IAN.] **A.** *sb.* A follower or adherent of the German mystic Valentin Weigel (1533–88). **B.** *adj.* Of or pertaining to Weigel, his opinions or followers.

1657 BAXTER *Present Th.* 4 The persons holding this third Opinion are the Paracelsians (under whom I comprehend the Weigelians and the rest of the Enthusiasts). **1676** W. HUBBARD *Happin. People* 28 No man, unless a Weigelian Sceptick, ever did account Moses less fit to be a Leader unto Israel because he was learned in all the wisdome of the Egyptians.

weigh (weɪ), *sb.*[1] Forms: 1 **wǽʒ(e, wéʒ, 2 wæiʒe, 3 weie, 4 waye, weih, weʒe, 4–5 weigh(e, 5, 9 wee, 5–7, 9** *dial.* **wey, 6 wye, 7–9 way, 9** *dial.* **weigh.** [OE. *wǽʒ* str. fem., *wǽʒe* wk. fem. (both meaning 'balance' and 'weight'; see WEY), corresp. to OS. *wâga* (MLG. *wâge*, MDu. *wâghe*, Du. *waag*; see WAW *sb.*[2]), OHG. *wâga* (MHG. *wâge*, mod.G. *wage*), ON. *vág*, (Sw. *våg*, Da. *vaag*):—OTeut. **wǣʒō-*, *-ōn-*, f. **wǣʒ-*(: **weʒ-*: **waʒ-*): see WEIGH *v.*]

†**1.** A weight. *Obs.* (For the word as the name of a particular denomination of weight, see WEY.)

c **1000** ÆLFRIC *Gram.* xxxii. (Z.) 58 *Pondus*, byrðen oððe wæʒe [*v.r.* wæʒ]. *c* **1200** *Vices & Vertues* 11 Godd us for-bett ðat we ne sculen habbe twifeald wæiʒe ne twifeald imett.

2. A balance, pair of scales.

†**a.** *sing. Obs.*

a **1050** *Liber Scintill.* xxiv. (1889) 97 Wordu soðlice snotera on wæʒe beoð aweʒene [*Ecclus.* xxi. 28 *statera ponderabuntur*]. *a* **1225** *Ancr. R.* 60 Auh seint Austin deð þeos two boðe in one weie, wilnen, & habe wille uorte beon iwilned. **1340** *Ayenb.* 255 Þe wordes of þe wyse byeþ y-weʒe ine þe waye. *c* **1350** *Will. Palerne* 947 Þou waltres al in a weih & wel y vnderstande whider þe belaunce bremliest bouwes al-gate. **1382** WYCLIF *Prov.* xi. 1 A treccherous weʒe [Vulg. *statera*] abominacioun is anent God. *a* **1450** *Mirk's Festial* 221 Then come thylke brennet dekon, and layde a grete pot on þe wey þe whech anon weyit vp al togedyr.

b. *plural* (sometimes construed as *sing.*). *Obs.* exc. *dial.* †Also, the zodiacal constellation Libra.

c **825** *Vesp. Psalter* lxi. 10 *Mendaces filii hominum in stateris*, lease bearn monna in weʒum. *c* **1100** *Gloss.* in Wr.-Wülcker 148/16 *Trutina*, wæʒa. **1340** HAMPOLE *Ps.* lxi. 9 Leighers in weighes, that is, on the weighes of rightwisnes. *c* **1400** tr. *Secreta Secret.*, *Gov. Lordsh.* 74 Heruest bygynnes whenne þe sonne entrys þe first degree of þe tokenynge of weighes. *c* **1425** WYNTOUN *Cron.* v. iv. 693 Pap Siluestir gert þaim be layide In til a weyis. **1480–1** *Durham Acc. Rolls* (Surtees) 97, j par Weez ligπ. cum ponderibus. **1533** *Extracts Aberd. Reg.* (1844) I. 451 Ane pair of woll weyiss, ane pair of ballendis of brass. **1552** LYNDESAY *Monarche* 2286 Sanct Mychaell, with his wyngis and weyis. **1573** *Extracts Aberd. Reg.* (1848) II. 10 A pair of weyis witht baikis, pryce xl. d. **1578** *Richmond Wills* (Surtees) 282 The kitchinge..A pair wyes and wyghts, iis. vjd. *c* **1587** MONTGOMERIE *Sonn.* xviii. 11 Hald evin the Weyis. **1609** SKENE *Reg. Maj.*, *Burrow Lawes* c. 125 §3 The heire..sall haue..ane flaill, the weyes [L. *stateram*], with the wechts, [etc.]. **1808** JAMIESON, *Weyes, Weyis*, a balance with scales for weighing. **1825** *Ibid.*, Weyes, Wees.

c. *Sc.* (See quot.)

1886 J. BARROWMAN *Sc. Mining Terms* 72 *Weighs*, a weigh-bridge; a waggon-weighing machine.

3. A pole borne on the shoulders of two men, for carrying a water-vessel. ? *Obs.* Also ***wey and bodkins*** (dial.): see quot.

1688 HOLME *Armoury* III. xiv. (Roxb.) 11/2 A Runge or Soe: which is a kind of vessell that Tanners, Glouers, and Beere-brewers use to carry Water in, being borne on a Way or pole betweene two men. **1844** W. BARNES *Poems Rural Life* Gloss. 368 *Wey an' bodkins*, a set of spreaders for hitching two horses to the same part of a sull or harrow. The first, the *Wey*, is fastened at its middle to the plough or harrow by a *cops*..and the *bodkins* are connected by a crook on their middle to *clipses* on the two ends of the wey.

weigh, *sb.*[2] In ***under weigh***, a common var. of *under way*, from erroneous association with the phr. 'to weigh anchor'. See WAY *sb.*[1] 38.

1777 E. DRAPER *Let.* 25 Aug. in *N. & Q.* (1944) 15 July 28/1, I can assure you on the authority of Mr. Sullivan, that he saw him underweigh in the Bessborough and for the East Indies several Weeks ago. **1785** CUMBERLAND *Observer* xii. [ix.] ¶7 This perverse wind has at last..come about to the east, so that we are all in high spirits getting under weigh. **1796** *Hist. Ned Evans* I. 182 Mr. Evans stood upon the beach till the packet got under weigh. **1840** R. H. DANA *Bef. Mast* xxiii, She got under weigh with very little fuss, and came so near us as to throw a letter on board. **1841** CATLIN *N. Amer. Ind.* xxxii. (1844) II. 2, I embarked..and was glad to get underweigh. **1855** F. C. ARMSTRONG *Warhawk* I. xii. 258 The following morning he embarked with his attendant, O'Regan, on board The Royal Anne, which got under weigh shortly after.

weigh (weɪ), *v.*[1] Pa. t. and pa. pple. weighed (weɪd). Forms: 1 **weʒan** (*3rd sing.* **wiʒeð, wihð; weʒeð, wehð**), 2–4 **weiʒe** (3 *3rd sing.* **weihð**), 3–4 **weʒe, weyʒe, 4 weghe, 6 weygh(e, waygh, 6–7 weighe, waigh(e, 6– weigh; 2–6 weie, 3–7 weye** (5 **wheyhe, 5–7** *Sc.* **veye), 4–7 (9** *Sc.*) **wey** (5–7 *Sc.* **vey); 4–7 waie, 5–7 waye** (5 **whaye), way, 6–7 weay; 5–6** *north.* and *Sc.* **wye** (5 **whye**), 7 *Sc.* **wie; 5 whe, 6** *Sc.* **we-, ve-, 9** *Sc.* **wee.** *Pa. t.* α. 1 **wæʒ,** *pl.* **wǽʒon, 3 way,** *pl.* **weʒe, 4 weʒ, wey, weyʒ(e, weygh, wayʒ, weghe, weie,** (? **woghe**). β. 3–4 **weide** (3 *pl.* **weiden**), 3–5 **weiede, 4 we(y)ʒed(e,** etc., 4–7 **weied, weyed, 6–7 wayed, waied, waighed,** etc., 6– **weighed.** *Pa. pple.* α. 1 **weʒen,** 2–3 **iwæiʒen, 4 yweʒe, weyen,** (i-), **(y)wey(e, (i)weie; 5 wawyn, wowyn, wowne.** β. 4 **yweid, (i)weied, weʒed, 4–7 weyed, 5 weiede, 5–6 weyd, 6 wei(e)d, wayed, wayd(e,** etc., 7– **weighed.** [A Com. Teut. strong verb: OE. *weʒan* (*wæʒ*, *wǽʒon*, *weʒen*) corresponds to OFris. *wega*, *weia* to move, weigh, OSax. *wegan* to weigh, (M)Du. *wegen* to weigh, OHG. *wegan* to move, shake, weigh (MHG. *wegen*; mod.G. has *bewegen* to move, while the simple verb is represented by the two verbs *wägen* trans., to weigh, *wiegen* intr., to weigh, be of a certain weight), ON. *vega* to lift, weigh (Sw. *väga*, Da. *veie*, to weigh), Goth. *ga-wigan* (only Luke vi. 38 in pa. pple. fem. *gawigana* shaken). The Teut. root **weʒ-*, **waʒ-*, **wǣʒ-* (for words representing the several grades see WAY *sb.*; WAG *v.*, WAGON, WAIN, WAW *sb.*[1] and *v.*[1]; WEIGH *sb.*[1], WEY) is:—Indogermanic **wegh-*, **wogh-*, **wēgh-*, found in Skr. *vah*, L. *vehĕre* to carry, Gr. ϝόχος, ὄχος vehicle.

The remarkably early appearance of the weak conjugation was prob. due to confusion with WEIGH *v.*[2]; the two OE. verbs *weʒan* and *wecgan* coincided in the form *weʒeð* of the 3rd sing. pres. (though the former verb had also the more normal *wiʒeð*). The strong inflexion of the pa. t. died out in the 14th century, and that of the pa. pple. in the 15th.]

I. To bear, carry, hold up; to heave up, lift.

†**1.** *trans.* To bear from one place to another; to carry, transport. *Obs.*

In quots. 13.. ? To carry round and serve (wine).

Beowulf 1207 He þa frætwe wæʒ..ofer yða ful. *c* **1000** *Narratiunculæ* (1861) 9 Micel mænigeo elpenda þa þe gold wæʒon & læddon. **13..** *E.E. Allit. P.* B. 1420 So faste þay weʒed to him wyne, hit warmed his hert. *Ibid.* 1508 Weʒe wyn in þis won, wassayl, he cryes. **13..** *Gaw. & Gr. Knt.* 1403 Wyʒez þe walle wyn weʒed to hem oft.

†**2.** To bear (arms); to wear (a robe, etc.). *Obs.*

c **897** ÆLFRED *Gregory's Past. C.* xiii. 77 On ðæm selfan hræʒle, ðe he on his breostum wæʒ. *c* **900** *Bæda's Hist* II. ix. (1890) 123 Hæfde he & wæʒ mid hine twiecge handseax ʒeættred. *c* **1205** LAY. 24471 Heo weʒe on heore honde feouwer sweord of golde. *Ibid.* 26279 Ælc weiede an sculdre sceld swiðe godne. *c* **1250** *Owl & Night.* 1022 (Cott.) He miʒte bet teche ane bore To weʒe [*Jes.* bere] boþe sheld & spere.

†**3.** With *up*: To hold up, support. *Obs.*

c **1200** *Vices & Virtues* 49 He ðe weiʒþ upp mid his fingre heuene and ierðe.

4. †**a.** With *up*: To hoist, to lift up. *Obs.*

1421–2 HOCCLEVE *Dialogue* 402 Right as a theef þat hath eschapid ones The roop, no dreede hath eft his art to vse, Til þat the trees him weye vp, body and bones. **1563–83** FOXE *A. & M.* 1472/2 They tooke the sayd Roode and weyed hym vppe and set him in his olde accustomed place. **1669** WORLIDGE *Syst. Agric.* viii. §1. 132 With which Tongs you may Beclip the [Hop-]Pole at the bottom, and resting the joynt thereof on a block of wood, you may weigh up the Pole.

†**b.** *fig.* To raise up, exalt. *Obs.*

c **1586** C'TESS PEMBROKE *Ps.* CVII. xiv, [God] from want the poore doth waigh.

c. *Naut.* To set up (a mast).

1841 DANA *Seaman's Man.* 134 *Weigh*, to lift up; as, to weigh an anchor or a mast.

5. a. *Naut.* To heave up (a ship's anchor) from the ground, before sailing. Now usually *to **weigh anchor*** (without art.). †Formerly also with *up*, *in*.

13.. *E.E. Allit. P.* C. 103 Cables þay fasten, Wiʒt at þe wyndas weʒen her ankres. ? *a* **1400** *Morte Arth.* 740 Wyghtly one þe wale thay wye up þaire ankers. **1492** *Acta Dom. Concil.* (1839) 245/1 Compelling of þe saidis Wegeantis seruitouris to wey þer ankeris. **1509** BARCLAY *Shyp of Folys* (1874) I. 108 Come to our shyp our ankers ar in wayde. *c* **1515** *Cocke Lorell's B.* (Percy Soc.) 14 Than Cocke wayed anker, and housed his sayle. *a* **1548** HALL *Chron.*, *Hen. V* 44 b, When the wynde was prosperous..they waied up the Ankers. **1556** W. TOWSON in Hakluyt *Voy.* (1589) 101 We wayed our Grapnel and went away. **1628** DIGBY *Voy. Mediterr.* (1868) 19, I weighed anchor and sett sayle. **1632** LITHGOW *Trav.* II. 45 The windes fauouring vs, we weighed Ankors. **1653** HOLCROFT *Procopius*, *Gothick Wars* I. 11 Constantianus wayed Anchor from Epidaurus. **1720** DE FOE *Capt. Singleton* x. (1840) 173 We weighed anchor the same tide, and stood out to sea. **1814** SCOTT *Ld. of Isles* III. iv, Cormac Doil..Hoisted his sail, his anchor weigh'd. **1835** SIR J. ROSS *Narr. 2nd Voy.* v. 77 We immediately weighed anchor.

b. *fig.*

1546 J. HEYWOOD *Prov.* (1867) 17, I will streight weie anker, and hoyse vp sayle. **1633** MASSINGER *Guardian* Prol., Our Author weighs up anchors, and once more Forsaking the security of the shore, Resolves to prove his fortune. **1650** R. STAPYLTON *Strada's Low C. Wars* II. 36 As often as this sacred Anchor [of Religion] is weighed, so often the Ship of the Common-Wealth is tossed. **1882** *Century Mag.* Sept. 707/2 He for whom the sexton has tolled the bell has 'weighed anchor'.

c. *absol.* = to weigh anchor. Hence, to sail (*from*, *out of* a port, etc.).

1513 SIR E. HOWARD in Ellis *Orig. Lett.* Ser. II. I. 215 We cowd ryd no lenger ther withowt gret danger,..we weyd to get us in to the Downes. **1549** *Compl. Scot.* vi. 40 The maister..bald the marynalis lay the cabil to the cabilstok, to veynde and veye. **1556** W. TOWSON in Hakluyt *Voy.* (1589) 101 Wee wayed and set saile. **1613** J. SARIS *Voy. Japan* (Hakl. Soc.) 1 The 14th in the morning we wayed out of the roade of Bantam for Japan. *a* **1647** PETTE in *Archaeologia* XII. 226 On Wednesday..we weighed from Limehouse, and anchored right against the Tower. **1748** *Anson's Voy.* I. iv. (ed. 4) 47 On the 3d of November we weighed from Madera. **1808** WELLINGTON in Gurw. *Desp.* IV. 193, I found about 60 of the convoy had lost their anchors in attempting to weigh. **1867** *Pall Mall Gaz.* 19 July 9/1 It would have been necessary for each ship to weigh singly, which would have occupied fifteen minutes each. **1893** H. M. DOUGHTY *Wherry in Wendish Lands* 20 In the morning we weighed early.

6. a. To raise (a sunk ship, gun, etc.) from the bottom of the water. Also with *up*.

a. *a* **1500** in *Arnolde's Chron.* (1811) 133 After tyme she was weyed and toued to the hauyn at Caleis. *a* **1548** HALL *Chron.*, *Hen. VIII* 26 Leuyng the gonne (because the master carpenter sayde yᵗ he woulde shortely way it out of the water). **1578** W. BOURNE *Treas. Trav.* IV. viii. 17 Then it will waygh or lyfte the sunken Shyppe from the bottome. **1669** STURMY *Mariner's Mag.* v. xii. 81 Rules to weigh Ships, or Guns, or any thing else in the Water. **1726** SHELVOCKE *Voy. round World* 239 [The diver] could find but one small gun, which he weigh'd and brought ashore. **1777** J. PUTNAM in Sparks *Corr. Amer. Rev.* (1853) II. 540 Should the enemy succeed in weighing the chevaux-de-frise, and proceed up the river. **1783** COWPER *Let. to J. Hill* 20 Oct., I must beg leave, however..to mourn..that the Royal George cannot be weighed.

b. **1545** DK. SUFFOLK in Hooker *Life Sir P. Carew* (1857) 129, I trust by Monday or Twisday..the Mary Rose shalbe wayed upp and saved. **1598** W. PHILLIP tr. *Linschoten* I. xcix. 194/2 The Reuenge had in her diuers faire brasse peeces, that were all sunke in the sea, which they of the Island were in good hope to waigh vp againe. **1643** BAKER *Chron.*, *Hen. VIII.* 7 A great Gunne..was overthrowne in a deep Pond of water;..the Master Carpenter taking with him a hundred labourers, went and weyed it up. *a* **1700** EVELYN *Diary* 6 June 1687, A vast treasure, which was sunk in a Spanish galloon..was now weigh'd up by some gentlemen. **1735** S. GALE in *Archaeologia* I. 189 *note*, One of these stakes, entire, was actually weighed up between two loaded barges at the time of a great flood. **1760** S. DERRICK *Lett.* (1767) I. 16 She being effectually sucked in by the heavy sandy bottom, all attempts to weigh her up have been ineffectual. **1782** COWPER *Loss of Royal George* 25 Weigh the vessel up..; Her timbers yet are sound, And she may float again. **1815** *Local Act 55 Geo. III* c. lv. §73 If any Boat..shall be sunk in any Part of the said Canal,..and the Owner ..shall not, without loss of Time, weigh or draw up the same.

†**b.** *intr.* for *refl.* To be raised *up*; to admit of being raised. *Obs.*

1655 W. HAMMOND *On death of Brother* (No. 2) Only this difference, that sunk downward, this Weigh'd up to bliss. **1669** STURMY *Mariner's Mag.* v. xii. 81 If the thing sunk be upon Sands or Rocks, it will weigh the better.

II. To balance in the scales; to ascertain the weight of; to consider or compare in this respect.

7. a. *trans.* To ascertain the exact heaviness of (an object or substance) by balancing it in a pair of scales, or on a steelyard, against a counterpoise of known amount.

c 1000 ÆLFRIC *Gram.* xiii. 84 Ælc þæra ðinga, þe man wihð on wæȝan. *c* 1000 *Sax. Leechd.* I. 374 Ðenim ȝeoluwne stan & salt stan & pipor & weh on wæȝe. *c* 1200 *Trin. Coll. Hom.* 213 Gif hit chepinge be, þe me shule meten oðer weien. *c* 1200 *Vices & Virtues* 17 He wile hes habben wel imotet and bi rihte wæiȝe wel iwæiȝen. 1340 *Ayenb.* 44 Huanne þo þet zelleþ be wyȝte purchaceþ and makeþ zuo moche þet þet þing þet me ssel weȝe ssseweþ more heuy. 1382 WYCLIF *2 Sam.* xiv. 26 He weiede [1388 weiȝide] the heeris of his heed with two hundred siclis be the comoun weiȝt. 1393 LANGL. *P. Pl.* C. x. 273 When..þe woolle worth weye, woo ys þe þenne. *a* 1400 *Eng. Gilds* (1870) 356 þe kynges by whas wyȝte hit be yweye. *c* 1440 *Promp. Parv.* 533/1 Wowyn, or weyyd, *ponderatus, libratus.* 1469 *Plumpton Corr.* (Camden) 21 The wheight stone that the wooll was weyed with. 1596 SHAKS. *Merch. V.* IV. i. 255 Are there ballance heere to weigh the flesh? 1613 J. SARIS *Voy. Japan* (Hakl. Soc.) 42 A Beame to waye spice with. 1617 MORYSON *Itin.* III. 98 They weigh the cheese when it is set on Table, and taken away, being paid by the weight. 1758 JOHNSON *Idler* No. 28 ¶9 Engines should be fixed in proper places to weigh chairs as they weigh waggons. 1765 *Museum Rust.* IV. 179 We have weighed it green, that is, just after mowing, against all the other pasture grasses, and it out-weighs them all. 1827 FARADAY *Chem. Manip.* xv. (1842) 387 A graduated transfer jar containing the gas to be weighed. 1863 MISS BRADDON *Aurora Floyd* xiii, While the numbers were going up, and jockeys being weighed. 1894 SIR J. ASTLEY *Fifty Yrs. Life* II. 212 When we weighed their riders after the morning's work, we found that Peter was giving Foxhall two stone and a half.

b. *absol.*

1362 LANGL. *P. Pl.* A. v. 118 Furst I leornede to lyȝe a lessun or tweyne, And wikkedliche for to weie was myn oþer lessun. 1390 GOWER *Conf.* III. 122 Libra..hath figure and resemblance Unto a man which a balance Berth in his hond as forto weie. 1474 CAXTON *Chesse* III. vii. (1883) 138 And by the potte and elle ben signefyed them that haue the charge to weye and mete and mesure truly.

c. ***to weigh*** (someone) ***against gold*** (or ***silver***): to perform the Indian ceremony in which (a rajah, etc.) is weighed and his weight in gold (or silver) distributed as largesse.

1696 J. OVINGTON *Voy. Suratt.* 179 The Moguls are sometimes weighed against Silver. 1934 *Times* 25 Aug. 13/2 The Maharajah .. will be weighed against gold... The gold-weigh ceremony is usually performed with gold supplied by the person being weighed... This amount will be distributed in charity. 1936 *Times* 14 Jan. 13/6 At this Durbar the Aga Khan will be weighed against gold, and it is expected that 20,000 guests will attend the function.

d. In Horse-racing. ***to weigh out, in***: to take the weight of (a jockey) respectively before and after a race. (Cf. 9.)

1890 *Rules of Racing* in *Encycl. Sport* (1898) II. 224 The Stakeholder shall not allow a jockey to be weighed out for any horse until such horse's stake [etc.] have been paid. *Ibid.* 225 The Clerk of the Scales..shall in all cases weigh in the riders of the horses.., and report to the Stewards any jockey not presenting himself to be weighed in.

e. ***to weigh off***: to punish; to convict or sentence. *slang* (orig. *Mil.*). Now chiefly *Criminals'*.

1925 FRASER & GIBBONS *Soldier & Sailor Words* 301 *Weighed off, to be,* to be brought up before an officer and punished. 1945 *Tee Emm* (Air Ministry) V. 54 P.O. Prune will have to investigate and deal with a charge..and possibly weigh off the first delinquent of his service career. 1958 F. NORMAN *Bang to Rights* i. 22 You just got weighed off yesterday? 1963 T. & P. MORRIS *Pentonville* ii. 20 One young man..commented that he had been 'weighed off at X Assizes by some old geezer togged up like Father Christmas'. 1978 B. NORMAN *To nick Good Body* x. 81 Another was in custody..waiting to be weighed off.

f. ***to weigh in***: to weigh (an air passenger's luggage) before departure; to subject (a passenger) to this procedure. See *excess luggage* s.v. EXCESS 6 b.

1934 RHYS-WILLIAMS *Diary* 1 Aug. (MS.), Left Eaton Place at 4.30 p.m. for Victoria, where we were 'weighed-in', and had our luggage weighed and labelled. 1961 L. DEIGHTON *Ipcress File* v. 30 She weighed in my wardrobe case. 1970 *New Yorker* 16 May 41/2 The porter..takes her bag and follows her to the desk to have it weighed in.

g. Angling. ***to weigh in***: of an angler, to have (one's catch) officially weighed at the end of a competition. Also *absol.*

[1928: see WEIGHER 3 a]. 1949 *Club Anglers' Jrnl.* Nov. 14/1 The river fished well and the winner weighed-in 6 lb. 4 oz. 12 drm. 1972 *Match Rules* (Nat. Fed. Anglers) in E. Marshall-Hardy *Angling Ways* (1973) xxxix. 306 No competitor may have his catch weighed in who has litter lying on the banks of his swim. 1976 *Wymondham & Attleborough Express* 17 Dec. 22/5 Only 10..competitors weighed in,..but..Frank Kilbourn..float fished to take 9-2 of good roach.

8. a. To measure a definite quantity of (a substance) on the scales. Usually with *out*: To portion out (a quantity measured by weight) from a larger mass; to apportion (such a quantity) *to* (a person or persons); †to measure exactly or to the full weight (*obs.*). Also with *in*, *into*: To introduce a specified weight of (a substance), to add as an ingredient.

c 1386 CHAUCER *Can. Yeom. Prol. & T.* 745 And of that coper [he] weyed out [*Cambr. MS.* vp] but an ounce. 1585 T. WASHINGTON tr. *Nicholay's Voy.* II. iii. 33 b, We began to way out the bisket vnto the gallie slaues. 1596 SPENSER *F.Q.* V. ii. 35 For at the first they all created were In goodly measure, by their Makers might, And weighed out in ballaunces so nere, That not a dram was missing of their right. 1615 R. COCKS *Diary* (Hakl. Soc.) I. 88 We wayed out the wax which came in the Hozeander, and fownd it want a tonne. 1616 *Ibid.* 111 We waid out the pepper to day for the king. *Ibid.* 217 He delivered or wayd out much more to Tomo Dono and Cushcron Dono. *a* 1646 BURROUGHES *Exp. Hosea* iii. (1652) 197 Never did any skilfull Physitian more carefully weigh out to every dram what the potion should be that is to be given to a child, than God doth weigh out every affliction that he sendeth upon his children. 1827 FARADAY *Chem. Manip.* iii. (1842) 75 No further difficulty will now arise in the way of graduating a tube. The 34.25 grains of mercury are to be weighed in... Another 34.25 grains of mercury are to be weighed into the tube to the metal already contained in it. *Ibid.* xii. 283 If it be found that as many parts of the acid have been used as of grains of the carbonate weighed out, the acid is of proper strength.

†**b.** To measure (a sum of money) by weight, in order to pay it *to* (a person). Chiefly in Biblical renderings. Also with *out*, *down*. *Obs.* (So OE. *aweȝan*, G. *wägen*, *dar-*, *zuwägen*.)

1382 WYCLIF *Zech.* xi. 12 And thei weyȝiden my meede, thritti platis of syluer. 1388 —— *Job* xxviii. 15 Nether siluer schal be weied [1382 peisid] in the chaungyng therof. 1535 COVERDALE *Jer.* xxxii. 10, I..weyed him there the money vpon the waightes. —— *Zech.* xi. 12 So they wayed downe xxx. syluer pens, ye value that I was prysed at. 1585 HIGINS *Junius' Nomencl.* 492/2 An officer that weyed out mony for soldiers wages. 1607 DEKKER & WEBSTER *Westw.-Hoe* II. i, Some [are] cutting purses, some cheating, some weying out bribes.

c. *fig.* To dispense or administer (justice) impartially.

c 1400 *26 Pol. Poems* i. 14 Weye o lawe in euenhede, Bytwen ffauour and vengeaunce. 1562 A. SCOTT *Poems* i. 29 (*To Q. Mary*) Waye iustice, equale without discrepance.

9. a. *intr.* in *Horse-racing.* Of a jockey: To take his place in the scales, in order that his declared weight may be verified by the clerk. ***to weigh out*** (***in***), to do this before and after a race. (Cf. 7 d.) Similarly in *Boxing*, ***to weigh in***, said of a boxer (turning the scales *at* a particular weight) before a fight. Hence in general colloq. use.

1805 *Weatherby's Racing Cal.* XXXII. p. xxxviii, That every person who shall ride at Newmarket for Plate, Sweepstakes, or Match, shall be obliged to weigh when he comes in. 1858 *Rules of Racing* §37 Jockies are required to weigh at the usual place of weighing, before the race,..and every rider is, immediately after the race, to ride his horse to the usual place of weighing,..and to weigh to the satisfaction of the person appointed for that purpose. 1868 WHYTE MELVILLE *White Rose* I. xiv. 174 Their riders are drinking sherry..preparatory to 'weighing in'. *Ibid.* 182 Mr. Snipe, returning to weigh after an easy victory. 1877 *Rules of Racing* §31 Weighing out and starting. *Ibid.* §34 Weighing in. 1879 J. RICE *Hist. Turf* I. 298 The rider of Musjid..is said to have weighed in and weighed out with a whip weighing 7 or 9 lbs. and to have exchanged it for a lighter whip before and after the race. 1909 'O. HENRY' *Roads of Destiny* xviii. 307 He was six feet four and weighed in at 135. 1920 MASEFIELD *Right Royal* 33 When the clock struck three and the men weighed out. *Ibid.* 119 Then the riders weighed-in, and the meeting was over. 1931 *Daily Express* 13 Oct. 1/7 Both boxers weighed in this afternoon. 1958 S. WILCOX *3 Days Running* vii. 79 When at last I was able..to 'weigh-in' ..I weighed five pounds more than at the beginning of the day. 1966 *Aviation Week & Space Technol.* 5 Dec. 6/1 The complete inertial package weighs in at only 14 pounds. 1979 *SLR Camera* Mar. 35/1 The compact 'Zuiko' 1000mm measures just 26 inches and weighs in at around eight and a half pounds.

b. Hence ***to weigh in with***: to introduce or produce (something that is additional or extra). *colloq.*

1885 *Daily News* Nov. (*Passing English*, 1909) The journal 'weighs in' with a prismatic Christmas number. 1901 *Macm. Mag.* Apr. 464/1 Carver..used to sit up and snort a bit when we weighed in with hock and seltzer instead of tea. 1921 D. MACKAIL *Romance to Rescue* i. 9 A Rhodes scholar weighed in with praise of Greenwich Village.

c. fig. ***to weigh in***: to bring one's weight or influence to bear; to enter a forceful contribution to a discussion, etc. *colloq.*

1909 G. B. SHAW *Let.* 31 July (1972) II. 854, I want you to ask the Chief Rabbi to weigh in. 1919 BEERBOHM *Seven Men* 147 A few weeks later the Anglo-Indians weigh in. In due course we have the help of our Australian cousins. 1938 E. BOWEN *Death of Heart* III. iii. 378 The telephone crisis.. had been the moment for Lilian to weigh in. 1956 A. L. ROWSE *Early Churchills* 221 The Princess Anne, in her constant rôle of fairy godmother to the Marlboroughs, weighed in; nor could it have been done with more tact and good feeling. 1976 *Milton Keynes Express* 4 June 38/4 Sim weighed in with 4-27 off eight overs.

d. To launch *into* and attack (a person, etc.). Also *fig. colloq.*

1941 BAKER *Dict. Austral. Slang* 81 *Weigh into someone*, to attack, wade into a person in a fight. 1976 F. WARNER *Killing Time* I. i. 8, I survived the war,..and then, if I was a minute after 9.30 in the evening, my Mother would weigh into me.

10. a. *trans.* To hold (an object) in the hand (or in both hands) in order to observe or estimate its weight; to balance an object in the hand (or hands) as if estimating its weight.

1540 PALSGR. *Acolastus* II. iii. M j b, Waye me this gyrdel heuy with moche golde .i. fele me this girdell, howe heuy it is with golde. 1781 COWPER *Expost.* 343 Who poises and proportions sea and land, Weighing them in the hollow of his hand. 1815 SCOTT *Guy M.* lvii, 'But why should he know of it?' said Glossin, slipping a couple of guineas into MacGuffog's hand. The turnkey weighed the gold, and looked sharp at Glossin. 1838 DICKENS *O. Twist* xxiii, Mr. Bumble ..counted the teaspoons, weighed the sugar-tongs. 1848 —— *Dombey* lvi, He remained before him weighing his white hat in both hands by the brim. 1911 H. W. & F. G. FOWLER *Concise Oxf. Dict.* s.v., [He] meditatively weighed his stick in his hand.

b. To keep (the wings) evenly outspread in flight. *poet.*

1667 MILTON *P.L.* II. 1046 Satan..in the emptier waste, resembling Air, Weighs his spread wings.

11. *fig.* (with more or less retention of the literal idea or expression): **a.** To estimate, assess the value of (a person, a condition, quality, etc.), as if by placing in the scales.

a 1200 *Moral Ode* 63 in *Lamb. Hom.* 163 þer me scal ure werkes weien biforan þe heuen king. 1362 LANGL. *P. Pl.* A. I. 152 þe same Mesure þat ȝe Meten A-mis oþer elles, ȝe schul be weyen þer-with whon ȝe wenden hennes. 1382 WYCLIF *Job* vi. 2 Wolde God, my synnes weren weȝed..in a balaunce. 1387 TREVISA *Higden* III. 129 þou art i-weye on a balaunce and i-founde þat þou hast lasse [Dan. v. 27]. 1526 *Pilgr. Perf.* (W. de W. 1531) 29 b, Our sayd lorde..at the houre of our iudgement shall ponder and wey euery mannes encrease or decrease. 1549 *Bk. Com. Prayer, Communion,* Not waiyng our merites, but pardonyng our offences. 1557 NORTH *Gueuara's Diall Pr.* Prol. A i, God doth not way us as we are, but as we desier to be. 1590 SPENSER *F.Q.* I. iv. 27 Accursed vsurie was all his trade, And right and wrong ylike in equall ballaunce waide. 1670 DRYDEN *1st Pt. Conq. Granada* III. (1672) 22 Friendship..weighs by th' lump, and, when the cause is light, Puts kindness in to set the Ballance right. 1736 BERKELEY *Discourse* Wks. III. 419 Were all men to be weighed in the exact scale of merit. 1744 M. BISHOP *Life* 97 Where such a cross-grain'd Piece of Stuff is concerned..one should ponder with inward Consultations, to be able to weigh him to a Hair. 1781 COWPER *Hope* 366 That heav'n will weigh man's virtues and his crimes With nice attention, in a righteous scale. 1815 BYRON *Hebrew Mel., Vis. Belshazzar* vi, He, in the balance weigh'd, Is light and worthless clay. 1872 BLACKIE *Lays Highl.* 134 God numbers not the heads, but weighs the hearts Of them that worship. 1897 'OUIDA' *Massarenes* xxii, [She] had mentally weighed him, and found him wanting.

b. To balance *with* or *against* (another object regarded as a counterpoise) in order to obtain a comparative estimate. Also ***to weigh together***.

1513 MORE *Rich. III*, Wks. 47/1 Waye the good that they dooe, with the hurte that commeth of them. 1549 *Bk. Com. Prayer* Pref., If those men will waye their labor, with the profite in knowlege, whiche dayely they shal obtein by readyng vpon the boke. 1592 SHAKS. *Rom. & Jul.* I. ii. 101 But in that Christall scales, let there be waid Your Ladies loue against some other Maid. 1596 SPENSER *F.Q.* V. ii. 45 For by no meanes the false will with the truth be wayd. 1609 DEKKER *Guls Horne-bk.* i. heading, The old world & the new waighed together. 1610 SHAKS. *Temp.* II. i. 8 Then wisely (good Sir) weigh Our sorrow with our comfort. 1647 COWLEY *Mistress, Love undiscovered* ii, Forbid it Heaven my Life should be Weigh'd with her least Conveniency. 1781 COWPER *Hope* 178 The fragrant grove, th' inestimable mine, Were light when weigh'd against one smile of thine. 1823 LAMB *Elia* Ser. II. *Tombs in Abbey*, While we had been weighing anxiously prudence against sentiment. 1829 NAPIER *Penins. War* II. 265 He anxiously weighed his own resources against those at the enemy's disposal. 1868 HELPS *Realmah* VI. x. (1876) 112 But of what weight was any mere earthly consideration of that kind when weighed against the danger of impiety? 1917 *Q. Rev.* Jan. 16 They held their lives to be of little price, when weighed against a nation's fidelity to its engagements.

c. To make equal, balance (the year; *i.e.* to make night and day of equal length). *poet.*

Cf. Columella x. 42 Cum..paribus Titan orbem librauerit horis.

1697 DRYDEN *Virg. Georg.* I. 419 Now sing we stormy Stars, when Autumn weighs The Year, and adds to Nights, and shortens Days. 1720 POPE *Iliad* XXII. 39 The Year when Autumn weighs.

12. a. To consider (a fact, circumstance, statement, etc.) in order to assess its value or importance; to ponder, estimate, examine, take due account of; to balance in the mind with a view to choice or preference.

c 1380 WYCLIF *Wks.* (1880) 323 ȝif we weyn aryht dispensis bi lore of þe hooly goost. *c* 1385 CHAUCER *L.G.W.* 384 (398) And weyen every thyng by equite. 14.. LYDG. *Horse, Goose & Sheep* 150 in *Pol. Rel. & L. Poems* (1903) 21 Ye prudent Iugis..Weieth this mater in your discrecioun. 1456 SIR G. HAYE *Gov. Princis* (S.T.S.) 147 Cast all thair counsailis ilkane till othir in thy mynde, and wey thame as thou thinkis the caus requeris. 1533 *Star Chamber Cases* (Selden Soc.) II. 300 They wayeing in thaire myndes the force of the saide acte. 1560 DAUS tr. *Sleidane's Comm.* 266 b, He desyreth them..that they would way the whole case diligently. 1590 SPENSER *F.Q.* I. ix. 20 She, now weighing the decayed plight And shrunken synewes of her chosen knight. 1613 SHAKS. *Hen. VIII*, II. iv. 197. 1653 W. RAMESEY *Astrol. Restored* 181 If thou hast seriously weighed the foregoing rules. 1697 DRYDEN *Æneis* XII. 70 Weigh in your Mind the various Chance of War. 1711 STEELE *Spect.* No. 43 ¶2, I have well weighed that Matter. 1742 FIELDING *J. Andrews* III. iii, I weighed the consequences on both sides as fairly as I could. 1775 SHERIDAN *Rivals* III. i, I have been likewise weighing and balancing what you were pleased to mention concerning duty. 1847 YEOWELL *Anct. Brit. Ch.* iii. 34 Let any thinking man weigh this singular circumstance. 1849 MACAULAY *Hist. Eng.* vi. II. 39 The jurymen,..being little accustomed to weigh evidence, followed without scruple the directions of the bench. 1855 *Poultry Chron.* III. 32 They never came to a decision without duly weighing the pros and cons. 1863 GEO. ELIOT *Romola* xx, The difficulty of the moment was too pressing for him to weigh distant consequences. 1870 MORRIS *Earthly Par.* III. II. 390 The king is wise; his wrath will well be weighed.

absol. 1796 WORDSW. *Borderers* II. 645 Men who are little given to sift and weigh.

b. To ponder and examine the force of (words or expressions). ***to weigh one's words***: to speak deliberately and in calculated terms.

1340 *Ayenb.* 255 Huo þet ne weȝþ his wordes ine þe waye of discrecion. *Ibid.* 256 Huer me ssel weȝe þet word er hit be yzed. **1576** GASCOIGNE *Steel Glas* 215 Words of worth, and worthy to be wayed. **1579** LODGE *Def. Plays* 16 If we way Poetes wordes and not ther meaning, our learning in them wilbe very mene. *a* **1584** MONTGOMERIE *Cherrie & Slae* 1164 Then Hope replyd,.. And wyselie weyd his words. *a* **1631** DONNE *Lett.* (1651) 309 The old King thought the preacher never had thought of his sermon, till he spoke it... I knew that he had weighed every syllable, for halfe a year before. **1655** in *Verney Mem.* (1907) II. 14, I must..weigh my words before they are sent abroad. **1725** POPE *Odyss.* XIII. 62 His words well-weigh'd, the gen'ral voice approv'd. **1846** J. MARTINEAU *Ess.* (1869) II. 64 The moralist..has far other work than to weigh expressions and analyze definitions. **1848** DICKENS *Dombey* xxii, Mr. Carker read this slowly; weighing the words as he went. **1877** HUXLEY *Techn. Educ.* Sci. & Cult. (1881) 82, I weigh my words when I say that if the nation could purchase a potential Watt, or Davy, or Faraday, at the cost of a hundred thousand pounds down, he would be dirt-cheap at the money.

c. with object-clause. Now *rare*.

Often ***to weigh by, with, within oneself***.

1526 *Pilgr. Perf.* (W. de W. 1531) 152 Ponderynge and weyenge also that of all vertues mercy is moost necessaryly requyred to this myserable worlde. **1549** E. ALLEN *Jude's Par. Rev.* xi. 16 Whether any suche thynge..maye hereafter happen, let euery true christen harte..well consyder and wey by himselfe. **1553** BRENDE *Q. Curtius* v. 81 They wayed also that both the sauegard of them, and of the king lay in the handes of one that was a prisoner. **1553** in Strype *Eccl. Mem.* (1721) III. App. XI. 30, I beseech yow..waye wyth your self, what a good Master our hevenlye Father ys unto yow. **1573** BEDINGFIELD tr. *Cardanus' Comf.* II. (1576) 18b, If they would waye wyth themselues, that all men..haue the vse of reason. **1578** WHETSTONE *2nd Pt. Promos & Cass.* v. v. M 1, Good Maddame way, by lawe, your Lord doth dye. *c* **1600** SHAKS. *Sonn.* cxx. 8 And I a tyrant haue no leasure taken To waigh how once I suffered in your crime. **1621** T. WILLIAMSON tr. *Goulart's Wise Vieillard* A2b, Well weighing with my selfe, that it was a Work might yeeld some profit to my Countrie men of England. **1675** DRYDEN *Aurengz.* v. (1676) 80 You thought me dead, and prudently did weigh Tears were but vain. **1683** *Pennsylv. Arch.* (1852) I. 75 We ye free People of ye Town..of Salem..weighing well in ourselves y[t] nothing can more readily conduce to our ..Happiness, then a fair and just settlement of our Foundations [etc.]. **1803** ELDON in Vesey *Chanc. Cases* (1827) VIII. 427 The Court ought to weigh, whether the doubt is so reasonable and fair, that the property is left in his hands not marketable. **1825** SCOTT *Talism.* iii, He weighed within himself, whether [etc.]. **1841** MYERS *Cath. Th.* III. §42. 161 Let any one weigh well what it is to translate such a collection of documents as constitute the Bible.

d. ***to weigh up***: to appraise, form an estimate of (a person). *colloq.*

1894 *Westm. Gaz.* 15 Feb. 5/1 The Liberal delegates were fervid only when 'weighing-up' the House of Peers and insisting upon its disestablishment. **1897** 'O. RHOSCOMYL' *White Rose Arno* 43, I will watch him closer for the future. I should have come up earlier now, but that I was weighing up his servant, an arrant Whig and a spy to boot. **1904** *Daily Chron.* 14 Jan. 7, 'I knew too much about her,' she said. 'I had weighed her up.'

†**13. a.** To esteem, value, think highly of; to count dear or precious; to ascribe value or importance to. Often with negative: (Not) to care for or regard. *Obs.*

a **1225** *Ancr. R.* 336 Kunde of gode heorte is to beon offeared of sunne, þer as non nis ofte; oðer weien swuðer his sunne summechere þen he þurfte. Weien hit to lutel is ase vuel, oðer wurse. *c* **1386** CHAUCER *Knt.'s T.* 923 That lord hath litel of discrecion, That in swich cas kan no diuision, But weyeth pride and humblesse after oon. **1449** PECOCK *Repr.* III. x. 335 Whi therfore schulen we ouer miche weie and apprise his seiyng? **1496–7** *Act 12 Hen. VII*, c. 12 Preamble, The same Kyng.., not fearyng Almyghty God in breking his seid promys nor weiyng his Honour in the same. **1567** HARMAN *Caveat* 64 Take no care for that, for I doe not greatly waye it; it was worth but three shyllinges foure pens. **1579** SPENSER *Sheph. Cal.* June 73 Nought weigh I, who my song doth prayse or blame. **1588** SHAKS. *L.L.L.* v. ii. 27 You waigh me not, O that's you care not for me. **1592** DANIEL *Compl. Rosamond* xxiii, Henry the second, that so highly weigh'd mee. **1595–7** LYLY *Wom. in Moon* III. ii. 289, I, he wayes more his flocke then me. **1633** MASSINGER *New Way* III. iii, My deeds, nephew, Shall speake my loue, what men report, I waigh not. **1676** SIR W. TEMPLE in *Essex Papers* (Camden) II. 81 The Estates would bee enough inclinable to it as weighing interest more than honour. **1681** W. ROBERTSON *Phraseol. Gen.* 1306/2, I do not weigh you a pin ..*Non ego te flocci facio.*

†**b.** with adj. compl. (*light*, *dear*, etc.). *Obs.*

c **1586** C'TESS PEMBROKE *Ps.* CXVI. v, Thy people all beholding, Who dear their deaths dost weigh. **1592** *Arden of Feversham* I. i. 361 To let them see how light I wey their words. *a* **1599** SPENSER *F.Q.* VII. vi. 55 Them all, and all that she so deare did way, Thence-forth she left. **1599** SHAKS. *Hen. V*, II. iv. 43 In cases of defence, 'tis best to weigh The Enemie more mightie then he seemes. **1601** —— *All's Well* III. iv. 32 Let euerie word waigh heauie of her worth, That he does waigh too light.

†**14.** *intr.* **a.** To pay heed or deference *to*. *Sc.*

1423 JAS. I *Kingis Q.* cxx, Myn effectis grete, Vnto the quhich ʒe aughten maist weye. **1456** SIR G. HAYE *Law Arms* (S.T.S.) 157 Suppos thai have na soverane to quham thai wey, bot anerly God allane.

†**b.** with *of*: To ponder, consider (something); to judge of, estimate, value, care for. *Obs.*

1573 *New Custom* D iij b, God waieth not..Of any vesture, or outward apparance a mite. **1577** HANMER *Anc. Eccl. Hist., Euseb.* v. v. 82 But weye of this euery man as pleaseth him. **1584** LODGE *Forbonius & Prisc.* 35 Solduvius, not..willing to weigh of the submissiue request of his daughter, interrupted her thus. **1596** SPENSER *F.Q.* VI. vii. 29 Vnworthy she to be belou'd so dere, That could not weigh of worthinesse aright.

†**c.** with negative: (Not) to hesitate *to* (do something). *Obs.*

1573 LLOID *Pilgr. Princes* 14 The women of Scithia called Amazones..wayed not to encounter with Hercules in the fielde.

III. To have heaviness or weight.

15. *intr.* Of a material object or substance: To have a greater or less degree of heaviness, as measured by the scales. **a.** To be equal to or balance (a specified weight) in the scales.

The specifying word is to be regarded as a predicative complement rather than as governed by the verb.

c **1000** *Sax. Leechd.* III. 92 Se sester sceal weȝan twa pund be sylfyr ȝewyht. *a* **1023** WULFSTAN *Hom.* xlv. (1883) 228 Ælc an haȝelstan weȝeð fif pund. **13..** *Sir Beues* 1424 A dede Beues binde to a ston gret, þat weʒ seue quarters of whet. *c* **1386** CHAUCER *Prol.* 454 Hir couerchiefs..I dorste swere they weyeden ten pound, That on a sonday weren vpon hir heed. **1387** TREVISA *Higden* III. 207 Oon of the hameres weiede tweie so moche as anoþer. **1474** CAXTON *Chesse* III. iv. (1883) 111 One framosian had promysed to hym as moche weyght of pure gold as the heed weyed. **1529** *Reg. Mag. Sig. Scot.* (1883) 177 Ane silver spune and a masar veand 3 uncis. **1553** EDEN *Treat. New Ind.* (Arb.) 34 The fleshe therof wayed .xlvij. pound weyght. **1590** SHAKS. *Com. Err.* IV. i. 28 Here's the note How much your Chaine weighs to the vtmost charect. **1655** MARQ. WORCESTER *Cent. Inv.* §69 A little..Key, not weighing a Shilling. **1675** R. VAUGHAN *Coin & Coinage* 75 They'd have it..so as the Pieces of Silver and Gold should weigh one the other. **1774** GOLDSM. *Nat. Hist.* IV. 44 Some of them [*sc.* marmots] are found to weigh above twenty pounds. **1838** T. THOMSON *Chem. Org. Bodies* 891 The gum weighed 3 per cent of the almonds analyzed. **1856** J. RICHARDSON *Recoll.* I. vi. 145 In person he was tall and corpulent, weighing something over twenty stone.

b. with adv. or pred. adj.

a **1225** *Ancr. R.* 232 Hwon two bereð one burðene ant te oðer bileaueð hit, þeonne mei þe þet holdeð hit up iuelen hu hit weihð. *c* **1290** *St. Michael* 395 in *S. Eng. Leg.* 311 Heouene geth al aboute þe eorþe, euene it mot weyʒe. *a* **1300** *Vox & Wolf* 237 in Hazl. *E.P.P.* I. 66 He lep in [the bucket], and way sumdel. **13..** *St. Cristofer* 364 in Horstm. *Altengl. Leg.* (1881) 458 The childe swa heuy woghe þat ofte-sythes one knees he hym droghe. *c* **1385** CHAUCER *L.G.W.* 1788 (Fairfax) And as she woke, hir bed she felt presse. What best ys that, quod she, that weyeth thus? *c* **1440** *York Myst.* xxx. 136 A! sir, yhe whe wele! *c* **1475** *Macro Plays, Mankind* 692 Ther ys to moche cloth, yt weys as ony lede. **1481** CAXTON *Godfrey* cxxxviii. 205 They..becam stronge, and delyuer in suche wyse that the armes that they bare weyed nothyng as them semed. **1581** A. HALL *Iliad* x. 174 His shield that waightie waied. **1586** WHITNEY *Choice Embl.* 41 The heauie loade, did weye so harde behinde. **1606** SHAKS. *Ant. & Cl.* IV. xv. 32 Heere's sport indeede: How heauy weighes my Lord? **1779** COWPER *Yearly Distress* 48 Like barrels with their bellies full, They only weigh the heavier. **1818** SCOTT *Br. Lamm.* x, His fingers fumbled as if..the other [*sc.* his beaver] had weighed equal with a stone of lead.

16. a. *fig.* (with more or less retention of the literal idea or expression).

a **1225** *Ancr. R.* 332 *Misericordia superexaltat judicium* [Jas. ii. 13]:..his merci touward us weieð euer more þen þet rihte nearuwe. **1340** *Ayenb.* 91 Loue is þe wyʒte ine þe balance..uor non oþer þing ne may weʒe, huanne me comþ to nime ech his ssepe, bote loue and charite. *c* **1386** CHAUCER *Monk's T.* 243 Thy regne is doon, thou weyest noght at al. **1390** GOWER *Conf.* II. 275 Ther ben manye of these Lovers, that thogh thei love a lyte, That scarsly wolde it weie a myte Yit wolde thei have a pound again, As doth Usure in his bargain. *c* **1440** *Jacob's Well* 4 3e weyin now in mennys hertys, in dreed of ʒoure myʒt, more þan all þe world, for all þe world dare noʒt wythstonde ʒou. *c* **1440** *Gesta Rom.* xlv. 177 For synne is not lyʒt, but it is hevy, and weythe more than lede. **1595** SHAKS. *John* II. i. 332 One must proue greatest. While they weigh so euen, We hold our Towne for neither: yet for both. **1599** —— *Much Ado* v. i. 93, I know them, yea And what they weigh, euen to the vtmost scruple, Scambling, out-facing, fashion-monging boyes. **1601** —— *All's Well* III. iv. 31 Let euerie word waigh heauie of her worth.

†**b.** To amount or be equivalent *to*. *Obs.*

1529 MORE *Dyaloge* IV. xi. 108 b/2 Yt gaue hym occasyon to dowt lest Luther ment not al thing so euyl as his wordys seme to way to. **1588** LAMBARDE *Eiren.* II. iv. (ed. 3) 152 Whether a man doe actually vse force in his entrie, or doe come so readily appointed and araied for it,..it seemeth to weigh to a violent (or *Forcible*) entrie.

†**c.** ***to weigh with*** (also ***even with***): to counterpoise in power, value, etc.; to be of equal value or importance with. *Obs.*

1597 SHAKS. *2 Hen. IV*, II. ii. 196 In euery thing, the purpose must weigh with the folly. **1607** —— *Timon* I. i. 146 Giue him thy Daughter, What you bestow, in him Ile counterpoize, And make him weigh with her. **1656** EARL MONM. tr. *Boccalini's Advts. fr. Parnass.* I. iii. (1674) 4 France may vie and weigh even with Greece it self, in point of Learning.

d. ***to weigh against***, †***again***: to counterbalance, countervail.

c **1410** [see 20]. **1590** GREENE *Never too late* II. (1600) K4b, Hee that seeketh to way against his owne will, oftentimes kicketh against the prick. **1597** SHAKS. *2 Hen. IV*, I. iii. 55 Much more, in this great worke..should we..know our owne estate, How able such a Worke to vndergo, To weigh against his Opposite? **1833** HT. MARTINEAU *Manch. Strike* iv. 47 Such evils..can neither be helped nor be allowed to weigh against the advantages of union. **1884** GILMOUR *Mongols* xviii. 216 He believes that every sin will weigh against him, and drag him down in the scale of being.

e. quasi-*trans.* To equal (something else) in weight or value; to counterbalance; †to be tantamount or equivalent to.

1583 GREENE *Mamillia* I. 6 b, So that eyther thou couldest sooth her with a frumpe, or els lay a loading carde on her backe, should wey a scoffe. **1588** SHAKS. *L.L.L.* v. ii. 26 Indeed I waigh not you, and therefore light. **1613** —— *Hen. VIII*, I. i. 11. *Ibid.* III. ii. 259 The heads of all thy Brother-Cardinals..Weigh'd not a haire of his. **1893** *Westm. Gaz.* 21 Mar. 3/2 There are difficulties..in the poem. Only they do not weigh the enormous difficulty of a multiplicity of Homers.

†**f.** *absol.* Of two things: To balance each other. *Obs.*

1523 BERNERS *Froiss.* (1812) I. xliii. 59 So that finally the good and the yuell wayed.

17. *intr.* To be of (much or little) value or account; to be regarded as considerable or important; to have influence *with* (a person) when he is forming an estimate or judgement.

c **1386** CHAUCER *Parson's T.* ¶367 (Hengwrt MS.) Dedly synne, whan the loue of any thyng weyeth in the herte of man as muche as the loue of god or moore. **1535** W. STEWART *Cron.* (Rolls) III. 313 And his command with him richt litill weyit. **1597** HOOKER *Eccl. Pol.* v. lxv. §5 Why things so light in their owne nature should waigh in the opinions of men so much. **1659** *Nicholas Papers* (Camden) IV. 179 Younge Darby [6th Earl], whoe nowe weighes much less then his name formerly hath donn. **1670** MILTON *Hist. Brit.* III. 107 Pleasing to God, or not pleasing, with them weighed alike; and the worse most an end the weightier. *a* **1700** EVELYN *Diary* 6 Dec. 1680, In truth, their testimonie did little weigh with me. **1705** ATTERBURY *Serm. bef. Queen* 28 Oct. 22 A Wise Man is then best satisfy'd..when he finds ..that the same Argument, which weighs with Him, hath weigh'd with Thousands..before him. **1744** KAMES *Decis. Crt. Sess. 1730–52* (1799) 79 Nor ought it to weigh that Murray run the hazard of his factor's bankruptcy. **1838** MACAULAY *Let. to Napier* in Trevelyan *Life* (1876) II. vii. 12 There is another consideration that weighs much with me. *a* **1853** ROBERTSON *Lect.* (1858) ii. 51, I have not the vanity to say..that my name had weight with many; but it did weigh with some. **1870** LOWELL *Among my Bks., Rousseau* 338 Every man feels instinctively that all the beautiful sentiments in the world weigh less than a single lovely action. **1899** DOYLE *Duet* xiv. 199 Holland is a sound man, and his opinion would weigh with any judge. **1910** BEET *Rise of Papacy* ii. 79 The Roman verdict weighed much throughout Christendom.

IV. To affect, or be affected, by weight.

18. a. *trans.* ***to weigh down***: to draw, force, or bend down by pressure of weight; *fig.* to depress, oppress, lie heavy on. Similarly, ***to weigh back***, †***on one side***, ***to the earth***.

a **1340** HAMPOLE *Psalter* vii. 17 He..likyd to be seruaunte of syn, swa þat his synn weghe him down, þat he neuer rise til þe rist of heuen. **1565** COOPER *Thesaurus* s.v. *Degrauo*, The vine lodeth and weigheth downe the elme. **1579** SPENSER *Sheph. Cal.* Feb. 232 The watrie wette weighed downe his head. **1595** DANIEL *Civ. Wars* IV. lxxvi, O could the mighty but giue bounds to pride And weigh backe fortune ere shee pull them downe. **1597** SHAKS. *2 Hen. IV*, III. i. 7 O gentle Sleepe..how haue I frighted thee, That thou no more wilt weigh my eye-lids downe..? **1598** GRENEWEY *Tacitus, Ann.* XIV. ii. 201 Then the rowers thought best to way the gallie on one side [L. *unum in latus inclinare*], and so to sincke her. **1611** BIBLE *Wisd.* ix. 15 The corruptible body presseth downe the soule, and the earthy tabernacle weigheth downe the minde that museth vpon many things. **1712** ADDISON *Spect.* No. 494 ¶4 There are many excellent Persons, who are weighed down by this habitual Sorrow of Heart. **1783** COWPER *The Rose* 4 The plentiful moisture incumber'd the flower, And weigh'd down its beautiful head. **1857** BUCKLE *Civiliz.* I. xi. 625 The people were weighed down by an insufferable taxation. **1858** DRAYSON *Sport. Scenes S. Afr.* 208 The Kaffirs returned, almost weighed down by the immense weight of meat. **1865** SWINBURNE *Atalanta* 1303 Falling and weighed back by clamorous arms Sharp rang the dead limbs of Eurytion. **1879** PATTISON *Milton* xiii. 215 Causes other than the inherent faults of the poem long continued to weigh down the reputation of *Paradise Lost*. **1884** *Contemp. Rev.* Feb. 252 What, then, was the *consuetudo carnalis* which thus weighed to the earth this soul of fire, striving to ascend to its true home?

†**b.** Without adv.: To depress, dispirit. *Obs. rare.*

1633 FLETCHER & SHIRLEY *Night-walker* I. (1640) B 3, You are light Gentlemen, Nothing to weigh your hearts.

†**19.** *intr.* **a.** Of the scale of a balance (with *up* or *down*): To rise or sink according as it holds the lesser or greater weight. Also *gen.* (with *down*): To sink through its own heaviness or load. *Obs.*

c **1375** *Sc. Leg. Saints* xxii. (*Laurence*) 750 A gret pot..in þat balance has he done; þane ourys veyt vpe tycht [*read* rycht] sone. ? **1566** W. P. tr. *Curio's Pasquin in Trance* 65 That Deuill..doth all that he can to make his parte [of the balance] way downe the heauier. *a* **1626** BACON *Sylva* §610 The Cause is the plenty of the Sap, and the Softnesse of the Stalke, which maketh the Bough, being ouer-loaden, and not stiffely vpheld, weigh downe.

†**b.** ***to weigh with***: to move with, follow the motion of (something that shifts or varies). ***to weigh against***: to strive to make head against (the wind). *Obs.*

1553 BRENDE *Q. Curtius* IV. 34 b, Waying with the worlde, according as the tyme should alter [*semper ex ancipiti mutatione temporum pendens*]. *a* **1557** MARY BASSET tr. *More's Treat. Pass.* M.'s Wks. 1372/1 A fainte harted mayster of a shippe..shrinketh from the sterne, and.. suffreth the ship alone to waye wyth the waues [*puppim permittit fluctibus*]. **1557** *Tottel's Misc.* (Arb.) 263 And where thou sekes a quiet port, Thou dost but weigh agaynst the winde.

20. *trans.* Of an object set in the scales (with *down*, *up*, †*out*; also †***to weigh to the beam***): To turn the scale when weighed against (something else); to outweigh, cause to rise in the scale. Also ***to weigh down*** (the balance or scale). Often *fig.*

1387 TREVISA *Higden* IV. 7 At þe laste þe stoon was leide in a balaunce, and he weieþ [*MSS.* α, β, γ, weygh, weyʒ, wayʒ] up al þat me myʒte leie aʒenst hym in þe oþer side. *c* **1410** HOCCLEVE *Mother of God* 21 Helpe me to weye Ageyn the feend, þat with his handes tweye, And his might, plukke wole at the balance To weye vs doun. *c* **1450** *Knt. de la Tour* 66 Her .. euell dedes .. weyed downe and ouercame her good dedes. *c* **1450** *Mirk's Festial* 221 When alle his synnys wern layde on þe balans and was nygh ouercomyn, then come thylke brennet dekon, and layde a grete pote on þe wey þe whech anon weyit vp al togedyr. **1593** SHAKS. *Rich. II*, III. iv. 89 But in the Ballance of great Bullingbrooke, Besides himselfe, are all the English Peeres, And with that oddes he weighes King Richard downe. **1596** SPENSER *F.Q.* IV. ix. 1 Hard is the doubt, and difficult to deeme, When all three kinds of loue together meet, And doe dispart the hart with powre extreme, Whether shall weigh the balance downe. *Ibid.* V. ii. 46 Yet all the wrongs could not a litle right downe way. **1601** SHAKS. *All's Well* II. iii. 162 We poizing vs in her defectiue scale, Shall weigh thee to the beame. **1613** —— *Hen. VIII*, III. i. 88 My Friends, They that must weigh out my afflictions. **1706** E. WARD *Wooden World Diss.* (1708) 14 Four Ounces of *Vigo* Dust, shall weigh him down more, than four Tun of Honesty. **1711** SWIFT *Examiner* No. 26 One Whig shall weigh down ten Tories. **1840** DICKENS *Old C. Shop* vii, Where all other inducements were wanting, the habitual carelessness of his disposition stepped in and still weighed down the scale on the same side. **1902** *Westm. Gaz.* 27 Mar. 7/3 Whose mistakes .. are a thousand times weighed up by his countless individual deeds of true friendship.

†**21.** *trans.* To sway or influence (a person); to induce (a person) *to* (do something). *Obs.*

1571 CAMPION *Hist. Irel.* 121 When these wordes waighed him nothing, his owne man .. began to reprove him for not relenting to so rich a proffer. **1586** J. HOOKER *Hist. Irel.* in *Holinshed* II. 83/2 By the procurement as well of the archbishop as of all the cleargie [the legate] was weighed to giue the citizens absolution.

22. *intr.* with *on* or *upon*. **a.** Of a thought, feeling, circumstance: To lie heavy on, depress (a person, his spirits, etc.). Also in indirect passive.

1775 SHERIDAN *Duenna* II. iv, If either of you had known how each moment of delay weighs upon the heart of her who loves. **1820** KEATS *Lamia* II. 43 Where am I now? Not in your heart while care weighs on your brow. **1832** TENNYSON *Lotos-eaters* 57 Why are we weigh'd upon with heaviness? **1838** LYTTON *Alice* II. ii, Something seemed to weigh upon her spirits. **1858** MRS. CARLYLE *Lett.* II. 387 This London atmosphere weighs on me. **1863** MARY HOWITT tr. *F. Bremer's Greece* II. xii. 47 The sceptre of despotism weighs oppressively on all free public life. **1909** J. L. ALLEN *Bride of Mistletoe* v. 147 The silence began to weigh upon her.

b. To insist or dwell *upon* (a fact, argument, etc.). *rare.*

1817 H. T. COLEBROOKE *Algebra*, etc. Notes & Illustr. p. xlii, These facts will be further weighed upon as we proceed. **1818** —— *Import Colonial Corn* 70 Without weighing upon this surmise.

23. The vb.-stem in combination: **weigh-balk** *north.* and *Sc.*, the beam of a pair of scales or steelyard; *pl.* scales; **weigh-bar** = *weigh-shaft*; **weigh-beam**, a balance or steelyard; **weigh-brods** *pl. Sc.*, boards used for the scales of a large balance; †**weigh-gilt** *Sc.*, a payment for weighing (after Du. *waaggeld*, G. *wage-*, *wägegeld*); †**weigh-leaf**, a board or plate used as a scale; **weigh-lock** *U.S.*, a canal-lock at which barges are weighed and their tonnage is settled; **weighman**, a man employed to weigh goods, etc.; in a colliery, one who weighs the tubs of coal as they leave the cage at the pit-mouth (for *check-weighman* see CHECK-); **weigh-master** (cf. G. *wagemeister*, Du. *waagmeester*), the official in charge of a weigh-house or public scales; **weigh-out**, the verification of a jockey's declared weight before a race (see 9); **weigh-shaft** = ROCK-SHAFT. Also WEIGH-BRIDGE, -HOUSE, -SCALE.

1485 *Inv.* in *Ripon Ch. Acts* (Surtees) 371, j *weybalke cum skales. **1593-4** *Burgh Rec. Stirling* (1889) II. 380 Quhat-sumever parson .. in tym cuming borrow the use of thair wey balk to wey irone or wther geir. **1608** in Cochran-Patrick *Early Rec. Mining Scot.* (1878) 150 Ane grit weybak with the balance brodis thereto for weying the ore. **1824** SCOTT *Redgauntlet* ch. xxiii, To see a' ane's warldly substance capering in the air in a pair of weigh-bauks, now up, now down. **1841** *Civil Engin. & Arch. Jrnl.* IV. 93/1 A lever is fixed upon the cross-head working in a link connected to a second lever fixed on a shaft or *weigh-bar across the engine, whereby a rocking motion is produced. **1890** W. J. GORDON *Foundry* 16 Beam-engine with its weigh-bar gearing. **1492** in Wadley *Notes Wills Bristol* (1886) 178 My *weybernes [? *read* -bemes] with all my weights of lede. **1804** *Local Act 44 Geo. III* c. lv. §1 To .. erect and set up .. Weighbeams, Cranes. **1833** N. ARNOTT *Physics* (ed. 5) II. 11 If we balance a quantity of ice in a delicate weigh-beam. **1578** *Inv. R. Wardrobe* (1815) 255 Ane pair of *wey broddis garnist with yron for weying of mettall with thair towis. **1497** HALYBURTON *Ledger* (1867) 74 Hous hir, 12, *veygylt, 4 g. **1498** *Ibid.* 213 Item veygilt, ilk sek 4. **1593** in *Archaeologia* (1853) XXXV. 436 For mending John Newarke's *way leaffe, broken in wayinge of lead, iij d. **1835** LIEBER *Stranger in Amer.* II. 140 The object of the greatest interest to me, in Utica, was a *weigh-lock—an American invention if I am not mistaken. The toll for freight on the canal is proportionate to weight. **1883** GRESLEY *Gloss. Coal-mining*, *Weighman.* See *Weigher.* **1907** [see WEIGH-HOUSE]. **1917** *Blackw. Mag.* Apr. 630/1 The bigger fish were weighed on an ingenious balance, consisting of a long steel rod with a sliding weight, the whole suspended on a bit of string held aloft by the weighman. **1617** in Heath *Grocers' Comp.* (1869) 428 The *Weymaster and his porters, which attended at the Guildhall. **1689** RAVENHILL *Acc. Comp. Grocers* 4 The Grocers .. may be well presumed (time out of Mind) to have had the management of the King's Beam, as an Office peculiar to them; .. thay having had all along .. the naming of the Weigh-Master, and the naming, placing, removing and governing of the four Porters, attending that Office, all to be elected out of their own Company. **1886** *Racing* (Badm. Libr.) 67 It was, indeed, this absolute certainty as to the accuracy of the *weigh-out, which led to the detection of the attempted fraud when Catch-em-alive won the Cambridgeshire. **1867-72** N. P. BURGH *Mod. Marine Engin.* 73 Motion is imparted to the lever *weigh shaft by a toothed quadrant keyed thereon. **1888** *Lockwood's Dict. Terms* 407 Weigh Shaft or Way Shaft.— .. Sometimes called a reversing shaft.

†**weigh**, *v.*[2] Only OE. and early ME. Forms: 1 **wecgan**, *3rd sing.* **weȝeð**, *pa. t.* **weȝ(e)de**, *pa. pple.* **ȝeweȝd**, 3 *3rd sing.* **weieð**, *pa. t.* **wæide**, 4 *pa. pple.* **yweid**. [OE. *węcgan* = OHG. *wegan*, MHG. *wegen* (weak vb., with umlaut *e*; distinct from OHG. *wegan*, MHG. *wegen* str. vb. = WEIGH *v.*[1]), Goth. *wagjan* to shake; f. Teut. root **waȝ-*, ablaut-var. of **weȝ-*: see WEIGH *v.*[1]] *trans.* To shake, toss, agitate, move about.

a **1000** *Boeth. Metr.* vii. 35 Wyrce him siðþan his modes hus, þær he mæȝe findan .. grundweal ȝearone: se to glidan ne þearf þeah hit wecge wind woruldearfoþa. *c* **1000** *Ags. Ps.* (Thorpe) cviii. 25 Hi weȝdan .. heora heafod. *c* **1205** LAY. 20137 Swa þe hæȝe wude, þenne wind wode weieð hine mid mæine. *Ibid.* 21869 Heo wæiden in hære ærmen heore children ærmen. *c* **1315** SHOREHAM *Poems* I. 370 þat makeþ man so hardiliche To stonde, and so merie Ine goste, þat he ne may nauȝt yweid be Wiþ blanding ne wiþ boste.

weighable, ('weɪəb(ə)l), *a.* [f. WEIGH *v.*[1] + -ABLE.] That can be weighed; heavy enough (or reckoned as heavy enough) to be weighed in scales.

1429 *Rolls of Parlt.* IV. 349/1 Woll, and al maner þinge weiable. **1570** DEE *Math.* Pref. cjb, Of euery one, the Content knowen, in your least waight, that is wayable. **1616** *Burgh Rec. Stirling* (1887) I. 144 All weyabill merchand waris, sic as lint, hemp, irn, woll. **1796** T. TWINING *Trav. Amer.* (1894) 161 It was applicable .. in every wholesale warehouse of weighable goods. **1854** DICKENS *Hard T.* III. vii, Anything so .. ridiculously shameful as the whelp in his comic livery, Mr. Gradgrind never could by any other means have believed in, weighable and measurable fact though it was. **1878** *N. Amer. Rev.* CXXVII. 50, I am not aware that the soul of Shakespeare or of Newton, when they died, added any weighable powers to the dust to which they returned. **1885** *Leeds Mercury* 5 Aug. 3/2 Where he found a weighable quantity was in the liver.

†'**weighage.** *Obs.* Also 7 **way-**, **weyage**, **-edge**. [f. WEIGH *v.*[1] + -AGE.] A duty or toll paid for the weighing of goods.

1547 *Charters rel. Glasgow* (1906) II. 511 All .. oure Custwmis of oure ciete and burgh of Glasgw, with mettage and weighage and all uther commoditeis pertenand thareto. **1603** *Reg. Mag. Sig. Scot.* 514/1 The pittie custumes .. togidder with the dewteis and custumes of weyage and metage. **1604** in *Rec. Convent. Burghs Scot.* (1870) II. 176 Thai tak na mair for weyage bot ane penny for the stane [of wool]. **1611** *S'hampton Crt. Leet Rec.* (1905) 441 We .. finde .. that the Towne is defrauded of that dew of wayage as it ought to receave by wayenge of goods saleable at the King's beame. **1632** *Sc. Acts Chas. I* (1817) V. 243 Weyages and heaven dewteis dew to be payed in harbereis. **1683** in *Somers' Tracts* (1748) I. 180 [London dues] Meetage, Weighage, Scavage, Hallage. *a* **1701** LEVINZ *Rep.* (1702) III. 37, 8 d. per Tonne pur chescun Tonne de Cheese port de ascun lieu en Angleterre al Port de London .. en nom de Weighage. **1824** CHITTY *Laws Commerce* II. 16 Weighage, called either *tronage* for weighing wool at the king's beam, or *pesage*, for weighing other avoirdupoise goods. **1856** BOUVIER *Law Dict. U.S.A.* (ed. 6) II. 647.

weighboard: see WAY-BOARD.

'**weigh-box.** **a.** One of a set of boxes, used in the operation of 'drawing' wool, in which the wool is more accurately weighed. **b.** A weigh-house. **c.** A chute which weighs and delivers coal at a railway coaling-station (*Cent. Dict.* Suppl. 1909).

1884 McLAREN *Spinning* vii. 120 (2) the spindle gill box; (3) the 4-spindle drawing box; (4) the 6-spindle weigh box. **1907** *Daily Chron.* 25 June 9/2 The following is a complete list of the cars which weighed in at the public weigh-box.

'**weigh-bridge.** [Cf. G. *brückenwage.*] A platform scale, flush with the road, for weighing vehicles, cattle, etc.

1796 R. SALMON in *Repert. Arts & Manuf.* VI. 74 Weigh-bridges or engines, with their apparatus, for the purpose of weighing carriages. **1825** in *Newton's Lond. Jrnl. Arts* (1828) XIV. 253 Certain improvements on Weighing Machines which Machines he [the patentee] denominates German Weigh Bridges. **1844** H. STEPHENS *Bk. Farm* III. 1194 The cart-steelyard or weigh-bridge. **1849** F. B. HEAD *Stokers & Pokers* viii. (1851) 75 [The] trucks .. are immediately drawn by horses first over a weighbridge. **1886** *Daily News* 26 July 2/2 The heaviest lamb turned 169lb. on the weighbridge.

fig. *a* **1834** COLERIDGE *Hints Th. Life* (1848) 21 The positions of science must be tried .. on the weigh-bridge of common opinion and vulgar usage.

weighed (weɪd), *ppl. a.* [f. WEIGH *v.*[1] + -ED.]

1. That has had its weight ascertained by the scales.

c **1440** *Promp. Parv.* 520/1 Weyd, or wowon, *ponderatus*, *libratus.* **1669** [see SQUASH *sb.*[2] 1]. **1827** FARADAY *Chem. Manip.* xxiv. (1842) 600 Then ascertain whether the weighed portions equipoise each other. **1857** MILLER *Elem. Chem.*, *Org.* 765 A weighed quantity of the solid .. is carefully introduced. **1886** JAGO *Chem. Wheat* etc. 407 Counterpoised and Weighed Filters.

2. Of judgement, opinion, etc.: Considered, balanced. †Of a person: Having a balanced and steady judgement. Cf. WELL-WEIGHED.

c **1645** HOWELL *Lett.* (1650) I. 349 Secretary Walsingham, and Secretary Cecil, a pair of the best weighed statesmen this island hath bred. **1647-8** COTTERELL *Davila's Hist. Fr.* (1678) 18 The Admiral, with more weighed Counsel, opposed the Princes opinion. **1675** DRYDEN *Aurengz.* I. i. (1676) 4 Aureng-Zebe, by no strong passion sway'd, Except his Love, more temp'rate is, and weigh'd. **1689** T. R. *View Govt. Europe* 67 Our English Ancestors have always been of a more steady principle, more wise, and more weigh'd, than to dance after their Politicks. **1909** *Westm. Gaz.* 23 Apr. 3/1 The weighed judgments of the staid 'councillor'.

3. With *down*: Depressed, downcast.

1822 BYRON *Werner* I. i. 509 'Tis past fatigue which gives my weigh'd-down spirit An outward show of thought. **1935** S. SPENDER in *London Mercury* May 8 The tall girl with her weighed-down head.

weigher ('weɪə(r)). Forms: 4 **wier**, **weir**, 4-5 **weiere**, **weyere**, 5 **weyor**, **-ar**, 5-6 **weyer**, 6 **waier**, **weygher**, 6-7 **wayer**, 6- **weigher**. [f. WEIGH *v.*[1] + -ER[1]. Cf. MLG., MHG. *weger.*]

†**1.** ? One who bears up or supports (a person).

a **1300** *Cursor M.* 22115 þe wicked gastes his wiers [*Gött.* weirs] Him foluand in al his afers.

2. One who heaves up or weighs (an anchor).

1598 FLORIO, *Salpatore*, a wayer or heauer of ankers. *a* **1818** M. G. LEWIS *Jrnl. W. Ind.* (1834) 5 The weigher of the anchor.

3. **a.** A person who is employed to weigh commodities; an official appointed to weigh or to supervise weighing, to test weights, etc. Also *weigher-in*.

14.. *Voc.* in Wr.-Wülcker 618/3 *Trutinator*, a weyere. **1463** *Cases bef. King's Council* (Selden Soc.) 111 Brouwurs weyers porters tresourers clerkys [etc.] of the Staple. **1476** *Stonor Papers* (Camden) II. 5 And whan I haue weyyde heme to .. pay .. to the weyor ffor euery sake j d. *a* **1513** FABYAN *Chron.* VII. (1811) 342 Where before tyme y[e] weyer vsyd to lene his draught towarde the marchaundyse, soo that the byar hadde by that meane .x. or .xii. li. in a draughte to his aduauntage. **1535** *Act 27 Hen. VIII*, c. 14 (§1) The waier of the Wolles within the said Porte. **1677** W. B. *Touch-stone Gold & Silver Wares* 20 Their Assay-Office, .. wherein is a Sworn Weigher. **1701** LUTTRELL *Brief Rel.* V. 79 Mr. Fitch, cheif weigher of the gold and silver at the Mint. **1794** GRIGGS *Agric. Essex* 26 Two men are nominated .. whom we call public weighers, whose business it is to .. examine the weights of all millers and shopkeepers. **1812** J. SMYTH *Pract. Customs* (1821) 11 At landing the Goods, the Weigher is to call out the full and true gross weight in the scale. **1855** H. G. DALTON *Hist. Brit. Guiana* II. 568 Licensed Weighers or Gaugers. **1880** 'MARK TWAIN' *Tramp Abroad* ii. 9 The crowd mash one another to pulp in the effort to get the weighers' attention to their trunks. **1886** *Act 49 & 50 Vict.* c. 49 §16 The Admiralty may appoint .. persons to be meters and weighers at and within the harbour. **1906** A. H. LEWIS *Confessions of Detective* I. i. 7 I've been weigher-in at the boxing tournaments for over ten years. **1928** *Daily Tel.* 25 Sept. 12/5 It is a rule that every fish caught must be kept alive, and after being weighed must be put back into the water by the official weigher-in. **1982** J. A. SHARWOOD in *Occasional Papers Univ. Sydney Austral. Lang. Res. Centre No. 20.* 20 He may be inclined to complain to the *boundary rider* .. about *the bloke with the short arm* being employed as the *weigher-in* there.

b. in fig. sense or context.

1388 WYCLIF *Prov.* xvi. 2 The Lord is a weiere [**1382** peisere] of spiritis. *c* **1430** *Pilgr. Lyf Manhode* III. xx. (Roxb.) 146 The time and the sunne j made myn owen and in my balaunce j putte hem. Bi myn outrage j haue maad my self weyere ther of and sellere. ? **1566** W. P. tr. *Curio's Pasquin in Trance* 64 b, *marg.*, Seint Michaell wayer of soules. **1759** [E. YOUNG] *Conj. Orig. Comp.* 72 Old Time, that best weigher of merits. **1875** JOWETT *Plato* (ed. 2) I. 171 Do you, like a skilful weigher, put into the balance the pleasures and pains. **1903** *Critic* (U.S.) XLIII. 360/1 Now that you are becoming a professional weigher of books yourself.

c. A machine for weighing.

1905 *Westm. Gaz.* 21 Aug. 4/1 The coal is then placed into a weigher, which dips at each quarter of a ton.

†**4.** Used to translate L. *æquator* (EQUATOR 1). Cf. WEIGH *v.*[1] 11 c. *Obs.*

c **1391** CHAUCER *Astrol.* I. §17 This same cercle [the equinoctial] is cleped also the weyere, *equator*, of the day.

Hence '**weighership**, the office of (public) weigher.

1885 *American* XI. 68 After all, Mr. Sterling seems likely to miss the Brooklyn weighership.

'**weigh-house.** [Cf. MLG. *wegehûs*, G. *wagehaus.*] A public building to which commodities are brought to be weighed.

1438 *Cal. Patent Rolls, Hen. VI* (1907) III. 192 [By the way which runs between] le Weyhous [of the said staple, and the said] Wolbrigge. **1463** *Bury Wills* (Camden) 35 Robert Basset, clerc of the Weyhous at London. **1530** TINDALE *Answ. More* Wks. (1572) 278/2 Thirty or forty sturdy lubbers, .. of which y[e] weakest shall be as strong in the belly when he commeth vnto the manger, as the mightiest porter in y[e] weyhouse. **1598** STOW *Surv.* 150 On the North side of this street [Cornhill] .. one large house is called the Wey house, where marchandizes brought from beyond the seas, are to bee weighed at the Kinges Beame. **1649** W. GREY *Chorogr.* 17 Under the Town-Court is a common Weigh-house for all sorts of Commodities. **1658** *Rec. Burgh Lanark* (1893) 170 The baillies and counsell ordaines the wechts in the wiehous. **1776** G. SEMPLE *Building in Water* 154 Public Stores and Weigh-houses. **1818** SCOTT *Rob Roy* xxxi, I might hae hung there till the day of judgment .. wi' my head hinging down on the tae side, and my heels on the tother, like the yarn scales in the weigh-house. **1829** HEATH *Grocers' Comp.* 186 The general Weighhouse and King's Beam were in Cornhill, upon the site of the present Sun-Court. **1833** *Act 3 & 4 Will. IV*, c. 46 §107 A weigh-house for the use of the inhabitants..with the necessary weights, scales, and measures. **1883** *Harper's Mag.* Apr. 692/1 Every scale in the weigh-house is painted some distinguishing color. **1907** *Daily Chron.* 18 Oct. 9/2 A large motor-car..backed into a public weigh-house at Blairgowrie (Perthshire)... The building was damaged and the steelyard destroyed... The weighman was in the house at the time, but was uninjured.

'weigh-in. [f. the vbl. phr. *to weigh in*: see WEIGH *v.*¹ 7, 9.] **1.** *Boxing.* The weighing-in of a boxer before a fight. See sense 9a of the vb.

1939 *Sun* (Baltimore) 28 June 15/1 The general might bring the subject up at the weigh-in and instruction period for the two fighters at noon to-morrow. **1946** *Daily Progress* (Charlottesville, Va.) 18 June 7/4 Louis expected to remain at Pompton Lakes until just before the weigh-in. **1952** L. A. G. STRONG *Darling Tom* 138 At the weigh-in, each man had received instructions to scow at the other. **1974** H. L. FOSTER *Ribbin', Jivin', & Playin' Dozens* vi. 251 Boxers at weigh-ins usually attempt to psych one another.

2. *Angling.* The weighing of the anglers' catch at the end of a competition. See sense 7g of the vb.

1949 *Club Anglers' Jrnl.* Oct. 14/2 A good weigh-in, topped by a splendid bag of roach. **1971** *Rocquaine Regatta: Programme* (Guernsey) 7 Event 1–8.00 a.m. Sea Angling. Start at Imperial Hotel 8.00 a.m.—weigh-in 10.30 a.m. **1972** *Shooting Times & Country Mag.* 1 July 16/1 The weigh-in caused great excitement as individual catches were very close.

weighing ('weɪɪŋ), *vbl. sb.* Forms: see the vb.; also 5 weyng(e. [f. WEIGH *v.*¹ + -ING¹.]

1. The action of lifting, raising, or hoisting. Also with *up*, †*out*, etc.

1485 *Naval Acc. Hen. VII* (1896) 27 Paid..for the weying of an Anker..ijᵈ. **1497** *Ibid.* 171 The brekyng vp of the dokke hede at Portesmouth weyng vt of the piles & shorys. **1545** in Hooker *Life Sir P. Carew* (1857) 131 My Lorde Admyrall..told me that he had a good hope of the waying upright of the Mary Rose this afternoe or to-morrow. *a* **1687** SIR W. PETTY in T. H[ale] *Acc. New Invent.* (1691) 119 The..weighing up of a Ship. **1755** in *Sixth Rep. Dep. Kpr. Rec.* App. II. 128 A Windlass, for the more easy weighing a Ship's Anchor at Sea.

2. The action or process of ascertaining the weight of an object.

1430 *Coventry Leet Bk.* 134 The ouersight of the weyng, and the sealyng of weightes. *c* **1440** *Promp. Parv.* 520/2 Weyynge, wythe whytys, *ponderacio, libracio.* *a* **1500** in *Arnolde's Chron.* (1502) 36 Whyinge appartayneth not vnto tronage. **1720** *Lond. Gaz.* No. 5869/2 Owners of Hops are to give Notice..of the..Hour of bagging and weighing. **1827** FARADAY *Chem. Manip.* ii. (1842) 65 The method of double weighing..invented by Borda. **1842** LOVER *Handy Andy* i, Certain weighing of soap and tobacco was going forward. **1857** MILLER *Elem. Chem.*, *Org.* 24 A second weighing gives the quantity of metallic lead. **1884** LD. KELVIN in S. P. Thompson *Life* xix. (1910) II. 801, I shall be greatly interested to hear more of your silver weighings.

b. *concr.* (See quot.)

1828 WEBSTER, *Weighing* 2. As much as is weighed at once; as, a weighing of beef.

3. *fig.* Balancing in the mind, pondering, considering.

c **1380** WYCLIF *Sel. Wks.* III. 364 And errour in weiyng of þis love makiþ many fals weddings. **1560** tr. *Fisher's Godlie Treat. Prayer* H 6 b, Ouerrunnyng a multitude of wordes with small consideration or weyghing of them. **1610** HOLLAND *Camden's Brit.* (1637) 636 After mature deliberation and weighing of the matter. **1660** JER. TAYLOR *Duct. Dubit.* III. v. rule 8 §12 The truth..is determinable by a just weighing of all that which very many wise Men have said, being put together. **1827** *J. J. Powell's Devises* (ed. 3) II. 151 If the 'weighing of inconveniences' were to be made on every particular will, the relative situation of the heir and devisee being thrown into the scale. **1848** MRS. GASKELL *Mary Barton* xv, Will's love had no blushings, no downcast eyes, no weighing of words. **1885** *Law Rep. 15 Q.B.D.* 137 The statute requires that there should be a real inquiry, a real weighing and sifting of evidence.

4. (Downward) pressure.

1398 TREVISA *Barth. De P.R.* VII. lv. (1495) r iv b, This skynne is deeled other slakyd somtyme..by to grete weyghte & weyenge dounwarde of the other membres.

5. *Comb.*, as ***weighing-cage***, ***-fee***, ***-house***, ***-room***, ***-scales***, ***-yard***; **weighing-engine**, **-machine**, an apparatus (e.g. a combination of levers, a spring-balance) for weighing heavy bodies; †**weighing-post**, a post on a race-course, indicating the place appointed for the weighing of the riders.

1819 REES *Cycl.*, **Weighing-Cage*,..an open box or cage, by means of which any small animal, such as a pig, sheep, calf,..may be..expeditiously weighed... It is constructed on the principle of the common steel-yard. **1796** *Repert. Arts & Manuf.* VI. 77 The main or long lever of the *weighing-engine. **1861** *Act 24 & 25 Vict.* c. 97 §34 Any House, Building, or Weighing Engine erected for the better Collection, Ascertainment, or Security of any such Toll. **1858** *Rules of Jockey Club* §30 The *weighing fee for plates and stakes is 10s. each horse, and 10s. extra for the winner. **1819** REES *Cycl.*, **Weighing-House*, a building furnished with a dock, and conveniences for gauging or ascertaining the tonnage of boats that are to be used on a canal. **1829** TYTLER *Hist. Scot.* vi. II. 155 It would be necessary to have some experienced person to attend in the weighing-house upon the part of the king, to superintend the annual payments. **1863** MISS BRADDON *Aurora Floyd* xiii, John was ..tumbling over small book-men in his agitation; dashing from the ring to the weighing-house. **1796** *Repert. Arts & Manuf.* VI. 75 (page-heading) Patent for an Improvement in *Weighing-Machines. **1844** H. STEPHENS *Bk. Farm* II. 343 The Weighing-machine is an important article of the barn furniture. **1864** MRS. CARLYLE *Lett.* III. 231 There is a weighing-machine at our green-grocer's. **1688** *Lond. Gaz.* No. 2312/4 Every Horse shall be shewn that day three weeks before the Race, at the *Weighing Post of Caythorp Course. **1734** CHENY *List Horse-Matches* 22 *Small-hopes* came in first, but the Rider alighting off before he came to the weighing Post, the Gelding was deem'd distanc'd. **1838** *Civil Engin. & Arch. Jrnl.* I. 116/2 There is an office for the clerk of the market, and a *weighing-room. *c* **1450** *Test. Ebor.* (Surtees) III. 99, j par *weyengscales de ligno, iiij d. **1891** 'R. BOLDREWOOD' *Sydney-side Sax.* xii, [After the race] Possie rode up to the *weighing yard with me.

†**'weighing,** *ppl. a.* [-ING².] Heavy. *Obs. rare.*

c **1400** tr. *Secreta Secret., Gov. Lordsh.* 71 Ley vpon þy wombe an hoot sherte and weyand [*camisiam calidam ponderosam*].

weighment ('weɪmənt). *Anglo-Indian.* [f. WEIGH *v.*¹ + -MENT, after *measurement*.] The action of weighing (commodities).

1878 J. INGLIS *Sport & Work* xii. 135 They..cheat in the weighments and measurements. **1889** V. BALL tr. *Tavernier's Trav.* II. 447 The methods of weighment employed by Tavernier and Schrauf respectively. **1903** C. BALD *Indian Tea* xiv. (1917) 215 A careful examination of leaf, load by load, before weighment. **1906** J. A. ELLIOTT in *Padri Elliott of Faizabad* 220 The Deputy Opium Agent.. let him set up a shop in the opium-camp during the two months that the weighments were on.

weigh-scale. Orig. *north.* In 4 weye scale, 5 weyscale, -scill, 6 weye skaile, weyskale. [ad. Du. *waagschaal* or MLG. *wageschale* (whence MSw. *väghskal*, Sw. *vågskål*, older Da. *væghskol*, Norw. *vaagskaal*) = G. *wagschale* (†*wage-*), OE. *wǣȝscalu* (once). See SCALE *sb.*¹ and next. In recent use perh. a new formation.] The pan of a balance; *pl.* a pair of scales.

13.. *Metr. Hom.* (Vernon MS.) in *Archiv Stud. neu. Spr.* LVII. 313 Þe ffendes leide in a weye scale Alle pers synnes grete and smale. *c* **1440** *Alphabet of Tales* 204 Hym þoght þer was fowle blakk men þatt putt all his ill dedis in a wey-skale. And on þe toder hand hym þoght þer was fayr men, bod þai wer passand hevy, & said þai had no gude dede of his to putt in þe toder wey-skale agayns his ill dedis. **1447–8** *Durham Acc. Rolls* (Surtees) 87 Pro uno drawghrape et uno smalrape pro Weyscill, 15d. **1459–60** *Ibid.* 89, j par del Weyscalez cum diversis ponderibus. **1582** *Durham Wills* (Surtees) II. 45, i paire of weye skailes. **1600** *Mem. St. Giles's, Durh.* (Surtees) 27 Paid for mendinge of a weyskale. **1897** KIPLING *Capt. Cour.* viii. 179 A tall woman who had been sitting on a weigh-scale dropped down into the schooner.

b. *to be on the weigh-scales*: to be undecided.

1886 M. MOORSOM *Thirteen all Told* 43 Elliot was still on the weigh-scales about going.

†**'weigh-shale** (5 weyschalle, weschale), var. of prec. (perh. directly representing OE. *wǣȝscalu*).

1465 *Priory of Finchale* (Surtees) p. ccxcviii, j par weschalis cum diversis ponderibus. *c* **1475** *Cath. Angl.* 412/2 (Addit. MS.) A Weyschalle, *vbi* A balane.

weight (weɪt), *sb.*¹ Forms: α. 1 ȝewiht, ȝewyht, 2 iwicht; 1–3 wiht, 3–5 wiht, wiȝt(e, 4–5 wyȝt(e, wyght(e, (4 wygthe), 4–6 whyght(e, 4–5 wighte, 4–7 wight (5 *Sc.* vycht); 4 wythe, 5 wyt(e, whyt(e, 4–5 witte, wytte. β. 3 *Orm.* wehht, 3–6 weght, 4–5 weghte, weȝt(e, 4– *Sc.* wecht (6 vecht); 3–4 weiht, 4–5 weyht(e, weiȝt(e, weyȝt(e, 4–6 weyght(e, 4–7 weighte (5 weigt-e, wheight-e; 5 *Sc.* weicht, 6 *Sc.* veicht, veycht, veyght, weycht), 4– weight; 5 waȝt-, 6–7 waight(e, wayght(e, (6 *Sc.* waicht, waycht, 7 wayht); 4–5 weit(e, (*pl.* wettes), 5 weyte, wheyt(e, weyth(e, wheith, whet(t)e, 6 waithe, 6 *pl.* waytts, 6–7 wait(e, 7 wayte. [OE. *wiht* (? fem.), = OFris. *wicht* (WFris. *wicht*, NFris. *wegt*, *wacht*), MDu. and Du. *wicht*, MLG. and LG. *wicht*, *wigt* (whence MDa. *vekt*, Da. *vægt*, Norw. *vegt*; MSw. *vekt*, *vikt*, Sw. *vigt*), G. (irreg.) *wucht*, ON. *vétt*, *vætt* fem.:—OTeut. type **weχti-z*, f. root **weȝ-*: see WEIGH *v.*¹ The more usual form in OE. was *ȝewiht(e* str. neut. = MDu. *ghewichte* (Du. *gewicht*), MLG. *gewichte*, *gewechte*, MHG. *gewichte* (G. *gewicht*):—OTeut. type **gaweχtjo-m.* As the prefix *i-*, *y-* (:—OE. *ȝe-*) in sbs. fell away in early ME., the two formations coalesced in the 12th c. The normal descendant in mod.English of the OE. *wiht* would be **wight*; the vowel of the β forms may be due partly to the influence of the prehistoric ON. **weht*, and partly to association with *weigh* vb.]

I. Measurement of quantity by means of weighing; quantity (in the abstract) as determined in this way.

1. *by weight*: as determined by weighing. †*without weight*: taken unweighed.

c **1000** *Sax. Leechd.* I. 146 Ðenim þas wyrte & swinen smeru..æȝþres ȝelice micel be wihte. [Cf. *Ibid.* I. 148 Ðenim..ealra þyssa wyrta ȝelice fela be ȝewihte.] *a* **1123** *O.E. Chron.* an. 1086 (Laud MS.) Maniȝ marc goldes & ma hundred punda seolfres. Ðet he nam be wihte..of his land-leode. *c* **1325** *Chron. Eng.* 503 (Ritson) He made thre condlen by wyht. **1340** *Ayenb.* 44 Huanne þo þet zelleþ be wyȝte purchaceþ and makeþ zuo moche þet [etc.]. *c* **1440** CAPGRAVE *Life St. Kath.* 1238 Alle soules..That shal to blisse, I peyse hem alle be wyte Whether in goodnesse thei ben heuy or lyghte. *c* **1460** *Contin. Brut.* 492 It was ordeyned þat þe gold in Englissh coygne shuld be weyed, & none receyved but by weght. **1539** BIBLE (Great) *2 Kings* xxv. 16 The brasse of all these vesselles was without wayght. **1585** T. WASHINGTON tr. *Nicholay's Voy.* II. i. 32 To distribute the bysket..by weight. **1601** F. TATE *Househ. Ord. Edw. II* §15 (1876) 13 The serjant chaundeler shal receve the wax & lightes bi waight from the clarke of the spicery. *c* **1612** *Turners Dish* in Rollins *Pepysian Garl.* (1922) 36 You that sel your wares by waight, and live vpon the trade. **1613** PURCHAS *Pilgrimage* II. iii. 98 Besides iewels, and brasse, and iron, without weight, with Cedars and stones without number. **1697** DRYDEN *Virg. Georg.* III. 561 With Axes first they cleave the Wine, and thence By Weight, the solid Portions they dispence. **1730** CONDUITT *Observ. Coins* (1774) 10 Foreigners who take our guineas in quantities only by weight, may melt down the heavy ones. **1811** A. T. THOMSON *Lond. Disp.* (1818) 440 The proportions of acid and water were equal by weight. **1815** W. H. IRELAND *Scribbleomania* 15 Of paper a pile..Which by weight had been purchas'd.

2. Associated with *measure* and *number*, esp. in figurative expressions referring to due proportion.

c **1250** *Gen. & Ex.* 439 Met of corn, and wiȝte of fe, And merke of felde, first fond he. **13..** *Cursor M.* 23564 (Edin.) Of his werkes es noht vnhale, bot al in mette and weiht and tale. **1340** HAMPOLE *Pr. Consc.* 7690 For he made alle thyng thurgh myght and sleght In certain noumbre and mesure and weght. *c* **1380** WYCLIF *Wks.* (1880) 321 It is good & resonable men to haue chirchis in mesure, & in numbre, & in weyhte, aftir þe hooly trinitee. *c* **1400** *26 Pol. Poems* xiv. 68 Let comon lawe his cours hold, Euene mesure, mett, and wyȝt. *c* **1480** HENRYSON *Swallow* 1666 All creature he maid for thi behufe..In number, wecht, and dew proportioun. **1551** CROWLEY *Pleas. & Payne* 562 You that by disceyte haue wonne, Were it in weyght or in measure. **1588** A. KING in *Cath. Tractates* (S.T.S.) 214 To vse falset in buying, selling or changing, in pryce, in weicht or mesure.

3. a. Ponderability, as a general property of material substances; relative heaviness.

Also *transf.* in Phrenology (see quot. 1860).

c **1385** CHAUCER *L.G.W.* Prol. 231 (Fairf. MS.) His gilte here was corowned with a sonne I-stede of golde for heuynesse and wyght. **1398** TREVISA *Barth. De P.R.* XIX. cxxx. (1495) 938 Two thynges makyth weyghte: lightnesse and heuynesse. **14..** LYDG. *Beware of Doubleness* 92 In balaunce whan they be peised, For lakke of weght they be bore down. *c* **1450** *Merlin* iii. 57 They..seide it was a thynge impossible to charge, they [the stones] were of soche gretnesse and wight. **1600** SHAKS. *All's Well* II. iii. 126 Our bloods Of colour, waight, and heat, pour'd all together, Would quite confound distinction. **1688** HOLME *Armoury* III. 315/1 The Axe for the cutting of the great and large Bones..hath weight and substance in it. **1728** POPE *Dunc.* I. 183 As clocks to weight their nimble motion owe, The wheels above urg'd by the load below. **1765** *Museum Rust.* IV. 74 The wool had then very likely gained weight considerably. *a* **1790** HENRY *Hist. Gt. Brit.* (1793) VI. 634 If the number of coins..did not actually make a pound in weight. **1858** LARDNER *Hand-bk. Nat. Phil.* 154 Air possesses, in common with all material substances, the qualities of impenetrability, inertia, and weight. **1860** MAYNE *Expos. Lex.*, *Weight* or *Resistance*,..a faculty common to man and to the lower animals..taking cognizance of weight and other kinds of mechanical force. *Phr.* **1857** G. A. LAWRENCE *Guy Liv.* i, He had slowly gravitated on into his present position, on the old Ring principle—'weight must tell'.

b. In *fig.* or *transf.* uses.

c **1374** CHAUCER *Boeth.* II. pr. iii. (1886) 25 Yif any frute of mortal thinges may han any weyhte or pris of welefulnesse. **1526** *Pilgr. Perf.* (W. de W. 1531) 41 b, In the weyght of this noble treasure, standeth all the effecte of the pilgrymage of perfeccyon. **1587** A. DAY *Daphnis & Chloe* (1890) title-p., Excellently describing the weight of affection, the simplicitie of loue. **1658** FLECKNOE *Enigm. Char.* 12 He hovers in his choice, like an empty Ballance with no waight of Judgement to incline him to either scale. **1787** WOLCOT (P. Pindar) *Ode upon Ode* Wks. 1812 I. 443 And really I would rather be knock'd down By weight of argument than weight of fist. **1891** CAYLEY *Math. Papers* (1897) XIII. 110 It is for this purpose convenient to introduce the notion of 'weight'; say a triangle has the weight 1, then a quadrangle, ..divisible into two triangles, has the weight 2.

c. Impetus (of a heavy falling body; also of a blow).

1375 BARBOUR *Bruce* XVII. 693 The gynour..swappit out the stane That evin toward the life is gane,..And with gret wecht syne duschit doune. *c* **1440** *Generydes* 2163 Ther strokes shuld come with grete wight.

d. In scientific use: (see quots.).

a **1721** KEILL *Maupertius' Diss.* (1734) 3 A secret Force, we call Weight or Gravity, attracts, urges or impels Bodies towards the Center of the Earth. **1806** O. GREGORY *Treat. Mechanics* I. 46 It will not be difficult to attach a just and scientific meaning to that which is commonly called weight: it is the effort necessary to prevent a body from falling. **1827** N. ARNOTT *Physics* I. 14 Weight, therefore, is merely general attraction acting everywhere.

e. *Prosody.* (See quot.)

1898 SWEET *A.S. Rdr.* Introd. (ed. 7) 86 Stress and quantity together constitute weight. *Ibid.* 92 This double alliteration is not essential to the metre like that caused by extra weight.

4. In various phrases (see also sense 1):

a. *in* (or †*of*) *weight*, added to adjs. such as *heavy*, *light*, *great*, etc.

c **1400** *Laud Troy Bk.* 4662 Semely dyght..With eglis faire and riche In syght, Off riche gold and mechel of wyght. **1484** CAXTON *Fables of Alfonce* vi, Thow wenest that within my bely shold be a precious stone more of weyght than I am. **1486** *Bk. St. Albans* d iij, That noon be heuyer then an other bot like of weyght. *a* **1500** in Arnolde *Chron.* (1811) 128 The said bales..were myche heuyer in weight than they shulde naturally haue ben. **1910** W. PARKER in *Encycl. Brit.* XI. 352/1 They [opossum skins] are..not only very light in weight and warm, but handsome.

fig. 1570 B. GOOGE *Popish Kingd.* 13b, The Dorekeeper instructed than, what things he ought to do Whenas this office great of waight he there doth come vnto.

†b. ***of weight*** (as adj. phrase): Heavy. *Obs.*

1374 CHAUCER *Troylus* II. 1385 (Campsall MS.) For swyfter cours cometh þyng þat is of wighte Whan it descendeth þan don þynges lyghte. *c* 1384 —— *H. Fame* 739 Any thinge that hevy be As stoon or lede or thynge of wight. *a* 1400–50 *Wars Alex.* 5473 Lamprays of weȝt Twa hundreth pond ay a pece. 1599 ALEX. HUME *Poems* (S.T.S.) *Hymn* vii. 113 Crosbowes of waight, and Gnosik gainyeis kein. 1663 GERBIER *Counsel* 47 Materials of weight, as Sauder, wherewith an unconscionable Plummer can ingrosse his Bill.

†c. ***of weight***: of full or standard weight. *Sc.*

1500 HALYBURTON *Ledger* (1867) 253 [Certain coins] all of vycht. 1524 in *Acts Parlt. Scot.* (1875) XII. 41/1 Þe gold sall have comone coursse . . þe Hary noble of Weiht for xl^{b} . . þe scottis demy of wecht xviij^{b}. 1597 *Reg. Mag. Sig. Scot.* 228/2 Rois nobilis of gold and wecht.

5. The amount which an article of given price or value ought to weigh. Chiefly *ellipt.* in predicative use = 4c. ***short weight***: see SHORT *a.* 15.

a 1400 *Eng. Gilds* 354 Ȝif þe ferþingloff is in defawte of wyȝte ouer twelf pans, þe bakere is in þe amercy. 1435 in Kingsford *Chron. Lond.* 73 That no man . . shulde putte fforth ne profre no golde . . but yff yt helde the weyht. 1530 PALSGR. 770/1, I pray you, go way this angell, and tell me and he be weygt [F. *de poyx*]. *a* 1585 in *Eng. Hist. Rev.* (1914) XXIX. 521 Spanishe gold of best and those [pieces] that be weight. 1623 FLETCHER & ROWLEY *Maid in Mill* IV. iii, We must be weight in love, no grain too light. 1640 QUARLES *Enchirid.* II. xlv, If thou finde him weight, make him thine owne. 1691 LOCKE *Consid. Lower. Interest* (1692) 149 Your heavy Money, (*i.e.* that which is weight according to its Denomination, by the Standard of the Mint). 1720 DE FOE *Capt. Singleton* vii. (1840) 119 It was near two ounces more than weight in a pound. 1802 MAR. EDGEWORTH *Pop. Tales, Murad* i, I . . protested . . that I had never furnished the people . . with bread that was not weight. *c* 1850 *Arab. Nts.* (Rtldg.) 212 The miller . . ordered her to bring the scales, to see if the money he was going to pay was weight.

†6. The action of weighing. *Obs. rare.*

a 1483 *Liber Niger* in *Househ. Ord.* (1790) 63 One of these clerkes dayly, to be at the weyghtes of wax in the chaundrey.

7. Ponderable matter; that which weighs.

1663 GERBIER *Counsel* 53 What resistance dust can be, when waight is laid upon it. 1755 CHAMBERLAYNE *Pres. St. Gt. Brit.* I. III. viii. 196 They are suffered to be over-charged with Weight laid upon them, that they expire presently. 1859 TENNYSON *Marr. Geraint* 526 Slowly falling as a scale that falls, When weight is added only grain by grain.

II. An amount determined or determinable by weighing; a definite quantity weighed or capable of being weighed.

8. a. A portion or quantity weighing a definite amount. Often preceded by an expression indicating the amount: in OE. in the genitive, as *anes pundes, þreora punda wiht*; now in attributive or appositional form, as ***one pound, three pounds weight***. Often abbreviated *wt.* ***weight for weight***: (see FOR *prep.* 25); also (with hyphens) used *attrib.*

c 1000 *Sax. Leechd.* I. 374 Ðenim . . of ælcere þisne wyrte xx peneȝa wiht. *a* 1300 *Cursor M.* 21429 If he his mone [= money] moght not gett, . . þat ilk weght þat þar was less, He suld yeild of his aun flexs. ? *a* 1366 CHAUCER *Rom. Rose* 1106 The barres were of gold ful fyne . . Full heuy gret and no thyng lyght, In eueriche was a besaunt wight. 1387 TREVISA *Higden* V. 397 Þe monkes . . took wiþ hem . . a weyȝte of brede for the iorney [L. *pondus panis diurni*]. *c* 1430 *Chev. Assigne* 155 She sente aftur a golde-smyȝte to forge here a cowpe; And . . delyuered hym his weyȝtes. 1494 *Acc. Ld. High Treas. Scot.* I. 314 For iij pund wecht foure vnce . . of gold. 1596 SHAKS. *Merch. V.* IV. i. 41 You'l aske me why I rather choose to haue A weight of carrion flesh, then to receiue Three thousand Ducats? 1655 MARQ. WORCESTER *Cent. Inv.* §99 How to make one pound weight to raise an hundred as high as one pound falleth. 1669 EARL SANDWICH tr. *Barba's Art of Metals* I. (1674) 12 Lemnian-Earth . . is esteemed as rich as Gold, and sold so weight for weight. 1728 E. S[MITH] *Compleat Housew.* (ed. 2) 164 Mix the Pulp and Meat together, and take the weight and half of Sugar. 1794 VANCOUVER *Agric. Cambridge* 55 The grass . . produced from the water-meadows, is chiefly inferior to that (weight for weight) which grows . . upon unwatered ground. 1827 STEUART *Planter's G.* (1828) 150 Close-planting, pruning, and other means are employed to obtain what is considered the greatest possible 'weight of wood'. 1845 DODD *Brit. Manuf.* v. 26 About 112 lbs. weight of biscuits are put into the oven at once. 1854 RONALDS & RICHARDSON *Chem. Techn.* (ed. 2) I. 236 The quantities of heat contained in equal weights of water and air at the same temperature. 1964 W. G. SMITH *Allergy & Tissue Metabolism* vi. 71 In the perfused cat hind limb it is as active as acetyl-choline on a weight-for-weight basis. 1968 *Times* 3 Dec. 10/8 Female rats were given daily doses reckoned to be about eight times as powerful on a weight-for-weight basis as those taken by the tribeswomen. 1974 *Brit. Med. Jrnl.* 19 Jan. 107/2 Special care needs to be taken over the use of Lanoxin brand [of digitalis], which is now twice as potent on a weight-for-weight basis as formerly.

fig. 1382 WYCLIF *2 Cor.* iv. 17 [The] liȝt thing of oure tribulacioun worchith . . the euerelasting weiȝte of glorie in vs. 1611 SHAKS. *Cymb.* III. v. 88 Is she with Posthumus? From whose so many waights of basenesse, cannot A dram of worth be drawne. 1706 PRIOR *Ode to Queen* x, Impartial Justice holds Her equal Scales; 'Till stronger Virtue does the Weight incline. 1852 TENNYSON *Ode Death Wellington* 240 One, upon whose hand and heart and brain Once the weight and fate of Europe hung.

transf. 1855 HOPKINS *Organ* II. 493 [In the New Organ] there are several reservoirs producing different weights of wind.

b. *ellipt.* A pennyweight of gold.

1890 *Melbourne Argus* 9 Aug. 4/6 Tried a crushing, and didn't get four weights to the ton.

c. ***to lose weight***: to become thinner or less corpulent; ***to put on weight***: see PUT *v.*^{1} 46f.

1961 M. SPARK *Prime of Miss Jean Brodie* iv. 114 She had lost weight through her sad passion for Mr. Lloyd. 1970 M. PATTEN *Bedsitter Cookery* 89/1 Most sensible people today are anxious to keep a slim figure and a well-planned diet is an essential towards either losing weight or maintaining a good weight. 1982 J. MANN et al. *Diabetics' Diet Bk.* I. 20 To lose weight you should aim to have only 1,300 calories a day.

9. ***its, his,*** etc. ***weight in*** or ***of gold, silver***, etc.: a quantity of gold, silver, etc. of the same weight. Chiefly in hyperbolical statements of value.

c 1205 LAY. 30835 For nauer neoðer nalde for his æfne wiht of golde þat þe king hit wuste þat [etc.]. *a* 1300 *Floriz & Bl.* 650 (Cambr. MS.) Ȝe habbeþ iherd of blauncheflur, Hu ihc hire boȝte . . For seuesiþe of gold hire wiȝt. 13.. *Sir Beues* 1725 An hors he hadde of gret pris . .; For him a ȝaf seluer wiȝt, Er he þat hors haue miȝt. 14.. *Guy Warw.* 8122 He wold have yove for the fyndyng [of the sword] The weyght of gold and of other thyng. *a* 1500 MEDWALL *Nature* (Brandl) II. 324 Thou art worth the weyght of gold. 16.. *Eger & Grine* 1154 in *Percy Fol. MS.* I. 390 He is worth to her his waight in gold. 1614 J. SARIS *Voy. Japan* etc. (Hakl. Soc.) 204 Muske, worth the wayht in Siluer. 1634 ? S. ROWLEY *Noble Soldier* II. i. D2, I would not drinke that infernall draught . . for the weight of the world in Diamonds. 1672 PETTY *Pol. Anat. Irel.* (1691) 68 Gold has been worth but twelve times its own weight in Silver. 1815 J. SMITH *Panorama Sci. & Art* II. 783 Add to the solution twelve times its weight of distilled water. 1854 PATMORE *Angel in Ho., Betrothal* 130 A Tasso worth its weight in gold. 1856 MISS YONGE *Daisy Chain* II. xxvi, The dear old nurse . . whom George Rivers would have paid with her weight in gold, for taking care of his new daughter.

10. a. The amount that something weighs; the quantity of a portion of matter as measured by the amount of its downward force due to gravitation; the amount of resistance offered by a body to forces tending to raise it. ***live weight***: see LIVE *a.* 7.

c 1385 CHAUCER *L.G.W.* 1118 Sakkis ful of gold of large weyghte. 1387 TREVISA *Higden* III. 205 Þanne he took heede þat þe hameres were of dyuers weiȝtes. 1398 —— *Barth. De P.R.* XVI. v. (Bodl. MS.), Þouȝe it [*sc.* gold] be in fire it wasteþ nouȝt, bi smokinge and vapoures noþer leseþ his weiȝt [L. *nec etiam in pondere minoratur*]. *c* 1400 MAUNDEV. (Roxb.) xviii. 84 Marchands sophisticatez peper, when it is alde . . and so by cause of þe weight it semes fresch and new. *c* 1475 *Pol. Poems* (Rolls) II. 286 The pore pepyll . . be oppressyd . . In yevyng theym to myche weythe into the spynnyng. 1597 SHAKS. *2 Hen. IV*, II. iv. 276 The weight of an hayre will turne the Scales betweene their Haber-de-pois. 1599 B. JONSON *Cynthia's Rev.* II. ii, To a friend in want, hee will not depart with the waight of a soldred groat. 1625 N. CARPENTER *Geogr. Del.* I. iv. (1635) 73 The parts are indowed with an equall waight. 1698 FLOYER *Asthma* (1717) 196 The Morning Weight [of the Asthmatic] was 178 Pound. 1715 tr. *Gregory's Astron.* (1726) I. 491 The Weights of homogeneous Bodies plac'd near one another. 1765 *Museum Rust.* IV. 74 The weight of this wool encreased from . . August 30, 1756, to Feb. 19, 1757, as 100 to 103¼. 1827 FARADAY *Chem. Manip.* ii. (1842) 25 Small weights cannot be appreciated in instruments intended for great quantities, because of the strength. 1855 BREWSTER *Newton* I. xii. 323 The weight of all bodies is diminished by the centrifugal force, so that the weight of any body is greater at the poles than it is at the equator. 1876 TAIT *Rec. Adv. Phys. Sci.* xiv. (1885) 357 The weight of a pound of matter varies from place to place on the earth's surface.

fig. 1390 GOWER *Conf.* II. 276 Mi weyhte of love and mi mesure Hath be mor large . . Than evere I tok of love ayein. 1571 CAMPION *Hist. Irel.* xiv. (1633) 46 When he was forced to silence with the waight of truth. 1586 A. DAY *Eng. Secretorie* II. (1595) 128 If men wold but throughly enter into the weight of their estates, and truly consider with them-selues what of duty appertaineth to very reputation. 1600 SHAKS. *A.Y.L.* I. ii. 9 Heerein I see thou lou'st mee not with the full waight that I loue thee.

transf. 1637 RUTHERFORD *Lett.* (1671) 128, I know not the weight of the pension the King will give me.

b. In phrases stating how much a thing weighs, as ***of two pounds weight***.

1389 *Eng. Gilds* 30 Also a knaue chyld . . beren a candel yat day, ye wygthe of to pound. ? 1449 *Paston Lett.* Suppl. (1901) 22, ij. tapers of wax of ij. lbs. wyght. 1479 *Cely Papers* (Camden) 19 And ij salt salers of sylver of the weyth of x unse or xj. 1553 EDEN *Treat. New Ind.* (Arb.) 34 The fleshe therof wayed .xlvij. pound weyght. 1557 RECORDE *Whetst.* Rj, A Cube of Brasse of 4 inches square, doth weighe 7 pounde weighte. 1599 SHAKS. *Much Ado* III. iv. 24 'Twill be heauier soone, by the waight of a man. 1758 *Payne's Universal Chron.* 29 July–5 Aug. 141/2 A Turtle of upwards of 500 lb. wt.

c. In figurative phrases. ***to pull (one's) weight***: see PULL *v.* 15b; ***to throw (chuck,*** etc.) ***one's weight about*** or ***around***: to assert oneself or one's authority, esp. in an objectionable way; to act officiously. *colloq.*

1617 MORYSON *Itin.* III. 37 The vastnesse of their Empire, falling with his owne weight. 1794 GOUV. MORRIS in Sparks *Life & Writ.* (1832) II. 395 We have seen such a system fall by its own weight. 1917 A. G. EMPEY *From Fire Step* 31 Don't chuck your weight about until you've been up the line and learnt something. 1921 *Brit. Weekly* 6 Oct. 2/3 There was a general . . belief that people round us were not pulling their weight. 1922 C. E. MONTAGUE *Disenchantment* viii. 104 Some typically stupid English General . . was clearly throwing his weight about, as they say, without any real understanding of anything. 1926 S. JAMESON *Three Kingdoms* xii. 348 'Come to that,' he said, 'Isabel has more right than any of you to fling her weight about.' 1941 J. P. MARQUAND *H. M. Pulham, Esq.* i. 10 Bill King . . always used to say that Bo-jo was a bastard, a big bastard. Perhaps he meant that Bo-jo sometimes threw his weight around. 1955 E. HILLARY *High Adventure* 163 A big, strong, swanking chap who had thrown his weight about a good deal lower down. 1966 N. MARSH *Death at Dolphin* (1967) vi. 145 Why hadn't he put his foot down? . . He should have thrown his weight about. 1982 'M. HEBDEN' *Pel & Staghound* xv. 176 Madame Rensselaer seemed to enjoy throwing her weight about.

d. Chem. ***atomic weight***: the relative weight of the atom of any element = *atomic mass* s.v. ATOMIC *a.* 1; similarly ***molecular weight***, the relative molecular mass of a molecule, equal to the sum of the atomic weights of the constituent atoms.

1820, etc. Atomic weight [see ATOMIC *a.* 1]. 1836–41 BRANDE *Chem.* (ed. 5) 236 A compound of 1 atom of hydrogen and 1 atom of chlorine, their respective weights being 1 and 36. 1838 T. THOMSON *Chem. Org. Bodies* 256 This would raise the atomic weight to 31·74. 1872 *Jrnl. Chem. Soc.* XXV. 949 The relative molecular weights of ether, alcohol and water. 1950 *Sci. News* XV. 88 Blue hæmocyanin. . . This molecule is the largest of any known substance, having a molecular weight of several millions. 1978 P. W. ATKINS *Physical Chem.* 11 We can determine how many elementary units we have by measuring the mass of the sample . . and knowing the relative molecular mass (R.M.M., the 'molecular weight').

e. *transf.* in *Mechanics.* (See quots.)

1810 *Encycl. Brit.* (ed. 4) XIII. 53/1 When two forces act against each other by the intervention of a machine, the one force is called the power, and the other the weight. 1829 *Chapters Phys. Sci.* 77 The *Inclined Plane* . . is always inclined obliquely to the *weight*, or the *resistance* to be overcome.

11. a. A heavy mass; usually, something heavy that is lifted or carried; a burden, load. Also *fig.*

c 1374 CHAUCER *Boeth.* II. met. v. (1886) 35 Allas what was he þat fyrst dalf vp the gobetes or the weyhtes of gold couered vndyr erthe. 1398 TREVISA *Barth. De P.R.* V. xxiii. (Bodl. MS.), A philosophir was preued whi an horrible man is more heuy þanne eny burþon oþir weiȝte [*ed.* 1495 wytte]. *c* 1440 *Gesta Rom.* xxxi. 117 Ther he was nye dreynte, for gret weyte of his burdon. 1523–34 FITZHERB. *Husb.* §20 With the weyght therof it pulleth the corne flatte to the erth. 1538 STARKEY *England* I. iii. 78 Not to lyue . . as an vnprofytabul weyght and burden of the erth. 1562 BP. PILKINGTON *Abdias* Pref. Aav, The greater weighte that is cast on, the soner it breakes. 1584–7 GREENE *Carde of Fancie* Wks. (Grosart) IV. 75, I found it built . . so slenderly, as ye least waight was able to pash it into innumerable peeces. *c* 1620 FLETCHER *False One* v. iv, My free mind, Like to the Palm-tree walling fruitful Nile, Shall grow up straighter and enlarge it self 'Spight of the envious weight that loads it with. 1642 *Docq. Lett. Pat. at Oxf.* (1837) 323 New invencions . . to raise ponderous weightes with. 1659 DRYDEN *Heroick Stanzas* xv, His palms, tho under Weights they did not stand, Still thriv'd. 1698 FLOYER *Asthma* iv. 127 All strait Cloaths, and the weight of Blankets hinder the Extention of the Breath. 1764 [J. BURTON] *Pres. St. Navig. Thames* 39 There will be no Occasion to penn up such a vast Weight of Water pressing on the Weir. 1792 *Jrnls. Ho. Comm.* XLVII. 363/2 It is an Absurdity . . to load the Extremities with more Weight of Metal than the Midships. 1814 SCOTT *Lord of Isles* v. xx, Strong are mine arms, and little care A weight so slight as thine to bear. 1852 MALPAS *Builder's Pocket-bk.* 57 The whole weight is thrown upon the beam. 1865 TYNDALL *Fragm. Sci.* (1871) 14 The simplest form of work is the raising of a weight.

transf. 1746 FRANCIS tr. *Hor., Sat.* I. x. 12 Let your sense be clear, Nor with a weight of words fatigue the ear. —— *Art of Poetry* 260 *note*, The Verses . . were so heavy with a Weight of Spondees.

b. Phr. ***to take the weight off (one's feet)***: to sit down and rest. Cf. *to take a load off (one's feet)* s.v. LOAD *sb.* 3h. *colloq.*

1936 'J. TEY' *Shilling for Candles* ix. 100 Waiters like to take the weight off their feet for a little. 1960 L. DAVIDSON *Night of Wenceslas* i. 19 We were at the seat now. 'Like to take the weight off?' I said. 1965 A. ROUDYBUSH *Season for Death* (1966) xxxii. 190, I stepped into the library . . to take the weight off my feet for a minute. 1973 H. MILLER *Open City* xv. 168 Sit down, take the weight off.

12. *spec.* **a.** In horse-racing or riding: The amount (expressed in stones and pounds) which the jockey or rider is required or expected to weigh, or which the mount can without difficulty carry. ***catch weights***: see CATCH- 4.

1692 *Lond. Gaz.* No. 2773/4 None but Gentlemen to ride; The weight 12 Stone. 1740 *Act 13 Geo. II*, c. 19 §3 Any Horse . . carrying less than the Weights herein before directed to be carried. 1771 [P. PARSONS] *Newmarket* I. 108 Who ever heard of a rider's throwing away part of his weight, or tearing his pocket that the shot might run out? 1858 *Rules of Racing* §38 Each jockey shall be allowed 2 lb above the weight specified for his horse to carry and no more. 1883 'RAPIER' *Types of Turf* 74, I remember how eagerly in a certain stable the weights were expected for last year's Cesarewitch.

b. Without article.

1734 CHENY *List Horse-Matches* 11 The highest Horse to carry 12 *st.* and all under his Size to be allow'd Weight for Inches. 1782 COWPER *Gilpin* 115 He carries weight! he rides a race! 1886 EARL SUFFOLK *Racing* 145 Weight for age is the basis of trials with old horses. 1889 BADEN-POWELL *Pigsticking* 117 The chief objections to an Arab are . . his frequent inability to jump and to carry weight. 1891 'R. BOLDREWOOD' *Sydney-side Sax.* viii, He was a dark brown horse . . up to weight, and good across country.

Comb. 1863 MISS BRADDON *Aur. Floyd* xiii, The bay filly which was to run in a weight-for-age race at the York Spring [meeting]. 1898 *Encycl. Sport* II. 196/2 Weight-for-age races are of three varieties.

c. *Boxing.* A match between boxers of a particular weight.

1914 *Varsity* 24 Feb. 15/1 An experienced boxer . . who won this weight last year at Cambridge. *Ibid.*, Selected to do duty in the two weights.

III. In figurative senses from the above.

13. a. A burden (of responsibility, obligation, suffering, years, etc.).

c **1380** WYCLIF *Sel. Eng. Wks.* I. 66 þei [the Jews] shal bere to þe ende of þe worlde the wiȝte of þe olde lawe. *c* **1450** CAPGRAVE *Life St. Gilbert* 90 He held him-self onworþi to þe birden of swech a wyte. **1539** BIBLE (Great) *Num.* xi. 11 Seynge that thou puttest yᵉ weyght of all this people vpon me. *a* **1586** SIDNEY *Ps.* v. iv, With heaped weights of their own sinns oppresse These most ungratefull rebells unto thee. **1590** SHAKS. *Com. Err.* II. i. 36 But were we burdned with like waight of paine, As much, or more, we should our selues complaine. **1632** SANDERSON *Serm.* 303 You that groane vnder the waight of Gods displeasure. **1661** F. HOWGILL in *Extr. S.P. rel. Friends* II. (1911) 129 The Imprisonment of Freinds lyes as a weight vppon the Nation. **1675** DRYDEN *Aurengz.* I. (1676) 2 The weight of seventy Winters prest him down. **1718** PRIOR *Power* 694 Permit me strength, my weight of woe to bear. **1719** DE FOE *Crusoe* II. (Globe) 540 For my Part I had a Weight taken off from my Heart. **1738** WESLEY *Ps.* CXLVII. vii, Ye, who bow with Age's Weight. **1811** BYRON *To Thyrza* 43 Oft have I borne the weight of ill, But never bent beneath till now! **1840** DICKENS *Old C. Shop* vi, The child, overpowered by the weight of her sorrows and anxieties.. burst into a passion of tears. **1883** S. C. HALL *Retrospect* I. 397 He was an aged man.. and seemed enfeebled by the weight of years.

b. Burden (of proof), onus.

1824 J. MARSHALL *Constit. Opin.* (1839) 312 The whole weight of proof.. is thrown upon him who would introduce a distinction.

14. a. The force of an onslaught or encounter in the field; pressure exerted by numbers.

c **1500** *Melusine* xix. 106 Wel ye wote that two knyghtes may not susteyne & bere the weight ayenst wel Lxxx. or houndred thousand paynemys. **1643** R. BAKER *Chron., Hen. III* (1653) 127 And so undertaking the main weight of the battell, [he] perished under it. **1697** DRYDEN *Æneis* IX. 1071 They bear him back; and whom by Might They cannot Conquer, they oppress with Weight. **1734** tr. *Rollin's Rom. Hist.* (1827) IX. 189 No longer able to support the weight of the enemy, they thought fit to retire. **1828** SCOTT *F.M. Perth* xi, The tumult.. forced asunder, by the weight and press of numbers, the Prince and Douglas.

b. *to feel the weight of*: to suffer from (by receiving a heavy blow or undergoing severe pressure). Freq. *fig.*

1553 *Respublica* 284 He that ones wincheth shall fele the waite of my fiste. **1617** MORYSON *Itin.* II. 98 He had felt the weight of her Majesties power. **1681** FLAVEL *Meth. Grace* xvii. 317 His enemies felt the weight of his prayers, and the church of God reaped the benefits thereof. **1701** ATTERBURY *Serm.* (1726) I. 268 They, who lately felt the weight of the English Arms. **1702** DE FOE *New Test Ch. Eng. Honesty* Writ. 1705 II. 306 The Church, who by this time began to feel the Weight of the King's Hand, had been Dispossess'd of Magdalen College in Oxford. **1880** MRS. PARR *Adam & Eve* II. 21 I've a made that great lutterputch feel the weight o' me hand.

†**c.** *to give a weight to*: to add force or vigour to.

1796 MME. D'ARBLAY *Camilla* VI. iv. III. 202 To see her thus completely disconcerted, gave a weight to the mischievous malice of Mrs. Arlbery.

d. *Mining.* (See quot.)

1892 *Labour Commission* Gloss., *Weight.* A weight is the gradual or sudden lowering of the roof of a mine after the coal has been worked on the long-wall system.

15. a. Importance, moment, claim to consideration; esp. (*a*) in phr. *of weight, of great* (*little,* etc.) *weight.*

(*a*) **1521** WOLSEY in Ellis *Orig. Lett.* Ser. I. I. 179 A smale conceylement.. of no regarde, weight, or importance. **1560** DAUS tr. *Sleidane's Comm.* 79 b, In matters of weight and difficultie. **1583** STUBBES *Anat. Abus.* II. 113 What obedience than is due to them in matters of small waight, of small importaunce. **1606** *Proc. agst. Late Traitors, Garnet* etc. 103 Such new matter as shallbe worth the hearing, as being indeed of waight and moment. **1642** D. ROGERS *Naaman* 50 So should we in our journeyes, travailes, attempts of weight,.. beseech him that his good hand might appeare. **1697** DRYDEN *Æneis* VII. 345 Pond'ring future Things of wond'rous Weight. **1729** LAW *Serious C.* xv. (1732) 274 It is certain, that all such bodily actions as affect the soul, are of great weight in Religion. *a* **1770** JORTIN *Serm.* (1771) II. xix. 377 This is an argument of weight. **1783** BURKE *Sp. Fox's E. India Bill* Wks. 1792 II. 417 The objection is of weight. **1851** HELPS *Comp. Solit.* xi. 214 The night-mares of care and trouble cease to weigh as if they were the only things of weight in the world.

(*b*) **1581** N. BURNE *Disput.* To King a v, As the importance and vecht of the mater requyris. **1597** HOOKER *Eccl. Pol.* v. lxv. §4 Ceremonies haue more in waight then in sight. **1614** RALEGH *Hist. World* IV. vii. §2. 299 Considering better.. the weight of the businesse, which he had taken in hand. **1662** HOWELL *New Engl. Gram.* 16 In French she [the letter Y] is of that weight that she makes somtimes a whole word of her self. **1708** SWIFT *Sacram. Test* Misc. (1711) 328 But there is no great weight in this. **1741** WATTS *Improv. Mind* II. iv, The weight and force of argument which should influence the mind. **1830** CUNNINGHAM *Brit. Paint.* I. 223 Yet weight must be allowed to the opinion of Northcote. **1849** MACAULAY *Hist. Eng.* iv. I. 513 Weight of moral character was indeed wanting to Edward Seymour. **1861** BUCKLE *Civiliz.* (1869) III. v. 324 Having no wealth to give him weight. **1888** BRYCE *Amer. Commw.* I. viii. 106 The two elections.. are the best evidence of the weight of this consideration.

b. *spec.* The relative value of an observation. More widely, a multiplying factor associated with each of a series of numerical quantities, esp. ones that are added together.

1825 *Phil. Mag.* LXV. 167 The arithmetical mean of a set of observations.. is the particular case when the weights a, a', a'' etc. are all equal, and the sum of the errors is equal to zero. **1838** DE MORGAN *Ess. Probab.* 138 The method of finding an average is this: multiply every observation by its weight and divide the sum of the products by the sum of the weights. **1868** J. C. WATSON *Theoret. Astron.* vii. 372 The relative accuracy of two or more observed values of a quantity may be expressed by means of what are called their weights. **1935** PAULING & WILSON *Introd. Quantum Mech.* iv. 100 The degree of degeneracy (the number of independent wave functions associated with a given energy level) is often called the quantum weight of the level. **1940** G. CROWTHER *Outl. Money* iii. 93 For some sorts of index numbers, weighting is essential... Weights that are correct at one time may be incorrect at other times. **1949** *Economist* 8 Oct. 775/1 If the estimate of the change in productivity had been based on calculations using post-war weights they would have indicated a larger increase in productivity in the United States. **1970** O. DOPPING *Computers & Data Processing* ii. 32 The number 491 means 4 × 100 + 9 × 10 + 1. The weights are 100, 10, and 1, respectively. **1983** *Personal Computer World* Dec. 142/2 When each digit is multiplied by its weight the sum of the products, including the check digit, whose weight is 1, is exactly divisible by 11 in a valid [Standard Book] number.

16. Persuasive or convincing power (of utterances, arguments, evidence); impressiveness (of matter or speech).

1534 BERNERS *Golden Bk. M. Aurel.* Prol. (1535) A iv, It suffiseth to gyue for the weyght the sentence. **1542** UDALL *Erasm. Apopth.* Erasm. Pref. **iiij b, A famous speaker.. geueth to the saiynges moche weight and grace also. **1586** A. DAY *Engl. Secretorie* I. (1625) 5 A matter of gravity is to be delivered with waight. **1630** PRYNNE *Anti-Armin.* 113 A Sentence of sufficient antiquity and weight to put a period to this Controuersie. **1716** ADDISON *Free-holder* No. 19 ¶3 Having nothing of any manner of weight to offer against the principles of their antagonists. **1783** BLAIR *Rhet.* xviii. I. 365 Nothing derogates more from the weight and dignity of any composition, than too great attention to ornament. **1829** SOUTHEY *Lett.* (1856) IV. 158 But this detracts not from the weight of your reasoning. **1849** MACAULAY *Hist. Eng.* ii. I. 172 No man spoke with more weight and dignity in council and in parliament. **1866** MRS. WHITNEY *L. Goldthw.* ii, The 'O father!' was not without its weight.

17. Weightiest or heaviest part; greatest stress or severity; preponderance, superior amount (of evidence, authority) on one side or the other of a question.

1568 GRAFTON *Chron.* II. 621, xv. thousand men, in whom consisted the waight and peyse of the whole enterprise. **1665** BRATHWAIT *Comment Two Tales* 199 Weight of Judgment has ever given Invention Priority before Language. **1722** DE FOE *Hist. Plague* (1754) 8 The Parish of St. Giles's, where still the Weight of the Infection lay. **1866** ROGERS *Agric. & Prices* I. x. 168 The weight of evidence is in favour of the latter hypothesis. **1883** *Law Rep.*, 11 Q.B.D. 591 An order.. for a new trial on the ground.. that the verdict was against the weight of evidence.

18. In various phrases:

a. *to lay weight upon*: †to urge (a person) to do something (*obs.*); to attach importance or value to.

(*a*) **1600** HOLLAND *Livy* XLIX. 1238 The woman laid great wait upon me to depart out of those quarters.

(*b*) **1708** SWIFT *Sacram. Test* Misc. (1711) 336 We are apt to lay some weight upon their Opinion. **1815** SCOTT *Guy M.* iv, We lay no weight whatever upon the pretended information thus conveyed. **1863** B. TAYLOR *Quaker Widow* xvi, And it was brought upon my mind.. That we on dress and outward things perhaps lay too much weight.

†**b.** *to hold weight with*: to vie in greatness with. *Obs.*

1641 J. SHUTE *Sarah & Hagar* (1649) 148 For there are but few deliverances temporall, that hold weight with the delivery from the paines of child-birth.

c. *to have weight*: to make an impression on, weigh *with* (those who judge a matter); to receive favourable consideration; to be recognized as valid or important. Similarly *to carry weight.*

1638 SIR K. DIGBY *Let. to Ld. G. Digby* (1651) 10, I conceive they are to have no more weight with those that have ability to examine them, then [etc.]. **1707** FREIND *Peterboro's Cond. Sp.* 108 The latter opinion had its weight, and prevail'd. **1748** RICHARDSON *Clarissa* (1768) I. 213 If.. such narrow motives have so little weight with me. **1771** *Junius Lett.* lix. 308 The conditions which constitute this right must be taken together. Separately, they have little weight. **1818** CRUISE *Digest* (ed. 2) I. 368 If the tenant.. were likely to be prejudiced by not being named, this objection would have weight. **1858** HAWTHORNE *Fr. & It. Jrnls.* (1872) I. 31 The *visé* of a minister carries more weight.

†**d.** *upon the weight of*: on the strength of, by relying on the value of. *Obs.*

1710 STEELE *Tatler* No. 4 Introd., I shall not pretend to raise a Credit to this Work, upon the Weight of my politic News only.

e. *to give* (full, due) *weight to*: to allow (a plea, argument, circumstance) its proper force; to weigh equitably; to treat as valid or important.

1885 *Manch. Exam.* 26 June 5/3 His Holiness has given due weight to the many conflicting aspects of the case. *Ibid.* 10 July 5/1 It is proper to give full weight to the exculpatory evidence adduced.

19. Influence or authority (of a person) due to character or ability, position, office, wealth, or the like. Freq. in phrases *of weight, of* (great, etc.) *weight*; also *to throw, put, one's weight behind* something, and varr.

1710 STEELE *Tatler* No. 4 ¶7 Those Persons at the Helm are so useful, and in themselves of such Weight. **1747** *Frauds & Abuses Coal-Dealers* (ed. 3) 5 In all popular Assemblies, it has been found necessary to place some Man of Weight and Dignity in the Chair. **1779** J. MOORE *View Soc. France* (1789) I. iv. 25 Their opinions have considerable weight on the manners and opinions of people of rank. **1855** MACAULAY *Hist. Eng.* xiii. III. 253 It could hardly be doubted that they were directed by some leader of great weight. **1885** *Manch. Exam.* 6 Nov. 5/3 Political economists of weight refused to join the Commission. **1938** 'G. ORWELL' *Homage to Catalonia* v. 65 The Communist Party, with Soviet Russia behind it, had thrown its whole weight against revolution. **1951** C. P. SNOW *Masters* xxxiii. 268, I can't do as much as I should like, but I shall throw in my weight wherever I can. **1976** *Southern Even. Echo* (Southampton) 11 Nov. 1/1 The floodgates opened on the fluoridation of water supplies.. when the.. Regional Health Authority put their weight behind the scheme.

IV. A standard of quantity determined by, or employed in, weighing.

20. †**a.** A standard of weight. *Obs.*

a **1000** *Laws Edgar* III. viii. in *Liebermann* 204 Gange an ȝemet and an ȝewihte swylce man on Lundenbyriȝ and on Wintanceastre healde. *a* **1200** *Moral Ode* 212 in *O.E. Hom.* I. 173 Godes wisdom is wel muchel.. & nis his milce naut lesse, ac bi þan ilke iwichte. *c* **1200** *Ibid.* 384 (Trin. MS.) *ibid.* II. 231 þar ne sullen [hi] habben god alle bi one wihte. *a* **1400** *Eng. Gilds* 356 þare þe kynges wyȝte by-lyþ. *Ibid.* 356 þe kinges by whas wyȝte hit be y-weye. **1429** *Rolls of Parlt.* IV. 349/1 It was ordeinid.. yat on weiȝte and on mesure be bi al ye Reme, as wel with oute ye Estaple as with ynne.

b. With addition of a distinguishing word, as in *troy, avoirdupois weight*: Any of the various systems (consisting of a series of units in fixed arithmetical relation to each other) used for stating the weight of a quantity of matter.

a **1500** in Arnolde *Chron.* (1811) 191 Ther beth iij maner weyghtis, that is to wete, troy weyght, auncell weyghtis, and lyggynge weyght. **1540** *Star Chamber Cases* (Selden Soc.) II. 222 Euery person.. shuld sell the same by liefull weight called Haberdepoys. **1545** *Rates Custom-ho.* d v, Fyrst of the waygth of Troye.. By thys wayght is bought and solde golde.. and iewels. **1656** BLOUNT *Glossogr.* s.v. *Weights*, There are two sorts.. in use with us; the one called Troy weight.. the other *Avoir-du-pois.* **1713** BERKELEY *Guardian* No. 35 ¶7 Ten Pound Averdupoise Weight of this Philosophical Snuff. **1724** SWIFT *Drapier* i. (1730) 15 Twenty Shillings will weigh Six Pounds Butter Weight. **1891** *Labour Commission* Gloss., Short, statute or imperial weight.—2,240 lbs. to the ton.. Long weight.—2,400 lbs. to the ton.

21. a. A unit or denominaton of ponderable quantity.

c **1200** ORMIN 7812 All þatt mann shollde biggen ut wiþþ fife wehhte [= shekels] off sillferr. *a* **1300** *Cursor M.* 28437 Again þe lagh.. haf i wysed fals weght and mette. **1398** TREVISA *Barth. De P.R.* VI. xvii. (MS. Addit. 27944) Mna is a certeyn wiȝte and valewe. **1623** COCKERAM II, A weight of three graines, *Kirat.* **1857** J. H. WALSH *Dom. Econ.* 620 The last mentioned goods may be sold either by the heaped measure, or by the standard weight. **1863** MISS BRADDON *Aur. Floyd* xxxi, She knew—to the smallest weight employed at Apothecaries' Hall.. how much sugar Mr. Bulstrode liked in his tea.

b. In pl. and coupled with *measures.*

1387 TREVISA *Higden* II. 227 Caym.. tornede symple lyuynge [of] men to fyndynge of mesures and of wyȝtes [L. *ponderum et mensurarum*]. **1596** (*title*) The Pathway to Knowledge. Conteyning certaine brief Tables of English waights, and Measures. **1656** BLOUNT *Glossogr.* s.v. *Weights*, One Phidon an Argive is said to have bin the first finder out of Weights and Measures. **1741–2** GRAY *Agrip.* 41 The power To judge of weights and measures. **1799** *Med. Jrnl.* I. 199 The operations relative to a general uniformity of weights and measures. **1844** H. STEPHENS *Bk. Farm* II. 393 The Weights and Measures Act (5th Geo. IV., c. 74).

†**c.** Used in various localities as a name for the customary unit for weighing particular commodities (e.g. wool, hemp, cheese, potatoes); the quantity denoted differs greatly in different places (see quots.). Cf. WEY, and MEASURE *sb.* 5 b. *Obs.*

1490 in *Somerset Med. Wills* (1901) 291, I have xviii weyghts of wulle besydes the bequestes aforeseyd. *a* **1500** in Arnolde *Chron.* (1811) 263 The weyght of Essex chese is.. CCC. weyght, fyue score xij. li. for the C. The weyght of Suffolk chese is xij. score and xvi. li. **1592** in *Rec. Convent. Burghs Scot.* (1870) I. 381 Ane neif full of ewirrie wecht of voll. **1656** H. PHILLIPS *Purch. Pattern* (ed. 3) 193 There are some other denominations of these weights in several places, as.. Rooves, Weights, Loads. **1687** A. LOVELL *Thevenot's Trav.* I. 98 The Inhabitants make Five thousand Weight of Silk yearly, with the Money whereof they pay their Tribute. **1881** RIMMER *Old Country Towns* 278 A 'weight' for some unexplained cause, was the Boston method of expressing 256 pounds. **1830** *Edin. Cycl.* VII. 221/2 [In Cork] Potatoes, when retailed in market, are sold by a measure called a weight, generally containing 21 lb. **1856** MORTON *Cycl. Agric.* II. 1127 (Dorsets.), of wool, a weigh or weight is 30 lbs., and ½ lb. or 1 lb. over in some places. Weight (Dorsets.), of hemp, 8 heads of 4 lbs., twisted and tied, making 32 lbs. (Somers.), of hemp, 30 lbs.

d. A measure of an illegal drug; hence, the drug. Also without article. *slang.*

1971 *Frendz* 21 May 11/2 Avoid carrying weight late at night. **1972** *Listener* 23 Mar. 359/3 Your hash dealer is usually a friendly happy freak who's managed.. to buy himself a weight and he deals it out to his friends. **1978** S. WILSON *Dealer's Move* i. 13 Neil was taking colossal risks, there'd be up to thirty weights sitting in the flat at one time.

22. a. A piece of metal or other substance, weighing a known amount and identical with one of the units or with a multiple or aliquot part of a unit in some recognized scale.

In early instances *false weights* is ambiguous, as it may be referred either to this sense or to 24 (pair of scales); probably the writers did not always distinguish, the virtual sense being 'fraudulent weighing'.

1340 *Ayenb.* 44 Huanne me heþ diuerse wyȝtes.. and beggeþ be þe gratteste wyȝtes.. and zelleþ by þe leste. **1398** TREVISA *Barth. De P.R.* XIX. cxxxi. (1495) 940 Somtyme massy thynges and heuy by the whyche the heuynesse is assayed is callyd a weyght. **1420** *E.E. Wills* (1882) 46, I ȝeve to þe sam William a beme þat I weye þer-wyth, and ij leuys, also iijᶜ of ledyn wyȝtis. *c* **1430** *Contin. Brut* 448 In þat tyme þe gold of þe realme went by weght; And euery man had a payr ballaunce And weghttes in hys sleve for þe gold. **1467** *Eng. Gilds* 383 That all other wightes wtyn the cite..be ensealed accordynge to the kynges standart. **1474** CAXTON *Chesse* III. iv, (1883) 107 A man holding in his ryght hand a balance And the weyght in the lifte hand. **1540** *Star Chamber Cases* (Selden Soc.) II. 222 Sufficient beames scales and weightes sealid..for true seruing of the byers. **1583** *Rates Custom ho.* Avj b, Brasse weights called pile weights the c, l. s. **1656** W. DU GARD tr. *Comenius' Gate Lat. Unl.* §536 The lightest little weight, giving motion to the Ballance, they call a Grain. **1784** TWAMLEY *Dairying* 59 Press it with a four pound weight, or..with a lighter weight. **1892** *Photogr. Ann.* II. p. cxvii, Scales and Weights.

b. *Athletics.* A heavy lump of stone, or ball of metal, which is thrown from one hand placed close to the shoulder. Commonly in the Sc. phr. ***putting the weight*** (see PUT *v.*[1] 2, PUTTING *vbl. sb.*[1] 8). Also *ellipt.* as the name of this sport.

1865 *Field* 21 Jan. 34/1 Throwing the hammer, putting the weight.

23. a. A block or lump of metal or other heavy substance, or a heavy object, used to pull or press down something, to give an impulse to machinery (e.g. in a clock), to act as a counterpoise, or the like. Cf. *letter-weight*, *paper-weight*, *sash weight*, JACK-WEIGHT.

c **1425** *Macro Plays, Cast. Persev.* 1943 Þis worthy, wylde werld, I wagge with a wyt [= wy3t]. **1515** in *Archæol. Cant.* XXXIII. 17 Payed for mendyng off the waithe off the clock ij d. **1535** COVERDALE *2 Kings* xxi. 13 Ouer Ierusalem wyll I stretch forth the lyne of Samaria, and the weighte of the house of Achab. **1606** *Shuttleworths' Acc.* (Chetham Soc.) 175 Payed for the jacke, the cordes and pullies, xxv; the weight and cheans, v. **1617** MORYSON *Itin.* III. 66 The dores likewise by waights are made to shut of themselves at the heeles of him that comes in. **1660** F. BROOKE tr. *Le Blanc's Trav.* 266 A delicate Clock with weights to it. **1774** M. MACKENZIE *Maritime Surv.* 48 Let the Weight at the End of the Line be pretty heavy. **1774** *Pennsylv. Gaz.* 9 Feb. Suppl. 2/3 Sash pullies, weights and lines. **1833** J. HOLLAND *Manuf. Metals* II. 299 A weight being attached to the hook *b*, the spring..is drawn downwards. **1838** HAWTHORNE *Amer. Note-bks.* (1868) I. 216 There was a clock without a case, the weights being visible.

fig. **1622** BACON *Hen. VII*, 189 By Gods wonderfull prouidence, that..hangeth great Weights vpon small Wyres. **1639** J. CLARKE *Parœm.* 109 Great weights hang on small wyers. **1641** GAUDEN *Love of Truth* 22 Love is the weight and motor of the soule.

†**b.** ***to go on weights*** (see quot.). *Obs.*

1597 A. M. tr. *Guillemeau's Fr. Chirurg.* 50/4 The small, thinne, and Hern-fashoned hippes and legges, wherof we commonlye say 'they goe one Wayghtes'.

V. A means of weighing.

†**24.** *pl.*, less commonly *sing.* (A pair of) scales, a balance. Also in figurative context. *Obs.*

a **1300** *E.E. Psalter* lxi. 10 Liyhers sones of men are ai In weghtes [L. *in stateris*]. **13..** *E.E. Allit. P.* B. 1734 Þy wale rengne is walt in we3tes to heng, & is funde ful fewe of hit fayth dedes. **1390** GOWER *Conf.* I. 332 If that I mihte finde a sleyhte, To leie al myn astat in weyhte. **1398** TREVISA *Barth. De P.R.* XIX. cxxx. (1495) nn iij, In this wyse..the thynge in the whyche a thynge is weyed is callyd a weyghte. **1437** *Rolls of Parlt.* IV. 508/2 Where ye Kings Weightes and his Beem ben sette. **1513** MORE in Grafton *Chron.* (1568) II. 763 The world would put her and her kindred in the wight, and say that they had.. broken the amitie and peace. **1555** EDEN *Decades* (Arb.) 220 One of these byrdes with her nest put in a paire of gold weightes,..hath waid no more than .ii. *Tomini.* **1596** SPENSER *F.Q.* v. ii. 45 The false he layd In th' other scale; but still it downe did slide, And by no meane could in the weight be stayd. *a* **1619** FOTHERBY *Atheom.* II. i. §3 (1622) 174 That..weigheth the mountaines in a waite. **1629** Z. BOYD *Last Battell* IV. 499 Dauid in his time put them in the weights together [Ps. lxii. 9].

VI. 25. a. *attrib.*, as ***weight balk, beam, -charge, -equivalent, -gain, limit, scale, sense, stone, thermometer***; ***weight-conscious*** adj.; **weight belt**, a belt to which weights are attached, designed to help divers and underwater swimmers stay submerged; **weight-clock**, a clock operated by weights; **weight cloth**, a cloth carried by a jockey to make up his riding-weight; also *fig.*; **weight function** *Physics*, a function that specifies the weight (sense 15 b) of some quantity; †**weight-house**, a weigh-house; **weight nail** (see quot.); **weight-plate**, a plate on which articles are set to be weighed in a weighing-machine; **weight training**, a method of physical training involving the use of weights.

1575 *Richmond Wills* (Surtees) 255, j olde *weight balke with skayles, ij d. **1462** *Maldon* (Essex) *Court Rolls* (Bundle 37, No. 4 b), A *weght beme de ferro, precii iiii *s.* [**1943** *Diving Man.* (U.S. Navy Dept.) x. 150 Next, the weighted belt is fastened on.] **1955** R. & B. CARRIER *Dive* iv. 111 *Weight belts should also provide for interchangeable weights to regulate buoyancy as needed. **1966** 'L. HOLTON' *Out of Depths* (1967) xii. 115 'Here. I'll show you a diver's gear.'.. He held up a weight belt. **1978** A. P. BALDER *Sport Diving* ii. 14 The purpose of the weight belt is to help the diver achieve the weightless state. **1898** *Daily News* 7 Dec. 2/7 The *weight-charge on packets above 1lb. in weight. **1850** DENISON *Clock & Watch-m.* 110 The great wheel of a *weight-clock rides on the barrel arbor. **1887** KIPLING *Plain Tales* (1888) 144 You can arrange the race with regard to 'Shackles' only. So long as you don't bury him under *weight-cloths, I don't mind. *Ibid.* 181 Maybe, Fate's weight-cloths are breaking his heart. **1889** *Daily News* 4 June 3/8 Before..her driver could return to weigh in, his weight cloths were abstracted from the sulky. **1974** *Radio Times* 28 Feb. 280/2 A nervously *weight-conscious society. **1897** SINGER & BERENS *Some Unrecognized Laws Nat.* 107 The volume-equivalent would be too great and the *weight-equivalent too small. **1930** *Weight function [see ORTHOGONALIZE *v.*]. **1974** G. REECE tr. *Hund's Hist. Quantum Theory* ii. 33 He made use of a weight function $G(E/\nu)$ for the enumeration of states. **1956** *Nature* 3 Mar. 423/2 (*caption*) Average *weight-gains of animals fed on lime-treated maize. **1981-2** *Deer Farmer* (N.Z.) Summer 3/1 (Wapiti) Crosses with reds; the hybrids also produce good velvet and weight-gains. **1714** *Fr. Bk. Rates* 300 Any of the Duties of the King's *Weight-House. **1961** *Engineering* 21 July 72/1 The new 1½ litre '*weight limit' formula came into effect..in May. *c* **1850** *Rudim. Navig.* (Weale) 134 **Weight nails* are similar to deck nails, but not so fine, have square heads, and are used for fastening cleats, &c. **1887** P. M'NEILL *Blawearie* 169 The colliery engineer was quickly on the ground, [and] the *weight-plate removed. **1849** NOAD *Electricity* (ed. 3) 357 A similar bow was formed on the back of the armature, to which the *weight scale was attached. **1899** *Allbutt's Syst. Med.* VI. 709 The *weight sense was lost in the hands as well as in the feet. **1469** *Plumpton Corr.* (Camden) 21, I have a counterpais wheith of the *weight stone that the wooll was weyed with. **1849** R. V. DIXON *Heat* I. 52 One an air thermometer,..the other a mercurial *weight thermometer. **1955** O. STATE *Weight Training for Athletics* i. 17 **Weight training*..implies training with light weights..for the purpose of improving one's performance in a particular sport. **1957** DUNCAN & BONE *Oxf. Pocket Bk. Athletic Training* (ed. 2) iii. 24 Weight training may now be regarded as an *essential* part of athletic training. **1976** E. DUNPHY *Only a Game?* v. 147 We have to do weights. I don't believe in weight-training.

b. *Comb.*, as ***weight-bearing*** (sb. and adj.), ***-carrier*** (*esp.* a horse that can carry a heavy rider), ***-carrying, -lifter, -lifting, -maker, -puller, -putting, -raising, -reducing*** (sb. and adj.), ***-resisting, -thrower, throwing***, †***-wiser*** (= indicator).

1954 MARTIN & HYNES *Clin. Endocrinol.* (ed. 2) ii. 50 Osteoarthritis of the hips, knees and spine develops from undue strains of excessive *weight-bearing as life advances. **1959** *Manch. Guardian* 9 July 5/7 We cannot even tell whether the heavy walls of the new buildings are the weight-bearing structures they look to be. **1977** P. A. RING in *Bone & Joint Dis.* (Brit. Med. Assoc.) 83 It may be better to strive for union in the relatively young patient, even at the risk of a period of protected weight-bearing. **1862** G. A. LAWRENCE *Barren Honour* xix. II. 90 Red Lancer is a very model of a fast *weight-carrier. **1893** F. F. MOORE *I Forbid Banns* (1899) 31 It has the build of a weight-carrier, that chair. **1883** MRS. E. KENNARD *Right Sort* xix, Mounted on a huge *weight-carrying hunter. **1897** *Daily News* 14 May 3/2 Our baggage animals—to the limit of their weight-carrying capacity. [**1884** *Nat. Police Gaz.* (U.S.) 12 Jan. 13/2 Alonzo Hiwanda, the..champion heavy-weight lifter.] **1897** *Ibid.* 26 May 3/4 Bothwell, of Glasgow, is well known as a powerful man, besides a *weight lifter. **1955** R. BANNISTER *First Four Minutes* 112 The waddling gait and breathlessness of a muscle-bound weight-lifter. **1980** *Sunday Times* (Colour Suppl.) 14 Sept. 99/2 A weightlifter complained that he did not like showing his tattoos in public. **1896** *Daily News* 6 Apr. 5/7 The London *Weight-lifting Club. **1902** *Daily Chron.* 28 Apr. 5/3 A series of weight-lifting competitions. **1647** in W. M. Williams *Ann. Founders' Co.* (1867) 103 No *Wayght Maker that doth cast Brass Wayghtes and..put them to sale. **1868** H. WOODRUFF *Trotting Horse* xxiii. 200 The *weight-pullers..are of medium weight. **1900** A. E. T. WATSON *Young Sportsman* 84 **Weight putting*—The weight should weigh 16 lbs., and in England must be of iron. **1948** *Sporting Mirror* 21 May 14/3 Giles had never done any weight putting when he went to Germany with the army. **1850** DENISON *Clock & Watch-m.* 245 The going part is also reduced..to a mere *weight-raising machine. **1922** *Times* 7 Oct. 13/5 Grilling is the great essential of the *weight-reducing diet. **1958** F. C. AVIS *Boxing Ref. Dict.*, *Weight reducing*, taking off superfluous weight, often by means of vapour baths, sweating exercises, etc. **1978** N. MARSH *Grave Mistake* ii. 42 She tried..to get Verity to fix a day when she would come to a weight-reducing luncheon. **1708** PHILIPS *Cyder* I. 265 Hazel, and *weight-resisting Palm. **1895** *Outing* XXVI. 461/2 Any one of her five *weight throwers could beat the best man at Cambridge. **1901** J. P. PARET *Woman's Bk. Sports* 163 *Weight-throwing has four or five variations. **1960** *Times* 29 Apr. 16/6 The investigation covered swimming, track running, weight-throwing. **1685** *Phil. Trans.* XV. 1003 We find, by several sorts of Baroscopes (or *weight-wisers) not only that [etc.].

weight (weɪt, *Sc.* wɛxt), *sb.*[2] *Sc.* and *north.* Forms: 2 wehit, (wheit), 4 wyeygt, whight, 4–5 weght, 8–9 wecht, 6– wecht. (See also *Eng. Dial. Dict.*) [Possibly a special application of prec. 21, orig. denoting a utensil capable of containing a certain weight of grain.] A farm utensil resembling a sieve in form, with a bottom of sheepskin or wood (unperforated), used for winnowing corn, also as a measure.

For *timbre wecht*: see TIMBRE *sb.*[1] b.

1183 *Boldon Bk.* (Surtees) 23 Et j. wheit de scatmalt, et j. wehit de farina, et j. wehit de avena. **1354** *Finchale Acc.* (Surtees) p. xxxvi, iiij wyeygtes. **1360** *Ibid.* p. lii, ij weghtes. **1371** *Durham Acc. Rolls* (Surtees) 129, iij riddils; j whight. **1483** *Cath. Angl.* 412/2 A Weght, *capisterium.* **1724** RAMSAY *Tea-t. Misc.* (1733) II. 181 My bairn has tocher of her awin ..A Wecht, a peet-creel and a cradle. *c* **1780** M. LONSDALE in S. Gilpin *Songs & Ballads Cumbld.* (1866) 279 Theer was whangs an' shives, thick an' thin, I' weights an' riddles putt'n. **1786** BURNS *Halloween* xxi, Meg fain wad to the Barn gaen, To winn three wechts o' naething. **1844** H. STEPHENS *Bk. Farm* II. 283 Wechts or maunds for taking up corn are made either of wood or of skin, attached to a rim of wood... Wechts should be made of [two] different sizes. **1898** J. COLVILLE *Sc. Vernacular* 12 When snow covered the ground, the barn wecht or close sieve was the favourite [bird] trap.

Hence **'wechtful**, the amount contained in a 'weight'. Also **wecht** *v. trans.*, to winnow (corn) with a 'weight'.

1804 TARRAS *Poems* 67 She wechts the corn anent the blaw. **1808** JAMIESON, *Wechtful*, as much as a wecht can contain. **1832** CARLYLE *Remin.* (1881) I. 29 Potatoes were little in use then; a 'wechtful' was stored up to be eaten perhaps about Halloween. **1844** H. STEPHENS *Bk. Farm* II. 273 Another woman, with a smaller wecht, takes up the good grain..and divides the wechtful between the other two women. *Ibid.* 283.

weight (weɪt), *v.* [f. WEIGHT *sb.*[1]]

†**1.** *trans.* To oppress (the mind); also *pass.*, to be oppressed in mind or spirit. *Sc. Obs.*

1647 R. BAILLIE *Lett.* (1842) III. 3 However this silence sometimes weighted my mind, yet I found it the best and wisest course. **1654** SIR A. JOHNSTON (Ld. Wariston) *Diary* 10 Apr. (S.H.S.) II. 230 Shoe told me my daughter Elizabeth had found under hir seaknesse a deserted condition and now shoe was weyghted with it. **1728** P. WALKER *Life Peden* (1827) I. 80 When he awak'd, he seem'd more than ordinary weighted, and groan'd heavily, saying, Sad Days for Scotland.

2. a. To load with a weight; to supply with an additional weight; to make weighty. Also with *down.*

1747 HOOSON *Miner's Dict.* G 3 b, If the Wholes be too soft, that we think it will let the Forks settle when they come to be weighted, we put a Sill under them. **1813** VANCOUVER *Agric. Devon* 65 The large masses [of stone] used for weighting the levers of the cider-presses. **1851-4** TOMLINSON *Cycl. Arts & Manuf.* II. 31/1 The boards..are ..filled with earth to weight them down. **1885** *Manch. Exam.* 10 Sept. 5/3 A bough is cut from a tree..weighted with a few heavy stones and then dragged over the soil.

fig. **1825** COLERIDGE *Aids Refl.* 78 We may see with complacency the Arrows of Satire feathered with Wit, weighted with Sense, and discharged by a strong Arm, fly home to their mark. **1860** MOTLEY *Netherl.* (1868) I. ii. 46 Intricate nets of diplomatic intrigue,..thoroughly weighted with Mexican gold.

b. *fig.* To oppress with weight, to weigh down; chiefly *pass.*, to be heavily burdened (*by* or *with* oppressive conditions or circumstances). Also with *down.*

1858 FROUDE *Hist. Eng.* III. xvii. 445 Weighted as he was with faults,..he fought his battle bravely. **1872** GEO. ELIOT *Middlem.* xlvi, It wants to have a House of Commons which is not weighted with nominees of the landed class. **1880** SWINBURNE *Study Shaks.* 236 The memory of Mr. Tennyson would be weighted and degraded by the ascription of whole volumes of pilfered and diluted verse.

c. *techn.* To add weight to (an inferior commodity) by the admixture or use of an adulterant.

1862 C. O'NEILL *Dict. Calico Printing & Dyeing* 19 A sulphate of baryta..is used for 'weighting;' that is, for giving weight and apparent body and firmness to inferior goods. **1886** *Daily Tel.* 24 June (Cassell) Dark arts are in certain quarters practised..in disguising and weighting teas. **1895** *Daily News* 1 Oct. 6/3 The ingenuity of the foreign dyer was such that he was able to 'weight' or adulterate his silk.

d. *Statistics.* To multiply the components of (an average) by compensating factors; to treat (the components of any numerical quantity) similarly.

1901 A. L. BOWLEY *Elem. Statist.* 111 The very important statistical method known as 'weighting the average'. *Ibid.*, Should we weight the numbers given by the total numbers of inhabitants of the contributing counties, or by their distance from London, or by some quantity derived from these? **1927** C. SPEARMAN *Abilities of Man* App. p. xviii, We urgently require to know how the single tests should be relatively 'weighted' in their combination. **1971** I. G. GASS et al. *Understanding Earth* v. 82 The individual data were weighted according to quality, so that a poorly determined result makes a smaller contribution to the mean than a precisely determined value. **1976** *Daily Record* (Glasgow) 30 Nov., Replies were weighted by age and General Election voting to make sure they were representative of all Record readers. **1977** *Whitaker's Almanack 1978* 1219 In working out the [cost-of-living] index figure, the price changes are 'weighted'—that is, given different degrees of importance —in accordance with the pattern of consumption of the average family.

3. To assign to (a horse) the weight he must carry in a handicap race. (Cf. WEIGHT *sb.*[1] 12 a.)

1846 DARVILL *Engl. Race Horse* (ed. 3) II. 286 Such horse is generally highly weighted, to bring him on a fair equality with the others. **1856** 'STONEHENGE' *Brit. Sports* II. I. i. §2 Horses are constantly entered and run solely with the view of inducing the handicapper to 'weight' them at a low scale. **1883** 'RAPIER' *Types of Turf* 73 A very bad colt..was weighted in a manner ludicrously disproportionate to his capacity.

fig. **1865** HUXLEY *Lay Serm.* ii. (1870) 30 So long as this potential motherhood is her lot, woman will be found to be fearfully weighted in the race of life. **1875** MERIVALE *Gen. Hist. Rome* v. 29 The plebeians, however unfairly weighted in the race for riches, could not be always kept in poverty.

4. a. (In senses of WEIGH *v.*[1]) *trans.* To ascertain the weight of (goods, etc.) by means of a weighing machine; to weigh. *lit.* and *fig.* Also *colloq.*, to feel the weight or heaviness of (something held in the hands).

1734 J. STEUART *Letter-Bk.* (1915) 378 Your meall to be weighted with the common standard weights of Mariebrugh. **1865-** [see WEIGHTING *vbl. sb.*]. **1898** L. QUILLER-COUCH *Span. Maid* xiv. 202 Why, there hasn' a-bin a touch of cold in the air..; an' heavy!—you can a-most weight it in yer hands.

b. Of a jockey: ***to weight out, in***, to undergo weighing before or after a race. = WEIGH *v.* 9.
1877 *Rules of Racing* §34 (iii), It is optional for the jockey to weight out or in with his bridle.

weight, obs. form of WAIT *sb.*, *v.*[1], WIGHT.

weightage ('weɪtɪdʒ). Chiefly *Pol.* or in *Pol.* contexts. [f. WEIGHT *v.* + -AGE.] The assignment of a weighting factor to compensate for some (numerical) disadvantage, esp. in favour of a sparsely populated area, or to a minority party, interest, etc.; the amount so added. See WEIGHTING *vbl. sb.* 3.
1906 in A. Husain *Fazl-i-Husain* (1946) vi. 96 Weightage, not by numerical strength but by political importance and value of the contribution made to the defence of the Empire. **1937** *Times* 24 Dec. 13/3 The Liberals [in Romania] only managed to secure 38 per cent. of the votes... They do not, therefore, qualify for the 'weightage' provided by the law of 1926. **1949** I. JENNINGS *Constitution of Ceylon* ii. 189 In agricultural countries like South Africa and Australia..the rural population, on whom the wealth of the country largely depends, must be given some weightage against the more concentrated and more highly organized urban population. **1957** L. F. R. WILLIAMS *State of Israel* 159 Does the present plan give these fractional groups a weightage in public affairs..which their relative unimportance cannot justify? **1971** *Queen's College* (Oxford) *Record* Dec. 22 The geographical distribution of men who have gone down does not reflect quite the same northern weightage as do schools of origin. **1980** *Sunday Mail* (Brisbane) 9 Nov. 25/1 The National Party yesterday reaffirmed its policy of electoral distribution based on the electoral 'weightage' principle.

weighted ('weɪtɪd), *ppl. a.* [f. WEIGHT *v.* + -ED[1].]
1. †**a.** Of one's mind or spirit: Overburdened, oppressed. *Obs.*
1660 [see WEIGHTEDNESS (below)]. *a* **1732** T. BOSTON *Crook in Lot* (1805) 168 Their weighted and sorrowful life will be succeeded with a fulness of joy.
b. Burdened with a heavy weight; loaded. Of the eyelids: Heavy with sleep.
1895 S. CRANE *Red Badge* xiii, His head fell forward..and his weighted lids went softly down over his eyes. **1905** 'J. OXENHAM' *White Fire* xiii, Their weighted progress was slow.
2. a. Furnished with a heavy substance to give additional weight.
1827 FARADAY *Chem. Manip.* xv. (1842) 360 When filled and covered with a weighted board, they [*sc.* the bladders] will supply a constant stream of gas. **1839** URE *Dict. Arts*, etc. 1286 The warp and web are kept longitudinally stretched by a weighted cord. **1872** *Abridgm. Specif. Patents, Raising* etc. (ed. 2) 182 A stationary rod, on which is mounted a weighted lever.
b. *fig.* Of words, etc.: Made weighty.
1879 *19th Cent.* Oct. 596 Supposing Mr. M.'s argument to be..that of a special pleader who uses weighted words even in preparing to open his discussion. **1914** D. MACMILLAN *Life R. Flint* xii. 344 Its objectivity is equally evident, if one compares it, say, with the more subjectively weighted definings.
c. ***weighted average***, an average in taking which each component is multiplied by a factor chosen to give it its proper importance. ***weighted*** is similarly used of numerical quantities other than averages.
1845 *Encycl. Metrop.* II. 443 We may..call the constant *c* the specific weight of the observations to which it applies, and $\Sigma cA \div \Sigma c$ the weighted mean. **1901** A. L. BOWLEY *Elem. Statist.* III. **1962** A. NISBETT *Technique Sound Studio* 277 Quoted noise levels are sometimes 'weighted' against bass according to standard loudness contours. Weighted and unweighted measurements may differ by 20 dB or more at low frequencies. **1970** G. K. WOODGATE *Elem. Atomic Struct.* vii. 137 The identity..simply states that the weighted mean of the energies of the levels belonging to a term coincides with the energy of the unperturbed term. **1972** *Times* 27 Sept. 2/2 (*heading*) 'Weighted' vote at Labour conference suggested.
Hence '**weightedness**, the condition of being weighted.
1660 J. DURHAM *Expos. Rev.* v. i. 284 Secondly, There is a disappointment, *vers.* 3. Thirdly, There is John's exceeding great heavinesse and weightednesse therewith, *vers.* 4.

†'**weightful**, *a. Obs.*[−0] [f. WEIGHT *sb.*[1] + -FUL.] Weighty.
1530 PALSGR. 329/1 Weyghtfull, *pondereux*.

weightily ('weɪtɪlɪ), *adv.* [f. WEIGHTY + -LY[2].] In a weighty manner; with or as with weight. Usually *fig.*
1552 HULOET, Weyghtelye, *pensiculate*. **1572** BOSSEWELL *Armorie* II. 25 b, It is very needefull..diligently to see, and weightely to consider the cote armors, whiche are put to them to bee paynted. *a* **1637** B. JONSON *Discov.* Wks. 1640 II. 101 No man ever spake more neatly, more presly, more weightily. **1667** H. MORE *Div. Dial.* II. xiv. (1668) 257 How few..do seriously spend their studies in any thing weightily Moral or Intellectual? **1725** BROOME *Pope's Odyss.* Notes VII. 379 II. 170 He makes his agents speak weightily and sententiously. **1856** FROUDE *Hist. Eng.* II. 409 Abuses, which..told most weightily on the serious judgment of the age. **1868** E. EDWARDS *Ralegh* I. xix. 410 There was some division of opinion upon the bench on the question thus weightily opened.

weightiness ('weɪtɪnɪs). [f. WEIGHTY *a.* + -NESS.] The quality or condition of being weighty: **a.** *fig.*, the fact of being of much weight, importance, or consequence; grave or serious character.
1530 PALSGR. 287/2 Weightynesse, *aggrauation*. **1560** DAUS tr. *Sleidane's Comm.* 152 b, The weightines of the cause also requireth, that many of vs should come to the counsell. **1596** LODGE *Marg. Amer.* 42 If thou faint through feeblenesse of bodie, I will default through waightinesse of discontent. **1618** *Barnevelt's Apol.* C 3, I had..complained ..of the weightinesse of the Office imposed vpon me. *a* **1665** J. GOODWIN *Filled w. the Spirit* (1867) 371 The weightiness or penetrating force of those arguments. *a* **1713** ELLWOOD *Autobiog.* (1714) 15 The Weightiness that was upon their Spirits and Countenances. **1744** M. BISHOP *Life* 14 Observing the Weightiness of the Concern, this was my Method of proceeding. **1905** 'J. OXENHAM' *White Fire* xvi. 161 'The matter is worth consideration,' he said, with an assumption of weightiness.
b. of material things.
1539 ELYOT *Cast. Helthe* III. vii, There is felt in the entrayles..a weyghtynesse with tension or thrustyng outwarde. **1591** SPENSER *Ruins of Time* 571 The Caue..with her owne weightinesse Vpon them fell. **1690** LOCKE *Hum. Und.* II. xxxi[i]. §18 The peculiar Weightiness, and yellow Colour of Gold. **1832** L. HUNT *Sir R. Esher* (1850) 33 It was relieved from an appearance of too much weight by the very weightiness of the hanging sleeves. **1839** BAILEY *Festus* 25 A deathless spirit's state, Freed from gross form and bodily weightiness.

weighting ('weɪtɪŋ), *vbl. sb.* [f. WEIGHT *v.* + -ING[1].]
1. a. The action of the verb.
1865 JANET HAMILTON *Poems* etc. (1870) 154 It's England mak's an' sign's the peace..; When Europe's balance gangs agee, She trims the scales for wechtin'.
b. *spec.* The action or process of fraudulently adding weight to textiles (see WEIGHT *v.* 2 c).
1904 *Tailor & Cutter* 4 Aug. 480/2 *Woollen Draper's Terms*, Weighting: A process by which sulphate of zinc and other metals is absorbed in wool, and so adding weight.
2. *concr.* Something used as a weight to press down, steady, or balance.
1875 KNIGHT *Dict. Mech.* 1464/1 *Weighting*. Blocks put on a flask to keep the cope down under the upward pressure of the body of iron poured into the mold. **1907** *Westm. Gaz.* 16 Feb. 13/1 Another evening frock..has weightings of jet and silver at the foot and about the décolletage.
3. The assignment of weights (WEIGHT *sb.* 15 b); the weights so used.
1905 *Westm. Gaz.* 12 Jan. 3/1 A different system of weighting,..&c., may cause a difference of 1, 2..per cent. in the index numbers. **1940** [see WEIGHT *sb.* 15 b]. **1965** PHILLIPS & WILLIAMS *Inorg. Chem.* I. iii. 75 One general technique for improving on the first approximation by the V.B. method is to include additional structures..in the complete wave function, with appropriate weighting factors. **1972** *Guardian* 18 Feb. 13/5 Rents and eating out..accounts for 22 per cent of the 'weighting' of the [retail price] index. **1983** *Personal Computer World* Dec. 142/2 Each of the eight digits of the base number is given a weighting.
4. An amount added to a salary for a special reason; esp. ***London weighting***, that paid to compensate for the higher cost of living in the London area.
1946 *Scheme of Conditions of Service* (National Joint Council for Local Authorities' Admin., Profess., Techn. & Clerical Services) 19 The salary scales shall be weighted, as follows, in favour of officers employed in the London area: ..£20 weighting with proportionate weighting of female scales. **1952** *Times* 25 Jan. 2/7 The wording of the statement relating to the award did not make clear whether the recommended increase was meant to be over and above the weekly 10s. 'weighting allowance' granted to London [fire]men. **1958** *Times* 5 Dec. 3/2 Salary (including London Weighting) according to age and experience. **1976** *Broadcast* Dec. 17/1 Brief consideration was given to a number of items including: weighting for major towns and cities other than London, London weighting, interest on monies owed to staff, [etc.]. **1982** *Daily Tel.* 20 Oct. 1/1 The government is to end the annual publication of the London weighting index which is widely used as the basis for calculating extra payments for employees in London.

weightless ('weɪtlɪs), *a.* [f. WEIGHT *sb.*[1] + -LESS.] **a.** Without weight, having comparatively little weight. Also (of a body having mass), not apparently acted on by gravity, either because the gravitational field is locally weak, or because both the body and its surroundings are freely and equally accelerating under the field (as in an orbiting satellite).
a **1547** SURREY *Æneid* II. 1054 But she was gone, And suttly fled into the weightlesse aire. **1597** SHAKS. *2 Hen. IV*, IV. v. 33 Did hee suspire, that light and weightlesse dowlne Perforce must moue. **1621** G. SANDYS *Ovid's Met.* x. (1626) 214 The Swans that drew Idalia's waightlesse chariot through the aire. **1652** BENLOWES *Theophila* III. xxx, Those lights..Who would portray, as soon may find A way to paint the viewless, poise the weightless wind. **1860** W. W. READE *Liberty Hall* I. v. 77 The captain of the Liberty Hall boat.. had long since observed young Saxon, his form slim therefore weightless. **1890** K. PEARSON in *Messenger Math.* XX. 28 Suppose the load at the free terminal not to be produced by a suspended load but by a weightless spring. **1929** *Science Wonder Q.* Fall 55/2 Do you mean that..we will be weightless as soon as you..set the lever at zero? **1950** *Jrnl. Aviation Med.* XXI. 396/2 A body is weightless as soon as it is allowed to move freely under the influence of gravity and of its own inertia. **1953** A. C. CLARKE *Prelude to Space* v. 28 The perfect [spaceship] pilot..must be capable of operating efficiently..when he was 'weightless'. **1978** *Nature* 20 July 236/1 We report here the results of an experiment in the weightless environment of space. **1983** A. MASON *Illusionist* i. 15 A man who could command his body to float weightless through the air could not command the necessities of life.
b. of immaterial things.
1608 J. ROBINSON in Bp. Hall *Apol. Brownists* (1610) 3 *margin*, [They] are oft times emboldened to roule vpon them as from aloft verye weake and weightlesse discourses. **1662** DRYDEN *To Ld. Chancellor* 155 The glorious course you have begun..must both weightless and immortal prove. **1855** SINGLETON *Virgil* VII. 814 For neither weightless was Amata's name. **1858** W. ARNOT *Laws fr. Heaven for Life on Earth* 2nd Ser. ii. 22 A voluble tongue..may..not add one grain to the stock of human wisdom by the imposing bulk of its weightless product.
Hence '**weightlessness**.
1884 E. FAWCETT *Rutherford* xvii. 195 The hand which she gave him had wasted into almost utter weightlessness. **1929** *Science Wonder Q.* Fall 58/2 If they had not already been accustomed to weightlessness, the first heedless step would have carried them far from the ship. **1932** D. LASSER *Conquest of Space* xiii. 192 The terrors of weightlessness. **1959** *Observer* 31 May 1/4 The two monkeys spent a number of minutes in a condition of weightlessness or zero G. **1974** R. ADAMS *Shardik* x. 74 Her stance gave a curious impression of weightlessness, as though she might actually be about to float down into the hollow. **1983** *Brit. Med. Jrnl.* 13 Aug. 479/2 The most important vestibular disturbance encountered in weightlessness is motion sickness.

Weight Watcher. orig. *U.S.* Also **weight-watcher.** [WEIGHT *sb.*[1]: see WATCH *v.* 12 d.]
1. *pl.* A proprietary name used esp. for (members of) an organization, Weight Watchers International Inc., formed to promote dietary control as a means of slimming, or any of its associated clubs. Occas. in *sing.*
1961 *Official Gaz.* (U.S. Patent Office) 28 Feb. TM 130/2 The Low Calorie Candy Co., Inc... Filed Mar. 14, 1960. *Weight Watcher*. For dessert and pie mixes sold in combination packages... First use Feb. 1, 1960. **1964** *N.Y. Herald Tribune* 1 Nov. II 4/3 Weight Watchers is an Alcoholics Anonymous for compulsive eaters. *Ibid.* (*caption*) Novice Weight Watchers line up for the first session of a new group. **1966** J. NIDETCH (*title*) The Weight Watchers Cookbook. **1966** *Sunday Tel.* 28 Aug. 2/4 A Long Island housewife has successfully tackled the American problem of compulsive eating with her movement Weight Watchers Incorporated, which now has hundreds of thousands of members in 15 States. **1967** *Business Week* 4 Mar. 106/3 They..transplant the Weight Watcher idea.. under a system of franchises. **1967** *Trade Marks Jrnl.* 25 Oct. 1628/2 *Weight Watchers*... Books, printed publications, stationery, diaries, printed matter and pocket portfolios..all containing data pertaining to dieting and weight control. Weight Watchers International Inc. **1967** *Official Gaz.* (U.S. Patent Office) 5 Sept. TM 21/2 I. B. Kleinert Rubber Company, New York... *Weight Watcher*. For girdles. **1968** *Ibid.* 16 Jan. TM 133/1 Weight Watchers International, Inc... Filed Sept. 26, 1967. *Weight Watchers*... For indicating membership in the applicant association. **1968** *Ibid.* 18 June TM 146/1 *Weight Watchers*. For planning, executing and supervising diet programs by means of group meetings, courses [etc.]... First use May 15, 1963. **1972** J. ANDERSON in *Clin. Endocrinol.* (1973) 80 Group therapy should not be derided and is probably one of the main reasons for the apparent success of 'Weight-Watchers' clubs. **1977** P. HILL *Liars* xi. 144 You should join Weightwatchers... They'd slim you down in no time. **1978** *Cornish Guardian* 27 Apr. 12/5 Mr. Arthur spoke of the health campaign in arranging a 'fun and jog' for all ages, involving the local Weight Watchers, Keep Fit Classes. **1984** S. MOODY *Penny Dreadful* xi. 144 Half the world starved while the other half joined Weight Watchers.
2. (With small initials.) A person who tries to lose weight, esp. by dieting; one who is weight-conscious.
1966 *Family Circle* Jan. (recto front cover), Meal plans for weight-watchers. **1968** *Sunday Times* 10 Nov. 35 Italians are not exactly the keenest weight-watchers in the world and hardly let a day go by without forking into the pasta. **1970** *Guardian* 6 June 12/5 What the intelligent weight watcher needs is a diet which keeps her fit. **1971** *New Scientist* 4 Feb. 231/3 The hint to weight-watchers is obvious: keep food out of sight, and it should stay out of mind. **1983** *Daily Tel.*, 9 Feb. 17/4 The old message that it was good for weight watchers to eat a slice of cheese on a cream cracker has gone out of the window.
Hence '**weight-watching** *ppl. a.* and *vbl. sb.*
1970 *Globe & Mail* (Toronto) 26 Sept. 29/2 (Advt.), Luncheon here is to be recommended..and for the weight watching girls..there are tempting light suggestions. **1978** *Dumfries Courier* 20 Oct. 28/3 Martin..decided that dieting or weight-watching were not for him. **1982** W. J. BURLEY *Wycliffe's Wild-Goose Chase* iv. 66 'Beef casserole with boiled potatoes and carrots.' Good! But not for weight watching.

weighty ('weɪtɪ), *a.* Forms: 5 wehty, 6 *Sc.* wegh-, vech-, vych-, wych-, waich-, waychtie, 6–7 *Sc.* wechtie, 7 *Sc.* weychtie, 6, 9 *Sc.* wechty; 6 weyghty(e, 6–7 weightie, 5– weighty; 6 wayghty, wai(h)ti, wayt(t)y, 6–7 waighty, -ie. [f. WEIGHT *sb.*[1] + -Y[1].]
I. 1. Of a considerable or appreciable weight; that weighs a good deal, heavy.
1500 *Ortus Vocab.*, *Onerosus*, heuy or wehty. **1535** COVERDALE *Prov.* xxvii. 3 The stone is heuy and the sonde weightie: but a fooles wrath is heuyer then they both. **1577** B. GOOGE *Heresbach's Husb.* I. 24 b, The best seede also is that which is waightiest. **1665** MANLEY *Grotius' Low C. Wars* 351 A very great Frost..had covered with Ice, both the Marshes and Rivers, that they would bear the greatest and most weighty Carriages. **1681** CHETHAM *Angler's Vade-m.* i. §4 Let all the Hasle Rods be..no weightier than you can easily manage with one Hand. **1697** DRYDEN *Æneis* XII. 1284 Now stern Æneas waves his weighty Spear Against his Foe. **1711** POPE *Temple Fame* 429 As weighty bodies to the centre tend. **1852** MALPAS *Builder's Pocketbk.* 43 Many ceilings..have heavy cornices, pendants, and other weighty

matters attached to them. **1879** J. C. Cox *Ch. of Derbysh.* IV. 141 He..lies buried under a weighty uninscribed tomb.
fig. **1641** J. JACKSON *True Evang. T.* I. 63 By that path, their Crowne of glory had neither been so certaine, nor so soone, nor so waighty.

b. Of persons or animals: Of more than the usual size, large or bulky of body, corpulent. †Of soldiers: Heavily armed or equipped.
1581 A. HALL *Iliad* II. Catal. Princes 39 And Iton breeder good Of waightie felterd felled sheepe. **1590** R. FERRIS *Dang. Adventure* B 2, We recouered him and got him vp againe (although he were a verie waightie man). **1670** MILTON *Hist. Brit.* II. 59 Ostorius..could hardly stay thir flight; till the waighty Legions coming on, at first poys'd the Battel, at length turn'd the Scale. *a* **1701** MAUNDRELL *Journ. Jerus.* (1732) 124 Upon the bough there sits a good weighty Fellow, to press it down to the bottom [of the water]. **1819** W. TENNANT *Papistry storm'd* (1827) 49 Auld Saunders Clerk, a man o' echty, Though eild-encumber't now and wechty.

c. Of great weight in proportion to its bulk, of high specific gravity.
1585 HIGINS *Junius' Nomencl.* 403/1 *Argentum graue*,.. weightie siluer, or siluer in bulleon, as they call it. *a* **1700** EVELYN *Diary* 22 June 1664, It look'd like a fungus, but was weighty like metall. **1748** J. HILL *Hist. Fossils* 13 Friable, weighty, fine red Bole. **1796** KIRWAN *Elem. Min.* (ed. 2) I. 138 Baroselenite..Rough and harsh, but appears weighty. **1839** URE *Dict. Arts* 816 The successive percussions that it receives, determine the weightier matters, and consequently those richest in metal, to accumulate towards its upper end.

†**d.** Of coin: Of full weight, of the standard or legal weight. *Obs.*
1617 MORYSON *Itin.* I. 294 He that brings a weighty French crowne *In specie* to the Gold-smyths, they will give him six shilling six pence for it. **1691** LOCKE *Consid. Lower. Interest* (1692) 156 He will..contract to be paid in weighty Money. **1730** CONDUITT *Observ. Coins* (1774) 52 If foreigners, who take our money in large parcels only by weight, are suffered to pour in light money upon us, at the same rate as if it were weighty.

2. Bearing down heavily as if weighted or of great weight; falling with force or violence.
1583 tr. *Maison Neuve's Gerileon* I. 61 b, If he had not by his agillitie and nimblenesse, eschewed the weightie blowes of the Giaunte. **1605** R. F. *Dedekind's Sch. Slovenrie* (1904) 101 Another must both brawling words and weightie blows abide. **1725** POPE *Odyss.* x. 198 Then leaning on the spear with both my hands, [I] Up-bore my load, and prest the sinking sands With weighty steps. **1738** WESLEY *Ps.* XXXII. viii, Whoe'er like Horse and Mule withstand,..I bruise beneath my weighty Hand.

II. 3. a. Of great gravity or significance; requiring earnest thought, consideration, or application; highly important, serious, grave, momentous.
1489 EARL OF NORTHUMBERLD. in *Plumpton Corr.* (Camden) 61 For right weighty consideration me moving concernyng the pleasure of the Kings highnes. **1503–4** *Act 19 Hen. VII*, c. 28 Preamble, Great and weyghtye maters concernyng the comen weale of this lande. **1548** HALL *Chron., Hen. VIII* 163 My lordes, we haue perceiued the kyng your masters requests, which be greate and of a waightie Importaunce. **1591** SHAKS. *1 Hen. VI*, II. i. 62 This was your default, That being Captaine of the Watch to Night, Did looke no better to that weightie Charge. **1606** STOCK tr. *Whitaker's Answ. Campian* 95 A waighty question ..concerning lawfull ceremonies. **1646** *Hamilton Papers* (Camden) 129 You may judge how gladly I would impart things of waightier and more pleasing consequence. **1693** W. FREKE *Sel. Ess.* xxvi. 154 By Dissimulation and Trifles, sometimes the Weightiest Matters haue been discouered. **1718** *Free-thinker* No. 65. 71 What weighty Negociations did He bring to a Conclusion! **1737** POPE *Hor. Epist.* II. i. 379 Or choose at least some Minister of Grace, Fit to bestow the Laureate's weighty place. **1769** BURKE *Observ. Late St. Nation* Wks. 1842 I. 80 The questions of war and peace, the most weighty of all questions. **1809** COLERIDGE *Friend* No. 7. 109 There are three weighty motives for a distinct exposition of this Theory. **1865** DICKENS *Mut. Fr.* III. iv, And now I am going seriously to tell you..four secrets. Mind! Serious, grave, weighty secrets.

b. Of a substantial or solid nature; ranking high in respect of importance or value.
In quot. 1744 employed sarcastically with allusion to sense 1.
1558 BP. WATSON *Seven Sacram.* xxx. 193 To exchaunge the short and light affections of thys tyme, wyth the eternall and weyghty ioyes in the Kyngdome of heauen. **1586** A. DAY *Eng. Secretorie* I. (1595) 49 The authority of Example is also very weighty. **1596** NASHE *Saffron-Walden* S 2, Were they weightie Treatises? **1653** W. RAMESEY *Astrol. Restored* 110 You are to know that a more weighty planet, or that which is superiour cannot apply unto the lighter or inferiour, except when he is retrograde. **1744** *Def. People* title-p., Full Confutation of the Pretended Facts, advanc'd in a late Huge, Angry Pamphlet... In a Letter to the Author of that weighty Performance. **1816** SINGER *Playing Cards* 165 Mr. Dibdin whose authority on the subject is the weightiest that could be possibly adduced. **1874** BLACKIE *Self-Cult.* 41 In these days, when the most weighty books may be had cheaply, in the lightest form. **1877** HUXLEY *Techn. Educ.* Sci. & Cult. (1881) 84 Steps which will have a weighty and a lasting influence on the growth and spread of sound and thorough teaching.

4. a. Of an argument, utterance, etc.: Producing a powerful effect; adapted to influence or convince; forcible, telling, potent.
1560 DAUS tr. *Sleidane's Comm.* 114 With moste weightie wordes. **1573** G. HARVEY *Letter Bk.* (Camden) 12 Your wurship hath harde what forcible and waiti reasons M. Nevil hath usid against me. **1594** SHAKS. *Rich. III*, I. i. 148 Lyes well steel'd with weighty Arguments. **1641** J. JACKSON *True Evang. T.* II. 133 A speech..so gnomicall and waighty, that S. Augustin highly commends it. **1717** PRIOR *Alma* III. 44 No fool Pythagoras was thought; Whilst he his weighty doctrines taught. **1759** ROBERTSON *Hist. Scot.* I. IV. 264 But on the other hand several weighty objections had to be urged. **1856** KINGSLEY *Misc.* (1859) I. ix. 331 Reflections very wise and weighty indeed. **1868** FREEMAN *Norm. Conq.* II. ix. 334 Few and weighty were the words which the great Earl spoke that day. **1890** *Law Times Rep.* LXIII. 684/1, I must adopt the evidence on the other side, which I think is more weighty.

b. Of persons: Having great authority or influence; important or impressive in respect of position, views, or utterance.
1662 HOWELL *New Engl. Gram.* To Rdr. 4 Mr. Ben Johnson a Weighty man and one who was as patient as hee was painfull in all his composures. **1666–7** PEPYS *Diary* 17 Feb., A mighty quick, ready man, but not so weighty as he should be. **1709** SWIFT *T. Tub* Author's Apol. ¶6 Since the weightiest men in the weightiest Stations are pleased to think it a more dangerous point to laugh at those corruptions in religion. **1729** BUTLER *Serm.* Wks. 1874 II. 49 There is not any necessity that men should aim at being important and weighty in every sentence they speak. **1853** LYTTON *My Novel* XI. v, The great commoner, the weighty speaker, the expert man of business. **1860** EMERSON *Cond. Life* v. (1861) 112 The argument is scouted, until by-and-bye it gets into the mind of some weighty person; then it begins to tell on the community. **1879** HUXLEY *Sensation* Sci. & Cult. (1881) 246 We sometimes hear it [this maxim] enunciated by weighty authorities, as if its natural consequence..had the force of a moral obligation.

5. Hard to bear or endure without failing or giving way; oppressive, burdensome, grievous.
1540 PALSGR. *Acolastus* v. iv. Z ij b, I am tourmented withinforthe..with so weighty a charge of conscience. **1568** GRAFTON *Chron.* II. 653 Like a wise prince, he alleged his insufficiencie for so great a rome and weyghty a burden. **1613** PURCHAS *Pilgrimage* I. xvi. 73 He was beholden to the Romanes, that eased him of so weighty a burthen, and lessened his cares of gouernement. **1712** STEELE *Spect.* No. 308 ¶1 The weighty Cares which you have thought fit to undergo for the publick Good. **1821** SCOTT *Kenilw.* xxii, I have lived ill, and the world has been too weighty with me. **1849** LEVER *Con Cregan* xviii, There are hundreds, here, whose weightiest evil would be that they awoke an hour earlier than their wont.

†**b.** Rigorous, severe. *Obs. rare.*
1607 SHAKS. *Timon* III. v. 102 We banish thee for euer.., If after two days shine, Athens containe thee, Attend our waightier Iudgement.

†**6.** Serious, grave; expressing seriousness or gravity, earnest, solemn. *Obs.*
1599 MARSTON *Antonio's Rev.* Prol., If any spirit breathes within this round, Vncapable of waightie passion. **1613** SHAKS. *Hen. VIII*, Prol. I. 2, I come no more to make you laugh, Things now, That beare a Weighty, and a serious Brow,..We now present. **1622** J. TAYLOR (Water P.) *Sir Greg. Nonsense* Wks. (1630) II. 3/1 With that the smug-fac'd Pluto shook his vestment, Deepe ruminating what the weighty Iest ment. **1677** PENN *Trav. Holland* etc. (1694) 212 The Countess..lookt upon me with a weighty countenance, and fetcht a deep sigh, crying out, O the cumber and entanglements of this vain World!

7. = HEAVY *a.* 20.
1828 W. IRVING *Life & Lett.* (1864) II. 337 My chief fear of the work is that..it may prove..in some parts heavy. I shall work it up, however, as much as possible, and endeavor to lighten it where it is weighty.

weih, var. WY. *Obs.*, man.

weiht, obs. f. WEIGHT, WIGHT.

weik(e, weiket, weikit, obs. ff. WEAK *a.*, WICK, WICKED, WICKET.

Weil (vaɪl). *Path.* [The name of H. A. *Weil* (1848–1916), German physician, who described the disease in 1886 (*Deutsch. Archiv f. Klin. Med.* XXXIX. 210).] ***Weil's disease***, a severe, sometimes fatal, form of leptospirosis that is characterized by fever, jaundice, and muscle pains and is acquired by infection from the urine of rats.
1889 *Brit. Med. Jrnl.* 6 July 11/1 (*heading*) Notes on a case of Weil's disease. **1934** [see LEPTOSPIROSIS]. **1961** R. D. BAKER *Essent. Path.* ix. 200 The mortality of Weil's disease (spirochetal jaundice), the common leptospirosis of man, is about 10 per cent. **1977** C. MCCULLOUGH *Thorn Birds* xii. 276 He looked thin, wrinkled and yellow... 'What is Weil's disease, Luke?'.. 'Oh, it's just some sort of jaundice most cutters get sooner or later. The cane rats carry it.'

weil, var. or obs. f. WEEL[1], WELL *adv.*, WHEEL, WHILE.

†**weila**, *int. Obs. rare.* [OE. *weᵹ lá*: see WELLAWAY, and cf. WELLA *int.*] Alas!
c **1000** *Ags. Ps.* lxix. 4 (Thorpe) Ealle..þe me word cwædon, Weᵹla, weᵹla [Vulg. *qui dicunt mihi, Euge, euge*]. *c* **1230** *Hali Meid.* (1922) 23 Weila þat reowðe. *Ibid.* 39 Weila [*v.r.* wala], lutel þarf þe carien for þin anes liuenеð.

weilaway, -awei, -awey, var. ff. WELLAWAY.

weilcum, obs. Sc. f. WELCOME *v.*

weild(e, obs. ff. WIELD.

weile, obs. f. WELL.

weil(e)fair, obs. Sc. ff. WELFARE.

Weil-Felix (vaɪl'fiːlɪks). *Med.* [The names of Edmund *Weil* (1880–1922), Austrian physician, and Arthur *Felix* (1887–1956), Polish bacteriologist, who described the reaction in 1916 (*Wien. klin. Wochenschr.* XXIX. 33).] ***Weil-Felix reaction***: an agglutination reaction which takes place when serum from a patient infected with typhus is added to certain strains of bacteria of the genus *Proteus*, used as a diagnostic test for the disease.
1919 *Public Health Rep.* (U.S.) XXXI. 2446 The Weil-Felix reaction..has recently come into use as a means of diagnosing typhus fever. **1956** *Nature* 11 Feb. 257/2 The Weil-Felix reaction..proved of immense value in the differential diagnosis of typhus from typhoid and other fevers of unknown origin, and stimulated a great deal of research to explain why it was possible to obtain a specific agglutination reaction with an organism playing apparently no part in the causation of the disease. **1978** *Jrnl. R. Soc. Med.* LXXI. 509 The Weil-Felix reaction, which is the only generally available diagnostic test, failed to detect over 50% of proven cases in several series.

weill, obs. f. VEAL *sb.*[1], WEEL, WELL.

weillaway(e, var. WELLAWAY.

weille, weill-fair, obs. Sc. ff. WELL *a.* and *adv.*, WELFARE.

weily, var. of (or error for) WELLY *adv.*
1731–8 SWIFT *Pol. Convers.* II. (1738) 170 Well; I'm welly [b]rosten, as they sayn in Lancashire.

Weimar ('vaɪmɑː(r)). The name of a city in Thuringia, Germany, where the democratic constitution under which Germany was governed from 1919 until the start of the Third Reich in 1933 was drawn up. Used *attrib.* and *absol.* with reference to the political, social, and cultural aspects of Germany during this period, esp. in phr. ***Weimar Republic***.
1932 *Internat. Affairs* XI. 770 The return pure and simple to the Weimar system. **1934** H. P. GREENWOOD *German Revolution* iii. 39 The National Assembly at Weimar epitomised..the whole Weimar Republic. **1958** *Listener* 20 Nov. 828/2 The liberal fancies of the Weimar Republic. **1963** W. H. CHAMBERLIN *German Phoenix* xiii. 244 In distinct contrast to the Weimar period, a political system based on free elections..has had time to strike deep roots. **1968** P. GAY *Weimar Culture* (1969) p. xiv, The dazzling array of these exiles..tempts us to idealize Weimar as unique, a culture without strains.., a true golden age... But to construct this flawless ideal is to trivialize the achievements of the Weimar Renaissance. **1974** W. LAQUEUR *Weimar* vii. 224 There was..a light side to Weimar culture: Fritzi Massary and Richard Tauber, Marlene Dietrich and the *White Horse Inn. Ibid.* ix. 273 The Weimar revival reached its apogee in the late 1960s with the rise of the New Left. **1982** S. G. DUFF *Parting of Ways* vii. 74 The Weimar Government tried to meet..obligations by printing money.

Weimaraner (vaɪmə'rɑːnə(r), waɪ-). [Ger., f. *Weimar* (see prec.) + *-aner* (something) of this place, region, etc.] A (breed of) grey, short-coated, drop-eared pointer, which was originally bred as a hunting dog in the Weimar region.
1943 *Amer. Kennel Gaz.* Jan. 77/1 The admission to registration of the Weimaraner..brings to 109 the breeds now recognized as pure-bred. **1952** L. ROSS *Picture* 35 He had..a pen for eight Weimaraner puppies. **1954** *Time* 1 Mar. 19/1 Republican speechwriters came to a point like so many Weimaraners last November. **1968** *Globe & Mail* (Toronto) 17 Feb. 49/5 (Advt.), Weimaraners are medium size sporting dogs. **1979** *Daily Mail* 26 Oct. 25/2 The upper middles have recently taken to foreign breeds—weimaraners and rotweilers.

†**weimer**. *Obs. rare*⁻¹. [Cf. WFris. (17th c.) *wemersang* 'song of woe'.] Lamentation.
c **1230** *Hali Meid.* (1922) 29 (Titus MS.) þeos ne schulen neauer song singen in heuene, ah schulen weimeres leod ai mare in helle.

weind, obs. form of WIND, WYND; Sc. var. WEND *v.*[2] (to ween).

†**weine**, *v. Obs.* [a. ON. *veina* = OE. *wánian* WONE *v.*] *intr.* To lament, wail.
c **1205** LAY. 25827 þa iherde he wepen, wunder ane swiðen, wepen and weinen. *c* **1400** *Pilgr. Sowle* (Caxton) I. xv. (1859) 12, I ne can nought done, but cryen, and weyne That charyte nought reckyth of my peyne.

weine pain, var. WAYNPAIN *Obs.*

weiner ('wiːnə(r)), var. of WIENER *sb.* a. Cf. WEENY *sb.*[2] *N. Amer.*
1961 in WEBSTER. **1965** P. TAMONY *Americanisms* (typescript) No. 10. 8 In Frankfurt small sausages were termed *Wein*; this turns up in American colloquialism as *weiner* and *weenie*. **1973** H. NIELSEN *Severed Key* iv. 45 We got a little cold beer and some weiners, and we thought we'd have us a picnic. **1980** J. M. BICKHAM *Regensburg Legacy* iv. 56 The hotel supper..sauerkraut, weiners, green beans.

weing, obs. Sc. f. WING.

weinscot, obs. f. WAINSCOT.

‖**Weinstube** ('vaɪnʃtuːbə). [Ger., f. *wein* WINE + *stube* STUBE, room.] A small German wine-bar or tavern. Cf. BIERSTUBE.
1899 F. NORRIS *McTeague* 126 Its place was taken by a German saloon, called a 'Wein Stube'. **1936** C. BEATON *Diary* Sept. in *Wandering Years* (1961) xvi. 297 We sit in the Weinstube drinking white wine. **1946** S. SPENDER *European Witness* 138 The Weinstube was one of those German drinking cellars which resemble a chapel. **1969** K. BENTON *Twenty-Fourth Level* vi. 101 He dined in a noisy, cheerful

German *Weinstube*. **1981** L. DEIGHTON *XPD* vi. 36 The wreckage of a German Weinstube.

‖**Wein, Weib, und Gesang** (vaɪn vaɪp ʊnt gə'zaŋ), *phr.* [Ger.] Wine, women, and song, proverbially considered the essential ingredients for carefree entertainment and pleasure by men.

First popularized as the title of a Strauss waltz (1869). Strauss prob. took it from the anon. couplet found in the Luther room at Wartburg: Wer nicht liebt Wein, Weib und Gesang /Der bleibt ein Narr sein Leben lang (see WINE *sb.*[1] 1 f(b), quot. 1862).

1885 G. B. SHAW in *Dramatic Rev.* 27 June 341/1 The '*Wein, Weib, und Gesang*' waltzes which the Inventions Council offer us as the flower of modern European music. **1924** G. B. STERN *Tents of Israel* vi. 87 Franz..was a typically Viennese Rakonitz, in the famous Wein-Weib-und-Gesang style. **1935** C. ISHERWOOD *Mr. Norris changes Trains* iii. 38, I shall..prepare myself to enjoy an evening of *Wein, Weib, und Gesang*. More particularly *Wein*. **1959** M. CROSLAND tr. *J. Rovan's Germany* 21 The famous trilogy '*Wein, Weib und Gesang*' (wine, woman and song) which form the subject of numerous drinking songs on both sides of the Rhine.

weipe, obs. Sc. f. WIPE *v.*

weir (wɪə(r)), *sb.* Forms: α. 1–2 **wer**, 3–8 **were**, 5 **werre**, 5–7 **weere**, 5–8 **weer**; 5, 7 **ware**, 6–8 **weare**, 7–9 **wear**; 6–7 **weire**, **weyre**, 7– **weir**; 6–8 **wier**. β. 6–7 **wyre**, (7 **wyer**), 7–8 **wire**. [OE. *wer* m., = OS. *werr*, MLG. *wer*, *weer*, *weir*, *were* (LG. *wêr*, *were*), MHG. *wer*, *were* (G. *wehr*, †*währ*; dial. *wier*) neut., f. the stem of OE. *werian* to dam up: see WERE *sb.* OIcel. *vǫr*, *var-*, landing-place, is possibly related.

Normally the standard modern form would have been *wear* (wɛə(r)); this is represented by the dialectal *wair*, *ware*. The late variant *wire* is difficult to account for.]

1. a. A barrier or dam to restrain water, *esp.* one placed across a river or canal in order to raise or divert the water for driving a mill wheel; also, the body of water retained by this means, a mill-dam; now gen., a dam, of which there are various forms, constructed on the reaches of a canal or navigable river, to retain the water and regulate its flow.

α. *c* **897** ÆLFRED *Gregory's Past. C.* xxxviii. 279 Se se ðe ðone wer bricð, & ðæt wæter utforlæt, se bið fruma ðæs ȝeflites. *c* **1460** *Oseney Reg.* 30 With all dwellynges þe which been vppon the were of þe milles. **1482** CAXTON *Higden* (Rolls) VIII. 543 The mayer of London..and the comynalte dyde do brake vp al the weerys that were bytwene Medewey and Kyngeston. **1491** *Cal. Anc. Rec. Dublin* (1889) 373 To arrest ther mill horses,..and to kepe them.. tyll they..make the saide werre. *a* **1550** LELAND *Itin.* (1769) IV. 92 A Damme or Were to serve the Kinges Milles a little lower then the Dammes. **1583** in W. H. Turner *Sel. Rec. Oxford* (1880) 434 A locke or weare by Rewlie lock, to bende the water in sommer and to drawe uppe in wynter. **1653** WALTON *Angler* iii. 89 [The trout] wil about (especially before) the time of his Spawning, get almost miraculously through Weires and Floud-Gates against the stream. **1695** *Act 6 & 7 Will. III*, c. 16 (title) An Act to prevent Exactions of the Occupiers of Locks and Wears upon the River of Thames Westward. **1722** DE FOE *Plague* (1756) 170 A Weer or Stop upon the River, made to raise the Water for the Barges which go up and down the River. **1792** A. YOUNG *Trav. France* 21 The navigation of the river in the town being absolutely impeded by the wear which is made across it in favour of the corn mills. **1813** VANCOUVER *Agric. Devon* 314 There are no other reservoirs than those which are formed by the dams or weirs by which the streams are raised for the purpose. **1859** H. KINGSLEY *G. Hamlyn* xiii, I'm the best swimmer in Devon. That was proved by my living in that weir in flood time. **1866** M. ARNOLD *Thyrsis* ii, The Vale, the three lone wears, the youthful Thames. **1877** HUXLEY *Physiogr.* 3 About 380 million gallons flow over the weir every four-and-twenty hours.

β. *a* **1722** LISLE *Husb.* (1757) 203 A good kiln ought to have such a draught as to roar like wires on a river. **1758** *Descr. Thames* 160 Farmer's Wires or Weirs..Day's Wires, [etc.]. **1776** G. SEMPLE *Building in Water* 33 There was..a Wire or a Stone Dike almost quite a-cross the River. **1875** H. R. ROBERTSON *Life Upper Thames* 40 A boat descending the stream meets with no impediment till it reaches the dam or 'weir' (pronounced 'wire' by the riverside people), as it is technically called.

b. *Her.* A charge representing a weir.

1780 EDMONDSON *Heraldry* II. Gloss., *Weare*, *Weir*, or *Dam, in Fesse*. It is made with stakes and osier twigs, wattled or interwoven as a fence against water.

2. a. A fence or enclosure of stakes made in a river, harbour, etc., for taking or preserving fish. (Cf. *fish-weir* FISH *sb.* 7.)

In OE. also used to render L. *captura* in the sense of a 'catch' of fish.

α. **839** in Birch *Cartul. Sax.* I. 598 Twyȝen weoras in fluvio qui dicitur Stur. **901** *Ibid.* II. 247 An wer on Ycenan. **996** in Kemble *Cod. Dipl.* VI. 136 Ðes healfan weres æt Bræȝentforda. **1052–67** *Ibid.* IV. 211 Al ðare þinge ðe ðarto mid richte ȝebirð..on waterin and on weren. *a* **1122** *O.E. Chron.* (Laud MS.) an. 963, þa twa dæl of Witlesmere mid watres & mid wæres & feonnes. *a* **1200** in Birch *Cartul. Sax.* I. 171 In captura..piscium quæ terræ illi adjacet, ubi sunt scilicet duo quod nostratim dicitur Weres. *c* **1374** CHAUCER *Troylus* III. 35 As why this fish, and nought that, cometh to were. *c* **1430** *Pilgr. Lyf Manhode* III. xxv. (1869) 150 It is maad as a were for fysh; Entree ther is, but issue nouht. **1459** *Rolls of Parlt.* V. 365/2 And a were called Petersam were.. to be had for evermore to the seid Priour and Monkes. **1523** *Act 14 & 15 Hen. VIII*, c. 13 Diuers weres & ingins for fisshynge, made & leuied in the same hauen. **1584** R. SCOT *Discov. Witchcr.* XII. xvii. 216 [He] robbed a millers weire and stole all his eeles. **1591** SYLVESTER *Du Bartas* I. v. 315 The delicate..Golden-eye, Kept in a Weyre, the widest space doth spy. **1610** HOLLAND *Camden's Brit.* (1637) 808 A very goodly Weare for the catching of Salmons. **1697** DAMPIER *Voy.* I. 465 Their only Food is a small sort of Fish, which they get by making Wares of stone, across little Coves, or branches of the Sea. **1724** *Col. Rec. Pennsylv.* III. 233 An act for demolishing..Fishing Dams, Wears & Kedles set across the River Schuylkill. **1791** W. H. MARSHALL *W. Eng.* (1796) II. 240 The [Salmon] Weir.. consists of a strong dam or breastwork, ten or twelve feet high, thrown across the river. **1859** R. F. BURTON *Centr. Afr.* in *Jrnl. Geog. Soc.* XXIX. 81 *note*, The Wigo, or weir, is like that of Western India. **1894** *Outing* Feb. 401/1 Close to the weir—a kind of circular fish-trap made by driving stakes into the bottom close together.

fig. **1548** UDALL, etc. *Erasm. Par. Luke* v. 4–7 Satan hath fishers of his owne too: who dooe..towle theim into the were and nette of damnacion.

β. **1624** CAPT. J. SMITH *Virginia* I. 7 The people were fled, but their wires afforded vs fish. **1638** SUCKLING *Aglaura* v. i. 35 Like wanton Salmons comming in with flouds, that leap o're wyres and nets, and make their way. **1697** DAMPIER *Voy.* I. 106 They carry them alive to Jamaica, where the Turtles have wires made with Stakes in the Sea to preserve them alive.

b. A weel for catching fish. †Also *Her.*, a representation of this, borne as a charge.

1611 COTGR., *Boissel d'ozier*. A weele, or weere of Ozier twigs. **1688** HOLME *Armoury* III. xvi. (Roxb.) 80/1 He beareth Azure, a Weele with its hoope vpward, Or. This is also termed a Fishard, or a Ware. **1834** WHITTIER *Mogg Megone* 841 The clear stream where The idle fisher sets his weir. **1845** *Peter Parley's Ann.* VI. 51 A weir is a basket loose and open at one end, and smaller at the other, into which the fish were driven.

3. A pond or pool. *Obs.* exc. *dial.*

For the forms *wayre*, *wair* see WAYOUR.

a **1300** *E.E. Psalter* cvi. 35 He set in weres ofe watres [L. *in stagna aquarum*] wildernes. *c* **1450** *Mirk's Festial* 143 And soo was hit hyd þer yn [to] þe tyme þat byschopys of þe tempull let make a were [*v.r.* wayre] yn þe same plas, forto wasch schepe yn. **1657** J. WATTS *Scribe*, etc. *Dipper Sprinkled* 31 To make choise of a common Pond or Weyr to dip your two new converted holy Sisters in. **1691** RAY *S. & E. Country Words*, *Were*, or *Wair*, a pond or pool of water. **1877** *Holderness Gloss.*, *Weir*, a pond.

4. *local.* **a.** A fence or embankment to prevent the encroachment of a river or sea-sand, or to turn the course of a stream.

1599 NASHE *Lenten Stuffe* 22 The burdensome detrimentes of our hauen, which euery twelue-month deuoures a Iustice of peace liuing, in weares and banckes to beate off the sand. **1680** *N. Riding Rec.* VII. 30 Roger Beckwith..and other of the adjoyning neighbours have taken care to make a weare to keep the said river in its antient channel. **1824** CARR *Craven Gloss.*, *Weer*, an embankment against its [*sc.* a river's] encroachment. **1846** BROCKETT *N.C. Words* (ed. 3), *Were*,..an embankment to prevent the encroachment, or turn the course of a stream. **1894** *Northumbld. Gloss.*, *Wear*, *weir*, a structure of stone mixed with rice (brushwood) for protecting a bank from the wash of a stream.

b. (See quot.)

1894 *Northumbld. Gloss.*, *Wear*, *Weer*, the landing place and fishing ground at a salmon-net fishery.

5. *Sc.* A hedge. (Cf. WEAR *v.* 23.)

1789 D. DAVIDSON *Seasons* 51 Now weir an' fence o' wattl'd rice, The hained fields inclose. *a* **1894** J. SHAW in R. Wallace *Country Schm.* (1899) 355 *Weir*,..a hedge.

6. *attrib.* and *Comb.*, as ***weir-bank***, ***-bridge***, ***-dam***, ***-frame***, ***-head***, ***-heck*** (HECK *sb.*[1] 2), ***-hole***, ***-pile***, ***-pool***, ***-stream***; ***weir-keeper***, ***-owner***; **weir-boat**, a boat kept at a weir for the use of the weir-keeper; † **weir-dike**, a bank that serves as a dam; **weir-hatch** [HATCH *sb.*[1] 6], the flood-gate or sluice of a weir; **weir-hedge**, a bank made on each side of a river to narrow and deepen its water; † **weir-hook** (see quot.); **weir house**, a trap for salmon at a salmon weir; † **weir-net**, a net for taking fish at or from a weir; **weir-shot net**, a fishing net that is shot or cast in a circular form, used in salmon fisheries on the Tweed (see quot. 1855).

1583 *Inquis. Sewers Linc.* (1851) 16 That all *weare banks & all other Bankes heretofore in Commission..& all close ditches & draines..shall be ditched sufficiently before Michaelmasse. **1436** *Catal. Anc. Deeds* IV. 273 (A. 8182) [Two boats called the] feriboot [and] a *wereboot. **1851** KINGSLEY *Yeast* iii, He found on the *weir-bridge two of the keepers. **1793** R. MYLNE *Rep. Thames* 22 Without a Lock in the said Cut, or a *Weir-dam in the bed of the River. **1518** *Sel. Pleas Star Chamber* (Selden Soc.) II. 130 A lytull grownde inclosyd in the fenne by Reasun of makyng of a *Weyr dyke. **1902** CORNISH *Naturalist Thames* 6 The holes and angles of the *weir-frame. **1898** HARDY *Wessex Poems* 204 As when a *weir-hatch is drawn, Her tears..With a rushing of sobs in a shower were strawn. **1817** SCOTT *Waverley* ix, A large brook..leapt in tumult over a strong dam, or *wear-head. *c* **1467–9** *Durham Acc. Rolls* (Surtees) 641 Pro extraccione et imposicione lez stapyls pro le *Warehek molendini. **1819** *Rees' Cycl.* VI. A a 4, s.v. *Canal*, Jetties, or *Weir-hedges have formerly been made, for diminishing the width of the river below the several shoals. **1841** HARTSHORNE *Salop. Antiq.* 610 **Ware-hole*, *Weirhole*, a hole into which the back water of a mill stream falls. **1688** HOLME *Armoury* III. xvi. (Roxb.) 86/2 A *Weare, or fish cage hooke. It is a large and strong Iron hooke with a sockett at the end, to be fixed on a long pole, or staffe, to take fish out of weares or cages. **1791** W. H. MARSHALL *W. Eng.* (1796) II. 256 The [Salmon] Weir..consists of a strong dam... At one end of the dam, is a '*weir house' or trap. **1791** R. MYLNE *2nd Rep. Thames Navig.* 15 By disuniting the Care of the Pound Locks from the Miller and the *Wear-Keeper. **1881** *Taunt's Thames Map* 66/1 The weir-keeper is another old hand on the river. **1585** HIGINS *Junius' Nomencl.* 256/2 *Excipulus*,..a *weare net. **1610** HOLLAND *Camden's Brit.* II. 18 In September they take in Weeles and Weere-nets an incredible number of most sweete and sauery eeles. **1656** W. DU GARD tr. *Comenius' Gate Lat. Unlocked* §358, p. 101 Part hee shutteth up in repositories, from whence when there is need hee taketh them out with a warenet. **1610** R. VAUGHAN *Water-Workes* H i b, *Weare-owners. **1864** MEREDITH *Sandra Belloni* xx, She saw the white *weir-piles shining. **1889** 'J. BICKERDYKE' *All-round Angler* III. 90 A man taking a chance day on the Thames has small chance of success unless he sticks to the *weirpools. **1855** *Archæol. Æliana* IV. 302 The *wear-shot net is rowed by means of a boat into the river in a circular form, and is immediately drawn to the shore. **1857** *Local Act 20 & 21 Vict.* c. cxlviii. §62 Every Person who shall shoot or work any Wear Shot Net in the River within the Distance of Thirty Yards of any other Wear Shot Net. **1889** J. K. JEROME *Three Men in Boat* ix. 143 We might have somehow got into the *weir stream, and be making for the falls. **1900** *Daily News* 1 Jan. 8/7 The well-known weir stream which skirts the grounds of Eton College.

weir (wɪə(r)), *v.* [f. WEIR *sb.*] *trans.* To provide with a weir. Chiefly in pa. pple.

1610 R. VAUGHAN *Water-Workes* G 2 b, The Riuer of Wie ..was.. so Weared & fortified, as if the Salmons therein.. had been forbidden their vsuall walkes. **1794–** [see WEIRING *vbl. sb.*]. **1828** CARR *Craven Gloss.* (ed. 2), *Weer*, to make a protection of a bank. **1904** *Times* 13 Feb. 13/6 The main channel was locked and weired for navigation.

weir, Sc. var. VERE *sb.* *Obs.*, WAR *sb.*[1], WERE *sb.* and *v.*, WIRE *sb.*

weirai, var. WARRAY *v.* *Obs.*

weird (wɪəd), *sb.* Forms: 1 **wyrd**, 3–5 **wird**, (4 **wired**, 5 **wirid**), **wirde**, 4–5 **wyrde**; 4 **wyerde**, **wierde**, 4–6 **werd** (5 **werid**), **werde**, 4– **weird** (5 *Sc.* **veird**), 7–8 (9 *Sc.*) **wierd**; *Sc.* 6 **waird**, 6–7 **weard**, 8 **weerd**. [OE. *wyrd* fem., = OS. *wurd* (pl. *wurdi*), OHG. *wurt*, ON. *urð-r*, from the weak grade of the stem *werþ-*, *warþ-*, *wurþ-* to become: see WORTH *v.*

The word is common in OE., but wanting in ME. until *c* 1300, and then occurs chiefly in northern texts, though employed also by Chaucer, Gower, and Langland. The normal later and modern form would have been *wird*, and the substitution of *werd*, *wērd* (which is natural in south-eastern ME.) is difficult to account for in the northern dialects. In senses now current the word is either Scottish or archaic (chiefly under the influence of Scottish writers).]

1. The principle, power, or agency by which events are predetermined; fate, destiny.

Beowulf 455 Gæð a wyrd swa hio scel. *Ibid.* 477 Hie wyrd forsweop on Grendles gryre. *c* **888** ÆLFRED *Boeth.* xxxix. §5 Ac þæt þæt we wyrd hatað, þæt bið Godes weorc þæt he ælce dæȝ wyrcð. *a* **1000** *Seafarer* 115 Wyrd biþ swiðre, meotud meahtiȝra, þonne ænȝes monnes ȝehyȝd. **13..** *E.E. Allit. P.* A. 249 What wyrde has hyder my iuel vayned. **13..** *Gaw. & Gr. Knt.* 2134 Worþe hit wele, oþer wo, as þe wyrde lykez hit hafe. *a* **1400–50** *Wars Alex.* 443 Þat sygnyfys þe same man þat sett is, be wird, So many prouynce to pas. *c* **1470** HENRY *Wallace* IX. 244 As werd will wyrk, thi fortoun mon thou tak. *c* **1585** MONTGOMERIE *Sonn.* xxxiii. 1 Vhom suld I warie bot my wicked weard, Vha span my thriftles thrauard fatall threed? **1603** *Philotus* c, Quhat wickit weird hes wrocht our wo? [**1895** W. MORRIS *Beowulf* 16 Weird wends as she willeth. *Ibid.* 17 Weird swept them away.]

b. Magical power, enchantment.

1813 HOGG *Queen's Wake* 79 He heard the world of awsome weird, And he saw their deedis of synn.

2. *pl.* The Fates, the three goddesses supposed to determine the course of human life.

c **725** *Corpus Gloss.* (Hessels) P. 15 *Parcae*, wyrde. *c* **1385** CHAUCER *L.G.W.*, *Hypermnestra* 19 The werdys that we clepyn destene Hath shapyn hire that she mot nedis be Pyetous sad. *c* **1450** *Crt. of Love* 1173, I mene, the three of fatall destinè, That be our werdes. **1483** *Cath. Angl.* 420/2 Wyrdis, *parce*. **1513** DOUGLAS *Æneis* I. i. 30 Gif werdis war nocht contrair [*si qua fata sinant*]. **1547** SURREY *Æneis* IV. 581 (Roxb.) F iij, The werdes withstande [*fata obstant*]. *a* **1585** MONTGOMERIE *Flyting* 326 'Woe worth', quoth the Weirds, 'the wights that thee wroght!' **1632** LITHGOW *Trav.* i. 5 And whilst from Phleg'ran fields, the weirds me call, I in Elisean plaines, am forc'd to fall. **1722** RAMSAY *Three Bonnets* II. 13 Ye're grown sae braw: now weirds defend me! **1855** SINGLETON *Virgil* I. 29 'Career ye on,' Have to their spindles cried..the Weirds [*Parcae*].

b. One pretending or supposed to have the power to foresee and to control future events; a witch or wizard, a soothsayer.

1625 HEYLIN *Microcosmos* (ed. 2) 509 These two..were mette by three Fairies, or Witches (Weirds the Scots call them). **1654** VILVAIN *Enchir. Epigr.* II. lxxx, The 2 Scots courtiers who met three Wierds or Witches which foretold their fortune. **1682** C. IRVINE *Hist. Scot. Nomencl.* 12 *Arioli*. Weards, Sooth-sayers, or Second-sighted-men. **1834** A. SMART *Rambling Rhymes* 164 Puir auld wives..Were seized in Superstition's clutches, An' brunt to death for wierds an' witches. **1899** J. SPENCE *Shetland Folk-lore* 143 With this green nettle And cross of metal I witches and wierds defy.

3. That which is destined or fated to happen to a particular person, etc.; what one will do or suffer; one's appointed lot or fortune, destiny.

Often in *to dree one's weird*: see DREE *v.* 2 c.

c **725** *Corpus Gloss.* (Hessels) S 433 *Sortem*, wyrd, *condicionem*. *c* **888** ÆLFRED *Boeth.* xl. §1 Ic wille secȝan þæt ælc wyrd bio good, sam hio monnum good þinc, sam hio him yfel þince. *a* **1300** *Cursor M.* 3453 Strang weird was giuen to þam o were þat þai moght noght þair strif for-bere. *Ibid.* 9968 Had neuer womman sa blisful wird..As maria maiden. **13..** *Gaw. & Gr. Knt.* 2418 Dalyda dalt hym hys wyrde. *c* **1400** *Ant. Arthur* xvi. (Irel. MS.) 'Ways me for thy wirde!'

cothe Waynor. *c* **1450** *St. Cuthbert* (Surtees) 4680 þai grett, þai sorowed þair sary werde. *c* **1470** HENRY *Wallace* IV. 761 My waryed werd in warld I mon fullfill. **1535** STEWART *Cron. Scot.* I. 109 Euerie ladie passit hame..Weipand full soir and wareand hir werd. **1563** SACKVILLE *Induct. Mirr. Mag.* lxiii, It made myne iyes in very teares consume: When I beheld the wofull werd befall, That by the wrathful wyl of Gods was come. *a* **1600** MONTGOMERIE *Misc. Poems* xlvi. 31 They haif wroght my weird Vnhappiest on eird. **1718** RAMSAY *Christ's Kirk Gr.* III. viii, It's a wise wife that kens her weird. *a* **1774** FERGUSSON *On Seeing Butterfly* Poems (1845) 18 Those Whose weird is still to creep, alas! Unnoticed, 'mang the humble grass. **1795** BURNS '*O tell na me*' iii, Let simple maid the lesson read, The weird may be her ain. **1818** SCOTT *Hrt. Midl.* xii, My weird maun be fulfilled, Mr. Butler. **1892** J. A. HENDERSON *Ann. Lower Deeside* 79 The weird of this kirk is that it will fall in time of worship. **1909** BELLOC *Marie Antoinette* 255 It was one more of those hammer-blows of Fate exactly coincident with the sequence of the Queen's weird.

b. *pl.* (often in reference to a single person).

a **1300** *Cursor M.* 15279 þe gait it es al graid, He mai sai wirdes warid þat forwit him es laid. **1320–30** *Horn Ch.* 456 Wiif thai toke, and duelled thare; In Inglond com thai no mare, Her werdes for to bide. *c* **1340** HAMPOLE *Psalter* lxxiv. 5 Sum says it was my werdis; sum says the sterne of my birth gert me syn. *c* **1374** CHAUCER *Boeth.* I. met. i. (1886) 1 The sorful wierdes of me olde man [*maesti mea fata senis*]. **1390** GOWER *Conf.* II. 94 Whan thei at mi nativite My weerdes setten as thei wolde. **1393** LANGL. *P. Pl.* C. IV. 241 As hus werdes [*v.r.* wirdus] were ordeined. **1423** JAS. I *Kingis Q.* ix, So vncouthly hir werdes sche deuideth. *c* **1470** HARDING *Chron.* LXXXV. iv, Fortune, false executryse of weerdes [= Chaucer *Troylus* III. 617], That euermore..To all debates thou strongly so enherdes. **1571** SIR J. MAITLAND in *Satir. Poems Reform.* xxvii. 102 Then warreitt war thy weirdis and wanhap. **1579** *Sc. Acts Jas. VI* (1814) III. 140/1 That they can tell þair weardis deathis & fortunes.

c. *spec.* An evil fate inflicted by supernatural power, esp. by way of retribution.

[*a* **1300** *Cursor M.* 8981 Bot hard it es, þe wird o sin þat yarked was til adam kin!] **1874** 'OUIDA' *Two little Wooden Shoes* 132 Swallows do not tell their secrets. They have the weird of Procne on them all. **1877** TRENCH *Lect. Med. Ch. Hist.* 178 But a weird was upon him and upon his race. **1885** JEAN INGELOW *Sleep of Sigismund* 7 The weird is on him to grope in the dark with endless Weariful feet for a goal that shifteth still.

4. a. A happening, event, occurrence.

Prov. ***after word comes weird***, the mention of a thing is followed by its occurrence or appearance.

a **900** *Cynewulf's Christ* 81 Ne we þære wyrde wenan þurfon toweard in tide. **971** *Blickl. Hom.* 221 þa ʒelamp wundorlic wyrd þæt se leʒ ongan slean & brecan onʒean þone wind. **1390** GOWER *Conf.* I. 340 It were a wonder wierde To sen a king become an hierde. *c* **1450** *St. Cuthbert* 5459 It befell þis wondir werde. **1721** J. KELLY *Sc. Prov.* 2 After Word comes Weird; fair fall them that call me Madam. **1883** HALL CAINE *Shadow Crime* xxxvi, Weel, weel; after word comes weird. That's why the constables are gone, and that's why Robbie's come.

b. That which is destined or fated to happen; predetermined events collectively.

c **1470** *Golagros & Gaw.* 1082 Thair wil nane wyis, that ar wis, wary the werd. **1513** DOUGLAS *Æneis* III. vii. 48 Bot we from werd to werd and chance mon wend. **1876** W. MORRIS *Sigurd* I. 3 A tale that the elders have told, A story of weird and of woe.

5. †**a.** A decree (of a god). *Obs.*

a **1400–50** *Wars Alex.* 270 þe werdes Of my gracious goddis, þe grettest on erde. **1513** DOUGLAS *Æneis* XII. xii. 202 And thou, Tellus, mast nobill God of erd, Hald fast the speris hed by ȝour werd.

†**b.** An omen or token significant of the nature of a future event; a prognostic. *Obs.*

1513 DOUGLAS *Æneis* XII. xiii. 150 Jove..bad hir hald doun baldly to the erd, For to resist Juturnais ire and werd [L. *omen*]. **1533** BELLENDEN *Livy* (S.T.S.) II. 233 þe senat ..said þai acceppit þe weird þat followit one þir wourdis.

c. A prediction of the fate which is to happen to a person; etc.; a prophecy.

1785 *Poems Buchan Dial.* 18 Altho' his mither, in her weirds, Foretald his death at Troy. **1802** C. GRAY *Poems* (1811) 73 Then, as to his fortin tellin',..he ne'er liket to be sellin' His weird for wind.

d. A supernatural or marvellous occurrence or tale.

1814 W. NICHOLSON *Poet. Wks.* (1897) 40 [She] Could tell her tale or lilt her sang,..Wi' weirds and witcheries aft atween, And unco sights that some had seen. *a* **1859** A. TAIT in Jas. Watson *Living Bards of Border* 151 What legends and weirds these fair scenes still awaken.

6. *Comb.*, as ***weird-fixed***, ***-set*** adjs.; **weird-licht** *Sc.* the light of destiny; †**weird-man**, a seer; **weird-woman**, a witch.

1819 W. TENNANT *Papistry Storm'd* (1827) 181 Now was come the *weird-fix't hour Ordain'd to break the Papish power. **1844** W. THOM *Rhymes & Recoll.* 54 There's a bricht e'e looks love to me, Like the *weird licht o'er me shining. **1806** JAMIESON *Pop. Ballads* I. 238 'Dire is the doom', the *wierd-man said; 'Nae mair, O lady, speir!' **1819** W. TENNANT *Papistry Storm'd* (1827) 46 The *weird-set day begins to daw. **1845** J. E. CARPENTER *Poems & Lyrics* 34 The *weird-woman had stol'n away.

weird (wɪəd), *a.* Also 5 **wyrde**, 5–6 *Sc.* **werd(e**, 6 **veird**, 7 **weyard (weyward)**, **weer'd**, 8 **weïrd**, 9 **weerd**. [Originally an attrib. use of prec. in *weird sisters* (see sense 1), the later currency and adjectival use being derived from the occurrence of this in the story of Macbeth.

The evolution of the forms found in Shakspere's *Macbeth* was app. from **weyrd* to *weyard* (retained in Acts III and IV in the First Folio) and *weyward* (used in Acts I and II); the latter was no doubt due to association with *wayward*, a word used many times by Shakspere. (The later folios retain the *weyward* spelling, and alter the other to this or to *wizard*.) In several passages the prosody clearly requires the word to be pronounced as two syllables; hence Theobald's use of the diæresis in his emendation *weïrd* (see quot. 1733 below), giving rise to the scansion of quot. 1755 in sense 1, and quot. 1820 in sense 4.]

1. Having the power to control the fate or destiny of human beings, etc.; later, claiming the supernatural power of dealing with fate or destiny.

Originally in ***the Weird Sisters*** = †(*a*) the Fates; (*b*) the witches in *Macbeth*.

c **1400** *Sc. Trojan War* II. 2818 Vþeris said sche was, I trow, A werde-sister, I wait neuir how. *c* **1420** WYNTOUN *Cron.* VI. xviii. 1862 þa women þan thoucht he Thre werd systeris mast lyk to be. *c* **1475** *Cath. Angl.* 420/2 (Addit. MS.) Wyrde systres, *parce*. **1513** DOUGLAS *Æneis* V. xiii. 74 Admit myne asking, gif so the fatis gidis,..Or ȝit werd sisteris list gif thaim that cuntre. **1549** *Compl. Scot.* vi. (1872) 64 The tail of the three veird systirs. **1577** HOLINSHED *Hist. Scot.* 243/2 *marg.*, The prophesie of three women supposing to be the weird sisters or feiries. **1605** SHAKS. *Macb.* I. iii. 32 The weyward Sisters, hand in hand, ..Thus doe goe, about, about. *Ibid.* III. i. 2 Thou hast it now, King, Cawdor, Glamis, all, As the weyard Women promis'd. *Ibid.* III. iv. 133, I will to morrow..to the weyard Sisters. *a* **1693** *Urquhart's Rabelais* III. xxviii. 237 The weer'd Sister Parques. **1733** THEOBALD *Shaks. Macb.* I. iii. *note*, In every passage..my Emendation must be embraced and we must read *weïrd* [ed. 1740 *Wierd*, or *Weïrd*]. **1755** J. G. COOPER *Tomb Shaks.* 99 Where three swart sisters of the weïrd band Were mutt'ring curses to the troublous wind. **1765** *Birth of St. George* 47 in Percy *Reliq.* III. 218 To the weïrd lady of the woods He purpos'd to repaire. **1807–8** W. IRVING *Salmagundi* (1824) 129 He had rather see one of the weird sisters flourish through his key-hole on a broom-stick. **1820** SHELLEY *Let. Maria Gisborne* 106 And here, like some weird Archimage sit I, Plotting dark spells. *a* **1854** H. REED *Lect. Brit. Poets* v. (1857) 189 The weird woman with beards meet to seal the deep damnation of their victim.

2. a. Partaking of or suggestive of the supernatural; of a mysterious or unearthly character; unaccountably or uncomfortably strange; uncanny.

1817 SHELLEY *Rev. Islam* IX. viii, Some said, I was a fiend from my weird cave, Who had stolen human shape. **1820** —— *Witch Atlas* 670 It is A tale more fit for the weird winter nights Than for these garish summer days. **1835** LYTTON *Rienzi* I. xii, This solitude has something in it weird and awful. **1847** TENNYSON *Princess* I. 14 Myself too had weird seizures, Heaven knows what. **1865** DICKENS *Mut. Fr.* I. i, Both men then looked with a weird unholy interest at the wake of Gaffer's boat. **1878** LUCY *Diary Two Parl.* (1885) I. 393, I hear a weird story in connection with the private history of the family.

absol. **1888** *Daily News* 30 Aug. 4/7 Miss Seward, according to Sir Walter Scott, was a mistress of the weird in oral narrative. **1899** SIR G. DOUGLAS *James Hogg* v. 101 Unlike the German's, Hogg's 'weird' is seldom or never morbid, fevered, hectic.

b. of sounds or voices.

1815 SHELLEY *Alastor* 30 In lone and silent hours, When night makes a weird sound of its own stillness. **1860** TYNDALL *Glac.* I. ii. 11 The weird rattle of the débris which fell at intervals. **1865** DICKENS *Mut. Fr.* II. i, The person of the house gave a weird little laugh here. **1876** SMILES *Sc. Natur.* vi. 100 He was awakened by a weird and unearthly moaning.

3. Of strange or unusual appearance, odd-looking.

1815 SHELLEY *Alastor* 448 Mutable As shapes in the weird clouds. **1861** H. MACMILLAN *Footn. Page Nat.* 23 The soft yielding carpets of greenest verdure and weirdest patterns, woven by these tiny plants on the floor of shadowy old forests. **1865** KINGSLEY *Herew.* Prel., He begins to people the weird places of the earth with weird beings. **1907** BP. A. ROBERTSON in *Trans. Devon Assoc.* 53 Bampfylde Moore Carew, King of the Gipsies, [not] the only weird, extravagant figure that has moved across Devon's stage.

4. a. Out of the ordinary course, strange, unusual; hence, odd, fantastic. (Freq. in recent use.)

1820 KEATS *Lamia* I. 107, I..bade her steep Her hair in weïrd syrops, that would keep Her loveliness invisible. **1849** LYTTON *K. Arthur* II. xxxvi, The prophet up the plain, Gathering weird simples, pass'd. **1855** DICKENS *Holly-Tree* i, He was a man with a weird belief in him that no one could count the stones of Stonehenge twice, and make the same number of them. **1912** *Eng. Hist. Rev.* Oct. 833 The 'Guacciadim' of p. 140 is a weird misprint for Guicciardini.

b. Colloq. phr. ***weird and wonderful***, marvellous in a strange or eccentric way; both remarkable and peculiar or unfathomable; exotic, outlandish. Freq. *iron.* or *derog.*

1859 J. H. STIRLING in *Meliora* Oct. 231 These [poems] are doubtless meant to be very weird and wonderful, but they are mere breath, and..barren as the wind. **1886** O. WILDE in *Pall Mall Gaz.* 1 Feb. 5/1 There is psychology of a weird and wonderful kind. **1908** T. E. LAWRENCE *Let.* 9 Aug. (1954) 70 Their food is weird and wonderful. **1946** VISCT. KNEBWORTH *Boxing* xiv. 176 The beginner so often gets the idea that he is going to do the most weird and wonderful movements. **1962** *Friend* 3 Aug. 947/1 Nearly all the weird and wonderful decorations were provided by a decorator member of the club. **1978** S. NAIPAUL *North of South* II. vi. 227 A weird and wonderful place is Jo'burg.

5. *Comb.*, as ***weird-looking*** adj.

1862 [ELIZ. JOHNSTON] *Gifts & Graces* xix. 184 All the trees grim and shadowy, every familiar object weird-looking. **1867** *Q. Rev.* Oct. 437 The Prophet first pointed out a weird-looking creature, a turnkey. **1888** F. HUME *Mme. Midas* I. Prol., A cruel, weird-looking scene, fantastic, unreal, and bizarre as one of Doré's marvellous conceptions.

weird (wɪəd), *v. Sc.* and †*north.* Also 4 **weirrd**, **werd**, **wired**, **wiird**, 6 **waird**, 8 **weerd**, 9 **wierd**; 7 *pa. pple.* **weard**. [f. WEIRD *sb.*]

1. *trans.* To preordain by the decree of fate; esp. in *pass.* to be destined or divinely appointed *to*, *into*, or *unto* (with inf. or sb.).

a **1300** *Cursor M.* 23368 Ne hert mai think þaa ioies sere, þat iesus crist has dight til his, þat weirrded er vnto þe bliss. *Ibid.* 25225 All þe men þat werded es for to be broght into þi blis. **1678** RAY *Prov.* (ed. 2) 360 (Sc. Prov.) A man may wooe where he will, but he will wed where he is weard [ed. 1, where his hap is]. **1742** R. FORBES *Ajax Sp.* (1755) 14 These darts that weerded were To tak the town o' Troy. **1885** J. LUMSDEN *Rural Rhymes* 236 Gin the gude Mr. Hootsman is weirdit to be married a third time neist week.

2. To assign to (a person) as his fate; to apportion as one's destiny or lot.

c **1550** *Clariodus* (Maitl. Club) I. 1030 The Waird Sisteris ..wairdit me, gif ane knave chyld war I, That efter I was sevin ȝeiris old To be transformit in ane lyoun bold. *a* **1800** *Kempion* iii. in Scott *Minstrelsy* (1802) II. 93, I weird ye to a fiery beast, And relieved sall ye never be, Till [etc.]. **1806** JAMIESON *Pop. Ballads* I. 238 Say..what the doom sae dire, that thou Doest wierd to mine or me? *a* **1869** C. SPENCE *Fr. Braes of Carse* (1898) 182 A lesson teaching poor and rich That nane should weird ill to a witch.

3. To warn or advise by the knowledge of coming fate.

1806 JAMIESON *Pop. Ballads* I. 237, I wierd ye, gangna there! *Ibid.* II. 174, I weird thee, to lat me be were best.

Hence '**weirded** *ppl. a.*; '**weirding** *vbl. sb.* in Comb. ***weirding peas***, peas employed in divination.

1804 TARRAS *Poems* 68 Jock Din is to the yard right sly, To saw his wierdin piz. **1820** SCOTT *Monast.* xvii, Say, what hath forged thy wierded [*footn.* fated] link of destiny with the House of Avenel?

'**weirddom**. [f. WEIRD *sb.* + -DOM.] The supernatural world.

1863 B. BRIERLEY *Chron. Waverlow* Introd. p. xv, Stories of eld and weirddom are vanishing too.

weirdie ('wɪədɪ). *slang.* Also **weirdy**. [f. WEIRD *a.* + -IE.] **1.** An odd or unconventional person; one who is considered 'weird'; *spec.* applied to any young man with long hair and a beard. Freq. in *pl.*

1894 A. S. ROBERTSON *Provost o' Glendookie* 101 'He's awa without his curran' loaf.' 'He's a weerdie.' **1949** W. R. BURNETT *Asphalt Jungle* (1950) ii. 19 Cobby..thought to himself: 'He's a weirdy, all right.' **1954** 'P. QUENTIN' *Wife of Ronald Sheldon* vii. 57 God, is that one a weirdie!.. There was a cobweb in her hair. **1959** *Listener* 3 Dec. 975/1 The weirdies that Kerouac seems always to meet wandering and muttering in the small hours. **1960**, **1961** [see BEARDIE 2]. **1962** *Punch* 14 Feb. 268/2 One [bedsitter]..advertiser.. added 'No Weirdies either'. **1966** *Daily Tel.* 17 Nov. 18/8 There was not an unwashed bearded weirdie in sight! **1974** K. MILLETT *Flying* (1975) I. 94 I'm not a friend, just the visiting weirdie.

2. Something that is 'weird', fantastic, bizarre, or grotesque. Freq. applied to a film, book, etc.

1948 *Astounding Sci. Fiction* Jan. 15 The *Cosmos* had one of its feature writers compose a weirdie about a world consisting of beings of pure mind. **1962** *Listener* 14 June 1043/3 *The Lake Lovers* is a weirdie. **1968** *Blues Unlimited* Nov. 25 Country Jim is a weirdie. **1969** R. PETRIE *Despatch of Dove* i. 26 No mistake, it was a weirdy of a day.

weirdish ('wɪədɪʃ), *a.* [f. WEIRD *a.* + -ISH.] Somewhat weird.

1863 DISRAELI in Monypenny & Buckle *Life* (1914) III. 472 A great number of owls have been disturbed..Their hooting at night is..louder than the south-west wind, which, indeed, is only the accompaniment to their weirdish arias. **1914** E. F. BENSON *Dodo the Second* iii. 68, I was always weirdish, and I am too old to change now.

weirdless ('wɪədlɪs), *a. Sc.* [f. WEIRD *sb.* + -LESS.] Destined to ill fortune, ill-fated, unlucky; hence unbusinesslike, incapable, worthless.

c **1800** *Mary Hamilton* iii. in Child *Ballads* III. 391/2 And wae be to that weirdless wicht. **1821** *Joseph the Book-Man* 99 Ye weirdless, naughty, spendthrift man. **1825** JAMIESON, *Weirdless* 2. Destitute of any capacity to manage worldly affairs, S. **1864** LATTO *Tam. Bodkin* x. 93 What could she think..but that I behooved to be some wild, weirdless, ne'er-do-weel?

Hence '**weirdlessness**.

1825 JAMIESON, *Weirdlessness*, wasteful mismanagement.

weird-like ('wɪədlaɪk), *a.* [f. WEIRD *sb.* + -LIKE.] Suggestive of the supernatural, ominous, eery, uncanny. Of a person: Uncanny-looking.

1854 GRACE GREENWOOD *Haps & Mishaps* 113 The almost deathly quiet, the oppressive loneliness, the strange deep, unearthly gloom of this mouldering city of the dead are things to be *felt* in all their melancholy and weird-like power. **1856** MISS MULOCK *J. Halifax* vi, Still I hear the awe-struck, questioning, weird-like tone. **1875** G. JACQUE *Hope* iii. 35 Along that dismal silent road A weirdlike man was seen to plod. **1884** W. C. SMITH *Kildrostan* 45 So weird-like was the feeling of the place.

weirdly ('wɪədlɪ), *a. Sc.* [f. WEIRD *sb.* + -LY[1].]

1. Favoured by fate, happy, prosperous.

1807 HOGG *Mtn. Bard* Poet. Wks. 1838 II. 211 Harden was a weirdly man. **1819** —— *Jacobite Relics* II. 189 In thy bien and weirdly nook Lie some stout Clan-Gillian banes.

2. Pertaining to, or suggestive of, witchcraft or the supernatural.

1831 Hogg *Magic Mirror* in *Blackw. Mag.* XXX. 650 A hill for weirdly deeds renowned. **1858** Masson *Milton* I. 538 In such studies and weirdly phantasies let the night pass. **1880** J. E. Watt *Poet. Sk.* 19 (E.D.D.) Though a warlock had waggit his weirdly wand To bring doon the lift on my head.

Hence ˈ**weirdliness.**

1859 Masson *Brit Novelists* 243 Passages . . to which, for visual weirdliness, there is nothing comparable in the pages of his rival.

ˈ**weirdly**, *adv.* [f. WEIRD *a.* + -LY^{2}.] In a weird or fantastic manner.

1859 Tennyson *Elaine* 840 Elaine . . past beneath the weirdly-sculptured gates. **1861** J. Thomson *Ladies of Death* xx, That face Of subtle loveliness though weirdly pale. **1888** Annie S. Swan *Doris Cheyne* iv. 71 A low, moaning wind . . waved the bare tree boughs weirdly to and fro.

ˈ**weirdness.** [f. WEIRD *a.* + -NESS.] The fact or quality of being weird.

1869 E. W. Benson in A. C. Benson *Life* (1899) I. 289 Then fell the weirdness that still comes betimes When, after earnest talk, I fall to talk For talking's sake. **1893** *Harper's Mag.* Dec. 44/2 The greatness, vastness, and, if the word be permissible, weirdness of an empire that is the ruler of countless millions.

weirdo (ˈwɪədəʊ), *sb.* and *a. slang.* [f. WEIRD *a.* + -O^{2}.] **A.** *sb.* = WEIRDIE 1.

1955 L. Feather *Encycl. Jazz* 347 *Weird-o*, a weird person. **1958** *Observer* 13 Apr. 15/3 He is worried by Press reports which represent him as 'a weirdo—there is another word for it'. **1967** *Courier-Mail* (Brisbane) 13 Apr. 22/3 Another set of weirdos using a slick philosophy of revolt against the established order as camouflage for a lazy or corrupt existence. **1972** J. McClure *Caterpillar Cop* iv. 45 A shock-haired, bearded weirdo in a tartan dressing-gown and wellington boots. **1976** M. Machlin *Pipeline* xli. 448 We are near the village and I go back a lot, but like I said, they all treat me like I was some weirdo. **1981** *London Rev. Bks.* 3–16 Sept. 3 Santa Fe is acknowledged as a milieu of aesthetes and weirdos. **1984** *Melody Maker* 6 Oct. 34/4 This record is for the real weirdos.

B. *adj.* Bizarre, eccentric, odd.

1962 *Sunday Times* 5 Aug. 20/6 Frankly, I'm sick of your whole weirdo line. Leave me alone. **1969** C. Burke *God is Beautiful, Man* (1970) 46 About halfway through the party a real weirdo thing happened. **1974** M. Moore *Silver Birch Country* 43 The lady I'm looking after is a dear old duck, completely weirdo, but she's got a terrible sense of humour, and I like her. **1979** *Tucson* (Arizona) *Citizen* 20 Sept. 2A/6 It . . makes us sound like some sort of weirdo fanatics opposed to all medicine.

ˈ**weirdsome,** *a.* [f. WEIRD *sb.* + -SOME.] Uncanny, mysterious.

1885 J. F. Molloy *Royalty Restored* I. 304 These dark and weirdsome gulphs. **1910** *Spectator* 9 July 51/2 She . . sent the animal on its weirdsome errand into the darkness of the night.

ˈ**weirdward,** *a.* [f. WEIRD *sb.* + -WARD.] Bordering upon or approaching the supernatural.

1866 J. B. Rose tr. *Ovid's Met.* XIII. 697 Unnumbered sisterhood Of wierdward birth.

ˈ**weirdy,** *a. Sc.* [f. WEIRD *sb.* + -Y.] Fateful.

1804 R. Couper *Poetry* II. 21 Life's ember suffers unco throwes—What will ye, weirdy time, disclose!

weire, Sc. var. WAR *sb.*^{1}

weirelyk, obs. Sc. var. WARLIKE *a.*

weiring (ˈwɪərɪŋ), *vbl. sb.* [f. WEIR *v.*] The constructing of a weir or of weirs; also, *concr.* materials used for making a weir or of which a weir is composed.

1794 W. H. Marshall *W. Eng.* (1796) II. 289 Hitherto, piles and planks had been used, to confine the rapid Tavey within its channel; much valuable timber having been used . . in 'weiring'. **1882** *Act 45 & 46 Vict.* c. 38 §25 The making . . of any works for any of the following purposes . . : (iv) Embanking or weiring from a river or lake. **1901** *Spectator* 27 July 119/1 In the canalised stream . . there were numbers [of crayfish], which made homes in . . sides of locks, and in the wood of the weiring.

weirlic, -lyk(e, obs. Sc. ff. WARLIKE.

weirlie, -ly, var. ff. WARLY *Obs.*

weirwal, var. WEREWALL *Sc. Obs.*

weische, obs. Sc. f. WASH.

weise, var. WASE; Sc. var. WISE *v.*

weisenheimer, var. WISENHEIMER.

weisht, Sc. var. WHISHT *sb.* and *int.*

weism (ˈwiːɪz(ə)m). [f. WE *pron.* + -ISM, after *egoism.*] The too frequent use of 'we' (see WE *pron.* 2 b) by a speaker or writer. Cf. WEGOTISM.

1800 *Anti-Jacobin Rev.* V. 58 What intolerable weism! more revolting than the worst species of egotism! **1833** *Fraser's Mag.* Apr. 505 His 'egotism', so offensive to the *we*-ism of the press.

ˈ**Weismannian,** *a.* and *sb.* [f. as next + -IAN.]

a. *adj.* Of or pertaining to Weismann or his biological theory. **b.** *sb.* One who accepts the theory of Weismannism.

1903 *Amer. Naturalist* May 349 The line of argument will probably not be convincing to even the milder Weismannians. **1903** *Science* 5 June 906/1 The method . . in which . . there is no reduction division in the Weismannian sense. **1905** *Westm. Gaz.* 30 Mar. 1/3 Objections to the Weismannian theories.

Weismannism (ˈvaɪsmənɪz(ə)m). [f. the name *Weismann* (see below) + -ISM.] The theory of evolution and heredity propounded by the German biologist, August Weismann, esp. in regard to the continuity of the germ-plasm and the non-transmission of acquired characteristics.

1894 H. Spencer in *Contemp. Rev.* Oct. 592 (*title*) Weismannism once more.

Weissenberg (ˈvaɪsənbɜːg). [The name of Karl *Weissenberg* (b. 1893), Austrian-born physicist.]

a. *Cryst.* Used *attrib.* with reference to a technique of single-crystal X-ray diffraction introduced by him, in which a metal shield allows the diffracted X-rays to produce only one set of parallel lines of spots which are recorded over the whole of the photographic film by rotating it synchronously with the crystal, enabling the Miller indices and other crystal parameters to be easily obtained.

1934 W. P. Davey *Study of Crystal Struct. & its Applic.* vii. 205 The Weissenberg camera may be used . . in the indexing of diffraction spots which are so thickly clustered on layer lines as to require otherwise a large number of oscillation photographs. **1962** Weissenberg photograph [see SALESITE]. **1976** D. Sherwood *Crystals, X-rays & Proteins* xiv. 507 To obtain full three-dimensional information, we may take a series of photographs corresponding to each layer line in which we are interested. This was realised by K. Weissenberg, and in 1924, he published an experimental method which enables this to be done. This is now known as the Weissenberg method.

b. *Physics.* ***Weissenberg effect***: an effect observed when a visco-elastic liquid is stirred, when the liquid rises in the centre and climbs the stirring rod rather than forming a concave surface like normal fluids.

1949 M. Reiner et al. in *Jrnl. Soc. Chem. Industry* LXVIII. 327/2 When a vertical rod is rotated in certain viscous elastic liquids, the liquid climbs up the rod and when a disc is rotated in such a liquid near the bottom of a beaker containing it, the liquid is drawn radially towards the centre. . . Freeman and Weissenberg claim that the first experimental observations were made by Weissenberg and Russell. . . In view of this it would seem justifiable to describe such phenomena as 'the Weissenberg Effect'. **1978** *Sci. Amer.* Nov. 148/2 If you would like to produce the Weissenberg effect, you might use a mixing bowl mounted on a turntable.

weissite^{1} (ˈvaɪsaɪt). *Min.* [Named (G. *weissit*) after C. S. *Weiss*, German crystallographer: see -ITE.] An altered form of iolite.

1836 T. Thomson *Outl. Min.* 282 Weissite occurs thinly scattered in a chlorite slate in kidney shaped pieces about the size of a hazel nut. **1849** J. Nicol *Min.* 263 Weissite, externally like fahlunite, but said to be monoclinohedric. **1868** Dana *Min.* (ed. 5) 301 Weissite, iberite, huronite, are supposed to be altered iolite.

weissite^{2} (ˈvaɪsaɪt). *Min.* [See quot. 1927 and -ITE^{1}.] A copper telluride, Cu_5Te_3, occurring (often in association with rickardite) as bluish black or bluish grey pseudocubic crystals with a metallic lustre that darken on exposure to air.

1927 W. P. Crawford in *Amer. Jrnl. Sci.* CCXIII. 346 The mineral is named Weissite after the late Loui Weiss, owner of the Good Hope mine [at Vulcan, Colorado]. **1980** *Mineral. Abstr.* XXXI. 354/1 Rickardite and weissite occur with pyrite, tetrahedrite, chalcopyrite, and altaite in this orebody in andesites and dacite porphyrites.

‖**Weisswurst** (ˈvaɪsvʊrst). [Ger., f. *weiss* white + *wurst* sausage.] (A) whitish German sausage made chiefly of veal.

1963 I. Fleming *On H.M. Secret Service* xxvi. 289 At the Franziskaner Keller . . they ate mounds of Weisswurst and drank four steins of beer each. **1970** *Sat. Rev.* (U.S.) 12 Sept. 107/3 Germany's never-stale variety of sausages, particularly . . the delicate Weisswurst. **1983** *N.Y. Times* 7 Sept. C7 Weisswurst, the great specialty of Munich, is generally made with veal, pork, bread crumbs, nutmeg, salt, pepper and, sometimes, lemon peel or parsley. It is also stuffed into casings before cooking.

weist, obs. f. WEST; var. WISHT *a. dial.*

weit, obs. Sc. f. WET; obs. f. WHITE, WIT *v.*; var. WITE *sb.*

weith, obs. f. WIGHT.

weive, obs. f. WAIVE *v.*^{1}, WEAVE; var. WAIVE *v.*^{2}

weize, var. WASE; Sc. var. WISE *v.*

wejack, earlier form of WOODCHUCK.

1796 S. Hearne *Journ. N. Ocean* 377 The Wejack and Skunk are never found in the Northern Indian country. **1829** J. Richardson *Fauna Bor.-Amer.* I. 52.

wek, obs. form of WEAK *a.*

weka (ˈweka, ˈweɪkə, ˈwiːkə). Also **waika.** [Maori, so named from its cry.] The native name for the flightless rails *Ocydromus australis* and *O. brachypterus* of New Zealand. Also called ***weka rail.***

1845 E. J. Wakefield *Adv. New Zealand* II. iv. 95 Two young *weka*, or wood-hens, about as large as sparrows. **1852** *Zoologist* X. 3400 The eggs of . . the Weka (*Ocydromus*), obtained in the Middle Island, New Zealand. **1873** *Ibis* Ser. III. (1874) IV. 97 Wood or Maori Hen. *Weka.* **1906** *Westm. Gaz.* 20 Jan. 9/2 The weka rails are also flightless. **1914** *Chamb. Jrnl.* Nov. 751/1 The weka . . is very common throughout the New Zealand bush.

†**weke,** *sb. Obs. rare.* [ad. ON. *veku, vøku*, obl. case of *vøkva* moisture.] Moisture; liquid.

a **1300** *Cursor M.* 4698 Tilmen . . Als þai war won þair sede had saun, Bot alkin weke it was wit-draun. *Ibid.* 11215 He þat þe walud wand moght ger In a night leif and fruit ber, Witvten weke or erth a-bute. *Ibid.* 24453 Bot als ferrsum i moght reke, To kis þat tre was blodi weke.

weke, obs. f. WEAK, WEEK *sb.*, WICK *sb.*^{1}; var. WEEK *int.*

weket, -ett, obs. ff. WICKET.

wekid, -it, wekir, obs. ff. WICKED, WICKER.

wekke, var. VECKE *Obs.*, WICK *a.*

wekked, wekker, wekyt, obs. ff. WICKED, WICKER, WICKET.

wel: see WAL, WEEL^{1}, WELL.

w'el, obs. contraction of *we will.*

1677 C. D'Avenant *Circe* IV. ii. 35 Let him dye, to his groans w'el dance and w'el sing.

wel-adaie, -aday, etc.: see WELLADAY.

welans (-anys), -ly, Sc. var. ff. VILLAINS *a.*, -LY. *Obs.*

welany, obs. Sc. f. VILLAINY.

welawei, -way, etc., **welawo:** see WELLAWAY, WELLAWO.

welawylle, -wynne: see WELLA *adv.*

welbede, -bode, obs. forms of WOUBIT.

wel bego(n, bigoo: see WELL BEGONE.

Welch, obs. form of WELSH.

welcome (ˈwɛlkəm), *sb.*^{1}, *int.*, and *a.* Forms: α. 1 wilcuma (wilcymo), 2–3 wilcume, (3 wilkume), 6 *Sc.* wylcum, wylcome; 1 wylcume, wylcyme, 3 wulcume, 3–5 wolcome. β. 2–3, 5 welcume, 3–4 wel come, 3–6 wel-come, welcum, 4 welkum, 4–7 welcom (5 *Sc.* velcom), 7 well come (7 *Sc.* weillcome), 7–8 well-come, 3– welcome. [Originally OE. *wilcuma* (f. *wil-*, *will-* will, desire, pleasure + *cuma* comer, guest) = OHG. *willicomo*, MHG. and MLG. *willekome*, *-kume* (whence OF. *wilecome*), with subsequent alteration of the first element to *wel-* WELL *adv.*, and identification of the second with the imperative or infinitive of the verb *come*, under the influence of OF. *bien venu*, *bien veigniez*, L. *bene venisti*, *bene venias*, etc., and possibly of the Scand. forms given below.

Parallel developments appear in the cognate languages, either with retention of the original form of the first element, and reduction or extension of the second, as in older G. *wille-*, *willkum(m)*, *-komm*, G. *willkomm*, LG. *willkâm*, MDu. *willecomen*, MLG. *willekomen* (LG. *willkamen*), MHG. *willechomen*, *-komen* (G. *willkommen*), or with substitution of *wel-* for *wil-*, as in MDu. *wellecome* (Du. *welkom*), *-comen*; also MLG. *wolkomen*, WFris. *wolkom*. It is not clear whether the ON. *velkominn* (Norw. *velkomen*; MSw. *vel-*, *välkomin*, Sw. *väl-*, Da. *velkommen*) is an independent formation or the result of LG. and Romanic influence.

The occasional ME. forms in *wol-* may represent either the southern *wul-* from *wyl-*, *wil-*, or the *wol* which appears as a variant of *wel* WELL *adv.*]

†**A.** *sb.* One whose coming is pleasing or desirable; an acceptable person or thing. *Obs.* (OE. only.)

Beowulf 1894 He . . cwæþ þæt wilcuman Wedera leodum scaþan scirhame to scipe foron. *c* **900** *Bæda's Hist.* IV. ix. (1890) 290 Me is, cwæð heo, þin cyme on miclum ðonce; & þu eart leof wilcuma [L. *et bene venisti*]. *a* **1000** *Riddles* IX. 11 (Gr.) Ic . . hæleþum bodiȝe wilcumena fela woþe minre.

B. In predicative use, passing into *adj.*

1. a. Of a person: Acceptable as a visitor, companion, etc.; also in phrase ***to make*** (a person) ***welcome.***

α. *Beowulf* 388 Ꝺesaȝa him eac wordum, þæt hie sint wilcuman Deniȝa leodum. *a* **1000** *Cædmon's Satan* 617 (Gr.) Ꝺe sind wilcuman! gað in wuldres leoht to heofona rice. *c* **1205** Lay. 8528 Wulcume ært þu Iulius. *Ibid.* 15995 Mærling þu ært wilcume. *a* **1225** *Ancr. R.* 394 Biturn þe and cum aȝean, wilkume schaltu beon me. *c* **1300** *Beket* (Percy Soc.) 1265 For ther nere hi noȝt wolcome: for the schame bifore, And the desclandre of Seint Thomas. *c* **1440** *Promp. Parv.* 532/1 Wolcome, *exceptus.* *c* **1560** A. Scott *Poems* (S.T.S.) xxvii. 38 Quhen schow growis meik and tame, Scho salbe wylcome hame.

β. *a* **1200** *Vices & Virtues* 99 Ȝif ðar cumþ ani þoht oðer ani word a godes half hie bieð hire swiðe welcume. *a* **1250** *Owl & Night.* 1600 Vor þan ic am hire wel welcume. **1297** R. Glouc. (Rolls) 10456 Þe king . . vel adoun akne . . To þe erchebissopes fet . . & sede leue fader wel come mote þou be. c 1350 *Will. Palerne* 3148 ȝe ben welcom to me bi crist þat me made. c 1386 CHAUCER *Sompn. T.* 103 Algates wel come be ye, by my fey. c 1400 *Destr. Troy* 9392 He . . was welcom I-wis to the weghes all. 1480 CAXTON *Chron. Eng.* ccxlii. 276 And no creature warned that feste, but alle were welcome. a 1533 BERNERS *Huon* lxviii. 253 They that gyue are euer welcome. 1551 CROWLEY *Pleas. & Pain* 597 In dede, very many do him entertayne Lyke as there were none more welcome then he. 1607 SHAKS. *Timon* I. ii. 23 *Timo.* O Apermantus, you are welcome. *Aper.* No: You shall not make me welcome: I come to haue thee thrust me out of doores. 1667 M. POOLE *Dialogue* 150 And the oftner they come to him, the welcomer they are. 1687 A. LOVELL tr. *Thevenot's Trav.* II. 83 Since for a little money all are welcom, one may eat as many as he pleases. 1749 FIELDING *Tom Jones* v. i, Harlequin . . was always welcome on the Stage. 1849 JAMES *Woodman* iv, Lord Chartley and his friends were right welcome. 1892 *Photogr. Ann.* II. 635 Visitors from abroad . . are always welcome.

b. In attributive use.

1579 TOMSON *Calvin's Serm. Tim.* 901/1 When we shall see them . . bee in credit and be the welcomest men in the world which fight against God and his trueth. 1718 PRIOR *Solomon* I. 312 They . . with full Mirth receive the welcome Guest. 1829 SOUTHEY *Sir T. More* (1831) I. 240 The kindest host, the welcomest guest. 1902 *Westm. Gaz.* 27 Jan. 8/2 A heartily-welcome member of the family.

2. a. Of a thing: Acceptable, agreeable, pleasing. †*to be evil welcome*: to be badly received.

a 1300 *Cursor M.* 24819 His presand welcum was and he, Als bringand wont was to be. c 1375 *Ibid.* 10276 (Fairf.) Thyne offeryng heþer is welcome. 1570 FOXE *A. & M.* (1583) 1620/1 As for death, if it come welcome bee it. 1579 TOMSON *Calvin's Serm. Tim.* 69/2 Dogs that barke against the seruants of God, seeking nothing so much as to . . cause their doctrine to be euill welcome. 1654 COCKAINE *Dianea* I. ii. 47 Knowing a full Relation will come the welcommest to me. 1657 in *Verney Mem.* (1894) III. 304 A few instructions would have beene welcome. 1758 JOHNSON *Idler* No. 1 ¶11 Praise is not so welcome to the Idler as quiet. 1821 SCOTT *Kenilw.* vii, I think fetters of gold are like no other fetters —they are ever the weightier the welcomer. 1838 LYTTON *Alice* I. ix, This letter was by no means welcome. 1851 CARLYLE *Sterling* I. i, Human Portraits, faithfully drawn, are of all pictures the welcomest on human walls.

Phrases. 1598 FERGUSSON *Sc. Prov.* (S.T.S.) 52 Of untymous persons. He is as welcome as water in a rivin ship. He is as welcome as snaw in harvest. 1659 HOWELL *Lex., Prov., Engl. Prov.* I. 11/1 As welcome as water into ones shoes. As welcome as Flowers in May. 1671 T. HUNT *Abeced.* 28 *Scholast.* 90 As welcome as Snow in the Harvest.

b. In attributive use.

1577 B. GOOGE *Heresbach's Husb.* IV. 189 b, Till the swallow with her appearing, promise a welcommer season. 1596 SHAKS. *1 Hen. IV*, I. i. 66 And he hath brought vs smooth and welcome newes. ? 1622 FLETCHER *Love's Cure* v. iii, Why this . . will be A welcomer present to our Master Philip Than the return from his Indies. 1660 BOYLE *New Exp. Phys. Mech.* xxxvii. 309 The People, upon a very well-come Occasion testified their Joy by numerous Bon-fires. 1697 DRYDEN *Æneis* I. 244 The Trojans, worn with Toils, and spent with Woes, Leap on the welcome Land. 1760 FAWKES tr. *Anacreon* Introd. p. vi, A Person of Anacreon's Character must . . meet with a welcome Reception wherever Wit and Pleasure were esteemed. 1839 FR. A. KEMBLE *Resid. in Georgia* (1863) 49 Port and bacon would prove a most welcome addition to their farinaceous diet. 1916 *Contemp. Rev.* Dec. 686 There are many other welcome signs of the drawing together of the Churches.

3. a. Freely permitted or allowed, cordially invited, (*to* do or *to* have something).

13.. *Seuyn Sages* (W.) 3822 He bad them say, That thai war welkum alway To soiorn in that same cetè. c 1400 *Sc. Trojan War* (Horstm.) II. 1924 To get þat golde . . Thai said he suld be richt welcume. c 1475 *Rauf Coilȝear* 71 Forsuith thow suld be wel-cum to pas hame with me. 1725 DE FOE *Voy. round World* (1840) 40 They were very welcome, if they thought fit, to go. 1729 P. WALKDEN *Diary* (1866) 40, I told him he was welcome to have the lend of it till Martinmas. 1840 DICKENS *Old C. Shop* xxv, You're very welcome to pass another night here. 1861 PALMERSTON in *Autob. Ld. C. Paget* (1896) Pref. p. vii, I must have 20 or 24 Iron-cased ships—you are quite welcome to have 40 or 48. 1882 'EDNA LYALL' *Donovan* xviii, He's welcome to call me what he pleases.

b. *and welcome*, added to a statement to imply: And he is (you are, etc.) freely permitted or cordially invited to do so, to have it, or the like.

1491 *Act 7 Hen. VII*, c. 22 Preamble, He may suerly comme hedir and welcome. 1562 J. HEYWOOD *Prov. & Epigr.* (1867) 104 So lo: now eate and welcome neighbour (quoth he). 1609 SHAKS. *Per.* II. iv. 22, I. *Lord.* Lord Hellicane, a word. *Hell.* With me? and welcome, happy day my Lords. 1755 *Man* No. 39. 5 And if this be done, let them judge and welcome. 1764 *Museum Rust.* III. 136 On the continent let them use the scythe and welcome, because there their weather is not so unsettled as ours. 1836 MRS. C. P. TRAILL *Backw. Canada* 75 Here are some cakes; . . take 'em, and welcome. 1869 LOWELL *Study Wind.* (1871) 2 Burgoyne may surrender and welcome.

c. Freely offered or open to all. *nonce-use.*

1772 PENNANT *Tour Scot.* (1774) 364 My hall was filled with my friends and kindred: . . and hecatombs of beeves and deer covered my rude but welcome tables.

d. *you are* (or *you're*) *welcome*: a polite formula used in response to an expression of thanks.

[1907 W. W. JACOBS *Short Cruises* ii. 34 'Thank you,' said the girl, with a pleasant smile. 'You're quite welcome,' said the skipper.] 1960 *Times* 14 Sept. 12/7 The coloured lift attendant in South Carolina who had that attractive way of saying, almost singing, 'You're welcome' whenever we thanked her. 1977 P. DICKINSON *Walking Dead* I. iv. 55 'Thanks,' said Foxe . . 'You're welcome,' said Dreiser. 1980 A. E. FISHER *Midnight Men* viii. 93 He dialled Directory Enquiries and asked the girl if she had a number. She gave him one and told him he was welcome.

e. *you are welcome* (*to* something): said ironically of something one is glad to be without.

1937 A. THIRKELL *Summer Half* i. 10 'Fine Old English Gentlemen,' said the applicant enthusiastically. 'You are welcome to him.' 1969 J. N. SMITH *Is he Dead, Miss ffinch?* xviii. 118 My Uncle Len and Aunty Marge live there in a caravan. (They're welcome.)

C. 1. a. Used in the vocative as a form of address to a visitor or guest; hence as *int.*, serving as an expression of good will or pleasure at the coming of a person. (Sometimes addressed to a thing personified or quasi-personified.)

α. c 890 WÆRFERTH tr. *Gregory's Dial.* 276 He ongan . . þus cweþan: 'wilcuman la, mine hlafordas, wilcuman la, mine hlafordas!' c 950 *Lindisf. Gosp.* Matt. xxv. 23 *Euge*, wilcymo. c 1100 *Gloss.* in Wr.-Wülcker 191/13 *Euax*, wilcume. c 1205 LAY. 22485 Wulcume sire Arður, wilcume lauerd [c 1275 wolcome]. 1500-20 DUNBAR *Poems* lxxv. 51 Now tak me be the hand, Wylcum! my golk of maireland. 1568 *Henryson's Orpheus & Eurydice* 155 (Bannatyne MS.) Fair weill my place . . And wylcum woddis wyld.

β. c 1150 *De Vita et Miraculis S. Godrici Heremitæ de Finchale* (Surtees) 306 Dixit enim hæc verba Anglica . . 'Welcume, Simund; welcume, Simund'. a 1240 *Sawles Warde* in *O.E. Hom.* I. 259 A seið warschipe, welcume, liues luue. a 1300 *Cursor M.* 8168 Alsuith sum he þat king had knaun, He said, 'sir welcum to þin aun'. 1362 LANGL. *P. Pl.* A. XII. 62 Al hayl, quod on þo, and I answered, welcome and with whom be ȝe. a 1450 *Mirk's Festial* 222 Welcom, my swete son and cosyn. c 1520 SKELTON *Magnyf.* 920 What! whom haue we here, Jenkyn Joly? Nowe welcom, by the God holy! 1552 HULOET, Welcome euen with all my herte, *optato aduenisti.* 1588 SHAKS. *L.L.L.* II. i. 92 Faire Princesse, welcom to the Court of Nauar. 1656 COWLEY *Misc.* 31 Welcome learn'd Cicero, whose blest Tongue and Wit Preserves Romes greatness yet. 1702 ROWE *Tamerl.* I. i, Wellcome! thou worthy partner of my laurels. 1766 GOLDSM. *Vicar W.* xii, Welcome, welcome, Moses! well, my boy, what haue you brought us from the fair? 1842 MACAULAY *Lays, Horatius* li, Now welcome, welcome, Sextus! Now welcome to thy home! 1865 SWINBURNE *Chastelard* II. i. 76 Look, Here come my riddle-readers. Welcome all. 1879 TENNYSON *Falcon* (1884) 105 Welcome to this poor cottage, my dear lady.

b. *to bid, wish* (a person) *welcome* (*home*): to tell (him) that he is gladly received (*home* or as a guest, etc.).

c 1375 *Cursor M.* 15060 (Fairf.) þe resceyues þine awen folk & biddis welcome hame [*Gött.* and biddes þe welcum hame]. 1598 SHAKS. *Merry W.* I. i. 201 Wife, bid these gentlemen welcome: come, we haue a hot Venison pasty to dinner. 1720 N. BLUNDELL *Diary* (1895) 162 My Wife sent Ned Howerd to Wooton to wish my Lady well-come-home.

c. The word 'welcome' displayed in letters.

1872 MARCH. DUFFERIN *Canad. Jrnl.* (1891) 42 The rooms were ornamented with 'welcomes' and wreaths of maple.

d. *welcome aboard*, said (in allusion to nautical usage) as a joc. greeting to someone joining a particular group, enterprise, etc.

1962 J. D. MACDONALD *Key to Suite* ii. 28 He put Hubbard's material in the envelope, hesitated, then scrawled across the front of it, 'Welcome aboard!' 1970 J. SANGSTER *Touchfeather, Too* iii. 79 We headed across the cool green lawn to the clubhouse. . . I was introduced to the manager . . [who] had once served . . in the navy. 'Welcome aboard, Miss Touchfeather,' he said. 1977 'J. LE CARRÉ' *Hon. Schoolboy* v. 111 'Welcome aboard,' said Guillam. . . They had reached the fifth floor.

2. †*welcome to our house*, a name for the Cypress Spurge, *Euphorbia Cyparissias.* Also *welcome-home-husband.*

1597 GERARDE *Herbal* II. cxxxii. 407 The fifth [is called in English] Cypresse Spurge, or among women, Welcome to our house. 1665 LOVELL *Herball* (ed. 2) 465 Welcome to our house, see Cypres spurge. 1828 CARR *Craven Gloss.*, *Welcome-home-husband*, Cypress Spurge.

welcome ('wɛlkəm), *sb.*[2] [f. prec. or next. Cf. Du. *welkom*, G. *willkomm*, MHG. *willekum.*]

1. a. An assurance to a visitor or stranger that he or she is welcome; a pleasant or hearty greeting or reception given to a person on arrival at a house or other place.

to outstay, or *overstay, one's welcome*: see the vbs.

1525 BERNERS *Froiss.* (1812) II. 433 She had neuer before ben at Parys, therfore the burgesses of Parys gaue her her welcome [Fr. *Si luy deuoient les bourgeois de Paris sa bien venue*]. 1610 SHAKS. *Temp.* v. i. 111 And to thee, and thy Company, I bid a hearty welcome. 1611 —— *Wint. T.* IV. iv. 560 Me thinkes I see Leontes opening his free Armes, and weeping His welcomes forth. 1649 J. TAYLOR (Water P.) *Wand. Wonders of West* 15 A house . . where I tooke a welcome, a supper and a bed, till the next morning. 1703 EARL ORRERY *As you find it* II. i. 20 I'll promise you nothing but an English-Dinner, and an English-Welcome. 1757 DYER *Fleece* I. 123 The little smiling cottage, where at eve He meets his rosy children at the door, Prattling their welcomes. 1814 BYRON *Lara* I. vii, Warm was his welcome to the haunts of men. 1846 MRS. A. MARSH *Father Darcy* II. xiv. 242 That he was the friend beloved by Everard, was sufficient to insure him a welcome from Evelyn. 1847 MARY HOWITT *Ballads* 144 Then the abbot he prayed them all be still, And let their welcomes wait. 1874 GREEN *Short Hist.* iii. §6. 145 The welcome of the townsmen made up . . for the ill-will . . of both clergy and monks.

b. *transf.* (esp. with *adjs.*) A greeting or reception of an unpleasant or unsatisfactory nature.

a 1548 HALL *Chron., Edw. IV* (1550) 39 b, But when they aproched the toune, the artillarie beganne to shote. . . This welcome semed very straung to kyng Edward, ponderynge together yestardayes promise, and this dayes doynge. c 1600 T. PONT *Topogr. Acc. Cunningham* (Maitl. Club) 10 Bot Vallace with a veill armed companey gifs them a very hote uelcome. 1633 T. STAFFORD *Pac. Hib.* I. xii. 78 The Invaders finding so ill a welcome, returned. 1725 P. WALKDEN *Diary* (1866) 11 We . . then went on to Mr. Jolly's, where we met but with a cold welcome.

†**c.** A special award in a lottery, made to the persons first drawing lots or blanks on the opening day or on each of the subsequent days. *Obs.*

1567 (Aug.) *Proclam. Gen. Lottery* (Arch. Bodl. F. c. 11, fol. 108), The first person to whome any Lot shall happen, shal haue for his welcome . . the value of fiftie poundes sterling. *Ibid.*, The Second . . shall haue . . for his welcome . . thirtie pounds. 1624 CAPT. J. SMITH *Virginia* IV. 118 Welcomes. To him that first shall be drawne out with a blanke, 100 Crownes. *Ibid.* 119 The prizes, welcomes, and rewards, shall be payed in ready Mony, Plate, or other goods.

2. a. *welcome home*, entertainment provided to celebrate the return home of a person; also, expressions of greeting made at a person's homecoming. Also *transf.* Also freq. *attrib.*

1530 TINDALE *Answ. More* IV. ii. Wks. (1572) 323/1 As when we call one that is new come home to breakfast and set a Capon before him and say, this is your welcome home. 1578 H. WOTTON *Courtlie Controv.* 296 She had good prouision of embracings, & wanton toyes, to feast him at his welcome home. 1603 HOLLAND *Plutarch's Mor.* VIII. vii. 776 Sylla of Carthage, upon my returne to Rome, after I had bene long absent, invited me to a supper for my welcome home. 1637 RUTHERFORD *Let. to J. Kennedy* Lett. (1664) 186 Our little inch of time-suffering is not worthy of our first night's welcome-home to heaven. 1680 LADY RUSSELL *Let.* 6 Mar. (1807) 3, I am very earnest to hear, . . how my brother is after his journey, and melancholy welcome home. 1885 'MRS. ALEXANDER' *Valerie's Fate* ii, I hope Madeleine has not forgotten my fire,' murmured Miss Riddell, as she walked . . down the Champs Elysées. 'Such evenings as these one wants a welcome home.' 1955 B. PYM *Less than Angels* vi. 71 We aren't getting on very fast with your welcome-home party. 1966 B. KIMENYE *Kalasanda Revisited* 32 He would take the creature up to the Musaka's and ask Miriamu to prepare it as a special 'welcome home' supper for Yosefu. 1974 M. BIRMINGHAM *You can help Me* viii. 178 It gives me the chance to be part of your welcome-home committee.

b. *Sc.* (See quots.)

1808 JAMIESON, *Welcome-haim*, the repast presented to a bride, when she enters the house of a bridegroom. 1818 *Edin. Mag.* Nov. 415/1 On Monday evening, just about gloamin, the husbands and wives of the village assemble at the house of the newly-married couple, to celebrate the welcome hame, by a good drink and funny crack.

c. *dial.* A bell tolled on the occasion of a person's death. Also *transf.*

1878 F. KILVERT *Jrnl.* 25 Dec. (1977) 328 The Welcome Home, as it chimed softly and slowly to greet the little pilgrim coming to his rest, sounded bleared and muffled through the thick snowy air. 1948 F. THOMPSON *Still glides Stream* xii. 226 It was a small, homely procession which . . accompanied Reuben on the last of his many journeys. The silvery sweet strain of a robin threaded the silence. 'The welcome home!' said Mrs. Finch.

3. Hearty or hospitable reception of a stranger or guest.

1590 SHAKS. *Com. Err.* III. i. 26 Small cheere and great welcome, makes a merrie feast. 1596 —— *Tam. Shr.* Ind. i. 103 Go sirra, take them to the Butterie, And giue them friendly welcome euerie one. 1641 *Nicholas Papers* (Camden) I. 39 It will much depend uppon what assurance of welcome we shall have from home in more then beare words. 1845 LINGARD *Anglo-Saxon Ch.* I. iii. 137 Edilwalch, king of Sussex, received him [Wilfrid] with welcome. 1859 TENNYSON *Enid* 387 A youth, that following with a costrel bore The means of goodly welcome, flesh and wine. 1879 —— *Falcon* (1884) 105 And welcome turns a cottage to a palace.

4. A welcoming salute. Also *attrib.*

1615 R. COCKS *Diary* (Hakl. Soc.) I. 63 The Duch envited the King of Firando abord their ship, and gave hym 3 pec. ordinance for a wellcom. 1808 SCOTT *Marm.* I. ix, The gunner held his linstock yare, For welcome shot prepar'd. *Ibid.* I. x, The cannon from the ramparts glanced, And thundering welcome gave.

†**5.** *powder of welcome*, a medicament for the eyes.

The origin is obscure: *welcome* is merely a rendering of the name used in the orig. L. of the quot. 1541, viz. *pulvis benvenuti.* Cf. *Treasure of Poore Men* (1540) 8 'Of pouder called Bonauenture'.

1541 R. COPLAND *Guydon's Form.* Y 1 b, Fyfthly is put the powdre of welcome, of myne owne makynge for all spottes of the eyes.

6. *attrib.* and *Comb.*, as **welcome mat** *U.S. colloq.*, a mat put out to greet welcome visitors; chiefly used in *fig.* phrs. to indicate a friendly welcome (cf. *red carpet* s.v. RED *a.* 19 a); **welcome song**: *spec.* the first ode composed by Purcell (see quots.); **welcome wagon** *N. Amer.*, a car bringing gifts and samples from local merchants to newcomers in a community; also *fig.*

1951 I. ASIMOV *Foundation* (1953) II. v. 73, I certainly don't intend to lay down the welcome mat. 1963 M. MCCARTHY *Group* iii. 50, I can only ask you to come here whenever you're in town. The welcome mat will be out. 1978 R. NIXON *Mem.* 622 The door will not only be open —I've been weaving a welcome mat. 1681 H. PURCELL (*song-title*) A Welcome Song in the year 1681 for the King. 1883 GROVE *Dict. Mus.* III. 47/1 In 1680 . . [Purcell] produced the first of his numerous odes, viz. 'An Ode or Welcome Song for his Royal Highness [the Duke of York] on his return from Scotland'. 1942 Welcome song [see *birthday ode* s.v. BIRTHDAY 3]. 1961 WEBSTER, Welcome wagon. 1970 A.

TOFFLER *Future Shock* (1971) vi. 104 We have in many American suburbs a commercial 'Welcome Wagon' service that accelerates the process by introducing newcomers to the chief stores and agencies in the community. **1971** H. T. WALDEN *Anchorage Northeast* 13 The welcome-wagon type of hospitality is not here. **1976** *Times Lit. Suppl.* 2 Jan. 4/3 He was never serious about moving to America, fearing perhaps that the American welcome wagon, by killing his habit of resentment with kindness and pelf, might stultify his..literary gifts.

welcome ('wɛlkəm), *v.*[1] Forms: α. 1 **(ʒe)wilcumian, wylcumian,** 3 **wil-, wulcumen, wolcume,** 4 **wolcome.** β. 1 **wellcumian,** 2 **welcumien,** 3 **-cumen,** 4–5 **welcum, -kum** (5 **whellcwm,** *Sc.* **velcum**); 3–5 **welcome** (6–7 *p. t.* **-commed**). [Originally OE. *wilcumian*, f. *wilcuma* WELCOME *sb.*[1], with later alteration of the first element in the same way as in the noun.]

1. *trans.* To greet (a person) with 'welcome!'; to receive (a visitor) gladly and hospitably; to accord a friendly reception to; to make welcome.

α. *c* **1000** *Ags. Gosp.* Matt. v. 47 Ʒif ʒe þæt an doð þæt ʒe eowre ʒebroðra wylcumiaþ. *c* **1000** ÆLFRIC *Saints' Lives* iii. 507 And basilius sende sona him to-ʒeanes and hine wylcumode. *c* **1205** LAY. 17098 þe king..ut him gon ride..to wulcumen Mærlin. *a* **1250** *Owl & Night.* 440 þe lilie mid hire faire wlite wolcomeþ [*Jesus MS.* welcumeþ] me. *c* **1300** *Beket* (Percy Soc.) 690 That folc to him drouȝ And wolcome him and makede feste. *c* **1350** *Will. Palerne* 4290 And worþili hire he wolcomed wen he hire mette.

β. *c* **1000** in *Engl. Studien* VIII. 478 Ðæt folc..wellcumiaþ Fenix. *c* **1160** *Ags. Gosp.* (Hatton) Matt. v. 47 Ʒyf ʒe þæt an doð þæt ʒe eowre ʒebroðre welcumieð. *c* **1250** *Gen. & Ex.* 1396 And laban cam to ðat welle ner, faiȝer welcumede he ðer eliezer. *c* **1290** *Beket* 696 in *S. Eng. Leg.* 126 þat folk sone to him drovȝ And welcomeden him. *a* **1300** *Cursor M.* 4015 He welcumd iacob selli fair, He wist he was his fader air. **13..** *Seuyn Sag.* (W.) 3850 Dame, in hert I am sary, That we haue noght al ful plenti, To welkum swilk a lord als he. *c* **1374** CHAUCER *Troylus* v. 849 Criseyde, at shorte wordes for to telle, Welcomed him, and doun by hir him sette. *c* **1400** *Rule St. Benet* (verse) 2411 For to welcum with wordes fre Euyr-ilk man in þer degre. *c* **1450** *Merlin* xxv. 447 [They ride] till thei come to logres the thirde day, and ther were thei richely welcomed. **1530** PALSGR. 779/1, I welcome with wordes or gentyll intreatyng. *Je bienuiengne.* **1557** TUSSER *100 Points Husb.*, July x, Then welcome thy haruest folke, seruauntes and all: with mirth and good chere, let them furnish thine hall. **1603** KNOLLES *Hist. Turks* (1638) 49 The yong Emperor..welcommed him full sore against his will. **1659** *Nicholas Papers* (Camden) IV. 130 Almost euery body would welcome the King and not a few expect him. **1725, 1732** [see SPEED *v.* 10d]. **1849** MACAULAY *Hist. Eng.* vii. II. 195 He would have found that the nation was not yet prepared to welcome an armed deliverer from a foreign country. **1874** GREEN *Short Hist.* vii. §6. 405 The exiled merchants of Antwerp were welcomed by the merchants of London.

b. Const. *to*, *into* (a place). Also with advs. of place, as *ashore*, *back*, *up*; esp. *to welcome home*.

c **1205** LAY. 10957 He nom forð rihtes six wise cnihtes, to Custance heom sende, & wilcumede hine to londe. *a* **1300** *Cursor M.* 15060 þe receiues þin aun folk, And welcums þe hame. *a* **1380** *S. Bernard* 1039 in Horstm. *Altengl. Leg.* (1878) 58/2 þe erchebisshop aȝein him sent A worþi clerk of good entent, Him to welcome curteisliche In to þat ilke bisschopriche. *a* **1450** *Mirk's Festial* 115 Welcomyng hym wyth songe into þe chirch, as þay welcomet hym syngyng into þe cyte of Ierusalem. **1594** SHAKS. *Rich. III*, IV. iv. 439 And there they hull, expecting but the aide Of Buckingham, to welcome them ashore. *Ibid.* v. iii. 260 Your wiues shall welcome home the Conquerors. **1610** HOLLAND *Camden's Brit.* 71 Probus was welcommed into Britaine. **1629** MILTON *Christ's Nativ.* 18 Hast thou no..solemn strein, To welcom him to this his new abode..? **1797** JANE AUSTEN *Sense & Sens.* vi, They were interrupted..by the entrance of their landlord, who called to welcome them to Barton. **1894** LADY M. VERNEY *Verney Mem.* III. 293 No one welcomed him back with the womanly love which mother and sister would have lavished upon him.

c. *fig.* Also with *in*.

1593 SHAKS. *Rich. II*, II. ii. 7 Yet I know no cause Why I should welcome such a guest as greefe. **1599** SHAKS. etc. *Pass. Pilgr.* 199 For she [the lark] doth welcome daylight with her ditte. **1785** COWPER *Task* IV. 41 So let us welcome peaceful ev'ning in.

d. Const. *to* (an entertainment).

1634 SIR T. HERBERT *Trav.* 51 Our Ambassadour, the Gentlemen his followers and Sea-captaines were welcommed to a very neat and curious Banquet.

2. To greet or receive *with* (or *by*) something (esp. of an unpleasant nature).

1590 SHAKS. *Com. Err.* IV. iv. 38, I am..driuen out of doores with it [*sc.* a beating] when I goe from home, welcom'd home with it when I returne. **1611** BIBLE *Transl. Pref.* ¶1 Zeale to promote the common good..is welcommed with suspicion in stead of loue, and with emulation in stead of thankes. **1639** DU VERGER tr. *Camus' Admir. Events* 2 Venon..at his returne found himselfe welcomed with two disasters. **1653** J. TAYLOR (Water P.) *Certain Trav.* 13 Good Mrs. Martin who welcom'd me with good whit wine. **1791** MRS. RADCLIFFE *Rom. Forest* i, If you return within an hour you will be welcomed by a brace of bullets.

3. a. To greet heartily or joyfully (the return of a person, etc.).

1697 DRYDEN *Virg. Georg.* II. 761 His little Children climbing for a Kiss, Welcome their Father's late Return at Night. **1815** SHELLEY *Alastor* 283 Thy sweet mate will..welcome thy return with eyes Bright in the lustre of their own fond joy. **1870** BRYANT *Iliad* v. 191 Since he no more should welcome their return From war.

b. To greet with pleasure the coming or occurring of (an event, etc).

1856 FROUDE *Hist. Eng.* I. ii. 131 He..would have welcomed an escape from the dilemma perhaps as warmly as Henry would have welcomed it himself. **1874** GREEN *Short Hist.* ii. §3. 68 The religious movement..was welcomed with an almost passionate fanaticism. **1884** GILMOUR *Mongols* xvii. 207 Such..difficulties..are welcomed..as subjects of debate.

†**welcome**, *v.*[2] *Obs. rare.* [f. WELCOME *sb.*[1] and *a.*] *intr.* To be welcome.

c **1450** LOVELICH *Grail* xlii. 278, 280 Ful lowde to hem they gonne to Crye, and seide 'welcometh' Al An hye..'Welcometh' quod Iosephes ful Sekerlye.

welcomed ('wɛlkəmd), *ppl. a.* [f. WELCOME *v.*[1] + -ED[1].] Made welcome; gladly received.

1583 MELBANCKE *Philotimus* Cc iij, Philotimus, my wished frend, and welcomde guest, how dost thou? **16..** W. BOSWORTH *Arcadius & Sepha* I. 553 This [wound] being slighted 'gan to fester in, And having got a newly welcom'd skin, Began to fester more. **1826** SHERER *Notes & Refl. Ramble Germany* 45 A man who had been drenched by the very same midnight rain, and..had been dried by the same welcomed sunbeams as myself.

'**welcomeless**, *a.* [f. WELCOME *sb.*[2] + -LESS.] Without a welcome; also, unwelcome.

1838 LYTTON *Alice* X. iii, Amidst blank and welcomeless faces, Maltravers passed into his study. **1848** —— *Harold* v. iii, The treasures of the King are well nigh drained in feeding these hungry and welcomeless visitors.

welcomely ('wɛlkəmlɪ), *adv.* [-LY[2].] In a welcome manner. **a.** With an expression or feeling of welcome; gladly, hospitably.

a **1595** SOUTHWELL *Hundred Medit.* (1873) 510, I shall..find the gates..wide open, and..shall be welcomely received. **1631** GOUGE *God's Arrows* v. §16. 428 Amitie with such Kingdomes will be earnestly desired, and welcomely embraced. **1649** J. TAYLOR (Water P.) *Wand. Wonders West* 9 There I stayd till the next day noone, being well and wellcomely entertained. **1693** W. FREKE *Sel. Ess., Art of War* 259 Such an Army [Militia] You may easily Disband..and, euery Man knowing his home is Welcomely receiued. **1776** in J. Rae *Adam Smith* (1895) 26 [In a letter of 22nd May 1776..the Glasgow Senatus tell the Master and Fellows of Balliol plainly that the Scotch students had never been] 'welcomely received' [at Balliol]. **1822** T. CHALMERS *Mem.* (1850) II. xiv. 359, I have been very kindly and welcomely entertained. **1884** *Westmorland Gaz.* 1 Nov. 5/6 Both were welcomely received by the husband's daughter.

b. In a manner that is welcomed; so as to gratify or please.

1646 SIR T. BROWNE *Pseud. Ep.* III. iv. 112 The same we meet with in Juvenal, who by an handsome and metricall expression more welcomely engrafts it in our junior memories. **1818** LADY MORGAN *Autobiog.* (1859) 100 The interesting guest who so unexpectedly, but so welcomely arrived. **1858** CARLYLE *Fredk. Gt.* x. v. (1873) III. 258 His Portrait (a welcomely good one, still to be found there). **1874** *Daily News* 22 May 5 Upon all the sun shone most welcomely.

†**welcomen**, obs. var. WELCOME *a.* 2.

c **1300** *Harrow. Hell* 150 (Digby MS.) Welcome, louerd, wel þou be,..fful welcomen art þou ous. **1432–50** tr. *Higden* I. 409 If thei wasche theire feete, thei thenke that thei be welle commen.

'**welcomeness.** [-NESS.] The state of being welcome or of being welcomed.

1620 *Swetnam Arraigned* (1880) 61 Oh, Madame, I haue such welcomenesse! For me, what is't? **1660** BOYLE *Seraph. Love* §xxv. (1700) 151 Yet will they [*sc.* our joys] really still continue new..upon the scores of their welcomness and Freshness. **1768** STERNE *Sent. Journ.* (1778) I. 113 (Montriul) The poor little fellow press'd it [the snuff-box] upon them with a nod of welcomeness..*Prenez en—prenez*, said he. **1977** [see *picnic party* s.v. PICNIC *sb.* 3].

welcomer ('wɛlkəmə(r)). [f. WELCOME *v.*[1] + -ER[1].] One who, or something which, welcomes or greets (a person or thing).

13.. *Pol. Rel. & L. Poems* (1903) 252 In prima porta..inuenient tres 'welcomeres' horribiles, videlicet..nakednesse Reminge feblesse. **1594** SHAKS. *Rich. III*, IV. i. 90 Farewell, thou wofull welcommer of glory. **1812** W. TAYLOR in *Monthly Rev.* LXVII. 529 Welcomers of libertinism, but not of impudence. **1829** C. ROSE *Four Years S. Africa* 306 Yes,—you [*sc.* a sea-fowl] are a fitting welcomer to my country. **1850** J. STRUTHERS *Poet. Wks.* Life, p. lxix, The welcome was acceptable, though the welcomer was not by any means promising or prepossessing. **1905** SIR A. LYALL *Marq. Dufferin* I. vii. 266 They were received by a concourse of welcomers and a profusion of banners.

welcoming ('wɛlkəmɪŋ), *vbl. sb.* [f. WELCOME *v.*[1] + -ING[1].] The action of greeting with welcome or of making welcome; a welcome.

1303 R. BRUNNE *Handl. Synne* 2858 Hys doghtyr was þe fyrste þyng þat mette hym and made hym welcomyng. **1390** GOWER *Conf.* II. 255 The king cam with his knichtes alle And maden him glad welcominge. *c* **1400** *Laud Troy Bk.* 14460 Thei..grete the kyng with wordes curteis; And he..thanked sone her wel-comyng. *c* **1440** *Generydes* 392 He came anon withoute taryeng, And curtesly gaue them ther welcomyng. **1525** BERNERS *Froiss.* II. clx. 177 And to his welcomyng to Dignon, many ladyes and damosels were come thyder to se hym. **1600** J. PORY tr. *Leo's Africa* VIII. 325 For the welcoming of whom [*sc.* all strangers] they bring up great store of doues, of chickens, and of such like commodities. **1670** MILTON *Hist. Eng.* Wks. 1851 V. 24 Elidure..runns to him with open Arms; and after many dear and sincere welcomings, convaies him to the Citty Alclud. **1798** COLERIDGE *Anc. Mar.* VI. xii, But soon there breathed a wind on me... It mingled strangely with my fears, Yet it felt like a welcoming. **1818** KEATS *Endym.* I. 377 Where every zephyr-sigh pouts, and endows Her lips with music for the welcoming. **1836** DICKENS *Sk. Boz, Tuggs's at Ramsgate*, Nothing was to be heard but talking, laughing, welcoming, and merriment. **1883** *Athenæum* 17 Nov. 627/1 The spontaneous welcoming of a given book by an audience that is in size and influence a public.

welcoming ('wɛlkəmɪŋ), *ppl. a.* [-ING[2].] That welcomes or gives a welcome.

1656 in *Nicholas Papers* (Camden) III. 285 Their famous new come preacher, makinge the wellcomming speech in the name of the rest. **1661** BOYLE *Style of Script.* (1675) 152 With how much more reason may God expect a welcoming entertainment for the least adorned parts of a Book, of which [etc.]. **1809** PINKNEY *Trav. France* 77 The returning husband, and the welcoming wife. **1821** CLARE *Vill. Minstr.* I. 161 Then as the glad sun breaks the clouds in a shower Tears melt in a welcoming smile. **1876** MISS BROUGHTON *Joan* I. x, Wolferstan stepping to meet her, with his low laugh and his welcoming eyes.

fig. **1863** KINGLAKE *Crimea* (1877) III. iv. 350 The happy-looking cottages, with their..welcoming porches.

Hence '**welcomingly** *adv.*

1884 *Century Mag.* Nov. 58/2 She..listened welcomingly to Juan's glad promises of the joy that was to be.

weld (wɛld), *sb.*[1] Forms: α. 4–6 **welde,** 6– **weld** (8 **wield**). β. 5–6 **wolde, (olde),** 5– **wold** (5 **oold**), 7–8 **would,** 8 **woold,** 8–9 **woald.** γ. *Sc.* 5– **wald.** [OE. **wealde*, Anglian **walde* = MLG. *walde* (*wolde*), *waude* (still in LG.), MDu. *woude*, *wouwe* (Du. *wouw*; hence G. *wau*, †*waube*, Sw. and Da. *vau*), possibly a derivative of *wald*, wood, forest. The Germanic word is the source of Sp. *gualda*, Pg. *gualde*, F. *gaude*.

The later forms of the word show the same development of the vowel as the West Saxon *weald* WEALD and Anglian *wald* WOLD.]

1. The plant *Reseda Luteola*, which yields a yellow dye. Also, the dye obtained from this plant.

α. *c* **1374** CHAUCER *Former Age* 17 No Madyr, welde, or wod no litestere Ne knewh. *c* **1440** *Promp. Parv.* 520/2 Welde, or wolde, herbe..*sandix, attriplex.* **1597** GERARDE *Herbal* II. cxxviii. 398 *Luteola*..in English Welde and Diers weede. *a* **1661** FULLER *Worthies, Kent* II. 57 Weld or Wold:—Know, Reader, that I borrow my Orthographie hereof (if it be so) from the Dyers themselves. **1676** *Phil. Trans.* XI. 795 Diarsweed, Weld or Would. **1707** [J. JOHNSON] *Clergyman's Vade Mecum* 217 Woad, Saffron, Wield, are all small Tythes. **1763** W. LEWIS *Chem. Philos.-Techn.* 412 The cloth..is then passed through a copper of weld or woold, prepared as for dying yellow, which is supposed to soften the cloth. **1789** *Trans. Soc. Arts* I. 207 A plat of weld I had planted the autumn before. **1815** J. SMITH *Panorama Sci. & Art* II. 539 Weld readily imparts its colour to water; it is used in the proportion of from three to six pounds for every pound of cloth. **1839** URE *Dict. Arts* 126 The boil of weld, by which the dye of black cloth is frequently finished. **1872** OLIVER *Elem. Bot.* II. 141 Dyer's Mignonette or Weld (R. Luteola) is cultivated for dyeing yellow.

β. **14..** in *Sax. Leechd.* III. 349/1 Wolde. *c* **1440** *Promp. Parv.* 532/1 Wold, herbe, or woode..*sandix.* **1496** *Bk. St. Albans, Fysshynge* h ij, Put therein two handfull of ooldys or of wyxen... Lete woode your heer in an woodsfatte a lyght plunket colour. And thenne sethe hym in olde or wyxin. **1530** PALSGR. 290/1 Wolde herbe. **1582** HAKLUYT *Voy.* (1599) II. I. 163 Yellowes and greenes are colours of small prices in this realme, by reason that Olde and Green-weed wherewith they be died be naturall here. *a* **1661, 1676** Wold, would [see α]. **1707** MORTIMER *Husb.* (1721) I. 165 Weld or Would is a rich Dyers Commodity. **1763** Woold [see α]. **1791** HAMILTON tr. *Berthollet's Dyeing* II. 259 Weld or woald is a plant yielding a yellow colour. **1855** SINGLETON *Virgil* I. 29 The ram shall..change his fleece, With now the sweetly-blushing purple dye, With now the saffron wold.

γ. **1498** HALYBURTON *Ledger* (1867) 223 Item sald hym a town of wald for 7 li. 15 s. **15..** *Aberd. Reg.* (MS.) XXIV, Thre half pokis of wald. **1672** *Sc. Acts Chas. II* (1814) VIII. 63/2 Noe vther incorporation..to buy or sell.. Wald and vther materialls for dying. **1743** R. MAXWELL *Sel. Trans. Agric.* 368 For every Pound of Yarn allow three fourths of a Pound good English Wald. **1808** JAMIESON.

†**b.** Applied to other species of *Reseda*. *Obs.*

1597 GERARDE *Herbal* II. cxxviii. 396 Of Sesamoides, or bastard Weld or Woade, out of Diosc... 3 *Sesamoides maius Scaligeri.* Barren Welde. 4 *Sesamoides paruum Mathioli.* Bucks horne Welde.

2. *attrib.* and *Comb.*, as ***weld plant, seed; weld-dyeing, liquor, vat, yellow***; **weldworts,** Lindley's name for the N.O. *Resedaceæ*.

1876 W. MORRIS in Mackail *Life* (1899) I. 325, I have found out and practised the art of *weld-dyeing. **1763** W. LEWIS *Chem. Philos.-Techn.* 413 The passing through *weld liquor, after scowering with soap, is entirely unnecessary. **1805** R. W. DICKSON *Pract. Agric.* II. 777 Sheep..will not touch the *weld plants. **1765** *Museum Rust.* IV. 147 The French sow their *weld-seed in July. **1899** MACKAIL *W. Morris* I. 317 Madder or *weld vats. **1845** LINDLEY *School Bot.* (new ed.) 72 Resedaceæ—*Weldworts. **1899** in Mackail *W. Morris* I. 312 Madder red, *wald yellow.

weld (wɛld), *sb.*[2] [f. WELD *v.*]

1. A joining or joint made by welding.

1831 J. HOLLAND *Manuf. Metal* I. 96 Should the bars of iron not be..long enough, they are to be welded, and the welds separated. **1862** *Fraser's Mag.* Nov. 634 Tires for locomotive engines are also exhibited, made without a weld. **1880** *Encycl. Brit.* XI. 279/2 Each barrel has a weld running down its whole length. **1892** *Profess. Papers Corps R. Engineers* 10 It was desirable, with such a weld, that the two surfaces should not be at an angle and this form of weld was called a 'butt' weld.

2. The act, process, or result of welding; the state or fact of being welded.

1862 *Times* 12 Aug. 9/4 Where soundness of weld might have been expected,..thin layers of interposed 'cinder' have ..prevented perfect union between contiguous laminæ of iron. **1884** LOCK *Workshop Rec.* Ser. III. 68/1 Copper phosphide would be formed, which would..effectually prevent a weld. **1884** W. H. GREENWOOD *Steel & Iron* i. 7 Under these conditions but moderate pressure is required to ensure a perfect weld.

3. Comb.: **weld decay**, (increased susceptibility to) corrosion in chromium-nickel stainless steel that has been kept at 600° to 900°C for a time (as in welding), owing to the precipitation of chromium carbide and the consequent lowering of the chromium content; **weld-iron**, wrought iron; **weld pool**, the pool of molten metal formed about a joint in welding; **weld-steel**, puddled steel.

1881 RAYMOND *Mining Gloss.*, Weld-iron. Weld-steel. **1884** LOCK *Workshop Rec.* Ser. III. 266/1 Steel which will harden from any cause..is termed weld-steel. **1932** E. GREGORY *Metallurgy* vii. 275 The heating of alloy steels of the 18 per cent chromium, 8 per cent nickel type in the range 650°–900°C. greatly decreases their corrosion resistance... This phenomenon is known as weld-decay. **1964** W. STEEDS *Engin. Materials, Machine Tools & Processes* (ed. 4) vii. 169 With coated electrodes too high a current..makes control of the weld pool difficult. **1973** A. PARRISH *Mech. Engineer's Ref. Bk.* v. 74 This local depletion of chromium causes lack of passivity in acid corrodants with consequent attack along grain boundaries (weld decay). **1975** BRAM & DOWNS *Manuf. Technol.* ii. 55 The arc and the weld pool are protected from atmospheric contamination.

weld (wɛld), *v.* [Alteration of WELL *v.*, prob. under the influence of the pa. pple.]

1. *intr.* To undergo junction by welding; to admit of being welded. Also *fig.*

1599 JAS. I *Basil. Doron* III. 153 Mixinge through..dailie conuersation, the men of euery kingdome with an other, as may with time make them to growe and weld [*orig. MS.* well] all in one. **1677** MOXON *Mech. Exerc.* i. 10 They say it makes the Iron weld, or incorporate the better. **1724** RAMSAY *Song, Widow* 21 Strike iron while 'tis het, if ye'd have it to wald. **1884** W. H. GREENWOOD *Steel & Iron* x. 204 When heated to whiteness..the particles cohere or weld together perfectly.

2. a. *trans.* To soften by heat and join together (pieces of metal, esp. iron, or iron and steel) in a solid mass, by hammering or by pressure; to forge (an article) by this method.

1677 MOXON *Mech. Exerc.* i. 9 And so weld, or work in the doubling into one another, and make it become one entire lump. **1680** ALSOP *Mischief Imposit.* vii. 51 A Cutler's boy.. was making a knife, and unluckily the steel fell off when he had welded it. **1823** P. NICHOLSON *Pract. Build.* 341 They are usually made of iron and steel welded together. **1832** BABBAGE *Econ. Manuf.* xxx. (ed. 3) 299 In this difficulty, the contractors resorted to a mode of welding the gun-barrel. **1848** LYTTON *Harold* I. i, I heard the smith welding arms on the anvil. **1880** *Encycl. Brit.* XI. 284 The bayonet consists of a steel blade welded to a wrought-iron socket.

b. *fig.* and *transf.* To unite intimately or inseparably; to join closely together.

(*a*) **1839** BAILEY *Festus* 243 Let us love, and die, And weld our souls together, night! **1860** GEO. ELIOT *Mill on Fl.* II. vi, If boys and men are to be welded together in the glow of transient feeling, they must be made of metal that will mix. **1890** 'R. BOLDREWOOD' *Col. Reformer* xi, Habits, inexorably welded into the being of the man.

(*b*) **1802** J. PLAYFAIR *Illustr. Huttonian Theory* 283 The *line* of separation..has, on the whole, been marked out with great precision; and, though the stones have been firmly united, or, as one may say, welded one upon another, yet, when a fresh fracture was obtained, the stratified and unstratified parts have rarely failed to be distinguished. **1859** MURCHISON *Siluria* xi. (ed. 3) 301 The lower part being welded on to the Upper Silurian by thin fissile strata. **1860** TYNDALL *Glac.* I. xx. 139 All the glaciers..are welded together to a common trunk. **1899** *Allbutt's Syst. Med.* VIII. 690 A hypertrophic condition of the horny layers of the epidermis—the cells becoming condensed or 'welded' together.

weld, obs. f. WEALD; obs. f. (and *pa. pple.*) of WIELD; var. WOLD *sb.*

weldability (wɛldəˈbɪlɪtɪ). [f. WELDABLE + -ITY.] The quality or property of being weldable.

1869 H. S. OSBORN *Metallurgy Iron & Steel* iii. 85 There is a degree of weldability in platinum which causes that metal to be classified with iron as a weldable metal. **1884** W. H. GREENWOOD *Steel & Iron* i. 8 The above-mentioned elements harden malleable iron, and probably affect its weldability. **1884** LOCK *Workshop Rec.* Ser. III. 300/2 Its weldability depends upon the viscosity it [*sc.* glass] assumes at a bright-red heat.

weldable (ˈwɛldəb(ə)l), *a.* [f. WELD *v.* + -ABLE.] **a.** Capable of being welded.

1855 D. LARDNER *Hand-bk. Nat. Philos.: Hydrostatics* III. v. 304 Weldable metals.—The metals capable of being welded soften before they are fused. **1864** *Reader* 9 Apr. 449/1 We have the various kinds of steel, which are highly elastic, malleable, ductile, forgeable, weldable. **1881** *Metal World* No. 24. 372 Pure malleable and weldable nickel. **1889** *Nature* 19 Sept. 510/2 Many metals not hitherto considered weldable, such as tool steel, copper, and aluminium are readily welded.

b. *transf.* Of plastic substances: Capable of being united in a solid mass.

1881 *Knowledge* 25 Nov. 67/1 Wax, pitch, resin, and all other solids that fuse, gradually cohere, are weldable..when near their fusing point. **1884** LOCK *Workshop Rec.* Ser. III. 300/2 Outside of the metals there is a multitude of weldable substances. Glass is a typical example of these.

weldar, obs. form of WIELDER.

weldbore, var. WILDBORE.

welde, obs. form of WIELD *sb.* and *v.*

welded (ˈwɛldɪd), *ppl. a.* [f. WELD *v.* + -ED[1].]

1. a. United by welding.

1869 *Scientific Opinion* 10 Feb. 270/1 The wire had been drawn from welded palladium. **1905** *Westm. Gaz.* 27 June 2/1 The immensely expensive welded-iron gun to which Sir W. Armstrong was wedded.

b. *transf.* and *fig.*

1837 SIR F. PALGRAVE *Merch. & Friar* (1844) Ded. 4 The welded mass of haut ton, or low ton. **1862** LYTTON *Str. Story* xxiii, The welded strength of its sinews was best shown in the lightness and grace of its movements. **1878** BROWNING *Poets Croisic* lxxi, Welded lines with clinch Of ending word and word. **1898** *Allbutt's Syst. Med.* V. 1008 The firm, thick, fibrous septum of the welded valve-structures.

2. *welded joint*, = *welted joint*: see WELT *v.*

1882 W. J. CHRISTY *Joints* 197 This variety [of overlapping joint] thus compactly rolled together is otherwise termed a welded joint.

3. *Geol.* **a.** Applied to pyroclastic rock formed by the union of small, heat-softened particles.

[**1802**: see WELD *v.* 2 b (*b*). **1899** J. P. IDDINGS in A. Hague et al. *Geol. Yellowstone Nat. Park* II. x. 406 The mass is compact of glass, but it consists of irregularly shaped streaks and patches of different color. These twist and curve about one another and appear like a perfectly welded mass of strips or ribbons and irregular fragments of variously colored glass.] **1909** —— *Igneous Rocks* I. i. viii. 333 These examples of welded pumice are from rhyolitic lavas in the Yellowstone National Park. **1935** *Trans. Amer. Geophysical Union* 309 Although commonly and perhaps generally associated with deposits of light-colored volcanic ash of rhyolitic composition, the welded tuff is not confined to this association but occurs also on older rocks. **1962, 1970** [see IGNIMBRITE]. **1977** A. HALLAM *Planet Earth* 74/1 There may also be intercalations of submarine pillow lavas or welded tuffs indicative of volcanic islands.

b. Applied to an intimate, close-fitting contact between two bodies of rock that have not been heat-softened or tectonically disrupted.

1939 *Q. Jrnl. Geol. Soc.* XCV. 354 The contact is, as usual, welded, and the base of the overlying sediments consists of current-bedded, brown-weathering, fine sandstone. **1948** R. R. SHROCK *Sequence in Layered Rocks* ii. 55 There are examples..where an entire geological system is represented by the hiatus along the welded contact. **1976** *Jrnl. Geol. Soc.* CXXXII. 125 The contact of the slump sheets with the overlying mega-beds is welded, i.e. depositional fit is present.

†**wel-dede.** *Obs.* Forms: 1 wel-dǣd, 2–4 weldede (wel-dede, wel dede). [OE. *weldǣd* = MDu. *weldaet* (Du. *weldaad*; LG. *woldâd*, WFris. *woldied*), OHG. *wolatât* (MHG. *woltât*, G. *wohltat*), Goth. *wailadēds*: see WELL *adv.* and DEED *sb.*] A good deed; a benefit.

a **1000** *Phœnix* 543 [Hie] stigað to wuldre wlitiȝe ȝewyrtad mid hyra wel-dædum. *c* **1000** ÆLFRIC *Hom.* II. 346 Do well on eallum ðinum life, and we siððan æfter ðinum wel-dædum bliðne ðe eft ȝenimað to us. *c* **1175** *Lamb. Hom.* 131 Vre lauerd seinte paul..muneged..to godes worde and to weldede. *c* **1205** LAY. 3160 Worðschepe haue þu þire wel-deda. **1362** LANGL. *P. Pl.* A. III. 62 For-þi I lere ȝou, lordynges, such writynge ȝe leue, To writen in Wyndouwes of ȝoure wel dedes.

weldende, weldent, var. ff. WALDEND *Obs.*

welder (ˈwɛldə(r)). [f. WELD *v.* + -ER[1].]

1. One who welds; spec., a smith employed exclusively in welding.

1828–32 WEBSTER. **1846** GREENER *Sci. Gunnery* 146 The spirals being thus formed, the welders commence their day's work. **1854** *B'ham P.O. Directory* 683/2 Of the gun trade are the following:..gun barrel borers, filers, welders, ribbers. **1918** *Chamb. Jrnl.* Aug. 532/2 This was done by engaging every available machinery welder and patcher.

2. A welding-machine.

1896 *Cyclist* 8 Jan. 25 A 40 kilowatt welder..occupies the following floor space.

welder, obs. form of WIELDER.

weldinde, var. f. WALDEND *Obs.*

welding (ˈwɛldɪŋ), *vbl. sb.*[1] [f. WELD *v.* + -ING[1].]

1. a. The action of the verb WELD; the process of joining with a weld.

1603 [see 2]. **1691** T. H[ALE] *Acc. New Invent.* 14 Their Pintells..never having had their due welding. *Ibid.* 23 To give it its due welding or working. **1815** J. SMITH *Panorama Sci. & Art* I. 11 The fire for welding should be free from sulphur. **1854** J. SCOFFERN in *Orr's Circ. Sci., Elem. Chem.* 438 The kaligenous metals, potassium and sodium,..readily admit of welding. **1881** J. EVANS *Anc. Bronze Implem.* 293 The term 'welding' is, however, inappropriate to a metal of the character of bronze.

b. Capacity for uniting under the operation of heat and pressure.

1825 J. NICHOLSON *Oper. Mech.* 784 *Welding.* The property of conjunction possessed by some metals at high temperatures. **1826** HENRY *Elem. Chem.* I. 556 The property of welding, which belongs to platinum and iron at a high degree of heat only, is possessed by this substance [sodium] at common temperatures. **1868** ROSCOE *Elem. Chem.* 236 When hot, it [wrought iron] possesses the peculiar property of 'welding'.

c. = *welding heat* (see 3).

1842 *Rep. Brit. Assoc.* 106 A piece of the same iron heated to welding, and left to cool, broke..in one blow.

2. *transf.* and *fig.* The action of uniting, or the fact of being united, closely or indissolubly.

1603 JAS. I *Basil. Doron* III. 149 The vniting and welding of them heerafter in one, by all sort of friendship, commerce, and alliance. **1857** I. TAYLOR *World of Mind* 669 These are solderings of the social system..but Love is a welding. **1874** SYMONDS *Sk. Italy & Greece* (1898) I. xi. 212 Nor was it in their welding of the bricks alone that these craftsmen showed their science. **1905** 'G. THORNE' *Lost Cause* xii, The harmonic welding of the order and traditions of our Lord's Own time with the full vivid life of the twentieth century.

3. *attrib.* and *Comb.*, as ***welding-machine, process, state, swage***; **welding heat**, the degree of heat to which iron is brought for welding; **welding point**, degree of heat requisite for welding; also *fig.*; **welding powder**, a flux used in welding; **welding torch**, a blow-pipe used in welding.

1710 J. HARRIS *Lex. Techn.* II, **Welding-Heat*, is a Degree of Heat which Smiths give their Iron in the Forge, when there is occasion to double up the Iron, and to Weld..the Doublings. **1776** *Phil. Trans.* LXVI. 510, I heated a piece of iron..to a white heat, or what the smiths call a welding heat. **1884** LOCK *Workshop Rec.* Ser. III. 301/2 Cast-steel requires a low welding-heat. **1874** KNIGHT *Dict. Mech.*, **Welding-machine*, one for uniting the edges of plates previously bent, [etc.]. **1868** JOYNSON *Metals* 69 Each quality of iron has a different *welding point. **1886** FROUDE *Oceana* i. 16 The feeling..may be a warm one, but not warm enough to heat us..to the welding point. **1873** SPON *Workshop Rec.* Ser. I. 361/1 The steel to be welded..is then dipped into the *welding powder, and again placed in the fire. **1907** E. WILSON & LYDALL *Electr. Traction* I. 95 The electric *welding process..welds the rails together. **1846** GREENER *Sci. Gunnery* 108 The parts first fused are gathered on the end of a similarly fabricated rod, in a *welding state. **1874** KNIGHT *Dict. Mech.*, **Welding-swage*, a block or fulling-tool for assisting the closure of a welded joint. **1921** *Engineering Index 1920* 417/2 A new carriage for *welding torches. **1975** BRAM & DOWNS *Manuf. Technol.* ii. 42 The welding torch used with these systems must be designed to aspirate the acetylene.

ˈ**welding,** *vbl. sb.*[2] [f. WELD *sb.*[1]] The process of dyeing with weld.

1815 J. SMITH *Panorama Sci. & Art* II. 550 The cloth is prepared as for welding, and dyed yellow.

Weldish, variant of WEALDISH *a. Obs.* [To this may belong the following:—

1336–7 *Acc. Exch. K.R.* 19/31 m. 6 In .C. Weldisbord' emptis ad eandem [bargiam]. **1419** *Will of Richard Hallum* (Somerset Ho.), Cum j pare linth[eaminum] de Weldysshclothe.]

weldless (ˈwɛldlɪs), *a.* [f. WELD *sb.*[2] + -LESS.] Made without a weld.

1865 *Athenæum* 30 Sept. 442/1 Weldless tyres. **1869** F. KOHN *Iron & Steel Manuf.* 182 Weldless Tubes. **1894** *Daily News* 14 June 6/4 The Triumph Weldless chain, an American invention.

weldment (ˈwɛldmənt). [f. WELD *v.* + -MENT.] A unit consisting of pieces welded together.

1945 in WEBSTER Add. **1950** *Engineering* 10 Feb. 149/1 In fabricated 'weldments'..it might not be necessary to stress-relieve. **1962** *B.S.I. News* Nov. 21/1 Fabricators may be taking a grave risk when they accept orders for weldments.. furnished to inadequate specifications. **1979** *Railway Age* 31 Dec. 50/2 New features include..use of alloy steel castings in place of weldments.

Weldmesh (ˈwɛldmɛʃ). Also **weldmesh.** [f. WELD *sb.*[2] or *v.* + MESH *sb.*] The proprietary name of wire mesh formed by welding together two series of parallel wires crossing at right angles. Freq. *attrib.*

1935 *Trade Marks Jrnl.* 24 Apr. 516/1 *Weldmesh*... screens, partitions, guards, frames, sieves and seatings, all made of welded steel wire. The British Reinforced Concrete Engineering Co. Limited,..Stafford; manufacturers and merchants. **1957** *Archit. Rev.* CXXI. 116 The balcony rail is of weld-mesh panels, with teak handrail. **1971** *Country Life* 11 Nov. 1255/1 It [*sc.* a cage] is made of weldmesh, used for tiger cages. **1978** *Cornish Guardian* 27 Apr. 10/3 (Advt.), 8 ft weldmesh pig lamps. **1984** *Times* 28 July 2/3 The committee recommended that the chain-link fence should be supplemented by weldmesh fencing which is more difficult to breach.

weldsomly: see WIL(D)SOMLY *adv.*

wele, obs. f. VEAL, WEAL *sb.*[1], WEEL, WELL *sb.*[1] and *adv.*, WHEEL.

†**wele,** *v. Obs.* [ad. ON. *velja*: cf. WALE *v.*[1]] *trans.* To choose, pick *out.*

c **1330** R. BRUNNE *Chron. Wace* (Rolls) 7340 Whan..Oure Prynces perceyue þer ar so fele, þe ȝonge dur þey nought out wele, Bot þulke of twenty wynter elde Or more. **13..** *Ibid.* (Petyt MS.) 2731 Sex hundred of hyse weled [*Lambeth MS.* colede] he out.

wele, we'le, contr. ff. *we will.*

1592 *Arden of Feversham* IV. iii. 74 Lyke louing frends, wele meete him on the way. **1677** C. DAVENANT *Circe* V. ix. 57 Then we'le retire.

weled, obs. pa. t. of WIELD *v.*

weleful, var. WEALFUL *Obs.*, WILFUL.

welew, obs. f. WILLOW.

welewe(n, var. ff. WALLOW *v.*[2]

weleygh(e, obs. ff. WILLOW.

welfare ('wɛlfɛə(r)), *sb.* Forms: α. 4– **welfare**, (4 **wilfare**), 4–8 **wellfare** (5 **wellefare**); 5 **welfar**, **whelfar**; 7 **welfaire**, **wellfair**. β. 4–5 **welefar(e**, (4 **weylfare**, 6 **-far**), 5 **weelfare**, *Sc.* **weillfair**, **weilfar(e**, **weill-**, **weyllfar**, **-fayr**, 5–6 *Sc.* **weil-**, **welefair**, (6 **veilfair**, **-fayr(e**, **-fare**). [f. the verbal phrase *wel fare* (see FARE *v.*[1] 7), the verb being replaced by the noun (FARE *sb.*[1]). Cf. ON. *velferð* (Sw. *välfärd*, Da. *velfærd*) welfare, *velfǫr* parting, leave-taking.]

1. a. The state or condition of doing or being well; good fortune, happiness, or well-being (of a person, community, or thing); thriving or successful progress in life, prosperity.

α. **1303** R. Brunne *Handl. Synne* 3928 Ȝyf þou euer haddyst sorow oþer kare Of þy neghëburs welfare. *c* **1369** Chaucer *Dethe Blaunche* (Fairf.) 582 My lyfe, my lustes, be me loothe, For al welfare and I be wroothe. **1390** Gower *Conf.* II. 116 So overcast is my welfare, That I am schapen al to strif. **1426** Lydg. *De Guil. Pilgr.* 9235 Thow art boundë to deuyse Hys goostly [h]elthë & wel-ffare. ? **1466** *Stonor Papers* (Camden) I. 77 Desyryng to here of yower wellefare and prosperyte of body and sawle. **1540** Palsgr. *Acolastus* I. i. D j b, I..had myne eye contynually vpon his welfare, I ouerpassed nothynge that myght profyt him. **1559** Aylmer *Harborowe* D 4 b, Whereupon dependeth either the welfare or ilfare of the whole realm. **1574** *Mirr. Mag.*, *Elstride* xxvii, [Thou] Didst liue a life deuoyde of all welfare. **1623** J. Taylor (Water P.) *Discov. by Sea* C 3 b, Your laudable endeuours for your welfare and commodity. **1684** J. S. *Profit & Pleas. United* 139 Above all let the King or Master Bee be Long, Shining, and Chearfull,..for upon his Success depends the wellfair of the whole Swarm. **1718** *Free-thinker* No. 65. 71 It was one continued Series of Actions, for the Welfare of the People. **1770** Goldsm. *Des. Vill.* 186 Their welfare pleas'd him, and their cares distress'd. **1838** Lytton *Alice* I. iii, Her first wish in life is for your happiness and welfare. **1847** Tennyson *Princess* III. 264 They know not, cannot guess How much their welfare is a passion to us. **1892** *Weekly Reporter* 17 Dec. 97/1 The welfare of the child—religious, moral, and social, as well as physical and pecuniary—is the paramount consideration for the court.

β. **1303** R. Brunne *Handl. Synne* 1715 Ȝyf þou fordost þe weylfare Betwyx þo þat weddyde are. **1357** *Lay Folks Catech.* 434 That our hert be noght to hegh for no welefare, Ne ouer mikel undir for nane yvel fare. *c* **1400** *Ywaine & Gaw.* 1354 Ful glad was sir Gawayne, Of the welefar of Sir Ywayne. *c* **1440** Lydg. *Hors, Shepe & G.* 495 Where pees restith, ther is al weelfare. *c* **1470** Henry *Wallace* v. 524 Spek I will off Wallace glaid weillfar. **1521** G. Douglas in Ellis *Orig. Lett.* Ser. III. I. 293 Concernyng ye weylfar and surte of his derrest nevo the Kyng. **1570** *Satir. Poems Reform.* xiii. 224 Pray..[that] Hir grace lang space may in gude weilfair stand. **1785** Burns *Cotter's Sat. Nt.* v, Brothers and sisters meet, And each for other's weelfare kindly spiers.

†**b.** As the name of a ship. *Obs.*

1310 *Rot. Scotiæ* 90/1 Will's le Fisshere de Gravesiende mag'r navis que vocatur la Welefare de Westm'.

†**2.** A source of well-being or happiness; *pl.* the good things of life. *Obs.*

c **1369** Chaucer *Dethe Blaunche* 1040 For certes she was.. My worldes welfare and my goddesse. *c* **1374** —— *Troylus* IV. 228 Lyth Troylus byraft of eche welfare I-bounde in þe blake bark of care. *c* **1440** *Alphabet of Tales* 450 Som tyme þer was a knyght þat lefte all his possessions & his wurshuppis and his welefaris, and made hym a monk.

†**3. a.** Good cheer, good living or entertainment.

c **1375** *Sc. Leg. Saints* xxix. (*Placidas*) 602, & ȝet þane til ane Inis haf þaim he can, & gert mak þaim welfare of al thing þat was necessare. **1377** Langl. *P. Pl.* B. XIX. 350 To wasten, on welfare and on wykked kepynge, Al þe worlde in a while þorw owre witte. *c* **1440** *Jacob's Well* 286 þe iiij. nyȝt, þei weryn herberwyd at an-oþer good mannys hows, & haddyn gret wel-fare. *a* **1470** H. Parker *Dives & Pauper* (W. de W. 1496) IV. ii. 162/1 Whan that yonge folke wexe rebelle ayenst fader & moder & gyue them to suche ryot & welfare & ydlenesse. **1528** Roy *Rede me* (Arb.) 45 Both in welfare and wede, With oute doute they farre excede The nobles of the region. **1577** W. Harrison *Descr. Scot.* i. 2/1 in *Holinshed*, Those that are giuen much vnto wine and such welfare.

†**b.** Abundance (*of* meat, drink). *Obs.*

c **1380** Wyclif *Wks.* (1880) 61 þei..han lordschipis, rentis, gaie houses & costy, & welfare of mete & drynk. *a* **1395** Hylton *Scala Perf.* I. lxxii. (W. de W. 1494), He that ..delytes in welfare of mete or drynke.

4. a. The maintenance of members of a group or community in a state of (esp. physical and economic) well-being, esp. as provided for and organized by legislation or social effort. See also sense 5.

1918 [see *rest room* s.v. REST *sb.*[1] 14 a]. **1965** A. J. P. Taylor *Eng. Hist. 1914–45* IV. 121 Free treatment of venereal disease was the sole innovation in 'welfare' directly attributable to the first World War. **1968** M. Pyke *Food & Society* v. 66 And a Western community converted to the principles of welfare will supply vitamins and much else without requiring profit. **1977** M. French *Women's Room* (1978) ii. 139 Welfare..was starting to be a big thing. A lot of Puerto Ricans coming up to New York to get a free handout.

b. *ellipt.* (Usu. with capital initial.) A welfare centre or office; (the officials of) a welfare department.

1928 [see PALLY]. **1960** D. Lessing *In Pursuit of English* IV. 135 Once she asked Welfare if Aurora could go to a council nursery. **1972** J. Mann *Mrs. Knox's Profession* vii. 57 That poor mite... The mother didn't ought to leave it like that. .. They ought to get the welfare to that woman. **1984** *Observer* (Colour Suppl.) 18 Mar. 6/2 First I rang the Welfare to make sure they would get me a flat.

c. = *welfare benefit*, sense 5 below. Esp. in phr. ***on* (*the*) *welfare***. orig. *U.S.*

1946 [see SNAG *v.*[2] 4]. **1964** S. M. Miller in I. L. Horowitz *New Sociol.* 295 Women on welfare strongly demonstrated against the cessation of allowances. **1970** *Toronto Daily Star* 24 Sept. 1/1 People receiving welfare in Metro broke all previous records. **1974** K. Millett *Flying* (1975) II. 141 Half the people I know feed on welfare. **1976** F. Zweig *New Acquisitive Society* II. v. 111 If a man with four children on supplementary benefits would only be better off working if he could earn about £75 a week, it would..need a very conscientious man, keen on his work, to resist the temptation to stay on welfare.

5. *Comb.* In recent use with sense of 'relating to or concerned with the welfare of' (workers, children, etc.) as ***welfare centre***, ***clinic***, ***committee***, ***department***, ***office***, ***officer***, ***policy***, ***service***, ***work***; also, provided by the State for those in need, as ***welfare benefit***, ***cheque***, ***food***, ***milk***; subsisting on benefits provided by the State, as ***welfare family***, ***mother***; **welfare capitalism**, a capitalist system seeking to combine a desire for profits with concern for the welfare of its employees; **welfare fund**, a fund or funds from which payments are made in time of sickness, etc.; **welfare hotel** *U.S.*, a hotel in which people on welfare are housed until more permanent quarters can be found for them; **welfare manager**, **worker**, a person engaged in looking after the welfare of people working in factories, mercantile establishments, etc.; **welfare roll** *N. Amer.*, a list of those entitled to welfare benefits from the State.

1977 M. Edelman *Political Lang.* vii. 125 Through disorder the poor have increased welfare benefits in the United States. **1960** *New Left Rev.* Sept.–Oct. 10/2 The very real achievements of 'welfare capitalism'. **1978** P. Bailey *Leisure & Class in Victorian Eng.* ii. 43 Robert Owen's New Lanark mills had included an annexe comprising a school, museum, music hall and ballroom.. and there were several other examples of this kind of welfare capitalism. **1917** *New Witness* 28 June 202/1 It is continually stated that Maternity Clinics and Infant Welfare Centres have met with the greatest success in France. **1941** J. S. Huxley *On Living in Revolution* (1944) 21 Communal feeding centres, crèches or welfare centres. **1947** *Sun* (Baltimore) 6 May 22/8 The cashing of four welfare checks sent to one of her male inmates after his death. **1976** *Billings* (Montana) *Gaz.* 17 June 1-D/2 When he got his Social Security and welfare checks. **1937** 'G. Orwell' *Road to Wigan Pier* v. 93 The baby was getting its weekly packets of milk from the Welfare Clinic. **1952** *Oxf. Jun. Encycl.* X. 282/1 The welfare committees also provide welfare services for the blind, deaf, dumb and crippled. **1922** S. Lewis *Babbitt* ii. 17, I wonder if I could get one of the department-stores to let me put in a welfare-department. **1977** M. Edelman *Political Lang.* v. 79 A welfare department or education department bears a name that is even less adequate in defining the priorities to which it must respond. **1977** *New Yorker* 27 June 88/3 The Spencers were far from being a welfare family; the house cost forty thousand dollars, which they could afford. **1948** *Ann. Reg. 1947* 487 There were..subsidies on animal feedingstuffs, welfare foods, milk in schools. **1958** Welfare food [see *family allowance* s.v. FAMILY *sb.* 11]. **1947** *Ann. Reg. 1946* 205 Mr Lewis [*sc.* a trade-union leader]..refused even to discuss his demands until he had been granted a 'welfare fund' financed by a royalty on coal. **1978** S. Sheldon *Bloodline* xxxix. 348 They were listed if they had paid taxes or drawn unemployment insurance or welfare funds. **1971** *Times* 8 Jan. 5/1 The scandal of the 'welfare hotels' [in New York] where the city places homeless families has been simmering for many weeks. **1977** *N.Y. Rev. Bks.* 15 Sept. 3/1 One welfare hotel in New York, the scene of repeated mayhem, is next to the local police station. **1906** *Daily Chron.* 6 Sept. 4/5 The camp was managed by the Men's Welfare League. **1904** *Century Mag.* Nov. 61 The welfare manager..who may be either a man or a woman, is a recognized intermediary between the employers and employees of mercantile houses and manufacturing plants. **1958** Welfare milk [see *family allowance* s.v. FAMILY *sb.* 11]. *a* **1974** R. Crossman *Diaries* (1976) II. 560 Increased family allowances with supplementary allowances and children's tax allowances, the price of school meals, the price of welfare milk, [etc.]. **1971** *N.Y. Times* 9 June 43 The needs of..the pressured pensioner, the welfare mother and the harried commuter in our cities involve the whole range of vital urban services. **1978** *Guardian Weekly* 8 Jan. 16/4 Welfare mothers should get off the dole and go to work. **1976** *National Observer* (U.S.) 12 June 4/3 I'd rather see people employed than at the welfare office. **1944** Welfare officer [see SAY *v.*[1] 1 c]. **1963** T. Parker *Unknown Citizen* ii. 58, I have been to see the C.A.C.A. welfare officer responsible for Smith's after-care. **1905** *Westm. Gaz.* 28 Jan. 11/1 Another scheme..is well described..by its title, 'the welfare policy'. The home of 'the welfare policy' is the city of Dayton, Ohio. **1970** *Toronto Daily Star* 24 Sept. 1/1 The number of family units on the welfare rolls has more than doubled in the past year. **1979** *United States 1980/81* (Penguin Travel Guides) 300 A city where the list of places that offer poor boy sandwiches is probably longer than the welfare rolls. **1952** Welfare service [see *welfare committee* above]. **1903** *Review of Reviews* July 79/1 The term 'industrial betterment', or 'welfare work', is used in a wider sense to include all of those services which an employer may render to his work people over and above the payment of wages. It has even been used to include the provision of homes for employees, kindergartens, schoolhouses [etc.]. **1916** *Daily Express* 29 Mar. 6/5 Welfare work tends to improve the conditions of life for women and girls employed in factories, etc. **1904** *Century Mag.* Nov. 63 The welfare worker of a large retail establishment.

†**'welfare**, *vbl. phr.* *Obs.* Also 6 **well fare**, 7 **wellfare**. [f. as prec. Cf. FAREWELL.] The optative phrase ***well fare*** (you, it, etc.), used either as a genuine expression of good wishes (= 'May it go well with', 'good luck to') or employed ironically.

1534 More *Comf. agst. Trib.* III. Wks. 1214/2 Welfare your hert, good Uncle, for this good counsell of yours. **1589** R. Harvey *Pl. Perc.* 2 Well fare London yet, for a policie besides water..pull downe the houses burning. **1590** Spenser *F.Q.* III. ii. 42 But thine my Deare (welfare thy heart my deare). **1612** T. James *Corrupt. Script.* III. 35 Yet welfare another learned Iesuit that had beene at Rome. **1625** Burges *Pers. Tithes* 32 Now welfare Brownist. **1672** S. Parker *Pref. to Bramhall's Vind.* a 2 Well fare poor Macedo for a modest Fool!

b. Used as sb. with *a*.

1642 Sir E. Dering *Sp. Relig.* 1 A well-fare to my Reader if he be either of *birth* or *breeding*: A farewell to the rest.

wel-farende, **welfaryng(e**: see WELL-FARING *ppl. a.* *Obs.*

'welfare state. Also **Welfare State.** [STATE *sb.* 30.] A country in which the welfare of members of the community is underwritten by means of State-run social services.

The term is sometimes said to have been coined by Sir Alfred Zimmern in the 1930s, but it has not been traced in his published writings.

1941 W. Temple *Citizen & Churchman* ii. 35 We have.. seen that in place of the conception of the Power-State we are led to that of the Welfare-State. **1948** *Economist* 24 Jan. 135/2 The welfare state got its start in the deepest depression this country [*sc.* the U.S.] has ever known. **1950** *Times* 19 May 5/3 This is one of the achievements for which the 'welfare State', with its vast apparatus of taxation, subsidies, family allowances, school meals, and other services, can claim credit. **1959** B. Wootton *Social Sci. & Social Path.* 16 The myth of the 'welfare state' has turned the minds of investigators away from the study of material want. **1967** M. Drabble *Jerusalem the Golden* ix. 214 She wondered whether she should fall on her knees and thank.. the Welfare State. **1976** *New Yorker* 22 Mar. 48/3 They came because Sweden, more than any other country in the industrial West, is a workers' state—not a Socialist state.. but a stunning experiment in welfare-state capitalism. **1977** M. Walker *National Front* 8 A scholarship kid who went to grammar schools and won a scholarship to Oxford because of the 1944 Education Act and the Welfare State. **1984** *Listener* 22 Mar. 9/3 Repeated assertions that the welfare state is to be dismantled and the counter-assertion that Mrs Thatcher's administration is committed to maintaining welfare expenditure. **1985** *New Statesman* 9 Aug. 3/1 The welfare state will have to retain the power to take away children from danger.

Hence ˌ**welfare-'statism** orig. *U.S.*, the social conditions or organization associated with a welfare state; ˌ**welfare-'statist**, one who advocates such organization. Cf. WELFARISM, WELFARIST 1.

1949 in *Amer. Speech* (1957) XXXII. 296 Welfare statism advanced slowly and gradually. **1958** *Spectator* 31 Jan. 143/1 The combined effects of high taxation, continuous inflation, welfare statism and the tempting array of consumer goods. *Ibid.* 13 June 761/1 The demands of the welfare-statists in Congress for increased Government spending and tax cuts are now only occasionally heard. **1971** P. Worsthorne *Socialist Myth* v. 76 Labour Governments have to make too many economic concessions to the rich.., which places very strict limits on the scope and scale of welfare-statism. **1980** *London Rev. Bks.* 3–16 July 15/3 'Welfare statism' came into being in the 1940s... It consisted in..the extension to the whole population of adequate health, education and social insurance.

welfarism ('wɛlfɛərɪz(ə)m). orig. *U.S.* [f. WELFARE *sb.* + -ISM.] The principles or policies associated with a welfare state; also = WELFARE-STATISM.

1949 *Life* 25 July 17/2 There must be safeguards so that welfarism does not end in economic or political tyranny. **1961** *Engineering* 17 Feb. 249/1 All Germans..also agree that the term 'welfarism' is likely to have widely different meanings in the U.K. and in Germany. **1962** *Times* 23 Jan. 9/7 Text-books..are slanted towards welfarism, socialism, and world government. **1968** P. B. Austin *On being Swedish* ix. 72 'The Swede,' said old Sundbärg, before welfarism or modern Swedish prosperity were born or thought of, 'would not mind Sweden being prosperous, providing that no one in it were better off than himself.' **1976** R. Delmar in Mitchell & Oakley *Rights & Wrongs of Women* ix. 283 State regulation of the family through welfarism (family allowances etc.)..means that the working class..has the law available to them. **1984** *Times* 21 Apr. 9/2 The proposition that the ills of Britain..are more or less the fault of capitalism is no more self-evident than the proposition that they are more or less the fault of welfarism.

welfarist ('wɛlfɛərɪst), *sb.* (*a.*) [f. as prec. + -IST.] **1.** One who is concerned with welfare, esp. that of animals. Also *attrib.* or as *adj.*

1941 I. Brown in *Manch. Guardian Weekly* 14 Mar. 214/3 There is in this country an enormous and semi-official bureaucracy which deals in social welfare and all manner of educational and uplifting matters. It is rapidly developing a jargon of its own... The Uplifters and Welfarists are assaulting us with the Scorpions of their Jargantuan. **1979** *Country Life* 15 Feb. 428/1 How does one define 'Animal Welfare'?.. To some the term 'welfarist' is almost one of contempt. **1980** *Times* 13 Feb. 3 The union has failed on our behalf to respond to the lies and unfair allegations of the welfarists. **1980** *Observer* (Colour Suppl.) 16 Mar. 41/3 The animal welfare movement—or the 'welfarist' movement as it is now widely called. **1983** *Sci. Amer.* Aug. 5/2 The pork producer of today generally is an animal protectionist and an animal welfarist in the best practical sense.

2. orig. *U.S.* One who supports the principles or policies associated with a welfare state. Also *attrib.* or as *adj.* Cf. WELFARE-STATIST.

1968 *New Yorker* 12 Oct. 201 The welfare state..is not incompatible with the police state. George Wallace is a welfarist, and so is Mayor Daley. **1977** *Daily Tel.* 30 June 16 Questions arise which, in recent years, have been rendered almost taboo by the near-universal acceptance of facile welfarist orthodoxy.. **1985** *Daily Tel.* 6 May 14/1 It has often been said..that he is the prisoner of a Californian perspective which scorns the moribund welfarist states of Western Europe for the growth and dynamism of the Pacific basin area.

welfed, obs. f. WELL-FED.

welful(l, var. ff. WEALFUL *a. Obs.*

welȝe, var. north. and Sc. form of VAIL *v.*^{1} *Obs.*

‖**weli, wely** (ˈwɛlɪ). Also 9 **wali, wullee.** [Arabic *walī*, *welī* friend (of God), saint.]

1. A Muslim saint or holy man.

1819 T. HOPE *Anast.* (1820) I. 341 Notes, *Hafeez*: holy, but in a less degree than the Wely or saint. **1840** J. B. FRASER *Trav. Koordistan* etc. I. 312 He..had on his head a magnificent turban of cashmere shawl—somewhat inconsistent in a dervish; but saints and *wullees* are now-a-days privileged people. **1876** STOBART *Islam* 204 Those faqirs who attain to great sanctity are called 'Walis'.

2. The tomb or shrine of a weli.

1838 E. ROBINSON *Res. Palestine* (1841) I. 322 Rachel's Tomb..is merely an ordinary Muslim Wely, or tomb of a holy person. **1871** FARRAR *Witn. Hist.* iii. 114 The white-domed wely of an obscure Mohammedan saint.

welk (wɛlk), *v.*^{1} *Obs.* exc. *dial.* Also 3 **welken,** 4–7 **welke,** 5 **wylke,** 7 **wilke;** *ppl. a.* 6 **wealked,** 9 *dial.* **wilkt.** [ME. *welken*, prob. of Continental origin: cf. (M)Du., LG., OHG. (MHG. and G.) *welken* (also OHG. *welhen*, MHG. *welchen*), in the same sense, and LG. *welk*, *wälk*, OHG. *welk*, *welc* (G. *welk*) adj., withered, flaccid, sere, etc.]

1. *intr.* Of a flower, plant, etc.: To lose freshness or greenness; to become flaccid or dry; to wilt, wither, fade. Also with *away*.

c **1250** [implied in WELKED *ppl. a.*]. *a* **1300** *E.E. Psalter* lxxxix. 6 It wites als gresse areli at dai;..At euen doun es it broght Vnlasʈes, and welkes and gas to noght. **1340** HAMPOLE *Pr. Consc.* 707 A man may likend be Til a flour, þat..Welkes and dwynes til it be noght. **1387** TREVISA *Higden* I. 77 No manere of tree leseþ þere his leues; no floures þere welkeþ. *c* **1440** *Jacob's Well* 262 Thou faryst as a vyne wyth brode levys that sone welkyn. *a* **1470** H. PARKER *Dives & Pauper* (W. de W. 1496) IV. xxiii. 189/1 They [the garlondes] shall alwaye be grene & fresshe, & neyther welke ne fade. **1577** HARRISON *England* III. xiv. 113 b, Saffron.. These flowers are gathered..before the rising of the Sunne, whych would cause them to welke or flitter. **1641** BEST *Farming Bks.* (Surtees) 31 Soe soone as the pennie-grass beginne to welke and seeme dry, then is it time to beginne to mowe. **1648** *Hunting of Fox* 7 Some particular vines..doe daily wilke and wither away. **1787** GROSE *Prov. Gloss.* s.v., Mown grass in drying for hay is said to welk. **1825** BROCKETT *N.C. Words*, *Welk*, to dry, to wither.

b. *transf.* and *fig.* (or in fig. context).

c **1340** HAMPOLE *Psalter* lxxii. 17 Behaulde the laste endinge of wicked men, when thair flour welkes, & wytes awaye. **1387–8** T. USK *Test. Love* II. xi. 105, I, as a seer tree, with-out burjoning or frute, alwaye welke. *a* **1425** tr. *Arderne's Treat. Fistula*, etc. 41 And so I quenchid þe forseid superfluites..so þat þai bigan to dry and to welk and fall away. **1625** K. LONG tr. *Barclay's Argenis* Pref. 4 For Bookes translated doe,..like remov'd Trees, welke. **1657** REEVE *God's Plea* 232 This world..can hold nothing in it long, the whitest flowers welk and drop.

†**2.** To become less, to diminish, to shrink. Of the sun or moon: To wane, lose brightness. *Obs.*

1390 GOWER *Conf.* I. 35 The See now ebbeth, now it floweth, The lond now welketh, now it groweth. [**1579** E. K. *Gloss. Spenser's Sheph. Cal.* Nov. 13 The Moone being in the waine is sayde of Lidgate to welk.] **1590** SPENSER *F.Q.* I. i. 23 When ruddy Phœbus gins to welke in west. **1631** QUARLES *Samson* xiii. 74 When the Sun was welking in the West. **1641** MILTON *Reform.* I. 29 The Church that before by insensible degrees welk't and impair'd, now with large steps went downe hill decaying.

3. *trans.* To cause to fade or wither.

1579 SPENSER *Sheph. Cal.* Nov., 13 But nowe sadde Winter welked hath the day. **1594** *Zepheria* xvi. C 4 b, Oh how hath black night welked vp this day? *a* **1825** FORBY *Voc. E. Anglia*, *Welk*... 2. To expose to sun and air, and turn over in order to be dried; as grass to be converted to hay.

Hence ˈ**welking** *vbl. sb.* and *ppl. a.*

a **1400** *Gloss.* in *Rel. Ant.* I. 6 *Emerceo*, to wex drie and welkynge. *c* **1440** *Promp. Parv.* 521/1 Welkynge, *marcor.* **1630** J. LANE *Contn. Squire's T.* IX. 225 (Ashm.) While welking Phoebus went down to the west.

†**welk,** *v.*^{2} *Obs. rare.* [Related to WALK *v.*^{1} and *v.*^{2}] *trans.* To roll or knead together.

a **1400** *Stockholm Med. MS.* i. 300 in *Anglia* XVIII. 302 Take garlek & hony & an eyis ȝelke, Do hem to-gedyr wel bete & welke. *a* **1825** FORBY *Voc. E. Anglia*, *Welk*,..To soak, roll, and macerate in a fluid.

welk(e, obs. forms of WHELK.

welk(e, obs. pa. t. of WALK *v.*

welked (wɛlkt), *ppl. a. Obs.* exc. *dial.* [f. WELK *v.*^{1}] **a.** Withered, faded, dried up. †**b.** Dulled in lustre.

c **1250** *Gen. & Ex.* 2107 And .vii. lene [ears] riȝt ðor-bi, welkede, and smale, and druȝte numen. *c* **1386** CHAUCER *Pard. T.* 410 For which ful pale and welked is my face. **1387–8** T. USK *Test. Love* III. v. 37 Mistrust with foly, with yvel wil medled, engendreth that welked padde. **1390** GOWER *Conf.* III. 357 That which was whilom grene gras, Is welked hey at time now. *c* **1425** tr. *Arderne's Treat. Fistula* etc. 71 Hyngyng in maner of a welked grape [*pendentes instar uvae marcidae*]. **1426** LYDG. *De Guil. Pilgr.* 16320 A drye stobyll, or..a welkyd leef. *Ibid.* 16325, I, the most wrechchyd Wyght off alle synners, and most dyffadyd and wylked with synne. *a* **1470** HARDING *Chron.* XCV. xii, The grasse and corne, that welked were afore..waxed grene and gan reuert. **1563** SACKVILLE *Induct. Mirr. Mag.* xii, Her wealked face with woful teares besprent. **1579** SPENSER *Sheph. Cal.* Jan. 73 By that, the welked Phœbus gan auaile His weary waine. **1594** NASHE *Terrors Nt.* Wks. (Grosart) III. 258 Our faces..are most deformedlye welked and crumpled. **1603** DRAYTON *Bar. Wars* VI. xxxix, There comes proude Phaeton tumbling through the cloudes,.. And setting fire vppon the welked shrowds [*ed.* 1619 His Chariot tumbling from the welked Shrowds]. **1879** CUSSANS *Hertfordsh.* III. 321 Shep likes tunnups better when they're wilkt.

†**welken,** *v. Obs.* [f. WELK *v.*^{1} + -EN^5.] *intr.* To wither, fade.

1398 TREVISA *Barth. De P.R.* XI. ix. (Tollemache MS.), Hore froste..makeþ herbes and floures up on þe which he falleþ welkenen. **14..** *A Goodly Balade* 52 in *Chaucer's Wks.* (1532) 234 b, Myn hert welkeneth thus sone.

Hence †ˈ**welkening** *vbl. sb. Obs.*

c **1450** *Mirour Saluacioun* (Roxb.) 144 There is the flouer of ȝouthede y^t neure shal knawe welknyng.

†**welken,** obs. var. WELKED *ppl. a.*

c **1440** *Promp. Parv.* 521/1 Welkyd, or walkyn [*Winch. MS.* welkyn], *marcidus.*

welkin (ˈwɛlkɪn). Forms: α. 1–2 **wolcen, wolcn** (2 **wlcn**), **wolc,** 2–3 **wolcne,** 3–4 **wolkne,** (1) 4 **wolken(e, wolkon;** *pl.* 1 **wolcnu, -na,** 2 **wolcne** (**wlcne**), **wolkne.** β. 2–3 **weolcne** (also *pl.*), 4 **weolkyn;** 3–5 **welkne,** 4–5 **welkene,** 4–7 **welken** (4 **welcon**); 4–6 **welkyn,** 5 **-yne,** 5, 7 **welkine,** 6– **welkin** (7 **-ing, wellkin, wilkin**). γ. 3–5 **walkne, walkene** (4 **-en**), 4–5 **walkyn(e.** [OE. *wolcen*, *wolcn* neut. = OFris. *wolcn-* (*olcn-*, *ulcn-*), *wolken* (*olken*, *ulken*; WFris. *wolken*, *wolk-e*, NFris. *wolk*), OS. *wolcan*, *wolcn-* (MLG. *wolke-n*, *wulke*, LG. *wolk-e*, *wulk-e*; MDu. *wolcke*, Du. *wolk*), OHG. *wolkan*, *wolchan* (MHG. *wolken*, G. *wolke*); the word is lacking in the Scand. group and not recorded in Gothic. A rare OE. *wolcne* wk. fem., is also represented in early ME.

The phonology of the ME. forms with *eo*, *e*, and *a* in the stem is irregular. It has been suggested that the *eo* and *e* are due to mutation, but there is no obvious reason for the change, and the explanation still leaves the forms with *a* unaccounted for. In a number of the early ME. instances it is difficult to decide whether the forms are to be taken as singular or plural.]

†**1.** A cloud. *Obs.*

In OE., esp. in poetry, freq. in plural, esp. in the phrase *under wolcnum* = under the sky or heaven (cf. sense 2).

Beowulf 651 Scaduhelma ʒesceapu scriðan cwoman, wan under wolcnum. *c* **825** *Vesp. Psalter* civ. 39 Aðeneð wolcen in ʒescildnisse heara. *c* **897** ÆLFRED *Gregory's Past. C.* xxxix. 285 Se ðe him ælc wolcn ondrædt, ne ripð se næfre. *Ibid.*, Se wind drifeð ðæt wolcn. **971** *Blickl. Hom.* 59 Ealle þa ʒewitaþ swa swa wolcn. *c* **1000** *Ags. Gosp.* Matt. xxvi. 64 Æfter þysum ʒe ʒeseoð mannes bearn..cumendne on heofones wolcnum. *c* **1050** *O.E. Chron.* (C.) an. 979 Þy ilcan ʒeare wæs ʒesewen blodiʒ wolcen on oft siðas on fyres ʒelicnesse. *c* **1205** LAY. 11974 Swurken vnder sunnen sweorte weolcnen. *Ibid.* 25592 Þa com þer..winden mid þan weolcnen a berninge drake.

2. The apparent arch or vault of heaven overhead; the sky, the firmament.

In later use (from 16th c.) only literary (chiefly *poet.*) and *dial.* (Lancs.).

α. **1122** *O.E. Chron.* (Laud MS.) Hi sæʒon on norð east fir micel & brad wið þone eorðe & weax on lengþe up on an to þam wolcne & se wolcne un dide on fower healfe and faht þær to ʒeanes. *c* **1200** *Trin. Coll. Hom.* 151 Þe sunne teð water from eorðe up to þe wolcne. *c* **1205** LAY. 27452 Þa wolcne gon to dunien, þa eo[r]ðe gon to biuien. **1297** R. GLOUC. (Rolls) App. E 4 Þer hi bigan his fliȝt, & fley him swiþe an hey Vp bi þe lofte fer, and þe wolkne was wel ney. *c* **1315** SHOREHAM VII. 68 Þe wolkne by-clepþ al þe molde. **1387** TREVISA *Higden* V. 399 Ethelbert spak wiþ hem out of house under þe wolken [*sub divo*].

β. *c* **1205** LAY. 2883 He ferde swiðe hehʒe þere weolcne he wes swiðe nih. *a* **1225** *Ancr. R.* 306 Al þene world leitende of swarte leite up into weolcne. *a* **1250** *Owl & Night.* 1682 (Jesus MS.) We habbe stefne brihte & sitteþ vnder welkne bi nyhte. *a* **1310** in Wright *Lyric P.* xlii. 114 Ase fele sythe ant oft..As sterres beth in welkne. **1377** LANGL. *P. Pl.* B. XVII. 160 Al þe wyde worlde... Bothe welkne and þe wynde, water and erthe, Heuene & helle. **1387** TREVISA *Higden* III. 459 It is ful likynge to us to beholde þe welkene and þe sterres of hevene. *c* **1420** *Anturs of Arth.* 328 (Douce MS.) Þe windes, þe weders, þe welkene vnhides. ? *a* **1500** *Chester Pl., Creation* 21 To be a divident to twyne the waters aye; Above the welkin, benethe also. **1529** MORE *Dyaloge* III. Wks. 1222/2 He..caste vp his eyen in to the welkin and wepte. **1551** RECORDE *Cast. Knowl.* (1556) 7 Whiche parte is aboue all the foure Elementes, and compasseth them about, and is called the Skie, or Welkin. **1591** SYLVESTER *Du Bartas* I. ii. 414 That lightly born..Safe through the Welkin I my course may take. **1632** LITHGOW *Trav.* III. 81 When the welkin had put aside the vizard of the night. **1662** HIBBERT *Syntagma Theol.* I. 29 Light..diffuseth in an instant the whole welkin over. **1678** VAUGHAN *Thalia Rediv.*, *Daphnis* 18 Not one Black cloud, no rags, nor spots did stain The Welkins beauty. **1714** GAY *Sheph. Week* I. 3 No chirping Lark the Welkin sheen invokes. **1748** THOMSON *Cast. Indol.* I. lviii, There would he linger, till the latest ray Of light sat trembling on the welkin's bound. **1817** SCOTT *Harold* I. ii, If a sail but gleam'd white 'gainst the welkin blue. **1857** LONGF. *Sandalphon* 44 When..the welkin above is all white, All throbbing and panting with stars.

fig. **1849** C. BRONTË *Shirley* xxviii, I..see a fine, perfect rainbow, bright with promise, gloriously spanning the beclouded welkin of life. **1868** LOWELL *Under Willows* 284 And all the heavens revolve In the small welkin of a drop of dew.

γ. *c* **1250** *Gen. & Ex.* 96 Ðo god bad ben ðe firmament, Al abuten ðis walkne sent. **13..** *K. Alis.* 1737 (Laud MS.), Ich haue moo kniȝttes to werren þan ben in þe walken sterren. **1377** LANGL. *P. Pl.* B. XV. 355 Shipmen and shepherdes.. Wisten by þe walkene, what shulde bityde. *c* **1407** LYDG. *Reson & Sens.* 1006 As sterris in the frosty nyght, Whanne walkne is most bryght, With-oute cloude or any skye. *c* **1450** *Cov. Myst., Creation* 86 The secunde day watyr I make The walkyn also ful fayr and bryth.

b. Considered as the abode of the Deity, or of the gods of heathen mythology: The celestial regions, heaven.

1559 *Mirr. Magistr., Hen. VI*, xiii, If..such as say the welken fortune warkes, Take Fortune for our fate. **1581** A. HALL *Iliad* I. 6 But Iuno hearde from Welkin high, this cruell iarre. *Ibid.* II. 31 Of Gods thou Ioue the soueraigne chiefe, and Lord of Welkin hie Of aire, and of this earth below. **1610** HOLLAND *Camden's Brit.* I. 327 How glittereth now this place of great request, Like to the seat of heavenly welkin hie? **1653** W. RAMESEY *Astrol. Restored* III. vii. 157 It is Nectar and Ambrosia such as will make the wilkin roar. **1852** KINGSLEY *Andromeda* 34 Far-seeing Apollo Watched well-pleased from the welkin.

c. in phrases descriptive of loud sounds, as ***to make the welkin ring, to rend the welkin***, etc.

1587 MARLOWE *1st Pt. Tamburl.* IV. ii. 1489 (Brooke) As when a fiery exhalation Wrapt in the bowels of a freezing cloude, Fighting for passage, makes the Welkin cracke. *a* **1593** MARLOWE & NASHE *Dido* IV. ii. 1103 O heare Iarbus plaining prayers, Whose hideous ecchoes make the welkin howle. **1596** SHAKS. *Tam. Shr.* Induct. ii. 47 Thy hounds shall make the Welkin answer them. **1635** QUARLES *Embl.* viii. 33 One frisks and sings,..and makes the Welkin rore. **1728** POPE *Dunc.* II. 246 Sound forth, my Brayers, and the welkin rend. **1735** SOMERVILLE *Chase* II. 157 The Welkin rings, Men, Dogs, Hills, Rocks, and Woods In the full Consort join. **1814** SOUTHEY *Roderick* III. 368 That shout, Which, like a thunder-peal, victorious Spain Sent through the welkin, rung within his soul Its deep prophetic echoes. **1818** WORDSW. *Inscr. Hermit's Cell* v. 10 When storms the welkin rend. **1837** CARLYLE *Fr. Rev.* III. I. vii, 'Live the Fatherland!' rings responsive to the welkin. **1854** SURTEES *Handley Cr.* i, Away they go full cry, making the welkin ring with the music of their deep-toned notes. **1874** DIXON *Two Queens* VII. i. II. 2 The citizens rent the welkin with their shouts.

d. in the asseveration ***by the welkin***.

1601 B. JONSON *Poetaster* I. i, This villanous poetrie will vndoe you, by the welkin. **1822** SCOTT *Peveril* xxxviii, Which, by the welkin and its stars, you would not be slow in avenging.

e. ***to the welkin***, 'to the skies' (SKY *sb.*^{1} 3 d).

c **1746** J. COLLIER (Tim Bobbin) *View Lancs. Dial.* Wks. (1862) 58 This Rascot..roost meh Bitch to the varra Welkin.

3. The upper atmosphere; the region of the air in which the clouds float, birds fly, etc.

13.. *Gaw. & Gr. Knt.* 525 Wroþe wynde of þe welkyn wrastelez with þe sunne. *c* **1369** CHAUCER *Dethe Blaunche* 343 Ne in al the welkyn was no clowde. *c* **1400** *Destr. Troy* 7621 Ouershotyng with shoures thurgh þere shene tenttes, As neuer water fro the welkyn hade waynit before. *a* **1450** *Mirk's Festial* 160 Men of all þe nacyons..werne comen togedyr ynto þe tempule for fere of þe berst þat þay herd yn þe welken. **1570** LEVINS *Manip.* 134/21 The Welkin, aire, *aura, aër.* **1582** STANYHURST *Æneis* III. (Arb.) 89 Thee stars imparted no light, thee welken is heauye. **1601** W. PERCY *Cuckqueanes & Cuckolds Errants* V. iv. (Roxb.) 69 Hold vp thy Lynk I say, I may obserue the state of the welking. Rayne or no Rayne? Ha. **1645** G. DANIEL *Poems* Wks. 1878 II. 42 The Royall Eagle, in the welkin towers. **16..** CHALKHILL *Thealma & Cl.* (1683) 160 One might perceive such changes in the King As hath th' inconstant wellkin in the Spring. **1713** CROXALL *Orig. Canto Spenser* x. (1714) 12 When the blasting Mildew's dreary Bane With noisom Breath infects the Welkin sheen. **1757** SMOLLETT *Reprisal* Epil., If this welkin angry clouds deform. **1853** C. BRONTE *Villette* xxxv, Down washed the rain, deep lowered the welkin. **1876** BLACKIE *Songs Relig.* 19 Breath that drew the rolling rivers From the welkin's dewy cells. **1880** WEBB *Goethe's Faust* I. ii. 67 The baleful powers of air, Which through the welkin stream.

fig. **1601** SHAKS. *Twel. N.* III. i. 65 Who you are, and what you would are out of my welkin, I might say Element, but the word is ouer-worne.

†**4.** In the Ptolemaic system: A 'heaven' or sphere. *Obs.*

c **1250** *Gen. & Ex.* 288 And euerilc on ðat helden wid him [Lucifer]..fellen ut of heuones liȝt In-to ðis middil walknes niȝt. **1387** TREVISA *Higden* II. 185 Þe planetes and þe neyþer wolkons moeueþ out of þe west in to þe est. *Ibid.*, The meouynge of þe ouermeste wolken out of þe est in to þe west.

5. *attrib.* and *Comb.*, as ***welkin-country, -dome, -way; welkin-high, -like*** adjs.; †**welkin-eye**, a heavenly or blue eye; **welkin-wise** *adv.*, after the fashion of the welkin; †**welkin-wizard**, an almanac-maker who makes astrological forecasts.

1581 A. HALL *Iliad* I. 15 The God his mansion keepes, In *Welkin Countrey he remaines. **1860** G. P. MORRIS *Poems* (ed. 15) 169 When victory rent the *welkin-dome He earned a sepulchre—at home. **1611** SHAKS. *Wint. T.* I. ii. 136 Come (Sir Page) Looke on me with your *Welkin eye. **1804** J. GRAHAME *Sabbath* 875 The joyous choir unseen, Poised *welkin-high, harmonious fills the air. **1839** BAILEY *Festus* 254 That high and *welkin-like infinity. **1590** SPENSER *F.Q.* I. iv. 9 He leaves the *welkin way most beaten playne, And, rapt with whirling wheeles, inflames the skyen With fire not made to burne. **1854** J. D. BURNS *Vision of Prophecy* 122 A luminous element of gladness Now vaults our sphere of being *welkin-wise. **1596** BARLOW tr. *Lavater's Three Serm.* i. 10 The coniectures of these *Welkin Wisards [*marg.* Almanacke makers], whose Prognostications of euerie yeares warres, diseases, heate, colde, [etc.]..proue either manifest vntruthes, or coniecturall ghesses.

welky, var. WHELKY *a.*[2]

well (wɛl), *sb.*[1] Forms: *α.* 1 **wælla** (**uælla**), 1, 3 **wælle** (1 **uælle**), 3–5 **walle**, 3–4 **wall**, 4–5 **wal**; *Sc.* and *north.* 6– **wall** (6 **vall**, 9 **wal**), 6–7 **woll** (6 **vol**). *β.* 1 **wella**, 1, 3–5 **welle** (4–5 **wele**), 1– **well**, 3–7 **wel**. *γ.* 1 **wylla**, **willa**, **wielle**, 1, 4 **wylle**, 1, 3–4 **wille**; 1 **wyl**, 1–4 **wyll**, 1, 5 **will**. [OE. *wielle* (*wylle*), **wiell* (*wyll*, *will*), str. masc., **wiella* (*wylla*, *willa*; Anglian *wælla*, *wella*), wk. masc., *wielle* (*wylle*, *wille*; Angl. *wælle*, *welle*), wk. fem., f. the stem of *weall-an* to boil or bubble up: see WALL *v.*[1] Cf. OHG. *wella* (G. *welle*) wave, ON. *vella* boiling heat.]

1. a. A spring of water rising to the surface of the earth and forming a small pool or flowing in a stream; a pool (or, rarely, a stream) fed by a spring. Now *arch.* or *dial.*

α. *c* **825** *Vesp. Psalter* xli. 2 Swe swe heorut ʒewillað to wællum wetra swe ʒewillað sawul min to ðe god. *c* **1205** LAY. 17025 Summe heo uerden a-nan þat heo comen to Alæban þat is a wælle. *a* **1240** [see 2 d.]. *c* **1440** *Floriz & Bl.* 291 (Cambr. MS.) Aboue þe walle stant atreo. *c* **1450** *Mirk's Festial* 179 Anon sprang a fayr walle. **1535** STEWART *Cron. Scot.* II. 219 Out of ane woll discendand fra ane spring, He send that tyme cald water for to bring. **1567** *Rec. Burgh Lanark* (1893) 39 That na personis wysche ony clathis..at the burne nor yit at Sanct Mungois wall. **1595** *Reg. Mag. Sig. Scot.* 91/2 Fra the said puill eist to ane wall callit the Dokand well. **1652** in *Edin. Topogr. & Antiq. Mag.* (1848) 152 Going..to the Kirktowne wall and washing of her daughter's eyen, & saying..All ye ill of my bairn's eyen in ye wall fall. **1775** *Companion to Map of Peebles* 107 There is a remarkable fine spring, called Geddes's wall, near the top [of Broad Law]. *a* **1806** R. JAMIESON *Pop. Ballads* I. 61 Tak me to yon wall fair; You'll wash my bluidy wounds o'er and o'er.

β. *c* **900** *Bæda's Hist.* v. x. (1890) 418 Is ðæt ec sæd þætte in ðere stowe, þer hio ofsleʒne weran, weolle an welle. *c* **1205** LAY. 19782 Heo comen to þare welle and heore bollen feolde. *c* **1220** *Bestiary* 62 A welle he sekeð ðat springeð ai boðe bi nigt and bi dai. **1297** R. GLOUC. (Rolls) 15 Vor engelonde is vol inoȝ of frut & ek of tren, Of wellen swete & colde. *a* **1300** *Cursor M.* 12470 Þe spring..o well,..þof it euer vte rinnand es þe wel es neuer mar þe less. ? *a* **1366** CHAUCER *Rom. Rose* 1417 About the brinkes of thise welles ..Sprang up the gras. **1390** GOWER *Conf.* I. 326 He strawhte him forto drinke Upon the freisshe welles brinke. **1422** YONGE tr. *Secreta Secret.* 245 [In autumn] Wellis wythdrawen ham, grene thynges fadyth, Frutes fallyth. *c* **1470** *Golagros & Gaw.* 40 Thay walkit be the syde of ane fair well. **1547** BOORDE *Introd. Knowl.* vi. (1870) 141 There be welles, the whyche doth tourne wood in to Irone. **1574** T. HILL *Art Garden.* II. *Bees*, etc. 69 And when ryuers and wels be shallower of water than customably, doe then declare raine to followe. **1603** STOW *Surv.* 11 Then was there 3. principall Fountaines, or wels in the other Suburbs, to wit Holy well, Clements well, and Clarkes well. Neare vnto this last named fountaine, were diuers other wels. **1663** R. LOWE *Lancs. Diary* (1876) 8, I went with Mary and other wenches to a well [at the] bottome of towne feild. **1775** R. CHANDLER *Trav. Asia M.* (1825) I. 121 At a well was a marble pedestal perforated, and serving as a mouth. **1832** W. IRVING *Alhambra* I. 249, I laid myself down one noon-tide, and slept under a palm-tree by the side of a scanty well. **1859** JEPHSON *Brittany* vi. 68 The well flows in a pure and abundant stream from the granite rock. **1870** *Handbk. Orkney Isl.* 94 There are several mineral wells in the island. **1892** J. A. HENDERSON *Ann. Lower Deeside* 169 He at last reached what proved to be a well of water.

γ. *c* **893** ÆLFRED *Oros.* IV. vii. §10 An wæs þæt on Piceno þæm wuda an wielle weol blode. *c* **900** *Bæda's Hist.* I. vii. (1890) 38 And þa sona hraðe beforan his fotum wæs wyl upp yrnende... And nu seo wylle & þæt wæter [etc.]. *c* **1000** *Sax. Leechd.* I. 116 Ðeos wyrt [watercress]..of hyre sylfre cenned bið, on wyllon & on brocen. *Ibid.* II. 32 And aþweah eft þa eaʒan on clænum wylle. *c* **1305** *St. Kenelm* 295 in *E.E.P.* 55 For þer is a wille fair ynouȝ..In þe stede as he lai on. *c* **1315** SHOREHAM *Poems* v. 55 Þe wylle þat hys in paradys Fol wel by-tokeneþ þys auys. **13..** *Cursor M.* 20212 (B. Mus. Add.) Sche dide of hure cloþes alle, and wasche hure with water of wille.

b. A miraculous spring of water (or oil); a spring of water supposed to be of miraculous origin or to have supernatural healing powers; also, in later use, a medicinal or mineral spring.

Freq. in proper names assigning the well to a particular saint.

854– [see HOLY WELL]. *c* **1305** *St. Kenelm* 295, 297 in *E.E.P.* (1862) 55 A wil spring vp þere stod..þat me clepeþ seint kenelmes welle: þat menie men haþ isoȝt. *c* **1440** *Stacyons of Rome* 828 in *Pol. Rel. & L. Poems* (1903) 171 Two wellis there bethe, I tell thee, that sprynggythe oyle. *c* **1450** *Mirk's Festial* 14 And whan he was buryet, at þe hed of þe tombe sprong a well of oyl þat dyd medysyn to all seke. **1581** *Sc. Acts Jas. VI*, III. 212/2 Aganis passing in pilgramage to chapellis wellis and croces. **1591** SHAKS. *Two Gent.* IV. ii. 84 *Th.* Where meete we? *Pro.* At Saint Gregories well. **1632** ROWZEE (*title*), The Queenes Welles. That is, A Treatise of the nature and vertues of Tunbridge Water. **1648** GAGE *West Ind.* 5 [Papists] encroaching upon many Houses and Farmes, enriching themselves, as namely at Winifreds Well (so termed by them) where they had bought an Inne. *a* **1774** FERGUSSON *Poems, Daft Days* 35 Reaming ale, Mair precious than the well o' Spa, Our hearts to heal. **1806** P. O'NEILL *Tour Orkney* etc. 26, I likewise visited the wells of Kildingie... These wells or springs, are situated in the Mill Bay. **1824** SCOTT (*title*), St. Ronan's Well. **1882** W. TAYLOR *Researches Hist. Tain* i. 27 *note*, A copious fountain of pure water situated on..the girth boundary in the heights of the parish..has from time immemorial borne the name of St. David's well. **1904** A. C. FRASER *Biog. Philos.* i. 26 The Priory..and the well and chapel of St. Modan on the hill, were my favourite haunts.

c. *pl.* A place where medicinal springs exist, to which invalids resort; a watering-place or spa.

1673 SHADWELL *Epsom-Wells* I. i, Enter Mrs. Woodly,.. to Toby and others, drinking at the Wells. **1707** in J. Ashton *Soc. Life Q. Anne* (1882) II. 113 The New Wells at Epsom, with variety of Raffling Shops, will be open'd on Easter Monday next. **1716** *Lond. Gaz.* No. 5459/1 The Princess set out..for the Wells of Medway. **1728** YOUNG *Love Fame* v. 23 Thro' every sign of vanity they run; Assemblies, Parks,.. Balls, Wells, Bedlams, [etc.].

†**d.** *Her.* The representation of a stream, used as a bearing. *Obs.*

1486 *Bk. St. Albans* Her. e vj b, And of hym y[t] beris thes armys ye most say..He berith of golde and .iij. Wellis.

e. A fountain fed by a spring; a structure erected above a spring for convenience in obtaining the water; a drinking-fountain. Chiefly *Sc.*

1575–6 in *Burgh Rec. Glasgow* (1876) 457 Item, to Johne Wilsoun for four geistis to the woll in Gallowgait..viij lib. **1630** *Ibid.* 373 The new woll in the Trongait to be sklaittet in the best forme. **1638** *Ibid.* 390 Ane warrand..for taking doun the wall at the Croce. **1656** *Ibid.* (1881) 351 The twa new wallis newlie buildit in Trongait and at the vennall. **1823** GALT *R. Gilhaize* III. 34 She was mobbet, and the wells pumped upon her by the enraged multitude. **1843** JAMES *Forest Days* i, It had on the south side, a well, and an iron ladle underneath.

2. *transf.* and *fig.* **a.** In allusive contexts directly suggestive of the nature (flowing, etc.) or uses (drinking, taking water) of a spring.

c **897** ÆLFRED *Gregory's Past. C.* vii. 49 (MS. Hatton) Hio [the speech] aweoll of anum wille [*Cott.* welle]; ðeah heo an tu tefleowe, ðeah wæs sio æspryng sio soðe lufu. *c* **1220** *Bestiary* 341 Ðanne we ðus brennen bihoueð us to rennen to cristes quike welle,..drinken his wissing. *a* **1225** *Ancr. R.* 282 In hire he heldeð nout one dropemele, auh ȝeoteð vlowinde wellen of his grace. *a* **1300** *Cursor M.* 310 Fader is he cald for-þi þat he is welle þat neuer sal dri. *Ibid.* 21023 O þe wel o witt he dranc. *c* **1315** SHOREHAM v. 61 Þys wulle hys god self man by-come, Of hym þys ioyen beþ alle y-nome. **13..** *Lay Folks' Catech.* (L.) 190 Crist was þe furst qwyk welle of grace. *c* **1420** *Prymer* 68 Mi soule þirstide to god, þat is a quyk welle! **1568** T. HOWELL *Arb. Amitie* (1879) 52 O noble hart whose Well of grace, shall spring and neuer drie. **1807** CRABBE *Par. Reg.* I. 98 Not one who, early by the Muse beguiled, Drank from her well the waters undefiled. **1840** LONGF. *Sp. Stud.* I. v, O sleep,..Holding unto our lips thy goblet filled Out of Oblivion's well, a healing draught! **1899** J. P. FITZPATRICK *Transvaal* i. 25 The effect of the annexation was to start the wells of plenty bubbling—with British Gold.

b. That from which something springs or arises; a source or origin.

α. *c* **825** *Vesp. Psalter* xxxv. 10 Forðon mid ðe is waelle lifes. *c* **825** *Vesp. Hymns* xi. in *O.E. Texts* 417 Leht lehtes & waelle lehtes. **1533** GAU *Richt Vay* (S.T.S.) 27 The bibil quhilk is the grund and vol of al godlie doctrine and hewinlie visdom. **1599** ALEX. HUME *Poems* (S.T.S.) *Hymn* vi. 110 He made the Sun a lampe of light, A woll of heate to shine by day.

β. *c* **1000** *Lambeth Psalter* xxxv. 10 Forðan þe mid þe is welle lifes. **1340** *Ayenb.* 80 Uayrhede, wyt, prouesse, myȝte, vridom and noblesse; þise byeþ zix wellen of ydelnesse. **1377** LANGL. *P. Pl.* B. xv. 30 And þat is wytte and wisdome, þe welle of alle craftes. *c* **1400** *Lanfranc's Cirurg.* 271 And fro diafragma it mai go to þe brayn, þat is þe welle of alle nerues. **1475** *Bk. Noblesse* (Roxb.) 51 Athenes, that was the welle of connyng and of wisdam. **1538** STARKEY *England* 180 Tyranny in al commynaltys ys the ground of al yl, the wel of al myschefe and mysordur. **1539** BIBLE (Great) *Prov.* xvi. 22 Understandyng is a well of lyfe vnto hym that hath it. **1667** MILTON *P.L.* XI. 416 [He] purg'd with Euphrasie and Rue The visual Nerve..; And from the Well of Life three drops instill'd. **1859** FITZGERALD *Omar* xxxiv, Then to this earthen Bowl did I adjourn My Lip the secret Well of Life to learn.

γ. *a* **1000** *Ags. Ps.* (Thorpe) xxxv. 9 Forþæm mid þe is lifes wylle. **1422** YONGE tr. *Secreta Secret.* 135 Vndyrstondynge is the begynnynge and will of al vertues.

c. Applied to persons regarded as a source or abundant manifestation of some quality or virtue.

a **1225** *St. Marher.* 11 Þu art walle of waisdom. *a* **1310** in Wright *Lyric P.* xxxiii. 94 Ofte y crie merci, of mylse thou art welle. **1377** *Pol. Poems* (Rolls) I. 218 Prince Edward That welle was of alle corage. *c* **1386** CHAUCER *Wife's Prol.* 107 Crist, that of perfeccion is welle. *c* **1400** *Pilgr. Sowle* v. i. (1859) 74 He is the welle of all manere of goodnes. *c* **1440** *Partonope* 226 That thay may say as ye passe by strete: Loo, yonder gothe the welle of gentylnesse. *c* **1450** tr. *De Imitatione* III. xi. 78 O þou welle of euerlasting loue. **1500–20** DUNBAR *Poems* lxxvii. 7 Oure lustie quein, The vall of velth, guid cheir, and mirrines. **1559** *Mirr. Mag., Edw. IV*, vi, A Salomon that was of wit the well. **1596** SPENSER *F.Q.* IV. ii. 32 Dan Chaucer, well of English vndefyled, On Fame's eternall beadroll worthie to be fyled.

d. A copious flow (of tears or blood). Also hyperbolically applied to a weeping person.

a **1225** *Ancr. R.* 156 For þui he [Jeremiah] bed welle of teares to his eien, þet heo ne adruweden nanmore þen welle. *a* **1240** *Ureisun* in *O.E. Hom.* I. 189 Þe ilke fif wallen [*v.r.* wellen] þet of þi blisfulle bodi sprungen and strike dun strondes of blode. **1382** WYCLIF *Jer.* ix. 1 Who shal ȝyue to myn hed watir, and to myn eȝen a welle of teres? *c* **1530** *Hickscorner* 19 She sawe her sone, all deed, Splayed on a crosse with the fyve welles of pyte. **1606** SHAKS. *Tr. & Cr.* v. x. 19 There is a word will Priam turne to stone; Make wels, and Niobes of the maides and wiues.

e. A whirlpool.

Applied spec. to certain whirlpools in the Orkneys as a rendering of the native designation *keld* = ON. *kelda* spring. Tennyson's use may either be independent or derived from Scott.

a **1654** BLAEU *Le Theatre du Monde* v. 159–60 Map, Orcades..Souna..the Welles. *Ibid.*, Spurness well. **1693** J. WALLACE *Descr. Orkney* 7 The Wells of Swinna, which are two Whirl-pools in the Sea. **1750** M. MACKENZIE *Orcades* 5/1 One of these Whirlpools or Wells, as they are called in Orkney. **1774** G. LOW *Tour Orkney* etc. (1879) 29 The whirlpools called the Wells of Swona, so long famous for the alledged danger in passing over or near them. **1821** SCOTT *Pirate* xxxviii, Even as the wells of Tuftiloe can wheel the stoutest vessel round and round, in despite of either sail or steerage.

1850 TENNYSON *In Mem.* x, If..the roaring wells Should gulf him fathom-deep in brine. *Ibid.* cviii, To scale the heaven's highest height, Or dive below the wells of Death.

3. a. A pit dug in the ground to obtain a supply of spring-water; spec. a vertical excavation, usually circular in form and lined with masonry, sunk to such a depth as to penetrate a water-bearing stratum.

α. *c* **950** *Lindisf. Gosp.* John iv. 6 Uæs..ðer uælle iacobes. *c* **1275** *Wom. Samaria* 12 in *O.E. Misc.* 84 Iesus at ore walle reste him seolf al one. *a* **1300** *Cursor M.* 13229 Here nu quat herodias did, In a wall his heued sco hid. *c* **1395** *Plowman's T.* 298 They folowe Christ that shedde his blodde To heven, as bucket in-to the wall. **1882** 'JACK ROBINSON' *Auld Tales* 11 (E.D.D.) T' horrator war prayan fer a girt wal et he cud drop intul.

β, γ. *c* **1000** *Ags. Gosp.* John iv. 6–7 Þær wæs iacobes wyl; Se hælend sæt æt ðam wylle. *c* **1250** *Gen. & Ex.* 2947 In euerilc welle, in euerilc trike, men funden blod al witterlike. *c* **1275** LAY. 19810 Þo wende to þan wille cnihtes swiþe snelle. *a* **1300** *Cursor M.* 11701 Mak vs a well for mine sake, þat all mai plente o water take. *c* **1385** CHAUCER *L.G.W.* 1584 Or as a welle that were botemeles Ryght so can fals Iason haue no pes ffor to desyryn [etc.]. *c* **1440** *Jacob's Well* 3 Whanne ȝoure welle is made..ȝe muste haue a wyndas, & a roop, & a bokett, a drawyn vp watyr to drynke, be-cause ȝoure welle is so deep. **1485** *Rec. St. Mary at Hill* 29 For the well a Bokett with a cheyne of yryn. **1530** PALSGR. 287/2 Well made of stone, *puis*, *putelle*. **1553** BRENDE *Q. Curtius* VII. 146 The ryuer of Oxus..being a water vnholsom to be dronke..the Macedons fell to digging of welles. **1592** SHAKS. *Rom. & Jul.* III. i. 99 No: 'tis not so deepe as a well, nor so wide as a Church doore, but 'tis inough. **1610** HOLLAND *Camden's Brit.* 281 A Well of an exceeding depth. **1625** N. CARPENTER *Geogr. Delin.* II. iv. (1635) 60 Starres from the darke bottome of a deepe Well or Mine will shew themselues at mid-day. **1698** FRYER *Acc. E. India & P.* 155 A little out of the Way is erected an high-wall'd Well. **1700** DRYDEN *Fables, Pal. & Arc.* II. 82 Now up, now down, as Buckets in a Well. **1745** tr. *Columella's Husb.* I. vi, The ground being dug after the manner of wells, which they call *siros*, receives the fruits. **1842** TENNYSON *St. Sim. Styl.* 63 For many weeks about my loins I wore The rope that haled the buckets from the well. **1858** HAWTHORNE *Fr. & It. Jrnls.* (1871) I. 337 There is no familiar object connected with daily life so interesting as a well. **1888** *Encycl. Brit.* XXIV. 402/2 When the population of a district is scattered it is possible to supply individual wants by means of streams, springs, or shallow wells.

fig. *c* **1400** *Lanfranc's Cirurg.* 193 Now we han medycyns drawen of .ij. wellis & of manie maistris. *a* **1591** H. SMITH *Serm.* (1592) 998 The well of Gods secrets is so deepe, that no bucket of man can sound it. **1611** BIBLE *Isaiah* xii. 3 With ioy shall yee draw water out of the wels of saluation. **1655** W. SPURSTOWE (*title*), The Wels of Salvation opened. **1781** COWPER *Convers.* 564 Hearts may be found..Whose wisdom, drawn from the deep well of life, Tastes of its healthful origin. **1848** DICKENS *Dombey* xviii, After stating this curious and unexpected fact, Mr. Toots fell into a deep well of silence.

b. *Her.* A bearing representing the stone curb or border of a well.

1780 *R. Glover's Ord. Arms Augm.* 49 in Edmondson *Her.* II. O, Gu. three wells ar. water az. **1828–40** BERRY *Encycl. Her.* I.

4. a. In various proverbial sayings or phrases. (See also PITCHER[1] 1 b.)

(*a*) **1546** J. HEYWOOD *Prov.* (1867) 70 Well well (quoth she) many wels, many buckets. **1757** B. FRANKLIN *Poor Richard* (1890) 278 Then as Poor Dick says, When the Well's dry, they know the Worth of Water. **1832** J. J. BLUNT *Reform. Eng.* 140 We know not, says the proverb, what the well is worth till it is dry. **1860** WHYTE MELVILLE *Mkt. Harb.* xiii, 'He's as deep as a well, is my master,' answered old Isaac.

(*b*) **1691** HARTCLIFFE *Virtues* 181 If Truth, as Democritus fansied, lies at the bottom of a deep Well. **1848** DICKENS *Dombey* xxxii, He tried a glass of grog; but melancholy truth was at the bottom of that well, and he couldn't finish it. **1888** J. M. COBBAN *By Telegraph* iv, The depth of the well at the bottom of which truth is hid was nothing to the unfathomableness of his designs.

b. *to put* (a person) *in the well* (see quot.). *slang.*

1812 VAUX *Vocab. Flash Lang.* (1819) s.v. *Garden*, To *put* a person *in the garden*..or *in the well*, are synonymous phrases, signifying to defraud him of his due share of booty by embezzling a part of the property, or the money it is fenced for.

5. *transf.* †**a.** = FONTANELLE 1 a. *Obs.*

c **1400** *Lanfranc's Cirurg.* 216 Make him .iij. cauterijs:.. oon bihinde þe nolle in þe welle þerof, [etc.]. *Ibid.* 309 Also in þe welle vnder þe eeris & bihinde þe eeris þou schalt make cauterijs for passiouns of iȝen.

b. *a well of a* (place): like a well, as being damp and cold or deep and dark.

1843 DICKENS *Chr. Carol* ii, He then conveyed him..into the veriest old well of a shivering best-parlour that ever was seen. **1869** BLACKMORE *Lorna D.* xliv, She had gotten it in a great well of a cupboard.

6. *Naut.* **a.** A vertical shaft protecting the pump below the lower (or upper) deck in a ship's hold. *to sound the well*, to ascertain, by means of a sounding-rod, the depth of water accumulated in the hold.

1611 Cotgr., *Lossec*, the sinke, or well, of the pumpe of a ship. 1626 Capt. J. Smith *Accid. Yng. Seamen* 11 The Pumpe, the pumpes-well, the pumpes brake, [etc.]. 1627 —— *Sea Gram.* ii. 9 The Dutch men vse a Burre pumpe.. to pumpe vp the Billage water that..cannot come to the well. 1750 Blanckley *Nav. Expositor.* 1762–9 Falconer *Shipwr.* ii. 464 They sound the well. 1825 T. Hook *Sayings* Ser. ii. *Passion & Princ.* xv. III. 401 The ship seemed rapidly settling..yet no one dared to sound the well. 1836 Marryat *Pirate* iv, The well was again sounded. Nine feet water in the hold. 1881 *Daily Tel.* 14 Feb., So long as the sounding-rod gave a dry well, the men's courage kept tolerably steadfast.

b. A cistern or tank in a fishing-boat, in which the catch of fish is preserved alive. Cf. WELL-BOAT 1.

1614 Gentleman *Eng. Way Wealth* 19 Fresh fish, which they of purpose do keepe aliue in their boates in Wells. 1720 De Foe *Capt. Singleton* ii. (1840) 37 This well [was of] the same kind which the small fisher-boats in England have to preserve their fish alive in. 1828 Davy *Salmonia* 49 He..is landed. A fine well-fed fish, not much less than 4 lbs. Throw him into the well. 1848 Johns *Week at Lizard* 259 The store-pot is emptied and its contents transferred to a well in the hold of the vessel. 1912 *Daily News* 29 Mar. 4 The Betsy was running for harbour for all she was worth. Her 'well' was full of live cod.

7. A shaft or pit bored or dug in the ground. In various specific applications.

a. An excavation for the storage of ice.

1681 *Cal. Treas. Bks.* 8 Building an ice well for his Majesty's use in Windsor Great Park. 1850 *Gardeners' Mag. of Bot.* I. 82 Section of ice well... *a*, well; *b*, porch. 1873 Spon *Workshop Rec.* Ser. i. 364/1 There must be perfect drainage insured from the bottom of the well, so that the ice will be kept dry.

†**b.** *Mil.* = SHAFT *sb.*[3] 2.

1702–11 *Milit. & Sea Dict.* (ed. 4) 1, *Well*, a Depth the Miner sinks into the Ground, and thence carries on the Branches, or Galeries, to find out, and disappoint the Enemies Mines, or to prepare one. 1736 J. Campbell *Milit. Hist. Pr. Eugene* etc. I. 217 We now began to perceive that their Miners were in search of our Mines, and that they worked in sinking Wells in order to get into our Galleries.

c. (See quot.)

1706 Phillips (ed. Kersey) s.v. *Observatory*, The Royal Observatory..furnish'd with all sorts of Instruments..and a dry Well for Discovery of the Stars in the Day-time.

d. A shaft sunk to obtain oil, brine, gas, etc.

1799 *Asiatic Researches* VI. 127 An Account of the Petroleum Wells in the Burmha Dominions. 1885 *Encycl. Brit.* XVIII. 713 In 1819 a well bored for brine in Wayne county, Kentucky, yielded so much black petroleum that it was abandoned. 1892 [see GUSHER 2]. 1901 *Munsey's Mag.* XXV. 743/2 The first flowing [petroleum] well, or 'gusher,' ..was struck in 1861.

e. A shaft to carry water through a retentive to a porous stratum or to a drain; a sink for sewage.

1856 J. C. Morton *Cycl. Agric.* I. 692 It will be proper.. to cut a drain of four feet in depth only, and then to sink small wells down to the watery bed. 1865 *Daily Tel.* 27 Oct. 5/2 The system of drainage adopted is that of running the pipes of each house into a dead well... These wells are made of bricks, without any cement.

f. *Engin.* A hollow cylinder or shaft of masonry sunk and filled in solid to form a foundation.

1885 L. F. Vernon-Harcourt *Harbours & Docks* I. 405 Where the thickness of the mud exceeded 13 feet, square masonry wells were sunk through it on to the rock... These wells, being..filled in solid with masonry, form piers for arches. 1920 in Webster.

8. a. The central open space, from roof to basement, of a winding, spiral, or elliptical staircase; the open space in which a lift operates.

*a*1700 Evelyn *Diary* 7 Nov. 1644, 2 paire of oval stayres all of stone and voide in the well. 1783 *Phil. Trans.* LXXIII. 138 Which, passing over pullies.., was fastened to a scale that descended into the well of an adjoining stair-case. 1817 J. Evans *Excurs. Windsor* etc. 161 In the well of the staircase, by a cord of black and yellow, hangs a Gothic lantern. 1848 Thackeray *Van. Fair* lxi, If you choose to consider it, and sit on the landing, looking up and down the well! 1886 Stevenson *Kidnapped* iv, The same passing brightness showed me the steps were of unequal length, and that one of my feet rested that moment within two inches of the well. 1890 B. Hall *Turnover Club* viii. 87 But Gean hustled the man out to the elevator shaft and dropped him into the well beneath. 1901 *Scotsman* 8 Mar. 6/8 Fall down a hoist well. *Ibid.*, The cage..was at the bottom of the well.

b. The space on the floor of a law-court (between the Judge's bench and the last row of seats occupied by Counsel) where the solicitors sit.

1853 Dickens *Bleak Ho.* i, The various solicitors in the cause..ranged in a line, in a long matted well..between the registrar's red table and the silk gowns. 1879 Escott *England* II. 209 In the 'well,' a seat a step below that of the Queen's counsel, sit the solicitors. 1883 D. C. Murray *Hearts* xxviii, Wigged heads went together in the well of the court, and papers were rustled to and fro on the table.

c. A deep narrow space formed by the surrounding walls of a building or buildings, serving for the access of light and air.

1859 Dickens *T. Two Cities* ii. v. (end), Climbing to a high chamber in a well of houses, he threw himself down in his clothes on a neglected bed. *a*1861 T. Winthrop *Cecil Dreeme* v. (1896) 64 Through a most unsavoury alley into a court, or rather space, serving as a well to light the rear range of a tenement house. 1915 *Spectator* 29 May 742/2 The back-rooms look south—into the well.

d. = *orchestra pit* s.v. ORCHESTRA 4.

1933 P. Godfrey *Back-Stage* i. 15 The orchestra are in position in the 'well'. 1951 *Oxf. Compan. Theatre* 836/2 The Orchestra Well for the accommodation of the theatre musicians is in front of and below the stage itself.

9. a. A space left, in stacking hay, to serve as a ventilating shaft. *dial.*

1710 Hilman *Tusser Rediv.* Aug. (1744) 102 Some prescribe leaving a Hole or Well in the Middle of the Mow ..by keeping therein a Basket or Barrel, and raising it as the Mow increases. 1842 C. W. Johnson *Farmer's Encycl.* 1261 *Well*, a..vent hole left in a rick or mow of hay or other similar materials, to prevent its overheating.

b. In *Ship-* and *Boat-building* applied to various vertical apertures: see quots.

1874 Thearle *Naval Archit.* §192 When it is not considered necessary to provide a well for raising the propellor. 1894 Paasch *From Keel to Truck* 108 Well. The deepening between the ends of two waterballast-tanks, or between the ends of a double-bottom and a bulkhead. 1897–8 *Encycl. Sport* I. 179 *Well*, the opening in a decked canoe to admit the putting in of cargo and to accommodate the crew.

10. a. A box-like receptacle in the body of a vehicle, for articles of luggage.

1783 *Morn. Chron.* 14 Mar. 4/2 Advt., A very roomy crane-necked Travelling Coach, with well to the bottom, and luggages behind. 1794 W. Felton *Carriages* (1801) II. 199 The Well of a Carriage is a strong box conveniently placed at the body to carry luggage. 1848 Thackeray *Van. Fair* lxvi, The baggage was strapped on. Francis came out with his master's sword, cane, and umbrella tied up together, and laid them in the well. 1911 Sir W. Butler *Autobiog.* xx. 354 He..took three or four brace of grouse from the bag, and..put the birds in the 'well' of the vehicle [an Irish car].

b. A comparatively deep receptacle at the bottom of a piece of furniture, esp. of one fitted with trays, drawers, compartments, etc.

1841 Savage *Dict. Printing.* 1842 Lytton *Zanoni* vii. ii, He peered into the well [of an escritoire], and opened the drawers. 1879 Miss Braddon *Vixen* III. 47 There was an old-fashioned work-table, with a faded red silk well, beside the open window. 1888 Jacobi *Printers' Vocab.*, *Well*, a receptacle under the cases in the upper part of a composing frame, for holding copy, etc. 1905 H. G. Wells *Kipps* iii. iii. §4 Kipps..draws out the marvellous till; here gold is to be, here silver, here copper—notes locked up in a cash-box in the well below.

11. A hole or cavity containing or to contain a liquid. In various applications.

a. The water-tank at the base of a shot-tower, into which the drops of melted lead fall.

1851–4 *Tomlinson's Cycl. Useful Arts* (1867) II. 514/1 For the carrying out of this invention shot-towers and shot-wells have been constructed. 1884 Lock *Workshop Rec.* Ser. iii. 362/1 They are sufficiently hardened by cooling to bear the shock of striking the surface of the water in the well below.

b. A cavity at the bottom of a furnace, into which the molten metal falls.

1864 Webster. 1881 Raymond *Mining Gloss.* s.v., *Well.* The crucible of a furnace.

c. A sunk receptacle for a liquid, as ink, etc.; also, an indentation or cavity in a dish, tray, etc.; *spec.* in *Ceramics*, the depressed central portion of a plate, saucer, or dish.

1873 Spon *Workshop Rec.* Ser. i. 166/2 The bath should be..larger than the well, which must be a square hole, a little larger than the plate, and about an inch deep. 1881 *Pharmaceut. Jrnl.* 165 A small glass 'naphtha well', set in the case, similar to an 'ink well'. 1937 *Crockery & Glass Jrnl.* Nov. 28 The Fleurette shape..with flower grouping in the well and repeated on the shoulder. 1971 *Country Life* 21 Oct. 1055/1 The saucer is decorated with a circular medallion of The Bull and the Mouse, its well with four sprigs of flowers, the bowl with the Bull and the Frogs.

12. *Physics.* = *potential well* s.v. POTENTIAL *sb.* 4c.

1942 *Rep. Progress Physics* VIII. 302 The..way to estimate the depth of the well is to postulate that the binding energy of the least strongly bound particle shall be equal to the experimental value for this quantity. 1972 *Sci. Amer.* Apr. 27/1 The original aim was to create a well so deep (from 10 to 20 million volts deep) that the ion-ion collisions could be energetic enough for nuclear transmutations to occur.

13. *attrib.* and *Comb.*, as ***well-conductor***, ***-covering***, ***-drill***, ***-grating***, ***-hook***, ***-mouth***, ***-plate***, ***-pulley***, ***-pump***, ***-roof***, ***-rope***, ***-shaft***, ***-side***, ***-site***, ***-stage***, ***-tubbing*** (TUBBING *vbl. sb.* 2), ***-yard***; ***well-maker***; ***well-like*** adj.

1974 *BP Shield Internat.* Oct. 2/1 The jacket..wraps round the *well-conductors which go down into the ground. 1845 G. Petrie *Eccl. Archit. Ireland* 449 *Well Coverings. 1875 Knight *Dict. Mech.*, **Well-drill*, a tool for boring wells. 1886 W. J. Tucker *E. Europe* 410 It is the duty..of the eldest boy in the school..to see that the *well gratings are closed. 1585 Higins *Junius' Nomencl.* 302/1 *Lupus*,..a *well hooke. 1854 Thoreau *Walden* 195 We have one other pond just like this, White Pond..but I do not know a third of this pure and *well-like character. 1910 Rider Haggard *Q. Sheba's Ring* xvi. 241 [He] pointed to a jagged, well-like hole blown out..by the recoil of the blast. 1666 *Despauterii Grammat. Instit.* vii. (Jam.) *Aquilex*,..a *wel maker. 1895 *Daily News* 21 Dec. 5/4 When the second slip took place, the well-maker was suffocated. 1537–8 *Rec. St. Mary at Hill* 377 Paid for j lode of bryk for his *well mowthe. 1869 Tozer *Highl. Turkey* II. 130 The well-mouth, from being dry, becomes full of water. 1888 *Lockwood's Dict. Mech. Engin.*, **Well Plate.* A cast-iron plate put over the mouth of a well to carry the pumps, &c. 1940 W. Faulkner *Hamlet* i. i. 18 He had already begun to hear the mournful..plaint of a rusted *well-pulley. 1889 *Daily News* 5 Aug. 2/7 A substantially constructed set of *well pumps, even if fitted down a well 100 or 200 feet from the ground level, may be utilised as a fire engine in large establishments. 1886 Mrs. Flor. Caddy *Footsteps Jeanne D'Arc* v. 88 Chemillé has a romanesque church and the usual domical stone *well-roofs. 1424 *Mem. Ripon* (Surtees) III. 151 It. Roberto Raper pro ij wellerapis. 1575 *Aldeburgh Rec.* in *N. & Q.* 12th Ser. VII. 227/1 For a bucket ye hoopes, and a *well Roape..xiiii[d]. 1752 *Rec. Elgin* (New Spald. Club 1903) I. 465 Rigwoodies, tethers, wallropes. 1908 *Westm. Gaz.* 21 July 2/1 He went to a well and clambered down the well-rope. 1857 Dickens *Dorrit* i. iv, In one corner of the hall.. there was a little waiting-room, like a *well shaft. 1656 Earl Monm. tr. *Boccalini's Advts. fr. Parnass.* i. xcvii. (1674) 131 The Rope which hung upon the Bucket by the *well-side. 1818 Scott *Br. Lamm.* xx, For all she can sit idle by a well-side the whole day, when she has a handsome young gentleman to prate with. 1972 L. M. Harris *Introd. Deepwater Floating Drilling Operations* iii. 22 The *wellsite geologist should..provide technical assistance to the drilling supervisor. 1979 *Jrnl. R. Soc. Arts* CXXVII. 406/2 This led in due time to the adoption of a system of deep ditches around the various well sites. 1888 *Lockwood's Dict. Mech. Engin.*, **Well Stage.* A framing of timber erected over the mouth of a well to carry the pumps and pipe connections. 1898 F. Davis *Silchester* 41 Roman wine casks that have served the purpose of *well tubbing. 1480 *Coventry Leet-bk.* 446 Their plum house by þe *well-yarde yate.

14. Special comb.: **well-basket**, a long deep basket formerly used by street-hawkers; **well-beam**, the wooden beam or roller over which the rope of a well-bucket runs; **well-borer**, (*a*) one who bores wells; (*b*) a machine or apparatus for boring a well; **well-boring** *vbl. sb.*, the process of sinking a well by drilling through earth or rock; also *concr.*, the shaft of a well; **well-brick** (see quot. 1889); **well-bullock**, one used (in India) to turn the windlass at a well; **well-cabin** (see quot.); †**well-carse** (see WELL-CRESS); **well-chapel**, one enclosing a holy well; **well-cistern**, one fed by a spring; **well crane** (see quot. 1888); †**well crank**, a windlass for raising and lowering a bucket at a well; **well-curb**, (*a*) the stone border round the mouth of a well; (*b*) see quot. 1892; **well-digger**, one who digs or bores wells as a profession; **well-dish**, a meat-dish with a depression at one end as a receptacle for gravy; **well-drag** (see quot.); **well-drain** *Agric.*, a drain for wet land, made after the manner of a well, with a boring through which the water rises to be carried off by the drain; **well-draining**, a system of land drainage (see quot. and prec.); hence **well-drain** *v.* (Webster 1847–54); **well-dresser**, one who takes part in well-dressing; **well-dressing** = *tap-dressing* (TAP *sb.*[1] 8); **well-eye** *Sc.* and *north.*, a spot in a bog where a spring rises to the surface; a small pool of spring-water; *fig.* a source; †**well fern**, the maiden-hair *Adiantum Capillus-Veneris*; **well-fire** = *well-grate* below; **well-flowering** = *tap-dressing* (TAP *sb.*[1] 8); **well-girse**, **-grass** *Sc.* = WELL-CRESS; **well-god**, a tutelary deity of a well; **well-grate** (see quot. 1910); **well-horse**, a horse that turns the windlass of a well; **well-house**, a small building or room enclosing a well and its apparatus; **well-karses**, **-kerses** *Sc.* and *north.* (see WELL-CRESS); **well-kerb** = *well-curb*; **well-kick**, the exerting by an oil-well of pressure in excess of that of the drilling fluid pumped into it, leading to loss of circulation; **well-packing** (see PACKING *vbl. sb.*[1] 2 note); †**well-pipe**, a conduit-pipe; in quot. *fig.*; **well plum**, a local name of the pochard, *Fuligula ferina*; **well-pole**, (*a*) a well-sweep; (*b*) see quot. 1893; †**well-reeve** (see quot. and REEVE *sb.*[1] 2); **well-rig** (see quot.); **well-room**, (*a*) the place on the floor of a boat or ship where the water collects, and lies until it is pumped out; (*b*) = *well-house*; (*c*) see quot. 1858; **well-shanker** *Sc.* = *well-sinker*; **well shrimp**, a fresh-water crustacean found in wells; **well-sinker** = *well-borer*, *-digger*; **well-sinking** *vbl. sb.* = *well-boring*; **well-smack** = WELL BOAT[1]; **well-spherometer**, 'a form of spherometer for accurately measuring the radius of curvature of a lens' (*Cent. Dict.* 1891); **well-staircase**, **-stairs**, **-stairway**, a winding or geometrical staircase with a well or open centre; **wellstead** [STEAD *sb.* 7], a site for a well; **well-sweep** (see SWEEP *sb.* 24); **well-tomb**, a prehistoric tomb having a well or shaft for an entrance; **well-trap**, (*a*) a depression in a drain, in which water lies and prevents the escape of foul air; (*b*) see quot. 1893; **well-tube**, the casing-pipe of a driven well; **well-way**, the shaft of a well; **well-wheel**, the wheel that turns the axle of a windlass at a well; **well-work**, the making of a well; **well-worship**, the worship of a well or its guardian spirit; also **well-worshipping** *vbl. sb.* and *ppl. a.* Also WELL-BOAT, -BUCKET, -CRESS, etc.

1851 Mayhew *Lond. Labour* (1861) II. 485/1, I give two shillings for a 'shallow'; that's a flat basket with two handles; they put 'em a top of '*well-baskets', them as can carry a good load. 1895 Kipling *Soldiers Three*, etc. (1917) 273 He will hang him by the heels from the *well-beam. 1786 *Phil. Trans.* LXXVII. 50 George Naylor, of Louth, in the County of Lincoln, *Well-borer. 1852 *Mechanics' Mag.* 6

Nov. 370 Thomson's Artesian Well-borer. **1884** *Lisbon* (Dakota) *Star* 10 Oct., Experienced well-borers..will endeavor to find petroleum. **1835** URE *Philos. Manuf.* 57 Mine and artesian *well-boring. **1890** *Hardwicke's Sci. Gossip* XXVI. 74/1 Many years ago, in a well-boring,..the flanks of the buried Primary rocks were reached at a depth of 1100 feet. **1784** *Phil. Trans.* LXXV. 3 To build a wall of clay against the morassy sides of the well, with a wall of *well-bricks internally, up to the top of it. **1889** *N.W. Linc. Gloss.*, *Well-bricks*, curved bricks used for lining wells. **1879** MRS. A. E. JAMES *Ind. Househ. Managem.* 72 One of the *well-bullocks had a violent attack of the malady. **1867** SMYTH *Sailor's Word-bk.*, **Well-cabins*, those in brigs and small vessels, which have no afterwindows or thorough draught. **1858** J. T. BLIGHT *Anc. Crosses E. Cornw.* 94 *Well-chapel, Menacuddle, St. Austell... The length of this building is 11 feet... The spring rises in the east end. **1898** *Dulbin Rev.* July 150 A *well-cistern of clear spring water. **1905** W. HOLMAN HUNT *Pre-Raphaelitism* II. xi. 289 To judge from the company round the well-cisterns..it [Cana of Galilee] was at the time a happy neighbourhood. **1849** J. GLYNN *Constr. Cranes* 35 The *well crane having been found inconvenient for raising great weights, because of the insufficient resistance of the ground at the well top. **1888** *Lockwood's Dict. Mech. Engin.*, *Well Crane*, a fixed post crane, one-half of whose post is above ground and the other sunk in a pit, or well, dug to receive it. *c* **1440** *Promp. Parv.* 520/2 *Welle crank, *tollinum*. **1877** TALMAGE *Fifty Serm.* 23 Will you sit down in front of the *well-curb, when a few more turns of the windlass might bring up the..buckets? **1886** KIPLING *Departm. Ditties*, etc. (1899) 56 We have trodden the mart and the well-curb. **1892** *Dict. Arch.* (Arch. Publ. Soc.), *Well-curb*. The ring of elm or metal upon which the lining of a well is built. **1693** MOXON *Mech. Exerc.* (1703) 254 A Borer (such as *Well-Diggers use). **1883** *Harper's Mag.* Oct. 708/2 By trade he is a well-digger. **1880** BLACKMORE *Mary Anerley* xlvii, When a coal comes to table in a *well-dish. **1857** WRIGHT *Obs. & Provinc. Dict.*, **Well-drag*, a three-pronged drag to bring the bucket up when it falls in. Leic. **1881** *Leicestersh. Gloss.* **1819** REES *Cycl.*, **Well-drain*, in Agriculture, that sort of vent or discharge for the wetness of land, which is constructed in somewhat the well or pit manner. *Ibid.*, **Well-draining*, that means of clearing lands from wetness, which..is accomplished by making large deep pits or wells. **1898** R. M. GILCHRIST *Willowbrake* i, Within five minutes the curtain would be drawn aside and the *well-dressers set free to join the turbulent outside revellers. **1860** *Well-dressing [see *tap-dressing*: TAP *sb.*[1] 8]. **1882** C. F. KEARY *Outl. Prim. Belief* ii. 87 Fetichism survives in the honours paid to wells and fountains,..in England known under the name of 'well-dressing'. **1536** BELLENDEN *Cron. Scot.* (1821) I. 170 Thay knew nocht the ground, and fell sometimes in swards of mossis, and sum time in *well-eys. **1820** *Marmaiden of Clyde* ii. in *Edin. Mag.* VI. 422 An' the marmaid's goun was green as grass In the cauld wall-ee that grows. **1826** GALT *Last of Lairds* xxxv, The cause o' our national decay, and agricultural distress,..come a' thegither frae anither well-ee. **1565** COOPER *Thesaurus*, *Adiantum*..It may be called Venus heare..other name it to be *well ferne. **1906** *Studio* XXXVIII. 127/1 *Well-fires are used in all the rooms. **1824** E. RHODES *Peak Scenery* 315 An ancient custom still prevails in the village of Tissington... It is denominated *Well-Flowering. **1874** *Murray's Handbk. Derbysh.* etc. (ed. 2) 188 An ancient..custom of dressing the 5 wells or springs of this village..is still kept up, and is known as 'Tap Dressing', or 'Well Flowering'. **1903** SECCOMBE & ALLEN *Age Shaks.* I. I. 44 His [Browne's] Devonshire has a large population of river-gods, *well-gods, and nymphs. **1673** D. WEDDERBURN *Voc.* 18 (Jam.) *Nasturtium aquaticum*, *well-grass. **1825** JAMIESON, *Well-grass*, *Well-girse*, *Well-kerses*, Water-cresses. **1910** *Encycl. Brit.* XII. 378/2 In the closing years of the 19th century a '*well-grate' was invented, in which the fire burns upon the hearth, combustion being aided by an air-chamber below. **1927** W. E. COLLINSON *Contemp. Eng.* 90 Fires..are more often well-grates (i.e. low) than basket-grates (with hobs for the kettle). **1894** MEREDITH *Lett.* (1912) II. 461, I am under an engagement..to deliver a novel in the Spring, and have to go the round of a *well-horse daily. **1354–5** *Durham Acc. Rolls* (Surtees) 555 In una sera reparanda pro le *Welhousdore. **1466–7** *Ibid.* 641 Pro punctuacione super stabulum hospitum et le Wellehouse infra abbathiam. **1597** in *Archaeologia* LXIV. 369, 1500 ston lat nail for ye well house. **1895** CROCKETT *Men of Moss-Hags* xxvii, I made a rush swiftly round the corner, and entered the well-house. **1889** KIPLING *Soldiers Three* (ed. 3) 67 Losson..lowered the cage [of the parrot] into the cool darkness of a well, and sat on the *well-kerb. **1972** L. M. HARRIS *Introd. Deepwater Floating Drilling Operations* x. 97 Closing in around the drill pipe and circulating a conventional *well kick. **1974** P. L. MOORE et al. *Drilling Practices Manual* xi. 277 Failure to recognize a well kick could be disastrous. **1875** KNIGHT *Dict. Mech.*, *Well-packing. **1540** COVERDALE *Fruitf. Lessons* T 4 b, Here are opened the conduites and *well pipes of life. **1862** JOHNS *Brit. Birds* 625 *Wellplum, the Red-headed Pochard. **1885** SWAINSON *Prov. Names Birds* 160 Well plum. **1826** LONGF. in S. Longfellow *Life* (1886) I. 86 There is so little..to remind one that he is out of town: no corn-fields..no slab-fences: no *well-poles. **1893** *S.E. Worc. Gloss.*, *Well-pole*, a pole having at the end a hook, with which the bucket is lowered into the well for the purpose of bringing up water. **1613** *Coventry Leet Bk.* II. 21 Apr. 11 Jas. I. leaf 63 (MS.) Such said aldermen..and such ten persons..shall choose and elect two persons dwelling in everie particular ward where any comon well is..to be *well-reeves for one whole year. **1875** KNIGHT *Dict. Mech.* 2759/1 **Well-rig* is the term applied to the whole *plant* for well-boring, consisting of the derrick, its engine [etc.]. **1769** FALCONER *Dict. Marine* (1780), s.v. *Limbers*. The water..is conveyed to the *well-room, where the pumps are fixed. **1852** *Hist. Co. Oxford* 278 A very curious well-room of the time of Henry II has been discovered in the centre of the keep tower. **1858** SIMMONDS *Dict. Trade*, *Well-room*, an apartment or building containing a mineral spring or spa, where the waters are drunk by invalids. **1882** *Well-shanker [see SHANKER 4]. **1853** *Gard. Chron.* 23 Apr. 260/2 A *Well Shrimp, a small white crustaceous animal, about half an inch long. **1914** *Brit. Mus. Return* 171 Well-shrimp. **1604** *Shuttleworths' Acc.* (Chetham Soc.) 156 A *well-sinker, vj days sinkinge the well..iij[s]. **1884** *B'ham Daily Post* 24 Jan. 3/4 Wanted..three good Well-sinkers. **1858** *Q. Rev.* Jan. 6 All sorts of earthwork, in embanking, boring, and *well-sinking. **1915** *Daily News* 20 Sept. 1 The authorities have requisitioned all workmen with a knowledge of well-sinking..and are sending them..to work on drilling artesian wells. **1765** *Museum Rust.* IV. 238 The *well-smacks employed in our cod-fisheries. **1840** DICKENS *Old C. Shop* xlviii, A little out-of-the-way door at the foot of the *well staircase flew briskly open. **1868** *Daily News* 4 Aug., If space is an object, two or three well-staircases..might be employed. **1892** *Dict. Arch.* (Arch. Publ. Soc.), *Well-stairs. **1883** *Harper's Mag.* Feb. 347/1 The central column around which these *well-stairways usually wind. **1546** *Yorks. Chantry Surv.* (Surtees) I. 152 For a *wellsteede..for a wellstede and a fysshyng. **1876** *Whitby Gloss.*, *Wellsteead*, the site of a well. **1828–32** WEBSTER, *Well-sweep. **1836** C. A. GOODRICH *Universal Traveller* (ed. 2) I. i. 27 Here and there, by the side of the older houses, may be seen a well-sweep, a primitive contrivance to draw up water by a pole, which is attached to a beam, moving up and down on an axle. *c* **1850–60** ALICE & PHŒBE CARY in M. C. Ames *Mem.* (1873) 252 A grape vine, shaggy and rough and red, Swings from the well-sweeps high, sharp head. **1886** E. S. MORSE *Jap. Homes* ii. 73 In this sketch a regular New England well-sweep is seen. **1889** *Nation* 11 Apr. 303/1 The graves belong to the type of '*well-tombs'. **1850** OGILVIE, **Well-trap*, the same as *stench-trap*. **1893** J. WATSON *Confess. Poacher* 133 The well-trap is a square, deep box, built into the ground opposite to a smoot-hole in the fence through which the rabbits run. As the rabbits run, the floor opens, and they drop into the well. **1875** KNIGHT *Dict. Mech.*, *Well-tube. **1753** HANWAY *Trav.* (1762) I. II. xvi. 69 The method of keeping them clear of water, is by a large scoop which is suspended..over the *well-way. **1900** *Engineering Mag.* XIX. 772/2 A sea-going hydraulic dredge having the ladder for the suction-pipe and cutter in a well-way in the centre. **1535** *MS. Rawl. D.* 777 fol. 84 b, ix new storoppes to staye the Rynge of the *well wheell to the spokes. **1542** UDALL *Erasm. Apoph.* 24 *marg.*, The scoldyng of brathels is no more to bee passed on, then the squekyng of welle wheles. **1895** *Atlantic Monthly* Mar. 308 You take insult like a donkey on a well wheel. **1858** SKYRING *Builders' Prices* 76 The digging will only be applicable to *Well-work, as that for Drains must of course depend upon their depth. **1810** C. O'CONOR *Columbanus's Third Let.* 84 Origin of Irish *Well-worship. **1882** *Proc. Berw. Nat. Club* IX. 510 Well-worship continues to this day, and votive gifts..are still thrown into the clear spring waters. **1810** C. O'CONOR *Columbanus's Third Let.* 79 *Well-worshipping was a Druidic superstition. **1892** *Catholic News* 23 July 5/5 A race of well-worshipping semi-pagans.

† **well**, *sb.*[2] *Obs.* [f. WELL *adv.*, substituted for WEAL *sb.*[1] under the influence of F. *bien*.]

1. Well-being, welfare, advantage, profit. **a.** In contrast to *woe*.

c **1385** CHAUCER *L.G.W.* 687 Neuere..ȝe nere out of myn hertis remembraunce For wel or wo, for carole or for daunce. *c* **1420** J. PAGE *Siege Rouen* in *Hist. Coll. Citizen Lond.* (Camden) 35 Thes were the syghtys of dyfferauns,.. That one of welle and þat othyr of wo. **1450–1530** *Myrr. Our Ladye* III. 320 For the soulle when yt ys departed fro the body by dethe receyueth anon welle or wo. **1550** CROWLEY *Last Trumpet* 160 But do thou nothing wickedly, Neyther for wel nor yet for wo. **1600** W. WATSON *Decacordon* (1602) 350 A resolute intent..in well, and in woe, to remaine constant.

b. In general use; freq. in *for the well of* —.

1424 *Coventry Leet Bk.* 72 ȝif it so be þat thei towche the well of the kyng..or his realme. **1440** in *Wars Eng. in France* (Rolls) II. 588 My saide lorde desireth that it like the king of his goode grace, for the grete welle of bothe his royaumes, to ordeyn,..that [etc.]. ? **1497** in *Lett. Rich. III & Hen. VII* (Rolls) II. 74 For the welle of hys saule he can noo lesse doo then sue for absolucion. **1509** BARCLAY *Shyp of Folys* 229 For worldy ryches, the trouth nat playne to tell, Puttynge bodely profyte before eternall well. **1525** BERNERS *Froiss.* II. xx. 17 b, For y[e] well of the peace..we desyre them to sette to their seales. **1590** SPENSER *F.Q.* I. ii. 43 That may restore you to your wonted well. **1632** LITHGOW *Trav.* IX. 414 Hungary aboundeth..in all things the earth can produce for the well of man. *a* **1645** LD. NAPIER *Mem.* (1793) 43 My Lord Lowdon..might have thought me willfull against my owne well.

2. *well public* = WEAL-PUBLIC 2. *rare*$^{-1}$.

1579 LODGE *Def. Plays* 6 Though Plato could wish the expulsion of Poetes from his well publiques,..yet the wisest had not all that same opinion.

3. Good or honourable report.

c **1500** *Melusine* 135 She..desired moche to see him for the well that it was said of hym. [**1802** COLERIDGE *Ode to Rain* 28 I'll nothing speak of you but well.]

well (wɛl), *a.* Forms: 3–7 **wel**, 4–6 **wele**, 5 **welle**, 5– **well**; *Sc.* and *north.* 5 **weyll**, 6–7 **weill** (6 **weil**), 6– **weel**. [From WELL *adv.* in predicative use: see sense 1.]

1. Used predicatively to denote a state of good fortune, welfare, or happiness: † **a.** With the dative of the personal pronouns, esp. in the formula ***well is me, thee, him***, etc., or ***well worth him***, etc. *Obs.* (Cf. L. *bene est mihi*, etc.)

Beowulf 186 Wel bið þæm þe mot æfter deaðdæȝe Drihten secan. *c* **825** *Vesp. Psalter* xxxiv. 21 [Hie] cwedon: wel ðe, wel ðe [L. *euge*]. *c* **1000** ÆLFRIC *Gen.* xii. 13 þæt me wel siȝ for þe, and min sawul lybbe for þinum intingan. *Ibid. Num.* xi. 18 Wel us wæs on Egipta lande. **12..** *Moral Ode* (Egerton MS.) 388 in *O.E. Hom.* I. 183 Of him to sene nis no[n] sed, wel hem is þe hine bi-healeð. *c* **1205** LAY. 13079 Wel wurðe þe Vortiger þat þu ært icumen her. *a* **1225** *Ancr. R.* 124 Wel is me uor mine gode, & wo is me þauh for þin vuel. *c* **1250** *Gen. & Ex.* 2387 'Wel me,' quað he, 'wel is me wel, ðat ic aue abiden ðus swil[c] sel!' **1297** R. GLOUC. (Rolls) 5751 A voys sede, as him þoȝte, þes wordes þoru þe soun, Wel is þe, wel is þe, as he vel adoun. *a* **1310** in Wright *Lyric P.* xviii. 59 Suete Jhesu, wel may him be, That the may in blisse se! *c* **1374** CHAUCER *Troylus* I. 350 Lord wel is hym þat may be of yow oon. *c* **1380** WYCLIF *Sel. Wks.* I. 256 And so at þe daie of dome, God shal not seie, Wel be þee. **1423** JAS. I. *Kingis Q.* liii, A! wele were him that now were In thy plyte! **1470–85** MALORY *Arthur* X. lxxxii. 558 Wel is me that I haue mette with yow. **1523** SKELTON *Garl. of Laurel* 718 O wele were hym that herof myght be sure. **1535** COVERDALE *Ps.* cxxviii. 2 O well is the, happie art thou. **1599** T. STORER *Life & D. Wolsey* B 3 b, But well is me where e're my ashes lie, If one teare drop from some religious eie. **1650** J. CARSTAIRES *Lett.* (1846) 63 If so, weils me for evermore. **1690** W. WALKER *Idiomat. Anglo-Lat.* 512 Well is me if this be true. **1825** BROCKETT *N.C. Words*, *Weel's-mon-thee*! God bless you.

† **b.** With nouns, orig. in the dative, but latterly (by loss of inflection) capable of being construed as nominatives. Also rarely with *to* or *for*. *Obs.*

c **1000** *Laws Cnut* lxxxiv. (Lieberm.) 368 Wel þære heorde ðe ȝefolȝað þam hyrde. *a* **1300** *Assump. Virg.* 99 Wel beo þe time þat þu were ibore, For al þis wordle were forlore. *c* **1330** R. BRUNNE *Chron. Wace* (Rolls) 1797 A place to pleye, ordeyned Brutus,—Corineus was wel of þat graunt—ffor to wrastle wyþ þat geaunt. *a* **1352** MINOT *Poems* ii. 5 It es wrokin, I wene, wele wurth þe while. *c* **1400** *Destr. Troy* 477 Well were that woman might weld hym for euer. *c* **1430** *How Good Wijf tauȝte hir Douȝtir* 213 in *Babees Bk.* (1868) 47 For weel is þe child þat wiþ synne wole not be filid. *c* **1450** *Merlin* xiv. 225 Well were that maiden that so feire a knyght wolde requere hir of love. **1509** BARCLAY *Shyp of Folys* 135 Well is that londe, and ioyous may it be, Whiche is defendyd by suche a noble estate. **1593** G. HARVEY *Pierces Super.* 141 Yet well-worth the Master-Ape. **1597** BP. HALL *Sat.* III. ii. 19 Well were thy name and thee Wert thou inditched in great secrecie. **1602** CAREW *Cornwall* I. 37 In times past.. Holdings were so plentifull and Holders so scarce, as well was the Land-lord who could get one to bee his Tenant. **1606** ROLLOCK *1 Thess.* 84 Well is that man in whose mouth this word is put: and well is that people that hes a man in whose mouth the Lord hes put his word. **1678** SPRAT *Serm. Gal. vi. 10*, 16 Charity..is made the constant Companion.. of all Virtues..and well it is for that Virtue, where it most enters, and longest stayes.

c. With the nominative forms of the personal pronouns, or with nouns clearly construed as nominatives.

In this usage freq. placed, like other adjectives, after the vb.

1297 R. GLOUC. (Rolls) 5765 He wende to heuene & was wel ynou. **1340** HAMPOLE *Pr. Consc.* 1452 Now er men wele, now er men wa. *a* **1375** *Joseph Arim.* 33 He þat ledes vs þis wei vre herborwe schal wisse. Þei founden hit newely, so wel weore þei neuere. *Ibid.* 659 We weore so wel of vr-self, we nuste what we duden. **1406** HOCCLEVE *La Male Regle* 12 Whil thy power [O Health!]..Regned in me & was my gouernour, Than was I wel, tho felte I no duresse. *c* **1450** *Cov. Myst.*, *Counc. Jews* 91 *Cayphas.* Fare wel, sere, and wel ȝe be. *c* **1489** CAXTON *Sonnes of Aymon* xxiv. 528 Now wold I be well in my ship in the myddes of the see, for if I abyde him, he shall make an ende of me. **1513** DOUGLAS *Æneis* VII. iii. 38 All haill our native goddis, weill ȝe be! *a* **1547** SURREY *Æneid* II. 301 And well were they whoes handes might touch the cordes. **1563–83** FOXE *A. & M.* 983 They fell to singyng. .. Well was he that could reache the hyest note. **1595** J. KING *Serm. Queen's Day* in *Lect. Jonas* (1597) 703 O well were wee in the daies of Queene Elizabeth. **1597** BEARD *Theatre God's Judgem.* 183 Wel was he that could hide himself in a corner. **1688** PENTON *Guardian's Instruction* 24 He was never well but when he was managing or talking of the Dogs. **1818** SHELLEY *To Mary* —— 11 Mary dear, come to me soon, I am not well whilst thou art far.

2. a. In favour, in good standing or estimation, on good terms, *with* (a person). Also rarely with *together*.

Originally with *to be* (see also the special senses below); now common only with *keep* or *stand* (see STAND *v.* 15 e), with approach to an adverbial force. The gap in the evidence between the 15th and 18th cent. is remarkable.

a **1300** *Cursor M.* 9521 He had an anlepe son, þat wit his fader was sa wele þat [he] wist his wisdom ilk dele. *c* **1300** *Havelok* 2878 She is fayr, and she is fre,..þertekene she is wel with me. **1377** LANGL. *P. Pl.* B. III. 152 There she [Meed] is wel with þe kynge, wo is þe rewme. *c* **1435** *Torr. Portugal* 1948 That man was well with god all-myȝt. *c* **1450** *Godstow Reg.* 26 She was fayre and comly, and well was with the kyng almyhty.

1709 MRS. MANLEY *Secret. Mem.* (1720) III. 76 There was nothing I outwardly omitted to be well with her Majesty. **1739** tr. *Rollin's Anc. Hist.* XVII. ii. (ed. 2) VIII. 30 Antigonus..had..intreated Philip to keep well with Aratus. **1741** CHESTERF. *Lett.* 8 Aug., The last [report] I had from Mr. Maittaire was so good a one, that you and I are at present extremely well together. **1750** *Ibid.* 26 Apr., He is well with..many people of the first distinction at Paris. **1753** RICHARDSON *Grandison* II. xii. 87 That he might stand well with a son, whose character..made his father half afraid of him. **1770** in Earl Malmesbury *Diaries & Corr.* (1844) I. 66 For although they are by no means well together, yet they would both find their advantages in a war. **1811** *Ora & Juliet* II. 66 She chose to keep well with the Dudleys in all appearance. **1881** MRS. LYNN LINTON *My Love* I. i. 13 He desired to keep well with Stella's father. **1883** D. C. MURRAY *Hearts* xiv, The new heir..had good reasons for standing well with his neighbours.

fig. **1820** T. BROWN *Lect. Philos. Human Mind* IV. c. 608 'The true secret of happiness', says Fontenelle, 'is to be well with our own mind.'

b. *spec.* On terms of intimate friendship or familiarity *with* (a woman).

1704 CIBBER *Careless Husb.* V. iii, But it's so natural for a prude to be malicious when a man endeavours to be well with anybody but herself. **1784** BAGE *Barham Downs* I. 91 You must know Sir, I have the honour to be well with Mrs. Gadbury, Lady Conollan's woman. **1809** MALKIN *Gil Blas* III. v. ¶2 All our set were well with some fine woman or other. *Ibid.* III. vii. ¶3 Do not suppose that you are well with a Duchess.

† **c.** Pleased or satisfied *with* (oneself). Also *well to do*. *Obs.*

1786 MRS. A. M. BENNETT *Juvenile Indiscr.* I. 11 He could not avoid being extremely well with himself. **1854** SURTEES *Handley Cr.* vii. (1901) I. 62 He went on 'Change with..a strut that plainly told how well he was to do with himself. **1865** 'Annie Thomas' *On Guard* I. iv. 61 His horses.. rattled over the stones..at a rate he would not have driven them had he been well with himself just then.

†**d.** Without const. In favour. *Obs.*

1694 M. Prior in *Lett. Lit. Men* (Camden) 213 Neither the Dauphin or Monsʳ Luxemberg are very well in Court. **1752** Chesterf. *Lett.* 22 Sept., However, be as well at court as you possibly can. *Ibid.*, In short, make yourself well there, without making yourself ill somewhere else. **1776** in Sparks *Corr. Amer. Rev.* (1853) I. 203, I have the pleasure to inform you that I am extremely well in the opinion of the senatorial part.

3. a. In a state of prosperity or affluence; more explicitly ***well in goods*** or ***cash, well in the world***; = well off 1 c. (See also well to do, to live, to pass.) Now *rare.* exc. in *well to do, well off.*

to leave (a person) ***well, to be well left***: to leave or be left well off by devise or inheritance.

c **1386** Chaucer *Knt.'s T.* 68 Thanked be ffortune and hire false wheel, That noon estat assureth to be weel. **1463** Ashby *Prisoner's Refl.* 78 Whiche greuyd me sore.. To be in pouert and of goodes bad, That before was well in goodes and rest. **1606** Dekker *Sev. Sinnes* v. (Arb.) 36 Richmens sonnes that were left well, and had more money giuen by will, then they had wit how to bestow it. **1682** in *N. & Q.* 12th Ser. IX. 436/2 He has left euery body that is related to him good Legaseys and his wife extreame well. **1686** tr. *Chardin's Coronat. Solyman* 130 A Family that is not very well in the World. **1746** W. Horsley *Fool* (1748) I. 189 Vanesius was well in Cash. **1780** *Mirror* No. 97 He imperceptibly became, 'in easy circumstances, well in the world, of great credit, [etc.]. **1809** Malkin *Gil Blas* II. vii. ¶4 He must be very well in the world. **1835** *Politeness & Good-breeding* 97 Two boys..the one high-born as to rank, and..the other well in the world as to riches. **1875** [see leave *v.*[1] 2 b].

†**b.** ***well and warm***: in comfortable and affluent circumstances. *Obs.*

1571 Campion *Hist. Irel.* II. ix. (1633) 114 But you are well and warme and so hold you. *a* **1670** Wood *Life* (O.H.S.) I. 129 A. W. seemed very sorry at this news, because he was well and warme where he was. **1673** Hickeringill *Greg. F. Greybeard* 4, I shall not get a penny by your custome; neither do I desire it. For I am well and warm.

c. Favourably circumstanced; having things as one wishes them to be; = well off 1 a. Now *rare.*

c **1440** *Partonôpe* 5281 When wymmen be well they can not cese. **1598** Shaks. *Merry W.* I. i. 278 *An.* Wil't please your worship to come in, Sir? *Sl.* No, I thank you forsooth, hartely; I am very well. **1606** —— *Ant. & Cl.* II. v. 33 We vse To say, the dead are well. **1643** Burroughes *Exp. 1st 3 ch. Hosea* II. v. 351 You who are thorough Gods mercy in his way, you are now well, know when you are well, and keep you wel. *c* **1645** Howell *Lett.* (1650) III. 24, I am afraid we have seen our best days, we knew not when we were well. **1784** Bage *Barham Downs* I. 64 But every body, Mrs. Susan, don't know when they are well. **1865** M. Arnould *Ess. Crit.*, *Academies* ¶2 Not without a little hesitation—for apparently they found themselves very well as they were.. —they consented.

4. In a sound or undamaged state; *spec.* in marine insurance, of a vessel.

c **1450** *St. Cuthbert* (Surtees) 475 God shewed meruaile in apert. Þe bell was wele al swythe. **1580** H. Smith in Hakluyt *Voy.* (1589) 470 Wee were afraid that she [the ship] had taken some hurt, but she was well. **1667** Earl Orrery *St. Lett.* (1742) 288 He..came..to inform me..that the Rupert was driven from them by force of weather, but doubts not, that she is well. **1848** J. Arnould *Marine Insur.* I. 586 In order to protect himself from liability to any loss before a given day, the underwriter frequently causes a warranty to be inserted in the policy that the ship was 'all safe', or 'well', on the day.

5. a. Sound in health; free or recovered from sickness or infirmity: more explicitly ***well in health.*** Const. *of* (a sickness, wound). Also ***not well*** (Sc. ***no weel***) = unwell *a.* 2 (†formerly with *of a sudden, o' th' sudden*).

1555 Card. Pole in *Eng. Hist. Rev.* (1913) July 529 Thoȝ my passage over the see was not so quyet..yet after I was londed I found myself very wel. **1560** Daus tr. *Sleidane's Comm.* 428 b, She was not very wel in health. **1596** Shaks. *Merch. V.* III. ii. 238 Not sicke my Lord, vnlesse it be in minde, Nor wel, vnlesse in minde. **1598** —— *Merry W.* I. i. 80 *M. Page.* I am glad to see your Worships well. **1599** —— *Much Ado* IV. i. 63 Is my Lord well, that he doth speake so wide? **1634** Milton *Comus* 1000 Where young Adonis oft reposes, Waxing well of his deep wound. **1650** Cromwell *Let.* 30 July in *Carlyle*, The Major-General will, I believe, within few days be well to take the field. **1711** Swift *Jrnl. to Stella* 1 Dec., He..drinks no claret yet, for fear of his rheumatism, of which he is almost well. **1782** Cowper *Gilpin* 220 This shall be yours when you bring back My husband safe and well. **1831** Scott *Ct. Robt.* xxxii, Ursel.. is restored to you well in health. **1853** Dickens *Bleak Ho.* xxiii, I hope you are well. I am happy to see you. **1864** Trollope *Small Ho. Allington* xx, 'The fact is this; I'm very well, you know;—as strong as a horse.' 'You look pretty well.'

(*b*) **1608** Middleton *Trick to catch Old-one* v. H 2 b, Troth I am not well of a suddaine. *a* **1616** Beaum. & Fl. *Wit without Money* III. i, A proper Gentleman: I am not well o' th' sudden. **1667** Dryden *Secret Love* I. iii, Dear Asteria lead me, I am not well o'th sudden. (*She faints.*)

†**b.** ***well in*** (one's) ***wits***: of sound mind. *Obs.*

1561 Hoby tr. *Castiglione's Courtier* I. (1900) 90 A manne may assuredly thinke him not to be wel in his wittes. **1577** tr. *Bullinger's Decades* II. viii. 206 What man that were wel in his wittes would say to kinges [etc.]. **1581** Pettie tr. *Guazzo's Civ. Conv.* I. (1586) 4 If I shuld say it, rather I (than you) might be thought scarce wel in my wits. **1645** Sir R. Weston *Husb. Brabant* (1652) 26 Such profitable Terms, as no man, that is well in his wits, but will venture at them. **1686** W. Clagett *17 Serm.* (1699) App. 18 No body, well in his wits can be misled by it. **1720** Waterland *Eight Serm.* 90 A Man would hardly be supposed well in his Wits, that should seriously entertain any the least Doubt..concerning it.

c. Used attributively, esp. as ***well man*** (†sometimes hyphened).

1628 Digby *Voy. Mediterr.* (Camden) 14, I tooke a view of my well men. **1654** Whitlock *Zootomia* 95 Our division of the living is not so much into Physitian, and Patient, as into well Physitian, and sick Physitian. **1666** Pepys *Diary* 12 Feb., In spite,..ill people would breathe in the faces, out of their windows, of well people going by. **1672** Wiseman *Wounds* II. vii. 50 He..could take no rest until his wounded finger was digested, yet his pain was not so great in his Wound, as in his well fingers. **1700** Dryden *Fables, Cock & Fox* 401 But neither Pills nor Laxatives I like, They only serve to make a well-man sick. **1737** B. Franklin *Poor Richard* (1890) 73 Poor Dick eats like a well man, and drinks like a sick. **1759** *Ann. Reg.* 62 One of the ships..with no more than 65 guns..and but 472 well men at quarters. **1841** Catlin *N. Amer. Ind.* (1844) II. xlv. 80 Of those who are alive, there are not well ones enough to take care of the sick. **1874** Howells *Chance Acquaint.* iv. (1882) 97 Calling Kitty's attention to his ingenuity by a pressure with her well foot. **1879** —— *L. Aroostook* (1883) II. 10 They welcomed him back to animation with the patronage with which well people hail a convalescent. **1900** 'Mark Twain' *Man that corrupted* etc. 128 Two days later he 'began to eat like a well man'.

(*b*) Comb., as **well-baby**, used *attrib.* to designate clinics or health care arrangements for routine checking of healthy children, as a form of preventive medicine; **well woman** (usu., with hyphen, *attrib.*), a woman who has undergone satisfactory gynæcological tests. orig. *N. Amer.*

1921 *Daily Colonist* (Victoria, B.C.) 5 Oct. 6/4 A well-baby clinic will be held at the Saanich Health Centre..An invitation is extended to all mothers to bring their infants. **1963** *Jrnl. Amer. Med. Assoc.* 2 Nov. 459/1 She had been advised to bring the child to the well-baby clinic. **1976** G. E. Godber *Brit. National Health Service* i. 5 Many of the elected councils of cities and counties had not used their powers to provide antenatal and well-baby care. **1977** *PEN Broadsheet* No. 3. 3/3 A range of leaflets on contraceptive methods, well-women care, sex-related diseases. **1980** *Brit. Med. Jrnl.* 29 Mar. 958/2 The new hospital will have a 40-bed gynaecological unit with a wide range of outpatient services and a specially designed 'well woman clinic' to provide urgently needed health screening. **1981** 'G. Gaunt' *Incomer* xxvi. 173 That Thursday's well-baby clinic functioned with the slick accuracy of a Jesuit mass. **1984** S. Townsend *Growing Pains A. Mole* 13 She says she needs the money for her 'Well Woman' test. She is having primary and secondary sexual organs checked. **1985** *Observer* (Colour Suppl.) 14 Apr. 23/3 She looked every inch the part of the world's most glamorous well-woman.

d. *absol.* (as pl.). Those who are sound in health.

1676 *Princ. Chymists Lond.* 104 For our S. P. never worketh on the Well, either by Vomit or Stool. **1783** Johnson *Let. Dr. Brocklesby* 29 Aug., in *Boswell*, It is great consolation to the well, and still greater to the sick. **1841** Catlin *N. Amer. Ind.* (1844) II. xlii. 69 Leaving about 30 sick, and about an equal number of well to take care of and protect them. **1886** Besant *Childr. Gibeon* xxv, Every body feels it, the sick and the well, the patient and the nurses. **1908** *Westm. Gaz.* 22 Feb. 16/1 It should be the business of the doctors to prevent the well from getting sick.

e. ***well day***: a day on which one is free from sickness, esp. from an attack of an intermittent disorder. (Sometimes hyphened.)

1652 Wood *Life* Aug. (O.H.S.) I. 176 What in the well-days his stomach had contracted, he would on the sick-day vomit it out. *a* **1657** R. Loveday *Lett.* (1663) 175, I scarce enjoy'd one well day in ten Weeks absence. **1719** De Foe *Crusoe* I. (Globe) 96 The 30th was my Well-day..and I went abroad with my Gun. **1760–72** H. Brooke *Fool of Qual.* (1809) II. 113 As it was one of his well days, he walked in without help. **1799** Underwood *Dis. Childhood* (ed. 4) I. 301 Repeated cold and hot fits..with one or more well-days between them. **1869** Carlyle *New Lett.* (1904) II. 251, I struggle to hang by my 'Work'..and generally do get a particle or two of it done every well-day.

f. Of a person's health or spirits: Sound, good. Of sickness: Cured.

1712 Swift *Jrnl. to Stella* 9 Oct., Lord-treasurer has had an ugly fit of the rheumatism, but it is now near quite well. **1760–2** Goldsm. *Cit. W.* v, His health, thank Heaven, is still pretty well. **1801** Eliz. Helme *St. Marg. Cave* III. 186 Your health is, I fear, not well. **1836** Southey *Cowper's Wks.* III. 137 Yet he described his spirits as tolerably well in the day. **1847** Surtees *Hawbuck Grange* iv. 74 Indeed he had fully determined, if his cold was well enough, to ride over to Snailswell.

6. In the phrase (*it is*) ***well*** (*that*) or *to*:

a. Advisable, desirable, to be recommended.

1475 *Bk. Noblesse* 82 It is welle to undrestonde that ye haue no protectoure, kepar, ne defendour but it come of God. **1605** Shaks. *Macb.* I. vii. 2 Then 'twer well, It were done quickly. **1820** Keats *Eve St. Agnes* xxxviii, If thou think'st well To trust, fair Madeline, to no rude infidel. **1848** Dickens *Dombey* xlvi, I never thought to look at him again, ..but it's well I should, perhaps. **1864** 'Annie Thomas' *D. Donne* III. 97 Suggestions as to the seat it would be well for him to take. **1910** *Encycl. Brit.* II. 28/1 When a trout rises it is well to count 'ten' before striking.

b. Gratifying, fortunate, lucky; forming a matter for satisfaction or thankfulness.

1665 Dk. Ormonde in *11th Rep. Hist. MSS. Comm.* App. v. 13 It is well wee have time to looke about us before the next assault. **1701** De Foe *Trueborn Eng.* 23 'Tis well that Virtue gives Nobility. **1717** Atterbury *Serm.* (1734) I. 161 It is well they afford us both these. **1779** Warner in Jesse *Selwyn & Contemp.* (1844) IV. 271 Such a dinner as we had to-day! it was well it was a christening! **1842** Dickens *Amer. Notes* xiv, It was well for us, that we were in this humour, for the road [etc.]. **1859** Tennyson *Guinevere* 421 Well is it that no child is born of thee. **1865** Le Fanu *Guy Deverell* III. 149 It is well when these sudden collapses of the overwrought nerves occur.

c. ***as well..if*** or ***that***, in preceding senses.

1753–4 Richardson *Grandison* II. xxvii. 209 Perhaps in this case..it were as well they did not. **1801** *Marvellous Love-Story* II. 288, I think it would be as well if John was to go off..this afternoon. **1889** Mrs. E. Kennard *Landing a Prize* vii, Perhaps it was just as well..that Ebenezer remained in his cabin.

7. a. Of a state of things, work, an undertaking, etc.: Satisfactory; of such a nature, or in such a condition, as to meet with approval or give content.

1381 in Knighton *Chron.* (Rolls) II. 139 For if the ende be wele, than is alle wele. **1523–34** Fitzherb. *Husb.* §14 If it be thynne, sowe thycker the nexte yere; and if it be well, holde his hande there other yeres. **1523** Skelton *Garl. Laurel* 763 He can neuer leue warke whylis it is wele. **1580** H. Smith in Hakluyt *Voy.* (1589) 471 We did tarrie for her to know whether all was well with her. **1581** A. Hall *Iliad* v. 76 The warre they deeme not well for them. **1604** Shaks. *Oth.* III. i. 45 Goodmorrow (good Lieutenant) I am sorrie For your displeasure: but all will sure be well. **1620** T. May *Heir* I. (1633) B 1, That's well, that's very well. **1746** Francis tr. *Hor., Sat.* II. vi. 10, I have enough in my possessing, 'Tis well. **1798–1803** Jane Austen *Northanger Abb.* x, Though it is vastly well to be here for a few weeks, we would not live here for millions. **1820** W. Irving *Sketch Bk., Wife* (1821) I. 35 She saw..with the quick eyes of affection, that all was not well with him. **1859** E. FitzGerald *Omar Khayam* lxiv, He's a Good Fellow, and 'twill all be well.

Prov. **1381** [see above]. **1562** J. Heywood *Prov.* (1867) 21 Well aunt (quoth Ales) All is well that endes well. **1600** F. L. *Ovid's Remedie of Love* etc., To Rdr. E 3 b, Yet take this old Prouerbe with a right application..All is well that endeth well. And so end I. **1724** P. Walker *Peden* (1827) Pref. p. xxvii, The old Saying holds, that All's well that ends well. **1905** 'G. Thorne' *Lost Cause* iv. 106 All's well that ends well! You won't have the services disturbed again.

b. of material things.

1562 J. Heywood *Prov. & Epigr.* (1867) 118 It [*sc.* a cheese] is, saith an other, well as can bee. **1595** in *Archaeologia* LXIV. 389 Because the walles ryse and be not well nor all of one collore, the most be wheyted at the plasterers charge. **1596** Shaks. *Tam. Shr.* IV. i. 172 *Kate.* The meate was well... *Pet.* I tell thee Kate, 'twas burnt and dried away. **1599** Minsheu *Span. Dial.* 3 This water is now well [*Ya esta buena est agua*], you may now wel wash Sir. **1600** Shaks. *Sonn.* ciii, Were it not sinfull then striuing to mend, To marre the subiect that before was well. **1761** Foote *Lyar* I. ii. (1786) 14 Do you know now, that..I honour the Park? forty thousand million of times preferable to the play house! Don't you think so, my dear? *Miss Godfrey.* They are both well in their way.

absol. **1589** Greene *Menaphon* (Arb.) 78 Sweet Censors take my silly worst for well.

c. ***to let*** (or ***leave***) ***well alone***: to refrain from trying to make better that which is already well.

1740 Cheyne *Regimen* Pract. Ess. p. xxxvi, When a Person is tolerably well, and is subject to no painful or dangerous Distemper, I think it his Duty..to let Well alone. **1830** [see let *v.* 18 b]. *a* **1865** Mrs. Gaskell *Wives & Dau.* xxxii, Why can't you leave well alone? **1883** D. C. Murray *Hearts* xii, Tom was very near yielding... But Mr. Carroll could not let well alone, and unfortunately he went on, 'Whom am I to believe, [etc.].'

d. ***all's well***: a sentry's reply when he has received the password in answer to his challenge. (See also quot. 1769.)

1769 Falconer *Dict. Marine* (1780), *All's well!* an acclamation of safety or security pronounced by a centinel.. at the time of striking the bell each half-hour during..the night watch. **1802** C. James *Milit. Dict.* s.v. *Pass, All's Well*, a term used by a British sentry after he has challenged a person that comes near his post, [etc.]. **1803** T. Dibdin *Engl. Fleet* III. ii. Duet, 'Who goes there? Stranger—quickly tell;' 'A friend,'—the word—'Good night—All's well'.

e. *Sc.* Quite ready. *rare.*

1805 A. Scott *Poems* 40 With hunger smit, may hap they seem to feel, Or cry, perhaps, oh! is the hodgil weel! **1825** Jamieson s.v. *Weill*, Is the denner weel?

8. a. In conformity with approved standards of action or conduct; right, proper. Now *arch.*

1534 *Star Chamber Cases* (Selden Soc.) II. 315 John.. toke the seid iiij horsez..and theym impounded, as well and lawfull it was..for hym to doo. **1540** Palsgr. *Acolastus* II. v. N ij, That is well, or well done, let hym be brought in. **1713** Addison *Cato* III. ii, O Portius, was this well!—to frown on her, That lives upon thy Smiles!

†**b.** qualifying a noun of action. *Obs.* (For the similar use with verbal sbs., see well *adv.* 30.)

1583 in Neal *Hist. Puritans* (1754) I. 267 The archbishop has power to make laws for the well government of the church. **1635** Strafford *Lett.* (1739) I. 482 That he see to the upholding of my Houses and well Usage of my Grounds. **1677** Earl Essex in *Essex Papers* (Camden) II. 148 The well payment of their Rents depending much upon the well paying of the Army.

c. Good; of a character or quality to which no exception can be taken. Now *arch.* or *Obs.*

1661 Marvell *Corr.* Wks. (Grosart) II. 70 The things [clauses in the Act] seem to me generally well and desirable. *Ibid.* 344 Which thing, as it hath a well and certain foundation, so it is your wisdome [etc.]. **1671** Milton *Samson* 1723 Nothing is here for tears,..no weakness, no contempt, Dispraise, or blame, nothing but well and fair. **1695** A. Charlett in Wood *Life* (O.H.S.) III. 499 His behaviour was very well during his Illnesse; was very patient and Quiet. **1766** Goldsm. *Vicar* xi, Our honest neighbour's goose and dumplings were fine... It is true, his manner of telling stories was not quite so well. **1773** —— *Stoops to Conq.* II. i, Yet the fellow, but for his unaccountable bashfulness, is pretty well too. He has good sense. **1780** Johnson in *Boswell* (1887) IV. 24 Yes, they *are* very well, Sir; but you may observe in what manner they are well. They are the forcible verses of a man of a strong mind, but not accustomed to write verse. **1798–1803** JANE AUSTEN *Northanger Abbey* v, It is really very well for a novel.

9. †**a.** Of good or satisfactory appearance. *Obs.*

1600 SHAKS. *A.Y.L.* III. v. 119 Hee'll make a proper man: ..His leg is but so so, and yet 'tis well. **1611** —— *Wint. T.* v. iii. 20 But here it [*sc.* a statue] is:..behold, and say 'tis well. *c* **1710** CELIA FIENNES *Diary* (1888) 248 In this parke stands another pallace St. James, wch is very well. **1742** RICHARDSON *Pamela* III. 162 He is a lively Gentleman, well enough in his Person. **1748** —— *Clarissa* (1768) I. 7 But then, stepping to the glass, she complimented herself, 'That she was very well'.

b. *well to see, well to be seen*: (of a person) good to look upon, comely. *rare.*

1804 R. ANDERSON *Cumbld. Ball.* (*c* 1850) 111 To be seer she's a sarvant, but weel to be seen. **1808–9** LAMB *Poetry for Children, Three Friends* 23 Well to do and well to see Were the parents of all three. **1902** CROCKETT *Dark o' Moon* vii. 43 In person she was short, well-to-see, rosy-cheeked, buxom.

10. In concessive use, followed by an objection or contrary view expressed or implied: **a.** *it is all very well*: it is right and proper in itself or under certain circumstances.

1560 DAUS tr. *Sleidane's Comm.* 82 And where as they saye that the Gospell must be taught after the interpretations approued by the churche (that is very well) but all the stryfe is, which is the trewe church. **1779** WARNER in Jesse *Selwyn & Contemp.* (1844) IV. 283 It is all very well, sir; I know what you will say—that you [etc.]. **1864** TROLLOPE *Small Ho. Allington* xxiii, That's all very well, Amelia. **1879** RUSKIN *Let.* 31 Oct. Wks. 1908 XXXIV. 238 Written contracts are all very well, but if the contractor stops payment—where are you? **1905** 'G. THORNE' *Lost Cause* v, Oh, it's all very well, vicar,..we know you never say anything against anyone.

b. *he* (*it*, etc.) *is all very well*: there is no fault to be found with him, it, etc.

For the force of the appended phrase *in his* (*her, its, their*) *way* see WAY *sb.* 14 f.

1835 DICKENS *Sk. Boz, Parish* ii, As to the curate, he was all very well; but..the curate wasn't a novelty, and the other clergyman was. **1837** *Partington's Brit. Cycl. Nat. Hist.* III. 746/2 As a curiosity the black swan is all very well..but it has none of the beauty and grace of the white swan. **1898** 'MERRIMAN' *Roden's Corner* xxvii. 288 Mr. Cornish is all very well in his way. But we're not fools.

c. Similarly with *well enough*.

1798 WORDSW. *Goody Blake* 37 'Twas well enough, when summer came... But when the ice [etc.]. **1823** SCOTT *Quentin D.* Introd., Their higher wines, indeed, are well enough..yet I cannot but remember the generous qualities of my sound old Oporto. **1842** DICKENS *Amer. Notes* xv, This is well enough, but nevertheless I cannot..incline towards the Shakers.

d. Without vb.: *well and good.* Also (? *Obs.* or *dial.*) *good and well.*

1699 BOYER *Royal Dict.*, Eng.-Fr., Well and good, *à la bonne heure.* **1749** SMOLLETT *Gil Blas* x. x. (1782) IV. 71 My mother's predictions were always favourable to those who solicited them: if they proved true, good and well; but when they came back to reproach her [etc.]. **1809** MALKIN *Gil Blas* x. x. (Rtldg.) 364 My mother always sold good luck for good money; if the accomplishment trod on the heels of the prediction, well and good. **1854** SURTEES *Handley Cr.* viii. (1901) I. 74 These people arrive to-day. If you..can find anything out about them, you know, well and good. **1888** 'R. BOLDREWOOD' *Robbery under Arms* vii, 'If you like to bow and scrape to rich people, well and good', I said.

e. For *very well*, without verb, see WELL *adv.* 25.

†**11.** Quite sufficient (as a statement). *Obs.*

1673 RAY *Journ. Low C.* 152, I have been often told that there are in Paris a million and a half of people, whereas it is well if there be half a million. *Ibid.* 379 A free State..as the Inhabitants boast, for above 1000 years, but its well if half so long.

12. Easy (to deal with). *rare*$^{-1}$.

1816 JANE AUSTEN *Persuasion* iii, In the way of business, gentleman of the navy are well to deal with.

well (wɛl), *v.*[1] *Pa. t.* and *pa. pple.* **welled** (weld). Forms: 1 wiellan, wyllan, wællan, 1–2 wellan, 4 wellen; 2–6 welle, (6 wel), 3– well (4 will); *Sc.* 9 wall. *Pa. t.* 3 welden (*pl.*), 4 wellyd, 4–5 wellyde, 5 wellede, 5–7 wellid, 6 weld, 4– welled. *Pa. pple.* 3 iweld, 3–4 iwelled, 4–5 wellid, wellyde, 5 wellyd, *Sc.* wellit, 4– welled. [OE. *wiellan* (*wyllan*; Anglian *wællan, wellan*), causative verb from the stem of *weallan* to boil, WALL *v.*[1] Cf. MDu. and Du., MLG. and LG., MHG. (and G. dial.) *wellen*, to cause to boil, to boil or well up, etc., WFris. *welje* to well up, NFris. *wêl* to boil, ON. and Icel. *vella* (p. t. *veldi*) to boil (trans.).

The form is appropriate only to the trans. senses; in the intr. it has taken the place of the original strong verb *wall*.]

†**1.** *trans.* To boil (a liquid, ingredients, etc.).

a **1000** *Sax. Leechd.* I. 72 Ðenim þa ylcan wyrte betonican & wyl on ealdan wine. *Ibid.* II. 22 Ðenim wudurofan & wudu merce..& wel on buteran. *Ibid.* 374 Ðepuna ða wyrte to somne & wæl to somne. *c* **1290** *St. Lucy* 145 in *S. Eng. Leg.* 105 Þo nomen huy pich and brumston, and welden it wel faste. ? *a* **1400** *Morte Arth.* 1736, I walde be wellyde alle qwyke, and quarterde in sondre, Bot I wyrke my dede. *c* **1420** *Liber Cocorum* 19 Take brede and peper and ale, And temper þo brothe..And welle hit to-geder. **14..** LYDG. *Horse, Goose & Sheep* 375 in *Pol. Rel. & L. Poems* (1903) 31 [Mutton] Wellid with growel.

†**b.** *fig.* (Cf. 3 b.) *Obs.*$^{-1}$

c **1450** HOLLAND *Houlate* 499 The wyis quhar the wicht went war in wa wellit.

†**c.** To thicken or curdle (a liquid, esp. milk) by boiling or heating. *Obs.*

c **1440** *Promp. Parv.* 520/2 Welle, mylke or oþer lycure, *coagulo.*

d. *spec.* (See quot.)

1876 *Whitby Gloss.* s.v. *Welling*, 'They're welling livers', obtaining the oil from the livers of fish, in the way of making it flow by an adapted heat.

†**2.** To liquefy (metal) by heat; to melt down, cast, found. *Obs.*

a **1225** *Ancr. R.* 284 Þe caliz þet was imelt iðe fure & stroncliche iwelled, and seoððen..so swuðe ueire afeited. *c* **1290** *St. Patrick's Purg.* 272 in *S. Eng. Leg.* 208 Þe feondes welden led and brass, and in heore mouþes caste. *a* **1300** *Holy Rood* (Ashm.) 501 He made him drynke led iweld. **138.** WYCLIF *Sel. Wks.* III. 136 Men schal welle [**1388** *Isa.* ii. 4 welle togidere: Vulg. *conflabunt*] hor swerde into plowgh-schares. **1388** —— *2 Chron.* xxxiv. 17 Thei han wellyd togidere [Vulg. *conflaverunt*] the siluere, which is foundun in the hous of the Lord. *c* **1440** *Promp. Parv.* 520/2 Welle, metel, *fundo.* **1570** LEVINS *Manip.* 55/14 To wel iron, *conflare.*

b. To soften (metal) by intense heat; to join while heated, to weld. *Obs.* exc. *dial.*

Du. and LG. *wellen* also have this sense.

1424 *Mem. Ripon* (Surtees) III. 152 Pro scharpyng et wellyng of wegges de ferro. *a* **1500** *Hist. K. Boccus & Sydracke* (?1510) R iij, As two peces of Iron fare In the fyre whan they wellyd are. Ley that one that other vpon And geue them a stroke anon, Throughe hete they together bynde. **1513** DOUGLAS *Æneis* VIII. vii. 174 A huge gret semely targat, or a scheild..In every place sevin ply thai well and call. **1599** *Churchw. Acc. Pittington*, etc. (Surtees) 275 For wellinge the springe and for makinge nailles to the cocke [clock ?] bordes, iij d. **1616** *Ibid.* 172 Pd to Thomas Pearson for mendinge the greate bell tounge, vj s...Pd.. about the wellinge and helpinge Thomas Pearson, xij d. **1808** JAMIESON s.v., *To wall*, To beat two masses into one. **1824** [CARR] *Craven Gloss.*, *Well*, to weld. **1825–** in various northern glossaries.

3. *intr.* To boil. (Said of a liquid, of ingredients, and also of the containing vessel.) Also with *up.*

a **1400** *Stockholm Med. MS.* 210 in *Archaeologia* XXX. 356 Take..ye whyte of tweyne eyre And a porcyon of rye mele, And late it well to geder welle. *c* **1420** *Liber Cocorum* 5 Take sope, cast in hys potage; Þenne wylle þe pot begyn to rage And welle on alle. *c* **1425** *Macro Plays, Cast. Persev.* 3594 Go þou to helle, þou devyl..In bras & brimston to welle! *c* **1450** *St. Cuthbert* (Surtees) 3371 When þe caldroun began to well þe tempest sest. **1483** *Cath. Angl.* 413/2 To Welle, *bullire, ebullire.* **1554–9** *Songs & Ball. Phil. & Mary* (Roxb.) 12 Full lean be thi pottage where the pote wellis. **1869** *Lonsdale Gloss.*, *Well*, to boil.

†**b.** *fig.* Chiefly in the phrase *to well in woe.*

Cf. *welling woe, welling wood*: WELLING *ppl. a.* 1 b, c.

a **1300** *Cursor M.* 23166 Gas to þe deuil, þar sal yee ga, for to well þar in his wa. *a* **1310** in Wright *Lyric P.* xi. 40 In such wondryng for wo y welle. *c* **1325** *Metr. Hom.* (1862) 29 Thar thai sal euermare duelle, And wafullic in pines welle. *a* **1400** *Min. Poems fr. Vernon MS.* xliv. 8 Þe Mon þat is taken in dedly synne, He may wel witen In wo to wellen. *c* **1440** *York Myst.* i. 131 For-thi efter þaire warkes were, in wo sall þai well.

†**c.** Of metal: To melt and boil up. *Obs.*

c **1430** *Chev. Assigne* 166 And I breke me a cheyne & halfe leyde in þe fyer, And it wexedde in my honde & wellede so faste, That I toke þe oþur fyve & fro þe fyer caste.

†**d.** *fig.* To unite as by welding.

159. JAS. I *Basil. Doron* III. (MS. = ed. 1599, p. 153) Mixing..the men of euerie Kingdome with another, as maye with tyme make thaime to grow & well all in ane. [Cf. WELD *v.* 1.]

4. Of liquids, esp. of a well or spring of water: To rise up to the surface (of the earth) and flow in a copious stream. Also with *up, out, forth.* †Const. *of.*

1387 TREVISA *Higden* II. 59 In þis citee welleþ vp and springeþ hote baþes. **1398** —— *Barth. De P.R.* XIII. i. (MS. Add. 27944) Other watir spryngeþ and welleþ owte of the ynner parties of the erthe as welles watir and pittes watir. ? *a* **1400** *Morte Arth.* 3377 Thane cho wente to the welle by the wode euis, That alle wellyde of wyne. *c* **1425** *Seven Sag.* (P.) 135 Fayre welles there wellyde fast. *a* **1500** *Hist. K. Boccus & Sydracke* U ij b, That [earth] turneth to brymstone Which wellyth vp somtyme anon. **1530** PALSGR. 778/2, I well up, as water that bobylleth, or cometh out of the yerthe. **1590** SPENSER *F.Q.* I. i. 34 Thereby a Christall streame did gently play, Which from a sacred fountaine welled forth alway. **1614** BP. HALL *Contempl.* v. iii. 62 Hee might (if he had pleased) haue caused a spring to well out of the plaine earth. **1727–46** THOMSON *Summer* 807 From his two springs,..Pure welling out, he..rolls his infant stream. **1787** BURNS *Death Sir J. H. Blair* ii, Lone as I..mus'd where limpid streams, once hallow'd, well. **1795** SOUTHEY *Joan of Arc* III. 21 Fast by a spring, which welling at his feet With many a winding crept along the mead. **1831** JAMES *Phil. Augustus* xvii, A clear small stream, that welled from a rock hard by. **1869** TOZER *Highl. Turkey* I. 39 The..fountains were..believed to well up from the Scamander. **1877** HUXLEY *Physiogr.* 190 The molten matter, which wells up the throat of a volcano.

fig. **1812** D'ISRAELI *Calam. Auth.* xxii. (1879) 178 A few of those public works whose waters silently welled from the spring of Leland's genius. **1838** LYTTON *Leila* I. ii, As the water glides from yonder rock,..I see the tide of empire welling from my hands. **1846** KEBLE *Lyra Innoc.* (1873) 71 O who may count The drops from that eternal Fount Of heavenly Intercession, welling night and day?

b. *transf.* of vapours, etc., that rise up to the surface, or flow forth in a stream; *poet.* of sound.

(*a*) **1842** DICKENS *Amer. Notes* iii, What sparkling bubbles glanced upon the waves, and welled up every moment to the surface. **1860** PUSEY *Min. Proph.* 82 The smoke..ascendeth, swelleth, welleth, vanisheth. **1863** DANA *Man. Geol.* 710 The heat as gradually welled up from below, penetrating the moist and yielding beds. **1895** S. CRANE *Red Badge* v, Smoke welled slowly through the leaves.

(*b*) **1848** KINGSLEY *Saint's Trag.* IV. iv, What sweet sounds from her fast-closed lips are welling. *a* **1849** POE *Bells* i, Keeping time..To the tintinabulation that so musically wells From the bells. **1867** MORRIS *Jason* XIV. 45 White bodies moving,..Wherefrom it seemed that lovely music welled.

c. *to well over*, to overflow. *lit.* and *fig.*

1843 JAMES *Forest Days* i, It had a pond, which was kept clear by a spring at the bottom, welling constantly over at the side next the road. **1883** D. C. MURRAY *Hearts* viii, His heart welled over with joy. **1885** 'MRS. ALEXANDER' *At Bay* i, The spring of imaginative passion..lay there, ready to bubble up and well over into a strong current at the touch of the divining-rod.

5. Of tears: To rise (*up*) to the eyes in a copious flood; to flow *down.*

c **1374** CHAUCER *Troylus* v. 215 But þo by-gan a lytel his herte vnswelle Thorugh teris which þat gonnen vp to welle. **1377** LANGL. *P. Pl.* B. XIX. 375 And þanne welled water for wikked werkes, Egerlich ernynge out of mennes eyen. **1600** FAIRFAX *Tasso* IV. xciv, Downe from her eies welled the pearles round, Vpon the bright Ennamell of her face. **1601** WEEVER *Mirr. Mart.* E 4, Still the pearles round Stil through her eies, and wel vpon her face. **1791** MRS. RADCLIFFE *Rom. Forest* iv, Tears welled into her eyes as she spoke these words. **1858** G. MACDONALD *Phantastes* xiii. 157 She lay with closed eyes, whence two large tears were just welling from beneath the veiling lids. **1863** MISS BRADDON *Aurora Floyd* ii, As she looked, the tears welled slowly up to her eyes which had been dry before. **1894** J. A. STEUART *In Day of Battle* vii, My heart welled into my eyes in thankfulness.

6. Of blood or corrupt matter: To flow from the body, a wound, or sore.

1387 TREVISA *Higden* IV. 287 Herodes..was..i-tormented..wiþ wormes þat welled þat sprang out of his prive harneys. *Ibid.* 289. **14..** *St. Mary of Oignies* (MS. Douce 114) in *Anglia* VIII. 140 Wormys wellynge oute of seint Symeouns woundes. **1532** MORE *Confut. Tindale* Wks. 491/2 As the water welled out wyth the blood oute of hys blessed heart vpon the crosse. **1590** SPENSER *F.Q.* I. viii. 47 Her dried dugs..Hong downe, and filthy matter from them weld. **1697** DRYDEN *Æneis* x. 1184 With clotted Locks, and Blood that well'd from out the Wound. **17..** BROOME *Iliad* x. Poems (1727) 128 Blood o'er the crimson Field Well'd from the Slain. **1777** POTTER *Æschylus, Agamem.* 271 When forth-welling from the wound, The purple-streaming blood shall fall. **1835–6** *Todd's Cycl. Anat.* I. 238/2 The blood..wells up abundantly from the bottom of the wound. **1858** G. MACDONALD *Phantastes* xiii. 182 His hand was pressed against his side... The blood was welling from between the fingers. **1890** *Brit. Med. Jrnl.* 29 Mar. 707 Many small cavities were exposed. They were tensely filled with foul pus, which welled out freely from them.

b. *transf.* of the source or a place. Const. *of.*

1387 TREVISA *Higden* V. 235 (MS. γ) He wellede ful of wormes. ? *a* **1400** *Morte Arth.* 3819 Alle wellys fulle of blode, thare he awaye passes. *c* **1482** *Monk of Evesham* (Arb.) 32 Also y behylde the right syde of the ymage of oure lordis body and hit wellid oute of blode.

7. *fig.* To spring or originate; to issue or flow *forth* or *out.* Of qualities, conditions: To emanate †*of, out of, from* a person or thing as a source.

13.. tr. *Ælred* in *Engl. Studien* VII. 311 Þyse ryueres beþ holy scriptures, þat welleþ out fro þe welle of wysdom, þat is Crist. **1387–8** T. USK *Test. Love* I. ii. 151 Trewly, al maner of blisse and preciousnesse in vertue out of thee springen and wellen. *c* **1400** *Pety Job* 438 in *26 Pol. Poems* XXV. 135 Vertues, lorde, though I haue none, Late thy grace in me now welle. *c* **1450** tr. *De Imitatione* III. x. 77 Considre all þinges as welling of þe hyest & most souereyn good. **1548** UDALL, etc. *Erasm. Par. Luke* iv. 20–24 The woordes whiche proceded from the mouth of Jesus..welled foorth from a brest replenished with the heauenly spirite of God. **1590** SPENSER *F.Q.* III. vi. 25 With sugred words and gentle blandishment, Which as a fountaine from her sweet lips went, And welled goodly forth. **1834** H. MILLER *Scenes & Leg.* xv. (1857) 223 Those old artless compositions which have welled out from time to time from among the people. **1846** *Eclectic Rev.* Feb. 134 The Pilgrim's Progress..welled up from the deep fountains of the author's own mind, and..flowed on without reserve. **1883** R. W. CHURCH *Spenser* v. 129 The abundance of his ideas, as they welled forth in his mind day by day.

8. *trans.* **a.** Of a spring: To pour forth (water, etc.). Also with adv., as *up.*

1387 TREVISA *Higden* VII. 391 Þis ȝere at Fynchamstede in Barrokschire a welle was i-seie welle blood fiftene dayes. *c* **1400** *Destr. Troy* 340 There was wellit to wale water full nobill, In yche place of the playne with plentius stremes. **1729** SAVAGE *Wanderer* v. 22 Rills..Meet in yon Mead, and well a River's Source. **1820** IRVING *Sketch Bk.* I. 32 Some classic fountain, that had once welled its pure waters in a sacred shade. **1853** G. JOHNSTON *Nat. Hist. E. Bord.* I. 227 Another green bank from which a spring wells up to the light its sparkling waters.

b. *fig.* To pour out (something) in or as a stream. Also with *out, forth, up.*

a **1425** *Cursor M.* 17076 (Trin.) Mary welle of mercy, wellyng [*Laud* willyng] euer pite. **1526** *Pilgr. Perf.* (W. de W. 1531) 112 Wherfore it is deuyded in two partes: on the one parte it welleth vp all mocyons of concupyscence. **1590** SPENSER *F.Q.* II. ii. 8 She sate, Welling out streames of teares. *Ibid.* x. 26 Behold the boyling Bathes at Cairbadon, Which seeth with secret fire eternally, And..to their people wealth they forth do well. **1610** G. FLETCHER *Christ's Vict. in Heaven* xlviii, How nimbly will the golden phrases flie, And shed forth streames of choycest rhetorie, Welling celestiall torrents out of poesie? **1834** DE QUINCEY *Autob. Sk.* Wks. 1853 I. 24 Deep is the solitude of millions who, with hearts welling forth love, have none to love them.

well, *v.*[2] [f. WELL *sb.*[1]]

1. *slang.* To defraud (one's confederates) by embezzling part of the booty; to conceal (booty) from one's confederates; to conceal (a portion of one's estate) from creditors.

1812 VAUX *Flash Dict.* (1819) s.v. *Well*, To *well* your accomplice, or *put him in the well.* **1823** EGAN *Grose's Dict.*

Vulgar Tongue, *Well*, to divide unfairly... A cant phrase used by thieves, where one of the party conceals some of the booty, instead of dividing it fairly amongst his confederates. **1824** *Compl. Hist. Murder Mr. Weare* 255 Probert frequently alluded to the money..and his apprehensions lest Thurtell should *well it* (meaning keep it to himself). **1893** *Illustr. Sporting & Dram. News* 22 July 766/1 Out of the salvage of my fortune—for something had been safely 'welled', you may be sure—I purchased a tricycle.

2. *Naut.* (See quot.)

1820 SCORESBY *Acc. Arctic Reg.* II. 450 To well the ship.—This operation [for stopping a leak], consisting in the building of a bulk-head or partition on the fore part of the leak, and caulking it, so as to confine the water within it.

well (wɛl), *adv.* Forms: α. 1–7 **wel** (1 **uel**, 3 **wuel**, **wæl**), 1, 5– **well** (2 **wæll**, 5 **whell**), 5 **welle**. β. 4–5 (8–9 *Sc.* and *north.*) **weel**, 4 **wiel**, *Sc.* 5 **veill**, 5–6 **weill**, 6 **wyell**, 7 **weell** (**weall**); 4–5, 7 (6 *Sc.*) **wele**, 5 **weile**, *Sc.* **veyle**, 6 **weele**. γ. (Chiefly *north.*) 4–5 **will** (5–6 **wyll**), 5 **wil**, 5–6 **wyl**; 4 **wille**, 5 **wile**, **wyle**, **wylle**. See also WOL *adv.* [Common Teutonic: OE. *wel*, *well* = OFris. *wel* (NFris. *wel*, *well*, WFris. *wel*, *wol*), MDu. and Du. *wel*, OS. *wel*, ON. and Icel. *vel* (Norw., Da. *vel*, Sw. *väl*); also OS. *wela*, *wola* (MLG. and LG. *wala*, *wal*), OHG. *wela*, *wala*, *wola*, *wol* (MHG. *wole*, *wol*, G. *wohl*), Goth. *waila*. The stem is regarded as identical with that of the verb WILL.

An early lengthening of the vowel is indicated by the ME. *weel* (*wiel*, *wele*, etc.), which appears in northern and Scottish texts from the 14th cent., and is still the current form in Scottish, northern, and north midland dialects. The forms *will* and WOL probably originated in unstressed positions.]

I. 1. a. In accordance with a good or high standard of conduct or morality; in a way which is morally good. Chiefly with *do* vb.

*c*825 *Vesp. Psalter* xxxv. 4 [He] nalde onȝeotan ðæt [he] wel dyde [L. *bene ageret*]. *a*1000 *Doomsday* 119 Welan ah in wuldre se nu wel þenceð! *a*1000 *Ags. Gosp.* Matt. xii. 12 Hyt ys alyfed on reste-daȝum wel to donne [L. *bene facere*]. *a*1122 *O.E. Chron.* (Laud) an. 1086 Litel rihtwisnesse wæs on þisum lande..buton mid munecan ane þær þær hi wæll ferdon. *c*1175 *Lamb. Hom.* 131 Ðe mon þe wel deð, he wel ifehð. *a*1200 *Moral Ode* 37 Ne scal na mon..slawen wel to done. *c*1300 *Relig. Songs* i. in *Owl & Night.* etc. (Percy Soc.) 63 Mon, let sunne and lustes thine; Wel thu do and wel thu thench. *c*1340 HAMPOLE *Pr. Consc.* 288 He says he has no wille to fele Ne to understand for to do wele. *Ibid.* 1987 Þe last day of man is hyd,..For he shuld kepe wele al þe other dayes. *c*1400 *Rule St. Benet* vii. 12 For þi lokys þat ye do wel. *c*1440 *Gesta Rom.* 1 Þerfore gouerne the wele the while til I come home aȝen. *c*1481 CAXTON *Dialogues* 47 *Qui bien fera bien aura*, Who doth well shall well haue. **1562** J. HEYWOOD *Prov.* (1867) 21 Doo well, and haue well, men say. *a*1591 H. SMITH *Serm.* (1601) 299 It is better to doe well then to doe good: for a man cannot offend in doing well. **1663** S. PATRICK *Parab. Pilgr.* (1687) 355 Let me see a Man that keeps his shop and buys and sells, and yet lives well and keeps the Laws of Christ. *a*1703 BURKITT *On N.T.* Mark x. 17 It is not talking well, and professing well, but doing well, that entitles us to heaven and eternal life. **1805** WORDSW. *Prelude* VIII. 527 That, by acting well, And understanding, I should learn to love The end of life. **1860** PUSEY *Min. Proph.* 606 If thou livest well and teachest well, thou wilt be a judge of all; if thou teachest well and livest ill, thine own only.

b. Satisfactorily in respect of conduct or action.

*a*1000 *Riddles* l[i]. 5 He him wel hereð, þeowaþ him geþwære. *c*1325 *Spec. Gy Warw.* 82 Wisdom in godes drede Vse wel, þat be my rede. *c*1386 CHAUCER *Knt.'s T.* 968 And they him sworen his axyng faire and weel. *c*1420 *Chron. Vilod.* 4838 To loue god & serue hym wyle. **1450–1530** *Myrr. Our Ladye* II. 65 Deuoute redyng..causeth moche grace and comforte to the soulle yf yt be well and dyscretely vsed. **1471** CAXTON *Recuyell* (Sommer) 60 The same Archas gouerned hym so wele and so wisely that [etc.]. **1526** TINDALE *1 Tim.* v. 17 The seniours that rule wele are worthy of double honoure. **1534** *Cal. Irish Chancery Rolls* I. 11 Ye swear that ye well and trulie shall serve our Sovraigne Lord the King. **1568** GRAFTON *Chron.* II. 349 If any charge do come vpon the king and his realme, howe it may be well and honourably supported. **1710** STEELE *Tatler* No. 212 ⁋4 A Woman must think well to look well. **1881** *Med. Temp. Jrnl.* XLIX. 13 He there worked well and never touched alcohol. **1883** WHITELAW *Sophocles, Antigone* 1323 'Tis counselled well, if well with ill can be.

†**c.** Justifiably, rightly. *Obs.*⁻¹

1382 WYCLIF *Jonah* iv. 4 And the Lord saide, Gessist thou, wher thou art wel [L. *bene*] wroth? *Ibid.* 9.

2. a. In such a manner as to constitute good treatment or confer a benefit; kindly, considerately; generously; charitably.

*c*825 *Vesp. Psalter* cxx[i]v. 4 Wel doa [L. *bene fac*], dryhten, godum & rehtum on heortan. *c*897 ÆLFRED *Gregory's Past C.* xli. 304 Far mid us, ðæt we ðe mæȝen wel don. *c*1000 *Ags. Gosp.* Matt. v. 44 Doð wel þam þe eow yfel doð. *c*1175 *Lamb. Hom.* 59 Þene Mon he lufede and welbiþohte. **1424** *E.E. Wills* 57 No man merueil þogh I do well to him, for, [etc.]. **1540** CROMWELL in Merriman *Life & Lett.* (1902) II. 270 Your grace was veray moch displeasyd Saying I am not well handelyd. **1565** COOPER *Thesaurus* s.v. *Bene*, To be well vsed for little coste. **1712** SWIFT *Jrnl. to Stella* 11 Oct., Opportunities will often fall in my way, if I am used well. **1896** GLADSTONE in *Daily Chron.* 8 Oct. (1903) 5/2 My danger is the danger of being too well used.. by my biographers.

b. *to deserve well of*: to be entitled to gratitude or good treatment from (a person). See DESERVE 3 b. Cf. L. *bene mereri de*, F. *bien mériter de*.

1585–6 EARL LEYCESTER *Corr.* (Camden) 423 He can tell you whether I dyd use Paul Buis, and deservyd well at his handes, or no. **1709** ADDISON *Tatler* No. 117 ⁋1 A great Man, who has deserved well of his Country. **1709–1840** [see DESERVE *v.* 3]. **1865** DICKENS *Mut. Fr.* III. ii, You do right, child,..to speak well of those who deserve well of you.

c. With verbs of greeting, receiving, etc.: In a kindly and friendly manner; with friendly words; with favour or welcome.

Cf. *to stand well with*, s.v. WELL *a.* 2.

*c*1000 in Kemble *Cod. Diplom.* IV. 214 Eadward king gret wel Willem biscop. *a*1122 *O.E. Chron.* (Laud) an. 675, Ic Agatho..grete wel seo wurðfulle Æðelred. *Ibid.* an. 1137, He for to Rome & þær wæs wæl underfangen fram þe pape. *c*1205 LAY. 15084 Uortigerne..grette wel Hengest. *c*1250 *Gen. & Ex.* 1420 Laban and his moder..fagneden wel ðis sondere man. *c*1325 *Spec. Gy Warw.* 52, [I] grete þe wel, fadyr myn. **1443** HEN. VI in Ellis *Orig. Lett.* Ser. III. I. 79 Right dere in God we grete you wele. **1483** RICH. III. *Ibid.* Ser. II. I. 159 Right reverend Fadre in God, right trusty and welbeloved, we grete you wele. **1706** tr. *De Piles' Art Painting* 336 He was well receiv'd at Court, and in favour with Four Kings successively. **1885** 'MRS. ALEXANDER' *At Bay* v, You receive him very well considering you do not like him?

d. With verbs denoting feeling or intention.

1659 *Nicholas Papers* (Camden) IV. 87 Not as intending well to the King, for they are vowed rebells. **1661** J. BARWICK in *Extr. S.P. rel. Friends* Ser. II. (1911) 128 A Gentleman that wishes well to the King. **1729** T. INNES *Crit. Ess.* (1879) 17 At least I meant well, and aimed only at truth. **1831** SCOTT *Cast. Dang.* iv, I am an Englishman, and wish dearly well to my country. **1836** DICKENS *Sk. Boz, Shops & Tenants*, We wished the man well, but we trembled for his success. **1847** MARRYAT *Childr. N. Forest* xxv, There is a great difference between wishing well to a cause and supporting it in person.

e. With verbs of thinking or speaking (†also of hearing) *of* a person, etc.

1445 tr. *Claudian* in *Anglia* XXVIII. 269 Easyly with the thus thi men live, thou seith of hem evir wele. *c*1450 tr. *De Imitatione* III. xxxiii. 102 Wheþer þei say wel, wheþer þei say evel, þou art not þerfore a noþer man. **1526** TINDALE *1 Tim.* v. 10 Soche a wone as was..well reported off in good workes. **1538** ELYOT *Dict.* Add., *Bene audire*, to be well spoken of. **1576** R. PETERSON *G. della Casa's Galateo* 22 Eache man desireth to bee well thought of. **1596** HARINGTON *Metam. Ajax* Answ. Let. A iv b, If you haue heard so well of my poore house. **1596** SHAKS. *Tam. Shr.* IV. iv. 37 Signior Baptista, of whom I heare so well. **1610** —— *Temp.* II. ii. 95 His forward voyce now is to speake well of his friend. **1698** M. HENRY *Christianity no Sect* (1847) 190 Ill-will never speaks well. **1753–4** RICHARDSON *Grandison* II. xlviii. 388 One would be willing to be well thought of by the worthy. **1848** DICKENS *Dombey* xliii, Papa thinks well of Mrs. Pipchin. **1865** [see 2 b]. **1895** *Bookman* Oct. 12/2 'The Ebb Tide' was practically by Mr. Stevenson himself, and he was disposed to think very well of it.

f. With equanimity or good nature; without resentment. Chiefly with *take*.

†*to take* (a thing) *well a worth*: see WORTH *sb.*

1753–4 RICHARDSON *Grandison* III. x. 133 They did not suffer her to go out of her chamber; which she took not well. **1923** R. A. FREEMAN *Dr. Thorndike's Case-Bk.* i. 31 'And how did the coloured gentleman take it?' 'Not very well.'

3. With courage and spirit; gallantly, bravely.

1338 R. BRUNNE *Chron.* (1725) 24 So many douhty dyntes was bituex tham tueye, Wele þei did togidere, better may noman seye. **1447** SHILLINGFORD *Lett.* (Camden) 20 Douryssh acquytted hym well. *c*1450 *Merlin* vi. 97 Alle the barouns that weren of valoure and wele hadde don. *Ibid.* xxxii. 654 Sir Gawein and his felowes dide merveiles and wele. **1600** SHAKS. *A.Y.L.* I. i. 134 Hee that escapes me without some broken limbe, shall acquit him well. **1667** MILTON *P.L.* VI. 29 Servant of God, well done, well hast thou fought The better fight. **1819** SCOTT *Ivanhoe* xxxi, Well and chivalrous did De Bracy that day maintain the fame he had acquired.

II. 4. Faithfully, heedfully, carefully, attentively: **a.** With verbs of holding, keeping, attending to, etc.

*c*831 in Sweet *O.E. Texts* 446 Ic..bebiade Eadwealde ..ðet he ðis wel healde. *a*900 CYNEWULF *Christ* 1236 Þreo tacen..þæs þe hi hyra þeodnes wel wordum and weorcum willan heoldon. **971** *Blickl. Hom.* 109 Hit is..nytlic þæt hie heora fulwiht-hadas wel ȝehealdan. *c*1200 ORMIN 1033 Þatt follkess haliȝdomess..wærenn inn an arrke þær Wel & wurrþlike ȝemmde. *c*1300 *Havelok* 209 And preide, he shulde yeme hire wel. *a*1300 *Cursor M.* 6849 Haldes þis wille [*Gött.* wele], i bid yow now. *c*1375 *Ibid.* 438 (Fairf.) He gaf an mast of al þat wele hif he coude a keppet hit weel. **1375** BARBOUR *Bruce* I. 118 Ȝe suld..Haiff chosyn ȝow a king, that mycht Have haldyn veyle the land in rycht. **1433** *Rolls of Parlt.* IV. 477/1 And well and truly kepe the seid godes. **1482** *Cely Papers* (Camden) 124 I hawhe promysyd hym a bow and I trwste that he wyll se whell to yowr hors. **1573–80** TUSSER *Husb.* (1878) 130 To cart gap and barne, set a guide to looke weele. **1577** B. GOOGE *Heresbach's Husb.* II. 53 Touchyng seede, this is to be well seen to. **1611** BIBLE *Jer.* xxxix. 12 Take him and looke well to him, and doe him no harme. **1782** BURNS *I'll go & be a Sodger* 6, I gat some gear wi' meikle care, I held it weel thegither.

b. With verbs of observing, considering, studying, etc.

971 *Blickl. Hom.* 203 Mid þy þe þa Cristenan leode þæt wel sceawodan, ða ȝesawon hie [etc.]. *c*1200 ORMIN 1829 Wel birrþ uss lokenn þær whatt uss þatt name maȝȝ bitacnenn. **1375** BARBOUR *Bruce* I. 202 And gyff ony thar-at war wrath, Thai watyt hym wele with gret scaith. *c*1385 CHAUCER *L.G.W.* (Fairf.) 335 Of thyn answere avise the ryght weel. *c*1400 *Rule of St. Benet* (Prose) 11 And tat ye recorde wel þe cumantemens of god. **1436** *Pol. Poems* (Rolls) II. 191 Loke wele aboute,..Unfayllyngly, unfeynynge, and unfeynte. **1513** BRADSHAW *St. Werburge* 1338 She well consydered with due dyscrecyon Of this present lyfe the great wretchydnesse. *a*1529 SKELTON *Agst. Garnesche* iii. 97 Note and marke wyl thys parcele. **1538** STARKEY *England* 117 Me thynke you pondur not al wel and depely. **1603** HARSNET *Popish Impost.* 36 Heere is her lesson read ouer: and marke the scholler how well she conned it. **1611** BIBLE *Prov.* xiv. 15 The prudent man looketh well to his going. **1746** FRANCIS tr. *Hor., Epist.* I. vii. 117 Philip, who well observ'd our simple Guest, Laughs in his Sleeve. **1849** MACAULAY *Hist. Eng.* v. I. 610 Feversham..had looked at himself well in the glass. **1873** *Punch* 4 Jan. 9/2 After thinking the matter well over, we have determined not to compete.

5. In a way appropriate to the facts or circumstances; fittingly, properly: **a.** With verbs of saying or speaking. †Also rarely in other contexts (quot. *c* 1175). ***well taken***: of a point in an argument, aptly or judiciously raised. (orig. *U.S.*).

To be distinguished from the phr. *to take* (someone's) *point*, where *take* = to understand the significance of.

*c*897 ÆLFRED *Gregory's Past. C.* xxi. 151 Be ðære ildinge suiðe wel Dryhten ðreade Iudeas, ða he ðurh ðone witȝan cuæð. *a*900 CYNEWULF *Christ* 547 Ðæt is wel cweden swa ȝewritu secgað, þæt [etc.]. *c*950 *Lindisf. Gosp.* John iv. 17 Cueð to hir se hælend, uel ðu cuede þætte ic ne hafu uer. **971** *Blick. Hom.* 9 Wel þæt wæs ȝecweden, forþon þe [etc.]. *c*1175 *Lamb. Hom.* 83 He com bi þis forwundede mon. Wel he com bi him, þa he bicom alswich alse he. **13..** *K. Alis.* 3097 Þou hast wel spoken, Dalmadas. **1340** *Ayenb.* 19 Zuych folie is wel y-clepede onwythede. **1382** WYCLIF *Matt.* xv. 7 Ysay, the prophete, propheciede wel of ȝou. *c*1440 *Generydes* 1835 Whanne the Sowdon had hard hym sey so will, 'Generydes', quod he, 'I geue yow grace'. **1470–85** MALORY *Arthur* X. xxxvi. 471 This is wel sayd, saide Morgan le fay. **1561** HOBY tr. *Castiglione's Courtier* I. (1900) 94 And you say wel, that [etc.]. **1590** MARLOWE *2nd Pt. Tamburl.* V. i, Wel said, let there be a fire presently. **1610** DONNE *Pseudo-Martyr* 170 Sepulueda..saies well..That the soule doth exercise *Herile Imperium* vpon the body. **1638** JUNIUS *Paint. Ancients* 7 It is well observed by an ancient Orator [etc.]. **1662** STILLINGFL. *Orig. Sacræ* III. ii. §1 If so, as Maimonides well observes, the whole Religion of Moses is overthrown. **1725** POPE *Odyss.* VIII. 153 Well hast thou spoke (Euryalus replies). **1779** *Mirror* No. 37 ⁋8 The delightful occupations of a country life, which Cicero well said..are next in kindred to true philosophy. **1809** ROLAND *Fencing* 119 It was well suggested..that it would be better [etc.]. **1855** PALEY *Æschylus* (1861) Pref. p. vi. *note*, Hermann himself well says of certain critics of the old school [etc.]. **1863** A. LINCOLN *Coll. Works* (1953) VI. 245 The point made in your paper is well taken. **1883** WHITELAW *Sophocles, Electra* 252 If I speak not well Have thou thy way. **1907** *Nation* (N.Y.) 14 Feb. 146 One of Mr. Hearst's points seems to us well taken. **1936** E. B. WHITE in *New Yorker* 14 Mar. 16/2 The question is well taken. **1943** [see POINT *sb.*[1] 28 c].

b. With verbs expressing fitness, suitability, etc.

*a*900 CYNEWULF *Christ* 3 Wel þe ȝeriseð, þæt þu heafod sie healle mærre. **971** *Blickl. Hom.* 13 Wel þæt ȝeras þæt heo wære eaðmod. *Ibid.*, Wel þæt eac ȝedafenaþ þæt he to eorðan astiȝe. *c*1050 *O.E. Chron.* (MS. C.) an. 1036 Syððan hine man byriȝde, swa him wel ȝebyrede, ful wurðlice, swa he wyrðe wæs. *c*1330 R. BRUNNE *Chron. Wace* (Rolls) 11914 Nys non on lyue..þat semeþ so wel his beryng. **13..** *E.E. Allit. P.* B. 793 Wlonk whit was her wede, & wel hit hem semed. **1375** BARBOUR *Bruce* I. 394 And in spek wlispyt he sum deill; Bot that sat him rycht wonder weill. ?*a*1400 *Morte Arth.* 170 Sone the senatour was sett, as hyme wel semyde, At the kyngez ownne borde. **1502** ATKYNSON tr. *De Imitatione* III. xxxiv. (1893) 223 It acordeth nat to well to my hert. **1513** DOUGLAS *Æneis* VII. Prol. 165 As our buik begouth his weirfair tell, So, weill according, dewlie bene annext Thow drery preambill. **1596** SHAKS. *Tam. Shr.* Induct. i. 126 An Onion wil do well for such a shift. **1600** —— *A.Y.L.* IV. ii. 4 It would doe well to set the Deares horns vpon his head. **1622** MABBE tr. *Aleman's Guzman d'Alf.* II. 167, I haue inlarged my selfe in speaking more already, then may well become mee. **1753–4** RICHARDSON *Grandison* II. xxiv. 185 She is dissatisfied with what she has written: But I tell her, I think it will do very well. **1832** G. R. PORTER *Porcelain & Gl.* 274 Almost any..inflammable vegetable matter will probably answer equally well. **1848** T. AIRD *Chr. Bride* II. i, Yea, well that forehead's beauty undebased Beseems the scion of a prince's side.

c. ***to do well***: to act prudently or sensibly. Also *ironically*.

1476 *Stonor Papers* (Camden) II. 12 Ye do Ryghte welle to set hyt in a suerete. *c*1489 CAXTON *Sonnes of Aymon* vii. 176 Ye have well doon, swete knyghte, for to have brought your horse here. *c*1530 BERNERS *Arth. Lyt. Bryt.* (1814) 535 It were well done that I sholde cause be armed v. hondred knightes. **1576** TURBERV. *Venerie* 192 The Huntsman.. shall do well to stop up his earthes if he can finde them. **1626** BACON *Sylva* §53 You shall doe well to put in some few Slices of Eryngium Roots. **1663** GERBIER *Counsel* 22 Roomes on moist grounds, do well to be Paved with Marble. **1673** DRYDEN *Amboyna* III. i, He do's well to take his time. **1725** DE FOE *Voy. round World* (1840) 180 Whoever shall follow the same, or a like track,..will do well to make a year of it. **1771** SMOLLETT *Humphry Cl.* (3rd) 14 June, You will do well to keep a watchful eye over..Villiams. **1818** SCOTT *Br. Lamm.* ix, Lord Bittlebrains would do weel to remember what his folk have been. **1856** MRS. OLIPHANT *Magd. Hepburn* I. 275 'Boy, thou dost well to beard me', cried Sir Roger. **1884** *Chr. Commw.* 1 May 688/3 Clergymen who have nothing better to do than incite to war would do well to seek some other calling.

6. a. Prosperously, successfully, fortunately, happily; without harm or accident. (Cf. 11.) Freq. with *do*, *fare*, *go*.

to be well rid of: cf. RID *v.* 3 c.

Beowulf 1045 Beowulfe..eoder Ingwina onwald ȝeteah wicga and wæpna; het hine wel brucan. *Ibid.* 2162 Bruc ealles well. *c*1000 ÆLFRIC *Gen.* xxxix. 2 Drihten wæs mid him; se man wæs wel donde on eallum þingum. *c*1300 *Havelok* 2983 Him stondes wel þat god child strenes. *c*1460 *Towneley Myst.* xxiv. 404 Well worth you all thre, most doughty in dede! **1535** COVERDALE *1 Sam.* xx. 7 Yf he saye then: It is good, then stondeth it well with thy seruant. —— *2 Kings* iv. 26 Axe her yf it go well with her. **1540** PALSGR. *Acolastus* III. iii. Pj, All hayle moche .i. god sende the well to fare. **1551** ROBINSON tr. *More's Utopia, P. Giles* (1895) p. c, Thus..I byd you most hartely well to fare. **1573–80** TUSSER *Husb.* (1878) 48 Too lustie of courage for wheat doth not well. **1607** SHAKS. *Cor.* IV. i. 21 Farewell my Wife,..Ile do well yet. **1611** Bible *2 Chron.* xii. 12 Also in Iudah things went well. **16..** Sir W. Mure *Ps.* xxxvii. 7 And fret not that his wayes go weell, Leud plotts to passe who brings. **1631** Shirley *Sch. Compl.* v. i. 68 Woo'd I were well rid of you. **1665** in *Spalding Club Misc.* I. 40, I am werie confident.. that the bussiness of our familie shall goe weall. **1712–13** Swift *Jrnl. to Stella* 17 Jan., This took well, and turned off the discourse. *a* **1718** Prior *Epitaph* 5 If Human Things went Ill or Well. **1842** Loudon *Suburban Hort.* 275 The gooseberry..and the common nightshade..succeed equally well. **1899** *Blackw. Mag.* Mar. 552 All went well as far as the foot of the ice-fall.

b. With verbs of going, bringing, getting, etc., and adverbial complement.

a **1300** *Cursor M.* 5024 Ledes wit yow beniamin, Godd giue yow þedir will [*Fairf.* wele] to wine. *c* **1470** *Stonor Papers* (Camden) I. 110 God ȝeve yow goode nyghte and brynge yow welle home and in schorte tyme. **1565** Cooper *Thesaurus* s.v. *Bene*, Good speede the, and send the well to returne. *Ibid.* s.v. *Ceres*, To call and praie to god to send well in our corne. **1636** Sanderson *Serm. Ad Aulam* iv. (1689) 415 So he came well off at the last, though he was dangerously engaged onward. **1708** S. Sewall *Diary* 18 Dec., Got home well in my slay, had much adoe to avoid slews. **1748** Richardson *Clarissa* (1768) VIII. 184 God send him well out of the kingdom! **1748** Smollett *R. Random* ix, We proceeded on our journey, blessing ourselves that we had come off so well. **1822** Scott *Nigel* xv, I wish you weel through, my lord, but it is an unequal fight. **1852** E. Warburton *Darien* I. xiii. (1860) 110 His regard for what was left of his reputation concurred with his greed of gold in wishing his guest well away. **1860** Sala *Badd. Peerage* I. xviii. 307 However, I'm well out of it, I don't mean Newgate, but my Spanish courtship. **1876** H. Brooks *Natal* 199 After he had got well off from the tribes in the old neighbourhood.

c. Successfully in some material respect; profitably; advantageously.

c **1450** *Godstow Reg.* 245 To be had and to be hold..frely quyetly..wele and in pease. **1604** E. G[rimstone] *D'Acosta's Hist. Indies* IV. ii. 208 What a father doth to marie his daughter wel, is to give her a great portion in mariage. **1673** Janeway *Heaven upon Earth* (1847) 79 Consider.. before you make light of this business, and know when you are well offered. **1729** T. Cooke *Tales* etc. 102 Monimia wrong'd the tender Soul shall move, And Anthony well lose the World for Love. **1753–4** Richardson *Grandison* II. xxx. 236 Will four thousand pounds be well laid out in a quarter-partnership? **1863** W. C. Baldwin *Afr. Hunting* vii. 231, I sold all my oxen well in Bloemfontein. **1864** Trollope *Small Ho. Allington* xxvi, 'Amelia has done very well [in her marriage], my dear.' 'Oh, if you call it doing well for your girls, I don't.' *a* **1865** Mrs. Gaskell *Wives & Dau.* xxxii, Mamma..always says you have done very well for yourself [in marriage].

†**d.** *spec.* Profitably for the seller or buyer; at a high or low price respectively. *Obs.*

c **1375** *Sc. Leg. Saints* xxviii. (*Margaret*) 6 And for þere prophetis thre we se it [the pearl] oft weile bocht be. **1480**, **1576** [see well-bought]. **1599** Hakluyt *Voy.* II. I. 59 They are exceeding fat [geese] & wel sold [L. *optimi fori*].

7. a. In a state of plenty or comfort. See also live *v.*[1] 4 d.

c **1000** *Ælfric's Colloq.* in Wright *Voc.* (1857) 9 Ʒe maȝon ..butan minon cræfte lif adreoȝan, ac na lancge ne to wel [L. *adeo bene*]. **1340–70** *Alex. & Dind.* 106 Þanne ferde þe worlde as a feld þat ful were of bestes, Whan eueri lud liche wel lyuede up-on erþe. **1874** Dasent *Tales fr. Fjeld* 302 He would be able to live well and good all his days.

b. Satisfactorily or excellently in respect of health or recovery from illness. Usually with *do*.

c **1440** *Alphabet of Tales* 251 A bruther of his askid hym how he did, and he said, wele. *a* **1478** *Stonor Papers* (Camden) II. 29, I trust to God þat he sal doo ryght weile, and so doth þe fessechane. **1530** Palsgr. 524/1, I do well: *ie me porte bien.* **1594** Shaks. *Rich. III*, II. iv. 40 How doth the Prince? *Mes.* Well Madam, and in health. *Ibid.* III. i. 96 How fares our Noble Brother? *Yorke.* Well, my deare Lord. **1611** Bible *John* xi. 12 Then said his disciples, Lord, if he sleepe, he shall doe well. **1711–12** Swift *Jrnl. to Stella* 17 Mar., Mrs. Percival's youngest daughter has got the small-pox, but will do well. **1841** H. Greville *Diary* Ser. I. (1883) 152 A fine child, and the Queen doing well. **1863** Longf. in *Life* (1891) III. 25 Bowditch is wounded through the arm; C. through both shoulders... Both doing well.

8. a. With good reason; naturally; as a natural result or consequence.

c **900** tr. *Bæda's Hist.* II. i. (Schipper) 110 Cwæð he: Wel þæt swa mæȝ, forþon hi englelice ansyne habbað. *c* **1205** Lay. 983 Wel ich hit mai suggen, to soþe ich hit wene. *c* **1380** Wyclif *Wks.* (1880) 26 Siþ lordis and men of grete statis.. ben so muche biholden to destroie it, & mowne welle don it in dede. *c* **1385** Chaucer *L.G.W.* 183 Men..wel it calle may The daisie, or elles the ye of day. **1423** Jas. I *Kingis Q.* xiv, Wist thou thy payne to cum..For sorow and drede wele myght thou wepe and waille. **1485** Caxton *Malory's Arthur* Pref. 2 In hym..myght wel be aretted grete folye and blyndenesse. **1508** Dunbar *Goldyn Targe* 279 Rude is thy wede,..Wele aucht thou be afiret of the licht. **1578** T. N. tr. *Conq. W. India* 60 Alleagyng..that he who had common 2000 leagues by Sea, mought well goe 70 leagues by lande. **1678** B. R. *Let. Pop. Friends* 3 Well may our Irish Friends, cry Oh Hone! Oh Hone! **1753–4** Richardson *Grandison* II. x. 70 What! are you confounded?—Well you may, if you cannot answer me as I wish! **1791** Cowper *Iliad* I. 319 Now Priam and his sons may well exult. **1816** Scott *Old Mort.* xliv, Ye could hardly weel be said to breakfast this morning. **1849** Macaulay *Hist. Eng.* iii. I. 368 The government did not venture..to enforce a regulation of which the legality might well be questioned. **1872** Morley *Voltaire* (1886) 5 Another might well have said of him what he..said of his famous contemporary. **1902** 'Violet Jacob' *Sheep-Stealers* viii, 'How do you get it all up to Abergavenny?' 'Ah, you may well ask.'

b. In clauses introduced by *and* or *as*.

a **1300** *Floriz & Bl.* 632 Þe children awoke þo anon..Sore hi beoþ offerd and wel maȝe. **1563–83** Foxe *A. & M.* 192/1 With thys vncomely outrage the King was much displeased (as he myght full well). **1650** Eliz. Cromwell *Let.* 27 Dec. in *Carlyle*, Which makes me think my writing is slighted; as well it may. **1667** Milton *P.L.* IX. 785 Back to the Thicket slunk The guiltie Serpent, and well might. *a* **1700** Evelyn *Diary* 5 May 1686, Which dispensation..gave umbrage (as well it might) to every good Protestant. **1753–4** Richardson *Grandison* III. viii. 119 The dear creature..took pride, as well she might, in her hair. **1852** Gladstone *Glean.* (1879) IV. 81 The capital was in amazement at the boldness of the Judges; and well it might. **1871** 'Mark Twain' *Eye-Openers* 87 All the high houses..were full, windows, roof, and all. And well they might be.

c. In concessive sense: Indeed, certainly. † *how well* (after F. *combien que*), although.

1470–85 Malory *Arthur* III. xiii. 116 Alas syr, sayd the lady..I must nedes reste me. Ye shal wel, said kyng Pellinore. **1471** Caxton *Recuyell* (Sommer) 93, I haue not Intencion for to obeye his comandement how well that he is my fader. **1474** —— *Chesse* I. iii. (1883) 15 How well that the lyon be the strengest beste, yet somtyme a lityll birde eteth hym. *Ibid.* II. iv. 47 How well he was kynge by right. **1585** T. Washington tr. *Nicholay's Voy.* I. xiv. 15 They do labour & til the ground, how wel there groweth no corne... But well there groweth certaine other graine and hearbes of small estimation. **1589** Puttenham *Engl. Poesie* I. i. (Arb.) 19 Who..may well be sayd a versifier, but not a Poet. **1634** Milton *Comus* 211 These thoughts may startle well, but not astound The vertuous mind.

9. a. Without difficulty or hindrance; readily, easily.

c **1000** *Canons of Ælfric* vii. in Thorpe *Laws* II. 346 Hy mihton þa wel habban wif on þam daȝum. **1154** *O.E. Chron.* (Laud MS.) an. 1137, Wel þu myhtes faren all a dæis fare, sculdest thu neure finden man in tune sittende. *c* **1250** *Prayer to Virgin* 19 in *O.E. Misc.* 196 Helpe þruh þin milde mod for wel þu mist [*rime* liht]. **13..** *Cursor M.* 20116 (Edin.) Alle þa leuedis þate þare wern, Ful wel þai miȝtin hir forberne. *a* **1352** Minot *Poems* i. 36 Þat lord of heuyn mot Edward lede And maintene him als he wele may. *c* **1400** Maundev. (Roxb.) xxv. 114 Þai may wele hafe swilk clathes, for þai er of lesse prys þare þan wollen clathez er here. *c* **1420** *Sir Amadace* (Camden) xxxix, For he that schope bothe sunne and mone, Fuile wele may pay for alle! *c* **1450** *Cursor M.* 19059 (Laud) Thow maiste wele se now our wone Yeftes haue we to the non. **1481** Caxton *Myrr.* I. xiii. 41 Who that myght haue the parfayt scyence therof, he myght wel knowe how the world was compassed. **1551** R. Robynson *More's Utopia* (1895) 53 All their housholde stuffe, whiche is verye lytle worth, though it myght well abyde the sale. **1803** *Med. Jrnl.* X. 203 With respect to this query,..I cannot so well answer. **1828** [G. C. Lewis] tr. *Boeckh's Pol. Econ. Athens* I. 318 These ambassadors remained absent three months, although they might have equally well returned at the end of one. **1849** Macaulay *Hist. Eng.* vi. II. 16 Nor were the refugees such as a country can well spare.

b. Used to denote the possibility or likelihood of an occurrence or fact.

? *a* **1400** *Morte Arth.* 1788 So may the wynde weile turnne, I quytte hym or ewyne. **1484** Caxton *Fables of Æsop* III. iii, He that is..atte vpperest of the whele of fortune, may wel falle doune. *a* **1547** Surrey *Æneis* II. 373 This right hand well mought have ben her defense. **1618** W. Lawson *New Orchard & Gard.* (1623) 7 The chilling cold may well some little time stay, or hinder the proud course of the sap. **1620** Quarles *Feast for Worms* xi. Ij, Was not this my Word,.. When this mis-hap mought well haue bin escaped? **1680** Moxon *Mech. Exerc.* x. 178 Though no size for the heighth of the Puppets can be well asserted. **1709** Berkeley *Ess. Vision* §144 A little consideration will shew us how this may well be. **1753–4** Richardson *Grandison* I. xii. 66 That a learned man and a linguist may very well be two persons. **1818** Cruise *Digest* (ed. 2) II. 188 This was as strong a case as could well come before the Court. **1874** Scrivener *Lect. Text N.T.* 5 No transcript..can well be found which does not differ from its prototype in some small points. **1887** 'L. Carroll' *Game of Logic* i. 10, I grant you they couldn't well be fewer. *Ibid.* 35 Your Premisses..are as fallacious as they can well be!

c. In negative or comparative clauses.

1523 Skelton *Garl. Laurel* 35, I can not wele tell you what was the occasyon. **1569** J. Sanford tr. *Agrippa's Van. Artes* 31 b, The thinge seemed graver unto him then that he mighte well speake of it. **1609** Bible (Douay) *4 Kings* xxv. Comm., There was so exceding much, that they wel could not, or did not weigh it. **1626** Bacon *Sylva* §173 The Base striketh more Aire, than it can well strike equally. **1642** *Tasman's Jrnl.* in *Acc. Sev. Late Voy.* I. (1694) 135 The Wind would not well suffer them to go to the Northward. **1686** [Allix] *Dissert.* i. in W. Hopkins *Ratramnus' Body & Bl.* (1688) 7 His Answer..could not be well written before the Year 868. **1711** Swift *Jrnl. to Stella* 27 Apr., I see not how they can well want him.., and he would make a troublesome enemy. **1768** Sterne *Sent. Journ.* II. 14 (*Passport, Paris*), By the time La Fleur had well told me, the master of the hotel came..to tell me the same thing. **1827** Disraeli *Viv. Grey* v. vii, Before Vivian could well finish his sentence. **1881** Jowett *Thucyd.* I. 192 He can praise a sharp remark before it is well out of another's mouth. **1898** 'Merriman' *Roden's Corner* xiii. 135 Appearing to know more of that abode of evil than she well could.

†**d.** At least, assuredly. *Obs.*

1825 Scott *Betrothed* xxi, Surely, if I am willing to confer such confidence, it is well thy part to answer it.

10. a. To all appearance; by good evidence.

a **1300** *Cursor M.* 17900 Þenne coom a mon..þat semed wel to haue ben eremyte. *c* **1386** Chaucer *Prol.* 369 Wel semed eche of hem a fair burgeys. **1450–1530** *Myrr. Our Ladye* II. 237 That yt appere wel that she ys hys mother. **1470–85** Malory *Arthur* VI. vii. 192 Thou semest wel to be a good knyght.

b. With acute reasoning; shrewdly.

c **1450** *Merlin* ii. 25 When thei herde these words, [they] supposed wele what he ment. **1523** Berners *Froiss.* I. xciv. 116 They supposed well before that the Kyng of Englande wolde come into Bretayne. *a* **1687** Cotton *Angler's Ballad* ii. Poems (1689) 76 And full well you may think, If you troll with a Pink, One too weak will be apt to miscarry.

III. 11. Effectively; successfully as regards result or progress.

Beowulf 2570 Scyld wel ȝebearȝ life and lice læssan hwile ..þonne his myne sohte. *c* **888** Ælfred *Boethius* xli. §4 Swiðe wel þu min hæfst ȝeholpen æt þære spræce. *c* **1200** *Trin. Coll. Hom.* 39 Þe childre þewuen wuel. *c* **1205** Lay. 23121 For ich hine wulle in Norwæȝe neowe king makien and hine wæl lere to witeȝen wel þa leoden. *c* **1375** *Sc. Leg. Saints* i. (*Petrus*) 322, I sal helpe þe wondire veill. *c* **1400** *Rom. Rose* 1911 But the oynement halpe me wele. *c* **1450** Lovelich *Grail* xiii. 270 Scheldes & hawberkis al to-broke, So wel they gonne there hem beweld. **1821** Southey *Lett.* (1856) III. 262 The printer gets on well with my History.

12. In a manner, or to an extent, approaching thoroughness or completeness.

c **1000** *Sax. Leechd.* II. 322 Ʒecnua [þa wyrta] wel. *c* **1200** Ormin 19308 He..haffde himm sellf wel filledd All þatt tatt cwiddedd haffde ben Off himm. *c* **1250** *Gen. & Ex.* 229 He ..heled him ðat side wel ðat it ne wrocte him neuere a del. *c* **1386** Chaucer *Reeve's T.* 388 Thise clerkes beete hym weel, and lete hym lye. ? *a* **1400** *Morte Arth.* 321 Now schalle we wreke fulle wele the wrethe of oure elders! *c* **1430** *Two Cookery-bks.* I. 6 Take otemele, an grynd it smal, an sethe it wyl. *Ibid.* 26 Menge hem wylle to-gederys. **1482** *Monk of Evesham* (Arb.) 23 Ageyne meruaylously the colowre of hys face was reuyuyd and welle shewyd. **1523–34** Fitzherb. *Husb.* §35 Corne,..if it be well wynowed or fande,..wyll be solde the derer. **1535** Coverdale *Ez.* xxiv. 5 Let it boyle well, & let the bones seyth well therin. **1565** Cooper *Thesaurus* s.v. *Bene*, Well accompanied or with a good companie. **1618** W. Lawson *New Orchard & Gard.* (1623) 12 All your labour..about an Orchard is lost vnlesse you fence well. **1639** Fuller *Holy War* I. xix. 31 Of late some English travellers climbing this mountain were well wetted. **1697** Dryden *Virg. Georg.* III. 295 This from his Weaning, let him well be taught. *Ibid.* IV. 191 Lab'ring Well his little Spot of Ground. **1703** Rowe *Ulysses* IV. i. (1706) 50 'Till.. that poor bleeding King be well reveng'd. **1799** G. S. Carey *Balnea* (ed. 2) 76 The market here is not very well supplied. **1814** Scott *Wav.* xlv, The pockets of the defunct..had been pretty well spung'd. **1820** Keats *Lamia* II. 301 She, as well As her weak hand could any meaning tell, Motion'd him to be silent. **1890** *Retrospect. Med.* CII. 307 After being well dried with an antiseptic sponge or dry gauze.

13. a. Used as an intensive to strengthen the idea implied in the verb, or to denote that the action, etc., indicated by it attains a high point or degree.

(*a*) *c* **888** Ælfred *Boeth.* v. §2 Ne meaht þu win wringan on mide winter, þeah ðe wel lyste wearmes mustes. *c* **1000** *Sax. Leechd.* I. 148 Syle him ðas ylcan wyrte wel drincan on wætere. *c* **1250** *Gen. & Ex.* 1521 Niðede ðat folk him fel wel, And deden him flitten hise ostel. *c* **1350** *Will. Palerne* 1266 Þan william wiȝtly, as he wel couþe, profered him þat prisoner. **1375** Barbour *Bruce* I. 21 Thai suld weill hawe pryss That in thar tyme war wycht and wyss. *Ibid.* XVIII. 87 Thai said weill at thai suld do sua. *c* **1449** Pecock *Repr.* Prol. 1 As resoun also it weel confermeth. **1876** *Coursing Calendar* 172 Mr. Deighton's bitch, who beat her opponent well at the finish. **1877** H. Smart *Bound to Win* III. 158 Ever since.. the twain had got on very well together.

(*b*) *c* **1200** Ormin 19300 Þiss birrþ þe full wel trowwenn. *a* **1352** Minot *Poems* i. 41 Gai þai war and wele þai thoght On þe Erle Morre and oþer ma. **1375** Barbour *Bruce* I. 149 He thocht weile..That he suld slely fynd the gate [etc.]. *c* **1400** *Ywaine & Gaw.* 2507 That may i noght do, Bileves wele, for me bus go. *c* **1430** *Chev. Assigne* 67 Þe kynge.. wente wele it were sothe alle þat she seyde. *c* **1450** *Merlin* xxxii. 655 Thei bothe fill to the erthe as he that trusted wele vpon his felowes. *c* **1460** *Townley Myst.* xxxi. 34 *Thomas.* Sir, What so euer ye bid vs do We aseent vs well ther to. **1476** *Stonor Papers* (Camden) II. 11 In trowthe I hadde wil hopide that your horsis shulde a ben here as þis night.

(*c*) **1542** Udall *Erasm. Apoph.* 215 b, Many moo then one to had well deserued to bee whipped. *a* **1669** [see deserve *v.* 3]. **1692** E. Walker tr. *Epictetus' Mor.* Ep. Ded., You were then pleas'd to express an high esteem for the Author, as he very well deserves it.

b. with verbs of pleasing (†*like*, *pay*), liking, or loving.

(*a*) *Beowulf* 639 Ðam wife þa word wel licodon. *a* **900** Cynewulf *Christ* 918 Þam þe him on mode ær..wel ȝecwemdun. *c* **950** *Lindisf. Gosp.* Matt. vi. 34 Wel mæȝ *vel* wel licas [L. *sufficit*] ðæm dæȝ weriȝnise his. **971** *Blickl. Hom.* 29 Þis is min se leofa sunu, on þæm me wel ȝelicode. ? *a* **1400** *Morte Arth.* 230 There ne es prelatte, ne pape,.. That he ne myghte be wele payede of thees pryce metes! **1596** Shaks. *Tam. Shr.* IV. iv. 39 Your plainnesse and your shortnesse please me well. **1753–4** Richardson *Grandison* I. li. 410 Sir Hargrave did not seem so well pleased.

(*b*) *a* **1300** *Cursor M.* 548 Wit bestes doumb man has his fele, O thyng man liks, il or welle. *c* **1430** *Chev. Assigne* 54 Sythen seche to þe courte.., And þou shalt lyke fulle wele yf þou may lyfe aftur. *c* **1450** *Merlin* xxx. 607 Kynge Ban..behilde the maydenys, and liked well theire companye. **1477** Earl Rivers (Caxton) *Dictes* 2 He trusted I shuld lyke it right wele. **1675** R. Burthogge *Causa Dei* 419 Perhaps, while some of us are for Martyn, and others for Luther,.. God likes well of us All. **1847** Riddell *Cottagers Glendale* III. xxv, Our Mary liket weel to stray Where clear the burn was rowin'.

(*c*) *a* **1300** *Cursor M.* 11310 O pouert na dedeigne had he þat biddes vs luue wel pouerte. **1338** R. Brunne *Chron.* (1810) 36 In Ingland neuer before was kyng lufed so wele. *c* **1386** Chaucer *C.T.* Prol. 634 Wel loued he garleek, oynons, and eek lekes. *c* **1412** Hoccleve *De Reg. Princ.* 3892 Thei love as vel as doth sustir & brothir. *c* **1450** Capgrave *St. Aug.* i. 3 We rede of hym..þat he hated þe Greke letteris and loued weel þe Latyn. **1593** Shaks. *2 Hen. VI*, IV. vii. 139 Let them kisse one another: For they lou'd well When they were aliue. **1818** Scott *Br. Lamm.* xx, It is a spot connected with the legendary lore which I love so well.

c. Placed before past pples. to denote a high degree of the state, etc., described. †Also occas. following the pple.

c **1205** Lay. 340 Þa wepmen weren iwexan, þa wimen wel iþowene. *c* **1300** *E.E. Poems* (1862) 153 Þis uers is ful wel iwroȝt. **1338** R. Brunne *Chron.* (1810) 242 Now I find þe here, wele set is my trauaile. *a* **1352** Minot *Poems* iii. 101 Þe Inglis men war armed wele Both in yren and in stele. *c* **1386** Chaucer *C.T.* Prol. 29 The chambres and the stables weren wyde And wel we weren esed atte beste. *a* 1425 *Cursor M.* 9900 (Trin.) A deep diche is þere aboute wel wrouȝte wiþouten doute. *c* 1449 PECOCK *Repr.* II. iii. 150 Eer thei be weel adauntid and weel schamed of her folie. *c* 1470 HENRY *Wallace* I. 112 Is nayne in warld, at scaithis ma do mar, Than weile trastyt in borne familiar. 1553 ASCHAM *Rept. Germany* 3 We were wel affrayd then, the sickenes would haue proued also to vs.. very contagious. 1560 DAUS tr. *Sleidane's Comm.* 231 Whan the number of Bysshoppes was wel increased, they beganne the Counsell. 1585 T. WASHINGTON tr. *Nicholay's Voy.* IV. xiii. 126b, A Leopardes skynne well spotted. *Ibid.*, The poleaxe at the point being well steeled. 1599 SHAKS. *Hen. V*, V. ii. 335 Maides well Sommer'd and warme kept, are like Flyes at Bartholomew-tyde. 1639 J. TAYLOR (Water P.) *Crabtree Lect.* 46, I am neither well litter'd, nor well provender'd.. nor well rubb'd, nor well curried, nor indeed well any thing'd. 1659 *Nicholas Papers* (Camden) IV. 171 Some say the Sweade is well beaten by the Dane and Dutch. 1746 FRANCIS tr. *Hor.*, *Sat.* I. iv. 190 Well fraught with numbers is the rhyming trade. 1771 MRS. HAYWOOD *New Present for Maid* 255 Wood-ashes well sifted. 1783 S. CHAPMAN in *Med. Commun.* I. 285 Tincture of roses, well acidulated. 1842 LOUDON *Suburban Hort.* 497 Pots.. either new or well cleaned in the inside. 1882 BESANT *All Sorts* xxvii, She had been drawn on into wider schemes, and could not retire until these.. were well started.

d. With past pples. followed by prepositions or adverbs.

1538 ELYOT *Dict.* Add., *Artitus*, well instructed in sciences. 1621 SANDERSON *Serm.*, *Ad Pop.* iv. (1689) 212 The land by that means well-purged of these overspreading Locusts. 1755 J. SHEBBEARE *Lydia* (1769) I. 178 Surgeon Macpherson being well learnt in northern knowledge. 1863 KINGLAKE *Crimea* (1876) I. xii. 198 He had not been kept well imbued with the policy which his Government was pursuing. 1899 *Daily News* 28 Oct. 7/1, I conceived that his system was not well-bottomed on facts.

e. With adjs. in *-ed* (cf. 32).

1486 *Bk. St. Albans* ej b, An hert heeded weele.

14. a. Clearly, definitely, without any doubt or uncertainty.

a 1250 *Owl & Night.* 95 Wel wostu þat hi doþ þar ynne. 1258 HEN. III *Proclam.* 18 Oct. §2 Þæt witen ȝe wel alle þæt we willen [etc.]. *c* 1290 *Beket* 119 in *S. Eng. Leg.* 110 For we it mowen wel i-wite.. Þat.. it is godes sonde. *a* 1300 *Harrow. Hell* (Digby MS.) 57 Þou miȝt wel witen bi mi play Þat ich wile hauen mine away. *a* 1300 *Cursor M.* 866, I sagh wel þat i misfard. 1340–70 *Alex. & Dind.* 91 Men seþ wel þat þe see seseþ & stinteþ. *a* 1366 CHAUCER *Rom. Rose* 1355 There were, and that wote I full well, Of pome garnettys a full gret dell. *c* 1386 —— *Merch. T.* Epil. 7 And from a sooth euere wol they weyue; By this Marchauntes tale it preueth weel. 1411 *Rolls of Parlt.* III. 650/1 He knoweth wel that.. he ne hath noght born hym as he sholde hav doon. *c* 1450 *Merlin* xxxii. 655 Segramor.. hadde well sein and parceyved whiche was Petrius. 1483 CAXTON *Golden Leg.* 429/1 The kyng theodoryk that wel wyste of it commaunded [etc.]. *c* 1483 SKELTON *Death Edw. IV*, 37, I se wyll, they leve that doble my ȝeris. 1526 TINDALE *John* iv. 26, I wot well Messias shall come. 1581 RICH *Farew. Milit. Prof.* Ep. Ded. a ij, Wisdome now hath warned me, that I well knowe Cheese from Chalke. 1585 T. WASHINGTON tr. *Nicholay's Voy.* I. xix. 22b, Which hee well perceiued, and smiling, tolde mee that he saw wel that I dissembled. 1624 BP. MOUNTAGU *Immed. Addr.* 95 As.. his most sacred Maiestie can well remember. 1638 BAKER tr. *Balzac's Lett.* II. 33 The number of my enemies is great, I see it well. 1667 MILTON *P.L.* IV. 926 Well thou knowst I stood Thy fiercest. 1711 STEELE *Spect.* No. 78 ¶7 We well know, Sir, you want no Motives to do Justice. 1741–2 GRAY *Agrippina* 60, I well remember too (for I was present). 1788 PRIESTLEY *Lect. Hist.* IV. xxiv. 191 Nor does it well appear that their kings did afterwards introduce any of another sort. 1837 WHEWELL *Hist. Induct. Sci.* (1857) II. 158 All is done by an impulsion which one does not well understand. 1849 MACAULAY *Hist. Eng.* vi. II. 24 He.. could well remember the political contests of the reign of James the First. 1895 *Law Times* XCIX. 544/1 The parties know perfectly well beforehand what are the points in dispute.

b. Intimately, familiarly; closely, in detail.

(*a*) *c* 1320 *Sir Tristr.* 225 Mi broþer wele it [a ring] knewe, Mi fader ȝaf it me. 1393 LANGL. *P. Pl.* C. XXI. 253 Peter þe apostel.. wel hym knewe. *c* 1400 *Destr. Troy* 13508 Wele his cosyn he knew, & kaght hym in armys. *c* 1420 *Avow. Arth.* xxx, The kinge his bugulle con blaw, His knyȝtus couthe hitte welle knaw. 1470–85 MALORY *Arthur* VI. iii. 186 We here knowe the wel that thou arte syre Launcelot du laake. 1535 COVERDALE *Gen.* xxix. 5 We knowe him well. 1596 SHAKS. *Merch. V.* I. i. 153 You know me well. 1697 DRYDEN *Virg. Georg.* III. 442 The Shepherd knows it well; and calls by Name Hippomanes. 1709 STEELE *Tatler* No. 58 ¶2 He being well known to us all. 1862 THACKERAY *Philip* xxvii, I know him.. too well to think he will ever apologize!

(*b*) *a* 1400–50 *Wars Alex.* 44 He couth.. wele as Aristotill þe artis all seuyn. 1422 YONGE tr. *Secreta Secret.* 122 Arystotle.. well kowth the lawes. *c* 1440 *Generydes* 3698 Be cause ye knowe so will this contre. 1602 *2nd Pt. Return fr. Parnassus* Prol. 46 Vnlesse you know the subiect well you may returne home as wise as you came. 1759 JOHNSON *Rasselas* vii, He thought himself happy in having found a man who knew the world so well. 1819 SCOTT *Ivanhoe* xxxiii, I can well of woodcraft.

15. a. In a skilful or expert manner.

c 825 *Vesp. Psalter* xxxii. 3 Wel singað [L. *bene psallite*] in wynsumnisse. *a* 900 CYNEWULF *Christ* 668 Sum mæᵹ fingrum wel.. hearpan stirᵹan. *a* 1200 *Moral Ode* 109 Ne mei him na Mon alsa wel demen ne alsa rihte. *c* 1205 LAY. 41 A Frenchis clerc, Wace wes ihoten, þe wel couþe writen. 1297 R. GLOUC. (Rolls) 3166 So wisliche he made hit & so wel þat me leuede him uaste. *c* 1386 CHAUCER *Prol.* 122 Ful weel she soong the seruice dyuyne. *Ibid.* 384 He koude.. Maken Mortreux and wel bake a pye. 1430–40 LYDG. *Bochas* II. 2368 This Tubal koude forge weel. 1529 MORE *Dialogue Heresyes* Wks. 108/2 And men mutter amonge them selfe, that yᵗ boke was not only faultles, but also very wel translated. *a* 1548 HALL *Chron.*, *Hen. VIII* 73 The same gate or tower.. well and warly was made ouer the gateloups. 1599 B. JONSON *Cynthia's Rev.* V. iii. 2nd Masque, How well Diana can distinguish times? 1626 —— *Staple of N.* IV. i, Well play'd, my Poet. 1656 STANLEY *Hist. Philos.* I. IV. iv. 3 A Man.. able to discourse wel. 1706 tr. *De Piles' Art Painting* 386 He was a universal Painter; he perform'd well alike in all kinds, Landskip only excepted. 1741 C'TESS POMFRET in *C'tess Hartford's Corr.* (1805) II. 277 Lord Strafford.. looks extremely young.. but talks very well. 1803 SCOTT *Cadyow Castle* xvii, Aim'd well, the Chieftain's lance has flown. 1857 RUSKIN *Pol. Econ. Art* ii. §102 A great work is only done when the painter.. determines to paint it as well as he can. 1875 JOWETT *Plato* (ed. 2) V. 381 Every one of these poets has said many things well and many things the reverse of well.

b. In a sufficient or satisfactory manner.

The exact sense varies in different contexts.

c 1250 *Gen. & Ex.* 1541 He seruede his fader wel Wið wines drinc and seles mel. 1375 BARBOUR *Bruce* XI. 50 God may richt weill our werdis deill. *c* 1386 CHAUCER *Squire's T.* 18 He.. kepte alwey so wel roial estat, That ther was nowher swich another man. *c* 1430 *Chev. Assigne* 2 Alle weldynge god.. Wele he wereth his werke with his owne honde. 1712 SWIFT *Jrnl. to Stella* 26 Mar., The quicksets.. do not grow so well as those famous ones on the ditch. 1853 *Jrnl. R. Agric. Soc.* XIV. II. 367 The machine.. could not cut laid corn well. 1855 *Poultry Chron.* II. 523 She appears moping, but eats very well. 1893 *Weekly Notes* 85/1 The existing practice has worked well, and.. ought to be maintained. 1908 [MISS E. FOWLER] *Betw. Trent & Ancholme* 40 Very fine Irises.. grow well in that garden.

c. With good appearance or effect; elegantly.

c 1330 R. BRUNNE *Chron. Wace* (Rolls) 196 After þe Inglis kynges he says þer pris Þat all in metir fulle wele lys. *c* 1386 CHAUCER *Clerk's T.* 332 This markis.. hir sette Upon an hors, snow-whyt, and wel ambling. *c* 1450 *Merlin* iii. 44 Thider come to hym a comely man wele araied. *a* 1529 SKELTON *Agst. Garnesche* iv. 135 Yt wold garnyche wyll thy face. 1710 STEELE *Tatler* No. 212 ¶4 A Woman must think well to look well. 1778 D. LOCH *Tour Scot.* 14 Upon the whole, it is a neat well laid out town. 1779 *Mirror* No. 11 That [science] of the serjeant, as it teaches a man to stand well on his legs. 1884 E. YATES *Recoll.* I. 142 The gardens were large and well laid out. 1898 A. BALFOUR *To Arms* vi, I was a big, strong fellow, carrying my six feet well.

IV. As an intensive with adjectives, numerals, adverbs, etc.

16. a. With adjectives. Formerly in common use, the sense varying from 'fully, completely' to 'fairly, considerably, rather'. Now *rare* exc. as in b.

c 888 ÆLFRED *Boeth.* xxv, Seo leo, þeah hio wel tam se,.. heo forᵹit sona hire niwan taman. *c* 900 tr. *Bæda's Hist.* IV. ii. 258 Wæron her stronge cyningas and wel cristene. 971 *Blickl. Hom.* 217 Þa wæs he þær daᵹas wel maniᵹe. *c* 1000 *Sax. Leechd.* II. 180 Pisan.. ᵹesodena.. on wine wel scearpum. *c* 1175 *Lamb. Hom.* 49 Ah leofemen godalmihtin haueð isceaweð us wel muchele grace. *c* 1205 LAY. 25694 We habbeð wið him iuohten wel feole siðen. *c* 1220 *Bestiary* 112 His muð is ȝet wel unkuð wið pater noster and crede. 1297 R. GLOUC. (Rolls) 1 Engelond his a wel god lond. *Ibid.* 7693 Þoru out al engelond he huld wel god pes. *c* 1315 SHOREHAM *Poems* i. 24 Be him wel siker, þer-to he schel. *c* 1350 *Will. Palerne* 4 In þat forest.. Þer woned a wel old cherl. 1362 LANGL. *P. Pl.* A. VII. 44 In a wel perilous place þat Purgatorie hette. 1387 TREVISA *Higden* I. 13, I haue peynt a wel faire man. *c* 1400 MAUNDEV. (Roxb.) ix. 35 A lytill citee and a narow, bot it es wele lang. *c* 1450 *Godstow Reg.* 160 Hit shold be wele lawfull to the same Abbesse. 1484 CAXTON *Fables of Avian* ii, Wel hyghe fro the ground. *a* 1533 BERNERS *Huon* lii. 176 He thought hymselfe ryght wel happy. 1577 HARRISON *England* II. ii. 62/1 in *Holinshed*, The Ogur or Gur.. is a welfaire streame. 1578 LYTE *Dodoens* IV. xxxi. 489 A branche of leaues, very well like to the leaues of the Lentil. 1599 MARSTON *Antonio's Rev.* V. iv, Tis well brim full. Euen I haue glut of blood. 1648 GAGE *West Ind.* 160 They have enough and more then is well sutable to their vow.. of poverty. 1664 H. MORE *Apol.* vi. in *Myst. Iniq.* 520 When he was once well warm in his Dignity. 1700 DRYDEN *Pal. & Arc.* I. 151 Nor well alive nor wholly dead they were. 1728 CHAMBERS *Cycl.* s.v. *Painting*, To Paint on a Wall: when well dry, they give it two or three Washes of boiling Oil. 1822 *Scoresby's Jrnl. Whale Fish.* (1823) 448 We.. made her well fast for another night's lodgings.

b. In modern use esp. in ***well able***, ***aware***, ***worth***, ***worthy***.

c 1420 *Sir Amadace* xxxi, Ȝe mone haue maysturs euyrqware, As wele wurthi ȝe ar soe. 1599 SHAKS. *Much Ado* I. i. 224 Amen, if you loue her, for the Ladie is verie well worthie. 1611 BIBLE *Num.* xiii. 30 Let vs goe vp at once and possesse it, for we are well able to ouercome it. 1612 R. CH. *Olde Thrift newly revived* 64 Though it be a seemely and large tree, and well worth the hauing, yet [etc.]. 1697 DRYDEN *Æneis* VII. 906 Himself well worthy of a happier Throne. 1711 STEELE *Spect.* No. 78 ¶9 You are well able to settle this affair. 1780 COXE *Russ. Discov.* 187 He was well aware that the only method [etc.]. 1804 ANNA SEWARD *Lett.* (1811) VI. 164 Every day produces letters as well worth attention as most of Cowper's. 1837 B. D. WALSH *Aristoph.*, *Knts.* I. iii, I was well aware that these intrigues were carpentered. 1885 *Law Times' Rep.* LII. 650/2 She thought the property was well worth that amount.

†17. With numerals, or terms of measurement, denoting fulness of the number, distance, etc. *Obs.*

c 1000 ÆLFRIC *Saints' Lives* xv. 37 Se godspellere.. ðær þurhwunode wel twa ᵹear mid him. *c* 1000 —— *On New T.* (Grein) 13 For þan þe ic ᵹesett hæbbe.. wel feowertiᵹ larspella on Engliscum ᵹereorde. *c* 1290 *St. Kenelm* 232 in *S. Eng. Leg.* 352 Folk þat þis wonder isaiȝ.. awaiteden wel a dai ȝware þe kou bicome. *c* 1300 *Havelok* 1747 He tok sone knithes ten, And wel sixti oþer men. *a* 1352 MINOT *Poems* vii. 57 Knightes war þare wele two score. *a* 1375 *Joseph Arim.* 521 Seraphe takes of heore men wel a two hundred. *c* 1400 MAUNDEV. (1919) xxii. 126 Wel a .iiij. quarteres of a furlong ore more. *c* 1425 *Engl. Conq. Ireland* xxi. 52 Wel thre þousand men. 1471 CAXTON *Recuyell* (Sommer) II. 446 He.. was there well thre owres seechyng yf he coude fynde ony hoole or caue. *c* 1489 —— *Sonnes of Aymon* i. 23 They were well an hondred men or more. 1523 BERNERS *Froiss.* I. xvi. 17 There was deed in the place, well to the nombre of ccc. 1582 N. LICHEFIELD tr. *Castanheda's Conq. E. Ind.* I. iii. 8 A great Harbour, which reacheth into the Lande sixe leagues, and at the entering it containeth well as much more.

18. †a. With adverbs. (Cf. 16.) *Obs.*

See also WELL-A-FINE, -MOST, -NEAR, -NIGH, and YWHERE *adv.*

a 1200 *Moral Ode* 8 Wel late ich habbe me bi-þocht; bute god me nu rede. *a* 1250 *Owl & Night.* 36 For þine wle lete Wel ofte ich my song furlete. *c* 1275 LAY. 25349 Folk þar com wel sone to þare borh of Rome. 13.. *Guy Warw.* (1891) 446 Wel wele y knowe,.. Herhaud, so god me rede. *c* 1350 *Will. Palerne* 4989, I hote þe in hert it liked him wel ille. 1377 LANGL. *P. Pl.* B. Prol. 67 The moste my[s]chief on molde is mountyng wel faste. *c* 1385 CHAUCER *L.G.W.* Prol. 33 There is wel onethe game non That from myne bokys maketh me to gon. *c* 1400 *Sowdone Bab.* 2513 Down to the erthe wele lowe thay loute. 1450–80 tr. *Secreta Secret.* xxi. 17 They beren it welle grevously ayens him. 1563 WINȜET tr. *Vincent. Lirin.* ix. Wks. (S.T.S.) II. 27 The writtingis of sum auld aunciant man weil dirklie setfurth.

b. With advs. and preps. of place or direction, in later use freq. in figurative phrases.

a 1300 *Cursor M.* 11027 Til elizabeth þan welforth stadd, Hir child in wamb [began] be gladd. *c* 1320 *Sir Tristrem* 22 His name, it sprong wel wide. 1387 TREVISA *Higden* I. 17 Þat is in oþer bookes iwrite welwyde. *c* 1400 *Ywaine & Gaw.* 549 He thoght to be wele on hys way Or it war passed the thryd day. *c* 1449 PECOCK *Repr.* I. iv. 20 Welnyȝ or weel toward the al hool lawe with which Cristen men ben chargid. 1473 *Paston Lett.* III. 92 Som men thynke it wysdom.. to be theer now weell owt off the weye. *c* 1489 CAXTON *Sonnes of Aymon* vii. 176 But or ever he was vnbounde, the other were well ferre. 1530 PALSGR. 862/1 Well forwarde, *bien auant*. 1625 PURCHAS *Pilgrims* II. 1132 Well within the banke we harboured. 1698 FRYER *Acc. E. India & P.* 173 Whose Force.. so gauled Seva Gi, that he wish'd him well off. 1788 J. WHITE *Jrnl. Voy. N.S. Wales* (1790) 109 Being well in with the westward-most point of a very large bay. 1840 R. H. DANA *Bef. Mast* xxxv. 133 The Captain stood well to the westward, to run inside the Bermudas. 1855 M. PATTISON in *Oxford Ess.* 287 Though not published till 1830, which was well into the second period. 1883 D. C. MURRAY *Hearts* xvii, She held her head well up. 1895 *Law Times' Rep.* LXXII. 817/1 A woman well past the age of childbearing.

†c. ***well at ease***: see EASE *sb.* 7a.

a 1300 *Cursor M.* 17651 He was gestend ful wel at es. 1377 LANGL. *P. Pl.* B. XIII. 42 Of þat men mys-wonne, þei made hem wel at ese. 1530 PALSGR. 844/1 Well at ease, *bien ayse*. 1551 T. WILSON *Logic* Dj, Nature hath denied some men health of body, that thei are neuer wel at ease. 1560 DAUS tr. *Sleidane's Comm.* 232 He felte hymselfe skant well at ease. 1706 tr. *De Piles' Art Painting* 229 By these high Prises Guido found himself, in a little while, very well at ease, and liv'd nobly. 1825 JENNINGS *Obs. Dial. W. Eng.*, *Well-at-ease*, hearty, healthy.

d. With various prepositional phrases or adverbs denoting a state or condition.

c 1425 *Macro Plays, Cast. Persev.* 2702 Þou art a party wele in age. 1605 SHAKS. *Macb.* IV. iii. 179 They were wel at peace, when I did leaue 'em. 1653 H. COGAN tr. *Pinto's Trav.* xlii. 168 A woman reasonably well in years. 1701 W. WOTTON *Hist. Rome* i. 17 Marcus went to Lectures to this Man.. when he was well in Years. 1861 HUGHES *Tom Brown at Oxf.* iv, It takes no mean qualities to keep a boat's crew well together and in order. 1879 MRS. ARGLES *Airy Fairy Lilian* III. 100 Taffy and Mabel Steyne can be seen a little lower down, holding well together.

e. *to be* (or *get*) ***well away***: to have (or obtain) a good start over one's pursuers; usu. *fig.*, to make good progress in an activity (esp. drinking). *colloq.*

1910 *Glasgow Herald* 7 Feb. 13/2 From the drop out Andrew got well away but Henry pulled him up. 1927 W. E. COLLINSON *Contemp. Eng.* 101 Expressions.. like.. 'he's well away' (he has got into his stride or into swing whether in tackling a meal or a flirtation or in drink). 1947 'N. SHUTE' *Chequer Board* iii. 51 Bristow had a bottle of whisky and I had one of gin so we were well away. 1950 J. CANNAN *Murder Included* vii. 141 'What's happened?'.. 'If we knew that, we should be well away.' 1956 C. BLACKSTOCK *Dewey Death* vi. 128 He paused again, but Sergeant Robins saw no point in making any comment; the young gentleman was plainly well away. 1973 J. PORTER *It's Murder with Dover* viii. 72 Many great men.. [can] drop off to sleep at any time.. and Chief Inspector was no exception. He was well away by the time MacGregor climbed back into the car. 1984 A. CARTER *Nights at Circus* III. v. 233 The Colonel.. overcomes his resistance to vodka to such an extent he is soon well away and sings songs of Old Kentucky.

†19. With comparative adjs. and advs. (esp. *bet* or *better*, *worse*, and *more*): Much, considerably, rather. *Obs.*

1297 R. GLOUC. (Rolls) 287 Man þou art iwis To winne ȝvt a kinedom wel betere þan min is. *a* 1300 *Cursor M.* 2438 Abram went ham and his wijf sare, He luued hir wil mare þan are. 1340 HAMPOLE *Pr. Consc.* 2359 Men sese noght ne knawes what it es, Þarfor men dredes it wele þe les. 1362 LANGL. *P. Pl.* A. v. 95, I deme men þat don ille, and ȝit I do wel worse. *c* 1400 *Beryn* 902 It had be wel bettir, he had be wele I-lernyd. *c* 1400 *Pilgr. Sowle* (Caxton) IV. xxxviii. (1859) 63 Thenne began she to wepe wel faster than byfore. *c* 1460 *Towneley Myst.* xxvi. 304, I was well wrother with Iudas. 1535 STEWART *Cron. Scot.* II. 199 Fra that tyme furth the weill les he thame dred. 1624 BEDELL *Lett.* xi. 141 Your next is well worse.

V. 20. as well as: a. In as good, efficient, satisfactory, (etc.) a way or manner as. (Also, in early use, simply ***well as***.)

a 1400–50 *Wars Alex.* 44 And wele as Aristotill [he couth] þe artis all seuyn. 1435 *Coventry Leet Bk.* (1907) 182 But neuer-the-later.. he makithe cardes ther-of as well as he may. 1530 PALSGR. 831/2 As well as is possyble,.. As well as can be or maye be. 1589 PUTTENHAM *Engl. Poesie* III. xxii. (Arb.) 267 Certaine propheticall rymes, which might be constred two or three wayes as well as to that one whereunto the rebels applied it. 1600 *Look about you* I 1b, I see Prince Iohn coorted as well as I. 1634 MILTON *Comus* 201 This is the place, as well as I may guess. 1634 MASSINGER *Very Woman* IV. i, *Ped.* How hast thou sped? *John.* My Lord, as well as wishes. **1793** *Piper of Peebles* 6 Fan cummers fled and hurl'd as weel On ice, as ony vady chiel. *a* **1809** J. PALMER *Like Master* (1811) I. xii. 174, I am left to rough it as well as I can. **1849** MACAULAY *Hist. Eng.* vi. II. 74 She affected.. to listen with civility while the Hydes excused their recent conduct, as well as they could.

b. To the same extent, in the same degree, as much, as.

OE. *eal swa wel.. swa swa* occurs in the same sense (Ælfric *Hom.* I. 274).

c **1440** *Alphabet of Tales* I. 75 He.. sayde he was a synner & mysterd forgyfnes of his syn als wele as sho did. **1474** CAXTON *Chesse* II. i. (1481) bj, He.. swore to hym.. that also wel he was and shold be his frend.. as euer he had ben tofore. **1547** *Homilies* I. *Swearing* II. G iv b, Aswell they vse the name of God in vayne.. as they whiche do promise [etc.]. **1628** BURTON *Anat. Mel.* II. ii. III. (ed. 3) 235 Why hath Daulis and Thebes no Swallowes.. as well as the rest of Greece. **1710** ADDISON *Whig Exam.* No. 4 ¶1 A man may as well hope to distinguish colours in the midst of darkness, as to find out what to approve and disapprove in nonsense. **1891** R. W. CHURCH *Oxf. Movement* xix. 347 The English Church was after all as well worth living in and fighting for as any other.

c. With weakened force, passing into the sense of 'both.. and', 'not only.. but also'. Also † *so well.. as*.

In early use the rendering 'not only.. but also' is applicable only if the two contrasted words or expressions are transposed.

c **1386** CHAUCER *Prol.* 49 And therto hadde he riden.. As wel in cristendom as in Hethenesse. **1390** GOWER *Conf.* I. 117 For al schal deie.. Als wel a Leoun as an asse, Als wel a beggere as a lord. *c* **1400** MAUNDEV. (Roxb.) vii. 25 Þus þai do als wele in winter as in somer. *c* **1425** tr. *Arderne's Treat. Fistula* etc. 60 Blode is norischyng of al membrez, als wele of sadde as of softe. ? **1467–8** *Stonor Papers* (Camden) I. 100 The Shireff shewyd ij comyssions of this graunt as well of the lordes as of the comyns. **1533** CRANMER *Let. to Dean of Arches* Misc. Writ. (Parker Soc.) II. 253 That you take all manner of depositions as well for the one part as for the other. **1571** DIGGES *Pantom.* I. xx. G j b, In equiangle triangles aswell the contayning as the subtending sides of equall angles are proportionall. **1588** PARKE tr. *Mendoza's Hist. China* 329 All of them as well the men as women and children were clothed with shamway skins. **1645** GATAKER *God's Eye on Israel* 50 Consisting of both sorts, as well unfaithfull as faithfull, as well bad as good. **1662** STILLINGFL. *Orig. Sacræ* II. iv. §2 Which.. must certainly comprehend as well the morall as the ceremoniall part of Moses his Law. **1718** HICKES & NELSON *J. Kettlewell* I. xiii. 38 Making Use as well of his Eye.. as of his Tongue. **1749** C. MIDDLETON *Free Inq.* Pref. p. xxxiii, It is allowed.. by all, as well friends as enemies. **1828** SCOTT *F.M. Perth* xiv, Our churchmen have become wealthy, as well by the gifts of pious persons, as by.. bribes.

(*b*) **1545** BALE *Image Both Ch.* xiii. (1550) d viij, Comprehending in him so wel Mahomyte as the Pope, so well the ragynge tyraunt as the styll hypocryte.

d. Used to denote the inclusion of one thing (person, etc.) or class with another.

c **1449** PECOCK *Repr.* III. vii. 316 The multitude of the lay peple, as weel as of clerkis. **1470–85** MALORY *Arthur* IX. xxxvi. 397 Whan men ben hote in dedes of armes ofte they hurte their frendes as wel as their foes. **1613** HIERON *Serm.* Wks. 1614 I. 335 Whereas the children of God in many things are trespassers aswell as the vngodly. **1649** HOWELL *Dodona's Grove* (ed. 3) 3 Nor is she lesse abounding in all things conducing to pleasure also, aswel as profit. **1655** *Nicholas Papers* (Camden) III. 221 My heart as well as pursse being quite sunck. **1702** ADDISON *Dial. Medals* ii. (1726) 37 I find.. the Latins mean Courage by the figure of Virtue, as well as by the word it self. **1715** DESAGULIERS *Fires Impr.* 127 The two first.. are made of Tin as well as the third. **1769** *Junius Lett.* ii. 13 Educated.. by.. a most spirited as well as excellent scholar. **1821** CRAIG *Lect. Drawing* etc. vii. 404 The back-ground as well as other parts is dotted or stippled. **1854** MRS. JAMESON *Comm.-pl. Bk.* (1877) 38 There are different sorts of strength as well as different degrees. **1896** *Law Times' Rep.* LXXIII. 615/1 A highway for carriages as well as for foot-passengers.

21. as well. a. Also, in addition; in the same way.

1303 R. BRUNNE *Handl. Synne* 536 As she dyde, he dyde yn dede;.. Ryȝt as she dede, he dede as weyl. **1549** *Compl. Scot.* Epist. 1 As veil it bringis furtht.. hoilsum frute of honour. *a* **1631** DONNE *Paradoxes* (1652) 60 They should love their brothers aswel. **1669–70** MARVELL *Corr.* Wks. (Grosart) II. 302 The next news will be, that.. they [the Lords] have as well complyed on their part also. **1875** *Economist* 23 Jan. 95/1 But the state of the French Exchange is such that gold is taken from London as well. **1882** BESANT *All Sorts* xxvii, Because she was a dressmaker, and lived at Stepney, he would be a workman and live there as well.

b. To the same extent.

c **1449** PECOCK *Repr.* II. ix. 199 Wherfore as weel or miche rather Cristen men ouȝten be waar forto entirmete with like ymagis. *Ibid.* II. xviii. 260 Wherfore as weel and as alloweabili y mai seie this speche.

c. With *may, might, had*, etc., implying the equivalence or equal result of one action in comparison with another.

c **1440** *York Myst.* xxix. 249 Sir, we myght als wele talke tille a tome tonne! **1608** DOD & CLEAVER *Expos. Prov. xi. and xii.* 87, I might as well haue thrown my mony down the riuer. **1652** SHIRLEY *Brothers* IV. v, He might as well have murdered me, for I Shall have no heart to live. **1692** E. WALKER tr. *Epictetus' Mor.* xviii, As well you might Wish Vice were Virtue, wish that Black were White. **1730** *Lett. to Sir W. Strickland rel. to Coal Trade* 25 Dyers.. buy wholly of the Lightermen, tho' they might as well.. buy of the Masters. **1768** STERNE *Sent. Journ., Le Patisser*, As I am at Versailles, thought I, I might as well take a view of the town. **1800** WORDSW. *Hart-Leap Well* II. ix, You might as well Hunt half a day for a forgotten dream. **1820** BYRON *Mar. Fal.* IV. ii, It had been As well had there been time to have got together, From my own fief.. more Of our retainers—but it is too late. **1870** J. E. T. ROGERS *Hist. Glean.* Ser. II. 151 He thought he might as well strive to promote his own ends. **1879** MISS BRADDON *Cloven Foot* xxxviii, You really may as well let me have a little food.

22. a. With qualifying adverb prefixed, as *too well, pretty well*.

Also freq. with *so, very, full* (see FULL *adv.* 1 c), *right* (see RIGHT *adv.* 9 a).

(*a*) *c* **888** ÆLFRED *Boethius* vii. §3 For ðæm þæt ðe ðissa woruldsælða to wel ne lyste. **971** *Blickl. Hom.* 185 Ic lærde þæt men.. uþgengra welena to wel ne truwodon. **1604** SHAKS. *Oth.* v. ii. 344 Then must you speake Of one that lou'd not wisely, but too well. **1753–4** RICHARDSON *Grandison* II. ix. 59 Those [facts], however, would too well justify him.

(*b*) **1599** MASSINGER etc. *Old Law* v. i, The Dutch Veny I swallowed pretty wel. **1737** BRACKEN *Farriery Impr.* (1756) I. 214 Give the Horse pretty well of my Cordial Ball. *Ibid.* 215 He has pretty well of Flesh upon his Back. **1753–4** RICHARDSON *Grandison* II. vii. 40 Their father.. by that time, had pretty well got over his grief. **1855** KINGSLEY *Westw. Ho!* ii, He.. had his heart pretty well hardened by long, baneful licence. **1882** BESANT *All Sorts* xxviii, They had got by this time pretty well all they clamoured for. **1888** 'J. S. WINTER' *Bootle's Childr.* xi, Lassie kept her composure pretty well. **1902** J. K. MANN *Hist. Popes* I. I. 417 The pallium.. had then.. pretty well its modern shape.

b. *well enough*: sufficiently well, adequately.

In the 16th cent. occasionally written as one word.

1390 GOWER *Conf.* II. 295 And thanne him thoghte wel ynouh, It was fantosme. *c* **1440** *Alphabet of Tales* 215 When sho saw þis maister of þe knyghtis, sho knew hym well enogh & he hur. *Ibid.* 414, I know þe not, bod I know þat gown well enogh. **1470–85** MALORY *Arthur* XXI. i. 839 And by cause of hyr fayre speche Syr Mordred trusted hyr wel ynough. **1579** J. STUBBES *Gaping Gulf* D 7, Which mought wel ynough be the cause why the Pope decked hym with hys title of most christian king. **1585** PARSONS *Chr. Exerc.* Pref. 4 The vulgar translation is known welinough. **1587** GOLDING *De Mornay* xxx. (1592) 473 But the Rabbines saw wellynough that the miracles of Iesus could not be denied. **1631** SHIRLEY *Sch. Compl.* v. i. 68 He gaue me two or three kicks, which I deseru'd well enough. **1710–11** SWIFT *Jrnl. to Stella* 11 Jan., The scheme.. would have done well enough in good hands. **1753–4** RICHARDSON *Grandison* I. xvii. 119 They liked not the humour he seemed to be in well enough to comply with his request.

c. With intensive (usu. *slang*) adv. or adj. prefixed, as ***bloody well, damn well***, etc.

1884 [see BLEEDING *ppl. a.* 6]. **1898** [see JOLLY *adv.* 2]. **1903** KIPLING *Five Nations* 117 We have had a jolly good lesson, and it serves us jolly well right. **1921** E. O'NEILL *Emperor Jones* i. 160 Ring the bell now an' you'll bloody well see what I means. **1928** E. WAUGH *Decline & Fall* III. iii. 240, I should bleeding well say there was. **1933** [see RUDDY *adv.*]. **1941** [see DAMN *a.* and *adv.*]. **1943** D. WELCH *Maiden Voyage* iii. 14 Someone in the next cell was shouting, 'Bloody well let me out, you bastards.' **1962** L. R. BANKS *End to Running* I. vi. 96 Because actually, as a matter of fact, don't y'know, I'm not sodding well coming.

VI. 23. a. Employed without construction to introduce a remark or statement, sometimes implying that the speaker or writer accepts a situation, etc., already expressed or indicated, or desires to qualify this in some way, but frequently used merely as a preliminary or resumptive word.

c **888** ÆLFRED *Boeth.* xl. §4 Wella, wisan men, wel, gað ealle on þone weᵹ [etc.]. *c* **1315** SHOREHAM *Poems* I. 285 Wel, broþer, Ne non ne may icristned be Ar he his boren of moder. [**1382** WYCLIF *Isaiah* xliv. 16 He.. is chaufid, and seide, Vah, or weel, I am hat. **1388** —— *Ezek.* xxvi. 2 Wel! the ȝatis of puplis ben brokun.] *c* **1420** ? LYDG. *Assembly of Gods* 505 'Well,' seyde Apollo, 'yef he on erthe bee, Wyth my brennyng chare I shall hym confound.' *c* **1450** *Cov. Myst., Counc. Jews* 76 Wel, serys, ȝe sal se.. I xal correcte hym for his trespas. **1529** MORE *Dyalogue* I. xxi. 27 b, Well quod I yet wold I wit one thyng more. **1550** CROWLEY *Way to Wealth* 320 Wel, loke to this geare be tyme. **1581** A. HALL *Iliad* I. 13 Wel, thee to please, I wil [go] to Ioue. **1589** [? LYLY] *Pappe w. Hatchet* B ij, Squirrilitie were a better word: well, let me alone to squirrell them. **1610** SHAKS. *Temp.* II. ii. 47 This is a very scuruy tune to sing at a mans Funerall: well, here's my comfort. *Drinkes.* **1652** H. BELL *Luther's Colloq. Mensalia* 293 They.. take from us what wee have. Well! they will repent it. **1691** tr. *Emiliane's Observ. Journ. Naples* 207 Well, (said he) I shall make a shift.. to eat them with my Fingers. **1711** SWIFT *Jrnl. to Stella* 3 Nov., Well, but as I was saying, what care I for your Mayor? **1766** GOLDSM *Vicar* xii, Well, my boy, what have you brought us from the fair? **1779** WARNER in Jesse *Selwyn & Contemp.* (1844) IV. 261 He asked, 'Well, and how is George?' **1826** GALT *Last of Lairds* xvii. 151 'I understood that Mr. Mailings.. was one of your most particular friends.' 'Well, and what of that?' **1863** MRS. CARLYLE *Lett.* III. 170 Well, I returned from that visit quite set up. **1894** FISKE *Holiday Stor.* 181 As works of art—well, they were rather too highly coloured for works of art.

b. *sb.* An instance of this use of the word.

1866 LOWELL *Biglow P.* Ser. II. Introd. (1912) 282 A friend.. told me that he once heard five 'wells'.. precede the answer to an inquiry. **1885** *Proc. Amer. Soc. Psych. Research* I. 312 (Cent.) The 'wells' and 'ahs', 'don't-you-know's' and other stop-gap interjections.

24. a. *well, well*, denoting surprise, resignation, or acquiescence.

[**1388** WYCLIF *Ps.* xxxiv. 21 Thei seiden, Wel, wel! oure iȝen han sien. *c* **1420** *Prymer* (1895) 66 (*Ps.* xl. 15) Bere þei her confusioun anoon, þat seien to me, 'wel! wel!'] *c* **1480** HENRYSON *Town & C. Mouse* x, 'Weill, weill, sister,' quod the rurale mous [etc.]. **1546** J. HEYWOOD *Prov.* (1867) 70 Well well (quoth she) many wels, many buckets. **1675** COTTON *Burlesque* 183 *Apol.* Well! well! but he were best take heed How he attaques my Maiden-head. **1712** STEELE *Spect.* No. 533 ¶1 Well, well, you may banter as long as you please. **1815** SCOTT *Guy M.* xlii, But well, well!—it will last my time. **1847** HELPS *Friends in C.* I. vii. 117 Well, well, we will leave these heights, and descend in little drops of criticism. **1883** D. C. MURRAY *Hearts* xv, 'Father',.. 'you must not talk like that.' 'Well, well, my dear,' said her father, 'well, well.'

b. with intervening noun (in vocative).

c **1550** R. WEVER *Lusty Juventus* (*c* 1560) D j b, Well wanton well, I wysse I can tel [etc.]. **1554** *Interl. Youth* (facs. Waley) B ij, Well wanton well, fye for shame. **1598** B. JONSON *Ev. Man in Hum.* I. (1601) B 1 b, Well Cosen well, I see you are e'ene past hope Of all reclaime. **1605** CHAPMAN *All Fooles* II. i. E 1, Well, wag, well, wilt thou still deceiue thy father..? *a* **1652** BROME *Mad Couple* I. i. (1653) B 6 b, Well wag well, you must not now put me off with my wife.

25. *very well*, denoting agreement, approval, or acquiescence.

In the absence of construction the distinction between the adverbial and adjectival use becomes obscured: cf. WELL *a.* 7 and 10.

1564 *Brief Exam.* D j b, You wyll say, we haue a commaundement of the Lorde... Very well. **1719** DE FOE *Crusoe* II. (Globe) 518 We were chas'd.. By five Sloops,.. says the Fellow... Very well, said I, then it is apparent there is something in it. **1815** SCOTT *Guy M.* xlvii, The Baronet, though highly offended, could only say, 'Very well, sir, it is very well.' **1866** GEO. ELIOT *F. Holt* xxxv, At last he said.. 'I agree—I must have time.' 'Very well. It is a bargain.' **1878** HARDY *Ret. Native* VI. iii, 'Very well, then,' sighed Thomasin, 'I will say no more.'

26. *well then*, introducing a conclusion or further statement, or implying that one can naturally be drawn or made.

c **1440** *York Myst.* xxxiii. 237 Wele þan, We sall frayst er they founde vs fer fro. **1509** HAWES *Past. Pleas.* XXIX. (Percy Soc.) 138 Well then, quod she, I shall you nowe tell Howe the case standeth. **1535** COVERDALE *Ezek.* iv. 15 Well than, I will graunte the to take cowes donge, for the donge off a man. **1542** RECORDE *Gr. Artes* N viij b, Well then go forthe, in the nexte space I fynd one counter, which I remoue forward. **1628** J. DOUGHTY *Serm.* 10 Well then, let both principles of Church tenents and Scripture stand in force. **1647** COWLEY *Mistress, Wish* i, Well then; I now do plainly see, This busie world and I shall ne're agree. **1679** DRYDEN *Œdipus* III. i. 34 *Dio.* Basely you kill'd him. *Adr.*.. Well then, I kill'd him basely. **1802–12** BENTHAM *Ration. Judic. Evid.* (1827) I. 136 *note*, Well then, since we must stop somewhere, we will stop at a trillion. **1844** DISRAELI *Coningsby* III. i, Well then, there were Bolingbroke and Pitt. **1884** B. L. FARJEON *Gt. Porter Sq.* (ed. 6) xxxvii. 290 'Well then!' she exclaimed; winding up the argument thus, as is the way with women.

27. With various additions, esp. ***well now, oh well, ah well***.

(*a*) **1599** B. JONSON *Ev. Man out of Hum.* IV. iv, Well now master Snip, let mee see your Bill. **1615** T. ADAMS *Spiritual Navig.* 19 Well yet, as salt and bitter as this Ocean the world is, there is some good wrought out of this ill. **1782** MISS BURNEY *Cecilia* VIII. iii, 'Well now,' said he, 'remember the sin of this breach of appointment lies wholly at your door.' **1889** 'J. S. WINTER' *Mrs. Bob* xix, 'What are you thinking about, Stevie?'.. 'Oh! well really, I can't say.'

(*b*) *a* **1779** D. GRAHAM *Writ.* (1883) II. 56 *Sawny.* A well a well then good day to you good-mither. **1814** SCOTT *Wav.* xxix, Aweel, Duncan—did ye say your name was Duncan or Donald? **1848** MRS. GASKELL *Mary Barton* xxxi, The old woman tried to comfort her, beginning with her accustomed —'Well-a-well!' **1868** LE FANU *Lost Name* I. xxii. 220 'Oh! well, after luncheon, then,' said he.

VII. *Comb.* The adverb *well* is extensively employed in combination with various parts of the verb, esp. the past and present participles, and in parasynthetic adjectives ending in *-ed*. In modern practice the latter are regularly hyphened. In attributive use the participial formations are properly hyphened, and the hyphen is also frequently employed even when the construction is predicative. On account of the large number of such combinations, all those of any standing (either by common or continued use, or in virtue of their source) are treated as main words, the less important or less common being printed in smaller type without definition, after the model of similar words in UN-. The normal insertion or omission of the hyphen, according to the construction of the word in the sentence, is indicated by printing it within parentheses, as *well(-)baked*.

In the following enumeration of the different types of combinations the illustration is chronological, and partly includes words more fully exemplified below.

28. With past pples., as ***well-born, -bred, -done***, etc., in predicative or attributive use.

Beowulf 1927 Hyᵹd swiðe ᵹeong, wis, welþungen. *c* **897** ÆLFRED *Gregory's Past. C.* xvii. 111 Ʒif hwæt welgedones bið. *c* **950** *Lindisf. Gosp.* Luke xix. 12 Monn sum welboren. *c* **975** *Rushw. Gosp.* John vi. 45 Alle larwas *vel* welgilærde. *c* **1375** BARBOUR *Bruce* I. 385 Bot off lymmys he was weill maid With.. schuldrys braid. *c* **1386** [see DISPOSED 2]. *c* **1449** PECOCK *Repr.* II. viii. 190 It is merytorie and weel doon forto ȝeue thilk ensaumple. **1474** SIR J. PASTON *Lett.* III. 107 He.. lefte a greet garnyson theer, weell ffornysshyd in vytayll, and all other thynge. **1525** BERNERS *Froiss.* II. clxviii. 469 A well trauelled knight and well knowen. **1577** B. GOOGE *Heresbach's Husb.* III. 128 His legges wel sette. *a* **1623** FLETCHER *Love's Cure* III. iv, *Cla.* 'Tis ill for a fair Lady to be idle. *Say.* She had better be well-busied. **1631** WEEVER *Anc. Funeral Mon.* 548 An ancient and well allied familie. **1661** BOYLE *Physiol. Ess.* (1669) 178 The hardness of a well-blown Bladder. **1746** FRANCIS tr. *Hor., Epist.* I. vi. 58 Venus decks the well-be-money'd Swain. **1793** HOLCROFT tr. *Lavater's Physiogn.* xxiii. 116 Well-arched and short foreheads are.. not of long duration. **1851** MAYNE REID *Scalp Hunters* xxi, This was said in well-accentuated.. English. **1890** 'R. BOLDREWOOD' *Miner's Right* xxxiii, The well-clothed, well-fed, well-amused passage through barren hours. **1959** W. ANDREW *Textbk. Compar. Histol.* iv. 113 (*caption*) The 'hairs', covered with well-vascularized epidermis, may be as much as 20 mm. long.

29. With present pples. in adjectival (predicative or attributive) use.

c **897** ÆLFRED *Gregory's Past. C.* xvii. 107 Onȝean ða godan & ða wellibbendan. *Ibid.* lvii. 439 Wyrta..swiðe welstincenda. *c* **1000** *Ags. Ps.* (Spelman) cl. 5 Heriað hine on cimbalum wel sweȝendum. **1382** WYCLIF *Ps.* xci. 15 Wel suffrende thei shul be. —— *Ecclus.* xlvii. 14 A son weel felende [*filius sensatus*]. **1432** *Rolls of Parlt.* IV. 405/2 The wynes..were..faire, fyne, wele drinking. *c* **1449** PECOCK *Repr.* II. xx. 274 Thilk word..is..so weel teching and dressing. **1477** *Paston Lett.* III. 182 If ther be among theym eny pric horse..in especiall that he be well trottyng. *a* **1586** SIDNEY *Apol. Poetrie* (Arb.) 40 Accompanied with..the well inchaunting skill of Musicke. **1597** A. M. tr. *Guillemeau's Fr. Chirurg.* 38/2 Then with a well-cuttinge sawe, sawe of the whole legge. **1660** INGELO *Bentiv. & Ur.* I. (1682) 148 The People express'd it with such exact harmony of well agreeing voices. **1670** EACHARD *Cont. Clergy* 12 If a lad has but a lusty and well-bearing memory..he proves a brave clergyman. **1844** W. H. MILL *Serm. Tempt. Christ* iii. 77 That..view, even when sobered to a well-calculating morality. **1864** DE COIN *Hist. & Cult. Cotton & Tobacco* 279 Sticks split from some good or well-splitting wood. **1884** MᶜLAREN *Spinning* (ed. 2) 36 A vessel..containing a well-closing lid. **1889** BADEN-POWELL *Pigsticking* 12 A sport which draws so well-paying a visitation on to their village.

30. a. With verbal sbs., as ***well-building, -guiding, -joining, -keeping***, etc.

The later tendency is to employ *good* with the vbl. sb., and restrict *well* to the gerund.

a **1300** *E.E. Psalter* cxviii. 91 With þi wele-setting [L. *ordinatione*] lastes dai. *a* **1568** ASCHAM *Scholem.* I. (Arb.) 49 Finding paine in ill doing, and pleasure in well studiyng. **1586** A. DAY *Eng. Secretorie* II. (1625) 14 Weeting of my well-deeming. **1600** FAIRFAX *Tasso* XVII. xcvi, Through my well guiding is your voiage donne. **1613** SHAKS. *Hen. VIII*, III. ii. 152 *Car.* And euer may your Highnesse yoake together..my doing well, With my well saying. **1623** J. TAYLOR (Water P.) *Discov. by Sea* C 2 b, A..large Armorie ..with other Weapons and munition, which for goodnesse, ..and well-keeping, is not second to any Noblemen in England. **1624** WOTTON *Elem. Archit.* 1 Well building hath three Conditions. **1641** SANDERSON *Serm., Ad Aulam* xiii. (1674) II. 195 In the well-joy[n]ing consisteth the strenth of structure.

b. Freq. with vbl. sbs. followed by *of*.

c **1440** HYLTON *Scala Perf.* (W. de W. 1494) I. lxiii, Vayne gladnes & wel payeng of thiselfe. *a* **1586** SIDNEY *Arcadia* I. iii. (1912) 19 The well bringing up of the people. **1596** HARINGTON *Anat. Metam. Ajax* Ep. Lij b, The wel handling of the matter. **1623** J. TAYLOR (Water P.) *Discov. by Sea* B 3 b, His goods are but lent him, by him that will one day call him to a reckoning, for the well or ill disposing of them. *a* **1639** W. WHATELEY *Prototypes* III. xxxix. (1640) 17 The wel-husbanding of abundance. **1655** D. DICKSON *Ps.* xcii. 4 in Spurgeon *Treas. David* IV. 272 One of the parts of the well-spending of the Sabbath. **1667** EARL ORRERY *St. Lett.* (1742) 305 For the well constituting of the said corporations. **1668** DRYDEN *Dram. Poesie* 46 The copiousness and well-knitting of the intrigues we have from Johnson. **1690** CHILD *Disc. Trade* (1698) 158 The well-making of our Woollen-Manufactures. **1691** T. H[ALE] *Acc. New Invent.* 119 The safety and well sailing of a Vessel. **1707** MORTIMER *Husb.* 48 In the well draining of Cornlands lies a main advantage. *Ibid.* 50 The well covering of the Seed must be of great advantage. **1739** TROWELL *Treat. Husb.* etc. 4 The well ploughing of the Land is a very great Advantage to all Seeds sown. **1766** *Complete Farmer* s.v. *Plough*, The well going of the plough wholly depends upon the placing of this.

c. With gerunds followed by an object or preposition.

? **1568** in Pettus *Fodinæ Reg.* (1670) 61 Rules and Ordinances for the well-governing the Affairs of the Society, etc. **1625** K. LONG tr. *Barclay's Argenis* v. xiv. 383 For the love of her..hee would not faile in well-looking to his charge. **1634** SIR T. HERBERT *Trav.* 138 Because of..the wel-seating it..he allured out of Babilon sixe hundred thousand soules. **1693** G. ST. LO *England's Safety* title-p., A Sure Method for..Raising Qualified Seamen for the well Manning Their Majesties Fleet on any Occasion. **1699** T. C[OCKMAN] tr. *Tully's Offices* 135 By Moderation..we mean ..the Knowledge of Well-timing whatever we do. **1765** GALE in *Phil. Trans.* LV. 197 The well-peopling the colonies, and securing our new acquisitions. **1766** *Complete Farmer* s.v. *Lucern*, The grand secret of well-managing a trading populous country. **1854** *Poultry Chron.* II. 351/2 The..all-important necessity of well matching the poultry. **1890** A. P. MORTON tr. *Le Roux' Acrobats & Mountebanks* 168 In well calculating the strength of the steed.

31. With verbs, as ***well-ally, -clothe, -employ***, etc. Now *rare*.

a **1300** *E.E. Psalter* civ. 9 He was mined..of his witeword hende..þat he weleset [Vulg. *disposuit*] for Abraham sake. **14..** *Voc.* in Wr.-Wülcker 602/23 *Persoleo*,..to welwone. **1563** MAN *Musculus' Commonpl.* 286 b, Seyng that the mystery of the holy Trinitye did not well lyke with that people. **1612** DRAYTON *Poly-olb.* xvii. 6 That of so great Descent, and of so large a Dower, Might well-allie their House. **1670** MILTON *Hist. Brit.* III. 129 Prowlers..intent upon all occasions..to pamper and well line themselves. **1851** (*title*) Robert Owen's Journal. Explanatory of the Means to Well-place and Well-feed, Well-clothe, Well-lodge, Well-employ, Well-govern, and Cordially unite the Populations of the World.

32. Forming parasynthetic adjectives in *-ed*, as ***well-ancestored, -dispositioned, -eared***, etc.

Cf. OE. *welwillednes.*

1530 PALSGR. 442/2 This sworde is well backed. **1568** GRAFTON *Chron.* II. 495 Of bodie he was slender,..well membred, and strongly made. **1571** GOLDING *Calvin on Ps.* xviii. 34, 63 He had bin a well-sinewed man. **1591** GREENE *Farew. Folly* (1617) I 4 b, The Gentleman is well forehanded and well foreheaded. **1630** BP. HALL *Occas. Medit.* xlii. 107 Why perfectly limmed; not a cripple? Why well-sensed; not a foole? **1671** WOODHEAD *St. Teresa* II. vii. 52 That those that shall be received, be thereto called by God, and be well-dispositioned. **1688** J. GRUBB *Brit. Heroes* vii, Castor the flame of fiery steed, With well-spur'd boots took down. **1704** *Hymn to Victory* lx. 41 Old English Courage scorns those trifling things, The Higher Ground, the Well-flank'd Wings. **1804** MITFORD *Inquiry* 372 A well-eared poet will of course avoid cacophony in rimes. **1855** *Poultry Chron.* III. 452 Her eggs are well formed and well-shelled. **1857** GOSSE *Omphalos* xi. 326 The formidable Shark,..a well-toothed adult. **1891** *Harper's Mag.* July 318/1 The well-ancestored, rich,..respectability from which she springs. **1894** *Outing* Sept. 427/2 The five brace of grand, plump, well-plumaged birds.

33. With adjectives.

a **1780** *Braes o Yarrow* vii. in Child *Ballads* IV. 165/1 Nine well-wight men lay waiting him. **1797–1803** JANE AUSTEN *Northanger Abbey* xxviii, The two girls..found themselves so well-sufficient..to themselves, that it was eleven o'clock ..before they quitted the supper-room. **1853** *Tait's Mag.* XX. 267 Its accession..would bring no well-wieldable strength with it. **1886** J. CORBETT *Fall of Asgard* I. 115 The charm of his face were the well-open eyes.

well, obs. dial. var. FELL *v.*

1511 *MS. Acc. St. John's Hosp., Canterb.*, Payd..for wellyng treys iii d. [See also WELLING.]

well, obs. f. WEEL, WILL *sb.* and *v.*

† **wella**, *int.* and *adv. Obs.* Forms: 1 wel lá, 3–4 **wella, wela, wele,** (3 **wælla, wælle, welle, wellen**). [OE. *wel lá* (see WELL *adv.* and LO *int.*[1]), partly confused with *wá lá* (see WALE *int.*) and *weȝ lá* (WEILA). Cf. also OE. *wel ȝá, weol ȝá*, glossing L. *heia* and *euge* respectively.]

A. *int.* **a.** Well then. **b.** Ah! alas!

Also followed by a sb. as object = alas for.., or a clause = alas *that*...

c **888** ÆLFRED *Boeth.* xxxiv. §8 Wella, men, wel. *c* **1000** ÆLFRIC *Saints' Lives* iii. 627 Hwæt þa se læce..cwæð mid wope: wella basilius, ȝif ðu sylf noldest, nære þu ȝit forðfaran. *c* **1205** LAY. 3456 Wallan, dæð, wela, deað, þat þu me nelt fordemen. *Ibid.* 7875 Welle broðer Nennius þat ich þe quic nabbe.

B. As *adv.* or intensive prefix: Very, exceedingly.

c **1205** LAY. 5970 Wælle muchel wes þa wop, þæ Belin þeonne wende. *Ibid.* 12805 þeder com þe ohte mon, wælla wel wes he ibon. *Ibid.* 29622 Welle uain [*c* **1275** wele glad] wes he þer uore. *Ibid.* 31258 Wellen henden wes þe mon Osric ihaten. **13..** *E.E. Allit. P.* B. 831 þe gestes gay & ful glad..Welawynnely wlonk. **13..** *Gaw. & Gr. Knt.* 518 Wela wynne is þe wort þat waxes þeroute. *Ibid.* 2084 Wela wylle was þe way, þer þay bi wod schulden. *a* **1400** *Wars Alex.* 1970 Wella [*v.r.* wele] wide ware þe wele,..Miȝt þou þe marches of Messedoyne mayntene þiselfe.

well-a'bused, *ppl. a.*

1879 HUXLEY *Hume* ii. 36 The offer..was particularly honourable to so well abused a man.

well-ac'cepted, *ppl. a.*

a **1763** SHENSTONE *Ess. Men & Manners* Wks. 1768 II. 42 He had such entire possession of the hearts as well as understandings of his friends, that he could soon make the most surprizing paradoxes believed and well-accepted.

† **well-a'ccomplished**, *ppl. a.*

1588 SHAKS. *L.L.L.* II. i. 56 A well accomplisht youth. **1650** WELDON *Crt. K. Jas.* 19 A wel accomplished Gentleman. **1792** A. MURPHY *Ess. Life & Genius Johnson* 141 At Mr. Thrale's he saw a constant succession of well-accomplished visitors. **1821** SCOTT *Kenilw.* x, I know you to be a worthy, kind, and well-accomplished gentlemen.

well-a'ccorded, *ppl. a.*

1581 SIDNEY *Def. Poetrie* (Arb.) 46 The Liricke,..with his tuned Lyre and wel accorded voyce. **1732** POPE *Ess. Man* II. 121 The lights and shades, whose well-accorded strife Gives all the strength and colour of our life.

well-a'ccording, *ppl. a.*

1814 BYRON *Lara* I. xx, Blest are the early hearts and gentle hands That mingle there in well according bands.

well-a'ccoutred, *ppl. a.*

1713 DERHAM *Phys.-Theol.* IV. xii. (1720) 225 When those [animals] that are able to shift for themselves, are left to their own Discretion and Diligence, but the Helpless well accouter'd and provided for. **1881** *Brit. Q. Rev.* Jan. 41 That the Tridentine dogma survives all the determined and well-accoutred assaults made thereon goes without saying.

well-a'ccredited, *ppl. a.*

1847 MRS. GORE *Castles in Air* xxix. (1857) 268 The subterfuges which tarnish many a well-accredited transaction on the turf.

well-a'ccustomed, *ppl. a.* Much frequented by customers. *Obs.* or *arch.*

1690, **1761** [see ACCUSTOMED 2]. **1736** ENTICK *Cant. Tales* Prol. 1 An Inn..noted for its great Trade, or as we say, a well-accustomed House. **1880** F. PEEL *Risings of Luddites* v. 24 The St. Crispin..was a well accustomed house, and the inner doors were swinging to and fro in the usual fashion.

well(-)a'cquainted, *ppl. a.*

† **1.** Familiarly known (to others). *Obs.*

1565 JEWEL *Repl. Harding* xiv. 509 These Authorities..be ..wel acquainted, and knowen vnto the World. **1590** SHAKS. *Com. Err.* IV. iii. 2 There's not a man I meete but doth salute me As if I were their well acquainted friend.

2. Having a good acquaintance *with* (= knowledge of) a person or thing; familiar *with*. Also without const. (of two or more persons).

1728 CIBBER *Provoked Husb.* I. i. 7 He is a Man too well-acquainted with the Female World to be brought into a high Opinion of any one Woman, without some well-examined Proof of her Merit. **1857** BUCKLE *Civiliz.* I. xii. 666 Mounier was well acquainted with our language. **1864** PUSEY *Daniel* (1876) 311 Habakkuk's hymn shows one well-acquainted with the Psalms. **1877** W. S. GILBERT *Sorcerer* I. Ballad, Time was when Love and I were well acquainted.

well-'acted, *ppl. a.*

1. Meritoriously conducted or lived.

1792 A. MURPHY *Ess. Life & Genius Johnson* 85, I boast no knowledge glean'd with toil and strife, That bright reward of a well-acted life.

2. Cleverly feigned or simulated.

1821 SCOTT *Kenilw.* xxxvi, 'Alas! my lord,' said Varney, with well-acted passion. **1883** D. C. MURRAY *Hearts* x, 'My dear Malfi', said Mark, in well-acted wonder and commiseration, 'what is the matter?'

3. Skilfully performed on the stage.

1890 'L. FALCONER' *Mlle Ixe* vi. 156 With far less emotion than a well-acted play would have excited in her.

well(-)a'dapted, *ppl. a.*

1713 STEELE etc. *Guardian* No. 64 ⁋18, I am charmed with his artificial Expressions in well adapted Similes. **1825** J. NEAL *Bro. Jonathan* II. 164 Her gown was a drab silk..of a cut well-adapted for the display of her fine shape. **1842** DICKENS *Amer. Notes* iii, With a rude eloquence, well adapted to the comprehension of his hearers.

welladay ('wɛlədeɪ), *int.* (*sb., v.*) Now *arch.* and *dial.* Forms: 6 **well a daye**, 6–7 **wel(l)-aday**, (8 **wel-a-day**), 6 **wellada**, 7 **wel-adaie, weleaday, welady, welody, welliday**, 7, 9 **well a-day**, 6– **well-a-day, welladay.** Also 6, 8–9 *Sc.* and *dial.* **wal(l)aday**; 6 **wer(e)aday**, 9 *dial.* **werraday.** [altered f. WELLAWAY, by substitution of DAY (or ADAY), as in *wo worth the day, lackaday.*]

A. *int.* An exclamation expressing sorrow or lamentation; = alas! Also with *ah* or *O* prefixed.

c **1570** W. ELDERTON in *Collect. B.L. Ballads* etc. (1867) 1 Well a daye, well a daye, well a daye, woe is me. **1570** LEVINS *Manip.* 196/42 Wel aday, *heu, hei.* **1591** SPENSER *Virg. Gnat* 417 Ah (waladay) there is no end of paine. **1592** SHAKS. *Rom. & Jul.* III. ii. 37 A weladay [Q. 2 weraday], hee's dead, hee's dead. *Ibid.* IV. v. 15 Oh weladay [Q. 2 wereaday], that euer I was borne. **1599** T. CUTWODE *Caltha Poet.* (Roxb.) xxxix, But walladay, he was not there aware of Cupids shaft. **1602** W. S. *Thomas Ld. Cromwell* IV. ii. 22 A, welliday for my Cowe! **1603** HOLLAND *Plutarch's Mor.* 198 Alas and weladay, what shall we doe? **1648** HERRICK *Hesper., Mad Maid's Song* iii, Alack and welladay! **1652** C. B. STAPYLTON *Herodian* xiii. 105 Then quire of Boys and Ladies sighing Welody, With Hymns and Pæans making dolefull Melody. **1719** D'URFEY *Pills* VI. 284 Alack and a welladay. **17..** *Gaberlunzie-man* v. in *Ramsay's Tea-t. Misc.* (1762) I. 79 She clapt her hand, cry'd, Waladay. **1781** COWPER *Hope* 428 Well-a-day, the title page was lost! **1798** COLERIDGE *Anc. Mar.* II. 135 [139] Ah wel-a-day! [*later* well a-day!] what evil looks Had I from old and young. **1813** MOORE *Two-penny Post Bag* viii. 35 Thou know'st the time, too, well-a-day! It takes to dance that chalk away. **1842** BARHAM *Ingol. Leg., Lay St. Cuthbert*, Well a day! Well a day! All he can say Is but just so much trouble and time thrown away. **1851** HAWTHORNE *Twice-told T.* I. viii. 154 But, welladay, we hear a shrill voice of affliction. **1888** *Sheffield Gloss.*, *Werraday*, welladay.

b. in reduplicated form *wella, welladay.*

1805 G. McINDOE *Poems* 92 The precious clay, Which in the tomb, with tears, I laid, Wella welladay! **1820** KEATS *Eve St. Agnes* xiii, And as she mutter'd 'Well-a—well-a-day!'

B. *sb.* The utterance of this exclamation; lamentation; a lament.

1582 T. WATSON *Centurie of Love* lxxxii. (Arb.) 118 At last, though late, farewell olde wellada. **1597** BEARD *Theatre God's Judgem.* I. xvi. 57 Their ioyfull song was turn'd to mournfull cries, And all their gladnesse chang'd to welladaies. **1598** PETOWE *2nd Pt. Hero & Leander* C iij b, This all alone sad Lady gan to play Framing sweet musick to her welladay. **1608** SHAKS. *Per.* IV. iv. 49 (1st Qo.) His daughters woe and heauie welladay. **1814** MRS. J. WEST *Alicia de Lacy* II. 291 Her ears were alternately assailed by the peccavis of penitence and the well-a-days of love.

transf. **1593** G. HARVEY *New Let. Notable Cont.* C 2 b, Let him be the *Falanta downe-didle* of Ryme, the *Hayhohalliday* of Prose, the *Walladay* of new writers.

C. *v. intr.* To cry 'welladay'. *nonce-use.*

1835 CLARE *Rural Muse* 153 The swains are sighing all, and well-a-daying.

well-a'djusted, *ppl. a.* **a.** In gen. use.

1735 THOMSON *Liberty* II. 330 The swelling mantle's well-adjusted flow. **1825** SCOTT *Talism.* xxi, The marabout raised his head gently from the ground,..moving with a well-adjusted precaution.

b. With reference to emotional adaptation. Cf. ADJUSTED *ppl. a.* 4.

1939 L. MACNEICE *Autumn Jrnl.* xii. 49 A civilised, articulate and well-adjusted Community where the mind is given its due But the body is not distrusted. **1940** [see ADJUSTED *ppl. a.*]. **1952** C. P. BLACKER *Eugenics: Galton & After* 307 Able and well-adjusted children. **1977** E. AMBLER *Send no More Roses* i. 11 The Able Criminal..may be presumed..to be emotionally stable and 'well-adjusted'.

well-a'dorned, *ppl. a.*

1616 CHAPMAN *Odyss.* VII. 239 He..Aduanc't him to a well-adorned Throne.

well(-)ad'vised, *ppl. a.* In 4–5 avised.

1. Of persons: Prudent, wary, cautious, circumspect.

In modern use chiefly predicative, as 'He would be well-advised to give up the idea'.

a. *c* **1386** CHAUCER *Melib.* ⁋2514 A man þat is wel auysed, he dredиþ his lest enemy. *c* **1430** LYDG. *Min. Poems* (Percy Soc.) 141 Hooly Awstyn, sad and wel avised, Kneuhe by signes this compleynt was no fable. *a* **1466** GREGORY *Chron.* in *Hist. Coll. Cit. Lond.* (Camden) 158 That Parlyment hadde an evylle faryng ende, to shamefully for to be namyd of any welavysyd man.

β. **1500–20** DUNBAR *Poems* xli. 2 Be ȝe ane luvar, think ȝe nocht ȝe suld Be weill adwysit in ȝour gouerning? **1585** T. WASHINGTON tr. *Nicholay's Voy.* I. 15 b, A most valiant & well aduised knight. **1594** SHAKS. *Rich III*, IV. iv. 517 Hath any well-aduised friend proclaym'd Reward to him that brings the Traytor in? **1603** KNOLLES *Hist. Turkes* (1638) 288 The well aduised and valiant captaine Kanacontes.

absol. **1560** BIBLE (Genev.) *Prov.* xiii. 10 With the wel aduised is wisedome. (And so **1611**.)

†**b.** with const. Careful or heedful *of* or *that*——.

c **1386** CHAUCER *Miller's T.* 398 Be well auysed on that ilke nyght.. That noon of vs ne speke nat a word. *c* **1400** *Master of Game* (MS. Digby 182) xviii, Also þat he be.. wele auysed of speche. *c* **1450** *Merlin* iii. 45 Quod the kynge, Be well avised that ye knowe it is he. And thei seide, We knowe verely it is he. **1579–80** NORTH *Plutarch, Lycurgus* (1595) 57 To another he put forth a question, who was to be well aduised of his aunswer.

†**c.** In one's right mind, sane. *Obs.*

1588 SHAKS. *L.L.L.* v. ii. 434 And were you well aduis'd? **1590** —— *Com. Err.* II. ii. 215 Am I.. Sleeping or waking, mad or well aduisde?

2. Of actions, etc.: Based on wise counsel or careful consideration.

a **1470** HARDING *Chron.* clxxvi. viii. (1812) 314 The kyng full sad, with wordes well auysed, Thanked them all. **1846** MRS. A. MARSH *Father Darcy* II. viii. 140, I hope I should not be found wanting either in spirit or perseverance to carry out well-advised plans. **1850** GROTE *Greece* II. lxiv. VIII. 203 Construing their studied and well-advised silence into a proof of oblivion.

Hence **well-ad'visedly** *adv.*

1587 GOLDING *De Mornay* ix. (1592) 127 He.. seemeth to speake discreetely and weladuisedly. **1648–58** HEXHAM II, *Wel-bedachtelick*, Well-advisedly, or Considerately.

well(-)a'ffected, *ppl. a.*

1. Favourably disposed, inclined to be favourable or friendly (*to* or *towards* a person or thing); *spec.*, well-disposed towards existing authority, loyal.

1563–83 FOXE *A. & M.* 150/2 If any good men were well affected or minded toward religion. **1609** R. I. *Nova Britannia* title-p., Nova Britannia: Offering most Excellent fruites by Planting in Virginia. Exciting all such as be well affected to further the same. **1611** SPEED *Theat. Gt. Brit.* To Rdr., To the well-affected and favourable Reader. **1664** D. FLEMING in *Extr. St. Papers Friends* III. (1912) 213 Hee Lives in a very well affected Towne, both to the church and State. **1671** R. MONTAGU in *Buccleuch MSS.* (Hist. MSS. Comm.) I. 502 The Presbyterian.. party.. never were well-affected to a French alliance. **1746** BP. SHERLOCK *Let.* 10 June in *10th Rep. Hist. MSS. Comm.* App. I. 291 The well-affected Clans. **1832** LYTTON *Eug. Aram* I. ix, I know you are an honest man, Bunting, and well affected to our family. **1878** BOSW. SMITH *Carthage* 359 Sicily.. was unlikely to give her further trouble, and that, not because she was well-affected, but simply because she was exhausted.

absol. **1643** [ANGIER] *Lanc. Vall. Achor* 10 Whilest the Siege lasted against Manchester, the heavens held a simpathy with the well-affected. **1658** *Dom. State Papers* 360 The petition of the well-affected of Gateshead. **1779** ARNOT *Hist. Edin.* I. vi. 206 It had been a common practice of government, to screen the well-affected from the punishment of their murders.

2. Adroitly assumed or simulated.

1907 *National Church* 15 Oct. 277/1 By this process in matters of religion the state will have washed its hands of any responsibility for the moral character of its citizens—a Gallio in its well-affected impartiality of indifference.

†**well-a'ffectionate**, *a. Obs.* [Cf. next.] Well disposed.

1590 SPENSER *F.Q.* III. iii. 62 Then each to other well affectionate, Friendship professed with vnfained hart.

well-a'ffectioned, *a.* [Cf. prec.] = WELL-AFFECTED 1. *Obs.* or *arch.*

1628 tr. *Mathieu's Powerfull Favorite* 127 A Senatour whom hee knew to bee a good Citizen and well affectioned to Tiberius. **1875** JOWETT *Plato* (ed. 2) III. 702 They were obedient to the laws, and well-affectioned towards the gods.

well-a-fine, *adv.* and *int. Obs.* exc. *dial.* [See AFINE *adv.*]

A. *adv.* Right well, well indeed; to good purpose, thoroughly.

c **1330** *Kyng of Tars* 780 Icham nou glad wel a fyn, Mai no mon blithur be. **1380** *Sir Ferumb.* 2752 Now y knowe wel-a-ffyn, þy message schendeth me. *c* **1400** *Rom. Rose* 3690 For no man.. maye.. of the reysyns haue the wyne, Tyl grapes rype and wel a fyne Be sore empressid. *c* **1400** *Beryn* 1393 The tale wol be ryff Of me, & of noon othir; I knowe riȝte wel a fyne. **1573** TUSSER *Husb.*, Author's Life xix. (1878) 210 A Moone,.. Which well a fine me thought did shine. **1746** *Exmoor Scolding* (E.D.S.) 81 Chem a laced well-a-fine aready. **1882** JAGO *Dial. Cornw.* 309 That's all well-a-fine. **1886** *W. Somerset Word-bk.*, *Well-a-fine*, adv. phr., very well; truly; indeed.

b. Altered to *well and fine*.

c **1400** *Gamelyn* 427 Anon as Gamelyn hadde eten wel and fyne. *c* **1400** *Beryn* 303 Fawnus lete hym clatir & cry wel & fyne. **14..** *Guy Warw.* (Camb. MS.) 9086 Gye lokyd theron wele and fyne. *c* **1450** LOVELICH *Merlin* 6860 This knowen ȝe alle wel and fyn.

B. *int.* (See quot. 1880.)

1880 *E. Cornw. Gloss.*, *Well-a-fyne*, a common interjection, meaning 'it's all very well'. **1892** 'Q' *Three Ships* ii. 33 Well-a-fine! What a teasin' armful is woman, afore the first-born comes!

†**wellage.** *Obs. rare*$^{-1}$. In quot. **welleage.** [f. WELL *sb.*^{1} + -AGE (denoting a material).] (See quot. and *press-ware* s.v. PRESS *sb.*^{1} 17.)

1612 STURTEVANT *Metallica* 92 Welleage is a kind of Presseware for the speedy making of Wells, farre cheaper then the rounds, which are made of Brick to keepe the earth from falling downe.

well-aged, *a.* Now *rare*. Advanced in years, of a good age.

c **1470** ASHBY *Active Policy* 815 Loke that youre counseil be rather godly set, Wele aged, of goode disposicion. **1535** COVERDALE *Josh.* xiii. 1 Thou art olde & well aged. *a* **1568** ASCHAM *Scholem.* II. (Arb.) 141 The Latin tong, concerning any part of purenesse of it,.. did not endure moch longer, than is the life of a well aged man. **1979** [see *road-bed* s.v. ROAD *sb.* 9 b].

well-aimed, *ppl. a.*

1598 CHAPMAN *Iliad* XI. 99 Atrides with his wel-aimde lance smote Isus on the brest. **1606** —— *Gentl. Usher* I. i, You come not neere him, but discharge aloofe Your wounding Pistoll, or well aymed Dart. **1667** MILTON *P.L.* IX. 173, I reck not, so it light well aim'd. **1725** POPE *Odyss.* XXI. 4 Who now can bend Ulysses' bow, and wing The well-aim'd arrow thro' the distant ring. **1819** SCOTT *Ivanhoe* xliii, The wearied horse of Ivanhoe, and its no less exhausted rider, went down.. before the well-aimed lance and vigorous steed of the Templar. **1867** AUGUSTA WILSON *Vashti* xxv, He retreated before a well-aimed blow. **1868** G. V. COX *Recoll. Oxford* 206 A well-aimed orange,.. thrown from the gallery, struck him forcibly on the face.

†**well-aired**, *a.* [f. AIR *sb.*] Having a sweet breath. *Obs.*

1505 in *Mem. Hen. VII* (Rolls) 233 The said queen is like for to be of a sweet savour and well eyred.

well(-)aired, *ppl. a.*

1. Thoroughly ventilated; favoured with good air.

1818 SCOTT *Hrt. Midl.* Note 3 The situation in the centre of the High Street rendered it [the Tolbooth] so particularly well-aired, that when the plague laid waste the city in 1645, it affected none within these melancholy precincts. **1843** R. J. GRAVES *Syst. Clin. Med.* v. 62 The bed-room of a patient labouring under fever should be well-aired. **1871** NAPHEYS *Prev. & Cure Dis.* I. i. 47 Well-aired locality.

2. Damp-freed by exposure to air or heat.

1789 H. NEWDIGATE *Let.* 1 July in A. E. Newdigate-Newdegate *Cheverels of Cheverel Manor* (1898) vi. 89, I came home to a well-air'd Comfortable Bed. **1848** MRS. GASKELL *Mary Barton* xxxi, She.. went on to assure Mary the bed was well aired.

well-a'llied, *ppl. a.*

1603 SHAKS. *Meas. for M.* III. ii. 109 The vice is of a great kindred; it is well allied. **1631** [see WELL *adv.* 28].

well-a'lly, *v. trans.*

1612 DRAYTON *Poly-olb.* xvii. 6 A Nymph.. That of so great Descent, and of so large a Dower, Might well-allie their House.

well-a'near, *int. Obs.* exc. *dial.* [app. altered f. WELLAWAY by substitution of ANEAR.] Alas! alack-a-day!

1600 *Look about you* ii. B 1 b, Now well a neere that ere I liu'd to see, Such patience and so much impiety. **1608** SHAKS. *Per.* III. Prol. 51 The Lady shreekes, and wel-a-neare, Do's fall in trauayle with her feare. **1640** J. D. *Knave in Grain* III. i. G 2, Wherefore was it? well a neare. **1677** W. NICOLSON in *Trans. R. Soc. Lit.* (1870) Ser. II. IX. 322 *Wellaneer*, well away, alack-a-day. **1787** GROSE *Prov. Gloss.*, *Wellaneer*. Alas. N. *a* **1836** in 'S. Gilpin' *Pop. Poetry Cumb.* (1875) 207 Bit, welleneer! when he sud tean his kiss,.. Hur elbow rease an' barr'd him fra his bliss.

So **well-a'nearing**, in same sense.

1683 G. M[ERITON] *Yorks. Dial.* 4 Wellaneerin, wellaneerin, run fast run, Hye thee Hobb, and bid my Mawgh Herry come. *Ibid.* 7 Ey wellaneerin, wilta gang and see. **1703** THORESBY *Let. to Ray*, *Wellaneering*, alas.

well-a'nnealed, *ppl. a.*

1831 BREWSTER *Optics* xxi. 184 Thin plates of well-annealed flint glass. **1854** *Pereira's Polarized Light* (ed. 2) 139 A well-annealed piece of glass, all of whose parts possess equal elasticity, is a single refractor.

well-a'nointed, *ppl. a.*

1746 FRANCIS tr. *Hor. Sat.* II. v. 142 Upon his naked back Her heir sustain'd the well-anointed pack [*cadaver unctum oleo largo*]. **1860** GEO. ELIOT *Mill on Fl.* I. ix, Mr. Rappit, the hairdresser, with his well-anointed coronal locks tending wavily upward.

well(-)a'paid, *ppl. a. Obs.* exc. *arch.* Heartily pleased or satisfied.

13.. *K. Alis.* 2031 Darie was wel apaied Of that Archelaus haveth ysaide. *c* **1350** *Will. Palerne* 1314 Whanne þemperour it wist, he was wel apayed. **1377** LANGL. *P. Pl.* B. VI. 198 And eche pore man [was] wel apayed to haue pesen for his huyre. **1387** TREVISA *Higden* III. 383 He cowþe feyne hym gracious and wel apaied when he were wrooþ, and wrooþ when he were wel apayed. **1470–85** MALORY *Arthur* XVIII. xxiii. 767, I am wel apayed, said sir Gareth, that I may knowe him. *c* **1500** H. MEDWALL *Fulgens & Lucres* E iv b, Be she wroth or well a payde. **1576** KNEWSTUB *Confut.*, *Serm.* Q 2 b, There is good cause, not only to be content, but also well appaide with it. **1590** SPENSER *F.Q.* III. ii. 47 She therewith well apayd, The drunken lampe downe in the oyle did steepe. **1611** R. FENTON *Treat. Usury* To Rdr. 3, I shall thinke my selfe well apaid, if I can cause them but to feele those wounds. **1643** TRAPP *Comm. Gen.* xxiv. 47 He joyeth over her with singing, as wel-apaid of his choyce. **1825** JENNINGS *Obs. Dial. W. Eng.*, *Well-apaid*, appeased; satisfied. **1870** MORRIS *Earthly Par.* III. II. 32 'Or all is nought Whereof I think,' at last a wanderer said, 'Or of my tale shall ye be well apaid'.

Hence †**well-a'paidness.** *Obs.*

1633 [D. ROGERS] *Treat. Sacr.* I. 190 This complacence and well apaiednesse of heart.

well(-)a'pparelled, *ppl. a.*

1530 PALSGR. 329/1 Well apparayled or well decked, *gorrier*. **1576** R. PETERSON *G. della Casa's Galateo* 18, I would haue euery man well appareled, meete for his age and calling. **1592** SHAKS. *Rom. & Jul.* I. ii. 27 When well apparel'd April on the heele Of limping Winter treads. **1821** LAMB *Elia* Ser. I. *All Fool's Day*, The goodly ornature of well-apparelled speech. **1860** LONGF. *Wayside Inn*, *K. Olaf* XIV. ix, Never, while they cruised and quarrelled, Old King Gorm, or Blue-Tooth Harald, Owned a ship so well apparelled.

well-a'pplied, *ppl. a.*

a **1586** SIDNEY *Arcadia* III. xviii. (1912) 463 By the diligent care of friends and well applied cunning of surgeons. **1625** K. LONG tr. *Barclay's Argenis* I. ii. 5 Timoclea, with well-applyed language, began to question her Guest. **1764** DODSLEY in *Shenstone's Wks.* (1768) II. 317 A stone seat.. with this well-applied inscription. **1768–74** TUCKER *Lt. Nat.* (1834) I. 646 A discreet and well-applied industry in the service of mankind. **1842** LOVER *Handy Andy* vi, Giving him a hearty cuff on the ear, which would have knocked him down, only that Oonah kept him up by an equally well applied box on the other.

well-a'ppointed, *ppl. a.* Properly equipped or fitted out.

1530 PALSGR. 844/1 Well apoynted, *bien a poynt*. **1535** COVERDALE *Jer.* vi. 22 They ride vpon horses wel apointed to yͤ batell agaynst the. **1597** SHAKS. *2 Hen. IV*, I. i. 190 The gentle Arch-bishop of Yorke is vp, With well-appointed Powres. *c* **1600** DRAYTON *Mis. Marg.* clxxviii, Ten thousand valient well-appointed men. **1656** COWLEY *Pindar. Odes*, *Brutus* iv, One would have thought t'had heard the morning crow, Or seen her well-appointed Star Come marching up the Eastern Hill afar. **1784** COWPER *Tiroc.* 676 In him thy well-appointed proxy see, Arm'd for a work too difficult for thee. **1807** WORDSW. *White Doe* 699 Nor wanted at this time rich store Of well-appointed chivalry. **1835** *Court Mag.* VI. 166/2 The well-appointed silk, waterproof, ivory-handled, umbrella of his friend. **1864** 'ANNIE THOMAS' *D. Donne* I. ii. 29 She saw that he had good horses and a well-appointed mail-phaeton. **1889** G. FINDLAY *Eng. Railway* 3 A well-appointed hotel.

Hence **well-a'ppointedness.**

1680 H. MORE *Apocal. Apoc.* 82 They have Breast-plates of Iron, which shows the courage of these Saracens, and their well-appointedness for War. **1890** H. JAMES *Tragic Muse* xxvi, He remembered too.. her actual smartness, as London people would call it, her well-appointedness.

well-a'pproved, *ppl. a.*

1590 SPENSER *F.Q.* II. x. 65 Hengist and Horsus, well approu'd in warre. **1596** SHAKS. *Tam. Shr.* I. i. 7 My trustie seruant well approu'd in all. *c* **1611** CHAPMAN *Iliad* XVII. 437 He cald to friend, these well-approu'd supplies; Th' Aiaces, and the Spartan king. **1684** BUNYAN *Pilgr.* II. (1900) 212 There dwelt also not far from thence one Mr. Skill, an antient and well approved Physician.

well-'argued, *ppl. a.*

1708 J. PHILIPS *Cyder* II. 20 With winning Rhetoric and well-argu'd Law. **1964** K. G. GRUBB *Layman looks at Church* iv. 100 Laymen make contributions in Assembly debates.. which are often serious and well-argued. **1975** *Amer. Speech 1971* XLVI. 261 Vennemann's paper is a well-argued proposal for modifying marking theory in TG grammar.

well-'armed, *ppl. a.*

1. Adequately armed for war or combat. Also *transf.* and *fig.*

c **1290** *St. Christopher* 143 in *S. Eng. Leg.* 275 Wel I-armede heo wenden forth. **13..** *K. Alis.* 2582 Faire chevalry him cam fro Mede, Wel y-armed, on heygh stede. **1340** *Ayenb.* 170 þet þe man by wel y-armed uor to ouercome parfitliche zenne. *c* **1425** WYNTOUN *Cron.* VIII. clxxix. 6723 His hors weill armyt wes. *c* **1460** *Towneley Myst.* xxvi. 469 A thousand shall I assay, and mo, well armed ilkon. **1592** SHAKS. *Rom. & Jul.* I. i. 216 In strong proofe of chastity well-arm'd. **1605** —— *Lear* III. vii. 20. **1635–56** COWLEY *Davideis* IV. 699 A vast, well-arm'd and glittering Host. **1791** COWPER *Iliad* IX. 96 Forth rush'd the guard well-armed. **1875** HIGGINSON *Hist. U.S.* xv. 133 The Indians' arrows did not put them on an equality with the well-armed Englishmen. **1901** *N. Amer. Rev.* Feb. 206 Create a regular and well disciplined army, and secure a well-armed diplomacy.

2. Furnished with a powerful armature.

1832 BREWSTER *Nat. Magic* xi. 273 A strong and well-armed loadstone.

well-'armoured, *a.*

1868 MORRIS *Earthly Par.* I. II. 578 The King's brave well-armoured folk.

well-a'rranged, *ppl. a.*

1798 SOPHIA LEE *Canterb. T.*, *Young Lady's T.* II. 377 Dr. Dalton listened, in mute astonishment, to this well-arranged, extravagant plan. **1823** SCOTT *Quentin D.* xxvii, A well-arranged and handsomely trimmed beard. **1842** DICKENS *Amer. Notes* ix, A well-arranged public library of some ten thousand volumes. **1905** *Athenæum* 7 Oct. 469/3 A good deal of interesting and well-arranged information will be found in the sections which come before the main list of biographies.

well(-)a'rrayed, *ppl. a.*

? *a* **1366** CHAUCER *Rom. Rose* 472 Al to selde iwys Is ony pouere man wel fedde Or wel araied. *c* **1374** —— *Troylus* II. 680 And also blisful Venus wel arayed Sat in hire seuenthe hous of heuene þo. **1387** TREVISA *Higden* VII. 359, I and þow be here allone, iliche wel i-horsed, and i-wepened, iliche wel arrayed. *c* **1425** WYNTOUN *Cron.* IX. xxv. 2826 Wiþ a nobyll company Weil arayit and dantely. **1470–85** MALORY *Arthur* I. x. 49 The two kynges were come ouer the see with thre hondred knyȝtes wel arayed both for the pees and for the werre. **1605** R. F. *Dedekind's Sch. Slovenrie* (1904) 16 At length, when thou art well araide, let both thy hose hang downe About thy heeles. **1742** YOUNG *Nt. Th.* II. 234 Ye well-array'd! Ye lilies of our land! Ye lilies male! who neither toil, nor spin.

† **well-'arted**, *a. Obs.* Artistically wrought.
c **1611** CHAPMAN *Iliad* XVIII. 356, I made A number of well-arted things; round bracelets, buttons braue.

well-ar'ticulated, *ppl. a.*
1951 W. K. MATTHEWS *Languages U.S.S.R.* iii. 33 Mordvin.. shares with Cheremiss a well-articulated system of word-formation. **1977** *Jrnl. Commonw. & Compar. Politics* XV. 5 Pre-unionists parties in some colonies and republics of South Africa were functionable, rather well-articulated units.

well-a'sserted, *ppl. a.*
1812 BYRON *Ch. Har.* I. xc, Not all the marvels of Barossa's fight,..Have won for Spain her well asserted right.

well-a'ssorted, *ppl. a.*
1790 BURKE *Fr. Rev.* (ed. 2) 15 The rich variety to be found in the well-assorted warehouses of the dissenting congregations. **1836** A. COMBE *Physiol. Digestion* (ed. 2) 302 The after-dinner small-talk of a well-assorted circle.

well-a'ssured, *ppl. a.*
1475 CAXTON *Jason* 78 During which time he helde him wel assured in his palais. **1898** *Westm. Gaz.* 16 Sept. 8/3 If they do not go out to well-assured situations they go to hunger, want, disease, and possibly death in a country which is wild and disappointing. **1899** CROCKETT *Kit Kennedy* xix. 131 With well-assured hearts the pair made themselves ready for what remained to be done.

well-a'ttempered, *ppl. a.*
1845 NEALE *Seaton. Poems* (1864) 9 Vain the trust in lance and mail And well-attemper'd sword. **1852** TENNYSON *Ode Wellington* 74 A man of well-attemper'd frame. **1866** FELTON *Anc. & Mod. Gr.* I. II. ix. 442 The soft and well-attempered air of spring.

well-a'ttended, *ppl. a.* Of a meeting: attended by a large number of people.
1946 *Nature* 21 Dec. 918/1 Dr. W. H. Taylor presided over a well-attended meeting. **1979** G. POTTINGER *Secretaries of State for Scotland 1926–76* xix. 193 The Scottish Covenant Movement..held two well-attended assemblies in 1947 and 1948.

well-a'ttending, *ppl. a.*
1725 POPE *Odyss.* III. 18 She..admonish'd thus his well-attending mind.

well-a'ttested, *ppl. a.*
1667 GLANVILL *Consid. Witches* etc. 5 Standing publick Records have been kept of these well attested Relations. **1756** BURKE *Vind. Nat. Soc.* 20 Other well-known and well-attested ones [*sc.* slaughters]. **1774** E. LONG *Jamaica* III. 874 There are well-attested instances in Jamaica of the voracity of the alligator. **1857** GEO. ELIOT *Ess.* (1884) 36 The well-attested facts of his life. **1871** NAPHEYS *Prev. & Cure Dis.* I. i. 45 A well-attested case of longevity.

well-a'ttired, *ppl. a. poet.*
† **1.** Properly equipped or furnished. *Obs.*
13.. *Sir Orfeo* 158 (Sisam) He..brouȝt me to his palays, Wele atird in ich ways.
2. Richly arrayed.
1637 MILTON *Lycidas* 146 The Musk-rose, and the well-attir'd Woodbine. **1791** COWPER *Iliad* XVIII. 473 Charis, Vulcan's well-attired spouse.

well-au'thenticated, *ppl. a.*
1786 POLWHELE tr. *Theocritus*, etc. (1792) II. 212 Amidst the legends of superstition, it is in vain we search for well-authenticated truths. **1820** W. IRVING *Sk. Bk., Spectre Bridegroom*, Events of the kind are extremely common in Germany, as many well authenticated histories bear witness. **1879** LUBBOCK *Sci. Lect.* v. 167, I have endeavoured to select only those arguments which rest on well-authenticated facts.

well-avised: see WELL-ADVISED.

wellaway ('wɛlə'weɪ), *int.* and *sb.* Now *arch.* Forms: α. **weȝ lá weȝ, wei lá wei** (2 **wí lá wei**), 3 **wæilawæi**, 3–4 **weilawei**, 3–5 **-wai** (6 *Sc.* **-wa**), 4–5 **weilawey**, 3–5 **-way**, 5–6 **weillaway** (5 **-weye**), 4–5 **weylaway** (5 **weyle-away, -awey**); 4–5 **weylowey** (**weyllo-**), **weyloway**, 5 **weilowey, -waie**; 4–5 **weile-, weyleway**. β. 3–4 **wailawai**, 3–5 **-way**; 3–4 **waile-wai**, 4 **-way**, 5 **-wey** (3–4 **wailwai**), 4–5 **wailoway**, 6 **waile a way**; 3–5 **wayla-**, 4–5 **wayle-, wayloway**. γ. 3–4 **walawai**, 4–5 **-waie, walewai(e**; 3–5 (9) **walaway**, 4–5 **-waye, -wey(e**, 4 **wale(a)way, woleway**; 4–5 **walo(w)way**; *Sc.* 6–7 **walla-**, 6 **wallo-**, 7 **wallouway**, 8 **walaways**, 9 **wally-wae**. δ. 3 **welawei**, 5 **-weie**, 4–5 **-wey**, 4 **-weye**; 4–7 **welaway**, 4–6 **-waye**, 5 **-waie, whela-, weloway**; 4–5 **well-, welle awey**, 5 **well y weye**, 5–6 **well-**, 6 **welle awaye**; 5–7 (9) **wellaway** (**well-away, well-a-way**); *Sc.* 6 **welloway**, 9 **wellawa**, 8–9 **williwa** (9 **will a waes**). ε. 4–5 **weleawey**, 4–6 **-away**, 6 *Sc.* **weill away**, 6–7 **wealaway, weale away**. [OE. *weȝ lá weȝ, wei lá wei*, an alteration of *wá lá wá* (see WELLAWO), by substitution of the OScand. interjection **wei* (ON. and Icel. *vei*; see WEILA) for OE. *wá*. The later forms are partly normal phonetic developments, partly the result of contamination with forms representing OE. *wá lá wá*, and partly due to the first element being identified with, or replaced by, *wel, wele* WELL *adv.* (cf. WELLA).]

A. *int.* An exclamation of sorrow or lamentation. (Cf. WELLADAY, -ANEAR, -A-WINS.)

Formerly often in phr. *to sing wellaway, my* (*his*, etc.) *song is wellaway*.

α. *c* **888** ÆLFRED *Boeth.* xxxv. §7 Weilawei [*Bodl.* wila wei]. *c* **1000** *Lambeth Ps.* xxxix. 16 *Qui dicunt mihi euge euge*, þa þe cweðaþ me weȝla weȝ *vel* wala wa *vel* eala eala. *c* **1205** LAY. 17918 Wæilawæi, wæilawæi,..muchel is þa sorȝe þe isiȝen is to londe. *a* **1225** *Ancr. R.* 64 Weilawei, min eie haueð irobbed al mine soule. **1297** R. GLOUC. (Rolls) 8193 De mount scabiouse was aslawe, weilaway. *c* **1330** R. BRUNNE *Chron. Wace* (Rolls) 12238 Biside þe toumbe þis womman lay, & often cried 'wey la way!' *c* **1386** CHAUCER *Reeve's T.* 152 Iohn..gan to crie: harrow and weylaway. **1412–20** LYDG. *Chron. Troy* IV. 4392 For now her trust of kynȝthod was away, Her worþi men slayen, weillaway! *c* **1440** *Ps. Penit.* (1894) 29 Defautes fele that me deface, Maketh me synge weylawey.

β. *a* **1250** *Owl & N.* 220 Þu singist aniȝht and noȝt adai & al þi song is wailawai [*Jesus MS.* waylaway]. *a* **1300** *Cursor M.* 8669 Bot wailawai! it sua bitide, Mi felaw smord hir barn in bedd. *c* **1400** *Gamelyn* 197 (Harl. MS.) And þer he herd a Frankeleyn wayloway syng. **1513** BRADSHAW *St. Werburge* II. 1614 Women and children cried 'out and waile-a-way'.

γ. *a* **1300** *Cursor M.* 9056 Has þou, coth þai, þi lau renaid? Yaa, soth haf i, walawai! he said. **13..** *Gosp. Nicod.* 1314 (Sion MS.) For come he here, I haue greete drede we sal say waloway. **1340** HAMPOLE *Pr. Consc.* 2434 Þan sal walaway be þi sang. *c* **1460** *Towneley Myst.* v. 36 Now, alas, and waloway! *c* **1480** HENRYSON *Fox & Wolf* 155 Now, quod the Foxe, allace and wallaway! *a* **1568** in *Bannatyne MS.* (Hunter. Club) 378 Now, walloway, is thair no help? **1724** RAMSAY *Tea-t. Misc.* (1775) I. 136 Walaways! I dow to do!

δ. *a* **1225** *Ancr. R.* 408 Louerd, wultu smiten?..Welawei! þu meiht wel. **1303** R. BRUNNE *Handl. Synne* 11214 'Welaweye' þey cry and sey. *c* **1374** CHAUCER *Anel. & Arc.* 338 But welawaye, to far ben thei to fecche. **14..** *Pol. Rel. & L. Poems* (1903) 125/63 Therfore my song is well-y-wey! *c* **1440** *Partonope* 6497 Hys songe was not but wellawaye. **15..** *Adam Bel* st. 99 in Child *Ballads* (1888) III. 27 Alas that euer I se this daye!..Alas and welawaye. **1553** BRADFORD *Serm. Repentance* (1574) Ev, But alas and welaway..Gods anger..hath taken him away by death. **1581** J. BELL *Haddon's Answ. Osor.* 410 Wellaway surely may Purgatory sing, if it have not better Proctour to uphold it, then Luther. **1590** SPENSER *F.Q.* II. viii. 46 Harrow and well away [ed. 1609 weal-away]. **1657** W. RAND tr. *Gassendi's Life Peiresc* II. 139 Alas and well away. **1818** SCOTT *Rob Roy* xxxii, There is not a farmer but shall sing well-a-wa over a burnt barnyard and an empty byre. **1820** [A. SUTHERLAND] *St. Kathleen* IV. 116 Will a waes, man, but ye hae a lang account to sattle. **1878** A. MARY F. ROBINSON *Handful Honeysuckle* 80 Alas, and Wellaway!

ε. **13..** *K. Alis.* 4481 (Laud. MS.) For Oxeatre & Darriadas He grade weleaway & allas. *c* **1412** HOCCLEVE *De Reg. Princ.* (Roxb.) 1958 But weleaway! so is myne hert wo. **1426** AUDELAY *Poems* 10 In hunger, in cold, in thrust, weleaway! Afftyr here almes ay waytyng. *c* **1495** *The Epitaffe* etc. in Skelton's *Wks.* (1843) II. 391 Alas for sorowe therefore! Oute and weleway. *c* **1530** *Hyckescorner* 549 We all may say weleaway For synne that is now-adaye. **1580** H. GIFFORD *Gilloflowers* (1875) 101 Her song was woe, and weale away. **1616** W. BROWNE *Brit. Past* II. i. 13 Alas and weale away, since now I stand In such a plight.

b. with *so* or *full* prefixed.
a **1300** *Cursor M.* 15366–7 He mai sai walawai Full walwa þan mai he sing. *Ibid.* 22703 Þis midelerth, ful wail wai [*Edinb.* ful wailewai, *Trin.* so weylaway], Al to noght sal brin awai. *c* **1369** CHAUCER *Bk. Duchesse* 729 Phyllis also for Demophon Henge hir selfe, so weylaway. *c* **1440** *York Myst.* vi. 24 For vs is wrought, so welaway, Doole endurand nyghte and day. **1513** DOUGLAS *Æneis* VI. i. 52 Quhair-in he porturit als, full welloway, The luif abhominable of quene Pasyphe.

c. followed by *that* and clause, expressing the ground or subject of lament. †Also with *what* = how!
c **1200** *Trin. Coll. Hom.* 183 A weilewei, þu fule hold, þat ich auere was to þe iteied. *c* **1205** LAY. 8031 Wæila wæi wæila wæi þæt he is þus i-faren awæi. *a* **1300** *Cursor M.* 17575 Walawai quat þai war blind. *c* **1330** *Arth. & Merl.* 6801 (Kölbing) Quaþ king Angvisaunt: Woleway, þat ich euer bot þis day. **1390** GOWER *Conf.* III. 286 Helas, mi Soster, waileway, That evere I sih this ilke day! *c* **1440** *York Myst.* xxxii. 309 So wala way þat euere I was in witte or wille þat tristy trewe for to be-traye. **1596** SPENSER *F.Q.* v. i. 15 Ah woe is me, and well away (quoth hee)..That euer I this dismall day did see.

† **d.** Followed by a sb. = alas for .., woe worth... Also with *to* or *for* + sb. *Obs.*
a **1300** *K. Horn* 956 Walawai þe stunde! Walaway þe while! **13..** *Guy Warw.* (1891) 400 Wayle-way þat stounde. *c* **1374** CHAUCER *Troylus* III. 1078 Allas þi wyle Serueth of nought, so wel-awey þe while. *Ibid.* 1695 But cruel day, so wel-awey þe stounde, Gan for to aproche. *c* **1400** *Emare* 812 He wepte and sayde, Welle-a-wey, For my sone so dere! *a* **1400–50** *Wars Alex.* 4564 Wailaway to wriches, & wa is ȝow in erthe. *c* **1440** *York Myst.* vi. 93 Sa welaway for harde peyne. **1579** SPENSER *Sheph. Cal.* Sept. 58 Wel-away the while I was so fonde.

B. *sb.* **1.** The utterance of this exclamation. Hence, lamentation, a lament.
a **1300** *K. Horn* 1478 (Camb.) He makede Rymenhilde lay, & heo makede walaway. *a* **1300** *Cursor M.* 24352 Bot quen i raxsild vp in rage, I ne wist bot wail wai [*Gött.* walaway, *Edinb.* walewai]. **1450** *Cov. Myst., Cain & Abel* 193 Now wyl I go wende my way With sore syeng and wel away. **1552** LYNDESAY *Monarche* 5474 With lowde allace and welaway. **1553** BRADFORD *Serm. Repent.* (1574) To Rdr. Bijb, Then was weale away, mourning and woe. **16..** J. D. *Mare of Collingtoun* in *Watson's Collect. Sc. Poems* (1706) I. 42 With mony a Shout and Wallaway. **1820** KEATS *Isabella* lxi, Spirits of grief, sing not your 'Well-a-way!' For Isabel, sweet Isabel, will die. **1823** GALT *Entail* II. 160, I wish that I was dead, but I'm no like to dee, as Jenny says in her wally-wae about her father's cow and auld Robin Gray. **1884** WOOLNER *Silenus* 22 Syrinx he saw..plunge in the stream And her young spirit pass into the reeds That now were whispering her sad well-away.

b. *transf.* A cause of lamentation.
1593 G. HARVEY *New Let. Notable Cont.* A3b, Who honoureth not..the very name of the renowned Lepanto:..the Halleluia of Christendome, & the Welaway of Turky?

† **2.** Sorrow, distress, misery, woe. *Obs.*
1303 R. BRUNNE *Handl. Synne* 11222 So, betwyxe fals and coueytous, ys welaweye broȝt to hous. *c* **1375** *Cursor M.* 22472 (Fairf.) Quar-to sulde we be borne to-day & se bot sorou & waleway. **1377** LANGL. *P. Pl.* B. XVIII. 227 Wote no wighte..what is witterly wel til weyllowey hym teche. **1402** *Fr. Daw Topias* in *Pol. Poems* (Rolls) II. 112 Thou shalt have the weleaway of Gelboth hilles, the sorowe of Sodome, and al sinful citeis. **1597** *Guistard & Sismond* I. B3b, Bringing forth the night, and care, and wele-away. **1640** SIR A. JOHNSTON (Ld. Wariston) *Diary* (S.H.S.) 240 Thou bad sorrou fall the, and another tyme wallouway fall the.

† **well away**, *compound adv. Obs.*
1. Qualifying a comparative: Far and away, much. Cf. WELLA B.
1362 LANGL. *P. Pl.* A. XI. 215 Þis is þe lif of þis lordis..And wel-a-wey wers and I shulde al telle. **1377** *Ibid.* B. XII. 263 Þe larke, þat is a lasse foule, is more louelich of ledne, And wel awey of wenge swifter þan þe pecok. ?*a* **1366** CHAUCER *Rom. Rose* 119 And somdele lasse it [the river] was than Seyn But it was strayghter wel away.

2. Used elliptically with *can* and a verb implied: *well away with* = put up with, tolerate, endure. Cf. AWAY 16.
1569 BLAGUE *Sch. Conceytes* 2 Whose pride I could not well away with. **1587** HOLINSHED *Chron.* III. 27/1 He..could well awaie with bodilie labour [1577 II. 334/2 could well endure trauaile and bodily labour]. **1612** T. TAYLOR *Comm. Titus* ii. 14. (1619) 532 They can well away with either religion, but care greatly for neither. **1622** GATAKER *Spirituall Watch* (ed. 2) 70 It is no small degree of euill, when a man can well away with euill in others. *a* **1629** HINDE *J. Bruen* xxxvii. (1641) 116 This Master Done being young and youthly,..could not well away with the strict observation of the Lords day.

b. To bear or submit *to* (do something).
1579–80 NORTH *Plutarch, Alcib.* (1595) 234 Notwithstanding the people of Athens could well away to liue like subiects vnder the gouernement of a fewe.

well-a-wins, *int. Sc.* In quots. **will-, weel-, wull-**. Altered form of WELLAWAY.
a **1774** FERGUSSON *Poems* (1789) II. 79 Ah! willawins for Scotland now. *a* **1800** *Lady Jane*, in Jamieson *Pop. Ballads* (1806) II. 81 O willawins! that graceless scorn Should love like mine repay. **1818** SCOTT *Br. Lamm.* xi, Wull a wins!—such a misfortune to befa' the House of Ravenswood, and I to live to see it! **1819** W. TENNANT *Papistry Storm'd* (1827) 51 But will-a-wins! Your hands are toom. **1871** W. ALEXANDER *Johnny Gibb* iii. 23 Weel-a-wuns, than, Jinsie,..we'se lat 'im rest's banes in peace an' quaetness.

† **wellawo**, *int.* and *sb. Obs.* Forms: α. 1 **wá lá wá**, 3–4 **walawa** (4 **walwa, walaiwa**). β. 3 **wala-**, 4 **walewo**; 3 **wola-**, 4 **wole-**, 5 **wolowo**. γ. 3, 5 **welawo**, 5 **wellawoo**; 4–5 **welleawoy, wellowoy**. δ. 4 **weilawo**, 4–5 **weylawo** (5 **weyle a woo**). [OE. *wá lá wá*, f. *wá* WOE *sb.* and *lá* LO *int.*[1]; cf. WALE *int.* In the γ-forms the first element has been assimilated to *wel* WELL *adv.* (cf. OE. *wel lá* WELLA), and in the δ-forms to ME. *wey-* in *weylawey*: see WELLAWAY.]

1. *int.* = WELLAWAY A.
α. *c* **888** ÆLFRED *Boeth.* xxxix. §1 Walawa þæt ða unȝesæliȝan menn na maȝon ȝebidon hwonne he him to cume. *c* **900** *Bæda's Hist.* II. i. (1890) 96 Wala wa: þæt is sarlic, þætte [etc.]. *a* **1122** *O.E. Chron.* (Laud MS.) an. 1086, Wala wa, þæt ænig man sceolde modiȝan swa. *c* **1205** LAY. 19632 Wa la wa [*c* **1275** Wo la wo] þat hit sculde iwurðen swa. *a* **1300** *Cursor M.* 15367 Ful walwa! þan mai he sing. *c* **1300** *Ibid.* 15279 (Gött.) He mai sai walawa his werd þat forwid him es laid.

β. *a* **1225** *Ancr. R.* 88 Weilawei & wolawo, heo seið. *a* **1250** *Owl & N.* 412 Þu singest a wynter wolawo. *c* **1330** *Arth. & Merl.* 742 (Kölbing) Wolewo, mi swete maide. *c* **1400** *Pride of Life* 327 (Brandl) Ȝe world is nou, so wo lo wo, in suc bal i bound.

γ, δ. **13..** *Minor Poems of Vernon MS.* xxxvii. 225 Weilawei & weilawo, þat synne was I-wrouȝt! *c* **1400** *Arth. & Merl.* 120 (Linc. Inn) Syngand allas and weylawo. *c* **1425** *Processional Nuns Chester* (1899) 31 Thy white body was blacke and bloo. Oure synnes it made so weyle A woo. *c* **1500** *Gest of Robyn Hode* st. 438 in Child *Ballads* (1888) III. 77 Alas and well a woo!

2. *sb.* = WELLAWAY B. 2.
c **1275** LAY. 26769 Welawo was ȝam ibore þat in hire wey were bivore. *c* **1330** *Arth. & Merl.* 142 (Kölbing) To Winchester þai flowen þo Wiþ mani siȝhing & walewo. **1377** LANGL. *P. Pl.* B. XIV. 235 He hath a greuous penaunce, þat is welawo whan he waketh.

well(-)baked, *ppl. a.*
1632 ROWZEE *Queenes Welles* 67 Bread of good pure wheate, well handled..and well baked. **1746** FRANCIS tr. *Hor. Sat.* II. viii. 89 A guest like me, polite to entertain With bread well baked, with sauces season'd right. **1811** *Regul. & Orders Army* 169 Each Soldier is to receive, as his Allowance for Four Days, a well-baked Loaf.

† **well-baken**, *ppl. a. Sc.* Well-baked.
1549 *Extracts Aberd. Reg.* (1844) I. 269 Breid, that be guid stuf,..and weill bakin.

well-'balanced, *ppl. a.*
This is prob. the true reading (as suggested by Rowe) in Shaks. *Meas. for M.* IV. iii. 104, for 'weale-ballanc'd' of the Folios.
1. Exactly poised or equilibrated.

1629 MILTON *Hymn Nativ.* xii, While the Creator Great His constellations set, And the well-ballanc't world on hinges hung.

2. Having an orderly or harmonious disposition of parts.

1859 J. WHITE *Hist. France* 69 A tumultuous republic of knights and barons had become a well-balanced kingdom.

3. Having or betokening a good balance of the mental faculties; sane and sensible; not flighty or eccentric.

1861 BUCKLE *Civiliz.* II. vi. 424 Hutcheson..rightly supposed, that an admiration of every kind of beauty..is essential to a complete and well-balanced mind. **1890** BESANT *Demoniac* i. 7 A perfectly healthy, steady, and well-balanced young man. **1912** *World* 7 May 679/1 Mr. Long's speech was a practical, well-balanced, and thoroughly sane fighting speech.

well-'beaten, *ppl. a.* (BEAT *v.*[1] 3, BEATEN 2.)

a **1704** LOCKE *Cond. Underst.* §28 Their Master's Rules.. mislead those who think it sufficient to excuse them, if they go out of their way in a well beaten Tract. **1860** TYNDALL *Glac.* I. xxiii. 165 Ascending the mountain by a well-beaten path. **1883** MISS BROUGHTON *Belinda* I. x, The well-beaten pathway.

well(-)be'coming, *ppl. a.* Highly befitting or suiting.

1530 PALSGR. 329/1 Well becommyng, *bien aduenant.* **1611** COTGR., *Bienseant*,..well-beseeming, well-becomming. **1662** GUNNING *Lent Fast* 44 This is the wel-becoming order which all Churches..do observe. **1697** DRYDEN *Æneis* XI. 94 A well becoming, but a weak Relief. **1831** SCOTT *Ct. Robt.* xxxiii, A fate well-becoming his odious crimes. **1864** BURTON *Scot Abr.* I. ii. 102 On the brow of the industrious crofter..we may yet see the well-becoming pride..that, in the fifteenth century, took the honours and distinctions of France as a natural right.

well-'bedded, *ppl. a.*

1616 SURFL. & MARKH. *Country Farm* v. xviii. 557 Then you shall lay it on a well-bedded kilne.

well-be'fitting, *ppl. a.*

1845 POE *Haunted Palace* 23 A throne where, sitting..In state his glory well-befitting, The ruler of the realm was seen.

†**well be'gone**, *ppl. a. Obs.* Also 4 **wel bigoo.** [See BEGO *v.* 8.]

1. Well-contented, cheerful, joyous.

?*a* **1366** CHAUCER *Rom. Rose* 693, I was neuer..So iolyf nor so wel bigoo Ne merye in herte as I was thoo. *c* **1381** —— *Parlt. Foules* 171 But lord, so I was glad and wel begoon.

2. Fortunate, well off.

c **1374** CHAUCER *Troylus* II. 294 Yif me youre hond, for yn þis world is noon, If þat you lyst, a wyght so wel begon. *c* **1400** *Rom. Rose* 5533 And certeyn he is wel bigone Among a thousand that fyndith oon. **1421-2** HOCCLEVE *Min. Poems* xx. 11 How welthye a man be or well be-gone, Endure it shall not. **1530** PALSGR. 844/1 Well bygone, *bien a poynt*, or *bien ayse.*

well(-)be'gun, *ppl. a.* Favourably or fully started. Chiefly in proverb (see quot. 1639).

1542 UDALL *Erasm. Apoph.* 38 For accordyng to our englishe prouerbe, a thyng well begoonne, is more then halfe dooen. **1639** J. CLARKE *Parœm.* 3 Well begun is halfe done. **1742** YOUNG *Nt. Th.* IX. 2066 And dost thou chuse what ends, ere well-begun?

well-be'hated, *ppl. a.*

1771 H. WALPOLE *Let. to Mann* 22 Oct., His cousin..is going to him with a commission from Louis the well-behated. [Instead of 'well-beloved'.]

well-be'haved, *ppl. a.* **1.** Displaying good conduct or manners; decorous.

1598 SHAKS. *Merry W.* II. i. 59 Hee..gaue such orderly and wel-behaued reproofe to al vncomelinesse. **1633** FORD *'Tis Pity* II. vi, A very modest welbehau'd young Maide. **1725** DE FOE *Voy. round World* (1840) 235 His sons were very pretty, wellbehaved youths. **1863** KINGSLEY *Water-Bab.* iii. 126, I have met one or two creatures like you before, and found them very agreeable and well-behaved.

absol. **1828** P. CUNNINGHAM *N.S. Wales* (ed. 3) II. 253 To give all due encouragement to the well-behaved.

2. *Math.* Applied to different entities with varying implications as to their susceptibility to manipulation, as continuity or differentiability (of a function), convergence (of a series).

1939 C. B. BOYER *Concepts of Calculus* vi. 246 Inasmuch as Euler restricted himself to well-behaved functions, he did not become involved in those subtle difficulties connected with the notions of infinity. **1965** PATTERSON & RUTHERFORD *Elem. Abstr. Algebra* iii. 60 Of the two operations in a ring *R*, addition is 'well-behaved' in that it satisfies the commutative and associative laws and there exist an identity element and inverses... Multiplication is not so well-behaved. **1968** FOX & MAYERS *Computing Methods for Scientists & Engineers* i. 13 Since $x = 0$, and $J_0(x)$ is perfectly 'well-behaved', then also $y'(0) = 0$.

3. Of a computer program: communicating with hardware via standard operating system calls rather than directly, and therefore able to be used on different machines.

1984 *Austral. Microcomputer Mag.* Jan. 42/1 The disk drives can read and write IBM-PC format disks, and of several programs tried on the system, those that were 'well behaved' worked and those, such as word processors, that tend to directly address the machine's hardware would not always work. **1984** *Austral. Personal Computer* May 65/3 PC mode handles all well-behaved programs... In the case of direct hardware calls, problems usually arise if a 'not quite IBM-compatible' machine is used.

well-being (ˌwɛlˈbiːɪŋ, older ˈwɛlˌbiːɪŋ), *vbl. sb.* [Cf. F. *bienêtre*, mod.L. *bene esse.*]

Occas. written without the hyphen, as one word or two.

The state of being or doing well in life; happy, healthy, or prosperous condition; moral or physical welfare (of a person or community).

a **1613** OVERBURY *A Wife*, etc. (1638) 46 Man did but the well-being of this life From Woman take; her Being she from Man. **1617** WOODALL *Surgeon's Mate* (1639) Pref. 1 So many waies in use for the health and wel-being of mankinde. **1646** BENBRIGGE *Usura Acc.* 8 The publicke-Weale wherein our owne Being, and Well-being are wrapped up. **1705** F. FULLER *Med. Gymn.* (ed. 2) 32 An erect Position is essential to the well being of the Body of Man. **1713** BERKELEY *Ess. Guardian* xiv. Wks. III. 191 That behaviour which best suits with the common well-being. **1741** A. MONRO *Anat. of Nerves* (ed. 3) 10 Circumstances.. necessary to the Being or Wellbeing of this or that particular Creature. **1756** C. LUCAS *Ess. Waters* I. 168 Water..is necessary to the well being of man in all ages. **1837** LOCKHART *Scott* IV. iv. 121 That paternal solicitude for the well-being of his rural dependants. **1849** COBDEN *Sp.* 56 High prices are incompatible with the well-being of this country. **1861** LOWELL *E Pluribus Unum* Writ. 1890 V. 46 A living fact with a direct bearing on the national well-being. **1865** PUSEY *Truth Engl. Ch.* 38 A body of faith,..which to 'know and believe', essential to the well-being of all Christians. **1883** J. M. FOTHERGILL *Indigestion* etc. 275 Most healthy persons feel..a sense of well-being after a meal.

b. Satisfactory condition (of a thing).

1702 CALAMY *Abridgm. Baxter's Life & Times* vii. 137 He says, That Imposition of Hands is..a proper means necessary not to the Being, but the Well-being of Ordination. **1837** DICKENS *Pickw.* xxii, His loudly-expressed anxiety at every stage, respecting the safety and well-being of the two bags, the leather hat-box, and the brown-paper parcel. **1849** RUSKIN *Seven Lamps* Introd. 4 The principles necessary to the well being of the art.

c. *pl.* (= individual instances of welfare).

a **1672** WILKINS *Nat. Relig.* 207 He is the Author of our beings and our well-beings. **1714** J. FORTESCUE-ALAND *Pref. Fortescue's Abs. & Lim. Mon.* 4 So that it may be said with Justice, that we owe our Beings to God, and under him our Well-beings to the Law.

†**well-be'known**, *ppl. a. Obs.* In 6 Sc. **weilbiknaw.** Well-known.

1513 DOUGLAS *Æneis* VII. ii. 17 On bankis weilbiknaw and fluidis bay.

†**well-be'lieving**, *ppl. a. Obs.* Easy of belief, credulous.

c **1710** CONGREVE tr. *Ovid* Wks. 1730 III. 314 But let not powder'd Heads, nor essenc'd Hair, Your well-believing, easie Hearts ensnare.

well-be'loved, *ppl. a.* and *sb.*

A. *ppl. adj.* **1.** Dearly loved, greatly beloved.

c **1386** CHAUCER *Prol.* 215 And wel biloued and famulier was he With frankeleyns ouer al in his contree. **1422** YONGE tr. *Secreta Secret.* 247 Wyth lefe and welbelowid Pepill lagh and Play. *c* **1440** tr. *Bonaventura* in *Hampole's Wks.* (1896) I. 218 Mari Mawdeleyne, þat wele-beluffed discypulas of Ihesu. **1526** *Pilgr. Perf.* (W. de W. 1531) 8 The chrysten man, as the welbeloued chylde of god. **1601** SHAKS. *Jul. C.* III. ii. 180 Through this [rent], the wel-beloued Brutus stabb'd. **1648** *Bury Wills* (Camden) 202 Susan Despotin, my well-beloued wife. **1799** HT. LEE *Canterb. T., Old Woman's T.* (ed. 2) I. 335 Lothaire..was the trusty and well-beloved page of Louis IX. **1831** SCOTT *Ct. Robt.* iii, Our well-beloved and highly-gifted daughter. **1850** TENNYSON *In Mem.* cii, We leave the well-beloved place Where first we gazed upon the sky.

2. In letters, decrees, etc., of a sovereign or lord, prefixed to the names or designations of the persons addressed or referred to. Usually '(right) trusty and well-beloved'; cf. TRUSTY *a.* 2. Also *absol.* (with omission of sb.), and †(*Sc.*) with plural ending.

1423 *Rolls of Parlt.* IV. 248/2 Ryght worshipfull and worshipfull Faders in God, oure ryght trusty and welebeloved. **1443** HEN. VI in Ellis *Orig. Lett.* Ser. III. I. 79 Our right trusty and right welbelouyd Cousin Therl of Suffolk. *c* **1450** *Godstow Reg.* 603 Our welbeloued in crist the Abbesse and Covent of Godestow. **1516** *Reg. Privy Seal Scot.* I. 423/2 Our welebelovit knycht and counsalour William Scot of Balwery. **1524** HEN. VIII in Ellis *Orig. Lett.* Ser. I. I. 239 Trusty and welbiloved we grete you wele. **1544** in Rymer *Foedera* (1719) XV. 19 Oure Welebelovittis Hew Cunnygahame, and Thomas Bischop. **1648** *Hamilton Papers* (Camden) 241 Our right trustie and right wellbeloued cousin the Earle of Lauderdaill. **1803** in *Nairne Peerage Evid.* (1874) 111 Our right trusty and wellbeloved George Keith baron Keith of Stone Haven. **1814** SCOTT *Let.* in *Lockhart* (1837) III. x. 311 He would tell you of my departure with our trusty and well-beloved Erskine. **1884** *Rep. Comm. Housing Working Classes* Pref. 3 Victoria [etc.]. To Our right trusty and well-beloved Councillor Sir C. W. Dilke. **1924** *Burke's Peerage* 2 Barons are..addressed officially by the Crown, 'Our Right trusty and well-beloved'. *Ibid.* 3 A Viscount..is officially addressed by the Crown as 'Our right trusty and well-beloved Cousin'.

B. *sb.* A dearly loved one.

1432-50 tr. *Higden* VI. 79 Technyge Beda his welbelovyde while that he lyvede. **1575** GASCOIGNE *Glasse of Govt.* III. iii. Wks. 1910 II. 47 Nowe my welbeloved, and what sayth the..Markgrave unto you? **1611** BIBLE *Cant.* i. 13 A bundle of myrrhe is my welbeloued vnto me. **1795-1814** WORDSW. *Excurs.* VII. 342 The great, the good, The well-beloved, the fortunate, the wise,—These titles emperors and chiefs have borne. *c* **1805** H. K. WHITE *Hymn, 'Awake, sweet harp'* iii, God sees his Well-beloved's face. **1891** KIPLING *Light that Failed* xv. 317 Then he comes back to me, for his well-beloved is here.

well-benched, *a.* [WELL *adv.* 32.] Used to render Homer's ἐύσσελμος, epithet of a ship.

1848 BUCKLEY *Iliad* II. 33 Let him lay hands upon his well-benched black ship. **1870** BRYANT *Iliad* VII. 522 From their well-benched ships The Achaians also issued. **1887** MORRIS *Odyss.* II. 414 They brought forth all and laid it within the well-benched keel.

well-'beneficed, *a.*

1791 BOSWELL *Johnson* (1904) I. 678 A wealthy well-beneficed clergyman.

well(-)be'seeming, *ppl. a.* = WELL-BECOMING. Hence **well-be'seemingly** *adv. rare*$^{-0}$.

1588 SHAKS. *Tit. A.* II. iii. 56 (Qo. 1600) Romes royall Empresse, Vnfurnisht of her well beseeming troope? **1596** —— *1 Hen. IV*, I. i. 14 In mutuall well-beseeming rankes. **1611** COTGR., *Bienseant*,..well-beseeming, well-becomming. *Ibid.*, *Bienseamment*, comelily, agreeably, well-beseemingly.

†**well be'seen**, *ppl. a. Obs.* Also 4 **bebiseye.** [See BESEE *v.* II.] Good-looking, of good appearance; well appointed or apparelled; well furnished *with*; versed or accomplished *in.*

?*a* **1366** CHAUCER *Rom. Rose* 821 Fetys he was and wel beseye [*Cointes fu et de bel atour*]. **1390** GOWER *Conf.* I. 302 My wif..Which is with reson wel besein. *Ibid.* III. 121 Sche [Virgo] is with sterres wel beseie. *c* **1440** *Generydes* 1978 Tentys large, full riche and wele besen. *c* **1470** HENRY *Wallace* I. 213 Likle he was, richt byge and weyle beseyne. **1530** PALSGR. 844/1 Well bysene, *bien accoustré.* **1576** R. PETERSON *G. della Casa's Galateo* 10 A Noble gentleman, courteous and well beseene in all good behauiour. *a* **1578** LINDESAY (Pitscottie) *Chron. Scot.* (S.T.S.) I. 147 Teodor Gaza ane weill besene man baitht in Lattine and greik. **1591** SPENSER *Virgil's Gnat* 651 Eftsoones he gins to fashion forth a place,..squaring it in compasse well beseene. **1596** —— *F.Q.* V. viii. 29 The Briton Prince him readie did awayte, In glistering armes right goodly well beseene. **1736** W. THOMPSON *Epithal.* xiv, Our dearling Prince to meet Augusta well-beseen. *a* **1911** Æ. J. G. MACKAY *Pitscottie Gloss.* s.v. *Beseine*, Still used. 'Ye are weel besene the day', *i.e.* well clothed or fit to look upon.

†**well be'spoken**, *ppl. a. Obs.* Fair-spoken, of courteous speech.

1471 CAXTON *Recuyell* (Sommer) I. 73 Archas..was right wise and well bespoken. **1474, 1483** —— [see BESPOKEN 1]. **1490** —— *Eneydos* x. C viij, Fayr and wel byspoken.

†**well-be'strutted**, *ppl. a. Obs.* Amply distended or plumped out.

1648 HERRICK *Hesper., Oberon's Feast* 34 He..eates the sagge And well-bestrutted Bees sweet bagge.

†**well-be'teemingness.** *Obs. rare*$^{-1}$. In quot. -beteam-. [BETEEM *v.*[1]] Readiness to vouchsafe or grant.

1642 D. ROGERS *Naaman* 178 That it [Grace] may appeare in all the excellency and fulnesse, freedome, bounty, unchangeablenesse and welbeteamingnesse thereof.

well-blacked, *ppl. a.*

1822 SCOTT *Nigel* ii, His low, flat..cap, and his well-blacked, shining shoes, indicated that he belonged to the city. **1860** G. H. KINGSLEY in Galton *Vac. Tour.* 140 A basin ..and a well blacked crock.

well-'blended, *ppl. a.*

1708 J. PHILIPS *Cyder* II. 663 Whose liquid Store Abundant, flowing in well blended Streams The Natives shall applaud.

†**well-'blooded**, *a. Obs.* Also 7 -**bloudied.** [See WELL *adv.* 32 and BLOODED *a.* 2.] Having plenty of blood.

16.. MIDDLETON, etc. *Old Law* v. i, Trust me, a lusty woman, able bodied, And well blooded cheeks. *Clo.* Oh she paints my Lord. *a* **1662** HEYLIN *Laud* (1668) 542 His Countenance chearful and well-bloudied.

'well-boat. [See WELL *sb.*[1] 6 b.]

1. A fishing-boat provided with a well or tank for the storage and transport of live fish.

c **1600** [see TODE *sb.*[1]]. **1614** GENTLEMAN *Engl. Way to win Wealth* 19 And these be Pinks and Wel-boats of the burthen of fourty Tunnes. **1653** H. COGAN tr. *Pinto's Trav.* xxx. 121 Others..get their living by selling fish alive, which to that purpose they keep in great well-boats. **1769** PENNANT *Brit. Zool.* III. 301 They [carp] are there a great article of commerce, and sent in well-boats to Sweden and Russia. **1800** COLQUHOUN *Comm. Thames* xv. 438 Fish wasting in Well-boats at Gravesend. **1883** *Fisheries Exhib. Catal.* 211 Severn Fisheries Board..Model of Trunk or Well Boat.

†**2.** A flat-bottomed boat for landing troops and stores. *Obs.*

1692 LUTTRELL *Brief Rel.* (1857) II. 482 The 40 well boates built at Deptford, which carry about 20 or 30 oars each, to land men in shoal water. **1693** *MSS. Ho. of Lords* (N.S.) I. 187 An able seaman to take charge of the well-boats at Portsmouth and the stores to be put on board them. **1693** *Lond. Gaz.* No. 2926/3 Three of the Bomb Ships, with the Brigantines and Well Boats went in and Anchored within half a Mile of the Town.

well-'boden, *ppl. a. Sc.* [See BODEN *ppl. a.*] Well provided or furnished; fully armed or equipped.

c **1425** WYNTOUN *Cron.* VIII. xxxviii. 6833 Weil bodyn Frankis men. **1496** *Extracts Aberd. Reg.* (1844) I. 60 That al fremen..compeir..at the Cunneger hill, welbodin and abilȝeit for weir in ther personis. **1598** FERGUSSON *Sc. Prov.* (S.T.S.) 49 He is weill bodden ther ben that neidis nather borrow nor lend. **1808** JAMIESON s.v. *Boden, Weil-boden*, or *ill-boden*, well or ill provided in whatever respect.

well-'bodied, *a.* [WELL *adv.* 32.] Having good bodily development.
1481 *Cely Papers* (Camden) 59 Sche ys as goodly a ȝeunge whomane as fayr as whelbodyd [etc.]. **1484** CAXTON *G. de la Tour* C iij b, Loo ther is a welbodyed woman which is wel worthy to be belouyd of somme knyght. **1594** *Knack to know a Knave* E 4, My Lord, she is.. Well bodied, but her face was something blacke, Lyke those that follow houshold businesse. *a* **1653** BINNING *Comm. Princ.* Wks. (1735) 28/2 By this he grew to the Stature of a tall and well-bodyed Christian. **1728** POPE *Dunc.* II. 42 All as a partridge plump, full-fed, and fair, She form'd this image of well-body'd air.

well-'boding, *ppl. a.*
1719 OLDISWORTH *Callipædia* II. 517 Or when the Lyon or the Centaur shines, Or the auspicious and well-boading Twins.

well-boiled, *ppl. a.*
1697 DRYDEN *Æneis* XI. 812 A knotty Lance of well-boil'd Oak he bore [*telum solidum nodis et robore cocto*].

well-boned, *a.* [WELL *adv.* 32.]
1. Having large or strong bones.
1297 R. GLOUC. (Rolls) 8571 þikke mon he was ynou.. wel iboned [*MS. γ* boned] & strong. **1530** PALSGR. 329/1 Well boned, *ossu.* **1553** ASCHAM *Rept. Germany* 16 Marches Albert is.. rather wel boned for strength, then ouerloded with flesh.
2. Properly stiffened with whalebone.
1871 [see BONED *ppl. a.* 2.]. **1901** *Daily News* 12 Jan. 6/7 It is made over a carefully fitted, well-boned lining.

well-'booted, *a.* [WELL *adv.* 32.]
1647 TRAPP *Comm. Ephes.* vi. 15 (1656) 772 As one that is well booted or buskind can walk unhurt amidst bryers and brambles. **178.** BURNS *Ronalds of Bennals* 41 Though I canna ride in weel-booted pride, And flee o'er the hills like a craw, man. **1894** A. LANG *Ban & Arrière Ban* 45 Lady, lady neat.. Wherefore dost thou hie, Stealthy, down the street, On well-booted feet?

well(-)born, *ppl. a.* [See BORN B. 1 d. Cf. Da. *velbaaren*, Du. *welgeboren*, G. *wohlgeboren* (MHG. *wolgeborn*).
The lack of examples in ME. is noticeable.]
1. Of good birth or lineage, of gentle blood.
c **950** *Lindisf. Gosp.* Luke xix. 12 Monn sum wel-boren [L. *nobilis*] foerde on lond un-neh. *c* **1000** ÆLFRIC *Deut.* i. 15 Ic nam wise menn and welborene [Vulg. *nobiles*].
1595 SHAKS. *John* II. i. 278 As many and as well-borne bloods as those. **1633** EARL MANCH. *Al Mondo* (1636) 146 To see well borne men to despise honest callings. **1667** DRYDEN *Secret Love* I. iii. (1668) 13 My Cousin is.. Valiant and wise; and handsome; and well born. *Qu.* But not of Royal bloud. **1749** FIELDING *Tom Jones* XIII. xii, There is a something in persons well-born, which others can never acquire. **1848** THACKERAY *Van. Fair* xlix, Mrs. Crawley is not very well born. **1905** R. BAGOT *Passport* xiii. 120 You would not be considered well-born enough nor rich enough.
b. *absol.*
the well-born: a nickname formerly given to the Federalists of the U.S., derisively adopted by their opponents from the serious use of the term by J. Adams (see quot. 1787).
1787 J. ADAMS *Def. Const. Govt. U.S.* Pref. I. p. x, The rich, the well-born, and the able, acquire an influence among the people, that will soon be too much for simple honesty and plain sense, in a house of representatives. **1788** *Amer. Museum* June (1792) 527 Under such a government, men of education, abilities, and property, commonly called *the well born*, will be the most likely to get into places of power and trust. **1841** HELPS *Ess., Domestic Rule* (1842) 52 The well-educated or the well-born. **1883** MCMASTER *People U.S.* I. 469 In most of the squibs and pasquinades that filled the papers the Federalists were reviled under the name of 'the well-born'.
2. Having the personal qualities naturally associated with good birth; noble in nature or character. (In early use after F. *bien né*.)
c **1450** *Knt. de la Tour* xii. 16 He herde that the king of Denmark had .iij. faire doughtres well born [*moult bien nées*].
1697 DRYDEN *Æneis* II. 455 Heav'n, that well-born Souls inspires, Prompts me.. To.. rush undaunted to defend the Walls. **1857** EMERSON *Poems, Celestial Love* 45 Counsel which the ages kept Shall the well-born soul accept.

well-'bottomed, *ppl. a.* Having a good foundation, firmly based.
1699 BOYER *Royal Dict., Eng.-Fr.*, Well-bottom'd, *bien fondé*. **1762** WILKES *Corr.* (1805) III. 33, I said.. that it would be soon seen how well-bottomed I was. **1874** MORLEY *Compromise* iii. 105 Obviously only three ways of dealing with the great problems of which we have spoken are compatible with a strong and well-bottomed character.

well-bought, *ppl. a.* †a. Bought at a fair price; worth the price paid. (See WELL *adv.* 6 d.) b. Valiantly won. (Cf. DEAR-BOUGHT.)
1480 *Cely Papers* (Camden) 56 Sum standerdes of mayll whelbhowte. **1576** *Ded. Verses* in Turberv. *Venerie*, A Booke well bought, God graunt it so be solde, For sure such Bookes are better worth than golde. **1811** SCOTT *Don Roderick* III. xiii, For never, upon gory battle-ground, With conquest's well-bought wreath were braver victors crown'd!

well-bound, *ppl. a.* Said of a book. Also *fig.*
1649 G. DANIEL *Trinarch, Hen. IV* st. 265 Whose Volumes Numberless Nature doth Summe In one Compendious Abstract; Well-bound Man! **1781** COWPER *Table-T.* 745 To see the name of idol self, Stamp'd on the well-bound quarto, grace the shelf. **1845** *Penny Cycl.* Suppl. I. 220/2 Most well-bound books have a little appendage at the top of the back-edge, called the 'head-band'. **1880** *Daily News* 19 Oct. 4/7 The rubbishy but well-bound book keeps its place on the shelves.

well-braced, *ppl. a.* Firmly or healthily strung up.
1785 T. DWIGHT *Conquest of Canäan* VI. 141 The well-brac'd buckler glittered o'er his breast. **1859** MEREDITH *R. Feverel* xix, The young ladies.. looked.. anything but well-braced.

well-branched, *a.* [WELL *adv.* 32.]
1649 C. WASE *Sophocles, Electra* 22 A spotted well-brancht Stag.

well-brawned, *a.* [WELL *adv.* 32.]
1577, 1609 [see BRAWNED 1]. **1585** HIGINS *Junius' Nomencl.* 448/2 *Torosus*,.. well flesht:.. well brawned. **1615** CHAPMAN *Odyss.* XIII. 155 From forth the hauens high crest, Branch the well-brawn'd armes of an Oliue tree.

well-breathed (-bri:ðd, -brɛθt), *a.* [WELL *adv.* 32 + BREATHED 1 and 6.] Sound or strong of wind; exercised so as to be in good wind; not out of breath.
1470–85 MALORY *Arthur* XVIII. xviii. 758 He is a noble knyghte, and a myghty man, and wel brethed. **1475** *Bk. Noblesse* (Roxb.) 76 To make hem hardie, deliver, and wele brethed. **1592** SHAKS. *Ven. & Ad.* 678 And on thy well-breathed horse keep with thy hounds. **1598** SYLVESTER *Du Bartas* II. iii. III. *Law* 182 A well-breath'd Body, nimble, sound, and strong. **1673** DRYDEN *Marr. à la Mode* IV. i. 54, I, take heat after heat, like a well-breath'd Courser. **1720** POPE *Iliad* XXII. 244 As through the forest.. The well-breath'd beagle drives the flying fawn. **1828–43** TYTLER *Hist. Scot.* (1864) I. 120 Bruce.. saw, too, that his own infantry were still fresh and well-breathed. **1849** J. FORBES *Physician's Holiday* ii. (1850) 13 The experienced, well-breathed, and robust traveller.
b. said of a speaker or reciter.
1647 N. WARD *Simple Cobler* (1843) 16 It is a most toylsome taske to run.. after a well-breath'd Opinionist. **1681** DRYDEN *Abs. & Achit.* I. 631 To speak the rest, who better are forgot, Would tire a well-breath'd Witness of the Plot. **1831** SCOTT *Cast. Dang.* ix, A less matter would hold a well-breathed minstrel in subject for recitation for a calendar month.

well-bred, *ppl. a.*
1. a. Of good family and bringing up. Usually: Displaying good breeding; having refined manners; courteous in speech and behaviour.
1597 SHAKS. *2 Hen. IV*, I. i. 26 A Gentleman well bred, and of good name. **1634** SIR T. HERBERT *Trav.* 2 If my thoughts haue wandred, I must intreat the well-bred Reader to remember, I haue wandred through many deserts. **1652** KIRKMAN *Clerio & Lozia* 100 Netling speeches, which well-bred women should avoyd as a dangerous Precipice. **1698** J. COLLIER *Immor. Stage* 60 A well Bred Man will no more Swear than Fight in the Company of Ladies. **1709** POPE *Ess. Crit.* 635 Tho' learn'd, well-bred; and tho' well-bred, sincere. **1752** CHESTERF. *Lett. to Son* 19 Sept., The officers, .. when of a certain rank and service, are generally very polite, well-bred people. **1781** COWPER *Conversat.* 193 A moral, sensible, and well-bred man Will not affront me, and no other can. **1813** JANE AUSTEN *Pride & Prej.* xlv, Whose endeavour to introduce some kind of discourse proved her to be more truly well bred than either of the others. **1886** RUSKIN *Præterita* I. x. 327 The first well-bred and well-dressed girls I had ever seen.
b. of speech, behaviour, etc.
1699 BENTLEY *Phal.* 251 I'll give him leave to tell me again in his well-bred way, That my head has no Brains in't. **1728** YOUNG *Love Fame* i. 115 It makes dear self on well-bred tongues prevail, And I the little hero of each tale. **1784** COWPER *Task* II. 413 With a well-bred whisper close the scene. **1808** MRS. C. KEMBLE *Day after Wedding* 27 You sit at such a well-bred distance from each other, one would swear you had been married 24 years, instead of 24 hours. **1818** SCOTT *Hrt. Midl.* l, Lady Staunton only answered this hint with a well-bred stare, which gave no sort of encouragement. **1867** LADY HERBERT *Cradle L.* vii. 173 His manner was grave to sadness, but extremely well-bred.
2. Of good breed or stock Said of animals.
1805 *Times* 7 Nov. 1/1 To be sold.. four capital well-bred hunters. **1815** *Sporting Mag.* XLVI. 118, I knew in their day, runners of fair repute, and as well bred as any horses upon earth. **1849** CLARIDGE *Cold Water Cure* 202 When the horse is well-bred, and his wind is unimpaired.

well-'breeched, *ppl. a.* Prosperous, well-to-do. Cf. BREECHED *ppl. a.* 4.
1821 P. EGAN *Life in London* II. ii. 178 Jerry is in Tip Street upon this occasion, and the Mollishers are all nutty upon him, putting it about, one to another, that he is a well breeched Swell. **1860** HOTTEN *Dict. Slang* (ed. 2) 104 *Breeched*, or *to have the bags off*, to have plenty of money; 'to be well breeched', to be in good circumstances. **1968** P. SCOTT *Day of Scorpion* I. ii. 64 Her first husband.. died well-breeched. **1980** *Jrnl. R. Soc. Arts* Apr. 266/1 That they had been able to become rich or well-breeched in a worldly sense is incidental. **1985** *Times* 22 Mar. 23/8 Britoil presents the spectacle of a fairly well-breeched oil group.

well(-)brewed, *ppl. a.*
1713 *Phil. Trans.* XXVIII. 135 A small and well brewed Beer. **1876** GEO. ELIOT *Dan. Deronda* i, It was near four o'clock on a September day, so that the atmosphere was well-brewed to a visible haze.

†**well(-)broke**, *ppl. a. Obs.*
1731 MILLER *Gard. Dict.* s.v. *Tulipa*, These do, in time, break into various beautiful Stripes, according to the Ground of their former Self-colour: but this must be intirely thrown off, otherwise they don't esteem a Flower well broke. **1796** C. MARSHALL *Garden.* viii. (1813) 104 Having thrown on a little good and well-broke mould.

well(-)broken, *ppl. a.*
1580 BLUNDEVIL *Art of Riding* II. x. 19 b, To say the truth, wearines and lack of breath, may cause anie horse, be he neuer so well broken, to do the same. **1728** MANDEVILLE *Fab. Bees* (1733) II. 316 All horses are ungovernable, that are not well-broken. **1857** *Putnam's Monthly Mag.* Feb. 173/1 Though his stud was not numerous or choice, it may be said to have been well broken. **1874** *Kennel Club Stud Bk.* 147 A brace of remarkably well-broken pointers.

well-brooked, *a.* Abounding in streams.
1887 MORRIS *Odyss.* XV. 295 And by Crouni was she running, and the well-brooked Chalcis' shore [*Χαλκίδα καλλιρέεθρον*].

well(-)brought-up, *ppl. a.* [See BRING *v.* 27 b.]
1611 COTGR., *Morigené*,.. well brought vp. **1827** EARL MOUNT-EDGCUMBE *Mus. Remin.* (ed. 2) 112 She was the daughter of an English gentleman.., and well brought up. **1861** MILL *Utilit.* iii. 40 An ordinarily well-brought up young person. **1896** MRS. CAFFYN *Quaker Grandmother* 6 She had an adaptable well-brought-up face.

well-browed, *a.* [See WELL-EYED 1483.]

well-browned, *ppl. a.*
1883 'ANNIE THOMAS' *Mod. Housewife* 59 A well-browned crust of bread. **1904** SLADEN *Lovers in Japan* ii. vi, 'Won't a cigarette do?' he asked, pulling out a well-browned leather case.

well-brushed, *ppl. a.*
1817 SCOTT *Chron. Canongate* vi, His clean linen and well-brushed coat. **1835** DICKENS *Sk. Boz, Parl. Sk.*, A well-brushed suit of black.

'well-,bucket. [WELL *sb.*[1] 3.] A bucket used to draw water from a well by means of a rope and pulley or windlass.
Often in pairs, one on each end of a rope, so arranged that the empty bucket descends while the filled one is raised.
1477–9 *Rec. St. Mary at Hill* 82 For a welbokette to harry Williamsons well, and for byndynge of the same, iij s. ij d. **1544** *Inv.* in *Surrey Archæol. Collect.* VII. 240 Itm a Well Bukket w[t] a rope & a Cheyne, xij[d]. **1688** HOLME *Armoury* III. 296/2 He beareth Argent, a Bucket, Sable, the Handle and Hoops, Or. This is termed for distinction, a Well Bucket. **1695** DRYDEN *Dufresnoy's Art Paint., Observ.* 120 The Muscles.. are so many Well-buckets; when one of them acts and draws, 'tis necessary that the other must obey. **1709** *Brit. Apollo* II. No. 6. 3/1 You like two Well-Buckets Appear, Which always must clash when they're near. **1823** COBBETT *Rur. Rides* (1885) I. 326, I saw a large well-bucket, and all the chains and wheels belonging to such a concern.

well-'builded, *ppl. a.* Also 4 -bild. = next.
c **1400** MAUNDEV. ix. (1919) 38 An Abbeye of Monkes wel bylded. *c* **1400** *Destr. Troy* 1569 Grete palis of prise, plenty of houses, Wele bild all aboute on the best wise. **1535** COVERDALE *Jer.* ii. 7 When I had brought you in to a pleasaunt welbuylded londe. *c* **1611** CHAPMAN *Iliad* XVIII. 332 Twentie Tripods.. To set for stooles about the sides of his well-builded hall. **1647** H. MORE *Song of Soul* II. App. xcvi. 215 Saving those few that were kept safe in store In that well builded ship.

well-built, *ppl. a.*
1. Of a house, town, ship, nest, etc.
c **1611** CHAPMAN *Iliad* VI. 14 Axilus, that did dwell In faire Arisbas well-built towres. **1615** —— *Odyss.* XIII. 152 The well-built Ships. **1708** J. PHILIPS *Cyder* I. 196 The bastion of a well-built city. **1822** SHELLEY '*When the Lamp*' 18 When hearts have once mingled, Love first leaves the well-built nest. **1858** W. ELLIS *Madagascar* xii. 329 The houses were all well-built, with clean swept court yards around them. **1872** JENKINSON *Guide Eng. Lakes* (1879) 239 On arriving at the well-built cairn, the prospect is magnificent.
2. *transf.* and *fig.* (e.g. of a person or animal, a suit of clothes, a poem).
1681 FLAVEL *Meth. Grace* xv. 292 This is well-built consolation which reaches the heart. **1706** [see BUILT *ppl. a.* 2]. **1707** PRIOR *Sat. Poets* 125 The Author then, whose daring hopes would strive With well-built Verse to keep his Fame alive. **1749** FIELDING *Tom Jones* I. x, This Gentleman .. was of a middle Size, and what is called well built. **1869** TOZER *Highl. Turkey* I. 269 His tall, well-built figure was shown off to advantage by his magnificent dress. **1881** BESANT & RICE *Chapl. of Fleet* I. iii, She was a strong, well-built woman, of about six or seven and twenty. **1888** 'J. S. WINTER' *Bootle's Childr.* vii, He was wearing a remarkably well-built suit of rough yellowish stuff.
Hence **well-'builtness**. *nonce-wd.*
1899 H. WRIGHT *Depopulation* 2 One saw the city standing out in all its strength of substantial well-builtness.

well-'burnished, *ppl. a.*
1787 BURNS *To W. Creech* 2 Auld chuckie Reekie's sair distress, Down droops her ance weel-burnish't crest.

well-burnt, -burned, *ppl. a.*
1727 DE FOE *Compl. Eng. Tradesman* I. iii. (1732) 33 The brick-maker's men.. turn'd their hands from the grey hard well-burnt bricks to the soft sammel half-burnt bricks. **1827** FARADAY *Chem. Manip.* xiii. (1842) 288 A piece of well-burned charcoal. **1890** J. WATSON *Conf. Poacher* (1893) 115 On a well-burnt moor the best poaching method is by using a silk net.

well-'calculated, *ppl. a.*
1884 J. TAIT *Mind in Matter* 157 Their convictions were matured by well-calculated expedients.

well-calved, *a.*
1744 *Essay on Acting* 14 A.. prominent Chest, and a well-calv'd Leg. **1825** T. HOOK *Sayings* Ser. II. *Man of Many Fr.* (Colburn) 136 A pair of superfine ladies' footmen, with well-calved legs and broad shoulders.

well-'cared-for, *ppl. a.* [See CARE *v.* 3.]
1942 W. FAULKNER *Go down, Moses* 129 He.. watched Lucas cross the Square,.. erect beneath the old, fine, well-cared-for hat. **1959** J. CARY *Captive & Free* 116 An envied minority of cherished, well-bred, well-educated, well-cared-for families. **1979** V. L. PANDIT *Scope of Happiness* xx. 136 A lovely well-cared-for garden.

well(-)carriaged, *a.* See CARRIAGED.

well-carved, *ppl. a.*
1615 CHAPMAN *Odyss.* VIII. 614 Nausicaa..Stood by a well-caru'd Columne of the roome.

well-caulked, *ppl. a.*
1697 DRYDEN *Æneis* IV. 575 And well calk'd Gallies in the Harbour ride. **1969** *Jane's Freight Containers 1968–69* 464/2 Liberal use of adhesives and sealants to provide a well-caulked box.

well-changed, *ppl. a.*
1635–56 COWLEY *Davideis* I. 30 Lo, with pure hands thy heav'enly Fires to take, My well-changed Muse I a chast Vestal make!

well-'characterized, *ppl. a.*
1839 MURCHISON *Silur. Syst.* I. xiv. 176 Further to the south..are flagstones, sandstones, and other well-characterized beds of the system. **1839** DE LA BECHE *Rep. Geol. Cornwall*, etc. ii. 31 Well-characterised hornblende slate.

†**well-cheered,** *a.* *Obs.* Of good cheer, cheerful.
a **1340** HAMPOLE *Psalter* i. 3 God lufis wele chered gifers. **1435** MISYN *Fire of Love* II. viii. 89 þer doutles welcheryd þa sal hym see.

†**well-choosing,** *ppl. a.* *Obs.*
a **1586** SIDNEY *Arcadia* IV. (1922) 110 Neither hath the one any feare, but a well choosing judgement.

†**well-chose,** *ppl. a.* *Obs.* = next.
1682 SHEFFIELD (Dk. Buckhm.) *Ess. Poetry* 139 Of well-chose words some take not care enough. **1751** WESLEY *Wks.* (1872) XIV. 188 Confirm it by a few well-chose arguments.

well(-)'chosen, *ppl. a.* **a.** Carefully or happily selected.
a **1586** SIDNEY *Arcadia* III. (1922) 12 The girle thy well chosen mistresse, perchaunce shall defend thee. **1593** SHAKS. *3 Hen. VI*, IV. i. 7 Heere comes the King. *Rich.* And his well-chosen Bride. **1635–56** COWLEY *Davideis* IV. last line, But, Lo! they 'arriv'ed now at th' appointed place; Well-chosen and well furnisht for the Chase. **1697** WALSH *Dryden's Virgil* Life *4 A well-chosen Library, which stood open to all comers of Learning and Merit. **1711** ADDISON *Spect.* No. 93 ¶10 The Mind never unbends itself so agreeably as in the Conversation of a well chosen Friend. **1755** YOUNG *Centaur* i. 5 Well-chosen Pleasure is a branch of happiness. **1784** COWPER *Task* III. 393 Then to his book, Well chosen, and not sullenly perus'd In selfish silence.
b. esp. of words or language. Freq. in phr. ***a few well-chosen words***, a short and telling speech or piece of writing; also *ironically*.
a **1704** LOCKE *Cond. Underst.* §31 Well-chosen Similies, Metaphors, and Allegories. **1733** *Trav. J. Massey* 21 The Terms in which he express'd himself were strong, and well-chosen. **1828** WHATELY *Rhet.* III. ii. §9. 243 A well-chosen epithet may often suggest..an entire Argument. **1845** LONGF. *Poets & P. Europe* (1871) 600 His language is simple, well-chosen, and beautiful. **1854** *Harper's Mag.* Feb. 423/2 Thomas Carlyle..has excelled all his contemporaries in the graphic pictures which he has painted in a few well-chosen and expressive words. **1912** BEERBOHM *Christmas Garland* 46 You figure him at the gate, shaking hands all round, and speaking perhaps a few well-chosen words about the future. **1957** D. ROBINS *Noble One* xix. 177, I can and shall go down and settle *her* with a few well-chosen words.

well-'circumstanced, *a.* In good circumstances, well off.
1861 M. ARNOLD *Pop. Educ. France* 99 Parents, even the well-circumstanced, receive gladly..this boon of free education for their children.

well(-)clad, *ppl. a.*
1484 CAXTON *Chivalry* vii. (Ellis) 91 To a Knyght apperteyneth..to haue fayr harnoys and to be wel cladde. **1684** *List Military* To Rdr., Four Thousand advantagiously Trained, and well clad Men. *a* **1796** BURNS *As on the banks* 19 When a' my weel-clad banks could see Their woody pictures in my tide. **1907** MCCARTHY *Needles & Pins* xx, You shall be well clad, well weaponed, well horsed.

well-cleansed, *ppl. a.*
1598 CHAPMAN *Seven Iliads* VII. 135 Which when he had infusde Into the greene wel-clensed wound,..the wound did bleede no more.

well-closed, *ppl. a.*
a **1586** SIDNEY *Arcadia* III. (1922) 27 But that it [her breath] hoped to bee drawne in againe to that well cloased paradise. **1656** EARL MONM. tr. *Boccalini's Advts. fr. Parnass.* II. xiv. (1674) 152 Each of them [draws] a Ball from forth a well-closed Urne. **1857** MILLER *Elem. Chem.* III. 18 The dry mass is..transferred to well-closed bottles.

well-clothed, *ppl. a.*
1636 CRASHAW *Temperance* 21 A well-cloth'd soul; that's not opprest Nor choak't with what she should be drest. **1727** SOMERVILLE *Occas. Poems* 353 He bow'd, obey'd, well-cloath'd, well-fed, And with his Patron's Children bred.

well-'coloured, *ppl. a.*
c **1400** [see COLOURED *ppl. a.* 2]. **1445–50** METHAM *Wks.* 92 Qwan the myd lyne ys..euyn and wele colouryd, yt sygnyfyth a mygthi stomake. **1535** COVERDALE *1 Sam.* xvii. 42 He was but a childe, well coloured, and beutyfull to loke vpon. **1591** SHAKS. *1 Hen. VI*, IV. ii. 37 These eyes that see thee now well coloured, Shall see thee withered, bloody, pale, and dead. **1662** CHARLETON *Myst. Vintners* (1675) 184 In which time the Wine usually becomes well-coloured and bright. **1731** POPE *Ep. Burlington* 153 The rich Buffet well-colour'd Serpents grace. **1913** *Oxford Mag.* 6 Nov. 67/1 The author writes..in a well-coloured and original style.

†**well-co'mmended,** *ppl. a.*
1603 R. PRICKET *Souldiers Wish* C 1, For God commands each welcommended means Be vsde to shield a kingdome from extreames.

well-com'pacted, *ppl. a.*
1628 VENNER *Baths of Bathe* 1 Bathe..is a little well-compacted Cittie. **1720** POPE *Iliad* XXII. 6 Advancing o'er the Fields Beneath one Roof of well-compacted Shields. **1725** —— *Odyss.* XXI. 253 At ev'ry portal let some matron wait, And each lock fast the well-compacted gate. **1825** SCOTT *Talism.* iii, The accuracy of proportion displayed in his nervous and well-compacted figure. **1854** MILMAN *Lat. Chr.* III. v. (1864) II. 11 The solid and well-compacted body of Roman law. **1874** GEO. ELIOT *Coll. Breakf.-P.* 815 Close by the stream where well-compacted boats Were moored.

†**well-com'plexioned,** *a.* *Obs.* Having a good complexion (constitution, colour, etc.).
1413 [see COMPLEXIONED 1]. **1622** S. WARD *Life of Faith in Death* (1627) 103 Such soules..as place all their felicitie to be in a full fedde, and well complexioned body. **1635** BRERETON *Trav.* (Chetham Soc.) 105 Proper, personable, well-complectioned men. **1688** COLLIER *Several Disc.* (1725) 15 And yet when Nature seems thus vigorous and strong, thus healthy and well complexion'd, 'twill then sicken, and sink on the sudden. **1715** [see COMPLEXIONED 3].

well(-)com'posed, *ppl. a.*
1606 SHAKS. *Tr. & Cr.* IV. iv. 79 The Grecian youths are ..well compos'd, with guift of nature. **1651** GATAKER *Ridley* in Fuller *Abel Rediv.* 194 His very outward making, promised a well-composed inside. **1792** BURKE *Let. Sir H. Langrishe* Wks. 1907 V. 210 It was a complete system,..well digested and well composed in all its parts.

well-con'cealed, *ppl. a.*
1925 F. SCOTT FITZGERALD *Great Gatsby* vii. 139 He put out his..hand with well-concealed dislike. 'I'm glad to see you, sir.' **1982** *N.Y. Times* 3 Feb. A 8/1 This correspondent visited the wellconcealed underground location of Venceremos radio in the mountains.

†**well(-)con'ceited,** *a.* *Obs.*
1. Displaying good fancy or invention; witty, ingenious.
1597 SHAKS. *2 Hen. IV*, v. i. 39 Well conceited, Dauy. **1598** MARSTON *Sco. Villanie* II. vi. E 6 b, Such straines of well-conceited poesie.
2. Of persons: Having a favourable opinion (*of* a person or thing).
1642 D. ROGERS *Naaman* 227 Weakely..affecting them who have beene..welconceited of me, tender and indulgent. **1649** [see CONCEITED *ppl. a.* 2]. **1673** RAY *Journ. Low C.* Ded., I am not..so well conceited of any Composition..of mine, as to think I shall do you any Honour by this Dedication. *a* **1677** [see CONCEITED *ppl. a.* 2].

well-con'ceived, *ppl. a.*
1836 J. S. MILL in *London Rev.* II. 368 A well-conceived and well-executed work of fiction. **1862** —— *Pol. Econ.* (ed. 5) II. v. ii. 395 Mr. Hubbard..whose well-conceived plan wants little of being..an approximation to a just settlement. **1919** W. S. CHURCHILL *Let.* 20 Jan. in M. Gilbert *Winston S. Churchill* (1977) IV. Compan. I. 472 Executive Heads of well-conceived Branches. **1979** *Jrnl. R. Soc. Arts* Apr. 259/2 The latter Council has gradually built up a series of well-sited, well-conceived and well-run centres.

well-con'certed, *ppl. a.*
1725 POPE *Odyss.* XXIII. 33 With well-concerted art to end his woes. **1742** YOUNG *Nt. Th.* I. 356 Death's subtle seed within..Smil'd at thy well-concerted scheme. **1768–74** TUCKER *Lt. Nat.* (1834) I. 483 Wisdom..pursues invariably one grand and well concerted design. **1846** MRS. A. MARSH *Father Darcy* II. xvii. 282 By a well-concerted opposition and peaceable exposure of their grievances.

well-con'cocted, *ppl. a.*
1676 WISEMAN *Surg.* IV. vi. 324, I opened it by Incision, and discharged a well-concocted Matter. **1697** DRYDEN *Virg. Georg.* Ded., Sobriety in our riper years is the effect of a well-concocted warmth. **1781** COWPER *Truth* 496 The well concocted juice.

well-con'corded, *ppl. a.* Duly harmonized.
1811 *Henry & Isabella* I. 227 Of all the utilities of this well concorded creation, the propriety of calamities..is one of the last which we learn to comprehend.

well-con'ditioned, *a.*
1. Of good disposition, morals, or behaviour; having good 'conditions' or qualities; right-minded.
c **1482** *Monk Evesham* (Arb.) 75 He yat was so honeste of leuyng and wele condycyonde in hys demening. *a* **1500** *Promp. Parv.* 521/1 (MSS. K., H.) Well condiciond or maneryd, *morosus, vel bene morigeratus.* *a* **1500** *Flower & Leaf* 581 Alle that good and wel-condicioned be. **1634** SIR T. HERBERT *Trav.* 30 Their King (then, sixteene yeares old, and well-conditioned). **1814** WORDSW. *Excurs.* v. p. 241 See, in this well conditioned Soul, A Third To match with your good Couple. **1835** POE *Hans Pfaall* (init.), The well-conditioned city of Rotterdam. **1860** EMERSON *Cond. Life, Worship* Wks. (Bohn) II. 398 See what allowance vice finds in the respectable and well-conditioned class. **1865** M. ARNOLD *Ess. Crit.* 285 (*M. Aurelius*) They sincerely regarded it [Christianity] much as well-conditioned people, with us, regard Mormonism. **1880** FROUDE *Bunyan* vii. 91 This book is wrought into the mind and memory of every well-conditioned English or American child. **1905** R. GARNETT *Shaks.* 56 And, for thy full assurance, I have feigned her Contrite and well-conditioned at the last.
2. a. Having a good physical condition; being in a sound, healthy, or satisfactory state.
a **1613** RALEGH *Let. to Pr. Henry* Sceptick, etc. (1651) 128 In a well conditioned Ship, these things are chiefly required. **1622** MABBE tr. *Aleman's Guzman d'Alf.* I. 240 Not a barrell that was missing, and..they were sound and well-conditioned. **1719** DE FOE *Crusoe* II. (Globe) 541 Father Simon..was a jolly well condition'd Man, very free in his Conversation. **1725** *Bradley's Family Dict.* II. s.v. *Sugar*, The other well-condition'd Boilings. **1753–4** RICHARDSON *Grandison* II. xxiii. 172 A pretty estate, which, tho' not large, was well-conditioned, and capable of improvement. **1755** MAGENS *Insurances* II. 5 The Goods are arrived and brought a-shore safe and well-conditioned at Ancona. **1851** MAYNE REID *Scalp Hunters* xxvii. 205 The devoted horse is in fact a well-conditioned animal. **1890** 'R. BOLDREWOOD' *Col. Reformer* xix, Surveying with an eye of satisfaction his ..well-conditioned cattle.
b. *spec.* in *Surg.*
1672 WISEMAN *Wounds* II. iii. 12 If you judge the Wound to be so well conditioned that there is neither fear of Putrefaction nor Mortification. **1676** —— *Surg.* II. i. 165 If the Constitution be good, and the Serum well-conditioned. **1883** OGILVIE (Annandale), *Well-conditioned*,..in *surg.* being in a state tending to health; as, a well-conditioned wound or sore.
c. *Surveying* and *Math.* Such that a small error in measurement or change in data gives rise to only a small change in the calculated result.
1882 J. L. ROBINSON *Treat. Marine Surveying* viii. 141 If the equilateral triangles are not obtainable, then they must be as 'well-conditioned' as possible, i.e. the angles must lie between 30° and 75°. **1952** D. R. HARTREE *Numerical Analysis* viii. 155 The normal equations are less well-conditioned than the original equations. **1973** C. W. GEAR *Introd. Computer Sci.* vi. 261 Is the problem of computing the hypotenuse of a right-angled triangle, given the other two sides, well-conditioned?
3. Established on good terms or conditions.
1645 FULLER *Gd. Th. in Bad T.* IV. vi. 205 A wel-conditioned Peace. **1876** GEO. ELIOT *Deronda* lxviii, An irksome submission to restraint, only made bearable by his thinking of it as a means of by-and-by securing a well-conditioned freedom.

well-con'ducted, *ppl. a.*
1. Properly directed, managed, or carried out.
1749 FRANCIS tr. *Horace, Art P.* 34 *note*, A regular well-conducted Piece. **1752** MASON *Elfrida, Lett. Drama* iii. p. ix, The advantage the Audience receiv'd from a well-conducted Chorus. **1803** CHALMERS in *Life* (1851) I. 479 A series of judicious and well-conducted experiments. **1842** J. AITON *Dom. Econ.* (1857) 185 Hence land, after a well-conducted fallow, is always more productive of good grain than when it has undergone any other preparation. **1884** E. YATES *Recoll.* I. 157 Every well-conducted restaurant nowadays is conducted on these principles.
2. Displaying exemplary conduct, well-behaved.
1838 DICKENS *Nickleby* iv, Whether you consider me a highly virtuous..and well-conducted man in private life. **1853** THACKERAY *Sorrows of Werther* 15 Charlotte..Like a well-conducted person, Went on cutting bread and butter. **1875** JOWETT *Plato* (ed. 2) III. 302 Well-conducted and meritorious citizens.

well(-)co'nnected, *ppl. a.*
1. Linked together in good order or sequence; exhibiting proper sequence or coherence of thought.
1734 BERKELEY *Analyst* ii. 5 When from the distinct Contemplation and Comparison of Figures, their Properties are derived, by a perpetual well-connected chain of Consequences. **1781** JOHNSON *L.P., Milton* I. 262 It [*Samson Agonistes*] wants that power of attracting the attention, which a well-connected plan produces. **1824** [see CONNECTED *ppl. a.* 2].
2. Of good family and connexions.
1840 [see CONNECTED *ppl. a.* 4]. **1856** MISS YONGE *Daisy Chain* I. i, He learnt from other sources that the Ernscliffes were well connected. **1871** LE FANU *Rose & Key* I. xiv. 126 The vicar is a well-connected old gentleman.
absol. **1882** W. S. GILBERT *Iolanthe* I. (*Ballad*), Spurn not the nobly born With love affected, Nor treat with virtuous scorn The well-connected.

well-conned, *ppl. a.*
1808 SCOTT *Marm.* III. Introd. 229 From me, thus nurtur'd, dost thou ask The classic poet's well-conned task?

†**well-'conscienced,** *a.* *Obs.* [WELL *adv.* 32.]
14.. *T. Beckington's Corr.* (Rolls) II. 168 Such wele consyenced persones. **1534** [see CONSCIENCED].

well-con'senting, *ppl. a.*
1715 POPE *Iliad* I. 370 Let both unite, with well-consenting mind.

well-con'sidered, *ppl. a.*
1. That has received due heed or consideration; carefully reflected on.
1769 BURROW *Rep. K.B.* (1776) IV. 2347 A solemn well-considered Determination. **1774** BURKE *Sp. Amer. Tax.* Sel. Wks. 1897 I. 107 We besought the King, in that well-considered address, to inquire into treasons. **1784** COWPER *Task.* v. 75 The cock..waiting at their head With well-consider'd steps. **1860** GEO. ELIOT *Mill on Fl.* III. iii, Mrs. Deane was a thin-lipped woman, who made small well-considered speeches on peculiar occasions. **1865** [see CONSIDERED *ppl. a.* 2].
2. Highly esteemed.
1886 STEVENSON *Kidnapped* xii. 112 He..was a well-considered poet in his own tongue.

well-con'sorted, *ppl. a.*
1590 SPENSER *F.Q.* II. iii. 11 So forth they pas, a well consorted paire.

well-'constituted, *ppl. a.* Of good make or constitution; rightly formed or framed.
a **1763** SHENSTONE *Ess.* Wks. 1768 II. 279 If we should strive to please a well-constituted taste. **1833** J. H. NEWMAN *Arians* II. i. (1876) 145 So reluctant is a well-constituted mind to reflect on its own motive principles. **1836** A. COMBE

Physiol. Digestion (ed. 2) 263 A healthy and well-constituted nurse. **1873** SYMONDS *Grk. Poets* iii. 74 When asked what made an orderly and well-constituted state, Solon answered, 'When the people obey the rulers, and the rulers obey the laws.

well-con'structed, *ppl. a.*
1784 COWPER *Tiroc.* 523 If shrewd, and of a well-constructed brain. **1893** W. S. GILBERT *Utopia (Limited)* I. 25 Oh admirable art! Oh neatly-planned intention! Oh happy intervention—Oh well-constructed plot! **1915** A. J. BALFOUR in M. Gilbert *Winston S. Churchill* (1972) III. Compan. II. 1281 Well-constructed trenches.

Hence **well-con'structedness.**
1975 *Studies in Eng. Lit.: Eng. Number* (Tokyo) 138 The defect of Mr. Halliburton's well-constructed volume, it seems to me, lies in its well-constructedness.

well(-)con'tent, *a.* Highly pleased, gratified, or satisfied.
c **1440** [see CONTENT *a.* 2]. *c* **1489** CAXTON *Sonnes of Aymon* xxvi. 557 Whan rowlande sawe that they were armed, he was not well contente wyth it. **1556** *Extracts Aberd. Reg.* (1844) I. 298 Off the quhilk sowme forsaid I grant me weill content, satisfiit, and pait. **1645** WALLER *Battle Summer Isl.* iii. 32 Now would the men with half their hoped pray Bee well content. **1784** COWPER *Task* III. 805 He that finds One drop of heav'n's sweet mercy in his cup, Can dig, beg, rot and perish, well content, So he may wrap himself in honest rags At his last gasp. **1786** [see CONTENT *a.* 2]. **1864** TENNYSON *En. Arden* 373 So Philip rested with her well-content.

well(-)con'tented, *ppl. a.*
1555 R. POWNALL *Musculus' Temporiser* iii. E j b, Being wel contented to suffre & indure al that the Lord hath ordeined for me, in that behalf. **1600** SHAKS. *Sonn.* xxxii, If thou suruiue my well contented daie. **1611** *Tarlton's Jests* (1638) B 2, The Gentleman noting his mad humour, went his way wel contented: for he knew not how to amend it. *a* **1661** HOLYDAY *Juvenal* xiii. (1673) 238 Then there was no such rout Of gods, as now: a few did serve throughout The well-contented skies. **1842** TENNYSON *Gard. Dau.* 88 From the woods Came voices of the well-contented doves. **1870** MORRIS *Earthly Par.* III. II. 431 Unless The dawn.. should creep Cold-footed o'er their well-contented sleep.

well-con'tenting, *ppl. a.*
1646 TRAPP *Comm. St. John* xxi. 24. 151 Humility.. would chuse to live and dye in its well-contenting secrecy.

well-con'tested, *ppl. a.*
1804 *Oxf. Jrnl.* 28 Jan. 1/2 Wimbledon Common,.. where Belcher has fought many a well-contested round. **1835** DICKENS *Sk. Boz, River,* A well-contested rowing-match on the Thames, is a very lively and interesting scene.

well-con'tinued, *ppl. a.* Diligently carried on or maintained.
1534 MORE *Comf. agst. Trib.* III. xvii. (1553) Q viij b, Howbeit, if this persecucion come, we be by this meditacion and well continued entente and purpose beefore, the better strengthed and confirmed. **1644** MILTON *Educ.* 2 Their untutor'd Anglicisms,.. not to be avoided without a well continu'd and 'udicious conversing among pure Authors.

well-con'trived, *ppl. a.*
1613 ZOUCHE *Dove* B 1 b, Like Natures rarest workmanship, the Eye, The well contriued instrument of seeing. **1622** [see SQUARE *sb.* 20 b]. **1715** LEONI *Palladio's Archit.* (1742) II. 56 The well-contriv'd Stair-case of the Castle of Chambor. **1784** COWPER *Task* III. 603 Nor taste alone and well-contriv'd display Suffice to give the marshall'd ranks the grace Of their complete effect. **1808** FORSYTH *Beauties Scot.* v. 23 A deep large well-contrived ditch secures it from the north.

well-con'trolled, *ppl. a.*
c **1611** CHAPMAN *Iliad* IX. 128 Twelue yong horse, well shap't and well controld.

well-cooked, *ppl. a.*
1611 [see COOK *v.* 2]. **1836** A. COMBE *Physiol. Digestion* (ed. 2) 285 Plain well-cooked animal food, not too recently killed. *a* **1865** MRS. GASKELL *Wives & Dau.* xxviii, Then the meals, light and well-cooked, suited his taste and delicate appetite so much better than [etc.].

well-co-'ordinated, *ppl. a.*
1940 W. FAULKNER *Hamlet* II. ii. 127 Precocious, well-coordinated and quick to learn.. he acquired enough credits in three years to enter college. **1983** *N.Y. Times* 7 May I. 14/5 A buoyant and wellcoordinated performance of the Vivaldi.

well-corked, *ppl. a.*
1774 E. LONG *Jamaica* III. 886 A scorpion, a house-spider, and a cockroach, were put all together for experiment into a well-corked phial.

well-corned, *ppl. a.*
†**1.** Covered with a good crop of corn. *Obs.*
1652 MAYNE tr. *Donne's Epigr.* Paradoxes 98 Glebes, which were long of sun and skie bereav'd, Now the Dutch Plowman sees wel corn'd & sheav'd.

2. Of cereals, beans, peas: Bearing a good head of grain or seeds.
1800, 1861 [see CORNED *a.*[1] 4].

3. Of beef: High-cured by salting.
1772 *Ann. Reg.* 221 While I, half-famished, ev'ry hour Biscuit and well-corn'd beef devour.

4. Exhilarated with liquor. *Sc.* and *dial.*
1825 JAMIESON s.v. CORN *v.* 2.

well-co'rrected, *ppl. a.* Properly disciplined or regulated.
1711 STEELE *Spect.* No. 100 ¶4 When a well-corrected lively Imagination and good Breeding are added to a sweet Disposition.

well-couched, *ppl. a.*
1. Of a structure; Firmly bedded or based.
1538 [see COUCH *v.*[1] 3 b]. **1608** BP. HALL *Char. Virtues & Vices* II. 104 He is the wheele of a well-couched fire-worke, that flies out on all sides, not without scorching it selfe. **1639** [see TRUNCHEON *sb.* 6]. **1675** [see COUCHED *ppl. a.*].

2. Of speech: Skilfully framed or expressed.
1625 K. LONG tr. *Barclay's Argenis* v. i. 325 He, in well-couched Language, beseeches Poliarchus to use his fortune moderately. **1644** MILTON *Educ.* 6 Logic.. with all her well coucht heads and Topics. **1649** —— *Eikon.* iv. 28 Wee have heer.. a neat and well-couch'd invective against Tumults. **1714** MANDEVILLE *Fab. Bees* (1723) I. 158 Whilst harmonious Musick and well-couch'd Flattery entertain his Hearing by Turns.

3. Skilfully or craftily planned.
1671 MILTON *P.R.* I. 97 Not force, but well couch't fraud, well woven snares.

well-'counterfeited, *ppl. a.*
1625 K. LONG tr. *Barclay's Argenis* I. xi. 29 With well-counterfeited griefe.

well-coupled: see COUPLED 3.

well-'covered, *ppl. a.* **a.** In *gen.* use; **b.** *spec.* thickly covered with flesh; hence in *colloq.* use of a person: plump, corpulent; cf. WELL-UPHOLSTERED *ppl. a.*
1697 WALSH *Dryden's Virgil* Life **2 In other Writers there is often well cover'd Ignorance; in Virgil, conceal'd Learning. **1791** BOSWELL *Johnson* an. 1776 (1904) II. 46 My worthy booksellers and friends, Messieurs Dilly in the Poultry, at whose hospitable and well-covered table I have seen a greater number of literary men, than at any other. **1853** SOYER *Pantropheon* 121 They are then cooked without water, in a well-covered vessel. *a* **1865** MRS. GASKELL *Wives & Dau.* xxxiii, Till he had placed him, nothing loth, at the well-covered dining-table. **1884** *Nonconf. & Indep.* 9 May 445/3 Thrusting his elbow into the well-covered ribs of Mr. W. H. Smith. **1943** D. WELCH *Maiden Voyage* xvii. 136 A mild, well-covered person, with crinkly hair and rather piggy eyes. **1972** 'E. FERRARS' *Breath of Suspicion* i. 7 He was rosy, bland and very well-covered.

well-'crafted, *ppl. a.* [CRAFT *v.* 2.]
1976 *Nature* 15 July 169/3 A well-crafted murder mystery. **1983** *Listener* 16 June 29/3 It is gripping, slick, well-crafted and beautifully shot.

well-crammed, *ppl. a.*
1743 BLAIR *Grave* 324 Where are thy boasted implements of art, And all thy well-cramm'd magazines of health?

well-'creamed, *ppl. a.*
1922 JOYCE *Ulysses* 527 Your wellcreamed braceletted hands.

†**well-created,** *ppl. a. Obs.* Noble, valiant. (Cf. obs. F. *bien créé.*)
a **1586** SIDNEY *Arcadia* IV. (1922) 130 She strengthened her well created heart.

well-cress. Now *dial.* [OE. *wyllecærse, -cerse*: see WELL *sb.*[1] and CRESS.] Water-cress, *Nasturtium officinale.*
c **1000** *Sax. Leechd.* I. 140 Seoð mid wylle cærsan [L. *cum fæno græco*]. *c* **1000** *Ags. Voc.* in Wr.-Wülcker 298/16 *Fenegrecio,* wyllecerse. **1393** LANGLAND *P. Pl.* C. VII. 292 Ȝut were me leuere.. lyue by welle-carse(s) þan haue my fode and my fyndynge of false menne wynnynges. **14..** *Voc.* in Wr.-Wülcker 597/24 *Nasturcium,* walcarse. *Ibid.* 712/17 *Hoc nastucium,* welcresse. **1597** in *Spalding Club Misc.* (1841) I. 105 Sche commandit the said Johne.. to eat valcarss. **1808** JAMIESON, *Well-kerses,* water-cresses, called also *wall-* or *well-grass.* **1894** *Northumbld. Gloss.* s.v. *Kars, Watter-kars,* water-cress; also called *well-karses.*

well(-)'crested, *a.* [WELL *adv.* 32.] Furnished with a good crest; *fig.* proud, high-spirited.
1642 HOWELL *For. Trav.* (Arb.) 76 It being the greatest glory of a King, to be King of a free and well-crested people. **1682** *Lond. Gaz.* No. 1768/4 A White grey Roan Gelding,.. well Crested.

well-cropped, *ppl. a.* Bearing a good crop.
1741 RICHARDSON *Pamela* (1824) I. 235 These rich meadows, and well-cropt acres.

well-crushed, *ppl. a.*
1860 GEO. ELIOT *Mill on Fl.* I. xii, The precious inland products, the well-crushed cheese and the soft fleeces.

well-'cultivated, *ppl. a.*
c **1710** CONGREVE tr. *Ovid* Wks. 1730 III. 304 And plenteous Crops of golden Grain are found, Alone, to grace well-cultivated Ground. **1755** SMOLLETT *Quix.* (1803) IV. 221 A student of acute parts, and a well-cultivated understanding. **1781** GIBBON *Decl. & F.* xxx. III. 171 The banks of the Rhine were crowned.. with elegant houses and well-cultivated farms. **1847** MRS. GORE *Castles in Air* I. ix. 181 The thriving, cheering aspect of our well-cultivated kingdom. **1879** MRS. HAWEIS *Art of Dress* 124 We are offending well-cultivated eyes and well-regulated minds.

well-'cultured, *ppl. a.*
1683 J. REID *Scots Gard'ner* (1907) 87 Kitchen-herbes and roots require very fat, light, warme, and well-cultured ground.

†**wellcurds** (also weale, wel-), obs. var. *welled curds*: see WELLED *ppl. a.*
1538 ELYOT *Dict., Schiston,* the mylke that remayneth after that the mylke is sodden, whiche is callyd well courdes. **1565** COOPER *Thesaurus, Schistum,* weale cruddes. **1577** B. GOOGE *Heresbach's Husb.* III. 148 Of the Whay that commeth from the Cheese, being sodde with a soft fyre, tyl the fatnesse of the Cheese swym aloft, are made Welcurdes [*Margin* Wellcurds].

well-cured, *ppl. a.*
1838 DICKENS *O. Twist* xvii (ed. 1), A side of streaky, well-cured bacon. **1875** 'S. BEAUCHAMP' *N. Hamilton* II. 256 The kitchen.. was well furnished, too, with well-cured hams and good thick sides of bacon.

well-curled, *ppl. a.*
1707 MORTIMER *Husb.* 177 See that they [*sc.* sheep].. have a soft greasie well curled close Wooll. **1833** T. HOOK *Parson's Dau.* I. xi, The well-curled damsels, standing at the shop-doors. **1859** *Habits Gd. Society* iv. 186 The feather.. should be full, well-curled, long and firm.

well-'curried, *ppl. a.*
1815 W. H. IRELAND *Scribbleomania* 1 My palfrey a long-ear'd and well-curried ass.

well-curved, *ppl. a.*
1813 VANCOUVER *Agric. Devon* 117 The light Dorset swing-plough.. has a well-curved iron breast.

well-'cushioned, *a.*
1862 MISS YONGE *C'tess Kate* i, Round, white, well-cushioned limbs. **1897** *Westm. Gaz.* 7 May 2/1 So he speedily settles down to his well-cushioned life.

well(-)'customed, *ppl. a.*
1594 PLAT *Jewell-ho.* I. 66 But this [trick of the vintners] is daungerous vnlesse it bee in a house well customed. **1681** *Lond. Gaz.* No. 1578/4 A Large and well customed Inn.

well(-)cut, *ppl. a.*
1635-56 COWLEY *Davideis* IV. 288 His Ephod, Mitre, well-cut Diadem on. *a* **1691** SIR G. MACKENZIE in *Watson's Collect. Sc. Poems* II. (1709) 79 A well cut Cristal, in a richer Case, Covers and Shews at once that Virgin's Face. **1721** in *New Collect. Poems by Prior* etc. (1725) 18 Close, Carver! by some well-cut Books, Let a thin Busto tell; In spight of plump and pamper'd Looks, How scantly Sense can dwell! **1841** EMERSON *Conservative* Wks. (Bohn) II. 274 Your roads are well cut and well paved. **1849** C. BRONTE *Shirley* xi, A well-cut, well-made gown. **1896** H. G. WELLS *Wheels of Chance* x, A well-cut holiday suit.

welld, obs. form of WIELD *v.*

well-'dealing, *ppl. a.* Fair in dealing or business with others.
1590 SHAKS. *Com. Err.* I. i. 7 The rancorous outrage of your Duke, To Merchants our well-dealing Countrimen.

well-dealt, *ppl. a.*
1859 *Habits Gd. Society* v. 191 One well-dealt blow settles the whole matter.

'well-deck. [WELL *sb.*[1] 9 b.] An open space on the main deck of a ship, lying at a lower level between the forecastle and poop; also *attrib.* Hence **'well-decked** *a.*, furnished with a well-deck. Also **'well-,decker,** a ship with a well-deck.
1888 *Daily Tel.* 22 Mar. 2/1 The objection to the well-deck ship is not due to structural form. **1888** *Engineer* 8 June 468/3 Steamers of the 'well-deck' type. **1888** *Iron* 22 June 554 A well-decked steamer of 270 feet length. **1888** *Ibid.* 20 July 65 The *Hurworth* has a poop, long raised quarter-deck, long bridge.., and a topgallant forecastle, leaving only a short well-deck. **1889** *Engineer* 1 Mar. 192/2 A large proportion of the steamers built and owned at West Hartlepool are 'well-deckers'. **1898** KIPLING *Day's Work* 83 The deck amidships, which was a well-deck sunk between high bulwarks.

well(-)decked, *ppl. a.* [DECKED *ppl. a.*]
1. Finely adorned.
? *a* **1500** [see DECKED *ppl. a.* 1]. **1530** PALSGR. 329/1 Well apparayled or well decked, *gorrier.* *c* **1611** CHAPMAN *Iliad* X. 4 As quicke lightnings flie From well-deckt-Iunos soueraigne, out of the thickned skie. **1865** [see DECKED *ppl. a.* 1].

2. Built with a good deck.
1887 MORRIS *Odyss.* IX. 127 The well-decked ships.

†**well-'deeded,** *a. Obs.* [f. WELL *adv.* 32 + DEEDED. Cf. WEL-DEDE.] Characterized by good deeds.
1612 R. CARPENTER *Soule's Sent.* 92 The witnes and inward testimony of a well-deeded life.. will relieue and comfort you in death. **1623** —— *Conscionable Chr.* 69 There is a reward in heauen for all well-deeded Christians prepared. **1650** TRAPP *Comm., Numb.* xxii. 18 A well-spoken and well-deeded person.

†**well-deemed,** *ppl. a. Obs.* Of good report, much accounted of.
1591-5 SPENSER *Colin Clout* 695 By slaundring his well deemed name.

†**well-de'fenced,** *ppl. a. Obs.*
1616 [see DEFENCED]. *a* **1618** RALEGH *Apol. Voy. Guiana* (1650) 15 From hence.. we sayled to Gomarrah, one of the strongest and well defenced places of all the Islands.

well-de'fended, *ppl. a.*
a **1586** SIDNEY *Arcadia* III. xxviii. (1912) 516 Pressing upon Zelmane in such a wel defended manner, that [etc.]. **1603** SHAKS. *Meas. for M.* v. i. 407 Whose salt imagination yet hath wrong'd Your well defended honor. *c* **1611** CHAPMAN *Iliad* XVIII. 244 Vaine entrie seeking vnderneath our well-defended wals. **1697** DRYDEN *Æneis* IX. 933 Soon repuls'd they fly, Or in the well-defended Pass they dye. **1829** SCOTT *Anne of G.* xxxiii, Instead of attempting to secure a well-defended frontier. **1870** BRYANT *Iliad* I. 169 We.. freely will appoint for thee Threefold and fourfold recompense, should Jove Give up to sack this well-defended Troy.

well-deˈfined, *ppl. a.* Clearly indicated, marked, or determined.

1704 NEWTON *Optics* II. I. (1721) 171 When the Rings.. appeared only black and white, they were very distinct and well defined. **1835** J. DUNCAN *Beetles* (Nat. Libr.) 154 A numerous and well-defined family, including nearly 200 known species. **1856** KANE *Arct. Expl.* II. xxviii. 279 There was one well-defined lead which..lost itself to seaward. **1865** LUBBOCK *Prehist. Times* 146 Its well-defined geographical and historical range. **1899** CROCKETT *Kit Kennedy* xxxix. 278 If Kit had looked closely he would have seen that his frankness had brought a well-defined blush to her cheek.

well-deˈlivered, *ppl. a.*

1869 BOUTELL *Arms & Armour* iii. 52 These cuirasses.. were not proof against a well-delivered thrust of the point of sword or spear.

well-deˈmeaned, *ppl. a.* Of good manners or behaviour.

1634 MASSINGER *Very Woman* III. v. (1655) 54 A very handsom fellow, And well demean'd. **1838** HALIBURTON *Clockm.* Ser. II. xii, The young queen..was..well-dressed and well-demeaned.

well(-)deˈrived, *ppl. a.* Of good descent or stock.

1591 SHAKS. *Two Gent.* V. iv. 146 Thou art a Gentleman, and well deriu'd. **1601** —— *All's Well* III. ii. 90 My sonne corrupts a well-deriued nature With his inducement.

well(-)deˈscended, *ppl. a.* Of good descent.

1611 SHAKS. *Cymb.* V. v. 303 Stay, Sir King. This man is better then the man he slew, As well descended as thy selfe. **1650** HEATH *Clarastella* 13 But she is high and well-discended; true; My birth stiles me as freeborn too. **1828** MISS MITFORD *Village* Ser. III. 269 A rich and well-descended country gentleman.

well(-)deˈserved, *ppl. a.* Rightfully merited or earned.

a **1586** SIDNEY *Arcadia* II. xxii. §9 We..caused the wicked Historian to conclude his history, with his owne well-deserued death. **1590** SPENSER *F.Q.* I. vi. 20 The lignage right, From whence he tooke his well deserued name. **1619** DRAYTON *Bar. Wars* II. xliv. 25 Your Bayes must be your well-deserued blame, For your ill actions quench my sacred flame. **1756** C. SMART tr. *Horace* (1826) II. 95 He who derived a well-deserved title from the destruction of Carthage. **1825** SCOTT *Talism.* v, Until his awful judge shall at length appoint the well-deserved sentence to be carried into execution. **1889** J. B. BURY *Later Rom. Emp.* I. 76 The Gildonic war, through which Stilicho won well-deserved laurels.

†**b.** In active sense or loose construction = 'having well deserved it.' *Obs.*

1601 SHAKS. *All's Well* II. i. 192 If I breake time, or flinch in property Of what I spoke, vnpittied let me die, And well deseru'd.

†**well-deˈserver.** *Obs.* One who deserves well (*of* another).

1617 A. NEWMAN *Pleasures Vision* 32 Then well-deseruers well regarded Would be. **1622** F. MARKHAM *Bk. War* I. vi. 22 This Reward of martiall excellence..extended fourth it-selfe, euen to the lowest souldier in his Campe and meanest wel-deseruer. **1697** DRYDEN *Virg. Georg.* Ded., The Court: A place of forgetfulness, at the best, for well deservers. **1709** STEELE & SWIFT *Tatler* No. 70 ¶6, I shall think my self a Well-Deserver of the Church, in recommending all the dumb Clergy to the famous speaking Doctor at Kensington.

†**well-deˈserving**, *vbl. sb. Obs.* Good desert.

1609 BIBLE (Douay) *3 Kings* vi. Contin. Ch. & Relig. 704 Booz..prayed God to render to Ruth a ful reward for her wel deserving. **1620** GAINSFORD *Glory Eng.* II. xxviii. (ed. 2) 331 Whether I flie with the wings of vaine-glorie, in the ampliation of our well deseruing. **1622** WITHER *Faire-Virtue* K4b, Shall a Womans Virtues moue, Me, to perish for her loue? Or, her well-deseruing knowne, Make me quite forget mine owne?

well-deˈserving, *ppl. a.* Highly meritorious or worthy.

1576 FLEMING *Panopl. Epist.* 117 How deepely the common wealth is growne in your debte, for your meritorious and wel deseruing behauiour. **1591** HARINGTON *Orl. Fur.* Apol. Poetrie ¶iij b, Traitors that sell their princes fauours, and rob weldeseruing seruitors of their reward. **1632** LITHGOW *Trav.* II. 66 The..Generals diuided innumerable spoyles, to their well-deseruing Captaines. **1697** DRYDEN *Virg. Georg.* III. 784 Now what avails his well-deserving Toil. **1798** WORDSW. *Peter Bell* 936 Calm is the well-deserving brute.

absol. **1634** SIR T. HERBERT *Trav.* 100 To defend and relieue the distrest and wel-deseruing. **1656** EARL MONM. tr. *Boccalini's Advts. fr. Parnass.* I. v. (1674) 8 Only the most vertuous and well-deserving commanded.

Hence **well-deservingness**.

1631 MABBE *Celestina* xii. 141 The gentlenesse and well-deservingnesse of Melibea.

well-deˈsigned, *ppl. a.*

1709 ATTERBURY *Serm.* (1726) II. 231 The Ill Success, that has been observed to attend well-design'd Charities. **1934** *Archit. Rev.* LXXV. 39/1 Well-designed manufactures are, after all, not so rare in England. **1975** *Language for Life* (Dept. Educ. & Sci.) xxvi. 540 There is evidence in some schools that well-designed measures can be successful.

well-deˈsigning, *ppl. a.*

1716 ADDISON *Free-holder* No. 14 ¶5 Under the name of Tories, I do not here comprehend multitudes of well-designing men, who were formerly included under that denomination, but are now in the interest of his Majesty and the present government.

well(-)deˈsired, *ppl. a.* Much sought after.

1604 SHAKS. *Oth.* II. i. 206 (Hony) you shall be well desir'd in Cyprus.

well-deˈtermined, *ppl. a.*

1905 W. JAMES *Ess. Radical Empiricism* (1912) iv. 128 Its successors differ from it in another well-determined way. **1968** FOX & MAYERS *Computing Methods for Scientists & Engineers* iii. 50 If the problem is well-conditioned the constants of this combination are well-determined.

well-deˈveloped, *ppl. a.*

1835-6 *Todd's Cycl. Anat.* I. 435/2 Well-developed systems of arteries. **1861** MILL *Utilit.* iii. (1863) 49 Any mind, of well developed feelings.

well-deˈvised, *ppl. a.*

1825 SCOTT *Talism.* xv, Some well-devised stratagem. **1861** BROUGHAM *Brit. Const.* v. (1862) 77 A well-devised system of registration.

well(-)dieted, *ppl. a.* Subjected to a good regimen of diet.

1475 J. PASTON in *P. Lett.* III. 142, I may not ete halff inough, when I have most hungyr, I am so well dyettyd. **1599** B. JONSON *Cynthia's Rev.* I. iv. 1 What! the wel-dieted Amorphus become a water-drinker? **1605** [see DIETED *ppl. a.*].

well(-)diˈgested, *ppl. a.*

†**1.** Of good digestion; *fig.* able to assimilate one's learning. *Obs.*

1601 B. JONSON *Poetaster* V. iii, If they should confidently praise their workes, In them it would appeare inflation: Which in a full, and wel-digested man Cannot receiue that foule abusiue name.

†**2.** Fully matured or ripened. *Obs.*

1657 JER. TAYLOR *Disc. Friendship* 12 Some have splendid fires, aromatic spices, rich wines, and well digested fruits. **1768-74** TUCKER *Lt. Nat.* (1834) II. 111 The strong tone of its vessels and its precipitant circulation drive on the juices before well digested, and are apt to throw crudities into the fruit.

3. Carefully and methodically arranged.

1708 J. CHAMBERLAYNE *St. Gt. Brit.* II. III. xi. 540 The College..has..a well digested Library. **1731** *Hist. Lit.* III. 255 At the end of each Volume [is] a copious well-digested Index. **1748** HARTLEY *Observ. Man* I. iii. §2. 354 Regular and well-digested Accounts of the Phaenomena of the Natural World.

4. Carefully pondered or thought out.

1768-74 TUCKER *Lt. Nat.* (1834) II. 284 Each man, whatever his peculiar notions be, if he has any serious well-digested ones, may find something in them, which [etc.]. **1826** *Art Brewing* (ed. 2) Pref., The well-digested plan which the large brewers have acted upon. **1867** A. BARRY *Sir C. Barry* viii. 281 A scheme..which will probably be thought to show well-digested principle.

well(-)diˈrected, *ppl. a.* Aimed, addressed, guided, conducted, with skill and care.

a **1586** SIDNEY *Arcadia* III. xi. §2 With a number of well directed Pioners. **1694** LOCKE *Hum. Und.* II. xx. §18 (ed. 2) 123 The pleasure..of well directed study in the search..of Truth. **1743** FRANCIS tr. *Hor., Odes* III. ii. 3 To hurl the well-directed spear. **1768-74** TUCKER *Lt. Nat.* (1834) II. 606 Any well-directed industry. **1781** COWPER *Expost.* 239 They breath'd in faith their well directed pray'rs. **1800** *Hull Advertiser* 7 June 2/4 The Penelope..whose well-directed fire..had shot away the main and mizentopmasts. **1836** A. COMBE *Physiol. Digestion* (ed. 2) 279 The power we possess of modifying the constitution by well-directed regimen is very great. **1855** MACAULAY *Hist. Eng.* xii. III. 236 The Dartmouth poured on them a well directed broad-side. *a* **1871** GROTE *Eth. Fragm.* ii. 36 If..we..explain it only as a well-directed choice and discretion on the part of the individual.

well(-)ˈdisciplined, *ppl. a.*

1. Kept under good discipline; strictly trained or controlled.

1595 [LEWKENOR] *Estate Engl. Fugitives* Riv, Like wel disciplined souldiours that keepe still good and warie watch, though they be neuer so farre from the enemie. **1642** EARL OF CORK in Earl Orrery *St. Lett.* (1742) 8 These seasoned and well disciplined companies. **1702** J. DENNIS *Ess. Navy* title-p., England's Advantage and Safety, prov'd Dependant on a Formidable and well-Disciplined Navy. **1768-74** TUCKER *Lt. Nat.* (1834) II. 339 A well-disciplined imagination. **1849** MACAULAY *Hist. Eng.* v. I. 528 The power of self-government which is characteristic of men trained in well disciplined camps to command and to obey. **1849** C. BRONTE *Shirley* x, At first sight, all but peculiarly well-disciplined minds were apt to turn from her with annoyance.

2. Soundly flogged.

1659-60 *Arsy Versy* vi, It did now, like a Truant's well-disciplined Bum, With the rod of affliction harder become.

well-disˈguised, *ppl. a.*

1724 FIDDES *Morality* Pref. p. lxxv, What we term public spiritedness..is nothing more than a refined and well-disguised hypocrisy.

well-diˈspersed, *ppl. a.*

1732 POPE *Ep. Bathurst* 236 In heaps, like Ambergrise, a stink it lies, But well-dispers'd, is Incense to the Skies.

well(-)diˈsposed, *ppl. a.*

†**1.** In good physical condition, healthy. *Obs.*

c **1386** [see DISPOSED 2]. **1398** TREVISA *Barth. De P.R.* v. xli. (1495) 157 Yf these [organs] ben in good state and yf they ben hoole and well dysposed, the beest is al hoole. **1422** YONGE tr. *Secreta Secret.* 247, I shall you say shortely What thynges makyth the body fat, moiste, and well dysposid. **1690** LOCKE *Hum. Und.* II. xxix. §4 Such a full and evident perception as it [the mind] does receive from an outward object operating duly on a well-disposed organ. *a* **1716** SOUTH *Serm.* (1842) III. 475 An healthful body and a sound mind, vigorous faculties and well-disposed organs.

†**b.** Of reason: ? Sound, sane. *Obs.*

c **1449** PECOCK *Repr.* II. iii. 148 Wherfore no doom of weel disposid resoun reproueth and weerneth the seid hauyng and vsing of ymagis in the chirche.

†**c.** Of the weather: ? Temperate, fair. *Obs.*

c **1477** CAXTON *Jason* 54 b, The fayr sonne shone clere.. and the weder was softe and well disposed.

2. Suitably or skilfully placed, arranged, or adjusted.

c **1470** ASHBY *Active Policy* 307 Be ye rather clept an executer Of wisdam..Than to be proclamed a wise speker, ..Of bothe, weldisposed, fame shal arise. **1576** R. PETERSON *G. della Casa's Galateo* 71 Long and continued talke: which would be well disposed, wel vttered & very wel set forth. **1725** *Bradley's Family Dict.* s.v. *Vine*, To plant an Acre of such Ground with Vines, in some well-disposed place on the declivity of an Hill. **1748** MELMOTH *Fitzosborne Lett.* lxi. (1749) II. 116 The grace and harmony of well-disposed lights and shades.

3. Of a good disposition; *esp.* disposed to be friendly or favourable, well-affected.

1455 *Rolls of Parlt.* V. 325/1 Every wele disposed persone of yis lande. **1456** *Paston Lett.* I. 392 The Comons of Kent ..er not all weel disposid. **1542** UDALL *Erasm. Apoph.* 15 b, An honeste or weldisposed manne. **1570** ELVIDEN *New Yr.'s Gift* (Huth 1875) Bij, Though the wicked syer Shoulde seeme for to prouoke His well disposed sonne to yll. *a* **1586** SIDNEY *Arcadia* II. xvii. (1912) 259 A certain sparke of honour, which rose in her well-disposed minde, made her feare to be alone with him, with whom alone she desired to be. **1593** SHAKS. *Rich. II*, II. i. 206 You loose a thousand well-disposed hearts. **1622** WITHER *Faire-Virtue* K4b, Should my heart be grieud..Cause I see a Woman kind? Or a well disposed Nature, Ioyned with a louely Feature? **1660** F. BROOKE tr. *Le Blanc's Trav.* 286, I was in a humour so well disposed that I accepted very willingly. **1665** BOYLE *Excell. Theol.* (1674) 139 Studious and well-dispos'd Readers may certainly understand such [truths] as are necessary for them to believe. **1709** SHAFTESB. *Charac.* (1711) II. 74 While he..stands so well-dispos'd towards the Laws and Government of his higher Country. **1776** ADAM SMITH *W.N.* I. ii, The charity of well disposed people.. supplies him with the whole fund of his subsistence. **1815** SCOTT *Guy M.* lii, An obliging, well-disposed, and civil neighbour of mine. **1856** *N. Brit. Rev.* XXVI. 95 The Government should have done their best to secure a well-disposed House.

absol. **1659** SOUTH *Serm.* (1679) 72 The Unprepossessed on the one hand, and the well disposed on the other. **1861** BROUGHAM *Brit. Const.* xv. 235 The indolence and timidity of the well-disposed enabled the enemies of the people to prevail.

Hence **well-diˈsposedness.** *rare.*

1621 BP. HALL *Heaven upon Earth* §10 By a well-disposednesse of mind, we may correct the iniquity of all hard euents.

well-diˈsputed, *ppl. a.*

1697 DRYDEN *Æneis* VIII. 902 Amid the Main, two mighty Fleets engage Their Brazen Beaks;..Actium surveys the well disputed Prize. **17..** CONGREVE *Homer's Hymn to Venus* Wks. 1730 III. 369 The Martial Maid..O'er War presides, and well-disputed Fights. **1728** POPE *Dunciad* II. 245 This well-disputed game.

well-diˈssected, *ppl. a.*

1708 J. PHILIPS *Cyder* I. 353 Thy Specular Orb Apply to well-dissected Kernels.

well-diˈssembled, *ppl. a.*

1693 *Dryden's Juvenal* iv. (1697) 84 Unhappy Youth! whom from his destin'd End, No well-dissembled Madness could defend. **1697** DRYDEN *Æneis* III. 394 The Grove it self resembles Ida's Wood; And Simoïs seem'd the well dissembl'd Flood. **17..** CONGREVE *Homer's Hymn to Venus* Wks. 1730 III. 370 While to conceal the Theft from Juno's Eyes, Some well-dissembled Shape the God belies. **1746** THOMSON *Spring* 383 The well-dissembled fly, The rod fine-tapering with elastic spring. **1765** COLMAN *Terence, Andrian* I. i. 15 Then! there! the frighted Pamphilus betrays His well-dissembled and long-hidden love. **1817** SCOTT *Ivanhoe* xiv, The cup went round amid the well-dissembled applause of the courtiers.

well-diˈstinguished, *ppl. a.*

1706 WATTS *Horæ Lyr.* (1727) 70 Lo, from afar the promis'd Day Shines with a well-distinguish'd Ray. **1878** STUBBS *Const. Hist.* III. xxi. 538 Servants, all arranged in well-distinguished grades.

well-diˈvided, *ppl. a.*

1606 SHAKS. *Ant. & Cl.* I. v. 53 He was nor sad nor merrie. *Cleo.* Oh well diuided disposition. **1634-40** HABINGTON *Castara* (Arb.) 21 If the Swans of Thames..Oth' sudden heare thy well-divided breath. [Cf. DIVIDE *v.* 11.]

well-ˈdocumented, *ppl. a.* Supported or attested by much documentary evidence.

1937 *Burlington Mag.* Apr. 156/1, 1465, in which year he [*sc.* Bellini] produced his first well-documented painting. **1946** *Nature* 30 Nov. 770/1 Well-documented studies of the Tehuelche and Puelche of Patagonia. **1978** *Jrnl. R. Soc. Med.* LXXI. 697/1 The well-documented increases in prescribing represent therapeutic irresponsibility.

well-doer (ˈwɛlˌduːə(r)). One who does well; one who lives virtuously or acts uprightly.

c **1450** *Mirk's Festial* 1 To bryng..weldoers to þe blys þat euer schall last. **1530** PALSGR. *Ep. to King* p. iv, Well doers in any kynde of vertue. **1648-58** HEXHAM II. s.v. *Wel, Een wel-doender, oft wel-dader*, a Benefactour or a Well-doer. **1684** *Contempl. St. Man* I. v. (1699) 51 Who is so general a well-doer, that no Body complains of him. **1961** NEW ENG. BIBLE *John* iii. 11 The well-doer is a child of God; the evil-doer has never seen God.

well-doing ('wɛl,duːɪŋ), *vbl. sb.*

1. The action or practice of doing good; virtuous life and behaviour.

1414 BRAMPTON *Penit. Ps.* (Percy Soc.) 62 Slownes is a cursid thing: For it is evere weri of weel doyng. *c* **1450** *Knt. de la Tour* 3 Ladies..that..were..honoured..for her weldoinge and goodnes. **1526** TINDALE *2 Thess.* iii. 13 Brethren be not weary in well doynge. **1574** HAKE *Touchstone* E i b, Of sinne commeth death: Of wel doing commeth life. **1663** PATRICK *Parab. Pilgr.* xv. (1687) 128 He suffered for well doing, and we for ill. **1736** BUTLER *Anal.* I. iii. Wks. 1874 I. 59 We are so made, that well-doing as such gives us satisfaction. **1824** SCOTT *St. Roman's* xiv, Laugh at your ain toom pouches—it will be lang or your weel-doing fill them. **1883** WHITELAW *Sophocles, Antigone* 703 Welldoing and fair fame of sire to son, Of son to sire, is noblest ornament.

†**b.** Valour, martial prowess. *Obs.*

c **1450** *Merlin* xxvii. 550 But the cristin ne myght but litill space endure, ne hadde be the well doinge of the v knyghtes of the reame of logres.

c. *pl.* Good deeds or actions.

1552 LATIMER *Serm., 1st Sund. Epiph.* (1584) 300 b, Seeing wee shall haue no rewarde for our well doynges.

2. Thriving condition; health, prosperity, welfare, success.

1387–8 T. USK *Test. Love* II. x. 120 In hope of weldoing, and of getting agayn the double of thy lesing. **1557** Q. MARY in Mary A. E. Wood *Lett. Roy. Ladies* (1846) III. 313 The lady Latimer, who, of a natural and motherly affection, doth tender the well-doing of her said daughter, hath been of late an humble suitor unto us for our letter, desiring [etc.]. **1579** *Manutius' Phrases Lat.* (1595) 154 Your welfare and weldoing reioyceth me as much as mine owne. **1625** LD. MOUNTAGU in *Buccleuch MSS.* (Hist. MSS. Comm.) I. 262 We are glad to hear of your well doing. **1659** B. HARRIS *Parival's Iron Age* 215 He began to make head again, and was in a way of well-doing, when he received the Kings command to disband. **1763** MILLS *Syst. Pract. Husb.* II. 415 For..the increase and well-doing of the plants. **1800** WORDSW. *Michael* 432 A good report did from their Kinsman come, Of Luke and his well-doing. **1854** *Poultry Chron.* II. 338 Houses..for fatting wild fowl,..whose well-doing was so considered, that [etc.]. **1924** ROSE MACAULAY *Orphan Island* ix. 93 'Our ten [children] have done well.'.. 'They certainly..seem to have had a fairly large allowance of descendants apiece, if that is well-doing.'

'well-,doing, *ppl. a.*

1. That does good or acquits oneself well; †valiant; diligent in performance of work or duty; well-behaved, respectable.

c **1330** *Arth. & Merl.* (Kölbing) 4773 Four score..Hardi & wele doinde kniȝtes. **1597** SHAKS. *Lover's Compl.* 112 And controuersie hence a question takes, Whether the horse by him became his deed, Or he his mannadg, by th' wel doing Steed. **1612** T. TAYLOR *Comm. Titus* ii. 1, 331 That his Master may find him doing, yea welldoing. **1822** BYRON *Heaven & Earth* I. iii, I am safe, not for my own deserts, but those Of a well-doing sire, who hath been found Righteous enough to save his children. **1888** D. GRANT *Sc. Stor.* 76 Sic an honest, weel-daen woman as I kent my wife to be!

2. *Sc.* Well-to-do, prosperous, thriving.

1821 GALT *Ann. Parish* v. 59 He was a douce and discreet man, fair and well-doing in the world. **1897** 'L. KEITH' *My Bonny Lady* vii. 67 'Do you know nothing of her folk?' 'Nothing, forby that they are well-doing in the world.'

well(-)done ('wɛl'dʌn), *ppl. a.*

†**1.** Wise, prudent, virtuous. *Obs.*

c **1200** *Trin. Coll. Hom.* 29 Ðu ert wel don man, and þarto wurðlich. *c* **1205** [see YDO(N].

2. a. Skilfully or rightly performed or executed.

c **1449** PECOCK *Repr.* II. viii. 190 It is a merytorie and a weel don deede. **1479** *Cely Papers* (Camden) 22 Hyt wher whell-doyn to enqwer..how he mythet be payd. **1601** SHAKS. *Twel. N.* I. v. 253 We will draw the Curtain, and shew you the picture..Ist not well done? **1606** —— *Ant. & Cl.* v. ii. 328–9 What worke is heere Charmian? Is this well done? *Char.* It is well done, and fitting for a Princesse. **1890** *Hardwicke's Sci.-Gossip* XXVI. 82 This is a clear and well-done translation. **1900** *Westm. Gaz.* 5 May 2/1 A well-done landscape of late autumn.

b. as an exclamation, expressing approval of what some one has done.

c **1460** *Towneley Myst.* xvi. 347 *Secundus Miles.* Well done! **1538** ELYOT *Dict., Euge*, well done. **1611** BIBLE *Matt.* xxv. 21 Well done, thou good and faithfull seruant. **1771** SMOLLETT *Humphry Cl.* 3 Oct., Well done, my dear boy!—O bravo! **1791** BURNS *Tam o' Shanter* 189 Tam..roars out, 'Weel done, Cutty-sark!' **1875** JOWETT *Plato* (ed. 2) I. 243 *Ion.* I obtained the first prize of all, Socrates. *Soc.* Well done.

c. quasi-*sb.* The utterance of this exclamation, as an expression of commendation.

1628 EARLE *Microcosm., Self-conceited Man* (Arb.) 32 Two excellent well-dones haue vndone him. **1790** *Proc. African Assoc.* 42 A single well-done from your Association has more worth in it to me, than all the trappings of the East. **1840** R. H. DANA *Two Yrs. bef. Mast* xi. (1854) 49 Fortunately I got through without any word from the officer, and heard the 'well done' of the mate, when the yard reached the deck.

†**d.** quasi-*sb.* What is well done. (In quot. personified.) *Obs.*

1602 WARNER *Alb. Eng.* IX. lii. 236 And curious thay That, dribling Almes by Arte, disband wel-Meant from wel-Dons pay.

3. Of meat: Thoroughly cooked.

1747 H. GLASSE *Art of Cookery* i. 4 Pork must be well done, or it is apt to Surfeit. **1846** SOYER *Gastron. Regen.* p. xxi, Veal and pork must be well done. Venison must be underdone.

well-'dowered, *ppl. a.*

1822 SCOTT *Nigel* iii, Unless you think rather of taking a pretty, well-dowered English lady. **1871** B. TAYLOR *Faust* II. III. 253 Then each shall dwell in homes well-dowered.

well-'drained, *ppl. a.*

1871 W. ROBINSON *Subtropical Garden* II. 198 A well-drained, sandy soil..is the best for this plant. **1912** J. W. WHITE *Flora of Bristol* 251 The well-drained banks of railway lines. **1960** *Farmer & Stockbreeder* 15 Mar. (Suppl.) 10/3 Most herbs will grow in any ordinary well-drained ground.

well(-)drawn, *ppl. a.*

1. Skilfully delineated. Also of the human form: Well modelled or proportioned.

1679 C. NESSE *Antichrist* Ded., As a dark soil in a well drawn picture. **1709** SHAFTESB. *Moralists* I. iii. 30 Not captivated by the Lineaments of a fair Face, or the well-drawn Proportions of a human Body. **1855** KINGSLEY *Glaucus* 162 Two little 'Popular' Histories..furnished..with well-drawn and coloured plates.

2. Strongly stretched, straightened out, etc.

1725 POPE *Odyss.* VIII. 262 In fighting fields as far the spear I throw, As flies an arrow from the well-drawn bow. **1864** *Jrnl. R. Agric. Soc.* XXV. 363 A thick coat of well-drawn dry wheat-straw is then laid over them [*sc.* the potatoes].

well(-)dressed, *ppl. a.*

1. Clothed in good and becoming attire.

1576 R. PETERSON *G. della Casa's Galateo* 20 They be neuer redie: euer a trimming: neuer well dressed to their mindes. **1712–14** POPE *Rape of Lock* ii. 5 Fair Nymphs and well-drest Youths around her shone. **1791** BOSWELL *Johnson* 19 Sept. 1777, A well-drest elderly housekeeper..shewed us the house. **1849** JAMES *Woodman* iv, This was no well-dressed and splendid assemblage. **1876** EMERSON *Lett. & Soc. Aims* ii. Wks. (Bohn) III. 177 The lady who declared 'that the sense of being perfectly well-dressed gives a feeling of inward tranquillity which religion is powerless to bestow'.

2. Properly prepared, cultivated, trimmed, cooked, etc.

1693 CONGREVE *Juv.* Sat. xi. 136 Scarce a Slave, but has to Dinner now, The well-dress'd Paps of a fat pregnant Sow. **1768** BOSWELL *Corsica* (ed. 2) 280 At dinner we had no less than twelve well-drest dishes. **1771** *Encycl. Brit.* (ed. 1) II. 211/2 The wool must be of a good quality, and well dressed. **1799** J. ROBERTSON *Agric. Perth* 465 The sloping banks of the Tay are finely wooded, with well-dressed walks on the top. *Ibid.* 470 Surrounded with well dressed fields to the south.

well-dried, *ppl. a.*

c **1624** CHAPMAN *Hymn to Hermes* 93 Seuen strings, of seuerall tunes,..Made of the Entrailes of a sheepe well dried. **1728** E. S[MITH] *Compleat Housew.* (ed. 2) 133 Then put in three quarters of a pound of Flour well dried. **1765** *Museum Rust.* IV. 467 The most proper fuel..for drying the flax, is either charcoal, or well-dried turf. **1880** C. R. MARKHAM *Peruv. Bark* xx. 225 At least 100,000 well-ripened and well-dried seeds were now gathered.

well-drilled, *ppl. a.* [See DRILL *v.*³]

1. Thoroughly trained, exercised, or disciplined.

1817 LADY MORGAN *France* I. 53 A certain mechanical immobility of the well-drilled countenances. **1864** BURTON *Scot Abr.* I. iv. 170 Immediately afterwards Richelieu handed over a well-drilled territory to Louis XIV. **1878** *N. Amer. Rev.* CXXVII. 257 Its vast and well-drilled army of Jesuits.

2. Skilfully pierced or perforated.

1873 W. PENGELLY *Cave Men Devon.* in *Manchester Sci. Lect.* Ser. v. & VI. 125 A bone needle with a well-drilled eye in it. **1896** KIPLING *Seven Seas, Story of Ung* 31 No store of well-drilled needles.

well-'driven, *ppl. a.*

1605 B. JONSON *Volpone* III. viii. (1607) H 3 b, *Mos.* O, that his well-driu'n sword Had beene so curteous to haue cleft me downe, Vnto the nauill, ere I liu'd to see [etc.]. *c* **1611** CHAPMAN *Iliad* XI. 386 This said, he threw quite through his shield, his fell and well-driuen lance.

well-dunged, *ppl. a.*

1577 GOOGE *Heresbach's Husb.* I. 33 b, The Beane delighteth in riche and wel dounged ground. **1760** R. BROWN *Compl. Farmer* II. 61 Barley, which delights in a well-dunged soil.

well-'dying, *vbl. sb.*

1633 EARL MANCH. *Al Mondo* (1636) 77 Seldome doth hee dye well that lives ill; therefore in the course of your life practise well doing, and, at parting you shall haue the comfort of well dying. **1693** *D'Emilianne's Hist. Monast. Orders* 209 Of the Order of the Fathers of Well-dying.

well-'dying, *ppl. a.*

1633 EARL MANCH. *Al Mondo* (1636) 104 But to assure there are joyes in Death, what saith the Scripture to well-dying men?

welle, obs. form of WEEL.

well(-)earned, *ppl. a.* Fully deserved or due; merited or acquired by good work or behaviour.

1730–46 THOMSON *Autumn* 343 The big hopes And well-earned treasures of the painful year. **1749** WARTON *Tri. Isis* 61 To wear the well-earn'd wreath that merit brings. **1814** WORDSW. *Excurs.* VIII. 593 The ruddy boys Withdrew, on summons to their well-earned meal. **1855** MACAULAY *Hist. Eng.* xi. III. 75 Yet William might have had a more tranquil reign if he had postponed for a time the well earned promotion of his chaplain. **1855** PALEY *Æschylus* (1861) Pref. vi, Its well-earned character for practical utility and careful editorial supervision. **1856** FROUDE *Hist. Eng.* II. viii. 305 No pirate who ever swung on a well-earned gallows had committed darker crimes.

welled, *ppl. a.*¹ [f. WELL *v.*¹ + -ED¹.]

†**a.** Of metal: Molten, cast. Also ***welled together***, rendering L. *conflatilis*. *Obs.*

c **1300** *Seyn Julian* 54 A chetel wol of iwelled bras biuore þis maide was ibroȝt. **1382** WYCLIF *Hab.* ii. 18 A wellid thing to gidre [Vulg. *conflatile*], and a fals ymage. *c* **1440** *Promp. Parv.* 520/2 Wellyd, as metel, *fusus*. *c* **1449** PECOCK *Repr.* II. vi. 173 And thilk ymage is clepid there a graued thing, and a wellid to gidere thing.

b. Of milk: Boiled, curdled. Of curds: Coagulated. Cf. WELLCURDS. *Obs.* exc. *dial.*

c **1420** *Liber Cocorum* 53 Melle white brede in dysshes aboute, Powre in wellyd mylke. *c* **1440** *Promp. Parv.* 520/2 Wellyd, as mylke, *coagulatus, concoctus*. **1552** HULOET, Welled curdes, *s[c]histon*. **1750** W. ELLIS *Mod. Husbandm.* III. I. viii. 138 From the Whey, if set on the Fire, will arise wild Curds by putting new Milk and sour Butter-milk to it. **1879** *Shropsh. Word-bk.* s.v. *Walled*, I toud yo' to wesh 'em i' the walled w'ey.

welled, *ppl. a.*² [f. WELL *sb.*¹ + -ED².]

1. Having a well or hollow on the surface, pitted.

1848 HARDY in *Proc. Berw. Nat. Club* II. 337 A series of ill-defined welled depressions. **1855** tr. *Labarte's Arts Mid. Ages* p. xxix, A broad flat border, with a welled centre, characterise this class of plates.

2. Having a tank or cistern in which fish are carried or preserved alive.

1864 *Rep. Comm. Sea Fisheries* (1866) II. 456 In the year 1712, at Harwich,..welled smacks were first constructed, suitable for fishing in the North Sea for cod-fish, &c. **1870** *Pall Mall Gaz.* 24 Aug. 4 Your fish..are brought to the city alive in welled fishing boats. **1874** H. MAYHEW *Lond. Characters* 335 These salmon mostly come..in welled steamers.

well-edged, *a.* Having a sharp edge.

1615 CHAPMAN *Odyss.* XI. 57 Then drew I from my Thy, My well-edg'd sword.

well-'educated, *ppl. a.*

1588 SHAKS. *L.L.L.* I. ii. 99 Define, define, well educated infant. **1704** SWIFT *T. Tub* iv. 103 Whoever went to take him by the Hand in the Way of Salutation, Peter with much Grace, like a well educated Spaniel, would present them with his Foot. **1828** LYTTON *Pelham* I. ii, I was reckoned an uncommonly well-educated boy. **1885** W. H. WHITE *M. Rutherford's Deliv.* iv, She was attractive and well-educated.

well-em'bodied, *ppl. a.*

1776 BRYANT *Anc. Mythol.* III. 55 Firm to their cause the Titans wide display'd A well-embodied phalanx. **1876** GEO. ELIOT *Deronda* vi, Being the outcome of a happy, well-embodied nature.

well-en'dowed, *ppl. a.* **a.** *gen.*

1690 LOCKE *Hum. Und.* IV. iii. §20 Whilst the Desire of Esteem, Riches, or Power, makes Men espouse the well-endow'd Opinions in fashion. **1809** MALKIN *Gil Blas* v. i. ¶65, I found myself a well-endowed widow. **1870** HULLAH *Speaking Voice* 4 A well-endowed but incomplete vocalist. **1876** GEO. ELIOT *Deronda* lviii, In Rex's well-endowed nature..the passionate stirring had gone deep.

b. *spec.* with reference to sexual potency or size of sexual organs. *colloq.*

1951 N. MONTSARRAT *Cruel Sea* v. 302 'I'm not rich.'.. 'You are doubtless well-endowed... It's better, really... A lot of women think so.' **1968** in H. & R. Greenwald *Sex Life Lett.* (1974) 79 By the age of ten, my member was already larger than that of a well-endowed adult. **1983** *Maledicta 1982* VI. 157 He says he has been well endowed and you must know this means 'heavily equipped sexually'.

†**well-'entered**, *ppl. a.* Duly initiated.

1601 SHAKS. *All's Well* II. i. 6 'Tis our hope sir, After well entred souldiers, to returne And finde your grace in health.

‖**Wellentheorie** ('vɛlənteori). *Philol.* [G., f. *welle* wave + *theorie* THEORY¹.] The theory that linguistic changes spread like waves over a speech-area and the dialects of adjacent districts resemble each other most; = *wave theory* (*b*) s.v. WAVE *sb.* 10.

1939 L. H. GRAY *Foundations of Lang.* ii. 42 To account for the spread and relationship of languages, two main hypotheses have been advanced, both, it is true, primarily for the Indo-European group, but, in principle, equally applicable to all others. These are the *pedigree-theory* (*Stammbaumtheorie*) advanced by August Schleicher in 1866 and the *wave-theory* (*Wellentheorie*) proposed by Johannes Schmidt in 1872. **1964** R. H. ROBINS *Gen. Linguistics* viii. 349 The theory of common characteristics resulting from the spreading of linguistic features 'in waves' over adjacent dialects within a family is called the 'Wellentheorie'. **1965** [see STAMMBAUM]. **1975** *Amer. Speech 1971* XLVI. 254 Real change..may in some sense be systematic (as in the analysis of style and social variables and the Wellentheorie of linguistic geographers).

well-en'titled, *ppl. a.* Obtained by good title.

1675 BROOKS *Golden Key* Wks. 1867 V. 519 The crown of life notes a well-entitled crown; a crown that comes by a true and noble title.

well-en'trenched, *ppl. a.*

1929 W. S. CHURCHILL *World Crisis* V. xix. 432 We had a rather restricted but well-entrenched and well-wired position. **1979** P. BUCKLAND *Factory of Grievances* v. 108 A handful of well-entrenched free-traders.

well-e'quipped, *ppl. a.*

a **1854** MILL *Early Draft Autobiogr.* (1961) 120 A well-equipped ship. **1875** J. FORREST *Explor. Australia* 79 A well-equipped vessel might have landed explorers at various points. **1890** *Hardwicke's Sci.-Gossip* XXVI. 254/2 A well-equipped observatory.

† **'weller.** *Obs.* Also 6 **wellar.** [f. WELL *v.*¹]

1. A caster or founder (of metal).

1388 WYCLIF *Jer.* vi. 29 Leed is waastid in the fier, the wellere [Vulg. *conflator*] wellide in veyn. *Ibid.* li. 17 [see WELLING *vbl. sb.* 2]. **1547** *Acts Privy Council* (1890) II. 445 The master wellar at xij^d the daye, and iij wellars with him at viij^d the daye.

2. A salt-boiler.

c **1440** *Promp. Parv.* 441/1 Saltare, or wellare of salt, *salinator.* [**1624**: see SALTWELLER.]

Wellerism ('wɛlərɪzm). Also **wellerism.** [f. the surname *Weller* (see below) + -ISM.] A speech or expression employed by, or typical of Sam Weller or his father, two celebrated characters in Dickens's *Pickwick Papers*; usu. *spec.*, a form of comparison in which a familiar saying or proverb is identified, often punningly, with what was said by someone in a specified but humorously inapposite situation.

1839 *Boston Morning Post* 9 Jan. 2/2 *Wellerisms.*—'It does one's heart good to look at you,' as the fox said to the chickens, when he found he couldn't get over the barn-yard wall, to eat them. **1854** *Yankee Notions* III. 142 (*heading*) Phrenological Wellerisms. **1886** (*title*) Wellerisms from 'Pickwick' and 'Master Humphrey's Clock'. **1931** A. TAYLOR *Proverb* IV. 219 Wellerisms involving a temporal clause, e.g. '*Much noise and little wool,' said the Devil when he sheared a pig*, are largely used of women. **1959** [see *knock-knock* sb., v., and int. s.v. KNOCK-.] **1975** *New Society* 25 Dec. 685/1 Sam Weller has joined Dr Spooner and fathered the wellerism: 'Meet you at the corner as one wall said to another,' but the wellerism can also be transformed into a riddle.

Also **Welleresque** (wɛlə'rɛsk), **Wellerian** (wɛ'lɪərɪən), *adjs.*, typical or reminiscent of either of these characters.

1839 DICKENS *Let.* 25 Jan. (1965) I. 359 Your agreement is—in Wellerian phraseology—gammon. **1868** LOUISA M. ALCOTT *Little Women* x, 'I'm the wretch that did it, sir,' said the new member, with a Welleresque nod to Mr. Pickwick. **1886** *Pall Mall Gaz.* 20 Feb. 5/2 Sam Weller's story of the muffins is not Wellerian at all.

† **wellesay.** *Obs.* Also **wele a saye, wyllossay.** [var. of WELLAWAY: for the ending cf. HARMESAY.] Alas!

14.. *Lamentacio Peccatoris* 52 in *Relig. Pieces fr. Thornton MS.* (1914) 117 Euer þer sang ys wyllossay. *c* **1440** *Bone Flor.* 1430 Sche caste up many a rewfull rerde, And seyde ofte Wele a saye! *c* **1440** *Pallad. on Husb.* VIII. 91 Breris.. This sely innocentis wole vnclothe And wellesay to tere her skynnys bothe.

well-e'stablished, *ppl. a.*

1709 SHAFTESB. *Inq. Virtue* Charac. (1711) II. 38 That sound and well-establish'd Reason, which alone can constitute..a uniform and steddy Will and Resolution. **1741** WATTS *Improv. Mind* I. viii. §27 We ought..to stand firm in such well-established principles, and not be tempted to change..for the sake of every difficulty. **1772** *Ann. Reg.* 188/1 There are therefore many well-established families in this last-mentioned place. **1865** LUBBOCK *Prehist. Times* xi. 337 Although there are some well-established cases of national decay. **1870** BOWEN *Logic* xii. 394 Any well-established Law of Nature. **1887** *Spons' Househ. Man.* 714 Some well-established shop, famed rather for the soundness of its goods than for their apparent cheapness.

well-e'steemed, *ppl. a.*

1749 CHETWOOD *Hist. Stage* 219 Mr. Sparks..has, by incessant Attention to the Drama, arrived to be a well-esteemed Person in the Business of the Theatre.

wellewerd, var. WOOLWARD.

well-e'xamined, *ppl. a.*

1728 CIBBER *Provoked Husb.* I. i. 7 He is a Man too well-acquainted with the Female World to be brought into a high Opinion of any one Woman, without some well-examin'd Proof of her Merit. **1748** MELMOTH *Fitzosborne Lett.* lvi. (1749) II. 76 To descend to truth thro' the tedious progression of well-examined deductions, is considered as a reproach to the quickness of understanding.

well-'executed, *ppl. a.*

1836 [see WELL-CONCEIVED *ppl. a.*]. **1978** R. LUDLUM *Holcroft Covenant* xxxvii. 425 It was a well-executed trap.

well-ex'perienced, *ppl. a.*

1599 HAKLUYT *Voy.* II. I. 59 Concerning the foresaid islands I inquired of diuers wel-experienced persons. **1608** SHAKS. *Per.* I. i. 164 Like an arrow shot from a well experienst Archer hits the marke. **1619** DRAYTON *Bar. Wars* IV. xv. 52 Men well experienc'd and of worthiest parts. **1662** GERBIER *Princ. Building* 22 A well-experienced Surveyor. **1765** BLACKSTONE *Comm.* Introd. §1. I. 10 This great and well-experienced judge. **1871** TYLOR *Prim. Cult.* I. 104 Of a well-experienced magician they say 'That is quite a Lapp'.

well-ex'pressed, *ppl. a.*

1845 MILL in *Westm. Rev.* XLIII. 331 It is a well-thought and well-expressed explanation. **1943** *Mind* LII. 354 What he [*sc.* Roger Bacon] has to say on *privatio* is sound and well-expressed.

† **well-eyed,** *a. Obs.* [WELL *adv.* 32.] Having good eyes; keen-sighted.

c **1400** *Master of Game* (MS. Digby 182) xviii, And also þat he be both in felde and at wode delyuere and wele y3ed and wele auysed of speche. **1483** CAXTON *Golden Leg.* 339/2 This ymage..was well eyed, well browed [etc.]. **1561** DAUS tr. *Bullinger on Apoc.* (1573) 59 Let the gallauntes of this worlde,..so well eyed, and gorgeously apparelled, marke these thynges well. **1571** GOLDING *Calvin on Ps.* lxxiii. 17 They doo nought else but dote, that wilbe wel eyed and quiksyghted of themselues. **1579** SPENSER *Sheph. Cal.* July 154 Shepheard mought be..well eyed, as Argus was. **1596** —— *State Irel.* Wks. (Globe) 626/1 Yet there appeareth amongest them some reliques of the true antiquitye, though disguised, which a well-eyed man may happely discover and find out.

well-'fabricated, *ppl. a.*

1709 SHAFTESB. *Moralists* III. ii. 215 But in Medals, and well-fabricated Pieces, you can discover Beauty, and admire the Kind.

† **well-faced,** *a. Obs.* [WELL *adv.* 32.] Having a fair face or good countenance. Also *fig.*

1553 ASCHAM *Rept. Germany* 29 He was now of the age of xxxii. yeares well faced. *a* **1569** KINGESMILL *Godly Advise* (1580) 13 Not so well faced as well lived, I meane not so well attired in the outward man as clothed in the inward manne. **1597** E. S. *Discov. Knts. Poste* A 4, If my credit be better then yours, with this my wel-faste hoastice. **1647** N. WARD *Simple Cobler* 2 Hee that hath any well-faced phansy in his Crowne. **1693** [? CALDER] *Sc. Presbyt. Eloq.* (ed. 2) Postscr. 102 A great Hantle of Bonnie braw well fac'd Lasses. **1707** *Lond. Gaz.* No. 4368/4 On the 15th Instant a pretty well Fac'd Boy..went away from School.

well-famed, *ppl. a.* Of good fame, famous.

1606 SHAKS. *Tr. & Cr.* IV. v. 173 My well-fam'd Lord of Troy. **1870** MORRIS *Earthly Par.* III. IV. 89 While he, forgetting clean The sorrow and the joy his eyes had seen, Lies quiet and well famed.

well-'fancied, *ppl. a.* Designed or devised with good invention and taste; displaying a happy fancy.

1710 STEELE *Tatler* No. 248 ¶1 She was mounted on a Pad, with a very well-fancied Furniture. **1751** ELIZA HEYWOOD *Betsy Thoughtless* II. 102 This happened to be the first day of her putting on a very rich, and extremely well-fancied gown. **1772** FOOTE *Nabob* II. Wks. 1799 II. 304 What think you of a bracelet, or a well-fancied aigret? **1779** WARNER in Jesse *Selwyn & Contemp.* (1844) IV. 311 Rendering odious a well-fancied oath from the mint of the metropolis by his vile provincial pronunciation. **1821** SCOTT *Kenilw.* xxx, The dress of Raleigh was a well-fancied and rich suit.

wellfare, obs. f. WELFARE.

well-'faring, *ppl. a. Obs.* exc. *arch.*

† **1.** Of handsome or well-favoured appearance; good-looking; also, robust, healthy. *Obs.*

c **1369** CHAUCER *Dethe Blaunche* 452 Than founde I sytte euen vpright A wonder welfaryng knyght. **1390** GOWER *Conf.* II. 240 Sche..thoghte hou nevere creature Was so wel farende as was he. *c* **1400** *26 Pol. Poems* ii. 51 Welfaryng men of armes. **1470–85** MALORY *Arthur* VI. i. 184 Hym thought he sawe neuer..soo wel farynge a man. *a* **1513** FABYAN *Chron.* VI. clvi. (1811) 144 He was fayre and welfarynge of body, and sterne of looke and of face. **1536** *Pilgr. Tale* 170 in *Thynne's Animadv.* 82 Ther I spyed walkyng a comely pryst, and a welfaryng. **1597** A. M. tr. *Guillemeau's Fr. Chirurg.* 47/3 The entralles of a sownde and welfaring man.

† **2.** Couched in proper or appropriate terms. *Obs.*

a **1400** *Isumbras* 333 A chartir was mad fulle wele farande, ..That thofe he never come in his lande, That scho solde qwene bee.

3. *arch.* Doing well, prosperous.

The spelling indicates association with *welfare.*

1888 DOUGHTY *Arabia Deserta* II. 116 If only his Lord would leave him here other two or three years!—then would he be fully at his ease, and a welfaring person.

well-farmed, *ppl. a.*

1848 MILL *Pol. Econ.* I. I. xii. 214 The careful cultivation of a well farmed district. **1955** P. C. WINTERTON *Fifty Tumultuous Years* 216 Well-farmed land.

well-'fashioned, (*ppl.*) *a.*

1. Of good make or fashion; well made.

1580 BLUNDEVIL *Art of Riding* I. iii. 3 His thighes large and long, with bones well fashioned. *a* **1700** DRYDEN *Ovid's Art of Love* I. 579 Wear well-fashion'd Cloaths, like other Men. **1887** MORRIS *Odyss.* XI. 108 When down in thy ship well-fashioned at last thou drawest anigh To the Three-horned Island.

† **2.** Of polite manners or demeanour. *Obs.*

1611 COTGR., *Morigené*,..well behaued, of good carriage, well fashioned. **1625** K. LONG tr. *Barclay's Argenis* IV. xvii. 396 Behaving himselfe with so well-fashioned modesty. **1693** LOCKE *Educ.* §143 (1699) 259 First, a disposition of the Mind not to offend others; and, Secondly, the most acceptable, and agreeable way of expressing that Disposition. From the one, Men are called *Civil*; from the other *Well-fashion'd.* *a* **1700** EVELYN *Diary* an. 1646 (Chandos) 189 His daughter, a pretty well-fashioned young woman. **1710** STEELE *Tatler* No. 198 ¶2 A young Man of Two and twenty, well-fashioned, learned, genteel.

well-'fatted, *ppl. a.*

1725 POPE *Odyss.* XVIII. 51 A Kid's well-fatted entrails (tasteful food!). **1791** COWPER *Iliad* IX. 578 Oxen and sheep they slaughter'd, many a plump Well-fatted brawn extended in the flames.

well-'favoured, *a.* **a.** Handsome or attractive in appearance, good-looking.

1420–22 LYDG. *Thebes* I. 754 He was a semly knyght, Wel fauoured in euery mannys sight. *c* **1430** —— *Min. Poems* (Percy Soc.) 40 Your weel favoured face. **1509** HAWES *Past. Pleas.* XIV. ii, Thy wel faverde and moost fayre lady. **1549** CHEKE *Hurt Sedit.* (1569) B iij b, If one be well fauourder than another, will ye punishe him bicause ye looke for an equalitie of all things? **1599** SHAKS. *Much Ado* III. iii. 15. **1633** C. FAREWELL *E.-India Colation* 15 A man of a liuely countenance and well fauored. **1684** BUNYAN *Pilgr.* II. (1900) 220 The Boy was in very mean Cloaths, but of a very fresh and well-favoured Countenance. **1787** BURNS *Song, There's a Youth* 3 He's bonie and braw, weel-favour'd withal. **1848** AKERMAN *Anc. & Mod. Coins* v. 89 A well-fed and well-favoured man. **1865** DICKENS *Mut. Fr.* I. vi, She was a tall, upright, well-favoured woman, though severe of countenance.

β. in Sc. form (**well** or **weel**) **faird, faur'd, far'd, far't, faurt,** etc.

1535 LYNDESAY *Satyre* 4333 Now, wallie fall that weill fairde mow! **15..** in *Bannatyne MS.* (Hunter. Club) 399 A weilfaird may. **1719** D'URFEY *Pills* III. 307 There I met with a welfar'd Lass. **1781** BURNS *'On Cessnock banks'* i. (var.) The graces of her weel-faur'd face. **1814** SCOTT *Wav.* xlii, He's vera weel,..but no naithing so well-far'd as your colonel. **1830** A. PICKEN *Dominie's Legacy* III. 32 The delinquent and his wife want to get their own infamous conduct shifted now over upon that well fard boy. **1894** CROCKETT *Raiders* xxiii. 277 I'll never deny that in the days o' yer youth ye war a weel-faured lass.

b. of an animal, a locality, a plant.

1539 BIBLE (Great) *Gen.* xli. 4 The euyll fauored & leane fleshed kyne did eate vp the seuen welfauored & fatt kyne. **1854** S. THOMSON *Wild Flowers* 112 The purple goat's-beard,..the corn blue-bottle are well-favoured plants. **1861** W. F. COLLIER *Hist. Eng. Lit.* 403 This ill-named and not very well-favoured spot formed the nucleus of Abbotsford.

† **c.** *transf.* (cf. WELL-FAVOUREDLY b).

1746 FRANCIS tr. *Hor., Sat.* I. v. 34 [He] bangs the mule at a well-favor'd rate.

† **well-'favouredly,** *adv. Obs.* In a well-favoured manner.

a. Beautifully, handsomely; attractively, gracefully.

1532 MORE *Confut. Tindale* Wks. 668/2 But now goeth Tindal wel fauoredly forth with a great face of another ful solucion. **1538** ELYOT *Dict.*, *Pulchre*, an aduerbe, signifyeth fayre, beautifully, well fauoredly. **1542** UDALL *Erasm. Apoph.* 7 We dooe not put images to makyng but onely to suche werkemenne of whom wee see some noumbre of images welfauouredly and mynionly made afore. **1545** ASCHAM *Toxoph.* (Arb.) 143 Teatche me to shoote as fayre, and welfauouredly as you can imagen. **1562** TURNER *Bathes* I b, He that had ben in Italye and Germany, and had sene howe costly and wellfauoredly the bathes are trimmed and appoynted there..woulde [etc.]. **1790** SHIRREFS *Poems* Gloss. 39/1 *Weelfar'dly*, cleverly, with a good grace. **1825** JAMIESON, *Weil-faur'tlie, adv.* 1. Handsomely, S.

b. Ironically, in reference to thrashing, punishment, etc.: Severely, soundly, 'handsomely'.

1542 UDALL *Erasm. Apoph.* 100 Diogenes..tooke abrode thongue..and the same wel fauouredly bestowed about ye ribbes and pate of Midias. **1565** *Kyng Daryus* 404 (Brandl) He wil not away til I canuis him wel fauoredly. **1579–80** NORTH *Plutarch, Antonius* (1595) 990 They them selues were oftentimes put to flight, and welfauoredly beaten. **1639** FULLER *Holy War* II. xxiv. (1640) 74 He would often give a smart jest,..and sometimes he was well-favouredly met with; as the best fencer in wits school hath now and then an unhappy blow dealt him. **1652** HEYLYN *Cosmogr.* II. 151 The [Russian] women..think themselves neither loved nor regarded, unlesse they be two or three times a day well favouredly swadled. *a* **1700** B. E. *Dict. Cant. Crew, I Swing'd him off*, I lay'd on and beat him well-favoredly.

c. ? Lavishly, liberally.

1563–87 FOXE *A. & M.* (1596) 259/1 About the sute whereof when much monie was bestowed on both sides welfauoredlie.

d. By good fortune, happily. *Sc.*

a **1774** FERGUSSON *Poems, Eclogue* 96 Whan I shoot my nose in, ten to ane If I weelfardly see my ane hearthstane.

well-'favouredness. Now *rare* or *Obs.* The quality or condition of being well-favoured; beauty, comeliness.

1545 ASCHAM *Toxoph.* (Arb.) 142 Nature it selfe taught men to ioyne alwayes welfauourednesse with profytablenesse. *a* **1575** tr. *Pol. Verg. Eng. Hist.* (Camden No. 36) 129 He is reported greatlie to have mervayled at their witte and welfaverdnes. **1607** MARKHAM *Caval.* I. (1617) 69 It maketh your Gelding haue a delicate fine leane head, of a comely shape, well-fauoredness and proportion. **1642** HOWELL *For. Trav.* (Arb.) 75 The longevity, well favourednesse and innated honesty of the people. **1780** M. MADAN *Thelyphthora* (1781) I. 213 A worthy man, who was in love with a married woman upon account of her modesty, and well-favouredness of her children. **1825** JAMIESON, *Weilfaur'tness*, handsomeness. **1885** BURTON *Arab. Nts.* (abr. ed.) III. 33 Khalid..was pleased with his well-favouredness and elegant aspect.

well-'feasted, *ppl. a.*

1671 MILTON *Samson* 1419 The well-feasted Priests [are] then soonest fir'd With zeal, if aught Religion seem concern'd.

well(-)'feathered, *ppl. a.*

1340–70 *Alisaunder* 269 Well feþered flon flonngen aboute. **1591** SPENSER *Visions Bellay* xi, A Bird all white, well feathered on each wing. **1639** FULLER *Holy War* II. x. (1640) 58 And herein he discovered his want of judgement, being indeed like an arrow well-feathered, but with a blunt pile; he flew swift, but did not sink deep. **1671** WOODHEAD *St. Teresa* I. xiii. 75 Like some young Bird, not so well-feathered. **1855** *Poultry Chron.* II. 419 Short, well feathered legs.

well-'featured, *a.* Having good features. Formerly also in wider sense: Well formed or shaped.

c **1500** *Three Kings Sons* 111 And many tyme he wold.. thinke yn his mynde that they were passing wele fetured and goodly folkes. **1590** *Tarlton's News out of Purg.* 11 A bare faced youth, well featured, of a liuely countenance. *c* **1600** IGNOTO in I. D. & C. M. *Epigr.* (?1830) D 5 b, Wel featurde lasse, Thou knowest I loue the deere. *a* **1618** J. DAVIES (Heref.) *Wits Pilgr.* etc. (Grosart) 27/2 Well featur'd Flesh too base a Subiect is For Sou'raign Loues diuine, ay-blest, imbrace. **1688** *Lond. Gaz.* No. 2354/8 An Indian Black, about 18 years of Age, well featur'd. **1787** BURNS *Song, 'There's a Youth'* 10 Weel-featur'd, weel-tocher'd, weel mounted and braw. **1860** WHYTE MELVILLE *Mkt. Harb.* v, Who, to do him justice, was a gentleman-like, well-featured fellow enough. **1874** MOTLEY *John Barnev.* II. xvii. 226 A tall, .. well-featured, mild, gentlemanlike man.

well(-)fed, *ppl. a.*

?*a* **1366** CHAUCER *Rom. Rose* 471 Al to selde iwys Is ony pouere man wel fedde. **1535** COVERDALE *Isa.* xxv. 6 Fat and welfed beastes. **1600** *Sir J. Oldcastle* III. i. 99 Weele strike the stagge our selues Shall fill our dishes with his wel-fed flesh. *c* **1611** CHAPMAN *Iliad* IX. 208 Then of a well fed swine A huge fat shoulder he cuts out. **1725** POPE *Odyss.* III. 535 Bid some swain to lead A well-fed bullock from the grassy mead. **1786** BURNS *The Vision* I. xiv, There, well-fed Irwine stately thuds. **1820** LAMB *Elia* I. *Christ's Hosp.*, Sleek well-fed blue-coat boys. **1828** DAVY *Salmonia* 49 A fine well-fed fish, not much less than 4 lbs. **1874** J. M. FOTHERGILL *Maintenance of Health* 344 Good meat has its red meat marbled or interstreaked with fat. This shows it is well-fed.

well-feed, -fee'd, *ppl. a.*

1684 *Contempl. St. Man* I. ix. (1699) 93 The rich Man shall not then have .. well-Fee'd Lawyers to defend his Process. **1897** *Westm. Gaz.* 28 Sept. 8/1 Twelve angry litigants, each assisted by bewigged and well-feed counsel.

well-'feeding, *ppl. a.*

c **1611** CHAPMAN *Iliad* III. 282 On Troyes well feeding soyle [ἐπὶ χθόνα πουλυβότειραν].

†**well-'feeling**, *ppl. a. Obs.* Sensible, intelligent.

1382 WYCLIF *Ecclus.* vii. 21 Wile thou not gone awei fro a wel felende womman [Vulg. *a muliere sensata*].

well-feigned, *ppl. a.*

1667 MILTON *P.L.* IX. 492 Under shew of Love well feign'd. **1725** POPE *Odyss.* XVIII. 57 Ulysses then with art, And fears well-feign'd, disguis'd his dauntless heart. **1813** SCOTT *Rokeby* V. xix, [He] look'd with well-feign'd fear around. **1825** T. HOOK *Sayings* Ser. II. *Man of Many Fr.* (Colburn) 136 The Colonel expressed a well-feigned astonishment at the appearance of the table.

well-fenced, *ppl. a.*

1705 MANDEVILLE *Grumbling Hive* 25 'Till some well-fenced Retreat is found; And here they die, or stand their Ground. **1719** DE FOE *Crusoe* (Globe) 148 Some enclosed Piece of Ground, well fenc'd either with Hedge or Pale.

well-'fended, *ppl. a.*

1865 ALLINGHAM 50 *Mod. Poems, Southwell Park* II. 118 The well-fended nunlike child.

well-fer'mented, *ppl. a.*

1731 ARBUTHNOT *Nat. Aliments* (1735) 193 Well fermented Bread, and well fermented Liquors.

well-filed, *ppl. a.*

1656 EARL MONM. tr. *Boccalini's Advts. fr. Parnass.* II. xviii. 251 The best Poets, with their well filed, and long studied verses.

well-filled, *ppl. a.*

1615 CHAPMAN *Odyss.* XXI. 574 Giue banquet; and the rest (Poeme and Harpe) that grace a wel-fill'd boorde. **1725** POPE *Odyss.* IX. 5 The well-fill'd palace, the perpetual feast. **1781** CRABBE *Library* 148 The dull red edging of the well-fill'd page. **1786** BURNS *To Auld Mare* xii, But thy auld tail thou wad hae whisket, An' spread abreed thy weel-fill'd brisket. **1832** LONGF. *Coplas de Manrique* lxi, He left no well-filled treasury. **1876** GEO. ELIOT *Deronda* xlii, Whose light-brown hair was set up in a small parallelogram above his well-filled forehead. **1878** J. BULLER *New Zealand* I. iv. 33 They came in fleets of their well-filled canoes.

well-'finished, *ppl. a.*

a **1763** SHENSTONE *Ess.* Wks. 1768 II. 173 One truly splendid action, or one well-finished composition, includes more than all the results from more trivial performances. **1901** *Scotsman* 3 Apr. 7/3 For cattle, well-finished animals met a brisk selling trade.

well(-)'fitted, *ppl. a.*

†**1.** Fully equipped or furnished. *Obs.*

1588 SHAKS. *L.L.L.* II. i. 45 A man of soueraigne parts he is esteem'd: Well fitted in Arts, glorious in Armes. **1656** COWLEY *Pindar. Odes, Resurrection* ii, Lo how the Years to come, a numerous and well-fitted Quire, All hand in hand do decently advance.

2. Exactly adjusted, shaped, or suited.

1791 COWPER *Iliad* XVIII. 758 A pond'rous helmet bright Well-fitted to his brows. **1839** AINSWORTH *Jack Sheppard* III. ii, It was a night well fitted to their enterprise—calm, still, and profoundly dark. **1904** A. C. FRASER *Biogr. Philos.* iv. 142 An easy flow of well-fitted words.

well-'fitting, *ppl. a.*

1857 DUFFERIN *Lett. High Lat.* vi. 59 A well-fitting white waistcoat. **1859** H. KINGSLEY *G. Hamlyn* xxvii, His well-fitting cord breeches. **1881** J. W. HAWARD *Orthop. Surg.* 72 Only well-fitting boots, with a sufficiently wide sole, should be worn.

well-fixed, *ppl. a.*

1. *lit.*

1718 P. RAE *Hist. Reb.* vi. 287 Followed by 40 or 50 stately Fellows .. arm'd each of 'em with a well fix'd Gun on his Shoulder. **1848** BAILEY *Festus* (ed. 3) 246 The complete Well-fixed necessity and end of all things.

2. *transf.* Reasonably affluent, comfortably off. *U.S. colloq.*

1822 A. D. MURPHEY *Let.* 22 Aug. in *Papers* (1914) I. 263 His Brother is well fixed, has one of the best tracts of land in Tennessee, and is growing rich *fast*. **1912** N. M. WOODROW *Sally Salt* 228 I'm well to do, Hilda, well fixed in the world. **1952** J. STEINBECK *East of Eden* ix. 78 He was better than well fixed—he was rich. **1970** J. BLACKBURN *Land of Promise* i. 11 He .. had become 'well fixed', as the family colloquialism expressed moderate wealth.

well(-)'flavoured, *ppl. a.* **a.** Having a good natural flavour. **b.** Mixed with an ingredient which imparts a good flavour.

1771 *Phil. Trans.* LXI. 311 The natural history of this well-flavoured fish. **1776** PENNANT *Brit. Zool.* III. 297 The flesh, when boiled, is of a pale red, but well flavored. **1868** *Epicure's Year-bk.* 185 Serve it with a well-flavoured sauce or purée. **1884** E. YATES *Recoll.* I. iv. 154 The culinary preparations .. were well flavoured, highly seasoned, and much relished by us.

well-fledged, *ppl. a.* Well-feathered.

1743 R. BLAIR *Grave* 767 The weary bird .. dozes till the dawn of day, Then claps his well-fledg'd wings, and bears away. **1870** BRYANT *Iliad* IV. 148 A well-fledged arrow that had never flown.

well(-)fleeced, *ppl. a.*

1616 W. BROWNE *Brit. Past.* II. ii. 46 Thou hast a well-fleec'd flocke feede to and fro. **1650** H. VAUGHAN *Silex Scint.* I. *The Search* 27 They .. drove home to the Tent Their well-fleec'd traine. **1724** [see FLEECED *ppl. a.*[2]].

well(-)fleshed, *ppl. a.*

1. Well furnished with flesh; plump, brawny. Also *fig.*

1585 HIGINS *Junius' Nomencl.* 448/2 *Torosus*, .. well flesht. **1858** [see FLESHED *ppl. a.* 1]. **1876** GEO. ELIOT *Deronda* lxix, Happiness is considered as a well-fleshed indifference to sorrow outside it. **1901** H. SUTCLIFFE *Mistr. Barbara Cunliffe* v. 76 Weel-fleshed men could niver stand up long agen an ale-pot.

2. Inured to or eager for bloodshed.

1586 T. B. *La Primaud. Fr. Acad.* I. (1594) 372 As gray-hounds well flesht follow after wilde beasts. **1693** DRYDEN *Epit. Sir P. Fairborne's Tomb* 11 Against the Moors his well-flesh'd Sword he draws.

well-fletched, *ppl. a.* Well-feathered.

1656 COWLEY *Pindar. Odes, 2nd Olymp.* x, Leave, wanton Muse, thy roving flight, To thy loud String the well-fletcht Arrow put.

well(-)floored, *ppl. a.*

1555 EDEN *Decades* (Arb.) 194 Chambers boorded after the maner of owre waynscotte and well flowred.

well(-)floured, *ppl. a.*

1728 E. S[MITH] *Compleat Housew.* (ed. 2) 108 Put under it two or three Sheets of Cap-Paper well floured. **1905** *Daily Chron.* 3 Oct. 8/1 The potatoes and flour are worked into dough on a well-floured board.

well(-)'flowered, *ppl. a.* **a.** Richly embellished with flowers or figures of flowers. **b.** Bearing a good head of flowers.

1592 SHAKS. *Rom. & Jul.* II. iv. 64 Why then is my Pump well flower'd. **1845** *Florist's Jrnl.* 135 Eriostemon cuspidatus, well flowered.

well-'followed, *ppl. a.* (FOLLOW *v.* 6 b.)

a **1586** SIDNEY *Arcadia* III. viii. (1912) 390 Thus with the well-followed valure of Amphialus were the other almost overthrowne.

well(-)fore'warning, *ppl. a.*

1593 SHAKS. *2 Hen. VI*, III. ii. 85 What boaded this? but well fore-warning winde Did seeme to say, seeke not a Scorpions Nest.

well-forged, *ppl. a.*

1791 COWPER *Iliad* XIII. 233 The well-forged helmet. **1813** SCOTT *Rokeby* VI. ix, He school'd us in a well-forged tale, Of scheme the Castle walls to scale. **1896** KIPLING *Seven Seas, Song of English, Victoria*, The tested chain holds fast, The well-forged link rings true!

well-formed, *ppl. a.*

a. of persons and material things.

c **1520** W. WALTER *Guystarde & Syg.* (Roxb.) A iij, Of shape and persone she was well fourmed. *a* **1586** SIDNEY *Arcadia* III. (1922) 58 The kissing of her welformed mouth. **1645** WALLER *Poems, Palamede to Zelinde* 1 Fairest piece of well form'd earth, Vrge not thus your haughty Birth. **1653** R. SANDERS *Physiogn.* 159 The well formed head is like a Mallet or a Sphear. **1788** MRS. HUGHES *Henry & Isab.* xviii. II. 88 Not a pleasing view, .. or a well-formed tree, was passed without furnishing matter for her observation. **1805** WORDSW. *Prelude* VII. 206 A range Of well-formed characters, with chalk inscribed Upon the smooth flat stones. **1831** JAMES *Phil. Augustus* iv, A man of thirty-two or thirty-three years of age, tall, well-formed, handsome. **1863** A. C. RAMSAY *Phys. Geog.* 160 Well-formed flint hatchets. **1883** D. C. MURRAY *Hearts* xi, He had a large and well-formed body, plump but not corpulent.

b. of immaterial things.

1643 DORNEY (*title*), A briefe and exact Relation of .. Passages that hapned in the late well-formed (and as valiently defended) Seige laid before the City of Glocester. **1725** WATTS *Logic* IV. Introd., A well-formed Proposition, or a just Argument. **1746** FRANCIS *Horace, A. P.* 230 The Child, who now with firmer Footing walks, And with unfaultering, well-form'd Accents talks. **1759** GOLDSM. *Pres. State Pol. Learn.* xi. (Globe) 444/2 In a well-formed education a course of history should ever precede a course of ethics. **1787** BURNS *Prol. spoken by Woods* 23 Well-form'd taste and sparkling wit.

(*b*) *spec.* formed according to stated grammatical rules.

1961 A. G. OETTINGER in *Proc. Symposia Appl. Math.* XII. 104 One important common problem is that of obtaining an algorithm for distinguishing sentences from nonsentences or .. well-formed strings from not well-formed strings. **1969** R. A. HALL in *Neuphilologische Mitteilungen* LXX. 204 The oft-repeated claim that all 'well-formed' sentences of a language are derivable from a single syntactic kernel is clearly unfounded. **1980** *Amer. Speech* LV. 90 'Le crabmeat cocktail' is well-formed in that *cocktail* has been borrowed into French as a masculine noun.

c. *Logic.* Applied to any sequence of symbols conforming to the formation rules of a logical system. Esp. as ***well-formed formula***.

1936 A. CHURCH in *Amer. Jrnl. Math.* LVIII. 346 We select a particular list of symbols... And we define the word *formula* to mean any finite sequence of symbols out of this list. The terms *well-formed formula*, [etc.], .. are then defined by induction. **1954** I. M. COPI *Symbolic Logic* vi. 184 In a logistic system .. any formulas which on the intended interpretation do *not* become significant statements are *not* well formed formulas. **1967** *Encycl. Philos.* V. 22/2 A formal language *L* is given by specifying (*a*) a list of *symbols* of *L* and (*b*) a set of *formation rules* for combining these symbols into acceptable, or well-formed, expressions (terms, formulas, sentences) of *L*. **1978** A. G. HAMILTON *Logic for Mathematicians* iii. 53 The use of parentheses in well-formed formulas is precisely given in the definition.

Hence **well-'formedness** (chiefly in *Linguistics*).

1957 *Encycl. Brit.* XIV. 306/1 The condition of well-formedness [in logical formulas]. **1961** N. CHOMSKY in *Word* XVII. 221 Information as to whether the sequence of phones is a properly formed or *grammatical* sentence and if not, in what respect it deviates from well-formedness. **1970** J. P. THORNE in J. Lyons *New Horizons in Linguistics* ix. 186 Between .. extremes of well-formedness occur sentences of varying degrees of grammaticalness. **1979** F. KERMODE *Genesis of Secrecy* iii. 64 We depend upon well-formedness .. in written language.

well-'formulated, *ppl. a.*

1968 C. G. KUPER *Introd. Theory Superconductivity* i. 2 A well-formulated problem. **1977** P. STREVENS *New Orientations Teaching of Eng.* ii. 23 Well-formulated propositions.

well(-)'fortified, *ppl. a.*

1538 [see FORTIFIED]. **1591** SHAKS. *1 Hen. VI*, IV. ii. 19 For I protest we are well fortified, And strong enough to issue out and fight. **1618** GAINSFORD *Glory Eng.* I. viii. 60 They can bring you into well fortified Cities. *a* **1625** MANWAYRING *Sea-mans Dict.* 68 If a Peece have much mettle in any part, they say, she is well fortified. **1692, 1757** [see FORTIFIED *ppl. a.*]. **1821** tr. *Iliad* II. I. 41 The well-fortified city of Ilium.

†**well-'fortunate**, *a. Obs.* = next.

1523 CROMWELL in Merriman *Life & Lett.* (1902) I. 34 The well fortunate and sawge Capetayn, the serife of Surrey. *a* **1533** BERNERS *Golden Bk. M. Aurel.* xliii. (1535) 84 Certaynly the princis are glorious, and the people well fortunate, and the senate happy, whan all agree in one councell.

†**well-'fortuned**, *ppl. a. Obs.* Favoured by fortune.

c **1374**, **1484** [see FORTUNED]. **1471** CAXTON *Recuyell* (Sommer) 249 Gretyng .. fro the esquyer vnknowen and well fortuned. **1530** PALSGR. 329/1 Well fortuned, *bien euré*. **1556** *Flores' Aurelio & Isab.* O 8, If anney ladey well fortunede founde you disposede in her fauour.

well-fought, *ppl. a.*

†**1.** Inured to fight. *Obs.*

1598 CHAPMAN *Seven Iliads* v. [IX.] 90 The Curets wars did hold With the well-fought Etolians [Αἰτωλοὶ μενεχάρμαι].

2. Valiantly contested.

1717 TICKELL *Epist. fr. Lady to Gent at Avignon* 74 Our Sex has .. purchased Fame in many a well-fought Street. **1725** POPE *Odyss.* XIV. 401 Oh! had he perish on some well-fought day. **1761** FOOTE *Lyar* I. ii. (1786) 17, I returned to reap the harvest of the well-fought field. **1814** SCOTT *Lord of Isles* IV. xx, Who in the well-fought conflict fell. **1818** NEWMAN *Poems* (1905) 48 The strange events of many a well-fought day.

†**well-'foughten**, *ppl. a. Obs.* = prec.

1599 SHAKS. *Hen. V*, IV. vi. 18 In this glorious and well-foughten field. **1622** DRAYTON *Poly-olb.* xxii. 1577 Broughton .. there lastly gaue his blood To that well-foughten Field.

well(-)found, *ppl. a.*

†**1. a.** Used in the vocative (like *welcome*) to greet a person when met. *Obs.*

c **1350** *Ipomadon* 6715 (Kölbing) Well founde, mayde Imayne. *c* **1350** *Lybeaus Disc.* (Ritson) 1660 The constable seyde, Well founde, Noble knyght of the table rounde.

†**2.** Of tried goodness, merit, or value; well-approved, commendable. *Obs.*

In quot. 1887 prob. an echo of Shakspere's use.

1601 SHAKS. *All's Well* II. i. 105 Gerard de Narbon was my father, In what he did professe, well found. **1607** —— *Cor.* II. ii. 48 In our well-found Successes. **1887** MRS. LYNN LINTON in *Fortn. Rev.* May 728 Many [of the Athenian hetæræ] lived comparatively well-found lives.

3. Fully furnished or equipped.

1793 [see FOUND *ppl. a.* 2]. **1864** BURTON *Scot Abr.* II. ii. 144 The garrison is large and well found. **1869** BLACKMORE *Lorna D.* x, He seemed very old, being over twenty, and well-found in beard. **1891** A. H. MARKHAM *Sir J. Franklin* 301 A well-found steamer.

well(-)'founded, *ppl. a.* **a.** Built on a good and solid base. *lit.* and *fig.*

c **1369** CHAUCER *Dethe Blaunche* 922 (Fairf.) And which a goodely softe speche Had that swete, .. So frendely, and so wel y-grounded, Vp al resoun so wely-founded [*Fondée sur toute raison*]. **1671** WOODHEAD *St. Teresa* I. xxiv. 164 My Prayer began to settle itself, like a well-founded Building. **1706** CONGREVE *Pindar. Ode to Queen* 5 Britain's Queen, .. Fix'd on the Base of Her well-founded State. **1821** CRAIG *Lect. Drawing*, etc. vii. 366 We will for this purpose establish a set of well-founded principles for our standard.

b. esp. of a belief, sentiment, statement, etc.: Having a foundation in fact; based on good or sure grounds or reasons.

1782 Miss Burney *Cecilia* viii. vii, Her jealousy, already but too well founded, received every hour the poisonous nourishment of fresh conviction. **1814** Scott *Wav.* xl, A well-founded disbelief in the co-operation of the English Jacobites kept many Scottish men of rank from his standard. **1827** —— *Two Drovers* ii, The Cumbrian Squire, who had entertained some suspicions of his manager's honesty, was taking occasional measures to ascertain how far they were well-founded. **1855** [see founded 1]. **1905** F. Harrison *Chatham* iii. 42 There was no personal malignity in his accusations, he believed them to be well-founded.

Hence **well-'foundedly** *adv.*; **well-'foundedness**.

1888 *Sat. Rev.* 27 Oct. 486/2 They had prided themselves, not too well-foundedly, that..they had far the better of England. **1920** *Glasgow Herald* 25 Feb. 9/3 There can be no discussion..with regard to..the well-foundedness of the charges. **1970** B. Brewster tr. *Althusser & Balibar's Reading Capital* (1975) iii. i. 212 Interpretations..whose well-foundedness will, I hope, emerge later in the paper.

well-framed, *ppl. a.* Well shaped, fashioned, constructed, or composed.

a **1586** Sidney *Arcadia* v. (1922) 146 Like a man whose best building was a well-framed conscience. **1625** K. Long tr. *Barclay's Argenis* iii. xi. 188 As soone as I shall come to shore..some wel-framed lye shall happely bring me to her. **1718** Prior *2nd Hymn Callim.* 73 In the well-fram'd Models,..Thou shew'dst, where Towers or Battlements should rise. **1791** Cowper *Iliad* ix. 70 Yet when thy speech is to the Kings of Greece It is well framed and prudent. **1876** Hardy *Ethelberta* xxxv, A well-framed reflective man with a grey beard.

well-fraught, *ppl. a.*

1674 N. Fairfax *Bulk & Selv.* To Rdr., That well-fraught world of words that answers works. **1708** J. Philips *Cyder* ii. 371 The well-fraught Bowl Circles incessant. **1808** Mrs. Iliff *Poems* (1818) 98 How wise Ulisses' well-fraught tale Did o'er Nausicaa's fears prevail.

well-'freckled, *ppl. a.*

1649 G. Daniel *Trinarch.* To Rdr. 140 For Leopard Learning is a finer Beast Then a Sire or Damme; well-freckled witts shew best. **1836** Marryat *Midsh. Easy* xxiv, He was broad-faced, broad-shouldered, well freckled, and pug-nosed.

well-'freighted, *ppl. a.*

1663 Cowley *Country Mouse* 82 Loe, in the midst of a well fraited Pye, They both at last glutted and wanton lye.

well-fre'quented, *ppl. a.*

1715 Pennecuik *Tweeddale* 10 An old and well frequented Inn. **1748** *Anson's Voy.* ii. xiii. 278 An amicable well frequented port. **1778** D. Loch *Tour Scot.* 5 A well-frequented weekly market each Thursday. **1824** Miss Mitford *Village* Ser. i. 289 The well-frequented Rose inn.

†**well-freshed**, *ppl. a. Obs.*

1598 Sylvester *Du Bartas* ii. iii. iii. *Law* 970 In a bucket, that [shepherd] (Well-fresht himselfe) bears some unto his Flock.

well(-)'fruited, *ppl. a.*

1626 Bp. Hall *Contempl.*, *O.T.* xx. xi. 251 So wee haue seene the kernell of a well fruited plant degenerate into that crab, or willow, which gaue the originall to his stocke. *a* **1703** Burkitt *On N.T.* Mark xii. 8 A vineyard is..a place well planted, well fruited.

wellful, var. wealful *Obs.*

well(-)'furnished, *ppl. a.* Amply provided, stocked, equipped, etc. (see furnished).

1474 *Paston Lett.* III. 107 He..lefte a greet garnyson theer, weell ffornysshyd in vytayll. **1553** [see furnished 2 c]. **1566** Painter (*title*), The Palace of Pleasure, Beautified adorned and well furnished with pleasaunt Histories and excellent Nouels. **1618** Gainsford *P. Warbeck* 45 The Kings Foreward being full of companie and well furnished. **1635-56** Cowley *Davideis* iv. end, Lo! they 'arriv'ed now at th' appointed place; Well-chosen and well furnisht for the Chase. **1687** *Lond. Gaz.* No. 2240/4 A thick well furnished grey Gelding, full aged. **1710** Congreve *Doris* 11 Wks. 1730 III. 293 Her sparkling Eyes she still retains, And Teeth in good Repair; And her well-furnish'd Front disdains To grace with borrow'd Hair. **1852** Grote *Greece* ii. lxix. (1862) VI. 193 A year's campaign..would enable them to return with a well-furnished purse.

b. *esp.* of a house or room.

1635-56 Cowley *Davideis* i. 681 Well-furnisht-Chambers, for in each there stood, A narrow Couch, Table and Chair of wood. **1829** *Anniversary* 122 He has..a fair estate,..a well furnished house, [etc.]. **1850** Lynch *Theoph. Trinal* vii. 133 A well-clad woman in a well-furnished room.

Hence **well-'furnishedness**.

1653 H. More *Conject. Cabbal.* (1662) 118 In respect of the fulness and well-furnishedness of the Earth.

well-furred, *ppl. a.*

1611 J. Davies (Heref.) *Scourge of Folly* (Grosart) 29/1 The well-furrd Deane. **1837** Sir F. Palgrave *Merch. & Friar* i. (1844) 22 These well-furred and awful plenipotentiaries. **1879** Geo. Eliot *Theo. Such* xviii. 329 Well-furred skins.

well-'gaited, *a.*

1712 [see *gaited ppl. a.* (gait *sb.*[1])]. **1825** Jamieson, *Weill-gaitit*,..applied to a horse that is thoroughly broke.

well(-)'garnished, *ppl. a.*

1597 [see garnished]. **1838** Marg. Fuller *Wom. 19th C.* (1862) 265 More than one well-garnished mansion.

well-geared, *ppl. a.*

c **1470** [see geared 1]. **1899** F. T. Bullen *Way Navy* 72 Like a well-geared piece of machinery.

well-'gifted, *a.*

1653 Gauden *Hierasp.* 20 Though Ministers might be well-gifted, and well-affected men. **1712** Arbuthnot *John Bull* iii. iii, Jack brag'd of greater Abilities than other Men; he was well-gifted, as he pretended.

well-girt, *ppl. a.* Firmly encircled or secured by a girdle or girth; esp., after Gr. εὔζωνος (ἀνήρ), girt up for exercise, in good trim for walking; hence *fig.* (of time) strenuously bestowed.

1647 N. Ward *Simple Cobler* 88 A well-girt houre gives every man content. **1798** Wordsw. *Idiot Boy* 39 The well-girt saddle. **1816** Southey *Poet's Pilgr.* i. iii. 1 Some three hours' journey for a well-girt man. **1845** Ford *Handbk. Spain* i. 57 To be Homerically well girt..is half the battle for the traveller in Spain. **1881** Saintsbury *Dryden* i. 3 A well-girt man can survey the whole in a day's walk.

b. *transf.* of a building or stronghold.

1756 Home *Douglas* iv. i, The trembling mothers, and their children [are] lodg'd In well-girt towers and castles.

†**well(-)'given**, *ppl. a. Obs.* Well-disposed.

1535 [see given 2]. **1579-80** North *Plutarch, Brutus* (1595) 1053 Cassius..was Brutus familiar friend, but not so well giuen, and conditioned as he. **1593** Shaks. *2 Hen. VI*, iii. i. 72 The Duke is vertuous, milde, and too well giuen, To dreame on euill, or to worke my downefall. **1607** Dekker & Webster *Westw. Ho* ii. ii, Why are you a burden to the worlds conscience, and an eie-sore to wel giuen men? *c* **1611** Chapman *Iliad* vii. 176 This said, the wel-giuen souldiers prayed.

well-glebed, *a.*

c **1645** W. E. in *Cleveland's Poems* (1677) 124 A well-gleb'd Vicarage.

well-glossed, *ppl. a.*

c **1611** Chapman *Iliad* vii. 264 By Telamon was giuen A faire well glossed purple waste.

well-gloved, *ppl. a.*

1864 'Annie Thomas' *D. Donne* III. 10 She laid her well-gloved hand on his arm.

well-'going, *ppl. a.* (Said of an animal, a machine, etc.)

1623 Lisle *Ælfric on O. & N. Test.* (Crawford) 66 Make me now ready a well going horse. **1786** Burns *Inventory* 10 My han' ahin's a weel gaun fillie. —— *Addr. Unco Guid* 5 Whase life is like a weel-gaun mill, Supply'd wi' store o' water. **1789** Cowper *Let. to S. Rose* 5 June, It seems they are well-going clocks, and cheap. **1895** Crockett *Men of Moss-Hags* xxxii. 236 Her well-going talk eased my heart in the midst of so many troubles.

well-'gotten, *ppl. a.* Obtained by good means, honourably gained. (Cf. ill-gotten.)

1530 Palsgr. 844/1 Well gotten, *de bon acquest.* *a* **1533** Berners *Huon* lxviii. 235 Duke Naymes wolde take neuer a peny, for he thought al that rychys was not wel goten. **1656** Cowley *Mistr.*, *Dialogue* ii, I'll the well-gotten Pleasure Safe in my Memo'ry Treasure. **1855** Tennyson *Maud* i. iv. iii, Your father has wealth well-gotten, and I am nameless and poor.

well-'governed, *ppl. a.*

1. Following a good rule of life and behaviour; controlled by reason.

c **1410** *Lantern of Light* 10 Whanne þi neiȝbour is wise, wel gouerned. *c* **1449** Pecock *Repr.* ii. vii. 179 Deuout and weel gouerned pilgrimes. **1592** Shaks. *Rom. & Jul.* i. v. 70 Verona brags of him, To be a vertuous and well gouern'd youth. **1598** F. Meres *Pallad. Tamia* 281 b, A man of vertuous disposition..and wel gouerned cariage. **1614** Bp. Hall *Contempl.*, *O.T.* v. vi. 137 How highly God doth esteeme a well gouerned zeale. **1634** Milton *Comus* 705 And that which is not good, is not delicious To a well-govern'd and wise appetite. **1865** Dickens *Mut. Fr.* ii. vii, Yes, but..a well-governed mind can be soured sitting!

2. Of a state or society of men: Ruled by a good government.

1570 *Homilies* ii. *Disobed. & Rebellion* iv. (1574) 590 In anye well gouerned common wealth, where good lawes are in force. **1656** Earl Monm. tr. *Boccalini's Advts. fr. Parnass.* i. xxv. (1674) 27 The rewards..which were practised in well-governed Common-wealths. **1748** *Anson's Voy.* iii. x. 413 The whole Empire was a well-governed affectionate family. **1816** Coleridge *Lay Serm.* i. (1852) 22 By the happy organisation of a well-governed society. **1875** Jowett *Plato* (ed. 2) I. 395 If you go away from well-governed states to..Thessaly, where there is great disorder and licence.

well-'governing, *vbl. sb.*

1649 Milton *Eikon.* xv. 141 Had he..known how to distinguish..between the wholsome heat of well Governing, and the fevorous rage of Tyrannizing. **1656** Earl Monm. tr. *Boccalini's Advts. fr. Parnass.* ii. li. (1674) 202 [His] Wit was miraculous in the well-governing of those people.

†**well-'government**. *Obs.*

1714 Fortescue-Aland *Pref. Fortescue's Abs. & Lim. Mon.* p. xvi, Positive Institutions for the Well-government of the People.

†**well-'governor**. *Obs.* One who governs well.

1388 Wyclif *1 Tim.* v. 17 The prestis that ben wel gouernoures [1382 that ben wel bifore, Vulg. *qui bene praesunt*].

well-gowned, *ppl. a.*

1920 E. Pound *Hugh Selwyn Mauberley* 20 Doubtful, somewhat, of the value Of well-gowned approbation Of literary effort. **1975** S. Milligan in C. Allen *Plain Tales from Raj* xv. 158 Always very pale and very beautiful and well-gowned and never moving very fast if they were on horses.

†**well-graced**, *a. Obs.* Full of grace or graces.

1593, **1605** [see graced].

well-'graded, *ppl. a.* Having easy gradients.

1857 [see graded 3]. **1878** J. S. Campion *Spain* xxi. (1879) 266 The well-graded waggon-road to Lerida.

well-grassed, (*ppl.*) *a.*

1731 [see grassed *ppl. a.* 1]. **1866** R. P. Whitworth *Bailliere's S. Austral. Gazetteer* Advts. p. xix, Large and well-grassed paddocks. **1890** 'R. Boldrewood' *Col. Reformer* viii, An open, thinly-timbered, well-grassed country.

well-'gravelled, *ppl. a.*

1799 G. S. Carey *Balnea* (ed. 2) 220 A beautiful well-gravelled walk.

well-greaved, *a.* Used to translate Homer's ἐϋκνήμιδες (pl.).

1848 Buckley *Iliad* ii. 331 But come, ye well-greaved Greeks, remain all here. **1870** Bryant *Iliad* i. 23 Well-greaved Achaians. **1887** Morris *Odyss.* ii. 402 Telemachus now already are thy well-greaved fellows there.

†**well-'grinded**, *ppl. a. Obs.* Well ground.

1651 Vaughan *Praise Countrie-life* ii. Wks. 1914 I. 127 In populous Cities their Corne is either mouldie, or not wel-grinded. **1670** Eachard *Cont. Clergy* 92 A soft and well-grinded pouch of meal.

well-groomed, *ppl. a.* **a.** *lit.* of a horse.

1890 'R. Boldrewood' *Miner's Right* xvi, The well-groomed, high-conditioned team..plunged at their collars. **1900** E. H. Cooper *Monk wins* vi. 40 Young men in smart riding suits on well-groomed hacks.

b. of persons: Neat and trim, spick and span, with hair, skin, etc. carefully tended.

1886 [see well-tailored]. **1889** *Daily News* 9 Dec. 5/5 He had a well-groomed air, though he seemed carelessly dressed. **1907** H. Wyndham *Flare of Footlights* i, Tables crowded with well-groomed men and pretty women.

Hence **well-'groomedness**.

1902 *Blackw. Mag.* Apr. 553/2 The first thing I observed, when he was shown in, was his well-groomedness.

well-'grounded, *ppl. a.* Of immaterial things: Based on good grounds, firmly founded, having a good basis or foundation.

c **1369** [see well-founded]. **1579** E. K. in *Spenser's Sheph. Cal.* Ded., What in most English wryters vseth to be loose, ..in this Authour is well grounded. **1611** A. Stafford *Niobe* i. 162, I would onely desire to see my natiue countrey voide of erronious doctrine, and flourish vnder a liuely, well grounded faith. **1644** (*title*) Humble Desires and Propositions for a Safe and Well-grounded Peace. **1648** [see grounded 1 b]. **1654** T. Brooks (*title*), Heaven on Earth, or a Serious Discourse touching a well-grounded Assurance of Mens Everlasting Happiness. **1671** T. Jordan *London's Resurr.* 11 A Vnion well-grounded no Malice can hurt. **1709** Berkeley *Ess. Vision* Ded., The great and well-grounded esteem I have conceived for you. **1753-4** Richardson *Grandison* I. xi. 60 No man.. can be well-grounded in any branch of learning, who has not been at one of our famous Universities. **1776** Lowth *Larger Confut. Bp. Hare* 58 The whole of this evidence must be laid together, before we can ..proceed to a well-grounded conclusion. **1837** Lockhart *Scott* II. ii. 38 His well-grounded knowledge of the jurisprudence of his country. **1840** Thirlwall *Greece* lvi. VII. 132 It was not through a paltry jealousy, but from a well-grounded anxiety. **1866** Lowell *Study Wind.*, *Swinburne's Trag.*, Indeed, we have some well-grounded doubts whether England [etc.]. **1888** Anna K. Green *Behind Closed Doors* ii, To determine whether our fears are well-grounded.

well-grown, *ppl. a.* Showing a satisfactory growth or development.

1597 Markham *Devoreux* 20 b, As..well-growne Cedars [exceed] marish-shaken Reeds. *c* **1611** Chapman *Iliad* iii. 219 A well growne Bel-weather. **1628** Ford *Lover's Mel.* iii. ii, Twines of Iuie round The well growne Oake. **1765** *Museum Rust.* IV. 213 Especially if his pasture be not large and well grown. **1801** *Farmer's Mag.* Aug. 359 The last Winter and Spring have been remarkably mild; and well-grown fleeces, and great crops of lambs are the consequence. **1842** Loudon *Suburban Hort.* 446 The leaves of any well-grown pine plant cannot be tied up without injuring them. **1881** J. M. Fothergill *Food we eat* 116 A well-grown, yet growing girl. **1907** J. H. Patterson *Man-Eaters of Tsavo* xvii. 189 The second rhino proved to be a well-grown youngster.

b. *Ship-building.* (See quot.)

1805 *Shipwright's Vade-M.* 141 *Well-grown.* This term implies that the grain of the wood follows the shape required, as in knee timber, &c. **1867** Smyth *Sailor's Word-bk.*

well-'guarded, *ppl. a.*

1632 Lithgow *Trav.* vi. 252 We set forward, being wellguarded round about with our keepers. **1720** Pope *Iliad* xxii. 651 Whom Ilion calls Astyanax, from her well-guarded Walls. **1846** *Commercial Mag.* Oct. 135 The compensation, to which the proprietors are as much entitled as his lordship is to his well-guarded purse.

well-'guided, *ppl. a.*

a **1586** Sidney *Arcadia* ii. xiii. (1912) 234 They set upon Tiridates campe, with so well-guided a fiercenes, that..he was like to be overthrowen. **1590** Spenser *F.Q.* i. vii. 42 His goodly reason, and well guided speach. *a* **1656** Bp. Hall *Soliloquies* xiv. Wks. 1662 III. 427 A tender, and well-guided Conscience. **1709** Prior *Cupid Mistaken* ii, Swift to His beauteous Parent's Heart The too well-guided Arrow flew.

well-'guiding, *vbl. sb.*
1600 FAIRFAX *Tasso* XVII. xcvi, Through my well guiding is your voiage donne.

well-'guiding, *ppl. a.*
1603 DRAYTON *Bar. Wars* III. xxxii. 59 Torleton.. On the Queenes part with all his might doth stand, To lay this charge on her well-guiding hand.

well-hained, *ppl. a. Sc.* **a.** Of a person: In good condition; well-preserved.
1722 W. HAMILTON *Wallace* 39 But English-Men, who wanted not for Gear, Were well hain'd Callans. and had ay good Chear. **1830** GALT *Lawrie T.* VI. x, Some buxom widow, or well-hained spinster.
b. Carefully saved up or hoarded.
1785 BURNS *Cotter's Sat. Nt.* xi, The Dame brings forth.. To grace the lad, her weel-hain'd kebbuck, fell. **1787** —— *Brigs of Ayr* 173 Wha waste your weel-hain'd gear on d—d new Brigs and Harbours!

well-haired, *ppl. a.* Having a good growth of hair.
c **1611** CHAPMAN *Iliad* XVIII. 339 Whom first, faire well-haird Charis saw. **1683** G. M[ERITON] *Yorks. Dial.* (1684) 76 As weel hair'd as thy sell. **1766** [see HAIRED *ppl. a.*]. **1897** O. THOMAS in *Proc. Zool. Soc.* 434 Tail well-haired.

†**well-haled,** *ppl. a. Obs.* Pulled up properly, drawn tight.
13.. *Gaw. & Gr. Knt.* 157 Heme wel-haled hose of þat same grene.

well-'hallowed, *ppl. a.*
1599 SHAKS. *Hen. V*, I. ii. 293 To put forth My rightfull hand in a wel-hallow'd cause.

well-'hammered, *ppl. a.*
1714 GAY *Trivia* I. 33 Let firm, well-hammer'd soles protect thy feet Thro' freezing snows.

well-'handed, *ppl. a. Obs.* exc. *dial.* Dexterous, clever.
c **1520** SKELTON *Magnyf.* 2230, I know well inough ye are bothe well handyd To grope a gardeuyaunce, though it be well bandyd. **1639** LD. DIGBY *Lett. conc. Relig.* (1651) 116 Giving us the right and well-handed interpretations of Scriptures. **1902** CROCKETT *Dark o' Moon* vii. 46 A weel-handed, through-gaun wife.

well-'handled, *ppl. a.*
1477 *Paston Lett.* III. 188, I thynke notte a mater happy, nor weell handelyd, nor poletykly dalte with, when it can never be fynysshyd with owte an inconvenyence. **1676** WISEMAN *Surg.* IV. iii. 254 If the Habit of Body be tolerably good and the Ulcers well-handled. **1900** *Westm. Gaz.* 27 Sept. 4/2 A small and well-handled force of mounted men.

†**well-hanged,** *ppl. a. Obs.* = WELL-HUNG 1 a.
1611 COTGR., *Couillatris*, well hangd (betweene the legs).

well-'hardened, *ppl. a.*
1663 COWLEY *Ess. Verse & Pr.* iv. (1906) 409 Here a well hard'ned active youth we see, Taught the great Art of chearful Poverty.

†**well(-)'harnessed,** *ppl. a. Obs.* Well armed or equipped.
c **1400** T. CHESTRE *Launfal* 377 Than come ther thorwgh the cyte ten Well yharneysyth men. **1480** *Cely Papers* (Camden) 55, I troste to Jhesu that I am whel-harnest to kepe London wt. **1535** COVERDALE *1 Macc.* iv. 7 They sawe that the Heithen were mightie and wel harnessed. **1606** [see WELL-HEARTED].

well-'havened, *a.* Provided with a good haven.
1790 COWPER *On Receipt Mother's Pict.* 90 As a gallant bark.. Shoots into port at some well-haven'd isle.

'well-head. [WELL *sb.*[1]]
1. a. The place at which a spring breaks out of the ground; the head-spring or source of a stream or river.
1340-1 *Durham Acc. Rolls* (Surtees) 539 In structura unius domuncule supra le Welleheved, 23*s.* 6*d.* **13..** *E.E. Allit. P.* B. 364 Waltes out vch walle-heued, in ful wode stremez. *Ibid.* 428 To-walten alle þyse welle-hedez & þe water flowed. **1398** TREVISA *Barth. De P.R.* XIII. iii. (1495) 441 Euery ryuer.. spryngith out in welle heedes. **1574** *Cal. Laing Charters* (1899) 225 Vp the face of the hill to ane lang veit welheid onder the craigis. **1590** SPENSER *F.Q.* II. ii. 6 Great Dame Nature, from whose fruitfull pap Their welheads spring. *a* **1628** PRESTON *New Covt.* (1629) 160 There would be different streames, there would be divers well-heads. **1832** TENNYSON *Eleanore* 16 From old well-heads of haunted rills. **1838** ARNOLD *Hist. Rome* I. xi. 195 By the well-head of the water of Ferentina. **1886** STEVENSON *Kidnapped* xxiv. 240 We.. travelled on eerie mountains and among the well-heads of wild rivers.
b. *Sc.* A spring in a marsh or morass.
1816 SCOTT *Old Mort.* xv, The charger on which he was mounted plunged up to the saddle-girths in a well-head, as the springs are called which supply the marshes. **1862** WHYTE MELVILLE *Queen's Maries* xxxi, The horse.. had got bogged up to the girths in a well-head, as those particularly soft pieces of morass are called, which abound on the Scottish moorland. **1884** SPEEDY *Sport in Highlands* xvii. 299 Extensive unfrozen marshes, abounding in 'well-heads'.
2. *fig.* The chief source or fountain-head of anything.
1542 BOORDE *Dyetary* Pref. (1870) 226, I.. beynge at the well-hed of Physycke [*sc.* at Montpelier]. **1587** GOLDING *De Mornay* ii. 18 The Veynes are spred foorth throughout the whole bodie, howbeit from one welhead, that is to say from the Liuer. **1596** SPENSER *F.Q.* v. ix. 26 Or that he likened was to a welhed Of euill words and wicked sclaunders by him shed. **1606** BRYSKETT *Civ. Life* 42 Knowing that the well bringing up of children, was the spring or wel-head of honest life. **1638** JUNIUS *Paint. Ancients* 309 We must suffer our understanding to be directed to the well-head of the history it selfe. **1654** PAGITT *Heresiogr.* (ed. 5) 141 Oxford, and Cambridge, two Well-heads of Divinity. **1820** HAZLITT *Lect. Dram. Lit.* 20 It was the spring, the well-head from which every thought and feeling gushed into act. **1842** BORROW *Bible in Spain* iii. 20 The Bible, which is the well-head of all that is useful and conducive to the happiness of society. **1854** PATMORE *Angel in Ho., Betrothal* 15 As Poets of grammar, Lovers are The well-heads of morality. **1890** *Spectator* 28 June, The County Council.. had better endeavour to find some well-head of money which has hitherto remained untapped.
3. a. The top of a draw-well. Also a more or less elaborate structure erected over this.
1613 J. SARIS *Voy. Japan* (Hakl. Soc.) 133 At euery fiftie paces there is a Well-head, fitted very substantially of free-stone, with buckets for the neighbours to fetch water. **1891** *Builder* 28 Nov. 403/1 Wrought-iron Well-head. **1908** W. C. GREEN *Old Cottages Surrey* 69 Fig. 102 shows one of these well heads with a rough roof over it. **1913** *Eng. Hist. Rev.* July 553 The thoroughly characteristic Italian well-head of the twelfth century in the Lateran cloister.
b. The structure surmounting an oil- or gas-well. Freq. *attrib.*
1951 *U.S. Rep. 1950* CCCXL. 180 The issue in this case is the power of a state to fix prices at the wellhead on natural gas. **1969** *Times* 16 Dec. (Bahrain Suppl.) p. iv/3 (Advt.), Well-head structures for undersea drilling. **1972** L. M. HARRIS *Introd. Deepwater Floating Drilling Operations* ix. 93 The wellhead is installed on top of, and run with, the conductor pipe. **1983** *Fortune* 13 June 60/2 For each $1 drop in the wellhead price, producers' net income falls only 25 cents.

well-'headed, *a.*
1610 MARKHAM *Master-piece* I. ci. 201 The Greeke horse.. is.. swift, bold, well headed. **1641** [see HEADED 3]. **1725** *Bradley's Family Dict.* s.v. *Potage*, Well-headed Cabbages.

well-'hearted, *a.*
†**1.** Stout-hearted, courageous. *Obs.*
1606 G. WOODCOCKE *Hist. Ivstine* XXXVIII. 121 The Scithians besides that they be well harnessed, and well harted [*praeter arma virtutemque animi*]. *a* **1614** J. MELVILL *Autob. & Diary* (Wodrow Soc.) 223 But nocht halff sa resolut and weill-harted to feght in the quarrell as our men war. **1714** R. SMITH *Poems of Controversy* (1853) 61 Athols souldiers,.. Quick, Swift, well hearted & most prompt in hands.
2. Well-disposed, kind-hearted, generous.
1766 LD. KAMES in *Complete Farmer*, s.v. *Flax* 3 M 1 b, This prospect must be agreeable to every well-hearted Briton. **1861** QUINN *Heather Lintie* (1863) 36 But then his son Is a weel-hearted winsome chiel, And's fond o' fun. **1920** MRS. HARKER *Montagu Wycherly* i. 22 Kind little girl! .. so transparently 'well-hearted' towards all the world.

well-'heated, *ppl. a.*
1845 ELIZA ACTON *Mod. Cookery* (ed. 2) 185 Bake the meat from five to six hours in a well-heated oven. **1886** W. J. TUCKER *E. Europe* xiv. 82 There were wooden benches round a well-heated earthenware stove.

well-heeled, *ppl. a.*: see HEELED *ppl. a.* 2 b.

†**well-'heling,** *vbl. sb. Obs.* [See HELING.] Good concealment (in quot. a personification).
c **1400** *Rom. Rose* 5857 Thanne shal delite and wel heelynge [Fr. *Bien-Celer*] Fonde shame adowne to brynge.

well-hewn, *ppl. a.*
1656 COWLEY *Pindar. Odes, Life & Fame* ii, A lasting Life in well-hew'en Stone they rear.

well-hinged, *ppl. a.*
1868-70 MORRIS *Earthly Par.* I. II. 510 And there he saw a door within the wall, Well-hinged, close shut.

†**well-hired,** *ppl. a. Obs.* Receiving a good salary.
1705 MANDEVILLE *Grumbling Hive* 20 That a poor Bee should Ten times come, To ask his Due,.. And by some well-hir'd Clerk be made, To give a Crown, or ne'er be paid.

well-'hoarded, *ppl. a.*
1786 BURNS *Halloween* vii, The auld Guidwife's weel-hoorded nits Are round an' round divided. **1842** D. VEDDER *Poems* 200 Sae Ranald shooled out, in the shape o' a fee, A weel-hoarded guinea frae out o' his spleuchan.

well-hole. [WELL *sb.*[1]]
1. a. An opening through a floor or series of floors, for a staircase, chimney-stack, or for the admission of light, etc.
1680 LEYBOURN *Primatt's City & Country Purchaser* III. 187 Note.. that.. you do afterwards take the dimensions of the Well-hole for the Stairs. **1690** —— *Curs. Math.* 901 In the measuring of flooring,.. you must deduct out of it the Well-holes for the Stairs and Chimneys. **1791** SMEATON *Edystone L.* (1793) §42 A Well Hole was begun to be left upon these courses for stairs in the center. **1819** REES *Cycl.*, *Well-hole*, in Building, is the hole left in a floor, for the stairs to come up through. **1892** *Dict. Arch.* (Arch. Publ. Soc.), *Well-hole*,.. the opening through a floor or floors, in a large warehouse, whereby light can be obtained from a glass roof over it, to each floor.
b. The empty space round which the stairs of a winding staircase turn.
1823 P. NICHOLSON *Pract. Builder* 185 Stairs that have a well-hole, or hollow in the centre, are called geometrical stairs. **1825** J. NICHOLSON *Oper. Mech.* 597 A cylinder.. of the size of the well-hole of the staircase. **1833** LOUDON *Encycl. Archit.* §423 The well-hole of the stair is shown at *m.*
c. A vertical passage-way (for machinery, a lift, etc.); a shaft.
1841 BREES *Gloss. Civil Engin.* 297 *Well-hole*, a hole connected with some mechanical contrivances, and adapted for the reception of a counterbalancing weight, and for other purposes. **1862** *Catal. Internat. Exhib.* II. x. 5 The uprights or guides of the shaft or well-hole [of a lift].
2. The compartment at the lower end of a ship's pump.
1774 *Phil. Trans.* LXIV. 412 If.. plates of copper.. were .. continued down the main-top-gallant-mast, the main-top-mast, and part of the main-mast, into the well-hole.

well-horned, *a.*
1725 POPE *Odyss.* XX. 368 Where to the pastern-bone by nerves combin'd, The well-horn'd foot indissolubly join'd. **1900** ELWORTHY *Horns of Honour* ii. 125 A bull with a human head, well-horned.

well(-)horsed, *ppl. a.* Furnished with, mounted on, drawn by a good horse or horses.
1387 TREVISA *Higden* VII. 359, I and þow be here allone, iliche wel i-horsed and i-wepened. *c* **1425** WYNTOUN *Cron.* VIII. xvi. 2484 Twenty thousande men Weil armyt and weil horssit. **1470-85** MALORY *Arthur* I. x. 48 Vlfyus and Brastias .. rode forth wel horsed and wel armed. *a* **1533** [see HORSED 1]. **1656** COWLEY *Pindar. Odes, To New Year* ii, His well-horst Troops, the Months, and Days, and Hours. **1666** EARL ORRERY *St. Lett.* (1742) 200 Nothing now being talked of but war, whoever has money will not spare it to be well horsed. **1884** [see HORSED 1 b]. **1899** *Scribner's Mag.* XXV. 66/2 The smart and well-horsed army service wagon. **1901** *Scotsman* 3 Apr. 8/2 The force was well-armed and well-horsed.

well-housed, *ppl. a.*
1838 DICKENS *O. Twist* xxiii, It was a night for the well-housed and fed to draw round the bright fire and thank God they were at home. **1846** MCCULLOCH *Acc. Brit. Empire* (1854) I. 445 A well-fed, well-clothed, and well-housed population.

well-hued, *a.*
a **1568** R. SEMPLE *Ballat* 75 in *Bannatyne MS.* (Hunter. Club) 357 With vlis to rennew it and mak it weill hewit. **1615** [see HUED].

†**well(-)'humoured,** *a. Obs.* [WELL *adv.* 32.] Good-humoured.
1683 DRYDEN *Life Plutarch* 12 As we say in English, a well humour'd man and a good companion. **1711** SHAFTESB. *Charac.* III. 108 He, who had the better of the Argument, wou'd be easy and well-humour'd.

well-hung, *ppl. a.*
1. a. Furnished with large pendent organs; *spec.* (of a man) having large genitals.
1611 COTGR., *Oreillé*, eared; well hung, or hangd; which hath great eares. **1681** DRYDEN *Abs. & Achit.* I. 574 In the name of Dulness be The well-hung Balaam and cold Caleb free. **1823** EGAN *Grose's Dict. Vulg. T.* **1868** *Index Expurgatorius of Martial* 3 In Rome well-hung youths made a good profit by their amours. **1958** L. DURRELL *Balthazar* v. 103 They love a well-hung diplomat. **1977** D. WILES *Death Flight* xviii. 177 Hey, man... You sure is well hung for a priest!
b. Decorated with rich hangings or tapestry.
a **1667** COWLEY *Ess. Verse & Pr.* i. (1906) 389 A painted Cage; Or the false Forest of a well-hung Room.
2. Of the tongue: Working readily and freely; glib, fluent.
1678 *Quack's Acad.* 6 If niggardly Nature or more penurious Education have not afforded you a Tongue well hung. **1790** J. FISHER *Poems* 57 Be sure to keep a well hung tongue, Your knav'ry to defend. **1853** HICKIE *Aristoph.* (1872) II. 576 Thou well-hung tongue.
3. Suspended or attached so as to hang well. Said, e.g., of a window-sash, a carriage, a gate, a lady's skirt.
1762 STERNE *Tr. Shandy* v. xvii, Susannah did not consider that nothing was well hung in our family,—so slap came the sash down like lightning upon us. **1771** SMOLLETT *Humphry Cl.* 26 June, The carriage is remarkably commodious and well hung. **1847** SURTEES *Hawbuck Grange* xi. 224 Some well-hung green gates. **1847** MRS. GORE *Castles in Air* I. x. 204 The light, easy, well-hung, well-finished barouche. **1896** *Daily News* 4 July 6/3 Nothing is fresher or prettier than a well-hung skirt of white or cream colour.
4. Of meat or game: Hung up for a sufficient time.
1877 *Cassell's Dict. Cookery* 1079/2 Well-hung four-year-old mutton. *Ibid.* 1080/1 A fine, well-hung neck of venison.

well-'husbanded, *ppl. a.*
1600 SURFLET *Country Farm* II. liv. 383 You shall plant their shootes after the same manner, in a well husbanded and digged ground. **1641** MILTON *Animadv.* 52 A well-husbanded nursery of plants and fruits. **1885** RUSKIN *Ulric Farm Serv.* Pref. p. v, In the quiet mornings of his well husbanded and well spent days.

wellie: see WELLY.

well-i'magined, *ppl. a.*
1798 SOPHIA LEE *Canterb. T., Young Lady's T.* II. 13 A well-imagined, or well-timed compliment. **1809** [see IMAGINED 1].

well-'imitated, *ppl. a.*
1744 ARMSTRONG *Preserv. Health* III. 91 With the well-imitated fly to hook The eager trout.

well-im'proved, *ppl. a.*
1641 [see IMPROVED 2]. **1709** T. MOLYNEUX in *Ir. Archæol. Soc. Misc.* (1846) I. 177 From thence to Moat, thro' a well improv'd, well planted country. **1735** BERKELEY *Querist* §413 A handsome Seat amidst well-improved Lands.

well-in, *adj. phr. Austral.* [f. dial. use of *in* = furnished, provided, 'off'.] Well-off, well-to-do.

1845 T. McCombie *Arabin* 241 They had a pretty little farm, and were well in. **1891** 'R. Boldrewood' *Sydney-side Sax.* Introd., He's a well-in squatter, that took up runs or bought them cheap before free selection.

well-in'clined, *ppl. a.* Of good natural inclination or disposition; well-disposed.

a **1586** Sidney *Arcadia* II. xxvii. (1912) 323 These words being spoken (like a furious storme) presently caried away their wel inclined braines. **1611** Rich *Honest. Age* (1615) 12 Zelous, and well inclined married wiues. **1615** Chapman *Odyss.* VII. 235 The well-inclin'd, And sacred order of Alcinous mind. **1683** H. Prideaux in *Lett. Lit. Men* (Camden) 185 We looke on him as a studious well-inclined yong Gentleman. **1709** Atterbury *Serm.* (1726) II. 237 For the sake of those, who..may be well-inclin'd to Works of Mercy. **1710** Steele *Tatler* No. 207 ⁋1 A well inclined young Man..must needs take Delight in being agreeable to his Elders. **1881** Gladstone *Let. to Forster* 8 Sept. in R. B. O'Brien *Life Parnell* (1898) I. 304 To reduce the following of Parnell by drawing away from him all well-inclined men.

well(-)in'formed, *ppl. a.* Well equipped with information; fully furnished with knowledge, whether of a special subject or of things in general; having a well-stored mind.

c **1440** [see informed *ppl. a.* 2b]. *c* **1611** Chapman *Iliad* Ep. Ded. 94 Great Princes, well inform'd and deckt With gracious vertue. **1614** [see informed *ppl. a.* 2b]. **1752** Chesterf. *Lett. to Son* 23 June, He is a very pretty and well-informed man. **1791** Boswell *Johnson* an. 1783 (1904) II. 485 This great man..was yet well-informed in the common affairs of life. **1794** Mrs. Radcliffe *Myst. Udolpho* i, A well-informed mind..is the best security against the contagion of folly and of vice. **1827** Sir J. Barrington *Pers. Sk.* I. 351 Colonel Burr was..a well-informed, sensible man. **1856** Ruskin *Mod. Painters* IV. v. §20 The perfect and well-informed decision of Albert Durer and his fellow-workmen. **1863** B. Woodcroft *Brief Biogr.* 18 Crompton..was intelligent, though not what is generally called 'well-informed'. **1898** Watts-Dunton *Aylwin* I. v, Her aunt, who was no doubt a well-informed woman, had been attending to her education.

absol. **1824** Landor *Imag. Conv., Bacon & Hooker* II. 65, I have observed, among the well informed and the ill informed, nearly the same quantity of infirmities and follies. **1842** Dickens *Amer. Notes* iii, Not to impress the thoughtful and the well-informed, but the ignorant and heedless. **1922** G. K. Chesterton *Man who knew* vii. 124 It startled the well-informed by being a new and fantastic idea they had never encountered.

welling ('wɛlɪŋ), *vbl. sb.*[1] [f. well *v.*[1] + -ing[1].]

1. The action of boiling or scalding. Also comb. **welling-lead**, a cauldron.

1371-3 *Durham Acc. Rolls* (Surtees) 577 In emendacione unius Wellynglede in pistrino. *c* **1440** *Promp. Parv.* 521/1 Wellynge, of mylke and oþer lycure, *coagulacio, decoccio.* **1588** L. M. tr. *Bk. Dyeing* 22 Take so much water as will go into the small kettle, so let it have a welling or two on the fire. **1691** Ray *S. & E. Co. Words*, 'Welling of whey' is heating it scalding hot, in order to the taking off the curds.

b. The boiling up (of a liquid in a pot).

c **1440** *Promp. Parv.* 521/1 Wellynge, or boylynge of playynge pottys, *ebullicio, bullicio.*

†**2. a.** The melting or founding of metals. *Obs.*

1388 Wyclif *Jer.* li. 17 Ech wellere togidere is schent in a grauun ymage; for his wellyng togidere is fals [Vulg. *quia mendax est conflatio eorum*]. *c* **1440** *Promp. Parv.* 521/1 Wellynge, of metel, *fusio.*

†**b.** = welding *vbl. sb.* Also *attrib. Obs.*

1660 tr. *Paracelsus' Archidoxis* I. vii. 109 Smiths.. compactly consolidated their Irons together as if they had been conglutinated with a true compaction, or welling. **1795** G. Pearson in *Phil. Trans.* LXXXV. 328 The substance made white hot, by the forge, had the glassy smooth surface of iron, in what is termed the welding or the welling state.

3. The bubbling *up* and overflowing (of water); the flowing *forth* or *out* (of a stream); the swelling (of flood-water, the sea).

c **1400** *Contin. Brut.* ccxxiv. 292 þere arose suche a sprynggynge and wellinge op of wateres and floodes, bothe of þe see and also of fresshe ryvers & sprynges, þat [etc.]. *c* **1440** *Promp. Parv.* 521/1 Wellynge, or boylynge vp as water fro þe erthe or sprynge, *scaturicio.* *a* **1500** *R. Bale's Chron.* in *Six Town Chron.* (1911) 135 The ix day of Octobre was such a wellyng and spring of waters..that [etc.]. **1867** Myers *St. Paul* (1896) 38 Welling of waves, disconsolate and tender, Sighed on the shore. **1871** Macduff *Mem. Patmos* xxiv. 326 The welling up of the Jordan in the cavern at the base of giant Mount Hermon.

b. *fig.*

1857 Livingstone *Trav.* xiv. 259 The notes..strike the mind by their loudness and variety, as the wellings forth from joyous hearts, of praise to Him who fills them with overflowing gladness. **1896** F. M. Crawford *Corleone* xxvii. (1897) II. 121 With a wild welling up of hope, Francesco galloped along the road. **1916** Mrs. H. Ward *Lady Connie* I. v. 95 It was a moment for her of strong reaction, of a welling-up and welling-back of life, after a kind of suspension.

'welling, *vbl. sb.*[2] [f. well *sb.*[1] + -ing[1].] The action of making a well or shaft; in quot. *concr.*, shaft-work.

1865 *Pall Mall Gaz.* 10 Oct. 7 He was assisting in placing a pile in the 'wellings' when the chain slipped from the 'crab'.

welling ('wɛlɪŋ), *ppl. a.* [f. well *v.*[1] + -ing[2].]

1. Boiling: said of a liquid, of molten metal, etc.; also of a pot. ***welling hot***, boiling hot.

a **1300** *Cursor M.* 21042 In a tun was welland hat fild of oyle he did him schott. *Ibid.* 26753 Alle your entrailles ilkon in welland pottes sal be don. **1303** R. Brunne *Handl. Synne* 6578 Whoso handlyth pycche wellyng hote He shal have fylthe thereof sumdeyl. **1340** Hampole *Pr. C.* 7126 It salle be hatter þan ever was Molten led or welland bras. **1370-80** *Visions of St. Paul* 134 in *O.E. Misc.* 227 And þei sodun euerichon In wellyng pich and Brumston. *a* **1400-50** *Wars Alex.* 4080 Till he come blesenand on a brym was welland hate. *c* **1440** *Gesta Rom.* lxviii. 385 Sone after come ij. deuyls yellyng, and broughtyn a Cawderon full of hote wellyng brasse.

†**b.** *fig.* in phr. ***welling woe*** (of hell). Cf. *to well in woe*, well *v.*[1] 3 b. *Obs.*

a **1300** *Cursor M.* 21836 He demed me in-till hell depe, Euer in welland wa to wepe. *c* **1375** *Sc. Leg. Saints* xvi. (*Magdalena*) 634 [Christ] tholit þare dyspituise ded, Fra welland wa vs al to led.

†**c.** ***welling wood***, raging mad. (Cf. walling *ppl. a.*[1] 1.) *Obs.*

13.. *St. Cristofer* 53 in Horstm. *Altengl. Leg.* (1881) 455 Bathe togedir away þay ȝode Als þay hade bene welland wode. *c* **1460** *Towneley Myst.* viii. 344 Thes folk shall flyt no far, If he go welland wode.

2. Of a spring, tears, etc.: Flowing abundantly, surging. Also *fig.*

1387-8 T. Usk *Test. Love* I. i. 86 Or els to see the sight that might al my wellinge sorowes voyde. **1388** Wyclif *Gen.* xxvi. 19 Thei diggiden in the stronde, and thei founden wellynge watir. **1548** Udall *Erasm. Par. N.T.* Pref. 7 He was a continual wellyng fountayne of eloquence,..a botomlesse spring of largesse. **1567** Turberv. *Ovid's Ep.* 50 Alongste my stayned cheekes eche houre the welling teares doe trill. **1819** S. Rogers *Human Life* 741 Their questions, their replies, Fresh as the welling waters, round him rise. **1850** Disraeli in G. E. Buckle *Life* (1914) III. viii. 238 There should be more variety in the movement. Something to break the low, tho' welling, chorus of the agrestic multitude. **1858** Farrar *Eric* I. xiii, Soft hair, tangled with welling blood. **1890** H. H. Johnston in *Nature* 13 Nov. 46 A welling, brackish pool.

3. That pours out a stream or streams. Of a wound, etc.: Bleeding copiously. Also *fig.*

1591 Sylvester *Du Bartas* I. iii. 181 The Sun..and Windes..Extract as much still of her humours thin, As weeping Aire, and welling Earth pours in. **1814** Byron *Lara* II. xvii, Kneels Kaled watchful o'er his welling side. **1910** *Sat. Rev.* 19 Feb. 225/1 His speeches..have the air of happy improvisation, as though they came from a welling heart.

welling, obs. dial. var. felling *vbl. sb.*

1513 *MS. Acc. St. John's Hosp., Canterb.*, For wellyng of ij elmys jd. **1520** *Ibid.*, Payd for wellyng off xv pyesys off tymber.

welling, obs. form of willing *vbl. sb.*

Wellington ('wɛlɪŋtən). Also **wellington**. [Named after Arthur, first duke of *Wellington*, 1769–1852.]

1. *attrib.* **a. *Wellington boot*** = sense 2 a and b.

1818 M. Birkbeck *Notes Journ. Amer.* (ed. 4) 88 Americans..in pantaloons and Wellington boots. **1839** Dickens *Nickleby* ii, Grey mixture pantaloons, and Wellington boots drawn over them. **1860** *All Year Round* No. 64. 331 The Wellington boot at present worn by our dragoons under their trousers. **1884** E. Yates *Recoll.* I. ii. 46 No gentleman could wear anything in the daytime but Wellington boots, high up the leg, over which the trousers fitted tightly, covering most of the foot, and secured underneath by a broad strap. **1971** [see delphinium b]. **1980** L. Lewis *Private Life of Country House* vi. 79 Snowboots.. were virtually superseded by rubber wellington boots, which I first saw when I was about eleven [i.e. *c.* 1920].

b. Used to designate other articles of clothing introduced by the Duke, or named after him, as ***Wellington coat, hat, trousers.***

1815 [see *half-dress* s.v. half- II. n]. **1818** Scott *Hrt. Midl.* i, The preposterous length of their great-coats, and the equally fashionable latitude and longitude of their Wellington trousers. **1828** Creevey *Papers* etc. (1904) II. 155 Yesterday morning he made his first appearance in a new 'Wellington' Coat (a kind of a half-and-half great Coat and undercoat, you know, meeting close and square below the knees). **1832** Marryat *N. Forster* xxxii, The above look much more scientific than Wellington trousers. **1893** Georg. Hill *Hist. Eng. Dress* II. 254 Wellington hat with the yeoman Crown.

c. *Wellington chest* (***of drawers***): a tall narrow chest of drawers used for keeping specimens. Occas. ellipt. as *Wellington.*

1953 'N. Blake' *Dreadful Hollow* iv. 50 There was the wellington to which Stanford Blick had directed him. Nigel opened one of its drawers. **1960** H. Hayward *Antique Coll.* 304/2 *Wellington chest*, a tall narrow chest containing about a dozen drawers which can be locked by a single hinged flap securing all the drawers. **1971** *Country Life* 7 Oct. (Suppl.) 23 (Advt.), A small antique mahogany Wellington chest of drawers measuring only 19½ inches wide, 14 inches deep and 41 inches high. **1982** 'J. Gash' *Firefly Gadroon* v. 53 There's a space where I used to have my Wellington chest before I flogged it for bread.

2. a. A high boot covering the knee in front and cut away behind. Also a somewhat shorter boot worn under the trousers.

1817 Moncrieff *Giovanni in Lond.* I. iv, And wear of wellingtons a pair, To shine from top to toe, sir! *a* **1821** Keats *Modern Love* 8 Miss's comb is made a pearl tiara, And common Wellingtons turn Romeo boots. **1854** C. Knight *Once upon a Time* II. 266 The tops lasted till Wellingtons and trousers drove them out. **1869** E. A. Parkes *Pract. Hygiene* (ed. 3) 416 The cavalry have Wellingtons and jackboots. **1906** *Stores' Price List*, 2 Pairs Calf Wellingtons.

b. A waterproof boot usu. reaching the knee, worn in wet or muddy conditions. Usu. *pl.*

1907 *Yesterday's Shopping* (1969) 326/1 Black glazed rubber boots. Ladies' Wellingtons. **1944** D. Welch *Jrnl.* 25 Jan. (1973) 107 He wore an old thick jersey, and grey flannels tucked into Wellingtons. **1984** *Brian Mills Catal.* Spring & Summer 337/4 Waterproof wellington in PVC.

3. A variety of cooking apple, large, roundish, and with yellowish white flesh. Also ***W. apple.***

1821 *Trans. Hort. Soc.* (1822) IV. 529 Mr. Richard Williams sent..specimens of an Apple called the *Wellington*, a very handsome and long keeping variety. **1839** C. McIntosh *Orchard* 18 Dumelow's Seedling [*Syn.* Wellington Apple, Dumelow's Crab]. **1882** *Garden* 18 Mar. 182/3 Cooks go generally for the Wellington as a cooking Apple.

wellingtonia (wɛlɪŋ'təʊnɪə). [Named by Lindley after Arthur, first duke of Wellington (1769–1852): see -ia[1].] The popular name in England of *Sequoia* (*Wellingtonia*) *gigantea*, a large coniferous tree, native of California; the 'big tree' or Washington cedar.

[**1853** *Gard. Chron.* 24 Dec. 820/1 Wellington stands as high above his contemporaries as the Californian tree above all the surrounding foresters. Let it then bear henceforward the name of *Wellingtonia gigantea*.] *Ibid.* 823/3 These considerations seem to leave no room for doubt that Wellingtonia is an entirely new coniferous form. **1868** *Morning Star* 18 June, A group composed of three gigantic Wellingtonias. **1880** Miss Braddon *Just as I am* xxvii, Gardens rich in monkey-trees, deodaras, Wellingtonias.

Wellingtonian (wɛlɪŋ'təʊnɪən), *a.* [See prec. and -ian.] Belonging to or characteristic of the duke of Wellington.

1854 *Poultry Chron.* I. 439/2 She performs this duty, too, in a true Wellingtonian spirit, coming off her nest with quiet dignity. **1889** *Academy* 14 Sept. 159/1 The Wellingtonian legend was once as strong in England as the Napoleonic in France. **1907** *Nation* 5 Oct. 9/1 There is a Wellingtonian vigour in his way of stating a case.

†**well-in'habited**, *ppl. a. Obs.* Populous.

1555 Eden *Decades* (Arb.) 286 The Ilande of saynt Laurence..beinge well inhabited and of temperate ayer. **1585** T. Washington tr. *Nicholay's Voy.* I. xvi. 17 The Bourg..[is] well inhabited. **1709** T. Molyneux in *Ir. Archæol. Soc. Misc.* (1846) I. 169 It seems to have been of old a well inhabited and thriving town. **1709** Shaftesb. *Moralists* II. i. 40 At its foot a River and well-inhabited Plain. **1780** Coxe *Russ. Discov.* 30 Two well-inhabited islands.

wellink ('wɛlɪŋk). *dial.* Also **wallink**. [app. worn down from **well* (well *sb.*[1]) *-lemke*: see lemeke and brooklime.] A provincial name of the Brooklime, *Veronica Beccabunga.*

1831 W. Patrick *Plants Lanark.* 46 Brooklime..The Wallink of the village herbalist. **1878** *Cumberld. Gloss.*, Well ink. **1881** *Hardwicke's Sci.-Gossip* XVII. 278 Brooklime. 'Wellink'...co. Antrim.

well-'instituted, *ppl. a.*

1644 Milton *Areop.* (Arb.) 49 No Nation, or well instituted State, if they valu'd books at all, did ever use this way of licencing.

well-in'structed, *ppl. a.*

1553 [see instructed]. **1560** Bible (Geneva) *Ecclus.* xxvi. 14 There is nothing so muche worthe as a woman wel instructed. **1781** Cowper *Conversat.* 903 But let the wise and well-instructed hand Once take the shell beneath his just command. **1835** *Court Mag.* VI. 224/2 A well-instructed appreciation of his public claims. **1838** Fr. A. Kemble *Jrnl. Resid. Georgia* (1863) 24 Mary's brother.. performs all the offices of a well-instructed waiter with great efficiency. **1865** Pusey *Truth Eng. Ch.* 224 Deadly sins could hardly be committed in ignorance by any one of well-instructed conscience.

Hence **well-in'structedness**. *rare*$^{-1}$.

1628 [see instructedness].

well-'integrated, *ppl. a.*

1943 *Mind* LII. 127 A well-integrated body of..laws. **1976** B. Gibson *Birmingham Bombs* ix. 74 They got on with their neighbours and most of them were regarded as well-integrated members of the community.

well-in'tended, *ppl. a.* Characterized by a right and sincere intention; well-meant.

a **1586** Sidney *Arcadia* III. xiv. (1912) 437 Especially setting forth their noble gratefulnes, in never forgetting wel-intended services. **1628** Feltham *Resolves* I. xxvi. 83 So, by bad circumstances, [we] poyson a well-intended principall. **1768-74** Tucker *Lt. Nat.* (1834) II. 263 The meanest, well-intended labours may claim thy patronage. **1777** Johnson *Let. to Dr. Dodd* 26 June in *Boswell*, In requital of those well-intended offices which you are pleased so emphatically to acknowledge. **1827** Higgins *Celtic Druids* 66 The perhaps well-intended but nonsensical and fruitless efforts of our priests. **1834** *Tait's Mag.* I. 208/2 The pamphlet is well-intended, sensible, and temperate.

†**well(-)intentionated**: see intentionated.

well-in'tentioned, *ppl. a.*

1. Of a person: Having good intentions.

1598 Parsons in *Archpriest Controv.* (Camden) I. 25 Yf the magistrates were knowen to be godly and well intentioned men. **1716** Addison *Freeholder* No. 50 ⁋2 Among us, This has been a mark of such well-intentioned persons, as would betray their country, if they were able. **1768-74** Tucker *Lt. Nat.* (1834) II. 681 Believing me a well-intentioned body, but a little bewildered by dealing too much among heathen authors. **1828** Miss Mitford *Village* Ser. III. 115 Dame Banks was in fact a well-intentioned, worthy woman. **1839** Burgon *Sir T. Gresham* I. ii. 65 The truth seems to be, that however well intentioned, he did not possess the requisite abilities for the office he filled. **1857** Buckle *Civiliz.* I. vii. 327 These well-intentioned, though mistaken, men.

2. Of actions, utterances, etc.: Due to or based upon good intentions.
1848 DICKENS *Dombey* iii, Polly triumphed not a little in the success of her well-intentioned scheme. **1875** JEVONS *Money* viii. 81 Many well-intentioned efforts to reform a currency have thus been frustrated. **1885** *American* XI. 44 A well-intentioned argument.
Hence **well-in'tentionedness**.
1799 COLERIDGE *Lett.* (1895) 315, I see enough of the boy to be fully convinced of his goodness and well-intentionedness.

well-in'vented, *ppl. a.* Cleverly fabricated or made up. Cf. It. *ben trovato*.
Well invented occurs as pa. t. in Spenser's *F.Q.* IV. ii. 2, IV. xii. 2.
1697 DRYDEN *Æneis* II. 206 He full of fraudful Arts This well invented Tale for Truth imparts. **17..** BYSSHE *Art Engl. Poetry* (1762) I. Pref. p. vii, The well-invented Fables of the Antients were design'd only to inculcate the Truth with more Delight.

wellish ('wɛlɪʃ), *adv. dial.* and *colloq.* [f. WELL *adv.* + -ISH.] Pretty well. ***wellish off***, fairly well to do. Also ***not wellish*** adj., rather unwell.
1737 BYROM *Rem.* (1856) II. I. 122 Mr. Lloyd complained of being hot, faint, not wellish. **1830** H. COCKBURN *Let.* 30 Dec. (1932) 30 How are you? All wellish here. **1856** D. G. ROSSETTI *Let.* 6 Mar. (1965) I. 293, I fancy it will pay wellish, too. **1875** 'S. BEAUCHAMP' *N. Hamilton* II. 134 They [the hops] looks moighty koind so fur, an they bin a taakin hold wellish. **1899** *Cumbld. Gloss.*, *Weelish off*, in easy circumstances. **1934** E. BOWEN *Cat Jumps* 230 '[Do you] know him fearfully well?' 'Wellish,' said Rachel.

† **well-i'toȝe(n, -i'towe(n**, *ppl. a. Obs.* [See TEE *v.*[1] and cf. UNTOWEN, WANTON.] Well trained or instructed; well-conditioned, modest.
c **1205** LAY. 10099 Luces wes wel itoȝen. *a* **1225** *Ancr. R.* 204 Þe Scorpiun of Lecherie.. haueð swuche kundles þet in one wel itowune muðe hore summes nome ne sit nout uorto nemnen; uor þe nome one muhte hurten alle wel itowune earen. *c* **1230** *Hali Meid.* (1922) 35 Muche dale laðluker þen eni wel-itohe muð for schome mahe seggen. *c* **1275** LAY. 12913 A child þat was wel itowe.

well-joined, *ppl. a.*
1553 ASCHAM *Rept. Germany* 1 If proper and naturall wordes, in well ioyned sentences do lyuely expresse the matter. *a* **1586** SIDNEY *Arcadia* II. xvii. (1912) 260 Alas, how painefull a thing it is to a devided minde to make a wel-joyned answere? *c* **1611** CHAPMAN *Iliad* XIII. 626 As through fallow fields, Blacke Oxen draw a well-ioyn'd plough. **1615** —— *Odyss.* XXI. 197 Thus, below A well-ioyn'd boord he laide it. **1645** MILTON *Tetrach.* 38 The intolerable yoake of a never well joyn'd wedlocke.

well-jointed, *ppl. a.*
1413 [see JOINTED]. **1874** J. M. FOTHERGILL *Maintenance of Health* 282 The rain should be collected into sufficient and well-jointed spouting.

well-judged, *ppl. a.* Marked by sound judgement, judicious; wisely estimated, correctly calculated.
1725 BERKELEY *Proposal* Wks. III. 230 An extensive and well-judged charity. **1780** COWPER *On Burning Ld. Mansfield's Libr.* 7 The well-judg'd purchase. **1841** ELPHINSTONE *Hist. India* II. 59 His next measure.. was perfectly rational and well-judged. **1868** GEO. ELIOT *Ess.* (1884) 325 A vast crop, that.. can be come at, not at all by hurried snatching, but only by a well-judged patient process. **1895** *Daily News* 7 Sept. 7/3 Stoddart being out to a well-judged catch at long-on.
Hence **well-'judgedly**, *adv.*
1768 MISS BURNEY *Early Diary* (1889) I. 18 Never was parent so properly, so well-judgedly affectionate!

well-'judging, *ppl. a.* Having or exercising or characterized by sound judgement.
1751 *Pope's Wks.* V. 240 *note*, An Age so distinguished for well-judging Patrons. **1755** YOUNG *Centaur* I. 5 Well-judging Wit is a flower of wisdom. **1789** COWPER *Catharina* 34 When the mind is endued With a well-judging taste from above. **1815** JANE AUSTEN *Emma* viii, He always speaks to the purpose; open, straight forward, and very well judging. **1815** SCOTT *Guy M.* xxxviii, A good and prudent and well-judging woman. **1868** GEO. ELIOT *Ess.* (1884) 334 The foresight, the conscience, that will make him well-judging and scrupulous in the use of it [*sc.* the franchise].

well-kempt, -kemmyt, *ppl. a.* Carefully combed. Also tidy, well cared for.
1513 DOUGLAS *Æneis* X. xiv. 13 Hys weyll kemmyt berd, hyngand full straucht Apon his breist. **1540** J. HEYWOOD *Four PP.* 878 Theyr hornes well gylt, theyr clowes full clene, Theyr taylles well kempt. **1922** JOYCE *Ulysses* 212 A wellkempt head, new-barbered. **1934** P. FLEMING *One's Company* II. xviii. 306 The numerous temples were so well-kempt. **1973** *Observer* (Colour Suppl.) 23 Sept. 43/1 Tall, improbably athletic, handsome, bearded, he looked like a well-kempt prophet.

well-kenned, -kent, *ppl. a. Sc.* Well-known, familiar.
a **1796** BURNS *On Willie Chalmers* 9, I doubt na, lass, that weel-kend name May cost a pair o' blushes. —— *Epigr. to Artist* 7 You'll easy draw a weel-kent face, But no sae weel a stranger. **1886** STEVENSON *Kidnapped* i, Others, all well-kenned gentlemen, had pleasure in his society. **1895** CROCKETT *Men of Moss-Hags* xxvii. 205 So I was here upon well-kenned ground.

well-kept, *ppl. a.* Carefully preserved or stored; faithfully observed or guarded; maintained in good order or condition.
14.. in *Rel. Ant.* I. 233 He shall never have good larder, fare gardeyn, nor wele kepte councell. **1613–16** W. BROWNE *Brit. Past.* I. ii. 43 That well kept Register wherein is writ All ils men doe. *c* **1670** O. HEYWOOD *Diaries* (1881) II. 348 How much reall comfort a Christian hath in a well-kept fast. **1763** *Museum Rust.* I. 143 A well-kept garden. **1865** *Dublin Univ. Mag.* I. 19 Ruddy as a well-kept apple. **1871** LE FANU *Rose & Key* II. 271 A well-kept road across a melancholy moor. **1898** MISS YONGE *Keble's Parishes* xiv. 157 Well-kept, picturesque cottages. **1915** *Edin. Rev.* July 101 The well-kept secrets of the older Gods.

well-knit, *ppl. a.*
1. Firmly conjoined or compacted; closely linked or connected.
1445 tr. *Claudian* 43 in *Anglia* XXVIII. 261 Ner for noise of litel offence [Fidelity] dissoluyth not knottis wele knytte. **1635–56** COWLEY *Davideis* I. 380 His spirit contains The well-knit Mass. **1708** J. PHILIPS *Cyder* II. 458 Anger-kindling Taunt, the certain Bane Of well-knit Fellowship. **1871** TYLOR *Prim. Cult.* II. xiv. 122 Declaring the will and answers of the gods.. in well-knit harangues.
2. Of a person, his frame: Strongly and compactly built, not loose-jointed.
1588 SHAKS. *L.L.L.* I. ii. 77 O well-knit Sampson, strong ioynted Sampson. **1674** COTTON tr. *B. de Montluc's Comm.* 179 He was.. strong and well knit. **1726** POPE *Odyss.* XVIII. 259 Thy well-knit frame. **1861** DICKENS *Gt. Expect.* iv, Joe was a well-knit, characteristic-looking blacksmith. **1890** 'R. BOLDREWOOD' *Col. Reformer* xv, The square form and well-knit figure of an ordinary English aristocrat.
fig. **1867** M. ARNOLD *Immortality* 13 His soul well-knit, and all his battles won.

well-'knotted, *ppl. a.*
1855 D. COSTELLO *Stories fr. Screen* 122 Bundles tied up in well-knotted handkerchiefs. **1888** F. H. WOODS tr. *Montelius' Civil. Sweden* 61 Upon the head was a well-knotted worsted net.

† **well-'knowing**, *ppl. a. Obs.* Intelligent and well-informed.
1674 N. FAIRFAX *Bulk & Selv.* 5 Most well-knowing men have been wary of speaking it out. **1709** SHAFTESB. *Moralists* I. iii. 30 Knowing as you are (continu'd I) well-knowing and experienc'd in all the Degrees and Orders of Beauty.

well-'knowledged, *ppl. a.* Furnished with sound knowledge.
1858 J. BROWN *Horæ Subs.* (1882) I. 407 He had the *momentum* of a strong, clear, well-knowledged mind.

well(-)known, *ppl. a.*
1. Known to many, widely or generally known.
c **1470** HENRY *Wallace* I. 11 It is weyle knawyne on mony diuers syde, How thai haff wrocht in to thair mychty pryde. **1479–80** *Paston Lett.* III. 269 He is well knowe in London. **1568** TURNER *Herbal* III. 8 Medewurte is an herbe well knowen unto all men. *a* **1586** SIDNEY *Arcadia* I. vii. §2 He by enquirie gotte to the wel-knowne house of Kalander. **1613** CHAPMAN *Rev. Bussy D'Ambois* III. i, Ile not wrong My well knowne Brother for Anonymos. **1621** BP. MOUNTAGU *Diatribæ* 19 The well-knowne and avowable practice of the Ancients. **1697** DRYDEN *Æneis* III. 141 The fruitful Isle of Crete, well known to Fame. **1711** ADDISON *Spect.* No. 127 ¶3 It is well known we have not had a more moderate Summer these many Years. **1780** *Mirror* No. 87 She instanced the well-known lines of Shakespeare. **1818** SCOTT *Hrt. Midl.* xxxiii, The well-known leader of the Porteous mob. **1837** *Penny Cycl.* IX. 163/1 Dry Rot, a well-known disease affecting timber. **1850** MCCOSH *Div. Govt.* II. i. (1874) 140 It is well known that art has in general preceded science. **1875** JOWETT *Plato* (ed. 2) I. 46 His father being a very well-known man. **1907** J. A. HODGES *Elem. Photogr.* (ed. 6) 95 Any well-known brand [of Bromide paper].
2. Intimately or thoroughly known.
1590 SPENSER *F.Q.* III. v. 17 A narrow foord, to them well knowne. **1596** *Ibid.* v. viii. 40 The dreadfull sight did them so sore affray, That their well knowen courses they forwent. **1697** DRYDEN *Virg. Georg.* III. 391 The Stallion snuffs the well-known Scent afar. **1711** STEELE *Spect.* No. 4 ¶2 There are.. many to whom my Person is as well known as that of their nearest Relations. **1726** POPE *Odyss.* XVI. 9 Some well-known friend (Eumæus) bends this way. **1796** MME. D'ARBLAY *Camilla* x. xii, A well-known voice reached her ears. **1805** SCOTT *Last Minstr.* IV. xxv, The boy.. Implor'd for aid each well-known face. **1867** MORRIS *Jason* II. 15 So lightly through the well-known woods he passed.
absol. **1890** *Hardwicke's Sci.-Gossip* XXVI. 158/2 It is always best to begin with the well-known, and proceed to the less known or altogether unknown.
Hence **well-'knownness**.
1961 D. J. BOORSTIN *Image* viii. 162 The star system.. puts a premium on well-knownness for its own sake. **1978** J. PEARSON *Façades* xxiii. 401 A celebrity has been defined by Daniel Boorstin as a person who is known for his well-knownness. **1984** *Listener* 15 Mar. 31/2 Telly persons are, as it were, well known for their well-known-ness.

wellkyn, var. WILKIN *Obs.*

well-'laboured, *ppl. a.* Skilfully wrought or elaborated; thoroughly tilled.
1708 J. PHILIPS *Cyder* I. 343 When they to the vocal Shell Warble melodious their well-labour'd Songs. **1718** POPE *Iliad* XXIV. 287 A large, well-labour'd bowl. **1835** URE *Philos. Manuf.* 41 Lancashire is the fertile and well-laboured soil in which the seed of factory knowledge will bring forth fruit one hundred fold.

well-'labouring, *ppl. a.*
1597 SHAKS. *2 Hen. IV*, I. i. 127 Whose well-labouring sword Had three times slaine th'appearance of the King.

well-laced, *ppl. a.* (See LACED 6.)
1826 J. F. COOPER *Last of Mohicans* vi, A powerful draught of the woodman's high flavoured and well-laced compound.

well-'laden, *ppl. a.*
1697 CONGREVE *Mourn. Bride* Epil. 22 Devoutly praying .. That some well-laden Ship may strike the Sands.

well-laid, *ppl. a.* Also with adv., as *in*, *on*.
1679 OLDHAM *Sat. Jesuits* I. (1681) 19 That damn'd Committee, whom the Fates ordain Of all our well-laid Plots to be the bane. **1826** GALT *Last of Lairds* iv. 31 A weel-laid-on whack o' the tawse. **1847** SURTEES *Hawbuck Grange* xii. 247 Our friends now got among nice, level, well-laid, well-pleached fences. **1854** —— *Handley Cr.* li. (1901) II. 92 Jorrocks, who is well-laid in on the road for a view, screeches and holloas them on.

† **well-'landed**, *ppl. a. Obs.* Possessed of much land.
1601 HOLLAND *Pliny* XVIII. iii. I. 550 Rich and substantiall men were tearmed in Latine, Locupletes, as one would say, Loci-pleni, [*i.* well-landed]. *a* **1623** CAMDEN *Rem.*, *Armories* (1636) 212 Ralph de Curva Spina or Creythorne, descended from an Ancestor well landed in Kent.

well-'languaged, *a.* Now *arch.* **a.** Having a good command of language. Also, skilled in languages.
1340–70 *Alex. & Dind.* 171 A wel-langaged lud. **1523** [see LANGUAGED 2]. **1561** T. HOBY tr. *Castiglione's Courtyer* I. (1577) E j b, *margin*, Men that will be demed to be well languaged. **1616** W. BROWNE *Brit. Past.* II. ii. 37 Well-languag'd Danyel. **1639** SALTMARSHE *Policy* 231 Where entreaties are of moment, use well languaged men; thus were the men of Lystra perswaded. **1671** [see LANGUAGED 1]. **1954** L. HOTSON *First Night of 'Twelfth Night'* i. 29 The well-languaged Elizabeth kept helping Lord Grey interpret the gist of it.
b. Expressed in good language, well-worded.
1692 WOOD *Ath. Oxon.* II. 169 His.. well languag'd Sermons. **1938** *Times Lit. Suppl.* 20 Aug. 548/2 Sir Robert Cordell, whose well-languaged seventeenth-century will.. makes interesting reading.

† **well-leared**, *ppl. a. Obs.* = next.
c **1400** *Rule of St. Benet* (Prose) 5 Euer sal be in his þoht þat his munkis be wel lered. *a* **1774** FERGUSSON *Poems, Drink Ecl.* 53 As weel-lear'd trav'llers tell.

well-learned, *ppl. a.* Now *rare*. Having sound knowledge or instruction; deeply read or versed (*in* a subject).
1426 *Paston Lett.* I. 25 Maister Iohn Blodwelle, a weel lerned man holden. *c* **1449** PECOCK *Repr.* I. xx. 129 A sad and weel leerned clerk in moral philsophie. **1594** SHAKS. *Rich. III*, III. v. 100 With reuerend Fathers and well-learned Bishops. *a* **1600** HOOKER *Eccl. Pol.* VII. xxiv. §5 And for discharge of a Bishops Office, to be well minded is not enough, no not to be well learned also. **1641** MILTON *Prel. Episc.* Wks. 1851 III. 90 He that thinks it the part of a well learned man.. to be no stranger to the volumes of the Fathers. **1709** STRYPE *Ann. Ref.* I. xxxiii. 336 A Man he was well learned in the Scripture. **1871** W. ALEXANDER *Johnny Gibb* xii. 90 He's a weel-meanin' man, an' a weel-leern't. **1887** MORRIS *Odyss.* XI. 432 She, well-learned in sin.
b. Of a weapon: Skilfully directed. *poet.*
1596 SPENSER *F.Q.* VI. vii. 11 His well learned speare Tooke surer hould.

well-leaved, *a.* Full of foliage.
1616 W. BROWNE *Brit. Past.* II. iii. 52 A little Robin Red-brest.. Sate sweetly singing on a well-leau'd Thorne. **1901** H. SEEBOHM *Birds of Siberia* xxx. 307 A well-leaved branch of a pine-tree.

well-led, *ppl. a.*
1633 BP. HALL *Hard Texts*, Heb. xiii. 7 Their well-led lives. **1678** DILLINGHAM *Serm. Funeral Lady Alston* 26 A Survey of an holy and well-led Life. **1890** KIPLING *Departm. Ditties*, etc. (ed. 4) 48 Ere two well-led cotillions Have danced themselves away.

well(-)left, *ppl. a.* (See LEAVE *v.*[1] 2 b.)
1620 T. MAY *Heir* I. (1633) B 1, I must expresse a griefe Not vsuall, not like a well left heire For his dead father. **1898** 'C. HARE' *Broken Arcs* viii. 102 A widow 'well left', who kept a small shop.

well-legged, *a.*
1552 HULOET, Brawned or well armed, or legged, *torosus*. **1593** *Pass. Morrice* (1876) 82 Some were.. perfect of bodie, yet ill legged; other, which were well legde, shaled with their feete. *a* **1779** D. GRAHAM *Writ.* (1883) II. 53 For his mither tell'd him the women look'd ay to the men's legs or they marry'd them, and the well-legged louns gade ay best aff.

well-'lettered, *ppl. a.* Having a good knowledge of letters; imbued with learning.
1303 R. BRUNNE *Handl. Synne* 7894 (Bodl. MS.) Prest weyl lettred ys to blame þat letteþ nat.. To pleye wyþ wymmen. *c* **1440** *Alphabet of Tales* 217 A bisshop þat was a passyng sutell clerk, & a well-letterd. **1483** CAXTON *Golden Leg.* 427/1 The which.. was.. also in theologye wel letterd. **1597** BEARD *Theatre God's Judgem.* (1612) 265 Quintius Valerius, a wise and well lettered man. **1858** GEN. P. THOMPSON *Audi Alt.* lvi. I. 220 Happy and well-lettered peasantry. **1870** DISRAELI *Lothair* xlii. 212 The Bishop.. would not himself have made a bad cardinal, being polished and plausible, well-lettered, yet quite a man of the world.

well-'lighted, *ppl. a.*
1631 MILTON *Epit. March. Winch.* 20 With a scarce-wel-lighted flame. *a* **1865** MRS. GASKELL *Wives & Dau.* xxvi, The rooms are not well-lighted to-night, are they, Mr. Preston? **1867** H. LATHAM *Black & White* 84 Each family occupies a separate corridor, high, well-lighted.

well-liked, *ppl. a.* [Cf. OE. *wel-ȝelícod*, glossing L. *beneplacitum*.] Regarded with much affection or approval. Also † ***well liked of***.
a **1586** SIDNEY *Arcadia* III. (1922) 12 This their well liked fellowship. **1670** COTTON *Espernon* I. IV. 174 To put himself

into possession of his new, and well lik'd of charge. **1820** A. McNay *Poet. Wks.* 33 (E.D.D.) The herd came rinnin' o'er the lea, His weel-liked cur to see. **1896** *McClure's Mag.* VI. 446/1 A good politician, and, on the whole, a very well-liked man.

†well-'liking, *vbl. sb. Obs.* [Cf. OE. *wellícung*, glossing L. *beneplacitum*.] Favourable regard, fondness; approbation or love (*of*).

1571 Golding *Calvin on Ps.* lv. 12. 214 All well-lyking of reason and honestie was quite banished. **1576** Fleming *Panopl. Epist.* 401 But this man lacking luck, did also lacke wel lyking. **1586** A. Day *Eng. Secretorie* II. (1625) 46 Whilest by an outragious well-liking of your selfe, you become ignorant of your owne mischiefes. **1603** Daniel *Def. Ryme* Wks. (1717) 6 Drawn farther on by the Well-liking and Approbation of my worthy Lord. **1654** Gataker *Disc. Apol.* 65 His approbation and wel-liking of those Innovations. **1679** Pepys *Let.* 6 May, Which you were pleased..to express your well-liking of.

well-'liking, *ppl. a.* [Cf. OE. *wel-lícendlic* adj., pleasing. For †*well like* v. see well *adv.* 31.]

1. In good condition and of lusty appearance; thriving, healthy, plump. *arch.*

13.. *Prose Psalter* xci. 14 Hij shul ben wele likand. ?*a* **1366** Chaucer *Rom. Rose* 1564 Aboute it is gras spryngyng, For moiste so thikke and wel likyng That it ne may in wynter dye. *c* **1440** *Partonope* 1087 Strong he was and wele lykyng. **1539** Bible (Great) *Ps.* xcii. 13 They.. shalbe fat and wel lyking [1611 flourishing]. **1561** Daus tr. *Bullinger on Apoc.* (1573) 119 The Popes clergie shal be well fed, faire and welliking. **1567** Maplet *Gr. Forest* 46 Houselike..is alwaies greene and well liking. **1621** Burton *Anat. Mel.* I. ii. II. i. 90 A Carthusian of a ruddy colour, and well likeing. **1685** H. More *Illustration* etc. 1 They refusing the King's portion, grow fair and well liking with pulse and water. **1753** Miss Collier *Art Torment.* Introd. 16 But be very careful daily to observe whether your patient continues in good health, and is fat and well-liken. **1795** *Jemima* I. 176 His Lordship..looks altogether smug and well-liking. **1865** Kingsley *Herew.* xxix, There came into the camp at Brandon, riding on an ambling pad, himself fat and well-liking, none other than Sir Deda. **1891** M. Muriel Dowie *Girl Karp.* 121 There was a tendency in the conditions at the farm to make one fat, lazy, and well-liking.

fig. **1588** Shaks. *L.L.L.* v. ii. 268 Wel-liking wits they haue, grosse, grosse, fat, fat. **1642** D. Rogers *Naaman* Ep. Ded. 3 To grow wel-liking and flourishing in goodnesse.

†2. Pleasant, agreeable. *Obs.*

1586 T. B. *La Primaud. Fr. Acad.* I. xlvii. 478 It beseemeth a man..to be well liking, gentle and acceptable [*se rendre plaisant, doux et aggreable*] to an honest and vertuous wife.

well-limbed, *a.* Having good or fine limbs.

1412–20 Lydg. *Chron. Troy* I. 2043 [Jason] So wel I-lemed and compact by mesure. **1555** Eden *Decades* (Arb.) 151 Thinhabitantes are of high and goodly stature, well lymmed and proportioned. **1626** *Maldon* (Essex) *Documents* Bundle 208 No. 9 A well-lymb'd gelding. **1634** Sir T. Herbert *Trav.* 14 The people are..well limmed and proper, nor want they courage..to their limmes. **1706** *Lond. Gaz.* No. 4249/4 Lost.., a..Horse,..a very strong well-limb'd Punch. **1792** *Ann. Reg., Charac.* 359 She was well limbed though so low of stature. **1876** Bancroft *Hist. U.S.* V. liv. 137 He was tall and slender, well-limbed, of a graceful address.

well-limned, *ppl. a. lit.* and *fig.* Also 7 -limb'd, lim'd, limmed. (See limn *v.* 3, 3 b.)

Quot. 1616 perh. belongs to well-limbed.

1597 Middleton *Wisd. Solomon* xiv. 18 The crafts-man ..makes the idoll comely, faire, and great, With well limnd visage, and best fashioned shape. **1616** W. Browne *Brit. Past.* II. i. 20 Neere this the curious Pencell did expresse A large and solitary wildernesse, Whose high well limmed Oakes in growing show'd As they would ease strong Atlas of his load. **1637** S. Marmion in T. Heywood *Descr. H.M. Ship* (1638) To Author A 3 b, Now for a Homer whose immortall Verse In well lim'd lines, and raptures might rehearse The bravery of this Vessell. **1652** *F. Grevil's Sidney* Ep. Ded., Both your Bloud and Vertues do so strongly Intitle you to this well-limb'd Piece. **1654** Whitlock *Zootomia* 468 It is the part of Poetry to have a judicious Reception of a well-lim'd Notion.

well-lined, *ppl. a.* [See line *v.*[1] 1, 3.] Furnished with a good lining. Also *fig.*

1562 Bullein *Bulw. Def., Sick Men* (1579) 6 The pacyent to haue light warme clothes, and slyppers, cleane, & well lyned. *c* **1611** Chapman *Iliad* xvi. 338 Well couer'd in a well-lin'd shield. **1784** Cowper *Task* II. 737 His cap well lin'd with logic not his own.

b. *spec.* Of a purse: Full of money. †Of a person: Affluent. *Obs.*

1611 Cotgr., *Aisé en son mesnage*, of good estate, well lined, well to liue. **1677** Miege *Fr.-Eng. Dict.* s.v. *Chaud*, He wants for nothing, he is warm, or well lined. **1691** [see lined *ppl. a.*[1]]. **1820** [see line *v.*[1] 3]. *a* **1832** Bentham *Constitut. Code* Wks. 1843 IX. 102 It is the interest of all highwaymen, not only that travellers should be numerous, but that their purses should be well-lined. **1831** James *Phil. Augustus* xxxvii, A well-lined pouch of chamois leather.

†well-'liquored, *ppl. a. Obs.* Stocked with liquor.

1623 J. Taylor (Water P.) *Praise of Hempseed* 6 His blushing Lattice would looke pale and wan, Nor could he long be a well liquord man.

well-lit, *ppl. a.*

1866 Geo. Eliot *Felix Holt* III. xlix. 249 Esther had to seat herself in the..drawing-room, in a well-lit solitude. **1931** W. S. Churchill *World Crisis* VI. xii. 179 Hindenburg, who was waiting in the 'well-lit station hall' at Hanover. **1965** *Motor* 17 July 5/1 Dipped headlights are probably of benefit on less well-lit roads.

well-'liveried, *a.*

1835 Lytton *Rienzi* II. iv, Thinking of his own well-liveried menials.

well-'living, *vbl. sb.* A virtuous manner of life.

c **1400** *Rule of St. Benet* (Verse) 243 For who to wele-lifing sall win, With greuauns grete þaim bus bigin. **1656** Stanley *Hist. Philos.* v. (1687) 162/2 The first [part of Philosophy], concerning well living.

well-'living, *ppl. a.* That leads a good life.

1377 Langl. *P. Pl.* B. x. 431 Þere aren witty and wel libbynge [*justi atque sapientes*], ac her werkes ben yhudde In þe hondes of almyȝty god. *c* **1400** *26 Pol. Poems* iii. 76 Wel lyuyng man [is] hardy of kynde. **1596** in *Spalding Club Misc.* I. 87 Thi self wsand thy witchecraft, altogidder contrarius to the natour of weill levand personis. **1870** Newman *Gram. Assent* I. iv. 55 The piously-minded and well-living people in all ranks of the community.

well-'loaded, *ppl. a.*

1781 Cowper *Conversat.* 196 Were I empow'r'd to regulate the lists, They should encounter with well-loaded fists. **1821** tr. *Iliad* IX. I. 275 When I have dragged to the sea my well-loaded vessels.

well-lodged, *ppl. a.*

1781 Cowper *Table-t.* 221 His form robust..Supplies with warm activity and force A mind well-lodg'd.

well-looked, *a. Obs.* exc. *Sc.* [See well *adv.* 32 and looked[2].] Of good appearance, good-looking.

1664 Pepys *Diary* 19 Aug., His lady..is a well-looked, fat, short, old Dutchwoman. **1722** W. Hamilton *Wallace* VIII. (1816) 145 Nine thousand Scots..All swinging, able, lusty, well look'd men. **1737** *Gentl. Mag.* VII. 651/2 The Officers were very apt to discharge an old Soldier, as often as they could find a clever well-look'd young Fellow ready to list in his Stead. **1756** Mrs. Calderwood in *Coltness Collect.* (Maitl. Club) 154 A very genteel well-looked man. *c* **1817** Hogg *Tales & Sk.* III. 126 A worthy excellent woman rather well looked. **1849** C. Brontë *Shirley* vii, A well-looked, well-meant, and..well-dispositioned girl. **1897** J. Willock *Shetland Minister* 30 (E.D.D.) Well-looked ladies.

well-'looking, *ppl. a.* Of good or attractive appearance, good-looking: **a.** of persons.

Formerly very common, but now less usual than good-looking.

1702 Steele *Funeral* I. i. 4 That Hale Well-looking Puppy! **1737** *Gentl. Mag.* VII. 176 A well-disciplin'd Army of above 7000 Collectors, and a peaceable well-looking one of 18000 Men. **1772** Graves *Spir. Quixote* III. ix. (1783) I. 151 A well-looking elderly gentleman. **1811–13** Jane Austen *Mansfield Park* xix, You should tell your father he is not above five feet eight, or he will be expecting a well-looking man. **1848** Thackeray *Van. Fair* xli, The sisters were rather well-looking young women. **1874** R. Tyrwhitt *Sketch. Club* 6 He was..well-bred, and something more than well-looking. **1895** J. G. Millais *Breath fr. Veldt* (1899) 66 His brother Piet (a fine well-looking fellow).

transf. **1773** Goldsm. *Stoops to Conquer* I, Tell me, Constance, how do I look this evening?.. Is it one of my well-looking days, child? am I in face to-day?

b. of an animal, plant, building, etc.

1772 *Ann. Reg.* 7 The blades..produced well-looking ears; but these were hollow, and totally destitute of grain. **1796** W. H. Marshall *Planting* II. 8 This [the horse-chesnut] is a large well looking tree. **1819** E. Rigby tr. *Chateauvieux' Italy* 76 Almost every farm maintains a well-looking horse, which goes in a small two-wheeled cart. **1832** G. C. Lewis *Lett.* (1870) 18 Avignon is a well-looking town. **1860** Geo. Eliot in Cross *Life* (1885) II. 171 The well-looking lines of building on each side of the Arno. **1886** Froude *Oceana* xi. 189 The houses of the wealthy and moderately wealthy classes are solid and well-looking.

c. *fig.* Of an idea: Specious, attractive.

1811 *Henry & Isabella* II. 174 The well looking idea of befriending an inexperienced young woman.

well(-)lost, *ppl. a.* Lost in a good cause or for a good consideration.

a **1586** Sidney *Arcadia* IV. (1922) 112 Never can God himselfe perswade me, that Pyrocles life is not well lost, for to preserve the most admirable Philoclea. **1601** Shaks. *All's Well* I. iii. 254 Would your honor But giue me leaue to trie successe, I'de venture The well lost life of mine, on his Graces cure, By such a day, an houre. **1678** Dryden (*title*) All for Love, or the World well Lost.

well-lotted: see lotted b.

well-loved, *ppl. a.* = well-beloved.

a **1300** *Cursor M.* 7288 Prophet he was, sir samuel, Wel luued wit godd, for he was lel. **1473** *Rental Bk. Cupar Angus* (1879) I. 166 Our landis of Cragnenady in Glenyleff to our welluvyt frend Wilzam coly. **1842** Tennyson *Ulysses* 35 This is my son, mine own Telemachus,.. Well-loved of me. **1887** Morris *Odyss.* II. 415 E'en so as they had been bidden by Odysseus' well-loved son. **1895** *Catholic Mag.* Aug. 228 St. Cuthbert's well-loved Melrose.

well-lunged, *a.* Furnished with good lungs.

1693 Dryden *Persius* v. 3 Whether to the well-lung'd Tragedians Rage They recommend their Labours of the Stage.

well-made, *ppl. a.* Also 5 -makyd.

1. Of a person or animal: Well-proportioned, of good build.

1297 R. Glouc. (Rolls) 8527 Quarre he was & wel ymad vor to be strong. *a* **1310** in Wright *Lyric P.* 36 Heo hath a mete myddel smal, Body ant brest wel mad al. *c* **1375** Barbour *Bruce* I. 385 Off lymmys he wes weill maid, With banys gret & schuldrys braid. **1422** Yonge tr. *Secreta Secret.* 226 Tho men whyche haue wel-makyd and synowy and stronge legges. *c* **1475** *Rauf Coilȝear* 486 War he ane manly man, as he is weill maid, He war full michtie. **1513** More in Grafton *Chron.* (1568) II. 786 She was..moderate of stature, well made, & very wise. **1664** Pepys *Diary* 15 Aug., He is a comely and well-made man. **1707** *Lond. Gaz.* No. 4391/4 A bay gelt Horse..well made and well ribb'd. **1783** Mrs. Cowley *Bold Stroke* v. (1784) 75 Let me see—a good air, and well made, you are the man for a dancer. **1849** C. Brontë *Shirley* iv, His stature was rather tall, and he was well-made and wiry. **1856** Kane *Arctic Explor.* II. xx. 204 She was a tall, well-made woman.

2. Of things: Skilfully fabricated, constructed, or contrived. Also ***well-made play*** [tr. F. *pièce bien faite*], a type of play written according to a prescribed formula and aiming at neatness of plot and dramatic incident rather than profundity of characterization, truth to nature, etc.

15.. Dunbar *Poems* xxviii. 21 Ȝe tailȝouris, with weilmaid clais Can mend the werst maid man that gais. **1577** Googe *Heresbach's Husb.* I. 42 b, We content ourselues with our earthen floores, wel made and of good earth. **1601** Shaks. *All's Well* IV. iii. 254 Halfe won is match well made. **1621** in Foster *Eng. Factories Ind.* (1906) 258 Greater qua[ntities] of well-made cloth. **1835** Dickens *Sk. Boz, Mr. Watkins Tottle* i, Her complexion..was as clear as that of a well-made wax doll. **1887** *Spons' Househ. Man.* 715 A well-made toque is graceful, becoming, and comfortable. [**1895** G. B. Shaw in *Sat. Rev.* 2 Nov. 576/1 Then 'The New Magdalen' was a fashionable and well-made piece.] **1897** *Daily News* 5 Jan. 6/1 There has been..a very decided reaction against the 'well-made' novel—that is the novel cunningly planned and ingeniously conducted to a definite dénouement. **1910** G. B. Shaw *Brieux* 13 Commercially, the classic play was supplanted by a nuisance which was not a failure: to wit, the 'well made play' of Scribe and his school. The manufacture of well made plays is not an art: it is an industry. **1962** *Listener* 11 Oct. 574/1 The merits and the demerits of a Galsworthian 'well-made' play.

well-'managed, *ppl. a.*

1. Carefully and skilfully controlled, handled, carried on, or dealt with.

1665 Waller *Upon H.M. New Buildings* 25 From a confin'd, well-manag'd Store, You both employ, and feed the Poor. **1677** Dryden *State Innoc.* I. 5 A well-manag'd War. **1784** Cowper *Task* III. 800 When his vote, Well-manag'd, shall have earn'd its worthy price. **1842** W. C. Taylor *Tour Manuf. Districts Lancs.* 137 The operatives in a well-managed country mill. **1845** *Florist's Jrnl.* 211 A collection of 15 stove and greenhouse plants..which contained many well-managed plants. **1876** Miss Yonge *Womankind* iii. 17 Many well-managed children are uncomfortable if they do not repeat 'their Catechism' straight through on the Sunday. **1884** E. Yates *Recoll.* I. 203 In those days the little Adelphi was a popular and well-managed resort.

2. Of a horse (see managed 1).

1697 Dryden *Æneis* x. 1226 His Courser..Well mouth'd, well manag'd. **1814** Scott *Wav.* xiii, The Baron..mounted on an active and well-managed horse.

well(-)manned, *ppl. a.* Equipped with a proper complement of men.

c **1450** *Contin. Brut* 469 Grete vessels,..stronge and well-manned. **1482–3** *Paston Lett.* III. 294 With ij. good carts well mannyd and horsyd. *a* **1586** Sidney *Arcadia* III. xviii. (1912) 460 A well-mand Galley. **1591** Sylvester *Du Bartas* I. ii. 191 Then should the sucking Elephant support Upon his shoulders a well-manned Fort. **1634** Sir T. Herbert *Trav.* 2 Six great and wel-mann'd ships. *a* **1684** R. Leighton *Comm. Pet.* i. 5 (1693) 64 So long as the place.. is of sufficient strength and well man'd..they are in safety. **1720** Ramsay *Prosp. Plenty* 181 A wood o' masts, wiel mann'd. **1835** Dickens *Sk. Boz, River*, A well-manned galley shoots through the arch. **1869** A. R. Wallace *Malay Archipelago* II. 59 Their long well-manned praus.

well-'mannered, *a.*

†1. Endowed with good morals, displaying virtuous conduct and behaviour. *Obs.*

1393 Langl. *P. Pl.* C. XI. 260 A mayde wel ymanered, of good men yspronge. *c* **1400** *Destr. Troy* 6320 Patroclus, þe proud kyng, was..Wel manert & meke. *c* **1450** tr. *De Imitatione* I. xxv. 37 Hou swete it is..to se fervent & deuoute breþren & wel manerd [*bene morigeratos*] & under discipline. *a* **1475** Ashby *Dicta Philos.* 113 Wele manered people bene of goode lif. **1526** *Pilgr. Perf.* (W. de W. 1531) 45 Whiche were in theyr conuersacyon ryght honest & well manerd. **1570** T. Norton tr. *Nowel's Catech.* 78 In Chirches well ordered and well mannered [*In ecclesiis bene institutis atque moratis*] there was [etc.]. **1596** Dalrymple tr. *Leslie's Hist. Scot.* I. 235 A man quha feiret God, and Was Weil maneret, and of singular conditiounis [*singulari morum probitate praedito*]. **1597** J. King *On Jonas* (1618) 382 To nurse you vp in a ciuil & well-mannered country.

2. Displaying good manners, courteous.

1547 Boorde *Introd. Knowl.* iii. (1870) 132 The people of the Englyshe pale be metely wel manerd,..but naturally they be testy. **1574** Hellowes *Guenara's Fam. Ep.* (1577) 74 Haue a care to be well manered: for with good manners, more than with any other thing we withdrawe our enimies, and do susteine our friends. **1682** Dryden *Medall* Ep. to Whigs, By which well-mannerd and charitable Expressions, I was certain of his Sect, before I knew his name. **1693** —— *Juv.* Ded. (1697) p. lxv, A Well-manner'd Court-Slave. **1714** Mrs. Manley *Adv. Rivella* 38, I was too well manner'd to take the Black, and leave none to attend your Ladyship. **1741** Richardson *Pamela* II. 227 Where's your well-manner'd Deceiver gone, Child? says she. **1847** Mrs. Gore *Castles in Air* vi, Though good-looking, and even well-mannered, because courteous and unaffected, they had no pretension to be ladies. **1847** Lytton *Lucretia* I. i, The boy..was so lively, yet so well mannered.

absol. **1856** Lever *Martins of Cro' Martin* xxiii. 244, I have given up association with the well-bred and the well-mannered, to rub shoulders with the coarse-minded, the rough-hearted, and the vulgar.

well-marked, *ppl. a.* Clearly defined or outlined, easy to distinguish or recognize.
1797 M. BAILLIE *Morb. Anat.* (ed. 2) 71 Any well marked example of this disease. **1830** WHEWELL *Archit. Notes German Ch.* 43 These arches have well-marked mouldings. **1855** *Orr's Circ. Sci., Inorg. Nat.* 74 Shells..of large size, and well-marked forms. **1861** PALEY *Æschylus* (ed. 2) *Supplices* 894 *note*, A play which has several well-marked resemblances to this. **1875** WHITNEY *Life Lang.* ix. 175 Even languages of so limited area as the Basque in the Pyrenees, have their well-marked dialectic forms. **1875** HUXLEY & MARTIN *Elem. Biol.* 243 Each [cell] has a well-marked oval nucleus. **1886** DRUCE *Flora Oxf.* 348 This well-marked plant occurs on wall-tops and dry banks.

well(-)'married, *ppl. a.* Fortunate in one's marriage. Also, †legally married.
1592 SHAKS. *Rom. & Jul.* IV. v. 77 Shee's not well married, that liues married long, But shee's best married, that dies married yong. **1600** —— *A.Y.L.* III. iii. 94 He is not like to marrie me wel: and not being wel married, it will be a good excuse for me heereafter, to leaue my wife. **1741** RICHARDSON *Pamela* (1824) I. xxii. 273 Is it not a sad thing to think of, that ladies, let them be young or old, well-married or ill-married, cannot live without intrigue?

well-'marshalled, *ppl. a.*
1645 WALLER *At Pens-hurst* II. 16 If shee walk, in even rankes they stand, Like some well marshall'd and obsequious band.

well-masked, *ppl. a.*
1860 PUSEY *Min. Proph.* 212 Vice imagines virtue to be well-masked vice.

well-matched, *ppl. a.*
1687 DRYDEN *Hind & P.* I. 356 And sacrilege and she, A well-match'd pair, got graceless heresie. **1749** G. WEST tr. *Pindar, Olymp. Odes* v. (1753) I. 46 The well-match'd Coursers. **1807** CRABBE *Par. Reg.* II. 358 Now to be wed a well-match'd couple came. **1837** DICKENS *Pickw.* liii, You are a well-matched pair of mean, rascally, pettifogging robbers. **1854** *Poultry Chron.* II. 310 All perhaps very good birds, but..not forming a well-matched pen.

well-'mated, *ppl. a.*
1899 CROCKETT *Kit Kennedy* xxi. 142 Then the well-mated pair proceeded to hold high discourse of fate and freewill.

well-ma'tured, *ppl. a.*
1676 EVELYN *Terra* 53 Cast..on this a layer of well-matur'd Dung. **1748** MELMOTH *Fitzosborne Lett.* lvi. (1749) II. 81 Sound thought and well-matured reflection. **1897** *Century Mag.* May 104 This quiet but intense thinking and the well-matured ideas which resulted from it.

†well-meaned, *a. Obs.* [See WELL *adv.* 32 and MEANED.] Furnished with considerable means.
1605 MARSTON *Dutch Courtezan* v. [iii.] H 2 b, He thats of faire bloud, well meand, of good breeding.

†well-meaned, *ppl. a. Obs.* [MEAN *v.*[1]]
1. Kindly disposed. *Sc.*
c **1470** HENRY *Wallace* XI. 1041, I haiff spokyn with lord Clyffurd that knycht, Wyth thair chyftanys weill menyt for your lyff.
2. = WELL-MEANT.
a **1711** KEN *Hymnarium* Poet. Wks. 1721 II. II. 94 Well-mean'd, tho' wandring Pray'rs. **1761** *Brit. Mag.* II. 606 *The Christian Common Prayer Book*... Sensible, moderate, and well-meaned.

well-'meaner. One who means well or is well-intentioned.
1654 WHITLOCK *Zootomia* To Rdr. A 6 b, With well-meaners even good Meanings and Aimes in Authors attone their Failings. **1683** DRYDEN *Vind. Dk. Guise* 59 Deluded well-meaners come over out of honesty, and small offendors out of common discretion, or fear. **1700** —— *Pal. & Arc.* III. 205 Well-meaners think no Harm. **1855** M. BRIDGES *Pop. Mod. Hist.* 432 On its benches sat many enthusiasts, no sages, a few well-meaners, and some colossal scoundrels.

well-'meaning, *vbl. sb.* Disposition to do what is right; good intentions.
1569 ELVIDEN *Closet of Counsels* (1573) To Rdr., I craue thy curtesie to respect of my well meaning, rather than of my abilitie. *a* **1586** SIDNEY *Arcadia* III. (1922) 57 The almightie powers, whom I inuoke as triers of mine innocencie and witnesses of my wel meaning. **1667** H. MORE *Div. Dial.* v. xxvi. (1713) 487 If that be at the bottom,..their well-meaning is commendable. **1703** EARL ORRERY *As you find it* III. ii. 38 Sir, your Deportment has been very surprizing to me,..but your Youth and Well-meaning may in a great measure excuse you. **1744** MASON *Musæus* (1748) 13 Let my well-meaning mend my ill essay. **1768** *Woman of Honor* I. 209 A few men of good sense, and real well-meaning. *a* **1849** H. COLERIDGE *Ess.* (1851) II. 254 Though I give the Bishop credit for well-meaning in his refusal of the pictures offered to St. Paul's.

well-'meaning, *ppl. a.* Having, or actuated by, good intentions; animated by a kindly purpose or friendly disposition.
Often with a somewhat derogatory implication of inefficiency or unwisdom.
1387-8 T. USK *Test. Love* II. v. 117 Right as see yeveth flood, so draweth see ebbe, and pulleth ayen under wawe al the firste out-throwe, but-if good pyles of noble governaunce in love, in wel-meninge maner, ben sadly grounded. **1555** EDEN *Decades* (Arb.) 124 And albeit that he were not lerned, yet was he a vertuous and well meanynge man. *a* **1557** GRIMALD in *Tottel's Misc.* (Arb.) 106 That nothyng hynder your welmeanyng minde. **1579** W. WILKINSON *Confut. Fam. Love* B ij, Take this briefe freindly and well meaning aunswere to your exceptions in good part. **1593** SHAKS. *Rich. II*, II. i. 128 My brother Gloucester, plaine well meaning soule. **1649** MILTON *Eikon.* xvii. 158 What a Cordial and well meaning helper they had of him abroad. **1673** *True Worship of God* p. iv, Some out of a well meaning mistake, thinking that which they call Preaching, the only means of Salvation. **1697** DRYDEN *Virg. Georg.* Ded. ¶ 1 'Tis the fault of many a well-meaning Man, to be officious in a wrong place. **1712** ADDISON *Spect.* No. 299 ¶ 3 She..treats me like a plain well-meaning Man, who does not know the World. **1828** LYTTON *Pelham* lxxxi, The annuity we have agreed upon, is only to be given in case of success—not merely for well meaning attempts. **1857** MRS. MATHEWS *Tea-Table Talk* I. 342 The well-intentioned but injudicious actions of what are called well-meaning people. **1919** *Eng. Hist. Rev.* July 440 The paternal attitude of the Tudor monarchy was at least well-meaning towards the education of the poor.
Hence **well-'meaningly** *adv.*; **well-'meaningness.**
1680 I. C. *Vind. Oaths & Swearing* (ed. 2) 37 That some expedient may be found out for their ease in this Point, to such especially as do erre ignorantly and well-meaningly. **1900** *Spectator* 13 Jan. 52/1 Sloppiness, mental and moral, and vague well-meaningness.

well-meant, *ppl. a.* **a.** Rightly, honestly, or kindly intended; said or done with good intention.
? **1476** J. PASTON in *P. Lett.* III. 159, I have herd oft tymys Rychard Stratton sey that ye can and wyll take every thyng well that is well ment. **1593** SHAKS. *3 Hen. VI*, III. iii. 67 His demand Springs not from Edwards well-meant honest Loue, But from Deceit, bred by Necessitie. **1628** R. HAYMAN in *Eng. Hist. Rev.* (1918) Jan. 31 The poore successe of diuers of these well meant generall treatises. **1707** ATTERBURY *Vind. Doctr. Funeral Serm. Bennet* 4 Had I err'd in this case, it had been a well-meant Mistake. **1816** SCOTT *Old Mort.* xxxviii, My ill-timed, though well-meant, request. **1886** BESANT *Childr. Gibeon* II. xxiv, Valentine's well-meant, but perhaps injudicious interference.
b. quasi-*sb.* (with personification).
1602 [see WELL-DONE 2 d].
c. Of persons: well-meaning. *rare.*
1849 C. BRONTË *Shirley* I. vii. 153 A well-looked, well-meant, and on the whole, well-dispositioned girl.

well-'measured, *ppl. a.*
1. Composed in good measure or rhythm.
c **1645** MILTON *Sonn. to Lawes* 1 Harry whose tuneful and well measur'd Song First taught our English Musick how to span Words with just note and accent. **1839** HALLAM *Hist. Lit.* II. II. vii. §9 Puttenham is perhaps the first who wrote a well-measured prose.
2. Wisely calculated or adjusted.
1839-40 WORDSW. *Punishm. Death* viii, Yet, as she may, for each peculiar case She [the State] plants well-measured terrors in the road Of wrongful acts.

well-meated: see MEATED *a.*

well-'merited, *ppl. a.*
1827 J. S. MILL in *Arch. für Sozialwissensch.* LXII. 456 Reformed patriots whose exertions in the cause of liberty have at length earned the well-merited award of a place. **1899** BELLOC *Moral Alphabet* 48 So he wrote, without stopping, for several days In terms of extreme but well-merited praise. **1946** *Nature* 26 Oct. 576/2 Under his wise guidance a well-merited reputation both in teaching and in research was rapidly built up.

well-met, *ppl. a.* (See also MEET *v.* 4 b and HAIL-FELLOW A. b.)
a **1586** SIDNEY *Arcadia* II. xi. (1912) 223 To stand upon the best defensive gard he could;..sometime with strong and well-met wards. **1707** E. SMITH *Phædra & Hipp.* v. 57 Haste then, let's joyn our well-met Hands together.

well-'metalled, *ppl. a.* Liberally supplied with precious metal; well paid or remunerated.
1609 J. DAVIES (Heref.) *Humours Heaven* (Grosart) 38/1 But, Fortune from the same these Scripts did pull, And in exchange fill'd either fist with Gold: For, while they had but Papers they were dull; But being wel-mettl'd they were blithe and bold. *a* **1734** [see METALLED 3].

†well-'mettled, *ppl. a.* [METTLED 1.]
1639 T. DE GREY *Compl. Horsem.* I. iv. (1656) 37 Horses..must have also good eyes, obedient mouthed, and well mettled. **1693** J. D. MARSH in Congreve *Old Batchelor* To Author, Like a well-metled Hawk you took your flight Quite out of reach.

well-'minded, *a.*
1. Having, or actuated by, a good disposition or intention; right-minded, loyal; †generously or favourably disposed, benevolent.
1522 MORE *De quat. Noviss.* Wks. 74/1 By whiche thy speache and talking, thou shalt not onely profite thy selfe as thou sholdest haue done by thy well minded sylence, but also [etc.]. **1524** Q. MARG. in Mary A. E. Wood *Lett. Roy. Ladies* (1846) I. 324 Your grace shall understand that there is many lords well-minded to the same. *a* **1586** SIDNEY *Arcadia* I. xiii. (1912) 88 An honest and well-minded gentleman. **1621** SANDERSON *Serm., Ad Pop.* iv. (1689) 211 By their affected poverty diverting the Charity of well-minded people from those that were truly poor. **1647** CLARENDON *Hist. Reb.* IV. §233 Sober, well-minded men, who were real lovers of the peace of the kingdom. **1651** GATAKER *Bale* in Fuller *Abel Rediv.* 507 Being ransomed by certaine charitable and well-minded Merchants. **1824** SOUTHEY *Life* (1849) I. 115 He was a well-minded boy, and has made a very respectable man. **1869** TROLLOPE *He knew* etc. I. ii. 12 Had he been perfectly well-minded in the matter, he would have gone too.
2. Wishful or determined (*to* do something).
1859 LD. LYTTON *Wanderer* 243 Forty thousand weather-cocks Each well-minded to keep his place.

well-'mingled, *ppl. a.*
1706 WATTS *Horæ Lyr.* II. (1727) 231 How blest the lovely Pair, Beyond Expression, if well-mingled Loves And Woes well-mingled could improve our Bliss!

well-mixed, *ppl. a.*
1599 SIR J. DAVIES *Nosce Teipsum* 10 Others thinke the name of Soule is vaine, And that we onely well mixt bodies are. **1680** OTWAY *Compl. Muse* xv, How to frame a Commonwealth, And Democracy, by stealth; To palliate it at first, and Cry 'Twas but a Well-mixt Monarchy. **1733** POPE *Ess. Man* iii. 294 Th' according music of a well-mix'd State.

well-'modelled, -'moduled, *ppl. adjs.*
1621 [see MODULE *v.* 2]. **1666** BURNET *Mem.* in *Miscell. Sc. Hist. Soc.* (1904) II. 340 We enjoy the purity of Religion under a well modelled government.

well-'modulated, *ppl. a.*
1845 POE in *Broadway Jrnl.* II. 354/2 The rhythm is..well-modulated. **1934** C. LAMBERT *Music Ho!* IV. 235 Mr. Christopher Stone whose well-modulated voice has doubtless given pleasure to millions.

†well-'moneyed, *a. Obs.* Well supplied with, having plenty of, money.
1479 [see MONEYED 1 b]. **1540** PALSGR. *Acolastus* II. i. I iij, The storer of some well moneyed myster [*cellarius cuiuspiam nummatioris domini*]. **1591** SAVILE *Tacitus, Hist.* II. lvi. 86 The soldiers..designed out the well moneyed masters [*dites dominos*] to pray vpon. **1639** FULLER *Holy War* IV. viii. 180 So well-moneyed he was, that for ten yeares together he might for every day expend an hundred marks. **1756** C. SMART tr. *Horace, Epist.* I. vi. 38 The goddesses, Persuasion and Venus, grace the well-monied man.

well-'moralized, *ppl. a.* Regulated by good morals.
1652 [see MORALIZED 3]. **1691** NORRIS *Pract. Disc.* 69 There are more Examples of ill Living than of ill Thinking, and a well-moralized Conversation, is a greater Rarity, than an Orthodox Head. **1727-46** THOMSON *Summer* 1578 Chaucer, whose native manners-painting verse, Well-moraliz'd, shines thro' the Gothic cloud.

†wellmost, *adv. Obs.* Also 6-7 **welmost(e.** [Formed after ALMOST, by substitution of *well* for *all*. See WELL *adv.* 18.] Almost, well-nigh.
1550 CROWLEY *Epigr.* 166 There are pore people, welmoste innumerable, That are dryuen to begge. *Ibid.* 324 They had boeth sore legges,..Al rawe from the fote welmost to the knee. **1556** T. HOBY tr. *Castiglione's Courtyer* Transl. Epist. A ij b, In this point..Englishmen are much inferiour to well most all other Nations. **1619** W. SCLATER *Exp. 1 Thess.* To Rdr., Which hath made me welmost a meere Peripateticke in my studies. **1622** R. HARRIS *Sermon* To Rdr., Our vnthankfulnes and vnfruitfulnes hath welmost vndone vs. **1626** —— *Hezekiah's Recov.* (1630) 30 It [sickness] turnes him well-most into an Image.

well-'motivated, *ppl. a.*
1965 N. CHOMSKY *Aspects of Theory of Syntax* 210 A stronger but rather well-motivated condition is proposed by Postal. **1977** P. STREVENS *New Orientations Teaching of Eng.* v. 59 A theory of language teaching, on the other hand, with well-motivated links to specific areas of linguistics and psychology—*that* might be attractive.

well-'motived, *ppl. a.*
1844 KINGLAKE *Eothen* xxv. 377 This villanous, though well-motived trick of his.

well-'moulded, *ppl. a.*
1847 TENNYSON *Princess* II. 91 A quick brunette, well-moulded, falcon-eyed. **1890** L. C. D'OYLE *Notches* 39 The well-moulded form in which those bones had once been encased.

well(-)'mounted, *ppl. a.*
1. Seated on a good horse.
1595 SHAKS. *John* v. vi. 42 These Lincolne-Washes haue deuoured them, My selfe, well mounted, hardly haue escap'd. **1630** CAPT. J. SMITH *True Trav.* vii. 12 Turbashaw with a noise of Howboyes entred the fields well mounted and armed. **1633** G. HERBERT *Temple, Dotage* i, Shadows well-mounted, dreams in a career. **1708** BOYER *Siege Toulon* II. 18 A Trooper well mounted and armed. **1818** SCOTT *Br. Lamm.* ix, He was accosted by a well-mounted stranger. **1841** DICKENS *Barn. Rudge* x, He was well-mounted upon a sturdy chestnut cob.
†2. ? Having a good bodily carriage, well-developed, 'well set up'. Also *fig. Obs.*
1607 BEAUM. & FL. *Woman-hater* IV. ii, A handsome, young, fair enough, and well mounted wench. **1621** FLETCHER *Wild-goose Chase* II. ii, Of a small body, she has a mind well mounted.
3. Fully equipped, well-appointed.
1846 MRS. GORE *Engl. Char.* (1852) 11 Sir Gordon Mosley and his white cravat are essential portions of every well mounted dinner-table. **1853** GROTE *Greece* II. lxxxviii. XI. 495 After all the wants of a well-mounted peace-establishment were satisfied.
4. Skilfully fixed or fitted.
1889 *Hardwicke's Sci.-Gossip* XXV. 47/2 Offered in exchange for two well-mounted slides, or other unmounted micro material.

well-mouthed, *a.* Having a good mouth (in various senses).
14.. in *Harrow. Hell* Introd. 25 The horss..well-mouthid, well-wyndyd. **1547** BALDWIN *Mor. Philos.* 73 b, The master that instructeth, ought first to giue to his scholler a strong bridle and sharpe bit, to the intent he may be well mouthed, so that no man take him with lies. **1590** COKAINE *Treat. Hunting* B 3 b, Hounds..well mouthed, cold nosed. **1606** CHAPMAN *Gentl. Usher* I. i, With harmonie Of well mouthed hounds. **1641** BEST *Farming Bks.* (Surtees) 13 Such [ewes] as are whole and well wool'd, and indifferent

well mouthed. **1685** *Lond. Gaz.* No. 2056/4 Sixteen Couple of middle sized Harriers, well mouthed. **1692** SIR W. HOPE *Fencing Master* 122 A well mouthed horse, that will answer your Bridle-Hand and spurres. **1737** POPE *Hor. Epist.* II. i. 123 One Tragic sentence.. Which.. well-mouth'd Booth with emphasis proclaims. **1842** J. AITON *Dom. Econ.* (1857) 237 The mutton of a well-mouthed wether is better than that of a young wether.

well(-)named, *ppl. a.*

1. Called by an appropriate or suitable name. **1445** tr. *Claudian* in *Anglia* XXVIII. 269 This damysel corrupcion is right wele namyd. **1861** L. CAMPBELL *Theætetus* p. vii, 'It was written' (so the last page informs us) 'by the hand of John', (well-named) 'Calligraphus'. **1879** SYMONDS *Shelley* v. 129 This poem [*Prometheus Unbound*], they cried, is well named, for who would bind it?

†**2.** Having a good name or reputation. *Obs.* **1390** [see NAME *v.*[1] 2 b]. *c* **1450** *Knt. de la Tour* ix. 12 A good woman, wel named and charitable. **1460** *Paston Lett.* I. 535, I comonyd late with a worschipful and a wele namyd, a good thrifty man of this cuntre. *a* **1533** [see NAME *v.*[1] 2 b].

well-'natured, *a. rare* (now chiefly *Sc.* and *dial.*).

1. a. Having, or showing, a good or benevolent disposition; kindly, good-natured. **1561** T. NORTON *Calvin's Inst.* II. 86 For which reason we feare not in common speache to call one man well natured, and an other of euell nature. **1579** TOMSON *Calvin's Serm. Tim.* 443/2 A quiet and well natured mind. *c* **1655** DOR. OSBORNE *Lett.* xlix. (1903) 222 If this be a fault in me, 'tis at least a well-natured one. *c* **1656** SIR H. CHOLMLEY *Mem.* (1787) 28 He was a well-natured man, charitable to the poor. **1677** DRYDEN *State Innoc.*, Apol. Her. Poetry c 1 b, These four lines, which have been sufficiently canvas'd by my well-natur'd Censors. *a* **1721** SHEFFIELD (Dk. Buckhm.) *Wks.* (1729) II. 212 This great satisfaction of mind in doing any generous well-natur'd action. **1759** ADAM SMITH *Theory Moral Sentim.* IV. i. (1781) 276 The social and well-natured James the First of Great-Britain. **1814** SCOTT *Wav.* xxv, His brother's disgrace seemed to have removed from his well-natured bosom all recollection of their differences. **1818** HALLAM *Mid. Ages* v. (1819) II. 97 Brave indeed, well-natured, and affable. **1888** D. GRANT *Sc. Stor.* 37, I ken that he's weel-natured an' richt kind-hairted. **1921** GALSWORTHY *To Let* II. i. 119 He went as a well-natured dog goes for a walk with its mistress, leaving a choice mutton-bone on the lawn.

b. *fig.* Accommodating, obliging. **1711** *Countrey-Man's Lett. Curat* 74 So well natur'd are some Arguments that they can equally serve two contending Parties.

†**2.** Of soil: Kindly, fertile. *Obs.* **1675** EVELYN *Terra* (1676) 51 This [trenching] is to be done in severals, as deep as you think fit, that is, so far, as you find the Earth well natur'd.

Hence **well-'naturedness**. **1679** PENN *Addr. Prot.* II. (1692) 225 You had better leave off valuing your selves upon the Mercy and Well-natur'dness of that Tenet.

well-near, *adv. Obs.* exc. *dial.* [Early ME. *wel-ner*, f. WELL *adv.* 18 + NEAR *adv.*[2]] = WELL-NIGH.

c **1200** ORMIN 15517 An wif, þatt wass þurrh blodless flod Well ner all brohht to dæþe. *a* **1300** *Cursor M.* 4760 þan iacob and his suns warn For defaut wel ner for-farn. **1338** R. BRUNNE *Chron.* (1810) 191 Welnere he com to late. **13..** *E.E. Allit. P.* B. 1585 So was þe wyȝe wytles, he wed wel ner. *c* **1460** *Towneley Myst.* xiii. 387 Welner at the fyrst cok. *c* **1470** HENRY *Wallace* I. 438 He for wo weyle ner worthit to weide. *a* **1547** SURREY in *Tottel's Misc.* (Arb.) 6 He lettes me to pursue a conquest welnere wonne. *c* **1578** in *Hakluyt's Voy.* (1600) III. 68 The day was welneere spent. **1623** FAVINE *Theat. Honour* II. i. 69 Who liued (well-neare) at the same time as the Geographer. **1627** DRAYTON *Nimphidia* 471 Who then had well-neere crack'd her spleene With very extreame laughter. **1656** HEYLIN *Surv. France* 298 Well-neer three miles in circuit. **1701** W. WOTTON *Hist. Rome* iv. 60 The Public Stock was well near exhausted. **1719** DE FOE *Crusoe* I. (Globe) 45 The last Time of these two had well near been fatal to me. **1869** STEWART *Rhymes* 5 (E.D.D.) Trees bow'd weel-near uprootin'. **1880** *W. Cornw. Gloss.* s.v., There were well-near a hundred people in the field. **1881** *Leicestersh. Gloss.*, *Well-near*, an occasional var. of *Welly*, but not nearly so common.

†**well-necked**, *a. Obs.*

1538 BALE *Thre Lawes* II. B vij b, The fellawe is wele decked, Dysgysed and wele necked. **1578** J. JONES *Preserv. Bodie & Soule* I. iii. 6 [The nurse shall be] broade breasted, and wel neckt.

wellness ('wɛlnɪs). [f. WELL *a.* + -NESS.] The state of being well or in good health.

Rather a nonce-wd. than of settled status like *illness*. **1654** SIR A. JOHNSTON (Ld. Wariston) *Diary* (S.H.S.) II. 197, I.. blessed God.. for my daughter's wealnesse. *c* **1655** DOR. OSBORNE *Lett.* xxviii. (1903) 126 You.. never send me any of the new phrases of the town... Pray what is meant by wellness and unwellness? **1791** T. TWINING *Recreat. & Stud.* (1882) 145 When I say 'well', I can't be supposed to mean the wellness that one should predicate of a professor who makes those instruments his study. **1836** CARLYLE *New Lett.* (1904) I. 33, I feel really very well at present; and could almost persuade myself it were the natural state of *wellness*. **1864** MRS. CARLYLE *Lett.* III. 210 Some weeks of such comparative ease and well-ness. **1896** MRS. DREW in A. C. Benson *Life Abp. Benson* (1899) II. 774 We were all struck by his *wellness*. **1905** H. H. COLVILL *Stepping Stone* 264 With an old man like that, wellness was illness, and illness didn't seem not so very different from wellness.

well-nigh ('wɛl'naɪ), *adv.* Also as one word or two. [OE. *wel néah, néh*, f. WELL *adv.* 18 + NIGH *adv.*] Very nearly, almost wholly or entirely.

a **1122** *O.E. Chron.* an. 999 (MS. F.) Welneah ealle West Cent. *a* **1135** —— an. 1132 (Laud MS.) Sua ðæt te king was wel-neh bepaht. *c* **1200** *Trin. Coll. Hom.* 33 Hie forwundeden him welneih to deaðe. *a* **1250** *Owl & Night.* 44 Hire horte was so gret, þat welneȝ hire fnast atschet. *c* **1275** *Passion our Lord* 477 in *O.E. Misc.* 50 Hit wes welneyh mydday þo þusternesse com. **1387** TREVISA *Higden* III. 281 Wel nyh alle his lyf tyme. *a* **1400–50** *Wars Alex.* 539 Of werke well ne I wede. **1449** PECOCK *Repr.* I. i. 7 Weelnyȝ thoruȝ al the chapiter. **1581** RICH *Farew. Milit. Prof.* P j, There was alreadie a whole yeare and a halfe welnie paste. **1599** SHAKS. *Much Ado* v. iv. 81 (Qo.) They swore that you were welnigh dead for me. **1604** T. WRIGHT *Passions* I. vi. 22 The experience is common (welnie) in all beasts. **1612** *Two Noble K.* III. ii, Tis now welnigh morning. *a* **1657** W. BURTON *Itin. Anton.* (1658) 34, I had wel-nigh forgotten the distance. **1780** S. J. PRATT *Emma Corbett* (ed. 4) I. 6 The blow which killed a son had well nigh killed a father also. **1848** WHITTIER *Pæan* 2 The dreary night has wellnigh passed. **1864** DASENT *Jest & Earnest* (1873) II. 263 Though before they were well-nigh beggars. **1896** *Law Times* C. 489/2 Suspicion pointed strongly, well-nigh overwhelmingly against the prisoner. **1920** *Eng. Hist. Rev.* Jan. 144 The amiable and wellnigh faultless hero.

†**well-nosed**, *a. Obs.* Keen-scented.

1611 COTGR., *Nazilleux*, well nosed. **1615** CHAPMAN *Odyss.* XVII. 433 He was a passing wise, and well-nos'd Hound. **1625, 1709** [see NOSED 1 b]. **1718** *Entertainer* No. 41. 280 Like a cunning and well-nosed Blood-Hound.

well-'noted, *ppl. a.*

1595 SHAKS. *John* IV. ii. 21 In this the Anticke, and well noted face Of plaine old forme, is much disfigured.

well-'nourished, *ppl. a.* [See further s.v. NOURISHED 1, 2.]

1422 YONGE tr. *Secreta Secret.* 237 The body.. may endure longe tyme, yf the kynde of man be Well y-noryschid .. by ettynge and drynkynge. **1883** J. M. FOTHERGILL *Indigestion* etc. 280 Stout, well-nourished persons do not die of wasting maladies. **1894** J. T. FOWLER *Adamnan* Introd. p. lxxv, His ruddy cheeks, and his well-nourished appearance.

well-'nurtured, *ppl. a.*

1535 COVERDALE *Ecclus.* xxvi. 14 A well nurtured mynde. **1605** R. F. *Dedekind's Sch. Slovenrie* (1904) 4 Well nurturde youth. **1781** COWPER *Table-T.* 634 A well-nurtur'd train Of abler votaries. **1850** THACKERAY *Pendennis* iii, A well-nurtured boy, brave and gentle.

well-oared, *a.*

1772 MURPHY *Grecian Dau.* I. 1, A well-oar'd galley. **1870** BRYANT *Iliad* II. 362 On board his well-oared bark.

well off, *adv.* and *a.* [See OFF *adv.* 11 and quot. 1636 in WELL *adv.* 6 b.]

1. In predicate, normally without hyphen: **a.** Favourably circumstanced, fortunately situated; **b.** well provided, having no lack (const. *for*, †*in*); *esp.* **c.** in easy circumstances, well-to-do.

a. 1733 *Trav. J. Massey* 18, I was well off if he only call'd me a Libertine. **1762** [see OFF *adv.* 11]. **1796** T. MORTON *Way to get Married* I. (1800) 5 Why don't you go to the other inn? I'll tell you—cause you know when you are well off, ha, ha! *a* **1865** MRS. GASKELL *Wives & Dau.* i, She was a silly little thing, and did not know when she was well off.

b. 1800 COLERIDGE *Let. to Poole* in J. D. Campbell *Life* (1894) 115 In gardens, etc., we are uncommonly well-off. **1879** MEREDITH *Egoist* viii, We are well-off for wild-flowers here.

c. 1849 LEVER *Con Cregan* vi, I began to conceive a great grudge against all who were well off in life. **1854** SURTEES *Handley Cr.* ii. (1901) I. 16 He was pretty well off, that is to say, he had more than he spent. **1866** TROLLOPE *Claverings* iv, If he dies, she will be well off, of course. **1889** 'J. S. WINTER' *Mrs. Bob* i, He was rich (or at least certainly well off).

2. *attrib.* or *adj.* (with hyphen). In sense 1 c. Also *absol.*

1884, 1888 [see OFF *adv.* 11]. **1893** FURNIVALL *Child-Marriages* Pref. 49 A well-off widow. **1899** *Allbutt's Syst. Med.* VIII. 301 The poor and hard-working are subject to mental upset during nursing in much larger numbers than the well-off. **1908** *Sociolog. Rev.* Apr. 131 The long-continued refusal of the well-off classes to enter public hospitals.

Hence **well-'offness**. *nonce-wd.* **1866** MRS. OLIPHANT *Madonna Mary* vi, Hesketh's well-off-ness.. was trying to a man. **1915** H. JAMES *Sense of Past* (1917) 289 His being in 1820 as 'rich' as he is, or was, in 1910 —which counts for an immense well-offness at the earlier period.

well-oiled, *ppl. a.* (*lit.* and *fig.*).

1740 SOMERVILLE *Hobbinol* ii. 34 The well-oil'd Champion shone. **1820** W. IRVING *Sketch Bk.* (1821) I. 54 Rip Van Winkle.. was one of those happy mortals, of foolish, well-oiled dispositions, who take the world easy. **1847** TENNYSON *Princess* III. 117 Sir, I was courteous, every phrase well-oil'd, As man's could be. **1897** *Outing* XXIX. 536/1 Since then she [the gun] has slumbered in well-oiled security. **1899** [see OILED *ppl. a.* 3].

well-'omened, *a.*

1754 FRANCIS *Constantine* v. v. 56 These well-omen'd Thunders.. Shall drown the Cries of Death. **1849** *Blackw. Mag.* Feb. 211 Not a very complimentary or well-omened name, certainly.

†**well-o'pinioned**, *a. Obs.* Having a good opinion (*of* oneself).

1615 T. ADAMS *White Devil* 61 The insolent hauty, well-opinioned of themselues. **1628** EARLE *Microcosm.* (Arb.) 47 He is not so well opinion'd of himselfe, as industrious to make other.

well-'orchestrated, *ppl. a.*

1947 A. EINSTEIN *Mus. Romantic Era* xvii. 315 The opinion that has become current with critics and with the public that the *Capriccio* is an unusually well-orchestrated piece is wrong: the Capriccio is a splendid composition for orchestra. **1979** *Wall St. Jrnl.* 20 Dec. 6/3 Why has such a well-orchestrated masking of political repressions been necessary?

well-'ordered, *ppl. a.*

1. Exhibiting good order; rightly regulated; carefully arranged; following good lines of conduct or procedure.

1606 SHAKS. *Tr. & Cr.* II. ii. 180 There is a Law in each well-ordred Nation To curbe those raging appetites that are Most disobedient and refracturie. **1615** CHAPMAN *Odyss.* XIX. 158 Nothing else, the cause Of all these blessings, but well order'd Lawes. **1668** R. STEELE *Husbandman's Calling* v. (1672) 96 Well-ordered charity makes no man poor. **1710** ATTERBURY *Serm.* (1734) I. 318 A Vertuous and Well-ordered Life. **1712** ADDISON *Spect.* No. 417 ¶ 5 The *Æneid* is like a well ordered Garden. **1768–74** TUCKER *Lt. Nat.* (1834) II. 23 It is of the utmost importance to have a well-ordered imagination. **1781** GIBBON *Decl. & F.* xviii. (1787) II. 116 The well-ordered ranks of Romans and Barbarians. **1841** DICKENS *Barn. Rudge* xl, White, well-ordered teeth. **1877** HUXLEY *Techn. Educ.* Sci. & Cult. (1881) 77 A well-ordered elementary school. **1886** PASCOE *London To-day* xx. (ed. 3) 193 To church or chapel in the morning, at least, is the custom of most well-ordered persons in London.

2. *Math.* [tr. G. *wohlgeordnet* (G. Cantor in *Math. Ann.* (1883) XXI. 548, (1898) XLIX. 207).] Of an ordered set: having the property that every non-empty subset of it has a first or least element.

1902 *Amer. Jrnl. Math.* II. 384 The usual notation $\alpha + \beta + \gamma + ..$ is only suitable for a finite, or at least for a well-ordered set of numbers. **1931** P. DIENES *Taylor Series* iii. 95 All these definitions.. extend to every type of transfinite sequence (well-ordered set) of numbers. **1975** R. A. SILVERMAN tr. *Kolmogorov & Formin's Introd. Real Analysis* i. 23 The set M of rational numbers in the interval [0, 1] is ordered but not well-ordered.

well-'ordering, *vbl. sb.* **a.** *gen.* The property of being well-ordered.

a **1586** SIDNEY *Apol. Poetrie* (Arb.) 21 The well ordering of a banquet. **1614** MARKHAM (*title*) Cheape and Good Husbandry, for the well-Ordering of all Beasts, and Fowles. **1668** PEPYS *Diary* 16 Sept., The well-ordering of the men [at a muster of the Guards].

b. *spec.* in *Math.*; also, a well-ordered set. Freq. *attrib.*

1941 BIRKHOFF & MACLANE *Survey Mod. Algebra* i. 9 The integers have one further important property, not characteristically algebraic and not shared by other number systems. This is the well-ordering principle. **1963** W. V. QUINE *Set Theory* 145 Well-orderings are notable for their exemplary behavior. **1966** *Math. Rev.* XXXI. 6/1 Only denumerable well-orderings are considered. **1970** A. G. HOWSON *Handbk. Terms Algebra & Analysis* xvi. 80 Zermelo's Well-Ordering Theorem states that if X is any set whatsoever, then there exists a well-ordering of X.

So **well-'order** *v. trans.*, to arrange the elements of (a set) in such an order as to produce a well-ordered set.

1944 *Ann. Math. Stud.* XIII. 117 For a finite set can be well-ordered in obvious fashion and hence must obey the axiom of choice. **1966** *McGraw-Hill Encycl. Sci. & Technol.* XII. 206/1 One considers the collection Z of all subsets of X, selects a point $x_\alpha = f(z_\alpha)$ from each element z_α of Z, and well orders X so that [etc.].

well-'ordering, *ppl. a.*

1668 R. STEELE *Husbandman's Calling* x. (1672) 246 The over-ruling and well-ordering hand of God.

well-'organized, *ppl. a.*

1857 RUSKIN *Pol. Econ. Art* I. §14 A well-organized nation. **1877** H. SMART *Bound to Win* III. 151 A well-organized robbery.

well-packed, *ppl. a.*[1] [PACKED[1].] Closely and compactly put together; in quot. of a horse = compactly or solidly built.

1842 J. AITON *Domest. Econ.* (1857) 243 A stumpy, sturdy, well-packed [horse].

well-packed, *ppl. a.*[2] [PACKED[2].] Skilfully selected or manipulated.

a **1716** SOUTH *Serm.* (1715) IV. 163 The Legerdemain of a well packed and paid Jury. **1834** AINSWORTH *Rookwood* IV. ii, 'Mod. Greek', Blind-hookey sees how well I squeeze The well-packed cards in shuffling.

well-'padded, *ppl. a.* Provided with sufficient padding. Also *transf.* and *fig.*

1933 J. BUCHAN *Prince of Captivity* II. ii. 190 What has become of the nice, easy-going, well-padded people with soft voices and wide smiles. **1945** WYNDHAM LEWIS *Let.* 29 June (1963) 384 However well-padded with dollar-bills you might be. **1976** 'R. GORDON' *Doctor on Job* vii. 62 Mr Clapper rocked back in his well-padded chair.

well(-)paid, *ppl. a.*

†**1.** Highly pleased or satisfied. Const. *of*. (See PAID 1, PAY *v.*[1] 1.) *Obs.*

c **1400** [see PAID 1]. *c* **1450** *Godstow Reg.* 166 Iohn, bisshop of exetur, was plesid & well paide of þe gifte. *c* **1460** *Towneley Myst.* xiii. 425, I hope they wyll nott be well payde when thay thare shepe lak. *a* **1846** in M. A. Richardson *Local Hist. Table-bk.*, *Leg.* III. 259 If he's struck my daughter I shall make him a weel-paid wife.

2. Liberally remunerated.
1590 SIR J. SMYTH *Disc. Weapons* Ded. 4 b, Souldiours well payd, and chiefly being subiects to the Prince that they serue. **1606** SHAKS. *Ant. & Cl.* III. i. 32 With his Banners, and his well paid ranks. *a* **1693** *Urquhart's Rabelais* III. xviii. 147 The well-payed Incomes of Regenting-Doctors. **1726** *Learned Diss. Dumpling* (ed. 4) 17 The Well-Fed, Well-Read, Well-Pay'd C—— J—— Esq. **1832** HT. MARTINEAU *Hill & Valley* iv. 63 It is the duty of well-paid labourers to become capitalists if they can. **1845** SYD. SMITH *Ir. R.C. Ch.* Wks. 1859 II. 334/1 A well-paid Protestant clergyman.

well-'painted, *ppl. a.* (*lit.* and *fig.*).
1593 SHAKS. *Lucr.* 1443 To this well painted peece is Lvcrece come. **1604** —— *Oth.* IV. i. 268 Oh well-painted passion. **1901** *J. Black's Carp. & Build., Home Handicr.* 67 The rule in building should be good joints and well-painted joints.

well-paired, *ppl. a.*
1617 MORYSON *Itin.* III. 18 Man and wife, like well paired Heyfers, beare all burthens together. **1725** POPE *Odyss.* xv. 98 The well-pair'd mules. **1729** JENYNS *Art of Dancing* III. 84 Rang'd on each side the well-pair'd Couples stand.

well-parked, *ppl. a.*
1760–72 H. BROOKE *Fool of Qual.* (1809) III. 115 A very beautiful and well-parked farm.

well-paved, *ppl. a.*
c **1611** CHAPMAN *Iliad* XXIV. 77 Of all that trod The well-pau'd Ilion. **1735** SOMERVILLE *Chase* I. 157 From the full Cistern lead the ductile Streams, To wash thy Court well-pav'd.

well-penned, *ppl. a.* Well written.
1598 MARSTON *Sco. Villanie* H 4, His huge long scraped stock Of well penn'd playes. **1603** J. DAVIES (Heref.) *Microcosm.* (Grosart) 81/2 A wel-pen'd Poem. **1622** FLETCHER *Beggars' Bush* I. ii, He will not..lend Upon the assurance of a well-pen'd Letter. **1757** [see PENNED *ppl. a.*[2] 1]. **1821** SCOTT *Kenilw.* xxx, The stranger then, in a well-penned speech, announced herself as that famous Lady of the Lake.

well-'peopled, *ppl. a.* Full of inhabitants; populous.
1588 [see PEOPLED b]. **1628** R. B[ELING] *Sixth Bk. Sidney's Arcadia* (1629) 504 The desolation of their wel-peopled country. **1718** LADY M. W. MONTAGU *Let. to Abbé Conti* 31 July, The Isle..is but ten miles in circuit, but in those days very rich and well-peopled. **1817** KIRBY & SP. *Entomol.* xx. II. 196 A well-peopled hive. *c* **1850** *Arab. Nts.* (Rtldg.) 279 Large, flourishing, and well-peopled towns.

well(-)placed, *ppl. a.* Set in a good place or position; rightly, fittingly, or judiciously placed.
1606 CHAPMAN *Gentl. Usher* IV. i, How strong an influence works in well plac'd words. **1607** B. JONSON *Volpone* v. iii, To cosen him of all, were but a cheat Well plac'd. **1635–56** COWLEY *Davideis* I. 595 A well-plac'ed Tapers light, Adds a becoming horror to the sight. **1674** *Barbette's Chirurg.* (ed. 2) 5 The Bone is well-placed, if in the second dressing, you find all even. **1753** MISS COLLIER *Art Torment.* I. iii. (1811) 86 Well-placed kindness. **1790** BURKE *Fr. Rev.* 96 They have perverted in themselves..all the well-placed sympathies of the human breast. **1876** *Coursing Calendar* 21 Filey..after losing ground at the start, got well placed.
b. Holding a good social position. In quot. *absol.*
1863 JEAFFRESON *Sir Everard's Dau.* 204 That distrust and commiserating disdain which the rich and well-placed are so prone to feel for the poor.

well-'placing, *vbl. sb.*
1672 DRYDEN *Conq. Granada*, Def. Epilogue 167 Well placing of Words for the sweetness of pronunciation was not known till Mr. Waller introduc'd it. **1674** *Barbette's Chirurg.* (ed. 2) 4 A broken Bone requireth four Manual Operations: Extention, Conjoyning, Ligature, Well-placing. **1715** LEONI *Palladio's Archit.* (1742) I. 34 Great care taken in the well-placing of Stair-cases.

well-planned, *ppl. a.*
1735 J. NIXON in Somerville *Chase* To Author, The well-plan'd System. **1890** 'R. BOLDREWOOD' *Col. Reformer* xviii, A large, strong, well-planned stockyard.

well-'planted, *ppl. a.*
1. Well stocked with growing plants.
a **1703** BURKITT *On N.T.* Mark xii. 8 A vineyard is a place enclosed, a place well planted, well fruited. **1872** GEO. ELIOT *Middlem.* lv, Where the fine old turf sloped..towards a lilied pool and well-planted mounds.
2. Of a blow or the like: Skilfully placed, directed, or delivered.
1755 SMOLLETT *Quix.* (1803) IV. 271 Sancho..held out his face and beard to the first, who treated him with a well-planted twitch. **1847** C. BRONTË *Jane Eyre* xxvi, He could have settled her with a well-planted blow.

well-pleased, *ppl. a.*
†**1.** Received with approval. *Obs.*[−1]
1382 WYCLIF *Ps.* cxl[i]. 5 In the wel plesid thingus of hem [Vulg. *in beneplacitis eorum*].
2. Highly gratified or satisfied.
c **1420** ? LYDG. *Assembly of Gods* 180, I am wellplesyd, quod thys Eolus. **1539** BIBLE (Great) *Matt.* iii. 17 This is my beloued sonne, in whom I am well pleased. **1593** SHAKS. *2 Hen. VI*, IV. x. 25 Sufficeth, that I haue maintaines my state, And sends the poore well pleased from my gate. **1619** DRAYTON *Bar. Wars* III. lxxxiv. 48 Where Welcome look'd with a well-pleased face. **1707** E. SMITH *Phædra & Hipp.* III. 26 The well pleas'd Sun With all his Beams survey'd their guiltless Flame. **1847** TENNYSON *Princess* Concl. 118 And home well-pleased we went. **1852** THACKERAY *Esmond* III. ix, 'I drink to my hostess and her family,' says the Prince, with no very well-pleased air.
Hence **well-'pleasedly** *adv.*, **well-'pleasedness**.
1633 D. R[OGERS] *Treat. Sacram.* ii. 36 So that former anger is turned into welpleasednesse. **1644** HAMMOND *Tracts, Consc.* §58 Serving God εὐαρέστως (*i.e.* either well pleasedly, cheerfully, willingly, or well pleasingly, so as God may and will accept). **1658** *Whole Duty Man* vii. §1. 158 This contentedness is a well-pleasedness with that condition.. that God hath placed us. **1701** BEVERLEY *Praise of Glory of Grace* 21 The pure and perfect Eudokia, or the Well-Pleasedness of his Will in it self.

well-'pleasing, *vbl. sb. rare.* The fact of being highly pleased, or of giving great pleasure.
1382 WYCLIF *Ps.* lxxxviii. 18 In thi wel plesing [Vulg. *in beneplacito tuo*] shal ben enhauncid oure horn. *c* **1450** tr. *De Imitatione* III. liv. 130 Ioy þou..in my welplesing & worship [*in mei solius beneplacito ac honore*]. **1625** BACON *Ess., Unity Relig.* (Arb.) 423 The Fruits of Vnity (next vnto the well Pleasing of God, which is All in All) are two.

well-'pleasing, *ppl. a.* Giving great pleasure or satisfaction.
1382 WYCLIF *Col.* iii. 20 This is wel plesynge to the Lord. **1607** *Statutes* in *Hist. Wakefield Gram. Sch.* (1892) 66 Thus the displeasinge hardnes of learninge shalbe made easie in the welpleasinge manner of teachinge. **1611** BIBLE *Phil.* iv. 18 A sacrifice acceptable, well pleasing to God. **1697** DRYDEN *Æneis* x. 856 My Sister Goddess, and well pleasing Wife. **1718–19** ATTERBURY *Serm.* (1734) II. 76 Upon such Principles and Grounds as are well-pleasing to God. **1875** MANNING *Mission H. Ghost* xii. 344 We ask the Holy Spirit of counsel to give us light to know what is right, what is well-pleasing.
Hence †**well-'pleasingly** *adv.*
1644 [see WELL-PLEASEDLY *adv.*].

well-'plenished, *ppl. a.*
1856 MERIVALE *Rom. Emp.* xlii. V. 56 Surely there was no room, behind so well-plenished an equipage, for the slave who [etc.]. **1897** 'SARAH TYTLER' *Lady Jean's Son* 274 A well-plenished dower-house.

†**well-'plighted,** *ppl. a. Obs.* [= *pleated*: see PLIGHT *v.*[2]]
1590 SPENSER *F.Q.* III. ix. 21 Her well plighted frock.

well-plucked, *a. colloq.* [PLUCKED *a.*] Plucky, fearless.
1873 M. A. BARKER *Station Amusements in N.Z.* 148 He was a well-plucked one... He told me it took five mortal hours to come the last mile. **1936** M. DE LA ROCHE *Whiteoak Harvest* xviii. 230 'That gray one is a 'andful for you'... 'I'm not afraid.' 'You're wot I call a well-plucked 'un.'

well-plumed, *ppl. a.*
1616 W. BROWNE *Brit. Past.* II. iii. 55 The well-plum'd Goshawke. **1743** R. BLAIR *Grave* 156 But see! the well-plum'd Herse comes nodding on Stately and slow.

'well-point. *Civil Engin.* [WELL *sb.*[1]] One of a system of pipes sunk into the ground around an excavated area in order to lower the water-table. Hence as *v. trans.*, to supply with well-points.
1951 *Engineering* 4 May 536/3 The consulting engineers considered..that lowering of the ground-water level by means of well-points would be the most efficient method of keeping the excavation dry. **1958** J. S. SCOTT *Dict. Civil Engin.* 409 An excavation in sand cannot become quick if effectively wellpointed. **1971** O. H. BULLITT *Search for Sybaris* xvii. 169 The most effective way of dewatering an area..would be by means of a well-point system.

well-'pointed, *ppl. a.*
1590 SPENSER *F.Q.* III. xi. 55 Her welpointed weapons. **1825** J. NICHOLSON *Operat. Mechanic* 349 A well-pointed punch of German steel.

well-poised, *ppl. a.* = WELL-BALANCED, WELL-WEIGHED (*lit.* and *fig.*).
1616 W. BROWNE *Brit. Past.* II. i. 14 The well poys'd Oares Of the poore Fisher-man that dwelt thereby. **1642** CHAS. I *Answ. XIX Propositions* 17 The ancient, equall, happy, well-poised..Constitution. **1663** PATRICK *Parab. Pilgrim* (1687) 409 Humility and Charity..are sufficient to carry us thorow this evil World with an equal and well-poised mind. **1678** DRYDEN *All for Love* Ep. Ded. A 2 b, We who have the happiness to be born under so equal, and so well-pois'd a Government. **1777** POTTER *Æschylus, Agamem.* 271 Comes sloth, and from her well-pois'd sling Scatters the piled up stores. **1781** COWPER *Hope* 611 By this he forms..His well-pois'd estimate of right and wrong. **1791** BURKE *Let. Member Nat. Assembly* (near end), They were offered a well-poised, free constitution. **1803** JANE PORTER *Thaddeus* ii, The well-poised mind of the veteran. **1864** BURTON *Scot Abr.* II. i. 30 Announcing the moral..in well-poised sentences.

†**well-policed,** *ppl. a. Obs.* = next.
1591 LAMBARDE *Archeion* (1635) 65 The necessitie of an Officer of this sort is inevitable in every well-polliced Kingdome. **1651** HOWELL *Venice* 198* This powerfull and so well policed Common-wealth.

†**well-'policied,** *ppl. a. Obs.* Having a good polity or government.
1647 COTTERELL *Davila's Hist. Fr.* I. 4 Well policied Government. **1662** PETTY *Taxes* 19 This, I conceive, were the worst of Taxes in a well policyed State. **1768–74** TUCKER *Lt. Nat.* (1834) II. 11 In every well-policied kingdom.

well-'polished, *ppl. a.* (*lit.* and *fig.*).
1615 CHAPMAN *Odyss.* v. 312 A faire wel polisht helme. **1625–8** tr. *Camden's Hist. Eliz.* II. (1675) 246 Campian was ..of a sweet Disposition, and a well-polished man. **1656** EARL MONM. tr. *Boccalini's Advts. fr. Parnass.* I. xxxiii. (1674) 39 You have lived in the well-polisht Court of Rome. **1661** WALLER *St. James's Park* 57 Here a well-polisht Mall gives us the joy To see our Prince his matchless force imploy. **1717** POPE *Ep. Jervas* 40 This small, well-polish'd Gem, the work of years. **1853** HICKIE tr. *Aristoph.* II. 577 Say something clever and well-polished.

†**well-po'ssessed,** *pa. pple. Obs.* Having large possessions.
1590 SHAKS. *Mids. N.* I. i. 100, I am my Lord, as well deriu'd as he, As well possesst.

well-'practised, *ppl. a.* Skilled through long or good practice.
1596 SPENSER *F.Q.* VI. ix. 43 He through long and perfect industry, Therein well practisd was. **1597** SHAKS. *2 Hen. IV*, V. ii. 121, I will..humble my Intents, To your well-practis'd, wise Directions. **1633** FORD *Love's Sacrif.* II. E 3 b, He's a well practiz'd gamester. **1634** MILTON *Comus* 310 Without the sure guess of well-practiz'd feet. **1701** NORRIS *Ideal World* I. i. 21 A well-practised Musitian. **1845** J. COULTER *Adv. Pacific* xii. 159 They..paddle [the canoe] with a well-practised arm. **1855** TENNYSON *Maud* I. IV. vii, An eye well-practised in nature.

well-pre'pared, *ppl. a.*
1596 SPENSER *F.Q.* V. iv. 37 With weapons well prepard. **1599** SHAKS. *Hen. V*, I. ii. 234 Now are we well prepar'd to know the pleasure Of our faire Cosin Dolphin. **1603** DRAYTON *To K. Jas.* A 3, Well-prepared pollicie. **1661** BOYLE *Physiol. Ess.* (1669) 67 A well-prepar'd Medicine of duly refin'd Silver. **1703** KELSEY *Serm.* 153 We bring not good, well-prepared Minds to them. **1868** GEO. ELIOT *Ess.* (1884) 325 He knows that for an article to be worth much.. there must be well-prepared material.

well-pre'served, *ppl. a.*
(Often used to describe elderly persons who carry their years well.)
1854 *Weekly Oregonian* Dec. 9 (Thornton) Antiquated gentleman.., well preserved, but somewhat wrinkled. **1859** GEO. ELIOT *Adam Bede* v, Her well-preserved faculties, and her old-fashioned dignity. *a* **1865** MRS. GASKELL *Wives & Dau.* vi, All the furniture in the room was as old-fashioned and as well-preserved as it could be. **1871** 'M. LEGRAND' *Cambr. Freshm.* 10 They were well-preserved women for their time of life.

well-primed, *ppl. a.* (See PRIMED, under PRIME *v.*[1]).
1705 TATE *Warriour's Welcome* xxxiv, Then try your Skill: a well-prim'd Canvass stretch.

well-'principled, *a.* Holding, actuated by, or founded upon, good principles.
1691 NORRIS *Pract. Disc.* 133 A Pious and well-principled Education. **1691** *Moralist* title-p., By way of Dialogue, between a Well-Principled Lay-man, and a Professor of Theology. **1791** BOSWELL *Johnson* an. 1754 The wild and pernicious ravings, under the name of Philosophy, which were thus ushered into the world, gave great offence to all well-principled men. **1828** P. CUNNINGHAM *N.S. Wales* (ed. 3) II. 60 An intelligent, spirited, and well-principled population. **1837** HT. MARTINEAU *Soc. Amer.* III. 157, I should like to see a well-principled reform in diet tried. **1873** MRS. BROOKFIELD *Not a Heroine* i. 5 Four children had grown up—amiable, well-principled, and good-looking.

well-printed, *ppl. a.*
1778 E. HARWOOD *Eds. Classics* (ed. 2) 53 This Edition of Polybius..is a well printed book, and very correct. **1852** COTTON *Eds. Bible* (ed. 2) 70 This is a well-printed book.

well-prized, *ppl. a.*
c **1611** CHAPMAN *Iliad.* XI. 478 Loth he should taint the wel-prisd fat, of any stall-fed steere.

†**well-pro'portionated,** *ppl. a. Obs.* = next.
1647 H. MORE *Song of Soul* II. App. lv. 205 Keeping a well-proportionated space One from another. **1657** [see next, quot. 1579–80].

well-pro'portioned, *ppl. a.* Having good or correct proportions.
c **1386** CHAUCER *Squire's T.* 184 The hors of bras..So wel proporcioned for to been strong. **1430–40** LYDG. *Bochas* III. 3293 He was..Weel proporciowned. **1538** ELYOT *Dict.* Add., *Amussitatus*, made by line, welle proporcyoned. **1579–80** NORTH *Plutarch, Lycurgus* (1595) 55 If they found him..well proportioned [ed. 1657 p. 41 well proportionated] of all his limmes. **1592** SHAKS. *Ven. & Ad.* 290 When a Painter would surpasse the life In limming out a well proportioned steed. **1661** COWLEY *O. Cromwell*, '*Curst be the man*' ii, Who would be rather a great Monster, than A well-proportion'd Man. **1663** GERBIER *Counsel* 18 Well proportioned Doores and Windowes. **1709** POPE *Ess. Crit.* 247 When we view some well-proportion'd dome. **1812** JANE AUSTEN *Pride & Prej.* xliii, A large, well-proportioned room, handsomely fitted up. **1831** SCOTT *Anne of G.* iii, A young man, unusually tall, well-proportioned and active. **1890** *Spectator* 3 May, He does not present us with a clear and well-proportioned historical sequence of events and dates.

well-proved, *ppl. a.*
c **1449** PECOCK *Repr.* III. viii. 331 Weel proued men in leernyng and in lyuyng. *Ibid.* V. x. 537 For such pretendid and weel proued causis. **1590** SPENSER *F.Q.* II. xi. 17 His well proued weapons. *c* **1611** CHAPMAN *Iliad* XII. 357 The well-prou'd mightie Lycian Chiefs. **1717** POPE *Iliad* x. 309 A well-'provd casque, with leather braces bound.

well-proven, *ppl. a.* = prec.
1877 RAYMOND *Statist. Mines* 283 Old and well-proven mines.

well-'provendered, *ppl. a.*
1584, 1707: see PROVENDER *v.* 2. **1861** LD. LYTTON & FANE *Tannhäuser* 79 When he [winter] Closed his well-provender'd days.

well(-)pro'vided, *ppl. a.*
1736 J. CAMPBELL *Milit. Hist. Pr. Eugene* etc. I. 385 The Garrison was far from being strong or well provided. **1799** HT. LEE *Canterb. T., Old Woman's T.* (ed. 2) I. 381 His eyes silently rested on..the height of the walls, the well-provided state of the ramparts.

well-'publicized, *ppl. a.*
1973 G. TALBOT *Ten Seconds from Now* xii. 165 The Queen's well-publicised love of horses. **1979** *Jrnl. R. Soc. Arts* CXXVII. 645/2 The discussion should be open and well-publicized.

well(-)'qualified, *ppl. a.*
1607 BEAUM. & FL. *Woman-hater* I. iii, You shall present me as a Gentleman well qualified, or one extraordinary seen in divers strange mysteries. **1621** *Relat. Exec. Prague* A 2, States-men Directors and other excellent and well qualified personages. **1720** T. INNES *Crit. Essay* (1879) 278 Among so many able and well qualified men. **1849** MACAULAY *Hist. Eng.* vi. II. 31 William Cavendish, Earl of Devonshire, took the lead in the Upper House; and he was well qualified to do so.

†**well-'qualitied**, *ppl. a.*
1600 [see QUALITIED *a.*]. **1689** N. LEE *Princ. Cleve* III. i. 36 Are your Wives handsome and well qualited? **1790** COWPER *Odyss.* XVIII. 335 A wife Well-qualitied and well-endow'd.

well-'quartered, *ppl. a.* (Said of animals.)
1641 BEST *Farm. Bks.* (Surtees) 3 Goode, fatte, and well-quartered lambes. **1682** *Lond. Gaz.* No. 1770/4 A thick well quartered Horse.

†**well-queme**, *a. Obs.* In 3 wel-, wilcweme. [f. WELL *adv.* 33 + QUEME *a.* (cf. OE. *wel-ȝecwéme*, *-ȝecwémness*), or *wil-* as in *wilcume* WELCOME.] Well-pleased, content, satisfied.
a **1225** *Leg. Kath.* 1744 Porphire & Auguste wurðen of þeos wordes..swiðe wilcweme [*v.r.* welcweme]. *a* **1225** *Juliana* 32 Ah habbich þin anes help, ich am wil cweme.
Also †**well-queme** *sb.*, **-quemeness**, that which is pleasing or agreeable to one. †**well-'queming** *ppl. a.*, pleasant, pleasing.
a **1300** *E.E. Psalter* lxxxviii. 18 In þi welequeme [*in beneplacito tuo*] vphouen bes oure horne. *Ibid.* xci. 15 Yhite felefold in elde ofe fulhed þai sal, And welquemand be. *Ibid.* cxl. 5 In welequemenesses ofe am [*in beneplacitis eorum*].

well-raised, *ppl. a.*
1581 SIDNEY *Apol. Poetrie* (Arb.) 65 The Tragedy shoulde be still maintained in a well raised admiration. *c* **1611** CHAPMAN *Iliad* II. 113 Not suffering well-raisd Troy to fall. **1649** [see COUPLED *ppl. a.* 3]. **1884** *Century Mag.* Apr. 919 The cleanliness, comfort, and well-raised foundation of the Fijian houses.

well-ranged, *ppl. a.*
1635–56 COWLEY *Davideis* I. 671 An inward Square by well-rang'd Trees was made. **1674** N. FAIRFAX *Bulk & Selv.* 74 A curious frame of well-ranged bulks. **1708** J. PHILIPS *Cyder* II. 61 The well-rang'd Files of Trees. **1752** 'SIR H. BEAUMONT' *Crito* 16 The Teeth should be middle-sized, white, well-ranged, and even. **1791** COWPER *Odyss.* IX. 666 They, all obedient, took their seats on board Well-ranged.

well(-)read, *ppl. a.*
1. Well-informed by reading, learned *in* (a subject). Also *gen.*, versed or skilled (*in*).
1596 SHAKS. *Tam. Shr.* I. ii, 170 This yong man..well read in Poetrie, And other bookes. **1607** BEAUM. & FL. *Woman-hater* I. iii, A Gentleman, well read, deeply learned, and thoroughly grounded in the hidden knowledge of all Sallads and Pot-herbs whatsoever. **1623** MASSINGER *Dk. Milan* III. i, We embrace you, As one well read in all the points of honor. **1670** G. H. *Hist. Cardinals* II. II. 150 All the world holds him very well read in the Art of dissembling. **1700** DRYDEN *Fables, Pythag. Philos.* 15 Then thus a Senior of the Place replies, (Well read, and curious of Antiquities). **1711** ADDISON *Spect.* No. 8 ¶7 As I am very well read in *Waller*, I repeated to her the four following Verses. **1756** BURKE *Subl. & B.* IV. xxiv, The author, so well read in human nature. **1772** BARRINGTON in *Phil. Trans.* LXII. 312 Not only a well-read naturalist, but an active sportsman. **1864** PUSEY *Daniel* (1876) 380 Well-read as he was in Greek. **1876** EMERSON *Lett. & Soc. Aims, Quot. & Orig.* Wks. (Bohn) III. 212 Our high respect for a well-read man is praise enough of literature.
2. Of a book: Attentively perused; read in a proper or profitable way.
1865 RUSKIN *Sesame* ii. §77, I speak therefore of good novels only... Well read, indeed, these books have serious use.

well-'readied, *ppl. a. Sc.* [READY *v.* 3 b.] Well-cooked.
1827 CARLYLE *Germ. Rom.* IV. 50 An old serving-maid brought in a well-readied meal.

†**well-reared**, *ppl. a. Obs.* [REAR *v.*[1] 1 b.]
a **1648** DIGBY *Closet Opened* (1671) 149 Put this into coffins of fine light well reared Crust.

well-'reasoned, *ppl. a.*
1834 J. S. MILL in *Monthly Repos.* VIII. 593 Lord Brougham..delivered a firm, steady, and well-reasoned opinion. **1856** KANE *Arct. Expl.* II. iii. 45 Whether from constitutional temperament, or well-reasoned argument, I find our state far from desperate. **1871** EARLE *Philol. Eng. Tongue* ix. 457 A well-reasoned book.

well-re'corded, *ppl. a.*
1812 BYRON *Ch. Har.* II. lxxxv, So perish all in turn, save well-recorded Worth.

well-reeved, *ppl. a.* Securely fastened.
1812 BYRON *Ch. Har.* II. xviii, The well-reeved guns, the netted canopy.

well(-)re'fined, *ppl. a.*
1600 SHAKS. *Sonn.* lxxxv, Euery Himne that able spirit affords, In polisht forme of well refined pen. **1611** BIBLE *Isa.* xxv. 6 A feast..of wines on the lees well refined.

well-re'formed, *ppl. a.*
1656 COWLEY *Pindar. Odes, Plagues Egypt* xvi, The sacred cheare That new begins their well-reformed Year. **1657** J. GAUDEN in J. Watts *Scribe* etc., To Rdr. 9 A bed-rid Church (whose once well reformed Religion seems not onely decayed, but dying and deplored).

well-re'freshing, *ppl. a.*
a **1586** SIDNEY *Arcadia* IV. (1922) 118 The noble Pamela having delivered over the burthen of her fearefull cares to the naturall ease of a well refreshing sleepe.

well-'regulated, *ppl. a.*
1709 SHAFTESB. *Moralists* II. iv. 108 If a liberal Education has form'd in us..well-regulated Appetites, and worthy Inclinations. **1714** R. FIDDES *Pract. Disc.* II. 250 The practice of all well regulated courts of justice in the world. **1812** J. JOYCE *Sci. Dial., Astron.* xii. II. 126 The equation of time..is the adjustment of the difference of time, as shown by a well-regulated clock and a true sun-dial. **1848** THACKERAY *Van. Fair* lviii, A remissness for which I am sure every well-regulated person will blame the Major. **1862** MRS. H. WOOD *Mrs. Hallib.* I. v. 27 It appeared, to her well-regulated mind, like a clandestine proceeding. **1894** *Pop. Sci. Monthly* June 165 The newspaper, a never wanting adjunct to every well-regulated American embryo city.

†**well re'leased**, *a. Obs.* [See RELEASE *sb.*[2], *v.*[2]] Clear in utterance, melodious.
a **1483** *Liber Niger* in *Househ. Ord.* (1790) 50 Chapleynes and clerkes of the Chapell..clene voysed, well releesed and pronouncynge.

†**well-'relished**, *a. Obs.* Savoury. (*lit.* and *fig.*)
1594 [see RELISHED *a.*]. **1687** MIEGE *Gt. Fr. Dict.* II. s.v. *Relish*, well relished, *qui a bon goût*.

†**well-'relishing**, *ppl. a. Obs.* Having a good flavour. (*lit.* and *fig.*)
1651 VAUGHAN *Praise Countrie-Life* ii. Wks. 1914 I. 127 The Husband-man..is alwaies furnished with wel-rellishing bread. **1656** EARL MONM. tr. *Boccalini's Advts. fr. Parnass.* II. xiv. (1674) 155 A well-relishing Latine Writer of the Annals of his times.

well(-)re'membered, *ppl. a.*
1. Appropriately or appositely brought to mind.
1482 J. PASTON in *P. Lett.* III. 290 And, well remembred, I wot well ye ought not to have me in jelusye. **1596** SHAKS. *Merch. V.* II. viii. 26 Marry well remembred. **1794** MRS. RADCLIFFE *Myst. Udolpho* xxxviii, 'Aye, that is well remembered,' said Dorothée.
2. Clearly or distinctly remembered.
1638 [see REMEMBERED *ppl. a.* 2]. **1760** A. MURPHY *Deserted Isl.* II. 18 Each well-remember'd object strikes my view. **1798** SOPHIA LEE *Canterb. T., Young Lady's T.* II. 446 Emily [was] going to hail the well-remembered old ferry-man. **1853** DICKENS *Bleak Ho.* xviii, The well-remembered voice of my godmother. **1890** 'R. BOLDREWOOD' *Col. Reformer* xiii, He whirled..along the well-remembered road.

well-re'plenished, *ppl. a.*
1616 W. BROWNE *Brit. Past.* II. iii. 53 Fly to the well-replenish'd Groues. **1829** *Anniversary* 115 A well replenished house.

well(-)re'puted, *ppl. a.* Held in good repute.
1591 SHAKS. *Two Gentl.* II. vii. 43 Fit me with such weedes As may beseeme some well reputed Page. **1601** —— *Jul. C.* II. i. 295 A Woman well reputed. **1642** MILTON *Apol. Smect.* viii. 37 The most of them being..of knowne and well reputed ancestry.

well-re'searched, *ppl. a.*
1958 *Times Lit. Suppl.* 15 Aug. 13 (Advt.), This well-researched book has been highly acclaimed. **1966** [see RESEARCHED *ppl. a.* 2]. **1978** *Jrnl. R. Soc. Med.* LXXI. 697/1 There is a respectable weight of well-researched evidence.

†**well(-)re'solved**, *ppl. a. Obs.* Resolute.
1613–16 W. BROWNE *Brit. Past.* I. v. 96 Like a valiant well resolued man. **1627** [? FALKLAND] *Hist. Edw. II* (1680) 114 Three hundred well-resolved Gallants. **1671** MILTON *Samson* 408 Who with a grain of manhood well resolv'd Might easily have shook off all her snares.

well(-)re'spected, *ppl. a.* † Duly considered or regarded (*obs.*); highly esteemed.
1596 SHAKS. *1 Hen. IV*, IV. iii. 10 If well-respected Honor bid me on. **1633** BP. HALL *Hard Texts, Hos.* xi. 4, I did to them, as a kind husbandman to his well-respected teame; I tooke off the yoke from them. **1829** *Anniversary* 122 He..is ..well connected, and well respected.

well-'rested, *ppl. a.*
1890 W. JAMES *Princ. Psychol.* II. xvii. 15 Successive contrast..can be avoided only by carefully fixating with the well-rested eye a point of one's field. **1965** J. A. MICHENER *Source* (1966) 798 At dusk on the afternoon of Tuesday, April 13, the Palmach men roused Ilana and her two well-rested companions.

well-ribbed, *a.*
1607 TOPSELL *Four-f. Beasts* 74 [Cows] wel ribbed. **1707** [see RIBBED *ppl. a.* 1]. **1847** W. C. L. MARTIN *Ox* 80/2 A heavy and well-ribbed carcass. **1908** *Westm. Gaz.* 25 Apr. 3/1 Large, well-ribbed umbrellas warranted not to blow inside out.

well-rigged, *ppl. a.*
1. Said of ships.
1502–9 [see RIGGED *ppl. a.*[1] 1]. **1590** SPENSER *F.Q.* ii. xi. 4 The Ferriman..With his well rigged boate. **1612** DRAYTON *Poly-olb.* ix. 313 Madock..Put forth his well-rigg'd Fleet. **1715** POPE *Iliad* I. 405 Mean time Atrides launch'd with num'rous Oars A well-rigg'd Ship.
2. Of a person: Well dressed or clothed.
a **1743** OZELL tr. *Brantôme's Sp. Rhodom.* (1744) 18 A well-rigg'd, spruce, proper Man. **1838** HALIBURTON *Clockm.* Ser. II. ii, A tidy, well-rigged nigger help.

well-ringed, *a.*
1838 LYTTON *Alice* XI. v, Warming his white and well-ringed hands by the fire.

well-'ripened, *ppl. a.*
1660 DRYDEN *Astræa Redux* 170 'Twas not the hasty product of a day, But the well ripened Fruit of wise delay. **1842** LOUDON *Suburban Hort.* 459 With good culture, in twelve months, they will have..4 feet of well-ripened cane.

well-'risen, *ppl. a.* †**a.** Of a horse or deer: ? Having an erect chest and well-carried neck. *Obs.* **b.** Of bread or paste (see RISE *v.* 10 c).
1639 T. DE GREY *Compl. Horsem.* I. iv. (1656) 37 Those three [properties] of a Hart, are to have lean and dry legs, to be well risen before, and a lean head. *Ibid.*, Horses..to have a great belly, well risen before, straight backt. **1728** E. S[MITH] *Compleat Housew.* (ed. 2) 133 When 'tis well risen, put in a pound of Carraway-comfits.

†**well-rode**, *ppl. a.* Skilled in riding.
c **1611** CHAPMAN *Iliad* III. 269 The wel-rode Peeres of Troy.

well-rolled, *ppl. a.*
1784 COWPER *Task* I. 351 We tread the wilderness, whose well-roll'd walks [etc.]. **1865** LUBBOCK *Prehist. T.* ix. 288 This layer..contains many well-rolled tertiary pebbles.

well-roofed, *ppl. a.*
1831 JAMES *Phil. Augustus* xxii, Like a heavy shower of hail upon some well-roofed building. **1845** SYD. SMITH *Ir. R.C. Ch.* Wks. 1859 II. 334/1 A well-windowed and well-roofed house.

well(-)'rooted, *ppl. a.* **a.** Firmly implanted. **b.** Well furnished with roots.
c **1611** CHAPMAN *Iliad* XII. 138 Two high hill-bred Okes, Well rooted in the binding earth. **1627** MAY *Lucan* I. A 3 b, And round about well rooted Trees doe grow. **1707** MORTIMER *Husb.* 4 A well rooted Set. **1842** LOUDON *Suburban Hort.* 253 The advantage of taking off cuttings in spring is, that they can be well rooted before winter.
fig. **1876** HARDY *Ethelberta* xxxiii, Well-rooted local people. **1878** [see ROOTED 2 *fig*].

well-'rotted, *ppl. a.*
1796 BOYS *Agric. Kent* (ed. 2) 120 Fifty cart-loads of well rotted farm-yard dung and mould. **1846** J. BAXTER *Libr. Pract. Agric.* (ed. 4) I. 91 Each pot is half filled with well-rotted manure. **1858** GLENNY *Everyday Bk.* 82/1 Top-dress Strawberry-beds with a coat of well-rotted dung.

well-'rounded, *ppl. a.* **a.** *lit.*
1752 'SIR H. BEAUMONT' *Crito* 17 The Knee should be even, and well-rounded. **1860** GEO. ELIOT *Mill on Fl.* III. vi, Such things bring lines in well-rounded faces.
b. *fig.* (Cf. ROUNDED 6, 6 b.) Of a person, his life: Complete and symmetrical. Of a period: Full and well turned.
18.. LONGFELLOW (Cent.) Something so complete and well-rounded in his..life. **1875** PLUMPTRE in *Expositor* I. 414 His well-rounded periods would be to such an one what the rhetorical morality of Cicero was to Augustine. **1889** GRETTON *Memory's Harkback* 277 Assuredly the preacher mistakes his errand..when he strives after fine phrases,.. well-rounded periods. **1897** PEERY *Gist of Japan* 224 The great variety of work necessitates a well-rounded man.

well-rowed, *ppl. a.*
1725 POPE *Odyss.* xv. 596 Swift to the town the well-row'd gally flew.

well-ruled, *ppl. a.* (See RULED 1 a.)

well-'ruling, *ppl. a.*
1596 SPENSER *F.Q.* v. v. 25 T'obay the heasts of mans well ruling hand.

well-run, *ppl. a.*
1876 *Coursing Cal.* 38 A well-run course of good length.

well-'running, *ppl. a.* (*lit.* and *fig.*).
c **1400** *Ywaine & Gaw.* 1067, I have a wele rinand page, Wil stirt thider right in a stage. **1697** DRYDEN *Æneis* Ded. (e) 2 If I shou'd instruct some of them to make well-running Verses, they want Genius to give them strength as well as sweetness.

well-'sailing, *ppl. a.*
1608 SHAKS. *Per.* IV. iv. 17 Well sayling ships, and bounteous winds Haue brought This king to Tharsus.

well-'sanded, *ppl. a.*
1707 [see SANDED *ppl. a.* 5 c]. **1843** *Chambers' Edin. Jrnl.* 45/2 A smiling infant..crawling over the well-sanded floor.

well-saved, *ppl. a.* Carefully kept, stored, or hoarded.
1600 SHAKS. *A.Y.L.* II. vii. 160 His youthfull hose well sau'd, a world too wide For his shrunke shanke. **1851** H. MELVILLE *Whale* xx. 107 She herself owned a score or two of well-saved dollars. **1890** 'R. BOLDREWOOD' *Col. Reformer* xiii, Their racks full of well-saved oaten hay.

well-'savouring, *ppl. a.* Sweet-scented.
c **1440** *Alphabet of Tales* 171 Many wele-saueryng spycis. **1551** TURNER *Herbal* I. E ij b, Folfoote is a well sauoringe herbe.

well-'saying, *vbl. sb. nonce-wd.*
1613 SHAKS. *Hen. VIII*, III. ii. 152 *King.* You haue said well. *Car.* And euer may your Highnesse yoake together.. my doing well With my well saying.

well-'scented, *ppl. a.* **a.** Keen-scented. **b.** Sweet-scented.

1579 [see SCENTED 1]. **1618** GAINSFORD *P. Warbeck* 105 Well-sented hounds. **1726** J. LAURENCE *Agric.* 268 Its beautiful well-sented Flowers.

well-schemed, *ppl. a.*

1728 FROWDE in *Theobald's Double Falsehood* Prol., Most modern Authors.. The well-schem'd Plan keep strict before their Eyes. **1909** H. BALFOUR in *Museums Jrnl.* IX. 14 A well-schemed plan of campaign.

well-scrubbed, *ppl. a.*

1916 JOYCE *Portrait of Artist* (1969) ii. 64 A well-scrubbed kitchen. **1949** C. FRY *Lady's not for Burning* II. 49 Always fornicate Between clean sheets and spit on a well-scrubbed floor. **1976** 'R. GORDON' *Doctor on Job* iii. 18 A small, round, well-scrubbed looking man.

well-'seasoned, *ppl. a.*

1. Said of meat or drink (see SEASON *v.* 1).

1684 EARL ROSCOM. *Ess. Transl. Verse* 248 Well-season'd Bowls the Gossyps Spirits raise. **1694** LOCKE *Hum. Und.* II. xxi. §69 The eating of a well season'd dish suited to a Man's pallate. **1851** D. JERROLD *St. Giles* xxxii. 330 He took the same pleasure in falsehood that an epicure receives from a well-seasoned dish.

2. Well matured and fit for use. Chiefly of timber: Thoroughly dried and hardened. Also *fig.*

1583 STUBBES *Anat. Abus.* I. D j b, These be well seasoned reasons, and substantiall asseuerations in deed. **1683** MOXON *Mech. Exerc., Printing* ii. 27 Letter-Boards.. ought to be made of clean and well-season'd Stuff. **1725** POPE *Odyss.* XIV. 26 To form strong buskins of well-season'd hyde. **1838** DICKENS *O. Twist* iv, Well-seasoned timber is an expensive article.

3. Of persons or animals: Fortified by training or experience. Also, inured *to*. (Cf. SEASONED 3 c.)

1756 C. SMART tr. *Horace, Sat.* II. v. 55 A well-seasoned lawyer. **1834** JAMES *J. Marston Hall* x, Our horses were strong and well-seasoned to hard work. **1849** —— *Woodman* iv, My well-seasoned staves would have drank the whole beer in the town without rolling. **1855** MOTLEY *Dutch Rep.* V. iv. (1866) 741 Twenty thousand well-seasoned and disciplined veterans.

well-'seated, *ppl. a.* Having a good seat or site.

1579–80 NORTH *Plutarch, Camillus* (1595) 150 Eighteene fayre great cities.. all of them very strong, and well seated. **1621–1720** [see SEATED 2]. **1705** MANDEVILLE *Grumbling Hive* 22 The once gay, Well-seated Houshold Gods.

well-seeing, *ppl. a.* Sharp-sighted.

1600 SHAKS. *Sonn.* cxlviii, O cunning loue, with teares thou keepst me blinde, Least eyes well seeing thy foule faults should finde.

well-'seeming, *ppl. a.* Presenting a good or specious appearance.

1592 SHAKS. *Rom. & Jul.* I. i. 185 Mishapen Chaos of welsee[m]ing formes. **1603** —— *Meas. for M.* III. i. 232 This well-seeming Angelo.

well(-)seen, *ppl. a.*

†**1.** Well provided or furnished. Const. *of*. *Obs.*

a **1300** *Cursor M.* 1011 O selenes es it [Paradise] wel sene. *c* **1450** [see SEEN 1 c].

2. Skilled, versed, proficient *in* (some subject or affair). Now *arch.*

1528 [see SEEN 2]. *c* **1545** J. HEYWOOD *Four P.* (W. Copland) B j, Syr, ye seme wel sene in womens causes. **1562** TURNER *Herbal* II. 80 Matthiolus a man otherwyse well sene in symples. **1639** FULLER *Holy War* II. xiv. 63 He was.. excellently well seen in all martiall affairs. *a* **1676** HALE *Prim. Orig. Man.* 13 A man well seen in Natural Causes and Effects. **1681** W. ROBERTSON *Phraseol. Gen.* 1107 Well-seen in a business, *callentissimus*. **1759, 1886** [see SEEN 2].

†**3.** Plainly visible, evident. *Obs.*

c **1386** CHAUCER *Knt.'s T.* 66 Now be we caytyues, as it is wel seene. **1535** COVERDALE *Ps.* lxvii[i]. 24 It is well sene (o God) how thou goest. *a* **1586** SIDNEY *Arcadia* III. (1922) 20 Her perfections then should have beene as well seene as Pamelas. **1725** RAMSAY *Gent. Sheph.* I. i, Daftly wad ye hide Your well-seen love and dorty Jenny's pride.

well-se'lected, *ppl. a.*

1808 SCOTT in *Lockhart* I. i. 54 There is generally, in a well-selected society of this nature, talent sufficient to meet the forwardest. **1848** THACKERAY *Van. Fair* lxi, My cellar of well-selected wine in Baker Street.

well-'selling, *ppl. a.*

1606 CHAPMAN *Gentl. Usher* III. i, Some words, pickt out of Proclamations,.. or well-selling Pamphlets.

well-served, *ppl. a.* [Cf. F. *bien servi.*]

1747 *Gentl. Mag.* XVII. 344 A numerous and well serv'd artillery. **1849** LEVER *Con Cregan* xviii, A well-served table. **1876** *Coursing Cal.* 26 A party of upwards of thirty sat down to a capital and well-served dinner. **1880** RUSKIN *Bible of Amiens* i. 1 At this halting-place.. there is a well-served buffet. **1882** SIR G. WOLSELEY in C. Royle *Egypt. Campaigns* (1886) I. 319 In full view of the enemy, and under the fire of his well-served artillery.

well(-)set, *ppl. a.*

1. Skilfully, fittingly, or happily placed, fixed, settled, arranged, or adjusted.

c **1369** CHAUCER *Dethe Blaunche* 828 So had she Surmountyd hem all of beaute.. Of stature and of well set gladnesse. *c* **1400** MAUNDEV. (1919) vi. 25 The town & the cytee weren full wel sett in a fair contree. **1456** SIR G. HAYE *Law Arms* (S.T.S.) 228 For that requeris obligacioun and trew consent, with wit seker and wele sett. **1475** *Bk. Noblesse* (Roxb.) 75 The peple that were welle set. **1513** MORE in Grafton *Chron.* (1568) II. 787 She verteously denied hym, but.. with so good maner & words so well set, that she rather kindled his desire then quenched it. **1535** COVERDALE *Isa.* iii. 24 For wellset hayre there shalbe baldnesse. *c* **1611** CHAPMAN *Iliad* XVIII. 51 Like a well-set plant In best soiles. **1635–56** COWLEY *Davideis* I. 348 Above the well-set Orbs soft Harmony. *a* **1743** SAVAGE *On False Historians* 129 Well-set in plan, and polish'd into style, Fair and more fair may finish'd fraud beguile. **1776** [see WELL-WRITTEN]. **1895** CROCKETT *Men of Moss-hags* xxxviii, The air of well-set distinction which marks the man of ancient family.

b. with *on*.

1639 T. DE GREY *Compl. Horsem.* I. iv. (1656) 41 The Trunchion small, long, well set on. **1854** SURTEES *Handley Cr.* i, A light, well-set-on head.

†**c.** Of a blow: Well planted or delivered. *Obs.*

a **1586** SIDNEY *Arcadia* III. viii. (1912) 391 While Ismenus doubled two or three more valiant, then well set blowes.

2. Of a person, animal, the limbs: Strongly built, firmly knit.

13.. *Guy Warw.* 6015 He was michel & wele y-sett. **1530** PALSGR. 715/2 The felowe is well sette, or well pyght. *a* **1548** HALL *Chron., Edw. IV*, 250 This kyng Edward was.. brode brested and well set. **1579** LYLY *Euphues* (Arb.) 115 If shee be well sette, then call hir a Bosse. **1607** TOPSELL *Four-f. Beasts* 74 [Cows] Wel set and compacted legs. *Ibid.* 666 A thicke, round, and well set Hogge. **1666** W. BOGHURST *Loimographia* (1894) 25 Strong well sett men dyed commonly in two dayes. **1727** A. HAMILTON *New Acc. E. Ind.* II. liii. 273 The Tartar was a lusty Man, and the Sailor short, but well set. **1774** *Pennsylv. Gaz.* 21 Dec. 4/2 Run away,.. a clever smart looking boy, well set. **1883** D. C. MURRAY *Hearts* i, His figure was well set.

b. Now usually ***well set-up***. (Cf. SET *ppl. a.* 10.)

1867 [see SET *ppl. a.* 10]. **1869** BLACKMORE *Lorna D.* xxvii, Very pretty damsels, and well set up. **1890** 'R. BOLDREWOOD' *Col. Reformer* xxii, The men's.. muscular, well set-up figures.

†**3.** Well-disposed. *Sc. Obs.*

1632 LITHGOW *Trav.* To Rdr., Referring the well set Reader to the History it selfe. *a* **1670** SPALDING *Troub. Chas. I* (Bannatyne Club) I. 5 The marquess of Huntly, and some weill sett freinds settled this feid.

†**4.** Of wine: Matured by keeping.

1720 RAMSAY *Edinb.'s Salut. Ld. Carnarvon* iv, The wale of well set ruby juice.. I can afford.

5. *Cricket.* Said of a batsman who is playing the bowling with ease and seems unlikely to get out.

1880 *J. Lillywhite's Cricketers' Annual* 62 There were only 49 runs left to get with six wickets to fall, one batsman thoroughly well set, and the ground by no means favourable for the bowlers. **1903** JEPHSON in Hutchinson *Cricket* 112 A bowler that.. might bowl a man at any period of his innings, however well set he might be.

well-'settled, *ppl. a.*

1600 FAIRFAX *Tasso* II. xxxi, She could not alter his well setled thought. **1625** K. LONG tr. *Barclay's Argenis* V. xiv. 382 He delivered this severe speech with so mild and well-settled a countenance. **1691** MAYDMAN *Nav. Spec.* 177 In all well-setled Governments. **1711** SHAFTESB. *Charac.* III. 4 In which the most confus'd Head, if fraught with a little Invention,.. might exert it-self to as much advantage, as the most orderly and well-settled Judgment.

well-'shading, *ppl. a.*

a **1586** SIDNEY *Arcadia* I. x. ¶7 The grasse (which plentifully grewe, brought vp vnder the care of those wel shading trees). **1616** W. BROWNE *Brit. Past.* II. iii. 64 Here the fine setting of well shading trees.

†**well-shape.** *Obs.* In 4–5 -schap(p. [irreg. f. WELL *adv.* + SHAPE *sb.*[1], perh. after *well-shape* pa. pple. (see below).] Shapeliness, beauty of figure.

c **1380** WYCLIF *Wks.* (1880) 4 Prowde of worldly goodes, of beaute, of welschap, of strengþe of body. *c* **1440** *Jacob's Well* 69 Prowde of þin herytage, & of þi bewte, & of þi wel-schapp.

well(-)shaped, *ppl. a.* Having a good shape, form, or figure.

1340–70 *Alisaunder* 186 Schuft shulders aright, well ischaped armes. *c* **1532** DU WES *Introd. Fr.* in *Palsgr.* 917 The man is well shaped. *c* **1611** CHAPMAN *Iliad* X. 372 Steeds More white then snow, huge, and well shap't. **1654** LIGON *Barbados* 72 This tree.. is well shap'd, her body straight, her branches well proportion'd. **1711** STEELE *Spect.* No. 53 ¶8 A delicate well-shaped Arm held a Fan over her Face. **1725** *Bradley's Family Dict.* s.v. *Pears*, A very large wellshaped Pear. **1831** JAMES *Phil. Augustus* xxxix, A.. small, well-shaped mouth. **1889** J. B. BURY *Later Rom. Emp.* I. 173 He was of middle height,.. well shaped, so that his body was neither too weak nor too weighty.

well(-)shapen, *ppl. a.* Now *arch.* Also 4–5 shape (schape, i-shape). = prec.

α. c **1374** CHAUCER *Troylus* III. 411 Be she neuere so faire or wel I-shape [*v.r.* wel schape]. **14..** in *Wr.-Wülcker* 584/14 *Formosus*, Welshape. *c* **1489** CAXTON *Sonnes of Aymon* ix. 232 Reynawde had xvi. fete of lengthe, & was well shape of body after yᵉ gretnes.

β. a **1425** tr. *Arderne's Treat. Fistula* etc. 6 Clene handes and wele shapen nailez. *c* **1500** *Melusine* xxxiii. 235 His fayre & wel shappen body. **1580** BLUNDEVIL *Order Dieting Horses* ix. 4 b, A well shapen horse. **1687** BLOME *Pres. St. Amer.* 41 Chusing them [*sc.* Negroes] as men do Horses in a Fair, and according as they are handsom, lusty, well shapen, and young. **1710** SHAFTESB. *Adv. Author* Charac. (1711) I. 164 'Tis the Unhappiness of those Wits,.. that.. they can bring nothing well-shapen or perfect into the World. **1859** GEO. ELIOT *Adam Bede* vi, A good-looking woman,.. well-shapen, light-footed.

well(-)sharpened, *ppl. a.*

1682 DRYDEN *Mac Flecknoe* 45 At thy well sharpned thumb from Shore to Shore The Treble squeaks for fear, the Bases roar. **1706** WATTS *Horæ Lyr.* II. (1727) 206 So whole Forests fall.. by one single Ax, And Steel well-sharpned. **1871** B. TAYLOR *Faust* II. III. 207 And let the knife, well-sharpened, fail not finally.

well-shaved, *ppl. a.* = WELL-SHAVEN *ppl. a.*

1940 W. FAULKNER *Hamlet* I. i. 15 He just sat there.. well-shaved and clean in his perfectly clean faded shirt.

well(-)'shaven, *ppl. a.*

1542–3 *Act 34 & 35 Hen. VIII*, c. 6 The Shanke [of the pin] well shaven, the pointe well and rounde fyled. **1842** D. VEDDER *Poems* 200 M'Lauchlan, the priest, wi' his weel-shaven crown.

well-'sheltered, *ppl. a.*

1796 MARSHALL *Planting* II. 14 The white-flowering Almond.. in well-sheltered places. **1880** C. R. MARKHAM *Peruv. Bark* 389 Lebong, a well-sheltered spur below Darjíling.

well-shod, *ppl. a.*

1580 BLUNDEVIL *Dieting of Horses* xix. 15 First then see that he be well shod, that is to say, with shooes that be neither too short nor too long. **1647** N. WARD *Simple Cobler* 22 It ill becomes Christians any thing well-shod with the preparation of the Gospel, to meditate flight from their deare Countrey. **1782** COWPER *Gilpin* 82 Finding soon a smoother road Beneath his well-shod feet. **1916** JOYCE *Portrait of Artist* (1969) v. 227 He.. passed out, his wellshod feet sounding flatly on the floor.

†**well-'shooted**, *ppl. a. Obs.* [app. f. *shooted*, irreg. wk. pa. pple. of SHOOT *v.*] Well grown or developed.

1633 T. ADAMS *Comm. 2 Pet.* i. 14. 270 A well shooted beard striving for length with the cassocke, makes not a Priest.

well-'showered, *ppl. a.*

1728–46 THOMSON *Spring* 186 Thus all day long the full-distended clouds Indulge their genial stores, and well-shower'd earth Is deep enrich'd with vegetable life.

Wellsian ('wɛlzɪən), *a.* (and *sb.*) Also **Wellsean.** [f. the name of H. G. *Wells* (1866–1946) + -IAN.] Of, pertaining to, or resembling the ideas and writings of H. G. Wells, esp. in his science fiction, social comment, etc. Occas. as *sb.*, a devotee or follower of H. G. Wells.

1912 *Westm. Gaz.* 9 Nov. 4/2 The delightful comments on the Wellsian philosophy. **1916** J. FREEMAN *Moderns* 93 The extension of such a rigid word as morality, until it includes its own contradictions, is typically Wellsean. **1916** G. B. SHAW *Pygmalion* 200 The new-born Wellsian had to find her bearings almost as ridiculously as a baby. **1923** A. HUXLEY *Antic Hay* iv. 55 'Let me put you down for a couple of pairs [of pneumatic trousers].' Mr. Mercaptan shook his head. 'Too Wellsian,' he said. 'Too horribly Utopian.' **1946** R. G. COLLINGWOOD *Idea of Hist.* 252 Some Wellsian machine for looking backwards through time. **1962** E. SNOW *Other Side of River* (1963) lxvi. 503 One Wellsian exhibit showed the long-range plan of a canal and river system which would virtually encircle China. **1977** M. DRABBLE *Ice Age* I. 69 He thought of a Wellsian paradise, a Welwyn Garden City, with neat boxes.

well-'sifted, *ppl. a.* (*lit.* and *fig.*).

1833 *Farm Rep.* 120 in *Lib. Usef. Knowl., Husb.* III, A coat of newly-slacked and well-sifted lime. **1901** *Daily Chron.* 9 Dec. 3/3 A veritable mine of well-sifted information.

†**well-'sighted**, *ppl. a. Obs.* Having good sight or mental discernment.

c **1522** SKELTON *Why nat to Courte* 531 Haue ye nat harde this, How an one eyed man is Well syghted when He is amonge blynde men? **1613** HAYWARD *Will. I*, 6 Hee was.. of a piercing wit, blind in no mans cause, and well sighted in his owne. **1630** LENNARD tr. *Charron's Wisd.* I. lix. (1670) 199 What good is it to a blind man, that his parents have been well-sighted? **1656** EARL MONM. tr. *Boccalini's Advts. fr. Parnass.* I. lix. (1674) 77 Good Officers.. known to be well-sighted in forbidding faults.

well-'sited, *ppl. a.*

1925 J. G. MACLEOD in *Oxf. Poetry* 27 Or that old solemn cormorant Who sits like a well-sited statue carved in black. **1979** [see WELL-CONCEIVED *ppl. a.*].

†**well(-)sitting**, *ppl. a. Obs.* See SITTING *ppl. a.* 1, 2.

well(-)'situated, *ppl. a.*

1618 GAINSFORD *Glory Eng.* I. xv. 129 A well scituated Castle. **1828–32** WEBSTER s.v. *Situated*, A town well situated for trade or manufactures.

well-sized, *ppl. a.* Of a good size.

1615 CHAPMAN *Odyss.* VIII. 589 A well-siz'd Caldron. **1642** MILTON *Apol. Smect.* iii. 28 Instead of well-siz'd periods, he greets us with a quantity of thum-ring posies. **1725** [see SIZED *ppl. a.*[1] 1 b]. **1833** T. HOOK *Parson's Dau.* II. xv, Only half a well-sized loaf remaining on the table.

well(-)skilled, *ppl. a.*

a **1553** UDALL *Royster D.* V. ii. (Arb.) 80 By your leaue I am not halfe well skilled in that arte. **1594** SHAKS. *Rich. III*, IV. iv. 116 O thou well skill'd in Curses, stay a-while, And teach me how to curse mine enemies. **1615** CHAPMAN *Odyss.* XI. 472 This then must stand, If while I liue, I rule in the command Of this well-skild-in-Nauigation State. **1634** MILTON *Comus* 620 A certain Shepherd Lad.. well skill'd In every vertuous plant and healing herb. **1715** POPE *Iliad* III. 477 She seem'd an ancient maid, well-skill'd to cull The snowy fleece. **1808** SCOTT *Marmion* VI. xx, O for one hour of Wallace wight, Or well-skill'd Bruce, to rule the fight.

absol. **1900** *Westm. Gaz.* 15 Jan. 1/3 Whist must be played by the unskilled as well as by the well-skilled.

well-ˈsmelling, *ppl. a. arch.* Fragrant.
c **1400** [see SMELLING *ppl. a.* 1]. **1534** BERNERS *Golden Bk. M. Aurel.* xviii. (1535) 31 He wolde washe his handes with very well smellyng waters. **1698** *Phil. Trans.* XX. 362 There were found many well-smelling Trees. **1887** MORRIS *Odyss.* II. 339 Well-smelling oil.

well-soled, *ppl. a.*
1663 BUTLER *Hud.* I. ii. 426 Well-sol'd Boots.

†**well-ˈsounding**, *vbl. sb. Obs.* Tunefulness.
1668 DRYDEN *Def. Ess. Dram. P.* Ess. (Ker) I. 118 The copiousness and well-sounding of our language.

well-ˈsounding, *ppl. a.*
c **1325**, **1486** [see SOUNDING *ppl. a.*[1] 1 b]. **1513** DOUGLAS *Æneis* VII. xii. 147 Weill soundand wriblis. **1600** FAIRFAX *Tasso* XIX. lviii, Trumpets, clarions, and well sounding bras. **1729** T. COOKE *Tales* etc. 204, I am certain that the passed Tenses of *sit* and *see*, which are *sat* and *saw*, will not be well sounding if this Rule is observed. **1781** [see SOUNDING *ppl. a.*[1] 1 b]. **1828** WHATELY *Rhet.* III. i. §5. 189 To be able to pour forth with fluency an unlimited quantity of well-sounding language. **1865** 'ANNIE THOMAS' *On Guard* III. 40 The phrase was a nice, magnanimous, well-sounding one.

well-ˈspaced, *ppl. a.* Of items that are neither too close nor too far apart from each other.
1939 M. SPRING RICE *Working-Class Wives* iv. 70 She.. has four children, well-spaced. **1962** E. SNOW *Other Side of River* (1963) lxxv. 576 Large blocks of well-spaced three-story apartments. **1977** N. SAHGAL *Situation in New Delhi* xiii. 128 Sometimes during a Cabinet meeting he said not more than five well-spaced words of one syllable each.

†**well-ˈspeaking**, *vbl. sb. Obs.* Eloquence; good delivery.
1557 CHEKE in Hoby tr. *Castiglione's Courtyer* ad fin., The roundnes of your saienges and welspeakinges of the saam. **1561** HOBY *Ibid.* I. I j b, I am sure he would muche sooner haue desired wel doing in himself then wel speaking in an other. **1634** W. TIRWHYT tr. *Balzac's Lett.* A iv, A man no less versed in the art of well-speaking then himself. **1694** LOCKE *Hum. Und.* III. vii. §2 *marg.*, In them [*sc.* the connecting particles] consists the art of well speaking.

†**well-ˈspeaking**, *ppl. a. Obs.* Eloquent. (See SPEAKING *ppl. a.* 1 b.)

well-sped, -speeding: see SPEED *v.* 7, SPEEDING *ppl. a.* 1.

well-spent, *ppl. a.*
1. Of time, life: Passed profitably and virtuously.
1534 MORE *Dial. Comfort* III. xvii. (1553) Q. viii b, The well spent time. **1662** G. WHARTON *Cal. Carol.* Feb. B 5 b, Who..laid down Their well spent Lives for Charles's Injur'd Crown. **1711** POPE *Temp. Fame* 330 The constant tenour of whose well-spent days No less deserv'd a just return of praise. **1780** *Mirror* No. 90 An old man, looking back on a well-spent life. **1848** THACKERAY *Van. Fair* lii, She beats all the women I have ever seen in the course of all my well-spent life.
2. Expended judiciously or to advantage.
1749 B. FRANKLIN *Poor Richard* (1890) 188 'T is a well spent penny that saves a groat.

well-spiced, *ppl. a.*
1644 MILTON *Areop.* (Arb.) 63 Some well spic't bruage. **1708** W. KING *Art of Cookery* (1709) 75 Well-spic'd Hippocras. **1829** A. CUNNINGHAM in *Anniversary* 137 Bowls well spiced and reeking.

well(-)ˈspoken, *ppl. a.* Also 5 -spoke.
1. Of a person: Gifted with good or ready speech; courteous and refined in speech.
c **1440** *Alphabet of Tales* 394 When þis chylde was waxen he was fayr & semely & wele-spoken. *c* **1440** *Promp. Parv.* 138/2 Eloquent, or welle spoke man or woman, *eloquens.* **1476** *Paston Lett.* III. 157 He is wel spokyn in Inglyshe, metly well in Frenshe. **1552** LATIMER *Serm. Christmas Day* (1584) 273 b, Shee did not as our welspoken dames do: Shee tooke not in hand to preach. **1594** SHAKS. *Rich. III*, I. iii. 348 For Clarence is well spoken, and perhappes May moue your hearts to pitty, if you marke him. **1604** BACON *Apol. Earl Essex* 37, I told her, my Lord was an eloquent and well spoken man. **1715** ADDISON *Drummer* v. end, Mr. Vellum, you are a well-spoken Man: Pray do you thank my Master and my Lady. **1816** JANE AUSTEN *Persuasion* iii, A very well-spoken, genteel, shrewd lady, she seemed to be. **1844** EMERSON *Ess., Nom. & Real.* ¶3 Strong, punctual, practical, well-spoken England. **1899** *Daily News* 5 June 4/7 A pretty, well-spoken girl of 18 years.
transf. **1594** SHAKS. *Rich. III*, I. i. 29 Since I cannot proue a Louer, To entertaine these faire well spoken dayes. **1599** B. JONSON *Ev. Man out of Hum.* Induct. i, I vrg'd it..the rather To giue these ignorant well-spoken daies Some tast of their abuse of this word Humor.
2. Of words: Spoken well or with propriety.
a **1592** GREENE & LODGE *Looking Gl.* (1598) E 1 b, Well spoken fellow in thine owne behalfe. **1602** SHAKS. *Ham.* II. ii. 488 Fore God, my Lord, well spoken, with good accent, and good discretion. **1605** —— *Lear* II. iv. 239 Is this well-spoken?
3. With *of*: Favourably mentioned.
1538 ELYOT *Dict.* Add., *Bene audire*, to be well spoken of. **1778** JOHNSON in *Boswell* (1904) II. 252, I have heard Henry's *History of Britain* well spoken of. **1963** WODEHOUSE *Stiff Upper Lip, Jeeves* ii. 18 Knowing where I could get a couple of tickets for a well-spoken-of musical.
Hence **well-spoken-of-ness.** *nonce-wd.*
1872 W. H. GILLESPIE *Argum. Being & Attrib. God* v. ii. (ed. 6) 179 The word *Blessedness*..may stand for consummate *Well-thought-of-ness*, or *Well-spoken-of-ness*.

well-spread, *ppl. a.*
1. Widely extended; †*spec.* of a horse, broad in the rear (*obs.*).
1577 B. GOOGE *Heresbach's Husb.* III. 115 b, If he be brode hanched, & well spred behind, and goeth wide, his pace wilbe the surer. **1592** GREENE *Black Book's Messenger* Wks. (Grosart) XI. 18 Hee was a faire large Gelding well spread and forheaded. **1610** HOLLAND *Camden's Brit.* (1637) 395 An ancient and well spred Family. **1639** T. DE GREY *Compl. Horsem.* I. iv. (1656) 37 He must have..large Thighes, round well spread Buttocks. **1676** WORLIDGE *Vinetum Brit.* 51 Any Fruit on a low well-spread Tree, is better and fairer than that on a tall Tree. **1685** *Lond. Gaz.* No. 2062/4 Lost a black Coach Mare.., well spread behind. **1708** ROWE *Royal Convert* II. i. 18, I took my usual Way, To seek the Coolness of the well-spread Shade. **1748** *Anson's Voy.* III. ii. 308 Woods of tall and well-spread trees.
2. Of a surface: Plentifully or elegantly covered with articles spread over it. Of a table: Laid out for a good meal.
1777 POTTER *Æschylus, Choeph.* 356 The well-spread couch Inviting soft repose. **1784** COWPER *Task* III. 408 Proud of his well-spread walls. **1825** SCOTT *Betrothed* viii, A well-spread bleaching-field! **1837** LOCKHART *Scott* IV. v. 166 The curious neophytes that surrounded the well-spread board. **1854** SURTEES *Handley Cr.* xxiv, The pawing of a horse..caused him to look up from his well-spread table.

ˈwell-spring. [OE. *welspryng, wylspring*: see WELL *sb.*[1] and SPRING *sb.*[1]]
1. The source or head-spring of a stream; a fountain-head.
c **1000** ÆLFRIC *Hom.* I. 22 God..asende ren of heofonum feowertiȝ daȝa togædere, and ȝeopenode þær toȝeanes ealle wyllspringas. *c* **1100** *Gloss.* in Wr.-Wülcker 178/9 *Latex*, welspreng. *c* **1250** *Gen. & Ex.* 1243 An angel..Taȝte her ðor a welle spring. *c* **1305** *St. Kenelm* 293 in *E.E.P.* (1862) 55 A wil spring vp þere stod Of þe stede þer he lai on. *c* **1450** *Merlin* xx. 338 A litill brooke that com rennynge of two welle sprynges of a mountayne. **1549–62** STERNHOLD & H. *Ps.* xlii. 1 Like as the hart doth breath and bray the well-springs to obtaine. **1613–16** W. BROWNE *Brit. Past.* I. i. 12 When of that streame he had discouered The fount, the well-spring, or the bubling head, He there would sit. **1645–50** BOATE *Ireland's Nat. Hist.* vii. (1652) 54 The water of these Well-springs is for the most part cool, clear, and pure. **1796** MARSHALL *Rur. Econ. Midl.* II. Gloss., Wall-spring. **1805** R. W. DICKSON *Pract. Agric.* I. 290 Such ditches..should be cut at the feet of the adjacent rising grounds..so as to intercept the wall-springs and land-floods. **1877** J. D. CHAMBERS *Div. Worship* 233 The Water..drawn recently from a well-spring.
2. *fig.* A source of perennial emanation or supply.
c **897** ÆLFRED *Gregory's Past. C.* lxv. 467 Ðæs wæterscipes welsprynge is on hefonrice. *c* **1000** ÆLFRIC *Hom.* I. 52 Seo soðe lufu is wylspring and ordfruma ealra godnyssa. *a* **1240** *Ureisun* in *O.E. Hom.* I. 195 Al englene were..Siggeð and singeð þet tu ert liues welspryng. **1534** MORE *Comf. agst. Trib.* II. Wks. 1208/1 Surely ye riche mannes substaunce, is ye welspring of the poore mannes liuing. **1577** tr. *Bullinger's Decades* I. vi. 54 True fayth is the welspryng and roote of all vertues. **1611** BIBLE *Prov.* xvi. 22 Vnderstanding is a well-spring of life vnto him that hath it. **1632** LITHGOW *Trav.* II. 75 This City was the Mother & Well-spring of all liberall Arts and Sciences. *c* **1710** PRIOR *My Birthday* 13 Well-spring of all my joy and woe, Clotilda. **1837** DICKENS *Pickw.* xxix, It was because they bore in their own hearts an inexhaustible well-spring of affection and devotion. **1876** BANCROFT *Hist. U.S.* II. xxii. 21 War for liberty became unexpectedly a well-spring of opulence.

well(-)squared, *ppl. a. lit.* and *fig.* (like Gr. *τετράγωνος*).
a **1586** SIDNEY *Arcadia* IV. (1922) 126 Thinking it want of a well squared judgement to leave any meane unassayed of saving their lives. **1613–16** W. BROWNE *Brit. Past.* I. iv. 79 A large well squared stone.

well-stacked, *ppl. a.*
1784 COWPER *Task* IV. 444 The well-stack'd pile of riven logs.

well-stained, *ppl. a.*
1742 YOUNG *Nt. Th.* IX. 70 The well-stain'd canvas, or the featur'd stone.

well-starred, *ppl. a.* Born under a lucky star, fortunate.
1867 M. ARNOLD *New Poems* 133 *Him*, I count *him*, well-starr'd. **1892** W. WATSON *Poems* 83 Friend, in whose friendship I am twice well-starred.

†**well(-)stayed**, *ppl. a. Obs.* Steady, sober.
1550 HARINGTON tr. *Cicero's Bk. Friendship* (1562) 33 A wel stayed mind. *Ibid.* 48 In full growen ages and well stayed wyttes.

well-steeled, *ppl. a.* Stoutly armed with steel.
1613 WITHER *Abuses* II. iv. S6, Let's trim our rusty Armes, and scoure Those long vn-vsed, well-steeld blades of our. **1751** [see STEELED *ppl. a.* 1]. **1867** MORRIS *Jason* II. 701 The well-steeled spears.

well-steered, *ppl. a.*
1749 G. WEST *Odes Pindar, Iphigenia in Tauris* II. (1753) I. 169 Swift the well-steer'd Vessel sails. **1809** WORDSW. *Epit. Chiabrera* iv, Fifty years Over the well-steered galleys did I rule.

well(-)stocked, *ppl. a.* [STOCKED 6.]
1634 MILTON *Comus* 152, I shall e're long Be well stock't with as fair a herd as graz'd About my Mother Circe. **1741** RICHARDSON *Pamela* (1824) I. 235 In this happy dwelling, and this well-stocked farm. **1796** BURNS *Hey for a Lass* 4 O, gie me the lass wi' the weel-stockit farms. **1832** G. DOWNES *Lett. Cont. Countries* I. 255 Several handsome, well-stocked shops. **1853** DICKENS *Bleak Ho.* xviii, A well-stocked orchard. **1876** C. GIBBON *Robin Gray* v, He had a well-stocked steading.

†**well-ˈstomached**, *ppl. a. Obs.*
1478 *Paston Lett.* III. 222, I wolde be gladde to have a weell stomakyd felawe that wolde for my sake everye daye see the seyde woodes..and to knowe iff any weer fellyd heer afftre. **1530** PALSGR. 329/1 Well stomaked, *bien encouraigé*.

well-stopped, *ppl. a.*
1626 T. H[AWKINS] *Caussin's Holy Crt.* 291 Keepe the vessell of your hart, as a wellstopped pot. **1774** E. LONG *Jamaica* III. 775 The fruit when..dried is packed in well-stopped bottles. **1836** J. M. GULLY *Magendie's Formul.* (ed. 2) 197 The lozenges should..be kept in a well-stopped glass.

well(-)stored, *ppl. a.* Amply stocked or furnished.
1591 SAVILE *Tacitus, Hist.* II. lvi. 86 The wellstoared groundes [*refertos agros*]. **1616** W. BROWNE *Brit. Past.* II. iii. 54 From one well-stor'd garden to another. **1656** COWLEY *Pindar. Odes, Plagues of Egypt* xii, The well-stored Egyptian year Began to cloath her Fields and Trees anew. **1667** MILTON *P.L.* IX. 184 His head..well stor'd with suttle wiles. *a* **1704** LOCKE *Cond. Underst.* §18 His Head was so well stor'd a Magazine. **1718** POPE *Iliad* XV. 520 The well-stor'd Quiver on his Shoulders hung. **1806–7** J. BERESFORD *Miseries Hum. Life* (1826) VII. lxx, While you are attentively listening to the information or opinion of a well-stored man. **1835** [see STORED *ppl. a.* 2].

†**well-strained**, *a. Obs.* [f. STRAIN *sb.*[1]] Coming of a good stock or breed.
a **1710** CONGREVE *To Earl Godolphin* 85 And now a while the well-strain'd coursers breathe.

well-strained, *ppl. a.* [f. STRAIN *v.*]
1867 MORRIS *Jason* XII. 264 And ye may hear across the well-strained shrouds The longed-for wind. **1883** 'ANNIE THOMAS' *Mod. Housewife* 53 Put a layer of well-strained boiled rice into the dish.

†**well-strand.** *north.* and *Sc. Obs.* [f. WELL *sb.*[1] + STRAND *sb.*[2]] A small stream flowing from a spring.
a **1400** *Pistill of Susan* 123 We wol wassche us..bi þis welle strende. *c* **1450** *Mirour Saluacioun* 4618 Of whilk like welle strondys thi blode brast out freely. **1802** C. FINDLATER *Agric. Peebles* 16 *note*, The designation of the smallest rill of water is a syke, or a well-strand, if from a spring-well. [**1898** LD. E. HAMILTON *Mawkin of Flow* ii. 21 The little well-strand that trickled into the burn at our feet.]

†**well-stream.** *Obs.* [OE. *wylle-stréam*: see WELL *sb.*[1] and STREAM *sb.*] A stream flowing from a spring.
a **1000** *Phœnix* 105 Swa se æþela fuȝel..wunað wylle-streamas. *c* **1205** LAY. 2849 King Bladud baðen iwrohte..mid ane stæn-cunne..þe he leide in ane walle stream. *c* **1330** *Arth. & Merl.* 6058 Þe blod of kniȝtes dede & of destrers & of stede Ran hem after al day so ȝerne, So water out of wel streme. *c* **1381** CHAUCER *Parl. Foules* 187 Colde welle stremys..That swemyn ful of smale fischis lite. **1390** GOWER *Conf.* III. 93 For wher the hulles ben most hyhe, Ther mai men welle stremes finde.

well-stricken, -strooken, -strucken (*in years* or *age*): see STRICKEN A., STRUCKEN A.
1526 TINDALE *Luke* i. 7 Booth were wele stricken in age. **1576** R. PETERSON *G. della Casa's Galateo* 11 The same gentleman..was a man well strooken in yeares.

well-ˈstructured, *ppl. a.*
1974 tr. *Wertheim's Evolution & Revolution* 97 To provide a model of an integrated, well-structured whole in which any conflict could be smoothed down. **1978** *Language* LIV. 205 There is a well-structured account for Korean by Martin 1962.

well-strung, *ppl. a.*
c **1600** DRAYTON *Mis. Margaret* xciv, Out goe the Browne Bills, with the well-strung Bowes. **1725** POPE *Odyss.* XVIII. 85 Gods! how his nerves..Swell o'er his well-strung limbs. **1875** HELPS *Soc. Press.* iii. 45 The man of hard, well-strung, healthy nerves.

well-ˈstudied, *ppl. a.*
1. Produced or devised by careful study.
1644 MILTON *Educ.* 7 While..the whole Symphony with artfull and unimaginable touches adorn and grace the well studied cords of some choise composer. **1717** POPE *Epist. Jervas* 33 Here thy well-study'd marbles fix our eye. **1853** KINGSLEY *Hypatia* xxii, Orestes..waved his hand for silence, and began his well-studied oration. **1855** PALEY *Æschylus* Pref. p. xxiv, The well-studied wisdom of iambic verses.
†**2.** Of a person: Well read, learned. Also, versed or proficient *in* (a subject). *Obs.*
1596, **1602** [see STUDIED 2]. **1639** FULLER *Holy War* II. ii. 45 An excellent book-man in reading of men, and otherwise well studied. **1651** FULLER etc. *Abel Rediv., Bolton* 587 He was also well studyed in Metaphysicks, Mathematicks, and School-Divinity. **1707** NORRIS *Treat. Humility* i. 9 A well-studied Divine. **1810** [see STUDIED 2].

well-stuffed, *ppl. a.*
1483 [see STUFFED *ppl. a.* 1]. **1612** DRAYTON *Poly-olb.* vii. 75 This stronglie to performe, a well stuft braine would need. **1824** W. IRVING *T. Trav.* III. (1848) 227 The carriage ..moved slowly under the weight of so many well-stuffed trunks and well-stuffed travellers.

†**well-sucˈceeding**, *ppl. a. Obs.* Having a happy issue.
a **1586** SIDNEY *Arcadia* II. xxi. §2 She vsing so straunge, and yet so well-succeeding a temper, that she made her people by peace, warlike.

well(-)'suited, *ppl. a.* **1.** [SUIT *v.* 10 b.]
The examples in quots. 1771 and 1837 can equally be analysed as *well* adv. + *suited* rather than as a ppl. adj.
1771, 1837 [see SUIT *v.*¹ 10 b]. **1950** T. S. ELIOT *Cocktail Party* II. 109, I consider That you are exceptionally well-suited to each other.
2. [SUITED *ppl. a.* 2.]
1855 W. WHITMAN *Leaves of Grass* 69 Do you think I could walk pleasantly and well-suited toward annihilation? **1980** D. K. CAMERON *Willie Gavin* xiii. 127 His likeness.. shows him as well-suited as any eminent Edwardian, the wide skirt of the jacket falling away from a high button.

well-sung, *ppl. a.*
1717 POPE *Eloisa to Abelard* 365 The well-sung woes will sooth my pensive ghost. **1785** BURNS *To W. Simpson* vi, Till echoes a' resound again Her weel-sung praise. **1818** BYRON *Ch. Har.* IV. xxx, Here repair Many familiar with his well-sung woes.

well-su'stained, *ppl. a.*
1742 YOUNG *Nt. Th.* IV. 41 Our Comment on the Comedy, Pleasing Reflections on Parts well-sustain'd, Or purpos'd Emendations. **1790** BURKE *Fr. Rev.* 249 A slow but well-sustained progress. **1842** LOVER *Handy Andy* lii, The bugler, lifting his instrument to his lips, gave one long well-sustained blast.

well-swelled, *ppl. a.*
1786 BURNS *To a Haggis* iv, Till a' their weel-swall'd kytes belyve Are bent like drums.

well-swollen, *ppl. a.*
1728 YOUNG *Love Fame* ii. 225 The well-swoln ties an equal homage claim.

well-'tailored, *ppl. a.*
1886 PASCOE *Lond. To-day* iv. (ed. 3) 60 For aught one can see in Rotten Row on a Midsummer morning, all the world may be prosperous, dignified, well-tailored, and well-groomed. **1899** T. M. ELLIS *Three Cat's-Eye Rings* 36 The .. well-tailored, dapper little man.

well-'taken, *ppl. a.* (In various senses: see e.g. TAKE *v.* 3, 33 b, 42.)
1639 DAVENPORT *Too late to call* 18 Times oft Wel-taken Lock. **1761** FOOTE *Liar* I. Wks. 1799 I. 288 Some compliments in verse.., well-tim'd, and, what was better, well-taken. **1788** MRS. HUGHES *Henry & Isab.* I. xii. 175 Mrs. Maitland's dressing-room was ornamented with many well-taken copies and elegant designs.

well-tamed, *ppl. a.*
1805 WORDSW. *Prelude* VI. 538 While Winter like a well-tamed lion walks.

well-tanned, *ppl. a.* Of skin, hide, etc. Now chiefly with sense 'tanned by the sun, sunburnt'.
1784 COWPER *Task* I. 51 The rest..content With base materials, sat on well-tann'd hides. **1867** W. WHITMAN *Leaves of Grass* (ed. 4) XLVII. 89 Preferring..those well-tann'd to those that keep out of the sun. **1892** 'MARK TWAIN' *Amer. Claimant* xvi. 164 He had a well-tanned complexion. **1916** JOYCE *Portrait of Artist* (1969) ii. 60 Uncle Charles was a hale old man with a welltanned skin.

well-'tasted, *a.* Now *rare.* [See TASTED B.]
1. Having a good taste or flavour.
1635–56 COWLEY *Davideis* I. 673 A pure, well-tasted, wholsome Fountain. *a* **1700** EVELYN *Diary* Aug. 1645, In this place are excellent oysters, small and well tasted like our Colchester. **1771** in *Phil. Trans.* LXI. 321 Carp..will grow within two Summers..to be fleshy and well-tasted. **1803** *A. Hunter's Georg. Ess.* I. 429 Sweet and well-tasted butter from the milk of cows fed upon turnips. **1850** GOSSE *Rivers of Bible* (1878) 232 The water was found by this traveller to be well-tasted.
fig. **1641** MILTON *Prel. Episc.* A 2 b, To uphold their now well-tasted Hierarchy by what faire pretext soever they could. **1746** YOUNG *Nt. Th.* IX. 2183 With thee bring, Not hideous visions, as of late; but draughts Delicious of well-tasted, cordial, rest; Man's rich restorative.
2. Of a person: Gifted with good taste.
1911 R. BROOKE in *Memoir* (1918) p. lxvii, So many intelligent and well-tasted people didn't seem to have any idea what I was driving at.

well-taught, *ppl. a.*
c **1386** CHAUCER *Prol.* 127 At mete, wel ytaught was she with alle. *c* **1470** HENRY *Wallace* I. 294 He was.. Nocht large of tong, weille taucht and debonayr. **1560** BIBLE (Geneva) *Ecclus.* xxxi. 19 How litle is sufficient for a man wel taught? **1594** KYD *Cornelia* v. 52 Our warie wel-taught troopes. **1605** B. JONSON *Volpone* IV. v, When that well-taught dame Had her Qu: giuen her, to crie out a rape. **1645** WALLER *Poems, To Flavia* ii, The graces of a well taught minde. **1711** POPE *Temp. Fame* 165 Wise Aurelius, in whose well-taught mind With boundless pow'r unbounded virtue join'd. **1854** *Poultry Chron.* II. 155 Some of the German birds are well-taught musicians.
absol. *a* **1879** GEO. ELIOT *Leaves fr. Note-bk.* Ess. (1884) 361 The well-taught, an increasing number.

well-taxed, *ppl. a.*
1775 BURKE *Sp. Concil. Amer.* Sel. Wks. 1897 I. 226 If you tax the import of that rebellious Colony, what do you tax but ..the goods of some other obedient and already well-taxed Colony? **1856** KANE *Arctic Expl.* II. v. 59, I labored..with all the ingenuity of a well-taxed mind, to keep up the spirits of my comrades.

well-'tempered, *ppl. a.*
1. †**a.** Having a good bodily 'temperament' or constitution. *Obs.*
1422 YONGE tr. *Secreta Secret.* 220 Rede coloure tokenyth complexcion wel temperit. **1625** K. LONG tr. *Barclay's Argenis* III. xi. 189 His wel-tempered veynes. *c* **1655** A. SYDNEY in *19th Cent.* (1884) Jan. 63 Like a strong well-tempered stomach. *a* **1716** SOUTH *Serm.* (1842) IV. 270 He sends them into the world with a well-tempered and rightly-disposed body.
b. Having a well-balanced mental temperament (*obs.*). In later use, good-tempered.
a **1586** SIDNEY *Arcadia* I. iii. (1912) 19 [Arcadia is noted for] the well tempered minds of the people. **1595** SPENSER *Amoretti* lxxxiv, Modest thoughts breathd from wel tempred sprites. **1633** P. FLETCHER *Pisc. Eclog.* VI. xx, Thy wel-temper'd soul. **1657** J. GAUDEN in J. Watts *Scribe* etc., To Rdr. 3 One of the most learned, judicious, grave, and well tempered Divines in this County of Essex. **1691** MAYDMAN *Nav. Spec.* 199 Therefore, I wish him to furnish himself with a well-tempered Disposition, To be as Wise as a Serpent, and as Harmless as a Dove. **1710** NORRIS *Chr. Prud.* viii. 347 Christian Wisdom..depends not so much upon great parts, as a willing and well-temper'd Mind. **1773** GOLDSM. *Stoops to Conquer* II, Yet she appears to me a pretty well-tempered girl. **1852** GROTE *Greece* II. lxxi. IX. 193 A discreet and well-tempered officer. **1883** *Harper's Mag.* Mar. 538/2 Crowds were walking in the middle of the roadway—merry and well-tempered.
transf. **1790** G. WALKER *Serm.* II. xxv. 216 Christianity is a mild, pleasant, and well-tempered religion.
†**2.** Of climate or season: Temperate. *Obs.*
1598 SYLVESTER *Du Bartas* II. ii. III. *Colonies* 65 Well-tempered Sumater Sub-equinoctiall. **1601** *Mary Magd. Lament.* vi. (Grosart) 123 A calme and bright well-tempred day. *a* **1628** F. GREVILLE *Sidney* ii. (1652) 30 That well-tempered, though over-zealous, and superstitious Region of Italy.
3. a. Of steel: Brought to the right degree of hardness and elasticity.
1597 C. MIDDLETON *Chinon* (1925) 18 His well tempered sword. *c* **1662** in *Verney Mem.* (1907) II. 263 A well-tempered Turkish or Persian Scymeterre. **1697** DRYDEN *Æneis* XI. 734 His Back and Breast, Well temper'd Steel and scaly Brass invest. **1807** SYD. SMITH *Lett. Catholics* i. Wks. 1859 II. 136/2 No power in Europe, but yourselves, has ever thought..of asking whether a bayonet is Catholic, or Presbyterian, or Lutheran; but whether it is sharp and well-tempered. **1815** J. SMITH *Panorama Sci. & Art* II. 735 The pallet-knife, is mostly a thin well-tempered blade of steel.
fig. **1662** GAUDEN in *Hooker's Wks.* Ep. to King A 3 b, Agreeable to right Reason and true Religion (which makes this well-tempered Peice a file capable to break the teeth of any that venture to bite it). **1726–46** THOMSON *Winter* 676 That wit..which with Attic point And kind well-tempered satire, smoothly keen, Steals through the soul, and without pain corrects.
b. Of clay or mortar: Well mixed or compounded.
1746 FRANCIS tr. *Horace, Epist.* II. ii. 9 Like Clay, well-temper'd with informing Skill, He may be moulded to what Shape you will. **1833** *Wauldby Farm Rep.* 120 in *Libr. Usef. Knowl., Husb.* III, On this lime a bed of well-tempered clay is directly laid. **1860** RUSKIN *Unto this Last* ii. §28 The builder who lays good bricks in well-tempered mortar.
4. *Mus.* Tuned in equal temperament.
Only in renderings of G. *das wohltemperirte Klavier*, the title of Bach's double set of 48 Preludes and Fugues in all the keys. Cf. TEMPERED 1 e.
1820 tr. *J. N. Forkel's Life John Sebastian Bach* 93 The well-tempered clavichord; or preludes and fugues in all the keys. **1884** CLARA BELL & FULLER-MAITLAND tr. Spitta *Bach* II. 6 *note*, The Well-tempered Clavier. **1889** *Grove's Dict. Mus.* IV. 482 The Well-tempered Clavichord.

well-'tended, *ppl. a.*
1795–1814 WORDSW. *Excurs.* II. 167 Many a sheltered and well-tended plant. **1869** TOZER *Highl. Turkey* I. 97 The sloping hill-side..is covered with well-tended vineyards.

wellthe, obs. form of WEALTH.

†**well-thewed**, *ppl. a.* *Obs.* [See THEWED.] Having a good character or disposition; well-conducted, well-mannered, virtuous.
c **1200** *Trin. Coll. Hom.* 41 Þe wise manne and þat wel-þeaud child habbeð boðe on laȝe. *c* **1250** *Gen. & Ex.* 1914 He wulde ðat he sulde hem ten ðat he wel-ðewed sulde ben. **1387** TREVISA *Higden* V. 89 Tweye ȝongelynges..wel i-þewed [*moribus compositos*]. **1390** GOWER *Conf.* I. 51 It sit a prest to be wel thewed, And schame it is if he be lewed. **1430–40** LYDG. *Bochas* IV. 1121 This Calistenes, in youthe riht weel thewed. **1483** *Cath. Angl.* 413/1 Wele thewyd, *morigeratus*. *a* **1529** SKELTON *Agst. Garnesche* iv. 147 Malapert, medyllar, nothyng well thewde. **1642–7** H. MORE *Song of Soul* II. i. I. xxiii, Well thewed minds the mind do alwayes setten free.
b. *transf.* of speech, etc.
c **1522** SKELTON *Why nat to Court?* 328 Thy tonge is nat wel thewde. **1579** SPENSER *Sheph. Cal.* Feb. 96 To nought more..my mind is bent, Then to heare nouells of his deuise: They bene so well thewed [E. K. *Glosse*, that is Bene moratæ, full of morall wisenesse]. **1594** *Zepheria* i. 2 Many their well thewd rimes doe fayre attemper Vnto their amours. **1624** BP. MOUNTAGU *Immed. Addr.* 35 The Prayers of the Church, in our Common Liturgies,..are very well thewed and composed for the nonce, to fit the dispositions and affections of men.

†**well-'thinking**, *ppl. a.* Judging rightly and fairly.
1593 '*Silence augmenteth grief*' 13 in R. S. *Phœnix Nest* 11 He was..to ech well thinking minde, A spotlesse friend, a matchles man.

well-thought, *ppl. a.* In comb. with a prep. or adv., as *of, on, upon, out.*
1579 GOOGE *Lopez de Mendoza's Prov.* Ep. Ded., This gentleman..deserueth of all men to be welthought of. *a* **1586** SIDNEY *Arcadia* v. (1922) 173 Philanax..beganne a well thought on discourse. **1611** COTGR., *Bienvoulu*, well beloued, well thought of. **1648–58** HEXHAM II, *Wel-bedacht*, Well-advised, or well-thought upon. **1865** tr. *Erckmann-Chatrian's Waterloo* ii. 10, I had rather remain poor and hardworking, than become rich and well-thought-of in this manner. **1901** E. PHILLPOTTS *Striking Hours* 250 You'm gwaine to blacken your awne name, an' that of a well-thought-on fam'ly. **1902** J. CHAMBERLAIN in *Scotsman* 13 Jan. 7/7 Well-thought-out plans.
Hence **well-thought-of-ness**.
1872 [see WELL-SPOKEN 3].

well-'thriven, *ppl. a.*
c **1375** *Cursor M.* 14806 (Fairf.) þis man is wele þriuen [*Cott.* fast es he throd and thriuen]. **1748** RICHARDSON *Clarissa* (1768) II. 7 Then I have a quarrel against his face, though in his person, for a well-thriven man, tolerably genteel. **1791** COWPER *Iliad* XVIII. 698 A well-thriven ox.

well-thumbed, *ppl. a.* Bearing marks of frequent handling.
1826 MISS MITFORD *Village* III. 271 She used to hear me read French out of a well-thumbed copy of Telemaque. **1840** DICKENS *Old C. Shop* xxvii, A couple of well-thumbed tambourines. **1884** E. YATES *Recoll.* I. 254 A large collection of greasy well-thumbed *Miscellany* volumes.

well-'timbered, *ppl. a.*
1. Strongly built or constructed of wood.
1596 SPENSER *F.Q.* V. xi. 29 As when the Mast of some well timbred hulke Is with the blast of some outragious storme Blowne downe. **1852** DUBOURG *Violin* (ed. 4) 344 Instruments..should be sufficiently *well-timbered*; their durability is much affected when they are finished off too weak in wood.
2. Having a good structure or constitution; well-framed, well-built. Chiefly of persons and animals.
1599 B. JONSON *Ev. Man out of Hum.* Ind. iii, A well-timberde fellow, hee woulde ha' made a good columne and he had been thought on when the house was a building. **1639** T. DE GREY *Compl. Horsem.* I. iv. (1656) 40 A well timbred Horse. **1668** R. L'ESTRANGE *Vis. Quev.* (1708) 269 The Devil of Subornation came next, which was a good-complexion'd, and a well-timber'd Devil. **1697** COLLIER *Ess. Mor. Subj.* II. 76 Let them [*sc.* the 'animal spirits'] be as Sleek and well Timber'd, as those Atoms Epicurus made his Soul of. **1769** *Stratford Jubilee* II. i, I'm as well timbered about the legs and face, as one can meet. **1816** SCOTT *Old Mort.* iv, Niel, a clean, tight, well-timbered, long-winded fellow. **1861** *Times* 27 Sept. 5/5 Cart-horses, young, and well-timbered, and quick walkers,..50 to 65 guineas.
3. Well-wooded.
1701 *Lond. Gaz.* No. 3724/4 Piggott's Farm..within a Mile of the Thames, being well Timbred, having a new-built House [etc.]. **1847** DISRAELI *Tancred* I. iv, You descend into a well-timbered enclosure. **1904** A. C. FRASER *Biogr. Philos.* i. 26 The charming well-timbered parks which surround it.

well-timed, *ppl. a.*
1. Occurring, done, or made at a good or fitting time; timely, opportune.
1635–56 COWLEY *Davideis* III. 839 But Jonathan..With well-tim'd zeal, and with an artful care, Restor'd, and better'd soon the nice affair. **1735** POPE *Ep. Lady* 225 But Wisdom's triumph is well-tim'd Retreat. **1766** GOLDSM. *Vicar W.* v, This well-timed present pleaded more powerfully in his favour, than anything I had to say could obviate. **1788** GIBBON *Decl. & F.* xli. IV. 504 Their well-timed and rapid charge decided the conflict. **1855** PALEY *Æschylus* Pref. p. xix, By a well-timed humility they might have escaped the curse of ancestral guilt. **1874** R. TYRWHITT *Sketch. Club* 149 A slight and well-timed frost next morning. **1902** J. BUCHAN *Watcher by Threshold* 76 The question was well-timed.
2. Actuated in regular time or at the right moment.
1697 TUTCHIN *Search Honesty* vi. 9 Two gentle Charons, Rowing, he espy'd, With Well-tym'd Oars, upon the Ebbing-Tyde. **1707** E. SMITH *Phædra & Hipp.* III. 26 Ev'n now the well tim'd Oars With sounding Stroaks divide the sparkling Waves. **1812** BYRON *Ch. Har.* I. lxxvi, With well-timed croupe the nimble coursers veer.

well-tochered *Sc.*: see under TOCHER *v.*

'well-to-'do, *adj. phr.* [See WELL *a.* 3.]
1. Possessed of a competency, in easy circumstances; thriving, prosperous:
a. as predicate (with or without hyphens).
1825 BROCKETT *N.C. Words* 230 *Weel-te-dee*, well to do —living comfortably. **1840** MARRYAT *Poor Jack* iii, Her husband had returned well, and *well to do.* *a* **1845** BARHAM *Ingol. Leg., Jerry Jarvis's Wig*, A reputable grazier of Ivychurch, worthy and well-to-do. **1864** TENNYSON *En. Arden* 310, I am rich and well-to-do. **1874** SYMONDS *Sk. Italy & Greece* (1898) I. vi. 119 For Corsicans they [the Napoleon family] were well-to-do.
b. in fuller form *well to do in the world.*
Cf. *well in the world*, WELL *a.* 3.
1825 MRS. CAMERON *Crooked Paths* (*Houlston Tracts* I. xxv.) 6 He is what is called very well to do in the world. **1854** SURTEES *Handley Cr.* xiii. (1901) I. 93 They are very respectable—that's to say..people well-to-do in the world. **1861** M. PATTISON *Ess.* (1889) I. 48 The Corporation of the Steelyard were too well to do in the world to be other than ..thoroughly Anglican. **1885** *Law Times Rep.* LII. 647/2 Both were well to do in the world.
c. *attrib.* (with hyphens).
1839 THACKERAY *Stubbs's Cal.* Jan., My father was..a well-to-do gentleman of Bungay. **1850** E. FITZGERALD *Lett.* (1889) I. 202 It is only idle and well-to-do people who kill themselves. **1865** TROLLOPE *Belton Est.* xiii. 143 The well-to-do squirearchy of England. **1892** GARDINER *Student's Hist. Eng.* 489 The Colony of Virginia grew into a tobacco-planting, well-to-do community.
d. *absol.* (as pl.).
1851 D. JERROLD *St. Giles* xiv. 136 He has strayed into the paradise of the well-to-do. **1891** MRS. OLIPHANT *Jerusalem* IV. ii. 441 The well-to-do of every village gathered conspicuous on the road.

e. *transf.* Indicative of easy circumstances, prosperous-looking.
1863 Mrs. Gaskell *Sylvia's L.* vi, Still, in spite of disorder like this, there was a well-to-do aspect about the place. **1883** D. C. Murray *Hearts* i, A comfortably furnished apartment, where shaded lamps and handsome curtains gave things a well-to-do and homelike look.

2. Of an animal or plant: Thriving.
1875 F. I. Scudamore *Day Dreams* 16 The cattle in the forestalls were sleek and well-to-do. **1881** *Leicestersh. Gloss.*, *Well-to do*,.. thriving, applied to trees, cattle, &c., as well as men. **1908** R. Bagot *A. Cuthbert* iii. 25 Fat and well-to-do rabbits.

3. Pleased or satisfied *with* oneself. *rare*$^{-1}$.
1854 [see well *a.* 2 c].

Hence **well-to-do-ism, well-to-do-ness,** prosperity.
1848 Clough *Poems* (1862) Mem. p. xv, Well-to-do-ism shakes her Egyptian scourge, to the tune of 'ye are idle, ye are idle'. **1849** Lytton *Caxtons* II. iii, The house had an air of solidity, and well-to-do-ness about it. **1882** Mrs. Oliphant *Lit. Hist. Eng.* III. 134 Even the poverty of wealth is better than the well-to-do-ness of the humble. **1887** E. Money *Dutch Maiden* xxii, 'It [an inheritance] is nothing wonderful,' he added, 'but well-to-doism for a fellow like myself.' **1925** J. Bone *London Perambulator* 127 All the nice well-flavoured old things [at a pastry-cook's in High Street] that suggested Kensington 'well-to-do-ness'.

well-told, *ppl. a.*
1713 Steele *Guardian* No. 42. ¶3 Yet the very same Occurrences shall please them in a well-told Story. **1884** J. Hall *Chr. Home* 88 It must be a well-told tale that holds its place in the memory for thirty or forty years.

well to live, *adj. phr.* Now *rare*; latterly *Sc.* and *U.S.* [See well *a.* 3.] Prosperous, well to do. Also ***well to live in the world.***
1579–80 North *Plutarch, Aristides* (1595) 349 And further-more, to shewe that hee was well to liue, and that his house was rich and wealthie, he bringeth foorth these proofes. **1596** Shaks. *Merch. V.* II. ii. 55 His Father..is an honest exceeding poore man, and God be thanked well to liue. **1622** Mabbe tr. *Aleman's Guzman d'Alf.* II. 95 Shee.. was married in the end to one of an honest condition, and well to liue. **1673** Ray *Journ. Low C.* 249 The Piemontese are generally well to live. **1796** *Hist. Ned Evans* I. 137 He was well to live, and was said to have plenty of money besides his stock. **1829** *Anniversary* 171 They were..well to live in the world, extensive dealers in corn and cattle. **1836** Carlyle in *Atlantic Monthly* (1898) Sept. 295/1 The Doctor looks very well and sonsy; he seems in good health and well to live.
attrib. **1897** *Boston* (Mass.) *Jrnl.* 4 Jan. 10/1 Unable to collect money from well-to-live people who have owed it to her for six months.

b. Partly intoxicated.
1619 R. Harris *Drunkard's Cup* Ep. Ded. A 2 b, One is coloured, another is foxt, a third is gone to the dogs, a fourth is well to live. **1825** Jamieson, *Weil to live.* 2. Tipsy, elevated with drink, half seas over. **1860** Bartlett *Dict. Amer.* [New England.]

well-toned, *a.* Having a good tone, in various senses: see toned.
c **1460**, **1742** [see toned 1 a, 1 b]. **1771** C. Burney *Pres. St. Mus. France & Italy* (1773) 145 The voice, which was a woman's, was well toned. **1827** Earl Mount-Edgcumbe *Mus. Remin.* (ed. 2) 74 David..was..the first tenor of his time, possessing a powerful and well-toned voice. **1874** H. H. Cole *Catal. Ind. Art S. Kens. Mus.* 213 Harmonious and well-toned colouring. **1879** H. Spencer *Data of Ethics* x. §64. 176 The..consequent discolouration, caused in a person of lax tissues by a blow which leaves in well-toned tissues no trace.

†**well-tongued,** *a. Obs.* Gifted with good speech.
1538 Elyot *Dict.*, *Benedicus*, a man wel tunged, or faire spoken. **1602** *Narcissus* (1893) 462, I was a well toung'd nimphe. **1603** J. Davies (Heref.) *Microcosm.* (Grosart) 95/1 Which wel-tongu'd Mercury shal faire relate.

†**well-took,** *ppl. a. Obs.* (See take *v.* A. 5 δ and B. 19 b.)
1602 Shaks. *Ham.* II. ii. 83 Meane time we thanke you, for your well-tooke Labour.

well to pass, *adj. phr.* Now *Sc.* [See well *a.* 3.]
a. In predicate: Well off, well to do. Also ***well to pass in the world.***
1610 T. Scott *Philomythie* (1616) A 7 His Mothers Husband..being rich and well to passe. *c* **1645** Howell *Lett.* v. xv. (1650) 152 Their Masters are both of them very wel to pass, and of good repute. **1702** W. J. tr. *Bruyn's Voy. Levant* ix. 29 Those who are well enough to pass in the World. **1784** R. Bage *Barham Downs* II. 100, I..am mistress of this inn, and thank God well to pass. **1815** Scott *Guy M.* xxxvii, Our poor friend has died well to pass in the world. **1901** G. Douglas *House with Green Shutters* 11 They were an able lot, and..most of them were well enough to pass. *Ibid.* 266 Johnny Coe, idle and well-to-pass.

b. *attrib.* (with hyphens).
1908 Ld. E. Hamilton *Mawkin of Flow* xvii. 228 With a neatness that any well-to-pass housewife might have envied, were ranged sack upon sack of oatmeal, barley and peas.

c. *absol.* (as pl.).
1902 Barrie *Little White Bird* xii. 124 They were children of the well-to-pass.

d. Well provided, well off *for* (something).
1809 E. S. Barrett *Setting Sun* I. 65 Charles XII. of Sweden (although himself a king, and not very well to pass for sense even among them).

Hence †**well-to-passer** *nonce-wd.*, a person of good estate.
1654 Whitlock *Zootomia* 504 Horace met with such Selfe-applauding well-to-passers, triumphing over anothers inferiority in Estate.

well-tossed, *ppl. a.*
a **1593** Marlowe *Ovid's Eleg.* III. ix. [x.] 31 When well-toss'd [*bene jactati*] mattocks did the ground prepare.

†**well-traced,** *a. Obs.* ? Having a good foot-print.
c **1400** *Master of Game* (MS. Digby 182) xxii, þer beth some hyndes wele traced, þe whiche haueth þe soole of þe foote as a staggard.

well-'traded, *a.* Having a good trade.
1585, **1610** [see traded 3]. **1687** Miege *Gt. Fr. Dict.* II. s.v. *Well*, A well-traded Town, *une Ville fort marchande.*

well(-)trained, *ppl. a.*
c **1611** Chapman *Iliad* IV. 350 His well-train'd Athenian troopes. **1618** Gainsford *Glory Eng.* II. ii. 164 A hundred well trained and ordered souldiers will beat a thousand of them. **1683** J. Reid *Scots Gard'ner* (1907) 103 Well-trained trees in a nurserie. **1735** Somerville *Chase* I. 297 A pilf'ring Race; well-train'd and skill'd In all the Mysteries of Theft. **1847** Disraeli *Tancred* II. xi, The well-trained ear of this guardian of the gate. **1868** Ruskin *Pol. Econ. Art* ii. §105 A well trained youth. **1894** *Pop. Sci. Monthly* June 184 Well-trained dogs transmit these qualities.

well-'travelled, *ppl. a.* That has travelled far; experienced in travel; also *fig.*
In the first quot. the word may be = well travailed; the Fr. probably means 'active', 'energetic'. Cf. also quot. *c* 1420 s.v. travailed.
1525 Berners *Froiss.* (1812) II. 469 Sir Johne Rosseau, who was a well trauelled knight and well knowen [*bien trauaillant et congneu en plusieurs terres*]. **1555** Eden *Decades* (Arb.) 208 Hystories..wrytten by wyttie and expert men well trauayled in the worlde. **1656** Cowley *Pindar. Odes, To Dr. Scarborough* iv, And Thy well-travell'd knowledge too does give No less account of th' Empire Sensitive. **1870** Dk. of Argyll *Iona* i. 2, I have heard well-travelled men declare that nothing they had seen in any part of the world had ever produced such an effect upon them [as Fingal's Cave].

†**well-tricked,** *ppl. a. Obs.* Artfully adorned.
1599 Drayton *Idea* Son. iii, Many there be excelling in this kind, Whose well trick'd rimes with all inuention swell.

well-tried, *ppl. a.* Often tried or tested with good result; thoroughly tried.
c **1449** Pecock *Repr.* III. vi. 312 Neither bi eny sufficient euydence of Holi Scripture or of other special and peculiar sure weel tried reuelacioun. **1590** Spenser *F.Q.* II. x. 40 [They] ransackt Greece well tryde, when they were wroth. *a* **1631** Donne *Eleg.* xiv. 60 The bright Signe of a lov'd and wel-try'd Inne. **1670** Eachard *Cont. Clergy* 33 Physick..is made up of severe reason, and well-tryed experiments. **1725** Pope *Odyss.* XVI. 263 Thy well-try'd wisdom, and thy martial fame. **1784** Cowper *Task* I. 148 Love, Confirm'd by long experience of thy worth And well-tried virtues. **1818** Scott *Rob Roy* xxxviii, A well-tried friend has appointed to meet me in this neighbourhood. **1856** Kane *Arctic Expl.* II. i. 20 Our sledge then is made of well-tried oak.

well-trimmed, *ppl. a.* (In various senses of trim *v.*)
1667 Dryden & Dk. Newcastle *Sir M. Mar-all* III. (1668) 26 A Woman's in a sad condition, that has nothing to trust to, but a Perriwig above, and a well-trim'd shoe below. **1728** Gardiner tr. *Rapin Of Gardens* II. (ed. 3) 90 When with a low and well-trim'd Head They [*sc.* cypresses] circling round adorn some flow'ry Mead. **1825** Scott *Talism.* xxiii, The mass of hair (now limited to a well-trimmed beard). **1840** Dickens *Old C. Shop* ix, A well-trimmed lamp. **1842** —— *Amer. Notes* v, The well-trimmed lawns and green meadows of home are not there. **1856** Kane *Arctic Expl.* I. xxx. 412 His coil of walrus-hide, a well-trimmed line of many fathoms' length.

well-trod, *ppl. a. poet.* = next.
1632 Milton *L'Allegro* 131 Then to the well-trod stage anon.

well-'trodden, *ppl. a.* Frequently trodden; much used to walk on. Also *fig.*
1825 Waterton *Wand. S. Amer.* 164 A smooth and well-trodden part of the road. **1825** J. Neal *Bro. Jonathan* II. 141 A solid, hot, stone pavement is not so agreeable..as the cool, fresh turf, or the well-trodden path. **1881** Tylor *Anthropol.* xv. 387 We need not go over the well-trodden ground of later history.

well-trussed, *ppl. a.*
†**1.** Of the human or animal frame: Well-knit; firmly and compactly built. Also with *together.*
1603 Florio *Montaigne* II. xxii. 392 Men of my stature, well-trust, short and tough. **1639** T. de Grey *Compl. Horsem.* I. iv. (1656) 37 He must have..a well-trussed together Body. **1741** *Compl. Family-Piece* II. i. 304 The Tumbler..is a well-truss'd Dog.

2. Securely tied in a bundle.
1633 Herbert *Temple, Ch.-porch* xxiv, Man is a shop of rules, a well truss'd pack, Whose every parcell under-writes a law.

well-'trusted, *ppl. a.*
a **1586** Sidney *Arcadia* III. (1922) 23 Like the clyent that committes the cause of all his worth to a well trusted advocate. *a* **1667** Cowley *Ess. Verse & Pr.* (1906) 412 (tr. '*Beatus ille*') How is he pleas'd th' encreasing Use to see Of his well trusted Labours bend the tree? **1856** Kane *Arctic Expl.* II. xxiii. 233 My well-trusted friend.

well-tuned, *ppl. a.* Melodious, in good tune.
1535 Coverdale *Ps.* cl. 5 Prayse him vpon the welltuned cymbals. **1588** Shaks. *Tit. A.* II. iii. 18 The Hounds, Replying shrilly to the well tun'd Hornes. **1591–5** Spenser *Colin Clout* 418 That well tuned song Which late he sung vnto a scornfull lasse. **1600** Shaks. *Sonn.* viii. 5 The true concord of well tuned sounds. **1653** H. More *Antid. Atheism* II. viii. (1712) 62 A Pack of well-tuned Hounds. **1660** J. Brookbank (*title*) The Well-tuned Organ. **1844** Mrs. Browning *Drama of Exile* 1212 What I see well-formed or hear well-tuned.
transf. **1613–16** W. Browne *Brit. Past.* I. ii. 41 Whose well-tun'd eares, chast-obiect-louing eyne Ne'er heard nor saw the workes of Aretine.

well-turned, *ppl. a.* [turn *v.* 4, 5.]
1. Skilfully turned or rounded.
[*a* **1700** Evelyn *Diary* 22 July 1670, The arches of the cellars beneath are well turn'd by Mr. Samuel the architect.] **1725** Pope *Odyss.* XVIII. 77 His nervous thighs By just degrees like well-turn'd columns rise. **1811** J. Milner *Eccles. Archit. Eng.* Pref. p. xv, The well-turned arches of the intercolumniations. **1813** Vancouver *Agric. Devon* 117 The slice, gradually ascending along this well-turned plate, operates with an equal friction on its whole surface.

2. Of the body or limbs: Symmetrically shaped or rounded.
1616 B. Jonson *Devil an Ass* II. vi, To play with this smooth, round, And well torn'd chin, as with the Billyard ball. **1687** *Lond. Gaz.* No. 2281/4 A large well turn'd Chesnut,..15 hands. **1693** Dryden *Ovid's Met.* I. 670 Her well-turn'd Neck he view'd. **1728** Ramsay *Bonny Kate* iv, How straight, how well-turn'd and genteel, are Her limbs! **1835** W. Irving *Tour Prairies* 29 They are a well-made race, ..with well-turned thighs and legs. **1886** J. Corbett *Fall of Asgard* ii. 66 Her well-turned form, so girlish and dainty still.

3. Of speech: Neatly finished, felicitously expressed.
1623 B. Jonson in *Shaks. Wks.* To Mem. Author 68 In his well torned, and true-filed lines. **1668** Dryden *Of Dram. Poesie* 59 The labour which is requir'd to well turn'd and polish'd Rhyme. **1714** Addison *Spect.* No. 556 ¶3, I made a Speech consisting of about half a Dozen well-turned Periods. **1773** Boswell *Tour Hebrides* 22 Oct. (1785) 431 It contains a just and well-turned compliment to my illustrious friend. **1888** Burgon *Twelve Good Men* I. 41 Enshrining the friend's name in a note, commonly with the addition of.. some well-turned phrase.

†**4.** Of the mind: Having a good bent, well disposed. *Obs.*
1798 Sophia Lee *Canterb. T., Young Lady's T.* II. 354 Nothing then remains, even in minds well turned, but a sense of mutual duty.

5. ***well turned-out***: smartly dressed, well-groomed.
1903 [see classy *a.*]. **1919** E. P. Oppenheim *Strange Case Mr. Jocelyn Thew* I. ii. 17 A very distinguished-looking and exceedingly well-turned-out caller. **1976** G. Ewart *No Fool* I. 20 Well-turned-out were the waisted women.

well-'tutored, *ppl. a.*
1648 J. Quarles *Fons Lachrym.* 41 Let thy well tutor'd grief Know rather how to purchase a relief, Than plagues and torments. **1784** Cowper *Tiroc.* 195 And thus, well-tutor'd only while we share A mother's lectures and a nurse's care. **1791** —— *Iliad* XVIII. 744 They, with well-tutor'd step, now, nimbly ran The circle.

well-'twisted, *ppl. a.*
c **1611** Chapman *Iliad* XXIII. 106 Well-twisted cords. **1616** W. Browne *Brit. Past.* II. iii. 81 Well-twisted threds. *a* **1687** Waller *Maid's Trag. altered* (1690) 42 Like a well twisted Cable, holding fast The anchor'd Vessel in the lowdest Blast.

well-under'stood, *ppl. a.*
a **1700** Evelyn *Diary* 25 Mar. 1644, A skreene.. accurately cutt in topiary worke, with well understood Architecture. **1792** Burke *Sp.* (1816) IV. 55 Without the guide and light of sound well-understood principles. **1845** G. Dodd *Brit. Manuf.* IV. 101 She only followed a well-understood practice among her countrywomen. **1868** Gladstone *Juv. Mundi* iv. 113 Homer may seem, then, to designate, though not as by absolute and well-understood synonyms, but rather with a certain vagueness, substantially the same persons.

well-up'holstered, *ppl. a.* Having soft and thick upholstery; usu. *transf.* in *colloq.* use, plump, 'well-covered'.
1932 H. R. Wakefield *Ghost Stories* 44 Mrs. C., a handsome well-upholstered matron, had a shrewd Scottish flair for entertainment. **1939** H. Hodge *Cab, Sir?* v. 48 She looks a bit second-hand, though she's well-upholstered. **1964** in Hamblett & Deverson *Generation X* 171, I have a preference for dark girls with warm brown eyes and I like them well-upholstered. **1971** E. Lemarchand *Death on Doomsday* ii. 26 Well-upholstered elderly women.

well-urged, *ppl. a.*
c **1611** Chapman *Iliad* x. 378 Till your well vrg'd and rich returne proue my relation sound. **1748** Thomson *Cast. Indol.* I. lxvii, Now the heart he shakes, And now with well-urg'd sense th' enlighten'd judgment takes.

wellus, var. vellous *Sc. Obs.*

well(-)used, *ppl. a.*
†**1.** Well practised or exercised. *Obs.*
c **1470** Henry *Wallace* III. 379 For thai war wicht, and weill wsyt in wer.

2. a. Rightly or effectively used.
1594 *Selimus* xx. H 2 b, A societie of puddings, did you marke that well vsed metaphor? **1667** Milton *P.L.* IV. 200 [He] only us'd For prospect, what well us'd had bin the pledge Of immortalitie. **1865** Dickens *Mut. Fr.* III. xvii, As she stands above him with her hardened manner, and her well-used eyes.

b. Much or often used.
1728–46 Thomson *Spring* 36 Where the well-us'd plough Lies in the furrow. **1835** Willis *Pencillings* I. viii. 54 A little further on was a baker's shop, with a well-used oven. **1840**

DICKENS *Old C. Shop* liii, That's the sexton's spade, and it's a well-used one, as you see.

well-ˈvaried, *ppl. a.*
1608 CHAPMAN *Byron's Trag.* I. i, In the well varyed seasons of the yeare. **1764** DODSLEY *Descr. Leasowes* in *Shenstone's Wks.* (1765) II. 293 A small lawn of well-varied ground.

well-ˈventilated, *ppl. a.*
1818 KITCHINER *Cook's Oracle* (ed. 2) Pref. p. xliv, A well-ventilated larder. **1887** *Spons' Househ. Man.* 39 A well-ventilated drain.

wellvet, obs. Sc. form of VELVET.

†**well-ˈvisaged**, *ppl. a. Obs.*
c **1420** *Prose Life Alex.* 74 Biȝonde þat riuere þay saw wonder faire & wele vesaged women cledd in foule clethyng. **1470–85** MALORY *Arthur* VII. i. 213 He was..brode in the sholders & wel vysaged.

†**well-voiced**, *a. Obs.* Having a good or powerful voice.
1634 SIR T. HERBERT *Trav.* 86 A well voiced boy..sings Eulogies to Mahomet. **1822** SCOTT *Nigel* i, The aforesaid..able-bodied and well-voiced apprentices.

†**well-ˈwaiting**, *ppl. a. Obs.* Compliant in attendance.
1581 SIDNEY *Apol. Poetrie* (Arb.) 38 Poetrie euer setteth vertue..out in her best cullours, making Fortune her wel-wayting hand-mayd.

well-waled, *ppl. a. Sc.* Well-chosen.
1718 RAMSAY *Christ's Kirk Gr.* III. xx, She her man like a lammy led Hame, wi' a well-wail'd wordy.

well-walled, *a.* Having good walls. (Cf. Gr. εὐτείχεος.)
c **1400** [see WALLED 1 b]. *c* **1611** CHAPMAN *Iliad* I. 130 The sacke of well-wall'd Troy. **1618** GAINSFORD *Glory Eng.* I. xv. 126 Valenciens..is very spacious, well walled, and full of ancient buildings. **1867** MORRIS *Jason* III. 153 Admetus from the well-walled Pheræ came.

well-wared, *ppl. a. Sc.* [See WARE *v.*² d.] Well spent or bestowed.
1637 RUTHERFORD *Let. to Parishioners* 13 July, O then wel-wared pained breast and sore back..in speaking early and late to you! **1856** G. HENDERSON *Pop. Rhymes Berwick* 14 The best fish i' the Tweed..Shall be thy weel war'd meed.

well-warmed, *ppl. a.*
1838 STERLING in Carlyle *Life* II. vii. (1872) 143 We slept ..at the Village of Simplon, in a very fair and well-warmed inn. **1891** KIPLING *Light that failed* 136 Men..who've done their work in a well-warmed studio all their lives. **1906** *Daily Chron.* 5 May 4/7 The sturdy beggars..who are just now making their annual exodus from well-warmed workhouses to a life of freedom on the road.

well-ˈwarranted, *ppl. a.* Authorized, guaranteed, or approved by good warrant.
1603 SHAKS. *Meas. for M.* V. i. 254 You, my noble and well-warranted Cosen. **1644** MILTON *Judgm. Bucer* Post-scr., A well-warranted rule. **1648** BP. HALL *Sel. Th.* lxxxi. 239 His well-warranted judgment. **1876** GEO. ELIOT *Dan. Deronda* xxxvii, He was rather ashamed that Hans's hopes caused him uneasiness in spite of his well-warranted conviction that they would never be fulfilled.

well-washed, *ppl. a.*
1727–46 THOMSON *Summer* 384 Repeated this, till deep the well-wash'd fleece Has drunk the flood. **1857** MILLER *Elem. Chem., Org.* 377 If a dilute solution of glycerin be mixed with well-washed yeast. **1900** H. LAWSON *On Track* 70 She wanted to make out she was nice, and wholesome, and well-washed, and particular.

ˈwell-ˌwater. [WELL *sb.*¹ Cf. WFris. *welwetter.*] Water issuing, or drawn, from a well or spring.
c **1000** *Sax. Leechd.* I. 330 Seoðe þonne his sceallan on yrnendum wylle wætere. *c* **1205** LAY. 19792 We habbeoð þe ibroht..cæld welle water. *c* **1375** *Sc. Leg. Saints* vi. (*Thomas*) 94 Vith þat þat servand mad hym ȝare,..þe velvatter for to brynge. *c* **1440** *Pallad. on Husb.* VIII. 129 For meth,..A sester of vnscomed hony do In sestris vj of welle water cleer. **1585** T. WASHINGTON tr. *Nicholay's Voy.* II. xi. 45 They haue none other water to drinke then well water. **1630** BP. HALL *Occas. Medit.* li. 123 All experience teacheth vs that Well-waters arising from deepe springs, are hoter in Winter, then in Summer. **1745** P. THOMAS *Jrnl. Anson's Voy.* 164 Well-water is to be found at a small Depth almost in every Part of the Island. **1860** *Family Economist* 28 Apr. 271/1 Some of the well waters of London contain eighty grains of chalk in a gallon. **1911** MARY JOHNSTON *Long Roll* v. 49 Lifting the gourd of well water to his lips.
fig. *c* **1175** *Lamb. Hom.* 159 þe ter þet Mon wepð for laðe of þisse liue is inemned welle water, for the welle of þe horte swa doð water of welle.

well-ˈwatered, *ppl. a.* [WELL *adv.* 28.] Plentifully supplied or moistened with water.
c **1450** *Bk. Curtasye* 438 in *Babees Bk.*, Litere..Wele watered, I-wrythen, be craft y-trode. **1611** BIBLE *Gen.* xiii. 10 Lot..beheld all the plaine of Iordane, that it was well watered euery where. **1621** [see SEATED *ppl. a.* 2]. **1784** COWPER *Task* I. 323 The Ouse, dividing the well-water'd land. **1867** MORRIS *Jason* III. 170 A plain well-watered, set with trees. **1919** *Q. Rev.* Apr. 347 The stirring population.. of well-wooded and well-watered Asturias and Galicia.

well-ˈweaponed, *ppl. a.*
c **1250** *Gen. & Ex.* 2479 He..bad him nimen him feres mide, Wel wopnede men. *c* **1425** *Eng. Conq. Ireland* 8 Knyghtes and þe skyers well I-horsed and well y-wepened. *c* **1450** *Robin Hood & Monk* viii. in Child *Ballads* III. 97/1 Take twelue of þi wyght ȝemen, Well weppynd, be þi side. **1586** J. HOOKER *Hist. Irel.* 162/2 in *Holinshed*, A thousand well weaponed and appointed men. **1655** FULLER *Ch. Hist.* IV. 108 The foresaid Arch-Bishops..attended with a numerous train of well-weaponed servants. **1670** MILTON *Hist. Brit.* II. 61 Thick upon the shoar stood several gross bands of men well weapn'd. **1917** KIPLING *Diversity of Creatures* 405 To the sound of trumpets shall their seed restore my Cities, Wealthy and well-weaponed.

well-ˈwearing, *ppl. a.* [WEAR *v.*¹ 15.]
a **1568** [see WEAR *v.*¹ 15]. **1803** SYD. SMITH *Wks.* (1859) I. 29/1 A man..composed of those well-wearing materials, which adapt a person for situations where genius and refinement would only prove a source of misery and of error. **1824** MISS MITFORD *Village* I. 55 One is never thoroughly sociable with flowers till they are..provided with decent, homely, well-wearing English names.

well-ˈweaving, *vbl. sb.*
a **1586** SIDNEY *Arcadia* II. xxv. (1912) 310 The same disdainefull scorne, which Pallas shewed to poore Arachne, that durst contende with her for the prize of well weaving.

well-weighed, *ppl. a.*
1. Carefully estimated; duly pondered or considered.
1581 SIDNEY *Apol. Poetrie* (Arb.) 70 Liuely to expresse diuers passions, by the low and lofty sounde of the well-weyed silable. *a* **1644** QUARLES *Sol. Recant.* vii. 34 The well-weigh'd works of the Almighties hand. **1649** MILTON *Eikon.* xxviii. 236 A deliberate and well-waighed Covnant. **1682** SIR T. BROWNE *Chr. Mor.* III. xviii. (1716) 106 The well weighed thoughts of their Hearts. **1697** DRYDEN *Æneis* Ded. (e) 4 A well-weigh'd Judicious Poem. *a* **1704** LOCKE *Cond. Underst.* §26 Well-weighed Reasons are to determine the Judgment. **1732** POPE *Ep. Bathurst* 229 To Worth or Want, well-weigh'd, be Bounty given. **1754** MISS BOOTHBY in *Life Johnson* (1805) 76 Not without deliberation and well-weighed choice. **1829** SOUTHEY *All for Love* IV. ix, Nor ever might light motive him From well-weigh'd purpose bend. **1855** MACAULAY *Hist. Eng.* xiii. III. 278 The well weighed and prudent letter of William was read. **1883** R. B. SMITH *Ld. Lawrence* II. 556 In this document he had set forth, in well-weighed language, alike his methods and his motives.
†**2.** Of persons: Displaying deliberate purpose and balanced judgement. *Obs.*
1701 COLLIER *M. Anton.* (1726) 135 He was a person modest, prudent, and well-weigh'd. **1709** STRYPE *Ann. Ref.* I. xlii. 428 This Bullinger was a right prudent, peaceable, well-weighed, and learned Man.

well-ˈweighing, *vbl. sb.*
1657 RAWLEY *Resusc. Bacon* Life (c 2), Which may be imputed..to the well weighing of his Sentence, by the Skales, of Truth, and Reason. **1767** MANSFIELD in Burrow *Rep. Cases* (1776) IV. 2016 Barbuit's Case..was solemnly argued before and determined by Lord Talbot, on considering and well-weighing..all the foreign Authorities.

well-ˈweighing, *ppl. a.* Heavy.
1601 SHAKS. *All's Well* IV. iii. 203 Or whether he thinkes it were not possible with well-waighing summes of gold to corrupt him to a reuolt.

well-whipped, *ppl. a.*
1738 POPE *Epil. Sat.* Dial. i. 70 All the well-whipt Cream of Courtly Sense. **1840** MARRYAT *Olla Podr.* (1849) 277 She spins round like a well-whipped top.

well-wigged, *ppl. a.*
1792 SOUTHEY *Lett.* (1856) I. 11 The well-wigged justices. **1832** GEN. P. THOMPSON *Exerc.* (1842) II. 177 Our well-wigged ancestors.

†**well-will**, *v. Obs. rare. trans.* To wish (one) well, to regard with favour.
a **1618** SYLVESTER *Maidens Blush* 688 Weening therefore these Augures all fulfill'd In Joseph now, him every one well-will'd. **1639** DU VERGER tr. *Camus' Admir. Events* 217 He..is well-knowne in Court, and well willed by great Ones.

well-willed, *a. Obs.* exc. *Sc.* and *north.* [See WILLED *a.* 2.] Kindly or favourably disposed.
1398 TREVISA *Barth. De P.R.* XVII. clxxxv. (1495) 727 Of good men and well wylled: dronkenesse makyth euyll men and wycked. *c* **1412** HOCCLEVE *De Reg. Princ.* 2186 Thogh I be nat wys, Wel-willed am I. **1484** RICH. III. in Ellis *Orig. Lett.* Ser. II. I. 166 Oure sayde soverayn Lord, as a wele-willed, diligent, and couragious Prince. **1530** PALSGR. 329/1 Wellwylled, *de bonne voulenté.* **1598** D. FERGUSON *Sc. Prov.* (S.T.S.) 82 Nothing is difficile to a well willit man. **1891** ATKINSON *Moorland Par.* 65 This was but one of the many exploits of a like nature achieved by this well-willed being. **1899** J. SPENCE *Shetld. Folk-lore* 212 The weel-willed man is the beggar's bridder.
b. Const. *to*, *unto*; also *to* (do something) or *that* (something be done).
1417 *E.E. Wills* (1882) 38 Y pray hem þat þey be well wyllet..to here. *c* **1440** *Alphabet of Tales* 295 And þuf all he war not welewillid þerto, yit he was compellid to drynk. *c* **1465** *Eng. Chron.* (Camden 1856) 5 All the Cite was vnto thaym frendly and wellwillid. **1465** MARG. PASTON in *P. Lett.* II. 202 As for the woman that made the clayme,..he ys wellwyllyd that she shold be seyn to in the way of almys. *c* **1473** *Plumpton Corr.* (Camden) 27, I will be as wellwilled to doe things for your pleasure. **1477** *Rolls of Parlt.* VI. 178/1 Wherunto the more partie of the inhabitaunts..be right welwilled and agreable. **1523** BERNERS *Froiss.* I. ccxi. 254 Certayne yonge knyghtes..well wylled to do some dede of armes. **1871** W. ALEXANDER *Johnny Gibb* xxii. 163 But see sic a han'le as that state o' maitters gies to them that's but owre weel-will't to be lords owre God's spiritual heritage.

ˈwell-ˈwiller. Now *rare.* [See WILLER 1 and cf. GOODWILLER.] One who bears good will or wishes well (to another, to a cause, etc.); one who is disposed to be kind or friendly.
In very frequent use from 1450 to 1700. Since then largely superseded by WELL-WISHER.
1448 *Paston Lett.* I. 69 All hys mene, and all that ben hys wele wyllers. **1470–85** MALORY *Arthur* X. xxxi. 465 Wherfore he thoughte to slee hym and alle his wel wyllars in that countrey. **1581** PETTIE tr. *Guazzo's Civ. Conv.* (1586) II. 78 Those with whome we are conuersant, being rather well-willers, than true friendes. **1583** BABINGTON *Commandm.* (1590) 121 Is the diuell our friende or our foe, our welwiller or our enemie? *a* **1586** SIDNEY *Arcadia* II. x. (1912) I. 209 No man durst shew himself a wel-willer of mine. **1604** T. WRIGHT *Passions* V. iv. 242 We may have many well-willers, but very few speciall friends: well-willers be generall friends. **1659** *Nicholas Papers* (Camden) IV. 148, I feare our inland friends will not be sufficyent, vnlesse our well-willers abroade clubb to yᵉ reckoninge. **1748** RICHARDSON *Clarissa* VI. 61 Every body and every-thing had a black and a white side, as ill-willers and well-willers were pleased to report. **1826** HOR. SMITH *Tor Hill* (1838) II. 101 Evil befall the foul fiend and all his well-willers. **1875** MORRIS *Æneids* VI. 280 And those Well-willers' iron beds [*ferreique Eumenidum thalami*]. **1908** HARDY *Dynasts* III. After Scene 351 The Well-willer, the kindly Might That balances the Vast for weal.
b. Const. *of*, *to* (*unto*, Sc. *till*).
1463 *Irish Acts 3 Edw. IV* c. 68 Gouuernyng..by theim that ben welwillers to the Kyng. *c* **1477** CAXTON *Jason* 78 b, Som of the welwillars of the king appollo. *a* **1568** ASCHAM *Scholem.* I. (Arb.) 82 They..scornefullie mocke his worde, and also spitefullie hate and hurte all well willers thereof. **1597** HOOKER *Eccl. Pol.* v. lxxii. §14 If now the Communion booke make for them too..it may be hoped that being found such a welwiller vnto their cause, they will more fauour it then they haue done. **1634** PEACHAM *Compl. Gentl.* v. (1906) 38 Give mee leave..as a well-willer unto you and your studies, to beare you company part of the way. **1638** JUNIUS *Paint. Ancients* 67 Lovers and Well-willers of Art. **1698** F. B. *Free but Modest Censure* 4 A friend and well-willer to that Cause. **1871** W. ALEXANDER *Johnny Gibb* xxxvi. 253 Ye ken brawly that I never was a weel-wuller till gyaun awa' fae the Pairis' Kirk. **1874** SWINBURNE *Bothw.* I. i. (1882) 6 Men Who are well-willers to this common state.
†**c.** One who is addicted or devoted *to* a study (esp. astrology). *Obs.*
1634 HEYWOOD & BROME *Lanc. Witches* v. L 2, Though he be no witch, he is a wel-willer to the infernal science. **1653** W. RAMESEY *Astrol. Restored* 18 For the satisfaction of the well-willers to Astrology. **1654** CLEVELAND *Char. Diurnal-maker* 5 He is the first tincture and rudiment of a Writer, dip't as yet in the preparative blew, like an Almanack well-willer. **1664** BUTLER *Hud.* II. iii. 240 [He] with the Moon was more familiar Than e'er was Almanack well willer. **1668** DRYDEN *Dram. Poesy* 4 One that is so much a well-willer to the Satire, that he spares no man. **1671** BLAGRAVE *Astrol. Pract. Physick* 188 To all such who are Students, and well-Willers unto this most excellent Science of Astrology. *a* **1680** BUTLER *Rem.* (1759) II. 185 A Virtuoso is a Well-willer to the Mathematics. **1686** GOAD *Celest. Bodies* II. vii. 245 To us Well-Willers nothing can be plainer, than that Comets are Flammeous, or Lucid Expirations.

†**ˈwell-ˈwilling**, *vbl. sb. Obs.*
1. The act of wishing well (to another); good will, favour, kindly regard.
a **1340** HAMPOLE *Psalter* cxlvi. 12 Wellwillynge is til lord on dredand him [*Beneplacitum est domino super timentes eum*]. *c* **1450** *Merlin* xxvii. 505 Better he cowde enforme hem of youre volunte, for he is with hem a-queynted and theire welwellinge. **1490** CAXTON *Eneydos* xviii. 67 By thy well wyllynge, and by the yeftes & alle other thynges that I haue doon vnto the. **1583** MELBANCKE *Philotimus* C cj, In those daies I wearied thee with my welwilling and yet I am not tired to procure thy wellfare. **1640** tr. *Verdere's Rom. of Rom.* II. xx. 75 It begot a well willing in her towards him. *a* **1708** BEVERIDGE *Thes. Theol.* (1710) I. 30 Benevolence, or Well-willing, to the Object beloved.
2. (One's) good pleasure; what it seems good to a person to do, intend, or allow.
a **1340** HAMPOLE *Psalter* cxl. 7 My prayere in þaire welewillyngis [*oracio mea in beneplacitis eorum*]. *c* **1449** PECOCK *Repr.* IV. iv. 439 This was doon..bi Goddis welwilling that it schulde be doon. *c* **1450** tr. *De Imitatione* II. ix. 50 He chose þe welwillyng of god [*divinum beneplacitum*] before mannys solace. *Ibid.* III. lv. 132 Do wiþ me þi desired welwilling [*desideratum beneplacitum tuum*].
3. Right or virtuous intention; willing what is good.
a **1340** HAMPOLE *Psalter* xvii. 27 Eftere my rightwisnes.. That is eftere my welwillynge þat is in my saule. **1390** GOWER *Conf.* I. 355 Pes to the men of welwillinge In erthe be among ous here [Lk. ii. 14]. **1597** HOOKER *Ecc. Pol.* v. lxxxi. §12 Simplie to will proceedeth from nature, but our welwilling is from grace.

ˈwell-ˈwilling, *a.* (and *sb.*) Now *rare* or *dial.* [Cf. Du. *welwillend.*]
A. *adj.* **a.** Wishing well to another; disposed to be kind or friendly; benevolent, propitious; loyal, well-affected.
c **1000** *Rule of Chrodegang* viii, Ne beon hiȝ modiȝe..ac.. welwyllende, & mildheorte. *c* **1000** ÆLFRIC *Saints' Lives* xxvi. 59 þæt he hraðe dælde þearfum and wædlum mid wel-willendum mode. **1375** BARBOUR *Bruce* v. 41 How that he fand nane weill willand, Bot all war fais that euir he fand. *c* **1430** LYDG. *Min. Poems* (Percy Soc.) 214 This fowle is sacred unto Jupiter, The lord of briddis in the highe heven, Wele willyng planete beholdyng from so ferre. **1448** HEN. VI *Will* in Willis & Clark *Cambridge* (1886) I. 379, I..pray my said heirs..that they shewe them self welwillyng feithful and tender lovers of my desire in this behalf. *a* **1533** FRITH *Disput. Purgat.* I. D iij b, Goddes law requyreth a thynge to be done wyth a well wyllynge harte. **1540** PALSGR. *Acolastus* Ep. Ded. A ij b, The louyng and well wyllyng subiectes. *a* **1578** LINDESAY (Pitscottie) *Chron. Scot.* (S.T.S.) I. 120 His folkis..was nocht so weill willing as he requyred. **1597** J. MELVILL *Autob. & Diary* (Wodrow Soc.) 410 They cam in a loving and weil-willing maner to inquyre. **1611** COTGR., *Bienvueillant*, well-willing, fauourable. **1931** *Times Lit. Suppl.* 20 Aug. 631/1 Not even the most well-willing of critics can escape from its two main flaws.

absol. c897 ÆLFRED *Gregory's Past. C.* xxxiv. 229 Ða welwillendan [L. *benevoli*]. **1569** *Reg. Privy Council Scot.* I. 677 That the weill willing may be rememberit, and the obstinat constrenit to thair dewitie.

b. Const. *to, towards, unto.*

1390 GOWER *Conf.* II. 18 It semeth love is welwillende To hem that [etc.]. c**1440** *Generydes* 964 To ther desire the kyng was welewillyng. **1461** *Paston Lett.* (1904) IV. 14, I knew..not whedyr they wer well wyllyng to yow or not. **1549** J. OLD *Erasm. Par., Ephes.* Prol. ℈ij, Sondry other curates & ministres..are honest and diligently well wyllynge towardes the trueth. **1579** W. WILKINSON *Confut. Fam. Love* 50b, Those which stand welwilling vnto his instructions. **1598** R. BERNARD *Terence, Hecyra* v. i. (1607) 338 Your speach hath made mee fauorable and welwilling towardes you now. **1599** A. M. tr. *Gabelhouer's Bk. Physicke* Transl. to Reader, Through the persuasions of diuers well-willinge Dutchmen to the English natione. **1888** STEVENSON *Black Arrow* Prol. 20 He was one of those who are.. ruggedly faithful and well-willing to their friends.

c. Ready or desirous *to* (do something).

c**1440** *Generydes* 2181 To wayte on hym ther were [they] well willyng. **1585** *Burgh Rec. Edin.* (1882) IV. 437 Sic persouns..as ar knawin to be..maist cairfull and weill willing to seik the saiftie and preseruatioun of the same.

†**B.** *sb.* One who is well disposed to another; a (person's) well-wisher or friend. *Obs.*

In pl., either unaltered or with *s*.

c**1330** R. BRUNNE *Chron. Wace* (Rolls) 8948 He spak so wyþ þe kyng of þat land, þat he was his wel willand Vpon Bretaigne a route to renge. **1340** *Ayenb.* 112 þe echedayes dol þet god yefþ to his wel wilynde. c**1375** *Lay-Folks Mass Bk.* (MS. B.) 368 Oure sib men and oure welewillandes. **1390** GOWER *Conf.* I. 299 If that thou wistest al, What Cheste doth in special To love and to his welwillinge. **1423** in *Reg. Mag. Sig. Scot. 1430*, 30/2 Til al lordis our frenddis and wele willand effectuusly we praye. c**1425** WYNTOUN *Cron.* VII. ix. 3048 Oþir gudis..þat langit til hym or til his men, Or til his weil willandis þen. c**1450** *Godstow Reg.* 12 To al oure frendes, and wel wyllynges. **1463** *Paston Lett.* II. 138 Wretyn..Be your welewylland, Abbot of Langeleye.

Hence †**well-willingness.**

c**1000** ÆLFRIC *Saints' Lives* xxxi. 44 Embe his efencempan he hæfde welwillendnysse and micele lufe. a**1390** *Wyclif Bible, Ecclus.* Prol., I monest ȝou to comen with wel willingnesse [Vulg. *cum benevolentia*].

well-'willy, *a. Obs.* exc. *dial.* [See WILLY *a.* Cf. Sw. *välvillig*, Da. *velvillig*.] Full of good will, benevolent, well-disposed, generous; = GOODWILLY *a.*

c**1374** CHAUCER *Troylus* III. 1257 Venus mene I, þe wel willy planete. c**1375** *Sc. Leg. Saints* iii. (*Andrew*) 807 Al þai þat vele wylly was to þe apostil. c**1402** LYDG. *Compl. Bl. Knt.* 627 A! fairë lady! welwilly founde at al. c**1425** *St. Mary of Oignies* II. iii. in *Anglia* VIII. 158 Pees in londe to men þat are wele willy. c**1449** PECOCK *Repr.* v. vii. 522 Wherfore ther mai not so greet a multitude be weel willi to religioun, if [etc.]. **1808** JAMIESON, *Weill-willie, Weill-willit*, Liberal, not niggardly. **1881** *Leic. Gloss., Well-willing*, and *Well-willy*, favourable to; having a kindly feeling towards; bearing good will towards.

well-'winded, *a.* Sound or strong of wind.

14.. in *Harrow. Hell* Introd. p. xxv, The horss hath xxv propertes... After the asse, well-mouthid, well-wyndyd.

well-'windowed, *a.*

1845 [see WELL-ROOFED].

well-winged, *a.*

1613-16 W. BROWNE *Brit. Past.* I. iv. 66 He past them o'er, quick, as..well-wing'd Shaft forth of a Parthian bowe. **1619** DRAYTON *Bar. Wars* II. xxxvi. 23 Those well-wing'd Weapons..Slip'd from the Bow-string, impotent and slacke. **1649** [see CANCELEER *sb.* b].

well-'winnowed, *ppl. a.*

1685 DRYDEN *Threnod. August.* xiii. 375 A plenteous Crop ..Of purest and well winow'd Grain. **1827** LYTTON *Pelham* ii, Seldom seen at large assemblies, she was eagerly sought after in the well-winnowed *soirées* of the elect.

well-wired, *a.*

1825 T. HOOK *Sayings* Ser. II. *Man of Many Fr.* (Colburn) 117 Artificial flowers were taught to twine round mock marble columns, and fragrant lights to spring spontaneously from well-wired boughs of trees.

well-wish, *sb.* Now *rare.* An act of wishing well to another; a good wish. Const. *to, for.*

1621 LADY M. WROTH *Urania* 435 If..these speeches haue proceeded only from your well-wishes to mee, I must be sorry for them. **1623** BP. HALL *Best Bargaine* Wks. (1625) 518 Our zealous well-wishes..for the vndoubted truth of our Maker and Redeemer. **1643** SIR T. BROWNE *Relig. Med.* II. §13 If this be true, I must confesse I am charitable only in my liberall intentions, and bountifull well-wishes. **1654** J. SHERMAN (*title*) White Salt: or, A Sober Correction of A Mad World, In some Wel-wishes to Goodness. **1708** ADDISON *Pres. St. War* 8 Any one that hath..a well Wish for his Friends or Posterity. **1709** HEARNE *Collect.* (O.H.S.) II. 288 Sends hearty wellwishes to Barnes'..design. **1816** KEATS *Lett.* Wks. 1889 III. 46 You know with what Reverence I would send my Well-wishes to him. **1872** MICHIE *Deeside Tales* xiv. (1908) 138 The bridegroom..got presents o' corn an' ither gear in token o' their well wishes. **1889** *Hardwicke's Sci.-Gossip* XXV. 226 Testifying their thanks and well-wishes to the captain and steward. **1908** *Westm. Gaz.* 5 June 2/2 The exhibition has received the well wishes of the Archbishop of Canterbury.

†**well-wish,** *v. Obs. intr.* To wish well *unto* (another).

1586 A. DAY *Engl. Secretorie* I. (1625) 14 Thinke how exceedingly I have always well-wished unto you.

†**well-wished,** *ppl. a. Obs.* Attended by good wishes.

1603 SHAKS. *Meas. for M.* II. iv. 27 Euen so The generall subiect to a wel-wisht King Quit their owne part, and in obsequious fondnesse Crowd to his presence.

'well-,wisher. One who wishes well to another, a cause, etc. Const. *to, of*, or with possessive.

1590 *Tarlton's Newes Purgatorie* 1 Amongst the rest of whose welwishers my selfe being not the least. **1639** G. PLATTES *Discov. Subterr. Treas.* To Rdr., So I take my leave and rest, Your hearty Well-wisher. G. P. **1670** EACHARD *Cont. Clergy* 8 All well-wishers either to the clergy or learning. **1711** ADDISON *Spect.* No. 10 ¶7, I know several of my Friends and Well-wishers are in great Pain for me. **1772** *Phil. Trans.* LXII. 356, I am..a constant well-wisher to the progress of arts and sciences. **1780** *Mirror* No. 82 Yet the tale has a moral, by no means flattering to the well-wishers of this country. **1788** MME. D'ARBLAY *Diary* 24 July, He seemed to feel that he spoke to a safe and a sympathising well-wisher. **1836** C. WORDSWORTH *Athens* xi. (1855) 66 Some wise well-wisher to the Areopagus. **1849** C. BRONTE *Shirley* i, It would be a nice opportunity for any of his well-wishers to pay him a visit. **1905** *Times* 10 May 10 Those who are not well-wishers of either country.

†**b.** One who aspires *to* (be or become). *Obs.*

1710-11 SWIFT *Jrnl. to Stella* 7 Mar., The latter has a good deal of learning, and he is a well-wisher to be an author.

well-wishing, *vbl. sb.* The action of wishing well to another; also, an expression of good wishes.

1569 ELVIDEN *Closet of Counsels* (1573) Ep. Ded., Wherefore..I haue beene bolde to offer you this same, as a token of my well wishing. **1586** A. DAY *Eng. Secretorie* I. (1625) 14 Not forgetting our accustomed greetings and interchangeable wel-wishings. **1617** MORYSON *Itin.* III. 29 Hee who knowes so to live with Italians..as he can gain their well-wishing. a**1672** WILKINS *Nat. Relig.* 326 Religion.. will teach them..to be generous and large in their well-wishing and their well-doing. **1909** J. R. HARRIS *Side-Lights N.T. Research* ii. 78 There is much hand-shaking and well-wishing. **1911** CRAIK *Clarendon* xxi. II. 190 Some one, 'who was believed to wish well to the King'—with that sort of well-wishing which characterized the time-serving of Bennet and his confederates.

well-wishing, *ppl. a.* That wishes well to others, benevolent; †loyal. Also *transf.*

1597 C. MIDDLETON *Chinon of Engl.* iii. (1925) 20 Flying with the fauorable fortune of well wishing windes. **1623** T. SCOT (*title*) An experimentall Discoverie of Spanish Practises or the Covnsell of a well-wishing Souldier. **1768-74** TUCKER *Lt. Nat.* (1834) II. 279 Thy candid well-wishing eye. **1842** LOVER *Handy Andy* xvii, And glass after glass they did drink in all sorts and shapes of well-wishing toasts. **1896** BLACK *Briseis* xviii. 229 Marked by a perfect self-possession—a self-possession sweet and serene and well-wishing.

†**well-'witted,** *a. Obs.* Gifted with good wits.

c**1450** METHAM *Wks.* 147 He that ys born that day schuld be trwe and wele-wyttyd. **1476** *Paston Lett.* III. 156 Thys man is..well wittyd, well manerd. **1529** *Commons' Petition* in Froude *Hist. Eng.* I. 198 Such subtle interrogatories..as are able quickly to trap a simple unlearned, or yet a well-witted layman without learning. **1552** HULOET, Able to receyue, or well wytted, *capax.*

well-won, *ppl. a.* Gained by hard or honourable effort.

1596 SHAKS. *Merch. V.* I. iii. 51 (Qq.) My well-won [Ff. -worne] thrift Which he cals interest. **1786** BURNS *To Auld Mare* iv, Tho' it was sma', 'twas weel-won gear. **1791** —— *To R. G. of F.* 43 His well-won bays, than life itself more dear. **1818** SCOTT *Hrt. Midl.* xxxix, I..will not lose weel-won gear with the like of him if it may be helped. **1842** J. AITON *Domest. Econ.* (1857) 59 A well-won penny is worth an ill-won pound. **1879** R. LOWE in *19th Cent.* June 992 The great and well-won reputation of Mr. Wallace as a scientific observer.

well-'wooded, *a.* Covered with growing trees.

a**1550** LELAND *Itin.* (1764) III. 28 The Soile..very good, and enclosid, and metely wel woddyd. **1741** RICHARDSON *Pamela* I. xi. (1824) 248 This pretty well-wooded and well-watered estate. **1780** COXE *Russ. Discov.* 211 Well-wooded mountains. **1885** E. P. WARREN & CLEVERLY *Wanderings 'Beetle'* 120 Past long well-wooded islands. **1914** D. MACMILLAN *Robert Flint* v. 111 The land is fertile and well-wooded.

well-'wooing, *ppl. a.*

1818 KEATS *Endym.* I. 101 Rain-scented eglantine Gave temperate sweets to that well-wooing sun.

†**well-woolled,** *a. Obs.* Having a thick or rich fleece.

1611 COTGR., *Mouton à la grande laine*, a Sheepe well-woolled, or of great burthen. **1641** BEST *Farm. Bks.* (Surtees) 13 A score of large and well-wold weathers.

†**well-word,** *v. Obs. trans.* To eulogize.

1605 J. DAVIES (Heref.) *Humours Heaven* 19 The other twaine..Whiles he was speaking, his speech seem'd to praise,..And now, by word, well-word they what he saies.

well-'worded, *a.* Couched in proper terms.

1656 COWLEY *Pindar. Odes, The Muse* i, Figures, Conceits, Raptures, and Sentences In a well-worded dress. **1841** LONGF. *Childr. Lord's Supper* 87 The fathers and mothers Stood behind them in tears, and were glad at the well-worded answer. **1865** PUSEY *Truth Eng. Ch.* 127 Yet even from Italy came a distinct, well-worded objection from the Bishop of Mondovi. **1907** J. H. MCCARTHY *Needles & Pins* x, I thought that some at least of what I said was rather well-worded.

well-worked, *ppl. a.* **a.** Thoroughly operated. **b.** Skilfully wrought.

1801 *Farmer's Mag.* Jan. 43 On very middling soils.. thirty bushels an acre is considered as only a decent crop, after tolerably well-worked fallow. **1865** LUBBOCK *Preh. Times* 195 The well-worked implements of the tumuli.

†**well-'worker.** *Obs.* One who does good.

c**1586** C'TESS PEMBROKE *Ps.* CXXV. iv, As the well-workers, soe the right beleevers, Lord favour further.

well-'working, *vbl. sb.* †**a.** Doing good, well-doing. *Obs.* **b.** Skilful fashioning or forging. **c.** Successful activity or operation.

1611 *Norton's Calvin's Inst.* Table of Contents X xx 1 b, Against all them which say that if this doctrine [of Predestination] take place, all endeuour of well working decaieth. **1691** T. H[ALE] *Acc. New Invent.* 79 According to the goodness and well working of the Iron, some prove of longer durance than other. **1879** SPENCER *Data of Ethics* vi. §34. 84 The well-working [of pleasure and pain] in essential matters is ignored; and the ill-working in unessential matters is alone recognized.

†**well-'working,** *ppl. a. Obs.* That does good, virtuous.

a**900** ÆLFRED *Blooms* I. in Cockayne *Shrine* (1864) 169 Ic þe halsie, ðu arfæsta, wel wilende & wel wyrcende drihten. c**1460** *Towneley Myst.* iii. 120 Thou was alway well wirkand, to me trew as stele.

well-worn, *ppl. a.*

1. Much worn or used; *fig.* trite, hackneyed.

1621 T. WILLIAMSON tr. *Goulart's Wise Vieillard* 53 It is a well worne saying, That [etc.]. **1786** BURNS *Tam Samson* Epit., Tam Samson's weel-worn clay here lies. **1818** SCOTT *Hrt. Midl.* xii, The old man was seated by the fire with his well-worn pocket Bible in his hands. **1842** TENNYSON *Gard. Dau.* 108 A well-worn pathway. **1849** SIR F. B. HEAD *Stokers & Pokers* iii. 39 That variety of free and easy well-worn costumes in which quiet-minded people usually travel. **1858** MERIVALE *Rom. Emp.* liv. (1863) VI. 411 The mind of the educated classes still flowed freely enough in the well-worn channels of literature. **1905** 'G. THORNE' *Lost Cause* v, It is a trite and well-worn aphorism that no event is trivial.

2. Becomingly carried or displayed.

1814 BYRON *Lara* I. xxvii, To whom he showed nor deference nor disdain, But that well-worn reserve which proved he knew No sympathy with that familiar crew.

well(-)'worthy, *a.* Worthy in a high degree.

1597 MARKHAM *Devoreux* 35b, Thou liuely worke of her great excellence, Wel-worthy Matter for her powre to frame. **1611** SPEED *Hist. Gt. Brit.* IX. ix. §91 Behold here good people, my Sonne Edmund..; how comely and well worthy he is of all your fauors. **1784** COWPER *Tiroc.* 918 Unless the world were all prepar'd t'embrace A plan well worthy to supply their place. **1796** *Seward's Anecdotes* III. 145 The Admiral [Coligny] approaching the Emperor with a reverence well-worthy of the greatness of the Prince..said [etc.].

wellwott, obs. Sc. form of VELVET.

†**well-'woulder.** *Obs. nonce-wd.* A conditional or would-be well-willer.

1643 *Plain English* 28 These are well-woulders to the Parliament and Kingdome.

†**well-wove,** *ppl. a. Obs.* = next.

c**1710** CONGREVE tr. *Ovid* Wks. 1730 III. 305 The well-wove Tours they wear, their own are thought; But only are their own, as what they've bought.

well-'woven, *ppl. a. lit.* and *fig.*

1591-5 SPENSER *Astrophel* 97 There his welwouen toyles and subtil traines He laid, the brutish nation to enwrap. **1663** SOUTH *Serm.* (1727) V. 206 No such Instrument to carry on a refined, and well-woven Rebellion, as a tender Conscience, and a sturdy Heart. **1671** MILTON *P.R.* I. 97 Not force, but well couch't fraud, well woven snares. **1768-74** TUCKER *Lt. Nat.* (1834) II. 279 When thy well-woven bands unite societies. **1791** COWPER *Iliad* XVIII. 741 Ev'ry maiden neat-attir'd In finest linen, and the youths in vests Well-woven. **1883** WHITELAW *Sophocles, Trachin.* 602 This well-woven robe. **1887** MORRIS *Odyss.* v. 58 The Nymph..of the hair well-woven.

well-wreathed, *ppl. a.* Skilfully twisted.

1615 CHAPMAN *Odyss.* II. 609 They..with well-wreath'd halsers hoise Their white sailes. *Ibid.* XXI. 543 As one..doth ..In tuning of his Instrument..lend To euery wel-wreath'd string, his perfect sound.

†**well-'writing,** *vbl. sb. Obs.*

1668 DRYDEN *Dram. Poesie* 33 All passions may be lively represented on the Stage, if to the well-writing of them the Actor supplies a good commanded voice.

well-'written, *ppl. a.*

1598 BARNFIELD *Poems* (Arb.) 119 Drayton, whose wel-written Tragedies, And sweete Epistles, soare thy fame to skies. **1776** BURNEY *Hist. Mus.* I. 171 A well-written and well-set scene of recitative. **1779** *Mirror* No. 36 A well-written preface. **1809** MALKIN *Gil Blas* XI. vi. (Rtldg.) 405 This well-written statement. **1911** G. B. SHAW *Blanco Posnet* Pref. 360 An able and well-written statement of the case.

well-wrought, *ppl. a.*

1. Well made or fashioned, skilfully constructed or put together: **a.** of material things.

1338 R. BRUNNE *Chron.* (1810) 341 To Westmynster þei hym brouht, Biside his fadere is laid in a toumbe wele wrouht. ?a**1366** CHAUCER *Rom. Rose* 1024 Hir nose, hir mouth, and eyhe and cheke Wel wrought [*bien fait*]. c**1400** *Destr. Troy* 1739 We haue a Cite..Well wroght for the werre, wallis full high. **1538** ELYOT *Dict.* Add., *Adfabrum*, well wrought. *c* **1611** CHAPMAN *Iliad* XI. 202 Yet pierc't it not his wel-wrought zone. **1640** HABINGTON *Castara* III. (Arb.) 120 And so I in thy favour dye, No memorie For me a well-wrought tombe prepare. **1723** MANDEVILLE *Fable Bees* (ed. 2) I. 185 From Caves..we are come to warm and well wrought Houses. **1732** POPE *Ess. Man* ii. 208 Tho' each by turns, the other's bound invade, As, in some well-wrought picture, light and shade. **1864** EARL DERBY *Iliad* v. 22 Idæus from the well-wrought chariot sprang.

b. of immaterial things, esp. literary or musical composition. Also with *out*.

c **1460** *Towneley Myst.* xvi. 370 This is well wroght gere that euer may be. **1668** DRYDEN *Dram. Poesie* 20 The Plots of their Plays being narrow, and the persons few, one of their Acts was written in a less compass then one of our well wrought Scenes. **1711** STEELE *Spect.* No. 11 ¶4 In Answer to your well-wrought Tale, I will give you..the History of Inkle and Yarico. **1849** HELPS *Friends in C.* II. i. (1854) I. 269 A store of goodly thoughts in well-wrought words. **1876** *Mus. Times* 1 June 492/1 Concluding his performance with a well-wrought-out fugue on this subject.

†**2.** Of ale: Thoroughly 'worked' or fermented.

1694 SALMON *Bate's Dispens.* (1713) 26/1 Put them in new well-wrought Beer or Ale.

†**3.** Of a convert: Fully persuaded. *Obs.*

1684 I. MATHER *Rec. Illustr. Provid.* ix. 291 He is..judged to be a well wrought Convert and real Christian.

welly ('wɛlɪ), *adv. dial.* [Colloquial reduction of WELL-NIGH.] Well-nigh, almost, nearly.

1615 W. GODDARD *Neaste of Waspes* No. 81 Shee screakes, cryes shees soe full, she burst-shall wellie. *Ibid.* No. 82 Shee scarce gone, hir back not turned wellie. **1641** BROME *Jovial Crew* III. (1652) G 4, Your Worships Charity to a poore Crytur welly starv'd. **1649** *Man in the Moon* No. 30. 235 Our long night of sorrow is now welly past over. **1717** *Obliging Husband* 10 You've welly gally'd me with ta'king on't. *c* **1746** J. COLLIER (Tim Bobbin) *View Lancs. Dial.* Wks. (1862) 40 Beleemy, Tummus, I welly lost my wynt. **1855** MRS. GASKELL *North & S.* xvii, A pack of spiritless, down-trodden men; welly clemmed to death. **1859** GEO. ELIOT *Adam Bede* lii, I should ha' been sure of her then, as she wouldn't go away from me to Snowfield, welly thirty mile off.

welly ('wɛlɪ), *sb.* Also **wellie**. Abbrev. of WELLINGTON 2 b. **a.** *colloq.* A wellington boot. Also *Comb.*, as ***welly-boot***.

1961 *Guardian* 2 June 9/5 The ground floor we converted back into a hall, for coats and wellies, etc. **1971** J. OSBORNE *West of Suez* I. 42 Huge surgeons who tower over you in green and rubber wellies. **1972** D. HASTON *In High Places* i. 15 We only have welly boots and gym-shoes. **1976** *Printing World* 30 Apr. 8/2 Wellington, who, as we all know, has a boot named after him... The influence of the child is apparent today as I gather it is now widely known as a 'wellie'. **1982** S. RADLEY *Talent for Destruction* iii. 20 Perhaps it wasn't done for a parson to wear welly boots under his cassock.

b. *slang.* A kick, acceleration. Also *fig.*

1977 *Daily Mirror* 10 May 23/1 The girl they call 'Daredevil Divi' gave the car a bit more wellie. In racing language, this meant she was stepping on the accelerator. **1979** *Guardian* 12 Feb. 20/3 The tactic most likely to succeed in the conditions was the long welly upfield. **1983** D. GETHIN *Wyatt & Moresby Legacy* xxv. 174 'When I say go, give it some welly... Go.'.. Explosions sounded.

Hence **welly** *v. trans.*, to kick or trip up with one's foot. *slang.*

1966 F. SHAW et al. *Lern Yerself Scouse* 48 *Eee wuz wellied*, he was kicked. **1980** D. MORRIS *Tribal Words* (typescript), *Wellied*, heavily tackled and brought down. To *welly* is to make a savage tackle, boot-first... 'He must expect to be wellied a few times' is a typical expression.

welm(e, var. ff. WALM *sb.*, *v.* and WHELM *v.*

†'**welmish**, *a. Obs. rare.* Also 7 **whelmish**. [Origin obscure. Cf. QUALM *sb.*[3]] Of colour: Pale, sickly (?).

1688 HOLME *Armoury* I. 13/1 Sky colour, or a light welmish Blew. *Ibid.* II. 23/2 If it [the rainbow] consist all of Yellow, this is palish; if white, its defiled, or whelmish. *Ibid.* III. 147/1 Green Verditer, a Welmish or Willow green.

welmost(e, var. forms of WELLMOST *adv.*

welogh, obs. form of WILLOW *sb.*

welonye, obs. form of VILLAINY.

welp, obs. form of WHELP.

wels (wɛls, vɛls). [a. Ger. *wels.*] = SHEAT-FISH.

1880 A. C. L. G. GÜNTHER *Introd. Study of Fishes* 565 The species which has given the name to the whole family is the 'Wels' of the Germans, *Silurus glanis.* **1905** D. S. JORDAN *Guide to Study of Fishes* II. ix. 182 The huge sheatfish, or wels,..next to the sturgeon, is the largest river fish in Europe. **1931** J. R. NORMAN *Hist. Fishes* vii. 138 The Wels or Glanis..of Europe normally feeds on fishes, frogs, and crustaceans. **1969** A. WHEELER *Fishes Brit. Isles & N.W. Europe* 221/2 Wels have been introduced in a number of private lakes in southern England.

Welsbach ('vɛlzbax). The name of Carl Auer Freiherr von *Welsbach* (1858–1929), Austrian chemist and engineer, used *attrib.* to designate the gas mantle (MANTLE *sb.* 5 g), invented by him, and the lamps employing it.

A proprietary name in the U.S.

1887 *Pall Mall Gaz.* 18 Mar. 12/1 The Welsbach burner would produce a purer light..with two cubic feet of gas per hour. **1901** *Daily Colonist* (Victoria, B.C.) 1 Oct. 5/4 The Victoria Gas Co., Ltd., are now installing complete Welsbach Lamps free of cost, charging the nominal sum of 5 cents per lamp per month for mantle renewal. **1912** A. BENNETT *Matador* 308 The Welsbach incandescent mantles on the chandelier saved thirty per cent in gas-bills while increasing the light by fifty per cent. **1964** *Official Gaz.* (U.S. Patent Office) 21 July TM 119/2 The Welsbach Corporation, Philadelphia, Pa... *Welsbach.* For gas lamps ..and gas mantles. **1980** *Sci. Amer.* May 123/2 The Welsbach mantle, a type of gas burner widely used for home lighting around the turn of the century, proved to be a rich source of N rays.

Welsh (wɛlʃ), *a.* and *sb.* Forms: *α.* 1 Wilisc, Wilsc, 1–2 Wylisc, 2 Wylsc. *β.* 1 Uuelesc, 1–3 Welisc, 4–5 Welische (Welisse); 2–3 Welsc, 4 Welsse, 6 Welshe (7 Welse), 6–9 Welch, 6– Welsh. *γ.* 1–2 Wælisc, 3 Walisc, 4 Walish, Walysch, 5 Walische, Walysshe, Wallish, Wallych, 6 Walyssh; 2 Wælsc, 3 Wailsc, 3–4 Wals, 4–5 Walsch(e, Walssh, 4–6 Walshe (6 Walche), 5 Walsshe, 6–7 Walsh. [OE. (West Saxon) *Wilisc*, *Wylisc*, (Anglian and Kentish) *Welisc*, *Wælisc*, f. *Wealh*, *Walh*, Celt, Briton, = OHG. *Walh*, *Walah* (MHG. *Walch*, G. *Wahle*) Celt, Roman, etc., ON. **Valr* (pl. *Valir*, Gauls, Frenchmen): see etym. note to WALNUT, and cf. WALACH and VLACH. To the English adj. correspond OHG. *wal(a)hisc*, *walesc* (MHG. *walh-*, *wälhisch*, *walsch*, etc., G. *wälsch*, *welsch*), Roman, Italian, French, Du. *waalsch* Walloon, ON. *valskr* Gaulish, French (MSw. *valskr*; Sw. *välsk*, Da. *vælsk* Italian, French, southern); cf. the note to WALSHNUT.

In OE. the final *h* of the stem normally disappeared before the adjectival ending. The West Saxon type **Wielisc* (from *Wealh*) did not survive beyond the OE. period; the two Anglian and Kentish types (from *Walh*) existed concurrently till the 16th cent., after which *Welsh* became the sole form in general use, *Walsh* remaining only as a surname. (The AF. *Waleis*, which is rarely employed in ME., also survives in the surname *Wallace*.)

The spelling *Welch* is retained in the title of the Royal Welch Fusiliers.]

A. *adj.*

1. Of persons: **a.** Originally: belonging to the native British population of England in contrast to the Anglo-Saxons. *Obs.* exc. *Hist.* **b.** In later use: belonging to Wales by birth and descent; forming (part of) the native population of Wales.

α. **688–695** *Laws Ine* §32 Be Wilisces monnes londhæfene. Ȝif Wilisc mon hæbbe hide londes [etc.]. *c* **1000** *Ags. Laws, Dunsetas* §3, 2, xii lahmen scylon riht tæcean Wealan & Ænglan: vi Englisce & vi Wylisce. *c* **1100** *O.E. Chron.* (MS. D.) an. 1052 Griffin se Wylisca cing. *Ibid.* (MS. C.) an. 1055 Tremerig se Wylsca biscop. *Ibid.* (Laud MS.) an. 1097 Ða Wylisce menn syððon hi fram þam cynge ȝebuȝon.

β. *c* **1100** *O.E. Chron.* (MS. C.) an. 1052 Eac man sloh Hris þæs Welscan cynges broþer. *c* **1205** LAY. 31632 þa iwærð abolȝen a Welisc king in þe hepe. **1360–1** *Durham Acc. Rolls* (Surtees) 562 Cuidam Welsharpour d'ni Will'i de Dalton, 3*s.* 4*d.* **1513** *Life Hen. V* (1911) 10 And this sufficeth of the Welsh conspiracies and battailes. **1598** SHAKS. *Merry W.* II. i. 209 Sir, there is a fray to be fought, betweene Sir Hugh the Welch Priest, and Caius the French Doctor. **1628** *Mad Pranks Robin Goodfellow* (Percy Soc.) 9 As infamous as a Welch-harper that playes for cheese and onions. **1647** CLARENDON *Hist. Reb.* VI. §135 Here a Welsh regiment of the King's..assaulted the works. **1796** MORSE *Amer. Geog.* II. 147 Henry I of England, planted a colony of Flemings on the frontiers of Wales,..none of the Welsh princes being powerful enough to oppose them. **1836** SOUTHEY *Lett.* (1856) IV. 475 Here I have found out who the Welsh attorney was who [etc.]. **1862** BORROW *Wales* xlix, Why, you told me you were of Welsh parents. **1905** 'G. THORNE' *Lost Cause* x, The sly Welsh girl was indubitably awed.

γ. *c* **1100** *O.E. Chron.* (MS. D.) an. 1050 Mid Gryfines fultume þæs Wæliscan cynges. **1338** R. BRUNNE *Chron.* (1725) 241 Had þei had a spie among þe Walssh oste..þei had bien men lyuand, þat þer to dede went. ? *a* **1400** *Morte Arth.* 320 'A! A!' sais the Walsche kynge 'wirchipid be Criste!' *c* **1420** *Contin. Brut* 368 þere was a man þat was clepid 'þe walsch clerke,' and apelyd a kniȝt..of treson. **1470–85** MALORY *Arthur* XVIII. xxiii. 767 And there with al he aspyed a walysshe knyghte where he was to repose him. [*a* **1577** SIR T. SMITH *Commonw. Eng.* I. xiii. (1583) 15 To defende themselues yet from them which were walsh and strangers,..[they] agreed..to consult in common.]

2. a. Of things: Of or pertaining to Wales or its inhabitants, †or to the British race in Anglo-Saxon times.

In OE. the wider sense of 'foreign' appears also to have been current, but clear instances are rare.

688–95 *Laws Ine* §46. 1 Gif hit ðonne bið Wilisc onstal, ne bið se að na ðy mara. *Ibid.* §70, xii ambra Wilisc ealað. **805–10** in Birch *Cartul. Sax.* I. 459 Selle mon..xxx. ombra godes uuelesces aloð. *a* **1122** *O.E. Chron.* (Laud MS.) an. 852 Wulfred scolde ȝifen..twa tunnan fulle hlutres aloð..& ten mittan Wælsces aloð. *c* **1205** LAY. 13021 Vortiger hafde Walisc [*c* **1275** Wals] lond. **1297** R. GLOUC. (Rolls) App. G. 146 Fram þe walische see ywis, Fram seint dauid to þe see. **1300–1400** *R. Gloucester's Chron.* (Rolls) App. XX. 591 Edward his sone..þat of þe welische londe clanliche al out I wan þe seignoriȝe. **1532** *Prayer & Compl. Ploweman* Fj, They haue enclosed it [God's leasow]..so hygh, there may no shepe come there within, but yef it be a walyssh lepre [= leaper] of the mountaynes. **1555** L. SAUNDERS in Coverdale *Lett. Martyrs* (1564) 188 Not in hope of rebellion or fulfillyng vnprofitable, yea pestilent welshe prophecies. **1599** SHAKS. *Hen. V*, IV. vii. 112 All the water in Wye, cannot wash your Maiesties Welsh plood out of your pody. *Ibid.* V. i. 83 Henceforth let a Welsh correction, teach you a good English condition. **1612** SELDEN *Illustr. Drayton's Poly-olb.* ix. 390 In the Welsh Prouerb *Mon mam Cymbry.* **1761** GOLDSM. *Ess.*, *Taste*, The native, genuine, and salutary taste of Welch beef. **1771** SMOLLETT *Humph. Cl.* 26 Apr. (1) At eight..we go..to the Pump-room; which is crowded like a Welsh fair. **1774** JOHNSON in Boswell *Life* (1904) II. 538 Yesterday I returned from my Welch journey. **1781** GIBBON *Decl. & F.* xxxviii. (1787) III. 623 Their subjects, of Welsh or Cambrian extraction, assume the respectable station of inferior freemen. **1862** BORROW *Wales* l, I reached a large village, the name of which, like those of most Welsh villages, began with Llan.

Proverbial (and allusively). *a* **1661** FULLER *Worthies, Wales* (1662) 7 As long as a Welsh pedigree. **1725** YOUNG *Love of Fame* III. 121 Till I surpass in length..A Welch descent. *a* **1764** CHURCHILL *Serm.* Ded. 60 (1771) p. iii, When thou art to thyself, thy Sire unknown, A whole Welsh genealogy alone?

b. In the names of various products of, and commodities obtained from, Wales, as †**Welsh cloth** (see *Welsh cotton*); **Welsh coal**, coal obtained from the South Wales coal-fields; anthracite; †**Welsh cotton**, a kind of woollen cloth with a nap; **Welsh dresser** (see quot. and DRESSER[1] 2); **Welsh flannel** (see quot. 1858); †**Welsh frieze** = *Welsh cotton*; **Welsh glaive** (see quot.); **Welsh lay**, a class of roofing-slates; †**Welsh lining**, a woollen cloth without a nap (cf. COTTON *sb.*[2] and FRIEZE *sb.*[1] 1); **Welsh lump**, a kind of fire-brick made in large pieces; **Welsh mutton**, mutton obtained from a small breed of sheep pastured on the Welsh mountains, highly esteemed for the delicacy of its flavour; **Welsh oilstone** (see quot.); †**Welsh plain** = *Welsh flannel*; **Welsh rag** = RAG *sb.*[2] 1 b; †**Welsh scarlet** (see SCARLET *sb.*[1]); **Welsh snuff** (see quot.); †**Welsh stone-coal** = *Welsh coal.* Also WELSH BILL, WELSH HOOK.

1566 *Act 8 Eliz.* c. 7 §1 *Welsh Clothe and Linyng, commonly called Cottons Fryzes and Playnes. *a* **1618** RALEGH *Invent. Shipping* 41 Our Newcastle, or our *Welsh Coales. **1743** *London & Country Brewer* III. (ed. 2) 177 At a famous Town in the West for brewing Beer, they burn this Welch Coal in a moveable Iron Grate. **1842** LOUDON *Suburban Hort.* 211 Welsh coal..is a very durable fuel, peculiarly well suited to these boilers. **1546–7** in Feuillerat *Revels Edw. VI* (1914) 5, iij yardes d. *wellshe Cotton at vj[d] yard. **1551–2** *Act 5 & 6 Edw. VI*, c. 6 §1 And that..Walshe Cottonne..shall not be streched on the Tentor..above a nayle of a yarde in bredith. **1580** Welsh cotton [see MANCHESTER 1]. **1910** *Encycl. Brit.* VIII. 578/1 A peculiarly effective combination of oak and mahogany is found in the dressers..made on the borders of Staffordshire and Shropshire... The expression '*Welsh dresser'..is now no more than a trade term,..applied to all dressers of this type. [**1598** Welsh flannel; used allusively in referring to a Welshman: see FLANNEL 1 d.] **1771** SMOLLETT *Humph. Cl.* I. 126 These sums she has more than doubled, by..dealing in cheese and *Welsh flannel, the produce of his flocks and dairy. **1858** SIMMONDS *Dict. Trade*, *Welsh-flannel*, the finest kind of flannel, made from the fleeces of the flocks of the Welsh mountains. **1860** HUNT *Ure's Dict. Arts*, etc. s.v. *Flannel*, Wales is the country in which flannel was originally made, and the Welsh flannel is still held in much estimation. **1551–2** *Act 5 & 6 Edw. VI*, c. 6 §1 All *Walshe Frices.. made and wrought within the Shires of Cardigan and Pembroke..or elsewhere of lyke makinge. **1786** GROSE *Anc. Armour* 56 The *Welch glaive is a kind of bill, sometimes reckoned among the pole axes. **1891** *Century Dict.* s.v. *Lay*[1] *n.* 8 **Welsh lay*, a slate measuring 3 by 2 feet. **1557–8** *Act 4 & 5 Phil. & Mar.* c. 5 §5 Everie Gode of *Welche lyning shall..be three quarters of a yarde in Breadthe. **1833** LOUDON *Encycl. Archit.* §599 The most convenient fire bricks are what are called *Welsh or Stourbridge lumps. **1842** GWILT *Archit.* §1826 Fire bricks... This sort of brick is made also in various parts of Wales, whence they are called Welsh lumps. **1892** *Dict. Arch.* (Arch. Publ. Soc.) *Welsh lump*... It can be had up to 3 ft. long, 10 ins. by 5 ins. thick. **1771** SMOLLETT *Humph. Cl.* II. 228, I dined upon a delicate leg of *Velsh mutton and cully-flower. **1830** LE KEUX *Illustr. Nat. Hist.* I. 141 The genuine Welsh mutton is highly esteemed. **1910** *Encycl. Brit.* XIII. 653/1 Idwal or *Welsh oilstone, used for small articles. **1584** in Feuillerat *Revels Q. Eliz.* (1908) 370 For ix yardes of *welshe playne. **1725** [see PLAIN *sb.*[1] 9]. **1823** NICHOLSON *Pract. Builder* 396 Patent slating was originally composed of slates called the *Welsh Rags. **1887** *Dict. Arch.* (Arch. Publ. Soc.), *Rag slate*, or *Welsh rag.* **14..** *Langland's P. Pl.* A. v. 113 (MS. T.), I may hit not leue He scholde wandre on þat *walsshe scarlet, so was it þred-bare. **1845** DODD *Brit. Manuf.* v. 148 There are many kinds of snuff called 'high-dried', such as '*Welsh' and 'Lundyfoot'. **1833** N. ARNOTT *Physics* (ed. 5) II. 143 *Welch stone-coal.

c. in the names of plants, beasts, insects, etc., indigenous to or found chiefly in Wales, as *Welsh cattle*, *pony*, *runt* (see RUNT *sb.* 2); **Welsh Black**, a black-coated ox or cow of a breed originally developed in north Wales, now usually kept for both meat and milk production; **Welsh clearwing**, **club-moss** (see quots.); **Welsh hound**, a dog similar to an English foxhound but wire-haired; **Welsh mountain (sheep)**, a small, hardy sheep of a breed developed in high regions of Wales; **Welsh poppy**, a perennial poppy of the genus *Meconopsis* (see POPPY *sb.* 3); **Welsh sorrel**, **speedwell**, **wave** (see quots.); **Welsh terrier**, a stocky, rough-coated, usually black and tan terrier with a square muzzle and drop ears, belonging to a breed originally developed in Wales to hunt vermin.

1919 K. J. J. MACKENZIE *Cattle* xi. 149 *Welsh Black Cattle. Some 20 years ago there were two distinct types of black cattle in Wales. **1953** A. FRASER *Beef Cattle Husbandry* ix. 134 The modern Welsh Black is the outcome of two types or breeds. **1977** *S. Wales Guardian* 27 Oct. 2/3 (Advt.), Welsh Black cow, 5th calver, with Cross-Friesian Steer calf at heel. **1747** H. GLASSE *Art of Cookery* xiii. 129 Take the leg of a fat but small Beef, the Fat Scotch or *Welch Cattle is best. **1834** YOUATT *Cattle* 47 Howell Dha.. describes some of the Welsh cattle in the tenth century, as being 'white with red ears'. **1869** E. NEWMAN *Brit. Moths* 15 The *Welsh Clearwing (*Sesia Scoliæformis*). **1796** WITHERING *Brit. Plants* (ed. 3) III. 759 *Pilularia annotinum*... *Welsh Clubmoss. On the mountains of Caernarvonshire. **1893** R. B. LEE *Mod. Dogs* (*Sporting Division*) iv. 86 The harrier is oftener coarser in his coat than the foxhound, which may be ascribed to crossing with a rough *Welsh hound that I believe is still to be found in some parts of the principality. **1930** J. D. D. EVANS in C. Frederick et al. *Foxhunting* xxxi. 306 The Welsh hound is probably in some degree of later origin. **1973** *Country Life* 27 Dec. 2173/2 The three Welsh hounds he is shown holding have long, hairy coats, whitish-grey in colour. **1899** W. J. MALDEN *Sheep Raising & Shepherding* ii. 5 Such breeds as the *Welsh Mountain.. have soft short wool. **1960** [see EXMOOR]. **1979** *Country Life* 7 June 1769/3 A black version of the Welsh Mountain sheep. **1771** SMOLLETT *Humph. Cl.* 26 Apr. (3), Patience is like a stout *Welsh poney; it bears a great deal, and trots a great way; but it will tire at the long run. **1831** YOUATT *Horse* 58 The Welsh pony.. has a small head, high withers, deep yet round barrel, short joints, flat legs, and good round feet. **1741** *Compl. Family-Piece* II. iii. 374 *Welsh-poppy. **1829** LOUDON *Encycl. Plants* (1836) 462 *Meconopsis cambrica* Vig. Welsh Poppy. **1882** *Garden* 20 May 353/1 A broad blue china bowl is brilliant with.. Welsh Poppy. **1659** HOWELL *Lex. Tetragl.*, *New Sayings* v. 8/1 He thrives as well as a *Welch Runt in Rumney Marsh. **1727** E. LAURENCE *Duty of Steward* 76 The Steward should be advis'd to stock the Ground with Scotch Keylys or Welch Runts. **1768**, **1886** [see RUNT *sb.* 2]. **1910** *Encycl. Brit.* V. 540/2 Welsh cattle are well known in the Midland counties.. where, under the name of 'Welsh runts', large herds of bullocks are fattened on the pastures. **1640** PARKINSON *Theat. Bot.* VI. x. 745 *Acetosa Cambro-Britanica Montana.* Mountaine *Welsh Sorrell. *c* **1710** PETIVER *Cat. Ray's Eng. Herbal* Tab. iii, Welsh Sorrel. **1731** MILLER *Gard. Dict.* s.v. *Veronica*, *Welsh spiked Speedwell, with a hairy Bugle Leaf. **1796** WITHERING *Brit. Plants* (ed. 3) II. 12 *Veronica hybrida*... Welsh Speedwell. Bugle-leaved Speedwell. **1885** *Kennel Chron. & Pedigree Register* VI. 161/1 *Welsh terriers.—*Dog*: 2nd, W. C. Whiskin (Welsh Dick). **1894** R. B. LEE *Mod. Dogs* (*Terriers*) x. 231 The dog of which I write as a Welsh terrier was unknown until some eight years.. ago. Then he appeared in some of our shows; he was given a place in the Stud Book; a club was formed in 1886 to look after his welfare. **1950** A. C. SMITH *Dogs since 1900* xi. 193 In 1942 Welsh Terriers came into prominence in the United States. **1980** E. LEATHER *Duveen Letter* i. 13 The Welsh terrier removed himself from the tapestry-covered Gainsborough chair. **1869** E. NEWMAN *Brit. Moths* 76 The *Welsh Wave (*Venusia cambricaria*).

d. in other collocations: **Welsh acre** (see quot.); **Welsh ambassador**, a name for (*a*) the cuckoo; †(*b*) the owl (cf. *Welsh falconer*); **Welsh aunt** (see quot.); **Welsh bait**, a rest, without other refreshment, given to a horse on reaching the top of a hill (see BAIT *sb.* 5); also *fig.*; **†Welsh brief** (meaning obscure); **Welsh cake**, a kind of individual spicy cake made in Wales with currants and ginger; **Welsh carpet** (see quot.); **†Welsh comb** (see quot.); hence **Welshcomb** *v. trans.*, to comb one's hair by using one's thumb and fingers instead of a comb; **Welsh cornice** (see quot.); **†Welsh cricket**, a louse; **Welsh diamond** (see quot.); **Welsh dragon**, a heraldic dragon as the emblem of Wales; also *fig.*; **Welsh drake**, the gadwall or gray duck, *Chaulelasmus streperus*; **†Welshdraper**, a maker of, or dealer in, 'Welsh cotton'; a woollen draper; **Welsh ejectment** (see quot.); **†Welsh falconer** = *Welsh ambassador* (*b*); **†Welsh fiddle** (see quot.); **Welsh groin, groining** *Arch.* (see quots.); **Welsh ham** (see quot.); **Welsh main** *Cockfighting* (see MAIN *sb.*[3] 3); **Welsh mile**, a distance of a mile and more; a long and tedious mile (chiefly proverbial); **Welsh mortgage** (see quot.); **Welsh Nationalist**, someone wanting home rule for Wales; *spec.* a member of the Welsh Nationalist Party; **Welsh niece**, a first cousin (cf. *Welsh aunt*, *W. uncle*); **Welsh Office**, an administrative department of the British Government with responsibility for Welsh affairs; the building where this is housed; **Welsh onion** = CHIBOL 1; **†Welsh parsley** (see quots.); **†Welsh pearl**, ? an inferior or counterfeit pearl; **†Welsh-pot shell** (see quot.); **Welsh road** (see quot.); **Welsh springer**, a kind of spaniel (see SPRINGER[1] 8 b); **Welsh uncle** (see UNCLE 1 d); **Welsh vault, vaulting** *Arch.* = *Welsh groin, groining*; **Welsh Wales** *colloq.*, the parts of Wales where Welsh culture is especially strong or which are most distinctively Welsh; **Welsh wig**, a worsted cap; **Welsh wizard** or **Wizard**, a nickname for David Lloyd George (1863–1945), Welsh politician and British prime minister. Also WELSH BEAN, WELSH HARP, WELSH RABBIT.

1704 *Dict. Rust.*, *Welch-acre*; it's usually two English Acres. **1608** MIDDLETON *Trick to catch Old One* IV. H 1, Thy Sound is like the cuckowe, the *welch Embassador. *c* **1620** *Welsh Embass.* IV. 1501 (Malone Soc.) Pray m^r Reese.. what is the reason that wee english men when the Cuckoe is vppon entrance saie the welsh embassador is Cominge. **1637** in *Retrosp. Rev.* (1853) I. 312 Two dozen of Welsh ambassodars. **1683–4** in Macray *Reg. Magd. Coll.* N.S. IV. (1904) 135 Mr. Clerke, commoner, complain'd of Sir Chernock, demy, for abusing him.., calling him foole, Welsh ambassadour (an expression for an owle). **1894** G. F. NORTHALL *Folk-phr. Four Counties* 25 The Welsh ambassador = The cuckoo. **1878** *N. & Q.* 10 Aug. 105/1 Some Radnorshire Words... **Welsh Aunt*, first cousin of father or mother. **1603** T. POWELL (*title*) *Welch Bayte to spare Prouender. Or, A looking backe vpon the Times past. **1658** HARRINGTON *Prerog. Pop. Govt.* I. vi. 32 In this place he takes a Welsh bait, and looking back makes a Muster of his Victories. *a* **1661** FULLER *Worthies*, *Wales* (1662) 7 The Proverbs... Give your horse a Welch-bait. **1626** B. JONSON *Staple of N.* v. i, It is a thing of greater consequence, Then to be borne about in a blacke boxe, Like a Low-countrey vorloffe or *Welsh-briefe. **1932** DYLAN THOMAS *Sel. Lett.* (1966) 6 Mother has made *Welshcakes. **1975** B. MEYRICK *Behind Light* xiv. 184 Sandwiches, spice buns, Welsh cakes and bread and margarine. **1980** B. FREEMAN *First catch your Peacock* viii. 163 *Welsh Cakes* (*Pice ar y maen*). There are two ways of making these traditional little spicy cakes. The most usual is on the bakestone or griddle, which produces them in a rather dry, biscuity form... The other method is to make them.. in a Dutch oven, and this produces cakes which are firm on the outside, soft and melting within. **1854** *Household Words* 2 Sept. 53/1 This *Welsh carpet is a pattern produced on the brick floor by staining the brick squares in figures with dockleaf juice. **1796** *Grose's Dict. Vulgar T.* (ed. 3), *Welch Comb, the thumb and four fingers. **1922** JOYCE *Ulysses* 125 He took off his silk hat and ..*welshcombed his hair with raking fingers. **1971** 'A. BURGESS' *MF* x. 111 Dressed and welshcombed, I pocketed my luggage and went downstairs. **1833** LOUDON *Encycl. Archit.* §459 These walls.. should have what is called a *Welsh cornice (two or three oversailing (protruding) courses of brickwork, one of which has dentils formed by the ends of bricks projecting at equal and regular distances) to finish with at top. **1592** GREENE *Upst. Courtier* D 2, A.. Gentle-man Marchant Tailor, giuing armes and the holye Lambe in his creast, where before he had no other cognisance, but a plaine Spanish needle with a *welsh cricket on the toppe. **1884** F. J. BRITTEN *Watch & Clockm.* 215 Rock crystal.. also known as 'Bristol', '*Welsh'.. or 'Irish' diamond, is also used by watch jewellers. **1857** C. M. YONGE *Dynevor Terrace* I. xxi. 349 If she had let the *Welsh dragon show his teeth in style, he would only have had to make unpleasant apologies. **1909** A. C. FOX-DAVIES *Compl. Guide Heraldry* xiii. 225 His Majesty the King has recently added the Welsh dragon differenced by a label of three points argent as an additional badge to the achievement of His Royal Highness the Prince of Wales. **1980** *Times* 16 Dec. 3/6 They.. see the Welsh dragon flying over public buildings in the principality. **1844** J. P. GIRAUD *Birds of Long Island* 306 At Egg Harbor a few [gadwalls] are seen.. and are there known by the name of '*Welsh Drake' or 'German Duck'. **1481** *Coventry Leet Bk.* 480 Hugh Walker ..*welch-draper. **1811** *Lex. Balatron.*, *Welsh Ejectment*, to unroof the house, a method practised by landlords in Wales to eject a bad tenant. *a* **1647** FLETCHER, etc. *Lovers Progr.* III, I hear by th' Owls, There are many of your *Welch falkoners about it [*sc.* a house]. *a* **1700** B. E. *Dict. Cant. Crew*, **Welsh-fiddle*, the Itch. **1778** W. PAIN *Carpenter's Repos.* Pl. 58 Make a semi-circular Arch.. that is commonly called a *Welch Groin. **1875** *Encycl. Brit.* II. 465/2 Groins, Welsh, or Underpitch... The system of vaulting is called underpitch groining, or, as termed by the workmen, *Welsh groining. *a* **1878** SIR G. SCOTT *Lect. Archit.* II. 173 Vaulting .. in which the side vaults.. cut the higher and main vault at a level lower than its crown.. is vulgarly known as 'Welsh' groining. **1877** *Cassell's Dict. Cookery* 1107 A *Welsh ham is simply the name given to a fat leg of mutton which has been cured and smoked like an ordinary ham. *c* **1450** *Merlin* xv. 247 All the contrey was of hem covered the length of a *walshe myle. **1652** J. TAYLOR (Water P.) *Journ. Wales* (1859) 21, I hired a guide who brought me to Swansey (sixteen well stretch'd Welch mountainous miles). **1796** *Grose's Dict. Vulgar T.* (ed. 3), *Welch Mile.* Like a Welch mile, long and narrow. His story is like a Welch mile, long and tedious. **1818** CRUISE *Digest* II. xv. i. §19 There is another kind of mortgage.. called a *Welsh mortgage, in which there is a perpetual right of redemption. **1911** *Encycl. Brit.* XVIII. 878/1 A Welsh mortgage is one in which.. a creditor.. takes the rents and profits in lieu of interest.., the estate being redeemable at any time on payment of the principal. **1891** *Dod's Parl. Compan.* 1890–91 246 George, David Lloyd... 'A *Welsh Nationalist', supporting 'Home Rule', 'Temperance', 'Disestablishment', and other items in the programme of the Advanced Liberal Party. **1925** *North Wales Observer* 13 Aug. 5/3 The proposals of the new Welsh Nationalist Party were calmly received.. at the Baptist Church, Pwllheli, on Thursday. **1937** W. H. JONES *What is happening in Wales?* iii. 9 What makes the Welsh Nationalist movement essentially a literary movement? **1966** M. WOODHOUSE *Tree Frog* xviii. 131 'Patriotism dictates,' he said. 'Don't give me that,' I said. 'I'm a Welsh Nationalist.' **1972** *Guardian* 19 June 24/8 Welsh Nationalists intend to set up a mobile pirate radio station. **1886** SIR F. H. DOYLE *Remin.* viii. 156 A young cousin, or rather.. *Welsh niece of mine. [**1964** *Times* 20 Nov. 6/7 Mr. Harold Wilson, Prime Minister.., in a statement defining the responsibilities of the Secretary of State for Wales, said:—. The interests of Wales are now represented in the Cabinet by the Secretary of State... He will have a Welsh office in Cardiff.. and a small ministerial office in London.] *Ibid.* 22 Dec. 10/4 Mr. Griffiths, Secretary of State for Wales, yesterday opened the first permanent home of the *Welsh Office in London. **1976** *S. Wales Echo* 26 Nov., Demonstrations by angry parents outside the Welsh Office now seem certain after South Glamorgan County Council's controversial decision to turn a Cardiff high school into a Welsh-speaking secondary. **1976** *Flintshire Leader* 10 Dec. 1/2 The call for a crossing did not meet Welsh Office conditions because there were not enough houses or people living in the village. **1977** *Western Mail* (Cardiff) 5 Mar. 3/2 The council has had to go to the Welsh Office for money for industrial development. **1731** MILLER *Gard. Dict.* s.v. *Cepa* M m/1 The *Welch Onions are only propagated for Spring Use also: These never make any Bulb, and are therefore only fit to be us'd green for Sallads, &c. **1824** LOUDON *Encycl. Gard.* (ed. 2) §3813 Welsh onion, or ciboule (*Allium fistulosum*, L). **1778**, **1832** [see CIBOL]. *a* **1625** FLETCHER *Elder Brother* I. ii, In tough *Welsh Parsly, which, in our vulgar Tongue, is strong Hempen Halters. **1638** RANDOLPH *Hey for Honesty* IV. i. (1651) 30 This is a Rascal deserves.. To dance in Hemp *Derricks Caranto*: Lets choke him with Welch Parsley. **1681** GREW *Musæum* I. §vi. ii. 146 *Welsh-Pearl... They are most of them flatish, and of a shining blackish colour. *c* **1711** PETIVER *Gazophyl.* VII. Tab. 69 Fig. 5 Carolina Lattice furrowed, *Welsh-pot Shell,.. Like our Garden Snail, but Lattice-furrowed and waved with yellow, like our Welsh Pot-ware. **1890** O. CRAWFURD *Round Calend. in Portugal* 212 The scent of those deep, damp lanes, green with ferns, which in this county [Monmouthshire] we call '*Welsh roads'. **1910** *Encycl. Brit.* VIII. 375/2 [Dogs.] *Sporting*... spaniel.. *Welsh springer. **1848** RICKMAN *Styles Archit. Eng.* p. liii, This [roof] is distinguished from the previous examples by having what are called *Welsh vaults over the clerestory windows. **1835** R. WILLIS *Archit. Mid. Ages* vii. 78 *note*, Such cells are termed *Welsh vaulting cells. **1858** *Ecclesiologist* XIX. 165 North transept, Welsh vaulting from circular shafts. **1954** G. DANIEL *Welcome Death* x. 125 'The Vale of Glamorgan is legally Wales, isn't it, although no one speaks any Welsh here?' 'Quite right... This is Wales, if not *Welsh Wales'. **1971** D. AYERST *Guardian* xxi. 290 In the hills behind the coastal resorts, Welsh Wales with its roots in the chapels had an intense cultural life of its own. **1983** A. BEEVOR *Faustian Pact.* i. 8 The sight of the sheep-cropped hills... There was Welsh Wales. **1842** J. WILSON *Chr. North* (1857) I. 2 Uncle Ben.. is seen galloping, in a *Welsh wig and strange apparel, in the rear of a pack of Lilliputian beagles. **1848** DICKENS *Dombey* iv, His Welsh wig.. was as plain and stubborn a Welsh wig as ever was worn. **1859** SALA *Gaslight & D.* xi. 129 Disguised in lamp-black, pomatum, Welsh wigs dyed black. **1917** M. MACDONAGH *Diary* 9 July in *London during Gt. War.* (1935) III. iv. 203 Is not 'L.G.' known as the '*Welsh Wizard'. **1922** *National Rev.* July 652 We are told.. that several of His Majesty's Ministers are acutely uncomfortable in the impasse into which they have allowed themselves to be manœuvred by the Welsh Wizard. **1976** W. J. BURLEY *Wycliffe & Schoolgirls* vii. 126 There had never been a real statesman since the little Welsh wizard.

3. As the designation of the language of the Welsh people; hence, written or spoken in the Welsh language; of or belonging to the language or literature of Wales.

1547 SALESBURY *Dict. Engl.-Welsh* Ded., Seyng ther is many of your graces subiectes in Wales that readethe parfytlye the welshe tonge.. I haue written a lytle englyshe dyctionary with the welshe interpretation. **1587** PENRY *Æquity Supplic.* 48 Vngodly welsh bookes are fraught with these Idolatries. *c* **1643** LD. HERBERT *Autobiog.* (1824) 32 Where I might learn the Welch tongue. **1682** W. RICHARDS *Wallogr.* 121 One in our Company.. having got a Welch Polysyllable into his Throat, was almost choak'd with Consonants. **1729** T. INNES *Crit. Ess.* (1879) 257 Mr. Edward Lhuyd, in his Welsh preface to his *Archæologia*. **1756–9** A. BUTLER *Lives Fathers, Beuno* (1821) IV. 226 Vawr, as the Welsh adjective Mawr great, is writ in several parts of Wales. *Ibid.*, *Wenefride* XI. 75 Lluydh, in his catalogue of Welch manuscripts. **1840** W. J. REES (*title-p.*) The Liber Landavensis... Published for The Welsh MSS. Society. **1877** RHYS (*title*) Lectures on Welsh Philology. **1888** JACOBI *Printers' Vocab.*, *Welsh cases*, cases of special lay for composing works in that language.

B. *sb.* (Elliptical uses of the adj.)

1. a. *pl.* The Britons as distinguished from the Anglo-Saxons. *Obs.* exc. *Hist.*

c **1100** *O.E. Chron.* (MS. D.) an. 1050 On þam ilcan ȝeare comon upp on Wylisce Axa of Yrlande. *a* **1122** *Ibid.* (Laud MS.) an. 1121 þa Wyliscean him onȝean coman. *c* **1205** LAY. 5574 Bruttes & Wailsce [*c* **1275** Walse]. *c* **1297** R. GLOUC. (Rolls) 9392 Of the welsse þat mid him beþ ne dorre ȝe noȝt drede. **1729** T. INNES *Crit. Ess.* (1879) 40 The old Midland Britains.. known.. by the name of Walenses (Welch, a common name to all that spoke the British language). **1839** KEIGHTLEY *Hist. Eng.* I. 14 The Britons or Welsh, as they were named by the conquerors, were thus driven back to the western side of the island.

b. The inhabitants or natives of Wales.

1338 R. BRUNNE *Chron.* (1725) 237 þe Walssh wer alle day slayn. **1530** TINDALE *Answ. More* II. xi. Wks. (1573) 299 Then he bringeth in how the wilde Irish and the Welch pray, when they go to steale. **1596** SPENSER *State Irel.* (Globe) 635/2 The same was also common amongest the Brittons, and is not yet altogither left of by the Welsh which are theyr posteritye. **1610** HOLLAND *Camden's Brit.* I. 652 These are distinctly knowen still from the Welsh, both by their speech and manners. **1612** SELDEN *Illustr. Drayton's Poly-olb.* ix. 320 So that the Welsh may challenge priority, of finding that new world, before the Spaniard. **1797** *Encycl. Brit.* (ed. 3) XVIII. 699/1 The Welsh, in their own language, call their country *Cymry*, and their language *Cymraeg*. **1825** SCOTT *Betrothed* viii, Two very strong bodies of Welsh attempted to carry the outer defences of the castle by storm. **1862** BORROW *Wales* lviii, Amongst the proverbial sayings of the Welsh, which are chiefly preserved in the shape of triads, is [etc.]. **1882** RHYS *Celtic Britain* 130 The more legendary traditions of the Welsh.

†c. *sing.* A Welshman. *Obs.*

1362 LANGL. *P. Pl.* A. v. 167 Godfrei of Garlesschire and Griffin þe walsche. **1387** TREVISA *Higden* VIII. 265 þe false Walsche David roos aȝenst kyng Edward in Palme Sonday. [**1601** F. TATE *Househ. Ord. Edw. II* §91 (1876) 55 Annote the walsh.] **1646** R. BAILLIE *Anabaptism* (1647) Epist. *4 At Naisby.. to beat nine thousand.. soldiers, the most part raw and new levied Welshes.

2. a. The Welsh language.

O.E. Chron. (Laud MS.) Pref., Her sind on þis iȝlande fif ȝeþeode: Englisc, & Brittisc, & Wilsc [*MS. D.* Bryt-wylsc], & Scyttisc [etc.]. ? *a* **1400** *Arthur* 7 Pendragon ys in walysch 'Dragones heed' on Englysch. **1470–85** CAXTON *Malory's Arthur* Pref. (Sommer) 3 Many noble volumes be made of hym.. which been not had in our maternal tongue, but in walsshe ben many & also in frensshe, & somme in englysshe. **1547** W. SALESBURY (*title*) A Dictionary in Englyshe and Welshe. *a* **1550** LELAND *Itin.* v. (1908) II. 82 It [Shrewsbury] is comonly caullyd now in Walche Moythik. Writers in Walsche caul it Penguern, *id est, caput Alneti.* **1596** SHAKS. *1 Hen. IV*, III. i. 193 My Wife can speake no English; I no Welsh. **1656** J. LEWIS in *Baxter's Certainty Worlds Spirits* (1691) 130 He could perceive the whisper of a Voice in Welch, bidding him hold his peace. **1668** SHADWELL *Sullen Lovers* IV. 74 If I don't..speak Spanish, Italian,..Welch and Irish. **1788** PRIESTLEY *Lect. Hist.* IV. xxv. 191 The next remains of the Britons, are Hoel Dha's Laws.. Of these there are several copies, both in Welch and Latin. **1820** SCOTT *Let. to C. Scott* 19 Dec. in *Lockhart*, You hear the Welsh spoken much about you. **1862** BORROW *Wales* lix, I learned to read Welsh and to write it at the same time. **1882** RHYS *Celtic Britain* 145 The latter [*sc.* Clyde], being..Clut in old Welsh, could only yield Clûd in later Welsh.

b. *transf.* A strange language; speech that one does not understand.

1648 WINYARD *Midsummer-Moon* 5 Hebrew to them is Welch. *a* **1661** FULLER *Worthies, Wales* (1662) 33 Amelcorne. This English Word (which I find in the English Cambden) is Welsh to me. **1888** *Sheffield Gloss.* Suppl. s.v. *Welsh*, 'He's talking Welsh!' 'That's Welsh!' means 'I don't understand you'.

3. Short for: Welsh coal.

1898 KIPLING *Fleet in Being* iv. 44 We're supposed to be burning No. 2 Welsh. **1905** *Blackw. Mag.* Jan. 26/2 Have you got that 'Welsh' trimmed?

C. Comb.: ***Welsh-begotten, -born, -English, -like, -rooted, -speaking, -wrought*** adjs.; **Welsh-Briton** = WELSHMAN 1 a; **Welsh-Keltic** *a.*, Cymric.

1615 J. STEPHENS *Satyr. Ess.* 291 He is the onely friend of Lawyers (if they be *Welch begotten). **1898** WATTS-DUNTON *Aylwin* XV. xii, I wonder whether any one who is not *Welsh-born can understand my delight. **1670** MILTON *Hist. Brit.* IV. 165 Kentwin the other West-Saxon King.. chac'd the *Welch-Britans..to the very Seashoar. **1759** T. RICHARDS (*title*) Antiquæ Linguæ Britannicæ Thesaurus: being a British, or *Welsh-English Dictionary. **1883** D. H. WHEELER *By-Ways Lit.* 100 It is believed that the *Welsh-Keltic manuscripts are unusually vicious in the texts. **1844** *Brereton's Trav.* (Chetham Soc.) 96 *note*, Of this *Welch-like name [Apthomas] I am unable to offer any explanation. **1863** W. BARNES *Dorset Gloss.* 8 Their *cadwyn* ..is a *Welsh-rooted word. **1893** *Harper's Mag.* Dec. 43/1 A *Welsh-speaking rebel against the tithes. **1876** MORRIS *Sigurd* III. 202 And they see the sheathed Wrath shimmer mid the restless *Welsh-wrought [= foreign] swords.

welsh (wɛlʃ), *v.* Also welch. [Of obscure origin.]

1. *trans.* To swindle (a person) out of money laid as a bet (see WELSHER[1]). Hence **welshing** *vbl. sb.* and *ppl. a. Racing.*

1857 *Morn. Chron.* 8 June 8/3 He got his living by 'welching' and taking in the 'flats'. **1867** *Sporting Life* 21 Sept., Money which people have been 'welshed' out of. **1868** *Morn. Star* 26 Mar., Some two or three of the prolific 'welshing' fraternity did manage to carry on their nefarious operations. **1887** *Daily Tel.* 12 Mar. 5/2 He will receive his winnings and run no risk of being 'welshed'. **1894** HENTY *Dorothy's Double* I. 57 He..had a narrow escape of being lynched by the crowd for welshing. **1902** *Times* 8 Mar. 14/3 In France..betting..had increased..because people were not now afraid of being welshed.

2. *intr.* Const. *on.* To fail to carry out one's promise to (a person); to fail to keep (an obligation).

1932 H. CRANE *Let.* ? Jan. (1965) 395, I really can't welsh on Eyler Simpson (who is equally responsible, since he signed the lease with me). **1971** H. WOUK *Winds of War* i. 4 The real shadow on this couple was that Commander Henry thought Rhoda had welshed on their courtship understanding. **1974** *Socialist Worker* 2 Nov. 5/1 When the brothers were captured on a bank raid, the British government welched on them, dropped them like a hot penny. **1978** *Lancashire Life* Apr. 73/4 Very few people welsh on paying their taxi fare. **1982** T. KENEALLY *Schindler's Ark* v. 72 Across his desk..had crossed copies of angry SS memoranda addressed to army officials and complaining that the army was welching on its arrangement.

†**Welsh bean.** *Obs.* Also 6 Welch. [ad. G. *welsche bohne*: see WELSH *a.* and BEAN *sb.*] The French or kidney bean (*Phaseolus vulgaris*).

1585 HIGINS *Junius' Nomencl.* 110/1 *Phaseolus, dolichus*,.. Welch beanes: beanes of Rome, or kidney beanes. **1598** FLORIO, *Faglioli, Fagiuoli*, a kind of pease like vnto a beane, called faseoles, french peason, welsh beanes, or kidney beanes.

†**Welsh bill.** *Obs.* In 5 Walshe, Wallish, Wallych, 7 Welch bill. [f. WELSH *a.* + BILL *sb.*[1] 4.] = WELSH HOOK.

1475 *Maldon* (Essex) *Court-Rolls* Bundle 49, No. 8 Insultum fecit..cum 1 Walshe byll, precii xx*d.* **1484** *Mem. Ripon* (Surtees) I. 310 Cum quodam Wallishbyll..in capite percussit. [Cf. *ibid.* 311 Cum quodam le Forest byll.] **1485** in *Sanctuarium Dunelm. & Beverlacense* (Surtees) 13 Jacobus Manfeeld..insultum fecit, et eundem in corpore cum uno le wallych byll felonice percussit. *a* **1625** FLETCHER *Nice Valour* IV. i, *Lapet.* Did not I say, this Whirrit, and this Bob, Should be both Pica Roman. *Clown.* So said I, Sir, both Picked Romans, And he has made 'em Welch Bills.

welsher[1] ('wɛlʃə(r)). Also †welcher. [Cf. WELSH *v.*] A bookmaker at a race-meeting, who takes money for a bet, and absconds or refuses to pay if he loses.

1860 LD. W. LENNOX *Pict. Sporting Life* I. 119 A gang of miscreants called Welchers, who make bets with the unwary, which they never dream of paying if they lose. **1868** E. YATES *Rocks Ahead* III. v, I know him, a defaulting ring-man, a mere common welsher. **1912** *Times* 24 Apr. 3/4 Counsel said..the real definite charge was that the plaintiff was a welsher.

transf. **1863** MISS BRADDON *Aurora Floyd* xvii, He was.. a 'welsher' in the matter of marbles and hardbake before his fifth birthday. **1904** SLADEN *Playing the Game* II. iii, The Japanese traders who dealt with them were, many of them, welshers who looked to repudiations for their profits.

'**Welsher**[2]. *nonce-wd.* [f. WELSH *a.* + -ER[1].] A Welshman.

1862 BORROW *Wales* I. v. 47 [A waggoner *loq.*] They are small men mostly, Measter, them Welshers.

Welsh harp. [WELSH *a.*] A name specifically applied to the triple-strung harp; also called ***Welsh triple harp.***

a **1637** B. JONSON *Masque, For Honour of Wales* Wks. (1641) 33 Yow s'all heare the true Pritan straines now, the ancient Welse Harpe. *a* **1700** EVELYN *Diary* 13 June 1649, With him was one Carew, who play'd incomparably on the Welsh Harp. **1753** *Scots Mag.* May 215/1 A Welch-harp. **1876** STAINER & BARRETT *Dict. Mus. Terms* s.v. *Harp*, The triple or Welsh harp, with three rows of strings, two rows tuned diatonically in unisons or octaves, the third or inner row arranged to supply the accidentals, sharps or flats. **1880** *Encycl. Brit.* XI. 489/2 The comparatively modern Welsh triple harp is always strung with gut. **1889** GROVE *Dict. Mus.* IV. 443 Welsh Triple Harp.

†**Welsh hook.** *Obs.* [WELSH *a.*] A billhook; a weapon of this form. Cf. WELSH BILL.

a **1593** MARLOWE *Edw. II*, IV. vi, [2nd Stage dir.] Enter with Welch hookes, Rice ap Howell, a Mower, and the Earle of Leicester. **1596** SHAKS. *1 Hen. IV*, II. iv. 372 Hee of Wales, that..swore the Deuill his true Liege-man vpon the Crosse of a Welch-hooke. **1599** G. SILVER *Paradoxes Def.* 31 The Welch hooke or Forrest bill, hath aduantage against all maner of weapons whatsoeuer. **1611** COTGR., *Riveran*,..a Welsh hooke, or hedging bill made with a hooke at the end. **1617** J. SWETNAM *Sch. Sci. Defence* 143 When you encounter with any man that hath a Staffe, a Welch-hooke, or a Halbert. **1618** J. TAYLOR (Water P.) *Penniless Pilgr.* B 4 b, A Watch-mans bill, or a Welch-hooke falles not halfe so heauy vpon a man. *a* **1637** B. JONSON *Masque, For Honour of Wales* Wks. (1641) 33 Owen Glendower, with a Welse hooke, and a Goats skinne on his backe. **1694** MOTTEUX *Rabelais* V. vii. 25 Their Claws..grow as crooked as a Welch Hook, or a Hedging Bill.

Welshie, var. WELSHY *sb.*

'**Welshify**, *v. nonce-wd.* [f. WELSH *a.* + -FY.] *trans.* To give a Welsh form to (a word).

1889 GRETTON *Memory's Harkback* 320 Are we to account for this, and so many other traces of Latin words Welshified, by the Roman occupation of the country?

'**Welshly**, *adv. nonce-wd.* [-LY[2].] In a Welsh manner.

The allusion is probably to the proverbially long Welsh mile (see WELSH *a.* 2 d).

1629 BP. FIELD in *St. Papers Dom.* Chas. I, CL. 110 A sooner journey willbe very cumbersome & jeopardous in regard of wayes, now deepe and dangerous, at all times steepe, craggy, and welshly tædious.

Welshman ('wɛlʃmən). Forms: see WELSH (also 4 Welss-, Weliss-, 6 Wealch, Welsch; 4 Walss-, Walis-, Walesch, 5 Wallissh-, 6 Walls-), and MAN *sb.* [f. WELSH *a.* + MAN *sb.*]

1. †**a.** A native Briton. *Obs.* **b.** A native of Wales.

In the early examples the adj. and noun are still separate words.

α. **688-95** *Laws Ine* § 32 Ʒif Wilisc mon hæbbe hide londes, his wer bið cxx scill. *c* **1000** *Ags. Laws, Dunsetas* § 6 Nah naðer to farenne ne Wilisc man on Ænglisc land ne Ænglisc on Wylisc ðe ma, butan gesettan landmen. *c* **1100** *O.E. Chron.* (MS. C) an. 1053 Eac Wylsce menn ʒeslogan mycelne dæl Englisces folces.

β. c **1205** LAY. 2120 Þat Cambrie wes ihaten þat is þat wilde lond þat Welsce [*c* 1275 Walse] men luuieð. **1297** R. GLOUC. (Rolls) 5140 Here we englisse men mowe yse some, Mid woche riȝte we beþ to þis lond ycome; Ac þe wrecche welissemen beþ of þe olde more. **1513** *Life Hen. V* (1911) 9 Manie Welshmen, and..the greater parte of all Wales, were confederate wth these rebbells. **1579** FULKE *Refut. Rastel* 764 The Welshmen that vnderstand not english, haue their common praier in their Welshe tongue. **1594** SHAKS. *Rich. III*, IV. iv. 477 You cannot guesse wherefore the Welchman comes. **1598** BASTARD *Chrestol.* III. xxxiii. 72 A Wealch and English man meete on the way. **1607** DEKKER & WEBSTER *Northw. Hoe* I. B 4, The Northerne man loues white-meates, ..the Welshman Leekes and Cheese. **1663-4** PEPYS *Diary* 22 Feb., The Duke of Monmouth's mother's brother.. being a Welchman. **1781** GIBBON *Decl. & F.* xxxviii. (1787) III. 625 *note*, The malicious Welshman [= Giraldus Cambrensis] insinuates, that [etc.]. **1851** MAYHEW *Lond. Labour* II. 250/2 The men..are about three-fifths Irishmen, a fifth Welchmen,..and the remainder Englishmen. **1882** RHYS *Celtic Britain* 145 The northern portion..is spoken of in the Saxon Chronicle as that of the Strathclyde Welshmen.

γ. c **1205** LAY. 2124 For þan duke Gualun Wælsce [*c* 1275 Walse] men me heom hateð. **1338** R. BRUNNE *Chron.* (1725) 35 Edgar..went to Kerlion, þe Walsch men he band With homage & feaute. **1387** TREVISA *Higden* II. 35 In Seint Edward his tyme Walsche men schulde not passe þat diche wiþ wepoun vppon a grete payne. *c* **1420** *Chron. Vilod.* 93 He commandede..alle þe Britones..To ben y-cleped Wallisshemen. *Ibid.* 96 Saxsones clepud hom..Walshemen. **1473** WARKW. *Chron.* (Camden) 6 Ther was the Erle of Pembroke takene..and two M^l^. Walschmenne slayne. **1513** BRADSHAW *St. Werburge* II. 510 Whiche kynge expulsed.. All brutes and walshemen clere out of his londe. **1565** STAPLETON *Fortr. Faith* 132 b, Inhabited by the olde Britons and walsh men.

2. *U.S.* A name applied locally to the black bass (*Micropterus*) and other fishes.

1714 J. LAWSON *Hist. Carolina* 159 The brown Pearch, which some call Welch-men, are the largest sort of Pearches that we have. **1884** *Century Mag.* Apr. 908/1 A black bass.. becomes..a 'welshman' in North Carolina. **1888** GOODE *Amer. Fishes* 55 On the Tar River of North Carolina, it [the Black Bass] is called 'Chubb', and on the Neuse, 'Welshman'.

3. Possessive combinations. **Welshman's button** = *hazel-fly* HAZEL[1] 4 c. †**Welshman's hose**, in phrases like ***to make a Welshman's hose of, to make like a Welshman's hose***, to stretch or wrest the meaning of (a word, sentence, etc.); cf. *shipman's hose* SHIPMAN 3 b. **Welshman's hug** (see quot.)

1787 BEST *Angling* (ed. 2) 117 The *Welchman's Button or Hasle comes on about the latter end of July. **1880** F. FRANCIS *Angling* vi. (ed. 5) 230 The Welshman's Button; where it is found, it is a capital fly. **1523** SKELTON *Garl. Laurel* 1239 And after conueyauns as the world goos, It is no foly to vse the *Walshemannys hoos. *a* **1529** —— *Col. Cloute* 780 A thousand thousande other, That.. make a Walshmans hose Of the texte and of the glose. **1559** *Mirr. Mag., Robt. Tresilian* xi, And wurds that wer most plaine whan thei by vs wer skande, We turned by construction lyke a welch-mans hose. **1583** *Leg. Bp. St. Androis* 737 Of omnigatherine now his glose: He maid it lyk a Wealchman hose: *Tempora mutantur* was his text. **1886** *W. Somerset Word-bk., Scotch-Fiddle.* 2. The itch, more commonly called the *Welshman's hug.

Welshness ('wɛlʃnɪs). [f. WELSH *a.* + -NESS.] Welsh character.

1682 W. RICHARDS *Wallogr.* 82 The shabbiness of their Bodies and the Baoticalness [? = Boeotian dullness] of their Souls, and that, which cannot any otherwise be exprest, the Welchness of both. **1797** T. TWINING in *Recreat. & Stud.* (1882) 203, I was much amused with the extreme Welshness of the good lady. **1894** *Athenæum* 22 Dec. 866/3 Prof. Rhys ..is not backward in recognizing what may be called the Welshness of the whole body of histories concerned with the 'blameless king' and his knights of the Round Table. **1912** AMELIA H. STIRLING *Life J. H. Stirling* iv. 68 In spite of the strangeness, the *Welshness*, of Pontypool, Stirling had been disappointed to find that it was not *in* Wales.

Welsh rabbit. [WELSH *a.* + RABBIT *sb.*[1] Cf. *Scotch rabbit* SCOTCH *a.* 4, and, for the jocular use of the noun, CAPON *sb.* 3.] A dish consisting of cheese and a little butter melted and mixed together, to which are added ale, cayenne pepper, and salt, the whole being stirred until it is creamy, and then poured over buttered toast: also, simply, slices of toasted cheese laid on toast.

1725 J. BYROM *Rem.* (1854) I. I. 108, I did not eat of the cold beef, but of Welsh rabbit and stewed cheese. *Ibid.* 109, I had a scollop shell and Welsh rabbit. **1747** MRS. GLASSE *Cookery* ix. 97 To make a Welch-Rabbit. Toast the Bread on both Sides, then toast the Cheese on one Side, and lay it on the Toast, and with a hot Iron brown the other Side. **1771** in Mme. D'Arblay *Early Diary* (1889) I. 130 When we meet to browse over a pot of Castalian Porter and a Welsh Rabbit. **1825** SCOTT 12 Oct. in *Fam. Lett.* (1894) II. xxiii. 354 A welch rabbit and a tankard of ale. **1854** THACKERAY *Newcomes* i, A desire for welsh-rabbits and good old glee-singing led us to the Cave of Harmony. **1876** FR. E. TROLLOPE *Charming Fellow* II. xi. 164 She had..prepared a welsh rabbit..for a little party of friends.

Welsh rarebit. [An etymologizing alteration of prec. There is no evidence of the independent use of *rarebit.*] = prec.

1785 GROSE *Dict. Vulgar T.*, *Rabbit*, a Welch rabbit, bread and cheese toasted, i.e. a Welch rare bit. **1845** ALB. SMITH *Fort. Scatterg. Fam.* xliii, One of those inextricable visions which are alone dependent upon love, or Welsh rare-bits, for their origin. **1865** *Morn. Star* 10 Apr., Then you advance to steaks,..thence to marrow-bones, thence to Welsh rarebit. **1905** H. G. WELLS *Kipps* I. vi. § 6 He had also eaten two Welsh rarebits—an unusual supper.

Welshry ('wɛlʃrɪ). Also 4 Walschrie; 7 Welshrye, 9 Welshery. [f. WELSH *a.* + -RY, or ad. med.L. *Walescheria* (1249).]

†**1.** Welshmen or Welsh people collectively. *Obs.*

1338 R. BRUNNE *Chron.* (1810) II. 244 After þam alle he sent, To fend þe Walschrie with him at þer powere.

2. That part of a town or county (inhabited by English and Welsh) which is appropriated to the Celtic population, as distinguished from the ENGLISHRY.

1603 G. OWEN *Pembrokeshire* iv. (1891) 38 This Shere is taken to be devided into two partes, that is to the Englishrie, and Welshrye as shall be more lardglie declared hereafter. **1804** J. EVANS *Tour S. Wales* 256 This country [in Pembrokeshire] is still divided into what is called the Englishry and Welshery; the latter, containing the original inhabitants. **1862** BORROW *Wales* II. xxx. 347, 'I have no Welsh, sir,' said she. 'How is that?' said I; 'this village is I think in the Welshery'. **1867** FREEMAN *Norm. Conq.* I. v. 338 Up to the time of Æthelstan Exeter had remained..a common possession of Teutonic and Celtic inhabitants. No doubt there was an English and a Welsh town, an Englishry and a Welshry.

3. Welsh origin or nationality.

1894 GRANT ALLEN in *Westm. Gaz.* 21 Sept. 2/1 Sometimes..I have even known them indignantly deny the imputation of Welshry.

Welshwoman (ˈwɛlʃˌwʊmən). Also **Welsh woman.** [f. WELSH *a.* + WOMAN *sb.*] A woman of Welsh nationality.

1442 *Rolls Parlt.* V. 45/1 So that the saide William to a Walsshwoman in no wise marie him. **1586** J. HOOKER *Girald. Irel.* in *Holinshed* II. 24/2 There came vnto him a Welsh or a Camber woman. **1656** S. HOLLAND *Zara* II. v. 112 Thy Mother sure was some Welsh woman, who instead of her own fostered thee with Mares Milk. **1801** MAR. EDGEWORTH *Moral T., Angelina* iii, Bartrand,—you have no ears, Welshwoman as you are! **1964** C. MACKENZIE *My Life & Times* III. 282 Nurse Williams..was a plump little Welshwoman from Rhyl.

Welshy (ˈwɛlʃɪ), *a. rare.* In 8 **Welchy.** [f. WELSH *a.* and *sb.* + -Y[1].] Resembling that of Wales or its inhabitants; Welsh-like.

1794 MRS. A. M. BENNETT *Ellen* II. 210 [Her name, Winifred] had such a welchy vulgar sound, she chose to be called Maria. **1848** *Bentley's Misc.* Jan. 106 Then we get towards a wild and Welshy country.

Welshy (ˈwɛlʃɪ), *sb. slang.* Also **Welshie.** [f. WELSH *a.* and *sb.* + -Y[6].] A Welshman or Welshwoman.

1951 E. COXHEAD *One Green Bottle* ii. 46 You'd think I was a Welshy by my name, Gwen Evans, but I'm a proper Cockney. **1978** E. MALPASS *Wind brings up Rain* ii. 23 Alice was still staring at her unblinking. 'You deep little Welshie', she said.

welsom(e, -sum: see WEALSOME, WILSOME *a.*[1]

welt (wɛlt), *sb.*[1] Forms: α. 5 **walt,** 6 **walte;** *Sc.* 6 **wat,** 6, 9 **waut,** 9 **waat;** *north. dial.* 9 **wolt, wote, woat, waut.** β. 5–6 **weltte, welte,** 6 **wealte,** 6– **welt.** [Of obscure origin; the variation in the vowel suggests an OE. **wealt*, with Anglian variant **walt*.]

1. *Shoemaking.* A strip of leather placed between and sewn to the edge of the sole and the turned-in edge of the upper in soling a boot or shoe.

α. **14..** *Garlande's Dict.* in Wright *Voc.* (1857) 125 *Pictaciarii* (clowtars) *viles sunt, qui consuunt sotulares veteres, renovandopictacia* (clowtys), *et intercucia* (waltys), *et soleas, et inpedeas.* **1500** *Ortus Vocab., Intercutium,* anglice a walte of a shoghe. **1508** DUNBAR *Flyting* 213 Stra wispis hingis owt [of thy boots], quhair that the wattis [*v.r.* waltis] ar worne. **1899** *Leeds Merc. Suppl.* 14 Oct. (E.D.D.) If tha doesn't mind, tha'll court thisen off o' t' walts.

β. *c* **1425** *Voc.* in Wr.-Wülcker 664/35 *Hoc intercucium,* weltte. *c* **1440** *Promp. Parv.* 521/1 Welte, of a schoo, *incucium, vel intercucium.* **1483** *Cath. Angl.* 414/1 A Welte, *intercucium.* **1530** PALSGR. 287/2 Welte of a shoe, *oureleure.* **1737** DYCHE & PARDON *Dict., Welt,* that Slip of Leather, or Part of a Shoe that joins and holds the Sole and upper Leather together. **1880** *Times* 21 Sept. 4/4 To attach a narrow strip of flexible stout leather (the welt) to the outer edge of the upper, and the two to the insole. **1895** *Boot Mending & Making* (ed. P. N. Hasluck) vi. 95 Whether the work is to be..left plain, which is called a 'blind-welt', or the stitch sunk, and the welt fudged to imitate stitching.

2. a. A narrow strip of material put on the edge of a garment, etc., as a border, binding, or hem; a frill, fringe, or trimming.

Frequently associated with GUARD (*sb.* 11).

α. **1506** *Acc. Ld. High Treas. Scot.* III. 115 Item, for ane waut of Rislis broun to it [a kirtle], iij s. **1804** W. TARRAS *Poems* 38 Gin onie chiel had coolie scaw't, Sic's groogl't crown, or raggit waut, Wad we na jeer't.

β. **1530** PALSGR. 287/2 Welt of a garment, *ourelet.* **1547** in Feuillerat *Revels Edw. VI* (1914) 9 One half having a border of black Letters & thother half having ij Rounde welttes of black vellett. **1582** BRETON *Flourish Fancy* etc. (Grosart) 15/1 Wherof good stoare of cloathe..in fashions may be spent: In gardes, in weltes, and iagges. **1611** SPEED *Hist. Gt. Brit.* VII. iv. §3. 202 Their Cassockes were..of linnen, trimmed and set out with very broad Gards or Welts. **1698** FRYER *Acc. E. India & P.* 355 A Scarlet Cloak, edg'd with a Welt, Was thrown him o're. **1748** *Earthquake Peru* i. 63 Their Habit is grey, with a purple Welt. **1820** SCOTT *Monast.* xxix, The unction with which he dilated upon welts, laces, slashes, and trimmings. **1831** CARLYLE *Sartor Res.* I. vii, Welts, a handbreadth thick,..waver round them by way of hem. **1894** J. DAVIDSON *Ballads & Songs* 113 Maid Marian's kirtle, somewhat old, A welt of red must now enhance. **1903** *Times* 8 Sept. 10/4 Very particular attention is devoted..to the welts on the undress overalls. Some Fusilier battalions substitute a narrow stripe stitched on in place of the orthodox welt.

fig. *a* **1637** B. JONSON *Discov.* (1641) 91 There are certaine *Scioli*..that are busie in the skirts..of Learning... They may have some edging, or trimming of a Scholler, a welt, or so: but it is no more.

†**b.** Phrase. ***without welt or guard***: without ornamentation or trimming. *Obs.*

1592 GREENE *Upst. Courtier* B 3 b, I saw they were a plaine payre of Cloth breeches, without eyther welt or garde. **1631** JORDAN *Nat. Bathes* Ded. (1669) 4 A plain sute of our Country Cloath; without welt or gard. **1679** *Hist. Jetzer* 36 He was cloath'd in a close Coat of coarse cloth, without welt or guard.

†**c.** *fig.* (Also ***without welt or cover.***)

c **1590** GREENE *Fr. Bacon* 2140 Marke you maisters, heers a plaine honest man, without welt or garde. **1594–1692** [see GUARD *sb.* 11 b]. **1603** HARSNET *Popish Impost.* 167 Loe heere ..plaine Gentilisme, without welt or couer. *a* **1734** NORTH *Examen* I. i. §7 (1740) 18 And of these irrefragable Authorities some he affords great Encomiums to, others pass without Welt or Guard.

d. Used by R. Holme (and hence by later compilers) as a heraldic term, in contrast to *border.*

1688 HOLME *Armoury* I. 31 An edg, or hem, or welt, only runs on the sides of the Ordinary; but the Border..goeth clear round the same. *c* **1828** BERRY *Encycl. Her.* I. Gloss., *Welt,* or *Edge,* a narrow kind of border to an ordinary, or charge, sometimes improperly called a fimbriation, but the cross..should have the fimbriation run all round it,..which the *welt* or *edge,* does not. [Hence in OGILVIE (1850) and in later Dicts.]

†**3.** A binding strip or band. *Obs.*

In quot. 1607 perhaps an error for 'netts'.

1607 TOPSELL *Four-f. Beasts* 215 Hauing found out the field or hill where the beasts are lodged, they compasse it.. with welts and toils inuented for that purpose. **1693** EVELYN *De la Quint. Compl. Gard.* I. III. xxi. 183 The Edges [of the baskets] both above and below [must] be so well wrought as not to unravel; There must be also a Welt round about the middle for the same reason. **1698** FROGER *Voy.* 133 Their Privy-parts, which they cover with a little Cotton-welt [Fr. *ceinture de coton*], that hangs down by their Legs.

4. a. A narrow ridge, a raised stripe. *Obs.*

1599 NASHE *Lenten Stuffe* 5 Their hauen..hauing but as it were a welte of land..betwixte it and the wide Maine. **1614** SYLVESTER *Bethulia's Rescue* IV. 375 Her muskie Mouth..A swelling Welt of Corall round behems, Which smiling shows two rows of orient Gems. **1614** MARKHAM *Cheap & Good Husb.* II. Of Hawks i. 137 And these Stones if they be full of crests and welts, they are the better. *a* **1682** SIR T. BROWNE *Tracts* I. (1683) 78 The Trunk or Body thereof [of the palm tree] is naturally contrived for ascension,..having many welts and eminencies. **1694** MOTTEUX tr. *Rabelais* V. xxiii. 107 Their dainty Chops and Gullets were lin'd through with Crimsin Satin with little Welts, and Gold Purls.

b. spec. in *Nat. Hist.* Now *rare.*

1578 LYTE *Dodoens* II. xxxv. 192 Of Floure Deluce or Iris. .. In the leaues [of the flower] that hang downewardes, there are certaine rough or hearie weltes lyke vnto a mans browes. **1597** GERARDE *Herbal* I. xxxv. §5. 50 Flowers of a purple or violet colour,..with a white hairie welt downe the middle. **1658** ROWLAND tr. *Moufet's Theat. Ins.* xiv. 958 Upon the shoulders [of the butterfly] there is a kinde of sandy dusky coloured roll or welt. **1698** FROGER *Voy.* 131 The Toucan,..whose bill is..all over nothing but black and white welts or streaks, like Ebony and Ivory interlaid. **1707** SLOANE *Jamaica* I. 94 On the upper margin of them, in a ferrugineous welt, lies the seed. **1713** PETIVER in *Phil. Trans.* XXVIII. 208 Its Leaves generally single,..with a large forked welt which saddles the Stalk. **1892** A. A. CROZIER *Dict. Bot. Terms, Welt,* a broad, raised stripe or ridge upon the surface of a fruit, as is occasionally seen in the orange and lemon.

c. A ridge on the flesh, esp. the mark of a healed wound; a seam.

1800 *Phil. Trans.* XCI. 8 The cicatrix formed a hard welt, tender to the touch. **1842** LOVER *Handy Andy* iv, From shoulder to flank, sir, I am one mass of welts and weals. **1876** *E. Wagner's Gen. Path.* 30 If the actual cautery be applied upon a corpse, there arise only..more or less hard or leathery welts. **1883** *Harper's Mag.* Mar. 534/1 The slight welt of a sabre cut on one cheek.

transf. and *fig.* **1882** G. F. PENTECOST *Out of Egypt* i. 12 Who can tell what the first hot and burning welt of pain was which followed the first stroke of passion's whip? **1892** KIPLING *Barrack-room Ballads* L'Envoi 53 O the blazing tropic night, when the wake's a welt of light.

5. Technical uses. **a.** A flange on a horse-shoe. **b.** *Saddle-making.* A narrow strip of leather stitched in between the skirts and the seat. **c.** *Glove-making.* (See quots.) **d.** *Knitting.* (See quots.) **e.** A strip or fillet laid over a seam or joint or placed in an angle to secure or strengthen it. **f.** The lap or fold of a welted joint (see WELTED *ppl. a.* 4). See also sense 1.

a. *c* **1770** T. FAIRFAX *Compl. Sportsm.* 21 [Horse] Shoes with swelling welts, or borders round about them, are used in Germany, &c. **1831** J. HOLLAND *Manuf. Metal* I. 171 Ordinary [horse] shoes..are either light flat disks,..or of much greater strength, with welts or knobs on the toes.

b. **1871** *Saddlers' Gaz.* 1 Nov. 10/1 The skirts being properly edged up, you will now make the welt and fix it to the skirt. **1904** *Saddlery* (ed. P. N. Hasluck) iii. 29 Place the thin hogskin welt along the upper edge of the seat and stitch the skirt and welt together... From the point to which the seat is stitched, a wider welt doubled like the narrow one must be stitched to the skirt.

c. **1883** S. W. BECK *Gloves* xii. 179 One minor..process, known as 'felling the slit-welt'—that is, the turning over and hemming of the welt on the edge of the opening of the gloves. **1886** *Chamb. Jrnl.* 10 Apr. 226/2 Out of the parts left he cuts pieces..for the binding round the top and the opening [of a glove]..which are called 'welts'.

d. **1869** *Lonsdale Gloss., Welt,* ribbed knitting. **1875** KNIGHT *Dict. Mech., Welt, (Knitting-machine)* a flap of work (as a heel-piece) disengaged laterally and knitted separately from the main body, and subsequently joined thereto by re-engagement of loops or by hand-knitting. **1879** *Shropsh. Word-bk.* s.v., The ribs of knitting at the top of a sock or stocking are called welts.

e. **1875** KNIGHT *Dict. Mech.* s.v. *Carvel-built,* The edges of the plates are brought flush together and riveted to a lap or welt in the rear. **1888** *Lockwood's Dict. Mech. Engin., Welt,* the covering strip used in butt riveting.

f. **1888** J. W. CLARKE *Plumbing Pract.* viii. 81 A mandrel must be fixed inside for the welt to be worked in quite closely.

6. A stroke with a lash or pliant stick; also, a heavy blow with the fist. (Cf. WELT *v.*[1] 5.)

1863 *Cornhill Mag.* VII. 453 There's thirteen of us to do the punishment, and we must have two welts a piece. **1900** A. MCILROY *By Lone Craig-Linnie Burn* v. 54 Every man claimed the right of bestowing a 'welt' on a restive horse with his ash 'plant' as he passed.

7. *attrib.* and *Comb.*, in the names of shoemakers' tools, appliances, and materials, as ***welt-beater, -cutter, file, -guide, -knife, -leather, -machine, -mill, shoulders*** (cf. SHOULDER *sb.* 5 b), ***-trimmer.*** **welt pocket,** a slot pocket having a welt on the lower edge that extends upward to cover the slit.

1812 *Sporting Mag.* XL. 14 Cobler's-wax and welt-leather. **1862** *Catal. Internat. Exhib.* Brit. II. No. 4671, Curried Welt Shoulders. **1875** KNIGHT *Dict. Mech.* 2760 Welt-cutter, -guide, -knife, -machine, -trimmer. **1895** *Boot Making* (ed. P. N. Hasluck) v. 83 If they are too thick, reduce them on the flesh side in a welt mill or skiving machine. *Ibid.* vii. 107 The welt file, used for smoothing the welt. **1897** C. T. DAVIS *Manuf. Leather* 637 To dress..welt leather and flexible splits. **1932** D. C. MINTER *Mod. Needlecraft* 134/1 Welt pocket... Mark opening with tack $4\frac{1}{2}$ inches long. Cut welt 5 inches long and width required. **1978** *Detroit Free Press* 5 Mar. A 16/2 (Advt.), Single-breasted styling with self-belt, epaulets, welt pockets.

†**welt,** *sb.*[2] *Obs. Cant.* (See RUM *a.*[1] 2 b.)

welt (wɛlt), *sb.*[3] *dial.* [Origin unknown.] The practice by which some members of a gang of dockers take an unauthorized break while the rest work, and so turn and turn about. Hence as *v. intr.*, to take a break thus; **'welting** *vbl. sb.*[3]

1964 *Guardian* 7 Dec. 4/1 It is 1.30 p.m...and the afternoon 'welt' is settling in. *Ibid.*, 'Welting'—the practice whereby part of a gang takes an unofficial break while the rest continues working—is firmly entrenched in Liverpool. **1965** *Wall St. Jrnl.* 13 Jan. 11 A visitor dropping into almost any waterfront cafe beside the forest of ship masts rising along the River Mersey in Liverpool will quickly discover one reason. He'll find stevedores 'welting' or enjoying their stout and porter at the bar on company time. Work crews allow members to 'welt' on a share-and-share alike basis. **1967** *Economist* 4 Nov. 490/1 Ending the welt would make possible higher basic rates of pay. **1977** *Guardian* 4 Sept. 2/2 In some docks..there is still tension because of managers' attempts..to crack down on the 'welt'.

welt (wɛlt), *v.*[1] Forms: α. 5 *Sc.* and *north.* **walte, waut,** 6 *Sc.* **walt, wawt, wate, vat.** β. 6 **welte, wealt,** 6– **welt.** [f. WELT *sb.*[1]]

1. *trans.* To furnish (shoes) with welts; to repair or renew the welts of.

α. **1483** *Cath. Angl.* 407/1 To Walte, *jntercuciare.* **1500** *Ortus Vocab., Intercutio,* to walte a schoghe.

β. **1729** P. WALKDEN *Diary* (1866) 49 Paid for welting and soling my shoes, 1s. 6d. **1854** G. BORROW in Shorter *B. & his Circle* xxxii. (1913) 374 My boots were worn up by the time I reached Swansea and was obliged to get them new soled and welted. **1914** *Daily News* 30 June 4, I cannot canonise the machine which stitches uppers and welts soles.

2. To border, hem, or ornament (a garment) with welts or strips of material. Also with *about.* Also *absol.* (Cf. WELTED *ppl. a.* 1 a.) Now *rare* or *Obs.*

α. **1489** *Acc. Ld. High Treas. Scot.* I. 162 Thre quartaris of veluus to waut hir gowne. **1541** *Ibid.* VIII. 22 For grene velvet to walt ane cote. **1546** *Ibid.* 438 Tua elnis..blak velvot..to walt the said goun and kirtill.

β. **1580** HOLLYBAND *Treas. Fr. Tong, Border & couvrir le bord,* to border, to welt. **1592** GREENE *Upst. Courtier* D 1 b, In making of veluet breeches, where there is required silke lace,..and such costly stuffe, to welt, gard, whip, stitch, edge, face, and draw out. **1755** JOHNSON, To *Welt,* to sew any thing with a border.

†**3.** ? To bind in strips. *Obs. rare.*

1613 PURCHAS *Pilgrimage* (1614) 412 If any be sicke, a speare is set vp in his Tent with blacke Felt welted about it.

4. Technical uses: **a.** To bind with strips or a strip of leather, spec. in *Glove-making* and *Carriage-building.*

1795 [see WELTING *vbl. sb.* 1 b]. **1862** MRS. H. WOOD *Mrs. Hallib.* I. xviii, Some welted, or hemmed the gloves round at the edge of the wrist.

b. *Plumbing.* To join (the ends of a pipe, etc.) by turning the edges one over the other and pressing them together. Cf. WELTED *ppl. a.* 4.

1888 J. W. CLARKE *Plumbing Pract.* viii. 81 At a sanitary exhibition..were exhibited some joints..made by welting the ends of the pipes together.

5. To beat, thrash.

1823 MOOR *Suffolk Words, Welt*...to beat severely—so as to raise wales or weals. **1837** HALIBURTON *Clockm.* Ser. II. xxii, And they gist fell to and welted him all the way into the town with the tip eend of their lassos. **1855** F. C. ARMSTRONG *Warhawk* I. xii. 248 I'll welt you with a rope's end if you don't mizzle. **1894** ASTLEY *50 Years Life* I. 105 My ribs ached as though they had been welted with a single-stick. **1901** E. PHILLPOTTS *Striking Hours* 12 Next time..I'll welt the hide off your bones.

welt, *v.*[2] *Obs.* exc. *dial.* Pa. t. 4–5 **welt(e.** [a. ON. **welta* intr. strong verb (Icel. and Norw. *velta,* MSw. *välta*), and trans. weak verb (Icel. and Norw. *velta,* MSw. and Sw. *välta,* Da. *vælte*); the latter corresponds to OE. *-wæltan* (Angl.), *wyltan,* OHG. *walzen, welzen* (MHG. *welzen,* G. *wälzen*), Goth. *waltjan,* f. the *a-* grade of the stem *welt-, walt-*: see WALT *a.* and *v.*]

1. *intr.* To roll or turn over (also with *over*); to fall over (also with *backward*); to sway or be unsteady.

13.. *St. Cristofer* 651 in Horstm. *Altengl. Leg.* (1881) 462 Whene þe kynge hade of hym syghte In his chayere he welte vpryghte. *c* **1400** *Destr. Troy* 7488 Philoc with felle angur frusshet to Remo, Till bothe welt backward of hor bare sadles. **1513** DOUGLAS *Æneis* X. x. 136 So tyll hys hart stoundis the prik of deith, He weltis our, and ȝaldis vp the breith. *Ibid.* XI. xii. 83 And stedis throwand on the ground that weltis. **1570** LEVINS *Manip.* 59/1 To Welt, *neuter, decidere.* **1703** THORESBY *Let. Ray, Welt,* to totter. **1876** *Whitby Gloss.* s.v., T' cart coup'd, an' we com welting into t' gutter. **1895** *Lakeland Gloss.*, *Welt*, to roll or roll over, to incline on one side.

fig. **13..** *E.E. Allit. P.* C. 115 Hit was a wenyng vn-war þat welt in his mynde. *c* **1400** *Destr. Troy* 4891 We, as vnwise men, welt into pride, Answarth hym awterwart with angur & skorne.

b. To gush *out*. Cf. WALT *v.* 4.

a **1400–50** *Wars Alex.* 839 (MS. Ashm.) So hard him hittis on the hede his hernes out weltid [*MS. Dublin* weltyn].

2. *trans.* To cast or throw *down*; to throw to the ground; to overturn; to beat down; also to roll, trundle. Cf. WALT *v.* 2.

? *a* **1400** *Morte Arth.* 3152 Walles he welte downe. *c* **1400** *Destr. Troy* 7490 Aither wegh other woundit, & welt to þe grene. **1513** Douglas *Æneis* IV. vii. 76 The burgeonit treis on buird thai bring for airis, Weltis down in woddis gret mastis. *Ibid.* IX. viii. 127 Down welting eik of huge wecht gret stanys. *Ibid.* X. iii. 21 Ane Agmon of Lyrnesya fast tharby Presys, wyth all the fors in his body, A felloune stone to welt the wallys tyll. **1570** Levins *Manip.* 59/1 To Welt, *actiue, euertere.* **1703** Thoresby *Let. Ray*, *Welt*,..overturn cart or wain. **1828** Carr *Craven Gloss.*, Grass or corn is said to be welted when it is beaten down by wind or rain, &c. **1869** *Lonsdale Gloss.*, *Welt*, v. t. to overset, to overturn. **1898** B. Kirkby *Lakeland Words*, *Welt*, upset.

welt (wɛlt), *v.*³ Chiefly *dial.* [? Alteration of WELK *v.* Cf. the earlier WELTER *v.*² and WILT *v.*] **a.** *trans.* Of the sun or weather: To wither (cut grass, etc.). Chiefly *pass.* **b.** *intr.* To become withered by exposure to the sun and air.

1764 *Museum Rust.* III. 333 That wheat which is mowed will require many days of hot weather to welt the grass and weeds. **1830** Spurdens *Forby's Voc. E. Anglia* App., *Wilted*, shrivelled as an apple. Also *Welted*: the same word. **1854** Miss A. E. Baker *Northampt. Gloss.* s.v. *Welted*, 'It is well welted:' or 'It is not fit to carry, it wants a good welting first'. **1863** *Jrnl. R. Agric. Soc.* XXIV. II. 350 Mown grass becomes first *welted*, then ferments. **1865** *Ibid.* 2nd Ser. I. II. 412 It is good management to give these turnips on grass, and to let them 'welt', or become dry from exposure to the sun and air.

Hence **ˈwelting** *vbl. sb.*

1766 *Museum Rust.* VI. 388 Cut the herb in the morning; and put it into the vats as soon as possible, in order to prevent its welting or heating. **1854** [see above].

welt, obs. form of WEALTH.

welt, welte, obs. contr. ff. *wieldeth*, *wielded*: see WIELD *v.*

‖**Weltanschauung** (vɛltanˈʃaʊʊŋ). Also with small initial. Pl. **-ungen**. [Ger., f. *welt* WORLD *sb.* + *anschauung* perception.] A particular philosophy or view of life; a concept of the world held by an individual or a group; = *world-view* s.v. WORLD *sb.* 26.

1868 W. James *Let.* in R. B. Perry *Tht. & Char. W. James* (1935) I. viii. 160, I remember your saying..that the characteristic of the Greek '*Weltanschauung*' was its optimism. **1906** *Nature* 10 May 26/2 In 1863 Haeckel entered the lists as the champion of the evolutionist 'Weltanschauung'. **1917** A. S. Pringle-Pattison *Idea of God* iv. 69 The intimate appreciation of living experience forms the basis of the whole *Weltanschauung* which he [*sc.* Bergson] offers us. **1934** M. Bodkin *Archetypal Patterns in Poetry* 326 A man's philosophy.. is his *Weltanschauung*—the individual vision, or perspective of reality. **1938** E. Quinn *Mission of Austria* iii. 30 Both Catholicism and National Socialism are *Weltanschauungen*. **1952** G. Sarton *Hist. Sci.* I. iv. 121 The creation of that astrological *Weltanschauung* which dominated late ancient and medieval thought and is not yet extinct today proves the survival through the Dark Interlude of some astronomical ideas of immemorial antiquity. **1958** J. Jocz *Theol. of Election* i. 11 The impact of the Christian *Weltanschauung* upon the Jewish mind. **1972** *Science* 2 June 988/1 The main reason why evolutionism..made such slow progress is that it was the replacement of one entire *weltanschauung* by a different one. **1978** N. Jardine in Hookway & Pettit *Action & Interpretation* 124 Speakers of different cultures, having different *Weltanschauungen*, ideologies, interests, paradigms, etc.

‖**Weltansicht** (ˈvɛltanzɪçt). *rare.* [Ger., f. as prec. + *ansicht* view.] A world view.

1892 W. James *Let.* 19 Sept. (1920) I. 324, I realized how exactly a philosophic *Weltansicht* resembles that from the top of a mountain. **1977** *Archivum Linguisticum* VIII. 49 The following statement that every language represents a 'Weltansicht' (world view) of its own also proves the significance of the non-uniformity of languages for von Humboldt.

‖**Weltbild** (ˈvɛltbɪlt). [Ger., f. as prec. + *bild* picture.] A view of life.

1934 L. Mumford in W. Frank et al. *Amer. & Alfred Stieglitz* ii. 47 Stieglitz..helped restore those values that had been left out of the narrow *Weltbild* of his contemporaries. **1963** J. Lyons *Structural Semantics* iii. 40 The suggestion that we are influenced in our 'Weltbild' by the language we have been brought up to speak is open to different interpretations. **1973** I. Robinson *Survival of Eng.* iii. 82 The automatic wage-increase is so much taken for granted as a necessary part of the world that it is perhaps more *Weltbild* than what is usually thought of as language. **1983** *Bull. Amer. Acad. Arts & Sci.* Oct. 35 Mahler's *Weltbild* bore the marks not only of intellectual populism but of his class and ethnic origins.

welted (ˈwɛltɪd), *ppl. a.* Also 8 **whelted**. [f. WELT *v.*¹ or *sb.* + -ED.]

1. a. Furnished with a welt as a border or edging. Of a gown, etc.: Adorned or trimmed with 'welts' (hence of a person with reference to this). ? *Obs.*

Freq. in 16th cent. in const. *welted with*.

(*a*) *c* **1507** in *Etoniana* (1865) 214 Servants cots of black cotton welted with yelowe. **1540** *Test. Ebor.* (Surtees) VI. 111 My blake gowne of cloth weltede with velvet. **1592** Greene *Upst. Courtier* G 1, I saw fiue fat fellowes all in damaske cotes and gownes welted with Veluet very braue. **1679** *Lond. Gaz.* No. 1378/4 A Bar Gown faced and welted with Velvet.

fig. **1631** J. Burges *Answ. Rejoined* 435 It stands..welted and guarded with so many reasons.

(*b*) **1595** Lodge *Fig for Momus* Sat. iv. E 4, They say thy welted gowne, and ruffes of lawne, When thou wert warden last was but a pawne. **1606** Dekker *Newes fr. Hell* Wks. (Grosart) II. 137 Hee shall meet a number there, who once went in black veluet coats, and welted gownes. **1606** —— *Seven Deadly Sins* 10 The welted Vsurer, and the politick Bankrupt. **1654** Gayton *Pleas. Notes* III. xii. 157 When in your gowne (not a Clericall habit of any Learning) but welted and crosse-lac'd.

b. Of boots or boot-soles: Furnished with a welt. ***welted work***: the making of welted boots.

1895 *Daily News* 20 Apr. 2/1 A piecework statement for welted work at Northampton should be prepared. **1905** *Westm. Gaz.* 30 Oct. 7/3 Hitherto America has produced practically all the machinery for the making of welted boots.

2. *Nat. Hist.* Furnished with a raised welt or projecting edge. ***welted thistle***: see THISTLE 3.

1597 Gerarde *Herbal* I. xxxv. §8. 50 The flower [of the Germaine Flower de-luce]..consisting of sixe great leaues, ..welted downe the middle. **1599** —— *Catal. Arb. in horto* 4 *Brassica fimbriata.* Welted Colewoorts. **1703** Petiver in *Phil. Trans.* XXIV. 1424 (2) These Leaves very much resemble the Virginian Sumach, with a winged or welted Stalk. **1712** J. Morton *Nat. Hist. Northampt.* 429 Fowls of the Fin-toed Tribe, that is, such as have their Toes welted or Finn'd, as it were, all along on each Side with appendant Membranes; but not webb'd together, by an intervening Skin, as are those of Ducks. **1713** *Phil. Trans.* XXVIII. 51 Its deep Scarlet Flowers, and square welted Pods.

b. Marked with a ridge or with ridges.

1899 Baring-Gould *Bk. West* II. v. 61 The face of the moor is in places welted to such an extent that it alters the character of the scene.

3. Marked with a welt or raised wound or mark of a lash.

1855 Wiseman *Fabiola* II. xxi, The mangled limbs, and welted backs, of the tortured Christians. **1908** *Westm. Gaz.* 15 Jan. 3/1 The unfortunate servant of the Christian was set free and given 5 dols. Hassani, to heal his welted skin.

4. ***welted joint***, a plumbers' joint made by turning the edges to be joined, one over the other, and pressing them together.

1888 J. W. Clarke *Plumbing Pract.* ix. 94 About two years ago, a series of lectures was given by a master plumber..and he showed a specimen of a welted joint. **1892** *Dict. Archit.* (Arch. Publ. Soc.), *Welted joint.* The old system of making a junction of the sides of two lengths of lead on a church roof, is preferred to the present system of a deal roll.

welter (ˈwɛltə(r)), *sb.*¹ [f. WELTER *v.* Rare before 19th cent.; cf. WALTER *sb.*]

1. A state of confusion, upheaval, or turmoil.

Freq. from *c* 1870, often with suggestion of 2 or 3.

1596 Dalrymple tr. *Leslie's Hist. Scot.* II. 277 He feiret be that coniunctione suld follow sum Welter in the religioune, casting doune of the Kirkes, Monasteries and siklike. *Ibid.* 465. **1619** Bp. Andrewes *96 Serm.*, *Nativ.* xiii. (1629) 125 Away with peace, *moveatur terra*, let all the earth be on a welter. **1837** Carlyle *Fr. Rev.* III. VI. ii. 355 [Danton] was heard to ejaculate..'I leave the whole business in a frightful welter (*gâchis épouvantable*): not one of them understands anything of government'. **1864** —— *Fredk. Gt.* XV. V. IV. 81 What a downrush of confusion there ensued... Belleisle himself must have paused uncertain over such a welter. **1888** *Sat. Rev.* 26 May 621 They are not precisely the strongest party in the present welter of English politics.

2. The rolling, tossing, or tumbling (of the sea or waves).

1849 Cupples *Green Hand* iv. (1856) 47 The long welter of the sea when the ship eased down. **1863** Whittier *Andrew Rykman's Prayer* 88 In the welter of this sea Nothing stable is but Thee. **1898** Kipling *Fleet in Being* i. 10 He..went out serenely to take his boat home through the dark and the dismal welter.

fig. **1873** Dowden in *Contemp. Rev.* XXII. 177 It is rather the oscillation, the refluence and welter of the great social and moral wave flung forward by the wind of revolution.

3. A surging or confused mass: **a.** of material things, persons, etc.

1857 Kingsley *Two Y. Ago* iii, A confused welter and quiver of mingled air, and rain, and spray. **1891** *Spectator* 18 July, A 'World's Fair' is apt to call up sickening recollections of..a vast welter of 'miscellaneous exhibits'. **1893** McCarthy *Red Diamonds* III. 235 Covered with the wreck and welter of the ruined building.

b. of immaterial things.

1851 Carlyle *Sterling* III. v. (1872) 206 His talk..went tumbling as if in mere welters of explosive unreason. **1864** Mitchell *Wet Days at Edgewood* 306 Losing point and force and efficiency in a welter of words. **1880** McCarthy *Own Times* IV. lxvii. 533 The historian is constantly involving himself in a welter of inconsistencies and errors.

welter (ˈwɛltə(r)), *sb.*² [f. WELT *sb.*¹ + -ER¹.] A worker who makes or inserts the welt (in a manufactured article).

1862 Mrs. H. Wood *Mrs. Hallib. Troub.* I. xviii, Some welted, or hemmed the gloves round at the edge of the wrist; these were called 'welters'. **1866** *Lond. Rev.* 27 Oct. 459/2 There are various epithets for shoemakers;..there are welters..clickers, blockers..closers. **1881** *Instr. Census Clerks* (1885) 75 Hosiery manufacture... Welter. *Ibid.* 76 Glover, glove maker... Welter.

welter (ˈwɛltə(r)), *sb.*³ [? f. WELT *v.*¹ 5.]

1. a. A heavy-weight horseman or pugilist. Cf. WELTER WEIGHT.

1804 *Sporting Mag.* XXIII. 293 The high weights, among the Subscribers called the Welters. **1863** E. Farmer *Scrap Book* (ed. 3) 61 Leaving 'Welters' and 'Craners' and 'slow-uns' behind. **1869** *Contemp. Rev.* XI. 365 There is a pleasing representation of the Tedsworth Hunt, who seem from it to be an awful lot of welters.

b. *Horse-racing.* Used attrib. with the meaning 'for heavy-weight riders', as ***Welter Cup***, ***Welter Stakes***; ***welter handicap***, ***race***. Also *ellipt.* (= welter race, etc.).

1820 *Sporting Mag.* VI. 2/1 A capital gentleman jockey for a *Welter* stake. **1843** W. Ruff *Guide to Turf* 36 The Welter Stakes of 20 sov. each. **1850** *Ibid.* 64 The Cheshire Welter Cup. **1880** W. Day *Racehorse in Training* 198 The runners in the welter races have surpassed those in the light-weight handicaps by two. **1897** N. Gould *Seeing him Through* xxv, The welter-handicap for amateur riders. *Ibid.*, There were ten starters for the amateur welter.

2. Something exceptionally big or heavy of its kind. *colloq.* and *dial.*

1865 J. Sleigh *Derbysh. Gloss.* in *Reliquary* (Jan. 1866) 171 *Welter*, a large person. **1888** *Sheffield Gloss.*, *Welter*, anything large, as a large stone. **1899** Kipling *Stalky* ii. 49 Then he gave us eight cuts apiece—welters.

welter (ˈwɛltə(r)), *v.*¹ Forms: 4–7 **weltre**, 4–6 *Sc.* **weltir**, 5–6 **weltyr**, 5– **welter** (5 *Sc.* **velter**). [a. MDu. *welteren* or MLG. (also LG.) *weltern* (hence NFris. *wälteri*, Sw. *vältra*), MHG. *welzern*, frequentative f. the stem *welt-*: see WELT *v.*² and cf. WALTER *v.*¹]

I. *intr.* **1.** To roll or twist the body; to turn or tumble about; to lie and roll about; to writhe, to wriggle. Also with *about*. Now *rare* or *Obs.*

a **1300** [implied in sense 2]. ? *a* **1400** *Morte Arth.* 890 He welterys, he wristeles, he wrynges hys handes! *Ibid.* 1142. *c* **1440** *Alphabet of Tales* 411 Sho was gretelye turment, to so muche at sho wold som tyme weltyr in þe fyre. *Ibid.* 488 He feld a blak myrk thyng welter betwix hym & his wyfe. **1470–85** Malory *Arthur* v. v. 168 And thenne Arthur weltred and wrong, that he was other whyle vnder and another tyme aboue. *Ibid.* XI. viii. 582 She wrythed and weltred as a mad woman. **1667** Milton *P.L.* I. 78 There [in Hell] the companions of his fall..He soon discerns, and weltring by his side One..nam'd Beëlzebub. **1727–46** Thomson *Summer* 265 They..weltering in the bowl, With powerless wings around them wrapt, expire. **1751** Chesterf. *Lett. to Son* 13 June, In mixed companies with your equals..you may..sit, stand, or occasionally walk, as you like; but I believe you would not think it very *bienséant* to..welter in an easy chair. **1815** Scott *Lord of Isles* IV. x, And the shy seal had quiet home, And welter'd in that wondrous dome.

b. To roll about (*in* the mire, etc.). Chiefly *fig.* Now *rare* or *Obs.*

1530 Palsgr. 779/2 Thou welterest in the myer, as thou were a sowe. **1583** Golding *Calvin on Deut.* xxi. 122 Verie fewe of them vouchsafed to consider that: for all of them lay weltring stil in their owne dung. **1603** Holland *Plutarch's Mor.* 264 Oftentimes he will welter and wallow in the mire, confessing..what sinnes..he hath committed. **1641** Milton *Church Govt.* II. 63 Such principles of earth as these wherein she [Prelaty, bred up in slime and mud] welters from a yong one. **1706** tr. *Liger's Compl. Florist* 167 Fowls are apt, after a great Drought, to welter in the Ground, or Dust, to cleanse their Feathers. *a* **1732** T. Boston *Crook in Lot* (1805) 110 Man threw himself into the mire at first, and now he is justly left weltering in it.

c. To roll or lie prostrate (*in* one's blood); hence (hyperbolically) to be soaked with blood or gore; also *fig.* of a nation, etc. Now only *poet.*

1590 Greene *Orl. Fur.* (1599) 10 Till all these Princes weltring in their bloods, The Crowne doe fall to Countie Sacrepant. *a* **1593** Marlowe *Edw. II*, II. v. 1181 Vpon my weapons point here shouldst thou fall, And welter in thy goare. **1643** *Decl. Commons Reb. Ireland* 26 Two Protestant Nations [were] ready to welter in each others blood. **1697** Dryden *Æneis* XI. 1218 Prostrate on the Plain, Welt'ring in Blood, she sees Camilla slain. **1744** P. Whitehead *Gymnasiad* III. 73 Down dropt the Hero, welt'ring in his Gore. **1783** Justamond tr. *Raynal's Hist. Indies* I. 252 Three successive generations were doomed to welter in their own blood. **1803** *Ann. Reg., Chron.* 4/2 The deceased..was weltering in his blood, and bore every indication of having been robbed as well as murdered. **1849** D. G. Mitchell *Battle Summer* (1852) 35 They lie—the fifty corpses—weltering in their blood. **1887** Bowen *Æneid* II. 667 Slaughtered, and weltering each in the blood from the others that flows.

2. *fig.* †**a.** To revel, live at ease. *Obs. rare.*

a **1300** *Cursor M.* 4503 Man þat weltres in his welis And, thoru his welth, na fautes felis. **1581** Mulcaster *Positions* xxxvi. (1887) 140 The midle sorte of parentes which neither welter in to much wealth, nor wrastle with to much want.

b. = WALLOW *v.*¹ 6. Now *rare.*

1535 Coverdale *Eccl.* xxiii. 12 But they yᵗ feare God, eschue all soch and lye not weltringe in synne. **1561** Daus tr. *Bullinger on Apoc.* (1573) 13 b, Who in the meane tyme swell with pride, and welter away in filthy pleasures. **1577–87** Holinshed *Chron.* I. 12/2 He suffered his owne bodie to welter in all vice and voluptuousnesse. **1611** Speed *Hist. Gt. Brit.* VII. i. 192 Numbers of them lay senslesse and weltring in wine. **1646** H. P. *Medit. Seige* 7 Luxury..in which thou hast weltred with securitie. **1867** Tennyson *Holy Grail* 767 Happier are those that welter in their sin.

c. To be sunk or deeply involved *in*.

1629 J. Cole *Of Death* 192 Let us then no longer lye weltring in sorrow, lest by overlong lamenting wee encrease Gods wrath. **1642** Prynne *Sov. Antidote* Pref., To make England in the selfesame desperate deplorable condition, as Ireland now lies weltring in. **1642** D. Rogers *Naaman* 16 Suffers them to welter in their fears, doubts and complaints.

1856 MERIVALE *Rom. Emp.* l. (1865) VI. 153 We seem, indeed, in perusing the narrative before us, to be weltering in a dream of horrors. *a* **1871** R. CHAMBERS in *Casq. Lit.* (1874) Ser. II. I. 264 They..leave you weltering in astonishment.

d. *transf.* of inanimate things.

1847 KINGSLEY *Poems, Sappho* 4 Upon the white horizon Atho's peak Weltered in burning haze. *a* **1849** BRYANT *Hymn of Sea* 42 The fertile plain Welters in shallows.

3. Of a ship: To roll to and fro (on the waves). Also *fig.* Cf. WALTER *v.* 1 b.

1423 JAS. I *Kingis Q.* xxiv, We pullit vp saile, and furth oure wayis went. Vpon the wawis weltering to and fro. **1609** HEALEY *Discov. New World* I. II. vii. 92 But our boat..did so welter from side to side. **1822–56** DE QUINCEY *Confess.* Wks. (1856) V. 266 My mind tossed, as it seemed, upon the billowy ocean, and weltered upon the weltering waves. **1876** J. SAUNDERS *Lion in Path* ix, The soldier's barque was weltering aimlessly, helplessly, hopelessly upon the waves. **1876** MORRIS *Sigurd* IV. 350 The keels roll down the sea-dale, and welter up the steep.

b. Of a dead body: To be tossed or tumbled about (on the waves); to roll or tumble about (in water). Also *fig.*

1593 NASHE *Christ's T.* 14 All the sinnes of the first World now welter, souse, & beate vnquietly in the Sea. **1637** MILTON *Lycidas* 13 He must not flote upon his watry bear Unwept, and welter to the parching wind. **1718** POPE *Odyss.* XIV. 155 But he whose name you crave Moulders in earth, or welters on the wave. **1791** COWPER *Odyss.* III. 115 Whether he on the continent hath fall'n By hostile hands, or by the waves o'erwhelm'd Of Amphitrite, welters in the Deep. **1806** SCOTT *Poems, Palmer* 40 A corpse amid the alders rank, The Palmer welter'd there. **1823** S. ROGERS *Italy* XXI. *Campagna of Florence* 149 Arno,..where, exulting, he had felt A swimmer's transport, there, alas, to float And welter.

4. To roll down in a stream; to flow.

c **1375** *Sc. Leg. Saints* xlii. (*Agatha*) 306 A gret hyl..brak owt in fyre & brynt don, weltrand, as a borne had bene. **1508** DUNBAR *Tua Mariit Wemen* 439 With that wateris myn ene, and welteris doune teris. **1835** LYTTON *Rienzi* I. xii, From the left arm..the blood weltered slowly. **1846** KEBLE *Lyra Innoc., Sleeping on Waters* 44 And Nile, soft weltering nigh, Sings him to sleep. *Ibid.*, *Bathing* 2 Around the rushy point comes weltering slow The brimming stream.

†**b.** To flutter (*down*). *rare*$^{-1}$.

c **1470** *Gol. & Gaw.* 290 [It] sall be licht as leif of the lynd lest, That welteris doun with the wynd, sa wauerand it is.

5. Of waves, the water, sea: To roll; to toss and tumble; to surge. Also *fig.* Now only *poet.*

1375 BARBOUR *Bruce* III. 700 The strem sa sturdy was, That wawys wyd (that) brekand war Weltryt as hillys her and thar. *c* **1480** HENRYSON *Paddock & Mouse* 179 The watter is the warld, ay welterand With mony wall of trubulatioun. **1581** A. HALL *Iliad* II. 23 As oft the seas we see The storme the boistrous surge to raise, weltring now low now hie. **1787–9** WORDSW. *Evening Walk* 122 There, waves that, hardly weltering, die away, Tip their smooth ridges with a softer ray. **1816** J. WILSON *City of Plague* II. i. 203 The sea that welters drearily Around the homeless earth! **1821** BRYANT *Ages* xviii, Till the North broke its flood-gates, and the waves Whelmed the degraded race, and weltered o'er their graves. **1865** SWINBURNE *Poems & B.*, *Song in Time of Order* 7 It swells and welters and swings, The pulse of the tide of the sea.

b. *transf.* Of a mass of persons or things: To be in a state of agitation, turmoil, or confusion.

1837 CARLYLE *Fr. Rev.* III. I. i, When a Nation..must now seek its wild way through the New, Chaotic,—where Force is not yet distinguished into Bidden and Forbidden, but Crime and Virtue welter unseparated. **1848** KINGSLEY *Saint's Trag.* II. iv, We sit in a cloud..while right below Welters the black fermenting heap of life On which our state is built. **1853** —— *Hypatia* xxix, The mob had weltered and howled ineffectually around the house for some half-hour. **1889** JEROME *Idle Thoughts* 128 Huddled like vermin in sewers, they welter, and sicken, and sleep. **1897** 'MARK TWAIN' *Man that corrupted* etc. (1900) 317 The whole Left was surging and weltering about the champion, all bent on wringing his hand.

6. †**a.** Of a vehicle: To sway or rock unsteadily; to overturn. *Obs. rare.*

1375 BARBOUR *Bruce* XI. 25 A litill stane oft, as men sayis, May ger weltir ane mekill wane. **1535** COVERDALE *Nahum* ii. 4 The charettes rolle vpon the stretes, & welter in the hye wayes.

b. To go with a heavy rolling gait; to flounder. Also *dial.*, to reel, stagger.

1595 R. JOHNSON *Seven Champions* II. (1608) 52 Oh that some ravenous harpey woulde welter from his denne. **1674–91** RAY *N.C. Words, Welter*, to goe aside, or heavily, as women with child, or fat people. **1785** *Bran New Wark* (E.D.S.) 188 Should a kraken welter up the sands..ye mud weel be astonished. **1822** SCOTT *Pirate* xvii, [The whale] was lying perfectly still, in a deep part of the voe into which it had weltered. **1851** MAYNE REID *Scalp Hunt.* xli. 324 With desperate energy I plunged and weltered through it [the water]. **1884** D. GRANT *Lays & Leg. North* 75 [She] Weltered hame through bogs an' hillocks Aifter mony a weary fa'.

fig. **1837** CARLYLE *New Lett.* (1904) I. 70 On the eighth day after this I am to make my appearance as a Lecturer!.. Some way or other we shall 'welter through it'.

II. *trans.* †**7.** To move, turn, or force by rolling. *Obs.*

? *a* **1400** *Morte Arth.* 1140 ȝitt es þe warlow so wyghte, he welters hyme vndere. **1513** DOUGLAS *Æneis* VI. ix. 183 For sum weltris a gret stane wp the bra. **1520** M. NISBET *N.T. Scots* Matt. xxvii. 60 He weltirit a gret staan to the dure of the beriele. **1535** COVERDALE *Prov.* xxvi. 27 And he yt weltreth a stone, shal stomble vpon it hymselfe.

refl. **1535** COVERDALE *Prov.* xxvi. 14 Like as the dore turneth aboute vpon the tresholde, euen so doth the slouthfull welter himself in his bedd. —— *Micah* i. 10 Thou at Betaphra, welter thy self in the dust and asshes.

†**b.** In pa. pple. with *in*. *Obs.* (Cf. 1 b, 2 b.)

1535 COVERDALE *Judith* xiv. 15 Then sawe he the deed body of Holofernes.., weltred in his bloude vpon the earth. **1578** BANISTER *Hist. Man* VIII. 110 In whiche absurditie many are weltred. **1632** J. HAYWARD tr. *Biondi's Eromena* 30 Foure bodies lying weltred in bloud. **1652** *Persuasive* 26 Princes, who are..weltered in their own blood. **1673** HICKERINGILL *Greg. Father Greybeard* 257 England, as well as other Countries, has been disciplin'd, 'till weltred in blood and ruine.

†**8.** To cause to roll; to toss up and down. *Obs.*

c **1425** *Macro Plays, Cast. Persev.* 2003 Byttyr balys þei [his enemies] brekyn on brode, Mankynde in wo to weltyr & waue. **1513** DOUGLAS *Æneis* III. iii. 90 The wyndis welteris the see continually. *a* **1547** SURREY *Æneid* II. 536 Fomy Nereus..From bottoms depth doth weltre up the seas. **1594** MARLOWE & NASHE *Dido* I. i. 223 And they so wrackt and weltred by the waues, As euery tide tilts twixt their oken sides.

9. To overthrow, overturn, upset: also with *down*. Chiefly *Sc.*

c **1450** *Gol. & Gaw.* 469 Wrightis welterand doune treis. *c* **1480** HENRYSON *Test. Cresseid* 436 All is decayit, thy weird is welterit so. **1513** DOUGLAS *Æneis* VII. xi. 51 This cruell dochtyr of the auld Saturn The marbyll hyrst can weltyr and ourturn. **1571** [see WALTER *v.*[1] 7]. *a* **1663** SANDERSON *Serm.* (1681) II. 257 Were it but an ox, or an ass..that lay weltred in a ditch. **1808** JAMIESON s.v., *To welter a cart*, to turn it upside down.

†**10.** To wear *out* (one's days) in a state of trouble or disquiet. *Obs.*$^{-1}$

1642 D. ROGERS *Naaman* 138 They returne to their old acquaintance with selfe, and so welter out their daies in utter misery.

Hence **'weltered** *ppl. a.*

1590 T. WATSON *Meliboeus* Poems (Arb.) 175 Castor and Pollux,..two welcome messengers, Conuey great comfort to the weltred minde.

'welter, *v.*[2] *Obs.* exc. *dial.* [Cf. WELT *v.*[3] and -ER[5]; the ending may have been suggested by *wither*. Cf. WILTER *v.*] *intr.* To wither. Hence **'weltered, 'weltering** *ppl. adjs.*

1645 BP. HALL *Remedy Discontentm.* v. 24 As for Beauty, what is it, but..a flower, which with one hot Sun gleam weltreth and fals? **1657** F. COCKIN *Div. Blossomes* 18 Your fading honour I esteem as dung, Earth's weltering glory as the dirt in street. **1855** DELAMER *Kitch. Gard.* (1861) 62 These vermin prefer weltered and flagging leaves to those that are quite fresh. **1860** I. TAYLOR *Ultimate Civiliz.* i. I. v. 40 The weltered hearts, and blighted memories of those whom we have..gathered from out of the..lost and wretched. **1887** *Kentish Gloss.*, *Welter*, to wither. 'The leaves begin to welter.'

weltering ('wɛltərɪŋ), *vbl. sb.* [f. WELTER *v.*[1] + -ING[1].]

1. The action of turning or twisting the body about (on the ground), rolling (in the mire), wallowing (in sin), etc. Now *rare* or *Obs.*

1448–9 METHAM *Amoryus & Cl.* 1631 This lyoun..Wypt on the gres hys blody mowth; and in hys welteryng Made alle blody Cleopes kerchyff in hys wypyng. **1520** M. NISBET *N.T. in Scots*, 2 Pet. ii. 22 The hound turnit agane to his spewing, and a sow [that] is weschin in weltring [*Wycl.* walwyng] in fenn. **1586** T. B. *La. Primaud. Fr. Acad.* I. 206 All kind of superfluitie, riot, and weltring in pleasures.

†**2.** The action of rolling or turning round; unstable condition; political agitation. *Obs.*

1423 JAS. I *Kingis Q.* clxiii, To se the sudayn weltering Of that Ilk quhele [of Fortune]. *a* **1586** SIDNEY *Astr. & Stella* Sonn. xxx, If in the Scottish Court be weltering yet. **1588** in *Rep. Commiss. Univ. Scot.* (1837) III. 193 In this confused tyme (quhen all folkis ar loukand to the weltering of the warld).

3. The rolling and tossing (of waves); the surging (of water, the sea). Also *fig.*

1805 WORDSW. *Prelude* VI. 138 The surpassing life..incapable of change, Nor touched by welterings of passion. **1827** POLLOK *Course T.* v. 595 And oft in dreams, the..sinner..heard the weltering of the waves of wrath. **1851** TRENCH *Poems* 73 'Mid the long weltering of the dreariest surge. **1867** MORRIS *Jason* IV. 681 A figure standing, with wide wings of gold, Upright, amid the weltering of the sea.

'weltering, *ppl. a.* [f. WELTER *v.*[1] + -ING[2].]

1. Of the sea: That tumbles and tosses; raging, surging.

1375 BARBOUR *Bruce* III. 719 The Se wald rys on sic maner, That off the wawys the weltrand hycht Wald refe thaim oft off thar sycht. *c* **1420** WYNTOUN *Cron.* IV. 203 Qwhil þe weltrande wawis keyn Sulde a part asswagit beyn. **1423** JAS. I *Kingis Q.* c, In the huge weltering wawis..Off lufis rage. **1587** TURBERV. *Trag. Tales, Epit.* etc. 170 No..wrath of weltring waues could stay, those martiall mates at home. **1629** MILTON *Hymn Nativ.* xii, While the Creator Great..bid the weltring waves their oozy channel keep. **1771** BEATTIE *Minstr.* I. liv, The deep roar Of the wide-weltering waves. **1820** W. IRVING *Sketch Bk.* (1859) 7 The straining and groaning of bulk-heads, as the ship laboured in the weltering sea. **1870** BRYANT *Iliad* XIV. 20 As when the face Of the great deep grows dark with weltering waves. **1897** F. T. BULLEN *Cruise of 'Cachalot'* 306, I trembled for his life in such a weltering whirl of rock-torn sea.

b. That is in a state of agitation, turmoil, or confusion.

1831 CARLYLE *Misc.*, *Nibelungen Lied* (1840) III. 71 A firm sunny island amid the weltering chaos of antique tradition. **1850** KINGSLEY *Alton Locke* xxviii, The weltering mass of bullocks, pigs, and human beings. **1879** FARRAR *St. Paul* I. xviii. 329 That vast weltering mass of idolatry and corruption. **1890** J. PULSFORD *Loyalty to Christ* I. 195 You restless, heaving, weltering kingdoms of Time, mock us not.

†**2.** *Sc.* **a.** Moving clumsily or unsteadily. **b.** Rolling. *Obs.*

c **1480** HENRYSON *Trial of Fox* 111 The wyld Once, the Buk, the Uelterand Brok. **1501** DOUGLAS *Pal. Hon.* III. xl, Thair micht I se..The welterand stone wirk Sisipho mich cair.

3. That is tossed about on or by the waves.

1609 HEALEY *Discov. New World* III. ii. 129 They..hold it fondnesse to hazard their liues either on a stumbling iade, or in a weltring barge. **1810** SCOTT *Lady of Lake* VI. xx, Another flash!—the spearman floats A weltering corse beside the boats. **1679** FARRAR *St. Paul* II. xliii. 377 They had drifted fourteen days, tossed up and down on the heaving waves of Adria, a weltering plaything for the gale.

4. Lying prostrate in blood; saturated with blood.

1816 BYRON *Ch. Har.* III. li, And Slaughter heap'd on high his weltering ranks. —— *Siege of Cor.* xvii, It is humbling to tread O'er the weltering field of the tombless dead.

welter weight. [WELTER *sb.*[3]]

1. †**a.** Heavy weight (of a horseman). *Obs. rare.*

1825 *Sporting Mag.* XVI. 280 He was always well mounted for his welter weight.

b. A heavy-weight rider.

1832 *Q. Rev.* XLVII. 240 'Out upon this great carcass of mine,' says one of the best of the welter-weights. **1850** 'H. HIEOVER' *Pract. Horsemanship* 191 A horse belonging to a friend, a welter weight. **1883** PENNELL-ELMHIRST *Cream Leicestersh.* 344 A welter weight never went better to hounds in a fast run. **1897** *Daily News* 12 Mar. 3/4 Horses equal to carrying a welter-weight of fifteen stone or more.

c. *Horse-racing.* An extra weight sometimes imposed in addition to weight for age.

1880 W. DAY *Racehorse in Training* 201 They have..added to other improvements the introduction of welter-weights; so that it only requires a little alteration—more long races with heavy weights, and fewer short courses with light weights—to complete the reform.

2. A boxer or wrestler whose weight is between that of a light-weight and a middle-weight. Also *attrib.*

1896 *Boston* (Mass.) *Jrnl.* 3 Oct. 3/1 Welterweight champion of California. **1903** *Daily Chron.* 19 Sept. 3/3 Not even an indomitable spirit will bring a bantam-weight and a welter-weight together. **1910** *Encycl. Brit.* IV. 351/2 The boxing rules of the American Amateur Athletic Association differ slightly from the British... The recognized classes by weight are: Bantam,..Feather,..Light,..Welter, 145 lb and under; Middle..and Heavy.

welthe, welht, obs. forms of WEALTH.

welting ('wɛltɪŋ), *vbl. sb.* Also *Sc.* and *north.* 6 **wawting**, 7 **valting**, 7–8 **walting**, 8 ? **waiting**; 7, 9 **waltin**, 9 **wattin**. [f. WELT *v.*[1] + -ING[1].]

1. The action of furnishing with a welt. **a.** The edging, binding, or ornamenting (a garment) with a welt or welts; chiefly *concr.*, an edging, a border, fringe.

1508 *Acc. Ld. High Treas. Scot.* IV. 135 Item, for grathing of foure sadilles..and wawting of thaim with wellus, xlviij s. **1552** in Feuillerat *Revels Edw. VI* (1914) 119 The garmentes welted aboute with blew & yellow gould tinsell conteyning xxxti yardes weltinge. **1558** —— *Revels Q. Eliz.* (1908) 23, viii plackardes of the same Maske and the welting and jagginge therof. **1600** ROWLANDS *Letting Humours Blood* ii. 54 The welting hath him in no chardges stood, Being the ruines of a cast French hood. **1647** *Caldwell Papers* (Maitl. Club) I. 100 Item for 4 elnes of Tours waltings to his claithes 0 10 0. **1737** *Ochtertyre House Booke of Accomps* (S.H.S. 1907) 80 For ⅞ of a yeard of cherry waiting [*sic: the Glossary gives* wating]. **1875** *Plain Needlework* 16 They can be stitched (like welting) and finished off with strings. **1881** *Leicestersh. Gloss.*, *Welting*,..a seam; a seaming.

transf. **1894** BLACKMORE *Perlycross* xxi, A westerly breeze played with the half ripe pods of gorse, and the brown welting of the heather.

b. in techn. senses, esp. in shoemaking.

1795 W. FELTON *Carriages* (1801) II. Gloss., *Welting* is the sewing a narrow strip of leather over the corner seams,..which..keeps out the wet. **1889** *Pall Mall Gaz.* 15 Jan. 6/2 [Shoe trade.] Welting machinery is making progress, and hand labour for welting is being trained. **1893** ELIZ. ROSEVEAR *Text-bk. Needlework* etc. 405 Welting or Ribbing is usually knitted at the top of stockings, socks, muffatees, and sometimes throughout a garment.

2. A beating, a thrashing.

1840 COCKTON *Val. Vox* xii, Do you want a good welting? ony say, and you shall catch, my dear, the blessedest rope's-ending you ever had any notion on yet. **1862** H. MARRYAT *Year in Sweden* I. 233 She received a sound welting..from her father. **1887** G. MEREDITH *Poet. Wks.* (1912) 191 He [a dog] bewhimpered his welting, and I Scarce thought it enough for him.

3. *attrib.*, as *welting cord*; †**welting stake**, some kind of armourer's anvil.

1660 in Meyrick *Ant. Armour* (1824) III. 128 Welting stakes. **1887** JAMIESON *Suppl.*, *Waltin-Cord, Wattin-Cord*, cord used in forming welts for seams and hems of gowns.

weltir, weltre, obs. forms of WELTER.

‖**Weltliteratur** ('vɛltlɪtera͵tuːr). Also **-litteratur.** [Ger., f. *welt* WORLD *sb.* + *literatur* LITERATURE.] A literature of all nations and peoples; a universal literature.

[**1827** GOETHE *Gespräche mit Eckermann* (1836) I. 325 National-Literatur will jetzt nicht viel sagen, die Epoche der Welt-Literatur ist an der Zeit.] **1913** E. POUND *Let.* 7 Nov. (1971) 24 Until 'we' accept what I've been insisting on for a decade, i.e., a universal standard which pays no attention to time or country—a Weltlitteratur standard—there is no hope. **1962** *Listener* 6 Sept. 358/2 It gives a new meaning to Goethe's dream of *Weltliteratur*. **1974** *Times Lit. Suppl.* 17 May 526/2 A truism, that Pound and Eliot were rebels against American provincialism and proponents of a *Weltliteratur*.

||**Weltpolitik** ('vɛltpoliˌtiːk). [Ger., f. as prec. + *politik* politics.] International politics; world affairs from a political standpoint; a particular country's policy towards the world at large.

1903 J. BAILEY *Diary* 19 Feb. (1935) 90 Lord George Hamilton said..that the one thing needed to make the U.S.A. friends with us was their going into *Welt Politik*. **1905** D. M. WALLACE *Russia* II. xxxviii. 428 Never, perhaps, has the construction of a single line [*sc.* the Trans-Siberian Railway] produced such deep and lasting changes in the sphere of *Weltpolitik*. **1941** *N. & Q.* 26 July 43/2 The ineffectiveness of the Kruger telegram opened German eyes to the need of a fleet if Germany was to play a successful, or even a real, part in *Weltpolitik*. **1979** G. ST. AUBYN *Edward VII* vii. 363 The Triple Entente was a direct reaction to Germany's *Weltpolitik*.

||**Weltschmerz** ('vɛlt-ʃmɛrts). Also **weltschmerz**. [Ger., f. as prec. + *schmerz* pain.] A weary or pessimistic feeling about life; an apathetic or vaguely yearning attitude.

1875 J. A. SYMONDS *Renaissance in Italy* I. iv. 232 The Weltschmerz did not exist for the men of the Renaissance. **1896** W. CALDWELL *Schopenhauer's System* 523 His philosophy is a study of the *Weltschmerz* that we all feel at times. **1923** A. HUXLEY *Let.* 2 Sept. (1969) 218, I have also been having a..jaundice lying on my liver, which reduced me to a fearful state of weltschmerz and incapacity to do anything. **1935** C. ISHERWOOD *Mr. Norris changes Trains* ix. 150 'What's the matter?' I asked. 'Things in general... The state of this wicked world. A touch of *Weltschmerz*, that's all.' **1947** [see ACCIDIA]. **1960** C. GEERTZ *Religion of Java* vi. 75 He said..the young good ones..die early, as a kind of reward, for it is a good thing to be dead. He spoke happily, not in any *Weltschmerz* mood. **1965** W. GOLDING *Hot Gates* 136 The sadness, the *weltschmerz* resulting from the constant movement of the ship. **1981** J. D. MACDONALD *Free Fall in Crimson* i. 6 'It is like *weltschmerz*.' 'Which, as you have so often told me, is homesickness for a place you have never seen.'

weluette, -uot, -wet, etc., obs. ff. VELVET.

||**Welwitschia** (wɛl'wɪtʃɪə). [mod.L., named by J. D. Hooker (1862) after Dr. Friedrich *Welwitsch* (1806–72), Austrian botanist: see -IA.] A genus of gymnospermous plants (N.O. *Gnetaceæ*) consisting of one species *W. mirabilis*, native to the sandy regions of western Africa.

1862 *Trans. Linnean Soc.* (1864) I. 1 On Welwitschia, a new Genus of Gnetaceæ. By Joseph Dalton Hooker. **1866** *Treas. Bot.*

welwot, obs. Sc. form of VELVET.

welwous, variant of VELLOUS (velvet).

wely, var. WEALY *a.*[1] *Obs.*; obs. form of WILY.

wem (wɛm), *sb. Obs.* exc. *arch.* Forms: 3– **wem** (5 *Sc.* **vem**), 3–7 **wemme**, 4 **wembe** (6 **wemb**), 4–6 **weme**, 6 **weam(e**. [ME. *wem*, substituted for OE. *wam(m*, *wom(m* (see WAM), under the influence of the verb.]

1. Moral defilement; stain (of sin). Chiefly in phr. ***without(en) wem*** = IMMACULATE *a.* 1. *Obs.* exc. *arch.*

(*a*) *a* **1225** *Ancr. R.* 10 Cleane religiun & wiðuten wem is iseon & helpen widewen [etc.]. *c* **1290** *St. Cecilia* 10 in *S. Eng. Leg.* 490 Lat, louerd, myn herte wiþoute wem be. *c* **1330** *Assump. Virg.* (B.M. MS.) 647 Marie..Clene maide and clene wyf, Clene widewe with oute wem. *a* **1340** HAMPOLE *Psalter* xviii. 14 If thar ware noght lordid of me, than i sall be withouten wem. *c* **1380** WYCLIF *Wks.* (1880) 304 Jamus telliþ of two religions; þe first is clene wit-oute wem...þe secounde is veyn religioun. *c* **1460** *Towneley Myst.* x. 37 My son shall in a madyn light..wythouten wem, os son thrugh glas. *c* **1475** *Partenay* 466 That god..of the virgyn unfold Was born without wemme in hir attamed. **1538** BP. LONGLAND *Serm. bef. King* in Foxe *A. & M.* (1570) 1253/2 Impollutus. He was vndefyled. He lyued cleane, without spotte or blotte, without wemme or stayne. **1561** DAUS *Bullinger on Apoc.* (1573) 29 Therefore was the Church of Smyrna right excellent, howbeit not vtterly without any wem. **1858** MORRIS *Def. Guenevere* etc. 123 Rapunzel sings..Mary, maid withouten wem, Keep me! (*b*) **1303** R. BRUNNE *Handl. Synne* 3111 Make not thy soule so wykked a wem To do wykkedness for pryde of hem. *Ibid.* 7446 þe þredde [sin] ys þe werste wem. **1387–8** T. USK *Test. Love* I. i. 74, I wot wel, wem ne spot may not abyde there so noble vertue haboundeth. *c* **1400** *Pilgr. Sowle* (Caxton 1483) I. xxii. (1859) 26 So clene of wem, that no thyng nedeth the To weyle, ne to wepe thy sinnes fore?

†**b.** With defining term, as *of sin*, etc. *Obs.*

a **1340** HAMPOLE *Psalter* xviii. 14, I sall be withouten wembe [*v.r.* wem] of dedly gilt. *c* **1340** —— *Prose Tr.* 38 For in hir [Mary] was full-hede of all vertus with-owttyne weme of synn. **1393** LANGL. *P. Pl. C.* XXI. 136 A mayde..Without wommanes wem in-to þis worlde brouhte hym. *a* **1425** *Cursor M.* 11208 (Trin.) Iesu hir childe bar she þore..Mayden wiþouten wem of flesshe. *a* **1450** *Mirk's Festial* 77 Oure Lord Ihesu Crist þat oure lady conceyuet of þe Holy Gost wythout wem of hyr body. *c* **1450** *Cov. Myst.* Prol. 5 Mary..wold not be defylyde With spot nor wem of man. **1519** HORMAN *Vulg.* 8 b, Our lady bare a chylde without any spot or wem of her virginite.

2. Material blemish, defect, injury, or stain. *Obs.* exc. *dial.*

a **1225** *Ancr. R.* 378 Hwon þe gost iwent ut..wið-ute bruche & wið-ute wem, of his two huses. **13..** *E.E. Allit. P.* A. 1003 Saffer helde þe secounde stale, þe calsydoyne þenne withouten wemme. ? *a* **1366** CHAUCER *Rom. Rose* 930 That other bowe was of a plante Withoute wem, I dar warante. **1387** TREVISA *Higden* I. 185 Vppon þat hulle lettres þat were i-write in poudre were i-founde wiþ oute wem [L. *illibatæ*] at þe ȝeres ende. *c* **1420** *Chron. Vilod.* 4228 Alle herre clothus ..were..clene wᵗouȝt spotte ore wemme. *c* **1440** *Pallad. on Husb.* IX. 157 Yf hit [water] be cleer apperyng like the skie, Withouten wem or signe of thingis vile. **1545** ASCHAM *Toxoph.* II. 114 A bowe..not marred with knot, gaule, wyndeshake, wem, freate or pynche. **1553** *Respublica* II. iii. 565 Naie, Honestie will not see a wemme on your Cote. **1565** STAPLETON tr. *Bede's Hist. Ch. Eng.* 151 All the clothes, that were about hym, semed..without wem or any blemish. **1657** C. BECK *Universal Char.* M 3 A wemme, v. *flaw*. **1691** RAY *S. & E.-Country Words*, *Wem*, a small fault, hole, decay, or blemish; especially in cloth, *Essex*. *a* **1825** FORBY *Voc. E. Anglia*, *Wem*, a small fretted place in a garment. **1889** *N.W. Linc. Gloss.* s.v., I'd no idee that tree was so full o' wems as I've fun it oot to be.

†**b.** Hurt, harm, injury. *Obs.*[−1]

1338 R. BRUNNE *Chron.* (1725) 76 So grete vengeance he nam of men of holy kirke, þat not did no wem tille him ne no trespas.

†**c.** *fig.* A break or pause (in time). *Obs.*

1599 NASHE *Lenten Stuffe* 43 This scuffling or bopeepe in the darke they had a while without weame or bracke.

3. Bodily blemish, disfigurement, or defect; also, the mark of a bodily injury, a cicatrix, a scar. *Obs.* exc. *arch.*

1297 R. GLOUC. (Rolls) 6897 ȝif..hire vet in eny wemme be ybroȝt, Holdeþ hom gulti of þe dede. *a* **1300** *Cursor M.* 19721 Men lete him dun Vte ouer þe walles o þe tun, Witvten ani wond or weme. *c* **1350** *Will. Palerne* 2460 þat barn þe best adoun sette Wiþoute eny maner wem þe worse it to greue. **1382** WYCLIF *Exod.* xii. 5 It shal ben a lombe with-outen wemme [Vulg. *absque macula*]. **1387** TREVISA *Higden* IV. 231 He schewed opounliche þe wemmes of the sore woundes [L. *vulnerum cicatrices*] þat he hadde i-fonge in Egipt. *c* **1400** *Lanfranc's Cirurg.* 247 Macula is a wem in a mannys iȝe. **1448–9** METHAM *Amoryus & Cl.* 1866 Hole and sound, with-owte wemme off yowre woundys, Nowe vpryse. *a* **1500** *Hist. K. Boccus & Sydracke* (? 1510) Z iij, If a man..haue a wemme in a lym Shal a man vpbreyde it hym. **1526** R. WHYTFORD *Martiloge* 122 b, A martyr slayne by yᵉ swerde, whose holy body..was founde .xl. dayes after his dethe..hole wᵗout wemme. **1577–87** HOLINSHED *Chron.* I. 92/1 There appeered in his head the signes and prints of ten wounds or more: all the which were growne into one wem. **1580** LYLY *Euphues* (Arb.) 463 This is the Glasse Ladies wher-in I woulde haue you..rubbe out the wrinckles of the minde, and be not curious about the weams in the face. *a* **1613** BREREWOOD *Lang. & Relig.* 196 Although the wound be in some sort healed, yet the wem or scar still remaineth. **1820** SCOTT *Monast.* x, 'It is even so,' he added,..'neither wem nor wound—not as much as a rent in his frock!'

fig. **1513** DOUGLAS *Æneis* IV. i. 46, I knaw and felis the wemmys and the way Of the ald fyre and flamb of luffis heit. **1623** BINGHAM *Xenophon, Comp. Rom. Manner of War* X 2 b, You spots and wems of noble Mars [tr. Lipsius *vos maculae et vibices generosi Martis*], which make the warres a refuge and sanctuarie for your villanies.

4. (By confusion with WEN[1].) A raised spot; a protuberance.

1567 MAPLET *Gr. Forest* 36 b, Theophrast sayth that it [the Cedar tree] is of marveylous highe growth,..about the bodie without wem or knot. **1584** D. FENNER *Def. Ministers* (1587) 123 Wemmes, bunches, and needlesse waightes of fatte. **1610** DONNE *Pseudo-Martyr* iv. §31. 138 The Reformers..thought to..take off euery Mole, and paire away euery Wemme.

wem, var. *whem* WHIM *sb.*[1]

1769 *Ann. Reg., Nat. Hist.* 101/1 Four horses,..at a common wem or engine, are sufficient to keep the mine clear.

†**wem**, *v. Obs.* Forms: 1 **wemman**, 3 **wemmy**, 5 **wemme**; *pa. t.* 1–2 **wemde**, 4–5 **wemmed**; *pa. pple.* 3 (*Orm.*) **wemmedd**, 3 **y-**, 4 **i-**, 4–6 **wemmed** (3 **y-wemned**); 3 **i-**, 4 **wemmid**, 4–5 **wemmyd**; 3 **i-wemmet**, 5 *Sc.* **wemmyt**; 4 **wemed**, 6 **wembde**. [OE. *wemman* (and *ȝewemman*), f. *wamm* WAM. Cf. AWEM *v.* and OHG. *bi-*, *giwemman*, Goth. *anawammjan* to blame.]

1. *trans.* To disfigure, mutilate (a person, his body); to impair (the mind); to injure (a thing).

c **900** tr. *Baeda's Hist.* IV. xxxii. (1890) 382 Wæs in ðæm mynstre sum ȝeong monn, ðam unwlitiȝ swyle & atolic his eaȝan wyrde & wemde. *a* **1225** *Leg. Kath.* 1426 Ah þæt wes miracle muchel, þæt nowðer nes iwemmet clað þæt ha hefden. *c* **1275** LAY. 6380 þat þorh his wraþþe his wit was i-wemmid. **1297** R. GLOUC. (Rolls) 6965 Ledeþ me þanne to mi sone, þat he mowe yse Min fet aboue & ek bineþe, wer hii ywemmed be. *a* **1300** *Cursor M.* 22824 If þat ani..Was wemed, or on fote or on hand,..it sal na wem o þam be sene. *a* **1375** *Joseph Arim.* 678 þenne com on fro þe fiht þat foule was wemmed, Was striken of þat on Arm and bar hit in þat oþer. **1387** TREVISA *Higden* V. 213 He ordeyned þat a man þat were i-wemmed in his body [L. *vitiatus corpore*] schulde fonge non ordres.

2. To desecrate or violate; to hurt or harm.

a **1000** *Ags. Ps.* (Spelm.) lxxxviii. 31 Ʒyf rihtwisnys min hi wemmaþ [L. *profanaverint*]. *a* **1000** *Ags. Laws* (Thorpe) II. 142 Ʒif he oðres ceorles wif wemme [L. *maculaverit*]. **1297** R. GLOUC. (Rolls) 4197, & þe wule he wolde þis tendre þing wemmy foule ynou. *c* **1375** *Cursor M.* 19504 (Fairf.) For god him gette, þat knawes al gode, þat he wemmed neuer sacles blode.

3. To spot or stain with sin or impurity.

c **1175** *Lamb. Hom.* 83 Alse þe liuendes godes sune in to þe meidene com & ho of hire meiden-had nawiht ne wemde. *c* **1200** ORMIN 2326 Sannte Marȝe sahh, þatt ȝho þa shollde wurrþenn Wiþþ childe, swa þatt ȝho þærþurrh Ne shollde nohht ben wemmedd. *a* **1300** *Cursor M.* 10021 Hir maiden-hed..neuer wemmed was a dele. **1387** TREVISA *Higden* V. 213 Also he seide þat Adam his synn wemmed [L. *laesit*] Adam alone. *c* **1449** PECOCK *Repr.* II. vi. 174 If the hous of Laban hadde be wemmed so cursidli as with the synne of ydolatrie. *a* **1500** *Hist. K. Boccus & Sydracke* (? 1510) G iij b, And she after chylde beryngе Shalbe wemmyd of nothynge.

4. To stain; to mark with spots.

1398 TREVISA *Barth. De P.R.* VIII. xxix. (Tollem. MS.) Whan sche [the moon] passeþ upwarde to þe heyer cerclis, sche is bryȝte and clene; and þan sche semeþ nouȝt wemmid with no splek and suttynge. **1567** DRANT *Hor. Art Poetrie* Ded. *iij, The verie Crownes and Scepters of best Monarks and princes had bene rustie, wembde, and warpde with obliuion.

Hence †**wemmed** *ppl. a.*

c **1375** *Sc. Leg. Saints* xxviii. (*Margaret*) 697 God forbed þat I With wenemyt [*read* wemmyt] handis sla þe in hy. **1382** WYCLIF *Deut.* xii. 15 Other vnclene it were, that is, wemmed and feble, other cleene, that is, hool and withouten wemme.

wem, obs. form of WAME.

†**wemay**, *int. Obs.* Also **wemo**, **wemmow**. [Cf. WE *int.*] An exclamation, app. denoting impatience or surprise.

c **1460** *Towneley Myst.* ii. 148 We! ryn on..Before! Wemay, man, I hold the mad! *Ibid.* 198 Wemo, wemo, foure [sheaves], lo, here! *Ibid.* xxvii. 291 *Lucas.* wemmow! where is this man becom?

wemb(e: see WAME, WEM *sb.*

wemble, var. WAMBLE.

weme: see WAME, WEM *sb.*

wemed, wemel: see WEMOD, WAMBLE.

women, obs. pl. of WOMAN.

†'**wemless**, *a. Obs.* [f. WEM *sb.* + -LESS. Cf. Icel. *vammlauss* faultless.]

1. Without stain of sin; undefiled, immaculate.

c **1275** *Orison Our Lord* 10 in *O.E. Misc.* 139 þo þu hire to come heo mayde wes, And mayde heo wes after wemme-les. *a* **1300** *E.E. Psalter* xiv. 2 Lauerd, in þi telde wha sal wone? .. Whilke þat incomes wemles, And ai wirkes rightwisenes. **13..** *Bonaventura's Medit.* 812 My sone ys slawe here afore myn ye þe whyche y bare wemles of my body. *a* **1400** *Pistill of Susan* 151 Are I þat worthliche wrethe, þat al þis world wrouȝt, Betere is wemles weende of þis world wyde. *c* **1420** LYDG. *Ballad* 104 Minor P. (1911) I. 258 O wemles mayden, enbelysshed with his byrthe.

2. Free from material blemish or imperfection; spotless.

a **1300** *Cursor M.* 18839 His for-hed fair, wemless to sight, Wit-vten ani runkel slight. **13..** *E.E. Allit. P.* A. 736 This makellez perle..is wemlez, clene & clere. **1398** TREVISA *Barth. De P.R.* VIII. xxviii. (1495) 338 Noo thynge [is] more Impassyble and wemles..than lyght.

3. Free from hurt or harm; uninjured.

c **1330** R. BRUNNE *Chron. Wace* (Rolls) 7906 He bar hym so in þat pres þat of wounde he was wem-les. *a* **1400** *Mirror St. Edmund* in *Hampole's Wks.* I. 222, I..þanke þe þat me ..þou hase kepid,..in þis nyghte..hale, safe, and wemles. *a* **1400–50** *Wars Alex.* 4066 [He] wendis a-way with that word & wemles þaim leuys. *c* **1470** *Gol. & Gaw.* 99 Bot thow mend hym that mys..Thow sall rew in thi ruse..Or thou wend of this wane wemeles away!

wemlock(e, var. forms of WAM-LOCK.

†'**wemming**, *vbl. sb. Obs.* Also 3 **wemmunge**, 3–4 **wemning(e, -ynge**, 4 **wemmyne**. [f. WEM *v.* + -ING[1].] The action of the verb; defilement; injury.

1100 *Aldhelm Gloss.* I. 4317 (Napier 113) *Lenocinii* wemminge. *c* **1230** *Hali Meid.* (1922) 19 Alswa deð meidenhad [preserve] meidenes cwike flesch, wiðute wemmunge halt alle hire limen & hire wittes. **1297** R. GLOUC. (Rolls) 6895 [Let them step on red-hot shares] & ȝif hire vet beþ þanne sauf wiþoute wemminge [*v.rr.* wemninge, wemnynge] Grauntеþ hom alle quit. *a* **1300** *Cursor M.* 11208 Ihesu crist hir barn sco bar,..and maiden neuer less, Wit-vten wemming of hir fless. **1300–1400** *Ibid.* App. XX. 236 Heo ȝaf out þe king & hadd hure broþer wiþoute wemning. *c* **1375** *Sc. Leg. Saints* xxvii. (*Machar*) 201 Angelis ..It kepit elyk fare fra wemmyne of þe fyr..oþir in body or in claith.

wemmow, wemo: see WEMAY *int.*

†**wemod**, *a. Obs.* Forms: α. 1 **wéamód**, 2–3 **wemod**, 3 **weamod**, 4 **waymot**. β. 3 **wamed**, **wemed**. [OE. *wéamód*, f. *wéa* affliction, trouble, malice + *-mód*: see MOOD *sb.* The β-forms may represent an OE. variant **wéaméde*.] Passionate, angry.

α. *c* **897** ÆLFRED *Gregory's Past. C.* xl. 289 Onȝean ðæt sint to manianne ða weamodan & ða grambæran [L. *iracundi*]. *c* **1175** *Lamb. Hom.* 5 Ne beo þu þereuore prud ne wilde ne sterc ne wemod ne ouer modi. *a* **1225** *Ancr. R.* 118 Pellican is..so weamod & so wreðful þet hit sleað ofte uor grome his owune briddes...þis pellican is þe weamode ancre. *c* **1290** *S. Eng. Leg.*, *St. George* 690 He is..Proud and wemod, and drinkare: and in wrathþe al-mest wod. **13..** *E.E. Allit. P.* C. 492 Why art þou so waymot wyȝe for so lyttel?

β. *c* **1205** LAY. 6368 Of alle þingen heo weore god ȝif heo neore to wamed. A-nan se he wes wrað wid eni mon i þan stude he hine wolde slæn. **13..** R. GLOUC. (Rolls) App. H 25 A knyȝt he was swiþe god, ac to wemed of ynou.

wempel, -pill, obs. forms of WIMPLE.

wen[1] (wɛn). Forms: 1 **wænn**, **wenn**, 2 **wean**, 4, 7–8 **wenn**, 5–7 **wenne**, 4– **wen**. [OE. *wen(n*, *wæn(n* = Du. *wen*, WFlem. *wan*, app. related to MLG. *wene* (1403), LG. *wehne*, *wähne* tumour, wart; the ultimate etym. is obscure.]

1. †**a.** A lump or protuberance on the body, a knot, bunch, wart. *Obs.* **b.** *Path.* A sebaceous cystic tumour under the skin, occurring chiefly on the head.

c **1000** *Sax. Leechd.* II. 34 Wiþ wenne on eaȝon ȝenim þa holan cersan [etc.]. *Ibid.* III. 46 Ȝif men synd wænnas ȝewunod on þæt heafod foran oððe on ða eaȝan. *c* **1050** *Voc.* in Wr.-Wülcker 422/2 *Impetigo*, eaȝan wenn. *c* **1400** *Lanfranc's Cirurg.* 8 In doynge awey þat is to myche skyn: as wertis or wennys. *c* **1440** *Promp. Parv.* 522/1 Wenne, *verucca*,..*gibbus*. *c* **1475** *Pict. Voc.* in Wr.-Wülcker 791/7 *Hic gibbus*, a wenne. **1555** Eden *Decades* (Arb.) 57 As he that wolde haue slaine Prometheus, wounded his wenne with his swoorde, whereby he was healed of that disease. **1597** Gerarde *Herbal* I. li. 72 The seede of Darnell..consumeth wens, hard lumps, and such like excrescence in any part of the body. **1626** Bacon *Sylva* §997 It would be tried, with Cornes and Wenns, and such other Excrescences. **1672** Wiseman *Treat. Wounds* II. ii. 10, I saw the Bullet lye like a small Wen or Scrophul, thrusting out under the Skin. **1711** Addison *Spect.* No. 59 ¶4 Cicero, who was so called from the Founder of his Family, that was marked on the Nose with a little Wen like a Vetch. **1794** R. J. Sulivan *View Nat.* I. 290 Others..exposed to fewer exhalations..will merely be deformed with wens and swellings about the joints. **1819** Keats *Otho* II. ii, Erminia has my shame fixed upon her, sure as a wen. **1840** Dickens *Old C. Shop* xi, A tall, meagre man, with a nose like a wen. **1884** T. Bryant *Pract. Surg.* (ed. 4) I. iii. 188 The acquired sebaceous cysts..are more common on the head and face than elsewhere..: when on the scalp they are known as 'wens'.

Comb. **1861** Wynter *Soc. Bees* 120 That cabinet of wen-like tumours.

c. Applied to the swelling on the throat characteristic of goitre. Also *Comb.*

1530 Palsgr. 287/2 Wenne in the throte, *gouoystre*, *gouistre*. **1617** Moryson *Itin.* I. 67 The men and women have great wens upon their throats, with drinking the waters that passe the Mines. *a* **1700** Evelyn *Diary* ? Apr. 1646 (Alps), People having monstrous gullets or wenns of fleshe growing to their throats. **1832** R. & J. Lander *Exped. Niger* I. v. 204 Others who have unseemly wens on the throat, as large as cocoa-nuts. **1852** *Meanderings of Mem.* I. 111 The wen-necked women.

d. An excrescence or tumour on the body of a horse.

1559 in *Richmond Wills* (Surtees) 133 One grey nagge with a wen in his side. **1600** Surflet *Country Farm* I. xxviii. 188 For the wen [Fr. *louppe*], open it when you shal perceiue it to be full of matter. **1649** J. Taylor (Water P.) *Wand. Wonders West* 19, I hired a Horse.., she had two wens as big as clusters of Grapes hung over both her eyes. **1677** *Lond. Gaz.* No. 1240/4 A black Coach Horse.., a wen upon the far foot behind. **1845** W. C. Spooner *Veterinary Art* 77 Wens are oval or round bodies, found floating loosely under the skin.

†**e.** An excrescence on a tree. *Obs.*

1538 Elyot *Dict.*, *Molluscum*, the wenne of a tree. **1577** B. Googe *Heresbach's Husb.* II. 108 With this wood [Maple] tables are couered..and other fine workes made, specially of the knobbes or wennes that growe out of it. **1707** Mortimer *Husb.* 330, I think those of eight or ten Inches circumference to grow better than smaller ones, provided the Bark be smooth, tender and void of Wens. **1725** T. Taylor in *Portland Papers* (Hist. MSS. Comm.) VI. 88 One old oak..had a kind of excrescence or wen upon it,..its semi-circle was thirty-two feet. **1791** Cowper *Yardley Oak* 66 And sides emboss'd With prominent wens globose.

f. *transf.* and *fig.*

Sometimes applied *spec.* to London: cf. quots. 1783, 1821.

1597 Shaks. *2 Hen. IV*, II. ii. 115 *Prince.* I do allow this Wen [Falstaff] to bee as familiar with me, as my dogge. **1640** Bastwick *Lord Bps.* iv. D 1 b, They are not the Body it selfe of the Church, but wennes, or swellings grown up, and..incorporated into the Body. **1649** J. Taylor (Water P.) *Wand. Wonders West* 12 Saint Michaels Mount..is a barren stony little wen or wart. **1678** Cudworth *Intell. Syst.* Pref. **1 b, This Digression of ours..is no Wen, or Excrescency, in the Body of this Book; but a Natural and Necessary Member thereof. **1765** in *Eliz. Carter's Lett.* 3 Sept. (1809) III. 118 This hot weather makes me languid... In Stoic language, I feel myself to be a wen. **1783** Tucker *Four Lett. Nat. Subj.* iii. 45 If..the Increase of Building [in London]..was looked upon to be no better than a Wen, or Excrescence, in the Body Politic. **1821** Cobbett *Rural Rides* (1885) I. 52 But what is to be the fate of the great wen of all? The monster, called..'the metropolis of the empire'? **1854** H. Rogers *Ess.* (1874) II. 6 Locke at once applies the knife to those huge wens of 'ontology'..which had so long impoverished..philosophy. **1871** Kingsley *At Last* iii, Port of Spain would be such another wen upon the face of God's earth as..the city of Havanna.

†**2.** A spot, blemish, stain. *lit.* and *fig.* *Obs.* (Confused with WEM *sb.*)

1340 *Ayenb.* 262 Þis boc is y-mad..Ham uor to berȝe uram alle manyere zen þet ine hare inwytte ne bleue no uoul wen. **1398** Trevisa *Barth. De P.R.* XVII. clxxviii. (1495) 720 The rote [of the wylde vyne] sod in reyne water and medlyd wyth wyne dooth awaye wennes [L. *maculas*]. **1535** Coverdale *Lev.* xxii. 22 Yf it be blynde, or broken, or wounded, or haue a wen..they shal offre none soch vnto the Lorde. **1552** Huloet, Wenne or fleshe spotte, *neuus*. *a* **1593** Marlowe *Ovid's Elegies* I. v. 18 Not one wen in her body could I spie.

3. Comb.: **wen-man** *nonce-wd.*, a city-dweller.

1937 Auden *Lett. from Iceland* viii. 102 The mountain-snob is a Wordsworthian fruit... He calls all those who live in cities wen-men.

wen[2]. Formerly the usual form of WYN, WYNN[2].

wen, repr. a pronunc. of WHEN *adv.* (*conj.*, *sb.*) in dialect or in uneducated speech.

1893 H. A. Shands *Some Peculiarities of Speech in Mississippi* 67 *Wen*, sometimes used by illiterate whites and negroes for *when*. **1901** M. Franklin *My Brilliant Career* iii. 16 It puts me in mind ev the time wen the black fellers made the gins do all the work. **1952** [see QUEEN *sb.* 5 e]. **1979** *Amer. Speech* LIV. 67 W'en you see the fire come from the brimstone..this earth ain' gon' be burnin'.

wen: see WEEN *sb.* and *v.*, WHEN, WHENNE.

†**wenbote**, var. WAINBOTE. *Obs.*

c **1250** *Rentalia Glaston.* (Somerset Rec. Soc.) 83 Debet habere wenbote, scilicet, unum quodque plaustrum, unum lignum. *Ibid.* 96, 133.

wench (wɛnʃ), *sb.* Forms: 3–7 **wenche**, (4 **weynche**, 5 **wenge**, 6 **wensche**, **whence**), 4– **wench**; *Sc.* 6 **winsch**, **wynch**, **vinche**, 8–9 **winch**. [ME. *wenche*, shortened form of early ME. *wenchel*: see WENCHEL.]

1. a. A girl, maid, young woman; a female child. Now *dial.*

c **1290** *S. Eng. Leg.*, *St. Kath.* 75 Nou is þis..gret schame..to sende a-boute..After þe gretteste Maistres, for-to despuyti a-ȝen a fol wenche. *a* **1300** *E.E. Psalter* lxvii. 27 Bifor come princes samened to singand þar, In midde wenches of timpans war. *c* **1350** *Will. Palerne* 1901 William & his worþi wenche [*sc.* Melior, his betrothed] þan were bliþe of þe help. *c* **1380** Wyclif *Serm.* Sel. Wks. I. 59 Crist came to þe hous of þis prince þat þe wenche lay deed inne. *a* **1450** *Mirk's Festial* 201 Then cryed þe fende and sayde: 'Alas,..al my myȝt ys lorne, now such a ȝeong wench hath ouercomen me'. **1519** *Interl. Four Elem.* (Percy Soc.) 25 Than we wyll have lytell Nell, A proper wenche, she daunsith well. **1548** Udall *Erasm. Par.*, *Luke* i. 57, 58 To whom it had been an happie chaunce to haue brought foorth a wenche, but a muche more luckie happe it was, to haue brought foorth a soonne. **1586** in Wadley *Bristol Wills* (1886) 250 If my wief be with Child whether it bee a Boye or a wenche I doe geve and bequeath vnto yt xx^{li}. **1606** Shaks. *Ant. & Cl.* I. ii. 36 Prythee how many Boyes and Wenches must I haue. **1648** Cromwell *Let. to Norton* 3 Apr., The money I shall need for my two little Wenches; and thereby I shall free my Son from being charged with them. **1665** Wood *Life* (O.H.S.) II. 53 One Mr. John Viccaridg his child (a wench) of 11 years old. **1787** Burns *Let. W. Nicol* 1 June, A clean-shankit, straught, tight, weel-far'd winch. **1860** Geo. Eliot *Mill on Fl.* I. ii, 'It seems a bit of a pity, though', said Mr. Tulliver, 'as the lad should take after the mother's side i'stead o' the little wench'. **1895** Crockett *Men of Moss Hags* xl. 287 For she was ever the most spirity wench in the world.

b. A girl of the rustic or working class.

1575 G. Harvey *Letter-bk.* (Camden) 145 She was but a milkmaide, and a plaine cuntrie wench. **1590** Spenser *F.Q.* I. iii. 11 She to her gan call,..But the rude wench her answer'd nought at all. **1620** Shelton *2nd Pt. Quix.* x. 59 Seeing none but the three wenches, he was somewhat troubled. **1717** Lady M. W. Montagu *Let. Pope* 1 Apr., These wenches [daughters of Greek gardeners]..pass their time at their looms. **1843** James *Forest Days* v, His taste lies amongst country wenches.

c. As a familiar or endearing form of address; used chiefly in addressing a daughter, wife, or sweetheart. Now only *dial.* or *arch.*

1581 A. Hall *Iliad* v. 97 [Juno to Pallas] Go we my wench, and let vs shew this dizarde here at ful, What power..we two haue. **1613** Shaks. *Hen. VIII*, IV. ii. 167 [Katharine to Patience, her woman.] When I am dead, good Wench, Let me be vs'd with Honor. **1826** Scott *Woodst.* ii, 'I fear ye lie, wench,' said her father. **1848** Mrs. Gaskell *Mary Barton* iii, Thou'lt have enough to do and to bear, poor wench, to-morrow. **1856** Mrs. Browning *Aur. Leigh* III. 1056 The mother held her tight, Saying..'Why wench, why wench, The squire speaks to you now'. **1885** J. Payn *Talk of Town* I. 189 Of course it annoyed me, wench, to see Frank so obstinate.

2. A wanton woman; a mistress. *Obs.* exc. *arch.*

More explicitly ***common, light,*** or ***wanton wench, wench of the stews***.

1362 Langl. *P. Pl.* A. Prol. 51 Ermytes on an hep wiþ hoteide staues, Wenten to Walsyngham & here wenchis aftir. **1377** *Ibid.* B. XIX. 433 Wenches of þe stuwes. *c* **1386** Chaucer *Merch. T.* 958, I am a gentil womman and no wenche. **1390** Gower *Conf.* I. 263 Envie..Is of the Court the comun wenche. *c* **1420** *Chron. Vilod.* 3360 Kyng Edgarus douȝter yche wene he was, Y-kete bot vpon a wenche. *a* **1529** Skelton *Col. Clout* 970 Vpon these beestes rydynge, Naked boyes strydynge, With wanton wenches winkyng. **1535** Coverdale *Isaiah* xxiii. 16 Take thy lute (saie men to her) and go aboute the citie, thou art yet an vnknowne wensche. **1590** Shaks. *Com. Err.* IV. iii. 55 Nay, she is worse, she is the diuels dam: And here she comes in the habit of a light wench. **1607** Dekker & Webster *Northw. Hoe* I. B 1, A lodging of your prouiding? to bee cal'd a Lieutenants, or a Captaines wench! **1666** Pepys *Diary* 6 Aug., Find my wife mightily out of order, and reproaching of Mrs. Pierce and Knipp as wenches, and I know not what. **1698** [see LIG-BY]. **1765** Francis tr. *Hor.*, *Sat.* (ed. 7) I. iv. 65 His spendthrift Son, who spurns the portion'd Bride, And keeps a common Wench. **1781** Johnson in *Boswell* 8 May, Chief Justice ——, who loved a wench, summed up favourably, and she was acquitted.

3. A female servant, maidservant, serving-maid; also †handmaid, †bondwoman.

1380 *Lay Folks Catech.* (L.) 861 Thy neyȝboris hows, wenche ne knaue Coueyte hem noȝt. *c* **1384** Chaucer *H. Fame* 206 Lord and lady, grome and wenche Of al the Troyan nacioun. *c* **1400** *Apol. Loll.* (Camden) 74 As God bad bi Sara, Kast out þe wench and her son. *c* **1491** *Chast. Goddes Chyld.* 89 He [Peter] that for a worde of a wenche forsoke hym. **1526** Tindale *Mark* xiv. 66 There cam won of the wenches off the hyest preste. **1578** T. N. tr. *Conq. W. India* 27 He determined to send one of the wenches to call her maister. **1659–60** Pepys *Diary* 10 Mar., My wife was late making of caps for me, and the wench making of a pair of stockings. **1710** Steele *Tatler* No. 248 ¶5 The Wench in the Kitchen sings and scowers from morning to night. **1740** Richardson *Pamela* (1824) I. iv. 19 O! said she, if the wench, (for so she calls us maiden-servants,) takes care of herself she'll improve. **1758** Johnson *Idler* No. 26 ¶3 Scarcely a wench was to be got for *all work*. **1819** Scott *Bride Lamm.* vi, It is the wench of the house clattering to the well in her pattens. **1843** Lefevre *Life Trav. Phys.* I. 8, I..was informed by a dirty looking wench who opened the door, that the young ladies were gone. **1883** Miss Broughton *Belinda* III. viii, Tea..is brought out to them, in an arbour overlooking the stream, by a stout wench.

attrib. **1552** Huloet, Wenche seruaunte, *ancilla*... A..maid seruaunte, or pore wenche seruaunt.

b. *U.S.* (See quots.)

1765 *Boston Gazette* 17 June (Thornton) 'Tis said the Fire was occasioned by a Negro Wench carrying a Quantity of Ashes. **1828–32** Webster, *Wench.* 3. In America, a black or colored female seryant; a negress. **1848** Bartlett *Dict. Amer.* **1891** *Century Dict.*, *Wench.* 3 (*c*) A colored woman of any age; a negress or mulattress, especially one in service. (Colloq.)

4. Comb.: **wench-like** *a.*, girlish.

1552 Huloet, Wenche lyke, *puellaris*. **1611** Shaks. *Cymb.* IV. ii. 230 Do not play in Wench-like words with that Which is so serious.

wench (wɛnʃ), *v.* *Obs.* exc. *arch.* [f. WENCH *sb.*] *intr.* To associate with common women. †*to wench out* (time): to spend (it) in wenching.

1599 Porter *Two Angry Wom. Abington* H 1, Indeed tis true, I am thus late a wenching, But I am forc'st to wench without a wench. *c* **1624** Chapman *Hymn to Hermes* 324 Tis better here to Imitate the Gods, And wine or wench out all times Periods. **1634** Peacham *Compl. Gentl.* i. (1906) 10 To be drunke, sweare, wench..are the attributes and markes now adayes of a great part of our Gentry. **1668** Dryden *Even. Love* IV. ii, As I am a Gentleman, a man of the Town, one who wears good Cloathes, Eates, Drinks, and Wenches abundantly. **1722** Steele *Conscious Lovers* IV. ii, Sir, I never saw a Man that wench'd soberly and discreetly, that ever left it off. **1809** Malkin *Gil Blas* IX. i. (Rtldg.) 311 Tell me where Signor de Santillane is fallible. Is he fond of play? does he wench?

†**wenchel.** *Obs.* Forms: 1, 3 **wencel**, (1 **wincel**), 3 **wenchel**, (*Orm.* **wennchell**), **wancel**. [OE. *wencel* n.:—**wankil-*, prob. related to *wancol* WANKLE *a.* The form *wincel* may represent a variant **winkil-*.] A child (of either sex); also, a servant or slave; also, a common woman.

c **890** Wæferth tr. *Gregory's Dial.* 11/20, & þa arn an wencel [L. *mancipium*] mid treowenum æscene.. to þære wyllan. *c* **1000** *St. Basil's Admonitio* ii. (1849) 34 And he for his wife ne for his wenclum ne dearr hine sylfne beladian. *c* **1200** Ormin 3356 Forr ȝuw iss borenn nu to daȝȝ Hælennde off ȝure sinness, An wennchell þatt iss Jesu Crist. *c* **1205** Lay. 31834 Quelæn þa wifmen, quelen þa wanclen. *a* **1225** *Ancr. R.* 334 And hu [he] biseinte Sodome & Gomorre, men & wummen & children [*MSS. T, C*, were & wif & wenchel]. *c* **1300** *11,000 Virg.* 98 in *E.E.P.* 68 His Cardynals were þeraȝen þat he his dignete gan reue Wiþ wenclen [*S. Eng. Leg.* 89/96 fole wummen] forto go.

wencher ('wɛnʃə(r)). Also 7 **wentcher**. [f. WENCH *v.* + -ER[1].] One who associates with common women.

1593 *Passionate Morrice* (1876) 82 Those I suspected to be wenchers. *a* **1625** Fletcher *Noble Gent.* I. i, I am a whoremaster, And such a one as dare be..pointed at to be a noble wencher. *a* **1654** Selden *Table Talk*, *Clergy* ¶5 Like the Fellow that was a great Wentcher. **1667** Pepys *Diary* 29 July, My cozen Roger told us..that the Archbishop of Canterbury, that now is, do keep a wench, and that he is as very a wencher as can be. **1701** Grew *Cosm. Sacra* II. vii. 76 He must be..no Gamester, Wencher, Fopp. **1712** Steele *Spect.* No. 274 ¶1 Impotent Wenchers.

wenching ('wɛnʃɪŋ), *vbl. sb.* [f. WENCH *v.* + -ING[1].] The action of the verb: also *attrib.*

1601 Holland *Pliny* XXXV. x. II. 545 Given he was exceedingly to wenching. *c* **1620** Fletcher *False One* IV. ii, You were told what this same whorson wenching long agoe would come to. **1672** Dryden *Assignation* II. i, Love alone, is either plain wenching, where every Curtizan is your Mistriss,..or else,..plain whining after one Woman. **1712** Addison *Spect.* No. 383 ¶5 [They asked] whether he was not ashamed to go a Wenching at his Years? **1775** Sheridan *St. Patrick's Day* II. i, Between ourselves, he is most confoundedly given to wenching. **1811** Byron *Hints fr. Horace* 706 The youth who trains..Must bear privations..Be call'd to labour when he thinks to dine, And, harder still, leave wenching and his wine. **1873** L. O. Pike *Hist. Crime* I. 93 In reality the Priest took to Money-getting and Wenching.

attrib. **1590** *Tarlton's Newes Purgatorie* 5 And some I can tell you haue come thither for wenching matters. **1592** *Def. Conny catching* in *Greene's Wks.* (Grosart) XI. 62, I omit Miles the Millers coossenage for wenching affaires. **1607** Dekker & Webster *Northw. Hoe* IV. i. E 3 b, I hope you thinke my wenching daies are past.

'**wenching**, *ppl. a.* [f. WENCH *v.* + -ING[2].] That habitually associates with common women.

1606 Shaks. *Tr. & Cr.* V. iv. 35 Whats become of the wenching rogues? **1719** D'Urfey *Pills* V. 268 To Wenching Smell-smocks give I these. **1913** *Sat. Rev.* 11 Oct. Suppl. p. iv/1 Fox was himself a gambling, drinking, wenching..rascal.

'**wenchless**, *a.* *rare*$^{-1}$. [f. WENCH *sb.* + -LESS.] Unprovided with a wench or wenches.

1608 Shaks. *Per.* IV. ii. 5 Mettelyne is full of gallants, wee lost too much money this mart by beeing too wenchlesse.

wencus, obs. Sc. form of VANQUISH *v.*

Wend (wɛnd), *sb.* Also **Vend**; 8 **Winde**. [ad. G. *Wende*, *Winde* (pl. *Wenden*, *Winden* = Da. *Vender*, ON. *Vindr*, OHG. *Winida*, OE. *Winedas*, *Weonod-*, med.L. *Venedi*, *Veneti*), of doubtful origin.]

1. A member of the Slavonic race now inhabiting Lusatia in the east of Saxony, but formerly extending over Northern Germany; a Sorb.

1786 tr. *J. R. Forster's Hist. Voy. North* 101 *note*, The Vandals mentioned here, are indubitably the Wends, or that tribe of the Sclavonians which opposed the Moguls and the Tartars. **1788** *Encycl. Brit.* (ed. 3) II. 700/1 (*Austria*), The

Windes, who are mixed with the Germans in these countries. **1830** *Encycl. Metrop.* XXI. 340 The Vends are a well-made, strong, courageous, and industrious people. **1843** *Penny Cycl.* XXVI. 206/1 The language of the Vends ..dates its first literature from the Reformation. **1861** PEARSON *Early & Mid. Ages* 155 Canute was still unable to subdue the Wends, who..made the Baltic a Slavonian lake. **1886** BARING-GOULD *Germany* xliii. 264 Henry I. had created the Margravate of Brandenburg as a bulwark against the heathen Wends, who lived on the Baltic.

2. ***Southern Wends***: (see quot.).

1822 *Encycl. Brit.* Suppl. V. 242 In 640, the Sclavonians took possession of Illyria,..and they still retain it, under the names of Servians, Croatians, and Southern Wends. *Ibid.*, The southern Wends..are now mixed with Germans in Carniola, Carinthia, and Lower Stiria.

wend (wɛnd), *v.*[1] *Pa. t.* and *pa. pple.* **wended** ('wɛndɪd). Forms: *Infin.* α. 1 **wendan** (*North.* **wœnda**), 2 **wænden** (**wanden**), 3-4 **wenden** (3 *Ormin* **wendenn**), 5 **wendyn**, *Sc.* **wendin**; 3-6 **wende** (4 **whende**), 4-5 *north.* and *Sc.* **vend**, 4- **wend**; 3 *sing. pres.* 1-4 **went** (2 **want**); β. 3 **wiende**, 4-5 **weende**, *north.* and *Sc.* 4-5 **weind**, **weynd**, 5 **weynde**; γ. 4 **winde**, **wind**, 5 **wynde**, **wynd**; δ. 4-6 **went**. *Pa. t.* 1-4 **wende** (3 *Ormin* **wennde**); 2 **wænte** (**wante**), 4-5 **wente**, 4- **went** (5 **whent**); *north.* 4 **weint**, 4-5 **wynt**; 6- **wended** (5 *north.* **weyndut**). *Pa. pple.* 1 **ʒewend**, 3-4 **iwend**, 4 **ywend**, **-e** (**wende**), 3-5 **wend** (3 *Ormin* **wennd**); 2 **i-want**, 3-5 **i-**, **iwent**, **went**, **wente**, 4 **y-**, **ywent**, 5 **i-wente**; *Sc.* 6 **wynt**; 1, 4, 6- **wended**. [Common Teutonic: OE. *wendan*, = OFris. *wenda* (WFris. *weine*, *wine*, NFris. *wên*, *wän*), MDu. (and Du.) *wenden*, OS. *wendian* (MLG. and LG. *wenden*, LG. *wennen*), OHG. *wentan* (MHG. and G. *wenden*), ON. and Icel. *venda* (Norw. *venda*; Sw. *vända*, Da. *vende*), Goth. *wandjan*; f. **wand-*, the preterite stem of *windan* WIND *v.*[1], of which *wendan* is the causative. The original forms of the pa. t. and pa. pple. are respectively *wende* and *wended*, *wend*, but the forms *wente*, *went* appear beside these from *c* 1200, and latterly become the more usual; in the refl. and intr. senses *went* finally replaced the older preterites belonging to *go*, and from *c* 1500 is most naturally regarded as the pa. t. of that verb, while *wend* was provided with the new form *wended*.

The following are illustrations of the less usual forms of the infinitive and present. The β-forms represent a normal lengthening of the vowel in certain dialects. The γ-forms are merely graphic (by confusion with WIND *v.*[1]), as the rhymes regularly indicate *wĕnd* or *wēnd*. The δ-form is due to the influence of the pa. t. and pa. pple. in the form *went(e*.

β. *c* **1290** *St. Silvester* 23 in *S. Eng. Leg.* 391 To-niȝht þou schalt..wiende to þe pine of helle. *a* **1300** *Cursor M.* 2363 Ȝee sal weind til a better land. **13..** *Northern Passion* 198 (Camb.) Vnto þat cite sone gan þai weynd. **1362** LANGL. *P. Pl.* A. x. 171 Elles schal al dye, and to helle weende. ?*a* **1400** *Morte Arth.* 450 Thow weyndez by Watlyng-strette, and by no waye elles. **1421** HOCCLEVE *Minor P.* xxii. 561 On my behalue to thy lady weende [*rhyme* seende = send]. *c* **1460** *Towneley Myst.* ii. 132 Good brother, let vs weynd sone.

γ. *a* **1300** *Cursor M.* 3564 Til vnwelth windes al his wald. *Ibid.* 8619 Haf god-dai, for nov wind i. *a* **1400** R. GLOUC. (Rolls) 805 (MS. B.) Þat ich was wond to wynde Mid so mony hondred knyȝtes a boute in eche ende. *a* **1400-50** *Wars Alex.* 2014 (Ashm.), I warne þe, or I wynd. *Ibid.* 2150, 2177, etc. *c* **1435** *Torr. Portugal* 107 He takythe leve at lorddys hend, And on hys wey gan he wynd. *a* **1500** *Coventry Corpus Chr. Pl.* i. 330 To hys blys that ye may wynd At your last day.

δ. *a* **1300** *Cursor M.* 27748 It wentes man fra godd his will. *Ibid.* 28681 Þou fand..all for to went his will. **1375** BARBOUR *Bruce* IV. 257 And thi Ferrand..Sall richt to Paris went. *c* **1400** *Rule St. Benet* 2027 When þai sal went in cuntre. *c* **1470** HENRY *Wallace* I. 330 Scho prayde he wald to the lord Persye went. **1560** ROLLAND *Seven Sages* 75 Thow seruis better for to haue punischement,..nor halie gaitis to went.]

I. Transitive and reflexive senses.

1. †**a.** To alter the position or direction of; to turn (something) round or over: also with *across*, *adown*, *away*. ***to wend down***: to overthrow, destroy. *Obs.*

c **888** ÆLFRED *Boeth.* I. §2 Þa wendon hi me heora bæc to. **971** *Blickl. Hom.* 191 Petrus cwæþ, þa he com to þære rode, ..'Wendaþ min heofod ofdune'. *a* **1000** *Sax. Leechd.* III. 16 Clæm ðonne on arfæt; læt standan nyȝon niht; wende man ælce dæȝe. *c* **1000** *Ags. Gosp.* Luke vi. 29 And þam ðe þe slyhð on þin ȝewenge, wend oðer onȝean. *c* **1050** *Voc.* in Wr.-Wülcker 377/18 *Conuoluens*, wendende. *c* **1200** *Trin. Coll. Hom.* 161 Hie wenden þe eorðe & wurpen god sad þaronne. *c* **1205** LAY. 46 Laȝamon leide þeos boc & þa leaf wende [*c* 1275 tornde]. *Ibid.* 26559 Bos..his hors wende wunder ane swiðe. *a* **1225** *Ancr. R.* 62 Louerd, seið Dauid, wend awei mine eien vrom þe worldes dweole. *Ibid.* 430 He ..went þe neruwe ende of þe horne to his owune muðe. *c* **1250** *Gen. & Ex.* 1649 Iacob wið hire wente ðat ston. *a* **1300** *E.E. Psalter* ix. 7 Þair cites doune dide þou wende. *c* **1330** *Assump. Virg.* 711 (Add. MS.) Here mouþes were to here nek went. **13..** *Gaw. & Gr. Knt.* 2152 Bi þat þe wyȝe in the wod wendez his brydel. **1398** TREVISA *Barth. De P.R.* XVII. lxxii. (1495) 646 Heye is ofte reysed torned and wended. *Ibid.* cxlvii. 702 It falleth to powder while it is tornyd and wende and kneden in the honde. *c* **1400** *Beryn* 2837 They made hir takelyng redy, & wend þe saill a-cros. *c* **1440** *Pallad. on Husb.* VI. 13 And yf the rayn bishoure, Wende hit [hay] not til hit be parfit drie. *a* **1450** *Le Morte Arth.* 1349 Bors de gawnes stille stode And wrothe a-way hys yȝen wente.

absol. **1475** *Partenay* 6566 Ho it metre will,..Be it in balede, uers, Rime, or prose, He most torn and wend, metrely to close.

†**b.** *fig.* To turn over, revolve (thoughts, etc., in the mind). *Obs.*

a **1225** *Ancr. R.* 98, & ȝet hwon he is forðe, heo went in hire þuhte ofte swuche wordes.

†**c.** ***to wend away***, to take away, remove. *Obs.*

c **1250** *Gen. & Ex.* 2613 Egipte wimmen..boden ðe childe letten ðer, Oc [ȝ]he wente it awei wið rem. *c* **1440** *York Myst.* ii. 42 Oway I will it wende full wyght. *Ibid.* 46 Now sene þe erthe þus ordand es,..to growe with gres, and wedis þat sone away bese went.

d. *Naut.* To turn (a ship's bow or head) to the opposite tack. Also with *about*, *aloof*. (Cf. 6 c below, and WIND *v.*[1] 8.)

to wend (a boat) ***off***: to float (a stranded boat) by this operation.

1556 J. HEYWOOD *Spider & Fly* lvii. 206 Better wende your ship a loofe: and take sea roome: Then roon here on rockes. **1622** R. HAWKINS *Voy. S. Sea* xxxiv. 84 And laying out an Anchor, we sought to wend her off. **1631** PELLHAM *Gods Power* 6 Some of our companie..were perswaded, to wend about the Boates head the second time, unto the Southwards. *Ibid.* 7 We wended the Shallop..unto the Northward. **1635** *Adm. Court Exam.* 52, 22 Oct., The Neptune being then newly wended from the Shoare. **1704** J. HARRIS *Lex. Techn.*, *Wending*, is a term for bringing a Ships' Head about. **1834** MARRYAT *P. Simple* xliv, He hauled-to the launch, and wending her bow to the privateer, directed her carronade..to where the Frenchmen were crowded the thickest. **1867** SMYTH *Sailor's Word-bk.*

†**2.** *fig.* **a.** To turn (one's mind, thoughts, will, etc.) in a new direction; to alter (one's mind or intention). Const. *from*, *to*. *Obs.*

c **888** ÆLFRED *Boeth.* xxxiii. §4 Ic wolde nu þæt ðu wende þin inȝeþonc from þæm leasum ȝesælðum. *Ibid.* xxxv. §7 Swa hwa swa..his mod went to ðæm yflum ðe he ær forlet. *c* **1205** LAY. 8836 Nu ich wulle wende mi mod, aȝenes uuel ich wulle don god. *c* **1290** *St. Kath.* 16 in *S. Eng. Leg.* 92 Sire, heo seide,..Þov scholdest þi wisdom and þi wit to some guode wende. *c* **1290** *Beket* 998 *Ibid.* 135 All we worþez i-brouȝt to nouȝte, bote þov þi þouȝt wende. *a* **1300** *Cursor M.* 10646 Al hir might and all hir tent To godds seruis had sco went. *c* **1330** R. BRUNNE *Chron. Wace* (Rolls) 7807 Anon tys wif his wille he went. **1390** GOWER *Conf.* I. 235 If hire lord his herte wente To love in eny other place.

†**b.** To turn (a person) *to* or *from* a course of life or condition; to alter (a person's will or purpose). *Obs.*

c **1200** ORMIN 3441 Forrþi þatt he þeȝȝm wollde þa To rihhte læfe wendenn. *a* **1225** *Ancr. R.* 110 Forte wenden us urommard þe licunge þet flesches lustes askeð. *c* **1250** *Gen. & Ex.* 693 To wenden men fro godes reed, To newe luue and to newe dred. **13..** *Cursor M.* 24824 (Gött.) Þaa þat he had na giftes till, wid hightes faire he went þair will. **1338** R. BRUNNE *Chron.* (1725) 194 My broþer..Is riche of tenement, his sonnes strong & stith, þer wille wille not be went.

†**3. a.** To change the character of; to alter. *Obs.*

Rarely also with adj. complement.

a **1000** *Guthlac* 730 [758] Þy læs þa tydran mod þa ȝewitnesse wendan þurfe. **1154** *O.E. Chron.* (Laud MS.) an. 1137 He..makede mani weorkes & wende þe tun betere þan it ær wæs. *c* **1205** LAY. 7128 Þe uncuðe weoren..wenden heore [*sc.* the burghs'] nomen. *c* **1230** *Juliana* 38 Ant he wende heowes & warð swuch as he her wes unwiht of helle. *c* **1290** *St. Kenelm* 60 in *S. Eng. Leg.* 347 Þe king of kent was þo kyng of al þe londe of kent, þat weren inne tweie bischopriches, and ȝeot nis it nouȝt i-went. **1390** GOWER *Conf.* II. 144 That sche ne mai..speke a word, ne ones loke, That he [a spy] ne wol it wende and croke And torne after his oghne entente.

†**b.** To 'turn' from one language into another; to translate. Const. *on* (= into), *till* (= to). *Obs.*

c **897** ÆLFRED *Gregory's Past. C.* Prol. 7 Ða ongan ic..ða boc wendan on Englisc. ?*c* **900** —— *Boeth.* Proem, Ælfred kuning wæs wealhstod ðisse bec, & hie of boclædene on englisc wende. *c* **1200** ORMIN Ded. 113 Ȝiff mann wile witenn..Whi icc till Ennglissh hafe wennd Goddspelless hallȝhe lare.

†**c.** To change the form or nature of; to transform, transmute, or turn *to*, *into*. *Obs.*

c **1000** ÆLFRIC *Hom.* (Thorpe) I. 168 Ȝif ðu Godes Sunu sy, wend þas stanas to hlafum and et. *a* **1000** *Ags. Ps.* (Thorpe) cxiii. 8 He wendeð stan on widne mere. *a* **1225** *Ancr. R.* 78 Þer, þurh hire bone, was water iwend to wine. *a* **1250** *Owl & Night.* 1464 (Cott.) Þat child bi me hit understond An his unred to red went. *c* **1275** in *O.E. Misc.* 90 Selcuþ dude vre dryhtin þat he water wende to win. *a* **1300** *K. Horn* (Cambr. MS.) 470 Þanne is mi þralhod Iwent in to kniȝthod. **1340** *Ayenb.* 60 Hi alle..wendeþ to guode al þet þe guodeman deþ oþer zayþ. *c* **1350** *Libeaus Desc.* (Kaluza) 2132 Þourȝ har chauntement To worme þey hadde me went.

†**d.** To bring (into a certain state). *Obs.*

c **1250** *Gen. & Ex.* 2896 Louered, qui was ic hider sent? Ðin folc is more in sorwe went.

†**4.** *refl.* To turn, direct, or betake (oneself). Freq. with advs. or preps. *Obs.*

Orig. in purely reflexive use, with the accusative of the pronoun, which is subsequently replaced by the dative.

c **888** ÆLFRED *Boeth.* xl. §1 Ic wolde..ðæt wit unc wenden sume hwile to þises folces spræce. *c* **893** —— *Oros.* III. vii. §4 [He] hiene siþþan wende on his þrie ȝebroðor. *a* **900** *O.E. Chron.* an. 894 Þa se cyning hine þa west wende. *c* **1000** ÆLFRIC *Gen.* xlii. 24 He wende hine lithwon fram him and weop. *c* **1200** ORMIN 6576 Þatt sume off ure little flocc.. Hemm wendenn oþerr stund fra Crist. *Ibid.* 11320 Forrþ-rihht se Jesuss fullhtnedd wass, He wennde him inntill wesste. *c* **1205** LAY. 24177 Wend þe hider Howeldin..haue þu Bulune. *a* **1225** *Ancr. R.* 18 Þer efter wendeð ou to vre Leafdi onlicnesse, and cneoleð mid fif auez. *c* **1250** *Kent. Serm.* in *O.E. Misc.* 27 Þo kinges hem wenten and hi segen þo sterre. *a* **1300** *Cursor M.* 5693 Þir wimmen went þam ham a-gain. *c* **1374** CHAUCER *Boeth.* III. met. xii. (1868) 107 He wente hym to þe houses of helle. **1390** GOWER *Conf.* II. 238 And fro his lond with Sail updrawe Thei wente hem forth. *c* **1425** *Eng. Conq. Irel.* 30 He went hym to þe kyng henry, & hym swith besoght [etc.]. **1586** J. HOOKER *Hist. Irel.* in *Holinshed* II. 11/2 He thought long yer he could wend himselfe ouer into Ireland. **1635** J. HAYWARD tr. *Biondi's Banish'd Virg.* 163, I know it stands us upon to wend us hence assoone as we conveniently can.

†**b.** *lit.* of a vane: To revolve (*with* the wind).

1340 *Ayenb.* 180 Hi byeþ ase þe wedercoc þet is ope þe steple, þet him went mid eche wynde.

II. Intransitive senses.

†**5.** Of events, etc., or impers. with *it*: To have or take a certain course; to take place, happen, or come about. *Obs.*

Beowulf 1739 Ac him eal worold wendeð on willan. *c* **888** ÆLFRED *Boeth.* xxxix. §2 Ac ic wundrie swiðe swiðlice forhwi hit swa went swa hit nu oft deð. **1297** R. GLOUC. (Rolls) 9400 Cuþeþ to day ȝoure manhede þat it mowe wende To ȝou & to ȝoure children to honour wiþouten ende. *a* **1300** *Cursor M.* 18789 Bot godd for-bede sua þat it weind, Þat we vr fa mak of ur freind. **13..** *Ibid.* 7662 (Gött.) Þare mani a man fel vnder schild, Bot wid dauid went þe feld. **1340** *Ayenb.* 262 Nou ich wille þet ye ywyte hou hit is y-went Þet þis boc is y-write mid engliss of kent. **1377** LANGL. *P. Pl.* B. III. 280 For so is þis worlde went wiþ hem þat han powere That who-so seyth hem sothes is sonnest yblamed. **1390** GOWER *Conf.* II. 276 If myn happ were so well went, That for the hole I mihte have half. *c* **1400** *Beryn* 1264 Then Beryn..seid, 'is this a sermon or a prechement? Yee were nat wont her-to, how is this I-went?'

6. †**a.** ***to wend again***: to turn back, to return. *lit.* and *fig.* *Obs.*

In OE. also without adv., and with *on bæc*.

O.E. Chron. an. 895 Þa hie ða eft ut of Norð Wealum wendon mid þære here hyðe þe hie ðær ȝenumen hæfdon. *c* **1000** *Ags. Gosp.* Luke xvii. 31 And se ðe bið on æcere ne went he on-bæc. *Ibid.* xxiv. 33 And hiȝ arison..& wendon [*c* 1160 *Hatton* wenten] to hierusalem. *c* **1205** LAY. 1590 He wende on ȝean sone & he ohtliche feaht. *c* **1250** *Gen. & Ex.* 979 An angel..bad hire sone wenden agen. *Ibid.* 3724 We wilen..wenden in-to egipte agen. *a* **1300** *Cursor M.* 3027 Þai went again to bersabee. *c* **1375** *Ibid.* 1867 (Fairf.) Agayne he dide þe waters wende, þe ship on lande bigan to lende. *c* **1430** *Chev. Assigne* 137 Wende þou aȝeyne, malkedras, & gete me þe cheynes.

†**b.** Of the wind: To change in direction. *Obs.*

c **1205** LAY. 9407 Þe wind wende forð riht framward þan stronde in to þissen londe. *c* **1400** *Gamelyn* 703 And sente.. For to seke Gamelyn..To telle him tydinges how the wind was went.

†**c.** *Naut.* Of a ship: To turn her head about (see 1 d above). *Obs.*

1297 R. GLOUC. (Rolls) 21 Wateres..Ȝware bi þe ssipes mowe come fram þe se & wende And bringe alonde god inoȝ. **1530** PALSGR. 779/2, I wende, I turne, as a shyppe dothe with the tyde. **1537** *Adm. Court Oyer & Term.* 73. No. 38 The said wood hoye..dyd wende abowte for to cum to an anker. *a* **1609** SIR F. VERE *Comm.* (1657) 32 About me the Gallions let slip Cable in the haulse, and with their top sails wended and drew towards the shore on the left hand of the Bay. *a* **1618** RALEGH *Observ. Royal Navy* (1650) 9 The lesser [ship] will turne her broad sides twice, before the greater can wend once. **1630** J. TAYLOR (Water P.) *Praise of Hempseed* Wks. III. 65 East and by South, West and by North she wends. **1704** J. HARRIS *Lex. Techn.* s.v. *Wending*,..They say, How wends the Ship? i.e. Which way does her Head lie?

†**7.** To turn from one condition or form to another; to change *to* or *into*. *Obs.*

c **888** ÆLFRED *Boeth.* iv, Forþan went nu fulneah eall moncyn on tweonunga, ȝif [etc.]. *c* **1000** *Sax. Leechd.* II. 248 Þonne ne maȝon þas þing helpan for þon ðe þæt wile wendan on wæter bollan. *c* **1250** *Gen. & Ex.* 321 [Lucifer] Wente in to a wirme, and tolde eue a tale. *a* **1300** *Cursor M.* 3564 His blode..wexus dri and cald, Til vnwelth windes [*v.r.* wendis] al his wald. **1340** *Ayenb.* 6 Þe wone is kueaduol and may wel wende to zenne dyadliche bot yef him ne loki. *Ibid.* 69 Þet him ssolde by triacle, to him went in to uenym. **1377** LANGL. *P. Pl.* B. XVIII. 202 Wo in-to wel mowe wende atte laste. **1422** YONGE tr. *Secreta Secret.* 153 Be-holde thy-Selfe, that thow arte Erthe and into Erthe thow shalte wende. **1579** SPENSER *Sheph. Cal.* Feb. 11 Must not the world wend in his commun course From good to badd, and from badde to worse?

†**8.** Of persons: To turn in thought or purpose *to* or *from* (a person, course of action, etc.); to betake oneself (*to* something different); to change or vary one's purpose. Said also of the heart. *Obs.*

For further illustration see 17 a.

c **888** ÆLFRED *Boeth.* xlii, Forðæm hit nis no unnet þæt we hopien to Gode, forðæm he ne went no swa swa we doð. *a* **1225** *Ancr. R.* 92 Euer so þe wittes beoð more ispreinde utwardes, se heo lesse wendet inwardes. *c* **1250** *Gen. & Ex.* 3510 Oc horedom ðat ðu ne do, Ne wend no lecherie to. *c* **1300** *Havelok* 1705 From him ne mithe [might] his herte wende, Ne fro him, ne fro his wif. **13..** *Cursor M.* 23049 (Edin.) [They] went vnto religioun, And did þair bodis in prison. **1340-70** *Alex. & Dind.* 804 For ȝe ben couaitouse kid & kunne nouht blinne, But euere wenden to winne wordliche godus. *c* **1400** *Rule St. Benet* (Verse) 313 Þair-for of þam I spek no fare, Bot to þe first I wend o-gayn. **1565** J. HALL *Crt. Vertue* 132 b, Can plague nor payne Make you refrayne, Nor from wickednes wende? **1567** *Gude & Godlie B.* (S.T.S.) 35 Christ..To saif vs is ful plyabill, Gif we repent and to him wend.

†**9.** To turn round, over, or from side to side; to turn or twist the body. *Obs.*

a **1310** in Wright *Lyric P.* vi. 28 Nihtes when y wende ant wake. *c* **1330** R. BRUNNE *Chron. Wace* (Rolls) 8197 When þey [the dragons] hadde longe to-gyder smyten,..Wyppyng wyþ wenges, ouer-wepen & went. **1390** GOWER *Conf.* I. 43

Forthi may no certeinete Be set upon his jugement, Bot as the whiel aboute went He yifth his graces undeserved. *c* **1475** *Partenay* 2905 In on estat ne myght he noght sogourn; Here on bakke laide, efte the bely vppon, Torning and wendyng euer enuiron. **15..** *Schole Ho. Women* 1014 in Hazl. *E.P.P.* IV. 115 Rub a scald horse vpon the gall, And he wil bite, wins and went. **1542** Udall *Erasm. Apoph.* Pref. *vj, [Wrestlers] haue..certain suer poinctes and wayes bothe to catche holde, and also to wend out of holde. **1561** Hollybush *Hom. Apoth.* 4 He wendeth and waltereth, and happely his head and fete do mete together.

fig. *c* **1374** Chaucer *Anel. & Arc.* 187 Hir daunger made him booþe bowe and beende, And as hir lyste made him tourne and wende.

†**b.** ***to wend to ground***, to fall from one's horse.

c **1430** *Chev. Assigne* 302 What yf grace be [that] we to grownde wenden?

10. To go off, away, or out; to depart. Also with preps., as *into*, *to*, *from*, or *to* with *inf.* Now *arch.*

In later use not clearly distinguishable from sense 13.

c **1000** Ælfric *Saints' Lives* xxv. 425 Oð þæt hi oncneowon þæt se cena iudas him wið-feohtende wæs and wendon ða to horsum. *c* **1200** *Trin. Coll. Hom.* 87 Ihc wile turnen agen to mine huse þe ich er ut of wende. *a* **1225** *Ancr. R.* 162 As ofte as ich euer was, he seið, among men, ich wende from ham [*L. recessi*] lesse mon þen ich er was. *c* **1290** *Beket* 840 in *S. Eng. Leg.* 130 Þo þov wendest of his seruise he ne Axede þe no-þing. *a* **1300** *Cursor M.* 860 Wen Adam sagh he had misdon He went to hide him al-son. *Ibid.* 14186 Yee sal Vnto Iude weind wit me nu. **1362** Langl. *P. Pl.* A. xi. 112, I..askede hire þe heiȝe wey wher Clergye dwelleþ, ..for tyme is þat I wende. *c* **1386** Chaucer *Prol.* 21 In Southwerk at the Tabard as I lay Redy to wenden on my pilgrymage. ?*a* **1400** *Morte Arth.* 2493 Thare salle weende to this viage sir Gawayne hym selfene. *c* **1400** *Beryn* 523 In soth, quod he, I woll nat fro þe dorre vend. *c* **1440** *Gesta Rom.* 246, & þere for withe owten lenger delay he made althinge Redy for to wende. *a* **1500** *Hist. K. Boccus & Sydracke* (? 1510) X j b, Whan the soule at the ende Shal out fro the body wende. **1568** Grafton *Chron.* II. 80, I may not wende out of my lande, for mine awne sonnes will rise against me, when I were absent. **1603** Shaks. *Meas. for M.* iv. iii. 150 Wend you with this Letter. **1819** Scott *Ivanhoe* xx, Wend on your way, in the name of God and St. Dunstan. **1879** Butcher & Lang *Odyss.* 11 To the end that after thou hast bathed..thou mayst wend to the ship joyful in spirit.

b. with advs., as *away*, *out*, *hence*.

c **1100** *O.E. Chron.* (MS. D.) an. 1050 Se cyng þa sende æfter þam scypum..þe ær ham wendon. *c* **1200** *Trin. Coll. Hom.* 161 *Hinc ex quo ueteres emigrauere coloni.* Aure seððen þe ealde tilie henne wenden. *a* **1225** *Ancr. R.* 50 Witeð þer our eien, leste þe heorte etfleo & wende ut. *c* **1250** *Gen. & Ex.* 623 He and hise wif wenten ut fre. *a* **1300** *Cursor M.* 6160 Quen þis time was al broght to end, Of egypte godds ost vte vend. *c* **1350** *Will. Palerne* 329 Seþþe þou schalt hennes wende, whanne þou komest to kourt..bere þe boxumly & bonure. **1377** Langl. *P. Pl.* B. xii. 82 Þe iewes knewe hemseluen Gultier..and wenten awey for schame.

c. In various obs. phrases, as ***to wend to bed***, ***to church***, ***to meat***, ***to seat***.

c **1300** *St. Brandan* 221 in *S. Eng. Leg.* 225 Þe monekes wende to bedde & slepe: þo soper was ido. **13..** *Cursor M.* 19046 (Gött.) Petre and iohn..went to kirc to make þair bone. **13..** *Gaw. & Gr. Knt.* 72 When þay had waschen, worþyly þay wenten to sete, Þe best burne ay abof. *c* **1400** *Destr. Troy* 2558 Than comaund the kyng the courtte for to ryse; Askit water wightly, wentton to meyte. *c* **1430** *Chev. Assigne* 161 And whenne it drowȝe to þe nyȝte he wendethe to bedde.

†**11.** To depart by death. Usu. with advb. phr., as ***to wend of*** or ***from life***, (***out***) ***of this world***, ***forth***, ***hence***, ***to death***, etc. (See also 17 d.) *Obs.*

971 *Blickl. Hom.* 195 Forþon ure yldran swultan & swiþe oft us from wendan. *a* **1250** *Prov. Alfred* 172 in *O.E. Misc.* 112 Not no mon..þene ende hwenne he schal heonne wende. *c* **1250** *Gen. & Ex.* 3884 Aaron ðo wente of liwe ðor. *a* **1300** *Cursor M.* 1272 Þou prai him þat he word me send Quen I sal o þis werld wend. *c* **1340** Hampole *Pr. Consc.* in *Archæologia* XIX. 323 The time of deth at our last end, When that we schul from henns wend. **1362** Langl. *P. Pl.* A. i. 152 For þe same Mesure þat ȝe Meten A-mis oþer elles, Ȝe schul be weyen þer-with whon ȝe wenden hennes. *c* **1400** *Pety Job* 652 in *26 Pol. Poems* 142 But oute of the world sone shal I wende. **1421** Hoccleve *Minor P.* xxiii. 136 Lord god shal y now die and hennes weende? *c* **1470** *Gol. & Gaw.* 1081 Quhasa with wourschip sall of this warld wende. **1563** B. Googe *Eglogs* etc. (Arb.) 73 The enuyous fates..in the mydst of all his toyle, dyd force hym hence to wende. **1567** *Gude & Godlie B.* (S.T.S.) 13 Grant vs grace, quhen we sall die, And fra this present lyfe we wend.

b. Similarly ***to wend to, into*** (heaven, hell, bliss, etc.).

c **1200** Ormin 8426, & siþþenn shall all Cristess hird Wiþþ Crist till heoffne wendenn. *c* **1250** in *O.E. Misc.* 186 Alle bac-biteres wendet [*c* **1275** wendeþ] to helle. *c* **1305** *St. Andrew* 99 in *E.E.P.* (1862) 101 Þat liȝt ileste iwis Forte þe holi soule wende þerwiþ to heuene blis. **1340** Hampole *Pr. Consc.* 3557 Þan sal his saul wende Til blis. **1340** *Ayenb.* 13 And uor þo scele wolde he efter his dyaþe wende in to helle. **1362** Langl. *P. Pl.* A. xi. 269 Ȝif I.. for here werkis & for here wyt wende to pyne, Þanne wrouȝte I vnwisly. *c* **1400** *Rule St. Benet* (Verse) 55 Þe whylk, yf þay dyde wele, myght wend To blys þat es with-outyn end. *c* **1480** Henryson *Sheep & Dog* 119 And efter deith [thay will] to lestand panis wend.

†**12.** *transf.* and *fig.* of things: To pass away; to disappear, perish, decay. Also with *away*. *Obs.*

For further illustration see 17 e.

a **1000** *Guthlac* 57 (Gollancz) Ðesihð he þa domas.. wonian & wendan of woruld-ryhte. *a* **1300** *Seven Sins* 46 in *E.E.P.* (1862) 19 To world-is wel nab þou no triste, hit went awei so doþ þe miste. *c* **1386** Chaucer *Knt.'s T.* 2167 The grete toures se we wane and wende. *c* **1480** Henryson *Age & Youth* 46 Quhen thy manheid sall wendin as the mone. **1560** Rolland *Seven Sages* 118 This being done, the well away sall went.

13. To go forward, proceed; to journey, travel; to take one's way. Now *arch.*

a **1122** *O.E. Chron.* (Laud MS.) an. 999 Her com se here eft abuton in to Temese & wendon þa up andlang Medewæȝan to Hrofe ceastre. *a* **1200** *Moral Ode* 86 He ane is eure an ilche stude, wende þer þu wende. *c* **1386** Chaucer *Prioress' T.* 6 And thurgh the strete men myghte ride or wende. **1393** Langl. *P. Pl.* C. xvi. 161 And bere hit in þy bosom abowte wher þou wendest. *c* **1400** *Parce Michi* 1 in *26 Pol. Poems* 143 By a forest syde, walkyng as I went, Disporte to take. *c* **1480** Henryson *Fox & Wolf* 96 Neid causis me to steill quhair euer I wend. **1600** Fairfax *Tasso* xii. xxxii, Downe from the tree I came in hast, And tooke thee vp and on my iourney wend. **1613–16** W. Browne *Brit. Past.* i. iii. 54 Vpon her walkes she all the day attends, And by her side she trips where ere she wends. **1775** J. Tait *Land of Liberty* i. xlvi. 23 The hero saw, amaz'd, A crowd of nobles o'er the country wend. **1814** Scott *Lord of Isles* iii. xxiv, For know, that on a pilgrimage Wend I. **1837** Carlyle *Fr. Rev.* I. i. ii, The Merovingian Kings, slowly wending on their bullock-carts through the streets of Paris. **1850** 'Sylvanus' *Bye-lanes & Downs* ii. 21 This 'racing-man'..to whose cottage I was wending so pleasantly.

b. with advs. Now *arch.*

c **1175** *Lamb. Hom.* 79 Ho him forwundeden..and wenden forð. *c* **1205** Lay. 29517 At Tanette he com hider in & swa he up is iwend. **1297** R. Glouc. (Rolls) 823 Þo þis King [Leir] adde iwend aboute in such soruol cas Attelaste he com to carric. *Ibid.* 11317 Þe king was among þe freres & hii manion Radde him vor to wenden in. *c* **1350** *Will. Palerne* 3338 Men..wendeþ ouȝt wiȝtli & wiþ ȝour fon meteþ. *c* **1380** Wyclif *Wks.* (1880) 427 Collegians wenden out & prechen & quykenen many partis of englond. *c* **1400** *Beryn* 675 The knyȝt & al the felisship, forward gon þey wende. *c* **1470** *Gol. & Gaw.* 790 Than schir Gawine the gay Prayt for the iournay, That he myght furth weynd. **1581** A. Hall *Iliad* ix. 171 Vlysse the wisest takes his leaue, and forth doth for-most wend. **1590** Spenser *F.Q* i. i. 28 Then mounted he vpon his Steede againe, And with the Lady backward sought to wend. **1635** J. Hayward tr. *Biondi's Banish'd Virg.* 13 Whither away wend you so late? *a* **1653** Chalkhill in Walton *Angler* iii. 76 Then care away, and wend along with me. **1796** Coleridge *Sonnet to Stanhope* i, Since scorning Faction's low and partial aim Aloof thou wendest in thy stately pace. **1841** Dickens *Barn. Rudge* xvi, It was not unusual for those who wended home alone at midnight, to keep the middle of the road. **1848** Lytton *Harold* i. v, When I depart, Rolf, thou wendest back to thy marches. **1865** Kingsley *Herew.* ix, To avoid which end the disappointed palmer wended homeward once more.

†**c.** With predicative adj.: To go or move about in a certain state. *Obs.*

1340–70 *Alex. & Dind.* 34 Nouht welde we now but naked we wende. **13..** *Gosp. Nicodemus* (G.) 476 We war vnclene, ȝe ken, hale thurgh his word we wend.

14. *transf.* and *fig.* of things: To move, flow, run (in a specified course or direction); to go *up* or *down*. Of a road: To extend or stretch in a continuous line.

c **1205** Lay. 29914 Alse þet watre Desse wendeð into þere sæ. **1297** R. Glouc. (Rolls) 179 Fos me clupeþ þilke wei þat bi mani a god toun deþ wende. *a* **1400–50** *Wars Alex.* 37 As wide as þe werd was, went worde of þaire teching. *c* **1400** tr. *Secreta Secret.* 80 And þanne it [the blood] wendys vp to þe haterell. **1433** *Rolls of Parlt.* IV. 447/2 He smote..his wiff on the hede, that the brayne wende oute. *c* **1450**, *a* **1500** [see 17 g]. **1622** Drayton *Poly-olb.* xxvi. 373 That assist Her weaker wandring Streame tow'rds Yorkeshire as she wends. **1816** Shelley *Sonn. Dante* 4 Ascend A magic ship, whose charmed sails should fly With winds at will where'er our thoughts might wend. **1821** Scott *Kenilw.* xxiii, Adieu, and may the blessing of God wend with you! **1863** Baring-Gould *Iceland* 230 A river wending towards a portal of black rock. **1866** J. B. Rose *Ovid's Met.* iii. 99 The hero started, as the tremors wend Through every vein.

15. With adverbial accusative, esp. *way*: To go or journey in a certain way or direction. Also, †to go on (an errand, voyage). Now only with possessive pron., ***to wend one's way*** (†***gate***, †***ride***), a phrase which was revived *c* 1800, and is now the most familiar use of the verb.

c **1250** [see 17 h]. *c* **1250** *Gen. & Ex.* 3950 To madian lond wente he his ride. *a* **1300** *Cursor M.* 10365 Quen þou again sal wend þi gate, þou sal mete at þi wijf anna. *Ibid.* 13087 Nu yee sal mine erand wend, Til þat gret lauerding iesu. *Ibid.* 14194 Qua has to wenden ani wai God es to go bi light o dai. *Ibid.* 14942 Sex dais forwit pask-dai Wit his he went þe strete. *c* **1325** *Song Deo Gratias* 41 in *E.E.P.* (1862) 125 Out of þat chirche i. went my way. *c* **1380** Wyclif *Wks.* (1880) 153, & so þei..maken þe peple..to wende þe weie to helle whanne þei wenen to goo to heuene. *a* **1400–50** *Wars Alex.* 428 And þen he went furth his way. *c* **1420** *Avow. Arth.* xli, I haue my ways for to weynde, For to speke with a frynde. *c* **1435** *Torr. Portugal* 115 He that schall wend soche a wey, Yt were nede for hym to pray. ?*a* **1500** *Chester Pl., Last Judgm.* 138 But well I wott that ilke way that Abraham went, weind I may. *a* **1547** Surrey *Æneid* iv. 616 She was left alone Uncompanied, great viages to wende In desert land. *a* **1586** Sidney *Arcadia* iii. (1922) 42 The turning of Zelmanes eye, was a strong sterne enough to all their motions, wending no way, but as the inchaunting force of it guided them. **1810** Scott *Lady of Lake* ii. xxvi, Now back they wend their watery way. **1829** G. Head *Forest Scenes N. Amer.* 109 We wended our way down the ravine. **1837** Dickens *Pickw.* xxxiii, Mr. Weller turned, and began wending his way towards Leadenhall Market. **1839** —— *Nickleby* xi, As she wended her way homewards. **1866** Neale *Sequences & Hymns* 186 Wending my way to the City. **1883** [see fairway]. **1885** Sladen *Poetry of Exiles* (ed. 2) I. 27 Pleasant it was to wend his way back to familiar Kent.

transf. and *fig.* *a* **1300** *Cursor M.* 29222 For-þi to weind þe seker wai, I rede we be in panance ai. **1860** Maury *Phys. Geog.* viii. §394 On the Australian side, an ice-bearing current is found wending its way from the Antarctic regions.

†**16.** *fig.* (of persons). To go to and fro on business or procedure; to busy oneself; to fare, 'get on'. *Obs.*

1297 R. Glouc. (Rolls) 4063 For ȝif we in þisse manere wendeþ, we ne fayleþ on none wyse þat we ne wolleþ abbe þe maistrie, wanne we defendz vre franchise. *a* **1400** Chaucer *Amorous Compl.* 78 (Skeat) Ever have I been, and shal, how-so I wende, Outher to live or dye, your humble trewe. *c* **1400** *Beryn* 1522 Fawnus had so goon a-bout I-turned & I-went, That he had brouȝt his sone to-fore þe Emperour [etc.].

†**17.** The compound tense *is*, *was*, etc. *went* (or *wend*), originally a true passive (= 'is, was turned'), was used as the perfect of the prec. intrans. senses = has, had gone, departed, etc.:

a. in sense 8.

1297 R. Glouc. (Rolls) 567 King lotrines herte was al & clene vp hire iwent. *a* **1300** *Cursor M.* 3113 In wrechedom er now all went, To lare o godd gif þai na tent. **1303** R. Brunne *Handl. Synne* 791 Þat shal y shewe when we be went Vnto þe þryde comaundement. *a* **1400** *Minor Poems Vernon MS.* xxi. 51 Whon I was went from him wiþ wronge. *c* **1400** *Rom. Rose* 6185 They ben fro clene Riligioun went.

b. in sense 10.

c **1205** Lay. 17574 To þere sæ beoð iwende Gillomar & Passen. **1297** R. Glouc. (Rolls) 1377 Androge þat was to rome mid þe emperour iwent. *Ibid.* 11857 [They] were in hor dedut iwend an hontinge. **1340–70** *Alex. & Dind.* 53 Þanne weren from hem went wifis & children. *c* **1386** Chaucer *Miller's T.* 479, I trow that he be went For tymber, ther our Abbot hath hym sent. *a* **1450** *Le Morte Arth.* 3025 To a wyldernesse he is went. *c* **1460** *Towneley Myst.* xxx. 116 All oure saules ar wente, and none ar in hell.

c. in sense 10 b.

1297 R. Glouc. (Rolls) 2599 Þo hii were alle henne ywend. *a* **1300** *Cursor M.* 5994 All þe fleies ware went awai. *c* **1380** Wyclif *Sel. Wks.* I. 119 Whan an unclene spirit is went out from a man. *c* **1386** Chaucer *Man of Law's T.* 75 Hoom to Surrye been they went ful fayn. *c* **1440** *York Myst.* xxii. 33 To wildernesse he is wente owte. **14..** in *Babees Book* (1868) 357 Whan he fro the ys wente A-way.

d. in sense 11.

1303 R. Brunne *Handl. Synne* 605 God ȝyue vs grace, or we be went, To kepe þys fyrst comaundment. *c* **1412** Hoccleve *De Reg. Princ.* 2876 Whan þat he is out of þis worlde went. *c* **1425** *Macro Plays, Cast. Persev.* 1664 Þe sekatouris schul seyn it is here be-houe to make us mery, for he is went, þat al þis good gan owle. **1600** Fairfax *Tasso* xii. lxx, But when he saw her gentle soul was went.

e. in sense 12.

a **1300** *Cursor M.* 1640 Al rightwisnes awai es went. *a* **1352** Minot *Poems* vi. 9 When all yowre wele es went. *a* **1400** in *Pol. Rel. & L. Poems* (1903) 257 Loue is out of lond iwent. **1426** Audelay *Poems* 19 When al the welth of this world is went from hem away. *c* **1440** *York Myst.* xli. 347 My age is went, I feyll no fray. *c* **1460** *Towneley Myst.* xxx. 388 This wykyd warld away is wente. *c* **1470** *Gol. & Gaw* 1132 As all his welthis in warld had ben away went. **1552** Lyndesay *Monarche* 4142 For, siclyke as the snaw doith melt in May,..Thir gret Impyris rychtso ar went away.

f. Of a period of time, a season, etc. = is gone, past, elapsed, or ended. Also with adv., as *out*, *over*.

13.. *Guy Warw.* 326 (Caius) Thus lyueth Guy in grete turmente Till the feest was ouer wente [*Auchinl.* was al to-went]. *c* **1386** Chaucer *Prioress's T.* 88, I wol do my diligence To konne it al er Cristemasse is went. *c* **1400** *Destr. Troy* 4586 Winter was went. *c* **1400** *Laud Troy-Bk.* 10045 The nyȝt is went, the day dawes. *Ibid.* 17071 Terme is went out of the trewe. **15..** *Tayis Bank* 42 (Bann. MS.), Wod Winter with his wallowand wynd But weir away wes went.

g. in sense 14.

c **1450** *St. Cuthbert* (Surtees) 1271 Þou hase so ferr to ryde þat þe sonn sall be went doune Or þou come whider þou ert boune. *a* **1500** *Hist. K. Boccus & Sydracke* (? 1510) Z j b, Whan some [stars] go doune, some up are went With meuyng of the fyrmament.

h. with *one's way*: see 15.

c **1250** *Gen. & Ex.* 1429 Eliezer is went his wei. *c* **1440** *York Myst.* xxxviii. 245 He is resen and wente his way.

†**wend**, *v.*[2] *Obs.* [f. *wend*(*e*, obs. pa. t. and pa. pple. of ween *v.*] *intr.* To think, suppose.

1581 A. Hall *Iliad* iv. 63 And that now of his enterprise none of them all should wende, He caused his souldiours hap him wel with buckler and with targe. *a* **1600** Montgomerie *Misc. Poems* xxxix. 39 Hir freindis ay weindis To caus hir to revok. *a* **1650** *Merline* 1280 in *Percy Folio MS.* I. 462 See yee nought the young man that the shoone hath bought? he wendes to liue them to weare.

wend(e, obs. pa. t. and pa. pple. of ween *v.*; obs. ff. wind *sb.*[1]

†**Wendagains-lane.** *Obs.* [f. wend *v.* (see 6 a) + genitival *agains* (see again).] The name of a cul-de-sac in London. Cf. *turn-again lane* s.v. turnagain 4.

1308–9 *Cal. Wills Crt. Husting, Lond.* i. (1889) 204 [The lane called] Wandayeneslane. **1328** *Ibid.* 335 Wendaȝenes-lane. **1337** *Ibid.* 422 Wandageynslane. **1348–9** *Ibid.* 531 Wendageyneslane.

wendage, var. vendage.

1496 *Dives & Pauper* vii. xiii. (W. de W.) s iij b, *Diues.* Of what thynge is a man bounde to tythe. *Pauper.* Of corn in heruest, of wyne in wendage, of fruyte, [etc.].

†**wenday.** *Obs.*[−1] [f. *wen-*, comb. f. ME. *wēn*, OE. *wǣn*, *wæȝn* wain *sb.* Cf. wenseves.] A day allowed to a tenant for preparing his wain in order to carry grain in harvest.

c **1250** *Rentalia Glaston.* (Somerset Rec. Soc.) 83 Et debet habere j wenday, scilicet, unum diem ad carrum suum preparandum antequam cariet, quietum de omni alio opere.

'wended, *ppl. a.* [f. WEND *v.* + -ED[1].] Twisted, plaited.
1719 D'URFEY *Pills* IV. 137 Her Bongrace of Wended Straw.

'Wendian. *rare*$^{-1}$. [f. WEND *sb.* + -IAN.] = WEND *sb.* 1.
1838 *Penny Cycl.* XII. 345/1 Russniaks, Slovacs, Croats, Wendians..(these four..are of Slavonian origin).

Wendic ('wɛndɪk), *a.* and *sb.* Also Windic. [f. WEND *sb.* + -IC. The form *Windic* is after G. *Winde*, var. of *Wende* WEND. Cf. *Windish* = WENDISH.] **a.** *adj.* Of or pertaining to the Wends. **b.** *sb.* The language of the Wends, Sorabian. (For a wider use see quot. 1861.)
1848 *Rep. Brit. Assoc. Adv. Sci. 1847* 267 The Old Slavonic of the Bible and of Nestor, the Russian, Servian, Croatic, and Wendic. **1856** MAX MÜLLER in *Oxford Ess.* i. 14 We know nothing of the Arian race, before it was broken up into different nationalities, such as Indian, German, Greek, Roman, Windic, Teutonic, and Celtic. **1861** —— *Lect. Sci. Lang.* 186 The fifth branch, which is commonly called *Slavonic*, I prefer to designate by the name *Windic*. *Ibid.* page-heading, Windic class. **1868** *Chamb. Encycl.* X. 139 Those remnants of the Slavic population of Lusatia who still speak the Wendic tongue. **1883** MORFILL *Slavonic Lit.* ii. 36 The Wendic mountains..are mentioned by the geographer Ptolemy.

wendigo, var. WINDIGO.

'wending, *vbl. sb. Obs.* [f. WEND *v.* + -ING[1].]
†**1.** The action of turning or changing; a change or turn. *Obs.*
c **897** ÆLFRED *Gregory's Past. C.* xlii. 306 Hit ȝedeð hit self him selfum suiðe unȝelic for ðære ȝelomlican wendinge. *a* **1050** *Liber Scintill.* xi. (1889) 63 Earfoðe ys færlic wendincg [L. *permutatio*]. *c* **1440** *Pallad. on Husb.* II. 12 But at the weendyng [L. *ubi ad versuram venerint*] slake The yook, thyn oxon nekkis forto cole.
2. The action of going; *esp.* a going away, departure.
13.. *K. Alis.* 920 Nis in this world so siker thyng So is deth, to olde and yyng! The time is nygh of heore wendyng! **13..** *Guy Warw.* 1218 He goþ him to his fader þo, þat for his wending was ful wo. *c* **1340** HAMPOLE *Psalter* civ. 36 Egipt was fayn in thaire wendynge [L. *in profectione eorum*]. *c* **1374** CHAUCER *Troylus* IV. 1630 And by my þryft my wendynge out of Troye A-noþer day shal torne vs alle to Ioye. —— *Boeth.* II. pr. i. (1868) 32 If þou wilt write a lawe of wendyng and of dwellyng to fortune. *c* **1430** *Syr Gener.* (Roxb.) 9967 She went ageyn with hir meigne; The third day aftir hir wending, [Generides] ther was crovned king.
†**3.** A journey. *Obs.*
13.. *K. Alis.* 3284 (Laud MS.), And þer he ordeyneþ his wendyng Toward Darrye þe riche kyng. **1338** R. BRUNNE *Chron.* (1810) 207 Jon dred þat wendyng, to France wild he nouht. *Ibid.* 260 þei hed redy wendyng, at Douer þei toke lond. [**1878** SEELEY *Stein* II. 489 Accordingly appeared 'My Wendings and Wanderings with the Imperial Baron'.]

'wending, *ppl. a.* [f. WEND *v.*] Going, proceeding. (In comb., as ***backward-wending***.)
1896 A. AUSTIN *England's Darling* I. i, Egbert's true grand-child..backward-wending pilgrims say, was seen [etc.].

Wendish ('wɛndɪʃ), *a.* and *sb.* Also 7, 9 **Windish**, 9 **Vendish, Vindish.** [f. WEND *sb.* + -ISH, or ad. G. *Wendisch, Windisch.*] **A.** *adj.* Of or pertaining to the Wends.
1614 [see VOIVODE β]. **1788** *Engl. Rev.* Dec. 479 The people ..are called in Saxony *Wenden*, i.e. Wendts, or Vandals, or Wendish. **1790** DORNFORD *Pütter's Develop. Germ. Emp.* III. Index, Wendish or Venedic countries. **1822** DOWNES *Lett. fr. Mecklenburg* 157 Pribislaus, a Wendish chief. **1822** *Encycl. Brit.* Suppl. V. 242 The Wendish dialect of the Sclavonian. **1892** DOUGHTY *Wherry in Wendish Lands* 113 Country places are still known by their Wendish names.
B. *sb.* The language of the Wends, esp. the Sorabian tongue spoken in Saxony.
1617 MORYSON *Itin.* I. 68 In the villages of Carinthia..the Countrey people speake Wendish, or the tongue of the old Vandals. **1788** *Engl. Rev.* Dec. 480 Every Saturday one of them preaches, in Wendish, a sermon in the university church. **1822** *Encycl. Brit.* Suppl. V. 243 A language consisting of a mixture of Wendish and German. **1887** MORFILL in *Encycl. Brit.* XXII. 150/1 The Slovenes are sometimes called 'Wends' and their language 'Windish' or 'Wendish'. **1915** *19th Century* Nov. 1045 Carniola, where Vendish, a Slav dialect, is spoken.

†**'wendling,** *sb. Obs.*$^{-1}$ (Possibly f. WEND *v.*, and = 'wanderer', 'vagabond', but more prob. an error for *findling* 'foundling'.)
c **1300** *K. Horn* (Hall) 729 (Laud MS.) Henne þou foule wendling [*Harl.* fundlyng] Out of boure flore.

Wendo- ('wɛndəʊ), combining form of WEND *sb.*
1853 FREUND in *Jrnl. Ethnol. Soc.* (1856) IV. 77 The boundary-line of Low-German and Wendo-Sclavonian. *Ibid.*, Wendo-Sclavonic cities.

wendoye, obs. form of WINDOW.

Wendy house. Also with small initial or hyphen. [Named after the small house built around Wendy in J. M. Barrie's play *Peter Pan* (1904).] A small house-like structure for children to play in.
1949 M. ATKINSON *Junior School Community* 11 Wendy house—made by a joiner: two large pieces of plywood hinged together. **1957** *Listener* 9 May 743 There is a Wendy-house in the corner [of the class room]. **1971** *Where* Dec. 356/1 They have performed wonders in getting the bus and re-equipping it with ladders, a wendy house and even a telephone. **1977** J. MCCLURE *Sunday Hangman* viii. 80 The rocking horse was legless.., the pedal car was a write-off, and the Wendy house had been trampled flat.

wene, pseudo-arch. var. WANE *sb.*[2]
1813 HOGG *Queen's Wake* II. (1814) 174 In yon green-wood there is a waik, And in that waik there is a wene. *Ibid.*, In that green wene Kilmeny lay.

wene: see WEAN *v.*, WEEN *sb.* and *v.*

wenem, -im, -ym, obs. forms of VENOM.

wenene, var. WHENNE *Obs.*, whence.

weneth(e, var. ff. UNEATH *adv.*
1422 YONGE tr. *Secreta Secret.* 136, 187.

weng(e, obs. forms of VENGE *v.*, WING.

†**wengand,** variant of (or error for) *wenyand* WANIAND.
1587 *Mirr. Mag., Sir N. Burdet* lii, Wylde wengand on such ire, wherby the realme doth lose.

wenge ('wɛŋgeɪ). [Local name in Zaïre.] The dark brown timber of *Millettia laurentii*, a tree of the family Leguminosæ found in Central Africa.
1963 *House & Garden* Feb. 60 (*caption*) Seating unit series ..teak and wenge frame, latex foam cushions. **1972** *Handbk. Hardwoods* (Building Res. Establishment) (ed. 2) 164 The timber wengé..from Zaire is generally similar in appearance and properties to panga panga.

wengeance, -aunce, obs. forms of VENGEANCE.

wenhill, obs. form of WEANEL, WENNEL.
1711 *B.N.C.* (Oxf.) *Docum.* A[3]. 20 One Bull, eight Wenhill Calves.

weniaunce, obs. form of VENGEANCE.

†**wening,** var. of WAINING or WONING *vbl. sb.*
c **1425** *Eng. Conq. Irel.* xxi. 54 Who-so had I-hard þe wepynge, & þe wenynge, & the sorow that thay mad.

‖**wên jên** (wən ʒən, wən rən). Also with hyphen. [Chinese *wénrén* man of letters, f. *wén* writing + *rén* (*jên* in Wade-Giles) man.] Chinese men of letters.
1958 W. WILLETTS *Chinese Art* II. vii. 509 From early Ming times until quite recently, the history of Chinese painting has been written by that highly articulate but alarmingly unanimous body of people, the *wên jên* or *literati*. **1970** *Oxf. Compan. Art* 232/2 Though *wên-jên*, many of them were also professional painters.

‖**wen li** (wən li). Also **wenli** and with capital initial. [Chinese *wén lǐ* grammar, literary style, f. *wén* writing + *lǐ* texture, reason.] = WEN-YEN.
The synonymy is based on a misconception of the Chinese meaning, and does not exist in that language.
1887 *Chinese Times* 11 June 502/1 The bishop's style, call it *Wen li* or *Mandarin*, is admirably clear and idiomatic. **1917** S. COULING *Encycl. Sinica* 597/2 The term *Wên li* is now in constant use especially among foreigners, to denote the Chinese literary style, which differs in degrees of conciseness or obscurity, and hence is sometimes divided into 'high' and 'low' *Wên li*. **1972** E. A. NIDA *Bk. of Thousand Tongues* 70/1 Wenli was a written language which could be used throughout the whole of China. **1977** C. F. & F. M. VOEGELIN *Classification & Index World's Lang.* 114 The descendant of an earlier form of Chinese known as Wen Yen or Wen Li continues to be used by all educated Chinese ..for special purposes.

†**wenlich,** *a. Obs.* [OE. *wénlic*, f. WEEN *sb.* + -LY[1]. Cf. OS. *wânlik* beautiful, MHG. *wænlich*, early mod.G. *wahnlich, wähnlich* probable, supposed.] **a.** Beautiful. **b.** ? Worthy, excellent.
c **1000** ÆLFRIC in Assman *Ags. Hom.* 108 Heo wæs swiðe wlitiȝ & wenlices hiwes. *c* **1200** *Trin. Coll. Hom.* 29 þe shadewe [i.e. her reflection in a mirror] hire tacheð hwu hie mai hire seluen wenlukest makien. *Ibid.* 83 And swo warð iturnd þat folc of ateliche to wenliche. *a* **1250** *Prov. Ælfred* 105 in *O.E. Misc.* 108 þe mon þe on his youhþe yeorne lerneþ..may beon on elde wenliche lorþeu.

Wenlock ('wɛnlɒk). The name of a town in Shropshire, used attributively in **Wenlock formation, group,** a formation of Upper Silurian age, typically developed near Wenlock. Also **Wenlock limestone, shale, slate.** In mod. use, the name of the middle of three divisions of the Silurian, lying below the Ludlovian and above the Valentian (Llandoverian); used *attrib.* and *absol.*
1834 MURCHISON in *Proc. Geol. Soc.* II. 14 The lower part of this formation is termed the 'Wenlock shale'. *Ibid.*, The shale beneath the Wenlock limestone. *Ibid.* 15 The Ludlow and Wenlock formations appear in the same escarpment. **1843** HUMBLE *Dict. Geol.* etc., *Wenlock slate.* Called also Wenlock shale. **1890** *Hardwicke's Sci.-Gossip* XXVI. 247 Splendid examples of Wenlock fossils. **1946** [see LUDLOVIAN *a.*]. **1969** BENNISON & WRIGHT *Geol. Hist. Brit. Isles* vi. 116 A great deal of relatively recent work has been done on the limestone and shale shelf-sea facies of Wenlock and Ludlow age in the Welsh Borders. **1979** R. ANDERTON et al. *Dynamic Stratigr. Brit. Isles* vii. 96/1 Turbidity currents deposited sands in a separate turbidite zone during the Wenlock and lower Ludlow.

Hence **wen'lockian** *a.*, of or belonging to the Wenlock formation or series. Freq. *absol.*
1855 J. PHILLIPS *Man. Geol.* 104 The genera being mostly Wenlockian and Ludlovian. **1946** [see LUDLOVIAN *a.*]. **1969** BENNISON & WRIGHT *Geol. Hist. Brit. Isles* vi. 124 The thickness of the Wenlockian strata may amount to about 25,000 feet. **1974** *Encycl. Brit. Macropædia* XVI. 774/2 The Llandoverian..saw the beginning of a sharp distinction between basin graptolitic shale facies and calcareous and.. sandy shelf facies. This distinction was well marked in the Wenlockian.

wenne: see WIN *sb.*[2], WHEN.

wennel: see WEANEL.

wennesone, obs. Sc. form of VENISON.

wennion, variant of WANION.

'wennish, *a. rare*$^{-1}$. [f. WEN[1] + -ISH.] Of the nature of a wen.
1614 WOTTON *Let.* 16 June *Reliq. W.* (1672) 434 The incision of a wennish tumour grown on his thigh.

wennome, obs. Sc. form of VENOM *sb.*

'wenny, *a.* Now *rare* or *Obs.* [f. WEN[1] + -Y.]
1. Of the nature of or similar to a wen.
1597 GERARDE *Herbal* II. clxvi. 463 A remedie against.. hard wennie swellings. **1611** COTGR. s.v. *Goitrons*, The wennie bags that breed vnder the throats of the most inhabitants of the Alpes. **1672** WISEMAN *Wounds* II. App. i. 79, I have had some persons..so deformed with these [cicatrices], as they have suspected them to be wenny. **1748** *Phil. Trans.* XLV. 536 Wenny Tumours of a monstrous Size. **1766** *Compl. Farmer* Dd 1, *Capellets*, in horses, are particular swellings..of a wenny nature, which grow on the heel of the hock, and on the point of the elbow.
2. Afflicted with wens; goitrous.
1630 *R. Johnson's Kingd. & Commw.* 60 The women are.. for the most part wenny, that is, having great bunches under their chinnes with drinking snow water. **1786** tr. *Beckford's Vathek* 110 Others..with hump-backs, wenny necks, and even horns.

wenomose, obs. Sc. form of VENOMOUS.

wenquis, obs. Sc. form of VANQUISH *v.*

wenscote, -skot(te, etc., obs. ff. WAINSCOT.

†**wenseves.** *Obs. rare.* [f. *wen-* (see WENDAY) + *seves* pl. of SHEAF *sb.*] Sheaves given as payment for carrying grain in harvest.
c **1250** *Rentalia Glaston.* (Somerset Rec. Soc.) 88 Nec aliud debet recipere..nisi wensenes [*read* wenseues] quando cariat bladum. *Ibid.* 135, ij garbas que vocantur wensewes.

wenskett, obs. form of WAINSCOT.

Wensleydale ('wɛnslɪdeɪl). The name of a district of North Yorkshire, used *attrib.*, and hence *ellipt.* as sb., to designate **a.** A breed of long-woolled sheep originally raised there; **b.** A local variety of blue-mould cheese; also, a white cheese (see quot. 1963).
1881 J. P. SHELDON *Dairy Farming* 250 Though the Wensleydale cheese are so small. **1893** J. WRIGHTSON *Sheep* 39 The Wensleydale is a large, high standing sheep, with a characteristic blue in the skin of the face and ears. **1896** J. BENSON & J. LONG *Cheese* 105 The Stilton-shaped Wensleydales are..classed as British blue mould cheeses. **1963** A. L. SIMON *Guide Good Food & Wines* 648/2 The best-known variety of Wensleydale cheese, cylindrical in shape, like Stilton, but of smaller dimensions, which grows 'blue' when ripe, like Stilton... The other sort of Wensleydale cheese is a flat-shaped, white cheese which is eaten fresh and does not generally go blue. **1985** D. CLARK *Performance* iv. 105 Brawn and Wensleydale cheese sandwiches.

went (wɛnt). *Obs.* exc. *dial.* Also 5 **weent,** 6 *Sc.* **vent,** 8 **wont,** 9 *dial.* **want, wint.** [Related to WEND *v.*[1]]
1. A course, path, way, or passage. *Obs.* exc. *dial.*
In later use esp. in pl. with *three* and *four*; also in combs. ***three-went-way*** THREE B. III. 2, and FOUR-WENT-WAY.
c **1250** *Gen. & Ex.* 136 Ilc sterre..He settes in ðe firmament, Al abuten ðis walkne went. *c* **1369** CHAUCER *Dethe Blaunche* 398 (Fairf.) Hyt forthe went Dovne by a floury grene went Ful thikke of gras. *c* **1384** —— *H. Fame* 182 In a forest, as they wente, At a turninge of a wente. **1418–20** J. PAGE *Siege Rouen* in *Hist. Coll. Citizen Lond.* (Camden) 17 Govnnys goode and redy bente, They were layde in many went. **1426** LYDG. *De Guil. Pilgr.* 10320 By peryllous weyes and by wentys I hadde had gret adversyte. **1513** DOUGLAS *Æneis* III. iv. 40 Ontill ane cave we went, Vndir a hingand hewch, in a derne vent. *Ibid.* 113 And followit furth the samyn went we haue, Quhar so the wynd and sterisman ws draue. **1570** LEVINS *Manip.* 66/8 A went, lane, *viculus*. **1596** SPENSER *F.Q.* IV. ii. 47 To the three fatall sisters house she went. Farre vnder ground from tract of liuing went. **1640** SOMNER *Antiq. Canterb.* 20 The Iron crosse, which sometime stood at the East-end of Castle-street, at the meeting of the foure wents. **1682** WHELER *Journ. Greece* VI. 475 Where these ways part was called by the ancients Τρεῖς Κεφαλαί, or, the Three Heads, signifying I suppose the same we do by *Three Wents*. **1854** W. GASKELL *Lect. Lancs. Dial.* 20 We have also..'wint',..a passage. *a* **1896** BARDSLEY *Dict. Surnames* (1901) 802 There are one or two wents, still so called, in my late parish [Ulverston].
fig. **1513** DOUGLAS *Æneis* I. Prol. 384 Logitianis knawis heirin myne entent, Ondir quhais boundis lurkis mony strange went.
†**b.** A journey, course of movement. *Obs.*

1430–40 LYDG. *Bochas* VIII. 2145 [They]..ful accordid be Thoruh Itaille for to make her went Toward Roome. **1596** SPENSER *F.Q.* IV. v. 46 But here my wearie teeme nigh ouer spent Shall breath it selfe awhile, after so long a went.

†**2.** A course of action or plan for attaining some end; a trick, contrivance, device. *Obs.*

1303 R. BRUNNE *Handl. Synne* 529 þe bysshop made a clerk þan wryte Al þat she seyd,..And alle how she made here went. **1390** GOWER *Conf.* II. 218 The Steward tok the gold and wente, Withinne his herte and many a wente Of coveitise thanne he caste. **1393** LANGL. *P. Pl.* C. VII. 263 Ich made meny wentes, How ich myght haue hit, al my wit ich caste. *c* **1440** CAPGRAVE *St. Kath.* IV. 929 Thanne do ye wrong ageyn her entent On what-maner wise ȝe make your weent.

†**3.** A turn or course of affairs; an occasion or chance. *Obs.*

1338 R. BRUNNE *Chron.* (1810) 63 Do him vnto þe suerd, withouten jugement, If ȝe may Griffyn take bityme at any went. **1513** DOUGLAS *Æneis* III. x. 123 Eneas..The fatis of goddis..Rehersing schew, and syndry strange wentis. **1596** SPENSER *F.Q.* VI. vi. 3 He knew the diuerse went of mortall wayes.

†**4.** A turn or change of direction; a turning about. *Obs.*

c **1374** CHAUCER *Troylus* II. 63 For which yn wo to bedde he wente, And made er it was day ful many a went. *Ibid.* V. 1194 Vp on þe walles made he many a wente. **1412–20** LYDG. *Troy Bk.* I. 2713 Vn-to hir chambre in hast sche is goon, Where vp and down sche made many went. **1471** CAXTON *Recuyell* (Sommer) 219 The monstre wente here and there, And made many wentes wyth oute seeyng and knowing where he wente.

†**b.** ? A turning or winding of a stair. *Obs.*

a **1548** HALL *Chron.*, *Hen. VIII* 73 b, The staier of the saied halpas was caste of passage by the wentes of brode steppes.

went, pa. t. (and pa. pple.) of WEND *v.*^{1}: now used as the pa. t. of GO *v.*

†**went**, app. used as pa. pple. of WIND *v.*

c **1500** *World and Child* 46 (Manly), I am not worthely wrapped nor went, But powerly prycked in pouerte.

†**wentle**, *v.* *Obs.* [ad. MDu. *wentelen* (also mod.Du.) = MLG. and LG. *wentelen*, G. dial. *wenzelen*.] *intr.* To roll or tumble about. (Used only by Caxton.)

1481 CAXTON *Reynard* viii. (Arb.) 18 Whan he was so wery, he wentled and tombled nyghe half a myle... And whan he was seen so comyng fro ferre, Some doubted what it myght be that cam so wentelyng. *c* **1489** —— *Sonnes of Aymon* xxii. 475 Al nyghte he coude not fall a slepe, but wentled in his bed without ony rest.

wentletrap (ˈwɛnt(ə)ltræp). Also 8 **ventle-**. [a. Du. *wenteltrap* winding stair, spiral shell, = G. *wendeltreppe*.] A marine shell of the genus *Scalaria* or the family *Scalariidæ*, esp. *Scalaria pretiosa*.

1758 H. WALPOLE *Lett. to Mann* 9 Feb., I have seen a little ugly shell called a Ventle-trap sold for twenty-seven guineas. **1776** MENDES DA COSTA *Elem. Conchol.* 151 Gualtieri ranks the famous Shell the Wentletrap, or Staircase, with Vermiculi. **1815** S. BROOKES *Introd. Conchol.* 157. **1851** S. P. WOODWARD *Mollusca* 16 *note*, A Wentle-trap which fetched 40 guineas in 1701 (Rumphius) was worth only 20 guineas in 1753, and now may be had for 5*s*.! **1861** P. P. CARPENTER in *Rep. Smithsonian Instit.* 1860, 188 Family *Scalariadæ*. (Wentle Traps).

†**Wentsunday**. *Obs.*$^{-1}$ [Of obscure origin.] The Sunday after Michaelmas.

c **1350** *Westminster Chapter Muniments* No. 27926 Usque diem dominicam proximam post festum Sancti Michaelis que dicitur Wentsounday.

wenyand(e, variant forms of WANIAND.

‖**wen-yen** (wən jɛn). Also **wenyan, wenyen**, and with capital initial. [Chinese *wényán*, f. *wén* writing + *yán* speech, words.] The traditional literary language or style of China, superseded in the twentieth century by PAI-HUA.

1936 N. WALES in E. Snow *Living China* 336 Until 1917 there existed in..stalemate three fairly distinct strata of literature: (1) the ancient cult of the *literati* in the dead *wen-yen* classical written language,..(2) the healthy parvenu *pai-hua*, 'plain speech', literature of the people in the spoken language, and..(3) the story-tellers' literature in the provincial dialects. **1964** *Anthropol. Linguistics* Mar. 31 Many words which require two characters in Han Chinese can be written with one character in Wenyen. **1968** [see PAI-HUA]. **1969** *Language* XLV. 690 One is the Classical Chinese, *wényán*, which has been used from antiquity up to recent years. **1980** *Times Lit. Suppl.* 27 June 725/1 He has been engaged..in an immense study of the ancient Chinese classics written in the elegant but archaic *wenyen* Chinese favoured by old-fashioned scholars—a language almost as remote from present-day speech as Latin from the modern European vernaculars.

wenym, obs. form of VENOM.

wenyson, wenysoune, obs. ff. VENISON.

weod, obs. form of WEED; variant of WOOD *a.*

weofud, -od, -ed: see WEVED *Obs.*, altar.

weol, obs. form of WHEEL.

weolde, obs. form of WIELD *v.*

weole, obs. form of WEAL *sb.*^{1}, WHEEL.

weolk, obs. pa. t. of WALK *v.*

weolthe, obs. form of WEALTH.

weoman, obs. form of WOMAN.

weonlete, variant of WAY-LEET *Obs.*

weonne, obs. form of WHEN.

weop(e, obs. forms of WEEP *v.*

weopmonne, variant of WAPMAN *Obs.*

weorc, obs. form of WORK.

weord, obs. form of WORD.

weore, obs. form of *were*: see BE *v.*

weor(e)ld(e, -uld, obs. forms of WORLD.

weork, obs. form of WORK.

†**weorne**, *v.* *Obs.* [OE. *weornian* (also *forweornian*), possibly related to *wisnian* to wizen.] *intr.* To wither.

a **1380** *Virg. Antioch* 215 in Horstm. *Altengl. Leg.* (1878) 29 þe riht hond..Of him weorned and wox al drie [L. *aruit*].

weorne, obs. form of WARN *v.*^{1}

weote, variant of WITE.

†**weothe**, *v.* *Obs.*$^{-1}$ [Of obscure origin.] *intr.* ? To rush.

c **1205** LAY. 6508 þat deor to-dede his chæfles and to þan king weoðede, and for-bat hine amidden a twa.

†**weothele**, *v.* *Obs.*$^{-1}$ [ME. *weoðelen, wiðelen*, = MHG. *wedeln* to flutter, etc.] *intr.* To become unsteady or uncertain.

c **1205** LAY. 2885 þe wind him com on wiðere, weoðeleden his fluhtes [*c* **1275** wiþeleode his fliþtes].

weouede, variant of WEVED.

weovil, obs. form of WEEVIL.

wep, obs. variant of WAP *v.*^{2}

c **1375** *Sc. Leg. Saints* xv. (*Barnabas*) 206 Al þe fyre..þai wepyt in a clath of lede. *Ibid.* xxvii. (*Machar*) 221 Weppit in clathis þe barn can lay.

wep(e, obs. forms of WEEP *v.*, WIPE *v.*

wepen(e, -in, obs. forms of WEAPON.

wepentake, obs. form of WAPENTAKE.

wepit, variant of WHIPPET *sb.*

wepman, -mon(ne, var. ff. WAPMAN *Obs.*

wepne, weppen, -on, -un, -yn: see WEAPON.

wept (wɛpt), *ppl. a.* [pa. pple. of WEEP *v.*]

a. Of tears: Shed in weeping. Also *fig.* of poetry. **b.** Of a person: Mourned for, lamented, with tears. Also *absol.*

1594 *Zepheria* ix. C 1, He wip't wept teares from Tellus bosome. *Ibid.* x. C 1 b, Since that, how often haue they sent wept Elegies To beg remorse at thy obdurat hart? **1729** SAVAGE *Wanderer* II. 83 Near the wept Fair, her Harp Cecilia strung. **1829** J. F. COOPER *Borderers* I. 1 *heading*, The Borderers; or the Wept of Wish-Ton-Wish.

wepte, weput, var. ff. *wiped* pa. t. of WIPE *v.*

wepun, -yn, obs. forms of WEAPON.

wepyntaille, -tale: see WAPENTAKE.

wer, dial. f. OUR; Sc. var. VER *sb.*^{1}; obs. f. WAR *sb.*^{1}, *v.*^{1}, WAR, WAUR *a.* and *adv.*, WARE *a.*, WEAR *v.*; var. WERE *sb.*^{2}, *sb.*^{3}, *v.*; var. *were*, pa. t. of BE *v.*; obs. f. WHERE, WHETHER.

wer-, variant of WERE-.

[**1802** SCOTT *Minstrelsy* II. 100 A wild story of a warwolf, or rather a war bear.] **1838** *Court Mag.* XIII. 261 A curious story of a *wer-bear*..is quoted by Sir Walter Scott. **1902** *Folk-lore* June 157 *note*, The wer-tiger beliefs, which are held..by the Peninsular Malays. **1904** G. C. KEIDEL *Man-Fox in Japanese Tradit.* 1 (MS.) The werfox, if we may so call him, is invisible. **1925** C. K. MEEK *North. Tribes Nigeria* I. 184 The villagers next day taxed the British officer with the death of the Galadima, who was known to be a wer-hyena.

weraly, obs. form of VERILY.

weratie, obs. Sc. form of VERITY.

weray, obs. Sc. f. VERY; var. WARY *v.* *Obs.*

werbi, -by, obs. forms of WHEREBY.

werble, -ul, variant forms of WARBLE *sb.*^{1}, *sb.*^{3}

1580 HOLLYBAND *Treas. Fr. Tong, Fusée, avec ses pesons*, the quill of threed, or the spindle and threed with the werble.

werc, obs. form of WORK.

werce, obs. form of WORSE.

werch, obs. Sc. form of WRETCH.

werch(e, werck, obs. ff. WORK.

†**wercock**. *Obs. rare*$^{-1}$. [f. COCK *sb.*, with obscure first element.] Some kind of bird.

1420 *Liber Cocorum* (1862) 36 Oþer smalle bryddes..As osel, smityng, laveroc gray, Pertryk, werkock.

werd, obs. form of WEIRD *sb.*, WORD, WORLD.

†**werde**, *v.* *Obs.* Also 1 **woerda**, 3 **weordenn**. [OE. (Anglian) *werdan* (Northumb. *wœrda*), = WS. **wierdan, wyrdan*, f. the stem *ward-* (WS. *weard-*), which appears also in OS. *a-wardian, -werdian*, OHG. *wart(i)an, wertan* (MHG. *werten*), *far-warten*, Goth. *fra-wardjan* to spoil, corrupt, injure, etc., with cognates in the Slavonic languages.] *trans.* To harm or injure.

c **725** *Corpus Gloss.* (Hessels) O 136 *Officit*, werdit. *c* **950** *Lindisf. Gosp.* Luke viii. 45 Ða meniᵹo ðec ᵹeðringað & woerdað [L. *affligunt*]. *c* **1000** *Ags. Ps.* (Thorpe) lxxvi. 4 Wæron eaᵹan mine eac mid wæcceum werded swyþe. *c* **1100** *Ælfred's Boeth.* (Bodl. MS.) xvi. §2 þa smalan wyrmas, þa ðone mon ᵹe innan ᵹe uton werdaþ [*Cott. MS.* wyrdaþ]. *c* **1200** ORMIN 4251 þe flæshess fule wille, þatt allre werrst.. Werdeþþ þe wrecche sawle. *Ibid.* 6249 Ne birrþ þe shendenn nani mann Ne weordenn þine þannkess.

werde, obs. pa. t. of WEAR *v.*, WERE *v.*; obs. f. WEIRD *sb.*, WORD, WORLD.

†**werder**. *Obs.*$^{-1}$ (Meaning obscure.)

c **1350** *Will. Palerne* 3185, I a-wede neieȝ of wit for þo werder bestes, þat folwe ȝour felachip, so ferli þei are.

werdingale, var. FARTHINGALE, VARDINGALE.

werdliche, obs. form of WORLDLY.

Werdnig-Hoffmann (ˈvɜːdnɪg). *Path.* The names of Guido *Werdnig*, 19th-century Austrian neurologist, and Johann *Hoffmann* (HOFFMANN 3), who described the disease in 1890 and 1893 respectively, used in the possessive and *attrib.* to designate a fatal familial disease that is present at birth or develops soon afterwards and is characterized by muscular atrophy, paralysis, and loss of sucking ability.

1903 *Trans. Clin. Soc.* XXXVI. 226 (*heading*) Three cases of family progressive spinal muscular atrophy (Werdnig-Hoffmann [*sic*] type). **1920** *Brain* XLIII. 170 The case was scarcely one of amyotonia congenita, but rather was related to Werdnig-Hoffmann's progressive muscular atrophy, in spite of there being no obvious element of heredity. **1978** *Arch. Dis. Childhood* LIII. 921/1 Werdnig-Hoffmann disease—the acute severe infantile form of spinal muscular atrophy—often presents in the neonatal period with profound weakness.

werdour, var. *verdour* VERDOUR *Obs.*

werdy, Sc. variant of WORTHY *a.*

†**were**, *sb.*^{1} *Obs.* Forms: 1 **wer**, 2–3 **were**. [Common Teutonic: OE. *wer* = OFris., OS., OHG. *wer*, ON. and Icel. *verr*, Goth. *wair* = L. *vir*, OIr. *fer* (Gael. *fear*), W. *gŵr*, related to Lith. *vyras*, Skr. *vīrá*, man, hero.]

1. A male person; a man.

Beowulf 993 Fela þæra wæs wera and wifa. *Ibid.* 1352 Oðer ..on weres wæstmum wræclastas træd. *c* **900** *Laws Ælfred* §21 ᵹif oxa ofhnite wer oððe wif. **971** *Blickl. Hom.* 11 Salomones reste wæs..ymbseted..mid syxtiᵹum werum. *c* **1000** *Sax. Leechd.* I. 156 þeos ylce wyrt ᵹedeþ þæt æᵹþer ᵹe wera ᵹe wifa feax wexeþ. *c* **1175** *Lamb. Hom.* 111 Wisdom biriseð weran. *Ibid.* 131 Bitwuxe were and wife nes nefre mare mon þenne he. *c* **1200** ORMIN 7615 þatt hallȝhe were Symeon Himm toc bitwenenn arrmess. *c* **1250** *Gen. & Ex.* 532 And on ðe sexte hundred ȝer Wimmen welten weres mester. *Ibid.* 3977 So was ðis were to wunder broȝt, ðhoȝ ðe asse spac, friȝtede he noȝt.

2. A husband.

c **893** ÆLFRED *Oros.* I. x. §1 Heora wif..sædon..hie him woldon oðerra wera ceosan. *a* **900** *Laws Ælfred-Ine* §38 (*title*) Be ðon ðe rihtᵹesamhiwan bearn habban, ond ðonne se wer ᵹewite. **971** *Blickling Hom.* 185 Wif ic lærde þæt hie heora weras lufedan. *c* **1000** ÆLFRIC *Exod.* xxi. 22 Bete swa micel swa ðæs wifes wer ᵹyrnð. *a* **1200** *Moral Ode* 31 Ne lipnie wif to hire were, ne were to his wive. *c* **1230** *Hali Meid.* 7 Hire latere were..lesse haueð þen hauede ear hire earre. *a* **1250** *Owl & Night.* 1341 For god wif may..Bet luuyen hire owe were, þan on oþer hire copinere. *c* **1275** *Wom. Samaria* 30 in *O.E. Misc.* 85 Go and clepe þine were and cumeþ hider y-mene.

were (wɪə(r)), *sb.*^{2} *Hist.* Also **wer**. [OE. *were*, var. of *wer* (dat. *were*), abbreviation of *were-*, *werᵹild*.] = WERGELD.

1607 COWEL *Interpr.* **1628** COKE *On Litt.* 127 *Wera* or *Were* sometimes signifieth amerciament or compensation. **1660** R. COKE *Power & Subj.* 190 Who shall commit perjury upon holy things, let him lose his hand, or half his *were*. **1819** LINGARD *Hist. Eng.* I. iii. 124 He paid the *were* for the death of Ælfwin. **1842** SIR H. TAYLOR *Edwin the Fair* II. v, He that within the palace draws his sword Doth forfeit an Earl's were. **1872** E. W. ROBERTSON *Hist. Ess.* 236 *note*, In later days it was a principle of Land-right that no free-man should be amerced 'above his wer'.

†**were**, *sb.*^{3} *Obs.* Forms: *α.* 3–5 **were** (5 *Sc.* **vere**), 4–5 **wer** (4 **werr**, 5 *Sc.* **ver**), 4, 5–6 *Sc.*, **weyr**, (9 *Sc.*) **weir** (5 *Sc.* **weyre, veir**), 5 **weere** (8 *Sc.* **weer**). *β.* 4 **wehere**, 4–5 **where**, 5 **wher, wheer**. *γ.* 5 **wyre**. [Of doubtful origin, but possibly the

same word as northern ME. and Sc. *were*, var. of ME. *werre* WAR *sb.*[1], retaining the original sense of 'confusion', 'perplexity', which is prominent in OHG. *werra*, etc. The form agrees with north-eastern OF. *were* (also *weire*, *wiere*, *wyere*), which is the immediate source of ME. and Sc. *were* 'war'.

In R. Brunne *Chron. Wace* (Rolls) 2126 and *Rom. Rose* 5699 the use of *were* is suggested by *guere* and *guerre* in the French originals. Although employed by some midland and southern writers, the word is chiefly characteristic of northern texts and latterly confined to Scottish use. Except in senses 5 b, 6, and 7, it most frequently occurs in the phrase *in (a) were*.]

1. Danger, peril, jeopardy.

c **1250** *Gen. & Ex.* 1788 Engel wirð a-gen him cam, Als it were wopnede here, Redi to silden him fro were. **1338** R. BRUNNE *Chron.* (1810) 319 His life was alle in wehere. He bed grete catelle, his lif forto saue. *c* **1375** *Sc. Leg. Saints* xxvii. (*Machar*) 274 He þat quyk sawit moyses..has defendit þis barne here, þat lyk was to be in gret were. *c* **1400** *Beryn* 2850 They had levir saille forth, þen put[ten] hem in were, Both lyve & goodis. *c* **1400** *Destr. Troy* 8266 All in wer for to walt, wayueronde he sote, But he held hym on horse. **1500–20** DUNBAR *Poems* xxxvi. 1 Sen thy lyfe is ay in weir, And deid is evir drawand neir.

b. ***in were of***, in danger of. Also Sc. ***in weres to*** (with inf.).

c **1400** *Destr. Troy* 7498 Bothe were þai bold men borne to þe grene, Woundit full wickedly in wer of hor lyues. *Ibid.* 13901. **1412–20** LYDG. *Chron. Troy* IV. 75 For outterly þei and her cyte Shal mor & mor in were of deth depende. **1804** TARRAS *Poems* 42 Lums [= chimneys] in wiers to get a dird [= shock] Or downward flung.

2. A condition of trouble or distress.

a **1300** *Cursor M.* 2425 Qui did þou vs þus in were, þat said þi wijf þi sister were? *c* **1330** R. BRUNNE *Chron. Wace* (Rolls) 828 He regned foure & þrytty ȝer In pes wyþouten wo & wer. **1352** MINOT *Poems* (ed. Hall) iii. 95 Þe Inglis men put þam to were Ful baldly, with bow and spere. *c* **1400** *Rom. Rose* 2827 Swete speche That hath to many oon be leche To bringe hem out of woo and were. *c* **1400** *Minot's Poems* (Hall) App. ii. 79 Þan sal þe land duel in were. *c* **1407** LYDG. *Reson & Sens.* 3061 Fro day to day most ful of moone, Solytarye, and allone, As a woman in gret wer. *c* **1460** *Towneley Myst.* iv. 22 Adam..liffyd..In sorow and in trauell strang, And euery day he was in were. *c* **1500** *Lancelot* 84 O woful wrech, that levis in to were.

b. A state of uncertainty or instability.

c **1375** *Sc. Leg. Saints* vi. (*Thomas*) 460 Þis present lyfe Is ..vndirlout to chansis sere, sa þat men liffis ay ine vere. **1390** GOWER *Conf.* I. 8 Bot we that duelle under the mone Stonde in this world upon a weer. *c* **1400** *Pety Job* 129 in *26 Pol. Poems* 125 Thus mannes tyme ys in a were; But thy tyme stondeth in oo degre.

3. Apprehension, fear, dread.

a **1300** *Sarmun* lix. in *E.E.P.* (1862) 7 Loke þat ȝe nab no were, for seue ȝer ȝe habbiþ to pardoun. **1338** R. BRUNNE *Chron.* (1810) 228 Þe Soudan was in wehere þe Cristen had suilk oste, Sir Edwarde's powere ouer alle he dred moste. *c* **1375** *Sc. Leg. Saints* i. (*Petrus*) 318 Sin eftir can crist appere To petir, at wes in sic were, and sad [etc.]. *a* **1400** *Pol. Rel. & L. Poems* (1903) 259, I am þi broþer, be nout in wer, be nout agast to come me ner. **1412–20** LYDG. *Chron. Troy* IV. 3420 He was boþe ferful & in were, In gret dispeire and inly ful of drede. **1426** —— *De Guil. Pilgr.* 21663 For dred off hyre, I was in were. *c* **1440** *York Myst.* ix. 146 Loke in and loke with-outen were. **15..** *Colkelbie Sow* 541 (Bann. MS.) Is nocht this a nyce caiss, That..in so mony dengeris, He eskapit with weris?

1808 JAMIESON s.v. *Were*, *I haif nae weir of that*, I have no fear of it, S.B.

b. A state of mental distress or trouble.

1303 R. BRUNNE *Handl. Synne* 5676 Pers..on hys dreme gan þynke, Syghyng with mornyng chere, As man þat was yn grete were. *c* **1385** CHAUCER *L.G.W.* 2686 (Fairf.) Drede of dethe doth hir so moche woo That thries doun she fele in swiche a were.

4. Perplexity; confusion of mind; doubt or uncertainty how to act or regard one's position, etc. Also with *a*.

(*a*) **1338** R. BRUNNE *Chron.* (1810) 81 William was in wehere, whan he herd þat tiþing. ? *a* **1400** *Hampole's Prose Tr.* 35 Be þou noghte in dowte ne in were when þou prayes or thynkes one Godd. *c* **1400** *Destr. Troy* 13160 A myst & a merknes mynget with rayn, þat wilt vs in were & our way lost. **1500–20** DUNBAR *Poems* xxx. 50 He vaneist away with stynk and fyrie smowk;..And I awoik as wy that wes in weir.

(*b*) **1377** LANGL. *P. Pl.* B. XI. 111 In a were gan I waxe and with my-self to dispute. **1390** GOWER *Conf.* I. 107 Ha, fader, be noght in a wer: I trowe ther be noman..That halt him lasse worth thanne I To be beloved. *c* **1400** *Pety Job* 129 in *26 Pol. Poems* 297 Thus he wandreth in a were As a man blynde. *c* **1407** LYDG. *Reson & Sens.* 2901 And thus I stood al in a rage..Wavering as in a were. **1412–20** —— *Chron. Troy* I. 4273 But in a were he abydynge longe, Aforn hym sawe þe myȝty Grekis stronge.

5. A (subjective) state of doubt or uncertainty with regard to the truth or reality of anything; undecidedness of belief or opinion. Const. *of*, *what*, *that*, etc. Also with *a* and pl.

(*a*) *a* **1300** *Cursor M.* 7069 Her-of thar naman be in were. *Ibid.* 17069 All men was in dute and wer bot þou, leue hali mai! **1338** R. BRUNNE *Chron.* (1810) 306 For þei were euer in wehere,..Whilk was best banere, with þat side forto hold. **1357** *Lay Folks Catech.* 294 If the prest be in were [*v.r.* dowte] of him that sal take it [baptisme] Whethir he be baptized or he be noght. **1412–20** LYDG. *Chron. Troy* III. 3993 So þat ȝe shal of no þing be in were Of al þat euere þat I seie ȝou here. **1426** —— *De Guil. Pilgr.* 22228, I stood in a maner wher, What tokenes that it myght be, The thynges that I dyde se. ? *a* **1500** *Chester Pl.* XXIII. 74 Fowle haue we leued many a year, and of our weninge bene in were. **1500–20** DUNBAR *Poems* lxxii. 89 In weir that he was ȝit on lyf, Thai ran ane rude speir in his syde.

(*b*) *c* **1350** *Will. Palerne* 3513 William was in a wer þat it were him-selue. **1377** LANGL. *P. Pl.* B. XVI. 3 Ac ȝet I am in a were, what charite is to mene. *a* **1395** HYLTON *Scala Perf.* II. xi. (W. de W. 1494), Therfore they falle ofte in suche weeres and doubtes of hemself. *c* **1420** ? LYDG. *Assembly of Gods* 1872 All that tyme stood I in a wyre [*rhyme* desyre] Whyche way furst myn hert wold yeue more To looke. **1500–20** DUNBAR *Poems* xc. 30 Sa that thi confessour be wyss and discreit, That can the discharge of every doute and weir.

b. ***to have no were***, to be in no doubt. Also Sc. ***to have weres***.

c **1375** *Cursor M.* 12135 (Fairf.) Of þine elde we haue na were; vnneþes artow of vij. ȝere. *c* **1430** *Hymns Virgin* (1867) 116 For of reward sche haþ no were þat þus abidiþ in charite. **1513** DOUGLAS *Æneis* Dyrect. Bk. 80 Of ȝour moblys and all other geyr Ȝe will me serf siklyke, I haue na weyr. **1535** W. STEWART *Cron. Scot.* I. 5 So that it be substantious of sentence In plane termis, thairof haif thow no weir. **1768** ROSS *Helenore*, *Songs* 129, I thought ere I died to have anes made a web, But still I had weers o' the spinning o't.

6. The condition of being (objectively) doubtful or uncertain; a state of affairs such as to give occasion for hesitation or uncertainty; a matter of doubt.

a **1300** *Cursor M.* 20794 Disput, he sais, es na mister Bituix te wis in swilk a wer. **13..** *Ibid.* 23824 (Edinb.) Þat ilke dai we se and here, we ah it noht to hald in were. **1303** R. BRUNNE *Handl. Synne* 462 Þan ys doute & grete were [*v.r.* weyr] To wyte where-of dremys come. *c* **1375** *Sc. Leg. Saints* ii. (*Paul*) 378 For-thy it is in wer gyff þis be paulis hewid or nocht. *c* **1475** *Rauf Coilȝear* 706 Ȝone is Wymond, I wait, it worthis na weir. ? *c* **1500** *Clariodus* I. 1320 Quhairfor this knicht we tuike in this maneir To save our aithes, traist weill this is no weir.

7. Often in phr. (usually introduced as a mere tag) ***but***, ***forouten***, ***out of***, ***without were***, without doubt. Also occas. with *any*.

(*a*) *a* **1300** *Cursor M.* 2157 Arphaxat liued wit-outen were Threhundret aght and tuenti ȝere. *c* **1340** HAMPOLE *Pr. Consc.* 2296 Þan er we certayn, with-outen were, þat at our last ende þai sal apere. *c* **1380** *Sir Ferumb.* 2872 Hast þou gode chere þy faire tour to gete aȝan wyþ-oute any where. *c* **1407** LYDG. *Reson & Sens.* 51 To yive me drynke of her tonne, Of which she hath, with-oute wer, Couched tweyn in hir celler. *c* **1485** *Digby Myst.* III. 1027 With-owtyn ony wyre, þer xall ye se hym. *c* **1530** *Songs, Carols*, etc. (E.E.T.S.) 83 This worde was wretyn withowt were For many a man, þat shuld drede. **1552** LYNDESAY *Monarche* 5288 Elie sayis, withouttin weir, The warld sall stand sax thousand ȝeir.

(*b*) *c* **1305** *Land Cokaygne* 21, I sigge for soþ, boute were, Þer nis lond on erthe is pere. *c* **1375** *Sc. Leg. Saints* xv. (*Barnabas*) 70 We lat ȝow wyt, but ony ver, þat of lord criste Ihesu,..we are þe seruandis & mene. **1456** SIR G. HAYE *Law Arms* (S.T.S.) 109 That he is his soverane.. is but were. *c* **1475** *Rauf Coilȝear* 499 For na gold on this ground wald I, but weir, Be fundin fals to the King. **1567** *Gude & Godlie B.* (S.T.S.) 37 Thay within ane lytill stound Began to myrrie be but weir. **1574** *Satir. Poems Reform.* xlii. 390 Thair suld be plantit throw this land At euerie Kirk..Ane Preichour at the leist but weir.

(*c*) **1375** BARBOUR *Bruce* IV. 222 Bot he wes fule, forouten weir, That gaf treuth to that Creature. *c* **1475** *Rauf Coilȝear* 288 He will be found in his fault that wants, foroutin weir.

(*d*) *a* **1425** *Cursor M.* 3799 (Trin.) He seide, oure lord out of were I wist not his wonyng here. *c* **1475** *Rauf Coilȝear* 230 'Out of weir', said the King, 'I wayndit neuer to tell'.

were, *sb.*[4] *rare.* [f. WERE *v.*]

†**1.** A defender, protector. *Obs.*

c **1250** *Gen. & Ex.* 2680 Moyses was louered of ðat here, ðor he wurð ðane egyptes were.

2. *Sc.* Defence.

a **1878** AINSLIE *Land of Burns* (1892) 237 At guard an wier lay Andro Keir—He faught to haud his ain.

were (wɪə(r)), *v. Obs.* exc. *Sc.* Forms: 1 **werian** (**werȝan**, **weriȝean**), 2–3 **werien** (3 **weriin**, 5 **weryyn**), 3–4 **werie**, 4 **werye(n)**; 2–3 **weren** (3 *Orm.* **werenn**), 4–5 **were**, **wer** (4 **werr**, 5 **werre**), 5 **weire**, 5–6, 9 *Sc.* **weir**, 6 **weere** (9 *dial.* **weer**), **weare**, 8–9 *Sc.* **wear**. *Pa. t.* 1–4 **werede** (1 **-ode**), 4 **wered**, **-id**, **werde**, 5 **werit** (*Sc.* **-yt**); 5 **were**, **wore**, *Sc.* **wor**. *Pa. pple.* 4 **werd**, 9 *dial.* **weard**. [Common Teut.: OE. *werian*, *werȝan* = OS. *werian*, *werean* (MLG. and LG. *weren*), OFris. *wera* (WFris. *weare*, *warre*; NFris. *weeri*, *wiare*), MDu. and Du. *weren*, OHG. *warian*, *werian*, etc. (MHG. *wergen*, *weren*, *wern*, G. *wehren*), ON. and Icel. *verja* (Norw. *verja*; Sw. *värja*, Da. *værge*, *verge*), Goth. *warjan*. The extent to which the two senses of preventing or checking, and defending or protecting, are represented, varies in the different languages; the greater currency of the second in English, though already prominent in OE., may have been assisted by the agreement with ON. *verja*.]

1. *trans.* To check or restrain; to ward off, repel. Also with *away*, *off*. Now *rare* or *Obs.*

a **900** *Andreas* 743 Stan..septe sacerdas sweotulum tacnum, witiȝ werede & worde cwæð. *c* **925** *Laws* II. *Edward* §4 Þæt ælc man hæbbe symle þa men ȝearowe.., ðe læden ða men ðe heora aȝen secan willen, and hy for nanum medsceattum ne werian. *c* **1220** *Bestiary* 102 [He] Of hise eȝen wereð ðe mist, wiles he drecceð ðore. *c* **1250** *Gen. & Ex.* 2898 Ic sal hem lesen fro, And here fon weren wið wo. *c* **1320** *Sir Tristr.* 2543 His gloue he put þer inne þe sonne to were oway. **13..** *Gaw. & Gr. Knt.* 2015 Fyrst he clad hym in his cloþez, þe colde for to were. *c* **1375** *Leg. Rood* viii. 297 Þe Cros I calle þe heerdes ȝerde,..And wiþ þe ȝerde þe wolf he werde. *a* **1470** HARDING *Chron.* XCVIII. xii. (1812) 181 By whiche he maye the wolf werre [*v.r.* bete] frome the gate. *c* **1480** HENRYSON *Test. Cress.* 182 Of his Father the wraith fra vs to weir.

1791 LEARMONT *Poems* 47 Lord wear aff the featour's blow Frae honest fock! **1829** BROCKETT *N.C. Words* (ed. 2), *Weer*, or *Wear*, to stop or oppose, to keep off, to guard.

2. To defend, guard, or protect from assault or injury.

Beowulf 1205 Siððan he under seȝne..wælreaf werede. *Ibid.* 1327 Ðonne we on orleȝe hafelan weredon. *a* **900** *O.E. Chron.* an. 755 Se cyning on þa duru eode, & þa unheanlice hine werede. **971** *Blickl. Hom.* vi. 79 Hie for þæm hungre þa burh werian ne mihton. *a* **1122** *O.E. Chron.* an. 1016 (Laud MS.), His rice he heardlice werode þa hwile þe his tima wæs. *c* **1175** *Lamb. Hom.* 81 Al þos godnesse hom ne mihte werien, þet ho ne wenden alle in to helle. *c* **1200** ORMIN 5305 Þa birrþ þe stanndenn þær onnȝæn, & werenn Cristess þeowwess. *c* **1205** LAY. 5696 And swiðe wel heom wereden þa walles of Rome. *a* **1250** *Owl & Night.* 834 Bute he can clymbe swiþe wel; þar myd he wereþ his greye vel. *a* **1300** *Cursor M.* 23766 Eth es for to win wit heer, þe ture þat nan es bute to were. **1340** *Ayenb.* 129 Þou hest kueade þeawes þet þe ssolle lede to þe dyaþe of helle bote þe grace of god þe ne werie. **1375** BARBOUR *Bruce* XX. 379 All tym had I Handis, myne hede for till were. *c* **1412** HOCCLEVE *De Reg. Princ.* 2546 He of iustice is bounden hem to were And to diffende. *c* **1440** *Promp. Parv.* 522/2 Weryyn', *idem quod* defendyn. *c* **1470** HENRY *Wallace* III. 183 Wallace..Wichtly him wor [*v.r.* did him weir], quhill he a suerd had tayne.

a **1800** in Chambers *Pop. Rhymes Scot.* (1870) 151 He tethered his tyke ayont the dike, And bade him weir the corn. **1807** J. STAGG *Misc. Poems* (1808) 40 For tho' wi' witch wood weard, yet weel They kend auld Hornie's tricks.

†**b.** Const. *with* or *against*, *from* (or *of*). *Obs.*

(*a*) *a* **1000** *Exodus* 237 Þa þe..ne mihton..breostnet wera wið flane feond folmum weriȝean. *c* **1175** *Lamb. Hom.* 13 Ic eou wille werien wið elcne herm. *c* **1200** ORMIN 10227 To fihhtenn forr þe leode, To werenn hemm wiþþ wiþerrþeod Þatt wollde hemm oferrganngenn. *c* **1315** SHOREHAM I. 1244 Þe þrydde hys icleped 'coniurement' Aȝenys þe foule þynge to werie þe. **1390** GOWER *Conf.* II. 248 Hir enchantement Ayein the Serpent scholde him were.

(*b*) *a* **1300** *Cursor M.* 11168 Hir sun he sal and fader baþe Be to wer his folk fra waþe. *c* **1400** *Ywaine & Gaw.* 3284 And fro my liown i sal the wer. **1402** *Pol. Poems* (Rolls) II. 44 For holy chirche hath us..happid with grace, to were us from wederes of wynteres stormes. *c* **1425** *Macro Plays*, *Cast. Persev.* 2046 Fro seuene synnys we schul hym were. *c* **1470** *Gol. & Gaw.* 58 Luke that wisly thow wirk, Criste were the fra wa!

(*c*) **1801** HOGG *Sc. Pastorals* 23 For wearin' corn of hens an cocks,..His match was never made.

†**c.** To defend, uphold, or give support to (a cause, etc.); to maintain (one's opinion). *Obs.*

c **1250** *Gen. & Ex.* 3714 Burȝes stronge and folc v[n-]friȝt, stalwurði to weren here riȝt. *a* **1300** *Cursor M.* 1476 Wit antecrist þan sal [Enoch] fight For to werye cristen right. **1340** *Ayenb.* 69 Þer byeþ zome..þet none guode techinge ne onderuongeþ, ak alneway weryeþ hare sentense huet þet hit by.

d. To keep or hold (a means of entrance or exit); †to have or possess as one's own.

c **1330** R. BRUNNE *Chron. Wace* (Rolls) 9312 Þe Erl ..þoughte no feyþ til [him] wold bere, But he in pes his wyf myght were. *c* **1470** HENRY *Wallace* IX. 1965 At Sterlyng bryg he ordand thaim full rycht, And thar to byd, the entre for to wer. **1802** *Fray of Suport* ii. in Scott *Minstrelsy* I. 187, I set him to wear the fore-door wi' the speir. *a* **1894** J. SHAW in R. Wallace *Country Schm.* (1899) 355 To wear a gate at sheep-shearing, to open and shut it.

†**e.** To protect or save by removing. *Obs.*

c **1460** *Towneley Myst.* viii. 151 If thay with wrong away wold wrast, outt of the way I shall the were.

†**3.** *refl.* To defend or guard (oneself, etc.); often followed by *against*, *from*. (Cf. 1 b.) *Obs.*

Beowulf 541 Wit unc wið hronfixas werian þohton. **993** *Battle of Maldon* 82 Ælfere & Maccus..hi fæstlice wið ða fynd weredon. *c* **1175** *Lamb. Hom.* 69 Crist..ȝeue us wepne ..Mid gode werkes for us to weren. *c* **1200** ORMIN 1406 Acc þu mihht werenn þe fra þeȝȝm Þurrh rihhte læfe o Criste. *a* **1225** *Ancr. R.* 400 Were þe, ȝif þu konst, aȝean me. *c* **1250** *Gen. & Ex.* 2083 Ðor-fore ic am in sorge and hagt, for ic ne migte me nogt weren. *a* **1300** *Cursor M.* 2227 Þai culd find on no manere How to wer þam fra þe flode. *c* **1315** SHOREHAM *Poems* I. 114 For we beþ of nonn power To weryen ous fro schame. *c* **1380** *Sir Ferumb.* 845 Olyuer tok is spere & eke ys scheld & heng hit on þer-wiþ him-self to were. *c* **1386** CHAUCER *Knt.'s T.* 1692 Foyne if hym list on foote, hym self to were. *c* **1407** LYDG. *Reson & Sens.* 1195 From al hir fon hir self to were, In her ryght honde she had a spere. *c* **1470** HENRY *Wallace* v. 901 A suerd he drew, rycht manlik him to wer.

†**4.** *absol.* **a.** To make a defence, to offer resistance. *Obs.*

c **1200** ORMIN 2046 Þuss mihhte ȝho bitellen wel & werenn þurrh þatt bisne. *c* **1200** *Mor. Ode* 325 in *Trin. Coll. Hom.* 230 Ne muȝe we werien naðer ne wið þurst ne wið hunger. *c* **1250** *Gen. & Ex.* 851 Fowre [kings] on-seken and fifue weren. **13..** *K. Alis.* 3533 The spies on bothe sydes goth, Of Alisaundre, and eke Darie, How eche schal from othir werye.

†**b.** To act as a shield or protection. *Obs.*

c **1375** *Cursor M.* 21840 (Fairf.) Hit is our shilde & our spere, a-gainis þe feinde for to were. *c* **1400** *Destr. Troy* 11108 Sho..Hade no helme on hir hede fro harmys to weire.

Hence †**'wering** *vbl. sb.*

a **1300** *E.E. Psalter* xxi. 20 And þou, lauerd, ne fer þi help fra me; At mi weringe bihald and se. **13..** *K. Alis.* 2798 The saut com so thikke and swithe, That no weryng ne myghte heom lithe. *a* **1310** in Wright *Lyric P.* xxv. 75 Send mi soule god weryyng.

were: see BE *v.* A. 6, 7.

were, var. or obs. f. VERE *sb.*, VERY, WAR *sb.*[1], *v.*, WAR, WAUR *a.* and *adv.*, WARE *a.*, WEAR *v.*, WEIR, WHERE, WHETHER, WIRE *sb.*

were- (wɪə(r)). The first element of WEREWOLF used in combination, chiefly with names of animals, to indicate a human being imagined to be transformed into a beast; as ***were-animal***, ***-ass***, ***-bear***, etc.; also ***were-man***. Cf. WER-. **ˈwere-jaguar**, in Olmec mythology, a creature partly human and partly feline.

1873 LONGF. *Wayside Inn* III. Interl. v. 4 The were-wolf is a legend old, But the were-ass is something new. **1883** J. F. M'LENNAN in *Encycl. Brit.* XV. 90 The Arcadians, or bear-tribe, sprang from the were-bear Callisto. *Ibid.*, In Ashango-land, . . a were-leopard was . . charged with murder and metamorphosis. **1894** *Sat. Rev.* 15 Sept. 289/2 The simple explanation . . that that beast was a were-calf. **1897** SIR H. H. JOHNSTON *Brit. Centr. Afr.* 439 In this respect the belief in 'were' animals . . is nearly universal. **1967** L. DEUEL *Conquistadors without Swords* xviii. 235 Today, . . more than 400 years after the Spanish Conquest and 2,000 . . years since its origin, the were-jaguar, the *nawal*, is still invoked to frighten children who will not go to sleep. **1967** E. P. BENSON *Maya World* ii. 24 Olmec art is full of creatures who are part human and part feline. . . Often they are a combination of human infant and jaguar. They are called 'were-jaguars'. **1979** E. ABRAMS tr. *H. Stierlin's Precolombian Civilizations* 68 This werejaguar figure tenoned into the wall of the pyramid at Chavín.

wereangel, -angle, var. forms of WARIANGLE.

†**wered.** *Obs.* Forms: α. 1 **werud, -od** (2 **wærod**), 1–3 **wered**; 1 **weorod**, 1, 3 **weored**; 1 *north.* **uorud**, 3 **wored**. β. 2–3 **werd**, 3 **word**, 3–4 **wird**, 4 **weird**. [OE. *werod*, *weorod*, etc., without parallels in the cognate languages.] A band, troop, company, host.

α. *c* **725** *Corpus Gloss.* (Hessels) A 407 *Agmen*, weorod. **971** *Blickl. Hom.* 131 Ac se heaþrym þæs Godes hades þæm englicum weorodum simle ondweard wæs. *c* **1000** *Ags. Gosp.* Matt. xiii. 34 Ealle þas þing se hælend spræc mid biȝ-spellum to þam weredum. —— Mark xv. 16 Hi tosomne eall werod clypedon. *c* **1205** LAY. 2598 He bi-com . . vppen ane weorede of wlfan awedde. *a* **1225** *Ancr. R.* 30 Ase þer beoð niene englene ordres [*MSS. B, C* weoredes]. *a* **1240** *Ureisun* in *Cott. Hom.* 195 Al englene were[d] and alle holie þing Siggeð and singeð þet tu ert liues welsprung.

Comb. *c* **1205** LAY. 509 Ʒif he heom mihte bi-winnen mid his wored strencðe.

β. *c* **1160** *Hatton Gosp.* Luke vi. 17 He stod on feldlicere stowe & micel werd hys leorningcnihte. *a* **1225** *St. Marher.* 22 Hali is . . þe lauerd of heouene riche wordes. *c* **1250** *Gen. & Ex.* 1786 Als he cam ner cananeam, Engel wirð [*sic*] a-gen him cam. *Ibid.* 1790 Ðor ðis wird of engeles metten him. *a* **1275** *Prov. Alfred* 697 in *O.E. Misc.* 138 Bi ford dages he is aferd of sticke & ston in huge werd. *a* **1300** *Cursor M.* 20282 He þat i bar, þat bligh brid, Sal me send of heuen wird [*Gött.* weird].

†ˈ**wereful**, *a.* *Sc.* *Obs.*$^{-1}$ [f. WERE *sb.*[3] + -FUL.] Doubtful.

1456 SIR G. HAY *Gov. Princes* Wks. (S.T.S.) II. 104 To geve the ensample and instructioun to wysly governe the in mony thingis that now ar werefull to the.

weregeld, -gild, var. forms of WERGELD.

wereit, obs. pa. t. and pa. pple. of WORRY.

†**werel.** *Obs.* *rare*$^{-1}$. [Of obscure origin: cf. MHG. *wedel*, *wegel*.] A fan or fly-whisk.

a **1390** *Wycliffite Bible, Job* Prol. II. 672 For the werelis, lepis, basketis [L. *pro flabello, calathis, sportellisque*], and litle ȝiftis of munkis, these spirituel . . ȝiftis . . taketh.

werelbone, obs. form of WHIRLBONE.

wereld(e, obs. forms of WORLD.

werelie, obs. Sc. form of VERILY and WARLY.

werelike, obs. Sc. form of WARLIKE.

werely, obs. Sc. var. WARLY *a.*

werena, *Sc.* = were not: see NA *adv.*[3]

weren't, colloq. contraction of 'were not'.

werew, obs. form of WORRY *v.*

†**werewall.** *Sc.* *Obs.* Also 5 **wer-**, 6 **weir-**. [f. WERE *v.* + WALL *sb.*] A bulwark, rampart. In quots. *fig.*

c **1450** HOLLAND *Howlat* 382 The armes of the Dowglass . . Of Scotland the wer wall. **1533** BELLENDEN *Livy* II. xxii. (S.T.S.) I. 222 Þai war campit to be ane were-wall for defence of Veanis. **1536** —— *Cron. Scot.* XIV. viii. (1821) II. 383 The . . surname of Dowglas, quhilkis war evir the sicker targe and weirwal of Scotland aganis Inglismen.

werewolf, werwolf (ˈwɪə-, ˈwɜːwʊlf). Forms: α. 1 **werewulf**, (3 **-wlf**), 7–9 **-wolf**; *pl.* 5 **-wolfes**, 9 **weir-**, **werewolves**. β. 4–7, 9 **werwolf** (6 *Sc.* **-woif**); *pl.* 4 **-wolfs**, **-wolues**, 9 **werwolves**. γ. 5–7 *Sc.*, 9 **warwolf**, 5–7 **-wolfe**, (7 *Sc.* **warewolf**, **warwoof**); *pl.* 6 *Sc.* **-wo(o)lfes**, 7 *Sc.* **-woophs**. δ. 9 **wehrwolf**. [OE. *werewulf* (once), = MDu. and Du. *weerwolf*, MHG. *werwolf* (G. *wer-*, *wehrwolf*), LG. *werwulf*; also WFris. *waerûl*, *warûle* (and *waerwolf* after Du.), Da. and Norw. *varulv*, Sw. *varulf*. The latter may represent an ON. **varulf-r*, whence ONF. *garwall* (Marie de France, *c* 1175), later *guaroul*, *-ou*, *garoul*, *-ou*, *warou*, *-eu* (mod.F. *loupgarou*); ON. *vargulf-r* (by association with *varg-r* wolf) occurs only in the translation of Marie's lay of Bisclavret.

The first element has usually been identified with OE. *wer* man WERE *sb.*[1], but the form *were-* in place of *wer-* (cf. however *were-* and *werȝild* WERGELD), and the variants in *war-*, *var-*, makes this somewhat doubtful.

Evidence for the real currency of the word (chiefly in the β and γ forms) is rare, and confined to Sc., after the 17th cent. In modern use it has been revived through folk-lore studies, and until recently the most usual form has been *werewolf*, and occas. *wehrwolf* from German.]

1. A person who (according to mediæval superstition) was transformed or was capable of transforming himself at times into a wolf; †also, an exceptionally large and ferocious wolf.

α. *c* **1000** *Laws Cnut* xxvi. (Lieberm.) Þæt se wodfreca werewulf to swyðe ne slite, ne to fela ne abite of godcundre heorde. *c* **1212** GERVASE OF TILBURY *Otia Imper.* xv. in Leibnitz *Script. Brunsv.* (1707) I. 895 Quod hominum genus *gerulfos* Galli nominant, Angli vero *Werewlf*, dicunt. *c* **1400** *Master of Game* (MS. Digby 182) vi, Þer beth some [wolves] þat eten children and men . . And þei be cleped werewolfes, for men shulde be were of hem, or þe mann see hem. **1605** VERSTEGAN *Dec. Intell.* 237 The were-wolues are certaine sorcerers, who hauing annoynted their bodyes, with an oyntment which they make by the instinct of the deuil; and putting on a certaine inchanted girdel, do not only vnto the view of others seeme as wolues, but to their own thinking haue both the shape and nature of wolues, so long as they weare the said girdel. [Hence in BLOUNT *Glossogr.* (1656), etc.] **1818** *Q. Rev.* XIX. 68 The weir-wolves of the wilds of Indiana. **1831** A. HERBERT in *Will. & Werwolf* (Roxb.) 4 As a punishment for his ferocity he [*sc.* Lycaon] was deprived by Jupiter of the human form, and ended his days a were-wolf. **1863** W. K. KELLY *Curios. Indo-Europ. Tradit.* 253 Stories about werewolves are still current in Germany. **1871** TYLOR *Prim. Cult.* I. iii. 77 The old doctrine of Werewolves, not yet extinct in Europe. **1891** FARRAR *Darkn. & Dawn* xxvi. 213 Stories of magic and vampires and were-wolves told them by travelled youths.

fig. **1872** LONGF. *Wayside Inn* II. Interl. i. 23 The brutes that wear our form and face, The were-wolves of the human race!

β. *c* **1350** *Will. Palerne* 15 Þat while was þe werwolf went a-boute his praye. *Ibid.* 3836, I wold him hunte as hard as euer hounde in erthe honted eny werwolf. *c* **1394** *P. Pl. Crede* 459 Þei ben wilde wer-wolues, þat wiln þe folk robben. **1470–85** MALORY *Arthur* XIX. xi. 793 His wyf . . made hym seuen yere a werwolf. **1508** KENNEDIE *Flyting w. Dunbar* 251 Wod werwolf [*v.r.* werwoif], worme and scorpion vennemous. ? **1605** DRAYTON *Poems Lyr. & Past., Man in Moone* G 8 b, About the fields religiously they went, with halowing charms the Werwolf thence to fray. **1816** SCOTT *Antiq.* xxv, All the German superstitions of nixies, oak-kings, wer-wolves, hob-goblins. **1868** LOWELL *Among my Bks.* Ser. I. (1870) 115 Lycaon, . . after passing through all the stages I have mentioned, becomes the ancestor of the werwolf. **1912** E. O'DONNELL *Werwolves* xiii. 212 As in France, the werwolf, in Belgium, is not restricted to one sex.

fig. **1902** *Spectator* 5 July 17/1 When from that underworld . . The werwolves of the darkness pour by night And show . . their misery and their guilt.

γ. *c* **1480** HENRYSON *Parl. Beasts* xiv, The warwolf and the pegase perillous. **1483** *Cath. Angl.* 409/1 A Warwolfe, *ravus*. *a* **1533** BERNERS *Huon* clvi *a.* 602 Huon the souerayne kyng of the fayry . . wolde condempne hym parpetually to be a warwolfe in the se [Fr. *luyton de mer*]. **1576** TURBERV. *Venerie* lxxv. 206 Some Wolues . . kill children and men sometimes: and then they neuer feede nor pray vpon any other thing afterwards. . . Such Wolues are called *War-wolues*, bicause a man had neede to beware of them. [Cf. *c* 1400 in α.] **1597** JAS. VI *Dæmonol.* III. i. 61 And are not war-woolfes one sorte of these spirites also . . ? *c* **1622** ROWLEY, etc. *Birth of Merlin* V. i. 106 Where no Night-hag shall walk, nor Ware-wolf tread. **1665** SIR J. LAUDER (Fountainhall) *Jrnl.* (1900) 83 Instead of our red dracons and giants they have *lougarous* or *warwoophs*. *a* **1800** *Kempion* xvii. in Scott *Minstrelsy* (1802) II. 96 O was it warwolf in the wood . . ? **1817** COLERIDGE *Zapolya* II. I. i. 337 Madam, that wood is haunted by the war-wolves. **1897** BARING-GOULD *Guavas* xvi, They hold Loup [a tamed wolf] to be naught else but a war-wolf.

δ. **1834** W. J. THOMS *Lays & Leg., France* 57 The Lay of Bisclavaret; or, the Wehr-wolf. **1855** D. COSTELLO in *Bentley's Misc.* XXXVIII. 361 Lycanthropy in London; or The Wehr-Wolf of Wilton-Crescent. **1884** J. DAVIDSON *Bruce* IV. iv, The wehrwolf, ravening in the warren, growls. **1913** R. HODDER *Vampire* viii. 43 The wehrwolf who discards his human form to bury his fangs in the throats of sleeping children.

2. *Sc. dial.* (See quot.)

1808 JAMIESON, *Warwolf* . . 2. A puny child or an ill-grown person of whatever age; pron. warwoof, Ang.

3. A member of a right-wing paramilitary German underground resistance movement.

1945 in *Amer. Speech* (1949) XXIV. 289/2 It boasted that . . underground killers—'Werewolves'—had carried out the sentence. **1946** E. LINKLATER *Private Angelo* xxi. 266 A company of Free Austrians who . . handed him over to a ridiculous little party of people who called themselves Werewolves. **1950** C. MACINNES *To Victors the Spoils* I. 111 Isn't it going to be dangerous . . ? What about the Gestapo and the werewolves? **1982** C. THOMAS *Jade Tiger* 48 The subject matter of the interrogation—local conditions, Werewolf units, SS and Gestapo individuals' whereabouts.

4. *attrib.*, as ***werewolf nails***, etc.; **werewolf girdle**, the enchanted girdle by means of which a man could transform himself into a wolf.

15.. *Rowll's Cursing* 192 (Bannatyne MS.), Dragoun heidis and warwolf nalis, With glowrane evne as glitterand glass. **1863** W. K. KELLY *Curios. Indo-Europ. Tradit.* 255 In Germany . . the skin of a man that has been hanged makes as good a werewolf girdle as the skin of a wolf. **1879** M. D. CONWAY *Demonol.* I. 158 The Were-wolf superstition, which exists still in Russia. **1883** STALLYBRASS *Grimm's Teut. Mythol.* III. 1096 Bodin's Dæmonomanie . . has several werewolf stories.

Hence ˈ**werewolfery**, = LYCANTHROPY 2; ˈ**werewolfish** *a.*; ˈ**werewolfism**, = LYCANTHROPY 2.

1831 A. HERBERT in *Will. & Werwolf* (Roxb.) 3 It is obvious to suspect that the most ancient Lycians were proficients in *werewolfery. **1912** E. O'DONNELL *Werwolves* i. 3 Persons accused of werwolfery. **1891** *Century Dict.*, *Werewolfish. **1865** BARING-GOULD *Werewolves* viii. 100 The traditional belief in *were-wolfism must, however, have remained long in the popular mind. **1901** *Edin. Rev.* July 198 In fact 'were-wolfism' is now known to have made the round of the globe.

‖**werf** (wɛrf). *S. African.* Also **werft**. [Older and dial. Du. *werf* (*werft*) = NFris. *werw*, *werrew*, LG. *warf*, in the same sense; orig., a raised plot on which a house is built, and identical with the same forms in the sense of 'wharf': see WHARF *sb.*[1]] The Cape-Dutch name for a homestead or the space surrounding a S. African farm.

1818 LATROBE *Jrnl. S. Afr.* 191 We therefore took leave, pitched the tent on the werft, and kindled a fire. **1861** ANDERSSON *Okavango River* xvi. 179 Five minutes' further walk brought us to a werft consisting of between twenty and thirty huts. **1888** A. BRIGG *Sunny Fountains* 231 A Dutchman calls his homestead his *werf*. **1895** *Times* 19 Jan. 5/3 They arrived at the deceased's werf on November 7, possessed themselves of the guns and arms on the werf . . and then shot Mr. Christie.

werfore, obs. form of WHEREFORE.

†**werg.** *dial.* *Obs.* (See quot.)

1707 E. LHUYD *Archæol. Brit.* I. 14/3 A Willow-Tree was Anciently call'd *Willig*; whence the Modern *Werg* [a Willow] us'd in Berkshire and some other Countreys, seems corrupted.

wergeld (ˈwɜːgɛld), **-gild**. *Hist.* Forms: α. 3 *Sc.* **weregeheld**, 5 **weregylt**, 7–9 **weregild**, 9 **-geld**. β. 5 *Sc.* **wargeld** (7 **vergelt**), 7, 9 **wergeld**; 9 **wehrgeld**. γ. 8–9 **wergild**. [ad. OE. (Anglian and Kentish) *werȝeld*, (WSaxon) *werȝield*, *-ȝild*, *-ȝyld*, late *wereȝild* (f. *wer* man WERE *sb.*[1] + *ȝeld*, *ȝield* YIELD *sb.*) = OFris. *wergeld*, *-ield*, OHG. *wer-*, *werigelt* (MHG. *wergelt*, G. *wer-*, *wehrgeld*, Du. *weergeld*); the equivalent ON. term is *manngjǫld*.

The three OE. types *werȝeld*, *werȝild*, and *wereȝild* are represented in the modern forms; the spelling *wehrgeld* is due to the incorrect German form.]

In ancient Teutonic and Old English law, the price set upon a man according to his rank, paid by way of compensation or fine in cases of homicide and certain other crimes to free the offender from further obligation or punishment.

α. *a* **1214** *Assise Will.* c. 14 in *Acts Parl. Scot.* (1844) I. 375 De weregehelde furis. De unoquoque fure per totam Scociam est weregehelde xxxiiij vacc. et dimid. **14..** *Ibid.*, Of þe law þat is callyt weregylt. **1614** SELDEN *Titles Honor* 389 *Were* is before deliuerd in *Weregild*, and is calld *pretium Redemptionis* in the laws of the Confessor. **1714** J. FORTESCUE-ALAND *Pref. Fortescue's Abs. & Lim. Mon.* 32 A Payment in Money called the *Veragelt*; from which no Body can doubt, but our Saxon Ancestors had their *Were-gild*. **1761** HUME *Hist. Eng.* (1762) I. App. I. 156 The price of the king's head, or his weregild, as it was then called, was by law 30,000 thrimsas. **1769** BLACKSTONE *Comm.* IV. xxiii. 308 In those times, when a private pecuniary transaction, called a *weregild*, was constantly paid to the party injured, or his relations. **1818** HALLAM *Mid. Ages* ii. II. (1819) I. 230 Such were the weregilds of the barbaric codes. **1848** LYTTON *Harold* V. vi, There is no weregeld for manslaying on the head of him who smiles so in death on his old comrades in life! **1863** H. COX *Inst.* II. x. 533 The Weregild, or compensation for murder was regulated according to the rank of the person slain. **1864** KINGSLEY *Rom. & Teut.* vii. 193 He . . died, like Samson, says old Paul, having got good weregeld for the loss of his eyes.

β. *a* **1250** *Reg. Maj.* IV. xii. in *Acts Parl. Scot.* (1844) I. 634 De unoquoque fure . . est wargeld triginta vacce et vna iuuenca. **1609** SKENE tr. *Reg. Maj.* IV. xix. 70 b, The Vergelt, or Ranson of ane theif, throw all Scotland is threttie kye; and ane zoung kow. **1614** SELDEN *Titles Honor* 204 This wergeld or werigeld is often met with in the Salique laws. **1848** MRS. HORROCKS tr. *Menzel's Hist. Ger.* I. 33 The Wergeld or fine seems to have been introduced at a later period. **1854** MILMAN *Lat. Chr.* III. v. I. 395 In the Burgundian law . . the life of every man . . is assessed . . at a certain value, and the wehrgeld may be received in atonement for his blood. **1902** F. SEEBOHM *Tribal Custom Ags. Law* i. 1 The Anglo-Saxon wergelds were stated, with perhaps one exception, in silver scillings.

γ. **1762** M. FOSTER *Rep. Proc. Surry* etc. 287 The Anglo-Saxons . . in Case of Homicide contented themselves with a pecuniary Compensation, which they called the *Wergild*, the Price of Blood. **1802** A. RANKEN *Hist. Fr.* II. 249 Culpable homicide was punished with banishment, besides the wargild [*sic*], or fine, paid to the nearest kin of the deceased. **1860** HOOK *Lives Archbps.* I. v. 243 His position in society was, according to the custom of the age, marked by the amount of his wer-gild. **1870** FREEMAN *Norm. Conq.* (ed. 2) I. App. 629 By this treaty provision is made for wergilds.

†**wergeldthief.** *Old Eng. Law.* *Obs.* Forms: 1 **werȝeldtheof** (**-ȝild-**), 3 **weregelt thef**; 3–5 **wer(e)gelthef** (4 **wergiltif**, 5 **werkelthef**). [OE., f. prec. + *þéof* THIEF.] A thief or other criminal whose 'wergeld' was paid as a satisfaction for his crime; also *ellipt.* jurisdiction over a thief of this description.

c **690** *Laws Ine* §72 Ʒif mon werȝildðeof ȝefehð. **781** in Birch *Cartul. Sax.* I. 334 Nec etiam fures illos quos Saxonice dicimus uuerȝeldtheouas alicui foras reddant.

1235 in *Cal. Charter Rolls* (1903) I. 208 [With] soc and sac, .. infangenthef, utfangenthef, wergeldthef, hamsocn [etc.]. *c* **1290** *Fleta* I. xlvii. (1647) 62 Weregelt thef, latronem qui redimi potest. **13..** HIGDEN *Polychron.* (Rolls) II. 94 De quibus [legibus] nonnulla vocabula adhuc frequentata. hic inserere dignum duxi: .. Wergelthef, id est, solte de laroun eschape. *c* **1437** JOHN BROMPTON in Twysden *Hist. Angl. Script.* (1652) 957 *Weregelthef* est solutio latronis evasi, i. soute de latrone eschape.

weri, var. WARY *sb. Obs.*, obs. f. WEARY *a.*

werid, var. WARIED *ppl. a. Obs.*; obs. pa. pple. of WEAR *v.*

werie, obs. f. or var. VERY, WARY *v. Obs.*, WEARY *a.*

werielie, werietie, obs. Sc. ff. VERILY *adv.*, VERITY.

werihede *Obs.*: see after WEARY *a.*

wering, obs. var. WARRING *vbl. sb.*

weris(s)he, obs. ff. WEARISH.

werius, obs. f. VERJUICE *sb.*

werk(e, obs. ff. WARK *sb.*[1] and *v.*, WORK.

†**werke.** *Obs. rare.* [a. MLG. *werk* (LG. *wark*): see WORK *sb.*] Honey-comb.

The quots. refer to Hanseatic traders of 1395–8.

1598 HAKLUYT *Voy.* I. 167 Fiue pieces of waxe, foure hundred of werke, and halfe a last of osmundes. *Ibid.*, Diuers goods and marchandizes, namely oyle, waxe, and werke, to the value of 300. pounds.

†**werkhop.** *Obs.* [Of obscure origin.] A measure containing two bushels and a half.

c **1300** *Battle Abbey Custumals* (Camden) 55 Cottarii maiores .. debent triturare .. unum werkhop, quod continet .ij. bussellos et dimidium, scilicet de frumento .. De ordeo vero, ij. werkhops ejusdem mensuræ.

werkyn, werkyng, obs. ff. WORK, WORKING.

werlaugh(e, werlaw(e, etc.: see WARLOCK[1].

werld(e. obs. forms of WORLD.

†**werle.** *Obs.*[−1] [?f. *were* WEAR *v.* + -LE.] ? Covering, attire.

13.. *E.E. Allit. P.* A. 209 A py3t coroune 3et wer þat gyrle, .. Hi3e pynakled of cler quyt perle, .. To hed hade ho non oþer werle.

werlik, werlot, obs. Sc. ff. WARLIKE, VARLET.

werlðe, obs. f. WORLD.

werlyng, var. WARLING *Obs.*

werm, obs. f. WORM.

†**wermod.** *Obs.* Forms: 1, 3–5 **wermod** (1 wær-, wyr-, 4 wr-), 2 **wermot**; 1, 5 **weremod**; 4–5 **wermode, wormod(e**. [OE. *wermod* = OS. *wer(i)môda, wermôde* (MLG. *wermede*), OHG. *wer(i)muota, wer-, wormôta*, etc. (MHG. *wermuote, -muot*, G. *wermut, -muth*, whence F. *vermout* VERMOUTH), of obscure origin.] = WORMWOOD.

c **725** *Corpus Gloss.* (Hessels) A 9 *Absinthium*, wermod. *a* **1000** *Riddles* xli. 60 Swylce ic eom wraþre þonne wermod sy. *c* **1000** *Sax. Leechd.* I. 216 Ðeos wyrt þe man absinthium & oþrum naman wermod nemneð. *a* **1100** *Voc.* in Wr.-Wülcker 296/24 Weremod. *a* **1200** *Ibid.* 544/35 Wermot. **1382** WYCLIF *Prov.* v. 4 Bitter as wormod. —— *Lam.* iii. 19 Recorde .. of wrmod [**1388** wermod] and of galle. **1402** *Friar Daw* in *Pol. Poems* (Rolls) II. 52 Wermode, Jak, moost verreli was Wiclif, 3our maister. *c* **1440** *Pallad. on Husb.* XI. 344 The soure almaund & wermode & feyn greek. *c* **1450** *Alphita* (Anecd. Oxon.) 1 Absinthium .. gallice aloine, anglice wermode.

wern(e, obs. ff. WARN *v.*[1]; var. ff. WARN *v.*[2] *Obs.*

wernage, Sc. var. VERNAGE, WARNAGE.

†**'wernard.** *Obs.* [a. AF. **wernard* = OF. *guernart* 'trompeur' (Godefroy).] A deceiver, liar.

1362 LANGL. *P. Pl.* A. II. 98 For wel 3e witen, wernardes, but 3if or wit fayle, þat fals is a faytur. *Ibid.* B. III. 179 Wel þow wost, wernard, but 3if þow wolt gabbe, þow hast hanged on myne half elleuene tymes. *c* **1386** CHAUCER *Wife's Prol.* 260 (Corpus) þus saistow, wernard, god 3iue þe meschaunce.

Werner ('wɜːnə(r), ‖'vɛrnər). *Path.* [The name of Carl W. O. *Werner* (b. 1879), German physician, who described the syndrome in 1904.] ***Werner's syndrome***: a rare hereditary syndrome whose symptoms include short stature, endocrine and vascular disorders, and premature ageing and death.

1934 OPPENHEIMER & KUGEL in *Trans. Assoc. Amer. Physicians* XLIX 359 After careful consideration we have selected the patronymic name, Werner's syndrome, rather than Rothmund's syndrome, for on reading Rothmund's original paper (1868) .. we are convinced that he described a quite different condition. **1962** A. SORSBY in A. Pirie *Lens Metabolism Rel. Cataract* 298 The association of cataract with such affections as .. Werner's syndrome has been known for many years. **1980** *Practitioner* Nov. 1170/2 Rapid whitening of scalp hair associated with rapid ageing of the face .. are features reported in Werner's syndrome, a heredo-familial disease in young adults who age rapidly.

Wernerian (wə'nɪərɪən), *a.* and *sb.* [See -IAN.]

A. *adj.* Of or relating to A. G. *Werner* (1750–1817), a German mineralogist and geologist, who advocated the theory of the aqueous origin of rocks; favouring Werner's views; agreeing with Werner's system or theory.

1811 *Edin. Rev.* XIX. 222 We cannot help thinking, that the Wernerian geology is faulty. **1842** SEDGWICK in *Hudson's Guide Lakes* (1843) 226 The Wernerian hypothesis has now passed away. **1859** J. HAMILTON *Mem. J. Wilson* i. 12 The discussion .. between Wernerian and Huttonian theorists.

B. *sb.* A supporter of Werner's theory; a Neptunian.

1815 W. PHILLIPS *Outl. Min. & Geol.* 183 These two parties are termed volcanists and neptunists; or more familiarly by geologists, Huttonians and Wernerians. **1858** SCROPE *Geol. Extinct Volcanos Central France* Pref. p. vi, The error of the Wernerians in undervaluing .. the influence of volcanic forces. **1890** *Nature* 3 July 218/1 The Wernerians were retreating before the Huttonians.

Hence **Wer'nerianism**, the Wernerian or Neptunian theory or system.

1892 *Athenæum* 6 Aug. 181/3 Ignoring the importance of volcanic action as a geological agent, Wernerianism saw even in such lava-like rocks as basalt nothing more than precipitates from aqueous solutions.

wernerite ('wɜːnəraɪt). *Min.* [Named in honour of A. G. *Werner* the German mineralogist: see -ITE.] Silicate of aluminium and calcium, the most important member of the scapolite group.

1811 PINKERTON *Petral.* I. 205 Wernerite is generally reddish. **1823** H. J. BROOKE *Crystallogr.* 489 Scapolite .. Wernerite. **1851** MANTELL *Petrifactions* iv. §1. 364 Felspathic substances. Triphane; .. Wernerite.

Wernicke (v-, 'wɜːnɪkə). *Path.* The name of Karl *Wernicke* (1848–1905), German neurologist, used in the possessive to designate:

a. A neurological disorder in which there is an inability to understand speech and, usually, to speak sensibly, caused by a lesion of ***Wernicke's area***, an area of the cerebral cortex comprising parts of the temporal and parietal lobes.

1887 VICKERY & KNAPP tr. *Strümpell's Text-bk. Med.* 679 The word, when it is heard, may fail to call up the appropriate mental image. Kussmaul has given this condition the name of word deafness (Wernicke's sensory aphasia). The patient is not really deaf, for he hears everything, but he no longer understands what he hears, and has forgotten what the words signify. **1907** *Practitioner* Oct. 545 In the Aphasia of Broca .. the cases .. closely resemble those of Wernicke's aphasia, with the difference that, in Broca's aphasia, the patient cannot speak. **1908** A. GORDON *Dis. Nervous Syst.* vii. 118 Pierre Marie .. holds that aphasia .. is caused by a lesion in the lenticular nucleus and in Wernicke's zone; the latter comprises the following portions: supra-marginal gyrus, angular gyrus, the posterior portions of the first two temporal convolutions. **1965** [see LOGORRHŒA, LOGORRHEA]. **1976** *New Yorker* 15 Nov. 152/2 There are two areas of the cortex that have been shown to be directly involved in speaking. Those areas—known since the late nineteenth century as Broca's area and Wernicke's area— are on the side of the brain (usually the left) that is dominant for speech. **1979** *Sci. Amer.* Sept. 161/1 In Wernicke's aphasia speech is phonetically and even grammatically normal, but it is semantically deviant.

b. An encephalopathy caused by vitamin B_1 deficiency and characterized by mental confusion and uncontrolled movements, esp. of the eyes. So ***Wernicke-Korsakoff*** [see KORSAKOFF], applied to Wernicke's syndrome and Korsakoff's syndrome when both are present in an individual.

1910 E. E. SOUTHARD in Osler & McCrae *Syst. Med.* VII. xiii. 631 (*heading*) Hemorrhagic superior poliencephalitis (Wernicke's disease). *Ibid.*, The non-alcoholic and the alcoholic forms of Wernicke's disease are considered. **1939** *Jrnl. Path. & Bacteriol.* XLVIII. 259 We suggest therefore that, as in chronic alcoholism so in pregnancy, B_1 deficiency may play a part in producing Wernicke's encephalopathy as well as polyneuritis. **1966** *Trans. Amer. Neurol. Assoc.* XCI. 31 The Wernicke-Korsakoff syndrome is .. both a clinical and a pathological entity. **1978** *Sci. Amer.* Oct. 76/3 The Wernicke-Korsakoff syndrome is a neurological disorder that begins with an acute phase characterized by palsy and poor muscular coordination; with treatment the acute phase gives way to a chronic phase, Korsakoff's psychosis, characterized by severe amnesia.

wernne, var. WARN *v.*[2] *Obs.*

wernysh-, obs. form of VARNISH *v.*

werowance ('wɛrəʊwɑːns, -æ-). Forms: 6–7 **wer-, wiroance, wiroans**, 7 **wyroaunce, -ance, wyroun(n)ce**, 7–9 **werowance.** [Amer.-Indian.] A chief of the Indians of Virginia and Maryland in early colonial days.

1588 HARRIOT *Brief Rep. Virginia* E 2, One onely towne belongeth to the gouernment of a Wiroans or chiefe Lorde. *Ibid.* E 3 b, What subtilty soeuer be in the Wiroances and Priestes, this opinion worketh so much [etc.]. *a* **1589** R. LANE in *Hakluyt's Voy.* 738 There be sundry Kings, whom they call Weroances. *c* **1608** E. M. WINGFIELD *Discourse Virginia* in *Capt. J. Smith's Wks.* (Arb.) I. p. lxxvi, Both these wyroaunces haue euer since remayned in peace and trade with vs. **1612** CAPT. J. SMITH *Map Virginia* Wks. (Arb.) I. 81 This word Werowance which we call and conster for a king, is a common worde whereby they call all commanders. **1635** *Relat. Maryland* 26 Their Government is Monarchicall, he that governes in chiefe, is called the Werowance. **1705** BEVERLEY *Hist. Virginia* III. xi. (1722) 194 A Werowance is a Military Officer, who of Course takes upon him the Command of all Parties.

1893 M. A. OWEN *Old Rabbit* i. 3 She was accepted as a child of the Werowances. **1899** *Atlantic Monthly* June 725/2 The canoe of the Nansemond werowance.

werp(e, obs. forms of WARP *sb.* and *v.*

werr, obs. f. WAR, WAUR *a.*, WEAR *v.*[2]

werra, -ly, -ment, obs. Sc. ff. VERY, VERILY, VERAMENT.

werrand: see WARRANT.

†**werrar**, *a. Obs. rare.* [f. *werr* WAR, WAUR *a.* + -ER.] = WORSER *a.*

c **1400** *Apol. Loll.* 49 þey semen werrar þan þe fend, þat asked stonis to be turnid in to bred.

werrate, obs. Sc. f. VERITY.

werray: see VERY *a.*, WARRAY *v.*

werrayour: see WARRIOR.

werre, variant of VERE *Obs.* spring-time.

1436 *Libel Eng. Policy* in *Pol. Poems* (Rolls) II. 194 In tyme of wynter and of werre [*v.r.* veer] Whan boistous wyndes put see-men into ferre.

werre, obs. f. VERY, WAR, WARE *a.*, WORRY *v.*

werrei, var. WERRAY *v. Obs*

werreles, obs. f. WARLESS *a.*

†**werrell.** *Obs.* (See *sea-poult* SEA *sb.* 23 d.)

1658 SIR T. BROWNE *Gard. Cyrus* iii. 53 The handsome Rhombusses of the Sea-poult or Werrell, on either side the Spine.

werrest, obs. f. WORST.

werrey, obs. f. VERY.

werrey(e, var. ff. WARRAY *v. Obs.*, WORRY *v.*

werreyoure, -iour, obs. ff. WARRIOR.

werrie, obs. Sc. f. VERY.

werrit ('wɛrɪt), *v. dial.* [Local variant of WHERRIT or WORRIT.] *trans.* To tease, annoy. Also **'werriting** *ppl. a.*

1808 E. WEETON *Let.* 5 Oct. in *Jrnl. of Governess* (1969) I. 111, I was laughed at, or found I had displeased. I had a most werreting life of it. **1825** BROCKETT *N.C. Words*, s.v., He would request not to be *werrited* so much about it. **1828** CARR *Craven Gloss.* **1865** W. S. BANKS *Wakefield Words* 80 *Werritin*, wearying; fretful and tiresome. 'What a werritin barn thah are!'

werrse, werrsenn, obs. ff. WORSE, WORSEN *v.*

werry, var. VERRY *a. Obs.*

1486 *Bk. St. Albans, Coat-arm.* b v b, The threde [coat-armour] is called werry, whan the felde is made like gobolettys of dyuerse colowris.

werry, obs. or dial. f. VERY; var. WARRAY *v. Obs.*, WARY *v. Obs.*; obs. f. WORRY *v.*

werryo(u)r, obs. f. WARRIOR.

wers(e, obs. ff. VERSE, WORSE.

wersell, obs. f. WRESTLE.

werset, obs. f. VERSET.

wersh (wɜːʃ; *Sc.* wɛrʃ, werʃ, warʃ), *a. Sc.* and *north dial.* Forms: 5 **warsch(e**, 6 **wairsche**, 7–9 **warsh**, 9 **wairsh, wearsh, whersh**, 8- **wersh.** [Prob. a contracted form of WEARISH. Cf. WERSHED *a.*]

1. a. Of persons: Sickly or feeble in appearance. Also Comb. ***wersh-like, -looking***.

c **1480** HENRYSON *Orpheus & Eur.* 233 Lene and dedelike, pitouse and pale of hewe, Rycht warsch [*v.r.* warsche] and wan, & walowit as a wede. **1842** CARLYLE in Froude *Mem.* (1884) I. 244 A harmless, intelligent enough, rather *wersh*-looking man. **1871** W. ALEXANDER *Johnny Gibb* xli. 289, I thocht she was luikin' warsh-like.

b. Physically weak or sickly; squeamish.

1755 R. FORBES *Ajax* etc. *Jrnl. to Portsmouth* 29 It was enough to gi' a warsh-stamack'd body a scunner. **1872** MRS. LYNN LINTON *Joshua Davidson* vi. 119 We were getting whersh and weak for want of food.

2. Destitute of savour; insipid, tasteless, or sickly-flavoured; unsalted. = WEARISH *a.* 1. Also *fig.*

fig. **1599** ROLLOCK *Serm. Epist. Paul* viii. Wks. 1849 I. 398 He callis it not simplie and bairlie with ane wairsche word, the gospell, .. bot he callis it the licht of the gospell. **1618** W. BARCLAY *Well at King-horne* A vij, So ceasing to prosecute this warsh matter of water, I will never cease to continue Your L. most humble and obedient seruitour. **1633** W. STRUTHER *True Happiness* 48 This was Balaams warsh wishing, his desires were so weak, that they pearced not his heart, how could they pearce the heaven? **1720** RAMSAY *Wealth* 133 And Helicon's wersh well thou ca's divine. **1820** *Blackw. Mag.* VIII. 80 As articles, they were not so musty as those of the old Scots Magazine..nor so wersh. **1884** SWINBURNE in *19th Cent.* Oct. 556 Charles Reade's Dominican is worth a dozen such 'wersh', ineffectual, invertebrate studies.

lit. **1823** J. WILSON *Marg. Lyndesay* xxix, Water's unco wersh, and does na sloken weel. **1831** *Blackw. Mag.* XXX. II. 345/2 Sage-stuffing and apple-sauce—without which indeed your goose is wersh. **1853** SHERER *Gold-Finder Australia* 261 It is my opinion, this mutton's unco wersh, Watty. Ha'e ye ony saut? **1861** E. B. RAMSAY *Remin.* Ser. II. 61 It's a' vera true, but a kiss and a tinniefu' o' cauld water maks a gey wersh breakfast. **1921** *Glasgow Herald* 2 May 8 To be sure, unfermented wine is wersh stuff.

3. Of weather or wind: Unrefreshing; raw.

1830 GALT *Lawrie T.* VII. vi, The breeze, as it comes from the surrounding lofty woods, is wersh. **1894** CROCKETT *Raiders* xl. 336 The yellow mist..had a wersh (raw) unkindly feel about it.

†**wershed**, *a. Obs.*$^{-1}$ [Cf. prec.] Tasteless.

1398 TREVISA *Barth. De P.R.* XVI. xcv. (Tollemache MS.) With oute salte nyȝe all mete is werschid [1535 werishe] and unsauery [*insipidus et insalsus*].

'**wershly**, *adv. Sc.* [f. WERSH *a.*] Insipidly; without animation or cordiality.

1633 W. STRUTHER *True Happiness* 101 The Scribes spake warshly, as men doing some other businesse; or as Boyes in the Schoole, rehearsing other mens inventions. **1676** ROW *Suppl. Blair's Autobiog.* xi. (1848) 364 The Moderator thanked him as slenderly and wershlie as before.

wersikill, obs. Sc. f. VERSICLE.

wersil, werssle, obs. ff. WARSLE.

wersslete, error for BERCELET *Obs.*, hunting dog.

c **1425** WYNTOUN *Cron.* VI. 1610 *note*.

werst, obs. 2 sing. pa. ind. and subj. of BE *v.*

werst, obs. f. FIRST, WORST.

werst(e, obs. ff. VERST.

werstil, -tle, obs. ff. WARSLE.

wert, 2 sing. pa. ind. and subj. of BE *v.*

wert(e, obs. ff. WART, WORT.

werteous, obs. f. VIRTUOUS.

Werterean, -ian, -ism: see WERTHERIAN, -ISM.

wertew, obs. f. VIRTUE.

‖**wertfrei** ('vɛrtfraɪ), *a.* [Ger., f. *wert* value, WORTH *sb.*[1] + *frei* FREE *a.*] Free of value-judgements; morally neutral. Hence '**wert-freiheit** (also with capital initial) [-HOOD], the quality of being *wertfrei*.

1909 W. M. URBAN *Valuation* xiv. 422 The more neutral or '*wertfrei*' judgments of science. **1944** H. A. HODGES *Wilhelm Dilthey* v. 80 It is generally recognized that the natural sciences have no interest in judgments of value. Their *Wertfreiheit* is one of their most treasured attributes. **1964** ROUSSEAS & FARGANIS in I. L. Horowitz *New Sociol.* 289 Max Weber distinguishes between science as being *wertfrei* and *wertlos*. *Wertfrei* is defined as being free from prevailing passion and prejudice. **1975** *Times Lit. Suppl.* 25 July 848/1 What specially distinguishes Ontology, American Style, however, is that it is far more *wertfrei*, uncommitted, cool, detached and technical. *c* **1978** C. R. TAME *Against New Mercantilism* 8 No one would abandon the heritage of *wertfreiheit* in economics and the social sciences.

werth(e: see WORTH *sb.*, *a.*, *v.*

Wertherian (vɜːˈtɪərɪən), *a.* Also **Werterian, -ean.** [f. G. *Werther*, the hero of Goethe's romance 'Die Leiden des jungen Werther' (1774) + -IAN.] Morbidly sentimental.

1831 CARLYLE *Sartor Res.* II. v, Their mad Petrarchan and Werterean ware. **1850** *Fraser's Mag.* Sept. 249 Some who are accustomed to consider that poem [*Locksley Hall*] as Werterian and unhealthy. **1850** THACKERAY *Pendennis* xli, The Byronic despair, the Wertherian despondency. **1857** TROLLOPE *Barch. T.* xxxiv, An ancient love-lorn swain.. full of imaginary sorrows and Wertherian grief.

Wertherism (ˈvɜːtərɪz(ə)m). Also **Werterism.** [f. as prec. + -ISM.] Morbid sentimentality.

1831 CARLYLE *Charact.* Ess. 1872 IV. 26 Werterism, Byronism, even Brummelism, each has its day. **1856** MRS. BROWNING *Aur. Leigh* III. 471 My German stopped At germane Wertherism. **1873** HAMERTON *Intell. Life* x. ii. 345 Goethe..cured himself very soon, and the author of 'Werther' had no indulgence for Wertherism.

wertow, wertu, obs. ff. VIRTUE.

wertual(l, wertuo(u)sse, obs. ff. VIRTUAL, VIRTUOUS.

'**werturn.** [var. of *wartern*, dial. f. QUARTERN *sb.*[2] 3 c (quot. 1883).] A particular weight of wool (see quots.).

1853 IBBERSON *Woollen Manuf. Guide* 13 Threads of slubbing, varying from 4 to 12 skeins per werturn. *Ibid.* 89, 1,520 yards are a standard skein. Six pounds, or 1,536 drams, are a standard werturn.

wertu(u)s, wertuwisse, wertuz, obs. ff. VIRTUOUS.

wertwale, var. WARTWALE.

werty, obs. f. WORTHY.

†**werve.** *Obs.* [OE. *weorf* (rare) a beast of burden.] A 'beast' for riding on.

c **1175** *Lamb. Hom.* 79 [He] bond his wunden & brohte him huppen his werue. *Ibid.* 85 Uppen his werue [= Lk. x. 34.]

wervel, variant of VARVEL.

werwolf: see WEREWOLF.

wery, obs. f. VERY; var. WARY *v.*; obs. f. WEARY, WORRY *v.*

weryauns, obs. f. VARIANCE.

†**weryer.** *Obs. rare*$^{-1}$. [f. ME. *werien* WERE *v.*] A defender, guardian.

c **1250** *Gen. & Ex.* 926 After ðis spac god to abram: 'ðin berȝ and tin werȝer [OE. *werȝend*; L. *protector*] ic ham.

weryfy, weryly, obs. ff. VERIFY *v.*, VERILY.

weryouns, obs. f. VARIANCE.

weryson, var. WARISON *Obs.*

weryte, obs. Sc. f. VERITY.

wes, obs. f. *was*, pa. t. of BE *v.*

wesage, obs. Sc. f. VISAGE.

Wesak, var. VESAK.

wesand(e, -a(u)nt, etc., obs. ff. WEASAND.

wesar, obs. Sc. f. VISOR.

wesch, obs. f. WASH.

weschael(le, -ail, -ale, -all, obs. Sc. ff. VESSEL.

weschcraft, obs. f. WITCHCRAFT.

wesche, obs. f. WASH, WISH.

weschel, -ele, -ell, etc., obs. Sc. ff. VESSEL.

wese, obs. pres. imper. of BE *v.*; obs. f. VIZY *v.*

we'se = *we shall*: see SHALL *v.* A. 5.

†**wesel.** *Obs. rare.* (Meaning obscure.)

c **1420** *Liber Cocorum* 52 For wesels. Fyrst grynde porke, temper in fere With egges [etc.].

wesel(e, obs. ff. WEASEL *sb.*

wesell, obs. f. WEASEL *sb.*; var. WEEZLE *Obs.*

‖**Wesen** (ˈveːzən). *rare.* [Ger.] **a.** A person's nature (as shown in characteristic behaviour).

1854-5 GEO. ELIOT in J. W. Cross *George Eliot's Life* (1885) I. vi. 353 Fräulein Solmar is..probably between fifty and sixty, but of that agreeable *Wesen* which is so free from anything startling in person or manner. **1884** MRS. H. WARD *Miss Bretherton* i. 10 And then her *Wesen* is so attractive; she is such a frank, unspoilt, good-hearted creature.

b. The distinctive nature or essence of anything.

1959 *Listener* 22 Oct. 689/2, I believe myself that it is only in the totality of its historic manifestations that Christianity can be understood, and that so long as it does survive, its *Wesen*, its nature, will continue to reveal new potentialities.

weser, rare obs. Sc. f. WIZARD.

wesh, dial. f. WASH *sb.* and *v.*

we-ship. *nonce-wd.* [f. WE *pron.* (2 b) + -SHIP (3 b).] ***his we-ship***, a mock title applied to a writer who has used the impersonal 'we'.

1673 MARVELL *Rehearsal Transp.* II. 105 'Tis most graciously done that his We-ship will allow them it.

wesil, obs. f. WEASEL *sb.*

wesill, obs. f. WEASEL *sb.*; var. WEEZLE *Obs.*

wesing, rare obs. f. WEASAND.

wesit, obs. Sc. f. VISIT *v.*

wesle, obs. f. WEASEL *sb.*

Wesleyan (ˈwɛslɪən, ˈwɛzlɪən, wɛzˈliːən), *a.* and *sb.* Also 8 **Weslean, Wesleian.** [f. the name of John *Wesley*, 1703–1791, originator of Methodism + -AN. The accepted pronunciation among Methodists is (ˈwɛslɪən).]

A. *adj.* Of or pertaining to Wesley or his teaching; belonging to the Wesleyans as a religious organization.

1771 J. W. FLETCHER *Checks to Antinom.* Wks. 1795 II. 277 Upon the scheme of what you call the 'Weslean orthodoxy', Christ is really the Saviour of all men. **1791** HAMPSON *Mem. Wesley* III. 77 A circumstance, in the Wesleian œconomy, as remarkable as any, is the admission of lay-preachers. **1843** THACKERAY *Irish Sk.-bk.* viii, A trim Wesleyan chapel, without any broken windows. **1872** MARCH. DUFFERIN *Canad. Jrnl.* (1891) 39 D. and I drove to see a fine Wesleyan church. **1878** *N. Amer. Rev.* CXXVII. 56 A Wesleyan meeting.

b. ***Wesleyan Methodist***, a member of the society of Methodists as constituted by John Wesley; also *attrib.* passing into *adj.*, of or pertaining to the Wesleyan Methodists as an organization. ***Wesleyan Methodism***, the religious principles, practice, and organization of the Wesleyan Methodists.

1796 MORSE *Amer. Univ. Geog.* I. 280 In 1788, the number of Wesleian Methodists in the United States, stood thus. **1839** *Penny Cycl.* XV. 142/2 Since his decease, the prevalence of Wesleyan Methodism in North America has been very great. *Ibid.*, The Wesleyan Methodist church in Upper Canada. **1858** [see METHODIST 4 a]. **1883** *Encycl. Brit.* XVI. 186/1 Herein was the actual and vital beginning of the Wesleyan Methodist Society, that is, of Wesleyan Methodism.

B. *sb.* A follower of John Wesley; a member of the Wesleyan Methodist Society, a Wesleyan Methodist.

1791 *Gentl. Mag.* LXI. I. 20/1 The Wesleyans found fault with the curate for the topics of his discourses. **1832** in Flor. M. Hawtrey *Hawtrey Family* (1903) II. 25 That John should leave the Westlians [*sic*] puzzles me. **1877** F. G. LEE *Gloss. Liturg. Terms, Wesleyan*, a person who belongs to the sect of Arminian Methodists founded by John Wesley.

Wesleyanism (ˈwɛslɪənɪz(ə)m). Also 8 **Wesleianism.** [f. WESLEYAN + -ISM.] The system of Arminian theology introduced and taught by John Wesley; the doctrines and church polity of the Wesleyans; Wesleyan Methodism.

1774 J. FLETCHER *Hist. Ess.* Wks. 1795 IV. 20 They have departed from what we call Christianity, and what you are at full liberty to call Wesleianism. **1842** PUSEY *Present Crisis* 163 Wesleyanism then was said to be 'degenerating into a developed heresy,' in that it substitutes for the Catholic teaching, a doctrine of justification, for which there is 'no warrant in the Word of God'. **1861** R. S. HAWKER in *Life* (1905) 345 No sooner did he find that Wesleyans formed the majority of —— Parish, than he began to preach and to talk Wesleyanism. **1904** *Q. Rev.* July 243 Wesleyanism was traditional in the family.

'**Wesleyanized**, *pa. pple.* [f. as prec. + -IZE + -ED.] Affected by Wesleyanism.

1849 KEBLE in J. T. Coleridge *Mem.* xv. (1869) 353 [Isle of Man] The clergy a nice set, but rather Wesleyanized. *c* **1905** J. HUNTER in L. S. Hunter *Life* (1921) 220 The English Congregational Union. Its churches and ministry.. are getting to be religiously more and more 'Wesleyanised'.

Wesleyism (ˈwɛslɪɪz(ə)m). *rare.* = WESLEYANISM.

1847 H. MILLER *First Impr. Eng.* xx. 394 Wesleyism also flourishes. **1904** *Daily Chron.* 22 Apr. 3/3 Wesleyism and Quakerism..had no hold on him.

'**Wesleyite.** *nonce-wd.* = WESLEYAN *sb.*

1807 J. HALL *Trav. Scot.* II. 594 Among the Wesleyites, and some other denominations of Dissenters.

weslyng, var. WISSELING *Obs. Sc.*

wesp, obs. form of WISP.

wess, obs. f. WASH *v.*

wessande, obs. f. WEASAND.

wessayle, obs. f. WASSAIL.

wessch, obs. f. WASH *v.*

wesschael(le, obs. Sc. ff. VESSEL.

wesse, obs. f. WASH *v.*; obs. pa. t. of BE *v.*

wessel, *adv. Sc.* Also **westle, wastle, wassel**, etc. [f. WEST *adv.*: cf. EASSEL.] Westward.

Awestill 'to the west of' occurs in 16th c. Sc.

1815, 1829 [see EASSEL]. **1897** LD. E. HAMILTON *Outlaws of Marches* xiv. 157 We was jickering along wessil, as I say, wi' our heads bent to the weather.

wessel(e, -ell(e, obs. ff. VESSEL.

Wessex (ˈwɛsɪks). [OE. *West Seaxe* West Saxons.] **1.** The name of a kingdom in south-west England in Anglo-Saxon times, used by Thomas Hardy as the name of the county in which his stories are set (corresponding approximately to Dorset, Somerset, Hampshire, and Wiltshire) and since used as a name for south-west England or this part of it.

1868 W. BARNES *Poems of Rural Life in Common Eng.* Pref., As I think that some people, beyond the bounds of Wessex, would allow me the pleasure of believing that they have deemed..my homely poems in our Dorset mother-speech to be worthy of their reading, I have written a few of a like kind, in common English. **1874** HARDY in *Cornh. Mag.* Nov. 624 Greenhill was the Nijnii Novgorod of Wessex; and the busiest..day of the whole statute number was the day of the sheep-fair. **1876** *Examiner* 15 July 794/1 The Wessex man knows that these passages have in them the real ring, all equally true to life and scenery. **1938** *Proc. Prehistoric Soc.* IV. 52 The work..was..undertaken with a view to examining the cultures of the geographical area usually comprised in the term 'Wessex' in the period immediately following the Beaker phase. **1979** *N. & Q.* June 193/2 All [volumes] share a chronology of the life and works, Hardy's General Preface to the Wessex Edition, and notes on Wessex and Wessex names.

2. *attrib.* = SADDLEBACK *sb.* 4h.

1919, etc. [see SADDLEBACK *sb.* 4h]. **1919** [see KILLER 4b]. **1978** A. WILLIAMS *Backyard Pig Farming* iv. 27 There used to be a Wessex Saddleback originating in Dorset; it had black back legs.

3. *Archæol.* Of, pertaining to, or designating an Early Bronze Age culture in southern England, *c* 2000–1500 B.C., represented by grave-goods of native and European provenance.

1938 S. PIGGOTT in *Proc. Prehistoric Soc.* IV. 52 Many elements..here described as typical of the Wessex Culture of the Bronze Age are..found in associations which are late and outside the main culture-area. **1954** *Antiquity* Mar. 28 The axes..of this broad-butted type,..characteristic..of Piggott's Wessex Culture. **1963** E. S. WOOD *Collins Field Guide to Archaeol.* I. iv. 64 The Wessex nobility seem to have come from Germany. **1975** *Times Lit. Suppl.* 14 Mar. 282/1 The unlikelihood of Mycenaean influence on Stonehenge and the 'Wessex culture' of southern England. **1983** P. A. CROWL *Prehist. Britain* i. 33 The Wessex urns..lacking the refinement one would have expected of this..culture.

wesseyl(e, obs. ff. WASSAIL.

wessh(e, obs. ff. WASH.

wessie, obs. f. VIZY *v. Sc.*

west (wɛst), *adv.*, *sb.*[1], and *a.* Forms: 1– **west** (1 **wæst**), 3 *Orm.* **wesst**, 3–7 **weste** (5 *Sc.* **veste**), *Sc.* 5, 7–9 **wast**, 6–7 **weast(e**, (6 *Sc.* **weist, weyst**, 7 *Sc.* **vaist**). [Com. Teutonic: OE. *west* adv. = OFris. *west* (WFris. *west*, NFris. *wêst*, *wâst*), OS. *-west* (in *north-*, *sûthwest*; MLG. and LG., MDu. and Du. *west*), OHG. *west-* (G. *west*), ON. and Icel. (with *r-* suffix; cf. *austr* EAST, etc.) *vestr* (MSw. *väster*, Sw. *vester*); MSw. *väst* (rare), Norw., Sw., Da. *vest* (prob. after LG.); not recorded in Gothic. The primitive Germanic stem **wes-t-* appears to be an extension of the **wes-* found in Gr. ἕσπερος, ἑσπέρα, L. *vesper*, *vespera* evening, west. In HG. dialects *abend* is similarly used for 'west'.

In OE. *west* occurs only as an adv., the use as noun and adj. being a later development. In the cognate languages it is usually (in some exclusively) a noun in the earlier periods, the adverbial use coming later, and the adjectival being represented only by the first element in compounds (OE. *west-* in *west-dǽl*, etc.).

The fact that the Romanic forms for 'east' (F. *est*, etc.) have been adopted from English indicates that this, rather than any other Germanic language, is also the source of F. *ouest* (OF. *west*), Sp. and Pg. *oeste*.]

A. *adv.* Towards or in the direction of that part of the horizon where the sun sets.

1. a. With reference to movement, extension, or direction.

In Sc. (and Anglo-Irish) use freq. added to verbs of going or coming to indicate the general direction: see quots. under (*b*).

(*a*) *O.E. Chron.* an. 886 Her for se here eft west þe ær east ʒelende. **944** *Charter of Eadmund* in Birch *Cartul. Sax.* II. 541 þonne west andlang weʒes on ðone lytlan beorʒ. *c* **995** *Battle of Maldon* 97 Wodon þa wælwulfas,..west ofer Pantan. **1033** in Kemble *Cod. Dipl.* IV. 45 Of ðam herpaðe west..on ðone stan; of ðon stane west..on Fiducforda. *c* **1205** LAY. 1278 Heo ferden forð & eeuer heo drowen west & norð. *c* **1350** *Libeaus Desc.* 1068 (Kaluza) Whan sche was take wiþ gile, He fliȝ for greet perile West into Wirhale. *c* **1440** *York Myst.* xxxvii. 333 *Sattan*..I schall walke este and weste, And garre þame werke wele werre. **1489** *Acc. Ld. High Treas. Scot.* I. 116 A man to pass to Edinburgh to haist the gunnis west. **1526** *Pilgr. Perf.* (W. de W. 1531) 35b, Where it weneth to go eest, it gothe west. **1581** BOROUGH *Discourse Var. Cumpas* (1585) Gj, The course set downe from Sillie to Cape Raso is due West. **1601** SHAKS. *Twel. N.* III. i. 145 There lies your way, due West. **1724** DE FOE *Tour Gt. Brit.* I. iii. 1, I intended once to have gone due West this Journey. **1760** R. ROGERS *Jrnls.* (1769) 197 We..kept the following courses:..west-by-north one mile, west two miles. **1848** B. WEBB *Cont. Ecclesiol.* 480 If the basilica orientated west. *Ibid.* 484 The remaining three..have their altars facing due west. **1859** H. KINGSLEY *G. Hamlyn* xxv, Splendid pastures, which stretch west farther than any man has been yet. **1892** KIPLING *Barrack-room Ballads* etc., L'Envoi, It's North you may run to the rime-ringed sun.. Or West to the Golden Gate.

(*b*) *a* **1724** *Ew-bughts, Marion* 32 in Ramsay *Tea-t. Misc.*, And soon as my chin has nae hair on, I shall come west, and see ye. *c* **1730** BURT *Lett. N. Scot.* viii. (1754) I. 181 He told us we must go West a Piece (though there was no Appearance of the Sun) and then incline to the North. **1887** ANNIE S. SWAN *Gates of Eden* i. 14 Weel a weel, tell them I'll come wast when I'm ready.

b. In special applications: (*a*) *to go west*, of the sun; also *fig.*, to die, perish, disappear. (*b*) To America, or to the Western States.

Also (*c*) in Highland Sc. and Anglo-Irish use freq. rendering Gael. *siar*, *iar* (= west, back) in the sense of 'back', 'away', 'up', or 'down'.

The immediate source of the modern use in (*a*), which became common during the Great War, has not been established.

(*a*) *c* **1400** *Laud Troy Bk.* 13365 For hit was nyght, the sonne goth west. *c* **1500** *Chaucer's L.G.W.* 61 (Trin. Camb.) Assone As the son gynneth go west. **15..** *Poems Gray MS.* vi. 42 (S.T.S.) 55 Women and mony wilsome wy as wynd or wattir ar gane west. **1915** E. CORRI *Thirty Yrs. Boxing Referee* 2, I shall once again be in the company of dear old friends now 'gone West'. **1919** J. B. MORTON *Barber of Putney* ix, 'All the Lewis guns gone west,' someone said. **1919** *Blackw. Mag.* Sept. 368/2 Their parcels..went persistently 'west'. **1925** COLE *Death of Millionaire* vi. 57 Wilson sighed. 'There's valuable evidence gone west', he said. 'It may be hard to pick up the trail now.'

(*b*) **1839** MRS. KIRKLAND *New Home* xviii. 122, I could not help thinking that one must come 'west' in order to learn a little of everything. **1851** J. L. B. SOULE in *Terre Haute Express* (Hoyt) Go West, young man! Go West. **1878** W. NASH *Oregon* 6 After some debate we settled to go West by the Pennsylvania railroad, going South..to Philadelphia, and thence West by way of Pittsburg. **1879** W. SAUNDERS *Through Light Cont.* 35 'Go West, young man,' was Horace Greeley's advice, and West I went accordingly.

(*c*) **1893** W. R. LE FANU *70 Yrs. Ir. Life* vii. (ed. 2) 90 'Why didn't you wash the back of your neck?' ''Twas too far west, my lady.'.. ''Tis not a cold I have at all..'tis a fly that's gone west in my stomach.'

2. a. With reference to place or location.

c **888** ÆLFRED *Boeth.* xxxix. §13 Se..æfensteorra, þonne he bið west ʒesewen, þonne tacnað he æfen. *a* **900** *O.E. Chron.* an. 894 þa he þa wið þone here þær wæst abisʒod wæs. **971** *Blickl. Hom.* 129 Ʒerusalem..is west þonon from þære stowe on anre mile. *c* **1200** ORMIN 12125 þa fowwre daless alle þatt Æst, & Wesst, & Suþ, & Norrþ þiss middellærd bilukenn. *a* **1250** *Owl & N.* 923 East & west, souþ & norþ, I do wel fayre my mester. *c* **1310** in Wright *Lyric P.* xviii. 59 Whether y be south other west. *c* **1350** *Libeaus Desc.* 2128 Est, west, norþ and souþe, Be maistris of har mouþe Many man couþ þey schende. **14..** *Sailing Directions* (Hakl. Soc. 1889) 18 Londay and the old hede of Hindilforde lye west and by north. **1559** CUNINGHAM *Cosmogr. Glass* 172 Fiue Ilandes..Of which that whiche is most west, is called properlye Ebuda. **1610** HOLLAND *Camden's Brit.* (1637) 459 Where it [Suffolk] lieth West and toward Cambridge-shire. *a* **1626** BACON *New Atlantis* 14 The Phœnicians..had great Fleetes. So had the Carthaginians their Colony, which is yet further West. **1719** DE FOE *Crusoe* II. (Globe) 379 One of the Islands which lay West. *a* **1788** BURNS *Ploughman* 9, I hae been east, I hae been west. **1890** *Hardwicke's Sci.-Gossip* XXVI. 256 Another imaginary line so many degrees east or west of the meridian of Greenwich. **1905** H. G. WELLS *Kipps* II. v. §1 We shall have a nice little flat somewhere, not too far west.

b. Followed by *of*.

1577 HARRISON *England* II. i. 49b/1 in *Holinshed*, The Kenet ryseth aboue Ouerton, v or vj myles west of Marleborow. **1597** SHAKS. *2 Hen. IV*, IV. i. 19 West of this Forrest, scarcely off a mile, In goodly forme, comes on the Enemie. **1728** [see WESTERLING]. **1784** FILSON *Kentucky* 22 Lees town is west of Lexington. **1807** SOUTHEY *Espriella's Lett.* II. 219 The Lakes..lay south-west, and west of Keswick. **1875** RUSKIN *Morn. Florence* i. 5 A few hundred yards west of you ..is the Baptistery of Florence.

c. *U.S.* In the West, out West. (Cf. C. 3b.)

1888 HOWELLS *Annie Kilburn* xi. 126 One of 'em married West, and her husband left her.

3. With modifying addition (in senses 1 and 2), as *west by south*, etc. Also WEST-NORTH-WEST, -SOUTH-WEST.

1577 HARRISON *England* II. i. 48b/1 in *Holinshed*, The Winrush..meeteth wyth the Isis west by south of Northmore. **1760** R. ROGERS *Jrnls.* (1769) 197 We..then steered ..west-by-south two miles, west-by-north four miles.

4. *Sc.* Ellipt. as *prep.* **a.** At, in, or to the west of. **b.** Towards the west along (a road, etc.).

1587 *Reg. Mag. Sig. Scot.* 480/2 Insuper creavit dictum Burgum de Anstruther super occidentali torrentis (west the burne). **1589** *Ibid.* 573/1 Strekand west the hie streit to the dyk. **1728** RAMSAY *Monk & Miller's Wife* 48 But step ye west the Kill A Bow-shot, and ye'll find my Hame. *Mod.* I saw him rinnin' wast the road. He bides wast the toun.

B. 1. Quasi-*sb.* = C.

c **1200** ORMIN 11258 All þiss middellærd iss ec O fowwre daless dæledd, Onn Æst, o Wesst, o Suþ, o Norrþ. *a* **1300** *Cursor M.* 22139 Fra est to west, fra north to soth, He sal do mak his sarmun cuth. *a* **1300** *K. Horn* 1177 (Camb. MS.) Ihc habbe go mani Mile, Wel feor bi ȝonde weste. *c* **1391** CHAUCER *Astrol.* I. §15 A longe croys in 4 quarters from est to West, fro sowth to north. *c* **1400** *26 Pol. Poems* xxiv. 208 Lord, whenne þou comest to deme so Al þe world be fyre, boþe est and west. **1500–20** DUNBAR *Poems* xxiv. 23 Thocht he this warld had eist and west, All wer pouertie but glaidness. **1575** A. FLEMING *Virg. Bucol.* II. 67 Th' increasing shadowes doubleth the sunne going downe at West. **1577** D. SETTLE *Frobisher's Voy.* Biij, Wee.. followed our course between West and Northwest, vntill the 4. of Iulie. **1611** SHAKS. *Cymb.* V. v. 471 The Romaine Eagle From South to West, on wing soaring aloft Lessen'd her selfe. **1648** T. SHEPARD *Clear Sun-shine of Gosp.* 30 A brighter day..wherein East & West shall sing the song of the Lambe. **1674** SIR J. MOORE *Math. Compend.* 93 From West to East the account is by degrees and parts, or by hours. **1789** S. SHAW *Tour W. Eng.* 444 The principal street extending from east to west is remarkably paved. **1819** KEATS *Song Four Faeries* 45 So you sometimes follow me To my home, far, far, in west. **1847** TENNYSON *Princess* II. 64 Our statues!—not of those that men desire,..Nor stunted squaws of West or East. **1892** KIPLING *Barrack-room Ballads* etc. 75 Oh, East is East, and West is West, and never the twain shall meet. **1904** H. BELLOC *Old Road* 31 Sea-going vessels..would have calm water..so long as the wind was south of west.

2. *by west*: †**a.** In the west; on the west side; also westward *of*. *Obs.*

13.. *K. Horn* 5 (Harl.) Kyng he wes by weste. *c* **1300** —— 1366 (Laud) He woneþ alby weste. *c* **1305** *St. Kenelm* 18 in *E.E.P.* (1862) 48 Temese into þe est see, & seuerne bi weste. *c* **1315** SHOREHAM VII. 64 By weste hy grendeþ, alle þyse, And comeþ aȝen þer hy aryse. *a* **1400** *Minor Poems Vernon MS.* (1901) 696 As I wandrede her bi weste ffaste vnder a forest syde. *c* **1470** *Golagros & Gaw.* 419 Quhare wourschip walkis be west. *a* **1550** LELAND *Itin.* (1764) III. 7 A Castel a Mile by West from Markesin. **1577** HARRISON *England* II. i. 50/1 in *Holinshed*, The Weie or the Waye rising by west, cometh from Olsted. *Ibid.* 53/2 By west of Auterton point also lyeth another hauen. **1596** SPENSER *F.Q.* V. vi. 22 Not farre away, but little wide by West, His dwelling was.

†**b.** As a compound prep.: On the west side of, to the west of (see BY *prep.* 9c). Also *fig.* (quot. 1612). *Obs.*

c **1275** LAY. 2136 Camber hafde al him seolf bi weste Seuarne. **14..** *Sailing Directions* (Hakl. Soc. 1889) 16 And by west belille and Ortingere southwest. **1482** *Rolls of Parlt.* VI. 203/1 In Southe Wales, by west the blak Montayne. **1525** in *Reg. Mag. Sig. Scot. 1527*, 96/1 Nixt befor Sanct Michaelis altar be West the said altar. **1612** DAVIES *Why Ireland* etc. (1787) 177 Whereupon grew that bye-word used by the Irish, viz. that they dwelt *by west the law*, which dwelt beyond the river of the Barrow. **1661** LAMONT *Diary* (Maitl. Club) 139 The Earle of Weyms be-ganne to bueld a new harbory for shipping, a little be west Saltgreine. **1714** R. SMITH *Poems of Controv.* (1853) 2 Let all be-west the Spittel come.

c. *Naut.* Indicating certain points of the compass (see BY *prep.* 9b).

14.. *Sailing Directions* (Hakl. Soc. 1889) 14 Huschaunt and the pople hope lien north and by west south. *Ibid.* 20 For cause of that Rok ye must go north and by west. **1598** W. PHILLIP tr. *Linschoten* I. xciii. 165 We held our course.. from thence south West and by West, vnto the cape *de Bona Speranza*. **1762** FALCONER *Shipwr.* II. 242 South and by west the threatening demon blew.

3. *Bridge.* (With capital initial.) The player sitting opposite and partnering East, and having South to his right.

1926 [see EAST *sb.* 4]. **1958** *Listener* 2 Oct. 541/1 West was a good enough player to have a chance of succeeding. **1974** *Country Life* 3 Oct. 975/1 Warned off Hearts and Clubs, West had to lead a Spade or a Diamond.

C. *sb.* (Usually with *the.*)

1. a. That one of the four cardinal points which lies opposite the east and at right angles to the north and the south; that part of the horizon or of the sky which is near the place of the sun's setting.

in the west, of the wind, = blowing from the west.

c **1180** *Newminster Cartul.* (Surtees) 118 Inde versus le West per viridem viam. *a* **1225** *Ancr. R.* 94 Ase is þe sunne gleam, þet smit from east into þe west. *c* **1290** *Brendan* 48 in *S. Eng. Leg.* 221 We comen to a watur..þat euere fram-ward þe est, toward þe west it droȝ. *c* **1305** *St. Kenelm* 13 in *E.E.P.* (1862) 48 Engelond..is..two hondred [miles] brod iwis Fram þe est in to þe west. **1382** WYCLIF *Exod.* x. 19 The Lord..made blow the moost hidows wynde fro the west. **1387** TREVISA *Higden* I. 45 þe lengþe of þe erþe þat men woneþ ynne from þe est to þe west, þat is from Ynde to Hercules is pilers. *c* **1400** MAUNDEV. (1839) v. 46 Toward the West, is the Contree of Coston. *a* **1450** *Mirk's Festial* 294/28 þan is hys hed leyde into þe west and hys fette into þe est. **1526** TINDALE *Luke* xii. 54 When ye se a cloude ryse out off the west, strayght waye ye saye: we shall have a shewer. **1577** GOOGE *Heresbach's Husb.* I. 42 Leauing open a space for twoo doores, a fore doore and a backe doore, but so, as neyther of them open to the West. **1614** E. WRIGHT *Dialling* C2, Your face being turned towards the North, your right hand sheweth the East, your left hand the West. **1667** DRYDEN *Ind. Emp.* V. ii, I in the Eastern Parts, and rising Sky, You in Heav'ns Downfal, and the West must lie. **1712** J. MORTON *Nat. Hist. Northampt.* 422 Pikes..never bite more freely, than when the Wind is in the West. *a* **1723** BINGHAM *Antiq. Chr. Ch.* XI. vii. §6 In renouncing the Devil they had their Faces to the West. *a* **1748** WATTS *Summer Evening* 5 Now the fair traveller's come to the west,..He paints the sky gay, as he sinks to his rest. **1805** SCOTT *Last Minstrel* III. xxiv, Her blue eyes sought the west afar. **1848** B. WEBB *Cont. Ecclesiol.* 156 A rood,..between which and the communion-table was a small prayer-desk facing the west, i.e. the people. **1876** BRIDGES *Growth of Love* xxix, I travel to thee with the sun's first rays, That lift the dark west and unwrap the night. **1925** J. METCALFE *Smoking Log*, etc. 116 When the wind was in the west.

transf. and *fig.* **1613** DONNE *Epithal.* 181 May never age, or error overthwart With any West, these radiant eyes, with any North, this heart. **1649** C. WASE *Sophocles, Electra* 47 O joyfull day! Thou hast restord our light, Wrapt up in constant night, In one continu'd West. **1655** FANSHAWE *Camoens' Lusiad* I. xxxii. 7 But now he fears that Glorie's neer it's West, In the black Water of Oblivion.

b. That quarter which with regard to the speaker or some particular place lies in a westerly direction.

1537 *Registr. Aberdon.* (Maitl. Club) I. 412 His tenment lyand in Auld Abirdene afornent þe cors of þe samynge one þe weist. **1671** MILTON *P.R.* IV. 448 A Sunny hill..Back'd on the North and West by a thick wood. **1773** NOORTHOUCK *Hist. Lond.* 597 Cordwainers-ward..is bounded..on the west by Bread-street-ward. *a* **1857** KEMBLE *Horæ Ferales* (1863) 25 The Lithuanians of Prussia on the west.

c. Followed by *of*.

1613 ZOUCHE *Dove* B6b, Aboue Iudæa, bord'ring on the West Of great Armenia, lesser Asia lyes. *a* **1660** *Contemp. Hist. Irel.* (Ir. Archæol. Soc.) I. 152 The armie marched to Bellaghnegrege on the weaste of Aleage. **1715** tr. *Gregory's Astron.* (1726) I. 318 According as the Meridian of the one lies to the East or to the West of the Meridian of the other. **1789** S. SHAW *Tour W. Eng.* 563 To the west of this..lies Overton. **1834** AINSWORTH *Rookwood* IV. ii, Harrow-on-the-Hill..lying to the west of the green on which they walked.

2. *spec.* **a.** The western part of the world. Now commonly, Europe as distinguished from Asia.

c **1205** LAY. 1231 Bi-ȝende France i þet west þu scalt finden a wunsum lond. **1297** R. GLOUC. (Rolls) 2 Engelond his.. Iset in þe on ende of þe worlde as al in þe west. **1382** WYCLIF *Matt.* viii. 11 Manye shulen come fro the est and west. *c* **1420** *Anturs of Arth.* 703 Waynour gared wisely write in þe west, To al þe religious to rede and to singe. **1593** SHAKS. *2 Hen. VI*, I. i. 154 All the wealthy Kingdomes of the West. **1613** ZOUCHE *Dove* B4, First Bacchus..set vp trophees in the conquer'd East: Oh would he had gone on as he begunne, And neuer turned to subdue the West! **1761** GRAY *Desc. Odin* 63 In the caverns of the west. **1784** COWPER *Task* VI. 811 Eastern Java there Kneels with the native of the farthest west. **1802** WORDSW. *Extinction of Venetian Rep.* 2 Once did She hold the gorgeous east in fee;

And was the safeguard of the west. **1864** TENNYSON *Aylmer's F.* 348 He never yet had set his daughter forth Here in the woman-markets of the west, Where our Caucasians let themselves be sold. **1892** KIPLING *Barrack-room Ballads* etc. 188 The Lords of Their Hands assembled; from the East and the West they drew. **1902** A. S. HURD *Naval Efficiency* 109 In the West there seems to be an impression that the fleet of Japan is a mere matter of show.

b. The western portion of the Roman world after its division into two empires in A.D. 395.

1577 HANMER *Anc. Eccl. Hist., Socrates Schol.* VI. i. 360 When yͤ Emperour Theodosius had departed this life..his sonnes tooke in hand the gouernment of the Romaine empire. Arcadius ruled the East and Honorius the West. **1610** R. FIELD *Fifth Bk. Ch.* xxxv. 194 The Bishop of Rome ..called a Synode of al the Bishops of the West. **1781** GIBBON *Decl. & F.* xxxiii. (1787) III. 327 Honorius, emperor of the West. **1790** PRIESTLEY *Gen. Hist. Chr. Ch.* II. 332 Having seen what was doing in the East, let us now turn our eyes towards the West, where Valentinian governed. **1840** MILMAN *Hist. Chr.* II. viii. II. 207 Of the persecution under Severus there are few, if any, traces in the West. **1865** BRYCE *Holy Rom. Emp.* iii. (1866) 27 Odoacer.. resolved to..extinguish the title and office of Emperor of the West.

c. The western parts of Europe.

1916 J. BUCHAN *Nelson's Hist. War* XIII. 121 A strong offensive in the West might induce the Allies to make a premature counter-attack.

3. The western part of a country, region, or area; *spec.* **a.** of England, Great Britain, Scotland, or Ireland.

14.. *Trevelyan Papers* (Camden) 67 The Boor' is farr in to the west, That shold vs helpe wͭ shild and sper'. **15..** *Ladye Bessie* (Percy Soc.) 53 When thou rydest into the weste, I pray the take noe companye But such as shall be of the beste. **1631** HEYWOOD (*title*) The Fair Maid of the West. **1651** J. NICOLL *Diary* (Bannatyne Club) 54 Thir ministeris..held thair awin secreit meetingis in the west. **1666** EARL ORRERY *St. Lett.* (1742) 158 From Kingsale I intend to go to Bandon to settle that town, and all the West. **1693-4** LUTTRELL *Brief Rel.* (1857) III. 248 Letters from the west say, our Streights fleet are clear of the Lands End. **1731** *Flying Post* 10 Aug. 2/1 Edinburgh... The Earl of Aberdeen is set out for the West to visit his daughter. *a* **1734** WODROW *Collect. Lives Reformers* (1834) I. 109 Mr. Willock was appointed.. Superintendant of the West. **1793** COLERIDGE *Sonn. River Otter* 1 Wild streamlet of the West! **1836** SOUTHEY *Lett.* (1856) IV. 465 My purpose is to..take Cuthbert with me into the West by way of Bristol. **1841** LEVER *O'Malley* xii, He was peaceably taking his departure from the West on Saturday. **1869** A. MACDONALD *Love, Law & Theol.* xii. 189 The aunt..resided in the vicinity of the capital of the west [i.e. Glasgow].

b. The western States of North America.

Formerly the country west of the original thirteen states, now usually taken to mean the country west (or north-west) of the Mississippi River. Sometimes limited, as *The Far, Middle West*. See also WILD WEST.

1796 G. WASHINGTON in *Claypoole's Amer. Daily Advertiser* 19 Sept. 2/2 The West derives from the East supplies requisite to its growth and comfort. **1829** EVERETT *Orat. & Sp.* (1850) I. 203, I have made a journey of between three and four thousand miles in the west. **1837** PECK *Gaz. Illinois* Introd. p. vi, No state in the 'Great West' has attracted so much attention..as that of Illinois. **1855** *Putnam's Monthly Mag.* Apr. 380/2, I am disgusted with the West. If ever you catch me at large, anywhere west of the Alleghanies, again, you may shoot me. **1872** SCHELE DE VERE *Americanisms* 165 The States west of the Mississippi continue to be called the West. **1878** H. H. VIVIAN *Notes Tour Amer.* 101 Omaha is the last city of the West. After you pass it you are in the 'Far West'—in the State of Nebraska. **1886** F. M. CRAWFORD *Tale Lonely Parish* v, In the mining districts of the West, in up-country stations in India.

c. The western part *of* a specified country, etc.

1613 ZOUCHE *Dove* B 5, The west of Asia, once Earths Paradice. **1789** S. SHAW (*title*) A Tour to the West of England. **1838** DOWLING *Introd. Eccl. Hist.* 37 The political and social condition of the west of Europe. **1840** DICKENS *Old C. Shop* xxxvii, Pretty nigh all over the West of England.

ellipt. **1894** C. VICKERMAN *Woollen Spinning* 232 Our super west cloths are all tender..when finished. [*Ibid.* 271 A plain super west of England cloth.]

d. The West End of London.

1823 W. T. MONCRIEFF *Tom & Jerry* III. iii, Let the West boast of their highflyers as they will, you'll find there are still some choice creatures of society left here. **1871** A. AUSTIN *Golden Age* 34 In one brief hour behold him curled and drest, And borne on wings of fashion to the West!

e. (With capital initial). The non-Communist states of Europe and America.

1946 H. NICOLSON *Diary* 22 Aug. (1967) 75 He is convinced that the Russians wish to dominate the world... The only way in which the West can counter this is to pool their philosophy of liberalism, put up a united front. **1951**, etc. [see EAST *sb.* 2 b]. **1957** *Ann. Reg. 1956* 228 Some 5,000 citizens a week continued to flee to the West. **1964** M. MCLUHAN *Understanding Media* (1967) ii. 40 Competitive sports between Russia and the West. **1979** T. BENN *Arguments for Socialism* i. 38 It is not only in the West that Marxism is seen as one of the main sources of democratic socialist philosophy.

4. *Ch. Hist.* The Catholic Church in the Western Roman Empire and countries adjacent to it; the Roman or Latin Church.

1586 [? J. CASE] *Praise Mus.* ix. 94 Look vpon the East and the West, the Greeke and Latine Churches, and you shall finde this to be true. **1652** E. SPARKE *Scint. Altaris* 4 Do not all the golden Fountains of the Fathers (both of the East and West, the Greek and Latine Church) flow with the same streams? **1790** PRIESTLEY *Gen. Hist. Chr. Ch.* II. 314 Though the bishops of the West had been deceived at Ariminum, they had all abjured the blasphemies of that council. **1850** NEALE *Hist. Eastern Ch.* I. Introd. 9, I shall constantly reckon among the Saints those whom the Eastern Church, whether with or without the consent of the West, so accounts. **1877** J. D. CHAMBERS *Div. Worship* 233 According to the universal custom of the West, this water should be cold.

5. a. The west wind.

1604 E. G[RIMSTONE] *D'Acosta's Hist. Indies* III. v. 133 They have reckoned two other windes, the East of summer, and the East of winter, and by consequence, two Weasts. **1725** POPE *Odyss.* XII. 478 Now out flies The gloomy West, and whistles in the skies. **1814** SCOTT *Lord of Isles* VI. xxi, Dark rolling like the ocean-tide, When the rough west hath chafed his pride. **1865** SWINBURNE *Poems & Ballads* Ser. I. 128 As roses, when the warm West blows, Break to full flower.

b. A westerly direction of the wind.

1842 DICKENS *Amer. Notes* xvi, Some nautical authority had told me a day or two previous, 'anything with west in it, will do'.

D. *adj.*

1. a. Lying towards the west; situated at or in the west; western, westerly. †Of a planet: Seen in the western part of the sky (tr. L. *occidentalis*).

c **1375** *Sc. Leg. Saints* ii. (*Paul*) 70 Syne Nero In þe weste partis has lattyn hym go. **1398** TREVISA *Barth. De P.R.* IX. xxiv. (1495) 361 A weste sterre that hyghte Vesperus. *c* **1400** MAUNDEV. (1839) v. 44 At Marrok, upon the West See, duelte the Calyffee of Barbaryenes. *c* **1460** *Oseney Reg.* 176, j. rodde of Arable londe vppon Otehulle at forthsheter, þat is to say, the more weste Rodde. **1482** *Rolls of Parlt.* VI. 204/1 Grete part of the Westbordures of Scotlande. *a* **1550** LELAND *Itin.* (1764) III. 9 The very Westeste Pointe of Cornewaulle. *Ibid.* 46 The Est and the West Gates be now the fairest. **1577** D. SETTLE *Frobisher's Voy.* title, A true reporte of the laste voyage into the West and Northwest regions. *Ibid.* B viij, On this West shoare we found a dead fishe floating. **1789** N. PORTLOCK *Voy.* 314 There is anchorage to the Northward of the West point of Morotoi. **1895** 'P. HEMINGWAY' *Out of Egypt* II. 185 The west sky grew pale and gold.

b. Of western Europe, as opposed to the east; *esp.* belonging to the Roman or Latin church; = WESTERN 4. Now *rare* or *Obs.*

1553 BECON *Reliques of Rome* (1563) 141 b, The Occidentall or weast Churches thorow out all Europe. **1565** HARDING *Answ. Jewel's Challenge* 86 b, Yet had they of that nation their Seruice then in Latine, as all the West churche had. **1577** HANMER *Anc. Eccl. Hist., Socrates Schol.* V. xxiv. 358 In the West empire there was one Eugenius, [etc.]. **1594** HOOKER *Eccl. Pol.* IV. xi. §12 The West Church vsing vnleauened bread, as the Iewes in their passouer did. **1628** BP. HALL *Old Relig.* xii. 116 The most eminent Diuines of both East and West Churches.

c. *spec.* **the West Bank**, a region west of the River Jordan and north-west of the Dead Sea which became part of Jordan in 1948 and was occupied by Israel in the Arab-Israeli War of 1967; hence **West Banker**, an inhabitant of the West Bank; †**west isles**, the western isles of Scotland; †**west world**, the new world, America.

1587 HARRISON *Descr. Eng.* I. x. 39/1 in *Holinshed*, The Iles that lie about the north coast of..Scotland..are either occidentals, the west Iles, [etc.]. **1613** S. DANIEL *1st Pt. Hist. Eng.* 5 As now, we see all the West world (lately discouered) to bee. **1967** *Times* 3 Aug. 16/7 Making the Israeli pound legal tender side by side with the Jordanian dinar on the Israeli-occupied West bank should go a long way towards increasing imports of goods from Britain. *Ibid.* 10 Aug. 7/1 Even those Israelis who would gladly abandon Sinai, Gaza and the West Bank would prefer to keep the Syrian heights overlooking the Sea of Galilee. **1968** *N.Y. Times* 22 Dec. IV. 4/6 The many interviews given by King Hussein who often refers to granting more self-government to the West Bankers. **1972** *Guardian* 10 Apr. 11/3 Hussein ..is seeking to prevent disaffected West Bankers..from reversing their links with the Hashemite throne. **1978** *Internat. Relations Dict.* (U.S. Dept. State Library) 35/2 These groups rejected..the establishment of a Palestinian state on the West Bank. **1983** 'J. LE CARRÉ' *Little Drummer Girl* ii. 32 Miss Bach had been talking wistfully of taking up the wagon-trail life of a West Bank settler.

d. Of or pertaining to the west.

1572 TWYNE *Dionysius' Surv. World* B vj b, Two winds,.. the Hesperian or Sicilian wynde, which is West, and the Southeaste, whiche bloweth from the sea Aegæum. **1697** DRYDEN *Virg. Georg.* III. 549 All the West Allies of stormy Boreas blow. **1900** H. S. HOLLAND *Old & New* 97 Whether East or West, we all with one consent excuse ourselves from our responsibilities.

2. With proper names: **a.** Denoting the western part of a country, district, etc., or the more westerly of two places having the same name.

1470-85 MALORY *Arthur* v. ii. 162 The lord of westwalis promysed to brynge xxx M men. **1530-1** *Act 22 Hen. VIII*, c. 17 §10 In West Depyng or Est Depyng yn the countie of Lyncoln. **1645** BOATE *Irel. Nat. Hist.* (1652) 6 East-Meath and Catherlogh or Carlo..West-Meath, Kildare, Kilkenny, [etc.]. **1646** R. BAILLIE *Lett.* (Bannatyne Club) II. 388 The French are like this year to have very bad successe, both in Italie, Spaine, and West Flanders. **1714** in *Jrnl. Friends Hist. Soc.* (1918) 27, I..set forward through west and East Jarsey. **1794** MORSE *Amer. Geog.* 566 The principal town in West Florida is Pensacola. **1811** WILLAN (*title*) A List of Ancient Words at present used in the mountainous district of the West Riding of Yorkshire. **1886** KINGTON OLIPHANT *New Engl.* I. 44 The term *wench* is used in the honourable sense of the West Midland.

b. Denoting the western division of a race, nation, or people. ***West Briton***: † (*a*) a native of Wales; (*b*) a native of Ireland; in mod. use, (chiefly derogatory) one who favours a close political connection with Great Britain; hence ***West Britonism***. Cf. WEST SAXON.

1561 DAUS *Bullinger on Apoc.* lxi. 430 The Westegothes possessed all Spayne. **1712** P. LEIGH *Life S. Wenefride* 46 Whatever this incredulous Age may think of..our Saint's Return to Life; it appear'd so evident to the West Britains.. that many Pagan People..came..to receive Baptism. **18..** T. C. LUBY *Life & Times O'Connell* 342/1 Thomas Spring Rice..was probably the first Irishman who nicknamed himself 'a West Briton'. **1816** J. GIFFARD *Let. to Sir Robert Peel* 19 Mar. (Brit. Library Add. MSS. 40,253, f. 258), The periphrastic Title of the United Kingdom of Great Britain and Ireland..goes out of its way—to remind people that they were once disunited and to keep them so—had the whole been called by one common name *Britain*—we should have had the Inhabitants proud of the glorious Title *Britons* and we West *Britons* would have been as much conciliated and attached as the North Britons are. **1836** D. O'CONNELL in J. O'Connor *Hist. Ireland 1798–1924* (1925) I. vii. 226 The people of Ireland are ready to become portion of the Empire, provided they be made so in reality and not in name alone; they are ready to become a kind of West Britons, if made so in benefits and justice; but if not, we are Irishmen again. **1909** JANE BARLOW *Irish Ways* 3 Not to believe in, at least, fairies, argues you a west-Briton, if nothing worse. **1910** D. HYDE in R. M. Dorson *Peasant Customs* (1968) II. 718 The men who..while protesting..against West Britonism, have helped..to assimilate us to England and the English. **1918** West Britonism [see SHONEEN]. **1925** in J. O'CONNOR *Hist. Ireland 1798–1924* II. xxiv. 368 The American friends of Irish liberty are both grieved and resentful at some of the recent exhibitions given there of the revival of West Britonism. **1944** JOYCE *Stephen Hero* xvii. 54 No West-Briton could speak worse of his Countrymen. **1960** C. C. O'BRIEN *Shaping of Mod. Ireland* 19 When Moran and his friends talked of West Britons they had in mind, I imagine, some archetype of a dentist's wife who collected crests, ate kedgeree for breakfast and displayed on her mantelpiece a portrait of the Dear Queen. **1962** B. INGLIS *West Briton* viii. 143, I never heard of West Briton being used except pejoratively. **1972** C. C. O'BRIEN *States of Ireland* iv. 77 Protestant loyalists—that is to say, most Protestants—also came inevitably under attack, usually as West Britons.

c. With sbs. and adjs. derived from the names of countries, districts, or peoples.

1614 SELDEN *Titles Honor* 80 Kings of West-gothique bloud. **1824** COLLIER & MACCARTHY (*title*) West-African sketches. **183.** GRAVES *Rom. Law* in *Encycl. Met.* (1845) II. 765/1 A manuscript of the Westgothic compilation, called the *Breviarium Aniani*. **1848** GOULD *Birds Australia* I. Pl. 18 West-Australian Gos-Hawk. **1852** HENFREY *Veget. Eur.* 169 Thus we get four sections of Germanic plants, viz.:..*c.* the west-Germanic. **1863** *Irish People* 5 Dec. 24/3 The West-British press chimed in. **1865** R. F. BURTON *Wit & Wisdom from W. Afr.* iii. 121 The practical selfishness and feelinglessness of the wild West African, who, when, tamed by slavery, becomes one of the most tender of men. **1877** *Cassell's Nat. Hist.* I. 363 The West African River Shrew. **1925** J. O'CONNOR *Hist. Ireland 1798–1924* II. xxiv. 373 People dance the same dances as were the fashion in the old West-British days. **1950** *New Yorker* 16 Sept. 83/1 They [*sc.* the Germans] think that German rearmament is inevitable, and suggest that a sort of Foreign Legion..be activated immediately, in which all West European men willing to go to war against Communism could volunteer. **1958** *Listener* 11 Dec. 977/2 He [*sc.* Herr Brandt] is coming gradually to symbolize for many West Berliners their determination to remain free. **1969** A. MARIN *Rise with Wind* (1970) vi. 75 Clay sank into a chair, his eyes fixed coldly on the West German. **1973** *Times* 27 Nov. 9/1 (*heading*) Fewer West Berliners visit the East. **1976** W. LAQUEUR in D. Villiers *Next Year in Jerusalem* 86 The non-Jewish Jew is a specifically West European phenomenon. **1976** M. BIRMINGHAM *Heat of Sun* iii. 34 To build a house in his home town, to which all West Africans dream of retiring. **1981** J. JOHNSTON *Christmas Tree* 114 It wasn't that I objected to De Valera's neutrality... I had no political feelings of being West British..no Crown fever. **1983** *Spectator* 14 May 8/1 It is unsettling to find a pillar of West German industry collecting Nazi memorabilia.

d. With abstract sbs. derived from the sbs. and adjs. of prec. sense.

1895 *Dundalk Examiner* 24 Aug. 2/6 A slogan cry which would..sound the death-knell of ascendancy and West Britishism in this country? **1971** J. SPENCER *Eng. Lang. W. Afr.* 28 There is certainly a sufficiency of terms and expressions peculiar to the use of English in this region to justify the term West Africanism. **1980** *English World-Wide* I. I. 76 AVE [*sc.* African Vernacular English] is.. characterized by a vocabulary adapted to its environment, which shows itself in oft-quoted West Africanisms.

3. *Eccl.* Situated in or at that part of a church (normally the actual west) which is farthest from the altar or high altar.

1412 *Catterick Ch. Contract* (1834) 9 The lenght of the body of the Kirke..with the thicknes of the west walle. *a* **1700** EVELYN *Diary* Aug. (end) 1641, There hang near the West window [of the church] two modells of shipps. **1773** NOORTHOUCK *Hist. Lond.* 629 The west front [of St. Paul's] is graced with a most magnificent portico. **1818** RICKMAN *Engl. Archit.* 72 The west doors of York are of the richest execution. *Ibid.* 92 The west window of St. George's, Windsor, has fifteen lights in three divisions. **1896** HARDY *Under Greenw. Tree* Pref., The Mellstock choir and its old established west-gallery musicians.

4. Facing to the west.

1593 T. FALE *Horolog.* 7 b, The making of the East and West Erect Dials. **1638** S. FOSTER *Art of Dialling* 13 Those plaines are called East and West incliners, whose horizontall line lyeth full North and South, and their inclination is directly towards either East or West. **1642** FULLER *Holy & Prof. St.* III. vii. 167 In a West-window in summer time towards night, the Sun grows low. **1832** *Planting* (Libr. Usef. Knowl.) 26 The soil of the nursery must be..under a south, east, or west exposure.

E. In combination: **a.** with vbl. sbs. and ppl. adjs. as †*west-coming*; *west-facing, -going*, †*-walling* adjs.

1592 in *Maitl. Club Misc.* I. 53 That thai report testimoniall heirintill agane thair first west cuming in this cuntrey. **1595** MARKHAM *Trag. Sir R. Grinvile* xxxiv, The great west-walling boisterous sea. **1866** *Good Words* I June 390/1 During the first two days we passed upwards of a hundred west-going waggons. **1898** *Contemp. Rev.* Aug. 181 A long.. west-facing gallery.

b. with advbs., as ***west-about***, ***-away***.

1579 in *Reg. Mag. Sig. Scot.* *1581* 73/1 Thairfra passand west about as the new stank braa lyis. **1891** *Century Dict.*, *West-about* adv., around toward the west; in a westerly direction. **1818** SCOTT *Rob Roy* xxvii, Will onybody.. grumble at the treaty that opened us a road west-awa' yonder? **1855** KINGSLEY *Westw. Ho!* xxx, If you sailed right west away far enough, you'd surely come to the edge, and fall over cleve. **1875** *Anderida* II. xi. 195 Three ships ran down the coast westaway.

c. With adjs., as **west-central** *a.*, belonging to the western half of the central postal division of London.

1860 *All Year Round* No. 66. 372 A small street off one of the west-central squares. **1865** 'ANNIE THOMAS' *On Guard* II. 265 The show-room of the west-central Mantalini for whom she worked.

west (wɛst), *sb.*[2] *Obs.* exc. *dial.* [Of obscure origin.] A sty or inflammatory swelling on the eyelid.

1569 ANDROSE tr. *Alexis' Secr.* IV. I. 4 To heale a West that riseth vpon the eye liddes. **1705** *Lond. Gaz.* No. 4185/4 A down Look, having a West in one of his Eyes. **1847** HALLIWELL. **1899** C. K. PAUL *Memories* 250, 'I have a west coming in my eye'.

west (wɛst), *v.* Also 4 **weste**. [f. WEST *adv.*] *intr.* To move towards the west. Chiefly of the sun: To draw near to the west, to sink in the west.

c **1381** CHAUCER *Parl. Foules* 266 On a bed of gold sche lay to reste Tyl that the hote sunne gan to weste. *c* **1385** —— *L.G.W.* 61 Whanne the sunne be-gynnys for to weste. **1596** SPENSER *F.Q.* v. Introd. viii, Foure times his place he shifted hath in sight, And twice has risen, where he now doth West, And wested twice, where he ought rise aright. **1607** WALKINGTON *Optic Glass* 162 Phœbus beginneth low to west. **1807** J. BARLOW *Columb.* x. 213 From Mohawk's mouth, far westing with the sun, Thro all the midlands recent channels run. **1888** DOUGHTY *Arabia Deserta* I. 443 The sun at length westing to the valley brow. **1889** in F. W. H. Myers *Human Personality* (1903) II. 340 A ship going round the world making east all the way would gain a day, and by westing would lose one.

west, obs. Sc. f. VEST *v.*; obs. pa. t. and pa. pple. of WIT *v.*[1]

westar, obs. Sc. form of WASTER *sb.*[1]

'west-bound, *a.* [WEST *adv.*] Travelling to the west or in a westerly direction; connected with travel in this direction.

Orig. *U.S.* of railway-trains. In more general use from *c* 1900, freq. of Transatlantic steamers.

1881 *Chicago Times* 12 Mar., The west-bound express was laid up all night at Kearney. **1889** *Pall Mall Gaz.* 3 Sept. 2/3 He will at once give you a west-bound ticket to Chicago. **1891** C. ROBERTS *Adrift Amer.* 67, I watched my chance.. and got on a west-bound freight train. **1902** *Westm. Gaz.* 22 Oct. 1/3 The West-bound traveller.. would choose his 'bus ..along the Embankment.

† **'Westbury apple.** *Obs.* (See quot. 1676.)

1676 WORLIDGE *Vinetum Brit.* 160 The Westberry-Apple, taking its name from Westberry in Hampshire,.. its one of the most solid Apples that grows, of a tough rind, [etc.]. **1707** MORTIMER *Husb.* 537 The Westberry Apple [**1721** The Westbury Apple]. **1747** MRS. GLASSE *Cookery* xxi. 164 Pippins,.. Westbury Apples, Russetting.

west-by(e ('wɛst'baɪ), *adv.* *Sc.* [f. WEST *adv.* + BY *adv.* I.] In a westerly direction, westwards.

1790 A. SHIRREFS *Poems* 72 We met wi' Bessy.. Wha taul's ye gaed west-by a wee before. **1864** LATTO *Tammas Bodkin* xxvii. 283 Tibbie's letters bein' aye left wastbye at Janet Wabster's to be forwarded.

west coast. 1. The western coast of a country or region; in some cases with capital initials as a proper name. Also *attrib.*

1377 LANGL. *P. Pl.* B. XVIII. 113 Þere I sawe sothely.. Out of þe west coste a wenche, as me thouȝte, Cam walkynge in þe way. **1689** *Acts Parlt. Scot.* (1875) XII. 54/2 That two friggetts be gott to cruse on the west coasts. **1801** M. DOWNIE *Observ. Atmosphere* 89 Those parts of the West coasts of Africa which lie between the Tropics. **1845** *N.Z. Jrnl.* 13 Sept. 234/2 Of the west coast of the Middle Island, commonly called by the whalers the 'West Side', we heard a good deal. **1850** *Calif. Courier* (San Francisco) 2 Dec. 2/1 Our position here on the West Coast has been and still is a peculiar one. **1862** *Jrnl. R. Geogr. Soc.* XXXII. 294 Arrangements entered into with the Provincial Government of Nelson for the survey of the West Coast district of that province. **1897** M. KINGSLEY *Trav. W. Afr.* 8 Sound knowledge.. collected during an acquaintance with the West Coast of over thirty years. **1926** A. HUXLEY *Jesting Pilate* IV. 287 The stranger coming to the West Coast will be astonished by the amount of casual embracement. **1959** A. MCLINTOCK *Descr. Atlas N.Z.* p. xvi, The road.. here swings in a northerly direction.. towards Arthur's Pass, 3,020ft, and thence to the West Coast. **1971** *Country Life* 9 Dec. 1642/2 Last year.. the west-coast herrings proved to be the only plentiful supply in northern Europe. **1977** H. FAST *Immigrants* II. 88 We're the lifeline, the West Coast, San Francisco.

2. (Usu. with capital initials.) Used *attrib.* with reference to a style of modern jazz playing that was centred on Los Angeles in the 1950s, typified by small ensembles, technical sophistication, and elaborate writing. orig. *U.S.*

Cf. *West Coaster* below, quot. 1954.

1954 *Downbeat* 7 Apr. 6/1 The latest example of this thinking-by-pigeonholes is the attempt to convince the populace that there is a growing west coast school of jazz. *Ibid.* 19 May 16/3 Nat Hentoff's comments on 'west coast jazz' aroused considerable comment. **1959** *News Chron.* 12 Aug. 6/5 He is not only benevolent about West Coast jazz but aware of its technical ins and outs. **1961** *Times* 4 Feb. 11/5 Music of considerable variety, ranging from some vigorous Dixieland.. to West Coast Jazz (with Palm Court cello). **1962** *Melody Maker* 21 July 7/1 Some of the 1954 tracks have a nostalgic, almost dated, appeal, in the writing, it is so typical of West Coast jazz of the time—neat, smooth and often very clever. **1980** *New Grove Dict. Mus.* XX. 371/2 Miles Davis's 1949–50 recordings were an initial influence as is shown by such archetypal West Coast performances as Rogers's *Didi* (1951).

3. Used *attrib.* to designate a kind of large rear-view mirror (see quot. 1963). orig. *U.S.*

1963 *Amer. Speech* XXXVIII. 46 *West coast mirror*,.. a large, square, rear-view mirror attached to the side of a cab. **1968** *Globe & Mail* (Toronto) 17 Feb. 41 (Advt.), Mercury ¾ ton pickup... 4 speed transmission, west coast mirrors. **1980** *Truck & Bus Transportation* (Austral.) Mar. 96/1 All-round vision is generally good, but Cronulla Carrying have gone one step further by replacing the meagre standard mirrors with the efficient west-coast type.

Hence **West Coaster**, (*a*) one who lives on the West Coast; *spec.* (*N.Z.*) = COASTER 3 c; (*b*) a player or devotee of West Coast jazz.

1896 *N.Z. Alpine Jrnl.* II. 157 He was.. not a native born West Coaster. **1936** 'R. HYDE' *Passport to Hell* ii. 54 He washed shirts for the brawny West Coasters. **1941** O. DUFF *N.Z. Now* v. 71 The people are never 'Southlanders'.. as the people of the West Coast are 'West Coasters'. **1949** M. STEEN *Twilight on Floods* II. ii. 198 Eighty-five per cent West Coasters die of fever, or return home total wrecks! **1954** *Time* 1 Feb. 38/2 Today, the liveliest center of developing jazz is California... The West Coasters include such names as.. Shelly Manne.., Shorty Rogers.., Gerry Mulligan and Stan Getz.., Dave Brubeck. **1958** K. GOODWIN in P. Gammond *Decca Bk. Jazz* xiii. 148 Groups from four to nine pieces have been most popular among the West Coasters. **1974** M. BRAITHWAITE *Ontario* ii. 7 It is nonsense to maintain that there are no special characteristics of Canadians from different regions of the country. West Coasters *are* different from those who live on the East Coast. **1977** *Times* 16 May 8/7 Their effect on humourless West Coasters [*sc.* in California] was.. devastating.

west country. [WEST *a.*] The western part of any country; the district or region towards the west; *spec.* of England or of Scotland.

Usually the remoter counties west (or south-west) of the speaker, or of London (in Scotland west of Edinburgh); sometimes *spec.* the south-western counties (Somerset, Devon, etc.).

1398 TREVISA *Barth. De P.R.* XI. iii. (Bodl. MS.) In þe est londes and contreyes is muche more plente of fruytes and floures þanne in þe northe and in þe weste contreys. *c* **1400** *Brut* ccxxviii. 301 In þe same ȝere, aboute þe Sowth-cuntreys and also in þe west cuntres, þere fell so much reyne ..þat [etc.]. *c* **1470** HENRY *Wallace* IV. 171 Our wast contre thar statute is so strang, Into the north my purposs is to gang. **1473** WARKW. *Chron.* (Camden) 10 The Erle of Warwyke londede in the west countre. **1534** CROMWELL in Merriman *Life & Lett.* (1902) I. 395 Ye do deteyne.. certeyne londes in the weste cuntrey contrary to all right. **1570–6** LAMBARDE *Peramb. Kent* (1596) 474 At Dartmouth in the West countrie. **1639** G. PLATTES *Discov. Subterr. Treas.* xi. 51 Every one may see in the west Country, where such a multitude of Firre trees doe lie covered so deepe in the earth, that [etc.]. **1827** SCOTT *Let.* in *Lockhart* (1837) I. v. 136, I had very little acquaintance.. with the gentry of the west country. **1845** CARLYLE *Cromwell* xliii. I. 359 The Whiggamore Raid, all the force of the West Country, 6,000 strong, is already there. **1906** J. E. VINCENT *Highways Berks.* ix. 241 It is a little strained, perhaps, to include Berkshire in the West country.

b. *attrib.* (Frequently hyphened.)

a **1653** BINNING *Usef. Case Consc.* (1693) 40 They think these Malignants better than the West-Countrey forces. **1678** T. JORDAN *Tri. Lond.* 14 Zome honest plain West-Country-mon. **1690** *Lond. Gaz.* No. 2579/2 Edinburgh... Several Thousands of the West-Country Men have offered to Serve Their Majesties against the Highlanders. **1720** *Ibid.* No. 5895/4 Speaks in a broad West-Country Dialect. **1805** R. W. DICKSON *Pract. Agric.* I. 435 Sheep.. of the Devonshire, or west-country breed. **1820** SCOTT *Monast.* Introd. Ep., A west-country whig frae Kilmarnock. **1865** KINGSLEY *Herew.* v, Why should he know our West country ways? **1879** *St. George's Hosp. Rep.* IX. 586 One branch of her family, living in a west-country town.

fig. **1853** W. D. COOPER *Sussex Gloss.* (ed. 2) 85 *West-country Parson*, the Hake; so called from the black streak on the back, and from its abundance along the West Coast.

† **westdeal.** *Obs.* In 1 **westdǽl**, 3 **westdel**, *Orm.* **wesstdale**. [See WEST *adv.* and DEAL *sb.*[1]] The western part or district, the west.

c **825** *Vesp. Psalter* lxxiv. 7 Ne from eastdæle ne from westdæle. **971** *Blickl. Hom.* 93 Þy fiftan dæȝe.. se heofon tobyrst from þæm eastdæle oþ þone westdæl. *c* **1200** ORMIN 16406 Wesstdale off all þiss werelld iss Dysiss bi name nemmnedd. *a* **1300** *E.E. Psalter* cii[i]. 12 Hou mikle estdel stand westdel fra, Fer made he fra vs oure wickenes swa.

† **weste,** *sb.* [Reduced form of OE. *wésten* (see WESTERN *sb.*[2]), or f. next.] A desert, wilderness.

c **1200** ORMIN 11747 Þær i þe wesste þær he wass Himm ane. *Ibid.* 17408 Alls he comm wiþþ all þe follc Inntill a wilde wesste. *c* **1200** *Trin. Coll. Hom.* 127 On his ȝuweðe he fleh fro folke to weste. *Ibid.*, Weste was his wunienge.

† **weste,** *a.* *Obs.* Also 3 **west**. [OE. *wéste*, earlier *wœ́ste* = OFris. *wôste* (WFris. *woast*), MDu. and Du. *woest*, OS. *wôsti* (MLG. *wôst*, *wûst*, LG. *wöst*), OHG. *wôsti*, *wuosti* (MHG. *wüeste*, G. *wüst*), f. the stem **wōst-*, related to L. *vāstus*: see WASTE *a.*]

1. Of places: Uninhabited and uncultivated or untended; desert, desolate, waste.

Beowulf 2456 [He] ȝesyhð sorhcearig.. winsele westne. *c* **825** *Vesp. Psalter* lxviii. 26 Sie eardung heara woestu. *Ibid.* lxxiv. 7 From woestum muntum. *c* **900** tr. *Bæda's Hist.* I. xv. 52 Is sæd of þære tide.. þæt hit [*sc.* þæt land] weste wuniȝe. *c* **1000** *Ags. Gosp.* Matt. xiv. 15 Ðeos stowe ys weste. *c* **1200** ORMIN 1417 All forrþi wass heoffness ærd Swa summ itt wesste wære. *c* **1200** *Trin. Coll. Hom.* 127 He.. þerfore ferde into weste wilderne. *c* **1205** LAY. 10591 Al þat lond heo makeden west. *Ibid.* 17330 Ich wulle.. maken him weste paðes & wildernes monie. *c* **1250** *Owl & Night.* 1528 Wowes weste [*v.r.* west] and lere huse. *a* **1300** *Maximian* 211 (MS. Digby 86) Þis world me þinkeþ west.

2. ***west(e) land***, waste land; desert.

c **1030** *Sherburn Surv.* in *Eng. Hist. Rev.* (1912) Jan. 18 Ond þys synd weste land: Ane is Sal-leȝe; oðer is Grante-leȝe. *c* **1200** ORMIN 9239 Sannt Johan i wessteland Wass wurrþenn cuþ þatt time. *Ibid.* 11429 All swa summ wessteland iss all Forrworrpenn & forrlætenn. *c* **1205** LAY. 16268 He funde west lond [*c* **1275** in west lond], leoden of-slæȝene.

† **weste,** *v.* *Obs.* [OE. *wéstan* (:—*wōstjan*: see WESTE *a.*) = OS. (*â*)*wôstian*, OHG. *wuostan* (MHG. *wuesten* G. *wüsten*).] *trans.* To lay waste.

c **893** ÆLFRED *Oros.* I. x. §1 Hie.. wæron fiftene ȝear þæt lond heriȝende & westende. *c* **1000** *Ags. Ps.* (Th.) lxxviii. 7 Hi.. his wic-stede westan. *Ibid.* lxxix. 13 Hine.. wilde deor westað and frettað. *c* **1205** LAY. 1754 Þus heo westen þat lond. *Ibid.* 20941 Heo.. sæiden þat heo wolden.. westen Arðures lond. *c* **1250** *Gen. & Ex.* 3915 Ðis folc.. his lond tok,.. And westen al to flum iordan.

weste, obs. pa. t. and pple. of WISH *v.*, WIT *v.*[1]

westecoateer, var. WAISTCOATEER.

westelur, var. WISSELER *Obs.*

† **'westen,** *a.* *Sc.* *Obs.*$^{-1}$ [f. WEST *adv.* Cf. EASTEN *a.*] Western.

1549 *Compl. Scot.* vi. 61 The feyrd cardinal vynd is callit fauonius or occidental, quhilk vulgaris callis vestin vynd.

† **westen,** *adv.* *Obs.* [OE. *westan* (f. *west* adv.) = OFris. *westa*, OS. *westan* (*wind*), ON. and Icel. (Norw., Sw.) *vestan* (Da. *vesten*): cf. WESTENE *adv.* and BEWEST.] From the west. Also with *fro*.

a **900** *Genesis* 806 Ȝif her wind cymð westan oððe eastan. *c* **1000** *Sax. Leechd.* III. 274 Se þridda heafod-wind.. blæwð westan. *c* **1250** *Gen. & Ex.* 3096 On wind cam fro westen, and ðo [h]opperes nam.

west end. [OE. *west-ende* (see WEST *adv.*) = Du. *westeinde*, WFris. *westein*, MLG., G. *westende*. In later use f. WEST *a.*]

1. The western end or extremity of anything.

c **893** ÆLFRED *Oros.* I. i. §3 Hire on westende is Scotland. *c* **1050** *O.E. Chron.* (MS. C) an. 1036 Syððan hine man byriȝde.. æt þam west ende, þam styple ful ȝehende. *a* **1225** *Ancr. R.* 244 Toward þe west ende of þe worlde. *a* **1400–50** *Wars Alex.* 1733 A selly nounbre Of wrichis & wirlingis out of the west endis. **1408–17** in *Rec. St. Mary at Hill* (1905) Introd. p. xcvi, A Tent withowt the west ende of the church yerd made of Clothe. *a* **1550** LELAND *Itin.* (1764) II. 7 The West Ende of Ewelm Paroche Chirch. *Ibid.* IV. 124 There be 2. Wooden Bridges at the West Ende of the Towne. **1591** SHAKS. *Two Gent.* v. iii. 9 Goe thou with her to the West end of the wood. *a* **1700** EVELYN *Diary* 25 Mar. 1644, Having two spires and middle lanterne at the West end. **1711** *Lond. Gaz.* No. 4906/3 We met an English Runner off the West-end of this Island [Jamaica]. **1782** MISS BURNEY *Cecilia* III. iv, He privately took a lodging at the west end of the town. **1818** SCOTT *Hrt. Midl.* vi, The west end of the defile formed by the Luckenbooths was secured in the same manner. **1847** [see RESPOND *sb.* 2]. **1848** DICKENS *Dombey* vii, A fashionable neighbourhood at the west end of the town. **1874** MICKLETHWAITE *Mod. Par. Churches* 59 The upper row of stalls.. at the west end of the chancel.

2. *spec.* ***the West End***, that part of London lying westward of Charing Cross and Regent St. and including the fashionable shopping district, Mayfair, and the Parks; also, those living within this area.

1776 *Gazetteer & New Daily Advertiser* 11 Sept. in Bond & McLeod *Newslett. to Newspapers* (1977) III. 186 A gentleman in a certain coffeehouse at the Westend of town. **1807** tr. *Goede's Trav.* I. 38 The devices at the west end, are usually crowns, stars, crescents. **1815** *Zeluca* III. 143 As you're staying with a relation at the west end.. there's no harm in making a genteel acquaintance—eh? **1835** DICKENS *Sk. Boz, Dancing Academy*, It was not in the West-end at all —it rather approximated to the eastern portion of London. **1863** O. W. HOLMES *Old Vol. Life* (1891) 97 We know what the West End of London wishes may be result of this controversy. **1882** BESANT *All Sorts* vii, She was setting up a dressmaker's shop;.. she had hopes of support, even from the West End, where she had friends.

b. The theatres of the West End, or their personnel.

1894 *Theatre* Oct. 155 The influence of the west end is felt both in the cheaper London houses and throughout the provinces. **1979** *Listener* 16 Aug. 206/3 No one wanted a National Theatre. The West End didn't want it because they feared a new rival.

3. *transf.* The fashionable or aristocratic quarter of a town or other place.

1823 BYRON *Juan* XI. xlv, The great world.. Meaneth the west or worst end of a city. **1830** CARLYLE *Misc. Ess.*, *Richter* (1872) III. 35 Richter, for his part, was quite excluded from the West-end of Hof: for Hof too has its West-end... So poor Richter could only be admitted to the West-end of the

Universe. **1840** HOOD *Up Rhine* 159 There was, however, a sort of West-end to the room, where the fashionables and the Vons seemed instinctively to congregate. **1854** tr. *Hettner's Athens & Pelop.* 28 This is the fashionable part, or 'west end' of New Athens. **1863** SPEKE *Source Nile* xii. 339 A number of huts.. were at once assigned to me, on the face of a hill... It was considered the 'West End'.

4. *attrib.* (from senses 2 and 3.) Also passing into *adj.*

1835 *Court Mag.* VI. 4/1 A refuge for the West-end destitute of all denominations. **1848** DICKENS *Dombey* i, Doctor Parker Pep's West End practice. **1863** MISS BRADDON *Aurora Floyd* xxxiii, A colour that West-End tailors had vainly striven to emulate. **1888** *Encycl. Brit.* XXIV. 28/1 Spacious west-end quarters in cities. **1889** LOWELL *Latest Lit. Ess.* (1891) 67 With that West-End view of the realities of life which Englishmen of a certain class feel it proper to take. **1890** G. B. SHAW *London Music 1888–89* (1937) 322 The more commercial atmosphere of the West-end theatre. **1890** O. WILDE *Pict. Dorian Gray* iii, in *Lippincott's Monthly Mag.* July 29, I will take a West-End theatre and bring her out properly. **1928** A. HUXLEY *Point Counter Point* x. 159 So well travelled, so brilliantly cosmopolitan and West-End. **1936** N. COWARD *To-Night at 8.30* I. 103 If you're so bloody West End why the hell did you leave it? **1954** 'M. COST' *Invitation from Minerva* 171, I got my first West-End engagement. Since then, I've never looked back. **1983** S. VIZINCZEY *Innocent Millionaire* iii. 14 Occasionally his London agent got him a part in the West End production of an American play.

Hence ˌ**West-ˈender**, one who lives at the west end of a town, *esp.* of London; ˌ**West-ˈendian** (*a*) *sb.* = prec.; (*b*) *adj.* = next; ˌ**West-ˈendy** *a.*, characteristic or suggestive of a west end, *spec.* that of London; ˌ**West-ˈendish** *a.*, of or characteristic of the West End; ˌ**West-ˈendism**, West-end quality or character.

1833 *Chambers's Jrnl.* 30 Mar. 66/2 There have been instances of '*west-enders' going on a tour of discovery.. within the precincts of Wapping. **1839** DICKENS *Nickleby* xxxvii, A pleasant fiction invented by jealous *West-enders. **1874** H. MAYHEW *Lond. Characters* 299 Already there is a sort of *esprit de locale*.. amongst the inhabitants of the new quarters that the old West Ender never dreamed of. **1825** HOR. SMITH *Gaieties & Grav.* II. 322 *West-endians and Bond-street loungers. **1856** J. M. LUDLOW *Let.* Nov. in C. L. Graves *Life & Lett. A. Macmillan* (1910) ii. 91 [A London shop] more West-endian than Bell's or Nutt's. **1909** *Daily Chron.* 9 June 5/4 An advanced..*West-endish sort of woman. **1875** BLACKIE *Introd. to C. Blackie's Etymol. Geog.* 33 Such-like apish mimicry of metropolitan *West Endism. **1911** J. BONE *Edin. Revisited* i. 12 A minister of the Gospel from the West Coast identified Edinburgh as an 'east-windy, *west-endy city'. **1959** *New Chron.* 25 July 4/5 Most of it proved too precious and West Endy for television.

†**westene**, *adv.* *Obs.* [OE. *westane* = OS. *westane*, OHG. *westana*: cf. WESTEN *adv.*] From the west.

c **893** ÆLFRED *Oros.* I. i. §24 Ða beorȝas..onȝinnað westane fram þæm Wendelsæ. *c* **1205** LAY. 25591 Þa com þer westene winden mid þan weolcnen a berninge drake.

wester (ˈwɛstə(r)), *a.* Chiefly *Sc.* Also 1 **westra**, *Sc.* 4 **westyr**, 4–6 **westir**, (5 **vestir**, 6 **vester**, **weister**), 7 **waster**. [OE. *westra* (f. *west* WEST *adv.*) = ON. and Icel. *vestri*, *vestari* (Norw., Sw., Da. *vestre*). The comparative ending is different from that which appears in OHG. *westar-*, MHG., LG., Du., Fris. *wester-*, western.] Lying (more) towards the west; western.

963 in Birch *Cartul. Sax.* III. 363 Se westra crochyrst. **967** *Ibid.* 486 Se westra east healh. **1365** *Antiq. Aberd. & Banff* (Spald. Club) IV. 158 Omnes terras.. de Westir Drummelochi. **1389** *Ibid.* III. 261 Terras de Westyr Badfothellis. **1438** *Exch. Rolls Scotl.* V. 56 De medietate terre de Westercloveth in Strathdone. **1474** *Acta Auditorum* (1839) 33/1 þe landis of þe wester part of Strathenry. **1490** *Acta Dom. Concil.* (1839) 131/1 þe landis of ester Copmalindy and Wester Copmanlindy. **1520** in *Laing Charters* (1899) 82 Of the whiche two chambres the oone is called the wester chambre. **1584** R. NORMAN tr. *Safegard of Sailers* 7 Keep off from the wester shore, for.. the easter shore is deeper. **1613** J. SARIS *Voy. Japan* (Hakl. Soc.) 43 He was gone to the Wester side of the Iland. **1633** T. JAMES *Voy.* 35 We had.. coasted the Wester side. **1680** A. HAIG in J. Russell *Haigs* xi. (1881) 309 The apple trees which is within the uppermost waster quarter. **1708** *Lond. Gaz.* No. 4430/5 The Magistrates and Town-Council of *Anstruther-Wester.* **1777** WATSON *Philip II* (1793) I. x. 448 From the Easter to the Wester Scheldt. **1891** *Hartland* (Devon) *Gloss.*, *Easter*, eastern. Similarly we have Wester, Nother, and Suther. Fields are frequently distinguished as Easter and Wester. **1898** A. BALFOUR *To Arms* vi, Away in the wilds of wester Dumfries.

†**b.** *Naut.* (Cf. EASTER *a.* and BOARD *sb.* 15.)

1697 DAMPIER *Voy.* I. 81 But the Winds hanging in the westerbord, and blowing hard, oft put us by our Topsails; so that we could not fetch it.

wester (ˈwɛstə(r)), *v.* [f. WEST *adv.* + -ER⁵.]

1. *intr.* Of the sun, moon, or a star: To travel westward in its course; to draw near the west. (Freq. after 1850.)

c **1374** CHAUCER *Troylus* II. 906 Þe sonne Gan westren faste. **1412–20** LYDG. *Chron. Troy* Prol. 136 And Esperus gan to wester dovn, To haste hir cours ageyn þe morwe graye. *Ibid.* I. 2674 Vp-on þe point whan Phebus with his liȝt I-westrid is.

1790 COWPER *Iliad* XXIII. 195 And now the lamp of day, Westering apace, had left them still in tears. **1837** CARLYLE *Fr. Rev.* III. I. ii, The Sun shines; serenely westering, in smokeless mackerel-sky. **1850** DOBELL *Roman* II. Poet. Wks. 1875 I. 36 The little star.. westers to its setting. **1889** CLARKE RUSSELL *Marooned* vi, The moon was westering and looking over our foretopsail yard-arm. **1922** A. E. HOUSMAN *Last Poems* xxvi, The half moon westers low.

fig. **1845** R. W. HAMILTON *Pop. Educ.* x. 330 Instead of turning to the sun of a once mighty prosperity as now fast westering and going down.

2. Of the wind: To shift to the west.

1580 H. SMITH in Hakluyt *Voy.* (1589) 468 The wind did Wester, so that we lay South southwest with a flawne sheete. **1628** DIGBY *Voy. Mediterr.* (Camden) 93 The wind northered vpon vs. Att night it westered againe. **1699** T. ALLISON *Voy. Archangel* 11 We.. began to consider.. as to our safety in that place, should the Wind Wester. **1823** SCORESBY *Jrnl.* 373 The wind having unfortunately westered. **1913** M. ROBERTS *Salt of Sea* x. 233 The wind westered so fast that I nearly jibed the mainboom.

3. To be moved farther west. *nonce-use.*

1803 W. TAYLOR in *Ann. Rev.* I. 361 Let Germany awake, and give herself a better constitution.. and the frontiers of France will wester again.

wester, var. WASTER *sb.*³

westeria, var. WISTARIA.

ˈ**westering**, *vbl. sb.* [f. WESTER *v.*] Westward movement, declension westwards.

c **1410** LYDG. *Life Our Lady* lxxi. (MS. Ashm. 39 lf. 89) This sterre.. To shewe hys light in euery showred & shade With oute westrynge or drawynge to declyne.

westering (ˈwɛstərɪŋ), *ppl. a.* [f. WESTER *v.*]

1. That declines from the meridian towards the west. (Said chiefly of the sun when it is nearing the western horizon.)

In very common use from *c* 1840.

1637 MILTON *Lycidas* 31 Oft till the Star that rose, at Ev'ning, bright Toward Heav'ns descent had slop'd his westering wheel. **1790** COWPER *Odyss.* XI. 19 Earthward he slopes again his westering wheels. **1795** SOUTHEY *Lett. Spain* (1799) 34 Hills beyond hills,.. part involved in shadow, and the more distant illumined by the westering sun. **1802** LEYDEN *Lord Soulis* xx, And bloody set the westering sun. **1831** MOORE *Summer Fête* 132 Warned.. by the daylight's westering beam. **1859** GEO. ELIOT *Adam Bede* liii, The low westering sun shone right on the shoulders of the old Binton Hills. **1894** BLACKMORE *Perlycross* vii. 56 By the light of the westering moon.

fig. **1851** MRS. BROWNING *Casa Guidi Wind.* I. 403 Learn The strong man's impulse.. and discern By his clear westering eye, the time of day. **1885–94** BRIDGES *Eros & Psyche* March xiv, Eros.. was Cupid named anew In westering aftertime of latin lore.

2. That moves in a westward direction. Of the wind: That shifts to the west.

1747 COLLINS *Ode Liberty* 84 Mona,.. Where thousand Elfin Shapes abide, And Wight who checks the west'ring Tide. **1871** SWINBURNE *Songs bef. Sunrise, Eve of Rev.* 66 Asia, that sawest their westering waters sweep With all the ships and spoils of time to carry. **1896** KIPLING *Seven Seas, Three Sealers* 142 There comes no good o' the westering wind that backs against the sun.

ˈ**westerliness.** [-NESS.] Westerly situation.

1730 BAILEY (Folio) s.v.; also s.v. *Occidentalness*. **1927** [see EASTERLINESS]

†ˈ**westerling.** *Obs.* [f. WESTER *a.* + -LING.] An inhabitant of a western country or district.

1630 CAPT. J. SMITH *True Trav., Adv., & Observ.* xxiii. (Arb.) 891 The Country being then reputed by your westerlings, a most rockie, barren, desolate desart. **1631** BYFIELD *Doctr. Sabb.* 85 The Westerlings, the Easterlings, the Europeans, and the Asians. **1687** A. LOVELL tr. *Thevenot's Trav.* I. 150 The Magrebins, or Westerlings, comprehending those of Barbary, Fez, and Morocco, who meet at Caire. **1728** MORGAN *Algiers* II. i. 215 The common appellation of Westerling, they [Turks] give to all such as inhabit West of Egypt. **1845** T. COOPER *Purgatory of Suicides* I. lxxx, Some hoary teacher.. Whose wisdom's lustre doth.. transcend The glimmering lights your westerlings revere.

westerly (ˈwɛstəlɪ), *a.* and *sb.* [f. WEST *adv.* Cf. *easterly*, etc., and next.]

A. *adj.*

1. Coming from the west.

1577 GOOGE *Heresbach's Husb.* I. 20 What time so euer it be doone, you must looke that the winde be Westerly. **1608** SHAKS. *Per.* IV. i. 51 Is this wind Westerlie that blowes? **1690** in Foster *Eng. Factories Ind.* (1906) 221 A fine gentle westerlie sea winde blowing. **1748** *Anson's Voy.* II. iii. 140 The westerly winds.. are almost perpetual in that part. **1849** MACAULAY *Hist. Eng.* x. II. 641 She.. had been detained in Holland.. by strong westerly winds. **1855** KINGSLEY *Westw. Ho!* xxxii, They got on a lee shore in Cardigan Bay, before a heavy westerly gale. **1886** STEVENSON *Kidnapped* xiii, She tore through the seas at a great rate, pitching and straining, and pursued by the westerly swell.

Comb. **1868** JOYNSON *Metals* 116 Even the weather has to be consulted,—a westerly-wind day is the best.

2. Situated in or towards the west.

1577 HARRISON *England* II. i. 49 b/1 in *Holinshed*, Two waters.. whereof the westerly called Basingwater, commeth from Basingstoke. **1584** R. NORMAN tr. *Safegard of Sailers* 10 The most westerly houses of Wieringhen. *a* **1609** SIR F. VERE *Comm.* (1657) 51 Flores and Corvo, the westerliest Islands of the Azores. **1610** HOLLAND *Camden's Brit.* (1637) 677 But the more Westerly part is not so fruitfull. **1669** STURMY *Mariner's Mag.* IV. iii. 147 This Table.. sheweth how much a Ship is more.. Easterly or Westerly, by sailing upon any Point.. of the Compass. **1765** R. ROGERS *Concise Acc. N. Amer.* title-p., The Interior, or Westerly Parts of the Country, upon the Rivers St. Laurence, the Mississippi, [etc.]. **1825** J. NEAL *Bro. Jonathan* III. 381 All the water on the westerly side of the town, was of a clear wine colour. **1870** *Daily News* 1 Feb., The eight twelve-pounders moved forward from one of the more westerly batteries.

b. Of a person: Dwelling in the west.

1865 W. G. PALGRAVE *Arabia* II. xiv. 241 Nor are more westerly historians always exempt from similar weaknesses.

3. Situated near the western horizon.

1801 SOUTHEY *Thalaba* VI. v, Nor stay'd he till over the westerly heaven The shadows of evening had spread. **1829** SCOTT *Anne of G.* xxx, The distant landscape, partly illumined, with ominous lustre, by the now westerly sun.

4. Extending towards the west; facing the west. Of motion, progress, etc.: Directed towards the west or the western horizon.

1637 R. NORWOOD *Sea-mans Pract.* ix. (1655) 115 Then shall you have.. the Latitudes and Longitudes of all Places as you saile, which may more easily and exactly be exprest upon this Chart, then the Easterly or Westerly distances. **1669** STURMY *Mariner's Mag.* IV. iii. 153 The Westerly [distance] is 16$\frac{85}{100}$ Leagues. **1802** C. FINDLATER *Agric. Peebles* 18 The hills.. of a southerly or westerly exposure, are generally more verdant. **1843** PRESCOTT *Mexico* (1850) I. 336 Where the vapours from the ocean, touching in their westerly progress, maintain a rich verdure throughout the year. **1878** NEWCOMB *Pop. Astron.* I. ii. 58 The westerly motion of the latter [planet]. **1897** MARY KINGSLEY *W. Africa* 362 This.. leads from Ntamo to the Atlantic in a nearly due westerly direction.

B. *sb. pl.* The prevailing westerly winds found in certain latitudes.

1876 SPRY *Cruise of 'Challenger'* 109 The strong westerlies caused the weather to be of such a boisterous character. **1897** F. T. BULLEN *Cruise of 'Cachalot'* 86 The dirty weather and variable squalls, which nearly always precede the 'westerlies'. **1898** *Jrnl. Sch. Geog.* (U.S.) Oct. 303 The beginning of the régime of the prevailing westerlies came at about latitude 40° S.

westerly (ˈwɛstəlɪ), *adv.* [f. as prec. Cf. ON. *vestarliga.*]

1. In a westward direction; towards the west.

1625 HYNMERS tr. *Blaeu's Sea-Mirr.* III. 3 You must goe first southwest or somwhat westerly to the Helder. **1669** STURMY *Mariner's Mag.* IV. iii. 154 S.W.b.W. ½ Westerly 190 Leagues. **1680** J. COLLINS *Plea Irish Cattell* etc. 7 Our Ships .. Westerly or Southerly bound, Victual here. **1722** DE FOE *Col. Jack* viii, We began to steer away westerly. **1771** *Cook's 1st Voy.* 26 A small white cloud.. from which a train of fire issued, extending itself westerly. **1795** VANCOUVER *Agric. Essex* 87 Crossing the great road, and proceeding thence westerly through Shenfield. **1835** W. IRVING *Tour Prairies* 70 Our plan was.. to keep westerly, until we should pass through.. the Cross Timber. **1863** *Daily Tel.* 6 Apr., The principal channel.. running in a straight line with the opening between the heads, westerly, out to sea. **1891** CLARK RUSSELL *Marriage at Sea* ii, We're going to get a breeze..; nothing to harm.. if it don't draw westerly.

2. (Blowing) from the west.

1708 *Lond. Gaz.* No. 4443/3 The Wind blowing fresh Westerly, oblig'd 'em to anchor. **1748** *Anson's Voy.* II. vii. 214 We found the wind to hang westerly. **1816** TUCKEY *Narr. Exped. R. Zaire* ii. (1818) 51 The winds now came more westerly.

†**westermore**, *adv.* *Sc.* In 5 **westermar**, 6 **westirmair.** [Cf. next and -MORE.] Farther west.

c **1470** HENRY *Wallace* I. 307 Wallace ansuerd, said; 'Westermar [**1570** Westir mair] we will.'

ˈ**westermost**, *a.* Now *rare* or *Obs.* [f. WESTER *a.* + -MOST.] Lying or situated farthest west; = WESTERNMOST.

1555 EDEN *Decades* (Arb.) 381 The Westermost poynte of the Trepoyntes. **1598** HAKLUYT *Voy.* I. 337 The riuer Ob is the most Westermost part thereof. **1625** N. CARPENTER *Geog. Del.* I. iii. (1635) 65 The Meridian about the Westermost of the Azores. **1697** DAMPIER *Voy.* I. 421 Three of the Islands were pretty large; the Westermost is the biggest. **1727** A. HAMILTON *New Acc. E. Ind.* II. 24 Sagor the wester-most Chanel of the Ganges. **1775** ROMANS *Florida* App. 37 At the east end of the westermost key is another channel 8 feet deep. **1821** SOUTHEY *Vis. Judgement* i. 10 From far Glaramara, Bleacrag, and Maidenmawr, to Grizedal and westermost Withop.

western (ˈwɛstən), *a.*, *sb.*¹, and *adv.* Forms: 1, 6–7 **westerne**, (1, 6 **weasterne**); 4–6 **westeren**, 6– **western**; 1 **wæstrene**, 2 **westrene**, 4–7 **westren**. [OE. *westerne* (f. *west* WEST *adv.* + -ERN): cf. OS. and OHG. *westrôni*, ON. *vestrœnn* (Norw. dial. *vestrøn*).]

A. *adj.*

1. Coming from the west. Of the wind, a gale, etc.: Blowing from the west. Of a current of water: Flowing from the west.

c **1050** *Bæda's Hist.* v. xix. (MS. B.) Sona ðæs þe he on scip eode, ða astah westerne wind & bleow. *a* **1100** *Aldhelm Gloss.* in Napier *O.E. Glosses* xxiii. 17 *Zepheri*, westernes windes. **1398** TREVISA *Barth De P.R.* XII. xv. (Bodl. MS.) Whanne þe westeren winde blowiþ. **1530** PALSGR. 288/1 Westerne wynde, *le vent daual.* **1581** A. HALL *Iliad* II. 23 When as the western winde doth meete a field of graine, In haruest time. **1604** E. G[RIMSTONE] tr. *Acosta's Hist. Indies* III. iv. 128 They saile with a westerne winde vntill they come to the burning Zone. **1613–16** W. BROWNE *Brit. Past.* I. iv. 79 A westerne milde, and pretty whispering gale. **1673** RAY *Journ. Low C.* Rome 386 The commixture of the warm Southerly and Western air, with the cold Northerly and Eastern. **1748** *Anson's Voy.* I. x. 103 The western winds which blew almost constantly there. *a* **1771** GRAY *Song* 9 Western gales and skies serene Speak not always winter past. **1796** NELSON *Let.* in Nicolas *Disp.* (1846) VII. Add. p. lix, I am endeavouring to get to the Eastward, but we have an amazing strong western current. **1802** LEYDEN *Mermaid* viii, Softly blow, thou western Breeze! **1827** STEUART *Planter's G.* (1828) 331 Removed Trees.. appearing unaffected by the western, and southwestern blasts. **1867** MORRIS *Jason* IV. 94 The piping of the following western breeze.

2. a. Dwelling in the west (of a country, esp. of England or Scotland); *spec.* living or originating in the 'West country' or south-western counties.

c **1100** *O.E. Chron.* (MS. D.) an. 1013, & com Æþelmær ealdorman þyder & þa wæstrena ðegenas mid him. **15..** *Ladye Bessie* (Percy Soc.) 61 Hee..drewe an eigle upon the entrye, That the westeren men myghte yt see. **1570** LAMBARDE *Peramb. Kent* (1576) 316 Muche are the Westerne men bound..to Polydore, who..remouing the infamous reuenge from Dorsetshyre, laieth it vpon our men of Kent. **1668** WILKINS *Real Char.* I. i. 4 A Western man [would speak it] thus, *Chud eat more cheese an chad it.* **1693** T. PITTS *New Martyrol.* (ed. 4) 527 The..Christian Courage of the Western Sufferers. **1822** SCOTT *Halidon Hill* I. ii. 497 O, were my western horsemen but come up, I would take part with you! **1841** LEVER *O'Malley* xiii, Few Western gentlemen were without constant intercourse with the Athlone attorney. **1869** A. MACDONALD *Love, Law & Theol.* xxv. 576 There was a respectable muster of western folks got up for the occasion.

b. Of things: Of or belonging to the south-western counties.

1545 *Rates Custom-ho.* d vj b, A dossen karsay, iij. A westerne dossen, ii. **1653** W. J. *True Gentlew. Delight* 85 To scald Milk after the Western Fashion. **1711** ADDISON *Spect.* No. 129 ¶3 Being a Lawyer of the Middle-Temple, a Cornishman by Birth, I generally ride the Western Circuit. **1782** R. LOCKE (*title*) The Western Rebellion. **1886** KINGTON OLIPHANT *New English* I. 564 The Western dialect appears, as *ch'am, ich cham, vilthy.*

3. a. Having a position relatively west; lying towards or in the west. ***Western Approaches***, the area of sea immediately to the west of Britain; ***Western hemisphere***: see HEMISPHERE 3; ***Western Islands*** = ***Western Isle*** (*a*), (*b*); ***Western Isle***, (*a*) *pl.*, the Hebrides; cf. *west isles* s.v. WEST *a.* 1 c; (*b*) *pl.*, the Azores; †(*c*) Ireland (*rare*$^{-1}$); ***Western Ocean***, the Atlantic.

1398 TREVISA *Barth. De P.R.* VIII. ix. (Tollemache MS.) Amonge þese tripliciteis of houses, þo þat beþ in þe Este ben strenger in here worchynge..þan þe Westren. **1584** POWEL *Lloyd's Cambria* 96 With a great armie out of Mercia and other westerne countries. **1610** HOLLAND *Camden's Brit.* 694 *Pennigent*, which among the Westerne hils mounteth aloft aboue the rest. **1649** J. TAYLOR (Water P.) *Wand. Wonders West* 14 The farthest Western Parish of.. Cornwall. **1671** MILTON *P.R.* IV. 25 He brought our Saviour to the western side Of that high mountain. **1691** SIR G. MACKENZIE *Vind. Govt. Scot.* 12 As to the bringing in the Highlanders on the Western shires..it is answered, that [etc.]. **1697** W. DAMPIER *New Voyage round World* v. 107 The most remarkable places that I did ever hear of for their breeding, is at an Island in the West Indies called Caimanes, and the Isle Ascention in the Western Ocean. **1748** *Anson's Voy.* II. ix. 224 Tempestuous weather from the western quarter. **1758** J. ARMSTRONG *Let.* 21 Oct. in *N. & Q.* (1979) Feb. 44/2, I hope you have had an agreeable View of the Western Isles. **1760** F. FAUQUIER *Let.* 28 Oct. in G. Reese *Official Papers* (1980) 422 The Vessel is cleared out for Gibraltar, and then under pretence of being drove by stress of Weather into Madeira or some of the western Isles. **1775** JOHNSON (*title*) Journey to the Western Islands of Scotland. **1776** GIBBON *Decl. & Fall* I. i. 5 The western isle might be improved into a valuable possession. **1784** COWPER *Task* VI. 484 Where England, stretch'd towards the setting sun,.. O'erlooks the western wave. **1805** in *Naval Documents U.S. Wars with Barbary Powers* (U.S. Office Naval Rec.) (1944) V. 366 It is my opinion, she is competent to be sent across the Western Ocean, and should it be deemed necessary to send her to the Mediterranean, she could be speedily equipped. **1810** J. E. CALDWELL *Tour through Part of Virginia* (ed. 2) (1951) 47 The Azores, or Western Islands, are nine in number. **1810** SCOTT *Lady of L.* I. viii, The Hunter marked that mountain high, The lone lake's western boundary. **1848** B. WEBB *Cont. Ecclesiol.* 117 The plan is quite basilican, containing a western bay between two western towers. **1870** W. H. KNIGHT *W. Australia* 1 The colony of Western Australia was founded on the 1st June, 1829. **1870** GODMAN (*title*) Natural History of the Azores, or Western Islands. **1886** STEVENSON *Kidnapped* xxiv, We were to pass through the western end of the country of Balquhidder. **1920** *Times* 1 Mar. 9/3 The title of Admiral Sir Reginald Tupper..has now been changed to Commander-in-Chief of the Western Approaches. There are three captains, R.N., in charge of Naval Areas under his orders. Captain Denis B. Crampton..commands the Irish Sea Area; Captain William D. Church..the Kingstown Area; and Captain E. G. Lowther-Crofton..the Buncrana Area. **1935** J. MASEFIELD *Victorious Troy* 8 Did you ever see a storm, a real storm, a Western Ocean Hurricane? **1946** W. S. CHURCHILL *Secret Session Speeches* 38 The powerful reinforcement of large-range aircraft..which were sent..to the Western Approaches are now active. **1961** G. FOULSER *Seaman's Voice* ii. 33 Western Ocean gales are notorious for their ferocity. **1976** *Mariner's Mirror* LXII. 177 Sometimes homeward-bound convoys would be routed away from the Western Approaches, the Bay of Biscay, and the English Channel. **1976** *Scotsman* 15 Dec., The rents of the 2000 local authority houses in the Western Isles are to be increased by £39 a year from April. **1979** *N. & Q.* Feb. 44/2 We can now be fairly certain that John Wilkes..also made a journey to the Western Islands of Scotland.

b. of the sky or the horizon, esp. as the place of the sun's setting; also of the sun, or the evening star (cf. WEST *a.* 1).

1591 SHAKS. *Two Gent.* V. i. 1 The Sun begins to guild the westerne skie. **1596** SPENSER *F.Q.* V. ix. 35 As the bright sunne, what time his fierie teme Towards the westerne brim begins to draw. **1633** P. FLETCHER *Purple Isl.* VI. lxxvii, But see, the stealing night, with softly pace, To flie the Westerne Sunne, creeps up the East. **1667** MILTON *P.L.* x. 92 Now was the Sun in Western cadence low From Noon. **1718** PRIOR *Solomon* II. 370 The Sun declin'd had shot his Western Ray. **1747** COLLINS *Ode to Evening* ii, The bright-hair'd Sun Sits in yon western Tent. **1805** SCOTT *Last Minstrel* III. xxiv, Her blue eyes sought the west afar, For lovers love the western star. **1853** A. SMITH *Life-Drama* iv. Poems (1854) 60 From yonder trees I've seen the western sky All washed with fire. **1860** TYNDALL *Glac.* I. xxi. 146 The sun was near the western horizon.

c. Of or belonging to the west; found or produced in the west.

1590 SHAKS. *Mids. N.* II. i. 166 Yet markt I where the bolt of Cupid fell. It fell vpon a little westerne flower. **1764** GOLDSM. *Trav.* 318 My genius spreads her wing, And flies where Britain courts the western spring. **1853** KANE *Grinnell Exp.* xxi. (1856) 161 He himself would take the western search.

†d. ***Western barge*** (***boat***, or ***wherry***), a barge, etc., used on the Thames westward of London. Hence ***Western bargee***, ***pug***, ***man***, a navigator of a Western barge or boat.

1505-6 *Will of J. Rede* (Somerset Ho.), My body..in the nyghte season..to be layde in..a bote or A westurne barge. **1591** LYLY *Endym.* IV. ii, In a Westerne barge, when with a good winde and lustie pugges one may goe ten miles in two daies. **1592-1611** Western pug [see PUG *sb.*[2] 3]. **1603-4** *Act 1 Jas. I* c. 16 §1 Westerne Barges Milboates and all other Vessells ordinarilie serving for other uses then the carryinge of Passengers. **1607** DEKKER & WEBSTER *West-w. Hoe* II. ii, The Lob has his Lasse,..the Westerne-man his Pug, [etc.]. **1666** Western bargee [see BARGEE]. *a* **1704** T. BROWN *Walk Lond. & Westm.* Wks. 1719 III. 324 A Western-Boat, stow'd with a Mixture of both Sexes. *Ibid.* 328 Others crowded into Boxes, like Passengers into a Western Wherry. *Ibid.* 329 He was a Western Bargeman.

e. in the specific names of animals or plants.

1784 PENNANT *Arctic Zool.* (1792) II. 289 Western Duck. *Anas Stelleri*, Pallas. **1824** STEPHENS in Shaw *Gen. Zool.* XII. II. 206 Western Pochard. (*Fuligula dispar.*) **1848** GOULD *Birds Australia* I. Pl. 12 *Ieracidea occidentalis*, Gould. Western Brown Hawk. **1876** F. G. WATERHOUSE in Harcus *S. Austral.* 288 Western gerygone. *Ibid.* 292 Western ground parrakeet.

f. ***Western Front***, the front in Belgium and northern France in the wars of 1914–18 and 1939–45.

[**1914** *Parl. Deb. Written Answers* (*Commons*) 12 Nov. 167 The British casualties in the Western area of the war up to 31st October are, approximately, 57,000. **1914** M. HANKEY *Memo.* 28 Dec. in M. Gilbert *Winston S. Churchill* (1972) III. Compan. I. 337 The remarkable deadlock which has occurred in the western theatre of war.] **1914** LLOYD GEORGE *Memo.* 31 Dec. in *Ibid.* 352 These objects cannot be accomplished by attacks on the Western Front. **1915** *Times* 7 Jan. 9/6 Lord Kitchener..explained that the operations on the Western front have for some time resolved themselves into a state of siege warfare. **1915** A. BENNETT (*title*) Over there: war scenes on the Western Front. **1917** *Weekly Dispatch* 3 June 1/3. (*heading*) Mystery of the Western Front. **1939** *War Weekly* 3 Nov. 35/1 The incalculable factor on the Western Front is the mind of Hitler. **1983** P. A. CROWL *Intelligent Traveller's Guide Historic Britain* x. 502 What was lost were thirty-six Czech divisions delivered to Hitler free of charge at Munich plus a greatly improved German position on her western front.

g. ***Western American***: = ***general American*** s.v. GENERAL *a.* 2 a.

1919 G. P. KRAPP *Pronunc. of Standard Eng. in Amer.* 147 If your own speech is of the Eastern American type, transcribe a passage illustrating it into Western American speech. **1925** —— *Eng. Lang. in Amer.* II. i. 30 The consonant *r* is more distinctly sounded in northern British and Western American. **1936** MENCKEN *Amer. Lang.* (ed. 4) vii. 358 The chief characters of Western, or General American and of New England and Southern American have been indicated. **1959** L. M. MYERS *Guide to Amer. Eng.* (ed. 2) ii. 30 Three major dialect areas have long been recognised in American English—New England, Western or General American, and Southern. Linguistic geographers now prefer the terms Northern, Midland, and Southern.

h. ***Western European Union***, an association formed in 1955 from the former Western Union, with the addition of Italy and (West) Germany, in order to coordinate defence and promote cooperation in economic matters and (until 1960) in social and cultural ones; abbrev. W.E.U. s.v. W 3; ***Western Union***, an association of West European nations (Belgium, France, Luxembourg, the Netherlands, and the United Kingdom) which was formed in 1948 for purposes of military and economic cooperation and became the Western European Union in 1955.

1948 E. BEVIN in *Hansard Commons* 22 Jan. 390 The European Recovery Programme brought all this to a head, and made us all face up to the problem of the future organisation. We did not press the Western Union..in the hope that when we got the German and Austrian peace settlements, agreement between the Four Powers would close the breach between East and West. **1950** *Times* 22 Aug. 4/6 About 50 squadrons of fighters and bombers will take part in the first Western Union air defence exercise. **1954** *Times* 11 Nov. 8/7 Some of the preparations for bringing the Western European Union into existence have been made by a committee in London. **1973** B. COCKS *European Parliament* viii. 67 The Assembly of the international organisation known as Western European Union has a close relationship with the Council of Europe since its entire membership is composed of the Representatives from the seven WEU countries to the Consultative Assembly. **1974** P. GORE-BOOTH *With Great Truth & Respect* 351 Mr Brown has recounted the strategem he employed at a Ministerial Western Union meeting to ensure that the application was formally presented in a way that could not run into procedural objections. **1976** J. WHEELER-BENNETT *Friends, Enemies & Sovereigns* iv. 125 He..expressed considerable concern as to what the effect would be of Germany's rearmament in accordance with her membership of the European Defence Community (or, as it turned out to be, the Western European Union).

4. a. Of or pertaining to the Western or European countries or races as distinguished from the Eastern or Oriental. In mod. use also *spec.* (*a*) applied to the countries of western Europe that opposed Germany in the wars of 1914–18 and 1939–45; (*b*) of, pertaining to, or designating the non-Communist states of Europe and America.

1600 FAIRFAX *Tasso* IV. xvi, These westren rebels, with your power withstand, Plucke vp these weedes, before they ouergroe The gentle garden of the Hebrewes land. **1601** R. JOHNSON *Kingd. & Commw.* (1603) 121 For such an other piece of ground..is not to be found againe in all our western world. **1704** ATTERBURY *Serm.* (1726) I. 339 Those Conspiracies and Rebellions, with which they have.. disturb'd the Quiet of this Western World. **1771** C. BURNEY *Pres. St. Mus. France & Italy* (1773) 272 *note*, As yet there is no regular catalogue of the western MSS. in the Vatican library. **1839** *Penny Cycl.* XIII. 307/1 The little intercourse that subsisted between the inhabitants of India and the Western nations. **1847** MRS. A. KERR tr. *Ranke's Hist. Servia* 449 They who are desirous of ascertaining..the reaction of Eastern on Western affairs, may examine the Egyptian question. **1883** T. WATTS in *19th Cent.* Mar. 413 The mystic type of all Eastern, and yet the mother of all Western, beauty.

(*a*) **1914** *Times* 23 Nov. 9/2 The appearance of Turkey as the ally of Germany and Austria against the Western Powers and Russia necessarily put an end to negotiations between Sofia and Constantinople. **1917** I. F. MARCOSSON *Rebirth of Russia* viii. 141 German imperialism, after having defeated our Western Allies, will turn against us the whole power of its arms. **1938** E. AMBLER *Cause for Alarm* viii. 132 The Nazis and the Fascisti..agreed to present a united front to the western powers. **1940** *Economist* 13 Jan. 51/2 The outbreak of open hostilities between the U.S.S.R. and the Western Powers. **1974** *Encycl. Brit. Macropædia* XIX. 958/1 The Russian Revolution of March..1917 dismayed the western Allies and delighted the Central Powers. *Ibid.* 1006/1 The western Allies' 'Operation Overlord'..took place on June 6, 1944.

(*b*) **1918** *Times* 4 June 5/2 The greatest question in the world to-day is whether Russia is to be abandoned, or whether she is to be saved; whether Western ideals are to prevail in the country whose potential power will be the balance in history. **1947** *Ann. Reg. 1946* 218 A pointed appeal to the Russian people to regard their two Western Allies [*sc.* Great Britain and the United States] as the only blot on the Soviet horizon. *Ibid.* 219 The need [of Russia] for an American loan and the consequent recognition of the desirability of making some concessions to the Western Powers. **1956** *B.B.C. Handbk. 1957* 60 The jamming..of certain language transmissions of the BBC and other Western Bloc broadcasters. **1959** *Daily Tel.* 18 Dec. 1 Expectations of some progress in Western politics rose in Paris to-night on the eve of the 'Western Summit' meetings which will take place here this weekend. **1982** *Ann. Reg. 1981* 67 The fourth [proposal] called on the Soviet Union to accept Western plans for reducing the risks of surprise attack.

Comb. **1880** L. WALLACE *Ben-Hur* 6 After years of residence with the Bedawin, the Western-born..will stop and wait the passing of the stately brute.

b. ***Western Church***, the Latin as distinguished from the Greek or Eastern Church; also, one or other of the early Churches of Western Europe.

1628 BP. HALL *Old Relig.* viii. 72 The Westerne, or Romane Church. **1659** H. THORNDIKE *Wks.* (1846) II. 557 Those controversies about which a settled division is once formed, as now in the western Church. **1838** W. PALMER *Ch. Christ* I. 276 The Western churches..were in communion ..with the great apostolical church of Rome. **1850** NEALE *Hist. Eastern Ch.* I. Introd. 9 The tendency of the Western Church..has been to embroil herself with the kings and kingdoms of this world.

c. Of or belonging to, connected with, characteristic of, the Western Church.

1699 BURNET *39 Articles* xxi. (1700) 201 All the First General Councils were made up for most part of Eastern Bishops; there being a very inconsiderable Number of the Western among any of them. **1755** AMORY *Mem.* (1769) I. 83 *note*, The eastern christians, called in contempt Arians by the western tritheists. **1790** PRIESTLEY *Gen. Hist. Chr. Ch.* II. 311 The Western bishops in general and Liberius himself at their head, were the avowed advocates of the Nicene faith. **1850** NEALE *Hist. Eastern Ch.* I. 317 The whole body of Eastern and Western Liturgies may be divided into four branches. **1853** C. HARDWICK *Chr. Ch., Mid. Age* 265 Gregory VII., who seems to have expected that Crusades, while strengthening his throne, would tend to reunite the Eastern and the Western Christians. **1880** A. P. STANLEY in *Fraser's Mag.* May 600 The Roman Church ..remains the great trunk from which the other communions have been divided in Western Christendom.

d. ***Western Empire***, the more westerly of the two parts into which the Roman Empire was divided in 395 A.D. So ***Western emperor***, etc.

1781 GIBBON *Decl. & F.* xxvii. (1787) III. 38 Maximus would have obtained, without a struggle, the sole possession of the western empire. **1790** PRIESTLEY *Gen. Hist. Chr. Ch.* II. 332 After the death of Constantine, the Western emperors were of the Nicene faith. **1840** MILMAN *Hist. Chr.* III. i. II. 343 In the Western provinces, Gaul, Spain, and Britain..the constitution of society was very different. **1865** BRYCE *Holy Rom. Emp.* 69 Odoacer..did not abolish the Western Empire as a separate power.

e. ***western man*** (also with either one or two initial capitals): man as shaped by the culture and civilization of Western Europe and North America.

1909 CHESTERTON *Orthodoxy* i. 14 An active and imaginative life,..a life such as western man at any rate always seems to have desired. **1927** WYNDHAM LEWIS (*title*) Time and western man. **1962** E. CLEAVER in A. Dundes *Mother Wit* (1973) 10/2 The traditional judgments which Western Man has made..are now..the cause of very serious maladjustments in our society and..the world at large. **1970** C. C. O'Brien *Camus* I. 27 The role often claimed for Camus, as an expression of the conscience of Western man. **1981** *Times Lit. Suppl.* 20 Mar. 321/2 Edward Bond's cloudy gropings towards a view of Western man.

5. a. With *States*: Constituting the more westerly of the United States of America: cf. WEST *sb.* 3 b.

1794 T. Cooper *Some Information respecting Amer.* 8 These parts..furnish yearly a very considerable number of emigrants to the middle and western states. **1829** Everett *Orat. & Sp.* (1850) I. 206 Allow me..to propose the following sentiment:—The Eastern and Western States. **1879** W. Saunders *Through Light Cont.* 131 The conditions under which first-class stall-fed beef may be produced in the Western States.

b. Of or belonging to the Western States. ***western equine encephalitis*** or ***encephalomyelitis***, a mosquito-borne viral encephalitis in the U.S., South America, and eastern Europe that affects chiefly horses but also people and is sometimes fatal, esp. to children; ***western roll*** (Athletics), a method of high-jumping in which the athlete jumps from the inside foot, swings up the other leg, and rolls across the bar on his side; ***Western saddle*** (see quot. 1946); ***western sandwich*** (N. Amer.), a sandwich in which the filling is an omelette containing onion and ham.

Freq. in the names of animals and plants resembling those of the Atlantic coast but whose habitat is west of the Mississippi.

1703 in *Mass. Hist. Soc. Coll.* (1838) 3rd Ser. VII. 61 Letters from Piscataqua come in the Western mail. **1784** G. Washington *Diary* 4 Oct. (1925) II. 326 The Western Settlers—from my own observation—stand as it were on a pivot. **1834** R. C. Sands *Writings* II. 179 One of the favorite and most expressive words of Western invention. **1835** C. F. Hoffman *Winter in West* I. 284 Adding, in western phraseology, 'The way in which folks'll stare, squire, will be a caution'. **1845** P. B. St. John *Trapper's Bride* 69 The Eutaws reined in as the two hunters faced them with the deadly western rifle levelled in their direction. **1871** *Leisure Hour* 336/1 A quality of tobacco, the 'stemmed' variety commonly called in the trade 'Western Strips'. **1880** *Fraser's Mag.* June 747 The changing conditions in agriculture caused by Western competition. **1929** G. M. Butler *Mod. Athletics* viii. 108 (*caption*) The 'western roll'. **1933** *Proc. Soc. Exper. Biol. & Med.* XXXI. 217 (*heading*) A serological difference between Eastern and Western Equine Encephalomyelitis virus. **1946** M. C. Self *Horseman's Encycl.* 346 The Western or cowboy saddle which is similar to that used..in all countries where men spend long hours in the saddle..is characterized by its deep seat, high cantle and pommel... The stirrups are set about midway and the cowboy rides with an almost straight leg. **1959** M. Callaghan in R. Weaver *Canad. Short Stories* (1968) 2nd Ser. 8 He thought of having a western sandwich in the café across the road from the hotel. **1959** *Jrnl. Infectious Dis.* CV. 295 A similar situation may exist with respect to western equine encephalitis infection in swine. **1961** *Canad. Jrnl. Microbiol.* VII. 295 Western equine encephalitis has been a disease of public health importance in Saskatchewan since it was first recognized in 1935. **1964** Western roll [see SCISSORS *sb. pl.* 2 b]. **1964** M. McLuhan *Understanding Media* (1967) xxxi. 341 The varied and rough textures of Western saddles, clothes, hides. **1973** D. Hughes *Along Side Road* xx. 155 He stopped to have a western sandwich and a cup of tea. **1976** *Western Mail* (Cardiff) 27 Nov. (Advt.), Just arrived from America: New selection of Western saddles. **1978** G. Wright *Illustr. Handbk. Sporting Terms* 23/3 The western roll is rarely practised today, the favoured methods being the straddle and the flop. **1983** *Amer. Rev. Respiratory Dis.* CXXVII. 132/3 We report here a patient with western equine encephalitis who developed hypoventilation. **1983** *Amer. Jrnl. Trop. Med. & Hygiene* XXXII. 1130 *Culex tarsalis* was a less competent vector of western equine encephalomyelitis (WEE) virus after 2–3 weeks' extrinsic incubation at 32°C than after incubation at 18° or 25°C.

c. ***western hemlock***, a conifer, *Tsuga heterophylla*, native to the western coast of North America; also, its light brown timber; ***western red cedar***, a large columnar conifer, *Thuja plicata*, native to western North America; also its reddish-brown timber; ***western white pine***, a pine with grey-green needles, *Pinus monticola*, native to high ground in western North America; ***western yellow pine*** = PONDEROSA.

1869 *Amer. Naturalist* III. 410 Western White Pine... I found scattered trees of this beautiful species on the highest parts of the Rocky Mountains. **1886** J. Macoun *Catal. Canad. Plants* I. 461 *J[uniperus] occidentalis*, Hook. Western Red Cedar... I place all our western 'red cedar' under this species. *Ibid.* 471 *T[suga] Mertensiana*, Carr. Western Hemlock... In the Selkirk Mountains it is a tall, beautiful tree, over 150 feet high. **1901** *World's Work* July 888/2 The wood of the western yellow pine..is used by them for mine timbers. **1905** *Bull. Bureau of Forestry* (U.S. Dept. Agric.) LXVI. 33 The rock pine, western red cedar,..have, without doubt, come down from the Rocky Mountains. **1908** N. L. Britton *N. Amer. Trees* 67 Western Hemlock..grows in rich, moist soil. **1923** Western yellow pine [see *heavy-wooded pine* s.v. HEAVY *a.*[1] 30]. **1957** *Handbk. of Softwoods* (Forest Products Res. Lab.) 22 Consignments of western hemlock frequently contain a percentage of fir. **1963** Western hemlock [see KAPUR]. **1969** Western red cedar [see RED CEDAR a]. **1977** *Weekly Times* (Melbourne) 19 Jan. 4/1 (Advt.), The following is included in your kit: Council plans and specifications, flooring,..glazed Western Red Cedar windows, [etc.]. **1978** W. H. Harlow et al. *Textbk. Dendrology* (ed. 6) 66 Western white pine was first observed along the banks of the Columbia and Spokane Rivers in 1831.

d. (Also with capital initial.) Applied to the films and novels called 'westerns' (see sense B. 4 below). orig. *U.S.*

[**1909** *Moving Picture World* 6 Nov. 638 The success of their Western series of last year was abundantly satisfying and added greatly to the reputation of the firm. *Ibid.*, Western subjects, in which the wild and woolly plays the leading part, have won immense popularity.] **1910** *Ibid.* 21 May 834/1 It is almost impossible to criticize these Wild Western films, because cowboys are likely to do almost anything. **1913** *Moving Picture Ann. 1912* 29 Many film makers still turn out great quantities of so-called Western and Indian pictures. **1931** *Ann. Reg. 1930* 49 Garry [*sic*] Cooper has revived the popularity of Western pictures. **1959** *News Chron.* 5 Aug. 6/4 Many Western novels are abominably written. **1967** M. Argyle *Psychol. Interpersonal Behaviour* i. 28 An indirect form of aggression will occur, which may consist of..mere aggression in fantasy, such as watching western films or wrestling matches. **1974** *Encycl. Brit. Micropædia* X. 624/2 The western film can be dated from *The Great Train Robbery* (1905).

6. Directed towards the west; facing westward.

1589 Hakluyt *Voy.* To Rdr. ¶7 Touching the westerne Nauigations, and trauailes of ours, they succeede naturallie in the thirde and last roome. **1706** London & Wise *Retir'd Gard'ner* I. 21 Of the Western Aspect... The Western Exposition begins at half an Hour after Eleven, and continues 'till the Sun sets. **1713** Addison *Guard.* No. 107 ¶8 A ship at sea has no certain method, in either her eastern or western voyages,..to know her Longitude. **1766** *Midnight Spy* vi. 52 The passengers on the western road must furnish him with his demands. **1784** Filson *Kentucky* (1793) 13 Salt river..runs a western course near ninety miles. **1795** Cowper *Moralizer Corrected* 18 Distant a little mile he spied A western bank's still sunny side. **1819** Keats *Eve of St. Mark* 6 And on the western window panes, The chilly sunset faintly told Of unmatur'd green vallies cold. **1886** *Lond. Society* Aug. 128 Hunstanton..is the only watering-place on the east coast of England with a western aspect.

7. *fig.* Of a person's life or days: Declining.

1615 Tomkis *Albumazar* v. vi, Fye, that a gentleman.. Crown'd with such reputation in your youth, Should in your Westerne dayes, loose th' good opinion Of all your friends. **1879** Longf. in *Life* (1891) III. 299 We, who are on the western side of life, must forget ourselves a little, and see with their eyes, who are looking out at the eastern windows.

8. Hinder, posterior. Cf. WEST *adv.* 1 b (*c*).

1829 Marryat *F. Mildmay* xxiv, What have you done to the western side of your gown? **1840** Haliburton *Clockm.* Ser. III. ix, I'd a-kicked them till I kicked their western eends up to their shoulders.

9. *Comb.* (chiefly in sense 4 a), as ***western-educated***, ***-European***, ***-style***, ***-trained***, ***-type*** adjs.

1933 N. Waln *House of Exile* I. vi. 96 A Western educated woman doctor. **1974** M. Fido *R. Kipling* 50/2 Kipling['s].. generation made 'Bengali' almost a synonym for 'western-educated Indian', and always used the word with a touch of contempt. **1949** M. Mead *Male & Female* vi. 132 Almost any Balinese male placed in a series of western-European males would look 'feminine'. **1969** 'E. Lathen' *When in Greece* ii. 17 Greece..was an associate in the Common Market, which would bring every Western European banker into the picture. **1895** *Montgomery Ward Catal.* Spring & Summer 330/1 Three-Horn Western Style Side Saddle. **1953** *Archit. Rev.* CXIV. 255/2 Peking of course offers a complete contrast to such cities as Shanghai where large areas have been covered with western-style multi-storey buildings. **1977** P. Johnson *Enemies of Society* xi. 160 The abolition of western-style academic research, and the substitution of acupuncture for standard medical practice. **1962** E. Snow *Other Side of River* (1963) xlii. 309 Since 1958 all Western-trained doctors have been required to devote at least six months to the study of Chinese medicine. **1958** *Times* 13 Aug. 12/4 In West Africa they hold to the traditional styles, though the more sophisticated often keep western-type frocks in their wardrobe.

B. *sb.*

1. A member of a Western race; a native or inhabitant of the West, as distinguished from an Oriental or Asiatic.

1708 Ockley *Hist. Saracens* (1848) 337 The folly of the Westerns in despising the wisdom of the Eastern nations. **1863** *Smith's Dict. Bible* II. 295/2 (*Medicine*) He [Hippocrates] extols the discernment of Orientals above Westerns, and of Asiatics above Europeans, in medical diagnosis. **1882** J. Neil *Palestine* 44 The former figure 'wings of the morning' to a Western is not a little obscure. **1884** *Athenæum* 12 Jan. 54/3 It may not be altogether superfluous to remind Westerns that Russia is now celebrating the three hundredth anniversary of her first printer, Ivan Fedorof. **1917** T. R. Glover *From Pericles to Philip* vii. 218 The employment of the camel in war strikes the Western oddly.

2. A member of the Western or Latin Church.

1860 W. Bright *Hist. Ch.* 313–451, 50 Among the bishops who had received the sympathy of the Westerns was Paul of Constantinople. **1865** Pusey *Truth Engl. Ch.* 60 S. Basil.. blamed the Westerns for their 'pride, haughtiness, precipitancy'. **1902** J. K. Mann *Hist. Popes* I. I. 30 Despite the express declaration of Justinian..some of the Westerns persisted in maintaining [etc.].

3. *U.S.* An inhabitant or native of the Western States.

1846 G. Warburton *Hochelaga* II. 22 There were Southerners and Northerners, Downeasters, and Westerns. **1888** Bryce *Amer. Commw.* III. lxv. II. 480 He was a raw rude Western, a man of the people.

4. (Also with capital initial.) A film or novel belonging to a distinct genre in which life in the American West in the nineteenth century is portrayed, usu. through idealized stock situations and characters, esp. cattlemen (cowboys) and gun-fights. Cf. sense A. 5 d above. orig. *U.S.*

1912 *Moving Picture World* 27 July 306 (Advt.), 'The Fight at The Mill'... A powerful Western, distinctly unusual among typical 'Westerns' containing a beautiful story and a dashing Indian battle that will interest and instruct. **1915** [see SUPE]. **1918** *Wells Fargo Messenger* VI. 178/1 What would the good old 'Western' be without the historic Wells Fargo stage coach and its treasure box? **1923** *Time* 11 June 15/1 Love stories are their first choice, comedies second, society life as known to the De Mille brothers third, and then come the Westerns. **1927** *Sat. Rev. Lit.* 15 Oct. 232 (Advt.), The Gun-Slinger by George M. Johnson. A Western with the kick of a .45. **1930** *Publishers' Weekly* 8 Feb. 689 (Advt.), Five sure-shot Westerns... Salesmen and booksellers everywhere report to us a keen and growing demand for this type of story. **1954** E. E. Cummings *Let.* 9 Mar. (1969) 227 'William S. Hart' was a vastly popular..hero of our early Westerns: i.e. melodramatic movies featuring terrific battles between noble & wicked hardriding sharpshooting super cowboys. **1958** *Listener* 9 Jan. 60/1 Twenty-five per cent of the best television time is still given over to 'Westerns'. **1962** L. Deighton *Ipcress File* xviii. 110 On the army table were a few books; German grammar..two paperback westerns. **1977** B. Pym *Quartet in Autumn* xviii. 171 Watching a Western on the other channel.

C. *adv.* *Equestrianism.* In the manner of a cowboy; in a relaxed style with a deep-seated saddle and almost straight legs.

1972 *Country Life* 5 Oct. 817/1 In a year Lady Sarah was so used to riding Western that she found it almost strange to revert to English for hunting. **1980** *Times* 28 June 13/7 Riding western is not like riding Badminton style.

†**western**, *sb.*[2] *Obs.* [Old Northumbrian *wœstern*, var. of OE. *wœsten*, *wésten*, f. the stem **wōst-*: cf. WESTE *a.* The ending *-ern* for *-en(n* also appears in *éfern* EVEN *sb.*, *fæstern* FASTEN *sb.* and **lenctern* LENTEN *sb.*] A desert, wilderness.

c **950** *Lindisf. Gosp.* Matt. iii. 1 In woestern iudeæ [*in deserto iudaeae*]. *Ibid.* Mark viii. 4 On woestern [*in solitudine*]. *c* **1200** *Trin. Coll. Hom.* 129 Ich am his steuene þe remeð in þis westerne. *Ibid.*, For þi is þis westren forgrouwen mid brimbles and mid þornes. *c* **1375** *Sc. Leg. Saints* xviii. (*Egipciane*) 1298 ȝarne he lukyt one ilke syd of þat westerne, brad & wyd.

†**western**, *sb.*[3] *Obs.* Also 6 **westorne**. [Of obscure origin.] The sand-martin, *Cotile riparia*.

1556 Withals *Dict.* (1562) 5/2 A westorne or marten, whiche breedeth in water bankes, *riparia*. **1589** Rider *Bibl. Schol.* I. 1702 Birds, A Marten, or westerne. *Ibid.* 1705 A westorne, vide marten. **1668** Charleton *Onomast.* 90 *Hirundo Riparia*..the Sand, or Bank Marten, or Western.

ˈ**western**, *v.* [f. WESTERN *a.*] *intr.* Of the sun: To decline in the west. (Cf. WESTER *v.* 1.) Hence ˈ**westerning** *ppl. a.*

1851 Pugin *Chancel Screens* 83 The warm tints of a westerning sun. **1904** *Daily Chron.* 28 Oct. 5/4 The sun was rapidly westerning.

†**westernais**, *adv.* *Obs.*$^{-1}$ [App. an alteration of OF. *bestorneis*.] Wrongfully, perversely.

13.. *E.E. Allit. P.* A. 307 ȝe setten hys wordez ful westernays þat louez no þynk [= thing] bot ȝe hit syȝe.

westerner (ˈwɛstənə(r)). [f. WESTERN *a.* + -ER.]

1. An inhabitant or native of the Western States of America.

1837 Ht. Martineau *Soc. Amer.* III. 21 'We are apt to think,' said a westerner to me, 'that..we are just as great and good.' **1872** Howells *Wedd. Journ.* (1892) 196 Those expressions of surprise at the existence of civilisation in a westerner which westerners find it so hard to receive graciously. **1888** *Century Mag.* Feb. 502/2 Cowboys, like most Westerners, occasionally show remarkable versatility in their tastes and pursuits.

2. One belonging to a western race, as distinguished from an Oriental.

1880 W. James in *Atlantic Monthly* Oct. 449/2 *Not* to fall back on the gods, where a proximate principle may be found, has with us Westerners long since become the sign of an efficient..intellect. **1910** *Times* 5 Mar. 6/1 The crowd crushing at the window at Peking clamouring for tickets..is a spectacle which affords constant amusement to the Westerner. **1919** Rihbany *Syrian Christ* 146 Some Westerners have an exaggerated idea of Oriental generosity.

3. One who lives in, or is a native of, the west part of a country.

1905 *Daily News* 24 Apr. 2 The Westerners [Gloucester and Bristol ringers] hope to eclipse this performance with a peal containing 12,345 changes.

4. *Hist.* An advocate of or believer in the concentration of forces on the Western Front during the war of 1914–18.

1928 F. B. Maurice *Rawlinson of Trent* p. xi, Upon the problems of the Great War, Rawlinson has naturally much light to throw. Who was right, the Easterner or the Westerner? **1931** W. S. Churchill *World Crisis* VI. xix. 282 Falkenhayn was a convinced and inveterate 'Westerner'. **1960** *Times Lit. Suppl.* 20 May 318/3 Captain Falls is a firm 'Westerner' although he believes that the Dardanelles enterprise was 'a well-inspired venture'. **1977** G. H. Cassar *Kitchener* xiv. 295 Kitchener's difficulties were exacerbated by the two prevailing schools of strategical thought, the Easterners and the Westerners.

5. a. *Hist.* A 19th-century Russian who adopted or advocated Western attitudes and behaviour.

1949 I. Deutscher *Stalin* vi. 207 But Lenin remained a 'Westerner' in several senses. **1950** E. H. Carr *Bolshevik Revolution* I. i. 8 The westerners held that it was the destiny of Russia, as a backward country, to learn from the west.

b. One belonging to the non-Communist West.

1964 M. McLuhan *Understanding Media* (1967) xxi. 222 Are we to suppose that this kind of media illiteracy is characteristic only of Westerners, and that Russians know how to correct the bias of the medium? **1975** P. Theroux *Great Railway Bazaar* xxx. 330, I was now the only Westerner on the train.

'westernism. [f. western *a.* + -ism.]

1. An idiom or expression peculiar to the Western States of America.

1838 *Knickerbocker* XI. 447, I now recollect but few specimens of Jack's *westernisms*, and these I think were not his best. **1884** *Home Missionary* (N.Y.) Jan., A Westernism originating in Nebraska, I believe. **1885** *American* IX. 378 It will become better known if he keeps his strength, as an alleged Westernism has it. **1886** *Harper's Mag.* Oct. 773 'It hasn't—ah—panned out.' He involuntarily made a droll face as he uttered this Westernism.

2. Western characteristics, practices, etc., as distinguished from Eastern or Oriental.

1892 W. W. Peyton *Memor. Jesus* 298 Our theology is too Eastern: we want our Westernism in it. **1907** *Daily Chron.* 20 Feb. 3/4 A great moral conflict between the teachings of two schools, the Slavophils and Westernism.

westernize ('wɛstənaɪz), *v.* [f. western *a.* + -ize.] **a.** *trans.* To make western in character; esp. to make (an eastern country or race) more western in regard to its institutions, ideas, etc.

1842 *Tait's Mag.* IX. 617 She herself pleads to having become so Westernized, as no longer to be a competent painter of Western peculiarities. **1848** *Eerie Laird* 247 A remnant of it [*sc.* the palace], rather clumsily Westernized, is now the official habitation of the British resident at Delhi. **1888** *Sat. Rev.* 22 Sept. 340/1 Bulgaria is being..more and more Westernized.

b. *intr.* To become western in character. *rare.*

1903 L. F. Ward *Pure Sociol.* 33 Some of the nations of the East, notably Japan, are rapidly westernizing.

Hence **'westernized** *ppl. a.*; **'westernizer**, one who makes a country or culture more Western; **'westernizing** *vbl. sb.* and *ppl. a.*; also **,westerni'zation.**

1893 *Sketch* 1 Feb. 38/2 The westernising of India is.. shown in the most curious ways. **1900** *Speaker* 9 June 284/2 The Young Turkish or Westernizing party. **1903** Fairbairn in *Camb. Mod. Hist.* II. xix. 701 He regarded Aristotle as a westernised Mohammadan rather than as a Greek. **1904** *Daily Chron.* 19 Feb. 3/3 The process that is generally called the Westernisation of Japan. **1935** *Times Lit. Suppl.* 2 May 287/2 French and English incursions.. entered [Afghanistan] from the East, and..carried Dravidian ideas with them against that tide of Westernizers of whom Alexander was one of the earliest. **1958** *Listener* 27 Nov. 864/2 Arab Westernizers. **1964** *Economist* 13 June 1251/2 Ch'en Tu-hsiu was a westerniser. **1976** *Times Lit. Suppl.* 23 Apr. 490/3 The dispute between Slavophiles and Westernizers, originally a literary controversy, spawned a vast secondary literature, first in Russia and then in the wider world.

westernly ('wɛstənlɪ), *a.* Now *rare.* [f. western *a.* + -ly[1]. Cf. westerly *a.*]

1. Situated in or towards the west.

1622 Blundevil *Exerc., Descr. Univ. Maps* (ed. 6) 790 The Westernly [1597 Westerly] 18 Meridians. **1657** J. Watts *Scribe* etc. *Dipper Sprinkled* 50 Our Westernly Northen Climate is colder much then those Easternly Southern.

2. Directed towards the west; extending westwards.

c **1595** Capt. Wyatt *Dudley's Voy.* (Hakl. Soc.) 52 Wee.. after altered that course and bear for the coste of Florida, a more westernlie course. **1643** G. Wilde *Serm. bef. Ho. Comm.* 3 Mar. 27 To look East upon the Rising Laity, and to reflect a Westernly Glance upon the declining Clergy. **1848** B. Webb *Cont. Ecclesiol.* 482 Thus nineteen [churches] have an easternly orientation:—and exactly nineteen also have a westernly direction. **1897** *Daily News* 21 May 5/5 The road..next turns in a westernly direction.

'westernly, *adv.* [f. western *a.* + -ly[2].]

†**1.** Towards the west. *Obs.*

1590 Greene *Never too late* (1600) B 3 b, France..beeing westernly seated neere great Brittaine. **1691** Ray *Creation* 136 Why the same Eclipse..should be seen to them that live one degree more Westernly.

2. In a Western manner.

1588 [see Kentishly *adv.*]. **1976** M. H. Kingston *Woman Warrior* (1977) 59 The one [Chinese] faculty member in the western suit smiles westernly. **1982** C. Thomas *Jade Tiger* iii. 59 A stylised, dignified, almost Westernly-handsome Chinese. **1983** *Christian Science Monitor* 15 Feb. 12/1 Dressing more stylishly—and often, more Westernly—is a preoccupation... Young Russians pass quick and critical judgement on the clothes of their peers.

'westernmost, *a.* [f. western *a.* + -most. Cf. westermost.] Farthest towards the west; most westerly.

1703 *Lond. Gaz.* No. 3937/3 The Westernmost Rocks of the Minques. **1778** Forster *Observ. Voy. World* 197 There is a small species of scorpion in the tropical isles of the South-Sea, but more common to the Westernmost than the Society Isles. **1846** G. Warburton *Hochelaga* II. 191 Not more than four thousand square miles of all this westernmost country is capable of cultivation. **1884** Helen Jackson *Ramona* ii, The two westernmost rooms had been added on. **1892** J. L. Allen *Blue-Grass Region* etc. (1900) 259 Pine Mountain, the westernmost ridge of the Alleghany system.

westernness ('wɛstənnɪs). Also with capital initial. [f. western *a.* + -ness.] The quality of belonging to a Western country or culture, or having Western attitudes and ideas.

1953 *Essays in Crit.* III. 132 We become aware..in the work of Conrad of the co-existence of two 'moralities': that derived from a simple tradition of 'Westernness'..and that derived from an awareness of the force..of *'égoïsme'* in a decaying order. **1977** P. Laslett *Family Life & Illicit Love in Earlier Generations* i. 13 Westernness or any other cultural attribute.

westerveldite ('wɛstəvɛldaɪt). *Min.* [f. the name of Jan *Westerveld* (1905–62), Dutch geologist + -ite[1].] An orthorhombic arsenide of iron or iron and nickel (see quot. 1972).

1972 I. S. Oen et al. in *Amer. Mineralogist* LVII. 354 A Co-bearing nickel-rich iron monoarsenide corresponding in composition and structure to a Ni-rich member of the orthorhombic FeAs-(Fe,Ni)As solid solution series of synthetic alloys occurs in chromite-niccolite ores from La Gallega, Spain. The name westerveldite is proposed for minerals in this solid solution series. **1977** *Neues Jahrb. f. Mineral. Abhandlungen* CXXX. 209 Recently westerveldite with the ideal composition FeAs was found at four localities within the Ilimaussaq alkaline intrusion in South Greenland.

westfalite ('wɛstfəlaɪt). Also -falit, -phalite. [ad. G. *Westfalit*, f. *Westfalisch-* (Westphalian), in the name of the original manufacturing company.] An explosive compound, used in three varieties, of which the principal ingredient was ammonium nitrate.

1896 *Glasgow Herald* 29 Feb. 7/7 The high explosives, ammonite..securite, and westfalit. **1896** *Daily News* 5 Dec. 7/4 The manufacture of the high explosive known as Westphalite. **1906** Sanford *Nitro-Explosives* (ed. 2) 294 West Falite No. 1. West Falite No. 2. **1909** Guttmann *Manuf. Explosives* 52 Saxonite..Bobbinite..Westfalite.

†**west-half.** *Obs.* [OE. *westhealf*: see west *adv.* and half *sb.*] The western side, the west.

c **893** Ælfred *Oros.* I. i. §8 On westhealfe [is] se sæ þe mon hætt Proponditis. *a* **1122** *O.E. Chron.* (Laud MS.) an. 1016 [Hie] droȝon heora scipa on west healfe þære brycge. *c* **1205** Lay. 29287 An æst halue, an west halue, wa wes Brutten þere. *a* **1300** *Cursor M.* 20993 On þe west half o þat cite Birid o cristen men was he. **13..** *K. Alis.* 6334 (Laud MS.) A Folk þer woneþ in þe west half þat eteþ noiþer Cow ne chalf. **1375** Barbour *Bruce* XVI. 550 Quhill thai, besyde Enuerkethyne, On vest half, toward Dunfermlyne, Tuk land.

West Highland. Used *attrib.* and *absol.* to designate animals associated with the West Highlands of Scotland, as (*a*) a breed of cattle also called kyloes (see kyloe); (*b*) a kind of terrier (see Poltalloch).

1875 *Encycl. Brit.* I. 389/1 The Kyloes or West Highland cattle are the most prominent of this group [*sc.* mountain breeds]. **1906** *Our Dogs* 15 Sept. 548/1 White West Highland Terriers.—Here truly may be written there is ample room for improvement. **1910** 'Saki' *Reginald in Russia* 28 A lady..was expressing to me..her interest in West Highland terriers. **1950** [see Poltalloch]. **1953** A. Fraser *Beef Cattle Husbandry* ix. 122 This breed, sometimes called the 'West Highland' or 'Kyloe', is descended from the native breed of the Scottish highlands. **1968** P. Dickinson *Skin Deep* ix. 174 She's a nice lass, Roedean, breeds West Highlands down at Sonning. **1976** *Daily Record* (Glasgow) 4 Dec. 25/3 (Advt.), West Highland pups..suitable for Christmas. **1978** *Country Life* 24 Aug. 489/3 The White West Highland was let out of the front door.

So **West Highlander**, a kyloe.

1832 *Chambers's Edin. Jrnl.* I. 70/2 On many farms I observed a variety..resembling the heavy class of our West Highlanders. **1882** [see kyloe]. **1979** *Country Life* 22 Nov. 1950/1 No breed of cattle more perfectly graces its native habitat than the West Highlander.

westie ('wɛstɪ). Also **westy.** [f. west *a.* + -ie, -y[6].] A West Highland white terrier.

1959 *Observer* 1 Feb. 12 The 'Westie' is one of the few terriers to maintain its position. **1978** *Country Life* 24 Aug. 489/3 The Westy returned and sat down. **1979** *Daily Mail* 26 Oct. 25/4 Mr Definitely-Disgusting..[is] particularly partial to 'Westies' as he calls West Highlands.

westinary, error for Westmony (q.v.).

West 'India. Now only *attrib.* Also 7 *pl.* India's. [west *a.* Cf. East India.]

†**1.** = West Indies. Also *pl. Obs.*

1555 Eden (*title*) The Decades of the newe worlde or west India. **1578** T. Nicholas (*title*) The Pleasant Historie of the Conquest of the Weast India, now called new Spayne. **1598** *Cures of Diseased* C, A great Fruit that growes in the West India, called *Pina.* **1648** Gage (*title*) The English-American his Travail by Sea and Land: or, A new Survey of the West India's.

2. *attrib.* (sometimes hyphened.) Of or pertaining to, connected with, the West Indies. ***West India Islands***, the islands lying between North and South America.

1656 Whitelocke *Mem.* (1853) IV. 281 An account of the engagement with the West India Spanish fleet. **1709** *Lond. Gaz.* No. 4522/3 Three other of the West-India Ships were also taken. **1731** Arbuthnot *Aliments* (1735) 177 The West-India dry Gripes are perhaps occasion'd by the too great Quantities of Acids. **1757** [Burke] *Europ. Settlem. Amer.* vii. xxviii. II. 273 All sorts of lumber for the West-India trade. **1774** E. Long *Jamaica* III. 806 West India Tea—*Capraria, erecta ramosa* &c. **1797** *Encycl. Brit.* (ed. 3) I. 644/1 In Jamaica and others of the West India islands. **1818** *Mathews's Bristol Directory* 28 West India Brokers. *Ibid.* 41 West India Merchants. **1847** C. Brontë *Jane Eyre* xxvii, The thin partitions of the West-India house.

West-'Indiaman. [f. prec. 2.] A vessel engaged in the West India trade.

1689 *Treas. P.* III. 196 (P.R.O.) The French Fleet has taken 5 dutch West Indiamen that came from Cuiresoe. **1769** *Ann. Reg.* 161 The steward of a West-Indiaman. **1794** *Plan London-Dock* 11 Whether the London-Dock..cannot be of extensive usefulness to West Indiamen..? **1818** Scott *Rob Roy* xxvii, A voluminous silk handkerchief, like the main-sail of one of his own West-Indiamen. **1861** Brougham *Brit. Const.* xx. 393 Compare the numbers of men in a West Indiaman and in a Baltic or Hamburgh trader.

West 'Indian, *sb.* and *a.* Also 9 (*vulgar*) -injine; 20— (as one word) **Westindian.** [f. West India.]

1. *sb.* †**a.** *pl.* The original inhabitants of the West Indies. *Obs.*

1584 R. Scot *Discov. Witchcr.* III. xv. 50 The West Indians doo the like. **1597** J. King *Jonas* (1618) 177 Those [cruelties] that were practiced by the Spanish nation vpon the west Indians. **1618** W. Lawson *New Orch. & Gard.* xii. (1623) 41 Also I read in the History of the West-Indians, out of Peter-Martyr, That [etc.]. **1658** Phillips, *Weroance*, a name given to any great Lord, among the West-Indians.

b. An inhabitant or native of the West Indies, of European origin or descent.

1661 E. Hickeringill *Jamaica* 100 The Major part of the Inhabitants being old West-Indians. **1757** [Burke] *Europ. Settlem. Amer.* vi. x. II. 112 In the foregoing manner the West-Indian would state some part of what he conceives to be his grievances. **1764** Foote *Patron* I. (1781) 11 This is one of Lofty's companions, a West-Indian of an over-grown fortune. **1771** Cumberland (*title*) The West Indian. **1817** Jane Austen *Sanditon* (1925) 78 And I have heard that's very much the case with your West-injines. **1873** B. Harte *Fiddletown*, etc. 97 Yet here sat that young West Indian.. Alexander Hamilton. **1876** Geo. Eliot *Deronda* I. iii, She had no notion how her maternal grandfather got the fortune inherited by his two daughters; but he had been a West Indian—which seemed to exclude further question.

c. A person of West Indian ancestry.

1928 *Times* 25 June 5/1 The out-cricket of the West Indians on Saturday indicates that the compliment, which has been paid to them, has not been prematurely offered. **1957** *Times* 18 Feb. 4/7 Statistics show that more than 26,000 West Indians migrated to Britain during 1956. **1961** *Ann. Reg. 1960* 122 In his message to West Indians on Christmas Day the Prime Minister of the Federation, Sir Grantly Adams, spoke of West Indian unity. **1971** *Observer* 21 Feb. 5/1 The Scots West Indian... Born in Edinburgh, he has Jamaican blood from his father's side. **1973** *Montserrat Mirror* 23 Mar. 5/2 Trinidad is the home of calypso but this form of music belongs to all Westindians. **1981** *Westindian World* 31 July 2/3 My findings demolished a myth about Westindians.

2. *adj.* **a.** Of or pertaining to, situated in, connected with, the West Indies.

1611 Cotgr., s.v. *Araroye*, A round..ornament of feathers, worne by the West-Indian Sauages at their backes. **1647** N. Ward *Simple Cobler* 4 The Sub-planters of a West-Indian Island. **1667** Earl Orrery *St. Lett.* (1742) 239 The West-Indian fleet consists of an hundred and thirty five sail. **1681** Grew *Musæum* I. §iv. iv. 80 A Great Nest of an other West-Indian Bird. *a* **1700** B. E. *Dict. Cant. Crew, Rum*,..a West-Indian Drink stronger than Brandy. **1754** H. Walpole *Let. to Bentley* 3 Nov., The West Indian war has thrown me into a new study. **1821** T. Dwight *Trav.* II. 458 Horses they sell at New-Haven and Hartford for the West-Indian market. **1835** Moodie *Ten Yrs. S. Afr.* I. 20 Some cold rum-punch..made..in the West Indian fashion. **1885** Tennyson *Wreck* iii. 6 A rich West-Indian isle.

b. in specific names.

1781 Latham *Synopsis Birds* I. I. 287 West Indian Green Parrot. **1804** Shaw *Gen. Zool.* V. 108 West Indian Pike. **1815** Burrow *Elem. Conchol.* 200 *Voluta Musica*, West Indian Music Shell. **1864** Grisebach *Flora W. Ind. Isl.* 788 West-Indian-bark, *Exostemma caribæum.*

Hence **West Indianness**, West Indian quality or character.

1953 *Caribbean Q.* III. III. 181 We are..still trying to discover what..makes us characteristically West Indian, or if you like, what is the essence of our West Indianness. **1972** Ramchand & Gray *West Indian Poetry* 89 The West Indian poet's confidence about his West Indian-ness.

West Indie, obs. var. West Indy.

West 'Indies. [west *a.* See Indies and cf. East Indies.] †**a.** The parts of America first discovered by Columbus and other early navigators. *Obs.* **b.** The West India Islands.

1555 Eden *Decades* (Arb.) 208 Suche thynges as I haue seene in yowre Empyre of the West Indies. **1577** Eden & Willes (*title*) The History of Trauayle in the West and East Indies. **1594** Blundevil *Exerc., Descr. Univ. Maps* (1597) 368 b, America, which we now call the West Indies. **1625** Bacon *Ess., Vicis. Things* ¶1 The great Burnings by Lightnings, which are often in the West Indies. **1647** Cowley *Mistr., Leaving Me* 15 Mine too her rich West-Indies were below, Where Mines of Gold and endless treasures grow. **1662** Stillingfl. *Orig. Sacræ* III. iv. §4 All those strange species of animals seen in the West-Indies. **1731** Miller *Gard. Dict.* s.v. *Melo*, Those Melons which are produc'd in the West-Indies are generally very large. **1766** Goldsm. *Vicar* xx, He was heir to a fortune..left him by an uncle in the West Indies. **1837** Dickens *Pickw.* xxvii, Providing the infant negroes in the West Indies with flannel waistcoats.

Comb. **1616** Capt. J. Smith *Descr. New Eng.* Wks. (Arb.) 225 The next was a West Indies man, of 160 tuns. [Cf. next and West Indiaman.]

West Indy, -ie, obs. or vulgar var. WEST INDIA.
West Indy man = WEST INDIAMAN.
1616 CAPT. J. SMITH *Descr. New Eng.* Wks. (Arb.) 225 Within two dayes after, we were haled by two West Indy men. *Ibid.* 226 Vnder the colour to take Pirats and West Indie men. **1642** HOWELL *For. Trav.* (Arb.) 45 Her West Indy Fleet..is subject to casualties of Sea. **1650** E. WILLIAMS *Virgo Triumphans* 42 The West Indie Potatoe. **1817** JANE AUSTEN *Sanditon* (1925) 77 A West Indy Family and a school. That sounds well.

westing ('wɛstɪŋ), *vbl. sb.* [f. WEST *adv.* or *v.*]
1. *Naut.* The net distance made by a vessel towards the west. (Cf. EASTING *sb.* 1.)
1628 DIGBY *Voy. Mediterr.* (Camden) 91 But for easting and westing, great diligence is required not to fall into error. **1669** STURMY *Mariner's Mag.* IV. xvii. 202 In the eighth, ninth, tenth, and eleventh Columns, set down the Northing, Southing, Easting, and Westing. **1690** LEYBOURN *Curs. Math.* 641 The Lesser Easting or Westing, subtracted from the Greater, shall give you the Departure. **1726** SHELVOCKE *Voy. round World* 384 The Westing we should gain in going to California would make amends for what we should lose. **1777** G. FORSTER *Voy. round World* II. 579 After leaving Ascension we made a good deal of westing. **1820** SCORESBY *Arctic Reg.* II. 369 A decrease of the variation of the compass, tends to give them more westing than they calculate upon. **1839** MARRYAT *Phantom Ship* ix, Their easting and westing could only be computed by dead reckoning. **1858** *Merc. Marine Mag.* V. 257 Furthest westing N. of Equator 26½° W.
2. Direction or course towards the west.
1825 SCOTT 29 June in *Fam. Lett.* (1894) II. 280 How sets the vane..? Due north I hope, with a westing towards Abbotsford. **1857** LIVINGSTONE *Trav.* xviii. 330 The westing we were making brought us among people who are frequently visited by the Mambari, as slave-dealers. **1872** —— *Let. to N.Y. Herald* (Feb.) in *Daily News* 29 July 5/6, I..at last found that the mighty river left its westing and flowed right away to the north.
b. *Astron.* Attainment of the western limit of the apparent course.
1883 PROCTOR *Gt. Pyramid* iii. 139 The easting, southing, westing, and northing of heavenly bodies.
3. Of winds: The fact of blowing from, or shifting to, the west.
1860 MAURY *Phys. Geog. Sea* (Low) iv. 79 Hitherto winds with westing in them have been most prevalent. *Ibid.* v. 127 The forces of diurnal rotation assist to give these winds their westing. **1883** *Encycl. Brit.* XVI. 144/1 The westing of these great aerial currents is due to..the rotation of the earth round its axis.

'westing, *ppl. a.* [f. as prec.] Tending towards the west.
1669 STURMY *Mariner's Mag.* IV. ii. 147 In the like manner you must do if your Course were North or Westing. **1836** *Scott. Monthly Mag.* July 207 The westing sun's beam Cast gold on the grass. **1880** MRS. WHITNEY *Odd or Even?* xxvi, A shade against the westing sun.

Westinghouse ('wɛstɪŋhaʊs). The name of George *Westinghouse* (1846–1914), U.S. inventor and manufacturer, used *attrib.* and *absol.* to designate a kind of air brake he invented in 1868 for use on railway trains, operated by compressed air on a fail-safe principle.
a **1877** KNIGHT *Dict. Mech.* I. 356/1 The Westinghouse Atmospheric Brake..was patented in 1869, and has been adopted on many railway lines in the United States and Europe. **1886** *Encycl. Brit.* XX. 248/2 The Westinghouse brake was greatly in advance of previously existing systems. **1933** *Times Lit. Suppl.* 2 Nov. 738/3 Many will regret the gradual abandonment of the Westinghouse brake on steam-hauled trains. **1949** D. M. DAVIN *Roads from Home* I. v. 75, I jammed on the Westinghouse, saying to myself I'd look a fine bloody fool if I'd stopped the train for nothing. **1967** G. F. FIENNES *I tried to run a Railway* iv. 40 Only the Stratford District had kept the Westinghouse brake.
Hence **Westing'housian** *a.* (*fig. nonce-use*).
1948 V. NABOKOV in *New Yorker* 31 July 20/1 The train stopped with a long-drawn Westinghousian sigh.

'westland. Chiefly *Sc.* Also *Sc.* 6 **vestland,** 6, 9 **wastland,** 8 **westlan'**. (Cf. WESTLIN *a.*) [f. WEST *a.* (or OE. *west-*) + LAND *sb.*[1]]
1. The western part of a country; *esp.* the West of Scotland.
1489 *Acc. Ld. High Treas. Scot.* I. 107 To pass with letteres of the Kingis for the Lordis of the Westlande. *a* **1578** LINDESAY (Pitscottie) *Chron. Scot.* (S.T.S.) I. 291 He passit ..to the toune of Air and to the pairtis of the wastland. **1818** SCOTT *Hrt. Midl.* xxxv, He uses maist partly the west-land of Scotland. **1894** K. HEWAT *Little Scot. World* v. 58 It was understood Montrose would make a descent on the Westland.
2. *attrib.* **a.** Of persons: Living in, coming from, the West of Scotland.
c **1470** HENRY *Wallace* VII. 776 A hundyr fyrst till him selff he has tayne, Off westland men. *Ibid.* x. 308. **1522** Q. MARGARET in *MS. Cott. Calig.* B. VI. fol. 270b, On the on syde, the vestland lordys and my lord of Angus vas forth. *a* **1578** LINDESAY (Pitscottie) *Chron. Scot.* (S.T.S.) I. 205 All the rest of the norland men and wastland men mett the King at Stirling. **1651** SIR A. JOHNSTON (Ld. Wariston) Diary (S.H.S.) II. 74 The vyle band which seven Westland gentle-men had subscryved. **1818** SCOTT *Br. Lamm.* xxiv, When he raised his militia..against the wrang-headed wastland whigs. **1827** —— *Two Drovers* i, The strong west-landman laughed aloud. **1828–43** TYTLER *Hist. Scot.* (1864) II. 239 On the rear division were the westland and Stirlingshire men.
b. Of places: Situated in the west.
1523 Q. MARGARET in *MS. Cott. Calig.* B. VI. fol. 440 The erl of Huntlay hath all the ruil of the north partys, the erl of Lenoss all the vestland part. **1650** J. NICOLL *Diary* (Bannatyne Club) 30 Ane Associatioun concludit and drawn up among the Westland schyres. *c* **1670** in *Jrnl. Friends Hist. Soc.* XXI. 69 Throwout the Westland presbiteries belonging to that synod [*sc.* Glasgow]. **1834** *Tait's Mag.* I. 608/1 Had she not given..reason to believe she thought them the greatest people on Westland ground. **1875** MORRIS *Æneids* VIII. 148 All the Westland earth beneath their yoke shall lie.
c. Proceeding from the west; blowing from the west, westerly.
1650 SIR A. JOHNSTON (Ld. Wariston) *Diary* (S.H.S.) II. 30 They censured the Westland Remonstrance mor nor Northland Band. **1847** EMERSON *Poems, Monadnoc* 136 Smoking in a squalid room Where yet the westland breezes come.
Hence **'westlander; -landways** *adv.*
a **1676** H. GUTHRIE *Mem.* (1702) 238 The West-Landers advanced towards Edinburgh. *Ibid.* 240 The Westlanders.. were all poor ignorant Creatures, taken from their Husbandry. **1814** SCOTT *Wav.* xxxvi, A few shots were exchanged betwixt them and the Westlanders. **1820** —— *Monast.* xxxv, Instead of that comes news that he has gone west-landways about some tuilzie in Ayrshire.

'westlin, *a. Sc.* Also 8 **-len.** [var. of *westlan'* WESTLAND 2.] Western; westerly.
17.. *Patie & Peggy* Chorus in Ramsay *Tea-t. Misc.*, Sun, gallop down the westlin skies. **1721** RAMSAY *Keitha* 27 Ye westlin Winds that gently us'd to play On her white Breast. **1728** —— *To Starrat* 6 Welcome, as Westlen Winds, or Berries ripe. **1785** BURNS *Ep. to Davie* 6 To..spin a verse or twa o' rhyme, In hamely, westlin' jingle. **1813** HOGG *Queen's Wake, Kilmeny* ii, When the fringe was red on the westlin hill. **1830** GALT *Lawrie T.* I. ii, The goodwill of the westlin winds. **1898** J. LUMSDEN *Edin. Poems & Songs* (1899) 168 A-doun the Westlin welkin.

'westlins, *adv. Sc. rare*$^{-1}$. [f. WEST + *-lins* -LING[2].] Westwards.
1718 RAMSAY *Christ's Kirk Gr.* III. i, Frae East Nook of Fife the Daw'n Speel'd Westlines up the Lift.

†**west-looker.** *Obs.*$^{-1}$ [f. WEST *adv.*] A name for the hare.
a **1300** *MS. Digby 86* fol. 168b, þe westlokere..þe sidlokere and eke þe roulekere [*read* -lokere].

†**westly,** *adv. Obs.*$^{-0}$ [f. WEST *adv.* Cf. MLG. *westelik*, G. *westlich*, Da. and Sw. *vestlig.*] Towards the west.
c **1440** *Promp. Parv.* 523/1 Westward, or westly, *occidentaliter.*

westm, var. WASTUM *Obs.*

Westmark ('wɛstmɑːk, ‖'vɛstmark). Also **west-mark, west mark.** [Ger., f. *west* WEST *sb.*[1] + *mark* MARK *sb.*[2] 2 c.] The currency unit of West (formerly western) Germany, as distinguished from the OSTMARK of East Germany.
1948 *Times* 2 Sept. 4/6 In view of the report that the east-mark is going to be recognized Berliners have been getting rid of the west-mark. **1959** [see OSTMARK]. **1964** L. DEIGHTON *Funeral in Berlin* v. 31 'How much money are you carrying?' I spread the few Westmarks and English pounds on the desk. **1980** A. SCHOLEFIELD *Berlin Blind* iii. 129, I have postcards in the bus which you may buy with Westmarks. **1980** *Times Lit. Suppl.* 31 Oct. 1230/3 In Germany..the Bundesrepublik offers 10,000 west-marks as the Thomas Mann prize, and the DDR 18,000 east-marks for the Heinrich Mann.

westment, obs. form of VESTMENT.

'Westminster.
1. a. The name of the abbey on the north bank of the Thames at London, used *attrib.*, esp. with reference to Westminster Hall as a court of justice, to the assembly of divines held in 1643, or to St. Peter's School.
1549 LATIMER *1st Serm. bef. Edw. VI* (Arb.) 28 Thus thys bargayne became a westminster matter; the lawyers gote twyse the value of the horse. *a* **1614** TIMME *Silver Watchbell* vii. (1634) 140 If his neighbor do damnifie him but the value of two pence, he will prouide a conserue of Westminster-hal wormewood for him out of hand. **1671** (*title*) Westminster Drollery. Or a choice Collection of the Newest Songs & Poems. **1691** *Hist. Rel. Late Presbyt. Gen. Assembly* 12 The Minister of Abbots-Hall was accused for neglecting the Catechism of the Westminster Divines. **1693** *Acc. Establ. Presbyt. Govt. Scot.* 43 Such a vast number of Propositions as are contained in the Westminster Confession. **1698** *Concubinage Disprov'd* 5 It does not appear by anything our Author says, that his Marriage with Mary Tomkins was any other than *Congressus Furtivus*, a Westminster Wedding. *a* **1700** B. E. *Dict. Cant. Crew*, *Westminster-Wedding*, a Whore and a Rogue Married together. **1719** *Collect. Conf. Faith Ch. Scot.* I. Pref. p. xi, Every body knows in what unhappy distracted Times, the Westminster Assembly met and compos'd that Confession of Faith. **1720** *Pref. to Addit. Westminster Confession* 182 Other catechisms, which..are for no other valuable quality any ways comparable to the Westminster Catechisms. **1747** MRS. GLASSE *Cookery* ix. 79 A Westminster-Fool. Take a Penny-loaf, cut it into thin Slices, wet them with Sack..: take a Quart of Cream, beat up six Eggs..[etc.]. **1837** DICKENS *Pickw.* xxxv, The waiters, from their costume, might be mistaken for Westminster boys. **1843** HETHERINGTON (*title*) History of the Westminster Assembly of Divines. **1856** SARA T. L. ROBINSON *Kansas* (ed. 3) 38 The old Westminster catechism allows works of necessity and mercy to be done on the Sabbath day. **1880** GOLDW. SMITH *Cowper* i. 13 The Nonsense Club, consisting of seven Westminster men who dined together every Thursday.
b. *ellipt.* A present or former pupil at Westminster School.
1690–1 SMALRIDGE in *Epist. Corr. Atterbury* (1783) I. 17, I suppose you expect to do little good but upon the Westminsters. **1880** GOLDW. SMITH *Cowper* i. 13 The set was strictly confined to Westminsters. Gray and Mason, being Etonians, were objects of its literary hostility. **1895** *Spectator* 23 Nov. 729 The Busby Trust, managed by thirteen trustees, who must be old Westminsters.
2. a. The Palace of Westminster; hence, Parliament, of which the Palace is the seat. Freq. *attrib.*
The present Palace of Westminster (built 1840–67) is more commonly known as the Houses of Parliament.
1807 *Morning Chron.* 13 Apr. 3/2 The Westminster Company of Independent Performers being lately dissolved. **1869** TROLLOPE *Phineas Finn* II. lxxiv. 306 The girl whom he loved..better even than Westminster and Downing Street. **1918** G. FRANKAU *One of Them* xvii. 127 What art thou, Westminster? A caucused lobby? An oratorial-acrobatic stadium..? Or art indeed the Common Weal's palladium? **1961** S. A. DE SMITH in *Jrnl. Commonwealth Political Stud.* I. 3 In its narrow sense the Westminster Model can be said to mean a constitutional system in which the head of state is not the effective head of government; [etc.]. **1972** *Guardian* 11 July 13/8 It is sometimes suggested that what de Gaulle did for France in Algeria, Westminster should do for Britain in Ulster. **1977** *Time* 27 June 20/1 One of the most frequently heard catch phrases has to do with moving away from the 'Westminster system' of parliamentary representation toward some form of presidential or federal system.
b. *Westminster chimes* or *quarters*: the pattern of chimes struck at successive quarters by Big Ben in the Palace of Westminster, and used for other clocks and (more recently) door chimes; it uses four bells struck in five different four-note sequences, each of which occurs twice in the course of an hour.
1860 E. B. DENISON *Rudimentary Treat. Clocks* (ed. 4) p. vii, Cambridge and Westminster chimes. *Ibid.* 191 A very grand G hour bell to the BAGD bells of the peel, on which the Cambridge and Westminster quarters might then be struck. **1923** W. I. MILHAM *Time & Timekeepers* xvii. 298 To make and place a clock..striking the hours and Westminster quarters on five bells. **1924** *Eng. Clocks & Watches* (Horol. Jrnl.) 42 The clock can be fitted with Whittington and Westminster Chimes. **1962** V. NABOKOV *Pale Fire* 43 Four hundred thousand times The tall clock with the hoarse Westminster chimes Has marked our common hour. **1967** 'R. SIMONS' *Taxed to Death* iv. 63 When Wace pressed the bell-button they heard Westminster chimes ringing in the hall. **1980** *New Grove Dict. Mus.* IV. 244/2 The best known of all clock chimes, the Westminster Quarters.., was derived from a quatrain in Handel's *Messiah*. In 1794 William Crotch wrote four variations on the fifth and sixth bars of 'I know that my Redeemer liveth'..for the new Cambridge University clock in Great St Mary's Church. They were accepted, and in 1845 were copied on the Royal Exchange clock, London. **1981** *Country Life* 12 Feb. 362 (Advt.), A superb clock..the three chimes, Westminster, Whittington and Winchester, obtainable at will.
Hence **'Westminsterism,** the principles characteristic of the Westminster Assembly of 1643.
1884 CALDERWOOD in *U.P. Mag.* July 366 Several things had occasioned opposition to the admission of the Cumberland Church, such as these:—its deliberate alteration of the Westminster Confession, its avowed antagonism to what was often named 'Westminsterism'.

Westmona'sterian. *rare*$^{-1}$. [f. *Westmonasterium*, Latinized f. WESTMINSTER.] One educated at Westminster School.
a **1695** WOOD *Life* (O.H.S.) I. 274 Richard Rhodes,..a confident Westmonasterian.

†**'Westmony.** *Obs.* [ad. Icel. *Vestmannaeyjar* (Da. *Vestmanøer.*] A group of islands off the south coast of Iceland. In quot. *attrib.*
Erroneously printed *Westinary* in Binnell *Descr. Thames* (1758) 260.
1663 *Act 15 Chas. II*, c. 7 §13 For the Encouragement of the Herring & North-Sea, Island [= Iceland], & Westmony Fisheries.

'westmost, *a.* Forms: 1 **westmæst,** 1, 6 *Sc.*, **westmest** (1 **weste-**), 6 *Sc.* **-mast,** 6–7 *Sc.* **-maist;** 3, 6– **westmost** (9 *Sc.* **wastmost**). [f. WEST *adv.* + -MOST.] Most westerly; westernmost.
825 in Birch *Cartul. Sax.* I. 542 Ærest of þam west mæstan æwylle..upp to þam eldan herepaðe. *c* **893** ÆLFRED *Oros.* VI. i, Romana [onweald]..is mæst & westmest. *Ibid.*, On þæm westemestan [onwealde], þæt is Roma. *c* **972** in Kemble *Cod. Dipl.* III. 262 þæs landes gemæra þe gebyriað into þære westmestan hide. **1297** R. GLOUC. (Rolls) 4495 Fram þe weste syde of þe world to þe est moste ende, þo adde king arþure ywonne fram þe west moste se. **1456** *Exch. Rolls Scot.* VI. 224 Onerat se..de ix li. de Mydmeststede de Warmwod. Et de ix li. de Westmeststede ejusdem. Et de ix li. de Estmeststede de Langhop. **1510** in *Laing Charters* (1899) 70 The haile foirland of the said tenement with the westmost 3harde. **1595** *Reg. Mag. Sig. Scot.* 90/2 To the westmest dyk of the eistmest cornefauld. **1632** LITHGOW *Trav.* I. 23 Gayetta, the West-most confine ..of the Neapolitan Kingdome. **1800** W. TAYLOR in *Monthly Mag.* VIII. 684 They are the westmost portion of the horde. **1805** *State, Leslie of Powis* etc. 56 (Jam.) That the westmost sight was above the Fluicky-shot. **1871** *Daily News* 27 Jan., A vague..attempt on the part of the French ..batteries at St. Ouen to enfilade our westmost one at Ormeson.

West Nile. *Med.* [f. WEST *a.* + name of the river *Nile.*] Used *attrib.* to designate a mosquito-borne virus and the disease it causes, usu. a mild fever but sometimes a fatal encephalitis.

1940 K. C. SMITHBURN et al. in *Amer. Jrnl. Tropical Med.* XX. 471 The purpose of this paper is to report the isolation of one such [infective] agent, which we call the West Nile virus, and to describe some of its properties. **1955** *Sci. Amer.* Mar. 64/3 He concluded that West Nile fever was predominantly a disease of childhood. **1961** M. HYNES *Med. Bacteriol.* (ed. 7) xxv. 392 Antigenically related viruses have a similar ecology..in central Africa (West Nile encephalitis). **1983** *Oxf. Textbk. Med.* I. v. 104/2 Recognizable disease due to West Nile virus infection has been observed in Israel... No vaccine is yet available.

west-north-west, *adv.*, etc. [See WEST *adv.* and NORTH-WEST. Cf. MLG. *westnortwest*, Du. *-noord-*, G. *-nord-*.] In or from the direction situated midway between west and north-west. Also as *sb.* and *adj.*

14.. *Sailing Directions* (Hakl. Soc., 1889) 11 The Ilonde and Berwik haven lien west north west and Est South est. *Ibid.* 18 The streemys of Briggewatir sit west norwest. *c* **1490** BOTONER *Itin.* (1778) 287 Anglice west-north-west versus Seynt Davyes. *a* **1550** LELAND *Itin.* (1764) III. 30 The secund [creke] lyith West North West. **1555** EDEN *Decades* (Arb.) 70 Proceadinge..at the lengthe towarde the weste northe weste. **1625** HYNMERS tr. *W. Blaeu's Sea Mirr.* II. 112 When that Lagernesse is westnorthwest from you, then goe on southeast. **1685** T. PHELPS *Acc. Captivity* 22 Our course by the North-Star was West-North-West. **1715** *Lond. Gaz.* No. 5360/5 With little Wind at West North West. **1725** DE FOE *Voy. round World* (1840) 111 The land lying away from the west-north-west to the south-east-by-south. **1855** KINGSLEY *Westw. Ho!* xxxi, A strong west-north-west breeze. **1883** R. H. SCOTT *Elem. Meteorol.* 359 The wind flies round to West, or West-north-west.

Hence **west-north-westerly** *a.*

1895 *Westm. Gaz.* 7 Oct. 5/2 She met with a tremendous west-north-westerly gale.

West of England. Also with hyphens. The name of a region of England, used *attrib.* and *absol.* to designate high-quality woollen broadcloth for which it has long been noted.

1843 *Penny Cycl.* XXVII. 555/2 In the West of England ..each workman confines himself exclusively to a particular branch of the manufacture; and this has been supposed to have led to the excellence of the West of England cloth. **1882** *Queen* 23 Dec. (Advt.), Homespuns, Tweeds,..West of England cloths. **1936** 'N. BLAKE' *Thou Shell of Death* i. 8 His waistcoat..[of] West-of-England cloth. **1972** E. KERRIDGE in J. G. Jenkins *Wool Textile Industry in Gt. Brit.* 33/1 The same [*sc.* a more intensive use of capital and skilled labour] was true to a lesser extent..of the new superfine West of Englands. **1976** F. GREENLAND *Misericordia Drop* i. vii. 49 He wore..grey West-of-England flannels.

Weston ('wɛstən). The name of Edward *Weston* (1850–1936) English-born electrical engineer, used *attrib.* **a.** In *Electr.*, designating a primary cell with electrodes of mercury and of cadmium amalgam and electrolyte of cadmium sulphate, used as a standard voltage source for calibrating electrical instruments.

1901 [see METASTABILITY]. **1963** G. L. PICKARD *Descriptive Physical Oceanogr.* vi. 94 The Weston cell has a limited sensitivity. **1972** *Physics Bull.* Jan. 40/2 The Bureau is.. interested in the Josephson effect for possible use in electrical standards, although for the moment the standard Weston cell is preferred for convenience.

b. In *Photogr.*, designating an obsolescent system of film speeds based on exposure meters made by the Weston Electrical Instrument Company or its successors.

1940 *Chambers's Techn. Dict.* 905/2 Weston film-speed. **1950** W. F. BERG *Exposure* 167 The introduction of Weston speed figures was of considerable importance. **1963** JERRARD & MCNEILL *Dict. Sci. Units* 105 The Weston number, the British Standards Institute speed number and the American Standards Association system also indicate the speed of the emulsion at its maximum sensitivity.

weston(e, obs. forms of WHETSTONE.

westour, obs. Sc. form of WASTER *sb.*[1]

Westphalia (wɛst'feılıə). Also 7 **Westfalia**. [med.L., f. OHG. *Westfalo* (G. *-fale, -phale*) an inhabitant of the district now called *Westfalen* in German.] The name of a region of West Germany (part of the *Land* of North Rhine-Westphalia) lying between the Netherlands, Hanover, Hessen, and the Rhine (formerly a Prussian province), used *attrib.* with *bacon*, *gammon*, or *ham*.

c **1650** TOWNSHEND *Poems* (1912) 8 Give us a salt Westphalia Gammon, Not meat to eat, but meat to drink. **1656** BLOUNT *Glossogr.*, Westphalia Bacon. **1664** F. HAWKINS *Youths Behav.* II. 178 A Westfalia Ham of Bacon. *Ibid.* 180 A Westphalia Ham. **1682** N. O. *Boileau's Lutrin* I. 178 His face..recalls the good Westphalia-Ham. **1710** P. LAMB *Royal Cookery* 66 To make a Westphalia-Ham. **1715** LADY G. BAILLIE *Househ. Bk.* (S.H.S.) 102 For 17¼ lb. westfalia hamb at 11d., 0 15 7.

West'phalian, *a.* and *sb.* [f. prec.] **A.** *adj.* Of or belonging to, connected with, Westphalia.

1604 MARSTON & WEBSTER *Malcontent* IV. iii, The sallo-westfalian-gamon-faced zaza. **1668** J. WILSON *Erasm. Praise of Folly* (1913) 25 As plump and round as a Westphalian Hogg. **1708** ADDISON *Present St. War* 34 The Westphalian Treaty. **1764** FALCONER *Poems, Demagogue* 128 Her vital blood, that pour'd from every vein, So late, to fill th' accurs'd Westphalian drain. **1820** *Mem. Crt. Westphalia* 220 The Westphalian troops performed miracles at Moskwa. **1824** BYRON *Juan* XV. lxv, They also set a glazed Westphalian ham on. **1842** BORROW *Bible in Spain* xviii, I have seen many a Westphalian hog quite as tall.

2. *Geol.* [ad. F. *westphalien* (A. de Lapparent *Traité de Géologie* (ed. 3, 1893) 819).] Of or belonging to a stratigraphic division of the Upper Carboniferous in Europe, above the Namurian and below the Stephanian. Also *absol.*

1901 [see STEPHANIAN *a.*]. **1915** C. SCHUCHERT *Text-bk. Geol.* II. xl. 729 The Coal Measures formation is again divided into two series, the earlier half, or Middle Carboniferous, being widely known as the Westphalian.. when coal bearing. **1969** BENNISON & WRIGHT *Geol. Hist. Brit. Isles* ix. 221 In Britain the greater part of the Coal Measures belongs to the Westphalian. **1976** *Nature* 22 July 277/1 The age of this late retrogression..is synchronous with the intrusion of younger Variscan granites, a major break in sedimentation and the main phase of Hercynian folding (Sudetic phase: Westphalian in age).

B. *sb.* A native or inhabitant of Westphalia.

1778 WARTON *Hist. Eng. Poetry* II. 311 Wernerus Rolewinck, a Westphalian. **1820** *Mem. Crt. Westphalia* 220 The Westphalians lost, in this battle, many valuable officers.

† **Westphalie, -phaly**, obs. varr. WESTPHALIA.

1577 GOOGE *Heresbach's Husb.* III. 148 The Gamonds of Fraunce,..which I suppose were none other but the flyches of Westphaly, so greatly esteemed at this day. **1661** RABISHA *Cookery* 20 A good piece of Westphalie Bacon. *Ibid.* 136 A Westphalie Gammon of Bacon. **1725** MANDEVILLE *Fable Bees* (ed. 4) I. 263 For the Small Beer they sent abroad, they receiv'd large Returns of Westphaly-Hams [etc.].

West-Pointer. *U.S.* [f. *West Point*, the name of a village on the west bank of the Hudson River in the state of New York.] An officer trained at the United States military academy at West Point.

1863 *Congr. Globe* 16 Jan. 327/3 There have been wounded since this war opened, from thirty to forty general officers. Many of them were West Pointers. **1878** *N. Amer. Rev.* CXXVI. 85 A West-Pointer enjoying the *soubriquet* of 'Shanks'. **1895** J. L. ALLEN *Kentucky Cardinal* xiii, The West-Pointer had been writing for some months in regard to the wild behaviour of his cousin.

Westralian (wɛ'streılıən), *a.* and *sb.* [f. *Westralia*, a telegraphic abbrev. of *West Australia.*] **a.** *adj.* Of or pertaining to West Australia. **b.** *sb.* A native or inhabitant of West Australia; *pl.* West Australian mining shares.

a. 1896 *Economist* 14 Mar. 325/1 The position of the Westralian Government in the matter is a serious one. *Ibid.* 25 Apr. 532/2 Westralian shares have been somewhat more freely dealt in. **1896** *19th Cent.* Nov. 711 (*title*) The Westralian Mining 'Boom'. **1900** *Speaker* 12 May 153/1 The Westralian Outlander complains that all the taxation falls on the gold-mines. **1904** *Blackw. Mag.* Mar. 398 Westralian finance copied the bad features of the Kaffir Circus.

b. 1896 *Economist* 20 June 809/2 Westralians have been weak on balance. **1896** *19th Cent.* Nov. 711 When..every department of the Stock Exchange was inactive, Westralians came to the rescue. **1900** *Westm. Gaz.* 17 Aug. 7/1 The boom in Westralians which does not come off.

Hence **We'stralianism.**

1905 *Westm. Gaz.* 1 May 9/1 Statements..on the subject of Westralianism. **1905** *Daily Report* 9 Sept. 6/1 Scandals, such as during recent years have made the term 'Westralianism' one of evil significance.

westre, obs. form of VESTRY.

westring, var. of WESTERING.

West 'Saxon, *sb.* and *a. Hist.* Also **West-Saxon.** [f. WEST *a.* + SAXON *sb.* and *a.*, after OE. *West-seaxan* pl.]

A. *sb.* **1.** *pl.* The division of the Saxons in England occupying the area south of the Thames and westward from Surrey and Sussex; also *sing.* an individual belonging to this group or area.

1387 TREVISA *Higden* VI. 403 Plegmundus..ordeyned.. fyve [bishops] to þe lond of Giweysys, þat beeþ West Saxons. **1432-50** tr. *Higden* VII. 99 Edmunde Irensyde.. subduede to hym the Westesaxons anoon. **1513** BRADSHAW *St. Werburge* I. 155 The thyrde [realm] was West Saxons, famous and myghty. **1596** DALRYMPLE tr. *Leslie's Hist. Scot.* I. 232 Aidan winnis the feild vpon the Pechtis and Westsaxonis. *a* **1643** BAKER *Chron.* (1653) 7 The third Kingdome of the Heptarchie, was of the West Saxons. **1714** ADDISON *Spect.* No. 569 ¶1, I was the other Day with honest Will. Funnell the West Saxon. **1728** CHAMBERS *Cycl.* s.v. *Money*, Ina King of the West-Saxons. **1781** GIBBON *Decl. & F.* xxxviii. (1787) III. 618 *note*, Cerdic, the West Saxon. **1877** TENNYSON *Harold* IV. i, Thou art but a West-Saxon: *we* are Danes!

2. The dialect of Old English used by the West Saxons.

1844 GARNETT in *Proc. Phil. Soc.* II. 17 The plural.. totally unknown in West-Saxon. *Ibid.* 18 The discrepancies from the ordinary West-Saxon are specified. **1876** SWEET *Ags. Reader* p. xii, The West Saxon of the eleventh century differs in many respects from that of Alfred's reign. **1893** A. C. CHAMPNEYS *Hist. English* 85 Northumbrian retains some very ancient forms not found in West Saxon.

B. *adj.* Of or pertaining to, characteristic of, the West Saxons or their speech.

1570 LAMBARDE *Peramb. Kent* (1576) 20 Kent was vnited by King Egbert..vnto the Westsaxon Kingdome,..and.. gouerned after the Westsaxon law. **1670** MILTON *Hist. Brit.* III. 121 Before the West-Saxon Kingdome. **1842** *Penny Cycl.* XXII. 231/2 During the West Saxon, Anglo-Saxon, and Anglo-Danish dynasties. **1848** LATHAM *Eng. Lang.* (ed. 2) 91 The Psalter also exhibits this West-Saxon form. **1876** SWEET *Ags. Reader* p. xii, The old Northumbrian poems were also copied in the West Saxon dialect. **1893** A. C. CHAMPNEYS *Hist. English* 86 The Southern or West Saxon plural, *-aþ.*

Hence † **West-'Saxonry**, the kingdom of the West Saxons.

1650 ELDERFIELD *Civil Right of Tythes* x. 70 Kenulph King of West-Saxon-rie.

† **West-sexene**, ME. form of OE. *West-se(a)xena*, gen. pl. of *West-se(a)xan* (see prec.).

? *a* **1300** *Shires Eng.* in *O.E. Misc.* 146 On is west-sexene lawe.

west side. Also **west-side.** [WEST *a.* Cf. WFris., MLG. *westside*, Du. *-zijde*, G. *-seite.*] **a.** The side situated in or lying towards the west.

c **1290** *Kenelm* 62 in *S. Eng. Leg.* 347 Þe bischopriche of Roucestre þat in þe west-side is next. **1340** HAMPOLE *Pr. Consc.* 5127 Als þe levenyng out gas in short tyde Fra þe est, and shewes it in þe west syde. *c* **1386** CHAUCER *Clerk's T.* 1 Ther is at the West syde of Ytaille..A lusty playne. *c* **1391** —— *Astrol.* I. §6 The west side is cleped the left side. **14..** *Sailing Directions* (Hakl. Soc. 1889) 17 On the west side of Milforde. **1503** *Surtees Misc.* (1890) 30 The utter west syde of his swynstye. **1597** *Reg. Mag. Sig. Scot.* 211/2 At the west syde of the Blak-tour. **1669** EARL WINCHILSEA *True Relat. Mt. Etna* 16 The two Torrents of Fire forward..had on the West-side branched it self into several Streams. **1681** in *Nairne Peerage Evid.* (1874) 6 The west syde of the high way. **1789** S. SHAW *Tour W. Eng.* 378 A pleasant little town on the west-side of a hill. **1896** BADEN-POWELL *Matabele Campaign* iv, On the west side of this road Umlugulu's impi was stationed.

b. *transf.* (Cf. WESTERN *a.* 8.)

1829 MARRYAT *F. Mildmay* xxv, Rubbing herself on her '*west*' side, as the Philadelphia ladies call it.

c. Also **West Side.** That district of New York City which lies on the west side of Manhattan. Also *attrib. U.S.*

1858 *Harper's Mag.* July 283/2 As our friend entered the door a well-known 'West side' operator made his bid. **1903** *Ibid.* July 213 The abysmal craving of New Yorkers—West Side or East Side—is for friends. **1958** A. LAURENTS (*title of play*) West Side story. **1976** BOTHAM & DONNELLY *Valentino* iii. 25 He left the West Side and moved into a stable garret adjoining the home of millionaire Cornelius Bliss. **1981** J. VALIN *Dead Letter* xix. 182 That region of worn houses..that is the westside ghetto.

West Sider. *U.S.* [-ER[1].] A resident of Manhattan's West Side.

1903 *N.Y. Even. Post* 14 Nov. 4 The persistence with which the West Siders have followed up this question of the Broadway trees. **1914** G. ATHERTON *Perch of Devil* I. 2 Ida, forced..to accept employment with a fashionable dressmaker and consumed with envy of the 'West Siders' whose measurements she took. **1980** *N.Y. Times* 21 July A-8/2 Because the West Sider usually has so much money and time tied up in his lawn, plants and trees..he finds himself in a constant struggle to keep growing things from turning brown.

† **west-south**, *sb. Obs. rare.* [See WEST *adv.* and SOUTH *adv.* OE. had *westsúðwind.*] The south-west.

1297 R. GLOUC. (Rolls) 476 To þe on ende of engelond, as in þe west souþ A lute bi norþe cornewaile.

west-south-west, *adv.* etc. [See WEST *adv.* and SOUTH-WEST. Cf. MLG. *westsütwest*, Du. *-zuid-*, G. *-süd-*.] In or from the direction situated midway between west and south-west. Also as *sb.* and *adj.*

a. *adv.* **14..** *Sailing Directions* (Hakl. Soc. 1889) 11 It flowith west southwest. *Ibid.* 13 Yif..the wynde be west south west. *c* **1440** *Pallad. on Husb.* III. 470 And west south-west [L. *in fauonium*] hem for to order best is. **1513** SIR E. HOWARD in Ellis *Orig. Lett.* Ser. II. I. 214 On mondey the wynd cam west sowth west. **1584** R. NORMAN tr. *Safe-gard of Sailers* 21 b, The floud sets east northeast, and the ebbe west southwest. **1698** HENNEPIN *New Discov. Amer.* I. 78 Steering our Course West-South-West, with a favourable Wind. **1760** R. ROGERS *Jrnls.* (1769) 197 We..kept the following courses: west-south-west two miles, west-north-west three miles. **1833-4** J. PHILLIPS *Geol.* in *Encycl. Metrop.* (1845) VI. 544/1 Less certain and continuous fissures passing nearly East North-East and West South-West.

b. *adj.* **1398** TREVISA *Barth. De P.R.* XI. iii. (1495) 386 The weste Southweste wynde hyghte Zephirus. **14..** *Sailing Directions* (Hakl. Soc. 1889) 14 All the havens be full at a west south west moone. *a* **1550** LELAND *Itin.* (1764) III. 12 An Hospital of S. John yet stonding at the West South West End of the Town. **1611** COTGR., *Vent d'aval*, a West South-west wind. **1632** LITHGOW *Trav.* III. 123 The West South west end of this once Regall Towne.

c. *sb.* **1555** EDEN *Decades* (Arb.) 77 The shores bended.. sumetyme towarde the Weste and westesouthwest. *a* **1592** GREENE & LODGE *Looking Gl.* (1598) E 1, Now the wind doth serue, And sweetly blowes a gale at West, Southwest. **1837** W. IRVING *Capt. Bonneville* I. iii. 61 One of these branches rises in the west south-west. **1839** DE LA BECHE *Rep. Geol. Cornwall*, etc. i. 8 On the west-south-west of the same district.

Hence **west-south-'westerly** *a.*

1881 W. POWELL in *Proc. R. Geog. Soc.* (N.S.) III. 92 A long straight piece of coast, running in a west-south-westerly direction.

westum, var. WASTUM *Obs.*

† **westvale.** *Obs.* Also 4 -fale, 4–5 -vall (-uall), 5 westevale. [a. MLG. *Westvale*, *-val*

Westphalian.] A variety of cloth of Westphalian origin.

1385 in S. Bentley *Excerpta Hist.* (1831) 139 Item lego ducentas vlnas de Westfale ad faciendum lintheamina. **1391** *Exped. Earl Derby* (Camden) 35 Pro ix vlnis Westuall.. emptis pro trussura dictorum pannorum. *Ibid.* 168 Pro coopertorio tele Westvall pro dresseur. **1396** *Will of Hervey of Kedwelly* (Comm. Ct. London), Lego Waltero Burtone vnum lectum de Westuale. **1397–8** *Exped. Earl Derby* 356 Westuall de worsted. **1403** *Will of R. de Chestrefeld* in *Lincoln Chapter Acts* (MS.), Cum vno Doser de Westvale steyned cum ymaginibus. **1423** *For. Acc. 1 Hen. VI*, I. (P.R.O.) Computat in..westevale, pellibus lanutis [etc.].

westward (ˈwɛstwəd), *adv.*, *sb.*, and *a.*[1] Also 5 **weste-**, 5–6 **westwarde**, 7 **westheard**. [OE. *westweard*, f. WEST *adv.* + -WARD. Cf. MLG. *westwart*, *-wert*, *-wort*.]

A. *adv.* **1.** Towards the west; in a westerly direction: **a.** Of motion or direction.

For *Westward ho!* see HO *int.*[1] 2 b.

a **900** *O.E. Chron.* an. 893, Her..for se micle here..of þæm eastrice westweard to Bunnan. *c* **1000** *Sax. Leechd.* III. 270 Þa seofon steorran..gangende eastan westweard. *O.E. Chron.* (Laud MS.) an. 1052 Hi..ȝewendon heom þa westweard oð þet hi comon to Portlande. **1297** R. GLOUC. (Rolls) 1039 So þat he drou him westward,..þe se he wende nei & bihuld west. **1377** LANGL. *P. Pl.* B. XVIII. 118 Her suster.. cam..Euene out of þe est, and westward she loked. *c* **1391** CHAUCER *Astrol.* II. §17 Espie diligently whan this same firste sterre passeth..westward. *c* **1400** MAUNDEV. (Roxb.) xxviii. 127 It lastez westward to þe ryuer of Phison. *c* **1407** LYDG. *Reson & Sens.* 658 Whan that he hath hys cours [y-]goon,..Ageyn westwarde he doth repaire. **1473** WARKW. *Chron.* (Camden) 9 Thei fledde westwarde to the see syde, and toke there here schippys. **1535** COVERDALE *Ezek.* xlv. 7 As farre as reacheth westwarde and eastwarde. **1593** T. FALE *Horolog.* 9 b, If the declination of your plat be West-ward, or from C. toward B. **1613** DONNE *Poems* (1633) 170 Goodfriday, 1613. Riding Westward. *a* **1661** FULLER *Worthies, Somerset* (1662) 32 Hence forward the Sun of the Kings cause declined, verging more and more Westward, till at last it set in Cornwal. **1697** DRYDEN *Æneis* XI. 1316 But westward to the Sea the Sun declin'd. **1752** BERKELEY *Verses Planting Arts & Learn. Amer.* 21 Westward the course of empire takes its way. **1783** J. KING *Thoughts Difficulties* iii. 29 We were told by a priest..that all the virtues were flying westward. **1816** KEATS *Ep. Geo. Keats* 141 Why westward turn? 'Twas but to say adieu! **1822** SCOTT *Nigel* v, The citizen..rode on westward along the Strand. **1848** B. WEBB *Cont. Ecclesiol.* 160 Projecting westward from the nave-arch is a stone rood-loft. **1877** RUSKIN *St. Mark's Rest* iii. 40 Look, as you recross its bridge, westward, along the broad-flowing stream.

b. Of relative position.

c **1386** CHAUCER *Knt.'s T.* 1036 Estward ther stood a gate of Marbul whit, Westward right swich another in the opposit. **1390** GOWER *Conf.* III. 103 And thanne upon that other syde westward..The brother..Aufrique nam. **1472–75** *Rolls of Parlt.* VI. 157/2 Almaner Woll..except Wolle to be shipped westward in Galees or Carrykkes, to be shipped and caried oute of this Reame, shal be conveyed to the Staple of Caleys. **1530** TINDALE *Exod.* xxvii. 12 And in the bredth of the courte westwarde, there shalbe hangynges of fyftye cubettes long. **1598** W. PHILLIP tr. *Linschoten* I. xciii. 171 We..compassed about yᵉ other corner that lay westward from vs. **1601** HOLLAND *Pliny* VI. xxx. I. 147 He telleth..that Westward there are people..whose king hath but one eie. **1631** WEEVER *Anc. Funeral Mon.* 642 A certaine holy Crosse, found farre Westward, and brought hither by miracle. **1773** NOORTHOUCK *Hist. Lond.* 742 From Bedford house on the same line westward, is Great Russel street Bloomsbury. **1810** SCOTT *Lady of L.* I. xxvi, Due westward, fronting to the green, A rural portico was seen. *a* **1861** CLOUGH *'Say not, the struggle nought availeth'* 16 In front, the sun climbs slow, how slowly, But westward, look, the land is bright!

c. Followed by *of*.

1691 *Hist. Rel. Late Presbyt. Gen. Assembly* 6 For twenty Miles Westward of Perth, there were but two or three Ministers. **1762** FALCONER *Shipwr.* III. 238 Westward of these..lies The long-lost isle of Ithacus the wise. **1821** *Acc. Peculations in Coal Trade* 4 Their papers should not be sent from the ship until she has arrived westward of Blackwall. **1842** BORROW *Bible in Spain* xxxvi, It is situated about twelve leagues..westward of Madrid.

d. *Comb.*, as ***westward-blowing***, ***-flowing***, etc.

1871 TENNYSON *Last Tourn.* 584 Those far-rolling, westward-smiling seas. **1875** *Encycl. Brit.* III. 105/1 The problem of the destination of the westward-flowing rivers. **1891** *Nation* (N.Y.) 19 Nov. 393/1 The westward-looking portion of this volume. **1895** *Daily News* 24 Dec. 6/1 That fierce westward-blowing gale of fire.

†**2.** *spec.* In allusive use: To Tyburn. *Obs.*

1600 *Looke about You* A 2 b, If they doe so, faith, westward then with Skinke. **1605** CHAPMAN etc. *Eastw. Hoe* II. i. B 3 b, *Touch.* Sir, Eastward hoe, will make you go Westward hoe. **1607** DEKKER & WEBSTER *Westw. Hoe* IV. ii. G 1 b, You..look as if you were going westward indeede. **1626** H. PARROT *Cures for the Itch* A 2 b, If any thing happen.., it must accrew from the next Sessions, prouided there be some to trauel westward. **1647** A. B. [? Brewer] *Countrie Girle* I 3 b, *Greg*... Is't not time he should now goe downward? *Hu.* And time, that you should goe Westward.

3. quasi-*sb.* = next.

1697 DRYDEN *Æneid* IX. 909 Like the Storm that flies From Westward, when the Show'ry Kids arise. **1810** SCOTT *Lady of L.* IV. vii, My followers guard each pass's mouth, To east, to westward, and to south.

B. *sb.* That direction or part which lies to the west of a place, etc.

1652 H. PHILLIPPES *Geometr. Sea-man* 79 Which..differs in longitude from the former place 90 degrees to the Westward. **1673** in Picton *L'pool Munic. Rec.* (1883) I. 316 To make cleare and pave the street on the cock of the Castell to the westheard. **1695** *Lond. Gaz.* No. 3099/3 The same day passed by the *Hastings*, with about 12 sail to the West-ward. **1725** DE FOE *Voy. round World* (1840) 308 They..saw two rockets rise up from the westward. **1762** FALCONER *Shipwr.* III. 571 The prow, swift wheeling, to the westward flies. **1838** STERLING in Carlyle *Life* II. vii. (1872) 145 The highest part..which commands a view..of the vale of the Arno to the westward. **1874** J. FORREST *Explor. Australia* (1875) 224 Sure enough there were the tracks of horses coming from the westward.

b. Const. *of*.

1766 SMOLLETT *Trav.* xii. I. 213 The river Var falls into the Mediterranean..about four miles to the westward of Nice. **1776** *Trial of Nundocomar* 60/1 *Q.* Where is that place? *A.* To the westward of Sasserum. **1796** MORSE *Amer. Geog.* I. 138 Directing his course to the westward of Cape Fare-well. **1896** BADEN-POWELL *Matabele Campaign* xv, About three miles to the westward of the mountain.

C. *adj.* Having a westerly situation or direction; lying, facing, moving, etc., towards the west.

1872 JENKINSON *Guide Eng. Lakes* (1879) 333 On completing the worst part of the climb, and obtaining a westward prospect. **1886** C. E. PASCOE *London To-day* xxvi. (ed. 3) 241 Let us retrace our steps..to the westward end of Cheap-side. **1896** HOWELLS *Impress. & Exp.* 282 One of the west-ward avenues. **1900** *Jrnl. Sch. Geog.* (U.S.) Apr. 134 A further link in the westward series..was finished in 1837.

†**westward**, *a.*[2] *Obs.* [OE. *westeweard*: cf. prec.] Westerly (= the west, or western part, of).

847 *Charter* in Sweet *O.E. Texts* 434 Ðonon on ða lytlan burȝ westewearde. *c* **893** ÆLFRED *Oros.* I. i. §3 Se westsuþende Europe..is in Ispania westeweardum. *c* **1205** LAY. 25657 He seide þat þer wes icumen a scaðe liðe of westward Spaine. *c* **1440** *Promp. Parv.* 523/1 Westward, *occidentalis*.

ˈ**westwardly**, *a.* [f. WESTWARD *adv.*]

1. a. Of wind: Blowing from the westward.

1653 *Nissena* 107 [They] hoist up their Sails, the wind being Westwardly, and good for their intended Navigation. **1706** LUTTRELL *Brief Rel.* (1857) VI. 10 The wind being westwardly, a general embarkation..is making at Harwich for Holland. **1805** *Phil. Trans.* XCVI. 249 *note*, He expected a continuance of fine, clear weather, with westwardly winds. **1876** DAVIS *Polaris Exp.* 259 The pack was driven in by a westwardly wind.

b. Moving or flowing westward.

1870 PROCTOR *Other Worlds* iv. 108 *note*, The relatively cold and westwardly equatorial currents.

2. Situated to the westward.

1704 *Phil. Trans.* XXV. 1634 The Section [seemed] to be a small matter more Westwardly. **1703** *Act 33 Geo. III* c. 131 title, The road leading from Uttoxeter to the westwardly part of Hardiwick heath.

ˈ**westwardly**, *adv.* [f. as prec.] In or to the westward; in a westerly direction.

1519 *Interl. Four Elem.* (Percy Soc.) 27 And next from them westwardly, Here by hymself, alone doth ly Ireland. *a* **1631** DONNE *Poems, Love-Lect. Shadow* 19 If love once faint, and westwardly declyne. **1756** TOLDERVY *Hist. 2 Orphans* IV. 76 After steering their course westwardly a few days, they met with a shabby company of strollers. **1794** VANCOUVER *Agric. Cambridge* 69 Thence extending westwardly. **1837** W. IRVING *Capt. Bonneville* I. v. 96 The travellers took final leave of the Sweet Water,..keeping westwardly. **1892** A. E. LEE *Hist. Columbus* (Ohio) I. 327 Westwardly..traveled an interminable caravan of emigrants.

ˈ**westwardmost**, *a.* [f. as prec. + -MOST.] Most westerly; farthest west.

1685 W. HEDGES *Diary* (Hakl. Soc.) I. 175 We..came to an anchor..on yᵉ Westwardmost Brace. **1788** J. WHITE *Jrnl. Voy. N.S. Wales* (1790) 109 The westward-most point of a very large bay. **1894** *Daily News* 7 May 6/3 They propose to commence at once on the westwardmost bay of the chapel.

ˈ**westwards**, *adv.* and *sb.* Also 6 **-wardes**. [f. WESTWARD *adv.* + -S[1]. Cf. Du. *westwaarts*, G. *westwärts*, and OE. *westweardes* (once).]

A. *adv.* = WESTWARD *adv.* 1 a.

1540 *Act 32 Hen. VIII* c. 17 The way from the barres in Holborne westwardes to the farre ende of high holborn. **1581** BOROUGH *Discourse Var. Cumpas* (1585) F iv, From hence Westwardes to Meta Incognita. **1614** E. WRIGHT *Dialling* E 1 An occidental Dial looketh directly Westwards. **1652** HEYLYN *Cosmogr.* IV. 96 He..informs us that he sailed not Westwards, but more towards the South. **1915** J. BUCHAN *Nelson's Hist. War* V. 126 The bulk of the Russian army went westwards to reinforce the van.

b. = WESTWARD *adv.* 1 b.

1585 T. WASHINGTON tr. *Nicholay's Voy.* II. vii. 37 b, A mountaine Westwards, and fiue miles from the Citie. **1599** E. WRIGHT *Haven-finding Art* 11 Helmshude (which place is Westwards from the North Cape of Finmark). **1854** tr. *Hettner's Athens & Pelop.* 162 Westwards yonder, towards the sea, lies Lerna.

B. *sb.* = WESTWARD *sb.* (Also with *of*.) Now *rare*.

1574 W. BOURNE *Regiment for Sea* 47 To the Westwardes of your towne. **1581** BOROUGH *Discourse Var. Cumpas* (1585) G ij, Wheras yᵉ Narue..should be from S. Nicholas ..to the Westwardes. **1584** R. NORMAN tr. *Safegard of Sailers* 37 Then he shall see the towne to the westwards before him. **1602** CAREW *Cornwall* 28 b, Vpon the North coast, and to the Westwards of Foy, few or none are taken. **1669** EARL WINCHILSEA *True Relat. Mt. Etna* 22 The other Torrent..in probability could not easily overflow to the Westwards. **1728** CHAMBERS *Cycl* s.v. *Wind*, The Easterly Trade-Winds blowing to the Westwards thereof.

west wind, west-wind. [OE. *westwind*, = OS., MLG., MDu., G. *westwind*, WFris. *westewyn*, NFris. *wästwinj*. OE. had also *westanwind* = ON. *vestanvindr* (Norw. *vestan-*, Da. *vestenvind*), MHG. *westenwint*.]

a. The (or a) wind blowing from the west. Also with *a* and *pl.*

c **900** *Bæda's Hist.* v. xix. (1890) 458 Sona þæs þe he on scyp eode..bleow westwind. *a* **1400** *Nominale* (Skeat) 567 *Vent galerne*..west-wynde. *c* **1440** *Promp. Parv.* 523/1 West wynde, *zephirus*. **1495** *Trevisa's Barth. De P.R.* XI. iii. 386 Fauonius, the Weste wynde arysyth in the Weste. **1535** COVERDALE *Exod.* x. 19 The Lorde turned a maruelous stronge west wynde. **1577** D. SETTLE *Frobisher's Voy.* B vij, Within foure dayes..the Northwest and West windes dispersed the yce into the Sea. **1634** MILTON *Comus* 989 And West winds, with musky wing About the cedar'n alleys fling Nard. **1645** BOATE *Irel. Nat. Hist.* (1652) 176 As the West-winds are much more common in Ireland,..than the East. **1715** POPE *Iliad.* IV. 319 The Cloud condensing as the West-Wind blows. **1819** WORDSW. *Sonn. 'Lone Flower'* 11 Bright jonquils, their odours lavishing On the soft west-wind and his frolic peers. **1892** KIPLING *Barrack-room Ballads* etc. 178 The West Wind called.

attrib. **1601** HOLLAND *Pliny* x. lx. I. 301 Some are of opinion that the wind will engender them: for which cause also they are called Zephyria [*i.* West-wind-egs].

b. (Usu. with capital initials.) One of the four 'tiles' or discs called winds in the game of mah-jong; the player who takes this tile at the beginning of the game and sits opposite East Wind, or a player who succeeds him in being so designated.

1922 R. E. LINDSELL *Ma-Cheuk or Mah-Jongg*, 13 East discards a West wind. North..exposes a pair of West winds. **1952** M. STEEN *Phoenix Rising* vii. 154 She slid the West Wind on to her ebony rack. **1960** [see EAST WIND b]. **1976** R. C. BELL *Discovering Mah-jong* 15 The third round is West Wind's round.

Hence **west-winded, west-windy** adjs.

1851 G. W. CURTIS *Nile Notes* xliv. 221 That west-winded, rose-odoured street. **1850** HAWTHORNE *Amer. Note-bks.* (1883) 379 It being a bright, westwindy, bracing day.

†**westy**, *a.*[1] *Obs.* Also 4 **wysty**. [OE. *wǽstiȝ*, *wéstiȝ*, f. *wǽste*, *wéste* WESTE *a.* Cf. WASTY *a.*[1]] Desolate, waste.

c **950** *Lindisf. Gosp.* Mark i. 35 [He] eode on woestiȝum stowum [*c* **975** *Rushw.* in westiȝe stowe]. *a* **1122** *O.E. Chron.* (Laud MS.) an. 449 Of Angle..se a syððan stod westiȝ betwix Iutum & Seaxum. *c* **1205** LAY. 1120 Leode nere þar nane, ne wapmen ne wifmen, bute westiȝe pædes [*c* **1275** weste paþes]. *c* **1230** *Hali Meid.* 42 (Bodley MS.) Þet tu.. schalt grenin godles in-wið westi [*Titus* wasti] wahes. **13..** *Gaw. & Gr. Knt.* 2189 Now iwysse, quoþ Wowayn, wysty is here; þis oritore is vgly.

ˈ**westy**, *a.*[2] *Obs.* exc. *dial.* [Of obscure origin.] Confused; giddy.

1599 BP. HALL *Sat.* IV. i. 158 While hee lies wallowing with a westie hed And palish carkasse, on his brothel-bed. **1674–91** RAY *N.C. Words*, *Westy*, dizzy, giddy. **1867** *Cornh. Mag.* XV. 741 He's a bit westy by times is Ashford. **1881** EVANS *Leicest. Gloss.* s.v., My head's very westy and bad.

westy, var. WESTIE.

wesy, obs. f. VIZY *v. Sc.*

wesyng, rare obs. f. WEASAND.

wesz, obs. f. *was*, pa. t. of BE *v.*

wet (wɛt), *sb.*[1] Forms: *α.* 1 **wǽt**, 3 **wet** (*dat.* **wete**), *Orm.* **wæt** (*dat.* **wæte**), 3–6 **wete**, (5 **whete**), 4–6 **weete**, 4–5, 6– *Sc.* **weet**, 6 **weat(e**, 5–6 *north.* and *Sc.* **weytt**, 5–7 *Sc.* **weit**. *β.* 4 *north.* **wat(e**. *γ.* 6– **wet**, 6 **wette**, 7 **wett**. *δ.* 9 *Sc.* **wat**. [OE. *wǽt* neut. (substantival use of *wǽt* adj., = WFris. *wiet*), giving normally ME. *wēt*, *wete*, *weete* and later *weat(e*. The other ME. and mod. forms are due to the influence of the adj. OE. had also *wǽta* wk. masc., represented in ME. by WETE; in later use the two become undistinguishable, and some of the examples given here (in sense 1) may really be survivals of *wǽta*.]

1. Moisture; liquid or moist substance.

In occasional use applied to water, blood, sweat, sap, etc.

α. *c* **888** ÆLFRED *Boeth.* xxxiii. §5 Swa þæt heora nan oðres mearce ne ofereode, & se cile ȝeþrowode wið ða hæto, & þæt wæt wið þam dryȝum. *c* **1220** *Bestiary* 73 Hise feðres fallen for ðe hete, And he dun mide to ðe wete Falleð in ðat welle grund. *a* **1240** *Ureisun* in *O.E. Hom.* I. 187 Hwa is þenne unwaschen þe haueþ þis halwende wet inwið his heorte. *c* **1290** *St. Michael* 668 in *S. Eng. Leg.* 318 Man hath of eorþe al is bodi, and of watere he hauez wete. *c* **1386** CHAUCER *Can. Yeom. Prol. & T.* 634, I se wel how ye swete, Haue heer a clooth, and wipe awey the wete. *c* **1400** *Beryn* 1022 [He] smote þe Damesell vndir þe ere, þe weet gon vpward spyn. **1412–20** LYDG. *Chron. Troy* IV. 3375 Whan he [Phoebus].. drieþ vp þe moysture & þe weete Of herbe & floure with his feruent hete. **1483** *Cath. Angl.* 415/1 Weytt, *maditas*. *a* **1500** *Hist. K. Boccus & Sydracke* (? 1510) M ij b, After a man hath in hym most Of wete of dryeth hete or colde Shall his complexcyon be tolde. **1523–34** FITZHERB. *Husb.* §124 The quyckeset wyll take no rote, excepte it haue greate weate.

γ. **1597** SHAKS. *Lover's Compl.* 40 Like vsery applying wet to wet. **1633** G. HERBERT *Temple, Providence* xxix, When th' earth was dry, thou mad'st a sea of wet. **1709** J. WARD *Yng. Math. Guide* (1734) 437 Divide the Sum of all those Dips or Wet Inches by the Number of Places you dipp'd in, and the Quotient will be the Mean Wet of all those Dips. **1784** TWAMLEY *Dairying* 32 If you cut the Cheese when young, you will find, that there is a Moisture, or Wet, in every Place where the Eye is,..which Wet or Moisture is called Tears. **1848** DICKENS *Dombey* liv, The foam was on his lips; the wet stood on his forehead. **1894** K. GRAHAME *Pagan P.* 129 The drippings made worms of wet in the thick dust of the road. 1897 MAX PEMBERTON *Queen of Jesters* iii. 105 The floor of the staircase was covered with wet and slime.

2. a. Rainy or damp weather.

α. c1200 *Trin. Coll. Hom.* 123 Man..þoleð..hwile druie and hwile wete, hwile chele, wile hete. 1362 LANGL. *P. Pl.* A. VI. 21, I haue walked ful wyde In weete and in druye. c1400 MAUNDEV. (Roxb.) vi. 23 Þer falles oft sithes grete derth of corne..by cause of ouer mykill wete. c1460 *Towneley Myst.* xii. 4 Now in hurt, now in heyll, now in weytt, now in blast. c1480 HENRYSON *Garm. Gude Ladeis* 24 Hir mantill of humilitie, To tholl bayth wind & weit. 1650 J. NICOLL *Diary* (Bann. Club) 27 That nicht being..full of wind and weit. *Ibid.* 32 Tempestis of weit and wind. 1790 BURNS *Young Jockie* iii, Thro' wind and weet, thro' frost and snaw.

β. a1300 *Cursor M.* 6365 Ne for na drught, ne for na wat, Changed neuer þai þare state. 1340 HAMPOLE *Pr. Consc.* 7611 In wate and drye, in hate and cald.

γ. 1573–80 TUSSER *Husb.* (1878) 92 By sowing in wet, is little to get. 1577 GOOGE *Heresbach's Husb.* I. 28 There is nothyng more hurtfull to Winter Corne,..then the wette of Winter. 1601 SHAKS. *All's Well* I. iii. 157 This distempered messenger of wet, The manie colour'd Iris. a1715 BURNET *Own Time* II. (1724) I. 801 Great numbers came to see him. But, after they had stood long in the wet, he disappointed them. 1801 WORDSW. *Sparrow's Nest* 8 The Sparrow's dwelling, which..in wet or dry My sister Emmeline and I Together visited. 1840 DICKENS *Old C. Shop* xviii, Make haste in out of the wet, Tom. 1860 FROUDE *Hist. Eng.* xxxiii. VI. 419 The sermon intended to be preached at the stake was adjourned, in consequence of the wet, to St. Mary's. 1905 *Sat. Rev.* 15 July 82/1 It is the alternation of wet and fine which brings every crop in its season.

b. Atmospheric moisture precipitated as rain, mist, or dew.

α. c1290 *St. Michael* 604 in *S. Eng. Leg.* 317 ȝwane þe sonne hath þudere idrawe þene mist for hete, It ne may no feor for þe colde, ake bicometh al to wete, And gaderez þare to one watur-cloude. 1533 BELLENDEN *Livy* I. vii. (S.T.S.) I. 41 Ane horribill tempest..made this nobil prince.. Invisibill with thik schoure of wete and myst. 1794 BURNS *My Nannie's Awa'* 6 And violets bathe in the weet o' the morn.

γ. 1613 T. CAMPION *Relat. Royal Entert.* A4b, Because some wet had fallen that day in the forenoone..all her footway was spred with broad cloth. 1617 MORYSON *Itin.* II. 68 The Pace of the Moyrye, by reason of much wet lately fallen, ..was hard to passe. 1671 MILTON *P.R.* IV. 433 And now the Sun..Had..dry'd the wet From drooping plant, or dropping tree. 1830 HERSCHEL *Study Nat. Phil.* II. vi. (1851) 159 When no rain or visible wet is falling. 1883 BLACK *Shandon Bells* xxiv, The silent thin wet that seemed to hang in the atmosphere like a vapour. 1901 A. M. FAIRBAIRN in Selbie *Life* (1913) 385 Nothing but wet and water fills the whole scene.

c. Rain, water, or damp regarded as deleterious or detrimental. Also, standing water which collects in pools, or which makes the ground muddy.

α. c1400 *Destr. Troy* 2006 Þre dayes þroly þai..duret vnder hacche, For wete of þe waghes þat wastis ouer hed. *Ibid.* 9653 [They] Turnit to þere tenttes..Thurgh the rug, & the rayn, þat raiked aboue, All wery for wete, & for wan strokes. c1480 HENRYSON *Swallow & Birds* 212 The woddis grene wer wallowit with the weit. 1523–34 FITZHERB. *Husb.* §54 Pelte-rotte..commeth of greatte wete, specyally in woode countreyes. 1545 *Acc. Ld. High. Treas. Scot.* VIII. 341, xxiiij pyonaris..quhilkis drew the cannonis and artalȝe ..withtin the munitioun hous to saife the stokis thairof from weit. 1595 in J. Bulloch *Pynours* (1887) 68 Salt and vther girnell guid subject to the perrell of weytt and rayn. a1670 SPALDING *Troub. Chas. I* (Bann. Club) I. 207 Monro caused bigg up betuixt the croces ane court de guard, for saiffeing his souldiers frae weitt and cauld on the night.

γ. 1684 J. S. *Profit & Pleasure united* 74 The Infirmitie of this Creature [the Ass] is mostly in the Feet, occasioned by standing or travelling in the wett. 1710 HILMAN *Tusser Rediv.* Feb. (1744) 16 The reason why unharrowed Beans set in Clay are apt to dye, is because the Wet fills the Holes and rots them. 1730 SWIFT *Panegyr. Dean* 109 Familiar grown to dirt and wet, Though daggled round, I scorn to fret. 1853 DICKENS *Bleak Ho.* lix, The wet had penetrated my dress. 1858 J. McD. STUART *Jrnls. Explor. Australia* (1864) 18 All our rations..being perfectly saturated with wet. 1862 H. MARRYAT *Year in Sweden* I. 74 On high, safe out of wet's way. 186. WHITMAN *Amer. Feuillage* Poems (1868) 95 Parties of snowy herons wading in the wet to seek worms. 1883 HARDY *Wessex Tales* (1888) I. 5 The gable-end of the cottage was stained with wet.

Comb. 1902 *Daily Chron.* 30 June 3/7 Wet-proof wire coverings.

d. (With *pl.*) A burst, storm, downpour, shower, or spell of rain.

α. c1440 *Alphabet of Tales* 217 On þe day at he was berid on, þer fell suche a wete and a rayn, þat ij dayes after þai mott nott berie hym. 1513 DOUGLAS *Æneis* V. xii. 53 A huge weit gan doun pour and tumbill. 1545 TAVERNER *Erasm. Prov.* 53 A mysselyng rayn gendreth a great weat. a1578 LINDESAY (Pitscottie) *Chron. Scot.* (S.T.S.) II. 312 Terribill windes with raine and weittis quhilk continewit xlviij houris togidder. 1606 in *Sel. Rec. Kirk Sess. Aberd.* (Spalding Club) 53 The gryt invndatioun of weittis liklie to rott the cornis. 1650 J. NICOLL *Diary* (Bann. Club) 8 Much unseasonable weather, the lyke quhairof wes not usuall for weittis, cold, frostes and tempestis. 1661 CHILDREY *Brit. Baconica* 65 Earthquakes always succeed great wets.

γ. 1611 SPEED *Hist. Gt. Brit.* IX. xxi. (1632) 1011 The weather extreame in wets and frosts. 1726 J. LAURENCE *Agric.* 281 Gardens which..are apt to be overflowed or soak'd with Water in the Winter, (for Summer Wets never hurt them). 1733 W. ELLIS *Chiltern & Vale Farm.* 47 The Wets that generally fall then. 1851 *Jrnl. R. Agric. Soc.* XII. II. 391 The weather often turning into sudden wets.

3. Liquor, drink. In mod. use only *slang*; esp. in ***heavy-wet***, malt liquor.

α. c960 ÆTHELWOLD *Bened. Rule* xliii. 69 Ac he ana ȝereorde..and be dæle æt and wæt ȝewanod sy. c1000 ÆLFRIC *Hom.* I. 66 He ne mæȝ ætes oððe wætes brucan. —— *Saints' Lives* xvi. 270 He..to micel nimð on æte oððe on wæte [c1175 *Lamb. Hom.* 103 on ete oðer on wete]. c1200 ORMIN 7852 Himm birrþ lokenn himm full wel Fra luffsumm æte & wæte.

γ. 1821 EGAN *Life in London* iii. 226 The soldiers and their *trulls* were seen tossing off the *heavy wet* and spirits. 1821 [? EGAN] *Real Life Lond.* I. xviii. 392 note, *Heavy wet*—A well-known appellation for beer, porter, or ale. 1839 J. GRANT *Trav. Town* I. 167 Pots of foaming heavy wet. 1894 ASTLEY *50 Years Life* II. 197 After a lot of talk and a certain amount of 'wet' he and I made three matches.

†4. Phr. ***without wet***, without being wetted. ***to take wet***, to be injured by damp. *Obs.*

a1300 *Cursor M.* 18547 Apon þe see wit-vten wete Gangand als apon a strete. 1513 [see TAKE *v.* 44b]. 1609 HOLLAND *Amm. Marcell.* 378 After they had beene weakened with this daungerous wet that they tooke. 1631 PELLHAM *Gods Power* 24 Wee found that all our Frittars of the Whale were almost spoyled with the wet that they had taken. 1693 LOCKE *Educ.* §7 He that considers how Mischievous and Mortal a thing, taking Wet in the Feet is to those, who have been bred nicely. 1712 [see TAKE *v.* 44b].

†5. ***in wet*** = in fresco (see FRESCO *sb.* 2). *Obs.*

1622 PEACHAM *Compl. Gent.* (1634) xii. 141 He wrought in distemper (as we call it) or wet with size, sixe histories of patient Iob. *Ibid.* 149 Making in his Cloyster many Histories in wet, after Masaccio's manner.

6. A 'wet' person (see WET *a.* 15b); *spec.* a politician with liberal or middle-of-the-road views on controversial issues (often applied to members of the Conservative Party opposed to the monetarist policies of Margaret Thatcher).

1931 F. L. ALLEN *Only Yesterday* x. 254 The Government putting wood alcohol and other poisons into industrial alcohol to prevent its diversion, and the wets thereupon charging the Government with murder. 1933 D. L. MURRAY *Eng. Family Robinson* vii. 159 He's quite right... You *are* a wet! Who does pay regularly? 1939 G. HEYER *No Wind of Blame* xvi. 299 He's a regular wet, that chap: doesn't hold with blood sports. 1948 C. DAY LEWIS *Otterbury Incident* ix. 111 Don't be a wet. We'll get off all right. 1961 C. WILLOCK *Death in Covert* xi. 201 'That wet,' said ffford, reverting to a school-boy expression. 'Wet he may be, but he knows about lighters.' 1974 I. MURDOCH *Sacred & Profane Love Machine* 76 You've made me into a bloody wet. I'm a fighter and you've made me into a weak person. 1976 S. BARSTOW *Right True End* III. xii. 180 She likes to throw out these challenges that put me to the test and make feel a weak-kneed wet. 1980 B. W. ALDISS *Life in West* ii. 42 He's a bit of a wet, but quite a sound art-historian.

1980 *Sunday Tel.* 6 Apr. 9 At least Sir Ian Gilmour and other political wets do not have their hair pulled. 1980 *Times* 7 Apr. 9/1 Mr James Prior, Secretary of State for Employment, is described in one Sunday paper as 'the champion of the Tory wets'. *Ibid.*, Who..are to be counted among the wets? The answer seems to be anybody who crosses the Prime Minister in fashioning a particular policy. 1980 W. WHITELAW in *Observer* 23 Nov. 11, I don't really know what a wet is. 1983 *Age* (Melbourne) 5 Oct. 13 [Of U.K. politics] In contrast to the expansionist, protectionist and welfare-oriented Wets, the Dries stand for small government, economic rationality and individual responsibility.

7. *U.S. slang.* = ***wetback*** s.v. WET *a.* 21.

1973 *Daily Tel.* (Colour Suppl.) 16 Feb. 13/1 In the past, unscrupulous employers would employ a 'wet' for a month, then denounce him to the Immigration authorities before pay day. 1979 *Time* 8 Oct. 33/1 A group of 'wets', or 'undocumented workers', as official jargon calls them. Most of the Mexican aliens are poor, frightened and docile people whose only crime is seeking to find work and a better life in the U.S. 1979 G. SWARTHOUT *Skeletons* 104 Why doesn't this [system] detect every wet who puts a toe across the line?

wet, *sb.*[2] *colloq.* [f. WET *v.*]

1. A drink or draught of some alcoholic beverage; a glass of liquor.

In the 18th c. app. sometimes confused with WHET *sb.* 2b.

1719 D'URFEY *Pills* V. 125 At Noon he gets up for a wet and to Dine. c1752 *Narr. Journ. Ir. Gentl. Eng.* (1869) 47 Valerius protested he could not walk back to dinner until he had taken a wet, as he called it: and..he went into a tavern ..and produced some cold roast beef, Cheshire cheese, and a cool tankard. 1789 *Trifler* No. xxxviii. 487 John Whip enquired of his knot of brethren on the roof whether they would take a wet. 1880 BARING-GOULD *Mehalah* xxiv, Do you, Elijah, hand a wet round. 1881 A. C. GRANT *Bush-Life Queensland* iii. (1882) 22 No bargain could be completed without a 'wet' over it. 1890 *Beeton's Christmas Ann.* 17 You look dry; let's have a wet. 1910 LOUISE GERARD *Golden Centipede* x, Chrys won't dare to hide the wets when there are visitors in the house.

2. *slang.* Urination, the act of urinating; urine. *rare.*

1925, 1975 [see WET *v.* 17].

wet (wɛt), *a.* Forms: α. 1–2 **wǽt** (**wát**), 1 *Anglian* **wét** (**uét**), 3–4 **wet**, 3–6 **wete**, 4–5, 9 *Sc.* **weet**, 4–6 **weete**, 5 **weiete**, *north.* **weytt**, 5–7 *Sc.* **weit**, 6 **weat(e**. β. 4 *north.* **wat**, 4–5 *north.* and *Sc.* **wate**, *midl.* **wote**, 5–6 *Sc.* **wait**. γ. 4– **wet**, 4–7 **wette**, 4–8 **wett**, (6 **whet**). δ. *Sc.* 6 **watt**, 6– **wat**. [Three distinct types are represented here: (1) the α-forms, originating in OE. *wǽt* adj. = OFris. *wêt* (WFris. *wiet*, dial. *weet*; NFris. *wiat*, *wīt*), ON. *vátr* (Icel. *votur*, Norw. *vaat*; Sw. *våt*, Da. *vaad*), a word not found outside of the Anglo-Frisian and Scandinavian groups; (2) the β-forms resulting from the adoption of the OScand. **wāt-* (ON. *vátr*), giving the common northern ME. *wate*, *wait*, and the rare midland *wote*; (3) the γ-forms, properly the pa. pple. of the verb, which finally supplant the others except in dialect. The Sc. *wat* may either be a variant of this or of the earlier *wate*.]

1. Consisting of moisture, liquid. Chiefly as a pleonastic rhetorical epithet of water or tears.

In OE. used with ref. to mediaeval physiology = MOIST 1d, HUMID b.

c888 ÆLFRED *Boeth.* xxxiii. §5 Sie eorðe is dryȝe & ceald, & þæt wæter wæt & ceald. c1000 ÆLFRIC *Saints' Lives* xxx. 441 Forȝif, drihten, þæt þyses fyres hæto sy ȝecyrred on wætne deaw. c1220 *Bestiary* 752 Al ðat eure smelleð swete, be it drie, be it wete. a1300 *Cursor M.* 23679 Waters renand alwais wat. 13.. *K. Horn* 970 (Harl. MS.) Horn..spec wiþ wete tearen. c1330 R. BRUNNE *Chron. Wace* 9952 Þre dayes hit was þey nought ete, Ne nought drank þat was wete. c1374 CHAUCER *Compl. Mars* 89 This cely Venus nygh dreynt in teres wete. —— *Troylus* v. 1109 Phebus with his hete Gan..to warmen of þe Est See þe wawes wete. 1513 DOUGLAS *Æneis* VII. v. 82 Careit throu feill large haw stremys wait. 1605 SHAKS. *Lear* IV. vii. 71 Be your teares wet? Yes faith: I pray weepe not. 1862 MRS. BROWNING *Last Poems, My Heart & I* iii, Our voice which thrilled you so, will let You sleep; our tears are only wet. 1894 *Pall Mall Gaz.* 20 Dec. 3/1 At Suez, Padishah gave way to tears—actual wet tears—when Potter became the owner of the birds. 1896 KIPLING *Seven Seas* 85 But, oh, the little cargo-boats, that sail the wet seas roun'.

Comb. 1597 MIDDLETON *Wisd. Solomon* xix. 18 The drie-land foule, did make the sea their nest, The wet-sea fish did make the land their rest.

2. a. Of weather, a period of time, a locality: Rainy.

c893 ÆLFRED *Oros.* III. iii. 102 Of untidlican ȝewideran, þæt is, of wætum sumerum, & of dryȝum wintrum. c1380 WYCLIF *Sel. Wks.* I. 96 As wete somers nurishen siche tares. c1461 *Bale's Chron.* in *Six Town Chron.* (1911) 145 Upon Thursday which was a wete day. 1577 GOOGE *Heresbach's Husb.* I. 21b, You must not plowe in wette weather. 1634 MILTON *Comus* 930 Wet Octobers torrent flood. 1685 in *Verney Mem.* (1907) II. 382 The wettest and windiest day that I have seene. a1700 EVELYN *Diary* 6 Oct. 1679, A very wet and sickly season. 1785 BURNS *Halloween* xv, The simmer had been cauld an' wat. 1849 C. BRONTË *Shirley* xii, They had passed a long wet day together without ennui. 1861 J. H. BENNET *Shores Medit.* I. vi. (1875) 161 [In] the Riviera..it is seldom or never, at the same time, cold and wet. 1863 [see SOAKING *ppl. a.* 6]. 1877 HUXLEY *Physiogr.* 46 The wettest spot in England being near Seathwaite in Cumberland.

b. Of the air, wind, etc.: Holding or carrying moisture in the form of vapour.

c1400 *Destr. Troy* 12474 Wintur vp wacknet with his wete aire. 1883 STEVENSON *Silverado Sq.* (1886) 42 In the tunnel a cold, wet draught..blew.

c. Of a star: Bringing rain.

c1425 *MS. Digby 233* lf. 225/1 At holy rode day.. bygynneth þe myȝt & þe strengþe of þe wete sterre arture.

d. *transf.* and *fig.* (Cf. RAINY 2b.)

a1661 FULLER *Worthies*, Gen. xi. (1662) 38 Ergo, saith the Miser, part with nothing, but keep all against a Wet day. 1691 NORRIS *Pract. Disc.* 34 The children of this World.. will [not] let slip any other advantage..of providing against a Wet Day. 1865 J. HATTON *Bitter Sweets* v, You'd most likely come down topsy-turvy, and have a werry wet welcome at the end of it. 1872 BLACK *Adv. Phaeton* xxix, Scotland was evidently bent on giving us a wet welcome.

e. *Comb.* (adj. + sb. used as an attrib. phr.).

1883 MISS BROUGHTON *Belinda* III. vi, It was an innocent enough wet-day amusement! 1897 MARY KINGSLEY *W. Africa* 96 The torrential downpour of the wet-season rain. 1901 C. HOLLAND *Mousmé* 323 Their huge wet-weather hats.

f. *absol.* = wet season. Freq. with def. article and also with capital initial. *colloq.* (chiefly *Austral.*).

1897 MARY KINGSLEY *W. Africa* 371 When the Ogowé and its neighbouring rivers come down in the 'long wet'. *Ibid.* 375 In February comes the short dry, then the short wet till May. 1908 MRS. A. GUNN *We of Never-Never* i. 5 He ..wired an inane suggestion about waiting till after the Wet. 1934 *Bulletin* (Sydney) 29 Aug. 20/4 In the 'wet' it became a miniature lake at which one cocky's horses were wont to drink. 1941 I. L. IDRIESS *Great Boomerang* vii. 51 An early and heavy wet would set in that would spill water for a thousand miles south-west. 1968 S. L. ELLIOTT *Rusty Bugles* in E. Hanger *Three Austral. Plays* I. ii. 41 That's what everyone tells me. Wait until you've done a Wet. 1981 P. CAREY *Bliss* iii. 135 Each year when the wet ended she found herself looking forward to it again.

3. a. Of land or soil: Holding water, saturated with water, heavy.

a900 *Leiden Riddle* 1 Mec se ueta uong, uundrum freoriȝ, ob his innaðae aerest caendæ. c1000 *Sax. Leechd.* I. 90 Ðeos wyrt..bið cenned ȝehwær on smeþum landum & on wætum. a1023 WULFSTAN *Hom.* (1883) 249 *Loca humentia*, þæt beoð wæte stowa. a1300 *Cursor M.* 1318 Gyson, fison, tigre, eufrate, Þis four mas al þis erth wate. 1375 BARBOUR *Bruce* XIX. 692 For I haf gert spy ws a gat. Suppos that it be sum-deill wat, A page of ouris we sall nocht tyne. 1377 LANGL. *P. Pl.* B. XIV. 41 Þe wylde worme vnder weet erthe. c1425 WYNTOUN *Cron.* I. xi. 968 Þe watyr of Nyle our fletis it all Withe mowynge spryngis wiþ outtyn spate, Qwhen Egipte nedis to be wate [*MS. W.* wait]. c1470 *Golagros & Gaw.* 35 Sa wundir wait wes the way. 1523–34 FITZHERB. *Husb.* §14 [Oats] wylle grow on weter grounde than any corne els. 1557 TUSSER *100 Points Husb.* §38 When pasture is gone, and the fildes mier and weate. 1596 DALRYMPLE tr. *Leslie's Hist. Scot.* (S.T.S.) II. 286 Thay contendet to cum out of that narow and watt place ful of dubis and myres. 1625 G. MARKHAM *Inrichment Weald Kent* 9 A cold, stiffe and wet clay. 1784 *Young's Annals Agric.* II. 43 In many of their fields they are troubled with springs; they call the wet spots *squalls*. 1842 BISCHOFF *Woollen Manuf.* II. 383 This is not, however, a turnip soil, being much too wet and heavy. 1847 [see SOAKING *ppl. a.* 6]. 1911 G. MACDONALD *Roman Wall Scot.* 132 The field at the bottom is still wet and marshy.

absol. 1824 SCOTT *St. Ronan's* viii, Miss Clara cares little for rough roads..Zounds! she can spank it over wet and dry.

fig. **1824** W. Irving *Tales Trav.* II. *Club Queer Fellows*, A good joke grows in a wet soil,..but withers on your d——d high dry grounds.

Comb. **1778** [W. Marshall] *Minutes Agric., Digest* 70 A wet-land Farm.

b. Of a crop: Grown in a moist or watery soil.

1885 W. W. Hunter *Imp. Gaz. India* (ed. 2) II. 63 The most valuable of the 'wet' crops is sugar-cane.

4. Made damp or moist by exposure to the elements or by falling in water; sprinkled, covered, or permeated with rain, dew, etc. Const. *with*, †*of*. **a.** of things, esp. clothing.

c **900** *Bæda's Hist.* v. xii. (1890) 436 Næfre he ða his wætan hræl & þa cealdan forlætan wolde, oðþæt hiȝ eft of his seolfes lichoman ȝewermedon & adruȝedon. *c* **1290** *St. Bridget* 39 in *S. Eng. Leg.* 193 So gret rein ore louerd to eorþe sende þat hire cloþes al wete weren. *c* **1385** Chaucer *L.G.W.* 775 Aurora with the stremys of hir hete Hadde dreyed vp the dew of erbis wete. *c* **1440** *Promp. Parv.* 523/1 Weet, wythe reyne, *complutus.* **1471** Caxton *Recuyell* (Sommer) 281 As for hercules all that he had vpon hym was weet and nothing drye. **1596** Ralegh *Discov. Guiana* 9 The weete clothes of so many men thrust together. **1597** Shaks. *2 Hen. IV*, v. i. 95 O you shall see him laugh, till his Face be like a wet Cloake, ill laid vp. **1725** Mandeville *Fab. Bees* (ed. 4) I. 271 In comes the nimble Messenger smoaking hot, with his Cloaths as wet as Dung with the Rain. **1800** Wordsw. *Two Thieves* 9 The traveller would hang his wet clothes on a chair. **1837** Dickens *Pickw.* li, The sky was dark and gloomy,..the streets wet and sloppy. **1853** —— *Bleak Ho.* xviii, She.. slipped off her shoes..and walked deliberately..through the wettest of the wet grass. **1866** Swinburne *Poems & B.*, *An Interlude* 2 In the greenest growth of the Maytime, I rode where the woods were wet, Between the dawn and the daytime. **1884** Pae *Eustace* 13 Eustace..was not long in divesting himself of his wet garments.

b. of persons (together with their clothes) or a part of the body. Also of animals.

c **1205** Lay. 28080 þa wes ich al wet, & weri of sorȝen and seoc. **1375** Barbour *Bruce* iv. 380 Thouch thai wate war and wery. *c* **1386** Chaucer *Reeve's T.* 187 Wery and weet as beest is in the reyn Comth sely Iohn. **1471** Caxton *Recuyell* (Sommer) 279 Wherof hercules and exione were all wette of the wasshing and springyng of the wawes. **1523** Berners *Froiss.* I. cccxxiv. 205 b, Suche as were wete & colde made fyers to warme them. **1597** Shaks. *2 Hen. IV*, iii. i. 27 Canst thou (O partiall Sleepe) giue thy Repose To the wet Sea-Boy, in an houre so rude. **1600** Fairfax *Tasso* i. xiv, He.. shooke his wings with roarie May-dewes wet. *a* **1700** Evelyn *Diary* 2 Oct. 1641, We were forced to walke on foote very wett and discompos'd. **1728** Ramsay *Anacr. Love* 8 A poor young wean a' wat! **1789** W. Blake *Songs of Innoc., Little Boy Lost* 6 The child was wet with dew. **1825** Cobbett *Rur. Rides* (1885) I. 399 The farm-house..from the warmth and good fare of which we do not mean to stir, until we can do it without the chance of a wet skin. **1849** James *Woodman* xlvi, Set me a seat by the fire,..and then call in the slave. He is wetter than we are. **1861** E. D. Cook *P. Foster's Dau.* i, Besides, I hate to get wet. **1918** *Chamb. Jrnl.* 1 Oct. 678/2 Mad as a wet hen because I refuse to take his word for it that the titles are O.K.

c. with prefixed intensive pple., as ***wringing*** (see wringing *ppl. a.*), ***dripping***, †***dropping wet***. ***wet through***, ***to the skin***: having one's clothes completely saturated (cf. wet *v.* 4 c).

a **1500** *Flower & Leaf* 406 Wherewith they made hem stately fyres grete To dry their clothes that were wringing wete. **1526** *A C. Merry Tales* No. 82 (facs.) 22 b, There fel a good showre of rayn that the skoler was well wasshyd and wete to yͤ skyn. **1591**, **1770** [see dropping *ppl. a.* 1 c]. **1611**, **1764** [see skin *sb.* 6 e]. **1798** Southey *Lett.* (1856) I. 61 But all this does not make it the more agreeable to get wet through. **1835** W. Irving *Tour Prairies* xiii, Some dripping wet, having fallen into the river. **1840** Longf. in *Life* (1891) I. 359 The last eighteen miles it rained like fury, and I reached Hartford wet through. **1859** F. E. Paget *Curate Cumberworth* 343 The rain set in..so heavily, that in half an hour I was wet to the skin.

d. absol. ***the wet*** = one's wet clothes.

17.. *The Ploughman* iii. in Herd *Songs* (1776) II. 145 Cast aff the wet, put on the dry, And gae to bed, my deary. **1816** Scott *Antiq.* xxvi, And then the man casts aff the wat and puts on the dry, and sits down..ahint the ingle.

e. Applied to a removable liner for the cylinder of an internal-combustion engine that has cooling water flowing between it and the cylinder wall.

1935 *Jrnl. R. Aeronaut. Soc.* XXXIX. 470 The four cylinders 63 m/m. bore by 120 m/m. stroke were steel jacketed, wet liners, having four valves per cylinder. **1959** *Motor* 14 Oct. 304/2 Cylinder blocks with individual wet liners of cast iron. **1975** M. J. Nunney *Automotive Engine* iii. 94 Positive sealing arrangements must be made with wet cylinder liners to prevent leakage of coolant into the crankcase. **1981** H. E. Ellinger *Automotive Engines* x. 157/2 Coolant flows around the cylinder sleeve, so this type of sleeve is called a wet sleeve.

5. a. Suffused with tears; moist with weeping or with being wept upon. Const. *with*, †*of*.

c **1205** Lay. 30268 Wete weoren his wongen. *a* **1225** *Ancr. R.* 278 Bihold mid wet eien þine scheomeful sunnen. *c* **1250** *Gen. & Ex.* 2356 Euerilc he kiste, on ilc he gret, Ilc here was of is teres wet. *a* **1300** *Cursor M.* 25999 þat þou mai sai al wit þe prophet, Mi weping mas mi bed al wet. *c* **1386** Chaucer *Knt's T.* 422 The pure fettres on his shynes grete Weren of his bittre salte teeres wete. **1390** Gower *Conf.* I. 98 Hire yhen smale and depe set, Hire chekes ben with teres wet. *c* **1489** Caxton *Sonnes of Aymon* ix. 226 His eyen wexed weete agen for pite. **1500–20** Dunbar *Poems* lxxii. 133 Repentence ay with cheikis wait, No pane nor pennence did eschew. **1611** Shaks. *Cymb.* v. v. 35 These her Women.. who with wet cheekes Were present when she finish'd. **1667** Dryden & Dk. Newcastle *Sir M. Mar-all* iv. i, Lord! her innocency makes me laugh my Cheeks all wet. **1785** Cowper *Task* iv. 17 Epistles wet With tears, that trickled down the writer's cheeks. **1871** Bryant *Odyss.* v. 105 Gazing with wet eyes upon the barren deep. **1885–94** Bridges *Eros & Psyche* May xxvi, And when at night her lover kisst her, lo! Her tender face was wet with tears of grief.

b. Suffused or covered with blood; dripping or oozing with blood. (Only of wounds, or with explicit mention of blood.)

a **1300** *Cursor M.* 15628 þat was blod þan of him ran, þe place was þar-wit wett. *Ibid.* 24082 His bodi al blodi wat. **13..** *Sir Orfeo* 80 Sche froted hir honden and hir fet, And crached hir visage, it bled wete. *c* **1320** *Cast. Love* 1433 þe woundes grene and weet, Wȝuche þat weoren on honden and feet. *c* **1400** *Destr. Troy* 1329 Wyde woundes & wete. *c* **1440** *York Myst.* xxxviii. 283 þat swete, þat for my loue tholed woundes wete. **1804** W. L. Bowles *Spir. Discov.* iv. 24 The evil of his march through cities stormed, And regions wet with blood!

c. Moist or damp with perspiration.

c **1400** *Laud Troy Bk.* 8436 Of his forhede barst the swote, That al his face ther-of was wote. **1803** *Med. Jrnl.* X. 84 After violent perspiration, a linen or cotton shirt becomes wet.

d. ***to get wet***: to lose one's temper, become angry. *Austral. slang* (? *Obs.*).

1898 *Bulletin* (Sydney) 17 Dec. Red Page, To *get narked* is to lose your temper; also expressed by *getting dead wet.* **1916** C. J. Dennis *Songs of Sentimental Bloke* 42 Romeo gits wet as 'ell. **1945** Baker *Austral. Lang.* 121 A man in a temper is said..*to get wet.*

e. ***to get*** (someone) ***wet***: to gain the upper hand over; to have at one's mercy. *N.Z. slang.*

c **1926** 'Mixer' *Transport Workers' Song Bk.* 29 He skites about in-fighting. Stick to him, Mick; you've got him wet. **1941** *Coast to Coast 1941* 124 'Got you wet, haven't they?' He flung the remark over his shoulder as he went over to his bed. **1945** F. Sargeson *When Wind Blows* vi. 40 Now we've got 'em wet.

f. Of those activities of intellignece organizations, esp. of the K.G.B., that involve assassination. *slang.*

1972 A. Price *Col. Butler's Wolf* vi. 58 The Russian slang for Spetsburo Thirteen was *Mokryye Dela*—'The department of wet affairs'..and to get wet was the feared, inevitable fate of traitors pursued by the special bureau. **1975** J. Grady *Shadow of Condor* ii. 47 'The courier made other mistakes... It was a wet affair.'.. Ryzhov like to use the old KGB liquid euphemism for executions. **1980** J. Gardner *Garden of Weapons* ii. vii. 191 He had seen men killed: and killed them himself: he had directed 'wet operations', as they used to be called.

6. a. Made moist or damp by dipping in, or sprinkling or smearing with, water or other liquid.

Freq. of new-printed matter (newspapers or books), esp. in the phr. ***wet from the press.***

1390 Gower *Conf.* II. 264 Tho lay ther certein wode cleft, Of which the pieces nou and eft Sche made hem in the pettes wete, And put hem in the fyri hete. **1398** Trevisa *Barth. De P.R.* vii. lxiv. (1495) 280 The water slydeth of as it were of a wete hyde. *c* **1430** *Two Cookery-bks.* 48 Wete þin dyssche in þe hony, & with þe wete dyssche ley þe malmenye & þe cofyns. **1432–50** tr. *Higden* I. 267 Then the white neckes schalle be humectate or made weiete with golde. *c* **1450** *Mirk's Festial* 191 Byd hym goo ynto þe chirch, and se how al þe pament ȝet ys wete of þe holy watyr. **1644** Milton *Areop.* (Arb.) 53 Do we not see..weekly that continu'd Court-libell..Printed, as the wet sheets can witnes, and dispers't among us for all that licencing can doe? **1721** E. Ward *Wand. Spy* i. (1729) 3 Then a wet Finger does its Duty, And robs the Bar-board of its Beauty. **1754** *Connoisseur* No. 29 ⁋1, I snatch up the favourite sheets wet from the press and devour every syllable. **1798** Coleridge *Recantation* xx, With the morning's wet newspaper. **1804** *Med. Jrnl.* XII. 494 It should be afterwards cleaned with a wet sponge. **1835** *New Monthly Mag.* XLIV. 337 Just published, and wet from the press, 'The Stranger's Guide through Little Pedlington'. **1838** Dickens *Mem. Grimaldi* I. vii. 186 No sooner did they arrive wet from the press, than men on horseback were immediately despatched with them to Canterbury. **1839** De Quincey *Wordsw. & Southey* Wks. 1889 II. 316 Wordsworth's habits of using books..were not vulgar; not the habits of those who turn over the page by means of a wet finger. **1850** F. K. Hunt *Fourth Estate* II. 220 Just as the wet Newspaper, fresh from the News-boy, is being opened at the eight o'clock breakfast table. **1859** FitzGerald *Omar* xxxvi, I watch'd the Potter thumping his wet Clay.

†**b.** (*a*) ***with a wet finger***: easily, with little effort. Also (*b*) readily, without hesitation; (*c*) slightly, lightly. *Obs.*

Perh. from the practice of wetting the first or second finger on one's tongue in order to facilitate turning over the leaves of a book or to rub out writing on a slate. Cf. quots. 1721 and 1839 in 6.

1542 Udall *Erasm. Apoph.* To Rdr. *iv, A large and plain table..whereby..to any good matier in the booke conteined, readie waye and recourse maye with a weet fynger easily bee found out. **1562** J. Heywood *Prov. & Epigr.* (1867) 78 With a wet fynger ye can fet, As much as maie easyly all this matter ease. **1589** *Rare Tri. Love & Fortune* iii. C 4, And I can finde One with a wet finger that is starke blinde. **1593** G. Harvey *Pierces Super.* 2, I hate brawles with my hart: and can turne-ouer A volume of wronges with a wett finger. **1600** *Wisd. Dr. Dodypoll* iii. E 3 b, *Flo.* Canst thou bring me thither? *Pea*[*sant*]. With a wet finger sir. **1644** Featly *Roma Ruens* 5, I could with a wet finger produce divers decrees of Popes..flat repugnant one to the other. **1690** C. Nesse *O. & N. Test.* I. 293 How easily ..even with a wet finger, (as we say) could God..have overturned Jacob. **1728** [De Foe] *Street-Robberies* 47 When our Tryal came on, we got clear with a wet Finger, as the Folks say. **1748** Richardson *Clarissa* (1768) V. 152 If thou likest her, I get her for thee with a wet finger, as the saying is! **1754** Foote *Knts.* i. 15 If Dame Winifred was here, she'd make 'em all out with a wet Finger; but they are above me. **1818** Scott *Hrt. Midl.* xii, If we could but find ony ane to say she had gien the least hint o' her condition, she wad be brought aff wi' a wat finger.

(*b*) **1583** Stubbes *Anat. Abus.* ii. 39 The broker will giue mony for them, with a wet finger. **1604** Dekker *Honest Wh.* i. A 4, If ever I stand in neede of a wenche that will come with a wet finger.

(*c*) **1586** [? J. Case] *Praise Mus.* vii. 79 To let passe all generalities which I touched before with a wet finger. **1624** Gataker *Transubst.* 45 The slightnesse and slendernesse of his Answeres, with a wet finger (as we say) passing by the manifold allegations produced.

c. in other proverbial expressions.

to cover oneself with a wet sack: see sack *sb.*[1] 3.

1561 tr. *Calvin's 4 Serm. Idol.* i. A iij b, Thinking that he is escaped when he is couered, as the common saying is, vnder a wette sack. **1578** H. Wotton *Courtlie Controv.* 61 For so many pleasures vanished, as an Ele through a wette hande. **1579**, *a* **1651** [see sack *sb.*[1] 3]. **1616** Draxe *Bibl. Scholast.* 218 He holdeth a wet eele by the taile. **1679** *Lett. Gent. Romish Rel. to Brother* 32 There being no more hold of them than of a wet Eel by the tail.

d. ***to come with a wet sail***: to make swift progress to victory, like a ship with sails wetted in order to keep close to the wind.

1876 *Coursing Calendar* 326 Westeria, coming with a wet sail, rushed by and ultimately killed. **1901** *Daily Express* 18 Mar. 8/1 Bury, who were expected to come with a wet sail, went down before their local rivals at Bolton.

7. Of timber: Full of sap, unseasoned.

c **1386** Chaucer *Knt.'s T.* 1480 And as it queynte, it made a whistlynge, As doon thise wete brondes in hir brennynge. **1468–9** *Stonor Papers* (Camden) I. 103 Let not hit be wete tymbyr in hond. **1900** Hueffer in *Academy* 18 Aug. 127/2 The wet-wood smoke drives us winking blind. **1906** H. Van Dyke *Ideals* xii. 266 Wet wood will not burn.

8. Of paint, varnish, ink: Not yet dry, sticky, liable to smudge.

1519 [see blotting-paper]. **1552–3** in Feuillerat *Revels Edw. VI* (1914) 139 For drying of stayning paynting and other wett pasted and mowlded woorkes. **1611** Shaks. *Wint. T.* v. iii. 81 The ruddinesse vpon her Lippe is wet: You'le marre it, if you kisse it. **1850** Miss Mulock *Olive* xx. (1890) 157 Ha! don't come near my picture. The paint's wet. Get away. **1883** M. E. James *How to Decorate* 19 Remember that tempera is many shades lighter when it is dry than when it is wet. **1914** 'Bartimeus' *Nav. Occas.* vii. (1916) 50 The younger girl wiped a foot of wet paint off the coaming of a hatch, and said sweetly it didn't matter in the least.

9. *Fort.* Of a ditch: Containing water.

For the sense cf. wet dock.

1590 Sir R. Williams *Discourse War* 50 No drie ditch can bee compared for strength vnto a wet ditch. **1813** *Ann. Reg.*, *App. to Chron.* 130 The whole of the fortification is surrounded by a wet ditch. **1869** Tozer *Highl. Turkey* II. 193 The citadel is separated from the mainland by a wet ditch of artificial construction.

10. Of fish: **a.** Cured with salt or brine. **b.** Fresh, not dried.

a. *c* **1580** in *Eng. Hist. Rev.* (1914) July 523 Wett newland fishe, ye c, 1 li. Drye fishe, the hondert, o li. 10 sh. **1580** R. Hitchcock *Polit. Plat* a iv, Twentie thousande of the beste and middle sort of wette fishe (at the leaste) called blanckfishe, and tenne thousande drie fishe. **1708** *Lond. Gaz.* No. 4421/7 The Cargo of the Prize-Ship Margaret of Nantz, consisting of about 11000 Wett, or Mud-fish. **1883** *Fisheries Exhib. Catal.* 64 The preparation of white herrings ..consists of packing the fish in salt, which soon turns to brine, and this method of preparation is termed the 'wet cure'.

b. **1851** Mayhew *Lond. Labour* I. 62/2 All fresh fish is 'wet'; all cured or salted fish, 'dry'. **1899** *Daily News* 14 Jan. 5/1 The inexpensive kinds of fish are cod, hake, skate, sprats, and 'wet' haddock.

11. Of confections: Preserved in syrup; of a syrupy nature. Of surgical or natural-history specimens: Bottled in spirits.

1612 *Sc. Bk. Rates* in *Halyburton's Ledger* (1867) 312 Wett confectionis—Preserved barbareis..Marmalad [etc.]. **1686** tr. *Chardin's Trav. Persia* 259 Sweat-meats Dry and Wet, upon small Porcelaine Plates. **1836** [Mrs. Traill] *Backw. Canada* 46 The American Crab, these beautiful little scarlet apples so often met with as a wet preserve among our sweetmeats at home. **1867** Latham *Black & White* 87 The 'wet specimens,' those bottled in spirits. **1891** *Century Dict.*, *Wet preparation*, a specimen of natural history immersed in alcohol.

12. Of measure: Used for liquid articles. ? *Obs.*

1597 Skene *De Verb. Signif.* s.v. *Gangiatores*, Al measures, & weichts, baith dry & weete. **1622** Malynes *Lex Mercat.* 39 The Romanes in times past, called the wet Measure by Ounces, as wee doe the weight. **1638** L. Roberts *Merch. Map Comm.* ii. 238 Wet Measures are also derived from this pound Troy.

13. *Med.* **a.** Designating certain diseases which are characterized by moist secretions.

1565 Blundevil *Curing Horses Dis.* lxix. (1580) 29, I call it the wet cough, bicause the horse in his coughing, will voide moiste matter at his mouth. *Ibid.* cxxvii. 58 Of the wet Spauen, or through Spauen. **1898** P. Manson *Trop. Diseases* xiv. 232 The paralytic-atrophic cases are designated 'dry beriberi' or beriberi atrophica; the dropsical cases, 'wet beriberi' or beriberi hydrops. **1899** *Syd. Soc. Lex.*, *Wet brain*, *Wet scald*, *Wet tetter*.

b. ***wet cup***, ***cupping***: see cupping *vbl. sb.* 1.

1897 *Allbutt's Syst. Med.* II. 175 Wet-cupping the loins to the extent of several ounces may be of service. **1913** Dorland *Med. Dict.*, *Wet-cup*, a cupping-glass to be used after scarification.

c. Designating various modes of hydropathic treatment, as in ***wet bandage***, ***compress***, ***pack***, ***packing***, ***sheet.***

1843 Sir C. Scudamore *Med. Visit Gräfenberg* 16 Wet Bandages. **1848**, **1870** [see compress *sb.* 1]. **1859**, **1899** [see pack *sb.*[1] 11]. **1874** [see packing *vbl. sb.*[1] 1 c]. **1874** Bucknill & Tuke *Psychol. Med.* (ed. 3) 754 The Wet Sheet or Wet Pack..acts as an energetic sudorific.

fig. *c* **1864** J. B. Paton in *Life* (1914) 85 We cannot submit to have these men..wrapped in the eternal wet-sheet of a monastic college.

14. *colloq.* **a.** Primed with liquor; more or less intoxicated. (Cf. WET *v.* 7 b.)

1704 PRIOR *Celia to Damon* 66 When my lost Lover the tall Ship ascends, With Musick gay, and wet with Iovial Friends. **1834** COLERIDGE *Table T.* 20 Jan., Some men are like musical glasses;—to produce their finest tones, you must keep them wet.

b. Addicted to drink.

a **1700** B. E. *Dict. Cant. Crew*, *Wet-Quaker*, a Drunkard of that Sect. *c* **1713** in Aitken *Steele* (1889) I. 395 It's a very wet town, and the voters are wet too. **1825** BROCKETT *N.C. Words*, *Wet-hand*, a drunken person. **1900** 'R. GUTHRIE' *Kitty Fagan* 207 It might keep some o' the wet hands oot o' the pub.

c. *transf.*

1592 NASHE *P. Penilesse* Wks. (Grosart) II. 57 Those that keep a wet corner for a friend, and will not thinke scorne to drinke with a good fellowe and a Souldior. **1805** [see BARGAIN *sb.*[1] 7]. **1824** W. IRVING *Tales Trav.* II. *Club Queer Fellows*, His jokes, it must be confessed, were rather wet, but they suited the circle over which he presided. **1848** THACKERAY *Van. Fair* xi, As he knew he should have a *wet night*, it was agreed that he might gallop back again in time for church on Sunday morning. **1905** VACHELL *The Hill* iii. 49 Some of us had a wet night of it, last night.

15. *colloq.* **a.** Of a Quaker: Not very strict in the observances of his sect. (See also 14 b.)

1700 T. BROWN *Amusem. Ser. & Com.* Wks. 1720 III. 29 Would you buy any naked Truth, or Light in a dark Lanthorn? Look in the Wet-Quakers Walk. *a* **1708** T. WARD *England's Reform.* II. (1710) 44 Quakers, and Wet-Quakers, or Merry-ones. **1785** GEO. A. BELLAMY *Apol. Life* (ed. 3) I. xiii. 78, I had not indeed dressed myself with the studied formality of a rigid Quaker, but only so plain and neat as to entitle me to the denomination of a wet Quaker; a distinction that arises chiefly from the latter's wearing ribbands, gauzes, and laces. **1838** *Bentley's Miscell.* IV. 297 Who has not heard of..a wet Quaker? who *thees* and *yays*, wears no collar to his coat..; but is in other respects..living that sort of life which, in England, is called that of a jolly dog. **1839** MARRYAT *Diary Amer.* Ser. I. I. 255 Mr. Buffum..was dressed as what is termed a wet Quaker. **1866** CARLYLE in Mrs. Carlyle *Lett.* II. 53 An enthusiastic young 'Wet-Quaker'.

transf. **1831** W. IRVING *Life & Lett.* (1864) II. 461 Mine host, the Rev. C. R. Reaston Rodes..is a kind of *wet* parson, if I may borrow that phrase from the Quakers. **1855** NEWMAN *Callista* vi. (1856) 48 Agellius is but a wet Christian;..not obstinate, like his brother there. **1876** MARCH. DUFFERIN *Canad. Jrnl.* (1891) 295, I believe our one friend here is a 'wet' Mormon, and at his house, where we spent the evening, we only met one-wifed men.

b. Inept, ineffectual, effete; also as quasi-*adv.* and in comb. ***wet fish***, a wet individual, a 'drip'. Also *spec.* in *Politics* (see quots. 1981 and 1983). Cf. WET *sb.*[1] 6.

1916 'TAFFRAIL' *Pincher Martin* ii. 27 I'll give yer a clip 'longside the ear'ole if you ain't careful. Don't act so wet. **1924** P. MARKS *Plastic Age* 94 They attended a performance of Shaw's 'Candida' given by the Dramatic Society and voted it a 'wet' show. *Ibid.* 192 A man is wet if he isn't a 'regular guy'; he is wet if he isn't 'smooth'; he is wet if he has intellectual interests..; and he is wet..if he is utterly stupid. **1938** E. BOWEN *Death of Heart* II. iv. 239 Cecil is so wet! Coming early like that, then sticking round like that. **1944** A. CHRISTIE *Towards Zero* 86 Audrey marry that wet fish? She's a lot too good for that. **1963** Wet fish [see MOOSE[1] c]. **1969** K. AMIS *Green Man* iv. 180 The Jesus of the Gospels can be a bit of a wet liberal at times. **1973** P. O'DONNELL *Silver Mistress* iv. 74 Don't talk wet, Jan. There's nothing you could do. **1980** *Times Lit. Suppl.* 28 Nov. 1355/2 The contrast between the splendid façade and the rather wet interior of the man [*sc.* Havelock Ellis], who was kind and gentle and distinguished, but also distressingly absent, indifferent and faint.

1981 *Observer* 26 July 12/3 The term 'Wet' was originally used by Mrs Thatcher, who meant it in the old sense of 'soppy', as in 'What do you mean the unions won't like it, Jim? Don't be so wet.' It meant feeble, liable to take the easy option, lacking intellectual and political hardness. Like so many insults, it was gleefully adopted by its victims, and so came by its present meaning of liberal, leftish, anti-ideological. **1982** *Listener* 23/30 Dec. 6/3 In considering the promotion of wet (or wettish) Ministers, she will tell herself that Pope was right. **1983** *Age* (Melbourne) 5 Oct. 13 Britain's Tory Prime Minister, Mrs Margaret Thatcher, began this vogue terminology by contemptously dismissing dewy-eyed dissenters from her arid Right-wing policies as 'wet'.

c. ***all wet***: mistaken, completely wrong. orig. and chiefly *U.S.*

1923 *N.Y. Times* 9 Sept. VII. 2/1 *All wet*, all wrong. **1931** *Kansas City Times* 29 Aug., Alfalfa Bill Murray may be 'all wet' in his state-line bridge and oil production controversies. **1940** G. ADE *Let.* 5 June (1973) 221 Regarding the Rotary Clubs, I..am an honorary member. I think the organization is alright and that Sinclair Lewis was all wet when he tried to poke fun at the small town booster. **1941** E. B. WHITE *Let.* Summer (1976) 216, I haven't had much time to think things over and I am probably all wet on a lot of things in here. **1951** A. BARON *Rosie Hogarth* 282 You're all wet if you think I'm giving up that easy.

d. ***wet behind the ears***: see EAR *sb.*[1] 1 c.

16. a. Consisting of alcoholic liquor.

1779 *Remembrancer* VIII. 277 Saturday last arrived here from Cadiz, a polacre, with a large and general assortment of dry and wet goods. **1837** J. COTTLE *Early Recoll.* I. 320, I think he carries on a snug business in the smuggling line, and..is on the look-out for some wet cargo. **1882** *Daily News* 31 Jan. 2/1 The central office for 'wet goods', i.e. wines and spirits. **1884** *Chamb. Jrnl.* 26 Jan. 58/2 Casks of vinous liquors, technically known as 'wet goods'.

b. Concerned with the sale and consumption of alcoholic liquor.

1892 [see DRY *a.* 11 a]. **1899** H. WYNDHAM *Queen's Service* 97 Canteens..are known as either 'wet' or 'dry'. In the former, beer, porter, and stout, but no spirits, are sold. *Ibid.* 98 The hours during which 'wet' Canteens are open. **1913** R. H. GRETTON *Mod. Hist. Engl. People* I. 90 Whereas at ports the customs arrangement allowed 'bonding' on a large scale, there was no such possibility in inland towns, except in some 'wet' trades.

c. orig. and chiefly *U.S.* Permitting the sale of alcoholic liquor: accepting or adhering to this as a principle; opposed to the prohibition of the liquor traffic. Freq. in recent use. Hence as quasi-*adv.* in phr. ***to go*** or ***vote wet***. Cf. DRY *a.* 11 a.

1870, etc. [see DRY *a.* 11 a]. **1888** BRYCE *Amer. Commw.* liv. II. 350 *note*, Some States, e.g. Georgia, have adopted a local option system, under which each county decides whether it will be 'wet' or 'dry' (i.e. permit or forbid the sale of intoxicants). **1888** *North American* (Philadelphia) 3 Apr. 1/1 Forty-nine counties have voted 'dry', and thirty-three 'wet'. .. Thirteen of twenty towns went 'dry', and seven 'wet'. **1908** *Westm. Gaz.* 20 May 12/1 A map of the United States, with prohibition States white, licence States black, and States partly 'dry' and partly 'wet' under local option indicated by shading. **1919** H. L. WILSON *Ma Pettengill* 36 Like a cow-hand with three month's pay hitting a wet town. **1954** K. AMIS *Lucky Jim* 109 The still recent tradition of a 'wet' Summer Ball. **1974** *Times* 7 Oct. 4/1 Flintshire, Radnorshire, Breconshire..voted to go wet. *Ibid.* 4/2 That poll ended the curious situation of one inn which straddled on the wet-dry border... The public bar was dry and empty, but the lounge bar was wet and crowded.

d. *absol.* or quasi-*sb.* (from prec. sense).

1888 *Battle Creek* (Michigan) *Weekly Jrnl.* 29 Feb., This is the first great victory for the 'wets'. **1896** [see DRY *sb.* 5]. **1906** *Mission Field* Aug. 144 The 'wets' would carry such cities as Guthrie, Oklahoma City and Shawnee. **1919** *Blackw. Mag.* Nov. 657/1 The party calling themselves 'The Wets' still believed that the President would intervene to avert such legislation. **1920** [A. G. GARDINER] *Windfalls* 17 The wasp..shares man's weakness for beer. In the language of America, he is a 'wet'. **1968** *Daily Tel.* 8 Nov. 1/4 The 'wets' gained three counties..in the Welsh referendum on Sunday drinking.

17. a. Designating various technical processes or operations.

1807 AIKIN *Dict. Chem.* II. 427 Tin is soluble in acid of tartar, and this solution is of importance in manufacture, as it is the method by which wet tinning is performed on copper and brass. **1854** C. TOMLINSON *Obj. Art-Manuf., Paper* 24 The paper..is subjected to a second pressure, called wet pressing, by which a further portion of the water is got rid of. **1859** REEVE *Brittany* 6 The wet collodion process. **1878** ABNEY *Treat. Photogr.* vii. 50 The following are collodions..for the wet process. **1882** *Imperial Dict.*, *Wet-puddling*, in metallurgy, pig-boiling. **1897** *Allbutt's Syst. Med.* II. 989 The dangers consequent upon the manufacture of arsenic have been much diminished..by what is technically known as the 'wet method'.

b. Designating chemical tests and analysis involving the use of solvents or other liquids; = HUMID *a.* c; so ***wet-chemical*** adj. Cf. WAY *sb.*[1] 14 c.

1800 tr. *Lagrange's Chem.* I. 398 Analysis by the wet way. **1858** *Phil. Mag.* XVI. 331 This method is particularly adapted..when the substances of this group occur in so small quantities that they are no longer recognizable in the wet way. **1887** *Encycl. Brit.* XXII. 70/2 A convenient wet-way method for small quantities is to boil the recently precipitated chloride..with caustic soda-ley. **1932** F. SODDY *Interpretation of Atom* xv. 253 Almost all the ordinary chemical tests for the common elements, by which they are identified in the ordinary reactions of 'wet' analysis, are not tests for the elements, but for their ions. **1967** *Electronics* 6 Mar. 29 (Advt.), You can be sure of a complete refinery service... Including, under one roof..laboratory facilities for wet chemical analysis and electrolytic methods of analysis. **1973** *Nature* 8 June 365/1 Since the Second World War, physical methods of analysis..have increasingly displaced wet chemistry from the industrial routine analytical laboratory. **1977** *New Scientist* 17 Feb. 384/1 Traditional methods of detecting nitrogen oxides as air pollutants monitor the change in colour of an acid permanganate solution as the oxides are absorbed. These wet-chemical methods..require relatively large samples of gases.

18. *Naut.* Of a vessel: Liable to ship water over the bows or gunwale.

1832 MARRYAT *N. Forster* x, She was what sailors term rather *a wet one*, and the sea broke continually over her bows. **1884** CLARK RUSSELL *Jack's Courtship* xvii, The *Strathmore*..had the reputation of being a very fast sailer, though what is termed a wet ship. **1891** M. ROBERTS *Land-travel & Sea-faring* 9 The *Seringapatam* was a very 'wet ship', that is, she was very much inclined to ship heavy seas.

19. Of natural gas: containing significant amounts of the vapour of higher hydrocarbons.

1926 *Daily Colonist* (Victoria, B.C.) 18 July 16/7 Wet gas flow of 3,000,000 feet a day was struck at McLeod No. 2 well in Turner Valley last night. **1948** *Petroleum Handbk.* (Shell Petroleum Co. Ltd.) (ed. 3) ix. 154 Gases produced in contact with oil can be either 'dry' or 'wet', depending on the nature of the crude oil and the method of separating the gas from the oil. **1982** *Shell Briefing Service* No. 5. 5/2 LPG is essentially a mixture of propane and butane stored at ambient temperature under moderate pressure. It can be derived from the gas associated with crude oil or from 'wet' natural gas directly at the well.

20. In combination with pa. pples.: **a.** predicative, as ***wet-crushed***, ***-picked***, ***-plucked***, ***salted***, ***situated***, ***spun***, ***woaded***.

1877 RAYMOND *Statist. Mines* 419 The cost of drying the *wet-crushed ore. **1885** *Encycl. Brit.* XVIII. 225/2 It [esparto] is again '*wet-picked' after boiling. **1960** *Farmer & Stockbreeder* 19 Jan. Suppl. 41/3 At slaughter the birds are all..*wet-plucked by machine and then eviscerated. **1969** R. ADLARD in R. Blythe *Akenfield* xiv. 234 The feathers are no use because the chickens [in factory farms] are wet-plucked, so there is only a mess. **1885** *Harper's Mag.* Jan. 274/1 Hides brought to the tannery in this condition are known as '*wet salted'. **1765** A. DICKSON *Treat. Agric.* (ed. 2) 471 When clay land is *wet situated. **1901** *Scotsman* 1 Apr. 11/1 The demand for *wet spun yarns. **1660** FULLER *Mixt Contempl.* xlix 76 What may be the cause why so much cloth so soon changeth colour? It is because it was never *wet wadded, which giveth the fixation to a colour.

b. parasynthetic, as ***wet-bottomed***, ***-eyed***, ***-feeted***, ***-footed***, ***-lipped***, ***mouthed***.

1812 SIR J. SINCLAIR *Syst. Husb. Scot.* I. 222 *Wet-bottomed land. **1886** C. SCOTT *Sheep-Farming* 89 Much wet-bottomed land..is ill suited for rearing lambs. **18..** LEIGH HUNT *Robin Hood & Outlaws* xvii, Never woman [came] for redress, And went away *wet-eyed. **1891** HARDY *Tess* xl, He knelt down at the bedside wet-eyed. **1864** DICKENS *Mrs. Lirriper's Legacy* i, It was in vain for me to..tell him he'd be..*wet-feeted to death by the slop and mess. **1833** HOOD *Public Dinner* 174 *Wet-footed, spoilt-beaver'd, ..You haste home to supper. **1856** MISS YONGE *Daisy Chain* I. vi, She has come home wet-footed and cold. **1870** MORRIS *Earthly Par.* III. IV. 232 The *wet-lipped west wind. **1951** DYLAN THOMAS *Sel. Lett.* (1966) 352 [Fresh recruits] see before them in the hot moonlight wetmouthed Persian girls from the bazaar.

21. Special collocations (see also 13 above): **wetback** orig. and chiefly *U.S.*, an illegal immigrant who crossed the Rio Grande from Mexico to the U.S.; also *attrib.* and *transf.*; **wet bar** *N. Amer.*, a bar or counter in a private house from which alcoholic drinks are served; **wet bargain** (see BARGAIN *sb.*[1] 7); **wet bob** [BOB *sb.*[7]], a boy at Eton who devotes himself to boating; also *gen.*; so **wet bob** *v. intr.*; **wet-bobbing** *vbl. sb.*; **wet-bulb**, designation of that one of the two thermometers of a psychrometer the bulb of which is covered with muslin, which is wetted at the time of observation so as to indicate the 'temperature of evaporation'; † **wet cloth**, cloth that has been wetted in the process of fulling; **wet cooper** (see COOPER *sb.*[1] 1); **wet diggings** orig. *U.S.*, gold diggings in or near a river or stream; cf. *dry diggings* s.v. DRY *a.* C. 3; **wet dream**, an erotic dream which causes a man or boy to have an involuntary sexual orgasm during sleep; also *fig.*; **wet-eared** = *wet behind the ears* s.v. EAR *sb.*[1] 1 c; **wet end**, that end of a paper-making or drying machine into which the wet material is passed; **wet fly** *Angling* (see quot. 1875); also *attrib.*; **wet frost**, a frost accompanied by damp air; † **wet glover** (see GLOVER[1] b); † **wet larder**, one where moist or liquid provisions were stored; **wet lease** (see quot. 1979); so **wet lease** *v. trans.*, **wet-leased** *ppl. a.*; **wet leg** *slang*, a self-pitying person; **wet look** [LOOK *sb.* 2 f], an appearance of a wet or shiny surface; usu. *attrib.*, esp. of fabrics (see quot. 1968); **wet meter**, a gas-meter in which the gas passes through a body of water; **wet pack**, a compact waterproof bag which folds or rolls up and is designed for carrying toilet articles; **wet plate** *Photogr.*, a sensitized collodion plate exposed in the camera while the collodion is moist; also *attrib.*; **wet-point** *a.*, of villages, settlements, etc.: having an available water supply; **wet process**, a manufacturing process involving the use of water or other liquid; freq. *attrib.*; **wet rent**, a levy paid to a brewery by a publican in a tied public house in proportion to the amount of beer sold (see also quot. 1907); **wet rot**, decay in timber caused by excessive moisture; † **wet-salter** (in contrast to DRY-SALTER); **wet shave**, a shave (SHAVE *sb.*[2] 2) carried out with the aid of a razor, soap, and water as opp. to a (usu. electric) razor alone; so **wet shaver**, someone who shaves by this method; **wet shaving** *vbl. sb.*; **wet smack** *slang* (chiefly *U.S.*), a spoil-sport; **wet spinning**, (*a*) spinning of natural fibres when they are wet from passage through a water bath; (*b*) spinning of man-made fibres in which the spinneret extrudes the streams of liquid into a coagulating bath; so **wet-spin** *v. trans.*, **wet-spun** *ppl. a.*; **wet steam** (see quot.); **wet strength**, the strength of paper and textiles when wet; **wet suit**, a suit, usu. of rubber, worn by divers, surfers, etc., to protect them from the cold; hence **wet-suited** *a.*; **wet time**, in the building trade, time during which work cannot be carried out owing to bad weather; **wet trade** (see quots.); **wet-weather** *a.*, (*a*) associated with or occurring in rainy weather; (*b*) designed for use in rainy weather; **wet-white**, liquid white theatrical make-up; **wet wing** *Aeronaut.* (see quot. 1969); usu. *attrib.*

1929 *Foreign Affairs* Oct. 101 The peon walks or swims across..and is welcomed by his countrymen here as a '*wet back'. **1972** *Observer* (Colour Suppl.) 28 May 28/1 Last year in California alone, border patrols turned back 27,000 wetbacks (the contemptuous name derives from their practice of swimming the Rio Grande to reach the US). **1978** *N.Y. Times Mag.* 23 July 23/2 Wetbacks (a derogation of Mexicans swimming the Rio Grande to slip into the U.S.) became illegal aliens, and are now referred to as undocumented persons. **1979** *Guardian* 8 June 5/2 Illegal migrants from South China . . are getting into Hong Kong . . usually swimming the last part of the trip. The total of Chinese 'wetbacks' intercepted . . in the first week of June alone came to 3,722. **1982** T. Beattie *Diamonds* xii. 100 It might be that wetback job I did... But they can't prove anything. **1968** *Globe & Mail* (Toronto) 15 Jan. 23/6 (Advt.), Panelled family room, games room, *wet bar. Real executive home! **1978** R. Thomas *Chinaman's Chance* xx. 206 Ploughman turned to find Reginald Simms standing by a small wet bar across the room. **1865**, **1886** *wet bob [see Bob *sb.*[7]]. **1872** *Daily News* 7 Aug., The 'wetbobs' of the Solent are not so absolutely the creatures of the weather office as the 'drybobs' of Canterbury. **1901** D. Sladen *My Son Richard* i, Only on the river they have this much mutual respect for each other—each recognises that the other is a good wetbob. **1884** J. Montagu *Let.* Mar. in Troubridge & Marshall *John Ld. Montagu of Beaulieu* (1930) 31, I have been out *wet-bobbing several times and am getting coached. **1901** G. Frankau *Eton Echoes* 40 (*heading*) Wet Bobbing. **1926** *Spectator* 3 July 11/1 Any alternative summer game or sport . . such as is provided by 'wet-bobbing' at a school like Eton. **1849** Eastwick *Dry Leaves* 228 The *wet-bulb Thermometer was generally 10° lower than the dry one till the beginning of June. **1916** *Lancet* 15 Jan. 142/2 A man . . can do far more work with less fatigue at a low wet-bulb temperature than at a high one. **1435** *Coventry Leet Bk.* 172 No walker . . Shall Rakke no Clothe on the Teyntur that schall be solde ffor *wette-clothe. **1439** *Rolls of Parlt.* V. 30/2 Mesurynge for the dosenne of wete Clothe xii yerdes and xii ynches, and of secce Clothe nought wete, xiiii yerdes and xiiii ynches. **1849** J. Wyld *Geogr. & Mineral. Notes* 21 The works are divided into two classes, —Dry Diggings and *Wet Diggings. **1862** J. L. C. Richardson *Sk. Otago* 48 See how the wet diggings will pay in the summer time. **1935** E. B. Buckbee *Saga Old Tuolumne* 11 He worked ceaselessly throughout the day lifting gold from the 'wet diggings'. **1965** G. J. Williams *Econ. Geol. N.Z.* vii. 72/1 The conglomerates accumulated on the slopes of the mountains are the proper field for the 'dry diggings', while from the gravel and sand of the beds of rivers and smaller streams the gold is obtained by 'wet diggings'. **1851** W. Acton *Pract. Treatise Diseases of Urinary Organs* (ed. 2) I. ii. 226 Spermatorrhœa . . is known . . as nocturnal or diurnal emissions, pollutions, *wet-dreams, [etc.]. **1921** H. Crane *Let.* 11 Feb. (1965) 53 The wet-dream explosions of Virgil Jordan and McAlmon. Their talk is all right—but what is true of it has been said adequately before. **1946** B. Marshall *George Brown's Schooldays* 170 Well, what are you standing there looking like a wet dream for? **1963** A. Heron *Towards Quaker View of Sex* ii. 16 It is at this stage that nocturnal emissions or 'wet dreams' as they are often called, are frequently the first clear sign of sexual maturity in the boy. **1971** B. W. Aldiss *Soldier Erect* 10 Jesus, what a wet dream of a party that was! **1978** A. Neave *Nuremburg* viii. 86 He was said by the prosecution to have boasted to his chauffeur of nightly wet dreams and exhibited the semen to prove it. **1967** E. McGirr *Hearse with Horses* iii. 50 If a race was fixed they wouldn't need a *wet-eared kid mixed up with it. **1971** F. Forsyth *Day of Jackal* I. i. 21 Apart from a few wet-eared ninnies who refused to come, Rodin led his entire battalion into the military putsch of April 1961. **1888** Cross & Bevan *Text-bk. Paper-Making* x. 154 This part of the machine, which is called the '*wet-end', is placed at a slight slope. **1927** T. Woodhouse *Artif. Silk* iii. 25 The wet pulp is now run on to the feed end, usually termed the 'wet-end', of the drying machine. **1962** Wet end [see *dry end* s.v. dry *a.* C. 3]. **1875** F. Francis in *Encycl. Brit.* II. 38/2 In the majority of instances it is the custom to let the tackle soak, and when fishing to allow the fly to sink a little under the surface—to fish with a '*wet fly', as it is called. **1904** Gallichan *Fishing Spain* 207 The ordinary winged patterns used for wet-fly fishing. **1832** Cobbett *Rur. Rides* (1885) II. 382 Wall-fruit is, when destroyed in the spring, never destroyed by dry-cold; but ninety-nine times out of a hundred, by *wet-frosts. **1688**, **1724** *wet glover [see glover[1] b]. **1726** *Dict. Rust.* (ed. 3) s.v., The Wet-glover is for Sheep, Goats, Lambs, and Castlings Skins . .; for the dressing whereof, he only uses Lime and Bran. **1544** *Inv.* in *Surrey Archæol. Collect.* VII. 238 The dry larder... The Kechyn... The *Whet larder. Itm in the Wett larder A musterd quern, iiij d. **1574** *Richmond Wills* (Surtees) 247 In the wett larder ii kymlinges, one trowghe. **1605** in *Archæologia* XIII. 330 The Clarcke of the Kittchine . . is to see into the wette and drie larders, what provisions there bee. **1962** *Aeroplane & Astronautics* CII. 88/2 Philippine Air Lines has *wet-leased (i.e., aircraft plus flight crew) a Boeing 707 from Pan American. **1977** *Indian Express* 18 May 1/2 The Airbus will be either wet leased or chartered by Air-India. **1979** *Daily Tel.* 8 June 36/6 Aircraft can be leased by the hour, day, week, month, quarterly or longer on a 'dry' lease which means that crews are not provided, or on a 'wet' lease which means that the owner of the aircraft also supplies crew and, in some cases, the necessary fuel. **1978** *Observer* 29 Jan. 1/5 These too will have to be taken out of service for modifications, and their place taken by '*wet leased' foreign aircraft (that is, planes taken complete with their own crews). **1922** D. H. Lawrence *Let.?* 12 Oct. (1962) II. 726 Being too much of a *wet-leg, as they say in England, nakedly to enter into the battle. **1929** —— *Pansies* 124 It is strange to think of the Annas, the Vronskys, the Pierres, all the Tolstoyan lot Wiped out... And the Tchekov wimbly-wambly wet-legs all wiped out. **1981** *Times Lit. Suppl.* 3 July 745/1 We know how much Auden hated wet-legs, how constantly he repeated his many litanies of his own good fortune. **1968** J. Ironside *Fashion Alphabet* 102 The '*Wet Look' is a chemical finish to fabrics to make them appear shiny and wet. **1969** *Times* 24 Nov. 16/2 Natural coloured python or wet-look patent are the most fashionable finishes for day. **1970** D. Uhnak *Ledger* (1971) ix. 114 Her lips, shining with a wet-look lipstick, quivered. **1971** *Daily Tel.* 2 Feb. 11 (*caption*) The chair and stool covered in white wet-look fabric. **1981** *Westindian World* 31 July 14/2 (Advt.), Hot & cold straightening, curly perm, wet look. *c* **1865** Letheby in *Wylde's Circ. Sci.* I. 127/1 There are two objections to the *wet meter, which are insurmountable. **1869-71** *Cassell's Househ. Guide* II. 17/2 The gas meters now in general use . . are known as 'wet' and 'dry' meters. **1928-9** *Army & Navy Stores Catal.* 419/1 *Wet Pack. Fitted with comb and nail file, etc. Size closed, $5\frac{1}{2} \times 4\frac{1}{2}$ in. . . Pigskin 12/-. **1974** *Harrods Christmas Catal.* 18/2 For travelling men... Two wet packs with waterproof linings. **1859** Reeve *Brittany* 123 Our camera, already charged with a *wet plate. **1878** Abney *Treat. Photogr.* xi. 77 Wet-plate photography. **1920** *Wet-point [see *dry-point village* s.v. dry *a.* C.3]. **1969** G. C. Dickinson *Maps & Air Photographs* xiv. 216 (*heading*) 'Wet-point' sites—i.e. places with an available water supply. **1909** Webster, *Wet... Chem., etc.* Employing, or done by means of, or in the presence of, water or other liquid... The **wet* process or way. **1930** *Engineering* 3 Jan. 18/3 The Assano Portland Cement Company's works at Nishitama. This is a wet-process plant. **1945** H. D. Smyth *Gen. Acct. Devel. Atomic Energy Mil. Purposes* vii. 75 Study of product recovery processes as a whole (wet processes, physical methods). **1969** Wet process [see by-product b]. **1907** F. E. E. Bell *At Works* v. 122 Some of the yearly benefit clubs of which the head-quarters are at public-houses demand . . an extra contribution, from 1d. to 3d., what is called the '*wet rent', which is quite deliberately allowed for drink each meeting-night. **1967** *Economist* 29 Apr. 480/2 The Jones board has implicitly accused the brewers of subsidising too many low volume country pubs, by charging less than the market rents but rather more for their beer, a practice known in the trade as a 'wet rent'. In actual fact, wet rents are steadily becoming proportionately less important, and the brewer's idea is to protect the publican against the ups and downs of trade by charging him, in effect, a rent that varies slightly with beer sales, thus identifying his interest more closely with that of the brewer. **1978** *Times* 3 May 19/6 The brewers . . continue phasing out 'wet' rents under which a tenant pays more or less to the brewery according to the amount of beer sold through the pub. **1865** Dickens *Mut. Fr.* I. viii, Sparrows were there, cats were there, dry-rot and *wet-rot were there. **1876** Preece & Sivewright *Telegraphy* 161 Wet-rot is the destructive agent at work more or less on all telegraph poles. **1726** De Foe *Eng. Tradesman* I. viii. 98 The orange-merchants and *wet-salters about Billingsgate. **1976** *NBR Marketplace* (Wellington, N.Z.) III. 2/1 Something over 50 per cent of the estimated 900,000 regular shavers in New Zealand prefer a *wet shave start to the day. *Ibid.* 2/3 About 94 per cent of wet shavers use the safety razor with double-edge blades or the modern single-edge blade systems. **1964** *Financial Times* 25 Feb. 11/8 The chief obstacle at present is the *wet-shaving industry's promotion of the new stainless steel blades. **1980** 'D. Kavanagh' *Duffy* iii. 44 They only took the television set and his electric razor. . . He went back to wet shaving. **1927** *Amer. Speech* III. 221 **Wet smack*, . . something unsatisfactory; applies particularly to an individual who spoils a party; a kill-joy. **1929** Wodehouse *Mr. Mulliner Speaking* i. 33 The man is beyond question a flat tyre and a wet smack. **1977** *Maledicta* Summer 17 If she is actually frigid, she's a *wet smack*. **1963** A. J. Hall *Textile Sci.* ii. 75 Some of these polymers are soluble in organic solvents . . and thus allow the preparation of solutions which can be *dry* spun . . or *wet spun—that is, extruded into a coagulating bath. **1973** *Materials & Technol.* VI. iv. 328 Polyacrylonitrile solutions have been wet-spun . . into a coagulating bath. **1864** *Wet spinning [see *dry spinning* s.v. dry *a.* C.3]. **1927** T. Woodhouse *Artif. Silk* 28 The coagulation by means of liquid of any kind has given rise to the term 'wet spinning', whereas the term 'dry-spinning' has been applied in all cases where the solvent is vaporized. **1969** A. J. Hall *Stand. Handbk. Textiles* (ed. 7) iii. 127 In wet spinning the roving is led through a trough of hot water . . so that the fibres are softened. **1973** *Materials & Technol.* VI. iv. 295 Another method of taking up the *wet spun yarn. **1858** R. Murray *Marine Engines* (ed. 3) 237 **Wet steam* is steam which holds watery particles in mechanical suspension. **1960** R. W. Marks *Dymaxion World of B. Fuller* 59/1 Even in 1954 Kraft paper having exceptional 'wet tensile strength' had been developed—'*wet strength' meaning the ability of the paper to retain its structural quality when saturated. **1962** J. T. Marsh *Self-Smoothing Fabrics* xiv. 211 These examples of dimensional stability are of some consequence, and indeed of great consequence with fibres of regenerated cellulose whose low wet-strength is a serious defect but one which is remedied by the crease-resisting process. **1973** *Nature* 27 Apr. 588/1 Cross linking has been used for over thirty years in making 'wet strength' papers. **1955** *Wet suit [see *dry suit* s.v. dry *a.* C.3]. **1964** *Skin Diver* Oct. 19 An American skin diver aboard an Irish fishing boat . . had a difficult time convincing the skipper that his 'wet' suit would save a man's life if he fell into the freezing water. **1970** *Daily Tel.* (Colour Suppl.) 18 Sept. 12 On deck three of us, clad in rubber wetsuits, prepared to slip over the side. **1972** *Islander* (Victoria, B.C.) 4 June 16/1 The wet suit, worn to keep the diver warm, is almost a necessity in these northern waters. **1984** S. Townsend *Growing Pains A. Mole* 78 She looked dead erotic in her black wetsuit and crash helmet. **1972** *Nat. Geographic* Oct. 584 *Wet-suited author examines the giant wraparound grin of a right whale. **1978** D. Williams *Treasure up in Smoke* xix. 174 The alerted wet-suited figure had . . waded to the beach. **1938** *Times* 5 May 10/4 For nearly 20 years the building trade operatives have . . claimed that for uncontrollable irregularities of employment . . there should be a scheme of compensation for loss of earnings. The phrase which they used to focus the claim was 'payment for *wet time'. **1952** *Economist* 12 July 118/2 Steel erectors on American building sites do not enjoy either a guaranteed week or payment for 'wet-time'. **1962** *Listener* 26 July 154/3 The 'do-it-yourself' enthusiast who is preparing to tackle garden operations involving the use of cement, lime, and water—the so-called '*wet trades'. **1973** *Times* 24 Feb. 13/1 The shortage of skilled workers, particularly in the 'wet trades' of bricklaying and plastering. **1858** T. S. Woodward *Let.* 20 Dec. in *Reminisc.* (1939) 157 Fortunately, we found a little *wet-weather spring near the top. **1901** [see wet *a.* 2 e]. **1922** M. A. von Arnim *Enchanted April* i. 8 Big grey eyes almost disappearing under a smashed-down wet-weather hat. **1934** M. V. Hughes *London Child* iii. 28 The boys were off on some long wet-weather tramp. **1978** 'D. Rutherford' *Collision Course* 182 I'm gambling on rain... We're giving you wet-weather tyres. **1922** M. Arlen *Piracy* III. xiv. 256 Just look how depraved they are! They are covered with verdigris, but they call it *wet-white! **1976** 'D. Fletcher' *Don't whistle 'Macbeth'* 51 The first time I sang Elvira, I had to cover myself from head to toe with wet-white. [**1958** *Flying Rev.* Oct. 37/1 Scheduled to Supplement earlier Stratofortresses currently serving with the Strategic Air Command, the B-52G employs a 'wet' integral-tank wing which substantially increases the bomber's unrefuelled range.] **1961** *Flight* LXXIX. 818/2 These new '*wet wing' versions, with greatly increased weight and machined-plank wing skins, have suffered local stresses greater than any experienced with the earlier versions of lower weight and performance. **1969** *New Scientist* 25 Sept. (Microbes in Industry Suppl.) 23/2 In modern 'wet-wing' aircraft, such as Concorde, the fuel is simply pumped into the wings which are coated internally with sealants. In older aircraft . . the fuel is contained in rubber bags in the wings.

wet (wɛt), *v.* Forms: α. *Inf.* 1 **wǽtan**, *Anglian* **wétan**, 3–6 **wete**, (5 *Sc.* **wet, vete**), 4–7 **weete**, (6 *pa. t.* **weeted**), 5–6 *Sc.* **weit**, 6 **weate**, 7 **weat**, 6– (chiefly *Sc.*) **weet**. *Pa. t.* 1 **wǽtte**, 3 **watte**, 4 **wat**, (5 *pl.* **watten**), 6– *Sc.* **wat**; 4–5 **wete**, (5 *Sc.* **vet**), 4–6 **wette**, 4–7 **wett**, 5– **wet**. *Pa. pple.* 4–5 **y-wet, y-wette**, 4–6 **i-wet, wette**, (5 *Sc.* **wete, vete**), 5–7 **wett**, 4– **wet**. β. *Inf.* 5–6 **wette**, 6–7 **wett**, 6– **wet**. *Pa. t.* and *pple.* 6– **wetted**. [OE. *wǽtan* (Angl. *wétan*), f. *wǽt* (*wét*) wet *a.*, = ON. *vǽta* (Icel., Norw. *væta*, Sw. *väta*, Da. *væde*). The normal shortening of the vowel in the pa. t. and pa. pple. in ME. was finally extended to the infin. and present.]

I. *trans.*

1. a. To make (an object) humid or moist by the application of water or other liquid; to suffuse, sprinkle, moisten, drench, bathe *with* (water, etc.); to dip, steep, soak *in*, †*on*.

a **950** *Guthlac* xxii. (Prose) Heo . . ᵹenam þa þæs ᵹehalᵹodan sealtes . . and wætte and drypte in þa eaᵹan. *a* **1000** *Riddles* xii[i]. 10 Hwilum mec . . dol druncmennen . . wæteð in wætre. *c* **1000** *Sax. Leechd.* II. 134 Wæt þæt liþ mid ecede. *Ibid.* 350 Wæt þæt ᵹewrit on þam drence. *c* **1275** *Passion of Our Lord* 103 in *O.E. Misc.* 40 Þat bred þat ich on wyne wete. *a* **1300** *Cursor M.* 17682 And wit a deu mi face he wette. *c* **1374** Chaucer *Troylus* III. 1115 Therwith his pows and pawmes of his hondes They gan to frote, and wete his temples tweyne. **1390** Gower *Conf.* III. 36 Send Lazar doun . . And do that he his finger wete In water. ? *a* **1400** *Morte Arth.* 2332 There barbours ware bownne, with basyns one lofte, With warme watire i-wys they wette theme fulle sone. *c* **1400** Maundev. xviii. [xiv.] (1919) 105 Ȝif a man . . wete hem with may dew ofte sithes. *c* **1430** *Two Cookery-bks.* 52 Take fayre Paynemayn y-wette in Wyne. ? **1550** W. P. tr. *Curio's Pasquin in Trance* 24 They . . wet the graue with vnholy water, and they perfumed it with Frankincense. **1560** Whitehorne *Ord. Souldiours* (1588) 39 b, A stoppell of cotten wet in oyle of gineper. **1677** J. White *Rich Cabinet* 143 You must let the Paper dry of it self after you have once wetted it. **1684** J. S. *Profit & Pleasure united* 23 Cleansing their mouths . . with a spung or Linnen cloath wett in Beer. **1707** *Ir. Act 4 Geo. I*, c 11. §13 If any of the persons aforesaid shall . . wet their hay, or use any other fraud or deceit to make any carr-load of hay to be of the weight prescribed. *c* **1770** T. Fairfax *Compl. Sportsm.* 31 Then having wetted your hand in water, rub his body all over. **1813** Southey *Nelson* I. 235 All the shrouds and sails of his ship, which were not absolutely necessary for its immediate management, were thoroughly wetted. **1859** *Handbk. Turning* 83 A small camel's-hair brush . . used for wetting postage stamps. **1869** Claridge *Cold Water Cure* 190 Her head, throat, and chest, were frequently wetted with cold water. **1907** J. A. Hodges *Elem. Photogr.* (ed. 6) 103 As soon as the paper is wetted with the solution.

Proverb. **1546** J. Heywood *Prov.* II. v. (1867) 58 He loueth well sheeps flesh, that wets his bred in the wul.

b. *Sci.* Of a liquid: to cover or penetrate (a substance or object) readily, so that a small quantity spreads uniformly over it rather than lying as droplets upon it.

A common criterion of wetting is the angle that the surface of a droplet makes, at its point of contact, with the surface on which it rests (as measured through the liquid): the liquid is said to wet or not to wet the surface according as the angle is less or greater than 90 degrees.

1855 D. Lardner *Hand-bk. Nat. Philos.: Hydrostatics* I. v. 69 If a liquid be poured into a vessel whose sides are of such a nature as to be wetted by it, the liquid . . will be curved upwards near the points where it touches the side. **1884** A. Daniell *Text Bk. Princ. Physics* xi. 246 Objects which are wetted by the liquid in which they float are thus apparently attracted by it; those which are not so are apparently repelled. **1932** *Phytopathology* XXII. 926 The presence of an appreciable quantity of sodium hydroxide . . increases the ease with which the leaves can be 'wetted' in the solution. **1967** M. Chandler *Ceramics in Mod. World* vi. 171 Silicon nitride . . is not wetted by molten metals. **1974** *Encycl. Brit. Macropædia* XI. 782/1 The adhesion of water to glass at an air-water-glass interface is greater than the cohesion of water, and hence water is said to wet the glass... The cohesion of mercury is greater than its adhesion to glass and it does not wet the glass. **1978** *Nature* 20 July 237/1 An example of this is a droplet of the liquid resting on a solid surface. When the contact angle is less that 90°, the liquid wets the solid. Molten beryllium does not wet BeO because the contact angle exceeds 90°.

2. To suffuse with tears, bedew with weeping. Also said of the tears.

c **825** *Vesp. Psalter* vi. 7 Mid tearum strene mine ic wetu. *a* **1300** *E.E. Psalter* vi. 6 With mi teres in mi bede Sal i wete mi liggynge-stede. *a* **1310** in Wright *Lyric P.* xv. 47 Unwunne haveth myn wonges wet. *c* **1375** *Sc. Leg. Saints* xviii. (*Egipciane*) 950 Quhen I had lange tyme gret, & al myn face with teris wete. **14..** *Sir Beues* p. 35 (MS. E.) So moche reweþe he hadde þere þat þe teres watten hys lere. **1596** Spenser *F.Q.* I. iii. 44 And all the way she wetts with flowing teares. *c* **1600** Shaks. *Sonn.* ix. 1 Is it for feare to wet a widdowes eye, That thou consum'st thy selfe in single life? **1614** J. Cooke *Greene's Tu Quoque* B 3 b, Giue not your friends cause to wet their handkerchers. **1616** B. Jonson *Epigr.* xxxiii, Who wets my graue, can be no friend of mine. **1682** Bunyan *Holy War* (1905) 289 Then they . . kissed his feet, and wetted them with tears. **1742** Fielding *J. Andrews* III. xii, A river of tears ran down her lovely cheeks, and wet the handkerchief which covered her bosom. **1836** Landor *Pericles & Asp.* lx, Her tears wetted my cheek. **1868** Louisa

M. ALCOTT *Little Women* xii, Laying her head on her arm, Jo wet her little romance with a few happy tears.

†**3.** Of wine: To moisten, fill with moist 'humours'. *Obs.*

c **1000** *Sax. Leechd.* II. 246 Ne þæt win is to þicgenne þætte hætеþ & wæteþ þone Innoþ. **1560** GOOGE tr. *Palingenius' Zodiac* III. (1561) Fiij, Apace we feede and scarce canne ryse, so wetes the wyne our brayne.

4. To make moist or damp by exposure to rain, by a fall into water, or the like. ***to wet through, to the skin***: to drench the clothes of (a person).

a. Said of water, rain, etc.

1297 R. GLOUC. (Rolls) 6578 þat water..wax euere uaste, ..& watte is sson & is vet. *a* **1300** *Cursor M.* 23685 Waters þat wete þan cristes flexs. **1387** TREVISA *Higden* II. 25 þe water wolde..wete [MS. γ weete] al her cloþes. *c* **1480** HENRYSON *Age & Youth* 4 Perly dropis of þe balmy schowris þir wodis grene hed with þe watter wet. **1530** PALSGR. 780/2 In the begynnyng of the yere the dewe weteth the grounde swetely. **1589** *Pappe w. Hatchet* in *Lyly's Wks.* (Bond) III. 394 We care not for a Scottish mist, though it wet vs to the skin. **1600** W. WATSON *Decacordon* (1602) 218 Men..of as bad a nature and base a moulde as euer water wette, or winde dried. **1658** *Nicholas Papers* (Camden) IV. 57 Wee had not above 4 shots of powder and that the worst that euer water wet. *a* **1700** EVELYN *Diary* an. 1646, These waters in some places breaking in the fall wett us as if we had pass'd through a mist. **1719** DE FOE *Crusoe* II. (Globe) 554 The Place was not deep, but it wetted me all over. **1795** SOUTHEY *Lett. fr. Spain* (1799) 60 The clouds wetted me as they passed along. **1816** TUCKEY *Narr. Exped. R. Zaire* v. (1818) 179 During the night we had two smart showers of rain, which..wetted us through. **1839** DICKENS *Nickleby* xiv, 'It doesn't take much to wet you and me through, Mr. Crowl,' said Newman, laying his hand upon the lappel of his threadbare coat. **1858** LARDNER *Hand-bk. Nat. Phil.* 73 If a capillary tube be plunged in a liquid which wets it. **1874** MARCH. DUFFERIN *Canad. Jrnl.* (1891) 171 A thunder-shower..which wetted us to the skin. **1884** *Law Times Rep.* LI. 229/2 The water..soaked under the wall and wetted the mud below it.

fig. *a* **1340** HAMPOLE *Psalter* xvii. 17 *Apparuerunt fontes aquarum*..þat is þe sothfastnes of prechours is seen, þat wetis men wiþ halesome lare. **1627** E. F. *Edw. II* (1680 fol.) 93 What can he do to England, which hath a wooden wall will wet his courage?

b. *absol.*

c **1330** R. BRUNNE *Chron. Wace* 10340 Wyþ rysyng wawes, ..Fer aboute hym wil he [the lake] wete. *Ibid.* 10343 þe wawes þat so wetes. *a* **1600** MONTGOMERIE *Misc. Poems* v. 44 All is not gold that gleitis..Nor water all that weitis. **1600** SHAKS. *A.Y.L.* III. ii. 27 The propertie of raine is to wet, and fire to burne. **1660** F. BROOKE tr. *Le Blanc's Trav.* 373 All they ever have is a dew, which is so slender it never wets at all. **1661** BOYLE *Physiol. Ess.* (1669) 187 Though every wetting Liquor be fluid, yet every fluid Body does not wet. **1756** C. LUCAS *Ess. Waters* I. 82 The purest water wets soonest and most.

c. *passive.* Often ***to be wet through***, (also †***thorough*** or ***through wet***), ***wet to the skin*** (cf. a).

The form *wet* of the pa. pple. is sometimes difficult to distinguish from WET *a.* 4 c.

c **1400** tr. *Higden* VII. 151 In processe of tyme þat body y-wette wiþ dewy droppes knewe þe comoun corrupcioun of dedly men. *c* **1400** *Laud Troy Bk.* 12942 So faste doun the water ȝet, That thei were alle thorow wet. **1497** *Naval Acc. Hen. VII* (1896) 129 The Newe making of a last of gonnepoudre wett in saltwater. **1535** COVERDALE *Dan.* iv. 15 With the dew of heauen shall he be wet. **1542** UDALL *Erasm. Apoph.* 99 b, But if he had been wetted from toppe to toe, no man standyng by to see it, then had he been miserable in veraye deede. **1589** PUTTENHAM *Eng. Poesie* III. xvii. (Arb.) 189 As the drie ground that thirstes after a showr Seemes to reioyce when it is well iwet. **1594** [see THROUGH *adv.* 4]. **1639** J. TAYLOR (Water P.) *Part Summers Trav.* 44 So that the miserable Stipend..will hardly buy wood to make a fire for him when hee comes home to dry him, when hee is through wet. **1659** in *Verney Mem.* (1907) II. 141 Hee..was wett to the skin before he came half way. **1759** JOHNSON *Idler* No. 71 ¶9 He..heard with great delight a shower, by which he was not wet, rattling among the branches. *a* **1766** MRS. F. SHERIDAN *Sidney Bidulph* (1796) IV. 53 The bottom of that vile ditch into which he had fallen was full of water, and he had been wet quite through. **1775** A. BURNABY *Trav. N. Amer.* 36, I had been wet to the skin in the afternoon. **1820** SOUTHEY *Wesley* I. 78 Having slept on the floor one night, because his bed had been wetted in a storm. **1842** *Min. Proc. Inst. Civil Engin.* II. 78 Some of the compressed trenails had been wetted by accident, and could not be afterwards driven into the holes in the chairs. **1856** HAWTHORNE *Engl. Note-bks.* (1870) II. 14 We were caught in two or three showers.. but got back..without being very much wetted. **1898** A. BALFOUR *To Arms* vii, The street was paved with large, rounded stones, which..were splashed and wetted by dirty water thrown from above. **1904** A. N. COOPER *Quaint Talks* 10 Few things have struck people as more wonderful than how I have survived being wet through so often.

5. a. Of a person or animal: To get (oneself, one's body or clothes, also another person or object) moist or damp by contact with, or immersion in, water or other liquid.

1338 R. BRUNNE *Chron.* (1810) 204 Sir kyng rise vp & skip, for þou has wette þi hater. *c* **1386** CHAUCER *Prol.* 129 She leet no morsel from hir lippes falle Ne wette hir fyngres in hir sauce depe. *c* **1400** MAUNDEV. (Roxb.) vi. 21 Þat wymmen schuld mow wade ouer and noȝt wete þaire kneesse. **1589** HAKLUYT *Voy.* 542 When they can flye no further [they] fall into the water, and hauing wette their wings take a newe flight againe. **1639** J. TAYLOR (Water P.) *Part Summers Trav.* 40 You know you need not wet your foot to seek them, they are your own already. **1770** C. JENNER *Placid Man* v. vii. II. 142 If you can be contented..to return at night,.. having in four or five hours tired a pair of coach-horses, wetted two servants to the skin [etc.]. **1816** G. S. FABER *Orig. Pagan Idol.* I. 398 Every morning they [certain aquatic birds] repaired to the sea, wetted their wings, and sprinkled the sacred edifice. **1818** SCOTT *Br. Lamm.* xiii, Twa finer dentier wild-ducks never wat a feather. **1846** MRS. A. MARSH *Father Darcy* xlv, In traversing the ford of the Stour ..they have wetted the bag of powder. **1873** MARCH. DUFFERIN *Canad. Jrnl.* (1891) 82 The gentlemen..in getting into the canoe..were upset, and wet all their clothes.

b. *Proverb.*

c **1384** CHAUCER *H. Fame* 1785 For ye be lyke the sweynte catte, That wolde haue fissh but..He wold no thinge wete his clowes. **1390** GOWER *Conf.* II. 39 As a cat wolde ete fisshes Withoute wetinge of his cles. *c* **1394** *P. Pl. Crede* 405 Þou woldest not weten þy fote, & woldest fich kacchen. **1545** TAVERNER *Erasm. Prov.* 59 b, The cat wold fyshe eate, but she woll not her fete weate. **1546** J. HEYWOOD *Prov.* I. xi. (1867) 28. **1639** J. CLARKE *Parœm.* 234 The Cat loves fish well, but is loath to wet her foot.

c. To void urine in (one's bed, clothes). ***to wet one's pants*** *fig.*, to become excited or upset (as if to the extent of involuntarily voiding urine).

1767 *Ordinary's Acc. Eliz. Brownrigg* 10 The deceased child had wetted the bed. **1899** *Allbutt's Syst. Med.* VIII. 259 The man who wets his bed, rather than take the trouble to get out and make water, is insanely idle. **1979** 'M. UNDERWOOD' *Smooth Justice* i. 35 There are quite a few people who'll wet their pants if I get sent down. **1981** A. PRICE *Soldier no More* 184 We did see the *Histories* season at Stratford, I grant you. But I don't remember any schoolgirls wetting their pants next to me.

d. *refl.* To urinate involuntarily. Also *fig.* (as at sense 5 c above).

1922 JOYCE *Ulysses* 730 What do I care with it dropping out of me and that black closed breeches he made me buy takes you half an hour to let them down wetting all myself. **1970** G. F. NEWMAN *Sir, You Bastard* 258 The Sunday editors would wet themselves; they liked nothing better than a sordid purge in an institution. **1976** *Times Lit. Suppl.* 30 Jan. 100/5 She also sweats, weeps, vomits and wets herself.

6. Of a river, sea, etc.: **a.** To water, irrigate (land).

1382 WYCLIF *Josh.* xiii. 3 The trubli flood that weetith [Vulg. *irrigat*] Egipt. *a* **1425** *Cursor M.* 1318 (Trin.) Fison, gison, tigre & eufrate, Al erþe þese weten erly & late. **1773** FERGUSSON *Leith Races* iv, I dwall amang the caller springs That weet the Land o' Cakes.

b. To lave, border with water (a coast, country). *rare.*

1572 T. TWYNE tr. *Dionysius' Surv. World* A v, The Sea.. which..wetting the countrie Issica..is called Issicum. *a* **1774** FERGUSSON *Auld Reekie* 319 As lang as Forth weets Lothian's shore.

7. a. ***to wet*** (one's) ***whistle, weasand, mouth, beak, beard***, etc.: to take a drink. See also CLAY *sb.* 4 b.

c **1386** [see WHISTLE *sb.* 2]. *c* **1460** *Towneley Myst.* xiii. 103 Had She oones Wett Hyr Whystyll She couth Syng full clere Hyr pater noster. **1530**, **1653** [see WHISTLE *sb.* 2]. **1611** COTGR., *Crocquer la pie*, to wet the whistle, or weason, throughly; to drinke hard. **1682** N. O. *Boileau's Lutrin* II. 154 Wetting their Whistles with the good Ale-pot. **1722** CROXALL *Fables Æsop* xcviii. 169 I'll give you a Dram to wet your Whistle. *a* **1774** FERGUSSON *Auld Reekie* 4 Whare couthy chiels at e'ening meet Their bizzing craigs and mous to weet. **1785** BURNS *Scotch Drink* xiv, Monie daily weet their weason Wi' liquors nice. **1850** DICKENS *Copperfield* vii, The wine shall be kept to wet your whistle. **1888** R. BUCHANAN *Heir of Linne* i, I ne'er can sing till my throat's wetted, Tammas. **1910** W. H. HUDSON *Sheph. Life* xi. 135 The starlings..singing and talking and swallowing elderberries between whiles to wet their whistles. **1939** T. S. ELIOT *Old Possum's Bk. Pract. Cats* 16 For to the Bell at Hampton he had gone to wet his beard. **1978** J. CARROLL *Mortal Friends* I. v. 53 Is there a public house here where a fellow could wet his beak?

†**b.** *passive.* To be primed with liquor. (Cf. WET *a.* 14 a.) *Obs.*

c **1440** *Partonope* 5198 And so they dronke þat boþe they bene Welle I-wette [*Rawl. MS.* Well wet]. **1540** HYRDE tr. *Vives' Instr. Chr. Wom.* III. i. (1557) 130 At bankettes and festes, whan they be well wette with drynke.

†**c.** *refl.* To imbibe liquor, take drink. *Obs.*

c **1440** *York Myst.* xxx. 94 Itt were appreue to my persone þat preuely ȝe paste me, Or ye wente fro this wones Or with wynne ȝe had wette yowe. **1672** R. WILD *Poet. Licentia* 27 And if the fiery trial should return, Most of you wet your selves too much to burn.

d. ***to wet the other*** (or ***t'other***) ***eye***: to drink one glass after another.

1745 *Life Bampfylde-Moore Carew* 89 The Officers.. filled him out a Bumper of Cherry Brandy, which when he had drank they forced another upon him, persuading him to wet the other Eye. **1840** J. T. J. HEWLETT *P. Priggins* xiii, Take one more jug of beer—wet t'other eye, we call it. **1840** DICKENS *Old C. Shop* lxii, Moisten your clay, wet the other eye, drink, man! *a* **1845** BARHAM *Ingol. Leg.*, *Hints Hist. Play* 47 There's not a drop left him to 'wet t'other eye'.

e. *absol.* To drink alcoholic liquor; to 'liquor up'.

1783 J. WOODFORDE *Diary* 9 Oct. (1926) II. 97 With the latter I walked to the Swan and there wetted with him that is, drank a glass of Wine. **1840** HALIBURTON *Clockm.* Ser. III. xi. 147 But come, let's liquour; I want to wet up. **1880** BARING-GOULD *Mehalah* xxi, I'm dry after my row and want a wet. As I wet I will talk.

f. To accompany (solid or dry food) with liquor.

1878 T. HARDY *Ret. Native* VI. iv, Maul down the victuals from corner-cupboard..and I'll draw a drop o' sommat to wet it with.

8. a. To celebrate by drinking; to have a drink over.

The earliest use is *to wet a commission* (in the Army or Navy).

a **1687** VILLIERS (Dk. Buckhm.) *Milit. Couple* Wks. 1715 I. 128 He was as Drunk as a Chaplain of the Army upon wetting his Commission. **1698** J. H. *Farquhar's Love & Bottle* Prol., Come on then; foot to foot be boldly set, And our young Author's new Commission wet. **1710** C. SHADWELL *Fair Quaker Deal* II. 27 *Crib.* Ay, the two Ships would serve us nicely. *Easey.* Then we should have Commissions to wet. **1711** STEELE *Spect.* No. 88 ¶4 Three Quarts to my new Lord for wetting his Title. **1829** MARRYAT *F. Mildmay* xvi, They..declared I should give them a dinner to wet my commission. *a* **1854** L. BEECHER *Lect. Intemperance* 23 Until in some places a man can scarcely wear an article of dress, or receive one of equipage or furniture, which has not been 'wetted'. **1876** HINDLEY *Cheap Jack* 268, I shall be back again shortly, when we will wet the deal. **1894** A. ROBERTSON *Nuggets* 16 Drinks is to be redooced to-day from a shillin' to sixpence, so we'll wet the occasion.

b. ***to wet the baby's head*** and varr.: to drink to celebrate the birth of a child. *colloq.*

1885 W. WESTALL *Old Factory* xxiv. 161 'We'll wet little Mabel's head with some of it.' 'What mean you?'.. 'Why my wife was brought to bed last night of a little lass as we are going to call Mabel, and I'd like us to drink to her health. That's what we call wetting a child's head in these parts.' **1924** LAWRENCE & SKINNER *Boy in Bush* xiv. 210 Come along in—all welcome!—an' wet the baby's eye. **1953** E. SIMON *Past Masters* III. v. 173 At the party given to 'wet the baby's head' the McGillivrays' friends and relations produced only large and expensive gifts. **1970** *Guardian* 2 May 3/7 If he had not been wetting the baby's head, and so been slightly above proof, he might have run for it.

9. †**a.** *Naut.* To cast or drop (an anchor). *Obs.*

a **1600** MONTGOMERIE *Misc. Poems* xlviii. 168 We wat ane anchor evin betuixt they tua. **1638** MAYNE *Lucian* (1664) 95 One Anchor more, perhappes, I have never yet cast, or wet, which is to pretend old age, sicknesse, [etc.].

b. ***to wet one's line***: to start fishing, to fish.

1653 WALTON *Angler* iii. 80, I have not yet wet my line since I came from home. **1898** G. A. B. DEWAR *In Pursuit of Trout* 165 On days when nothing was doing..he might not rarely be heard remarking that he had not wetted his line.

10. a. To steep or soak (grain) in water in order to convert it into malt.

1695 *Lond. Gaz.* No. 3076/4 A large Mault House that wets 700 Quarters per Annum. **1742** *Lond. & Country Brew.* I. (ed. 4) 22 In a great Brew-house..they wetted or used a considerable Quantity of Malt in one Week. **1844** J. T. HEWLETT *Parsons & W.* xxv, The farmer would get a good price for his barley, the poor man would be able to 'wet' and convert into malt enough for his family.

b. To infuse (tea) by pouring boiling water on the leaves; also with tea-leaves as *obj. dial.* and *colloq.*

1902 *Cornh. Mag.* Dec. 776, I ha' wetted th' tea pretty nigh half-an-hour ago. **1905** H. G. WELLS *Kipps* III. ii. §3 Ann..stooped with the kettle-holder to wet the tea. **1916** *Blackw. Mag.* Apr. 499/1 'Aye, aye, sir,' replies the duty servant. 'Tea just being wetted.' (We never 'make' tea, we always 'wet' it!) **1939** JOYCE *Finnegan's Wake* 585 You never wet the tea! **1944** M. LASKI *Love on Supertax* viii. 77 Make yourself at home, and I'll just wet the tea-leaves. **1978** I. MURDOCH *Sea* 419 'I'll wet the tea,' said Hartley and disappeared into the kitchen.

11. ***to wet down***, to damp (sails, paper, embers) with water.

1840 R. H. DANA *Bef. Mast* iv, We..continued wetting down the sails by buckets of water whipped up to the mast-head. **1888** JACOBI *Printers' Vocab.*, *Wetting down*, the process of damping paper for printing purposes. **1891** *Daily News* 26 Sept. 2/5 Holland said that when he came on his watch there was no supply of coal in the bunkers, and that Jensen would not wet down his ashes.

12. *Dyeing.* ***to wet out***, to soak in water.

1882 CROOKES *Dyeing* 106 The yarns or pieces are first wetted out uniformly with water. **1900** *Jrnl. Soc. Dyers* XVI. 8 Before dyeing, the bodies [of hats] are well wetted-out in boiling water.

13. *Glass-making.* ***to wet off, up.*** (See quots. and cf. WETTER 1 b, WETTING *vbl. sb.* 3 d.)

1849 A. PELLATT *Curios. Glass Making* 85 The pontil secures the whole preparatory to its being whetted [*sic*] off the bowl..by the touch of the cold pucellas. **1908** ROSENHAIN *Glass Manuf.* 57 The virgin clay and chamotte having been intimately mixed, the whole mass is 'wet up' by the addition of a proper proportion of water and prolonged ..kneading. *Ibid.* 99 The blower..detaches the bottle from the pipe..by locally chilling the glass—a process known by the descriptive term of 'wetting off'.

II. *intr.*

14. To become wet. Also ***to wet through.***

a **1310** in Wright *Lyric P.* ix. 36 The water that it [*sc.* a stone] wetes yn, Y-wis hit wortheth al to wyn. **1757** in *Phil. Trans.* L. 361 The millers do not deny..that *some* whiting is carried to all the great mills. The excuse alleged for it is, that it makes the flour *wet*, and consequently *bake*, the better. **1902** S. E. WHITE *Blazed Trail* xviii, I thought any leather would wet through in the snow!

15. To rain, drizzle. *dial.*

1740 RICHARDSON *Pamela* II. 88 Dont you think that yonder Cloud may give us a small Shower? and it did a little begin to wet. **1825** JAMIESON, *To weit, weet*, to rain. **1828** CARR *Craven Gloss.*, *Wit*, to rain gently. **1886** *Chesh. Gloss.*, *Weet* or *wet*, to rain slightly.

16. *Naut.* Of a vessel: To ship water.

1875 BEDFORD *Sailor's Pocket Bk.* vi. 214 A reef should be taken in directly the boat begins to wet.

17. To urinate. Also *fig.*

1925 D. H. LAWRENCE *Novel* in *Reflections on Death of Porcupine* 122 But see old Leo Tolstoi wetting on the flame. As if even his wet were absolute! **1935** V. WOOLF *Let.* 21 June (1979) V. 403 The marmoset is just about to wet on my shoulder. **1954** J. STEINBECK *Sweet Thursday* xiv. 82 House-broken dogs wet on the parlor rug. **1975** J. CLEARY *Safe House* ii. 71 The children want to wet... Come on, love. Have your wet.

III. 18. The vb. stem in comb., as **wet-bed** = *bed-wetter* s.v. BED *sb.* 19.

1934 'J. SPENSER' *Limey breaks In* iv. 61, I lay awake for so long that I heard the night watchman come to call the wet-beds. **1960** J. STROUD *Shorn Lamb* xviii. 204 Does he enurete?.. I've got four chronic wet-beds already.

wet, *adv. rare*$^{-1}$. [f. WET *a.* in WET NURSE.] As a wet nurse.

1697 VANBURGH *Relapse* v. v, I who had suckled it, and swadled it, and nurst it both wet and dry.

wet, obs. form of WHAT, WIT *v.*

weta ('wɛtə). *N.Z.* [Maori.] Any of several wingless orthopteran insects of the genus *Deinacrida*, *Pachyrhamma*, or *Hemideina*.

1843 E. DIEFFENBACH *Trav. N.Z.* II. III. 396 Weta—an insect so called. **1857** C. HURSTHOUSE *N.Z.* I. v. 123 The Weta, a suspicious-looking scorpion-like creature, apparently replete with 'high concocted venom', but perfectly harmless. **1863** S. BUTLER *First Year in Canterbury Settlement* ix. 441 One of the ugliest-looking creatures.. is called 'weta', and is of tawny scorpion-like colour, with long antennae and great eyes, and nasty squashy-looking body, with (I think) six legs. **1888** *Trans. N.Z. Inst.* XXI. 41 Not a sound was heard in that lonely forest, except.. the sharp noise produced by the *weta*. **1949** [see HUHU]. **1961** R. PARK *Hole in Hill* (1962) xiv. 115 A giant glistening black insect.. waving its antennae... 'It's only a *weta*!' **1975** E. HILLARY *Nothing Venture, Nothing Win* ii. 40 When I was making up the bed I found a huge weta.. in one of the blankets.

wetale, obs. Sc. form of VICTUAL.

wet blanket.

1. A blanket that has been drenched in water; esp. one used for quenching a conflagration. Chiefly in allusive use.

1662 ATWELL *Faithf. Surveyor* 95 Of quenching an house on fire. The Instruments.. are.. forks, wet-blankets, ladders,.. pails, &c. *Ibid.* 97 Cover the out-side with wet blankets, hair-cloths, &c. that neither the flame get out nor air get in. **1702** BAYNARD *Cold Bathing* II. (1709) 264 At Whitny in Oxfordshire, those who work at the Blanket-Mills, carry wet Blankets in their Arms next their Breast, Winter and Summer, and never catch Cold. **1772** CUMBERLAND *Fashionable Lover* I. i. 4 His humours damp all mirth and merriment, as a wet blanket does a fire. **1821** BYRON *Juan* III. xxxvi, Lambro's reception at his people's banquet Was such as fire accords to a wet blanket. **1838** PUSEY in Liddon *Life* (1893) II. xxi. 54 It seems like a wet blanket cast upon all the fire we have been fanning.

2. *fig.* **a.** Something that acts as a damper to activity, enthusiasm, or cheerfulness.

1810 SIR G. JACKSON *Diaries & Lett.* (1873) I. 143 It would have been a cruel stroke of fate.. if.. a wet blanket [had] been thrown over them [*sc.* gaieties]. **1829** *Sporting Mag.* XXIII. 426 All was in readiness.. when a wet blanket was thrown upon all their hopes. **1848** MRS. GASKELL *Mary Barton* ii, It was an unlucky toast or sentiment... It was a wet blanket to the evening. **1894** JESSOPP *Rand. Roaming* vi. 195 That chilling maxim—the wet-blanket of enthusiasm.

b. A person who has a depressing or dispiriting effect on those around him.

1857 MRS. MATHEWS *Tea-Table T.* I. 185 Such people may be termed the wet blankets of society. **1875** S. BEAUCHAMP *N. Hamilton* II. 18 As he is of course the wet blanket of the party, they are none of them sorry when he leaves again. **1883** MISS BROUGHTON *Belinda* II. iv, She would spoil the whole thing; she is such a wet blanket. **1897** MRS. OLIPHANT *W. Blackwood* I. iii. 128 Sometimes he called her a wet blanket, when she thus damped his ardour.

Hence **wet-'blanket** *v. trans.*, to throw a damper on, discourage, depress. Also (*nonce-wds.*) **wet-'blanketing** *ppl. a.*; **wet-'blanketiveness**; **wet-'blanketty** *a.*

1866 J. D. COLERIDGE *Let.* in *Life Ld. Coleridge* (1904) II. 140, I think any one would have felt *wet-blanketed by the utter commonplaceness of the whole affair. **1868** LOUISA M. ALCOTT *Little Women* xxi, I know Meg would wet-blanket such a proposal, but I thought you had more spirit. **1893** W. A. SHEE *My Contemp.* iii. 47 Such people.. should.. not be allowed to wet-blanket the world with their stolid stare. **1901** *Scotsman* 12 Mar. 9/5 Power traction.. had been effectively wetblanketed for fully two generations. **1843** J. F. MURRAY *World of London* I. 131 The impossible-mongering, cold-water-throwing, *wet-blanketting-fellows, howled in this way about the Thames tunnel. **1834** *Fraser's Mag.* X. 412 Throwing off the '*wet-blanketiveness' which usually extinguishes your social qualities. **1848** *Zoologist* VI. 2048 Adapting my phraseology to the author's, I would say such parts of the book are very '*wet-blanketty'.

wetche, obs. form of WATCH.

wetched, -et, obs. forms of WATCHET.

wet dock. (In contrast to DRY DOCK.)

†**1.** = DOCK *sb.*^{3} 1 (where see quot. 1627). *Obs.*

2. (See DOCK *sb.*^{3} 4.)

1661-2 [see DOCK *sb.*^{3} 4]. **1689** *Lond. Gaz.* No. 2512/4 A Pink about 30 Tun, lying in the Wet-Dock at Deptford. **1724** *Ibid.* No. 6321/3 The great wet Dock in Rotherhith. **1753** HANWAY *Trav.* (1762) I. VII. lxxxvi. 400 The harbour or wet-dock.. will contain eighty men of war. **1814** SCOTT *Wav.* xviii, The little inlet of water.. where, as in a wet-dock, the skiff.. was still lying moored. **1839** *Civil Engin. & Arch. Jrnl.* II. 26/1 It is proposed to construct a ship canal from Newhaven Harbour to Lewes. with a wet-dock and basin at Lewes. **1880** *Encycl. Brit.* XI. 466.

†**wete.** *Obs.* [OE. *wǽta* wk. masc. In later ME. merged in WET *sb.*^{1} 1.] Moisture; a liquid, liquor, drink.

c **897** ÆLFRED *Gregory's Past. C.* xi. 73 Se wæta ðara innoða [*humor viscerum*]. **971** *Blickl. Hom.* 209 Swiþe wynsum ond hluttor wæta utflowende. *c* **1000** *Ags. Gosp.* Luke viii. 6 Hit forscranc forþam þe hit wætan nafde. *c* **1000** ÆLFRIC *Hom.* II. 298 Ne dranc he wines drenc, ne nan ðæra wætena þe druncennysse styriað. *c* **1205** LAY. 19769 Vt heo droȝen sone amppullen scone ifulled mid attere, weten alre bitterest. *a* **1225** *Ancr. R.* 164 Hwo þet bere a deorewurðe licur, oðer a deorewurðe wete, as is bame, in a feble uetles.

wete, obs. f. WEET *v.*^{1}, WET, WHEAT, WIT.

weter, obs. f. WATER *sb.*

weteri, -y, obs. ff. WATER *v.*

weterly, var. WITTERLY.

wetewold, obs. f. WITTOL.

†**weth**, var. WAITH *sb.*^{2}

1602 *Reg. Mag. Sig. Scot.* 476/1 Cum parvis custumis,.. wrak, wair, weth et proficuis quibuscumque. **1631** *Ibid.* 633 Cum lie gressingis, scheillingis, multuris wraik, wair, weth.

†**wethe**, *v. Obs. rare.* [Of obscure origin; perh. an alteration of *weve* (cf. BIWEVE *v.*^{1} 2), or related to south-western dial. *weath* pliant, supple.] *trans.* To twist or twine.

1398 TREVISA *Barth. De P.R.* XVII. cxliv. (Bodl. MS.), Som weþies beþ.. so pliaunte þat þei brekeþ nought but beþ made stronge wiþ weþing [*ed.* 1495 weuynge] and windinge as þrede is wᵗ twynyng. *c* **1440** *Pallad. on Husb.* IV. 676 Too bowes.. they take And bynde, and wethe [L. *torques*] hem so that germynynge Commixt vp go.

wethe, obs. form of WITHY.

†**'wethead.** *Obs. rare.* In 4-5 **wetehed(e.** [f. WET *a.* + -HEAD.] Wetness.

1379 *Glouc. Cath. MS.* 19 No. I. I. iv. 11 b, And wirketh as frost doth in the wetehede. *c* **1440** *Jacob's Well* 238 Moysture, wetehed, softhed & neschhed.

wethen, var. WHETHEN *Obs.*, whence.

wether ('wɛðə(r)). Forms: α. 1, 3 **weðer**, 3-4 **weþer**, 4-5 **wethur, -ir**, 5 **wethyr, -ire**, 6 **wethar**, 6-9 **weather**, 4- **wether**; 4-5 **whethir, -ur**, 4-6 **whether**, 5 **whetther**. β. 4, 6 **weder, wedir**, 5 **wedyr, wedor**; 5-9 **wedder** (5 **-ur, -yr**); *Sc.* 5-6 **vedder, weddir**, 6 **wadder, wodder, weadder**. [Common Teutonic: OE. *weðer* = OFris. **wether* (NFris. *wether*, WFris. *weer*), OLFrank. *wither* (MDu. *weder*, Du. *weer*), OS. *withar, -er* (MLG. *weder, wêr*, LG. *weer*), OHG. *widar, -er, -ir* (MHG. *wider*, G. *widder*), ON. and Icel. *veðr* (Norw. *veder, ver*; MSw. *väþur, wädhur*, etc., Sw. *vädur*, Da. *væder*), Goth. *wiþrus* (= lamb), prob. related to L. *vitulus* calf.]

1. A male sheep, a ram; esp. a castrated ram. See also BELL-WETHER.

α. *c* **890** WÆRFERTH tr. *Gregory's Dial.* 34 He breac on þam hælftre for bridelse & weþera fella for sadole. *c* **1000** ÆLFRIC *Hom.* II. 576 His biȝleofa wæs ælce dæȝ.. hundteontiȝ weðera. *c* **1250** *Gen. & Ex.* 3998 On ilc alter fier alðerneðer, And ðoron an calf and a weðer. **1297** R. GLOUC. (Rolls) 1210 Vourti þousend of ruþeren he let quelle þer to, & of fatte weþeren an hondred þousend al so. *a* **1300** *Cursor M.* 11649 Wolf and weþer, leon and ox, Sal comen samen, and lamb and fox. **1382** WYCLIF *Gen.* xxx. 35 And he seuerde that day the she geyt, and the sheep, and the hyeȝ geyt, and the wetheres. **1398** TREVISA *Barth. De P. R.* VIII. x. (1495) 310 As a whetther in lyenge vpon oo syde tornyth and chaungyth by egall tymes. *c* **1450** *Mirour Saluacioun* (Roxb.) 81 Ysaac .. was delyvred fro dede And a wethire cleving in breres sacrified in his stede. **1533** in Weaver *Wells Wills* (1890) 2 John Horley oon whether,.. ii yewes. **1588** LAMBARDE *Eiren., Precedents* (1591) Y yj b, Tres oues castratas (anglicè vocatas Weathers). *a* **1589** MASCALL *Cattle, Sheep* (1596) 236 In some places they doe.. point the wethers, the yeaws, and the lambes ech by themselues. **1599** SHAKS. etc. *Pass. Pilgr.* 272 My weathers bell rings dolefull knell. **1616** W. BROWNE *Brit. Past.* II. iv. 95 The Weathers bell that leads our flocke around. **1671** MILTON *Samson* 538 Who shore me Like a tame Weather, all my precious fleece. **1676** *Lond. Gaz.* No. 1122/4 Lost or stolen.. 45 Sheep, called Western Weathers. **1727-46** THOMSON *Summer* 409 Some mingling stir the melted tar..; Others the unwilling wether drag along. **1747** SMOLLETT *Reproof* 71 All senior members of the horned race.—The weather, goat, ram, elk and ox were there. **1807** CRABBE *Par. Reg.* II. 343 Two pigs, a cow, and wethers half a score, Increased his stock. **1861** *Times* 7 Oct., For wethers the average prices obtained were 38s. to 56s. **1870** BRYANT *Iliad* XII. 541 As when a shepherd carries home with ease A wether's fleece.

β. *a* **1340** HAMPOLE *Psalter* lxiv. 14 Cled ere wedirs of shepe. **1375** BARBOUR *Bruce* VII. 115 And ane of thame apon his hals A mekill bundyn weddir bare. *Ibid.* 152 Thai slew the veddir at thai bar. **1387** TREVISA *Higden* III. 127 Daniel seiȝ þe fifte siȝt and visioun of þe weder þat hadde hornes nouȝt al i-liche. *c* **1425** *Non-Cycle Mystery Plays* (1909) 33 Turn þe & take þat wedyr there, & sacrifye hym on þat awtere. *c* **1440** *Alphabet of Tales* 290 At ans he wolde ete a quarter of a weddur, or ij hennys, or a guse. **1479** *Bury Wills* (Camden) 53 And also the same Edmund haue cccc weders in my flokke of Ryngmer. **1523-34** FITZHERB. *Husb.* §53 It is than best tyme to.. seuer theym in dyuers sortes,.. the lambes by theym-selfe, wedders and the rammes by them-self. **1552** LYNDESAY *Monarche* 5443 Quhat holynes is thare within Ane wolf cled in ane Wodderis skin? *a* **1585** MONTGOMERIE *Flyting* 205 Fore store of lambes and lang-tailde wedders. *c* **1610** SIR J. MELVILLE *Mem.* (Bannatyne Club) 382 Bot some yearly nomber of wethers wilbe easely granted, be them that possess presently the saidis stoir rowmes. **1681** COLVIL *Whigs Supplic.* (1751) 85 Two three beggars,.. Who stealing public geese and wedders, Were freed, by rendering skin and feathers. **1796** W. MARSHALL *West Eng.* I. 263 The wedders, of the best sort, fat perfectly well, at two years old. **1830** *Cumb. Farm. Rep.* 55 in *Libr. Usef. Knowl., Husb.* III, Sheep generally fed off by turnips are the best description of Cheviot wedders. **1861** *Times* 16 Oct., Wedders commonly clip 7$\frac{1}{2}$lb. of wool. **1888** J. INGLIS *Tent Life Tigerland* 96 What might be the price of wedders now in Australy?

b. *transf.* of a man; *spec.* a eunuch.

1548 HALL *Chron., Hen. VIII* (1550) 187 b, So the great wether which is of late fallen.. so craftely, so scabedly, ye & so vntruly iuggled wyth the kynge, that [etc.]. **1596** SHAKS. *Merch. V.* IV. i. 114, I am a tainted Weather of the flocke, Meetest for death. **1724** GAY *Captives* Epil. 19 But the soft voice of an Italian weather, Makes them all languish three whole hours together.

†**2.** Occasional uses. **a.** A battering ram. **b.** The zodiacal sign of the Ram.

14.. *MS. Digby 233* lf. 182/1 As þe instrument þat hatte þe wether smyteþ þe walles of a cyte þat is byseged. **1565** GOOGE tr. *Palingenius' Zodiac* XI. PP vij, The other by the Balance runnes, and by the Wethers face.

3. ***grey wethers***: boulders of hard sandstone found lying on the surface of the Downs in Wiltshire and Devon.

1661 CHILDREY *Brit. Baconica* 49 Upon the Downs between Marleborough and Aubury.. are to be found abundance of great stones, commonly called by the Country thereabout, the Gray Weathers. **1681** GREW *Musæum* III. 291 A course sort of Jasper Stones, knockt off from those in Wilts-shire near Marleborough, called The Grey-Weathers. **1743** STUKELEY *Abury* 48 An infinite quantity of immense stones, or sarsens, or gray-weathers. **1801** H. SKRINE *Rivers Gt. Brit.* 331 Those vast stones called 'The Grey Withers [*sic*]', are scattered irregularly about the country. **1835-95** [see GREY *a.* 8].

4. *Comm.* The fleece obtained from the second or any subsequent shearing of a sheep.

1879 *Cassell's Techn. Educ.* IV. 260/1 (Wool) To good, healthy, sound fleeces more than one year old the term 'wethers' is given. **1895** *Agric. Gaz.* 17 June 538/3 Super-super wethers, 9$\frac{1}{2}$d.;.. selected Yorkshire wethers, 7$\frac{3}{4}$d.; deep wethers, 9*d*.

5. *attrib.* and *Comb.*, as ***wether fleece, -flock, haggis, -mutton, -skin***; **wedderbouk** *Sc.*, the carcass of a wether; **wether-gammon**, a leg of mutton; †**wether gang** *Sc.*, a pasture or right of pasturage for wethers (see GANG *sb.*^{1} 4 c); **wether-getter**, a ram kept for breeding wethers; †**wether goat**, a castrated goat; **wether head**, a sheep's head; *fig.* a stupid person; **wether hog**, a male sheep (castrated or not) before its first shearing; also ***wether hog sheep*** (cf. HOG *sb.*^{1} 4); chiefly *Sc.* and *north.*; **wether lamb**, a male lamb; †**wether-silver** *Sc.*, money in lieu of a wether paid as a customary rent or tax; **wether teg** = *wether hog*. Also WETHER SHEEP.

15.. *Aberd. Reg.* (Jam.), ijs. Scottis for half ane *wedder-bouk. **1422** YONGE tr. *Secreta Secret.* (1898) 163 Pelleus.. Sende.. Iason.. into the Ile of Calcos to wyn the *wethyr fleis of golde. *a* **1722** LISLE *Husb.* (1757) 321 In favour rather of keeping a *weather-flock than an ewe-flock on the hill-country. **1886** C. SCOTT *Sheep-farming* 31 Wedder flocks are generally kept on the highest hirsel of the farm. **1890** 'R. BOLDREWOOD' *Col. Reformer* xi, The wether flock which had been lost. *a* **1774** FERGUSSON *Poems, Drink Eclogue* 84 Wi' skelps like this fock sit but seenil down To *wether-gammon. **1561** in *Dunfermline Reg.* (Bannatyne Club) 427 Item the bouplaces and *wedder gangis within the parrochin of Dunfermling, lxxxxvj. li. **1609** in *Reg. Mag. Sig. Scot. 1610*, 154/1 Cum pastura super Pidmidle et lie Weddergang earundem. **1790** W. MARSHALL *Midland Co.* I. 422 The characteristic difference between what is called a 'ramgetter', and a '*weddergetter' or a 'good grazier's sheep'. **1671** T. HUNT *Abeced. Scholast.* 52 *Caper*, a *Weather-Goat. **1772** NUGENT *Hist. Friar Gerund* I. 35 To drub this Signior Barbi-castron, this false-bearded wether-goat. **1789** BURNS '*Ken ye ought*' 8 Is he slain by Highlan' bodies?.. And eaten like a *wether haggis? *a* **1796** —— *Grace bef. Dinner*, And send us from thy bounteous store A tup or *weather head! **1869** LE FANU *Wyvern Myst.* II. 102 Why didn't ye tell me, ye d——d wetherhead? **1537** *N.C. Wills* (Surtees 1908) 103, I geve unto.. John half a hundreth of share *wedder hogges. **1541** in Gage *Hengrave* (1822) 118 Item, lix wether hogg shepe at xiiij*d*. the pece. **1614, 1794** [see HOG *sb.*^{1} 4 b]. **1776** *Compl. Grazier* (ed. 4) 149 So of the male sheep, we may reckon them wedder or wedder hogs, after they are.. of a year's growth. **1844** H. STEPHENS *Bk. Farm* II. 38 [In Scotland] a female is called a *ewe-hogg*, a male a *tup-hogg*, and a castrated male a *wether-hogg*. *c* **1475** *Pict. Voc.* in Wr.-Wülcker 758/12 *Hic agnus*, a *wedyrlombe. **1595** *Nottingham Rec.* IV. 62 Unus agniculus (Anglice 'a wether lambe'). **1801** *Farmer's Mag.* Aug. 360 Wedder lambs.. are selling from 10s. to 12s. and 13s. per head. **1815** *Sporting Mag.* XLV. 227 She.. gave me a detail of their management in buying their wether lambs and fattening their wethers. **1886** C. SCOTT *Sheep-farming* 115 The best ewe lambs.. are retained, and all the wether and the second ewe lambs are sent to the market. **1707** J. STEVENS tr. *Quevedo's Com. Wks.* (1709) 171 She never dress'd *Weather-Mutton, when she could get Ewe or Goat. **1824** in *Spirit Publ. Jrnls.* (1825) 281 Does Mr. Giblet, the butcher, reserve his.. weather-mutton for better customers? **1844** H. STEPHENS *Bk. Farm* II. 100 Wether-mutton is the meat in perfection. **1557** in *Reg. Mag. Sig. Scot. 1598*, 223/1 Custum-mert-sylver, custum-*wadder-silver. *c* **1560** A. SCOTT *Poems* ii. 128 Bettir we bath wer byand hyddis And *weddir skynnis at hame. **1917** *Blackw. Mag.* Nov. 676/2 [*temp.* 1750-90] Wood and wedder-skins and grain packed for export to the South. **1550** in Phillipps *Wills* (*c* 1830) 180 Forty *Wether Teggs. **1844** H. STEPHENS *Bk. Farm* II. 39 In England.. sheep bear the name of lamb until 8 months old, after which they are called ewe and wether teggs until once clipped.

wether, obs. f. WEATHER, WHETHER, WHITHER.

wethering(e, obs. forms of WEATHERING.

wether sheep. = WETHER 1.

13.. *St. Peter & Paul* 244 in Horstm. *Altengl. Leg.* (1881) 79 Þan Nero gart his heuede of strike, For þe wedir schepe was him like. **1504** *Acc. Ld. High Treas. Scot.* II. 449 For tedderis to tua wedder scheip..xxj d. **1563** HYLL *Art Garden.* (1593) 31 If that you take the maw of a weather sheepe new killed. **1583** in Phillipps *Wills* (*c* 1830) 273, I bequeath unto my Sonne..six wether shepe. **1607** TOPSELL *Four-f. Beasts* 638 Of the Weather-sheepe... Al Nations do distinguish him from the ram, because of one property or defect in him, for that hee is not fit for generation. **1669** STURMY *Mariner's Mag., Penalties* 5 Such Weather-sheep.. as are..for the Ships use. **1733** W. ELLIS *Chiltern & Vale Farm.* 284 Fatting of Oxen, or Wether Sheep. **1834** *Brit. Husb.* I. 506 The next year it carried upwards of forty wether sheep.

wetherun, wetherwine, var. ff. WITHERWIN *Obs.*

wethewinde, obs. f. WITHWIND.

wethir, obs. f. WEATHER, WETHER, WHETHER.

wethirwyne, var. WITHERWIN *Obs.*

wethring, obs. f. WEATHERING.

wethy, obs. f. WITHY.

wethyr, obs. f. WEATHER, WETHER.

weting(e, obs. ff. WEETING, WETTING.

wetish, var. WETTISH.

wetland (ˈwɛtlænd). [f. WET *a.* + LAND *sb.*] An area of land that is usually saturated with water, often a marsh or swamp. Also *attrib.* Also *pl.* (sometimes const. as *sing.*).

1743 M. CATESBY *Nat. Hist. Carolina* II. p. iv, On this wet Land grows a variety of Evergreen Trees and Shrubs. **1847** H. HOWE *Hist. Coll. Ohio* 98 'Wet land'..by judicious cultivation..rapidly improves in fertility. **1955** *Sci. News Let.* 29 Oct. 281/2 The wetland partridge is about twice the size of the valley quail. **1965** *New Scientist* 17 June 763/3 Wetlands are defined to include marshes, bogs, swamps and any still water less than six metres deep. **1969** *Nature* 19 Apr. 239/2 Wetland ecosystems in the limited sense of this work are defined as ecosystems with a watertable, above, at or very near the substrate surface, the substrate remaining saturated throughout the year. **1979** *Daily Tel.* 25 Oct. 11/4 Plans to protect the Somerset wetlands—an area of rare wildlife, whose future has been in dispute—are to be prepared. **1980** *National Trust* Spring 16/3 We intend to preserve this swamp area in its natural state as a haven not only for wetland flora but also for birds and animals. **1985** *Daily Hampshire Gaz.* (Northampton, Mass.) 9 Aug. 17/5 Under state law construction can not take place on a wetlands unless there are plans to replace the wetlands.

ˈwetly, *adv.* Also 6 weatly. [f. WET *a.*] In a wet manner or state.

α. **1562** J. HEYWOOD *Prov. & Epigr.* Dd iv b, Walke thou weatly, walke thou dryly: In thy walke, walke not hyly.
β. **1822** BYRON *Werner* I. i. 254 *Iden.* How fares he? *Gab.* Wetly and wearily, but out of peril. **1866** R. BUCHANAN *Poems* (1884) 163 For the world rolls on with air and ocean Wetly and windily round and round. **1890** MISS BROUGHTON *Alas!* II. vii, February has come wetly in, with rain wildly weeping against the casements. **1893** J. A. BARRY *Steve Brown's Bunyip* 3 The immense beast, black, shining wetly. **1975** *Times Lit. Suppl.* 12 Dec. 1486/3 Raffles's relations with his accomplice, Boswell, and room-mate, the wet and unendearing Bunny. Bunny..went to prison..to shield A. J., who rather let him down; but Bunny wetly forgave him. **1978** *Guardian Weekly* 12 Mar. 21/3 A peaceable fellow-officer, played slightly wetly by the American Beau Bridges.

Wetmore (ˈwɛtmɔə(r)). The name of Alexander *Wetmore* (1886–1978), American ornithologist, used *attrib.* in *Wetmore order* to designate the system of bird classification developed by him.

1965 *Jrnl. Lancs. Dial. Soc.* Jan. 5 They are listed in Wetmore Order, i.e. the system of classification which is generally accepted in modern bird books. **1979** *Nature* 29 Mar. 490/1 Indeed Wetmore's name has become a household word among ornithologists, for his classification of the birds of the world, forming the basis for the well known 'Wetmore order', has, with modifications necessitated by new knowledge, become the generally accepted arrangement, as adopted in Peters' *Checklist of Birds of the World* and other authoritative compilations.

ˈwetness. Also 1 wétnis, 5–6 wetenes, 6 -ness(e, 7 weatness; 4–6 wette-, wetnes(se. [f. WET *a.* + -NESS.] **a.** The fact or condition of being wet; also *concr.*, moisture, wet.

α. *c* **950** *Lindisf. Gosp.* Luke viii. 6 Oðer feall ofer stan and ..fordrugade forðon ne hæbde wetnise. *c* **1430** *Syr Gener.* (Roxb.) 546 The king..of that wetenes [*sc.* tears] was affraied That by his arme and his shuldres ran. **1530** PALSGR. 288/1 Wetenesse, *moilleure, moisteure.* **1546** *Yorks. Chantry Surv.* (Surtees) 285 The weteness of the grounde and grete inundations of waters. **1573** *Kent & Surrey Sewers Comm.* (1909) 163 These men..were extreamly hindred thorowe the extreamenes of the wetenesse of the wether. **1664** J. CARSTAIRES *Lett.* (1846) 149 See that it be kept verie dry, the least weatness will much prejudice me.
β. *c* **1330** R. BRUNNE *Chron. Wace* 10352 Schal he neuere take scathe, Ne haue wetynge [*Petyt MS.* haf wettenes] ne waþe. *c* **1400** tr. *Higden* (Rolls) VII. 149 A lanterne..þat myȝt nouȝt be quenched nouþer wiþ wynde ne wiþ none moysture ne wetnes. **1573–80** TUSSER *Husb.* (1878) 99 What worser for barlie than wetnes and cold? **1577** GOOGE *Heresbach's Husb.* III. 141 b, The wettenesse hereof doth not onely hurt..their feete, but also spoyleth their coates. **1645–50** BOATE *Ireland's Nat. Hist.* xxi. §3 (1652) 165 Which inconstancy and wetness of the weather is..troublesome to men. **1699** MEAGER *New Art Garden.* 42 If the Vine stands against damp Walls, the wetness perishes the Clusters that touch it. **1765** A. DICKSON *Treat. Agric.* (ed. 2) 136 The wetness of land from its situation may be prevented. **1794** VANCOUVER *Agric. Cambridge* 57 This meadow land..in that state of wetness. **1846** *J. Baxter's Libr. Pract. Agric.* (ed. 4) I. 229 The suffocating wetness and cold of the furrows. **1871** B. STEWART *Heat* §152 The sensation of dryness or wetness does not depend upon the absolute amount of aqueous vapour present in one cubic foot of air.

b. A wet spot or patch of ground.

1805 R. W. DICKSON *Pract. Agric.* I. Pl. XLVI, The plan of draining wetnesses on the tops of hills and banks.

c. Feebleness, ineptness. Cf. WET *a.* 15 b.

1977 *Times* 29 Sept. 4/1 It was surely not Liberal 'wetness', as the incoming president, Mr. Gruffydd Evans, termed their traditional virtues of niceness and fairmindedness. **1981** R. D. EDWARDS *Corridors of Death* vii. 33 A profession which regards loyalty as weakness and decency as wetness. **1983** *Times* 4 Nov. 7/1 The idea that an ally has a right to independent judgment is too easily dismissed as what Mrs Thatcher might describe..as wetness.

wet nurse, wet-nurse, *sb.* A woman who is hired to suckle and nurse another woman's child. Cf. DRY-NURSE.

1620 MIDDLETON *Chaste Maid* II. ii, I call the Wet Nurse hither. *a* **1633** AUSTIN *Medit.* (1635) 45 Shee was both wet-Nurse, and dry-Nurse herselfe. And yet this his handmaid was his Mother. **1689** *Full Answ. Depos. Birth Pr. Wales* 7 Query, Whether she did not use to provide a Wet-Nurse, at her other Deliveries. **1776** *Pennsylvania Even. Post* 8 Feb. 70/2 Wants a place, as Wet Nurse, a young woman with a good breast of milk. **1888** MISS BRADDON *Fatal Three* I. iii, A wet-nurse being wanted at the great house.
transf. and *fig.* **1826** HOOD *Irish Schoolm.* xxi, How Romulus was bred in savage wood, By wet-nurse wolf, devoid of wolfish rage. **1884** GILMOUR *Mongols* xxxii. 375 China has acted the wet-nurse to Mongolia, and discharged her duty well.

wet-nurse, *v. trans.* To serve as wet nurse to, suckle (another woman's infant). Also *transf.*

1784 *Morn. Chron.* 13 Apr. 4/4 Advt., Wanted, a Child to Wet Nurse, by a Young Woman, with a good breast of milk. **1786** MRS. A. M. BENNETT *Juvenile Indiscr.* III. 62 At the house of the woman who had wet-nursed him. **1860** O. W. HOLMES *Professor* i. 25 A *mythus*..Such as Livy told about the wolf that wet-nursed Romulus and Remus.

b. *fig.* To treat tenderly or take under special care, as if helpless.

1873 *Siliad* 109 A curious youth..Who, ere his whiskers had completely grown, Possessed a comic paper of his own; But though wet-nursed by someone in Debrett, It died quite young. **1891** *Telegr. Jrnl.* 13 Feb. 205/2 The system of wet-nursing adopted by the Post Office authorities in the case of the telegraph service has not been one of uniform success. **1893** *Westm. Gaz.* 7 Feb. 6/1 A member of independent spirit—not wet-nursed for party purposes by political gold. **1917** *Blackw. Mag.* Nov. 584/1, I was wet-nursed by an elderly old buffer of a General.

wet-saffe, obs. form of VOUCHSAFE.

wet-shod (†**-shoed**), *a. Obs.* exc. *dial.* Forms: α. 4–5 **wete-schood, -shoed, -shode**; 5 **wet-schoede, -schode, -shood** (**whetshood**), 6 **-shoode**, 7 **-shooed**; 5 **watschoed, -schood.** β. 4–6 **wete-shodde**, 5 **wate-shodd**; 5– **wet-shod** (5 **-schod**, 7 **-shodde**; 5 **wadsshod**, 7 ? **wet-shot**). (Also in many dialect forms: see *Eng. Dial. Dict.*) [f. *wete, wate* WET *a.* + SHOED, SHOD, *ppl. adjs.*] Having the feet wet.

α. **1377** LANGL. *P. Pl.* B. XVIII. 1 Wolleward and wete-shoed went I forth after. **1393** *Ibid.* C. XVII. 14 And ȝut is wynter for hem wors, for wet-shood þei gangen. ? *a* **1400** *Arthur* 469 þere men were watschoede All of brayn & of blode. *a* **1470** GREGORY *Chron.* in *Hist. Collect. Cit. Lond.* (Camden) 207 They fulle ungoodely smote owte the heddys of the pypys and hoggs hedys of wyne, that men wente wete-schode in wyne. **1650** FULLER *Pisgah* II. v. §2 Moses foretold that he should be wetshooed in oile.
β. **1377** LANGL. *P. Pl.* B. XIV. 161 And ȝit is wynter for hem worse, for wete-shodde thei gange. **1393** *Ibid.* C. XXI. 1 Wo-werie and wetschod wente ich forth after. *c* **1440** *Alphabet of Tales* 172 A preste þat hight Stephan on a tyme was wate-shodd. *a* **1510** STANBRIDGE *Vulgaria* (W. de W.) B vj, I am wete shodde, *Pedes humectant.* **1542** BOORDE *Dyetary* xxx. (1870) 293 Beware of takyng colde in the legge, or rydinge, or goynge wetshod. **1592** LYLY *Gallathea* I. iv. 10 Ile warrant by this time he is wetshod. **1627** DRAYTON *Agincourt* cxcii, Scarse a man but wet-shod went in gore. **1657** T. M. *Life Sat. Puppy Nim* 10 They which followed the Coffin to buriall, went wetshod in those affectionate Teares. **1684** BUNYAN *Pilgr.* II. (1900) 235 So he went over [the river] at last, not much above wet-shod. **1742** RICHARDSON *Pamela* IV. 320 Your Billy has not yet been accustom'd to be wet-shod. **1775** CHANDLER *Trav. Asia Minor* 41, I passed the stream several times without being wet-shod. **1825–** in many dialect glossaries (cf. *Eng. Dial. Dict.*).

b. *fig.* (or in figurative context).

1575 FENTON *Golden Epist.* (1582) 249 You seeme..to wade continually wetshoode in the laake of this miserable worlde. **1589** ? LYLY *Pappe w. Hatchet* B j b, He will make their wits wetshod, if the ale haue his swift currant. **1622** MASSINGER & DEKKER *Virg. Martyr* III. iii, All my hopes are seam-rent, and go wet-shod. *a* **1652** BROME *City Wit* IV. i, Virtue goes often wetshod, and is forc'd to be cobled up with base means, to hold out water and cold necessity. **16..** *Times* I in *Cleveland's Wks.* (1687) 239 To speak in wet-shod Eyes, and drowned Looks.

wetshode, obs. form of WATCHET.

ˈwettable, *a.* [f. WET *v.*] Admitting of being wetted.

1885 H. O. FORBES *Nat. Wand. E. Archip.* 484 His only wettable garment being his loin-cloth. **1903** W. R. FISHER tr. *Schimper's Plant-Geogr.* III. i. 225 The foliage in a constantly humid climate is as a rule easily wettable. **1955** [see CAPTAN]. **1976** *McGraw-Hill Yearbk. Sci. & Technol.* 208/2 Spraying the wettable powder or flowable formulation results in distribution patterns that are particulate in form rather than lamellar.

Hence **wettaˈbility**, the property of being wettable; the degree to which something may be wetted (WET *v.* 1 b).

1913 *Chem. Abstr.* VII. 3441 The wetting of glass by different pairs of liquids was investigated with special reference to the effect of prolonged wetting upon the 'wetability'. **1933** *Amer. Jrnl. Sci.* XXV. 329 The 'wettability' of the particle in water. **1973** *Nature* 2 Mar. 14/1 The wettability of leaf surfaces is influenced by the fine structure and chemical composition of the wax. **1977** J. L. HARPER *Population Biol. Plants* xi. 379 *Larrea* affects the water relations of the soil surrounding the plants, reducing soil wettability.

wette, var. WIT *sb.* and *v.*

ˈwetted, *ppl. a.* [f. WET *v.*]

1. Made wet; moistened, damped.

1615 CHAPMAN *Odyss.* XXII. 561 Clense each boord & Throne With wetted Sponges. **1719** *Phil. Trans.* XXX. 1084, I touch'd the end A with a wetted Finger. **1762** FALCONER *Shipwr.* II. 249 They sound the well, and..Along the line four wetted feet appear. **1774** GOLDSM. *Nat. Hist.* VI. 402 The eggs are covered with a tough white skin, like wetted parchment. **1848** MRS. GASKELL *Mary Barton* xxxiii, He saw her sitting up in bed,..her head bound round with wetted cloths. **1887** *Harper's Mag.* July 170/1 Spreading over it a strip of wetted paper.

2. *Aeronaut.* Of an aircraft surface: in contact with the moving airflow.

1916 F. W. LANCHESTER *Flying Machine from Engin. Standpoint* 110 If the direct resistance is properly assessed on the basis of 'wetted' surface, whether we call it a *surface* coefficient or a *skin-frictional* coefficient is merely a question of terminology. **1958** *Observer* 11 May 13/4 The plan form of the 'nicked delta' or delta with the inner middle rear part cut out, was adopted to reduce to a minimum the 'wetted' area or part over which air flows, without reducing the part that does useful work. **1983** D. STINTON *Design of Aeroplane* v. 208 When an aeroplane is very clean and highly streamlined, parasite drag may be attributed to skin friction drag... For this we need to work out wetted area.

ˈwetter. [f. WET *v.*]

1. One who wets; *spec.* one who damps paper to be used in printing.

1737 CHAMBERLAYNE *St. Gt. Brit.* (ed. 33) II. 93 Wetters of paper for [rolling-press]. **1760** *Court & City Reg.* 130, 7 Layers of Paper, and 2 Wetters of ditto. **1888** JACOBI *Printers' Vocab.*, *Wetter*, the workman whose duty it is to 'wet down' paper preparatory to printing.

b. *wetter-off*, in glass-making, a workman who detaches glass by wetting it. (Cf. WET *v.* 13.)

1883 H. J. POWELL *Glass-making* 86 If the bottle be large it is handed, whilst still attached to the blowing-iron, to the 'wetter off', who detaches it by applying a moistened tool to the neck. **1888** *Daily News* 14 Feb. 6/7 The glass is never attached to any part of the machine, and so the 'wetter-off' is dispensed with.

2. *colloq.* A wetting, soaking.

1885 SLADEN *Poetry of Exiles* (ed. 2) I. 28 Unheedful of the dew..Until a shiver told him that he'd 'had a thorough wetter'.

wetter, dial. form of WATER; var. WITTER *sb.*[2]

wetterly, var. WITTERLY *adv. Obs.*

ˈwetting, *vbl. sb.* [f. WET *v.*]

1. The action of making wet, or the fact of becoming wet; also (with *a* and pl.), an instance of this: **a.** Of persons, esp. by rain or falling into water.

c **1290** *S. Eng. Leg.* 268 Þo Marie hadde i-blessed þat watur with hire honde, With-oute wetingue þare-ouer heo ȝeode. *c* **1330** [see WETNESS β]. *c* **1400** *Destr. Troy* 1579 Pight vp with pilers..[for] Weghis into walke for wetyng of rayn. **1610** SHAKS. *Temp.* IV. i. 211 That's more to me then my wetting. **1645** BP. HALL *Remedy Discont.* 149 It must be our wisedome..some whiles to abide a wetting; that, if need be, wee may endure a drenching also. *a* **1700** EVELYN *Diary* 5 May 1645, So that one can hardly step without wetting to the skin. **1836** SOUTHEY *Lett.* (1856) IV. 490 At the cost of a thorough wetting under a succession of heavy showers. **1849** C. BRONTË *Shirley* xxvi, Many a wetting we got amongst the mountains. **1876** SMILES *Sc. Natur.* xii. (ed. 4) 250 The sea was like a sheet of glass; so that he had little fear of getting a wetting during his few hours' stay.

b. In general use. Also in fig. context.

a **1340** HAMPOLE *Psalter* i. 3 He sall be as a tre that..has ay wetynge of the watirs of grace. *c* **1380** WYCLIF *Sel. Wks.* III. 27 Þat men þoru hem moun take weetynge of hevenly deew to her drie hertis. **1390** GOWER *Conf.* II. 39 As a cat wolde ete fisshes withoute wetinge of his cles. *c* **1440** *Promp. Parv.* 523/2 Wetynge, *madefaccio, madidacio.* **1577** GOOGE *Heresbach's Husb.* III. 119 b, Your stable must be buylt in a dry place, for wetting the Horses hoofe. **1623** in Foster *Eng. Factories Ind.* (1908) II. 285 The wettinge and late cominge downe of thier goods. **1693** EVELYN *De la Quint. Compl. Gard.* II. 59 The second thing that is to be done, after having remov'd Fig-Trees out of the Conservatory,..is (to use the Phrase of Gard'ners) to give them a good Wetting in every Case; which is, one good substantial Watering. **1725** *Bradley's Family Dict.* s.v. *Narcissus of Japan*, They must have a sound wetting, steeping the Pots in Water until you find it swims upon the Surface. **1789** T. WRIGHT *Meth. Watering Meadows* (1790) 23 It can be of no service to the lowest parts of the meadow, unless as a wetting in Spring or Summer. **1815** J. SMITH *Panorama Sci. & Art* I. 255 The wetting of the slate was merely superficial. **1863** P. BARRY

Dockyard Econ. 197 The only sensible effect is the wetting of the wires. **1886** *Athenæum* 20 Feb. 268/1 It is functionally protective against undue wetting by rain.

2. The action of moistening the throat with liquid; a small quantity of water or liquor used for this purpose.

1340–70 *Alex. & Dind.* 1033 Drink may him helpe, A litil wetinge of watur his wo wol amende. **1835** J. M. WILSON *Tales of Border* I. 118 It is seldom a thimblefu' that fa's to my share,.. mony a time, no a weetin'. **1884** *Punch* 11 Oct. 180/1 'Twas like the free run of a Bar, And Politics wants lots o' wetting. **1906** *Times* 6 Mar. 9/6 Drinks and 'wetting', ruinous to health and morals, are part of the business plant.

3. The action of making wet or moist as part of a special process: **a.** Of cloth. (Also in fig. contexts.)

1463–4 *Rolls of Parlt.* V. 501/2 That every Cloth of Kersey .. be parfitly wette, and after that wetyng redy to the sale,.. conteigne in lengh xviii yerdes. **1540, 1592** [see SHRINK *v.* 2 b]. **1593** GREENE *Mamillia* II. E 4, The cloath is not knowne till it come to the weeting. **1616** DRAXE *Bibl. Scholast.* 189 He will not abide the touchstone. He shrinketh in the wetting. **1627** J. TAYLOR (Water P.) *Navy Land Ships* B 5, Like No[r]therne Cloth shrunke in the wetting. **1631** R. BOLTON *Comf. Affl. Consc.* iv. (1635) 16 A professour of the truest and heavenliest dye that holds out in the wetting and shrinkes not in the Day of adversitie. **1875** KNIGHT *Dict. Mech.* 2415/2 The stretch is taken out of it by repeated wettings and stretchings.

b. The steeping of barley in the process of malting; the quantity steeped at one time.

1467 *Bury Wills* (Camden) 46 That the occupier.. shall haue his wetyng of his barley in the fate of the seid Denyse during maltyng tyme,.. the seid Denyse on wetyng and the seid occupier an other wetyng. **1702** *Lond. Gaz.* No. 3790/4 Every Cistern.. or other Vessel,.. made use of for the Wetting or Steeping of Corn. **1720** *Ibid.* No. 5864/2 The intire wetting.. shall be charged with the Duty of 6d. per Bushel.

c. *fig.* (Cf. WET *v.* 11.)

1706 E. WARD *Wooden World Diss.* (1708) 53 He must have his double Jug, before he weighs,.. because wetting of his Sails, will make him run the faster.

d. *Glass-making.* (See quot. and WET *v.* 13.)

1888 *Daily News* 14 Feb. 6/5 The bottle is.. cut off from the blow pipe by means of a steel chisel and cold water. This is called 'wetting' or 'wetting off'.

4. *concr.* A liquid mixture employed to wet something else. (See also *E.D.D.*, *Wetting* sb. 3.)

1728 E. S[MITH] *Compleat Housew.* (ed. 2) 134 Make a Hole in the midst of the Flour, and pour all the wetting in.

5. Urination, usu. resulting from incontinence or stress.

1943 [see SOILING *vbl. sb.*[1] 1 b]. **1960** I. BENNETT *Delinquent & Neurotic Children* viii. 252 Soiling, wetting, and difficult behaviour.

6. *attrib.*, as ***wetting-board, -machine, -place, -trough.***

1790 *Act 31 Geo. III*, c. 7, § 18 The Cistern, Uting-fat, or other Wetting-place or Utensil. **1800** *Act 41 Geo. III* c. 6 § 3 Damaged Barley in the Cistern,.. or other wetting Place. **1888** JACOBI *Printers' Vocab.*, *Wetting boards*, the boards placed between the different reams in the press in the wetting department. *Ibid.*, Wetting machines. *Ibid.*, Wetting trough.

'wetting, *ppl. a.* [f. WET *v.*]

a. That makes wet or moist.

1661 BOYLE *Physiol. Ess.* (1669) 187 The distinction betwixt a fluid Body and a wetting Liquor. *a* **1668** LASSELS *Voy. Italy* (1698) I. 134 Here you have the Grotto of Cupid with the wetting-stools, upon which sitting down, a great spout of water comes full in your face. *Ibid.* 159 The great variety of water-works, grots, and wetting sports. **1718** ROWE tr. *Lucan* I. 403 The wetting winds had thaw'd the Alpine snows. **1842** LOUDON *Suburban Hort.* 397 The plant .. is regularly drenched with heavy wetting dews. **1854** H. MILLER *Sch. & Schm.* vi. (1858) 120 There came on a thick, wetting drizzle. **1902** MABEL BARNES-GRUNDY *Thames Camp* 296 The chilly evenings and the heavy wetting mists in the morning. **1948** *Nature* 28 Feb. 313/2 A non-polar 'wetting' liquid such as carbon tetrachloride is floated on mercury in the reservoir beneath the U-tube. **1980** *Brit. Med. Jrnl.* 18 Oct. 1047/2 A wetting solution coats a hard lens with a chemical that permits water to spread and form a surface that is less traumatic to eye tissues.

b. ***wetting agent***, a chemical that can be added to a liquid to reduce its surface tension and make it more effective at wetting.

1927 *Chem. Abstr.* XXI. 414 The Na salts of the products may be used as wetting agents. **1950** *Engineering* 5 May 517/1 The success of Teepol as a wetting agent is due to its effectiveness in reducing the surface tension of water. **1977** J. HEDGECOE *Photographer's Handbk.* 39 Rinsing the film in 'wetting agent' (weak detergent) at the end of washing helps to prevent the accumulation of drops of water.

'wettish, *a.* [f. WET *a.* + -ISH.] Somewhat wet.

1648 R. JOSSELIN *Diary* (Camden 1908) 53 A wett night, and wettish day. **1651** in *Hartlib's Legacy* (1655) 99, I have been with Doctor D. about Lucern, who tells me that it groweth best in wettish grounds. **1733** W. ELLIS *Chiltern & Vale Farm.* 47 This loose Earth.. should be ploughed and sowed in a wettish Time. **1764** J. FERGUSON *Lect.* 59 Wettish or sandy ground. **1788** LD. AUCKLAND *Corr.* (1861) II. 98 It continues wettish and windy. **1812** W. TAYLOR in *Monthly Mag.* XXXIV. 16 Flowers are odoriferous in wettish air. **1828** CARLYLE in Froude *Life* (1882) I. 424 She looked.. eastward with wettish eyes. **1871** —— in *Mrs. Carlyle's Lett.* III. 192 Weather mild though dim and wettish. **1882** *Garden* 6 May 305/1 Particularly in deep, wettish soils.

Hence **'wettishness.**

1727 BAILEY (vol. II), *Moistness*, wettishness, dampness.

wettrien, obs. f. WATER *v.*

wetty, obs. f. WITTY *a.*

weturly, var. WITTERLY *adv. Obs.*

wetware ('wɛtwɛə(r)). [f. WET *a.* after *hardware, software.*] Chemical materials organized so as to perform arithmetic or logical operations; brain substance, as having this ability.

1975 *Nature* 23 Oct. 634/1 An electronic computer is made up of hardware and software; a chemical automaton needs an additional component, a chemical reaction system which might be called 'wetware'. **1977** *N.Y. Times* 8 May I. 34/6 Computer scientists have lately begun talking about 'wetware', which is the human brain. **1984** *Times Lit. Suppl.* 14 Dec. 1442/3 There is no obvious reason why biological 'wetware' should be any better at imbuing internal structures with semantic significance than silicon 'hardware'. **1985** *Listener* 10 Jan. 9/3 The whole claim of strong AI is that the physical and chemical hardware or wetware of the system are quite irrelevant.

wetye, var. WITIE *v. Obs.*

wetyng(ly, obs. ff. WEETING(LY.

weuch, Sc. var. WOUGH *sb. Obs.*

we-uns ('wiːʌnz), *pron. U.S. dial.* Also **we uns, we'uns.** [f. WE *pron.* + *uns*, dial. var. *ones* (ONE *pron.*).] Used in place of WE or US *prons.*

1864 *Harper's Mag.* Dec. 16/2 'What for you uns', said they, in their barbaric dialect, 'come down here to fight we uns?' **1865** O. L. JACKSON *Colonel's Diary* (1922) 208 If we 'uns were to go down to Goldbro or Raleigh, do you think we 'uns could get any old creetur?.. A horse or a mule? **1907** H. B. WRIGHT *Shepherd of Hills* xi. 105 You can get out o' these hills an' be somebody like we'uns. *Ibid.* xii. 109 He sure talks so we'uns can understand. **1913** H. KEPHART *Our Southern Highlanders* xiii. 286 Let's we-uns all go over to youerunses house. **1938** C. H. MATSCHAT *Suwannee River* iii. 53 We-uns'll.. light for home.

†**weve,** *sb. Obs.*[−1] [f. next.] A short or quick movement. ***in little weve***, in a moment.

a **1300** *Cursor M.* 22927 All þe flexs þat was o þe man.. sal be delt in littel weue [*Edinb.* wefe]; þat was o best [= beast] al sal bileue [= remain].

†**weve,** *v.*[1] *Obs.* Forms: 3–5 **weve,** 4–5 **wefe;** *pa. t.* 3 **wefde, weft;** *pa. pple.* 4 **y-, i-weved, veved.** [Perh. a dial. var. of WAIVE *v.*[2] (a. ON. *veifa*); possibly repr. an unrecorded OE. **wǽfan* = ON. *veifa*. Cf. BIWEVE *v.*[2] Although disappearing from literary use in ME., the verb appears to have survived in speech, and to be represented in mod.Eng. by WEAVE *v.*[2]]

1. *intr.* Of persons: To go from one place to another; to travel, wander, pass.

c **1200** *Trin. Coll. Hom.* 85 Ðenne þe iuele gost fareð ut of þe manne and weueð wide.. sechende reste. *c* **1290** *Beket* 2053 in *S. Eng. Leg.* 165 Into þe cloistre of Caunterburi with grete noyse heo comen weue. **1297** R. GLOUC. (Rolls) 1475 Ȝef he com mid is ost in to þis lond weue. **13..** *E.E. Allit. P.* A. 318 Þou wylnez ouer þys water to weue.

b. Of things: To go, pass, make way.

c **1275** LAY. 28049 And ich ig[rap] my gode sweord.. and smot of Modred his hefd, þat hit wefde [*c* 1205 wond] a [the] felde. *c* **1400** *Rowland & O.* 545 He hitt hym a-bown appon þe heuede, þat to þe scholdire þe swerde wefede. *Ibid.* 564 Otuell says 'my suerde kan schere', & in to þe erthe it weuede.

c. To move to and fro; to toss about.

a **1300** *Cursor M.* 24839 þe weder.. son bigan to rug and reth, þat ilk wau til oþer weft, And bremli to þo barges beft. *c* **1300** *Metr. Hom.* 40 But thurt him noht haf tint his heued, Yef he als red [= reed] wald haf weuid. *c* **1350** *Will. Palerne* 4368 To cold coles sche schal be brent ȝit or come eue, & þe aschis of hire body with þe wind weue.

2. *trans.* To move or remove from one place to another; to convey or bring; to strike *down*.

13.. *K. Alis.* 3807 With his sweord he wolde his heved Fro the body have y-weved [*Bodl. MS.* yreued]. **13..** *Sir Beues* 954 A leide on wiþ þe bor is heued, Til þat hii were adoun i-weued. *c* **1325** *Metr. Hom.* 40 Gif me in a disce weued Sain Jon the Baptist heued. **13..** *E.E. Allit. P.* A. 976, I an-endez þe on þis syde Schal sve [= follow], tyl þou to a hil be veued.

b. To wave or brandish (a weapon). Also *absol.*, to beckon, make signals.

c **1325** *Metr. Hom.* (1862) 122 Hir ald fader bird hir lefe, And on hir lemman clep and wefe. *Ibid.* 123. *c* **1325** *Metr. Hom.* (MS. Ashmole 42) fol. 100 Borne he was bothe doumbe & defe and peres on him gon call & wefe. *c* **1350** *Libeaus Desc.* 544 His brond aboute he weved; All þat he hitte he cleved. *c* **1440** [cf. WEVING *vbl. sb.* below].

c. ? To toss about, trouble.

c **1350** *Will. Palerne* 922 Auntrose is þin euel, ful wonderliche it þe weues; wel i wot þe soþe.

3. a. ***to weve up***: to open (a window, a gate): = WAIVE *v.*[2] 2. **b.** ***to weve off***: to throw off (a garment). Cf. WAIVE *v.*[2] 4 a.

a. *c* **1205** LAY. 19003 þa cnihtes weoren swide [*sic*] whæte, and wefden up þa castles ȝæte, & letten hine binnen fare. *c* **1350** *Will. Palerne* 2978 [She] weued vp a window þat was toward þe place.

b. *c* **1290** *Beket* 951 in *S. Eng. Leg.* 133 þo seint thomas hadde is masse i-songue: his chesible he gan of weue.

4. To give (to a person).

13.. *Gaw. & Gr. Knt.* 1976 þe lorde Gawayn con þonk, Such worchip he wolde hym weue. *Ibid.* 2359 Hit is my wede þat þou werez,.. Myn owen wyf hit þe weued, I wot wel for soþe.

Hence †**weving** *vbl. sb.*

c **1440** *Promp. Parv.* 523/2 Wevynge, or mevynge wythe tokne, *annutus*.

†**weve,** *v.*[2] *Obs.*[−1] [OE. *wǽfan* to wrap. Cf. BIWEVE *v.*[1]] *trans.* To wrap up, cover.

1398 TREVISA *Barth. De P. R.* II. viii. (1495) b v b/2 The name of Seraphyn menyth thynge that is not weyled [= veiled] neyther weuyd.

weve, obs. form of WEAVE *v.*

we've, contracted f. *we have* (HAVE *v.* A 2 d).

1742 RICHARDSON *Pamela* III. 313 When, too late, we see what we've miss'd. **1882** BESANT *All Sorts* xxvi, Do you mean to say that we've got to have dinner?

†**'weved.** *Obs.* Forms: *α.* 1 **wio-, weobud, weofud, -od, weofed-,** 3 **weofed** (*dat.* **weofde**), **weoued.** *β.* 1 **wefod,** 3–4 **wefed** (*dat.* **wefde**), 3–5 **weued** (4 **-yd**), 4 **wyeued** (*dat.* **wyefde**). [OE. *wéofud, -od*, earlier *wéo-, wíobud*, f. *wéoh-, wíoh-, wíh-* (*wíȝ-*) holy, sacred + *béod* (masc.) table. In OE., however, the second element very commonly appears as *-bed* (in the forms *wio-, wéo-, wíȝ-, wíbed*) and was evidently identified with the noun *bed*, being sometimes inflected *-beddes*, etc.; in agreement with this the usual gender of *wéofod* is neuter. As an independent word the first element in OE. is a noun meaning 'idol', corresponding to OS. *wîh*, ON. *vé* holy place, sanctuary, and OHG. *wîh* (MHG. *wîch*, G. *weih-*), Goth. *weihs* adj. holy.] An altar.

α. *c* **897** ÆLFRED *Gregory's Past. C.* 217 Ðif se weobud ufan hol nære. *Ibid.*, Hwæt elles ȝetacnað ðæt weobud buton ryhtwisra monna saula? *c* **960** ÆTHELWOLD *Bened. Rule* lxii. 113 Healde he simle þone styde.. butan þære þenunge anre þæs halȝan weofodes. *c* **1000** *Ags. Gosp.* Matt. xxiii. 35 Zacharias.. þone ȝe ofslogon betweox þam temple and þam weofode. *c* **1205** LAY. 31951 He Peteres weofed þere wunliche isohte. *a* **1225** *Ancr. R.* 346 Ualleð biuoren ower weoued a creoix to þer eorðe. *a* **1240** *Lofsong* in *O.E. Hom.* I. 209 Ich.. bi-seche þe.. þurh þine eadi flesche and þine iblescede blode i-sacred oðe weouede.

β. *c* **1000** *Ags. Gosp.* Matt. v. 23 Ðif þu bringst þine lac to wefode.. læt þær þine lac beforan þam altare. *c* **1130** *O.E. Chron.* an. 1125, He sang ðone hehmesse on Eastren dæi æt Cristes wefod. *c* **1205** LAY. 28747 Meleon.. fleh to are chirche and forð riht anan wende forn to ane wefde. *c* **1290** *Beket* 1082 in *S. Eng. Leg.* 137 He let maken is bed.. Op in þe heie chirche bi-twene twei weuedes. **1297** R. GLOUC. (Rolls) 4593 At glastinbury.. at uore þe heye weued amydde þe quer. **1340** *Ayenb.* 14 þe sacrement of þe wyefde. *Ibid.* 236 Godes table is þe wyeued. **1387** TREVISA *Higden* I. 161 þe auters and weuedes of þat peple. *c* **1425** *Eng. Conq. Ireland* xviii. 42 Yn the modyr chyrche,.. & to-for the weued.

wevede, obs. pa. t. and pa. pple. of WEAVE *v.*

wevel(l, wever(e, obs. ff. WEEVIL, WEAVER.

†**wevesterte.** *Obs.* In quot. **wewestrete.** [f. WEVE *v.* + START *sb.*[1] Cf. WAGSTART.] The wagtail.

14.. in Wr.-Wülcker 617/44 *Truga, quedam avis*, a wewestrete.

'wevet. *south-west. dial.* [f. WEAVE *v.* Cf. WEFT *sb.*[1]] A cobweb. †Also *collect.*

1499–1500 *Churchw. Acc. S. Edmund, Sarum* (1896) 51 To Will. Belrynger for Strykyng downe of the Weuet in the Churche. **1581** J. BELL *Haddon's Answ. Osor.* 56 b, Ye skyppe over the open Oracles of truth, and are entangled in the wevett of errour. [Cf. *spider-wevet* s.v. SPIDER 10.] **1825** JENNINGS *Observ. Dial. W. Eng.* 134 Tha church war durty. —Wevets here Hang'd danglin vrom tha ruf. **1886** W. BARNES *Dorset Gloss.*, *Wevvet, wivet*, a cobweb.

wevil(l, -yl(l, obs. forms of WEEVIL.

wew, obs. Sc. f. VIEW; var. WHEW *int.*

wewe, obs. f. VIEW *sb.*, WEAVE *v.*

wewell, obs. form of WEEVIL.

wex(e, obs. ff. VEX *v.*, WAX *sb.* and *v.*

wexin, obs. f. WAXEN.

wey[1] (weɪ). Forms: 1 **wǽȝ** (**wéȝ**), **wǽȝe,** 4–8 **weye,** 5– **wey** (5 **wegh**), 5–7 **way** (6 **waye, waie**), 7 **waigh(e,** 7– **weigh.** [Identical in origin with WEIGH *sb.*[1] Cf. WAY *sb.*[2] and WAW *sb.*[2]]

1. A standard of dry-goods weight, varying greatly with different commodities. (See quots.)

a. Of cheese.

805–10 in Birch *Cartul. Sax.* I. 459 Ðif hit ðonne festen dæȝ sie, selle mon uuæge cæsa & fisces. *c* **833** *Ibid.* 577 An weȝ spices & ceses. **1377** LANGL. *P. Pl.* B. v. 93, I wolde be gladder.. Than þouȝe I had þis woke ywonne a weye of essex chese. **1542** RECORDE *Gr. Arts* K v b, The very weights of it [*sc.* cheese] are cloues and weies, so that a cloue shoulde contayne 7 pounde: and a wey 32 cloues, that is 224 poundes. **1590** PAYNE *Brief Descr. Irel.* (1841) 8 You may haue yeerely .. fortie great wayes of cheese, of the milke gathered betwixt May and Michaelmas. **1596** *Recorde's Gr. Arts* 162 And so much [256 pound] weyeth the weigh of Suffolke cheese... The Wey of Essex Cheese containeth 16 score, and 16 pound. **1638** L. ROBERTS *Merch. Map Comm.* II. 239 The true weight of cheese and butter, called the Waighe. *Ibid.*, The Waighe of Suffolk cheese being 256 li. and the waighe of Essex cheese 336 li. averdupois. **1725** *Bradley's Family Dict.* s.v. *Clove*, In Suffolk they allow forty two of these Cloves or three hundred thirty six pounds to the Wey. **1846** *J. Baxter's Libr. Pract. Agric.* (ed. 4) II. 429 A wey in Suffolk 32 cloves, or 256 lbs. A wey in Essex 42 cloves, or 336 lbs.

b. Of wool.

a **975** *Laws Edgar* III. §8 Ga seo wæȝe [*v.r.* wæȝ] wulle to cxx. p[enninga]. [*c* **1300** *Fleta* II. xii. (1647) 73 Et duæ wayæ lanæ faciunt unum saccum.] *a* **1500** *Arnolde's Chron.* (1811) 100 Of the sac wulle goyng out of London of iij. weys,.. the Sheref owᵗ to haue xi.d'. **1638** L. ROBERTS *Merch. Map Comm.* II. 239 The sacke of wooll formerly so famoused by the staplers, did weigh 364 li. averdupois, two waighes of wooll make a sacke, and 12 sacks make a laste. **1665** W. SHEPPARD *Office Clerk of Market* 65 The Sarplar is the Case wherein the Wooll is, and the Waigh respecteth the quantity of the Wooll it self. **1688** HOLME *Armoury* III. 261/1 A Wey [of Wool] contains six Tods and a half. **1844** H. STEPHENS *Bk. Farm* III. 888 Wool.. is weighed out in double stones of 48 lb., each being called a weigh.

c. Of salt.

1443 *Durham Acc. Rolls* (Surtees) 83 In 2 Wegh et di. grossi salis empt., 50s. **1451** *Paston Lett.* I. 228 That ye sold a wey salt but for xxs. that she might hafe had xls for every wey. **1459** *Maldon* (Essex) *Court Rolls* Bundle 34 No. 1, vi weyes do baysalt, prec. le wey xxvis. viii*d.* **1533–4** *Durham Househ. Bk.* (Surtees) 255, 2½ qu. [salis] vocata ½ wey. **1545** *Rates Custome ho.* cvb, Salte called baysalt the waye xiii.s. iiii.d. *a* **1585** in *Eng. Hist. Rev.* (1914) XXIX. 517 You must lade for every thousand fishe a weye of salte or rather more. **1611** in Picton *L'pool. Munic. Rec.* (1883) I. 179 Ev'ry Way of Salt, conteyning by measure x barrells. **1615** E. S. *Britain's Buss* in Arber *Garner* III. 635 Likewise, the Buss cannot conveniently stow, at once, above ten Weys of salt. **1638** L. ROBERTS *Merch. Map Comm.* II. 248 A tunne of Salt at Plimouth is greater than a weigh of London by 32 gallons. **1674** JEAKE *Arith.* (1696) 70 Salt is reckoned by the Hundred and Wey. In 1 Hundred of Salt 10½ Weyes, in 1 Wey 40 Bushels. **1704** *Lond. Gaz.* No. 4060/5 About 50 Weigh of Salt, out of the La Senie. **1748** W. BROWNRIGG *Art making Salt* 214 The law now allows three bushels duty free, for every wey (or forty bushels) of British salt carried coastwise.

d. Of coal, corn, etc., or in general use.

?*c* **1300** in *Rep. Comm. Weights & Meas.* (1758) 19, xiv petræ faciunt unum pondus, quod Anglice dicitur weye. *a* **1400** *Rel. Ant.* I. 70 Sevene waxpund makiet onleve ponde one waye, twelf weyen on fothir. **1471** *Churchw. Acc. Yatton* (Somerset Rec. Soc.) 107 For ij wey cole, xˢ. **1542–3** *Act 34 & 35 Hen. VIII*, c. 9. §5 The said common meater to haue for the measuring of euery way of corne .ii.d. **1560** *MS. Acc. Bk. Butchers' Co., Lond.*, The price of a Waie of tallowe was this yere Rated.. at 30/. **1656** BLOUNT *Glossogr.*, *Weigh*,.. in some parts of this land it signifies a quantity of Corn (most commonly of Barley or Malt) containing six quarters. **1660** F. BROOKE tr. *Le Blanc's Trav.* 385 Out of the Mounts of Libani in Cuba, there was one [piece of gold] taken weighing 3310 weighs. **1706** PHILLIPS (ed. Kersey), *Wey*, the greatest Measure for dry things, containing five Chaldron: *Weys* or *Weighs*, are also 165 Pounds, 180 Pounds, or 200 Pounds and a half for a Charge. **1725** *Bradley's Family Dict.* s.v. *Wey*, A Weigh of Barley or Malt, is six Quarters or forty eight Bushels. **1813** VANCOUVER *Agric. Devon* 54 During which time five or six weys of culm were raised. **1823** J. GUY *Tutor's Assist.* 51 How many weys and bushels, in 72 lasts? *Ans.* 144 weys, 5760 bus. **1891** L. CLARK *Dict. Metric Measures* 97 *Wey*, or *Load* (dry measure) = 40 bushels = 5 quarters.

attrib. **1603** G. OWEN *Pembrokeshire* (1892) 137 Neither ys the Cranoke or Wey measures vsed in selling thereof [corn].

†**2.** ? A pound. (Vulg. *libras centum.*)

a **1225** *Ancr. R.* 372 Nicodemus brouhte uorte smurien mid ure Louerd an hundred weien of mirre & of aloes.

†**wey.**[2] *Obs. rare.* [Of obscure origin; the variation in the stem-vowel would normally indicate an OE. *wǽȝ*, *wáȝ-*.] ? A bill or halberd.

c **1205** LAY. 30982 Breken bræde weiȝes [*c* **1275** weyes], brustleden scaftes. *Ibid.* 21505 Cheorles.. mid clubben swiðen græte, mid spæren and mid græte waȝen. *Ibid.* 21596 Moni cniht mid heore wahȝen [*c* **1275** wawes].. ualden heom to grunden.

wey, obs. f. WAY *sb.*, WEIGH *v.*, var. WY *Obs.*, man.

weyard, obs. var. WEIRD *a.*

wey-bit, var. WAY-BIT *Obs.*

weybred, obs. var. WAYBREAD.

weyche, obs. Sc. f. WITCH *sb.*

weycht, obs. Sc. f. WEIGHT, WIGHT.

weydde, obs. f. WEED *v.*[1]

weyde, obs. f. WIDE *adv.*

weydraught, obs. f. WITHDRAUGHT.

†**weye**, *v. Obs. rare.* Also waye. [OE. *wǽȝan* to delude, deceive.]

1. *trans.* To deceive, lead astray.

c **1315** SHOREHAM *Poems* I. 370 Þat he ne may nauȝt yweid be Wiþ blanding ne wiþ boste. *Ibid.* VII. 648 The deuel.. dorste nauȝt adam asaylly, Al for to waye.

2. *intr.* To go astray.

c **1315** SHOREHAM *Poems* I. 301 Bote hi ariȝt icristned be, Fram heuene euere hi weyeþ.

weye, obs. f. WAY *sb.*[1], WEIGH *v.*, WHEY; var. WY (man) *Obs.*

weyfe, obs. f. WAIF *sb.*[1], WAIVE *v.*[1]

weyffe, obs. f. WIFE.

weyghe, weyghte, obs. ff. WEIGH(T.

wey-hey, var. WEHEE *v.*

weyhte, obs. f. WEIGHT.

weyit, obs. Sc. f. WET *v.*

weyk(e, obs. ff. WEAK *a.*, WICK.

weylawey, obs. f. WELLAWAY.

weyld, obs. f. WIELD *v.*

weyle, obs. f. WAIL *v.*, WALE *v.*[1], WEEL[2].

weyle a woo, var. WELLAWO *Obs.*

weylecott, var. WYLIECOAT *Sc.*

†**weyleyship.** *Obs.*[−1] [f. *wey* WEIGH *v.* Cf. METLEYSHIP.] The office of weigher.

1587 LD. BURGHLEY in *12th Rep. Hist. MSS. Comm.* App. VII. (1890) 12 [Concerning the office of the] weyleyship and metleyship [in Penrith].

weylico(i)tt, obs. ff. WYLIECOAT *Sc.*

weylsum, var. WEALSOME *a. Obs.*

weyme, obs. f. WAME.

weymen, obs. pl. WOMAN.

weyment(e, var. ff. WAYMENT.

Weymouth (ˈweɪməθ). **1.** [The title of the first Lord *Weymouth*, by whom the tree was extensively planted after its introduction into England in 1705] ***Weymouth Pine***, the American white pine, *Pinus Strobus*.

[**1731** P. MILLER *Gard. Dict.* s.v. *Pinus, Pinus Americana*,.. Lord Weymouth's Pine.] **1766** *Complete Farmer* s.v. *Aphernousli*, The white Canada-pine, which is better known in England by the name of Weymouth-pine. **1781** *Westminster Mag.* IX. 133 The Weymouth-pine has been long naturalized here; the patriarch plant still existing at Longleat. **1791** W. GILPIN *Forest Scenery* I. 82 The Weymouth-pine has very little picturesque beauty to recommend it. **1862** ANSTED *Channel Isl.* IV. xxi. (ed. 2) 496 The Weymouth pine, the stone pine,.. and the larch, are all occasionally seen. **1882** *Garden* 16 Sept. 251/2 Weymouth Pine, Scotch Spruce, and Silver Fir timber sold at a low figure.

2. *Horseriding.* Designating a type of curb bit (see quot. 1963) or a double bridle comprising this bit and a snaffle with two sets of reins.

1792 T. H. MORLAND *Every Man his Own Judge* 70 A Weymouth bridle, with bit, and bradoon, is in my opinion preferable to any other sort for the road. **1919** R. S. TIMMIS *Notes on Riding & Driving* iii. 39 A few good snaffles, both racing and exercising (with cross-pieces outside the cheek), and a Weymouth or a Pelham bit and bridoon are all that are necessary for practically all horses. **1938** F. C. HITCHCOCK *To Horse!* ix. 274 The only objection to a double bridle is that its use entails two separate mouthpieces in the horse's mouth. The usual pattern bit used is called the Weymouth. **1946** M. C. SELF *Horseman's Encycl.* 433 The Weymouth bridle consists of a bit and bridoon. It is the bridle most usually used for the finished saddle horse. **1963** BLOODGOOD & SANTINI *Horseman's Dict.* 21 *Weymouth or Ward Union bit*, bit consisting of straight, moderately long cheek-pieces, stationary or sliding mouthpiece, either straight or with a slight Muller or Cambridge port. Simplest of all curb bits and most generally used. **1965** C. E. G. HOPE *Riding* v. 59 The curb used with a double bridle, known as the Weymouth or Ward Union, invariably has a plain port mouth.

weyn, obs. f. VAIN *a.*; north. f. WEEN *sb.*, *v.*

weynd(e, obs. ff. WEND *v.*

weyne, obs. f. VEIN, WAIN *sb.*[1], WINE; north. f. WEEN *sb.*, *v.*

weyng(e, obs. ff. WING.

weynscot, -scotte, skot, obs. ff. WAINSCOT.

weynt, ? var. *queynt*, pa. pple. of QUENCH *v.*

a **1450** MYRC *Par. Pr.* 1102 Hast þou for slowþe I-be so feynt Þat al þy wylle has be weynt.

weype, obs. form of WIPE *v.*

†**weyr.** *Obs.* [Of obscure origin.] Some piece of timber in the structure or fittings of a vessel.

1296 *Acc. Exch. K.R.* 5/20 m. 2b, In xiiij lignis de longitudine .l. pedum emptis.. ad Weyres. *Ibid.* m. 3b, In duobus Weyris ad Bargiam emptis de Henrico de Wermue. *Ibid.* m. 4b, In Weyris Spurchis et aliis emendacionibus factis in Galea et Bargia.

weyr, Sc. var. VER spring. *Obs.*

weyre, Sc. var. WERE *sb.* doubt, etc.

weyrly, var. WARLY.

weysand(e, obs. ff. WEASAND.

weysse, obs. f. WISE *a.*

weyst, obs. Sc. f. WEST.

weyte, obs. f. WHITE.

weyth, obs. f. WITHE.

†**weythernoy**, error for *vethervoy, south-western var. *fetherfoy*: see FEATHERFEW.

1597 GERARDE *Herbal* Suppl., Weythernoy is Feuerfew. [**1665** LOVELL *Herball* (ed. 2) 465 Weyther-ney, see Feaverfew.]

weythwynde, obs. f. WITHWIND.

weyve, obs. f. WAIVE *v.*[1]; var. WAIVE *v.*[2] *Obs.*; obs. f. WEAVE *v.*

weyward, = *weyard* obs. var. WEIRD *a.*

wezand, wezen, wezzand, obs. ff. WEASAND.

wezeer, obs. f. VIZIER.

wezill, var. WEEZLE *Obs.*

wez(z)on, obs. ff. WEASAND.

wh, a consonantal digraph, normally represents initial *hw* in words of OE. origin, as in *hwæt* what, *hwisprian* to whisper. In words of other origin, its occurrence may be due to analogy resting on the supposed phonetic appropriateness of the 'aspirate' sound, as in *whip*, *whisk*; it sometimes varies with *h* or simple *w*; e.g. *whortleberry* and *hurtleberry*, *whoop* and *hoop*, *whelked* and *welked*. Historically OE. initial *hw* represents OTeut. *χw* (under which Indo-Eur. *qʷ* and *kw* were levelled), which appears as *hw* in the early forms of the Germanic languages, but is variously modified in their modern forms, appearing in High and Low German as *w*, in the Scandinavian languages, according to dialect, as *hv*, *kv*, and *v*, in English as *wh*. For typical forms see WHAT.

The normal OE. spelling *hw* was generally preserved in early ME. till late in the 13th century, e.g. in the Nero MS. of Ancren Riwle (with occas. variants in *w*, as *wase* whoso), and the pieces contained in An Old English Miscellany (E.E.T.S.); it persists in the Ayenbite of Inwyt in the form *hu*, as *huich*. The modern spelling *wh* is found first in regular use in the Ormulum, e.g. *whillc* which; it is the commoner spelling in the earlier text of Layamon's Brut (with frequent variants in *w*), the Harl. MS. of King Horn, and the earliest MS. of Robert of Gloucester's Chronicle, and continues thence without interruption to the present day; sporadic anticipations occur in the 11th century in the interlinear Rule of St. Benedict, as in *æiwhepera* (ed. E.E.T.S., p. 81), *whænne* (ib. 103), and in the 12th century in the Peterborough Chronicle (e.g. *whilc*, an. 675), and the Lambeth and Cotton Homilies. A few instances of the omission of *h* occur in some early texts (e.g. *sinuurbul* 'teres' in Epinal Gloss., *wilum* 'nunc' in 9th century Bede Glosses), and there are some in the 11th century Rule of St. Benedict (e.g. *wylce* which, *wanon* whence); it becomes more frequent in the 12th century, chiefly in words of the interrogative class, e.g. *wilc*, *ȝewilcum*, *wat*, *wænne*, and (*sum*)*wile*, for *hwilc*, *ȝewhilcum*, *hwæt*, *hwænne*, and *hwíle* (Cato Glosses, Canterbury Psalter, Peterborough Chronicle, Homilies, etc.). Many examples of simple *w* are to be found in the two versions of Layamon and other 13th century texts, and this variant spelling continues in widespread use till 1500.

Strong enunciation of the back (guttural) element in the pronunciation of (hw) is shown by the spellings *chua*, *chuæt*, *chwæm*, *chuelc* = *hwá*, etc. of the Lindisfarne Gosp., and began to be denoted in ME. of the 13th century by the use of *qu* (*quu*, *qw*), first in East Anglian texts (once in the Bestiary, *qual* whale; regularly but not exclusively in Genesis and Exodus). It remained a feature of East Anglian spelling till *c* 1450 (as in the Paston Letters and the works of John Metham), but after 1300 it became more especially a characteristic feature of northern English, surviving in Scottish, esp. in the form *quh*, till the 18th century. (For the converse use of *wh* for *qu* (kw), see the letter Q.)

Early in the 15th century appear spellings with *wh* of words with initial *h* followed by an *o*-sound. It occurs first before *ǭ* (:—*ā*), e.g. *whom* for *hǭm* (OE. *hám*) in Brut *c* 1420 (E.E.T.S.), pp. 346, 370, *wholle* for *hǭle* (OE. *hál*) in Chron. Vilod. *c* 1420, 3368, and Camb. MS. of Guy of Warwick 3422, *whote* for *hǭt* (OE. *hát*) in Partonope, *whore* for *hǭre* hoar (OE. *hár*) in Revel. Monk of Evesham (1482); *wholy* for *hǭly* is used by Tindale, 1526. Later, other words normally spelt with initial *ho-* (of whatever origin) became subject to the same variation of spelling; e.g. *whore* for *hǭre* (OE. *hóre*), *whole* for *hǭle* (OE. *hol*), *whood* for *hood* (OE. *hód*), *whoord* for *hǭrd* 'hoard' (OE. *hord*). Some of these spellings were especially frequent in the 16th century; thus *whood* 'hood' is used by Hall the chronicler, Nashe, Harvey, John Davies of Hereford, and Sylvester. The *wh*-spelling has become standardized in two of these words, viz. *whole* and *whore*, and their derivatives, in which it became common *c* 1600. The corresponding labialized pronunciation is current dialectally only in *whole*, but it survives in several other words where the standard form has preserved the original *ho-*, as in *hoard*, *hold*, *hole*, *home*, *hot*; in *home*, pronunciations such as (wɔm), (wʊəm), (wʌm) cover a wide area. For details of the evidence see the various words in this Dict. and Eng. Dial. Dict.

Spellings of HOW *adv.* with initial *hw*, *wh*, and (consequently) *quh* are on a different footing, as they are due in the first place to association of the word with the interrogative *why*, *where*, etc.

From the fourteenth century onwards there are sporadic instances of initial *whr* for *wr*, as *whrightes* (R. Brunne's Chron. Wace 8711), *whrassid* 'wrested' (St. Cuthbert, 6041), *whretchedly* (Bale, 1560). For the relationship of *hurlpool*, *hurlwind*, *hurtleberry* to *whirlpool*, *whirlwind*, *whortleberry*, etc., and of *thwack*, *thwang* to *whack*, *whang*, etc., see these words.

Pronunciation. In OE. the pronunciation symbolized by *hw* was probably in the earliest periods a voiced bilabial consonant preceded by a breath. This was developed in two different directions: (1) it was reduced to a simple voiced consonant (w); (2) by the influence of the accompanying breath, the voiced (w) became unvoiced. The first of these pronunciations (w) probably became current first in southern ME. under the influence of French speakers, whence it spread northwards (but ME. orthography gives no reliable evidence on this point). It is now universal in English dialect speech except in the four northernmost counties and north Yorkshire, and is the prevailing pronunciation among educated speakers. The second pronunciation, denoted in this Dictionary by the conventional symbol (hw), and otherwise variously denoted by phoneticians, (w*h*), (*w*), (w̥), (ʍ), is general in Scotland, Ireland, and America, and is used by a large proportion of educated speakers in England, either from social or educational tradition, or from a preference for what is considered a careful or correct pronunciation.

The 15th or 16th century Welsh transcript of the English Hymn to the Virgin (E.D.S. Misc. 3, p. 27) shows the voiceless pronunciation, rendering *where* by *hwier*, and the evidence of the 16th century and later orthoepists goes to show that this was the prevailing pronunciation among cultured speakers, but there are indications that it was not of universal currency. Towards the end of the 18th century the voiceless was ousted by the voiced sound, and the lexicographer John Walker (1791) notes that in London speech 'the aspirate *h* is often sunk', and includes the voiced pronunciation of *wh* among the four faults of the speech of the metropolis. The restoration of the voiceless pronunciation which took place in the 19th century was due in part to Scottish and Irish influence, and in part to conscious reference to the spelling. Some early orthoepists admitted a pronunciation of *whole*, *wholesome* with (hw). This must have been familiar to Samuel Johnson, for in the Grammar prefixed to his Dictionary he remarks that 'in *whore* only, and sometimes in *wholesome*, *wh* is sounded like a simple *h*.' The dialectal pron. (woːl, wʊl) are widespread.

In Sc. dialects north of the Tay the voiceless bilabial (hw) has become the voiceless labio-dental (f) in interrog. prons. and advs., as *fa* who, *fat* what, *fan* when; in Aberdeen and Banff in other words also, as *fite* white, *folp* whelp, *fup* whip. (Cf. FALL *sb.*[3]).

1. (Also **wh-, wh'**) Informal written abbrev. of WHICH *a.* and *pron.*, in relative use.

c **1858** E. DICKINSON *Poems* (1955) I. 16 Sleep is the station grand Down wh', on either hand The hosts of witness stand! **1865** HARDY *Let.* 20 Oct. (1978) I. 5 You will know wh. part of the Abbey I mean if you think of Salisbury Cathedral & of the row of small arches over the large arches. **1889** W. WHITMAN *Daybks. & Notebks.* (1978) II. 528 Paid $3.15 for insurance for $300 on stock at 1213 Filbert st. wh- is continued on to Feb: 8 '90.

2. *Linguistics.* A symbol representing an interrogative or relative pronoun (most of which begin with the digraph *wh*). Freq. *Comb.*, as ***wh-clause***, ***-question***, ***-transformation***, etc.

1957 N. CHOMSKY *Syntactic Struct.* vii. 69 In the morphophonemics of English we shall have rules: *wh* + *he*→/huw/, *wh* + *him*→/huwm/, *wh* + *it*→/wat/. **1960** *Internat. Jrnl. Amer. Linguistics* XXVI. III. ii. 36 Again adopting Chomsky's excellent analysis of interrogative sentences, we wish now to produce those structures introduced by words beginning, for the most part, with *wh-*, i.e. WH-questions and their affirmative counterparts, relative clauses and question-word clauses. **1962** N. CHOMSKY in *3rd Texas Conf. Probl. Linguistic Anal. in Eng.* 147 Application of the *wh*-transformation is conditional on the interrogative transformation 3. **1964** *Language* XL. 5 The interrogative specifier *Wh* can remain unattached or can have attached to it (indicated by +) various elements of the sentence. **1966** G. N. LEECH *Eng. in Advertising* vi. 61 It is the type which consists of an embedded *wh-* clause. **1975** J. GOULET *Oh's Profit* v. 31 *Trabasso*: You mean he demonstrates nonkernel sentences? *Liedlich*: Passive, interrogative, imperative, and he's beginning to get the hang of WH-subordination, too. **1980** B. NEWMAN in *Bible Translator* XXXI. 326 Lengthy sentences are found throughout NIV... Romans I. 1-4 is a single sentence consisting of 72 words, involving at least one case of ellipsis, one dash, one colon, two 'wh'-clauses, and several appositions. **1981** R. BURCHFIELD *Spoken Word* 30 *Wh*-questions: Which hotel is he staying *at*? Who are you voting *for*?

wha(a, dial. forms of WHO; var. WHAU *int.*

whaaped, var. WHAPED *pa. pple. Obs.*, WHAUP.

whack (hwæk), *sb. colloq.* Also 8-9 *Sc.* **whawk, whauk**, 9 **wack**. [? Echoic: perh. an alteration of THWACK.]

1. a. A vigorous stroke with a stick or the like; a heavy resounding blow; also the sound of this.

1737 RAMSAY *Sc. Prov.* (1750) 13 As sair greets the bairn that's paid at e'en, as he that gets his whawks in the morning. **1823** E. MOOR *Suffolk Words* 477 *Whack*, a blow, a thump. **1832** BARRINGTON *Pers. Sk.* III. xviii. 242, I never saw .. any dangerous contusion from what they called 'whacks' of the shillelah. **1854** SURTEES *Handley Cr.* lxxiii, Bill gave the boy two or three more hearty whacks, and then kicked him into the hosier's shop. **1860** THACKERAY *Lovel* v, Bessy's 'Ah!' or little cry was followed by a *whack*, which I heard as clear as anything I ever heard in my life.

b. ***to have*** or ***take a whack at***: to make an attempt or attack upon. *U.S.*

1891 *Boston* (Mass.) *Jrnl.* 22 June 2/2 There are thousands ..who..are anxious to have a whack, at the polls, at the party that deceived them. **1894** *Advance* (Chicago) 20 Dec. 418/1 Mother's got over her long weak spell, and is able to take a whack at doings.

2. a. A portion, share, allowance; *esp.* a full share, a large portion or amount.

Chiefly in phr. ***to get, have, take one's whack***.

1785 GROSE *Dict. Vulgar T.*, *Whack*, a share of a booty obtained by fraud. **1790** ALEX. WILSON in *Poems & Lit. Prose* (1876) II. 51 Whauks o' guid ait-farll cowins Synet down wi' whey. **1805** C. PAGET in *P. Papers* (1896) II. 162 My whack of prize money..will be about fifty thousand Pounds. **1830** MARRYAT *King's Own* xxxiv, 'I'll punish the port to-morrow.'.. 'I'll take my whack to-day.' **1874** *Slang Dict.* 338 To go whacks, to divide equally; to enter into partnership. **1894** ASTLEY *Fifty Yrs. Life* II. 119 He could not trust himself to take a fair whack of liquor without taking too much. **1918** *Blackw. Mag.* July 43/2 I've had a run for my money this whack of leave.

b. A dividing *up* of accounts. Also more generally, a sharing-up or distribution.

1885 HORNADAY *Two Yrs. in Jungle* xxiv. 284 When the Colombo rice merchants, shopmen, the hotel-keepers have their quarterly 'whack-up' with the government. **1896** ADE *Artie* xii. 107 He hadn't been in on the whack-up six weeks till he was wearing one o' them bicycle lamps in his neck-tie. **1912** R. A. WASON *Friar Tuck* xi. 85 'What ya goin' to kill her with?' he asked, his eyes dancin' like an Injun's at the beef whack-up.

c. *U.S.* A bargain or agreement. Esp. in phr. ***it's*** (or ***that's***) ***a whack***.

1860 *Johnson's Orig. Comic Songs* (ed. 2) 45, I axed her for to marry me, she said it was a whack. **1876** 'MARK TWAIN' *Tom Sawyer* vi. 70 I'll stay if you will.' 'Good—that's a whack'. **1884** J. HAY *Bread-Winners* x. 149 Say the word, and it's a whack. **1903** A. D. MCFAUL *Ike Glidden in Maine* xviii. 146 'I'll guarantee to get him to take you to Grand Menan with him.' 'It's a whack,' said Jim. **1911** *Dialect Notes* III. 540 *Whack*,..an agreement, a 'go'; e.g., 'That's a whack!'

3. As *int.* or *adv.*: With a whack (in sense 1).

1812 H. & J. SMITH *Rej. Addr.*, *Archit. Atoms*, Jill..bobbs plump against him, whack! **1836** MARRYAT *Midsh. Easy* v, Whack came the cane on Johnny's shoulders. **1857** HUGHES *Tom Brown* I. ii, Whack, whack, whack, come his blows.

4. ***out of whack***: disordered, malfunctioning; out of order or alignment. Cf. WACKY *a.* Chiefly *U.S.* **a.** Of a person or a part of the body.

1885 C. A. SIRINGO *Texas Cowboy* v. 33, I was too weak to walk that far on account of my back being out of whack. **1899** ADE *Doc' Horne* viii. 79 My stomach seems to be out of whack. **1903** A. M. BINSTEAD *Pitcher in Paradise* vi. 146 At last he utterly gets his thinker out of whack an' goes back to the villa. **1918** H. A. VACHELL *Some Happenings* xii. 205 His liver is out of whack and no mistake. **1969** 'V. PACKER' *Don't rely on Gemini* (1970) xviii. 150 Margaret had had symptoms of early menopause last winter: that had thrown her way out of whack, could conceivably explain such erratic and erotic behaviour.

b. Of a mechanism.

1906 *McClure's Mag.* Feb. 34 Being able to get at any part of the mechanism which may be 'out of whack' is important. **1934** D. HAMMETT *Thin Man* xi. 77 The phone in the apartment was out of whack. **1949** *Time* 30 May 53/2 With normal vibration a lot of them would have gone out of whack. **1975** *New Yorker* 28 Apr. 40/3 He sends no message on the tape recorder to the little boys, because they have already put the machine out of whack. **1985** *Mail on Sunday* (Colour Suppl.) 3 Mar. 20/2 The body's like an automobile. You have to rest and repair it, not run with the motor out of whack.

c. *fig.*

1952 C. ARMSTRONG *Black-Eyed Stranger* xiv. 117 Ambielli's got principles. They are a little off, slightly out of whack. **1973** in G. Gibson *Eleven Canad. Novelists* 123, I don't know whether it is because my own sense of sexual timing or whatever is out of 'whack' with everybody else's. **1975** M. AMIS *Dead Babies* v. 33 Everything is out of whack at Appleseed Rectory; its rooms are without bearing and without certainty. **1978** S. BRILL *Teamsters* vi. 250 In the next decade..the bad loans and poor investment management would..start to throw the cash-flow projections out of whack.

whack (hwæk), *v. colloq.* Also 8-9 *Sc.* **whauk**. [See prec.]

1. a. *trans.* To beat or strike vigorously, as with a stick; to thrash.

1721 *Ramsay's Poems* I. Gloss. **1742** RICHARDSON *Pamela* III. 334 Many and many a good time have I whacked the Rascal's Jacket. **1847** ALB. SMITH *Chr. Tadpole* Introd. (1879) 3 The sheriffs..whacked each other soundly with their wands. **1897** MARY KINGSLEY *W. Africa* 225 When the husband loses his temper,..he whacks his wife.

absol. or *intr.* **1852** C. W. DAY *Five Yrs.' Resid. W. Indies* I. 304 Whacking away, I finally severed his head from his body. **1898** M. MURIEL DOWIE *Crook of Bough* xxiii, Her tough tweeds whacked on the ivory lintel.

b. *fig.* To beat in a contest.

1877 *Holderness Gloss.* s.v., Ah can whack him onny day at sums.

2. *transf.* and *fig.* Substituted for 'put', 'bring', 'get', etc., with implication of vigorous or violent action; cf. *knock up*.

1719 RAMSAY *3rd Answ. to Hamilton* viii, Why should we ..thole sae aft the Spleen to whauk us Out of our Reason? **1861** J. BARR *Poems* 154 (E.D.D.) A rotten stump my brain had rackit.. Till Doctor Manning oot did whack it. **1872** C. KING *Mountain. Sierra Nev.* x. 219 If I design to paint a head, or a foot, or an arm, I get my little old Sarah Jane to peel the particular charm, and just whack her in on the canvas. **1897** KIPLING *Capt. Cour.* v. 115 When they whacked up a match 'twix' his sister Hitty an' Lorin' Jerauld. **1903** —— *Their Lawful Occas.* I. in *Traffics & Discov.* 117 Can we whack her [*sc.* a torpedo-boat] up to fifteen, d'you think?

3. [See prec. 2.] To share, divide. Also with *up*.

1812 J. H. VAUX *Flash Dict.*, *Wack*, to share or divide any thing equally. **1821** *Life D. Haggart* (ed. 2) 94 We got twenty-two screaves by this adventure, which we whacked. **1888** 'R. BOLDREWOOD' *Robbery under Arms* xlviii, We hadn't much trouble dividing the gold, and what cash there was we could whack easy enough. **1893** H. A. SHANDS *Some Peculiarities of Speech in Mississippi* 77 *Whack up*, an expression employed by all classes, probably as semi-slang, to mean *to divide*, *to share*. **1961** *Coast to Coast 1959-60* 126 I'll whack up the breakfast, then, and see how poor bloody Bill's getting on. **1981** *Amer. Speech* LVI. 27 The DARE project has turned up *whack it up*, *whack up* (two informants for each).

4. *intr.* With *off*: to masturbate. *U.S. slang.*

1969 P. ROTH *Portnoy's Complaint* 78 Did I mention that when I was fifteen I took it out of my pants and whacked off on the 107 bus from New York? **1969** *Listener* 17 Apr. 538/3 Fellatio with the Monkey does not present the same practical difficulties as whacking off in Momma's bathroom. **1977** *Transatlantic Rev.* LX. 36 'What-in-hell you do for sex anyway?' he asked the boy one night. 'Whack off into the tin pot where they keep the mashed potatoes?'

whack, dial. form of QUACK *v.*[2]

1807 HOGG *Mountain Bard*, *Pedlar* xxiv, The ducks they whackit, the dogs they yowled.

whack, var. WACK.

whacked (hwækd), *ppl. a. slang.* [f. WHACK *v.* + -ED[1].] **1.** Tired out, exhausted.

1919 *Athenæum* 15 Aug. 759/1 'Whacked to the wide' means to be tired out. **1952** J. CANNON *Body in Beck* v. 82 He had been on the job since dawn, was whacked and must call it a day. **1960** L. MEYNELL *Bandaberry* vi. 100 I'm whacked. How far have we done? **1976** J. SNOW *Cricket Rebel* 118 In addition to recovering from the injury to my right hand I was whacked when I arrived back in England from the MCC tour.

2. ***whacked out***: mad, crazy; *spec.* intoxicated with drugs. Cf. WACKY *a. U.S.*

1969 *Current Slang* (Univ. S. Dakota) Summer 17 *Whacked out*, unorthodox; inclined toward foolish acts. **1969** 'V. PACKER' *Don't rely on Gemini* (1970) i. 8 You Cancers are whacked out because the moon rules you. **1975** *High Times* Dec. 68/3 Then there's the pilot who was whacked out of his skull and landed a hundred-grand rented Cessna 411 gear up in Las Vegas. **1980** W. SAFIRE in *N.Y. Times Mag.* 14 Sept. 11/2 In America, the term 'whacked-out' is current, as an intensified form of 'spaced out' or 'zonked out', meaning soft-headed after prolonged and excessive use of drugs.

whacker ('hwækə(r)). *colloq.* [f. WHACK *v.* + -ER[1].]

1. a. A heavy blow. *dial.*

1823 E. MOOR *Suffolk Words* 477 *Whacker*, a blow, a thump.

b. A driver of animals, a drover. *U.S.*

1880 *Harper's Mag.* LX. 679 The whacker's long whip cracking..as he lashes his unwieldy beasts [*sc.* oxen] into position. **1889** H. O'REILLY *Fifty Yrs. on Trail* xvi. 172 To search round for bull-whackers to drive them over.

2. Anything abnormally large of its kind; *esp.* a 'thumping' lie; a 'whopper'.

1825 BROCKETT *N.C. Gloss.*, *Whacker*, a lie. **1828** *Sporting Mag.* (N.S.) XXII. 416 Though the fences are whackers, the brooks they are small. **1857** HUGHES *Tom Brown* II. iv, Oh, there's a whacker!..we haven't been within a hundred yards of his barn. **1872** J. R. GREEN *Let. to E. A. Freeman* 18 Sept., The Dome which ought to be a whacker is a poor wee thing.

whacking ('hwækɪŋ), *vbl. sb. colloq.* [f. WHACK *v.* + -ING[1].] The action of the verb WHACK.

1. a. Beating.

1862 MRS. H. WOOD *Channings* i, Then take your whacking! **1887** *Pall Mall Gaz.* 14 Nov. 2/2 There is a sound of the whacking of staves and sticks.

attrib. **1886** *Pall Mall Gaz.* 19 June 5/1 We turned away followed by the beaters, one of whom tucked his long whacking-stick under his chin.

b. *transf.* A beating or defeat in a contest; a 'thrashing'.

1951 *Sport* 27 Apr.–3 May 3/2 If Wednesday gets a whacking from Spurs this time.. they can hardly grumble.

2. Dividing up or sharing.

1851 MAYHEW *Lond. Labour* II. 154 At last Long J—— and I got to quarrel about the 'whacking'; there was cheatin' a-goin' on.

whacking ('hwækɪŋ), *ppl. a. colloq.* [f. WHACK(ER + -ING².] That is a 'whacker'; abnormally large; 'thumping', 'whopping'.

Often quasi-advb. in *whacking big, great.*

1806 J. DAVIS *Post Captain* iv. 19 She looks.. like a whacking frigate. **1819** J. THOMSON *Poems* (ed. 2) 201 A whakin' fee gets tauld them down for sorry haet, I trow. **1823** SCOTT *Quentin D.* Introd. ¶7 A certain whacking priest in our neighbourhood. **1829** —— *Jrnl.* 16 Apr. (1890) II. 268 This whacking reason. **1853** G. J. CAYLEY *Las Alforjas* II. 193 We saw a whacking great building. **1873** C. M. DAVIES *Unorth. Lond., Walworth Jumpers* 91 A good whacking kiss that echoed all over the archway.

whacko (stress variable), *int.* Also **wacko.** [f. WHACK *sb.* + -O².] An exclamation of delight or excitement: Splendid! Excellent! Hurrah!

1941 BAKER *Dict. Austral. Slang* 81 *Whacko*, good! Hurrah! A popular ejaculation. **1944** A. F. BRUNO *Desert Daze* 7 Chips let his [Mills bomb] go.. Whacko! **1961** J. MACLAREN-ROSS *Doomsday Book* I. vii. 74 'All's well,' Marsh said elatedly.. 'Whacko!' Eustace cried. **1967** *Southerly* XXVII. 75 This is the message. 'Home Friday. Wacko.' **1978** L. DAVIDSON *Chelsea Murders* xvii. 94 After all it was only two days to—whacko!—Monday.

whacko, whacky, varr. WACKO, WACKY.

whad, whaddie: see WHAT, WADDY¹.

whadd(a)ya, etc., repr. colloq. pronunc. of 'what do you'.

1927 C. HOPLEY-WOOLRICH *Children of Ritz* iv. 72 Gaffney shook hands. 'Whaddya know, eh?' he greeted him breezily. **1945** A. KOBER *Parm Me* 33 'Waddeya mean,' she says back to mē. **1952** E. WILSON *Equations of Love* 34 'Well, whaddaya know!' exclaimed Mort. **1955** W. GADDIS *Recognitions* II. iv. 446 Whadda you say? **1967** J. WAINWRIGHT *Talent for Murder* 205 Wadya mean, copper? **1975** *New Yorker* 20 Oct. 38/2 'Hey, hey, whaddya say!' he shouts. **1981** J. D. MACDONALD *Free Fall in Crimson* xiii. 147 'Peter Kesner in, please?' 'Whaddaya want with him?'

whaey, whafer, whaff, whaffle: see WHEYEY, WAFER *sb.*, WAFF *v.*¹, WAFFLE *v.*

whahoo, variant of WAHOO¹.

whaies: see WHY.

whaiet, obs. dial. f. QUIET.

1581 N. WOODES *Confl. Consc.* III. iv, Ay wawd he wer brunt that ay mawght be whaiet.

whaile, obs. var. QUAIL *v.*², to curdle.

c **1440** *Anc. Cookery* in *Househ. Ord.* (1790) 453 At the first boyling take hom off the fyre that they whaile noght.

whaint, whair(e, whaish, whais(h)le, whaizle, whaite, whake: see QUAINT, WHERE, WHEYISH, WHEEZE, WHEEZLE, WAIT *v.*¹, QUAKE.

‖**whakapapa** (faka'papa). [Maori.] (Maori) genealogy; a genealogical table.

1960 N. HILLIARD in C. K. Stead *N.Z. Short Stories* (1966) 249 You don't even know your own *whakapapa*! **1966** *Encycl. N.Z.* II. 438/2 Most Maori traditional narrative includes some whakapapa or genealogical record of a connection between the characters in the story. The web of the tale is often so entwined as to require the explanation afforded by the whakapapa. **1974** *N.Z. Listener* 20 July 10/4, I can.. make a brief and somewhat tentative reference to the links in our whakapapa, between our tribes they are a long way back. **1975** D. BAGLEY *Snow Tiger* iv. 53 Turi's *whakapapa* stick, his most prized possession,.. which gave his ancestry.

Whaker, north. dial. form of QUAKER.

1700 in Sir C. Sharp *Chron. Mirab.* (1841) 51 Att ye Whakers metting house. **1802** R. ANDERSON *Ball. Cumbld.* (1805) 22 The neist was a Whaker, caw'd Jacob, He turn'd up the wheyte o' his een.

whale (hweɪl), *sb.* Forms: 1 hwæl, 3–4 whal, wal, 4–5 wall, 5 wale, 5–6 whalle, 7 whaill, wheal, 4– whale; chiefly *Sc.* and *north.* 3 qual, 4 quale, 5 qwal, qwall(e, qwaylle, 5–6 quhail(l, 6 quhale, quhell. [OE. *hwæl*, corresp. to OHG., MHG. *wal* (G. *walfisch* WHALEFISH, q.v.), ON. *hvalr* (Sw., Da. *hval*), related to OHG. *wâlira, welira*, MHG. *wâlre*, and MHG., G. *wels* (:—**χwalis*) sheath-fish; cf. Pruss. *kalis* sheath-fish.

The present form *whale* represents oblique forms (OE. *hwalas*, etc.); the OE. nom. *hwæl* gave 14th–17th cent. *whall* (cf. *small, awl*, †*all*, from *smæl, æl*).]

1. a. Any of the larger fish-like marine mammals of the order *Cetacea*, which have fore-limbs like fins and a tail with horizontal flukes, and are hunted for their oil and whalebone; in wider (scientific) use, any cetacean of the groups *Mystacoceti* or whalebone-whales, and *Odontoceti* or toothed whales (which are distinguished by the names dolphin, grampus, porpoise, etc.).

c **893** ÆLFRED *Oros.* I. i. §16 Se hwæl bið micle læssa þonne oðre hwalas. *c* **1000** ÆLFRIC *Gen.* i. 21 God ȝesceop þa þa micelan hwalas and eall libbende fisc-cinn. *c* **1055** *Byrhtferth's Handboc* in *Anglia* VIII. 310 Þa myclan hwælas, & þa lytlan sprottas. *c* **1220** *Bestiary* 735 He is blac so bro of qual. *c* **1300** *Havelok* 753 He tok þe sturgiun, and þe qual. *c* **1325** *Metr. Hom.* 136 Riht als the quale fars wit the elringe, And riht als sturioun etes merling. *c* **1330** *Arth. & Merl.* 1495 He hadde a bodi as a whal. *c* **1386** CHAUCER *Sompn. T.* 222 Me thynketh they been lyk Iovinyan Fat as a whale and walkynge as a swan. **14..** *Metr. Voc.* in Wr.-Wülcker 625/11 Wale, *cete.* **14..** *Nom.* ibid. 704/15 *Hic cetus*, a whalle. *c* **1440** *Promp. Parv.* 523 Whale, or qwal, grete fysche. **1513** DOUGLAS *Æneis* VII. Prol. 23 Fludis monstreis, sic as meirs wyne or quhailis. **1606** SHAKS. *Tr. & Cr.* V. v. 23 And there they flye or dye, like scaled sculs, Before the belching Whale. **1707** *Curios. Husb. & Gard.* 140 Steep your Corn, or any other Seed, in Oil of Whale. **1769** PENNANT *Brit. Zool.* III. 35 Whales are still seen one hundred and sixty feet long. **1843** *Penny Cycl.* XXVII. 272/2 The Toothed Whales are subdivided into those which have teeth in both jaws and those which have teeth in the lower jaw. **1860** GOSSE *Rom. Nat. Hist.* x. 259 The pursuit of the whale, whether that species which our hardy mariners seek amidst the ice-floes of the Polar Seas, or the still huger kind which wallows in the boundless Pacific.

collective sing. **1637** I. JONES & DAVENANT *Brit. Tri.* 15 And then on Rock he [*sc.* the giant] stood to bob for Whale. **1845** COULTER *Adv. Pacific* vii. 78 While cruising for whale, the look-outs are on the cross trees.

b. (*a*) With defining words for various species: e.g. BOTTLE-NOSE(D *w.*, CA'ING-WHALE, FIN-, FINBACK(ED, FINNER, GREENLAND, GREY (*a.* 8 b), HUMPBACK, ICE-¹, PIKE-, PIKED, PIKE-HEADED, PILOT, ROSTRATED, *round-lipped* (ROUND *a.* 16 b), SCRAG (*sb.*¹ 5), SPERMACETI *w.*, SPERM WHALE, WHALEBONE-, WHITE *w.* Also **beaked, black, bowhead, Sowerby's whale**: see quots.

1755 tr. *Pontoppidan's Nat. Hist. Norway* II. 123, I shall call it Balæna rostrata, or Nebbe-hval, the *Beaked Whale. **1920** *Brit. Mus. Return* 89 Cuvier's Beaked Whale (*Ziphius cavirostris*). **1831** in R. McNab *Old Whaling Days* (1913) i. 3 The *black whales visit the bays and coasts of New Zealand for the purpose of calving. **1834** DEWHURST *Cetacea* 16 *note, La Baleine Franche*,.. Common Black Whale. **1840** MARRYAT *Poor Jack* vi, The sparmacitty don't take the harpoon quite so quietly as the black whale does. **1843** *Penny Cycl.* XXVII. 296/1 The Whalebone Whale or Black Whale of the South Seas. **1883** *Fisheries Exhib. Catal.* (ed. 4) 201 Slabs of whalebone of *Bowhead Whale. **1920** *Brit. Mus. Return* 101 Tooth of a *Sowerby's Whale (*Mesoplodon bidens*).

(*b*) **right whale**, a whalebone-whale, esp. of the genus *Balæna*. Hence *right-whaling, right-whaler*, etc.

1725 P. DUDLEY in *Phil. Trans.* XXXIII. 256 The Right or Whalebone Whale is a large Fish, measuring sixty or seventy Feet in Length. **1824** J. F. COOPER *Pilot* xvii, 'Tis a right whale,.. I saw his spout. **1849** H. MELVILLE *Mardi* I. i. 5 This horrid and indecent Right Whaling.. is as the butchery of white bears upon blank Greenland icebergs. **1874** DARWIN *Desc. Man* II. xvii. (ed. 2) 516 The males of the right-whales do not fight together. **1888** *Encycl. Brit.* XXIV. 527/2 A right whale fishery of great importance. **1895** *Pall Mall Gaz.* 16 Dec. 2/1 Just before I took to 'right' whaling.

2. Applied to the 'great fish' which swallowed Jonah (*Jonah* i. 17).

c **950** *Lindisf. Gosp.* Matt. xii. 40 Suæ forðon wæs ionas in innað *vel* in wom huales ðrim dagum & ðrim næhtum. [**1382** WYCLIF As Jonas was in the womb of a whall three days and three niȝtis]. **13..** *E.E. Allit. P.* C. 247 Now is ionas þe Iwe iugged to drowne;.. A wylde walterande whal.. bi þat bot flotte. *c* **1450** *St. Cuthbert* (Surtees) 572 Grete god.. þat saued þe prophete with in þe whall. **1548** UDALL, etc. *Erasm. Par. Acts* ii. 22–28 Euen as did yᵉ whale reuomit the prophet Ionas. *a* **1586** MONTGOMERIE *Misc. Poems* xxxi. 35 Ionas, in þe quhellis bellie, þow safit thre dayis. **1687** A. LOVELL tr. *Thevenot's Trav.* I. 41 Jona's Whale is also to go to Paradise.

†**3.** *whale of the river, river-whale*: = SHEAT-FISH¹, a large freshwater fish, *Silurus glanis. Obs.*

1585 HIGINS *Junius' Nomencl.* 69/2 *Silurus*,.. a fish much like a Sturgeon: a sheathfishe; a whale of the riuer. **1611** COTGR., *Silure*, the rauening sheat fish, or Whall of the riuer.

4. *transf.* (from 1). An object resembling a whale; *Astron.* (with cap.) the constellation *Cetus.*

1551 RECORDE *Cast. Knowl.* (1556) 267 The greate Whale, contaynyng 22 starres. **1664** *Phil. Trans.* I. 5 In the evening of that day it [*sc.* a comet] was to come into the jaw of the Whale. **1760** *Ann. Reg., Chron.* 66/1 The comet.. passed.. toward the whale's jaw. **1866** LOCKYER *Guillemin's Heavens* (ed. 2) 356. **1905** F. M. CRAWFORD *Glean. Venet. Hist.* I. 5 When the first fugitives, blind with terror, stumbled ashore upon the back of one of the sand whales in the lagoon.

5. Allusive, proverbial, transf., and fig. uses of sense 1. **a.** Prov. phr. *(to throw out) a tub to the whale*: see TUB *sb.* 9 b. *very like a whale* (after Shaks. *Ham.* III. ii. 398): see quot. 1859.

[**1591** *1st Pt. Troub. Raigne K. John* (1611) C3b, The mariner, Spying the hugie Whale, whose monstrous bulke Doth beare the waues like mountaines fore the wind, That throwes out emptie vessels, so to stay His fury.]

1859 *Slang Dict.* 115 *Very like a whale*, said of anything that is very improbable.

b. *allusively.*

1601 SHAKS. *All's Well* IV. iii. 249 A.. lasciuious boy, who is a whale to Virginity, and deuours vp all the fry it finds. **1606** DEKKER *Seuen Deadly Sinnes* Wks. (Grosart) II. 27 Be wise therefore,.. play with these Whales of the Sea, till you escape them that are deuourers of your Merchants. **1914** MARRIOTT in *Edin. Rev.* July 1 Amid a shoal of minnows they promptly pose as authoritative whales.

c. fig. phr. *a whale on...*, having a great capacity or appetite for..., very good at or keen on... *a whale of* (orig. *U.S.*): 'no end of'. *colloq.*

1893 MCCARTHY *Red Diamonds* xxiii, He was not, as he put it himself graphically, a whale on geography. **1899** A. MARSHALL *Peter Binney* xvi. 326, I should be a whale on parental authority myself if I were in your place. **1913** *19th Cent.* Sept. 621 [They] had what the Americans call 'a whale of a good time'. **1921** *Chambers's Jrnl.* May 308/1 He had come here to have one whale of a time. **1938** G. HEYER *Blunt Instrument* iii. 45 It doesn't look such a whale of a case to me. **1954** J. B. PRIESTLEY *Magicians* i. 15 An equally dashing, whale-of-a-fellow, R.A.F. type. **1963** N. MARSH *Dead Water* (1964) i. 22 She's having a whale of a time with Mr. Joyce. **1980** B. CASTLE *Castle Diaries* 363 They regaled us with drinks and a superb buffet and we had a whale of a time.

6. a. *attrib.* and *Comb.*, as *whale-blubber* [BLUBBER *sb.*¹ 4], *-butt, -calf* [CALF¹ 3], *-catching, -cry, -cub, -cutter, -drive* [DRIVE *sb.* 1 c], *-duty, -ground, -guts, -hole, -hunt, -hunter* (cf. OE. *hwælhunta*), *-hunting* (cf. OE. *hwælhuntaþ*), *-killer, -killing, -kind, -meat, -spoilt, -steak, -striker, -striking, -trade, -vessel*; also in names of weapons, etc. used in hunting whales, as *whale-gun, -lance, -line, -net, -pike, -pole, -rope, -spade*; also *whale-blue, -like, -mouthed, -shaped, -tailed* adjs. **b.** Spec. Combs.: **whale-acorn-shell** (see quot.); **whale-barnacle** = CORONULE 2; **whale-brit** [BRIT *sb.*¹] = *whale-food*; **whale-deep** = *whale-hole*; **whale-feed** = *whale-food*; **whale('s) food** [tr. G. *walfischaas*, 1747], a general name for the small animals upon which whales feed; *spec.* a mollusc, *Clio borealis*; **whale-foots** [FOOT *sb.* 22], the refuse in refining whale-oil, used by soap-makers and tanners; **whale-gull**, the ivory gull (GULL *sb.*¹); **whale-head**, the shoebill or whale-headed stork, *Balæniceps rex*; also called **whale-headed stork**; †**whale-horn**, whalebone; **whale-laid** *a.* of a rope (see quot.); **whale-louse**, a small crustacean of the genus *Cyamus*, parasitic on whales; **whale-mouse** = *whale's guide*; **whale-pool** *humorous*, the Atlantic ocean (cf. *herring-pond*); **whale's belly, -tail**, etc., stars in the constellation *Cetus* (see 4); †**whale's guide**, the animal called by Pliny *musculus piscis* (cf. note s.v. MYSTICETE¹); **whale-shark**, (*a*) a very large shark, *Rhinodon typicus*; (*b*) the basking-shark (BASKING *ppl. a.* 2); **whale-ship** = WHALE-BOAT; †**whale-shot** [SHOT *sb.*¹ 19], spermaceti. Also WHALEBACK, -BIRD, -BOAT, -BONE, -FIN, etc.

1815 BURROW *Elem. Conchol.* 194 *Balanoides*, Small, striated Acorn S[hell]. *Diadema*, *Whale Do. **1854** A. ADAMS, etc. *Man. Nat. Hist.* 305 *Whale-Barnacles (*Coronulidæ*). **1844** H. STEPHENS *Bk. Farm* II. 646 *Whale-blubber.. forms a good compost for turnips. **1845** DARWIN *Voy. Nat.* x. 214 A piece of putrid whales-blubber. **1946** DYLAN THOMAS *Deaths & Entrances* 55 The coast Blackened with birds took a last look At his thrashing hair and *whale-blue eye. **1835** BATMAN in K. Cornwallis *New World* (1859) I. 369 The 'Belinda', of Sydney, with a cargo of *whale-butts. **1867** SMYTH *Sailor's Word-bk.*, **Whale-calf*, the young whale. **1685** R. TURNER in W. Penn *Furth. Acc. Pennsylv.* 13 Three Companies for *Whale catching. **1851** H. MELVILLE *Moby Dick* II. xii. 78 The ancient *whale-cry upon first sighting a whale from the mast-head. **1885** J. G. WOOD in *Longm. Mag.* Mar. 552 The *whale-cub, when first formed, has no baleen. **1631** PELLHAM *Gods Power* A 4 b, Thomas Ayers, *Whale-cutter. **1668** PRYNNE *Aurum Reg.* 127 This *Whale Duty hath been totally suspended.. from the death of King Henry the 8, till the first year of King James, for want of a Queen Consort. **1853** *Househ. Words* VI. 402/1 The little red creatures ("*whale feed', sailors call them) are retained by the fringe [of the baleen]. **1767** tr. *Crantz' Hist. Greenland* I. 109 This *whale's-food is found in the greatest quantity between Spitzberg.. and Greenland. **1865** GOSSE *Land & Sea* 166 The immense aggregations of close-packed swimming invertebrata so well known to mariners in Arctic regions under the appellation of 'whale-food'. **1851** *Whale-ground [see *oil-ship* s.v. OIL *sb.*¹ 6 e]. **1852** MACGILLIVRAY *Brit. Birds* V. 508 *Cetosparactes eburneus.* The Ivory *Whale-gull. **1858** *Merc. Marine Mag.* V. 149 The crew.. murdered the Captain and third officer by shooting them with a *whale-gun. **1780** COXE *Russ. Discov.* 256 Cloaks,.. made of thin *whale guts. **1884** COUES *Key N. Amer. Birds* (ed. 2) 654 *Balæniceps rex*, the Shoe-bill or *Whale-head, of Africa. **1875** *Encycl. Brit.* III. 759/1 The gigantic *Whale-headed Stork, *Balæniceps rex.* **1897** KIPLING *Captains Courageous* v. 111 '*Whale-hole.'.. He had led them to the edge of the barren Whale-deep, the blank hole of the Grand Bank. **1562** in *Inv. Mary Q. Scots* (Bannatyne Club) Pref. p. xxviii. *note*, xij bowtis of *quhaill horne. **1851** H. MELVILLE *Moby Dick* III. xix. 134 The far different nature of the *whale-hunt. **1598** HAKLUYT *Voy.* I. 4 He was come as far towards the North, as commonly the *whale hunters vse to trauell. **1851** H. MELVILLE *Whale* xvi, Some of these same Quakers are the most sanguinary of all sailors and whale-hunters. **1615** *Trade's Incr.* 52 The Greenland company, out of the pretence of their first *Whale-hunting. **1868** GORRIE *Summ. & Wint. in Orkneys* viii. 323 The whale-hunting fleet. **1613** *Voy. Spitzbergen* in *Archæol. Amer.* (1860) IV. 305 When he enters into the sounds, our *whal-killers doe presentlie sallie forth to meet him. **1625** PURCHAS *Pilgrims* III. III. 461 The first setled, ordinary, and orderly Voyages for the *Whale killing. **1703** DAMPIER *Voy.* III. ii. 57 About Christmas these are mostly imployed in Whale-killing. **1706** PHILLIPS (ed. Kersey), *Manati*, a Fish of the *Whale-kind that breeds about the Island of Hispaniola. **1812** MANBY *Ess. Preserv. Shipwr. Persons* 17 It may likewise be coiled in the manner used in the whale fishery. *Whale laid. **1823** SCORESBY *Voy. N. Whale-fishery* 112 Armed only with a *whale-lance, he.. set out on his adventurous exploit. **1608** SYLVESTER *Du Bartas* II. iv. *Schisme* 1016 This mighty Fish, of *Whale-like hugenesse. **1855** LEIFCHILD *Cornwall* 166 The large whale-like back of a prostrate pillar. **1785** *Act 25 Geo. III* c. 56 §2 Short Chucking, Half Clean, *Whale-line, or other Toppings. **1897** F. T. BULLEN *Cruise of 'Cachalot'* 12 The whale-line, manilla rope like yellow silk, 1½ inch round, was brought on deck. **1774** GOLDSM. *Nat. Hist.* (1824) III. 21 A small animal, of the shell-fish kind, called the *Whale-louse, that sticks to its body. **1916** R. C. ANDREWS *Whale Hunting* xxi. 248 This growth [on the snout of the right whale] is produced by whale lice. **1952** J. FISHER *Fulmar* xviii. 423 He writes of the fulmars 'searching out' whale-lice. **1972** *Nat. Geographic* Oct. 579 (*caption*) Communities of whale lice.. some of them half an inch long, cling to the growths [on the head of each right whale]. **1875** KNIGHT *Dict. Mech.* s.v. *Whalebone*, Time has passed since the people of England reveled in *whale meat. **1607** TOPSELL *Four-f. Beasts* 504 A little fishe called..in Greeke Mystocetos, the *Whale-mouse. **1656** OSBORN *Adv. Son* (ed. 4) To Rdr., As I did then, in imitation of Sea-men by designe, so I may perhaps now cast out some empty stuffe, to find play for the *Whale-mouth'd gapers after Levity. **1952** L. MACNEICE *Ten Burnt Offerings* ii. 23 The whale-mouthed arch the bones of the future. **1853** KANE *Grinnell Exp.* xlvi. (1856) 426 Stalwart fellows, practiced in the kayack, and the sledge, and the *whale-net. **1851** H. MELVILLE *Moby Dick* II. xii. 94 The valiant Captain danced up and down with a *whale-pike. *Ibid.* xiv. 124 The flag of capture lazily hanging from the *whale-pole inserted into his spout-hole. *a* **1876** M. COLLINS *Pen Sketches* (1879) II. 145 This is one of the good turns for which I am grateful to our friends across the *whale-pool. **1849** H. MELVILLE *Redburn* I. xx. 194 Coiled away in a tub. Like a *whale-rope. **1857** in Trevelyan *Compet. Wallah* (1866) 342 A coil of whale rope. **1573** W. BOURNE *Regim. Sea* (1580) 59 b, The names of the Starres..*Whales backe. Whales belly... Whales tayle. **1668** CHARLETON *Onomast.* 125 *Cetorum Dux*..the *Whales Guide. **1706** PHILLIPS (ed. 6), *Mysticetus*, a Fish, call'd the Whale's Guide. **1930** *Times Educ. Suppl.* 25 Oct. p. iv/1 In the *whale-shaped head is a window for the driver. **1978** M. PUZO *Fools Die* ii. 16 White-dotted red square dice were dazzling flying fish over the whale-shaped crap tables. **1884–5** *Riverside Nat. Hist.* (1888) III. 78 The Rhinodontidæ embraces only two species of large sharks, one of which well deserves the name *whale-shark, which is applied to it. **1820** SCORESBY *Acc. Arctic Reg.* II. 199 The crew of a *whale-ship usually consists of 40 to 50 men. **1612** *Sc. Bk. Rates* in *Halyburton's Ledger* (1867) 332 *Whale shote the barrell, xx li. **1852** MUNDY *Antipodes* (1857) 104 The harpoon, the axe, the lance, and the *whale-spade. **1836** *Uncle Philip's Convers. Whale Fishery* 349 They heard *whale-spouts near them. **1851** H. MELVILLE *Moby Dick* II. xii. 166 Don't I always say that to be good, a *whale-steak must be tough? **1969** *Listener* 14 Aug. 206/3 What *did* we eat? Well, we ate whale-steak for one thing. **1613** *Voy. Spitzbergen* in *Archæol. Amer.* (1860) IV. 289 Then the Basks, our *whale-strikers, went presentlie back againe to the Foreland wth their shallops. **1821** SCOTT *Pirate* xx, No *whale-striking, bird-nesting favourite for me. **1781** PENNANT *Hist. Quadrup.* II. 537 *Whale-tailed Manati. **1840** R. H. DANA *Bef. Mast* v, He had been forty years in the *whale-trade. **1821** SCOTT *Pirate* xxxviii, A garland of faded ribbons, such as are used to decorate *whale-vessels.

whale (hweɪl), *v.*[1] [f. prec.] *intr.* To engage in whale-fishing; see also WHALING *vbl. sb.*[1]

c **1700** in *Cheever's Whalem. Adv.* i. (1850) 5 [To] whale out in the deep for sperm whales. **1812** *Sydney Gaz.* in *O'Hara's Hist. N.S. Wales* (1817) 386 The brig Active..was at Frederick Henry Bay whaling.

whale, *v.*[2] Now *U.S. colloq.* [Of obscure origin. Commonly regarded as a spelling of WALE *v.*[1], but there are difficulties of form, chronology, and meaning. Perhaps orig. = to thrash with a whalebone whip (see WHALEBONE 3 b).]

1. *trans.* To beat, flog, thrash.

1790 GROSE *Prov. Gloss.* (ed. 2), *Whale*, to beat with a horsewhip or pliant stick. **1801** COL. G. HANGER *Life* II. 162 Whaleing a gentleman is but a vulgar revenge. **1884** 'MARK TWAIN' *Huck. Finn* iii, He used to always whale me when he was sober and could get his hands on me.

2. *transf. intr.* To do something implied by the context continuously or vehemently.

a **1852** F. M. WHITCHER *Widow Bedott Papers* (1883) vi. 67 You remember that one that come round a spell ago a whalin' away about human rights. **1886** *Harper's Mag.* July 322/1 In tones of wrath..he whaled it at his opponent throughout the fifteen minutes alloted to him. **1897** BARRÈRE & LELAND *Dict. Slang*, *To whale away*, (Amer.), to preach, talk, or lecture away continuously or vehemently. **1908** H. DAY *King Spruce* xxiv, You don't think I've whaled up here..to..talk about women, do you? **1915** *Morning Post* 1 June 4/4 They ..snatched these rifles up, and whaled away at our chaps.

whale, var. WALE.

whaleback (ˈhweɪlbæk). [f. WHALE *sb.* + BACK *sb.*]

1. An arched structure over the deck of a steamer; = TURTLE-BACK 1.

1886 *Times* 20 Apr. 10/2 He was standing under the whaleback.

2. A kind of steam vessel having a spoon bow and the main decks covered in and rounded over, suggesting the back of a whale.

1891 *Pall Mall Gaz.* 10 June 2/2 The Americans claim that, in Captain Macdougall's steel 'whalebacks', they possess the universal ship of the future.

3. *Geol.* A large mound of the shape of the back of a whale. More widely, any land form or land mass likened to the back of a whale; *spec.* (*a*) = ROCHE MOUTONNÉE; (*b*) an elongated sand dune.

1893 HOWORTH *Glacial Nightmare* II. 774 Glaciers cannot explain the mounds called eskers, kames, or whalebacks. **1913** *Proc. Geologists' Assoc.* XXIV. 247 A characteristic rounded form resembling..the 'whale-back' of glaciated areas. **1918** *Geogr. Jrnl.* LI. 23 In these whalebacks and crescents the cross-section that has the longest base passes through the summit of the dune. **1928** *Chambers's Jrnl.* Jan. 1/2 Behind all, a dim whale-back that might be Stroma, or Ultima Thule. **1933** *Geogr. Jrnl.* LXXXII. 125 A whaleback is a flat-topped ridge of sand anything up to 100 miles in length, of the order of half a mile wide, and up to 100 feet high. **1952** V. CANNING *House of Seven Flies* xi. 155 A long stretch of sand.. the long ridges of wave marks from the last tide shadowed across the rising whaleback. **1955** *Geogr. Jrnl.* CXXI. 476 Some British whalebacks are undoubtedly *roches moutonnées*, some others, and probably many tropical examples, are genetically related to tors. **1974** M. GILBERT *Flash Point* x. 82 Behind the whaleback of Kinder Low and Edale Head a storm was brewing up. **1977** A. HALLAM *Planet Earth* 67/2 Where folds can be traced in three dimensions, it is found that the structures die out along their fold axis and where suitably exposed, form whalebacks.

4. *attrib.* or as *adj.* Furnished with a whaleback (sense 1); of the shape of the back of a whale.

1891 *Daily Graphic* 24 July 14/1 The first 'whaleback' boat which has crossed the Atlantic arrived at Liverpool on Monday. **1894** *Engineer* 13 July 33/3 A new craft is expected to take part in the yacht races at Galveston. She was built in Fort Worth, and may be classed as a whale-back yacht. **1908** *Daily Chron.* 29 July 4/4 Beneath a hot sun Belgrade lies bleaching on her whaleback promontory.

Hence **ˈwhalebacked** *a.*, shaped like a whale's back; **ˈwhalebacker**, a whaleback steamer.

1869 'MARK TWAIN' *Innoc. Abroad* 441 We can see the long, whale-backed ridge of Mount Hermon projecting above the eastern hills. **1879** *Daily News* 8 Nov. 5/7 Whale-backed station of the London and South Eastern Railway Company. **1891** *Daily Graphic* 24 July 14/1 These 'Whalebackers' as they are termed offer very little resistance to the sea. **1903** KIPLING *Five Nations, Sussex* 19 Our blunt, bow-headed, whale-backed Downs.

ˈwhale-bird. Name of various birds which inhabit the places where whales are found, or which feed on their oil or offal: (*a*) a petrel of the genus *Prion* or *Procellaria*; (*b*) the turnstone, *Strepsilas interpres*; (*c*) the red or grey phalarope; (*d*) the ivory gull.

1768 *Phil. Trans.* LX. 117 Another bird, not much unlike a quail, which they call here the whale-bird, from its feeding on the offal of those fish. **1867** SMYTH *Sailor's Word-bk.*, *Whale-bird*, a beautiful little bird seen hovering in flocks over the Southern Ocean. **1875** MELLISS *St. Helena* 200 The Whale Bird (*Procellaria glacialoides*). **1879** *Bulletin U.S. Nat. Mus.* No. 15. 85 *Phalaropus fulicarius*,..'Shatgak', Cumberland Eskimo. 'Whale-bird', or 'Bow-head Bird', of whalemen.

ˈwhale-boat. A long carvel-built boat, sharp at both ends, and steered with a rudder or an oar, used in whale-fishing. **b.** A boat of this kind carried as a life-boat by large passenger-steamers and warships.

1756 R. ROGERS *Jrnls.* (1769) 13 Our rendezvous was appointed at Albany, from thence to proceed in four whale-boats to lake George. **1824** W. IRVING *T. Trav.* IV. iv. (1849) 415 A picked crew of daring fellows set off for her in a whale-boat. **1871** *Good Words* 713 Having come to her moorings, she is immediately surrounded by a multitude of whale-boats.

whalebone (ˈhweɪlbəʊn), *sb.* Forms: see WHALE *sb.* and BONE *sb.*; also 4 **huelbon**, 7 **whel-**, **whal-**, **whealbone**, **quhallbon**; (in sense 1) **whales bone**, etc.

†**1.** Ivory from the walrus or some similar animal confused with the whale: chiefly in phr. ***white as whale's bone***. *Obs.*

c **1205** LAY. 2363 Þe walles of stone, þe duren of whales bone [*c* **1275** wales bone]. *a* **1310** in Wright *Lyric P.* xi. 38 A wayle whyt as whalles bon. **13..** *E.E. Allit. P.* A. 212 Her ble more blaȝt þen whallez bon. *a* **1400** *Sqr. lowe Degre* 537 Lady, as whyte as whales bone. ? **1467** *Paston Lett.* II. 298 But yef ye purposid to falle hastely in my Lady Anne P. lappe, as white as whales bon, &c. *c* **1520** SKELTON *Garl. Laurel* 472 An hundred steppis mountyng to the halle, One of iasper, another of whalis bone. **1567** TURBERV. *Epit.*, etc. 138 Hir Mouth so small, hir Teeth so white as any Whale his bone. **1588** SHAKS. *L.L.L.* v. ii. 332 This is the flower that smiles on euerie one, To shew his teeth as white as Whales bone. **1590** GREENE *Never too Late* Wks. (Grosart) VIII. 213 Legges as white as whales bone. **1610** TOFTE *Hon. Acad.* IV. 162 Her hands were white, as Whale his bone. **1848** KINGSLEY *Saint's Trag.* III. i, Purer than white whales' bone.

β. **13..** *Coer de L.* 62 All it was whyt of huel-bon. *c* **1400** *Destr. Troy* 3055 Alse qwyte & qwem as any qwalle bon. **1500–20** DUNBAR *Poems* xxi. 46 Toungis now are maid of quhyte quhaill bone, And hairtis ar maid of hard flynt stone.

2. The elastic horny substance which grows in a series of thin parallel plates in the upper jaw of certain whales in place of teeth; baleen: used esp. for stiffening parts of the dress, etc.

Formerly supposed to be obtained from the whale's fins.

1604 *Lismore Papers* Ser. II. (1887) I. 107 For whelbone to ye bodes ix^d^. **1613** *Voy. Spitzbergen* in *Archæol. Amer.* (1860) IV. 311 They cut of his head, containing his toung and his finnes, commonlie called whalbone. **1711** ADDISON *Spect.* No. 127 ¶4 A Female who is thus invested in Whalebone is sufficiently secured against the Approaches of an ill-bred Fellow. **1712** BUDGELL *ibid.* 277 ¶8 The Petticoat has no Whale-bone. **1820** SCORESBY *Acc. Arctic Reg.* I. 457 Fifteen feet is the greatest length of the whalebone. **1878** J. W. HAYES *Draper & Haberd.* (ed. 4) 87 Stay Whale-bone is prepared and cut into suitable lengths for corsets. *Ibid.*, Dress Whalebone is sold in lengths varying between 27 in. and 54 in. **1887** RUSKIN *Præterita* II. xi. 390 At a Christmas party, [she] acted any part—that depended on whalebone [*i.e.* stays]—admirably.

3. a. A strip of whalebone, esp. used as stiffening in women's stays, dresses, etc.

1601 [? MARSTON] *Jack Drums Entert.* IV. F 4, Oh I could crack my Whalebones, breake my Buske, to think what laughter may arise from this. *a* **1635** CORBET *Iter Bor.* 391 She was barr'd up in Whale-bones that did leese None of the Whales length, for they reach'd her knees. **1674** tr. *Scheffer's Lapland* 107 If they fish with a Cane or Whale-bone. **1712–14** POPE *Rape Lock* v. 40 Fans clap, silks rustle, and tough whalebones crack. **1871** *Figure Training* 106 In order to insure a good fit, and to keep it perfectly in place, the busk in front, and the whalebones behind, are made somewhat longer than the present fashion.

b. A riding-whip of whalebone.

1842 LOVER *Handy Andy* iii, Smarting under a sense of injury and whalebone. **1867** A. L. GORDON *Poems* (1912) 96 Ah! there goes Fred's whalebone a flanker.

4. The jaw-bone of a whale. (Cf. G. *walfischbein*.)

1846 R. E. E. WARBURTON *Hunting Songs* viii. 25 Where 'twixt the whalebones the widow [*sc.* Maria Hollingsworth, a German by birth] sat down.

5. a. *attrib.* and *Comb.*, as ***whalebone-cutter***, ***-kind***, ***-man***; **whalebone-hair**, the hairy fringe of whalebone; **whalebone-tree**, an Australian urticaceous tree, *Pseudomorus brunoniana*; **whalebone-whale**, a whale of the family *Balænidæ*, having plates of whalebone developed from the palate instead of teeth; a right whale.

1761 *Brit. Mag.* II. 672 Philip Benton, of Gainsborough, ..*whalebone-cutter and merchant. **1820** SCORESBY *Acc. Arctic Reg.* II. 451 Large shreds of old thin canvas, *whalebone-hair, and a quantity of ashes. **1708** J. CHAMBERLAYNE *St. Gt. Brit.* II. I. iii. (1743) 331 Great whales of the Baleen, or *whale bone kind. *a* **1637** B. JONSON *Underwoods* lx. Wks. (1641) 208 The *whale-bone man That quilts those bodies, I have leave to span. **1889** MAIDEN *Useful Pl. Australia* 591 *Pseudomorus Brunoniana*,..called *Whalebone Tree in Southern New South Wales. **1725** *Whalebone whale [see WHALE *sb.* 1 b (*b*)]. **1843** *Penny Cycl.* XXVII. 272/2 The Toothless or Whalebone Whales.

b. as *adj.* Stiffened with strips of whalebone; made of or containing whalebone; also *fig.*, 'stiff', affected.

1601 B. JONSON *Poetaster* II. i. (1905) 28 Your whale-bone-bodies. **1603** in *10th Rep. Hist. MSS. Comm.* App. I. 31 Ane par of quhallbon bodis. **1650** BULWER *Anthropomet.* 193 And to that end..shut up their Wastes in a Whale-bone prison. **1711** SWIFT *Jrnl. to Stella* 10 Nov., Have you got the whalebone petticoats among you yet?..a woman here may hide a moderate gallant under them. **17..** in *Lyra Elegant.* (1867) l. 3 Last Sunday at St. James's prayers I, drest in all my whale-bone airs. **1802** MARIA EDGEWORTH *Moral T.*, *Good Fr. Gov.*, A few words in defence of sacks, long waists, and whalebone stays. **1807** W. IRVING *Salmag.* No. 6 (1811) I. 119 A plentiful stock of whims, and oddities, and whalebone habits. **1866** LE FANU *All in Dark* lxviii, To make his bow before the world in the picturesque long robe and whalebone wig which everyone of taste admires. **1908** [ELIZ. FOWLER] *Betw. Trent & Ancholme* 382 A light umbrella was one not made with whalebone ribs.

Hence **whaleboned** (ˈhweɪlbəʊnd) *pa. pple.* and *ppl. a.*, stiffened with whalebone; **ˈwhaleboning**, a beating with a piece of whalebone (sense 3).

1641 J. DAY *Parl. Bees* (1881) 29 Such whale-bon'd-bodied rascals. **1835** *Court Mag.* VI. p. vii/2 A mantelet.. whale-boned in such a manner as to prevent it from crushing the dress. **1851** H. MELVILLE *Moby Dick* I. xxx. 205 Only a whaleboning that he gave me—not a base kick. **1908** EDITH WHARTON *Hermit*, etc. IV. 150 A laced, whaleboned, frizzle-headed, high-heeled daughter of iniquity.

whale-eyde, obs. f. WALL-EYED.

ˈwhale-fin. ? *Obs.* Also 7 **whales-finne**. Whalebone, formerly supposed to be the fin of the whale.

1612 *Sc. Bk. Rates* in *Halyburton's Ledger* (1867) 332 Whale fin the fin, xl s. **1614** PURCHAS *Pilgrimage* IV. xvii. (ed. 2) 433 The Inhabitantes holde trade with other Samoeds.. for..Beauers, Downe, Whales-Finnes. **1741** *Daily Post* 11 Apr. 1/3 On Tuesday was imported..from Holland 9 C. Whale-fins. **1809** KENDALL *Trav.* II. lii. 207 By whale-fin has always been meant the barb, from which the whale-bone is really obtained. **1820** SCORESBY *Acc. Arctic Reg.* II. 415 Whale-bone, or whale-fins, as the substance is sometimes, though incorrectly named.

†**whalefish.** *Obs.* Also 6 **wall-**, **whal(le)-**, 6–7 **wale-**. [repr. unrecorded OE. *_hwælfisc_, or a. MLG., MDu., Du. *walvisch* = OHG. *walvisc* (MHG. *-visch*, G. *walfisch*), ON. *hvalfiskr*: see WHALE *sb.* and FISH *sb.*[1]] A whale.

c **1511** *1st Eng. Bk. Amer.* (Arb.) Introd. 28/1 There by be many walefysshes & flyinge fysshes. **1535** COVERDALE *Ps.* cxlviii. 7 Prayse the Lorde vpon earth, ye whalfishes and all depes. **1546** *Gassar's Prognost.* A v b, The Son in the same euening shall go doune or set with the tayle of the Whalle fish. **1582** N. LICHEFIELD tr. *Castanheda's Conq. E. Ind.* I. ii. 6 b, These people doe mainteine themselues with rootes of hearbes, with Sea Woulfes, and Whale fish. **1615** R. COCKS *Diary* (Hakl. Soc.) I. 91, 2 pec. wale fyshe. **1635** R. JOHNSON *Hist. Tom a Lincolne* (1828) 105 The whale fishes lay wallowing in the waves. **1712** *Phil. Trans.* XXVII. 440

About two Years ago there came a Stranger to me, who had two Penis's of the Whale Fish.

ˈwhale-ˌfisher. [f. WHALE-FISHING: see -ER[1].] = WHALER 1. So **ˈwhalefisherman**, = WHALER 1 and 2; **ˈwhale-fishery**, (*a*) the occupation or industry of whale-fishing; (*b*) a locality where whale-fishing is carried on or where whales abound.

1773 BERRIDGE *Chr. World Unmasked* (1805) 43 In Greenland among the *whale-fishers. **1820** SCORESBY *Acc. Arctic Reg.* I. 271 The salt in the sea.. destroys the tenacity of the bay-ice,.. and, in the language of the whale-fisher, completely rots it. **1874** A. H. MARKHAM *Whaling Cruise* i. 1 Hither [*sc.* to the Arctic Regions] our brave whale-fishers have annually ventured for many years. **1724** *Phil. Trans.* XXXIII. 193 Our *Whale Fishermen of Nantucket. **1820** SCORESBY *Acc. Arctic Reg.* II. 74 Foreign Protestants also, who had served three years on board of any British whale-fishermen. **1704** *Phil. Trans.* XXIV. 1723 When our Ships return'd from the *Whale-Fishery. **1752** J. HILL *Hist. Anim.* 555 About Greenland, and in other places where there are whale-fisheries. **1820** SCORESBY *Acc. Arctic Reg.* II. 76 The British whale-fishery of 1758 was very unsuccessful. **1874** A. H. MARKHAM *Whaling Cruise* i. 8 The ships engaged in the whale fishery are all most substantially built.

ˈwhale-ˌfishing. [f. WHALE *sb.* + FISHING *vbl. sb.*] The occupation of taking whales, whaling.

1580 in Hakluyt *Voy.* (1589) 460 To the end we may turne our new found land fishing or Island fishing or our whale-fishing that way. **1699** T. ALLISON *Voy. Archangel* 109 A Flemish Fly-boat bound to Greenland, for Whale-fishing. **1722** ELKING *View Greenland Trade* (1859) 95 We can.. carry on the whale-fishing trade.. much cheaper than the Hollanders. **1820** SCORESBY *Acc. Arctic Reg.* I. 257 Ice becomes exceedingly fragile towards the close of the whale-fishing season. **1889** C. EDWARDES *Sardinia* xviii. 345 The industry [of tunny-fishing] is as speculative as whale-fishing or silver-mining.

whal eie, obs. f. WALL EYE.

whaleman (ˈhweɪlmən). [MAN *sb.*[1] 4 p, 14.]

1. = WHALER 1.

1716 B. CHURCH *Hist. Philip's War* (1867) II. 133 And Whale-men then will be very serviceable in this Expedition, which having a promise made to them, that they shall be released in good season to go home a Whaling in the Fall. **1850** H. MELVILLE *White Jacket* I. iv. 21 He launched out.. into tremendous laudations of whalemen; declaring that whalemen alone deserved the name of sailors. **1898** F. T. BULLEN *Cruise of 'Cachalot'* xvi. 198 A smarter whaleman than Mistah Jones did not live.

2. = WHALER 2.

1767 M. CUTLER in *Life*, etc. (1888) I. 19 Whalemen fitted out for the Straits of Belle Isle, and Davis Straits. **1840** R. H. DANA *Bef. Mast* vii, The ship was the Cortes, whaleman, of New Bedford. **1860** *Merc. Marine Mag.* VII. 254 There were two or three whalemen in port.

ˈwhale-oil. Oil obtained from whale-blubber.

1435–6 in Heath *Grocers' Comp.* (1869) 418, ii shippes of waloill, conteynyng xlviij.[0] iii. v. oyll. *c* **1580** in *Engl. Hist. Rev.* (1914) July 520 Whale oyles that come frome newfound Land. **1672** *Act 25 Chas. II* c. 7 §4 Noe English built Shipp.. importing Whale oyle or Blubber or other Fish, Oyle. **1712** tr. *Pomet's Hist. Drugs* I. 157 We have Oil of Camomile and Linseed.. when Train or Whale-Oil is dear. **1896** BRANNT *Anim. & Veg. Fats* (ed. 2) II. 57 The pure whale oils, pale, brownish-yellow or brown.

attrib. **1853** *Zoologist* XI. 4044 Syringing the young tree well with whale-oil-soap. **1885** *Harper's Mag.* Feb. 368/2 Flavilla lit the.. whale-oil lamp.

whaler (ˈhweɪlə(r)). [f. WHALE *sb.* or *v.*[1] + -ER[1].]

1. A person engaged in whaling; a whale-catcher.

1684 *Roxb. Ball.* (1885) V. 457 Without you do now imploy the Wheelers to do 't, Ye ne'r will be able to bring all about. **1775** ROMANS *Florida* App. 79 The North, or Grand Bahama bank, is little frequented but by whalers and turtlers. **1843** *Penny Cycl.* XXVII. 752/1 The whalers kill the calves in order to capture the mother. **1895** GORE-BOOTH *Sea Fishing* (Badm. Libr.) xvi. 476 Two bollard heads (pronounced 'bullet heads' by the Scotch whalers).

2. a. A vessel used in whale-fishing. **b.** = WHALE-BOAT b.

1806 *Sydney Gaz.* in *O'Hara's Hist. N.S. Wales* (1817) 270 Arrived.. same day, the Aurora south whaler. **1817** BYRON *Beppo* lxi, Stopp'd by the elements, like a whaler. **1893** *Times* 3 July 6/2 Some loose oars.. with which I supported myself until picked up by the Dreadnought's whaler. **1898** KIPLING *Fleet in Being* v. 62 The First Lieutenant.. had the whaler's crew sleeping all handy by. **1909** *Athenæum* 13 Mar. 320/1 The original plan was to descend the Mackenzie to the Beaufort Sea, leaving the stores to come round by whaler.

3. Anything unusually large of its kind; a 'whacker', 'whopper'. *U.S. slang.*

a **1860** *Georgia Scenes* 184 (Bartlett) 'He's a whaler!' said Rory; 'but his face is mighty little for his body and legs.' **1873** LELAND *Egypt. Sketch-Bk.* 25, I shared.. a cabin with a captain who had been a whaler for forty years; and he *was* a whaler! and great at 'whalers'.

4. Also **waler.** [ellipt. f. *Murrumbidgee w(h)aler* s.v. MURRUMBIDGEE: (see also quot. 1945).] A tramp or 'sundowner'. *Austral. slang.*

1883 R. E. N. TWOPENY *Town Life in Australia* 244 A 'waler' is a bushman who is 'on the loaf'. He 'humps his drum', or 'swag', and 'starts on the wallaby track'. **1886** F. COWAN *Australia* 31 The Whaler: of the Murrumbidgee and the Darling; when it suits his pleasure and convenience, a dolce-far-niente outcast in the fertile valleys of the rivers named, beyond the running of a warrant or a writ. **1903** 'T. COLLINS' *Such is Life* 4 Willoughby, who was travelling loose with Thompson and Cooper, was a whaler. **1945** BAKER *Austral. Lang.* v. 102 According to an old-timer correspondent: 'They were so apt to lie about the size of the 'whales' they caught that a generic name for this class of unemployable traveller came into being.' This explanation is open to some doubt... In our early days New South Welsh horses exported to India for army use were known as *walers*. The original *Murrumbidgee whalers* may therefore have been N.S.W. tramps... Blood brethren of the *whaler* (this spelling is retained because tradition holds mainly to the 'whale' theory).. are the *Domain dosser*, [etc.]. **1963** A. MARSHALL *In Mine Own Heart* (1964) xx. 164 The whaler, a term that had originated from the name given to those swagmen who in the early days spent their time moving up and down the Murrumbidgee River.. now applied to those who walked from town to town in preference to jumping trains. **1965** B. WANNAN *Fair Go, Spinner* II. 53 After drinking some Wilcannia beer, a whaler I once saw got up and started to fight with himself.

5. Special Combs. **whalerman** = WHALER 1; **whaler shark**, any of several sharks of the genus *Galeolemma*, found in Australasian waters.

1891 R. L. STEVENSON *In South Seas* (1896) I. xiii. 128 Captain Chase, they called him, an old whaler-man. **1963** *Times* 18 May 9/7 The first big bang was at night and the Norwegian whalermen heard it six miles away. **1974** G. JENKINS *Bridge of Magpies* ii. 33 Old whaler-men's graves in New England. [**1882** J. E. TENISON-WOODS *Fish New South Wales* iv. 92 The following list [of sharks] includes all that are known to occur in our seas:.. the Whaler, [etc.].] **1937** Z. GREY *Amer. Angler in Austral.* vii. 70 Among the trawlers it was not unusual to see a dozen whaler sharks all in a bunch. **1972** *Islander* (Victoria, B.C.) 9 Apr. 7/1 A whaler shark darting over the reef flat with a sudden burst of speed.

whalery (ˈhweɪlərɪ). [f. WHALE *sb.* + -ERY.]

1. The industry of whale-fishing, or the establishment for carrying it on.

1683 W. PENN *Let. to Free Soc. Traders* 9 The Whalery [is conveniently posted] for a sound and fruitful Bank. **1685** —— *Furth. Acc. Pennsylv.* 8 We justly hope a considerable profit by a Whalery. **1878** SUSAN PHILLIPS *On Seaboard* 15 Since I sailed away to the whalery, When I was a bit of a lad. **1899** *Daily News* 2 Dec. 6/4 South Sea whaleries.

2. A tank to keep a whale in.

a **1880** F. T. BUCKLAND *Notes & Jottings* (1882) 345 When the whale had been in his whalery about three hours, he had quite recovered himself both in mind and body.

whales bone: see WHALEBONE.

whaling (ˈhweɪlɪŋ), *vbl. sb.*[1] [f. WHALE *sb.* or *v.*[1] + -ING[1].] **1. a.** The action, practice, or business of catching whales.

1716 B. CHURCH *Hist. Philip's War* (1867) II. 133 Whale-men.. having a promise made to them, that they shall be released in good season to go home a Whaling in the Fall. **1851** H. MELVILLE *Whale* xvi, 'But what takes thee a-whaling?'.. 'Well, sir I want to see what whaling is.' **1895** GORE-BOOTH *Sea Fishing* (Badm. Libr.) xvi. 497 The Arctics seem to have an extraordinary and incomprehensible attraction for some people; and when it is coupled with whaling, to the author it becomes almost irresistible.

b. *attrib.* or as *ppl. a.*

1722 *New-England Courant* 18 June 2/2 Huffey of Nantucket.. went out from thence on the Whaling Account. **1767** M. CUTLER in W. P. & J. P. Cutler *Life & Corr. M. Cutler* (1888) I. i. 19 Our whaling vessels sailed for the Western Islands. **1782** 'J. H. ST JOHN DE CRÈVECŒUR' *Lett. from Amer. Farmer* v. 158 They have greatly cheapened the fitting out of their whaling fleets. **1821** SCOTT *Pirate* v, Ill-faur'd tools they had in their hands, whaaling knives they ca'ed them. **1823** SCORESBY *Voy. N. Whale-fishery* 34 The practice of such kinds of harmless frolic, as the circumstances of a whaling voyage will admit. **1836** *Uncle Philip's Convers. Whale Fishery* 6 There was a whaling ship fitting out for her voyage. **1843** *Penny Cycl.* XXVII. 752/1 The number of whales has greatly decreased on the whaling-ground. **1860** WRAXALL *Life in Sea* ii. 33 He listened to the brilliant promises of a whaling captain. **1863** MRS. GASKELL *Sylvia's Lovers* xvi, Stores had to be purchased by the whaling-masters. **1890** 'R. BOLDREWOOD' *Col. Reformer* xvi, The barque was empty and the whaling gear in trim.

2. Comb. **whaling station**, a land base where whales which have been caught are flenched and rendered.

1874 C. M. SCAMMON *Marine Mammals N.W. Coast N. Amer.* III. v. 247 At the point where the enormous carcass was stripped of its fat, arose the 'whaling station', whose trypots were set in rude furnaces.. and capacious vats were made of planks, to receive the blubber. **1930** L. G. D. ACLAND *Early Canterbury Runs* 1st Ser. vi. 116 The country .. was accessible on foot from the old shore whaling station. **1963** L. DIACK *Labrador Nurse* v. 25 One night we tied up at a whaling station. **1977** C. MCCULLOUGH *Thorn Birds* ii. 20 The eleven men.. came out at the whaling station of Hobart.

ˈwhaling, *vbl. sb.*[2] *dial.* and *U.S.* [f. WHALE *v.*[2] + -ING[1].] Beating, thrashing.

1852 MRS. STOWE *Uncle Tom's C.* xxxvi, How did yer whaling agree with yer, Tom? **1885** 'C. E. CRADDOCK' *Proph. Gt. Smoky Mts.* ii. 44 From fear of a whaling by his active parent.

whalish (ˈhweɪlɪʃ), *a. rare.* [f. WHALE *sb.* + -ISH[1].] Of the nature of or resembling a whale.

a **1892** G. H. KINGSLEY *Sport & Trav.* (1900) 424 A big, wide-flippered whalish-looking creature.

whalke, whall(e: see WALK *sb.*[1], WALL.

whallabee, var. WALLABY.

whallup, obs. f. WALLOP *v.*

whally (ˈhwɔːlɪ), *a. rare.* Also 9 **-ey.** [? f. *whall*, WALL *sb.*[3], 'whally eyes' being equivalent to 'eyes of wall', i.e. wall-eyes.] Of the eyes: ? Showing much white, glaring.

1590 SPENSER *F.Q.* I. iv. 24 A bearded Goat, whose.. whally eyes (the signe of gelosy). **1828** J. WILSON in *Blackw. Mag.* XXIV. 669 His low vile forehead, whalley eyes, pendulous cheeks.

whalm, whalp: see WALM, WHELM, WHELP.

whaly (ˈhweɪlɪ), *a. rare.* [f. WHALE *sb.* + -Y[1].] Of whales.

1600 TOURNEUR *Transf. Metam.* xxxix, The ocean's monarch.. The great controller of the whaly ranckes.

† **wham,** *sb.*[1] *Obs. nonce-wd.* [A factitious word made by altering the vowel of WHIM.] A whimsical or fantastic person.

1691 WOOD *Ath. Oxon.* II. 253 The Author of it was a whim and a wham, a Fellow that invented ridiculous Principles.

wham (hwæm), *sb.*[2] *colloq.* [Echoic. Cf. WHAM *v.*] **1.** A heavy blow; the sound of a heavy blow (or of an explosion, etc.). Also, a resounding success, a 'knock-out'; an attempt *at* something (cf. WHACK *sb.* 1 b).

1923 *N.Y. Times* 9 Sept. VII. 2 *Wham*, a success, a knock-out. **1924** *Dialect Notes* V. 257 Onomatopoetic words.. bam, blam, ca-blam, slam, wham, zam.. (all = sound of blow). **1949** J. R. COLE *It was so Late* 90 The occasional echoing wham of a charge of gelly. **1957** 'J. WYNDHAM' *Midwich Cuckoos* iv. 38 Might be a good idea to have a wham at it. **1973** C. BONINGTON *Next Horizon* viii. 121 Have another try... This time the peg held, another half-dozen whams of the hammer, and it was in to the hilt.

2. As *int.* or *adv.*: with a wham.

1924 E. HEMINGWAY *In our Time* 10 The bull rammed him wham against the wall. **1934** J. M. CAIN *Postman always rings Twice* xi. 126 And then, wham, I pleaded her guilty. **1948** 'J. TEY' *Franchise Affair* viii. 90 They go that short step too far and wham! out comes that business-like paw. **1958** P. MORTIMER *Daddy's gone a-Hunting* xxx. 170 He.. walked through the front door and wham. She did it with a clock. **1965** M. FRAYN *Tin Men* xxvi. 144 When the iron was hot, wham!—he would come out like a tiger and knock it for six. **1975** A. AYCKBOURN *Norman Conquests* 5 It was just wham, thump and there we both were on the rug.

wham (hwæm), *v. colloq.* [Echoic. Cf. WHAM *sb.*[2]]

1. *trans.* To strike violently; to propel with great force, by hitting, throwing, kicking, etc. Also *fig.*

1925 *Sat. Even. Post* 14 Feb. 16 The wow finish, properly, is the legitimate successor to the old apple-sauce flag-waving finish for whamming an audience. **1930** E. FERBER *Cimarron* xxi. 349 Standing Bear whams it out so straight and so far that he makes the [golf] pro look like a ping-pong player. **1933** J. THURBER *My Life & Hard Times* iv. 57 She.. picked up a shoe, and whammed it through a pane of glass across the narrow space that separated the two houses. **1950** A. BUCKERIDGE *Jennings goes to School* xii. 239 You must have put all your weight behind it, or you wouldn't have gone down flat like that, after you'd whammed it in. **1951** *Sport* 7–13 Jan. 15/2 Basically the same team, which had been languishing generally on the wrong side,.. whammed in six against Derry. **1962–3** E. BIRNEY *Sel. Poems* (1966) II. 59 Nine shoeboys wham their boxes Slap at my newshined feet. **1971** C. BONINGTON *Annapurna South Face* xiii. 161 He whammed in the ice-hammer, pulled up on it, kicking with the two front points of his crampons into the ice.

2. *intr.* To pound or strike violently; to move with speed, violence, or noise. Also *fig.*

1948 W. C. WILLIAMS in *Poetry* June 147 Each time he'd swing the axe and I heard it wham into the wood, I'd let out a wild cackle of delight. **1948** D. BALLANTYNE *Cunninghams* 135 The nausea rushes that made his head wham. **1954** A. C. CLARKE *Silence Please* in *Tales from White Hart* (1957) 3 Bert's blast whammed overhead. **1962** K. KESEY *One flew over Cuckoo's Nest* I. 51 The black boy whammed flat against the wall and stuck, then slid down to the floor. **1973** P. WHITE *Eye of Storm* xii. 586 A partition of the door still in motion whammed against an ear and sent his hat spinning. **1980** *Daily Tel.* 27 Aug. 2 (Advt.), The incredible Casio FX39.. whams through complicated equations and elementary statistical formulae.

wham, Sc. and north. dial. form of WHOM.

wham-bam, -bang, *adv.* (or *int.*), *a.*, (*sb.*). [f. WHAM *sb.*[2] 2 + BAM *int.* or BANG *v.* 8.]

A. *adv.* or *int.* With a wham and a bang: used to denote a sudden or forceful effect (*lit.* or *fig.*); *spec.* with reference to sexual intercourse conducted quickly and without tenderness, esp. in phr. ***wham, bam, thank you ma'am.***

1956 B. HOLIDAY *Lady sings Blues* (1973) ii. 22 With my regular white customers, it was a cinch. They had wives and kids to go home to. When they came to see me it was wham, bang, they gave me the money and were gone. *Ibid.* 25 'I thought I was giving you a chance,' she spouted at me. 'But you turned out to be a girl of bad character.' Wham, bang, four months she handed me. **1971** S. FIRESTONE *Dialectic of Sex* vi. 152 Men are interested in nothing but a screw (wham, bam, thank you M'am!). **1977** *Ripped & Torn* VI. 9/1 We play a set that starts at the beginning and goes Wham Bam Bam to the end. **1977** *Playgirl* May 13/1 Not all men are 'wham bam thank you ma'am' types.

B. *adj.* Loud, violent, forceful (see also quot. 1960).

1960 WENTWORTH & FLEXNER *Dict. Amer. Slang* 573/1 *Wham-bam*, quick(ly) and rough(ly); displaying more energy than finesse. **1976** *Publishers Weekly* 4 Oct. 65/2 Harbinson on Elvis.. ticks off the outrageous 'Hound Dog' of pop music in wham-bam style. **1977** *Listener* 20 Oct.

498/3 Screenwriters..know that it's mainly wham-bang shock effect that sells.

C. *sb.* A sudden, violent effect.

1975 *Listener* 17 July 68/3 Now it is the big wham-bang of sudden [price] rises.

whamble, var. WHEMMEL *Sc.*, overturn.

whame. *Obs.* or *dial.* A gadfly.

1658 ROWLAND tr. *Moufet's Theat. Ins.* 937 This Fly [*Curvicauda*] the English in their proper tongue call a Whame and a Burrell-fly. **1775** ROMANS *Florida* App. 51 *note, Tabona* [*sic*] is Spanish for a whame or horsefly. **1829** *Glover's Hist. Derby* I. 177 *Oestrus Bovis*, Whame or Burrel Fly. **1881** BLACKMORE *Christowell* ii, He mistook a large stone-fly..for a genuine oestrus, a bot-fly, whame, or tabanus.

whamera, var. WOOMERA.

whamire, dial. var. QUAMIRE *Obs.*

whammel, var. WHEMMEL *Sc.*, overturn.

whammer (ˈhwæmə(r)). *Mountaineering.* [f. WHAM *v.* + -ER[1].] A kind of piton hammer.

1971 [see *piton hammer* s.v. PITON 3]. **1974** H. MACINNES *Climb to Lost World* ix. 142 The Whillans 'Whammer'—a multi-purpose piton hammer.

whammo (hwæməʊ: stress variable), *int.* Also **whamo.** [f. WHAM *sb.*[2] + -O[2].] = WHAM *sb.*[2] 2; an exclamation suggesting a sudden violent blow or surprising event, etc.

1932 *Fitchburg* (Mass.) *Sentinel* 7 May, But the heavy comes to, and Whamo! The boy goes down bam. **1945** *Record* (Philadelphia) 4 July 11/1 'Ring out the tidings, Grandpa!' and the old gent spit on his hands, and Whammo! went the Liberty Bell. **1959** N. MAILER *Advts. for Myself* (1961) 97 They meet again in New York..and whammo do they get together. I mean drinking and making love, nothing can stop them. **1969** P. DICKINSON *Pride of Heroes* I. 45 Everyone a bit nervy for about a fortnight, and then, whammo, something happens. **1981** *Daily Express* 24 July 14/4, I put the telephone down and whammo! Another 'little twinge'.

whammy (ˈhwæmɪ). *colloq.* (orig. and chiefly *U.S.*). [f. WHAM *sb.*[2] + -Y[6].] An evil influence or 'hex'. From the 1950s, often with reference to the comic strip Li'l Abner (see quot. 1951), esp. in phr. ***a double whammy*** and varr. Hence, an intense or powerful look, etc.; something effective, upsetting, problematic, etc.

1940 J. R. TUNIS *Kid from Tomkinsville* x. 151 Interest round the field now centered in the Kid's chances for a no-hit game... On the bench everyone realized it too, but everyone kept discreetly quiet on account of the Whammy. Mustn't put the Whammy on him! **1951** *Al Capp's Li'l Abner* July, *Evil-Eye Fleegle* is th' name, an' th' '*whammy*' is my game. Mudder Nature endowed me wit' eyes which can putrefy citizens t' th' spot!.. There is th' '*single whammy*'! *That*, friend, is th' full, *pure power o' one* o' my evil eyes! It's *dynamite*, friend, an' I do not t'row it around lightly!.. And, lastly—th' '*double whammy*'—namely, th' *full power o' both eyes*—which I hopes I never *hafta* use. **1952** B. MALAMUD *Natural* 75 They were afflicted with more than the usual number of hexes and whammies and practised all sorts of magic to undo them. **1964** J. MASTERS *Trial at Monomoy* ii. 66 You heard that our local witch has put her whammy on you now? **1970** *Daily Tel.* (Colour Suppl.) 30 Oct. 19/2 That smile, a huge, sweet, melting smile, a whammy of an MRA smile, a West-Coast switched-on-sincere smile, which envelops just everybody. **1976** *New Yorker* 16 Feb. 107/1 In the Germany scenes, Wertmuller achieves the effect of liveliness through one whammy after another. The starving prisoners in the camp are beaten and murdered to the tune of the Ride of the Valkyries. **1979** C. JAMES *Pillars of Hercules* III. xi. 122 Holmes was a nonconformist in a conformist age, yet still won all the conformist rewards. It was a double whammy.

whampee, var. WAMPEE.

whan, obs. f. WHEN, WHOM; obs. pa. t. of WIN.

whand, Sc. var. WAND *sb.*

whane, whanene: see WHEN, WHENNE.

whang (hwaŋ), *sb.*[1] Also **wang.** Also 6 *Sc.* **quhayng, quhaing,** 7 **whange,** 9 *Sc.* **quhang;** 7 **whanck,** 7- **whank.** [Variant of *thwang*, THONG.]

1. = THONG *sb. Sc.* and *dial.*

1536 BELLENDEN *Cron. Scot.* (1821) II. 32 Quhen Hengist had gottin the grant of sa mekill land as he micht circle about with ane bull hide, he schure it in maist crafty and subtell quhaingis. *a* **1578** LINDESAY (Pitscottie) *Chron. Scot.* (S.T.S.) I. 117 Ane gret scheiff of arrowis knet together in ane quhange of leathir. *a* **1598** D. FERGUSSON *Scot. Prov.* (1785) 647 Mony ane tines the haff-merk whinger for the halfpenny whang. **1670** RAY *Prov.* 289 Of other mens lether, men takes large whanges. **1691** —— *Coll. Words* (ed. 2) 151 Shoe-whang. **1717** DE FOE *Mem. Ch. Scot.* III. 268, I had not the worth of a Spur Whang of any Man's, but was mounted of Horse and Arms of my own. **1737-8** *MS. Par. Bk., Pannal, Yks.*, Church gate mending a beast face and Whangs, 1s. od. **1818** SCOTT *Rob Roy* xxxiii, Never weigh a MacGregor's bluid against a broken whang o' leather. **1837** SIR F. PALGRAVE *Merch. & Friar* i. 16 Their sacks..tightly bound by many a whang and thong.

2. A large or thick slice, esp. of cheese, bread, etc. *Sc.* and *dial.*

1684 MERITON *Yorksh. Dial.* 57 What a whanck's there. *a* **1700** *Gaberlunzie Man* viii. in Ramsay *Tea-t. Misc.* (1733) I. 86 The twa, with kindly sport and glee, Cut frae a new cheese a whang. **1818** HOGG *Tales & Sk., Adv. Allan Gordon* (1836) I. 264 A good whang of solid fish. **1866** W. HENDERSON *Folk Lore N. Counties* 3 The whang must be taken from the edge of the cheese, and divided into portions. **1879** STEVENSON *Trav. Cevennes* 33 With a glass, a whang of bread, and an iron fork, the table is completely laid.

3. The penis. *slang* (orig. and chiefly *U.S.*).

1935 H. L. DAVIS *Honey in Horn* iii. 34 Leave them horses alone or I'll cut your whang off. **1949** H. MILLER *Sexus* viii. 250 You say he's got a terrific wang, Bill. I don't know how he ever gets it in there. **1952** N. MAILER *Barbary Shore* x. 89 Guinevere..went on at length with one of her inexhaustible stories about a lover and his whang. **1959** M. RICHLER *Apprenticeship D. Kravitz* I. x. 60 He's got a whang that could choke a horse. I know, we had a leak together once. **1969** K. VONNEGUT *Slaughterhouse-Five* v. 115 Montana was naked, and so was Billy, of course. He had a tremendous wang. **1981** G. HAMMOND *Revenge Game* ix. 102 Maybe you're not as ready with your whang as you were, or maybe you couldn't keep it up——.

whang, *sb.*[2] Chiefly *dial.* [Echoic. Cf. WHANG *v.*[2]] A resounding blow or stroke, or the sound of such a blow; a bang.

1824 MACTAGGART *Gallovid. Encycl.*, *Whang*..a blow, or rather a lash with a whip. **1868** KINGLAKE *Crimea* IV. v. 279 The 'whang' of the round-shot. **1889** 'Q' *Splendid Spur* ix. 130 Soon the whang-whang! of the hammer below rous'd me. **1891** *Century Mag.* Dec. 246 Our gear came down with a whang as the ship forged ahead.

whang, *v.*[1] Also **wang.** [Variant of THONG *v.*; cf. WHANG *sb.*[1]]

1. a. *trans.* To beat as with a thong; to lash (also *fig.*); *gen.* to beat, strike, hit or knock violently. *Sc.* and *dial.*

1684 MERITON *Yorksh. Dial.* 54 If she hear she'l whang me varra sayer. **1786** BURNS *Ordination* iii, Heresy is in her pow'r, And gloriously she'll whang her. **1889** BADEN-POWELL *Pigsticking* 21 A savage would consider it the height of sport to go and whang a pig on the head.

b. To throw, drive, pull, etc. with force or with violent impact. *trans.* and *intr. dial.* and *colloq.*

1820 CLARE *Rural Life* (ed. 2) 60 I'd just streak'd down, and with a swish Whang'd off my hat soak'd like a fish. **1899** CROCKETT *Black Douglas* xix, Whang the steel bolt through his ribs. *Ibid.* xxxiv, Bring back every true lad that can whang bow, or gar sword-iron whistle. **1905** in *Eng. Dial. Dict.* VI. 439/2 He wanged a stone at me. **1914** C. MACKENZIE *Sinister Street* II. III. i. 500 The governor wanged them into my lap. **1965** *Punch* 22 Sept. 420/1 Anybody wanting to wang up a skyscraper or indeed any building of size and importance will have to publish a comprehensible model or drawing. **1980** D. BOGARDE *Gentle Occupation* ix. 249 Suddenly a stone spun out of nowhere and whanged harmlessly against the bonnet of the car. **1984** *New Yorker* 23 Apr. 80/3 Bad bush pilots..cross the margins of heavy weather and whang into mountains. *Ibid.* 29 Oct. 140/3 Mondale was ready for him and whanged the line back.

2. To cut in 'whangs' or large slices. Also *absol.* or *intr. Sc.* and *dial.*

a **1743** *Argyll is my name* in Whitelaw *Bk. Scot. Song* (1866) 224 I'll aff to the Highlands as hard's I can reel. And whang at the bannocks o' barley meal. **1801** W. BEATTIE *Tales* (1813) 8 At last, came cheese..My uncle set it to his breast And whang'd it down.

whang, *v.*[2] Also **wang.** [Cf. WHANG *sb.*[2]] **a.** *intr.* To make a loud resounding noise, as of a heavy blow or explosion, of shot flying through the air, of a loudspeaker, of a speeding car, etc.

1875 KINGLAKE *Crimea* V. vi. 426 Another of the mighty 18-pounder shot flew whanging over the heads of our soldiery. **1912** MASEFIELD *Widow in Bye Street* II. liv, The organ whangs, the giddy horses reel. **1952** *Observer* 2 Nov. 3/5 The words from the loudspeaker wang back from the quiet village houses, but the doors remain closed. **1977** *Motor* 19 Feb. 24/1 You rush from the pits just as the leading Porsches wang past.

b. The vb.-stem used adverbially: cf. BANG *v.* 8.

1844 KINGLAKE *Eothen* xxi. 335, I..went falling, and falling through air till my crown came whang against the ground. **1855** BROWNING *Up at a Villa* ix, Bang, whang, whang goes the drum.

whang, dial. f. WANG[1].

whangdoodle, whang-doodle. *N. Amer.* Also **whangydoodle.** [Fanciful.] **a.** An imaginary creature. **b.** Something unspecified, a 'thingummy'. (See also quot. 1904.)

1858 H. T. LEWIS in *Salem* (Illinois) *Advocate* 27 Jan. 1/2 They shall..flee unto the mountains of Hepsidam, where the lion roareth and the wang-doodle [*Yankee Notions* Feb. 52/1 whang doodle] mourneth for his first-born. **1870** *Punchinello* (N.Y.) 9 Apr. 30/1 In his own State the Ku-Klux raged, together with the fierce whang-doodle. **1890** *Boston Jrnl.* 24 July 2/5 The rougher element among the boys..formed the 'Whang Doodle' Club for the purpose of settling him. **1904** R. F. FOSTER *Practical Poker* 11 The 'whangdoodle', a round of compulsory jack-pots after a big hand has been shown. **1923** *Nation* (N.Y.) 22 Aug. 179 The downtrodden and oppressed force on the *Gazette*..has to live with this old whang-doodle and listen to his preterbacious scandulations. **1931** *Amer. Speech* VI. 259 Whangdoodle, whangy-doodle, what have you, whatsis, whatsit, [etc.]. **1979** *Globe & Mail* (Toronto) 24 Jan. 6/1 In 1976... A new company sprang to the fore in Quebec... PQ Productions claimed to have invented the whangdoodle.

whangee (hwæŋˈgiː). Also **w(h)anghee.** [Chinese *huang* bamboo sprouts too old for eating, a hard white-skinned bamboo (Giles).] A cane made of the stem of one or other species of *Phyllostachys*, Chinese and Japanese plants allied to and resembling bamboos. Also ***whangee-cane.***

1790 in W. Roughead *Bad Companions* (1930) 6 He..sometimes wears a cocked hat,..and generally carries a Wangee cane in his hand. **1813** W. MILBURN *Oriental Comm.* II. 545 Wanghees, sometimes called Japan canes, should be chosen pliable, tough, round and taper. **1836** *Act 3 & 4 Will. IV*, c. 56 Duties of Customs Inwards... Canes, *viz.*.. Whangees, Jumboo..and other Walking Canes or Sticks, the 1,000..0.5.0. **1891** A. DOBSON *Hogarth* ii. 31 A short-trowsered tar of the Tom Bowling era is deliberately executing a nautical *pas seul*..with the aid of a whangee. **1906** OXENHAM *Profit & Loss* vi, A tough flexible whangee cane.

whanger (ˈhwæŋə(r)), *sb.*[1] [f. WHANG *v.*[1] + -ER[1].] (See quot.)

1867 SMYTH *Sailor's Word-bk.*, *Whangers*, or Cod-whangers. Fish-curers of Newfoundland. An old term for a large sword.

whanger (ˈhwæŋə(r)), *sb.*[2] *U.S. slang.* Also **wanger.** [f. WHANG *v.*[1] + -ER[1].] = WHANG *sb.*[1] 3.

1939 J. STEINBECK *Grapes of Wrath* ii. 14 An' there we spied a nigger, with a trigger that was bigger than an elephant's proboscis or the whanger of a whale. **1976** M. MACHLIN *Pipeline* xiv. 160 She didn't get the idea so fast, so he whipped the old wanger out of his union suit and laid it on the table in front of her.

whanhope, obs. form of WANHOPE.

whank, whanker, occas. varr. WANK, WANKER.

whanne, obs. f. WHEN; var. *wan*, obs. pa. t. of WIN *v.*

whannen, var. WHENNE *Obs.*, whence.

whannes, obs. f. WHENCE.

†**whannow**, *int. Obs.* Also **wannowe.** [? f. WHAT + NOW. Cf. WHAU, which is similarly used.] What! I say! Come, come!

c **1450** *Northern Passion* (MS. Addit.) 147/59* 'Wannowe', sayde kayme, 'her es Envy; My smoke gose down and thyne gose hye.' *c* **1460** *Towneley Myst.* xxviii. 184 *Thomas.* Whannow, peter! art thou mad?

whanse, var. WANZE *v. Obs.*

whante, whantite, obs. ff. QUANT, WANT, QUANTITY.

whap, var. WAP *v.*[3] *Obs.*, to bark, WHAUP *Sc.*, curlew, WHOP.

†**whaped**, *pa. pple. Obs.* Also 4 **whaaped,** 5 **waped.** [Cf. AWHAPE.] Bewildered, dismayed.

c **1374** CHAUCER *Anel. & Arc.* 215 Turnid is in quakynge all my daunce My suretee in a whaaped [*v.rr.* waped, wayped, whaped] countenaunce. *c* **1403** LYDG. *Temple of Glas* 401 That þei wiþ derknes were waped & amate. **1426** —— *De Guil. Pilgr.* 1297, I was so whapyd & amaat.

whapper, etc.: see WHOPPER, etc.

whappet (ˈhwɒpɪt). *dial.* Also 9 **wappet.** [f. **whap*, WAP *sb.*[2] + -ET[1].] A small dog addicted to 'wapping' or yelping.

1577 HARRISON *England* III. vii. (1878) 48 The whappet or prick-eard curre. **1622** S. WARD *Life of Faith* (1627) 62 As the sturdie Steede dashes out the little Whappets braines, so easily doth Death with the least kicke..the stoutest Constitution. *a* **1825** FORBY *Voc. E. Anglia*, *Wappet*, a yelping cur.

whapple, var. WARPLE.

whapto, var. WAPPATO(O.

whar, obs. f. *were*, pl. pa. t. indic. of BE *v.*; obs. f. WARE *a.*; Sc. and n. dial. f. WHERE; obs. contr. f. WHETHER.

†**whar**, *v. Obs.* Imitative of a rumbling sound.

13.. *Gaw. & Gr. Knt.* 2203 What! hit wharred, & whette, as water at a mulne.

‖**whare** (ˈfare, ˈhwɒrɪ, ˈwɒrɪ). Also 9- **wurrie, ware, warree, warré, wharre, wharry.** [Maori *whare, ware* house.] **1.** A Maori hut or native dwelling.

1807 J. SAVAGE *Some Acct. N.Z.* xi. 77 *Wurrie*, a house, or hut. **1817** J. L. NICHOLAS *Voyage to N.Z.* I. xii. 352 A young woman..beckoned to me to accompany her to her *warree* or hut. **1833** H. WILLIAMS in H. Carleton *H.W.* (1874) 151 The Europeans, who were near us in a raupo whare (rush house). **1852** MUNDY *Antipodes* (1857) 179 A capital breakfast..was served in a handsome glass-windowed and carpeted warree. **1865** *Pall Mall Gaz.* 28 Sept. 9/2 Lounging among the wharres of a pah. **1875** WOOD & LAPHAM *Waiting for Mail* 31 He pulled up..beside a wharry. **1892** E. REEVES *Homeward Bound* 63 A smart man he, and transacted his business in a very handsome wharè.

2. Hence *gen.*, a hut or shed; *spec.* on a sheep station, a building where the hands sleep or eat. Also with defining word.

1853 A. S. ATKINSON *Jrnl.* 26 Oct. in *Richmond-Atkinson Papers* (1960) I. 135 James and I went to the site chosen for our new whare. **1853** J. M. RICHMOND *Let.* 11 Nov. in *Ibid.* 133 Their 'wharre', as it is called, is a most romantic tho' not v. commodious dwelling;..it is in fact a roof on the ground, thatched with nikau, a palm, the only one in N.Z. **1891** R. WALLACE *Rural Econ. Austral. & N.Z.* xv. 225 Pioneering, or cutting a place out of the bush and building a log 'wharë', is extremely rough and lonely work. **1904** 'G. B. LANCASTER' *Sons o' Men* 4 He scudded across the tussock flat to the eating-wharé; burst open the door, and cast the word loose on the boys. **1926** A. F. WEBB in D. M. Davin *N.Z. Short Stories* (1953) 205 We had dinner at twelve and made a plum duff because there was time to cook it while we were all about the whare. **1939** J. MULGAN *Man Alone* viii. 95 You'll be sleeping in the *whare* down there... There's no room in the house. **1963** B. PEARSON *Coal Flat* vii. 141 Eventually Miss Dane said: 'Time I got back to the *whare*.' **1972** M. SHADBOLT *Strangers & Journeys* i. 29 They found he had built a whare. A one-room shack of roughly-split timber.

3. Special combinations. **whare puni**, a (Maori) family sleeping-house (see also quot. 1911); **whare runanga** [RUNANGA], a Maori council chamber.

1911 W. H. KOEBEL *In Maoriland Bush* xx. 262 It is regrettable that the interpretations of the carvings upon the beams and panels of the old *whare-punis* or meeting-houses have been lost. **1926** H. GUTHRIE-SMITH *Tutira* (ed. 2) 86 A *whare-puni* or sleeping-house. **1950** *N.Z. Jrnl. Agric.* May 502/2 The great michi, the barge boards of a whare-puni (a sleeping house). **1891** R. WALLACE *Rural Econ. Austral. & N.Z.* xiv. 218 A special house of assembly, the *whare runanga*..is set apart in which to receive and entertain strangers. **1910** J. COWAN *Maoris of N.Z.* xii. 163 Most Maori villages of any importance contain at least one *whare-whakairo*, a large house..used as the communal assembly hall, council-place (*whare-runanga*),..and guest-house (*whare-manuhiri*). **1955** W. J. PHILLIPS *Maori Carving Illustr.* 40 The Assembly House or whare runanga is often well adorned with carvings.

whare, obs. shortened form of WHARROW.

1688 HOLME *Armoury* III. 272/1 A Ropers Whare or Wharve, or Wheele Spindle.

whare, obs. form of WHERE.

wharel, obs. f. QUARREL *sb.*[2], quarry.

c **1356** *Durham Acc. Rolls* (Surtees) 557 Wharel-wegges.

wharf (hwɔːf), *sb.*[1] Pl. **wharfs** (hwɔːfs), **wharves** (hwɔːvz). Forms: 1 **hwearf, wearf, hwerf**, 1, 4 **warf**, 4 **wherf(e, warffe, wharghffe, quarf**, 5 **qwerf**, 5–7 **warff, wharff(e**, 5–8 **wharfe**, 6 **quarfe, (wharthe)**, 7 **hwarf**, 7– **wharf**. [Late OE. *hwearf* (cf. earlier poetical comp. *merehwearf* sea-shore), corresp. to MLG. *warf, werf* mole, dam, wharf, raised site protected from flooding (LG. *warf*), whence EFris. *warf, werf*, Du. *werf* shipyard, G. *werf* wharf, pier, *werft* dockyard. Ultimately related to WHARF *sb.*[2], WHARVE *sb.* and *v.*

'Mr. Pickering notices this form of the plural of *wharf*, as peculiar to Americans. The English say *wharfs*. In the Colony and Province Laws of Massachusetts, Mr. Pickering says he has observed the plural *wharfs* (or *wharfes*) as late as the year 1735; but after that period the form *wharves* is used' (Bartlett *Dict. Amer.*, 1848).]

1. A substantial structure of timber, stone, etc., built along the water's edge, so that ships may lie alongside for loading and unloading.

Often with prefixed sb., as *fish-wharf, gun-wharf*.

10.. *Charter of Eadweard* in Kemble *Cod. Dipl.* IV. 221 Ic wille ðat sainte Petre and ða ȝebroðera in Westminstre habben ðat land and ðone wearf..ðe Ulf and his wif..ȝafon. **1067** in *Charter Roll 9 Edw. III*, m. 18 De uno hwearfo quod est ad applicationem navium ad capud pontis illius civitatis [*sc.* London]. **1080–5** in H. W. C. Davis *Regesta Regum Anglo-Norm.* (1913) 126 Unum warf quod est ad caput pontis Londonie. *c* **1320** *Domesday of St. Paul's* (Camden) 158* An qwarvæ sive kayæ, muri sive wallæ..debite reparentur. **1320** *Rolls of Parlt.* I. 370/2 In shopis suis super Warfam predictam. **1397** *Ibid.* III. 371/1 De la novell Keye autrement appelle le Wherf [**1432** *Act 10 Hen. VI*, c. 5 §2 Qwerf] a le cost du dit Port de Caleys. **1442** *Ibid.* V. 54/2 Diverse Wharves and Keyes beyng by the water sides. **1485** *Cal. Pat. Rolls* 6 [Keeping the] hawes and wharfes of Walton and Waybrigge. **1503–4** *Act 19 Hen. VII*, c. 37 §5 Too Cotages or Meses wyth Howses & Wharfes..in Stepeney. **1669** STURMY *Mariner's Mag., Pen. & Forf.* 8 If any Custom-house Officer..keep any Wharfe, or hold any Hostelry, or Tavern. *a* **1700** EVELYN *Diary* 17 Aug. 1654, A wharfe of hewn stone, which makes the river appeare very neate. **1815** J. SMITH *Panorama Sci. & Art* I. 241 Its [*sc.* Blackfriars bridge] length, from wharf to wharf, is about nine hundred and ninety-five feet. **1834** DICKENS *Sk. Boz, Steam Excurs.*, The bell at London-bridge Wharf rang; and a Margate boat was just starting. **1878** NARES *Polar Sea* I. i. 1 H.M. ships 'Alert' and 'Discovery' cast off from the dockyard wharf, Portsmouth. **1882** J. RHYS *Celtic Brit.* ii. 46 The wharfs for the tin-barges were erected.

†**2. a.** An embankment, mole, or dam. *Obs.*

1038 *Charter of Harold* in Thorpe *Charters* 341 þa ȝyrnde he þæt he moste macian foran gen Mildryþe æker ænne hwerf wið þon wodan to werianne. **1567** GOLDING *Ovid's Met.* xv. 196 b, Untill that hee the bowwing wharf besyde the hauen tooke [orig. *Tendit ad incurvo munitos aggere portus*]. **1600** HOLLAND *Livy* XL. li. 1091 Lepidus..raised the great causey or wharfe at Tarracina. **1601** —— *Pliny* VI. xxviii. I. 140 The Apamians..set open the sluces, and breake up the wharfes and bankes that keepe these two rivers asunder.

†**b.** A terrace or raised platform. *Obs.*

1533 in W. H. St. John Hope *Windsor Castle* (1913) I. 249 The makyng off a new wharff upon the north syde of the said Castell. **1535** *Ibid.* 262 The buttresses made on the bakesyde of the new Wharffe.

c. †The bank of a river (*obs.*); also, a gravel or sandbank.

1602 SHAKS. *Ham.* I. v. 33 The fat weede That rots it selfe in ease, on Lethe Wharfe. **1606** —— *Ant. & Cl.* II. ii. 218 From the Barge A strange inuisible perfume, hits the sense Of the adiacent Wharfes. **1867** SMYTH *Sailor's Word-bk.*, *Wharf*, in hydrography, is a scar, a rocky or gravelly concretion, or frequently a sandbank,..where the tides throw up dangerous ripples and overfalls.

†**d.** A large raft. *Obs. rare.*

1662 J. BARGRAVE *Pope Alex. VII* (1867) 119 They were brought upon warffs or raffts of many pines and firs.

e. A place raised or otherwise marked out on which stuff is deposited for subsequent removal to another place.

1725 in *Dig. Proc. Crt.-leet Savoy* (1789) 22 For making a dung wharfe or lay stall at the lower end of Fountain Court.

3. *attrib.* and *Comb.*, as ***wharf-end, -frontage, -head, -holder, -house, -labourer, -land, -man, -master, -measure, -property, -shed, -side, -stead, -wall***; **wharf-boat**, (*a*) *U.S.* a boat supporting a platform and moored at a bank, used as a wharf; (*b*) a boat employed about a wharf; **wharf crane**, a crane fixed in position on a wharf (see quot. 1968); a wharf-side crane; †**wharf-gelt**, ? an impost levied on shipping for the use of a wharf; **wharf-lumper** *Austral.* [LUMPER *sb.* 1 a], a wharf-labourer; **wharf-rat**, (*a*) the common brown rat, *Mus decumanus*, which infests wharfs; (*b*) a man or boy who loafs about wharfs, often with the intention of stealing (*slang*).

1849 LYELL *2nd Visit U.S.* II. 227 In the *wharf-boat..I expected to find a bed for the first night. **1860** BARTLETT *Dict. Amer.* s.v., On the Western rivers the height of the water is so variable that a fixed wharf would be useless. In its place is used a rectangular float... It is generally aground on the shore side, and is entered by a plank or movable platform. This is a *wharf-boat*. **1878** *N. Amer. Rev.* CXXVII. 225 She was used as a 'wharf-boat' or store-ship. **1893** K. P. DAHLSTROM tr. *Weisbach & Herrmann's Mech. Hoisting Machinery* vi. 243 The ordinary *wharf crane with capacity to lift 100 to 200 cwt. **1903** J. HORNER *Elem. Treat. Hoisting Machinery* xvii. 195 There is a class of fixed jib cranes which have no other name than that which designates the nature of their service, fixed wharf cranes... But by the term wharf crane, a broad type only is understood. **1968** *Gloss. Terms Materials Handling* (*B.S.I.*) IV. 14 *Dockside or wharf crane*, a jib crane designed for loading and unloading ships, consisting of a full or semi-portal, fixed or rail mounted, supporting a revolving superstructure and jib. **1897** KIPLING *Capt. Cour.* iv. 95 Her rigging flew knotted and tangled like weed at a *wharf-end. *Ibid.* x. 216 Statistics of boats, gear, *wharf-frontage, capital invested,..and profits. **1505** *Cal. Pat. Rolls Hen. VII*, 404 [Without paying any] sandegelt, *wharfgelt. **1800** *Asiat. Ann. Reg., Chron.* 35/1 All goods whatsoever, that are not disembarked at the *Wharf Head. **1883** *Law Rep. 11 Q.B. Div.* 486 Whether the persons for whom the weighing was done were *wharfholders or not. **1698** in *Hertford Sess. Rolls* (1905) I. 428 [Encroaching upon the river Lea] by building a *wharfe house..thereon. **1890** *Evening Post* (Wellington, N.Z.) 11 July 2 A *wharf-labourer who stands charged with the theft of an oil skin coat... The accused was at work discharging coal on the Mawhera. *a* **1948** L. G. D. ACLAND *Early Canterbury Runs* (1951) xi. 321 Trouble with wharf labourers..kept them six weeks in Auckland. **1895** *Daily Tel.* 5 Aug. 5/3 Converting a piece of *wharfland on the Isle of Dogs into a public pleasure-ground. **1906** E. DYSON *Fact'ry 'Ands* iii. 39 Three weeks..later, Sarah was married to a *wharf-lumper..and Fuzzy's dream of love was over. **1951** V. PALMER in *Landfall* V. 292 In Victoria..it was read by nearly everybody, from wharflumpers to politicians. **1848** MILL *Pol. Econ.* I. ii. §6 Bargemen, sailors, *wharfmen. *a* **1618** RALEIGH in *Rem.* (1661) 179 From any Port Town..the Bridge-master or the *Wharfmaster..will deliver a true Note of the number of Lasts of Herrings brought to their Wharfes. **1836** J. M. PECK *New Guide for Emigrants to West* xii. 320 The following, from the register of a wharf master, will exhibit the commerce for 1835. **1968** M. M. SIBLEY *Port of Houston* iii. 59 Wharfmaster Daniel G. Wheeler reported that in that year [*sc.* 1844] 6.892 bales passed over the Houston wharves. **1821** *Acc. Peculat. Coal Trade* 13 All coals sent out, *wharf measure. **1877** BURROUGHS *Taxation* 140 The whole *wharf property..was liable to be taxed. **1823** J. F. COOPER *Pilot* II. i. 13 To burrow like a rabbit, or jump from hole to hole, like a *wharf-rat. **1836** *Franklin Repository* (Chambersburg, Pa.) 4 Oct. 1/3 I've an idea, my man, that you are one of the wharf rats; and, if so, the less lip you give me the better. **1860** BARTLETT *Dict. Amer.*, *Wharf-Rats.* 1. Rats that inhabit wharves. 2. Thieves that infest the wharves of seaport towns. **1863** HAWTHORNE *Our Old Home, Boston* I. 269 Lolling on long-boats,..as sailors and old wharf rats are accustomed to do. **1952** R. FINLAYSON *Schooner came to Atia* xi. 61 In the..market place by the *wharfshed. **1842** DICKENS *Amer. Notes* xi, A crowd of high-pressure steam-boats, clustered together by a *wharf-side. **1891** MEREDITH *One of our Conq.* xxv, A hanged heavy look, suggestive of a wharfside crane. **1828** *Craven Gloss.*, **Wharf-steead*, a ford in a river. In Ray, it is *warstead*, q.d. waterstead. **1831–3** in *Encycl. Metrop.* (1845) VIII. 604/1 A *wharf wall..at the East end of His Majesty's dock-yard, Woolwich.

†**wharf,** *sb.*[2] *Obs.* [OE. *hwearf* (poet., alliterating on *w*), corresp. to OS. *hwarf* crowd, MLG. *warf, werf* circle, assembly sitting in a circle, court of justice, OHG. *warb* (MHG. *warp, warf*): cf. prec.] A crowd, assembly.

In the first quot. from Laȝamon's *Brut* perh. = change (OE. *hwearf*: cf. OFris. *hwarf, werf*, OHG. *warba*, MHG. *warbe* (with numerals) time(s, (M)LG. *werf, warf*, (*-ve*) turn, time; cf. WHARVE *v.*).

a **1000** *Guthlac* 234 Beorȝ ymbstodan hwearfum wræcmæcgas. *c* **1205** LAY. 2070 Þus is þis eitlond igon from honde to hond, þet alle þa burhȝes þe Brutus iwrohte..beoð swiðe afelled þurh warf of þon folke. *Ibid.* 17485 Þider com Aurilie..& al his folc mid him. Whiten-sunendæie he þer wærf makede [Wace *Altre gent assés assambla Feste tint*].

wharf (hwɔːf), *v.* Also 7 **warfe**. [f. WHARF *sb.*[1]]

†**1.** *trans.* To strengthen or make firm (e.g. the bank of a river) with a wall of timber or stone. *Obs.*

1569 *Surrey & Kent Sewers Comm.* (1909) 6 To..cope and wharfe xxiiij[te] roddes of the walle. **1615** *Crt.-roll of Gt. Waltham Manor, Essex* (MS.), Preceptum est..sufficienter cumulare (Anglicè, to wharfe) fossatum suum. **1618** in F. Devon *Issues Exch.* (1836) 335 For three bridges to go over the sewers, and for wharfing the sides with strong timber. **1674** JOSSELYN *Two Voy. New-Eng.* 162 The houses are for the most part raised on the Sea-banks and wharfed out with great industry and cost. *a* **1700** EVELYN *Diary* 6 Mar. 1667, I proposed to my Lo. Chancellor Monsieur Kiviet's undertaking to warfe the whole river of Thames, or Key, from the Temple to the Tower..with brick. **1724** [see WHARFING 2]. **1793** R. MYLNE *Rep. Thames* 37 The Road ought to be raised and wharfed.

transf. **1628** WITHER *Brit. Rememb.* I. 192 Is this that Iland, which our love..Did wharfe about (within her watry Dike) With mighty Rocks, and Cliffes?

2. To bring to shore or discharge at a wharf.

1629 WADSWORTH *Pilgr.* viii. 87 A Master of an English Barke..who had wharft ouer a hundred French. **1694** *Lond. Gaz.* No. 3024/4 Goods will be Wharfed here at easier Rates than heretofore. **1798** in *Spirit Publ. Jrnls.* (1799) II. 351 Every species of property (whether landed, funded, wharfed, warehoused, or shipped). **1803** W. TATHAM *Rep. Imped. Thames* 73 Nor would it be a very difficult matter to dock or wharf the whole of their commerce.

3. To accommodate (vessels) at a wharf.

1902 *Times* 1 Nov. 5/6 A large stone basin, capable of wharfing a dozen battleships of the first class.

4. *intr.* To come to wharf.

1891 *Voice* (N.Y.) 1 Jan., When the Mayflower wharfed at Plymouth Rock. **1901** *Daily Chron.* 4 June 3/4 The Royal Squadron wharfed..at half-past seven.

wharfage ('hwɔːfɪdʒ). Also [3 **wheruagium**, 4 **querfage, werphagium**], 5, 8 **wharffage**, 6 **warfeage**, 8 **warf(f)age**. [f. WHARF *sb.*[1] + -AGE.]

1. The provision of or accommodation at a wharf; the stowage of goods on, or loading or unloading at, a wharf.

[**1295** *Memoranda K. R.* 23 & 24 Edw. I (P.R.O.), In cariagio dicte lane..vsque London..cum wharuagio et portagio eiusdem. **1376** *Rolls of Parlt.* II. 351/1 Ore sont ils constreintz de paier pur Messuage de chescune Sarp' ob. Et un autre ob. pur Querfage. **1395** *Compotus Will. Chert custodis collegii Cantuar. Oxon.* (1881) 28 Item pro werphagio eiusdem (meremii capelle) iijs. iiij*d*.] **1469–71** *Stonor Papers* (Camden) I. 106 Paid..for C and vj li. of Iren, iiij.s. v.d, for the wharfage, j d., for bringyng of the seid stuffe to Derteford, vj.d. *a* **1552** LELAND *Itin.* (1768) II. 29 There is great Warfeage of Timbre and fier Wood on the West Ende of the Bridge. *c* **1640** J. SMYTH *Lives Berkeleys* (1883) I. 341 Renting out the Toll or profit of the wharfage. **1687–8** in Willis & Clark *Cambridge* (1886) II. 545 Expences for sawing, carriage, and wharfage of Cedar. **1795** J. PHILLIPS *Hist. Inland Nav.* Addenda 109 For wharfage exceeding six months, to make a reasonable recompence. **1848** MILL *Pol. Econ.* III. v. §3 The rents of wharfage, dock and harbour room. **1885** *Law Times* LXXIX. 189/2 Duties for defraying the expenses of pilotage, wharfage, lighthouses, and lights and buoys.

2. The charge or dues exacted for the use of a wharf.

1535 *Act 27 Hen. VIII*, c. 26 §23 Lordes Marches..shall have within..their said Lordeshipps..wreke de mere, wharfage and customes of Strangers. **1598** HAKLUYT *Voy.* I. 135 All marchants..may come into our kingdome..without paying wharfage, pontage, or pannage. *c* **1683** *Citizens Loss* in Somers *Tracts* (1748) I. 180 Wharfage, with Power to distrain for the same. **1715** *Lond. Gaz.* No. 5387/3 The Wharfage, Duties, and Profits arising..by and out of Billingsgate-Dock. **1795** J. PHILLIPS *Hist. Inland Nav.* Addenda 105 Wharfage for more than twenty-four hours, to be a reasonable allowance. **1894** *Times* 25 Aug. 5/4 The company is gradually issuing through rates, inclusive of Ship Canal toll and wharfage.

3. Wharfs collectively; wharf accommodation.

1807 *Ann. Reg., Chron.* 406 The company assembled on the insular wharfage. **1836** JESSE *Angler's Rambles* 295 The little secluded harbour, with its small planked wharfage. **1848** MILL *Pol. Econ.* I. i. §4 The wharfage or harbour-room. **1899** *Westm. Gaz.* 26 Sept. 9/1 At the terminus of the railway the Dominion Government is erecting complete wharfages to make the harbour suitable for oil vessels.

4. *attrib.*

1714 LADY G. BAILLIE *Househ. Bk.* (S.H.S.) 30 For warfage porters carts to the Lodging etc., 1. 9. 1... For warfage bale and cariing to the Lodgine, 0. 2. 6. **1862** G. T. LLOYD *33 Yrs. Tasmania* xvi. 415 Wharfage accommodation. **1867** SMYTH *Sailor's Word-bk.*, *Wharfage dues*, the dues for landing or shipping goods at a wharf; customs charges in particular... Wharfage charges are demanded even from a ship of war!

Wharfe (hwɔːf). Short for **Wharfedale** (*machine*): see quots.

1888 JACOBI *Printers' Vocab.*, *Wharfedale machine*, a cylindrical machine manufactured in Yorkshire and called after the place of that name. *Wharfe*, short term for the Wharfedale printing machine. **1890** W. J. GORDON *Foundry* 210 The Wharfedales, Bremners, and other machines on which is printed most illustrated work. **1901** *Daily Chron.* 3 Dec. 9/7 Printer's Minder, 31, seeks Situation; Wharfes., platens, gas engine.

wharfie ('hwɔːfɪ). *Austral.* and *N.Z. colloq.* [f. WHARF *sb.*[1] + -IE.] A wharf-labourer; a stevedore or docker.

1912 *Lone Hand* 1 May 40 The best testimonial to Hughes' ability is the fact that he has so often swayed the unruly 'wharfies', and controlled their organisation for so long. **1926** J. DEVANNY *Lenore Divine* vii. 47 Imagine Holly haranguing the wharfies from the soap-box. **1928** *Bulletin*

(Sydney) 21 Mar. 12/1 'Twas Bill the wharfie grinned and stuck his hook into his belt. **1938** W. E. DEXTER *Rope Yarns* 234 Ships arrived [at Melbourne] with general cargo—oddments from a needle to an anchor—and were looked upon as legitimate prey by the warfies and lumpers. **1949** D. M. DAVIN *Roads from Home* 226 They..watched the wharfies unloading. **1963** B. PEARSON *Coal Flat* xx. 355 Sid Holland would put those bloody wharfies and miners in their place. **1978** B. MASON in *Islands* (N.Z.) Aug. 18 But one of his wharfie mates had given him a ticket for his birthday. **1981** *National Times* (Austral.) 25–31 Jan. 24/2 A lazy wharfie would be known as 'the Judge' because he was always sitting on a case, and another 'the London Fog' because he would never lift.

wharfing ('hwɔːfɪŋ). [f. WHARF *sb.*[1] + -ING[1].]
†**1.** = WHARFAGE 1, 2. *Obs. rare.*
1466–7 *Mann. & Househ. Exp.* (Roxb.) 392 Item, fore warffenge at the keye, ob.
2. A structure in the form of a wharf; materials of which a wharf is constructed; the facing of sea-walls, etc. by planks secured by ties.
1691 T. H[ALE] *Acc. New Invent.* p. lxxviii, To go into the Thames..will cost a Man 300l. with the slighter sort of Wharfing. *a* **1700** EVELYN *Sylva* I. ii. (1776) 49 A..strong stone-wall, which was a kind of wharfing against a river running by it. **1724** DE FOE *Tour Gt. Brit.* I. III. 87 The Mill Tayl, or Floor for the Water below the Wheels is Wharft up on either Side with Stone,..at the End of this Wharfing is a Grating of Wood. **1791** R. MYLNE *2nd Rep. Thames* 7 An old Wharfing, bent over into the Stream, which formerly supported a Parish Road along the Shore. **1809** *Naval Chron.* XXIII. 81 The destruction of the wharfing of the basin. **1897** *Jrnl. R. Agric. Soc.* Dec. 612 Wharfing along the sides with short posts and rough boards.

wharfinger ('hwɔːfɪndʒə(r)). Also 8 **wharfenger**. [app. for earlier **wharfager* (f. WHARFAGE + -ER[1]), like *harbinger*, *passenger*, *messenger* for earlier *harbeger*, *passager*, *messager*.] An owner or keeper of a wharf.
1552–3 *Act 7 Edw. VI*, c. 7 §3 No person..shall buy any suche Wood Coles or Fuell but onelye suche as will..consume the same,..without fraude or covine, or Wharfingers or Bargemen. **1642** *Two Orders of Lds. & Comm.* 3 Dec. 2 No Carrier, Waggoner, Watchman, Wharfinger. **1704** *Lond. Gaz.* No. 4024/4 Francis Haslewood, of London, Cornfactor, and Wharfenger. **1761** *Ann. Reg., Chron.* 119 Whether the wharfingers are accountable for the thefts committed on board their lighters. **1858** REDFIELD *Law Railways* xvi. §7. 250 *note*, A delivery to the wharfinger without notice, if warranted by the usage of the place, was sufficient. **1911** SIR H. CRAIK *Life Clarendon* I. ii. 42 Their goods were thus delayed at the caprice of the wharfinger.

wharfless ('hwɔːflɪs), *a.* [f. WHARF *sb.*[1] + -LESS.] Having no wharf.
1822 W. TAYLOR in *Monthly Rev.* XCVII. 35 Wharfless shores. **1906** *Daily Chron.* 10 Mar. 1/7 Exercises in embarkation and disembarkation on a wharfless beach.

wharl (hwɑːl), *v.* Also 5 **warl-**. [Imitative.] *intr.* To pronounce the letter *r* with a burr or guttural sound; = BURR *v.*[3] 1. Hence **wharl** *sb.* = BURR *sb.*[6], **'wharler**, **'wharling** *vbl. sb.*
c **1440** *Promp. Parv.* 37/2 Blaffoorde or warlare, *traulus*. (P. *Traulus peccat in R, peccat in S sidunus.*) *Ibid.* 523/2 Wha[r]lare, in speche. **1610** HOLLAND *Camden's Brit.* I. 517 As for Carleton, as one would say, the husband-mens towne, ..wherein..all in maner that are borne,..have an ilfavoured, untunable, and harsh maner of speech, fetching their words with very much adoe deepe from out of the throat, with a certaine kind of wharling. **1634** W. WOOD *New Eng. Prosp.* II. xviii. 92 The Tarrenteens, whose Tongues runne so much upon *R*, that they wharle much in pronunciation. **1656** DUCH. NEWC. *Natures Pict.* etc. 376 Not stuttering, nor wharling in the throat, or speaking through the Nose. **1661** CHILDREY *Brit. Baconica* 109, I have heard from some that were this Country [Leicestershire] men, that it is Breson that is the Town of the Wharlers, and not Carleton. **1769** *De Foe's Tour Gt. Brit.* (ed. 7) III. 251 The Northumberland R, or Wharle. **1825** JAMIESON.

wharl(e: see QUARREL *sb.*[1], [2], WHORL.

Wharncliffe ('hwɔːnklɪf). The name of James Archibald Stuart-Wortley-Mackenzie, 1st Baron *Wharncliffe* (1776–1845), used *attrib.* and in the possessive to designate a standing order in Parliament which requires the directors of a company wishing to promote any private Bill for the extension of the company's powers to secure the consent of its members or shareholders, or a meeting at which this consent is sought.
1846 *Hansard Lords* 23 Apr. 874 Their Lordships had already required further securities, in particular cases, by the Order called Lord Wharncliffe's Order, which required in the case of established companies, if they..demanded powers beyond their original powers—that..a meeting consisting of three-fifths of the company should have sanctioned the proposed alteration. **1851** ERSKINE MAY *Law of Parl.* (ed. 2) xxvii. 560 It is directed by an order commonly known as 'Lord Wharncliffe's order'. **1887** F. CLIFFORD *Hist. Private Bill Legislation* II. xx. 784 In order to prevent directors of companies from promoting Bills without the knowledge or sanction of shareholders, the House of Lords framed, in 1846, a series of Orders, under which 'Wharncliffe meetings', as they were afterwards termed, must be held, to consider each Bill so promoted. **1923** *Daily Mail* 24 Feb. 3/2 Your approval will be asked at a Wharncliffe Meeting which will be held in the near future. **1948** O. C. WILLIAMS *Hist. Devel. Private Bill Procedure* I. vi. 166 The Wharncliffe Order, then, was *not* first framed in 1846, as Clifford says, but in 1838; it was *not* one of a series of orders, but developed into a series by processes of division and addition; its object was *not* simply to prevent directors of companies from promoting bills without the knowledge and sanction of shareholders but to prevent the promotion of bills to obtain further powers (especially to construct branch lines—always a speculative project) without such sanction.

wharp, erron. form of WARP *sb.* (sense 6).

wharre, wharry, wharrel, var. WHARE, QUARREL *sb.*[2], quarry.

wharrow ('hwærəʊ). Also 6 **whar(r)owe, wherrow(e**, 9 **worra**. [By-form of WHARVE *sb.*] = WHARVE *sb. Obs.* exc. *dial.* (= grooved pulley in spinning-wheel). Also attrib. ***wharrow-spindle*** (a heraldic bearing).
[*c* **1475** *Pict. Voc.* in Wr.-Wülcker 794/18 *Hoc vertebrum*, a aworowylle.] **1519** HORMAN *Vulg.* 149 b, I wotte nat where is my spyndel with the wharowe. *a* **1529** SKELTON *E. Rummyng* 298 Theyr wharrowe, Theyr rybskyn and theyr spyndell. **1578** LYTE *Dodoens* VI. xxix. 695 The fruite whiche is large, and almost fashioned lyke to a wherrowe or buckler. **1610** GUILLIM *Heraldry* IV. vii. 204 The round Ball at the lower end serueth to the fast twisting of the threed, and is called a Wharrow: and thereof this is called a Wharrow Spindle. **1716** S. KENT *Gram. Her.* s.v. *Trefuses of Cornwall*, A Chevron between three Wharrow Spindles Sable. **1825** JENNINGS *Obs. Dial. W. Eng.* 84 The spill and worra are attached to the common spinning-wheel. *c* **1828** BERRY *Encycl. Her.* I. Gloss., *Wharrow-Spindle* is represented in heraldry with a hook at the end, to spin with a distaff.

wharry, dial. f. QUARRY *sb.*[2]

whart(e, wharter, whartfull: see QUART, THWART, WART, QUARTER, QUARTFUL *a.*

wharth, obs. var. WARTH.
c **1450** *St. Cuthbert* (Surtees) 5717 How anes at eland at full se, On þe wharth sodanly, A way wex dry. *Ibid.* 5797–9.

Whartonian (hwɔːˈtəʊnɪən), *a. Anat.* Applied to certain structures discovered or described by Thomas Wharton, English anatomist (1610–73), as ***Whartonian*** (also ***Wharton's***) ***duct, gelatine (jelly)***: see quots.
1840 W. J. E. WILSON *Anat. Vade M.* 474 The excretory duct (Wharton's) of the submaxillary gland commences upon the papilla, by the side of the frænum linguæ. **1857** BULLOCK tr. *Cazeaux' Midwifery* 209 These vessels are surrounded by a gelatinous substance called Wharton's gelatine. **1860** MAYNE *Expos. Lex.*, Whartonian Duct. **1874** C. H. JONES & SIEV. *Path. Anat.* (ed. 2) 137 The Whartonian jelly of the umbilical cord.

wharve (hwɔːv), *sb.* Forms: 1 **hweorfa**, 5–7 **wherve**, (5, 7, 9 **warve**, 9 **warf**), 9 **wharve**. [OE. *hweorfa* = OHG. *werbo*, *werfo* wk. masc., *werbâ* wk. fem. rotating object, whirl, vortex :—**χwerbon*, f. *χwerb-*, as in OE. *hweorfan*, Goth. *hwairban* (see next).] The whorl of a spindle.
c **1000** *Sax. Leechd.* II. 310 Wið ceoc adle, nim þone hweorfan þe wif mid spinnað. **14..** *Lat.-Eng. Voc.* in Wr.-Wülcker 618/46 *Vertebrum*, a wherve, or a reele. **14..** *Metr. Voc.* ibid. 627 Colus cum fuso uertebrum [*glossed* warve, *misprinted* warbe] filum, alabrumque. **1538** ELYOT, *Spondilus*, a wherue, whyche is a rounde thynge of stone, or wodde, or leadde, put on a spyndell to make it runne rounde. **1582** STANYHURST *Æneis*, etc. 95 Three wheru's [orig. *radios*] fyerd glystring, with Soutwynds rufflered huffling. **1590** BARROUGH *Meth. Phisick* v. xxiv. (1596) 339 He did lay and bind vnto Ganglium, a thick round peece of lead like vnto a wherue. **1601** HOLLAND *Pliny* XI. xxiv. I. 323 So fine ..a thread she [*sc.* the spider] spinnes, hanging thereunto her selfe, and using the weight of her owne bodie in stead of a wherve. **1688** HOLME *Armoury* III. xxi. (Roxb.) 266/2 The Warve or small Pullas. *a* **1693** *Urquhart's Rabelais* III. xxviii. 237 Wouldst thou..blunt the Spindles, joynt the Wherves, slander the Spinning Quills,..of the weer'd Sister Parques? **1805** in *Abridgm. Specif. Patents Spinning* (1866) 125 The making the haft or warf at times to shift or remove from off the spindle. **1831** *Ibid.* 236 The warve is driven by a band passing round it and round the spindle drum. **1884** W. S. B. MCLAREN *Spinning* (ed. 2) 171 The wharve, B, together with sliding tube, C, runs loosely on the spindle and carries the bobbin.

†**wharve**, *v. Obs.* Forms: 1 **hwearfian, hweorfan, hwierfan, hwerfan, hwyrfan**, 2 **hwærfan**, 3 **whærfen, whæruen, weruen, hwarefen, warfen**, (*Orm.*) **wharrfenn**. [Three (for the most part) synonymous vbs. existed in OE.: (1) *hweorfan* = OFris. *hwerva* to turn, OS. *hwerban* to turn, change (MLG. *werven* to be active or busy, gain, obtain), OHG. *hwerban*, *hwerfan* (MHG. *werben*, *werfen*) to be active, turn, return, set or be in motion, ON. *hverfa* to turn, return, disappear, Goth. *hwairban* to go; (2) *hwearfian* = OS. *hwarbôn*, OHG. *warbôn*, *warpôn* to wander, proceed, ON. *hvarfa* to turn round, wander, Goth. *hwarbôn*; (3) *hwierfan*, *hwirfan*, etc. = OS. *gihwerbian* to turn, change, OHG. *hwarban*, *hwerban* (MHG. *werben*) to turn, roll, return, *giwerben* to turn, divert, ON. *hverfa* to cause to turn: all f. *χwerb-*: *χwarb-* to turn (cf. prec. and WHARF *sbs.*[1] and [2]).]
1. *trans.* To change, turn. Cf. BLINDWHARVED.
c **897** ÆLFRED *Gregory's Past. C.* xxxvi. 256 He hwierfde his stemne nalles his mod. *c* **1200** ORMIN 13289 & forrþi wass he wurrþ þatt Crist Hiss name himm shollde wharrfenn. *Ibid.* 14137 Forr þatt he wollde..þurrh þe ȝife off Haliȝ Gast Uss wharrfenn all fra sinne. *c* **1200** *Trin. Coll. Hom.* 173 Gief hie wuniende hwarefeð, hie turneð fram iuele to werse. *c* **1205** LAY. 6319 Alfred..whærfde hire nome on his dæȝe and cleopede heo Mærcene laȝe. *Ibid.* 30738 Wið him warfte Brien al his iweden. [**13..** *Gaw. & Gr. Knt.* 2220 He rusched on þat rurde,..& wyth quettyng a-wharf, er he wolde lyȝt.]
2. *intr.* To turn, revolve.
c **888** ÆLFRED *Boeth.* xxxix. §3 þære eaxe þe eall þes rodor on hwerfð. *c* **1200** ORMIN 3641 All þiss middellærdess þing Aȝȝ turrneþþ her & wharrfeþþ..swa summ þe wheol.
3. To roam, wander.
c **890** WÆRFERTH tr. *Gregory's Dial.* IV. lix. (1900) 347 Swa oft swa he wæs hwearfiende mid þam ilcan scipe. *c* **1200** *Trin. Coll. Hom.* 87 He wandrede wide weruende longe sechende him. *c* **1205** LAY. 31680 Eiðer freten oðer, swa hund deð his broðer, and leten heore whelpes whæruen heom bi-sides elc oðer quelle.
4. To proceed, turn out, happen.
c **888** ÆLFRED *Boeth.* iv, ðif seo wyrd swa hweorfan mot on yfelra manna ȝewill. *c* **1200** ORMIN 8420 Swa shall itt tanne wharrfenn Bitwenenn Cristess hallȝhe þeod & deofless laþe genge.
Hence † **wharfed** (*wherrfedd*, *warrfedd*) *ppl. a.*, perverse; whence †'**wharfedlaik**, perversity, error.
c **1200** ORMIN 9721 Forrþi þatt wherrfedd follc hemm hallt Forr gode & forr rihhtwise. *Ibid.* 9825 & tatt wass mikell wherrfeddleȝȝc þatt dide hemm swa to wenenn.

wharve(s: see WHARF *sb.*[1]

whas, obs. f. *was*, pa. t. of BE, WASH *v.*

whas(e: see WHOSE, WHOSO.

whasche, etc.: see WASH *v.*

whasp(e, obs. ff. WASP *sb.*[1]

whassa ('hwɒsə). Also **wassa**. Repr. colloq. or careless pronunc. of 'what is the (matter, etc.)'. Cf. WHAT'SA MATTER.
1906 E. NESBIT *Railway Children* ii. 28 Roberta woke Phyllis... 'Wassermarrer?' asked Phyllis. **1942** BERREY & VAN DEN BARK *Amer. Thes. Slang* §256/14 *What's the matter?*..wha'sa mat?, wha'sa matter?..wazzo maro? **1951** C. M. KORNBLUTH *Marching Morons* in *Best of C. M. Kornbluth* (1977) 156 'Wassamatter?' snorted her husband. **1967** 'W. WRIGHT' *Shadows don't Bleed* v. 84 Whassa matter? You don' believe me? **1973** J. DRUMMOND *Bang! Bang! You're Dead!* xxv. 86 'Wassermatter?' 'I want to join, is all.' **1978** M. KENYON *Deep Pocket* ix. 102 'Whassa time?' A quarter to three.

what (hwɒt), *pron.*, *a.*[1], *adv.*, *conj.*, *int.* (*sb.*) Forms: 1 **hwæt, huæt, huæd**, 1–4 **hwet**, 2–4 **hwat, wet**, 2–5 **wat**, 3 (*Orm.*) **watt, whæt, wæt**, (**waht, wæht, whæht, weht, ȝwat**), 3–4 **whet**, (4 **huet, wad**), 3 (*Orm.*), 5 **whatt**, 3–6 **whate**, (5 **whad, wath**), 5–6 **whatte**, (9 *dial.* or *vulgar* **wot**), 3– **what**; 3–5 *north.* **quat**, (3 **quuat**, 4–5 **quatt, qwat**, 5 **qhat**), 4–8 *Sc.* **quhat**. [OE. *hwæt* = OFris. *hwet*, *wet*, *haet*, *hat*, etc. (Fris. *wæt*, *wat*, *wut*, *haet*, etc.), OS. *huat*, (M)LG., (M)Du. *wat*, OHG. *hwaz*, *waz* (MHG. *waz*, G. *was*), ON. *hvat* (Sw. *vad*, Da. *hvad*), Goth. *hwa*:—OTeut. **χwat*:—Indo-eur. **qʷod* (cf. L. *quod*), neut. sing. of the interrog. pron. **qʷos* WHO, q.v.]
Of the various possible arrangements of the uses of this word the following has been adopted as likely to be most convenient to the reader. The main classification is according to meaning: Branch A. comprises the uses of *what* as an Interrogative, B. as an Exclamatory word, C. as a Relative, D. as an Indefinite (non-relative), and E. as a Substantive. Within these divisions meanings and uses are arranged according to the part of speech; the following is a key to this arrangement:—Pronominal and substantival uses, A. 1–12, B. 6, C. 1–7, D. 1, E. 1–3; Adjectival, A. 13–18, B. 5, C. 8–10; Adverbial or Conjunctional, A. 19–21, B. 4, C. 11–12, D. 2; Interjectional, B. 1–3.
A. Interrogative and allied uses.
I. *pron.* * In direct questions.
1. As the ordinary interrogative pronoun of neuter gender, orig. sing., in later use also pl., used of a thing or things: corresponding to the demonstrative *that* (THAT *dem. pron.* B. 1 a).
c **888** ÆLFRED *Boeth.* xvi. §1 Hwæt mæȝ ic þy mare secgan be þæm weorðscipe..þisse woruldе? **971** *Blickl. Hom.* 15 Hwæt wilt þu þæt ic þe do? *a* **1000** *Sal. & Sat.* xix. (1848) 184 Hwæt hatte Noes wif? *a* **1175** *Cott. Hom.* 233 Unwraste man, wat lacede ȝeu an alle mire rice? *c* **1200** ORMIN 10970 Whatt wass þatt te Faderr sellf þær off hiss Sune seȝȝde? *c* **1205** LAY. 3004 Waet seist tu? *Ibid.* 29623–4 Whæt þenchest þu, Austin, what þenchest þu, leof min? **12..** *Moral Ode* 46 (Egerton MS.) Wet sulle hi segge oþer don at þe muchele dome? **1340** *Ayenb.* 265 Sleȝþe zayþ, 'God, wet ssolle we do?' *a* **1400** *Pistill of Susan* 287 What signefyes, gode sone, þese sawus þat þou seis? *c* **1440** *Alphabet of Tales* 50 þe furste question was þis, What was þe grettest mervayle & fayrest þing þat evur God made in leste rowme? **1470–85** MALORY *Arthur* VI. xiv. 205 What is your broders name? *c* **1485** *Digby Myst.* III. 1249 Qwat sey ȝe? **1560** *Bible* (Geneva) Ezra v. 4 What are the names of the men..? —— Zech. xiii. 6 What are these woundes in thine hands? **1582**

ALLEN *Martyrdom Campion* (1908) 65 One demaunded, 'What do you meane by Catholike Religion?' **1697** DRYDEN *Æneis* x. 949 What will they say of their deserting Chief? **1749** FIELDING *Tom Jones* VIII. xii, 'Nubbing Cheat', cries Partridge, 'pray, Sir, what is that?' *Ibid.* XV. xii, 'What is the Name of the Street?' cries Jones. **1782** MISS BURNEY *Cecilia* VII. ii, Odd people? and in what are we so very odd? **1853** MISS YONGE *Heir of Redclyffe* xxv, What has come to you? **1863** THACKERAY *Round. Papers, Autour de mon Chapeau*, What are the technical words..? **1884** W. S. GILBERT *Princ. Ida* II, *Flo.* But what are these? *Hil.*.. Why, Academic robes, Worn by the lady undergraduates, When they matriculate. **1905** R. BAGOT *Passport* xx, I do not find the female society of Montefiano very—what shall I say?—sharpening to the intellect.

2. Of a person (or persons), in predicative use (cf. THAT *dem. pron.* B. 1 b): formerly generally, in reference to name or identity, and thus equivalent to *who*; in later use only in reference to nature, character, function, or the like. Also in phr. †***what for a*** ... = what kind of: see FOR *prep.* 19 c.

For the OE. construction with a partitive gen. see 13.

c **1000** *Ags. Ps.* (Th.) xxiii[i]. 10 Hwæt is se ʒewuldroda kyning? [L. *Quis est iste rex gloriæ?*] **1000** ÆLFRIC *Gen.* xxvii. 32 Þa cwæð Isaac: Hwæt eart þu? He andwirde and cwæð: Ic eom Esau. *c* **1200** *Trin. Coll. Hom.* 167 Hwat is þis þe astihȝð alse dai rieme? *c* **1205** LAY. 25869 Whæt ært þu, fære wiht [*MS.* whit]? eært þu angel, eært [þu] cnih[t]? *Ibid.* 27372 What beoð þeos ut-laȝen? *a* **1300** *Cursor M.* 3685 'And quat art þou?' þe fader said, 'Sir, i esau, þi met es graithid.' *Ibid.* 13592 'Quat haldes þou þat man?' said þai. 'A prophet,' said he. **1362** LANGL. *P. Pl.* A. II. 15 'What is þis wommon', quod I, 'þus wonderliche A-tyret?' *c* **1400** *Sowdone Bab.* 1623 What be ye, That make here this ruly moone? *c* **1430**, *c* **1440**, **1470–85** [see HIGHT *v.*[1] B. 5 β b, d]. *c* **1489** CAXTON *Sonnes of Aymon* iv. 120 What ben ye, lordes, that are soo countrefayt, are ye paynemes, or of what countrey ben ye? **1526** TINDALE *Rev.* vii. 13 What are these which are arayed in longe whyte garmentes? *a* **1596** *Sir T. More* I. i. 47 What art thou that talkest of reuendge? **1596** SHAKS. *Tam. Shr.* IV. ii. 62 *Tra.* What is he Biondello? *Bion.* Master, a Marcantant, or a pedant, I know not what. **1604** —— *Oth.* I. i. 94 *Bra.*.. What are you? *Rod.* My name is Rodorigo. **1691** in J. Russell *Haigs* (1881) 325 For it is not now as it was of old, *What is he?*..but, *What has he?* **1753** FOOTE *Englishm. in Paris* I. i, *Buck*...And what are you, hey? *Barb.* Je suis Peruquier, Monsieur. **1781** COWPER *Hope* 497 What were they? what some fools are made by art, They were by nature, atheists. **1860** DICKENS *Uncomm. Trav.* v, 'You noticed that young man, sir, in at Darby's?' 'Yes. What is he?' 'Deserter, sir.' **1871** TENNYSON *Last Tourn.* 755 About his feet A voice clung sobbing till he question'd it, 'What art thou?'

3. a. In rhetorical questions, implying an emphatic contrary assertion.

what am I but..? is equivalent to 'I am nothing but..', ***what did he*** (*do*) ***but..?*** to 'He actually did..', ***what can he not do?*** to 'He can do anything'.

c **1000** ÆLFRIC *Hom.* I. 346 Hwæt sind þas buton ðrymsetl heora Scyppendes, on ðam ðe he wuniʒende mannum demð? *c* **1175** *Lamb. Hom.* 17 Hwet halt þe wredðe? **1340** *Ayenb.* 137 Huet am ich bote esssse and spearken? *c* **1384** CHAUCER *H. Fame* III. 546 What did this Eolus but he Toke out hys blake trumpe of bras. *c* **1440** LYDG. *Hors, Shepe & G.* 420 What but thi wolle was cause of al the striff? *c* **1440** *Gesta Rom.* xl. 159 What dude he but purveyde him of so muche mony? **1535** COVERDALE *2 Esdras* xvi. 5 Plages are sent vnto you, & what is he that wyl dryue them awaye? **1593** SHAKS. *Lucr.* 414 What could he see but mightily he noted? What did he note, but strongly he desired? **1599** NASHE *Lenten Stuffe* 48 What did me he, but..chopt aloft. **1611** *Bible* Judges xiv. 18 What is sweeter then honie? and what is stronger then a Lion? **1681** DRYDEN *Abs. & Achit.* I. 303 What cannot Praise effect in Mighty Minds? **1780** *Mirror* No. 96 ¶6 Give a young woman admiration, and what more can she wish for? **1798** WORDSW. *We are Seven* 4 A simple Child, That lightly draws its breath,..What should it know of death? **1866** GEO. ELIOT *Ess.* (1884) 329 What else is the meaning of our Trades-Unions?

b. In predicative quasi-adj. use: Of what account, consequence, value, or force?

c **825** *Vesp. Ps.* cxliii[i]. 3 *Quid est homo quia innotuisti ei?* hwet is monn ðæt ðu cuðades him? **1388** WYCLIF *2 Sam.* vii. 18 Who am Y, my Lord God, and what is myn hows, that thou brouȝtist me hidur to? **1546** J. HEYWOOD *Prov.* (1867) 77 What is a woorkman, without his tooles? **1734** POPE *Ess. Man* IV. 237 What's Fame? a fancy'd life in others' breath. **1781** COWPER *Truth* 107 Your sentence and mine differ. What's a name? **1841** BROWNING *Pippa passes* III. ad fin. (*Song*), What's death? You'll love me yet! **1851** *Househ. Words* 6 Sept. 553/1 What are my strength and weight compared with that one pillar? **1885** 'MRS. ALEXANDER' *At Bay* ix, I am an Englishman of unblemished character. What would your assertion be against mine?

4. a. With ellipsis, esp. of the remainder of the question; hence (*colloq.*) short for 'What did you say?' or 'What is it?'

13.. *Seuyn Sag.* (W.) 2193 'On the falle..swich a maner vileynie, As hadde the burgeis for his pie.' 'O, maister, he saide, what? what? I the praie, tel me that.' *c* **1460** *Towneley Myst.* iv. 183 *Isaac.* A, good sir, abide; ffader! *Abraham*, What son? *Isaac.* to do youre will I am redy. **1534** MORE *Comf. agst. Trib.* III. Wks. 1224/1 Why wife quod her housebande what woulde you doe? What? by God goe forwarde with the beste. **1667** MILTON *P.L.* II. 165 What when we fled amain,..and besought The Deep to shelter us? **1834** DICKENS *Sk. Boz, Steam Excurs.*, 'Oh! oh!—I'm so frightened!' 'What at, dear?—what at?' said the mother. **1837** —— *Pickw.* xix, 'What's your name?' 'Cold punch', murmured Mr. Pickwick, as he sunk to sleep again. 'What?' demanded Captain Boldwig. No reply. **1898** M. M. DOWIE *Crook of Bough* i, 'That's a queer start o' young Sam's', said one voice. 'Wot is?' said another.

b. Substituted for a word or phrase of which explanation is asked.

1676 SHADWELL *Virtuoso* I. 11 *Sir Sam.* Gad I'll do't instantly, in the twinkling of a Bed-staff... *Bruce.* In the twinkling of what? *a* **1814** *Manœuvring* I. i. in *New Brit. Theatre* II. 78 Sure enough, my lady's the greatest policizer under the sun. *Kit.* Polly what? **1825** T. HOOK *Sayings* Ser. II. *Passion & Princ.* xi. III. 218 'Here, Sir, take away the Tiffin'. 'The what, Sir Frederick?' said the principal waiter. 'The Tiffin, Sir', repeated his Excellency, in a voice of thunder. **1837** DICKENS *Pickw.* xlii, 'Your chummage ticket will be on twenty-seven, in the third.' 'Oh', said Mr. Pickwick. 'My what, did you say?' **1880** MRS. PARR *Adam & Eve* II. 47 'Bacause—' 'Because what?'.. 'Because you've —' but before the sentence could be finished, Eve had flown upstairs.

c. As an interrogative expletive (sometimes with *eh*) usually at the end of a sentence, esp. in recent trivial or affected colloq. use.

1785 MME. D'ARBLAY *Diary* 19 Dec., He [*sc.* George III] said, 'What? what?'—meaning, what say you?.. 'it is not possible. Do you think it is?—what?' **1850** *Househ. Words* 16 Nov. 177/2 What is all that about the—eh—what—law of ex—what?—pansion—eh? *c* **1891** 'J. S. WINTER' *Lumley* xv, But then, she's so beastly *chic*, dontcherknow—eh, what! **1906** MANSFIELD *Girl & Gods* xvi, Good-bye, Miss Thornton, awfully jolly evening—what? **1914** A. N. LYONS *Simple Simon* I. i. 16 Can't say I've read it. It's a bit too literary for me. What? But they say it's jolly clever. You had it at school, I dare say. What?

5. Phrases. a. In elliptical phr. with adv., conj., or prep., the precise sense of which varies with and may usually be inferred from the context or circumstances: cf. defs. below.

what else? what else should be the case?; used as an emphatic affirmative reply: = certainly! †***what for-thy?*** what of that? (see FOR-THY *conj.* b); also parenthetically as advb. phr. = in spite of that, nevertheless. ***what if*** (†***what and, what an***(*d if* arch.)..? what is or would be the case if..? what will or would happen if..? what does it matter if..? etc.; often expressing a hypothesis or proposal: = 'suppose..', 'supposing..'. ***what of..?*** what is to be said of..? what do you think of..? what comes of or follows from..? etc. ***what then?*** what happens or would happen in that case? what of that? (see THEN *adv.* 4); so ***what next?*** ***what though..?*** (somewhat *arch.*) what happens or would happen in view of the fact that, or on the supposition that..? (nearly = *what if..?*, but implying some opposition between the circumstance mentioned and the possible one implied: cf. THOUGH 4); †also absol. ***what though?*** what if it is (or were) so? what does it matter? what then? See also WHAT-NOT.

c **1200** ORMIN 8105 Acc whatt forrþi nass þatt nohht don. *c* **1290** *S. Eng. Leg.* 18/591 'Ȝwat nou?' quath þis bolde maister: 'ȝwy ne habbe ȝe him i-brouȝt?' *c* **1420** *Wyclif's Bible, Pref. Ep. St. Jerome* ii. 63 What if thilk beest ȝe hadden herd tellinge his owne wordis! *c* **1440** *Alphabet of Tales* 74 Saynt Basll sayd; 'what & I dye nott or tomorn?' **1509** HAWES *Past. Pleas.* xvi. (1555) Kj, What thoughe quod he, draw you not abacke. **1513** DOUGLAS *Æneis* IV. Prol. 200 Quhat of bewte, quhar honestie lyis deid? **1564** [see THEN *adv.* 4]. **1588** SHAKS. *Tit. A.* IV. iv. 9 What and if His sorrowes haue so ouerwhelm'd his wits? **1590** —— *Mids. N.* I. i. 228, I am thought as faire as she. But what of that? Demetrius thinkes not so. **1591** LYLY *Midas* IV. iii, *Pet.* Wel, tis hard to haue ones browes imbroidered with bugle. *Licio.* But canst thou blowe it? *Hunts.* What els? *Min.* But not away. **1600** SHAKS. *A.Y.L.* III. iii. 51 Heere wee haue no Temple but the wood... But what though? Courage. **1667** MILTON *P.L.* II. 174 What if all Her stores were op'n'd, and this Firmament Of Hell should spout her Cataracts of Fire. **1742** POPE *Dunc.* IV. 255 What tho' we let some better sort of fool Thrid ev'ry science, run thro' ev'ry school? **1766** GOLDSM. *Vicar W.* xx, My ship sails to-morrow;..what if you go in her as a passenger? **1819** KEATS *Otho* I. i, To me! What of me, ha? **1827** HEBER *Hymn, 'From Greenland's Icy Mountains'* ii, What though the spicy breezes Blow soft o'er Ceylon's isle... In vain with lavish kindness The gifts of God are strown. **1847** C. BRONTE *Jane Eyre* xix, But if..they ..dropped off and left me one by one, what then? **1876** BROWNING *Fears & Scruples* x, What, and if your friend at home play tricks? **1889** 'J. S. WINTER' *Mrs. Bob* ii, 'Did anybody tell you about the Manor Lodge?' 'No, not a word; what about it?' **1914** 'IAN HAY' *Knt. on Wheels* xiii. §5 Game and rubber..! Now, what about bed?

b. In various other phr. (See also 8, 10, 11.)

†***what is thee?*** [THEE *pron.* 1 b], what is the matter with thee? †***what lack you?*** or ***what do you lack?*** [LACK *v.*[1] 3], a salesman's cry; hence as an appellation for an itinerant vendor or pedlar. ***what say you*** (mod. ***what do you say***) ***to..? what think you*** (mod. ***what do you think***) ***of..?*** are you inclined for..? how would you like..? ***what say?*** (*slang*, orig. *U.S.*), what did (or do) you say? shall we? (cf. SAY *v.*[1] 2 m). ***what's my thought?*** a guessing game (the same as *yes and no*: see YES 1 b). ***what's with..?*** (*colloq.*, orig. and chiefly *U.S.*), what's the matter with..?, what has happened to? (see also quot. 1962). See also WHAT-D'YE-CALL, WHAT'S-HIS-NAME.

1297 R. GLOUC. (Rolls) 2720 Þo sede on to an oþer, merlin, wat is þe? Þou faderlese ssrewe, wy misdostou me? *c* **1300** *Havelok* 1951 Bernard, hwat is þe? Hwo haues þe þus ille maked?

1589 GREENE *Menaphon* Wks. (Grosart) VI. 14 A secular wit that hath liued all daies of his life by what doo you lacke. **1597** BRETON *Wit's Trenchmour* Wks. (Grosart) II. 16/2 The sonne of What lacke you, was become the onely right worshipfull. **1614** J. COOKE *Greene's Tu Quoque* B 1, What lacke you sir? faire stuffes or veluets? **1663** KILLIGREW *Parson's Wedd.* I. i, His Father was a..Pedler, a what do you lack, Sir.

1596 SHAKS. *Tam. Shr.* IV. iii. 17 What say you to a Neats foote? **1649** DK. NEWCASTLE *Country Capt.* II. i. 23 Betweene us too, what thinke you of a wench? **1749** FIELDING *Tom Jones* X. iv, 'What think you of some Eggs and Bacon, Madam?', said the Landlady. **1793** COWPER *Beau's Reply* 27 What think you, Sir, of killing Time With verse address'd to me?

1825 J. NEAL *Bro. Jonathan* I. 357 'Was he hurt, uncle Harwood?' 'What say?' **1855** W. G. SIMMS *Forayers* 52 What 'say, boys—won't a back-and-rush of the nags do it? **1934** S. LEWIS *Work of Art* 294, I think it would be fun to run up the Hudson to Ye Bunche of Grapes some noon. What say? **1966** *New Yorker* 24 Dec. 25 What say we skip a few 'fa-la-la's'? **1972** 'B. GRAEME' *Tomorrow's Yesterday* iii. 32 What say we have coffee at home for once?

1847 TENNYSON *Princess* Prol. 188 We..like as many girls ..play'd Charades..And *what's my thought* and *when and where and how*.

1940 J. O'HARA *Pal Joey* 125 Nick what's with the free food? Explain. **1960** 'E. MCBAIN' *Killer's Choice* ix. 97 'What's with this kosher bit?' he asked. 'Get me some butter.' **1962** *Amer. Speech* XXXVII. 203 The elliptical 'What's with..?' (*Vos iz mit..?*) also has occurred, not only in the sense of 'What's new?'..but also as a substitute for 'What's the matter with..?' (a sense common in Yiddish). **1976** *National Observer* (U.S.) 24 Jan. 1/1 But it's not easy, because an interloper keeps asking depressing questions—such as: How do you feel about the state of the country? What's with the economy? **1977** H. FAST *Immigrants* III. 172 There are ways to find out what's with Jake.

¶ ***but what?*** (a Gallicism = *mais quoi?*): but, after all.

1586 T. B. *La Primaud. Fr. Acad.* I. 59 Ye shall have verie few, but saie, that they are enimies to evill... But what? As they never knew what goodnes ment, so they know as litle of the contrarie. **1605** ERONDELLE *Fr. Gard.* N 7 b, O Marguerite!..thou hast beene heeretofore greatly esteemed in France, but what? all other thinges doe wither,..as well as flowers.

c. ***what about it?***: an enquiry as to the course of action to be adopted.

1927 H. A. VACHELL *Dew of Sea* 259 Your head keeper says we must have two guns apiece. Now—what about it? **1935** D. L. SAYERS *Gaudy Night* viii. 163 'I say,' said Mr. Farringdon, '.. you simply *must* come.'.. 'What about it?' said Harriet, deferring to Mr. Pomfret.

** In dependent clauses. (In early use occas. followed by *that* (THAT *conj.* 6).)

Here the interrogative force varies according to the nature of the principal clause; after verbs or phrases of asking, wondering, or the like, the dependent clause is more or less explicitly an indirect question (e.g. 'I asked him what he meant' = 'I asked him "What do you mean?"'); after verbs or phrases of knowing, saying, or the like, it is only implicitly so, but the sense is essentially the same, and is to be distinguished from the compound relative (= 'that which': see C. I.* below), which however it sometimes closely approaches, the construction being often identical; cf. 'I did not know what he meant' (which implies the mental question 'What did he mean?') with 'I did not hear what he said' (where *what* simply = 'that which').

The dependent clause may by inversion of construction become a subject-clause: e.g. 'What he meant was unknown to me' = 'I did not know what he meant.' (Cf. quot. 1766 s.v. HOW *adv.* 8 a.)

6. In indirect questions, and clauses of similar meaning (see remarks above): corresponding to the direct use in 1. Of a thing: either (*a*) in finite clause, or (*b*) as obj. of a following infinitive (cf. TO *prep.* B. 16).

735 BÆDA *Death song* 4 To ymbhycggannae..huaet his gastae..doemid uueorthae. *c* **897** ÆLFRED *Gregory's Past. C.* lii. 405 He..him ʒetæhte hwæt hi on ðæm don sceolden, hwæt ne scolden. **1154** *O.E. Chron.* (Laud MS.) an. 1137 Nu we willen sæʒen sumdel wat belamp on Stephnes kinges time. *a* **1200** *Moral Ode* 79 He wat wet þenkeð and hwet doð alle quike wihte. *c* **1200** ORMIN 2904 Josæp..mikell ummbeþohhte, Off whatt himm wære bettst to don. *Ibid.* 2992, 3 Þatt birrþ uss lokenn whatt itt iss & whatt itt wile seggenn. *c* **1205** LAY. 25334 Ær heom mihte iwurðen waht heo don wolde. *a* **1250** *Owl & Night.* 1441 Hit nuste neauer hwat hit was. *c* **1290** *S. Eng. Leg.* 11/350 He..Axede heom of þe croyz ȝwat were þe tokningue. **1297** R. GLOUC. (Rolls) 9249 To loke wat were best to do. **1340** *Ayenb.* 264 Me him acseþ huo he ys, huannes he comþ, huet he heþ ysoȝe. **1390** GOWER *Conf.* I. 3 What schal befalle hierafterward God wot. **1450** *Paston Lett.* Suppl. (1901) 31 Qhat the cawse is I wote nott. **1501** DOUGLAS *Pal. Hon.* I. lxii, He demandit my answer, quhat I said? **1533** GAU *Richt Vay* 7 It is neidful first to ane seik man to knaw quhat is his seiknes. **1568** GRAFTON *Chron.* II. 89 Demaunding of them what the matter was. **1588** SHAKS. *L.L.L.* III. i. 160 O thou knowest not what it is. **1601** —— *Twel. N.* III. iii. 9 Iealousie, what might befall your trauell. **1671** MILTON *Samson* 1346, I am sorry what this stoutness will produce. **1749** FIELDING *Tom Jones* XV. vii, No to be sure, it signifies nothing what becomes of them. **1773** GOLDSM. *Stoops to Conq.* II. i, I believe they are in actual consultation upon what's for supper. **1782** MISS BURNEY *Cecilia* X. ii, Something strange..must have happened, but what, she had no means to know. **1849** MACAULAY *Hist. Eng.* V. I. 540 What such a force..could effect..was proved, a few years later, at Killiecrankie. **1850** *Househ. Words* 15 June 285/1 It will be time enough then to think what next. **1889** STEVENSON *Master of Ballantrae* vi. 186 Has it never come in upon your mind what you are doing? **1891** *Speaker* 2 May 532/2 The Socialist no longer thinks of dictating to society what it ought to be.

(*b*) *c* **1400** *R. Gloucester's Chron.* (Rolls) 9237 (MS. B.) Hii nuste wat to do. **1581** MARBECK *Bk. Notes* 1171 Haue alwaies what to doe in your hands. **1624** CAPT. J. SMITH *Virginia* I. 16 We tooke more Cod then we knew what to doe with. **1697** DRYDEN *Æneis* IV. 423 Jove will inspire him, when, and what to say. **1713** BERKELEY *Hylas & Phil.* I. (1725) 47, I know not what to think of it. **1883** D. C. MURRAY *Hearts* ii, Cousin Mark was not burdened with more money than he knew what to do with.

7. Of a person, in predicative use (with distinctions of sense as in 2).

c **897** ÆLFRED *Gregory's Past. C.* xxi. 158 Ðonne eow misliciað þa medtrymnessa þe ʒe on oðrum monnum ʒesioð, ðonne ʒeðence ʒe hwæt ʒe sien & hwelce ʒe sien. *c* **1290** *St. Brandan* 627 in *S. Eng. Leg.* 237 Ich eschte him ȝwat he were. He seide, 'ich am þin Abbot.' **1297** R. GLOUC. (Rolls) 919 Þe king eschte wat hii were. *a* **1300** *Cursor M.* 4931 Þe folk asked quat þai suld be, 'Theues,' coth ioseph. *c* **1386** CHAUCER *Can. Yeom. Prol. & T.* 63 Is he a clerk or noon? telle what he is. *c* **1489** CAXTON *Blanchardyn* xxvi. 99 The kynge, that gretli desired to knowe of his estate, asked of hym what he was, of what lande and of what lynage. **1542** UDALL *Erasm. Apoph.* Table X iij, Athlete [= -æ], what they be that are so called. **1596** [see 2]. **1604** SHAKS. *Oth.* IV. i. 74 And knowing what I am, I know what she shallbe. **1605** in Dixon *Tower* (1870) II. xi. 104 To ansoure to formall interrogatours..as quhat he is, for I can neuer yett heare of any man that knowis him. **1697** DAMPIER *Voy.* I. 301 To write a Letter to the Governor, to inform him what we were, and on what account we came. **1697** DRYDEN *Æneis* VI. 1194 He..ask'd his airy Guide, What, and of whence was he. **1832** DISRAELI *Cont. Fleming* vii, I was to be something great, and glorious, and dazzling; but what, we could not determine. **1854** R. S. SURTEES *Handley Cr.* ii, Who or what he was,..no one ever cared to inquire.

8. Phrases. **a.** ***to know what's what*** [KNOW *v.* 15]: to understand the qualities or values of things; to have a good judgement or apprehension; to have clear or full knowledge of the matter in hand, or of the state of the case; to know what is fitting or profitable. So with other verbs, as *perceive*, *show*, etc. *colloq.*

c **1400** *Ywaine & Gaw.* 432 Ful sarily than thare i sat, For wa i wist noght what was what. **1421-2** HOCCLEVE *Dial.* 778 in *Min. Poems* 138 They me oghten haue in greet cheertee, And elles woot I neuere what is what. *a* **1500** *Chaucer's Dreme* 1296 Neither knew I kirke ne saint Ne what was what ne who was who. *a* **1553** UDALL *Royster D.* I. ii. (Arb.) 17 Enamoured quod you? haue ye spied out that? Ah sir, mary nowe I see you know what is what. **1600** ROWLANDS *Lett. Humours Blood* Epigr. xxv. 31 Tut, tell me not whats what; I know the law. **1663** BUTLER *Hud.* I. I. 149 He knew what's what, and that's as high As Metaphysick Wit can fly. **1737** BRACKEN *Farriery Impr.* (1757) II. 215, I dare venture to say ..that not a common Farrier in the Universe knows what's what. **1860** THACKERAY *Lovel* v, I had so much claret on board, I did not much know what was what. **1911** *Times* 26 Oct. 8/4 My distinguished friend..who appeared as a witness had told me what was what.

b. Phrases used as sbs. ***I know*** or ***wot not*** (mod. ***I don't know***) ***what***, ***Lord*** or ***God knows what*** (LORD *sb.* 6b, GOD 10b), ***who knows what?*** †***know-not-what*** (see KNOW-), ***watna what*** (see WATNA), etc.: something unknown or only vaguely apprehended or suggested; cf. L. *nescio quid*, F. *je ne sais quoi*. So ...***and*** (***I don't know***) ***what all*** (*colloq.*) = '...and various other things unknown or unspecified', '...and all sorts of things besides'. ***you know what***, †(***you***) ***wot what***: something that need not be specified (see YOU 11).

a **1000** *Riddles* liv. [lv], Hyse..hrand under gyrdels hyre stondendre stiþes nathwæt. *c* **1560** A. SCOTT *Poems* (S.T.S.) xxx. 39 Thay luve no man effeminat, And haldis thame, bot I wat not quhat, That can nocht be w^tout thame. **1568** GRAFTON *Chron.* II. 765 Sent, no man wist whether, to be done wyth, God wot what. **1570** *Satir. Poems Reform* xv. 115 ȝe worke maist lyke ȝe wat not quhat With your Politick heidis. **1587** in W. M. Williams *Ann. Founders' Co.* (1867) 70 Which when they did see they putt theyre hands they could not tell to whatt. **1603** HOLLAND *Plutarch's Mor.* 154 When he was about to speake (I wot not what) as touching painting-craft. **1662** *Rump Songs* I. 52 Next come those idle Twittle-twats, Which calls me many God-knows-whats. **1701** WALLIS in *Collect.* (O.H.S.) I. 330 Under penalty of ..(who knows what?). **1702** S. PARKER tr. *Cicero's De Finibus* Transl. Pref., The Grandeur, Eloquence, Neatness, and I know not what all, of an Author's Expression. **1823** [see GOD 10b]. **1840** THACKERAY *Barber Cox* Aug., Shouting out, 'Aha!' and '*Sapprrrristie!*' and I don't know what. **1856** THOREAU *Let. to Mr. B.* 21 May, So we shall save some of our money..and lose—I do not know what. **1859** DICKENS *Haunted House* vii. 33/1 There's examins, and catechizes, and I dunno what all for him to be put through. **1901** H. SUTCLIFFE *Barbara Cunliffe* 9 Some reckon Tib helps him wi' his black magic, an' his turning stones to gold, an' what all. **1942** W. FAULKNER *Go down, Moses* 76 My mind gonter change about whatall I seed. **1947** E. MEYNELL *Sussex* ix. 225 Sheep are most unfortunate creatures in the infections to which they are liable—the foot rot..and the liver-fluke and what all. **1957** J. KEROUAC *On Road* (1958) III. iv. 202 Weariness and..sorrow and what-all was on his mind. **1962** A. LURIE *Love & Friendship* vii. 123 That old Mr Higginson... Got his house full of bird dirt and what-all.

c. ***to know what it is***: to apprehend what it implies or may involve; hence, to have had experience of it. Usually with *inf.*

1592 SHAKS. *Ven. & Ad.* 615 Thou know'st not what it is, With iauelings point a churlish swine to goare. **1608** KELLISON *Reply to Sotcliffe's Answ.* Ep. Ded. a v, Till miserie had taught the prodigal Sonne wit, he neuer knew what it was to liue at home in his Fathers howse. **1711** ADDISON *Spect.* No. 26 ¶7 Though I am always serious, I do not know what it is to be melancholy. **1860** THACKERAY *Round. Papers, On Two Children in Black*, As for the first night at a strange school, we most of us remember what *that* is. **1901** W. R. H. TROWBRIDGE *Lett. her Mother To Eliz.* xiii. 58 To know what dust is, you must come to Switzerland in August; the road was like driving through sand.

d. *ellipt.* for 'what it is', 'what is the truth of the matter', 'what is the thing to do', or the like, in ***I('ll) tell you what*** (and similar phrases now *obs.* or *dial.*), used to emphasize or call special attention to what is said (= 'let me tell you'), or (*mod. colloq.*) in making a proposal. Also ***that's what; you know what?***

c **1384** CHAUCER *H. Fame* III. 694 Ye be lyke the swynt catte That wolde haue fisshe, but wostow whatte He wold no thinge wete his clowes. **1576** GASCOIGNE *Steele Glas* (Arb.) 78 Disdaine him not: for shal I tel you what? Such clime to heauen, before the shauen crownes. **1592** SHAKS. *Rom. & Jul.* I. v. 86 This tricke may chance to scath you, I know what, You must contrary me. **1594** —— *Rich. III*, III. ii. 92 Wot you what, my Lord, To day the Lords you talke of, are beheaded. **1596** —— *Merch. V.* I. i. 86, I tell thee what Anthonio, I loue thee. **1657** in *Brand's Pop. Antiq.* (Bohn) I. 121 I'le tell thee what, To-morrow thou shalt see Me weare the willow. **1773** G. A. STEVENS *Trip Portsm.* i. 10 *Sir Flimsey.* I'll tell you *what*, madam—. *Miss Flirt.* And I'll tell you *when*, Sir Flimsey. When you take a lady out with you, don't domineer so. **1872** *Routledge's Ev. Boy's Ann.* June 442/1 I'll tell you what, we'll row down. **1899** H. WYNDHAM *Soldiers of Queen* viii. 176 Tell you what, Bill, you can start your stock with one of my old shirts for the price of a quart. **1902** *Dialect Notes* II. 247 *That's what*, exclamation of affirmation or assent. **1908** L. M. MONTGOMERY *Anne of Green Gables* xv. 165 She'll..be ready enough to go back of her own accord, that's what. **1960** H. PINTER *Room* 98 You know what though? It looks a bit better. It's not so windy. **1965** 'LAUCHMONEN' *Old Thom's Harvest* ii. 29 'You don't bring anybody.'..'Oh—oh. That's what. **1982** H. ENGEL *Murder on Location* xviii. 164 'You know what, Chris?' 'What?' 'You know it stinks to heaven as well as I do.'

*** Various special uses and collocations (in direct questions or in dependent clauses). See also 17.

For *what becomes* (*is become*, etc.) *of*... see BECOME *v.* 4.

9. With intensive additions, as ***what the deuce*** (***devil, dickens***, etc.), ***what in the name of***..., ***what in the world, what on earth***, etc.: see also the sbs. (Cf. HOW *adv.* 1b.)

c **1385-** [see DEVIL *sb.* 20]. **1596-** [see PLAGUE *sb.* 3d]. **1600-** [see DICKENS a.]. **1614** JACKSON *Creed* II. 133 What a Gods name, hinders him from doing it? **1709** STEELE & ADDISON *Tatler* No. 110 ¶4 What-a-Pox hast thou to do with Ladies and Lovers? **1757-** [see DEUCE² b¹.]. **1818** SHELLEY *Ess. & Lett.* (1852) II. 116 What on earth does he mean by some of his inferences? **1829** SCOTT *Anne of G.* xii, Thinking what in the universe it could be made of. **1836** [see HELL *sb.* 9]. **1897** S. CRANE *Third Violet* xv. 101 What the mischief have I done? *Ibid.* xvi. 105, I wonder what in blue thunder you mean.

10. Of quantity, amount, or price: How much, how many. So of the time of day, in ***what's o'clock, what's the time*** (see CLOCK *sb.*¹ 3, 5, TIME *sb.* 13).

The orig. use was with partitive gen.; later, partitive *of* occurs.

c **1000** *Ags. 'Ps.'* (Th.) cxviii[i]. 84 Hwæt synt þinum esne ealra dagena? *c* **1420** *Avow. Arth.* xxxiii, Quat is thi rawunsun opon ry3te? *c* **1425** *Crafte Nombrynge* (E.E.T.S.) 26 Yf þou wold wete qwat is 4 hundryth times 4. **1508** DUNBAR *Gold. Targe* 274, I knaw quhat thou of rethorike hes spent. *c* **1525** *Vox Populi* 374 in Hazl. *E.P.P.* III. 281, I knowe not whates a clocke, But by the countre cocke. **1557** *Order of Hospitalls* C vij b, That there be geven Warrants.. what shall be paid to any such Pencioner wekly. **1600** SHAKS. *A.Y.L.* III. ii. 319, I pray you, what i'st a clocke? **1669** STURMY *Mariner's Mag.* I. ii. 34 As 16 to 7: So is 8 to what? **1814** *J. H. Moore's Pract. Navig.* (ed. 19) 130 What is Greenwich Time when it is Noon 75°, or Five Hours, West of Greenwich? **1816** SCOTT *Bl. Dwarf* ix, But I'll see what o' them can be gotten back. **1835** DICKENS *Sk. Boz, Parlour Orator*, He can tell what's o'clock by an eight-day, without looking at the minute hand, he can. **1859** *Habits Gd. Soc.* xi. 305 What of that essential harmony..can there possibly be between a hundred..people? **1904** SIR H. HAWKINS *Remin.* II. 2 Lloyd must have made £20,000 a year..; what I made is of no consequence.

11. a. ***what for*** (introducing a clause (a non-standard use); sometimes written as one word; Sc. and north. dial.; earlier north. ME. †*for what*, replacing OE. *for hwan*); now, in polite colloq. use, only ***what...for*** (in independent or dependent clause), or ***what for?***: for what purpose, with what object? for what reason, why, wherefore? Also †***through what***: how? So †***what to*** (***till***): to what end, whereto.

c **1200** ORMIN 199 Þurrh whatt ma33 icc nu witenn þiss? *Ibid.* 4814, 5 Forr whatt iss Drihhtin me þuss wraþ? *Ibid.* 14113 Forr all mannkinn to shæwenn swa Forr whatt he comm onn erþe. *c* **1250** *Gen. & Ex.* 1657 Iacob tolde him for quat he swanc So fer. **1375** BARBOUR *Bruce* XI. 28 (Camb. MS.) God..wat quhat-to [*Edin. MS.* quhat-till] all thing efferis. *c* **1760** D. HUME in *Ramsay's Remin.* v. (ed. 18) 116 What for should I burn a' my..bukies? **1799** BURNS '*What ails ye now*', ix, 'Geld you!' quo' he, 'and whatfor no?' **1823** GALT *R. Gilhaize* lx, The children wondered whatfor an honest man should be brought to punishment. **1857** HUGHES *Tom Brown* II. i, The boot he had just pulled off flew straight at the head of the bully..'Confound you, Brown, what's that for?' **1879** F. W. ROBINSON *Coward Consc.* I. viii, What are you staring at a fellow like that for? **1948** E. WAUGH *Loved One* 51 What for you want new ideas? **1984** J. PLATT et al. *New Englishes* vii. 127 *What for* you want to do that?

b. When subordinated ***what...for*** comes to mean 'the reason why'.

1714 R. FIDDES *Pract. Disc.* II. 236 But what I cited all these passages for is to show [etc.].

c. As sb. phr. in the slang phr. ***to give*** (one) ***what for*** = to inflict severe pain or chastisement. Also, ***to show*** (someone) ***what for***: to make him take notice; to show who is in charge.

1873 *Routledge's Yng. Gentl. Mag.* Feb. 137/1 It'll give you what for if it touches your lips. **1894** DU MAURIER *Trilby* I. 31 Taffy..was a match for any *maître d'armes* in the whole French army, and Svengali got 'what for'. **1960** N. HILLIARD *Maori Girl* 142 If a man came here I took a liking to, I'd show him what-for soon enough. **1966** *Listener* 18 Aug. 229/1 The stereotype of 'the wily oriental gentleman.. the half-civilized levantine.. the type of fellow who must be shown what for'.

12. As indefinite final alternative in a disjunctive question. Chiefly *colloq.*

1766 J. ADAMS *Diary* 29 July, Wks. 1856 II. 198 In what is this man conspicuous?—in reasoning, in imagination, in painting, in the pathetic, or what? **1769** G. WHITE *Selborne, To Pennant* 28 Feb., Is it owing to the vast, massy buildings of that place, to the many waters round it, or to what else? **1842** E. FITZGERALD *Let. to Barton* 16 Sept., Have you supposed me dead or what? **1884** tr. *Lotze's Logic* 341 We shall further discover whether the true path is a circle, an ellipse, an oval, or what.

II. *adj.*

13. a. (*a*) As the ordinary interrogative adjective, sing. or pl., used of a thing or things, a person or persons, in direct questions: often with ellipsis, as ***what cheer?*** (CHEER *sb.*¹ 3b), ***what news?*** etc.

The meaning was expressed in OE. by *hwæt* with a partitive gen.

[*Beowulf* 237 Hwæt syndon ȝe searohæbbendra byrnum werede? *c* **897** ÆLFRED *Gregory's Past. C.* xxi. 164 Hwæt is ðinga þe biterre sie on ðæs lareowes mode..ðonne se anda ðe for ryhtwisnesse bið upahafen?] *a* **1225** *St. Marher.* 4 Hwet godd heiestu ant hersumest? *a* **1300** *Cursor M.* 29034 Quat bote is fra mete to min And dedeli for to lig in sin? **1382** WYCLIF *1 John* iii. 12 And for what thing slew he him? *c* **1384** CHAUCER *H. Fame* II. 525 'And what sovne is it lyke?' quod hee. *Ibid.* III. 1058 And eueryche cried, what thing is that? And somme sayde, I not neuer what. *a* **1400-50** *Wars Alex.* 683 Quat sterne is it at ȝe stody on? *a* **1425** *Cursor M.* 13154 (Trin.) What maner þing. *c* **1440-** [see CHEER *sb.*¹ 3b]. **1500-20** DUNBAR *Poems* xiii. 3 Quhat tydingis gossep, peax or weir? *a* **1586** SIDNEY *Arcadia* I. ii. (1912) 14 What cause then..made you venter to leave this sweete life? *a* **1596** *Sir T. More* I. iii. 71 Sirra, what newes? **1610** SHAKS. *Temp.* II. i. 88 What impossible matter wil he make easy next? **1749** FIELDING *Tom Jones* x. ix, What saucy Fellow..told you any Thing of my Lady? **1815** SCOTT *Guy M.* xi, 'What Mr. Bertram?'..'not Mr. Bertram of Ellangowan, I hope?' **1853** C. BRONTE *Villette* xxxvii, A story! What story? **1880** 'MARK TWAIN' *Tramp Abr.* xxii, But what good would it do?

(*b*) ***what way*** (Sc. and north.): how? why?

1570 LEVINS *Manip.* 197/3 Whatway, *quà, quomodò?* **1719** RAMSAY *To Arbuckle* 6 [He] disna care for A how, a what way, or a wherefore. **1799** MITCHELL *Scotticisms* 95 What way did it happen? **1902** J. J. BELL *Wee Macgregor* v, Macgreegor,..whit wey did ye strike puir Wullie Thomson?

b. In rhetorical questions, implying a contrary assertion: cf. 3.

c **1420** *Sir Amadace* (Camden) xxviii, Quat wundur were hit, thaȝhe him were wo? **1513** DOUGLAS *Æneis* VI. Prol. 105 Quhat cristnit clerk suld hym haue consalit bettir, Althocht he nevir was catholik wight? **1592** SHAKS. *Ven. & Ad.* 565 What waxe so frozen but dissolues with tempring? **1697** DRYDEN *Æneis* XI. 770 With what becoming Thanks can I reply! **1790** BURNS *Ball. Dumfries Election* xx, What Whig but wails the good Sir James Dear to his country by the names, Friend, Patron, Benefactor! **1821** SHELLEY *Hellas* 387 What hope of refuge, or retreat, or aid? **1848** KINGSLEY *Yeast* xiii, What wonder if the children take them at their word and act accordingly?

14. a. In indirect questions, and dependent clauses of similar meaning, with varying interrogative force, sometimes approaching the compound relative use (C. 8): cf. I.** above.

c **1200** ORMIN 722 Godess enngell se33de himm þær, Whatt name he shollde settenn Uppo þatt illke child. *a* **1300** *Cursor M.* 34 Bot be the fruit may scilwis se, O quat vertu is ilka tre. *c* **1330** R. BRUNNE *Chron. Wace* (Rolls) 2746 Þey ȝede spiande her & þer In what bataille þe kynges wer. *c* **1450** *Mirk's Festial* 33 Tell þes men whad þou hast yseyne, and whad joy þes men han lost. **1470-85** MALORY *Arthur* x. xxix. 460 Thenne sire Tristram lete deuyse the bataille in what manere that it sholde be. **1548-9** (Mar.) *Bk. Com. Prayer, Collect 1st Sund. after Epiph.*, Graunt that they maye both perceyue and knowe what thynges they ought to do. **1597** HOOKER *Eccl. Pol.* v. xlviii. §2 To examine..what dependencie it hath on God. **1667** MILTON *P.L.* II. 741 Till first I know of thee, What thing thou art. *c* **1720** DE FOE *Mem. Cavalier* (1840) 25 They called frequent councils of war what course to take. **1835** DICKENS *Sk. Boz, Mr. Watkins Tottle* ii, How, or at what hour, Mr. Watkins Tottle returned..is unknown. **1918** *Cornh. Mag.* June 637 He made no attempt..to suggest upon what lines that future might be shaped.

b. ***I know not what, Heaven knows what***, etc. used as adj. phr. = some unknown or undefined ..., some...or other: cf. 8b.

a **1635** in *Cath. Rec. Soc. Publ.* (1906) III. 43 There was present on horse-backe, I knowe not what poetical preacher, named Pourcase. **1670** G. H. *Hist. Cardinals* II. III. 205 There has been already some disgusts.., about I know not what reducement of the Light-horse. **1824** SCOTT *St. Ronan's* viii, And I know not what other menaces of formidable import.

15. In reference to quality or character: = What kind of (= L. *qualis*). Also followed by *a* (*dial.*).

†***what done, what dones***: see DONE *ppl. a.* 2.

1297 R. GLOUC. (Rolls) 225 He wolde iwite ȝwat man þe child ssolde be. *Ibid.* 315 Brut sende vp þere þre hondred men..to loke ȝwat lond þat were. *c* **1385** CHAUCER *L.G.W.* 1305 *Dido*, Allas what weman wele ȝe of me make? *a* **1400** *Pistill of Susan* 314 Tel nou me trewly, vnder what tre? **1445** in *Anglia* XXVIII. 269 Þou..askist what life this man hath had. **1577** GOOGE tr. *Heresbach's Husb.* 17b, It is to be learned..in planting, what ground is best for Uines, what for other trees. **1605** A. WARREN *Poor Man's Pass.* etc. H 2, I dare not call thee Asse, but aske thy selfe, What eares thou hast. *a* **1715** BURNET *Own Time* (1724) I. II. 318 It was a common piece of raillery in the Court, upon the death of any Prince, to ask what a person his widow was. **1853** MAURICE *Proph. & Kings* vi. 98 He wants a God as the support of his authority; what God he cares very little. **1879** F. W. ROBINSON *Coward Consc.* I. vi, 'What wine is this, Fisher?' 'Johannisberg, sir.'

16. In reference to quantity or amount: How much, how many.

Cf. the OE. use with partitive gen. (10 above).

1375 BARBOUR *Bruce* XIX. 293 'Quhat folk ar thai?' 'Schir, mony men.' **1605** SHAKS. *Macb.* III. iv. 126 *Macb.*... What is the night? *La.* Almost at odds with morning, which is which. **1654** *Kirk Sess. Rec.* in Jas. Campbell *Balmerino* (1899) 408 To stent and sie what bolls of victuall everie heritor was. **1820** DIBDIN *Ivanhoe* II. i, Pray thee what money hast thou brought? **1867** SMYTH *Sailor's Word-bk.*

728 What water have you? The question to the man sounding, as to the depth of water which the lead-line gives. *Mod. colloq.* What pudding is there left?

17. In predicative use, corresponding to a predicative adj. in direct statement: usually referring to quality (cf. 15) = of what kind, character, or disposition.

Syntactically indistinguishable from the pron., but essentially adjectival in meaning, and sometimes implying ellipsis of sb.: e.g. in quot. *a* 1450 *whad..more* = 'what more wits'.

1340 *Ayenb.* 264 'And huet is helle?'.. 'Helle is wyd wyþ-oute metinge, dyep wyþ-oute botme.' *c* **1400** *Anturs Arth.* viii, What is þi good rede? *a* **1450** MYRC 1333 Here ben þe wyttus fyue, How þey ben spende, telle me blyue, And whad þou hast in herte more. **1526** TINDALE *James* i. 24 He goeth his waye, and hath immediately forgotten what his fassion was. **1601** SHAKS. *Twel. N.* I. v. 269, I see you what you are, you are too proud. **1605** —— *Lear* II. ii. 121 What was th' offence you gaue him? **1697** DRYDEN *Æneis* VII. 178 To search the Land, and where the Cities lye, And what the Men [Virg. *quive habeant homines*]. *Ibid.* XI. 516 Noble his Mother was,.. But what his Father's Parentage, unknown. **1828** DUPPA *Trav. Italy*, etc. 3 What the Transfiguration may have been, as to execution and colouring, I cannot tell. **1905** R. BAGOT *Passport* xvi, You know what he is about anything disagreeable—how he simply ignores its existence.

18. In parasynthetic compounds, as ***what-fashioned, -natured*** adjs. (= of what fashion, nature). So ***what countryman*** (= a man of what country): see COUNTRYMAN 1.

1559 AYLMER *Harborowe* P 1 b, Some of you knowe what natured men they be. **1607** R. C[AREW] tr. *Estienne's World of Wonders* 237 [One] may well doubt whether locke-smithes ..vsed files..or rather what fashioned files they had. **1622** MABBE tr. *Aleman's Guzman d'Alf.* II. 302 He began to aske of me what Country-man I was? I told him that I was of Sevill. **1796** SOUTHEY *Lett. fr. Spain* (1799) 196 Turning round to Manuel, he asked him what countryman he was. **1807** [see COUNTRYMAN 1].

III. *adv.*

† **19.** For what cause or reason? for what end or purpose? why? *Obs.*

what need(s: see NEED *v.*[2] 1 b, 2 b, 5 b.

c **888** ÆLFRED *Boeth.* xiv. §2 Hwæt murcnast þu þonn[e] æfter þam þe þu forlure? **971** *Blickl. Hom.* 137 Hwæt secestu minne naman, forþon he is mycel & wundorlic? *c* **1205** LAY. 13632 Whæht [*c* 1275 wi] is þæt þu murnest. *c* **1385** CHAUCER *L.G.W.* 2218 *Ariadne*, What shulde I more telle hire compleynynge? *c* **1400** *Rom. Rose* 5097 Withoute more (what shulde I glose?). *c* **1449** PECOCK *Repr.* II. v. 162 What ben ȝe greuose to this womman? **1579** FULKE *Heskins' Parl.* 148 But what stand we trifling about this testimonie? **1611** *Bible* Transl. Pref. ¶4 But what mention wee three or foure vses of the Scripture? **1667** MILTON *P.L.* II. 329 What sit we then projecting Peace and Warr? *a* **1677** BARROW *Serm.* I. 7 What should I mention beauty; that fading toy?

20. a. In what way? in what respect? how? *Obs.* or *arch.* (See also AIL *v.* 4, quots. *c* 1450–*c* 1817.)

c **1200** ORMIN 14018 Ure Laferrd Jesu Crist þuss seȝȝde till hiss moderr; Whatt falleþþ þiss till me wiþþ þe, Wifmann, þiss þatt tu mælesst? **1382** WYCLIF *Gen.* xx. 9 What han we synned in thee? *a* **1400–50** *Wars Alex.* 2523 Quat knawis þou þat? **1457** HARDING *Chron.* in *Engl. Hist. Rev.* (1912) Oct. 744 What hath Englonde so felly the offende, This noble prynce.. To Rauysshe so fro vs? *c* **1460** in *Pol. Rel. & L. Poems* (1866) 250 A, ihesu! quat hast þou gylt? **1535** COVERDALE *Baruch* iv. 17 But alas, what can I helpe you? **1816** SCOTT *Antiq.* xv, It just cam open o' free will in my hand—what could I help it? **1842** TENNYSON *Morte d'Arth.* 250 For what are men better than sheep or goats..If, knowing God, they lift not hands of prayer..?

b. To what extent or degree? how much?

Chiefly with such verbs as *avail, care, matter, signify*, or with *the* and comparative, as *the better*; cf. NOTHING B. 1, 2 c, NONE C. 1 b. Also † *quhat fele* (Sc. obs.) = how many?

1382 WYCLIF *Gen.* xxxvii. 26 What shal it profit vs if we sleen oure brother? *c* **1420** ? LYDG. *Assembly of Gods* 1664 What were they bothe amendyd that day? *c* **1450** HOLLAND *Howlat* 627 Quhat fele armes on loft,.. The said persewant bure. *a* **1535** FISHER *Spir. Consol.* Wks. (1876) 357 And what am I now the better for all this? **1592** SHAKS. *Ven. & Ad.* 207 What were thy lips the worse for one poore kis? *Ibid.* 285 What cares he now, for curbe, or pricking spurre? **1697** DRYDEN *Virg. Georg.* III. 784 Now what avails his well-deserving Toil! **1757** [see SIGNIFY 7]. **1865** RUSKIN *Sesame* i. §32 What do we, as a nation, care about books?

21. As mere sign of interrogation, introducing a question. *Obs.* exc. *dial.* (see *Eng. Dial. Dict.*).

Often taken as interjection (cf. B. 1), and printed with following comma or mark of exclamation.

c **1000** *Lamb. Ps.* Cant. vi, Hwæt la [Vulg. *Numquid*] nis he fæder þin? *a* **1300** *Cursor M.* 5182 Quat ha yee broght him wit yow hider? **13..** *Gaw. & Gr. Knt.* 309 'What, is þis Arþures hous,' quod þe haþel þenne. **1592** MARLOWE *Mass. Paris* 938 Come on sirs, what, are you resolutely bent? **1592** SHAKS. *Rom. & Jul.* I. v. 57 What dares the slaue Come hither..To fleere and scorne at our Solemnitie? **1602** —— *Ham.* I. i. 19 Say, what is Horatio there? **1677** RAVENSCROFT *Wrangling Lovers* II. i. 13 What's he a Spy too? **1741** tr. *D'Argens' Chinese Lett.* xxxii. 243 What have they been extinguish'd by Sorcerers, as they had been form'd by supernatural Prodigies?

B. Exclamatory and allied uses.

I. *int.* † **1.** Used to introduce or call attention to a statement: Lo; now; well. *Obs.*

Beowulf 1 Hwæt! we Gar-Dena in ȝeardaȝum, þeodcyninga þrym ȝefrunon. *c* **1000** ÆLFRIC *Hom.* II. 130 Hwæt ða ȝelyfdon for wel meniȝe, and on Godes naman ȝefullode wurdon. *c* **1386** CHAUCER *Prol.* 856 He seyde syn I shal bigynne the game What welcome be the cut a goddes name.

2. a. As an exclamation of surprise or astonishment (sometimes mixed with indignation): usually followed by a question.

c **1200** ORMIN 19429 Whatt Abraham, whatt Moysæs, Whatt tiss & tatt profete, Ne sæȝhenn þeȝȝ nohht Drihhtin Godd Inn hiss goddcunnde kinde? *a* **1250** *Owl & Night.* 1298 Hwat, heo seyde, vle, artu wod? **13..** *Cursor M.* 10456 (Gött.) Quat? wenis þu i be a fole? **1377** LANGL. *P. Pl.* B. XIII. 184 'What?' quod clergye to conscience 'ar ȝe coueitouse nouthe After ȝeresȝyues?' **1412–20** LYDG. *Chron. Troy* I. 2900 What, hath sche nat fro deth and fro distresse Preserued þe, and ȝit þou takest noon hede? **1589** R. HARVEY *Pl. Perc.* (1590) 5 What, what, latine in the mouth of a plaine fellow? **1633** FORD *'Tis Pity* IV. iii, What, crying, old Mistresse! **1639** J. CLARKE *Parœm.* 303 What againe? quoth Paul when his wife made him cuckold the second time. **1749** FIELDING *Tom Jones* XV. vii, 'O, Mr. Jones, I have lost my Lady for ever.'—'How! what! for Heaven's Sake tell me.' **1810** CRABBE *Borough* xxii. 74 None put the question,—'Peter, dost thou give The boy his food?—What, man! the lad must live.' **1847** TENNYSON *Princess* II. 33 What! are the ladies of your land so tall? **1886** BARING-GOULD *Crt. Royal* xii, 'What!—not Sunday clothes?' 'Sunday is nothing to us.' 'What! no go-to-meeting clothes?'

b. With intensive additions, as in A. 9 (of which use this may be partly an elliptical variant).

c **1420** ? LYDG. *Assembly of Gods* 425 'Ys hit thus!' quod Attropos, 'what in the deuyllys date!' *c* **1520** SKELTON *Magnyf.* 795 What the deuyll! can ye agre no better? **1754** RICHARDSON in J. Duncombe *Lett.* (1773) III. 13 What a duce, must a man be always writing! **1865** DICKENS *Mut. Fr.* I. iii, If there is a word..that I abominate, it is energy... What the deuce! Am I to rush out into the street [etc.].

3. Used to hail, summon, or call the attention of a person; also formerly for incitement, or as an expression of excitement or exultation. *arch.* and *dial.* Earlier in phr. WHAT HO!

c **1386**, etc. [see WHAT HO *int.*]. *a* **1553** UDALL *Royster D.* I. iii. (Arb.) 22 What Tibet, what Annot, what Margerie. Ye sleepe, but we doe not. **1581** A. HALL *Iliad* II. 29 What? courage sirs my felowes al. **1592** SHAKS. *Rom. & Jul.* I. iii. 3, 4 *Nurse*..I bad her come, what Lamb: what Ladi-bird, God forbid, Where's this Girle? what Iuliet? **1607** DEKKER & WEBSTER *Northw. Hoe* V. i, Chamberlain, call in the music, ..What! we'll make a night of it. **1610** SHAKS. *Temp.* IV. i. 33 What Ariell; my industrious seruant Ariell. *Ar.* What would my potent master? here I am. **1633** B. JONSON *Tale Tub* I. iii, Here they are both! What Sirs, disputin. **1878** HARDY *Ret. Native* III. viii, What, Diggory? You are having a lonely walk.

II. 4. *adv.* To what an extent! in what a way! = HOW *adv.* 7. *Obs.* exc. *dial.*

Beowulf 530 Hwæt þu worn fela..beore druncen ymb Brecan spræce! *a* **900** CYNEWULF *Juliana* 167 Juliana! hwæt þu glæm hafast. **971** *Blickl. Hom.* 33 Eala hwæt Drihten deofles costunga ȝeþyldelice abær. ? *c* **1250** in *E.E. Lyrics* (1907) 1 Ei, ei, what this nicht is long! *a* **1300** *Cursor M.* 23175 Quat he war wijs þat moght Stedfast hald þis dai in thoght! **13..** *Gaw. & Gr. Knt.* 2203 What hit wharred, & whette, as water at a mulne. **1340** *Ayenb.* 51 A god huet we hedde guod wyn yesteneuen and guode metes. **1375** BARBOUR *Bruce* I. 215 A! quhat thai dempt thaim felonly! *c* **1440** *York Myst.* xiv. 71 A! lorde, what the wedir is colde! **1556** *Chron. Grey Friars* (Camden) 60 What rebellyous they were. *Mod. Sc.* What bonny!

III. 5. a. *adj.* Used (as *sing.* or *pl.*) to express the surprising or striking nature of the thing(s) or person(s) denoted by the sb.; in *sing.* usually, now always, followed by the indef. art., exc. with a sb. in collective or abstract sense. Often with ellipsis (cf. A. 4, 13).

Formerly usually, and still in archaic style, with inverted construction as in a direct question; being distinguished from this by intonation, and in the (non-collective) sing. by the presence of the indef. art.; cf. 'What a place is this!' (mod. 'What a place this is!') with 'What place is this?'

c **1315** SHOREHAM II. 119 O swete leuedy, wat þe was wo, þo ihesus deyde on rode! *a* **1450** *Le Morte Arth.* 530 O, worthy god, what wele is me! **1450–1530** *Myrr. our Ladye* II. 119 O wyth what reuerence,.. wyth what inwarde deuocyon ..oughte we to haue vs in euery place. *c* **1485** *Digby Myst.* IV. 1157 What a fawte it was, The seruaunte, alas, His master to forsake! **1509** BARCLAY *Shyp of Folys* (1874) II. 105 O what a Cyte, and what a se royall Hath had first name of pore men and rurall. **1590** SHAKS. *Com. Err.* III. i. 48 What a coile is there Dromio? who are those at the gate? **1596** —— *Merch. V.* I. iii. 161 O father Abram, what these Christians are. **1601** —— *Jul. C.* I. iii. 42 Cassius, what Night is this? **1602** —— *Ham.* II. ii. 315 What a piece of worke is a man! **1611** —— *Cymb.* IV. i. 16 What Mortalitie is? **1615** W. LAWSON *Country Housew. Garden* (1626) 32 What rottennesse? what hollownesse? **1633** A. STAFFORD *Fem. Glory* 133 O what proficients in Faith did these rusticall Swaines prove in a moment! **1705** ADDISON *Italy* 307 What a strain'd unnatural Similitude must this seem to a Modern Reader? **1776** EARL CARLISLE in Jesse *Selwyn & Contemp.* (1844) III. 160 What a house! What people! what manners! **1798** G. HAY in *Ushaw Mag.* (1913) Dec. 288 What shocking times we live in! **1825** SCOTT *Talism.* i, What was the surprise of the Saracen, when, dismounting to examine the condition of his prostrate enemy, he found [etc.]. **1847** C. BRONTË *Jane Eyre* ii, What a consternation of soul was mine that dreary afternoon!.. Yet in what darkness, what dense ignorance, was the mental battle fought! **1855** BROWNING *A Lovers' Quarrel* i, Oh, what a dawn of day! How the March sun feels like May! **1888** RIDER HAGGARD *Col. Quaritch* xli, What rubbish you talk.

b. In dependent clauses, after verbs of thinking or perceiving.

Here the exclamatory force varies as the interrogative force does in the corresponding interrogative use (A. 14), with which this often nearly coincides: cf. remarks under A. I.**

a **1300** *Cursor M.* 1610 Quat was his reut [= ruth] þan all mai see. **1554** in *Engl. Hist. Rev.* (1913) July 528 When I consydere ever what servants of God they were and so dyed. **1594** SHAKS. *Rich. III*, I. iv. 21 Me thought what paine it was to drowne. **1610** —— *Temp.* I. ii. 251 Do'st thou forget From what a torment I did free thee? **1708** *Caldwell Papers* (Maitland Club) I. 216 You cannot imagine what a parcel of cheating brutes the work people here are. **1713** ADDISON *Guardian* No. 119 ¶1 We may see after what a different manner Strada proceeds. **1808** SCOTT *Marm.* II. vi, See what a woful look was given. **1840** DICKENS *Old C. Shop* lxix, You may judge with what devotion he..clung to this girl. **1916** SANDAY *In View of End* 93 Let..the ordinary church-goer call to mind what a large proportion of the best of our hymn-tunes are German.

IV. † **6.** *pron.* Used in exclamation to denote something surprising or striking; sometimes with inverted construction, as in 5. *Obs.*

1382 WYCLIF *Num.* xxiii. 23 In his tymes it shal be seide to Jacob and to Yrael, What the Lord hath wrouȝt! [Vulg. *quid operatus sit Deus*; **1611** What hath God wrought!] **1390** GOWER *Conf.* I. 54 Lo now, my Sone, what it is A man to caste his yhe amis. *c* **1460** *Wisdom* 1121 in *Macro Plays* 72 Haue mynde, Soule, wat Gode hath do!

C. Relative and allied uses. (In early use often followed by *that* (THAT *conj.* 6), rarely *as*.)

I. *pron.* * as compound relative (combining antecedent and relative).

1. a. (*a*) That which, the thing which. (Sometimes with pleonastic correlative *that*.) Also *occas.* (*b*) more generally, A thing which, something that.

Not used of persons, exc. in the idiomatic phr. *but what*: see 5 below.

The line of division between the dependent interrog. use (see A. I **) and the pure relative use is in certain conditions, esp. in the early periods, difficult or impossible to draw.

c **1200** *Trin. Coll. Hom.* 191 *Quod pungit ueneno afficit*... Hie..attreð hwat heo prikeð. *c* **1205** LAY. 31618 ȝe habbeoð alle iherd whæt Penda king hafueð iseid. *c* **1350** *Will. Palerne* 2578 Mekli þan to meliors he munged what he þouȝt. *c* **1410** *Master of Game* (MS. Digby 182) Prol. 12 This booke tretith of what shalbe in euery sesoun moste durable. *c* **1449** PECOCK *Repr.* II. vi. 172 That thou wolt folewe Holi Writt, and take for the lawe and seruice of God what that Holi Writ allowith. **1521** *Perth Hammermen Book* (1889) 16 Item giffin to Andro Scot of quhat was awand him,.. iiij s. **1592** SHAKS. *Ven. & Ad.* 88 So offers he to giue what she did craue. **1596** DANETT tr. *Comines* (1614) 219 Notwithstanding what I haue heard, that I will report. **1599** *George a Greene* G j b, What as Bradford holdes of me in chiefe, I giue it frankely vnto thee for euer. **1649** MILTON *Eikon.* iv. 36 He..justifi'd and abetted them in what they did. **1724** RAMSAY *Vision* xii, I ken sum mair than ye..Of quhat sall afterwart befall. **1731–8** SWIFT *Pol. Conversat.* Introd. p. lxxxi, So incurable is the Love of Detraction, perhaps beyond what the charitable Reader will easily believe. **1850** TENNYSON *In Mem.* cxxiv, And what I am beheld again What is. **1851** *Househ. Words* 6 Sept. 560/1, I was going to ask you to dine with me on what I have left. **1865** RUSKIN *Sesame* i. §20 Milton means what he says. **1884** W. S. GILBERT *Princ. Ida* II, What we have Of hair, is all our own. **1886** *Law Rep.* 32 *Chanc. Div.* 71 It appears to me that they acted very resonably in what they did. **1889** MRS. E. KENNARD *Landing a Prize* i. (1891) 2 His duties were performed with the precision of an automaton. What he did one day, that he did the next.

(*b*) **1697** J. LEWIS *Mem. Dk. Glocester* (1789) 56 Dr. Radcliffe..finding him feverish, prescribed what restored him to health in five days. **1784** COWPER *Task* I. 55 If cushion might be call'd, what harder seem'd Than the firm oak of which the frame was form'd.

b. In reference to a prec. sb., esp. after *but, except, only, than, like*, etc., with quasi-adj. force: The one which; chiefly as *pl.* those which; †also (*rare*) of persons, those who.

1597 SHAKS. *2 Hen. IV*, IV. iv. 4, Wee will..draw no Swords, but what are sanctify'd. **1611** *Bible* 2 Cor. i. 13 We write none other things vnto you, then what you reade or acknowledge. **1664** PEPYS *Diary* 2 Jan., To the King's house, and saw *The Usurper*, which is no good play, though better than what I saw yesterday. **1676** DRYDEN *Aurengz.* II. i, An easier yoke than what you put on me. **1677** *Essex Papers* (Camden) II. 118 Ye Parties which lost it now was greater than wt carried it when ye perpetuating clause was lately ordered. **1681** M. FOX in *Jrnl. Friends' Hist. Soc.* (1912) July 139 Hauing noe body to bee with at home but what is noe Friends. **1758** S. HAYWARD *Serm.* xvi. 475 He was under no obligations to take human nature, only what arose from his free..promise. **1762** KAMES *Elem. Crit.* (1774) I. i. 24 We feel a gradual dilatation..of mind, like what is felt in an ascending series. **1824** L. MURRAY *Engl. Gram.* (ed. 5) I. 233 All fevers, except what are called nervous. **1868** M. ARNOLD *Sch. & Univ. Cont.* 21 The Revolution made a clean sweep of all old endowments; what exist date from a time since the Revolution.

2. With special implications. **a.** Expressing quantity or amount (cf. A. 10): So much (or many) as, as much as.

1646 in M. Sellers *Eastland Co.* (Camden) Introd. 66 They desire, that what as hath allready bene equallie disburst,..be brought to accompt, and what as remayned in Cash be returned up. **1664** PEPYS *Diary* 18 Mar., Their service was six biscuits a-piece, and what they pleased of burnt claret. **1718** *Free-thinker* No. 62. 44 The Romans learnt, what they knew of this Mysterious Doctrine, from the Etrurians. **1789** *Massachusetts Spy* 9 Apr. 3/2 What of the votes in Newhampshire for President, we have seen, are nearly equally divided.

b. Expressing quality or character (cf. A. 2, 15, 17): Such as; the kind of thing (or person) that.

a **1658** CLEVELAND *Rustick Ramp.* 114 He delighted to be ..acknowledged for what he was. **1697** DRYDEN *Æneis* X. 901 And what Æneas was, such seem'd the Shade. **1756–7** tr. *Keysler's Trav.* (1760) IV. 468 The court is still very splendid, though much altered from what it was in the year 1716. **1849** MACAULAY *Hist. Eng.* ii. I. 185 The country was not what it had been twenty-two years before. **1861** THACKERAY *Round. Papers, On being Found Out*, Would you have your wife and children know you exactly for what you are? **1891** *Speaker* 2 May 533/1 The book is very much what might have been expected from the author.

c. Expressing parallel relation or correspondence (with *to* in principal clause and in relative clause).

1673–4 GREW *Anat. Pl.* III. (1682) 127 And what the Mouth is, to an Animal; that the Root is to a Plant. **1732** BERKELEY *Alciphr.* IV. §21 Intellect is to the mind what sight is to the body. **1853** RUSKIN *Stones Venice* III. iv. §11 What the elm and oak are to England, the olive is to Italy. **1914** *Month* Dec. 608 Jingoism is to true patriotism what bigotry is to true religion.

3. a. In a parenthetic phrase (chiefly with *call*) qualifying a following word or phrase; equivalent to an adjective phrase, or to a following phrase with *as*: e.g. *what is called*... = 'the so-called...', or '..., as it is called'.

1697 J. LEWIS *Mem. Dk. Glocester* (1789) 15 A fortification, mounted with small guns, and what were stiled his great ones, which were four little brass cannon. **1794** in *Jrnl. Friends' Hist. Soc.* (1918) 8 Other demonstrations of what they call Loyalty. **1801** COLERIDGE *Lett.* (1895) 346 Calvert is..what is well called a handy man. **1828** *Life Planter Jamaica* 211 A very small pea,..a kind of what is called squashies. **1856** MRS. BROWNING *Aur. Leigh* I. 9, I, writing thus, am still what men call young. **1908** R. BAGOT *A. Cuthbert* v. 40 She is what she calls 'taking your measure'.

b. Introducing a prefatory (usually parenthetic) qualifying clause, equivalent to a following clause with *which* (or to an adv., e.g. *what is more* = furthermore, still more).

1697 DAMPIER *Voy.* I. 5 Where we saw (what we always feared) a Ship [etc.]. **1713** POPE in Earl Orrery *Rem. Swift* (1752) 36 If it be true, what I have heard often affirmed by innocent people, That [etc.]. **1743** BULKELEY & CUMMINS *Voy. S. Seas* 40 And, what was reck'on'd very odd, the Cabbin-Bell came ashore. **1818** SCOTT *Rob Roy* v, She wore, what was then somewhat unusual, a coat, vest, and hat, resembling those of a man. **1839** THACKERAY *Fatal Boots* Feb., I got from him..a..silver-laced waistcoat,..and, what's more, I had no less than three golden guineas in the pocket of it. **1966** I. MURDOCH *Time of Angels* iii. 32 Pattie resented too, what before she had scarcely noticed, Carel's assumption that Muriel and Elizabeth were socially her superiors. **1970** C. W. K. MUNDLE *Critique Linguistic Philos.* 16 Their claim is sometimes that so and so is..incorrect English, sometimes (what is very different) that it is absurd or meaningless. **1976** *Times* 7 June 14/6 To this he added, what could hardly be encouraging to other aspirants to riches, 'In building a large fortune it pays to be born at the right time.'

4. a. (*a*) In generalized or indefinite sense: Anything that: = WHATEVER 2 a. Now only in such phrases as ***what you please, come what may***, or esp. (*b*) ***for what I know, care, can tell.*** †Formerly also in a qualifying dependent clause: = WHATEVER 3 a.

c **1315** SHOREHAM IV. 159 Ac tyde þe what by-tyde. **1340** *Ayenb.* 43 Oþer be uenym, oþer ine oþre manere, huet þet hit by. **1340–70** *Alex. & Dind.* 68 What it be þat 3e bidde, 3our bonus i graunte. *a* **1425** *Cursor M.* 13148 (Trin.) He bad hir aske what [*Cott.* quatsum, *Fairf.* quateuer] she wolde. **1469** *Bury Wills* (Camden) 50 To make therof qwat that he can. **1535** COVERDALE *Gen.* i. 24 Catell, wormes and what as hath life vpon earth. **1601** SHAKS. (*title of play*) Twelfe Night, Or what you will. **1655** VAUGHAN *Silex Scint., Mt. Olives* i, Such ill-plac'd wit, Conceit, or call it what you please, Is the braines fit, And meere disease. **1670** in *Marvell's Corr.* Wks. (Grosart) II. 299 Its therefore my request to you to..be assisting to him with your Certificates, or in what else you can serve him. **1680** MOXON *Mech. Exerc.* xii. 208 With your Flat Chissel or Gouge, (or what is nearest at hand) knock softly. **1749** HARTLEY *Observ. Man* I. i. §1. 20 Be the Cause what it will. **1859** H. KINGSLEY *G. Hamlyn* ix, One thing she was determined on, not to give up her lover, come what would. **1908** S. E. WHITE *Riverman* xix, To sacrifice his pride, his ambition, his what-you-will.

(*b*) **1697** J. LEWIS *Mem. Dk. Glocester* (1789) 55 You may have half a dozen [legs] for what I know, as it is difficult to discover any under the petticoats you wear! **1798** CHARLOTTE SMITH *Yng. Philos.* I. 22 She may die for what you know. **1818** SCOTT *Hrt. Midl.* xxii, It may have been murdered, for what I can tell. **1875** RUSKIN *Fors Clav.* lx. 332 You may think, for what I care, what you please in such matters.

†**b.** Of a person or persons: Whoever. *Obs.*

c **1340** HAMPOLE *Prose Treat.* 43 Ilke man, what þat he be, þat in-calles þe name of Godd, þat es to say askes saluacione by Ihesu and by his passione. *c* **1430** *Freemasonry* (1840) 445 And what he be, let hym be sow3ht. **1448–9** METHAM *Amoryus & Cl.* 916 He redy schuld be For hys lady sake to iuste, ayens yche knyght in general,..and qwat he were myght yeue hym a falle. **1591** SHAKS. *1 Hen. VI*, v. iii. 45 Be what thou wilt, thou art my prisoner. **1613** —— *Hen. VIII*, v. iii. 47 That..my Accusers, Be what they will, may stand forth face to face.

c. with the indefinite sense indicated by *ever, so*, etc. following (now only immediately following: see WHATEVER, WHATSO, etc.): cf. 9 b below.

c **1200** ORMIN 2504, & all wass mænelike þing Whatt littless se þe33 haffdenn. **1390** GOWER *Conf.* I. 20 What as eny man accuse. *Ibid.* 103 What as evere that ye seie. **1464** *Stonor Papers* (Camden) I. 68 What that euer he wer to by straw, he must pay in honde. ? **1481** CAXTON *Chesse* III. iv. (ed. 2) g v, To alle trewe marchauntis and other what that som-euer [*ed.* 1474 other what som euyr] they be.

d. *what else*: orig. ellipt. = whatever else there may be; hence, with loss of the relative force, anything else, anything and everything.

1579 *Expos. Termes Law* s.v. *Reservation*, Theyr reseruations were as wel..in vittailis, whether flesh, fishe, corne, bread, drinke, or what els, as in money. **1585–6** EARL LEYCESTER *Corr.* (Camden) 85 Impostes, customes, and what ells that yeld them money. **1593** SHAKS. *3 Hen. VI*, III. i. 51 Warwicke..in conclusion winnes the King from her, With promise of his Sister, and what else, To strengthen and support King Edwards place. **1659** in *Engl. Hist. Rev.* (1919) July 287 That..you will afford the best of your assistance..and what elce needfull. **1873** RUSKIN *Crown Wild Olive* App. xi. 201 The right to keep everything and every place about you in as good order as you can—Prussia, Poland, or what else.

e. *what have you*: anything else (similar) that there may be, or that one can think of. orig. *U.S.*

1925 *New Yorker* 10 Oct. 28/2 New Yorker, Newarker, or what have you? **1930** H. CRADDOCK *Savoy Cocktail Bk.* I. 113 Fill the said tumbler with Water, Ginger Ale, or What Have You, until almost to the top. **1944** AUDEN *For Time Being* (1945) 115 Disguising himself as a swan or a bull or a shower of rain or what-have-you. **1956** A. WILSON *Anglo-Saxon Attitudes* 163 Too busy or going on leave or what-have-you. **1968** K. WEATHERLY *Roo Shooter* 110, I must have been away about two hours, buying the stores and what-have-you. **1973** C. BONINGTON *Next Horizon* iv. 66, I was eager to snatch at every opportunity to get myself established as a writer, film-maker, what-have-you, in an effort to find a clearly defined career.

5. a. *but what* (after a negative expressed or implied): except what (or who); which (or who)..not (= BUT C. 12 b): see also BUT C. 30.

1596 SHAKS. *Tam. Shr.* v. ii. 14 Padua affords nothing but what is kinde. **1662** EVELYN *Sculptura* Table, Never any of the Antients excelled in these Arts, but what were Gentlemen. **1688** SOUTH *Serm., Matt.* xxii. 12 (1697) II. 333 Few are Confident, but what are first Careless. **1747** *Gentl. Mag.* 247/2 Of the sails that were left, I believe there is not a cloth but what has a shot through it. **1780** BENTHAM *Introd. Mor. & Legisl.* xiv. (1789) p. clxxxv. *note*, There are few madmen but what are observed to be afraid of the strait waistcoat. **1796** CHARLOTTE SMITH *Marchmont* IV. 133 Not one of these insinuations but what gathered something from malevolence.

b. *loosely* as conjunctional phr.: But that, that..not (= BUT C. 12): see also BUT C. 30. *colloq.*

¶In quot. 1807 exceptionally without preceding negative: = BUT C. 11 a.

1662 [see BUT C. 30]. **1753** A. MURPHY *Gray's Inn Jrnl.* No. 43 There hardly arose an Incident, but what our Fellow-Traveller would repeat twenty or thirty Verses in a Breath. **1807** W. IRVING *Salmag.* No. 9 (1824) 144 In vain did the wind whistle and the storm beat—my aunt would waddle through mud and mire, over the whole town, but what she would visit them. *c* **1883** E. FITZGERALD *Let.* in A. C. Benson *E. Fitzgerald* (1905) i. 19 Never having read his father's [poems]..till drawn to them by me... Not but what he loved and admired his father in every shape but that. **1894** DU MAURIER *Trilby* VI. (1895) 284 Not but what many changes had been wrought. **1908** R. BAGOT *A. Cuthbert* xxi. 257 You should have kept quiet in the house to-day. Not but what you are certainly looking better than you did early this morning.

6. Used redundantly after *than* or *as* introducing a clause. *dial.* or *vulgar.*

1818 SCOTT *Hrt. Midl.* xxx, I think I laughed heartier then than what I do now. **1960** M. SPARK *Ballad Peckham Rye* iii. 29 'He's the same as what we are,' Dixie said. **1966** P. WILLMOTT *Adolescent Boys* ii. 26 They're all about the same age as what we are.

** **7.** As simple relative (*sing.* or *pl.*): Which (or who); that. **a.** referring to a pron. (demonstr. or indef.), occas. to a noun; orig. introducing a dependent question in apposition with it (A. 6); esp., in later use only, in ***all what*** (now *dial.* or *vulgar*).

Apparent instances in OE. are due to imitation of Latin: [*c* **1000** *Ags. Gosp.* Luke vi. 3 Ne rædde ȝe þæt hwæt dauid dyde? (Vulg. *nec hoc legistis quod fecit D.*?). **11..** *Ælfred's Boethius* xl. §7 (Bodl. MS.) Eall hwæt [*Cott. MS.* þ] he willniaþ hi biȝitaþ.] *c* **1200** ORMIN 1115 Nu icc wile shæwenn 3uw all þatt whatt itt bitacneþþ. **1297** R. GLOUC. (Rolls) 4862 þe king..wende toward bangor þo To destruye þe brutons, wat he founde mo. *c* **1440** *Alphabet of Tales* 86 He told þaim all what at he saw. *c* **1449** PECOCK *Repr.* II. ix. 191 Aftir al this what is tretid upon the firste.. gouernauncis. **1532** TINDALE *Expos. Matt. v–vii* (*c* 1550) 20 b, Here seist thou ye vttermoost what a christen man must looke for. **1557** NORTH *Gueuara's Diall Pr.* 244 They do al thinges what they lyst, and nothing what they ought. **1597** G. HARVEY *Trimming of Nashe* Wks. (Grosart) III. 53 The beast Ephemeron, which because shee hath but one day to liue, hath manie legs, foure wings, and all what Nature can afford, to giue her expedition to see about the world. **1645** FULLER *Good Th. in Bad T.* (1841) 36 For matter of language there is nothing what grace doth do, but wit can act. **1657** S. TITUS *Killing no Murder* 9 They..thought it not adultery what was committed with her. **1718** HICKES & NELSON *J. Kettlewell* III. §78 He continued Unmoveable in all what he Believed to be his Duty. **1740** RICHARDSON *Pamela* xxiii. I. 57 Do you think that so dutiful a Son as our Neighbour.. does not pride himself, for all what he said at Table, in such a pretty Maiden? **1919** J. B. MORTON *Barber of Putney* xv, If I sat down to write a book, I'd want to shove in all what I saw.

†**b.** in dependence on a prep.; spec. in phr. ***for what*** (replacing OE. *for hwon*) = for which purpose or reason, wherefore. *Obs.*

c **1175** *Lamb. Hom.* 81 Þis monne me mei sermonen mid godes worde, for hwat he scal his sunne uor-saken and bileuen. *c* **1200** ORMIN 2831 Ure preost..nohht ne mihhte trowwenn þatt word tatt himm þurrh Gabriæl Wass se33d o Godess hallfe, Forr whatt himm wass hiss spæche..þurrh Drihhtin all biræfedd. *c* **1200** *Vices & Virtues* 39 Gif ðu na þing ne luuest..ðurh hwat ðu miht forliesen godes luue. *a* **1225** *Ancr. R.* 66 Kumeð þe coue..& fret al þet of hwat heo schulde uorð bringen hir cwike briddes. *Ibid.* 382 He..bid me ofte techen him sum þing mid hwat he muhte his licome deruen. **1297** R. GLOUC. (Rolls) 2533 Hengist..him grantede..is do3ter abbe to wif, Vor 3wat þe king 3eue him þe contreie of kent. *a* **1300** *R. Gloucester's Chron.* 3451 (MS. B.) Hii vnder 3ete a welle..Of wat [*MS. A.* wan] þe king ofte dronk. *a* **1300** *Seven Sins* 11 in *E.E.P.* (1862) 19 Þi fair schrute mid whate þou art ischrid aboute.

c. *gen.* (Now *dial.* or *vulgar.*)

a **1568** ASCHAM *Scholem.* II. (Arb.) 121 In folowyng so preciselie, either the matter what other men wrote, or els the maner how other men wrote. **1621** ELSING *Debates Ho. Lords* (Camden) 34 To add that to the weight what the washers had taken away. **1668** WILKINS *Real Char.* 122 That incisure or resemblance of cutting what is common to most of them [*sc.* insects]. *c* **1842** in T. W. Reid *Life Forster* (1888) I. v. 144 Be like Long Forster, what walked to Colne and back before breakfast. **1865** DICKENS *Mut. Fr.* III. ii, Them's her lights, Miss Abbey, wot you see a-blinking yonder.

II. *adj.* (*sing.* or *pl.*, of things or persons; always as compound relative exc. in 10 b.)

8. That (or those)..which (or who); such..as; often expressing quantity, So much (or many).. as: cf. C. 1, 2 a.

c **1350** *Will. Palerne* 1114 Fondes to do þe duk what duresse 3e may. *a* **1400** *Minor Poems fr. Vernon MS.* 608 Tak what þing þe profred is Whon þou mai3t redi haue. **1579** FULKE *Heskins' Parl.* 150 By what things I was conioyned vnto you, those things..I haue giuen vnto you. **1605** SHAKS. *Lear* III. vi. 2, I will peece out the comfort with what addition I can. **1677** in *12th Rep. Hist. MSS. Comm.* App. v. 36 Lord Purbecke makes what hast he can to consume his ladie's fortune by gameing. **1710** STEELE *Tatler* No. 169 ⁋1 Do we..destroy the use of what organs we have? **1795** SOUTHEY *Joan of Arc* VI. 388 What few to guard the town Unwilling had remained, haste forth to meet The triumph. **1874** RUSKIN *Fors Clav.* xlii. 129, I will take what indulgence the..reader will give me.

9. a. In generalized sense: Any..which (or who), any..that: = WHATEVER 2 b. Now only in certain collocations: cf. C. 4. Also = WHATEVER 3 b.

c **1380** WYCLIF *Wks.* (1880) 311 What man seiþ heyl to siche antecristis shal haue part of heere werkis for assent þat he 3iueþ. **1393** LANGL. *P. Pl.* C. III. 34 What man þat me louyeþ and my wille folweþ, Shal haue grace. **1422** *E.E. Wills* (1882) 50, I bequeth to what thenge þat is most necessary in þ^e^ same Chirch, v. marc. **1470–85** MALORY *Arthur* x. xxxviii. 475 What Knyghte maye ouercome that Knyght..shal haue me and alle my landes. **1567** MAPLET *Gr. Forest* 101 Into what cleare Fountaine or Riuer he swimmeth, he infecteth it. **1592** SHAKS. *Rom. & Jul.* II. vi. 3 Come what sorrow can. **1665** HOOKE *Microgr.* 149 Provide a good large Box..and of what depth you shall judge convenient. **1712–14** POPE *Rape Lock* I. 70 Spirits..Assume what sexes and what shapes they please. **1852** THOREAU *Summer* 23 June, The red color of cattle also is agreeable in a landscape, or let them be what color they may. **1891** MORRIS *Poems by Way* 126 Unmoved I stand what wind may blow.

b. with the generalized sense indicated by *ever, so, soever*, or *somever* following (now only, exc. with *soever*, immediately following: see WHATEVER, WHATSO, WHATSOEVER, WHATSOMEVER).

c **1200** ORMIN 10111 Whatt mann se itt iss þatt hafeþþ twe33enn kirrtless, 3ife he þatt an þatt illke mann þatt iss wiþþutenn kirrtell. **13..** *Cursor M.* 1149 (Gött.) To quat contre so þu wend, Sal þu na man find to freind. *c* **1440** *Gesta Rom.* i. 1 (Harl. MS.) That knyʒt shall dye by my crafte, yn what cuntre of the wordle so euer þat he be ynne. *c* **1450** *Merlin* i. 5 In what nede that euer ye haue. **1470–85** MALORY *Arthur* x. xli. 481 What knyght someuer he were that smote doune sir Palomydes shold haue his damoysel to hym self. **1472** in P. H. Hore *Hist. Wexford* (1900) I. 230 A strange marchaunt..what that ever condicion he be of. **1558** Q. KENNEDY in *Wodrow Soc. Misc.* (1844) 98 Quhat sect or opinioun that evir thou be of. **1588** SHAKS. *Tit. A.* v. i. 82 By that same God, what God so ere it be. **1676** SHADWELL *Virtuoso* IV. 66 Let what harmony soever be between Lovers at first, in a short time it turns to scurvy jangling. **1716** POPE *Iliad* VIII. 567 What Pow'r soe'er provokes our lifted Hand. **1822** K. H. DIGBY *Broadstone Hon.* Pref. p. v, The Gentlemen of England, of what rank or estate soever they may be. **1868** MORRIS *Earthly Par.* (1870) I. II. 460 All people ceased What talk they held soever.

c. Usually with *soever*, in indef. (non-relative) sense (cf. 4 d): Any..at all, any whatever: = WHATEVER 4 a, WHATSOEVER 3 a.

In first quot. 1856 = some..or other.

1597 J. PAYNE *Royal Exch.* 18 Let all right belevers..be of good comforth vnder what cross or distress soever. **1608** CHAPMAN *Byron's Conspir.* v. i. Plays 1873 II. 243 Rise then for euer Quit of what guilt soeuer. **1611** SHAKS. *Wint. T.* I. ii. 44, I loue thee not a Iarre o' th' Clock, behind What Lady she her Lord. **1664** POWER *Exp. Philos.* II. 91 At which Angle of Inclination the perpendicular will be equal to 29 inches, let the Tube be of what length soever. **1725** DE FOE *Voy. round World* (1840) 197 Not to come any nearer, upon what occasion soever. **1736** *Gentl. Mag.* Dec. 721/2 Goods, Chattels, and Things of what Nature or Value soever. **1825** SCOTT *Talism.* xx, She wore not upon her person any female ornament of what kind soever. **1856** EMERSON *Eng. Traits, First Visit Eng.*, Mr. Landor..has a wonderful brain,..by what chance converted to letters. *Ibid.*, Whatever is didactic —what theories of society, and so on,—might perish quickly. **1881** SWINBURNE *Mary Stuart* I. ii. (1899) 52 We took in hand to cut this peril off By what close mean soe'er and what foul hands Unwashed of treason.

10. a. *what time* (later also † ***at what time***), as conj. phr.: At the time, or at any time, at which; when; whenever. So ***what day, what while.*** Now only *poet.*

1357 *Lay Folks' Catech.* (T.) 65 Teche tham thair childir ..What tyme so thai er of eld to lere tham. *c* **1380** *Antecrist* in Todd *Three Treat. Wyclif* (1851) 124 Seynt Jon..seide what tyme he lyved þat þenne weren many antecristis. *c* **1440** *Generydes* 4225 What tyme that eny kyng weddid shuld be,..The kyng and she shuld neuer togeder mete. **1535** COVERDALE *Zech.* viii. 14 Like as I deuysed to punysh you, what tyme as youre fathers prouoked me vnto wrath. **1637** MILTON *Lycidas* 28 What time the Gray-fly winds her sultry horn. **1648** EVELYN *Let. to R. Browne* 18 Dec., Abstaining from using uncivil terms at what time they differed in judgment. **1791** COWPER *Iliad* xx. 190 What time the monster of the Deep pursued The Hero. **1861** D. G. ROSSETTI tr. *Dante's Vita Nuova* in *Early Italian Poets* II. 299 It is your fickleness..makes me tremble thus What while a lady greets me with her eyes. *c* **1882** G. M. HOPKINS *Poems* (1967) 93 Walked with the wind what while we slept. **1885–94** R. BRIDGES *Eros & Psyche* Sept. ii, Was the trial waged What day the Sirens with the Muses strove. **1936** W. B. PEMBERTON *Carteret* ix. 253 He and his brother were quietly mobilising their forces what time a rollicking.. Carteret dictated optimistic despatches. **1945** R. HARGREAVES *Enemy at Gate* 24 One side getting ready for the next time what-time the other as carefully and methodically prepared themselves to fight the last.

†**b.** (with *what* as simple rel.): At which time; when; and then. *Obs.*

1568 GRAFTON *Chron.* II. 65 The kinges Ambassadors repulsed of the French king returned, at what tyme he sent another Ambassade vpon the lyke cause. **1630** *R. Johnson's Kingd. & Commw.* 128, I read..that it was builded..in the time of Edward the third of England; at what time our Kings ..had as yet nothing to doe in this Citie. **1653** H. MORE *Antid. Ath.* III. ix. §3 He gave up the Ghost about the third hour of the night, at what time a black Cat..ran to his bed.

III. *conj.*

†**11. a.** During the time that; while. *Obs. rare.*

c **1175** *Lamb. Hom.* 11 Muchel is us þenne neod.., wet we on þisse middelerd liuien, sod scrift.

†**b.** Up to the time that; till, until. (See also ALLWHAT.) *Obs.*

a **1175** *Cott. Hom.* 235 Si laȝe..adiliȝede..wat hit com to þa time þe god sende þe halie witiȝe. *c* **1250** *Kent. Serm.* in *O.E. Misc.* 30 Þu hest i-hialde þet beste wyn wat nu. *c* **1315** SHOREHAM v. 245 Fram crystes resurreccioun, Wat comeþ hys ascensioun. **13..** *Guy Warw.* (A.) 4902 In þat cite þai bi-leued þere What Tirry was hole & fere. *c* **1330** *Arth. & Merl.* 5022 No fined þai neuer swiche a sleiȝt, What þai to Gaheriet com riȝt. **1340** *Ayenb.* 87 Wyþoute comynge ayen of huyche þinges, non ne is ury in þise wordle, huet hi is y-do.

12. To the extent that; as much as, so far as. (Cf. C. 2 a, 8.) *Obs.* exc. *dial.*

c **1374** CHAUCER *Troylus* IV. 35 Ector..Caste on a day wiþ Grekes for to fighte As he was woned to greue hem what he myghte. *c* **1400** *Destr. Troy* 1794 He..welcomyt hym worthely as a wegh noble, And fraynit hym with frendship qwat the fre wold. **1561** T. HOBY tr. *Castiglione's Courtyer* III. (1577) Q viij b, As though shee woulde..allure what she can the eyes and affection of whoso beholdeth hyr. **1647** WARD *Simple Cobler* (1843) 52, I speak these things to excuse, what I may, my Countrymen in the hearts of all. **1690** PENN *Rise & Progr. Quakers* (1834) 6 They changed what they could, the kingdom of Christ..into a worldly kingdom.

†**13.** (? after F. *que..ou.*) Whether (with correl. *or*).

c **1550** ROLLAND *Crt. Venus* I. 797 Befoir my Maiestie..Or my deputis quhat thay be greit or small.

D. Indefinite (non-relative) uses.

I. *pron.* (*sb.*). †**1.** Something; anything: only OE. exc. as surviving in phrases in which *what* is qualified by a quantitative or identifying word, (sometimes a genitive), e.g. ANYWHAT, ELSEWHAT (OE. *elles hwæt*), LITTLE-WHAT (OE. *lýtles hwæt*, ME. *litles what*, *what litles*, LITTLE B. 3 c), MANYWHAT, MOST*what*, MUCHWHAT (also *mickle what*, MICKLE A. 3), NOWHAT, OTHERWHAT, SOMEWHAT, q.v., whence was evolved a subst. use of *what* = thing. *all what*: all sorts of things. *Obs.*

c **1200** ORMIN 9035, & ȝet forr all an oþerr whatt Seȝȝde þe laffdiȝ Marȝe, þatt Josæp Cristess faderr wass. *Ibid.* 18553 Þatt all þatt strenedd iss off Godd, Off Godess aȝhenn kinde, All iss itt all þatt illke whatt Þatt Godd iss inn himm sellfenn. *c* **1290** *St. Edmund* 408 in *S. Eng. Leg.* 442 Ȝwat lutles it was þat he et, was al of grete þingue. **1303** R. BRUNNE *Handl. Synne* 5963 Ȝyf þou receyuedyst any what Of one þat hys þyng forgat. *c* **1374** CHAUCER *Boeth.* IV. pr. vi. 104 (Camb. MS.) She a lytel what smylynge. **1390** GOWER *Conf.* I. 98 Florent..syh this vecke wher sche sat, Which was the lothlieste what That evere man caste on his yhe. *a* **1400–50** *Wars Alex.* 3046 So fell fliȝt was of flanys..Of arrows & of all quat. **1562** J. HEYWOOD *Prov. & Epigr.* (1867) 112 Doo, say, or syng, in any what, Thou art a minion marmsat. **1579** SPENSER *Sheph. Cal.* July 31 Come downe, and learne the little what, that Thomalin can sayne. **1596** —— *F.Q.* VI. ix. 7 They..gaue him for to feed Such homely what, as serues the simple clowne.

II. *adv.* or *conj.*

(Often, esp. in early examples, capable of being construed as a pronoun = 'some'.)

2. a. Introducing (*a*) each, or (*b*) only the first, of two or more alternative or co-ordinate words or phrases: (*a*) ***what..what***, (*b*) ***what..and*** (†*as*, †*so*) = Some..others; both..and; including..and; as well..as; partly..partly. Now *rare* exc. with special implication (see b).

(*a*) *a* **1175** *Cott. Hom.* 237 Of þe folce we siggeð þat hit cumþ fastlice..wat frend, wat fa. **1297** R. GLOUC. (Rolls) 1152 Hor folc hii lore..Wat in bataile, wat in þe se, and hore hors nei echon. *Ibid.* 5548 Wat þoru is stalward-hede, wat þoru godes grace, Mony was þe gode body, þat he slou. *Ibid.* 8289 Wat adreint, wat aslawe, tuelf princes þer were ded. *a* **1300** *Cursor M.* 2293 Quat for luue and quat for doute. *Ibid.* 3907 Quat of his wiues tuin in spus, And wat of hand wimmen in hus, Tuelue suns had he o þaa. *c* **1330** *Arth. & Merl.* 8873 What wiþ wristling, wat wiþ togging, What wiþ smiteing & wiþ skirminge, On boþe half so þai wrouȝten, Her kinges on hors þai brouȝten. *c* **1384** CHAUCER *H. Fame* III. 968 The thinges that I herde there What a lovde, and what in ere. *c* **1400** MAUNDEV. (Roxb.) xxv. 118 Fyfty comacy of men, what of hors men, what of fote men. *c* **1449** PECOCK *Repr.* II. viii. 189 He schal, what in the firste partie, and what in the ijᵉ. partie, fynde herto proof ynouȝ. **1531** TINDALE *Prol. Jonas* Wks. (1573) 28/2 All the noble bloud was slayne vp, and halfe the commons thereto, what in Fraunce, and what with their owne sword, in fightyng among them selues for the crowne. *a* **1548** HALL *Chron.*, *Hen. IV* 13 b, These Lordes had much people folowing them what for feare and what for entreatie. **1610** HOLLAND *Camden's Brit.* I. 634 The Severn sea..what beeing driven backe..with a Southwest winde, and what with a verie strong pirrie from the sea troubling it, swelled [etc.]. **1654** EARL MONM. tr. *Bentivoglio's Wars Flanders* 122 Most of the Kings ships which, what great, what little, were about forty. **1670** COTTON *Espernon* II. VIII. 350 A hundred and fifty Horse (what Gentlemen, and what of his own Guards). *a* **1693** *Urquhart's Rabelais* III. i. 19 Seven Children at the least (what Male what Female) were brought forth. **1819** SCOTT *Ivanhoe* xxvi, I conceive they may be—what of yeomen—what of commons, at least five hundred men.

(*b*) *c* **1400** MAUNDEV. (1919) xxviii. 170 What on horse & on fote, mo þan CC. Mł. persones. **1442** *Beckington's Jrnl.* (1828) 101 There is in pypes, what in the towne so in the castel, moo than CC legge herneys. *c* **1450** *Brut* II. 483 What of rayne, thondere and lightnyng and hayll. *c* **1500** *Melusine* 240 Many riche rayments..were made what for the spouse as for the ladyes & damoyselles. *Ibid.* 266 About xviii. C what balesters as Archers. **1509** HAWES *Past. Pleas.* III. iii, The very perfect bryghtnes, What of the tower, and of the cleare sunne. **1523** LD. BERNERS *Froiss.* I. ccxxiv. 119 b/1 They rode so long what night and day. **1670** COTTON *Espernon* III. IX. 441 They had been mann'd out with above four hundred and fifty, what Mariners, and Souldiers.

b. Introducing advb. phrases formed with prepositions (in the earliest periods chiefly *for*, later usually, now almost always, *with*), implying (in early use only contextually) 'in consequence of, on account of, as a result of; in view of, considering (one thing and another)'.

In quot. 1591 without alternative: ***whatfor*** simply = 'for, because of'.

(*a*) *c* **1175** *Lamb. Hom.* 145 Alle we beoð in monifald wawe ..hwat for ure eldere werkes, hwat for ure aȝene gultes. *c* **1290** *Beket* 391 in *S. Eng. Leg.* I. 117 Ȝwat for eiȝe, ȝwat for loue, no man him ne with-seide. **1340** HAMPOLE *Pr. Consc.* 7100 What for sorow, and what thurgh smoke And what thurgh cald, and what thurgh hete..þai salle ay grete. *c* **1450** *St. Cuthbert* (Surtees) 1743 What for hungyr, what for thriste, þe shipmen of na lykyng lyste. **1476** *Paston Lett.* III. 161, I ame somewhat crased, what with the see and what wythe thys dyet heer. **1551** ROBINSON tr. *More's Utopia* II. (1895) 116 The .ii. corners, what wythe fordys and shelues, and what with rockes, be very ieoperdous. **1570** FOXE *A. & M.* (ed. 2) 209/2 What for the pillage of the Danes, and what by inward theues and bribers: this land was brought into great affliction. **1603** SHAKS. *Meas. for M.* I. ii. 83 What with the war; what with the sweat, what with the gallowes, and what with pouerty, I am Custom-shrunke. *a* **1672** WILKINS *Nat. Relig.* I. iii. (1675) 36 What through their vicious affections..; what through their inadvertency or neglect.. they are not to be convinced. **1673** MARVELL *Reh. Transp.* II. 181 The Penalty of the Bonds should have differ'd, what in case he run the Subject only into Errour, and what in case of Sin. **1678** J. WILLIAMS *Hist. Gunp.-Treas.* 18 What for avoiding the Report of too much Credulity,..what from the care of doing any thing that might redound to the blemish of the Earl of Northumberland,..it was resolved [etc.]. **1756** *Monitor* No. 35. I. 325 What by..diminution of trade: what by the immense weight of taxes;..some were actually ruined. **1819** SCOTT *Ivanhoe* xliv, Athelstane's spirit of revenge, what between the natural indolent kindness of his own disposition, what through the prayers of his mother Edith..had terminated [etc.]. **1842** DE QUINCEY *Mod. Greece* Wks. 1890 VII. 331 What through banks, and what through policemen, the concern has dwindled to nothing. **1865** KINGSLEY *Herew.* ii, The track, what with pack-horses' feet, and what with the wear and tear of five hundred years' rainfall, was a rut three feet deep and two feet broad.

(*b*) *c* **1386** CHAUCER *Sqr.'s T.* 46 The foweles..What for the seson and the yonge grene Ful loude songen hire affeccions. **1393** LANGL. *P. Pl.* C. XVIII. 85 What þorw werre and wrake and wycked hyfdes. *a* **1400–50** *Wars Alex.* 781 Quat of stamping of stedis & stering of bernes, All dymed þe dale. *c* **1420** *Chron. Vilod.* 3173 What by-cause of þe hele of þis gode wyff, & also of þe meracle þe whiche þer was do. *c* **1440** *Alphabet of Tales* 13 What for calde & for holdyng in þe watir, I was nere-hand slayn. **1579** TWYNE *Phis. agst. Fort.* I. xxx. 41 What by the wonderfulnesse and number of the woorkes, there was nothyng in all the whole world to be wondered at, but Rome. **1591** GREENE *Maiden's Dream* 154 She..wrong out sighes so sore: That what for grief her tongue could speak no more. **1665** SIR T. HERBERT *Trav.* (1677) 166 What by Themistocles on shore, and Leonidas at Sea, at Salamis and Thermopylæ, his huge Army melted away. **1702** DE FOE *Shortest Way w. Dissenters* 29 Alas the Church of England! What with Popery on one Hand, and Schismaticks on the other; Now has she been Crucify'd between two Thieves. **1768** STERNE *Sent. Journ.*, *Fragment* I. 106 What for poisons, conspiracies and assassinations.., there was no going there by day—'twas worse by night. **1822** COBBETT *Cott. Econ.* (1823) §108 What of Excise Laws and Custom Laws and Combination Laws and Libel Laws, a human being..scarcely knows what he dares do or..say. **1867** PARKMAN *Jesuits in N. Amer.* xxiii. (1875) 346 What with hunting, fishing, canoe-making, and bad weather, the progress of the august travellers was so slow. **1870** DASENT *Ann. Eventf. Life* xxxvi, Aunt Mandeville,..what between the White Lady and the warm verses, was quite upset.

⁂ For other indefinite (non-relative) uses see C. 4 d, 9 c.

E. Substantival nonce-uses (from A., B., C.).

1. The question 'What?', 'What is it?', or the like, or the answer to such question; the essence or substance of the thing in question.

1656 COWLEY *Pindar. Odes*, *Extasie* vi, An unexhausted Ocean of delight Swallows my senses quite, And drowns all What, or How, or Where. **1796** MME. D'ARBLAY *Camilla* v. vi, 'What, ma'am?—how?—what?—' 'Nay, nay, don't be frightened. Come down to dinner, and we'll talk over the hows? and the whats? afterwards.' **1832** MOTLEY in *Corr.* (1889) I. 18, I was summoned before the Senate of the University, and then wrote my name and my whences and whats, etc., etc., in a great book. **1844** L. HUNT *Blue-Stocking Revels* II. 171 Poems 114 My lady will know all the what and the why. **1861** J. BROWN *Horæ Subsec.* Ser. II. 101 Desiring to divine the essences rather than the appearances of things—in search of the *what* chiefly in order to question it, make it give up at whatever cost the secret of its *why*. **1884** tr. *Lotze's Metaph.* 431 It must seem utterly inconceivable that we should ask for the 'what' of a thing, and yet look for the answer in anything except that which this thing is and does.

2. A something.

1654 WHITLOCK *Zootomia* 149 We have seen the Pittifull who's, and in short the slender whats are against modest Learning in Religious Division. **1903** A. MACLAREN *Last Sheaves* 54 We are not seeking a What; we are seeking a Whom.

3. An instance of the exclamation 'What!'

1779 WARNER in Jesse *Selwyn & Contemp.* (1844) IV. 254 His partner..gave..a 'What!' of such sharp, shrill astonishment, that you could not but have laughed at it. **1785** MME. D'ARBLAY *Diary* 16 Dec., The *What!* was then repeated.

†**what**, *a.*[2] *Obs.* Forms: 1 hwæt, 3 hwat, whæt, wat. [OE. *hwæt* = OS. *hwat* keen, bold, OHG. *hwaz*, *waz* sharp, rough, severe, ON. *hvatr* bold, vigorous: related to WHET *v.*, q.v.] Quick, active; stout, brave.

Beowulf 1601 Næs ofgeafon hwate Scyldingas. *a* **1000** *Bi Monna Cræftum* 81 Sum biþ to horse hwæt. *c* **1200** *Trin. Coll. Hom.* 183 To gode þu ware slau and let; and to euele spac and hwat. *c* **1205** LAY. 7137 Þer weoren eorles swiðe whæte [*c* **1275** wate] and leiden þene king bi ane ȝate.

what, Sc. f. WHET *v.*

whata, var. FUTTAH.

whatabout(s (ˈhwɒtəbaʊt(s). *rare.* [f. WHAT *pron.*, after *whereabout(s).*] What one is about; doings, occupations.

1830 SOUTHEY *Lett.* (1856) IV. 170 Then you might know of all my..whatabouts and whereabouts from Henry Taylor. **1841** N. HAWTHORNE in *N. H. & Wife* (1885) I. 227, I bethink me that you may have no objections to hear something of my whereabout and whatabout. **1868** ELIZ. PRENTISS *Life & Lett.* (1882) 244, I was right glad..to learn of your whereabouts and whatabouts.

†**what-call-ye-him.** *Obs.* Also simply **what-call.** = WHAT-D'YE-CALL-'EM (-UM), -HER, -HIM, -IT.

1473 SIR J. PASTON in *P. Lett.* III. 104 Ber the cuppe evyn, as What-calle-ye-hym seyde to Aslake. **1592** NASHE *P. Penilesse* Wks. (Grosart) II. 130 His Page shal say..he is so busie with my L. How-call-ye him, and my L. What-call-ye him. **1598** *Seruingman's Comf.* (1868) 166 M. what-call-you-hims man. **1609** *Ravenscroft's Deuteromelia* 21 This other day I start a hare On what-call Hill.

whatcha (ˈwɒtʃə, ˈhw-), repr. a colloq. or vulgar pronunciation of *what do* (or *are*, or *have*) *you*? See WATCHA.

1934 J. T. FARRELL *Calico Shoes* 43 H'lo, baby! Whatcha say, kid! **1966** M. & G. GORDON *Undercover Cat prowls Again* (1967) v. 44 Whatcha getting me today, Tim? **1973** *Black World* June 65 Awwwwh, Baby what'cha done to me-ee. **1978** 'M. CRAIG' *Were he a Stranger* xvi. 128 'Whatcha want?'..'We're looking for a man,' Ted called.

whatchamacallit (ˈwɒtʃəmə͵kɔːlɪt, ˈhw-), repr. a pronunciation of *what-you-may-call-it* (see WHAT-D'YE-CALL-'EM, etc. γ). Chiefly *U.S.*

[**1928** M. OSTENSO *Mad Carews* xii. 160 It's your—whatcha-may-call-it—your dowry!] **1942** BERREY & VAN DEN BARK *Amer. Thes. Slang* §75/4 *Contrivance*..*gadget*, whatchamacallit. **1974** R. B. PARKER *God save Child* (1975) ii. 13 A pet whatchamacallit... Guinea pig. **1979** *Globe & Mail* (Toronto) 24 Jan. 6/2 Wouldn't everyone feel silly if it turned out..that the whang-doodle was just a whatchamacallit with speed stripes?

what-d'ye-call-'em (-um), -her, -him, -it (ˈhwɒtdjə-, ˈwɒtʃəkɔːləm, ɛtc). *colloq.* Less commonly **what-do-you-call-'em**, etc.; also variously abbreviated (see quots.); also simply 7–8 **what-d'ye-call.** See also *β.* below. [WHAT *pron.* A. 1.] An appellation for a thing or person whose name the speaker forgets, does not know or wish to mention, or thinks not worth mentioning. Also *occas.* substituted for any word (e.g. an adjective) which the speaker fails to recall.

1639 [J. TAYLOR (Water-P.)] *Divers Crabtree Lect.* 217, I ..gave her a sound spurnne upon the Buttocks:..O my what doe you call't, said shee. **1641** COWLEY *Guardian* v. v, *Dog.*..How the what-d'ye-call-'um runs? What do ye call it? *Pun.* Time, Sir. *c* **1646** MILTON *Sonn.*, *On new forcers Consc.* 12 By shallow Edwards and Scotch what d'ye call. **1678** DRYDEN *Kind Keeper* III. i, His Father was Squire what-d'you call him, of what d'you call 'em Shire. **1704** SWIFT *T. Tub* Pref. 17 Spoken by Mr. Whatdicall'um. **1752** FOOTE *Taste* II, She was a kind of a what d' ye call 'em..a sort of a Queen or Wife, or something or other to somebody, that liv'd a damn'd while ago. **1765** STERNE *Tr. Shandy* VIII. xix, There being so many tendons and what d'ye call-'ems all about it. **1773** H. WALPOLE *Let. to W. Cole* 8 Jan., Mr. What-d'ye-call-him's pamphlet. **1779** MME. D'ARBLAY *Diary* 16 June, Miss What-d'ye-call-her. **1806** SURR *Winter in Lond.* III. 257 We..went to that public house or what-d'ye-call, in Piccadilly. **1827** SCOTT *Chron. Canongate* iii, There is good accommodation at the what-d'ye-call-'em arms. **1838** DICKENS *Nich. Nick.* xxv, To break up old associations and what-do-you-callems of that kind. **1870** LOWELL *Study Wind.* 74 As legitimate a subject of human study as the glacial period or the silurian what-d'ye-call-ems. **1875** F. E. TROLLOPE *Charm. Fellow* i, College is out of the question..unless he entered himself as a what-do-you-call-it?..A sizar.

†β. In contracted forms **whatd'ecalt, what d'ee cal't, what-d'ye-caw't, whatchicalt, what-sha-callum**, etc. (cf. WASHICAL): sometimes analysed as = *what shall I call..? Obs.*

1593 G. HARVEY *Pierce's Super.* Wks. (Grosart) II. 57 Hollinsheads engrosing; some-bodies abridging; and what-chicaltes translating. **1598** B. JONSON *Ev. Man in Hum.* I. ii. (1601) B4, Didst thou not see a fellow here in a what-sha-callum doublet? **1632** BROME *North. Lasse* v. v, Your great acquaintance, and alliance in the Whatshicall Court *Non obstante.* **1641** —— *Jov. Crew* II. (1661) F 1, Rogue enough though, to offer us his whatd'ecalts? his Doxies. **1654** WHITLOCK *Zootomia* 121 What think you Sir of your what-sha'come Water and Diascord? **1658** A. FOX tr. *Würtz' Surg.* II. xxviii. 188 It is called also the not-named, or (a whats you call) an unknown Sore, no body knows what it is. **1673** *S'too him Bayes* 55, I came onely to..be a witness for the orthodoxness of what d'ee cal't. **1691** MRS. D'ANVERS *Academia* 10 'Tis, let me see, now, whach'ee call, Syncategorematical. *a* **1807** J. SKINNER *Songs & Poems* (1859) 43 That camsteary—what-d'ye-caw't? (I think it's genius, walie fa't). **1820** SCOTT *Abbot* xxvi, My Lady What-shall-call 'um's powder.

γ. So **what-ye** (*or* **-you**) **-call(-it**, etc.), later usually **what-you-may-call-it** [WHAT *pron.* C. 4].

1598 CHAPMAN *Blinde Beg. Alexandria* Plays 1873 I. 28 *Eli.* Why hees a what you calt. *Mar.* A what you call it can you not name it. **1600** SHAKS. *A.Y.L.* III. iii. 74 Good euen good Mr what ye cal't. **16..** MIDDLETON, etc. *Old Law* III. ii, *Lis.* Heeres your first weapon ducks meat. *Sim.* How, a dutch what you call em, Stead of a German falchion. **1848** DICKENS *Dombey* xxvii, There is no What's-his-name but Thingummy, and What-you-may-call-it is his prophet! **1870** MARY BRIDGMAN *Robt. Lynne* xxiv, Fine place, Bob; built by the what-you-may-call-its. **1891** KIPLING *Light that Failed* ix, Say good-bye to the what-you-call-um girl.

†**whate**, *sb. Obs.* Forms: 1 *pl.* **hwata**, 3 **hwat**, 3–4 **quate**, 3–5 **wat(e**, **what(e**, 5 **qwate**. [OE. pl. *hwata*, **hwatan* (gen. *hwatena*), related to *hwata* augur, *hwatung* divination.]

1. Divination, augury; ? foreboding.

c **1000** ÆLFRIC *Lev.* xix. 26 Ne eton ʒe blod, ne ne ʒimon hwata ne swefna! *c* **1200** *Trin. Coll. Hom.* 11 Warienge, and handselne, and time, and hwate, and fele swilche deueles craftes. *c* **1250** *Gen. & Ex.* 1054 ȝet sat loth at ðe burȝes gate, After sum geste stod him quake [*read* quate]. *c* **1375** *Cursor M.* 19567 (Fairf.) Of wate he [*sc.* Simon Magus] was ful wonder wise.

2. Fortune, destiny, fate, luck.

c **1200** *Trin. Coll. Hom.* 105 þe unbileffulle..Werpeð þat gilt..uppen hwate, and seið, nahte ich no betere wate. **1297** R. GLOUC. (Rolls) 802 Alas alas þou luþer wate [*MS.* δ fortune], þat vilest me þus one. *Ibid.* 8519 Vor gode wate afterward he nadde in none dede. **13..** *St. Gregory* (Vernon MS.) 294 þis is a child of goode whate. *c* **1400** *Destr. Troy* 13681 þen fortune his fall felli aspies, Vnqwemys his qwate, & þe qwele turnys. **14..** *MS. Cantab. Ff.* v. *48*, lf. 94 (Halliw.) To bilde he hade gode quate.

b. ? Good fortune, luck.

c **1330** *Florice & Bl.* (1857) 14 And be hit erli and be hit late To thi wille thou schalt haue whate.

†**whate**, *adv. Obs.* [f. WHAT *a.*[2]] Quickly.

The identity of the word in the phr. *alse (h)wat se* (= as soon as) is uncertain.

c **1175** *Lamb. Hom.* 79 Al se hwat se he forgulte wes..þet him er luuede ho him for wundeden. *c* **1200** *Trin. Coll. Hom.* 71 Alse wat swo þe man his sinne sore bimurneð, ure drihten leðeð þe sinne bendes. **13..** *K. Alis.* 2639 (Laud MS.) To Tebes ward hij wendeþ whate, Hij sheteþ aȝeins hym þe gate. *a* **1400** *Lybeaus Disc.* 1741 Lambard ladde hym forth well whate.

whate, obs. north. f. WOT.

whatever (hwɒtˈɛvə(r)), *pron.* and *a.* Also *poet.* **whate'er** (hwɒtˈɛə(r)); 6–7 **whatere**. [Orig. two words, WHAT A., B. and EVER *adv.* 8 e.]

1. *interrog.* An emphatic extension of *what*, used in a question (direct or indirect), implying perplexity or surprise. Now *colloq.*

(More properly written as two words: see EVER *adv.* 8 d.)

a. *pron.*

13.. *Seuyn Sag.* (W.) 3514 Son, what may al this noys be, ..Whateuer sal it sygnyfy? **14..** in *Anglia* XXVII. 285 Scho..thoght: what euer menes þis message to me. *c* **1440** *York Myst.* xxiii. 85 *Petrus.* Brethir, what euere ȝone brightnes be? **1823** *Spirit Publ. Jrnls.* 409 Whatever possessed her, I know no more than the child unborn. **1856** F. E. PAGET *Owlet of Owlst.* xiv. 143 'Gracious heart alive, whatever in all the world was that?' asks one. **1880** MRS. OLIPHANT *He that will not* etc. xxiii, Whatever can you want to emigrate for?

b. *adj.*

Mod. Whatever [*or* What ever] contrivance is that? I wonder whatever [*or* what ever] queer thing he'll do next.

2. As compound relative, in a generalized or indefinite sense: see EVER *adv.* 8 e. (Occas. with correl. demonstrative following.) **a.** *pron.* Anything at all which, anything that; sometimes contextually (esp. *poet.*), all that, everything that.

c **1375** *Cursor M.* 321 (Fairf.) Quat euer þe haly gaste wille, þe fader and sone wil tyte fulfil. *c* **1450** *Godstow Reg.* 31 Holdynge ferme & stable what euyr he wolde do ther-with. **1456** SIR G. HAYE *Law Arms* (S.T.S.) 228 Quhatever sik men dois, it is comperit to the dede of a beste. **1567** *Gude & Godlie B.* (S.T.S.) 39 Quhat euer I haif, all that is thyne. **1592** SHAKS. *Ven. & Ad.* 623 Being mou'd he [*sc.* the boar] strikes, whatere is in his way. **1671** MILTON *P.R.* I. 149 Whose constant perseverance overcame Whate're his cruel malice could invent. **1726** SWIFT *Gulliver* IV. v, It is a Maxim among these Men, That whatever has been done before may legally be done again. **1832** HT. MARTINEAU *Life in Wilds* vii. 88 In a few months we shall have stores of whatever we want. **1883** D. C. MURRAY *Hearts* i, We'll lay in whatever you want to-morrow.

b. *adj.* (*sing.* or *pl.*, of things or persons): Any ..at all which (or who), any..that; sometimes (*poet.*), all or every..that.

c **1380** WYCLIF *Sel. Wks.* III. 343 Whatever reasoun men maken of Crist, of Petir, or oþer good ground, it goiþ opinli aȝen sich a pope. **1382** —— *Ezek.* xxxiii. 12 The riȝtwijsnesse of a iust man shal not delyuere hym, in whateuer day he shal synne. *c* **1449** PECOCK *Repr.* IV. viii. 463 What euer gouernaunce God in his Holi Scripture of the Newe Testament blameth. **1596** DALRYMPLE tr. *Leslie's Hist. Scot.* I. 29 Quhateuir thing the handis of men had twechet,..frome al sik thay absteined mony dayes thaireftir. **1692** BENTLEY *Boyle Lect.* vi. 22 What-ever successive Duration, shall be bounded at one end, and be all past and present, must come infinitely short of Infinity. **1764** GOLDSM. *Trav.* 113–117 Whatever fruits in different climes were found,..Whatever blooms in torrid tracts appear... Whatever sweets salute the northern sky..; These, here [*sc.* in Italy] disporting, own the kindred soil. **1821–2** SHELLEY *Chas. I*, II. 374 They will hear homilies of whatever length Or form they please. **1887** GOLDW. SMITH in *Contemp. Rev.* July 3 The Governor-General has been stripped of whatever little authority he retained.

3. Introducing a qualifying dependent clause equivalent to a conditional or disjunctive clause, often with verb in subjunctive (*whatever happen* = 'if any (sort of) thing happen', 'whether one thing or another happen'). **a.** *pron.* = 'No matter what'; frequently implying opposition (equivalent to a conditional clause with *though*): = 'Notwithstanding anything that'.

As predicate sometimes (esp. of persons) expressing quality or character, and thus approaching a pred. adj. (cf. WHAT A. 17). Often with ellipsis (*whatever its merits* = 'whatever its merits may be').

13.. *Minor Poems fr. Vernon MS.* xlix. 344 Whon þe þef passeþ quyt a-way, þe trewe mon haþ schome, what-euer men sai. *a* **1425** *Cursor M.* 11143 (Trin.) But whateuer he had in þouȝt Mis-likyng chere had he nouȝt. **1559** *Mirr. Mag., Jack Cade* i, Whateuer it were this one poynt sure I know. **1591** SHAKS. *Two Gent.* III. i. 100 Take no repulse, what euer she doth say. *c* **1600** —— *Sonn.* cxiii. 11 Whatere thy thoughts, or thy hearts workings be, Thy lookes should nothing thence, but sweetnesse tell. **1600** —— *A.Y.L.* II. vii. 109 What ere you are That in this desert..Loose, and neglect the creeping houres of time. **1606** —— *Tr. & Cr.* IV. v. 77 *Æne.* If not Achilles sir, what is your name? *Achil.* If not Achilles, nothing. *Æne.* Therefore Achilles: but what ere, know this. **1623** HEMINGE & CONDELL *1st Folio Shaks.* A 3, But, what euer you do, Buy. **1667** MILTON *P.L.* II. 162 Whatever doing, what can we suffer more..? **1668** DRYDEN *Secret Love* I. iii, *Phil.* And yet, there is a thing, which time may give me The confidence to name. *Lys.* 'Tis yours whatever. **1697** —— *Æneis* VI. 526 Mortal, what e're, who this forbidden Path In Arms presum'st to tread, I charge thee stand. **1712** STEELE *Spect.* No. 497 ¶3 Whether it were from Vanity,..or whatever it was, he carried it so far, that [etc.]. **1780** WARNER in Jesse *Selwyn & Contemp.* (1844) IV. 342, I am glad to hear you speak of a little horse, what-ever his colour be. **1840** DICKENS *Old C. Shop* lxxiii, So Richard asked her; whatever she said, it wasn't No. **1842** —— *Amer. Notes* iii, Whatever the defects of American universities may be, they disseminate no prejudices. **1856** NEWMAN *Univ. Sk.* (1902) 191 Men of one idea and nothing more, whatever their merit, must be to a certain extent narrow-minded. **1857** MRS. CARLYLE *Lett.* II. 326, I have had nothing to suffer from heat, whatever else.

b. *adj.* = 'No matter what..'; often implying opposition: = 'Notwithstanding any..that'.

Also (after a prep.) with ellipsis, passing into sense 4 a (*a*).

1561 WINȜET *Bk. Questions* Wks. (S.T.S.) I. 77 We addict our selfis to the doctrine of na man, of quhateuir leirning and auctoritie he be. **1595** SHAKS. *John* IV. i. 84. **1692** BENTLEY *Boyle Lect.* v. 17 What-ever Considerations of this nature you propose to this Atheist,..he hath this one subterfuge from them all. **1751** JOHNSON *Rambler* No. 142 ¶10 Money, in whatever hands, will confer power. **1794** PALEY *Evid.* (1825) II. 74 Whatever fables they have mixed with the narrative, they preserve the material parts. **1889** *Nature* 19 Sept., Rocks of whatever origin, crushed and ground to pieces,..reconstruct themselves into new forms. **1906** H. BELLOC *Hills & Sea* 176 In whatever place a man may be the spring will come to him.

c. *adv.* Whatever may be the case, at all events. *dial.* (and *colloq.*).

1870 'R. PIKETAH' *Forness Folk* 15, I cuddent leave t' pleass whativver wi'out seein' her. **1900** 'A. RAINE' *Garthowen* 93 She's got a tidy pair of ankles, whatever. **1933** 'R. CONNOR' *Girl from Glengarry* 120, I am doing my utmost whatever. **1960** R. WILLIAMS *Border Country* I. ii. 58 What do it matter it's down?.. He is Will whatever. **1962** *Amer. N. & Q.* I. 15/1 Whatever, from the early 1700s to the present day..it was the musical that struck root as an indigenous form. **1980** *New Musical Express* 12 Jan. 33/1 Whatever, the myth looks momentous in its sleek new American threads.

4. As indefinite adj. or pron., with loss of the relative force: cf. WHAT D.

a. *adj.* (*sing.* or *pl.*, of things or persons); Any ..at all. †(*a*) preceding the sb.: cf. WHAT C. 9 c. *Obs.* or merged in the elliptical use under 3 b.

c **1383** in *Engl. Hist. Rev.* (1911) Oct. 742 Prelatis curatis & preestis or what euere clerkis: shulen not do symonie. *c* **1449** PECOCK *Repr.* I. xvii. 99 Lete hem not come into what euer examynacioun of argumentis whiche mowe be mad ther upon. **1620–55** I. JONES *Stone-Heng* (1725) 11 Accounting it their chiefest Glory to be wholly ignorant in whatever Arts. **1667** MILTON *P.L.* II. 442 If thence he scape into what ever world, Or unknown Region. **1709** SHAFTESB. *Charac.* II. II. I. iii. 93 The Bull alone makes head against the Lion, or whatever other invading Beast of Prey.

(*b*) following the sb.: usually, now only, after *any*, *no*, *all* (*anything*, *nothing*), etc., which it qualifies like an adv. = 'at all': cf. EVER 8.

1623 N. ROGERS *Str. Vineyard* 78 We see that the Barke of the Vine seemeth more withered and dry than the..Barke of any other Tree whateuer. **1681** CHETHAM *Angler's Vade-m.* iv. §13 (1689) 42 The most holding Bait of all other whatever. **1718** PRIOR *Poems* Ded. (1905) p. xx, He was so strict an Observer of his Word, that no Consideration whatever, could make him break it. **1749** FIELDING *Tom Jones* II. i, I shall not look on myself as accountable to any Court of Critical Jurisdiction whatever. **1823** SCOTT *Quentin D.* xvii, Fortifying her strong castle against all assailants whatever. **1853** DICKENS *Bleak Ho.* iv, I know nothing whatever of Mr. Jellyby. **1855** BAIN *Senses & Int.* I. ii. 195 All bodies whatever are liable to the state of sonorous vibration. **1884** *Marshall's Tennis Cuts* 94 That a player using a racket had no chance whatever against an opponent catching and throwing the ball.

b. *pron.* Anything at all: cf. WHAT D. 1. *rare.*

1637 EARL MONM. tr. *Malvezzi's Romulus & Tarquin* 211, I surely should not put this behinde what ever else. **1892** M. DODS *Gosp. John* II. xiv. 218 The torrent bursts in on me and pours over my wasted bulwarks, resolves, high aims, and whatever else.

c. ***or whatever***: used after a noun (or nouns) to suggest that some other unspecified term might be employed instead, as being more usual, preferable for any reason, or more applicable; or something similar; or the like. *colloq.*

1905 W. JAMES *Let.* 25 Apr. (1920) II. 225 Poor Professor De Sanctis, the Vice President or Secretary or whatever. **1913** E. POUND *Let.* 7 Nov. (1971) 24 *If* Chicago (or the U.S.A. or whatever) will slough off its provincialism, if it will begin to be aware of Paris (or of any other centre save London),..there is no reason for Chicago or *Poetry* or whatever not being the standard. **1917** H. JAMES *Sense of Past* II. 83 One of those concentrated terms of pious self-dedication or whatever by which the aspirants of the ages of faith used to earn their knighthood. **1958** P. SCOTT *Mark of Warrior* II. 167 I'd get on to battalion or brigade, or whatever, and tell 'em. **1964** [see KIWANIS]. **1975** I. MURDOCH *Word Child* 47 And even if we are all thoughts in the mind of God or whatever why should you be able to become God? **1981** 'M. INNES' *Lord Mullion's Secret* ii. 21 There isn't a handy second title around. Viscount Tom Noddy, or whatever. **1984** J. BARNES *Flaubert's Parrot* x. 129 Bourgeois monarchy, or bureaucratised totalitarianism, or anarchy, or whatever.

d. Similarly replacing other parts of speech.

1947 *Periodical* XXVII. 93 It was in one with a brown (or whatever) cover. **1976** *Church Times* 6 Aug. 9/1 Now that the Archbishop of Canterbury has 'relinquished', 'delegated' or whatever his metropolitical authority to the local Arab Anglicans.., is it not proper [etc.].

what ho (hwɒtˈhəʊ), *int.* and *a.* **A.** *int.* An exclamation used to call the attention of a person, or as an expression of excitement or exultation. Cf. WHAT B. I. 3. Now *arch.* or *affected.*

c **1386** CHAUCER *Miller's T.* 251 What how, what do ye maister Nicholay? **1579** SPENSER *Sheph. Cal.* July 5 What ho, thou iollye shepheards swayne, Come vp the hyll to me. *c* **1590** MARLOWE *Faustus* III. iv. (1616), What ho, Officers, Gentlemen, Hye to the presence to attend the Emperour. **1610** SHAKS. *Temp.* I. ii. 313 What hoa: slaue: Caliban. **1810** SCOTT *Lady of L.* II. xxxv, 'Malise, what ho!'—his henchman came. **1864** BALLANTYNE *Lifeboat* x, 'What ho! Coleman,' cried Bax,..'have you actually acquired the art of sleeping on a donkey?' **1899** H. WYNDHAM *Soldiers of Queen* vi. 137 'What ho! Did you get your bloomin' ticket this time?' demands a brother 'Lancer'.

B. (hyphened) as *adj.* Superior, smart, stylish; designating the type of person supposed to use the exclamation, esp. the heartier kind of officer and gentleman.

1937 in *Amer. Speech* (1938) XIII. 239/1 At the time of their installation the elevators at the Ritz Carlton were considered the What-ho-iest in town. **1973** *Times Lit. Suppl.* 21 Sept. 1074/3 Those who survive to be relieved by what-ho young soldiers in scarlet tunics and white bandoliers. **1977** *Time* 22 Aug. 37/1 The Legionnaires are a carefully assorted lot,..a soulful French musician, a what-ho English blueblood, a hulking Russian who once guarded the Czar's family, and so on.

what-if (ˈhwɒtɪf), *a.* and *sb.* [An extended use of the phr. *what if..?*: see WHAT A. I. 5 a.] (That involves) speculation as to what might have been, had antecedent conditions been different; an instance of this.

1973 *Nation Rev.* (Melbourne) 31 Aug. 1455/1 The whatif game, a futile exercise in hindsight, poses such unanswerable questions as whatif Romulus and Remus had fallen foul of a hostile..wolf? **1974** J. IRVING *158-Pound Marriage* (1980) III. 57 Joseph Stalin..was himself a figure surrounded by a horde of *what if's*. **1977** *New Yorker* 29 Aug. 66/2 'The Eagle Has Landed', one of the current unalarming terror films about what-if, the what-if being, in this case, what if the Germans had tried to capture Churchill? **1982** *Times* 14 Jan. (Information Technology Suppl.) p. v/4 *What-If Games.* Computer software is available which allows users to change one variable in a set of data, and see how this affects all the other variables. **1984** *Computers in Teaching* No. 1. 29 All of the models are theoretically realistic and allow the undergraduate student to pose the 'What if..?' kinds of question, which are so difficult to answer without recourse to simulation.

what-is-it, var. WHATSIT.

†**whatkin**, *sb. Obs. rare*⁻¹. [f. WHAT D. 1 + -KIN.] A little 'something'; a minute particle.

1674 N. FAIRFAX *Bulk & Selv.* 112 It self [*sc.* a leasting or atom] being an unthroughfaresom whatkin.

†'**whatkin, -kins,** *a. Sc.* and *n. dial. Obs.* (Sometimes as two words.) Forms: see WHAT *pron.* and KIN *sb.*[1]; also 5 **what skynnes.** [f. WHAT *a.*[1] + KIN *sb.*[1] 6 b. In later use Sc.; cf. WHAT'N.]

1. Interrogative or exclamatory: Of what kind; what kind or sort of; what.

a **1300** *Cursor M.* 963 Tell me.. Howgat and wit quatkin-thing, I sal couer þi saghteling. **13..** *E.E. Allit. P.* A. 771 Quat-kyn þyng may be þat lambe, þat þe wolde wedde vnto hys vyf? **13..** *Gosp. Nicodemus* (G.) 28 We wate wele Ioseph was a wright,.. and mari vs menes his moder hight, we, whatkin goddes er þise? *c* **1400** MAUNDEV. (Roxb.) xvi. 76 If ȝe will wit whatkyn letters þai vse, here ȝe may here þam. *c* **1425** WYNTOUN *Cron.* II. Prol. 1 Now haf ȝhe herd on qwhatkyn wyse I haf contenyt þis tretyis. *c* **1475** *Rauf Coilȝear* 592 Quhat kin a fallow was that ane? **1561** WINȜET *Bk. Questions* Wks. (S.T.S.) I. 60 Quha declaris expreslie quhatkin a faith thai haif in God.

β. **13..** *Cursor M.* 3687 (Gött.) 'Sir,.. þi mete es graid.' 'And quatkines mete?' 'sir, venisun.' *Ibid.* 10442 Ne wate þu noght.. Quatkines a fest it es to day? *a* **1450** MYRC *Par. Pr.* 1526 Take gode hede on hys de-gre, Of what skynnes lyuynge þat he be. **1457** HARDING *Chron.* in *Engl. Hist. Rev.* (1912) Oct. 751 To spye.. whatkyns passage wer for an hoste to ryde.

2. Relative: That kind of.. which, such.. as; usually in generalized sense (sometimes with *so* or *soever*): Whatever.

a **1300** *E.E. Psalter* lv. 10 [lvi. 9] In what-kin dai I cal the nou, Loke, I knew that mi God art þou. *c* **1380** WYCLIF *Sel. Wks.* III 515 Men clepid men of holi Chirche may.. do what kynne sinne, what kynne tresoun, likeþ hem. **1435** MISYN *Fire of Love* I. vii. 14 Slike one & so grete he is, whatkyns or so mykill none odyr is, no neuer may be. *a* **1450** MYRC *Par. Pr.* 210 On what skynnes maner so hyt be wroȝt, Dedly synne hyt ys forthe broght.

†**whatliche,** *adv. Obs.* Forms: 1 **hwætlice,** 3 **hwatliche,** *Orm.* **whattlike;** *comp.* 3 **watloker,** 4 **whatloker(e, -likere;** *sup.* 4 **whatlokest.** [OE. *hwætlíce*, f. *hwæt* WHAT *a.*[2] + *-líce* -LY[2].] Quickly.

a **1000** *Ags. Ps.* (Th.) cxxxvii[i]. 4 [3] Ðehyr me hwætlice. *c* **1200** ORMIN 12166 Þatt deofell let te Laferrd seon Whattlike inn an hanndwhile Off all þiss wide middellærd Þe kinedomess alle. *a* **1250** *Owl & Night.* 1708 Þeos hule spac wel baldeliche, For þah heo nadde swo hwatliche Ifare after hire here, Heo walde neoþeles ȝefe answere.

b. *comp.* Sooner, more readily, rather; *sup.* soonest.

c **1200** *Vices & Virtues* 87 Bute ðu iswik, ðe hwatliker hit te scall æure ma rewen. **1297** R. GLOUC. (Rolls) 8846 Worri he wolde watloker mid worde þan mid arme. *c* **1300** *Beket* (Percy Soc.) 1249 And whatlokere [*v.r.* wel raþur] scholde such an heȝ man ne come he noȝt so sone, And nother ich ne he habbeth with oure bischops to done. *a* **1305** *St. Kenelm* 315 in *E.E.P.* (1862) 56 Wheþer of þuse tuei schires whatlokest miȝte awake Al sauf scholde wende forþ. **13..** *Leg. Rood* 30/142 Þe raþer [*v.r.* whatlikere] it him was uorȝeue.

what-like, *interrog. a.* (*sb.*) *arch.* and *dial.* (Also as two words.) [orig. Sc.: f. WHAT *pron.* + LIKE *a.* (q.v. 1 b ¶), as in '*What* is he *like*?', after SUCH-LIKE.] **a.** Of what appearance or aspect; of what kind or character. (Usually predicative.)

1719 A. RAMSAY *Poems* (1945) I. 214 To speer what like a Carlie is he. **1810** R. H. CROMEK *Remains of Nithsdale & Galloway Song* 37 What like may your lassie be? **1821** SCOTT *Kenilw.* xi, I should be glad to know myself what like the fellow was. **1857** JAS. HAMILTON *Less. Gt. Biog.* 309 It would be interesting to know what like man was in the primeval paradise. **1861** DICKENS *Gt. Expect.* ix, What like is Miss Havisham? **1865** DICKENS *Mut. Fr.* II. III. ii. 16 She knows Miss Abbey of old, remind her, and she knows what-like the home, and what-like the friend, is likely to turn out. **1876** MORRIS *Æneids* I. 751 Meanwhile unhappy Dido.. asked.. With what-like arms Aurora's son had come unto the King. **1905** in *Eng. Dial. Dict.* VI. 443/1 What-like hat had he on? **1953** 'N. BLAKE' *Dreadful Hollow* xii. 150 Now you tell me —what like are the Blick laddies?

b. as *sb.* Aspect, appearance. *nonce-use.*

1853 C. C. LEITCH in *Mem.* (1856) 125 The.. questions of the whereabouts and the what-like of a new bungalow.

Whatman ('hwɒtmən). [From the name of the maker.] In full ***Whatman paper***: the proprietary name for a kind of paper, made in various qualities, used for drawings, engravings, etc.

[**1876** *Trade Marks Jrnl.* 8 Nov. 748 *J. Whatman*... W. and R. Balston, Springfield, Maidstone, Kent; Paper Manufacturers... Writing paper and drawing paper.] **1880** *Macm. Mag.* No. 245. 380 For rapid sketching, thin rough Whatman, properly stretched upon a board, is as good as any other paper. **1886** H. R. ROBERTSON *Art of Pen-and-Ink Drawing* 37 Some old Whatman paper. **1916** *Trade Marks Jrnl.* 26 July 763 W. E. R. Balston Limited Genuine Whatman folded filter papers. **1976** *Ibid.* 28 Apr. 890/2 *Whatman*.. paper and paper articles.. not including printed publications. Whatman Limited, Springfield Mill, Maidstone, Kent, Paper manufacturers.

what'n, whatten ('hwɒt(ə)n), *a. Sc.* and *n. dial.* Forms: 6 **quhaten, quhattane, -in(e, whattin,** 9 **whaten, -an, whatten.** Also *β.* (with indef. art.) **what'n a, whatna.** [Reduced form of WHATKIN *a.*; cf. THAT'N, THISSEN.] Properly, What kind of; hence, what.

a **1510** DOUGLAS *K. Hart* I. 245 Quhat will ȝe saye me now for quhaten plycht? *c* **1560** A. SCOTT *Poems* (S.T.S.) xxviii. 16 Quhattane ane glaikit fule am I. **1561** WINȜET *Bk. Questions* Wks. (S.T.S.) I. 57 Quhattin a Papist I am in this samin ruid Buik of Questionis.. I tak on hand to preue.. the maist haly Martyris,.. to hef bene the samin Papistis. **1600** [? LYLY] *Maydes Metam.* III. ii, Priapus quoth a? Whattin a God might that bee? **1818** SCOTT *Hrt. Midl.* xxxix, I wish I had whaten books ye wanted. **1825** BROCKETT *N.C. Gloss.*, Whatten o'clock is't? **1891** MORRIS *Poems by the Way* 157 And whatten a bed for me?

β. *a* **1796** BURNS '*There was a lad*', But what'n a day o' what'n a style I doubt it's hardly worth the while To be sae nice wi' Robin. **1816** SCOTT *Antiq.* xxxix, But whatna wife's this, wi' her creel on her back? **1899** CROCKETT *Kit Kennedy* ix, Think, oot o' whatna pit the laddie has been digged.

whatness ('hwɒtnɪs). [f. WHAT *pron.* + -NESS; transl. L. *quidditās* QUIDDITY.] That which makes a thing what it is; essential nature, essence: = QUIDDITY I.

1611 FLORIO, *Quidità*, the whatnesse of any thing. **1627** W. SCLATER *Expos. 2 Thess.* (1629) 39 The kinde or quality, or if you'l so terme it, whatnesse of it. **1656** [? J. SERGEANT] tr. *T. White's Peripat. Inst.* 198 The Understandablenesse of a thing, or the quiddity, the Whatnesse. **1870** MORLEY *Stud. Lit.* (1891) 266 Pressing for definition, you never get much further than that each given quiddity means a certain Whatness. **1889** MIVART *Truth* 212 We must.. have the conception of the kind of thing the object is—'what' it is, or the idea of its 'whatness'.

†**b.** Used by N. Fairfax for: Statement of what a thing is, definition. *Obs. nonce-use.*

1674 N. FAIRFAX *Bulk & Selv.* 80 The definition or whatness of a thing ought to be of a thing as a thing.

what-not, whatnot ('hwɒtnɒt). [Properly an ellipt. interrog. phr. (see first quot. below, and cf. WHAT A. 5).]

1. a. Usually and preferably as two words ('hwɒt'nɒt): Anything whatever; everything; 'anything and everything'; 'all sorts of things': mostly, now only, as final item of an enumeration: = anything else, various things besides; 'whatever you like to call it'. (Also occas. of persons.)

1540 PALSGR. *Acolastus* v. ii. Y iij b, Excesse of fleshely pleasures.. hath taken awaye all thynges.. my goodes or substance, my name .i. my good name and fame, my frendes, my glory .i. my renoume or estimation, what not? .i. what thyng is it that she hath not taken from me? **1576** FLEMING *Panopl. Epist.* 185 His minde was so altered, his conditions so changed, and what not in him so alienated. **1596** SHAKS. *Tam. Shr.* v. ii. 110 Marrie peace it boads, and loue, and quiet life, An awfull rule, and right supremicie: And to be short, what not, that's sweete and happie. **1602** MARSTON *Antonio's Rev.* v. iv, I have.. Borne out the shock of war, and done, what not, That valour durst. **1663** PEPYS *Diary* 21 Dec., The strange variety of people.. bakers, brewers, butchers, draymen, and what not. **1718** POPE *Lett.* (1735) I. 263 Our evening Walks in the Park, our amusing Voyages on the Water, our Philosophical Suppers, our Lectures, our Dissertations, our Gravities, our Reveries, our Fooleries, our what not? **1741** RICHARDSON *Pamela* I. xix. 46 A Gentleman.. who is my Master, and thinks himself intitled to call me Bold-face and what not. **1849** in B. Gregory *Side Lights* (1898) 462 Well off with the profits of his books and whatnot. **1852** THACKERAY *Esmond* II. iii, The blessed king's rosaries, the medals which he wore, the locks of his hair, or what not. **1872** BLACK *Adv. Phaeton* xxix. 391 We had our chops and what not in the parlour of the inn. **1876** E. W. HEAP *Diary* 11 June in *Publ. Amer. Dial. Soc.* (1969) LII. 56 [We] all started out on our grand excursion Picnic fishing party or what not. **1890** 'R. BOLDREWOOD' *Col. Reformer* xiii, Fencing, dam-making, cattle-droving, what not. **1911** *Athenæum* 24 June 711/1 They were too apt to go to law and fight over their lands and fishing rights and what-not.

b. A thing or person that may be variously named or described; a nondescript. *rare.*

1602 *How Chuse Good Wife* v. i. I 2, Why you Iacke sawce, you Cuckold, you what not. **1903** ALICE M. EARLE *Two Cent. Costume Amer.* II. 481 Besides the furbelows and *prétintailles*, or 'whatnots', were hurly-burlies and *fanfreluches*.

¶ Confusedly used in *pl.* for 'various things'.

a **1861** T. WINTHROP *Life in Open Air* (1863) 53 Passengers who are constantly to make portages will not encumber themselves with what-nots. **1862** THACKERAY *Philip* ix, I profess to be an impartial chronicler of poor Phil's fortunes, misfortunes, friendships, and what-nots.

c. Used as a euphemism for something the speaker does not wish to name.

1964 in Hamblett & Deverson *Generation X* 85 By the time I was fourteen I'd been a court witness in an indecent exposure case after an Indian doctor had been caught flashing his whatnot at me in an Adventure Playground. **1977** *Custom Car* Nov. 28/2 What ho, a twace of the fairer whatnot in the old Panther eh? **1977** M. RILEY *Ideal Friend* iv. 30 She said.. tapping the Cellophane-covered éclairs, 'I don't know about you but these always put me in mind of nignogs' whatnots.'

2. An article of furniture consisting of an open stand with shelves one above another, for keeping or displaying various objects, as ornaments, curiosities, books, papers, etc.

1808 SARAH, LADY LYTTELTON *Corr.* (1902) 54 The old chairs, tables, what-nots, and sofas. **1831-4** R. S. SURTEES *Jorrocks's Jaunts* (1838) 330 There was a 'what not' on the right of the fire-place. **1862** *Catal. Internat. Exhib., Brit.* II. No. 5674, Canterbury what-not. **1863** HAWTHORNE *Our Old Home, About Warwick* I. 140 Such delicate trifles as we put upon a drawing-room table.. or a whatnot.

Hence '**whatnotism**, any or every kind of 'ism' (as a final term in an enumeration of 'isms').

1915 GALSWORTHY in *Fortn. Rev.* 1 Nov. 928 What is wanted in a work of art is an.. adequate correspondence between fancy and form.. so that one shall not be distracted by its naturalism, mysticism, cubism, whatnotism. **1951** KOESTLER *Age of Longing* I. v. 113 Those convicted of formalism, neo-Kantianism,.. and whatnotism were given their deserved punishment.

what-now. *nonce-wd.* = QUIDNUNC.

1890 C. MARTYN *W. Phillips* 236 The wits of the pot-house and the what-nows of society were.. mightily amused.

what reck, whatreck, *interrog. phr.* (*adv.*) *Sc.* Also 6 **quhat ra(c)k, quhattrak, quattrack,** 9 **foutrack.** [f. WHAT *a.*[1] (13 b) + RECK *sb.*[1] 2.] What matter? what does it matter? Also parenthetically as *adv.*: For all that, nevertheless.

1500-20 DUNBAR *Poems* xxviii. 30 Thocht a man haif a brokin bak, Haif he a gude crafty telȝour, quhattrak, That can it cuver with craftis slie. **1535** LYNDESAY *Satyre* 3292 The Mers sould find me beif and kaill. Quhat rak of bread! *a* **1586** MONTGOMERIE *Poems* (S.T.S.) 280 'And thow steill a cow, cairle, thair they will hang the.' 'Quattrack, Lord, of that? For anis mon I die.' **1787** BURNS *When Guilford good our Pilot stood* ii, But yet, whatreck, he, at Quebec, Montgomery-like did fa', man. **1808** A. SCOTT *Poems* 114 Yet they whatreck in population spread. **1825** JAMIESON s.v. *Foutrack*, One, who hears any unexpected news, exclaims, Foutrack! i.e., Indeed! Is it really as you say? **1847** J. HALLIDAY *Rustic Bard* 165 But yet, what reck?

So **whatrecks** (6 **quhatt rax,** 9 *Sc.* **fatrecks**) [WHAT *adv.* (20) + RECK *v.* 8 b] in same sense.

1535 LYNDESAY *Satyre* 1540 (Bann. MS.) Now quhill the king is sound sleipand, Quhatt rax to steill his box? **1724** RAMSAY *Tea-t. Misc.* (1733) I. 108 Her mill into some hole had fawn Whatrecks, quoth she, let it be gawn. **1804** TARRAS *Poems* 12'Fatrecks!' quo' Will, 'it needs nae badder.'

whatsaile, -saill, obs. ff. WASSAIL.

what'sa matter (,wɒtsə'mætə(r), ,wh-). Also **whatsamatter,** etc. Repr. colloq. or careless pronunciation of 'what is the matter?' Cf. WHASSA.

1935 *New Yorker* 12 Jan. 18/3 What'sa metta with Kitty Shapiro? **1950** *Commentary* Sept. 255/2'Whatsa-matter,' he shouted at Rosa, 'you want her blood?' **1960** 'E. MCBAIN' *Heckler* (1962) xiv. 136 Whattsa matter? Something wrong? **1977** D. E. WESTLAKE *Nobody's Perfect* (1978) II. i. 102 Whatsa matter don't you wanna go home!!!

what-sha-callum, what-sha'-come, etc.: see WHAT-D'YE-CALL-'EM.

what's-her-face ('wɒtsəfeɪs, 'hw-), occas. U.S. var. *what's-her-name* s.v. WHAT'S-HIS-NAME. Cf. WHATSISFACE.

1980 in S. Terkel *Amer. Dreams* 5 Several times during my year as what's-her-face I had seen the movie *The Sting*.

what's-his-name ('hwɒtshɪzneɪm). *colloq.* Also **whatsisname.** Substituted for the name of a man or boy (loosely, of a thing) which the speaker forgets, does not know, or is unwilling to mention. So **what's-her-name** (of a woman or girl), **what's-its-name** (of a thing), **what's-your-name** (of a person addressed).

whatsename (quot. 1866) represents an ambiguous form which is not uncommon. *what's-their-names* (quot. 1773) is very rare.

1697 DRYDEN *Virg. Past.* III. 61 Two Figures on the sides emboss'd appear; Conon, and what's his Name who made the Sphere. **1757** FOOTE *Author* I, Look ye here, Mr. What's-your-name? **1773** G. A. STEVENS *Trip Portsm.* ii. 28 The what's-their-names at uproars squall. **1816** SCOTT *Old Mort.* Concl., 'And what became of old Mrs What's her name, the housekeeper?' 'Mrs Wilson, madam', answered I. **1829** MARRYAT *Frank Mildmay* xxiii, Mr. Thingamy, you will take the what's-his-name. **1838** DICKENS *Nich. Nick.* xxxi, Those great folks in what's-its-name Place. **1846** —— *Cricket on Hearth* i, There was soon the very What's-his-name to pay. **1848** —— *Dombey* xxi, 'But seclusion and contemplation are my what's-his-name—' 'If you mean Paradise, Mamma, you had better say so, to render yourself intelligible.' **1866** READE *Griffith Gaunt* xv, He.. almost persuaded Whatsename, another heathen gentleman, to be a Christian. **1872** EARL PEMBR. & G. H. KINGSLEY *S. Sea Bubbles* i. 29 The back-sliding individual is looked upon.. by the more.. decent of the community as little better than one of the what's-his-names. **1880** 'OUIDA' *Moths* i, It makes one feel like What's-her-name in the 'Trovatore'. **1942** W. FAULKNER *Go down, Moses* 87 Is that so? Look here, Mister What's-your-name—. **1943** K. TENNANT *Ride on Stranger* x. 114 And then Bleeby.. accusing me.. of turning Whatsisname against him. **1979** S. WILSON *Glad Hand* I. i. 11 *Marilyn.* What is going on? *Brian.* Same old thing: raising the whatsis-name—the Antichrist.

whatsisface ('wɒtsɪzfeɪs, 'hw-), U.S. var. WHAT'S-HIS-NAME.

1967 *Current Slang* (Univ. S. Dakota) Spring 5, [1964] *What's his face*, one whose name is forgotten. **1977** J. WAMBAUGH *Black Marble* (1978) vi. 79 They're having another Save Harry Whatzisface party there today. **1978** *N.Y. Times Mag.* 23 July 23/3 The derivation of some vogue phrases is a mystery:.. What visual need caused the unforgettable 'whatsisname' to become whatsisface?

whatsit ('wɒtsɪt, 'hw-). *colloq.* Also **what-is-it, what's-it,** and (*U.S.*) **whassit.** [The phr. 'what is it?' used as a sb.: see WHAT A. I. 1.] = WHAT'S-

HIS-NAME, WHAT'S-ITS-NAME, etc. (used variously of a person or thing); a 'thingummy'.

a **1882** *Philad. Times* in *Dict. Americanisms* (1951) II. 1855/1 The two negro girls, who figure as 'what-is-its', are paid $200 a week. **1898** J. D. BRAYSHAW *Slum Silhouettes* 158 'Now,' said Joe, 'who says pudden? Mister What's It—a little piece?' **1922** S. LEWIS *Babbitt* vi. 77 He's a what-is-it from Columbia. **1931** *Kansas City Times* 29 Sept., A Whassit. Excitement.. Friday afternoon was caused by the appearance of an insect which [etc.]. **1954** P. FRANKAU *Wreath for Enemy* III. v. 215, I couldn't even walk along the passage to the whatsit. **1979** P. ALEXANDER *Show me Hero* xvii. 178 Suddenly you're a man. Not just because you happen to have a couple of whatsits, but because you *feel* it. **1984** B. FRANCIS *AA Car Duffer's Guide* 14 Do you think I ought to check the strength of the whatsit—electrolyte—while I'm at it?

whatso ('hwɒtsəʊ), *pron.* and *a. arch.*, chiefly *poet.* [ME. *w(h)at so*, *quatso*, *hwat se*, (Orm.) *whattse*, reduced form of OE. *swá hwæt swá*, early ME. *swa hwet swa*, generalized form of *hwæt* WHAT *pron.*: see SO *adv.* 17 d.]

1. a. *pron.* = WHATEVER 2 a.

c **1200** ORMIN 426 Forr swa we don unnhaȝherrliȝ Whattse we don to gode. *c* **1250** *Gen. & Ex.* 1324 Oc abraham it wulde wel Quat-so god bad. *c* **1275** LAY. 25703 We leteþ him one don wat so [*c* 1205 Faren heu swa] he wolle. **13..** *Gaw. & Gr. Knt.* 255, & quat so þy wylle is, we schal wyt after. **1340–70** *Alex. & Dind.* 359 What so we worchen in þis worlde,.. For his sake þat it sente soþli we worchin. **1399** LANGL. *Rich. Redeles* Prol. 36 Mekely to suffre what so him sente were. *c* **1475** *Rauf Coilȝear* 511 And thow mat me ony mair, cum efter quhat sa may, Thow and I sall dyntis deill. **1594** R. C[AREW] *Tasso* (1881) 7 When Sire eternall.. Lookes downe, and.. in one vew, Comprizeth all what so the world can shew. **1622** WITHER *Faire-Virtue* N 2 b, And, my Care, it addes not to What-so, others say, or doe. **1795** SOUTHEY *Joan of Arc* I. 70 And whatso He commands, that I must speak. **1876** MORRIS *Æneids* XII. 182 Whatsoever God Is in the air, or whatso rules the blue sea with its rod. **1900** BEECHING *Confer. Bks. & Men* Ded., Despatches, sermons,—whatso goes Into their brain comes out as prose.

b. *adj.* = WHATEVER 2 b.

1591 SPENSER *Virg. Gnat* 682 And whatso other hearb.. The ioyous Spring.. brings forth.. He planted there. **1868** MORRIS *Earthly Par.* I. Prol. 17 His fleet held whatso keel could swim From Jutland to Land's End. **1891** C. E. NORTON *Dante's Hell* vii. 31 Whatso power he have.

2. a. *pron.* = WHATEVER 3 a.

a **1300** *Cursor M.* 9036 Ne [er] þe gode þe wers to prais, Quat-so men o þe wick sais. **13..** *Gaw. & Gr. Knt.* 382 Gawan I hatte, þat bede þe þis buffet, quat-so bi-fallez after. **1377** LANGL. *P. Pl.* B. x. 128 Al worth as þow wolte, what so we dispute. **1457** HARDING *Chron.* in *Engl. Hist. Rev.* (1912) Oct. 747 What so men gat couetyse noght hym fylde. *a* **1542** WYATT *Poems, Synce loue wyll nedes* iii, Whatso befall, till that I sterve By proof full well it shall be known. **1600** FAIRFAX *Tasso* v. lxxviii, Loue calles it follie, what so wisdome saith. **1868** MORRIS *Earthly Par.* (1870) I. I. 445 And fearless will I enter here And meet my fate, whatso it be. **1870** *Ibid.* L'Envoi (1890) 444/1, I love thee, whatso time or men may say.

†**b.** Of a person: Whoever. *Obs.*

c **1205** LAY. 6555 What se [*c* 1275 wose] hæfde richedom, he hine makede wræcche mon. *a* **1225** *Ancr. R.* 66 Ancre, hwat se heo beo, alse muchel ase heo euer con & mei, holde hire stille. *c* **1386** CHAUCER *Prol.* 522 But it were any persone obstinat, What so he were, of heigh or lough estat Hym wolde he snybben. **1412** in *Laing Charters* (1899) 24 The forsaid lord or his ayris qwhat sa thai be for the tyme. **1565** J. HALL *Crt. of Virtue* 103 b, The poore man,.. As well as he, What so he be, That ryches doth endue.

c. *adj.* = WHATEVER 3 b.

1867 MORRIS *Jason* VI. 456 Whatso thing the next day bring, Right merrily shall pass these coming hours.

3. *adj.* = WHATEVER 4 a.

1902 A. AUSTIN *Crowning of Kingship* ii, And, like the sea, let whatso tempests shrill, One, world-wide,.. and free.

whatsoever (hwɒtsəʊ'ɛvə(r)), *pron.* and *a.* Also *poet.* **whatsoe'er** (hwɒtsəʊ'ɛə(r)). Also 5 **quatsever**, 6 **whats'ever**. (In early use often as two words or three.) [f. WHATSO + EVER *adv.* 8 e; cf. SOEVER.]

1. a. *pron.* = WHATEVER 2 a.

c **1250** *Gen. & Ex.* 270 Wisdom ðe made ilc ðing of noȝt, Quuat-so-euere on heuone or her is wroȝt. *c* **1320** *Cast. Love* 420 Riht ne spareþ for to jugge What-so-euere Soþ wol sugge. *c* **1420** *Sir Amadace* (Camden) xlvii, Quat-seuer ȝe wille with the kingus men do. **1509** FISHER *Funeral Serm. C'tess Richmond* Wks. (1876) 301 What so euer thou wylt aske of god thy fader I knowe wel he wyll graunte it vnto the. **1526** TINDALE *John* xiv. 13 Whatsoever ye axe in my name, that will I do. **1591** SYLVESTER *Du Bartas* I. i. 252 Whats'ever now the Heav'ns wide arms embrace. **1597** HOOKER *Eccl. Pol.* v. xlvii. §2 Whosoeuer hath the name of a mortal man, there is in him whatsoeuer the name of vanitie doth comprehend. **1664** BUTLER *Hud.* II. iii. 297 He knew whats'ever's to be known. **1817** SHELLEY *Rev. Islam* IV. xii, Whatsoe'er my wakened thoughts create. **1874** PUSEY *Lenten Serm.* 103 More grievous will be that fire, than whatsoever man can suffer in this life.

b. *adj.* = WHATEVER 2 b.

1484 CAXTON *Fables of Æsop* VI. ii, None, for what so euer myght that he haue ought not to despreyse the other. **1526** TINDALE *Phil.* iv. 8 Whatsoever thyngs are true, whatsoever thyngs are honest,.. those same have ye in youre mynde. **1564** BULLEIN *Dial. agst. Pest.* (1888) 139 Whatsoeuer thinges are seen with bodily iyen. **1667** MILTON *P.L.* IV. 587 In whatsoever shape he lurk, of whom Thou telst. **1868** MORRIS *Earthly Par.* (1870) I. I. 71 Whatsoever things We asked for,.. those were ours.

2. a. *pron.* = WHATEVER 3 a.

13.. *Cursor M.* 10508 (Gött.) Þu ma gode chere Quat so euer þu se or here. *c* **1450** *Merlin* ii. 37, I will knowe the soth, what-so-euer it coste. *a* **1533** LD. BERNERS *Huon* xliii. 143, I woll not be dyspleased what so euer thou sayest. **1582** ALLEN *Martyrdom Campion* (1908) 16 Meaning by the state (whatsoeuer they otherwise pretende).. the welfare of some few.. upholden by this new religion. **1676** DRYDEN *Aurengz.* IV. 61 And, whatsoe'r my Letter did pretend, I made this meeting for no other end. **1681** —— *Abs. & Achit.* 797 Whatsoe'r their Sufferings were before, That Change they Covet makes them suffer more. **1794** R. J. SULIVAN *View Nat.* I. 113 Any force by which bodies tend towards each other, whatsoever be the cause. **1825** J. NEAL *Bro. Jonathan* III. 187 They froze me, or affronted me.. whatsoever I did.

†**b.** Whoever: = prec. 2 b. *Obs.*

c **1430** LYDG. in *Pol. Rel. & L. Poems* (1903) 46, I Counsell, what-so-euer thow be. **1573** TUSSER *Husb.* (1878) 122 Pay iustly thy tithes whatsoeuer thou bee. **1588** A. KING tr. *Canisius' Catech.* 69 Quhatsaeuer ȝe be yat ar baptized in Christ ȝe haue put on Christ. **1601** SHAKS. *Twel. N.* I. iii. 124. **1628** FELTHAM *Resolves* II. [I.] xi. 29 Could'st thou that readest this, whatsoeuer thou art..?

c. *adj.* = WHATEVER 3 b.

a **1533** LD. BERNERS *Huon* cxlix. 568 Ye ought to praise our lord god, what so euer losse ye haue had. **1546** in Lindesay (Pitscottie) *Chron. Scot.* (S.T.S.) II. 68 Quhat-soevir estait or ordour he be of. **1596** DALRYMPLE tr. *Leslie's Hist. Scot.* I. 1 Afore the eyne baith of our Nobilitie, and of the lai people, in quhatsaeuir state or degrie. **1711** ADDISON *Spect.* No. 125 ¶8 Those whom they ought to look upon as their Common Enemies, whatsoever Side they may belong to. **1849** RUSKIN *Seven Lamps* i. (1885) 7 The art which so disposes and adorns the edifices raised by man, for whatsoever uses, that [etc.]. **1874** L. MORRIS *Songs of Two Worlds* Ser. II. *Reply* ii, Whatsoever chance befall, Of myself I'd die possest.

3. a. *adj.* †(*a*) = WHATEVER 4 a (*a*). *Obs.*

1589 in *Cath. Rec. Soc. Publ.* V. 177, I wil put it in practice, nothwithstanding whatsoeuer inclination to the contrary. **1605** A. WOTTON *Answ. Popish Pamph.* 76 [We] who submitt whatsoeuer our expositions to be compared with the Scriptures. **1611** *Bible* Transl. Pref. ¶3 He would not suffer it to be broken off for whatsoeuer speaches or practises. **1611** W. SCLATER *Key* (1629) 125 Fornication.. is any what-soeuer breach of Chastitie. **1678** CUDWORTH *Intell. Syst.* 232 One True God, from whom is all Whatsoever Nature. *a* **1679** HOBBES *Rhet.* Pref., The Art of speaking, which.. is able to bring about whatsoever Interest.

(*b*) = WHATEVER 4 a (*b*).

1472–3 *Rolls of Parlt.* VI. 34/1 In this Parlement, or any other Parlement afore this tyme holden whatsoever notwithstondyng. **1549** WRIOTHESLEY *Chron.* (Camden) II. 9 This realme of Englande and other the Kinges dominions whatsoeauer. **1582** in Allen *Martyrdom Campion* (1908) 80, I build not my faith upon any one man whatsoever. **1596** SHAKS. *Tam. Shr.* I. ii. 216, I promist we would be Contributors, And beare his charge of wooing whatsoere. **1692** HICKERINGILL *Good Old Cause* Wks. 1716 II. 535 You may easily know to get an Antidote against Death, and Losses, and Crosses, whatsoever. **1792** ALMON *Anecd. W. Pitt* II. xxix. 127 In every circumstance of government and legislation whatsoever. **1865** KINGSLEY *Herew.* ix, He felt in himself no title whatsoever to that epithet.

†**b.** *pron.* = WHATEVER 4 b. *Obs.*

1579 TOMSON *Calvin's Serm. Tim.* 1023/1 Other wil become horne madde and be at defiance with whatsoeuer. **1583** STOCKER *Civ. Warres Lowe C.* III. 134 It was also well furnished.. with whatsoeuer els necessary for a Trenche. **1641** EARL MONM. tr. *Biondi's Civil Wars* III. 152 The pompe and solemnity exceeded whatsoever of former times.

†**whatsome**, *pron. Obs.* In 4 **quat-sum, -sim.** [f. WHAT *pron.* + SUM *rel. adv.*] Whatever.

a **1300** *Cursor M.* 792 Quat sum first þar was gain saw, Al for noght þai ette it bath. *c* **1375** *Ibid.* 9036 (Fairf.) Quat-sim men of þe wikked saise.

whatsomever (hwɒtsəm'ɛvə(r)), *pron.* and *a. Obs.* exc. *dial.* (In early use often as two words or three.) [f. prec. + EVER *adv.* 8 e.]

1. a. *pron.* = WHATEVER 2 a.

c **1400** MAUNDEV. (Roxb.) xxvi. 123 Þai will graunt þam what sum euer þai asch. *c* **1530** in Ellis *Orig. Lett.* Ser. II. I. 312 Yff your Grace wold witsaffe to wryght iij. wordes to the sayd Archibishope shewyng hyme, whatt so mever hathe ben wrytyn. **1581** *Satir. Poems Reform.* xliv. 274 The vther number of the congregation, Redaris, exhortaris, or quhatsumeuir thay be. **1602** SHAKS. *Ham.* I. ii. 249 And what someuer els shall hap to night, Giue it an vnderstanding but no tongue. **1648** EARL WESTMLD. *Otia Sacra* 67 Whatsome'r both Earth and Air afford.

b. *adj.* = WHATEVER 2 b.

c **1400** *Rom. Rose* 5041 But what some euer woo they fele, They wole not pleyne. **1523–34** FITZHERB. *Husb.* §168 Whatsomeuer thynge is gyuen vnto them for the loue of hym, he taketh it as it were done to hym-selfe. **1588** A. KING tr. *Canisius' Catech.* 58 Quhatsumeuer things ar treue, quhatsumeuer things ar honest. *c* **1610** SIR J. MELVIL *Mem.* (1683) b 2 b, Favourites.. who.. take pleasure of whatsomever Recreation they find the Prince inclined to. **1634** in J. Russell *Haigs* (1881) 207 Whatsomever bonds are in Moneys in my behoof.

2. a. *pron.* = WHATEVER 3 a.

a **1300** *Cursor M.* 10508 'Anna,' he said, 'þou ma god chere Quat-sum euer þou se or here.' *c* **1430** *Syr Gener.* (Roxb.) 2804 Wel am I wroken on the, What som euer fal on me. *c* **1485** *Digby Myst.* III. 1235 Whatt-so-mewer yow be-tyde. **1508** FISHER 7 *Penit. Ps.* ii. Wks. (1876) 35 Alwaye content what someuer god sent vnto them. **1523** LD. BERNERS *Froiss.* I. ccxii. 106 b/2 Our subiectes, comons, colleges, vniuersities, or syngular personnes, what someuer they be. **1603** *Philotus* lxxvii, Quhat sumeur me befall.

†**b.** Whoever: = WHATSO 2 b. *Obs.*

c **1450** in *Three 15th Cent. Chron.* (Camden) 98 That the justice may do upon them trew jugement, what some evar they be. *c* **1475** *Rauf Coilȝear* 398 Quhat sumeuer that he be, Bring him haistely to me. **1535** STEWART *Cron. Scot.* (Rolls) I. 641 Nor na other, quhatsumeuir that thai be, Haldis of ȝow or ȝour auctoritie. **1601** SHAKS. *All's Well* III. v. 54 What somere he is He's brauely taken heere.

c. *adj.* = WHATEVER 3 b.

1482 CAXTON *Trevisa's Higden* (Rolls) I. 363 No man.. schal be i-saued, but he be verrey repentaunt, what sommeuer penaunce he doo. **1523** LD. BERNERS *Froiss.* I. ccxii. 107 b/1 Subiectes, (whatsomeuer estate or condicion they be of). **1533** BELLENDEN *Livy* I. Prol. (S.T.S.) I. 7 In quhatsumeuir way It sall happin. **1606** SHAKS. *Ant. & Cl.* II. vi. 102 All mens faces are true, whatsomere their hands are.

3. a. *adj.* = WHATEVER 4 a.

1429 in *15th Rep. Hist. MSS. Comm.* App. VIII. 10 Any other accyons qwatesumewer be twyx thaim. **1482** in *Charters Edin.* (1871) 155 Ony vther place quhatsumeuer neidful, or amangis quhatsumeuir merchandis. **1588** in *J. Melvill's Autob. & Diary* (Wodrow Soc.) 266 All and whatsumever persones, avowit or suspected to be Papists. **1678** G. MACKENZIE *Crim. Laws Scot.* II. xi. §5, (1699) 202 In all the Courts of Bishops, Abbots, and the Lords whatsomever. **1711** in *Nairne Peerage Evid.* (1874) 132 Him his heirs and successors whatsomever. **1842** BARHAM *Ingol. Leg.* Ser. II. *Dead Drummer*, I can't see no Drummer-boy here whatsumdever. **1894** CROCKETT *Raiders* xviii, Silver Sand had no cloak or plaid whatsomever.

†**b.** *pron.* = WHATEVER 4 b. *Obs.*

1648 EARL WESTMLD. *Otia Sacra* 54 Our Lust, our Pride, Ambition, Or whatsome'r beside.

whatstane, obs. form of WHETSTONE.

whatte, obs. form of WOT.

whatten, -in: see WHAT'N.

ˌ**what-the-'hell**, *v. slang.* [The phr. 'what the hell?' used as an expression of irritation: see HELL *sb.* 9.] *intr.* To exclaim 'what the hell..?'; to make an angry demand for an explanation.

1924 WODEHOUSE *Leave it to Psmith* x. 211 While everybody's cutting up and what-the-helling. **1939** H. HODGE *Cab, Sir?* 181 The yawper, of course, is convinced that if he doesn't what-the-hell a little.. we shall deliberately go a long way round. **1963** WODEHOUSE *Stiff Upper Lip, Jeeves* xvii. 132 This telephone call was Aunt Dahlia what-the-helling.

ˌ**what-the-'hell**, *adj. phr. slang.* [Cf. prec.] Casual, insouciant, devil-may-care.

1968 *Listener* 1 Aug. 130/1 Much of this is due to his casual 'What the hell?' attitude to the over-familiar pomposities of public life. **1977** *Time* 19 Dec. 47/2 The only real stumbling block is fear of failure. In cooking you've got to have a what-the-hell attitude.

whatway: see WHAT A. 13 (*b*).

what-wise, *adv. phr. rare.* [Properly two words, WHAT *a.* (13) + WISE *sb.*] In what manner; how. Also *in whatwise*.

a **1300** *Cursor M.* 20398 Of vs es nan þat wat for quam, Ne wat quat-wis we heder cam. *c* **1350** *Will. Palerne* 904 Seie me in what wise þat þat hache þe haldes. *c* **1460** *Towneley Myst.* xxix. 36, I shall you tell what-wyse and how. **1513** DOUGLAS *Æneis* IV. Prol. 188 With Venus henvifis quhat wyse may I flite? **1905** J. B. BURY *Life St. Patrick* vii. 139 Tell us how we may know him, in what-wise he will appear.

what-you-(may-)call-it, etc.: see WHAT-D'YE-CALL-'EM.

whau, *int. north. dial.* Also **wha, whaugh.** [A natural exclamation; perh. also contained in WHANNOW.] Well! Why! Also = WAUGH a.

1589 'MARPRELATE' *Hay any Work* 30 Whau, whau, but where haue I bin al this while. **1684** MERITON *Yorksh. Dial.* Gloss., *Whaugh*, a word of Admiration, as God bless us, etc. **1828** *Craven Gloss.*, *Wha*, well. **1832** LYTTON *Eugene Aram* IV. ix, Depend on it, they are two of a trade—augh!—bother!—whaugh! **1847** HALLIWELL, *Whau*, why; yes. *North.*

whau (faʊ, waʊ), *sb. N.Z.* Also **wou.** [Maori.] A shrub or small tree, *Entelea arborescens*, of the family Tiliaceæ, native to New Zealand and bearing serrate leaves and clusters of small white flowers; = CORKWOOD 2. Also, the light wood of this tree.

1840 J. S. POLACK *Manners & Customs New Zealanders* 263 The *Pongo* and *Wou*.. are varieties of the cork-tree. **1868** *Trans. N.Z. Inst.* I. III. 35 For floats, the light wood of the small tree Whau.. was used. **1889, 1946** [see CORKWOOD 2]. **1980** J. T. SALMON *Native Trees N.Z.* 120 Whau is an attractive New Zealand tree with an unusual, almost tropical appearance.

whaule eyed, obs. form of WALL-EYED.

whaup (hwɔːp, hwɑːp), *sb. Sc.* and *north.* Forms: 6 **quha(i)p**, 7 **whoup**, 7–9 **whap**, 8–9 **whaap**, 8– **whaup**, (8 **whape, wap**, 9 **whawp, quhaup**). [Perhaps for **whalp* and allied to OE. *huilpe* (Seafarer 21), = early WS. **hwielpe*:—**χwalpjon-*, f. *χwalp-* : *χwelp-* a stem imitative of the bird's cry, and represented also in LG. *regenwilp*, *-wölp* sandpiper, WFris. (*greate*) *wylp* curlew (*reen-*, *wetterwylp*, *lytse wylp* Numenius phæopus), Du. *wulp*, *wilp* curlew. (WFris. *wettergulp*, LG. *regengilp* show a variant with *g*.) The dial. name *curlew-help* may be for **curlew-whelp*, and so attest the former existence of a variant **whelp*; but cf. the form *hilpe* (1530 in *Ancestor* XI. 179).] The larger curlew, *Numenius arquata*.

Also †*great whaup*, *stock whaup* (see STOCK *sb.*[1] 64).

1538 *Burgh Rec. Edin.* (1871) II. 92 A quhap that is greitt xij d. **1553** *Ibid.* 185 The best quhaip viij d. **1549** *Compl.*

Scot. vi. 39 Quhilk gart the quhapis for fleyitnes fle far fra hame. **1683** ALEX. GARDEN in *Macfarlane's Geogr. Collect.* (S.H.S.) II. 133 The Whap also uses to be eaten. **1733** T. GIFFORD *Zetland Isl.* (1786) 26 Wild fowl.. such as pluvers, whapes. **1793** *Statist. Acc. Scot.* V. 188 The wild land fowls are plovers, pigeons, curlews, (commonly called whaap). **1839** STODDART *Songs & P.* 18 An' his dirges lang and dreary Pipes the grey whaup to the morn. **1895** CROCKETT *Men of Moss-Hags* xxxix, Not so much as a whaup came near me on that great, wide, dappled hill.

whaur, Sc. f. WHERE.

wha(u)ve (hwɔːv), *v. dial.* Also 7 whoave, 9 wauve. [ad. ON. *hvalfa, holfa*: see WHELVE.]

1. *trans.* To turn upside down; to turn (pottery) when drying.

1611 COTGR. s.v. *Dent, Mettre vn pot &c. à dents*, to turne it vpside-down, to whauve it with the mouth downewards. **1686** PLOT *Staffordsh.* 123 When the Potter has wrought the clay either into hollow or flat ware, they are set abroad to dry.. turning them as they see occasion, which they call whaving.

2. a. *trans.* To cover over. **b.** *intr.* To hang over.

1674 RAY *N.C. Words*, To Whoave; *Chesh.* to cover or whelm over. We will not kill but whoave. *Prov. Chesh.* ab A.S. *Hwolf, Hwalf*, a covering or canopy; Verb. *Hwalfian*, camerare, fornicare. **1828** *Craven Gloss.*, *Whauve*,.. to whelm. **1847** HALLIWELL, *Whave*, to cover, or hang over.

Hence **whauve** *sb.*, (*a*) *techn.* the amount of the dish (DISH *sb.* 5) of a wheel; (*b*) *dial.* the arched covering of turf over a grave (*Shropsh. Word-bk.*); **'whaver** (in quoits: see quot. 1818).

1674 WHAVER [see RINER]. **1818** WILBRAHAM *Gloss. Cheshire* 25 in *Archæologia* XIX, A Riner is when the Quoit touches the peg or mark. A whaver is when it rests upon the peg, and hangs over. **1869** *Eng. Mech.* 31 Dec. 389/3 Add to this twice the wauve (dish) of the wheels, *i.e.* 5 in.

whaw, obs. form of VAU.

1758 WISE *Some Enq. Eur.* 137 *note*, The Hebrew ו Vau or Whaw.

whawl, whax, whay, whayle, whaynt, whayte, whazle, whe, wheadle: see WAUL, WAX, WAY, WHEY, WHOLE, QUAIL, QUAINT, WAIT, WHEEZLE, WE, WHO, WHEEDLE.

wheak, *v. dial.* Also 6 qu(h)aik, 6, 9 wheek, 9 weak, week. [Imitative.] *intr.* To squeak, whine. So **wheak** *sb.*, a squeak or whine.

1513 DOUGLAS *Æneis* VII. ix. 79 With mony pant, and felloun hauchis and quhaikis. **1584** R. SCOT *Discov. Witchcr.* XIII. viii. (1886) 245 The wheeking of a little pig. **1828** *Craven Gloss.*, Wheek.

†**wheal** (hwiːl), *sb.*[1] *Obs.* Forms: 5-6 whele, (5 whelle, wheel, 6 wheell, wele), 6-7 wheale, 7-8 wheal. [OE. **hwele* (Somner), related to WHEAL *v.*[1]: cf. WHELK[2].] A pimple, pustule.

c **1440** *Promp. Parv.* 523/2 Whele, or whelke, soore (*K.* whelle, *S.* qwelke, *P.* wheel), *pustula*. **1530** PALSGR. 288/1 Whele in the hande, *boubette, bubette*; uessie. **1545** RAYNALDE *Byrth Mankynde* 120 Sumetymes happeneth to yᵉ chyldren wheles and blysters on theyr tounges and mouth. *c* **1550** LLOYD *Treas. Health* U vj, Applye it to the scruphules and weles, it kylleth and brekyth them. **1594** NASHE *Unfort. Trav.* K 3, I durst not let out a wheale for feare through it I should bleede to death. **1601** HOLLAND *Pliny* XXXII. vi. II. 437 It killeth the itch, and healeth angrie wheals. **1623** HART *Arraignm. Ur.* II. iii. 46 Small wheales like the small Poxe. **1706** *Phil. Trans.* XXV. 2317 When she scratched the little Pimples or Wheals that arose on its surface.

fig. **1542** UDALL *Erasm. Apoph.* 71 The assemblees of yᵉ people swarmyng about the same oratours, he called the pymples or little wheales of glorie.

b. *attrib.* **wheal-worm**, an insect producing wheals, as the itch-mite or harvest-bug.

1648 WILKINS *Math. Magick* I. xvi. 115 What strang discoveries of extream minute bodies (as lice wheal-worms, mites, and the like). **1658** ROWLAND tr. *Moufet's Theat. Ins.* 1095 The most vertuous Lady of Penruddock.. was for ten years troubled with these wheal-worms. **1668** CHARLETON *Onomast.* 56 Syrones in cute, Wheal-worms. [**1829** GOOD *Study Med.* (ed. 3) V. 663 From the glossy wheals which its [*sc.* the harvest-bug's] bite produces, it has sometimes been called Wheal-Worm.]

Hence †**whealy** *a.*, pimply.

1611 COTGR., *Bothoral*, whealie, poukie, pushie.

wheal (hwiːl), *sb.*[2] [Misspelt form of WEAL *sb.*[2] Cf. WHEAL *v.*[2]] **a.** The ridge raised on the flesh by a blow: = WALE *sb.*[1] 2, WEAL *sb.*[2]

1811 L. M. HAWKINS *C'tess & Gertr.* I. 26 Cover her neck over that I may not see the wheals on it. **1825** *Gentl. Mag.* May 396/2 Each blow raised a wheal upon the place where it fell. **1836** MARRYAT *Midsh. Easy* v, Without supper—covered with wheals. **1887** RIDER HAGGARD *Jess* ix, Across his face was a blue wheal where the whip had fallen.

b. In modern medical use, a flat, usually circular, hard elevation of the skin, esp. that characteristic of urticaria.

So called because resembling the 'wheal' raised on the skin by a blow.

1808 WILLAN *Cutan. Dis.* I. p. xi, Wheal; a rounded, or longitudinal elevation.. with a white summit,.. not containing a fluid, nor tending to suppuration. **1818-20** E. THOMPSON tr. *Cullen's Nosologia* (ed. 3) 326 It [*sc.* Urticaria] is distinguished by those elevations of the cuticle, which are usually denominated wheals. **1876** BRISTOWE *Theory & Pract. Med.* 290 A wheal may be regarded as a form of tubercle.

Comb. **1876** BRISTOWE *Theory & Pract. Med.* 542 The internal coat of translucent wheal-like thickenings.

c. *gen.* A ridge.

1855 NEWMAN *Callista* xv, They [*sc.* locusts] moved right on like soldiers in their ranks..; they carried a broad furrow or wheal all across the country. **1898** H. G. WELLS *War of Worlds* xii, The water in its track rose in a boiling wheal crested with steam.

wheal, *sb.*[3] *local.* [Cornish *huel.*] A mine.

1830 *Eng. & For. Mining Gloss.* **1857** C. M. YONGE *Dynevor Terrace* I. iii. 38 The last unfortunate wheal failed when the rope broke.

†**wheal**, *v.*[1] *Obs.* Forms: 1 hwelian, 5 whelyn, 6 whele, 6-7 wheale, 6- wheal. [Late OE. *hwelian*; pa. pple. *ȝehweled*, f. **hwele* WHEAL *sb.*[1]]

1. *intr.* To suppurate, gather; to develop or become affected with wheals.

c **1000** *Sax. Leechd.* II. 282 ȝif þæt lic heard si, utan leȝe on þane læcedom þe þæt heard forði hweliȝe. *a* **1050** *Liber Scintill.* xv. (1889) 77 *Multi.. de bonorum profectibus inuidie liuore tabescunt*, Mæniȝe.. be goddra fremum andan mid wunde hwеliað. *c* **1440** *Promp. Parv.* 523/2 Whelyn, as soorys.., *pustulo*. **1530** PALSGR. 780/2 Outher you have many wormes, or els you be nat well in your lyver, for your handes wheale a pace. **1602** MARSTON *Antonio's Rev.* V. i, Now gin the leprous cores of ulcered sins Wheale to a heade. **1829** BROCKETT *N.C. Gloss.* (ed. 2).

2. *trans.* To suppurate or bring to a head; to affect with wheals. Only in *pa. pple.* suppurated, pustuled, pimpled.

c **897** ÆLFRED *Gregory's Past. C.* 275 Forðamðe hie [*sc.* speech].. ðæt ȝehwelede on ðæm oðrum ȝeopenað & utforlæt. *c* **1000** *Sax. Leechd.* II. 208 Siþþan þæt ȝeswel biþ ȝehweled & tobyrst. **1522** SKELTON *Why not to Court* 1182 Domingos nose that was wheled. **1556** WITHALS *Dict.* 76 b/2 Matter, as in a wounde when it is whealed, *pus*. **1607** TOPSELL *Four-f. Beasts* 651 If they be whealed and filled with matter. **1676** WISEMAN *Surg.* I. xiii. 63, I.. washt the Parts whealed and swelled with *spir. vini*.

Hence †**whealing** *vbl. sb.*, suppuration.

c **1440** [see VENTOSING *vbl. sb.*]. *c* **1440** *Promp. Parv.* 523/2 Whelynge, of sorys, *pustulacio*.

wheal (hwiːl), *v.*[2] [Misspelt form of WEAL *v.*]

1. *trans.* To mark with wales or weals.

1698 FRYER *Acc. E. India & P.* 135 Batts and Wasps.. following their Aggressors till they have Whealed them into Contrition for their unadvised Provocation. **1701** STANHOPE *Pious Breathings* VII. xii. 339 His Body rent and whealed with Scourges. **1813** *Sporting Mag.* XLI. 24 The horse.. would have been whipped and whealed. **1845** S. JUDD *Margaret* I. ii, His eyes were bloodshot, his cheeks whealed and puffed. **1868** BROWNING *Ring & Bk.* V. 135, I.. now am whealed, one wide wound all of me.

2. *intr.* To be marked with weals or ridges.

1570 GOOGE *Pop. Kingd.* III. 34 b, The bloud sprang out a pace, and eke their backe did swell and wheale With multitude of stripes.

wheale, whealke, wheam, whean, wheang, whear: see WEAL, WHEEL, WHELK, QUEME, QUEAN, WHEEN, WHANG, WHERE.

†**whease**, *v. Obs.* [?] *trans.* To signal.

1602 R. CAREW *Cornwall* I. 32 b, By crying with a lowd voice, whistling through his fingers, and wheazing certing diuersified signes, with a bush, which hee holdeth in his hand. **1650** J. REYNOLDS *Flower Fidel.* 151 The Master upon the Poop with his silver Sword to whease them to Lee-ward.

whease, wheasle: see WHEEZE, WHEEZLE.

wheat (hwiːt), *sb.* Forms: 1 hwæte, 2-3 hwete, 3-6 wete, 4-5 wheet(e, whet, 4-6 whete, 6-7 wheate, (1 huæte, 3 whæte, hweate, 4 huete, whyte, wit, 5 wheytt, white, 5-6 whett(e, whyt, 6 wheitt, whaytt, whiett, wett(e, weate), 6- wheat; *Sc.* and *north. dial.* 4-5 quhet, qwet, 5-6 quhete, qwheit, 5-7 quheit (4 quete, 5 qw(h)ete, qwheet, qhete, qwete, qwyte, qwyet, quhe(y)t, 6 quheitt, quhait, quheite, qwheytte, queat, quhyt(t, vhyt). [OE. *hwǽte* str. m. = OFris. *(*h*)*wête* (NFris. *wête*), OS. *hwêti* (MDu. *weite*, Du. *weit*), MLG. *weiten, wêten* (LG. *weten*), OHG. *weizzi*, (MHG. *weize, weitze*, G. *weizen*), ON. *hveiti* (Sw. *vete*, Da. *hvede*), Goth. *hwaiteis*:— OTeut. **χwaitjaz*, derivative of **χwīt-* WHITE.]

1. a. The grain of a cereal (see sense 2), furnishing a meal or flour which constitutes the chief breadstuff in temperate countries.

c **825** *Vesp. Ps.* lxiv. 14 [lxv. 13] *Convalles abundabunt frumento*, dene ȝenyhtsumiað hwæte. *c* **1000** *Ags. Gosp.* Matt. iii. 12 He ȝegaderað hys hwæte on his bern. *c* **1200** ORMIN 10527, I þa þatt swelltenn winndweþþ Crist & clennseþþ here hiss whæte. *c* **1220** *Bestiary* 292 in *O.E. Misc.* 10 Ðe mire suneð ðe barlic, Ðanne ȝe fint te wete. *a* **1225** *Ancr. R.* 270 Ane wummon.. þet windwede hweate. **1297** R. GLOUC. (Rolls) 18 Vor engelonde is vol inoȝ, of frut, & ek of tren, Of wit [*v. rr.* whyte, whyt] & of wolle god. **1303** R. BRUNNE *Handl. Synne* 10091 Þe vble ys made of whete, þe louelyest corne þat men ete. **13..** *Cursor M.* 22327 (Gött.) Þe mett of qwet, als it es tald, For a peni it sal be sald. *c* **1375** *Sc. Leg. Saints* xxvi. (*Nycholas*) 214 In þe hawine schipis gret Ware arywit, chargit with quhet. *c* **1480** HENRYSON *Two Mice* 361 Full benelie stuffit.. Of beinis, and nuttis, peiss, ry, and quhite. **1485** in *10th Rep. Hist. MSS. Comm.* App. v. 291 The busshell of whette be boghte for xii. *d.* *c* **1489** CAXTON *Sonnes of Aymon* viii. 187 The rasour of whete was solde for fourty shelynges and twenty pence. **1550-3** *Decaye Eng.* in S. Fish *Supplic.*, etc. (1871) 99 Allowe to euery person ij. quarters of weate. **1556** *Chron. Grey Friars* (Camden) 4 Thys yere a bushelle of wett was at five shillings. **1569** *Richmond Wills* (Surtees) 218, L. stroke queat unbarrowed. **1603** DEKKER *Batchelars Banquet* Wks. (Grosart) I. 176, I can tell you their mouthes will not be stopt with a bushell of wheat that speake it. **1833** TENNYSON *Lotos Eaters* 167 An ill-used race of men.. Storing yearly little dues of wheat, and wine and oil.

b. in allusive and proverbial use: often opposed to *chaff, tares.*

a **1225** *Juliana* 79 Hwen drihtin o domes dei windweð his hweate. **1390** GOWER *Conf.* II. 59 It were a schort beyete To winne chaf and lese whete. **1561** WINȜET *Bk. Questions* Wks. (S.T.S.) I. 120 Guid and euill, expressit in the Euangell, be the similitude of quheit and fitcheis. **1611** COTGR. s.v. *Pain*, *Quiers tu meilleur pain que de fourment*? Wouldst thou haue better bread then's made of wheat? **1639** J. CLARKE *Paræm.* 46 Malt is above the wheat with him. *Cylicum remiges.* **1874** *Sankey's Sacred Songs* (1878) 11 Let us keep the wheat and roses, Casting out the thorns and chaff. **1874** C. E. NORTON *Lett.* (1913) II. 38 He had now got a good handful of pure wheat to offer in the place of his common sackful of the most unnutritious chaff.

2. a. The cereal plant (closely related to barley and rye) which yields this grain, esp. common wheat, *Triticum vulgare* (*sativum*), cultivated in temperate climates.

With qualification denoting a particular kind, as DUCKBILL *wheat, goat's-wheat* (GOAT 4 c), GUINEA *wheat, Indian wheat* (INDIAN *a.* 4 b), *Lammas-wheat* (LAMMAS *sb.* 4), POLAND[1] *wheat, pollard wheat* (POLLARD *sb.*[2] B. 1), RED WHEAT, *rivet-wheat* (RIVET *sb.*[2] b), *spelt-wheat* (SPELT *sb.*[1] 2), *summer wheat* (SUMMER *sb.*[1] 4 c), TURKEY WHEAT, WHITE *wheat*, WINTER *wheat*; also applied to some plants of other genera, as BUCKWHEAT, COW-WHEAT, *French wheat* (FRENCH *a.* 5).

c **950** *Lindisf. Gosp.* Matt. xiii. 25 Mið ðy uutedlice ȝeslepdon.. ða menn cuom fiond his & ofer-ȝeseawu.. sifðe In middum hwæte. **1340-70** *Alex. & Dind.* 692 Hue tilede in hur time on þe touh erþe, & whete soþliche sew. **1398** TREVISA *Barth. De P.R.* XVII. clxviii. (W. de W.) Vij/2 Of whete is dowble kynde: One manere kynde is red wythout.. and is moost whyte wythin, & heuy... The other manere whete is yelowe wythout and clere and whyte wythin: and is lyghte. *c* **1400** MAUNDEV. (Roxb.) xxx. 134 In þis cuntree es lytill qwheet or barly. **1513** DOUGLAS *Æneis* VII. xi. 80 Sithis, and all hukis that scheris quheit. **1580** TUSSER *Husb.* (1878) 49 Graie wheat is the grosest, yet good for the clay... Much like vnto rie be his properties found. **1590** SHAKS. *Mids. N.* I. i. 185 When wheate is greene, when hauthorne buds appeare. **1603** G. OWEN *Pembrokeshire* (1892) 60 A third kinde of wheate.. which is called holie wheate or sommer wheate. **1632** LITHGOW *Trav.* IX. 415, I found the Wheat here growing higher then my head. **1797** *Encycl. Brit.* (ed. 3) XVIII. 846/1 The three principal kinds of bad wheat are, the blighted, the smutty, and the worm-eaten. **1867** H. MACMILLAN *Bible Teach.* v. (1870) 103 Wheat will not thrive in hot climates. **1868** MORRIS *Earthly Par.* (1870) I. II. 587 The tall wheat, coloured by the August fire Grew heavy-headed.

b. The pale gold colour of ripe wheat. Also ***wheat-gold.***

1915 WODEHOUSE *Something Fresh* iii. 83 Joan Valentine was a tall girl, with wheat-gold hair. **1965** [see *French roll* s.v. FRENCH 3 b]. **1970** *New Yorker* 8 Aug. 1 (Advt.), Great embroidered coat of cotton-polyester in wheat with pumpernickel trim. **1977** M. HERR *Dispatches* 175 He was wearing a denim workshirt and wheat jeans. **1983** *Harrods Mag.* Spring & Summer 104/2 Cotton trousers in White, Wheat, Slate Blue or Navy. **1984** H. HIRT *Heat of Winter* i. 2 His face was.. very fair—what the Indian matrimonial advertisements describe as a 'wheat' complexion.

3. *pl.* Wheat-plants; crops of wheat; kinds of wheat.

1795 *Scots Mag.* LVII. 544/1 In Lancashire.. their wheats are not yet on the bloom. **1797** *Sporting Mag.* X. 297 The new Wheats already thrashed out. **1805** R. W. DICKSON *Pract. Agric.* I. 429 They are frequently also sown on the young wheats and clovers in the spring. **1812** SIR J. SINCLAIR *Syst. Husb. Scot.* I. 339 The bread of Perth in particular, where those wheats are alone used, equals any in the united kingdom. **1888** *Daily News* 13 Oct. 2/6 Foreign white wheats.. have hardened to a small advance on the week. **1894** *Times* 22 Jan. 4/1 The young wheats.. looking little or none the worse for their week beneath the snow.

4. a. *attrib.* and *Comb.*, as ***wheat-acre, -area, -awn, -barn, -belt*** (BELT *sb.*[1] 5 a), ***-blade, -blossom, -blossoming, -braird, -bran, -bread, -breeder, -breeding, -cake, -chaff, -close*** (CLOSE *sb.*[1] 2), ***cocky*** Austral. (COCKY *sb.*[2] 2), ***-colour, country, -crop, -crust, -drill, -eddish, -fallow, -farm, -farmer, -farming, -feed, -field, -firlot, -flour, futures*** (FUTURE *sb.* 6), ***-garner, -glean*** (GLEAN *sb.*[1] 1), ***-grain, -ground, -grower, -harvest, -haulm, -house, -loaf, -loft, -lumper, -lumping, -malt, -mill, -mow, -pit*** (PIT *sb.*[1] 11), ***-plant, -producer, -production, ranch, rancher, -reed*** (REED *sb.*[1] 2 c), ***-rick, -ridge, -riping, -screenings*** (cf. SCREEN *sb.*[1] 5), ***-scrip*** (SCRIP *sb.*[4]), ***-seed, -seeding, -sheaf, -sowing, -stack, -stalk, -starch, -straw, -stubble, -threave, -wine; wheat-bellied, -blazing, -coloured, -fed, -growing, -hid*** adjs.; applied to insects, fungi, etc. destructive to wheat, as ***wheat-bug, -caterpillar, -gall-fly, -gnat, -insect, -joint-worm, -louse, -maggot, -midge, -mildew, -mite, -moth, -plant-louse, -weevil, -worm***; applied to implements used in obtaining or preparing the wheat-grain, as ***wheat-brush, -dryer, -flail, -heater, -ridder, -riddle, -separator, -sieve.*** **b.** Special Combs.: **wheat-barley** = *naked barley* (NAKED *a.* 12 c); **wheat berry**, the grain of wheat; **wheat-bird**, a bird that feeds on wheat, esp. the chaffinch; also, in North America, the horned lark, *Eremophila alpestris*; **wheat bulb fly**, the larva of a muscid fly, *Hylemyia coarctata*, which attacks the base of wheat stems; **wheat-duck**, the American widgeon, *Mareca americana*, found in flocks in wheat-fields; **wheat-fish**, the squeteague; **wheatflakes** *sb. pl.* (orig. *U.S.*), a breakfast cereal made from flaked and flavoured wheat (cf. *cornflakes* sb. pl. s.v. CORN *sb.*[1] 11); **wheat-fly**, name for various insects whose larvæ infest the wheat plant, as the Hessian fly, the wheat-midge, etc.; **wheat germ**, the embryo of the wheat grain, extracted during milling, and valued as a source of vitamins; **wheat-grass**, (*a*) name for various species of the genus *Triticum*, esp. couch-grass, *T. repens*; (*b*) a creeping perennial grass of the genus *Agropyron*; **wheat-lay** *dial.*, the sowing of land with wheat; **wheat-rent**, in the Channel Islands, wheat paid as rent (cf. QUARTER *sb.* 4 b); **wheat roll**, a roll made of wheatmeal bread; **Wheat State**, in the U.S., a popular nickname for Kansas or Minnesota; also used of South Australia. See also WHEAT-CORN, etc.

1876 G. M. HOPKINS *Poems* (1967) 177 The blue *wheat-acre is underneath. **1884** *Spectator* No. 2932. 1165 Whether the *wheat-area of the world will be maintained. **1869** BLACKMORE *Lorna D.* lxxiv, I caught a limb, and tore it (like a *wheat-awn) from the socket. **1578** LYTE *Dodoens* IV. viii. 460 *Hordeum Nudum.* Naked or bare Barley, *Wheate Barley. **1377** in *Cal. Close Rolls* 509 [The grange called the] *wheteberne. **1474–5** *Durham Acc. Rolls* (Surtees) 156 Pro tectura..super le Whetebarn Manerii de Eluet. **1543** *Richmond Wills* (Surtees) 42 In the whiett barne, whyatt and rye. **1922** JOYCE *Ulysses* 196 Eve. Naked *wheatbellied sin. **1863** *Harper's Mag.* Oct. 718/1 The enterprising town..is the wheat-market for a considerable section of the *wheat-belt of the state. **1910** *Chambers's Jrnl.* Mar. 205/2 The laying out of ready-made farms in the wheat-belts of North-West Canada. **1980** *Jrnl. R. Soc. Arts* Mar. 175/2 In the wheat belts in the USA and Australia there were..large areas still undeveloped. **1848** *Rep. Comm. Patents 1847* (U.S.) 373 Taking the outer coating or bran from the *wheat berry previous to grinding produces the following important results. **1905** *Westm. Gaz.* 20 Sept. 8/1 The wheatberry, to become blood, bone, and flesh, must be broken up. **1746–7** M. CATESBY in *Phil. Trans.* XLIV. 444 They [*sc.* exotic Birds] arrive [in Virginia] annually at the time that Wheat..is at a certain Degree of Maturity... They have attain'd the Name of *Wheat-Birds. **1865** Wheat bird [see PEABODY]. **1917** T. G. PEARSON *Birds Amer.* II. 212 Horned Lark..[also called] Prairie Bird; Road Trotter; Wheat Bird. **1867** EMERSON *Poems, May-day* 201 The dead log touched bursts into leaf, The *wheat-blade whispers of the sheaf. **1937** BLUNDEN *Elegy* 60 Seek the wide *wheat-blazing plain. **1733** TULL *Horse-hoeing Husb.* xiii. 154 The nipping Winds..which..might destroy the tender *Wheat Blossoms. *a* **1722** LISLE *Husb.* (1757) 299 The cows milk abates about *wheat-blossoming time. **1825** HONE *Every-day Bk.* I. 150 The *wheat-braird was strong. **14..** *Sir Beues* (C.) 1622 + 21 3yt was he wonte before eche day, ..Of *whyte brawne to haue a messe. *a* **1425** tr. *Arderne's Treat. Fistula* etc. 75 Tak whete branne als myche as sufficeþ. **1707** MORTIMER *Husb.* 257 If a little Wheat-bran is boiled in our ordinary Beer. **1946** *Nature* 31 Aug. 293/1 The fungus was grown in various modifications of Czapek-Dox medium with addition of manganese sulphate, in some cases with..autoclaved wheat-bran extract. **1377** LANGL. *P. Pl.* B. VII. 120 Þough *whete bred me faille. **1552** *2nd Prayer-bk. Edw. VI, Commun.* rubric, The best and purest wheate bread, that conueniently maye be gotten. **1703** J. BRAND *Descr. Orkney* 18 As for Wheat-bread it is rare. **1862** M. D. COLT *Went to Kansas* 83, I live entirely on food made of corn ..leaving the wheat bread for grand-ma and grand-pa. **1880** [see SOUTHERN *a.* 4 c]. **1978** *Listener* 10 Aug. 180/3 Oatcakes, potato cakes and wheat bread were cooked deliciously on a griddle. **1912** *Rep. 13th Meeting Australasian Assoc. Adv. Sci.* 536 (*heading*) The realization of the aims of William J. Farrer, *wheat breeder. **1974** *Encycl. Brit. Macropædia* III. 1157/2 Wheat breeders regularly produce new varieties. **1898** W. J. FARRER *Let.* 30 Aug. in R. Archer *William James Farrer* (1949) xiv. 109, I should continue to carry on the *wheat-breeding work at Lambrigg. **1965** *Austral. Encycl.* IX. 284B (*caption*) Wheat-breeding plots at the Temora Experiment Farm. **1884** KNIGHT *Dict. Mech.* Suppl. 945/1 **Wheat Brush*, a device for scouring grain. **1860** CURTIS *Farm Insects* Index, *Wheat-bugs. *Miris tritici* and *M. erraticus*. **1883** E. A. ORMEROD *Rep. Observations Injurious Insects 1882* 20 *Wheat-bulb fly..was observable early in March. **1921** *Jrnl. Agric. Sci.* XI. 98 Wheat-bulb fly..does not appear to do much harm in a wet, cold, or damp summer. **1975** *N.Z. Jrnl. Agric.* Sept. 67/1 The topics covered in the first few months of the scheme include cereal mildew, wheat bulb fly, yellow rust. **1772** M. PATTEN *Diary* (1903) 293 His wife baked a parcel of *Wheat Cakes for me when I went up to Cockermouth. **1865** A. D. WHITNEY *Gayworthys* 218 There are wheat-cakes and maple syrup for your breakfast. **1981** J. DUNNING *Deadline* (1982) xix. 191 Trudy fixed him a breakfast of eggs and bacon and wheat cakes. **1826** KIRBY & SP. *Entomol.* xxxi. III. 277 This door is to serve the moth for its exit, like that formed by the *wheat-caterpillar. **1573–80** TUSSER *Husb.* (1878) 46 *Wheat chaffe lay vp drie. **1847** W. C. L. MARTIN *Ox* 149/1 Supposing that the stomach be distended by light materials, as wheat-chaff, chopped straw. **1599** *George a Greene* C j b, Madge pointed to meete me in your *wheate close. **1818** SCOTT *Hrt. Midl.* xxix, He's in Gaffer Gabblewood's wheat-close. **1933** *Bulletin* (Sydney) 1 Mar. 13 A good, typical S. Australian public man—a *wheat cocky. **1941** K. TENNANT *Battlers* xxi. 228 Like many another broken 'wheat cocky'.. Jim might be packing his kids and wife into his old truck any time now. **1711** HEARNE *Collect.* (O.H.S.) III. 150 The hair on the upper [lip] being thin and short of a *wheat Colour. **1898** *Westm. Gaz.* 10 Mar. 3/2 The *wheat-coloured straw. **1776** *New-York Gaz.* 24 June 3/3 To be Sold..a very good Grist-Mill..in a very good *Wheat Country. **1890** *Stock Grower & Farmer* 29 Mar. 5/3 The panhandle country..is a fine wheat country. **1979** TANOUS & RUBINSTEIN *Wheat Killing* (1980) ix. 55 We were in the flat wheat country drained by the Missouri River. **1581** *Durham Wills* (Surtees) II. 42 All the *wheat crope, that is sowen upon my farmhold. **1765** *Museum Rust.* IV. 338 That my wheat-crops would be hurt by the north-easterly winds. **1857** MILLER *Elem. Chem., Org.* (1862) xiii. §1. 834 Land which might have been supposed to have been exhausted of its phosphates by a previous wheat-crop. **1615** MARKHAM *Eng. Housew.* II. ii. 65 Your course *wheat-crust would bee kneaded with hot-water. **1733** TULL *Horse-hoeing Husb.* xxii. 318 In the Side of a Mortise of a *Wheat-Drill. **1884** *Health Exhib. Catal.* 113/1 Model of the Patent *Wheat Dryer. **1888** G. Trumbull *Names & Portraits of Birds* 21 He found this species [*sc.* the American widgeon] in enormous flocks on the wheat-fields, and..it was there called the *wheat-duck. **1917** T. G. PEARSON *Birds Amer.* I. 120 Wheat Duck..is very fond of wild celery. **1980** *Hunting Ann. 1981* 40/3 A wigeon in one region would be called a baldpate in another area or wheatduck in another. **1764** *Museum Rust.* II. xxiv. 76 Immediately after harvest I turn them on the *wheat eddishes. *a* **1722** LISLE *Husb.* (1757) 20 They..will not allow a load of..dung at harvest to come through their *wheat-fallow. **1958** *Publ. Amer. Dial. Soc.* xxx. 6 Farmers who have large *wheat-farms. **1870** *Rep. Comm. Agric. 1869* (U.S. Dept. Agric.) 5 The *wheat farmer ..is not joyous over his market returns. **1959** *Cape Times* 18 July 2/5 Wheat farmers welcomed the good rains. **1965** *Austral. Encycl.* IX. 285/2 The most spectacular change in *wheat-farming practice in recent years. **1892** *Times* (weekly ed.) 2 Feb. 89/3 The *wheat-fed pork of the North West. **1932** *Daily Tel.* 8 Oct. 4/2 Oats quiet of sale... Millers' *wheatfeed quiet. **1960** *Farmer & Stockbreeder* 29 Mar. 4/2 Demand for wheatfeed is steady. **1425** in *Rep. MSS. Ld. Middleton* (1911) 108 That no man take away his bestes fro the comyn herd..to go in the *qwete feld to lese the qwete. **1603** HOLLAND *Plutarch's Mor.* 209 By laying corne-grounds and wheat-fields to his owne demaines. **1840** LONGF. *Sp. Stud.* III. i, Over the wheat-fields, where the shadows sail. **1771** *Encycl. Brit.* II. 706/2 That the *wheat firlot shall contain 19 pints and two joucattes. **1888** GOODE *Amer. Fishes* 111 The Squeteague.. Some old authorities use the name '*Wheat-fish'. **1903** *Bull. Maine Agric. Exper. Station* No. 84, 143 Fruen's Best *Wheat Flakes, 'made from the best Pacific Coast White Wheat'. **1939** G. GREENE *Lawless Roads* ii. 45 He looked up from his dry wheat flakes. **1970** M. KELLY *Spinifex* ii. 37 A grocer size wheatflakes box. *a* **1425** tr. *Arderne's Treat. Fistula* etc. 31 When..þer is added þerto white of eiren and oyle, wiþ wax and *whete floure. **1535** COVERDALE *Ps.* lxxx[i]. 16 He shulde fede them with the fynest wheate floure. **1639** O. WOOD *Alph. Bk. Secrets* 102 Fry them together till they be thick with a little wheatflower. **1766** *Phil. Trans.* LVII. 456 A mucilaginous vegetable paste..as wheat-flower and water. **1847** W. C. L. MARTIN *Ox* 175/1 Gruel made of fine wheat-flour. **1798** NEMNICH *Polygl.-Lex., Virginian *Wheat fly*, a mischievous insect in the American state: It eats the grain, and is a moth in a perfect state. **1844** H. STEPHENS *Bk. Farm* III. 951 The wheat-fly, *Cecidomyia tritici*. **1908** 'O. HENRY' *Strictly Business* 252 After I had taken some $9,000,000 out of the soap business I made the rest in corn and *wheat futures. **1979** TANOUS & RUBINSTEIN *Wheat Killing* (1980) ii. 13 The rise in the wheat price will mean a fortune to them if they own the wheat futures. **1453–4** *Durham Acc. Rolls* (Surtees) 634 Operanti..super..emendacionem de le *Whet-garner. **1897** *Sears, Roebuck Catal.* 15/3 *Wheat Germ Meal... Cooked in 5 minutes. **1933** *Discovery* May 160/1 The richest source of vitamin E is wheat germ. **1980** *Sunday Times* (Colour Suppl.) 20 Jan. 57/3 Wheatgerm Loaf. A good hearty farmhouse loaf. *c* **1430** LYDG. *Min. Poems* (Percy Soc.) 96 The *whete glene crowned above the greyne. **1826** KIRBY & SP. *Entomol.* xliv. IV. 221 The Ichneumon of the *wheat-gnat. *c* **1400** *Rom. Rose* 5590 An hundred mavis [? mowis] of *whete greyne. **1837** CARLYLE *Fr. Rev.* I. IV. iii, It has now..sifted out the true wheat-grains of National Deputies. **1918** *Chamb. Jrnl.* Aug. 520/1 For years millers have laboured to provide us with a perfectly white loaf, throwing away some of the most valuable parts of the wheat-grain in so doing. **1668** WILKINS *Real Char.* 73 *Wheat-grass..either the greater used for the making of frails: or the lesser. **1762** W. HUDSON *Flora Anglica* 45 Common Wheat-grass, Dog's-grass, Quick-grass or Couch-grass. **1766** *Museum Rust.* VI. 442 Common Wheat-grass, or Couch-grass. **1796** WITHERING *Brit. Plants* (ed. 3) II. 173 Sea Wheat-grass. Rush Wheat. **1871** *Harper's Mag.* July 187/2 Among the more important of these plants the wheat-grass stands pre-eminent. **1968** F. W. GOULD *Grass Systematics* 186 Several species of *Agropyron* are important forage grasses on western rangelands, outstanding among which are..bluebunch wheatgrass, and..western wheatgrass. *a* **1722** LISLE *Husb.* (1757) 17 He sows on his *wheat-ground ..about February. **1765** *Museum Rust.* IV. 348 That is a profit more than the rent of the ground, and half as much again above the profit of the *wheat-grower. **1868** *Rep. U.S. Comm. Agric.* (1869) 18 The pioneer upon the prairie is a wheat-grower. **1840** BUEL *Farmer's Comp.* 23 Pennsylvania, then one of the best *wheat-growing States. **1382** WYCLIF *Gen.* xxx. 14 And Ruben goon out in tyme of *wheet heruest into the feeld. **1733** TULL *Horse-hoeing Husb.* xiii. 154 If their Wheat Harvest in Sicily be about the 20th of May. *c* **1000** *Sax. Leechd.* II. 130 ðenim gate tord & *hwæte healm gebærn to duste. **1748** *Lond. & Country Brewer* IV. (ed. 2) 255 Wheat Straw under a Hair-Cloth is reckoned the best Fuel by most, Rye-Straw next, and Wheat-Haulm worse. **1827** CLARE *Sheph. Cal.* 50 And lonely chirp the *wheat-hid quails. **1559** in Willis & Clark *Cambridge* (1886) I. 143 For covering y[e] *whete house ut patet per billam. **1710** HILMAN *Tusser Rediv.* June (1744) 72 Lay it in the best Place you have, for which the Wheat-Houses now in request..are I think the best. **1819** D. B. WARDEN *Acc. United States* II. 53 The Hessian fly, or *wheat insect (*Tipula tritici*). *a* **1722** LISLE *Husb.* (1757) 324 It may be proper to fold till Christmas, and then go on the *wheat-lay. **1534** *Star Chamber Cases* (Selden Soc.) II. 208 The Baillye..Weyed ageyn his bredde wiche was to leight in the 1[d] *Whete loffe iiij ounces. **1587** in Willis & Clark *Cambridge* (1886) I. 26 [A] *wheate loft. **1934** *Bulletin* (Sydney) 3 Jan. 14/3 Harrison, a Wallendbeen (N.S.W.) *wheat-lumper, carried 1170 bags of wheat the other day. **1957** *Wheat-lumping [see RING *v.*[1] 11]. **1452** *Cal. Anc. Rec. Dublin* (1889) 275 Drege malte, pese, benes, *whetemalte. **1743** *Lond. & Country Brewer* II. (ed. 2) 93 Wheat-Malt also differs much from Barley-Malt. **1840** J. & M. LOUDON tr. *Köllar's Treat. Insects* II. 123 The *Wheat Midge... The perfect insect has a distant [*sic*] resemblance to the common midge, but is smaller. **1843** *Penny Cycl.* XXVII. 304 The wheat-midge (*Cecidomyia tritici*). **1931** K. M. SMITH *Textbk. Agric. Entomol.* xi. 169 Wheat midge was especially destructive in 1926 in the eastern counties. **1585** HIGINS *Junius' Nomencl.* 185/1 *Chondrocopium farreum*,..a *wheate mill or (as some say) an otemeale mill. **1860** CURTIS *Farm Insects* Index, *Wheat-mite. An acarus infesting stored corn. **1862** T. W. HARRIS *Insects Injur. Veget.* (ed. 3) Index, *Wheat moths. *c* **1700** *Bagford Ballads* (1876) I. 66 Both his *Wheat Mows & his Hay, By Flames of Fire are consum'd away. **1808** COBBETT in *Friendsh. Mary R. Mitford* (1882) I. 43 The hares will be heard squeaking like rats on the breaking up of a wheat-mow. **1884** DEPEW in *Harper's Mag.* (1886) XII. 217 In the *Wheat Pit at Chicago in a single year was buried more of the future prosperity of this republic than the sum of all the traffic which flows through that great city in a decade. **1733** TULL *Horse-hoeing Husb.* xi. 112 If the How-Plow goes so near to the Rows as it ought, it would be apt to tear out the *Wheat-Plants along with the Stubble. **1868** *Rep. U.S. Comm. Agric.* (1869) 17 A disposition to increase the breadth of *wheat-planting. **1860** CURTIS *Farm Insects* Index, *Wheat plant-louse, *Aphis granaria*. **1908** *Westm. Gaz.* 1 July 6/3 Canada aims at being the great *wheat-producer of the world. **1884** *Spectator* No. 2932. 1165/2 To increase *wheat-production in India. **1874** *Wheat ranch [see *sheep ranch* s.v. SHEEP *sb.* 7 c]. **1947** *Mazama* Dec. 1/1 An overnight trip to the 500-acre wheat and stock ranch..near Wamic. **1947** *Chicago Tribune* 1 Nov. 11/4 A former life term prisoner..admitted the..slaying of a retired Canadian *wheat rancher. **1977** J. GILLIS *Killers of Starfish* (1979) v. 32 Maybe he was a big wheat rancher. **1813** T. DAVIS *Agric. Wilts* Gloss., **Wheat-reed*, straw preserved unthrashed for thatching. **1682** WARBURTON *Guernsey* (1822) 94 A man, that has either house or land which he wishes to dispose of, ..sells it to another to hold to him and his heirs for ever, paying yearly so many quarters..of *wheat rent. **1694** FALLE *Jersey* iii. 95 Together with several Parcels of Lands and Meadows, Wheat-Rents, Escheats. *a* **1722** LISLE *Husb.* (1757) 182 In that fashion, without thatching, they make *wheat-reeks in the Isle of Wight. **1823** COBBETT *Rural Rides* (1885) I. 255 A..farm-house,..with a wheat-rick standing in the yard. *c* **1430** *Two Cookery-bks.* 32 Take a seve or a *wheterydoun. **1733** W. ELLIS *Chiltern & Vale Farm.* 200 Our Wheat-ridder Sieves. **1479–80** *Priory of Finchale* (Surtees) p. cccxlvii, ij *whetridils, iij haveridils, et ij cribris. **1729** WALKDEN *Diary* (1866) 45 Windowed my wheat the chaff out of it, but, for want of a wheat riddle, we could dress it no further. **1844** H. STEPHENS *Bk. Farm* II. 281 A wheat-riddle of wood. **1733** TULL *Horse-hoeing Husb.* xi. 110, I find by measuring my *Wheat Ridges in the Spring, that none of them are quite a Foot High. **1860** R. S. HAWKER in *Life* (1905) 323 No one ever remembers the aspect of the wheat-ridges so mournfully unpromising. **1382** WYCLIF *Judges* xv. 1 Whanne the dais of *whete ripynge stooden yn. **1962** E. SNOW *Other Side of River* (1963) lix. 447 The dining room I saw was serving *wheat rolls, turnips, cabbage and spinach which looked adequate and wholesome. **1978** H. MCLEAVE *Borderline Case* (1979) iv. 49 Shigo brought hot coffee, wheat rolls baked on the spot, butter. **1855** *Poultry Chron.* III. 343 *Wheat-screenings, cracked corn,..or buckwheat, may be added to their diet. **1733** W. ELLIS *Chiltern & Vale Farm.* 309 The..*Wheat-seed Plough. **1810** *Sporting Mag.* XXXVI. 225 He..had worked with other horses all the wheat-seed time. **1631** WEEVER *Anc. Funeral Mon.* 724 Certaine waxe candles, which euer and onely they vsed to light in *wheat-seeding. **1729** WALKDEN *Diary* (1866) 44 When he ended his wheat seeding. **1884** KNIGHT *Dict. Mech.* Suppl. 946/1 **Wheat Separator.* The separation of mustard, cockle, and grass seed from the wheat is effected by passing the mixed grains over inclined plates perforated with holes. *c* **1530** in Gutch *Coll. Cur.* II. 329 Item a greate Bason withe a *Wheyte Sheffe in the bottom. **1600** NASHE *Summers Last Will* Wks. (Grosart) VI. 127 God knowes who shal pay goodman Yeomans, for his wheat sheafe. **1782** HIGHMORE *Ramble Coast Sussex* (1873) 15 Nature..shewed us her Wheatsheaf —and her Autumn Horn. **1846** J. BAXTER *Libr. Pract. Agric.* (ed. 4) II. 403 A wheat-sheaf should never contain more than two or three handsful. **1897** *Allbutt's Syst. Med.* IV. 375 The cones [of the kidney] which are often compressed in their centres to the well-known wheat-sheaf shape. **1834** *Brit. Husb.* I. 390 It should be pounded till it will run through a *wheat-sieve. **1557** TUSSER *100 Points Husb.* xxv, October for *wheate sowing, calleth as fast. **1825** COBBETT *Rural Rides* (1885) II. 178 Wheat-sowing is yet going on, on the Wold. **1778** [W. MARSHALL] *Minutes Agric., Digest* 126 To-day..nine men,—three boys,—three teams,—and four carriages, have made a very handsome *Wheat-Stack of eighteen harvest loads. **1577** GOOGE tr. *Heresbach's Husb.* I. 28 The stalke or steale thereof [*sc.* of rye] is smaller then the *Wheate stalke. **1733** TULL *Horse-hoeing Husb.* xiii. 158 The lower parts of the Wheat-stalks must receive the greater share of Heat. **1880** MEREDITH *Pheobus with Admetus* iv, Stately stood the wheatstalk, with head bent high. **1585** HIGINS *Junius' Nomencl.* 109/2 *Amylon*,..*wheatestarch. **1854** *Pereira's Polarized Light* (ed. 2) 154 Tapioca-meal, East Indian arrow-root..wheat-starch. **1911** D. MALLOCH *Resawed Fables* 65 He had a Friend in the Retail Lumber Business..and he sent him enough Money to get Home to the *Wheat State. **1945** BAKER *Austral. Lang.* x. 187 Popular names for the various Australian states are:..South Australia: the Wheat State. **1950** R. MEYER *Festivals U.S.A.* 225 Kansas is sometimes called the Wheat State, but it is more familiarly known as the Sunflower State. **14..** *Stockholm Med. MS.* ii. 755 in *Anglia* XVIII. 325 His stalke is gret as *whete-stro. **1523–34** FITZHERB. *Husb.* §27 The wheate strawe, that they pourpose to make thacke of. **1789** T. WRIGHT *Meth. Watering Meadows* (1790) 43 The hay is almost as long, coarse, and dry, as wheat-straw. **1813** VANCOUVER *Agric. Devon* 90, 100 sheaves of wheat-straw reed. **1830** LINDLEY *Nat. Syst. Bot.* 303 It is..said that Wheat-straw may be melted into a colourless glass with the blow-pipe. *c* **1903** O. READ in *Library Southern Lit.* (1909) X. 4374 The Squatter, with his wheat-straw beard, his hay hair and his autumn leaf complexion. **1941** L. B. LYON *Tomorrow is Revealing* 44 A son with a bird's glint, and wheat-straw hair. **1760** R. BROWN *Compl. Farmer* II. 48 They plough in the *wheat stubble in December. **1846** J. BAXTER *Libr. Pract. Agric.* (ed. 4) II. 337 The wheat stubbles are ploughed as soon as the wheat sowing is over. **1812** SIR J. SINCLAIR *Syst. Husb. Scot.* I. 330 The *wheatthreave consists of twenty-eight sheaves. **1862** T. W. HARRIS *Insects Injur. Veget.* (ed. 3) 83 The true grain-weevil or *wheat-weevil of Europe. **1954** E. POUND *Cantos* liii. 281 With gold cup of *wheat-wine that he go afield to spring ploughing. **1982** C. THOMAS *Jade Tiger* 52 Wheat wine, almost pure alcohol. **1862** T. W. HARRIS *Insects Injur. Veget.* (ed. 3) 453 They have been called *wheat-worms, gray worms, and brown weevils... The name of grain-worms has likewise sometimes been applied to them.

Hence **'wheatless** *a.*, having no wheat.

1868 LYNCH *Rivulet* CXXXVII. iii, I opened many a..book, ..But all the leaves were wheatless straws. **1870** LOWELL *Among my Bks.* Ser. I. (1873) 336 The laity look on while theologians thrash their wheatless straw. **1917** *Times* 30 May 7/4 What will be the attitude of those portions of Greece..if they remain wheatless.

wheat, *v.* [f. prec.] *trans.* To crop with wheat.

1847 *Jrnl. R. Agric. Soc.* VIII. I. 61 The land must not be wheated oftener than the soil will admit.

wheat, obs. form of WHITE.

'wheat-corn. Now *rare.* [OE. *hwǣtecorn* = MHG. *weiz(en)korn* (G. *weizenkorn*), ON. *hveitikorn* (MSw. *hvetekorn*, etc.): see CORN *sb.*[1]]

1. A grain of wheat.

c **1000** *Sax. Leechd.* II. 34 Ȝenim hnutcyrnla & hwæte corn. *a* **1175** *Cott. Hom.* 241 Þis bread was imaced of ane hwete corne. **13..** *Propr. Sanct.* (Vernon MS.) in Herrig's *Archiv* LXXXI. 102/4 But ȝif þat a whete-corn ffalle into þe eorþe lowe. *c* **1440** *Alphabet of Tales* 165 He vsid to putt whete-cornys in his ere, & he lernyd a white dowffe to stand opon his shulder & take þaim oute. **1526** TINDALE *John* xii. 24 Except the wheate corne fall into the grounde and deye, it bydeth alone. **1601** HOLLAND *Pliny* XXVII. xiii. II. 291 Little berries..of the bignesse of wheat corns. **1854** SPENCER in *Brit. Q. Rev.* July 140 Our own systems [of weights], both troy and avoirdupois, are derived primarily from wheat-corns.

†**2.** = WHEAT *sb.* 1. *Obs.*

1425 in *Rep. MSS. Ld. Middleton* (1911) 108 Nother comyn herd ne sched herd com in the qwyte corn feld to the korn be lad awey. **1764** *Museum Rust.* III. I. 1 The wheat-corn was remarkably backward, though it, in general, promised to be a good crop.

wheatear[1] ('hwi:tɪə(r)). [EAR *sb.*[2]] **1.** An ear of wheat.

c **1400** MAUNDEV. (Roxb.) vii. 27 Þe seuen barayne ȝeres þat ware betakned by þe seuen deed qwhete eres. [**1688** HOLME *Armoury* I. 103/3 Our old English terms were these ..Whet-herys, Wheat Ears.] **1798** BLOOMFIELD *Farmer's Boy, Summer* 52 Shot up from broad rank blades that droop below, The nodding wheat-ear forms a graceful bow. *c* **1840** ELIZA COOK *Song of Sun* iv, Who else can purple the grape on the vine, Or flush the wheat-ear with gold? **1878** MEREDITH *Love in Valley* 158 Slain are the poppies that shot their random scarlet Quick amid the wheatears.

2. A pattern in embroidery, lace, weaving, etc., or an ornament in wood-carving, etc., resembling an ear of wheat.

1882 CAULFEILD & SAWARD *Dict. Needlework* 195/2 *Wheatear Stitch.* This stitch is a combination of Point Natté and Chain Stitch. **1911** *Encycl. Brit.* XIII. 306/1 The backs of Hepplewhite chairs were often adorned with galleries and festoons of wheat-ears or pointed fern leaves. **1919** T. WRIGHT *Romance Lace Pillow* ix. 83 The ancient pattern called the *Wheat-ear and Cornflower*..is still made. **1955** R. W. MILLAR tr. *Daniel-Rops' Jesus in His Time* ix. 366 Heavy columns of porphyry with rather ungainly capitals carved with grapes and wheat-ears. **1957** SIMPSON & WEIR *Weaver's Craft* xii. 151 The patterns most generally used for tweeds are..Twill..Goose eye..Wheatear. **1977** *Penguin Dict. Decorative Arts* 374/2 Typical of the [Hepplewhite] style are..wheat-ears with which the central splat of shield-back and other chairs are decorated.

Hence **'wheat-eared** *a.*, full of wheat-ears.

1792 *Ess. towards new Ed. Tibullus* 11 Be thine, blond Ceres, from my wheat-ear'd field, A pendant crown thy temple's doors to grace.

wheatear[2] ('hwi:tɪə(r)). Also 6 **whekere** (?), 7 **wheat ears, wheatgear** (?). [Early evidence wanting prob. on account of local origin; but the orig. form is app. still represented in the 17th cent. by *wheatears* (*a* 1661) for **whiteeres*, f. *whit-*, WHITE *a.* (cf. for the phonology the place-name *Whittern*, OE. *hwītærn*) + *eeres, ers*, ARSE, the name being given in allusion to the bird's white rump; cf. Cornish dial. form *whiteass*, the similar dial. names *white rump, wittol* = *white-tail* (in Cotgr. *whittaile*, glossing F. *culblanc* 'white-rump'), and Du. *witstaart*, G. *weiss-schwanz*. From *wheatears*, taken as pl., a supposed sing. *wheatear* was inferred, and association with WHEAT *sb.* (see quot. 1653, etc.) established the spelling of the first syllable.]

A small passerine bird, *Saxicola œnanthe*, widely distributed over the Old World, having a bluish-grey back, white belly, rump, and upper tail-coverts, and blackish wings; esteemed as a delicacy.

1591 *Shuttleworths' Acc.* (Chetham Soc.) 70 A courleve xvj[d]; thrie whekeres [*so printed*], xvj[d]; larkes and yowloringes, iiij[d]. **1653** J. TAYLOR (Water P.) *Cert. Trav. Uncert. Journ.* 17 There were rare Birds I never saw before. .. Th'are called *Wheat ears*, less then Lark or Sparrow... The name of *Wheat ears*, on them is ycleap'd, Because they come when wheat is yearly reap'd. *a* **1661** FULLER *Worthies* (1662) III. 98 Wheat-ears is a bird peculiar to this County [*i.e.* Sussex], hardly found out of it. It is so called, because fattest when Wheat is ripe, whereon it feeds... That Palateman shall pass in silence, who being seriously demanded his judgment concerning the abilities of a great Lord, concluded him a man of very weak parts, because once he saw him at a great Feast feed on Chickens when there were Wheat-Ears on the Table. *a* **1700** B. E. *Dict. Cant. Crew, Wheat-gear*, a Bird smaller than a Dottrel. **1724** DE FOE *Tour Gt. Brit.* I. II. 57 The Bird call'd a Wheatear, or as we may call them, the English Ortolans. **1770** CUMBERLAND *West Indian* III. ii, A hot-brain'd headlong spark, that would run into our trap, like a wheat-ear under a turf. **1883** *Century Mag.* XXVII. 111 The wheat-ear uncovered its white rump as it flitted from rock to rock. **1894** R. B. SHARPE *Hand-bk. Birds Gt. Brit.* I. 291 The winter home of the Wheatear extends from the North-western Himalayas to Persia, and also to North-eastern and Eastern Africa, as well as to Senegambia.

wheaten ('hwi:t(ə)n), *a.* Forms: 1 **hwæten, huaeten,** 3 **ȝweten,** 4 **hueten,** 5, 6 **whetyn,** 6 **whettyn, whe(a)ton,** 7 **wheten,** 6- **wheaten.** [OE. *hwǣten* = MDu. *weiten*, MHG. *weizīn*: see WHEAT *sb.* and -EN[4].]

1. Composed of the grain or flour of wheat. Sometimes applied *spec.* to bread made of the whole grain ('wholemeal') as distinct from white bread.

805-31 in Sweet *O.E. Texts* 444, cxx huaetenra hlafa & xxx clenra. *c* **1000** *Sax. Leechd.* I. 322 Mid hwætenan meluwe. *c* **1290** *St. Cuthbert* 52 in *S. Eng. Leg.* 360 Clene ȝwetene flour. **1340** *Ayenb.* 82 Þe wyfman grat myd childe, þet more hi uynt smak in ane zoure epple þanne ine ane huetene lhoue. *c* **1430** *Two Cookery-bks.* 33 Bynd hym vppe with fflour of Rys, oþer with whetyn floure. **1530** PALSGR. 288/1 Whetynbreed, *pain bourgois.* *c* **1530** *Songs, Carols*, etc. (E.E.T.S.) 120, I clynge as doth a wheton cake. **1577** HARRISON *England* III. i. 95 b/1 in *Holinshed*, Wheaton bread, so named because the colour..resembleth the graie wheat. **1608** in J. Nicholl *Comp. Ironm.* (1866) 140 Wheate ..to be ground into meal and baked into white and wheten bread, and the wheaten to contayne xj oz. the penny wheten loffe, and the three-halfpenny white loves after the same rate. **1638** PENKETHMAN *Artach.* H 2, The Law doth appoint three sorts of Bread only to be made, *viz.* white, wheaten, and houshold. **1709** *Act 8 Anne* c. 19 Table, The White Loaves are One Half, and the Wheaten Three Quarters of the Weight of Household Loaves. **1727** DE FOE *Syst. Magic* I. i. (1840) 4 Our penny wheaten brown bread loaves. **1818** COLEBROOKE *Import Colon. Corn* 69 The bread made of this mixed flour is found to be..better..than that made with plain wheaten meal. **1844** H. STEPHENS *Bk. Farm* II. 367 Rye-bread is denser than wheaten-bread. **1857** MILLER *Elem. Chem., Org.* (1862) xiii. §2. 839 Bread made from wheaten flour. **1919** *Q. Rev.* July 182 The food and fuel regulations respecting wheaten bread, sugar, and 'lightless nights' had been withdrawn. **1922** JOYCE *Ulysses* 503 Wheatenmeal with honey and nutmeg. **1944** L. MUMFORD *Condition of Man* vi. 202 Wheaten bread.

2. Of or belonging to wheat as a plant; made of the stalks or straw of wheat.

c **1000** *Ags. Gosp.* John xii. 24 Þæt hwætene corn wunað ana, buton hyt fealle on eorþan & sy dead. **1552** HULOET, Wheaten branne. **1565** GOLDING *Ovid's Met.* II. (1587) 17 There waited summer naked starke all saue a wheaten hat. **1597** GERARDE *Herbal* I. i. 1 Apparent shew of wheaten leaues. **1602** SHAKS. *Ham.* v. ii. 41 As Peace should still her wheaten Garland weare. **1681** GREW *Musæum* IV. iii. 376 The Stalk as thick as a Wheaten-straw. **1730** THOMSON *Autumn* 1 Crown'd with the sickle and the wheaten sheaf. **1827** CLARE *Sheph. Cal.* 49 Oft making 'love-knots' in the shade, Of blue-green oat or wheaten blade. **1865** SWINBURNE *Poems & Ball., In Mem. Landor* 9 In many a tender wheaten plot Flowers that were dead Live.

†**3.** ***wheaten plum*** = WHEAT-PLUM. *Obs.*

1542 [see WHEAT-PLUM, quot. 1538]. **1552** HULOET, Wheaten plummes, whiche be whyte or yelowe plummes, *cærea pruna.* **1594** BARNFIELD *Affect. Sheph.* II. xlii, Bullas and wheaton Plumbs.

4. Of a pale honey colour. ***wheaten terrier***, a soft-coated terrier belonging to a breed originally developed in Ireland and distinguished by its pale golden wavy coat. Also *absol.* as *sb.* denoting the dog (also, the colour).

1943 *Our Dogs* 5 Mar. 234/5 The soft-coated Wheaten Terrier has now been recognised by the English Kennel Club. *Ibid.* 19 Mar. 281/2 There were 30 entries of Wheatens at the Irish Kennel Club show. **1945** C. L. B. HUBBARD *Observer's Bk. Dogs* 146 Wheaten-coloured Terriers of soft coats have existed in Ireland for a considerable time. **1959** *Times* 14 Aug. 1/7 (Advt.), Soft-coated Wheaten Terrier puppies. **1971** F. HAMILTON *World Encycl. Dogs* 480 The mature Wheaten is an attractive, compact, well-built dog, strong and energetic. **1975** *Country Life* 6 Feb. 311 The Border terrier..coat of either wheaten, red, grizzle and tan, or blue and tan.

Wheaties ('hwi:tɪz), *sb. pl.* Also **wheaties.** [f. WHEAT *sb.* + -IE.] The name of a breakfast cereal made from wheat.

A proprietary name in the United States.

1925 *Official Gaz.* (U.S. Patent Office) 24 Mar. 738/2 Washburn Crosby Company, Minneapolis, Minn. *Wheaties* ..Cereal food products. **1935** *Good Housekeeping* (N.Y.) June (Advt., rear cover), Wheaties bring real whole wheat.. in a ready-to-serve form that children adore. **1952** *Galaxy* Sept. 50/1 An institution is where they put Aunt Maggy when she started collecting Wheaties in a stamp album. **1968** *Shakes. Q.* Winter 38 For Ryot..to tempt Youthe with archery, would be as if Gluttony tried to corrupt his appetite with a bowl of wheaties. **1981** I. ST. JAMES *Balfour Conspiracy* vii. 241 Their morning wheaties came wrapped in a..Press Release.

'wheat-land. Land on which wheat is grown or suitable for growing wheat on.

977 *Charter of Oswald* in Kemble *Cod. Dipl.* III. 159 Buton .lx. æcran ðæt hæft se arcebisceop ȝenumen into Cymesige to his hame him to hwæte-lande. **1573-80** TUSSER *Husb.* (1878) 128 Thry fallow once ended, go strike by and by, Both wheat land and barlie. **1603** G. OWEN *Pembrokeshire* (1892) 59 *marg.*, Wheate lande howe dressed. **1763** MILLS *Pract. Husb.* II. 12 He gave five plowings to a piece of wheat-land. **1821** CLARE *Vill. Minstrel* I. 173 The same Power..That browns the wheat-lands in their summer-stain. **1916** *Times* 27 Nov. 10/4 Many thousand acres of our richest wheatland is to-day totally uncultivated.

wheatmeal ('hwi:tmi:l). [OE. *hwǣtemelu* = MHG. *weiz(en)mel* (G. *weizenmehl*), ON. *hveitimiol* (MSw. *hvetemiol*, etc.): see MEAL *sb.*[1]] Meal or flour of wheat. Also *attrib.*

c **1000** *Sax. Leechd.* II. 354 Ȝebriw wel swiþne briw þær on mid hwæte melwe. **1382** WYCLIF *Exod.* xxix. 2 Of puyr whete meele thow shalt make alle thingis. **1398** TREVISA *Barth. De P.R.* XVII. clviii. (W. de W.) T viij b/1 The flowur of whete meele hyghte Simula: and is the cheyf meele of whete. *a* **1425** tr. *Arderne's Treat. Fistula*, etc. 72 Tak cow mylk, and put þerto a subtile whete meel. **1579** in J. Nicholl *Comp. Ironm.* (1866) 103 Wheat meale the best iij[s] the bushell. **1681** GREW *Musæum* II. ii. 222 It must be mixed nothing near so stiff as our Wheat-Meal. **1767** *Ann. Reg., Hist. Eur.* 61 The bill to continue..the free importation of wheat and wheat-meal. **1870** *Daily News* 6 Dec., The mixed diet of linseed cake, barley, beanmeal, wheatmeal, peameal. **1915** *Ibid.* 5 Jan. 4 It is specially necessary that the sick and wounded should not go short of wheatmeal bread.

†**wheat-plum.** *Obs.* (or *dial.*) [orig. a misinterpretation of L. *cēræa prūna* waxen or wax-coloured plums (Virgil, *Ecl.* ii. 53), *cēræa* being misapprehended as **cěrea* wheaten (f. *Ceres* wheat, corn); subsequent association with *white* is probable (cf. WHEATEAR[2] and Du. *witte pruim*).] Name of a supposed variety of plum.

1538 ELYOT Addit., *Cerea pruna*, wheate [*ed.* 1542 wheaten] plummes. **1573-80** TUSSER *Husb.* (1878) 76 Januaries abstract. Of trees or fruites to be set or remoued. .. Wheat plums. **1577** GOOGE *Heresbach's Husb.* II. 96 Wheate Plomes, and horse Plomes, wherewith they vse to fatte Hogges. **1611** COTGR., *Prune blanche*, the wheat, or white Plumme. **1657** C. BECK *Univ. Char.* M 3, A wheat plum-tree. **1676** *Phil. Trans.* XI. 629 There groweth wild in some places of the Woods a Plum somewhat like our Wheat-Plum. **1793** M. CUTLER in *Life*, etc. (1888) II. 294, I am uncertain what he intends by the Wheat-plum. **1847** HALLIWELL, *Wheat-plum*, a large fleshy plum, sometimes called a bastard Orleans plum. *Linc.*

Wheatstone ('hwi:tstən). [Called after Sir Charles *Wheatstone*, who in 1843 brought into notice the 'differential arrangement' apparatus, which had been invented by S. Hunter Christie in 1833.] **a.** In full, ***Wheatstone('s) bridge***: a simple circuit for measuring a resistance by connecting it so as to form a quadrilateral with three known resistances and applying a voltage between a pair of opposite corners: a galvanometer connected between the other two corners registers no current when the ratios of the two pairs of adjacent resistances are equal.

1872 *Jrnl. Soc. Telegr. Eng.* 8 May 196 A Differential Resistance Measurer,—or, as it is commonly called, a 'Wheatstone's Bridge'. **1885** WATSON & BURBURY *Math. Th. Electr.* I. 221 The principle of the instrument known as Wheatstone's Bridge. **1901** *Phil. Trans. R. Soc.* A. CXCVI. 29 The two grids A and A' formed two arms of a Wheatstone bridge. **1953** A. SMITH *Blind White Fish in Persia* i. 25 He had with him..a Wheatstone's bridge—a gadget of complex appearance for measuring the electrical resistance of the soil. **1979** E. N. LURCH *Electric Circuit Fundamentals* ix. 296 The Wheatstone bridge..is the elementary bridge circuit that is the prototype of all the more complex bridges used in electric circuit analysis.

b. Used in the possessive, *attrib.*, and *absol.* to denote forms of electric telegraph invented by Wheatstone.

1858 FARADAY in *Notices of Proc. R. Inst.* II. 555 (*heading*) On Wheatstone's electric telegraph in relation to science. **1881** *Ibid.* IX. 302, I found that one of our Wheatstone instruments was actually working at the rate of 180 or 190 words a minute. **1898** *Daily News* 21 May 7/4 The clicking of the needles, the tapping of the Wheatstones. **1922** GLAZEBROOK *Dict. Appl. Physics* II. 788/2 Wheatstone simplex circuits are used extensively for the transmission of press telegrams to all parts of Great Britain. **1949** *Brit. Jrnl. Psychol.* XL. 37 A Wheatstone transmitter was driven at 6 and 14 words a minute by a variable speed gear.

'wheaty, *a.* [f. WHEAT *sb.* + -Y[1].]

†**a.** Containing grains of wheat. *Obs.*

1598 YONG *Diana* 259 Ripening fruit, and wheatie eares. **1611** COTGR., *Fourmentier*, wheat-yeelding, wheatie. *a* **1623** H. AINSWORTH *Annot. Deut.* xxxii. 14. Ee 2 b/2 With fat of wheaty kidneys fine [see KIDNEY 4].

b. Of or pertaining to wheat.

1933 L. I. WILDER *Farmer Boy* vii. 47 The wheaty smell of new bread.

wheay, wheaze, whech(e, whecker, whed(d)er, whed(d)le: see WHO, WHEASE, WHEEZE, WHICH, WHITCH, WITCH, WHICKER, WEATHER, WHETHER, WHITHER, WHEEDLE.

whee (hwi:), *int.* [Echoic.] An exclamation of joy, exhilaration, astonishment, etc. Occas. as *sb.*, a high-pitched sound resembling this.

[**1918** E. A. MACKINTOSH *War, the Liberator* IV. 145 Whee-ee-ee-errump! The air was full of dust and smoke from a little way up the trench.] **1920** S. LEWIS in *Sat. Even. Post* 11 Dec. 10/1 'Whee!'.. He sprang up, posed like the Statue of Liberty, hurled a pillow at her. **1944** E. S. GARDNER *Case of Black-Eyed Blonde* (1948) xx. 205 The little boy shrieked with delight. 'Whee-eee-ee,' he cried. **1960** M. MACDONALD in G. Maxwell *Ring of Bright Water* xii. 168 Her [*sc.* the otter's] basic conversational vocabulary was a high-pitched whistling 'Whee'. With loud and soft, short and long and other variations of 'Whees' she had quite a lot to say. **1978** N. Freeling *Night Lords* v. 24 Whee, thought Castang: he has worked fast. **1981** *Studia Mystica* IV. iv. 34 A cry of 'Whee!'

whee (hwiː), *v.* [f. prec.] **a.** *trans.* With *up.* To stimulate, excite. *U.S. colloq.* **b.** *intr.* To utter a high-pitched sound.

1949 *Sat. Even. Post* 3 Dec. 3/3 And did that whee him up to do his Christmas shopping early? **1960** M. Macdonald in G. Maxwell *Ring of Bright Water* xii. 171 She [*sc.* an otter] would lie on the floor..'wheeing' plaintively. **1966** *N.Y. Times* 17 Apr. v. 2, I was all wheed up, feeling great, I knew I would win. **1971** *Atlantic Monthly* Mar. 36, I got so patriotically wheed up that I ended by calling for three cheers for General Douglas MacArthur.

whee: see QUEY.

wheedle ('hwiːd(ə)l), *sb.* Now *rare.* Forms: see the vb. [f. next.]

1. An act or instance of wheedling; a piece of insinuating flattery or cajolery; also *gen.* wheedling speech.

1668 Etheredge *She wou'd if she cou'd* I. i, Dost thou think to pass these gross Wheadles on me too? **1681** Hickeringill *Black Non-Conf.* vii. Wks. 1716 II. 61 It looks like a Wheedle, or a Trepan, to drill a Man into a Court by Process in a feigned Suit. **1687** Sedley *Bellamira* IV. i, You have several times talked to me of a sister of mine, lost from our house in Devonshire; but I always look'd upon it as a meer wheedle. *a* **1708** T. Ward *Eng. Ref.* II. (1710) 87 In Cant and Wheedle most Expert They were. **1755** Shebbeare *Lydia* (1769) II. 284 She.., by a soft insinuating wheedle, took possession of the divine's good opinion. *a* **1814** *Word of Honor* III. i. in *New Brit. Theatre* I. 368, I cannot stand this wheedle. **1861** Thackeray *Round. Papers, Ogres,* So were the Sirens ogres—pretty blue-eyed things..singing their melodious wheedles.

†**2.** A wheedler. *Obs.*

1673 Wycherley *Gent. Dancing-Master* IV. i, *Hipp.* You saw I cou'd dissemble with my Father, Why shou'd you think I cou'd not with you? *Ger.* So young a Wheadle? **1681** Otway *Soldier's Fort.* III. i, Dainty Wheadle, here's a Fellow for ye. *a* **1700** B. E. *Dict. Cant. Crew, Parasite,* a Trencher Friend, a meer Wheedle. *Ibid., Wheadle,* a Sharper.

wheedle ('hwiːd(ə)l), *v.* Also 7 **whed(d)le,** 7–9 **wheadle.** [Origin obscure. Possibly a survival in a specialized application of OE. *wǽdlian* to beg, orig. to be poor, f. *wǽdl* poverty.]

1. *trans.* To entice or persuade by soft flattering words; to gain over or take in by coaxing or cajolery.

1661 Blount *Glossogr.* (ed. 2), *Whead* or *Wheadle,* is a late word of fancy, and signifies to draw one in, by fair words or subtile insinuation, to act any thing of disadvantage or reproof. **1668** Shadwell *Sullen Lovers* IV. 52 Come Sir, don't think to Wheadle me at this rate! **1675** Tully *Let. to Baxter* 23 To be wheadl'd with bare Talke. **1726** De Foe *Hist. Devil* I. i. (1840) 12 He wheedled Eve, deluded Adam. **1814** Wordsw. *Excurs.* II. 254 Smooth words he had to wheedle simple souls. **1850** Dickens *Dav. Copp.* xxxii, He was crossing you and wheedling you. **1888** Bryce *Amer. Commw.* xxxix. II. 78 The citizens are too numerous to be all wheedled or threatened.

b. with various preps. and advs., or with inf.: To bring into a specified condition by such action.

1667 *Leathermore: Advice conc. Gaming* (1668) 7 If the Winner be bubbleable, they will..wheadle him into play and win all his Money. **1669** Worlidge *Syst. Agric.* (1681) 247 By laying the Net in such haunts, and wheedling them [*sc.* pigeons, etc.] in by a Stale. **1672** Marvell *Reh. Transp.* I. 129 To wheedle one almost to make himself away. **1673** Dryden *Amboyna* Prol., Religion wheedled you to Civil War. **1687** in *Magd. Coll.* (O.H.S.) 167 They were wheedled off of it by some few sugar words. **1722** De Foe *Col. Jack* i. (1840) 12 The major..was wheedled away by a couple of young rogues. **1726** —— *Hist. Devil* I. i. (1840) 12 How he wheedled the people..into the absurd..undertaking of building a Babel. **1860** Dickens *Uncomm. Trav.* i, I.. should have no idea..how to wheedle a man into ordering something he doesn't want. **1869** Mrs. Stowe *Oldtown Folks* xl. (1870) 467 He has a tongue that could wheedle a bird out of a tree. **1876** C. M. Davies *Unorth. Lond.* (ed. 2) 184 Whom he wheedled over not to betray him. **1891** Kipling *Light that Failed* xii. 232, I have seen you wheedle an angry Mahdieh woman into giving you dates.

2. To do (a person) *out of* a thing, or to get (a thing) *out of* a person, by such action.

1670 Wood *Life* (O.H.S.) II. 196 The M[asters] are whedled out of one [Act]. **1700** Congreve *Way of World* III. xviii, I have already a deed of Settlement of the best part of her Estate; which I wheadl'd out of her. **1759** Franklin *Hist. Penn.* Wks. 1840 III. 529 These proprietaries..would have either bullied or wheedled the inhabitants out of the privileges they were born to. **1816** Scott *Antiq.* iii, I wheedled an old woman out of these [ballads]. **1831** —— *Cast. Dang.* xi, I suffered the abbess to wheedle the secret out of me. **1886** Stevenson *Kidnapped* xxiv, Wheedling my money from me while I lay half conscious.

3. *absol.* or *intr.* To use soft flattering words; (of an animal) to fawn; † ***to wheedle in with,*** to curry favour with; † ***to wheedle with*** = sense 1.

1664 Butler *Hud.* II. iii. 335 His bus'ness was to pump and wheedle. **1712** Hearne *Collect.* (O.H.S.) III. 290 Lancaster goes down to the Dean of Xt. Church, and began to wheedle with him. **1716** Swift *Phyllis* 87 Johnny wheedled, threaten'd, fawn'd, Till Phyllis all her trinkets pawn'd. **1726** De Foe *Hist. Devil* II. i. (1840) 183 Secretly wheedling in with the dignified clergy. **1811** *Ora & Juliet* I. 204 She wheedled with the housekeeper, till she insured a glass of cordial from her. **1847** Tennyson *Princ.* v. 151 Wheedling and siding with them! **1865** Swinburne *Poems & Ball., Satia te Sanguine* xiv, As a tame beast writhes and wheedles.

b. *Cant.* = WHIDDLE *v.*

1710 Palmer *Proverbs* 197 Sing in the Proverb, is the same that our Newgate-Birds call Wheedle; which is, when one of the Gang Tattles, Confesses, and Accuses the Rest.

Hence '**wheedled** *ppl. a.*; '**wheedling** *vbl. sb.* and *ppl. a.* (chiefly of conduct, manner, etc.); whence '**wheedlingly** *adv.*; also '**wheedler**; '**wheedlery,** wheedling; '**wheedlesome,** '**wheedly** *adjs.*, of a wheedling character.

1675 R. Head *Proteus Rediv.* 226 His gulled or *Wheedled Patient. **1773** *Ainsworth's Lat. Dict.* II, *Delinitor,*..a cajoler, or *wheedler. *a* **1861** T. Winthrop *Life in Open Air* (1863) 41 Smith, wheedler of trout. **1868** L. M. Alcott *Little Women* xiv, You get everything you want out of people... you are a born wheedler. **1909** 'G. G.' *Winkles* 58 The fond daughter continued her *wheedleries. **1863** L. M. Alcott *Hosp. Sk.,* etc. 94 Anything more irresistibly *wheedlesome I never saw. **1674** R. Head *Jackson's Recant.* Bjb, Incomparable at the Art of *wheedling, which some call Complaisance. **1702** Pope *Wife of Bath* 163 By murm'ring, wheedling, stratagem, and force, I still prevail'd. **1837** Dickens *Pickw.* v, Notwithstanding all kinds of coaxing and wheedling, there were Mr. Winkle and the horse going round and round each other for ten minutes. **1859** Meredith *R. Feverel* xxxi, Wheedling availed as little as argument. **1668** Shadwell *Sullen Lovers* IV. 60 Pox on't what a *wheadling Rogue art thou now? **1694** F. Bragge *Disc. Parables* II. 41 His sly and wheedling insinuations. **1713** Rowe *Jane Shore* I. i, A laughing, toying, wheadling, whimpering she. **1848** Dickens *Dombey* lii, 'I wonder Master didn't take you with him, Rob,' said the old woman in a wheedling voice. **1856** Meredith *Shav. Shagpat* i. 18 *Wheedlingly she looked at him. **1904** W. S. Gilbert *Fairy's Dilemma* i, *Al.* (*wheedlingly*). What am I to get for this, eh? **1838** Sarah, Lady Lyttelton *Corr.* (1912) 282 The maids of honour..are very coaxy and *wheedly with me.

wheef(f)le, Sc. forms of WHIFFLE.

wheel (hwiːl), *sb.* Forms: 1 **hweoȝol, -ul, -el, hweowol, -ul, hweowl, hweohl,** 1–3 **hweol, hwel,** 3–4 **weole, wel,** 3–6 **whel,** 3–7 **whele,** 4–5 **wele,** (**whiel**), *north.* **quele,** 4–6 *Sc.* **quhele,** 4–7 **wheele,** *Sc.* **quheill,** (1 **hwiol,** 3 **wheol, weol, ȝweol, ȝwele,** 4 **wheole, woele, hueȝel, whewel,** *north.* **quel, quile, quil,** *Sc.* **quhel,** 5 **wheyle, whelle, whyll, wyle,** *north.* **quheyll, qweyll, qwell,** 5–6 **wheylle,** *north.* **qwhele, qwele, quheil(e, quhell,** 6 **wheill, whefyll, wheale, whieale, weil, whyl(l)e, qwyl,** *Sc.* **vheill, vhel(e, while,** 7 *Sc.* **quheele**), 4– **wheel.** [OE. *hweoȝol, hweowol, hwéol* = OFris. **hwêl* (EFris. *weel, wêil,* NFris. *well*), (M)LG. *wêl,* (M)Du. *wiel* (whence G. *wiel* in technical senses), ON. *hjól* (Sw., Da. *hjul*), *hvél*:—OTeut. **χwe(ȝ)ula-,* **χweχula-*:— Indo-Eur. **q^{w}eq^{w}lo-* repr. by Skr. *cakrá-* circle, wheel, Zend *caχrəm,* Gr. κύκλος; reduplicated f. **q^{w}elo-*: **q^{w}olo-,* repr. by ON. *hvel, hvela* (Norw. *kvel*), OPruss. *kelan* wheel, Gr. πόλος axis, pole, ploughed-up land, L. *colus* distaff, OSl. *kolo* wheel; the root meaning of *q^{w}el-* is 'to turn' (cf. Skr. *cárati* to move, Zend *čaraiti* 'versatur', Gr. πέλεσθαι to be in motion, L. *colere* to till, *in-quil-īnus* sojourner).]

I. 1. A circular frame of wood, metal, or other hard substance (sometimes in the form of a solid disc, but usually of a ring (*rim* or *felloe*) with spokes radiating from the central part or *nave*) attached or capable of being attached at its centre to an axle around which it revolves; used, in many different forms and sizes, for communicating, facilitating, or equalizing motion, and for other purposes.

a. In a vehicle, plough, locomotive engine, etc., each of two or more such appliances which support it and, by rolling upon the ground or other surface, enable it to move along with the least possible friction.

at or ***in the wheel,*** of horses, next to the carriage, in the place of the wheelers (see WHEELER 3) as opposed to the leaders. ***on the wheel, on wheels,*** riding in wheeled vehicles. (See also 13 b.)

c **888** Ælfred *Boeth.* xxxix. §7 Swa swa on wænes eaxe hwearfiað þa hweol. *a* **900** *O.E. Martyrol.* 26 Dec. 8 An pleȝende cild arn under wænes hweowol ond wearð sona dead. *c* **1000** *Sax. Leechd.* III. 270 Se firmamentum went on ðam twam steorran swa swa hweoȝel [*v. rr.* hweoȝul, hweowul] tyrnð on eaxe. *a* **1225** *Ancr. R.* 356 Elies hweoles þet weren furene. **1297** R. Glouc. (Rolls) 8437 An quointe tour hii lete make..Vpe four woeles..it was idriue. *a* **1300** *Cursor M.* 21267, I sal tell..Quat mai be yock, and quat quele [*Fairf.* quile, *Trin.* wheel] mai be, Bridel quat es, and quat axeltre. *c* **1315** Shoreham IV. 223 Me makeþ prynses þe host to gouerni, And ase whewelen þe linses To-gadere heldeþ hy. *c* **1400** Maundev. (Roxb.) xxv. 118 He rydez in a chariot with foure whelez. **1523–34** Fitzherb. *Husb.* §2 In Kente they haue other maner of plowes, somme goo with wheles, as they doo in many other places. **1573–80** Tusser *Husb.* (1878) 130 Hoy out (sir carter) the hog fro thy wheele. **1599** *Lanc. Wills* (Chetham Soc.) III. 9 Two turfe waynes furnished wth whiles axeltries. *a* **1600** Montgomerie *Misc. Poems* xlviii. 185 The bouand dolphin, tumbland lik a vhele. **1630** *R. Johnson's Kingd. & Commw.* 490 They..have moving houses built on wheeles. **1782** Cowper *John Gilpin* 41 Smack went the whip, round went the wheels. **1820** A. Sutherland *St. Kathleen* III. 216 It widna be Christian-like to stay cosie at hame, an' a' the countryside on the Wheel. **1883** E. Pennell-Elmhirst *Cream Leicestersh.* 223 Noble lords were now and again to be seen following the chase on wheels. **1884** J. E. T. Rogers *Work & Wages* 23 Plain wheels—that is, wheels formed from the trunk of a tree, with holes bored through them for the axles to run on. **1890** 'R. Boldrewood' *Col. Reformer* xiii, Three leaders and a pair of great upstanding half-bred horses at the wheel. **1893** Dunmore *Pamirs* II. 298, I took my tarantass with five horses attached, three in the wheel and two leaders.

b. Generally, in machinery or mechanical apparatus of any kind.

a **1100** *Aldhelm Gloss.* I. 502 (Napier 15/1) *Rota hauritoria,* hlædtrendle, hweowla, hweowl. **14..** *Voc.* in Wr.-Wülcker 600 *Panus, virgula illa circa quam trama involvitur. Idem et canellus dicitur,* a Quele. **14..** *Nom.* ibid. 696/10 *Hoc vertubrum,* a whelle. *c* **1440** *Jacob's Well* 260 A carte-qweel, drye & vngrecyd, cryeth lowdest of oþere qwelys. **1479–81** *Rec. St. Mary at Hill* 101 Nayle to amende the whele of the Sanctus bell. **1483** *Cath. Angl.* 415/2 A Wheylle of A drawe wele, *anclea.* **1495** *Naval Acc. Hen. VII.* (1896) 189 Wheles for to wynde up the Mayne Sayle. **1516** *Stratton Churchw. Acc.* in *Archæologia* XLVI. 204 A new whefyll for the gret bell. **1545** *Ludlow Churchw. Acc.* (Camden) 21 A while to the secounde tenor. **1590** Sir J. Smythe *Disc. Weapons* 47 Whereby they should faile to strike iust vpon the wheeles being fire-lockes. **1616** T. Scot *Philomythie* H 6, Some wheels were taken off..And some stood vselesse, so the Clock was spoild. **1768** Tucker *Lt. Nat.* I. I. iii. 59 A curious engine compounded of wheels screws and pulleys whereby a lady with a single hair of her head might raise a stone of two hundred weight. **1803** Mrs. P. L. Powys *Pass. fr. Diaries* (1899) 354 Before you enter the [silk-]manufactory you pass an immense wheel; by that one 99,947 other wheels are all turn'd. **1845** G. Dodd *Brit. Manuf.* IV. 185 Other wheel and pinion work..modifies this motion.

c. ***wheel and axle*** (or †***axis***), as one of the mechanical powers: see POWER *sb.*[1] 12.

1773 W. Emerson *Princ. Mech.* (ed. 3) 284 *Wheel and axle,* a machine to raise weights. One of the mechanic powers. **1799** Jas. Wood *Princ. Mech.* iv. (ed. 2) 63 The wheel and axle consists of two parts, a cylinder *AB* moveable about it's axis *CD,* and a circle *EF* so attached to the cylinder that the axis *CD* passes through it's center, and is perpendicular to it's plane. **1821** *R. Turner's Arts & Sci.* 85 In using the wheel and axis as the weight is raised, the rope coils round the axis and enlarges the diameter, hence the advantage of the power is diminished. **1862** Spencer *First Princ.* II. xiv. §114 (1875) 325 The advance from the lever to the wheel-and-axle is an advance from a simple agent to an agent made up of several simple ones.

d. With prefixed defining words indicating kind, structure, use, etc.

There are numerous compounds, as CART-WHEEL *sb.*, COG-WHEEL, DRIVING-WHEEL, FLY-WHEEL, etc., etc. ***fifth wheel, idle wheel***: see FIFTH A. 1 c, C, IDLE *a.* 5 b.

II. A wheel or wheel-like structure, or an instrument or appliance having a wheel as its essential part, used for some specific purpose.

2. a. A large wheel, or contrivance resembling one, used in various ways as an instrument of torture or punishment. ***to break on the wheel***: see BREAK *v.* 7 b.

c **888** Ælfred *Boeth.* xxxv. §7 þæt unstille hweol ðe Ixion wæs to ȝebunden. *c* **1000** Ælfric *Saints' Lives* xiv. 86 Het se arleasa casere ȝebindan georium on anum bradum hweowle. *a* **1225** *Leg. Kath.* 1965 Ha schal beon tohwiðeret, wið þe hweoles swa, in an hondhwile. *c* **1290** *St. George* 58 in *S. Eng. Leg.* 295 So sone ase huy þis guode man a-boue þusse ȝweole brouȝte, þat ȝweol to-brac. *c* **1375** *Sc. Leg. Saints* xxxiii. (*George*) 545 þare brocht wes a quhele made Awfule & hye, & in it hade Sharpe swerdis scherand in al syde. *c* **1450** *Mirk's Festial* 134 A whele set full of howkes yn þat on syde of þe whele, and swerde poyntys in þat oþyr syde aȝeyne þat. **1578** H. Wotton *Courtlie Controv.* 111 By the same iudgement was Ponifre..broken vpon a wheele. **1608** Dekker *Dead Tearme* Wks. (Grosart) IV. 11 As if hee were a Male-factor, and hadde beene tortured on the Germaine Wheele. **1709–10** Addison *Tatler* No. 133 ¶ 3 To rescue him from the Ignominy of the Wheel. **1764** Goldsm. *Trav.* 435 The lifted axe, the agonizing wheel. **1821** Scott *Kenilw.* xli, He was swoln like a corpse three days exposed on the wheel.

b. ***wheel of Ixion*** (Astron.): see quot.

1590 T. Hood *Use of Celestial Globe* 39 b, *Corona Austrina,* the South garland..Others call it the wheele of Ixion.

3. Various mechanical contrivances. **a.** The revolving part of a turning-lathe, or of a potter's lathe (***potter's wheel***: see POTTER *sb.*[1] 3); also allusively, as in phr. ***on the wheel*** = in process of being fashioned, in the making. **b.** = MILL-WHEEL. **c.** = SPINNING-WHEEL. **d.** = TREAD-WHEEL; also, a treadmill. † **e.** ***musical wheel,*** the revolving barrel of a barrel-organ or musical box. **f.** An instrument for measuring distances: = PERAMBULATOR 2. **g.** = *grinding-wheel*: see GRINDING *vbl. sb.* 2. **h.** *Naut.*, etc. = *steering-wheel*: see STEERING *vbl. sb.* 3 b. Now usu. of the steering-wheel of a motor vehicle. **i.** = PADDLE-WHEEL.

a. **1382** Wyclif *Jer.* xviii. 3 And Y cam doun in to the hous of the crockere, and lo! he made a werc vp on a whel. **1540** Palsgr. *Acolastus* III. v. R ij b, As well proportioned as if it had ben made of a tourners hande, at his wheele. **1677** Gilpin *Dæmonol.* I. xviii. 153 While they are upon the Wheel (as a Potters Vessel in the Prophet) they are often marred. **1695** J. Sage *Fund. Charter Presbytery* (1697) 9 Our Reformation was on the Wheel. **1728** Chambers *Cycl.* s.v. *Pottery,* The Wheel and Lathe are the Chief, almost the only Instruments, used in Pottery. **1875** Jowett *Plato* (ed. 2) III. 47 Potters..have their wheel at hand, that they may work a little when they please.

b. *c* **1400** *Pilgr. Sowle* (Caxton) I. xxv. (1859) 30 The whele of a mylle lyghtly torneth alwey to ther that he bygan. **1484**

CAXTON *Fables of Æsop* v. x, For the swyftnesse of the water he must nedes passe vnder the whele of the mylle. **1609** SKENE *Reg. Maj.* I. 115 b, Of ane milne and ane man slane with the quheill thereof. **1833** TENNYSON *Miller's Dau.* 102, I loved the..dark round of the dripping wheel.

c. **1467** *Maldon, Essex, Crt. Rolls*, Bundle 43, no. 14 (MS.) vii cusshones, I whyll, I par cardarum, I hemper. *c* **1525** *Richmond Wills* (Surtees) 10 Item j qwele, j par of kayrds, j rakyncrok, xij^d^. **1617** in W. F. Shaw *Mem. Eastry* (1870) 229 One payer of wollen cards two wollen whiles. **1651** J. NICOLL *Diary* (Bann. Club) 61 Sum pure pepill quha wer spyning that day loist thair quheillis and wer brokin. **1729** WALKDEN *Diary* (1866) 57 A Jersey wheel to wind spoyles on. **1834** D. CROCKETT *Life* iv. 32 My wife had a good wheel, and knowed exactly how to use it. **1890** HARTLAND *Sci. Fairy Tales* i. (1891) 7 The women at their wheels; and while they spin they sing love ditties.

d. **1623** J. TAYLOR (Water P.) *New Discov.* A6, In a Wheele I saw a comely Asse..draw as it were from the infernall pit..So..coole a water. **1697** COLLIER *Ess. Mor. Subj.* II. (1703) 114 Envy is..a vice they say which keeps no holydays, but is always in the wheel, and working upon its own despair. **1742** YOUNG *Nt. Th.* III. 331 To climb daily Life's worn wheel, Which draws up nothing new. **1827** SCOTT *Jrnl.* 22 Mar., It..makes one feel like a dog in a wheel, always moving and never advancing. **1835** DICKENS *Sk. Boz, Last Cab-driver*, He positively refused to work on the wheel; so after many trials, I was compelled to order him into solitary confinement.

e. **1659** LEAK *Waterwks.* I ij b, Let there be a Musical Wheel..so when the said water Wheel shall turn it shall cause the Musical Wheel to turn.

f. **1696** *Phil. Trans.* XIX. 319 One by the Wheel was Sixteen Perches round, another in walking Seventy six Paces. **1774** M. MACKENZIE *Marit. Surv.* iii. 7 Some Surveyors measure their Distances by a Wheel.

g. **1707** J. STEVENS tr. *Quevedo's Com. Wks.* (1709) 433 Running at the Grinder, [he] made him quit his Wheel. **1831** J. HOLLAND *Manuf. Metal* I. 289 The blades, after being hardened, are directly carried to the grinding-mill, or wheel, as the establishment is called.

h. **1743** BULKELEY & CUMMINS *Voy. S. Seas* 8 There broke a Sea in the Ship, which carried me over the Wheel. **1840** R. H. DANA *Bef. Mast* xxxiii, It took two men at the wheel to steer her. **1883** D. C. MURRAY *Hearts* xxxiii, Most of the people were below, and the few on deck were clustered near the wheel. **1906** C. N. & A. M. WILLIAMSON *Car of Destiny* xxxiii, Taking the wheel himself,..he backed the big, reddish-brown car off the barricade. **1929** J. B. PRIESTLEY *Good Compan.* I. ii. 67 For the next hour she sat at the wheel under his tuition. **1972** T. P. MCMAHON *Issue of Bishop's Blood* (1973) xvi. 229 The long-haul truckers drove themselves right into a ditch after too many hours at the wheel.

i. **1842** DICKENS *Amer. Notes* i, The two great wheels turn fiercely round for the first time; and the noble ship..breaks proudly through the..water.

†**4.** A turnstile or similar contrivance at the entrance of a convent. Also ***turning-wheel*** (TURNING *ppl. a.* 7). *Obs.*

14.. in Aungier *Syon* (1840) 257 The kepers of the wheyles, grates, gates, or entres into the clausures. *a* **1652** BROME *City Wit* III. i, He never sung to the wheele in Saint Brides Nunnery yonder. **1669** WOODHEAD *St. Teresa* II. xxxi. 192, I wished him to go, and put up a Wheele, and a Grate, in the House appointed for the Nuns dwelling.

5. In full ***wheel of fortune*** (see 12 a): = *lottery-wheel*: see LOTTERY 5. Also *allusively*.

1698 *Post Boy* 3 Jan. in Hone *Every-day Bk.* (1827) II. 1422 We have divers wheels agoing. **1750** *New Jersey Archives* Ser. I. (1895) XII. 640 The [Lottery] Ticketts will be putting into the wheels on Wednesday. **1763** *Brit. Mag.* IV. 548 Beware the Wheel of Fortune—'tis a gin, You'll lose a dozen times for once you win. **1774** FOOTE *Cozeners* II, I believe Toby will hardly thank me for going into the wheel. **1801** T. MOORE *To the Large & Beaut. Miss* —— 4 But how comes it that you, such a capital prize, Should so long have remained in the wheel? **1834** L. RITCHIE *Wand. Seine* 167 Stalls, provided with wheels-of-fortune, at which the Norman lass boldly ventures her solid sous for empty hopes. **1880** *A. McKay's Hist. Kilmarnock* (ed. 4) 121 Wheel-of-fortune men, offering to make all rich in a jiffie.

6. **a.** A rotatory firework in the form of a wheel. (See also CATHERINE WHEEL 3, PIN-WHEEL 2.) **b.** ***wheel of colour***: = CHROMATROPE. **c.** ***wheel of life***: = ZOETROPE.

1629 in Hodgkin *Rariora* (1904) III. *Fireworks* 16 Girondelles or Fierie Wheeles. **1653** *Van Etten's Math. Recreat.* 272 How to make Wheels of Fire. **1826** HOOD *Vauxhall* 13 Wheels whiz—smash crackers—serpents twist. **1872** Wheel of life [see ZOOTROPE]. **1877** WOOD *Nature's Teach., Optics* ii. 306 The Chromatrope, or Wheel of Colour.

7. **a.** orig. and esp. *U.S.* A bicycle or tricycle; also *abstr.* (with def. art.) the practice of riding on one, cycling; (with indef. art.) a cycle-ride.

1880 *Scribner's Monthly* Feb. 483/1 A few possessors of the birotate chariot, numbering some forty odd, enjoyed a 'wheel around the Hub'. **1882** *Wheelman* I. 13 'I love my wheel,' he said, 'as the yachtsman loves his boat.' **1884** *Harper's Mag.* Jan. 305/1 The wheel was a new thing in New York ways. **1888** P. FURNIVALL *Phys. Training* 3, I am more accustomed to the wheel than the pen. **1893** *Outing* (U.S.) XXII. 140/2 It would have been a most lovely wheel had we chosen to explore it on bicycles. **1896** H. G. WELLS *Wheels of Chance* vii, Hoopdriver..felt a pleasing sense of having duly asserted the wide sympathy that binds all cyclists together, of having behaved himself as becomes one of the brotherhood of the wheel.

b. ***to be on someone's wheel***: to be close behind someone, to be on his track; to put pressure on someone (to do something). *slang* (chiefly *Austral.*).

1941 V. DAVIS *Phenomena in Crime* vi. 78 Don't come here if there's a busy on your wheel! **1954** V. KELLY *Shadow* 89 Down there the cops'll give you a go. Here they're on your wheel all the time. **1959** A. UPFIELD *Bony & Mouse* 104 I'll be ready for it. I'm going to be right on Tony's wheel when it happens. **1969** O. WHITE *Under Iron Rainbow* 118 The inspector's been on my wheel to trace him.

c. *pl.* A car. *slang* (orig. *U.S.*).

1959 *Esquire* Nov. 70J, *Wheels*, car. **1970** K. PLATT *Pushbutton Butterfly* (1971) v. 51 'Can I drive you to where you're agitating today?' 'Beautiful. I don't have wheels,' he said. **1971** 'H. CARMICHAEL' *Quiet Woman* iv. 33 I'd be out and about if I had wheels. Damn car won't be ready until tomorrow. **1982** G. LYALL *Conduct of Major Maxim* xxv. 222 'Did you find me some wheels?'.. 'Yep: a Renault 16TX.'

8. ***we had one but the wheel came off***, joc. phr. used to indicate that the speaker has not understood the subject of the foregoing conversation.

1937 PARTRIDGE *Dict. Slang* 366/1 *Had one and* (or *but*) *the wheel came off* (*,we*), a lower-class and military c.p. directed at an unintelligible speaker or speech. **1974** P. WRIGHT *Lang. Brit. Industry* xiv. 128 If asked for something foolish, you can say,..'I had one but the wheels came off.'

III. Something resembling a wheel in form or movement.

9. An object having the form or figure of a wheel; a circle, or something circular; a disc. *spec.* **a.** (*a*) in *Needlework*, an open pattern or decoration with radiating threads; (*b*) in *Arch.* an ornament with radiating tracery (cf. *wheel-window* in 19); (*c*) in *Zool.* a wheel-like structure, as the *wheel-organ* of a rotifer, or a *wheel-spicule* in an echinoderm or sponge.

a **900** *O.E. Martyrol.* 5 May 74 He sæde þæt þa drihtnes fotlastas wæron beworht mid ærne hweole. *c* **1000** *Hymns* (Surtees) 22/25 þære sunnan hweogul [orig. *solis rotam*]. *c* **1384** CHAUCER *H. Fame* II. 286 Yf that thow Thorwe on water now a stoon Wel wost thou hyt wol make anoon A litel roundell..And..thow shalt see wel That whele sercle wol cause another whele. *a* **1500** *Assemb. Ladies* 55 With stayres going doun Inmiddes the place, with turning wheel, certayn. **1556** *Aurelio & Isab.* (1608) F vj, The pecocke puttes in a whylle his geltede fethers. **1611** COTGR., *Rouë de mer*, the sea-wheele; a huge, round, and monstrous sea-fish. *a* **1651** SIR J. SKEFFINGTON *Heroe of Lorenzo* (1652) 71 Let the Peacock please himself with the glorious wheel of his train. **1835** R. WILLIS *Archit. Mid. Ages* vi. 64 Wheels occur mixed with the tracery and pannelling of the Italian Gothic. **1888** ROLLESTON & JACKSON *Forms Anim. Life* 550 The calcareous deposits..are..represented..by wheels (= rotulae), e.g. in *Chirodota*. **1903** *Daily Chron.* 3 Oct. 8/3 Trimmed with smart wheels and tassels of brown silk.

b. *U.S. slang.* A dollar; = CARTWHEEL 2.

1807 H. TUFTS in E. Pearson *Autobiogr. of Criminal* (1930) II. iv. 293 *Wheel*, a dollar. **1825** J. NEAL *Brother Jonathan* I. 160, I shows him a double handful o' the royal goold; the ginooine yeller stuff—wheels. **1902** W. N. HARBEN *Abner Daniel* 143 How will fifteen hundred round wheels strike you? **1907** C. E. MULFORD *Bar-20* v. 47, I paid twenty wheels for that eight years ago.

c. A whole cheese, flan, or other food which is made with a circular form but may be cut into sections. Usu. with *of* and defining term.

1977 *New Yorker* 3 Oct. 53/3 A feast of varied delicacies, its principal ornament a small wheel of Camembert. **1978** C. CONRAN *British Cooking* 233/2 On May Day in the city of Gloucester a huge golden wheel of cheese, festively garlanded, used to be carried in procession round the town. **1978** *Neiman-Marcus Christmas Bk.* 93 A full three pound wheel, covered with protective black wax. **1982** M. BABSON *Death warmed Up* viii. 75 The wheels of pizza and quiche lorraine in the makeshift rack. **1985** *Sci. Amer.* May 67/1 The semisoft, blue-mold cheese is made from sheep's milk and formed into wheels weighing about 2·5 kilograms (5·5 pounds) each.

10. The celestial sphere or firmament, or one of the spheres of the planets, etc. in the ancient astronomy, regarded as revolving like a wheel. *Obs.* or merged in figurative senses (see 13, 14).

c **1200** ORMIN 17531 þurrh whatt wass heffness whel forrgarrt To dreȝhenn helle pine? *c* **1374** CHAUCER *Boeth.* I. met. v. (1868) 21 O þou maker of þe whele þat bereþ þe sterres. **1387–8** T. USK *Test. Love* II. i. (Skeat) l. 124 The shyning sonne of vertue in bright whele of this Margaryte beholde. *c* **1430** *Pilgr. Lyf Manhode* I. xl. (1869) 24 The wheel in whiche the moone goeth alwei aboute. *c* **1449** PECOCK *Repr.* II. xvi. 242 The fix sterris with her orbe or whele. **1814** CARY *Dante, Parad.* I. 62 Her eyes fast fix'd on the eternal wheels [*i.e.* the heavens].

11. One of the wards of a lock, which are rotated by the key. *techn.*

1784 BRAMAH in *Repert. Arts & Manuf.* (1796) V. 218 The inserting..between the key-hole and the bolt, a greater or less number of wheels or wards. **1846** *Penny Cycl.* Suppl. II. 212/1 These prominent rings are the *wards*, or in technical language, *wheels*, which impede the introduction of a false key.

IV. Figurative, allusive, and abstract uses.

12. **a.** The wheel which Fortune is fabled to turn, an emblem of mutability. (See also 5.) So ***wheel of Providence*** (rare).

Phr. *to set* or *sit high on the wheel* (of Fortune): to make or be highly fortunate; *the wheel has come full circle* and varr. (in allusion to SHAKES. *King Lear* v. iii. 174), the same situation has come about again, things have returned to their original position.

c **888** ÆLFRED *Boeth.* vii. §2 Wenst þu þæt ðu þæt hwerfende hweol þonne hit on ryne wyrð mæȝe oncerran? *a* **1300** *Cursor M.* 23719 Dame fortune turnes þan hir quele. **1340** *Ayenb.* 24 Huanne þe lheuedi of hap heþ hire hueȝel y-went. **1375** BARBOUR *Bruce* XIII. 637 Fortoune... This mychty kyng of Yngland Scho had set on her quheill on hicht. *c* **1386** CHAUCER *Knt.'s T.* 67 Thanked be ffortune and hire false wheel. *a* **1400–50** *Wars Alex.* 4660 þe qwele of qwistounes ȝoure qualite encreses. **1448–9** METHAM *Amoryus & Cl.* 389 O fortune,..Qwy chongyddyst thow thi qwele causeles? **1596** T. WILSON *Diana* (1921) 34 Ffortunes turning whyle. **1610** HOLLAND *Camden's Brit.* I. 448 Fortune turned her wheele and downe went this Colony. **1622** BACON *Hen. VII* 228 So fatall a thing it is, for the greatest and straitest Amities of Kings, at one time or other to haue a little of the Wheele. *c* **1645** HOWELL *Lett.* IV. xxix. (1890) 608 Till the great Wheel of Providence turn up another spoke. **1760–2** GOLDSM. *Cit. W.* vii, The wheel of fortune turns incessantly round. **1859** TENNYSON *Marr. Geraint* 347 Turn, Fortune, turn thy wheel and lower the proud. **1916** L. TRACY *Day of Wrath* v, The turn of fortune's wheel was distinctly favourable. **1944** W. S. MAUGHAM *Razor's Edge* v. 176 The wheel comes full circle. .. There was a time when the black sheep of the family was sent from my country to America; now apparently he's sent from your country [*sc.* America] to Europe. **1954** J. A. SHEARD *Words we Use* iv. 158 Old English had a derivative noun, *godspellere*, but this..was later replaced by a foreign loan-word,..*evangelist*... But in recent years the wheel has come full circle, and by a new process of derivation the Americans have their *hot gospellers*! **1966** W. H. LEWIS in *Lett. C. S. Lewis* 24 The wheel had come full circle: once again we were together in the little end room at home. **1977** J. CROSBY *Company of Friends* xviii. 117 The wheel was coming full circle. The public was fed to the teeth with disclosure. It yearned for the security of secrecy.

b. With allusion to the wheels of the chariot of the Sun. *poet.*

1557 PHAER *Æneid* VII. (1558) S ij b, The golden morning bright with roset wheles dyd mounting ryse. **1727** BROOME *Iliad* XI. Poems 177 While with his morning Wheels, the God of Day Climb'd up the Steep of Heav'n.

13. In direct fig. use from 1, esp. 1 a, chiefly in reference to the course or sequence of events, procedure, the passage of time. **a.** from 1 a.

a **1340** HAMPOLE *Psalter* xix. 8 þai ere draghen aboute with þe whels of couatys. **1390** GOWER *Conf.* I. 18 Whos carte goth upon the wheiles Of coveitise and worldes Pride. ?**1613** J. TAYLOR (Water P.) *Wks.* (1630) II. 174/2 The wheele of Time would turne. *a* **1628** F. GREVIL *Cælica* viii, Furrowes not worne by time, but wheeles of anguish. **1668** PEPYS *Diary* 27 Dec., All they can hope for to do out of the King's revenue being but to keep our wheels a-going on present services. **1675** OWEN *Indwelling Sin* xvi. (1732) 219 To oyl the Wheels of Mens utmost Endeavours. **1679** EVERARD *Disc.* 20 All these States may be in a condition to nail the Wheel, and to produce an Universal Peace in Christendom. **1698** FRYER *Acc. E. India & P.* 86 On these Wheels moves the Traffick of the East, and has succeeded better than any Corporation preceding. *a* **1716** SOUTH *Serm., Luke xii.* 15 Wks. 1727 IV. 438 Covetousness has been..the principal..Spring of Motion; and..hypocritical Prayers and Fastings, the sure Wheels, by which the great Work..has still gone forward. **1776** ADAM SMITH *W.N.* II. ii. I. 346 The great wheel of circulation [*sc.* money] is altogether different from the goods which are circulated by means of it. **1821** LAMB *Elia* Ser. I. *South sea House*, Night's wheels are rattling fast over me. **1857** HUGHES *Tom Brown* i, This present writer..is anxious..to help the wheel over, and throw his stone on to the pile. **1884** J. PARKER *Apost. Life* III. 73 A little recognition of merit, a kindly reference to loving service done..helps the wheel of life to run round more smoothly. **1907** *Standard* 19 Jan. 6/6 The wheels of progress might be unduly impeded.

b. ***on wheels***: (*a*) With rapid and continuous movement or action; chiefly in phr. ***to go*** or ***run on wheels***, to proceed swiftly or uninterruptedly; to go smoothly, make good progress; to go on actively or incessantly; (humorously, of a clock) to go too fast or irregularly; (*b*) In working order, in normal condition for action (*dial.*); (*c*) used as an intensive: in the extreme.

1547 GARDINER in Foxe *A. & M.* (1563) 734/2 The euell willers of the realme will take corage and make accompt.. that all goeth on wheles. **1591** SHAKS. *Two Gent.* III. i. 317 Then may I set the world on wheeles, when she can spin for her liuing. **1600** BRETON *Pasquil's Passe* Wks. (Grosart) I. 8/2 From the blaines and kibes vpon my heeles; And from a madding wit that runnes on wheeles,.. The blessed Lord of heau'n deliuer me. **1675** HOBBES *Odyssey* XVIII. 31 While his tongue Thus runs on wheels. **1731–8** SWIFT *Pol. Conversat.* 108 *Col.* Pray, my Lord, what's a Clock by your Oracle? *Ld. Sparkish.* Faith, I can't tell, I think my Watch runs upon Wheels. **1820** J. CLARE *Poems* 89 If fate's so kind to let's be doing, That's—just keep cart on wheels a going. **1831** MRS. SHERWOOD *Henry Milner* III. xv. 307, I can..let my jointure run up to liquidate debts; and then, when it is clear, we shall be on our four wheels again. **1914** [see JOB *sb.*[3] 4 d]. **1943** S. LEWIS *Gideon Planish* 127 Looks just like a sweet little ivory statue, but is she hell on wheels! **1958** M. DICKENS *Man Overboard* iv. 59 It was his wife. She's a bitch on wheels, from what he tells me. **1970** 'D. HALLIDAY' *Dolly & Cookie Bird* iv. 42 Look at the time... If you're going to show us your balloons, you'll have to do it on wheels. **1978** S. BRILL *Teamsters* vii. 275 In the 1930s and '40s and into the '50s, truck driving was sweatshop labor on wheels. **1980** N. FREELING *Castang's City* xxv. 174 Local wine-shipper in quite a high-class way... The business ran on wheels.

†**c.** ***a word on its*** (or ***upon the***) ***wheels***: an echo of the marginal 'Heb. spoken vpon his wheeles' in the A.V. of Proverbs xxv. 11, where the text has 'fitly spoken'. *Obs.*

Heb. *'ophnāw* (dual or pl.) of this passage is now regarded as ἅπαξ λεγόμενον, and *'al-'ophnāw* interpreted as 'in its turns', 'in (right) circumstances'; formerly referred to *'ōphen* a wheel.

1655 GURNALL *Chr. in Arm.* I. (1669) 36/1 A word in season is a word on its wheels. *c* **1657** P. HENRY in *Life* (1699) 23 There never was Truth..more seasonable to any than this was to me: It was a word upon the Wheels.

d. ***silly as a wheel***: extremely silly. *Austral. slang.*

1952 T. A. G. HUNGERFORD *Ridge & River* 57 Oscar was sound, but silly as a wheel. **1966** J. MORRISON in *Coast to Coast 1965–66* 157, I warned Rose. She was as silly as a wheel, too, but a man's got to do what he can to protect his daughters.

14. a. With allusion to sense 1 b, denoting a constituent part or element of something figured as a machine.

1625 Bacon *Ess., Seditions* (Arb.) 405 So that if these three wheeles goe, Wealth will flow as in a Spring tide. *a* 1628 Preston *Saints Daily Exerc.* (1629) 116 It sets all the wheeles of the soul the right way. 1692 W. Lloyd *Pret. Fr. Invas.* 15 The French King (the main Wheel in this designed Restauration). 1768 Tucker *Lt. Nat.* (1834) II. 363 Nor does He find the wickedness of men improper wheels for carrying on His most important designs among them. 1771 Wesley *Jrnl.* 31 Mar. (1827) III. 415 In the Methodist discipline, the wheels regularly stand thus: the Assistant, the Preachers, the Stewards, the Leaders, the people. 1916 *19th Cent.* Apr. 822 The protagonist sets the wheels of fate in motion.

b. ***wheels within wheels***, less usually ***a wheel within a wheel*** (after Ezek. i. 16): a complexity of forces or influences; a complication of motives, designs, or plots; also *gen.* any complexity.

1679 Prance *Add. Narr.* 32 Yet the Wheel within the wheel moved upon other grounds, God making use of his Soveraignty over his Creatures, in raising and stirring up One Nation or Person to punish the Evils of Another. 1709 Shaftesb. *Charac.* (1711) I. 114 Thus we have Wheels within Wheels. And in some National Constitutions.. we have one Empire within another. *a* 1754 E. Erskine *Serm. Wrath of Man* Wks. (1791) 711/2 There is a wheel within a wheel, which will turn matters about so, as the wrath of man shall praise God, and advance his interest, instead of ruining it. 1824 L. Murray *Engl. Gram.* (ed. 5) I. 457 They are wheels within wheels; sentences in the midst of sentences. 1854 Miss Baker *Northampt. Gloss.* s.v., There's a wheel within a wheel, or you wouldn't have got that. 1861 Gurowski *Diary* (1862) 75 McClellan ought to.. have direct action; and not refer to Scott. What is this wheel within a wheel? 1900 'H. S. Merriman' *Isle of Unrest* vi, There are wheels within wheels.. in the social world of Paris.

c. ***to see*** (***what makes***) ***the wheels go round*** and varr: to see how things work; chiefly *fig.* with reference to the operation of a business, organization, etc. *colloq.*

[1876 J. Habberton *Helen's Babies* 11 'I want to see the wheels go round,' said Budge.] 1922 *Broadcaster* Oct. 149/1 The natural indifference of the fair sex to any knowledge of what 'makes the wheels go round.' 1923 R. D. Paine *Comrades of Rolling Ocean* ix. 160, I want to watch a supercargo and see his wheels go round. 1979 P. Levi *Head in Soup* iii. 58 How amateur we were. Those who know how the wheels turn are always bored. 1980 N. Freeling *Castang's City* xv. 100 There's any amount of what makes the wheels go round... Feather-bedding and barrel-rolling.

d. = *big shot* s.v. SHOT *sb.*[1] 22 c. Cf. *big wheel* (*b*) s.v. BIG *a.* B. 2. *slang* (orig. and chiefly *U.S.*).

1933 *Amer. Speech* VIII. ii. 55/2 *Wheels*, substitute for big shots, leaders of a gang. 1956 B. Holiday *Lady sings Blues* (1973) xviii. 149 After I got to be a wheel in the kitchen, I used to take care of Marietta by saving her the best of the food. 1963 J. N. Harris *Weird World Wes Beattie* (1966) iii. 36 Well, in business, Howie is a sort of minor wheel... He owns pieces of things. Radio stations, a commercial film company, a night club. 1975 *Globe & Mail* (Toronto) 12 Sept. 27/8 If politicians and business people and other wheels don't like it, he couldn't care less. 1980 A. Fox *Kingfisher Scream* vi. 94 Some Pentagon wheel's flying in and Don feels he has to travel up there with him.

15. *fig.* A reiterated or recurring course of actions, events, or time; an endless round or cycle.

a 1225 *Ancr. R.* 322 Uorte leren us þet we of þe worldes torpelnesse, & of sunne hweol, ofte gon to schrifte. *a* 1340 Hampole *Psalter* xi. 9 Erthly godes þat tornes wiþ þe whele of seuen dayes. 1382 Wyclif *James* iii. 6 The tunge.. set afijre of helle, enflaumeth the wheel of oure birthe. 1871 Alabaster *Wheel of Law* Pref. p. xiii, All Buddhists.. call their religion the doctrine of 'The Wheel of the Law'.

†**b.** *Alch.* A series of operations by which one element was supposed to be converted into another.

1471 Ripley *Comp. Alch.* in Ashmole (1652) 133 The Wheele of Elements thou canst turne about. *Ibid.* 187 Then to wyn to thy desyre thou needst not be in dowte, For the Whele of our Phylosophy thou hast turnyd abowte. 1610 B. Jonson *Alch.* II. iii, I' haue another worke;.. That three dayes since, past the Philosophers wheele, In the lent heat of Athanor; and 's become Sulphur o' nature.

†**c.** = TURN *sb.* 28. *Obs. rare.*

1422 Yonge tr. *Secr. Secr.* 214 Me sholde ordeyne that euery gouernoure had tene Vicaries in his hoste, and euery vicarie ten lederis in his whele.

16. [Partly f. WHEEL *v.*] A movement like that of a wheel. **a.** A movement in a circular or curved course; a circling motion (usually, through a single complete circle); a revolution.

1604 E. G[rimstone] *D'Acosta's Hist. Indies* VI. xxviii. 493 In these daunces they made twoo circles or wheeles [orig. *dos ruedas de gente*]. 1667 Milton *P.L.* III. 741 Satan .. Throws his steep flight in many an Aerie wheele. 1805 Cary *Dante, Inf.* XVI. 21 They.. Whirl'd round together in one restless wheel. 1810 Scott *Lady of L.* II. xxxi, Amid his senses' giddy wheel. 1815 —— *Guy M.* xxii, A rough terrier dog.. scampered at large in a thousand wheels round the heath. 1847 Longf. *Ev.* I. iv. 34 Merrily whirled the wheels of the dizzying dances.

b. A movement about an axis or centre; a rotation; a turn (usually, not completely around); *spec.* (*Mil.*) such a movement of a rank or body of troops about a pivot (PIVOT *sb.* 2); occas. = CART-WHEEL *sb.* 3.

a 1660 *Contemp. Hist. Irel.* (Ir. Archæol. Soc.) I. 69 The captain mountinge on a white horse, did leade the musketires, without any wheeles, but went the high beaten way. 1672 T. Venn *Milit. Discipl.* 19 There may be a Counter-march for the gaining of Ground; but I conceive them wholly useless but where you have not ground to make your Wheels. 1788 D. Dundas *Princ. Mil. Movem.* App. 5 All wheels or filings made from the halt into column or line, are made at a quick step. 1797 J. Bailey & Culley *Agric. Northumbld.* 123 At the first appearance of any person they set off in full gallop; and at the distance of two or three hundred yards, make a wheel round, and come boldly up again. 1832 *Prop. Reg. Instr. Cavalry* II. 10 Right Wheel. 1854 R. S. Surtees *Handley Cr.* xl, Tea and coffee were enlivened by a collision between the footboys. Stiffneck with the tea-tray made a sudden wheel upon No. 2 with the coffee-tray. 1890 'R. Boldrewood' *Col. Reformer* xxviii, The reckless speed and practised wheel of the trained stock horses. 1904 Johnston *H. P. Liddon* xi. 301 The 'gamins', who used to wheedle pennies from him by making 'wheels' for his amusement.

c. In *Rugby Football.* (See quot. 1897.)

1897 [see BACK *a.* 1]. 1927 H. Walpole *Jeremy at Crale* xvi. 284 Back they went, down again, the ball flung in. The Callendar forwards had it and manœuvred the finest wheel of the match, swinging round against all opposition.

17. *Prosody.* A set of short lines forming the concluding part of a stanza, usually five in number, varying in form and length, but generally having the first line riming with the last, and often the intervening three riming with each other; the first line in some types is very short, and is then called the *bob*.

1838 Guest *Engl. Rhythms* II. 290 Besides the staves which originated in mixed and continuous rhime, there are others, which have sprung from the use of the Wheel and Burthen. By the latter of these terms I would understand the return of the same words at the close of each stave, and by the former the return of some marked and peculiar rhythm. *Ibid.* 332. 1906 Saintsbury *Hist. Engl. Prosody* I. 105 The bob being of two syllables, and the wheel an irregular but unmistakable ballad-quatrain.

V. Combinations.

18. General: **a.** *attrib.* Of, pertaining to, consisting of, or connected with a wheel or wheels, as ***wheel alignment***, ***arch***, ***bearing***, ***-belt***, ***-box***, ***-boy*** (cf. WHEELMAN 1), ***brake***, ***-cage***, ***-case***, ***-circle***, ***-coulter***, ***-flange***, ***-grease***, ***-lathe***, ***-mark***, ***-nave***, ***-rim***, ***-ring***, ***-road***, ***-rod***, ***-rut***, ***-spoke***, ***-sweep*** (SWEEP *sb.* 17 c), ***-timber***, ***-tire***, ***-tooth***, ***-top***, ***-track***, ***-train*** (TRAIN *sb.*[1] 15), ***-tread*** (TREAD *sb.* 10 b), ***trim***, etc.; furnished with or moving on a wheel or wheels (of vehicles = 'wheeled'), as ***wheel-arquebus***, ***-bier***, ***-bridge***, ***-clock***, ***-crane***, ***-harrow***, ***hoe***, ***loader***, ***-machine***, ***mail***, ***-sled***, ***-vehicle***.

1908 *Motor Man.* (ed. 10) vi. 165 (*heading*) To test *wheel alignment. 1971 'D. Rutherford' *Clear Fast Lane* 70 I'm not going on till we've had the wheel-alignment checked. There's.. a service station ten kilometres on. 1935 *Automobile & Carriage Builders' Jrnl.* Mar. 45 (*caption*) Details of the *wheelarch, scuttle ventilator and rear locker. 1983 *Buses* Feb. 57/1 Longitudinal seating provided over the rear wheelarches. 1855 tr. *Labarte's Arts Mid. Ages* x. 369 These arms were denominated *wheel-arquebuses [F. *arquebuses à rouet*]. 1892 *Photogr. Ann.* II. 390 The castors at the front feet work upon *wheel bearings. 1884 W. S. B. McLaren *Spinning* (ed. 2) 158 There can be no slipping of the twine *wheel-belt. 1898 F. D. How *Bp. Walsham How* 371 A simple *wheel-bier decorated with flowers received the coffin. 1853 Dickens *Bleak Ho.* liii, [A carriage] with silver *wheel-boxes. 1892 Black *Wolfenberg* xi, The solitary figure slowly pacing up and down by the wheel-box [of a ship]. 1825 J. Nicholson *Oper. Mech.* 423 Little or no attendance is required from *wheel-boys or followers. 1936 *Discovery* July 228/2 The average pilot regards his *wheel brakes as an assistance to ground taxying rather than as a means of arresting his run. 1974 *Encycl. Brit. Macropædia* I. 378/1 Wheel brakes are generally hydraulically operated. *a* 1700 Evelyn *Diary* 7 Aug. 1641, The *wheel-bridg, which engine his Excellency had made to run over the moate when they storm'd the castle. 1889 Mivart *Orig. Hum. Reas.* 268 A squirrel or white mouse which turns in its *wheel-cage. 1875 Knight *Dict. Mech.*, **Wheel-case*, a stout paper case, .. filled with composition,.. tied to the rim of a wheel or rotating piece of fire-works. *c* 1384 *Whele sercle [see 8]. 1671 Hunt *Abeced. Schol.* 110 By the Press we make men immortal, by *Wheel-clocks we are made companions of time. 1839 Ure *Dict. Arts* 77 Automata.. are certainly not older than wheel-clocks. 1875 Knight *Dict. Mech.*, **Wheel-colter*, a sharp-edged wheel running in advance of the breast of the plow, to cut the sod or weeds in the line of the furrow. 1769 Falconer *Dict. Marine* (1780) II, *Crone*, a *wheel-crane, built on a wharf. *a* 1663 Killigrew *Parson's Wedd.* II. vi. (1664) 99 Ever since yellow starch and *wheel Fardingales were cry'd down. 1859 *Newton's Lond. Jrnl. Arts* 1 Feb. 115 The pressure of the *wheel-flange will tend to crush any obstructing substance upon the chairs. 1585 Higins *Junius' Nomencl.* 269/1 *Axungia*,.. *wheele grease. 1901 *Academy* 8 June 495/2 Derby, with its locomotives and everlasting Midland wheel-grease. 1404 *Durham Acc. Rolls* (Surtees) 399, j *qwhele harow. 1858 C. Flint *Milch Cows* 193 In weeding, a little *wheel-hoe is invaluable. 1911 *Daily Colonist* (Victoria, B.C.) 22 Apr. 9/6 (Advt.), We carry a full line of Garden Drills, Double and Single Wheel Hoes. 1875 Knight *Dict. Mech.*, **Wheel-lathe*, a lathe for turning railway-wheels and other large work. 1971 *Wheel loader [see DOZER[2]]. 1770 Forbes *Jrnl.* (1886) 288 A Wooden Bridge .. by which Horses and *Wheel-machines do easily Cross the Water. 1890 'R. Boldrewood' *Col. Reformer* xxvii, It was problematical whether the contractor was running a *wheel mail or not. 1854 R. S. Surtees *Handley Cr.* xxxix, Following the old *wheel-marks on the gravel. 1707 Mortimer *Husb.* 332 The Witch-Elm.. is good for *Wheel-naves. 1513 Douglas *Æneis* XII. Prol. 162 The payntit povne.. Kest vp his taill, a provd plesand *quheil rym. 1893 *Outing* (U.S.) XXII. 133/2 My rear wheel-rim. 1766 *Complete Farmer* s.v. *Fence*, This timber is of excellent service.. for ploughs, axle-trees, *wheel-rings, harrows, &c. 1824 Scott *St. Ronan's* i, To my own contemporaries, who have known *wheel-road, bridle-way, and footpath for thirty years. 1882 Morris in Mackail *W.M.* (1899) II. 67 The wheel-roads across the downs are doubtful. 1598 Hakluyt *Voy.* I. 95 The breadth betweene the *wheele-ruts of one of their cartes. 1829 Carlyle *Misc.* (1857) II. 59 Little is laid open to us but two wheel-ruts and two hedges. 1570 *Rec. Inverness* (New Spalding Club) I. 195 That na *quheill sleddis.. cum vpon the brig. 1556 Withals *Dict.* (1562) 19/1 A *whele spoke, *radius vel modiolus*. 1707 Mortimer *Husb.* 326 Oak.. for.. Shingles, Wainscott, Wheel Spoakes. 1891 Hardy *Tess* xxxiii, It had stout wheel-spokes, and heavy felloes. 1833 Loudon *Encycl. Archit.* §1244 The Pulborough stone paving of the *wheel sweep. 1376 *Durham Acc. Rolls* (Surtees) 584 Rob'o Yoill, carpentario, culpanti *qweltimber. 1573 *Lanc. Wills* (Chetham Soc. 1893) 139 Item bords cowper tymber wheles and whele tymber. 1662 Atwell *Faithf. Surveyour* 132 Plow-timber, cart-timber, wheel-timber. 1792 *Descr. Kentucky* 41 In 1787 were exported Sets of wheel timbers 1,056. 1831 J. Holland *Manuf. Metal* I. 145 According as the metal is intended to be reduced to the strength of *wheel-tyre, hoop-iron, or different sized bars. 1825 J. Nicholson *Oper. Mech.* 509 The points of the *wheel-teeth must not be rounded off. 1509 Hawes *Past. Pleas.* XXVII. (Percy Soc.) 118 Beholdynge Mars how wonderly he stode, On a *whele top with a lady of pryde. 1552 Huloet, *Whele tracte or rutte, *orbita*. *c* 1820 S. Rogers *Italy, Naples* 115 The wheel-track worn for centuries. 1859 Hawthorne *Fr. & It. Note-bks.* (1871) II. 285 A vineyard, with a wheel-track through the midst of it. 1888 *Cassell's Encycl. Dict.*, **Wheel-train*, a number of wheels so arranged that the revolution of one causes the revolution of all. 1735–6 *Wheel-tread [see TREAD *sb.* 10 b]. 1976 *Ilkeston Advertiser* 10 Dec. 3/4 (Advt.), Morris 1800 (Princess style) Saloon (1975 'P')... Fitted radio, *wheel-trims etc. 1983 *Which?* Sept. 435/2 However, all of the 'MG' wheel trims fell off at some time. 1734 J. Rowe (*title*) All sorts of wheel-carriage improved;.. Waggons, Carts, Coaches, and all other *Wheel-Vehicles. 1836 Carlyle *New Lett.* (1904) I. 48 The wheel-vehicles making no noise.

b. Objective, as ***wheel-bearer*** (= ROTIFER), ***-cutter***, ***-maker***, ***-tapper***, ***-turner***; ***wheel-bearing***, ***-changing***, ***-cutting***, ***-greasing***, ***-resembling***, ***-turning*** sbs. and adjs.; instrumental, as ***wheel-driven***, ***-going***, ***-made***, ***-marked***, ***-smashed***, ***-spun***, ***-turned***, ***-worn*** adjs.; similative, parasynthetic, etc., as ***wheel-broad***, ***-footed***, ***-like*** adjs.

1861 H. J. Slack *Marv. Pond-life* 23 Following the Protozoa, come the Rotifera, or *Wheel-bearers. 1877 Wood *Nature's Teach., Optics* ii. 306 Soon after the powers of the microscope became known, these Wheel-bearers were discovered. 1846 Patterson *Zool.* 6 The order itself Rotifera, or *wheel-bearing. 1974 *Harrod's Christmas Catal.* 69/2 Lotus.. scale model: complete with *wheel brace for wheel changing. 1670 Dryden *Conq. Granada* I. Prol., *Wheel-broad hats. 1843 *Penny Cycl.* XXVII. 308/2 *Wheel-cutting.. comprehends the modes of cutting the teeth in the wheels used by watch and clock makers. 1884 F. J. Britten *Watch & Clockm.* 88 The circular brass plate in a wheel-cutting engine. 1972 *Wheel-driven [see SALT *a.*[1] 1 c]. 1788 Cowper *Gratitude* 9 This *wheel-footed studying chair. 1844 Kinglake *Eothen* i, At Semlin.. I had come, as it were, to the end of this *wheel-going Europe. 1835–6 *Todd's Cycl. Anat.* I. 607/1 The cilia constitute the .. *wheel-like organs of the Rotiferous Infusoria. 1888 *Jrnl. Derbysh. Archæol. Soc.* X. 50 *Wheel-made pottery in the barrows of the district. 14.. *Nom.* in Wr.-Wülcker 688/15 *Hic rotarius*, *whelmaker. 1844 H. Stephens *Bk. Farm* III. 1154 The principle which directs the modern wheel-maker. 1894 *Outing* (U.S.) XXIV. 398/1 Along a wide and *wheel-marked trail. 1596 R. Linche *Diella* (1877) 68 Great Gouernour of (*wheele-resembling) Heauen. *a* 1825 Forby *Voc. E. Anglia*, **Wheelspun*, very stout worsted yarn, spun on the common large wheel. 1881 *Instr. Census Clerks* (1885) Index 178 *Wheel tapper. 1837 Wheelwright tr. *Aristophanes* II. 293 O thou clear lustre of the *wheel-turn'd lamp. 1875 Knight *Dict. Mech.*, **Wheel-turning Lathe*, one with two very solid head-stocks with large face-plates, and two slide-rests operated by a ratchet-feed from an overhead rock-shaft. 1727 Broome *Jason & Medea* Poems 242 Along the *Wheel worn Road they hold their way. 1781 Cowper *Expost.* 21 The chariots bounding in her wheel-worn streets. 1944 Blunden *Shells by Stream* 13 Its kingdom is the farm, the farmer's lane Its wheelworn churchway from the lonely road.

19. Special Combinations: **wheel-animal**, **-animalcule** = ROTIFER; **wheel arrangement**, the relative positioning of driving wheels and idle wheels on a locomotive; **wheel-assembler**, one who fits together the parts of the wheels of bicycles, etc.; so **wheel-assembly**, the operation of doing this; **wheel-back**, a back resembling a wheel, characteristic of chairs made by Heppelwhite about 1775; also a chair with such a back; **wheel balance** *Mech.*, an even distribution of mass about the axis of a wheel so that it rotates without wobbling or vibrating; so **wheel balancing**, the process of achieving this for the wheels of a motor vehicle; **wheel-barometer**, a mercurial barometer having a float attached to a string passing over a pulley-wheel on which the index turns; **wheel-base**, the distance between the points of contact of the front and back wheels of a vehicle, as a bicycle or railway-carriage, with the ground or rail; **wheel bay** = *wheel well* below; †**wheel-bed**, a trundle-bed; **wheel-bird**, a local name for the night-jar or goat-sucker, from its cry suggesting the noise of a spinning-wheel; **wheel-boat**, a boat with wheels, *esp.* (*Sc.*) a steamboat with paddle-wheels; **wheel brace**, (*a*) a tool for screwing and unscrewing nuts on the wheel of a vehicle; (*b*) a kind of hand drill worked by the turning of a wheel; **wheel-bug**, a large reduviid insect (*Prionidus cristatus*) of the southern United States and W. Indies, with a semicircular serrated crest suggesting a cog-wheel; **wheel car**, a simple farm-cart (see quot. 1931); **wheel-chain** (see quot.); **wheel clamp**, a clamp designed to be locked to one of the wheels of an illegally parked motor vehicle to immobilize it; hence as *v. trans.*; so **wheel clamping** *vbl. sb.* and *ppl. a.*; **wheel-cross**, a variety of ring-cross with arms radiating from a small circle in the centre of the ring; **wheel-dog** *Canad.*, the dog harnessed nearest to the sleigh in a dog team; **wheel-draught**, a current of smoke and hot air in a steam-engine, circulating continuously in one direction; **wheel-dwelling, -hut** *Archæol.* = WHEEL-HOUSE 3; †**wheel-fire** [mod.L. *ignis rotæ*], in *Old Chem.*, a fire completely encompassing a crucible; **wheel-guard**, (*a*) a circular guard on a sword or dagger; (*b*) a guard to protect a wheel from dirt or injury, or to prevent it from chafing some other part of the vehicle or machine; **wheel-head**, (*a*) the nave or central part of a wheel; (*b*) 'the headstock of a spinning-mule' (*Eng. Dial. Dict.*); (*c*) 'the lathe-head of a seal-engraver's engine' (*Cent. Dict.*); **wheel-horse**, a horse harnessed between the shafts of a vehicle, next to the wheels, as distinguished from a *leader*; *fig.* a person who bears the chief burden of a business; **wheel-insect** = *wheel-animal*; **wheel-iron** (see quot. 1837); **wheel-ladder** (see quot. 1888); **wheel landing** *Aeronaut.*, a landing (of an aircraft with a tail-wheel or tail-skid) in which the main wheels touch down first, followed by the tail; **wheel-map** (see quot. 1899); **wheel-money**, name for certain prehistoric metallic objects, supposed by some to be money, made in the form of a wheel, i.e. of a cross surrounded by a ring; **wheel-organ** *Zool.*, the trochal disc of a rotifer; **wheel-pair**, a pair of wheel-horses; **wheel pants** *Aeronaut.* (see quot. 1956); **wheel pen**, a pen with a small toothed wheel instead of nibs, for tracing dotted lines (Webster 1920); **wheel-piece**, (*a*) a lateral part of a car-truck, supporting the pedestals or axle-boxes; (*b*) a post fixed beneath a door-sill on each side, to take the strain of the wheels of a vehicle when passing over it; **wheel-pit**, (*a*) a space enclosed by masonry for a large wheel, as a fly-wheel or turbine, to turn in; (*b*) *dial.* a whirlpool; **wheel-plate**, (*a*) the part of a solid wheel between the rim and the hub; (*b*) see quot. 1892; **wheel-plough**, a plough having wheels running on the ground to reduce the friction or regulate the depth of the furrow; **wheel-press**, (*a*) a form of rotary printing-press; (*b*) a hydraulic press for moulding a solid wheel, or for fixing it on the axle; **wheel-race**, the part of a mill-race in which the mill-wheel is fixed; **wheel-rood** = *wheel-cross*; **wheel-rope**, *Naut.*, †(*a*) cf. quot. 1495 in 1 b; (*b*) a rope passing round the barrel of the steering-wheel to the tiller; **wheel-seat**, the part of an axle encircled by the wheel (Knight *Dict. Mech.* 1884); **wheel-set**, a pair of wheels attached to an axle; **wheel-shaped** *a.*, having the shape of a wheel; *spec.* in *Bot.* = ROTATE *a.*; †**wheel-sick** *a.*, giddy; **wheel-skate**, a roller-skate; so ***wheel-skater, -skating***; **wheel slip**, the failure of the wheels of a vehicle to grip the surface on which they are travelling, so that they slip instead of rolling; also (*rare*) as *v. intr.*; **wheel-spicule**, *Zool.* one of certain disk-shaped calcareous concretions, with an appearance of radiating spokes, in the skin of some holothurians; also, a wheel-shaped spicule in sponges; **wheel spin**, the spinning of the wheels of a vehicle, caused by hard acceleration of the engine combined with the failure of the wheels to take a grip on a slippery surface; **wheel-spur** (ME. **-spore**), the ridge on the inner side of a wheel-rut (cf. SPOOR *sb.*[1], and *cart-spur* s.v. CART *sb.* 6); **wheel-stitch** (see quot.); **wheel-stock** (*local*), (*a*) the nave of a wheel, or timber to be used for this; (*b*) wood materials for wheel-making; **wheel-stone**, a fossil consisting of a detached joint of the stem of an encrinite, and having the form of a circular disk with a central perforation; an entrochite; **wheel-swarf** [SWARF *sb.*[2]], the pasty substance produced by the friction of a grindstone and the cutlery ground upon it, consisting of a mixture of particles of stone and steel, and used as an air-tight coating in steel-manufacture; **wheel-tax**, a tax on wheeled carriages; **wheel-tracery**, tracery radiating from a centre, as in a *wheel-window*; **wheel-tree**, (*a*) a S. American tree (*Aspidosperma excelsum*), also called *paddle-wood* (cf. quot. 1866 s.v. PADDLE *sb.* 11); (*b*) an Australian tree (*Stenocarpus sinuatus*) with flowers in circular clusters; (*c*) *Mining* (see quot. 1886); **wheel vat**, in *Tanning* = PIN-WHEEL *sb.* 3; **wheel-way**, a way, road, or track along which wheeled vehicles run; also *fig.* (cf. RUT *sb.*[2] 1 c); **wheel well**, the recess, under the wing of a vehicle, into which the wheel fits, or, on an aircraft, into which the landing gear is retracted; †**wheel-whirl** (see quot.); **wheel-window**, a circular window with mullions radiating from the centre like the spokes of a wheel (= CATHERINE WHEEL 2); **wheel-wise** *adv.*, in the manner or form of a wheel; (of swimming) with the arms moving like the spokes of a wheel; **wheel wobble**, vibration of the wheels of a vehicle in motion, usu. when travelling at some speed; also *fig.* See also WHEEL-BAND, WHEELBARROW, etc.

1788 *Encycl. Brit.* II. 28/1 The *Wheel-Animal, or Vorticella..is found in rain water that has stood some days. **1834** *Lancet* 24 May 290/2 We see in this *wheel-animalcule, the *hydatina senta*, many of those muscular bands passing down longitudinally from the head, nearly as we saw in the large holothuria. **1912** *Railway Mag.* Mar. 203/1 Of the total number of engines mentioned, 80 were of the 2-2-2-0 *wheel arrangement. **1966** K. MÖLLER *Amer. & Brit. Railway English* 43, 0-8-0 is a notation for a wheel arrangement of eight driving wheels and no leading or trailing wheels. A great number of wheel arrangements have special names, originating with the railway on which they were first used. **1897** *Outing* (U.S.) XXX. 277/2 All through the arts of the *wheel-assemblers. *Ibid.* 279/2 They are then sent to the *wheel-assembly department, to receive the bearings, spokes and rims. **1902** W. H. HACKETT *Decorative Furnit.* xi. 133 A set of six typical Heppelwhite [*sic*] chairs.. had '*wheel' backs, on taper legs, with cross stretchers. **1909** G. O. WHEELER *Old Engl. Furnit.* (ed. 2) 489 Heppelwhite's wheel-back chair..may be found with cabriole legs, and later with typical straight tapered ones. **1927** W. E. COLLINSON *Contemp. Eng.* 90 The revival of Welsh dressers, wheel-backs and ladderbacks. **1968** J. ARNOLD *Shell Bk. Country Crafts* 133 In the hand-made 'wheel-back' there is the vestigial hub in the centre, but for economy this is absent from the factory-made splat. **1946** W. H. CROUSE *Automotive Mech.* xxiv. 533 *Wheel balance can be checked in several ways. **1962** *Which? Car Suppl.* Oct. 139/2 Severe vibration developed throughout the car at speeds over 65 mph and a further check of wheel balance failed to overcome this. **1951** I. FRAZEE et al. *Automotive Suspensions* x. 276 (*heading*) *Wheel balancing. **1977** Wheel balancing [see SHIMMY *sb.*[2] 2]. **1665–6** *Phil. Trans.* I. 155 My *Wheel-barometer I could never fill so exactly with Mercury, as to exclude all Air. **1840** *Hutton's Recr. Math.* 652 Several expedients have been adopted for lengthening the scale of the barometer... The most popular expedient is that adopted in what is called the wheel barometer. **1886** *Jrnl. Franklin Inst.* Mar. 201 The distance between the supporting wheels is four feet, which thus forms the rigid *wheel-base of the truck. **1976** 'A. HALL' *Kobra Manifesto* xv. 200 The problem was to keep my body arched against the curved top of the *wheelbay, giving me a chance of escaping the wheels when they slammed home and locked. **1556** *Richmond Wills* (Surtees) 92 On pare of bed stocks, one pare for a *qwele bedd. **1589** *Lanc. Wills* (Chetham Soc. 1860) 206 One standinge bedd and a wheelebed in y[e] parlor. **1619** *Shuttleworths' Acc.* (Chetham Soc.) 238 For a wheele bedd vj[s]. **1817** STEPHENS in Shaw *Gen. Zool.* X. I. 147 This species [European Goatsucker] makes a..noise, which has been compared to that of a large spinning wheel,..and has on that account been called the *wheel bird. **1862** [see WHEELER 6]. **1834** MARRYAT *Peter Simple* viii, 'How did you come from Glasgow?' 'By the *wheel-boat, or steam-boat, as they ca'd it, to Lunnon.' **1864** WEBSTER, *Wheel-boat*, a boat with wheels, to be used either on water or upon inclined planes or railways. **1920** *Motor Man.* (ed. 23) xiv. 144 The most popular form of fitting is by means of separate bolts carried on the fixed hub, to which the pressed-steel wheel is held by a number of capped nuts which can be detached by a *wheel brace. **1964** F. PRESTON *Man makes Hole* 6/2 The hand drill or wheel brace is of fairly recent origin, although it derives from the so-called bevel drill widely made in Germany. **1974** Wheel brace [see *wheel changing*, sense 18 b above]. **1975** R. A. SALAMAN *Dict. Tools* 187/2 *Drill, hand* (Wheel Brace..).. The modern form of Hand Drill was an American innovation of about 1870 which reached this country about the turn of the century. **1984** B. FRANCIS *AA Car Duffer's Guide* 38/2 Then, with the wheelbrace, slacken off all the wheel nuts about half a turn. **1815** KIRBY & SP. *Entomol.* iv. (1818) I. 110 The *wheel-bug can.. communicate an electric shock to the person whose flesh it touches. **1868** *Rep. U.S. Comm. Agric.* (1869) 316 The *Reduvius*, or wheel-bug, is found in gardens, feeding voraciously upon caterpillars. **1931** *Antiquity* June 185 The special features of the *wheel-car are..(a) the great length.. of the body..; (b) the position of the axle tree *above*..the main beams of the frame; (c) the bumpers..; and (d) the embryo cart structure. **1968** J. ARNOLD *Shell Bk. Country Crafts* xi. 163 Round about Clun, they knew it [*sc.* a gambo] as a wheel-car. **1891** H. PATTERSON *Naut. Dict.* 194 **Wheel Chains*, chains used in place of the rope for connecting the steering wheel and the tiller. **1980** *Daily Tel.* 2 Jan. 3 (*heading*) Car park offenders face *wheel clamps. **1981** *Times* 19 Nov. 3 Illegal parking in London has become so widespread that the Government may bow to police demands to be allowed to use wheel clamps to immobilize offending vehicles. **1983** *Daily Tel.* 14 July 19/1 Cars belonging to diplomats will no longer be wheel-clamped. **1980** *Daily Tel.* 2 Jan. 3/2 More officers will be available to tow away dangerously parked vehicles and the use of the 'Denver Shoe' a *wheel clamping device, is being considered. **1983** *Sunday Tel.* 15 May 3/1 The wheel clamping team..will consist of one sergeant, eight police constables, 28 vehicle removal officers and eight traffic wardens. **1882** WORSAAE *Industr. Arts Denmark* 66 The ring-cross was sometimes employed indiscriminately with the *wheel-cross to indicate the wheels of the sun-carriage. **1922** G. C. F. PRINGLE *Tillicums* 85, I put a smaller dog..in the lead and hitched Steal up next the sleigh as my '*wheel-dog'. **1965** A. V. WILSON *No Man stands Alone* 29, I firmly believe that the 'wheel-dog', next to the sled, can upset one any time he wishes. **1871** *Routledge's Ev. Boy's Ann.* 529 A *wheel-draught; that is to say, the current of flame and smoke, after passing along the bottom of the boiler, rises up at the end. **1931** V. G. CHILDE *Skara Brae* vii. 174 The Jarlshof hut..illustrates..the normal construction of a *wheel-dwelling. **1662** R. MATHEW *Unl. Alch.* 165 Make a good fire of Charcole about it, wch is called a *Wheel-fire of cementation. **1860** HEWITT *Anc. Armour* II. 258 The guard took a variety of forms, as the cross-guard, that composed of two knobs, and the *wheel-guard. **1875** KNIGHT *Dict. Mech.*, *Wheel-guard Plate*, (*Ordnance*), an iron plate on each side of the stock of a..gun-carriage to prevent its being chafed by the wheels when turning. **1845** S. JUDD *Margaret* I. vi, On naked beams above were suspended..*wheelheads, &c. **1900** *Daily News* 17 Jan. 7/1 The wheel-head crosses of Ireland. **1708** *Lond. Gaz.* No. 4424/1 Which enjoins Waggoners to draw with a Pole between the *Wheel-Horses. **1827** HARE *Guesses* Ser. I. 10 He falls into it as certainly as a new wheel-horse in a mail. **1911** H. S. HARRISON *Queed* xxvii, The only speech was made by the Solon who had the bill called up, a familiar organization wheelhorse. **1931** V. G. CHILDE *Skara Brae* vii. 173 The relics from the *wheel-huts round the broch of Jarlshof cannot be distinguished from those from the broch itself. **1800** J. ANDERSON *Recreat.* II. 257 There has been discovered among the *animalcula infusoria*, one which..has been called by the English, the *wheel insect. **1829** *Sporting Mag.* (N.S.) XXIII. 388 What we call a *wheel-iron, placed, as usual on the nose of an axle-tree. **1837** W. B. ADAMS *Carriages* 87 Splinter Bar Stays, to resist the action of the draught. Formerly these were affixed to the ends of the axles, and called 'wheel irons'. **1573–80** TUSSER *Husb.* (1878) 36 *Wheele ladder for haruest. **1710** HILMAN *Tusser Rediv.* Sept. (1744) 117 Cart Ladders and Wheel Ladders are Frames on the Sides and Tail, to support light Loads as Hay, &c. **1888** ELWORTHY *W. Somerset Word-bk.*, *Wheel-ladder*, a lade for the back part of a wagon, having a small roller or windlass attached, by which the ropes for binding the load can be strained tight. **1928** N. MACMILLAN *Art of Flying* x. 142 With many aeroplanes.. too slow speed of approach makes the elevator unable to apply the necessary load quickly enough. This results in a *wheel landing with the tail up. **1942** *R.A.F. Jrnl.* 13 June 8 The second pilot..said that the impact was no worse than a bad wheel landing. **1899** *Geog. Jrnl.* Mar. 226 The mediæval *wheel-maps, in which Jerusalem was accepted as the centre of the world, whence the main geographical lines radiated like the spokes of a wheel. **1907** T. C. MIDDLETON *Geogr. Knowl. Discov. Amer.* 18 The 'wheel-maps' of the globe, devised by St. Isidore. **1861** *Archæol. Cambrensis* Ser. III. VII. 215 These specimens of *wheel and ring money, which were fabricated in the latter place [*sc.* Caltu]. **1878** BELL tr. *Gegenbaur's Comp. Anat.* 138 This *wheel-organ—so-called from the movement of its cilia—varies greatly in character. **1794** in *Chamb. Jrnl.* (1858) 9 Oct. 234/1 The postilion so managed the *wheel-pair, that the princesses.. were..enabled to leap from the carriage without injury. **1956** *U.S. Air Force Dict.* 567/1 **wheel pants*, a set of streamlined fairings around each wheel in certain fixed landing gears. **1971** *Flying* Apr. 40/1 The 172 did appear with clean, 175-style wheel-pants. **1833** LOUDON *Encycl. Archit.* §889 The sill of the door..sunk level with the threshing-floor, and supported by two stout posts or *wheel-pieces. **1828** *Craven Gloss.*, **Wheel-pit*, a whirlpool. **1850** S. JUDD *R. Edney* iii. 43 The subordinate branches were carried on below, under the 'bed' or main floor of the mill, near the wheel-pit. **1875** KNIGHT *Dict. Mech.*, *Wheel-pit*, a walled hole for the heavy fly-wheel of a train of rolls, etc. **1859** *Carriage Builders' Art Jrnl.* I. 7/2 In Broughams,..when a *wheel-plate twenty-two inches in diameter is used, a shortening of nine inches is gained between the fore and hind wheels. **1881** J. W. BURGESS *Coach-Building* 92 The central circle is the wheel-plate, or, as the Americans term it, the fifth wheel. **1892** *Lockwood's Dict. Terms Mech. Engin.*, *Quadrant Plate, or Wheel Plate.* —The plate which carries the stud wheels in the change wheel series for screw cutting in the lathe. **1707** MORTIMER *Husb.* 38 The Hertfordshire *Wheel-Plough. **1710** HILMAN *Tusser Rediv.* Sept. (1744) 119 A Wheel-Plough for Stony, and a Swing Plough for Clay. **1844** H. STEPHENS *Bk. Farm* I. 646 It must be admitted, even by the advocates of the wheel-plough, that..they cannot by any means be brought so handily to follow the undulations of the surface. **1875** KNIGHT *Dict. Mech.*, **Wheel-press*, a hydrostatic press for forcing car-wheels on to their axles and removing them. **1890** W. J. GORDON *Foundry* 185 The wheel-press of Benjamin Dearborn. **1825** J. NICHOLSON *Oper. Mech.* 104 The *wheel-race should always be built in a substantial manner with masonry. **1862** H. MARRYAT *Year in Sweden* II. 259 Here, above the chancel arch, hung a *wheel-rood of exceeding beauty. **1485** *Naval Acc. Hen. VII.* (1896) 37 *Whele Ropes feble..j. **1820** SCORESBY *Acc. Arctic Reg.* II. 483 The pressure of the helm strained a new wheel-rope. **1823** —— *Jrnl.* 358 We lay to under a close-reefed main top sail, until new wheel-ropes were arranged. **1969** *Jane's Freight Containers 1968–69* 102/1 Provision has to be made for *wheelsets to be available at the destination terminal. **1980** *Sci. Amer.* Aug. 33/3 A revolutionary bogie design which prevents wear on the wheel flange as the train negotiates a bend. No longer is the wheelset banging from side to side, abrading the flanges. **1775** J. JENKINSON tr. *Linnæus' Brit. Plants* 231 *Wheel-shaped. **1895** R. DAVEY *Sultan & Subj.* (1897) I. 15 An enormous wheel-shaped box, divided into compartments. **1670** BAXTER *Cure Ch. Div.* 141 As boyes when they have made themselves *wheel-sick with turning round will lay hold on the next post to keep them from falling. **1870** *Routledge's Ev. Boy's Ann.* Suppl. 8/1 A pair of *wheel skates. **1876** 'OUIDA' *Winter City* vi, The *wheelskaters, and poker-players..of our time. **1875** *Field* 2 Jan. 1/3 The *wheel-skating at Brighton and at Prince's. **1945** H. J. MASSINGHAM *Wisdom of Fields* x. 193 A tractor was ploughing in the stubble... The machine was wheel-slipping. *Wheel-slip means [*sc.* causes] soil-panning and winter-souring of it;..it means waste. **1960** *Times* 14

Mar. 21/2 Wheel-slip, with wheeled tractors, can be an intolerable nuisance. **1983** *Austral. Transport* Feb. 21/2 The locomotives are equipped with greatly improved wheel slip controls. **1877** *Encycl. Brit.* VII. 639/2 *Wheel-spicule of *Chirodota vitiensis.* **1928** *Daily Tel.* 11 Sept. 15/6 He took a grassy approach too wide, and had a *wheel spin, from which he cleverly recovered. **1937** *Times* 13 Apr. p. xvi/4 On a sandy gradient of about 1 in 2, the vehicle was stopped and started, ascending and descending. No wheel spin or baulking was noticed. **1956** *Railway Mag.* Nov. 722/1 Steps already had been taken to check wheelspin. **1979** R. Lewis *Violent Death* i. 7 The van came lurching.. from under the trees... Wheel-spin threw up a mist of pine needles. *c* **1440** *Promp. Parv.* 524/1 *Whele spore (*K., H.* welspore), *orbita.* *a* **1825** Forby *Voc. E. Anglia* s.v., If, to avoid the deep rut, a carriage drawn by a single horse was ventured upon the quarter, the horse was obliged to make the wheel-spur his path, often a very unsafe one, particularly in stiff soils. **1882** Caulfeild & Saward *Dict. Needlework* 195/2 **Wheel Stitch*, a stitch resembling a spider's web, and worked into the material, and not over an open space, like English wheel and other lace Wheels. **1835** Dav. Webster *Rhymes* 11 (E.D.D.) My mither.. bang'd her bobbin down on the *wheel stock. **1884** C. S. Sargent *Rep. Forests N. Amer.* 515 Manufacturers of cooperage and wheel stock. **1888** Elworthy *W. Somerset Word-bk., Wheel-stock*.. the nave of a wheel. **1846** Patterson *Zool.* 46 The detached vertebræ are well described by the common English name of '*wheel-stones'. **1831** J. Holland *Manuf. Metal* I. 229 In Sheffield, a mass of the stiff ferruginous mud, called *wheelswarf,.. is generally used. **1780** A. Young *Tour in Ireland* II. xvii. 75 Taxes are inconsiderable, for there is no land tax, no poor rates.. only half a *wheel tax. **1888** *Daily News* 5 Dec. 5/4 There had been enough of this sort of wheel-tax policy tried in other places. **1913** M. Barrett *Scott. Monast. of Old* II. v. 178 The west window contained a splendid specimen of *wheel tracery. **1882** J. Smith *Dict. Pop. Names Plants* 438 *Wheel Tree, or Paddle-wood (*Aspidosperma excelsum*).. when cut transversely the section has the appearance of the rays of a wheel. **1886** J. Barrowman *Sc. Mining Terms* 72 *Wheel-tree*, a prop to which the pulley on a short self-acting incline is fastened. **1885** *Wheel vat [see wheel *v.* 17]. *a* **785** *Charter of Offa* in Birch *Cartul. Sax.* I. 342 And on *hweoȝel weȝ to þan rahheȝe. **1829** I. Taylor *Enthus.* vi. (1867) 114 To lie supine in the ruinous wheel-way of chance. **1889** *Century Mag.* Aug. 570/2 Nearer the wheelway and upon the outer edges of the public road. **1919** F. D. Adams *Aeronaut. Dict.* 181/2 **Wheel well*, a recess or hollow in a wing, fuselage, etc. for a retractable landing-gear wheel. **1961** N. D. van Sickle *Mod. Airmanship* (ed. 2) iv. 103 Having the openings closed while the gear is down is advantageous because the tires will not throw foreign matter into the wheel well during ground movement. **1974** *Hot Rod Yearbk.* XIV. 219/1 Epoxy paint.. was also sprayed on rear inner wheel wells. **1975** *Times* 31 Mar. 4/1 (*caption*) A Boeing 727 arrives at Saigon airport.. with the body of a South Vietnamese soldier hanging from the wheelwell. **1608** Topsell *Serpents* 213 The tayle [of the Newt] standeth out betwixt the hinder-legges in the midle, like the figure of a *wheele-whirle [tr. Gesner: *rhombi figuræ quadam similitudine*]. **1821** M. Browne *Jrnl.* 2 May in *Diary of Girl in France* (1905) 25 There are [in Amiens Cathedral] two pretty painted *wheel-windows. **1835** R. Willis *Archit. Mid. Ages* vi. 63 Wheel windows are exceedingly prevalent in Italy; unfortunately the tracery is often removed. **1594** Nashe *Unfort. Trav.* Wks. (Grosart) V. 105 Embossed christall eies affixed, wherein *wheelewise were circularly ingrafted sharpe pointed diamonds. **1859** W. H. Gregory *Egypt* I. 276 Swimming as schoolboys call it wheel-wise. **1930** *Engineering* 7 Feb. 163/1 Concerned with problems of suspension and *wheel wobble and shimmy. **1961** *Times* 17 Jan. 14/1 Apart from an alarming wheelwobble early in their second innings West Indies have had by far the best of today's play. **1978** A. Waugh *Best Wine Last* vii. 56 It [*sc.* a car] developed a wheel wobble at between forty-eight and fifty miles an hour.

wheel, *v.* Forms: see prec. [f. wheel *sb.*]

I. To move like a wheel (and connected senses).

* **1. a.** *intr.* To turn or revolve about an axis or centre, like a wheel on its axle; to rotate; to whirl.

a **1225** *Ancr. R.* 356 Heo beoð her hweolinde ase hweoles þet ouerturneð sone, and ne lesteð none hwule. *c* **1586** C'tess Pembroke *Ps.* cvii. x, Now shipp with men do touch the skies:.. For now the whirlwinde makes them wheele: Now stop'd in midst of broken round As drunckards use, they staggring reele. *c* **1645** Howell *Lett.* I. v. xi. (1890) 262 His Glory sound thou first Mobile, which mak'st all wheel In circle round. **1796** H. Hunter tr. *St. Pierre's Study Nat.* (1799) I. 426 If the Earth wheels around it's axis. **1813** Scott *Trierm.* III. xxi, When the whirlwind's gusts are wheeling. **1819** Shelley *Mask of Anarchy* lxxviii, Let the horsemen's scimitars Wheel and flash, like sphereless stars. **1886** F. Harrison *Choice of Bks.* i. 23 The gates which lead to the Elysian fields may slowly wheel back on their adamantine hinges.

b. *fig.* of time, the seasons.

1660 Stanley *Hist. Philos.* XIII. (1687) 859/2 When they beheld the course of the Heavens, and the various Seasons of the year, to wheel about, and return in certain order. *a* **1849** Mangan *Poems* (1859) 35 When Years have wheeled. **1871** B. Taylor *Faust* (1875) II. II. iii, I wait, and Time around me wheels.

c. To reel, as from giddiness; to be affected with giddiness. Also *fig.*

1593 Nashe *Christ's T.* Wks. (Grosart) IV. 183 Why doe not all thinges wheele and swarue topsie-turuy? **1620** [G. Brydges] *Horæ Subs.* 116 If these giddy goers bee forced to giue a reason for their wheeling vp and downe the streets. **1638** 'R. Junius' *Drunkard's Char.* 154 No man ever saw mee so much as wheele in the streets; I am therefore no drunkard. **1832** Marryat *Newton Forster* xxvi, [His] head wheeled with the sudden change in his prospects.

2. a. *trans.* To turn (something) on or as on a wheel; to cause to revolve about an axis; to rotate; to cause to move in a circle or cycle.

Used with variety of context, lit. and fig.

c **1374** Chaucer *Troylus* I. 139 Fortune on loft And vnder eft gan hem to whielen bothe. *c* **1480** Henryson *Fox, Wolf & Husb.* xxvii, This fair is of fortoun: As ane cummis vp, scho quheillis ane vther doun. **1593** Q. Eliz. *Boeth.* III. met. ix. 3 Thou.. who time from first Bidst go, and stable stedy all elz dost while. **1613** Purchas *Pilgrimage* III. xvii. 284 In the execution of their rites, shaking and wheeling their heads like madde men. **1635** R. N. tr. *Camden's Hist. Eliz.* IV. 532 Affaires in Court were not long wheeled about upon one Axell-tree. **1654** Sir A. Johnston *Diary* (S.H.S.) II. 197 The Lord semes to be wheeling al things about to the re-establishing of that Covenant agayne. **1667** Milton *P.L.* VII. 501 Now Heav'n.. rowld Her motions, as the great first-Movers hand First wheeld thir course. **1668** Culpepper & Cole *Barthol. Anat.* IV. ii. 161 Others will have the Arm to be wheeled about by the *Infraspinatus.* **1820** Keats *Lamia* II. 64 While through the thronged streets your bridal car Wheels round its dazzling spokes. **1855** E. Forbes *Lit. Papers* ix. 250 The Lamas, whose temples, modes of worship,.. compendious methods of wheeling their prayers, [etc.]. **1875** Browning *Aristoph. Apol., Herakles* 1397, I shall play Ixion's part quite out, the chained and wheeled.

b. *spec.* To twirl or flourish (a stick) in menace or challenge. Also *absol.* (in Irish use).

1617 Moryson *Itin.* I. 243 If at any time we went slowly, hee wheeled his cudgell about his head, and crying *Wohowe Rooe* [etc.]. **1875** *Daily News* 26 Feb., 'Wheeling,' said he, 'is one of those challenges which is given by this energetic population to express their own anxiety for a free fight.' **1893** Le Fanu *70 Yrs. Irish Life* iii. 32 One man 'wheeled,' as they called it, for his party; that is, he marched up and down, flourishing his blackthorn, and shouting the battle-cry of his faction.

3. *Mil.* **a.** *intr.* Of a rank or body of troops: To turn, with a movement like that of the spokes of a wheel, about a pivot (pivot *sb.* 2), so as to change front.

1579 Digges *Stratiot.* 111 The Ruyters vse to Wheele about with their whole Troupe. **1671** Milton *P.R.* III. 323 He saw them in thir forms of battell rang'd, How quick they wheel'd. **1672** Venn *Milit. Discipl.* 62 Right half ranks, wheel about to the right until they be even a breast with the front half files. **1744** M. Bishop *Life* 212 The Colonel.. said, wheel to the left of the Battalion. **1815** Scott *Guy M.* xlvii, Leading file, to the right wheel—trot. **1859** F. A. Griffiths *Artil. Man.* (1862) 9 Left wheel into line. Quick march.

b. *trans.* To cause (a rank or body of troops) to turn in this way.

1634 Peacham *Compl. Gentl.* xx. 245 *marg.*, Wheele the Body to the right hand. *c* **1720** De Foe *Mem. Cavalier* (1840) 104, I wheeled off my troop. **1814** Scott *Wav.* xxxix, He wheeled his little body of cavalry round the base of the castle. **1833** *Regul. Instr. Cavalry* I. 34 The ranks are then wheeled up.

4. a. *intr.* To turn so as to face in a different direction; to turn round or aside, esp. quickly or suddenly. Often with *round, about, †off.*

1639 Fuller *Holy War* III. xi. 127 The French and English wheeling about, charged the Turks most furiously. **1644** Symonds *Diary* (Camden) 148 The rebells wheeled off behind their owne cannon and musqueteers. **1735** Somerville *Chase* III. 105 How to the Head they press, Justling in close Array, then more diffuse Obliquely wheel. **1784** Cowper *Task* VI. 518 His steed Declin'd the death, and wheeling swiftly round.. Baffled his rider. **1827** Scott *Highl. Widow* v, A party of five Highland soldiers.. wheeled suddenly into sight. **1867** J. T. Headley *Farragut & Nav. Comm.* 575 [The captain] wheeled out of line and ran with a full head of steam on straight into the ironclad monster. **1888** 'J. S. Winter' *Bootle's Childr.* vii, He wheeled round from the window as if he was about to confront Halliday and offer to fight him on the spot.

b. *fig.* To change or reverse one's opinion, attitude, or course of action; to turn aside, deviate, decline *from* some course or attitude.

1632 G. Herbert *Church Militant* 54 Plato and Aristotle were at a losse, And wheel'd about again to spell Christ-Crosse. **1663** Heath *Flagellum* (1672) 27 Who had wheeled from his Loyalty during the War. *a* **1716** South *Serm., 2 Thess. ii. 11* II. Wks. 1727 IV. 413 From Independents they improved into Anabaptists. From Anabaptists into Quakers: From whence being able to advance no farther, they are in a fair Way to wheel about to the other Extreme of Popery. **1784** P. Wright *New Bk. Martyrs* 807/2 Jeffreys summed up the evidence against the parson, but wheeled at last into this.

c. *trans.* To turn (a person, animal, or thing) round or aside.

1805 Scott *Last Minstr.* II. viii, So had he seen, in fair Castile, The youth in glittering squadrons start, Sudden the flying jennet wheel, And hurl the unexpected dart. **1829** G. Head *Forest Scenes N. Amer.* 121 Wheeled round every now and then by the wind, we were enveloped in clouds. **1842** Lover *Handy Andy* xix, Wheeling his horse suddenly round, he charged along the advancing front of the people.

** **5. a.** *intr.* To move like a point in the circumference of a wheel; to move in a circle, spiral, or similar curve; to circle, revolve; to go round about.

1600 Holland *Livy* xxxiv. xiv, He commaunded two elect cohorts of footmen to wheele about the right flanke of the enemies. **1607** Shaks. *Cor.* I. vi. 19, I was forc'd to wheele Three or four miles about. **1617** Moryson *Itin.* I. 185, I might see him send two horsemen after me, who wheeling about the mountaines,.. suddenly rushed vpon me. **1665** *Phil. Trans.* I. 72 These two Planets have Moons wheeling about them. **1703** Pope *Thebais* 441 The son of May.. wheeling down the steep of heav'n he flies, And draws a radiant circle o'er the skies. **1726–46** Thomson *Winter* 145 The cormorant on high Wheels from the deep. **1850** Tennyson *In Mem.* xcviii, When all is gay.. With sport and song,.. And wheels the circled dance. **1863** Dickens *Uncomm. Trav.* xxiv, The gulls that wheel and dip around me. **1892** Kipling *Barrack-room Ballads, L'Envoi* ix, The old lost stars wheel back, dear lass, That blaze in the velvet blue.

fig. **1661** J. Stephens *Procurations* 128 But I wheel too far about. **1698** Fryer *Acc. E. India & P.* 132 Those occurrences which wheeled in their Sphere. **1749** Smollett *Regic.* IV. ii, Love, Jealousy, implacable Despair In Tempests wheel.

b. *trans.* To cause (something) to move in this way; to perform (a movement), trace (a course), spend (a time) in this way.

1725 Pope *Odyss.* IV. 704 'Till the twelfth moon had wheel'd her pale career. **1750** Gray *Elegy* ii, Save where the beetle wheels his droning flight. **1808** Scott *Marm.* VI. xx, Wheeling their march, and circling still, Around the base of Flodden hill. **1817** Coleridge *Sibyl. Leaves, Happy Husband* iii, Transient joys, that.. into tenderness soon dying, Wheel out their giddy moment. **1839** Kemble *Resid. Georgia* (1863) 21 Hawks of every sort and size wheel their steady rounds above the rice-fields. **1846** Tennyson *Golden Year* 24 The Sun flies forward to his brother Sun; The dark Earth follows, wheel'd in her ellipse.

6. *transf.* **a.** *intr.* To extend in a circle or curve. ? *Obs. rare.*

1648 Gage *West Ind.* xvii. 114 In a narrow passage where the way went wheeling. **1789** J. Williams *Min. Kingd.* I. 112 Coal and coal metals.. wave and wheel. **1791** W. Gilpin *Rem. Forest Scenery* II. 120 A forest-lawn,.. which wheeled around us in the form of a crescent.

†**b.** *trans.* To encircle, surround, encompass. *Obs. rare.*

1582 Stanyhurst *Æneis* II. (Arb.) 55 He spyed his person with Troian coompanye wheeled. **1667** Milton *P.L.* IV. 783 Half these draw off, and coast the South With strictest watch; these other wheel the North.

*** **7.** *intr.* To roll along like a wheel. *rare.*

1667 Milton *P.L.* XII. 183 Haile mixt with fire must rend th' Egyptian skie And wheel on th' Earth, devouring where it rouls. **1875** F. T. Buckland *Log-Bk.* 355 The waves at the outer end wheeled at a swift gallop.

II. To move on, or by means of, wheels.

* **8. a.** *trans.* To convey in a wheeled vehicle, or on a chair, sofa, etc. moving on wheels.

1601 *Shuttleworths' Acc.* (Chetham Soc.) 139 For whellinge forth xxv quarters of colles, vj[d]. **1740** Mrs. E. Montagu *Corr.* (1906) I. 41 Lord Berkshire was wheeled into the rooms on Thursday night, where he saluted me with much snuff and civility. **1761** Colman *Jealous Wife* I. 22 You shall clap Her into a Post-Chaise,.. wheel Her down to Scotland. **1853** Dickens *Bleak Ho.* xxix, Let the gardener.. press the leaves into full barrows, and wheel them off, still they lie ankle-deep. **1888** 'J. S. Winter' *Bootle's Childr.* vi, She was able to totter to the sofa and be wheeled into the adjoining room.

b. *fig.* To pass or convey easily or smoothly, as if on wheels. *rare.*

1658 Harrington *Oceana* 23 Through the paucity of her Citizens, her greater Magistracies are continually wheeled through a few hands. **1689** Hickeringill *Ceremony Monger* vi. Wks. 1716 II. 444 We'll have as many Organs.. if we have nothing else to do with our Money; or cannot tell how to wheel off an hour or two in Devotions. **1851** Mrs. Browning *Casa Guidi Wind.* II. 309 As some smooth river which has overflowed Will slow and silent down its current wheel A loosened forest.

c. *colloq.* To bring (someone) *in*, as for an interview, meeting, performance, etc. Also, with similar meaning, const. *on, out.* Also *fig.*

1970 *New Yorker* 28 Feb. 29/3 The Administration wheels out what are at the moment issues.. which everyone can agree on. **1977** M. Allen *Spence in Petal Park* xviii. 78 Wheel Prendergast straight in when he arrives. **1978** *Daily Mirror* 12 Jan. 2/4 The agreed quota for Japanese car imports in 1977 should be wheeled out again for 1978. **1983** *Listener* 20 Oct. 27/1 'Celebrities' were wheeled in before a studio audience. **1984** *Times* 9 Feb. 11/5 This new element is wheeled in when cousins come to stay. *Ibid.* 15 Aug. 11/1 Kenny Everett.. was wheeled on with other celebrities to warm up a Conservative rally for the Leader in the course of last year's general election campaign here. *Ibid.* 8 Dec. 6/4 Although his field is limited to southern France from the fourteenth to the eighteenth century, the French media wheels him out to make pronouncements on Giscard's reign, his reservations about Mitterand's regime, or whether Nazi war criminals like Barbie should be executed.

9. *intr.* To travel in or drive a wheeled vehicle; to go along on wheels, as a vehicle; *mod. colloq.* to ride a bicycle or tricycle, to 'cycle'.

1721 Ramsay *Content* 351 He found he could not walk,.. and wheel'd away. **1768** Sterne *Sent. Journ., The Address*, By the time he [*sc.* a coachman] had wheel'd round the court, and brought me up to the door. **1798** Jane Austen *Northang. Abb.* xx, The chaise and four wheeled off with some grandeur. **1884** *Century Mag.* Sept. 643/2 A youth on a bicycle, who wheeled attentively by her side. **1898** Hamblen *Gen. Manager's Story* v. 48 Both trains were wheeling down under the bridge at a forty-mile gait.

10. a. *trans.* To push or draw (something) on wheels.

1784 Cowper *Task* IV. 37 Let fall the curtains, wheel the sofa round. **1832** Lytton *Eugene Aram* I. v, The sofa was wheeled into the hall where they dined. **1848** Dickens *Dombey* xlix, He wheeled the table close against Florence on the sofa. **1885** *Law Times* LXXIX. 47/1 A porter.. put all the luggage on a trolley.. and wheeled the trolley on to the platform. **1896** H. G. Wells *Wheels of Chance* ix, The other man in brown had a bad puncture and was wheeling his machine.

b. To drive a car slowly, as when manœuvring into or out of a car park.

1962 R. Unekis *Chase* (1963) vii. 20 Grozzo wheeled the Olds into the big parking area. **1974** N. Freeling *Dressing of Diamond* 182 It was Castang who wheeled the Citroën out of the parking-lot. **1976** *National Observer* (U.S.) 11 Dec. 8/2, I wheeled the bright-blue test car into a parking space.

** †**11.** ? To wind *up* the mechanism of: in quot. *fig. Obs. rare.*

1632 *Mason's Turke* (ed. 2) Argt., There are other passages of Triuiall Inferior persons, Interwouen into this peice, which serue as a foyle to the Brauery and hight of the Tragedy, yet are Instruments aptly set going to wheele vp the worke.

III. Miscellaneous uses.

†**12.** *intr.* Of a peacock: To spread the tail in a circular form like a wheel. Also *trans.* with the tail as *obj. Obs.*

1513 BRADSHAW *St. Werburge* I. 1805 Prowde as a Pecocke whelynge full bryght. **1600** SURFLET *Country Farm* I. xix. 115 You neede no other signe then his [*sc.* the peacock's] viewing of himselfe, and couering of his whole bodie with the feathers of his taile, and then we say hee wheeleth. **1656** W. DU GARD tr. *Comenius' Gate Lat. Unl.* §137 The most fair is the Peacock, ever and anon wheeling his glorious tail. **1745** tr. *Columella's Husb.* VIII. xi.

13. *trans.* To make like a wheel; to give a circular or curved form to. *rare.*

1656 W. DU GARD tr. *Comenius' Gate Lat. Unl.* §203 The hair covereth the chiefest part of the head, being wheeled on the crown [*capilli..rotati in vertice*]. **1808** SCOTT *Marm.* v. vi, At every turn, with dinning clang, The armourer's anvil clash'd and rang; Or toil'd the swarthy smith, to wheel The bar that arms the charger's heel.

14. To furnish with a wheel or wheels.

1661, 1898 [see WHEELING *vbl. sb.* f]. **1802** H. MARTIN *Helen of Glenross* I. 46 She begged leave to paint, glaze, new carpet, and new wheel the old coach.

†**15.** To torture or 'break' on a wheel. *Obs. rare.*

1611 [implied in WHEELING *vbl. sb.* h].

16. To form or shape on a wheel, as pottery.

17. *Tanning.* = PIN-WHEEL *v.*

1885 C. T. DAVIS *Manuf. Leather* 530 The skins next go into the England wheel vat..and are 'wheeled' in sumach liquor.

wheel: see WEEL, WHEAL.

wheelage (ˈhwiːlɪdʒ). [f. WHEEL *sb.* + -AGE.]

1. A toll paid for the passage of wheeled vehicles; cost of carriage in a wheeled vehicle, cartage. *Hist.*

1611 COTGR., *Droict de Roüage*, wheelage. **1672** (*title*) Deed between William Osbolston..and the Mayor and Corporation of London, relates to the Collection of Tolls, or Wheelage over Old London Bridge (MS.). **1765** *Lond. Chron.* 25 Apr. 398 The Committee..lett..the toll of carts and wheelage over London-Bridge. **1808** *Hist. Worcester* 93 A ton of coal, threepence for wheelage. **1894** C. WELCH *Tower Bridge* 48 The Sheriffs never had anything to do with the wheelage, which was collected by a City-officer.

†**2.** Wheel-making. *Obs. rare*$^{-0}$.

1681 W. ROBERTSON *Phraseol. Gen.* 1312 Wheelage, or wheel-work, *rotarum fabricatio*.

wheel and ˈdeal, *v. colloq.* (orig. and chiefly *U.S.*). Pa. t. **wheeled and dealed.** [f. WHEEL *sb.* 14d + DEAL *v.*] **1.** *intr.* To engage in scheming or shrewd bargaining, esp. of a political or commercial nature. Cf. WHEELER-DEALER.

1961 WEBSTER, *Wheel and deal*, to take the part of a leader or wheel and to take charge of affairs or arrangements (showed the town how an absolute dictator wheels and deals —*Newsweek*). **1962** 'K. ORVIS' *Damned & Destroyed* vii. 53 You don't act like you really know where to wheel-and-deal yet. **1967** *National Observer* (U.S.) 3 July 13 Reagan could break loose votes from the Democrats if he really wanted to. You can always wheel-and-deal and get at least part of what you want. **1967** *Listener* 24 Aug. 250/1 Frost is wheeling and dealing off camera. **1974** *Publishers Weekly* 24 June 58/1 Lads who..wheeled and dealed with megacorporations. **1976** J. I. M. STEWART *Memorial Service* xiv. 234 'What's in the wind is a little quiet wheeling and dealing about the black sheep of the family.'..'Why should the Provost wheel and deal about you?'

2. *trans.* To obtain by scheming; to deal or bargain in.

1971 R. DENTRY *Encounter at Kharmel* xii. 217 In other words, if we agree to shut up, you'll wheel and deal some pin money for us. **1974** *Scottish Daily Express* 16 Apr. 4/3 Dr. Henry Kissinger, due here shortly to wheel and deal his way to stilling the guns. **1979** *Tucson Mag.* Mar. 49/1 The Inn was originally built to wheel and deal Arizona land.

Hence **wheeling and ˈdealing** *vbl. sb.* Cf. *wheeler-dealing* vbl. sb. s.v. WHEELER-DEALER.

1969 *Listener* 9 Jan. 60/3 As a proof of his mischievous intentions, he [*sc.* Henry II] invites the devious King of France to this gathering. It would need a Norman Mailer to describe accurately the wheeling and dealing that follows. **1976** [see sense 1 above]. **1981** *Beautiful Brit. Columbia* Summer 9 When silver prices rode the crest and silver-miners and promoters flocked to the Slocan..the streets of New Denver..were alive with wheeling and dealing.

ˈwheel-band. [f. WHEEL *sb.* + BAND *sb.*²]

†**1.** The tire of a wheel. *Obs.*

1392-3 *Earl Derby's Exp.* (Camden) 202 Item pro j whele-band, j scho pro curru, et emendacione currus, v gr. **1557** *Richmond Wills* (Surtees) 93 In the hay housse..iiij. qwele bannes. **1598** CHAPMAN *Iliad* VII. R3b, [XI. 466] The chariote tree was drownd in bloode, and th' arches by the seat Disperpled from the horses houes, and from the wheelbandes beate.

2. A band or strap that goes round a wheel, as the driving band of a spinning-wheel. *dial.*

*a***1656** *Roxb. Ball.* (1881) IV. 101 It is a well twined Wheelband. **1693** C. MATHER *Wond. Invis. World* (1862) 159 One Susanna Sheldon..had her hands Unaccountably ty'd together with a Wheel-band. **1705** *Phil. Trans.* XXV. 2166 To prevent the Recipients being drawn from its place by the motion and tug of the Wheel-band.

wheelbarrow (ˈhwiːlˌbærəʊ), *sb.* Forms: see WHEEL *sb.* and BARROW *sb.*³; also 4 **wil-**, 6 **whil-**; 4 **-bargh**, 5 **-berghe**, **-berwe**, 6 **-barugh**, **-berow**, 7 **-barrough**. A barrow or shallow open box mounted between two shafts that receive the axle of a wheel at the front ends, the rear ends being shaped into handles and having legs on which it rests; also applied to similar contrivances with more than one wheel.

*c***1340** *Nominale* (Skeat) 218 Sikeman lith in hors-bere.. And the crepul in the wilbarewe. **1394** in *Archaeologia* XXIV. 308 Et in j welbargh empt' pro stauro Maner' xij d. **14..** *Voc.* in Wr.-Wülcker 572/1 *Cenovectorium rotatum*, a whelberwe. **1533** *MS. Rawl. D.* 776 lf. 149 Whele-barrowes ffor laborers to serve bryklayers with. *c***1563** *Jack Juggler* (1912) B iv b, I shall make thee not able to goo nor ryde But in a dungcart or a whilberow liyng on on syde. **1598** BARRET *Theor. Warres* v. ii. 131 Hand-barrowes, and wheele-barrowes to carrie earth. **1678** OTWAY *Friendship in F.* III. i, I can act the rumbling of a Wheelbarrow. **1700** T. BROWN tr. *Fresny's Amusem.* 20 Another Fellow driving a Wheel-Barrow of Nuts. **1855** DELAMER *Kitch. Gard.* (1861) 8 Two doors,..wide enough to admit a wheel-barrow, or a small cart.

†**b.** *transf.* applied to a light carriage. *Obs.*

*c***1600** DAY *Begg. Bednall Gr.* v. (1881) 114 To be jaunted up and down London Streets in a lethern wheelbarrow. **1625** B. JONSON *Staple of News* II. iii, You thinke I can runne like light-foot Ralph, Or keep a wheele-barrow, with a sayle in towne here To whirle me to you. **1778** *Eng. Gazetteer* (ed. 2) s.v. *Yarmouth*, People are carried here all over the town ..for 6d. in what they call a coach, but it is only a wheel-barrow, drawn by one horse. **1794** WOLCOT (P. Pindar) *Pindariana, Hymn to Adversity*, Morality..may..Throw by his wheel-barrow, and keep a carriage. **1819** SCOTT *Let.* in *Lockhart* (1837) IV. 290 You know of old how I detest that mania of driving wheel-barrows up and down, when a man has a handsome horse and can ride him.

c. In allusive and proverbial phr.: see quots.

1597 BRETON *Wits Trenchmour* Wks. (Grosart) II. 9/1 It is not a little treason in youth, to catch age in a wheele-barrow. **1618** T. ADAMS *Gods Bountie* i. Wks. 864 This oppressor must needs goe to heauen,..But it will bee, as the by-word is, in a Wheele-barrow; the fiends, and not the Angels will take hold on him. **1675** COTTON *Burlesque upon B.* 128 When drunk as Drum, or Wheelbarrow. **1677** W. HUGHES *Man of Sin* II. ii. 36 Behold the Reason of the Wheelbarrow! That goes to rumble. *Ibid.* x. 159 The Believing Collier whirles right to Heaven in a Wheel-barrow. **1709** [see DRUNK *ppl. a.* 1 b].

d. *attrib.* and *Comb.*, as ***wheelbarrow-load***, ***-man***, ***race***, ***tub***; ***wheelbarrow fashion*** advb. phr.; **wheelbarrow-machine** (see quot.).

1834 M. SCOTT *Cruise Midge* xviii, Laying hold of the navigator *wheelbarrow fashion. **1863** HAWTHORNE *Our Old Home, Outside Glimpses Engl. Pov.*, The wealthier inhabitants purchased their coal by the *wheelbarrow-load. **1856** *Jrnl. Soc. Arts* IV. 402 Mr. Applegarth..has also invented a beautiful little machine for printing the borders on silk handkerchiefs, called the *wheelbarrow machine, from its being worked by the hand round the cloth, which remains stationary. **1712** J. JAMES tr. *Le Blond's Gardening* 109 The *Wheelbarrow-Men make five or six Stages, according to the Length of the Way. **1788** *Massachusetts Spy* 26 Nov. 2/1 It is said the perpetrators were of that class called wheelbarrow men, but this is rather improbable, as their object did not appear to be plunder. **1837** D. WALKER *Sports & Games* 341 *Wheelbarrow Race... Along this course, over the bridge, and up to the goal, the candidates must drive their barrows blindfolded—if they can. **1833** LOUDON *Encycl. Archit.* §731 More economical to convey the milk thither in *wheelbarrow tubs.

Hence **wheelbarrow** *v. trans.*, to convey in a wheelbarrow (whence **ˈwheelbarrower**); **ˈwheelbarrowful**, as much as a wheelbarrow holds. See also WHEELBARROWING *vbl. sb.*

1721 AMHERST *Terræ Fil.* No. 44 (1726) 244 The greatest part of his heavy compliments are *wheel-barrow'd from the lime-kiln. **1887** BARING-GOULD *Gaverocks* xiv, Onions.. wheelbarrowed into the town. **1893** W. WALLACE *Scot. Yest.* 73 He became the regular *wheelbarrower at the Castle. **1837** THACKERAY *Ravenswing* viii, The theatre servants wheeled away a *wheelbarrow-full. **1851** *B'ham & Midl. Gard. Mag.* Apr. 31 At the rate of one wheelbarrow full to every twelve of soil.

ˈwheelbarrowing, *vbl. sb.* [f. WHEELBARROW *sb.* + -ING¹.] **1.** Conveyance in a wheelbarrow.

1893 W. WALLACE *Scot. Yest.* 74 Often I saw him pausing in his wheelbarrowing.

2. *Aeronaut.* Landing where only the nose-wheel (of an aircraft with a tricycle undercarriage) is in contact with the ground.

1977 *Flight* 13 Aug. 480/2 We found the nose could be held up. We thought that there could be little excuse for nosewheel landings or wheelbarrowing. **1983** D. STINTON *Design of Aeroplane* x. 370 Sloppier landing habits, failure to get the tail down on landing..cause too many ballooning, wheelbarrowing and mishandling incidents.

ˈwheel-ˌcarriage.

1. Carriage (CARRIAGE 1) or conveyance by wheeled vehicles.

1733 W. ELLIS *Chiltern & Vale Farm.* 30 Ashes or Soot.. are seldom used, because they generally lie too distant for Wheel Carriage from London. **1765** *Museum Rust.* IV. 247 Where the country proves clay, marl, or rich or spungy soil, ..and yet much wheel-carriage necessary, and no turnpike.

2. A carriage (CARRIAGE 23) moving on wheels, a wheeled vehicle; also as a part of a machine (CARRIAGE 29).

1733 W. ELLIS *Chiltern & Vale Farm.* 319 Its fore-part lying on the Stock of the Wheel-Carriage as the Fallow-plough does. **1756** WASHINGTON *Lett. Writ.* 1889 I. 369 The only gap of the Alleghany at present made passable for wheel-carriages. **1845** G. DODD *Brit. Manuf.* IV. 123 The wheel-carriage on which the roller rests is then wheeled onward. **1883** S. C. HALL *Retrospect* II. 304 The roads.. that led from town to town were barely passable to wheel-carriages.

wheel-chair. [f. WHEEL *sb.* + CHAIR *sb.*¹] Also **wheelchair, wheel chair. 1.** A chair on wheels used by invalids or the disabled; also = *Bath-chair* s.v. BATH *sb.*² 2.

*a***1700** EVELYN *Diary* 11 Jan. 1662, My Lord Aubignie.. shew'd us..his wheele-chaire for ease and motion. **1817** JANE AUSTEN *Let.* ? May (1952) 497, I..am to..be promoted to a wheel-chair as the weather serves. **1841** THACKERAY *Second Funeral of Napoleon* iii. 77 A servant passes, pushing..a shabby wheel-chair. **1890** *Harper's Mag.* Mar. 613/1 Mrs. Aydler flitted backward and forward in her wheel chair. **1904** LEE *Recoll. Gen. R. E. Lee* 196 When put in her wheel-chair, she could propel herself on a level floor. **1958** *Times* 15 Sept. 11/1, I was in no condition to register the details of arriving in the hospital ward in a wheelchair. **1977** *Whitaker's Almanack 1978* 584/2 Britain banned a team of 5 White and 5 Black young Rhodesians confined to wheelchairs from coming to the U.K. to participate in games for the disabled at Stoke Mandeville, Bucks. **1981** *Sunday Times* 14 June 86 A lot of people seem slightly on edge at meeting me in a wheelchair but my main aim is to dispel this straight away.

2. *attrib.* and *Comb.*, as ***wheelchair patient***, ***wounded***; ***wheelchair-bound***, ***-ridden*** adjs.; also with reference to sporting events for those confined to wheelchairs, as ***wheelchair athlete***, ***games***, ***Olympics***, ***slalom***.

1972 Wheelchair athlete [see *wheelchair games* below]. **1981** *Daily Mail* 17 June 38/5, I am fortunate enough not to be wheelchair-bound. **1972** R. C. ADAMS et al. *Games, Sports & Exercises* (ed. 2) iii. 10/2, 1960..marked the first time the wheelchair games were held along with the Olympic Games... Wheelchair athletes from all over the globe were greeted by the Pope. **1972** *Even. Telegram* (St. John's, Newfoundland) 5 Aug. 18/1 The Wheelchair Olympics..were started after the Second World War for crippled war veterans. They have since become games for athletes with spinal cord injuries or those who have been paralysed by polio. **1970** *Stoke Mandeville Dict. Managem. Paraplegic Patients* 4 Occasionally indicated on the stiff hip or knee of wheelchair-patients. **1968** T. STOPPARD *Real Inspector Hound* 16 Magnus, the wheelchair-ridden half-brother to her ladyship's husband Lord Albert Muldoon. **1964** *Times* 12 Nov. 11/3 Carol Bryant..won a gold medal in the wheelchair slalom. **1982** *Daily Tel.* 5 Oct. 15/1 He would not change his mind about excluding 'wheelchair wounded' from the Falklands victory parade.

Hence **ˈwheel-chaired** *a.*, in or confined to a wheelchair.

1938 *Amer. Speech* XIII. 196 Wheel-chaired. **1973** *Times* 11 Apr. 8/6 A mini-bus is used in one of our split-site comprehensives to carry wheelchaired pupils from building to building. **1977** *New Scientist* 3 Mar. 499/1 Another council decision..caused the AAAS's wheel-chaired delegates to wheel themselves out of the room in disgust.

wheeldom (ˈhwiːldəm). *nonce-wd.* [f. WHEEL *sb.* + -DOM.] The domain or 'world' of wheeled vehicles, esp. bicycles or users of them.

1887 *Cycl. Tour. Club Monthly Gaz.* Mar. 123 A prominent interest in matters pertaining to wheeldom.

wheeled (hwiːld, *poet.* ˈhwiːlɪd), *a.* Also 7 **wheeld, whilde.** [f. WHEEL *sb.* + -ED². (In OE. in parasynthetic comb. *fýrhweohlod* four-wheeled, *héhhwíolad* high-wheeled.)]

1. a. Furnished with a wheel or wheels, or with any revolving disc; *esp.* of a vehicle, mounted or moving on wheels. Also in parasynthetic comb., as ***two-wheeled***, etc. Also freq. in ***wheeled chair***, = WHEEL-CHAIR.

1606 SHAKS. *Ant. & Cl.* IV. xiv. 75 The wheel'd seate Of Fortunate Cæsar. **1633** T. STAFFORD *Pac. Hib.* III. viii. (1821) 322 Pickaxes and Whildebarrowes. **1765** A. DICKSON *Treat. Agric.* (ed. 2) 219 The wheeled plough. **1815** ELPHINSTONE *Acc. Caubul* (1842) I. 378 An inland country, destitute of navigable rivers, and not suited to wheeled carriages. **1836** PRICHARD *Phys. Hist. Man.* (ed. 3) I. 258 Ever shifting their wheeled houses. **1847** DICKENS *Dombey & Son* (1848) xxx. 300 Withers the page, released..from the propulsion of the wheeled-chair. **1855** HEWITT *Anc. Armour* I. p. xxii, The knights appear to have rejected with particular obstinacy the innovation of the wheeled spur. **1856** STANLEY *Sinai & Pal.* ii. 134 Roads for wheeled vehicles are now unknown in any part of Palestine. **1875** REYNARDSON *Down the Road* 107 A tinker with one of those wheeled grinding-stones. **1911** F. H. BURNETT *Secret Garden* xx. 213 The strongest footman in the house carried Colin down-stairs and put him in his wheeled chair. **1981** J. MANN *Funeral Sites* i. 11 I'm too fat for an operation, they say... It's endurance or a wheeled chair.

b. *transf.* Effected on wheels or by wheeled vehicles.

1845 STOCQUELER *Handbk. Brit. India* (1854) 348 Wheeled carriage is unknown:..no wheeled conveyances could be used. **1882** T. G. BOWLES *Flotsam & Jetsam* 110 The almost entire absence of wheeled traffic. **1906** *Blackw. Mag.* May 640/2 The country through which we passed in our wheeled pilgrimage to Land's End.

2. Of the form of a wheel. *poet. rare.*

1820 SHELLEY *Prometh. Unb.* IV. 233, I see a chariot... Its wheels are solid clouds,..A guiding power directs the chariot's prow Over its wheelèd clouds.

ˈwheel-engraving. [f. WHEEL *sb.* + ENGRAVING *vbl. sb.*] The art or craft of engraving patterns, etc., on glass by means of a rotating copper wheel and an abrasive mixture of emery and oil, sand and water, or the like.

1884 KNIGHT *Dict. Mech.* Suppl. 946/1 *Wheel Engraving.* .. As distinguished from sand-blast engraving or acid etching. See *Glass Engraving.* **1929** W. BUCKLEY *Diamond Engraved Glasses of 16th Cent.* 8 Wheel engraving became common before the end of the 17th century and superseded the use of the diamond as the usual method of engraving glasses. **1957** *Encycl. Brit.* X. 413/1 By the end of the [17th] century this type of diamond point work was superseded in popularity by wheel engraving. **1975** *Oxf. Compan. Decorative Arts* 403/2 English glass..was greatly in demand in the Netherlands for the flourishing school of wheel-engraving in the German manner.

Hence (as a back-formation) **'wheel-engrave** *v. trans.*; also **'wheel-engraved** *ppl. a.*; **'wheel-engraver**.

1926 B. RACKHAM in W. Buckley *European Glass* p. x, The wonderful skill of technique shown in the finest German wheel-engraved glasses may make up..for the loss of nobility involved. **1937** *Burlington Mag.* Nov. 221/1 The lines are crudely wheel-engraved. **1961** E. M. ELVILLE *Collector's Dict. Glass* 55/2 There are quite a number of diamond point and wheel engravers today who have constant employment in such work. **1972** *Country Life* 30 Nov. 1499/1 A later tumbler in the same sale was wheel-engraved with a bust portrait of Prince Charles Edward. **1979** *Homes & Gardens* June 83/1 Often these declare their purpose at a glance, with wheel-engraved patterns of the ale brewer's hop leaves and barley.

wheeler ('hwi:lə(r)). Also 4 **whelere**, 5–6 **wheler**. [f. WHEEL *sb.* and *v.* + -ER[1].]

I. Senses derived from the sb.

†**1.** ***wheeler dog***, ? orig. a turnspit dog; *transf.* a roasting-jack or similar instrument. *Obs. rare.*

1379 *Will of Carter* (Comm. Crt. London), Vnum instrumentum vocatum a whelere dogge.

2. A wheelwright or wheel-maker.

1497 *Naval Acc. Hen. VII* (1896) 109 Whelers and Smythes toles. **1549** *MSS. Dk. Rutland* (Hist. MSS. Comm.) IV. 570 A wheler to make wheles. **1666** *Bedloe's Narr. Popish Plot* 6 A Paper with a Ball of Wild-fire,..was found in the Nave of a Wheel, in a Wheelers-yard. **1733** W. ELLIS *Chiltern & Vale Farm.* 19 The Stones that..ever will be the Cause of a greater Charge of Smith's and Wheeler's Bills. **1830** MISS MITFORD *Village* Ser. IV. 84 The wheeler's shop, always picturesque, with its tools, and its work. **1876** VOYLE & STEVENSON *Milit. Dict.* 468/1 *Wheelers*,..the mechanics of a battery engaged in setting up the wheels of the gun-carriages. **1901** *Daily Chron.* 8 May 11/2 Wheelwrights.—Wanted 2 good wheelers.

3. A wheel-horse (see WHEEL *sb.* 19) or other draught-animal in the same position; often opp. to *leader* (LEADER[1] 6 b).

1813 COL. HAWKER *Diary* (1893) I. 82 My leader took fright..but luckily I kept my wheeler in. **1842** DICKENS *Amer. Notes* xiv, Now, the coach was lying on the tails of the two wheelers; and now it was rearing up in the air. **1885** *New Bk. Sports* 171 Few things are more distressing than to see..one wheeler hanging away from the pole, and the other hugging it.

4. One who attends to the wheel in a spinning-machine.

1876 SMILES *Sc. Natur.* iii. 47 Each spinner had three boys under him—the wheeler, the pointer, and the stripper.

5. *Needlework.* One who makes 'wheels': see WHEEL *sb.* 9 a (*a*).

6. = *wheel-bird*: see WHEEL *sb.* 19.

1862 JOHNS *Brit. Birds* 625 Wheel-bird, or Wheeler, the Nightjar.

7. Something, as a vehicle, a boat, etc. furnished with a wheel or wheels: chiefly in compounds, as FOUR-WHEELER, STERNWHEELER, etc.

1886 A. WATT *Electro-Depos.* 314 The whole bicycle fraternity, who had been accustomed to plain steel or painted wheelers.

8. ? A nail used in fixing the parts of a wheel.

1873 *Iron* 1 Feb. 75/1 Nails..Wrought..Best Derby Countersunk Dub deep Wheelers, 3 [lbs.], 2/9.

II. Senses derived from the verb.

9. One who wheels a vehicle, or conveys something in a wheeled vehicle (esp. a wheelbarrow).

1683 J. REID *Scots Gard'ner* (1907) 55 With wheel-barrows; three barrows for two wheelers and one filler sometimes doth well. **1688** HOLME *Armoury* III. 261/1 *Wheeler*, is him that carryeth the Clay from the Pit, to the Moulding Board foot. **1862** SMILES *Engineers* III. iii. 24 The younger boys worked as wheelers or pickers on the bank-tops. **1884** C. T. DAVIS *Bricks, Tiles* etc. (1889) 131 The wheeler gathers the stones and hard lumps of clay that have been thrown out..and wheels them to some out of the way place.

†**10.** One of a series of projecting stones in a battlement: see quot. *Obs. rare.*

1688 HOLME *Armoury* III. 470/2 A Tower with a plain Battlement; that is, the Battlement is not made with Wheelers and Kneelers, but is straight, and even in the Walk of the Wall. *Ibid.* 472/1 (Terms of the Fractable on a Gable end) A Wheeler, are wrought stones that ly levell and streight, yet make outward Angles when other stones are ioyned to them.

11. *Mil.* The man at the outermost end of the rank in wheeling.

1798 SIR W. YOUNG *Instr. Armed Yeom.* 13 The man on the other Flank, or Wheeler, will move round square, to Dress by the Pivot Man.

12. One who turns so as to face another way; *fig.* one who changes his opinion or attitude, a turncoat, a 'weathercock'.

1836 *Tait's Mag.* III. 40 He..is one of the most notorious wheelers in Parliament.

13. One who rides a bicycle or tricycle, a cyclist. *colloq.*

1886 H. BAUMANN *Londinismen* 232/1 *Wheeler*, velocipedist. **1897** BARRÈRE & LELAND *Dict. Slang.* **1929** *Newport & Market Drayton Advertiser* 28 June 3/4 Shropshire wheelers. Sunday's run to Bala. **1979** *Guardian* 8 Aug. 7/4 A posh camping shop..no shop for humble wheelers.

wheeler-'dealer. *colloq.* (orig. and chiefly *U.S.*). [f. WHEEL AND DEAL *v.*: cf. -ER[1].] A schemer, esp. in business or politics; one who wheels and deals (see quot. 1960).

1960 WENTWORTH & FLEXNER *Dict. Amer. Slang* 574/2 *Wheeler-dealer*..one who wheels and deals; an adroit, quick-witted, scheming person; a person with many business or social interests. **1963** *Economist* 24 Aug. 666/1 Two Dallas oil millionaires,..described as 'a pair of old-line Texas wheeler-dealers'. **1968** G. WYCKOFF *Image Candidates* iii. 20 Ted had been known as the Wheeler-Dealer because he always had important phone calls to make from his hotel room when we arrived on location. **1973** *Guardian* 23 Mar. 15/3 Old-style American corruption of the wheeler-dealer variety. **1978** L. HEREN *Growing up on The Times* ix. 301 He [*sc.* Lyndon Johnson] was a shop-soiled old politico, a wheeler dealer, and past master of consensus politics.

Hence **wheeler-'dealing**, the activity of a wheeler-dealer; = *wheeling and dealing* vbl. sb. s.v. WHEEL AND DEAL *v.*

1968 *N.Y. Times* 1 Feb. 42 Wondering what wheeler-dealing was going on over telephone lines among the various managements. **1976** *Listener* 5 Feb. 135/3 To ensure that.. councils (or the community) got the upper hand in any wheeler-dealing between councils and developers. **1979** *Daily Tel.* 27 Apr. 36/6 Mr Prior also stressed that voting liberal could mean another 'hung' Parliament which would mean more 'wheeler dealing' at Westminster. **1984** *Listener* 22 Mar. 4/1 It is here in the intricate wheeler-dealing of the Common Market, the Atlantic alliance and international trade and finance that the 'diplomatic' reputations of the future will be made.

wheelerite ('hwi:lərait). *Min.* [Named from Lieut. G. M. *Wheeler*, of the U.S. Army: see -ITE[1].] A yellowish fossil resin occurring in lignite in the cretaceous strata of New Mexico.

1874 *Amer. Jrnl. Sci.* Ser. III. VII. 571.

wheelery ('hwi:ləri). *rare.* [f. WHEEL *v.* + -ERY.] Wheeling, circumgyration.

1847 BARHAM *Ingol. Leg.* Ser. III. *Truants*, With curlings and twistings, and twirls and wheeleries.

'wheel-house. Also **wheel house, wheelhouse**.

1. A structure enclosing a large wheel, *e.g.* a water-wheel; *spec.* a house or superstructure containing the steering-wheel, a pilot-house; also, the paddle-box of a steam-boat.

1835 J. H. INGRAHAM *South-West* I. xxiii. 247 The pilot (as the helms-man is here called) stands in his lonely wheel-house. **1846** A. HAWKINS *Let.* 20 Nov. in N. E. Eliason *Tarheel Talk* (1956) 304 The carpenter in coming out of the wheel house whare he had been mending the wheel dropd the candle on some loose cotton. **1850** B. TAYLOR *Eldorado* i. (1862) 3 On the morning of July 5th, I took a station on the wheel-house. **1883** GRESLEY *Gloss. Coal-Mining* 285. **1892** J. S. FLETCHER *When Chas. I was King* (1896) 26 The mill at Wentbridge, where the stream was pouring through the wheel-house like a cataract. **1906** 'MARK TWAIN' *Autobiogr.* I. 310 Rush..astern to the solitary lifeboat lashed aft the wheelhouse on the port side. **1976** *Southern Even. Echo* (Southampton) 2 Nov. 20/1 On the roof of the main building is a full size replica of a ship's wheelhouse which is used for training.

2. a. A building in which cart-wheels are stored.

1813 VANCOUVER *Agric. Devon* 472 The wheel-house under the barn, 25 feet square.

b. = ROUND-HOUSE *sb.* 3 a.

1971 [see ROUND-HOUSE *sb.* 3 a].

3. *Archæol.* A circular stone dwelling of the late Iron Age of a type widespread in northern and western Scotland, having partition walls radiating from the centre. Cf. *wheel-dwelling, -hut* s.v. WHEEL *sb.* 19.

1935 V. G. CHILDE *Prehist. Scotland* x. 217 A wheel-house is in essence a walled area roughly circular or oval..divided up into a number of voussoir-shaped rooms or compartments by radial walls arranged like the spokes of a wheel. **1957** T. C. LETHBRIDGE *Gogmagog* viii. 149 A considerable mass of pottery of what must be considered Iron Age culture, though of Roman date, has now been recovered from brochs and wheel-houses in the Hebrides. **1970** BRAY & TRUMP *Dict. Archaeol.* 254/2 Wheelhouses survived well into the Roman period as dwellings and farmhouses.

wheelie ('hwi:li). *slang.* Also (*rare*) **wheely**. [f. WHEEL *sb.* + -IE.] **1.** orig. *U.S.* **a.** The stunt of raising the front wheel off the ground while riding a bicycle or motor-cycle.

1966 *N.Y. Times* 12 Nov. 45 A popular sport for young bicycle riders is 'doing a wheelie'. This means lifting the front wheel off the ground and balancing on the rear wheel alone. **1969** *Oz* Apr. 31/1 Odd Job tries to do a few wheelies but can't quite get the front wheel off the ground. **1975** *Courier-Mail* (Brisbane) 6 Dec. 2/4 Wheelies are no trouble to the world 125cc motocross champion... But..it's a technique he uses strictly off the road. **1982** *Daily Tel.* 25 June 6/7 Acquitting a motor-cyclist..of careless driving by performing a 'wheelie'—driving with his front wheel off the road. **1985** *Daily Mail* 6 Apr. 25/1 That's the bike seen on TV with crash-hatted kids doing wheelies.

b. *transf.* In skateboarding, the stunt of riding on only one pair of wheels, with either the nose or tail of the board in the air. (In quot. 1978 further *transf.*)

1976 A. CASSORLA *Skateboarder's Bible* 10 Many of the tricks now popular originated that year, including nose and tail wheelies. **1978** *Evening Standard* 10 May 8/1 Wheelies centre rolls to a close. A pioneer skateboard centre is closing through lack of support. **1979** W. JONES in *Voices 20* Autumn 43 Down the subway he doth go..Out the other end and into a wheely.

2. A sharp U-turn made by a motor vehicle, causing skidding of the wheels. orig. *Austral.*

1973 *Sunday Mail* (Brisbane) 29 July 3/1 'Hoons' felt free to do 'wheelies'—making U-turns at high speed to make their tyres scream. **1977** *Custom Car* Nov. 63/2 One of the most hair-raising wheelies I've ever seen..necessitating an extensive chassis rebuild. **1982** J. S. BORTHWICK *Case of Hook-Billed Kites* xxxvi. 122 Tom did a wheelie into Route 77.

3. *Austral.* A person in or confined to a wheelchair.

1977 *Courier-Mail* (Brisbane) 14 Nov. 2/3 Terry Valentine braces the wheelchair as wheelie-shotputter Rene Ahrens..prepares to make his toss. **1978** *Sunday Mail* (Brisbane) 10 Sept. 34/3 So many places and things are inaccessible to the 'wheelie'. **1981** *Telegraph* (Brisbane) 14 Jan. 44/2 The wheelie symbol on selected parking spaces.. is often ignored.

wheeling ('hwi:lɪŋ), *vbl. sb.* [f. WHEEL *v.* + -ING[1].] The action of the verb WHEEL, in various senses.

a. Turning or revolution about an axis or centre; rotation. Also *fig.* **b.** *Mil.* (See WHEEL *v.* 3.) Also *attrib.* **c.** A turning aside or in a different direction, deviation; also *fig.* **d.** Motion (or *transf.* extension) in a circle or curve; circling, circuitous movement; also *fig.* **e.** Conveyance of something in a wheelbarrow or the like; travelling in a wheeled vehicle, or (*colloq.*) on a bicycle or tricycle; also, the condition of a road suitable for the passage of (wheeled) vehicles. Also *attrib.* **f.** Furnishing or fitting with a wheel or wheels. **g.** *Needlework.* The making or working of 'wheels': see WHEEL *sb.* 9 a (*a*); *attrib.* as in ***wheeling stitch, yarn***, etc. †**h.** Torturing or 'breaking' on a wheel. *Obs.* **i.** The process of shaping or forming something by means of a wheel; in quots. *attrib.* **j.** ***wheeling and dealing***: see WHEEL AND DEAL *v.* Also **wheeling-dealing** *vbl. sb.* and *ppl. a.*

a. *a* **1483** EARL RIVERS *Ball.* 6 in Ritson *Anc. Songs* (1877) 150 This world being Of such whelyng Me contrarieng. **1587** GOLDING *De Mornay* xiii. 223 The wheelings about of the Skye. **1594** NASHE *Terrors Nt.* Wks. (Grosart) III. 269 As the firmament is still mouing and working, so vncessant is the wheeling and rolling on of our braines. *a* **1680** BUTLER *Rem.* (1759) I. 318 All Rotations and Wheelings cause a kind of Giddiness in the Brain. **1773** MRS. GRANT *Lett. fr. Mount.* (1807) I. xiii. 105 The 'boiling' and 'wheeling' of the waters below.

b. 1623 'JACK DAWE' *Vox Graculi* 38 What wheelings, what windings, what summoning to parlees. **1625** MARKHAM *Souldiers Accid.* 22 Wheeling (as by conversion or turning to either hand). **1796** *Instr. & Reg. Cavalry* (1813) 15 In division Wheelings, the whole keep closed lightly towards the hand they wheel to, and must avoid pressing the pivot man off his ground. **1832** *Prop. Regul. Instr. Cavalry* II. 10 Wheeling should at first be practised in single rank. **1833** *Regul. Instr. Cavalry* I. 20 The Wheeling Step, or March, is 120 steps of 30 inches each, or 300 feet in a minute. **1894** *Outing* (U.S.) XXIV. 236/1 The wheelings and dress are fully equal to the best regular regiments.

c. *a* **1660** *Contemp. Hist. Irel.* (Ir. Archæol. Soc.) I. 182 His unconstant whilinges to Ormond. *a* **1711** KEN *Anodynes* Poet. Wks. 1721 III. 431, I sooner cou'd of shifting Wind, The Rise, Recess, and Wheelings find, Than of my heart detect the Wiles.

d. 1674 N. FAIRFAX *Bulk & Selv.* 24 After all this wheeling about, we are not a step further than we were. **1789** J. WILLIAMS *Min. Kingd.* I. 15 A different dip or declivity of the strata, which is occasioned by the waving and wheeling of the strata. **1839** MRS. KIRKLAND *New Home* xvi. 101 We had been watching the wheelings and flittings of a flock of prairie hens. **1876** GEO. ELIOT *Dan. Der.* xxx, The hovering and wheeling of Grandcourt's caprice.

e. 1805 R. W. DICKSON *Pract. Agric.* I. 113 When stones can be got within a wheeling distance, or about sixty or seventy yards. **1850** L. SAWYER *Jrnl.* 3 July in *Way Sketches* (1926) v. 81 Our road lay over deep barren sand, which rendered the wheeling very difficult. **1864** *Ret. Agric. Soc. Maine* 52 The January thaw..gives us bare hills and wheeling. **1873** 'G. HAMILTON' *Twelve Miles* ii. 25 He told her he would give her a sleigh-ride when it came wheeling. **1882** *Prospectus Cycle Touring Club*, The encouragement of all that is admirable in the art of wheeling. **1883** *Harper's Mag.* Oct. 727/2 Travelling in the saddle was..a necessity, wheeling is now everywhere easy.

f. 1661 in Swayne *Churchw. Acc. Sarum* (1896) 334 Stocking and wheeling of the same [*sc.* bells]. **1875** *Carpentry & Join.* 120 Far more suitable for amateurs than building or 'wheeling' as it is termed. **1898** *Daily News* 21 Feb. 6/5 The gearing and wheeling of the cars.

g. 1808 JAMIESON, *Wheelin*, coarse worsted. **1862** *Catal. Internat. Exhib., Brit.* II. No. 4032, Fingering, lambs-wool, and wheeling hosiery. **1880** *Plain Hints Needlework* 29 Wheeling yarn.

h. 1611 CORYAT *Crudities* 388 The fifth and last punishment is wheeling, which is onely for murderers.

i. 1882 *Standard* 16 Sept. 8/2 Brickmakers' plant and stock, comprising..iron wheeling plates. **1884** *B'ham Daily Post* 23 Feb. 2/4 Tin and Iron-plate workers, &c... Wireing, Swaging and Wheeling Machines.

j. 1973 *Guardian* 21 June 2/3 The cliché of the moment is that Mr Brezhnev is..a sort of wheeling-dealing gladhander. **1977** *Guardian Weekly* 28 Aug. 22/4 The wheeling-dealing that went on within the tribunal when it came to considering the verdicts.

wheeling (ˈhwiːlɪŋ), *ppl. a.* [f. WHEEL *v.* + -ING².] That wheels, in various senses.

a. Turning like a wheel; revolving about an axis; rotating, rolling, whirling, swirling. Also *fig.* of a recurring or 'revolving' period of time. **b.** *Mil.* (See WHEEL *v.* 3.) *wheeling flank*, the outward flank in wheeling, which describes the largest curve. **c.** Turning round or aside; changing direction. **d.** Moving, or executed as a movement, in a circle or similar curve; circling. †In first quot., wandering about, roving. **e.** Moving on wheels.

a. **1628** MILTON *Vac. Exerc.* 34 Where the deep transported mind may soare Above the wheeling poles. **1635** L. FOXE *N.-W. Fox* 187 Wheeling streames like edie tides. **1636** W. CARTWRIGHT *Royal Slave* v. ii, Hemm'd in on every side With Beauties, which his wheeling eye runs o're All in a Minute. **1725** RAMSAY *Gentle Sheph.* IV. ii, With Patience then I'll wait each wheeling Year. **1742** YOUNG *Nt. Th.* IX. 1274 What arm Almighty put these wheeling globes In motion? **1818** SCOTT *Rob Roy* xxxiii, The deep and wheeling stream of the river.

b. **1796** *Instr. & Reg. Cavalry* (1813) 41 An officer or under officer from the wheeling flank..of each squadron. **1833** *Reg. Instr. Cavalry* I. 23 The outward wheeling man.. lengthens his step.

c. **1716** POPE *Iliad* v. 53 As he to Flight his wheeling Car addrest. *a* **1769** FALCONER *Shipwr.* III. 388 The pilots..Still with the wheeling stern their force repel. **1882** 'OUIDA' *Bimbi* vi. 186 He endeavoured to soothe his fretting and wheeling beast.

d. **1604** SHAKS. *Oth.* I. i. 137 Tying her Dutie, Beautie, Wit, and Fortunes In an extrauagant, and wheeling Stranger. **1650** BULWER *Anthropomet.* 263 We are faine to use a wheeling-stride, and go as it were in orbe. **1697** DRYDEN *Virg. Georg.* IV. 803 Dark as a Cloud they make a wheeling Flight. **1730–46** THOMSON *Autumn* 487 Happy he who tops the wheeling chase. **1805–6** CARY *Dante, Inf.* III. 93 Around whose eyes glared wheeling flames. **1827** KEBLE *Chr. Y., 20th Sunday after Trin.*, The wheeling kite's wild solitary cry. **1905** TREVES *Other Side of Lantern* II. xxii. 142 Pigeons sweep round this square in wheeling flocks.

e. **1596** SIR J. DAVIES *Orchestra* cxv, A wheeling Cart. **1637** WHITING *Albino & Bellama* 21 Goe harnesse straight my wheeling chaire. **1773** LADY MARY COKE *Jrnl.* 22 Aug. (1896) IV. 225 He was placed in a wheeling chair, as he has not the use of his legs. **1902** *Brit. Med. Jrnl.* 12 Apr. 907/2 A new stretcher, which could be used either as a light portable or as a wheeling stretcher.

Hence **ˈwheelingly** *adv.* on wheels. *rare.*

1611 FLORIO, *A ruóta*, wheelingly.

wheelless (ˈhwiːllɪs), *a.* [f. WHEEL *sb.* + -LESS.] Without a wheel or wheels; having no wheels; not adapted to wheeled vehicles.

1824 MISS FERRIER *Inher.* xxvii, The carpet..was.. strewed with headless dolls, tailless horses, wheelless carts. **1848** DICKENS *Dombey* xxxvii, Withers..stood upright.. behind her wheel-less chair at dinner-time. **1897** *Q. Rev.* Oct. 470 In many a rollicking expedition in wheelless Liddesdale.

ˈwheel-lock. [f. WHEEL *sb.* + LOCK *sb.*²]

1. A form of gun-lock in which the powder was fired by the friction of a small wheel (wound up with a spring) against a piece of iron pyrites. Also *attrib.*

1670 COTTON *Espernon.* I. IV. 181 The wheel-lock of a Pistol, ready wound up. **1677** PLOT *Oxfordsh.* 71 These.. have been much used for Carabines and Pistols, whil'st Wheel-locks were in fashion. **1821** EDGEWORTH *Mem.* (ed. 2) I. 279 Guns,..some with old match-locks,..and others with wheel-locks. **1860** HEWITT *Anc. Armour* III. 589 Their [*sc.* German Reiters' or pistoliers'] characteristic arm, the wheel-lock pistol. **1904** TYLOR *Anthropol.* i. 17 The match-lock led up to the wheel-lock, and that again to the flint-lock musket.

2. A form of letter-lock (see LETTER *sb.*¹ 9) with a series of wheels or disks upon the edges of which the letters were inscribed.

1875 KNIGHT *Dict. Mech.*

3. a. (See quot.)

1875 KNIGHT *Dict. Mech.*, *Wheel-lock*, a wagon-lock, to retard the revolution of the wheels in descending a hill.

b. = LOCK *sb.*² 15.

1927 *Observer* 20 Feb. 21/3 The majority of our fire-fighting appliances are not provided with adequate wheel-locks.

wheelman (ˈhwiːlmən). Pl. **-men.** Also **wheelsman.** [f. WHEEL *sb.* + MAN *sb.*¹]

1. A man who attends to a wheel in some piece of mechanism; *U.S.* a helmsman.

1865 *Oregon State Jrnl.* 12 Aug. 2/5 The wheelman says that large fragments of the bottom and a part of the rudder were afterwards seen alongside the wreck. **1866** 'MARK TWAIN' *Lett. from Hawaii* (1967) 195 Four other gentlemen and the wheelsman were all assembled on the little after portion of the deck. **1885** *Harper's Mag.* Mar. 643/1 The.. wheelsman..tries to entice her up to his pilot-box, which towers above the vessel. **1886** J. BARROWMAN *Sc. Mining Terms* 72.

2. A man who rides a bicycle or tricycle; a male cyclist. *colloq.*

1881 *Tribune* (N.Y.) 5 Apr., An enthusiastic wheelman of Boston had not up to January 1, missed but one day riding on his 'steely steed' since the winter season commenced. **1887** *Morning Post* 8 Apr., A reconnaissance can be carried out more quickly..by wheelmen than by horsemen.

3. A driver, *spec.* (*Criminals' slang*) the driver of a getaway vehicle. orig. *U.S.*

1935 J. HARGAN *Gloss. Prison Lang.* 8 *Wheelman*, driver of a getaway car. **1962** 'K. ORVIS' *Damned & Destroyed* xii. 80 Later on,..he began driving a cab. Also being a wheel-man for the mobs. **1967** M. PROCTER *Exercise Hoodwink* vi. 44 The thieves had locked themselves in, and when they had emptied the safe, they had phoned for their wheel man like calling for a taxi. **1975** *Publishers Weekly* 27 Jan. 283/3 (Advt.), When a young California hoodlum blew the brains out of a helpless store clerk last year Ken Pestana was the unwitting wheelman waiting outside.

So **ˈwheel,woman**, a female cyclist.

1884 *Pall Mall Gaz.* 5 Sept. 11/2 Wheelmen and wheel-women.

wheelwork (ˈhwiːlwɜːk). [f. WHEEL *sb.* + WORK *sb.*] **a.** A set of connected wheels forming part of a machine or mechanical contrivance.

1670 EVELYN *Sylva* xxiii. (ed. 2) 115 The Cornel-tree..is exceedingly commended for its durablenesse, and use in Wheel-work, Pinns, and Wedges. **1772** C. HUTTON *Bridges* 99 Pile Driver, is an engine for driving down the piles... It is worked..either with or without wheel work. **1825** J. NICHOLSON *Oper. Mech.* 347 These spindles are connected with wheel-work. **1845** G. DODD *Brit. Manuf.* IV. 29 This axle, by the aid of intervening wheel-work, is set into rotation.

b. Applied to the trochal apparatus of a rotifer or *wheel-animalcule.*

1778 *Encycl. Brit.* (ed. 2) I. 448/2 The most remarkable part of this animalcule is its wheel-work.

c. Applied to the works of a watch or other time-piece. Also *fig.*

1843 *Penny Cycl.* XXVII. 107/2 In a repeater there is an additional train of wheels between the frame-plates, called the runners, or little wheel-work. **1868** *Chambers's Encycl.* X. 82/1 The arrangement of the wheel-work in a watch. **1890** W. JAMES *Princ. Psychol.* II. xix. 112 There seem no good grounds for supposing this additional wheelwork in the mind. **1981** *Times* 2 May 15/4 Examination of the instrument reveals nothing inconsistent with it being a bench-timer, possibly contrived from an early frame and wheel work.

wheelwright (ˈhwiːlraɪt). Forms: see WHEEL *sb.* and WRIGHT.

1. A man who makes wheels and wheeled vehicles.

1281 *Pat. 9 Edw. I* m. 22 d. in *50th Rep. Dep. Kpr. Rec.* 22 Richard le Whelwryht. **1482** *Howard Househ. Bks.* (Roxb.) 198 To the whele wryte of Boxford for exyng of a carte v.d. **1483** *Cath. Angl.* 415/2 A Whele wryght, *rotarius.* **1523–34** FITZHERB. *Husb.* §134 If there be asshes in it, [I advise thee] to sell.. the gret asshes to whele-wryghtes. **1534** *Nottingham Rec.* III. 373 Thomas Hobe..the qwyl-wryght. **1662** in *Proc. Suffolk Inst. Archæol.* (1883) VI. 90 To Jno Blomfield Whealewright as by his bill, 01 05 00. **1799** *Monthly Rev.* XXX. 486 They carry with them only their best wood for spars and wheelwright's work. **1866** GEO. ELIOT *F. Holt* Introd., The wheelwright putting the last touch to a blue cart with red wheels.

†**2.** One who works at or turns a wheel: applied to Fortune (cf. WHEEL *sb.* 12 a). *Obs.*

a **1300** *Poem on Fortune* v. in *Rel. Ant.* II. 8 A wifman of so much myȝth, So wonder a whelwryȝth, Sey I nevere with syȝth. *c* **1420** *Anturs of Arth.* xxi. (Thornton MS.) False fortune in fyghte, That wondirfulle whele wryghte.

Hence **ˈwheel,wrighting**, the business of a wheelwright: the making of wheels and wheeled vehicles.

1883 *Rep. Indian Affairs* (U.S.) 253 Carpentry, harness-making, wheelwrighting. **1894** *Review of Rev.* Apr. 441/2 Wheel-wrighting also grows of necessity out of the making and care of the wagons and other vehicles of the farm.

wheely (ˈhwiːlɪ), *a. rare.* [f. WHEEL *sb.* + -Y¹.] Of or pertaining to a wheel.

c **1626** BOSWORTH *Arcadius & Sepha* I. 957 Fortune (whose continual wheely force Keeps constant course). **1708** J. PHILIPS *Cyder* II. 80 To exercise the pointed Steel On the hard Rock, and give a wheely Form, To the expected Grinder.

wheem(e, dial. forms of QUEME *a.*

wheen (hwiːn), *a.* and *sb. Sc.* and *north. dial.* Forms: 4–5 **quheine, qwheyn(e**, 4–6 **quheyn(e, -en(e**, (5 **qwhayne**, 7 **whein, wheene**, 9 **whean**), 7–9 **whin**, 7– **wheen.** [Represents OE. *hwéne* (*hwǽne, hwǽne*) in some degree, somewhat, instrumental case of *hwón* WHON = (a) few, the meanings of which it took over in ME.]

1. Few, not many.

1375 BARBOUR *Bruce* II. 244 Thocht thai war qwheyn, thai war worthy. *Ibid.* XI. 605 Quhenar be full fer war thai Than thair fayis. *c* **1400** *Sc. Trojan War* (Horstm.) II. 2283 Þe quheyne folk þat ware Liffand. **1513** DOUGLAS *Æneis* I. iii. 43 On the huge deip quhen salaris did appear. **1557** *Extr. Aberd. Reg.* (1844) I. 303 Within thir quheyne last immediat yeiris. **1894** *Northumbld. Gloss.* s.v., Aa hevn't seen him these wheen days.

absol. *c* **1375** *Sc. Leg. Saints* xl. (*Ninian*) 921 þe best part of þaim ves slane, &..quheine eschapit. *c* **1425** WYNTOUN *Cron.* IV. vii. 740 Qwhayne had toyme þar aynde to draw. **1500–20** DUNBAR *Poems* xiv. 14 So quhene the Psalme and Testament to reid Within this land was nevir hard nor sene.

2. *a wheen* (*of*), a few: in recent use = a 'good few', a fair number.

1375 BARBOUR *Bruce* VIII. 368 The king..With a quheyn [*Edin. MS.* quhone] lik poueralȝe, Vencust him vith a gret menȝe. **1513** DOUGLAS *Æneis* III. vi. 45 Of mony wordis, schortlie, a quhene sall I Declair. **1680** in *Proc. Soc. Antiq. Scot.* XLV. 237 A wheen of..canny wise professors. *Ibid.* 241 A whin knaves. **1682** PEDEN *Lord's Trumpet* 20 O sirs! Christ had a whein noble worthies in Scotland. **1814** SCOTT *Wav.* lxv, What use has my father for a whin bits o' scarted paper? **1816** —— *Antiq.* xxiv, There will be a wheen idle gowks coming to glower at the hole as lang as it is day-light. **1886** STEVENSON *Kidnapped* iii. 23, I wouldnae like the Balfours to be humbled before a wheen Hieland Campbells. **1901** G. DOUGLAS *Ho. w. Gr. Shutters* 71 'Have the carriers a big load?' 'Andy has just a wheen parcels, but Elshie's as fu' as he can haud.'

3. *a wheen* as advb. phr.: A little, somewhat.

1869 C. GIBBON *Robin Gray* x, The auld wife's a wheen better.

wheen(e, obs. or dial. ff. QUEEN *sb.*

1340 HAMPOLE *Pr. Consc.* v. 4463 Þe qwene [*MS. Bowes 136* wheene] of Amazons.

wheen, wheenerd, wheenge: see WHINE, WINNARD, WHINGE.

whee-oh, -oo. Imitative of the cry of some birds, of a bullet whistling through the air.

1892 LOWNDES *Camping Sk.* 19 The shrill 'whee-oh' of the widgeon. **1915** *Chamb. Jrnl.* 5 June 426/1 Whee-oo! whistled a bullet..uncomfortably close to my head.

wheep, *sb.* [Echoic.] A long-drawn sound of a steel weapon drawn from its sheath.

1891 KIPLING *Life's Hand., Head Distr.* v, The soft wheep, wheep of unscabbarded knives. **1905** CROCKETT *Cherry Ribband* xlvi, With the long clean wheep of steel leaving steel, he unsheathed his sword.

wheep (hwiːp), *v. Sc.* and *north. dial.* [Imitative.] = WHEEPLE *v.*

1808 JAMIESON, *To Wheep*, 1. To give a sharp whistle at intervals. 2. To squeak. **1894** A. REID *Sangs o' Heatherld.* 39 The plover wheepit owre the lea.

wheep, Sc. form of WHIP.

wheeple (ˈhwiːp(ə)l), *v. Sc.* and *north. dial.* [Imitative.] *intr.* To utter a somewhat protracted shrill cry, like the curlew or plover; also, to whistle feebly (*intr.* and *trans.*). So **wheeple** *sb.*

1793 *Statist. Acc. Scot.* VII. 601 *note*, I wad na' gie the wheeple of a whaup for a the nightingales that ever sang. **1818** HOGG *Brownie of Bodsbeck, Hunt of Eildon* v, Like Redwings wheepling through the mist. *a* **1837** R. NICOLL *Poems* (1843) 284 We've a' been heathens—now we pray, And sing and wheeple. **1901** G. DOUGLAS *Ho. w. Gr. Shutters* 80 He sometimes wheepled a tune.

wheer, wheese, wheesh, wheesht, wheest, Wheeson: see WHERE, WEESE, WHEEZE, WHISH, WHISHT, WHIST *int.*¹, WHITSUN.

wheetle (ˈhwiːt(ə)l), *v.* Chiefly *Sc.* [Imitative: cf. *wheeple.*] *intr.* To whistle shrilly. Also reduplicated.

1825 JAMIESON, *Wheetle*, sharp peeping sound made by young birds. **1849** CUPPLES *Green Hand* xvi, A loud clear wheetle-wheetling note from some curious fowl. **1865** H. KINGSLEY *Hillyars & Burtons* l, Parrots..who, crowded in long rows, kissed one another, and wheetled idiotically.

wheetle, Sc. var. WHEEDLE.

wheeze (hwiːz), *sb.* [f. next.]

1. An act of wheezing; a whistling sound caused by difficult breathing.

1834 *Good's Study Med.* (ed. 4) I. 477 *note*, A loud sibilant or dry sonorous rhoncus, corresponding with the loud sighing wheeze, audible by the naked ear. **1848** DICKENS *Dombey* xx, A wheeze very like the cough of a horse. **1872** CALVERLEY *Fly Leaves* 90 A ladylike sneeze, Or a portly papa's more elaborate wheeze.

b. *transf.* A sound resembling this.

1835 LONGF. *Outre-Mer, Vill. Auteuil* (1886) 55 The last wheeze of the clarionet died upon my ear. **1880** SWINBURNE *Stud. Shaks.* 220 A somewhat hoarse and reedy wheeze from the scrannel-pipe of a lesser player than Pan.

c. *Phonetics.* A whisper (see WHISPER *sb.*) intensified by further contraction of the glottis.

1890 SWEET *Primer of Phonetics* (1902) 12 Wheeze. If we strongly exaggerate an ordinary whisper, we get that hoarse, wheezy sound known as the 'wheezing' or 'stage whisper'.

2. orig. *Theatr. slang*, A joke or comic gag introduced into the performance of a piece by a clown or comedian, esp. a comic phrase or saying introduced repeatedly; hence, (*gen. slang* or *colloq.*) a catch phrase constantly repeated; more widely, a trick or dodge frequently used; also, a piece of special information, a 'tip'.

1864 P. PATERSON *Glimpses Real Life* 131 The art of getting up 'wheezes', as the clown's jokes are called. **1884** G. MOORE *Mummer's Wife* xiv, Up to the present, only one 'wheeze' had been found. **1885** *Longm. Mag.* Nov. 18 He [*sc.* the comedian]..would, for a quarter of an hour together, improvise 'wheezes' to keep the house in a roar. **1890** *Spectator* 17 May 698/2 The now hackneyed wheeze, 'A sudden thought strikes me, let us swear eternal friendship,' is taken from 'The Rovers'. **1903** *Blackw. Mag.* Oct. 534/1 He is now wisely convinced that this wheeze is played out. **1906** *Daily Chron.* 30 Aug. 2/6 Someone gave the defendant the wheeze. **1910** *Dundee Adv.* 2 July 6 The old wheeze about one touch of nature making the whole world kin.

wheeze (hwiːz), *v.* Forms: 5 **whese**, 6 **whiese, wease**, 6–8 **whease, wheese**, 6–9 **wheaze**, 8 **wheez**, 7– **wheeze.** [prob. a. ON. *hvæsa* to hiss (MSw., Sw. *hväsa*, Da. *hvæse*). (There is no connexion with OE. *hwósan*, 3rd pers. pres. ind. *hwést*, pa. t. *hwéos* to cough, dial. HOOSE.)]

1. *intr.* To breathe hard with a whistling sound from dryness or obstruction in the throat, as in asthma.

c **1460** *Towneley Myst.* xvi. 472, I lagh that I whese. **1538**, etc. [see WHEEZING *vbl. sb.* and *ppl. a.*]. *c* **1611** CHAPMAN *Iliad* xv. 222 Not stretcht upon his bed, Nor wheasing with a stopt-up spirit. **1648** WINYARD *Mids.-Moon* 6 Hee'l shortly be a Baptist without a voice, and wheases already, as if he fed on nothing but Locusts and Grashoppers. **1679** DRYDEN *Troil. & Cress.* I. i, Tickling his spleen, and laughing till he wheeze. **1684** SOUTHERNE *Disappointm.* II. i, I must laugh at him; not sooth him in his vanity, nor tickle him, till he wheeze. **1697** R. PEIRCE *Bath Mem.* II. ii. 278 She.. wheesed, as they vulgarly term it here, when the Windpipe makes a Noise in Breathing. **1809** W. IRVING *Knickerb.* VII. ix, Wheezing as he went with corpulency and terror. **1869** TROLLOPE *He knew*, etc. li. (1878) 281 'I'm not a bit afraid to die', said the old woman, wheezing. **1875** WHYTE-MELVILLE *Katerfelto* xiv, He chatted, he chuckled, he coughed and wheezed, and told his stories.

b. *transf.* To make a similar sound.

1854 G. W. CURTIS *Potiphar Papers* iv. (1866) 127 That elegant youth has pumped life dry, and now the pump only wheezes. **1895** S. CRANE *Red Badge* v, Like a firework... It wheezed and banged with a mighty power.

2. *trans.* To utter with a sound of wheezing.

1849 LEVER *Con Cregan* xiv, 'If you'll look in that glass yonder, which is opposite the mirror, you'll soon see!' wheezed out the old man, maliciously. **1880** P. LUDLOW *Nick Hardy at Coll.* vi, A hand-organ grinder.. began to wheeze forth the entrancing strains of 'Old Dog Tray'. **1905** A. T. SHEPPARD *Red Cravat* III. x. 362 A barrack clock, wheezing out the hour. **1905** F. YOUNG *Sands Pleas.* II. vii, Listening to the strain of *Dies Irae* wheezed out on an old harmonium.

3. *Comb.*, as ***wheeze-belly*** used attrib.

1728 VANBR. & CIBBER *Prov. Husb.* I. i, We were in hopes to ha' come Yesterday, an' it had no' been that th' owld Wheaze-belly Horse tyr'd.

wheeze, obs. form of WEESE, to ooze.

wheezer ('hwiːzə(r)). [f. WHEEZE *v.* + -ER[1].] One who wheezes; *esp.* a broken-winded horse.

1831 YOUATT *Horse* x. 196 The Wheezer utters a sound not unlike that of an asthmatic person when a little hurried. **1844** H. STEPHENS *Bk. Farm* II. 227.

transf. **1915** *Blackw. Mag.* Aug. 259/1 Beastly cold on top of this old wheezer [*sc.* omnibus].

wheezing ('hwiːzɪŋ), *vbl. sb.* [f. WHEEZE *v.* + -ING[1].] The action of the verb WHEEZE.

1538 ELYOT Addit., *Asthma*.. a sycknesse, where one maye not fetche his wynde but with moche difficultie, with weasynge [**1565** COOPER wheesing] of the breast. **1576** [T. TWYNE] *Schoolem.* I. xxviii. D iij b, Cresses.. clense the Lunges, and take away the wheesing. **1683** TRYON *Way to Health* 178 Coughs, Wheesings, Shortness of Breath. **1758** *Phil. Trans.* L. 572 She had a frequent and severe cough, with great shortness of breath and a wheezing. **1848** DICKENS *Dombey* xxvi, The Major.. fell into a fit of wheezing. **1898** *Allbutt's Syst. Med.* V. 283 In the treatment of the attacks of wheezing, so often met with in emphysema.

transf. **1862** SMILES *Engineers* III. 9 The working of a Newcomen engine is.. accompanied by an extraordinary amount of wheezing, sighing, creaking, and bumping.

wheezing ('hwiːzɪŋ), *ppl. a.* [f. WHEEZE *v.* + -ING[2].] That wheezes; characterized by wheezing.

1560 GOOGE tr. *Palingenius' Zodiac* III. (1561) F iv, Heare soundes with wheasyng noyse, The boxen shalme. **16..** MIDDLETON, etc. *Old Law* II. ii, A cough o' the lungs, or say a wheezing matter. **1697** DRYDEN *Virg. Georg.* III. 745 The wheasing Swine With Coughs is choak'd. **1730** SWIFT *Panegyr. Dean* 278 Wheezing asthma, loth to stir. **1874** LISLE CARR *Judith Gwynne* i, The.. dismal droning of the wheezing old organ. **1905** TREVES *Other Side Lant.* II. xii. 90, I entered the hallowed town in a wheezing carriage.

Hence '**wheezingly** *adv.*

1886 *Homilet. Rev.* (U.S.) Nov. 412 Wheezingly saying to himself in secret, 'Soul, be of good cheer'. **1895** ZANGWILL *Master* II. ix. 233 He laughed wheezingly.

wheezle ('hwiːz(ə)l), *v.* Chiefly *Sc.* and *north. dial.* Also 8–9 **wheazle, whaizle**, 9 **wha(i)sle, wheasle, wheezel, whazle, whozzle**, etc. [f. WHEEZE *v.* + -LE.] *intr.* To wheeze. Hence '**wheezling** *vbl. sb.* and *ppl. a.*

1779 *Mirror* No. 40 ¶3 One of your damnation apoplectics kill'd him in the chucking of a bumper; you could scarce have heard him wheazle! **1786** BURNS *Auld Farmer's Salut. Mare* x, But sax Scotch miles thou try't their mettle, An' gart them whaizle. **1808** MAYNE *Siller Gun* II. xxii, Tho' whozzling sair and cruppen down Auld Saunders seem'd. **1839** *Whistle-Binkie* Ser. I. 83 Gin the win' were out o' your whaisling hauze, I'd marry again and be voggie, O. **1880** *Antrim & Down Gloss.* s.v. *Wasslin'*, Do you hear the chile wasslin' in his chest?

So '**wheezle** *sb.*, a wheeze.

1822 HOGG *Perils of Man* II. 346 My voice went away to a perfect wheezle. **1825** BROCKETT *N.C. Gloss.*, *Whazle*, an indication of asthma.

wheezy ('hwiːzɪ), *a.* [f. WHEEZE + -Y[1].] Characterized by wheezing; resembling a wheeze.

1818 KEATS *To a Cat* 10 The wheezy asthma. **1822** GOOD *Study Med.* I. 466 Many persons have a thick or wheezy respiration. **1843** THACKERAY *Fitz-Boodle's Conf.*, *Ottilia* ii, The Chancellor is.. too fat and wheezy to preside at the Privy Council. **1892** 'F. ANSTEY' *Voces Pop.* Ser. II. 13 A couple of Matrons converse in wheezy whispers.

b. *transf.* Making a wheezing sound.

1847 THACKERAY *Love Songs, Cane-bottomed Chair*, The rickety, ramshackle, wheezy spinet. **1859** H. KINGSLEY *G. Hamlyn* xii, A lean, wheezy old clock. **1889** JEROME *Three Men in Boat* ix, The strains of 'He's got 'em on', jerked.. out of a wheezy accordion.

Hence '**wheezily** *adv.*, '**wheeziness**.

1884 *Punch* 27 Dec. 306/2 Breath that comes not wheezily. **1898** *Allbutt's Syst. Med.* V. 288 More or less wheeziness and constriction of the chest.

wheft, variant of WAFT *sb.*[1]

whefyll, obs. form of WHEEL.

whegh, var. WIE, WY, man.

wheill, obs. form of WHEEL.

whein, wheint, obs. dial. ff. QUEAN, QUAINT *a.*

wheire, obs. form of CHOIR, QUIRE.

1528 *Test. Ebor.* (Surtees) V. 248 In the hie wheire of oure Blisside Ladie in the pariche church of Ellughton.

wheisht, wheit, wheither: see WHISHT, WEIGHT *sb.*[2], WHET, WHETHER.

whel, whele, obs. forms of WEEL, WHEAL, WHEEL, WHILE.

whelk[1] (hwɛlk). Forms: α. 1 **wioloc, wiloc, wyloc**, (2 **wilque**), 4–5 **wylke**, 4–8 **wilke**, 5–9 **wilk**. β. 7–9 **whilk**. γ. 1 **weoloc, -uc**, (2 **welche**), 2–7 **welke**, 4–7 **welk**, 6 **wealk**. δ. 5–6 **whelke**, 7– **whelk**. ε. 5 **wolke**, 5–6 **walke**. [OE. *wioloc, weoloc* = WFlem. *willok, wullok* (whence OF. *willo*): of obscure origin. The unetymological spelling with *wh* begins in the 15th cent.] **a.** A marine gastropod mollusc of the genus *Buccinum*, having a turbinate shell, esp. *B. undatum*, common on the European and North American coasts, much used for food.

Also applied, esp. with qualifying word, to molluscs of allied genera, as the hairy or ribbon whelks of the genera *Fulgur* and *Sycotypus*, the red whelk (*Chrysodomus antiquus*), the rough whelk (*Urosalpinx cinerea*), the DOG-WHELK of the genus *Nassa*; see also quots.

α. *c* **725** *Corpus Gloss.* (Hessels) C 865 *Coccum*, wioloc. *c* **875** *Erfurt Gloss.* 267 *Coc[h]leas*, uuylocas. **1312–13** *Durham Acc. Rolls* (Surtees) 10 In lempetis, Wylkes. *c* **1425** *Voc.* in Wr.-Wülcker 642/6 *Hec tortuga*, wylke. **1500–20** DUNBAR *Poems* lxxxii. 24 At your hie Croce,.. thair is bot crudis and milk; And at ȝour Trone bot cokill and wilk. **1565** GOOGE tr. *Palingenius' Zodiac* VII. A aj, Scallops of the baye, And Wilks, & Irchin eke. **1624** CAPT. J. SMITH *Virginia* v. 180 One.. hid himselfe in the Woods, and liued onely on Wilkes and land Crabs. **1782** P. H. BRUCE *Mem.* XII. 424 Their shell-fish are conques, perriwinkles, coneys, sogers, wilkes, etc. **1835** DICKENS *Sk. Boz, Greenwich Fair*, Divers specimens of a species of snail (*wilks*, we think they are called). **1841** J. T. HEWLETT *Parish Clerk* III. 232 Searching for.. wilks, periwinkles, and other shellfish.

β. **1668** CHARLETON *Onomast.* 182 *Cochleæ*, Sea-Snails, Whilks, or Porwinkles, & Periwinkles. **1713** TYLDESLEY *Diary* (1873) 79 Cos Tom Carus and his lady sup[d] with us on whilkes in the shell. **1773** JOHNSON *Let. to Mrs. Thrale* 30 Sept., Muscles and whilks in their natural state. **1823** E. MOOR *Suffolk Words*, Whilk or Whelk.

γ. *c* **900** tr. *Bæda's Hist.* I. i. (1890) 26 Her beoð swyþe ȝenihtsume weolocas, of þam bið ȝeweorht se weolocreada tælgh. *c* **1050** in Wr.-Wülcker 293/25 *Coclea*, weoluc. *c* **1170** MARIE DE FRANCE *Fables* xii. 3 Une welke [*v. rr.* welche, wilque] truva entiere. **1290** in *Archaeologia* XV. 352 Pro ij lampred' iij[s] pro welkes vi[d]. **13..** *Liber Albus* (Rolls) I. 244 Oysters, welkes, muskeles ou soel. **1339** *Little Red Bk. Bristol* (1900) II. 23/1 De anguillis, ostriis, conchiris, welkes, floundris et aliis quibuscunque minutis piscibus venalibus. *c* **1420** *Liber Cocorum* (1862) 17 Take welkes and wasshe fayre. **1555** EDEN *Decades* (Arb.) 237 The shelles of certeyne great welkes. **1606** N. B[AXTER] *Sydney's Ourania* D 1 b, There growen the Scallop, Cockle, Welke, and Oyster. **1668** WILKINS *Real Char.* II. v. §7. 129.

δ. **14..** *Metr. Voc.* in Wr.-Wülcker 625 Whelke, *concha.* **1583** in Feuillerat *Revels Q. Eliz.* (1908) 361 For mendinge of iiij whelkes shelles and Couloringe them. **1655** MOUFET & BENNET *Health's Improv.* 164 Perwinckles or Whelks, are nothing but sea-snails, feeding upon the finest mud of the shore and the best weeds. *c* **1711** PETIVER *Gazophyl.* viii. 77 Limington Bottle Whelk. **1815** S. BROOKES *Conchol.* 202 *Strombus Lucifer*, Spiked Whelk. **1862** *Macm. Mag.* Oct. 503 The whelks, clams,.. and occasionally the crabs, are used by the fishermen as bait for their white fish lines. **1874** A. H. MARKHAM *Whaling Cruise* ii. 19 By way of supper I was initiated into the mysteries of 'whelks'.

ε. *c* **1430** *Two Cookery-bks.* 23 Take Walkys an sethe in Ale. **1444** *Maldon, Essex Crt.-rolls* Bundle 26 No. 1 b (MS.) Vendidit in mercato pisces fetentes, viz. wolkis. **1589** RIDER *Bibl. Schol.* I. 1724 A walke, or wrinkle, *turbo.*

†**b.** The shell of this mollusc, or a representation of it. *Obs.*

1575 LANEHAM *Let.* (1907) 52 Tunneyz, Conchs, & wealks: all engrauen by exquisit deuize and skill. **1605** JONSON *Masques, Of Blacknesse* Wks. (1616) 894 Torch-bearers.. all hauing their lights burning out of whelks, or murex shells.

†**c.** A structure resembling a whelk-shell; a testudo. *Obs.*

1408–9 tr. *Vegetius' De Re Milit.* IV. xiv. (Roy MS. 18 A. XII) lf. 105 The gynne that is clepede the snayle or the welke.

d. *attrib.* and *Comb.*, as ***whelk-boat, -man, -pot*** (POT *sb.*[1] 5 b), ***-shell, -snail, -tribe***; ***whelk-like, -shaped*** adjs.; **whelk-stall**, a stall at which whelks are sold; freq. in phr. ***to be unable to run a whelk stall*** and varr., to be incompetent, esp. in business; **whelk-tingle**, = TINGLE *sb.*[3]

1419 *Liber Albus* (Rolls) I. 343 Item, quantum dabit *welkbot de v tandles. **1900** *Daily News* 17 Aug. 7/1 Two fishermen went off in a whelk boat. **1861** P. P. CARPENTER in *Rep. Smithsonian Inst.* 1860, 180 A *whelk-like dentition. **1851** MAYHEW *Lond. Labour* I. 163/2 The *whelkmen, who are the biggest rogues in Billingsgate. **1883** *Fisheries Exhib. Catal.* 10 Set of *Whelk Pots with Gear. **1861** P. P. CARPENTER in *Rep. Smithsonian Inst.* 1860, 185 One group.. in which the shell is thin and *whelk-shaped. *c* **725** *Corpus Gloss.* (Hessels) C 530 *Conquilium*, *wiloc scel. *c* **1440** *Astron. Cal.* (MS. Ashm. 391), Capricorne þat is þe signe of a goot in a welke shelle. **1681** GREW *Musæum* I. VI. i. 131 'Tis usual to give Drink to Children that have the Chin-Cough, out of a Wilk-shell. **1891** *Science-Gossip* XXVII. 71 The hermit crab.. which always lives in empty whelk shells. **1681** GREW *Musæum* I. VI. i. 131 The *Wilk-Snail winding, from the Mouth towards the right Hand. **1842** *Punch* III. 74/2 The adjacent *whelk-stall. **1894** J. BURNS in *South-Western Star* 13 Jan. 3/4 From whom am I to take my marching orders? From men who fancy they are Admirable Crichtons,.. but who have not got sufficient brains and ability to run a whelk stall? **1928** 'N. SHUTE' *So Disdained* iv. 159 If you try to run him as a manager as well, then your luck'll be out... He couldn't run a whelk stall to make it pay. **1960** C. STORR *Marianne & Mark* iii. 42 The beaches and the whelk stalls. **1965** O. MANNING *Friends & Heroes* xiv. 148, I said we were all disgusted at the way the School had gone down; and I said things would be no better under Callard. I said Callard couldn't run a whelk-stall. **1966** *Hansard Commons* 22 Nov. 1283 The great majority of hon. Gentlemen opposite have not the qualifications to run a whelk stall profitably. **1980** M. DRABBLE *Middle Ground* 25 Which should she pick?.. vain Albert from the whelk stall? **1981** *Financial Times* 1 Apr. 15/2 None of them [*sc.* the 364 economists] has had enough practical experience to run the proverbial whelk stall. **1882** *Standard* 26 Sept. 2/2 The dog-whelk or '*whelk tingle'. **1959** *Times* 25 Aug. 5/6 A survey of the damage done on English oyster beds by the American whelk tingle.. has just been concluded. **1835** KIRBY *Hab. & Inst. Anim.* I. ix. 279 The Buccinidan or *Whelk tribe.

whelk[2] (hwɛlk). Forms: 1 **hwylca**, 4–7 **whelke**, 5 **qwælke**, 5–6 **welke**, 6 **whealke**, 8–9 **welk**, 9 *dial.* **w(h)ilk**, 5– **whelk**. [Late OE. (WS.) *hwylca*, prob. for **hwelca* (cf. late *hwylp* for *hwelp*), f. *hwelian* WHEAL *v.*[1] For the formation cf. *swelca* swelling, f. *swellan* to swell.]

1. A pustule, pimple; = WHEAL *sb.*[1]

c **1000** ÆLFRIC *Gloss.* in Wr.-Wülcker 161/17 *Uarix*, cwydele, *uel* hwylca. *c* **1386** CHAUCER *Prol.* 632 Ne oynement that wolde clense and byte, That hym myghte helpen of the whelkes white. **1388** WYCLIF *Lev.* xiv. 56 This is the lawe of al lepre.. and of litle whelkis [1382 bleynes; Vulg. *papularum*] brekynge out. **1398** TREVISA *Barth. De P.R.* VII. lxiv. (1495) s j b/2 In the face ben redde pymples & whelkes, out of whom ofte renne blood & matere. *c* **1400** *Lanfranc's Cirurg.* 241 *Obtolmia* is clepid a whit' welke or a reed poynt'. **1545** RAYNALDE *Byrth Mankynde* 116 Whelkes or bladders on the body. **1599** SHAKS. *Hen. V*, III. vi. 108 His face is all bubukles and whelkes, and knobs, and flames a fire. **1612** WOODALL *Surg. Mate* Wks. (1653) 198 If the patient sick of the Collick have certaine small whelks or pushes arising upon his belly. **1632** tr. *Bruel's Praxis Med.* 398 Purple colour spots, or else little whelks arise. **1865** R. HUNT *Pop. Rom. W. Eng.* Ser. II. 240 Those little gatherings which occur on the eye-lids of children, locally called 'wilks'.

Comb. **1585** HIGINS *Junius' Nomencl.* 72/2 *Mordella*,.. a whelke flie, or blister flie.

2. Used by confusion for WEAL *sb.*[2], WALE *sb.*[1]

a **1761** CAWTHORN *Poems, Wit & Learn.* (1771) 153 I'll lay thee, miscreant! on my knee, And print such welks thy naked seat on. **1791** COWPER *Iliad* XXIII. 894 And on their flanks and shoulders, red The whelks arose. *a* **1825** FORBY *Voc. E. Anglia*, *Welk, welt*.. to give a sound beating, which is likely to raise weals, welks, or welts. **1870** BRYANT *Homer* I. II. 47 A bloody whelk Rose where the golden sceptre fell.

whelked, welked (hwɛlkt, wɛlkt), *ppl. a.* Also 7 **welkt, welk't, wealked**. [f. WHELK[1] + -ED[2].]

1. Formed like a whelk; twisted, convoluted, or ridged like the shell of a whelk.

a **1560** PHAER *Æneid* x. (1562) Ggj b, Him Triton combrous bare that galeon blew w[t] whelkid shell [orig. *concha*]. **1567** GOLDING *Ovid's Met.* v. 61 b, With crooked welked [orig. *recurvis*] hornes that inward still doe terue. **1605** SHAKS. *Lear* IV. vi. 71 Hornes wealk'd [*Qos.* welkt, welk't], and waued like the enraged [*Qos.* enridged] Sea. **1627** [R. NICCOLS] *Beggers Ape* A 4, He with.. shaggy beard And welked hornes so Satir-like appeard. **1876** A. S. PALMER *Leaves Word-Hunter's Note-Bk.* iv. 73 Look up at its [*sc.* the tree's] towering expanse of branches, observe its whelked and furrowed bole.

2. Marked with ridges on the flesh, waled, wealed: cf. WHELK[2] 2. (Sometimes as pa. pple. of an assumed verb **welk*: see also below.)

1727 GAY *Fables* I. xliv, The smacking lash he smartly plies; His ribs all welk'd, with howling tone The puppy thus expressed his moan. **1812** W. TAYLOR in *Monthly Mag.* XXXIV. 235 Stripes from the fiend attain her heart, And the whelk'd bosom scar. **1828** SCOTT *F.M. Perth* xxii, The labour of their welked hands. **1829** —— *Anne of G.* xxx, My hand has been too much welk'd and hardened by practice of the bow.

¶ In the following Scott uses *welk* as an intr. verb (? = rise in ridges) in the collocation *welk and wave* based on a misunderstanding of Shaks. *Lear* IV. vi. 71, which he echoes directly in quot. 1827.

1821 SCOTT *Pirate* ii, The.. boatmen saw the horns of the monstrous leviathan welking and waving amidst wreaths of mist. **1827** —— *Napoleon* I. viii. 331 Looking out upon the tumultuary sea of pikes, agitated by the fifty thousand hands, as they rose and sunk, welked and waved.

†'**whelky**, *a.*[1] *Obs. nonce-wd.* [f. WHELK[1] + -Y[1].] Formed in a shell.

1591 SPENSER *Virg. Gnat* 105 Ne ought the whelky pearles [orig. *conchea bacca*] esteemeth hee, Which are from Indian seas brought far away.

whelky ('hwɛlkɪ), *a.*[2] *rare.* Also **welky**. [f. WHELK[2] + -Y[1].] Pimply.

1822–29 *Good's Study Med.* (ed. 3) II. 357 A welky or bubukled face. **1845** S. JUDD *Margaret* I. xvii, His shining bald pate and whelky red face streaming with moisture.

whell(e: see QUELL *v.*[1], WHEEL, WHILE.

whelm (hwɛlm), *sb.* Also 6 **whealme**, 6–7 **whelme**. [f. WHELM *v.*]

1. A wooden drain-pipe: orig. a tree-trunk halved vertically, hollowed, and 'whelmed down' or turned with the concavity downwards to form an arched watercourse. Now *dial.*

c **1576** in *Catal. Archives All Souls' Coll.* (1877) 37 Quidam truncus vocatus a whelme. **1584** *Crt.-roll Wormingford, Essex* (MS.), Cursus aquae vocat. The whealme est in decasu. **1613** *Ibid.*, [To place] sufficientem truncam (Anglicè a whelme) in regia via. **1797** A. YOUNG *Agric. Suffolk* 157, I strongly recommend these carrier ditches to be open, though at the expence of a whelm at the bottom of a field where a cart-way is necessary. **1823** E. MOOR *Suffolk Words* 478.

2. The overwhelming surge of waters. *poet.*

1842 *Blackw. Mag.* LII. 287 Dark yawn'd a cleft in the midst of the whelm. **1888** SWINBURNE *Armada* VI. iii. Poems 1904 III. 203 They sink in the whelm of the waters.

whelm (hwɛlm), *v.* Forms: 3–5 **quelm**, 4 **welme**, 4–7 **whelme**, 5–6 *Sc.* **quhelm**, 8–9 **'whelm**, 5– **whelm**; 9 *dial.* **whalm**, **whawm**, **welm**. Also WHEMMEL. [? representing OE. **hwelman*, parallel to **hwelfan* WHELVE.]

†**1.** *intr.* To overturn, capsize. *Obs.*

In second quot. perh. pass. of sense 4.

a **1300** *Cursor M.* 24862 Þaa sori loked ai sua for-suonken, Quen þe scip suld quelm and drunken. *a* **1513** FABYAN *Chron.* VII. (1811) 599 By the mysgydynge of the sterysman, he was set vpon the pylys of the brydge, and the barge whelmyd.

2. *trans.* To turn (a hollow vessel) upside down, or *over* or *upon* something so as to cover it; to turn with the concave side downwards. Now *dial.*

c **1340** *Nominale* (Skeat) 360 *Apres beyuer hanap endente*, welme the cuppe. *c* **1440** *Promp. Parv.* 524/1 Whelmyn a vessel, *suppino*. **14..** *Med. Receipts in MS. Lincoln A.* i. 17, lf. 285 (Halliw.) Tak a bryghte bacyne, and anoynte it with mylke reme, and whelme it over a prene. **1513** DOUGLAS *Æneis* VI. xii. 18 And, with that word, his helm Befoir thair feit all void down did he quhelm. **1530** PALSGR. 780/2 Whelme a platter upon it, to save it from flyes. **1590** LUCAR *Lucarsolace* IV. i. 147 Whelme a new elme bole in the bottome of the said hole. **1604** N. F. *Fruit. Secr.* 18 Whelme downe the maunds, emptying them gently, into small baskets. **1618** BOLTON *Florus* (1636) 201 The barbarous whelmed their shields over their heads. **1643** LIGHTFOOT *Glean. Ex.* (1648) 47 On the top..lay a golden dish whelmed downe. **1657** S. PURCHAS *Pol. Flying-Ins.* 178 A tub..which as soon as you have emptied, suddenly whelm it upside down. **1687** SETTLE *Refl. Dryden* 2 That the Earth is like a Trencher, and the Heavens a Dish whelmed over it. **1712** *Phil. Trans.* XXVIII. 254 It was found with the Mouth whelm'd downward. **1796** TROUTBECK *Scilly Isl.* 171 Their ovens are large iron pots which they whelm over things to be baked, upon heated iron plates. **1842** *Florist's Jrnl.* (1846) III. 24 Pansies that were planted out in the autumn, should be protected by whelming a small pot over each plant. **1854** MISS BAKER *Northampt. Gloss.* s.v., Whelm that dish over them currants.

†**b.** *gen.* To turn downwards: in quots. with reference to Fortune's wheel. *Obs.*

c **1470** *Gol. & Gaw.* 1225 Quhan on-fortone quhelmys the quheil. **1532** *Chaucer's Wks.*, *Troylus* I. 139 And thus Fortune a lofte And vnder efte gan hem to whelmen [*MSS.* whielen, weyle(n] bothe.

†**c.** To cover (a thing) by turning a vessel, etc. upside down over it. *Obs.*

a **1400–50** *Bk. Curtasye* 703 in *Babees Bk.*, A qwyte cuppe of tre þer-by schalle be, þer-with þo water assay schalle he; Quelmes hit agayn by-fore alle men. **1532** TINDALE *Expos. Matt.* v. (*c* 1550) 24 b, As men lyghte no candle to whelme it vnder a bushell. *a* **1651** GATAKER *Parker* in Fuller *Abel Rediv.* 524 Those that are wont to wrap up their talent in a towell, and whelm their light under a bushell.

d. To throw (something) over violently or in a heap upon something else, esp. so as to cover or to crush or smother it.

1624 DONNE *Serm.* xix. (1640) 185 Hill upon hill whelmed upon it. **1637** POCKLINGTON *Altare Christianum* 96 This Milstone of a consequence the Author has whelmed upon himselfe. **1686** PLOT *Staffordsh.* 166 Fig. 3. is to be whelmed upon Fig. 2. so that A. in Fig. 3. touch A. in Fig. 2. **1752** YOUNG *Brothers* I. i, Not seals of adamant, not mountains whelm'd On guilty secrets, can exclude the day. **1888** *Sheffield Gloss.* s.v. *Whawm*, Whawm that cloth over that pancheon. **1894** BLACKMORE *Perlycross* vi, With..a broad hat whelmed down upon his hairless white face.

†**e.** To turn *over* (soil, etc.) so as to expose the under parts. Also *absol. Obs.*

1652 BLITHE *Eng. Improver Impr.* xxviii. 193 The phin made broad, descending or whelming to the right hand. **1759** MILLS tr. *Duhamel's Husb.* I. ix. 49 In this plough, the place of breast-board must be supplied by an iron plate, which..is..carried back, and gradually brought to whelm, as if it would fall upon the furrow. **1795** VANCOUVER *Agric. Essex* 180 To bury every weed by whelming the slice or furrow completely over.

†**3.** *intr.* (*poet.*) To come or pass over something so as to cover it. *Obs.*

c **1440** *Bone Flor.* 683 Garcy hyt Otes on the helme, That upon hys hedd hyt can whelme. **1690** DRYDEN *Don Sebastian* I. i, The Waves whelm'd over him. **1697** —— *Æneis* IX. 725 The Tow'r that follow'd on the fallen Crew, Whelm'd o're their Heads, and bury'd whom it slew. **1700** BLACKMORE *Job* 98 Dismal floods of grief whelm o'er thy head.

4. *trans.* **a.** To cover completely with water or other fluid so as to ruin or destroy; to submerge, drown; occas. to sink (a boat).

1555 PHAER *Æneid.* I. (1558) A ij, Let out thy windes & all their ships do drown wt waters wylde, Disperse them all to sondrie shores or whelme them downe wt deepe. **1598** SHAKS. *Merry W.* II. ii. 143 Giue fire: she is my prize, or Ocean whelme them all. **1697** DRYDEN *Æneis* VI. 455 He saw his Friends, who whelm'd beneath the Waves, Their Fun'ral Honours claim'd. **1725** POPE *Odyss.* IV. 658 Whelm'd in the bottom of the monstrous deep. **1818** SCOTT *Battle of Sempach* xxxvi, He 'whelmed the boat, and as they strove, He stunn'd them with his oar. **1830** LYELL *Princ. Geol.* I. 295 Marsh land..has at last been over-flowed, and thousands of the inhabitants whelmed in the waves. **1889** JESSOPP *Coming of Friars* ii. 105 Flocks, and herds, and corn and hay being whelmed in the deluge.

b. To bury under a load of earth, snow, or the like.

1555 WATREMAN *Fardle Facions* I. iii. 35 So whelmed in sande and grauell, that there is nothing but mere barreinesse. **1583** MELBANCKE *Philotimus* X iv, Whelmed be the World with fire and brimstone, that [etc.]. **1601** HOLLAND *Pliny* XXXII. vi. II. 437 To coole oisters forsooth, they must needs whelme and cover them all over with snow. **1611** SPEED *Hist. Gt. Brit.* IX. xiii. §60. 601 A couragious Esquier of Yorkeshire, whom the sodaine ruine of a Tower ..whelmed and slew outright. **1668** CULPEPPER & COLE *Barthol. Anat.* I. xiii. 32 The Pancreas doth lie out of the reach of Medicaments, being deeply whelmed among the Bowels. **1793–** AIKIN & MRS. BARBAULD *Even. at Home* (1805) IV. 3 He..dug over the whole bed, and whelmed all the relics of his flowers deep under the soil. **1801** *Farmer's Mag.* Jan. 52 A size of furrow-slice is raised sufficient to overlap or whelm up all the weeds. **1883** MISS BROUGHTON *Belinda* II. viii, A day that wrecks ships by fleets;..that whelms trains in snowdrifts.

5. *transf.* To engulf or bear down like a flood, storm, avalanche, etc.; hence, to involve in destruction or ruin. **a.** in material sense.

1667 MILTON *P.L.* VI. 141 Who..with solitarie hand..at one blow Unaided could have finisht thee, and whelmd Thy Legions under darkness. **1740** DYER *Ruins Rome* 529 The Goth and Vandal..Rush, as the Breach of waters, whelming all Their Domes. **1817** SHELLEY *Rev. Islam* VI. vi, The files compact Whelmed me. **1847** TENNYSON *Princess* Prol. 45 Some were whelm'd with missiles of the wall. **1864** —— *En. Ard.* 668 Where either haven open'd on the deeps, Roll'd a sea-haze and whelm'd the world in gray. **1883** *Fortn. Rev.* Feb. 162 The wind that would whelm the wilderness.

b. in immaterial sense.

1553 *Primer Edw. VI, Prayer for ryche menne*, Lustes, whyche whelme men into perdicion and destruction. **1571** GOLDING *Calvin on Ps.* xliii. 2 The light of lyfe drieuth away the mist vnder which wee were whelmed in heauinesse. **1598** R. BERNARD tr. *Terence, Andria* V. iv, My minde is so whelmed with feare, hope, ioy. **1622** MABBE tr. *Aleman's Guzman d' Alf.* II. 265, I lay buryed and whelmed-over head and eares in a well of miseries. **1791** COWPER *Iliad* II. 204 Sorrow whelm'd his soul. **1832** CAMPBELL *Ode to Germans* ii, And the tyrants now that whelm Half the world shall quail and flee. **1860** J. P. KENNEDY *Life W. Wirt* I. xx. 302 Many other ladies were also whelmed in this awful catastrophe. **1891** A. P. PEABODY *King's Chapel Serm., Acts xiv. 11.* 138 Christ..whelmed with his forgiving love the penitent who wept at his feet.

Hence **whelmed** *ppl. a.*, **'whelming** *vbl. sb.* and *ppl. a.*

1819 KEATS *Otho* I. i, In my grave, Or side by side with *'whelmed mariners. **1842** LOUDON *Suburban Hort.* 145 A common saucer and whelmed pot. **1898** MEREDITH *Odes Fr. Hist.* 75 These tortures to distract her [*sc.* France] underneath Her whelmed Aurora's shade. *c* **1440** *Promp. Parv.* 524/1 *Whelmynge, *suppinacio*. **1670** RAY *Prov.* 282 (Scott. Prov.) If I can get his cairt at a whelming [**1678**, p. 379 at a wolter], I shall lend it a put. **1637** MILTON *Lycidas* 157 Under the *whelming tide. **1652** BLITHE *Eng. Improv. Impr.* xxviii. 194 The Coumb or Wing so fixed..to the Share, with its true whelming, hollow, cross winding, compass, just answring the cast or turn of the Furrow. **1658** W. BURTON *Itin. Antonin.* 92 The all-whelming deluge of Time. **1725** POPE *Odyss.* I. 210 Doom'd to welter in the whelming main. **1792** WORDSW. *Descrip. Sketches* 207 By Him who saves Alike in whelming snows and roaring winds. **1799** COWPER *Castaway* 13 Not long beneath the whelming brine, Expert to swim, he lay. **1821** CLARE *Vill. Minstr.* cxviii, If he may live for joys or sink in 'whelming pain. **1861** BERESF. HOPE *Eng. Cathedr. 19th C.* 166 At a crisis of growing darkness and whelming confusion. **1891** ATKINSON *Last of Giant-Killers* 145 Hidden by a whelming mass shot down from the hill above.

whelm, variant of WALM *v. Obs.*

†**whelmer.** *Archit. Obs.* [? f. WHELM *v.* + -ER[1].] ? A stone placed horizontally. (But cf. WHEELER 10.)

1618 in Willis & Clark *Cambridge* (1886) I. 207 Doresteds with..whitestone heads with whelmers and kneelers over the same of free stone. **1688** HOLME *Armoury* III. 472/2 A Wall whose Door head, Cap, or Cover is called a Square, or a Cover of Whelmers and Kneelers.

whelp (hwɛlp), *sb.*[1] Forms: 1 **hwelp**, (**hwoelp**, **huoelp**, **hwealp**, **hwylp**), 1, 4 **welp**, 3 **hweolp**, **ȝwelp**, (*Orm.*) **whellp**, **wheollp**, 3–7 **whelpe**, 4–5 **welpe**, 6 **wheleppe**, 4– **whelp**; *Sc.* and *north.* 4 **quelp(e**, **quilp(e**, 4–7 **quhelp(e**, 5 **qwelp(e**, **quhalp**, **quholp(e**, 8–9 **whalp**. [OE. *hwelp* = OS. *hwelp*, (M)LG., (M)Du. *welp*, OHG. (*h*)*welf* (MHG., G. *welf*), ON. *hvelpr* (Sw. *valp*, Da. *hvalp*): further relations uncertain.]

1. The young of the dog. Now little used, superseded by *puppy*.

c **950** *Lindisf. Gosp.* Matt. xv. 27 Soð hiu cweð ȝee drihten forðon & huoelpas brucas of screadungum ða ðe falles of bead hlaferda hiora. *c* **1000** *Sax. Leechd.* I. 368 Ðyf þu on foreweardon sumera þiȝest hwylcne hwelpan þonne ȝyt unȝeseondne. *Ibid.* II. 172 Ðif þu wille þæt wif cild hæbbe oþþe tife hwelp. *c* **1000** *Ags. Voc.* in Wright *Voc.* 78 *Catulus*, hwylp. *c* **1205** LAY. 31679 Let þu þa hundes..eiðer freten oðer swa hund deð his broðer, and leten heore whelpes whæruen heom bi-sides. *c* **1375** *Sc. Leg. Saints* xxxiii. (*George*) 278 He folouyt hyre as it had bene þe mekeste quhelpe wes euir sene. *c* **1430** *Chev. Assigne* 61 Seuenne whelpes she sawe sowkynge þe damme. **1579** GOSSON *Sch. Abuse* (Arb.) 19 So must I disprayse his methode in writing, which following the course of amarous Poets, dwelleth longest in those pointes, that profite least; and like a wanton whelpe, leaueth the game, to runne riot. **1607** TOPSELL *Four-f. Beasts* 139 That Whelpes..of one and the same Bitch, be neuer suffered to couple. *a* **1682** SIR T. BROWNE *Tracts* V. (1684) 119, I kept an Eagle two years, which fed upon Kats, Kittlings, Whelps and Ratts. **1709** STEELE *Tatler* No. 37 ¶2 Trips, a Whelp just set in. **1765** GOLDSM. *Elegy on Mad Dog* iv, Both mongrel, puppy, whelp, and hound. **1816** SCOTT *Let. to Terry* 18 Apr. in *Lockhart*, His whole pack rushed out upon the man of execution, and Dandie followed them..exclaiming, 'the tae hauf o' them is but whalps, man.' **1859** GEO. ELIOT *Adam Bede* I. v, I want to call at the Hall Farm on my way, to look at the whelps Poyser is keeping for me. **1894** KIPLING *The 'Mary Gloster'* Verse 1919 I. 175 Mean as a collier's whelp Nosing for scraps in the galley.

b. †(*great*) *with whelp*, now *in whelp*: (of a bitch) pregnant, in pup.

1398 TREVISA *Barth. De P.R.* XVIII. xxv. (Bodl. MS.) lf. 260 b/2 Þe bitche goþ wiþ whelpe in here wombe iiijxx daies. **1562** J. HEYWOOD *Prov. & Epigr.* (1867) 203 Thy bytch great with whelpe. **1634** BRERETON *Trav.* (Chetham Soc.) 37 A bitch in whelp. **1887** *Field* 19 Feb. 227/2 All the bitches that missed last year have this season got in whelp, and mostly to the same dogs.

2. The young of various wild animals, *esp.* and now only (chiefly as a literary archaism) of such as the lion, tiger, bear, and wolf, to the young of which the name *cub* is now usually applied.

c **825** *Vesp. Psalter* xvi[i]. 12 Swe swe hwelp leon eardiende in deȝulnissum. *a* **1050** *Liber Scintill.* xxiv. (1889) 95 *Raptis foetibus*, ȝegripenum hwealpum. *c* **1200** ORMIN 5838 Forr leness whellp þær þær itt iss Whellpedd, tær liþ itt stille þre daȝhess. *c* **1290** *St. Edmund* 72 in *S. Eng. Leg.* 299 And riȝt ase he [*sc.* a wolf] wolde is owene ȝwelp with wilde bestes it wuste. *a* **1300** *Cursor M.* 7103 A lion quilpe þat ran ouer-thuert, Rampand to sampson he stert. *c* **1386** CHAUCER *Sqr.'s T.* 491 As by the whelpe chasted is the leon. **1398** TREVISA *Barth. De P.R.* XIII. xxvi. (Bodl. MS.) lf. 137 b/1 [The whale] loueþ his whelpes with a wonder loue. *c* **1440** *Alphabet of Tales* 307 þer was wulfe-whelpis þerin. *Ibid.* 478 þe propurtie of þe ape is to hafe ij whelpis. *c* **1440** *Gesta Rom.* lix. 243 (Harl. MS.) We haue longe tyme fedde þere with þe serpente & hir whelpes. *a* **1578** LINDESAY (Pitscottie) *Chron. Scot.* (S.T.S.) II. 302 Ane kow of Sauchie that calffit xxv grew quholpis. **1677** N. COX *Gentl. Recr.* I. (ed. 2) 134 When the she-Bear perceiveth her self with whelp, she withdraws her self into some Cave. **1774** GOLDSM. *Nat. Hist.* (1776) III. 233 To let the lioness suckle her own whelps. **1825** J. NEAL *Bro. Jonathan* III. 265 The whelp of a bitch-catamount. **1859** DARWIN *Orig. Spec.* xiii. 439 Stripes can be plainly distinguished in the whelp of the lion. **1870** BRYANT *Iliad* XVII. 161 Firm as stands A lion o'er his whelps.

b. *transf.* A young child; a boy or girl. Now only *jocular*.

1483 CAXTON *Gold. Leg.* 265/1 Thou arte moder of a right noble whelp. **1573–80** TUSSER *Husb.* (1878) 185 Not rod in mad braines hand is that can helpe, But gentle skill doth make the proper whelpe. **1591** MORYSON *Let* in *Itin.* (1617) I. 14 Imbrace in my name our common friend G. B. and of my loving hosts family let not a whelpe goe unsaluted. *c* **1591** *Rob Stene's Dream* (Maitl. Club) 5 Bot ȝe sowld cheifly mene his caice, To quhalpis ar of his nobill raice. **1852** KINGSLEY *Let.* in *Life* x. (1879) I. 273, I and my gardener George, and my little whelp Maurice and Dandy, Went out this afternoon fishing.

c. *fig.* (from 1 or 2) with literal language retained, often with implication as in 3.

lion's whelp is used allusively, partly after Shaks. *1 Hen. IV.* III. iii. 167, *Hen. V.* I. ii. 109, for 'a valorous youth sprung from a valorous race'.

a **1225** *Ancr. R.* 200 Þe Unicorne of Wreððe..haueð six hweolpes. Þe uormest is Cheaste, oðer Strif. **13..** *Sir Beues* (A.) 1733 'A-ȝilt þe,' a seide, 'þow fox welp.' *c* **1450** *Cov. Myst.* v. (Shaks. Soc.) 51 And save thi servaunt from helle qwelp. **1588** SHAKS. *Tit. A.* II. iii. 281 Two of thy whelpes, fell Curs of bloody kind Haue heere bereft my brother of his life. **1596–7** *Min. Archd. Colchester* (MS.) lf. 147 Calling them [*sc.* neighbours] doggs, slye whelpes, and that they might have barked before they had bitt. **1631** A. WILSON *Swisser* II. i, And ther's a whelp [*points at Alcidonus*] wo'd haue a Marybone. **1663** COWLEY *Cutter Coleman St.* IV. vi, This bouncing Bear of a Colonel will break the Back of my little Whelp of a Captain. **1831** JAMES *Philip Aug.* xxvii, You were but a whelp, where you are now a lion! **1922** *Times Lit. Suppl.* 23 Feb. 123/1 A time when young Englishmen were just as formidable lion's whelps as they are to-day.

3. a. Applied depreciatingly to the offspring of a noxious creature or being. (Cf. *son of a bitch*.)

1338 R. BRUNNE *Chron.* (1725) 281 Cambinhoy beres him coy, þat fendes whelp. *a* **1340** HAMPOLE *Psalter* lvi. 5 Warldis lufers þat ere the whelpis of deuels. **1560** BECON *New Catech.* Wks. (1564) I. 497 Those whelpes of Rome. **1580** H. GIFFORD *Gilloflowers* (1875) 6, I would..liken all such whelpes of Zoilus, to that..canckerly naturde curre. **1590** GREENE *Mourn. Garm.* (1616) C 2, Use not dice, for they be fortunes whelpes. **1610** SHAKS. *Temp.* I. ii. 283 The Son, that she did littour heere, A frekelld whelpe, hag-borne. **1634** CANNE *Necess. Separ.* 105 Their vngracious Bishops, these whelpes of Antichrist.

b. An ill-conditioned or low fellow; later, in milder use, and esp. of a boy or young man: A saucy or impertinent young fellow; an 'unlicked cub', a 'puppy'. Also *attrib.*

c **1330** *Arth. & Merl.* 4516 Him to helpe, To fiȝt oȝain þe Sarrazin welpe. *c* **1460** *Towneley Myst.* xii. 426 Thou art an yll qwelp ffor angre. **1611** B. JONSON *Catiline* I. i, Let me but finde you againe with such a face: You Whelpe. **1710** *Brit. Apollo* III. No. 20. 3/2 He's..a Silly Whelp. **1711** SWIFT *Lett.* (1767) III. 161 Sir Thomas Mansel and Tom Harley met me in the Park, and made me walk with them till nine, like unreasonable whelps. **1741** RICHARDSON *Pamela* (1824) I. 11 When she was beginning to complain of the whelp lord's impertinence. **1768** GOLDSM. *Goodn. Man* II. i, Stupid whelp! But I don't wonder: the boy takes entirely after his mother. **1809** SCOTT *Let.* 7 Aug. in *Lockhart*, It is funny enough to see a whelp of a young Lord Byron abusing me. **1823** 'JON BEE' *Dict. Turf* 192 *Whelp*, a boy with dog's-tricks. **1834** MARRYAT *Peter Simple* iii, Bad company, you whelp! **1866** MISS BRADDON *Lady's Mile* i, The shabby whelp gambling for marbles in the gutter. **1888** *Sat. Rev.* 20 Oct. 458/1 These whelps have been before the magistrates charged on their own confession with murder.

4. *Naut.* One of the longitudinal projections on the barrel of a capstan or the drum of a windlass.

The object designated in the first quot. is uncertain.

1356 in *Pipe Roll 32 Edw. III* m. 34/1 Idem computat expendisse.. in factura .iij. Whelpes .j. grossi Wynche..c. lb. *a* **1625** *Nomenclator Navalis* (Harl. MS. 2301), The Whelps are like Brackettes, sett to the bodie of the Capstaine close vnder the Barrs, downe to the Decke, and are theie which giue the Sweepe to the Capstaine. Theis are made soe in partes that the Cabell maie not be so apt to surge, as it would if it did run vpon a whole round bodie. **1627** CAPT. J. SMITH *Sea Gram.* ii. 8 The Whelps are short peeces of wood made fast to it, to keepe the Cable from coming too high in the turning about. **1769** FALCONER *Dict. Marine* (1776) s.v. *Capstern.* **1847** KEY *Recov. H.M.S. Gorgon* 19 The space between which had been filled up with wood, like the whelps of a capstan.

b. One of the teeth of a sprocket-wheel (Knight *Dict. Mech.* 1875).

†**5.** *Naut.* One of a fleet of auxiliary war vessels established in Charles I's reign, app. orig. so called because designed to attend upon H.M.S. Lion. *Obs.*

1628-9 *Cal. St. Papers, Dom.* (1859) 455 [When she [*sc.* a small man-of-war] heard] our Whelps bark so loud and saucy, and saw them put up the King's colours, [she endeavoured to escape]. **1631** SIR J. PENNINGTON *Jrnl.* in *10th Rep. Hist. MSS. Comm.* App. IV. 276 Our whole fleete being 4 sayle in all, viz[t] the Convertive, Admirall, the Assurance, Vize Admirall, the Tenth Whelpe, and the Second Whelpe. **1634** BRERETON *Trav.* (Chetham Soc.) 158 Here we saw the 9th Whelp lying at anchor, to guard the fleet which now is ready to go hence to Bristoll fair. **1641** PRYNNE *Disc. Prel. Tyrr.* ii. 135 Being imbarqued.. in one of the Kinges Whelpes,.. he landed at Dover. **1660** BURNEY *Κέρδιστον Δῶρον* 53 When he visits the Navy, and even boards the Whelps and Frigots. **1894** C. N. ROBINSON *Brit. Fleet* 227 A class of smaller craft, each of 185 tons, was decided on. They were called 'whelps', and were vessels built for sweeps as well as sails.

6. *Comb.*, as ***whelp-robbed*** adj.

1627 MAY *Lucan* v. H 8 b, Swifter then whelpe-robb'd Tyger.

Hence '**whelphood**, the condition of being a whelp; '**whelpish** *a.*, of, resembling, or characteristic of a whelp; '**whelpless** *a.*, having no whelps, deprived of whelps; †'**whelplich** [-LY[2]] *adv.*, like a whelp; '**whelpling**, a young whelp; also *contemptuously* of a person.

1847 E. BRONTË *Wuthering Heights* I. xiii. 325 It [*sc.* a dog] had spent its *whelphood at the Grange. **1886** SWINBURNE *Misc.* 211 A vapid and effeminate rhymester in the sickly stage of whelphood. **1586** WHITNEY *Choice Emblems* 49 Though *whelpishe daies, his nature did disguise Yet time at length vnto my euell lucke Bewray'de his harte. **1687** MIÉGE *Gt. Fr. Dict.*, Whelpish, *mechant, mauvais.* **1711** G. CARY *Phys. Phylactic* 334 You mightily hugged this whelpish Thought. **1883** J. CHRISTIE in *Mod. Scott. Poets* Ser. VI. 263 Thou gar'd the rocks and hallows ring Wi' whalpish glee. **1598** YONG *Diana* 9 Angry more then *whelplesse Beare. **1814** BYRON *Lara* II. xxv, Her eye shot forth with all the living fire That haunts the tigress in her whelpless ire. **1847** TENNYSON *Princess* VI. 83 The old lion, glaring with his whelpless eye. *c* **1400** *Beryn* 481 He.. scrapid the dorr *welplich. *a* **1618** SYLVESTER *Profit of Imprisonment* Wks. (1621) 625 As, when the Lion fierce.. Runnes midst a million swords, his *whelplings to defend. **1782** ELPHINSTON *Martial* XII. clxxi. [I. lxxxiii.] 460 On thy lov'd lips, the whelpling lambent hung. **1889** FARRAR *Lives of Fathers* I. v. 222 That whelpling [L. *canicula*] Diogenes sought to find a man.

whelp, *sb.*[2] Erron. for WELT *sb.*[1]

1912 in *Dialect Notes* III. 593 She whipped the horse till she raised great whelps on him. **1952** *Publ. Amer. Dial. Soc.* XVII. 34 Time was in the upcountry when the teacher would, with a hickory, raise whelps on the legs of a recalcitrant pupil. **1962** W. FAULKNER *Reivers* viii. 181 How the hell did Sugar Boy ever let him get this far without at least one whelp on him? **1980** *Verbatim* Autumn 17/2 A quite common mispronunciation is 'whelp' for 'welt': 'He has some big whelps on his arm.'

whelp (hwɛlp), *v.* [f. WHELP *sb.*[1]]

1. *trans.* To bring forth (a whelp or whelps).

c **1200** ORMIN 6029 Þatt deor þatt wass i leoness like, þatt riseþþ o þe þridde daʒʒ Affterr þatt itt iss wheollpedd. *a* **1225** *Ancr. R.* 200 Monie mo hweolpes þen ich habbe inempned haueð þe Liun of Prude ihweolped. **1398** TREVISA *Barth. De P.R.* XVIII. i. (Bodl. MS.) lf. 241 b/2 Þe female wolfe whelpiþ manye whelpes as þe bitche doþe. **1493** *Festivall* (W. de W. 1515) 145 Whan a lyon hath yonge whelpes they shall lye as deed thre dayes after y[t] they ben whelped. **1577** GOOGE *Heresbach's Husb.* III. 155 b, As soone as they be Whelped, cast away such as you mislike. **1677** N. COX *Gentl. Recr.* I. (ed. 2) 135 [Bears] are whelped most commonly in March, sometimes two, and not above five in number. **1731** *Gentl. Mag.* Aug. 352/2 A Litter of young Lions was whelped at the Tower, from a Lioness and Lion whelp'd there 6 years before. **1775** *Phil. Trans.* LXVI. 103 They all come on shore in December, to whelp their young. **1861** HUGHES *Tom Brown at Oxf.* iii, Jack's the dog as can draw a brock.. agin any Lonnun dog as ever was whelped. **1892** *Brit. Fancier* 19 Feb. 71/2 His bitch Dainty.. has just whelped a.. fine litter to Mrs. Dainty's Dictator.

b. *transf.* and *fig.* To bring forth: often with contemptuous implication.

1581 J. BELL *Haddon's Answ. Osor.* 82 b, Two detestable lyes whelped at one lytter (so pregnant is this worme). **1599** B. JONSON *Cynthia's Rev.* II. iv, Vnlesse shee had whelpt it her selfe, shee could not haue lou'd a thing better. *a* **1641** BP. MOUNTAGU *Acts & Mon.* (1642) 422 Antignus, Boethus, Sadoc, and such mungrels were scarce whelped in Epiphanius his dayes. **1675** HOBBES *Odyss.* VIII. 472 Sing now of the Horse of Wood.. Which in Troy-Town destruction to it whelpt. **1781** COWPER *Table-T.* 536 Having whelped a prologue with great pains. **1821** SCOTT *Kenilw.* xix, Out, you diminutive pint-pot, whelped of an overgrown reckoning! **1902** WISTER *Virginian* xv, None of 'em was whelped savage enough to sing himself bloodthirsty.

2. *intr.* To bring forth whelps.

1398 TREVISA *Barth. De P.R.* XVIII. lxxiv. (Bodl. MS.), Þat wesels conceyue atte mouþe and whelpiþ atte ere. *a* **1400** *Octouian* 470 The tygre aftyr thys batayle, Whelpede sone for hyr trauayle. **1605** B. JONSON *Volpone* II. i, Your lyons whelping, in the Tower. **1660** BOYLE *New Exp. Phys.-Mech.* Digress. 368 A Bitch that was said to be almost ready to whelp. **1798** W. TAYLOR in *Monthly Mag.* V. 208 On Paris' tomb The flocks insulting frisk, And whelps the lioness in Priam's hall. **1887** SWINBURNE *Locrine* IV. ii. 98 No she-wolf whelps upon the wold Whose brood is like thy mother's.
fig. **1821** SHELLEY *Hellas* 874 The foliage in which Fame, the eagle, built Her aerie, while Dominion whelped below.

Hence **whelped** *ppl. a.*, **whelping** *vbl. sb.* (also in ***whelping ice*** (see quots.)).

1398 TREVISA *Barth. De P.R.* XVIII. xxvi. (Bodl. MS.), In bicches melk is founde many daies bifore þe whelpinge. **1625** K. LONG tr. *Barclay's Argenis* II. xiii. 105 She was then lately dead in whelping. **1804** W. TAYLOR in Robberds *Mem.* (1843) I. 491 Licking the whelped bears into courtliness at one's leisure. *c* **1900** J. P. HOWLEY in *Regional Lang. Stud.—Newfoundland* (1978) VIII. 23 Whelping ice. The part of an ice field where they [*sc.* seals] bring forth their young. **1907** R. LEIGHTON *New Bk. Dog* 578 Breeding and Whelping. **1919** W. T. GRENFELL *Labrador Doctor* (1920) ix. 174 The smoother, whiter variety known as 'whelping ice'—that is, the Arctic shore ice.. on which the seals give birth to their pups. **1969** H. HORWOOD *Newfoundland* xii. 83 The drift ice where they [*sc.* seals] give birth to their young is the whelping ice.

whels, obs. form of WHILES.

whelve (hwɛlv), *v.* *Obs.* exc. *dial.* Forms: 1 **hwylfan**, 3 **hwelfen**, 5- **whelve**, (9 **whilve**). [Late OE. *hwylfan* = **hwielfan*, Anglian **hwelfan* (also in compounds *á-*, *be-*, *ofhwylfan*) = OS. *bihwelbian* to cover over, (M)Du., (M)LG. *welven*, OHG., MHG. *welben*, *welwen* (G. *wölben*) to vault, arch, ON. *hvelfa* to arch, turn upside down:—OTeut. **χwalbjan*, causative vb. f. *χwalb-* (: *χwelb-*, *χulb-*), whence OE. *hwealf* sb., arch, vault, adj. vaulted, OHG. *walbe* (MHG. *walbe*), curved object, gutter-tile, roof-gutter, *walbî* 'volubilitas', *walbên* to roll, ON. *hvalf* vault, concavity, *hvalfa*, *holfa* to capsize (see WHAUVE); further related to Goth. *hwilftri* coffin, Gr. *κόλπος* bosom: the radical notion being 'rounded, arched'.]

1. *trans.* To turn (a vessel, etc.) upside down so as to cover something; *gen.* to turn or roll over, overturn; to upheave. ***to whelve over***, to overwhelm: = OVERWHELVE.

c **1000** in *Techmer's Zeitschr.* (1885) II. 125 Ðonne þu hlid habban wylle, þonne hafa þu þine wynstran hand samlocene and eac swa þa swyþran and hwylf hy syþþan ofer þa wynstran eal swylce þu cuppan hlide. [*c* **1000** *Regius-Psalter* etc. (Roeder) 276 Cneoris min alæd & ofhwylfed [Vulg. *conuoluta*] is fram me.] *c* **1275** *Passion our Lord* 513 in *O.E. Misc.* 51 He hwelfde at þare sepulchre-dure enne grete ston. [*c* **1374** CHAUCER *Boeth.* II. met. iii. (1868) 39 Þe horrible wynde aquilon moeueþ boylyng tempestes and ouer whelweþ þe see.] *c* **1440** *Pallad. on Husb.* I. 161 For harm & stryf of that vpon thy selue May rise, yhe & perchaunce ouer thee whelue [*v.r.* the overwhelve]. **1854** *Trans. Philol. Soc.* 84 (Surrey) I'll whelve a pot over 'em, to keep off the sun. **1854** *N. & Q.* 1st Ser. X. 479 (Cornwall) *Whelve* or *Whilve*, to turn upside down any hollow vessel.

†**2.** To cover over with anything; to hide, bury.

c **1440** *Pallad. on Husb.* IV. 393 Ek whelue a seriol ther-out that haue Grauel vp to the myddes. **1566** W. P. tr. *Curio's Pasquine in Traunce* To Rdr., The candell whelued vnder the Busshell wil burne a hole throughe. **1706** PHILLIPS (ed. Kersey), To *Whelm* or *Whelve*, to cover.

wheme, var. QUEME *sb.* and *v.* *Obs.*

whemen, obs. f. *women*, pl. of WOMAN.

whemmel ('hwɛm(ə)l), *sb.* *Sc.* and *dial.* Forms: see next. [f. next.] An overturn, upset, overthrow; a state of confusion.

1818 SCOTT *Rob Roy* xxii, Nae doubt, nay doubt—ay, ay—it's an awfu' whummle—and for ane that held his head sae high too. **1822** GALT *Sir A. Wylie* civ, The chaise made a clean whamle, and the Laird was lowermost. **1830** —— *Lawrie T.* III. v, Many a joint-dislocking jolt, and almost headlong whamle. **1887** *Jamieson's Sc. Dict.* Suppl., *Quhemle*.. a rock, toss; a rocking, tossing. **1895** CROCKETT *Men of Moss-Hags* xlviii, His horse also fell from rock to rock, and among a great whammel of stones, reached the bottom of the defile.

whemmel ('hwɛm(ə)l), *v.* *Sc.* and *dial.* Forms: 6, 9 **quhemle**, **quhomle**, 7-9 **whemmel**, 8-9 **whomel**, **whemble**, 9 **w(h)emmle**, **whammle**, **wham(b)le**, **whommle**, **whum(m)el**, etc. (see *Eng. Dial. Dict.*). [Metathetic form of WHELM *v.*]

1. *trans.* To turn upside down; to overturn, capsize; to drink off (liquor) to the bottom; also *transf.* and *fig.* to upset, throw into confusion.

1536 BELLENDEN *Cron.* Proheme ii. (1541) F iv, And schyll Triton with his wyndy horne Ouir quhemlit all the flowand ocean. **1684** [MERITON] *Yorksh. Dial.* 47, I whemmeld Dubler owr'th Meat, To keep it seaf and warm for you to Eat. **1715** RAMSAY *Christ's Kirk Gr.* II. xix, On whomelt tubs lay twa lang dails. **1721** —— *Prospect of Plenty* 196 Healthfou hearts shall own their honest flame, With reaming quaff, and whomelt to her name. **1816** SCOTT *Antiq.* xl, I think I see the coble whombled keel up. *Ibid.* xli, He took the curbstane, and he's whomled her as I wad whomle a toom bicker. *c* **1850** *Denham Tracts* (1895) II. 31 Put into a wheelbarrow and whemmeled over upon the muck-midden. **1883** *Trans. Amer. Philol. Soc.* 55 *Whommle*, 'to turn a trough, or any vessel, bottom upwards, so that it will drain well'; used in West Virginia.

b. To cover (something) by turning a vessel, etc. upside down over it.

1790 GROSE *Prov. Gloss.* (ed. 2), *Whemble*, to cover with a bowl. **1824** MACTAGGART *Gallovid. Encycl.* s.v. *Whommled*, To be whommled beneath a bushel. **1855** [J. D. BURN] *Autobiog. Beggar Boy* (1859) 57, I was, like the turkey, whomalled under a tub.

2. To submerge in or as in a flood; to drown.

1567 *Satir. Poems Reform.* iv. 51 Quhomlit in sorow and plungeit in cair. **1824** MACTAGGART *Gallovid. Encycl.* s.v. *Whommled*, 'To be whommled by a wave,' to be whelmed in the deep.

3. *intr.* To tumble over, capsize; also, to move unsteadily, stumble about.

1895 CROCKETT *Men of Moss-Hags* xxiii, The deil whummelt on his hearthstane! **1897** —— *Lads' Love* iii, When.. your hoggs [are] whammelin' in the black hags by the score.

when (hwɛn), *adv.* (*conj.*, *sb.*) Forms: α. 1-3 **hwonne**, (1 **huonne**), 3 **wonne**, 3-4 **whonne**, 6 *Sc.* **quhone**. β. 1-3 **hwanne**, 3 **wæne**, **quanne**, (**quuanne**, **ʒwanne**, **ʒwane**), 3-4 **wane**, 3-5 **whanne**, **wanne**, **quane**, 4 **huanne**, 6 **whane**, *Sc.* **quhane**. γ. 1 **hwenne**, **hwænne**, (**hoenne**), 2-3 **wenne**, 3 **hwenne**, **weonne**, 3-5 **whenne**, 4 **quenne**, **qwenne**, **quene**, *Sc.* **qwene**, **qwhene**, 4-6 *Sc.* **quhene**, 5 **whene**. δ. 3-4 **hwon**, **won**, (4 **wʒon**), 4-5 **whon**, 5 **qwon**. ε. 3-4 **hwan**, (3 **quuan**, **quæn**), 3-5 **wan**, **quan**, 3-6 **whan**, (4 **van**, 5 **whann**), 5-6 *Sc.* **quhan**. ζ. 3 **hwen**, 3-5 **wen**, 4-5 **quen**, (4 **qwheyn**, 5 **qwen**, **qwhen**), 4-8 *Sc.* **quhen**, 4- **when**. [OE. *hwanne*, *hwǫnne*, *hwenne*, (Nth. *hwœnne*), late WS. *hwænne*, corresp. to OFris. *wanne*, (*h*)*wenne* until, if (Fris. *wan* when, if), OS. *hwan* when, *hwanna* at some time, when, (MLG. *wan*, *wen*, *wanne*, *wenne*, MDu. *wan*, *wen*, surviving in Du. *wanneer* when = OS. *hwan êr* as soon as), OHG. *wanne*, *wenni*, *-e* (MHG. *wanne*, *wenne*, G. *wann* when, *wenn* if), Goth. *hwan* when, how: a derivative of the interrog. stem *χwa-* WHO, WHAT, as *then* is of the demonstrative *þa-*; cf. Avestic *kəm* how, L. *quom*, *cum* when, OPruss. *kan* if, OIr. *can*, W. *pan*.

The formations present points of difficulty; the following related forms have a dental suffix: OFris. *hwande*, *hwante*, *wande*, *want*, *hwende*, *hwent*(*e* (Fris. *want*) for, because, as, OS. *hwanda*, *hwand* when, for, because (MLG. *wande*), OHG. (*h*)*wanta* why, L. *quando* when (cf. Skr. *kadā́* when, Lith. *kadà* where, etc.).]

I. Interrogative uses.

1. a. In a direct question: At what time? on what occasion? Sometimes passing into the sense: In what case or circumstances? (cf. 8). Also with ellipsis of the remainder of the question (see also b).

c **1000** *Ags. Gosp.* Matt. xxv. 37 Hwænne ʒesawe we ðe hingriʒende, & we ðe feddon? *c* **1000** *Ags. Ps.* (Th.) xl[i]. 5 Hwonne ær he beo dead, oþþe hwænne his nama aspringe? *c* **1175** *Lamb. Hom.* 65 Wenne scal þos bode us god don? **1382** WYCLIF *Ps.* xli[i]. 3 Whan I shal comen, and apere befor the face of God? *c* **1412** HOCCLEVE *De Reg. Princ.* 864 Whan schol ye þre to vs be reconsiled? **1540** PALSGR. *Acolastus* IV. v. V j b, Thou shalt haue gold tolde out to the. *La.* Whan, at the Grekish calendes? **1590** SHAKS. *Com. Err.* II. ii. 13 When spake I such a word? **1681** DRYDEN *Abs. & Achit.* I. 387 When should People strive their Bonds to break, If not when Kings are Negligent or Weak? **1742** YOUNG *Nt. Th.* III. 537 When shall I die?—when shall I live for ever? **1841** *Punch* 24 July 21/2 When is a horse like a herring?—When he's hard rode. **1865** DICKENS *Mut. Fr.* III. xiv, When shall I come to see you, Mr. Boffin? **1867** TENNYSON *Holy Grail* 255 Who shall blazon it? when and how?

†**b.** *ellipt.* as an exclamation of impatience. *Obs.*

1592 KYD *Sp. Trag.* III. i. 47 No more, I say: to the tortures, when! **1596** SHAKS. *Tam. Shr.* IV. i. 147 Off with my boots, you rogues: you villaines, when? **1623** MIDDLETON *More Dissemblers* V. i. (1657) 66 Why when? begin Sir: I must stay your leisure.

2. In a dependent question or clause of similar meaning: At what time; on what occasion; in what case or circumstances. Also *ellipt.*

say when, colloq. formula used by a person pouring out drink for another, to ask him to say when he shall stop; also *ellipt.*, as a reply to this formula.

c **1000** *Ags. Gosp.* Matt. ii. 7 Herodes.. befran hi ʒeorne, hwænne se steorra hym æteowde. *a* **1300** *Cursor M.* 5446

Nou rek i neuer quen i dei. *c* **1375** in Horstmann *Altengl. Leg.* (1878) 124/1 Alle ȝe haue herd told & How & whanne god þis world mad. **1535** COVERDALE *Lev.* xiv. 57 That it maye be knowne, whan eny thinge is vncleane or cleane. **1676** N. FRENCH *Vnkinde Desertor* i. 22 To know when to speake, and when to be silent. **1710** SWIFT *Jrnl. to Stella* 7 Oct., I wonder when this letter will be finished. **1854** R. S. SURTEES *Handley Cr.* i. (1901) I. 11 He knew when to lay hold of his hounds, and when to let them alone. **1865** DICKENS *Mut. Fr.* IV. iii, Say when you've put it safe back, Mr. Venus.

a **1225** *Ancr. R.* 144 Deað þet we beoð siker of & unsiker hwonne. *c* **1400** *Pol. Rel. & L. Poems* (1903) 263 Deȝe we ssulin sikerliche; bot god wot wanne & were. **1545** ASCHAM *Toxoph.* II. (Arb.) 125 Whych matter was onse excellentlye disputed vpon, in the Scooles, you knowe when. **1590** SHAKS. *Com. Err.* III. i. 39 Ile tell you when, and you'll tell me wherefore. **1667** MILTON *P.L.* x. 499, I am to bruise his heel; His Seed, when is not set, shall bruise my head. **1779** H. WALPOLE *Let. to Selwyn* 5 July, Can you tell me if the Duchess of Leinster still goes to Aubigny; and, if she does, when? **1828** HAZLITT *Self Love & Benev.* Sk. & Ess. (1872) 104 What might be the consequence to myself the Lord knows when? **1883** STEVENSON *Treas. Isl.* xi, Well, now, if you want to know, I'll tell you when. The last moment I can manage; and that's when. **1888** 'J. S. WINTER' *Bootle's Childr.* ii, I haven't seen such food I don't know when. **1889** *Mod. Society* 6 June (Farmer's *Slang*) 'Say when,' said Bonko, taking up a flagon of whiskey and commencing to pour out the spirit into my glass. **1911** *Maclean's Mag.* Oct. 297/2 'Say when?' I held the glass with a shaking hand: 'When.' **1931** A. POWELL *Afternoon Men* I. 13 'Say when, sir,' said the waiter. 'When,' said Pringle. **1948** E. WAUGH *Loved One* 3 'When,' he added aside to the young man, who helped him to whisky. 'Right up with soda, please.'

3. After a prep. (esp. *since, till*), in a direct or a dependent question: = What time?

Cf. F. *depuis quand*, G. *seit wann.*

a **1300** *Cursor M.* 5670 Sin quen was þou vr dempster? **1583** MELBANCKE *Philotimus* N iv, If any circumstance of where, or when, or whome, may make a probable Argument. **1828** SCOTT *F.M. Perth* xiv, Since when is it, good Father, that the principal libertine has altered his morals so much? **1861** H. KINGSLEY *Ravenshoe* xix, 'Since when have you missed her?' 'Since yesterday afternoon.'

II. Relative and conjunctive uses.

Formerly (now *arch.*) also followed by *that* (THAT *conj.* 6).

4. As compound relative (cf. WHAT C.*), or as correlative to *then* (implied and sometimes expressed): At the (or a) time at which; on the (or an) occasion on which.

Also *ellipt.* with only the predicate expressed, e.g. ***when a boy*** = when he (I, etc.) was a boy; ***when cold*** = when it is cold.

a. In reference to a definite actual occurrence or fact, chiefly with verb in past tense: At the time that, on the occasion that; sometimes with verb in present tense = now that (sometimes with mixture of sense 9 a).

a **1000** *Guthlac* 209 Hwonne hy mid menᵹu maran cwome, þa þe for his life lyt sorᵹedon. *c* **1250** *Gen. & Ex.* 576 Sexe hundred ȝer noe was hold Quan he dede him in ðe archewold. *a* **1300** *Cursor M.* 8958 Quen þat sco to þe cite com Sco com in at þat ilk yatte, þar þis tre lai in hir gatt. *c* **1350** *Will. Palerne* 2484 Wan þei þider come, þei founde al awei fare. *c* **1400** *Destr. Troy* 1689 Qwhen this Citie was set ..Then meuyt to his mynde [etc.]. *c* **1420** *Sir Amadace* xxix, Qwen he was gone on this kin wise, Thenne iche mon sayd thayre deuise. **1470–85** MALORY *Arthur* x. lxx. 536 Whanne he saw her make suche chere he ferd lyke a lyon that there myghte no man withstande hym. **1533** BELLENDEN *Livy* v. xxiv. (S.T.S.) II. 230 We suld nocht leif oure ciete now quhen It hes sa mony ruynouss housis. **1577** HANMER *Anc. Eccl. Hist.* 239 When that he was certified..that the Ethnicks offred sacrifice..in that place..he sharply rebuked Eusebius. **1581** *Satir. Poems Reform.* xliii. 154 Sone efter that the Counsell cround ȝoursell, Quhan godly Murray as a regent rang. **1605** SHAKS. *Macb.* II. ii. 27 Listning their feare, I could not say Amen, When they did say God blesse vs. **1763** J. BROWN *Poetry & Mus.* v. 67 Music had then its greatest Power, when the Melody was most confined in its Compass. **1775** HARRIS *Philos. Arrangem.* Wks. (1841) 339 It was by being attacked when asleep..that the gigantic Polypheme fell a sacrifice to Ulysses. **1779** *Mirror* No. 23. ¶3 He lost his father when an infant. **1848** THACKERAY *Van. Fair* liii, It was ten o'clock when he woke up. **1863** DICKENS *Uncomm. Trav.* xxvi, When I was a child..I used to think that I should like to play at Chinese Enchanter. **1894** BARING-GOULD *Bk. Fairy T.* 70 It is not the time for violets, when the snow lies deep?

(*b*) With ellipsis of following clause: in the past, in the old days (*N. Amer. colloq.*).

1962 M. RICHLER in *Kenyon Rev.* Winter 88 Six months from now..I'll be saying I knew you when. **1968** H. WAUGH *'30' Manhattan East* (1969) 163 She needn't try those airs with me. I knew her when. **1984** M. HINXMAN *Night they murdered Chelsea* viii. 65 The Hearst newspaper group are even flying in Gloria Beesley to cover the case. She knew Charlotte when.

b. In reference to a future time (whether in the present or the past).

971 *Blickl. Hom.* 97 He sceal winnan & sorᵹian, hwonne se dæᵹ cume. *c* **1275** LAY. 643 He..þrettede þan castle, and þat folk wið ine, wanne he hit mihte awinne. *c* **1350** *Leg. Rood* (1871) 21 Vr lord bi-het me þere Wiþ Oyle of Milce smere me whonne hit tyme were. *c* **1420** *Avow. Arth.* xxiv, Quen thou art armut in thi gere, Take thi schild and thi spere. **1560** *Bible* (Geneva) 1 Sam. iii. 12 When I begin, I wil also make an end. **1588** SHAKS. *L.L.L.* IV. iii. 145 What will Berowne say when that he shall heare Faith infringed? **1646** in Row *Hist. Kirk* (Wodrow Soc.) p. xxxi, I desyrit our people to convein quhen the bellis suld be rung. **1769** MRS. RAFFALD *Eng. Housekpr.* (1805) 109 When your head is boiled, rub it over with the yolk of an egg. *a* **1814** [see THAT *conj.* 6]. **1865** KINGSLEY *Herew.* xxxi, Pray St. Etheldreda to be with us when the day shall come. **1889** TENNYSON *Crossing the Bar* 16, I hope to see my Pilot face to face When I have crost the bar. **1915** 'IAN HAY' *First Hundred Thou.* II. xx. 303 The Oxford Dictionary of the English Language will have to be revised and enlarged when this war is over.

c. Indefinitely or generally: At any time, or at the several times, at which; on any occasion that: most commonly with vb. in pres. tense.

c **1200** *Trin. Coll. Hom.* 147 Wanne hie seȝen men wanred þolien oðer on sinne bifallen..þer-of hie hadden reuðe. *c* **1220** *Bestiary* 16 in *O.E. Misc.* 1 Wanne he is ikindled Stille lið ðe leun. *a* **1250** *Owl & Night.* 324 Ich singe an eue a riȝte time & soþþe won hit is bedtime. **1340** *Ayenb.* 27 Huanne he yziȝþ oþer yherþ þe guod of oþren..þanne him comþ a zorȝe to þe herte. **1461** PASTON *Lett.* I. 541 To see that the contre be allweys redy to come bothe fote men and hors men, qwen they be sent for. **1553** *Respublica* 894 Solace we muste nedes have whan that we are werie. **1591–5** SPENSER *Astrophel* 29 There was no pleasure nor delightfull play, When Astrophel so euer was away. **1639** J. CLARKE *Parœm.* 87 When God will, all winds bring raine. **1711** ADDISON *Spect.* No. 26 ¶7 When I look upon the tombs of the great, every emotion of envy dies in me. *a* **1774** GOLDSM. *Elegy Mrs. Mary Blaize* 16 She never slumbered in her pew,—But when she shut her eyes. **1827** SCOTT *Highl. Widow* v, The answers which he received from him, when conversing on religious topics. **1860** DICKENS *Uncomm. Trav.* ii, I am overpowered when I think of you and your hospitable home.

5. Introducing a clause as the object of a verb, or (later) governed by a preposition: = The or a time at which; †a case in which (cf. 8).

This use arises from the dependent interrog. use (sense 2), and the OE. examples are only particular cases of this.

971 *Blickl. Hom.* 227 Hine ðæs heardost langode hwanne he of ðisse worulde moste. *a* **1000** *Cædmon's Gen.* 1433 Hæleð langode..hwonne hie of nearwe..stæppan mosten. *c* **1375** *Cursor M.* 5939 (Fairf.) Sette us terme & quenne [*Cott.* term wen] we salle pray for þe & þi men. *c* **1412** HOCCLEVE *De Reg. Princ.* 113 Passe ouer whanne þis stormy nyght was gon, And day gan at my wyndowe in to prye. **1487** *Cely Papers* (Camden) 166 They loke euery owre when the comens of the town schall ryse. **1568** [see LOOK *v.* 3 c]. **1603** SHAKS. *Meas. for M.* II. ii. 11, I haue seene When after execution, Iudgement hath Repented ore his doome. **1648** HERRICK *Hesper., To the Lark*, And know thy when To say, Amen. **1689** MILWARD *Selden's Table-t.* Ded., In your Fancy carry along with you, the *When* and the *Why* many of these things were spoken. **1838** S. SHARPE *Hist. Egypt under Ptol.* 186 As to the when, the why, or by whom the pyramids were built. **1867** MORRIS *Jason* XVII. 100 Since when I am dead, By none but him the people shall be led. **1868** —— *Earthly Par.* Prol. 202 Expecting when our turn shall come to die. **1884** *Dailys of Sodden Fen* x, I was a grown young man of twenty by when it happened.

6. a. As simple relative (cf. WHAT C.**): At which time, on which occasion; and then. Sometimes implying suddenness: = and just then, and at that moment.

a **1000** *Cædmon's Gen.* 1265 Siððan hundtwelftiᵹ ᵹeteled rime wintra on worulde wræce bisᵹedon fæᵹe þeoda; hwonne frea wolde on wærloᵹan wite settan. **1461** PASTON *Lett.* I. 541 Wrytyn the xxiij. day of Janware in haste, wan I was not well at hesse. **1562** WINȜET *Cert. Tractates* Wks. (S.T.S.) I. 2 Haistelie maid one Pasche twisday,..1562, quhen thair apperit ane daingerous seditioun in Edinburgh. **1592** SHAKS. *Ven. & Ad.* 320 His testie maister goeth about to take him, When lo the vnbackt breeder full of feare,..swiftly doth forsake him. **1634** FORD *Perkin Warbeck* II. E 2 b, There haue been Irish-Hubbubs, when I haue made one too. **1711** BUDGELL *Spect.* No. 77 ¶1 We took a turn or two more, when, to my great Surprize, I saw him squirr away his Watch a considerable way into the Thames. **1780** *Mirror* No. 78 ¶3, I had not been above three years at college, when the death of an uncle put me in possession of a very considerable estate. **1820** KEATS *Lamia* II. 26 There came reposed,..When from the slope side of a suburb hill, ..came a thrill Of trumpets. **1893** *Law Times* XCV. 62/2 An inspector..tested the drain, when he found that the joints of the pipes were not properly cemented. **1894** BARING-GOULD *Bk. Fairy T.* 58 Scarcely had she touched the spindle when she pierced her hand with it.

b. As *quasi*-pronoun after a preposition (esp. *since* or *till*): = which time.

13.. *Cursor M.* 20180 (B.M. Add. MS.) Haueþ he me sette any day Aȝens when I me greithe may? **1581** A. HALL *Iliad* I. 12 But then a suter will I be, til when I wish (my child) You from the battayle do absteine. **1593** SHAKS. *3 Hen. VI* II. ii. 89 *Ed.* I was adopted Heire by his consent. *Cla.* Since when, his Oath is broke. **1634** SIR T. HERBERT *Trav.* 145 Since when it [*sc.* Persia] was vanquished by Tangrolipix the Turke, an. 1030. **1712** MRS. CENTLIVRE *Perplex'd Lovers* III. i, Till when, thou Charmer of my Soul, Farewel. **1820** SHELLEY *Prometh. Unb.* III. ii. 40 Thy steeds will pause at even, till when farewell.

7. With *time, day*, etc. as antecedent: = at or on which.

The following OE. quot. exemplifies the kind of context out of which this constr. might arise:—*Guthlac* 82 Fyrst was on godes dome, hwonne Guðlace on his ondᵹietan engel sealde þæt [etc.].

c **1200** ORMIN 133 Att ænne time whanne hiss lott Wass cumenn upp to þeowwtenn. *a* **1300** *Cursor M.* 19716 To wait þe time Quen þai moght cum to murther him. **1362** LANGL. *P. Pl.* A. Prol. 1 In A somer sesun whon softe was þe sonne. **1406** HOCCLEVE *La Male Regle* 326 Nat tell I can the tyme Whan they to bedde goon, it is so late. *c* **1440** *Gesta Rom.* xii. 38 (Harl. MS.) A day was set whanne the king shuld come and see hire. **1596** SPENSER *F.Q.* VI. vii. 32 On a day when Cupid kept his court. **1697** DRYDEN *Virg. Georg.* III. 79 A time will come, when my maturer Muse, In Cæsar's Wars, a Nobler Theme shall chuse. **1788** COWPER *Let. to S. Rose* 29 Mar., At all times, when it shall suit you to give us your company. **1845** M. PATTISON *Ess.* (1889) I. 9 The ages of faith, the ages when the Church bore sway over every action of life. **1865** NEWMAN *Hist. Relig. Opin.* iv. 201 Charges.. which..I fully believed at the time when I made them. **1876** SWINBURNE *Note Engl. Repub.* 16 Time was when England herself might have claimed..this noblest of human rights. **1876** MEREDITH *Beauch. Career* iv, There are times when an example is needed.

8. a. With the notion of time modified by or merged in that of mere connexion: In the, or any, case or circumstances in which; sometimes nearly = if. Often *ellipt.* with only the predicate expressed.

The clause with *when* is often equivalent to a phrase with preposition and gerund (***when he sees*** or ***saw*** = 'on seeing'; ***when he says*** or ***said*** = 'in saying').

c **1175** *Lamb. Hom.* 153 Mildheortnesse me kuð him soluen, h[w]enne he him biþengð þet he isuneȝed haueð and þet sare bimurneð. *c* **1220** *Bestiary* 502 in *O.E. Misc.* 16 Ȝef ðu it soȝe wan it flet. **1357** *Lay Folk's Catech.* (T.) 518 That is when we will noght do to god almighten,..That us augh for to do. **1370–80** *Visions St. Paul* 198 in *O.E. Misc.* 228 He opened þe Mouþ of þat put, Hit stonk foule wȝon hit was vn-schut. *c* **1400** tr. *Secr. Secr., Gov. Lordsh.* 63 Ȝers and reals dedys shal bettir come to a kynges mynde whon enhyed. *c* **1460** FORTESCUE *Abs. & Lim. Mon.* iv. (1885) 117 Whan a kynge rulith his reaume only to his owne profite..he is a tyrant. **1588** A. KING tr. *Canisius' Catech.* 181 The quhilk thing the scriptur meanes quhen it sayis [etc.]. **1591** SHAKS. *Two Gent.* v. iv. 44 Oh tis the curse in Loue..When women cannot loue, where they're belou'd. **1643** TRAPP *Comm. Gen.* xxxv. 1 God..takes his opportunity, (for we are best, when at worst). **1724** DE FOE *Tour Gt. Brit.* 15 When I have said this, I think I have done Malden Justice. **1781** COWPER *Table-T.* 148 Most confident, when palpably most wrong. **1859** RUSKIN *Two Paths* i. §42 A painter designs when he chooses some things, refuses others, and arranges all. **1890** J. CHAMBERLAIN *Sp.* 7 May in W. S. Lilly *1st Princ. Pol.* 161 *note*, When great national interests are at stake,..the party system breaks down.

b. As simple relative (cf. 6): †(*a*) with *case* as antecedent: = in which: (*b*) in which case; whereupon; and then.

1526 *Pilgr. Perf.* (W. de W. 1531) 2 Except in case whan you vnderstande not yᵗ ye rede therin. **1803** *Med. Jrnl.* X. 564 It may be opened with a lancet or a needle, when the fluid will run out. **1880** *Encycl. Brit.* XI. 695/1 The ribbon ..is sometimes couped or cut short, when it becomes a *bâton*.

9. With the notion of time passing into that of cause or contrast. **a.** It being the case that, seeing that, considering that, inasmuch as, since. (Often, and now only, with implication of opposition or contrast, thus approaching b.)

c **1230** *Hali Meid.* 9 Hwen þus is of þe riche, hwat wenes tu of the poure? **1297** R. GLOUC. (Rolls) 2215 Wanne ȝe abbeþ fourme of men, beþ men an alle wise. *a* **1330** *Otuel* 1272 Otuwel, whan it is so, Tak þe bataille a godes name. *c* **1420** *Sir Amadace* xxviii, Quat wundur were hit, thaȝhe him were wo, Quen alle his godus were spendutte him fro. **1591** SHAKS. *1 Hen. VI*, IV. i. 112 What madnesse rules in braine-sicke men, When for so slight..a cause, Such factious æmulations shall arise? *a* **1637** B. JONSON *Timber* Wks. (1641) 118 And indeed when the attaining of them [*sc.* all knowledges] is possible, it were a sluggish and base thing to despaire. **1764** GOLDSM. *Trav.* 64 But where to find that happiest spot below, Who can direct, when all pretend to know? **1865** DICKENS *Mut. Fr.* IV. iii, What's the good of my pretending to stand out, when I can't help myself? **1886** [E. H. DERING] *In Light of 20th Cent.* iv. 85 'If you would only ..look at the question without prejudice—' 'Prejudice! I like that, when you are full of prejudices about it.'

b. In adversative sense: While on the other hand, while on the contrary, whereas.

†In quot. *c* 1489 = although.

1297 R. GLOUC. (Rolls) 7770 Hii wolde euere abbe ynou, wanne þe pouere adde wo. *c* **1489** CAXTON *Sonnes of Aymon* vi. 153 And whan the kyng gaaff you not his suster but a simple damoysell, yet oughte you to beleve hym. *a* **1568** ASCHAM *Scholem.* II. (Arb.) 145 To follow rather the Gothes in Ryming, than the Greekes in trew versifiyng, were euen to eate ackornes with swyne, when we may freely eate wheate bread emonges men. **1610** SHAKS. *Temp.* II. i. 139 You rub the sore, When you should bring the plaister. *a* **1654** SELDEN *Table-T.* (1689) 26 Little things do great works, when great things will not. **1725** RAMSAY *Gentle Sheph.* IV. ii, An estate like yours yields braw content, When we but pike it scantly on the bent. **1836** MARRYAT *Japhet* lvii, I..received fifty shillings, when I ought to have received, at least, ten pounds. **1888** F. HARRISON *Cromwell* vi. 118 He was solemnly debating a treaty, when he never intended to keep any treaty at all.

III. Indefinite and substantival uses.

†**10. a.** *adv.* At some time (only OE. with *nú, seld(um)*; ***when and when***, at one time and another, now and then. *Obs. rare.*

c **900** tr. *Bæda's Hist.* II. i. (1890) 94 He nu hwonne on þam ilcan bið on wuldre arisende mid oþrum hyrdum þære halᵹan cyricean. *c* **1470** HARDING *Chron.* CXXI. iv, And Scottes also that false wer when and when.

b. As the second element of a compound: see ANYWHEN, AYWHEN, ELSEWHEN, EVERYWHEN, NOWHEN, SELD-*when*, SOMEWHEN.

11. as *sb.* The time at which something happens (or did or will happen): = *time when* (see 7); also *vaguely*, Time, duration.

Often conjoined with *where* or *how* similarly used.

1616 B. JONSON *Epigr.* xxxiii. Wks. 777 Thou art but gone before, Whither the world must follow. And I, now, Breathe to expect my *when*, and make my *how*. **1765** STERNE *Tr. Shandy* VII. xxi, The gardener..troubled his head very little with the *hows* and *whens* of life. **1819** SHELLEY *Ode to Heaven* 6 Deep, immeasurable vast, Which art now, and which wert then Of the Present and the Past, Of the eternal Where and When. **1864** NEWMAN *Apol.* VI. 362, I have very little reason to doubt about the issue of things, but the when and the how are known to Him. **1867** CARLYLE *E. Irving* in *Remin.* (1881) 101 The *when* of my first call there I do not now remember. **1885** TENNYSON *Anc. Sage* 104 Thin minds, who creep from thought to thought, Break into 'Thens' and 'Whens' the Eternal Now.

when, var. WHENNE *Obs.*, whence.

whenabouts ('hwɛnəbaʊts). *nonce-wd.* [f. WHEN, after *whereabouts*.] The time (or the approximate time) at which a thing happened. Also *interrog.*

1898 L. A. TOLLEMACHE *Talks with Gladstone* i. 19 The whereabouts and the whenabouts of my interviews with him. **1952** V. GOLLANCZ *My Dear Timothy* 74 By eighteen hundred and ninety-eight, when or whenabouts I first heard it. **1966** A. E. LINDOP *I start Counting* xx. 247 'When? Whenabouts?' '..Lemme see. Be about four o'clock in the afternoon.'

whenas, when as (hwɛn'æz, 'hwɛn æz), *adv.*, *conj. arch.* [f. WHEN + AS *adv.* 27.]

1. At the, or a, time at which; in a case in which: = WHEN 4, 8.

1423 JAS. I *Kingis Q.* ii, Quhen as I lay In bed allone waking,.. Fell me to mynd of many diuerse thing. **1550** LEVER *Serm. 4th Sund. Lent* A vij b, Ye shall heare, when as much people commynge vnto Iesus,.. what Iesus did. **1574** T. HILL *Art Garden., Bees* 66 This is a great token of raine to follow, when as the Sunne in the day time, and the Moone in the night, do appeare pale, or blackish of colour. **1602** KYD *Sp. Trag.* III. H 2 b, At the mid of noone, When as the Sun-God rides in all his glorie. **1638** QUARLES *Hieroglyph.* VII. iv, Subjects must vail, whenas their Sov'reigne's by. **1748** THOMSON *Cast. Indol.* I. lxv, Whenas we found he would not here be pent, To him the better sort this friendly message sent. **1808** SCOTT *Marm.* I. xxviii, Whenas the Palmer came in hall, Nor lord, nor knight, was there more tall. **1904** M. HEWLETT *Queen's Quair* II. vi, Whenas he hesitated..she came forward in a pretty, shy way.

†**b.** At which time; and then; whereupon: = WHEN 6. *Obs.*

1553 in Feuillerat *Revels Q. Mary* (1914) 159 Vntill the xxviijth daye of the same monethe wen as the same.. surseased. **1631** WEEVER *Anc. Funeral Mon.* 254 Hugh had scarce continued one yeare of probation, when as the fore-said Abbot Wido departed the world. **1697** J. SERGEANT *Solid Philos.* 205 Where's that Other Duration or Succession before Time,.. whenas 'tis confessed there was none.

2. a. Seeing that, inasmuch as: = WHEN 9 a.

1551 TURNER *Herbal* I. B ij b, When as the greater Galanga is..without any..euell sauoure I wold rather take great Galanga for Acorus, then the comon calamus. **1644** MILTON *Areop.* (Arb.) 57 How can he be a Doctor in his book.. whenas all he teaches..is but under..the correction of his patriarchal licencer? **1728** in *Sewall's Letter-bk.* (1886) II. 240, I may well condole the bereavement, whenas so much personal friendship is therewithall vanished. **1899** C. W. DOYLE *Taming of Jungle* i, Whenas my back smarted..from the blows of the chuprassi's shoe,.. I took the oil from my chirag and anointed my back therewith.

b. In adversative sense: Whereas: = WHEN 9 b.

1578 TIMME *Calvin on Gen.* 95 They doe verie childishly erre, which do consider originall sinne onely..in the inordinate motion of appetites: when as it fulfilleth the seate of reason and the whole hart. **1593** SHAKS. *3 Hen. VI*, v. vii. 34 So Iudas kist his master, And cried all haile, when as he meant all harme. **1699** BENTLEY *Phal.* 272 He brings in this Date of Solon's Death, out of Phanias: as if it was a point uncontroverted, and allow'd by Plutarch himself. Whenas Plutarch barely mentions it. **1711** SEWALL *Diary* 14 May (1879) II. 311 Through the Goodness of God I had little or no hurt, when as my Horse's Nose bled for it.

whence (hwɛns), *adv.*, *conj.* (*sb.*) Forms: 4–5 **whannes, whennes,** (4 **huannes, wannes, whennus, -ys**), 4–6 **whens,** 5 **qwens,** 6 **whense,** *Sc.* **quhens, quhence,** 6– **whence.** [13th c. ME. *whannes*, *whennes*, f. *whanne*, WHENNE + -S *suffix*[1]. In all senses often preceded by redundant *from*, †*fro* (FROM 15 a), occas. *of* (obs. or arch.).]

I. Interrogative uses. (Now replaced in ordinary colloquial speech by *where...from.*)

1. From what place? **a.** in a direct question.

a **1300** *K. Horn* 161 (Camb. MS.) Whannes beo ȝe, faire gumes, þat her to londe beoþ icume. **1382** WYCLIF *Gen.* xvi. 8 Whens comyst thow, and whithir gost thow? *c* **1430** *Syr Tryam.* 431 What do ye here, madam? Fro whens come ye? [*ed. Copland* (*c* 1550) Of whens be you..?]. **1526** TINDALE *John* vi. 5 Whence shall we bye breed that these might eate? **1540** PALSGR. *Acolastus* II. v. N ij, From whense haste thou brought hym hyther? **1547** BOORDE *Introd. Knowl.* xxvii. (1870) 192 Of whens be you? I am of England. **1596** SHAKS. *Tam. Shr.* II. i. 103 Of whence, I pray? *Tra.* Of Pisa, sir. **1697** DRYDEN *Æneis* x. 945 Whence am I forc'd, and whether am I born? **1720** DELANY *News fr. Parnass.* 19 From whence is this Fool? **1773** GOLDSM. *Stoops to Conq.* v, My wife, as I'm a Christian. From whence can she come? **1855** TENNYSON *The Brook* 22 O babbling brook,.. Whence come you?

b. in an indirect question.

c **1300** *St. Brandan* 288 We nuteth noȝt bote thurf God whannes hit is i-brouȝt. **1377** LANGL. *P. Pl.* B. v. 532 Þis folke frayned hym firste fro whennes he come. *c* **1450** *Merlin* 44 They axed hym of whens he was. **1526** TINDALE *John* ix. 29 Thys felowe, we knowe not from whence he ys. **1579** SPENSER *Sheph. Cal.* May 261 The Kidd..Asked..who, and whence that he were. **1697** DRYDEN *Æneis* VI. 1193 He ..ask'd his airy Guide, What, and of whence was he. *Ibid.* VIII. 150 Resolve me, Strangers, whence, and what you are. **1710** DE FOE *Ess. Public Credit* 6 We..hardly know whence it [*sc.* the wind] comes, or whither it goes. **1802** MARIA EDGEWORTH *Moral T., Forester* v, He inquired whence the water came. **1886** STEVENSON *Kidnapped* xxv, There was no question put of whence I came or whither I was going.

2. *gen.* and *transf.* From what source, origin, or cause? **a.** in a direct question.

c **1305** *Pop. Treat. Sci.* (1841) 139 Loke hou crokede thu were ther,.. Whannes [*earlier text* Fra ȝwam] cometh hit siththe to bere the so heȝe? **1382** WYCLIF *Matt.* xxi. 25 Of whennes was the baptem of Joon; of heuene, or of men? **1526** TINDALE *Luke* i. 43 Whens hapeneth this to me, that the mother off my lorde shulde come to me? **1697** DRYDEN *Æneis* x. 9 From whence these Murmurs, and this change of Mind? **1759** STERNE *Tr. Shandy* II. xvii, But whence..have you concluded..that the writer is of our church? **1853** DICKENS *Bleak Ho.* xix, From whence have we derived that spiritual profit?

b. in an indirect question.

1485 CAXTON *Chas. Gt.* 53, I am wel admeruaylled fro whens that cometh to the suche presumpcion to speke so hastyly. **1599** *Broughton's Lett.* viii. 28 There are some that can tell..from whence you borrow..your much bragd-of Concent. **1667** MILTON *P.L.* v. 856 Strange point and new! Doctrin which we would know whence learnt. **1718** PRIOR *Solomon* I. 459 Ask Reason now, whence Light and Shade were giv'n. **1781** COWPER *Truth* 237 An apt similitude shall show Whence springs the conduct that offends you so. **1849** C. BRONTE *Shirley* vii, The laughter and mirth of her uncle, and Hannah, and Mary, she could not tell whence originating. **1859** TENNYSON *Pelleas* 520 For so the words were flash'd into his heart He knew not whence or wherefore. **1867** F. HARRISON in *Questions Ref. Parlt.* 255 No man can say from whence the greater danger to order arises.

II. Relative or conjunctive uses.

3. From which place; from or out of which.

Also with ellipsis of *there* or *thither* in the main clause.

1382 WYCLIF *Ps.* cxx[i]. 1, I rered vp myn eȝen in to the mounteynes; whennys [**1388** fro whannus] shal come helpe to me. **1535** COVERDALE *Deut.* xi. 10 The londe of Egipte, whence ye came out. **1560** *Bible* (Geneva) Isa. li. 1 Loke vnto the rocke, whence ye are hewen. *a* **1700** EVELYN *Diary* 30 June 1644, A dreadfull cliff, from whence the country and river yeald a most incomparable prospect. **1728–46** THOMSON *Spring* 910 Mossy rocks, Whence on each hand the gushing waters play. **1838** DICKENS *O. Twist* xxxiv, The little room..looked into a garden, whence a wicket-gate opened into a small paddock. **1887** SWINBURNE *Stud. Prose & Poetry* (1894) 141 The quarter from whence the following lucubration is addressed.

1590 SHAKS. *Com. Err.* III. i. 37 Let him walke from whence he came. **1591** —— *Two Gent.* II. iv. 122 Now tell me: how do al from whence you came? **1611** *Bible* Job x. 21 Let me alone that I may take comfort a litle, Before I goe whence [COVERDALE thyther, from whence] I shall not returne.

†**b.** as *compound relative*: From the place in which, from where. *poet. Obs. rare.*

1601 SHAKS. *All's Well* III. ii. 124 Come thou home Rossillion, Whence honor but of danger winnes a scarre, As oft it looses all. **1607** —— *Timon* I. i. 22 Our Poesie is as a Goume [*printed* Gowne] which vses [*i.e.* oozes] From whence 'tis nourisht.

4. *gen.* and *transf.* From which source or origin (as a product); from which cause (as a result); from which fact or circumstance (as an inference).

a **1568** ASCHAM *Scholem.* I. (Arb.) 61 This opinion is not French, but plaine Turckishe: from whens, som French fetche moe faultes, than this. **1590** SPENSER *F.Q.* III. iii. 1 Vertue..Whence spring all noble deeds and neuer dying fame. **1678** CUDWORTH *Intell. Syst.* 32 To lay down such Principles, as from whence it would follow, that any Real Entity in Nature did come from Nothing and go to Nothing. **1731–8** SWIFT *Pol. Conversat.* Introd. 29 From whence I did then conclude..that Wine doth not inspire Politeness. **1781** COWPER *Expost.* 111 Faith, the root whence only can arise The graces of a life that wins the skies. **1859** JEPHSON *Brittany* vi. 81 St. Ive..became a successful advocate, whence he is now venerated by Breton lawyers as their patron. **1885** GOODALE *Physiol. Bot.* 400 During its revolution a tip bows or nods successively to all points of the compass; whence the name nutation.

III. 5. as *sb.* (*nonce-use.*) That from which something comes or arises; place of origin; source.

1832 MOTLEY in *Corr.* (1889) I. 18, I was summoned before the Senate of the University, and then wrote my name and my whences and whats, etc., etc., in a great book. **1869** MRS. WHITNEY *Hitherto* xviii. 242 We start from some whence, and are expressed through to somewhere. **1875** E. WHITE *Life in Christ* I. iv. (1878) 30 Uncertain as to the Whence and Whither of humanity.

whenceforth, *adv. rare.* [Properly two words, WHENCE and FORTH *adv.* 3.] †**a.** Forth from which. **b.** From which time onward: cf. *henceforth.* (With redundant *from.*)

1590 SPENSER *Muiopot.* 316 The God of Seas..strikes the rockes with his three-forked mace; Whenceforth issues a warlike steed in sight. **1658** HARRINGTON *Prerog. Pop. Govt.* 34 From whenceforth God proposeth unto the People no otherwise then by Moses.

whence'forward, *adv. rare.* [Properly two words, WHENCE and FORWARD *adv.*; cf. HENCEFORWARD, THENCEFORWARD.] **a.** = prec. **b. b.** From which place onward.

a **1661** FULLER *Worthies, Shropshire* (1662) III. 16 Whence forward and not before, his Forces deserved the name of an Army. **1899** *Daily News* 1 July 4/6 From hence it is no great way to Woodford, whenceforward the return journey is but a repetition of the outward.

†**whence-from**, *adv. Obs.* [An inversion of *from whence*: cf. HENCE-FROM, THENCE-FROM.]

1. *interrog.* = WHENCE I.

1579 TOMSON *Calvin's Serm. Tim.* 29/2 Whence-from did our Lord Iesus Christe and his Apostles drawe their doctrine, but out of Moses? **1598** SYLVESTER *Du Bartas* II. ii. *Ark* 306 Whence (shall I say) then, whence-from comes it.. That [etc.]. **1604** T. WRIGHT *Passions* Pref., I have divers times weighed with my selfe, whencefrom it should proceed [etc.].

2. *rel.* = WHENCE II.

1666 J. SMITH *Old Age* (1676) 236 Whereunto all the blood..doth naturally tend;..and whence-from it will in no wise depart.

whenceness ('hwɛnsnɪs). *rare.* [f. WHENCE *adv.*, *conj.* (*sb.*) + -NESS.] The place or source from which something comes or arises; place of origin.

1922 JOYCE *Ulysses* 388 All is hidden when we would backward see from what region of remoteness the whatness of our whoness hath fetched his whenceness. **1980** *Dædalus* Spring 248 Given the group's oblique disposition, the 'whenceness' of this saved soul seems unmistakable.

whencesoever (hwɛnssəʊ'ɛvə(r)), *adv.*, *conj.* Also *poet.* **-soe'er** (-səʊ'ɛə(r)). (In early use as two words.) [f. WHENCE + SOEVER.] From whatever place or source; wherever...from. (Also with redundant *from.*)

1511 *Guylforde's Pilgr.* (Camden) 22 This Cytie of Jherusalem..stondeth vpon suche a grounde that from whens soever a man commyth theder he must nede ascende. **1593** SHAKS. *Rich. II*, II. iii. 22 It is my Sonne, young Harry Percie, Sent from my Brother Worcester: Whence soeuer. **1610** HOLLAND *Camden's Brit.* 208 (1) Whencesoever the name came, it is antient. **1670** DRYDEN *1st Pt. Conq. Granada* IV. ii, From whence-soe're their Hate our Houses drew, I blush to tell you, I have none for you. **1759** JOHNSON *Rasselas* xxxviii, Whoever or whencesoever you are. **1842** MANNING *Serm.* i. (1848) I. 2 Whatsoever or whencesoever be the origin of Sin. **1887** MORRIS *Odyssey* I. 10 O Goddess, ..from whencesoever ye may, Gather the tale. **1912** G. B. GRAY *Crit. Introd. O.T.* 200 He re-moulds his material, whencesoever derived.

whencever (hwɛns'ɛvə(r)), *adv.*, *conj.* Also *poet.* **whence'er** (hwɛns'ɛə(r)). Earlier as two words, **whence ever.** [See EVER *adv.* 8 e.] = prec.

1718 PRIOR *Solomon* II. 793 Whence ever I thy cruel Essence bring, I own thy Influence. **1888** CLOUGH *Poems, Fragm. Myst. Fall* xii, A thing, whence'er it came, To be forgotten and considered not. **1899** BELLOC *Danton* iv. 119 The enthusiasms which, from whencever they blow, are the fresh winds of the soul.

†**whenceward**, *adv. Obs. rare*[−1]. [f. WHENCE + -WARD: cf. THENCEWARD.] *From* whence.

1701 RAY *Creation* II. (ed. 3) 366 In those Ponds from whenceward they steered their course.

whench, variant of QUENCH *v.*

†**whene**, *v. Obs.* Also **wene, ȝwene.** [Aphetic f. AWHENE (OE. *âhwǽnan*).] *trans.* To afflict, trouble, offend.

a **1310** in Wright *Lyric P.* 49 Lyare wes mi latymer, Sleuthe ant slep my bedyuer [= bed-fellow; *printed* bedyner], that weneth me unbe-while. Umbe-while y am to whene, when y shal murthes metan. *c* **1315** SHOREHAM I. 1908 And þaȝ þat lawe for-bede nauȝt þat man and wyf ymene Toe-hebbe a child, ȝet scholdy nauȝt Honestete so ȝwene. *c* **1330** R. BRUNNE *Chron. Wace* (Rolls) 6887 'Lord,' he seyde, 'ȝow þar nought wene, Why y am comen ȝe may wel mene.'

whene, obs. f. QUEEN, WAIN, WHEN.

whenever (hwɛn'ɛvə(r)), *adv.*, *conj.* (In early use as two words.) Also *poet.* **whene'er** (hwɛn'ɛə(r)). [f. WHEN + EVER (see below).]

I. As relative adverb or conjunction: cf. WHEN 4.

1. [EVER *adv.* 8 e.] At any time when; every time that, as often as. In a qualifying (conditional) clause, the meaning becomes: At whatever time, no matter when. Also with the idea of time weakened or lost (cf. WHEN 8): In any or every case in which. Also as adv. with loss of relative force: at whatever time (*colloq.*).

c **1380** WYCLIF *Sel. Wks.* III. 354 As þe popis clerkis feynen þat þei done miraclis whanne evere þei syngen, moo and more woundirful þan ever dide Crist or his apostlis. *c* **1440** *Generydes* 1245 Ser, on to hir loggyng, When euer it please yow, I shall be your gyde. *c* **1449** PECOCK *Repr.* Prol. 2 Whanne euer he takith vpon him for to..correpte his Cristen neiȝbour. **1509** *Reg. Privy Seal Scot.* I. 293/2 Landis ..that sall happin to cum in the Kingis hands..throu the said Henrys deceis quhenevir it sall happin. **1588** SHAKS. *Tit. A.* IV. ii. 15 When euer you haue need, You may be armed and appointed well. **1667** MILTON *P.L.* x. 771 His doom is fair, That dust I am, and shall to dust returne: O welcom hour whenever! **1678** *Yng. Man's Call.* p. xiv, So might you welcom your death with pleasant smiles when ere it comes. **1766** GOLDSM. *Vicar W.* xxx, You may, at a minute's warning, send them over England whenever your honour thinks fit. **1842** DICKENS *Amer. Notes* ix, Whenever an Englishman would cry 'All right!' an American cries 'Go ahead!' **1865** RUSKIN *Sesame* i. §25 Roguery and lying..are instantly to be flogged out of the way whenever discovered. **1891** FARRAR *Darkn. & Dawn* xiv, She still had access to the Emperor whenever she desired. **1917** H. JAMES *Ivory Tower* in *Amer. Novels* III. v. 221, I said to myself..three weeks ago, or whenever, that it wasn't for that I was going to come over. **1921** *Oxford Mag.* 28 Jan. 163/1 When the official story..is published, whenever that may be, minor details.. will require correction. **1982** J. D. MACDONALD *Cinnamon Skin* xi. 107 Maybe we can leave it that you can come over to Lauderdale when-ever.

2. [EVER 8 c.] At the very time or moment when; as soon as. (Now only in *Sc.* and *Irish* use.)

1655 tr. *Sorel's Com. Hist. Francion* VIII. 7 He gave me a good supper last night when ever I came within his doors. **1800** *Monthly Mag.* IX. 323/2 We will go to our dinner whenever the clock strikes two. **1839** URE *Dict. Arts* 589

One-third of the mixture is introduced at first; whenever this is melted, the second third is thrown in. **1875** A. Wilson *Abode of Snow* xxxviii. 360 And whenever my tent was set up I went to sleep in spite of the wind.

II. 3. As interrogative adverb, an emphatic extension of *when*. (Properly two words, and usually so written: see EVER 8 d.) Now *colloq.*

1713 Addison *Cato* I. i, When-e're did Juba, or did Portius, show A Virtue that has cast me at a Distance? *Mod.* When ever I did I say that? I waited and waited, and wondered when ever he would come.

†**whenne, when,** *adv.*, *conj. Obs.* Forms: *α.* 1 **hwanone,** 3 **hwanene, whanene, wanene, hweonene, wheonene, wenene, whonene, whonnene, wonene, (whænnenen).** *β.* 2 **hwonne,** 3 **hweonne, whone, wanne,** 3–5 **whenne,** 4 *Sc.* **quhene.** *γ.* 1 **hwanon, -an, -un, hwonan, -on,** 3 **hwannen, whannen, -in, wannen, wanen.** *δ.* 1 **huona, hwona.** *ε.* 4 **wen, wan,** *north.* **quen,** *Sc.* **quhen,** 4–5 **when.** See also WHYNE. [OE. *hwanone, hwanon, hwonan* = OS. *hwanon, -en*, whence (*nêthwanen* from somewhere or other), OHG. *(h)wanana, wanân, wannen* (MHG. *swannen* = **sô wannen sô* whencesoever): a derivative of the interrog. stem *χwa-* WHO, WHAT, as HEN, HENNE (= hence) is of *χi-* HE, and THENNE, THEN (= thence) of *þa-*.]

1. *interrog.* = WHENCE 1, 2.

Beowulf 333 Hwanon ferigeað ȝe fætte scyldas? *Ibid.* 2403 Hæfde þa ȝefrunen, hwanan sio fæhð aras. *c* **888** Ælfred *Boeth.* v. §3 Wast þu hwonan ælc wuht cume? *c* **950** *Lindisf. Gosp.* Luke i. 43 *Unde hoc mihi ut ueniat mater domini mei ad me*, huona [*Rushw.* hwona; *Ags.* hwanun; *Hatton* hwanen] ðis me þætte cyme moder drihtnes mines to me? *a* **1000** *Gosp. Nicod.* iv. (Thwaites) 2 Hwanone sceoldest þu specan on Hebreisc? *c* **1200** *Vices & Virtues* 69 Ic ðe warni.. ðat tu.. understande and lierne fastliche ða ȝekyndes of sinnes, hwannen and hwanne hie cumen. *c* **1205** Lay. 1430 Whonene [*c* **1275** Wanene] beo ȝe cnihtes? *Ibid.* 6193 He.. hæhte heom suggen wannen heo weoren. **1297** R. Glouc. (Rolls) 2407 He esste hom wanen [*v.r.* of wanne] hi were & wo him þider broȝte. **13..** *Guy Warw.* (A.) 1724 Gij.. seyd, 'wen comestow, pilgrim?' **1362** Langl. *P. Pl.* A. xii. 75 He.. asked him after, Of when þat he were. *c* **1380** *Sir Ferumb.* 2547 'Ihesu lord', quaþ Olyuere; 'fro wan comeþ al þis gold?' **1390** Gower *Conf.* I. 265 Of Envie noman knoweth Fro whenne he cam bot out of helle. *a* **1425** *Cursor M.* 13929 (Trin.) Whenne he shal com shal noon knowe. **1483** *Cath. Angl.* 416/1 Whenne, *vnde*.

2. *rel.* or *conj.* = WHENCE 3, 4.

c **1000** *Ags. Gosp.* Matt. xviii. 25 þa he næfde hwanon he hyt agulde. *c* **1175** *Lamb. Hom.* 61 Parais, from hwonne þe engles a-dun follon. *c* **1205** Lay. 2034 He hire sette name on.. to munien his ikunde whone he icomen weore. **1297** R. Glouc. (Rolls) 4298 Toward þe wode wanene [*v.r.* fram wanne] hii come þe brutons gonne to fle. **1390** Gower *Conf.* I. 212 To.. go.. To Rome, whenne that sche cam.

b. Qualified by *ever*: = WHENCESOEVER.

1390 Gower *Conf.* I. 156 He which was a Bacheler, Mi fader, is now mad a Pier; So whenne as evere that I cam, An Erles dowhter now I am. *c* **1440** *Ipomydon* 497 Where [*v.r.* when] he euer come or what he is.

whenne, whennes, -us, obs. ff. WHEN, WHENCE.

ˈ**whenness.** *nonce-wd.* [f. WHEN + -NESS.] Condition in respect of time.

1710 De Foe *Ess. Public Credit* 6 It has no Whereness, or Whenness, Scite, or Habit.

whens, whense, obs. ff. WHENCE.

whenso (ˈhwɛnsəʊ), *adv.*, *conj.* Forms: see WHEN and SO *adv.* and *conj.* [ME. *hwense*, representing OE. **swá hwanne swá*: see WHEN and SO *adv.* 17 d.]

†**1.** = WHEN 4. *Obs.*

c **1175** *Lamb. Hom.* 85 In þe deie of liureisun hwense god almihtin wule windwin þet er wes iþorschen. *c* **1205** Lay. 15054 Weonne so ich beo uorð faren, Hengest eow wul makien kare. *a* **1225** *Ancr. R.* 412 Ȝe ȝet moten chaungen ham hwonse ȝe euer willeð. **1423** Jas. I *Kingis Q.* cxviii, Quhen so my teris dropen on the ground,.. the lytill birdis smale Styntith thaire song. **1567** *Reg. Privy Council Scot.* I. 522 Quhen swa this cruell murthour wes committit,.. nevir ceissit he of his wickit.. pretense.

2. = WHENEVER 1. *arch.*

c **1200** Ormin 1466 Whannse þu forrȝifesst tuss þin wraþþe & ec þin wræche, Aȝȝ þanne lakesst tu þin Godd Gastlike i þine þæwess. *c* **1400** *Rule St. Benet* (verse) 861 When so we ȝern ony thing þat may fall vnto flesch likyng, Thinke we god waites vs weterly! *c* **1425** *Cast. Persev.* 2542 in *Macro Plays* 153 It is good, whon-so þe wynde blowe, A man to haue sum-what of his owe. **1473** *Rental Bk. Cupar-Angus* (1879) I. 178 He sal haue the fredome of hoslary quhenswa at it be sufficiand. **1591** Spenser *M. Hubberd* 829 Whenso loue of letters did inspire Their gentle wits. **1866** Neale *Sequences, Hymns*, etc. 216 Whenso that battle seems going against us, remember the legend. **1879** Butcher & Lang *Odyssey* III. 40 Phrontis,.. who excelled the tribes of men in piloting a ship, whenso the storm winds were hurrying by.

whensoever (hwɛnsəʊˈɛvə(r)), *adv.*, *conj.* Also *poet.* **whensoe'er** (-ˈɛə(r)). [f. prec. + EVER *adv.*; cf. SOEVER.] = WHENEVER 1.

c **1320** *Cast. Love* (Halliw.) 177 Thet whensoever the appul he ȝete, Thet sholde deth that lyfe he shulde forlete. *c* **1450** *Godstow Reg.* 532 To.. whom-so-euer or which-so-euer and whan-so-euer he wolde yeve bequeth.. hit. **1486** *Bk. St. Albans* d ij b, Whensoeuer and whersoeuer thay se any tame Dookes. **1526** Tindale *Mark* xiv. 7 Ye shall have povre with you all wayes: and when soever ye will, ye maye do them goode. **1603** Shaks. *Meas. for M.* v. i. 158 What he with.. all probation will make vp full cleare Whensoeuer he's conuented. *a* **1716** South *Serm., James iii. 16* Wks. 1727 V. 397 Whensoever the Romans conquered an Enemy, it was indeed the General himself only, who was said to triumph. **1815** W. H. Ireland *Scribbleomania* 20 Whensoever Mr. Southey issues from the press, we find him arrayed in a different costume. **1819** Shelley *Peter Bell 3rd* v. x. 3 Whensoever he should please, He could speak of rocks and trees In poetic metre. **1853** Rock *Ch. Fathers* III. II. 51 The bishop first blessed the attire with which those ministers were to be arrayed whensoever they had to go about their holy office.

b. *ellipt.* with loss of relative force: At any time.

1604 Shaks. *Ham.* v. ii. 210 (Qo. 2) If his fitnes speakes, mine is ready: now or when soeuer, prouided I be so able as now. **1651** tr. *Life Father Paul Sarpi* 10 Either rising from the board, or from his bed at midnight, or whensoever applying himself wholly.. to the subject.

whensomever (hwɛnsəmˈɛvə(r)), *adv.*, *conj.* Now *dial.* or *vulgar*. [See SOMEVER 2.] = prec.

a **1425** tr. *Arderne's Treat. Fistula* etc. 61 When-someuer þe pacient feleþ tyklyng or ychyng or prykkyng in þe lure. **1507** *Cov. Leet Bk.* 608 When-sume-euer and as often as the case shall require. **1558** Q. Kennedy *Compend. Tract.* in *Wodrow Soc. Misc.* (1844) 99 Quhensumevir questioun or debait rysis. **1611** in *10th Rep. Hist. MSS. Comm.* App. I. 547 The next degree I expecte is some violent fryars and Jesuites inciting.. the Catholick Princes against hereticks.. Which whensomever it bee I confidently beleeve you shall see yᵉ tragedie begin in France. **1810** *Splendid Follies* III. 112 You have my consent, sir, to marry the girl whensumdever it's convenient.

whent, wheoder, wheol(e: see QUAINT *a.*, WHETHER, WHEEL.

wher, obs. f. *were*, pa. t. indic. pl. of BE *v.*; obs. f. WHERE; obs. or dial. contr. f. WHETHER.

wherble, obs. form of WARBLE.

where (hwɛə(r)), *adv.* and *conj.* Forms.: *α.* 1–2 **hwær,** (1 **huoer, hwoer, wær, uer),** 1–3 **hwer,** 1–4 **huer,** (3 **whær(e, wær),** 3–5 **wer,** 3–6 **wher,** 4 **hwere,** 4–6 **were,** 6 **whear,** *Sc.* **vher,** 6–7 **wheare,** 7 (9 *dial.*) **wheer,** 4– **where;** *Sc.* and *north. dial.* 3–5 **quer,** 4–5 **quere,** 5 **qwer(e, qwher,** 6 **quheir,** 7 **quher(e.** *β.* 1–3 **hwar,** (1 **hwara),** 2–4 **war,** (3 **wahr, ȝwar, ȝware),** 3–5 **ware,** (8 *Sc.*) **whare,** (8–9 *Sc.*) **whar,** 4 **hware,** 5 **whaire,** 6–7 **vhair,** (9 *Sc.*) **whair,** 9 *Sc.* **whaur;** *Sc.* and *north. dial.* 3–4 **quar,** 4–5 **quare,** 4–6 **quhar, quhare,** 5 **qwar, qware, qwhar, qwhare;** 5–6 **quair,** 5–8 **quhair,** 6–7 **quhaire.** *γ.* 3 **wor, quor, quuor,** 4 **hwore, quore,** 4–5 **whore,** 5 **whor.** *δ.* *n.e. Sc.* 6 **for,** 9 **faur** (*Irish* far). [OE. *hwǽr, hwár*, corresp. to OFris. *hwêr*, OS. *hwâr* (MLG. *wâr*, LG. *waar, woor*, MDu., Du. *waar*), OHG. *(h)wâr, wâ*, MHG. *wâ*, G. *wo* (*wâr* surviving in G. *warum*). A disyllabic OE. form *hwára* (ME. *whǭre*) also existed; cf. *þára* there. Forms with short vowel appear in OE. *hwar, hwara*, (ME. *whar, whare*), OS. *hwar*, OHG. *wara*, MHG. *ware, war* whither, ON. *hvar* (Sw. *var*, Da. *hvor*), Goth. *hwar* where.

Derived from the interrog. stem *χwa-*, as HERE is from *χi-* HE, and THERE from *þa-*; cf. Lith. *kur̃* where, L. *cūr* (:—**quōr*) why, Skr. *kár-hi* when.]

I. Interrogative uses.

In dependent clauses formerly sometimes followed by *that*: see THAT *conj.* 6. For the distinction between the dependent interrogative and the relative use, cf. WHAT A. I.**

1. In or at what place (region, country, etc.)? **a.** in direct questions.

c **825** *Vesp. Psalter* xli. 4 [xlii. 3] Hwer is god ðin? *c* **1000** Ælfric *Gen.* iii. 9 God.. cwæð: Adam, hwar eart þu? *a* **1175** *Cott. Hom.* 241 þis is hare bread, hwer scule we win finden? *c* **1200** Ormin 12734 Lef maȝȝstre, whære biggesst tu? *c* **1205** Lay. 4454 Whær beo ȝe mine cnihtes, whar beo ȝe mine kempen? *c* **1250** *Gen. & Ex.* 356 Ðu, nu, quor art, adam, adam? *Ibid.* 1311 Quar sal ben taken ðe offrende ðat ðu wilt maken? *a* **1300** *Cursor M.* 1123 Caym ware es þi broiþer abell? **1382** Wyclif *Gen.* iii. 9 The Lord God clepide Adam, and seide to hym, Where art thow? *a* **1400–50** *Wars Alex.* 683 Quat sterne is it at ȝe stody on, quare stekis it in heuyn? **1456** Sir G. Haye *Law Arms* (S.T.S.) 6 The secounde questioun that is to say quhare was bataill first fundyn. *c* **1460** *Towneley Myst.* xiii. 402 *Primus pastor.* Bot I will go before, let vs mete. *ijus pastor.* whore? *iijus pastor.* At the crokyd thorne. *a* **1600** Montgomerie *Sonn.* lvi. 13 Vhair go they then? **1637** Milton *Lycidas* 50 Where were ye Nymphs when the remorseless deep Clos'd o're the head of your lov'd Lycidas? **1779** Warner in Jesse *Selwyn & Contemp.* (1844) IV. 285, I have been preaching this morning, and am going to dine,—where?—in the afternoon. **1838** P. Egan *Pilgr. Thames* 259 Where the deuce am I? **1848** Dickens *Dombey* xxvi, My dearest Edith,.. where on earth have you been? **1896** Barrie *Sentim. Tommy* iii. 34 Whaur heard you that name?

b. (*a*) in dependent clauses.

c **893** Ælfred *Oros.* IV. x. §3 Ðesecgað me nu Romane, cwæð Orosius, hwonne þæt ȝewurde oþþe hwara [etc.]. **971** *Blickl. Hom.* 241 þine stefne ic ȝehiere, ac ic ne wat hwær þu eart. *c* **1200** *Trin. Coll. Hom.* 143 Ȝe hereð, ware heo com to ure helende. *a* **1240** *Ureisun* 106 in *O.E. Hom.* I. 197 Ful wel þu me iseie.. Hwar ich was and hwat i dude. *c* **1290** *S. Eng. Leg.* 10/325 He wuste ȝware þe rode lai. *a* **1300** *Cursor M.* 157 Hit sal be reddynn þanne.. How he was born and quen and ware [*v.rr.* quare, whare]. *Ibid.* 17288 + 223 þai haf taken my lord,.. and doyne him Ine wote whore. **13..** *E.E. Allit. P.* A. 65, I ne wyste in þis worlde quere þat hit wace. **1461** *Paston Lett.* II. 17, I have knowelege quere the shippyng chall be. **1470–85** Malory *Arthur* x. lvii. 511 Yet wold not sire Launcelot telle me certeynte of you where I shold fynde yow. **1573–80** Tusser *Husb.* (1878) 117 Where hops will growe, here learne to knowe. **1645** in *Spalding Club Misc.* I. 56 Ye will certanly knaw whair to find ws with the Regiementis. **1648** Cromwell *Let. to T. Saunders* 17 June in *Carlyle*, You may send to Colonel Herbert,.. who will certainly acquaint you where he is. **1724** Ramsay *Vision* vii, I.. Speird, quhair he had been sae lang? **1784** Cowper *Ep. to J. Hill* 47 An emp'ror, a wise man—No matter where, in China or Japan. **1822** Scott *Nigel* iii, You did not tell him where I lived, you knave? **1860** Dickens *Uncomm. Trav.* ii, Little does it signify to us, when the soul has departed, where this poor body lies. **1882** Besant *All Sorts* xv, You come from no one knows where; you live no one knows how.

(*b*) in dependence on an int. or vb. of looking: ***lo, see, look, behold where*** (he comes) = Here or there (he comes)! *arch.*

c **1205** Lay. 5029 Leo wær here þa wombe þe þu læie inne swa longe. *c* **1420** *Chron. Vilod.* 3117 Lowe where is a lomb! a fayre whyte lomb! lo! lo! **1591** Shaks. *Two Gent.* v. i. 7 See where she comes. **1593** —— *3 Hen. VI*, I. i. 50 My Lords, looke where the sturdie Rebell sits. **1605** —— *Macb.* v. viii. 55 Behold where stands Th' Vsurpers cursed head. **1681** Dryden *Abs. & Achit.* II. 1125 See where the Princely Barque in loosest Pride, With all her Guardian Fleet, Adorns the Tide! **1742** Gray *Spring* i, Lo! where the rosy-bosom'd Hours, Fair Venus' train, appear. **1839** Hood *Quakers' Conversaz.* II. 29 Lo! where the Soldier walks, alas! With Scars received on foreign Grounds.

c. *colloq.* with *from* or *to* at the end of the sentence or clause: ***where...from?*** = whence? ***where...to?*** = whither?

1760–72 H. Brooke *Fool of Qual.* (1809) II. 103, I must go suddenly, but where to? **1835** Dickens *Sk. Boz, Parish* iii, Where on earth the husband came from. **1914** 'Ian Hay' *Knt. on Wheels* xiii, Where do these brats hail from?

2. In general and fig. senses: In what position, situation, or circumstances? at what point or stage (of action, speech, or thought)? in what passage or part (of a writing)? in what particular? in what respect? in what? also (contextually, with *get*, etc.) from what source?

a **1225** *Ancr. R.* 8 Askeð him, Hwat beo ordre, & hwar he ifinde in holi write religiun openluker descriued.. þen in sein Iames canoniel epistle? *a* **1250** *Owl & Night.* 892 & þan sunfulle ic helpe al so Vor ic him teche hwar is wo. *a* **1300** *Cursor M.* 2800 Godd.. þat made þat sinful folk sa madd, þat þai ne wist war þai war stad. *c* **1450** *Mirk's Festial* 4 Hys angyll.. tellyng hym redely wher and how oft he haþe don amys. **1531** Elyot *Gov.* I. xiii. (1883) I. 131 In defendynge of oratours and poetes I had all moste forgoten where I was. **1599** Shaks. *Hen. V*, III. v. 15 Where haue they this mettell? Is not their Clymate foggy, raw, and dull? **1600** —— *A.Y.L.* v. ii. 32 O, I know where you are. **1641** Milton *Ch. Govt.* I. vii. 28 If there were no opposition where were the triall of an unfained goodnesse and magnanimity? **1728** Law *Serious C.* ix, You must not deceive yourself with saying, Where can be the harm of clothes? **1847** C. Bronte *Jane Eyre* xxxii, 'But where is the use of going on,' I asked. **1882** Besant *All Sorts* xxii, 'I see.. You were attracted by the ancient inscriptions?' 'Naturally: without inscriptions, where are you?' **1908** R. Bagot *A. Cuthbert* v. 47 That is all very well; but where do I come in?

3. To what place? Now, in ordinary use, taking the place of WHITHER; cf. HERE *adv.* 7, THERE 8. (Formerly freq. with BECOME, q.v. 1 b.)

c **1000** *Wanderer* 92 Hwær cwom mearȝ? hwær cwom maȝo? *c* **1205** Lay. 21913 Wær scullen we bicumen? *a* **1300** *Cursor M.* 13748 Quar ar þai cummen, þin wiþerwins þat þe had nummen? **1303** R. Brunne *Handl. Synne* 7492 þat þrostel sagh he no more; Hyt become, he ne wyst whore. **1377** Langl. *P. Pl.* B. Prol. 166 Were þere a belle on here beiȝ... Men myȝte wite where þei went and awei renne! **1470–85** Malory *Arthur* xxi. iv. 846 Where are al my noble knyghtes becomen? **1587** Harrison *England* I. xi. 47/1 in *Holinshed*, Whose eies are so blinded with the thicknesse of that element, that they cannot see where to become. **1590** Shaks. *Mids. N.* III. i. 166 Where shall we go? **1611** —— *Wint. T.* IV. iv. 304 *Aut.* Get you hence, for I must goe Where it fits not you to know. *Dor.* Whether? *a* **1708** T. Ward *Eng. Ref.* I. (1710) 86 His Soul departed, God knows where. **1730** A. Gordon *Maffei's Amphith.* 289 We shall now mention where every one of those Entries.. lead. **1809** Malkin *Gil Blas* III. iii. ¶8 Unconscionable dogs! Where do they expect to go when they die? **1860** Dickens *Uncomm. Trav.* iii, Who departed this life I don't know when, and whose coaches are all gone I don't know where.

4. In rhetorical questions having the effect of emphatic negations (cf. WHAT A. 3): e.g. *where is* ——? implying or suggesting '—— has vanished' or 'there is no —— anywhere'; *where not* = everywhere (cf. WHAT NOT).

c **888** Ælfred *Boeth.* xix, Hwær synt nu þæs Welondes ban, oððe hwa wat nu hwær hi wæron? *c* **1000** *Ags. Gosp.* Luke viii. 25 Ða cwæþ se hælend, hwar is eower ȝeleafa? *c* **1300** *Havelok* 1083 Hwere mithe i finden ani so hey So hauelok is, or so sley? *c* **1430** *Hymns Virgin* (1867) 86 Where is bicome cesar, þat lorde was of al? *c* **1520** Skelton *Magnyf.* 2055 Where is nowe my Welth and my noble estate? **1567** *Satir. Poems Reform.* iv. 174 Quhair sall men find steidfast Stabilnes? **1600** W. Watson *Decacordon* (1602) 34 All went to wracke in England, Scotland, Flanders, Germanie, Polony, and where not. **1709** Prior *Henry & Emma* 282 And where is Emma's Joy, if Henry flies? **1842** Mrs. Trollope *Vis. Italy* I. iii. 49 As to pictures, where could I find foolscap enough to catalogue the multitude I have seen? **1865** Dickens *Mut. Fr.* I. v, Where would be the good of Mrs. Boffin and me quarrelling over it? **1906** Bigg *Wayside Sk.* vi. 154 Where shall we find him [*sc.* the perfect reformer] except in the Son of Man?

II. Relative and conjunctive uses.

Formerly often followed by *that* (THAT *conj.* 6).

* In senses referring to physical position.

5. as compound relative, or as correlative to *there* (implied and sometimes expressed; cf. WHAT C.*, WHEN 4): In or at the (or a) place in or at which; at the part at which.

[c950 *Lindisf. Gosp.* Matt. vi. 21 *Ubi enim est thesaurus tuus ibi est et cor tuum*, ðer *vel* huer forðon is strion ðin, ðer is & hearta ðin.] **13..** *Northern Passion* I. 138 þei souhte anoþer where þei myhte. **1338** R. Brunne *Chron.* (1725) I. 22 þer where he was schotte. **c1400** tr. *Secr. Secr., Gov. Lordsh.* 89 A hors shal neuer henny whore he dwellys. **1483** *Acta Audit.* in *Acta Dom. Conc.* II. Introd. 102 The Lordis ..ordanis that letters be writin to the schireffis quhar the said landis liis. **1548–9** [see THITHER 1 c]. **1583** Melbancke *Philotimus* Ej, Wher God buildes a church, the deuill builds a chappell. **a1592** Greene *Orpharion* Wks. (Grosart) XII. 33 Where the sea is most deepe, there it is most calme. **1639** J. Clarke *Parœm.* 48 He is where he would be. **1779** Cowper *A Tale*, '*Where Humber*', Where Humber pours his rich commercial stream, There dwelt a wretch, who breath'd but to blaspheme. **1810** Crabbe *Borough* ii. 45 Where the common eye Can but the bare and rocky bed descry, There Science loves to trace her tribes minute. **1859** Ruskin *Two Paths* i. §2 Inverness, placed where it might ennoble one of the sweetest landscapes. **1893** Max Pemberton *Iron Pirate* iv, I shall stay where I am.

b. To the (or a) place in or at which (= *thither where*).

[c950 *Lindisf. Gosp.* John xi. 32 *Cum uenisset ubi erat iesus*, Miððy cuome ðer *vel* huoer uæs se hælend.] **c1375** *Sc. Leg. Saints* i. (*Petrus*) 100 To þe prince sa spak he þane, þat quhare petire wes, he wane. **a1500** *Hist. K. Boccus & Sydracke* (? 1510) Nj, They fare as a lefe on the tre That turnes whare the wynd wylbe. **c1586** C'tess Pembroke *Ps.* lxxxiv. iii, Me seemes I see them going Where mulberies are growing. **1671** Milton *P.R.* iii. 244, I will bring thee where thou soon shalt quit Those rudiments. **1697** Dryden *Æneis* xi. 44 He took his Way, Where, new in Death, lamented Pallas lay. *Mod.* I'll take you where we shall get a better view.

6. Introducing a clause as obj. of a verb or prep., or as predicate: = a or the place in (or to) which.

Originating in, and not always distinguishable from, the use in indirect questions (1 b).

[c950 *Lindisf. Gosp.* Matt. viii. 20 *Filius..hominis non habet ubi caput reclinet*, Sunu..monnes ne hæfis huer [*Rushw.* wær] heafud ȝehlutes; **1382** Wyclif but mannes sone hath nat wher he reste his heued.] **c1200** Ormin 12985 þeȝȝ tokenn þær to fraȝȝnenn Crist Off whære he wass att hame. **1579** W. Wilkinson *Confut. Fam. Love* Brief Descr., Not hauyng where they durst at any tyme rest. **1590** Spenser *F.Q.* iii. iii. 27 From where the day out of the sea doth spring, Vntill the closure of the Euening. **1613** Purchas *Pilgrimage* ii. xvii. 170 The Iewes will not quite empty any place of water, that on the Sabbath these fierie soules may finde where to coole them. **1766** Goldsm. *Vicar W.* v, Within about twenty paces of where we were sitting. **1766** —— *Hermit* 3 And guide my lonely way To where yon taper cheers the vale With hospitable ray. **1876** Tennyson *Harold* v. i, I can see it From where we stand. **1882** Besant *All Sorts* iv. (1898) 42 He..showed her where the liquor stood to ferment.

7. as simple relative. **a.** With antecedent *place*, or some sb. denoting a place or receptacle; introducing a defining or restrictive clause completing the sense: In or at which.

c1250 *Kent. Serm.* in *O.E. Misc.* 27 Al-wat hi kam over þo huse war ure louerd was. **1390** Gower *Conf.* III. 324 He bad his man to gon and spire A place wher sche myhte abyde. **c1400** *Rule St. Benet* (verse) 1666 And honest place for to be in, Whor þai may sit with-outyn dyn. **1457** *Test. Ebor.* (Surtees) II. 207 Att Saynt Nicholas auter before the stall quer I sitt at mese. **1539** in *Extr. Aberd. Reg.* (1844) I. 159, I sell leid the to the place for the freir swewyt the. **1567** *Sc. Acts Jas. VI* (1814) III. 23/2 The Superintendent, and Ministeris of that Prouince quhair the benefice lyis. **a1600** Montgomerie *Sonn.* xlviii. 2 In hauthornes vher thou hyds thy self and hants. **1697** Dryden *Virg. Georg.* iv. 752 Th' unhappy Climes, where Spring was never known. **1788** Picken *Poems* 27 At yon burnie..Whar the shinan peebles lie. **1835** Marryat *Jacob Faithful* xlv, I hastened to the black hole where Tom was confined. **1893** Max Pemberton *Iron Pirate* iii, Looking for all the world like some great dog that has entered a house where dogs are forbidden.

b. Introducing an additional statement, the sense being complete without the relative clause: In or at which place; and there.

a1300 *Cursor M.* 950 Vnto þe wreched werld to gang, Quare þou sal thinc þou liues to lang. **1375** Barbour *Bruce* i. 354 To Sanct Androws he come..Quhar the byschop..Resavyt him. **c1420** *Anturs Arth.* xxxvii, By þat on plumtone land a palais was piȝte, Were neuer freke opone folde had fouȝtene biforne. **1526** *Pilgr. Perf.* (W. de W. 1531) 5b, Theyr probacyon in deserte, where god proued theyr fayth and hope. **a1586** Montgomerie *Misc. Poems* xlviii. 222 Then to the Douns, vhair that we raid a space. **1632** Milton *L'Allegro* 72 Russet Lawns, and Fallows Gray, Where the nibling flocks do stray. **1766** Goldsm. *Vicar W.* xiv, We were shewn into a little back room, where there was only a venerable old man. **1820** Keats *Lamia* i. 380 A pillar'd porch..Where hung a silver lamp. **1882** Besant *All Sorts* xxviii, I have been in America, where, if anywhere, the people have it their own way.

8. as compound or simple relative: (In, or to, the place) to which; whither.

13.. *Cursor M.* 1154 (Gött.) Wid all þu sal biholden vile, Quar þu wendis in exile. **1508** *Reg. Privy Seal Scot.* I. 250/2 Quhether the saidis P. and J. pass in the realme of France or uther partis quhare ples thaim. **1594** Shaks. *Rich. III*, i. ii. 106 He is in heauen, where thou shalt neuer come. **1655** in *Nicholas Papers* (Camden) III. 209 A letter..which..hee vndertooke to transmitt where it was directed. **1774** Chesterf. *Lett.* I. i. 2 Holland, where you are going, is, by far, the finest..of the Seven United Provinces. **1852** Mrs. Stowe *Uncle Tom's C.* xxvi, Tom..looked up for help where he had always been used to look. **1893** Max Pemberton *Iron Pirate* i, Him I am going to meet in this Paris where I go without aim.

9. In generalized or indef. sense: In, or to, any (or every) place in, or to, which; wherever.

The indef. sense is more explicitly expressed by the addition of *ever*, *so*, †*sum*: see WHEREVER, WHERESO, WHERESOME, WHERESOMEVER.

c1200 Ormin 5904 Whære o lande summ itt iss þatt mann off Goddspell spelleþþ. **c1205** Lay. 3320 Lete we sum þis mochele folc fare wher [*later text* woder] ha wulleð. **1297** R. Glouc. (Rolls) 6617 Euere ware he com gode lawes he broȝte. **13..** *Cursor M.* 6136 (Gött.) Mas sacrifis ȝour lauerd vntill, Quar and hou so þat ȝe will. **a1352** Minot *Poems* (ed. Hall) ix. 20 None letes him þe way to wende whore he will. **1395** *E.E. Wills* 8 Ware that euer I deye. **14..** in *Tundale's Vis.* (1843) 99 Lett thi name wher we rydy or gon..Be owre defence ageyn owre mortal fon. **1552** Huloet, Where you will, *ubilibet*. **1605** Shaks. *Lear* iv. v. 10 Where he arriues, he moues All hearts against vs. **1781** Cowper *Table T.* 298 Sing where you please. **1865** Dickens *Mut. Fr.* iii. viii, I won't stand in your way. Go where you like.

** In general and figurative senses.

10. as compound relative. **a.** In the passage or part (of a writing) in which; at, or to, the point or stage (of action, speech, etc.) at which.

c1400 *Rule St. Benet* (verse) 206 In his godspel, whaire he says þus: 'Nolo mortem peccatoris'. **c1450** Capgrave *Life St. Aug.* Prol., In þe first capitle Ad Romanos, where he saide þat he was dettour on-to wise men and onwise. **1580** R. Parsons *Brief Disc.* 40 Throughe out the scripture, where Idoles are forbidden, they translate it Images. **1622** Peacham *Compl. Gent.* xi. 97 But we returne where we left. **1661** in *Extr. St. Papers rel. Friends* Ser. ii. (1911) 126, I marked the booke where there is a passage full of treason. **1907** *Blackw. Mag.* Jan. 136/2 Where Powell parted company most fiercely from the Radicals was in his steadfast patriotism.

b. (*a*) In a or the case in which (often nearly = WHEN 8); in the circumstances, position, or condition in which; in that respect or particular in which. (Sometimes with implication of contrast or opposition: cf. 12 b.)

1387 Trevisa *Higden* (Rolls) V. 227 Were þe socour of the watir faillede þere men schulde defende hem in þe lond by help of þe wal. **c1420** ? Lydg. *Assembly of Gods* 1634 He wold deele where he had no charge. **1513** Douglas *Æneis* iv. Prol. 199 Quhar schame is lost quyte schent is womanheid. **1591** Shaks. *Two Gent.* v. iv. 44 When women cannot loue, where they're belou'd. **1635** Quarles *Embl.* i. xii, Ther's nothing wholsome, where the whole's infected. **1766** Fordyce *Serm. Yng. Women* (1767) I. v. 192 We cannot be easy, where we are not safe. **1824** Scott *St. Ronan's* xxii, 'By my soul, Clara, I will make you repent this!' said Mowbray, with more violence than he usually exhibited where his sister was concerned. **1850** Newman *Diff. Anglicans* ix. 221 They are rude where they should be reverent. **1918** *Act 8 Geo. V* c. 5. §1 (1) Where it is proposed to make any such Order..a draft of the Order shall be presented to each House of Parliament.

(*b*) Contextually indicating a person or persons as the object of love or marriage.

1611 Beaum. & Fl. *King & No K.* iii. i, O she is far from any stubbornness,..and no doubt will like Where you would have her. **1859** Geo. Eliot *Adam Bede* i. iv, Thee know'st we canna love just where other folks 'ud have us. **1878** Hardy *Ret. Native* i. iv, I saw that..it would be better she should marry where she wished.

c. with construction as in 6: = †a case in which; †a person to whom; the point or particular in which. (Cf. WHEN 5.)

a1300 *K. Horn* 691 (Camb. MS.), Ihc herde whar he sede, & his swerd forþ leide, To bringe þe of lyue. **1375** Barbour *Bruce* xi. 39, I herd neuir quhar so lang varnyng Wes gevin. **1601** Shaks. *Jul. C.* i. ii. 59, I haue heard, Where many of the best respect in Rome..Haue wish'd that Noble Brutus had his eyes. **1611** —— *Cymb.* ii. iv. 111 The Vowes of Women, Of no more bondage be, to where they are made, Then they are to their Vertues. *Mod.* That was where he failed. (*colloq.*) That's just where it is!

(*b*) In U.S. use freq. equivalent to THAT *conj.* (see also quot. 1931).

1927 E. O'Neill *Marco Millions* ii. ii. 122, I can see where I'll have to be telling her what to do every second. **1931** G. O. Curme *Syntax* 245 This old use of *where* with the force of a noun + *in which* is still heard in colloquial speech: 'This morning I read in the Tribune *where* (in the literary language *an account in which*) *a boy killed his father*.' **1938** D. Runyon *Furthermore* iii. 51, I see by the papers where three Brooklyn citizens are scragged. **1958** T. Capote *Breakfast at Tiffany's* 110 [I] had read where the Trawlers were countersuing for divorce. **1965** *New Yorker* 15 May 45, I see where the St. Regis has changed hands again. **1976** *National Observer* (U.S.) 14 Aug. 2/4, I can see where people might think that Kelley doesn't know what's going on in his own organization.

d. In *colloq.* phr. ***where it's*** (***he's, she's***) ***at***: the true or essential nature of a situation (or person); the true state of affairs; a place of central activity. Cf. AT *prep.* 1 d. orig. *U.S.*

1903 [see AT *prep.* 1 d]. **1965** *Daily Mail* 2 Oct. 5/2 What's the phrase you use for being in touch?..Where it's at. **1967** *Listener* 26 Oct. 522/3 As Dylan says, 'I'll let you be in my dream, if I can be in yours.' I think I know where he's at. **1971** *Melody Maker* 9 Oct. 17/5 The musicians frequently became frustrated..not really believing their own bands were where it was at. **1974** R. M. Pirsig *Zen & Art of Motorcycle Maintenance* x. 117 That, today, is where it is at, and will continue to be at for a long time to come. **1977** W. J. Weatherby *Home in Dark* xiii. 69 She was always a housewife at heart. She just took too long to find out where she was at.

e. *U.S. dial.* ***to where***, to or at a point, position, etc., such that; to such an extent that. Occas. with omission of *to*.

1933 M. K. Rawlings *South Moon Under* xvi. 157 Is your loggin' to where you kin leave it for a whiles? **1938** —— *Yearling* xvi. 181 My grand-pappy got hisself stung oncet to where he was in the bed a fortnight. **1960** H. Lee *To kill Mockingbird* xi. 109 Having developed my talent to where I could throw up a stick and almost catch it coming down. **1969** B. K. Green *Wild Cow Tales* 247, I would pitch a rope over a steer's neck and give it a whip-like motion to where the knot would come back under his neck on the ground back on my side. **1974** N. Guidici in S. Terkel *Working* vi. 316, I want to have enough money where I wouldn't have to be a bum on the street.

11. as simple relative. **a.** Introducing a defining or restrictive clause (cf. 7 a): In or at which; †*rarely* with person as antecedent, In whom.

c1500 *Melusine* 238 She consyderyng the daunger where bothe she & her peple had be. **1585** Jas. VI *Ess. Poesie* (Arb.) 53 Ignorants obdurde, quhair wilful errour lyis. **1593** Shaks. *Rich. II*, v. ii. 5 *York.* Where did I leaue? *Duch.* At that sad stoppe, my Lord, Where rude misgouern'd hands..Threw dust..on King Richards head. **1692** Dryden *St. Euremont's Ess.* 98 There is no life so regular, where particular Actions don't sometimes exceed the general habit and conduct. **1792** *Jrnl. Ho. Comm.* XLVII. 641/1 In a Case where the Officers had broken into a Bedchamber. **1887** W. P. Frith *Autobiogr.* I. xxi. 284 It is difficult to put one's finger on the precise spot where confidence merges into conceit.

b. Introducing an additional statement (cf. 7 b): In or at which; and there; hence, †whereupon, and then.

1377 Langl. *P. Pl.* B. v. 283 Who so leueth nouȝte þis be soth loke in þe sauter glose, In *miserere mei deus*, where I mene treuthe. **1423** Jas. I *Kingis Q.* lxi, With that anon ryght sche toke vp a sang, Quhare come anon mo birdis and alight. **1591** Shaks. *Two Gent.* i. i. 29 To be in loue; where scorne is bought with grones. **1634** Sir T. Herbert *Trav.* 67 The Agent for the English Merchants inuited vs to a Banquet, where he shewed a heartie Entertainment. **1694** tr. *Marten's Voy. Spitzbergen* in *Acc. Sev. Late Voy.* ii. 128 The Seamen let them alone until the Whale be killed, where they take him without any trouble. **1781** Cowper *Truth* 372 The controversial field, Where deists, always foil'd, yet scorn to yield. **1831** Scott *Kenilw.* Introd., The Yorkshire Tragedy, a play erroneously ascribed to Shakspeare, where a Rake..throws his wife down stairs.

c. ***to the point where***, to a situation, condition, extent, etc., such that.

1938 F. Scott Fitzgerald *Let.* 22 Feb. (1964) 569 If it ever came to the point where you thought you ought to lay up under medical care, his is the sanitarium which I should choose. **1960** *Radio Amateur's Handbk.* (ed. 37) 190/2 Adjust the potentiometer..to the point where the oscillator cannot be heard between dots and dashes at normal keying speed. **1968** Chomsky & Halle *Sound Pattern Eng.* 329 Our investigations of these features have not progressed to a point where a discussion in print would be useful. **1970** P. Whittle *Probability* v. 100 Models which can be simple, without being idealized to the point where they have no practical value.

12. †**a.** It being the case that; in view of the fact that; forasmuch as, inasmuch as: = WHEREAS 2; cf. WHEN 9 a. (Chiefly in legal or other formal documents.) *Obs.*

1411 *Rolls of Parlt.* III. 650/1 First, where the forsaid Lord the Roos..compleyneth hym by a Bille, surmettyng on the same Robert [etc.]. **c1450** *Godstow Reg.* 25 Women of relygyone, in redynge bokys of latyn, byn excusyd of grete vndurstondyng, where it is not her modyr tonge. **1548–9** (Mar.) *Bk. Com. Prayer* Pref., And where heretofore, there hath been great diuersitie..within this realme: Now from henceforth, [etc.]. **1562–3** *N.C. Wills* (Surtees) II. 36 Where that..Hadoile the smythe hathe gyven to me his eldest sonne Christopher as my owne, I will he be put unto the schoale. **1599** in *10th Rep. Hist. MSS. Comm.* App. v. 336 Where it is considered by the Maior, Sheriffs, and cittizens of this citie how greatly the city is impoverished. **1637** *Bk. Com. Pr. Scot.* Table & Kal., And where [1662 whereas] the Cxix. psalme is divided into xxij. portions,..it is so ordered [etc.].

b. In adversative sense: While on the contrary: = WHEN 9 b, WHEREAS 3.

c1380 Wyclif *Sel. Wks.* III. 358 It fordoiþ Cristis privylege, þat where Cristene men shulden be free, now þei ben nedid to hire a preest. **c1440** *Generydes* 1134 Now A dayis I lese all that I wanne, Where here before I was a threfty man. **1542** Udall *Erasm. Apoph.* 62 Purple in those dayes was for the wearyng of none but kynges & princes, wher now it is communely taken vp with euery sowter. **1596** *Edw. III* iv. iii, And, where tofore I loued thee as Villeirs, Heereafter Ile embrace thee as my selfe. **1668** Rolle *Abridgm., Action sur Case* 40 He swore, that the Wood was worth 40s. where it was dear of 13s. 4d. **1681** in Pepys *Diary & Corr.* 11 Apr., All Baptist's bases are singable, where many of Pedro's are not so. **1929** R. A. Cram *Catholic Church & Art* iv. 57 Where the pagan architecture had been an *exterior* art..and where Roman and Byzantine art had striven to achieve space in its simplest form, the North worked for interior space.

III. Indefinite and substantival uses.

13. With preceding qualifying words (*one*, *other*, etc.), forming adverbial phrases: In or at (one, another, etc.) place.

Chiefly as second element in compounds: see ALLWHERE, ANYWHERE, AYWHERE, EACHWHERE, ELSEWHERE, EVERYWHERE, MANYWHERE, NOWHERE, ONEWHERE, OTHERWHERE, SOMEWHERE, WIDE-WHERE.

1508 in *Dunbar's Poems* (S.T.S.) II. 321 Suth it is, and sene in all our quhare, No erdly thing bot for a tyme may lest. **1526** Tindale *Luke* xiii. 33 For it cannott be that a prophet perisshe eny other where save att Jerusalem. **1528** —— *Obed. Chr. Man* 74 We must stere vp some warre one where or a nother. **c1550** *Syr Tryam.* in Utterson *E.P.P.* (1817) I. 58 They hunted and rode many a where. **c1586** C'tess Pembroke *Ps.* cvii. xii, How many where doth he convert Well watred grounds to thirsty sand? **1650**

AMBROSE *Ultima* (1659) 186 His Apostles are scattered in the garden, his garments at the Crosse, his blood how many wheres! *a* **1694** TILLOTSON *Serm.* VII. 108 Though they be very active, yet they can be but one where at once. **1722** DE FOE *Col. Jack* i. (1809) 10 He got victuals enough one where or other. **1815** J. FOSTER in *Life & Corr.* (1846) I. 453, I still preach, one where or other.

14. as *sb.* Place, locality; in mod. use *esp.* the place at which the thing spoken of is or happens.

1443–9 PECOCK *Donet* xvi. (1921) 92 More of þis mater.. may be seen.. in þe book of dyuyne office in manye a wher. *c* **1449** —— *Repr.* I. v. 27 In othere wheris of my writingis. **1560** PHAER *Æneid.* IX. 58 He troub[l]ous vewes their wals, & ryding sekes ech entring where. **1563** SACKVILLE *Induct. Mirr. Mag.* lxvi, In euery where or sworde or fyer they taste. **1590** SPENSER *F.Q.* III. iv. 19 Finding the Nymph a sleepe in secret wheare. **1635** J. HAYWARD tr. *Biondi's Banish'd Virg.* 36 Resolved to leave no where thereabouts unsearched for her. **1720** DE FOE *Ser. Refl. Crusoe, Vis. Angelic World* iv. (1801) 223 For if we are to be, we must have a where. **1813** BYRON *Corsair* I. xiv, The why—the where—what boots it now to tell? **1863** LONGF. tr. *Dante, Parad.* XXVII. 109 In this heaven there is no other Where Than in the Mind Divine. **1896** A. AUSTIN *England's Darling* I. i, While he roams abroad,.. Spying the where and whither of his foes.

IV. 15. In senses of branches I and II, in comb. with advs. and preps.

For history of this use see HERE *adv.* 16; cf. THERE 17.

a. With advs., as †***whereforth***; ***whereaway***, whither, in what direction. **b.** With preps.: = what or which (†*occas.* whom), as ***whereagainst***, ***wherealong***, ***whereamong(st***, †***wherenigh***, ***whereover***, ***whereround***, †***wherewithout***. See also main words, WHEREABOUT to WHEREWITHAL.

1526 TINDALE *Luke* xxi. 15, I will geve you a mouth and wysdom *were agaynste all youre adversarys shall not be able to speake. **1607** SHAKS. *Cor.* IV. v. 113 That body, where against My grained Ash an hundred times hath broke. **1622** MABBE tr. *Aleman's Guzman d'Alf.* I. 251, I was.. driven to seeke out some Wall, where-against to leane. **1768** TUCKER *Lt. Nat.* I. I. vii. 201 The organs or other channels *wherealong they pass. **1582** MUNDAY *Engl. Rom. Lyfe* v. 55 Reliques, *where among he named the Nayles, that nailed Christe on the Crosse. **1620** tr. *Boccaccio's Decam.* 160 Isabella fell into abundance of teares, where-among she mingled many sighes and groanes. **1929** R. BRIDGES *Testament of Beauty* I. 17 Where-among hath the sceptic honourable place. **1578** LYTE *Dodoens* IV. xxviii. 485 Growing almost as high as the wheat or corne ..*whereamongst it groweth. **1535** STEWART *Cron. Scot.* (Rolls) II. 637 And *quhair awa, quhither to hevin or hell. **1842** *Whistle-binkie* Ser. III. 84 He daunert on, ne'er thinkin' whar-awa. **1867** SMYTH *Sailor's Word-bk., Where away?* in what bearing? a question to the man at the mast-head to designate in what direction a strange sail lies. **1885** *Harper's Mag.* Jan. 212/2 Much pondering where-away The Northeast Passage lay. *c* **1290** *St. Cuthbert* 77 in *S. Eng. Leg.* 361 He ne miȝte nouȝt finde is fore, *ȝware-forth he wende a-wei in snowe ne in þe flore. **1393** LANGL. *P. Pl.* C. XVII. 339 Ac þorw werkes þou myght wite wher forþ he walkeþ. **1642** *Iack Puffe* 16 in Hazl. *E.P.P.* IV. 315 The shockt mount, whereforth a Mouse did clime. **1658** BURTON *Comm. Itin. Antoninus* 90 Our learned Antiquary therefore hath shewed very good judgement in descrying the ground, *where-nigh it stood of yore. **1475** *Bk. Noblesse* (Roxb.) 72 It was never seen that any countre.. did encrece welle *wherover many nedeles officers.. was reignyng.. over theym. **1583** STUBBES *Anat. Abus.* II. (1882) 74 Wherouer the holie Ghost hath made them ouerseers. **1853** T. PARKER *Disc. Death Webster* Wks. 1865 XII. 18 A great gulf.., whereover neither Dives nor Abraham, nor yet Moses himself, can pass. **1883** SWINBURNE *Cent. Roundels* 68 Love lies bleeding in the bed whereover Roses lean. **1910** *Spectator* 4 June 927/2 The storm-grey Manse, *Where-round tall rhododendrons dance. **1567** JEWEL *Def. Apol.* v. xiii. 572 The conductes of Water, *wherewithout menne cannot commodiously liue. **1578** *Bk. Chr. Prayers* B ij, Thou light, wherewithout all things are deepe darcknesse. **1899** BEERBOHM *More* 95 Mere masses of colour, crude intensity of conception, wherewithout posters fail, were quite unnecessary.

where, obs. f. CHOIR, WERE, WHETHER.

whereabout (ˈhwɛərəˈbaʊt: stress var.), *interrog.* and *rel. adv.*, *sb.* [f. WHERE 15 + ABOUT.]

1. a. *interrog.* About where? in or near what place, part, situation, or position? Now *rare*: replaced by WHEREABOUTS 1.

a **1300** *Cursor M.* 15429 Quar abute abide yee nu? **1484** CAXTON *Fables of Æsop* IV. xiii, My broder and my frend where aboute is thy sore? *c* **1566** J. ALDAY tr. *Boaystuau's Theat. World* (1581) K iij, My shooe is new,.. wel made, but you know not where about it doeth hurt & grieue me. **1665** *Phil. Trans.* I. 39 His Ephemerides directing where-about it is to be. **1720** S. SEWALL *Diary* 4 Nov. (1882) III. 274, I ask'd her Whereabout we left off last time. **1736** BUTLER *Anal.* I. iv, One irregularity after another embarrasses things to such a degree that they know not whereabout they are. *c* **1850** *Arab. Nts.* (Rtldg.) 175, I desired the owner of the ass to enquire whereabout the house.. was. **1861** H. KINGSLEY *Ravenshoe* xviii, She.. used to look over to where the ship lay beneath the sea, and wonder whereabout it was. **1908** KIPLING *Lett. Trav.* (1920) 188 'And where-about do they go?' I asked. 'Oh, all about anywheres.'

(*b*) Contextually, with *love*: cf. WHERE 10 b (*b*).

15.. in *Dunbar's Poems* (S.T.S.) 308 Fane wald I luve, bot quhair abowt? Thair is so mony luvaris thairowt, That thair is left no place to me.

†**b.** *rel.* About or near which place; in the neighbourhood of which. *Obs. rare.*

1722 WHISTON *The. Earth* II. 218 At.. Pekin.. whereabout probably Noah liv'd immediately before the Deluge.

2. †**a.** *interrog.* About or concerning what? on what business or occupation? *Obs.*

13.. *Northern Passion* (1913) I. 85/2 We wist noght whare obout þou went. *c* **1425** *Cast. Persev.* 2367 in *Macro Plays* 148 Where-a-bowte stonde ȝe al day? **1560** *Bible* (Geneva) 1 Sam. xxi. 2 Let no man knowe whereabout I send thee. **1596** SHAKS. *1 Hen. IV*, II. iii. 107, I must not haue you henceforth, question me, Whether I go: nor reason whereabout. **1598** R. BERNARD tr. *Terence, Andria* IV. iii, Whereabout goest thou?

b. *rel.* About, concerning, or in regard to which. ? *Obs.*

1538 ELYOT *Dict.*, *Operatio*, the wark, or that wherabowte a man laboureth. **1597** HOOKER *Eccl. Pol.* v. lxvii. §12 Those things whereabout they differ. *a* **1653** BINNING *Serm.*, *Rom.* viii. 2 Wks. (1735) 200 That whereabout the Thoughts and Discourses of Men now run.

3. *rel.* About or around which. ? *Obs.*

1585 HIGINS *Junius' Nomencl.* 267/2 *Axis*,.. the axeltree or the axetree where about the wheeles turne.

4. as *sb.* (ˈhwɛərəbaʊt). [from 1.] With possessive or *of*: The place in or near which a person or thing is; (approximate) position or situation. Now replaced by WHEREABOUTS 3.

1605 SHAKS. *Macb.* II. i. 58 For feare Thy very stones prate of my where-about. **1786** COWPER *Let. to Bagot* 17 Nov., Wks. 1836 II. 263 That.. I shall derive considerable advantage.. from the alteration made in my *where-about*. **1814** CARY *Dante, Parad.* XII. 27 A voice That made me seem like needle to the star, In turning to its whereabout. **1831** CARLYLE *Sart. Res.* III. ix, By degrees, the eye grows accustomed to its new Whereabout. **1861** MUSGRAVE *By-Roads & Battle-F.* 170 Both armies.. were then within a few days of each other's whereabout.

'wherea'bouts (stress var.), *adv.*, *sb.* [f. prec. + advb. *-s*: cf. HEREABOUTS, THEREABOUTS.]

1. a. *interrog.* = prec. 1 a. Also *fig.*

c **1450** *Mirk's Festial* 167 Sonne, whereaboutes art þow? **1540** PALSGR. *Acolastus* II. v. N j b, Wheraboutes is our hostes house? **1621** I. C. in *T. Bedford's Sin unto Death* ¶ vj, Except they know.. whereabouts the daunger is. **1648** DUPPA *Soules Solil.* 2 Many.. go away informed.. where abouts the Spleen lies, or where the Liver. **1791** GOUV. MORRIS in Sparks *Life & Writ.* (1832) I. 357, I ask him whereabouts he is with the claims of the German Princes. **1837** DICKENS *Pickw.* liii, Whereabouts were your apartments, Mr. Pickwick? **1893** SELOUS *Trav. S.E. Africa* 97 The natives pointed out to me whereabouts they passed in the valley below.

†**b.** *rel.* About the amount at which. (Cf. THEREABOUTS 2 b.) *Obs. rare.*

1766 J. INGERSOLL *Lett. rel. Stamp-Act* 6 *note*, The Parliament have.. settled the above Duties just whereabouts they are stated in the above Letter.

†**2.** *interrog.* and *rel.* = prec. 2 a, b. *Obs.*

1540 PALSGR. *Acolastus* I. i. D j, What studyeth he .i. wheraboutes gothe he? **1576** FLEMING *Panopl. Epist.* 224 Neyther had I any thing at all, where abouts to occupie my penne. **1630** BEDELL in *Ussher's Life*, etc. (1686) 452 Only he labours about Kildromfarten: Whereabouts I purposed to have spoken with your Grace.

3. as *sb.* (ˈhwɛərəbaʊts). [from 1.] = prec. 4. Also *fig.*

1795 T. TWINING *Let. to Parr* 15 Feb. in *P.'s Wks.* (1828) VIII. 273 By way of giving you the whereabouts of my present political opinions. **1836** DICKENS *Sk. Boz, Scot.-Yard*, Not all his knowledge of the history of the past.. may help him to the whereabouts.. of Scotland-yard. **1878** BAYNE *Purit. Rev.* i. 12 Bunyan wrote the Pilgrim's Progress .. without giving a hint of his ecclesiastical where-abouts. **1903** *Times* 3 May 3/6 The prisoner.. succeeded in concealing his whereabouts.

whereafter (hwɛəˈrɑːftə(r), -æ-), *rel. adv.* Now formal or *arch.* [WHERE 15.] After which.

c **1375** *Sc. Leg. Saints* xxii. (*Laurentius*) 113 He tane had halely þe tresoure, Quhare-eftyre socht þe emperoure. *c* **1410** *Master of Game* (MS. Digby 182) Prol. 7 He hath ynogh at done.. to loke wherafter he hunteth. **1577** T. KENDALL *Flowers Epigr.* 78 So loste he that he had, and that where-after he did snatche. **1631** WEEVER *Anc. Funeral Mon.* 819 The Parish and Lordship of Clipesby.. gave name .. to a familie of ancient note.. whereof there hath beene diuers Knights; where after it had passed in the names of Algar, Elfled, and Odberd, all sirnamed de Clipesby. *a* **1641** BP. MOUNTAGU *Acts & Mon.* viii. (1642) 489 The image and similitude of God, whereafter God made man at first. **1847** HARE *Vict. Faith* 68 Whereafter in another generation Consciousness was asserted to be the ground of all existence. **1885** SWINBURNE *Misc.* (1886) 163 The judicious Dr. Nott has written in the margin 'This is much too unqualified': whereon—or at least, as I presume, whereafter—a pen was struck through the last fourteen words.

So †**where'afterward** *rel. adv. Obs. rare*$^{-1}$.

1483 CAXTON *Gold. Leg.* 354 b/1 Wherafterward.. it was shewed.. that by cause that place was ouer lytil.. they shold do make.. another chirche.

whereagainst, -along, etc.: see WHERE 15.

whereanent (hwɛərəˈnɛnt), *rel. adv.* Orig. and chiefly *Sc.* [f. WHERE 15 + ANENT *prep.* 11.] Anent or concerning which.

1579 *Sc. Acts Jas. VI.* lxii. (1814) III. 182/2 The auld fundationis.. notwᵗstanding qʳanent his maᵗⁱᵉ.. dispenssis. **1609** SKENE *Reg. Maj.* I. 7 b, The debaitable matter, quhairanent the summons is made. **1681** in *Nairne Peerage Evid.* (1874) 15 That the said letters.. passe the great seale per saltum whereanent these presents shall be a sufficient warrant. **1899** tr. *Dante's Paradiso* XXXI. 379 To question my Lady concerning things whereanent my mind was in suspense.

whereas (hwɛəˈræz), *rel. adv.*, *conj.* (*sb.*). In early use as two words.

I. As relative adv. or advb. phr.: cf. *where that* s.v. WHERE II.

†**1.** = WHERE 5, 7–11. *Obs.* or *rare arch.*

c **1350** *Will. Palerne* 1782 þei.. tok forþ here wey.. to sum wildernesse where as þei bredde. *c* **1386** CHAUCER *Frankl. T.* 74 Nat fer fro Pedmark ther his dwellyng was Where as he lyueth. *c* **1400** *Rom. Rose* 1966 The helthe of loue[rs] mut be founde Where as they token firste hir wounde. *c* **1450** *Merlin* 242 The grete distruxion where-as the kynge Aguysanx hadde I-be. **1548–9** (Mar.) *Bk. Com. Prayer*, Collect 4th Sund. aft. Easter, That.. oure heartes may surely there be fixed, where as true ioyes are to be founde. **1567** J. SANFORD *Epictetus* 23 Whereas vtilitie is, there is pietie. **1578** LYTE *Dodoens* II. xx. 172 Auicularia groweth.. in fields amongst wheate, or where as wheate hath growen. **1578** *Bible* (Geneva) To Rdr., Whereas the Ebrewe speache seemed hardly to agree with ours, we haue noted it in the margent. **1601** HOLLAND *Pliny* II. lxxxv. I. 39 All that levell whereas the river Mæander now runneth by goodly medowes. **1663** GERBIER *Counsel* 12 Ornaments on that upright, whereas the Southerly windes raise much dust. **1868** MORRIS *Earthly Par.* (1870) I. II. 655 And quickly too he gat Unto the place whereas the lady sat.

II. As illative or adversative conjunction.

2. In view or consideration of the fact that; seeing that, considering that, forasmuch as, inasmuch as. (Chiefly, now only, introducing a preamble or recital in a legal or other formal document.)

1424 *Information against Walter Aslak* in *Paston Lett.* I. 16 Where as the seyd William Paston, by assignement and commaundement of the seyd Duk of Norffolk.. was the Styward of the seyd Duc of Norffolk. **1488–9** *Act 4 Hen. VII* c. 2 Where as it was of old tyme.., that ther was for the weale of the Kyng.. Fynours and parters of Gold and Silver [etc.]. *a* **1533** LD. BERNERS *Huon* civ. 345 Where as thou sayest I am a traytoure I shall shewe the how thou lyest. **1539** *Bible* (Great) 1 Kings viii. 18 Where as it was thyne hert to buylde an house vnto my name, thou dyddest well, that thou wast so mynded. **1635** R. N. tr. *Camden's Hist. Eliz.* I. 31 Whereas the Emperour and the Catholicke Princes by many Letters made intercession, that the displaced Bishops might be mercifully dealt withall.. shee answered [etc.]. **1713** *Act 13 Anne* c. 28 §1 Whereas Part of the Highway.. is become so very ruinous that [etc.]. **1918** *Act 8 Geo. V* c. 6 Preamble, And whereas the Army Act will expire in the year, one thousand nine hundred and eighteen on the following days.

3. Introducing a statement of fact in contrast or opposition to that expressed by the principal clause: While on the contrary; the fact on the other hand being that. (The principal clause usually precedes, but sometimes follows as in 2.)

†In quot. 1542, Notwithstanding that; though (*obs.*).

1535 COVERDALE *2 Esdras* vii. 5 There are layed vp for vs dwellynges of health & fredome, where as we haue lyued euell. **1542** UDALL *Erasm. Apoph.* 7 This knaue, wheras he is the greattest glutton.. that maye bee, yet is he the moste idle lubber. **1591** SHAKS. *1 Hen. VI*, II. v. 76, I deriued am From Lionel Duke of Clarence..; whereas hee, From Iohn of Gaunt doth bring his Pedigree. **1631** WEEVER *Anc. Funeral Mon.* 520 Hee might haue worne the Diadem many yeares, whereas he bare the title of King no longer than two moneths. **1749** FIELDING *Tom Jones* x. iii, Whereas he had received a very handsome fortune with his wife, he had now spent every penny of it. **1849** C. BRONTE *Shirley* xxvi, 'Yet, they are great whiskered fellows, six feet high each.' 'Whereas.., Harry, you will never be anything more than a little pale lameter.' **1882** BESANT *All Sorts* xxiv, I brought him up in ignorance of his father, whom he had always imagined to be a gentleman; whereas he was only a sergeant in a Line regiment. **1892** *Photogr. Ann.* II. 519 Whereas a pinhole has no focus, every lens has a focus.

III. 4. as *sb.* (from 2). A statement introduced by 'whereas'; the preamble of a formal document.

1795 COLERIDGE *Plot Discov.* 23 While the contrary remains unproved, such a Whereas must be a most inadequate ground for the present Bill. **1796** GROSE *Dict. Vulgar T.* (ed. 3) s.v., To follow a whereas; to become a bankrupt..: the notice given in the Gazette that a commission of bankruptcy is issued out against any trader, always beginning with the word whereas. **1804** F. L. HOLT *Land we live in* II. i. (1805) 30, I am as long-winded as the *Whereas* of a proclamation. **1863** GUROWSKI *Diary* 18 Oct. (1864) 347 A new *whereas* calling for three hundred thousand volunteers.

whereat (hwɛərˈæt), *adv.* Now formal or *arch.* [f. WHERE 15 + AT *prep.*]

1. *interrog.*: At what? *rare.*

In first quot. app. = for what cause or reason, wherefore: cf. AT *sb.* 34, 37.

c **1250** *Gen. & Ex.* 3237 Qvað god, 'quor-at calles ðu me?' *c* **1480** HENRYSON *Cock & Fox* 563 Now Iuge ȝe all quhairat Schir Lowrence leuch. **15..** *Adam Bel & Clym of Clough* cxlvii, 'I hold hym neuer no good archar That shuteth at buttes so wyde.' 'Wherat?' then sayd our kyng. **1540** PALSGR. *Acolastus* I. iii. G j, Thou wottest fulle lyttell wherat thou reioysest. **1755** JOHNSON s.v., Whereat are you offended?

2. *rel.* At which. **a.** in local and allied senses.

c **1400** MAUNDEV. (Roxb.) xxvi. 121 A wyndowe, whare at þe light commez in. **1513** DOUGLAS *Æneis* II. viii. 33 A litle ȝett.. Quhairat was wont alane Andromacha To entir. **1588** A. KING tr. *Canisius' Catech.* h iv, Giff ȝow wald knaw ye dominicall lettre of ony hundereth ȝere, quhairat ye ordre of ye first table according to ye awld kallendar is interrupted. **1613** PURCHAS *Pilgrimage* v. xi. 425 At this Cart hang many .. Ropes, whereat all the people hale and pull. **1626** GOUGE *Serm. Dignity Chivalry* §1 Take notice of the generall Scope whereat the Holy Ghost aimeth in this Chapter. **1688** HOLME *Armoury* II. 84/2 The Pit or Hole, from the Body, or stock there is whereat the branches sprout out. **1865**

SWINBURNE *Chastelard* II. i. 78 Albeit I think Ye have caught the mark whereat my heart is bent. **1891** C. JAMES *Rom. Rigmarole* 27, I returned to the spot whereat the Squire kept dreary watch.

b. in reference to occasion or cause.

1535 JOYE *Apol. Tindale* (Arb.) 11 Wherat many were offended. **1599** T. STORER *Life & D. Wolsey* F 4, What had the wiser sort whereat to smile? **1667** MILTON *P.L.* II. 389 With full assent They vote: whereat his speech he thus renews. **1782** COWPER *Gilpin* 205 Whereat his horse did snort, as he Had heard a lion roar. **1840** DICKENS *Old C. Shop* xlvi, Nell could not help weeping..; whereat..the simple schoolmaster shed a few tears himself. **1897** J. L. ALLEN *Choir Invis.* ii, The inventor..said..that..he would demonstrate by his own model that some day navigation would be by steam: whereat they all laughed kindly at him for a dreamer.

whereaway: see WHERE 15.

wherebole, obs. form of CUIR-BOUILLI.

a **1400** *Warres of Jewes* (MS. Cott. Calig. A. ii) in Warton *Hist. Eng. Poetry* Sect. x. (1840) II. 106 Whippes of wherebole [*Laud MS.* quyrbole] bywent his white sides.

whereby (hwɛə'baɪ), *adv.* [f. WHERE 15 + BY *prep.*]

I. 1. *interrog.* **a.** By, beside, or near what? in what direction? **b.** By what means? how? (BY 29, 30.) †**c.** For what reason? why? (BY 36).

a **1300** *Cursor M.* 7801 þat þai bath er slain, quar-bi Wat þou it es sua? *c* **1350** *Will. Palerne* 2256 Wharbi seistow so so þe god help? **1377** LANGL. *P. Pl.* B. x. 436 Wherby wote men whiche is whyte if alle þinge blake were? *a* **1450** MYRC *Par. Pr.* 4 In-to þe dyche þey fallen boo, For þey ne sen whare by to go. **1470–85** MALORY *Arthur* VIII. xvi. 297 Be ye a knyght of Cornewaile? where by aske ye hit? said sir Tristram. **1526** TINDALE *Luke* i. 18 Wherby shall I knowe this? **1604** SHAKS. *Oth.* III. i. 9 *Clo.* Thereby hangs a tale. *Mus.* Whereby hangs a tale, sir? **1755** JOHNSON s.v., Whereby wilt thou accomplish thy design?

II. *rel.* **2.** By means of or by the agency of which; from which (as a source of information); according to which, in the matter of which, etc.

c **1200** *Trin. Coll. Hom.* 81 We wolden sen sum fortocne of þe, Warbi we mihten cnowen ȝif it soð were þat þu seist. *c* **1250** *Gen. & Ex.* 573 Mete quorbi ðei miȝten liuen. **1377** LANGL. *P. Pl.* B. XIV. 40 Lyflode.. Wher-of or wherfore or where-by to lybbe. **1390** GOWER *Conf.* II. 294 A staf, wherby, he seide, he wolde That Adrian him scholde holde. *c* **1450** *Mirk's Festial* 195 Summe spyritual visyon wherby þat he myȝt haue ben confortyd yn sowle. **1450–1520** *Myrr. our Ladye* II. 234 A starre of Iacob wherby ys vnderstonde oure lorde iesu cryste. **1560** *Bible* (Geneva) Jer. xxxiii. 8, I will cleanse them from all their iniquitie, whereby they haue sinned against me. **1584** J. MELVILL *Autob. & Diary* (Wodrow Soc.) 192 The absolut power, wharbe..the haill privileges of the thrie Esteates of the Realme is weakned. **1662** STILLINGFL. *Orig. Sacræ* II. iii. §3 The rationall evidence of that divine authority whereby Moses acted. **1667** MILTON *P.L.* v. 411 Every lower facultie Of sense, whereby they hear, see, smell, touch, taste. **1697** in *Col. Rec. Pennsylv.* I. 516 His Return of rep[re]sentatives for Council was produced, qrby it appeared [etc.]. **1709** BERKELEY *Th. Vision* §61 Stated Lengths, whereby we measure Objects. **1794** R. J. SULIVAN *View Nat.* II. 92 An universal plastic power, whereby every body in nature receives its..specific form. **1883** WHITELAW *Sophocles, Ajax* 1025 This..sword-point—this whereby Ebbed out thy life. **1918** *Times Lit. Suppl.* 14 Mar. 122/2 There is no convention in war whereby the loser can convert disaster into stalemate.

3. In consequence of, as a result of, or owing to which; from which (as a cause or reason); wherefore; sometimes practically equivalent to 'so that', 'in order that'. *Obs.* exc. *dial.*

c **1380** WYCLIF *Wks.* (1880) 310 þise men lousen crist þat maken hise membris heere special patrouns, & leuen to haue crist oonliche heere patroun, werbi þei louen lasse crist. **1523** LD. BERNERS *Froiss.* I. c. 49 b/1 The table rounde, wherby sprange the fame of so many noble knightes through out all the worlde. **1526** *Pilgr. Perf.* (W. de W. 1531) 1 b, It was put in to my mynde to drawe it in the englysshe tonge, wherby it myght be the more accepte to many. **1596** SHAKS. *1 Hen. IV*, v. i. 67 We were inforc'd for safety sake, to..raise this present Head, Whereby we stand opposed by such meanes As you your selfe haue forg'd against your selfe. **1632** LITHGOW *Trav.* v. 232 Wee buried the slayne people in deep graues, whereby Iackals should not open vp their graues. **1678** WANLEY *Wond. Lit. World* v. ii. §81. 472/2 He was suddenly seised with a Cancer in the Reins of his back, whereby he rotted above ground. **1844** HOOD *Univ. Feud* 105 Whereby it so may happen as that neither of them Scholars May be the proper Chairman for the Glorious Apollers! **1890** 'R. BOLDREWOOD' *Col. Reformer* xv, I ought to be..going peacefully to bed, whereby I should wake up with a clear head.

b. Upon which, whereupon. *dial.* ? *Obs.*

1597 SHAKS. *2 Hen. IV*, II. i. 104 Goodwife Keech.. telling vs she had a good dish of Prawnes; whereby yᵘ didst desire to eat some: whereby I told thee they were ill for a greene wound. **1748** SMOLLETT *Rod. Random* xxiv, Whereby he told the captain that..he would heave him overboard. *Ibid.*, We heard firing, whereby we made for the place.

4. Beside or near which; along, through, or over which. Now *rare*.

1297 R. GLOUC. (Rolls) 21 Wateres..Ȝware bi þe ssipes mowe come fram þe se. **14..** *Master of Game* xix. (MS. Digby 182), A kenell shulde haue a gutter or two, wherby alle þe pisse of þe houndes..may renne oute. **1586** LLOYD *Pilgr. Princes* 154 b, Hee..hideth him selfe vnder some.. rocke, or any other place, whereby hee semeth to bee. **1596** DALRYMPLE tr. *Leslie's Hist. Scot.* v. I. 293 He occupies and standes in a way quhairby the men of weir fled. **1818** BYRON *Ch. Har.* IV. xxxiii, The brawling brook, where-by..glide the sauntering hours With a calm languor. **1847** TENNYSON *Princess* IV. 359 Fear..wing'd Her transit to the throne, whereby she fell Delivering seal'd dispatches. **1885–94** R. BRIDGES *Eros & Psyche* Feb. 10 At Aphrodite's golden gate —whereby They came as night was close on twilight dim.

where-ever: see WHEREVER.

wherefore ('hwɛəfə(r)), **wherefor** (hwɛə'fɔː(r)), *adv.* (*sb.*) Forms: α. 2–3 **hwarfore**, 3 **waruore, quor-fore**, 4 **quar-fore, quer-fore, huervore, werfore**, 4–5 **warfore**, 4–7 **wherfore**, 5 **wharfore, wher-ffore, qw(h)erf(f)ore**, *Sc.* **qwharfore**, 5–6 *Sc.* **quharfore**, 6 *Sc.* **quhairfore**. β. 3 **werefore, ware uore**, 4 **warefore, where-fore**, 5 **wharefore, qwereffore**, *Sc.* **quharefore**, 6 *Sc.* **quherefore**, 5– **wherefore**. γ. 4 **wharfor, quarfor, querfor**, 4–5 **warfor**, 4–6 *Sc.* **quharfor**, 5 **werfor, qwer for**, 5–6 **wherf(f)or**, 6 *Sc.* **qwarfor, quhairfoir**, 6–8 *Sc.* **quhairfor**, 7 *Sc.* **quherfoer**. δ. 4 **quere-for**, 6, 9 **wherefor**. [f. WHERE 15 + FOR *prep.* Cf. Du. *waarvoor*, ON. *hvar fyrir*, MSw. *hvarfore*, Sw. *varfor*, Da. *hvorfor*, G. *wofür*. For the spellings cf. THEREFORE.]

I. Interrogative uses.

For the dependent or indirect interrogative use, and its distinction from the relative, cf. WHAT A. I.**

1. For what? *esp.* for what purpose or end? (Often scarcely distinguishable from 2.)

c **1200** *Vices & Virtues* 45 þu finst feawe ðe wile ȝiuen ðe ani þing, bute hie witen hwarfore. *a* **1300** *Cursor M.* 1296 Seth þen sette him spell o-nend And tald him warfor þat he was send. **13..** *Ibid.* 1734 (Gött.), He teld þat resun to mani a man, Quarfor he suilk a schip bigan. **1476** *Stonor Papers* (Camden) II. 12 (MS.) I vnderstonde there schalle be a gret Counsell, whereffore I wat nere. **1555** in Feuillerat *Revels Q. Mary* (1914) 199 As herunder the partyes names and somes of monye due and wherfore perticlerly ensue. **1590** SHAKS. *Com. Err.* III. i. 40 *E. Ant.*.. Open the dore. *S. Dro.* Right sir, Ile tell you when, and you'll tell me wherefore. *Ant.* Wherefore? for my dinner. **1593** —— *Rich. II*, II. iii. 122 Wherefore was I borne? **1667** MILTON *P.L.* IV. 657 But wherfore all night long shine these..? **1846** MRS. A. MARSH *Fr. Darcy* xxix, Here I am—wherefore come, I have to learn.

2. For what cause or reason? on what account? why? (Freq. with ellipsis; often coupled with *why* for emphasis.)

c **1230** *Hali Meid.* 15 þe feondes flan fleoð awei aȝain on him seluen, and loke hwarfore. *c* **1250** *Gen. & Ex.* 1632 Iacob calde ðat stede betel; Quor-fore he it dede, he wiste wel. *c* **1325** *Metr. Hom.* 31 His felau thoht herof ferly, And asked him quarfor and qui. **1423** JAS. I *Kingis Q.* ii, As I lay In bed allone waking,..Fell me to mynd of many diuerse thing, Off this and that; can I noght say quharfore. **1535** COVERDALE *2 Sam.* xii. 23 Now that it is deed, wherfore shulde I fast? **1585** JAS. I *Ess. Poesie* (Arb.) 54 Ze may maruell paraventure, quhairfore I sould haue writtin in that mater. **1663** BUTLER *Hud.* I. i. 8 Whose honesty they all durst swear for, Though not a man of them knew wherefore. **1781** COWPER *Truth* 12 Hard lot of man—to toil for the reward Of virtue, and yet lose it! Wherefore hard? **1809** MALKIN *Gil Blas* x. ix. (Rtldg.) 362 You..ran away.. without leaving me word why or wherefore. **1853** DICKENS *Bleak Ho.* xx, If he be ever asked how, why, when, or wherefore, he shuts up one eye and shakes his head. **1873** LONGF. *Michael Ang.* I. IV, But wherefore should I jest?

II. Relative uses.

3. For which. Now distinguished by stress and spelling (*where'for*).

†***without anything wherefore***, without a return or equivalent; †***to do wherefore***, to make a return, give an equivalent.

1297 R. GLOUC. (Rolls) 7526 Willam hit sende hire vaire inou wiþoute eny þing ware uore. **1377** [see WHEREBY 2]. *a* **1400** in *Engl. Gilds* (1870) 353 No wollemongere..ne may habbe no stal in þe heye-stret of Wynchestre bote he do warfore. *c* **1400** *Rule St. Benet* (prose) 27/22 þa þat serue sal ta yeme til þam þat etes, þat tay haue na defaute of þat tay sal haue, wharfore þai make na noise. **1530** TINDALE *Answ. More* III. i. Wks. (1573) 304/1 That we be bounde to beleue the church in thinges, wherefore they haue no scripture. **1551** CROWLEY *Pleas. & Payne* 62, I..gaue you that wherefore ye sought. **1599** SHAKS. *Hen. V*, v. ii. 1 Peace to this meeting, wherefore we are met. **1913** *Act 3 & 4 Geo. V* c. 20 §118 (1)(d) All sums (not exceeding..one hundred pounds) due in respect of compensation under the Workmen's Compensation Act, 1906, the liability wherefor accrued before the said date.

4. On account of or because of which; in consequence or as a result of which. Chiefly with sb. (esp. *reason* or *cause*) as antecedent. *arch.*

c **1250** *Kent. Serm.* in *O.E. Misc.* 28 Gode werkes þet bieth þo offringes..werefore se christenman..of-seruet þo blisce of heuene. *a* **1300** *Cursor M.* 10784 þar es resuns..Quar-for godd wald sco spused were. **1340** *Ayenb.* 45 Greate blasfemies of god and of his halȝen hueruore god him wreþeþ. *c* **1400** MAUNDEV. (Roxb.) xxxii. 145 þou schall fynd na thing with vs wharfore þou schuld werray apon vs. **1474** CAXTON *Chesse* I. iii. (1883) 13 The causes wherfore this playe was founden ben thre. **1495** *Liber Festivalis* v iij/2, I denounse..all tho that purchasen lettres of ony lordes courte wherfore letynge is made in cristen courte. **1597** HOOKER *Eccl. Pol.* v. lxiii. §1 The true reason wherfore Christ doth loue belieuers is because their belief is the gift of God. **1829** SOUTHEY *Sir T. More* II. 187 The reason is sufficiently manifest wherefore a preference for republican institutions should hitherto have been shown.

5. Introducing a clause expressing a consequence or inference from what has just been stated: On which account; for which reason; which being the case; and therefore. (Now always '*wherefore*.)

a **1300** *Cursor M.* 16806 þen com word to sir pilat..Of all thingez þat by-fell, Wharfor he wex radd. **1340** HAMPOLE *Pr. Consc.* 1194 Whar-for worldes worshepe may be cald Noght elles. **1456** SIR G. HAYE *Law Arms* (S.T.S.) 232 This barne is all innocent.., quharefore he aw nocht to be grevit. *c* **1500** *Melusine* 361 And ryght forth said geffray, 'I chalenge the, wherfor deffende the.' **1500–20** DUNBAR *Poems* xxviii. 15 Sowtaris, with schone weill maid and meit, Ȝe mend the faltis of ill maid feit, Quhairfoir to Hevin ȝour saulis will fle. *c* **1620** A. HUME *Brit. Tongue* (1865) 10 Quherfoer in this case I wald commend to our men the imitation of the greek and latin. **1766** GOLDSM. *Vic. Wakef.* xxii, I could not continue a silent spectator of her distress: wherefore, assuming a degree of severity in my voice and manner [etc.]. **1842** TENNYSON *Morte d'Arth.* 248 More things are wrought by prayer Than this world dreams of. Wherefore, let thy voice Rise like a fountain for me night and day. **1882** BESANT *All Sorts* xxix, A person, you see, is an individual, or an indivisible thing. Wherefore, let us not despise our neighbour.

†**b.** Followed by *soever*: For whatever reason; on whatever account. *Obs. rare.*

c **1230** *Hali Meid.* 61 Sone so þu telles te betere þen an oðer —beo it hwerfore se hit eauer beo,..þu marres ti meidenhad. *c* **1530** LD. BERNERS *Arth. Lyt. Bryt.* lxxv. (1814) 331 He is in a great study, wherfore so euer it be. **1587** GOLDING *De Mornay* xxxii. (1592) 514 But come they once in Question, wherefore soeuer it bee, let them not escape.

III. 6. as *sb.* A question beginning with *wherefore*, or (more usually) the answer to such question; cause, reason. Often following *why* similarly used.

1590 SHAKS. *Com. Err.* II. ii. 45 *Ant.* Shall I tell you why? *S. Dro.* I sir, and wherefore; for they say, euery why hath a wherefore. **1624** FLETCHER *Rule a Wife* III. i, Such as are understanding in their draughts, And dispute learnedly the whyes and wherefores. **1641** 'SMECTYMNUUS' *Vind. Answ.* xiii. 144 But let him first answer our *Therefores*, and wee will quickly answer his *Wherefores*. **1719** RAMSAY *To Arbuckle* 6 [He] disna care for A how, a what way, or a wherefore. **1838** DICKENS *O. Twist* xxxi, They *will* have the why and the wherefore, and will take nothing for granted. **1884** ANNIE S. SWAN *Dor. Kirke* xiv, I am carried back to the days when I rebelled and demanded the wherefore of all God's dealings with me.

†**where'fro**, *adv.* Chiefly *Sc. Obs.* (quhairfra). [f. WHERE 15 + FRO *prep.*]

1. *rel.* = next.

In quot. 1585 *ellipt.* = to the place whence.

c **1449** PECOCK *Repr.* IV. viii. 467 The occasioun wherbi and wherfro the goostli harme and synne comen. **1508** DUNBAR *Gold. Targe* 57 Amang the grene rispis and the redis, Arrivit sche, quhar fro anonn thare landis Ane hundreth ladyes. **1541** COPLAND *Galyen's Terap.* B j b, The thyng wherfro nothyng can be taken, nor put to it. **1585** JAS. I *Ess. Poesie* (Arb.) 48 He tolde me then, how she flew bak againe, Where fra she came. **1588** A. KING tr. *Canisius' Catech.* h iv, It behoueth ye cowrse of ye dominicall lettre to be Interrupted, euerie hundereth ȝere quhairfra is subduced ane day. **1643** *Reg. Privy Council Scot.* Ser. II. VIII. 66 Thomas Irwing..being verie seik in Quondale, quherfra he was flitting.

2. *indirect interrog.* = WHENCE 1 b.

1513 DOUGLAS *Æneis* IX. vii. 106 To se quhayrfra the grundyn dart dyd glyde. **1596** DALRYMPLE tr. *Leslie's Hist. Scot.* I. 25 This guse ȝeirlie in the spring tyme returnes to ws: quhairfra can na man tell.

wherefrom (hwɛə'frɒm), *adv.* Now formal or *arch.* [f. WHERE 15 + FROM *prep.*] From which; whence.

1490 CAXTON *Eneydos* xii. 45 There is the Region of thire, wherfrom we haue wythdrawen..all this people. **1621** SANDERSON *Serm., 1 Cor. vii. 24* (1674) I. 205 Some Calling; wherefrom he may be altogether averse, and whereto altogether unfit. **1768** TUCKER *Lt. Nat.* (1834) II. 40 We have none others wherefrom to describe anything conceivable to our imagination. **1837** CARLYLE *Fr. Rev.* I. IV. iv, Lofty galleries; wherefrom dames of honour..may sit and look. **1865** KINGSLEY *Herew.* xvi, Wherefrom Hereward opined that Gilbert had need of him. **1893** J. CAIRD *Fundam. Ideas Chr.* vii, Akin to the infinite source wherefrom they proceed.

†**wherehen, -hence**, *adv. Obs.* Forms: α. 4 **whar hanne**. β. 6 **wherhens, wherhence**, 6–7 **where-hence, wherehence**. [f. WHERE 15 + HENNE, HENCE. Cf. HEREHENCE, THEREHENCE.]

1. *interrog.* = WHENCE 1, 2.

c **1400** *R. Glouc. Chron.* (Rolls) 7726 Wonder it was whar hanne [*v.rr.* wanene, whannen, whens] it com. *c* **1475** *Partenay* 3383 Off norreles Anon gan hym to enquere; Where-hens he cam. **1567** JEWEL *Def. Apol.* III. ii. 336 Where hence haue Schismes, and Heresies spronge vp, or where-hence doo they springe, onlesse [etc.]. **1584** *Copie of a Letter* 78 And wherhence (I pray you) ensueth al this?

2. *rel.* = WHENCE 3, 4.

c **1475** *Partenay* 5489 Where-hens thay shull noght depart veryly Fro thys vnto the day of Iugement. **1548** UDALL *Erasm. Par. Luke* ii. 24 b, Not after the fleshe onely (wherhens in dede the begynnyng of this saluacion hath proceded). **1575** TURBERV. *Faulconrie* 27 But wherehence soeuer the name is deriued, this is moste assured, that of all other birds of pray, the Falcon is most excellent. **1603** J. DAVIES *Microcosmos* Wks. (Grosart) I. 31/2 Dust of the earth ..Wherehence we came, and wherevnto we must. **1611** CORYAT *Crudities* 448 This part of the country..was.. inhabited by a kinde of people called Triboces,..wherehence it was called *Tribocum regio*. **1647** TRAPP *Comm. Matt.* vii. 5 God will lay them in the slimy valleyes,..wherehence also they shall be brought forth to the day of wrath.

wherein (hwɛər'ɪn), *adv.* Now formal or *arch.* [f. WHERE 15 + IN *prep.* Cf. Du. *waarin*, G. *worin*, MSw. *hvarinne*, Sw. *vari*, Da. *hvori*.]

I. Interrogative. **1.** In what (thing, matter, respect, etc.)?

In quot. 1600 = in what dress? (IN *prep.* 6.)

For the distinction between the use in dependent clauses and the relative use, cf. WHAT A. I ** note.

c **1230** *Hali Meid.* 39 Hare confort & hare delit, hwerin is hit? *c* **1460** METHAM *Wks.* (1916) 46 Clerkys wryte, off gret and smal, Her namys and naturys, and qwere-in thei noy be kend natural. **1509** FISHER *Funeral Serm. C'tess Richmond* Wks. (1876) 289 To shewe wherin this.. prynces may wel be lykened.. vnto the blessyd woman Martha. **1535** COVERDALE *Exod.* xxii. 27 His rayment is his onely couerynge of his skynne: wherin he slepeth. **1600** SHAKS. *A.Y.L.* III. ii. 234 How look'd he? Wherein went he? **1611** *Bible* Isa. ii. 22 Wherein is hee to be accounted of? **1671** MILTON *Samson* 564 To what can I be useful, wherein serve My Nation? **1728** LAW *Serious C.* x, Wherein does the sinfulness of this behaviour consist? **1850** McCOSH *Div. Govt.* I. iii. (1874) 60 It is not needful to show wherein the weakness of this theory lies. **1891** FARRAR *Darkn. & Dawn* xxii, Oh, Britannicus! wherein have we offended?

II. Relative. **2.** In which (place, material thing, writing, etc.); where.

c **1400** MAUNDEV. (Roxb.) vii. 26 A felde whare in bawme growes apon smale brusches. **1484** CAXTON *Fables of Alfonce* iv, A grete purse wherin were a thousand Crownes. **1523** LD. BERNERS *Froiss.* I. lxxv. 39 b/2 The cytie.. was destroyed, and the churches of godde wherin that god was honoured. *c* **1620** A. HUME *Brit. Tongue* (1865) 14 Anie latin word, quharein now we sound c as s. **1634** MILTON *Comus* 135 Stay thy cloudy Ebon chair, Wherin thou rid'st with Hecat'. **1711** STEELE *Spect.* No. 158. ¶5 Your Paper, wherein you fall upon us whom you envy. **1859** GWILT *Archit.* (ed. 4) 1027 A species of building wherein the faces of the stones are.. picked with the point of a hammer. **1888** 'J. S. WINTER' *Bootle's Childr.* ii, Peering keenly into the shadow wherein she stood.

(*b*) with ellipsis of antecedent: cf. WHEREWITH 2 b.

1674 N. FAIRFAX *Bulk & Selv.* 99 The world is made as much for stirring in its kind, as any share of it, if it had but a wherein to stir.

b. In, at, during, or in the course of which (time).

1535 COVERDALE *Ps.* lxxxix. [xc.] 15 The yeares wherin we haue suffred aduersite. **1597** MORLEY *Introd. Mus.* Ded., We liue in those daies wherein enuie raigneth. **1629** MILTON *Nativity* i, This is the Month, and this the happy morn Wherin the Son of Heav'ns eternal King.. Our great redemption from above did bring. **1733** BERKELEY *Th. Vision Vind.* §70 In an Age wherein we hear so much of Thinking and Reasoning. **1819** SHELLEY *Cenci* I. i. 32 Length of days Wherein to act the deeds which are the stewards Of their revenue.

3. In which (matter, fact, action, condition, etc.); in respect of which.

c **1400** *Apol. Loll.* 88 He haþ god þis þat he moost lufiþ, and wer in he tristiþ, as in God. *c* **1440** *Alphabet of Tales* cli. 105 þies er sophyms & subtelties, whare-in I wastis all my dayes. **1526** TINDALE *Luke* xi. 22 He taketh from him his harnes wherin he trusted. **1611** *Bible* Luke i. 4 That thou mightest know the certainetie of those things wherein thou hast bene instructed. **1711** STEELE *Spect.* No. 33. ¶ 1 Poor Daphne was seldom submitted to in a Debate wherein she was concerned. *a* **1774** GOLDSM. *Hist. Greece* I. 265 A very sharp action ensued, wherein.. the Athenians got the better. **1865** SWINBURNE *Chastelard* v. ii. 205 Whate'er this be wherein you were aggrieved. **1889** 'J. S. WINTER' *Mrs. Bob* xiv, There began a round of pleasure for Julia wherein she was the central figure.

(*b*) *ellipt.* or as *comp. rel.* = in that respect in which; that (one, something) in which.

1590 SHAKS. *Mids. N.* III. ii. 179 Wherein it doth impaire the seeing sense, It paies the hearing double recompence. **1597** HOOKER *Eccl. Pol.* v. xlvi. §2 There is wherein to exercise patience. **1628** in *Engl. Hist. Rev.* (1918) Jan. 30 Your Wisdome will supply it, wherein it is defectiue. **1728** H. HOME *Decis. Crt. Sess. 1716–28* To Rdr., No Decision is taken Notice of, but wherein some new Point is established. **1894** *Forum* (N.Y.) Oct. 248 This is wherein a bracing climate.. accounts for much with the New Englanders.

4. Into which: = WHEREINTO 1.

c **1400** *Pilgr. Sowle* (Caxton 1483) IV. xxxiii. 81 A coufre wherin that men shal put pryue thynges. **1526** TINDALE *John* vi. 22 There was none other shyppe there save that won wher in his disciples were entred. **1585** T. WASHINGTON tr. *Nicholay's Voy.* II. x. 44 We came to an anker very nigh the castle, wherin when our patrone would followe vs [etc.].

† **whereinne**, *adv.* *Obs.* [f. WHERE 15 + INE, INNE. In later instances perh. only a variant spelling of *wherein*.]

1. *interrog.* = prec. 1.

1382 WYCLIF *Matt.* v. 13 ȝif the salt shal vanyshe awey, wherynne shal it be saltid? *a* **1425** *Cursor M.* 7208 (Trin.) Til she þe soþe made him say Wher ynne al his strengþe lay.

2. *rel.* = prec. 2, 3, 4.

c **1275** LAY. 26336 Ear hii come ride anon to þe tealdes dore war ine was þe caisere. **1297** R. GLOUC. (Rolls) 5026 An chirche of sein Martin.. War inne me ssolde godes seruise do. **1340** *Ayenb.* 23 þis zenne is þe dyeules panne of helle, huerinne he makeþ his friinges. *Ibid.* 109 þe þridde bene huerinne we byddeþ oure uader of heuene þet his wyl by ydo. *Ibid.* 178 Uor þe zennes uenials huerine me ualþ ofte. **1387** TREVISA *Higden* (Rolls) III. 475 þou hast not wereynne to doo suche a ȝifte, for þyn soule is ful of covetise. *c* **1400** *Rule St. Benet* (prose) 38 þis es þe rihte gate whare-inne þu salle life.

whereinso'ever, *adv.* Now formal or *arch.* [f. WHEREIN + SOEVER.] In whatever matter, respect, etc.

1526 TINDALE *2 Cor.* xi. 21 Wherin soever eny man dare be bolde.. I dare be bolde also. **1552** *Bk. Com. Prayer, Communion* Exhortation, To examine your lyues.. and wherinsoeuer ye shall perceyue your selues to haue offended,.. there bewaile your owne synful lyues. **1768** TUCKER *Lt. Nat.* (1834) II. 456 That their own person, whereinsoever it consists, shall be made accountable for the actions performed by it in this life. **1845** KEBLE in *Newman's Lett.* (1891) II. 472 The impression.. of its being my own fault, not theirs, whereinsoever I am found wanting. **1870** MYERS *Poems* 56 Whereinsoever breath may rise and die Their generations follow on.

† **wherein'till**, *adv.* *Sc.* *Obs.* In 6–7 quha(i)r-. [f. WHERE 15 + INTILL.] Wherein.

1516 in *Acts Parlt. Scot.* (1875) XII. 36/2 For ye surty of oure Soveranis person quharintill we confess we above all utheris bundin & oblist. **1567** *Abstr. Protocols Town Clerks of Glasgow* (1896) III. 99 The.. land of Craiginfeoch quhairintill the saidis Lyoune was infeft. **1652** Z. BOYD *Zion's Flowers* (1855) App. 24/2 Bands quhairintill hir name is insert.

whereinto (hwɛərɪn'tuː, hwɛər'ɪntuː), *adv.* *arch.* [f. WHERE 15 + INTO.]

1. Into which.

1539 *Bible* (Great) John vi. 22 None other shyp.. saue that one wher into his disciples were entred. **1569** GOLDING tr. *Heminge's Postill* Ded. a vij b, The death whereintoo all mankynde was falne. **1641** J. JACKSON *True Evang. T.* III. 211 Proverbs, and Apophthegmes, whereinto a great deale of wisedome is abridged. *a* **1676** HALE *Prim. Orig. Man.* (1677) 9 They find.. some things which they call by these Names, to be that whereinto Bodies are dissolved. **1768** TUCKER *Lt. Nat.* (1834) I. 519 Voluntary agents.. can.. change the course whereinto bodies had been thrown by impulse. **1865** CHR. ROSSETTI *Memory* II. i, I have a room whereinto no one enters Save I myself alone.

†**2.** In which (cf. INTO 22). *Sc. Obs.*

1560 *Diurn. Occurr.* (Bannatyne Cl.) 63 Ane buik, quhairinto was contenit, that thair sould be in this realme tuelf superattendentis.

† **wheremid, -mide,** *adv.* *Obs.* [f. WHERE 15 + MID *prep.*[1], MIDE. Cf. Du. *waarme(d)e*, MSw. *hvarmädh*, Sw. *varmed*, Da. *hvormed*.] With which, by means of which, wherewith.

c **1160** *Hatton Gosp.* Matt. xviii. 25 þa he næfde hwær-mid he hyt agulde. *a* **1240** *Lofsong* in *O.E. Hom.* I. 211 Nab ich waremide leden mi lif i þisse worlde. *c* **1300** *Vox & Wolf* in *Rel. Ant.* II. 274 Nothing he ne founde.. Wermide his honger aquenche miȝtte. **1340** *Ayenb.* 266 þe toknen of þe passion he heþ ine his bodye, huermyde he ous boȝte.

whereness ('hwɛənɪs). [f. WHERE + -NESS: cf. HERENESS, THERENESS.] The condition, quality, or fact of being where it is; position, situation, location, *ubi* (as an attribute of something, or *vaguely* of things generally).

1674 N. FAIRFAX *Bulk & Selv.* 43 It would crack my brain to find so many whernesses there, to stow each of them in. **1701** GREW *Cosmol.* I. iii. 11 A Point.. hath no Dimensions, but only a Whereness. **1733** WATTS *Philos. Ess.* VI. v. (1734) 165 The *Ubi* or Whereness of a Spirit. *a* **1843** SOUTHEY *Doctor* cxcii. (1848) 509, I.. can never be lost till I get out of Whereness itself into Nowhere. **1887** *Mind* Jan. 18 Any special whereness or thereness. **1895** G. MACDONALD *Lilith* iii, You know nothing about whereness.

wherenigh: see WHERE 15.

whereof (hwɛər'ɒv), *adv.* Now formal or *arch.* [f. WHERE 15 + OF *prep.* Cf. (M)Sw. *hveraf*, Da. *hvoraf*; Du. *waarvan*.]

I. *Interrogative.* Of what.

1. †**a.** in various obsolete senses of OF: *esp.* From what source, whence; to what purpose, what.. for; for what reason, wherefore.

c **1200** ORMIN 2931 He sahh þatt ȝho wiþþ childe wass, & nisste he nohht whæroffe. *c* **1250** *Gen. & Ex.* 3530 Hu he sulen maken Ðe tabernacle, and wor-of taken Ðe gold, and siluer. *a* **1300** *Cursor M.* 9687 Quar-of serues ani a-sise Of sothfastnes, or of iustise, Bot for to yeme þe pes in land. *c* **1400** *Pety Job* 283 in *26 Pol. Poems* 130 Wherof than shulde I presume To be hygh-herted or lyghtly wroth? **1528** MORE *Dyaloge* IV. Wks. 273/2 Wherof shal reason serue if man had no power of himself towarde the direccion of his own workes? **1579–80** NORTH *Plutarch* (1595) 19 *marg.*, Manipulares whereof so called.

b. in various current senses of OF.

c **1400** *26 Pol. Poems* 64 Where-of is mad al mankynde? *c* **1400** MAUNDEV. (Roxb.) xxxiii. 150 Whare off þe wall es made, can na man tell. *c* **1400** *Pilgr. Sowle* (Caxton) V. i. (1859) 71, I not what to asken, ne wherof for to speke. **15..** in *Dunbar's Poems* (S.T.S.) II. 310 Thus wait I nocht quhairof to wryte. **1596** SHAKS. *Merch. V.* I. i. 4 What stuffe 'tis made of, whereof it is borne, I am to learne. **1605** —— *Lear* I. iv. 312 Now Gods that we adore, Whereof comes this? **1667** MILTON *P.L.* VII. 64 To know.. how this World.. first began, When, and whereof created. **1755** JOHNSON s.v., Whereof was the house built?

II. *Relative.* Of which.

2. a. From or out of which (as source or origin, in the way of result or consequence, liberation or privation, etc.), whence (OF I–III).

a **1225** *Ancr. R.* 12 Auh hwarse wummon liueð oðer mon bi him one.. of þincges wiðuten hwarof scandle ne kume, nis nout muche strencðe. *c* **1275** LAY. 26090 Telle of þine cunne war of þou hart ispronge. **1393** LANGL. *P. Pl.* C. IV. 60 A cours of kynde wher-of we comen alle. **1481** CAXTON *Godfrey* ccix. 305 The holy sepulcre where he laye deed in, and out wherof he aroos fro deth to lyf. **1562** TURNER *Herbal* II. 96 b, [Polygala] hath sede besyde euery lefe, wherof it is called the male. **1567** *Satir. Poems Reform.* iv. 5 The ruite quhair of I did spring. **1611** *Bible* Deut. xxviii. 27 The itch, whereof thou canst not bee healed. **1613** W. COWPER *Holy Alph.* 236 Wherof we learn, that.. if when we haue fallen, we rise & repent, it is euer to be imputed to God that teacheth vs. **1688** HOLME *Armoury* III. 259/2 By Avoir-du-pois Weight is weighed.. all things whereof comes waste.

b. Of which material substance (OF VII).

a **1300** *Cursor M.* 368 þe mater of þe four elements.. Quar of was serenes siþen scapen. **1594** T. B. *La Primaud. Fr. Acad.* II. 49 That matter whereof Kernels are made. *c* **1620** A. HUME *Brit. Tongue* (1865) 10 These and al other diphthonges I wald counsel the teacheres not to name be the vouales quherof they are maed. **1667** MILTON *P.L.* VI. 518 Mineral and Stone, Whereof to found thir Engins. **1794** R. J. SULIVAN *View Nat.* I. 107 The pre-existent.. matter whereof bodies are formed.

3. For, by reason of, because of, or on account of which; wherefore (OF 13, 14). Chiefly in constructional dependence on certain classes of words.

a **1325** *MS. Rawl. B.* 520 lf. 80 b, Send .iiij.i. chosene kniȝttes.. to seon were he be sik ware of he soined him of sik bedde. **1411** *Rolls of Parlt.* III. 650/2, I knowe wele that I haue failled.. yow,.. wherof I beseke yow of grace and mercy. **1484** CAXTON *Fables of Auian* xi, [He] oughte to doo good.. wherof other may preyse hym. *c* **1489** —— *Sonnes of Aymon* iii. 106 He knewe well that they were of his faders folke. Werof he was full sory for it. *a* **1533** LD. BERNERS *Huon* lxii. 215 Huon gaue her a ryche gyft, wherof humbly she thanked hym. **1539** *Bible* (Great) Ps. cxxvi. 3 The Lorde hath done greate thynges for vs all ready, wherof we reioyse. **1606** SHAKS. *Tr. & Cr.* I. iii. 139 The Feauer, whereof all our power is sicke. **1618** *Southampton Crt. Leet Rec.* (1907) III. 544 The wall.. is much impared & verye daungerous whereof wee desier the same to be amendyd verye speedelye.

4. By means of which, with which, whereby, wherewith (OF VI). *Obs.* or *rare arch.* exc. with *full*, etc. (= of which).

Also with ellipsis of antecedent as obj. of a vb.: = that by which, that with which: cf. WHEREWITH 2 b. WHEREWITHAL 2 b.

1340 *Ayenb.* 119 þise byeþ þe graces huer-of he wes al uol. **1377** [see WHEREBY 2]. *c* **1400** MAUNDEV. (Roxb.) Pref. 2 For þe whilk land ilke a gude Cristen man þat may, and has wharoff, suld enforce him for to conquere oure right heritage. *c* **1450** *Mirk's Festial* 4 ȝe hadden ynogh wherof to haue fed me. **1585** T. WASHINGTON tr. *Nicholay's Voy.* IV. xxxi. 154 [They] kept their wyues.. vnder lock and key, for feare least they should gette of theyr neyghbours, whereof sometymes theyr iealous husbandes could not furnish them. *c* **1592** MARLOWE *Jew of Malta* III. iv, Borgia's wine, Whereof his sire.. was poyson'd. **1607** SHAKS. *Timon* IV. iii. 194 Dry vp thy Marrowes, Vines, and Plough-torne Leas, Whereof ingratefull man.. greases his pure minde.

5. a. About or concerning which; in regard to or in respect of which (OF VIII, IX, XI).

In quot. *c* 1400 *ellipt.* or as *comp. rel.* = in that in respect of which.

a **1300** *Cursor M.* 1624 Als it in noe flod be-fell, Quare of i sal yow siþen tell. *c* **1400** *Rom. Rose* 2311 Where of that thou be vertuous, Ne be not straunge ne daungerous. **1526** TINDALE *Acts* xvii. 19 Thys newe doctrine wher off thou speakest. **1560** T. WILSON *Rhet.* Prol. to Rdr., That I was in farther perill, then wherof I was aware. **1585** T. WASHINGTON tr. *Nicholay's Voy.* I. xvii. 19 b, He had vnderstanding, that the Frigate.. was of Malta, whereof he thought very straunge. **1611** *Bible* 1 John iv. 3 This is that spirit of Antichrist, whereof you haue heard, that it should come. **1672** MARVELL *Corr.* Wks. (Grosart) II. 408 We shall now shortly come to a good issue. Whereof therefore you may please to advertise your worthy Society. **1742** H. WALPOLE *Let. to Mann* 25 Sept., Our Duke goes.. they say, to marry a Princess of Prussia, whereof great preparations have been making. **1868** MORRIS *Earthly Par.* (1870) I. I. 382 More precious gifts.. Whereof not e'en in dreams they could have thought.

b. Phr. ***to know whereof one speaks*** (or ***writes***, etc.): to know what one is talking about, to speak from experience.

1922 H. VAN LOON *Story of Mankind* xliii. 256 He [*sc.* Erasmus] had travelled a great deal and knew whereof he wrote. **1967** R. STEIN *Great Cars* 165/1 Ettore Bugatti knew whereof he spoke when he advised people griping about hard starting to keep their cars in heated garages. **1975** *Publishers Weekly* 24 Mar. 42/2 Fischer has been a lifelong reporter on public affairs and was on LBJ's Commission on Rural Poverty, so he knows whereof he writes.

6. Of which, in *objective* senses (OF X).

1469 *Bury Wills* (Camden) 50 In wittenesse qwherof I haue set to myn seele. **1561** T. NORTON *Calvin's Inst.* I. To Rdr., Whereof I geue to the godly reders a new profe in this setting fourth of this boke. **1592** SHAKS. *Ven. & Ad.* 880 Like one that spies an adder,.. iust in his way, The feare whereof doth make him shake, & shudder. **1647** CLARENDON *Hist. Reb.* I. §18 In dispensing whereof, he was guided more by the rules of Appetite, than of Judgement. **1676** RAY *Corr.* (1848) 123 Reputation (to the vanity of any affectation whereof I desire to be wholly mortified). **1827** HOOD *Plea Mids. Fairies* xxxv, We be the handmaids of the Spring, In sign whereof, May.. Hath wrought her samplers on our gauzy wing.

7. Of which or whom, in *partitive* sense (OF XIII).

Also with ellipsis of antecedent as obj. of a vb.: = some or something of which (OF 45).

c **1390** in *Rel. Ant.* II. 54 To han wherof to spenden on these myraclis. **1459** *Paston Lett.* I. 473, xiij. spones, wherof oon is gilt, weiyng xvij. unces. **1535** COVERDALE *Gen.* iii. 11 Hast thou not eaten of the tre, wherof I commaunded the, y[t] thou shuldest not eate? **1593** SHAKS. *Rich. II*, I. ii. 11 Edwards seuen sonnes (whereof thy selfe art one). **1610** —— *Temp.* v. i. 38 The greene sowre Ringlets.. Whereof the Ewe not bites. **1667** MILTON *P.L.* II. 584 Lethe the River of Oblivion.., whereof who drinks, Forthwith his former state and being forgets. **1726** SWIFT *Gulliver* II. vii, Civil Wars, the last whereof was happily put an end to by this Prince's Grandfather. **1827** LYTTON *Pelham* lxix, I presume that you have many titles, whereof some are more grateful to your ears than others. **1865** DICKENS *Mut. Fr.* I. iv, The two bottles: whereof one held Scotch ale and the other rum.

8. Of which, in *possessive* and related senses (OF XIV).

a **1400–50** *Wars Alex.* 4380 þe faire floryscht filds of floures & of herbys, Quare-of þe breth as of bawme blawis in oure noose. **1554** in Strype *Eccl. Mem.* (1721) III. App. xvii. 43 By reason wherof we affirm Purgatory.. to be the Doctrin of Antichrist. **1576** TURBERV. *Venerie* xxviii. 72 You shal seke the hart in heaths and broomie places, wherof they then delight to crop the flowers and toppes. **1661** J. CHILDREY

Brit. Baconica 23 Bodmin . . hath one street . . on the South side whereof it hath a great high hill. **1753** *Stewart's Trial* 219 In the eyes of those tenants whereof he had assumed to be protector. **1821** SCOTT *Kenilw.* xviii, Dangerous sickness, the issue whereof is in the will of Heaven. **1882** BESANT *All Sorts* xxxiii, All that work for your grandfather whereof you now sweetly reap the benefit.

†**9.** To which, whereto (OF 58). *Obs. rare*$^{-1}$.

1659 LEAK *Waterwks.* 25 Let there be a water wheel to the Axtree, whereof let there be fastned a Wheel of thirty six Teeth or more.

Hence †**where-'offen** *adv.*, in quot. in sense 5.

c **1450** LOVELICH *Grail* xxxvii. 11 Where-offen they spoken ful pleyn.

whereon (hwɛər'ɒn), *adv.* Now *formal* or *arch.* [f. WHERE 15 + ON *prep.* Cf. Du. *waaraan*, G. *woran.*]

I. 1. *Interrogative.* On what?

c **1205** LAY. 15516 Ne mihten heo nauere finden . . whær on hit weore ilong. *c* **1250** *Gen. & Ex.* 1310 Ðo wurð ðe child witter and war Ðat ðor sal offrende ben don, Oc ne wiste he quuat, ne quor-on. *a* **1400–50** *Wars Alex.* 268 Quare-on muse ȝe sa mekill, maister? **1600** SHAKS. *A.Y.L.* I. iii. 59 Tell me whereon the likelihood depends? **1602** —— *Ham.* III. iv. 124 Whereon do you looke? **1611** *Bible* 2 Chron. xxxii. 10 Whereon doe ye trust, that yee abide in the siege in Ierusalem? **1755** JOHNSON s.v., Whereon did he sit?

II. *Relative.* On which. **2.** Of local position (ON *prep.* 1–4).

a **1300** *Cursor M.* 16762 + 116 Til our lord in erth so mikel was not leued, Whar on þat he miȝt rest on is wery heued. *c* **1400** MAUNDEV. (Roxb.) xi. 48 A stane wharon oure Lord satt and preched. *a* **1508** DUNBAR *Tua Mariit Wemen* 5 Ane gudlie grene garth, . . Hegeit . . with hawthorne treis; Quhairon ane bird . . birst out hir notis. **1539** *Bible* (Great) Exod. iii. 5 Y^{e} place whereon thou stondest is holy grounde. **1603** SHAKS. *Meas. for M.* I. ii. 164 A horse whereon the Gouernor doth ride. **1667** MILTON *P.L.* IX. 526 He [*sc.* the Serpent] lick'd the ground whereon she trod. **1812** BYRON *Ch. Har.* I. xlix, On yon long level plain, at distance crown'd With crags, whereon those Moorish turrets rest. **1896** A. MORRISON *Child Jago* xiv, The ground was bought whereon should be built a church.

3. Of time, esp. with antecedent *day* (ON *prep.* 6).

1588 A. KING tr. *Canisius' Catech.* h vj, The astrologians estiming ye haill varieteis of ye change to tak end in 19 ȝeres and returne yairefter to ye same dayes quhairon yai fell before. **1595** SHAKS. *John* IV. ii. 156 On that day at noone, whereon he sayes, I shall yeeld vp my Crowne. **1600** J. PORY tr. *Leo's Africa* III. 138 Vpon eight seuerall daies of the yeere besides, whereon the Moores feastes are solemnized. **1817** SHELLEY *Rev. Islam* V. xxxvii, The eve of that great day Whereon the many nations . . Decreed to hold a sacred Festival. **1883** WHITELAW *Sophocles, Electra* 278 That fatal day whereon Our father by her treachery she slew.

4. Of immediately subsequent or consequent action (ON *prep.* 7). Now more usually WHEREUPON (sense 4).

1597 SHAKS. *2 Hen. IV*, V. ii. 81 Your Highnesse . . strooke me . . Whereon (as an Offender to your Father) I . . did commit you. **1685** FOUNTAINHALL *Hist. Obs.* (Bannatyne Club) 146 He . . had very near shot Douglas himselfe dead, had not the Whig's carabine misgiven, wheron Douglas pistoled him presently. **1863** KINGSLEY *Water-Bab.* iii, Whereon she curled up her lip. **1885–94** R. BRIDGES *Eros & Psyche* Mar. xxi, Whereon she quickly led him down on earth, And show'd him Psyche.

5. Of motion or direction to or towards (ON *prep.* 14–16): Onto which.

a **1300** *Cursor M.* 1896 Noe . . Lete vte a doue þat tok hir flight And fand na sted quare-on to light. *a* **1578** LINDESAY (Pitscottie) *Chron. Scot.* (S.T.S.) I. 310 Ane skaffald quhairon they pat this innocent man. **1667** MILTON *P.L.* XI. 897 He . . will therein set His triple-colour'd Bow, whereon to look And call to mind his Cov'nant. **1728** CHAMBERS *Cycl.* s.v. *Glass*, The Table, whereon the Glass is to be run, is of Pot Metal. **1800** BLOOMFIELD *Farmer's Boy, Spring* 259 The oaken shelf whereon 'tis laid.

6. In reference to the object of an action, feeling, etc., and in various constructional uses (ON *prep.* 20–22, 29).

1340 *Ayenb.* 176 Verst be þe heauede, hueran me zet ofte grat cost. **1526** TINDALE *John* iv. 38, I sent you to repe that wheron ye bestowed no laboure. **1591** SHAKS. *1 Hen. VI*, II. iii. 47 To thinke, that you haue ought but Talbots shadow, Whereon to practise your seueritie. **1594** HOOKER *Eccl. Pol.* I. iii. §3 If the string whereon he striketh chaunce to be vncapable of harmonie. **1611** SHAKS. *Wint. T.* I. i. 2 If you shall chance . . to visit Bohemia, on the like occasion whereon my seruices are now on-foot. **1781** COWPER *Conversat.* 676 Fly-blown flesh whereon the maggot feeds. **1821** SHELLEY *Ginevra* 193 A corpse whereon A vulture has just feasted. **1850** TENNYSON *In Mem.* xxi, I take the grasses of the grave, And make them pipes whereon to blow.

†**7.** Of which, whereof (ON *prep.* 27). *Obs.*

c **1420** ? LYDG. *Assembly of Gods* 48 To declare her greefe of the gret offence To theym done by Eolus, wheron they compleynyd. **1525** LD. BERNERS *Froiss.* II. ccxxxiv. [ccxxx.] 303 b/2 The duke fell sycke, wheron he dyed. **1583** STOCKER *Civ. Warres Lowe C.* III. 112 No milke to be solde, whereon butter might be made. **1624** QUARLES *Job Militant* Medit. 17 The parts, whereon the World consists.

whereout (hwɛər'aʊt), *adv. arch.* [f. WHERE 15 + OUT *adv.* Cf. Du. *waaruit*, G. *woraus.*] Out of which, out from which (in various senses: see OUT *adv.* and OUT OF).

1340 *Ayenb.* 242 Lottes wyf lokede behinde hire þe cite þet bernde, huerout hi wes iguo. **1375** in Horstmann *Altengl. Leg.* (1878) 132/1 þe tre of mercy . . Where out renneþ oyle of lyf. *c* **1489** CAXTON *Sonnes of Aymon* xix. 428 He hath betrapped me wythin his gynnes wheroute I can not scape. **1535** COVERDALE *Micah* ii. 3, I deuysed a plage, wherout ye shal not plucke youre neckes. **1578** in Feuillerat *Revels Q. Eliz.* (1908) 300 In the whole—lxviij^{s} ij^{d}. whereout abate vj^{s}. viij^{d}. **1606** SHAKS. *Tr. & Cr.* IV. v. 245 The very breach, where-out Hectors great spirit flaw. **1641** EARL MONM. tr. *Biondi's Civil Wars* VII. 75, I have not whereout to frame a History. **1768** TUCKER *Lt. Nat.* (1834) I. 615 The general good becomes the root whereout all our schemes and contrivances . . are to branch. **1885** TENNYSON *Anc. Sage* 13 The heavens Whereby the cloud was moulded, and whereout The cloud descended.

†**b.** From which, whence (as an inference). *Obs.*

1569 J. ROGERS *Glasse Godly Love* (New Shaks. Soc.) 179 The wife must bee obediente vnto her husband, as vnto Christ himselfe; whereout it foloweth, that the saide obedience extendeth not vnto any wickednesse or euill. *a* **1626** W. SCLATER *Exp. 4th Ch. Rom.* (1650) 92 The end was, that he might be Father of Believers in both people: where-out amounts the conclusion intended.

†**c.** Also *whereout of* (cf. WHEREINTO). *Obs.*

1574 tr. *Marlorat's Apoc.* 21 Yet did hee sauour of the earth, wherout of his bodie was taken, and wherin hee was placed to liue. **1583** GOLDING *Calvin on Deut.* xxiv. 142 Being humbled in our selues by beholding the miseries wher-out of we be waded. *c* **1632** in G. Barry *Orkney* (1805) 474 The Baillie of the paroch whereout of he has fled, shall cause him be jogged at the church.

whereover, whereround: see WHERE 15.

whereso ('hwɛəsəʊ), *adv., conj. arch.* [ME. *whær swa, se*, representing OE. *swá hwǽr swá*: see WHERE and SO *adv.* 17 d; Ormin's form *whærs* is influenced by ON. *hvars* = *hvar* where + *es* rel. particle.]

1. = WHEREVER 2, 5.

1154 *O.E. Chron.* (Laud MS.) an. 1137 War sæ me tuede þe erthe ne bar nan corn. *c* **1200** ORMIN 1574, & whærs itt iss. *Ibid.* 4874, & whærse icc amm bitwenenn menn Icc hutedd amm & þutedd. *c* **1205** LAY. 9202 Ah whære swa he fonde enne gume: þe of Rome weore hider icumen, he lette smiten him of þet hæfde. *c* **1300** *Havelok* 1349 þou maght til he aren quike, Hwore so he o worde aren. *c* **1374** CHAUCER *Troylus* v. 1797 And red wher so þou be or elles songe, That þow be vnderstonde god beseche. **1393** LANGL. *P. Pl.* C. VII. 99 þenne was ich a-redy . . to lacke myn neghebores, Here werkes, here wordes wher-so ich sete. *c* **1460** *Play Sacram.* 337 Syr Almyghty god mott be yow^{r} gyde And glad yow where soo ye rest. *a* **1542** WYATT *How to vse the court* 53 Stay him by the arme where so he walke or goo. **1590** SPENSER *F.Q.* II. i. 18 That short reuenge the man may ouertake, Where so he be. *a* **1850** ROSSETTI *Dante & Circle* I. (1874) 118 Since I find not one . . Whereso I be or whitherso I turn. **1870** W. MORRIS *Earthly Par.* IV. 163 Few indeed were there Who did not pray that well he still might fare Whereso he was. **1893** F. THOMPSON *Poems, Carrier Song* iv, Whereso you keep your state Heaven is pitched over you.

2. = WHEREVER 3.

c **1290** *Beket* 1363 in *S. Eng. Leg.* I. 145 To spene to him and alle his ȝware-so heo euere come. *a* **1300** *Cursor M.* 1154 Quar-sa þou wendes in exile. *c* **1386** CHAUCER *Sqr.'s T.* 118 Wher so yow lyst . . Beren youre body in to euery place. **1596** SPENSER *F.Q.* VI. vi. 29 Ne would the Prince him euer foot forsake, Where so he went. **1600** FAIRFAX *Tasso* IX. xii, I follow thee, where so thee list to goe. **1851** NEALE *Med. Hymns* 154 On must the faithful warrior go Whereso the Chief precedeth.

3. = WHEREVER 4.

a **1225** Hwarse [see WHEREOF 2]. *c* **1340** HAMPOLE *Prose Treat.* 2 Whare-so I be, whare-so I sytt, what-so I doo. *c* **1407** LYDG. *Reson & Sens.* 3201 Wher so as her sort was set, The knot never was vnknet. *a* **1547** SURREY *Poems*, '*Set me wheras the sonne*' 11 Thrawle, or at large, aliue whersoo I dwell; Sike, or in healthe. **1667** MILTON *P.L.* XI. 722 Hee oft Frequented thir Assemblies, whereso met. **1868** MORRIS *Earthly Par.* Prol. 89 To seek your own land, whereso that may be.

4. = WHERE 1 b. *Obs.* exc. *arch. rare.*

13.. *Cursor M.* 8456 (Gött.) þe kind of thinges lered he, Bath of tres and grisses fele, Quilk war þair vertus lele . . Quer-so þai grew in wode or playn. **1889** 'MARK TWAIN' *Connecticut Yankee* xi. 130 Whereso if ye be minded . . it is in the east.

wheresoever (hwɛəsəʊ'ɛvə(r)), *adv., conj.* Now formal or *arch.* Also *poet.* **wheresoe'er** (-'ɛə(r)); 7 -ere, -e're; also 4–5 *contr.* **wher(e)sere.** [f. WHERESO + EVER; cf. SOEVER.]

1. = WHEREVER 2, 5.

13.. *Cursor M.* 8931 (Gött.) Bot quar-sua-euer [*Cott.* quar-sum-euer] þis tre lay, God schued þar-on his mihtes ay. **13..** *Gaw. & Gr. Knt.* 644 Quere-so-euer þys mon in melly was stad, His þro þoȝt was in þat, þurȝ alle oþer þyngez. *a* **1400–50** *Bk. Curtasye* 105 in *Babees Bk.* 302 Where-sere þou sitt at mete in borde, Avoide þe cat. **1526** TINDALE *Matt.* xxvi. 13 Wheresoever this gospell shalbe preached . . , there shall also thys thatt she hath done, be tolde for a memoriall of her. **1588** A. KING tr. *Canisius' Catech.* 35 We worschipe Christ him Selffe and his Sancts, quhairsoewir thay ar repræsentit vnto ws be thair images. **1671** MILTON *P.R.* III. 79 Conquerours, who leave behind Nothing but ruin wheresoe're they rove. **1733** WATTS *Philos. Ess.* I. x. (1734) 35 Wheresoever Body is, there Space is not. **1859** RUSKIN *Two Paths* i. §23 Wheresoever the search after truth begins, there life begins. **1890** BRIDGES *Shorter Poems* IV. xxv, But wheresoe'er he take his way, He killeth our delight.

b. *ellipt.* = WHEREVER 2 b.

1561 T. HOBY tr. *Castiglione's Courtyer* II. (1577) H j b, Meeting in the market place or wheresoever anye friende. **1597** HOOKER *Eccl. Pol.* v. lv. §7 The person of Christ is whole, perfect God and perfect man wheresoeuer. **1633** J. DONE *Hist. Septuagint* 58 In all the Treasors, neyther in all the Cabinets, or other wheresoeuer, was not to bee found any thing so rich.

2. = WHEREVER 3.

c **1320** *Cast. Love* (ed. Hall.) 431 Ne helpyth him nothyng whersere he wynde. *c* **1400** *Rule St. Benet* (verse) 2215 And whor so euer þai gang o-boute, þe ȝonger sal þe elder loute. **1535** COVERDALE *Mark* xiv. 14 Where so euer he goeth in, there saye ye to the good man of the house [etc.]. **1600** SHAKS. *A.Y.L.* I. iii. 77 And wheresoere we went, like Iunos Swans, Still we went coupled and inseperable. **1697** DRYDEN *Æneis* XI. 1124 This way and that his winding Course he bends; And wheresoe're she turns, her Steps attends. **1711** STEELE *Spect.* No. 134 ⁋6 [She] still goes on laying waste wheresoever she comes. **1818** SHELLEY *Eugan. Hills* 30 Wander wheresoe'er he may. **1865** TENNYSON *Captain* 20 He . . Hoped to make the name Of his vessel great in story, Wheresoe'er he came.

3. = WHEREVER 4.

a **1450** MYRC *Par. Pr.* etc. 64 Hit is to tyȝe [= tyþe] . . Off hey, where-sere hit growes. *c* **1475** *Rauf Coilȝear* 759 The nixt vacant . . That hapnis in France, quhair sa euer it fall, . . I gif the heir heritabilly. **1573** D. P. *Cert. Rules Geog.* A iv, Where so euer you are, imagine a poynt or pricke directly ouer your head, which is called Zenith. **1645** VANE *Lost Sheepe* 267 Wheresoere they are, or whatsoeuer doing, they soe behaue themselues, as if with Saint Hierome, they heard the sound of the Archangells trump. **1853** KINGSLEY *Hypatia* xxx, Wulf, too, had gone to his own place, wheresoever that may be.

†**wheresome,** *adv., conj. Obs.* [f. WHERE + -SOME^{3}, SUM *rel. adv.* 2.] = WHEREVER.

c **1200** ORMIN 6411 Sone summ ȝe findenn himm, Whær summ he beoþ onn eorþe, Wiþþ ȝure maddmess lakeþþ himm. *a* **1300** *Cursor M.* 18957 þat ilk tung quar-sum þai war, Til ilk lede þai gaf ansuar. *c* **1400** *Ywaine & Gaw.* 30 On ilka syde wharesum þai yede.

wheresomever (hwɛəsəm'ɛvə(r)), *adv., conj. Obs.* exc. *dial.* [f. WHERE + SOMEVER.]

1. = WHEREVER 2, 2 b.

a **1300** *Cursor M.* 8931 Bot quar-sum-euer þis tre lai, Godd sceud þar-on his mightes ai. **1452** *Reg. Mag. Sig. Scot.* 131/1 All and sindri my landis . . within the realme of Scotland quharesumever. **1490** CAXTON *Eneydos* xvi. 62 Hys grete wynges . . that bare hym . . hyghe and lowe, where som-euere he wolde be. *c* **1500** *Melusine* xxxvi. 275 And take there your lodgys tofore them wheresomeuer it playse you. **1502** ATKYNSON tr. *De Imitatione* II. i. (1893) 179 Wheresomeuer we be in this worlde, we be as pylgryms and straungers. **1619** J. WILLIAMS *Serm. Apparell* (1620) 30 The soules house is there, wheresomeuer it worketh.

2. = WHEREVER 3.

1470–85 MALORY *Arthur* VII. vi. 221 Where someuer ye goo I wylle folowe you. **1501** in *Lett. Rich. III & Hen. VII* (Rolls) I. 136 Wheresomever it shuld please the king to sende theym. *a* **1592** GREENE *Alphonsus* I. ii, Arragon, Who . . Doth play the diuell where some ere he comes.

3. = WHEREVER 4.

1477 EARL RIVERS (Caxton) *Dictes* 21 Whersomeuer one dye the weye to the other worlde is alle like. *c* **1489** CAXTON *Sonnes of Aymon* xxiv. 533 Mawgys habandouned never reynawd whersomever he went. **1599** SHAKS. *Hen. V*, II. iii. 7 Would I were with him, wheresomere hee is. **1837** R. BIRD *Nick of Woods* iii. 43 He haunts about our woods . . and kills 'em [*sc.* Indians] wheresomever he catches 'em.

†**where'thorough,** *adv. Obs.* [f. WHERE 15 + THOROUGH *prep.*] = next.

a **1225** *Ancr. R.* 210 þeo þet dronc eni drunch, oðer el þing dude hwarðuruh no childe ne schulde beon of hire istreoned. **1297** R. GLOUC. (Rolls) 1393 Echman paide a peni, . . War þoru he wuste hou moni men in al þe worlde were. *Ibid.* 2463 Tounes grete & heye Ware þoru him & is men in vair warison he broȝte. *Ibid.* 7493 He nadde no wounde war þoru he ssedde an drope blod. *a* **1300** *Cursor M.* 6446 (Cott.) Ietro gaue him consail Vnder baillis for to sett, Quar thoru in right þai suld be gett. *c* **1375** *Ibid.* 984 (Fairf.) Quen he con breke þe comandement Quar þorow his ospringe was shent. *c* **1440** *Gesta Rom.* liii. 234 (Harl. MS.) And thenne yaf him medesyne, wherthorowe he was hole. *a* **1450** *Knt. de la Tour* 45 Hit happed on a day her chapelein was sike that he might not synge, wherthorugh she must go home withoute masse. **1470–85** MALORY *Arthur* x. xxxviii. 475 A posterne where thorou he shold flee. **1503–4** *Act 19 Hen. VII* c. 34 §10 Offices and inquisicions dailly be founde . . wherethorough suche Maners . . be seased into the Kinges handes. **1583** STUBBES *Anat. Abus.* I. (1879) 80 The Authors of these new toyes, wherthorow they offended, shalbe giltie of their deathes. **1627** SPEED *England* x. §2 The ayre . . is cleansed . . by the Billowes that ever worke from off her environing Seas, where-thorow it becommeth pure and subtill.

wherethrough (hwɛə'θruː), *adv.* Now *formal* or *arch.* [f. WHERE 15 + THROUGH *prep.* Cf. Du. *waardoor*, G. *wodurch.*] Through which (in various senses of THROUGH *prep.*).

1. In reference to movement or direction in space, etc., or to duration in time (THROUGH *prep.* 1–4).

1297 R. GLOUC. (Rolls) 170 Veire weies . . ȝwar þorȝ me mai wende Fram þe on ende of engelond vorþ to þe oþer ende. *c* **1400** MAUNDEV. (Roxb.) viii. 30 Him behoues passe by þe Reed See . . whare thurgh þe childer of Israel went drye fote. **1568** *Bible* (Bishops') Wisd. xix. 8 The drye earth appeared . . ; Wherethrough all the people went that were defended with thy hande. *c* **1600** SHAKS. *Sonn.* xxiv, Mine eyes haue drawne thy shape, and thine for me Are windowes to my brest, where-through the Sun Delights to peepe, to gaze therein on thee. **1632** LITHGOW *Trav.* VI. 281 The top is couered, and hath three holes, where-through they let the dead Christians fall downe. **1842** TENNYSON *Ulysses* 19 All experience is an arch wherethro' Gleams that untravell'd world, whose margin fades For ever and for ever when I move. **1870** MORRIS *Earthly Par.* II. III. 349 The many years Wherethrough thou waitedst. **1896** A. MORRISON *Child Jago* v, A hole where-through a very small boy might squeeze.

2. In reference to agency or instrumentality (THROUGH *prep.* 7): By means of which, whereby, wherewith. Now *rare* or *Obs.*

13.. *Northern Passion* I. 25/222 It es my fless þat I ȝow gif, Whar thurgh ȝe may þe better lif. **13..** *Gosp. Nicodemus* (G.) 284 We say a spirit enclosed he has, wharthurth all thinges he wate. **1422** YONGE tr. *Secr. Secr.* 128 Force of Powere, wher-throgh he may his reme kepe, mayntene, and defende. **1470–85** MALORY *Arthur* XIII. xviii. 638 Whanne shalle the holy vessel come by me where thurgh I shalle be blessid. **1577** HOLINSHED *Chron.* II. 1868/2 A great tempest.. wherethrough sixe houses in that towne were borne downe. **1678** R. BARCLAY *Apol. Quakers* xiii. §2. 446 That.. Spiritual Body of Christ; whereby, and wherethrough, he communicateth Life to Men.

3. In reference to reason or cause: By reason of which, on account of which, wherefore; in consequence of which, from which, whereby, whence (as result or inference); *rarely* referring to a person = by whom: cf. THROUGH *prep.* 8. *arch.*

c **1220** *Bestiary* 779 in *O.E. Misc.* 25 Amonges men a swete smel He let her of his holi spel, Wor-ðurȝ we muȝen folȝen him In-to his godcundnesse fin. *a* **1225** *Leg. Kath.* 236 Ne nis na þing hwerþurh monnes muchele madschipe wreððeð him wið mare. *c* **1300** *Beket* 839 Whar thurf me thingth that of nothing thu ne schalt ansuere noȝt. **1375** BARBOUR *Bruce* I. 170 Schir Ihon the Balleoll.. Assentyt till him, in all his will; Quhar-throuch fell eftir mekill ill. *Ibid.* VII. 89 Quhar-throu. **1500–20** DUNBAR *Poems* xxvii. 103 For lawchtir neir I brist; Quhairthrow I walknit of my trance. *a* **1578** LINDESAY (Pitscottie) *Chron. Scot.* (S.T.S.) I. 27 This was done without the chancellaris counsall quhair throw he was hichlie offendit. **1638** PENKETHMAN *Artach.* I 3, There could be none found for money, where-through many poore people were constrained to eat Barks of Trees. **1819** SCOTT *Leg. Montrose* ii, Your Spaniard..is a person altogether unparalleled in his own conceit, wherethrough he maketh not fit account of such foreign cavaliers of valour as are pleased to take service with him. **1870** MORRIS *Earthly Par.* II. III. 7 Folk cried the name Of him wherethrough the weary struggle came.

wheretill (hwɛəˈtɪl), *adv.* In later use *Sc.* [f. WHERE 15 + TILL *prep.* Cf. (M)Sw. *hvartill*, Da. *hvortil.*]

1. *interrog.* †**a.** = next, 2. *Obs.*

a **1300** *Cursor M.* 7291 'Lauerdinges,' he said, 'sais me quartill Haf yee me fott?' *c* **1400** tr. *Secr. Secr., Gov. Lordsh.* 113 þis ys þe ffygure of wys ypocras; whare-tyll haue ȝe askyd me þerof?

b. To what place, whither.

1819 W. TENNANT *Papistry Storm'd* (1827) 31 She tauld the friskie fairy thing Whairtill to flee on rapid wing.

2. *rel.* = next, 3.

1423 JAS. I *Kingis Q.* clxx, Though thy begynnyng hath bene retrograde, Be froward opposyt quhare till aspert, Now sall thai turn, and luken on the dert. **1535** STEWART *Cron. Scot.* (Rolls) I. 562 How Carentius schew his Desyre to thir Tua Kingis, quhairtill thai grantit baith richt glaidlie.

whereto (hwɛəˈtuː), *adv.* Now *formal* or *arch.* [f. WHERE 15 + TO *prep.* Cf. Du. *waartoe.*]

I. Interrogative.

1. To what? (in various senses of TO *prep.*); in what direction, whither?

a **1300** *Cursor M.* 24488 Quen i sagh son warto þai tight, Al mi licam can þai light, And mi mode a-mend. *c* **1400** *Rule St. Benet* (verse) 293 Whar-to so þai turn pair mode. *Ibid.* (prose) 38 þan sal man rede hir þe reule, þat sho may wite witerli whar-to sho salle halde hir. *c* **1400** in *26 Pol. Poems* 149 Wherto ys a man more lyke, Then to a floure that spryngeth in may? **1484** *Cely Papers* (Camden) 152 Wherto thys schall growe I can nott saye. **1570** LEVINS *Manip.* 154/40 Wherto, *quorsum.* **1590** SHAKS. *Mids. N.* III. ii. 256 Lysander, whereto tends all this? **1855** EMERSON *Misc.* vii. 56 What is matter? Whence is it? and Whereto?

†**2.** [TO *prep.* 8.] To what end? for what purpose? for what reason? wherefore? what.. for? *Obs.* exc. *arch.*

a **1225** *St. Marher.* 16 Hwerto schuld i tellen þe..of ure cunde? *a* **1250** *Owl & Night.* 464 Wan min erende is ido, Sholde ich bileue? nai: war to? **1382** WYCLIF *Matt.* xxvi. 50 Jhesus seide to hym, Frend, wherto art thou comen? **1390** GOWER *Conf.* I. 287 How sche that scharpe swerdes blad Receive scholde and do withal So as sche wot wherto it schal. *c* **1400** MAUNDEV. (Roxb.) xxxii. 145 Qwhare to þan..gaders þou þe ricches of þis werld? *c* **1420** *Prose Life Alex.* 46, I ame ..sent vn-to þe fra kyng Alexander to wiete where to þou taries to come till hym to gyffe hym batelle. *c* **1470** HENRY *Wallace* XI. 311 Quhar to suld I her off lang process mak? **1484** CAXTON *Fables of Poge* iv, What is that whiche thou berest on thy fyste and wher to is it [*sc.* a spere-hawk] good. **1561** NORTON & SACKV. *Gorboduc* IV. ii, We marueyle muche wherto this lingeryng staie Falles out so longe. *a* **1585** MONTGOMERIE *Cherrie & Slae* 653 Quhairto suld he come heir? **1602** SHAKS. *Ham.* III. iii. 46 Whereto serues mercy, But to confront the visage of Offence? **1790** SHIRREFS *Poems Sc. Dial.* 144 But whare-to did ye't, oman, lat me hear? **1900** A. MEYNELL *John Ruskin* vii. 119 Whereto, then, is the persuasion of this book directed?

II. Relative.

3. a. To which (in various senses of TO *prep.*).

1340 *Ayenb.* 169 þeruore is þe zeuende stape of þise uirtue þe ilke þet oure mayster Iesu crist deþ þerto huerto þe filozofes ne miȝte come. *c* **1440** *Gesta Rom.* xxxiii. 352 The sone of a maide hath not wherto he may lay his hede. **1526** *Pilgr. Perf.* (W. de W. 1531) 21 b, The fruytes of the heuenly countre, wherto they go. **1592** SHAKS. *Rom. & Jul.* I. ii. 21 This night I hold an old accustom'd Feast, Whereto I haue inuited many a Guest. **1602** —— *Ham.* v. i. 234 That Lome (whereto he was conuerted). **1667** MILTON *P.L.* VIII. 398 Whereto th' Almighty answer'd, not displeas'd. **1768** TUCKER *Lt. Nat.* (1834) II. 356 The perfection whereto their natures are destined. **1810** VINCE *Astron.* xxi. 230 A matter whereto I gave not all the attention requisite. **1887** MORRIS *Odyss.* XII. 162 The mast-step, whereto shall the cords be tied.

†**b.** In addition to or besides which (TO *prep.* 15).

1568 *Satir. Poems Reform.* xlvi. 27 Quhairto, till deif ȝow wᵗ tome clatter, Ar nane sic in the floit as scho.

†**4.** For which (purpose): cf. TO *prep.* 8. *Obs.*

1535 COVERDALE *Isa.* lv. 11 The worde also that commeth out of my mouth..shal..prospere in the thinge, wherto I sende it.

Hence **whereto'ever, wheretoso'ever** *advbs.*, to whatever place, whithersoever. *rare.*

1609 *Bible* (Douay) *1 Sam.* xviii. 5 David also went forth to al thinges wheretosoever Saul sent him. **1635** PERSON *Varieties* I. 5 Because the Heavens, of all the parts of the World are most conspicuous, as that wheretoever we bend our eyes, being the most glorious Creature.

whereunder (hwɛərˈʌndə(r)), *adv. arch.* [f. WHERE 15 + UNDER *prep.* Cf. Du. *waaronder*, Da. *hvorunder*, G. *worunter.*] Under which.

a **1300** *Cursor M.* 1348 Him thoght it raght fra erth til hell, Quare vnder he sagh his broþer abell. **1340** *Ayenb.* 221 þe mayde marie made of spoushod hire mentel hueronder wolde by godes zone y-conceyued and y-bore. **1550** BALE *Image Both Ch.* II. Dj b, Thus haue we heere what is done already, and what is it to come vnder this sixt trompet blowyng (where vnder we are now) which al belongeth to the second wo. **1600** FAIRFAX *Tasso* XV. lxii, Her amber tresses ..Where vnder loue himselfe in ambush placed. **1615** *Southampton Crt. Leet Rec.* (1907) III. 493 He ought to shutt downe the Scluce where vnder the water Runeth. **1627** W. SCLATER *Expos. 2 Thess.* (1629) 162 The miserable bondage vnder sinne and Satan, whereunder who groanes not? **1836** LANDOR *Pericles & Aspasia* I. xxiv. 49 The flowery bank of youth, whereunder runs the stream that passes irreversibly! **1888** 'H. S. MERRIMAN' *Yng. Mistley* x, Snowy froth whereunder lay the wise trout.

whereuntil (hwɛərʌnˈtɪl), *adv. dial.* [f. WHERE 15 + UNTIL.] = next.

1588 SHAKS. *L.L.L.* v. ii. 493 Wee know where-vntill it doth amount. **1818** SCOTT *Hrt. Midl.* xxxix, This victim, who is rescued from the horns of the altar, whereuntil she was fast bound by the chains of human law.

whereunto (hwɛərʌnˈtuː, -ˈʌntuː), *adv.* Now *formal* or *arch.* [f. WHERE 15 + UNTO.]

1. *interrog.* Unto what? †to what end? for what purpose? wherefore? = WHERETO 1, 2.

1423 JAS. I *Kingis Q.* lxviii, Than said I thus, 'quhare-unto lyve I langer?' **1490** CAXTON *Eneydos* liv. 149 Alle they that ben here, knowe well wheronto the thynge is come. **1526** TINDALE *Matt.* xi. 16 But whearevnto shall y lyken this generacion? —— *Acts* v. 24 When..the hye prestes herde these thynges, they doubted off them, where vnto this wolde growe. **1552** LATIMER *Serm., St. Andrew's Day* (1562) 119 When Andrew hearde wherunto Christ was come, he forsoke his maister Iohn, and came to Christe. **1865** PUSEY *Eirenicon* 174 Which, whereunto it may lead, one had rather not think.

2. *rel.* Unto which: = WHERETO 3.

1490 CAXTON *Eneydos* xxix. 111 The operacyons and wodnesses of helle..wherunto she hath subdued and submytted herself. **1526** TINDALE *Acts* xiii. 2 Seperat me Barnabas and Saul for the worke where vnto I have called them. *Ibid.* xxvii. 8 A place called Goode porte. Neye where vnto was a citte called Lasea. **1530** in Leadam *Sel. Cases Star Chamber* (Selden Soc.) II. 50 Decrees..whervnto the seid Abbott was neuer partye. **1560** *Bible* (Genev.) Deut. iv. 26 The land, whereunto ye go ouer Iorden to possesse it. **1596** DALRYMPLE tr. *Leslie's Hist. Scot.* I. 24 The Water of fforth is ane arme of the Sea, and a place quhairwnto the sey flowis and ebbis. **1611** SHAKS. *Cymb.* III. vii. 13 With those Legions Which I haue spoke of whereunto your leuie Must be suppliant. **1646** SIR T. BROWNE *Pseud. Ep.* I. ii. 6 The omnisciency of God, whereunto there is nothing concealable. *a* **1687** PETTY *Pol. Arith.* iv. (1690) 76 It is also material to examin, how many of them do get more than they spend, and how many less. In order whereunto it is to be considered, that [etc.]. **1760–72** H. BROOKE *Fool of Qual.* (1809) IV. 128 Your family-vault,..whereunto even my Harry must finally adjourn. **1832** G. R. PORTER *Porcelain & Gl.* xiv. 302 The too sudden variations of temperature where-unto the glass would be subjected. **1846** TRENCH *Mirac.* xxxiii. (1862) 464 Unlike as was his outward appearance to that whereunto their eyes were accustomed. **1871** T. R. JONES *Anim. Kingd.* (ed. 4) 552 The lower valve of the shell being fixed immediately to the rock whereunto the animal is attached.

whereup (hwɛərˈʌp), *adv.* (*conj.*) *rare.* [f. WHERE 15 + UP *prep.*]

†**1.** = WHEREUPON 2, 3 b. *Obs.*

1340 *Ayenb.* 251 Hy comþ doun of þe heȝe roche hueroppe hi ys yzet. **1425** *Paston Lett.* I. 21 Wher up... I prey yow hertily to sette al these matieres in continuaunce.

2. Up which; upwards along which.

1880 *Athenæum* 17 Apr. 502/3 The spiral track Whereup ..flash perfect Souls. **1916** H. E. G. ROPE *Relig. Ancilla* 29 The never-ending ranks of vine..Whereup the purple haze of even climbs.

whereupon (hwɛərəˈpɒn), *adv.* Now *arch.* or *formal* exc. in sense 4. [f. WHERE 15 + UPON.]

I. 1. *Interrogative.* Upon what? = WHEREON 1; †in early use = at what? about or concerning what? upon what ground, wherefore?

13.. *Cursor M.* 18774 (Gött.) God men of galile, Quar-apon sua wonder ȝe? **1535** COVERDALE *Job* xxxviii. 6 Where wast thou, when I layed yᵉ foundacions of the earth?.. Where vpon stonde the pilers of it? **1581** A. HALL *Iliad* x. 183 So that I to him brought From out your campe some certain newes, & whervpon you thought, Whether you meant to take the sea, or to your tackle stand. **1596** SHAKS. *1 Hen. IV*, IV. iii. 42 The King hath sent to know The nature of your Griefes, and whereupon You coniure from the Brest of Ciuill Peace, Such bold Hostilitie. **1597** —— *2 Hen. IV*, II. iv. 99 Neighbour Quickly (sayes hee) receiue those that are Ciuill; for (sayth hee) you are in an ill Name: now hee said so, I can tell whereupon. **1666** MARVELL *Corr.* Wks. (Grosart) II. 192 The sense of the nation's extreme necessity makes us exceeding tender whereupon to fasten our resolutions.

II. *Relative.* Upon which.

2. Of local position: = WHEREON 2. (In first quot. *fig.*)

1390 GOWER *Conf.* I. 42, I thenke..speke of thing [*sc.* love]..wherupon the worlde mot stonde, And hath don sithen it began. *c* **1400** MAUNDEV. (Roxb.) xxxiv. 154 In þe myddes..es a lytill hill, whare apon es a lytil palace. *c* **1460** *Towneley Myst.* xxiii. 259 Godys son..hase not where apon his hede to rest. **1535** COVERDALE *Judges* xvi. 26 The pilers wher vpon the house stondeth. **1585** HIGINS *Junius' Nomencl.* 51/1 *Ouum vrinum*,..an addle egge, whereupon the hen sitteth not. *c* **1660** in *Verney Mem.* (1907) II. 262 A small hill whereupon is built a strong castle. **1853** G. JOHNSTON *Nat. Hist. E. Bord.* I. 20 The site whereupon stood the Bastle.

†**b.** Over which, as superior. *Obs. rare*$^{-1}$.

1450–1530 *Myrr. our Ladye* 97 Thys monastery of Syon, where vpon our lady is chyef lady & quyene.

3. Upon which as a basis of action, argument, etc., and in various constructional uses.

1521 FISHER *Serm. agst. Luther* i. Wks. (1876) 313, .iij. great groundes wher vpon Martyn dothe stable in maner all his articles. **1566** in *Maitl. Club Misc.* I. 46 For payment of the sowmis quhairvpoun the samin [landis] lyis in wadset. *a* **1572** KNOX *Hist. Ref.* Wks. 1846 I. 55 In his death..he fand the mercy of his God, whareupoun he ever exhorted all men to depend. **1596** DALRYMPLE tr. *Leslie's Hist. Scot.* I. 114 Our king..hes, of ȝeirlie rentis, quhairvpon he royallie may susteine his court. **1610** HEALEY *St. Aug. Citie of God* XVII. iv. 625 The text wherevpon all this prophetesses words haue dependance. **1643** in *Spalding Club Misc.* I. 15, I haue at this place found a very concerning occasion wheyrvpon to renew my desyre. **1710** in *Nairne Peerage Evid.* (1874) 152 We declare that the not delivery herof..shall be no.. ground whereupon to reduce quarrell.

†**b.** (with clause as antecedent.) On which account, for which reason, wherefore; (of derivation or inference) from which, whence. *Obs.*

1456 SIR G. HAYE *Law Arms* (S.T.S.) 80 Force is ane of the principale foundementis of bataill, quhareapon men suld wit that syndry folk..has the body rycht lytill, and ȝit thai have the hert and the curage grete. **1567** MAPLET *Gr. Forest* 17 Panteron is a stone of all colours..wherevpon it is so named. **1611** SHAKS. *Wint. T.* IV. iv. 763 One that will eyther push-on, or pluck-back, thy Businesse there: where-upon I command thee to open thy Affaire. **1617** MORYSON *Itin.* III. 137 It seemes a worke hanging in the Ayre, where-upon it is called Stoneheng vulgarly, and is reputed among Miracles. **1674** PLAYFORD *Skill Mus.* (ed. 7) I. xi. 46 In the which [*sc.* Airy Musicks]..that liveliness of Singing is in that place to be omitted, and not any Passion to be used which savoureth of Languishment. Whereupon we see how necessary a certain judgment is for a Musician.

4. Upon (the occurrence or occasion of) which; immediately after and in consequence of which; and when that happened, or was done or said.

The chief current sense; resembling 3 b in having a clause or statement as antecedent, but expressing a different shade of meaning.

1461 *Paston Lett.* II. 17 The said the Kyng hade wreton to dyvers persones here quych hade promysed men, quer-uppon I promysed a man. **1582** *N. T.* (Rhem.) Matt. xiv. 7 The daughter of Herodias daunced before them: and pleased Herod. Wherevpon [TINDALE, Wherefor] he promised with an othe, to giue her whatsoeuer she would aske of him. **1634** SIR T. HERBERT *Trav.* 121 Sultan Tokomac..assailed him, whereupon ensued a most bloudy and furious battaile. **1727** DE FOE *Engl. Tradesm.* ii. (ed. 2) 18 Last month I receiv'd my fortune..; whereupon I have taken a house in one of the principal streets of the town of ——. **1818** CRUISE *Digest* (ed. 2) V. 269 The lord of the manor..sold the lands to John Podger in fee, who..died two years after; whereupon the estate descended to his son Marmaduke. **1885** SWINBURNE *Misc.* (1886) 331 She assented on condition that the divorce could be lawfully effected without impeachment of her son's legitimacy; whereupon Lethington undertook..that she should be rid of her husband without any prejudice to the child.

5. Upon the subject of which; about, as to, or concerning which. Now *rare.*

a **1533** LD. BERNERS *Huon* iii. 4 Then they..shewyd hym there conclusyon where a pon they were agreyd. **1611** *Bible* Acts xxvi. 12, I persecuted them euen vnto strange cities. Whereupon [TINDALE, About the which thynges; R.V. 1881 *margin*, On which errand], as I went to Damascus [etc.]. **1613** SHAKS. *Hen. VIII*, II. iv. 201, I did steere Toward this remedy, whereupon we are Now present heere together.

6. Of motion or direction towards something, etc.: = WHEREON 5, 6.

1560 *Bible* (Genev.) Amos iv. 7 One piece was rained vpon, and the piece whereupon it rained not, withered. *c* **1600** SHAKS. *Sonn.* xx. 6 An eye..Gilding the obiect where-vpon it gazeth. **1611** *Bible* Ezek. xxiv. 25 The desire of their eyes, and that whereupon they set their minds. **1640** tr. *Verdere's Rom. of Rom.* II. 22 This young Prince..took infinite delight in the object of this picture, whereupon his eies were incessantly fixed.

wherever (hwɛərˈɛvə(r)), *adv.*, *conj.* contr. (*poet.*) where'er (hwɛərˈɛə(r)). Orginally as two words (and so still in sense 1); subsequently often with hyphen, *where-ever* (*where-e'er*), etc.; now always in contracted spelling *wherever* (*where'er*), the final *e* of *where* coalescing with the initial *e* of *ever*. [f. WHERE + EVER *adv.* 8 d, e.]

1. *interrog.* An emphatic extension of *where?* implying perplexity or surprise. Now *colloq.*

More properly written as two words: see EVER *adv.* 8 d.

[**971** *Blickl. Hom.* 167 Hwær aȝylte he æfre on his ȝeȝerelan, se þe mid þon anum hræȝle wæs ȝeȝyrwed þe of olfenda hærum awunden wæs?] *c* **1275** LAY. 26127 þo hii þat heued iseȝen, sellich heom þohten ware euere onder heauene soch heued were ikenned. *c* **1435** *Torr. Portyngale* 625

'Seynt Marre', seyd the chyld so fre, 'Wher euyr my jentyll squyer myght be, That I with me to wod browght?' 1864 T. A. TROLLOPE *Beppo* III. vi, Where ever am I to find a girl that can pull me up out of my chair in the way you do? 1875 PARISH *Sussex Dial.* s.v. *Mask*, Why! you're one mask! Wherever have you been? 1890 'R. BOLDREWOOD' *Col. Reformer* xvii, Wherever did the cayenne come from?

2. a. *rel.* At (or to) any place at which.

Occas. introducing a subject-clause = any place at which; also with correlative *there, thither*.

a 1300 *Cursor M.* 4672 Ioseph..Did gader sariantz and squier..Quar-euer þat [*Gött.* Quare þat euer] þai funden were. 1382 WYCLIF *Luke* xvii. 37 Where euere the body schal be, also the eglis schulen be gederid to gidere thidur. 1508 DUNBAR *Flyting* 67 Quhair evir we meit thairto my hand I hecht, To red thy rebald ryming with a rowt. 1593 SHAKS. *Rich. II*, v. iii. 141 Good Vnckle helpe to order seuerall powres To Oxford, or where ere these Traitors are. 1712 STEELE *Spect.* No. 423 ¶2 Where-ever you are Damon appears also. 1796 BURNEY *Mem. Metastasio* I. 227 Wherever a great personage happens to be, will become the principal place. 1857 PUSEY *Real Pres. Doctr. Engl. Ch.* iii. 325 Wherever our Lord and Saviour is, there He is to be adored. 1882 BESANT *All Sorts* xxviii, Wherever there are Englishmen, working, fighting, or sporting, there are some of those families among them.

b. *ellipt.* (with loss of relative force): At any place whatever, at some place or other. Now usu. preceded by *or*, whatever place. Cf. WHATEVER *pron.* and *a.* 4 c; WHENEVER *adv.*, *conj.* 1. *colloq.*

1667 MILTON *P.L.* XII. 449 Not onely to the Sons of Abrahams Loines..but to the Sons Of Abrahams Faith wherever through the world. 1671 —— *P.R.* IV. 404 Our Saviour..Hungry and cold betook him to his rest, Wherever, under some concourse of shades Whose branching arms..might shield..his shelter'd head. 1917 H. JAMES *Sense of Past* IV. iii. 242 A pot of about the size..of that one ..on the cabinet or wherever. 1952 A. HOCKING *Best Laid Plans* vi. 90 This committee will now adjourn to The Pig and Whistle or wherever, for liquid refreshment. 1976 *Bookseller* 24 Apr. 2088/1 A jet flies off to London, New York, Paris, or wherever. 1978 *Jrnl. R. Soc. Arts* CXXVI. 220/1 In time of trouble, whether in Cyprus, or Karachi, or wherever, you would see everybody tuning in to the BBC. 1981 W. BRONK *Life Supports* 31 The terrible world where hollow catastrophe Hangs wherever.

3. To (or at) any place to which; whithersoever.

c 1375 *Sc. Leg. Saints* xviii. (*Egipciane*) 741 Send me quhare-ewyr þu wil. *c* 1375 *Cursor M.* 1154 (Fairf.) Wiþ al þou sal be halden vile Quare-euer [*Cott.* Quarsa] þou comys in exile. *c* 1450 *Mirk's Festial* 302 Myn arme is roted awey þat was wont to peynte an ymage of þe whereuer I went. *a* 1578 LINDESAY (Pitscottie) *Chron. Scot.* (S.T.S.) I. 25 Quhair evir he raid he was convoyit with ane thowsand horsmen. 1692 PRIOR *Ode Imit. Hor.* x, Where-e'er old Rhine his fruitful Water turns. 1740 GRAY *Let. to his Mother* 2 Apr., I desire you to give my duty to my father, and wherever else it is due. 1849 MACAULAY *Hist. Eng.* i. I. 147 Wherever he came, the gentry flocked round him. 1853 DICKENS *Bleak Ho.* iii, 'Don't you want to go there?' 'Where, sir?' 'Where? Why, wherever you are going,' said the gentleman.

4. Introducing a qualifying (equivalent to conditional or disjunctive) dependent clause, often with verb in subjunctive: In (or to) whatever place; whether at one place or another; no matter where.

c 1430 *Syr Tryam.* 1461 In worlde where ever he be bestedd, And he wyste of thys case, Hyddur he wolde take hys pase. 1579 SPENSER *Sheph. Cal.* June 99 Flye to my loue, where euer that she bee. 1667 MILTON *P.L.* VIII. 170 Of other Creatures, as him pleases best, Wherever plac't, let him dispose. 1703 EARL ORRERY *As you find it* II. ii. 28 Where-ever they come from,..they have perform'd very well. 1771 MRS. GRIFFITH *Hist. Lady Barton* I. 45, I should not chuse to be farther removed from that blessed spot, where ere it be. 1854 J. S. C. ABBOTT *Napoleon* (1855) I. xxii. 352 England claimed the right of visiting and searching merchant ships, to whatever nation belonging, whatever the cargoes, wher-ever the destination. 1854 MRS. JAMESON *Comm.-pl. Bk.* 69 Unhappy that nation, wherever it may be, where the question is yet pending between servitude and civil war!

5. *gen.* or *fig.* In any case, condition, or circumstances in which (cf. WHERE 10 b).

1600 SHAKS. *A.Y.L.* III. v. 87 *Phe.* Why I am sorry for thee gentle Siluius. *Sil.* Where euer sorrow is, reliefe would be. 1695 WOODWARD *Nat. Hist. Earth* VI. 246 Where-ever he hath receded from the Mosaick Account of that Earth, he hath..receded from Nature, and Matter of Fact. 1766 GOLDSM. *Vicar W.* xx, For wherever there is genius there is pride. 1799 *Med. Jrnl.* I. 422 Whereever the state of the patient's strength is sufficient to undergo the process.., it ought frequently to be practised. 1884 FAIRBAIRN in *Congregationalist* Apr. 288 Wherever the laws of mechanics rule, necessity rules; wherever necessity rules, freedom is absent.

wherewith (hwɛə'wɪð), *adv.* (*sb.*) Now *formal* or *arch.* [f. WHERE 15 + WITH *prep.*]

I. 1. *Interrogative.* With what?

c 1200 ORMIN 1718 & tiss me birrþ nu shæwenn ȝuw Whatt itt ȝuw maȝȝ bitacnenn, & whærwiþþ itt maȝȝ fesstnenn ȝuw Inn ȝure rihhte læfe. *c* 1386 CHAUCER *Wife's T.* Prol. 131 Wher with sholde he make his paiement If he ne vsed his sely Instrument? 1539 *Bible* (Great) Judges vi. 15 Oh Lord, wher with shall I saue Israel? 1577 *N.T.* (Genev.) Matt. v. 13 But if the salte haue lost his sauour wher with shal one salt? 1588 SHAKS. *L.L.L.* I. i. 264 Which with, O with, but with this I passion to say wherewith.

II. *Relative.* With which.

2. In instrumental and allied senses: By means of which; whereby.

Sometimes followed by *to* and inf. (see TO *prep.* B. 16, and cf. b c below).

1297 R. GLOUC. (Rolls) 585 Min handax..Ȝware wiþ ich abbe geans & maniman aslawe. *a* 1300 *Cursor M.* 5399 Now haue we noght ware-wit we mai Lenght our liue wit fra þis dai. 1340 HAMPOLE *Pr. Consc.* 3835 Þe pape þe kays bers, Whar-with he bathe opens and spers. 1390 GOWER *Conf.* II. 214 Sche..hath ynow wherwith to plese Of worldes good whom that hire liste. 1484 CAXTON *Fables of Æsop* v. vii, He brake the cord wherwith he was bounden. 1526 TINDALE *Eph.* ii. 4 The greate love wherwith he loved vs. 1605 SHAKS. *Macb.* I. vi. 17 Those honors..Wherewith your Maiestie loades our House. *c* 1730 RAMSAY *Wyfe of Auchtermuchty* x, He gat water in a pan, Quherwith he slokend out the fyre. 1880 SWINBURNE *Stud. Shaks.* 29 That royal robe of heroic verse wherewith he had clothed the ungrown limbs of limping..tragedy. 1904 J. T. FOWLER *Durh. Univ.* 5 Without even a shirt of his own wherewith to cover his body.

b. With ellipsis of antecedent, or as compound relative involving antecedent (cf. WHAT C. I.*): That, or something, with which; the means by which. (*a*) with following clause, usu. with *to* and inf.; (*b*) with ellipsis of following clause.

(*a*) *c* 1230 *Hali Meid.* 11 As gentille wimmen mest alle nu o worlde þat nabbeð hwerwið buggen ham brudgume. *c* 1290 *S. Eng. Leg.* 419/46 Me þinchez..þe feste feble were Bote Men hadden ȝware-with þe wombe Ioye a-rere. *c* 1386 CHAUCER *Prol.* 302 And bisily gan for the soules preye Of hem þat yaf hym wher with to scoleye. *c* 1400 *Rom. Rose* 6710, I wole..Telle how a man may begge at nede That hath not wherwith hym to fede. *a* 1533 LD. BERNERS *Huon* liv. 181 He had not wherwith to arme him. 1611 *Bible* Ps. cxix. 42 So shall I haue wherewith to answere him that reprocheth me. 1788 PRIESTLEY *Lect. Hist.* v. lviii. 460 They will have wherewith to purchase the produce of other countries. 1856 MISS YONGE *Daisy Chain* II. iv, Here is wherewith to build the school. *a* 1891 R. W. BARBOUR *Thoughts* (1900) 80 Where is one to get wherewith to help another if not from the healed scars in himself?

(*b*) 1393 LANGL. *P. Pl.* C. VII. 317 Roberd þe ryfeler on *reddite* lokede, And for þer was nat wher-with he wepte ful sore. 1523 LD. BERNERS *Froiss.* I. ccv. 99 They..taryed..to refresshe theym..for they founde in that abbey well wherwith. 1550 CROWLEY *Way to Wealth* 21 Holde the candle to them that haue wherewyth, and wyll sette lustily to it.

c. = WHEREWITHAL 2 c, which is more usual.

(*a*) 1674 N. FAIRFAX *Bulk & Selv.* 99 A least bitling is made as much for cleaving, if it had but a wherewith to be cloven. 1876 SPENCER *Princ. Sociol.* §15. I. 19 Heavily taxed in providing the wherewith to meet excessive loss by radiation.

(*b*) 1825 JENNINGS *Obs. Dial. W. Eng.*, *Wherewi'*, property, estate; money.

3. With which as cause or occasion; in consequence of which; on account of or by reason of which, whereat; by the agency or effect of which, whereby.

c 1440 *Generydes* 3577 Where with the Sowdon was full wele apayde. 1561 WINȜET *Bk. Questions* Wks. (S.T.S.) I. 67 In ony controuersie affirmit be zou, quharewith thai be offendit. 1651 in Fuller *Abel Rediv.*, *Melancthon* 239 He fell into an Ague, wherewith in few dayes he dyed. 1663 PATRICK *Parab. Pilgr.* (1687) 346 The World will need such a good example, to reform the evil wherewith it abounds. 1814 SCOTT *Let.* in *Lockhart* (1837) III. x. 313 Every body that I see talks highly of your steady interest with the public, wherewith..I am pleased but not surprised. 1891 FARRAR *Darkn. & Dawn* xxiii, I have far too much wherewith to reproach myself.

4. Along with or together with which; against which; in addition to or besides which.

14.. *Ephyphanye* in *Tundale's Vis.* (1843) 123 Saf among we knele among the racke Wherewith the son was somtyme thi plesaunce. 1611 *Bible* 2 Chron. xxxv. 21, I come not against thee this day, but against the house, wherewith I haue warre. 1658 EARL MONM. tr. *Paruta's Wars Cyprus* 81 To boot wherewith, he had secret instructions given him.

b. With which occurrence, act, etc.: whereat, whereupon, 'and with that'. *arch.*

a 1533 LD. BERNERS *Huon* lvii. 193 As sone as the lady saw Gerames she knew him, wherwith she began to chaunge coloure. 1575 *Bp. T. Cooper's Reg.* (Linc. Episc. Rec. 1912) 123 He gott her neck under his arme & with his leyshe woulde have bound her wherwith she cried out. 1581 A. HALL *Iliad* IV. 61 Yet after this he wils hir hast, wherewith such speed she makes. 1648 GAGE *West Ind.* 187 We saw the monster stir and move,..wherewith we made hast from him. 1871 ROSSETTI *Poems, Last Confess.* 133 Then all the blessed maidens..laughed up at once..Wherewith I woke.

wherewithal (hwɛəwɪ'ðɔːl), *adv.* (*sb.*) [f. WHERE 15 + WITHAL.]

I. 1. *Interrogative.* = prec. 1. *arch.*

1535 COVERDALE *Ps.* cxviii[i]. 9 Where withall shall a yonge man clense his waye? 1540 PALSGR. *Acolastus* II. iii. M ij b, Where withal I beseche the..shall men bye or make prouysion for our cates? 1611 *Bible* Matt. vi. 31 Wherewithall shall wee be clothed? 1798 CHARLOTTE SMITH *Yng. Philos.* III. 96 He never was so hard run for money. Knew not wherewithal to pay his duties.

II. *Relative.*

2. = prec. 2. *arch.*

1578 LYTE *Dodoens* III. xxvii. 353 The iuyce of Aloë.. openeth the belly, in purging..humours, especially suche wherewithal the stomacke is burdened. 1593 SHAKS. *Rich. II*, v. i. 55 Northumberland, thou Ladder wherewithall The mounting Bullingbrooke ascends my Throne. 1615 WITHER *Sheph. Hunt.* IV. E 5, The rest Wherewithall thy minde is blest. *a* 1673 HORTON *Expos. Ps. lxiii.* 7 (1675) 590 He is not like the Egyptian Task-masters, which require brick, and give no straw wherewithal to make it. 1769 ROBERTSON *Chas. V*, VIII. III. 88 The..marks of his good-will and gratitude wherewithal they had been honoured. 1848 DICKENS *Dombey* xxxi, Mrs. Miff has heard..that the lady hasn't got a sixpence wherewithal to bless herself. 1870 MORRIS *Earthly Par.* II. III. 344 The love I had therefor was not so much above That wherewithal I loved the silver ring.

b. With ellipsis of antecedent, or as compound relative: = prec. 2 b. (*a*) followed by inf. with *to*; (*b*) with ellipsis of inf. (See also c.) *arch.*

(*a*) 1583 STUBBES *Anat. Abus.* II. (1882) 93 If he haue not wherewithall to maintaine his estate. 1659 MILTON *Hirelings* 32 No people to pay him tithes, but his own children and servants, who had not wherewithall to pay him, but of his own. 1693 *Mem. Count Teckely* III. 66 Teckely being in the Neighbourhood, without having wherewithal to attempt any thing by force. 1742 FIELDING *J. Andrews* IV. i, When your ladyship's livery was stript off, he had not wherewithal to buy a coat. 1855 KINGSLEY *Westw. Ho!* xxxi, They gave him what they had, and hulled him with every shot... He had not wherewithal to return the compliment.

(*b*) 1605 *Lond. Prodigal* I. ii, The charge is small charge, syr; I thanke God my father left me wherewithal. 1613 SHAKS. *Hen. VIII*, I. iii. 59 That Churchman Beares a bounteous minde indeed... His dewes fall euery where... *L. San.* He may, my Lord, H'as wherewithall. 1663 DRYDEN *Wild Gallant* I. ii, My husband and I cannot live by Love, as they say; we must have wherewithal, as they say. 1730 RAMSAY *Fables* VI. 21 Them that wanted wherewitha', He dang them back. 1865 KINGSLEY *Herew.* xix, 'Here is wherewithal', said Martin.

c. Preceded by the definite (rarely the indefinite) article, which qualifies the omitted or implied antecedent: (*a*) followed by inf. with *to* = means by which, resource with which (*to do* something); (*b*) with ellipsis of inf. (chiefly *colloq.*), thus becoming a *sb.* = means, *esp.* pecuniary means; resource or supply (esp. money) needed for the purpose in view.

(*a*) 1809 MALKIN *Gil Blas* I. viii. ¶2 There is a wherewithal to satisfy your craving. 1833 HT. MARTINEAU *Manch. Strike* xii. 127 A..hope..that this day's post would have brought the wherewithal to build up new expectations. 1917 *Engl. Hist. Rev.* Oct. 490 To supply him with the wherewithal to pay for the defence of the border.

(*b*) 1809 MALKIN *Gil Blas* VII. xii. ¶13 How the devil does she mean that I should get the wherewithal? 1861 MUSGRAVE *By-Roads & Battle-F.* 14 The design comprised a harbour for vessels carrying forty guns; but the wherewithal failed. 1890 BESANT *Demoniac* iii, Our English girls, when they have got the wherewithal, do in the second generation easily assume the aristocratic manner and appearance.

†**3.** = prec. 3. *Obs.*

1607 TOPSELL *Four-f. Beasts* 695 He forgot Diana, wherewithall she was very angry. 1640 tr. *Verdere's Rom. of Rom.* II. 23 The accents of the voice..made him conclude that they proceeded from a person very much afflicted: wherewithall he was so moved to pity, [etc.].

4. = prec. 4. *Obs.* or *rare arch.*

1618 WITHER *Motto, Nec Curo* 193 A knowledge wherewithall He is prepar'd for whatsoe're may fall. 1846 HAWTHORNE *Mosses* II. *P.'s Corr.*, With precisely the same complacency of conscience, wherewithal he contemplates the volume of discourses above-mentioned.

†**b.** = prec. 4 b. *Obs.*

a 1542 WYATT *Poems*, '*The longe love, that in my thought*' 9 Where with all, vntoo the herte forrest hee fleith. 1640 tr. *Verdere's Rom. of Rom.* II. 39 Wherewithall considering the ..obligation wherein he was bound to her affection, he resolved to let her see how sensible he was of a benefit.

wherewithout: see WHERE 15.

wheritte, wherk: see WHERRET, WORK.

wherk, dial. var. QUIRK *sb.*[1]

1747 HOOSON *Miner's Dict.* Y 2 b, *Wherk* [is] a small and unlooked for turning in the Stone, Side, or Ore.

wherken, dial. var. QUERKEN, to suffocate.

wherl, etc.: see WHIRL, etc.

¶ **whern(e,** error for *wheru(e*, WHARVE *sb.*

1552 HULOET, *Wherne.* Loke in whorle. 1631 ANCHORAN *Comenius' Gate Tongues* 98 [They] draw their threads, whether it be with a reele, or with a spindle, and a wherne. 1668 WILKINS *Real Char.* Alph. Dict., Wherl, Whern.

wherne, obs. form of QUERN[1].

wherpole, -pool, obs. ff. WHIRLPOOL.

wherret ('hwɛrɪt), *sb.* Now *dial.* Forms: 6 **wheritte, whyrit, -rret,** 6–8 **whirrit,** 6–9 **whirret,** 7 **wheret, -it,** 7–9 **wherrit,** 7– **wherret.** [? Echoic.] A sharp blow; esp. a box on the ear or slap on the face.

1577 KENDALL *Flowers Epigr.* 17 b, Thou fearst a pat on pate, or els a whirrit on the eare. 1581 RICH *Farew.* (1846) 208 And with this up with his fiste, and gave Phylotus a sure wheritte on the eare. 1589 [? NASHE] *Martins Months Minde* Ep. Ded. A 2, I haue giuen them both now one Cuffe more: which albeit in truth bee but a whirret. 1621 MOLLE *Camerar. Liv. Libr.* v. ii. 324 He..gaue one of them such a whirret with his sword-hilts, that [etc.]. 1664 [J. SCUDAMORE] *Homer à la Mode* 25 She striking him two or three wherets O'th ears, tooke hold of's bunch of carrets. 1727 'S. BRUNT' *Voy. to Cackl.* 67, I returned the Compliment with a Wherret of my Fist, which knock'd him over. 1881 *Isle of Wight Gloss.* s.v., I'll ghee thee a wherret in the chops.

fig. 1715 *C'tess D'Aunoy's Wks.* 116 Let her Conduct be never so void of Offence, she cannot shun the Whirrits of their Malice.

b. *Comb.*: † **wherret-stopper**, a contrivance on a boat to prevent injury from collision, etc.

1708 *Constit. Watermen's Co.* liii, Owners..shall Mark and Number..Boats, with plain Figures on the Linings on each side, just abaft the Wherrit-Stoppers of every Boat.

wherret ('hwɛrɪt), *v.* Now *rare.* [Cf. prec.] *trans.* To give a blow or slap to; †occas. *transf.* with the blow as object. Also *fig.*

1599 MINSHEU, *Cacheteádo*, whirreted on the cheeke. **1678** LITTLETON *Lat. Dict.* II. s.v. *Pugnus*, To box or wherret one. *a* **1693** *Urquhart's Rabelais* III. vi. 59 Their most considerable Knocks had been..jerked and whirrited within the Curtines of his Sweet-heart. **1711** SWIFT *Jrnl. to Stella* 30 Sept., The Whigs are in a rage about the peace, but we'll wherret them, I warrant. **1866** WHITTIER *Marg. Smith's Jrnl.* Prose Wks. 1889 I. 49 The Deacon..seeing him in this way, wherreted him smartly with his cane.

'**wherrit,** *v. dial.* [Possibly local form of *thwert*, THWART *v.* Cf. dial. *whart* and *whartle* (beside *thwartle*, *thurtle*). See WERRIT.] *trans.* To tease, pester, annoy.

1762 BICKERSTAFF *Love in Village* I. ix. (1763) 17 Find some other road, can't you? and dont keep wherreting me with your nonsense. **1767** *Woman of Fashion* I. 35 What the dickens! Must I be wherretted with your Advice too? **1787** GROSE *Prov. Gloss.*, *Wherrited*, teazed. **1888** FENN *Dick o' the Fens* xxi, With..the missus a-nigh wherritted to death wi' trouble.

wherrow, var. WHARROW.

1578 LYTE *Dodoens* V. xxiii. 579 The roote is rounde lyke a wherrow or wherle, or rather like a litle round appel.

wherry ('hwɛrɪ), *sb.*[1] Also 5–6 **whery(e**, 6 **wherrye, -ey, where, whirie, whyr(i)e, whyrry(e, -ie, wheary**, 6–7 **wherie, whirr(e)y, -ie**, 7 **wheery**, 9 **whurry**. [Etymology obscure; perh. f. WHIRR with suggestion of rapid movement.]

1. A light rowing-boat used chiefly on rivers to carry passengers and goods.

1443 *For. Acc. 21 Hen. VI* G *dorso* (P.R.O.), Vnius Batelle vocate Whery. *c* **1515** *Cocke Lorell's B.* 6 There came suche a winde fro wynchester That blewe these women ouer the ryuer, In wherye. **1534** WRIOTHESLEY *Chron.* (Camden) I. 24 For murderinge of two straungers in a wherie in the Thames. **1536** *MSS. Dk. Rutland* (Hist. MSS. Comm.) IV. 277 Payd to Robert Day..for 1 day with his where with my Lady,..viij *d.* **1555** *Act 2 & 3 Phil. & Mary* c. 16 Preamble, The Whiries & Boates nowe occupied & used and of late tyme made for Rowing upon the said Ryver [Thames]. **1568** GRAFTON *Chron.* II. 635 He toke a Whirry, and so escaped to London. *a* **1591** H. SMITH *Six Serm.* (1594) 83 They tremble for feare, like women that shrike at euery stir in the whirry. **1666** PEPYS *Diary* 13 Sept., My pictures and fine things, that I will bring home in wherrys. **1689** WOOD *Life* (O.H.S.) III. 302 John Temple..flung himself over a wherry when it was shooting London bridge. **1723** SWIFT *Judge Boat* 24 Our Boat is now sail'd to the Stygian Ferry, There to supply old Charon's leaky Wherry. **1759** *Universal Chron.* 14–21 July 231/1 Two young fellows going up the Isis in a wherry with a sail, were overset by a sudden gust of wind. **1780** FALCONER *Dict. Marine*, *Yawl*, a wherry or small ship's boat, usually rowed by four or six oars. **1857** DICKENS *Dorrit* II. ix, Nothing moving on the stream but watermen's wherries and coal-lighters. **1861** *Chamb. Encycl.* II. 177/2 The Thames wherry..is stoutly built and is constructed to carry about eight passengers. It is usually managed by one sculler or two oarsmen. **1877** BLACK *Green Past.* xxvii, Smaller craft—wherries, steam-launches, tenders, and what not.

2. A large boat of the barge kind: see quots. *local.*

a **1589** R. LANE in *Hakluyt's Voy.* 740, I tooke a resolution with my selfe..to enter presently so farre into that Riuer with two double whirries, and fourtie persons one or other. **1691** *Lond. Gaz.* No. 2672/3 Four large Wheries..which we brought..from Dublin, in which were put 150 Granadiers. *a* **1788** in *Orig. Forty-Five* (S.H.S. 1916) 260 They were alarmed by five wherries, the same, as they supposed, that landed the Campbells the night before... The wherries sailed by to the southward without ever stopping. **1829** BROCKETT *N.C. Gloss.* (ed. 2), *Whurry, wherry*, a large boat—a sort of barge or lighter. **1857** WRIGHT *Prov. Dict.* s.v., A wherry..on the East-Norfolk and East-Suffolk rivers it is a large sailing boat, carrying from 15 to 35 tons of merchandise. **1867** SMYTH *Sailor's Word-bk.*, *Wherry*,..a decked vessel used in fishing in different parts of Great Britain and Ireland. **1891** *Daily News* 3 Oct. 3/8 A coal wherry belonging to Atkinson, Shields.

3. A large four-wheeled dray or cart without sides. *local.*

1881 [see *wherry driver* in 4]. **1886** *Leeds Mercury* 1 Apr., One new light Spring Wherry, carry one ton.

4. *attrib.* and *Comb.*, as (sense 1) ***wherry-boat***, ***-rower***, ***-slave***, ***-wharf***, (sense 2) ***wherry yacht***, (sense 3) ***wherry-driver***. Also WHERRYMAN.

1538 FITZHERB. *Just. Peas* 134 Passynge the riuers of Thames or Medwaye by barge or *wheribote. **1600** HOLLAND *Livy* XXV. x, The Captaine..escaped to the key, where he tooke a small barge or whirrie-bote. **1881** *Instr. Census Clerks* (1885) Index 178 *Wherry driver. *c* **1515** *Cocke Lorell's B.* 11 Bargemen, *whery rowers, and dysers. **1569** JEWEL *Def. Apol.* (1571) 202 You maie remember, that Iulius the 2..from a *whearyslaue, not longe sithence became a Pope. **1884** 'H. COLLINGWOOD' *Under Meteor Flag* xxiv, We reached the *wherry-wharf at Kingston. **1896** *Daily News* 3 June 5/6 At Lowestoft..Dr. Jameson..boarded a *wherry yacht.

Hence '**wherry** *v. trans.*, to carry in or as in a wherry; '**wherrying** *vbl. sb.*, the plying of a wherry.

1827 MONTGOMERY *Pelican Isl.* I. 244 Buoyant shells, On stormless voyages..Wherried their tiny mariners. **1902** *Longm. Mag.* Nov. 41, I chucked up th' wherryen' and went deek-drawen'. **1909** *Daily Chron.* 30 Dec. 3/1 [They] are men who have always picked up their living by wild fowling, poaching, wherrying.

'**wherry,** *sb.*[2] *dial.* = WHERRET *sb.*

1726 VANBRUGH *Journ. Lond.* I. (1728) 14 Somewhat fetcht me such a wherry a-cross the Shins, that dawn came I flop o' my Feace.

wherry, obs. var. WHIRRY *v.*

wherryman ('hwɛrɪmən). Pl. **-men.** Forms: see WHERRY *sb.*[1]; also 6 **whirriman**, 6–7 **wherriman.** [f. WHERRY *sb.*[1] + MAN *sb.*[1] 4 p.] A man employed on a wherry (sense 1 or 2).

1535 COVERDALE *Ezek.* xxvii. 28 All whirry men, and all maryners vpon the see. **1542** in *Sel. Pleas Crt. Admiralty* (Selden Soc.) I. 116 John Peers..of the parishe of Sainte Olyff in the Burge of Sowthwerke wherryman. **1549** LATIMER *6th Serm. bef. Edw. VI* (Arb.) 176 There is neuer a whirriman at Westminster brydge, but he can answere to thys. **1593** BACON *Let. to Earl of Essex* 10 Nov., As he that is an excellent wherryman, who you know looketh towards the bridge when he pulleth towards Westminster. **1661** in *Extr. St. Papers rel. Friends* Ser. II. (1911) 130 Thomas Tracey of Great Yarmouth..wherryman. **1766** ENTICK *London* IV. 145 The society of watermen and wherrymen. **1905** A. I. SHAND *Days of Past* ii. 19 They had run the old wherrymen and scullers off the Thames.

1881 *Instr. Census Clerks* (1885) Index 178. **1893** P. H. EMERSON (*title*) On English Lagoons, being an account of the Voyage of Two Amateur Wherrymen on the Norfolk and Suffolk Rivers and Broads. **1897** *Daily News* 14 Dec. 5/3 Wherrymen and anglers report the destruction of large numbers of coarse fish in the lower reaches of the Norfolk tidal rivers.

whersere, obs. contr. f. WHERESOEVER.

whersh, variant of WERSH *a.*

whert, var. QUART, QUERT *a.* and *sb.*[1] *Obs.*

wherve, variant of WHARVE.

wherwille, whery, whes, Whesen, whesille, whess, whest, whestion, wheston: see WHIRL, VERY, WHOSE, WHITSUN, WEASEL *sb.*, WASH *v.*, QUEST *sb.*[1], QUESTION, WHETSTONE.

whet (hwɛt), *sb.* [f. WHET *v.*]

1. An act of sharpening; *transf.* the interval between two sharpenings of a scythe, etc.; also *fig.* an occasion, turn, 'go'. Now *dial.*

a **1628** J. PRESTON *Saints Daily Exerc.* (1629) 32 The whetting of the sithe, though there be a stop in the work for a time, yet, as our common saying is, a whet is no let. **1641** BEST *Farm. Bks.* (Surtees) 32 A good mower will goe the breadth of those broade-landes with a whette. **1849** C. BRONTE *Shirley* xxx, If the afflatus comes, give way, Robert; never heed me: I'll bear it this whet (time). **1892** HOLE *Mem.* xvi. (1893) 194 'Well, Booth,' a visitor said to his sick neighbour, 'thee'd like to get better, wouldn't thee, Booth? But thee mun dee, this whet.'

2. *fig.* Something that incites or stimulates desire; an incitement or inducement to action.

1698 FRYER *Acc. E. India & P.* 112 *marg.*, The sloth of the Moors a whet to the Banyans. **1710** S. PALMER *Proverbs* 6 Diversion shou'd never be any more than a Whet in order to the better..Pursuit of our Work. **1770** *Ann. Reg., Hist. Eur.* 32/2 The carnage at Patras gave a new whet, which was not at all wanted, to the..revenge of the Greeks. **1846** LOWER *Hand-bk. Lewes* 24 Should any facts I may state serve as a whet for the visitor's curiosity. **1880** J. CAIRD *Univ. Addr.* (1898) 134 For some minds..the whet of society is indispensable in order to the attainment of the right temper and use of their powers. **1882** STEVENSON *Across the Plains* iii. (1892) 123 Solitude: an excellent thing in itself, and a good whet for company.

b. Something that whets the appetite; chiefly, light refreshment taken as an appetizer or to stave off hunger till the next meal; *esp.* an appetizer in the form of a small draught of liquor; a dram, a drink (cf. *wet*).

1688 SHADWELL *Sqr. Alsatia* II. 23 Let's whett; bring some Wine. Come on; I love a Whett. **1692** RAY *Disc.* II. v. (1693) 191 The President of the Council..engaged me to take a Glass of Wormwood Wine as a whet before dinner. **1693** CONGREVE in *Dryden's Juvenal* xi. 209 An Iv'ry Table is a certain whet; You would not think how heartily he'll eat. **1698** FRYER *Acc. E. India & P.* 279 Fruit, Wine, Tobacco, and Salt Bits for a Whet, being placed before them, they continue Drinking till Midnight. **1736** FIELDING *Pasquin* I. 6, I have brought the Colonel to take a Morning's Whet with you. **1741** RICHARDSON *Pamela* (1785) III. 360 They whipt out two Bottles of Champaigne instantly, for a Whet, as they called it. **1769** MRS. RAFFALD *Engl. Housekpr.* (1778) 139 To make a nice Whet before Dinner. Cut some slices of bread.., fry them in butter, [etc.]. **1771** SMOLLETT *Humphry Cl.*, *To Sir W. Phillips* 8 Aug., I have seen turnips make their appearance, not as a dessert, but by way of *hors d'œuvres*, or whets. **1803** *Med. Jrnl.* X. 477 As he walks out in the morning he takes what is called a small glass (half a gill) of bitters..at the first grog-shop he passes; and commonly takes a second whet (another half gill) before he gets to work. **1833** in F. D. Palmer *Diary of C. J. P.* (1892) 112 The Corporation gave a 'whet' at the Town Hall. **1852** W. JERDAN *Autobiogr.* I. xxiii. 189 He..swallowed his two dozen of green oysters as a whet, and proceeded to dine. **1879** STEVENSON *Trav. Cevennes* 90 Father Michael..gave me a glass of liqueur to stay me until dinner... The whet administered, I was left alone.

whet (hwɛt), *v.* Forms: 1 **hwettan**, 4 **quette**, 4–7 **whette**, 5–7 **whett**, (5 **wete, qwete**, *Sc.* **quhete**, 6 **wette, wheit**), 7–8 **wet**, 6– **whet**; *pa. t.* 1 **hwette**, 3 **whætte, ȝwette**, 4 **wette**, 4–6 **whette**, 6–7 **whet**, 8 *Sc.* **whatt**; *pa. pple.* 3 **iwhæt**, 4–5 **ywhet(t, whette**, 4–8 **whet**; *pa. t.* and *pa. pple.* 4–5 **whettid**, 5– **whetted.** [OE. *hwęttan* = (M)Du., (M)LG. *wetten*, OHG. *wezzan* (MHG. *wezzen*, G. *wetzen*), ON. *hvetja* (Sw. *vässa*, Da. *hvæsse*):—OTeut. **χwatjan*, f. *χwat-* (whence OE. *hwæt*, etc.: see WHAT *a.*[2]).]

1. a. *trans.* To sharpen, put a sharp edge or point upon.

c **897** ÆLFRED *Gregory's Past. C.* xxvi. 186 Swæ se læce grapað, & stracað, & hyt his seax & hwett [*v.r.* hwæt]. **971** *Blickl. Gloss.* 259 Hy hwetton, *exacuerunt*. *c* **1205** LAY. 14215 He..whætte his særes alse he schæren wolde. *c* **1290** *St. George* 84 in *S. Eng. Leg.* 296 Heore wepne huy drowen forth and ȝwetten hem. *c* **1374** CHAUCER *Troylus* v. 1760 Ofte tyme I fynde þat þey mette with blody strokes.. Assayinge how here speres were whette. **1412–20** LYDG. *Chron. Troy* I. 4306 A swerde, scharp[e] grounde & whet. **1530** PALSGR. 780/2, I love better whettynge of knyves afore a good dyner than whettynge of swordes and bylles. **1594** SHAKS. *Rich. III*, I. iii. 244 Foole, foole, thou whet'st a Knife to kill thy selfe. **1596** in *Archaeologia* LXIV. 379 For a fylle to wheit the blakstone saw iiii d. **1605** BACON *Adv. Learn.* I. viii. 42 b, Like an ill Mower, that mowes on still, and neuer whets his Syth. **1698** *Phil. Trans.* XX. 418 It became very hot towards the Point, the Edge being whet away to a Wire. *Ibid.* 419, I whet it again strongly in the same manner, and it changed again. **1721** E. WARD *Merry Trav.* I. (1729) 12 The Butchers..Some wetting Knives upon a Steel. **1728** YOUNG *Love of Fame* II. 121 As in smooth oil the razor best is whet. **1825** SCOTT *Talism.* iii, Thou whett'st our very banquet-knives To tools of death and war. **1865** SWINBURNE *Chastelard* IV. i. 115 You do not think It is my wrath or will that whets this axe Against his neck?

b. Of a boar or other animal sharpening its tusks or teeth in preparation for an attack.

c **1000** *Eccl. Inst.* in Thorpe *Anc. Laws* (1840) II. 396/6 Of ..þæm undeadlicum wyrmum þa hwettað hyra blodiȝan teð to þon þet hiȝ..urne lichoman wundian. **13..** *K. Alis.* 6607 (Laud MS.) In her mouþ ben teeþ trebble sshet, None bores better ywhett. *c* **1440** *Alphabet of Tales* 178 Þai whettid þer tethe agayns þaim. **1553** EDEN *Treat. Newe Ind.* (Arb.) 16 He fyleth and whetteth his horne on a stone. **1697** DRYDEN *Virg. Georg.* III. 387 Boars whet their Tusks; to battel Tygers move. **1747** W. DUNKIN in Francis tr. *Hor., Ep.* II. ii. 42 A very Wolf..Now whetting keen his wide devouring Jaw. **1799** SOUTHEY *God's Judgem. Wicked Bp.* 77 They have whetted their teeth against the stones, And now they pick the Bishop's bones. **1812** BYRON *Ch. Har.* II. xlii, The eagle whets his beak.

c. In allusive and fig. phrases (in which the literal language is freq. retained, e.g. *to whet the teeth, the sword*, etc.) usually expressing preparation for attack; often in echoes of Ps. lxiv. 3, cxl. 3.

c **1000** *Ags. Ps.* (Spelman) cxxxix. [cxl.] 3 Hi hwetton tungan heora swa swa nædran. *c* **1374** CHAUCER *Anel. & Arc.* 212 Þe swerd of sorowe whett with fals plesaunce. **14..** *Tundale's Vis.* (1843) 95 For to skape the cruell vyolence Of nedis swyrd whettyng with violence. **1563** *Homilies* II. *Worthy receauing Sacr.* I, Therfore (saith Ciprian) when we do these thynges, we nede not to whet our teeth. **1573** G. HARVEY *Letter-bk.* (Camden) 6 A hie point forsooth for them to whet there tungs about. **1581** PETTIE tr. *Guazzo's Civ. Conv.* (1586) 7 They..had not yet whetted their tongues to slaunder their neighbours, gaue not their mindes to cruelties. **1633** COWLEY *Poet. Blossoms, Constantia & Philetus* 74 Yet hee by chance had hit his heart aright, And on Constantia's eye his Arrow whet. **1674** W. SHERLOCK *Disc. Knowl. Christ* 56 That now we may look Justice in the face, and whet our Knife at the Counter door, all our Debts being discharged by Christ. **1796** H. HUNTER tr. *St. Pierre's Study Nat.* (1799) III. 266 'Combined Nations,' says she, 'and formidable cities whet the sword against me.' **1833** I. TAYLOR *Fanat.* ii. 26 The writer who is seen to be thus whetting afresh his words. **1866** LIDDON *Divin. Our Lord* vii. (1875) 357 The edge and point of every weapon that might be forged or whetted by the ingenuity of passionate animosity.

d. *absol.*; also *fig.* to get ready for an attack (like a boar whetting his tusks).

1398 [see WHETSTONE 1]. *c* **1460** *Towneley Myst.* xvi. 318, I mon whett lyke a bore. **1642** D. ROGERS *Naaman* 19 Those who cease whetting at Gods secrets..(as not belonging to them)..have a marke upon them of such as shall be saved. **1680** DRYDEN *Limberham* IV. i. 47 I have been whetting all this while. **1682** —— *Medall* 240 They..grin and whet like a Croatian band.

†**2.** *fig.* To incite, instigate, egg or urge *on to* or *to do* something. *Obs.*

Beowulf 204 Ðone siðfæt him snotere ceorlas lythwon loȝon,..hwetton hiȝerofne. *a* **1000** *Sal. & Sat.* 493 Oðer [gast] hine tyhteð & on tæso læreð..& ðurh ðæt his mod hweteð. *c* **1000** *Malchus* in Cockayne *Shrine* (1864) 41 Þa ȝehyrde hio fram me þæt ic hiȝ hwette to fleanne. *c* **1330** R. BRUNNE *Chron. Wace* (Rolls) 2828 On was þer þat ful euele spak To whette Brenne to reyse contak. **1412–20** LYDG. *Chron. Troy* IV. 1354 Liche a lyoun whetted wiþ woodnes. **1560** DAUS tr. *Sleidane's Comm.* 461 b, Certen biting libelles ..wherin were some thinges to whet the people. **1579** W. WILKINSON *Confut. Fam. Love* 26 b, By Dauid George his Maisters whettyng him forward..he became the sonne of perdition. **1595** SHAKS. *John* III. iv. 181 Now that their soules are topfull of offence,..I will whet on the King. **1621** SANDERSON *Serm., Ad Clerum* II. (1689) 37 If he would whet them up to the battle. **1624** QUARLES *Job Militant* Medit. 3 A gloomie night Whets on the morning, to returne more bright. **1649** MILTON *Eikon.* xxvii. 214 They..are but whetted and inrag'd by what they suffer'd, against those whom they look upon as them that caus'd thir suffrings. **1718** HICKES & NELSON *J. Kettlewell* I. §8 He would be often discoursing..about Points..of Religion, that he might thereby whet those who sat at Table with him. **1761** CHURCHILL *Rosciad* 491 When she to murther whets the tim'rous Thane.

3. To sharpen, render (more) acute, keen, or eager (a person's wits, appetite, interest, curiosity, etc.). Also with *up*.

a **1400–50** *Wars Alex.* 2420, I attellyd neuer athens with armes to entre, Bot you questions to enquire to wete [*Ashm.*

qwete] with my wittes. c1400 *Rom. Rose* 6197 How high that euere his heed he shere With resoun whetted neuer so kene. 1402 HOCCLEVE *Let. Cupid* 243 They that to wommen ben ywhett so kene. 1561 T. NORTON tr. *Calvin's Inst.* III. 262b, The very weight of ye thing it self shal whet our endeuor. 1579 LYLY *Euphues* (Arb.) 187 Diuers coulours offende the eyes, yet hauing greene among them, whette the sight. 1601 SHAKS. *Twel. N.* III. i. 116 Madam, I come to whet your gentle thoughts On his be-halfe. 1612 DEKKER *If it be not good* Wks. 1873 III. 282 [He] seekes new wayes to whet dull appetite. 1617 MORYSON *Itin.* III. 9 Aduersities doe often whet our wits. 1648 W. MOUNTAGU in *Buccleuch MSS.* (Hist. MSS. Comm.) I. 309 This I confess whets my prayers for your Lordship's health. 1752 HUME *Pol. Disc.* iii. 48 Their industry only whetted by so much new gain. 1759 —— *Hist. Eng., Tudors* II. *Eliz.* iii. 547 Theological controversy daily whetted the animosity of the sects. 1823 T. BEWICK *Memoir* (1975) xii. 105 The extreme interest I had always felt in the hope of administering to the pleasures & amusement of youth..whetted me up & stimulated me to proceed. 1840 DICKENS *Old C. Shop* xxxii, Efforts to stimulate the popular taste and whet the popular curiosity. 1861 BUCKLE *Civiliz.* II. iii. 210 The desire of revenge whetted their exertions.

absol. 1626 BACON *Sylva* §831 The Cause, why Onions, and Salt, and Pepper, in Baked Meats, moue Appetite, it is by Vellication of those Nerues; For Motion whetteth. 1877 'MARK TWAIN' in *Atlantic Monthly* Nov. 586/2 You see 'em begin to whet up whenever they smell argument in the air. 1893 —— in *Century Mag.* Jan. 342/2 The people were still in the drawing-room, whetting up for dinner.

†4. In renderings of Deut. vi. 7 and echoes of it, translating Heb. *shānan* lit. to sharpen, fig. to inculcate. (Const. *on*, *upon*.) *Obs.*

1528 TINDALE *Obed. Chr. Man* To Rdr. 13 Moyses saith Deutro. vj. Heare Israel let these wordes which I commaunde the this daye steke fast in thine herte, and whette them on thi childerne. 1548 BECON *Sol. Soul* Wks. 1564 II. 115b, And euer bee whettynge of that in thy mynde. 1612 BRINSLEY *Lud. Lit.* xxii. (1627) 255 Use all diligence to apply every piece unto them, to whet it upon them. a1665 J. GOODWIN *Being filled with the Spirit* (1867) 229 Was it thoroughly known, and frequently whetted upon the thoughts and minds of men [etc.].

†5. Of a bird: To preen (the feathers). *rare.*

a1678 MARVELL *Garden* 54 There like a Bird it sits, and sings, Then whets, and combs its silver Wings.

6. †a. *intr.* To take an appetizer. b. *trans.* in phr. ***to whet one's whistle*** (in which *whet* has been substituted for the earlier *wet*): to clear the throat or voice by taking a drink.

1674 FLATMAN *Belly God* 46 First whet thy whistle with some good Metheglin. 1688 [see WHET *sb.* 2b]. 1742 FIELDING *J. Andrews* II. xi, Give the gentleman a glass to whet his whistle before he begins. 1809 in *Sir G. Jackson's Diaries & Lett.* (1873) I. 20 Punch..served very agreeably to wet, or whet, my whistle. 1908 HARDY *Dynasts* III. III. vi, See that they have plenty of Madeira to whet their whistles with.

7. *Comb.*: **whetsaw**, a bird allied to the cuckoo, so called from its making a noise like the whetting of a saw; **whet-slate**, a hard slate used for hones; novaculite.

1778 J. CARVER *Trav. N. Amer.* xviii. 475 The Whetsaw is of the cuckow kind, being like that a solitary bird, and scarcely ever seen,..it makes a noise like the filing of a saw. 1839 URE *Dict. Arts* 1141 *Whet-slate*, or *Turkey hone*, is a slaty rock, containing a great proportion of quartz. 1856 PAGE *Adv. Text-bk. Geol.* viii. (1876) 161 Among the minor products may be mentioned whet-slate and ragstone.

whet, obs. f. WAIT *sb.*, WHAT, WHEAT.

whetblowe, obs. f. WHITLOW.

whete, obs. f. WET, WHEAT.

†**'whethen**, *adv. Obs.* Forms: 3 **weðen, queðen,** 4 **wheþin, -yn, whethene, queþen, quiþen, queiþin, queyþen, weþen, wethen, wythenne,** 4–5 **wheþen(e, whethen, quethen,** 5 **wheþon, whethyn, whythene, -yne, quethin, qu-, qwethun.** [a. ON. *hvaðan* (MSw. *hwädhan*, MDa. *hvæden*; f. root of WHO + *ðan* as in *heðan*, *þeðan*), with vowel-assimilation to HETHEN, THETHEN.] = WHENCE; and, like that word, often preceded by redundant *fro* (occas. *of*).

1. *interrog.* = WHENCE 1, 2.

c1200 *Trin. Coll. Hom.* 127 Weðen is me cumen þat mi louerdes moder cumeð to me? c1250 *Gen. & Ex.* 1401 Al he tolde hem fro queðen he cam. 13.. *Cursor M.* 2619 (Gött.) 'Agar,' he said, 'queþen comes þou, Or queþerward wil þu ga nou?' 13.. *Gaw. & Gr. Knt.* 461 Neuermore þen þay wyste fram queþen he was wonnen. c1400 *Anturs Arth.* xxviii, Wheþene [*v.r.* whythene] is þe comli kniȝte? c1420 *Chron. Vilod.* 535 þe kynge askede anone what was his name And what mon And whethen þat he wasse.

2. *rel.* = WHENCE 3.

a1340 HAMPOLE *Psalter* cxx. 1, I liftid myn eghyn in hillis wheþen help cum till me. 1340 —— *Pr. Consc.* 5205 Ierusalem..fra whethen þe crosse for yhow I bare. c1400 *Laud Troy Bk.* 4118 That he was lord of that kyndome Fro whethen alle that riches is come.

b. In generalized or indefinite sense: From whatever place, whencesoever.

13.. *Gaw. & Gr. Knt.* 871 Wheþen in worlde he were, Hit semed as he myȝt Be prynce with-outen pere.

Hence †**'whethenward** *adv. Obs.*, in phr. ***fra whethenward*** [cf. -WARD 4, 7], from whence, whence.

c1200 ORMIN 16668 þu ne mahht nohht witenn..Fra wheþennwarrd gast cumeþþ forþ.

whether ('hwɛðə(r)), *pron.*, *adj.*, *conj.* (*sb.*) Forms: see below. [OE. *hwæþer* and *hweþer*, corresp. to OFris. *hwed(d)er*, *hw(w)oder*, *ho(e)r* (NFris. *wader*), OS. *hweðar* one of two, whether, OHG. *hwedar*, *wedar* which of two, neut. whether, either, (MHG. *weder*, surviving in G. *weder* neither), ON. *hvaðarr*, nom. pl. *hvárer* (whence sing. *hvárr*), which of two, each, neut. whether (Sw. *hvar* each, mod.Icel. *hvorr*), Goth. *hwaþar* which of two:—OTeut. **χwaþaraz*, **χwe-*, f. *χwa-*, *χwe-* WHO + comp. suffix (Indo-eur. *-tero-*) as in OTHER (cf. Skr. *katará-*, Gr. πότερος, Lith. *katràs*). *Either* (OE. *ǽȝhwæþer*) is a compound of *whether*. With forms of the *γ*-type cf. OHG. *diu hwiduru*, *thohwidaro* THOUGH-WHETHER, early mod.G. *wider* neither; with forms of the δ-type OFris. *hwoder*; and with forms of the ε-type OFris. *hoer*, *hor* (but in ME. north. texts *hwor* may represent ON. *hvárr*).]

A. Illustration of Forms.

α. 1 **hwæðer, -þer, -der,** 1–3 **hwaþer,** 3 **whæðer, whaðer, -der, (wahðer),** 3–4 **waþer,** 4 **quaþer.**

8.. in *O.E. Texts* 444 Sue hwaeder suae. *Ibid.* 452 Hwaðer. 900–30 *O.E. Chron.* an. 894 (Parker MS.) Bi swa hwaþerre efes swa hit þonne fierdleas wæs. c1000 *Ags. Gosp.* John iv. 33 Hwæðer ænig man him mete brohte? c1205 LAY. 20877 Whæðer [c1275 waþer] swa ich wulle don oðer slæn oðer ahon. *Ibid.* 23593–5 Whaðer unkere..wahðer vinkere. 13.. *Cursor M.* 13596 (Gött.) To mistrouu..Quaþer forwid blind al had he bene. c1380 *Sir Ferumb.* 486 Waþer þe wil or no.

β. 1 **hueðer,** 1–3 **hweðer, -þer,** 3 **weðer, -þer, queðer, (ȝweðer, -ur),** *Orm.* **wheþþr,** 4 **wheiþer, queþer, quedir, -ur,** *Sc.* **quhethyr(e,** 4–5 **wheþer, -ire, -ur(e, whethere, -ir(e, -yr, wethir, quether, -þir, whedir, -ur, queder,** 4–6 **wheder,** *Sc.* **quhethir, quhedir,** 4–7 **wheither,** 5 **whethur, wheithir, whedere, -yr(e, wedir, quethire, -ur, qweþer, -ther, -þire,** *Sc.* **quheþer, -ir, quheythir, qwheþir, -dyr, -yar,** 5–6 **wheddur,** 6, 9 *dial.* **-er,** *Sc.* **quhether,** 4– **whether.**

c825 *Vesp. Ps.* cxxxviii[i]. 24 *Et vide si via iniquitatis in me est*, & ȝeseh hweðer weȝ unrehtwisnisse in me is. c950 *Lindisf. Gosp.* Matt. xxvii. 17 *Quem uultis dimittam uobis*, hueðerne wallas ȝie ic forleto iowh? a1122 *O.E. Chron.* (Laud MS.) an. 1101 Loc hweðer þæra ȝebroðra oðerne oferbide. c1200 ORMIN 526 Illc an hird wel wisste inoh, Wheþþr itt to serrfenn sholde [etc.]. c1200 *Trin. Coll. Hom.* 155 On is weðer þe eorðe beo bicumeliche to þe sede, þat oðer weðer hit beo riht time þer to. c1250 *Gen. & Ex.* 1471 Queðer here sulde birðen bi-foren. c1290 *St. Austin* 60 in *S. Eng. Leg.* 25 Are ich habbe more vnderȝite: ȝweþur þis Message beo trewe. a1300 *Cursor M.* 44 Quedur [*v.rr.* queþer, wheþer] þai be worthi or bale or bote. c1300 *Havelok* 2098 Betere is i go miself, and se Hweþer he sitten nou, and wesseylen. 13.. *Gaw. & Gr. Knt.* 1109 Sware with trawþe, Queþer, leude, so lymp lere oþer better. 13.. *Northern Passion* 1006 (Camb. Gg. 5. 31) Wheder he will hym safe or spyll. c1325 *Spec. Gy Warw.* 272 Wheiþer þeih wolen, or þeih nelle. 1340 HAMPOLE *Pr. Consc.* 1829 He es uncertayne Whether he sal wend til ioy or payne. c1375 *Sc. Leg. Saints* i. (*Petrus*) 421 Quhedir he A lele man or a lear be. c1420 *Pol. Rel. & L. Poems* (1903) 276 þo iewys kestyn at þe dys Qweþer xuld han hys cloth. 1456 SIR G. HAYE *Law Arms* (S.T.S.) 5 The ferde questioun is quheythir bataill be lefull to be done. c1500 *Lancelot* 1186 Qwheyar if yone bee Our presoner, my consell Is we see. 1523 LD. BERNERS *Froiss.* I. cccxiv. 195b/1 The kynge lende or gaue him I can nat tell wheder, a .lx. thousande frankes. 1526 TINDALE *Matt.* xxi. 31 Whedder of these ij fulfylled there fathers wyll? 1533 GAU *Richt Vay* 80 Quhedir he be pape or patriarch. 1585 JAS. I *Ess. Poesie* (Arb.) 60 Quhether the lyne be lang or short.

γ. (1 **hwiðer),** 4 **whydyr,** 5 **whyder, qwydyr,** 5–6 *Sc.* **quhither,** 5–7 *Sc.* **quhidder,** 6 **whidder, quhiddir, qwhider,** 6–7 **whither,** 7 *Sc.* **quither.**

9.. ÆLFRED *Gregory's Past. C.* xliv. 330 (Cott. MS.) Hwonne bið ðæt, ðæt ðu nyte hwiðer ðu maran wilniȝe? 13.. *Lay Folks' Catech.* (L.) 1258 Noman wot whydyr he may be worþy to haue hate or loue of god. c1400 *Rule St. Benet* (verse) 92 Here may we chese, Whyder we our-self wyll saue or lese. 1450–1530 *Myrr. our Ladye* I. xviii. 48 Whither comest thow to chyrche to slepe or to wake? c1460 METHAM *Wks.* (1916) 146 Qwydyr y[t] schuld preue fayr or foule. c1480 HENRYSON *Sheep & Dog* 1199 (Harl. MS.) Quhidder the scheip suld answer in iugement Before the wolf. 1535 STEWART *Cron. Scot.* (Rolls) II. 144 Quhither it wes, thairof haif I no feill. 1546 *Suppl. Poore Commons* (E.E.T.S.) 4 Whither this lawe be indifferent or not. 1583 *Leg. Bp. St. Androis* 285 Whidder hir malisone tuike effect, Or gif it was the gude wyne sect. 1614 SIR W. MURE *Misc. Poems* iii. (*title*), Ane reply to I cair not quither I get hir or no. a1699 J. BEAUMONT *Psyche* XVIII. cix, Yet whither you will bow down your Consent To our meek Doctrines.

δ. 4 **woþer, wother.**

13.. *Northern Passion* 1984 (Camb. Gg. I. 1) Ihesus..bad scho suld to Petir gane..Wother a been in boure or halle. a1400 R. *Glouc. Chron.* (1724) 388 Woþer of hem tueye lenger alyue were.

ε. *contr.* 3 **whær, wer(e, ware,** 3–5 **whar,** 4 **hwere, hwor, war, quer(e,** 4–7 **wher,** (9 *dial.*) **where,** 5 **wherr', quar, quare,** 7 **wher'.**

Editors of Shakespeare have printed *whêr*, *whe'er*, and *whe'r*, with no authority from the folios or quartos.

c1205 LAY. 13839 Of eou ich wulle iwiten..whar ȝe wullen beon treowe. *Ibid.* 18545 Ah inæt whær [c1275 ware] heo hine luuede. 1297 R. GLOUC. (Rolls) 2747 He esste at is clerkes, were it to leue were. *Ibid.* 6923 þe king hire esste sturneliche wer heo wolde þe dom do. a1300 *Cursor M.* 13451, I dar noght sai Quere þis was þat ilk or nai. *Ibid.* 23803 We haf us forwit waies tua, þe tan to wel, þat toþer wa, Quer we will freli mai we ta. c1300 *Havelok* 1119 Godrich ..seyde, 'hwor þou wilt be Quen and leuedi ouer me?' c1380 WYCLIF *Wks.* (1880) 84 Ony synful wrecche, þat wot neuere where he schal be dampnyd or sauyd. c1380 *Sir Ferumb.* 1381 þat mayde..askede war he hed On his body any wounde. c1386 CHAUCER *Knt.'s T.* 1539 Ne reccheth neuere wher I synke or fleete. ?1462 *Stonor Papers* (Camden) I. 55 Where ye wil come in to Devenshire to abide other no. 1567 TURBERV. *Ovid's Ep.* xv. (? 1580) Miv, I doubtfull stoode where powre or vertue were the best of twaine. 1595 SHAKS. *John* I. i. 75 But where I be as true begot or no. 1618 WITHER *Motto, Nec Habeo* 196, I care not wher' they thinke I loue or no. 1660 WOOD *Life* (O.H.S.) I. 334 The captain..asked him where he was willing to shed blood. 1825 JENNINGS *Obs. Dial. W. Eng.* 180 I'll hirn auver an zee where I can't help 'em.

B. Signification.

I. *pron.* and *adj.* Which of the two. *Obs.*, *arch.*, or *dial.*

Occas. used loosely of more than two: cf. EITHER A. 2c, 4c. The pron. is occas. found with the gen. inflexion *-es*, *-s*.

1. In direct questions. a. *pron.*

c1000 *Ags. Gosp.* Matt. xxi. 31 Hwæðer þara tweȝra dyde þæs fæder willan? a1225 *Ancr. R.* 284 Hweðeres fere wult tu beon? *Ibid.* 364 Of two men, hweðer is wisure? a1300 *Cursor M.* 14045 Queþer o þir tua aght luue him mare? c1400 *Laud Troy Bk.* 3477 And whether schulde Mayster be, Thei of Grece or Troye Cite? 1528 MORE *Dyaloge* I. Wks. 163/2 Whether of them would ye beleue best? 1583 STUBBES *Anat. Abus.* II. (1882) 73 There is both a reading and a preaching ministerie: whether doe you prefer before the other? 1601 SHAKS. *All's Well* IV. v. 23 Whether doest thou professe thy selfe, a knaue, or a foole? 1662 H. MORE *Antid. Ath.* II. xi. §13 (1712) 78 Whether of them, think you, is the plainer pledge of a knowing and a designing Providence? 1753 RICHARDSON *Grandison* (1754) II. v. 71 Perturbations delightful, or undelightful, Harriet, whether? 1872 TENNYSON *Gareth & Lynette* 333 Whether would ye? gold or field?

b. *adj.* (*rare.*)

1629 GAULE *Pract. Theories Christ* 115 We know which Sex Fell first; whether can boast of more honour in the Recouerie? 1671 H. M. tr. *Erasm. Colloq.* 524 Whether thing is heavier water or wine?

2. In indirect questions, or dependent clauses of similar meaning. (Cf. note s.v. WHAT A. I **.)

a. *pron.*

c1000 ÆLFRIC *Hom.* I. 256 Ðif man openað deaddra manna byrgynu, nast ðu hwæðer beoð þæs rican mannes ban, hwæðer þæs ðearfan. c1055 *Byrhtferth's Handboc* in *Anglia* VIII. 303 Cweð hwæðer þe selre þince. c1200 *Moral Ode* 240 (Trin. Coll. MS.) Niten hweðer hem doð wers. 1297 R. GLOUC. (Rolls) 2564 Me nuste to weþer hii bicome þe children þat hii bere. 1357 *Lay Folks' Catech.* (L.) 970 Ilke man þat haþ resun wot wheþer ys better to chese. 1424 *Stonor Papers* (Camden) I. 35 þe processe is..retournable at þe oeptes or þe quinzisme, I not qwether. 1470–85 MALORY *Arthur* VII. xvii. 238 There was none that beheld them myghte knowe whether was lyke to wynne the bataill. a1568 ASCHAM *Scholem.* I. (Arb.) 82 Now new, now olde, now both, now neither, To serue the worldes course, they care not with whether. 1613 JACKSON *Creed* I. II. x. §3 They did not rightly apprehend the manner of the worlds destruction by them, nor whethers course was first passed. 1624 MASSINGER *Parlt. Love* I. v, I am troubled With the toothach, or with love, I know not whether. 1726 SWIFT *Gulliver* II. i, We came in full View of a great Island or Continent, (for we knew not whether). a1794 SIR W. JONES in *Parr's Wks.* (1828) VII. 210 It is indifferent to me, as a friend to the people, whether of the two sit in Parliament. 1852 ROBERTSON *Serm.* Ser. III. xii. (1857) 172 The question ..whether of the two sections held the abstract right.

b. *adj.*

c893 ÆLFRED *Oros.* III. i. §6 þæt is mid Crecum þeaw þæt mid ðæm worde bið ȝecyþed hwæðer healf hæfð þonne siȝe. 1297 R. GLOUC. (Rolls) 773 He nuste to ȝweþer doȝter betere truste þo. 1390 GOWER *Conf.* I. 217 Whan the fader..sih to whether side it drowh. 1432–50 tr. *Higden* (Rolls) V. 405 The manifestacion of a notable signe wheder parte awe to be folowede. 1598 SYLVESTER *Du Bartas* II. i. I. *Eden* 655 What children there [*sc.* in Eden] they earned, and how many, Of whether sex. 1613 DAY *Dyall* ix. (1614) 218 A controversie there is which they that are in whither Table. 1656 BRAMHALL *Replic.* i. 43 Whether the separation be criminous, whether party made the first separation,.. whether side gave the cause,..is not so easy to be discerned. 1690 T. BURNET *Rev. Th. Earth* 46 You know in whether Scale the Natural Reasons are to be laid. 1702 H. DODWELL *Apol.* in S. Parker *Cicero's De Finibus* a8, The Dispute.. whether Life is the more to be preferred, the Active, or the Contemplative.

c. Phr. ***whether is whether***, which is which (of the two). *Obs.* or *dial.*

1303 R. BRUNNE *Handl. Synne* 3447 þan wete men neuer, wheþer ys wheþer. c1375 *Cursor M.* 9290 (Fairf.) Wele salle he knaw queþer is quilk. 1596 SPENSER *F.Q.* IV. ix. 10 She vneath discerned, whether whether weare. 1828 *Craven Gloss.* s.v. *Whether*, I cannot tell whether is whether.

3. In generalized or indef. sense: Whichever of the two: (*a*) as *comp. relative*, the implied antecedent belonging to the principal clause; (*b*) introducing a qualifying clause: No matter which of the two. a. *pron.*

(*a*) c1205 LAY. 23593 Whaðer unkere swa beoð þere sone he bið þe laðere. 1297 R. GLOUC. (Rolls) 7967 Hii acordede ..þat weþer of hom tueye lengore aliue were þat he ssolde be oþeres eir. 13.. *Cursor M.* 7463 (Gött.) And queþer may oþer ouercome in feild, þe toþer folk all to him helde. c1386 CHAUCER *Wife's T.* 371 Now chese your seluen wheither þat yow liketh. c1430 *Two Cookery-bks.* 33 Serue it forth for a potage, or for a gode Bakyn mete, wheder þat þou wolt. 1551 ROBINSON tr. *More's Utopia* I. (1895) 86 To kepe still the one of this .ii. kingdomes, whether he would. 1611 *Bible* Ecclus. xv. 17 Before man is life and death, and whether him liketh shalbe giuen him. 1663 in Picton *L'pool Munic. Rec.* (1883) I. 333 You are to p'sent noe..p'son both for lands and goods, but for whethr you estimate to be of the better value.

1692 BENTLEY *Boyle Lect.* v. 29 Let them take whether they will. **1764** ELIZA MOXON *Engl. Housew.* (ed. 9) 123 Put it into your sillabub-glasses or pots, whether you have.

(*b*) *a* **1300** *Cursor M.* 2463 Queder þou ches, on right or left, I sal ta me þat þou haues left. *c* **1400** *Gamelyn* 249 Weþer þat it be, He þat comes ones in þine hande schal he neuer þe. **1583** GREENE *Mamillia* I It was in doubt, whether he wanne more fauour for his wit, or feare for his ryches: . . but sure whether it were, he had gayned the heartes of all the people. **1632** BROME *Novella* II. ii, There is some hidden vertue in this fellow, Or dangerous ill: but whether let it be.

b. *adj.*

c **1380** WYCLIF *Sel. Wks.* II. 404 Wheþer pope men nennen, þei bileven not þat he is Cristis viker. *c* **1430** *Hymns Virgin* 32 Bothe ȝonge & oolde, wheþir ȝe be, in cristis name good cheer ȝe make. **1523–34** FITZHERB. *Husb.* §144 Nowe arte thou at thy lyberty, to chose whether waye thou wylt. **1600** HOLLAND *Livy* v. i. 179 It seemed, whether part were vanquished, should come to finall destruction. **1654** GATAKER *Disc. Apol.* 15 But cal the day by which, or whether term of them you please. **1671** J. WEBSTER *Metallogr.* i. 3 Whether way soever it be taken, it is apparent [etc.].

†**c.** With the indef. sense expressed by adding an intensive adv.: see WHETHEREVER, WHETHERSO, WHETHERSOEVER, WHETHERSUM. *Obs.*

II. *conj.*

1. As an interrogative particle introducing a disjunctive direct question, expressing a doubt between alternatives. Usually with correlative *or*; occas. repeated before the second alternative (cf. 3). *Obs.* or *rare arch.*

c **1000** *Ags. Gosp.* Matt. xxi. 25 Hwæðer wæs iohannes fulluht, þe of heofonum, þe of mannum? *Ibid.* Luke v. 23 Hwæðer is eðre to cweþenne, þe synd þine synna forȝyfene; hwæþer þe cweþan, aris & ga? *a* **1300** *Cursor M.* 12292 Leif sun, me sai, Queþer þou put barn or nai? **1382** WYCLIF *Matt.* xxvii. 17 Whom wole ȝee, I leeue, or delyuere, to ȝou? wher Barabas, or Jhesu. *c* **1400** *Pilgr. Sowle* (Caxton) I. xxx. (1859) 34 Whether shal the lord refuse this seruaunt either els he shal receyue hym? **1535** LYNDESAY *Satyre* 2255 Sir, quhidder is ȝour pardon black, or blew? **1595** SHAKS. *John* I. i. 134 Whether hadst thou rather be a Faulconbridge, . . Or the reputed sonne of Cordelion? **1596** —— *Merch. V.* III. ii. 117 Moue these eies? Or whether riding on the bals of mine Seeme they in motion? **1610** HEALEY *St. Aug. Citie of God* x. xxvi. (1620) 375 Whether would he haue us subiect to those Angels that declare the wil of the Father vpon earth, or vnto him whose will they declare? **1713** BERKELEY *Hylas & Phil.* I. (1725) 5 Whether does Doubting consist in embracing the Affirmative or Negative Side of a Question? *a* **1822** SHELLEY *Ion* Pr. Wks. 1888 II. 115 Whether do you demonstrate these things better in Homer or Hesiod?

†**b.** Introducing an alternative statement, or standing at the end of a disjunctive question or phrase with *or* (cf. EITHER B. 5). *Obs. rare.*

13.. *Gaw. & Gr. Knt.* 203 Wheþer hade he no helme ne hawbergh nauþer, . . Ne no schafte, ne no schelde, . . Bot in his on honde he hade a holyn bobbe. **1599** SHAKS., etc. *Pass. Pilgr.* vii. 17 Was this a louer, or a Letcher whether? **1608** BP. HALL *Pharis. & Chr.* (1609) B 3, The Sect (or order whether) of the Phariseis ceassed with the Temple.

†**2.** Introducing a simple direct question, thus becoming a mere sign of interrogation (but often with verb in subjunctive, and almost always without inversion of subject and verb, as if depending on a principal clause understood: cf. 4). *Obs.*

c **1000** *Ags. Gosp.* Matt. xx. 15 Hwæþer þe þin eaȝe manful ys, forþam þe ic god eom? *a* **1300** *Cursor M.* 5178 Lauerd! quer i sal him euer se? *c* **1300** *Havelok* 292 Godrich . . seyde, 'Hweþer she sholde be Quen and leuedi ouer me?' **13..** *Bonaventura's Medit.* 102 Eche loked on ouþer . . And seyd, 'lorde wheþer hyt be y?' **1382** WYCLIF *Matt.* xiii. 55 Wher is nat this the sone of a smyth, or carpenter? Wher his modir be nat seid Marie? *c* **1420** *Chron. Vilod.* 1213 Wher þe holy gost wolnot as gladlyche wone Vnder a mantyl y-furned wᵗ beuer . . As vnder a mantyl y-furned wᵗ a row gotus felle? **1483** *Cath. Angl.* 415/2 Whedirnot, *eciam, numquid, nonne.* **1549** LATIMER *1st Serm. bef. Edw. VI* (Arb.) 38 Whither wyl he alowe a subiect to much? . . Whether haue any man here in England to much? **1588** A. KING tr. *Canisius' Catech.* 67 Quhat is Baptisme? and quhidder it be necessare to all mankynd?

3. Introducing a disjunctive dependent question or its equivalent expressing doubt, choice, etc. between alternatives: usually with correlative *or* (†*other*, †*þe*, etc.). Sometimes repeated after (or without) *or* before the second or later alternative. Often with verb in subjunctive (and so in following senses); also with *to* and inf.

c **1000** ÆLFRIC *Hom.* II. 120 Eft ða Gregorius befran, hwæðer þæs landes folc cristen wære ðe hæðen. *c* **1205** LAY. 905 þer wes moni riche mon þe cuðe lutel reden weðer [*c* **1275** waþer] heom weore wnsumre to faren þe to wonien. *a* **1225** *Leg. Kath.* 2312 Loke nu . . hweðer þe beo leouere don þat ich þe leare . . oðer þis ilke dei . . deien. *c* **1250** *Gen. & Exod.* 3272 Egipcienes woren in twired wen queðer he sulden folȝen or flen. **1297** R. GLOUC. (Rolls) 4507 In woch half turne he nuste þo weþer est þe west. *a* **1300** *Cursor M.* 4918 Now wel is sene Queþer þat yee be fule or clene. *Ibid.* 13451 [see A. ɛ]. **1377** LANGL. *P. Pl.* B. XII. 268 And where he be sauf or nouȝt sauf þe sothe wote no clergye. *c* **1385** CHAUCER *L.G.W.* Prol. 499 [487] 'Wostow' quod he 'wher this be wif or maide?' **1412–20** LYDG. *Chron. Troy* III. 4866 She lokkid hym vnder swiche a keye, þat he wot nat wher to lyue or deye. **1528** MORE *Dyaloge* II. Wks. 177/2 There was principally in question whither woorshyppyng of ymages . . were lawfull or not. **1535** STEWART *Cron. Scot.* (Rolls) II. 172 The Scottis than weill wist nocht in that caice, Quhidder to byde or follow on the chace. **1580** LYLY *Euphues* Wks. 1902 II. 176 If I shoulde aske you whether in the making of a good sworde, yron were more to bee required, or steele. **1610** SHAKS. *Temp.* v. i. 123 Whether this be, Or be not, I'le not sweare. **1658** W. BURTON *Anton. Itin.* 102 There remain yet two doubts: First: whether this Prætenture, or Wall, was made of Stone, or of Turfs. **1707** MORTIMER *Husb.* (1721) I. 63 He does not remember whether every Grain came up or not. **1819** SHELLEY *Lett.* Prose Wks. 1888 II. 292, I am exceedingly interested in the question of whether this attempt of mine will succeed or no. **1849** MACAULAY *Hist. Eng.* iv. I. 464 His neighbours might well doubt whether it were more dangerous to be at war or at peace with him. **1872** MORLEY *Voltaire* i. 3 More than two generations had almost ceased to care whether there be any moral order or not.

4. By suppression of the second alternative, *whether* comes to introduce a simple dependent question, and becomes the ordinary sign of indirect interrogation = IF 9.

c **1000** *Ags. Gosp.* Matt. xxvi. 25 Cwyst þu, lareow, hwæðer ic hyt si? *Ibid.* xxvii. 49 Utun ȝeseon hwæþer helias cume & wylle hyne alysan. *a* **1023** WULFSTAN *Hom.* xlvi. (1883) 233 Ðonne se ðe oðerne tælan wille, þonne . . beþence [he] hine sylfne . . hwæðer hine ne mæge ænig man ȝetælan. *c* **1175** *Lamb. Hom.* 121 Lokiað hweðer enies monnes sar beo iliche mine sare. **1297** R. GLOUC. (Rolls) 6471 Me ne dar noȝt esse, weþer he were kene þo & prout. *a* **1300** *Cursor M.* 13097 Yee ask him if he be þat gom þat for man sauue suld com, . . Or his word he send vs þan Queþer we sal bide a-noþer man? *c* **1386** CHAUCER *Squire's T.* 571 Wher me was wo, that is no question I kan nat make of it discripsion. *c* **1395** *Plowman's T.* 834 Ech man loke whether that I ly. **1470–85** MALORY *Arthur* VII. xx. 244 He mette with a poure man . . & asked hym whether he mette not with a knyghte. **1521** FISHER *Serm. agst. Luther* iv. Wks. (1876) 317 Se now here wheder chryst was not the mouthe of Peter whan he promoted his cause. **1597** HOOKER *Eccl. Pol.* v. lxxvii. §9 Some are doubtfull whether any man may seeke for it [*sc.* the ministry] without offence. **1616** B. JONSON *Epigr.* xcvi, Who shall doubt, Donne, where I a Poet bee, When I dare send my Epigrammes to thee? **1676** RAY *Corr.* (1848) 122 Tell me whether any such bird be known to you. **1712** ADDISON *Spect.* No. 383 ¶1 A loud chearful Voice enquiring whether the Philosopher was at Home. **1818** SCOTT *Br. Lamm.* xxxi, Uncertainty . . whether her letter had been ever forwarded. **1849** MACAULAY *Hist. Eng.* iii. I. 390 Thither the Londoners flocked . . to hear whether there was any news.

5. Introducing a disjunctive clause (usually with correlative *or*) having a qualifying or conditional force, and standing in adverbial relation to the main sentence (cf. WHATEVER 3, WHEREVER 4): *whether . . or* = whichever of the alternative possibilities or suppositions be the case; in either of the cases mentioned; if on the one hand . . and likewise if on the other hand.

Sometimes repeated with each alternative (occas. with omission of *or*, or substitution of *and*); but most frequently with ellipsis in the second alternative, the *or* connecting two predicates, objects, etc., or the second alternative being reduced to a simple negative or the like (*or not, or otherwise,* etc.; see also NO *adv.*[1] 2, and 6 b below).

a **1250** *Owl & Night.* 1360, 1362 (Cotton MS.) Wummon mai pleie under cloþe Weþer [*Jesus MS.* hweþer] heo wile wel þe wroþe & heo mai do bi mine songe Hwaþer [*Jesus MS.* hweþer] heo wule wel þe wronge. *a* **1300** *Cursor M.* 6618 O þis watur he gert ilkan Drinc, quer he wald or nan. **13..** *Ibid.* 10205 (Gött.) If þai ani child miht haue, Queþer þat it ware scho or he. *c* **1380** WYCLIF *Sel. Wks.* I. 321 þat þis world is beterid bi everyþing þat fallip þerinne, where þat it be good or yvel. **1470–85** MALORY *Arthur* II. v. 81 Ye shal abyde whether ye will or nyll. **1590** SHAKS. *Mids. N.* III. i. 156 Thou shalt remaine here, whether thou wilt or no. **1611** *Bible* Rom. xiv. 8 Whether [TINDALE yf] we liue, we liue vnto the Lord: and whether [TINDALE yf] wee die, we die vnto the Lord; whether [so in TINDALE] wee liue therefore or die, we are the Lords. **1678** BUTLER *Hud.* III. ii. 174 For Loyalty is still the same, Whether it win or lose the Game. **1732** POPE *Ess. Man* II. 12 Alike in ignorance, his reason such, Whether he thinks too little, or too much. **1796** BURNEY *Mem. Metastasio* II. 389 Now I am forced to finish my letter, whether I will or no. **1818** COLERIDGE *Friend* I. 335 That Reason which remains always one and the same, whether it speaks through this or that person. **1857** BUCKLE *Civiliz.* I. vii. 347 Whether it is fair, or whether it is wet, he pursues his labours with equal success.

b. with ellipsis in both alternatives: often virtually equivalent to *either.*

c **1205** [see WHETHER A. a]. **1594** WILLOBIE *Avisa* XXXIII. vi, But what to me? where false or true, Where liue or die, for aye Adue. **1606** BP. HALL *Medit. & Vows* I. x, So great distrust is there in man, whether from his impotencie or faithlesnes. **1667** MILTON *P.L.* III. 523 The Stairs were then let down, whether to dare The Fiend by easie ascent, or aggravate His sad exclusion from the dores of Bliss. **1732** BERKELEY *Alciphr.* VII. §11 This, I say, whether right or wrong. **1766** GOLDSM. *Vicar W.* iii, I knew he would act a good part whether vanquished or victorious. **1849** MACAULAY *Hist. Eng.* iv. I. 463 All other governments, whether republican or monarchical, whether Protestant or Roman Catholic. **1867** FREEMAN *Norm. Conq.* I. App. D. 627 William, whether by accident or by design, was not admitted. **1913** *Daily Graphic* 19 Feb. 8/1 The increase in the number of officials . . , which should give pause to every man, whether Liberal or Tory.

6. *whether or no* (NO *adv.*[1] 2), less freq. *not.* **a.** as *conj. phr.* introducing a dependent interrog. clause, as in 3.

1650 SANDERSON *Cases* (1678) 93 The next enquiry must be, Whether or no the words of the Engagement will reasonably bear such a construction. *a* **1657** SIR W. MURE *Ho. Rowallane* Wks. (S.T.S.) II. 240 Not verie certaine wheyʳ or not brethren yʳof at one & the same time, do beare the armes of the paternall coat. **1711** ADDISON *Spect.* No. 92 ¶5 Whether or no they are real Husbands or personated ones I cannot tell. **1852** THACKERAY *Esmond* I. ix, What matters whether or no I make my way in life. **1871** MORLEY *Crit. Misc.* Ser. I. 174 As Protestants always ask of so much of Catholicism as they have dropped, whether or no it is true.

b. introducing a qualifying clause, as in 5.

1665 BOYLE *Occas. Refl.* II. iv. 27 They . . help to make the man good, whether or no they make his style be thought so. **1868** SWINBURNE *Blake* 88 The shape or style of workmanship each artist is bound to look to, whether or no he may . . trouble himself about the moral . . bearings of his work.

c. *ellipt.* as *adv. phr.* In any case, at all events.

1784 *Unfortunate Sensibility* I. 182 Whether or no, this coat shall be my favourite coat. **1840** DICKENS *Old C. Shop* lxviii, Was it natural that at that instant, without any previous impulse or design, Kit should kiss Barbara? He did it, whether or no. **1873** MORLEY *Struggle Nat. Educ.* 79 You may say that this is to degrade the state. Possibly. But whether or no, this is the principle already . . acted upon. **1904** WEYMAN *Abb. Vlaye* xiii, 'God help us whether or no!' the Vicomte answered in senile anger.

7. *whether for a penny*: undecided, uncertain. *dial.*

1672 W. WALKER *Parœm.* 28, I am unresolved; I am whether for a penny.

8. as *sb.*, with pl. *whethers.* **a.** In phr. *at whethers*: see quot. *dial.*

1828 *Craven Gloss.* s.v. *Whethers*, 'To be at whethers', to be in a state of doubt or uncertainty. 'I stend at whethers'.

b. *nonce-use* (from 4).

1827 HOOD *Kangaroos* 68 In weighing every why and whether. **1836** DICKENS *Sk. Boz, Sentiment*, Whether she was engaged, whether she was pretty, . . and many other *whethers* of equal importance.

†**whether**, *adv. Obs.* Forms: 1 **hwæþ(e)re**, 2 **hweðer(e**, 4–5 **queþer**, **qwhethir**, 5 **qwhedyr**, **queder**. [OE. *hwæþ(e)re*, advb. formation from *hwæþer* WHETHER *pron.*] Nevertheless, however, and yet, for all that.

Beowulf 555 Hwæþre me ȝyfeþe wearð, þæt ic aglæcan orde ȝeræhte, hildebille. *c* **1000** *Sax. Leechd.* II. 256 Ne sceal mon hwæþere þisne drincan sellan on foreweardne þone ece. *a* **1175** *Cott. Hom.* 225 He cweð þat him of-þuhte þat he efre mancinn ȝesceop þa wes hweðere an man richwis et-foran gode. **13..** *Cursor M.* 4622 (Gött.) 'Do queþer,' he said, 'þar-of na strijf.' **13..** *S. Erkenwolde* 153 in Horstm. *Altengl. Leg.* (1881) 269 Queþer mony porer in þis place is putte into graue. *a* **1400–50** *Wars Alex.* 581 Queþer ȝit, for any quat a quyle latt him kepe. *c* **1425** WYNTOUN *Cron.* VIII. xxviii. 4791 He said: 'Na hast'; qwhedyr perfay His folk walde fayne haf beyn away.

b. in comb. THOUGH-WHETHER (*the-whether*), q.v.

12.. *Moral Ode* 131 (Egerton MS.) þeh [*v.r.* þeih] hweðer we it iluuet wel. *a* **1300** *Cursor M.* 11009 þair modres þo-queþer bath mild, Yoede at ans wit þair child. **1375** BARBOUR *Bruce* I. 332 The quhethir he glaid was and ioly. *c* **1425** WYNTOUN *Cron.* VIII. xxxix. 6949 þe qwheþir oft ryot walde þai ma To preik and poynde.

¶ *never þe queder*: app. a confusion of *nevertheless* and *the-whether.*

a **1400–50** *Bk. Curtasye* 715 in *Babees Bk.* 323 The ouer bassyn þay halde neuer þe queder, Quylle þo keruer powre water in-to þe nedur.

c. app. as *adversative conj.* Although.

a **1400–50** *Wars Alex.* 2090 Quethire days thre þurȝe-out thraly we foȝten, . . And ȝit þe lawest at þe last vs limpid to bee.

whether, obs. f. WEATHER, WETHER, WHITHER.

'**whethered**, *ppl. a. dial.* So **whethering** *vbl. sb.* (See quots.)

1614 MARKHAM *Cheap Husb.*, *Bull* etc. xxxvi. 60 Of a Cow that is whethered. This disease is when a Cow after her caluing cannot cast her cleaning. **1847–54** WEBSTER, *Whethering*, the retention of the after-birth in cows. *Gardner.*

†**whether'ever**, *pron. Obs.* [WHETHER *pron.* + EVER *adv.* 8 e.] Whichever of the two.

1621 BP. HALL *Heav. upon Earth* §23 Whether euer ouercommeth, is troubled both with resistance and victorie. **1632** SANDERSON *Serm.* 13 But whether ever beginneth, he may be sure the other will follow.

†'**whetherso**, *pron.* and *conj. Obs.* (Mostly as two words.) [WHETHER + SO *adv.* 17 d. In OE. *swá hwæþer swá*, reduced to *swæþer* (*swá*).]

1. *pron.* = prec.

c **1200** *Vices & Virtues* 113 He hadde auȝene kere to donne hwaðer swo he wolde. **1357** *Lay Folks Catech.* (L.) 482 Ylke man answere for his owne dedys and be dampnyd or sauyd wheþer-so [*v.r.* whethir-sum] þey haue seruyd. **1389** *Engl. Gilds* (1870) 74 To come to þe exsequies of hym or of hir þat is deede, whethir-so it be. *c* **1400** *Cursor M.* 28788 (Cott. Galba) Whether so askes more rightwisly, Sall be herd of god almighty.

2. *conj.* = WHETHER B. 5 (the addition of *so* emphasizing the idea of indefiniteness).

c **1220** *Bestiary* 357 in *O.E. Misc.* 12 Alle ðe oðre foleȝen, weðer so he swimmeð er he wadeð. *c* **1250** *Gen. & Ex.* 491 Queðer so it ðhoȝte hem iuel or good. *c* **1325** *Song Deo Gratias* 59 in *E.E.P.* (1862) 126 Wheþer so þou beo in bale or blis. *c* **1386** CHAUCER *Frankl. T.* 50 Ye shul it lerne wher so ye wole or noon. **1426** LYDG. *De Guil. Pilgr.* 2560 Whereso be he yong or old. *c* **1475** *Rauf Coilȝear* 381 Quhidder sa it gang to greif or to gawin.

ˌ**whetherso'ever**, *pron.* and *conj.* Now *rare* or *Obs.* [See SOEVER.]

1. *pron.* = prec. I.

1531 TINDALE *Expos. 1 John* v. 1–3 (1538) 70 b, So that whether so euer I fele fyrst, the same certifyeth me of the other. **1600** W. WATSON *Decacordon* (1602) 307 Whether soeuer or who else besides winne it by conquest. **1613** DAY *Dyall* ix. (1614) 238 Whether soever of you had beene slaine in that quarrell. **1630** BP. HALL *Occas. Medit.* 219 What matters it whether I go for a flower, or a weed, here;

whethersoever, I must wither. **1679** Cheyney *Vind. Oaths* 19 Whethersoever be named, both are included.

2. *conj.* = prec. 2.

13.. *E.E. Allit. P.* A. 606 Queþer-so-euer he dele nesch oþer harde. *c* **1400** *Rule St. Benet* (verse) 1763 Wheder so euer þai sit or stand. **1747** Hooson *Miner's Dict.* R2, Whethersoever the Lids be Stone, Mixt-beds, &c.

† '**whethersum,** *pron.* and *conj. Obs.* [See sum *rel. adv.* and *conj.*] = prec.

a **1300** *Cursor M.* 10205 Queþer-sum it war sco or he. *Ibid.* 10503 Quersum i haf, maiden or knaue. **1357** [see whetherso 1].

whetile, whetned, whetsaw: see witwall, whetten, whet *v.* 7.

whetstone ('hwɛtstəʊn). Forms: see whet *v.* and stone *sb.*; also 4 **whestoun,** 4–5 **wheston, weston(e,** 4–6 **whestone,** 5 **whestoon, watstone, quetstone,** 5–6 **whatstane;** *β.* 6 *Sc.* **quhitstane,** 7 **whitston,** 8 **whitstone.** [OE. *hwetstán* (*huete-, huetistán*) = (M)Du. *wetsteen*, MLG. *wettestên* (LG. *wettstein*), OHG. *wez(z)istein* (MHG. *wetz(e)stein*, G. *wetzstein*): f. whet *v.* + stone *sb.*]

1. A shaped stone used for giving a smooth edge to cutting tools when they have been ground.

c **725** *Corpus Gloss.* (Hessels) C746 *Cox*, huetestan. *c* **893** Ælfred *Oros.* iv. xiii. §5 Hit biþ eac ȝeornlic þæt mon heardlice gnide þone hnescestan mealmstan æfter þæm þæt he þence þone soelestan hwetstan on to ȝeræceanne. *c* **1374** Chaucer *Troylus* i. 631 A wheston [*v.r.* weston] is no keruyng Instrument, And yet it maketh sharpe keruyng tolys. **1398** Trevisa *Barth. De P.R.* xvi. xxiii. (Tollem. MS.), Ben diuerse maner of whetstones, and some neden water and some neden oyle for-to whette. **1472** *Durham Acc. Rolls* (Surtees) 247, j whatstane. **1573–80** Tusser *Husb.* (1878) 61 Get grindstone and whetstone, for toole that is dull. **1584** Cogan *Haven Health* cxcii. 150 And, as it is saide a good Cooke can make you good meate of a whet-stone. **1587** Holinshed *Chron.* III. 916/1, I am .. taken suddenlie with a thing about my stomach, that lieth there along as cold as a whetstone. **1606** Dekker *Newes from Hell* Wks. (Grosart) II. 99 Some pittifull fellowes (that haue .. wittes colde as Whetstones, and more blunt). **1692** South *Serm., John vii. 17* (1697) I. 270 Diligence is to the Understanding, as the Whetstone to the Razor. **1794** Kirwan *Elem. Min.* (ed. 2) I. 239 Some argillites and sandstones; these last form the coarser whet-stones. **1857** Miller *Elem. Chem., Org.* xi. §2. (1862) 775 The .. skins .. are carefully smoothed with a whetstone upon a beam. **1896** J. Davidson *Fleet St. Ecl.* Ser. ii. 14 Still and anon The whetstone shrieked against the curving blade.

β. **1513** Douglas *Æneis* vii. xi. 62 Sum .. on quhitstanis thair axis scharpis at hame. **1533** Bellenden *Livy* i. xv. (S.T.S.) I. 84 Þow suld cut þat quhitstane in þi hand with ane rasoure.

b. Any hard fine-grained rock, as novaculite, of which whetstones are made; hone-stone.

1578 T. Proctor *Gorg. Gallery* H iij b, Like as what stone, .. hardiest is with toole to bee graue, Doth sooner breake in peeces, then it bendeth. **1661** J. Childrey *Brit. Baconica* 111 This shire is well stored with Milstones, Crystal, Alabaster and Whetstone. **1788, 1806** [see hone *sb.*[1] 3, 4]. **1894** *Northumbld. Gloss., Whetstone*, or *Whetstone-sill*, strata of argillaceous and siliceous hazle-stone in the carboniferous limestone formation.

c. *transf.* (See quots.)

1580 T. Newton *Approved Med.* 93b, A Mole in a womans body, otherwise called a whetston, or a moone Calfe [*i.e.* a false conception]. **1683** Thoresby *Diary* (ed. Hunter) I. 155 This place [Grantham] is .. chiefly noted of travellers, for a peculiar sort of thin cake, called Grantham Whetstones. **1886** *Cheshire Gloss., Whetstun*, .. any hard swelling. **1887** *S. Cheshire Gloss., Whetstone*, a lump in the udder of a cow, consequent upon the ducts having been overcharged.

2. Allusive and fig. uses. **a.** *gen.* with reference to the use of a whetstone.

1387 Trevisa *Higden* (Rolls) VII. 341 He .. whette þe rude soules to goode wiþ þe whestoun of vertues. **1547–64** Bauldwin *Mor. Philos.* (Palfr.) 111 Except the sinful heart of man .. be often scoured with the whetstone of aduersity. **1589** Nashe *Martin Marprel.* Wks. (Grosart) I. 157 Shooting out their venemous shafts, with mischeeuous heads, sharpened vpon Martins most malicious whetstone. **1603** Dekker *Wond. Year* Wks. (Grosart) I. 147 The very name of Londoners being worse then ten whetstones to sharpen the sword of Iustice against them. **1654** Whitlock *Zootomia* 165 Rhetoricall Topicks are such Whetstones, that even the Sword of the Spirit (that two-edged Sword) hath often used. **1763** Colman *Jealous Wife* iv. 59 He serves for nothing but a mere Whetstone of your Ill-humour. **1818** Byron *Ch. Har.* iv. xxxviii, Boileau, whose rash envy could allow No strain which shamed his country's creaking lyre, That whetstone of the teeth—monotony in wire! **1821** Scott *Kenilw.* xv, The face of the Sovereign was a whetstone to the soldier's sword.

b. in allusion to the former custom of hanging a whetstone round the neck of a liar; esp. in phr. ***to lie for the whetstone***, to be a great liar.

[**1364** *Liber Albus* (Rolls) iv. 601 Juggement de Pillorie par iii heures, ove un ague pier entour soun col, pur mensonges controeves.] **1418** *Cal. Let.-Bks. Lond., Let.-Bk. I* (1909) 197 He, as a fals lyere .. shal stonde .. upon þe pillorye .. wiþ a Westone aboute his necke. *c* **1460** *Towneley Myst.* xxi. 80 A, good sir, lett hym oone; he lyes for the quetstone, I gyf hym the pryce. **1472** *Cov. Leet Bk.* 372 Nor that they frohensfurth enbrase eny jure, vppon the peyn to lese at þe first defalt, C s., and at þe ij de defalt to haue the wheston aboute their nekkes. **1570** Foxe *A. & M.* (ed. 2) 196/1 Peraduenture he that was the inuentor fyrst of thys tale of the stone, was disposed to lie for the whetstone: Wherfore in my mynde he is worthy to haue it. **1577** Fulke *Confut. Purg.* 437 You haue sayd enough, M. Allen, to winne the whetstone, if it were as bigge as any mountaine in the worlde. **1579** —— *Confut. Sanders* 596 Of all the lowde lyes that euer I heard, this may goe for the whetstone. **1592** Nashe *Strange Newes* Wks. (Grosart) II. 267 Ware stumbling of whetstones in the darke there, my maisters. **1593** G. Harvey *Pierce's Super.* Wks. (Grosart) II. 211 He might .. for his labour challenge to be preferred to the Clarkship of the whetstone. *Ibid.* 215 Our worshipfull Clarkes of the whetstone, Doctour Clare [etc.] .. diuers late Historiologers, and .. this new Tale-founder himselfe. **1600** Nashe *Summer's Last Will* Wks. (Grosart) VI. 98 O intolerable lying villayne, that was never begotten without the consent of a whetstone! **1607** Topsell *Four-f. Beasts* 639 They wil presently giue both these Authors and me the Whet-stone for rare vntruths. **1658** [H. Edmundson] *Fellow-trav.* 285 A great Person .. had in a frolick set on some wanton wits to lye for the Whetstone. **1709** Mrs. Centlivre *Busie Body* iii. iv, If you be not as errant a Cuckold, as e're drove Bargain upon the Exchange, .. I am the Son of a Whet-stone. **1792** Budworth *Ramble to Lakes* vi. **1881** *Leic. Gloss.*

β. **1778** *Exmoor Courtship* (E.D.S.) 79 What a gurt Lee es thate! .. thek Man shou'd a' had the Whitstone.

c. Something that sharpens the wits, desires, etc., or incites to action.

1551 T. Wilson *Logic* Ep. A iij, I professe it to be but a spurre, or a whetstone, to sharpe the pens of some other. **1551** Recorde *Pathw. Knowl.* Ep. to King, By the readyng of wyttie artes (which be as the whette stones of witte). **1583** Greene *Mamillia* 8b, The court Mamillia, is yᵉ whet-ston of lust, the baite of vanity, the call of Cupid. **1588** —— *Pandosto* B 1 b, Preferment to a meane man, is a whetstone to courage. **1618** J. Taylor (Water P.) *Pennyles Pilgr.* B3, Wits whetstone, want. **1657** R. Ligon *Barbadoes* (1673) 37 For a whetstone, to pull on a cup of wine, we have dryed Neats tongues. **1691** Wood *Ath. Oxon.* I. 358 The Wits .. made him their Whetstone. **1752** Hume *Pol. Disc.* ii. 31 Anger, which is said to be the whetstone of courage. **1821** Shelley *Epipsych., Passages* etc. 100 Let them read Shakespeare's sonnets, taking thence A whetstone for their dull intelligence. *a* **1857** R. A. Vaughan *Ess. & Rem.* (1858) I. 7 Their wit could content itself with no less royal a whetstone than himself and his son Pius.

β. **1617** R. Cocks *Diary* (Hakl. Soc.) I. 240, I am of opinion that Goresano, our late *jurebasso*, is a whitston to egg hym on against us.

3. *attrib.* and *Comb.*, as ***whetstone-mountain***; ***whetstone-shaped*** adj.; † **whetstone-leasing** (leasing *sb.*): cf. 2b above.

1598 Bp. Hall *Sat.* iv. vi, *Whet-stone leasings of olde Maundeuile. **1851** B. Thorpe *Northern Mythol.* I. 71 The club was dashed in pieces, of which one portion fell on the earth, whence come all the *whetstone mountains. **1883** *Encycl. Brit.* XVI. 680/1 *Whetstone-shaped crystals. **1888** Rolleston & Jackson *Anim. Life* 114 The mucus .. contains whetstone-shaped bodies.

† **Whetstones-park.** *Obs.* (See quot. *a* 1700.) Hence † **Whetstone whore.**

1682 *News fr. France* 4 You may as soon make those of Whetstones-park among you blush, as put them out of countenance. **1684** Dryden *Ovid's Amours* ii. xix. 31 Let him who loves an easie Whetstone Whore, Pluck leaves from Trees, and drink the Common Shore. *a* **1700** B. E. *Dict. Cant. Crew, Whet-stones-park*, a Lane betwixt Holborn and Lincolns-Inn-fields, fam'd for a Nest of Wenches, now de-park'd.

whett, obs. form of wheat.

whetted ('hwɛtɪd), *ppl. a.* [f. whet *v.* + -ed[1].] Sharpened.

1563 *Mirr. Mag., Hastings* lxx, The whetted tuske, and furrowed forhead hye. **1693** Dryden *Juvenal* x. 365 One, who at sight of Supper open'd wide His Jaws before, and whetted Grinders try'd. **1794** Coleridge *Fall of Robespierre* i. 185 Who from a bad man's bosom wards the blow Reserves the whetted dagger for his own. **1870** Morris *Earthly Par.* II. iii. 391 Then light the torch, and draw the whetted sword! **1876** Miss Broughton *Joan* ii. iv, Every one else .. beginning to eat with the whetted appetite that going to church always seems to engender.

whet-tell, dial. form of witwall.

† **whetten,** *v. Obs.* [f. whet *v.* + -en[5].] *trans.* To whet.

1582 Stanyhurst *Æneis* iii. (Arb.) 79 My mynd was greedelye whetned Too parle with the Regent. **1597** J. Payne *Royal Exch.* 22 Sathan now whettens his hornes .. to goore the more dyrefully. **1624** Burton *Anat. Mel.* iii. ii. ii[i]. iv. (ed. 2) 386 To .. make him .. more iealous, to whetten his loue.

whetter ('hwɛtə(r)). [f. whet *v.* + -er[1].]

1. A sharpener of an instrument.

1556 Withals *Dict.* (1562) 20a/2 A whetter, *acutor, qui instrumenta acuit.* **1611** Cotgr., *Affileur*, a whetter, or sharpener of edg'd tooles. **1781** J. Moore *View Soc. It.* lxxi. II. 363. **1875** Knight *Dict. Mech., Whetter*, a sharpener; as a whetstone, hone. **1881** *Instr. Census Clerks* (1885) 45 Blade Whetter.

† **2.** *fig.* One who urges *on. Obs.*

1579 Fenton *Guicciard.* xviii. 1096 The blacke bands .. serued as good examples and whetters on of the residue of his armye.

3. *fig.* One who or that which sharpens, stimulates, or incites the intellect, desires, appetite, etc.

1617 Fletcher *Valentinian* iv. i, You whetters of my follies. **1653** H. More *Antid. Ath.* ii. xii. Wks. (1712) 82 Sympathy and Antipathy .. are notable whetters and quickeners of the Spirit of Life in all Animals. **1695** Congreve *Love for L.* i. i, The Air upon Banstead Downs is nothing to it for a Whetter. **1742** Fielding *J. Andrews* iii. ii, Love, like other sweet things, is no whetter of the stomach. **1830** Scott *Jrnl.* 11 July (1890) II. 348 No whetter of genius is necessity, though said to be the mother of invention.

b. *spec.* A habitual drinker of 'whets' (whet *sb.* 2b); a dram-drinker. ? *Obs.*

1709 Steele *Tatler* No. 138 ⁋4 A sort of Persons commonly known by the Name of Whetters, who drink themselves into an intermediate State of being neither drunk or sober before the Hours of 'Change. **1725** *View Lond. & Westm.* 38 Here is likewise a religious Ambulatory for the Whetters and Wenchers.

c. = whet *sb.* 2b. ? *Obs.*

1755 *Connoisseur* No. 87 ⁋1 They frequently have recourse to whetters and provocatives, to anticipate the call of hunger. **1824** in *Spirit Publ. Jrnls.* (1825) 205 Fifty verses we've sung—and we scarce can do better, Than to finish our ditty by taking a whetter.

whetting ('hwɛtɪŋ), *vbl. sb.* [f. whet *v.* + -ing[1].] The action of the verb whet.

1398 Trevisa *Barth. De P.R.* xvi. xxiii. (Bodl. MS.), Þe whestone haþ þre propretees þᵗ it serueþ anoþre þinge in whettinge and wasteþ hym silfe some and some. *c* **1440** *Promp. Parv.* 524/1 Whettynge, or scharpynge, *acucio.* **1574** W. Bourne *Regim. Sea* vi. (1577) 28b, I would not wish them to meddle with .. whettyng of the side of the needle. **1616** Draxe *Bibl. Scholast.* 176 Whetting (viz. of kniues and sithes) is no letting. [Cf. quot. *a* 1628 s.v. whet *sb.* 1.] **1633** Bp. Hall *Occas. Medit.* (ed. 2) §131 Recreation is intended to the minde, as whetting is to the sithe. **1667** *Decay Chr. Piety* xiv. 344 That we should sacrifice the one [*sc.* the Churches peace] .. to the whetting and inflaming of the other [*sc.* curiosity]. **1774** G. White *Selborne, To Pennant* 2 Sept., The titmouse .. early in February begins to make two quaint notes, like the whetting of a saw. **1852** M. Arnold *Empedocles* ii. 164 With one arm over his head, Watching how the whetting sped.

attrib. **1678** Moxon *Mech. Exerc., Join.* v. ⁋26 They wedge the blade of the Saw hard into the *Whetting Block. **1825** Hone *Every-day Bk.* I. 1081 It .. furnishes shoemakers with .. *whetting-boards to smooth the edges of their knives upon. **1706** Farquhar *Twin Rivals* i. i, I have brought you a *Whetting-Glass, the best Old Hock in Europe; I know 'tis your drink in a Morning. **1432–50** tr. *Higden* (Rolls) I. 417 A *qwettenge-ston.

whettle, dial. form of whittle.

whew (hwjuː, hjuː, wjuː), *sb.*[1] Forms: 5 *Sc.* **qwe, whewe,** 6 *Sc.* **quhew,** 7, 9 *dial.* **whue,** 9 **wheugh,** 7– **whew.** [Echoic.]

† **1.** A musical instrument, a pipe. *Obs.*

c **1400** *Destr. Troy* 6051 For to wacche and to wake for wothis of harme, With qwistlis & qwes, & other qwaint gere. *c* **1475** *Cath. Angl.* 415/2 (Addit. MS.), A Whewe, *fistula.*

2. a. A sound as of whistling or of something rushing through the air; *spec.* the cry of the plover.

1513 Douglas *Æneis* vii. xi. 46 Than from the hevin dovne quhyrland wyth a quhew Come queyne Juno. *c* **1610** *Robin Hood & Curtall Fryer* xxxi. (Ritson), The fryer set his fist to his mouth, And whuted whues three. **1710** Ruddiman *Gloss. Douglas's Æneis, Quhew*, the sound which a bird's wings make in the air. Scot. Bor. *a Few*, vox ex sono conficta. *a* **1784** *Rookhope Ryde* x. in Scott *Minstrelsy*, Then oer the moss, where as they came, With many a brank and whew. **1837** Carlyle *Fr. Rev.* i. v. vi, The whew of lead still singing in their ears. **1845** Darwin *Voy. Nat.* xiii. 289 The yelping of the guid-guid, and the sudden whew-whew of the cheucau. **1851** H. Stephens *Bk. Farm* (ed. 2) II. 22 The shrill whew of the plover.

b. *dial.* A factory hooter.

1869 J. Hartley *Halifax Clock Almanack* 48 Yond's th' whew, soa we mun goa an' do another bit for th' maister. **1929** J. B. Priestley *Good Compan.* iv. 118 Bruddersford has an elaborate system of factory buzzers—usually known as whews. **1934** —— *Eng. Journey* vi. 194 Time for them had been marked by the sound of its [*sc.* the mill's] hooter—locally known as a 'whew'.

3. An utterance of the interjection *whew!*

1751 Smollett *Per. Pickle* xxii. [xix], He uttered a long and loud whew! which was succeeded by an exclamation of 'Damn my old shoes! a bite by G——!' **1847** Helps *Friends in C.* i. iii, A sound from the old oak, like an 'ah' or a 'whew'. **1855** Kingsley *Westw. Ho!* xix, At sight of which Yeo gave a long wheugh.

4. (Also ***whew-duck***) = whewer.

1804 Bewick *Brit. Birds* II. 352 Wigeon. Whewer, Whim, or Pandled Whew. **1852** Macgillivray *Brit. Birds* V. 83 *Mareca Penelope.* The European Wigeon. Common Wigeon. Whew Duck. Pandle-Whew.

whew, *sb.*[2] *dial.* [f. whew *v.*[2]] A hurry; *esp.* in phr. ***all of a whew***, in a hurry, impatient or excited.

1905 in *Eng. Dial. Dict.* VI. 453/1 Sec a whew he's in. **1922** A. Brown *Old Crow* xi. 119 He wants me to go down in his river pastur', choppin'. All of a whew to git at it.

whew (hwjuː, hjuː, wjuː), *v.*[1] Also 6 *Sc.* **quhew.** [Echoic.] *intr.* To whistle; to make a whistling or rustling noise; to utter the interjection *whew!* Hence '**whewing** *vbl. sb.*

c **1475** *Cath. Angl.* 415/2 (Addit. MS.), To Whewe, *fistulare.* **1590** Burel in Watson *Coll. Sc. Poems* (1709) ii. 31 Evrus .. With quhewing, renewing, His bitter blasts againe. **1609** Dekker *Gull's Horn-bk.* vi. 32 Mewe at passionate speeches, blare at merrie, .. whew at the childrens Action, whistle at the songs. **1765** [see whew *int.*]. **1801** Robt. Walker (Tim Bobbin 2nd) *Plebeian Pol.* 23, I met two pa's'ns weh grete geawns on, whewink i' th' wind. **1818** Hogg *Brownie of Bodsbeck* iii, I heard them [*sc.* the plovers] aye whewing e'en an' morn. **1848** Aird *Mother's Blessing* i. i, Down all at once a wind Came whewing from the hollow of the hill. **1896** *Idler* Mar. 324 Friend: 'Whew——w!' Man in Love (irritably) 'Don't go "whewing" all over the place like that.'

whew (hwjuː, wjuː), *v.*[2] Also **wheugh, whue, whiew.** [perh. the same as prec.] **a.** *intr.* To move quickly; to hurry away, depart abruptly (*dial.*); to bustle about (*U.S.*).

1684 OTWAY *Atheist* III. i, Methought indeed the Coach whew'd it away a little faster than ordinary. *a* **1743** RELPH *Misc. Poems* (1747) 17 See! owr the field the whurlin sunshine whiews. **1828** *Craven Gloss.* s.v., 'To whew off,' to turn off abruptly, to depart without ceremony. **1873** MRS. WHITNEY *Other Girls* xxxiii. (1876) 427 Bel Bree had not been brought up in a New England farm-house, and seen her capable stepmother 'whew round', to be hard put to it now over half a dozen cups and tumblers more or less.

whew (hwjuː, hjuː), *int.* Forms: 5 *Sc.* **quhewe**, 7 **wheu heu**, 7–8 **wheu**, 8 **whieu**, **whu**, 8–9 **whuh**, 9 **wheugh**, 6– **whew**. An exclamation of the nature of a whistle uttered by a person as a sign of astonishment, disgust, dismay, etc.

The identity of the word in the first quot. is uncertain.

c **1425** WYNTOUN *Cron.* VIII. xxix. 4949 (MS. Auchinl.) ȝhit þai wiþin set wp a schout And cryit lowde and said 'Quhewe! [*v.r.* Quhow] Now haif we heire the Montagew'. **1596** SHAKS. *1 Hen. IV*, II. ii. 30 A plague vpon't, when Theeues cannot be true one to another. *They Whistle.* Whew: a plague light vpon you all. **1601** W. PERCY *Cuckqueanes* etc. III. iv. (Roxb.) 38 *Don*... Come on thy ways. *Joi.* I come. *Pig.* Wheu heu, wheu heu, now goe thy wayes. **1728** RAMSAY *The Lure* 110 Whieu,—Whieu,—he whistled. **1765** STERNE *Tr. Shandy* VII. xxii, Whu—v—w—whew—w—w—whuved Margarita. **1766** *Ibid.* IX. xxxiii, Wheu—u—u— cried my father; beginning the sentence with an exclamatory whistle. **1770** CUMBERLAND *West Indian* II. viii, Whuh! What's the hurry the man's in? **1800** E. D. CLARKE in *Life* (1824) v. 433 And now let the scene change—Whew!—away with inscriptions! **1815** SCOTT *Guy M.* xxxix, 'But how did your joint production look the next morning?'.. 'Wheugh! capital—not three words required to be altered.' **1838** DICKENS *O. Twist* xliv, Whew! said the housebreaker, wiping the perspiration from his face. **1898** 'H. S. MERRIMAN' *Roden's Corner* xxxii, 'Whew!' ejaculated Roden, when the danger seemed to be past, and they could breathe again.

whew, obs. form of HUE *sb.*^{1}

whewellite (ˈhjuːəlaɪt). *Min.* [f. the name of Professor William *Whewell* (1794–1866) + -ITE^{1}.] Calcium oxalate, occurring in colourless or white monoclinic crystals.

1852 BROOKE & MILLER *Phillips' Elem. Introd. Min.* 623.

whewer (ˈhwjuːə(r)). *dial.* [app. f. WHEW *v.*^{1} + -ER^{1}.] The female wigeon, *Mareca penelope*.

1634 *Althorp MS.* in Simpkinson *Washingtons* (1860) p. xxiii, Peckards 3—broadbills 5—whewers 2. **1668** CHARLETON *Onomast.* 100 *Boscas*, aliis *Anas Fistularis*.. the Whewer, or Whistling Widgeon. **1674** in *Corr. J. Ray* (1848) 16, I have put up in a box..a Widgeon and a Whewer. **1734** ALBIN *Nat. Hist. Birds* II. 88. **1804** [see WHEW *sb.*^{1} 4].

whewl (hwjuːl, wjuːl), *v.* Now *dial.* Forms: 6 **whewl**, 7, 9 **whule**, 9 **wewl**. [Echoic.] *intr.* To cry plaintively, moan, whine, howl. Hence ˈ**whewling** *vbl. sb.* and *ppl. a.*

a **1560** PHAER *Æneid* x. (1562) Dd 4 b, Whiles whewling sad he sat. **1567** GOLDING *Ovid's Met.* VII. 497 Lamenting for his sonnes mischaunce with whewling in the Aire. **1609** *Old Meg of Herefordsh.* Ded. (1816), Tweire-pipe that famous Southren Taberer..who for whuling hath beene famous through the Globe of the world. **1615** CHAPMAN *Odyss.* XII. 135 For here, the whuling Scylla, shrowds her face. **1616** S. S. *Honest Lawyer* II. D 4 b, A Virgin..Could not with whuling nay's be so peruerse. *Ibid.* IV. H 4 b, You know the Iayle. Ha you neuer bin hir'd to yawle for the whole prison? and whule to the passengers? **1847** HALLIWELL, *Whule*, to whine; to howl. *Suffolk.* **1895** *E. Anglian Gloss.*, *Wewling*, a plaintive note in crying, commonly with a view to excite charity.

whey (hweɪ), *sb.* Forms: 1 **hwæʒ**, **hweʒ**, **hwæiʒ**, 3 **weȝe**, **wei**, **hwey**, 4 **qwhey**, 4–5 **wheye**, 5–6 **way**, 5–7 (9 *dial.*) **whay**, 6 **qway**, **quay**, *Sc.* **quhay(e**, 6–7 **whaye**, **wey**, 9 *dial.* **whew**, 5– **whey**. [OE. *hwæʒ*, *hweʒ* = OFris. **wei*, (WFris. *waei*, NFris. *wâi*, EFris. *wôi*), MDu. *wey* (Du. *wei*, LG. *wei*, *waje*):—OTeut. **χwajo-*, of which an ablaut-variant is found in MLG. *huy*, *hoie* (LG. *hui*, *hoi*, Du. *hui*):—**χujo-*.]

1. a. The serum or watery part of milk which remains after the separation of the curd by coagulation, esp. in the manufacture of cheese.

c **725** *Corpus Gloss.* (Hessels) S 272 *Serum*, hwæʒ. *a* **1050** *Rect. Sing. Pers.* §14 (Liebermann) 451 Sceaphyrdes riht is, þæt he hæbbe..blede fulle hweʒes oððe syringe ealne sumor. **12..** *Sidonius Glosses* (Anecd. Oxon.) I. v. 34/3 *Hoc serum*, i. weȝe. *a* **1250** *Owl & Night.* 1009 (Cotton MS.) Hi drinkeþ milc & wei [*Jesus MS.* hwey] þar to. **13..** in *Rel. Ant.* I. 9/2 *Cerum, i. quidam liquor*, qwhey. *c* **1400** *Lanfranc's Cirurg.* 200 A purgacioun with gotis whey. *c* **1430** *Two Cookery-bks.* 56 Take croddys of þe deye, & wryng owt þe whey. **1549** *Compl. Scot.* vi. 43 Thai maid grit cheir of.. curdis and quhaye. **1587** MASCALL *Cattle, Oxen* (1596) 56 See..that your cheese be well and close gathered, in pressing foorth cleane all the whay. **1600** SURFLET *Country Farm* I. xiv. 90 The whaie may serue for the feeding of the hogs and dogs. **1732** ARBUTHNOT *Rules of Diet* in *Aliments*, etc. I. 252 Of all Drinks, Whey is the most relaxing. **1791** SCOTT *Let.* in *Lockhart* (1837) I. vi. 183 My uncle drinks the whey here, as I do ever since I understood it was brought to his bedside every morning at six, by a very pretty dairy-maid. **1893** J. P. SHELDON *Brit. Dairying* xv. 163 On dairy farms where cheese and butter are made, pigs are useful to consume whey and skim-milk.

b. with qualification: ***whey of butter***, buttermilk; ***alum whey***, whey formed in the coagulation of milk by powdered alum; ***celery whey***, ***mustard whey*** (MUSTARD *sb.* 4 c), ***sack whey*** (SACK *sb.*^{3} 2), ***wine whey***, names of beverages or medicinal drinks; ***white whey*** (see quot. 1837).

1530 PALSGR. 288/1 Whay of butter, *babeure.* **1733** CHEYNE *Engl. Malady* III. i. (1734) 268 To drink plentifully of small Sack Whey, or Water-Gruel. **1747** WESLEY *Prim. Physick* (1762) 80 Drink half a Pint of Cellery Whey. **1769** MRS. RAFFALD *Engl. Housekpr.* (1778) 313 To make Wine Whey. Put a pint of skimmed milk, and half a pint of white wine into a bason. **1784** J. POTTER *Virt. Villagers* II. 88 Wine and mustard wheys. **1837** *Brit. Husb.* II. 424 (Libr. Usef. Knowl.), That which is pressed by hand from the curd, is termed 'white whey', and contains a considerable portion of oily matter. **1856** EMERSON *Engl. Traits* xiv. 246 The making a better sick-chair and a better wine-whey for an invalid. **1883** MRS. G. L. BANKS *Forbidden to Marry* viii, To prepare a whey of alum-and-milk.

†**2.** The serum of the blood. *Obs.*

1578 BANISTER *Hist. Man* v. 82 The whay of bloud ought by the reynes to be strayned out. **1615** CROOKE *Body of Man* 95 The whey is deriued by the vreters into the bladder. **1718** CHAMBERLAYNE *Relig. Philos.* I. v. §4 The afore-mention'd Food mixes itself with another Humour, Water, or Whey, which the Anatomists call the *Lympha*.

3. a. *attrib.* and *Comb.*, as ***whey-bath***, ***-colour***, ***-curd***, ***-house***, ***-lead*** (LEAD *sb.*^{1} 5), ***-pot***, ***-tub***; ***whey-drinker***; ***whey-colour***(***ed***), ***-hued***, ***-like***, ***-sour*** adjs.; in reference to the pale colour of whey, as ***whey beard***, ***countenance***, ***face***; ***whey-bearded***, ***-pale*** adjs.; **whey-bacon**, bacon from a *whey-pig*; **whey-beard**, (*a*) a person having a 'whey beard'; (*b*) the whitethroat, *Sylvia cinerea*; **whey-bird**, the woodlark, *Alauda arborea*; also = *whey-beard* (*b*); † **whey-blooded** *a.*, cowardly; † **whey-brained** *a.*, weak-brained; **whey-brose**, brose made with whey instead of water; **whey-butter**, butter made from whey or from *whey-cream*; **whey-cream**, the cream which remains in the whey after the curd has been removed; **whey-drop**, **-eye**, a hole in an imperfectly pressed cheese in which the whey collects; **whey-face**, a person having a pale face; so **whey-faced** *a.*; **wheygoose** *nonce-wd.*, used as a term of opprobrium; **whey-pig**, a pig fed with whey; **whey-porridge**, porridge made with whey instead of water; **whey-spring** = *whey-drop* above; **whey-whig**, a beverage made of whey flavoured with herbs; **whey-worm**, see quot. 1828; *fig.* a whim; hence **whey-wormed** *a.*, marked with whey-worms.

a **1722** LISLE *Husb.* (1757) 431 The latter end of November or December, when all the *whey-bacon is gone. **1888** RAE *Austrian Health Res.* viii. 169 The spoiled daughters of luxury..indulge in *whey baths. **1614** R. TAILOR *Hog hath lost Pearl* IV. F 3 b, Father *whay-beard. **1647** LILLY *Chr. Astrol.* xv. 84 He is leane, crooked, or beetle-browed, a thin whay Beard. **1831** RENNIE *Montagu's Ornith. Dict.*, *Whey beard*, a name for the White Throat. **1553** GRIMALDE *Cicero's Offices* I. (1556) 46 b, As soone as he waxed *whey-berded. **1825** JAMIESON, **Whey-bird*, the wood-lark,..Lanarks. **1862** JOHNS *Brit. Birds* 625 Whey-bird, the Whitethroat. **1675** DUFFETT *Mock Tempest* I. i, The *Whey-Blooded Rogue looks as if his heart were melted into his Breeches. **1660** TATHAM *Rump* I. i, A *Whey-brain'd fellow. **1894** LATTO *Tam. Bodkin* viii, The *whey-brose was perfection. *a* **1722** LISLE *Husb.* (1757) 406 They skimmed the cream off to make *whey-butter. **1846** J. BAXTER *Libr. Pract. Agric.* (ed. 4) I. 211 The quantity of whey-butter per cow is about half a pound per week. **1662** R. VENABLES *Exper. Angler* ix. 89 When..the river.. looketh of a *whay colour. **1684** J. S. *Profit & Pleas. United* 171 If the weather be dark or Whey-colour. **1845** JAMES *Arrah Neil* ii, That indistinct hue which may be called whey-colour. **1602** SHAKS. *Merry Wives* B iii, I take it hee is somewhat a weakly man: And he has as it were a *whay coloured beard. *a* **1735** ARBUTHNOT *Diss. Dumpling* Misc. Wks. 1751 I. 67 A goodly Whey-colour'd Beard. **1836** COMBE *Digestion* I. v, A semi-transparent whey-coloured fluid. **1604** T. M. *Black Bk.* E 1 b, A *whay countenance, short stooppes, and earthen dampish-voyce. **1750** W. ELLIS *Mod. Husb.* IV. I. 170 When Butter is wholly made with *Whey-cream, it is then justly named Whey-butter. **1591** PERCIVALL *Sp. Dict.*, *Requeson*, *whey cruds. **1740** BAYNARD *Health* (ed. 6) 20 Such a Tormenter never rages 'mong *Whey-Drinkers in poor cottages. **1811** W. AITON *Agric. Surv. Ayrs.* 452 (Jam.) Putrifying holes, which, in the dairy language of Ayrshire, are termed *whey-drops. *Ibid.* 455 Whey-springs, or *eyes, are seldom met with in the cheeses of Ayrshire. **1605** SHAKS. *Macb.* v. iii. 17 *Macb.*..What Soldiers, Patch?.. What Soldiers *Whay-face? *Ser.* The English Force, so please you. **1753** JANE COLLIER *Art Torment.* I. ii. 46 If her complexion is fair, call her Whey-face. **1824** MISS MITFORD *Village* Ser. I. *Mrs. Mosse*, A little ..man, with a Jerry-Sneak expression in his pale whey-face. **1649** DAVENANT *Love & Hon.* IV. iv. 20 Marke, sir, that *whey-fac'd fellow in the red. **1697** PRIOR *Ep. to Sir F. Sheppard* 49 That sneaking Whey-fac'd God Apollo. **1753** FOOTE *Englishm. in Paris* I. i, One whey-fac'd Son of a Bitch ..call'd me *Bête.* **1847** C. BRONTE *Jane Eyre* xvii, Your tutor, whey-faced Mr. Vining. **1949** C. FRY *Lady's not for Burning* I. 8 What shall I do With this nattering *wheygoose, Alizon? Shall I knock him down? **1663** PEPYS *Diary* 10 June, To the Royal Theatre... Thence to the *whay-house, and drank a great deal of whay. *a* **1915** JOYCE *Giacomo Joyce* (1968) 2 Smitten by the hot creamy light, grey *wheyhued shadows under the jawbones. **1872–4** JEFFERIES *Toilers of Field* (1892) 164 Against one wall are the *whey-leads. **1796** WITHERING *Brit. Plants* (ed. 3) IV. 174 A *whey-like juice. **1822** GOOD *Study Med.* II. 189 Whey-like urine. **1916** JOYCE *Portrait of Artist* v. 193 He saw in a moment the student's *wheypale face. **1978** H. WOUK *War & Remembrance* xiii. 129 Ascher's whey-pale face wanly lit up at the comparison. **1585** HIGINS *Junius' Nomencl.* 51/1 *Porcus serarius*,..a *whey pig. **14..** *Metr. Voc.* in Wr.-Wülcker 624/4 Whey i. olla *whey potte. **1922** JOYCE *Ulysses* 29 With her weak blood and *wheysour milk she had fed him. **1784** TWAMLEY *Dairying Exempl.* 13 Faults..in Cheese such as..*Whey Springs. **1811** [see *whey-eye*]. **1813** RUDGE *Agric. Glouc.* 299 Butter-milk..is sometimes saved in the *whey-tub. **1811** WILLAN in *Archaeologia* XVII. 163 **Whey-Whig*, whey impregnated with mint, balm, and walnut leaves. *a* **1548** HALL *Chron.*, *Edw. IV* 222 The Essex men hauynge wylde *whaye wormes in their heddes. **1828** *Craven Gloss.*, *Whey-worms*, pimples, from which exudes a wheylike moisture. *a* **1529** SKELTON *E. Rummyng* 553 A sory face *Wheywormed about.

b. as *adj.* Whey-coloured (cf. *whey beard*).

1663 BUTLER *Hud.* I. I. 245 His tawny Beard..The upper part thereof was Whey, The nether Orange mixt with Grey.

† **whey**, *v.* *Obs.* [f. prec.] *trans.* To separate the whey from (milk); hence in *vbl. sb. attrib.*, as ***wheying cloth***; also, to make (the blood) wheyish or thin.

1660 in *Sir R. Sadler's St. Papers* (1809) III. 358 Two fleeting dishes, six turning cloathes, and five wheying cloathes. **1661** FELTHAM *Resolves* (ed. 8) II. xi. 201 It is most true that in matters unjust, Christian Religion wheyes the bloud and makes a Coward of man. **1716** M. DAVIES *Athen. Brit.* III. 73 The Idolatry of Covetousness..had so whey'd or coagulated all it's Mass of Blood. **1728** E. SMITH *Compl. Housew.* (ed. 2) 85 Take the Curd of a gallon of Milk, and whey it well. *Ibid.* 105 Take a gallon of new Milk, set it as for a Cheese, and gently whey it.

whey, north. f. QUEY, heifer, WAY *int.*

wheyey (ˈhweɪɪ), *a.* Forms: 6 **wheye**, 6–7 **whayey**, 7 **whayie**, **wheyie**, **whaey**, 7– **wheyey**. [f. WHEY *sb.* + -Y^{1}.] Of the nature of whey; consisting of, containing, or resembling whey.

1547 RECORDE *Judic. Uryne* 13 b, Urine is the superfluitie or wheye substaunce of the bloude in the hollow vayne. **1572** J. JONES *Buckstones Bathes Benefyte* 18 The whayey, thinne, and subtyle humoures. **1615** CROOKE *Body of Man* 95 The serous or wheyie part of the bloud. **1708** *Brit. Apollo* No. 23. 2/1 The more Wheyey Parts of the Chyle. **1778** PENNANT *Tour in Wales* (1883) I. 54 Discolored by a wheyey tinge. **1822** GOOD *Study Med.* IV. 81 The surface of which [*sc.* the bladder] pours forth a cheesy or wheyey fluid. **1847** W. C. L. MARTIN *Ox* 29/1 A separation of the buttery and wheyey parts.

Hence ˈ**wheyiness**, wheyey quality.

1662 J. CHANDLER *Van Helmont's Oriat.* 220 They prefer Asses milk before the rest, by reason of its thin substance, and very much wheyinesse.

wheyish (ˈhweɪɪʃ), *a.* Also 6 **whaish**, 6–7 **whayish(e**. [f. WHEY *sb.* + -ISH^{1}.] Having the nature or quality of whey; like or resembling whey in consistence, colour, or other quality; watery, thin; palish.

1565 RAYNALDE *Byrth Mankynde* 46 b, The vayne.. whiche bryngeth the whayishe humour into the left kydney. **1572** TWYNE *Dionysius' Surv. World* E viij, A wheyish Topase. **1585** BANISTER *Tumors* xxxiv. Wks. (1633) 114 A watrish or whayish and unprofitable substance. **1625** B. JONSON *Staple of News* II. 2nd Intermeane, If it be fresh and sweet butter; but say it be sower and wheyish? **1683** TRYON *Way to Health* 150 Some River-Water will look of a wheyish whiteish Colour. *a* **1722** LISLE *Husb.* (1757) 295 A cow.. lately had the yellows, and the first coming of them to be known was by her milk being wheyish. **1801** BEDDOES *Hygeia* VI. (1802) 43 These break..and discharge the ill-conditioned, wheyish, and curdy matter. **1807** JAS. HALL *Trav. Scot.* II. 327 The liquid oozing from the roof in a few minutes seems to be formed into a wheyish substance.

Hence ˈ**wheyishness**, wheyish quality; also *fig.*

1637 MARKHAM *Engl. Housew.* II. (ed. 5) 107 To prevent the wheyishnesse of the Custard. **1803** SOUTHEY in Robberds *Mem. W. Taylor* (1843) I. 453, I have read Cowper's 'Odyssey'..to cure my poetry of its wheyishness.

wheyl(l)e, obs. forms of WHEEL.

wheyn, var. WHYNE *Obs.* whence.

wheynte, obs. f. QUAINT *a.*

wheyte, north. f. QUIT *v.*

whhi-hhee: see WEHEE.

whi: see WEHEE, WHY, WIE.

whib(b)le, etc., obs. variants of QUIBBLE, etc.

1604 BABINGTON *Comf. Notes Exod.* ii. 25 Whiblers and pratling pick-thanks, tatlers, and tale-tellars. **1624** GEE *Foot out of Snare* (ed. 3) 82, I doe not heare, that any of those snarling whibbling Curres can barke. If they dare open their snapping mouthes, let them doe it whilest men liue that may refute them. *a* **1626** MIDDLETON *Mayor Quinb.* v. i. (1661) 63, *2 Cheat.* The Whirligig, the Whibble, the Carwidgen. *Sym.* Hey day, what names are these! *2 Cheat.* New names of late.

whibibbe, obs. form of CUBEB.

1355–6 *Durham Acc. Rolls* (Surtees) 555 Et in una libra de Whibibbes prec. iiij s.

† **whiblin.** *Obs.* Of doubtful origin and meaning; perh. a slang term denoting 'thingumbob', 'what-d'ye-call-it'; but cf. WHIBBLE and QUIBLIN.

With quot. 1604 cf. WHIFLING, WHIMLING.

1604 DEKKER *Honest Wh.* I. I. ii, Hees a very mandrake, or else..one a these whiblins, and thats worse, and then all the children that he gets lawfully of your body sister, are bastards by a statute. **1613** MARSTON *Insat. C'tess* II. D j b,

A rare whiblin, To be reueng'd, and yet gaine pleasure in't. 1623 J. Taylor (Water P.) *World runs on Wheels* Wks. (1630) II. 234/1 Proiects..of planting the Ile of Dogs with Whiblins, Corwhichets, Mushromes and Tobacco. *a*1652 Brome *Lovesick Court* v. i, Come, Sir, let go your whiblin. (*Dis.* snatcheth his sword away.)

whicche: see WHITCH, WITCH.

which (hwɪtʃ), *a.* and *pron.* Forms: see below. [OE. *hwelc*, *hwilc*, *hwylc* corresp. to OFris. *hwelik*, *hwel(e)k*, *hwek*, *hulk*, *huk*, *hok* (Fris. *wolk*, *wæk*, *huk*, etc.), OS. *hwilîc*, MLG. *welik*, *welk*, MDu. *welc*, (LG., Du. *welk*), OHG. **hwalîh*, *uualîh*, *hwelîh*, *welîh*, *-ich*, *-eh* (MHG. *welh*, *welch*, G. *welch*), Goth. *hwileiks*:—OTeut. **χwalīk-*, **χwilīk-* 'of what form', f. *χwa-*, *χwi-* (Indo-eur. $q^{w}o$-, $q^{w}i$- WHO, etc.) + **līko-* body, form (cf. LIKE *a.*). OE. *hwelc* (OWS. and Anglian), *hwælc* (Northumb.) and *hwilc* (chiefly WS.), represent primitive **hwalīk-* and **hwilīk-* respectively; later OE. has a rounded form *hwylc* of *hwilc*. The three OE. types *hwelc*, *hwilc*, *hwylc* gave three ME. types **hwelch*, *hwilch*, *hwülch*, which became, by loss of *l* (cf. SUCH), *hwech*, *hwich*, *hwüch*; the second of these types alone has survived in mod.English, the other two not remaining current after the 15th century. The forms with non-palatalization of the final consonant *whilk* (*quhilk*), occas. *quhik*, are northern (in ME. also East Anglian): cf. SWILK, SIC. Forms showing the absorption of *w* as in *hulch*, *huch* (cf. *such* for *swuch*, and OFris. *huk*) are rare.

Certain continental forms are compounded with other derivatives of the same pronominal stem; Goth. *hwēleiks* with the instrumental *hwē* (cf. *hwēlaups* how great); ON. *hvílíkr* (MSw. *hviliken*, *huilkin*, *hu(l)kin*, Sw., Da. *hvilken*) with the locative *hwī*; OHG. *hwêolîh*, *wiolîh* (MHG. *wielich*) with the adv. *hweo*, *weo* (G. *wie*) how.

For the compounds *ᵹehwilc*, *ǽᵹhwilc*, see EACH.]

A. Illustration of Forms.

1. 1 **hwelc, huelc, hwælc, huælc, huoelc,** 3 **hwælch,** 4–5 **wheche, weche,** 5 **whech, qwech(e, queche, (qheche);** 3 **qwel,** 4 **quelk.**

[*c*725 *Corpus Gloss.* Q74 *Quo cumque modo*, ᵹehwelci weᵹa.] *c*825 *Vesp. Psalter* xviii. 13 [xix. 12] *Delicta quis intellegit*, scylde hwelc onᵹeteð? *c*950 *Lindisf. Gosp.* Mark ix. 34 *Disputauerant quis esset illorum maior*, ..ᵹeflioton hua *vel* huelc woere hiora mara. *Ibid.* xii. 19 *Si cuius frater mortuus fuerit*, ..ᵹef huælc *vel* æniᵹ broðer dead sie *vel* bið. *c*1200 *Vices & Virtues* 21 An hwælche wise ic mihte betst sahtlin wið mine halend Criste. *c*1250 qwel [see B. 8]. *c*1375 *Cursor M.* 27236 (Fairf.) þe prest agh spire..Of men þat ar in religioun Quelk reccheles prelatis is. 1387 *E.E. Wills* (1882) 2 The cheste..weche they haue of myn. 1418 *Ibid.* 44 þe money þe qweche Oliuer hath in his hand. 14.. *Cast. Love* 578 (MS. Bodl. Add. B. 107), Herkeneth wheche loue, wych bucsomnesse, Whiche grace & whiche swetnesse, That good from hevyn to alyȝht ches! 1449 Marg. Paston in *P. Lett.* I. 82 Abok of sofystre..the qheche my seyd brother behestid my moder. *c*1450 Capgrave *Life St. Aug.* xxxii, þat þei schuld not denye o tyme whech þei graunted anoþer tyme. 1461 *Paston Lett.* II. 10, I am enformyd, ye schall recuver of hard and but a part, the qwech schuld be dere of the sute.

2. *a.* 1–3 **hwilc, wilc,** 3 **hwilch, w(h)ilch, whilc,** *Orm.* **whillc** (*gen.* **whillkess,** *pl.* **whillke**), 3–4 **wilk,** 4 **wylke,** 4–5 **whylke,** 4–6 **whilke,** 4–6, 7–9 *dial.* **whilk,** 5 **wilke,** 5–7 *dial.* **whylk,** (6 *Sc.* **vhilk,** *pl.* **vhilks,** 6–8 *Sc. pl.* **whilks**); 3–4 **quilc, quilke,** 4 **qwilk, quylk, quhylk, (quil),** 4–5 **quilk,** 4–8 *Sc.* **quhilk** (*pl.* 5–7 **quhilkis,** 6 **quhilks**).

*a*950 *Ælfred's Boeth.* xxxiv. §10 Hwilc ure mæᵹ areccan medemlice ures scyppendes willan? *c*975 *Rushw. Gosp.* Matt. xxi. 24 Ic ek eow sæcge in wilce mæh[t]e ic þas do. *c*1200 Ormin 471 whillc [see B. 4]. *Ibid.* 5283 O whillkess kinness wise. *c*1200 *Vices & Virtues* 77 Whilch lean aust ðu te hauen of godd? *Ibid.* 125 ȝif þu wilt witen wilke eiȝene ðe hierte muȝe habben. *c*1200 *Trin. Coll. Hom.* 179 Hlisteð nu for hwat and o wilche wise. 13.. quhylk [see B. 7 a]. 13.. *Northern Passion* 256 (MS. Camb. Gg. 5. 31), þai lukyd.. Whylke [*v.r.* wylke] of þayme it myght be fall. 1424 *E.E. Wills* (1882) 57, I wul my wyf haf my best ambeler, and my sone..wylk him likeþ best. 1585 Jas. I *Ess. Poesie* (Arb.) 14 The vapouris..Whilks syne in cloudds are keiped closs and well. *c*1634 W. Cartwright *Ordinary* IV. i, Lere me whylk way he wended. 1711 in *Nairne Peerage Evid.* (1874) 132 To be..granted to the said deceast Robert lord Nairn and the airs male of his body whilks failzieing to the said Margaret now lady Nairn his daughter. 1819 Scott *Leg. Montrose* iii, Their damnable skirlin' pipes, whilk they themselves pretend to understand.

*c*1250 *Gen. & Ex.* 2350 Seið him quilke min blisses ben. *Ibid.* 3631 Quilc frud, quat offrende, quilc [*MS.* quil] laȝe. *a*1300 *Cursor M.* 4788 Lok quilk of us sal tak on hand For vs alle do þis trauail. *Ibid.* 8454 þe kind o thinges lerd he,.. Quil war þair mightes soth and lele. 1387 in *Edin. Charters* (1871) 35 In fourme the quylk eftir folowys. 1456 Sir G. Haye *Law Arms* 1 The rubryis..be the quhilkis men may better knaw [etc.]. *a*1592 whilke [see B. 2 b]. 1637–50 Row *Hist. Kirk* (Wodrow Soc.) 123 The bukes of the Assemblie, all quhilkis I had preserved hole. 1724 Ramsay *Vision* xvii, Starrie gleims, Quhilk prinkled.

β. 2 **hwic, wic,** 2–3 **hwich, (ȝwich),** 3–6 **wyche, wich,** 4 **hwych,** *pl.* **huiche,** 4–5 **wiche,** 4–6 **whiche, whyche, wych,** 5 **whych, (wycche,** 6 **wycch,** *Sc.* **vich, vhich),** 4– **which;** 4–5 **quiche, quyche,** 5 **quich, quych, qwiche, qwyche(e,** 5–6 *Sc.* **quhich;** 5 *Sc.* **quhik.**

*a*1175 *Cott. Hom.* 238 Wic ȝeie, wic drednesse wurð þer. *Ibid.* 243 Hwic scule beon ure sceld, sanctus paulus hus seið. *a*1200 *Moral Ode* 136 Lutel he hit scaweð hwice hete is þer þa saule wuneð. *c*1200 *Trin. Coll. Hom.* 141 Lusteð..wiche wise hie hine bisohte and hwich andswere he hire giaf. 1297 R. Glouc. (Rolls) 326 Vor to wite in ȝwiche stede is wonii[n]gge were. *c*1300 *Beket* (Percy Soc.) 974 In whiche manere. 1340 *Ayenb.* 129 Yziȝ wrechche ine huiche zorȝes and ine huiche perils þou art. *c*1375 *Cursor M.* 21136 (Fairf.) þat folk ilkane walde oþer steyuen Quiche muȝt come titist to heyuen. *c*1380 *Sir Ferumb.* 511 A costrel.. hwych ys ful of þat bame cler. 1390 which [see B. 7 b]. 1415 in *43rd Rep. Dep. Kpr. Publ. Rec.* 584 On ye morou ye Fryday ye quich was yis day fourteneghte. 1471 *Paston Lett.* Suppl. (1901) 138 Wycche mony I pray zow that [ye] bestowe yt as I wryth to zow. *a*1500 *Bernard. de cura rei fam.* 215 A mane,..quhik al his fantasy Has geffyne to vice. 1551 Crowley *Pleas. & Payne* 63 Ye..Wych wythout me had come to nought. 1585 T. Washington tr. *Nicholay's Voy.* I. vii. 6 The master of my skiffe, whiche presently..was made fast by the leg. *a*1600 Montgomerie *Sonn.* lvi. 6 My teirs vhich so abound.

3. *a.* 1 **hwylc,** 2 **hwulch, hulch,** 2–3 **wulc,** 3 **whulc(h, wulch,** 5 **whulche.**

871–889 *Charter* in *O.E. Texts* 452/52 Swa hwylc mon swa hio wonie & breoce. *c*1175 *Lamb. Hom.* 15 Hwulc mon is þet nauet to broken elche dei þas godes laȝe þe ic eou nu cweð. *Ibid.* 27 hulche [see B. 6]. *Ibid.* 49 Nu ȝe habbeð iherd wulc hit is for to iheren godes weordes and heom ethalden. *c*1205 Lay. 2303 þu nast of whulche londe heo com heder liðen. *Ibid.* 20735 For whulches cunnes þinge ligge we þus here. *c*1400 *St. Alexius* (Vernon MS.) 207, I wolde fayn, & i wuste whulche.

β. 3 **hwuc, hwu(c)ch, wucch,** 3–5 **wuch(e, woch(e,** 4 **whuche, (wȝuch),** 4–5 **whuch, whoche,** 5 **whoch, huch.**

*c*1200 *Trin. Coll. Hom.* 189 And to-ȝenes hwuch fo man agh furðien seið þe holi apostle. *Ibid.* 219 For woche þinge he nemnede [etc.]. *a*1225 hwuc [see B. 1]. *a*1250 *Owl & Night.* 1378 Bo wuch ho bo. *c*1320 *Cast. Love* 110 Allas wȝuch serue and deol þer wes! *c*1400 *Beryn* 176 Huch þe Pardoner, & he, pryuely in hir pouchis þey put hem aftirward. 1401 *26 Pol. Poems* iii. 36 Whoche party may strengere be. 1422 Yonge tr. *Secr. Secr.* 143 Wylde bestis, amonge woche euery olt hym abow hym to whome he is prere [? pere].

B. Signification.

I. Interrogative and allied uses.

For the distinction between the dependent interrogative and the relative, cf. note s.v. WHAT A. I.**

†**1.** *adj.* Most usually *predicative*: Of what kind, quality, or character; also *attrib.* what kind of: = L. *qualis*. (The interrogative corresponding to the demonstrative SUCH.) *Obs.*

In attrib. use (in *sing.*) sometimes followed by *a*.

*c*897 Ælfred *Gregory's Past. C.* lxv. 467 Ðær ic hæbbe ᵹetæht hwelc hierde bion sceal. *c*1000 *Ags. Gosp.* Luke vii. 39 He wiste hwæt & hwylc þis wif wære.., þæt heo synful is. *c*1205 Lay. 10120 Men..talden him tiðende of alle þere fore þe Petrus dude in Rome, and whulcne [*c*1275 wochne] martirdom Petrus hauede vnder-fon. *a*1225 *Ancr. R.* 64 Hwon Godes prophete makede swuche mone of eien, hwuc mone wenestu is to moni mon..icumen..of hore eien? *c*1250 *Gen. & Ex.* 3212 Ðor he stunden for to sen Quilc pharaon wið hem sal ben. 1297 R. Glouc. (Rolls) 1189 So hii miȝte lerni wiche brutons were. *c*1320 *Cast. Love* 53 To wȝuche a Castel he alihte, þo he wolde here for vs fihte. 1388 Wyclif *James* i. 24 Anoon he forȝat which he was. *c*1400 tr. *Secr. Secr., Gov. Lordsh.* 104 Whiche ys þy fayth, and þy lawe? *a*1400–50 *Bk. Curtasye* 301 in *Babees Bk.*, To aske his nome, and qweche he be.

2. As general interrogative. (Mostly *Obs.*) †**a.** *adj.* = WHAT A. 13, 14. *Obs.* (or merged in 3 a.)

*c*900 tr. *Bæda's Hist.* IV. xx[i]v. (1890) 348 Hwylc þearf is ðe husles? *c*1000 *Ags. Gosp.* Matt. xxiv. 3 Seᵹe us..hwilc tacn si þines to-cymys. *c*1200 *Trin. Coll. Hom.* 33 þe engel ..seweð a whilche wise and þuregh hwam þis blisse cumen sholde. *c*1290 *Beket* 2323 in *S. Eng. Leg.* 173 In ȝwat manere he was a-slawe and ȝwuch tyme he was ded. *c*1305 *Jud. Isc.* 101 in *E.E.P.* (1862) 110 Siþþe ic fond mie louerd aslawe y not in whiche wise. *a*1340 Hampole *Psalter* Cant. 515 He leryd him in whilk degre,..and how he sould luf him. 1588 Shaks. *L.L.L.* IV. i. 105 *Clo.* From my Lord to my Lady. *Qu.* From which Lord, to which Lady? 1715 Leoni *Palladio's Archit.* (1745) II. 65 Nor ought any one to wonder, which way such vast Quantities of earthen Ware came here. 1752 Chesterf. *Lett.* ccxcvi. (1792) IV. 6 In some congratulatory poem prefixed to some work, I have forgot which.

b. *pron.* = WHAT A. 1, 6. Also (OE. and occas. later) = Who. *Obs.* exc. as a *dial.* or humorous substitute for *what*.

971 *Blickl. Hom.* 169 Hwylc æteowde eow to fleonne fram ðon toweardan Godes erre? *c*1290 *St. Brendan* 569 in *S. Eng. Leg.* 235 Man mai i-seo ȝwuch it is to ȝyuen oþur mannes þing with wouȝ. *a*1400 *Minor Poems fr. Vernon MS.* 240/738 Afftur þis schaltou witen þen Wȝuche ben þe comaundemens ten. *c*1400 *Brut* 22 (*heading*), How iiij kynges curteisely helde al Britaigne; and whiche beth here names. 1548–9 *Bk. Com. Prayer, Catech.*, Tell me how many [commandments] there bee... Tenne. Whiche be they? *a*1592 Greene *Jas. IV*, I. 657 Sike is the werld, but whilke is he I sawe? 1599 Shaks. *Much Ado* II. i. 107, I haue manie ill qualities? *Bene.* Which is one? *Mar.* I say my prayers alowd. 1648 *G. Sandys's Par. Ps.* cxiv. 9 Recoyling Seas, which [*ed.* 1638 what] caus'd your dread?

1835 A. Parker *Trip to West & Texas* 88 Ask a question, and if they do not understand you, they reply '*which*?' 1848 Dickens *Dombey* xxxviii, 'I want a so-and-so' he says—some hard name or other. 'A which?' says the Captain. 1891 Kipling *Light that Failed* ix, Who's interfering with which? 1910 P. W. Joyce *Eng. as we speak it in Ireland* 348 When a person does not quite catch what another says, there is generally a query... Our people often express this query by the single word 'which?' 1938 W. Faulkner *Unvanquished* 83 Yankee say, 'Sartoris, John Sartoris,' and Marse John say, 'Which? Say which?' 1950 —— *Coll. Stories* 752 'Here,' Weddel said, extending the tumbler... The Negro stopped. .. 'Which?' he said. He looked at the glass.

3. In limited sense, expressing a request for selection from a definite number: What one (or ones) of a (stated or implied) set of persons, things, or alternatives. (The current use.) **a.** *adj.*

Sometimes, as in *which way*, indistinguishable from 2 a.

*c*1000 *Ags. Gosp.* Matt. vii. 9 Hwylc man is of eow ᵹyf his sunu hyne bit hlafes sylst þu him stan? *c*1386 Chaucer *Reeve's T.* 158 Whilk way is he geen? *c*1400 *Destr. Troy* 12659 þen þai fraynet qwiche freke, þat schuld first enter. 1535 Coverdale *2 Kings* iii. 8 Which waye wil we go vp? 1562 J. Heywood *Prov. & Epigr.* I iv, I know on which syde my bread is buttred. 1596 Shaks. *Merch. V.* II. ix. 11 Neuer to vnfold to any one Which casket 'twas I chose. 1667 Milton *P.L.* IV. 73 Which way shall I flie? 1770 Foote *Lame Lover* II, A wise man should well weigh which party to take for. 1882 Besant *All Sorts* xxi, Bound for some American port—I forget which. 1916 T. R. Glover *The Jesus of Hist.* iv. 70 When the question is asked, 'Was Jesus the Messiah?' the obvious reply is, 'Which Messiah?'

b. *pron.* (†occas., in dependent clause, with *the*.)

*c*950 *Lindisf. Gosp.* Matt. vi. 27 *Quis autem uestrum*.. huælc uutetlice iurre? *c*1000 *Ags. Gosp.* John xix. 24 Ne slite we hy, ac uton hleotan hwylces ures heo sy. 1297 R. Glouc. (Rolls) 928 Among hom..strif me miȝte ise Woch mest maisters were. *a*1300 *Cursor M.* 15275 Ful wel i wat þe quilk o yow þe tresun has puruaid. 13.. *St. Alexius* 207 (MS. Laud 108) Lauedi, I wille ful fayn, and I wiste wilk. 1402 *Jack Upland* 28 Frere, how many orders be in erthe, and which is the perfitest order? *c*1470 *Gol. & Gaw.* 919 Quhilk that happynnit the lak, Couth na leid say! 1526 Tindale *John* viii. 46 Which of you can rebuke me off synne? 1573–80 Tusser *Husb.* (1878) 77 In making or mending as needeth thy ditch, get set to quick set it, learne cunningly whitch. 1599 Shaks. *Much Ado* v. iv. 72 Which is Beatrice? *Beat.* I answer to that name. 1601 R. Johnson *Kingd. & Commw.* 2 Of these two I doe not know which to prefer. 1611 Shaks. *Wint. T.* IV. iii. 94, I cannot tell..for which of his Vertues it was. 1660 Fuller *Mixt Contempl.* xiii. 21 Two young Gentlemen were comparing their revenues together, vying which of them were the best. 1791 Cowper *Let. to W. Bagot* 18 Mar., Indisposed..with gout or rheumatism, (for it seems uncertain which). 1857 Ruskin *Pol. Econ. Art* Addenda 191 *note*, The contest between them is not..which shall get everything for himself. 1889 Stevenson *Ballantrae* iii, But which is it to be? Fight or make friends?

4. *adj.* and *pron.* Repeated (in sense 3): **a.** in each of two (or more) separate clauses, usually connected by a conj.

*c*897 Ælfred *Gregory's Past. C.* lix. 451 He us ᵹetacnode for hwelcum ðingum we sceolden ure godan weorc helan, & for hwelcum we hi sceolden cyðan. *c*1200 Ormin 471–2 Prestess..& dæcness..Shifftedenn hemm bitwenenn Whillc here shollde serrfenn firrst, Whillc siþþenn i þe temmple. 1297 R. Glouc. (Rolls) 2562 Me nuste Woch was on ne woch was oþer. *c*1330 R. Brunne *Chron. Wace* (Rolls) Prol. 17 To here.. whilk were foles, & whilk were wyse. 1575 Turberv. *Faulconrie* 159 To note the naturall disposition of his Hawkes: as, whiche will flee beeing high .., and whiche best, when she is kepte lowe, whiche will flee best when she is set most sharpe and eager, and whyche contrary, and whiche in a meane betweene both. 1849 Macaulay *Hist. Eng.* iii. I. 407 Which ballot boxes were to be green and which red, which balls were to be of gold and which of silver..and a hundred more such trifles, were gravely considered. 1880 Shorthouse *John Inglesant* xxvii, Trying..to make out..which was noble and which was groom.

b. in the same clause, in abbreviated expressions, esp. ***which is which*** = which is the one and which is the other; so ***which goes with which***, etc.; also with another interrog., as ***who is to have which***.

A jocular variant is contained in the phr. ***to tell tother from which***.

*a*1300 *Cursor M.* 9290 Wel sal he cun knau quilk es quilk, Fra the wick þe god to scil. 1398 Trevisa *Barth. De P.R.* XII. iii. (Bodl. MS.), þe furste manere hawkes takeþ onelich here praie fleinge briddes and þe secunde manere haukes..reeseþ on briddes þ[t] setteþ one þe grounde. And þe briddes knowiþ whiche is whiche. *c*1412 Hoccleve *De Reg. Princ.* 445 Som tyme, afer men myghten lordes knowe By there array, from oþer folke; but now A man schal..musen a long throwe Whiche is whiche. 1559 Aylmer *Harborowe* K 4, It was not to bee iudged by the greatnes or smalnes, but which was whose. 1564 Harding *Answ. Jewel* 73 It is hard to fynde which keye serueth which locke. 1582 *N.T.* (Rhem.) Mark xv. 24 Casting lottes vpon them, who should take which. 1605 Shaks. *Macb.* III. iv. 127 What is the night? Almost at oddes with morning, which is which. 1711 Steele *Spect.* No. 41 ¶4 There does not need any great Discernment to judge which are which. 1849 C. Bronte *Shirley* xxiii, Caroline, looking round, met a new Robert,—the real Robert... 'Well,' said he,..'which is which?' 1881 Miss Braddon *Asphodel* xii, To see which went best with which.

II. Exclamatory use.

†**5.** *adj.* (in non-collective sing. followed by *a*): = WHAT B. 5, 5 b. *Obs.*

*c*888 Ælfred *Boeth.* xvi. §2 Ᵹif ᵹe nu ᵹesawan hwelce mus þæt wære hlaford ofer oðre mys,..mid hwelce hleahtre ᵹe woldon bion astered. *a*1175 [see A. 2 *β*]. *c*1175 *Lamb. Hom.* 19 Nimað ȝeme..hwilche ȝife he us ȝefeð. *a*1225 *Ancr. R.* 134 þenc hwuch pinen he þolede. 1297 R. Glouc. (Rolls) 7237 Hii seye þe soþnesse In wuch lecherie & oþer sunne þe prestes songe hor messe. *c*1305 *11,000 Virgins* 62 in *E.E.P.* (1862) 67 Louerd, which a cumpaignye of clene maidenes was þere. 1377 Langl. *P. Pl.* B. x. 27 Whiche lordes beth þis shrewes! *c*1386 Chaucer *Frankl. T.* 714 Lo which a wyf was Alcestem. *a*1400–50 *Wars Alex.* 1807 He tellis quyche a tunne of tresoure he hauys. *c*1430 *Pilgr. Lyf Manhode* III. v. (1869) 139 Harrow, which gret wood-shipe is þis. *c*1440 *Jacob's Well* 102 Lo, whiche a worschip sche hadde, & whiche a ioye.

III. Relative uses. * as simple relative.

6. *adj.* The ordinary relative adj.

Formerly in Sc. with pl. inflexion *-s*, *-is*: see A. 2*a*. For the construction with a prep., cf. 7a.

c **1175** *Lamb. Hom.* 27 þesne mon ic habbe itaken to mine aȝene bihofþe. Ma monna ic scolde biȝeten swa, bi hulche monna seið drihten in his spelle þa he þus cweþ [etc.]. *c* **1250** *Kent. Serm.* in *O.E. Misc.* 30 Lecherie, spusbreche, Roberie,..and alle oþre euele deden, þurch wyche þinkes man ofserueth þet fer of helle. **13..** *Northern Passion* 1309 (MS. Camb. Gg. I. 1) þe tre of lif On woche [*v.r.* whilke] tre þat appil grewe. *c* **1400** *Brut* 229 His flesshe was restorede aȝein,..for whiche miracle þe good man & his frendes louede God and Seint Thomas. **1432–50** tr. *Higden* (Rolls) II. 101 The thrydde realme was of Estesex..The kynges of whiche place..were obediente to other kynges. **1460** CAPGRAVE *Chron.* (Rolls) 166 He fond him ontretable; for whech cause the bischop cursid him. **1526** TINDALE *Col.* iii. 6 Fornicacion, vnclennes,..and covetousnes..: for which thynges sakes the wrath of god falleth on the chyldren off vnbeleve. **1585** JAS. I *Ess. Poesie* (Arb.) 55 They are figures of Rhetorique and Dialectique, quhilkis airtis I professe nocht. **1610** SHAKS. *Temp.* I. ii. 277 She did confine thee.. Into a clouen Pyne, within which rift Imprison'd, thou didst painefully remaine A dozen yeeres. **1719** DE FOE *Crusoe* I. (Globe) 71 It rain'd all Night and all Day,..during which time the Ship broke in pieces. **1800** WORDSW. *Hart-Leap Well*, The monuments spoken of in the second Part of the following Poem, which monuments do now exist as I have there described them. **1831** CARLYLE *Sart. Res.* I. i, Concerning which last, indeed. **1892** *Photogr. Ann.* II. 883 A 5 × 4 camera..(which size is now the most popular).

7. *pron.* The ordinary relative pronoun introducing an additional statement about the antecedent, the sense of the principal clause being complete without the relative clause; thus sometimes equivalent to 'and that (it, they, etc.)'. (Cf. THAT *rel. pron.* 2.)

In this and following senses formerly sometimes followed by *that* (THAT *conj.* 6), occas. by *as* (cf. AS *adv.* B. 27).

a. As obj. of a prep., which usually precedes *which*, but occas. stands at the end of the clause.

If the prep. depends on some other word (e.g. a sb. or numeral), that word (with any that qualify or govern it) usually stands immediately before the prep.

c **1175** *Lamb. Hom.* 11 Drihten him bi-tahte twa stanene tables breode on hwulche godalmihti heofde iwriten þa ten laȝe. **13..** *Cursor M.* 9540 (Gött.) Ilk-an gaf he substance an,..Widuten quhylk on nan manere Miht he in pes his kingriche ȝeme. **1423** JAS. I *Kingis Q.* iii, A boke..Off quhich the name Is clepit.. Boece. **1451** *Paston Lett.* Suppl. (1901) 35 A letter..qwych I send yow a copy of. **1590** SPENSER *F.Q.* I. xi. 29 A springing well, From which fast trickled forth a siluer flood. **1603** in Gage *Hengrave* (1822) 32 One payer of little orgaynes wth a board w^h^ they stand on. **1687** A. LOVELL tr. *Thevenot's Trav.* I. 17 Our Ship stuck a ground, with the noise of which, our Captain awoke. **1726** *Adv. Capt. R. Boyle* (1768) 113 Their Beards & Mustachoes ..which they take a particular Pride in the Length or Largeness of. **1858** CARLYLE *Fredk. Gt.* II. vii. I. 131 The Pope..being held..at a distance: the result of which was what we see. **1893** MAX PEMBERTON *Iron Pirate* ii, A.. Scotsman, who carried the economy of his race even to the extent of flesh, of which he was sparse.

b. As subject or object of a verb.

Formerly sometimes used where *as* is now idiomatic, as in quot. 1688: cf. 10.

a **1300** *E.E. Psalter* ix. 16 In þis snare whilke þai hid swa. **1390** GOWER *Conf.* III. 132 His herbe propre is Rosmarine, Which schapen is for his covine. *c* **1400** *Cursor M.* 25391 (Cott. Galba) þe blis of heuyn, Whilk seuyn vertuse vntill vs wins, And als fordose seuyn dedly sins. **1485** CAXTON *Chas. Gt.* 193 Eche took an hors..which ranne at al aduenture. *c* **1550** ROLLAND *Crt. Venus* Prol. 11 Complexiounis.. Quhilkis ar thir four:..Phlegmatike..Sanguineane.. Colerike..Melancolie, Quhilkis of nature ar wonder different. **1552** LYNDESAY *Monarche* 4373 This is ane maruellous Monarche, Quhilk hes power Imperiall Boith of the body and the Saull. *a* **1613** BREREWOOD *Lang. & Relig.* (1622) 201 The Italian, French, and Spanish: all which in a barbarous word haue beene called Romanse. **1650** FULLER *Pisgah* I. xiii. 41 The Hebrews measuring their land by a bow-shot,..which..admits of variation. **1688** HOLME *Armoury* III. 331/2 The Pitchfork (or Pikel, which we vulgarly call it). **1719** DE FOE *Crusoe* I. (Globe) 48, I spy'd a small Piece of a Rope, which I wonder'd I did not see at first. **1825** T. HOOK *Sayings* Ser. II. *Passion & Princ.* x. III. 209 'And so good night': saying which, he urbanely shook hands. **1872** MORLEY *Voltaire* i. 3 Ideas..whose forms were old.., but which were full of seemingly inexhaustible novelty. **1875** JEVONS *Money* xix. 246 The United States government tried a similar experiment, which was soon discontinued.

c. Referring to a fact, circumstance, or statement. Now very common in spoken English.

Quot. 1950 is a mixed construction. Cf. AND *conj.* 11 a.

1390 GOWER *Conf.* I. 12 To make pes betwen the kynges ..Which is the propre duete Belongende unto the presthode. **1516** in E. Lodge *Illustr.* (1838) I. 17 He would advise me to get me to some little house, with a few persons with me, which I have done. **1521** in *Essex Rev.* XIII. 221 If she [*sc.* the ship] come not well home, which God forfende. **1597** SHAKS. *2 Hen. IV*, v. ii. 34 You must now speake Sir Iohn Falstaffe faire, Which swimmes against your streame of Quality. **1669** BOYLE *Contn. New Exper.* I. xxxiv. 118, I order'd the Air to be let in very leisurely, upon which we could plainly see [etc.]. **1699** BENTLEY *Phal.* xii. 320 The last part of the Sentence not..answering to the first; which is the proper definition of a Solœcism. **1760** STERNE *Tr. Shandy* III. xxiv, I dragged her after me, by means of which she fell backwards soss against the bridge. **1787** J. FEA *Fish. Sc. Isl.* 31 We have no Methodists settled amongst us, which is very fortunate. **1836** DICKENS *Sk. Boz*, *Sentiment*, Looking as amiable as they possibly could— which, by the by, is not saying much for them. **1839** URE *Dict. Arts* 1076 Yellow rosin contains some water, which black rosin does not. **1886** [E. H. DERING] *In Light of 20th Cent.* iv. 65 Observation..only shows what is visible, which life is not. **1902** H. JAMES *Wings of Dove* I. iv. 85 He imaged it—which was enough as some proved vanity. **1914** 'IAN HAY' *Knt. on Wheels* xiii. § 3 They conformed to the rules, ..observing the spirit rather than the letter of the law. Which was just as well. **1950** PATTERSON & CONRAD *Scottsboro Boy* II. v. 122 He..said, 'Haven't I told you black sons of bitches about talking after bed hours?' 'I wasn't talking,' I said. And which I wasn't. **1981** *London Rev. Bks.* 19 Feb.–4 Mar. 9/2 To be fair, Frances Partridge is concerned in this book to put the record straight on the central episode of Carrington's suicide: to emphasize Ralph Partridge's fear that this would happen, and his desperate efforts to avert it. Which is reasonable enough.

d. With a conjunction in the relative clause, usually following *which*, rarely preceding. *arch.*

In early use more frequently with pleonastic personal pronoun (see 14). For sylleptic uses see 15.

[**1510**: see 13 b.] *a* **1548** HALL *Chron.*, *Edw. IV* 214 b, To conuey hym selfe into some other place, without delay, which if he did they assured hym, y^t^ he should haue neither hurte nor damage. *c* **1643** LD. HERBERT *Autobiog.* (1824) 193 Oliver Herbert was forced to fly France, which, that he might do the better, I paid the said fencer 200 crowns. **1752** FIELDING *Amelia* III. viii, The tears began to overflow— which, when he perceived, he stopt. **1796** MRS. INCHBALD *Nature & Art* xi. (1820) 29 Explanations followed all these questions; but which..require no recital here. **1835** CHATTO *Rambles Northumbld.* 106 A girl..returning home from milking..saw many fairies gamboling in the fields, but which were invisible to her companions. **1871** RUSKIN *Fors Clav.* iii. 14 It was not [then] esteemed of absolute necessity to put agreements between Christians in writing! Which if it were not now, you know we might save a great deal of money. **1883** R. W. DIXON *Mano* II. iv. 76 Which when he saw, thither full fast ran he.

e. Introducing a parenthetic qualifying clause inserted in the principal clause. (Cf. sense 11, quots. 1599, 1719.)

1560 ROLLAND *Seven Sages* (Bann. Club) 50 He purposit, quhilk was wors, My awin Lady..to defors. **1611** BEAUM. & FL. *Maid's Trag.* III. ii, Are not you, Which is above all joyes, my constant friend? **1640** E. REYNOLDS *Passions* xvi. 174 Strange Sinnes too (which is the curiositie and corruption of Nature) are marvellous attractive. **1862** RUSKIN *Unto this Last* ii. 40 Primarily, which is very notable and curious, I observe that men of business rarely know the meaning of the word 'rich'. **1882** BESANT *All Sorts* vii, When, which happened every day, they forgot their disguises for a while, they talked quite freely.

8. a. Introducing a clause defining or restricting the antecedent and thus completing the sense. Regularly so used after the antecedent *that* (THAT *dem. pron.* 6), or after a prep. (see b); in other cases the more regular relative is *thăt* (THAT *rel. pron.* 1).

In modern printing usually distinguished from 7 by the absence of a comma before the relative (as in speech by the absence of a pause).

†***all which*** continued in literary use till *c* 1850.

c **1250** *Gen. & Ex.* 170 So made god..Al erue, and wrim, and wilde der, Qwel man mai sen on werlde her. *c* **1320** *Cast. Love* 1434 þe woundes..Wȝuche þat weoren on honden and feet. *c* **1400** *Apol. Loll.* 42 Man was maad to lord in alle creaturis, and forfetid not þat wyche synniþ not. **1598** B. JONSON *Ev. Man in Hum.* II. ii. (1601 Qo.), That land or nation best doth thriue, Which to smooth-fronted peace is most procliue. **1610** SHAKS. *Temp.* v. i. 204 It is you, that haue chalk'd forth the way Which brought vs hither. **1611** *Bible* Gen. i. 7 God..diuided the waters, which were vnder the firmament, from the waters, which were aboue the firmament. **1619** in *Hales' Gold. Rem.* II. (1673) 125 This is all which is done this week. **1774** GOLDSM. *Nat. Hist.* (1776) II. 335 Repairing the destruction, which they must often suffer, by their quick reproduction. **1824** L. MURRAY *Engl. Gram.* (ed. 5) I. 74 After all which can be done, to render the definitions..comprehensive and accurate. **1834** NEWMAN *Par. Serm.* I. xix. 293 This is the path which leads to death. **1848** PUSEY *Paroch. Serm.* I. iv. (1873) 71 All which we are, except sin, He became. **1875** JEVONS *Money* xx. 254 Let us suppose that there is a town which is able to support two banks. **1918** *Act 8 Geo. V* c. 5 §4 (2), If any person..makes ..any statement which is false.

b. As obj. of a prep., which usually precedes the relative as in 7 a.

c **1250** *Kent. Serm.* in *O.E. Misc.* 31 Alle þo sennen þurch wiche me liest þo luue of gode almichti. *a* **1300** *Cursor M.* 17288 + 74 þat friday was our leuedy day On wilk our lord slayn was. *c* **1386** CHAUCER *Sqr.'s T.* 17, 18 And of the secte of which þat he was born He kepte his lay to which þat he was sworn. *c* **1450** *Merlin* ii. 32, I moste go in to that contre ffro whiche these be come to fecche me. **1663** *Extr. St. Papers rel. Friends* Ser. II. (1911) 173 Many more thinges which the controuersy of the Lord is against. **1700** CONGREVE *Way of World* II. iii, The Guilt with which you wou'd asperse me. **1830** MACAULAY *Ess.*, *Moore's Life Byron* (1843) I. 336 They wrote concerning things the thought of which set their hearts on fire. **1839** DE LA BECHE *Rep. Geol. Cornw.*, etc. xiv. 459 A bar upon which the sea breaks occurs at the entrance of the Kingsbridge estuary.

¶ **c.** In anacoluthic construction, as in THAT *rel. pron.* 8. *rare.*

1729 LAW *Serious C.* ix, Direct your common actions to that end which they did.

9. Used of persons. Now only *dial.* except in speaking of people in a body, the ordinary word being *who* (objective *whom*) or (in sense b) *that*.

a. Introducing an additional statement, as in 7: thus sometimes = 'and he (they, etc.)'.

a **1300** *E.E. Psalter* cxlv[i]. 3 Traiste never..in men sones, in whilk hele es nane. *c* **1386** CHAUCER *Frankl. T.* 94 Hire freendes whiche þat knewe hir heuy thoght Conforten hire. —— *Shipman's T.* 153 Yow which I haue loued specially. **1447** BOKENHAM *Seyntys*, *Caecilia* 201 Lord Jhesu Cryst, wych al thyng knowyst. *a* **1450** *Knt. de la Tour* 65 The holy man whiche had pitee of his neuew, sorufull he yede into his chapell. *c* **1489** CAXTON *Sonnes of Aymon* xxvi. 547 Charlemagn toke a messager whiche he sente to reynawde. **1526** TINDALE *1 Cor.* xv. 57 Thankes be vnto God, whych hath geven vs victory. **1548–9** *Bk. Com. Prayer*, *Matins* 2nd Collect, O God, which art author of peace, and louer of concorde. **1610** SHAKS. *Temp.* I. ii. 342, I am all the Subiects that you haue, Which first was min owne King. **1692** O. WALKER *Grk. & Rom. Hist.* II. 310 He had nine Wives, all which he cast off successively. **1703** MOXON *Mech. Exerc.* 254 The Master-Bricklayer, or else his Foreman (which ought to be an ingenious Workman). *a* **1774** GOLDSM. tr. *Scarron's Com. Rom.* (1775) I. 200 A couple of women..one of which..leaned on the other's shoulder. **1837** DICKENS *Pickw.* xxxiv, Had been told it herself by Mrs. Mudberry which kept a mangle, and Mrs. Bunkin which clear-starched. **1899** *Scribner's Mag.* XXV. 114/1 His mother had ten children, of which he was the oldest.

b. Introducing a defining clause, as in 8.

1338 R. BRUNNE *Chron.* (1810) 224 Whan þei were inowe, on whilk þei mot afie. *c* **1386** CHAUCER *Pars. T.* ¶981 If ther be a confessour to which he may shriuen hym. **1483** *Acta Audit.* in *Acta Dom. Conc.* II. Introd. 106 Because he mariit without his consent quhilk is his ourlord. **1526** TINDALE *Matt.* v. 10 Blessed are they which suffre persecucion for rightewesnes sake. *a* **1548** HALL *Chron.*, *Hen. IV* 28 b, Entendyng to be reuenged on them whiche he sought for. **1600** SURFLET *Country Farm* VI. xxii. 803 The reader which is carefull of his health, may learne to make choise of such wine. **1605** SHAKS. *Lear* IV. vi. 215 Euery one heares that, which can distinguish sound. *a* **1703** BURKITT *On N.T.* Luke iv. 24 That Minister which prostitutes his Authority, frustrates the end of his Ministry. **1774** J. BRYANT *Mythol.* I. p. xiv, Those people which, I term Amonians. **1836** JAS. GRANT *Random Recoll. Ho. Lords* x. 224 Dugald Stewart, one of the greatest men which Scotland has produced. **1841** ALISON *Hist. Eur.* IX. lxix. 202 The wounded, which were carried past.., never failed to salute the Emperor. **1909** *Westm. Gaz.* 9 July 2/2 He is on the high road to get all the men for which he has asked.

c. Still regularly used of a person in reference to character, function, or the like, in which case the sense is really 7 or 8.

1645 HOWELL *Twelve Treat.* (1661) 233 The subject of this Discours were more proper to One of the long-Robe, which I am not. **1797** BP. WATSON *Apol. Christ.* vi. (ed. 6) 180 He put two maid servants, which were called ministers, to the torture. **1842** BORROW *Bible in Spain* (1843) II. x. 208 He was by no means the profound philologist which the notary had represented him to be. **1855** NEWMAN *Callista* xii. 108 He was not quite the craven..which she thought him.

10. Rarely used after an antecedent to which the ordinary correlative is *as*. **a.** after *same*: = THAT *rel. pron.* 4. **b.** after *so* or *such*: often equivalent to 'that it (he, etc.)'.

1340, etc. [see SAME A. 1 a]. *c* **1386** [see SUCH B. 12]. **1550** VERON *Godly Sayings* Ep. Ded. (1846) 19 Who is so dul,.. whiche..would not be moued too thankefulnes? **1596** 'L. PIOT' *Silvayn's Orator* 401 No man ought to bind himselfe vnto such couenants which hee cannot..accomplish. **1605** CAMDEN *Rem.*, *Names* 45 *Barvch*, *Hebr.* the same which Bennet, blessed. **1607** TOPSELL *Four-f. Beasts* 326 A kind of wilde horsse which hath hornes like a Hart, and therefore I take it to bee the same which is called Hypellaphus. **1709**, **1888** [see SUCH B. 12]. **1802–12** BENTHAM *Ration. Judic. Evid.* (1827) V. 321 There is not any argument so absurd, which is not daily received.

** as compound relative (or with ellipsis of antecedent).

† **11.** *pron.* That which, one which, something that: = WHAT C. 1, 3 a; also of a person, One who; *pl.* Those which or who. *Obs.*

c **1205** LAY. 2167 Al Albanakes folc folden i-scohten Buten whilc þat þer at-wond þurh wode burȝe. *c* **1430** *Syr Gener.* (Roxb.) 8837 He dremed of you which him affrayed. *c* **1470** HENRY *Wallace* XI. 321 Na men he tuk bot quhilk he hydder brocht. **1548** UDALL, etc. *Erasm. Par. John* vii. 31 Should he do greater thynges then whiche this man doeth? **1579** FULKE *Heskins' Parl.* 105 They interprete literally, which the doctors did write figuratiuely. **1599** SHAKS. *Much Ado* IV. ii. 83, I am a wise fellow, and which is more, an officer, and which is more, a housholder. **1643** DIGGES *Unlawf. Taking up Arms* 8, I shall desire one thing especially may be remembred, as which hath great influence upon all cases. **1654** Z. COKE *Logick* 16 An ambiguous word is which indistinctly signifieth things that in nature are divers. **1719** DE FOE *Crusoe* I. (Globe) 75, I had the loose Earth to carry out; and which was of more Importance, I had the Cieling to prop up.

12. In generalized sense (*adj.* or *pron.*), with or without qualifying adv. (*ever*, *so*, etc.): Any (person or thing) that, whatever; usually, now always, with limitation of reference, as in 3: = WHICHEVER 1; also (with *ever* or *soever*) = WHICHEVER 2.

OE. *swá hwilc* (*swá*), ME. *hwilch..so*, *se* (see WHICH-SO), north. *quilk sum*, were ultimately superseded by *which ever*, *soever* (see WHICHEVER, WHICHSOEVER).

a **890** *Charter* in *O.E. Texts* 451 Swa hwylc minra fædrenmeȝa swa ðæt sio. **900–30** *O.E. Chron.* an. 755 (Parker MS.), þæs cyninges þeȝnas..þider urnon swa hwelc swa þonne ȝearo wearþ. *c* **1000** *Ags. Ps.* (Th.) cxxxvii[i]. 4 [3] Swahwylce daȝa ic þe deorne ciȝe. *c* **1220** *Bestiary* 5 in *O.E. Misc.* 1 Bi wilc weie so he wile. *a* **1225** *Ancr. R.* 8 O hwuche wise se heo euer wule. **1297** R. GLOUC. (Rolls) 497 Brut bad corineus for to chese of ech contrei..ȝwich..him likede best. *a* **1300** *Cursor M.* 16373 Ask quilk sum yee will haue. *c* **1400** *Rule St. Benet* (prose) liii. 35 þabbesse..ouþir a-noþir nunne, wilke sam sho cumandis. **1464–5** in *Acts Parlt. Scot.* (1874) XII. 31/1 Thai personis..sall outhir entire þe kingis ward..or thane dewoide þe realmes..quhilk þat salbe seine maist expedient. **1523** LD. BERNERS *Froiss.* I. cccxli. 217/2 Whiche of them y^t^ euer should breake this peace.. shoulde rynne in the sentence of the pope. **1545** RAYNALDE *Byrth Mankynde* 134 Whiche of these wayes so euer it cume it shall be very good to bathe the chylde. **1602** SHAKS. *Ham.* IV. vii. 13 My Vertue or my Plague, be it either which. **1633** G. HERBERT *Temple*, *Home* ix, Nothing but drought and dearth,..Which way so-e're I look, I see. **1667** MILTON *P.L.* IV. 75 Which way I flie is Hell; my self am Hell. **1690** CHILD *Disc. Trade* (1698) 10 Which way ever we take our measures, to me it seems evident [etc.]. **1753** Johnson *Adventurer* No. 69 ⁋10 Which way soever he turned his thoughts, impossibility and absurdity arose in opposition. **1824** Scott *St. Ronan's* xvi, [He] lets a'things about the manse gang whilk gate they will. **1844** S. R. Maitland *Dark Ages* xv. 243 The table was so large that, place it which way they would, it could not be prevented from shewing above water. **1877** Tennyson *Harold* II. ii. 141 But wherefore is the wind, Which way soever the vane-arrow swing, Not ever fair for England?

*** **13. the which**. *arch.* **a.** as *adj.* = 6.

13.. *Cursor M.* 9434 (Gött.) þe first law was cald 'of kinde,'..þe toþer has 'possitiue' to name; þe whilk lawe was forbed Adam. Forto ete þat fruit. **1447–8** J. Shillingford *Lett.* (Camden 1871) 26 The whiche copies all y pray yow avysely to over rede. **1526** Tindale *Heb.* x. 10 By the which will we are sanctified. **1607** Topsell *Four-f. Beasts* 466 There was a lionesse which had whelpes in her den, the which den was obserued by a Beare, the which Beare on a day finding the den vnfortified,..entred..and slew the Lions whelpes. **1820** Byron *Mar. Fal.* note, Wks. (1842) 193/1 Finished copying August..1820; the which copying makes ten times the toil of composing. *a* **1850** Rossetti *Dante & Circle* I. (1874) 98 Of the which thing I bethought me to speak unto her.

b. as *pron.* (*a*) = 7.

1340–70 *Alex. & Dind.* 1127 Wo & wikkede paine, þe whiche þe heie godus haten. **1461** *Paston Lett.* II. 42 Desieryng to herre of ȝour welfar and good prosperite, the gwyche [*sic*] I pray God encresse. **1510** in Leadam *Sel. Cases Star Chamber* (Selden Soc.) II. 69 If the whiche shuld contynewe..your seid Towne..shall wexe empty. **1526** Tindale *Gal.* v. 21 The dedes of the flesshe..off the which I tell you before, as I have tolde you in tyme past. **1590** Spenser *F.Q.* I. i. 36 Sweet slombring deaw, the which to sleepe them biddes. **1682** Bunyan *Holy War* iii. (1905) 209 He told too, the which I had almost forgot, how Diabolus had put the Town of Mansoul into Arms. **1812** Cary *Dante, Parad.* XXII. 146 [This world] o'er the which we stride So fiercely. **1884** Tennyson *Becket* Prol., He holp the King to break down our castles, for the which I hate him.

(*b*) = 8.

a **1300** *Cursor M.* 146 How god bigan þe law hym gyfe þe quilk the Iuus in suld life. **1470–85** Malory *Arthur* XX. vii. 809, I told hym the peryls the which ben now fallen. **1526** Tindale *Acts* xxvi. 16 To make the..a witnes both off the thynges which thou hast sene and off tho thynges in the which I will apere vnto the. **1611** *Bible* James ii. 7 Doe not they blaspheme that worthy Name, by the which ye are called?

†**c.** as compound relative: = 11. Also qualified by *soever*: = 12. *Obs.*

1523 Ld. Berners *Froiss.* I. xx. 11/2, I knowe y^{t} the most worthy..knight of my realme shall acheue for me, the whyche I coulde neuer attayne vnto. **1551** Robinson tr. *More's Utopia* I. (1895) 89 For there is no waye so proffytable..as the whiche hath a shewe and coloure of iustice. **1581** J. Bell *Haddon's Answ. Osor.* 67 We follow not your fayth, as the which we have tasted to bee..most detestable. **1660** Heylin *Hist. Quinquart.* II. 7 To put his hunting spear amongst them, and the which of them soever should lay hold upon it, should be..drawn out of the water.

†**d.** Of persons: = 9.

1338 R. Brunne *Chron.* (1810) 52 Emme þe quene..of þe whilk was born Alfred & Edward. *c* **1386** Chaucer *Frankl. T.* 452 This Briton clerk hym asked of felawes The whiche þat he had knowe in olde dawes. **1470–85** Malory *Arthur* I. xviii. 64 Kynge Ryence of North walys the whiche was a myghty man of men. *c* **1500** *Lancelot* 184 The metire and the cuning..Quhilk I submyt to the correccioune Of yaim the quhich that is discret & wys. **1567** *Gude & Godlie B.* (S.T.S.) 172 Geue Christ, the quhilk hes me redrest, Be on my syde. **1596** Shaks. *1 Hen. IV*, II. i. 78 There are other Troians that y^{u} dream'st not of, the which (for sport sake) are content to doe the Profession some grace. **1606** G. W[oodcocke] *Hist. Ivstine* XXIII. 85 He the which was Lord of infinit riches to daie, was scarce maister of any to morrow.

**** Peculiar constructions. (See also 7 d, 8 c.)

14. a. (as *pron.* or *adj.*) With pleonastic personal pronoun or equivalent in the latter part of the relative clause, referring to the antecedent, *which* thus serving merely to link the clauses together: (*a*) with the pers. pron. (or the antecedent noun repeated) as subj. or obj. to a verb (principal or subordinate) in the relative clause, which is usually complex; (*b*) with genitive of pers. pron. (or equivalent, as *thereof*), *which* together with this being equivalent to the genitive of the relative (*whose*, *of which*): cf. that *rel. pron.* 9.

(*a*) *c* **1374** Chaucer *Troylus* II. 654 Þis is he, which þat myn vncle swereth he mot be ded. **1449** *Paston Lett.* I. 84 Yowr wurschupfull ustate, the whyche All myghte God mayntayne hyt. **1481** *Cov. Leet Bk.* 493 Which yf it so be, we haue gret cause of displeasure. **1526** Tindale *John* xxi. 25 There are also many other thynges which Jesus did, the which yff they shulde be written every won, I suppose [etc.]. **1589** Puttenham *Engl. Poesie* III. iv. (Arb.) 159 Ye finde these words, *penetrate*, *penetrable*, *indignitie*, which I cannot see how we may spare them. **1655** Fuller *Ch. Hist.* IX. vi. §27. 175 A Schedule containing his heresies, (which what they were may be collected by that which ensueth). **1690** Locke *Govt.* II. v. §42 (1694) 196 Provisions..which how much they exceed the other in value,..he will then see. **1726** Shelvocke *Voy. round World* Pref. p. vii, Scandalous and unjust Aspersions..which, how far I deserve them, I shall leave to the candid opinion of every unprejudiced Reader. **1768** Sterne *Sent. Journ.* II. *Fragment*, The history of myself, which, I could not die in peace unless I left it as a legacy to the world.

(*b*) *c* **1374** Chaucer *Troylus* II. 318 Þe kynges dere sone,..which alwey for to do wel is his wone. **1470–85** Malory *Arthur* XVII. xi. 705 Ther is in this Castel a gentylwoman whiche we and this castel is hers. *c* **1530** Ld. Berners *Arth. Lyt. Bryt.* (1814) 270 To do many thynges, the whyche the hurte therof lyghteth on theyr owne neckes. **1622** Mabbe tr. *Aleman's Guzman d'Alf.* II. 164 Take away..mens credits, and estates.., which lies not afterwards in their power to make restitution thereof. **1721** Bradley *Philos. Acc. Wks. Nat.* 90 Bulbous-rooted Plants, which when the Leaves of them decay, a new framed Root..supplies their Loss.

¶**b.** Hence, in vulgar use, without any antecedent, as a mere connective or introductory particle.

1723 Swift *Mary the Cook-Maid's Let.* 13 Which, and I am sure I have been his servant four years since October, And he never call'd me worse than sweetheart, drunk or sober. **1862** Thackeray *Philip* xvi, 'That noble young fellow', says my general... Which noble his conduct I own it has been. **1870** Bret Harte *Truthful James, Answ. to Let.* viii, Which I have a small favor to ask you, As concerns a bull-pup, which the same,—If the duty would not overtask you,—You would please to procure for me, game. **1905** *Daily Chron.* 21 Oct. 4/7 If anything 'appens to you—which God be between you and 'arm—I'll look after the kids.

¶**15.** In sylleptic construction, e.g. as obj. of two different verbs, or of a prep. and a verb, or as obj. of one verb and subj. of another; giving the effect of ellipsis of a personal pronoun (*it*, *them*).

1687 Wood *Life* (O.H.S.) III. 238 Dr. Dolbein..did read much of his sermon before the king..which the king telling him of, he never after did. *a* **1697** Horneck *Gt. Law Consid.* v. (1702) 302 To see me roll Sisyphus his Stone, which when I have brought to such a pitch, rolls down again. **1741** *Johnson's Debates* (1787) I. 390 A quality..which, if we could obtain, would add nothing to our honour. **1796** Eliza Hamilton *Lett. Hindoo Rajah* (1811) II. 271 They still retained an authority over his mind, at which, though his pride revolted, his understanding could not conquer. **1818** H. F. Clinton *Lit. Rem.* (1854) 24 These were works which, though I often inspected, I did not accurately study.

16. Preceded by *and*. **a.** in regular construction, *and* connecting two relative clauses, or an adjectival phrase and a relative clause, qualifying the same sb.

1579–80 North *Plutarch, J. Cæsar* (1595) 771 An army vnuincible, & which they could not possibly withstand. **1668** Dryden *Dram. Poesy* Ess. 1900 I. 78 We have many plays of ours as regular as any of theirs, and which, besides, have more variety of plot and characters. **1779** Johnson *L.P., Addison* (1868) 225 Two books yet celebrated..for purity and elegance, and which, if they are now less read, are neglected only because [etc.]. **1804–6** Syd. Smith *Mor. Philos.* (1850) 284 The habit of contradicting, into which young men..are apt to fall; and which is a habit extremely injurious to the powers of the understanding. **1810** Southey *Ess.* (1832) I. 40 The subject..was one of great difficulty and which required very serious consideration. **1876** Ruskin *Fors Clav.* lxx. VI. 315 If the dog have the good fortune to find a master, he has a possession..better than bones; and which, indeed, he will..leave, not his meat only, but his life for.

¶**b.** in erroneous or illogical use, either *and* or *which* being superfluous.

1606 G. W[oodcocke] *Hist. Ivstine* etc. L13, Galeaze..who had conquered a great part of Italy, and which inheritance discended to his Nephews. **1608** Topsell *Serpents* 288 His forefeet being like hands, are forked and twisted very strong, & with which it fighteth and taketh his prey. **1748** G. White in *Jrnl. Sacred Lit.* (1863) July 299 For the proper return to virtue and Good-works is Honour, & Love; this is their Due, and which ought to be rendered to them by all people. **1796** Mrs. Inchbald *Nature & Art* xvi. (1820) 42 The dean had just published a pamphlet in his own name, and in which that of his friend the bishop was only mentioned with thanks for hints. **1848** W. Templeton *Locomot. Eng.* (ed. 2) 71 A recent occurrence..seems..to have established the fact of steam being highly charged with electricity, and which may..be the means of increasing our knowledge [etc.]. **1861** Dasent *Burnt Njal* I. p. lviii, Every temple must contain a ring of at least two ounces in weight, and which the priest was to bear on his arm.

'which-a-way, *pron. U.S. colloq.* and *dial.* [Cf. which *a.* and *pron.* B. 12; *every which way* s.v. every *a.* 1 f.] Which way, in what direction. Cf. that-a-way *adv.*

1909 *Dialect Notes* III. 381 *Which-a-way*,..which way. **1938** M. K. Rawlings *Yearling* i. 13 Which-a-way will we begin huntin' him? **1968** O. Spann in P. Oliver *Screening Blues* iii. 125 Well, you know I'm so mad this morning, don't know whichaway to go.

which(ch)e, var. whitch *Obs.*, chest.

whichever (hwɪtʃ'ɛvə(r)), *a.* and *pron.* [Orig. two words, which and ever *adv.* 8 e.]

1. As compound relative: Any or either (of a definite set of persons or things, expresssed or implied) that...; that one (or those) who or which (with implication that it is unknown or undetermined which). †Formerly also without restriction to a definite set: = whatever 2.

Often following, and in apposition with, a pair or set of alternatives connected by *or*; the construction is then app. identical with that in 2, but is really different, and distinguished by intonation.

1388 Wyclif *Ps.* i. 3 Alle thingis which euere [*first vers.* what euere] he schal do schulen haue prosperite. **1418** in *Engl. Gilds* 445 Þat the bretheren and susteren..ȝerely chese on Alderman and Maistres,..qwicheuer [hem] thinketh most best. *c* **1449** Pecock *Repr.* I. xix. 112 He..allowith which euer of thilk weies and meenis be take. **1754** in *Nairne Peerage Evid.* (1874) 48 Upon their attaining their respective ages of eighteen years compleat or their being lawfully married whichever of these events should first happen. **1802** Maria Edgeworth *Moral T., Forester* xi, At a walk, trot, or gallop, whichever you please. **1844** Alb. Smith *Adv. Mr. Ledbury* xlii, They were..permitted to go whichever way they chose. **1872** Black *Adv. Phaeton* x. 145 To dinner—or supper, whichever it ought to be called. **1880** Hardy *Trumpet-Major* I. ix. 178 Whichever of us she likes best, he shall take her home. **1911** *Act 1 & 2 Geo. V* c. 46 §16 (1) Copyright shall subsist during the life of the author who first dies and for a term of fifty years after his death, or during the life of the author who dies last, whichever period is the longer. **1919** G. B. Shaw *Inca of Perusalem* in *Heartbreak House* 205 The Inca is to come and look at me, and pick out whichever of his sons he thinks will suit.

2. Introducing a qualifying dependent clause: Whether one or another (of a definite set); no matter which.

1690 Locke *Hum. Und.* II. xvii. §3 Which-ever [*ed.* 1714 Whichsoever] of these he takes, and how often soever he doubles..it, he finds [etc.]. **1704** Swift *Batt. Bks.* Misc. (1711) 226 Both Sides hang out their Trophies too, which ever comes by the worst. **1769** *Junius Lett.* xxiii. (1788) 135 Whichever way he flies, the Hue and Cry of the country pursues him. **1847** De Quincey *Joan of Arc* Wks. 1890 V. 390 On whichever side of the border chance had thrown Joanna, the same love to France would have been nurtured. **1856** Merivale *Rom. Emp.* xlii. V. 29 To whichever of the two camps..he should repair, his own jealous nature feared to awaken the jealousy of the other. **1882** Besant *All Sorts* xxviii, In politics you are used as the counters of a game... You get nothing, whichever side is in.

†**'which-like**, *a. Obs.* $rare^{-1}$. [f. which + like *a.*, after *such-like*.] Of which kind.

1641 Sanderson *Sermons* (1681) II. 4 By long accustoming themselves to which-like outward observances, they had almost lost the vigor and soul of true religion.

'which-so, *pron. arch.* [= which and so *adv.* 17 d.] †**a.** Whoever, whatever. **b.** Whichever.

c **1230** *Hali Meid.* 26 Hwuch-se wule beon of þe lut of his leoueste freond. *Ibid.* 45 Beo he cangun oðer crupel, beo he hwuch-se he eauer beo. **1297** R. Glouc. (Rolls) 771 He is kniȝtes echone, Vor coust binome him, bote an vif men one, Wuche so hii were to serui him. *a* **1325** *MS. Rawl. B. 520* lf. 31 Wuche so a uinden þer of gulti, a sullen punissen hoem. **1890** W. Morris in *Engl. Illustr. Mag.* June 695 Let the Hoary One..carry me to life or death, which-so he will.

whichso'ever, *pron. arch.* [f. which: see soever.]

1. = whichever 1.

c **1450** *Godstow Reg.* 532 To the said Alisaundre and molde his wyf and to ther heires or ther assignes or whom-so-euer or which-so-euer and whan-so-euer he wolde yeve bequeth selle or assigne hit. **1795** Washington *Let.* Writ. 1892 XIII. 65 To go to whichsoever [side] their interest, convenience, or inclination, might prompt them. *a* **1843** Southey *Cid* II. xiv, Saying that to whichsoever God should give the victory, to him also would he give up the kingdom. **1862** Johns *Brit. Birds* 235 Hunting..for whichsoever article of their diet happens to be in season.

2. = whichever 2.

a **1533** Ld. Berners *Huon* xxi. 64 Whiche so euer way ye take, it shall not be without me. **1691** T. H[ale] *Acc. New Invent.* f9, [The] Proposal of an obvious..Remedy to the said Evil, to whichsoever of the supposed Causes the same should be found imputable. **1714** [see quot. 1690 s.v. whichever 2]. **1769** Robertson *Chas. V* x. III. 248 Whichsoever of these authors an intelligent person takes for his guide.., he must discover [etc.]. **1828** Scott *Tales of Grandfather* Ser. I. (ed. 6) II. 274 To whichsoever he might attach himself, he was sure to become an object of hatred and suspicion to the other. **1853** Dickens *Repr. Pieces, Noble Savage*, Yielding to whichsoever of these agreeable eccentricities, he is a savage. **1853** —— *Bleak Ho.* x, With whichsoever of the many tongues of Rumour this frothy report originated, it..never reached..the ears of young Snagsby.

'whichway(s, *adv.* Chiefly *U.S.* = *every which way* s.v. every *a.* 1 f. Often prec. by *all*.

1961 in Webster, Leaving her towel and brush and comb lying whichway. **1968** 'J. Welcome' *Hell is where you find It* xiv. 166 He told me they [*sc.* drugs] took everyone all whichways. If you'd ever had a drink or two before, you want a lot more where you were on the pills kick—sometimes. **1975** 'Miss Read' *Battles at Thrush Green* i. 16 What chance is there of pushin' a mower up these 'ere paths with the graves all going which-way? *Ibid.* xix. 223 He was on a bike far too big for him—sawing away he was, wobbling all whichways. **1978** *People's Friend* 13 May 19/1 She pictured the scene and winced at the idea of Gregory seeing her without make-up, her hair all-which-way from the steam.

†**whick**, *v. Obs. rare.* [Imitative.] *intr.* To squeak, as a pig.

a **1693** *Urquhart's Rabelais* III. xiii. 107 The..whicking of Pigs, gushing of Hogs.

whick(e, etc.: see quick, etc.; wick *a.*[2]

whicker ('hwɪkə(r)), *v. dial.* and *U.S.* Also 9 **wicker, whecker, whihher**. [Imitative. Cf. *nicker*, *snicker*, and MHG. *wiheren* (G. *wiehern*).]

1. *intr.* To utter a half-suppressed laugh; to snigger, titter.

a **1656** Ussher *Ann.* VI. (1658) 284 Having never seen the like done before, he fell a whickering. *c* **1730** Haynes *Dorset. Voc.* in *N. & Q.* 6th Ser. (1883) VIII. 45/2 To *whicker*, to laugh. **1808** Jamieson, *Whihher*,..to titter. **1891** Hardy *Tess* l, The green-spangled fairies that 'whickered' at you as you passed.

2. Of a horse: To whinny; also of a sheep or goat, to bleat, of a dog, to whine, etc.

1753 J. Poulter *Discoveries* (ed. 5) 7 The Horse, as soon as the others past began to whicker, so that we were obliged to gag him. **1808** Jamieson, *Whihher*..to *wicker*, to neigh or whinny. **1825** Jennings *Obs. Dial. W. Eng.*, To *Whecker*,..to neigh. **1888** Elworthy *W. Somerset Word-bk.* s.v. *Wickery*. **1893** Kipling *Many Invent.* 215 The mare whickered. **1912** Masefield *Widow in Bye St.* VI. xxxii, The wall-top grasses whickered in the breeze.

3. To make a sound as of something hurtling through or beating the air.

1926 *Spectator* 28 Aug. 313/2 Bid Jove send down a thunderbolt to whicker through the sky. **1965** G. Maxwell *House of Elrig* xiii. 167 My aunt's black-and-white nun pigeons whickered past my window and drank at the bird-table.

So **'whicker** *sb.*, a snigger; a whinny; also, the sound of something beating the air; hence **'whickering** *vbl. sb.* and *ppl. a.*

1882 *Harper's Mag.* June 53 The whicker of old Molly at the foot of the lane, and the answer of the colt in the lot. **1899** Somerville & 'Ross' *Some Experiences Irish R.M.* xi. 277 A pale, yellow foal sprinted up beside us, with shrill whickerings of joy. **1909** 'O. Henry' *Roads of Destiny* ix, Through the intense silence, he heard the whicker of a horse. **1920** J. Masefield *Right Royal* 73 Far over his head with a whicker of wings Came a wisp of five snipe from a field full of springs. **1937** E. Sitwell *I live under Black Sun* i. iii. 48 The door of her room..opened with a dark strawy noise like the wickering voice of a bear. **1940** H. Spring *Fame is Spur* i. 11 And so great was the silence that the whickering of banners could be heard. **1965** G. Maxwell *House of Elrig* ii. 27 Black rock cliffs with deep mysterious caves full of the whicker of rock-pigeons' wings.

whid (hwɪd), *sb.*[1] Forms: 6 whydd, 7– whid, 9 *Sc.* whud. [Origin uncertain. That it is a dial. variant of OE. *cwide* speech (otherwise not represented in the language) is possible, but the absence of parallels is a serious objection. The sense-development is remarkably similar to that of yed.]

1. A word. (Usually in *pl.*). *Thieves' cant.*

1567 Harman *Caveat* (1869) 84 To cutte bene whydds, to speake or geue good wordes, to cutte quyre whyddes, to geue euell wordes or euell language. *Ibid.* 86 Stowe your bene, cofe, and cut benat whydds. **1673** R. Head *Canting Acad.* 49 Be wary. Stow your whids. **1728** [De Foe] *Street Robberies Consider'd* 34 Plant the Whids, take Care what you say. **1821** Scott *Kenilw.* x, The swaggering vein will not pass here, you must cut boon whids. **1861** Reade *Cloister & H.* lv, I pray Heaven thou mayest prove to paint better than thou cuttest whids.

2. A lie, fib, falsehood; an exaggerated story. *Sc.*

1791 Burns *Death & Dr. Hornbook* i, Ev'n Ministers, they hae been kenn'd,.. A rousing whid, at times, to vend, And nail't wi' Scripture. **1863** M. Dods *Early Lett.* (1910) 330 Your πρῶτον ψεῦδος, *i.e.* Your fundamental whid. **1894** Crockett *Raiders* xlvi, Kennedy thinks no more o' tellin' a whud (lie) than o' slappin' a cleg that nips him on the hench bane.

3. A dispute, quarrel. *dial.*

1847 Halliwell, *Whid*, a dispute; a quarrel. *East.*

whid (hwɪd), *sb.*[2] *Sc.* Forms: 6 quhyd, 8–9 whid, whud. [? a. ON. *hviða* squall = OE. *hwiþa*.]

†**1.** A squall, blast of wind. *Obs.*

1590 Burel in Watson *Coll. Sc. Poems* ii. (1709) 24 The wind, with mony quhyd, Maist bitterly thair blew.

2. A quick noiseless movement, esp. of a hare. *in* or *wi' a whid*, in a trice.

1719 Ramsay *2nd Answ. to Hamilton* i, Wi' a Whid,.. She'll rin red-wood. **1785** Burns *To W. S*******n* xii, Jinkin hares, in amorous whids. **1788** R. Galloway *Glasgow Fair* ii. vi, He lent a blow at Jonny's eye, That rais'd it, in a whid.

whid (hwɪd), *v.*[1] *Sc.* Also whud. [f. whid *sb.*[1]] *intr.* To talk cant; to lie, fib. Chiefly in *vbl. sb.* and *ppl. a.*

1823 Egan *Grose's Dict. Vulgar T.*, *Whidding*, talking cant. *Scotch cant.* **1881** Walford *Dick Netherby* v, A fair-farrend, whuddin' youngster. **1891** 'H. Haliburton' *Ochil Idylls* 90 Whiddin's an airt.

whid (hwɪd), *v.*[2] *Sc.* Also 9 whud. [f. whid *sb.*[2]] *intr.* To move nimbly without noise.

c **1730** Ramsay *1st Answ. to Somerville* 94 You range After the fox or whidding hare. **1790** Burns *Elegy on Capt. M——H——* vi, Ye maukins whiddin thro' the glade. **1816** Scott *Bl. Dwarf* iii, Ye see yon other light that's gaun whiddin' back and forrit.

whidah, whydah ('hwɪdə). [Name of a town in Dahomey, West Africa. *Whidah bird* is an alteration of widow-bird, q.v., due to association with this as one of the habitats of these birds.]

1. In full ***whidah-bird***, etc.: = widow-bird.

1783 Latham *Gen. Synopsis Birds* II. i. 178 Whidah B[unting]... Rather less than a Hedge Sparrow. *Ibid.*, *note*, Whidah Bird. **1872** Livingstone *Last Jrnls.* 19 June (1874) II. vii. 199 The young whydah birds crouch closely together at night for heat. *Ibid.*, Whydahs, though full fledged, still gladly take a feed from their dam. **1896** G. E. Shelley *For. Finches* 273 The Whydahs..form a natural group of Finches, nearly allied to the Weavers.

2. whidaw goat, a West-African species of goat, *Capra reversa*. **w. thrush**, *Pholidauges leucogaster*.

1781 Pennant *Hist. Quadrup.* I. 57 Goat..Whidaw. Capra reversa... From Juda or Whidaw, in Africa. A small kind: the horns short, smooth, and turn a little forwards. **1783** Latham *Gen. Synopsis Birds* II. i. 58 Whidah Thr[ush]. Size of a Lark, or rather less:..the plumage in general is violet, excepting the belly, which is white... Inhabits the kingdom of Whidah, in Africa.

whiddelynge, obs. f. whitling.

whidder: see whether, whither *sb.* and *v.*

whiddle ('hwɪd(ə)l), *v. slang.* Also 8 whidle, whidel, widdle. [? f. whid *sb.*[1]] *intr.* **a.** To divulge a secret, turn informer, 'peach'. **b.** See quot. 1725. Hence **'whiddler**.

c **1661** *Marq. Argyle's Last Will* in *Harl. Misc.* (1746) VIII. 28/1, I understand..he hath made so large a Progress in Discovering, that he can pay it now to himself—The Devil was in me to suffer such a pitiful Fellow to whiddle before me. *a* **1700** B. E. *Dict. Cant. Crew*, *Whiddler*, a Peacher (or rather Impeacher) of his Gang. **1725** *New Cant. Dict.*, *To Whiddle*, to enter into a Parley, to compound with, or take off by a Bribe. **1756** J. Cox *Narr. Thief-takers* 66 The Prisoner..then swore he wished he had cut off his Head, for then he would not have whidelled again. **1781** G. Parker *View Soc.* ii. 133 About Darkey [*i.e.* twilight], or when Oliver don't widdle [*footn.* The Moon not up]. **1812** J. H. Vaux *Flash Dict.* s.v., Don't you whiddle about so and so, that is, don't mention it.

whider, whie, whieale, whiel, whiet, whieu, whiew, whife: see whither, quey, why, wheel, quiet, white, whew, wife.

Whieldon ('hwiːldən). The name of Thomas *Whieldon* (1719–95), Staffordshire potter, used *attrib.* to designate the kind of coloured earthenware made in his factory (founded 1740). Also *Comb.*, as ***Whieldon-type*** adj., resembling this ware.

1869 C. Schreiber *Jrnl.* 1 Oct. (1911) I. 42 One Wheildon [*sic*] Ware plate. **1900** F. Litchfield *Pott. & Porc.* vii. 317 Whieldon ware is peculiarly light and the articles well potted. **1929** H. Read *Staffordshire Pottery Figures* Pl. 14 (*caption*) The term 'Whieldon type' [is used] when the figure depends entirely for its decoration on coloured glazes. **1942** *Burlington Mag.* Oct. 260/1 Most dangerous are the increasingly skilful fakes of Astbury and Whieldon figures. **1968** *Canad. Antiques Collector* July 13/1 What is Whieldon Ware? This is a term referring to all types of ware of a mottled, cloudy or splashed character. **1978** *Times* 28 Jan. 12/6 (*caption*) A Whieldon-type teapot and cover, c. 1765. **1983** *Country Life* 2 Dec. (Suppl.) 72/2 A Whieldon pottery horse, decorated in underglaze colours of green, yellow and brown.

whiff (hwɪf), *sb.*[1] Also 6–7 whiffe, 8–9 whif. [? Partly an alteration of ME. weffe (= offensive odour or taste, vapour, hoisted signal), partly a new onomatopœic formation. The senses are in part identical with those of waff *sb.* and waft *sb.*[1]]

I. 1. a. A slight puff or gust of wind, a breath.

1591 Sylvester *Du Bartas* i. iv. 334 The Winde..Whirls with a whiff the sails of swelling clout. **1602** Shaks. *Ham.* ii. ii. 495 With the whiffe and winde of his fell Sword, Th' vnnerued Father fals. **1610** Holland *Camden's Brit.* i. 195 Their ensignes..Waue to and fro with whiffes of wind. **1786** in *Mme. D'Arblay's Diary* 6 Oct., A whiff [of wind] from the King's stairs, enough to blow you half a mile off! **1838** Dickens *O. Twist* xxxix, Give her a whiff of fresh air with the bellows, Charley.

b. *transf.* and *fig.* A 'breath', 'blast', 'burst'.

1644 Milton *Areop.* 24 That the whiffe of every new pamphlet should stagger them out of their catechism. **1649** —— *Eikon.* xxvii. 222 Deny'd and repuls'd by the single whiffe of a negative. **1766** Sterne *Tr. Shandy* IX. ii, A whiff of military pride had puffed out his shirt at the wrist. **1817** Byron *Beppo* liii, They had their little differences, too; Those jealous whiffs, which never any change meant. **1851** Brimley *Ess.*, *Wordsw.* (1858) 174 The Quarterly Review.. issued a mild whiff of qualified approval. **1878** Hardy *Ret. Native* v. ix, There seemed to be not a whiff of life left in either of the bodies. **1883** Stevenson *Treas. Isl.* xx, This little whiff of temper seemed to cool Silver down. **1912** *Times Lit. Suppl.* 13 June 241/1 Factories..brought with them the first whiff of cotton-spinning democracy.

c. A slight attack, 'touch'; = waff *sb.* 3 b.

1837 Carlyle *New Lett.* (1904) I. 58, I have twice had flying whiffs of cold.

d. *U.S. slang.* A miss, a failure to hit (a ball).

1952 *N.Y. Herald Tribune* 15 May 21/6 On the first tee he took a careful stance and then fanned the air four times. After the fourth whiff he growled, 'This is the hardest course I ever played.'

2. a. An inhalation of tobacco-smoke; smoke so inhaled; in early use also, †the 'taking' of tobacco, smoking (***to take the whiff***, to smoke).

1599 B. Jonson *Ev. Man out of Hum.* Dram. pers., His chiefe exercises are taking the Whiffe, squiring a Cocatrice, and making priuy searches for Imparters. *Ibid.* iii. i, *Sog.*.. Doe you professe these sleights in Tabacco?.. *Punt.* But you cannot bring him to the Whiffe so soon? **1600** Marston, etc. *Jack Drums Entert.* i. (1601) B 3, Iust like a whiffe of Tabacco, no sooner in at the mouth, but out at the nose. **1603–37** Breton *Poste with Packet Lett.* Wks. (Grosart) II. 35/2 Tobacco is like to grow a great commoditie, for there is not an Ostler nor a Tapster, but will be at his whiffe or two. **1607** Walkington *Optic Glass* ix. 54 Tobacco..must needs be very pernicious in regard of the immoderate & too ordinary whiffe. **1690** J. Stevens *Jrnl.* (1912) 139 Seven or eight will gather to the smoking of a pipe and each taking two or three whiffs gives it to his neighbour. *a* **1718** Prior *Epigr.*, *Frank carves very ill*, Four Pipes after Dinner he constantly smokes; And seasons his Whifs with impertinent Jokes. **1742** Fielding *J. Andrews* iv. xvi, Gaffer Andrews.. complained bitterly that he wanted his pipe, not having had a whiff that morning. **1812** Heyne *Tracts on India* (1814) 392 The Malays..roll a little tobacco in a small piece of plantain leaf,..and after it is lighted, take only a few whifs, and throw the rest away. **1841** Dickens *Barn. Rudge* i, He had taken his pipe from his lips, after a very long whiff to keep it alight. **1886** G. R. Sims *Ring o' Bells* Prol. i He took a couple of whiffs at his long churchwarden.

†**b.** A sip or draught of liquor. *Obs.*

1605 *Tryall Chev.* iii. i. E j b, I had but a whiffe or two; for I was passing dry. **1624** Bp. Hall *True Peacemaker* Wks. (1625) 539 In beds of lust, chests of Mammon, whiffes and draughts of intoxication. **1653** Urquhart *Rabelais* i. vi. 31, I will yet go drink one whiffe more [orig. *encores quelque veguade*].

3. a. A wave or waft of (usually unsavoury) odour.

1668 R. L'Estrange *Vis. Quev.* (1708) 137 The Poysonous Whiffs she sends from her Toes and Arm-Pits. **1731** Swift *Strephon & Chloe* 12 No noisom Whiffs or sweaty Streams..Could from her taintless body flow. **1774** Burke *Sp. Amer. Tax.* Wks. 1842 I. 172 To whom a single whiff of incense withheld gave much greater pain, than he received delight in the clouds of it. **1784** Cowper *Task* iv. 469 A whiff Of stale debauch. **1844** Dickens *Mart. Chuz.* v, That whiff of russia leather, too, and all those rows on rows of volumes, neatly ranged within. **1872** Black *Adv. Phaeton* xiii. 182 A whiff of honeysuckle was borne to us as we passed. **1884** Mrs. C. Praed *Zero* i, Is not the very name Monte Carlo like a whiff of some intoxicating draught?

b. *fig.* Flavour, savour.

1872 Morley *Voltaire* vii. 321 Apologising for some whiffs of orthodoxy which Voltaire scented. **1895** Rashdall *Univ. Eur.* II. 514 *note*, There is a whiff of the Renaissance about the very words of the Statute.

4. a. A puff of smoke or vapour, esp. of tobacco-smoke.

1714 Addison *Spect.* No. 568 ⁋ 1, I lighted it at a little wax candle..and, after having thrown in two or three whiffs among them, sat down. **1752** *Lady's Curiosity* 10 He.. knocks you down with a whiff, or a f—, if you ask for an argument. **1839** Longf. *Wreck of Hesperus* 19 The skipper he blew a whiff from his pipe. **1875** Howells *Foregone Conclus.* vii, The..heaven, in whose vast blue depths hung light whiffs of pinkish cloud.

b. *transf.* A cigarette or small cigar.

1881 *Instr. Census Clerks* (1885) 60 Cheroot Maker... Whiff Maker. **1896** *Daily News* 9 Mar. 5/4 The popular form of these daintily-got-up cigarettes is a 'whiff' of about two inches in length.

5. a. A puffing or whistling sound, as of a puff or gust of wind through a small opening; a short or gentle whistle; hence freq. = whew (also as *int.*).

1712 Arbuthnot *John Bull* iv. i, Nic...pull'd out a Boat-swain's Whistle; upon the first Whiff, the Tradesmen came jumping into the Room. **1828** Lytton *Pelham* xxxi[i], Sir Willoughby..made..no other reply than a long whiff, and a 'Well, Russelton, dash my wig..but you're a queer fellow.' **1847** Tennyson *Princess* Concl. 58 But yonder, whiff! there comes a sudden heat. **1854** R. S. Surtees *Handley Cr.* ix, Now we read the 'Hercules' on the engine, and anon it pulls up with a whiff, a puff, and a whistle. **1869** Lowell *Cathedral* 74 Sunshine, whose quick charm..wiled the bluebird to his whiff of song. **1876** Bristowe *Theory & Pract. Med.* (1878) 387 A like whiff or blowing sound follows each sonorous expiratory shock of cough.

b. A discharge of shot or explosive.

1837 Carlyle *Fr. Rev.* III. vii. vii, Six years ago, this Whiff of Grapeshot was promised. **1870** *Routledge's Ev. Boy's Ann.* Feb. 90 He might clear the gangway for the boarders with a 'whiff' of this terrible projectile [*i.e.* grape-shot]. **1915** 'Ian Hay' *First Hundred Thou.* ii. xviii. 251 A whiff o' shrapnel.

6. ***in a whiff***: in a short time, in a jiffy. *dial.*

1800 M. Edgeworth *Parent's Assistant* (ed. 3) VI. 158 Lean on my arm, madam, and we'll have you in and at home in a whiff. **1825** Brockett *N.C. Gloss.* s.v., In a whiff, in a short time. **1888** *Lippincott's Mag.* Apr. 454 All this passed through his mind in a whiff.

II. 7. A flag hoisted as a signal.

Cf. waff *sb.* 1 b, waft *sb.*[1] 6, waif *sb.*[2] 2, weffe, whiffler[2] 3, whift *sb.* 2.

1693 Lyde *Retaking Ship* 20, I took a Sash from one of them,..and put it out for a Whiff. **1832** Marryat *N. Forster* xlviii, The stranger..hoisted a whiff, half-mast down.

III. 8. A light kind of outrigged boat for one sculler, used on the Thames.

1859 *Guardian* 13 Apr. 331/1 The accidental upsetting of a pleasure-boat, called a 'whiff', on the river Cherwell. **1875** H. R. Robertson *Life Upper Thames* 209 A funny is an open, out-rigged sculling-boat, having stem and stern alike, the keel falling away in a sloping curve from either end. A whiff resembles a funny in every point, except that the stern is upright, and not sloped away as the bows are. **1880** *Daily News* 2 Mar. 5/1 Every Etonian who has passed an examination in swimming may boat..in skiffs or whiffs, gigs and outriggers. **1910** *Encycl. Brit.* IV. 100/1 Whiff. Length. 20' to 23'. Beam. 1' 4" to 1' 6"... Whiff Gigs. 19' to 20'. 2' 8" to 2' 10".

whiff, *sb.*[2] [? Same word as prec.] A name for various flat-fishes or flounders, as the sail-fluke or mary-sole, *Rhombus megastoma*, the smear-dab, *Pleuronectes microcephalus*.

1713 Jago in *Ray's Synopsis Piscium* 163 Passer Cornubiensis asper, magno oris hiatu. A Whiff. **1836** Yarrell *Brit. Fishes* II. 251 The Whiff. The Carter, *Cornwall*. **1867** Smyth *Sailor's Word-bk.*, *Whiff*, the *Rhombus cardina*, a passable fish of the pleuronect genus. **1873** T. Gill *Catal. Fishes E. Coast N. Amer.* 17 Citharichthys microstomus... Whiff.

whiff, *v.*[1] [f. whiff *sb.*[1]]

1. a. *intr.* To blow with a whiff or slight blast; to move with or make the sound of this. Chiefly in *vbl. sb.* and *ppl. a.*

1591 Sylvester *Du Bartas* i. ii. 545 When through their green boughs whiffing winds do whirl With wanton puffs their waving locks to curl. **1608** *Ibid.* ii. iv. *Schism* 620 A sudden whirl-winde, with a whiffing Fire. *Ibid.*, *Decay* 652 The whiffing flashes of this Sword so quick. **1645** Z. Boyd *Holy Songs in Zion's Flowers* (1855) App. 12/2 Their head on neck could not abide, off chop't with whiffing steele. **1851** Walshe *Dis. Lungs* 93 The character of the murmurs is hollow, whiffing, and moderately metallic. **1866** J. MACGREGOR *Rob Roy on Baltic* x, The whiffing of the strong wings of the wild goose. **1890** *Daily News* 12 Dec. 3/1 A raw and biting breeze whiffing about his grey hairs.

b. *trans.* To utter with a whiff or puff of air.

1765 STERNE *Tr. Shandy* VIII. xxvi, Then whiffing out a sentimental heigh ho! **1889** 'MARK TWAIN' *Yankee Crt. K. Arth.* xxvi, They crossed themselves, and whiffed out a protective prayer or two.

2. a. *trans.* To drive or carry by or as by a whiff; to puff or blow *away*, etc.

1601 W. PERCY *Cuckqueanes & Cuck. Err.* I. ii. (Roxb.) 11, I take him by the sleeue,..bid him looke to himself, Then round as a Jugler's boxe, whiffe his vpper vestment, and away. *Ibid.* I. iii. 16 Neither keene knife, nor yet Thumbe, May whiff him by slit or by numbe. **1615** SYLVESTER *Job Triumph.* II. 395 How oft, as Straw before the winde, are They, And as the Chaff with Tempest whift away? **1620** B. JONSON *News from New World* Wks. (1641) 42 The smoake took him and whift him up into the Moone. **1657** FARINDON *Serm.* v. 108 That joy which is..raised as a Meteor out of dung and is whiffed up and down by every wind and breath. **1812** W. TENNANT *Anster F.* II. xii, John Frost..Whiff'd off the clouds that the pure blue conceal'd. **1837** CARLYLE *Fr. Rev.* I. v. ii, And then his 'sincere attachment', how was it scornfully whiffed aside! *Ibid.* vi, A rabble to be whiffed with grapeshot. **1916** *Blackw. Mag.* Jan. 59/1 Troops would not always remain in the open to be whiffed out of existence by shrapnel.

b. *intr.* To move with or as with a puff of air.

1686 GOAD *Celest. Bodies* I. xvi. 105 The Index hath whiffed round all the points of the Compass. **1889** STEVENSON *Master of Ballantrae* ii, I have sought to stay myself..against what looked to be a solid trunk, and the whole thing has whiffed away at my touch like a sheet of paper.

3. a. *trans.* To puff out tobacco-smoke from a pipe, etc.; hence, to smoke. (With the smoke or the pipe, etc. as object.) Also *fig.*

1616 R. C. *Times' Whistle* v. 2218 Every..skip-iacke now will have his pipe of smoke, And whiff it bravely till hee's like to choke. **1617** BRATHWAIT *Sol. Jov. Disput.* etc. 171 These smokers of our Age; they whiffe me [Time] out in fume. **1628** *Mad Pranks Robin Goodf.* (Percy Soc.) 34 She whift her pipe, she drunke her can. **1646** QUARLES *Judgem. & Mercy* Medit. 16 What pleasure tak'st thou in that breath, which draws and whiffs perpetuall fears? **1756** MRS. CALDERWOOD in *Coltness Collect.* (Maitland Cl.) 166 He put his pipe in the cheek next him, and whifed it in his face. **1859** MEREDITH *R. Feverel* xxii, Richard..found him furtively whiffing tobacco. **1867** *Good Cheer* 7 These formal toasts.. having been all drunk, the men whiffed their pipes.

b. *absol.* or *intr.*

1602 DEKKER *Satirom.* C4b, Morrow, Captaine Tucca, will you whiffe this morning? **1639** JUNIUS *Sin Stigmatized* 269 They are bound..to be powring in at their mouths, or whiffing out at their noses. **1713** TYLDESLEY *Diary* (1873) 88, I found honest Tho. Barton very harty and ffree, but the 2 Wadsworths only whiffed. **1714** tr. *Joutel's Jrnl. Voy. Mexico* (1719) 148 Then they made us all smoke round, and every one of them whiff'd in his Turn. **1862** H. A. KENNEDY *Waifs & Strays* 205 Luxuriously whiffing away at my after-breakfast cheroot.

†**4.** *trans.* To imbibe, drink (liquor). Also *fig.*

1609 DEKKER *Gull's Horn-bk.* iv. 18 Hee..that would striue to fashion his legges to his silke stockins, and his proud gate to his broad garters, let him whiffe downe these obseruations. **1650** TRAPP *Comm. Num.* vi. 20 The most generous wine in Lovain and Paris, is known by the name of *vinum theologicum*: the divines (those Sorbonists) do so whiffe it off. *a* **1693** *Urquhart's Rabelais* III. xvii. 141 She whiffed off a..good Draught.

5. a. To inhale, sniff; also *intr.* to smell, sniff.

1635 QUARLES *Embl.* IV. vii. (1718) 213 Let us both retire, And whiff the dainties of the fragrant field. **1646** —— *Sheph. Oracles* x. Wks. (Grosart) III. 231/1 Which like a Sun in this our Orbe, Whiffes up the Belgick fumes. **1854** R. S. SURTEES *Handley Cr.* lviii, The pack..now whiffing with curious nose round the hollies, and now trying up the rides. *Mod.* (*slang*), What a horrid smell! Can't you whiff it?

b. *intr.* To emit an unpleasant odour. *slang.*

1899 KIPLING *Stalky* iii. 79 Then she'll whiff. Golly, how she'll whiff!

6. *U.S. slang.* **a.** *intr.* Of a batter in Baseball or a golfer: to miss the ball. Cf. FAN *v.* 8b.

1913 *Wells Fargo Messenger* I. 93/2 When he has to line 'er out he does, but he doesn't whiff at random. **1926** *Amer. Speech* I. 369/2 He [*sc.* a baseball player] 'whiffs' when he fails to hit. **1942** BERREY & VAN DEN BARK *Amer. Thes. Slang* §677/34 *Miss the ball*,..whiff.

b. *trans.* = FAN *v.* 8a.

1914 R. LARDNER in *Sat. Even. Post* 7 Mar. 7/2, I whiffed eight men in five innings in Frisco yesterday. **1941** *Nebraska State Jrnl.* 20 June (*heading*), Hurler whiffs 20. **1951** in Wentworth & Flexner *Dict. Amer. Slang* (1960) 575/1 Vic Raschi whiffed twelve batters in gaining his 15th win of the year.

Hence '**whiffing** *vbl. sb.*[1] (also *attrib.*) and *ppl. a.*; also '**whiffer**, one who whiffs.

1591–1866 [see sense 1]. *c* **1614** Tobacco-whiffer [see TOBACCO 3]. **1632** LITHGOW *Trav.* x. 435 The Alehouse is their Church.., their singing of Psalmes the whiffing of Tobacco. **1811** *Sporting Mag.* XXXVIII. 191 Opening his tobacco-box, soon commenced his whiffing operation.

whiff, *v.*[2] *Angling.* [Perhaps same as prec.] *intr.* To angle for mackerel, etc. from a swiftly moving boat with a hand-line towing the bait near the surface. Hence '**whiffing** *vbl. sb.*[2] (also *attrib.*).

1836 YARRELL *Brit. Fishes* II. 172 Hand-line fishing for Pollacks is called whiffing. **1863** JOHNS *Home Walks* 164 We generally threw out our whiffing lines as we cruised about. **1886** *Globe* 22 July 3/1 When you 'whiff' at Scilly, you whiff for pollack.

whiffet ('hwɪfɪt). *U.S.* Also **whiffit, wiffet.** [? f. WHIFF *sb.*[1] + -ET[1].]

1. (Also ***whiffet dog.***) A small dog.

1801 *Olio* (Philad.) 41 (Thornton) Who heeds the Whiffit's bark, when tempests howl? **1848** *Ladies' Repository* VIII. 315 The best protection to a house, with a family in it that can be named—that is, a little, barking, noisy, cowardly, whiffet dog. **1879** J. BURROUGHS *Locusts & Wild Honey* 30 The king-bird will worry the hawk as a whiffet dog will worry a bear.

2. *transf.* An insignificant person; a whipper-snapper. *colloq.* (Cf. WHIFLING.)

1839 *Congress. Globe* Jan., App. 105/3 There was not a Whig whiffet in the country but could ask [etc.]. **1876** WHITMAN *Specimen Days* 1 Sept., Writ. 1902 IV. 157 This gusty-temper'd little whiffet, man. **1883** L. A. LAMBERT *Notes on Ingersoll* xxii. 200 We hold ourselves responsible to him, and to all the glib little whiffets of his shallow school.

¶The sense 'a little whiff or puff' given in Webster 1864 is not authenticated.

whiffle ('hwɪf(ə)l), *sb.* [f. WHIFF *sb.*[1] + -LE.]

†**1.** Something light or insignificant; a trifle.

1680 H. MORE *Apocal. Apoc.* 253 Such a childish trifle or sleight whiffle.

2. An act of whiffling; a slight blast of air; a veering *round.*

1842 in Gosse *Birds Jamaica* (1847) 366 At first two or three whiffles make darkened tracks on the glassy waters. **1870** MISS ALCOTT *Good Wives* xxi, Amy keeps me pointing due west most of the time, with only an occasional whiffle round to the south. **1909** BEGBIE *Cage* x, The whiffle in the air grew more distinct.

3. A soft sound as of gently moving air or water.

1972 F. FORD *Atush Inlet* i. 9 Their subdued cries could be heard faintly against the gentle whiffle of falling water. **1976** J. CROSBY *Snake* (1977) xxx. 179 She listened to..the soft whiffle of her breathing.

4. *Comb.*, as **whiffle-ball** *U.S.*, a light hollow ball used for playing a variety of baseball; also, a game played with such a ball; cf. WIFFLE; **whiffle-minded** *a.* (*U.K.* and *U.S. dial.*), changeable, fickle.

[**1931** *Official Gaz.* (U.S. Patent Office) 17 Nov. 573/2 *Whiffle.* For game apparatus of the type having ball receiving and discharging mechanism.] **1965** F. KNEBEL *Night of Camp David* xvii. 273 The boys of Saybrook were playing whiffle ball. **1970** *New Yorker* 11 July 20 Kids playing with whiffleballs and baseballs. **1976** WOODWARD & BERNSTEIN *Final Days* 242 He would get a whiffleball game going on the White House tennis court. **1980** *N.Y. Sunday News Mag.* 2 Mar. 12/2, I would chase the whiffleball across the street. **1985** T. BOYLE *Only Dead know Brooklyn* xvii. 133 Clusters of Puerto Ricans..swung plastic bats at whiffle balls. **1902** H. F. DAY *Pine Tree Ballads* 47 Hate to act so whiffle-minded, but my father used to say, 'Men would sometimes change opinions; mules would stick the same old way'. **1905** in *Eng. Dial. Dict.* VI. 456/1 'e's so w'iffle-minded—'e dunna know 'is own mind two minutes together.

whiffle ('hwɪf(ə)l), *v.*[1] Also 6 **wyffle**, 7 **whifle.** [f. WHIFF *v.*[1] + -LE. Cf. Flem. *weyfelen* 'vacillare' (Kilian).]

1. *intr.* To blow in puffs or slight gusts; hence, to veer or shift *about* (of the wind; hence, of a ship). Often *fig.* or in fig. context: To vacillate, to be variable or evasive. Now chiefly *dial.*

1568 [see WHIFFLING *ppl. a.*[1] 1]. **1671** R. BOHUN *Wind* 56 Near mountainous Islands, or shoares, they [*sc.* winds] whiffle up and down, and shift from one point of the Compasse to another. **1697** DAMPIER *Voy.* I. 413 The Wind had been whiffling about from one part of the Compass to another. **1699** *Ibid.* II. III. 61 If the Winds also whiffle about to the South. **1737** OZELL *Rabelais* III. xxxv. 236 *note*, A Man who is continually turning and whiffling about to all the Points of the Compass. **1768** TUCKER *Lt. Nat.* (1834) I. 155 Were we to give a full latitude to sympathy, we should whiffle about with every wind. **1801** *Spirit Publ. Jrnls.* IX. 370 She yaws and whiffles about like a weathercock. **1812** TENNANT *Anster F.* IV. liv, The whizzing wind..whiffling through the wooden tubes so small. **1840** [LADY BURY] *Hist. Flirt* xii, They whiffle about like a weathercock. **1854** MISS BAKER *Northampt. Gloss.* s.v., The wind whiffles about so. **1881** *Nation* (N.Y.) XXXII. 400 Who like a manly man, will not whiffle, or quibble, or evade. **1903** F. HARRISON in *Westm. Gaz.* 24 Nov. 1/3 If he finally whiffle round to tax foreign food.

2. *trans.* To blow or drive with or as with a puff of air. Often *fig.*

1641 TRAPP *Theol. Theol.* viii. 335 Whiffled and tossed too and fro with every wind of doctrine. **1655** tr. *Sorel's Com. Hist. Francion* IV. 3, I so whiffled him on the face with my Torch [orig. *je lui passe le flambeau par devant le nez*] that I burned off allmost all his beard. **1660** S. FISHER *Rusticus ad Acad.* Wks. (1679) 152 Like men in a Ship that are whiffled up and down in a troubled Sea. **1664** H. MORE *Expos. 7 Epist.* ix. 163 Such as would whiffle away all these Truths by resolving them into a mere moral Allegorie. **1684** HOWE *Redeemer's Tears* Pref., Swollen with the conceit, that they have whiffled Christianity away, quite off the stage, with their profane breath. **1817** MARIA EDGEWORTH *Ormond* xxvi, No easy dupe, to be whiffled off and on, the sport of a coquette. **1843** MIALL in *Nonconf.* III. 225 The world is not destined to be whiffled out of its own independent reason by a handful of priests and statesmen.

b. *fig.* To dismiss by evasion; to say or state evasively.

1654 VILVAIN *Theorem. Theol.* Suppl. 227 This he whiffles off slightly, that 'tis a Parabol. **1676** MARVELL *Mr. Smirke* 43 He whiffles, those were the Jewish Ceremonies.

3. *intr.* To move lightly as if blown by a puff of air; to flicker or flutter as if stirred by the wind. Often *fig.*

1662 HIBBERT *Body Div.* II. 26 Any anabaptistical humorist, who hath a company of phanatique toyes whiffling about his understanding. *a* **1680** GLANVILL *Sadducismus* II. (1726) 452 A mind that useth to whiffle up and down in the levities of fancy. *a* **1774** HARTE *Poems, Eulogius* 546 Just as int'rest whiffled on his mind, He Anatolians left, or Thracians join'd. **1817** J. GILCHRIST *Intell. Patrim.* 148 Better chirp with the cricket, or chatter with the sparrow, than whiffle round this eternal monotony of futility. **1818** HAZLITT *Engl. Comic Writers* viii. (1907) 216 He whiffles about the stage with considerable volubility. **1866** MRS. H. WOOD *St. Martin's Eve* xvi, Suddenly the flame inside began to whiffle. **1870** JULIE P. SMITH *Widow Goldsmith's Dau.* xxxvii, She would whiffle and whirl up and down like a withered leaf.

4. *intr.* To talk idly; to trifle. *dial.* (See also WHIFFLING *ppl. a.*[1] 3.)

1706 PHILLIPS (ed. Kersey), *To Whiffle*, to trick one out of a thing, to stand trifling. **1847** HALLIWELL, *Whiffle*, to talk idly. *North.*

5. *intr.* To make a light whistling sound; *trans.* to utter with such a sound.

1832 *Fraser's Mag.* VI. 262 The two strangers whiffled and hissed together, in an unknown very rapid tongue. **1863** COWDEN CLARKE *Shaks. Char.* xvii. 448 Master Silence whiffling his scraps of ballads. **1893** *Daily News* 13 Feb. 6/1 Where a keen cold blast whiffles and blusters about the black and sullen monsters. **1909** *Ibid.* 14 Sept. 3 When a bear comes 'whiffling' about your snow hut. **1915** *Glasgow Herald* 9 Aug. 8 Shells flew 'whiffling' over our heads.

†**6. a.** *trans.* To smoke (tobacco). **b.** *absol.* To drink. *Obs.* (Cf. WHIFF *v.*[1] 3, 4.)

1683 TRYON *Way to Health* 165 The constant and common whiffling it [*sc.* tobacco]. *a* **1693** *Urquhart's Rabelais* III. Prol. 15 Those..importunate sots who.. constrain an easy, good-natured fellow to whiffle, quaff, carouse [orig. *trinquer, voire caros et alluz*].

Hence '**whiffling** *vbl. sb.*[1]

a **1677** BARROW *Serm.* v. Wks. 1687 I. 65 Such as are.. versatile whifflings and dodgings. **1681** J. SCOTT *Chr. Life* iv. 367 Too much whifling up and down in the little levities of Fancy. **1692** L'ESTRANGE *Josephus, Antiq.* VII. ix. Wks. (1702) 203 In her Course, upon the whifling of the Air, a snagged Bough of a Tree took hold of his Hair. **1841** J. F. COOPER *Deerslayer* I. i. 23, I would carry the gal off to the Mohawk by force, make her marry me in spite of her whiffling. **1866** MRS. H. WOOD *St. Martin's Eve* xvi, The whiffling of the flame was remedied now. **1882** 'F. ANSTEY' *Vice Versa* iv, This infernal whiffling and sniffing, sir, I will not put up with. **1906** *Springfield* (Mass.) *Weekly Republ.* 18 Oct. 3 This outcome of a week of doubt and whiffling will be viewed with mixed emotions. **1984** *Daily Tel.* 13 Feb. 12/5 When first I heard these whifflings, a couple of years ago, I thought they must be satiric.

'**whiffle**, *v.*[2] *nonce-wd.* [Back-formation f. WHIFFLER[1].] *intr.* To act as a whiffler.

1857 BORROW *Romany Rye* App. viii, Nobody can use his fists without being taught the use of them,..no more than any one can 'whiffle' without being taught by a master of the art... The last of the whifflers hanged himself about a fortnight ago..there being no demand for whiffling since the discontinuation of Guildhall banquets;..let any one take up the old chap's sword and try to whiffle.

whiffled ('hwɪf(ə)ld), *a. slang.* [Origin obscure: cf. SQUIFFY *a.*] Intoxicated, drunk.

1927 WODEHOUSE *Meet Mr. Mulliner* vi. 191 Intoxicated? The word did not express it by a mile. He was oiled, boiled, fried..whiffled, sozzled, and blotto. **1930** —— *Very Good, Jeeves!* ii. 46 'Have you forgotten that I did thirty days..for punching a policeman..on Boat-Race night?' 'But you were whiffled at the time.' **1956** J. D. CARR *Patrick Butler for Defence* xiv. 157 Helen..was much too clear-headed..ever to let herself get whiffled.

'**whifflegig**, *a. colloq.* Trifling, 'whiffling'. Also '**whiffmagig** = WHIFFLER[2] 2.

1830 H. LEE *Mem. Manager* I. i. 10 Not one of your puny punsters, or..whiffle-gig word-snappers. **1871** MEREDITH *H. Richmond* liv, Plenty of foreign whiffmagigs are to be found, but you won't come upon a fellow like that.

whiffler[1] ('hwɪflə(r)). *Obs.* exc. *Hist.* Forms: 6 **viffleur, wyffler, wyff-, wiffeler, wyfler, weffler,** 6–7 **wiffler, whiffeler,** 6–8 **wifler,** 7 **whyfler,** 7–8 **whifler,** 6– **whiffler.** [f. WIFLE javelin, axe + -ER[1]; the spelling with *wh* is prob. due to association with WHIFF and WHIFFLE *v.*[1]] One of a body of attendants armed with a javelin, battle-axe, sword, or staff, and wearing a chain, employed to keep the way clear for a procession or at some public spectacle.

Whifflers formed a regular part of the Corporation procession at Norwich till 1835; they were employed also on 11 Sept. 1848, when the then Duke of Cambridge attended the triennial musical festival.

1539 in *Archaeologia* XXXII. 33 The chamberlayn & councellors of the cytye, & the aldermens deputyes whiche were assigned to be wyffelers on horsebacke, were all yn cotes of whyte damaske..w[t] great chaynes abowte theyre necks, & propre javilyns or battle axes yn theyre hands... The wyffelers on fote were iiij. C propre lyght persones apparellyd yn whyte sylke or buffe jerkyns,..every man havyng a slaugh sworde or a javelyn to kepe the people yn araye, w[t] chaynes abowte theyre necks. **1544** in Rymer *Foedera* (1719) XV. 53 [At the King's departure from Calais] Furst, the Drommes and Viffleurs, then the Trompets, then [etc.]. **1544** in *Lett. & Papers Hen. VIII*, XIX. II. 305 The captain of the Spaniards..asketh allowance for the wages of himself, his petty captain, his standard bearer, drum, fife, wifler, surgeon and priest. **1556** J. HEYWOOD *Spider & F.* LII. v, Drums, fiffes, flags, and wiflers. **1560–1** in *Old City Acc. Bk.* (Archæol. Jrnl. XLIII), Payde for iij staves ffor wefflers. **1599** SHAKS. *Hen. V* v. Chorus 12 The deep-mouth'd Sea, Which like a mightie Whiffler 'fore the King, Seemes to prepare his way.

1605 BACON *Adv. Learn.* II. xiii. 50 They..were..scornefull toward particulars, which their manner was to vse..as.. Sargeants and Wifflers..to make way..for their opinions. **1618** BP. HALL *Righteous Mammon* Wks. (1625) 701 Some vaine whiffler, that is proud of a borrowed chaine. **1641** MILTON *Animadv.* iv. 30 His former transition was in the faire about the Jugglers, now he is at the Pageants among the Whifflers. *a* **1658** CLEVELAND *Poems*, etc. (1677) 112 First as a Whifler before the show enter Stamford, one that trod the Stage with the first, travers'd his ground, made a Leg and Exit. **1707** E. WARD *Hud. Rediv.* VI. II. 23 The Colours that their Whifflers wear, And diff'rent Ensigns that they bear. **1712** ADDISON *Spect.* No. 536 ¶5 Our fine young Ladies.. retain in their Service..as great a Number as they can of supernumerary..Fellows, which they use like Whiflers. **1787** GROSE *Prov. Gloss.*, *Whifflers*, men who make way for the corporation of Norwich, by flourishing their swords.

b. *transf.* A swaggerer, braggadocio.

1581 J. BELL *Haddon's Answ. Osor.* 113 Yet another place of S. Paule out of the whiche this wylde wiffler may rushe upon us with his leaden dagger. **1607** DEKKER & WEBSTER *Northw. Hoe* II. i, Your right whiffler..hangs himselfe in Saint Martins, and not in Cheape-side. **1644** FEATLEY *Levites Scourge* To Rdr., They fight..rather like whifflers with vizards on their faces. **1881** SHORTHOUSE *John Inglesant* ix, A motley company of mummers, masquers, fantastic phantoms, whifflers, thieves, rufflers. **1889** 'Q' *Splendid Spur* xiii, The crew of gipsies, whifflers, mountebanks, fortune-tellers.

¶ The sense 'piper, fifer' found in Dicts. from Kersey's ed. of Phillips (1706) onwards is baseless.

whiffler[2] ('hwɪflə(r)). [f. WHIFFLE *v.*[1] + -ER[1].]

†**1.** A smoker of tobacco. *Obs.* (Cf. WHIFFER.)

1617 MIDDLETON & ROWLEY *Fair Quarrel* IV. i, How likest thou this, whiffler? **1836** HOR. SMITH *Tin Trump.* 117 So may we allow Vesuvius and Etna to smoke, without conceding that privilege to every puny whiffler.

2. A trifler; an insignificant or contemptible fellow (cf. WHIFFLING *ppl. a.*[1] 3); also, a shifty or evasive person.

1659 *Lady Alimony* v. iv, Such Whifflers are below my scorn, and beneath my spite. **1675** COVEL in *Early Voy. Levant* (Hakl. Soc.) 279 Here are every year abundance of Whiflers in those scraps of learning. **1678** H. MORE in Glanvill *Sadducismus* Postscript (1681) 45 O the impudent profaneness..of perverse shufflers and whifflers. *a* **1745** SWIFT *Public Absurd. Eng.* Wks. 1841 II. 311/1 It is a common topic of satire, which you will hear..from the mouths..of every whiffler in office. **1809–12** MARIA EDGEWORTH *Absentee* iv, He was not a whiffler to stand upon ceremony about disturbing a gentleman in his last moments. **1866** J. MARTINEAU *Ess.* I. 187 These metaphysical whifflers draw no blood. **1896** *Advance* (Chicago) 25 June 935/2 [Giving the Gospel message] requires single-mindedness; no whiffler can succeed.

†**3.** A flag. *Obs. rare.* (Cf. WHIFF *sb.*[1] 7.)

1759 DURAND *Mem. Capt. Thurot* (Percy Soc.) 28 The commodore and second vessel carried white whifflers or pendants forward.

4. The whistlewing or golden-eye duck, *Clangula glaucion*. *local U.S.*

1888 G. TRUMBULL *Names of Birds* 79.

whifflery ('hwɪflərɪ). *nonce-wd.* [f. prec.: see -ERY.] Action characteristic of a whiffler; trifling.

1835 CARLYLE in Froude *T.C.* (1884) I. 60 Life is no frivolity, or hypothetical coquetry or whifflery.

whiffletree, U.S. variant of WHIPPLETREE.

1842 W. P. HAWES *Sporting Scenes* II. 69 Our whiffle-tree became detached from the vehicle, and fell upon the horse's heels. **1855** BRISTED in *Cambr. Ess.* 65 Whiffle-tree, the invariable American for splinter-bar. **1868** *Rep. U.S. Comm. Agric.* (1869) 256 A boy can lead a horse, with a suitable chain attached to the whiffletree. **1896** *Century Mag.* Nov. 23 With trace-chains rattling and whiffletrees snapping over the stumps of trees.

whiffling, *vbl. sb.*[1]: see WHIFFLE *v.*[1]

'**whiffling**, *vbl. sb.*[2] [f. WHIFFL(ER[1] + -ING[1].] The action of a whiffler in clearing the way; also *attrib.* or as *ppl. a.*, used by, or acting as, a whiffler.

1618 in J. Nicholl *Comp. Ironm.* (1866) 183 For 14 doz. of whiffling staves and 1 doz. of truncheons..2 *li.* 5 *s.* 0 *d.* **1675** V. ALSOP *Anti-Sozzo* iii. §2. 156 These whiffling Slanders do but make way for the Show. **1683** [J. NORRIS] *Murnival of Knaves* 16 The Rabbles Darling, small Birch-rod Of Loyalty, a Whifling Blade.

whiffling ('hwɪflɪŋ), *ppl. a.*[1] [f. WHIFFLE *v.*[1] + -ING[2].]

1. That whiffles; blowing, or blown, in light puffs; moving lightly as if driven by gusts of wind.

1568 T. HOWELL *Arb. Amitie* (1879) 68 Vphoyst by wyffling windes. **1660** INGELO *Bentiv. & Ur.* II. (1682) 205 The whiffling dust which flies in the faces of Travellers. **1685** WOOD *Life* (O.H.S.) III. 135 No raine fell from the 26 Jan..., only a little whiffling snow. **1713** ROWE *Jane Shore* IV. i, Like a dry leaf, an idle straw, a feather, The Sport of every whiffling Blast that blows. **1765** STERNE *Tr. Shandy* VII. xvi, Those whiffling vexations which come puffing across a man's canvas. **1800** HURDIS *Fav. Village* 32 The whiffling breeze..among the bents. **1845** S. JUDD *Margaret* xvii, Where the whiffling winds had left the earth nearly bare [of snow].

b. Making or characterized by a light whistling sound.

1831 CARLYLE *Sart. Res.* I. iv, Some whiffling husky cachinnation. **1911** GALSWORTHY *Patrician* xix, Rain, which the wind drove horizontally with a cold whiffling murmur.

2. Inconstant, shifting; evasive.

a **1680** BUTLER *Rem.* (1759) II. 109 This puts him upon perpetual Apologies..in a Kind of whiffling Strain. **1741** WATTS *Improv. Mind* ix. (1801) 79 A person of a whiffling and unsteady turn of mind, who cannot keep close to a point of controversy, but wanders from it perpetually. **1800** *Asiat. Ann. Reg., Proc. E. Ind. Ho.* 139/1 That it should be got rid of by the whiffling way of an adjournment. **1818** HAZLITT *Pol. Ess.* (1819) 343 A whiffling turncoat. **1835** W. IRVING *Tour Prairies* iv, Hee had..a whiffling double voice, shifting abruptly from a treble to a thorough-bass. **1856** EMERSON *Engl. Traits* viii. 143 The national temper, in the civil history, is not flashy or whiffling. **1914** *Contemp. Rev.* Sept. 323 The whiffling and unsteady frame of mind of the Imperial workman.

3. Trifling, pettifogging, fiddling, fussy; (passing into) paltry, insignificant, 'piffling'.

1613 HOBY *Counter-snarle* 3 Some vile blurr, and maleuolous aspersion, from one or other her suborned Pandars and whifling agents. **1671** CROWNE *Juliana* I. 8 A pittiful whiffling small-beer Duke. **1678** CUDWORTH *Intell. Syst.* I. v. 847 A meer Whifling, Evanid, and Phantastick thing. **1710** *Brit. Apollo* III. No. 7. 3/1 Whiffling, Noisy Whelp apace Barks. **1719** D'URFEY *Pills* (1872) IV. 107 The whiffling Gallants of the Inns of Court, Do hinder their Studies certainly. **1817** HAZLITT *Times Newsp.* Wks. 1902 III. 171 The low, whiffling, contemptible gratification of their literary jealousy. **1854** MISS BAKER *Northampt. Gloss.*, *Whifling*, slight, slender, insignificant. 'A little whiffling fellow.' **1903** R. BRIDGES *To a Socialist in Lond.* 111 The least petty whiffling ephemeral insect.

Hence '**whifflingly** *adv.*, in a trifling manner.

1668 H. MORE *Div. Dial.* II. 482 All the Articles of our Faith..might be most frivolously and whifflingly allegorized into a mere..Fable.

whiffling, *ppl. a.*[2]: see WHIFFLING *vbl. sb.*[2]

whifflow ('hwɪfləʊ). *Naut. slang.* [Fanciful formation.] (See quot. 1961.)

1961 F. H. BURGESS *Dict. Sailing* 222 *Whifflow*, an unnamed gadget; used when a proper name is forgotten. **1971** 'A. BURGESS' *MF* v. 64 The cabin was still a mess of smashed and battered whifflows.

whiffmagig: see WHIFFLEGIG.

whiffy ('hwɪfɪ), *a. slang.* [f. WHIFF *sb.*[1] + -Y[1].] Having an unpleasant smell. Also *fig.*

1849 H. MELVILLE *Mardi* II. xxvii. 109 A pithy, whiffy sentence or two. **1905** R. MARSH *Spoiler of Men* xvii. 149 It [*sc.* his tobacco] is a bit whiffy, ain't it? **1934** R. MACAULAY *Going Abroad* xi. 77 'A bit whiffy,' Hero said, as they passed among the cottages that encircled the muddy..pool. **1962** AUDEN *Dyer's Hand* (1963) 520, I have always found the atmosphere of *Twelfth Night* a bit whiffy. **1978** *Birds* Summer 45/2 The area is dusty and whiffy with lorries arriving to tip every four minutes.

†**whiffling.** *Obs.* [f. WHIFF *sb.*[1] + -LING.] An insignificant creature. (Cf. WHIFFLER[2] 2.)

1635 GLAPTHORNE *Hollander* I. i, Hang him young whifling, he know a Lady, pity of his life first.

whift (hwɪft), *sb. Obs.* exc. *dial.* Also wift. [var. of WHIFF *sb.*[1] with excrescent *-t*.]

1. A whiff or slight blast of wind, etc.; a snatch (of song).

1614 GORGES *Lucan* v. 202 So hauing said, the surging whifts The ship ten times together lifts. **1855** BROWNING *Fra Lippo Lippi* 52 A sweep of lute-strings, laughs, and whifts of song. **1905** *Westm. Gaz.* 16 June 2/1 A wift of white foam.

2. A small signal flag. (Cf. WHIFF *sb.*[1] 7.)

1644 *True Narr. Seige Plymouth* 5 Having..given a signe ..by hanging out a Wift, that he was in distresse. **1839** BEALE *Nat. Hist. Sperm Whale* xii. 155 Two or three small flags, called 'whifts', which are inserted in the dead whale, in case the boats should leave it in chase of others. **1846** YOUNG *Naut. Dict.* 359 *Waft, Weft*, or *Whift*, a signal (most frequently for a boat) made by hoisting a flag rolled up lengthways and bound together with a few stops. **1901** W. CLARK RUSSELL *Ship's Adv.* vii, There's the barque that fouled us last night, sir. She's got a wift at her mizzen-peak.

†**whift**, *a. Obs. rare.* [f. WHIFF *v.*[1] (cf. sense 4) + *-t* = -ED[2].] Drunk, intoxicated.

1611 COTGR., *Entrebeu*, halfe drunke, almost whift.

whig (hwɪg), *sb.*[1] Now *Sc.* and *dial.* Forms: 6 whyg(ge, 6–7 whigge, 6–7, 8–9 *Sc.* wig, 7, 9 *Sc.* whigg, 7, 8–9 *Sc.* wigg, 9 *Sc.* quhig, 6– whig. [Of unascertained origin, but presumably related to WHEY. (The variation of *whig* and *wig* in Sc. is remarkable.)] Variously applied to (*a*) sour milk or cream, (*b*) whey, (*c*) buttermilk, (*d*) a beverage consisting of whey fermented and flavoured with herbs.

1528 ROY *Rede me* (Arb.) 100 Lyvynge on mylke, whyg, and whey. **1561** B. GOOGE tr. *Palingenius' Zodiac* IV. Hv, My lusty gotes with kid they swel, ne want I whigge, nor whay. **1589** [? LYLY] *Pappe w. Hatchet* Wks. 1902 III. 406 Martins conscience hath a periwig; therefore to good men he is more sower than wig. **1615** MARKHAM *Country Contentm.* II. iv. 114 As for the Whey you may keepe it also in a sweet stone vessell: for it is that which is called Whigge, and is an excellent coole drinke and a wholsome. **1633** HART *Diet of Diseased* II. xvii. 209 Sowre whey..is in very great request in the Northerne parts of this Iland, where it is called of some whigge, and of others wigge. **1684** [MERITON] *Yorksh. Ale* Gloss. 114 *Whig* is Clarified Whey, put up with Herbs to drink. **1688** HOLME *Armoury* II. 173/1 Thick Milk, Butter-milk made thick through the heat of Summer, the bottom part falling to a Whigg. **1799** *Statist. Acc. Scot.* XXI. 142 Cream, too long kept, and purified by drawing off the thin part, or wig, for drink, was converted into butter. **1834** *Tait's Mag.* I. 736/1 *Whig*..is the provincial name in the south-west of Scotland for that blue-and-yellowish, thin sub-acid liquid which gathers on the surface of whey or butter milk.

fig. **1661** NEDHAM *Hist. Engl. Reb.* xlii, There lies the Cream of all the Cause; Religion is but Whig.

Whig (hwɪg), *sb.*[2] and *a.* Forms: 7 whige, whigh, whigue, *Sc.* uhig, uig, 7–8 wig(g, 8 quig, 7–9 whigg, 7– whig. [Origin unascertained; prob. shortening of *whiggamer*, WHIGGAMORE; the occurrence of sense 1 (if it belongs to this word) some years before the date of the 'whiggamore raid' points to the existence of *whig* in a general sense before that event.

The supposition that this word is identical with WHIG *sb.*[1] (cf. the following quots.) has no historical foundation.

1717 DE FOE *Mem. Ch. Scot.* III. (1844) 68/2 The word is said to be taken from a mixt Drink the poor Men drank in their Wanderings compos'd of Water and sour Milk. **1721** WODROW *Hist. Suff. Ch. Scot.* II. ii. I. 263 The poor honest People, who were in Railery called Whiggs, from a Kind of Milk they were forced to drink in their Wandrings and Straits. *a* **1734** NORTH *Exam.* II. v. §10 (1740) 321 This [*sc.* the name Birmingham Protestants] held a considerable Time; but the word was not fluent enough for hasty Repartee; and, after diverse Changes, the Lot fell upon Whig, which was very significative, as well as ready, being vernacular in Scotland, (from whence it was borrowed) for corrupt and sour Whey. Immediately the Train took, and, upon the first Touch of the Experiment, it run like wild Fire, and became general. And so the Account of Tory was ballanced, and soon began to run up a sharp Score on the other Side.]

A. *sb.* †**1.** A yokel, country bumpkin. *Obs. rare.*

c **1645** T. TULLY *Siege of Carlisle* (1840) 3 And needs he [*sc.* Leslie] would retreat to Newcastle, till great Barwise set himself first into the water; and the rest, following him, so frighted y[e] fresh water countrie whiggs, y[t] all of them answered the Motto, *veni, vidi, fugi.* *c* **1655** J. GWYNNE *Mil. Mem. Gt. Civil War* II. (1822) 90 Most of them were no souldiers, but countrey bumkins, there called Whigs.

2. An adherent of the Presbyterian cause in Scotland in the seventeenth century; applied orig. to the Covenanters in the West of Scotland who in 1648 wrested the government from the Royalist party and marched as rebels to Edinburgh; in later years, to the extreme section of the Covenanting party who were regarded as rebels. *Hist.*

'By rigid Episcopalians, it is still given to Presbyterians in general; and, in the West of S[cotland], even by the latter, to those who, in a state of separation from the established church, profess to adhere more strictly to Presbyterian principles' (Jamieson, 1808).

1657 in Jas. Campbell *Balmerino* (1867) 213 Having fallen in among the Whigs of Kilmany. **1666** NICOLL *Diary* (Bannatyne Club) 452 The Generall [Dalyell] having marched towards the West, he took and killed sindrie persones, callit The Whigs. **1666** *Cal. State Papers, Dom.* *1666–7* (1864) 301 Now not one [*sc.* of the rebels] dares call himself a Whig. **1667** *Lond. Gaz.* No. 121/1 We were informed that the Whigs had privately in the night stollen down the heads of 4 of the Rebels that were set up in Glasgow. **1679** *Lauderdale Papers* (Camden 1885) III. 163 The Whiggs horse and foot fell in pell, mell, upon the Dragoons. **1683** CLAVERHOUSE in *Clavers, the Despot's Champion* (1889) xii. 142, I am as sorry to see a man day, even a whigue, as any of themselfs. **1684** *Buccleuch MSS.* (Hist. MSS. Comm. 1903) II. 196 The bearer wil tell you the kindness the Whighs has for your lordship, which is no ill argument of your lordship's zeal in the King's service. *a* **1699** KIRKTON *Hist. Ch. Scot.* (1817) 46 This was done at the Whiggs' Road, as was called. **1708** in Brand *Hist. Newc.* (1789) I. 424 *note*, [In St. Andrew's Register, November 1708, this burying-ground for dissenters is called] the Quigs buring-place. *a* **1715** BURNET *Own Time* I. (1724) I. 43 Those in the west [of Scotland] come in the summer to buy at Lieth the stores that come from the north: And from a word Whiggam, used in driving their horses all that drove were called the Whiggamors, and shorter the Whiggs. **1875** tr. *Ranke's Hist. Eng.* XVI. ix. IV. 121 Doubtless, in Scotland also, the republican tendencies appeared; for instance, in October 1680, the King and the Duke were excommunicated with due form;..These were, however, rather Anabaptist than Presbyterian views; their adherents were indeed called Whigs, but 'wild Whigs'. **1888** M. MORRIS *Claverhouse* ix. 159 The men of the hill-sides and moorlands of the West, the wild Western Whigs, who feared ..the name of Claverhouse.

3. a. Applied to the Exclusioners (*c* 1679) who opposed the succession of James, Duke of York, to the crown, on the ground of his being a Roman Catholic. *Hist.* (Opposed to TORY A. 2.)

1679 WOOD *Life* (O.H.S.) II. 431 After the breaking out of the popish plot severall of our scholars were tried and at length were discovered to be whiggs, viz... Georg Reynell of C.C.C., looked upon as always a round-head. **1681** LUTTRELL *Brief Rel.* (1857) I. 124 The latter party have been called by the former, whigs, fanaticks, covenanteers, bromigham protestants, &c.; and the former are called by the latter, tories, tantivies, Yorkists, high flown church men. **1682** *Tories Confess.* vi, What pimping Whig shall dare controule, or check the lawfull Heir. **1683** [J. NORRIS] *Murnival of Knaves* 2 Whig and Tory..The one of Caledonian Race, T'other has an Hibernian Face. **1691** WOOD *Ath. Oxon.* II. 652 In 1678..he closed with the Whiggs, supposing that party would carry all before them. *a* **1734** [see etymology above]. **1827** HALLAM *Const. Hist.* xii. (1876) II. 439. **1905** C. S. TERRY *Pentland Rising* 84 The.. controversies which cleft the Whigs in 1679, to the paralysis of serious military achievement, were absent in 1666.

b. *fig.* A rebel.

1682 Dryden *Another Epil. Dk. Guise* 22 When Sighs and Prayers their ladies cannot move, They rail, write Treason, and turn Whigs to love.

4. Hence, from 1689, an adherent of one of the two great parliamentary and political parties in England, and (at length) in Great Britain. (Opposed to Tory A. 3.)

Since the middle of the 19th century mostly superseded (exc. as a historical term) by *Liberal* (see liberal A. 5, B. 1 b), but used occas. since then to express adherence to moderate or antiquated Liberal principles.

1702 *Clarendon's Hist. Reb.* I. Pref. p. viii, We have lived ..to see the two great Parties, of late known by the Names of *Whig* and *Tory*, directly change their ground. **1704** C. Leslie *The Wolf Stript* 82 A Whigg is a State-Enthusiast, as a Dissenter is an Ecclesiastical. **1713** *Guardian* No. 1. ¶4, I am, with relation to the government of the Church, a Tory, with regard to the State, a Whig. *a* **1715** Burnet *Own Time* I. (1724) I. 43 All that opposed the Court came in contempt to be called Whiggs. **1741** Hume *Ess., Parties Gt. Brit.* 131 A Whig may be defin'd to be a Lover of Liberty, tho' without renouncing Monarchy; and a Friend to the Settlement in the Protestant Line. **1778** Johnson 28 Apr. in *Boswell*, 'And I have always said, the first Whig was the Devil.' *Boswell.* 'He certainly was, Sir. The Devil was impatient of subordination.' **1791** Burke (*title*) An Appeal from the New to the Old Whigs, in consequence of some late discussions in Parliament, relative to the Reflections on the French Revolution. **1844** Disraeli *Coningsby* vi. iii, 'I look upon an Orangeman,' said Coningsby, 'as a pure Whig.' **1852** Ld. J. Russell in S. Walpole *Life* (1889) II. 156 *note*, The term Whig..has the convenience of expressing in one syllable what Conservative Liberal expresses in seven; and Whiggism, in two syllables, means what Conservative Progress means in other six. **1883** *Sat. Rev.* 21 July 67/2 The Gladstonian Moderate, the 'Whig' as he is locally called, has ceased to have a reason for existence in Irish politics. **1911** B. Holland *Spencer Compton* II. 129 Until this moment [1886] the word 'Whig' was still in common use to denote a connection loosely bound together, the moderate Liberals, led by the chiefs of certain families of long standing. Since 1886, the word has been used in a purely historical sense, while 'Tory' has still a living meaning.

5. *Amer. Hist.* **a.** An American colonist who supported the American Revolution.

1768 *New York Gaz.* 14 Mar., (*title of article*) The American Whig. **1768** *Boston Gaz.* 11 Apr. 3/1 On reading, in the American Mercury, an advertisement of a weekly paper to be published, under the title of *A Whip for the American Whig*; I could not help falling into a train of serious reflections, on the persecuting genius that inspires the high flying Tory party, in the episcopal church. **1775** Thacher *Mil. Jrnl. Amer. Rev.* (1823) 12 The..majority.. are united in resolution to oppose..the wicked attempts of the English Cabinet. This class of people have assumed the appellation of Whigs. **1775** Johnson in *Boswell* 21 Mar., When the Whigs of America are thus multiplied, let the Princes of the earth tremble in their palaces. **1812** *Niles' Weekly Reg.* 6 June 240/1 A great battle is said to have been fought about the 1st May, between the 'whigs' of Caracos and 'tories' of Coro, the latter being aided by some 'regulars' from Porto Rico. **1884** A. Johnston *Hist. Amer. Pol.* (ed. 2) 6 As soon as independence was announced, in 1776, to be the final object of the contest, the names Whig and Tory lost, in America, whatever of British significance they had ever possessed.

b. A member of a party formed in 1834 from a fusion of the National Republicans and other elements opposed to the Democrats; it favoured a protective tariff and a strong national or central government, and was succeeded in 1856 by the Republican party. (See quot. 1905.)

1834 *Niles' Weekly Reg.* 12 Apr. 101/2 In New York and Connecticut the term 'whigs' is now used by the opponents of the administration when speaking of themselves, and they call the 'Jackson men' by the offensive name of 'tories'. **1839** *Congress. Globe* Jan., App. 105/1 In 1796,..Whig..was synonymous with Democrat,..or, in the Federal language of the times, was fit for the common people;..but now for political effect, the same party have taken the term Whig to themselves. **1888** Bryce *Amer. Commw.* III. liii. II. 340 The majesty and beneficent activity of the National government ..was generally in fact represented by the Federalists of the first period, the Whigs of the second, the Republicans of the third. **1905** *A. Johnston's Amer. Pol. Hist.* II. 239 His [*sc.* James Watson Webb's] newspaper, the *Courier and Enquirer*, had originally supported Jackson, and had been driven into the opposition by the President's course. In February, 1834, he baptized the new party with the name of 'Whig', with the idea that the name implied resistance to executive usurpation, to that of the Crown in England and in the American Revolution, and to that of the President in the United States of 1834.

B. *adj.* That is a Whig; of, pertaining to, or characteristic of a Whig or Whigs: holding the opinions or principles of a Whig.

1681 T. Flatman *Heraclitus Ridens* No. 32 (1713) I. 205 Oh there's a thick Disguise they say upon Affairs, and unless you have a pair of Whig-spectacles, there's no seeing through it. **1683** Dryden *Vind. Dk. Guise* 22 As for Knave, and Sycophant, and Rascal, and Impudent, and Devil, and old Serpent,..I take them to be only names of Parties: And cou'd return Murtherer and Cheat, and Whig-napper. **1683** Luttrell *Brief Rel.* (1857) I. 279 Commenting on several proceedings of those called the whig party. **1719** T. Gordon *Char. Indep. Whig* (ed. 2) 19 Let them not..give up Whig Boroughs into Jacobite Hands. **1732** P. Walker *Cargill* in *Biogr. Presbyt.* (1827) II. 100 They said 'Take up the old damn'd Whig-Bitch.' **1768** *Boston Gaz.* 21 Mar. 3/1 May the best of Heaven's Blessings ever attend the Whig Cause. **1818** Scott *Br. Lamm.* x, Free and safe as a whig bailie on the causeway of his own borough, or a canting presbyterian minister in his own pulpit. **1837** Syd. Smith *Let. Archd. Singleton* Wks. 1859 II. 276/2 Lord John Russell, the Whig leader. **1839** Whittier *Pr. Wks.* (1889) II. 323 The late Whig defeat in New York. **1888** Bryce *Amer. Commw.* III. liii. II. 333 The other section, which called itself at first the National Republican, ultimately the Whig party. **1912** G. O. Trevelyan *Geo. III & Fox* I. 292 A rallying point for the hardy Whig militiamen of the Carolinas.

C. *Comb.*, as ***Whig-Radical*** sb. and adj.; ***Whig-defeating***, ***-hunting*** adjs.; **Whig historian**, a historian who interprets history as the continuing and inevitable victory of progress over reaction; **Whig history**, history written by or from the point of view of a Whig historian. †**Whigland** (*obs. slang*), the land of Whigs, esp. Scotland; hence †**Whiglander**, a native or inhabitant of 'Whigland'.

1682 T. Flatman *Heraclitus Ridens* No. 65 (1713) II. 152 A Cause-confounding, *Whig-defeating..Dispensation. **1924** G. B. Shaw *Saint Joan* Pref. p. x, Her [*sc.* Joan's] ideal biographer..must understand the Middle Ages..much more intimately than our *Whig historians have ever understood them. **1980** H. Trevelyan *Public & Private* 149 George Macaulay Trevelyan..was essentially a Whig historian, thus continuing the family tradition derived from his father and his kinsman Macaulay. **1931** H. C. Butterfield *Whig Interpretation of Hist.* i. 6 The truth is that there is a tendency for all history to veer over into *whig history. **1973** *Listener* 28 June 869/1 Macaulay..wrote consciously Whig history: yet..enunciated the principles of historical criticism which explains why Whig history is a distortion. **1905** C. S. Terry *Pentland Rising* 2 The familiar *Whig-hunting duty of Claverhouse. **1681** T. Flatman *Heraclitus Ridens* No. 45 (1713) II. 39 The Territories of *Whigg-land. **1683** [J. Norris] *Murnival of Knaves* 16 Patron of all Dissenters, and The Demogorgon of Whigland. *a* **1700** B. E. *Dict. Cant. Crew*, *Whig-land*, Scotland. **1682** *Ballad, Happy Ret. Old Dutch Miller* i, I am so Zealous for *Whiglanders Crew, I'l cure their Distempers with one Turn or Two. **1820** J. Rickman *Extr. Life & Lett.* 10 Feb. 215 The address of the Yorkshire *Whig Radicals.

Hence (mostly *humorous* or *contemptuous nonce-wds.*) '**Whiggarchy** (-ɑːkɪ) [Gr. ἀρχή rule], government by Whigs; '**Whiggess**, a female Whig; '**Whiggify** *v.*, *trans.* to make Whig or whiggish (so ˌ**Whiggifi'cation**); **Whi'ggissimi** [jocular f. with L. superl. ending], extreme or absolute Whigs; '**Whiggize** *v.*, *intr.* to act like a Whig, play the Whig; **Whiggo'logical** *a.*, relating to Whig principles; '**Whiglet**, '**Whigling**, a small or petty Whig (also *attrib.*); **Whi'gocracy** [-cracy], government by Whigs; *concr.* a body of Whig rulers; '**Whigship**, the personality or quality of a Whig; †'**Whigster** [-ster], a contemptuous appellation for a Whig.

1712–13 Swift *App. to Cond. Allies* Wks. 1841 I. 437/1 That they will not recognize any other government in Great Britain but *Whiggarchy only. **1776** *Pennsylvania Even. Post* 2 Jan. 3/2 A reasonable *Whiggess scorns all implicit faith in the state as well as the church. **1839** Lady Lytton *Cheveley* v, Whigesses always make their 'début' later than other girls. **1832** J. Wilson in *Blackw. Mag.* Sept. 387 We were all along against the *whiggification of the Tory System. **1682** 'Philanax Misopappas' *Tory Plot* II. 3 If he preach up nothing but Hell and Heaven, and a good Life,.. D - - - me, says he, this Fellow's *Whiggefi'd. **1835** *Fraser's Mag.* XI. 364 They may aid..in whiggifying some of the propositions of the government. **1841** *Tait's Mag.* VIII. 484 A whiggified Radical is a jobber. **1725** Swift *Let. to Sheridan* 25 Sept., Because they are above suspicions, as *Whiggissimi and Unsuspectissimi. **1832** J. Rickman *Extr. Life & Lett.* 18 Apr. 294 Whigs, Whiggamores, Whiggissimi. **1832** J. Wilson in *Blackw. Mag.* XXXII. 708, I don't like a Whig..but..I have even less affection for a *Whiggizing Tory. **1817** *Q. Rev.* Oct. 135 Mr. Bentham will no doubt be thankful for so striking an illustration of his *whiggological theories. **1681** T. Flatman *Heraclitus Ridens* No. 36 (1713) I. 232 Some tolerable Reasons why the little *Whiglets engag'd themselves in such an Affair. **1821** *Blackw. Mag.* X. 221 You have made some of the Radicals and Whiglets, both of Edinburgh and Glasgow, feel. *Ibid.* 3 Tears of joy and gratitude at beholding the *whiglings placed so near his Majesty's seat of honour. **1834** *Oxf. Univ. Mag.* I. 41 The carping jibes of Whigling envy. **1883** J. Wilson *Ess. Hist. & Biogr.* xvi. 289 The whole breed of Radicals, and Whiglings, and Cockneys. **1836** *Fraser's Mag.* XIII. 568 Any of the *Whigocracy. *a* **1796** Burns *Stanzas on Naething* 37 Her *whigship was wonderful pleased. **1846** Landor *Imag. Conv., Johnson & John Horne* (*Tooke*) Wks. I. 166/1 People of your cast in politics are fond of vilifying our country. Is this your whigship? **1683** *Romulus & Hersilia* Prol., Now I dare swear, some of you *Whigsters say, Come on, now for a swinging Tory Play.

whig, *v.*^{1} *Sc.* [Cf. *fig* (vb.^{3}), *frig*, *jig*.]

1. *trans.* To urge forward, drive briskly.

1666–7 G. Blackhal *Brief Narr.* (1844) §8. 163, I did sie the contrie people whigging their meres, to be tymously at the kirk.

2. *intr.* To jog along.

c **1690** *Killiecrankie* in C. Mackay *Jacobite Songs* (1861) 38 The solemn league and covenant, Cam whigging up the hills, man. **1701** De Foe *Trueborn Eng.* I. 222 Scots from the northern frozen banks of Tay, With packs and plods came whigging all away. **1815** Scott *Guy M.* xxiv, Just when I.. was whigging cannily awa hame.

Whig, *v.*^{2} [f. Whig *sb.*^{2}] *trans.* To behave like a Whig towards; *intr.* to play the Whig.

1681 T. Flatman *Heraclitus Ridens* No. 39 (1713) I. 258 They will Whig us bravely indeed, if by the Pretences of the Fear of Popery and Arbitrary Government, Flanders and Germany should..fall into the Scale of France. **1695** in C. Mackay *Jacobite Songs* (1861) 43 Say, was it foul, or was it fair, To come a hunder mile and mair, For to ding out my daddy's heir, And dash him wi' the whiggin o't. **1816** Scott *Old Mort.* xxxvi, I think he will hardly neglect the parade of the feudal retainers, or go a-whigging a second time. **1832** Lytton in *Life*, etc. (1883) II. viii. i. 280 They Whigged everything they touched. They gauged and docketed all the objects of Poetry.

whig, *v.*^{3} *dial.* [f. whig *sb.*^{1}] *trans.* and *intr.* To turn sour; to curdle.

1756 F. Home *Exper. Bleaching* 196 The milk is whigged, and still pretty sour. **1825** Jamieson s.v., Stale churned milk, when it throws off a sediment, is said to whig. **1835** De Quincey *Tory's Acc. Toryism*, etc., Wks. 1863 XV. 224 If you pour milk upon rum, and do it so slowly or so unskilfully as to coagulate the mixture, you are said 'to whig it.'

whig(g, variants of wig *sb.*^{1}, kind of bun.

whiggamore ('hwɪgəmɔə(r)). *Hist.* Forms: 7 **whigimyre**, **whiggamaire**, **-mer**, **whigmuir**, **wickhamer**, **wiggomer**, 7– **whiggamore**, 8 **whiggamor**, **whigamoor**, 9 **whigamore**. [The form *whig(g)amore*, used by Bp. Burnet in the often cited passage given s.v. Whig *sb.*^{2} 2, and later popularized by Scott, is app. an erratic form (like *whigmuir*, *whigimyre*) of *wiggomer*, *whiggamaire*, which is prob. f. whig *v.*^{1} + *mere*, mare *sb.*^{1}

The word *whiggam* adduced by Burnet as a term used in driving horses is unsupported by evidence.]

Originally, One of a body of insurgents of the West of Scotland who in 1648 marched on Edinburgh, their expedition being called the 'whiggamore raid, road, or inroad'; later (*contemptuous*), = Whig *sb.*^{2} 2. Also *attrib.*

1649 Sir Jas. Balfour *Hist. Wks.* (1825) III. 388 Anent the Scotts last going into England, and the Englishe, with Cromwell and Lambert, ther heir-coming at the Whiggamaire roade. *Ibid.* 420 Since Julij last, 1649, and the Whigamore road. **1654** in *R. Baillie's Lett. & Jrnls.* (Bann. Club) III. 568 Some hes maid a report..that wee wer raysing a Whigimyre road vnder Argyle. **1662** in Wodrow *Hist. Suff. Ch. Scot.* I. iii. (1721) I. 151 There was another Statue in a Whigmuir's Habit, having the Remonstrance in his Hand. **1666** *Cal. State Papers, Dom. 1666–7* (1864) 302, 68 of the Wickhamers. **1666** in *Dom. State Papers Chas. II* CLXXIX. lf. 136 (MS.), The Wiggomers, for so they call the mutineers, being a middle sort betwixt Anabaptist and Presbyterian, are quite quelld onely that they shifft their quarters as they heare they are pursued. **1670** Sir Jas. Turner *Mem.* (1829) 68 So soone as the news of our defeate [*sc.* of the Scots at Preston] came to Scotland, Argile and the Kirks partie rose in armes everie mothers sonne; and this was calld the Whiggamer rode. *a* **1715** [see Whig *sb.*^{2} 2]. **1816** Scott *Old Mort.* viii, There's a thousand merks on the murdering whigamore's head. **1818** —— *Rob Roy* xxv, It isna good for my health to come in the gate o' the whigamore bailie bodies. **1821** —— *Pirate* iv, 'Hear to him,' said an old whigamore carline. **1830** J. Rickman *Extr. Life & Lett.* 17 Sept. 267, I hear the Whiggamores begin to be frightened. **1886** Stevenson *Kidnapped* ix. 77 *note*, Whig or Whigamore was the cant name for those who were loyal to King George [an. 1751]. **1891** Gardiner *Hist. Civil War* lxvi. III. 491 The Whiggamore leaders constituted themselves..into a Committee of Estates. **1898** W. S. Douglas *Cromwell's Sc. Camp.* 9 It is certain that after the events of 1648 they must have considered the 'Whiggamores' more closely bound to their interest than that body proved to be.

Whiggery ('hwɪgərɪ). [f. Whig *sb.*^{2} + -ery.] Whig principles or practice; Whiggism. (Mostly *hostile* or *contemptuous*.)

1682 T. Flatman *Heraclitus Ridens* No. 66 (1713) II. 161 What other Whiggery have you? **1714** G. Lockhart *Mem. Scot.* (ed. 3) 128 The first of these was..after the Revolution, raised to the Bench upon Account of his Whiggery and Disloyalty. **1814** Scott *Wav.* xxx, That's a' your Whiggery, and your presbytery, ye cut-lugged, graning carles! **1843** E. Quincy *Life of W. L. Garrison* iii. 92 Great opposition was made to David Lee Child on account of his bias towards Whiggery. **1849** Macaulay *Hist. Eng.* ii. I. 275 Noisy zealots, whose only claim to promotion was that they were always drinking confusion to Whiggery, and lighting bonfires to burn the Exclusion Bill. **1876** *N. Amer. Rev.* CXXIII. 213 Whiggery meant sound views on the tariff. **1885** Courthope *Lib. Movem. Engl. Lit.* ii. 50 Whiggery, in Burke's days, meant simply adherence to the principles of the Revolution of 1688. **1908** *Sat. Rev.* 9 May 586/2 We must congratulate Mr. Asquith on disregarding the shrill cries of antiquated whiggery.

b. *fig.* Rebellion. (Cf. Whig *sb.*^{2} 3 b.)

1826 Galt *Last of Lairds* i. 3 When the day happened to be wet, the poultry were accustomed to murmur their sullen and envious whiggery against the same weather [etc.].

'**whiggish**, *a.*^{1} *rare.* In 6 **whighish**. [f. whig *sb.*^{1} + -ish^{1}.] Pale as whey.

1590 Fenne *Frutes, Hecuba's Mishaps* Cc4, Whose whighish skin the muddy mire with filthy spots had hild.

Whiggish ('hwɪgɪʃ), *a.*^{2} Also 7–8 **whigish**, 8 **wiggish**. [f. Whig *sb.*^{2} + -ish^{1}.] = Whig *a.*; also, Having or indicating something of the character of a Whig, inclined to Whiggism. (Formerly usually *hostile* or *contemptuous*; now usu. with reference to historical interpretation: see *Whig historian*, *history* s.v. Whig *sb.*^{2} and *a.* C.)

1680 *Roxb. Ball.* (1883) IV. 637 Great York in favour does remain, In spight of all the Whigish train. **1681** T. Flatman *Heraclitus Ridens* No. 23 (1713) I. 150, I scorn the Trade of Lying, if it were for nothing else, but that it makes a Man look so Whiggish. **1684** in T. Hutchinson *Hist. Mass.* (1795) I. 308 *note*, I suspect you, of the Massachusetts, are more whiggish, and your neighbours more toryish, to express it in the language of late in use. **1705** E. Ward *Hud. Rediv.* II. 20 Mix'd with some High Church Vindications Against false Whiggish Defamations. **1779** Burke *Corr.* (1844) II. 270 Your liberal, wise, and truly whiggish principles. **1790**

BURNS *Epit. Capt. M—— H——* viii, If ony whiggish whingin sot, To blame poor Matthew dare, man. **1813** MISS MITFORD 11 Apr. in L'Estrange *Life* (1870) I. vii. 229 If not a Reformer I am nothing; for I have as pretty a contempt for the ministers as my whiggish papa. **1816** SCOTT *Antiq.* v, The whiggish and perverse opposition to established rank and privilege. **1975** *Times Lit. Suppl.* 28 Nov. 1404/3 The danger, ever-present in women's history (as in labour history) of whiggish perspectives: of self-indulgently allowing enthusiasm for the women's cause today to obstruct sensitive understanding of women's situation yesterday.

†**b.** *fig.* Rebellious, factious. *Obs. slang.*

a **1700** B. E. *Dict. Cant. Crew, Whiggish,* Factious, Seditious, Restless, Uneasy.

c. *transf.* Liberal, 'broad': cf. LIBERAL *a.* 4 b.

1715 M. DAVIES *Athen. Brit.* I. Pref. 17 In the same fourth Century there were some Whiggish Pamphlets publish'd by some Moderate Heathens. **1907** P. T. FORSYTH *Positive Preaching* iv. 120 They gave the gnostics a huge advantage over the whiggish apologists and their liberal Christianity.

Hence **'Whiggishly** *adv.*, **'Whiggishness.**

1681 T. FLATMAN *Heraclitus Ridens* No. 32 (1713) I. 209 That was as *Whiggishly objected as ever I heard in my Life. **1684** LUTTRELL *Brief Rel.* (1857) I. 295 There have been commissioners appointed, who .. have turn'd out those persons in hospitalls and other publick places who are whiggishly inclined. **1728** SWIFT *Let. to Sheridan* 18 Sept., I fancy you may do some good with the Primate, .. if you wheedle him and talk a little Whiggishly. **1818** HOGG *Brownie of Bodsbeck* xii, Whiggishly inclined. **1975** *University* (Princeton Univ.) Winter 4/1 This is not to say whiggishly that science at any juncture has been the only description of physical reality that was historically possible. **1980** *Times Lit. Suppl.* 25 July 837/1 Authors tend to win a place in the history of social and political thought by making what is usually, and whiggishly, referred to as a 'theoretical contribution'. **1889** *Academy* 16 Nov. 311/1 Mr. Walpole has himself that trait of *Whiggishness which peculiarly fits him to paint the portrait of the chief of the Whigs. **1920** *Blackw. Mag.* Mar. 402/2 Johnson would have tolerated his coxcombry as little as he would have borne with his inveterate Whiggishness.

Whiggism ('hwɪgɪz(ə)m). Also 7–8 **Whigism.** [f. as prec. + -ISM.] The principles, tenets, or methods of the Whigs; moderate or antiquated Liberalism. (Opposed to TORYISM.)

? **1666** *Cal. State Papers, Dom. 1666–7* (1864) 415 Extract of a Scotch letter, by M. L'Estrange; whiggism and treason. **1683** WOOD *Life* (O.H.S.) III. 6 Sept., To expell Mr. Parkinson from the University for whiggisme. **1702** DE FOE *Shortest Way with Dissenters* 15 We can never enjoy a settled uninterrupted Union and Tranquility in this Nation, till the Spirit of Whiggisme, Faction, and Schism is melted down like the Old-Money. **1776** J. ADAMS *Let. to Sergeant* 21 July, Wks. 1854 IX. 425 But when persons come to see there is greater danger to their persons and property from toryism than whiggism, the same avarice and pusillanimity will make them whigs. **1813** W. TAYLOR in *Monthly Rev.* LXXII. 275 An account of the Kit-cat club, throws light on the history of Whiggism. **1844** DISRAELI *Coningsby* VI. iii, I look upon an Orangeman .. as .. the only professor and practiser of unadulterated Whiggism. **1844** *Punch* VI. 46/1 The velocity with which Lord Brougham turns round from Whiggism to Toryism. **1880** GREEN *Hist. Eng. People* IV. IX. i. 220 The King [*sc.* Geo. III] still called himself a Whig, yet he was reviving a system of absolutism which Whiggism .. had long made impossible.

b. (with *pl.*) A Whiggish principle or tenet.

1830 GEN. P. THOMPSON *Exerc.* (1842) I. 222 The whiggisms that are abroad upon this question of representation.

whighen, obs. form of QUICKEN *sb.*[1]

whighhie, var. f. WEHEE.

whight, whiȝt: obs. forms of WEIGHT *sb.*[2], WHITE, WIGHT.

whigmaleery ('hwɪgməlɪərɪ). *Sc.* Also **-me-, -ie.** [Origin obscure.] Anything fanciful or whimsical; a fantastic notion, whim, crotchet; a fanciful ornament, contrivance, etc. Also *attrib.*

1730 RAMSAY *Man with Twa Wives* 18 But Bess the whig .. Took figmaliries, and wald jump. **1786** BURNS *Brigs of Ayr* 96 Gin ye be a Brig as auld as me, .. There'll be, if that day come, I'll wad a boddle, Some fewer whigmeleeries in your noddle. **1793** —— *Lett. to Mrs. Dunlop* 5 Jan., I had two worthy fellows dining with me the other day, when I .. produced my whigmaleerie cup. **1818** SCOTT *Rob Roy* xix, It's a brave kirk—nane o' yere whigmaleeries and curlie-wurlies and open-steek hems about it. **1878** MRS. OLIPHANT *Primrose Path* vii, A' the whigmaleeries of the auld steeple.

whigwham, variant of WIGWAM.

whiht, obs. form of WIGHT.

whik(k, -en, obs. dial. ff. QUICK, QUICKEN.

whil, whilberow, whilc, whilch, whilde, obs. ff. WHILE, WHEELBARROW, WHICH, WILD.

while (hwaɪl), *sb.* Forms: 1, 4 **hwil,** (1 **huil**), 2–5 **wil,** 3 **hwile,** (**ȝwile, ȝwyle, ȝuile**), 3–5, 7 **whil,** 4 **huile,** (**wyel**), 4–5 **whyl, whylle,** 4–6 **whyll, wyle,** 4–7 **whyle,** (chiefly *Sc.*) **whill,** 4–5 **wile,** 5 **wyl, wyll,** (**weil, whylghe**), 5, 7 **whille,** 6 **wylle, will,** (**whyell, vyl,** *Sc.* **vhyle, vhill**), 3– **while;** 3–4 **quil,** 3–5 **quile,** 4 **quyl, quyle, quille,** 4–6 *Sc.* **quhile, qwhil,** 4–7 *Sc.* **quhil,** (9 *arch.*) **quhill,** 4–8 *Sc.* **quhyle,** 5 **qwile, qwyle, qwil, qwill,** *Sc.* **qwhile,** (**qwhiel**), **qwhill(e, quhille,** 5, 6 *Sc.* **qwyl,** 5–6 *Sc.* **quhyl, qwhyl,** 6 *Sc.* **quhyll.** *β.* 3 **hwule, whule, wule.** [OE. *hwíl* str. fem. = OFris. *hwîle, wîle* (Fris. *wîl*), OS. *hwîl, hwîla* time (MDu. *wîle* hour, moment, Du. *wijl*), OHG. *hwîl,* (*h*)*wîla* point or period of time (MHG. *wîle,* G. *weile*), ON. *hvíla* bed (Sw. *hvila,* Da. *hvile* repose, refreshment), Goth. *hweila* time:—OTeut. **χwīlō,* the first syllable of which derives from Indo-eur. *qʷi-,* represented by L. *quiēs* rest, *tranquillus* (= *-*quilnos*) quiet, OSl. *počiti* to rest; cf. the sense of ON. *hvíla* and *hvíld* rest, repose, and of the continental forms of the verb.]

I. 1. a. A portion of time, considered with respect to its duration; = TIME *sb.* 1, 2, rarely 4 or 6. Now almost exclusively in certain connexions (see below), the ordinary word being *time.* Formerly with gen. *while's.* Rarely *pl.*

971 *Blickl. Hom.* 125 Hwilce hwile hine wille Drihten her on worlde lætan. *a* **1250** *Owl & Night.* 1591 And swuþe longe hire is þe hwile, An ek steape hire þunþ a mile. *a* **1300** *Cursor M.* 22161 Als symon magus in his quile Right sua sal he þe folk bigile. **1303** R. BRUNNE *Handl. Synne* 12562 Holy cherche, despyse and fyle, þat wyl y bleþly, alle my whyle. **1390** GOWER *Conf.* I. 221 He despeired for the while. **1473** *Paston Lett.* III. 89 They shall dwell ther I wot no whylghe. **1485** CAXTON *Paris & V.* (1868) 82 After a whyle of tyme. **1533** MORE *Answ. Poys. Bk.* Wks. 1053/2 Though ye see euery man dye here for the whyle, yet I shall .. reyse them all vp .. at the last day. **1547–8** in Feuillerat *Revels Edw. VI* (1914) 32 During the whiles thies maskes were a makyng. *a* **1613** OVERBURY *A Wife,* etc. (1638) 277 Have but that while's patience, you may passe it drie-foot. **1644** DIGBY *Nat. Bodies* xv. §7. 135 The fire, in all this while of continuall application to the body it thus anatomiseth [etc.]. *a* **1683** OLDHAM *On Morwent* Wks. (1686) 75 Thy prudent Conduct had so learnt to measure The different whiles of Toil and Leisure. **1828** SOUTHEY in *Corr. w. C. Bowles* (1881) 133, I am now .. stealing whiles of time for the *Colloquies,* which are approaching to their close. **1829** CARLYLE *Ess., Novalis* (1840) II. 228 After short whiles, all is again swimming vaguely before them. **1841** CATLIN *N. Amer. Ind.* liv, Filling up the while with nonsensical garrulity. **1894** in Milne *Rom. Pro-consul* (1911) 26 We had a capital while together.

b. with adj. expressing quantity, as *good* (GOOD *a.* 19), *great, little, long, short;* also *any, no, some:* forming esp. advb. phr. = for a (long, etc.) time.

Beowulf 146 Wæs seo hwil micel. *a* **1000** *Cædmon's Gen.* 486 Lytle hwile sceolde he his lifes niotan. *a* **1175** *Cott. Hom.* 221 He wes to sume wile anstandende. *c* **1200** ORMIN 2392 Ʒho bilæf wiþþ hire frend Ʒet affterr þatt summ while. *c* **1290** *St. Dunstan* 51 in *S. Eng. Leg.* 20 A guode ȝwyle it was a-gon. *a* **1300** *Cursor M.* 3124 He began to luf him sua þat he moght na quil him for-ga. **1340** HAMPOLE *Pr. Consc.* 632 Whether he lyf lang or short while. *c* **1450** *Mankind* 574 in *Macro Plays* 22 Ewynsonge hath be in þe saynge, I trow, a fayer wyll; I am yrke of yt. **1533** ELYOT *Cast. Helthe* II. xxviii. (1541) 45 To liue lesse while than other men. **1542** UDALL *Erasm. Apoph.* 175 b, Philippus .. had slept a great long while together. **1597** MORLEY *Introd. Mus.* 81 The shorter while you staie vpon the discord, the lesse offence you giue. **1610** HOLLAND *Camden's Brit.* I. 506 Having enjoied these honors a small while. **1711** STEELE *Spect.* No. 33 ¶ 1, I do not know any thing that has pleased me so much a great while. **1796** BURNEY *Mem. Metastasio* II. 201, I have not written to you a long while. **1836** NEWMAN *Lett.* (1891) II. 197, I am not more lonely than I have been a long while. **1871** RUSKIN *Fors Clav.* ii. 15 A little while since, I was paying a visit in Ireland. **1897** FLOR. MONTGOMERY *Tony* i, The two sat for a little while at the other end of the carriage.

c. ***a while*** (also rarely ***one while***): (*a*) as sb. phr., a time, *esp.* a short or moderate time (chiefly with certain preps., viz. *after, for, in,* †*within*); contextually = a considerable time, some time, as in ***quite a while*** (colloq.). (*b*) as advb. phr. = for a (short or moderate) time (see also AWHILE).

once in a while: see ONCE 8 c.

(*a*) [*c* **950** *Lindisf. Gosp.* Luke iv. 5 *In momento temporis,* in huil tides.] *a* **1300** *Havelok* 722 Ne were neuere but ane hwile þat it ne gan a wind to rise. **13..** *E.E. Allit. P.* B. 1620 Þe burne byfore baltazar was broȝt in a whyle. *c* **1380** *Sir Ferumb.* 4573 Wyþinne a wyle þer wer y-dyȝt, Mo þan ten þousant of Sarȝyns wyȝt. **1470–85** MALORY *Arthur* VII. x. 226 Within a whyle they sawe a toure as whyte as ony snowe. **1513** DOUGLAS *Æneis* IV. iv. 29 Quhen Apollo list .. leif the flude Exanthus, for a quhile, To vesy Delos. **1526** TINDALE *John* xvi. 16 After a whyle ye shall nott se me. *a* **1533** LD. BERNERS *Huon* lxi. 213 They were within a whyell far fro ye londes of y^e .ii. admyralles sarazyns. **1561** T. HOBY tr. *Castiglione's Courtyer* IV. (1577) V viij b, After a whiles silence. **1621** LADY M. WROTH *Urania* 218 Pleasantly they passed a while together. **1718** HUTCHINSON *Witchcraft* xv. (1720) 232 After a while's Practice. **1847** HALLIWELL s.v., A while's work, work requiring a certain time. **1853** DICKENS *Bleak Ho.* xliv, It is to be forgotten now; to be forgotten for a while. **1870** FREEMAN *Norm. Conq.* (ed. 2) I. App. YY 700 So Eadwig escapes, at least for one while. **1900** *Longman's Mag.* Mar. 450 She .. rather enjoyed getting wet through once in a while. **1905** ELINOR GLYN *Viciss. Evang.* 149 It was quite a while before he elicited the facts from me.

(*b*) **1297** R. GLOUC. (Rolls) 2352 He sede he moste wende a wule out of þis lond. *a* **1300** *Cursor M.* 1309 Quen seth a quil had loked in, He sagh .. mikel welth and win. *Ibid.* 3622 A wyel sco hir vmbithogt. **1423** JAS. I *Kingis Q.* ii, I .. toke a boke to rede apon a quhile. **1568** GRAFTON *Chron.* II. 97 The sayde league continued but a while. **1667** MILTON *P.L.* II. 918 The warie fiend Stood on the brink of Hell and look'd a while, Pondering his Voyage. **1733** FIELDING *Don Quix. in Eng.* II. xiv, My landlord and the coachman won't overtake them one while, I warrant. **1781** JOHNSON *L.P., Fenton,* He was a while secretary to Charles earl of Orrery. **1816** J. WILSON *City of Plague* II. ii, I will sit down a while. **1873** SPENCER *Study Sociol.* vii. (1877) 148 The Smallpox epidemic, which a while since so unaccountably spread.

d. with demonstr. adj. *that* or *this* (now only with *all* preceding), forming advb. phr.

c **1480** HENRYSON *Robene & Makyne* 59 Makyne, I haif bene heir this quhyle; at hame god gif I wair. **1590** SPENSER *F.Q.* II. ii. 16 Her other sisters .., Who all this while were at their wanton rest. **1604** SHAKS. *Oth.* III. iv. 177, I haue this while with leaden thoughts beene prest. **1629** GAULE *Pract. Theories Christ* 355 The Iewes rested that Sabbath now; Christ rested that while in his Graue. **1711** STEELE *Spect.* No. 51 ¶ 8 He would see he has been mistaken all this while. **1871** SMILES *Charac.* ii. (1876) 34 All this while, too, the training of the character is in progress.

e. with qualifying sb.: The duration of, or time needed for (what is denoted by the sb.). *Obs.* or *arch.*

breathing-while, life-while, minute while, paternoster while, etc.: see the sbs.

13.. [see TWELVEMONTH 3]. **1377, 1591** [see MINUTE *sb.*[1] 1]. *c* **1430** *Chev. Assigne* 286 To speke with hym but a speche whyle. *c* **1450** in Aungier *Syon* (1840) 274 Al the bellys schal be ronge one *Miserere* whyle at leste, and than the chaptyr belle schal be ronge oo *Pater noster* while. **1593, 1873** [see BREATHING *vbl. sb.* 10]. **1676** WYCHERLEY *Pl. Dealer* III. i, Stay but a making Water while, (as one may say) and I'll be with you again.

2. a. ***the while*** (OE. *þá hwíle* accus.): (*a*) as advb. phr.: During the time, in the meantime, meanwhile; (*b*) followed by conj. †*the* or *that,* and later with ellipsis. *arch.* = WHILE *conj.* 1. **b.** ***all the while*** (with constructions as above): During the whole time (that). †**c.** ***to while*** (with constructions as above): For a time; for the time, meanwhile; for the time that, while. So *þer hwile,* etc.: see THEREWHILE. *Obs.* †**d.** ***in the while:*** in the mean time, meanwhile. *Obs.* (For *in the mean while* see MEAN WHILE.) †**e.** ***most while*** (cf. MOST C.): on most occasions, for the most part. †**f.** ***by while:*** on occasion, from time to time. ***over while:*** at times. Cf. UMQUHILE.

a. (*a*) *c* **960** ÆTHELWOLD *Rule St. Benet* (Schröer) ix. 33 Man þreo rædinga ræde and þry ræpsas, and ealle þa ȝebroþra þa hwile sittan. **1297** R. GLOUC. (Rolls) 1273 Þe king þe wule londone bisegede uaste. **1362** LANGL. *P. Pl.* A. VII. 8 What schul we wimmen worche þe while? *a* **1425** *Cursor M.* 3889 (Trin.) Þe while [*Cott.* to quils] holde lya in bedde þenne shal þou rachel wedde. **1593** SHAKS. *Rich. II* II. i. 211 Ile not be by the while. **1610** —— *Temp.* III. i. 24 If you'l sit downe Ile beare your Logges the while. **1772** MACKENZIE *Man World* I. xi, 'I will go,' said she, sobbing, 'and pray for him the while.' **1840** DICKENS *Old C. Shop* xx, Mr. Chuckster .. telling him he was wanted inside, bade him go in and he would mind the chaise the while. **1891** 'J. S. WINTER' *Lumley* iv, Wouldn't you like some lollipops to eat the while?

(*b*) *c* **888** ÆLFRED *Boethius* x, Eall hie [*sc.* earfoðnesse] us þyncað þy leohtran ða hwile þe þa oncras fæste bioð. **971** *Blickl. Hom.* 35 Swa we sceolan þa hwile þe we lifȝaþ her on worlde. *c* **1175** *Lamb. Hom.* 7 Þis witeȝede dauid þe þe salm scop in þe saltere muchel erdþon þa wile he liuede. *c* **1290** *St. Cuthbert* 3 in *S. Eng. Leg.* 359 Þe ȝwyle þat he was a ȝong child. **1297** R. GLOUC. (Rolls) 1962 Þo was traen al a louerd þe wule it wolde ylaste. *c* **1425** *Engl. Conq. Irel.* 16 The whill the host was thus in Ossory. **1594** MARLOWE & NASHE *Dido* I. i. A4, The while thine eyes attract their sought for ioyes. **1605** SHAKS. *Macb.* III. ii. 32 Vnsafe the while, that wee must laue Our Honors in these flattering streames. **1633** G. HERBERT *Temple, Sacrifice* xxxviii, I for both have wept When all my tears were bloud, the while you slept. **1650** CARSTAIRES *Lett.* (1846) 68 Not the whyle I was at home with you nor since. **1820** KEATS *Lamia* II. 68 Beseeching him, the while his hand she wrung, To change his purpose. **1870** MORRIS *Earthly Par.* III. 380 The while his right [hand] did shade His eyes from the bright sun.

b. *a* **1400** *Minor Poems fr. Vernon MS.* xxix. v. 49 For al þe while he was so seek, He feled neuere lisse ne lith, þerfore hym þouȝte beter legles. **1482** *Cely Papers* (Camden) 109 Hyt was not comen to Bregys all the whyle he wus there. **1539** *Bible* (Great) 1 Sam. xxii. 4 They dwelt w^t him all the whyle that Dauid kepte him selfe in hold. **1600** J. MELVILL *Autob. & Diary* (Wodrow Soc.) 485 He remeanit in the town all the whyll. **1654–66** EARL ORRERY *Parthen.* (1676) 685 All the while I was speaking, I was much concern'd in Statira's looks. **1667** MILTON *P.L.* I. 539 All the while Sonorous mettal blowing Martial sounds. **1700** HICKES in *Pepys's Diary,* etc. (1879) VI. 206 She was shut up all the while we were there. **1844** DISRAELI *Coningsby* VIII. vi, The rogue had an eye all the while to quarter-day. *a* **1864** HAWTHORNE *Septimius* (1872) 152 But all the while he was gone there was the mark of a bloody footstep impressed upon the stone doorstep of the Hall.

c. *c* **950** *Lindisf. Gosp.* Luke viii. 13 *Qui ad tempus credunt,* ðaðe to tid *vel* to huil ȝelefað. *c* **1000** *Sax. Leechd.* II. 348 Þonne meaht þu hine betan to hwile. *c* **1250** *Gen. & Ex.* 1104 We sulen it fren, Ðor quile ðu wilt ðor-inne ben. **13..** *Cursor M.* 22060 (Edinb.) An angel .. To þe dragune suiþ he wanne, .. And in þat pitte him sperid faste, To-quile a thusande ȝier to laste. *c* **1330** R. BRUNNE *Chron. Wace* (Rolls) 4141 To whyle þe kyng & his cosyns In loue loken ar þer lynes, Richesse þey hadde ynow to wylle. **1338** —— *Chron.* (1810) 71 To while þat he was fresch þei fond him fulle austere.

d. **1542** UDALL *Erasm. Apoph.* 77 Yet in ye while, thei would neuer the more foloe the steppes of thesame good menne. **1605** B. JONSON *Sejanus* II. ii, In the while, Take from their strength some one or twaine, or more Of the maine Fautors. *a* **1617** BAYNE *Lect.* (1634) 11 In the while, wee must labour to keepe a watch over our soules. **1760–72** H. BROOKE *Fool of Qual.* (1809) II. 111 Mary, in the while, being frighted almost to death.

e. *c* **1383** in *Eng. Hist. Rev.* Oct. (1911) 742 Neiþir preestis neiþir dekenis shulden ben occupied in ony seculer office in lordis courtis most whil seculer men ben sufficient to do suche seculer office.

f. **13..** *Orfeo* 8 Sum [layes ben] of happes þat fallen by whyle. *c* **1400** *Apol. Loll.* 97 He cessiþ to harme hem, or fendiþ hem ouer wyl.

3. *spec.* The time spent (connoting the trouble taken or labour performed) in doing something. †**a.** in phrases such as ***to quit*** or ***yield*** (one) ***his while***, to repay (him) for his trouble, also ironically, to 'pay (him) out'; ***to lose*** or ***spill*** one's ***while***, to waste one's time or effort. *Obs.*

c **1175** *Lamb. Hom.* 137 Mon sullðe his elmesse ðenne he heo ȝefeð sulche monne þe him deð.. wiken and cherres and ðencheð mid his elmesse forȝelden him ðeo hwile. *a* **1250** *Owl & Night.* 1020 He miȝte bet sitte stille Vor al his wile he sholde spille. **1297** R. Glouc. (Rolls) 2476 Send after help.. & icholle hor wule ȝelde. *c* **1386** Chaucer *Miller's T.* 113 A clerk hadde litherly biset his whyle But if he koude a Carpenter bigyle. **1390** Gower *Conf.* III. 151 The proverbe is, who that is trewe, Him schal his while nevere rewe. *c* **1400** *Rom. Rose* 4392 If Ielousie doth thee payne, Quyte hym his while thus agayne. *c* **1430** *How Good Wife taught Dau.* 111 in *Babees Bk.*, And he þat weel dooþ, þou qwite him weel his whyle.

b. Now only in phr. ***worth the while*** (now rare or arch.), ***worth*** one's ***while***, ***worth while***: often merely = worth doing, profitable, advantageous (the notion of time being weakened or lost). ***to make it worth*** (a person's) ***while***, to give (him) sufficient recompense.

1387 Trevisa *Higden* (Rolls) IV. 355 The queene.. beet Iudas ful ofte, but al for nouȝt, ffor it was not worþ þe while. **1639** Ld. Digby *Lett. Conc. Relig.* (1651) 123, I would not think my pains lost, or study of the Fathers not worth the while. **1662** Stillingfl. *Orig. Sacræ* III. i. §18 It had not been worth while for the soul to have been in the body. **1672** Marvell *Reh. Transp.* I. 166 Nor is it worth ones while to teach him out of other Authors. **1755** Mrs. F. Brooke *Old Maid* No. 4. 24 In one word, madam, make it worth my while. **1842** Lever *Jack Hinton* xxvii, It is worth while being a soldier in Ireland. **1861** Mrs. H. Wood *East Lynne* III. xix, 'Keep dark upon it, Bethel,' he said; 'I will make it worth your while.' **1877** Huxley *Physiogr.* 93 It may be worth while to explain the kind of information which they give.

†**4.** (without article.) Sufficient or available time, leisure for doing something: = TIME *sb.* 8.

a **1225** *Ancr. R.* 32 3if ȝe habbeð hwule, siggeð þesne psalm, 'Levavi oculos meos'. **1387** Trevisa *Higden* (Rolls) IV. 87 Whanne he myȝte have while he wroot fables. *c* **1450** *Mirk's Festial* 125 On Settyrday þay myȝt not haue whyll. **1600** Holland *Livy* VI. x, If they might have had while and time as well to follow it. *a* **1639** W. Whateley *Prototypes* I. xix. (1640) 233 He can have while to ruminate upon the evil things which Satan and the fleshe doe stirre up.

†**5. a.** Term or period of office; *transf.* office, function, 'place'. *Obs. rare.*

c **1375** *Sc. Leg. Saints* xii. (*Mathias*) 351 Schaw quhilk of þire twa sal ve ches To supple þe quhyle of Iudas. *c* **1449** Pecock *Repr.* III. xvi. 386 Thouȝ this man which now lyueth performe not the deede for his while.

¶**b.** Used in the Wycliffite Bible to render L. *vicissitudo* in senses of *turn*: (*a*) a service rendered (= TURN *sb.* 23); (*b*) ***by whiles***, by turns (TURN *sb.* 28). *Obs. rare.*

1382 Wyclif *1 Sam.* xxiv. 20 The Lord ȝeelde to thee this while [Vulg. *vicissitudinem hanc*], for that, that to day thou hast wrouȝt in me. **1388** —— *1 Kings* v. 14 So that in twei monethis bi whilis thei weren in her howsis.

II. 6. a. Time at which something happens or is done; occasion; †proper or suitable time; †season: = TIME *sb.* 13–15. *Obs.* exc. *arch.* or *dial.* (or as in e below).

Mostly with qualifying word, either with prep. preceding, or with ellipsis of prep. forming advb. phr. (cf. 1 b–d, 2), e.g. ***that while*** = at that time, on that occasion, then; ***another while*** = 'another time', on another occasion; ***every while*** (also as one word, after *everywhere*), †at every time, always (*obs.*): every time, on every occasion (*dial.*). See also below, and OTHERWHILE, SOMEWHILE.

c **950** *Lindisf. Gosp.* Matt. xxvi. 55 *In illa hora..*, in ðæm tid *vel* in ðære huile. *c* **1200** *Trin. Coll. Hom.* 51 Þat israelisshe folc was walkende toward ierusalem,.. and þo wile was hersum godes hese. *c* **1375** *Cursor M.* 13130 (Fairf.) Seynt Iohn þis quile in prisoun lay. *c* **1380** *Sir Ferumb.* 2140 Þus wyle was he on halle sittyng with is puple atte mete, þan com þer an heþene kyng rydynge atte ȝete. *c* **1400** *MS. Serm.* (Tollem. MS.), We been not sufficiaunt to knowe þe tymes or þe whilis þat þe fadir of þe Trynyte haþ put in his owne power. **1418–20** J. Page *Siege Rouen* in *Hist. Coll. Cit. Lond.* (Camden) 33 The Fraynysche men in the same whyle, Forthe they went with Umfrevyle. *c* **1440** *Pallad. on Husb.* VIII. 3 Whete heruest now in tempur lond is while Forto conclude. **1470–85** Malory *Arthur* VII. v. 218 Hope ye so that I maye ony whyle stand a proued knyght. **1503** Dunbar *Thistle & Rose* vi, Thow did promyt, in Mayis lusty quhyle, For to discryve the Ross. **1552–3** in Feuillerat *Revels Edw. VI* (1914) 129 At dyuers other tymes betwene those whiles. **1579–80** North *Plutarch* (1595) 842 The [dragon's] taile on a time fell out with the head, and complained, saying, it would another while go before, & would not alwaies come behind. **1648** Crashaw *Steps, Hymn Epiph.* 30 But every where, and every while, Is one consistent solid smile. **1671** H. M. tr. *Erasm. Colloq.* 149 *Eu.* Were those women who encouraged thee with thee that while? *a* **1850** Rossetti *Dante & Circle* I. (1874) 100 What while a lady greets me with her eyes. **1884** *Cheshire Gloss.*, *Every while stitch*, every now and then; at times. **1886** Stevenson *Kidnapped* xxii, There are whiles.. when ye are altogether too canny and Whiggish to be company for a gentleman like me.

b. ***one while*** (adv. phr.): †(*a*) at one time, on one occasion, in one case (usually opp. to ***another while***, sometimes to *then*, *again*, *anon*); also rarely = on some future occasion, 'some time' (*Obs.*); (*b*) *U.S.*, a long time.

1470–85 Malory *Arthur* XVI. xvii. 688 Soo wente they douneward in the see one whyle bakward another whyle forward. **1575** *Gammer Gurton* II. iii. 21 One whyle his tonge it ran and paltered of a cat; Another whyle he stammered styll vppon a rat. **1598** Sylvester *Du Bartas* II. i. III. *Furies* 450 One-while the Boulime, then the Anorexie, Then the Dog-hunger. **1664** South *Serm., John xv. 15* (1697) II. 86 Those, who are one while courteous.. and obliging,.. but within a small time after, are so supercilious, sharp, [etc.]. **1744** Eliza Haywood *Female Spect.* v. (1748) I. 262 One while we are transmogrified into milk-maids—then into a kind of Amazonians. **1815** Kirby & Sp. *Entomol.* iii. (1818) I. 73 One while a silky fluid should be secreted, at another none. **1836** T. C. Haliburton *Clockmaker* (1837) 1st Ser. xvi. 136 You'll search one while.. afore you'll find a man that.. is equal to one of your free and enlightened citizens. **1852** Mrs. Stowe *Uncle Tom's Cabin* I. xi. 159 I'd mark him ..so that he'd carry it *one* while. **1897** 'Mark Twain' *Following Equator* liii. 511 If India knows about nothing else American, she knows about those, and will keep them in mind one while.

†**c.** With qualifying sb. (cf. TIME *sb.* 13 b), as ***dinner while***, ***mass while***, ***service while***, ***supper while***, etc.: see also the sbs. (Sometimes including the idea of duration, as in 1 e.) *Obs.* (or *rare arch.*).

13.. [see MASS *sb.*[1] 7]. **1435** Misyn *Fire of Love* II. x, With desire in meet qwhiel to ȝerne. **1557** Machyn *Diary* (Camden) 148 My lord of London begane the durge, with ys myter [on] alle the durge wylle. **1597** Beard *Theatre God's Judgem.* (1612) 119 The gouernour of Mascon, a Magitian, whom the diuell snatched vp in dinnerwhile. *a* **1667** C. Hoole *Accidence* (1671) 110 *Inter cœnandum*, at supper while. **1868** Browning *Ring & Bk.* I. 311 Be it but a straw 'twixt work and whistling-while.

d. In exclamations of grief: cf. similar use of *day*, *time*. Chiefly *poet. Obs.* or *arch.*

c **1402** Lydg. *Compl. Bl. Knt.* 244 This is the cold that wolde the fyr abate Of trewe mening; alas! the harde whyle! *c* **1440** *York Myst.* vi. 51 That we shulde haue alle welthis in walde, wa worthe þe whyle! **1513** Douglas *Æneis* VI. viii. 77 Alace the quhile! *a* **1586** Montgomerie *Misc. Poems* xxi. 25 O! waryit be the vhyle That euer we wer acquent! **1596** Shaks. *1 Hen. IV*, II. iv. 146 God helpe the while, a bad world I say. **1810** Scott *Lady of L.* II. xv, Woe the while That brought such wanderer to our isle! **1825** —— *Talism.* x, He conceives himself, God help the while, ungratefully treated.

e. Phr. with pl.: ***at whiles***, at times, sometimes, at intervals. ***between*** (***betwixt*** obs. or arch.) ***whiles***: see BETWEEN-WHILES.

[*c* **1449** Pecock *Repr.* II. xx. 273 Good and profitable to be had at certein whilis.] **1540** Palsgr. *Acolastus* V. i. X iv b, Me semeth now and than, or at whiles that [etc.]. **1647** Trapp *Comm. Rom.* ii. 15 Meanwhile, or, Betwixt whiles. **1717** Berkeley in *Mem.* (1784) 61 A sort of.. dashing (as it were) of waves, and between whiles, a noise like that of thunder. **1802** Mrs. Radcliffe *Gaston de Blond.* Wks. 1826 II. 62 To drive away the gloom, that yet, at whiles, hung upon his brow. **1865** Swinburne *Chastelard* II. i. 66 To think what grievous fear I have 'twixt whiles Of mine own self and of base men.

while (hwaɪl), *adv.* (*adj.*), *conj.* (*prep.*) Forms: 1–3 **hwile**; from *c* 1300 onwards as in WHILE *sb.*; also 4 quel, 5 **whele**, *Sc.* **quhel**, 6 **whel**, 8 **wile**, 9 *dial.* **whell**; 6 vhol, 9 *dial.* **wol(l**. [As adv., OE. *hwíle*, accus. of *hwíl* WHILE *sb.*; as conj., abbreviation of OE. phr. *þá hwíle þe*, ME. *þe while þat* = 'during the time that' (see WHILE *sb.* 2 a), = OHG. *dia wîla* (*unz*) so long as (MHG. *die wîle* while, G. *dieweil* while, because), Du. *dewijl*; similar abbreviation has given G. *weil* because, Du. *wijl*, NFris. *wîl*.

In senses A. 1 and 2, ME. *while* may be in some texts a reduced form of *whilen*, WHILOM.]

A. *adv.* (*adj.*)

†**1.** At a time or times, sometimes; *esp.* introducing each of two or more parallel phrases or clauses: At one time... at another time; now ...then: = WHILOM 1. *Obs.*

a **1000** *Hymns* iii. 44, 5 (Gr.) Hwile mid weorce, hwile mid worde, hwile mid ȝeþohte þearle scyldi. *c* **1175** *Lamb. Hom.* 133 Ure helend saweð his halie word hwile þurh his aȝene muðe and hwile þurh ðere apostlene muðe. *c* **1200** *Trin. Coll. Hom.* 207 Eȝen bihelden þat he ne sholden, wile idel, wile unnut, wile ifel. *a* **1300** *Cursor M.* 7433 Quil wit gleu, and quil wit sang,.. þus he serued saul lang. **1375** Barbour *Bruce* I. 338 For knawlage off mony statis May quhile awailȝe full mony gatis. *c* **1425** Wyntoun *Cron.* (Royal MS.) I. Prol. 32 For Romans to rede is delytabyle, Suppose that thai be quhyle bot fable. *c* **1470** Henry *Wallace* v. 611 Quhill wald he think to luff hyr our the laiff, And othir quhill he thocht on his dissaiff. *c* **1560** A. Scott *Poems* (S.T.S.) xxxi. 24 Lufe sall him hald W[t]in the dungeoun of dispair; Quhyle hett, quhyle cald. **1584** Hudson *Du Bartas' Judith* VI. 91 While vp he lifts his head, while lets it fall. **1632** J. Hayward tr. *Biondi's Eromena* 184 The intellect (fixing it selfe, while on one, and while on another wonder of matter and workemanship).

†**2. a.** At one time, formerly, once: = WHILOM 2.

c **1000** *Deor's Compl.* 36 (Gr.) Ic bi me sylfum secȝan wille, þæt ic hwile wæs Heodeninga scop. *c* **1175** *Lamb. Hom.* 17 Ne do þu þin uuel on-gein uuel swa me dude hwile. *a* **1250** *Owl & Night.* 1016 Þeȝ eni god man to hom come, So wile dude sum from rome. *c* **1305** *St. Andrew* 29 in *E.E.P.* (1862) 99 Þe gywes while nome And slowe him as he worþie was. *c* **1380** *Sir Ferumb.* 2580 Þat god of miȝt.. Hwich of marie þat mayde briȝt while tok flechs & blode. *c* **1425** Wyntoun *Cron.* I. Prol. 15 Thai þat set haly þare delite Gestis or storyis for to write,.. As Gwydo de Calumpna quhile.

†**b.** as *adj.* That formerly existed, occurred, etc.; former, 'late': = UMQUHILE B., WHILOM 2 b.

1399 Langl. *Rich. Redeles* III. 363 Þey.. were y-dubbid of a duke ffor her while domes. *c* **1425** Wyntoun *Cron.* II. viii. 756 For honoure of his modyr qwhile.

†**3.** For a or the time, temporarily; at the same time, meanwhile. (See also THEREWHILE.) *Obs. rare.*

a **1500** *Colkelbie Sow* 828 (Bann. MS.), Thocht he wald preve the thrid penny quhyle hid, Quhilk for the tyme no fruct nor proffeit did. **1508** Kennedie *Flyting w. Dunbar* 428 Thow beggit with a pardoun in all kirkis,.. And ondir nycht quhyle stall thou staggis et stirkis. *c* **1645** Howell *Lett.* I. II. x. (1690) 110 Yours while J. Howell.

B. *conj.* (or in *conj. phr.*) and *prep.*

1. a. ***while*** (***that***): during the time that. (Now expressed by *while* alone: cf. THAT *conj.* 7.)

Often with ellipsis before a pple. or other predicative word or phrase, e.g. *while walking*, *while at rest*, *while an infant*.

1154 *O.E. Chron.* (Laud MS.) an. 1137 Ðet lastede þa .xix. wintre wile Stephne was king. *c* **1200** Ormin 2393 Whil þatt ȝho wass Wiþþ hire kinn att hame. *c* **1275** Lay. 14873 Þat we solle hatie wile þat we libbeþ [*c* **1205** þa while þa we luuien]. **13..** *Cursor M.* 6088 (Gött.) Ne hones noght quile ȝe er etand. *c* **1350** *Will. Palerne* 2537 While men hunted after hem þai han a-wai schaped. *c* **1400** *Pilgr. Sowle* (Caxton) II. lvii. (1859) 55 While that thou and I were coupled to geders, thou madest me to lede a ful vnthryfty lyf. **1513** Douglas *Æneis* I. v. 71 Quhill that of Troy and Ilion stude the ring. **1599** Shaks. *Hen. V*, I. ii. 178 While that the Armed hand doth fight abroad, Th' aduised head defends it selfe at home. **1611** Sir W. Mure *Misc. Poems* ii. 67 Quhil in this weak estait, ail meanes I soght To be aweng'd on him. **1667** Milton *P.L.* IV. 977 While thus he spake, th' Angelic Squadron bright Turnd fierie red. **1779** *Mirror* No. 32 ¶6 While we were sitting together, talking of old stories,.. John entered. **1849** Macaulay *Hist. Eng.* v. I. 662 Cornish was arrested while transacting business on the Exchange. **1882** Besant *All Sorts* xv, While he was laughing the door opened.

b. With special reference (*a*) to the extent of the time: During the whole, or until the end, of the time that; as long as (see also 2 a); (*b*) to the limits of the time: Within, or before the end of, the time that.

(*a*) *c* **1230** *Hali Meid.* 6 He wule carie for hire.. hwil ha riht luueð him. *c* **1300** *Havelok* 301 Daþeit hwo it hire yeue Euere-more hwil i liue! *a* **1400–50** *Wars Alex.* 2255 Yf it worth sall to wy whil þe world standes. **1422** Yonge tr. *Secr. Secr.* 161 Whyle an hooke is a yonge Spyre, hit may be wonde into a wyth. *c* **1430** *Two Cookery-bks.* 23 Wasshem.. whele þey ben slepyr. *c* **1440** *Promp. Parv.* 74/2 Chylde, whyle hyt can not speke, *proles*. **1529** More *Dyaloge* I. xv. 20/1, I shall loue her ye worse whyle I lyue. **1610** Shaks. *Temp.* III. ii. 120 While thou liu'st keepe a good tongue in thy head. **1706** Prior *Ode to Queen* xix, Nought done the Hero deem'd, while ought undone remain'd. **1742** Fielding *J. Andrews* II. iv, She told her 'while there was life there was hope.' **1848** Dickens *Dombey* xxxii, The confidence of this house.. is not to be abused.. while I have eyes and ears.

(*b*) *c* **1300** *Havelok* 363 Him for to hoslen, and forto shriue, Hwil his bodi were on liue. **1393** Langl. *P. Pl.* C. XI. 287 Whil þow art ȝong and ȝep, and þy wepne kene, Awreke þe þerwith. *c* **1450** *Mirk's Festial* 5 Wherfor, syrs,.. whyll ȝe byn here, makyth amendes for your mys-dedys. *c* **1450** *Mankind* 77 in *Macro Plays* 4 Lett ws be mery wyll we be here! *c* **1550** Lyndesay *Tragedie* 303 Amend ȝour lyfe now, quhill ȝour day Induris. **1697** Dryden *Virg. Georg.* III. 263 Set him betimes to School.. While yet his youth is flexible and green. **1825** T. Hook *Sayings* Ser. II. *Passion & Princ.* xi. III. 253, I wish.. that to-morrow.. you would step down to the Tower;.. while you are there, you might just go to the London Docks. **1866** Ruskin *Crown Wild Olive* iii. 203 All the greatness she [*sc.* England] ever had,.. she won while her fields were green and her faces ruddy.

†**c.** Without necessarily implying duration: At the time that; when. *Obs.*

a **1300** *Fragm. Pop. Sci.* (Wright) 62 As me mai the mone i-seo while heo is nue riȝt. *c* **1320** *Cast. Love* (ed. Hall.) 403 For in tyme whill he fre was, He hede with him bothe Merci and Pes. *a* **1425** *Cursor M.* 15461 (Trin.) Whil ȝe se me kisse him Leye hondes on him allone. **1477** *Rental Bk. Cupar-Angus* (1879) I. 209 We half grantyt to the forsad Paton and Jonat the tak of Rechy Jak quhel it ma vake.

d. During which time; and meanwhile.

c **1400** *Warres of the Jewes* in Warton *Hist. Eng. Poetry* (1774) I. x. 311 In Tyberyus tyme the trewe emperour Syr Sesar hym sulf saysed in Rome Whyle Pylot was provost under that prynce ryche. **1697** Dryden *Virg. Georg.* IV. 809 Thus have I sung of Fields, and Flocks, and Trees,.. While mighty Cæsar, thund'ring from afar, Seeks on Euphrates Banks the Spoils of War. **1766** Goldsm. *Vicar W.* vi, Moses sate reading, while I taught the little ones. **1820** Keats *Lamia* I. 242 He pass'd,.. while her eyes Follow'd his steps. **1905** Elinor Glyn *Viciss. Evang.* 79 Mr. Montgomerie said rather gallant things to me,.. while the girls looked shocked.

2. *transf.* with various connotations. **a.** As long as, so long as (implying 'provided that', 'if only').

1375 Barbour *Bruce* I. 60 Thar mycht succed na female, Quhill foundyn mycht be ony male. *c* **1400** *Apol. Loll.* 14 Þe kirk may not iustli priue þe comyning of cristun men, nor taking of þe sacraments.. wyle he is iust. **1597** Hooker *Eccl. Pol.* v. xlvii. §4 Neither boldnes can make vs presume as long as we are kept vnder with the sense of our owne wretchednes; nor, while we trust in the mercie of God through Christ Iesus, feare be able to tyrannize ouer vs. **1849** Macaulay *Hist. Eng.* i. I. 47 The encroachments of the ecclesiastical power.. produced much more happiness than misery, while the ecclesiastical power was in the hands of the only class that had studied history.

b. At the same time that (implying opposition or contrast); *adversatively*, when on the contrary or on the other hand, whereas; *concessively*, it being granted that; sometimes nearly = although.

1588 Shaks. *L.L.L.* I. i. 74 Painefully to poare vpon a Booke, To seeke the light of truth, while truth the while

Doth falsely blinde the eye-sight of his looke. **1617** SIR W. MURE *Misc. Poems* xxi. 23 Whill others aime at greatnes boght with blood, Not to bee great thou stryves, bot to bee good. **1662** STILLINGFL. *Orig. Sacræ* III. i. §7 While they deny a Deity, they assert other things on far less reason. **1719** WATTS *Ps.* xxiii, There would I find a settled Rest, (While others go and come). **1749** HARTLEY *Observ. Man* I. i. §2. 75 White is vulgarly thought to be the most uncompounded of all Colours, while yet it really arises from a certain Proportion of the Seven primary Colours. **1857** BUCKLE *Civiliz.* I. x. 608 While the object of the people was to free themselves from the yoke, the object of the nobles was merely to find new sources of excitement. **1864** BRYCE *Holy Rom. Emp.* v. (1875) 52 In rude and unsettled states of society men respect forms and obey facts, while careless of rules and principles. **1908** R. BAGOT *A. Cuthbert* vi. 51 While regretting the sorrow which had fallen upon him, Miss Cuthbert was nevertheless glad that her brother was free.

c. In modern colourless use: At the same time that, besides that, in addition to the fact that; often = and at the same time, and besides.

[**1750** SHENSTONE *Ode Rural Eleg.* 161 There, while the seeds of future blossoms dwell, 'Tis colour'd for the sight, perfum'd to please the smell.] **1860** LÖWENTHAL *Morphy's Games Chess* 165 A very good move, for while it brings the Queen into a more attacking position, it at the same time defends White's Queen's Pawn. **1904** *Times* 25 May 3/6 The walls..are decorated with white enamelled panelling, while the frieze and ceiling are in modelled plaster.

3. a. (†Also with *that*, *at*.) Up to the time that; till, until. Now *dial.* (chiefly *north.*).

Occas. with reference to place, etc.: †***while it come to*** = as far as, up to.

13.. *Seuyn Sages* (W.) 1644 Dwelle thou, wil ich arisen be. **1375** BARBOUR *Bruce* IV. 763 Man is in-to dreding..of thingis to cum, quhill he Haue of the end the certante. **1419** *Munim. de Melros* (Bann. Club) 502 þe qwhilkis Indentours þe forsaid Nychole has delyuerit till þe said abbot and Conuent..qwhile at þai be fullely assythit of þe said fowrty pund. *c* **1420** *Liber Cocorum* (1862) 46 Fyrst sethe þy mustuls quyl shel of lepe In water. *c* **1460** *Battle of Otterburn* liv. (Child *Ball.* VI. 298, They swapped together whyll that they swette. *c* **1480** HENRYSON *Bludy Serk* 40 To fecht with him..Quhill ane wer dungin doun. **1524** Q. MARG. in *St. Papers Hen. VIII*, IV. 129, I thowt best to put them both in the castel of Edynbrou, vhol that thay fynd a vay how the Bodarz may be vel reulyd. *a* **1578** LINDESAY (Pitscottie) *Chron. Scot.* (S.T.S.) I. 7 Thair was nevir perfytt stabillitie quhill that the Douglas was perisch deid and gane. **1586** MARLOWE *1st Pt. Tamburl.* IV. iv, Faste and welcome sir, while hunger make you eat. **1589** NASHE *Martin Marprel.* Wks. (Grosart) I. 117 Let him swell while he burst. **1688** BUNYAN *Heavenly Footman* (1724) 77 Run sweet Babe, while thou art weary, and then I will take thee up and carry thee. **1759** R. BROWN *Compl. Farmer* 9 Take horse-aloes.. give him the purge.., and ride him out again while he purges. **1813** HOGG *Queen's Wake* 81 They drank of the byshopis wyne Quhill they culde drynk ne mair. **1825** BROCKETT *N.C. Gloss.* s.v., Stay while I come back. **1872** *J. Hartley's Yorksh. Ditties* Ser. II. 17 We blushed wol us faces wor all in a blaze.

b. as *prep.* Up to (a time), up to the time of; till, until. Now *dial.* (chiefly *north.*).

c **1450** *St. Cuthbert* (Surtees) 1276 þat þou fast noȝt whil to morne. **1464–5** in *Acts Parlt. Scot.* (1874) XII. 30/2 þt þe lew be proclamit to xiij s. iiij d. fra fasterin sewyn furth next tocum and quhill thane to haue course as thai haue now. **1559** in *Wodrow Soc. Misc.* (1844) 268 Thay..wald not beleif me..quhill now. **1587** GREENE *Euphues* Wks. (Grosart) VI. 251 Their commaunds were dated but while death. **1605** SHAKS. *Macb.* III. i. 44 While then, God be with you. **1662** GURNALL *Chr. in Arm.* III. xxiii. §4 The Apothecary gathers his simples in Summer, which haply he may not use while Winter. **1720** *Lett. Lond. Jrnl.* (1721) 14 Tho' he sweat and scrub while Doomsday. **1722** in *Rutland Gloss.* (1891) 39, I was 2 dayes; And my Son was 2 days. And the third day wile three a Clock. **1854** MISS BAKER *Northampt. Gloss.* s.v., It wants a quarter while nine o'clock.

4. ***while as*** (also occas. as one word, cf. WHENAS, WHEREAS). **a.** = 1. *Obs.* or *rare arch.*

1563 GOOGE *Eglogs* etc. (Arb.) 69 Whyle as the rauenyng Wolues he prayed his gylteles lyfe to saue. **1593** SHAKS. *2 Hen. VI*, I. i. 225 Pirates may make cheape penyworths of their pillage,..While as the silly Owner of the goods Weepes ouer them. *c* **1620** Z. BOYD *Zion's Flowers* (1855) 138 Hee spares while as the faults of men are young. *c* **1690** N. BURN in *Roxb. Ball.* (1888) VI. 608 Burn cannot his grief asswage, whileas his dayes endureth. **1786** *Har'st Rig* (1801) xci, But now, whileas the show'r does last, 'Tis no thought proper they shud fast. **1812** CARY *Dante, Parad.* xxv. 79 Whileas I spake. **1918** W. DE LA MARE *Motley* 68 How do the days press on, and lay Their fallen locks at evening down, Whileas the stars in darkness play.

†**b.** = 2 b. *Obs. rare.*

1625 HART *Anat. Ur.* I. ii. 13 The chiefe..part of Physicke diagnosticke..is..neglected; while as the ordinarie sort of Physitians do onely labour to know..the nature..of the disease by the..indication of the..vrine. **1646** R. BAILLIE *Anabaptism* (1647) 98 To Christ they give but one nature, while as all Divines since his Incarnation give him two.

C. Combinations: †**while-being** *a.* temporary, or temporal (*rare*); **while-ever (whilever)** *conj.* [see EVER *adv.* 8 e; for the abbreviated spelling cf. *wherever*], as long as (*rare*); **while-you-wait** *adj.* or *adv. phr.* (orig. *U.S.*), designating a service that is performed immediately (as opp. to one for which the customer must leave his property and collect it later); also *fig.*; also *absol.* as *sb.*, an establishment providing such a service; freq. (in advertisements) spelt *while-u-wait.*

1674 N. FAIRFAX *Bulk & Selv.* 40 This time-lasting World, and every while-being thing in it. **1776** *Ann. Reg., Hist. Eur.* 73/1 He solemnly declared, that while-ever he sate in that house, he would not endure such language. **1878** JAS. THOMSON *Plenipotent. Key* 19 She had had her husbands five, And would have more whilever she was alive. **1929** *Amer. Speech* V. 24 Those who are selling 'service' are fond of using expressions of this sort:..Shine While U Wait, Hats Cleaned While U Wait, [etc.]. **1936** MENCKEN *Amer. Lang.* (ed. 4) 209 Q-room.., While-U-wait, and Bar-B-Q.., all of them familiar signs. **1965** H. GOLD *Man who was not with It* xxix. 271 We were at a low office block.., shoe repair and while-you-wait. **1972** *Guardian* 11 July 10/6 The..catalogue essay..is a masterpiece of myth-making, art history while-u-wait. **1972** *Times* 9 Aug. 12/7 (*caption*) A while-you-wait parts replacement service. **1977** *Evening Gaz.* (Middlesbrough) 11 Jan. 13/2 (Advt.), M.O.T. test while-u-wait.

while, *v.* [f. WHILE *sb.*

A new formation, having no continuity with early ME. I-HWULEN to have leisure, or connexion with the continental forms OHG. *wîlôn* (MHG. *wîlen*, G. *weilen* to stay, linger), ON. *hvíla* (Sw. *hvila*, Da. *hvile*) to rest, Goth. *hveilan* to pause, cease (cf. WHILE *sb.* etym.).]

†**1.** *trans.* To occupy or engage (a person) for a time, or for the time; to fill up the time of. *Obs.*

1606 BP. HALL *Medit. & Vows* I. §88 Hee findes not-any worthy employment to while himselfe withall. **1613** PURCHAS *Pilgrimage* VII. xi. 592 The..still Lakes, thicke Woods, and varietie of the Continent-obseruations, haue thus long whiled vs. *a* **1659** OSBORN *Misc.* Pref. B 8, The First Cause of their projection, being rather, for the intent to While my Selfe, then Busie others.

†**2.** with *it*: To keep it up, 'stick it out'. *Obs.*

a **1617** BAYNE *Lect.* (1634) 137 They are poore, not brought up to it, not able to while it, wife and children might begge, [etc.].

3. To cause (time) to pass without wearisomeness; to pass or get through (a vacant time), esp. by some idle or trivial occupation. Also, to divert the attention from, 'beguile' (sorrow, pain). Usually, now almost always, with *away*.

Possibly developed from sense 1 by transference of the object from the person to the time. Association with such phr. as *beguile the day, the time* (Shaks.), L. *diem decipere*, F. *tromper le temps*, has led to the substitution of WILE *v.* by some modern writers.

1635 QUARLES *Embl.* III. xiii. 34 Nor do I beg this slender inch, to while The time away, or falsly to beguile My thoughts with joy. *a* **1644** —— *Sol. Recant.* solil. II. 36 And like a pain-afflicted stripling, play With some new Toy, to while thy grief away. **1706** BRAGGE *Disc. Parables* (ed. 3) I. i. 17 Those..who frequent our Religious Assemblies..to while away the Time that lies useless upon their Hands. **1726** POPE *Let. to Bethel* 9 Aug., Let us while away this life; and (if we can) meet in another. **1769** WESLEY *Wks.* (1872) XII. 374 There will be a danger likewise of whiling away time. **1796** MME. D'ARBLAY *Camilla* X. iii, Such dangerous expedients to while away chagrin. *a* **1800** PEGGE *Anecd. Engl. Lang.* (1814) 229 To while away so much time in perusing this Disquisition. **1807** W. IRVING *Salmag.* No. 13 (1811) II. 75 These moments of mental gloom, whiled away by the cheerful exercise of our pen. **1809** MALKIN *Gil Blas* XII. viii. (Rtldg.) 434 A delightful residence, where he whiled away three weeks. **1813** BYRON *Corsair* I. xiv, Then shall my handmaids while the time along. **1840** DICKENS *Old C. Shop* ix, When she left her own little room to while away the tedious hours. **1882** *Mrs. Raven's Temptation* I. 5 There was nothing for the young traveller to while the time with.

b. *intr.* Of time: To pass tediously. Now *dial.*

1712 [see WHILING *ppl. a.*]. **1898** HARDY *Wessex Poems* 106 All that year and the next year whiled, And I still went thitherward.

†**4.** ***while off***: to put (a person) off for the time.

1646 LOCKYER *Serm.* 31 If you cast them off too, when they have cast off all for you, or if you shall while them off, when they tell you, Sir, this is our last meale in the barrell [etc.].

while, obs. f. WHEEL, WILE.

whileas: see WHILE *conj.* 4.

†**whilemeal**, *adv.* In 4 **whilmele**. [f. WHILE *sb.* + -MEAL.] Used to render L. *vicissim* by turns.

1382 WYCLIF *1 Kings* v. 14 Ten thousand bi eche moneth whilmele [1388 bi whilis].

whilen, obs. form of WHILOM.

†**whilend**, *a. Obs.* [OE. *hwílende*, rare var. of *hwílwende* (cf. WHILWENDLIC), f. *hwíl* WHILE *sb.* + *wend-* to turn, WEND *v.*] Temporary.

a **1050** *Liber Scintill.* ix. (1889) 49 Hi na to þære hwilendre mihtan dædbote becuman. *c* **1175** *Lamb. Hom.* 7 þeos world is whilende and ontful and swiðe lewe. *a* **1225** *Ancr. R.* 182 Vorte beon martirs efning, þuruh a wilninde [*v.r.* hwilinde] wo. *c* **1230** *Hali Meid.* 35 For þat hwilende [*v.r.* hwilinde] lust. *a* **1272** *O.E. Misc.* 94 þis world fareþ hwilynde hwenne on cumeþ an oþer goþ.

†**whileness.** *Obs. rare.* [Abnormally f. WHILE *sb.* + -NESS.] Used to render L. *vicissitudo* in senses (*a*) = TURN *sb.* 23 (cf. WHILE *sb.* 3 a, 5 b); (*b*) change, variation.

1382 WYCLIF *Joel* iii. 4, Y shal ȝeelde the whilnesse to ȝou on ȝour hed. —— *James* i. 17 The fadir of liȝtis, anentis whom is not ouerchaunginge, nether schadewing of whileness, or tyme.

whilere (hwaɪl'ɛə(r)), *adv. arch.* [Orig. two words, WHILE *adv.* 2 and ERE; for the abbreviated spelling cf. *wherever*.] A while before; some time ago: = EREWHILE.

a **1000** *Judith* 214 þa þe hwile ær elðeodigra edwit þoledon. *c* **1386** CHAUCER *Can. Yeom. Prol. & T.* 775 Helpeth me now as a dide yow whil eer. *c* **1412** HOCCLEVE *De Reg. Princ.* 1317 Whyl er, my sone, tolde I naght to þe What habundance in youth I hadde of good. *c* **1460** J. RUSSELL *Bk. Nurture* 377 Son, take þy knyfe as y taught þe whileere, Kut bravne in þe dische riȝt as hit liethe there. **1590** SPENSER *F.Q.* I. ix. 28 That cursed wight, from whom I scapt whyleare. **1610** SHAKS. *Temp.* III. ii. 127 Will you troule the Catch You taught me but whileare? **1630** MILTON *Circumcision* 10 He who with all Heavn's heraldry whileare Enter'd the world, now bleeds to give us ease. *a* **1652** BROME *Weeding of Cov.-Garden* I. i, Mark how he stands, as if he had learn't a posture at Knightsbridge spittle as we came along while-eare. **1767** MICKLE *Concub.* I. ii, Melodious Mulla! when, full oft whyleare, Thy gliding Murmurs soothd the gentle Brest Of hapless Spenser. **1808** SCOTT *Marmion* v. Introd. 139 My harp..Whose Anglo-Norman tones whilere Could win the royal Henry's ear. **1884** J. PAYNE *Tales from Arabic* I. 225 How joyous and how solaceful was life in them whilere!

whiles (hwaɪlz), *sb.* (*advb. gen.*), *conj.* (*prep.*), *adv. Obs.* or *arch.* Forms: 3 **hwihles**, 3–4 **wiles**, 4–5 **whilis, whylys, whilles, whils**, 4–6 **whyls**, 4–8 **whyles**, 5 **whilez, whilys, whylis, whyllys, wilis, wylys, whills, (whels)**, 5–6 **whilse**, 6 **whylse**, 4– **whiles**; 3–4 **quiles**, 4 **quyles, quilis, quylis, qwylys, quils, qwhylles**, *Sc.* **quhillez**, 4–6 *Sc.* **quhilis**, 6 *Sc.* **quhillis, quhylis, quhyles, quhyls**, 7–8 *Sc.* **quhiles**. [orig. in advb. and conj. phr., as *sumehwiles* formerly, *oðerhwiles* at times, *þerhwiles* while, meanwhile, formed with advb. -s on *sumhwile*, *oðerhwile*, *þerhwile* (see SOMEWHILE(S, OTHERWHILE(S, THEREWHILE(S); on this type were modelled the expressions *þis* or *þat quiles*, *to quiles*, *long whiles*, *a* (*good*) *whiles*, etc. and the simple conj. *whiles*.]

I. †**1.** Preceded by a demonstrative adj., indefinite article, or other qualifying word, forming advb. phrases: e.g. ***that whiles***, at or during that time; ***long whiles***, for a long while, etc. *Obs.*

13.. *Cursor M.* 5495 (Gött.) þat quiles ras þar a neu king. *Ibid.* 5713 þis quilis [*Fairf.* alle þis quyle] was in israel þe folk ledd in mekil vnwele. *c* **1330** R. BRUNNE *Chron. Wace* (Rolls) 10198 In þat louh ar sexti iles—In þo þe dwelte longe whyles. *c* **1430** *Two Cookery-bks.* 42 Lat it seþe esyli,..a good whylys. *c* **1450** LOVELICH *Merlin* 9833 Thanne schal neuere kyng Arthewr..his lond jn pes thanne non whyles holde. *c* **1540** tr. *Pol. Verg. Engl. Hist.* (Camden 1846) 254 In the meane whiles. **1594** R. ASHLEY tr. *Loys le Roy* 85 b, It endured but a whiles. **1607** J. CARPENTER *Plaine Mans Plough* 233 Ye haue beene as sheepe going a great whiles astray. **1633** PRYNNE *Histrio-m.* I. 52 All which, if our Actors ..would but a whiles consider [etc.]. **1651** H. L'ESTRANGE *Answ. Mrq. Worc.* 91 Where God one whiles insinuates himself into the conscience in the language of a familiar Friend, another while reclaims it with the indignation of an incensed Judge. **1654** GAYTON *Pleas. Notes* IV. 289 Nor have the Wardens ventur'd all this whiles, To lay, except my selfe, one in those Iles.

2. ***the whiles***, advb. and conj. phr. = *the while*, WHILE *sb.* 2 a, b. †Also (rarely) ***in whiles*** as conj.

a **1300** *Cursor M.* 3309 Bot ai þe quils he ne fan To behald þat leue maidan. **13..** *Ibid.* 1729 (Gött.) Bot euer þe quilis þat he [*sc.* Noah] wroght, þe folk to preche forgat he noght. **1375** BARBOUR *Bruce* III. 435 The king, the quhilis..Red to thaim..Romanys off worthi Ferambrace. **14..** *Northern Passion* 430 (Camb. Ii. 4. 9) Here ȝe schuln me A byde þe qwylys [*v.rr.* to whyls, whils] I go here be syde. **1540** PALSGR. *Acolastus* III. v. R j b, We wyll walke vp and downe ..the whyles. **1583** STOCKER *Civ. Warres Lowe C.* IV. 4 b, All suche pointes, as thei could iustly finde them selues agreeued, and in whiles he gouerned, deminished. **1590** SPENSER *F.Q.* II. vii. 62 The whiles my hands I washt in puritie, The whiles my soule was soyld with foule iniquitie. **1609** HOLLAND *Amm. Marcell.* XIX. xii. 141 Paulus all the whiles was the prompter..of these cruell enterludes. **1632** HOLLAND *Cyrupædia* 144 Perceiving..draught-beasts to draw other things, and feeding the whiles. **1759** COLMAN *Ode* in *Prose Sev. Occas.* (1787) II. 277 His heel Sparkles refulgent with elastic steel: The whiles he wins his whiffling way. **1808** SCOTT *Marmion* I. xiii, They feasted..The whiles a Northern harper rude Chanted a rhime of deadly feud.

†**3.** ***to whiles***, advb. and conj. phr. = 2. Also as conj., to the time that, until. *Obs.*

a **1300** *Cursor M.* 1729 Ai to-quils þat [noe] sa wroght þe folk to preche for-gate he noght. *Ibid.* 3889 To quils haa lya in þi bedd, For-soth þan sal þou rachel wedd. *Ibid.* 4923 þan war þaa breþer..prisund til þe thrid morn,..To-quils sent ioseph þe yepe Men þair harnais for to kepe. **1338** R. BRUNNE *Chron.* (1810) 220 Suilk ribaudie þei led,..To-whils Sir Edward had seisid alle Euesham. **1357** *Lay Folks Catech.* (T.) 139 To whiles that his bodi lai in the graue, The saule with the godhede went untill hell. *a* **1400** *R. Brunne's Chron. Wace* (Rolls) 2645 þe while [*Petyt MS.* Towhils] þer fader was on lyue For þe royalme gon þey to stryue. *c* **1400** *Ywaine & Gaw.* 1079, I dar yow hight, To have him her or the thrid nyght; Towhils efter yowr kownsayl send.

II. 4. *conj.* = WHILE *conj.* 1; also with *that*, †*as*.

c **1220** *Bestiary* 256 in *O.E. Misc.* 8 Ðus ȝe tileð ðar, wiles ȝe time haueð. *c* **1275** *Ibid.* 144 We schulde..vs ibidde nyht and day hwihles þat we libbe. *a* **1300** *Cursor M.* 1833 For quils þat godd þam raght his grace, Littel roght þam of his manance. *Ibid.* 1948 To lof leute quils þou mai lif. ? *a* **1400** *Morte Arth.* 3651 Thies ware the cheefe armes Of Arthure ..qwhylles he in erthe lengede. *c* **1440** *Generydes* 4037 Whels he sleppe this cursyd creature Full trayturly with hir is goo. *c* **1465** *Chevy Chase* xxxvii, Fyghte ye, my myrry men, whyllys ye may. **1526** TINDALE *Matt.* v. 25 Agre with thine adversary at once, whiles thou arte in the waye with hym. **1551** TURNER *Herbal* I. Prol. A ij b, He that whilse other men feight, standeth in the top of a tre. **1572** *Satir. Poems Reform.* xxxiii. 108 Thir vertewis all scho had, quhyls scho stude aw Of God Eterne. **1593** SHAKS. *3 Hen. VI*, III. i. 39 The Tyger will be milde, whiles she doth mourne. **1633** PRYNNE *Histrio-m.* I. Ep. Ded., The pressing importunity..drew me whiles I was yet a novice. *a* **1648** DIGBY *Closet Opened* (1669) 156 No longer then whiles you can say the Miserere Psalm very leisurely. **1756** MRS. CALDERWOOD in *Coltness Collect.* (Maitland Club) 189

Whiles Mr Calderwood went through the colledge..with the fathers, Daniel attended me. **1858** MORRIS *Welland River* 230, I pray you, nurse-tend me, my knight, Whiles that I have my breath.

†**b.** *transf.* = WHILE *conj.* 2. *Obs.*

1551 TURNER *Herbal* I. Prol. A iij b, For now (say they) euery man with out any study..will become a Phisician... Whilse by occasyon of thys boke, euery man, nay euery old wyfe will presume not without the mordre of many, to practyse Phisick. **1580** FULKE *Retentive, Discov. Dang. Rock* xii. 248 Whiles the one will vrge a prerogatiue of Peter, the other will forge a Byshoplike office in the Apostles. **1610** HOLLAND *Camden's Brit.* I. 71 Whiles Gallienus..gave himselfe over to..riotousnesse, the State of Rome..lay dismembred as it were. **1665** EVELYN *Let. to Sir W. Coventry* 2 Oct., Sir William D'Oyly and myself have near ten thousand upon our care, whiles there seems to be no care of us.

†**5.** *conj.* and *prep.* Till, until: = WHILE *conj.* 3.

1398 *Munim. de Melros* (Bannatyne Cl.) 489 To be..haldene..qvhillez þ[t]..satisfactioun and payement..be..made. *a* **1400** *Pistill of Susan* 177 Whiles þe Morwen to Middai and mare. *c* **1450** *St. Cuthbert* (Surtees) 7492 þare he bade whils he ware deede. **1526** *Pilgr. Perf.* (W. de W. 1531) 259 Whyles the nexte matyns. **1545** ASCHAM *Toxoph.* I. 37 b, I coulde..reken vp suche a rable of shoters that be named..in poetes, as wolde holde vs talkyng whyles tomorowe. **1601** SHAKS. *Twel. N.* IV. iii. 29 He shall conceale it Whiles you are willing it shall come to note.

6. *adv.* †**a.** Formerly: = WHILE *adv.* 2. *Sc. Obs.*

c **1375** *Sc. Leg. Saints* xxxvii. (*Vincencius*) 3 þis name vincensius to say Is man þat ourcumys ay, As sancte vincent quhilis dide Thru his pacience. **1573** *Satir. Poems Reform.* xli. 94 That Bogill thair that ȝe hard blaw, With quhome quhyles ȝe wer small content.

b. Sometimes: = WHILE *adv.* 1. Chiefly *Sc.*

In mod. use apprehended as sb. pl.: cf. WHILE *sb.* 6 e.

c **1480** HENRYSON *Two Mice* 7 Quhyle vnder busk, quhyle vnder breir, Quhylis in the corne. *c* **1550** ROLLAND *Crt. Venus* I. 356 Lufe..alteris ay to euerie kinde and stait: Quhylis to, quhylis fra. *a* **1557** GRIMALDE in *Tottel's Misc.* (Arb.) 103 Italian whiles, and Spanish you do hear, and know full well. **1661** R. BAILLIE in *Lauderdale Papers* (Camden 1884) I. 96 My hert whiles trimbles for you. *a* **1722** FOUNTAINHALL in M. P. Brown *Suppl. Dict. Decis.* (1826) II. 460 She took whiles fits of distraction. **1829** BROCKETT *N.C. Gloss.* (ed. 2) s.v., It rains whiles. **1830** NEWMAN *Verses Var. Occas.* (1868) 42 Keen regret and tearful yearning, Whiles unfelt, and whiles returning. **1886** STEVENSON *Kidnapped* xxvi, So we lay.., whiles whispering, whiles lying still.

whilest, obs. form of WHILST.

whilie ('hwaɪlɪ). *Sc. dial.* Also **whiley, whyllie.** [f. WHILE *sb.* + -IE.] A short time.

1819 J. BURNESS *Plays* 29 Master Clinton is out a whyllie syne. **1908** *Old-Lore Misc.* I. IV. 183 After it was burned a whiley. **1920** J. L. WAUGH *Heroes* 18 When ye've been a whilie here. **1951** N. M. GUNN *Well at World's End* xxiv. 214 'Be quiet!' she said... 'I just came for a whilie to see them.' **1981** G. HAMMOND *Revenge Game* vi. 55 The inspector's house..was let to a retired couple for a whilie, but they moved away up to Inverness.

whiling ('hwaɪlɪŋ), *ppl. a.* [f. WHILE *v.* + -ING[2].] Of time: Passing tediously, tedious: see WHILE *v.* 3 b.

1712 STEELE *Spect.* No. 448 ¶1 The whiling Time, the gathering together, and waiting a little before Dinner, is the most awkwardly passed away of any Part in the four and twenty hours. *Ibid.* 522 ¶1 To pass away the whiling Moments and Intervals of Life.

whilk (hwɪlk). [?.] Local name for the scoter, a species of wild duck.

a **1705** RAY *Syn. Avium* (1713) 138 *Anser maximus niger*, The Whilk dictus, ineunte Bruma primum adveniens. [Hence in later books.]

whilk, var. WHELK; dial. f. WHICH.

whill, obs. form of WHILE.

whillaloo ('hwɪləluː), *sb.* (*int.*, *v.*) *dial.* Also 7 **fuillilaloo,** 8 **whilly lou,** 9 **whillaluh, whillilu, whillilew, whillalew.** [Ir. *uileliugh.* Cf. ULULU.] A cry or song of lamentation; an outcry, uproar, hubbub. Also as *int.* and *v. intr.* Cf. PILLALOO *sb.* (*int.*).

1663 R. HEAD *Hic et Ubique* I. vi. 18 Enter Patrick crying ..Fuillilaloo! **1790** JAS. FISHER *Poems* 65 She's sleeping now! Yet wakens wi' a greeting eye, An' whilly lou. **1800** MARIA EDGEWORTH *Castle Rackrent* Tales 1832 I. 5 Then such a fine Whillaluh! you might have heard it to the farthest end of the county. [*Ibid.* 100 The declining taste for the Ullaloo in Ireland.] **1820** HOGG *Winter Even. Tales* I. 162 What whillilu is that, Thou keep'st a trilling at? **1841** LEVER *O'Malley* lxxx, And sure I set up a whillilew myself. **1899** [see PILLALOO *sb.* (*int.*)]. **1977** *Times Lit. Suppl.* 22 Apr. 480/4 All those uncles trailing their coats and shouting whillaloo and clear the way.

Whillans ('hwɪlənz). The name of Don *Whillans* (1933–85), mountaineer, used *attrib.* of objects devised by him for the assistance of climbers, as ***Whillans box***, a kind of frame tent (see quot. 1971[1]); ***Whillans harness***, a harness designed for use by mountaineers climbing fixed ropes; ***Whillans whammer***, a kind of peg hammer or piton.

1971 C. BONINGTON *Annapurna South Face* v. 66 At this stage, Base Camp was no more than a staging camp, with a two-man tent and two Whillans Boxes... We had been worried that ordinary tents might prove inadequate on the very steep ground... Don had come up with the solution, designing a prefabricated, box-like structure, with a framework of timber and an outer covering of proofed nylon. *Ibid.* xii. 147 This [*sc.* being on an ice cliff] was one place where Dougal found a use for the Whillans Whammer, Don's space-age climbing tool, for its squat, triangular-shaped pick proved ideal for this type of ice. **1972** D. HASTON *In High Places* xi. 118 Huddled into the back of the Whillans box—a super-strong frame tent designed by Don —we could only sit and wait. **1974** H. MACINNES *Climb to Lost World* ix. 137 It was ironic that the designer of the Whillans harness was the only member of the expedition who didn't have..one which would fit his ample girth. **1978** P. GILLMAN *Fitness on Foot* v. 73 The Willans harness is manufactured by the Lancashire company Troll.

whille, -ll(e)s, -llest, -llom(e, -llon, obs. ff. WHILE, WHILES, WHILST, WHILOM.

whilly ('hwɪlɪ), *v. Sc.* [? Short for WHILLYWHA *v.*] *trans.* = WHILLYWHA *v.*

1721 RAMSAY *Addr. to Town-Council Edin.* 10 They..The honest Lieges whilly'd. **1737** —— *Sc. Prov.* (1797) 91 Wise men may be whilly'd wi' wiles. **1820** SCOTT *Abbot* xvi, These baptized idols..whillied the old women out of their corn and their candle ends.

whillywha ('hwɪlɪhwɑː, -ɔː), *sb. Sc.* Also **-whaw, -whaa, -wa, whilli(e)wha, whullywha.** [Of obscure origin.]

1. A wheedling or insinuating person; a flattering deceiver. Also *attrib.*

c **1680** [F. SEMPILL] *Banishm. Poverty* in Watson *Coll. Sc. Poems* (1706) I. 12 We fear'd no Reavers for our Money, Nor Whilly-whaes to grip our Gear. **1714** RAMSAY *Elegy on Cowper* v, He gather'd Gear..and left it a'! May be to some sad Whilliwhaw O' fremit Blood. **1824** SCOTT *Redgauntlet* ch. xii, He's a whilly-whaw body and has a plausible tongue of his own. **1890** SERVICE *Notandums* xix, Ony whillywha o' an Englisher.

2. Wheedling speech, flattery, cajolery.

1816 SCOTT *Old Mort.* v, I wish ye binna beginning to learn the way of blawing in a woman's lug wi' a' your whillywha's. **1843** BALLANTINE *Gaberlunzie's Wallet* x. 225 'Gae wa' wi' your whillywhaws,' said Nanny.

whillywha, *v. Sc.* [See prec.] *trans.* To take in or persuade by flattery; to wheedle, coax, cajole.

1816 SCOTT *Old Mort.* xl, He canna whilliwha me as he has dune mony a ane. **1893** STEVENSON *Catriona* xv, The fower lads..tried to whillywha him to be quiet.

whilmele, -nesse: see WHILEMEAL, -NESS.

whilom ('hwaɪləm), *adv.* (*adj.*), *conj.* Forms: 1 **hwilum, -on, -an, -un, wilum,** 3 (*Orm.*) **whilumm, hwilem, (h)wylem, hwylen, ȝwilene, wilen,** 3–4 **whilen,** 4 **whylon, (whilhom),** 4–5 **whilum,** 4–6 **whylome,** 4–7 **whylom,** 5 **whylum, whilene,** 6 **whillon,** (*Sc.* **vhylome**), 7 *Sc.* **whillome,** 8 **whillom,** 4– **whilome, whilom;** 3–4 **quilum,** 4 *Sc.* **qwhilom,** 4–5 *Sc.* **quhilom,** 4–6 *Sc.* **quhilum, quhylum,** 5 *Sc.* **qwhilum, qwhylum, qwylum,** 6 **quilome.** [OE. *hwílum*, later *-on*, *-an*, = OS. *hwîlon* at times (MDu., MLG. *wîlen* formerly, Du. *wijlen* late = deceased), OHG. *hwîlôn*, *-on* (MHG. *wîlen*, *wîlent*, G. *weiland* formerly) dat. pl. of WHILE *sb.*]

A. *adv.* (*adj.*)

†**1.** At times: = WHILE *adv.* 1, WHILES 6 b. *Obs.*

a **900** *O.E. Martyrol.* 7 July, Ymb tweȝen daȝas, hwilum ymb þry, hwilum æfter ealre wucan. *a* **1000** *Boeth. Metr.* xxix. 53 Hwilum cerreð eft on uprodor ælbeorhta leȝ, leoht lyfte; liȝeð him behindan hefiȝ hrusan dæl, þeah hit hwilan ær eorðe sio cealde oninnan hire heold. *a* **1300** *Cursor M.* 25166 þar es resun qui vr bon Es noght granted us quilum sun. *c* **1350** *Will. Palerne* 1788 Whilum þei went on alle four ..& whan þei wery were þei went vp-riȝttes. ? *a* **1400** *Morte Arth.* 1145 Thai tiltine to-gederz; Whilome Arthure ouer, and other-while vndyre. ? *a* **1550** *Freiris Berwik* 353 in *Maitland Folio MS.* (S.T.S.) 143 And quhylum he sat still in ane studeying, And quhylum on his buik he was reyding. *a* **1600** MONTGOMERIE *Misc. Poems* xlii. 24 Flie vhylome love, and it will folou thee.

2. At some past time; some time before or ago; once upon a time: = WHILE *adv.* 2, WHILES 6 a. *arch.*

c **1200** ORMIN 4868 Ure Laferrd Crist himm sellf Uss ȝaff heroffe bisne, þær þær he seȝȝde himm sellf whilumm þurrh hiss prophetess tunge. *c* **1205** LAY. 28633 þa wes hit iwurðen þat Merlin seide whilen. *c* **1250** *Kent. Serm.* in *O.E. Misc.* 27 Hi offrede Stor, þet me offrede wylem be þo ialde laghe to here godes sacrefise. *a* **1300** *Cursor M.* 6786 To cumlinges do yee right na suike, For quilum war yee seluen slike. *c* **1386** CHAUCER *Knt.'s T.* 1 Whilom as olde stories tellen vs Ther was a duc þat highte Theseus. *c* **1425** WYNTOUN *Cron.* II. Prol. 22 As Orosius qwhilum wrate. **1513** BRADSHAW *St. Werburge* II. 2021 Auncient poetes..Whilom flouryng in eloquence facundious. **1581** A. HALL *Iliad* IV. 66 Oyntments ..T'aswage the paine: the which whilom the cunning Chyron taughte To Esculape. **1582** STANYHURST *Æneis* III. (Arb.) 72 This Polydor whillon..Too king Treicius was sent. **1656** EARL MONM. tr. *Boccalini's Advts. fr. Parnass.* II. lxi. (1674) 213 The whilome powerful Kingdom of Hungary. **1682** DRYDEN *Mac Flecknoe* 35 The Lute I whilom strung. **1749** FIELDING *Tom Jones* x. viii, The 'squire..began to roar forth the name of Sophia as loudly.. as whilom did Hercules that of Hylas. **1808** SCOTT *Marmion* IV. xi, Where oft whilom were captives pent. **1879** JEFFERIES *Wild Life in S. Co.* i. 10 The wistful eyes which whilom glanced down..upon the sweet clover fields.

b. as *adj.* That existed, or was such, at a former time; former; †of a person, 'late', deceased (*obs.*): = WHILE *adv.* 2 b. *arch.*

1452 in Tytler *Hist. Scot.* (1864) II. 387 All them that had arte or parte of the slaughter..of whylum William, Earle of Douglas, my brother. **1581** A. HALL *Iliad* IV. 70 Thy whilome sire..neuer quaild in mortal ioyne. *a* **1657** SIR W. MURE *Hist.* Wks. (S.T.S.) II. 249 Designeing her the wife to whillome S[r] Adame Mure. **1837** CARLYLE *Fr. Rev.* III. v. iii, General Doppet, a whilom Medical man. **1868** G. DUFF *Pol. Surv.* 151 Mexico..that whilom dependency of the Spanish Crown. **1888** BRYCE *Amer. Commw.* lxxvii. III. 17 When superstition and the habit of submission have vanished from the whilome subjects.

†**3.** At a future time, some time; in future.

a **1300** *Cursor M.* 17732 Quilum sal þis ilk barn Be to sum men in uprising, Til oþer sum in dun falling. **1513** BRADSHAW *St. Werburge* I. 81 Therfore I purpose..All suche ydlenes whylom to refuse.

B. *conj.* = WHILE *conj.* 1, 3. *dial.*

1616 R. C. *Times' Whistle*, etc. 121 A man..With whom his father held much conversation Whilome he livde. **1647** WARD *Simple Cobler* 51 Subjects their King, the King his Subjects greets, Whilome the Scepter and the Plough-staffe meets. **1854** MISS BAKER *Northampt. Gloss.*, *Whilom*, whilst, during which time. 'Stay whilom I come.'

¶ Aberrant uses. ***of whilom***: for some time past. So ***this whilom***.

1619 FLETCHER *Mons. Thomas* IV. ii, This mony I do give ye, because of whilom You have been thought my son. *c* **1620** Z. BOYD *Zion's Flowers* (1855) 72, I wot not, what in mee is come to pass, In mee this whilome who most gladely was.

Hence [with *-s*, after WHILES] †**whiloms** *adv. Sc. Obs.* (5 **quhillumys,** 6 **quhyllum(m)is, quhylomis;** cf. WFris. *wilens*), at times, sometimes.

a **1500** *Bernard. de cura rei fam.* 219 Gef quhillumys pleseis ioculatoris,..Fenȝe þe þar fantasy to here. *a* **1585** MONTGOMERIE *Flyting* 508 In þe bark of ane bowrtrie, quhyllumis they bed it. **1768** ROSS *Helenore* I. 69 Whiloms they tented, an' sometimes they plaid.

whilse, obs. form of WHILES.

whilst (hwaɪlst), *adv.*, *conj.* (*prep.*) Forms: 4 **quilest, -ist, quylest, -ist,** 5 **qwhilste, whylst,** 5–6 **whylest,** 6 **whillest, whylyst, wylst,** *Sc.* **quhylest,** 6–7 **whilest,** 7 **whil'st,** 6– **whilst.** [f. WHILES + *-t* as in *amongst*, *amidst*.]

1. a. In advb. phr. *the whilst* (obs. or rare arch.), also (rare) †***to whilst, in the whilst***, or as simple adv. *whilst* (obs. exc. dial.): During that time, meanwhile. Also †***a whilst***: for a time.

c **1375** *Cursor M.* 6417 (Fairf.) þe quilest moises helde vp his hende Hit was wele in þe batel kende, For ay to quilest witerly Had goddis folk þe ouer maistri. **1595** in Ellis *Orig. Lett.* Ser. III. IV. 116, I served a whilest with the late Erle of Leycester. **1601** SHAKS. *Twel. N.* IV. ii. 4 Doe it quickly. Ile call sir Toby the whilst. **1613** BEAUM. & FL. *Cupid's Rev.* II. v, Go run, And tell the Duke; And whilst I'll close her eyes. **1646** H. LAWRENCE *Commun. Angels* 113 If God would doe all, and men might sleepe the whilest. **1671** H. M. tr. *Erasm. Colloq.* 228 Alway, except that in the whilest at the first, I lived four years at Padua. *c* **1672** *Roxb. Ball.* (1888) VI. 500 Though present you be, all the whilst that they dine. **1683** in *10th Vol. Walpole Soc.* (1922) 67 Pray..forget not the proposal of Sr: Yours Really whilst F. Place. **1819** SCOTT *Ivanhoe* x, But a small sum; something in hand the whilst. **1895** JAS. PRIOR *Renie* xxi, Why don't you send for the p'liceman whilst?

b. ***the whilst***, conj. phr. (also with *that*): During the time that, while; †when. *Obs.* or *rare arch.*

c **1375** *Cursor M.* 2966 (Fairf.) þe folk ware ful of pride þe quylest he dwelled ham bi-side. *Ibid.* 15461 þe quilist þat ȝe me se him kis Lay hande on him. **1582** STANYHURST *Æneis* III. (Arb.) 79 Thee whilst fayre Phœbus thee yeers course roundlye reuolued. **1595** SHAKS. *John* IV. ii. 194, I saw a Smith stand with his hammer (thus) The whilst his Iron did on the Anuile coole. **1625** FLETCHER & SHIRLEY *Nt. Walker* I. i, Make your mirth, the whilst I bear my misery. **1798** *Anti-Jacobin* No. 25 (1799) II. 237 Each his head..Shakes, the whilst his tale is told.

2. *conj.* (†also with *that*) = WHILE *conj.* 1, b, d, WHILES 4.

c **1375** *Cursor M.* 2085 (Fairf.) He liued lelly quylist he moȝt. *Ibid.* 5491 Quylest atte Ioseph regned þare His breþer in egipte regnande ware. **1435** MISYN *Fire of Love* II. ix. 91 Slike frenschyp is fenyd, for it may not last bot qwhilste lust & profett bydis. *c* **1450** in Aungier *Syon* (1840) 308 A clothe, up on the which the professours must lygh prostrat whylst the letany is in syngyng aftyr masse. **1569** *Reg. Privy Council Scot.* Ser. I. II. 4 The parliament held quhylest scho wes in Lochlevin. **1579** LYLY *Euphues* I. P ij b, Whilest that the childe is young, let him be instructed in vertue and lyterature. **1598** SHAKS. *Merry W.* I. i. 186 Ile nere be drunk whilst I liue againe, but in honest, ciuill, godly company. *a* **1631** DONNE *Serm., Ps. xxxii. 6* (1640) 597 Woe unto us, if we seeke him not whilest he affords us these helpes. **1635** JACKSON *Creed* VIII. viii. 73 During the time of his humiliation here on earth, or whilest hee became hostage for our Redemption. **1669** WORLIDGE *Syst. Agric.* 222 The Trees..and Fields are now naked, unless cloathed in white, whilest the Countrey-man sits at home, and enjoyes the Fruit of his past labours. **1703** DE FOE *More Reform.* 12 With lame pretences they revive Those Lines when Dead, he blush'd at whilst alive. **1782** ELIZ. BLOWER *Geo. Bateman* III. 7 All in less time than whilst one could cry—'A good riddance'. **1818** SCOTT *Br. Lamm.* xxi, Fetch us up a bottle of the Burgundy,..And I say, Craigie, you may fetch up half-a-dozen whilst you are about it. **1848** THACKERAY *Van. Fair* xxv, Be quiet whilst the tempest lasts. **1918** *Act 8 & 9 Geo. V* c. 17 Sched. I. ii, Such revocation shall not be made whilst the Bill..is pending in either House.

†**b.** *prep.* During. *Obs. rare*$^{-1}$.

1591 SPARRY tr. *Cattan's Geomancie* 186 Whilest the time that the Emperour Charles the fift was at Nece..I was requested..to make him a fygure.

3. *transf.* = WHILE *conj.* 2 a, b, c.
1548 UDALL, etc. *Erasm. Par. Matt.* vi. 26 Whilest they catche after a vayne reward here, they be disapointed of that, whiche onelye aught to be desyred. **1586** T. B. *La Primaud. Fr. Acad.* I. 15 Whilest they [*sc.* the Stoics] granted to mans power such an excellent and divine disposition, they lift him up in a vain presumption. **1590** SHAKS. *Com. Err.* II. i. 88 His company must do his minions grace, Whil'st I at home starue for a merrie looke. *c* **1600** —— *Sonn.* xxxvii. 10, I am not lame, poore, nor dispis'd, Whilst that this shadow doth such substance giue. **1655** FULLER *Ch. Hist.* I. i There is a place..where..thousands of the Heads of Oxen were digged up, whereat the Ignorant wondred, whilest the Learned well understood them to be the proper Sacrifices to Diana. **1699** GARTH *Dispens.* II. 20 Portia..Laments her barren Curse, and begs a Son. Whilst Iris, his cosmetick Wash, must try, To make her Bloom revive, and Lovers dye. **1741** MIDDLETON *Cicero* I. iii. 152 The Knights.. considered him as the pride and ornament of their order, whilst he, to ingratiate himself the more with them, affected always..to boast of that extraction. **1848** THACKERAY *Van. Fair* xxix, Whilst her appearance was an utter failure..Mrs. Rawdon Crawley's *début* was, on the contrary, very brilliant. **1890** L. C. D'OYLE *Notches* 4 One day the right leg would be disabled, whilst the next day it would be the left leg that suffered. **1907** *Athenæum* 3 Aug. 129/2 It is not to be found in the Boston,..or the Congress Libraries, whilst the copy at Harvard is imperfect.

4. *conj.* Till, until: = WHILE *conj.* 3, WHILES 5. *Obs.* exc. *dial.*
c **1520** SKELTON *Magnyf.* 324, I pray you, Larges, here to remayne, Whylest I knowe what this letter dothe contayne. *Ibid.* 685 Tary whylyst that I come agayne. **1594** GREENE & LODGE *Looking Gl. Lond.* 451 My wife might blow whilst she burst. **1653** *Cloria & Narcissus* I. 308 There to remaine,.. whilst she heard some newes of Narcissus.

whilt(e, obs. north. ff. QUILT *sb.*[1]

whilum, obs. form of WHILOM.

†**whilwendlic,** *a. Obs.* [OE. *hwīlwendlic*, f. *hwīl* WHILE *sb.* + stem of *wendan* to turn, WEND *v.* + *-lic* -LY[1].] Lasting for a time, temporary.
c **1000** *Ags. Gosp.* Matt. xiii. 21 Hyt næfþ þone wyrtrum on him ac is hwilwendlic. *c* **1200** ORMIN 18825 þatt arrke iss whilwendlike þing & eldeþþ & forrwurrþeþþ.

whilwh, whily, obs. ff. WILLOW, WILY.

whim (hwɪm), *sb.*[1] Also 8 **whym.** [See WHIM-WHAM. The transference of meaning from branch I to branch II is similar to that in ENGINE and GIN *sb.*[1]]

I. †**1.** A pun or play on words; a double meaning. *Obs.*
1641 BROME *Jov. Crew* I. (1652) B 1 b, There was the whim, or double meaning on't. *Ibid.*, One told a Gentleman His son should be a man-killer, and hang'd for't; Who, after prov'd a great and rich Physician, And with great Fame ith' Universitie Hang'd up in Picture for a grave example. There was the whim of that. Quite contrary! *Ibid.* B 2 b, Shall Squire Oldrent's Daughters Weare old rents in their Garments? (there's a whim too).

2. †**a.** A fanciful or fantastic creation; a whimsical object. *Obs.*
1678 BUTLER *Hud.* III. i. 108 When he..Had rifled all his Pokes and Fobs Of Gimcracks, Whims and Jiggumbobs. **1712–13** SWIFT *Jrnl. to Stella* 16 Jan., I came home at seven, and began a little whim, which just came into my head; and will make a threepenny pamphlet. **1731** CHENY *List Horse-Matches* 89 This Prize is call'd a Whim or whimsical Plate, because the Conditions of running for the same, are different from those of all other Prizes. **1752** HUME *Ess. & Treat.* (1777) I. 275 Were the testimony of history less positive..such a Government [as that of Sparta] would appear a mere philosophical whim or fiction. **1821** CLARE *Vill. Minstrel* I. 111 Some may praise the grass-plat whims, Which the gard'ner weekly trims.

†**b.** A whimsical fellow. *Obs.*
1712 ADDISON *Spect.* No. 371 ¶2 That sort of Men who are called Whims and Humourists.

c. In ombre, the deciding on the trump suit by turning up the top card of the stock.
1874 H. H. GIBBS *Ombre* 41 *note*, Voltereta, though known in England (under the name of the Whim), was not appreciated there.

3. A capricious notion or fancy; a fantastic or freakish idea; an odd fancy.
1697 VANBRUGH *Prov. Wife* II. ii, Walking pretty late in the Park..A Whim took me to sing Chevy-Chace. **1702** SAVERY *Miner's Friend* 80 Many such like Whims [as perpetual motion] are pretended to by Designing Men. **1713** HEARNE *Collect.* (O.H.S.) IV. 254 The New-Printing House just erected, w[ch] is (it seems, out of a Whim) to be called Typographeum Clarendonianum. **1781** COWPER *Truth* 89 See the sage hermit,..Wearing out life in his religious whim, Till his religious whimsy wears out him. **1832** HT. MARTINEAU *Ella of Gar.* viii, The scheme was no whim of the moment. **1848** DICKENS *Dombey* xlii, Mrs. Dombey may be in earnest, or she may be pursuing a whim, or she may be opposing me. **1899** CONAN DOYLE *Duet, Confessions*, There are all..degrees of love, some just the whim of a moment, and others the passion of a lifetime.

b. In generalized sense: Capricious humour or disposition of mind.
a **1721** PRIOR *Enigma*, 'Form'd half beneath, etc.' 7 They [*sc.* skates] serve the poor for use, the rich for whim. **1728** POPE *Dunc.* III. 153 Sneering Goode, half malice and half whim. **1809** MALKIN *Gil Blas* XII. i. (Rtldg.) 423, I came up to pay my devotions; but whim, or perhaps revenge.. determined her to put on the stranger. **1884** STEVENSON *Mem. & Portraits* xvi. (1887) 275 Mr. Besant so genial,.. with so persuasive and humorous a vein of whim.

c. *Comb.*
1647 WARD *Simple Cobler* 25 These whimm' Crown'd shees, these fashion-fansying wits. **1786** BURNS *Bard's Epit.* i, Is there a whim-inspir'd fool, Owre fast for thought, owre hot for rule,..Let him draw near.

II. 4. A machine, used esp. for raising ore or water from a mine, consisting of a vertical shaft carrying a large drum with one or more radiating arms or beams to which a horse or horses, etc. may be yoked and by which it may be turned, the rope being wound on the drum by the horse's motion. Also *horse-whim.*
1738 *MSS. Dk. Portland* (Hist. MSS. Comm.) VI. 177 This Lord has destroyed the old ridiculous water works and whims that were then when made much in vogue. **1759** B. MARTIN *Nat. Hist.* I. *Cornwall* 11 A Wheel and Axle, (which they call a Whim). **1778** PRYCE *Min. Cornub.* 143 A proper working Shaft, upon which a Whym may be erected. **1859** H. KINGSLEY *G. Hamlyn* xxxvi, They above..were rigging a rope to an old horse-whim. **1890** 'R. BOLDREWOOD' *Miner's Right* xliv, The whole plant, the whim, the tools,.. —every mortal thing down to a worn-out hide bucket—was sold.

b. *attrib.* and *Comb.*, as ***whim-driver, -engine, -gin, -horse, -house, -kibble, -rope, -round, -shaft.***
1757 BORLASE in *Phil. Trans.* L. 504 The whim-house shook so terribly, that a man there at work ran out of it, concluding it to be falling. **1778** PRYCE *Min. Cornub.* 144 A whym Shaft to draw the Deads and Ore from the Sump of the Mine. *Ibid.* 150 Two horses..go round upon a platform named the Whym-round. *Ibid.* 165 In deep Mines, some whym ropes cost fifty or sixty pounds. *Ibid.* Gloss. s.v. *Kibbal*, A Whym-Kibbal is a larger [bucket], which..serves to draw water with, or bring up the Ore to grass. **1789** BRAND *Hist. Newc.* II. 684 In a whim gin the ropes run upon two wheel pullies over the shaft. **1834** *2nd Rep. Cornwall Polytechn. Soc.* 41 The Steam Whim Engine. **1855** LEIFCHILD *Cornwall* 139 Shafts..intended for the extraction of ores (called whim-shafts where horse-whims are employed for extracting the produce). **1881** *Instr. Census Clerks* (1885) 84 Whim Driver. **1896** J. HOCKING *Fields of Fair Renown* i, The boy who drove the 'whim horse' cracked his whip.

¶ In sense 4 a variant *whin* is found.
1838 SIMMS *Publ. Wks. Gt. Brit.* II. 3 Cutting the whin ropes nearly through. **1884** KNIGHT *Dict. Mech.* Suppl., *Whin* (Mining), a machine for raising ores and refuse. **1897** *Westm. Gaz.* 9 June 5/3 Rolling a large oak tree with a timber whin.

Hence **whimmed** *a.*, ? possessed with a whim or odd fancy; **'whimmery**, a piece of whimsicality; **'whimship**, mock title for a whimsical person.
1654 GAYTON *Pleas. Notes* I. viii. 29 Our Don (or if Sancho had the braines, for the Squires were *whim'd in the whiske) might very well from that encounter have stil'd himself a Knight of Millan. **1837** *Fraser's Mag.* XV. 333 Had not Mr. Pugin's attention been too exclusively engrossed by that architectural *whimmery. **1906** T. SINTON *Poetry of Lochaber* 182 We can imagine the swing of his bow with many a pause and twirl carrying through the whimeries of the rhyme. **1793** *Ann. Reg., Projects* 337 You're sure to find his *Whimship there.

whim, *sb.*[2] [Of unknown origin.] The European wigeon.
a **1705** RAY *Syn. Avium* (1713) 146 *Penelope* Aldrov. An *Anas fistularis*? The Wigeon, or Whewer, or Whim. [Hence in later works.]

whim (hwɪm), *v.* [f. WHIM *sb.*[1]]
1. †**a.** *intr.* with *it*: To play the whimsical fellow. †**b.** *trans.* To put *off* by a whim or fancy. **c.** To desire capriciously, to have an odd fancy for. Hence **'whimming** *ppl. a.*, whimsical, capricious.
1704 T. BAKER *Act at Oxf.* III. ii. 32 *Blo.* [*Aside*] The Rogue whims it rarely. **1710** R. WARD *Life H. More* 216 He knew not, how he came to be whimm'd off from it (as his expression was). **1787** HOWIE *Plain Reas. Diss.* 215 [The motion] was rejected on the whimming pretence there was no present danger. **1842** MRS. TROLLOPE *Vis. Italy* I. x. 153 What he whimmed to will, that he had power to do. **1860** S. MARTIN *Westm. Chapel Pulpit* ii. 15 He expects us to do not what we whim.

2. *intr.* Of the head: To be giddy, to 'swim'. Now *dial.*
1700 CONGREVE *Way of World* IV. 61 My head begins to whim it about—Why dost thou not speak? thou art both as drunk and as mute as a Fish. **1716–20** *Lett. Mist's Jrnl.* (1722) I. 88 The first Night he retired to his Chamber, his Head whimm'd immediately.

whim, var. QUEME *a.*, WHIN, WIM *v.*

whimberry ('hwɪmbərɪ). *local.* Forms: 1 **winberiȝe,** 5 **wynneberie,** 7 **win(ne)berry,** 8 **wind-berry,** 9 **whinberry, w(h)imberry.** [Assimilated f. *whinberry*, alteration of *winberry* (representing, with normal vowel-shortening, OE. *wīnberiȝe*; cf. WINEBERRY) by association with WHIN[1].] The bilberry or whortleberry.
a **1100** in Napier *O.E. Glosses* 132/5194 *Bacciniarum*, winberiȝena. *c* **1460** J. RUSSELL *Bk. Nurture* 78 Aftur mete peeres, nottys, strawberies, wynneberies, and hardchese. **1610** *Shuttleworths' Acc.* (Chetham Soc.) 189 Given to a wenche which brought winberries from Burneley woode, iiij[d]. **1611** COTGR., *Morets*, winne-berries, hurtle-berries. **1634–5** BRERETON *Trav.* (Chetham Soc.) I. 131 Winberries made me subject to fainting also, and are churlish things for the stomach. **1776** WITHERING *Bot. Arrangem.* 228 Blackworts... Biberries [*sic*]. Wind-berry. **1847** HALLIWELL, *Whimberries*, bilberries. **1857** PRATT *Flower. Pl.* III. 351 Bilberry, or Whortleberry..This elegant shrub ..is sometimes called also Whinberry. **1860** W. WHITE *Wrekin* viii. 74 Bilberries,—wimberries, as the rustics call them. **1862** KINGSLEY *Water Bab.* i, The heath was full of bilberries and whimberries. **1882** LEES & CLUTTERBUCK *Three in Norway* xxi. 177 Four wimberry tarts..and a venison pie. **1906** *Westm. Gaz.* 24 Aug. 10/1 Bilberry..is merely the midland name for the bleaberry of the North, the whortleberry of the West, and the whinberry of the Welsh Border.

whimble: see WIMBLE, WIMPLE.

whimbrel ('hwɪmbrəl). Forms: 6 **whympernell** (?), 7, 9 **wimbrel,** 9 **whimbrell,** 7– **whimbrel.** [? f. WHIMP or WHIMPER *v.*, from the bird's cry. Cf. for the ending *dotterel, titterel.*] Applied to various small species of curlew, esp. the European *Numenius phæopus.*
1530–1 *Durham Househ. Bk.* (Surtees) 46, 3 curleus et 1 whympernell 13*d.* **1678** RAY *Willughby's Ornith.* 294 The Whimbrel: Arquata minor,..Mr. Johnson of Brignal, in his Papers communicated to us, describes this Bird by the name of a Whimbrel thus. It is less by half than the Curlew, hath a crooked Bill, but shorter by an inch and more. **1688** *Phil. Trans.* XVII. 997 Curlews something less than our English, tho' bigger than a Wimbrel. **1768** PENNANT *Brit. Zool.* II. 514 The Whimbrel entirely leaves England in the Spring. **1863** BARING-GOULD *Iceland* vi. 100 Whimbrel and golden plover pipe and wail in all directions. **1897** *Spectator* 14 Aug. 210/1 On the fringe of a muddy creek..were some thirty whimbrel..with three or four curlews. **1898** J. A. GIBBS *Cotswold Village* 102 There are wimbrels and curlews that have been shot here..stuffed and hung up in glass cases.

†**whimling.** *Obs.* Also 7 **-len.** [Cf. WHIFLING and *whinnelling* s.v. WHINDLE.] A miserable or insignificant creature.
1612 BEAUM. & FL. *Coxcomb* IV. i, Go whimling, and fetch two or three grating loaves out of the Kitching. **1616** B. JONSON *Masques, Love Restored*, Before I could procure my properties, alarum came, that some o' the whimlen's had too much.

whimmy ('hwɪmɪ), *a.* Also 9 **whimy.** [f. WHIM *sb.*[1] + -Y[1].] Of the nature of a whim; full of whims; whimsical, capricious.
1785 *Strother's Jrnl.* (1912) 66 A whimmy thought struck him that Aram was following him for the bone. **1827** COLERIDGE in *Lit. Rem.* (1839) IV. 314 The study of Rabbinical literature either finds a man *whimmy*, or makes him so. **1880** ADEL. SARTORIS *Past Hours* I. 162 She is very uncertain and whimmy, and has an immense *amour propre* about it. **1889** MARY E. CARTER *Mrs. Severn* II. iv, 'Perhaps it is only a whim,' said Anna. 'She's not a whimy body'.

whimp (hwɪmp), *v. local.* In 6 **whympe,** 9 **wimp.** [Echoic.] *intr.* To whimper. Hence as *sb.*
1549 LATIMER *3rd Serm. bef. Edw. VI* (Arb.) 77 Sainte Paule sayed. There shall be intractabiles, that wil whympe and whine. **1890** *Glouc. Gloss.*, *Wimp*, to whine; of a dog. **1925** *Blackw. Mag.* Aug. 169/2 'Don't whimp,' I said to Irene. 'I am not whimping, daddy.' *Ibid.* 173/1 This was something beyond a whimp.

whimper ('hwɪmpə(r)), *sb.* [f. next.]
1. a. A feeble, broken cry, as of a child about to burst into tears; a fretful cry expressive of complaint or grief.
a **1700** B. E. *Dict. Cant. Crew*, *Whimper*, a low, or small Cry. *a* **1734** NORTH *Exam.* III. vii. §63. (1740) 550 After a few Whimpers and a Wipe, he said..That..he knew..he was in the Wrong. **1839** CARLYLE *Ess.*, *Sinking of Vengeur* (1857) IV. 218 Some vague faint murmur or whimper of admission. **1874** BURNAND *My time* xxvii. 256 A whimper in her voice expressive of utter helplessness.

b. A similar cry of dogs, etc.
1810 SCOTT *Lady of L.* II. xxiv, The loved caresses of the maid The dogs with crouch and whimper paid. **1852** R. S. SURTEES *Sponge's Sp. Tour* lxviii. 383 The scent improved a little, and..a hound or two indulged in a whimper. **1859** BURTON *Centr. Africa* in *Jrnl. Geog. Soc.* XXIX. 83 The hyena's whimper, and the fox's whining bark. **1906** TREVES *Highways Dorset* xiii. 197 The voice of the preacher is apt to be interrupted by the whimper of circling seagulls.

c. *transf.* Of inanimate things.
1895 W. WATSON *Hymn to Sea* 6 Braying of arrogant brass, whimper of querulous reeds. **1897** 'O. RHOSCOMYL' *White Rose Arno* xxii, The clank of capstan and the whimper of sheaves.

2. ***not with a bang but a whimper***: see BANG *sb.*[1] 2 a.

whimper ('hwɪmpə(r)), *v.* Also 6 **whymper, wimper,** *Sc.* **quhymper.** [Echoic. Cf. WHIMP.]
1. *intr.* To utter a feeble, whining, broken cry, as a child about to burst into tears; to make a low complaining sound.
1513 DOUGLAS *Æneis* II. xii. 14 The ȝing childring, and frayit matrounis eik, Stude all on raw, with mony peteous screik..quhymperand woundir sair. **1530** PALSGR. 781/1 The poore boye whympereth a lytell, but he dare nat wepe for his lyfe. **1589** NASHE *Martin Marprelate* Wks. (Grosart) I. 184 He whimpered and put finger in the eye. **1644** QUARLES *Sheph. Oracles* VII. (1646) 84 We..compose Strange rufull faces; whimper in the nose. **1727** GAY *Begg. Op.* I. xiii, The Boy, thus, when his Sparrow's flown.. Whines, whimpers, sobs and cries. **1840** DICKENS *Old C. Shop* iii, Get you away now you have said your lesson. You needn't whimper. **1912** MRS. ALLEN HARKER *Mr. Wycherly's Wards* xiv. 202 Baby began to whimper.

b. *fig.* To complain pulingly; to 'whine': esp. *for, after,* †*to* something.
1549 LATIMER *3rd Serm. bef. Edw. VI* (Arb.) 76 Was there euer yet preachers, but ther were gaynsaiars..yat whympered agaynste him? **1644** QUARLES *Sheph. Oracles* VII. (1646) 76 Time was, Adelphus, that my wants would whine And whimper in poore rags as well as thine. *a* **1653** G.

Daniel *Idyll.* iii. 43, I..whimper to the Teat, though Strong enough To digest meat. **1815** W. H. Ireland *Scribbleomania* 190 The great Grecian youth, Who whimper'd for more worlds to conquer. **1828** Scott *F.M. Perth* viii, Proudfute..began to cry for assistance..and almost in the same breath to whimper for mercy. **1842** Peel in *Croker Papers* 27 July (1884) II. 383 Farmers..were whimpering over advertisements offering fresh meat [etc.]. **1848** Thackeray *Van. Fair* lxvii, She is still whimpering after that gaby of a husband—dead..these fifteen years. **1894** Jessopp *Rand. Roam.* vi. 196 For ever whimpering for the days that are gone.

c. *trans.* To utter or express in a whimper.

1784 Cowper *Task* iv. 429 But poverty, with most who whimper forth Their long complaints, is self-inflicted woe. **1819** Scott *Ivanhoe* xxviii, 'You deal with me better than your word, noble knight,' whimpered forth poor Wamba. **1820** Hogg *Tales, Allan Gordon* (1837) I. 314 The generous animal whined and whimpered her joy. **1891** Farrar *Darkn. & Dawn* lxv, He still kept whimpering, 'Only to think that such an artist as I am must perish!'

2. *intr.* Of an animal, esp. a dog: To utter a feeble querulous cry.

1576 Turberv. *Venerie* xxxix. 108 He [*sc.* a hound] will streyne and lappyse, or whymper, or sometime call on plainely. **1641** W. Cartwright *Siege* i. iv, Whimpering at The Chamber door, like to the little Spaniel. **1825** J. Neal *Bro. Jonathan* I. 335 The dog stopped; whimpered; looked him in the face. **1898** M. Hewlett *Forest Lovers* xxx, The dogs whimpered and tugged at the leash; they doubtless knew that there was blood in her.

3. Of running water or the wind: To make a continuous plaintive murmur. Also *trans.*

1795 H. Macneill *Will & Jean* i. xx, In a howm, wha's bonnie burnie Whimperin row'd its crystal flood. **1820** W. Irving *Sketch Bk.* II. 358 The little brook that whimpered by his school-house. **1821** Clare *Vill. Minstrel* II. 106 The brook mourns drippling o'er its pebbly bed, And whimpers soothingly a calm serene. **1891** Kipling *Engl. Flag* i. Verse 1919 I. 290 Winds of the World, give answer! They are whimpering to and fro—And what should they know of England who only England know?

Hence **'whimpered** *ppl. a.* (sense 1 c).

1892 G. Meredith *Teaching of Nude* i. Poet. Wks. (1912) 410 A Satyr..fetching whimpered tunes For words.

whimperer ('hwɪmpərə(r)). [f. prec. + -er[1].] One who whimpers.

1737 Ozell *Rabelais* ii. vii. 66 *note, Marmiteux*, a Whimperer. *a* **1739** Jarvis *Don Quix.* i. i. (1742) I. 3 No finical gentleman, nor such a whimperer as his brother. **1841** Emerson *Ess.* Ser. i. ii. 75 We are become timorous, desponding whimperers. **1863** Holme Lee *A. Warleigh* III. 241 When her wee whimperer would allow any voice but his own to be heard.

whimpering ('hwɪmpərɪŋ), *vbl. sb.* [f. prec. vb. + -ing[1].] The action of the verb whimper.

1522 More *De quat. Noviss.* Wks. 89 Yf we..liue in puling & whimpering & heuines of hert. **1621** T. Granger *Eccles.* xii. 4. 320 The noise of little birds, the whimpering of mice, euery small stirrage waketh them. **1621** Markham *Hungers Prevention* 274 A kinde of whimpering and whining in his [*sc.* the dog's] voice. **1660** H. More *Myst. Godl.* x. vii. 509 He will not..be put off with solemn whimperings, Hypocritical Confessions, ruful faces. **1735** Somerville *Chase* i. 225 The..Hound..Bounds o'er the Lawn to seize his panting Prey And in imperfect Whimp'rings speaks his Joy. **1832** W. Irving *Alhambra* II. 102 His wife received him..with whimperings and repinings. **1851** D. Jerrold *St. Giles* viii. 78 There was no sham whimpering..but the boy's heart seemed touched. **1902** L. Stephen *Stud. Biogr.* IV. v. 188 Many men of business..enjoy in strict privacy a little whimpering over a novel.

whimpering ('hwɪmpərɪŋ), *ppl. a.* [f. prec. vb. + -ing[2].] That whimpers, in various senses.

1598 E. Guilpin *Skial.* (1878) 29 Their whimpring Sonnets, puling Elegies Slaunder the Muses. **1622** Massinger & Dekker *Virg. Mart.* ii. i, Our whimpring Lady and Mistresse sent mee. **1648** Herrick *Hesp., To Primroses fill'd with Morning Dew* ii, Speak, whimp'ring Younglings, and make known The reason, why Ye droop, and weep. **1735** R. Savage *Progr. Divine* Wks. 1777 II. 121 Be yours the blubb'ring lip, and whimp'ring eye! **1810** Scott *Lady of L.* i. xxiv, With heads erect, and whimpering cry, The hounds behind their passage ply. **1840** Thackeray *Paris Sk.-bk., Mme. Sand*, Any one can see why Rousseau should be such a whimpering reformer. **1879** Browning *Ivan Ivanovitch* 205 The whimperingest cub that ever squeezed the teat!

Hence **'whimperingly** *adv.*

1878 Stevenson *Inland Voy.* 157 He would suddenly break away and begin whimperingly to commiserate the poor.

whimple, whimsey: see wimple, whimsy.

†**whimseycado.** *Obs. nonce-wd.* [f. whimsical + *-ado* Sp. suffix = -ate[1].] (?) A whim.

1654 Gayton *Pleas. Notes* iv. v. 201 If *Amadis du Gaul* and *Palmerin* Be lies, what whimsey-cados are we in?

†**whimsic,** *a. Obs. rare.* [f. as next + -ic.] ***whimsic chair*** = whimsy *sb.* 5.

1684 *Ballads illustr. Gt. Frost* (Percy Soc.) 29 Dutch whirling, whimsic chair, Turning more swift than unrestrained air.

whimsical ('hwɪmzɪkəl), *a.* (*sb.*) Also 7 whym-. [f. whims(y + -ical.]

1. Of persons, their actions, thoughts, etc.: Full of, subject to, or characterized by a whim or whims; actuated by or depending upon whim or caprice.

1653 W. Ramesey *Astrol. Rest.* To Rdr. 10 So they fell to words and at last (to end this Whimsical controversie) they resolved to kill one another. *Ibid.* 11 Were not they better be ..grave, sober, serious, then whymiscal, fickle and fantastical? **1690** C. Nesse *O. & N. Test.* I. 251 So do the whimsical Enthusiasts..make long relations of strange dreams. **1703** Earl Orrery *As you find it* iii. i. 35 A Man with a fantastical, whimsical Stomach may starve in the midst of Plenty, not for want of Food, but such as he likes. **1711** Addison *Spect.* No. 101 ¶7 One Sir Roger de Coverley, a whimsical Country Knight. **1756** Burke *Subl. & Beaut.* iii. xi. (1759) 208 It has given rise to an infinite deal of whimsical theory. **1809** Malkin *Gil Blas* iv. vii. ¶2 One of those old codgers who have been a little whimsical or so in their youth. **1839** Hallam *Lit. Eur.* ii. vii. §20 It would be rather whimsical to deny this to be a principal merit in a comparison. **1875** J. E. T. Rogers *Protests of Lords* I. Pref. p. lvi, Two whimsical dissents from Lords Radnor and Abingdon.

2. Characterized by deviation from the ordinary as if determined by mere caprice; fantastic, fanciful; freakish, odd, comical.

1675 E. Wilson *Spadacr. Dunelm.* Pref. B 5 b, Panacæa's, Universal Medicines, Secrets, and such like whimsical Remedies. **1687** T. Brown *Saints in Uproar* Wks. 1730 I. 79 The most whimsical scene of the farce is still behind. *a* **1700** Evelyn *Diary* 29 Nov. 1644, A whimsical chayre, which folded into so many varieties as to turn into a bed, a bolster, a table, or a couch. **1710** Swift *Lett.* (1767) III. 57 Is it not whimsical that the dean has never once written to me? **1769** Burke *Corr.* (1844) I. 165 Matters here are in a situation whimsical enough. **1773** Wesley *Jrnl.* 29 Nov., Wks. 1830 IV. 5, I went..to Sheerness; over that whimsical ferry, where footmen and horses pay nothing. **1826** F. Reynolds *Life & Times* I. 193 The Germans are whimsical animals in their appearance. **1836** Brande *Chem.* (ed. 4) 17 Alembics, stills, retorts, receivers, and a variety of whimsical and complex vessels. **1852** Mrs. Stowe *Uncle Tom's C.* ix. 66 Our senator..looked after his little wife with a whimsical mixture of amusement and vexation. **1890** *Science-Gossip* XXVI. 85 All these whimsical prescriptions gradually fell out of the Pharmacopœias.

absol. **1740** Cibber *Apol.* (1756) I. 112 Who..delighted more in the whimsical than the natural. **1838** Dickens *Nich. Nick.* xxiv, Hesitating between the respect he ought to assume, and his love of the whimsical.

†**b.** Subject to uncertainty or the 'caprice of fortune'. *Obs.*

1654 Whitlock *Zootomia* 151 Must the bread of Life be ground only by the winde of every Doctrine? and whimsicall Wind-Mills? **1700** Congreve *Way of World* ii. vii, A Fellow that lives in a Windmill has not a more whimsical Dwelling than the Heart of a Man that is lodg'd in a Woman. There is no Point of the Compass to which they cannot turn. **1716** Addison *Freeholder* No. 18 ¶3, I shall only take notice of the whimsical circumstances a people must lie under, who can be thus made poor or rich by an edict. **1748** Richardson *Clarissa* (1768) III. 191 Poor man! he stands a whimsical chance between us.

B. *sb.* (in *pl.*) A cant name for a section of the Tories in the reign of Queen Anne: see quots.

1714 Swift *Pres. St. Aff.* Wks. 1841 I. 492/2 That race of politicians, who in the cant phrase are called the whimsicals. **1818** Scott *Br. Lamm.* xxvii, Many of the High Church party..affected to separate their principles from those of the Jacobites, and, on that account, obtained the denomination of Whimsicals.

whimsi'cality. [f. prec. adj. + -ity.] The quality or state of being whimsical; whimsicalness; oddity, fantasticalness. Also with *a* and *pl.*

1760 Sterne *Tr. Shandy* III. xxxiii, The whimsicality of my father's brain was far from having the whole honour of this. **1800** Maria Edgeworth *Belinda* ii, Lady Delacour.. laughed affectedly at her own whimsicalities. **1844** Hood (*title*) Whimsicalities, a periodical gathering. **1850** L. Hunt *Autobiogr.* vi. (1860) 117 Lewis was a comedian of the rarest order, for he combined whimsicality with elegance, and levity with heart. **1898** R. Hichens *Londoners* ii, The expression of curious whimsicality that stole into her face.

'whimsically, *adv.* [f. prec. adj. + -ly[2].] In a whimsical manner; capriciously; oddly, fantastically.

1711 Steele *Spect.* No. 100 ¶4, I thought it was whimsically said of a Gentleman, That if Varilas had Wit, it would be the best Wit in the World. **1742** Fielding *J. Andrews* i. xviii, Her passions..were not so whimsically capricious that one man only could lay them. **1775** Sheridan *Duenna* ii. iv, Was ever truant daughter so whimsically circumstanced as I am? **1821** Croker in *C. Papers* 1 Aug. (1884) I. 199 Our supper whimsically served; the first dish being green peas alone. *a* **1861** T. Winthrop *Life in Open Air* (1863) 103 The mist, white and delicate where we stood, but thick and black above, opened whimsically and delusively. **1888** Burgon *Lives 12 Gd. Men* II. v. 65 How whimsically Wilberforce was capable of blending the pathetic and the playful.

'whimsicalness. [f. prec. adj. + -ness.] The quality of being whimsical; whimsicality.

1714 tr. *à Kempis' Chr. Exerc.* iv. xiv. 250 Lest Meditation should decline..into Melancholy and Whimsicalness. **1747** Hoadly *Suspicious Husb.* v. ii, I cannot sufficiently admire at the Whimsicalness of my good Fortune, in being so instrumental to this general Happiness. **1865** Mrs. Whitney *Gayworthys* xxxii, 'Did you think I would?' cried Joanna, lifting up her head suddenly, with something of the old spirit of whimsicalness.

†**'whimsied,** *pa. pple.* or *a. Obs. rare.* [f. whimsy + -ed.] Filled with whims; made whimsical.

1624 Fletcher *Rule a Wife* ii. i, To have a mans brains whimsied with his wealth. **1628** Ford *Lover's Mel.* ii. ii, You are but a little staring—there's difference betweene staring and starke mad. You are but whymsed, yet crotchetted, coundroun'd, or so. **1835** Willis *Pencillings* I. xxiii. 162 A whimsied madman.

whimsily, whimsiness: see after whimsy.

whimstone, variant of whinstone.

1822 Conybeare & Phillips *Outl. Geol. Eng.* i. 204 Concretions are frequent..and are called whim-stones or potlids.

whimsy, whimsey ('hwɪmzɪ), *sb.* (*a.*) Forms: 7 whim-, whymzie, whimsee, 7–8 whimzy, 8 whymsey, 7–9 whimsie, whims(e)y. [See whim-wham.]

A. *sb.* **I.** †**1.** Dizziness, giddiness, vertigo. *Obs.*

16.. Middleton, etc. *Old Law* iii. ii, I ha' got the scotomy in my head already, The whimsey: you all turn round. **1656** Blount *Glossogr., Scotomatical*, that is troubled with such a whimsey in the head.

†**2.** A wench. *Obs. rare.*

1614 B. Jonson *Barth. Fair* ii. iv, And shall we ha' smockes Vrsla, and good whimsies, ha? *a* **1625** Fletcher *Bloody Brother* iv. ii, You'l pick a bottle open, or a whimsey, As soon as the best of us.

3. a. = whim *sb.*[1] 3.

1605 B. Jonson *Volpone* iii. i, I can feele A whimsey i' my bloud: (I know not how) Successe hath made me wanton. **1628** Venner *Baths of Bathe* (1650) 365 Such as have their pates full of outlandish whimsies. **1646** J. Hall *Horæ Vac.* 31 That whimsey of Pythagoras of the transmigration of Soules. **1713** Derham *Phys.-Theol.* i. i. 7 *note*, Our Inability to live in too rare and light an Air may discourage those vain Attempts of Flying, and Whimsies of passing to the Moon. **1803** Jefferson *Writ.* (1830) III. 508 Plato, who only used the name of Socrates to cover the whimsies of his own brain. **1849** Macaulay *Hist. Eng.* ii. I. 164 Both had what seemed extravagant whimsies about dress, diversions, and postures. **1891** Besant *St. Katherine's* i. vi, Why, I was young once, and had my own whimsies like the rest.

b. = whim *sb.*[1] 3 b. *arch.*

a **1680** Glanvill *Sadducismus* ii. (1681) 50 All this is Whimsey and Fiction. **1709** Shaftesb. *Charac.* (1711) II. 337 In One there are the Marks of Wisdom and Determination; in the other, of Whimsy and Conceit. **1775** Wraxall *Tour N. Eur.* 121 It may just as well be called an European structure, where whimsy and caprice form the predominant character. **1881** Blackmore *Christowell* xlviii, They winnow my gatherings on every wind of whimsy.

4. = whim *sb.*[1] 2 a.

1712 *H. More's Antid. Ath.* iii. ix. §2. Schol. 169 Engrav'd with Characters, and other Magical whimsies of this sort. **1785** J. Collier *Mus. Trav.* (ed. 4) 62 The Italian whimsies and tweedle-dums, that people played upon in these days. **1791** Cowper *Yardley Oak* 118 Thy root..A quarry of stout spurs, and knotted fangs,..crook'd into a thousand whimsies. **1860–1** D. Coleridge in *Phil. Soc. Trans.* 164 The proposed Dictionary..must include many a mere whimsey and many a gross corruption. **1906** E. V. Lucas *Wand. in Lond.* i. 14 The lodge in the garden of the Record Office. This little architectural whimsy might be the abode of an urban fairy or gnome.

II. †**5.** A merry-go-round, roundabout. *Obs.*

1684 *Ballads illustr. Gt. Frost* (Percy Soc.) 4 There were Dutch whimsies turned swiftly round Faster then horses run on level ground.

6. a. = whim *sb.*[1] 4. *local.*

1789 J. Williams *Min. Kingd.* I. 430 This may be done.. with a small horse-gin or whimsy, instead of a windlass, for drawing the water and work in sinking. **1836** *Hull & Selby Railw. Act* 44 To make use of any gins, whimsies, tackling, ropes, machines. **1875** *Ure's Dict. Arts* III. 319 In Cornwall, a kibble, in which the ore is raised in the shafts, by machines called whims or whimseys.

b. (See quot.)

1867 Smyth *Sailor's Word-bk., Whimsey*, a small crane for hoisting goods to the upper stories of warehouses.

7. a. *Glass-making.* (See quot.)

1856 H. Chance in *Jrnl. Soc. Arts* IV. 224/2 Still whirling, the table [of crown glass], as it is now called, is carried off, laid flat upon a support called a whimsey, detached by shears from the ponty, [etc.].

b. A small object made by a glass-maker or potter for his own amusement.

1938 A. Fleming *Scottish & Jacobite Glass* ix. 109 Dame Fashion..seems to settle upon glass as a favourite and satisfactory medium of decoration. Other 'wimsies' are cheap little fantastic groups of figures, fruit and flowers delicately made from a tube modelled by a tool with infallible dexterity. **1976** *Canadian Collector* (Toronto) Mar.–Apr. 23/1 We were able to locate several more examples of the whimseys produced by the last potter.

B. *adj.* Whimsical.

1632 Shirley *Hyde Park* ii. ii, Ieere on, my whimsy Lady. **1867** Lanier *Strange Jokes* 7 Poems (1892) 217 Once in a whimsey mood he sat. **1913** Mrs. Stratton-Porter *Laddie* xiv, Laddie studied the sky, a whimsy smile on his lips.

C. *attrib.* and *Comb.*, as ***whimsy-pate, -shaft***; ***whimsy-headed*** adj.; †***whimsy-board***, ? a board or table used in some game of chance, or on which different objects were carried about for sale.

a **1704** T. Brown *Lett. Living to Dead* Wks. 1720 II. 19, I am sometimes a small Retainer to a Billiard-Table, and sometimes, when the Master on't is sick, earn a Penny by a *Whimsy-Board. **1708** W. King *Art of Cookery* (1709) 99 Then Pippins did in Wheel-barrows abound, And Oranges in Whimsey-boards went round. **1710** *Lond. Gaz.* No. 4659/3 He frequents the Cock Pits and Gaming Houses, Whimsy Boards. **1698** E. Ward *Lond. Spy* iii. (1706) 63 The first *Whimsie-headed Wretch of this Lunatick Family. **1682** Winyard *Mercurius Menip.* 6 His *Whimsie-Meagrim must be an Ecstasie. **1654** Gayton *Pleas. Notes* iii. iv. 88 What a company..doth this phantasticall *whimzy-pate gather. **1821** W. Forster *Section of Strata* (ed. 2) 331 *Whimsey Shafts may be sunk to the depth of ten ..fathoms.

Hence **'whimsily** *adv.*, **'whimsiness.**

1654 Gayton *Pleas. Notes* iv. iii. 188, I love Toboso, and I know not why, Only I say, I love her (whimsyly). **1909**

Daily Chron. 14 Sept. 5/3 To..indulge his political whimsiness. **1980** P. MOYES *Angel Death* xviii. 237 The whimsily-drawn pamphlet which they gave to visitors.

whimsy-whamsy. [f. WHIMSY after next.] = next, 2. Also *attrib.*

1807 SOUTHEY *Lett. from England* III. lix. 109 An old Welsh baronet..chose some years ago to set up a heresy of his own... He himself called it Rational Whist; his friends, in a word of contemptuous fabrication, denominated it his *whimsy-whamsy*. **1871** CADDELL *Never Forgotten* ii, Maude always was obstinate when she had one of her religious whimsey whamseys in her head. **1900** 'ANTHONY HOPE' *Quisanté* v, The real reason..why the Dean hasn't risen higher is because he always has some whimsy-whamsy in his head. **1931** *Time & Tide* 26 Sept. 1118 Have we not whimsy-whamsy authors of our own without importing the too, too, quaint devices of foreign playwrights? **1945** S. LEWIS *Cass Timberlane* xl. 302 Sure, the jolly little playboy, and underneath his whimsy-whamsy, he's the coldest-hearted rich-man's lawyer. **1951** MCLUHAN *Mech. Bride* (1967) 101/1 It is not a laughter or comedy to be compared with the whimsy-whamsy article of James Thurber.

whim-wham ('hwɪmhwæm). Also 6–7 **whym wham**, 7 **whimwhom**, 8–9 **whimwam**, 9 **wimwam**, **whim-**, **wim-wom**. [A reduplication with vowel-variation, like *flim-flam*, *jim-jam*, *trim-tram*, all of which are similarly applied to trivial or frivolous things.

The history of the group of words of which WHIM *sb.*[1], WHIMSY, and this word are the chief members, is not clear. The existence in ON. of *hvima* to wander with the eyes as with the fugitive look of a frightened or silly person, and *hvimsa* to be taken aback or discomfited, suggests the possibility of an ultimate Scand. origin; but, seeing that *whim-wham* is the earliest recorded of the group (contemporaneously with the similar reduplicated forms mentioned above), an indigenous symbolic origin is more likely; in which case *whimsy* may be related to *whim-wham* as *flimsy* to *flim-flam*.]

1. A fanciful or fantastic object; *fig.* a trifle; in early use chiefly, a trifling ornament of dress, a trinket; later in various local uses (see quots.).

a **1529** SKELTON *E. Rummyng* 75 After the Sarasyns gyse, With a whym wham, Knyt with a trym tram, Vpon her brayne pan. **1602** DEKKER *Satirom.* F 2, Dost loue that mother Mumble-crust, dost thou? dost long for that whim-wham? **1621** J. TAYLOR (Water P.) *Superbiæ Flagellum* C 7 b, Whimwhams & whirligiggs to please Baboones. **1625** FLETCHER & SHIRLEY *Nt. Walker* I. i, They'll pull ye all to pieces, for your whim-whams, Your garters and your gloves. **1641** J. TAYLOR (Water P.) *Reply as true as Steel* (1877) 6 He caus'd some formes of flowers..'twixt the Beast legges be painted To hide his whim wham. **1659** TORRIANO, *Tencone*, ..a mans whim-wham. **1691** MRS. D'ANVERS *Academia* 17 The Yat's [= gate's] all hung about with whimwhoms, As Fishes Bones, and other thingums. **1721** RAMSAY *Scriblers Lash'd* 197 Dealers in small Ware, Clinks, Whim Whams. **1808** HAN. MORE *Cœlebs* (1809) II. 183, I have spent 700 pounds..for her to learn music and whim-whams. **1818** SCOTT *Br. Lamm.* xi, Florentine and flams—bacon, wi' reverence, and a' the sweet confections and whim-whams. *a* **1842** HAWTHORNE *Twice-told T.* (1851) I. ix. 163 So much for the commencement of this long whim-wham. **1854** MISS BAKER *Northampt. Gloss.*, *Whim-wom*, a bird-boy's clackers for frightening birds from fruit or corn. **1860** *Slang Dict.*, *Whim-wham*, an alliterative term, synonymous with fiddle-faddle, riff-raff, etc., denoting nonsense, rubbish, etc.

2. A fantastic notion, odd fancy; = WHIM *sb.*[1] 3.

1580 FULKE *Stapleton Confut.* II. viii. 117 Voluntarie pouertie in Augustine not found in the first planters of this newe trim tram. A matter worthie to be aunswered with a whim wham. **1588** J. HARVEY *Disc. Probl.* 40 Such blind vnreasonable whimwhams. **1621** FLETCHER *Wild-Goose Chase* III. i, Your studied Whim-whams; and your fine set faces. **1759** STERNE *Tr. Shandy* I. vii, Who..not only hit upon this dainty amendment, but coaxed many of the old-licensed matrons..to open their faculties afresh, in order to have this whim-wham of his inserted. **1807–8** W. IRVING *Salmag.* (1824) 123 He declared he would humour the weather no longer in its whim-whams. **1832** ROWL. HILL in *Life* (1834) 382 The pure and simple gospel of Christ, but not intermixed with the whim-whams of the present day. **1882** C. D. WARNER *W. Irving* iv. 50 The follies and 'whim-whams' of the metropolis.

whimy: see WHIMMY.

whin[1] (hwɪn). Forms: 5 **quyn**, **qwynne**, **wyne**, 5–7 **whyn(ne**, 6 **whyne**, *Sc.* **quyin**, 6–7 **whinne**, **whine**, *Sc.* **quhinn(e**, 7 **win**, **whimme**, (9 *dial.*) **whim**, *Sc.* (9 *dial.*) **quhin**, 8 (9 *dial.*) **whinn**, 8–9 *Sc.* and *dial.* **whun**, 6– **whin**. [app. orig. northern, and prob. of Scand. origin (cf. Sw. *hven*, early Da. *hvine*, *hvinegræs*, *-strå*, Norw. *hvine*, *hvén*, *kvein*, applied to certain grasses); the evidence goes to show that gorse was formerly of economic importance in the areas of special Scand. influence.

This origin is more probable than that which has been proposed from OWelsh *chwynn* weeds (mod. *chwyn*), cognate with Breton *chouenna* to hoe, weed.]

1. The common furze or gorse, *Ulex europæus.* Often *collect. pl.* and *sing.* for a clump or mass of the shrub, or a quantity of it used for fuel, fencing, etc.

c **1400** *Ywaine & Gaw.* 159 A strete, Ful thik and hard,.. With thornes, breres, and moni a quyn. *c* **1425** *Voc.* in Wr.-Wülcker 643/32 *Hec saliunca*, wyne. *c* **1440** *Promp. Parv.* 524/2 Whynne, *saliunca.* **1538** TURNER *Libellus*, *Paliurus, uarias habet subspecies, quarum una est frutex ille quem all[i]oqui* a whyn *allij* a furre *nominant.* **1549** *MSS. Dk. Rutland* (Hist. MSS. Comm.) IV. 352 For fellyng and ledyng of xj lodes of whynnes..iijs. viij*d.* **1573–80** TUSSER *Husb.* (1878) 119 With whinnes or with furzes thy houell renew. **1578** LYTE *Dodoens* VI. ix. 669 The common Whyn, or great Furze. **1606** in *Trans. Cumbld. & Westmld. Archaeol. Soc.* (1903) III. 152 That none..shall cutt any whinne to burne upon paine of vi*d.* **1610** MARKHAM *Masterp.* II. xxiv. 258 Rough hay, full of whims [*ed.* **1636** whimmes, **1675** whins], thistels, or other pricking stuffe. **1698** A. DE LA PRYME *Diary* (Surtees 1869) 178 When all their fother was done, they took green whinz,..stampt them ..to bruise all their pricles, and then gave them to their beasts. **1721** RAMSAY *Ode to the Ph——* ii, Driving their Baws frae Whins or Tee, There's no ae Gowfer to be seen. **1815** J. SMITH *Panorama Sci. & Art* II. 597 Whins or common furze make a valuable fence. **1859** H. KINGSLEY *G. Hamlyn* v, Down beyond down, a vast sheet of purple heath and golden whin. **1878** SUSAN PHILLIPS *On Seaboard* 254 Between the whin and the workhouse they pulled the old fox down. **1882** *Garden* 13 May 324/3 The double flowering Whin (Furze).

2. Applied to other prickly or thorny shrubs, as rest-harrow and buckthorn; also to heather.

1530 PALSGR. 288/1 Whynne, *bruiere.* Whynnes or hethe, *bruiere.* **1548** TURNER *Names Herbes* (E.D.S.) 13 Anonis called also Ononis is called..in Cambryge Shyre a whyne. **1570** LEVINS *Manip.* 133/14 A Whin, *rhamnus.* **1706** PHILLIPS (ed. Kersey), *Whin* or Petty Whin, a Shrub, otherwise call'd Knee-holm. **1854** MISS BAKER *Northampt. Gloss.*, *Whin*, the rest-harrow.

3. With distinctive additions, in local names of various prickly shrubs:

cammock, **lady-**, **land-whin** = petty whin (*a*); **cat('s) whin** = petty whin; also dwarf furze, dog-rose, burnet-rose; **heather-**, **moor-**, **moss-**, **needle-whin** = petty whin (*b*); **petty whin**, (*a*) Turner's name for the Rest-harrow, *Ononis arvensis*; (*b*) the Needle-furze, *Genista anglica.*

14.. *MS. Laud 553*, lf. 18 Reta bouis is an herbe þt me clepuþ cammok whynne or calketrap. **1551** TURNER *Herbal* I. D j, Petye Whyne, or grounde Whyne, or lytle Whyne is called in latyn, & Greke ononis, and anonis... In cambryge shyre thys herbe is called a whyne, but I putt pety to it, to make dyfference betwene thys herbe, and a fur: whyche in manye places of Englande is also called a Whyne. **1579** LANGHAM *Gard. Health* 527 Restharrow, Cammok, or Petywhin. **1650** [W. HOWE] *Phytol. Brit.* 45 Genistella.. Needle Furze or Petty Whin. **1684** MERITON *Praise Ale* 108 (E.D.S.) Our Land is tewgh, and full of..Cat-whins. **1763** *Museum Rust.* I. lxxxv. 377 Such barren sandy heaths where petty-whin, heather, and short furze, plentifully grow. **1788** W. MARSHALL *E. Yorksh.* II. Gloss. (E.D.S.) Cat-whin, sb. *rosa spinosissima*, burnet rose. *a* **1825** FORBY *Voc. E. Anglia*, *Land-whin*, s., the rest-harrow. **1853** G. JOHNSTON *Bot. E. Bord.* 51 *G[enista] anglica.* Moor-Whin: Heather-Whin: Moss-Whin. **1878** *Cumbld. Gloss.*, *Cat-whin*, the dwarf whin. *Ulex nanus.* **1886** BRITTEN & HOLLAND *Plant-n.*, Lady-whin, *Ononis arvensis*,..Encyclopædia of Agriculture.

4. *attrib.* and *Comb.*, as ***whin-bloom***, ***-covert***, ***-cow*** (COW *sb.*[2]), ***-fence***, ***-flower***, ***-hack*** (HACK *sb.*[1]), ***-pod***, ***-prick***, ***-prickle***, ***-root***, ***-seed***; **whin-kid**, a bundle of whin; hence ***whin-kid*** vb., to fence or thatch with whin; **whin-linnet** (see quots.); **whin-mill**, a mill for crushing whin for horse-feed; **whin-thrush**, a local name for the redwing, = WINNARD; **whin-wrack**, a species of grass (see quot.).

1824 MACTAGGART *Gallovid. Encycl.*, **Whun blooms*, the yellow blooms of the whin. **1865** ALLINGHAM *50 Mod. Poems, Among the Heather* ii, Your mountain air is sweet.. When..the whinbloom smells like honey. **1843** *Zoologist* I. 80 Walking through a straggling *whin-covert. **1826** SCOTT *Jrnl.* 28 Feb. in *Lockhart*, If you would have a horse kick, make a crupper out of a *whin-cow. **1797** J. BAILEY & CULLEY *Agric. Cumberld.* 185 Large tracts..inclosed by *whin-fences. **1897** WATTS-DUNTON *Aylwin* xvii, Making the gold coins round her neck shine like dewy *whin-flowers struck by the sunrise. **1585–6** *Wills & Inv. Durham* (Surtees) II. 131, iij *whine hackes. **1651** *N. Riding Rec.* V. 90 Six *whyn kidds. **1841** *Instit. Civil Eng. Min. Proc.* I. 141 The author..has lately been..warping silt, with whin or gorse kids, laid horizontally. **1876** *Mid-Yorks. Gloss.* s.v., The parcels of land [are]..whin-kydded about. **1837** MACGILLIVRAY *Brit. Birds* I. 371 *Linaria cannabina.* The Brown Linnet... *Whin Linnet. Greater Redpoll. **1862** JOHNS *Brit. Birds* 625 Whin Linnet, the Common Linnet. **1793** in *Trans. Buchan Field Club* (1935) XIV. 76 Carrying wood for the *whine mile. **1893** C. A. MOLLYSON *Parish of Fordoun* 188 With a plentiful supply of oilcake and other nutritious feeding stuffs there is no place now for the whin-mill. **1957** E. E. EVANS *Irish Folk Ways* viii. 110 The knocking stones..where the whins were 'melled' with a wooden maul, are sometimes to be seen in the farmyard, and there were a few water-driven 'whin-mills'. **1874** STEVENSON *Ess. Trav., On Unpleas. Places* 246 The.. crackling of the *whin-pods in the afternoon sun. **1664** POWER *Exp. Philos.* I. 13 The little white Field-Spider.. imboss'd all over with black Knobs, out of..which grow bristles or prickles like *whin-pricks. **1899** CROCKETT *Kit Kennedy* xxxvi, As if they had been sitting on *whin prickles. **1586** *Depos. Durham* (Surtees) 320 My good man's horse fest at a *whinne roote. **1824** MACTAGGART *Gallovid. Encycl.* 28 Harrows wi' teeth o' whunroots. **1765** A. DICKSON *Treat. Agric.* (ed. 2) 122 Every time that the land is turned into grass, the *whin-seeds near the surface will vegetate. **1848** *Zoologist* VI. 2290 The redwing is in G[loucestershire] a '*whin thrush'. **1853** G. JOHNSTON *Bot. E. Bord.* 212 *Holcus mollis...* *Whin-wrack,—so called because it is found to occupy places whence Whins have been removed.

whin[2] (hwɪn). *Sc.* and *north. dial.* Forms: 4 **quin**, 6 *Sc.* **quhin**, **quhyn(e**, 6, 9 **whun**, 8 **whyn(n**, 8– **whin**, (9 **whinn**, *Sc.* **whunn**, **fin**). [Origin obscure.] = WHINSTONE.

a **1300** *Cursor M.* 7531 He tok fiue stans rond o quin, And put þam in his scrip wit-in. **1513** DOUGLAS *Æneis* IV. vii. 8 Of ane cald hard quhyn, The clekkit that horrible mont, Caucasus hait. **1535** STEWART *Cron. Scot.* (Rolls) I. 56 Greit cragis of quhin. **1599** ALEX. HUME *Hymnes* iii. 133 The blew paymented whun [*rime* sun]. **1708** J. C. *Compl. Collier* (1845) 12 If a Whin (which is the hardest sort of Stone..) lye in the way. **1799** KENDAL *Geol. Ess.* 310 Carbonated wood is frequently found under trap, whin, or basalt. **1864** A. MILLER *Coatbridge* ii. 8 Where the Ironstone comes into conjunction with whin it is..much impregnated with pyrites.

b. *attrib.* and *Comb.*, as ***whin boulder***, ***-dike*** (DIKE *sb.*[1] 9 b), ***-float*** (FLOAT *sb.* 20 a), ***gravel***; **whin-rock**, whinstone; **whin-sill**, a sill or layer of whinstone; also as a name for whinstone.

1873 GEIKIE *Gt. Ice Age* xi. 152 Gravel and stones with large '*whin' boulders. **1789** J. WILLIAMS *Min. Kingd.* I. 29 Dykes of basaltes, or other hard stone, which are commonly called *whin dykes. **1825** E. MACKENZIE *View Northumbld.* (ed. 2) I. 81 The Whin-dikes are filled with basalt, which has apparently issued hot from the interior parts of the earth. **1845** J. PHILLIPS *Geol.* in *Encycl. Metrop.* VI. 619/1 A few faults in the magnesian limestone range of Durham and Yorkshire, as along the line of the great whindyke. **1883** GRESLEY *Gloss. Coal-m.*, **Whin-float*, a kind of greenstone, basalt, or trap, occurring in coal measures. **1799** *Trans. Soc. Arts* XVII. 246 Clayey loams, limestone gravel, *whin gravel. **1683** G. SINCLAIR *Nat. Philos.* 277 An impregnable *Whin-Rock, or Flinty Stone. **1785** BURNS *Death & Dr. Hornbook* xviii, I might as weel hae try'd a quarry O' hard whin rock. **1806** FORSYTH *Beauties Scot.* IV. 58 All the hills are whin-rock. **1839** URE *Dict. Arts* 748 In Cumberland the metalliferous limestone includes a bed of trap, designated under the name of *whinsill. **1845** J. PHILLIPS *Geol.* in *Encycl. Metrop.* VI. 756/1 The origin of the whin-sill. **1869** PHILLIPS *Vesuv.* iv. 128 The toadstone in Derbyshire, or the whinsill in Teesdale.

whin: see WHEEN, WHIM *sb.*[1] ¶.

whinberry: see WHIMBERRY.

'whin-bush. Forms: see WHIN[1] and BUSH *sb.*[1]; also 6 **wyn-**, 7 **wine-**. A furze-bush.

1483 *Cath. Angl.* 416/1 A Whyn buske..*salivnca, saliuncula, paliurus.* **1563** FOXE *A. & M.* 1728/1 He tost a faggot at his face..and set a wynbushe of thornes vnder his feete. **1644** W. CAVENDISH (Dk. Newc.) *Let.* Life (1886) 352 Through some fields of furze and whin bushes. **1721** RAMSAY *To the Whin-Bush Club* 19 To come beneath your Whin-Bush Shade. **1881** J. GRANT *Cameronians* iv, Masses of whin-bush (or gorse as it is called in England). **1889** CONAN DOYLE *Micah Clarke* x, The gentle murmur of the breeze amongst the whin-bushes.

whinch, obs. form of WINCE.

whinchat ('hwɪntʃæt). [f. WHIN[1] + CHAT *sb.*[2]] A small European bird, *Pratincola rubetra*, closely allied to the stonechat.

Also called locally *furze-chat*, *gorse-chat*.

1678 RAY *Willughby's Ornith.* 234 The Whin-chat,..In bigness it scarce exceeds a Wagtail... The *Anthus* or *Florus* of Aristotle..differs from our Whin-chat in the colour of its Bill, and in the place where it lives; sith our Chat abides especially in heaths, and among Furze-bushes. *c* **1775** G. WHITE *Selborne, To Pennant* xli. (1789) 107 How the wheat-ear and whin-chat support themselves in winter cannot be so easily ascertained, since they spend their time on wild heaths and warrens. **1843** *Penny Cycl.* XXVII. 324/1 The flight of the Whinchat is undulating. **1894** R. B. SHARPE *Handbk. Birds Gt. Brit.* I. 300 As in Great Britain, the Whinchat is a summer visitor to most parts of Europe.

whinder, obs. var. WINDER *sb.*, wigeon; var. WINDER *v. Obs.* to wither, etc.

whindle ('hwɪnd(ə)l), *v. Obs.* exc. *dial.* Also 7 **whinil**, 7–9 **whinnel**. [app. f. WHINE *v.* + -LE.] *intr.* To whine, whimper. Hence **'whindling** *vbl. sb.*; **'whindling** *ppl. a.*, weak, pining, puny; *fig.* trifling, petty. So **'whindle** *sb.*, (*a*) a whining creature; (*b*) a low cry, a whine.

1601 MUNDAY & CHETTLE *Death Earl of Huntington* I. iii. B 2 b, He keepes a paltry whinling girle, And will not bed, forsooth, before he bride. **1609** B. JONSON *Silent Wom.* IV. v. (1620) L 2, The other a whiniling dastard. **1647** TRAPP *Comm. 1 Thess.* v. 16 [*Rejoice evermore*] A duty..little practised by many of Gods whinnels, who are ever puling and putting finger in the eye. **1648** in *Verney Mem.* (1907) I. 397 [He had intended to go with her to coast, but..his wife's] 'whinnelling'..[stopped him]. *a* **1652** BROME *Damoiselle* II. i, *Val.* Wee'll end the difference. *Broo.* By the Sword; no otherwise; No whinnelling satisfaction. *a* **1700** B. E. *Dict. Cant. Crew*, *Whindle*, a low or feigned Crying. **1709** *Mem. Signor Rozelli* 61 All the Women..fell a howling and whinneling. **1728** [DE FOE] *Street Robb. Consid.* 10, I [*sc.* an abandoned baby] began to Whindle, and Tune my Pipes. **1854** MISS BAKER *Northampt. Gloss.*, *Whindle*, to whine as a child.

whindle, variant of WINDLE, the redwing.

whine (hwaɪn), *sb.* [f. next.] An act of whining; a low somewhat shrill protracted cry, usually expressive of pain or distress; a suppressed nasal tone, as of feeble, mean, or undignified complaint; a complaint uttered in this tone. Also *transf.* a sound resembling this.

1633 P. FLETCHER *Pisc. Ecl.* I. xxii, The whistling windes joyn'd with the seas to plain, And o're his boat in whines lamenting creep. **1691** SOUTH *Serm.*, *1 John iii. 21* (1697) II. 470 By a few demure Looks, and affected Whines, set off with some odd, devotional Postures and Grimaces. **1751** JOHNSON *Rambler* No. 133 ¶ 2 The whine of condolance, or the growl of anger. **1808** SCOTT *Marm.* IV. Introd. 70 With dejected look and whine, To leave the hearth his dogs repine. **1822** HAZLITT *Table-t.* Ser. II. i. (1869) 17 A peevish whine in his voice like a beaten schoolboy. **1853** KANE *Grinnell Exp.* xxix. (1856) 244 The low whine which the ice gives out when we cut it at right angles with a sharp knife. **1897** *Allbutt's Syst. Med.* III. 623 The child utters a short cry or whine. **1928** E. WALLACE *Double* xx. 295 They heard the whine of a car draw up on the ground below. **1942** W. FAULKNER *Go down, Moses* 143 The air pulsed with..the whine and clang of the saw. **1962** *Which? Car Suppl.* Oct. 127/2 Other noises of which our drivers complained were rear axle whine in all the cars.

whine (hwaɪn), *v.* Forms: 1 **hwinan**, 4–7 **whyne**, 5–6 **wyne**, 6 *Sc.* **quhyn**, (7 **wheen**), 8 **wine**, 4– **whine**. [OE. *hwínan* (only in *Wídsíð* 128, of the whizzing of an arrow) = ON. *hvína* (Sw. *hvina*, Da. *hvine*) to whiz, whistle in the air; the weak grade of the stem is represented in ON. *hvinr* whiz, late OE. *hwinsian* (of dogs) to whine (see WHINGE).]

1. *intr.* To utter a low somewhat shrill protracted sound or cry, usually expressive of pain or distress; to cry in a subdued plaintive tone: also occasionally merely referring to the tone. **a.** of persons.

c **1275** *Sinners Beware* 310 in *O.E. Misc.* 82 For chele hy gunne hwyne. For hunger hi hedde pyne. **13..** in *Rel. Ant.* II. 245 Ich rede tha come nou to me, anaunter last ha whyne. **1526** *Pilgr. Perf.* (W. de W. 1531) 158 Not chauntyng nor brekyng your notes, nor whynynge in ye nose as many women done. **1534** MORE *Comf. agst. Trib.* II. Wks. 1182/2 Yet canne thys peuyshe gyrl neuer ceace whining and pulyng for fear. *c* **1590** J. STEWART *Poems* (S.T.S.) II. 54 Scho quhyns, Scho schrinks, Scho vreyis, Scho vips for vo. **1606** SHAKS. *Ant. & Cl.* III. xiii. 101 Whip him.. Till like a Boy you see him crindge his face, And whine aloud for mercy. *a* **1654** SELDEN *Table-T.* (Arb.) 92 If a Man should make love in an ordinary Tone, his Mistress would not regard him; and therefore he must whine. *a* **1700** B. E. *Dict. Cant. Crew*, To *Whine*, to cry squeekingly, as at Conventicles. **1727** GAY *Begg. Op.* I. xiii, The Boy thus, when his Sparrow's flown,.. Whines, whimpers, sobs and cries. **1852** THACKERAY *Esmond* II. xiii, The crowd of beggars.. whining for alms. **1868** LOUISA M. ALCOTT *Little Women* viii, You can't go, Amy; so don't be a baby and whine about it.

b. of animals, esp. dogs; also formerly, to whinny as a horse, or to cry as an otter.

13.. *Guy Warw.* (A.) 1336 Þe helmes þai seyen briȝt schine, þe stedes nyen, and togider whine. *c* **1386** CHAUCER *Wife's Prol.* 386 As an hors I koude byte and whyne [*v.r.* whine]. *c* **1400** *Beryn* 481 He.. scrapid the dorr welplich, & wynyd with his mowith, Aftir a doggis lyden. **1481** CAXTON *Reynard* xxxiv. (Arb.) 97, I saide I was also hongry, thenne wente we.. and fond nothyng, tho whyned he and cryed. **1576** TURBERV. *Venerie* 238 An Otter whineth. **1577** WHETSTONE *Gascoigne* xxix, The horse.. will neither winch nor whine. **1605** SHAKS. *Macb.* IV. i. 2 Thrice the brinded Cat hath mew'd.. Thrice, and once the Hedge-Pigge whin'd. **1735** SOMERVILLE *Chase* II. 118 Let each Lash Bite to the Quick, 'till howling he return And whining creep amid the trembling Crowd. **1812** BYRON *Ch. Har.* I. Song 'Good Night' ix, Perchance my dog will whine in vain, Till fed by stranger hands. **1835** W. IRVING *Tour Prairies* 272 Occasionally a scoundrel wolf would scour off.. and.. sit down and howl and whine.

c. *transf.* of inanimate objects.

1874 J. G. HOLLAND *Mistr. Manse* xviii. 52 Till the old chimney howled and whined. **1885** TENNYSON *Balin & Balan* 341 The canker'd boughs.. Whined in the wood. **1901** *Munsey's Mag.* XXIV. 555/1 The bullets.. whined through the air. **1962** *Which? Car Suppl.* Oct. 140/1 Engine always whined when started from cold. **1972** *Daily Tel.* 16 May 9 Two minutes after the jet engines whine to a standstill she walked slowly down the special lateral gangplank. **1974** S. MIDDLETON *Holiday* iv. 42 Lawn-mowers whined.

2. To utter complaints in a low querulous tone; to complain in a feeble, mean, or undignified way.

1530 TINDALE *Num.* xi. 18 Ye haue whyned in the eares of the Lorde saynge: who shall geue vs flesh to eate? **1568** *Hist. Jacob & Esau* II. iv, See and the knaue be not for his dinner whining. **1654** WHITLOCK *Zootomia* 29 Since Life is but as a Game at Tables, if the fore-game be not to thy wish; neither whine nor Curse, but rowse thy care to an after-Game. **1756** JOHNSON in *Boswell*, I know not why any one but a school-boy in his declamation should whine over the Common-wealth of Rome. **1769** *Ibid.*, A man knows it [*sc.* death] must be so, and submits. It will do him no good to whine. **1880** DIXON *Windsor* III. xxiv. 238 He had whined and begged for liberty. **1891** KIPLING *Light that Failed* x, I won't whine when my punishment comes.

3. *trans.* **a.** To cause to pass *away* by whining; to waste in whining.

1607 SHAKS. *Cor.* V. vi. 98 At his Nurses teares He whin'd and roar'd away your Victory. **1656** OSBORN *Adv. Son* iii. (ed. 4) 100 That Taylor, reported to have whin'd away himselfe for the love of Queen Elizabeth.

b. To utter in a whining tone.

1698 FRYER *Acc. E. India & P.* 282 At the Reading the Epistle and Gospel, they change their Cope, Mantle, and Hood, and Whine them forth. *a* **1699** J. BEAUMONT *Psyche* I. ccxxiv, To sigh, and weep, and whine Out long complaints. **1781** COWPER *Conversat.* 577 Canting and whining out all day the word. **1848** DICKENS *Dombey* xxx, 'If one is to go on living through continual scenes like this,' she whined. **1880** MISS BRADDON *Just as I am* iii, Tomorrow morning he will be whining his recantation.

whine = *why not*: see WHY.

whineard, obs. form of WHINYARD.

whiner ('hwaɪnə(r)). [f. WHINE *v.* + -ER[1].] A person or animal that whines.

1603 FLORIO *Montaigne* I. xix. (1632) 39 An armie of Physitians and whiners [F. *pleureurs*]. **1607** TOPSELL *Four-f. Beasts* 504 The Epithets of myce.. whiner, biter. **1684** J. S. *Profit & Pleas. United* 156 In the Composing your Kenell, some whiners and treble crys will not do amiss, to make the opening of the Pack the more Musicall. *a* **1734** NORTH *Life Ld. Kpr. North* (1742) 216 From a Whiner for Favour to Criminals, he proved the veriest Butcher of a Judge. **1832** HT. MARTINEAU *Homes Abroad* iii. 47 Don't have anything to say to the whiners at the gate. **1886** CORBETT *Fall of Asgard* II. 244 A cheery man fares better than a whiner.

whiney: see WHINY.

whing (hwɪŋ), *int.* and *sb.* [Imitative.] A word expressing a high-pitched ringing sound.

1912 FLORA A. STEEL *King-Errant* I. ix, The toneless treble of the old voice whining away like the fine whing of a mosquito. **1919** J. J. BENNETT *Dover Patrol* xi. 130 'Whing,' 'whing,' sings the shrapnel.

whing (hwɪŋ), *v.* [Onomatopœic; initial *wh-* (expressing forcible movement, as in *whack*, *whirl*) combined with the *-ing* of *fling*, *swing*.] *trans.* and *intr.* To move with great force or impetus.

[**1673** *Sackfull of Newes* in *Shaks. Jest-Bks.* (1864) II. 176 Lob, I pray thee what was that the priest went so whinging whanging withal? Why Hob (qd the other),.. It is frankincense.] **1882** FLOYER *Unexpl. Baluch.* 185 He whings the heavy mallet back over his head at arms' length. **1896** KIPLING *Seven Seas, McAndrews' Hymn* 43 Her time, her own appointed time, the rocking link-head bides, Till—hear that note?—the rod's return whings glimmerin' through the guides.

whing, obs. form of WING.

whinge (hwɪndʒ), *sb.* orig. *Sc.* and *dial.* [f. next.] A whine, *esp.* a peevish complaint.

1500–20 DUNBAR *Poems* xxxii. 10 He [*sc.* a fox].. schuk his taill, with quhinge and ȝelp. **1825** CROKER *Fairy Leg. Irel.* I. 48 The whinge, and the yelp, and the screech, and the yowl. **1852** *Meanderings of Mem.* I. 170 With cur-like whinge to such soft cutting whip. **1938** S. BECKETT *Murphy* iii. 37 He threw his voice into an infant's whinge. 'I cudden do anything, Maaaammy.' **1947** I. L. IDRIESS *Isles of Despair* xxxviii. 254 The bull [whale] complained with a stupid little grumbling whinge and edged a few yards farther away. **1963** [see PEANUT 2 b]. **1973** P. WHITE *Eye of Storm* i. 64 'You're so *unfair*!' A whinge developed through a moan into a downright blub. **1981** *Listener* 4 June 749/1 This is not just an envious whinge. **1982** J. THOMSON *To make a Killing* xiii. 231, I knew bloody well he'd shop me and make a fuss... He'd already had a whinge about the rubbish I'd left. **1985** *Times* 10 Jan. 10/6 In my one-but-last whinge I was going on about the burdensome duties of The Talk.

whinge (hwɪndʒ), *v.* orig. *Sc.* and *north. dial.* Forms: 6 **quhinge, quhynge**, 9 **winge, wheenge**, 8 **whindge**, 7– **whinge**, 20 **winge**. [North. form of OE. *hwinsian*, corresp. to OHG. *win(i)sôn* (MHG. *winsen*; cf. MHG., G. *winseln*) :—OTeut. **χwinisōjan*, f. root of *hwínan* to WHINE. For the suffix cf. OE. *clǽnsian* to CLEANSE, *bletsian* to BLESS, *rícsian* to rule, ON. *hreinsa* to cleanse; for the phonology of the form *whinge* cf. CLENGE, *ringe*, north. forms of CLEANSE, RINSE.] *intr.* To whine; *esp.* to complain peevishly. Hence '**whinging** (also **w(h)ingeing**) *vbl. sb.* and *ppl. a.*

a **1150** *MS. C.C.C. Camb. 303* 125/7 Mid hwinsunge & mid dreoriȝum mode hio [*sc.* the dogs] cerdon ealle onȝean to þan hunten. *Ibid.* 126/14 Þa hundes ne ȝeswicon to hwinsianne midceariendre stæmne. **1513** DOUGLAS *Æneis* XIII. iii. 28 The remanent of that questing sort,.. about the master hunteir With quhyngeand mouthis quaikand standis for feir. *Ibid.* 32 Thai hald thar mowthis still, Thar quhingeing and thar questing at his will Refrenis. **1562** WINȜET *Cert. Tractates* Wks. (S.T.S.) I. 8 Dum doggis, quha.. dar nother quhryne nor quhynge. **1720** C'TESS COWPER *Diary* (1864) 152 The second Time she said, whingeing [etc.]. **1725** RAMSAY *Gentle Sheph.* I. i, Daft Gowk! leave off that silly whindging Way. **1727** P. WALKER *Life Semple* etc. (1827) 316 You will die honourably before many Witnesses,.. and I will die whinging upon a Pickle Straw. **1728** RAMSAY *Last Sp. Miser* xviii, The mair they whing'd, it gart me hug My swelling Purses. **1760–72** H. BROOKE *Fool of Qual.* (1792) I. v. 159 A little beggar boy,.. whinging and shivering with cold. **1790** BURNS *Elegy Capt. M— H—* Epit. viii, Ony whiggish whingin' sot. *a* **1837** R. NICOLL *Poems* (1842) 17, I needna greet, What gude on earth wad whingeing do? **1867** P. FITZGERALD *Seventy-five Brooke St.* I. xxi, This mean, whinging fellow. **1907** J. M. SYNGE *Let.* 31 Mar. (1971) 121 Forgive this contemptible sort of whinging. I am so lonely and miserable I cant help it. **1922** JOYCE *Ulysses* 10 You crossed her last wish in death and yet you sulk with me because I don't whinge like some hired mute from Lalouette's. **1946** K. TENNANT *Lost Haven* (1947) xvii. 272 She had lifted up her brief skirt.. to exhibit her sand-fly bites... 'You don't want to whinge about them. .. You had a good time, didn't you?' **1955** S. BECKETT *Molloy* II. 172, I forgot that my son would be at my side,.. whinging for food. **1965** *Listener* 2 Sept. 339/2 There is a stinging phrase in use, 'wingeing Poms' (translate into 'complaining English'). **1969** *Advertiser* (Adelaide) 12 May 5/4 Stop whingeing and give a bloke a go, mates. **1973** B. BAINBRIDGE *Dressmaker* 8 If that girl didn't stop her wingeing, the neighbours would be banging on the wall. **1983** *Times Lit. Suppl.* 11 Mar. 236/1 In 1849, Arnold whinged to Clough that the age was '..unpoetical'. **1983** *Sunday Times* 31 July 33/1 'What sort of people do Australians hate most?' 'The whingeing Pom... Poms that come over and do nothing but whinge.' **1984** *Times* 20 Jan. 10/7 This is not the month for whingeing criticisms. **1984** *Sunday Times* 9 Dec. 7/1 All must drill most Tuesday nights ..and not whinge when the trousers of their best suits are crumpled and smutted under the uniform.

whinger ('hwɪŋ(g)ə(r), 'hwɪndʒə(r)), *sb.*[1] Chiefly *Sc. Obs.* exc. *Hist.* Forms: 6 *Sc.* **quhingar, -ger, -gre, quhinȝear, -yeir, whingear**, 6, 8 **whingar**, 9 *dial.* **whinjer**, 6– **whinger**. [Presumably related to the earlier synonymous WHINYARD. The pronunciation with (ŋ) or (ŋg) is vouched for by several instances in rime; that with (dʒ) is indicated by the spelling *whinjer* (quot. 1823) and implied by the form of Gael. *cuinnsear* dagger, sword, which is a loan-word from Sc.] = WHINYARD.

1540 *Rec. Elgin* (New Spald. Cl. 1903) I. 49 The quhingar ..quhairwith the said bluid was drawin. **1560** ROLLAND *Seven Sages* (Bann. Club) 313 Incontinent his quhinȝear furth he drew. **1566** *Diurn. Occurr.* (ibid.) 101 My lord gaif him twa straikis with ane quhingar at the paip. **1681** COLVIL *Whigs Supplic.* I. (1710) 7 Some had Cross-Bows, some were Slingers; Some had only Knives and Whingers. *Ibid.* 52 And other some get bloudy Fingers, By grasping naked Knives and Whingers. **1715** *Act 1 Geo. I*, c. 54 §1 Poynard, Whingar, or Durk. *c* **1730** RAMSAY *Highland Lassie* v, I can wield my trusty sword, Or frae my side whisk out a whinger [*rime* finger]. **1820** SCOTT *Monast.* xxvii, If there were a man left.. who could draw a whinger. **1823** E. MOOR *Suffolk Words*, *Whinjer*, a weapon, especially a large sword.

Hence '**whinger** *v. trans.*, to stab with a whinger.

1892 *Longman's Mag.* Apr. 687 He and his brother were 'whingered' upon the spot.

whinger ('hwɪndʒə(r)), *sb.*[2] orig. *Sc.* or *dial.* [f. WHINGE *v.* + -ER[1].] A whiner.

1791 LEARMONT *Poems* 312 I'll nae act the whinger's part, Like bairnies discontentit. **1934** *Bulletin* (Sydney) 27 June 11/2 Touching the query about 'whinger'.., 'winjer' was accepted slang for 'grumbler' at Q. Uni. a few years ago, and probably still is. I have seldom heard it elsewhere, and no one who uses it seems to know the derivation. **1959** I. & P. OPIE *Lore & Lang. Schoolch.* x. 186 Other local terms for crying... In Dublin the usual word is 'whinging', hence 'whinger', a term also still used in Cumberland, and occasionally heard in Liverpool. **1983** *Listener* 14 Apr. 17/2 Certainly, no whinger like me will ever turn Simon into a dissident.

whiniard, obs. form of WHINYARD.

whinid: see FINEWED.

whinil, obs. f. WHINDLE *v.*, to whine.

whining ('hwaɪnɪŋ), *vbl. sb.* [f. WHINE *v.* + -ING[1].] The action of the verb WHINE; the uttering of a low somewhat shrill cry or sound, or of a complaint in a low querulous tone.

c **1440** *Promp. Parv.* 524/2 Whynynge, *ululatus*. **1508** DUNBAR *Test. A. Kennedy* 65 My fenȝeing, and my fals wynyng, *Relinquo falsis fratribus*. **1542** UDALL *Erasm. Apoph.* 14 A bodye.. maketh a great whynyng, if he haue had any losse. **1605** SHAKS. *Lear* II. ii. 25 One whom I will beate into clamor[ou]s whining. **1607** TOPSELL *Four-f. Beasts* 138 The louder and shriller voice of a Dogge, is called barking, the lower and stiller, is called whining, or fawning. **1618** FLETCHER *Loyal Subj.* I. iii, Here will be trim piping anon and whining, Like so many Pigs in a storm. **1626** DONNE *Serm., John xi. 21* (1640) 820 For the ratling of a Coach, for the whining of a doore. *a* **1693** *Urquhart's Rabelais* III. xiii. 107 The.. wheening of Whelps. **1765** GOLDSM. *Ess., Eng. Clergy*, I am not for whining at the depravity of the times. **1853** KANE *Grinnell Exp.* xlii. (1856) 386 A whining as of young puppies. **1859** JEPHSON *Brittany* vii. 86 The unmanly whining of disappointed vanity or morbid sentiment. **1897** *Allbutt's Syst. Med.* II. 908 The voice is enfeebled to whinings and fretful pulings.

b. *attrib.* ***whining cross*** = WEEPING *cross*.

1602 BRETON *Wonders worth Hearing* Wks. (Grosart) II. 12/1 These yong men.. will.. leaue vs to make our prayers at whining crosse.

'**whining**, *ppl. a.* [f. as prec. + -ING[2].] That whines; characterized by whining. (*lit.* and *fig.*)

In some technical uses (quots. 1625, 1679) = WEEPING *ppl. a.*

15.. COSOWARTH in Farr *S.P. Eliz.* (1845) II. 406 This did my whyninge life endure awhile. *a* **1586** SIDNEY *Arcadia* I. x. (1912) 60 The houndes.. with a whining Accent craving libertie. **1600** SHAKS. *A.Y.L.* II. vii. 145 The whining Schoole-boy with his Satchell. **1625** MARKHAM *Inrichm. Weald of Kent* 9 Winter-springs, or teares of water (for, which some call such, A whining or weeping ground). **1660** *Nicholas Papers* (Camden) IV. 254 A whining puritanicall tubb preacher. **1678** OTWAY *Friendship in F.* II. i, To have us two such whining crop-sick Lovers. **1679** EVELYN *Sylva* xx. (ed. 3) 87 Whyning, or shrivell'd-Gelster. **1711** STEELE *Spect.* No. 142 ¶2 A Man of Honour, not a Romantick Hero or a Whining Coxcomb. **1773** GOLDSM. *Stoops to Conq.* v, The whining end of a modern novel. **1841** BORROW *Zincali* I. II. iv. 278 The whining, canting tones peculiar to the Gypsies. **1888** *Times* 2 Oct. 9/1 The English masses.. cannot be got to take much interest in a whining poltroon. **1897** KIPLING *Capt. Cour.* v, The whining wheel.

Hence '**whiningly** *adv.*

1660 INGELO *Bentiv. & Ur.* II. (1682) 21 [They] talk whiningly. **1689** T. PLUNKET *Char. Gd. Comm.* Prol., Making those swearers (whiningly) to yield. **1814** BYRON *Let. to Moore* 3 Aug., I have seriously and not whiningly neither hopes, nor prospects. **1888** GUNTER *Mr. Potter* xx, The dog becomes so fearfully restless and whiningly uneasy.

† **whinion**, obscure obs. var. WHINYARD.

1654 GAYTON *Pleas. Notes* I. iii. 12 Be not afraid To gird thy whinion to thy trusty Thigh.

whinling, whinnel: see WHINDLE.

whinner ('hwɪnə(r)), *v. local.* [Frequentative of WHINE *v.*: see -ER[5].] *intr.* To whine (feebly). Hence '**whinnering** *vbl. sb.* and *ppl. a.*; '**whinner** *sb.*, a feeble whine.

c **1700** KENNETT *MS. Lansd. 1033.* **1840** MRS. CARLYLE *Lett.* (1883) I. 124 Lying on the floor insensible, or occasionally sitting up.. executing a sort of whinner. **1854** THOREAU *Walden* xii. (1886) 227, I formerly saw the racoon in the woods,..and..heard their whinnering at night. **1866** CARLYLE *Remin.* (1881) II. 212 Poor whinnering old moneyed women. **1888** *Lippincott's Mag.* Apr. 453 A fitful, whinnering gust.

whinnock^{1} ('hwɪnək). *dial.* Also 6 **qwenock, whinock.** [Celtic (Gael. *cuin(n)eag*, Ir. *cuinneog*, W. *cunnog*).] A pail, *esp.* a milk-pail.

1555 *Inv. R. Robinson, Kendal* (Somerset Ho.), A Qwenock & a skyll. **1594** *Inv. Cowper, Kendal* (ibid.), 2 flesh whinocks. **1691** RAY *Coll. Words* (ed. 2) 138 A *Whinnock* or Kit, a Pail to carry Milk in. **1787** GROSE *Prov. Gloss.*

'**whinnock**^{2}. *dial.* Also 9 **whinock, winnick.** [? f. the root of WHINE *v.* + -OCK.] The smallest pig in a litter.

1691 RAY *S. & E.C. Words* (ed. 2) 92 A *Cadma*, the least of the Pigs which a Sow hath at one fare;..it is also called the Whinnock. **1864** WEBSTER, *Whinock*..the small pig of a litter. (*local U.S.*) **1905** *Eng. Dial. Dict.*, *Winnick*... 2. The smallest pig of a farrow. Wil.

whinny ('hwɪnɪ), *sb.*^{1} [f. WHINNY *v.*] An act of whinnying; a (low or gentle) neigh, or similar sound.

1823 E. MOOR *Suffolk Words*, *Whinny*, the half neigh, half nigger, of a horse, mare, or colt. **1847** TENNYSON *Princess* v. 442 The gray mare Is ill to live with, when her whinny shrills From tile to scullery. **1870** MEREDITH *Let. to J. Morley* 27 Jan., Out flaps the big girl with a whinny, Fire! Fire! **1871** WHYTE-MELVILLE *Sarchedon* ii, A troop of wild asses standing at gaze for a moment, to disappear with snort and whinny. **1894** CROCKETT *Raiders* xli, I set my hands to my mouth,..and made the whinny of the heatherbleat [= snipe] palpitate across the moor.

'**whinny**, *sb.*^{2} *rare.* [f. WHIN^{1}, ? after *spinney*.] A thicket of whins or furze-bushes.

1896 *Westm. Gaz.* 4 Nov. 4/1 Portions of the common.. retain the thick covering of gorse whinnies.

whinny ('hwɪnɪ), *a.*^{1} [f. WHIN^{1} + -Y^{1}.] Covered or abounding with whins or furze-bushes.

1482-3 *Durham Acc. Rolls* (Surtees) 648 Circa manuram de le Whynnyclose. **1607** MARKHAM *Cavel.* VII. xxx. 49 Hay which growing in whinnie grounds is ful of sharp prickes and stumpes. **1761** STERNE *Tr. Shandy* IV. xxxi, The Oxmoor..was a fine, large, whinny, undrained, unimproved common. **1824** MISS FERRIER *Inher.* xliv, The whinny braes of his native land. **1826** GALT *Last of Lairds* xxxv. 320 I've had a notion..that there's a mine o' copper ore aneath the whinny-knowes.

whinny ('hwɪnɪ), *a.*^{2} [f. WHIN^{2} + -Y^{1}.] Of the nature of or containing whin or whinstone.

1789 J. WILLIAMS *Min. Kingd.* II. 6 The whinny and the argillaceous regularly stratified mountain rock.

whinny ('hwɪnɪ), *v.* Forms: 6 **whyn(n)ye, whiny, wynny, -ie,** 7–9 **whinney,** 9 **winny,** 6– **whinny.** [Imitative; cf. the earlier *whine* (14th cent.), *whrinny* (15th cent.), and L. *hinnīre*.]

1. *intr.* Of a horse: To neigh, esp. in a low or gentle way; also occasionally of other animals, as calves or certain birds, or of inanimate objects making a similar noise.

1530 PALSGR. 781/1 My horse whynyeth cherfully this mornyng. *Ibid.* 782/2, I wynny, as a horse dothe. **1592** [? GREENE] *Def. Conny Catch.* (1859) 19 After an amorous weke or two, as old Jades wynnie when they cannot wagge the tayle. **1676** HOBBES *Iliad* XII. (1686) 173 The Horses when upon the Brink they were, Boggl'd and whinny'd, and refus'd to pass. **1683** SNAPE *Anat. Horse* II. ix. (1686) 93 Does the horse neigh, or whinney as they call it in some Countrys? **1815** SCOTT *Guy M.* xxiii, Dumple..walked to his own stable-door, and there pawed and whinnied for admission. **1855** KINGSLEY *Westw. Ho!* vii, The colts in the horse-park..whinnied as they played together. **1858** O. W. HOLMES *Aut. Breakf.-t.* xii, French horns whinnied. **1885** MRS. C. PRAED *Head Station* xlvi, The calves whinnied in their pen as she approached. **1893** KIPLING *Many Invent.*, *Finest Story* 124 The gas-jet puffed and whinnied. **1894** CROCKETT *Raiders* xxxvii, Again the bird [*sc.* snipe] whinnied in the air.

2. *trans.* To utter with a whinnying sound; to express by whinnying.

1815 SCOTT *Guy M.* li, 'He who shot young Hazlewood —ha, ha, ho!' burst forth the Dominie, with a laugh that sounded like neighing... 'Accidental! ho, ho, ha!' again whinnied Sampson. **1859** MEREDITH *R. Feverel* xxiv, 'I can't move.' Benson made a resolute halt. 'I must be fetched', he whinnied. **1888** GUNTER *Mr. Potter* iv. 45 The donkeys.. whinny their pleasure as they drink.

Hence '**whinnying** *vbl. sb.* and *ppl. a.* (†also quasi-*adv.*).

1585 HIGINS *Junius' Nomencl.* 358/2 *Hinnitus*,..the neying or whinying of an horse or mare. **1595** NORTH *Plutarch, Sylla* 514 A sharpe voyce like the neying of a horse, or whynnying of a goate. **1607** MARKHAM *Cavel.* I. xvi. 63 Where they may neither heare the noyse of their dams, nor their dams heare their whinneing. **1675** COTTON *Burlesque upon B.* 40, I..run whynnying mad, For every woman that I see. **1819** SCOTT *Leg. Montrose* viii, His low whinnying neigh, his pricked ears [etc.]. **1837** W. IRVING *Bonneville* xli, The elk kept up a continual whinnying or squealing. **1876** GEO. ELIOT *Dan. Der.* lxx, Several small, whinnying laughs. **1881** MRS. C. PRAED *Policy & P.* xvi, There was a whinnying call from one horse to another. **1895** CROCKETT *Men of Moss-Hags* xxv, The whinnying of swords as they whistled through the air.

†**whinny-whanny.** *Obs.* [Cf. WHIM-WHAM, WHIMSY-WHAMSY.] ? A trivial thing, trifle.

1673 *S'too him Bayes* 54 You may make an Egregious Play with the rest of your Whinny-whanneys but where's the Plot?

whinse, obs. form of WINCE.

whinstone ('hwɪnstəʊn). Also WHIMSTONE. [f. WHIN^{2} + STONE *sb.*] A name for various very hard dark-coloured rocks or stones, as greenstone, basalt, chert, or quartzose sandstone.

1513 DOUGLAS *Æneis* VII. Prol. 39 On raggit rolkis of hard harsk quhyne stane. **1763** W. LEWIS *Phil. Comm. Techn.* 441 The stone called whynn stone, with which some of the streets of London have been lately paved. **1791** BEDDOES in *Phil. Trans.* LXXXI. 65 Whether the basaltes proceeds southward..till it join the Elvin or whinstone, and granite of Devonshire and Cornwall. **1802** PLAYFAIR *Illustr. Hutton. The.* 66 The strata are intersected by veins of whinstone, porphyry and granite. **1823** P. NICHOLSON *Pract. Builder* 289 In Scotland, whole towns are built of whin-stone. **1879** G. MACDONALD *Sir Gibbie* xxi, Granite red and grey, blue whinstone, yellow ironstone, were all mingled.

b. A boulder or slab of this rock. Often used *fig.* or *allusively*.

a **1585** MONTGOMERIE *Flyting* 744 Except I wer to force the with quhin staneis. **1803** *Gazetteer Scot.* s.v. *Girvan*, The coast is generally flat and sandy, interspersed with large whinstones, with which most of the houses are built. **1816** SCOTT *Bl. Dwarf* xi, The despair he felt..was..such as would have melted the heart of a whinstane. **1827** —— *Jrnl.* 15 Aug. in *Lockhart*, You might have been as well employed in buttering a whin-stone. **1865** G. MACDONALD *Alec Forbes* xiv, He's a blue whunstane that's hard to dress. **1899** CROCKETT *Kit Kennedy* xlvi, An old man..that you told me was breaking whin-stones on the roadside.

c. *attrib.* Pertaining to or consisting of whinstone; also *fig.* hard, tough.

1834 H. MILLER *Scenes & Leg.* xi. (1857) 167 The castle —a grey whinstone building. **1874** GREEN *Short Hist.* i. §3. 25 The scant herbage scarce veils the whinstone rock. **1910** BUCHAN *Prester John* v, I haven't your whinstone nerve.

whinta(i)ne, obs. forms of QUINTAIN^{1}.

whiny ('hwaɪnɪ), *a.* Also **whiney**. [f. WHINE *sb.* or *v.* + -Y^{2}.] Characterized by whining; disposed to whine, fretful. Also ***whin(e)y pin(e)y***; so ***whiney-pine*** vb. intr., to make whining noises.

1854 MISS BAKER *Northampt. Gloss.*, *Whiny piny*, fretful, complaining. **1885** T. MOZLEY *Remin. Towns*, etc. I. 377 The sweet but rather whiny sing-song of Northamptonshire. **1897** SARAH GRAND *Beth Bk.* iv. (1898) 29 Beth, you really are a whiny child, you always have a grievance. **1920** 'K. MANSFIELD' *Let.* 27 Sept. (1977) 182 Two infant wasps..each caught hold of a side of a *leaf* and began to tug... They became furious. They whimpered, whiney-pined—snatched at each other—wouldn't give way.

whinyard ('hwɪnjəd). Now *Hist.* Forms: 5 **whyneherd, whyneard,** 6 **whynarde, whinyeard, winniard,** 7 **whineyard, -yeard, whineard, whyniard, whinniard,** 7–8 **whiniard,** 6– **whinyard.** [Of obscure origin; cf. WHINGER *sb.*^{1}] A short-sword, a hanger.

1478 *Nottingham Rec.* II. 296 *Cum quodam armicudio vulgariter nuncupato Anglice* 'a whyneherd'. **1499** *Will of Love* (Somerset Ho.), A whyneard with a chape of siluer. *a* **1529** SKELTON *Bouge of Court* 363 And by his syde his whynarde and his pouche. **1653** GATAKER *Vind. Annot. Jer.* 136 We shall not need to borrow great Alexanders whiniard to cut this Gordian knot. **1663** BUTLER *Hud.* I. III. 480 His Pistol next he cockt anew, And out his nut-brown Whiniard drew. **1719** D'URFEY *Pills* III. 320 Who wav'd his Whinyard o'er her Loyn, as if he'd gone to Knight him. **1810** SCOTT *Lady of L.* I. viii, The hunter..For the death-wound..Muster'd his breath, his whinyard drew. **1856-9** R. BUCHANAN *Trag. Dramas*, *Wallace* I. viii, I'd liefer Plunge this Scots whinyard in thy felon breast, Than in the heart of Turk or Saracen.

†**b.** ? A subtle 'blade'. *Obs. nonce-use.*

1611 CHAPMAN *May-Day* I. i, *Lor.* It is not Hector but Paris, not the full armefull, but the sweet handfull that Ladies delight in. *Ang.* O notable old whyniard.

whio ('fiɔ, 'wiːəʊ). *N.Z.* Also 9 **wihu, wio.** [Maori.] The blue duck, *Hymenolaimus malacorhynchos*, native to New Zealand.

1847 T. BRUNNER *Jrnl.* 2 Apr. in N. M. Taylor *Early Travellers N.Z.* (1959) 272 Shot a *wihu*, or blue duck. **1855** R. TAYLOR *Te Ika a Maui* xxv. 407 *Wio*,..the blue duck, is found abundantly in the mountain streams of the south part of the North Island..; it takes its name from its cry. **1880** J. C. CRAWFORD *Trav. N.Z. & Austral.* 122 At Kai-inanga, Deighton shot a pair of *whio*, or blue-ducks. **1966** *Encycl. N.Z.* I. 499/2 The most peculiar is undoubtedly the blue duck, mountain duck, or *whio*.

whip (hwɪp), *sb.* Forms: 4–6 **wippe, quippe,** 4–7 **whippe,** 5–6 **wyppe, whyppe, whyp,** *Sc.* **quhippe,** (4 **quyppe,** 5 **whhipp,** *Sc.* **qwype, quhipe,** 6 *Sc.* **quhyp, quhipp, whupe),** 5–7 *Sc.* **quhip,** 6–7 **whipp,** (9 *Sc.* **whup),** 5– **whip.** [Partly f. WHIP *v.*, q.v.; partly a. (M)LG. *wippe*, *wip* quick movement, leap, moment of time, lift for raising a well-bucket or hoisting cargo, lever, = Du. *wip* see-saw, strappado, swipe, skip (*in een wip* in an instant, *met een wip* at one sweep), OHG. *wipph* (MHG. *wipf*, *wif*) quick movement. Fris. *wip*, *wipp*, in some of these senses, also = mousetrap, Sw. *vipp* pump-gear, early Da. *vip*, *vippe*, also *hvip* leap, skip, short distance, moment, swipe, flap, lappet, Da. *vippe* swipe, G. *wippe* see-saw, crane, swipe, windlass, pliable pole, etc. are from LG. (Early Flem. *wippe* whip, in Kilian, is dubious.)]

I. The instrument of flagellation, and connected senses.

1. a. An instrument for flogging or beating, consisting either of a rigid rod or stick with a lash of cord, leather, etc. attached, or of a flexible switch with or without a lash, used for driving horses, chastising human beings, and other purposes.

c **1325** *Gloss. W. de Bibbesw.* in Wright *Voc.* 154 Ses chivaus deyt le charetter De sa fowette [*gloss* a quippe] ou de sa ryote gyer [*gloss* haling-wippe]. *c* **1340** *Nominale* (Skeat) 886 *Chareter ad sa reorte*, Carter hathe his wippe. *c* **1386** CHAUCER *Sec. Nun's T.* 406 For which Almachius dide hym so bete With whippe of leed, til he the lif gan lete. *c* **1450** *Cov. Myst.* (Shaks. Soc.) 315 Bynde hym to a pelere,..Than skorge hym with qwyppys. **1535** COVERDALE *Prov.* xxvi. 3 Vnto the horse belongeth a whyppe, to the Asse a brydle, and a rodde to the fooles backe. **1567** *Aldeburgh Rec.* in *N. & Q.* 12th Ser. VII. 142/2 P^{d} to Sponer for his attendans at ye churche wth ye whyppe..x^{d}. **1597** in *J. Melvill's Autob. & Diary* (Wodrow Soc.) 432 Into thy youthe, rejose to tholl the whupe. **1651** *Maldon, Essex, Burgh Deeds* Bundle 82 No. 2 (MS.), xii*d.* paid Samuell Sturgeon for punishing of three persons by the whipp. **1735** SOMERVILLE *Chase* II. 112 The clust'ring Pack..hear with respect thy Whip Loud-clanging. **1807** SOUTHEY *Espriella's Lett.* II. 48 The coachman smacked his whip. **1868** F. E. PAGET *Lucretia* 173 Flick, flick, flick, went the whip.

b. In fig. or allusive use: cf. SCOURGE *sb.* 2, 3.

c **1386** CHAUCER *Merch. T.* 427 She may be youre purgatorie She may be goddes meene and goddes whippe. **1406** HOCCLEVE *La Male Regle* 118 Seeknesse, y meene, riotoures whippe. *a* **1548** HALL *Chron.*, *Hen. VIII* 234 This act established chiefly sixe articles, wherof..of some it was named the whip with sixe strynges. **1588** SHAKS. *L.L.L.* III. i. 176 And I forsooth in loue, I that haue beene loues whip! **1625** DEKKER *Rod for Run-awayes* Wks. (Grosart) IV. 278 Iehouah, when he is angry, holds three Whips..the Sword, Pestilence, and famine. **1647** (*title*) A Fresh Whip for all scandalous Lyers. **1700** ROWE *Amb. Step-Mother* III. iii, Revenge shall..with her Iron whips Lash forth this lazy Ague from my Blood. **1817** D'ISRAELI *Cur. Lit.* III. 312 Fanatics, who had..smarted under the satirical whips of the Dramatists. **1881** SHELDON *Dairy Farming* 177/3 Artificial manures act as 'whips' or stimulants.

c. *transf.* The occupation or art of driving horses; coachmanship.

1792 HOLCROFT *Road to Ruin* II. 25 You may challenge the whole fraternity of the whip to match you. **1818** SCOTT *Br. Lamm.* xxii, The coachman of the Marquis,..observing the rival charioteer was mending his pace, resolved, like a true brother of the whip,..to vindicate his right of precedence. **1851** APPERLEY *The Road* 58 The taste for the whip has undoubtedly declined.

d. Phrases. ***a fair crack of the whip*** (*colloq.*): a fair chance to participate or act. †***to drink*** or ***lick*** (***up***) ***on the whip***: to have a 'taste' of the whip, to get a flogging. †***a whip and a bell***: something that detracts from one's comfort or pleasure (in allusion to the ancient Roman custom of attaching a whip and a bell to the chariot of a triumphing general, to drive away evil). ***whip and spur*** (advb., usually with *ride*): using both the whip and the spur to urge the horse on; at one's utmost speed, at a furious pace: cf. SPUR *sb.*^{1} 2 a. ***whip behind!***, a cry to the driver of a horse vehicle calling his attention to the presence of some one riding on the back of the vehicle without his knowledge.

c **1460** *Towneley Myst.* iii. 378 For youre long taryyng Ye shal lik on the whyp. **1576** GASCOIGNE *Steele Glas* 688 He shal be sure, to drinke upon the whippe. **1644** CLEVELAND *Char. Lond. Diurn.* 4 In all this Triumph there is a whip and a Bell. **1681** T. FLATMAN *Heraclitus Ridens* No. 19 (1713) I. 127 Care and the compleat Character-Man are riding Whip and Spur who shall have the next Vacancy in Bedlam. **1684** OTWAY *Atheist* I. i, To get rid of that Whip and a Bell, call'd thy Wife. **1742** POPE *Dunc.* IV. 197 Each fierce Logician.. Came whip and spur, and dash'd thro' thin and thick. **1814** SCOTT *Wav.* lxvi, I rode whip and spur to fetch the Chevalier. **1835** CARRICK etc. *Laird of Logan* (1841) 307 Some wandeidy weans cried 'whip behind! whip behind!' **1929** K. S. PRICHARD *Coonardoo* 179 I'll see you get a fair crack of the whip now, Mr. Watt. **1944** L. GLASSOP *We were Rats* 2, I am sorry to have to tell you that the Lord's had a fair crack of the whip and He's missed the bus. **1957** *Technology* Oct. 271/1 We should give the technical high school a trial..with a fair crack of the whip when the talent is being handed round. **1971** *Radio Times* 19 Aug. 50/1 It is the first time in $4\frac{1}{2}$ years that those opposing the present abortion law have been given a really fair crack of the whip on a B.B.C. panel.

2. a. An object resembling a whip: a slender flexible branch of a plant; a twig, sprig, switch; a collection or growth of such branches.

1585 HIGINS *Junius' Nomencl.* 146/1 *Flagellum*,..the whip or smal toptwig of the vine. **1881** E. INGERSOLL *Oyster-Industry* 250 *Whips*, slender branches used to mark the bounds of oyster-beds. (Connecticut.) **1908** S. E. WHITE *Riverman* xv, What, in the early year, had been merely a whip of brush, now had become a screen.

b. = *whip aerial* s.v. WHIP- 1 c.

1940 *Electronics* July 68/2 The whip is used to increase the capacitance and to carry some current to greater heights. **1960** *Practical Wireless* XXXVI. 342/2 The aerial is an 8 ft. 'whip' which is swung into the vertical on arrival at a stopping place, being attached to the side of the caravan permanently, on an insulator. **1976** *S9* (N.Y.) Feb. 34/1 They are factory pretuned..and will take up to 500 watts of power, radiating from a 46-inch stainless steel whip.

3. a. A blow or stroke with, or as with, a whip; a lash, stripe; *pl.* a flogging. Now only *Sc.*

c **1425** WYNTOUN *Cron.* III. ii. 294 Wiþe a cheik bane of ane as,..He let about hym qwype for qwype. **1545** ASCHAM *Toxoph.* (Arb.) 145 He wyll gyue hym a whip. **1567** *Satir. Poems Reform.* v. 38 It war weill wairit he gat his quhippis. **1602** SHAKS. *Ham.* III. i. 70 For who would beare the Whips and Scornes of time? **1879** G. MACDONALD *Sir Gibbie* xxi, He's a coorse cratur, an' maun hae's whups.

b. *fig.* An attack, access (of illness or calamity). *Sc.* (Cf. WHIFF *sb.*[1] 1 c.)

1891 'H. HALIBURTON' *Ochil Idylls* 89 Ye chose me—at a whip o' dearth—To represent ye. **1894** 'IAN MACLAREN' *Bonnie Brier Bush, Lachlan Campbell* iii, If a body hes a bit whup o' illness.

c. *pl.* Abundance, 'lots'. *dial.*, *Austral.*, and *N.Z.* (Cf. LASHING *vbl. sb.*[1] b.)

1888 G. G. B. SPROAT *Rose o' Dalma Linn* 242 He'll hae whups o' tabacca. **1897** I. SCOTT *How I stole 10,000 Sheep* vii. 29, I was glad to hear Jim come cantering up with 'whips' of bread, cheese, beer and horse-feed. **1904** *Blackw. Mag.* Apr. 558/2, I must have lost 'whips' of blood. **1928** 'BRENT OF BIN BIN' *Up Country* xi. 183 Whips of room for us both. **1948** R. FINLAYSON *Tidal Creek* I. vi. 59 'Didn't think old Podder would ever bother about that bit of land,' says Uncle Ted. 'Got whips of land.' **1961** G. FARWELL *Vanishing Australian* 182 Then you want capital—whips of it.

4. a. One who wields a driving-whip; a driver of horses, a coachman. (Usually with descriptive adj. or phr. expressing skill or style.)

1775 SHERIDAN *Rivals* I. i, None of the London whips of any degree of *ton* wear wigs now. **1837** DICKENS *Pickw.* xiii, You're a wery good whip, and can do what you like with your horses. **1855** SMEDLEY *H. Coverdale* v, The old boy is nothing of a whip. **1884** EARL MALMESBURY *Mem.* I. 16 He ..drove four-in-hand better than any whip between Windsor and London.

b. *Printing.* A compositor who sets type speedily.

1890 BARRÈRE & LELAND *Dict. Slang* II. 409/1 *Whip*... (Printers), quick setter of type. *a* **1974** P. EVETT in J. Burnett *Useful Toil* (1974) III. 333, I was put into the piece 'ship' on the paper, where I can truly say I held my own, though I was no whip. **1978** *Times Lit. Suppl.* 15 Sept. 1022/4 An average compositor at that time would have set a thousand characters or ens an hour, and a 'whip', or fast setter on piece-work, would have set upwards of fifteen hundred.

5. *Hunting.* = *whipper-in* 1.

1848 THACKERAY *Van. Fair* xlv, The two whips.. possessing marvellous dexterity in casting the points of their long heavy whips at the thinnest part of any dog's skin who dares to straggle. **1860** LD. W. LENNOX *Pict. Sporting Life* I. 197 Gentlemen, I have been with you thirty-two years—one year as second whip, five as first whip, and twenty-six as huntsman.

6. A member of a particular party in Parliament whose duty it is to secure the attendance of members of that party on the occasion of an important division. Originally called *whipper-in* (WHIPPER-IN 2).

There is a variable number of Government Whips (under a Chief Whip) in both Houses of Parliament, who receive salaries paid out of public money. The Chief Whip in the Commons is the Parliamentary Secretary to the Treasury. In 1964, the additional post of Assistant Government Whip was created, several of whom are appointed.

1850 THACKERAY *Pendennis* II. vi. 52 Captain Raff, the honourable member for Epsom,..retired after the last Goodwood races, having accepted, as Mr. Hotspur, the whip of the party, said, a mission to the Levant. **1853** DICKENS *Bleak Ho.* lviii, The Whip for his party hands it about..to keep men together who want to be off. **1855** LD. LONSDALE in *Croker Papers* (1884) III. 323 There never was a division where the calculators and whips were more out of their reckoning. **1884** D. ANDERSON *'Scenes' in Commons* 214 Mr. Sheil, a Parnellite Whip. **1888** BRYCE *Amer. Commw.* I. xiv. 198 There is neither Government nor Opposition; neither leaders nor whips.

7. a. The action of 'whipping *up*' the members of a party for a Parliamentary division, or any body of persons for some united action.

1828 ELLENBOROUGH *Diary* (1881) I. 42, I hear Planta did not send out the notes for the division to-night till yesterday evening, so that there was a general idea it was not to be made a Government question... On the other side there is a perfect whip. **1832** LD. LYTTELTON in *Corr. Sarah Lady L.* (1912) 271 The latter was *shut out*, consequently there would have been 152. There must have been a great *Whip.* **1862** STANHOPE *Pitt* IV. 157 An anxious *whip* was made by *both* parties. **1884** E. W. HAMILTON *Diary* 2 May (1972) II. 608 It was carried..by a majority of 2 to 1, owing no doubt in great measure to the whip-up which the Prince of Wales had made. **1894** *Westm. Gaz.* 8 Oct. 2/2 As a demonstration of Parnellism..it was mainly drawn from Dublin. The whip-up from the country was even less successful than formerly.

b. A call or appeal to a number of persons for contributions to a sum or fund; now usu. *whip-round.*

1861 HUGHES *Tom Brown at Oxf.* iv, If they would stand a whip of ten shillings a man, they might have a new boat. **1865** *Slang Dict.*, *Whip*, after the usual allowance of wine is drunk at mess, those who wish for more put a shilling each into a glass handed round to procure a further supply. **1874** JEFFERIES *Toilers of the Field* (1892) 26 Wine 'whips' are formed, and the sherry circulates freely. **1874** HOTTEN *Slang Dict.* 339 Whip-round. **1887** *Echo* 23 Nov. 4/4 Neighbours, who knew that she had no money, instituted a 'whip round', and soon raised the necessary amount. **1888** *Daily News* 27 Dec. 3/7 A 'whip round'..for the Robin Dinner Fund for poor children in London. **1948** M. LASKI *Tory Heaven* i. 12 The whip-round for garments and the ladies' little cries when they were told that clothes were rationed at home. **1977** *Centuryan* (Office Cleaning Services) Christmas 2/3 It appears a whip-round for the drinks was suggested. **1980** A. MORICE *Death in Round* xiv. 107 She..handed over the money that had been raised by the whip round. **1985** *Times* 14 June 5 The extra money will have to be found by a nonrepayable whip-round among member states.

c. The written appeal or circular letter issued by a Parliament 'whip' to summon the members of his party.

1879 T. H. S. ESCOTT *England* II. 149 Having issued the whip, the great thing for the whip himself is to see that members do not slip through his fingers. **1884** *L'pool Mercury* 18 Feb. 5/6 The following five-lined whip, headed 'Most important,' has been issued to members of the Opposition.

d. *the whip*: the discipline that goes with being a member of a party in Parliament; an MP's membership of a party.

1950 THEIMER & CAMPBELL *Encycl. World Politics* 458/2 To decline the whip is a method of resignation from the party. **1955** *Times* 24 May 15/1 Some effort had been made to arrive at a non-intervention arrangement, but it broke down when Mr. Walker was asked if he would accept the Conservative whip. **1966** *Listener* 25 Aug. 289/1 If he is a member of the Labour Party, he is bound by the standing orders of the Parliamentary Labour Party... To defy the standing orders may involve the withdrawal of the whip. **1980** B. CASTLE *Castle Diaries* 12 The bitterness intensified when, in October 1971, sixty-nine Labour MPs, headed by Roy Jenkins, defied the Labour whip and voted for Mr. Heath's motion.

8. A preparation of whipped cream, eggs, or the like.

1756 *World* No. 201. ¶3 If he will not be satisfied with whips and creams, he may carry his voraciousness to more liberal tables. **1813** *Sk. Char.* (ed. 2) I. 86 There's cold meat for the men, soups for the married ladies, and puffs and whips for the girls. **1883** *Amer. Dishes* 157 Chocolate Whips.

9. a. (associated or identified with sense 3.) A movement as of a whip or switch; a lashing motion; *spec.* a slight bending movement produced by sudden strain, as in a piece of mechanism, or in the barrel of a gun when fired.

1889 MRS. E. KENNARD *Landing a Prize* xv. (1891) 113 Harry gave one backward whip of the [fishing-] rod. **1898** *Jrnl. R. U.S. Instit.* Oct. 1140 The whip of the barrel when fired. **1907** *Westm. Gaz.* 5 Dec. 4/2 The..frame [of a motor-car] is deepened in the centre to prevent whip.

b. *Cricket.* A whipping or springy action of the batsman's or bowler's wrist in playing or delivering the ball.

1903 [see FLICK *sb.*[1] 1 d]. **1923** *Cricketer Ann. 1922-3* 78 Kilner bowls left hand slow..has a good action with a nice 'whip' in it.

II. A movement, and connected senses.

†10. a. A sudden, brisk, or hasty movement; a start; *occas.* a sudden gust. *Obs.* (Cf. WHIP *int.*)

†*with a whip Sir John*: 'before you can say Jack Robinson'.

a **1553** UDALL *Royster D.* I. iii. (Arb.) 20 No haste but good, Madge Mumblecrust, for whip and whurre The olde prouerbe doth say, neuer made good furre. **1562** J. HEYWOOD *Prov. & Epigr.* (1867) 94 The hare at pinche turnth from him at a whip. *a* **1578** LINDESAY (Pitscottie) *Chron. Scot.* (S.T.S.) I. 259 This man..wanischit away as he had bene..ane quhipe of the whirle wind. **1583** H. HOWARD *Defensative* E4b, The sodaine whippes of the wheele of fortune. **1631** MABBE *Celestina* III. 39 With a whip-Sir Iohn, e'r you could scarce say this, shee was heere againe.

b. *Fencing.* A thrust in which the blade slides along the adversary's blade.

1771 LONNERGAN *Fencer's Guide* 86.

11. The brief time taken by a sudden movement; a moment, instant. *Obs.* exc. *Sc.*

c **1450** *St. Cuthbert* (Surtees) 4577 Thre wawes..þe whilk in to rede blode þan War turned with'in a whhipp. **1808** JAMIESON s.v., *In a whip*, in a moment. **1836** M. MACKINTOSH *Cottager's Dau.* 65 Syne in a whip she let him in.

III. Something moved briskly.

†12. A 'spring trap' for catching vermin, etc.

1590 M[ASCALL] *Bk. Fishing*, etc. 63 The whippe or spring trappe. This Engine, is called the whip or spring. *Ibid.* 85 A whippe spring, made..to take Buzardes and Kites.

†13. *Naut.* A handle attached to the tiller, formerly used in small ships: = WHIPSTAFF 2. *Obs.*

1611 COTGR. s.v. *Barre, La barre du timon*, the whip of the Rudder (of a ship). *Ibid.*, *Molinet*,..the roll wherein the whip of a Rudders tiller goes. *a* **1625** *Nomenclator Navalis* (Harl. MS. 2301), The Whippe is that staff which the Steeres-man dooth houlde in his hand, whereby he gouernes the helme..... In greate shipps they are not vsed.

14. Each of the arms or radii carrying the sails in a windmill.

1759 SMEATON in *Phil. Trans.* LI. 149 *note*, The extreme bar is 1-3d of the radius (or whip, as it is called by the workmen), and is divided by the whip in the proportion of 3 to 5. **1888** *Encycl. Brit.* XXIV. 599/1 In all the older windmills a shaft..carried four to six arms or whips on which long rectangular narrow sails were spread.

15. a. A simple kind of tackle or pulley, consisting of a single block with a rope rove through it (*single whip*); used on board ship, and in mining, etc. for hoisting, esp. light objects.

A *double whip*, *whip on whip*, or *whip and runner* consists of a standing block and a running block, the 'fall' or rope of the former being attached to the latter. *whip and derry* = WHIPSY-DERRY.

1769 FALCONER *Dict. Marine*, *Whip*, a sort of small tackle, ..generally used to hoist up light bodies, as empty casks, &c. out of a ship's hold, which is accordingly called whipping them up. **1778** PRYCE *Min. Cornub.* 179 In this winding by the whip, a strict attention should be paid to the filling the kibbals to the brim. **1834** MARRYAT *Peter Simple* xxviii, He ..made a whip, and lowered me on deck. **1846** A. YOUNG *Naut. Dict.* 367 *Whip-upon-whip*, or a double Whip, is one whip applied to the fall of another. **1875** KNIGHT *Dict. Mech.*, *Whip and Derry*, an arrangement for raising the kibble, by means of a rope merely passing over a pulley and attached to a horse. **1904** FITCHETT *Commander of 'Hirondelle'* xvii. 191 A whip was being rigged from the mainyard to hoist in the wounded.

b. (See quot.)

1808 JAMIESON, *Wheeps*, the name given to the instrument used for raising, what are called the bridgeheads of a mill.

16. A fairground roundabout in which a continuous revolving chain carries a number of cars or tubs round an oval track, the tubs being pivoted so as to swing freely about their point of attachment to the chain.

A proprietary name in the U.S.

1925 WODEHOUSE *Carry on, Jeeves!* vi. 152, I could hardly drag him away from the Whip, and as for the Switchback, he looked like spending the rest of his life on it. **1937** HULL & WHITLOCK *Far-Distant Oxus* xx. 277 Bridget, Anthony, and Peter went off for a ride on the 'Whip'. **1969** L. MOODY *Ruthless Ones* ix. 96 They went into the fun fair and tried the big dipper, the wheel, the whip. **1976** *Official Gaz.* (U.S. Patent Office) 8 June TM89 A. G. Mangels Co., Inc., Bay Shore, N.Y... *Whip.* For carnival type amusement ride... First use since at least as early as 1914. **1979** C. WOOD *Bond & Moonraker* v. 61 'The Whip' of his childhood days, but revolving at a speed that would have..hurled it half-way across the fairground.

IV. 17. *Needlework.* A stitch of the kind described s.v. WHIP *v.* 18; an overcast stitch; the projecting portion of the stuff between such stitches.

1592 GREENE *Greene's Vision* Wks. (Grosart) XII. 226 A Stomacher of Tuft Mockado, and a Partlet cast ouer with a prittie whippe. **1706** PHILLIPS (ed. Kersey), *Whip*,..a round sort of a Stitch in Sowing. **1882** CAULFEILD & SAWARD *Dict. Needlework* 519 Take up every Whip, or portion of the roll, between the stitches.

18. *Weaving.* (See quots.)

1825 J. NICHOLSON *Oper. Mech.* 415 In the weaving of ribands and other ornamental works, many extraneous substances, totally unconnected with the warp or weft, are thrown in... These substances are merely held in the fabric by the intersection of..the warp and the weft, and are by the weavers denominated whips. **1863** J. WATSON *Weaving* vi. 206 Whip is the name given to that kind of yarn which is used for making the figures in lappet weaving, and it is made by twisting together so many ends of common yarn.

V. †19. A bandage. *Sc. Obs.*

1504 *Acc. Ld. High Treas. Scot.* II. 465 For claith to be wippes to Johne Balfouris sair leg. **1507** *Ibid.* IV. 15 For iiij elne Holland clath quhilk wes wippes to the Kingis arm that wes hurt.

†20. A wreath, garland. *Sc. Obs.*

1513 DOUGLAS *Æneis* XII. iii. 19 Thar hedis dycht In wyppis of the haly herb vervane.

whip (hwɪp), *v.* Pa. t. and pple. **whipped** (hwɪpt), **whipt.** Forms: 3 **wippen, hwippen,** 4 **wippe, wype,** 4–6 **wyppe, whippe,** 5 **whype,** 5–6 **whyppe,** 6 **quip, wyp,** *Sc.* **quhip(pe, quhyppe,** 8–9 *Sc.* **wheep,** 9 *Sc.* and *dial.* **wip,** 8- *Sc.* and *U.S. dial.* **whup,** 6- **whip.** [The early history of this verb and its related sb. is uncertain. The senses of both no doubt represent several independent adoptions or formations. With the earliest uses of the vb. cf. (M)LG., Du. *wippen* to move up and down or to and fro, swing, oscillate, leap, dance, = MHG. *wipfen* to dance; from LG. are app. derived early Da. *vippe* to raise with a swipe, clip coin, also †*hvippe* to move quickly, leap, beat with a whip (?), Da. *vippe* to toss, see-saw, Sw. *vippa*, G. *wippen* to rock, tilt, see-saw, strappado, WFris. *wippe*, *wipje* to move quickly. The base *wip-* is also represented by forms cited s.v. WHIP *adv.*, and by several compounds, as (M)LG. *wipgalge*, Du. *wipgalg*, early Da. *vippegalge* strappado, Du. *wipbrug*, early Da. *vippebrygge* drawbridge, Du. *wipplank* see-saw, *wipstaart* wagtail, *wipvisite* flying visit, (M)LG. (G.) *wipper* money-clipper, LG. *wipwap* see-saw; and prob. G. *wipfel* tree-top, summit; Goth. *wipja* 'crown' represents a sense-development ('wind or bind round', branch III below) which is more extensively exemplified by the form derived from the variants *weip-*, *waip-* (Goth. *waips* wreath, crown, *weipan* to crown, ON. *veipr* head-dress, OHG. *weif* bandage; cf. WIPE). Cf. the parallel *sw*-formations s.v. SWEPE *sb.*[1], SWIP *v.*, SWOPE. The spelling with *wh* was presumably adopted as being symbolic.]

I. To move briskly, etc.

1. *intr.* **†a.** To flap violently with the wings.

a **1250** *Owl & Night.* 1066 (Cotton MS.) Þi song mai bo so longe genge Þat þu shalt wippen [*v.r.* hwippen] on a sprenge. *c* **1330** R. BRUNNE *Chron. Wace* (Rolls) 8197 When þey hadde longe to-gyder smyten,..Wyppyng wyþ wenges,.. Cracchyng wiþ clawes.

b. *gen.* (†occas. *refl.*) To make a sudden brisk movement; to move hastily or nimbly; to slip or shift quickly; almost always with adverbial extension (*about*, *in*, *off*, *out*, etc.).

c **1440** *Alphabet of Tales* 363 Sho . . saw þe dure was oppyn, & whippid in & lokkid þe dure faste. **1542** Udall *Erasm. Apoph.* 69 b, When he by chaunce sawe a mous rennyng and whippyng about from place to place. **1548** —— etc. *Erasm. Par. Mark* ii. 13–17 The sicke of the palsey, when he whipt out of his bed, and went home vnto his house. **1592** Greene *Disput.* B 4, Why then quoth shee, steppe into this Closet, hee whipt in hastely. **1599** Shaks. *Much Ado* i. iii. 63, I whipt [*Qo.* whipt me] behind the Arras. *a* **1604** Hanmer *Chron. Irel.* (1633) 189 The Bishop seeing . . the imminent danger, whipt out at a backe doore. **1748** Richardson *Clarissa* (1768) IV. 261, I can land these Ladies in France; whip over before they can get a passage back, [etc.]. **1773** Goldsm. *Stoops to Conq.* v. ii, If your own horses be ready, you may whip off with cousin. **1786** Burns *Ordination* vii, Oh rare! to see our elbucks wheep, And a' like lamb-tails flyin. **1852** Mrs. Stowe *Uncle Tom's C.* xxxix, We'll whip in at the back door. **1876** *Coursing Calendar* 19 The hare then whipped downhill. **1883** Stevenson *Treas. Isl.* xiii, He whipped out of sight in a moment. **1907** J. H. Patterson *Man-Eaters of Tsavo* xvii. 186 The moment he [*sc.* a rhinoceros] got wind of me, he whipped round in his tracks like a cat and came for me.

†**c.** with *it*, in same sense (see also WHIPPET *v.*); also *fig.* in phr. ***to whip it in with***, ? to ingratiate oneself with. *Obs.*

1540 Palsgr. *Acolastus* ii. iv. M iv b, Whipping it aboute for ioye. **1694** Motteux *Rabelais* iv. lv. 216 Let's whip it away. *a* **1704** T. Brown *Amusem.* iii. (1709) 40, I found my Neighbour K—— . . was made a Commission-Officer by the Name of Captain Whip 'em, I . . judg'd he had been Whipping it in with the Gentlewomen before mention'd.

2. a. *trans.* To move (something) in some way suddenly or briskly; to take, put, pull, push, strike, cut, flourish, etc. with a sudden vigorous movement or action; *fig.* to 'come *out* with', utter suddenly. Almost always with adverbial extension (*away*, *off*, *out*, *up*, etc.).

13.. *Gaw. & Gr. Knt.* 2249 When þou wypped of my hede at a wap one. *c* **1380** *Sir Ferumbras* 1617 Wyþ þat strok A wypede of his heued. *c* **1450** *Mankind* 788 in *Macro Plays* 29, I wyppe yt in þi cote; a-non yt wer don. **1513** Douglas *Æneis* x. vii. 128 With hys brycht brand his rycht hand he of quhyppyt. *c* **1540** *Bk. Fayre Gentyl-woman* B j, She [*sc.* Fortune] whyppeth her wheele about. **1570** Foxe *A. & M.* (ed. 2) 2173/2, I stirred out of my bed & whipt on my hose. **1600** *1st Pt. Sir J. Oldcastle* i. iii. 202 He . . leapes behind me, whippes my purse away. **1602** Shaks. *Ham.* iv. i. 10 Hearing something stirre, He whips his Rapier out. *a* **1704** T. Brown *Char. Jacobite Clergy* Wks. 1711 IV. 262 If they can but get to be a Lord's Chaplain, they immediately whip on a long Scarf. **1740** Richardson *Pamela* I. 165, I popt down, and whipt my fingers under the upper Tile. **1773** Goldsm. *Stoops to Conq.* ii. ad fin., I'll engage to whip her off to France. **1821** *Life D. Haggart* (ed. 2) 98, I wheep't out my chive. **1827** Lytton *Pelham* iii, 'Ah! Grant, Grant!' said Lord Vincent, eagerly, who saw another opportunity of whipping in a pun. **1829** Gen. P. Thompson *Exerc.* (1842) I. 6 When the Protestants found themselves in danger of being oppressed . . they whipt another king upon the throne, and kept him there. **1852** Thackeray *Esmond* iii. v, Whipping a dozen into prison or into the pillory. **1889** W. Clark Russell *Marooned* ii. (1891) 6 These considerations . . made me whip out, 'Miss Grant, it is settled. We sail together.'

b. *slang.* To drink quickly, 'toss off'. Usually with *off* or *up*. Hence *fig.* (see quot. 1687).

a **1600** Deloney *Gentle Craft* Wks. (1912) 164 When they had whipt off two or three quarts of wine. **1653** Urquhart *Rabelais* i. v. 24 Whip me off this glasse neatly [Fr. *Fouette moy ce verre qualentement*]. **1687** Miege *Gt. Fr. Dict.* ii, To whip off a Thing, to make short work with it, *expedier* (*depecher promtement*) *quêque Chose.* **1692** L'Estrange *Fables, Life Æsop* 11 The Fellow . . Whips up the Drink, and gives Xanthus the Pott again Empty. **1814** *Sporting Mag.* XLIV. 188 Two honest quarts . . down gullet whips he.

c. To make *up* quickly or hastily.

1611 Cotgr., *Fesse-breviaire*, a Priest that quickly whips ouer, or mumbles vp, his Breuiarie. **1697** Vanbrugh *2nd Pt. Æsop* 6 Fix upon the place of Treaty, . . and whip up the Peace Like an Oyster. **1711** Hearne *Collect.* (O.H.S.) III. 133 The Dedication to the Master was whipp'd up. **1861** Flor. Nightingale *Nursing* 48 [The clever nurse] will not bring in the bad article, but not to disappoint the patient, she will whip up something else in a few minutes.

d. To pinch or steal, to make off with; †to swindle. *slang* (orig. *Criminals'*).

1859 G. W. Matsell *Vocabulum* 95 *Whipped*, cheated out of a share, or equal part of the plunder. **1904** 'No. 1500' *Life in Sing Sing* xiii. 259 *Holding the mark till the tool whips his stone.* Engaging a person's attention till the thief succeeds in stealing his diamond. **1946** G. Kersh *Clean, Bright & Slightly Oiled* ii. 11 Hi, you, you give me back that dog-end you whipped. **1958** M. K. Joseph *I'll soldier no More* 19 'Where's your hat, Barnett?' . . 'Dunno, Someone musta whipped it.' **1976** A. Miller *Inside Outside* xi. 173 One of them was rightly furious as the escaper had whipped (stolen) his overcoat. **1981** P. O'Donnell *Xanadu Talisman* ix. 182 The Shah must've whipped this... Stashed it away in a Swiss bank.

†**3.** To pierce with a sword-thrust; to run *through*. *Obs. slang.*

a **1700** B. E. *Dict. Cant. Crew*, *Whipt through the Lungs*, run through the Body with a Sword. **1710** Addison *Tatler* No. 256 ⁋ 1 To make the sun shine through the criminal, or, . . to whip him through the lungs. **1842** C. Whitehead *R. Savage* xx, Why, you're not going there? . . This . . fellow . . would make nothing of whipping you through the body.

4. *Fencing. intr.* To make a thrust in which the blade slides along the opponent's blade. Also *trans.* with the blade as obj.

1771 Lonnergan *Fencer's Guide* 90 By disengaging after you whip, you have Quarte-over-the-arm. **1861** G. Chapman *Foil Practice* 13 Some fencers . . perform the Parries of Quarte and Tierce by whipping the blade, with a forward action, along that of the adversary's. **1889** W. H. Pollock *Fencing* iv. (Badm. Libr.) 82 The point must be raised towards the left shoulder, the hand drawn back a little towards the fencer's left breast, so that he may whip his blade neatly over the adversary's point.

5. *Naut.*, etc. *trans.* To hoist or lower with a whip (WHIP *sb.* 15).

1769 [see WHIP *sb.* 15]. **1835** [see WHIPPING *vbl. sb.* 3 c]. **1872** *Routledge's Ev. Boy's Ann.* 336 The chair was 'whipped' up again instantly.

II. To use a whip, strike with a whip.

6. *trans.* To strike or beat with or as with a whip. **a.** To punish or chastise with a whip or rod; to scourge, flog. Also *loosely*, to beat (esp. a child) with the hand or otherwise, to spank.

c **1386** Chaucer *Pars. T.* ⁋ 716 Eek Dauid seith: that . . they shul nat been whipped with men. **1483** *Cath. Angl.* 416/1 To Whype, *flagellare.* **1583** *Aldeburgh Rec.* in *N. & Q.* 12th Ser. VII. 367/1 P[d] for a cart th[t] gromes maide was whipte at vi[d]. **1590** Shaks. *Mids. N.* iii. ii. 410 Come thou childe, Ile whip thee with a rod. **1605** —— *Lear* i. iv. 199 And you lie sirrah, wee'l haue you whipt. **1617** Moryson *Itin.* i. 85 The pictures of Christ whipped, of Christ carrying his crosse, and of Christ praying in the garden. **1624** Burton *Anat. Mel.* iii. ii. i. i. (ed. 2) 356 She . . whipped him [*sc.* Cupid] . . on the bare buttocks with her pantophle. **1664** in *Verney Mem.* (1904) II. 214 If the 'Whelps meddle with Sheepe, they must be tied to any Dead sheepe, and whipped soundly'. **1709** Steele *Tatler* No. 76 ⁋ 1, I must whip my children for going into bad company. **1726–31** Waldron *Descr. Isle of Man* (1865) 32 Two or three of them seized her, and pulling up her clothes, whipped her heartily: . . she ran home . . , telling what had befallen her, and showing her buttocks on which were the prints of several small hands. **1752** Chesterf. *Let. to Dayrolles* 18 Oct., If a poor child is to be whipped equally for telling a lie, or for a snotty nose, he must of course think them equally criminal. **1813** E. S. Barrett *Heroine* iii. (1909) 17 Master Bobby . . mewed like a cat, when he was whipt. **1859** Thackeray *Virgin.* lxii, She deserves to be whipped, and sent to bed. **1868** Browning *Ring & Bk.* ii. 1243 Ah, being young and pretty, 't were a shame To have her whipped in public.

1893 H. A. Shands *Some Peculiarities of Speech in Mississippi* 68 *Whup*, . . Negro for *whip*. **1929** W. Faulkner *Sanctuary* (1981) xi. 132 You done whupped him. **1939** J. Steinbeck *Grapes of Wrath* xxviii. 504 Whyn't ya whup her, Ma? . . Go on, give her a whup. **1950** Patterson & Conrad *Scottsboro Boy* iii. ii. 193, I told the warden I was not guilty of the charge and didn't want to be whupped. **1972** J. Gores *Dead Skip* v. 31 He might have come after Bart . . because he wanted to whup a nigger?

b. To drive *away*, *out*, etc. with a whip. Also *fig.*

1567 *Stanford Churchw. Acc.* in *Antiquary* XVII. 169/2 For whipping dogges from y[e] churche. **1599** Shaks. *Hen. V* i. i. 29 Consideration like an Angell came, And whipt th' offending Adam out of him. **1667** Poole *Dial. betw. Prot. & Papist* (1735) 100 Tho' he whipt some out of the Temple, yet he never whipt any into his Church. **1711** Steele *Spect.* No. 157 ⁋ 1 We have so many Hundred unaccountable Creatures every Age whipped up into great Scholars. **1712** —— *Ibid.* No. 509 ⁋ 2 The . . boys . . were whipped away by a beadle. **1821–2** Shelley *Chas. I*, ii. 58 If all turncoats were whipped out of palaces, poor Archy would be disgraced in good company. **1878** Robt. Dick in Smiles *R. D.* viii. 82 The storm fairly whipped six vessels out of Scrabster Roads.

c. To drive or urge on (a horse, etc.) with strokes of a whip. Also (occas.) *absol.*

1587 Mascall *Cattle, Horses* (1596) 118 Let him neuer vse to beat them [*sc.* horses] with the stock of the whip, but to whip them with the lash. **1598** Chapman *Iliad* iv. [viii.] 70 Saturnia whipt her horse, And heauen gates guarded by the Howers, opte by their proper force. *c* **1611** *Ibid.* xv. 319 All whipt their chariots on. **1794** Mrs. Radcliffe *Myst. Udolpho* vi, The man whipped his mules till they went as fast as possible. **1838** Dickens *Nich. Nick.* xix, The coach, and the coachman, and the horses, rattled and jangled and whipped. **1852** Thackeray *Esmond* i. xiii, Your lordship will upset the carriage if you whip so hotly. **1859** H. Kingsley *G. Hamlyn* xiii, So, whipping up his horse, he drove there. **1889** Gunter *That Frenchman* xiii. 164 The driver . . sees a chance to dodge through an opening in the crowded street, and suddenly whips up for the effort.

d. Hunting. ***whip in***: to drive (hounds) with the whip back into the pack so as to prevent them from straying; *absol.* to act as whipper-in. ***whip off***: to drive (the hounds) with the whip away from the chase; *absol.* to give over the chase.

1739 [implied in WHIPPER-IN 1]. **1859** *Sporting Mag.* Feb. 80 The hounds were whipped off, as the evening was closing on us. **1862** *Ibid.* Dec. 438 James Stacey . . formerly whipped-in to the late Lord Fitzhardinge's hounds. **1887** *Field* 19 Feb. 231/1 Morris Hills, who whipped in to the Queen's Stag-hounds under Davis and King.

e. To spin (a top) by striking it with a whip.

1588 Shaks. *L.L.L.* v. i. 69 Thou disputes like an Infant: goe whip thy Gigge. **1598** —— *Merry W.* v. i. 27 Since I . . plaide Trewant, and whipt Top. **1697** Dryden *Æneis* vii. 528 As young Striplings whip the Top for sport. **1874** Ruskin *Fors Clav.* xxxvii. (1896) II. 273 A nice little girl whipping a top on the pavement.

7. a. *Confectionery*, etc. To beat up into a froth (cream, eggs, etc.) with a fork, spoon, or other instrument; to prepare (a fancy dish) in this way; also *fig.* See also quot. 1845.

1673, **1691** [see WHIPPED *ppl. a.* 3]. **1764** Eliza Moxon *Engl. Housew.* (ed. 9) 123 Whip it with a whisk, take off the froth as it rises. **1845** G. E. Day tr. *Simon's Anim. Chem.* I. 177 If the blood be whipt with due care, the fibrin is obtained as a thick . . mass, surrounding the twigs of the rod. **1849** C. Bronte *Shirley* xxxvi, When did I whip up syllabub sonnets? **1895** Montrésor *One who looked on* 7, I went to the kitchen to whip a strawberry cream.

b. *intr.* Of cream: to be capable of being whipped.

1943 *Mod. Lang. Notes* LVIII. 13 Cream *whips* quickly. **1979** A. Parker *County Recipe Notebk.* viii. 108 Single cream . . will not whip.

8. *Angling.* To cast the line upon the water with a movement like the stroke of a whip; to draw a fly or other bait along the surface by such a movement; *intr.*, or *trans.* with the bait or (usually) the water as obj.

1653 [see WHIPPING *vbl. sb.* 1 d]. **1832** Lytton *Eugene Aram* i. ix, Now he whipped it [*sc.* the fly] lightly on the wave; now he slid it coquettishly along the surface. **1838** James *Robber* ii, He prepared to ascend the stream, whipping it as he went with the light fly. **1883** Black *Shandon Bells* xxix, He worked away, whipping industriously and mechanically. **1904** Bindloss *League of Leopard* ii, [He] whipped several pools unsuccessfully.

9. a. *trans.* To strike like a whip, lash; to move or drive in this way.

1699 Dampier *Voy.* II. iii. 69 The Wind . . blew so violently . . that the Boughs of the Trees whipt them . . before they got thither. **1796** [see WHIPPING *vbl. sb.* 1 b]. **1799** W. Nicol *Pract. Planter* iv. §9. 219 Suffer no plant to overtop or whip another; keep the extremities of all side branches just touching one another. **1848** Thackeray *Van. Fair* xxii, One gusty, raw day, . . the rain whipping the pavement. **1869** Ld. Lytton *Orval* 67 On the wind That whips one through this wither'd waste. **1882** *Garden* 14 Jan. 25/3 The foliage . . whipped by the branches of other trees. **1884** Marsden *Cotton Spinning* 90 The primitive method of whipping the cotton with willow wands.

b. *intr.* To lash, swish; also, to bend or spring like a whip or switch.

1872 *Routledge's Ev. Boy's Ann.* 44/1 Lest the twigs should whip back into my face. **1893** H. M. Doughty *Our Wherry* 76 We could see the mast . . whip with the weight. **1894** Crockett *Raiders* iii, The chill wind whipping about my shanks.

10. *trans.* To bring, get, render, make, or produce by whipping (*lit.* or *fig.*).

1635 J. Taylor (Water P.) *Old, Old Man* D 3, Those Royall Opinions were whip'd out of him. *a* **1716** South *Serm.* (1744) IX. 154 Those . . whose religion lies no deeper than their skin, may whip themselves holy. **1740** J. Clarke *Educ. Youth* (ed. 3) 26 Having had *Lily* whipp'd into them at School. **1825** Hone *Every-day Bk.* I. 1190 A clown going round and whipping a ring: that is, making a circular space amongst the spectators with a whip. **1884** Haweis *My Musical Life* I. 42 He taught me how to whip instead of scraping the sound out [of the violin]. **1889** *Cornhill Mag.* Apr. 356 The cold has whipped red roses on her cheeks.

11. *fig.* To vex, afflict, torment; to punish, chastise; to administer severe satire or reproof to, 'lash', 'castigate'.

1530 Palsgr. 781/1, I whyppe with a shrode tourne, *je baille belle.* *a* **1548** Hall *Chron., Hen. VI* 178 b, With what great tormentes & afflictions God hath whypped & scorged this miserable Isle. **1588** Shaks. *L.L.L.* iv. iii. 151 Now step I forth to whip hypocrisie. **1651** H. More *Enthus. Tri.* (1656) 71 So unmercifully to whip poor Aristotle. **1831** James *Philip Aug.* xxx, More likely . . that some little unforeseen accident . . should prove our best calculations false, and whip us with our own policy! **1891** Kipling *Light that Failed* xiv, He pressed the girl more closely to himself because the pain whipped him.

†**b.** esp. *imper.* as a mild execration: = 'confound', 'hang'. *Obs.*

1604 Shaks. *Oth.* i. i. 49 Whip me such honest knaues. **1608** —— *Per.* iv. ii. 91 Marie whip the Gosseling. **1759** *Compl. Letter-writer* (ed. 6) 221 And yet, whip it, there is a satisfaction in reflecting [etc.]. **1872** Spilling *Giles's Trip* ix. (1920) 109 Tarnin' round I'll be whipped if the same mischievous brute han't managed to get it throw them wires.

12. To overcome, vanquish, defeat; to surpass, outdo: = BEAT *v.*[1] 10. Now *U.S. colloq.* Phr. ***to whip one's weight in wildcats*** and varr.: (to be able) to fight vigorously; to be fit and strong. Chiefly *U.S.* ? *Obs.*

1571 Campion *Hist. Irel.* ii. i. (1633) 64 Reymond . . whipped the Rebells, quieted Leinster. **1571** *Satir. Poems Reform.* xxvi. 100 ȝe neid na ma bot Gedionis thre hunder To quhip your fais. **1638** Baker tr. *Balzac's Lett.* (vol. II.) 17 You will whip the Spaniards in point of generousness. **1828** *Spirit of Seventy-Six* (Frankfort, Kentucky) 17 Jan. 3/5, I can ride upon a streak of lightning, whip my weight in wild cats. **1834** *Sk. David Crockett* xiii. 164 I'm that same David Crockett, fresh from the backwoods, . . ; can whip my weight in wild cats. **1836** Haliburton *Clockm.* Ser. i. xxvi, The British can whip the whole airth, and we can whip the British. **1852** H. C. Watson *Nights in Block-House* 20 Not as long as I can whip my weight in catamounts or bar, I'll never give in. **1861** Lever *One of them* xl, We can whip all cre-ātion. **1870** G. H. Lewes *Let.* 17 May in *Geo. Eliot Lett.* (1956) V. 96 We hope to see you both come back ready to 'whip your weight in polecats'. You will not find us in that vigorous condition! **1878** [see ONCE *adv.* A. γ]. **1901** R. S. Warren Bell *Tales of Greyhouse* 18 If Eccles uses his weight cleverly, Wardour will be whipped to a cert. **1906** *Dialect Notes* III. 164 *Whup*, . . to vanquish, to punish, to tire. 'That *whups* me.' **1968** *Punch* 25 Sept. 451/2 The Matt Dillon urge to 'whup' the Commies.

13. To urge, incite, rouse; to restore to energy or vitality, revive.

1573 Hatton *Let.* in Ld. Campbell *Chancellors* xlv. (1857) II. 265 Shame whippeth me forward. **1815** H. M. Williams *Narr. Events France* xi. 234 Their dormant patriotism was now awakened, bribed or whipped up. **1835** C. F. Greville *Mem.* 18 July (1875) III. xxviii. 280 On this occasion I whipped up the old friendship. **1894** A. Robertson *Nuggets* 29 He cuffed and whipped his brains to no purpose.

14. (orig. *fig.* from 6 d.) To summon to attend, as the members of a party for a division in Parliament, or any body of persons for some united action. Const. *in*, *up*; also simply or *absol.* Cf. WHIP *sb.* 6.

1742 H. FINCH *Let.* 18 Nov. in P. D. G. Thomas *House of Commons in 18th Cent.* (1971) vi. 114 The Whigs for once in their lives have whipped in better than the Tories. **1769** (May 8) BURKE in Sir H. Cavendish *Debates Ho. Comm.* (1841) I. 426/1 [Here Mr. Burke mentioned the ministry's sending for their friends to the north and to Paris,] whipping them in; [than which, he said, there could not be a better phrase]. **1805** M. CUTLER in *Life*, etc. (1888) II. 191 On the question of the Georgia claims.. he undertook to whip in his party. **1833** MACAULAY *Let.* 28 Oct. in Trevelyan *Life & Lett.* (1876) I. v. 336 Lord Essex was there,.. whipping up for a dinner-party. **1857** TOULMIN SMITH *Parish* 62 With no room for trickery or cajolery, or whipping-up uninformed voters. **1886** *Pall Mall Gaz.* 4 Sept. 9/1 The Liberals will probably support it and whip for it. **1898** J. HOLLINGSHEAD *Gaiety Chron.* i. 23 A literary friend.. whipped up a small syndicate of companions to support me.

†**15.** *pa. pple.* Streaked, striped. (After F. *fouetté.*) *Obs.*

1693 EVELYN *De la Quint. Compl. Gard.* I. 137 Another sort [of fig].. is pretty black, having only its Skin a little whipt with gray. **1699** L. MEAGER *Art of Gardening* 139 It hath white Leafs edged and whiped about, and feathered in the middle with a deep brown purple. **1721** MORTIMER *Husb.* II. 241 [Tulip] of a sad Red-colour about the Edges, whipped with Crimson.

16. Phrases. **a.** ***to whip the cat***: used (chiefly *dial.* or *techn. colloq.*) in various senses, some of which are not satisfactorily explained.

†(*a*) To get drunk; ? = 'to shoot the cat'. (*b*) ? To lay the blame of one's offences on some one else. (*c*) To work as an itinerant tailor, carpenter, etc. at private houses by the day. (*d*) To play a practical joke, for description of which see CAT *sb.*[1] 14. (*e*) To practise extreme parsimony. (*f*) To shirk work on Monday. (*g*) *Cards.* (See quot. 1854.) (*h*) *Austral.* and *N.Z.* To complain or moan. Cf. *whip-cat* (under WHIP- 2).

1622 J. TAYLOR (Water P.) *Arrant Thiefe* (1625) C 2 b, To be a Drunkard, and the cat to whip, Is call'd the king of all good Fellowship. **1793** *Philadelphia Ledger* 19 June in *Daily Chron.* (1902) 5 July 5/1 'Whipping the Cat!':—'Mirabeau's ashes were dispersed as belonging to a traitor, by the patriot Brissot, who is styled a villain by the patriot Egalité,' [etc.]. *a* **1825** FORBY *Voc. E. Anglia, To whip the cat*, to practise the most pinching parsimony, grudging even shreds and scraps to the cat. In Suffolk the phrase.. is applied to a practice.. of the village tailor going from house to house to work. **1845** S. JUDD *Margaret* iii, Made shoes, a trade he prosecuted in an itinerating manner from house to house—'whipping the cat,' as it was termed. **1854** MISS BAKER *Northampt. Gloss.* s.v., When one of the players at the game of whist wins all the tricks in one deal, he is said to whip the cat. **1859** *Slang Dict.*, *Whipping the cat*, when an operative works at a private house by the day,—term amongst tailors and carpenters. **1892** *Bulletin* (Sydney) 7 May 10/3 Now he only 'whips the cat' at the bottom of the Carlton poll. **1897** BARRÈRE & LELAND *Dict. Slang*, To *whip the cat* is modern working-men's slang for shirking work and enjoying oneself on Monday. **1909** H. THOMPSON *Ballads about Business* 12 You could make tenners den like vinkin', dough Now you are vippin' der cat. **1911** *Triad* 10 June 18 Tell him [*sc.* a misled person] he has leave to go and whip the cat. **1948** V. PALMER *Golconda* xxiii. 194 If there's anything wants doing you've only got to ask Macy Donovan... And he makes light of it, too. No whipping the cat: no setting himself up as a little tin god.

b. ***to whip the devil round the post*** (*U.S.* ***around the stump***): see DEVIL *sb.* 22 n.

1786 *Belknap Papers* I. (1877) 427 What the Virginians call 'whipping the devil round a stump'. **1841** *Congr. Globe* 7 July 132/3 Many men in the State Legislatures.. have run their constituents so deeply in debt, that now they want to whip the devil around the stump, and get somebody else to tax them. **1887** *Japan Mail* in J. M. Dixon *Dict. Idiom. Phr.* s.v. *Devil*, It is asserted.. that the devil might be whipped round the Tientsin Convention.

III. To bind round or over. (This group of senses is prob. represented earlier in the compound WHIPCORD, which appears 1318–19.)

17. a. *trans.* To overlay (a rope, string, or other object) with cord, thread, or the like wound closely and regularly round and round; to bind round or 'serve' (SERVE *v.*[1] 54 a) with cord, etc. Also, to bind (cord, etc.) in this way round something.

c **1440** *Promp. Parv.* 524/2 Whyppyn, as sylke womene (*K.*, *P.* whyppyn or closyn threde in sylke), *obvolvo.* **1561** *Ludlow Churchw. Acc.* (Camden) 102 For whippinge the seconde belle rope.. ij d. **1581** STYWARD *Mart. Discipl.* I. 44 They must haue.. their [bow-]stringes whipped & waxed ouer with glew. **1616** SURFL. & MARKH. *Country Farm* IV. xvi. 512 Then with a silke thred, of the colour of your line, whip and warpe the hooke round about. **1651** T. BARKER *Art of Angling* (1820) 15 Lay.. the poynt of the feather towards the shank of the hook, then whip it three or four time[s] about the hook with the.. silk. **1676** COTTON *Angler* II. v. 39 Take a strong small silk.. and then whip it twice or thrice about the bare hook. **1681** CHETHAM *Angler's Vade-m.* i. §2. (1689) 2 Whale-bone made round & taper, & whip'd with Shoomaker's Wax, and Silk. **1769** FALCONER *Dict. Marine*, *To Whip*,.. to tie a piece of pack-thread, spun-yarn, &c. about the end of a rope, to prevent it from being untwisted. **1770** LUCKOMBE *Hist. Printing* 330 He begin[s] at the opposite.. corner of the Plattin, and lashes and whips that. **1836** RONALDS *Fly-Fisher's Entom.* 28 Holding a fine thread well waxed.. in one hand, whip a part of it three or four times round the end of the shank of the hook. **1887** RIDER HAGGARD *Allan Quatermain* iv, It was whipped round at intervals.. with copper wire.

b. To fasten or 'seize' (SEIZE *v.* 10 b) by binding in this way.

1760 SIR J. HAWKINS *Walton's Angler* 254 *note*, For whipping on a Hook take the following directions. **1787** BEST *Angling* (ed. 2) 10 Cut about six inches off the top of the rod, and in its place whip on a smooth, round and taper piece of whalebone. **1884** *St. James's Gaz.* 21 June 6/2 The old method of whipping on the wings.. is objectionable for wet-fly fishing. **1885** LENO *Boot & Shoemaking* ix. 67 The side linings [of a Wellington] are whipped or hemmed on with either awl or needle.

18. *Needlework.* †**a.** ? To trim or ornament with embroidery (*obs.*). **b.** To sew over and over, to overcast. **c.** To draw into gathers, as a frill, by a combination of overcast and running stitch.

a **1548** [see WHIPPED *ppl. a.* 1]. **1592** GREENE *Upst. Courtier* Wks. (Grosart) XI. 221 Veluet-breeches,.. drawn ouer with the best Spanish Satine, and.. curiously ouer whipt with gold twist. **1612** WEBSTER *White Devil* K 2, A Lawyer In a gowne whipt with veluet. **17..** DRURY *Rival Milliners* I. ii, All the Day We're forc'd to whip and stitch the Time away. **1840** BARHAM *Ingol. Leg.* Ser. II. *Aunt Fanny* 61 Whipping the Frill. **1853** KANE *Grinnell Exp.* xlvi. (1856) 425 They have been busy.. whipping and stitching the seal-skins with reindeer tendon thread.

†**19.** *trans.* To bind about, wreathe, entwine. *Sc. Obs.*

c **1500** KENNEDY *Passion of Christ* 8 Haill, in my Hert with Lufe wippit Intern! **1508** DUNBAR *Gold. Targe* vii, Thair brycht hairis.. In tressis clere, wyppit [*Bann. MS.* wypit] wyth goldyn thredis. **1513** DOUGLAS *Æneis* VII. vii. 114 To the, Bacchus, scho raisit.. Gret lang speris,.. Wyth wyne tre branchis wyppit. [**1802** SIBBALD *Chron. Scot. Poetry* IV. Gloss., *Quhip*, *Wipp*, *Wipe*, to bind about.]

†**whip**, *int.* and *adv.* *Obs.* [The vb. stem used as int. and adv.; cf. Du. *wip* (e.g. in *en wip was hij weg!*), and LG. *wip(p)s.*] Suddenly, forthwith, instantly, in a trice; quick! presto! Also in comb., as ***whip-dash***, ***-slap***.

c **1460** *Wisdom* 518 in *Macro Plays* 52 'Farewell', quod I; 'þe deuyll ys wppe!' *Ibid.* 554 Wyppe wyrre & care a-wey! [Cf. quot. *a* 1553 *s.v.* WHIP *sb.* 11.] **1525** W. SMITH *Wyddow Edyth* (1573) F j, Whip quod Thomas and got him down ward And commeth agayne with the cup full. **1588** SHAKS. *L.L.L.* v. ii. 309 Whip to our Tents. **1676** SHADWELL *Virtuoso* II. 19 You should see how I wou'd shew my parts, Whip-slap dash. *Ibid.* 26 With a helter-skelter, whip-dash. **1699** A. ROBERTS *Voy. Levant* 5 If any one happen to say anything amiss, whip 'tis at the Captains ears. **1748** RICHARDSON *Clarissa* VII. 341 When I came, whip, was the key turned upon their girls. **1806** *Simple Narr.* I. 167 But whip, before I could say Jack Robinson, he sprung into the chaise.

whip- in combination.

1. Combinations of the sb. **a.** General attrib., as ***whip-crack***, ***-flick***, ***-leather***, ***-mark***, ***-stroke***, ***-thong***. **b.** Instrumental, objective, similative, etc., as ***whip-cracking*** (*sb.* and *adj.*), ***-maker***, ***-making***, ***-minder***, ***-smacking***; ***whip-corrected***, ***-like***, ***-scarred***, ***-shaped***, ***-wielding*** adjs. **c.** Special combs.: **whip aerial**, **antenna**, an aerial in the form of a flexible wire or rod with a connection at one end; **whip-beam**, the white-beam (cf. *whip-crop* below); **whip-bird**, an Australian bird (*Psodophes crepitans*) with a note resembling the crack of a whip; also called *coach-whip bird*; †**whip-broth** (*obs. humorous nonce-wd.*), a 'taste of the whip', a flogging; †**whip-cart** (see quot.; cf. LG. ? *wipkarre*); **whip-club**, a driving-club (also *attrib.*); hence **whip-clubbist**, a member of a whip-club; **whip-craft**, the art of, or skill in, driving; **whip-crane**, a crane with a 'whip' (WHIP *sb.* 15) for hoisting; **whip-crop**, a local name for several shrubs or trees whose stems are used for whipstocks, as the white-beam (*Pyrus Aria*) and the wayfaring tree (*Viburnum Lantana*); **whip-fish**, a chætodont fish, *Heniochus macrolepidotus*, having a dorsal spine elongated into a filament like a whip-lash; **whip gin** = WHIP *sb.* 15; **whip-grass**, a species of *Scleria* (see quot. 1858); **whip-handle**, the handle of a whip, a whipstock; also *fig.* (see quot. 1653; with quot. 1861 cf. WHIP-HAND 2); **whip-hanger** = *whip-rack*; **whip-hem**, *Needlework*, a hem formed by 'whipping' or overcasting (see WHIP *sb.* 16, *v.* 18 b); **whip-hold**, control (cf. WHIP-HAND 2); **whip-horse**, a horse employed in hoisting by means of a 'whip' (WHIP *sb.* 15); †**whip-lade** [? LADE *sb.*[3]] = *whip-cart*; **whip-land** (*local*): see quot.; **whip line**, (*a*) = WHIPCORD 1; (*b*) the line or rope of a 'whip' (WHIP *sb.* 15); **whip-net**, technical name of a simple kind of network; **whip-rack**, a rack with notches for hanging whips upon; **whip-ray**, a fish of the family *Trygonidæ*, having a long slender flexible tail resembling the lash of a whip, and armed with a serrated spine; a sting-ray; **whip-roll**, *Weaving* (see quot. 1875); **whip-scorpion**, an arachnid of the order Pedipalpida, having a flattened abdomen and long flagella attached to the first pair of legs; **whip-shaft** = WHIPSTOCK 1; †**whip-sloven**, ? a sloven who deserves whipping; **whip-socket**, a socket fixed to the dash-board of a horse-drawn vehicle to hold the butt-end of the whip; **whip-stall** *Aeronaut.*, a stall in which an aircraft changes suddenly from a nose-up attitude to a nose-down one; **whip-stick**, (*a*) a whipstock, or a pliant stick used as a whip; (*b*) applied in Australia to a dwarf species of *Eucalyptus*; **whip tail**, a (dog's or horse's) tail resembling a whip (see also WHIPTAIL); **whip-thread**, †**whip-wood** (see quots.); **whip-worm**, a parasitic nematoid worm of the genus *Trichocephalus*, consisting of a stout posterior and slender anterior part, like a whipstock with a lash.

1941 *Electronics* Jan. 60/2 It was necessary to vary the height of the *whip aerial which was mounted on the top of the solenoid. **1979** A. JUTE *Reverse Negative* (1980) 42 The car had a prominent whip aerial of the kind police mobile patrols use mounted on its rear fender. **1943** F. E. TERMAN *Radio Engineers' Handbk.* 1019/2 (Index), *Whip antennas. **1974** R. B. PARKER *Godwulf Manuscript* xviii. 141 An aggressively nondescript car made noticeable by the big whip antenna folded forward over the roof and clipped down. **1733** W. ELLIS *Chiltern & Vale Farm.* 180 A Sallow Hedge has the Advantage of most.. others,.. because it may be thickned at Pleasure..; Beech and Hornbean [*sic*] will grow after this manner;.. Ash worse, Maple and *Whip-bean [*sic*] not at all. **1845** R. HOWITT *Australia* 177 The *whip-bird, which surprised I hear. **1893** MRS. C. PRAED *Outlaw & Lawmaker* xxx, The bell-bird rang its silvery peal, and the whip-bird gave its coachman's click. **1615** J. TAYLOR (Water P.) *Taylors Rev.* Wks. 1630 II. 143 Where I was ill thought of.. and.. in a greater puzzell then the blinde Beare in the midst of all her *whip-broth. **1677** PLOT *Oxfordsh.* 257 A sort of Cart they call a Whip-lade, or *Whip-cart, whose hinder part is made up with boards after the manner of a Dung-cart, having also a head of boards..; which head being made so as to be taken out or left in, the Cart may be indifferently used to carry.. dung, when the head is in, and Corn, etc. when taken out. **1808** *Monthly Pantheon* I. 416/1 A new *Whip-club is now about to be established. **1815** *Sporting Mag.* XLVI. 94 The 'Whip-club-blade' with four in hand 'handles the ribbons gay'. **1908** *Blackw. Mag.* Oct. 433 They belonged to a Spanish whip-club. **1809** E. S. BARRETT *Setting Sun* III. 39 If the nobility of France had not degenerated into *whip-clubbists, and opera-house committee-men. **1859** DICKENS *T. Two Cities* II. xxi, As an unruly charger *whip-corrected. **1893** F. ADAMS *New Egypt* 130 With.. a cascade of *whip-cracks, the two light-footed Arab horses are at once *en route.* **1775** J. JEKYLL *Corr.* (1894) 62 An Englishman at Tours who took a lesson of *whip-cracking every day from a postillion. **1875** W. S. HAYWARD *Love agst. World* ii, The whip-crackings, and shouts of the whips as they encouraged.. the hounds. **1934** WEBSTER, Whip-cracking, *adj.* **1939** R. CAMPBELL *Flowering Rifle* I. 17 For whom I sent the gay whip-cracking words To round them up in flabbergasted herds. **1976** A. MURRAY *Stomping Blues* ix. 166 He also behaves for all the world like a whip-cracking trail driver. **1865** *Athenæum* 4 Feb. 171/3 Divers turnings and *whipcraft feats. **1883** *19th Cent.* July 151 Half a dozen *whip-cranes.. would.. pull up these boxes with great rapidity. *a* **1850** BROMFIELD *Flora Vectensis* (1856) 167 *P[yrus] Aria*,.. White Beam-tree. Vect. *Whipcrop,.. The long, straight and very tough shoots are cut for whip-handles by waggoners. *Ibid.* 235 The slender stems [of *Viburnum Lantana*] are used.. for whip-handles,.. as might be inferred from the vernacular name of Whipcrop. **1960** C. DAY LEWIS *Buried Day* vi. 126 Our instructor.. was a.. man with.. a word of command like a *whip-flick. **1976** *Sunday Sun* (Brisbane) 23 May 115/1 *The whip flick.* Done in a tight finish. You flick your whip across the other horse's nose, up goes his head and you have the advantage in the photo. **1884** KNIGHT *Dict. Mech.* Suppl., **Whip Gin*, a simple tackle-block, over which a hoisting-rope runs. **1814** O. RICH *Synopsis Genera Amer. Plants* 106 Scleria... *Whip-Grass. **1818** T. NUTTALL *Genera N. Amer. Plants* II. 205 *Scleria*, Gærtner (Whip-grass). [Cf. **1858** HOGG *Veg. Kingd.* 808 The long, straight leaves of *S[cleria] flagellum* are armed with fine sharp-cutting teeth, and are made into whips for flogging negro slaves in the West Indies.] **1653** URQUHART *Rabelais* II. xxvii. 176 These little ends of men and dandiprats, whom in Scotland they call *whiphandles [orig. *manches d'estrilles*]. **1861** in *Century Mag.* (1889) Oct. 932/2 They know that we shall keep the whip-handle. **1911** BEAN *'Dreadnought' of Darling* xxxv, Joe Fagan.. had taught him to make whip-handles. **1875** KNIGHT *Dict. Mech.*, **Whip-hanger*, an annular rim or bracket provided with notches, into which the ends of the suspended whips fit. **1866** MRS. WHITNEY *Leslie Goldthwaite* i, The bits of ruffling.. with their edges in almost invisible *whip-hems. **1895** ANNA M. STODDART *J. S. Blackie* I. 211 He had recourse to.. fines sternly imposed, and so kept moderate *whip-hold of the team. **1890** 'R. BOLDREWOOD' *Miner's Right* viii, We.. bought a '*whip horse'.. which staunch and well-trained animal drew up the precious gravel. **1677** *Whip-lade [see *whip-cart*]. **1811** T. DAVIS *Agric. Wilts* 259 **Whip Land*, land.. measured out (when ploughed) by the whip's length. **1829** GEN. P. THOMPSON *Exerc.* (1842) I. 138 They could not pay for their *whip-leather. **1847–9** *Todd's Cycl. Anat.* IV. 8/2 A *whip-like moveable proboscis. **1883** SAVILLE-KENT in *Fisheries Bahamas* 40 The whiplike appendages or flagella of the cells. **1582** in Feuillerat *Revels Q. Eliz.* (1908) 353 For *whip lyne. **1894** *Times* (weekly ed.) 2 Feb. 91/3 The whip line of the apparatus [*sc.* breeches buoy].. got round the neck of the seaman. **1690** *Lond. Gaz.* No. 2579/4 Mr. Richard Weller, *Whip-maker. **1859** H. KINGSLEY *G. Hamlyn* xxxix, The most accomplished whipmaker. **1884** KNIGHT *Dict. Mech.* Suppl. 947/2 The main items of expense in *whip making material are rattan and whalebone. **1898** H. G. WELLS *War of Worlds* I. xvi, With the cabman's *whip-marks red across his face and hands. **1928** R. NEVILL *Romantic London* vii. 143 A quaint old-world calling.. was that of '*whip-minder'; a number of people formerly making a living by looking after the whips of drivers of vehicles, while the latter were engaged on pleasure or business. **1961** *Times* 23 Mar. 17/3 When Covent Garden boasted 'whip minders'. **1839** URE *Dict. Arts* 1235 The mail-net.. is.. a combination of common gauze and the *whip-net in the same fabric. **1875** KNIGHT *Dict. Mech.*, *Whip-rack. **1699** DAMPIER *Voy.* II. II. 73 The

*Whipray differs from the other two sorts, having a . . longer Tail and ending with a Knob, shaped like a Harpoon. **1873** T. GILL *Catal. Fishes E. Coast N. Amer.* 34 *Trygon centrura*. . . Sting-ray; whip-ray; stingaree. **1863** J. WATSON *Weaving* vi. 219 Below the yarn beam, on each side of the loom, the brackets are fixed for the gudgeons of the *whip rolls to run in. **1875** KNIGHT *Dict. Mech.*, *Whip-roll* (Weaving), a roller or bar over which the yarn passes from the yarn-beam to the reed. **1849** J. R. LOWELL *King Retro* in *Nat. Anti-Slavery Standard* 10 May 199/2 From *whip-scarred flesh the soul can soar To him who made and sees us. **1966** R. HAYDEN in S. Henderson *Understanding New Black Poetry* (1973) 158 Harriet Tubman, Woman of earth, whipscarred, A summoning, a shining. **1912** J. H. COMSTOCK *Spider Book* i. 16 The common name *whip-scorpions was doubtless suggested by the slender caudal appendages of the Thelyphonidæ. **1981** *Sci. Amer.* Dec. 32/1 Watch out for the fungus-ridden whip scorpion and the vampire bats. **1849** CUPPLES *Green Hand* xiv, The masts trembled, and the spars aloft bent like *whip-shafts. **1866** *Treas. Bot.*, **Whip-shaped*, flagelliform. *a* **1529** SKELTON *Agst. Garnesche* ii. 38 Thes twayne *whyp-slouens. **1845** POE in *Broadway Jrnl.* 2 Aug. 60/2 The 'Katherine and Petruchio' of Niblo's, is absolutely beneath contempt—a mere jumble of unmeaning rant, fuss, *whip-smacking, crockery-cracking, and other Tom-Foolery. **1879** ATCHERLEY *Trip Boërland* 259 He . . set up an infernal whip-smacking. **1875** KNIGHT *Dict. Mech.*, *Whip-socket. **1900** 'H. S. MERRIMAN' *Isle Unrest* xvii, He twisted the reins round the whip-socket. **1927** C. A. LINDBERGH *We* ii. 33 For an instant we hung motionless in the perfect position for a *whipstall. **1936** *Aircraft Engin.* Apr. 111/1 The mechanics of the whip-stall or uncontrollable nose dive are simple. **1953** C. A. LINDBERGH *Spirit of St. Louis* II. vi. 326 A whipstall at 1500 feet, with nothing but needles by which to orient myself! **1782** J. ADAMS *Diary* 26 July, Wks. 1851 III. 297 One of the grooms ran up to us with three *whip-sticks. **1850** R. G. CUMMING *Hunter's Life S. Afr.* xxx. II. 278, I resolved to have some fishing; . . and sallied forth with one of the waggon whip-sticks for a rod, and some string for a line. **1874** M. C. *Explorers* 123 (Morris) A patch of whip-stick scrub. **1889** 'MARK TWAIN' *Connecticut Yankee* xxvii. 354 A precaution which had been suggested by the *whip-stroke that had fallen to my share. **1958** L. DURRELL *Mountolive* xii. 229 Nessun felt the heat of the whip-stroke on his hand though the lash had not touched him. **1709** *Lond. Gaz.* No. 4523/4 When taken away he had a *whip Tail. **1885** *Bazaar* 30 Mar. 1258/2 Black and tan toy terrier dog . . whip tail. **1827** *Hallowell* (Maine) *Gaz.* 20 June 4/5 They have also received a large supply of . . Whips and *Whipthongs. **1897** *Outing* (U.S.) XXX. 252/2 If your whip thong gets caught in the harness. **1883** C. P. BROWN *Cotton Manuf.* 168 **Whip-thread*, the crossing thread in gauze. **1838** W. TENNANT *Anster F.* I. xxxvi, An ass, With stout *whip-wielding [*ed.* 1812 whip-cracking] rider on his back. **1696** PLUKENET *Almagestum* Opera 1769 II. 395 Xylomastix arbor Americana *Whip-wood. **1875** T. S. COBBOLD *Tapeworms* (ed. 3) 70 My treatment not only expelled an ordinary tapeworm but also a solitary *whipworm.

2. Combinations of the vb. **a.** with second element in objective relation: †**whip-arse**, a schoolmaster (1611 s.v. ARSE 1 b); **whip-belly (-vengeance)**, *slang*, weak thin beer or other liquor; †**whip-can** [see WHIP *v.* 2 b], a toper, tippler, 'toss-pot'; **whip-cat**, †*adj.* drunken [see WHIP *v.* 16 a (*a*)]; *sb.* (also ***whip-the-cat***), a tailor or other workman who 'whips the cat' [see WHIP *v.* 16 a (*c*)]; †**whip-king**, one who drives or controls kings (as one does horses with a whip), a 'king-maker'. **b.** in attributive relation to second element: (*a*) = *whipping-*: **whip-boy** (*rare*$^{-1}$) = WHIPPING-BOY; **whip-gig** = *whip-top*; **whip-post** = WHIPPING-*post*; **whip-top** = WHIPPING-*top* (also *fig.*); (*b*) = *whipped*: **whip-pan** *Cinemat.* and *Television*, a panning movement fast enough to give a blurred picture; also as *v. intr.*; **whip-rod**, a fishing-rod 'whipped' or wound round with twine [WHIP *v.* 17]; **whip-sillabub**, whipped sillabub [WHIPPED *ppl. a.* 3]; also *fig.*

1731–8 SWIFT *Pol. Conversat.* ii. 166 Faith, it is mere *Whip-Belly-Vengeance. **1847** HALLIWELL, *Whip-belly*, thin weak liquor. **1845** JANE ROBINSON *Whitehall* iii, He had been . . '*whip-boy' to the young heir. **1611** COTGR., *Bourrachon*, a tipler, quaffer, tossepot, *whip-canne. **1653** URQUHART *Rabelais* I. viii. 40 He would prove an especial good fellow, and singular whip-can [orig. *fesse-pinthe*]. **1694** MOTTEUX *Rabelais* v. Prognost. v. 236 Topers, Quaffers, Whipcans, Tosspots. **1582** STANYHURST *Æneis* III. (Arb.) 81 With *whip cat bowling they kept a myrry carousing. **1611** FLORIO, *Parlàre brianzésco*, to speake tipple, drunken or whip-cat language. **1851** MAYHEW *Lond. Labour* (1861) II. 366 A tailor who 'whipped the cat', . . the '*whip cat's' meals. **1912** R. M. FERGUSSON *Ochil Fairy T.* 34 He plied his trade as a 'whup-the-cat' for fivepence a day and 'his meat'. **1781** COWPER *Hope* 190 The puny tyrant burns to subjugate The free republic of the *whip-gig state. **1610** HOLLAND *Camden's Brit.* I. 570 Richard Nevil, that *whip-king (as some tearmed him). **1960** D. DAVIS *Grammar of Television Production* 33 The '*whip pan', a device . . whereby the camera sees one object, then pans very quickly and sees another, is . . legitimate because it does what the eye does and blurs the intervening detail. **1965** P. JONES *Technique of Television Cameraman* x. 136 Some television directors . . instruct the cameraman to whip pan across a scene, but cut to the next static shot on another camera before the pan has ceased. **1979** *Observer* 26 Aug. 20/8 The cameras . . zooming in and out, whip-panning, busying about the place looking for new angles. **1980** *Times Lit. Suppl.* 3 Oct. 1098/3 Unlike Brian De Palma in his movie version of King's earlier novel, *Carrie*, Kubrick doesn't use whip-pans, sudden zooms on neck-wrenching shocks: the horrors are revealed discreetly, almost lovingly. **1740** RICHARDSON *Pamela* (1824) I. 6 Or rather Frenchify our English solidity into froth and *whip-syllabub. **1843** *P. Parley's Ann.* IV. 2 His snowy beard foaming on his bosom like whip syllabub. **1801** STRUTT *Sports & Past.* IV. iv. §6. 288 We have hitherto been speaking of the *whip-top [under the name of 'top']; for the peg-top . . must be ranked among the modern inventions. **1887** STEVENSON *Misadvent. J. Nicholson* iv, A man who was a mere whiptop for calamity.

whipcord ('hwɪpkɔːd), *sb.* [? f. WHIP *v.* III, with later association of WHIP *sb.* I + CORD *sb.*[1]]

1. a. A thin tough kind of hempen cord, of which whip-lashes or the ends of them are made; in allusive use, the material of whip-lashes.

Perh. orig. Fine cord or twine for 'whipping' or binding closely round something.

1318–19 in G. Oliver *Lives Bps. Exeter* etc. (1861) 381 Wyppe-cord, 3d. **1362–3** *Durham Acc. Rolls* (Surtees) 565 In xij peciis de Qwypcord empt. pro carectar. iiij d. **1465** MARG. PASTON in *P. Lett.* II. 215 Thei . . bownde his armes be hynde hym with whippe cord like a theffe. **1487–8** *Rec. St. Mary at Hill* (1904) 131 For lyne and whippcorde to serve the same clothe, ij d. **1541** in *Essex Rev.* XXI. 145 Payd for whipcorde for the pascall, ii *d.* *c* **1616** FLETCHER *Thierry & Theod.* v. i, Beg, beg, and keep Constables waking, wear out stocks and whipcord. **1675** *Three Inhumane Murthers* 6 The Judge Caus'd his Thumbs to be ty'd fast together with whipcord. **1824** SCOTT *Redgauntlet* ch. xix, He will neither spare whipcord nor spur-rowel. **1861** HUGHES *Tom Brown at Oxf.* xxxii, He looks as hard as iron, and tough as whipcord.

b. A piece of this material, as a whip-lash or its extremity.

? *a* **1500** *Chester Pl.* (E.E.T.S.) xvi. 430 Takes him here bounden fast, While a whipcord here will last. **1592** NASHE *P. Penilesse* (ed. 2) 17 As far as the whipcord would stretch. *a* **1700** EVELYN *Diary* 11 Apr. 1645, Dashing the knotted and ravelled whipcord over their shoulders. **1825** J. NICHOLSON *Oper. Mech.* 63 One may break a whip-cord . . with one's hand . . by bringing one part of the rope to cut the other. **1856** KANE *Arctic Expl.* I. vi. 58 Our eight-inch hawser parted like a whip-cord.

c. *attrib.* Tough as whipcord.

1879 BROWNING *Halbert & Hob* 27 One whipcord nerve in the muscly mass from neck to shoulder-blade.

2. *transf.* **a.** A kind of catgut.

1880 *Spon's Encycl. Manuf.* II. 609 To produce a cord—known as 'whipcord'—from these intestines.

b. A close-woven ribbed worsted material used for dresses, riding breeches, etc. Also *attrib.*

1895 *Montgomery Ward Catal.* Spring & Summer 4/2 All Wool Black Whipcord Suiting . . shows fine raised satin finished cords running diagonally through the cloth. **1897** *Daily News* 9 Mar. 6/3 Whipcord coatings, bengalines in silk and wool. **1900** *Ibid.* 16 Apr. 7/3, 60,000 pairs of whip-cord riding trousers. **1915** R. BEAUMONT *Woollen & Worsted* 305 Warp Twills. Fancy Twills—Included in the former are the standard makes of fabric known as whip cords.

3. Applied (simply or attrib.) to **a.** species of willow with very flexible shoots, as *Salix purpurea* or *S. vitellina*; **b.** species of seaweed with long slender fronds, as *Chorda Filum* or *Chordaria flagelliformis*.

1812 J. WALKER *Hebrides* II. 273 Salix vitellina . . is called . . the whip-cord willow because its shoots are so tough and flexible, that they can be wrapt round the finger like a whip-cord. **1850** MISS PRATT *Comm. Things of Sea-side* ii. 125 The Whipcord Fucus (*Chordaria flagelliformis*).

Hence '**whipcord** *v. trans.*, to furnish with whipcord; '**whip,cordy** *a.*, resembling whip-cord, sinewy.

1784 R. ROBINSON *Jrnl.* 26 May in *Belfast Monthly Mag.* (1809) June 435/1 Whip-corded the boys' plough whips. **1863** MRS. GASKELL *Cousin Phillis* i, in *Cornh. Mag.* Nov. 627 He has often to whip-cord the plough-whips. **1856** S. WILBERFORCE in *Life* (1881) II. 336 The Bishop (Exeter) wonderfully hale and *whipcordy.

'**whip-,grafting.** *Hort.* Also †**-graffing.** [f. WHIP *v.* 2.] (See quot. 1878.) Hence **whip-graft** *v., trans.* to graft in this way.

1657 R. AUSTEN *Fruit-Trees* (ed. 2) 47 *marg.*, Second Way of Grafting, called whip-Grafting. **1660** SHARROCK *Vegetables* 63 The one of these wayes is called shoulder-grafting. . . The other Whip-grafting, because the operator only makes his streight-down right cut and tarryes not to indent it at all. **1675** WORLIDGE *Syst. Agric.* (ed. 2) 115 Taking a Graft or Sprig of the Tree you designe to propagate, and a small piece of the Root of another Tree of the same kinde, . . Whip-graft them together. **1719** (see *tongue-grafting* s.v. TONGUE *sb.* 16]. **1815**, **1842** [see *splice-grafting* s.v. SPLICE *sb.* 3]. **1878** BALTET *Grafting* etc. 112 The old-fashioned system of 'whip-grafting', employed in England in the case of some kinds of trees in preference to budding, on account of the inclemency of the climate. The stock is headed down and cut on one side only to receive the scion, which is cut with a long splice-cut and partially cleft or notched.

whip-hand ('hwɪp'hænd). [f. WHIP *sb.* 1.]

1. The hand in which the whip is held in driving or riding; the driver's or rider's right hand.

1806 *Ann. Reg. 1804* 413/1 For a morning's ride this might be *complimentary*; but it was here depriving me of the *whip hand.* **1809** CHRISTIAN *Blackstone's Comm.* I. 74 The law of the road, viz. that horses and carriages should . . keep the left side of the road, and consequently . . pass each other on the whip-hand. **1838** *Bentley's Misc.* IV. 601 A thick gold ring on the little finger of his whip-hand. **1887** R. H. ROBERTS *In the Shires* ii. 27 Raising his whip-hand, which brings the cavalcade to a halt.

2. fig. phr. ***to have the whip-hand*** (*of*): to have the advantage or upper hand (of), control. Hence in similar phr.

1680 ALSOP *Mischief Impos.* ii. 8 When once they are got into the Saddle, and have the whip-hand of the poor Laity. **1690** CHILD *Disc. Trade* Pref. C 8, Before the Dutch get too much the whip-hand of us. **1694** ECHARD *Plautus* 204 A silent Woman has always the whip Hand of a Talker. **1849** DE QUINCEY *Engl. Mail-Coach* Wks. 1890 XIII. 307 In the art of conversation, . . he admitted that I had the whip-hand of him. **1863** COWDEN CLARKE *Shaks. Char.* viii. 200 He has a secret of her own, and this gives him the whip-hand of her. **1884** RIDER HAGGARD *Dawn* xiv, For the sake of my own safety, I dare not abandon the whip hand I have of you. **1947** *Sun* (Baltimore) 22 Dec. 2/1 Its objective will be to outstrip the Marshall plan and so to gain the political whiphand over Europe. **1951** F. YERBY *Woman called Fancy* (1952) xvi. 302 In that election year of 1894, the white vote was so hopelessly divided that the blacks . . held the whip hand. **1974** *Howard Jrnl.* XIV. 49 The white population who have for so many centuries held, both literally and metaphorically, the whip hand. **1977** M. THATCHER in *Observer* 25 Sept. 10/1 If trade unions hold the whip hand, upon whose back does the lash fall? **1985** *Times* 26 Jan. 21/2 Sir Owen, however, still has the whip hand: he has the money and can bail the banks out of the whole complex exercise.

whip-her-ginny, -jenny: see WHIPPER-GINNIE.

†**whip-jack** ('hwɪpdʒæk). *Obs.* [app. f. WHIP *v.* 6 + JACK *sb.*[1]] A vagabond or beggar who pretends to be a distressed sailor. Also *gen.*

a **1556** PONET in *Maitland's Ess. Ref.* (1849) 74 One Boner (a bare whippe Iacke) for lucre of money toke vpon him to be thy father. **1561** AWDELAY *Frat. Vacab.* (1869) 4 A Whypiacke is one that by coulor of a counterfaite Lisence doth use to beg lyke a Maryner. **1608** DEKKER *Belman of London* Wks. (Grosart) III. 102 Another sort of . . knaues . . are called Whipiacks: who talke of nothing but fights at Sea, piracies, drownings and shipwracks. **1753** RICHARDSON *Grandison* VI. xxv. 142 Sir Charles Grandison is none of your gew-gaw whip-jacks. [**1834** AINSWORTH *Rookwood* III. v, 'And a rum'un he be', . . returned the whip-jack, or sham sailor.]

b. Humorously applied to a book in blue binding. *nonce-use.*

1624 in *Cosin's Corr.* (Surtees) I. 33 He also sent me a little whipjack in a blew jackett, caled A Gagg for the newe Gospell.

'**whip-lash,** *sb.* Also **whiplash.** [f. WHIP *sb.* 1 + LASH *sb.*[1] 2.]

1. The lash of a whip. Also *allusively* and *fig.*

1573–80 TUSSER *Husb.* (1878) 36 Whiplash wel knotted, and cartrope ynough. **1774** *Pennsylv. Gaz.* 9 Feb. Suppl. 2/3 Silk whip-lashes. **1838** DICKENS *Nich. Nick.* xxxii, He let out his whip-lash and touched up a little boy on the calves of his legs. **1891** KIPLING *Light that Failed* iv, 'He wants the whip-lash.' 'Lay it on with science, then.' **1894** *Athenæum* 11 Aug. 195/2 Nothing escapes the whip-lash of the 'college wit'. **1915** M. BAILLIE SAUNDERS *Captain the Curé* v, Listening to the sharp whip-lash of furious voices in the room below.

2. *transf.* An object resembling the lash of a whip, as the *vibraculum* of certain polyzoans; *spec.* a species of seaweed with long narrow fronds.

1850 MISS PRATT *Comm. Things of Sea-side* ii. 124 The two species of Sea Whiplash, . . One kind of this whiplash (*Chorda filum*) grows attached to rocks and stones. **1857** GOSSE *Omphalos* 146 The long and tough whip-lash in which the point of each leaf terminates. **1865** —— *Land & Sea* 225 In the Scuparia . . there are some special organs of defence. . . One of these is called the vibraculum, or the whiplash.

3. An injury to the head, neck, or spine caused by the head's being dashed to and fro on the less mobile trunk when a seated person is jerked forwards or backwards, as in a car accident. Usu. *attrib.*, esp. in ***whiplash injury***.

1955 *Jrnl. Amer. Med. Assoc.* 5 Nov. 983/2 Poor seat-design accounts for thousands of so-called whiplash injuries. **1962** *Times* 23 Jan. 5/5 They discount arguments that 'whiplash' injury is common among safety belt wearers. **1971** H. PACY *Road Accidents* i. 21 In damage to rear of vehicle think of whiplash. **1975** *Year Bk. Ear, Nose & Throat* 14 This article documents another useful study regarding the effects of cervical spine trauma, or 'whiplash' trauma. **1977** *Woman's Day* (Austral.) 24 Oct. 47/1 My husand had a car accident at the beginning of last year and received a whiplash injury. **1983** *Which?* Sept. 402/3 If no effective head restraint is provided, the head tends to get left behind, causing major bending and straining of the neck —'whiplash' injuries.

whiplash ('hwɪplæʃ), *v.* [f. prec. sb.]

1. *trans.* **a.** To inflict sudden or severe harm on.

1957 A. MACNAB *Bulls of Iberia* viii. 83 The bull's trajectory is accordingly also bent in an arc. . . The bull is not now being violently whip-lashed as in the 'benders', but is being smoothly worn down. **1975** *Business Week* 14 July 50 Whether such a complex plan can be managed effectively, or whether it will be whiplashed by the short-term interest of elected officials and mired in a new superbureaucracy is perhaps the most important unanswered question. **1980** *N.Y. Times* 28 June 9/5 Much of the playing was perfunctory. Mr. Getz had a ghastly time, whiplashed between feedback and reed trouble that led to a classic climactic squeak. **1982** *Christian Sci. Monitor* 5 Oct. B 2/2 Oil field service companies have been 'whiplashed' as profit-starved major oil companies have sharply cut back drilling programs.

b. To jerk in a contrary direction; *spec.* to cause a whiplash injury to.

1971 *Daily Colonist* (Victoria, B.C.) 27 May 55/1 Parents who shake their babies in a fit of temper are threatening their lives, a surgeon has warned. Severe shaking can 'whiplash' the baby's head, causing blood clots on the brain. **1980** *Washington Post Mag.* 30 Nov. 53/1 (*caption*) The final solution to the problem of the hook on your tape measure slipping off the edge of the credenza to which you've attached it, whiplashing the tape into your eye. **1982** J. GARDNER *For Special Services* xiii. 133 The force of impact had whiplashed the man's head, breaking his neck.

2. *intr.* To move suddenly and forcefully, like a whip that is cracked. Also *fig.*

1963 *Lebende Sprachen* VIII. 169/3 [Drivers' vocabulary.] To whiplash. 1. his head whiplashed. 2. the trailer whiplashed. **1971** *Daily Tel.* 13 Dec. 3/2 The Environment Department is investigating methods used to fix posts for motorway crash barriers. It fears that if they have not been planted deep enough, a crash might uproot them and allow a stretch of high-tension metal barrier to 'whiplash' across the carriageways. **1972** D. DELMAN *Sudden Death* (1973) iii. 77 He set us against each other. And he figures.. one of us ..is going to whiplash with something he can use. **1977** *Washington Post Mag.* 27 Nov. 40/3 Conservatives say they can't do or say anything because it will hurt their careers. It's like the old backlash has whiplashed. **1983** *Washington Post* 20 Feb. G3/6 The cable that catches the planes when they come in snapped. It whiplashed around the deck and caught the Chief in the spine. **1983** D. BOGGIS *Women they sent to Fight* xxxviii. 220 Margaret released her... Zelaszny whiplashed round.. terrified.

'whipless, *a.* [-LESS.] Of a Member of Parliament: having resigned, or having been deprived of, the whip.

1962 *Guardian* 13 Dec. 2/3 Mr Emrys Hughes, the 'whipless' Labour member for South Ayrshire. **1967** R. BUTT *Power of Parliament* xii. 317 Opinions varied as to how far the 'Whipless' MPs suffered from social or other pressures from the parties they had deserted during their period in isolation. **1976** *Times* 23 Feb. 13/2 A small and whipless group of independent Labour MPs.

†**whipling,** *vbl. sb. Obs. rare*$^{-1}$. [Cf. WHEEPLE *v.*] ? A 'piping' noise.

1522 SKELTON *Why not to Court* 347 There is a whyspring and a whipling, He shulde be hyder brought.

whipman ('hwɪpmən). Now *rare.* Pl. **-men.** [f. WHIP *sb.* 1.] A man who wields a whip; a driver of horses; *dial.* a carter. Hence **'whipmanship,** the character or skill of a 'whipman', the art of driving.

1797 *Sporting Mag.* IX. 50 The school of whipmanship, for the young nobility and gentry. *Ibid.* X. 288 No sooner were the whipmen passed than the void part was filled. *a* **1825** DUFF *Poems, Old Horse* 84 (Jam.) Routhless whipmen, scant o' grace. **1834** *Proc. Berw. Nat. Club* I. No. 2. 45 The whip-men (carters) bought it.

'whip,master. [f. WHIP *sb.* 1.] A master who uses the whip; a flogger.

1725 BAILEY *Erasm. Colloq.* (1878) I. 103 Wo to our Back-Sides, he's a greater Whip-Master [L. *flagellator*] than Busby himself. **1893** K. GRAHAME *Pagan Papers* 96 These whipmasters of ours.

whippable ('hwɪpəb(ə)l), *a.* [f. WHIP *v.* 6 + -ABLE.] Liable to be whipped.

1853 *Blackw. Mag.* Dec. 643 Two sorrowful, whippable *alumni* stood each beside a 'tree of knowledge'. **1881** PHIL ROBINSON *Under the Punkah* 216 The distinctive feature of this period of life [*sc.* boyhood], is popularly supposed to be that it is a whippable age.

'whippant, *a. humorous nonce-wd.* [f. as prec., after heraldic terms in -ANT.] That is frequently whipped.

1652 [see STOCKANT].

whipped (hwɪpt), *ppl. a.* Also 5-7 **whipt.** [f. WHIP *v.* + -ED^{1}.]

1. *Needlework.* (See WHIP *v.* 18.)

a **1548** HALL *Chron., Hen. VIII* 207 b, Frettes of whipped gold of damaske very riche. **1716** GAY *Trivia* II. 339 In half-whipt Muslin Needles useless lye.

†**2. a.** (See quot.) *Obs. nonce-use.*

1562 V. LEIGH *Survey.* (1588) O iij, I call it.. the whipped line, because I haue formed it.. like a little whipcorde. **1619** H. LYTE *Art of Tens* 20 In the table on the left hand of the whipped line.

b. Bound with cord closely wound round: see WHIP *v.* 17.

1886 J. H. KEENE *Fishing Tackle* 159 Twisting a hackle.. round the shank of a whipped hook.

3. *Confectionery,* etc. Beaten into a froth: see WHIP *v.* 7. Hence in figurative expressions denoting something 'frothy', flimsy, or unsubstantial.

1673 DRYDEN *Marr. à la Mode* IV. iii, The dull French Poetry,.. so thin, that it is the very Leaf-gold of Wit, the very Wafers and whip'd Cream of sense. **1691** SHADWELL *Scourers* II. i, To make clouted cream, and whipt Sillabubs. **1725** *Fam. Dict.* s.v. *Sugar,* The White of a whipt Egg. **1748** RICHARDSON *Clarissa* lxxxv. VII. 117 To distinguish the froth and whipt-syllabub in them [*sc.* letters] from the cream. **1781** COWPER *Table-T.* 551 Summoning the Muse to such a theme, The fruit of all her labour is whipped cream. **1828** SCOTT *Jrnl.* 23 Apr. in *Lockhart,* Who cares for the whipp'd cream of London society? **1846** SOYER *Cookery* 209 Add a gill of whipped cream.

4. a. Beaten with or as with a whip; scourged, flogged, lashed.

1713 *Guardian* No. 8 ¶4 Saying, That it became not the Condition of a whipt Rascal to travel on Horseback. **1842** BORROW *Bible in Spain* xiv. 138 The two nationals, who sneaked away like whipped hounds. **1842** *Congr. Globe* 29 Jan. 183/2 A whipped cur was ever the most fawning dog.

b. *Farriery.* Of a horse: see quot.

1737 BRACKEN *Farriery Impr.* (1757) Pref. p. xi, You shall hear many a Horse praised for being a thorow-winded one, and a brave whipt-horse. *Ibid.* II. 122 He is a good whip'd Horse, that is, he will answer the Whip well.

5. *Fencing.* (See WHIP *v.* 4.)

1771 LONNERGAN *Fencer's Guide* 90 If I whip along your Tierce-side, parry round with a whipped Quarte.

6. With *up*: Made up artificially, factitious.

1900 *Daily News* 8 Feb. 3/4 The recent agitation was a whipped-up thing. **1902** J. H. ROSE *Napoleon I,* I. xii. 274 His keen instinct for reality, which led him to scorn such whipped-up creeds as Robespierre's Supreme Being.

¶ **7.** Used for WHIP-.

1680 *Lond. Gaz.* No. 1561/4 Two Mares, one of them.. whipt Tail'd, and Grizled. **1688** HOLME *Armoury* III. iii. 94/2 Little round holes whipt-stitched about.

8. Subject to a Parliamentary whip.

1970 P. G. RICHARDS *Parliament & Conscience* iii. 60 This was duly debated and defeated on a straight party whipped vote. **1976** *Times Lit. Suppl.* 12 Mar. 300/2 In the 1970–74 Parliament, two thirds of the Conservative members voted against their party whip on at least one occasion, and one (Enoch Powell) did so in 113 whipped divisions. **1981** MARSH & CHAMBERS *Abortion Politics* vii. 194 MPs.. are subject to constituency and interest group pressure on whipped issues.

whippence: see WHIPPIN.

whipper ('hwɪpə(r)). [f. WHIP *v.* + -ER^{1}.] One who or that which whips, in various senses.

1. One who beats or chastises with (or as with) a whip; a scourger, flogger; *spec.* an official who inflicts whipping as a legal punishment. Also *fig.*

1552 HULOET, Whypper who whyppeth beggers and vacaboundes, or others, *plagiarius.* **1601** B. JONSON *Poetaster* v. iii, Ambitiously, affecting the title of the vntrussers, or whippers of the age. **1628** FELTHAM *Resolves* II. [I.] I. 147 It is the basest Office Man can fall into, to make his tongue the Whipper of the Worthy man. **1697** J. PARTRIDGE (*title*) Flagitiosus Mercurius flagellatus; or the Whipper whipp'd. **1813** E. S. BARRETT *Heroine* xvi. (1909) 88 At last, marrying some honest gentleman,... she degenerates into a dangler of keys and whipper of children. **1841** ORDERSON *Creoleana* ix. 96 The brutal hand of the mercenary whipper. **1886** *8th Rep. Prison Comm. Scot.* 6 The case against the boy was accordingly delayed,.. because a whipper could not be found.

b. = FLAGELLANT A. 1.

a **1656** BP. HALL *Serm. 1 Cor. xi. 10* Wks. 1808 V. 487 A brood of mad heretics,.. whom they called Flagellantes, 'the whippers'; which went about.. lashing themselves to blood. **1782** PRIESTLEY *Corrupt. Chr.* II. IX. 213 The whippers.. ran about in promiscuous multitudes.

c. = WHIPPER-IN 1, 2. ? *Obs.*

1826 *Sporting Mag.* (N.S.) XVII. 366 John Roberts the huntsman, and Will Veale the whipper. **1884** GLADSTONE in *Western Daily Press* 12 July 8/1 The authority, for every loyal Liberal, of the whipper.

d. A kind of fishing-rod: see quot., and cf. WHIP *v.* 8.

1688 HOLME *Armoury* III. iii. 103/1 A Whipper, or Whipping Rod is a slender top Rod, that is weak in the middle and top heavy, but all slender and fine.

2. A person or thing that surpasses others. (Cf. WHIP *v.* 12.) ? *Obs.* exc. *dial.* applied to a big active person.

c **1520** *Boke of Mayd Emlyn* 356 in Hazlitt *Early Pop. Poetry* IV. 94 Bycause he coude clepe her, She called hym a whypper. **1540** J. HEYWOOD *Four PP.* C i b, This relyke, her is a whipper.. here is a slypper Of one of the seuen slepers.

3. A workman who hoists coal with a 'whip': = COAL-WHIPPER. (Cf. WHIP *v.* 5.)

1835–6 BARLOW in *Encycl. Metrop.* (1845) VIII. 87/1 The four whippers now run up a sort of step-ladder. **1836–9,** etc. [see COAL-WHIPPER]. **1887** R. NEWMAN in *Charity Org. Rev.* July 275 Coal-whipping.. has now all but ceased; but a similar class of men.. are probably as numerous as were the whippers of twenty years ago.

4. One who runs the coloured thread along the edge of a blanket. (Cf. WHIP *v.* 18.)

1881 *Instr. Census Clerks* (1885) 66 Blanket Manufacture; .. Tucker. Whipper. Binder.

whipperee (hwɪpə'riː). *U.S.* Corrupt form of *whip-ray* (see WHIP- 1 c): cf. STINGAREE.

†**whipperginnie.** *Obs. slang.* Also 6 **whipper-ienny,** 7 **whip her Ginny, whip-her-ginny,** 8 **whip-her-jenny.** [Of obscure origin.]

1. A term of reprobation or abuse applied to a woman.

1593 *Tell-trothe's N.Y. Gift* (1876) 13 Shee fals so hot to scoulding with the whipperginne her ostice. *Ibid.* 21 That fornicators (after they had obtained their desires..) should .. seeking other wenches, meet with whipper ginnies. **1599** PORTER *Angry Wom. Abingt.* (Percy Soc.) 103 What needst thou to care, whipper-ienny, tripe-cheeks?

2. ***the land of whipperginnie,*** app. a nickname for purgatory.

1594 NASHE *Unfort. Trav.* C 3 b, What newes from heauen, hell, and the land of whipperginnie.

3. Name of an old game at cards. *Obs.* exc. *arch.*

1622 J. TAYLOR (Water P.) *O'Toole* Wks. (1630) II. 19/2 Thou hold'st it Valours ignominy, To spend thy dayes in peacefull whip her Ginny. **1629** —— *Wit & Mirth* xix. ibid. 181/2 An vnhappy boy.. would fall to Cards at the Cambrian game of whip-her-ginny, or English one and thirty. **1737** *Poor Robin* Dec. B 7 b, Maw, Whip-her-jenny, Poor and Rich, With other fruitless Pastimes. **1923** R. GRAVES *Whipperginny* 45 The minds of these two princes Were of such subtlety and such nimbleness That Whipperginny on the fall of a card Changed to Bèzique or Cribbage or Piquet.

'whipper-'in. [f. the phr. *to whip in*: see WHIP *v.* 6 d.]

1. a. A huntsman's assistant who keeps the hounds from straying by driving them back with the whip into the main body of the pack. Also called shortly a *whip* (WHIP *sb.* 5), or formerly occas. a *whipper* (WHIPPER 1 c).

1739 *Ess. Better Regul. Free-Thinking* 7 Should.. the Postilion turn Cook, and the Whipper in resolve to be nothing less than Steward or Butler. **1742** FIELDING *J. Andrews* I. ii, He was soon transplanted from the Fields into the Dog-kennel, where he was placed under the Hunts-man, and made what Sportsmen term a Whipper-in. **1875** W. S. HAYWARD *Love agst. World* i, The brothers.. ordered their whipper-in.. to unkennel the hounds.

fig. c **1771** S. FOOTE *Maid of Bath* Prol. p. vi, To change the figure—formerly I've been To straggling follies only *whipper-in.* **1785** WOLCOT (P. Pindar) *Lyric Odes* iv. Wks. 1812 I. 87 My Muse is whipper-in. **1836** E. HOWARD *R. Reefer* xxxv, One of the two.. brigs that was to accompany us as whippers-in to the convoy.

b. In the game of hare and hounds, a runner whose business it is to keep the hounds in order.

1855 'G. FORREST' *Every Boy's Bk.* 11 The Hare should not be the best runner, but should be daring, and.. prudent. .. A Huntsman and Whipper-in are then chosen... The Hare then starts, and has about seven minutes' grace, at the expiration of which time the Huntsman blows a horn.. and sets off, the Hounds keeping nearly in Indian file, the Whipper-in bringing up the rear. **1901** R. S. WARREN BELL *Tales of Greyhouse* 47 The too impetuous hounds had to be curbed by the whippers-in.

c. *Racing slang.* The horse last in a race or at any given moment of a race.

1892 *Daily News* 8 Sept. 3/5 The field began to break up, and the whippers in became Curio and El Diablo.

2. In parliamentary use, = WHIP *sb.* 6. *Obs.* exc. *Hist.*

1771 *Ann. Reg., Misc. Ess.* 196/1 He was first a whipper-in to the Premier, and then became Premier himself. **1792** *J. Pearson's Pol. Dict., Whipper-in,* a fellow that sends for Members to carry a question when the Minister is hard run. **1835** DICKENS *Sk. Boz, Parl. Sk.,* He.. will tell you how Sir Somebody Something, when he was whipper-in for the Government, brought four men out of their beds to vote in the majority. **1903** *Westm. Gaz.* 9 Oct. 12/1 At the beginning of the Canadian 'Parliamentary Companion' a whole page is headed in large capitals, 'Whippers-in.' Then follow the names of the various party 'Whips,' as we would call them.

'whipper-snap, *v.* [Back-formation f. WHIPPER-SNAPPER.] *intr.* To behave like a whipper-snapper; to be impertinent. Hence **'whipper-snapping** (and varr.) *vbl. sb.* and *ppl. a.*

1908 W. DE MORGAN *Somehow Good* xi. 100 The lines they might elect to whipper-snap on were not to be those of sentimental nonsense. **1913** D. H. LAWRENCE *Sons & Lovers* xiii. 349 Think I'm goin' ter have *you* whipperty-snappin' round? **1925** —— *Refl. Death Porcupine* 231 Oh, the universe has a terrible hole in the middle of it, an oubliette for all of you, whipper-snappering mongrels. **1973** *Times* 11 Apr. 13/5 Jackie Rea, a former champion, there to match whipper-snapping with an old dog's tricks.

'whipper-,snapper. [? A jingling extension of **whip-snapper,* a cracker of whips (see WHIP *sb.* 1, SNAP *v.* 12), on the model of the earlier *snipper-snapper.*] A diminutive or insignificant person, *esp.* a sprightly or impertinent young fellow. Also rarely applied to a thing.

†In quot. 1674 app. A violent or dangerous person, a 'rough': cf. quot. 1589 s.v. WHIPSTER 1 a.

1674 HEAD *Jackson's Recant.* C 2 b, Have a care of Marlbrough Downs, there are a parcel of whipper Snappers have been very busie there of late. *a* **1700** B. E. *Dict. Cant. Crew, Whipper-snapper,* a very small but sprightly Boy. **1700** T. BROWN *Amusem.* xi. 136 A Grave Old Gentleman.. thus repremanded our Saucy Whipper-Snapper. **1827** SCOTT *Surg. Dau.* ii, A whipper-snapper of an attorney's apprentice,.. I'll teach him to speak with more reverence of the learned professions. **1840** THACKERAY *Paris Sk.-bk.* (1869) 15 Not that he feared such fellows as these—little whipper-snappers—our men would eat them. **1866** MRS. GASKELL *Wives & Dau.* xxii, A little whipper-snapper of a French watch. **1876** BLACK *Madcap Violet* xxxviii, It is only the whipper-snapper in criticism who is always crying out for a grand and tremendous motive.

attrib. **1742** FIELDING *J. Andrews* IV. vi, A Parcel of Whipper-snapper Sparks. **1856** MISS YONGE *Daisy Chain* I. xxix, A whipper-snapper school-boy.

whippet ('hwɪpɪt), *sb.* Also 6 **wepit, whippett,** 9 **whippit, wippet.** [? partly f. WHIP *sb.* or *v.* + -ET^{1}, partly f. WHIPPET *v.*]

†**1.** ? Some light wine. *Obs.*

c **1500** *Blowbol's Test.* 50 (MS. Rawl. C. 86 lf. 107 b) Good drynke he louyd better than he did wepit. *Ibid.* 337. 112 Malmasyes, Tires, and Rumneys,.. Whippett and Pyngmedo.

2. A lively young woman; a light wench; now *dial.* a nimble, diminutive, or puny person.

1550 CROWLEY *Epigr.* 1331 All modeste matrons I truste wyll take my parte, As for nice whippets, wordes Shall not come nye my hert. **1596** NASHE *Saffron Walden* Wks. (Grosart) III. 158 Those worthlesse Whippets and Iack Strawes hee could get, he would seeme to enable and compare with the highest. **1597** BRETON *Wit's Trenchmour* Wks. (Grosart) II. 15/1 Why, quoth this Whippet, if I should tell you I loue you [etc.].

†**3.** A sudden brisk movement. *Obs. rare*$^{-1}$.

a **1603** T. CARTWRIGHT *Confut. Rhem. N.T.* (1618) 431 As soone as ever [the dog] seeth [the rost] taken from the fire, he giveth a whippet from his wheele.

4. a. A small breed of dog; now *spec.* a cross between a greyhound and a terrier or spaniel, used for coursing and racing, esp. in the north of England.

With the earliest examples cf. WHAPPET.

a **1610** HEALEY *Theophrastus* (1616) 75 If a little dog or whippet of his dye, ô hee makes him a tombe. *c* **1615** W. GODDARD *Mastiff Whelp* G 3, Too loude thou barkest Whelpe, I must haue whippets now, that doe but yelpe. **1630** J. TAYLOR (Water P.) *Dogge of Warre* Wks. II. 232 The little Curre, Whippet, or House-dogge. **1645** MILTON *Colast.* 26 If a man cannot peaceably walk into the world, but must bee infested..with bauling whippets, and shinbarkers. **1665** in *Sporting Mag.* XLII. 10 To seize..all such greyhounds, beagles, or whipperts [*sic*]. **1841** HARTSHORNE *Salopia Antiqua* 614 *Whippet*, a dog bred betwixt a greyhound and a spaniel. **1884** *St. James's Gaz.* 18 Oct. 6/2, I found a man training a wiry racing-dog... The 'whippet' strode along with great earnestness.

attrib. and *Comb.* **1885** *Bazaar* 30 Mar. 1260/3 Fawn whippet bitch for sale. **1894** F. LLOYD *Whippet & Race-Dog* viii. 45 The National Whippet-racing Club. *Ibid.* xi. 73 A most important personage on the Whippet-track is the clerk of the scales.

b. *transf. Mil.* The Medium Mark A 'tank', a light kind of 'tank' used in the war of 1914–18. Also called *chaser.* Usually *attrib.* as ***whippet tank.***

1918 *Times* 15 Aug. 7/6 The..capture of Morlancourt, where light Tanks or whippets were used. **1918** E. W. FARROW *Dict. Mil. Terms* 664 *Whippet tank*, an English armored car equipped with caterpillar treads. **1920** J. C. F. FULLER *Tanks in Gt. War* 176 March 26 [1918] is an interesting date in the history of the Tank Corps, for, on the afternoon of this day, the Whippet Tanks made their debut. **1938** G. GREENE in *Spectator* 22 July 139/2 Whippet tanks—camouflaged as in war. **1946** *New Yorker* 9 Mar. 83/1 Solid city blocks of whippet and giant tanks.

†**5.** A little whip. *Obs. rare*$^{-1}$.

1616 SURFL. & MARKH. *Country Farm* I. xxviii. 132 He shall not vse anie thing else to ride him [*sc.* horse] with, saue onely his whippet and trench.

†**6.** 'A short light petticoat' (Forby). *dial. Obs.*

Hence **whippe'teer, 'whippeter**, a person who keeps a whippet (sense 4); **'whippeting,** *sb.* the breeding, training, etc. of whippets; *a.* engaged in this.

1894 SIR J. ASTLEY *Fifty Yrs. Life* II. 337 The principal whippeteers are colliers in Lancashire. **1894** F. LLOYD *Whippet & Race-Dog* vii. 44 Everything connected with Whippeting. *Ibid.* ix. 58 Some Whippeting people. *Ibid.* xxiv. 174 Common names have been given by Whippeters to the dogs.

†**'whippet,** *v. Obs.* Also 6 -yt. [app. the phr. *whip it* written as one word: see WHIP *v.* 1 c.] *intr.* To move briskly, bestir oneself, frisk.

1540 PALSGR. *Acolastus* III. i. N iv, Lest he a camell shulde not skyp or whippyt about. *c* **1550** *Pryde & Abuse Wom.* 57 in Hazl. *E.P.P.* IV. 234 Wyth whippet a whyle, lyttle pretyone Prancke it, and hagge it well. *a* **1553** UDALL *Royster D.* I. iii. (Arb.) 22 Nowe whippet apace for the maystrie. **1599** NASHE *Lenten Stuffe* Wks. (Grosart) V. 270 Whippet, turne to a new lesson, and strike wee vp Iohn for the King.

whippin ('hwɪpɪn). *dial.* Also 7 wippin, 8 whipping, 9 w(h)ippon, whippence. [Origin obscure.] = WHIPPLETREE². Also ***whippintree.***

1697 in *Sussex Archæol. Collect.* VI. 195 One wagon Ready to Runn..Six yoakes..Five wippins. *a* **1722** LISLE *Husb.* (1757) 72 The plough-beam, sprinter, whippings, and traces must often break when they come against a great stone. **1778** [W. MARSHALL] *Minutes Agric.* 29 July 1775, I ..intend that he..shall attend to the spread-bats and whippins. *Ibid.* 26 Dec. 1775, 7 Iron trace whippins, 2 Setts of hempen trace ditto. **1811** T. DAVIS *Agric. Wilts* 263 Whippence, viz. the weigh-beam and bodkins, the fore carriage of a plough, as also of the harrow and drag. **1855** *Jrnl. R. Agric. Soc.* XVI. I. 113 They [*sc.* horses drawing a plough] should be worked abreast (the attachment being by means of 'wippons'). **1884** *West Sussex Gaz.* 25 Sept., 10 sets of drag and small harrows, whippons and traces. **1919** R. P. CHOPE *Some Old Farm Implements* 13 The modern harrows are made entirely of iron, and the parts are not hinged together, but to a wooden cross-beam which is connected to the whippintree.

†**whippincrust.** *Obs. rare*$^{-1}$. Some kind of wine; ? a perversion of HIPPOCRAS.

1616 *Marlowe's Faustus* Wks. (1910) 197 *Rob.* [the ostler]. If thou't go but to the Tauerne with me, I'le giue thee.. Sacke, Muskadine, Malmesey and Whippincrust.

whippiness ('hwɪpɪnɪs). [f. WHIPPY *a.* + -NESS.] Pliable quality; flexibility.

1881 *Sportsman's Year-bk.* 70 Some successful anglers use the two extremes of whippiness and stiffness [in fly-rods]. **1913** W. E. DOMMETT *Motor Car Mech.* 130 This control has the objection..that the gear box has to be long with possible whippiness of the shafting. **1975** *Daily Tel.* 5 Apr. 8/1 All you have to do is to choose a branch of sufficient whippiness to be pulled down to the ground and fixed there.

whipping ('hwɪpɪŋ), *vbl. sb.* Also (sense 2) *Sc.* wippen. [f. WHIP *v.* + -ING¹.]

1. The action of striking with or as with a whip.

a. The, or an, infliction of corporal punishment by strokes of a whip or rod; scourging, flogging, flagellation; *loosely*, beating with the hand or otherwise, slapping, spanking. Also *fig.* chastisement, disciplinary correction; defeat, 'beating' (*U.S. colloq.*).

1566 *Aldeburgh Rec.* in *N. & Q.* 12th Ser. VII. 142/1 Pᵈ for whyppynge of a man xiiᵈ. **1602** SHAKS. *Ham.* II. ii. 556 Vse euerie man after his desart, and who should scape whipping. **1630** DONNE *Serm., Matt.* iv. *18–20* (1640) 733, I am not bound..to teare my flesh by inhumane whippings, and flagellations. **1642** FULLER *Holy & Prof. St.* II. xvi. 110 To such a lad a frown may be a whipping. **1720** SWIFT *Mod. Educ.* Wks. 1755 II. II. 34 Whipping breaks the spirits of lads well born. **1752** CHESTERF. *Let. to Dayrolles* 18 Oct., Pray let my godson never know what a blow or a whipping is, unless for those things for which, were he a man, he would deserve them. **1835** F. A. CHARDON *Jrnl.* 10 July (1932) 37 Went to the Medicine dance last—Came back late and got a whipping from my Wife for my bad behaviour. **1866** MRS. H. WOOD *Elster's Folly* xxxiii, She put him across her knee, pulled off an old slipper she was wearing, and gave him a sound whipping with its fat sole. **1880** MEREDITH *Tragic Com.* xii, If a letter had been withheld by her father it was a part of her whipping. **1916** *Contemp. Rev.* Nov. 623 The savage whippings of criminals. **1948** A. LOMAX in A. Dundes *Mother Wit* (1973) 481/1 Give him a whuppin'. **1974** W. GARNER *Big enough Wreath* vii. 94 You swore there never was a whupping could make you holler.

b. *gen.* or in other connexions, e.g. the driving of a horse, or spinning of a top, with a whip.

1577 GOOGE tr. *Heresbach's Husb.* 119 b, It must be sene to, that they [*sc.* horses drawing together] be euen matched, least the stronger spoyle the weaker, while he dreadeth the rating, and whipping. *a* **1628** F. GREVIL *Let. Hon. Lady* iv, Our flesh being like a Toppe which only goes vpright with whipping. **1796** MARSHALL *Planting* I. 150 The plants..will ..become liable to lash each other's tops, with every blast of wind. This evil is called whipping of tops. **1917** 'JOHN OXENHAM' *Loosing Lion's Whelps* 21 Faces..bleached and sodden with the whipping of the wind.

c. *Confectionery*, etc. (See WHIP *v.* 7.)

1845 G. E. DAY tr. *Simon's Anim. Chem.* I. 156 The blood contains a certain amount of fibrin,..which on whipping is separated in..stringy masses. **1854** R. S. SURTEES *Handley Cr.* iv, The whipping of creams, the stiffening of jellies, [etc.].

d. *Angling.* (See WHIP *v.* 8.)

1653 WALTON *Angler* xi. 205 There is no better sport then whipping for Bleaks in a boat in a Summers evening. **1787** BEST *Angling* (ed. 2) 60 To initiate a young angler..by his whipping for them in a hot summer's evening. **1844** J. T. HEWLETT *Parsons & Widows* v, What state is the river in?.. Will it do for whipping?

e. (See WHIP *v.* 6 d, 14.)

1834 in Dk. Buckingham *Crts. Will. IV. & Vict.* (1861) II. 115, I rather think the Government, as they knew they would be weak, considered it..best..to take no pains in whipping. **1880** TREVELYAN *C. J. Fox* v. 196 It was an allusion which Burke made in the course of the evening to the industry of the Treasury officials that first rendered the term 'whipping in' classical. **1892** *Pall Mall Gaz.* 20 June 6/2 The Government is entitled to whatever credit is due to a good piece of whipping. **1901** R. S. WARREN BELL *Tales of Greyhouse* 48 Wardour, a trifle weary of the arduous task of whipping-in, had forged ahead. **1903** *Times* 30 Mar. 7/6 Extra zeal..in the whipping-in of audiences.

f. The action of stirring *up* strong feelings or the like (see WHIP *v.* 13).

1952 C. DAY LEWIS *Grand Manner* 12 This whipping-up of words into a frenzy. **1955** *Times* 18 July 4/7 He had emphasized that the 'whipping up' of public opinion against South Africa..would..estrange the great majority of South Africans. **1959** *Daily Tel.* 29 Dec. 6 This prospect suggests a possible explanation for his deliberate whipping-up of patriotic frenzy.

2. a. The action of overlaying or binding with cord or the like wound closely round and round; *concr.* the cord, etc. so wound around something (or each turn of it).

1540 *Ludlow Churchw. Acc.* (Camden) 4 Payd for whyppynge of roopes..viij d. **1673** *Wedderburn's Vocab.* 38 (Jam.) *Baculi caulis*, the club shaft. *Baculi manubrium*, the handle where the wippen is. *Baculi filum*, the wippen. **1683** MOXON *Mech. Exerc., Printing* xxii. ¶ 5 [He] whips the Cord again about the Page.., taking care that the several whippings lye parallel. **1688** HOLME *Armoury* III. xvii. (Roxb.) 117/1 The whipping of the string, is that part where the arrow is set on. **1770** LUCKOMBE *Hist. Printing* 330 The lashings..will yield no longer to his whipping and pulling. *c* **1860** H. STUART *Seaman's Catech.* 28 For splicing an eye put on a good whipping. **1883** *Man. Seamanship for Boys* 112 To whip the end of a rope..The turns of the whipping are always passed up towards the end of the rope. **1887** J. H. KEENE *Fishing Tackle* 90 The whipping of hooks on gimp.

b. *Needlework.* (See WHIP *v.* 18.)

1814 MISS MITFORD in L'Estrange *Life* (1870) I. 274 Tell Mrs. Haw..to prepare for plenty of hemming and whipping. **1866** MRS. WHITNEY *Leslie Goldthwaite* ix, All kinds of stitches—embroidery, and plain over-and-over, and whippings, and darns. **1882** CAULFEILD & SAWARD *Dict. Needlework* 519 *Whipping*, a term..denoting a method of drawing up a piece of frilling..into gathers, by..sewing loosely over a delicately rolled edge of the same.

3. †**a.** = WHIP-GRAFTING. *Obs.*

1629 PARKINSON *Parad.* III. vi. 547 For whipping, the time is somewhat later then grafting in the stocke.

b. Hoisting with a 'whip' (WHIP *sb.* 15).

1835–6 *Encycl. Metrop.* (1845) VIII. 87/1 There is no occasion in this case, in unloading a vessel of coals, to be confined to..what is called whipping. **1861, 1887** [see COAL-WHIPPING].

4. *attrib.* and *Comb.* **a.** in sense 1, as ***whipping-audit*** (AUDIT *sb.* 3), ***-bout, -day,*** etc.; **whipping-bench**, a bench on which offenders are laid to be whipped; **whipping-block**, a block on which offenders are laid to be whipped; †**whipping-cheer** (*humorous*), flogging, flagellation; **whipping cream**, a grade of cream suitable for whipping; **whipping-girl** (cf. WHIPPING-BOY); **whipping-hand** = WHIP-HAND; **whipping-house** *U.S.*, a building in which at one time Blacks were whipped; **whipping-place**, a place at which offenders are or were publicly whipped; **whipping-pole** = next; **whipping-post**, a post set up, usually in a public place, to which offenders are or were tied to be whipped; **whipping-stock,** (*a*) = WHIPPINCRUST; (*b*) a person who is frequently whipped (cf. *laughing-stock*); **whipping-top**, a top spun by whipping; also *fig.*; **whipping-trade** (*sarcastic*), the occupation of a schoolmaster.

a **1658** CLEVELAND *Char. Country-Comm.-man* Wks. (1687) 77 His Fate..is..a *whipping Audit, when he is wrung in the Withers by a Committee of Examinations. **1906** CROCKETT *White Plumes* xiv, The *whipping-bench and a good dozen spare rods are what they want. *a* **1877** SWINBURNE *Lesbia Brandon* (1952) 504 He..begged..that he might not be hoist across the *whipping-block by a servant. **1953** R. GRAVES *Poems* 26 And taught St. Dominic's to baulk At gown and hood and whipping-block. **1772** NUGENT *Hist. Fr. Gerund* I. 160 Her husband had still the marks of a *whipping-bout. **1578** WHETSTONE *1st Pt. Promos & Cass.* IV. i. 2 She fearde of late, of *whipping cheere to smell. **1647** HERRICK *Noble Numbers, Hell*, Hell is the place where whipping-cheer abounds. **1683–4** *Thamasis's Advice to Painter* 40 For his Cheat, the Man will pay full dear, Condemned by my Lord to Whipping Chear. **1924** *Techn. Bull. N. Y. State Agric. Exper. Station* No. 113. 3 Good whipping cream gave a reduced volume of whipped cream when compared to poor *whipping cream. **1978** *Chicago* June 248/2 Pure whipping cream for coffee and batters. **1712–13** SWIFT *Jrnl. to Stella* 9 Jan., To-morrow.. is his [*sc.* the Lord Treasurer's] day when all the ministers dine with him. He calls it *whipping-day...we do indeed usually rally him about his faults on that day. **1896** *Daily News* 30 Dec. 5/1 There will always be a devotee ready to stand as *whipping-girl between him and the strokes of fate. **1906** MRS. CROKER *Youngest Miss Mowbray* viii, Ella did not speak; she did not even cry out, while she acted as the whipping-girl of her enemy. **1681** HICKERINGILL *Black Non-Conf.* Postscr. Y, You have got the *whipping hand of him. **1852** MRS. STOWE *Uncle Tom's Cabin* II. xxix. 147 It was the universal custom to send women and young girls to *whipping-houses. **1631** *Aldeburgh Rec.* in *N. & Q.* 12th Ser. VIII. 427/2 The *whippinge place in the Markett. **1836** DICKENS *Sk. Boz, Crim. Crts.*, Often have we strayed here, in sessions time, to catch a glimpse of the whipping-place. **1862** H. MARRYAT *Year in Sweden* I. 360 *note*, In after times the Kaken or *whipping-pole, stood on the Stortorg. **1600** *Newe Metamorphosis* (Nares) Be brought to th' *whipping post..And as a rogue stande ready to be whipt. **1741** TAILFER etc. *Narr. Georgia* 37 Irons, Whipping-Posts, Gibbets, &c. were provided. **1849** THACKERAY *Pendennis* ii, He never was flogged, but it was a wonder how he escaped the whipping-post. **1854** —— *Newcomes* ii, No whipping post..could have been leaner than Mrs. Newcome. **1703** DE FOE *Hymn to Pillory* 250 In vain he struggl'd, he harangu'd in vain, To bring in *Whipping Sentences again. **1615** BRATHWAIT *Strappado* (1878) 174 Send them to th' *whipping-stocke. **1678** PENN in *Life*, Wks. 1782 I. p. lxii, We have been as the wool-sacks, and common whipping-stock of the kingdom. **1809** MALKIN *Gil Blas* VII. i. (Rtldg.) 225, I am born to be the mere *whipping-top of fortune. **1885** MOZLEY *Remin. Towns* etc. II. 249 A boy's whipping-top. *a* **1704** *T. Brown's Wks.* (1711) IV. 185 By Nature meant, by Want a Pedant made, Bl——re at first profess'd the *Whipping-trade.

b. in sense 2, as ***whipping cotton, silk, twine.***

1769 FALCONER *Dict. Marine* French terms, *Fisolle*, or *Ficelle*, whipping-twine. **1887** J. H. KEENE *Fishing Tackle* 102 A piece of gold tinsel is..secured by one turn of the loose whipping silk. **1893** ROSEVEAR *Text-bk. Needlework* 208 Whipping cotton must be very..strong, and yet fine.

c. in sense 3 c, as ***whipping-hoist, -jigger.***

1875 KNIGHT *Dict. Mech.*, *Whipping-hoist*, a steam hoisting-device for use in buildings. **1895** *Daily News* 13 July 5/4 A crane lifting eight tons, fitted with 'whipping jigger'.

d. whipping side *Austral.* (see quot. 1965).

1957 STEWART & KEESING *Old Bush Songs* IX. 259 You see our ringer already turned and he's on the whipping side. **1965** J. S. GUNN *Terminol. Shearing Industry* II. 37 *Whipping side*, the name given to the last side of the sheep to be shorn and the blow here is down from the shoulder.

'whipping, *ppl. a.* [f. WHIP *v.* + -ING².] That whips, in various senses.

1. Moving briskly or nimbly; acting vigorously or violently; characterized by such movement or action. (See senses of WHIP *v.* I.)

[**1530**: see WHIPPINGLY below.] **1600** W. WATSON *Decacordon* (1602) 17 A whipping Mistresse H. (whose toung goeth like the clacke of a Mill). **1656** (*title*) Divine Fire-works..hinting what the Almighty Emanuel is doing in these whipping times. **1700** R. CROMWELL in *Engl. Hist. Rev.* (1898) XIII. 120 A whippinge sneezing cold. **1741** RICHARDSON *Pamela* xxxiii. III. 323, I have a whipping Stomach, and were there fifty Dishes, I always taste of every one. **1895** MEREDITH *Amazing Marr.* xviii, At a whipping pace.

2. Beating with or as with a whip; flogging; lashing; also *fig.*

1598 R. BERNARD tr. *Terence, Andria* I The master of the rogues, a whipping Bedle. **1628** FELTHAM *Resolves* II. [I.] xxvi. 84 The whipping Satyrist. **1904** R. CULLUM *Hound from North* ii, The whipping snow lashed their faces. **1919** *19th Cent.* Nov. 968 To become the drilling and whipping masters of the despised soldiery.

b. ***Whipping Tom***: a man who whips others or flagellates himself (see quots. for various uses).

1681 HICKERINGILL *Vind. Naked Truth* II. 2 A furious chastizing Pædagogue, another Whipping-Tom, that took pleasure to lash and slash. **1715** M. DAVIES *Athen. Brit.* I. Pref. 21 A Detachment of the same Croisade, or Holy War, call'd *Flagellantes* or Whipping-Toms. *a* **1728** W. KENNETT in *Aubrey's Rem. Gentilisme* (1881) 59 A Whipping Tom in Kent who disciplined the wandring Maids and Women till they were afraid to walk abroad. **1791** THROSBY *Leicester* 356 These whip-men, called Whipping-Toms, are preceded by a bell-man [etc.]. **1846** *Local Act* (Leicester) *9 Vict.* c. 29 §41. **1923** S. H. SKILLINGTON *Let. to Editor*, Early on Shrove Tuesday a crowd assembled in the Newarke, Leicester. At the sound of the 'Pancake Bell' a number of men and youths began a game of hockey or shinney. About 1 o'clock the 'Whipping Toms', three men in blue smocks with very long wagon whips, began to try to drive the shinney players out with their whips. The game was suppressed by Parliament in 1846.

Hence **whippingly** *adv.*

1530 PALSGR. 844/1 Whyppyngly, hastely, *hastiuement*. Whyppingly, gorgyasly, *gorgiasement*.

'whipping-boy. A boy educated together with a young prince or royal personage, and flogged in his stead when he committed a fault that was considered to deserve flogging. Hence *allusively*.

1647 TRAPP *Comm. 1 Tim.* v. 20 Rebuke before all: yet not as if they were whipping boyes. *a* **1715** BURNET *Own Time* I. (1724) I. 59 William Murray of the bed-chamber, that had been whipping boy to King Charles the first. **1822** SCOTT *Nigel* vi, Sir Mungo had been..attached to Court in the capacity of whipping-boy..to King James the Sixth. **1841** HELPS *Ess., On Choice of Agents*, The choice of agents is a difficult matter,..for you have to choose persons for whose faults you are to be punished; to whom you are to be the whipping-boy. **1914** PETRIE in *Anc. Egypt* 32 With some writers..Manetho is the whipping-boy, who must always be flogged whenever anything is not understood.

'whipping-ˌsnapping, *a. nonce-wd.* [Fanciful f. WHIPPER-SNAPPER.] Diminutive, insignificant.

1861 THACKERAY *Round. Papers, Ogres*, Though they had seven-leagued boots,..all sorts of little whipping-snapping Tomb [*sic*] Thumbs used to elude and out-run them.

Whipple ('hwɪp(ə)l). *Path.* [The name of George Hoyt *Whipple* (b. 1878), U.S. pathologist, who described the disease in 1907 (*Bull. Johns Hopkins Hosp.* XVIII. 382).] ***Whipple's disease***: = *intestinal lipodystrophy* s.v. LIPODYSTROPHY.

[**1939** *Amer. Jrnl. Path.* XV. 483 (*heading*) Malabsorption of fat (intestinal lipodystrophy of Whipple).] **1945** *Ibid.* XXI. 1079 The pathologic findings in Whipple's disease are characterized by deposits of fat and fatty acids in the small intestine and mesenteric lymph nodes. **1978** *Price's Textbk. Pract. Med.* (ed. 12) VIII. 652/2 Whipple's disease, characterized by fever, joint pains, wasting, and diarrhoea, can initially be suspected [in cases of Crohn's disease].

†**'whippletree**[1]. *Obs.* Of uncertain origin and meaning.

Usually glossed 'cornel-tree' and compared with MLG. *wipelbôm*, which, with *wiepen-* and *weipkenbôm*, glosses L. *cornus*. (In the absence of a French gloss in quot. 1530, the identity of the word intended is doubtful.)

c **1386** CHAUCER *Knt.'s T.* 2065 Mapul, thorn, bech, hasel, Ew, whippeltre [*v.rr.* Whippul-, -il-, whipil-, wypul-]. **1530** PALSGR. 288/1 Whypple tree.

whippletree[2] ('hwɪp(ə)ltri:). [The first element is app. f. WHIP; cf. WHIPPIN.] = SWINGLETREE 2.

1733 W. ELLIS *Chiltern & Vale Farm.* 319 Two Whippletrees of two Foot sixteen Inches each, that the Horses draw by. **1790** *Trans. Soc. Arts* VIII. 244 A Spring and Index fixed to a Whipple-tree for ascertaining the force exerted in the Draught of Carriages. **1834** *Brit. Husb.* I. 165 These carts are capable of being drawn either by two horses abreast, or by the same number at length; for which purpose there are suitable staples fixed for hanging the whipple-tree upon. **1891** MALDEN *Tillage* 110 Iron Whippletrees for Two Horses Abreast.

'whip-poor-'will. Also 8 **whipper-**, 9 **wipper-**, **-vill**, **whippo-**. [Echoic, from the bird's note.] Popular name in U.S. and Canada for a species of Goatsucker, *Antrostomus* (*Caprimulgus*) *vociferus*.

1709 J. LAWSON *New Voy. Carolina* 146 Whippoo-Will, so nam'd, because it makes those Words exactly. **1747** G. EDWARDS *Nat. Hist. Birds* II. 63 The Whip-Poor-Will, or lesser Goat-Sucker... It is called in Virginia, Whip-Poor-Will, from its Cry. **1778** J. CARVER *Trav. N. Amer.* xviii. 468 The Whipperwill, or as it is termed by the Indians, the Muckawiss..acquires its name by the noise it makes. **1809** W. IRVING *Knickerb.* VI. iv. (1861) 198 The melancholy plaint of the Whip-poor-will, who, perched on some lone tree, wearied the ear of night with his incessant moanings. **1822** J. WOODS *Two Yrs. Resid. Illinois* 197 Wipperwill, or whip-poor-will, or wippervill,—a brown bird..is generally heard of an evening in spring and summer. **1884** 'MARK TWAIN' *Huck. Finn* i, I heard..a Whippowill and a dog crying about somebody that was going to die. **1920** W. D. HOWELLS *Vacation of Kelwyns* 42 The whippoor-wills.. whirred through the cool, damp air. **1938** J. M. GORDON *Canad. Mosaic* (1939) ix. 218 Dreamily lying with prairie for pillow Clear I hear calling the lone whip-poor-will. **1960** R. T. PETERSON *Field Guide Birds of Texas* 134 Whip-poor-will... Best known by its vigorous cry repeated in endless succession at night.

whippy ('hwɪpɪ), *a.* [f. WHIP *sb.* + -Y[1].] Resembling a whip; *esp.* bending like a whip, flexible, springy.

1867 F. FRANCIS *Bk. Angling* ix. 277 The Irish spliced rods are..rather too whippy or flexible. **1898** *Cycling* 25 An unduly whippy machine should be let alone.

whip-saw ('hwɪpsɔ:), *sb.* Also **whipsaw**. [f. WHIP *sb.* or *v.* + SAW *sb.*]

1. A frame-saw with a narrow blade, used esp. for curved work.

1538 ELYOT, *Runcina*, a whypsawe, wherwith tymber is sawen. **1552** in P. H. Hore *Wexford* (1901) 243 In the Storehouse at the Mynes..a whypp sawe. **1556** *Richmond Wills* (Surtees) 100 In Maid's chamber..11 old wood chests and a whype sawe. **1657** R. LIGON *Barbadoes* (1673) 107 Three whip-sawes, going all at once in a Frame or Pit. **1678** MOXON *Mech. Exerc.* vi. 99 The Whip-Saw is used..to Saw such greater peeces of Stuff that the Hand-Saw will not easily reach through;..two men takes each an handle of the Saw. **1846** HOLTZAPFFEL *Turning* II. 701 The long saw, pit saw, or whip saw. *Ibid.* 703 The blade [of the pit frame-saw] is usually five or six feet long, and thinner than that of the whip saw. **1903** NANCY H. BANKS *Round Anvil Rock* ii, The rich dark wood of its walls and floor—all rudely smoothed with the broadaxe and the whip-saw.

2. *fig.* Something that is disadvantageous in two ways. orig. and chiefly *U.S.*

1873 *Kansas Mag.* Mar. 232/1 There was fifteen hundred on the turn—seven hundred and fifty on each side of it—and the run was tray, ace; a whipsaw. **1929** L. F. CARR *Amer. Challenged* 79 The whip-saw of paying high prices for what they bought and being forced to receive low prices for what they sold. **1967** *Listener* 23 Nov. 656/3 The wage push..and the rising interest rates..have together caught the American economy in a cruel and sharp whipsaw... The worst sort of inflation of costs and the worst sort of deflation of values. **1977** *Time* 25 July 48/3 By the spring of 1974, the whipsaw effect of recession and rising costs—particularly for oil which fuels 80% of Con Ed's generating capacity—left the company strapped.

Hence **whip-saw** *v.*, *intr.* to work a whip-saw; *trans.* to cut with a whip-saw; *fig.* (*U.S. slang*) to have or get the advantage of thoroughly, to overcome completely, 'cut up'; also **whip-sawing** *vbl. sb.* (lit. and *fig.*); **whip-sawyer**, a man who works a whip-saw.

1842 *Amer. Pioneer* I. 83 Dwellinghouses, made of wood, whip-sawed into timbers, four inches thick, and of the requisite width and length. **1873** *Kansas Mag.* June 497/1 On the next Budd whipsawed him, and that closed that deal. **1881** *Lumber World* (U.S.) Mar., Some of the first saw mills built in England..were destroyed..on the ground that it would ruin the occupation of the whip sawyers. **1884** *Hartford* (Conn.) *Post* Sept., Had Braddock been half as prudent as he was brave, he could..have whipsawed the French and Indians in that campaign. **1885** *Mag. Amer. Hist.* May 496/1 *Whip-sawing*, the acceptance of fees or bribes from two opposing persons or parties. **1903** *Sun* (N.Y.) 8 Nov. 10 The speculators have subjected themselves to the process known in Wall Street as whipsawing, that is, they have bought when the market was strong and sold when the market was weak, and found each time that they bought at the top and sold at the bottom. **1904** ELIZ. ROBINS *Magnetic North* ii. 26 He would..show us how to whip-saw. **1918** R. DOLLAR *Mem.* vi. 63 These [trees] are hewn in the woods either on two or four sides, and are then whip-sawn by the natives at the place of consumption. **1930** H. A. INNIS *Fur Trade in Canada* II. v. 140 Men were engaged in cutting, squaring, whipsawing, and hauling timber for the construction and repair of the forts. **1957** *Listener* 12 Dec. 970/1 Mr [Adlai] Stevenson has been whip-sawed by conflicting advice. **1958** F. G. SLAUGHTER *Daybreak* III. xiii. 176 The tendency to whipsaw all society into robots who work, think and eat alike is hardly an end product of intelligence. **1969** D. BAGLEY *Spoilers* ii. 58 'Okay, so you've whipsawed me,' said Follet sourly. **1975** *Weekend Mag.* (Montreal) 12/1 Whip-sawing, industrial relations slang for the union practice of wringing a high settlement from a weak company and then using that settlement as a floor for bargaining with a big company, was rampant. **1976** *Billings* (Montana) *Gaz.* 27 June 8-C/3 A major problem occurs when one small union negotiates a salary increase for its workers and all other state employes in the same job classification want the same increase. The effect is to 'whipsaw' the state between their competing demands. **1979** C. E. SCHORSKE *Fin-de-Siècle Vienna* vii. 351 Schoenberg whipsaws us upward out of the crepuscular calm.

whipsey-, -sider(r)y: see WHIPSY-DERRY.

whipship ('hwɪpʃɪp). *nonce-wd.* [f. WHIP *sb.* + -SHIP.] **a.** (with poss. pron.) Humorous title for a coachman. **b.** The post of a parliamentary 'whip'.

1817 KEATS *Let. to Fanny Keats* 10 Sept., I disembark'd from his Whipship's Coach. **1907** *Sat. Rev.* 1 June 671/2 Lord Ribblesdale has flung up the whipship of his party.

'whip-snake. Name for various serpents of long slender form like a whip-lash, as *Masticophis flagelliformis* of N. America, *Philodryas viridissimus* of Brazil, *Hoplocephalus flagellum* of Australia. In southern Africa, a grass or sand snake of the genus *Psammophis*, esp. *P. notostictus*.

1774 GOLDSM. *Nat. Hist.* (1776) VII. 203 In the tropical climates, the rattle-snake, the whip-snake, and the cobra di capello, are the most formidable. **1813** J. FORBES *Oriental Mem.* I. 199 The Concan abounds with serpents..: one of the most dangerous is a long snake of a beautiful green; in form resembling the lash of a coach-whip, from whence it is called the whip-snake. **1825** WATERTON *Wand. S. Amer.* I. (1903) 9 The whipsnake, of a beautiful changing green,.. may be handled with safety. **1880** J. NIXON *Among Boers* ii. 45 He had all but put his foot upon a whip snake. These snakes are small and slender, being only as thick as the little finger. **1887** R. M. PRAED *Longleat Kooralbyn* xx, A whip-snake..made a dart at Barrington's arm. **1898** E. D. COPE *Crocodil.*, etc. *N. Amer.* (1900) 789 The species of this genus [*sc.* Zamenis] are elongate in form and active in movement, so that the popular names of 'whip-snake' and 'racer' are appropriate. **1912** F. W. FITZSIMONS *Snakes S. Afr.* (new ed.) 462 The Grass and Sand Snake, when alarmed, glide off over the stunted herbage... Colonists know these as Whip Snakes. **1952** *Cape Times* 24 Apr. 9/2 As schoolboys were walking along the road..they saw a whipsnake.

whipstaff ('hwɪpstɑ:f, -æ-). [STAFF *sb.*]

1. = WHIPSTOCK 1.

1599 MIDDLETON *Micro-cynicon* B4b, With nailed shooes, and whipstaffe in his hand.

†**2.** *Naut.* = WHIP *sb.* 13. *Obs.*

1627 CAPT. J. SMITH *Sea Gram.* ii. 12 The Whip-staffe is that peece of wood like a strong staffe the..Helmesman hath alwaies in his hand..made fast to the Tiller with a Ring. **1726** SHELVOCKE *Voy. round World* 305 My land Gentlemen ..were now forced to learn to steer, and take their turns at the Whipstaff. **1769** FALCONER *Dict. Marine* French terms, *Manuelle*, the whip-staff of a helm;..now entirely disused.

whipstalk ('hwɪpstɔ:k). *dial.* = WHIPSTOCK 1.

1592 KYD *Sp. Trag.* III. (1602) G, Bought you a whistle and a whipstalke too. **1856** OLMSTED *Slave States* 329 Horrid belaboring of the poor horses' backs, with the butt-end of a hickory whip-stalk.

†**whipstart.** *Obs. rare*$^{-1}$. [? f. WHIP *v.* Cf. UPSTART.] app. = next, 1 c.

1581 J. BELL *Haddon's Answ. Osor.* 437b, Whiles this whipstart [*sc.* a priest] alone have played all the partes of the Pageaunt.

whipster ('hwɪpstə(r)). [app. f. WHIP *v.* + -STER. Cf. prec. and WHIPPING *ppl. a.* 1.]

1. A vague term of reproach, contempt, or the like, with various shades of meaning. **a.** A lively, smart, reckless, violent, or mischievous person. *Obs.* or *dial.*

1589 R. HARVEY *Pl. Perc.* 3 They had neede be large long Spoons..if I come to feed with such whipsters. **1593** G. HARVEY *Pierce's Super.* Wks. (Grosart) II. 63 You that intende to be fine companionable gentlemen, smirkinge wittes, and whipsters in the world. **1683** KENNETT tr. *Erasm. on Folly* 18 Cupid feigned as a boy,..because he is an underwitted whipster [*orig.* nugator], that neither acts nor thinks any thing with discretion. *a* **1700** B. E. *Dict. Cant. Crew*, *Whipster*, a sharp, or subtil Fellow. **1822** W. IRVING *Braceb. Hall* (1845) 223 The whipsters roam in truant bands about the neighbourhood. **1906** SINTON *Poetry of Badenoch* 432 Like a whipster from school.

b. A wanton, lascivious, or licentious person, a debauchee. *Obs.* or *dial.*

1593 *Passionate Morrice* (1876) 81, I should quite fray away many of M. Anthonies companions from bestowing their affections on so liberall whipsters. **1667** DRYDEN & DK. NEWCASTLE *Sir M. Mar-all* IV. i, There were Whipsters abroad, i' faith, Padders of Maiden-heads. **1697** VANBRUGH *Prov. Wife* v. iii, To deliver up her fair Body, to be tumbled and mumbled, by that young Liquorish Whipster. [**1898** R. BLAKEBOROUGH *Wit*, etc. *N. Riding Yorkshire* Gloss., *Whipster*, a doubtful character.]

c. A slight, insignificant, or contemptible person. (The current literary sense, often with the epithet *puny*, after Shaks.)

1604 SHAKS. *Oth.* v. ii. 244, I am not valiant neither: But euery Punie whipster gets my Sword. **1682** D'URFEY *Inj. Princ.* IV. iv, A plaguy little Whipster this. **1708** ROWE *Royal Convert* Prol., Each puny Whipster here, is Wit enough. **1838** DICKENS *Nich. Nick.* xxxiv, When I first saw this whipster. **1840** THACKERAY *Paris Sk.-bk.* (1869) 42 Every little whipster of a French poet. **1882** STEVENSON *Across the Plains* iii. (1892) 141 No tearful whipster.

2. One who wields a whip: **a.** a driver of horses; **b.** one addicted to whipping or flogging, a scourger, lasher (also *fig.*). ? *Obs.*

1651 CLEVELAND *News from Newc.* 29 He'd leave the trotting Whipster, and prefer Our profound Vulcan 'bove that Wagoner. **1670** *Comenius Janua Ling.* §504. 132 A school master should take care of being curst (a whipster). **1707** J. STEVENS tr. *Quevedo's Com. Wks.* (1709) R2, The Whipsters..laid aside their Disciplines. **1825** LAMB *Ass* Wks. 1903 I. 304 To see one of those refiners in discipline himself at the cart's tail, with just such a convenient spot laid bare to the tender mercies of the whipster.

whip-stitch ('hwɪpstɪtʃ), *sb.* (*adv.*) [f. WHIP *sb.* 16, *v.* 18 + STITCH *sb.*]

1. *Needlework.* A stitch of the kind described s.v. WHIP *v.* 18; an overcast stitch: = WHIP *sb.* 17.

1640 J. TAYLOR (Water P.) *Praise Needle* A2, The smarting Whip-stitch, Back-stitch, & the Crosse-stitch. **1880** *Plain Hints Needlework* 22 Whip-stitch. This should be formed of a very neat tight roll, the raw edge being completely rolled in. **1885** LENO *Boot & Shoemaking* x. 88 When lasted, the upper is braced round with a single thread with a whip-stitch. **1893** ROSEVEAR *Text-bk. Needlework* 204 The stitch makes the roll on the material look like a whip-cord, and..this is probably the origin of the name of whip-stitch.

2. Phr. (*at*) ***every whip-stitch***, at short or frequent intervals. Also (without *at*), each item without exception; 'every last thing'. *dial.* and *U.S.*

1824 P. HOBBY *Life of Marion* p. i, What can one do, when one's friends are..calling out at every whipstitch..'Well, but sir, where's Marion?' **1888** F. R. STOCKTON *Dusantes* III. 130 Every whip-stitch of his bag and baggage shall be trundled after him. **1890** J. D. ROBERTSON *Gloss. Glouc.* s.v., 'He was in and out every whip-stitch,' meaning 'every now and then'. **1899** *Atlantic Monthly* LXXXIII. 757/2 Feast days occur at every whipstitch.

†**3.** as *adv.* or *int.* expressing sudden movement or action. *Obs. slang* or *colloq.*

1676 SHADWELL *Virtuoso* IV. 74 I'll slide down from the window..and, Whip Stich, your Nose in my Breech, Sir Nicholas. I'll leave my Cloaths behind me. **1706** E. WARD

Wooden World Diss. (1708) 80 He shall cast ye a Knot, whip stich, in a Twinkling, as intricate as the Gordion one.

whip-stitch, *v. Needlework.* [Cf. prec.] *trans.* To sew with a whip-stitch: = WHIP *v.* 18.

1592 GREENE *Upstart Courtier* Wks. (Grosart) XI. 240 Silcke lace, cloth of golde, of siluer, and such costly stuffe, to welte, garde, whippstitch, edge, face, and draw out. **1887** *Harper's Mag.* July 179/2 If 'inserts' or 'plates' of single sheets are to form part of the book, these are usually pasted or 'whip-stitched' by hand upon or within the folded sheet.

whipstock ('hwɪpstɒk). [STOCK *sb.*[1]]

1. a. The stick or staff to which the lash of a whip is attached; the handle of a whip.

1530 PALSGR. 288/1 Whypstocke, *manche dung fouet.* **1608** SHAKS. *Per.* II. ii. 51 He appeares To haue practis'd more the Whipstocke, then the Launce. **1655** [G. HALL] *Tri. Rome* vi. 75 The Baalites spared their flesh lesse then her cruellest whip-stocks. **1850** 'SYLVANUS' *Bye-lanes & Downs* iv. 52 Beating out the brains of one ruffian with a whip-stock he always carried. **1881** BESANT & RICE *Chapl. Fleet* I. ii, Sitting down and leaning his chin upon his whipstock. **1895** J. G. MILLAIS *Breath from Veldt* 62 Having fishing material with us.. I soon had the two whipstocks rigged up.

b. *transf.* A man who drives horses. *contemptuous.*

1615 TOMKIS *Albumazar* IV. iv, Out Carter. Hence durtie whipstocke.

†2. A whipping-post (= *whipping-stock* (*a*), WHIPPING *vbl. sb.* 4 a). *Obs.*

1619 H. HUTTON *Follie's Anat.* B 4b, The beggers whip-stock, or the Gallowes hire. **1638** BRATHWAIT *Barnabees Jrnl.* III. (1818) 113 Suspected for a picklock Th' beedle led me to the whip-stock.

†3. A person who is frequently whipped (= *whipping-stock* (*b*), WHIPPING *vbl. sb.* 4 a); in quot. = FLAGELLANT *sb. Obs.*

1640 BP. HALL *Chr. Moder.* I. iii. 24 Such were the famous whip-stocks in the time of Gregory the tenth.

†4. *Naut.* = WHIPSTAFF 2, WHIP *sb.* 13. *Obs.*

1682 WHELER *Journ. to Greece* III. 286 In this Storm we broke the Whip-stock, and split the Stern.

5. *Oil Industry.* A long, tapered steel wedge which can be placed at the bottom of a hole to cause the drilling bit to deviate sideways, e.g. in directional drilling.

1903 *Dialect Notes* II. 345 *Whip-stock, n.*, an implement used in drilling past a set of tools when fast. **1935** *Econ. Geol.* XXX. 740 Controlled deflection of a hole toward a specific objective through the use of whipstocks, knuckle-joints and improved methods of well surveying has given added flexibility to rotary tools. **1973** J. W. JENNER in Hobson & Pohl *Mod. Petroleum Technol.* (ed. 4) iv. 128 The whipstock had to be pulled out of the hole and reset every 25 ft or so.. in order to achieve sufficient angle build up.

6. *attrib.*: **whipstock wise** *adv. phr.*, in the manner of a whipstock: in quot. applied to WHIP-GRAFTING.

1608 PLAT *Garden of Eden* (1653) 117 Grafting whipstock wise, and letting in the cions into the stock by a slit, is good for young trees.

whipstress ('hwɪpstrɪs). *rare*⁻¹. [f. WHIPSTER 2 b: see -STRESS.] A female flogger.

1707 tr. *Wks. C'tess D'Anois* (1715) 366 The Whipstresses [orig. *fouetteuses*].. had so tir'd themselves, that they could no longer stir their Arms.

whipsy-derry. Also **whipsider(r)y, whipsey-derry.** [app. connected with WHIP *sb.* 15 and DERRICK *sb.*] A contrivance for hoisting (esp. ore in shallow mines), consisting of a derrick with a 'whip' or simple pulley attached, and worked by a horse or horses. Also simply *whipsy* and *whip and derry* (WHIP *sb.* 15).

1865 TREGELLAS *Tales* 146 (E.D.D.) 'What is a whipsiderry, sir?' said I. 'A whipsiderry,' said he, 'es a thing for rising traade, 'tes a sort of whem.' **1866** THORNBURY *Greatheart* xxxiv, Two waggons, laden with.. whipsidery pulleys, disjointed fragments of steam-engines, and miners' gads and crowbars. **1866** R. P. WHITWORTH *Bailliere's S. Austral. Gazetteer* 116 There are.. 2 double whipseys, and several single whipseys. **1875** J. H. COLLINS *Metal Mining* 76 With the 'derrick' or 'whipsey-derry' the cost will be a little more than with the horse-whim.

whiptail ('hwɪpteɪl). [f. WHIP *sb.* 1 + TAIL *sb.*[1]] Name used (simply or attrib.) for any one of various animals having a long slender tail like a whip-lash: see quots.

1771 J. R. FORSTER *Flora Amer. Septentr.* To Rdr. p. vii, Whiptail forked Fistularia tabaccaria [tobacco-pipe fish]. **1887** TYRWHITT *New Chum Queensland Bush* 145 (Morris) Kangaroos.. of.. different kinds,.. the smaller kind, known as pretty faces or whip tails. **1887** *Buck's Handbk. Med. Sci.* V. 748/1 The genus *Thelyphonus* (Whip-tail, Nigger Killer, Mule Killer..) [= whip-scorpion]. **1898** MORRIS *Austral Eng.*, *Tasmanian Whiptail*,.. *Coryphænoides tasmaniæ*,.. an altogether different fish from *Myliobatis aquila*, the Eagle or Whiptail Ray [= whip-ray].

whip-tom-kelly. [Imitative, from the bird's note: cf. WHIP-POOR-WILL.] Popular name for the Red-eyed Greenlet or 'Flycatcher' (*Vireo olivaceus* or *Vireosylvia olivacea*) of eastern N. America, and the Black-whiskered Greenlet (*Vireo barbatulus* or *Vireosylvia calidris*) of the W. Indies, Bahamas, and Florida.

1756 P. BROWNE *Jamaica* 476 Whip-tom-kelly. I believe this to be a bird of passage. **1864-5** WOOD *Homes without H.* xii. 247 The Red-Eyed Flycatcher (Muscicapa olivacea) popularly known as 'Whip-Tom-Kelly,' from its peculiar articulate cry. **1872** COUES *Key N. Amer. Birds* 120 *Vireo altiloquus* var. *barbatulus*. Black-whiskered Vireo. Whip-tom-kelly.

whir, *sb.* and *v.*: see WHIRR.

whirche, obs. var. WORK *v.*

whirken, obs. f. QUERKEN *v.*, to suffocate.

c **1440** *Alphabet of Tales* 101 Þai war bothe whirkenid þer-with & deyid.

whirl (hwɜːl), *sb.* Forms: 5 **qwherel, qwerle, wherwille,** *Sc.* **quhirl(l,** 6 **whiruel(l, wherle, whyrle, whirroll,** 6–7 **whurle,** 6–8 **whirle,** 7 **wervell, whurl,** 6– **whirl.** [Partly a. MLG., MDu. *wervel* or ON. *hvirfill* (see WHIRL *v.*), partly f. the verb itself. Cf. WHORL.]

I. Denoting a material object.

1. a. The fly-wheel or pulley of a spindle: = WHORL *sb.* 1.

1411 *Nottingham Rec.* II. 86, x. qwerles. **1479** *Paston Lett.* III. 270, vj. soketes, with branches to remeve. iij. wherwilles to the same. **1483** *Cath. Angl.* 298/2 A Qwherel of A spyndylle [*A.* A Qworle of A roke), *giraculum, neopellum, vertibrum.* **1510** STANBRIDGE *Vocabula* (W. de W.) C j b, *Verticillum*, a wherle [1525, a whorle]. *a* **1553** UDALL *Royster D.* I. iii. (Arb.) 20 Nourse medle you with your spyndle and your whirle. **1556** WITHALS *Dict.* (1562) 35/1 A whiruell, *verticulum, verticulus, spondilus.* **1585** W. WHITAKER *Answ. to Rainolds* 160 Among the other praises of a woorthy.. woman that is one, that she putteth hir hande to the wherle. **1598** FLORIO, *Aspo*,.. a whirroll. **1659** TORRIANO, *Cócca*, the wervell or button of a spindle. **1825** J. NICHOLSON *Oper. Mech.* 389 The revolution of the wheel,.. conveyed by a band to the whirl, or pulley on the spindle.

†b. *transf.* A skein of thread sufficient to fill a spindle. *Obs.*

1560 W. BALDWIN *Funeralles Edw. VI*, *Death playnt* iii, Atropos did knap in two the string, Before her sisters sixtene whurles had spun.

c. *Rope-making.* A cylindrical piece of wood furnished with a hook on which the ends of the fibre are hung in spinning.

1794 *Rigging & Seamanship* I. 58 Whirls are of beech or ash,.. cylindrically formed, and fixed on iron spindles in the heads of wheels, with a hook at one end for the spinner to hang his hemp on. They are likewise used to hang the yarn on for hardening and laying ropes. **1797** [see *whirl-hook* under WHIRL-]. **1886** *Encycl. Brit.* XX. 844/1 The point of the prolonged axis of the whirl is bent into a hook.

†2. = WHIRL-WORM 1. *Obs.*

1658 ROWLAND tr. *Moufet's Theat. Ins.* 1042 A Whirl or little hairy Worm with many feet. *Ibid.*, I collect that there is a house Whurl like to *Silphius*.

3. *Bot.* and *Zool.* = WHORL *sb.* 2.

1713 PETIVER in *Phil. Trans.* XXVIII. 194 The upper Whirls are guarded with round pointed Leaves. **1796** WITHERING *Brit. Plants* (ed. 3) II. 189 Whirls of leaves often so thickly set as partly to tile the stems. **1883** *Harper's Mag.* Jan. 187/2 The numberless animals of the colony are grouped in whirls.

4. *Conch.* **a.** = WHORL *sb.* 3.

1681 GREW *Musæum* I. VI. i. 125 A Shell.. with a Knobed Turban or Whirle. **1851** WOODWARD *Mollusca* 45 The whirls of spiral shells are sometimes separated by the interference of foreign substances. **1861** P. P. CARPENTER in *Rep. Smithsonian Inst.* 1860, 186 In *Triforis*, the whirls turn the wrong way.

b. = TOP *sb.*[2] 2.

1708 *Phil. Trans.* XXVI. 79 Trochites, The Whirle, or Top-shell.

5. A convolution, curl, spiral; = WHORL *sb.* 4.

1862 BURTON *Bk. Hunter* (1863) 399 The noses, the tails, the feet of the characteristic monster of the sculptured stones, all end in a whirl. **1884** *Jrnl. Frankl. Inst.* June 418 The reduction of friction and of whirls in the wheel.

6. *Angling.* A spinning bait.

1888 GOODE *Amer. Fishes* 71 Using two lines with spoon-baits or 'whirl'.

7. *Electr.* (See quots.)

1842 FRANCIS *Dict. Arts, Whirl, Electrical.* (See *Flyer.*) **1862** *Catal. Internat. Exhib., Brit.* II. No. 5598, Series of apparatus.. including Leyden jars.. swan, spider, whirl or fly. **1893** SLOANE *Electr. Dict.* 577 A conductor carrying an electric current is surrounded by circular lines of force, which are sometimes termed an electric whirl.

II. Denoting a movement (and derived senses).

8. a. The action, or an act, of whirling; (swift) rotatory or circling movement, rotation, circumvolution, gyration; a (rapid) turn, as of a wheel, around an axis or centre.

spec. in *Fencing*: cf. quot. 1771 s.v. WHIRL *v.* 3. In *Kinematics*, a uniform rotation of a fluid about a fixed axis.

c **1480** HENRYSON *Orpheus & Eurydice* 370 Wardly men sum tyme ar castin hie Apon the quhele, in grete prosperitee, And wyth a quhirl, vnwarly, or thai witte, Ar thravin doun to pure & law estate. **1598** MARSTON *Sco. Villanie* III. x. H 3, The whirle on toe, The turne aboue ground. **1609** *Bible* (Douay) 1 Sam. xxv. 29 In violence, and whurle of a sling. **1621** FLETCHER *Pilgrim* III. vi, What flaws, and whirles of weather. **1742** YOUNG *Nt. Th.* IV. 562 The good man.. bids earth roll, nor feels her idle whirl. **1771** LONNERGAN *Fencer's Guide* 87 This [wrenching] differs from whirling; because you limit it not as you do the whirl, to get a good Repost. **1829** C. ROSE *Four Yrs. S. Africa* 146 A wild kind of dance, the principal motion of which was a whirl. **1856** KANE *Arctic Expl.* I. xvi. 186 The howling of the wind and the whirl of the snow-drift. **1878** W. K. CLIFFORD *Kinematic* 214 Whirls. Suppose next that the lines of flow are circles having their centres on a fixed axis, and their planes perpendicular to it, and that there is no spin except at the axis, and no expansion anywhere. **1894** *Phil. Trans.* CLXXXV. I. 281 In an unloaded shaft, the period of whirl coincides with the natural period of lateral vibration. **1908** S. E. WHITE *Riverman* xxvi, A whirl of the wheel to the right, a turn to the left.

b. Something, as a body of water or air, in (rapid) circling motion, or the part at which this takes place; an eddy, a vortex.

a **1547** SURREY *Æneis* II. 531 As wrastling windes out of dispersed whirl [orig. *rupto turbine*] Befight themselues. **1726** LEONI *Alberti's Archit.* II. 118/1 These whirls and eddies in a River.. have.. the nature and force of a Screw. **1753** FRANKLIN *Lett.* Wks. 1840 VI. 155 Still the tube or whirl of air may remain entire. **1798** COLERIDGE *Anc. Mar.* VII. x, Upon the whirl, where sank the ship, The boat spun round and round. **1847** STODDART *Angler's Comp.* 146 Trout .. are found.. close below banks, among side-runs and small whirls. **1902** *Words of Eye-witness* 101 A whirl of rifle-bullets beat upon the wet ground.

9. In extended use: Swift or violent movement, as of something hurled or flung, or of a wheeled vehicle, etc.; rapid course; rush, hurry. Also *fig.*

1649 G. DANIEL *Trinarch., Rich. II.* cix, The Noble Vere springs at a double whirle, Marquesse and Duke. **1725** POPE *Odyss.* x. 52 Snatch'd in the whirl, the hurried navy flew. **1842** DICKENS *Amer. Notes* vi, The lively whirl of carriages is exchanged for the deep rumble of carts and waggons. **1882** T. G. BOWLES *Flotsam & Jetsam* 97 Such a wretched device for filling their holidays as a whirl from one place to another, and a whirl back.

10. *fig.* Confused and hurried activity of any kind; disturbance, commotion; tumult, bustle.

1552 HULOET, Whyrle or rage of a battayle. **1620** I. C. *Two Merry Milk-maids* I. iii. C 4 b, What whirle's this? **1780** MRS. COWLEY *Belle's Stratagem* II. i, The feelings of Wife, and Mother, are lost in the whirl of dissipation. **1827** KEBLE *Chr. Y., Whit-Sunday* x, A giddy whirl of sin Fills ear and brain. **1840** DICKENS *Old C. Shop* xxxix, Tomorrow was to be a half-holiday devoted to a whirl of entertainment. **1889** 'J. S. WINTER' *Mrs. Bob* vi, Those who live in the whirl of London Society.

b. A confused, disturbed, distracted, or dizzy state of mind or feeling.

1707 ADDISON *Rosamond* III. iii, My soul is.. in the whirle of passion lost. **1848** THACKERAY *Van. Fair* iv, In a whirl of wonder at the theatre. **1854** R. S. SURTEES *Handley Cr.* lxv, His head was in a complete whirl. **1905** H. G. WELLS *Kipps* III. iii. §6 He departed in a whirl, to secure a copy of every morning paper.

11. *colloq.* (orig. *U.S.*). An attempt, esp. an initial or tentative attempt. Freq. in phr. *give it* (and varr.) ***a whirl***. Cf. BURL *sb.*[2] 2.

1884 C. B. LEWIS *Sawed-Off Sk.* 277 After licking the best man in his own camp he came down to give us a whirl. **1889** 'MARK TWAIN' *Connecticut Yankee* xix. 234 No sound and legitimate business can be established on a basis of speculation. A successful whirl in the knight-errantry line. .. It's just a corner in pork, that's all, and you can't make anything else out of it. **1904** 'O. HENRY' *Sixes & Sevens* (1911) 75 I'd been saving up for a year to give this New York a whirl. **1922** S. LEWIS *Babbitt* vi. 90 But—I wish I could've had a whirl at law and politics. **1923** WODEHOUSE in *Strand Mag.* Apr. 335 Jeeves, if he cared to take a whirl at it, could be Prime Minister or something to-morrow. **1949** A. MILLER *Death of Salesman* I. 66 Come on up. Tell that to Dad. Let's give him a whirl. **1965** K. ROBERTS in J. Carnell *New Writings in S-F* III. 127 I'm going up again next weekend. Give it another whirl. **1979** S. WILSON *Greenish Man* 11 You've nothing to lose. Give it a whirl, try it for a month. **1985** *Times* 28 Feb. 20/2 John Syer came to me and said he could help... So I thought I would give it a whirl.

whirl (hwɜːl), *v.* Forms: 3 **ȝwirle,** 4 **wyrle,** 4–6 **whyrle,** 4–7 **whirle,** 5 **quirle,** 6 **whyrl,** *Sc.* **quherle, quhirl(l)e, vhirle,** 6–7 **whorle, whurl(e,** 6– **whirl.** [prob. a. ON. *hvirfla* to turn about, whirl (Sw. *virfla*, obs. Da. *hvirle*, Da. *hvirvle*), related to ON. *hvirfill* circle, ring, esp. crown of the head, top, summit, pole of the heavens (MSw. *hvirvil* crown of the head, Sw. *virvel*, obs. Da. *hvirrel*, Da. *hvirvel* eddy, etc.) = (M)Du., (M)LG. *wervel* †whirlpool, †spindle, vertebra, swivel, bolt, OHG. *wirbil, wirvil* whirlwind (MHG., G. *wirbel* whirlwind, whirlpool, giddiness, vertebra, swivel, sheave, tumult; cf. *wirbeln* to whirl, trill, *wirblig* rotatory, giddy):—OTeut. **χwerbil-*, f. *χwerb-* to rotate: see WHARVE *v.*, -EL[1], -LE I, 3.

ON. *hwearflian, hwearftlian* 'errare' (Northumb. *hwærflung* 'error', 'vicissitudo') and **hwierflian, hwyrftlian* to rotate, do not appear to have survived; they are app. based on the variant *χwarb-*, which is otherwise widely represented (cf. late Northumb. *huarf* 'error', OE. **hwierfel, wirfel* in place names, OHG. *werbil* 'sistrum, plectrum', *warbelōn* 'rotari, versari', *warblich* 'versatilis', and forms s.v. WHARVE *v.*).

Contamination with *hurl* is seen in sense 6, as also in the variants HURLPOOL, HURLWIND of WHIRLPOOL, WHIRLWIND. Cf. similarly THIRLPOOL (association with THIRL, THRILL).]

1. *intr.* To move in a circle or similar curve, to circle, circulate; more vaguely, to move about in various directions, esp. with rapidity or force; to go (wander, fly, etc.) *about*; to be in commotion.

c **1290** *S. Eng. Leg.* 211/387 Þe kniȝt ȝwirlede op in þis blast, ase speldene doth, wel wide. **1412-20** LYDG. *Chron. Troy* I. 1873 As þe blase whirleth of a fire, So to and fro þei fleen. *c* **1440** *Promp. Parv.* 525/1 Whyrlyn a-bowte, yn ydylnesse.. *vagor.* *a* **1475** ASHBY *Dicta Philos.* 259 This world is not certeine ne stable, But whirlyng a bowte and mutable. **1563** GOOGE *Eglogs, Cupido* 648 That vyle deformed Churle Whose foggy Mates.. do thycke aboute him whurle. **1602** MARSTON *Antonio's Rev.* v. v, Then wil I daunce and whirle about the ayre. **1676** MACE *Musick's Mon.* 53 Let the Strings have scope enough to whirle about with clearness of Sound. **1719** De Foe *Crusoe* II. (Globe) 331 His Spirits whirl'd about faster than the Vessels could convey them. **1853** Kane *Grinnell Exp.* v. (1856) 36 Rocks, about which the sea-swallow and kittiwake were whirling in endless rounds. **1860** Tyndall *Glac.* I. xxvii. 210 Dense clouds of snow rose, whirling in the air.

b. *fig.*

1582 Bentley *Mon. Matrones* II. 3 His spirit whurling in my hart, greater than I can declare. **1834** Whittier *Mogg Megone* I. 426 What thoughts of horror and madness whirl Through the burning brain of that fallen girl! **1859** W. Collins *Q. of Hearts* i, A child of the new generation, with all the modern ideas whirling together in her pretty head. **1862** Carlyle *Fredk. Gt.* XII. ix. (1872) IV. 195 Breslau.. is whirling with business.

2. To turn, esp. swiftly, around an axis, like a wheel; to revolve or rotate (rapidly); to spin.

In quot. 1588 *fig.* with allusion to the wheel of Fortune. In *Mech.* used *spec.* of a shaft revolving at excessive speed so as to become bent by the centrifugal force: see quot. 1894 s.v. whirling *vbl. sb.* 1.

c **1384** Chaucer *H. Fame* III. 916 This hous.. was shapen lyke a cage.. I the telle That but I bringe the therinne Ne shalt thou neuer kunne gynne To come in to hyt.. So faste hit whirleth [*v.rr.* whyrleth, whirlyth] lo aboute. **1398** Trevisa *Barth. De P.R.* XIII. xvii. (1495) C vij b, For his depnesse he [*sc.* the whirlpool] meuyth rounde aboute, whyrlynge & reboundyng. Therfore swymmers ben oft perisshyd. *a* **1400–50** *Wars Alex.* 5294 Twenti tamed Olifants turned it a-boute, Quirland all on queles. **1513** Douglas *Æneis* VII. viii. 88 As sum tyme sclentis the round top of tre, Hit with the twynit quhyp, dois quherle. **1563** *Mirr. Mag.* II. *Collingbourne* iv, We knowe.. the course of Fortunes wheele, Howe constantly it whyrleth styll about. **1588** Shaks. *L.L.L.* IV. iii. 384 Iustice alwaies whirles in equall measure. *a* **1600** Montgomerie *Misc. Poems* xlviii. 148 Ȝon is Charybdis that vhirlis ay about. **1633** T. James *Voy.* 14 The eddies whirle into twenty manners. **1799** G. Smith *Laboratory* I. 29 A fire wheel which is to whirl horizontally in the water. **1833** Tennyson *Palace of Art* 15 While Saturn whirls, his stedfast shade Sleeps on his luminous ring. **1840** Dickens *Old C. Shop* xli, Round whirled the wheels, and off they rattled. **1853** Mrs. Gaskell *Ruth* vii, She sat down and could not speak—the room whirled round and round.

b. To turn round or aside quickly: = wheel *v.* 4.

a **1861** T. Winthrop *Life in Open Air* xii. (1863) 91 Instantly at the lucky hackle something darted, seized it, and whirled to fly.. up the [river]. **1884** 'Mark Twain' *Huck. Finn* xxvii, The king whirls on me and rips out: 'None o' your business!' **1916** S. E. White *Bobby Orde* xii, 'What's this?' asked Mr. Kincaid's quiet voice. The man whirled about.

3. *trans.* To cause to rotate or revolve, esp. swiftly or forcibly; to move (something) around an axis, or in a circle or the like: with various shades of meaning: to turn (a wheel, etc.), †twirl (a light object held in the hand), †roll (the eyes), flourish or swing round (a weapon, sling, etc.); *spec.* in *Fencing* (see quot. 1771).

? *a* **1400** *Morte Arth.* 3261 A-bowte cho whirllide a whele with hir whitte hondez. *c* **1440** *Promp. Parv.* 525/1 Whyrlyn, as spynners wythe the whele. **1579** Rice *Invect. Vices* C iv, Seruantes lacke worke, and stande whirlyng their knife aboute their fingers. **1614** Gorges *Lucan* IX. 404 We crosse the Axle of the world, And with the sphere about are whorled. *a* **1633** G. Herbert *Jacula Prudentum* (1640) 717 To whirle the eyes too much shewes a Kites braine. **1697** Dryden *Æneis* IX. 905 They whirl their Slings around. **1771** Lonnergan *Fencer's Guide* Index, *Whirling*, is to whirl your adversary's blade about to the same parade again; that is, when you parry with a Half-circle, to whirl his blade round to a Tierce, and into a Half-circle again; or, you may whirl from one parade to another, as from a Quinte to a Quarte, ..&c. **1774** tr. *Helvetius' Child Nat.* lix. II. 308 Richard blushed through stupidity, and, whirling his hat, said he would please me. **1807** Crabbe *Par. Reg.* II. 489 One with whom oft he whirled the bounding flail. **1823** J. Wilson *Marg. Lyndsay* xix. 148 Widow Alison.. was.. whirling down a yard of twine from the roller, to tie a two-pound parcel of brown-sugar. **1830** Herschel *Study Nat. Phil.* II. vi. (1851) 149 A stone whirled round in a sling. **1835** Dickens *Sk. Boz, Greenwich Fair*, The gentlemen.. go down the middle and up again,.. and whirl their partners round.

†**b.** To twist or twine around something. *Obs.*

1676 Cotton *Angler* II. vii. 64 The dubbing of a Bears dun whirl'd upon yellow silk.

4. *intr.* To move along swiftly on or as if on wheels; to travel fast in a wheeled vehicle; *gen.* to go swiftly or impetuously, rush or sweep along.

13.. *E.E. Allit. P.* B. 475 Ho [*sc.* the dove] wyrle[d] out on þe weder on wyngez ful scharpe. **13..** *Gaw. & Gr. Knt.* 2222 Whyrlande out of a wro, wyth a felle weppen. *c* **1400** *Laud Troy Bk.* 13457 To Menelaus Troylus whirled. *a* **1547** Surrey *Æneis* IV. 563 Whither whirles he? **1553** *Douglas's Æneis* XII. xiii. 158 The schaft thrawin, that quhirllis [*v.r.* quhirris] throw the skye. **1581** A. Hall *Iliad* x. 177 The Lyons.. downe whirling from the rocke,.. for to assault the sheepe. **1588** Shaks. *Tit. A.* v. ii. 49 Ile come and be thy Waggoner, And whirle along with thee about the Globes. **1697** Dryden *Æneis* IX. 956 A knotted Lance,.. Which roar'd like Thunder as it whirl'd along. *a* **1716** South *Serm.* (1727) VI. 216 But the Report of it shall whirl and rattle over a whole Nation. **1722** E. Ward *Wand. Spy* II. 47 A Hackney Chaise came whirling by. **1816** Scott *Antiq.* xx, Wha suld come whirling there in a post-chaise, but Monkbarns. **1859** Kingsley *Misc.* II. v. 230 Travellers.. within an hour's run of the greatest metropolis in the world, whirling through miles of desert. **1877** Black *Green Past.* iii, The beautiful landscapes through which the train whirled. **1879** E. O'Donovan *Merv Oasis* xxiv. (1882) I. 415 Turcoman cavalry whirling down in their usual loose order.

†**b.** *trans.* To go swiftly about or around (a place). *Obs. rare*⁻¹.

1649 G. Daniel *Trinarch., Hen. V*, cccxc, While he lay Full at the Seige, the Dolphin whirles the Coast.

5. *trans.* To drive (a wheeled vehicle), or convey in a wheeled vehicle, swiftly; *gen.* to drive, impel, carry, or urge along impetuously, as a strong wind or stream (often and now only with implication of circular movement, as in 7).

c **1386** Chaucer *Squire's T.* 663 Appollo whirleth vp his Chaar so hye. *c* **1400** *Rom. Rose* 4362 She [*sc.* Fortune] canne .. whirle adown, and ouer turne Who sittith hieghst. **1513** Douglas *Æneis* XII. Prol. 30 So fast Phaeton wyth the quhip him quhirlys. **1616** S. S. *Honest Lawyer* II. D 4 b, A Coach, And prauncing Coursers, that shall whirle thee through The popular streetes. **1725** Ramsay *Gentle Sheph.* IV. i, Frae his Pouch he whirled forth a Book. **1781** Cowper *Retirem.* 393 He steps into the welcome chaise.. behind four handsome bays, That whirl away from business and debate The disincumber'd Atlas of the state. **1835** Lytton *Rienzi* I. iii, In popular commotions, each man is whirled along with the herd. **1848** Dickens *Dombey* xx, The.. speed at which the train was whirled along. **1850** Tennyson *In Mem.* xv. 3 The winds begin to rise..; The last red leaf is whirl'd away. **1854** G. W. Curtis *Potiphar Papers* iv. (1866) 126 He whirled her off into the dance. **1873** Black *Pr. Thule* ii, The gallant little horses that whirled them.. into the open country. **1879** Froude *Cæsar* xxiii. 398 He had been as a leaf whirled upon a winter torrent. **1907** J. H. Patterson *Man-Eaters of Tsavo* x. 111 The river.. becoming a raging.. torrent, tearing up trees by the roots and whirling them along like straws.

b. *fig.*

1578 Whetstone *Promos & Cass.* II. iv. ii, Such dunghyll churles, Such newes, as is in market tounes, about the country whorles. **1656** Earl Monm. tr. *Boccalini's Advts. fr. Parnass.* I. lxxxvi. (1674) 114 The.. fetches, by which unhappy mankind.. is.. with such publick calamity whirld about. **1837** Hallam *Lit. Eur.* II. vi. §46 Juliet is a child, whose intoxication in loving and being loved whirls away the little reason she may have possessed.

6. To throw or cast with violence, fling, hurl (esp. with rotatory movement, as from a sling). Also *absol.*

Formerly app. sometimes used by confusion for *hurl* (cf. *per contra* hurlpit, -pool, -wind).

c **1440** *Wyclif's Bible* 1 Sam. xvii. 49 (MS. Bodl. 277) Dauid.. took o stoon, and he castide [*v.r.* whirlide] with the slynge. **1542** Udall *Erasm. Apoph.* 79 b, He taught theim.. to whurle with a slyng, and to.. cast a darte. *Ibid.* 138 b, A .. boye.. was whurleyng litle stones emong the thickest of yᵉ people. **1563** P. Whitehorne *Onosandro Platon.* 78 Molested of the weapons whorlde from farre of. **1579–80** North *Plutarch, Crassus* (1595) 611 Who gallowping vp and down the plaine, whirled vp the sand hils from the bottome with their horse feete. **1591** Sylvester *Du Bartas* I. vi. 795 The boistrous Winde, that.. proudest Turrets to the ground hath whurld. **1682** Bunyan *Holy War* 104 Twelve slings, to whirle stones withal. **1718** Pope *Iliad* XVI. 585 Sarpedon whirl'd his weighty Lance. **1742** Gray *Eton* 72 Whirl the wretch from high.

†**b.** *Gaming.* To cast (the dice). Also *absol.*

1579 Rice *Invect. Vices* E ij, Ye plaie naughteilye, whorle, take vp, the tricke is mine, shamfully caste. **1772** Foote *Nabob* II. (1778) 26 When you want to throw off six and four, .. you must.. whirl the dice to the end of the table. *Ibid.* 27, I shall be able to tap, stamp, dribble, and whirl, with any man in the club.

7. *intr.* To be affected with giddiness, to reel: usually (now only) of the head or brain.

1561 Hollybush *Hom. Apoth.* 5 b, Many are whom the heade whyrleth so sore yᵗ he thinketh the earth turneth vpsyde-doune. *Ibid.* 42 A.. feuer.. wherewith men do whyrle and be dismade. **1820** Shelley *Witch Atl.* v, The dim brain whirls dizzy with delight. **1880** 'Ouida' *Moths* vi, You make my head whirl.

b. *trans.* To affect with giddiness; to put in a whirl or tumult. ? *Obs.*

1593 Q. Eliz. *Boeth.* IV. met. v. 90 Hydden causes whyrls yᵉ mynd. **1606** Shaks. *Tr. & Cr.* III. ii. 19, I am giddy: expectation whirles me round. **1685** F. Spence tr. *Varillas' Ho. Medicis* 456 If he had not been whirl'd with a crotchet to buy a house. *a* **1769** Falconer *Shipwr.* III. 627 Nor let this total ruin whirl my brain! **1829** Good *Study Med.* (ed. 3) IV. 540 Precipices, the sight of which has whirled all his brains while awake.

whirl(e, obs. var. harl *sb.*¹, herl.

1676 Cotton *Angler* II. vii. 64 A flie call'd the Peacock-flie; the body made of a whirl of a Peacocks feather.

whirl-, the sb. or vb.-stem in Combination: **whirl-brain**, a giddy-brained person (cf. G. *wirbelgeist* scatter-brain); †**whirl-crowned** *a.*, giddy-brained; †**whirl-fire**, a poetic or rhetorical name for lightning (? as associated with violent storms or whirlwinds); †**whirl-gate**, a turnstile; **whirl-hook**, in *Rope-making*, each of the hooks of a 'whirl' (see whirl *sb.* 1 c); †**whirl-jack** = whirligig 1 (*c*); †**whirl-mint**, ? = whorled water-mint; **whirl-pillar, -spout**, a rotating column of water or dust, a waterspout or dust-whirl; **whirl-shaped** *a.*, whorled; †**whirl-snail**, †**whirl-stone** (see quots.); †**whirl-whale**, some kind of whale (cf. whirl-about 1, whirlpool¹); **whirl-wheel** (tr. Fr. *rouet volant*), a kind of water-wheel (see quot.).

1817 Coleridge *Biog. Lit.* I. x. 179 He is a *whirl-brain that talks whatever comes uppermost. **1648** N. Ward *Petit. Eastern Assoc.* 20 Many *whirl-crown'd, and bragg-braind Opinionists. **1605** Sylvester *Du Bartas* II. iii. *Law* 1011 The smoaking storms, the *whirl-fire's crackling clash. *c* **1620** Z. Boyd *Zion's Flowers* (1855) 104 The whirle fire shall flash. **1550** *Ludlow Churchw. Acc.* (Camden) 44 The *whirle yate anont the college dore. **1797** *Encycl. Brit.* (ed. 3) XVI. 483/2 This second spinner attaches his own hemp to the *whirl hook. **1653** Urquhart *Rabelais* I. xi. 57 That he [*sc.* Gargantua] might play.. after the manner of the other little children.., they made him a faire weather *whirljack [1694 whirle-gig], of the wings of the windmill. *c* **1710** Petiver *Cat. Ray's Eng. Herbal* Tab. xxxi, Water *Whirl-mint. Cross Whirl-mint. *c* **1850** *Rudim. Navig.* (Weale) 83 In some parts of the ocean the water-spout or *whirl-pillar is occasionally met with. **1761** *Phil. Trans.* LII. 359 Each series is of equal length, and placed in a wheel or *whirl-shaped form like the equisetum or horse-tail plant. **1681** Grew *Musæum* I. vi. i. 132 The *Whirle-Snail. *Turbocochlea.* **1737** [S. Berington] *G. di Lucca's Mem.* (1738) 93 We saw.. Ten Thousand little *Whirl-spouts of Sand. **1681** Grew *Musæum* III. i. i. 262 The Short *Whirle-Stone. *Trochites.* **1605** Sylvester *Du Bartas* II. iii. *Law* 732 Another, swallowed in a *Whirl-Whale's womb, Is laid a-live within a living Toomb. **1853** Glynn *Treat. Power Water* 37 An elaborate series of experiments and an excellent report on the useful effect of the ordinary horizontal water-wheel at present used in France. Those on which the experiments were made are at Toulouse... These wheels are of two kinds: those situate on the rivers are called bucket-wheels (*à cuve*)..; those which are placed on the canal are called *whirl-wheels (*rouets volants*),.. and are turned by the percussion of the water upon curved floats.

'whirl-about.

†**1.** A name for some kind of whale: cf. *whirl-whale* (whirl- in Comb.), whirlpool¹. *rare*⁻¹.

1591 Sylvester *Du Bartas* I. v. 98 The monstrous Whirl-about [F. *l'énorme Senedete*], Which in the Sea another Sea doth spout.

2. The action of whirling about; something that whirls about, or is in a whirl; *attrib.* or *adj.* characterized by whirling about.

1786 C. Morris *Songs* (1788) 8 While thro' this whirl-about journey [*sc.* life] we reel. **1857** Palgrave *Norm. & Eng.* II. 30 There is such a whirlabout amongst the parties in these transactions, always changing sides. **1863** Kingsley *Water-Bab.* vii, His little whirl-about of a head.

whirlary: see whirlery.

†**'whirlbat, 'whorlbat.** *Obs.* Forms: α. 6–7 **whorle-**, 7 **whoorl-**, 7–8 **whorlbat**. β. 7–8 **whirl(e)bat**. [Alteration of hurlbat by substitution of whirl for the first syllable.]

1. Used in the 16th and 17th c. to render L. *cæstus*, which was defined as 'a weapon with plummettes of leade, vsed in games for exercise' (Cooper's *Thesaurus*) and 'a certain game.. among the ancients, wherein they whirled leaden plummets at one another' (Phillips, 1658); also in renderings of Gr. πύξ.

α. **1565** Cooper *Thesaurus* s.v. *Cæstus*, *Bellare cæstu*, to play as it were at the whorle bat. **1574** *Withals' Dict.* 51/2 *Cæstus*, an whorle batte, an instrument of leather couered with leade, to buffet one another. **1601** Holland *Pliny* XI. xxxvii. I. 331 All the sort of Rams he armed with crooked hornes,.. as if they were gantlets or whorlebats [*cæstus*], given them by Nature to thumpe and jurre withall. *c* **1611** Chapman *Iliad* XXIII. 538 Your shoulders must not vndergo the churlish whoorlbats fall [οὐ γὰρ πύξ γε μαχήσεαι]. **1614** Raleigh *Hist. World* II. xiii. §6 He.. compelled all strangers to fight with him, at whorlebattes. **1656** Cowley *Pindar. Odes, Praise of Pindar* Note 3, The Cestus, or Whorle-bats. **1697** Dryden *Virg. Georg.* III. 30 The Whorlbat, and the rapid Race, shall be Reserv'd for Cæsar.

β. **1615** Chapman *Odyss.* VIII. 285 At wrestling, buffets, whirlbat, speed of race [ἢ πὺξ ἠὲ πάλῃ ἢ καὶ ποσίν]. *Ibid.* XI. 406 Pollux, that exceld, in whirlbat fight [πὺξ ἀγαθὸν Πολυδεύκεα]. **1617** Minsheu *Ductor* 371 A Plummet, or whirle-bat, that vaulters, leapers, and dauncers vse. **1650** Horn & Rob. *Gate Lang. Unl., Foundation* C. §3 Slain by thee with the whirlbat [*a te cestu cæsum*]. **1685** Cotton tr. *Montaigne* I. xxii. (1711) I. 130 Fencers, inur'd to beating, when bang'd almost to Pulp with Clubs and Whirl-bats [tr. Cicero *pugiles cæstibus contusi*]. **1700** Dryden *Fables* Pref. *D 2, He rejected them as Dares did the Whirl-bats of Eryx.

2. A club.

1791 Cowper *Iliad* VII. 167 Where him his iron whirl-bat [κορύνῃ] nought avail'd.

'whirl-blast. [f. whirl- + blast *sb.*¹; app. a word of the Cumberland dialect, for which Wordsworth is the earliest literary authority.] A whirlwind, hurricane. Also *fig.*

1798 Wordsw. *Poems of Fancy* iii, A whirl-blast from behind the hill Rushed o'er the wood. **1807** Stagg *Misc. Poems, Return* xvi, Hark, the whurlblast loudly blusters. **1813** Coleridge *Nt.-Scene* 77 The whirl-blast comes, the desert-sands rise up. **1820** Shelley *Witch Atl.* xlviii, Which rain could never bend, or whirl-blast shake. **1851** Mayne Reid *Scalp Hunters* xi, Vast towers of sand, borne up by the whirlblast, rise vertically. **1904** Dowden *Browning* 246 There is a fixity of grief which is more appalling than this whirlblast.

whirl-bone ('hwɜːlbəʊn). *Obs.* or *dial.* Forms: 4–8 **whirlebone**, 5 **whirle-, wherle-, whyrlebon, wherl-, werel-, qwhirl-, qworle-, qvyrlebone**, 5–6 **whyrl-, whorlebone**, 5–7 **whyrlebone**, 6 **whurle bone**, (7 **whall-bone**), 8 **hurle bone**, *dial.* **whirly booan**, 9 *Sc.* **whorle-bane**, 6– **whirlbone**. (Also with hyphen, or as two words.) [Replacing OE. *hweorf-*, *hwyrfbán*, *hwe(o)rbán* knee-cap, by substitution of whirl for the first element; cf. MLG. *wervel(bên)*, G. *wirbelbein* vertebra.]

1. The round head of a bone turning in the socket of another bone; *spec.* that of the thigh-bone at the hip-joint (in later use esp. in the horse).

1398 Trevisa *Barth. De P.R.* v. xxvii. (Bodl. MS.), þei [*sc.* bones of the arms] beþ ykeuered with ioyntes whirlebones and grustel bones. [Mistranslation; *ed.* **1582** They are covered in joynts and whirlbones with gristles; L. *in iuncturis et vertebris cartillagine vestiuntur*.] *c* **1440** *Promp. Parv.* 421/1 Qvyrlylebone, yn a ioynt, *ancha*. *Ibid.* 524/2 Whyrlebone, or hole of a ioynt (*S.* whylbone), *anca, vertebrum, vertibulum, condulus*. **1548–77** VICARY *Anat.* ix. (1888) 75 Ech of these two bones..hath a great rounde hole, into the whiche is receyued the bone called *Vertebra*, or The whorle bone. *Ibid.* x. 84 *Vertebrum*, or Whurle bone,..and is receyued into the boxe or hole of the hanche bone. **1685** *Lond. Gaz.* No. 2046/4 A Black brown Gelding..a Strain in his Whirlebone. **1728** CHAMBERS *Cycl.*, *Hurle Bone*, in an Horse, is a Bone near the Middle of the Buttocks very apt to go out of its Sockets with a Slip or Strain. **1753** J. BARTLET *Gentl. Farriery* xxix. (1754) 240 A lameness in the whirle bone and hip, is discovered by the horse's dragging his leg after him. **1814** J. WHITE *Vet. Med.* (ed. 2) III. 192 Injury of the Hip Joint, commonly called Whirl, or Hurdle Bone, or Round Bone. **1825** JAMIESON, *Whorle-bane*, the hip-bone or joint, Fife.

2. The round bone of the knee; the knee-pan, patella.

14.. *Voc.* in Wr.-Wülcker 590/19 *Internodium*,..the knepanne, or wherlebon. **1530** PALSGR. 288/1 Whyrlbone of ones kne, *pallette de genouil*. **1587** HARRISON *England* I. v. 11 in *Holinshed*, When the bodie of Aiax was found, the whirlebone of his knee was adiudged so broad as a pretie dish. **1611** COTGR., *La charniere des genoux*, the whall-bone, or whirle-bone, of the knees. **1634** T. JOHNSON tr. *Parey's Chirurg.* xv. xxii. (1678) 340 The Patella, or Whirl-bone of the Knee..is oft-times contused. *c* **1746** J. COLLIER (Tim Bobbin) *View Lanc. Dial.* Wks. (1862) 52 He geete fro his Whirly booans, and sed..while his Heart beeots an his Blood sarclates there's Hopes. **1828** *Craven Gloss.*, *Whirlbaan*, the cap of the knee.

†**3.** A vertebra of the spine. *Obs.*

c **1400** *Lanfranc's Cirurg.* 3 Cap. vj. of woundis of þe rigboon & of whirlebones [*v.r.* whirle bonys] of þe rigge. *Ibid.* 104 Make smale cauteries..bitwene ech whirlebon of þe necke. **1668** CULPEPPER & COLE *Barthol. Anat.* Man. IV. xiv. 349 Five Vertebræ or Whirle-bones of the Spina.

whirled (hwɜːld), *a.*

1. [f. WHIRL *sb.* + -ED[2]. Cf. OE. *hwyrfled* round.] = WHORLED.

1715 *Phil. Trans.* XXIX. 307 Shells, whirled and single. **1796** WITHERING *Brit. Plants* (ed. 3) 823 Leaves expanding, a little bowed back at the ends; somewhat whirled. **1851** WOODWARD *Mollusca* 163 H[elix] epistylium, Pl. XII. fig. 7. Imperforate, globosely conoid, close-whirled, aperture lamellate within, lip sharp.

2. [f. WHIRL *v.* + -ED[1].] Rotated rapidly, etc.

1875 FARRAR *Silence & Voices* iv. 76 Could we..judge rightly of the..sun..if we only saw it glaring luridly through the whirled sands of the desert? **1895** MEREDITH *Amaz. Marr.* xlv, Lord Fleetwood's yet undocked old associates vowed he 'smelt strong' of the fumes of the whirled silver censer-balls.

whirler (ˈhwɜːlə(r)). [f. WHIRL *v.* + -ER[1].]

I. A person who whirls.

1. One who turns or spins rapidly round; †one who wanders about (*obs.*); a 'whirling' dervish.

c **1440** *Promp. Parv.* 524/2 Whyrlare a-bowte, or goare a-bowte in ydylnesse..; *girovagus*. **1815** *Tweddell's Rem.* 229 *plate*, Dervish of the Order of Whirlers. **1832** LD. JEFFREY *Let. to Mrs. Rutherfurd* 1 Apr., The only chance is for one pair to cling close, like waltzers, and whirl lovingly among the whirlers. *a* **1843** SOUTHEY *Comm.-pl. Bk.* Ser. III. (1850) 391/1 Sect of dancers and whirlers. **1873** LELAND *Egypt. Sketch-Bk.* 101 He promenaded around the performers, and taking his place in the ring began to spin—for there were during the entire performance one or two whirlers at work.

2. One who whirls something; †one who hurls or flings something, a hurler (*obs.*); one who turns a wheel or other revolving piece of mechanism.

1563 P. WHITEHORNE *Onosandro Platon.* 74 The whorlers of darts. **1825** J. NICHOLSON *Oper. Mech.* 466 For wash-bowls, dishes, or plates, the workman, called the whirler, uses a vertical spindle. **1889** LIPSCOMB in *Land Agent's Rec.* 6 Apr. 316 When flails were whirling for six months..in the tithe barns, while the whirlers and their families ate barley bread.

II. A thing that whirls.

†**3.** ? A whirlwind. *Obs. rare*[−1].

1606 SYLVESTER *Du Bartas* II. iv. *Magnificence* 396 What boystrous lungs the roaring whirlers blown: What burning wings the Lightning rides upon.

4. A revolving piece of mechanism.

spec. **a.** A potter's whirling-table. **b.** An apparatus invented by Troughton to serve as an artificial horizon at sea, consisting of a rapidly rotating top with a mirror attached: also called *Troughton's top*. **c.** A device by which the strands are twisted together in spinning; in *Rope-making*, each of the rotating hooks by which the hemp or other fibre is twisted into yarn.

1860 W. WHITE *Wrekin* xxxi. 377 A revolving pedestal or 'whirler', on which the article to be ornamented is placed. **1867** SMYTH *Sailor's Word-bk.*, Whirler, or Troughton's Top. **1875** KNIGHT *Dict. Mech.* **1884** *Girl's Own Paper* Nov. 4/3 The females busy with a bunch of camel's hair and a 'whirler', making..the coarse..thread with which much of their rough sewing is done. **1898** BINNS *Story of Potter* 198 The wheel..at which he [*sc.* potter] stands is called, when revolved by some other power than himself, a 'jigger'; that which he turns with his own hand..is a 'whirler'. **1918** *Pall Mall Gaz.* 29 June 8/5 Lithographic plate whirler.

†ˈ**whirlery.** *Obs. rare.* Also 6 -ary. [f. WHIRL *v.* + -ERY.] Whirling, circling flight (or ? roaring noise: cf. WHURL *v.*). In first quot. as part of a jingling refrain.

c **1560** *Doctour Doubble Ale* 436 in Hazl. *E.P.P.* III. 321 Fare well and a dewe; With a whirlary whewe, And a tirlary typpe. **1582** STANYHURST *Æneis* III. (Arb.) 77 With gagling whirlerye flapping Theyr wings.

whirley, var. HURLY[2], influenced by WHIRL.

1886 J. BARROWMAN *Sc. Mining Terms* 72 *Whirley*, a hutch, hurley, or tub. **1886** HODDER *Life 7th Earl Shaftesb.* I. x. 413 A little child,..whose duty it was, on hearing the approach of a whirley, or coal-carriage, to pull open the door.

whirley: see WHIRLY.

ˈ**whirlicote.** *Obs.* exc. *Hist.* Forms: 5 whirlecole, whirlecote, wherlecote, 6 wherli-, whirlicote, 8–9 whirlicot. [Form doubtful; app. orig. *whirlecole*, f. WHIRL *v.* + an unidentified element; recorded by Stow in the form *whirlicote*, whence in later use.] A coach, carriage.

c **1381** *Anominalle Cron.* (MS. Stowe 1047) lf. 68 b, Le roy mesmes vient al mile ende et ouecque luy sa meir en vn whirlecole. *c* **1450** *Brut* II. 386 þe Lorde Powys meyne brouȝt hym out of Walis to London yn a whirlecole [*sic MSS. Camb. and Reg.*; *MS. B. Mus. Add.* whirlecote; *ed. Caxton* (1480) wherlecote]. **1598** STOW *Surv.* 65 Of old time coatches were not knowne in this Island, but chariots, or Whirlicotes..: I reade that Rychard the second being threatened by the rebelles of Kent, rode from the Tower of London to the Myles end, and with him his mother in a Wherlicote. *a* **1800** PEGGE *Curialia Misc.* (1818) 270. **1860** *Our Engl. Home* 75 The wheels of my lady's whirlicot or the franklin's plough were repaired in the kitchen. **1888** FREEMAN in Stephens *Life & Lett.* (1895) II. x. 385, I can't do much walking, but I go about in a whirli-cot. Is not that the oldest name for a coach or landau?

whirligig (ˈhwɜːlɪgɪg), *sb.* Forms: 5 whyrlegyge, (whirlegogge), 5–7 whirlegigg, 6 whirlygigge, whyrlegygge, worlegyg(g, 6–7 whirligigg, 6–8 whirlegig, 7 whirlegigg(e, whirligig(g)e, whirliegig, 7–8 whirly(-)gig, (8 whirlagig, 9 whirlgig), 6– whirligig. [orig. (and still to some extent dial.) two words, f. WHIRL- and WHIRLY- + GIG *sb.*[1]]

1. a. Name of various toys that are whirled, twirled, or spun round; *spec.* †(*a*) a top or teetotum (cf. GIG *sb.*[1] 1); (*b*) a toy consisting of a small spindle turned by means of a string; (*c*) a toy with four arms like miniature windmill-sails, which whirl round when it is moved through the air.

c **1440** *Promp. Parv.* 525/1 Whyrlegyge, chyldys game, *giraculum*. **1530** PALSGR. 288/2 Whirlygigge to play with, *pyrouette*. **1591** SYLVESTER *Du Bartas* I. iii. 191 As a turning Whirli-gig goes round [Fr. *Comme la pirouette animee se tourne*]. **1659** MOXON *Tutor Astron.* v. 148 The Gnomon must appear on both sides like the stick in a Whirli-gig, which children use. **1686** BLOME *Gentl. Recr.* II. 148 Pulling the Line you may make the Looking-Glass play in and out as Children do a Whirlegig... Keep it turning that the twinkling of the Glass against the Sun may provoke the Larks to come to view it. **1687** A. LOVELL tr. *Thevenot's Trav.* III. 43 The Pummel [of the sword]..is neither Round nor Oval, but is flat above and below like a Whirligigg. **1728** POPE *Dunc.* III. 57 As..whirligigs, twirl'd round by skilful swain, Suck the thread in, then yield it out again. **1801** STRUTT *Sports & Past.* IV. iv. §6. 288 The peg-top..probably originated from the te-totums and whirligigs. **1811** *Sporting Mag.* XXXVIII. 220 They hold each other tight by the middle, and so go round like whirligigs. **1908** [ELIZ. FOWLER] *Betw. Trent & Ancholme* 77 A..figure of The Christ-Child playing with a 'Whirligig'.

b. *fig.* 'Plaything', 'sport'.

1624 BURTON *Anat. Mel.* III. ii. I. i. (ed. 2) 356 Thou art Cupids whirlegigge. *a* **1677** BARROW *Serm.* (1683) II. 12 Turning him into..a whirlegig of fate or chance.

2. Applied to various mechanical contrivances having a whirling or rotatory movement; *spec.* †(*a*) an instrument of punishment formerly used, consisting of a large cage suspended so as to turn on a pivot; (*b*) a roundabout or merry-go-round.

In quot. 1601 ? = GIG *sb.*[1] 2; in quot. 1623 ? allusively applied to a carriage; in quot. 1822 to a clock.

1477–8 in Swayne *Churchw. Acc. Sarum* (1896) 22 Pro vna pecia maeremii de nouo empto pro le Whirlegigg'. *Ibid.* 23 For a pece of Tymber to the Whirlegogge. **1554** in Sir W. Parker *Hist. Long Melford* (1873) 365 Payde to Newman for mending of Hall Myll Bridge, and makyng of a worlegyg, 22[d]. **1601** DEACON & WALKER *Spirits & Divels* 230 The silie poore birdes sit prying at, and playing with the whirligig. [Cf. quot. 1686 in 1.] **1617** J. TAYLOR (Water P.) *Three Weekes Observ.* E 2, It is hanged on a turning Gybbet, like a Crane:..It is bigge enough to hold two men, and..if any one or more doe rob gardens..he or they are put into this same whirligigge, or kickumbob, and the gybbet being turned, the offender hangs in this Cage..some 12 or 14 foot from the water,..and with a tricke..the bottome of the cage drops out, and the thiefe fals sodenly into the water. **1623** —— *World runs on Wheels* Wks. (1630) II. 238/2 The last Proclamations concerning the retiring of the Gentry out of the City into their Countries..how it cleered the Streetes of these way-stopping Whirligigges! **1788** GROSE *Milit. Antiq.* II. 204 One [punishment] formerly very common, for trifling offences,..was the whirligig;..a kind of circular wooden cage, which turn'd on a pivot; and..whirled round with such an amazing velocity, that the delinquent became extremely sick. **1816** E. WEETON *Let.* 22 May in *Jrnl. of Governess* (1969) II. 145 Large caravans enter the town with ..wooden horses, whirligigs, gambling tables, barrel organs. **1822** SCOTT *Nigel* v, Yonder hall-clock at Theobald's, and that other whirligig that you made for the Duke of Buckingham. **1839–41** LANE *Arab. Nts.* I. 71 In the outskirts of the cemeteries, swings and whirligigs are erected. **1853** LYTTON *My Novel* II. viii, One of those rotatory entertainments commonly seen in fairs, and known by the name of 'whirligigs' or 'roundabouts'.

3. a. *gen.* and *fig.*, in various applications: (*a*) Something that is continually whirling, or in constant movement or activity of any kind; †(*b*) a fantastic notion, a crotchet (*obs.*); (*c*) circling course, revolution (of time or events); (*d*) a lively or irregular proceeding, an antic; (*e*) a circling movement, or condition figured as such, a whirl.

1589 *Pasquil's Ret.* B iv b, Euery one that had a whirlegig in his braine, wold haue his own conceit to goe currant. **1599** NASHE *Lenten Stuffe* Wks. (Grosart) V. 237 *Quot capita tot sententiæ*, so many heades, so many whirlegigs. **1601** SHAKS. *Twel. N.* v. i. 385 And thus the whirlegigge of time brings in his reuenges. **1631** WEEVER *Anc. Funeral Mon.* 11 The heathen gods and goddesses, with all their whirligiggs. **1635** SHIRLEY *Coronation* III. (1640) E 2, *Phi.* Tis a strange turne. *Lisa.* The whirligigs of women. **1654** GAYTON *Pleas. Notes* III. ii. 73 His braines..being as vertiginous as a whirle-poole, presented ten thousand whirlygigs, Windmils, and Turne-pikes to his errantick soule. **1660** HEXHAM, *De Key Lotert hem*, he hath a Whirlegigg in his head. *a* **1670** HACKET *Abp. Williams* I. (1693) 181 The Whirly-Gig of the Dispensation, which run round from Pope to Pope, and never could be said to settle. **1704** PRIOR *Ladle* 6 Since They [*sc.* the gods] gave Things their Beginning; And set this Whirligig a Spinning. **1781** JOHNSON in *Boswell* 1 Apr., She is the first woman in the world, could she but restrain that wicked tongue of hers;..could she but command that little whirligig. **1796** MME. D'ARBLAY *Camilla* VII. xiii, You'll put my poor head quite into a whirligig. **1809** MALKIN *Gil Blas* VII. xvi. ¶2 This ridiculous baboon..got back again to his old tricks and whirligigs. **1862** HUXLEY in *Life* (1900) I. xv. 198, I was..glad to get your letter at that whirligig of an association meeting. **1874** SYMONDS *Sk. Italy & Greece* (1898) I. ix. 186 The whirligig of events restored Francesco Sforza to his duchy. **1897** MRS. RAYNER *Type-writer Girl* xviii, Water-beetles who dart and dance..in interlacing whirligigs. **1911** MARETT *Anthropol.* vii. 186 When the whirligig of social change brings the uneducated temporarily to the fore.

b. A fickle, inconstant, giddy, or flighty person (cf. GIG *sb.*[1] 4); also, one who turns round or moves about actively, as in a dance.

1602 DEKKER *Satirom.* L 3, No whirligig, one of his faithfull fighters. **1605** CHAPMAN *All Fooles* I. i. 281 To maintaine a wanton whirly-gig, Worth nothing more then she brings on her back. *a* **1704** T. BROWN tr. *Æneas Sylvius Lett.* lxxxii. Wks. 1709 III. II. 81 Woman is the Whirly-Gig of Nature; she changes so often and swiftly. **1711** BUDGELL *Spect.* No. 67 ¶9 An impudent young Dog..ran to his Partner [in a dance],..and whisked her round..; just as my Girl was going to be made a Whirligig, I ran in, seized on the Child, and carried her home. **1796** MME. D'ARBLAY *Camilla* II. iii, Knowing you to be such a merry little whirligig. **1822** T. MITCHELL *Com. Aristoph.* II. 317 Give way, and make room for their play,..We'll sit here..and mark how these whirligigs whisk it!

4. A water-beetle of the family *Gyrinidæ*, esp. the common species *Gyrinus natator*, found in large numbers circling rapidly over the surface of the water in ponds and ditches. Also ***whirligig beetle***.

1713 PETIVER *Aquat. Anim. Amboinæ* Tab. iv, *Trochus Pyramidalis Indicus*..Indian Whirligig. **1855** *Poultry Chron.* III. 378 The Gyrinidæ, or whirligig beetles. **1874** WOOD *Insects Abr.* 69 The Gyrinidæ, or Whirligig Beetles, of foreign countries..being scarcely larger than our familiar British species. **1877** F. P. PASCOE *Zool. Classif.* 110 Gyrinus (Whirlgig).

5. *advb.* Like a whirligig; with rapid circling movement.

1598 E. GUILPIN *Skial.* (1878) 51 His head..Wherein ten thousand thoughts runne whirligigge. **1828** SCOTT *Jrnl.* 16 June, To dress my sails to every wind;..and spin round, whirligig.

6. *attrib.* Resembling a whirligig; characterized by a whirling movement (*lit.* and *fig.*). See also 4.

1582 STANYHURST *Æneis* IV. (Arb.) 120 With whirlygig eyesight Vp to the sky staring. **1614** PURCHAS *Pilgrimage* III. xiii. (ed. 2) 307 Continuing their whirlegigg-deuotions with continuall turnings (fitly agreeing to so giddie and brainsicke a Religion). **1688** HOLME *Armoury* IV. xiii. (Roxb.) 521/2 The memory of the heathen gods and Godesses, with all their whirligig fancies. **1807** W. IRVING *Salmag.* No. 13 (1811) II. 74 That intoxicating, inflammatory, and whirligig dance, the waltz. **1816** SCOTT *Antiq.* xiii, The changes of this trumpery whirligig world. **1840** HOOD *Kilmansegg, Fancy Ball* xxx, She finished off with a whirligig bout. **1879** *Punch* 31 May 256 The whirligig whims of the moment.

Hence ˈ**whirligig** *v.*, *intr.* (also with *it*), to turn like a whirligig, to whirl or spin round (whence **whirligigging** *ppl. a.*).

1598 E. GUILPIN *Skial.* (1878) 35 This mad-cap world, this whirlygigging age. **1687** A. LOVELL *Bergerac's Com. Hist.* 57 These..have been constrained to whirlegig it. **1840** HOOD *Up Rhine* 188 Half a score of bouncing girls, ballad singing, and whirligigging. **1872** 'ALIPH CHEEM' (Yeldham) *Lays of Ind* (1876) 6 The dancers..postured, bobbed, whirligigged, wriggled.

whirligoround: see WHIRLY-.

whirling (ˈhwɜːlɪŋ), *vbl. sb.* [f. WHIRL *v.* + -ING[1].] The action of the verb WHIRL.

1. A turning (swiftly) round; (rapid) rotation, revolution, or circling movement: *spec.* of air or water, as in a whirlwind or eddy; also of persons in a dance, etc.

spec. in *Mech.* (quot. 1894): see WHIRL *v.* 2.

c **1398** CHAUCER *Fortune* 11 So mochel hath yit thy whirlynge vp and down I-tawht me. **1423** JAS. I *Kingis Q.* clxv, Sum were slungin, Be quhirlyng of the quhele, vnto the ground. **1496** *Bk. St. Albans, Fishing* h v, Yf that there be a manere whyrlynge of water. **1582** Bentley *Mon. Matrones* II. 3 This the same vnknowne gift or whurling in my hart, doth bring mee a new desire. **1616** Holyday *Persius, Sat.* v. 138 A base horse-keeper.. whom if's Master turne about, I' th' moment of the Whirling he goes out. **1633** T. James *Voy.* 9 We came amongst the most strangest whirlings of the sea. **1636** in *Ann. Dubrensia* (1877) 7 The countrie Wakes, and whirlings have appeer'd.. like forraine pastimes. **1699** Dampier *Voy.* II. I. 170 The Sholes probably caused some whirling about of the Tide. **1825** T. Hook *Sayings* Ser. II. *Passion & Princ.* vii. III. 89 The rapid, and as he thought perilous, whirling of the.. vehicle. **1835** Hood *United Family* ix, We none of us that whirling [*sc.* the waltz] love, Which both our parents disapprove. **1838** Hawthorne *Amer. Note-bks.* (1868) I. 187 Where the whirlings of the stream had left the marks of its eddies in the solid marble. **1894** *Phil. Trans.* CLXXXV. I. 279 The Whirling and Vibration of Shafts.

2. Giddiness, vertigo.

1561 Hollybush *Hom. Apoth.* 42 The same driueth away .. the whirling in the head. **1892** Meredith *Poems, Empty Purse* 107 A whirling seized thy head.

3. Hurling, flinging.

1579 Rice *Invect. Vices* B iij, The whorlyng of the Pottes about the house, the Cardes into the fire.

¶ Misused for hurling *vbl. sb.* 2 a.

a **1721** Prior *Ess. Opin.* Wks. 1907 II. 201 Bodmin or Truro shal break more Bones at a Whirling in Cornwal than the ablest Surgeon in London shal be able to set.

4. *attrib.* and *Comb.*, as ***whirling speed***; **whirling disease**, a disease of trout caused by the parasitic sporozoan *Myxosoma cerebralis*, which affects the balance of the fish it attacks.

1961 J. I. Lengy et al. tr. A. V. Uspenskaya in G. P. Petrusheveski *Parasites & Dis. Fish* 47 One of the most dangerous of the known parasitic diseases is the so-called 'whirling disease'. **1962** *Spec. Sci. Rep. U.S. Fish & Wildlife Service* No. 427. 2/2 Whirling disease appeared in brook trout at the Benner Spring Fish Research Station.. in 1956. **1982** *Times* 12 Feb. 4/5 Whirling disease.. is a parasite which gets into the skull of trout fry, causing a fish to lose its balance so that it swims round and round until it eventually dies. **1894** *Phil. Trans. R. Soc.* CLXXXV. 283 The whirling speed was taken to be at the commencement of whirl, that is to say, the lowest speed at which the shaft definitely whirled.

'whirling, *ppl. a.* [f. as prec. + -ING[2].] That whirls, in various senses of the verb; turning (rapidly) round, rotating, revolving, circling (swiftly); eddying; moving impetuously, etc.

1382 Wyclif *2 Peter* ii. 17 Cloudis..driuun with whirlinge wijndis. **1387** Trevisa *Higden* (Rolls) II. 51 Woodnesse of.. whirlynge water casteþ vp.. grete hepes of grauel. *c* **1450** *Mirk's Festial* 138 What by þondyr and by layte,.. by whyrlyng-wynde, by mystes. **1545** [see plat *sb.*[2] 7]. **1572** Bossewell *Armorie* II. 90 b, The blinde goddesse Fortune, with her doble visage, and whirlynge whele. **1581** Mulcaster *Positions* xix. (1888) 80 Children when they had their whirling gigges vnder the deuotion of their scourges. **1622** J. Taylor (Water P.) *Farew. Tower-Bottles* A 2 b, The whirling wheele of fickle Fate. **1630** Bp. Hall *Occas. Medit.* §13 That whirling Globe of earth. **1697** Dryden *Æneis* x. 1264 A whirling Dart he sent. **1762** Cowper *To Miss Macartney* 34 Some Alpine mountain.. Thus braves the whirling blast. **1839** Ure *Dict. Arts* 1296 The whirling public so blindly follows fashionable caprice in the choice of a carriage. **1872** Yeats *Techn. Hist. Comm.* 273 The whirling and complicated machinery. **1885** T. P. Hughes *Dict. Islam* 118/1 [The Maulawīyah] are called by Europeans.. the 'dancing', or 'whirling' darweshes.

b. *fig.*

1602 Shaks. *Ham.* I. v. 133 (Qo. 1) These are but wild and wherling [1623 hurling] words, my Lord. **1633** Bp. Hall *Occas. Medit.* §140 Those hurrying and whirling judgements of God. **1684** Creech *Odes Hor.* III. xxx, Nor whirling Time, nor flight of Years. **1853** Dickens *Bleak Ho.* xxxvi, I cannot say what was in my whirling thoughts. **1855** Milman in *Mem.* (1900) 189 Quiet, though in the midst of the whirling city.

c. Special collocations: **whirling blue, whirling dun**, names of artificial flies used in angling; **whirling-board** = *whirling-table* (*a*); **whirling chair**, a chair contrived to rotate rapidly, used in the treatment of insane patients; **whirling-machine** = *whirling-table* (*a*); **whirling plant**, the 'telegraph-plant', *Desmodium gyrans* (see telegraph *sb.* 8); **whirling-table**, (*a*) a machine consisting essentially of a table contrived to revolve rapidly, used for experiments or demonstrations in dynamics or other branches of science; (*b*) a horizontally rotating disk in a potter's lathe, carrying a mould which shapes the inside of a plate, cup, or other circular piece of ware, while the outside is shaped by a templet above it.

1747 Bowlker *Art Angling* 73 The little *Whirling Blue. .. This Fly is only to be Fish'd with.. in warm Weather. **1764** J. Ferguson *Lect.* ii. 19 Which weight.. will draw the ball from the edge of the *whirling-board to its center. **1799** Underwood *Dis. Childhood* (ed. 4) II. 50 Exciting vertigo by placing the patient in a *whirling chair. **1676** Cotton *Angler* II. vii. 61 About the twelfth of this Month [Apr.] comes in the Flie call'd the *whirling Dun. **1843** *Penny Cycl.* XXVII. 326/1 **Whirling-machine* is an apparatus.. for the purpose of determining the resistance of the air. **1866** *Treas. Bot.* 1232/1 *Whirling Plant, *Desmodium gyrans*. **1764** J. Ferguson *Lect.* ii. 18 The *whirling-table is a machine contrived for shewing experiments of this nature. **1830** Kater & Lardner *Mech.* viii. 100 An apparatus called a whirling table.. for the purpose of exhibiting illustrations of the laws of centrifugal force. **1840** *Penny Cycl.* XVIII. 473/1 The workman stands at a bench provided with a whirling-table.., which has its motion given by a horizontal pulley or jigger. **1879** Prescott *Sp. Telephone* 262 An attachment to the whirling-table for projecting sound-curves upon a screen.

Hence **'whirlingly** *adv.*, with whirling movement (also *fig.*).

1812 W. Tennant *Anster F.* II. lix, As they trip it whirlingly. **1902** S. E. White *Blazed Trail* viii, The forces of nature.. so whirlingly contemptuous of puny human effort.

† whirling-bone. *Obs.* = whirl-bone.

14.. *Voc. Lat.-Angl. in MS. Harl. 1002* (Varnhagen) 3/172 *Vertebra*, þe whyrlyngbone of the kne.

† 'whirlpit. *Obs.* [f. whirl- + pit *sb.*[1]] = whirlpool[2] 1.

1570 Foxe *A. & M.* (ed. 2) I. 94/2 [He] ranne into a whurlepyt, where he was drowned. **1599** B. Jonson *Ev. Man out of Hum.* II. iii. (1600) G, The deepest whirlepit of the rau'nous Seas. *a* **1632** T. Taylor *God's Judgem.* I. I. ix. (1642) 22 To escape the hands of his enemies, he ran into a whirlepit and his body was never found. **1724** De Foe *Tour Gt. Brit.* I. 92 As if the Water had at once ingulph'd itself in a Chasm of the Earth, or sunk in a Whirlpit.

fig. **1560** Becon *New Catech.* IV. Wks. 1564 I. 420 b, To throwe vs headlong into the whourlepytte of euerlasting dampnation. **1610** Holland *Camden's Brit.* I. 143 England recovered out of the whirlepit of calamities.

† 'whirlpool[1]. *Obs.* Also 6 **wherpole, w(h)orpoul**, etc. [app. an alteration, by popular etymology, of thirlepoll, q.v.] ? The large blowing whale.

c **1450** *Brut* II. 603 Ther wer sene in þe Temys at Londen, many whyrlepolys, & anoþer tyme a whale. **1508** Stanbridge *Vulgaria* (W. de W.) B j, *Balena*, a whyrlepole. **1541** in *Lincoln Chapter Acts* II. 49 (Linc. Rec. Soc. XII.), Sturgion, seale, porpoise, wherpole, and such like. **1558** Gesner *Hist. Anim.* IV. 853. **1601** Holland *Pliny* IX. iii. I. 235 The Whales and Whirlepooles called Balænæ. **1678** *Yng. Man's Call.* 301 At Quinborough three great dolphins were taken,.. and a while after three other fishes, called whirlpools were taken at Gravesend. **1694** Motteux *Rabelais* IV. xxxiii. 131 A huge monstrous Physetere, a sort of a Whale (which some call a Whirl pool).

whirlpool[2] ('hwɜːlpuːl). Also 6 **whirpole, whoorlpool**, etc. [f. whirl- + pool *sb.*[1] Cf. late OE. *hwyrfepól* and *wirfelmere*.]

1. a. A place in, or part of, a river or the sea, where the water is in constant (and usually rapid) circular movement, due to the configuration of the channel or bottom, to some obstruction, or to the meeting of adverse currents or wind and tide; a (large and violent) eddy or vortex.

1530 Palsgr. 288/1 Whirpole a depe place in a ryver, where the water tourneth rounde. **1555** Eden *Decades* (Arb.) 75 Many whorlepooles and shelfes. **1613** J. Saris *Voy. Japan* (Hakl. Soc.) 66 Drowned in a wherlpoole. **1642** Fuller *Holy & Prof. St.* II. xi. 94 A guilty conscience is like a whirlpool, drawing in all to it self which otherwise would passe by. **1774** Pennant *Tour Scot. in 1772*, 359 Eddies and whirlpools rising.. with furious boilings. **1815** Elphinstone *Acc. Caubul* (1842) I. 150 The river of Caubul .. forms numerous rapids and whirlpools. **1880** Geikie *Phys. Geog.* iii. 154 Where the tide is thrown from side to side against sunken rocks, or where two opposing currents meet.., the water forms whirlpools.

transf. **1674** N. Fairfax *Bulk & Selv.* 30 The whirl-pool of the spirits in the blood. **1799** W. Tooke *View Russ. Emp.* I. 65 Which.. buries both men and cattle in whirl-pools of snow and sand. **1903** Agnes M. Clerke *Probl. Astrophysics* 446 Those cosmic 'whirlpools', every trait of which testifies to the counterplay of multiple activities.

b. *fig.* in various applications: *esp.* a destructive or absorbing agency by which something is figured as engulfed or swallowed up; a scene of confused and turbulent activity.

1529 S. Fish *Supplic. Beggers* 10 Howe all the substaunce of your Realme.. rynneth hedlong ynto the insaciabill whyrlepole of these gredi goulafres. **1555** Eden *Decades* (Arb.) 63 Drowned in the whirlepoole of obliuion. **1571** Golding *Calvin on Ps.* lxix. 4 In ye deepest whoorlpools of aduersities, faith may hold vs vp. **1642** Milton *Apol. Smect.* x. Wks. 1851 III. 307 The non-resident.. Prelats, the gulphs and whirle pooles of benefices, but the dry pits of all sound doctrine. **1654** Whitlock *Zootomia* 419 In the middest of the Whirl-pooles of Change. *a* **1704** T. Brown *Walk round Lond., Coffee-Houses* (1709) 36 The Whirl-pool of Poetry suck'd me in, and I fell a Rhiming. **1831** James *Philip Aug.* xliii, What a whirlpool of contending feelings! **1863** Dickens *Uncomm. Trav.* xxii, You may revolve in a whirlpool of red shirts, shaggy beards [etc.]. **1888** Bryce *Amer. Commw.* xcvii. III. 362 Europeans.. have assumed.. that public life will draw.. enough of the highest ability into its whirlpool.

c. A bath or pool with underwater jets of hot, usu. aerated, water, used for purposes of physiotherapy or relaxation; also, a pumping unit for producing such jets. orig. *U.S.*

1975 *Sports Illustrated* Aug. 41 Sportswriters let you know they are on such intimate terms with an athlete that they can interview him in 'the whirlpool'. *Ibid.* 42/3 Last year Underwriters' Laboratories.. dropped its long-standing approval of portable whirlpools whose unit, motor and all, goes into the water. **1976** *Billings* (Montana) *Gaz.* 16 June 8-A/3 (Advt.), Relaxing, soothing whirlpool... Directional nozzle, aerator, timer, handle. **1978** *Detroit Free Press* 5 Mar. D17/2 (Advt.), Entertainment and dancing in the Wharf Lounge. Indoor pool, sauna, whirlpool, charming restaurants. **1980** D. Williams *Murder for Treasure* ix. 86 The heated indoor whirlpool.. measures twelve feet across. **1985** *Brit. Med. Jrnl.* 6 Apr. 1024/1 The whirlpool or Jacuzzi is a North American invention which has flourished there since the early 1970s but has only recently been introduced into Britain. Hot water is agitated mechanically through pressurised jets in a large tub and gives the bather a pleasurable sensation. Bathing in the company of others is usual.

2. *attrib.* and *Comb.*

1602 Marston *Antonio's Rev.* IV. ii, They have.. sunke the tossed galleasse in depth Of whirlepoole scorne. **1647** H. More *Song of Soul* IV. *Oracle* 34 Bitter wave of troubled flesh, And whirl-pool-turnings of the lower spright. **1664** Power *Exp. Philos.* III. 159 To recoyl by a double whirl-pool-motion. **1902** *Westm. Gaz.* 6 Mar. 6/2 The whirl-pool rapids [of the Niagara].

b. (In sense 1 c above.)

1950 *Life & Health* Oct. 8/2 Whirlpool baths have stimulating effects. **1972** 'E. Lathen' *Murder without Icing* (1973) xii. 113 It's more like a country club.. saunas and whirlpool baths, cocktail bars and singles nights. **1975** *Sports Illustrated* Aug. 42/2 Doctors generally agree on the salubrious effects of whirlpool therapy. **1978** *Official Gaz.* (U.S. Patent Office) 13 June TM 88/1 Jacuzzi Bros Inc., Little Rock, Ark... *Jacuzzi*... For hydro-therapy products .. therapeutic whirlpool baths and parts thereof. **1984** *Miami Herald* 6 Apr. 15D/5 (Advt.), Bayside pool, sundeck and whirlpool spa. **1984** *Listener* 19 July 17/4 (Advt.), For couples who want to get away together.. 4 poster beds, water beds—with whirlpool bath en suite.

Hence **'whirlpooling** *ppl. a.*, circling or eddying like a whirlpool.

a **1861** T. Winthrop *Life in Open Air* (1863) 48 A birch [canoe].. lies, light as a leaf, on whirlpooling surfaces.

'whirl-puff. *Obs.* exc. *dial.* (also **whirli-puff**). [f. whirl- + puff *sb.* after whirlwind.] A puff or gust of wind such as raises dust in a whirl or eddy; also †a whirlwind. Also *fig.*

1382 Wyclif *Wisd.* v. 24 As a whirle puff of wind. **1601** Holland *Pliny* II. xlviii. I. 24 A whirlepuffe or ghust called Typhon. **1609** —— *Amm. Marcell.* 41 Whiles some.. pestiferous whirle-puffe raiseth up still these miseries of common mischiefes in the State. **1637** Whiting *Albino & Bellama* 116 A shuffling whirle-puffe roar'd amongst the trees. **1640** G. Abbot *Job Paraphr.* 183 As the whirlepuft [*sic*] lifts up the dust. **1854** Miss Baker *Northampt. Gloss.*, *Whirli-puff*, a sudden gust of wind driving the dust into an eddy. **1899** Dickinson & Prevost *Cumbld. Gloss.*, *Whirl-puff*, a small whirl-wind such as will form dust spirals on a dusty road in summer.

† whirlwater. *Obs.* [f. whirl- + water *sb.*] A waterspout.

1626 in *Crt. & Times Chas. I.* (1848) I. 114, I hear of a whirlwater upon the Thames. *Ibid.*, The breaking.. of the whirlwater, or, as some call it, the water-pillar.

whirlwig ('hwɜːlwɪg). = whirligig 4.

1816 Kirby & Sp. *Entomol.* xvi. (1818) II. 4 The little beetles called whirlwigs (*Gyrinus*, L.),.. seem to.. form their assemblies.. to enjoy together.. the mazy dance. **1826** *Ibid.* xxix. III. 80 The whirlwig-beetle (*Gyrinus natator*). **1877** Wood *Nature's Teach., Nautical* ii. 22 The common Whirlwig-beetle.. may be found in nearly every puddle.

whirlwind ('hwɜːlwɪnd), *sb.* [f. whirl- + wind *sb.*, prob. after ON. *hvirfilvindr* (obs. Da. *hverrelwind*, Da. *hvirvelwind*, Sw. *virvelvind*), whence Du. *wervelwind*, G. *wirbelwind*.]

1. A whirling or rotating wind; an atmospheric eddy or vortex; a body of air moving rapidly in a circular or upward spiral course around a vertical or slightly inclined axis which has also a progressive motion over the surface of land or water.

In its larger forms it constitutes a violent and destructive storm, as a cyclone or tornado; over a body of water it sometimes causes a waterspout, over a sandy or dusty region a sand-pillar or dust-whirl.

a **1340** Hampole *Psalter* Cant. 511 Cumand as whirlwynd to skatire me. **1387** Trevisa *Higden* (Rolls) VII. 159 Sodenly a whirlewynd comynge caste doun the dores. *a* **1400** *Gloss.* in *Rel. Ant.* I. 6/2 *Turbo*, the qwyrlewynde. *c* **1440** *Alphabet of Tales* 321 Þe fend flow away in liknes of a whorle-wynd. **1585** Forman *Argt.* (MS. Ashm. 208, lf. 239 b) Elyas was taken up Within a whorrell-winde. **1596** *Edw. III*, III. i, As when a wherle winde takes the Summer dust And scatters it. **1611** *Bible* Job xxxviii. 1 Then the Lord answered Iob out of the whirlewind. **1633** G. Herbert *Temple, Giddinesse* iv, As if a whirlwinde blew And crusht the building. **1706** Prior *Ode to Queen* vii, Swift as the Whirlwind drives Arabia's scatter'd Sands. **1764** Goldsm. *Trav.* 207 The loud torrent, and the whirlwind's roar. **1858** Maury *Phys. Geog. Sea* ii. §94 All boys are familiar with miniature whirlwinds on shore,.. sweeping along the roads .., raising columns of dust, leaves, etc., which.. gyrate about the.. axis of the storm. **1882** 'Ouida' *In Maremma* viii, Herds of buffaloes.. rushed, like a whirlwind themselves,.. towards the shelter of the thickets.

2. *transf.* and *fig.* Something rushing impetuously like a whirlwind; a violent or destructive agency; a confused and tumultuous process or condition.

to sow the wind and reap the whirlwind (Hos. viii. 7): to indulge in reckless wickedness or folly, and suffer the disastrous consequences.

1382 Wyclif *Hosea* viii. 7 Thei shuln sowe wynd, and repe whirlwynd. **1590** *Tarlton's Newes Purgatorie* 3 Either a mans soule must in post haste goe presently to God, or else with a whirlewind and a vengeance goe to the diuell. **1609** Holland *Amm. Marcell.* xv. iv. 35 A tempestuous whirlewind of new calamities. **1667** Milton *P.L.* I. 77 O'rewhelm'd With Floods and Whirlwinds of tempestuous fire. **1714** [Blanch] *Beaux Merchant* II. 18 What my Landlady put into her Soup, I can't tell; but.. I had a Whirlwind in my Belly. **1816** Scott *Bl. Dwarf* xviii, It is sowing the wind to reap the whirlwind. **1837** Dickens *Pickw.* xxviii, Mr. Pickwick concluded amidst a whirlwind of applause. **1840** Alison *Hist. Eur.* lxii. VIII. 353 The foot soldiers in the rear..were instantly enveloped by a whirlwind of horse. **1855** KINGSLEY *Glaucus* 3 Free from the cares of town business, and the whirlwind of town pleasure. **1857** BUCKLE *Civiliz.* I. xii. 699 To see whether they who had raised the storm could ride the whirlwind. **1918** *Times Lit. Suppl.* 21 Mar. 139/1 The verbal whirlwind of his [*sc.* Swinburne's] later utterance.

3. *attrib.* Of or pertaining to a whirlwind; resembling a whirlwind, violent, impetuous; *spec.* applied to something done in great haste.

1614 GORGES *Lucan* v. 199 Rockes..ouerturn'd with whirle-wind shocks. **1750** GRAY *Long Story* 60 Upstairs in a whirlwind rattle. **1828** CARLYLE *Misc.* (1857) I. 120 With a whirlwind impetuosity he rushes forth. **1865** PARKMAN *Huguenots* ix. (1875) 157 A whirlwind visitation—to ravage, ruin, and vanish. **1942** [see ROMANCE *sb.* 5]. **1952** J. L. WATEN *Alien Son* 87 Auntie Fanny lived her own life, never commenting on her husband's whirlwind comings and goings. **1969** 'D. SHANNON' *Crime on their Hands* vii. 99 We only got engaged last week. It was a whirlwind romance. **1977** D. E. WESTLAKE *Nobody's Perfect* 65 Jet-setter Arnold Chauncey, just back from his whirlwind tour of Brasilia. **1984** *Times* 20 Feb. 10/2 His whirlwind investigation of NHS management.

4. *Comb.*, as ***whirlwind-footed***, ***-peopled***, ***-rifted*** adjs.; ***whirlwind-like*** adj. and adv.

1820 SHELLEY *Prometh. Unb.* III. iii. 77 *Whirlwind-footed coursers. **1876** SWINBURNE *Erechtheus* 433 A whirlwind-footed bridegroom. **1598** SYLVESTER *Du Bartas* II. i. *Handycrafts* 448 The flying ayre he catches, Born *whirl-winde-like. **1670** DRYDEN *Tyrannick Love* v. i, Who ..Whirlwind-like, around him drove the Air. **1837** CARLYLE *Fr. Rev.* I. I. ii, Democracy announcing,..that she is born, and whirlwind-like, will envelope the whole world. **1840** *Chamb. Jrnl.* 18 Apr. 104/2 He had heard a whirlwind-like noise. **1820** SHELLEY *Prometh. Unb.* I. 204 'Mid *whirlwind-peopled mountains. **1818** —— *Rosal. & Helen* 1158 *Whirlwind-rifted clouds.

Hence (*nonce-wds.*) **'whirlwind** *v.*, *intr.* to rush impetuously like a whirlwind; **'whirlwindish, 'whirlwindy** *adjs.*, resembling a whirlwind.

1892 BLACK *Wolfenberg* xxii, Thus bereft of her usual whirlwindish activity. **1894** 'MARK TWAIN' *Let.* 22 Dec. (1917) II. 617 These salvation-notions that were whirlwinding through my head. **1895** HOLMAN-HUNT in *Daily News* 14 Aug. 6/2 Paris, where young professors go whirlwinding in what they call study for a time. **1903** *Blackw. Mag.* Apr. 473/1 Its whirlwindy approach.

whirl-worm ('hwɜːlwɜːm). Also 7 **whurl(e-**. [f. WHIRL- + WORM *sb.*]

†**1.** An insect larva destructive to plants. *Obs.*

In quot. 1643 tr. L. *convolvulus* a caterpillar that rolls itself up in a leaf; in quot. 1658 tr. mod.L. *verticillus*, Gr. σφονδύλη.

1643 HORN & ROB. *Gate Lang. Unl.* (1650) xix. §217 Earth-worms gnaw upon muck-hils.., moths on garments, ..whirl-worms [*margin*, The divels gold-ring] on vines. **1658** ROWLAND tr. *Moufet's Theat. Ins.* 1042 The Northern English call it Andever; the Southern, Whurlworm, that is, a Whirl or little hairy Worm with many feet:..I..collect.. that there are two kindes of Whurlworms; one about houses, another in the fields.

2. A turbellarian worm. *rare*$^{-0}$. (? An error.)

1891 in *Cent. Dict.*

whirly ('hwɜːlɪ), *a. rare.* Also **-ey**. [f. WHIRL *sb.* or *v.* + -Y[1].] Characterized by whirling or rotatory movement.

1806 *Spirit Publ. Jrnls.* X. 170 Thames, in whirly dimples flowing. **1887** MEREDITH *Poems, Last Contention* vii, A whirly tune These winds will pipe. **1895** —— *Amazing Marr.* xxxvii, A skimming sense of a drop upon a funny, whirly world.

'whirly-, obs. or dial. var. of *whirl-* in comb., as †**whirly-bat**, †**whirly-pool**, **whirly-wind** = WHIRLBAT, -POOL, -WIND (cf. *whirligig* and *whirlgig*); also **whirly-go-round** (also **whirligoround**), a merry-go-round; †**whirly-hole** (see quot.); †**whirly-rock**, a spiral or turbinate fossil shell; **whirly-whirly**, (*a*) a dentist's drill (*nonce-use*); (*b*) *Austral.*, a whirling air current or dust cloud.

1725 BAILEY *Erasm. Colloq.* (1733) 42 The fighting with *Whirly-bats. **1865** MEREDITH *Rhoda Fleming* xliii, He was a faithful servant, till one day he got up on a regular *whirly-go-round, and ever since...such a little boy! **1871** —— *Harry Richmond* xlvi, Like one who has been gazing on the whirligoround, he saw the whole of women running or.. waiting..to run the giddy ring to perdition. **1686** PLOT *Staffordsh.* 172 At Kinfare Towne,..there goes another hole into the rock,..call'd *whirleyhole, from the Eddy of water the River makes at the mouth of it. **1727** BAILEY (Vol. II.), *Whirly-pool. **1892** MEREDITH *Ode, To Comic Spirit* 87 These..Would keep our life the whirly pool Of turbid stuff. **1904** RICKERT *Reaper* xix, There's often whirly-pools in the sea. **1681** GREW *Musæum* III. I. i. 265 A piece of *Whirly-Rock. *Turbinites Saxum.* **1928** A. P. HERBERT *Trials of Topsy* xii. 73 He *thrust* the *whirly-whirly *inch* by *inch* into the very *dome* of a girl's head. **1930** V. PALMER *Men are Human* xiii. 112 A cool breeze..raised little whirly-whirlies of dust. **1959** *Listener* 15 Jan. 113/1 The dust whirls and capers into fantastic whirlie-whirlies. **1972** *Southerly* XXXII. 4 A small whirly-whirly swept down the verandah, lifting dust and lolly papers in a mini-spiral. **14..** *Trevisa's Barth. De P.R.* XI. iv. (Bodl. MS.), *Whirly winde and a raynye cloude.

whirlybird ('hwɜːlɪbɜːd). *slang* (orig. *U.S.*). [f. WHIRLY- + BIRD *sb.*] A helicopter.

1951 *Air Facts* 1 July 30/1 The biggest untold story out of Korea is of a few score unarmed American helicopters and a handful of pilots who have flown themselves and their 'whirlybirds' into military history. **1959** *Sunday Times* 26 Apr. 31/4 The noise which piston-engined 'whirly-birds' inevitably make causes no nuisance to workers in London. **1983** *Chicago Sun-Times* 28 July 82/1 The Bellwood-based whirlybird company has asked Civil Aeronautics Board approval to operate regularly scheduled flights.

whirne, obs. form of QUERN *sb.*[1]

1588 *Wills & Inv. Durham* (Surtees) II. 328, j paire off pepper whirnes.

whirr, whir (hwɜː(r)), *sb.* Forms: 5 *Sc.* **qwirre**, 6 *Sc.* **quhir**, 6–7 **whurre**, 7 **whirre**, 7–8 **whur**, 8–9 **whurr**, 9 **whirr**, **whir**. [See next.]

†**1.** Violent or rapid movement, rush, hurry; the force or impetus of such movement. *Obs.*

Sometimes approaching sense 2; but in early use the stress is on the movement rather than the sound.

*a***1400–50** *Wars Alex.* 560 All flames þe flode as it fire were,..And þan ouer-qwelmys in a qwirre. *Ibid.* 1854 In a qwirre [*v.r.* whirre] as þe quele turnes. **1513** DOUGLAS *Æneis* XII. v. 114 The sovir schaft flaw quhisland wyth a quhir. *a***1553** UDALL *Royster D.* I. iii. (Arb.) 20 No haste but good, ..for whip and whurre The olde prouerbe doth say, neuer made good furre.

†**b.** *fig.* Commotion of mind or feeling; a mental or nervous shock. *Obs.*

1628 FELTHAM *Resolves* II. [I.] xl. 121 Knowing himselfe chollericke, and in that whirre of the mind, apt to rush vpon foule transgression. **1702** VANBRUGH *False Friend* v. i, I'm mightily muddled with a Whur—round about in my head. **1728** VANBR. & CIB. *Prov. Husb.* II. i, They slupt the Door full in my Feace, and gave me such a whurr here—I thought they had beaten my brains out!

2. A continuous vibratory sound, such as that made by the rapid fluttering of a bird's or insect's wings, by a wheel turning swiftly, or by a body rushing through the air.

1677 N. COX *Gentl. Recr.* II. 168 Whur is the rising and fluttering of Partridge or Pheasant. **1774** GOLDSM. *Nat. Hist.* (1824) II. 346 The Goat-sucker..makes a loud singular noise, like the whirr of a spinning-wheel. **1829** SOUTHEY *All for Love* II. x, A whirr of unseen wings he heard. **1837** CARLYLE *Fr. Rev.* II. II. iii, The wide simultaneous whirr of shouldered muskets. **1847** LONGF. *Ev.* I. i. 23 Shuttles..Mingled their sound with the whir of the wheels. **1887** HALL CAINE *Son of Hagar* III. v, Between the whirrs of the wind he heard the tinkle of the signal bell. **1893** TOUT *Edw. I*, xi. (1896) 196 The king's horse took fright at the whirr of the sails of a windmill.

fig. **1874** MEREDITH *Let. to Capt. Maxse* 5 Aug., I do not see my way out of the encircling whirr of work.

whirr, whir, *v.* (*adv.*, *int.*) Forms: 5 *Sc.* **quirr(e**, **quir**, **quhir**, 5–7 **whirre**, 6 *Sc.* **quhirr(e**, **quhyrr(e**, 7 **whurre**, 7, 9 **whurr**, 8 **whur**, 7– **whirr**, **whir**. [The early occurrence of this vb. and the related sb. in northern texts makes a Scandinavian origin probable; cf. Da. *hvirre*:—**hvirve*, Norw. *kvirra*, Sw. dial. *hvirra*, app. assimilated forms of a verb **hvirfa* (cf. ON. *hverfa* WHARVE *v.*), related to *hvirfill*, *hvirfla* WHIRL. In later use the Eng. verb has been reinforced by onomatopœia.]

1. *trans.* †**a.** To throw or cast with violence and noise; to fling, hurl. *Obs.*

*a***1400–50** *Wars Alex.* 2226 Othire athils of armes Albastis bendis, Quirys [*v.r.* whirres] out quarrels. **1605** SYLVESTER *Du Bartas* II. iii. *Captains* 516 The formost Ranks it [*sc.* hailshot] whirr'd Upon the next, the second on the third.

b. To carry or hurry along, to move or stir, with a rushing or vibratory sound. (In mod. use *causal* from 2.)

1608 SHAKS. *Per.* IV. i. 21 A lasting storme, whirring me from my friends. **1909** *Nation* 27 Nov. 363/1 They whirred their wings. **1921** A. F. ROBERTSON *Story of Pam* ix, As he was 'whirred' through the night.

2. *intr.* To move swiftly in some way (rush, fly, dart, flutter, turn, etc.) with a continuous vibratory sound, as various birds, rapidly revolving wheels, bodies flying quickly through the air, etc.

*a***1400–50** *Wars Alex.* 1556 All þe cite..felowis him eftir, Quirris [*v.r.* whirrez] furth all in quite. **1513** DOUGLAS *Æneis* XII. xiv. 96 Furth flaw the schaft..And quhirrand smait him throw the thee. **1605** SYLVESTER *Du Bartas* II. iii. III. *Law* 779 As the poor Partridge, cover'd with the net, In vain doth strive,..For, the close meshes..Suffer the same no more to whurre aloft. **1606** CHAPMAN *Gentl. Usher* III. ii. 14 The great wheeles, Turning but softly, make the lesse to whirre About their businesse. **1728–46** THOMSON *Spring* 692 With stealthy wing,..Amid a neighbouring bush they silent drop, And whirring thence,..deceive The unfeeling school-boy. **1830** LYTTON *Paul Clifford* xii, The distant wheel of a carriage whirred on the ear. **1859** H. KINGSLEY *G. Hamlyn* xxviii, Through the grassy flat, where the quail whirred before them. **1864** SKEAT tr. *Uhland's Poems* 356 Hark! arrows are whirring, swords clash in the fray. **1899** WERNER *Captain of Locusts* 25 The locusts whirred up round his horse's hoofs.

3. Without implication of onward movement: To make or emit a vibratory sound.

1804 A. WILSON in *Poems & Lit. Prose* (1876) II. 359 The squirrel chipped, the tree frog whirred. **1886** STEVENSON *Kidnapped* xxii, Grasshoppers whirring in the grass. **1899** J. L. WILLIAMS *Stolen Story* etc. 154 The telephone bell whirred. **1905** A. C. BENSON *Upton Lett.* 83 The casements whirr, the organ speaks.

b. *dial.* To snarl or growl; to purr.

1706 PHILLIPS (ed. Kersey), *To Whur*, to snarl, as a Dog does. **1843** J. BALLANTINE *Gaberlunzie's Wallet* 209 At your feet..Whurrs your wee catty. **1847** HALLIWELL, *Whurr*, to growl, as a dog.

4. The verb-stem as *int.* or *adv.*, expressing a sudden or rapid movement with vibratory sound.

1600 *Dr. Dodypoll* III. D 4 b, Whirre, I haue strooke him vnder the shorte ribs. *a***1625** FLETCHER *Fair Maid Inn* v. i, You demand if I am guilty, whir says my cloak by a trick of Legerdemain, now I am not guilty. **1826** DISRAELI *Viv. Grey* VI. i, Whirr! the exploded cork whizzed through the air. **1836** T. HOOK *G. Gurney* v. (1850) I. 87 Whurr went the pheasants—bang went the barrels. **1844** KINGLAKE *Eothen* i, Whirr! whirr! all by wheels!—whiz! whiz! all by steam! **1858** THACKERAY *Virgin.* xxxix, Whirr came the wheels—the carriage stopped at the very door.

whirra ('hwɪrə). [f. WHIRR, WHIR *sb.*] A whirring sound that varies in quality. (The examples are *Austral.*)

1929 K. S. PRICHARD *Coonardoo* i. 14 The pigeon flew off with a whirra of grey silken wings. **1969** H. WILLARD in P. A. Smith *Folklore Austral. Railwaymen* 174 Within two minutes whirra whirra whirra, the spears and boomerangs were coming over our heads.

whirra, -oo, whirret: see WIRRA, WHERRET.

whirrick, variant of WHERRET.

1760–72 H. BROOKE *Fool of Qual.* (1809) I. iii. 17 Harry.. gave master such a whirrick, that his cries instantly sounded the *ne plus ultra* to such kind of diversions.

whirring ('hwɜːrɪŋ), *vbl. sb.* [f. WHIRR *v.* + -ING[1].] The action of the verb WHIRR; a continuous vibratory sound, or movement with such a sound.

1581 A. HALL *Iliad* II. 30 This speech..doth greatly ioy the Greekes, They such a noyse and whirring made. **1598** SYLVESTER *Du Bartas* II. i. *Furies* 115 The first-mov'd heav'n (in't self it self stil stirring) Rapts with his course (quicker then windes swift whirring) All th' other Sphears. **1811** SHELLEY *St. Irvyne* ix. Pr. Wks. 1888 I. 190 Save by the whirrings of the bats, the stillness..was uninterrupted. **1840** THACKERAY *George Cruikshank* (1869) 305 What a pious whirring of bible leaves one hears all over the church. **1863** BATES *Nat. Amazons* I. i. 9 The whirring of cicadas. **1918** H. BINDLOSS *Agatha's Fortune* ii, An electric fan made an unpleasant whirring.

'whirring, *ppl. a.* [f. as prec. + -ING[2].] That whirrs; moving with or making a vibratory sound; also said of the sound.

*c***1480** HENRYSON *Trial of Fox* 116 The quhuirand [*v.r.* quhrynand] quhitret with the quhasill went. *c***1611** CHAPMAN *Iliad* XVII. 399 The whirring chariot. **1611** COTGR., *Roncé*, hurled; or making a whurring noise, as a stone, &c., cast with violence. **1704** POPE *Windsor Forest* 111 From the brake the whirring pheasant springs. **1783** BURNS '*Now westlin winds*' i, The moorcock springs, on whirring wings, Amang the blooming heather. **1830** TENNYSON *Owl* i, The whirring sail goes round. **1841** JAMES *Corse de Leon* iii, The whirring scream of the night hawk.

whirrit, whirroll, obs. ff. WHERRET, WHIRL *sb.*

'whirry, *sb.* ? *Obs.* In 7 **wherry**, **whurrie**. [Cf. next.] **a.** A rapid or sudden movement. **b.** Activity.

1611 COTGR., *Bacule*, a square, and heauie dore..let fal (as a Portcullis) in a trice, with a whurrie. **1622** MABBE tr. *Aleman's Guzman d'Alf.* I. 229 A company of beetle-heads, dull-spirited fellowes, that had no wherry in them. **1675** COVEL in *Early Voy. Levant* (Hakl. Soc.) 214 At last, with a merry wherry of their musick, they turn round (as the Dervises) a long time.

whirry ('hwɪrɪ), *v.* Now *Sc.* Forms: 6 **whirrye**, **-ie**, 7 **whurry**, **wherry**, 7, 9 *Sc.* **whirry**. [? f. WHIRR + -Y, after *hurry*.]

1. *trans.* To carry or drive swiftly; to hurry along. Also *fig.*

1582 STANYHURST *Æneis* III. (Arb.) 89 Hoyse me hence.. too sum oother countrye me whirrye. **1621** T. BEDFORD *Sin unto Death* 29 The..sea that is..whirryed and tossed with a tempestuous winde. **1660** BONDE *Scut. Reg.* 51 As the unruly quadrupedes whirried about the Chariot,..untill they had set the whole world on fire. *a***1756** HALKET in W. Walker *Bards Bon-Accord* (1887) 205 Ill boding comets blaze o'erhead, O whirry whigs awa', man. **1820** SCOTT *Monast.* Introd. Ep., 'Some of the quality, that were o' his ain unhappy persuasion, had the corpse whirried away up the water.'

fig. **1619** SCLATER *Expos. 1 Thess.* v. 21. 548 Giddie and inconstant people, whirried about with euery blast of vaine Doctrine. **1621** T. WILLIAMSON tr. *Goulart's Wise Vieillard* 58 Whurried about with intemperate lusts and desires. **1675** T. BROOKS *Gold. Key* 4 A Christian is sometimes wherried and whirled away by sin before he is a ware.

2. *intr.* To move or go rapidly, hurry.

*c***1630** *Robin Goodfellow* in *Roxb. Ball.* (1874) II. 82 Through pooles and ponds, I whirry, laughing, ho, ho, ho! **1691** SIR T. P. BLOUNT *Ess.* 103 When once the spoke of the Wheel is uppermost, it soon whurries to the bottom. **1818** SCOTT *Hrt. Midl.* xviii, Her and the gudeman will be whirrying through the blue lift on a broom-shank. **1920** BLUNDEN *Waggoner* 24, I whirry through the dark.

whirry ('hwɜːrɪ), *a.* [f. WHIRR, WHIR *sb.* + -Y[1].] Characterized by, or of the nature of, a whirr.

1936 E. DARK *Return to Coolami* xiv. 142 There are the locusts beginning... A nice noise, whirry, hot, drowsy. **1982** *Financial Times* 25 Sept. 6/6 Intal suffered from the disadvantage that it could only be taken by the patient by means of a rather complex, whirry machine called the 'Spinhaler'.

whirry, obs. form of QUARRY *sb.*[1]

whirtle, variant of WORTLE.

whiruel(l, obs. forms of WHIRL *sb.*

whish (hwɪʃ), *sb.* [Imitative.] A soft sibilant sound, as that of something moving rapidly through the air or over the surface of water. Cf. SWISH *sb.*[1] 1.

1808 JAMIESON, *Whish, whush*, a rushing or whizzing sound. **1850** MAYNE REID *Rifle Rangers* I. viii. 103 The 'whish' of a rocket attracted our attention. **1863** POWER *Arab. Days & Nts.* 25 The noises on deck, and the whish of the water through which we were rapidly..cutting our way. **1890** HALLETT *Thous. Miles* 453 The howls of these poor creatures, together with the whish of the cane, is heard through the city.

whish, *a.*[1] *Obs.* exc. *dial.* [Cf. WHISHT and WHUSH.] Hushed, silent: = WHISHT *a.*[1], WHIST *a.*[1]

a **1612** HARINGTON *Epigr.* I. xxvii. (1618) B 7, You tooke my answer well, and all was whish.

whish, *a.*[2] (*dial.*): see WISHT.

whish (hwɪʃ), *v.*[1] Also 6 **whysshe.** [Imitative.] Hence **whishing** *vbl. sb.* and *ppl. a.*

1. *intr.* To utter the syllable 'whish' or a sound resembling it; *trans.* to drive or chase by crying 'whish!'

1518 *Sel. Cases Star Chamber* (Selden Soc.) II. 133 [He] whysshyd them booth owte of the churche. **1538** BALE *Thre Lawes* B iij b, With whysperynges and whysshynges. **1842** *Blackw. Mag.* Aug. 243/1 He [*sc.* an ostler] had relieved the process of whish—whishing at the horses, in imparting [etc.]. **1897** J. HOCKING *Birthright* ii, We heard them 'whishing' up the sheep.

2. To make a soft sibilant sound of this kind, as a body rushing through air or water, or the wind among trees, etc.

1540 PALSGR. *Acolastus* Aa iv b, What a whishynge of the wynde is yonder. **1565** COOPER *Thesaurus, Bruma spirans*.. whishyng with winde. **1856** S. ROGERS *Table-Talk* 11 You could hear the whishing sound of the ladies' trains. **1860** O. W. HOLMES *Prof. Breakf.-t.* vi, The lightning-express-train whishes by a station. **1929** R. GRAVES *Good-bye to all That* xiii. 153, I heard one shell whish-whishing towards me. **1939** L. MACNEICE *Autumn Jrnl.* xiv. 54 The wheels whished in the wet. **1959** R. BRADBURY *Day it rained Forever* 214 Wouldn't it be nice to take a Sunday walk the way we used to do, with your silk parasol and your long dress whishing along?

whish, *v.*[2] Now *dial.* Also 6 **whysh.** [f. WHISH *int.*[1]; cf. WHISHT *v.*, WHIST *v.*[1]]

1. *trans.* To silence, put to silence, hush.

1542 UDALL *Erasm. Apoph.* 287 b, Pompeius cooled & whyshed hym in this wyse. **1684** O. HEYWOOD *Diaries* (1885) IV. 111 Sir Jo. Kay silenced and whisht him.

2. *intr.* To be silent or quiet.

1607 TOMKIS *Lingua* IV. viii, Why do you whish thus? here's none to heare you. **1876** BLACKMORE *Cripps* xlix, Whish!—can't 'ee whish, with my name so pat?

whish, *int.*[1] Now *dial.* Also 9 *Sc.* **wheesh.** [Cf. HUSH *int.*, WHISHT *int.*] An exclamation to command silence: Hush!

1635 QUARLES *Embl.* II. viii. 9 Whish, lullaby,..What ayles my Babe to cry? **1675** COVEL in *Early Voy. Levant* (Hakluyt Soc.) 194 All the waiters cry'd: Whish, whish, etc. in token of silence. **1858** TROLLOPE *Dr. Thorne* xix, 'A good dinner now and then is a very good thing.' 'Yes; but I don't like eating it with hogs.' 'Whish-h; softly, softly, Mr. Gresham, or you'll disturb Mr. Apjohn's digestion.' **1876** [see prec. 2].

whish, *int.*[2] Also 6 *Sc.* **quhisch.** Imitation of a soft sibilant or rushing sound, as of something moving rapidly through the air, etc.

1535 LYNDESAY *Satyre* 1920 Gif that ȝour mawkine cryis quhisch. **1692** D. LAWSON in G. L. Burr *Narr. Witchcraft Cases* (1914) 153 Makeing as if she would fly, stretching up her arms as high as she could, and crying 'Whish, Whish, Whish!' **1839** HOOD *Sonn. to Vauxhall* 9 Whish—ish!—On high The rocket rushes. **1849** CUPPLES *Green Hand* vii, Whish! rush! came the rain in sheets and bucketfuls. **1894** FENN *Real Gold* xxiii, Whish, whirr, came a peculiar sound.

whishin, obs. form of CUSHION.

whisht (hwɪʃt), *sb.* Also 9 *Sc.* **wheesht, wheisht.** [f. WHISHT *int.*]

1. An utterance of 'whisht!' to enjoin silence: cf. WHIST *sb.*[2] 1.

1553 T. WILSON *Rhet.* 106 A Whisht is when we bid them holde their peace that haue least cause to speake. **1908** WEYMAN *Wild Geese* viii, What do you mean with your 'whishts' and your nods?

2. Silence; in phr. ***to hold one's whisht***, to keep silence. *Sc.*

1785 BURNS *Vision* I. 43, I held my whisht; The infant aith, half-form'd, was crusht. **1824** MACTAGGART *Gallovid. Encycl.* s.v. *Wheesht*, Haud your wheesht, be silent. **1895** CROCKETT *Men of Moss-Hags* xxxv, You ken naught about it. You had better hold your wheesht.

3. A whisper; with negative = 'not a whisper', not the least utterance. *Sc.*

a **1774** FERGUSSON *Ecl.* Poet. Wks. (1800) 89 Be you as calm's a mouse, Nor let your whisht be heard. **1881** WALFORD *Dick Netherby* v, There is na a wheesht against him.

whisht (hwɪʃt), *a.*[1] Now *dial.* Also 6 **whysht(e,** 9 *Sc.* **wheesht.** [A variant of WHIST *a.*[1]; cf. WHISHT *int.*] Silent, quiet, still, hushed.

1570 T. WILSON *Demosth. Orat., Life* 117 He desired..to tell them a merie tale. Where vpon when euery man was whisht and still, he sayde thus. **1615** BRIGHTMAN *Rev.* 143 Reprehensions are whisht, wickednes raigneth. **1802** R. ANDERSON *Cumbld. Ball.* (1805) 5 As whisht as a mouse. **1893** STEVENSON *Catriona* xv, Nights..when he was here on sentry, the place a' wheesht.

Hence **'whishtly** *adv.*, silently, quietly.

1548 UDALL, etc. *Erasm. Par. John* xvi. 23-28, I shall than speake vnto you whishtlye and without woordes.

whisht, *a.*[2] (*dial.*): see WISHT.

whisht, *v.* Now *dial.* Also 9 *Sc.* **wheesht.** [f. WHISHT *int.* Cf. WHISH *v.*[2], WHIST *v.*[1]]

1. *intr.* To be silent, keep silence.

1815 SCOTT *Guy M.* xlviii, Wasp—Wasp, whisht, hinny.. and let's hear what they're doing.—Deil's in ye, will ye whisht? **1894** 'J. S. WINTER' *Red Coats* 50 'Whisht, woman, whisht,' interposed Trueman..'No, I just won't whisht, William Trueman.'

2. *trans.* To put to silence, silence, hush.

1804 R. COUPER *Poetry* II. 11 (Eng. Dial. Dict.) A weel-claw'd luif whishts the harangue. **1897** C. M. CAMPBELL *Deilie Jock* iv, Wheesht your gab.

whisht (hwɪʃt), *int.* Now *dial.* Also 5 **whischt,** 7-9 **wheesht.** [A natural utterance, nearly identical with the 16th c. *huissht* (see HUSHT *int.*[1]), and with WHIST *int.*[1]] An exclamation enjoining silence: Hush!

14.. Whisht, whischt [see quot. 1382 s.v. WHIST *int.*[1]]. **1684** [MERITON] *Yorksh. Dial.* 53 Wheesht, wheesht, my Mother's coming up. **1725** RAMSAY *Gentle Sheph.* III. i. Prol., But whisht! it is the Knight in Masquerade, That comes. **1815** SCOTT *Guy M.* xlv, But whisht, I hear the keeper coming. **1893** STEVENSON *Catriona* xxx, 'Wheesht!' said he, 'this is my affairs'.

whisk (hwɪsk), *sb.*[1] Forms: 4-6 *Sc.* **wysk,** 5-6 *Sc.* **quhisk,** 5-9 **wisk,** 6 **whysk,** 6-7 **whiske,** 7 **wiske,** 6- **whisk.** [orig. *wisk, wysk*, and first in Sc. texts; partly f. WHISK *v.*, partly ad. Scandinavian sb. represented by ON. *visk* wisp, Sw. *viska* besom, wisp, swab, Norw. *visk* wisp, cluster, pull, tug = OHG. *wisc* (MHG., G. *wisch*) wisp of hay, dish-clout, (M)DU. *wisch* wisp, LG. *wisk* quick movement, moment of time: see WHISK *v.*]

I. 1. A brief rapid sweeping movement; a sudden light stroke, rush, dart, etc.; a light stroke of a brush or other sweeping implement. Also *transf.* and *fig.*

In later use regarded as noun of action from the verb (*quasi* an act of whisking); but evidenced in quots. earlier than the verb.

with a whisk becomes phrasal = in an instant, in a flash: similarly ***in a whisk.***

1375 BARBOUR *Bruce* v. 641 The king..Vatit the sper.. And with a wysk the hed of-strak. *c* **1480** HENRYSON *Paddock & Mouse* 122 With ane wisk..He claucht his cluik betuix thame. *a* **1510** DOUGLAS *K. Hart* I. 199 Fresche Bewtie with ane wysk come vp belyve. **1577** STANYHURST *Descr. Irel.* 18/1 in *Holinshed*, Sodaynly it [*sc.* a salmon] fetcheth such a round Whiske, that at a trice it skippeth to the top of the rocke. *a* **1586** MONTGOMERIE *Misc. Poems* iii. 28 Quhen with a quhisk sho [*sc.* Fortune] quhirlis about hir quheill. **1589** [? LYLY] *Pappe w. Hatchet* To Rdr., To giue them a whiske with their owne wand. *a* **1625** FLETCHER *Noble Gent.* v. i, This first sad whisk [of the sword] Takes off thy Dukedom. **1644** BULWER *Chirol.* 94 [He] brings in Cæsar in the whiske of one of his Epigrams. *a* **1693** *Urquhart's Rabelais* III. xvii. 141 Three Whisks of a Broom Besom. **1821** SCOTT *Pirate* xxi, Come and gae like a glance of the sun, or the whisk of a whirlwind. **1853** LYTTON *My Novel* IV. xi, The pad [mare]..giving a petulant whisk of her tail. **1863** LOWELL *Two Scenes from Life of Blondel* II. v, If a whisk of Fate's broom snap your cobweb asunder. **1863** *Reader* 7 Nov. 538 His [*sc.* tiger's] tail looks as if it had a wisk in it still. **1869** MRS. STOWE *Oldtown Folks* xxxiv. (1870) 407 These wild, sudden whisks of gaiety. **1896** CONAN DOYLE *Rodney Stone* xiii, He walked up and down the room.. turning with a whisk upon his heel every now and then. **1900** ZANGWILL *Mantle of Elijah* II. xv, You see it all in a whisk.

II. 2. A neckerchief worn by women in the latter half of the 17th century. *Obs.* exc. *Hist.*

1654 in Jeaffreson *Midsx. County Rec.* (1888) III. 225 Six Corle Whiskes worth seventeen shillings, six Corle Gorgetts worth fourteen shillings, [etc.] *a* **1658** CLEVELAND *Zealous Disc.* Wks. (1687) 382 Pray rectifie my Gorget, smooth my Whisk. **1660** PEPYS *Diary* 22 Nov., My wife..bought her a white whisk and put it on. **1688** HOLME *Armoury* III. ii. 17/1 A Womans Neck Whisk..is used both Plain and Laced, and is called of most a Gorgett or a falling Whisk. **1706** E. WARD *Hud. Rediv.* (Nares) With whisks of lawn, by grannums wore.

3. An instrument, now freq. a bundle of wires, for beating up eggs, cream, or the like.

1666 BOYLE *Orig. Formes & Qual.* 111 By beating the White of an Egge well with a Whisk, you may reduce it from a somewhat Tenacious into a Fluid Body. **1747** MRS. GLASSE *Cookery* xv. 140 First beat the Whites of the Eggs up well with a Whisk. **1882** *Worc. Exhib. Catal.* III. 38 Egg whisk for confectioners.

4. A bundle or tuft of twigs, hair, feathers etc. fixed on a handle, used for brushing or dusting; also, a water-sprinkler.

1729 SWIFT *Direct. Serv.* viii. (1745) 75 If you happen to break any China with the Top of the Wisk. **1772** T. SIMPSON *Vermin-Killer* 18 With a whisk, sprinkle the corn..with it. **1834** MARRYAT *Peter Simple* xiii, Father M'Grath seized hold of the pot of holy water, and dipping in the little whisk, began to sprinkle the room. **1844** G. DODD *Textile Manuf.* vi. 176 The reeler then takes a whisk of fine twigs bound together.

b. A slender hair-like or bristle-like part or appendage, as those on the tails of certain insects.

(In first quot. app. used for 'sting'.)

a **1618** SYLVESTER *Tobacco Battered* 290 The..piercing Poyson of a Dragon's Whisk, Or deadly Ey-shot of a Basilisk. **1676** COTTON *Angler* II. viii. 72 This..Stone-Flie ..has two or three whisks..at the tag of his tail. **1747** BOWLKER *Art Angling* 64 The May Fly..with a long forked Tail made with the Hair or Whisks of a Fitchow's Tail. **1859** KINGSLEY *Glaucus* (ed. 4) 198 The Ephemeræ..throwing off the whole of their skins (even..to the skin of the eyes and wings, and the delicate 'whisks' at their tail). **1886** F. M. HALFORD *Floating Flies* 38 If the fly to be imitated has setæ or whisks. **1887** J. H. KEENE *Fishing Tackle* 181 Two whisks from a long fibre hackle, or two rabbit's whiskers.

c. The panicle or other part of certain plants used for making into brushes or brooms; *esp.* the panicle of the common millet or 'broom-corn' (*Sorghum vulgare*); hence, the plant itself.

1757 [see *whisk seed* in 7]. **1805** *Trans. Soc. Arts* XXIII. 258 Whisk, the article of which carpet brushes are formed. **1874** *Treas. Bot.* Suppl., *Whisk*, a trade name for the flower-spikes of *Sorghum vulgare*. **1893** *Let. to Editor from Director of Kew Gardens*, The fibrous root received for identification is that of *Chrysopogon Gryllus*, Trin. known as the Venetian or French Whisk. **1902** HANNAN *Textile Fibres* 157 Whisk, Mexican (*Epicampes macroura*). *Ibid.* 160 Whisk, Italian (*Sorghum*).

d. A small bunch, tuft, wisp.

1845 S. JUDD *Margaret* II. xi, The ceiling was divided by whisks of flowers. **1862** SMILES *Engineers* III. 318 Holding over their work large whisks of straw..to protect the bricks and cement.

e. A swarm of insects whisking or moving briskly about. *rare*$^{-1}$.

1867 F. FRANCIS *Bk. Angling* vi. 202 The Fœtid Brown, or mushroom fly..may be seen in small whisks or swarms skipping up and down over the water.

5. A name for various mechanical appliances having a whisking movement. **a.** A kind of winnowing-machine. **b.** A machine for winding yarn. **c.** A cooper's plane for levelling the chimes of casks.

1813 VANCOUVER *Agric. Devon* 127 Few winnowing-machines, saving a common whisk or fly, are used in this county. **1825** JAMIESON, *Whisks*, a machine for winding yarn on a quill or clue. **1863** J. WATSON *Weaving* ii. 57 In winding warp from the hank, swifts or whisks are used. **1875** KNIGHT *Dict. Mech.*, *Whisk*, a cooper's plane.

III. †**6.** A whipper-snapper. *Obs. slang.*

1628 FORD *Lover's Mel.* III. i, No quarrels, good'ee Whiske. *a* **1652** BROME *Novella* IV. ii. L 7 b, *Nic.* This is the Gentleman. *Pi.* Tis the proud Braches whiske! *a* **1700** B. E. *Dict. Cant. Crew*, *Whisk*, a little inconsiderable impertinent Fellow.

IV. 7. *attrib.* and *Comb.* (Some of these may be regarded as attrib. uses of the stem of WHISK *v.*) **whisk broom** = sense 4; †**whisk-comb** (see quot.); †**whisk rod**, a rod consisting of twigs or the like (cf. WHISK *v.* 4); **whisk seed**, millet-seed (see 4 c); **whisk tail**, a tail that is or may be whisked; hence **whisk-tailed** *a.*, having a whisk tail.

1857 *Local Act 20 & 21 Vict.* c. cxlii. Sched. (B) *Whisk Brooms, loose, per 1,000 0 0 9. **1897** *Army & Navy Co-op. Soc., Ltd.* No. 4 Dept. Special List 193 Whisk Broom, Leather bound with handle. **1688** HOLME *Armoury* III. xiv. (Roxb.) 13/1 The *Wiske combe, haue teeth on one side, and are wide and slender. *Ibid.* vii. 312/1 The *Whisk Rod is used to correct Rebellious Youths. **1757** FRANKLIN *Lett.* Wks. 1887 II. 494, I enclose you some *whisk seed; it is a kind of corn, good for creatures. **1675** *Lond. Gaz.* No. 976/4 One Bay Mare,..with a *whisk Tayl. **1697** *Flying Post* 19-21 Oct. 2/2 A small Spaniel Lap-Dog,..a short whisk Tail. **1720** *Lond. Gaz.* No. 5836/4 A well spread Mare,.. with a short whisk Tail. **1675** *Ibid.* No. 952/4 Two Geldings, ..both *whisk Tail'd. **1859** CHRISTINA ROSSETTI *Goblin Market* 107 The whisk-tailed merchant bade her taste.

whisk, *sb.*[2] *Obs.* or *dial.* [? f. WHISK *v.*] The earlier name of the card-game now called whist (WHIST *sb.*[3]). Also *attrib.* Hence †**'whisker** (**wisker**) *nonce-wd.*, a whist-player.

1621 J. TAYLOR (Water P.) *Motto* D 4, He flings his money free..At One and thirty, or at Poore and rich, Ruffe, slam, Trump, nody, whisk. **1674** COTTON *Compl. Gamester* v. (1680) 61 The elder begins and younger follows suit as at Whisk. [*Elsewhere in the book* Whist.] **1704** T. BAKER *Act at Oxf.* III. ii. 33 We'll sit down to Ombre, Picquet, Wisk, and Swabbers; or One and Thirty Bone-ace. **1723** LADY BRISTOL in *Lett.-bks. J. Hervey, 1st Earl of Bristol* (1894) II. 278 The wiskers have promised me some diversion. *Ibid.* 287, I reign Queen of the whisk party. *Ibid.* 291 He will be missd..as a whisk player. **1728** [see SWABBER[2]]. **1810** *Sporting Mag.* XXXVI. 75 Playing at whisk in an obscure village, in the Christmas holidays. **1829** BROCKETT *N.C. Gloss.* (ed. 2), *Whisk*, a vulgar pronunciation of whist. **1854** MISS BAKER *Northampt. Gloss.*, *Whisk*, whist, a game at cards. **1880** [see SWAB *sb.*[2]].

whisk, *v.* (*adv.*, *int.*) Forms: see WHISK *sb.*[1] [In early use Sc.; prob. of Scandinavian origin: cf. Sw. *viska* to whisk (off), sponge, Da. *viske* to wipe, whisk, rub, sponge (a gun), Norw. *viska* to put straw, etc. together in a bundle = OHG. *wisken* (MHG., G. *wischen*) to wipe, †intr. to move lightly or briskly, LG. *wisken* to move quickly, wipe off, etc.: cf. WHISK *sb.*[1] The spelling with *wh* was adopted as being symbolic (cf. *whip*).]

1. a. *intr.* To move with a light rapid sweeping motion; to make a single sudden movement of this kind, to rush or dart nimbly; to move about or travel swiftly or briskly (occas. with *it*).

c **1480** HENRYSON *Swallow* xliii, Like to the mow before the face of wind Quhiskis away. **1513** DOUGLAS *Æneis* III. iv. 68 Suddanlie away thai [*sc.* harpies] wisk ilk ane, Furth of our sicht, heich wp in the sky. *Ibid.* XII. xii. 172 Lyke as befor the hund wyskis the hair. **1549** COVERDALE, etc. *Erasm. Par. James* iv. 7–17 You..whiske about by sea and by lande, to get pelfe. **1592** R. D. *Hypnerotomachia* 12 b, Their vestures whisking vp and flying abroad. **1623** JOBSON *Golden Trade* 35 Beasts..will wiske with their tayles,..to auoyde or be rid of them [*sc.* flies]. *a* **1699** J. BEAUMONT *Psyche* XX. cxlvii, Sweets which each silly Wind that whisketh by, Snatcheth, and scattereth. **1710** STEELE *Tatler* No. 144 ¶2 We..watch an Opportunity to whisk cross a Passage, very thankful that we are not run over. **1719** D'URFEY *Pills* I. 172 Prickets from Thickets, Come whisk it and frisk it. **1800** MRS. HERVEY *Mourtray Fam.* III. 272 In whisking round a sharp angle, they over-set the carriage. **1837** W. IRVING *Capt. Bonneville* II. 133 The..beavers..chasing each other about the pond, dodging and whisking about on the surface. **1868** LOUISA M. ALCOTT *Little Women* iii, As Meg appeared, Scrabble [the pet rat] whisked into his hole. **1872** BLACK *Adv. Phaeton* xviii. 254 We whisked through Maghull village.

b. The vb.-stem used as *adv.* or *int.*: With a whisk, or sudden light movement.

1750 GRAY *Long Story* 79 Out of the window, whisk, they flew. **1840** DICKENS *Old C. Shop* xlvii, He carried in his pocket..a fire-box of mysterious..construction; and as sure as ever Kit's mother closed her eyes, so surely—whisk, rattle, fizz—there was the single gentleman consulting his watch by a flame of fire. **1916** 'BOYD CABLE' *Action Front* 12, I heard..something else goin' *whisk* like a cane switched past your ear. **1919** H. WALPOLE *Secret City* II. v. 353 A beautiful fruit just within his grasp... He's going to taste it, when whisk! it's gone.

2. a. *trans.* To move (something) *about*, *away*, *back*, etc. with a light sweeping motion.

1513 DOUGLAS *Æneis* VIII. Prol. 163 Quhen I walkynnit, all that welth was wiskyt away. **1594** MARLOWE & NASHE *Dido* II. C 1 b, He..whiskt his sword about. **1675** HOBBES *Odyssey* XI. 576 A sudden winde..whiskt away the Twigs. **1711** BUDGELL *Spect.* No. 67. ¶9 [He] ran to his Partner,..and whisked her round cleverly above ground. **1768** TUCKER *Lt. Nat.* (1834) I. 83 Burning a small stick at the end..and whisking it round to make gold lace, as we called it. **1784** COWPER *Task* VI. 317 The squirrel..there whisks his brush, And perks his ears. **1837** DICKENS *Pickw.* iv, The horses..whisked their tails about. **1884** *Manch. Exam.* 24 Nov. 6/3 One cannot always guard against a whirlpool catching the rudder..and whisking the boat round. **1916** A. B. REEVE *Pois. Pen* iii, I forgot about it as I was whisked up in the elevator.

b. in reference to rapid travel: cf. *whirl*.

1694 N. H. *Ladies Dict.* 436 They whisk her to Bath, to Bristol. **1801** G. COLMAN *Poor Gentl.* IV. i. 59 There are four spanking greys..that shall whisk you to town in a minute. **1817** W. T. MONCRIEFF *Giovanni in Lond.* I. ii, Ply your oar, and wisk me over to the other side. **1872** BLACK *Adv. Phaeton* ii, A solitary omnibus, which daily whisks a few country people..down to Uxbridge.

3. To brush or sweep lightly and rapidly from a surface, esp. with a light instrument, as a feather or small brush.

1621 G. SANDYS *Ovid's Met.* x. (1626) 214 Their tufted tailes Whiske vp the dust. *c* **1790** *Imison's Sch. Arts* II. 26 Having drawn the outline..faintly with charcoal, whisking out the faulty part with a feather. **1822** W. IRVING *Braceb. Hall* II. 259 His..horse stood, stamping and whisking off the flies. **1838** DICKENS *O. Twist* xxiii, The beadle..finished a piece of toast; whisked the crumbs off his knees [etc.]. **1881** WALFORD *Dick Netherby* v, 'An' shame on you for thinkin' sae.' Mrs. M'Clintock whisked her apron from her eyes.

4. To beat or whip with a rod of twigs or the like. *Obs.* in *gen.* sense: in later use, To stir or beat up (eggs, cream, etc.) with a light rapid movement (= WHIP *v.* 7), esp. by means of a whisk (see WHISK *sb.*[1] 3).

1530 R. WHYTFORD *Werke for Housholders* E i, Yf any chylde be..stubburne,..let it..be whysked with a good rodde. **1703** [implied in WHISKING *vbl.sb.*]. **1710** T. FULLER *Pharmacopœia* 325 Whites of Eggs beat up and whisk'd 'till it stand all in froth. **1836** MOLLARD *Art of Cookery* 265 A tea spoonful of Gum Dragon whisked to a solid froth. **1846** SOYER *Cookery* 49 Using three whole and three yolks of eggs, but omitting the whisked whites. **1904** *Cassell's New Dict. Cookery* s.v. *Cream, Whipped*, Double cream may be simply whipped by whisking it with a wire whisk until it thickens.

†**5.** *fig.* app. To hoax. (Cf. FRISK *v.* 4 b.)

1674 J. HOWARD *Engl. Mounsieur* v. iv, Hark ye Mr. Frenchlove, I believe you and I are whisk't with a couple of Wives, for Mr. Welbred, and Mr. Comely pretended to be in love with them, and the Devil a bit there's any such thing.

whisker (ˈhwɪskə(r)), *sb.*[1] Forms: 5–7 **wisker**, 6 **whysker**, (7 **whisquer**), 9 **whiscar**), 7– **whisker**. [f. WHISK *v.* + -ER[1]. Cf. Sw. *viskare* sponge, swab, LG. *wisker* a rubber, duster, G. *wischer* rubber, clout, (fig.) reprimand.]

1. Something that whisks or is used for whisking: applied to various objects, as a fan; a rod or switch; a bunch of feathers used as a brush (cf. WHISK *sb.*[1] 4); etc. *Obs.* or *dial.*

c **1425** *St. Mary of Oignies* II. iii. in *Anglia* VIII. 155 She sawe oure lady..as wiþ a wisker waftynge wynde vpon hir. **1567** HARMAN *Caveat* (1869) 89 A whyp is a whysker, that wyll wrest out blood. **1611** COTGR., *Houssine*, a Switch, or Whisker. **1825** JAMIESON, *Whisker, whiscar*, a bunch of feathers for sweeping anything.

†**2.** A person who whisks or moves briskly about; a lively young gallant: cf. WHISKING *ppl. a.* 1 c.

1595 GOSSON *Pleas. Quippes* vii, When yoong wiskers..in no good sort will spend the day, But be prophane, more then a Turke.

3. *slang* or *colloq.* Something great or excessive, a 'whopper' (cf. WHISKING *ppl. a.* 2); esp. a great lie, a 'bang'. Now *rare* or *Obs.*

1668 WILKINS *Real Char.* 32 Relations belonging to Quantity..Greatness, Magnitude, ample, large, vast, huge,..whisker,..magnifie, aggravate, exaggerate. **1672** EACHARD *Hobbs's State Nat., Let.* 35 It may be convenient for you to call this..a flam, a whisker, a caprice. **1694** ECHARD *Plautus* 9 Suppose I tell her some damn'd Wisker. [**1858** WRIGHT *Dict. Obs. & Prov. Engl.* s.v., 'The dam of that was a whisker', a phrase used when a great falsehood was uttered.]

†**b.** A 'whisking' or blustering wind: see WHISKING *ppl. a.* 1 b. *Obs.*

1670 RAY *Prov.* 288 March whisquer was never a good fisher.

4. The hair that grows on an adult man's face; formerly commonly applied to that on the upper lip, now called *moustache*, and sometimes to (or including) that on the chin (*beard*); now usu. restricted to that on the cheeks or sides of the face. **a.** *pl.*: usually collective; sometimes distributive, as ***a pair of whiskers***, denoting the hair on the two sides.

c **1600** *Timon* II. ii. (1842) 27 My wiskers hanging o're the ouerlipp. **1622** MABBE tr. *Aleman's Guzman d'Alf.* II. 259 Some spruce yonker, with a starcht beard, and his whiskers turn'd vp. **1650** BULWER *Anthropomet.* Pref., The rank Mustachos into whiskers grown. **1698** FRYER *Acc. E. India & P.* 390 His [*sc.* Persian's] Beard is Cut neatly, and the Whiskers..encouraged from one Ear to the other, in fashion of an Half-Moon on the upper Lip, with only a decent Peak on the under. **1719** DE FOE *Crusoe* I. (Globe) 152 What grew on my upper Lip..I had trimm'd into a large Pair of Mahometan Whiskers. **1808** W. WILSON *Hist. Diss. Ch.* I. 141 The men members wore whiskers upon their upper lips. **1823** E. MOOR *Suffolk Words, Whiskers*, the hair on the upper lip, as until lately, I believe, all over England. Now, the hair under the ears, sometimes under the eyes also, bear[s] this term, and the labial comæ, are called moustaches. **1837** DICKENS *Pickw.* xli, A tall fellow, with..very thick bushy whiskers meeting under his chin. **1854** R. S. SURTEES *Handley Cr.* iii, He grew whiskers under his chin. **1878** BESANT & RICE *Celia's Arb.* ii, His whiskers..were cut to the old-fashioned regulation 'mutton-chop'. They advanced into the middle of the cheek, and were then squared off in a line which met the large stiff collar below at an angle of forty-five.

b. *sing.*: in earlier use, a moustache; now, the hair on one side of the face; also collectively.

1706 PHILLIPS (ed. Kersey), *Whisker*, a tuft of Hair on the Upper Lip of a Man. **1762** STERNE *Tr. Shandy* V. i, La Fosseuse..traced the outline of a small whisker..upon one side of her upper lip. **1836** H. GREVILLE *Diary* 24 June (1883) 91 The ball lodged in the lining of the carriage, and some of the wadding in his whisker. **1848** DICKENS *Dombey* ii, He was a..shaggy fellow,..with a good deal of hair and whisker. **1851** in Kinglake *Crimea* (1863) I. xiv. 267 A mere lad without whisker or moustache. **1875** H. JAMES *Rod. Hudson* v. 173 A tall..gentleman..with a carefully brushed whisker.

†**c.** Applied to a lady's curl hanging over the cheek. (Cf. *whiskerette* below.) *Obs.*

1786 *Pogonologia* 55 About a century ago [in France] the ladies..curls hung down their cheeks as far as their bosom. These curls went by the name of whiskers.

d. Phr. ***to have whiskers*** and varr.: (of news, a subject, etc.) to be no longer novel or fresh; similarly ***to grow whiskers***. Also concr., of food: to become contaminated with mould.

1935 D. L. SAYERS *Gaudy Night* viii. 182 That old story...It's got whiskers on it—it's six years old. **1951** M. KENNEDY *Lucy Carmichael* VII. i. 345, I am putting on Capek's *R.U.R.* But it has got whiskers. It was quite a novelty when it was first put on. **1959** *Times* 6 May 4/6 The subject is beginning to grow whiskers. **1977** D. FRANCIS *Risk* vii. 78 The steak in the fridge had grown whiskers. **1977** D. O'SULLIVAN in D. Marcus *Best Irish Short Stories* II. 90 'Did I ever tell you the one about the Scotsman and the octopus?'..'It has whiskers.'

5. a. Each of a set of projecting hairs or bristles growing on the upper lip or about the mouth of certain animals; also applied to a similar set of feathers in certain birds, and to mystacial markings.

1678 *Lond. Gaz.* No. 1342/4 A light gray Gelding,..with an iron mark of a G. on the near Buttock, and two whiskers on the upper lip. **1712** E. COOKE *Voy. S. Sea* 329 The Raccoon has..Whiskers and Nose like a Pig. **1747** GRAY *Cat* iv, A whisker first and then a claw. **1752** J. HILL *Hist. Anim.* 352 The lesser Butcher-bird,..there are about the angles of the beak certain rigid bristles or hairs, which serve as whiskers. **1830** M. DONOVAN *Dom. Econ.* II. 85 The sea-otter is a large animal;..the eyes are small; the whiskers are white, strong, and numerous. **1879** HUXLEY *Sensation* Sci. & Cult. (1881) 266 The 'whiskers' of cats owe their functional importance to the abundant supply of nerves to the follicles in which their bases are lodged.

b. *fig.* A very small distance or amount, a fraction: used chiefly in comparisons. *colloq.* (orig. *U.S.*).

1913 *Dialect Notes* IV. 6 *Whisker, n.*, a little; a trifle. 'Move it just a whisker.' **1953** *Wall St. Jrnl.* 11 Aug. 1/5 The London price is still a whisker below the 30 cents a pound charged by major U.S. producers. **1973** P. O'DONNELL *Silver Mistress* i. 13 Sooner or later they would go on a job and not come back... Even in the past year they had come within a whisker of it twice. **1980** *Jrnl. R. Soc. Arts* Mar. 236/2 In these storms at sea, sunsets, sunrises, cloud formations and light conditions, Turner was within a whisker of pre-empting the great Monet himself. **1983** *Times* 15 July 18/3 Yesterday the shares rose 2p to 99p—a whisker from the year's high. **1984** *Listener* 14 June 15/3 Someone shoots for goal, and he either misses it by a whisker or by miles.

c. *Electr.* A wire used to form a rectifying contact with the surface of a semiconductor; cf. *cat's whisker* s.v. CAT *sb.*[1] 18 and 19.

1915, etc. [see *cat(s') whisker* s.v. CAT *sb.*[1] 18 and 19]. **1949** *Ann. Reg. 1948* 418 By the addition of a second wire whisker touching the germanium within a few thousands of an inch of the first the diode was converted into a triode. **1959** K. HENNEY *Radio Engin. Handbk.* (ed. 5) ix. 15 These diodes are representative of a family of germanium point-contact diodes using unplated whiskers. **1975** D. G. FINK *Electronics Engineers' Handbk.* IX. 62 Until 1965 point contact diodes were fabricated utilizing moderately low resistivity material with the rectifying contact established by contacting the semiconductor surface with a metal whisker.

6. *Naut.* **a.** Each of two wooden or iron spars extending laterally on each side of the bowsprit, for spreading the guys of the jib-boom.

1844 MRS. HOUSTON *Yacht Voy. Texas* II. 15 Our fore-top-mast was carried away, as well as the larboard whisker. **1885** LADY BRASSEY *The Trades* 382 It was found that the whiskers of the jibboom had carried away. **1913** M. ROBERTS *Salt of the Sea* viii. 208 Between the whiskers and the fore-mast.

b. A lever for exploding a torpedo.

1880 SLEEMAN *Torpedoes* 135 In addition to the nose piece, horizontal and vertical levers, or whiskers, may also be used.

7. A single crystal that has grown in a filamentous form a few microns thick, characterized by a tensile strength much greater than the bulk material and used in quantity as reinforcing agents.

1946 *Monthly Rev. Amer. Electroplaters' Soc.* Jan. 28/1 The growth of needle-crystals on cadmium deposits has caused considerable annoyance in the radio industry. These crystals are known as 'whiskers'. They grow between condenser plates of variable condensers, and, being electrical conductors, actually short-circuit the plates. **1951** *Corrosion* VII. 329/1 An attempt was made to develop whisker growths in the laboratory. **1961** *New Scientist* 28 Dec. 776/3 Whiskers, the hair-like crystals which are far stronger than steel, are now being incorporated in bonding materials: for example, General Electric's silver reinforced with sapphire whiskers. **1973** *Sci. Amer.* July 44/2 Alumina whiskers have a tensile strength of up to three million pounds per square inch and a modulus of 62 million pounds per square inch.

8. *attrib.* and *Comb.* (in sense 4). **whisker pole** *Naut.* (see quot. 1976); = sense 6 a.

1785 GROSE *Dict. Vulgar T.*, *Wisker splitter*, a man of intrigue. **1786** *Pogonologia* 80 It was then [*sc.* in Lewis XIV's reign] no uncommon thing for a..lover to have his whiskers..combed, and pomatumed by his mistress; and..a man of fashion took care to be..provided with..whisker-wax. **1813** MOORE *Post-Bag* viii. 14 When the rich rouge-pot..Tips even thy whisker-tops with red. **1853** 'C. BEDE' *Verdant Green* I. xi, He told Verdant, that his claret had been repeatedly tapped,..his whisker-bed [*i.e.* face] napped heavily. **1954** *Motor Boating* Dec. 27/1 *Iris* was flying all her kites—main, mizzen, genoa winged out on the whisker pole, and mizzen staysails. **1960** J. J. ROWLANDS *Spindrift* 204 On the yacht-club float a girl..is rubbing down the last coat of varnish on a whisker pole. **1976** *Oxf. Compan. Ships & Sea* 938/1 *Whisker pole*, a short bearing-out spar used in yachts and sailing dinghies to bear out the clew of the jib on the opposite side of the mainsail when running before the wind, thus obtaining some of the advantage which would be gained in a larger vessel when she sets a spinnaker. **1980** *Yachts & Yachting* 29 Feb. 651/2 'American Express' carried two poles that extended from 11.5 ft to 18 ft plus a standard pole of 7.5 ft. The long ones were used as a spinnaker pole in the collapsed position, as whisker pole in the fully extended position, and as a bowsprit in the 14ft length.

Hence **ˈwhisker** *v.* (*nonce-wd.*), *trans.* to furnish with whiskers; **ˈwhiskerage**, whiskers collectively, a growth of whiskers; **ˈwhiskerer** (*nonce-wd.*), a man who wears whiskers; **whiskeˈrette**, a small whisker; a curl at the side of a girl's face (cf. sense 4 c above); **ˈwhiskerless** *a.*, destitute of whiskers.

1812 *Examiner* 5 Oct. 632/2 Deliberating how still further to Germanize and to *whisker out British soldiers. **1858** CARLYLE *Fredk. Gt.* I. i. (1872) I. 6 Fellows..with such a breadth of sabre, extent of *whiskerage [etc.]. **1859** MEREDITH *R. Feverel* xxxvi, The trim of their whiskerage. **1717** *Entertainer* No. 1. 4 We are no *Whiskerers of the Order of St. Jacobs. **1880** *Athenæum* 2 Oct. 440 Her hair is trimly curled in '*whiskerettes'. **1896** *Columbus* (Ohio) *Dispatch* 23 Sept., A man wearing whiskers,..his chin shaven and allowing two distinct whiskerettes to be plainly discerned. **1843** DICKENS *Mart. Chuz.* (1844) ii. 10 His very throat was moral... Serene and *whiskerless. **1848** —— *Dombey* xxxi, Mr. Towlinson is whiskerless.

whisker, *sb.*[2], whist-player: see WHISK *sb.*[2]

whiskerandos (hwɪskəˈrændɒs). *humorous.* [f. WHISKER, with ending in imitation of Spanish words.] Name of a character (*Don Ferolo Whiskerandos*) in Sheridan's play 'The Critic' (1779): hence *allusively* (more commonly in the form **whiskerando**, the *-s* being taken as sign of pl.), a (heavily) whiskered man. Hence **whiskerandoed** (-dəʊd) *a.*, whiskered.

1807 *Sporting Mag.* XXIX. 179 The mustachio salute is not only sanctioned now by the dowagers of the whiskerando tribe, but even voted by the young smooth-lipped belles to be 'funny enough'. **1831** JEKYLL *Corr.* (1894) 287 To the great dismay of a whiskerandos, second brother of my lord. **1838** SOUTHEY *Doctor* clvi. V. 227 To.. what extravangances would the whiskerandoed macaronies of Bond Street.. proceed, if the beard.. were.. to 'make the man!' **1894** STEVENSON *St. Ives* ii, Some of these old whiskerandos, originally peasants, trained since boyhood in victorious armies,.. could ill brook their change of circumstance.

whiskered ('hwɪskəd), *a.* [f. WHISKER *sb.*[1] + ED[2].]

1. Having whiskers. **a.** Of men: see WHISKER *sb.*[1] 4.

1769 T. WARTON *Let.* 10 Oct. in D. Garrick *Private Corr.* (1831) I. 369, I went on board one of the Russian ships, and had the pleasure of being surrounded with a thousand whiskered sailors and soldiers from Archangel. **1784** COWPER *Task* III. 768 Our forefathers—a grave whisker'd race. **1809** W. IRVING *Knickerb.* v. vii, To have seen him.. in martial array—booted to the middle—sashed to the chin—collared to the ears—whiskered to the teeth. **1840** THACKERAY *Shabby-Genteel Story* vii, A tall whiskered man, who.. looked like a field-marshal.

b. Of animals: see WHISKER *sb.*[1] 5; *spec.* as a descriptive appellation of particular species, as ***whiskered auk, fly-catcher, shrike, tern.***

1764 GRAINGER *Sugar Cane* II. 62 The whisker'd vermin race. **1783** LATHAM *Gen. Syn. Birds* II. I. 364 Whiskered Fl[ycatcher]. **1788** COWPER *Death of Mrs. Throckmorton's Bulfinch* 35 A beast.. Long-back'd, long-tail'd, with whisker'd snout. **1809** SHAW *Gen. Zool.* VII. 298 Whiskered Shrike. **1826** KIRBY & SP. *Entomol.* xlvi. IV. 309 Whiskered (*Mystacinum*), when the upper lip is furnished with whiskers (*Mystax*), or bearded. **1872** COUES *N. Amer. Birds* 342 Whiskered Auk.. two series.. of filamentous white feathers on each side of head. **1897** R. B. SHARPE *Handbk. Birds Gt. Brit.* IV. 8 The Whiskered Tern is an accidental visitor to the British Islands.

2. Formed into or constituting whiskers. *rare*$^{-1}$.

1737 M. GREEN *Spleen* 761 Preferring sense, from chin that's bare, To nonsense thron'd in whisker'd hair.

whiskery, *a.* [f. WHISKER *sb.*[1]]

1. Having large whiskers.

1848 THACKERAY *Bk. Snobs* xxxiv, The old lady is.. as tall and whiskery as a grenadier.

2. Suggestive of or resembling whiskers or a whisker; having whiskers.

1927 H. V. MORTON *In Search of England* v. 98 The dark room smelt of.. that indefinite whiskery smell of old men. **1959** *Times* 4 May 4/5 They fluffed a chip out of whiskery grass. **1984** *Listener* 10 May 3/1 Streets with a few measly roadside stalls peddling second-rate oranges and whiskery root vegetables.

whisket, var. WISKET *dial.*, a basket.

whiskey: see WHISKY.

whiskful ('hwɪskfʊl). [f. WHISK *sb.*[1] + -FUL 2.] As much as a whisk will carry: see WHISK *sb.*[1] 4.

1840 *Dairy of a Nun* I. xiv. 200 As the animals are brought up.. to be blessed, the priest mutters a few Latin words, and dashes a whiskful of water in their faces.

whiskied ('hwɪskɪd), *a. rare.* Also **-keyed.** [f. WHISKY *sb.*[1] + -ED[2].] Saturated or tainted with whisky.

1850 THACKERAY *Pendennis* lvi, In his whiskeyed blood there was not a black drop, nor in his muddled brains a bitter feeling. **1919** *Blackw. Mag.* Dec. 767/2 He breathed whiskied breath at me.

whiskified ('hwɪskɪfaɪd), *a.* Also **-k(e)y-**, *Sc.* **whus-**. [f. WHISKY *sb.*[1] + *-fied*, pa. ppl. ending corresp. to -FY.] Affected by excessive drinking of whisky.

1802 H. MARTIN *Helen of Glenross* III. 128 Paddy was only a little whiskified. **1850** THACKERAY *Pendennis* v, Fact and fiction reeled together in his muzzy, whiskified brain. **1864** LATTO *Tam. Bodkin* xiii. 126 'I shay—hic—open the door, will ye?'.. quoth the whuskifeed voice. **1872** HOWELLS *Wedd. Journ.* viii, That poor, whiskeyfied, Irish tatterdemalion.

whiskijack, -john, var. WHISKY JACK, etc.

†'**whiskin**[1]. *north. dial. Obs.* [Of unascertained origin.] A shallow kind of drinking-vessel.

1635 HEYWOOD *Philocoth.* 45 Noggins, Whiskins, Piggins. **1640** BRATHWAIT *Two Lanc. Lovers* 19 Wee will han a whiskin at every rushbearing. *a* **1700** B. E. *Dict. Cant. Crew, Whiskins*, shallow, brown Bowls to Drink out off. **1818** SCOTT *Hrt. Midl.* xxxii, A whole whiskin, or black pot of sufficient double ale.

†'**whiskin**[2]. *slang. Obs.* [Cf. *pimp-whisk(in.*] A pander.

1632 BROME *Northern Lasse* I. iv, Farewell old Whiskin. **1635** SHIRLEY *Lady Pleas.* IV. (1637) G 3 b, I am promis'd a convenient whiskin,.. That has read all Sir Pandarus workes. **1640** H. MILL *Nights Search* 145 To make him whiskin.

whisking ('hwɪskɪŋ), *vbl. sb.* [f. WHISK *v.* + -ING[1].] The action of the verb WHISK, in various senses.

a **1553** UDALL *Royster D.* II. iv. (Arb.) 37 Is all your delite and ioy In whiskyng and ramping abroade like a Tom boy? **1594** MARLOWE & NASHE *Dido* II. C 3, The crye of beasts, the ratling of the windes, Or whisking of these leaues. *a* **1625** FLETCHER *Noble Gent.* v. i, With the whisking of my sword about. **1668** DRYDEN *Even. Love* I. i, The whisking of a Silk-Gown, and the rash of a Tabby-Pettycoat. **1703** THORESBY *Let. to Ray* (E.D.S.), *Whisking*, is also switching; 'there will be whisking for't'. **1797** MRS. INCHBALD *Wives as they were* II. i. 30 The whisking of a woman's gown made me give a sudden start! **1853** DICKENS *Bleak Ho.* xlix, A rattling of tin mugs, a whisking of brooms. **1876** MISS BROUGHTON *Joan* I. i, A herd of deer.. trooping from one glade to another, with a tossing of great horns and whisking of tiny tails.

'**whisking,** *ppl. a.* [f. as prec. + -ING[2].]

1. That whisks, in various senses: see the verb.

1522 SKELTON *Why not to Court* 1161, I suppose that he is Of Ieremy the whyskynge rod, The flayle, the scourge of almighty God. **1591** SYLVESTER *Du Bartas* I. ii. 637 With whisking broom they brush and sweep. **1690** C. NESSE *O. & N. Test.* I. 268 This whisking tail of the dragon.. may cast down some doctors of the church.

†**b.** Of the wind: Blowing briskly, forcibly, or freshly. *Obs.*

1545 ASCHAM *Toxoph.* (Arb.) 156 A litle winde in a moystie day, stoppeth a shafte more than a good whiskynge wynde in a clere daye. **1591** SYLVESTER *Du Bartas* I. i. 817 As swiftly whirling as the whisking winde. **1635** SWAN *Spec. Mundi* v. §2. (1643) 171 If the exhalation be little, tenuous or thin, then we have onely a pleasant whisking wind,.. by which the aire is gently moved. **1697** in *Nat. Hist. Irel.* (1726) 113 The air was somewhat troubled with little whisking winds, seeming to meet contrary ways.

c. Of a person: Moving actively, brisk, lively, smart. *slang* or *colloq.* ? *Obs.*

1611 MIDDLETON & DEKKER *Roaring Girl* I 1, What are your whisking gallants to our husbands. **1681** T. FLATMAN *Heraclitus Ridens* No. 40. (1713) II. 2 If you talk of Rubbers and Whiskers,.. he's a whisking Rubber for you;.. he can rub one Man into two. **1824** CARLYLE *Let. to Miss Welsh* 23 June, Captain Smith was.. brisk,.. whisking, smart of speech.

2. Great, excessive, 'bouncing', 'whopping'. *slang* or *colloq.* (now only *dial.*).

1673 R. HEAD *Canting Acad.* 166 They have whisking water-works for evacuation. **1681** HICKERINGILL *News fr. Colchester* Wks. 1716 I. 394 With what astonishment the People.. were struck, when they read.. this Whisking Lye. **1706** PHILLIPS (ed. Kersey), *Rousing Lie*, a whisking great one. **1792** BURNS *Willie's Wife* ii, A whiskin' beard about her mou'.

†'**whiskish,** *a. Obs. rare*$^{-1}$. [f. WHISK *sb.*[1] or *v.* + -ISH[1].] Lively, frisky.

1599 *Sir Clyom.* xv. in *Peele's Wks.* (1888) II. 172 The whores be so whiskish.

whisky, whiskey ('hwɪskɪ), *sb.*[1] Also 8 **-kie, -kee.** [Short for WHISKYBAE, etc. (Gael. *uisgebeatha* lit. 'water of life'), though this is not actually evidenced so early (but Ramsay has *usque* for USQUEBAUGH, q.v., in 1728). In modern trade usage, Scotch *whisky* and Irish *whiskey* are thus distinguished in spelling; *whisky* is the usual spelling in Britain and *whiskey* that in the U.S.]

a. A spirituous liquor distilled originally in Ireland and Scotland, and in the British Isles still chiefly, from malted barley (with or without unmalted barley or other cereals), in U.S. chiefly from maize or rye. With *a* and *pl.*, a drink of whisky.

Also in ***whisky-and-milk, -soda, -water*** (often so hyphened), denoting mixed or diluted drinks.

1715 in Maidment *Bk. Scot. Pasquils* (1868) 404 Whiskie shall put our brains in rage. **1746** M. HUGHES *Jrnl. Late Reb.* 46 A double Portion of Oatmeal and Whisky. *note*, Whisky is a hot Malt Spirit. **1753** *Gray's Inn Jrnl.* No. 48 Whiskee—Po!—Give me a Glass of that Rhenish. **1753** *Gentl. Mag.* Aug. 391/2 In one dram shop only in this town [*sc.* Dublin], there are 120 gallons of that accursed spirit, whiskey, sold. **1827** *Whitehall* II. iii, The Major then mixed himself a glass of whiskey and water in equal portions. **1835** DICKENS *Sk. Boz, Parl. Sk.*, He.. went home.. for his whiskey-and-water. **1884** G. MOORE *Mummer's Wife* xvi, 'I think I'll have a whisky.' 'Scotch or Irish?' asked the barman. **1894** K. GRAHAME *Pagan Papers* 76 Those of us who were left being assembled to drink a parting whisky-and-milk. **1898** G. B. SHAW *Mrs. Warren's Profession* II. 177, I could do with a whisky and soda now very well. **1903** *Times* 31 July 13/6 In less than an hour he sold 22 whiskies. **1924** H. CRANE *Let.* 30 Nov. (1965) 195 As whiskey and soda was served I quickly revived. **1979** G. ST. AUBYN *Edward VII* vi. 316 Offering him a whisky-and-soda and a cigar.

b. *attrib.* and *Comb.*, as ***whisky bottle, -brose*** (cf. BROSE b), ***-can, -cocktail, decanter, -drinker, -drinking*** sb. and adj., ***-gill, glass, -peg*** (PEG *sb.*[1] 6), ***-punch, -shop, -still, -toddy***; ***whisky-gold, -soaked, -sodden*** adjs.; **whisky-head** *U.S. slang*, one who consumes a great deal of whisky; **whisky-house** *Obs.*, a place where whisky is sold; **whisky insurrection** or **rebellion** *U.S. Hist.*, an outbreak in Pennsylvania in 1794 against an excise duty on spirits imposed by Congress in 1791; **whisky mac** (also **Whisky Mac**), whisky and ginger wine mixed in equal proportions; a drink of this; **whisky money** *Hist.*, the proportion of the beer and spirit duty which was allocated to technical education by the Local Taxation (Customs and Excise) Act of 1890; **whisky-poker** (see quot.); **whisky priest**, an habitually drunken priest; **whisky ring** *U.S. Hist.*, a combination of distillers and revenue officers formed in 1872 to defraud the government of part of the tax on spirits; **whisky-skin** *U.S. slang*, a drink containing whisky; **whisky-soda** (not in U.K. use), whisky-and-soda; **whisky sour** orig. *U.S.*, a drink of whisky acidulated with the juice of citrus fruit; **whisky-straight** *U.S. slang*, whisky without water; **whisky voice**, a hoarse or alcoholic voice; **whisky-water** = *whisky-and-water*.

1843 'R. CARLTON' *New Purchase* II. lvi. 242 He abstained.. from his *whisky bottle. **1981** M. HATFIELD *Spy Fever* I. vi. 53 The whisky bottle was still in play, though its contents.. had not shrunk catastrophically. **1822** A. CUNNINGHAM *Trad. Tales, Allan-a-Maut* (1887) 136 *Whisky-brose shall be my breakfast, and my supper shall be the untaken-down spirit. **1845** ELIZA COOK *Poems, Fisher Boat* 12 Jolly mates, a *whiskey-can, and trusty nets for me! **1862** JERRY THOMAS *How to mix Drinks* Contents, *Whiskey Cobbler, Cocktail. **1931** M. ALLINGHAM *Police at Funeral* xi. 151 He.. shot a hopeless glance at the *whisky decanter. **1976** E. WARD *Hanged Man* xxi. 129 Galbraith placed the whisky decanter within reach. **1771** WESLEY *Jrnl.* 18 June (1827) III. 424 The house.. was filled with *whisky drinkers. **1905** ROLLESTON *Dis. Liver* 178 Hobnailed, Gin, or Whiskey-drinker's liver. **1883** 'MARK TWAIN' *Life on Mississippi* lviii. 571 *Whiskey-drinking, breakdown-dancing rapscallions. **1884** —— *Huck. Finn* xxi. 212 There was considerable whisky drinking going on. **1891** C. ROBERTS *Adrift Amer.* 34 The row was the outcome of whiskey drinking. **1785** BURNS *Holy Fair* xix, Be't *whisky gill, or penny wheep, Or ony stronger potion. **1940** R. CHANDLER *Farewell my Lovely* xiii. 82 She wore a hat with a crown the size of a *whisky glass. **1918** E. SITWELL *Clown's Houses* 15 The sunlight pours all *whisky-gold. **1944** S. BELLOW *Dangling Man* 179 'Took you in it at last, didn't I!' I exclaimed. 'You damned old *whisky-head.' **1968** P. OLIVER *Screening Blues* 23 Blues about liquor and the 'whisky-head man', about prostitution, gambling, vagrancy and intended violence, figure in the work of singers of all generations. **1767** *Scots Mag.* Apr. 222 Grant kept a *whisky-house. **1835** R. M. BIRD *Hawks of Hawk-Hollow* II. 6 You would have some of the wherewithall smuggled up to this identical old woman's whiskey-house! **1824** *Mass. Spy* 28 July (Thornton *Amer. Gloss.*), Tinctured with the duelling or *whiskey-insurrection mania. **1960** *Spectator* 14 Oct. 579 It [*sc.* Stone's Ginger Wine] is a little cloying taken neat, but mixed with an equal quantity of whisky it becomes '*Whisky Mac'. **1961** L. PAYNE *Nose on my Face* iv. 63, I.. said I'd have a whiskey mac. **1976** *Liverpool Echo* 22 Nov. 7/5 A thief stole a £45 cask of whisky mac from an off-licence in Pasture Road, Moreton. **1982** BARR & YORK *Official Sloane Ranger Handbk.* 92/2 You drink beer, whisky macs, cherry brandy, sloe gin—or neat whisky. **1911** *Encycl. Brit.* XXVI. 495/1 If the '*whisky' money.. were found to be well and carefully expended, no future Chancellor would be able to divert it to any other purpose. **1937** G. A. N. LOWNDES *Silent Social Revolution* ii. 39 Action taken by the Technical Education Committees of the County Councils.. to encourage the formation of classes and guarantee them financial support out of the 'Whiskey Money'. **1973** L. HOLCOMBE *Victorian Ladies at Work* ii. 30 A portion of the 'whisky money', the proceeds from the increased duties on beer and spirits, to be spent on technical education by the county and county borough councils. **1889** CONAN DOYLE *Sign of Four* xii, There he sat.. drinking *whisky-pegs and smoking cheroots. **1878** J. S. CAMPION *On Frontier* (ed. 2) 25 *Whisky-poker, a harmless non-gambling game, in which the winner gets a drink and the losers a smell at the cork of the bottle. **1939** G. GREENE *Lawless Roads* vi. 161 'He was just what we call a *whisky priest.'.. He had taken one of his sons to be baptized, but the priest was drunk. **1971** H. C. RAE *Marksman* I. iii. 19 With cheap striped pyjamas buttoned close around his throat Doyle looked like a whisky priest in a penal settlement. **1977** *Times* 4 Aug. 10/5 The communist equivalent of one of those Greeneland fables wherein a whisky priest rallies.. to strike a blow for the God he no longer believes in. **1785** BURNS *Scotch Drink* xvii, A glass o' *Whisky-punch. **1850** THACKERAY *Pendennis* xlii[i], His.. utterance began to fail him, over his sixth tumbler of whisky-punch. **1863** in Thornton *Amer. Gloss.* s.v., The *whisky rebellion of Pennsylvania. **1884** *Boston* (Mass.) *Jrnl.* 25 Sept., The candidate of the *whisky ring. **1804** LEWIS & CLARK *Orig. Jrnls. Lewis & Clark Expedition* (1904) I. 10 Such as have made hunting.. a pretext to cover their design of visiting a neighbouring *whiskey shop. **1868** A. K. H. BOYD *Less. Middle Age* 29 The sight of a whisky-shop or a gin-palace is to such an overwhelming temptation. **1856** *Yale Lit. Mag.* XXI. 146 (Th.), Nine *whisky skins, and our spirits rushed together. **1891** *Sunday Times* 22 Feb. 2/3, I heard of the contemplated establishment of a London American club, the scheme of which seemed to comprise unlimited cocktails, whiskey skins, corpse revivers, [etc.]. *a* **1910** 'MARK TWAIN' *Autobiogr.* (1924) I. 209 Some old *whisky-soaked, profane.. infidel of a tramp captain. **1978** R. LUDLUM *Holcroft Covenant* xiii. 153 Ellis made arrangements for the whiskey-soaked clothes to be picked up by the cleaners and returned by mid afternoon. **1915** H. L. WILSON *Ruggles of Red Gap* 50 Here, Charley, *veesky-soda! **1975** O. SELA *Bengali Inheritance* xxv. 220 Shaking heads over their whisky-sodas saying, what could you expect. **1883** 'MARK TWAIN' *Life on Mississippi* lvi. 548 A harmless *whiskey-sodden tramp. **1891** E. KINGLAKE *Australian at H.* 102 You whisky-sodden old miscreant. **1889** *Cent. Dict.*, *Whisky sour. **1904** R. M. LOVETT *Richard Gresham* 186 Bring a couple o' whiskey sours there, barkeep. **1975** D. LODGE *Changing Places* iii. 116 The lavish whisky-sours and daiquiris being prepared by the host. **1980** L. BIRNBACH et al. *Official Preppy Handbk.* 102/2 Tailgate picnics, whiskey sours in the stadium, and the general complexity of the sport guarantee that nobody knows what is going on. **1785** BURNS *Scotch Drink* xx, Thae curst horse-leeches o' th' Excise, Wha mak the *Whisky Stells their prize! **1864** *Congressional Globe* 21 Apr. 1876/2 From the impassioned tone of the gentleman from Illinois.. one would suppose that he had been investing in *whisky straight. **1872** 'MARK TWAIN' *Innoc. Abr.* xv. 106 We will take a whisky-straight. **1812** COL. HAWKER *Diary* (1893) I. 59, I sat down with some *whisky toddy. **1964** J. C. CATFORD in D. Abercrombie et al. *Daniel Jones* 32 Simultaneous whisper + voice + creak: one form of 'beery' or '*whisky' voice. **1978** J. UPDIKE *Coup* (1979) vii. 294 The women in the souk, with those long red finger-nails and blue hair in bandanas and those cracked whiskey voices. **1919** 'ETIENNE' *Strange Tales from Fleet* 5 'Thank you,' said the Captain, 'a *whisky water, please.' **1978** T. WILLIS *Buckingham Palace Connection* i. 7 The ice-machine had broken down and I had to put up with a tepid whisky-water.

Hence **whisky** *v.*, *trans.* to supply with whisky, to give a drink of whisky to.

1830 G. COLMAN *Random Rec.* II. 139 Post-boys and waggoners water'd their horses, and *whisky'd* themselves. **1862** B. TAYLOR *Home & Abr.* Ser. II. 120 The horses were changed, and the passengers whiskied. **1882** [LEES & CLUTTERBUCK] *Three in Norway* ix. (1888) 65 We 'whisky' every one who turns up at camp.

whisky, whiskey, *sb.*^{2} [app. f. WHISK *v.* + -Y^1, from its swift movement.] A kind of light two-wheeled one-horse carriage, used in England and America in the late 18th and early 19th c. Also called TIMWHISKY.

1769 *Lloyd's Even. Post* 3–5 July 15 As a Gentleman was returning to Battersea, in his whisky, his horse took fright, and ran away. **1784** ELIZ. CARTER *Let. to Mrs. Vesey* 30 July, Travelling over hill and dale in a whisky. **1794** W. FELTON *Carriages* (1801) I. 58 The gig from the whiskey also differs materially, the whiskey being constructed on the most simple plan, with the body united to the carriage. **1824** SCOTT *St. Ronan's* xiv, It was a two-wheeled vehicle, which ..aspired only to the humble name of that almost forgotten accommodation, a whiskey. **1837** W. B. ADAMS *Carriages* 245 The old One-horse Chaise, or Whiskey, was as heavy as the modern Cabriolet, without its grace of form. **1844** T. WEBSTER *Encycl. Dom. Econ.* §6672 A whiskey or chair is a small chair, not hung by braces, but placed on the shafts, having springs of some kind interposed between them and the axles... It is made low, and very light. **1879** LOUISA POTTER *Lanc. Mem.* 139 [She] but rarely went out of her own grounds except to church, in a machine which ninety years ago was called a 'whiskey'.

'whisky, *a. rare.* [f. WHISK *v.* + -Y^1: cf. prec.] Light and lively, flighty.

1782 MISS BURNEY *Cecilia* IX. iii, Talking in such a whisky frisky manner that nobody can understand him.

b. *Comb.* **whisky-bobby**, angler's name for some kind of artificial bait.

1904 F. WHISHAW *Lovers at Fault* vi, Flies, minnows or whisky-bobbies might be used.

whiskybae, whisquy-beath, var. USQUEBAUGH. (Cf. 16th cent. *iskiebae.*)

1792 GALLOWAY *Poems* 72, I told him I ne'er drank no Whiskybae. **1792** *Statist. Acc. Scot.* III. 525 A refreshment ..consisting generally of whisquy-beath, or some foreign liquor, butter and cheese.

whiskyish ('hwɪskɪɪʃ), *a. rare.* [f. WHISKY, WHISKEY *sb.*^{1} + -ISH^1.] **a.** Inclined for whisky. **b.** Tainted with whisky.

1929 W. DEEPING *Roper's Row* ii. 11 Don't be in a 'urry, my lad. Wait till they're warm. If they're whiskyish, wait till the whisky's got 'em. **1929** E. BOWEN *Last September* vi. 73 Some one tried to kiss you with whiskyish breath.

whisky jack ('hwɪskɪ dʒæk), Also 8 **whiski-jack,** 9 **whiskey jack**; also with hyphen. [Altered form of next by substitution of *jack* for *john* (cf. JACK *sb.*^{1}).] A popular name for the common grey jay of Canada, *Perisoreus canadensis.*

1772 Whiskijack [see next]. **1873** *Forest & Stream* 11 Dec. 273/3 Two whisky jacks are driven into camp, and now sit on the palisades over the fire. **1888** LEES & CLUTTERBUCK *B.C. 1887* xxviii. (1892) 320 Those delightful birds known as the Camp Robbers or Whisky Jacks.

whisky john ('hwɪskɪ dʒɒn). In 8 **whiski-**; 20 **wiskajon.** [Corruption of the American Indian name (Cree *wiskatjan*, Montagnais *wishkutshan*).] = prec.

1772 *Phil. Trans.* LXII. 386 *Lanius...Excubitor...* Great Butcher-bird... Cinereous Shrike... White Whiskijohn at Hudson's Bay... *Corvus..Canadensis...* Cinereous Crow. .. These birds are called Whiskijohn and Whiskijack at the Hudson's Bay. **1856** BALLANTYNE *Fur Traders* xi, Whisky-johns are the most impudent, puffy, conceited, little birds that exist. **1912** E. T. SETON *Arctic Prairies* 301 Each morning..gray Wiskajon and his mate..came wailing through the woods.

whisle, -ler, -ling, obs. ff. WHISTLE, etc.

whisp, *sb. rare.* [Echoic: cf. WHISPER.] A slight blast or puff (of wind) or sprinkle (of rain). So **whisp** *v.*, implied in **whisping** *vbl. sb.*, used of a slight blast or a low rustling sound: see quots.

1379 *Glouc. Cath. MS. 19. No. I.* I. iii. lf. 5 b, The ers hole by egestion.i. schityng Crackynge & Whispynge by nethe is purgynge propirly of the guttys. **1884** *19th Cent.* Feb. 241 A whisp or two of cold wind. **1901** *Daily News* 2 Feb. 5/7 Nothing broke the stillness but the whisping of the waters. **1923** *Times* 27 Apr. 12/1 A whisp of rain,..too light to be called a shower, touched the crowd here and there.

whisp, variant of WISP.

whisper ('hwɪspə(r)), *sb.* [f. WHISPER *v.*]

1. a. An act, or the action, of whispering, or speaking 'under one's breath'; the low non-resonant quality of voice which characterizes this (esp. in phr. ***in a whisper***).

In *Phonetics* (equivalently), Speech or vocal sound without the musical or resonant tone produced by vibration of the vocal cords; a 'breath' sound, as distinguished from 'voice' (see BREATH 10, VOICE *sb.* 1 g); in strict use implying also contraction of the glottis: see also 4.

1608 SHAKS. *Per.* III. i. 9 The sea-mans Whistle Is as a whisper in the eares of death, Vnheard. **1626** BACON *Sylva* §174 The Inward Voice or Whisper can neuer giue a Tone. **1758** JOHNSON *Idler* No. 10 ¶9 Secrets which he always communicates in a whisper. **1778** MISS BURNEY *Evelina* (1791) I. xxiii. 124, I heard him say..in an audible whisper, —which is a mode of speech very distressing and disagreeable to by-standers [etc.]. **1836** DICKENS *Sk. Boz, Crim. Crts.*, Conversing in low whispers. **1837** —— *Pickw.* xlv, Mr. Weller delivered this..with great vehemence of whisper. **1855** BAIN *Senses & Int.* II. iv. §35 (1864) 319 In a whisper there is no musical sound. **1877** SWEET *Handbk. Phonetics* 5 Whisper in popular language simply means speech without voice. Phonetically whisper implies not merely absence of voice, but a definite contraction of the glottis. **1882** BESANT *All Sorts* xxii, 'Mind, it's a secret.' He lowered his voice to a whisper.

b. A whispered word, phrase, remark, or speech.

1599 SHAKS. *Hen. V*, IV. Chor. 7 From Camp to Camp,.. The Humme of eyther Army stilly sounds; That the fixt Centinels almost receiue The secret Whispers of each others Watch. **1624** MASSINGER *Parl. Love* v. i, She has put The judges to their whisper. **1770** GOLDSM. *Des. Vill.* 203 Full well the busy whisper, circling round, Convey'd the dismal tidings when he frown'd. **1821** BYRON *Sardanap.* III. i. 424 What, at whispers With my stern brother? **1829** SCOTT *Anne of G.* xi, The sage Persian comforted him by a long whisper, of which the last part only was heard. **1833** HT. MARTINEAU *Demerara* xi, Some relaxation of discipline allowed them to exchange a whisper from time to time.

c. ***pig's whisper***: see PIG *sb.*^{1} 14 c. ***stage whisper***: see STAGE *sb.* 14.

2. A secret or slight utterance, mention, or report; a suggestion, insinuation, hint, light rumour (communicated in a whispering voice, or *fig.* by a soft rustling sound (cf. 3) or mentally); with negative, the slightest mention, the 'least word'.

1596 DALRYMPLE tr. *Leslie's Hist. Scot.* II. 178 Not a word, nor quhisper in thair contrare. **1602** SHAKS. *Ham.* I. i. 80 At least the whisper goes so. *Ibid.* IV. v. 82 The people ..vnwholsome in their thoughts, and whispers For good Polonius death. **1664** in *Extr. St. Papers rel. Friends* Ser. II. (1911) 191 Some whispers that the Judges would not proceede against any of the Quakers. **1677** W. HUBBARD *Pres. St. New Eng.* 43 The bullet passing through his own hair, by that whisper telling him that death was very near. **1711** STEELE *Spect.* No. 64 ¶1 He [*sc.* a Courtier] deals much in Whispers, and you may see he dresses according to the best Intelligence. **1780** BENTHAM *Introd. Mor. & Legisl.* xvii. §11 (1789) 313 If the thunders of the law prove impotent, the whispers of simple morality can have but little influence. **1823** SCOTT *Quentin D.* vi, A whisper from those recesses of the heart in which lies much that the owner does not know of. **1827** J. W. CROKER in *C. Papers* 17 Apr. (1884) I. 374 No one raises even a whisper of reproach against Peel. **1846** MRS. A. MARSH *Fr. Darcy* xxviii, He rejected the pleadings of pity—the whispers of conscience. **1873** BURTON *Hist. Scot.* VI. lxxii. 292 There were whispers that he was to be put to death without trial.

3. *fig.* A soft rustling sound resembling or suggesting that of a whispering voice.

1637 MILTON *Lycidas* 136 The milde whispers..Of shades and wanton winds, and gushing brooks. **1798** COLERIDGE *Anc. Mar.* III. xiii, With far-heard whisper, o'er the sea, Off shot the spectre-bark. **1842** TENNYSON *Gard. Dau.* 248 Whispers, like the whispers of the leaves That tremble round a nightingale. **1898** 'H. S. MERRIMAN' *Roden's Corner* v, A silence, broken only by the whisper of the wind through the rigging.

4. *attrib.* Uttered in a whisper; in *Phonetics*, uttered without the vocal murmur, 'breath' (see BREATH 10); ***whisper-like, -proof*** adjs.; **whisper-shot** *nonce-wd.* [after *ear-shot*], the distance within which a whisper can be heard.

1626 BRETON *Fantasticks* Wks. (Grosart) II. 6/2 The leaues of the trees are in whisper talkes. **1838** E. GUEST *Engl. Rhythms* I. 9 It is..doubtful if there ever was a language which had its whisper letters perfect. *Ibid.* 10 The whisper sounds of the two liquids *l, r*, constitute two distinct letters in Welsh. **1846** *Proc. Philol. Soc.* III. 4 The sound of *th*, whether whisper or vocal. **1876** LANIER in *Atlantic Monthly* (1899) LXXXIII. 799/1 I..inserted a whisper chorus..to prepare by its straining pianissimo for the outburst of jubilation. **1876** *Gentl. Mag.* Sept. 339 To ascertain whether..our boasted right of asylum was really whisper-proof. **1890** W. S. GILBERT *Foggerty's Fairy* etc. 152 Informing everybody within whisper-shot..that this was my first brief. **1904** W. H. HUDSON *Green Mansions* iii. 45 The mysterious melody began... It was uttered by the same being heard on former occasions..that low, whisper-like talking. **1936** N. STREATFEILD *Ballet Shoes* xviii. 278 Petrova looked round to see that Posy was out of whisper-shot. **1964** J. C. CATFORD in D. Abercrombie et al. *Daniel Jones* 37 What *feels* like *breath*..begins to *sound* more whisper-like at rates of flow above about 300 cl/sec.

Hence **'whisperhood** *nonce-wd.*, the condition of being a whisper (in sense 2); **'whisperless** *a.*, not uttering a whisper, or in which no whisper is heard; absolutely silent; **'whisperous** (whence **'whisperously** *adv.*), **'whispery** *adjs.*, full of or characterized by whispers; resembling a whisper.

1710 SWIFT *Examiner* No. 15 ¶5, I know a Lie that now disturbs half the Kingdom with its Noise, which..I can remember in its *Whisper-hood. **1863** P. S. WORSLEY *Poems & Transl.* 19 Crouching *whisperless. **1911** R. BROOKE *Coll. Poems* (1918) 74 The secret deeps are whisperless. **1884** LD. LYTTON in *19th Cent.* Dec. 898 The *whisperous, awe-struck tone of the voice. **1892** —— *King Poppy* viii. 8 Waves that, hid in whisperous shadows, heaved. **1858** LYTTON *What will he do?* v. viii, The Duchess..sinks her voice, and gabbles on—*whisperously. **1834** MRS. HEMANS *Zegri Maid* ii. Wks. 1843 VII. 25 In the *whispery olive shade. **1844** LOWELL *Columbus* 5 The reeling sea..falling Crumbled to whispery foam. **1861** L. L. NOBLE *Icebergs* 254 The whispery, hissing sound of smoothly sliding waters.

'whisper, *v.* Forms: 1 **hwisprian,** 5 **qu-, qwysper,** 5–6 **whysper,** 6 *Sc.* **quhisper,** 7 **wisper,** 6– **whisper.** [OE. *hwisprian* (only Northumb.) = Early Flem. *wisperen* (Kilian), G. *wispern*; cf. MLG., MDu. *wispelen*, OHG. *(h)wispalôn* (MHG. *wispeln*). ON. has *hviskra*, Da. *hviske*, Sw. *viska* to whisper.]

1. a. *intr.* To speak softly 'under one's breath', i.e. without the resonant tone produced by vibration of the vocal cords; to talk or converse in this way, esp. in the ear of another, for the sake of secrecy. (See also 4 a.)

c **950** *Lindisf. Gosp.* John p. 4 *Murmurantes*, hwisprendo. *c* **975** *Rushw. Gosp.* Luke xix. 7 And miððy ȝeseȝon alle hwispredon [Vulg. *murmurabant*]. *c* **1440** *Promp. Parv.* 421/1 Quysperon.., *mussito. Ibid.* 525/1 Whysperyn. *c* **1530** H. RHODES *Bk. Nurture* 373 in *Babees-bk.* 81 Whysper not thou with thy fellowes oft. **1601** SHAKS. *All's Well* IV. iii. 329 Ile whisper with the Generall, and knowe his pleasure. **1610** —— *Temp.* IV. i. 125 Iuno and Ceres whisper seriously. **1676** *Hatton Corr.* (Camden) I. 136 Ld Wharton, and Ld Mohun sat..wispring together. **1709** STEELE *Tatler* No. 38 ¶8 He immediately runs into Secrets, and falls a whispering. **1848** THACKERAY *Van. Fair* xlviii, Many ladies round about whispered and talked, and many gentlemen nodded and whispered.

b. *trans.* with *adv.* To bring by whispering.

1692 DRYDEN *Eleonora* 318 Her Soul was whisper'd out, with God's still Voice. **1855** KINGSLEY *Westw. Ho!* xxiv, Cary..returned, and whispered Amyas away.

2. a. *trans.* To say, tell, communicate, utter, or express by whispering. (With simple obj. or obj. clause; often with the actual words uttered as obj.) See also 4 b.

1588 SHAKS. *L.L.L.* v. ii. 436 What did you whisper in your Ladies eare? **1601** —— *Jul. C.* II. ii. 100 If Cæsar hide himselfe, shall they not whisper Loe Cæsar is affraid? *a* **1678** MARVELL *Last Instr. Painter* 937 His Fathers Ghost too whisper'd him one Note, That who does cut his Purse will cut his Throat. **1697** DRYDEN *Æneis* XII. 324 Rising Fears are whisper'd thro' the Crowd. **1712** MRS. CENTLIVRE *Perplex'd Lovers* I. i, She..whispers out her words, least I shou'd hear her. **1827** LYTTON *Pelham* viii, I took the opportunity..to approach Lady Roseville and whisper my adieus. **1836** E. B. BROWNING *Poet's Vow* v, in *New Monthly Mag.* XLVIII. 217 They whispered oft, 'she sleepeth soft'. **1891** 'J. S. WINTER' *Lumley* iii, 'What is it?' he asked, in a loud whisper. 'Gooseberry', she whispered back—'come and sit here by me.'

b. *intr.* for *passive. rare.*

1850 TENNYSON *In Mem.* iii, O Sorrow,..What whispers from thy lying lip?

3. With the person, etc. as obj.: To address in a whisper; (with following clause or inf.) to tell, inform, bid, or ask in a whisper.

1540 PALSGR. *Acolastus* I. i. D iij b, He hath whyspered the in the eare, or taught the thy lesson in a corner. *a* **1591** H. SMITH *Serm., Satan's Compass.* (1592) 988 He will whisper the poore howe they shall come by riches. **1599** SHAKS. *Much Ado* III. i. 4 Whisper her eare, and tell her I and Vrsula, Walke in the Orchard. **1611** —— *Wint. T.* IV. iv. 827 Ile..whisper him in your behalfes. **1626** BACON *Sylva* §946 He did first whisper the Man in the Eare, that such a Man should thinke such a Card. **1711** ADDISON *Spect.* No. 117 ¶5 He whispered me in the Ear to take notice of a Tabby Cat. **1758** GOLDSM. *Mem. Prot.* (1895) I. 34, I whispered my Companion softly, that as the Night was very dark, we might give him the Slip. **1777** SHERIDAN *Sch. Scandal* IV. iii, Re-enter Servant and whispers Joseph Surface. **1796** MORSE *Amer. Geog.* II. 35 By whispering the rein-deer in the ear, they know the place of their destination. **1840** DICKENS *Old C. Shop* viii, Miss Jane..whispered her sister to observe how jealous Mr. Cheggs was. **1898** BESANT *Orange Girl* II. xxi, The Lord Mayor whispered the Judge again.

4. With special connotations. **a.** *intr.* To speak or converse quietly or secretly about something (usually implying hostility, malice, conspiracy, etc.); also (with negative) to speak ever so slightly, to say 'the least thing' about something.

1515 BARCLAY *Egloges* ii. (1570) B iv/1 That when other talke and speake what they will, Thou dare not whisper. **1539** *Bible* (Great) Ps. xli. 7 All myne enemyes whisper together agaynst me. **1555** EDEN *Decades* (Arb.) 108 His companyons whyspered and muttered ageynste hym. **1667** PEPYS *Diary* 28 June, And ne'er a prince in France dare whisper against it. **1824** MRS. HOFLAND *Patience* vii. 111 Mrs. Masterman..whispers every where about your wife's covetousness.

b. *trans.* To say, report, communicate, or utter quietly, secretly, or confidentially; also (with negative) to utter ever so slightly, to say the least word of. (With simple obj. or obj. clause; often in passive.)

1562 *Reg. Privy Council Scot.* I. 209 It is quhisperit and murmurrit that sum sold forgett thair devoyr. **1593** SHAKS. *Rich. II*, II. iv. 11 Leane-look'd Prophets whisper fearefull change. **1628** in Foster *Engl. Factories India* (1909) III. 202 This newes was first wispered here the 19th November. *a* **1708** T. WARD *Eng. Ref.* II. (1710) 38 This Matter whisper'd up and down, Was quickly spread thro' all the Town. **1815** SCOTT *Guy M.* lii, It is whispered about..that there is such a plan. **1840** DICKENS *Old C. Shop* lii, Some vague rumour..which had been whispered abroad. **1845** DISRAELI *Sybil* IV. xii, Whisper nothings that sound like something. **1887** R. H. ROBERTS *In the Shires* xiv. 246 It was whispered that a man answering to his description was keeping a very lucrative gambling-house in San Francisco.

c. *trans.* with *adv.* or *advb. phr.* To bring *into* or *out of* something, or to take *away*, by secret (esp. malicious or slanderous) speech.

1631 *Star Chamber Cases* (Camden) 24 He is to be admonished..not to whisper away the fame and credit of Deputies and governors. **1783** BURKE *Sp. Fox's East India Bill* 99 They cannot be whispered out of their duty,..their public conduct cannot be censured without a public discussion. **1840** DICKENS *Old C. Shop* lviii, Are characters to be whispered away like this? **1872** BUSHNELL *Serm. Living Subj.* xiii. 257 The great majority..are led, drawn, beckoned, whispered into their calling.

5. *intr.* (*fig.* from 1.) To make a soft rustling sound resembling or suggesting a whisper.

1653 WALTON *Angler* ix. 185 There will the River wispering run. **1697** DRYDEN *Æneis* IV. 759 The Winds no longer whisper through the Woods. **1766** GRAY *Kingsgate* 10 No tree is heard to whisper, bird to sing. **1846** MRS. A. MARSH *Fr. Darcy* xxxiv, The autumn wind whispered low among the branches.

6. a. *trans.* (*fig.* from 2.) To suggest secretly to the mind; also, to express or communicate by a soft rustling sound (cf. 5).

1640 S. HARDING *Sicily & Naples* III. i. 33 This day (There's something whispers to me) will prove fatall. **1667** MILTON *P.L.* IV. 158 Gentle gales..dispense Native perfumes, and whisper whence they stole Those balmie spoiles. **1751** GRAY *Spring* 8 Whisp'ring pleasure as they fly, Cool zephyrs..Their gather'd fragrance fling. **1823** LAMB *Elia* Ser. II. *Old Margate hoy*, The waves to him whispered more pleasant stories. **1837** DISRAELI *Venetia* II. i, A strange sympathy which whispers convictions that no evidence can authorise. **1878** BROWNING *La Saisiaz* 150 Truth is truth in each degree, Thunderpealed by God to Nature, whispered by my soul to me.

b. with the person, etc. as obj. (*fig.* from 3).

1605 SHAKS. *Macb.* IV. iii. 210 Giue sorrow words; the griefe that do's not speake, Whispers the o're-fraught heart, and bids it breake. **1713** ADDISON *Cato* II. i, Something whispers me All is not right. **1761** A. MURPHY *All in Wrong* I. i What devil whispered thee to marry such a woman? **1771** GOLDSM. *Hist. Eng.* II. 394 Adulation had whispered the king with such an opinion of his own ability. **1832** DISRAELI *Cont. Fleming* v, Nature seemed to whisper me the folly of learning words instead of ideas. **1849** T. WOOLNER *My Beautiful Lady, Noon* iv, Western wind..Whisper deliciously the trembling flowers.

Hence (*nonce-wds.*) **ˈwhisperable** *a.*, that can be whispered; **whispeˈration**, whispering.

1830 *Blackw. Mag.* XXVIII. 893 All speak—talk—whisper—or smile, of all the speakable, talkable, *whisperable, and smileable..affairs. **1710** C. SHADWELL *Fair Quaker Deal* III. 37 *Coxen.* Ah—when the Captain and Purser whispers, our Guts ought to grumble. *6 Sailor.* Ay, Coxen, those *Whisperations are many an Ounce of Butter and Cheese out of our Way.

whispered (ˈhwɪspəd), *ppl. a.* [f. prec. + -ED[1].]

1. Uttered, said, or told in a whisper.

1567 *Gude & Godlie B.* (S.T.S.) 201 The quhisperit sinnis, callit eir Confessioun. **1746** CAWTHORN *Poems* (1771) 59 The whisper'd tale. **1821** T. W. HILL *Sel. Papers* (1860) 26 Making the whispered *z* serve..for an unwhispered *s*. **1848** MRS. GASKELL *Mary Barton* xvi, A whispered earnest consultation took place. **1890** SWEET *Primer Spoken Engl.* I In whispered sounds [the vocal chords] are brought closer together, but without vibration.

2. Said or reported quietly or secretly; (with negative) uttered ever so slightly.

1605 SHAKS. *Lear* II. i. 8 You haue heard of the newes abroad, I meane the whisper'd ones. **1748** RICHARDSON *Clarissa* (1768) V. 35 Like a whispered scandal, it passed through several canals. **1897** *Daily News* 4 June 5/6 There is not even a whispered suggestion of repealing it.

whisperer (ˈhwɪspərə(r)). [f. as prec. + -ER[1].] One who whispers.

1. One who speaks in a whisper.

1567 MAPLET *Gr. Forest* 79 b, The Crane by proper name should be called whisperer, or flackerer. **1711** STEELE *Spect.* No. 148 ⁋4 Next to these Bawlers, is a troublesome Creature who comes with the Air of.. your Intimate, and that is your Whisperer. **1740** RICHARDSON *Pamela* (1785) II. 375 As we walk'd up the Church..we had abundance of Gazers and Whisperers. **1832** BREWSTER *Nat. Magic* ix. 225 Where the whisperer is in the focus of one reflecting surface, and the hearer in the focus of another. **1876** J. SAUNDERS *Lion in Path* v, 'Hush', exclaims one of the whisperers to his neighbour.

b. An appellation for certain celebrated horse-breakers, said to have obtained obedience by whispering to the horses.

1810 H. TOWNSEND *Stat. Surv. Co. Cork* 439 He was an awkward, ignorant rustic.., his name James Sullivan, but better known by the appellation of the whisperer,..from a vulgar notion of his being able to communicate to the animal what he wished, by means of a whisper. **1842** BORROW *Bible in Spain* xv, One who is an expert whisperer and horse-sorcerer.

2. One who communicates something quietly or secretly; *esp.* a secret slanderer or tale-bearer.

1547–50 BAULDWIN *Mor. Philos.* II. Liij, Caste whysperers and tale bearers, out of thy company. **1611** *Bible* Prov. xvi. 28 A whisperer separateth chiefe friends. **1675** TEMPLE *Let. to King* Wks. 1731 II. 328 The Whisperers of this Story. **1707** NASH in Goldsm. *Life* (1762) 33 Whisperers of lies and scandal. **1751** JOHNSON *Rambler* No. 180 ⁋10 The most officious of the whisperers of greatness. **1819** KEATS *Otho* IV. i, Whisperers..Hungry for evidence to ruin me. **1876** BESANT & RICE *Golden Butterfly* xviii, To be a Great Man's whisperer is a position coveted by many.

whisperhood: see after WHISPER *sb.*

whispering (ˈhwɪspərɪŋ), *vbl. sb.* [f. as prec. + -ING[1].] The action of the verb WHISPER.

1. The action of speaking in a whisper; speech without vibration of the vocal cords; whispered talk or conversation.

c **975** *Rushw. Gosp.* John vii. 12 Hwisprunge micle [Vulg. *murmur multum*] wæs..in ðreote. **1412–20** LYDG. *Chron. Troy* I. 2785 Whan sche heryth wispring eny-where. **1526** *Pilgr. Perf.* (W. de W. 1531) 159 b, Noyse of whisperyng with the lyppes. **1611** SHAKS. *Wint. T.* I. ii. 284 Is whispering nothing? Is leaning Cheeke to Cheeke? **1740** RICHARDSON *Pamela* (1785) II. 375, I was much less concerned..at the Gazings and Whisperings of the Ladies and Gentlemen. **1837** DICKENS *Pickw.* xxviii, After a little whispering with the other young ladies. **1863** A. M. BELL *Princ. Speech* 164 This whispering of the Voice Articulations is a remarkable characteristic of Gaelic, Welsh, and Irish speakers.

2. The action of saying or reporting something quietly or secretly; suggestion or insinuation (by whispered speech); faint mention or rumour; *esp.* (*obs.* or *arch.*) malicious insinuation, secret slander or detraction, backbiting.

c **1384** CHAUCER *H. Fame* III. 868 That place..filde ful of tydynges Other lovde or of wisprynges. *c* **1450** *Mirk's Festial* 279 Now hit ys made an hous..of whisperyng and rownyng. **1526** TINDALE *2 Cor.* xii. 20, I feare lest there be founde amonge you..whisperynges, swellynges and debate. **1546** W. THOMAS *Peregryne* Wks. 1774 I. 115 He had herd a whysperyng amonge the souldieres how the sayde Earle.. had gotten promes of ayde. *a* **1548** HALL *Chron., Rich. III* 53 Sekynge after his compagynie and yet not once herynge any noyse or whysperynge of theim. *a* **1586** [see WHISPERINGNESS]. **1605** SHAKS. *Macb.* V. i. 79 Foule whisp'rings are abroad. **1734** tr. *Rollin's Anc. Hist.* IV. 207 By false reports, whispering and calumny. **1828–43** TYTLER *Hist. Scot.* (1864) IV. 33 Rumours of war, and whisperings of the intrigues and conspiracies.

3. *fig.* **a.** Soft rustling sound resembling or suggesting whispered speech.

1610 HOLLAND *Camden's Brit.* I. 564 The river..making a..gentle whispering. **1821** SCOTT *Kenilw.* xxvii, The garden..was silent, but for the whispering of the leaves,.. and the plashing of the fountains. **1849** T. WOOLNER *My Beautiful Lady, Night* viii, The..hushed whispering of the vines. **1904** FITCHETT *Commander of 'Hirondelle'* xx. 230 Her voice fell into the key of the mystical whispering of the sea.

b. Mental suggestion or intimation figured as whispered speech.

1672 SIR T. BROWNE *Let. Friend* §2 Some secret sense or intimation thereof by dreams, thoughtful whisperings, [etc.]. **1811** SHELLEY *Poems fr. St. Irvyne* I. iii, Conscience in low, noiseless whispering spoke. **1848** MRS. GASKELL *Mary Barton* xv, The whisperings of her womanly nature.. caused her to shrink from any unmaidenly action.

4. *attrib.*: **whispering campaign**, a systematic circulation of rumours, esp. in order to denigrate someone or something (orig. in *U.S. Politics*); **whispering-closet**, satirically for a private consulting-room; **whispering-gallery**, a gallery or dome, usually of circular or elliptical plan, in which a whisper or other faint sound at some point can be heard by reflexion at a distant point where the direct sound is inaudible; **whispering-hole**, a hole through which one whispers; **whispering-office**, nickname for a confessional; † **whispering-place**, = *whispering-gallery*; † **whispering-room**, a room for private interviews or consultations; † **whispering-trumpet** (*obs.*), **whispering-tube** = SPEAKING-TUBE 1; **whispering Willie** *slang* (see quots.).

1920 *Nation* (N.Y.) 10 Nov. 517/1 The scandalous underhandedness of the *whispering campaign of the Democrats..only prove[s] the spuriousness of all their protestations of belief in equal rights for black and white. **1949** 'R. WEST' *Meaning of Treason* I. vi. 118 A whispering campaign designed to weaken public confidence. **1962** D. LESSING *Golden Notebk.* I. 139 He was desperately depressed —a whispering campaign around the party and near-party circles, that he was and had been 'A capitalist spy'. **1978** D. BLOODWORTH *Crosstalk* viii. 69 The Chinese have been mounting a whispering campaign against the Soviet Union, quite distinct from their overt anti-Soviet propaganda. **1808** BENTHAM *Sc. Reform* 80 The Judge's *whispering-closet: from which all who have any interest in the discovery of the truth are carefully excluded. *a* **1700** EVELYN *Diary* 31 July 1654, The Minster is indeede a noble fabric. The *whispering gallery is rare, being thro' a passage of 25 yards, in a many-angled cloister. **1812** *Examiner* 28 Dec. 827/2 The whispering gallery in St. Paul's. **1663** BUTLER *Hud.* I. I. 518 Speaks..As though a Trunk, or *whisp'ring hole. **1712** ADDISON *Spect.* No. 457 ⁋3 Peter Hush has a whispering Hole in most of the great Coffee-houses about Town. **1704** SWIFT *T. Tub* iv, The erecting of a *Whispering-Office. **1635** BRERETON *Trav.* (Chetham Soc.) I. 180 This *whispering place..is a vault or gallery. **1682** SIR T. BROWNE *Chr. Mor.* iii. §13 (1716) 97 The voice of Prophecies is like that of Whispering-places: They who are near or at a little distance hear nothing, those at the farthest extremity will understand all. **1746** *Phil. Trans.* XLIV. 219 As for whispering Places, the best I ever saw was that at Gloucester: But in Italy..I saw, in an Inn, a Room with a square Vault, where whispering, you could easily hear it at the opposite Corner. **1623** WEBSTER *Duchess Malfi* I. ii, A Vizor and a Masque are *whispering roomes That were neu'r built for goodnesse. *Ibid.* III. ii, His breast was fill'd with all perfection, And yet it seem'd a priuate whispering roome It made so little noyse of 't. **1688** HOLME *Armoury* III. xvi. (Roxb.) 75/2 In the Base of this square, runing into the next, is a *Whispering Trumpett, a long streight hollow pipe. **1857** DUFFERIN *Lett. High Lat.* vi. (ed. 3) 65 The voices..became thin and low, as though they reached me through a *whispering tube. **1918** H. W. MCBRIDE *Emma Gees* 135 The..'*Whispering Willies' belong to the class of large caliber, long range naval gun shells which pass over the front line so high that only a sort of whistling sound is heard. **1937** PARTRIDGE *Dict. Slang* 952/2 *Whispering Willie*, a type of big naval gun used by the Germans: East African campaign of the G.W.

ˈwhispering, *ppl. a.* [f. as prec. + -ING[2].]

1. That whispers; speaking in a whisper.

1596 SHAKS. *Merch. V.* I. iii. 125 With bated breath, and whispring humblenesse. **1716** LADY M. W. MONTAGU *Toilet* 46 Her Face may boast the Peach's Bloom; But does her nearer whisp'ring Breath perfume? **1770** GOLDSM. *Des. Vill.* 14 The hawthorn bush, with seats beneath the shade, For talking age and whispering lovers made! **1890** 'R. BOLDREWOOD' *Col. Reformer* xv, A dozen smiling and whispering girls.

b. Uttered in, or of the nature of, a whisper.

1592 SHAKS. *Rom. & Jul.* I. v. 25, I..could tell A whispering tale in a faire Ladies eare. **1649** J. TAYLOR (Water P.) *Wand. Wonders West* 19, I spake to him..in a low whispering voice. **1760–72** H. BROOKE *Fool of Qual.* (1809) III. 89 He held with them a long and whispering kind of conversation. **1846** MRS. A. MARSH *Fr. Darcy* xxxiv, In a low, whispering voice, rendered..faltering by their emotions.

2. Reporting something secretly or confidentially; *esp.* secretly slanderous, talebearing, backbiting.

1581 MUNDAY (*title*) An Aduertisement and defence for Trueth against her Backbiters, and specially against the whispring Fauourers..of Campians. **1603** B. JONSON *Sejanus* II. ii. Wks. (1616) 378 Whispring fame Knowledge, and proofe doth to the iealous giue. **1800** COLERIDGE *Christabel* 409 Whispering tongues can poison truth.

3. Making a soft rustling sound like a whisper. Also said of the sound.

a **1547** SURREY *Æneis* II. 963 Eche whispring wind hath power now to fray..my doutfull mind. **1575** A. F. *Virg. Bucol.* vii. 20 Vnder the whispering hollye. **1671** MILTON *P.R.* IV. 250 There Ilissus rouls His whispering stream. **1770** GOLDSM. *Des. Vill.* 121 The watch-dog's voice that bayed the whispering wind. **1784** COWPER *Poplar-Field* 2 The whispering sound of the cool colonnade. **1795–1814** WORDSW. *Excurs.* IV. 1170 The whispering air Sends inspiration from the shadowy heights. **1847** LONGF. *Ev.* I. iv. 137 She heard the whispering rain fall. **1850** TENNYSON *In Mem.* c, Low morass and whispering reed. **1890** 'R. BOLDREWOOD' *Col. Reformer* xxiii, The sighing, whispering, sad-voiced water-oaks.

Hence **ˈwhisperingly** *adv.*, with a whispering voice or sound, in a whisper; † **ˈwhisperingness**, whispering quality or character (in quot. in sense 2).

1580 in *Liturgies Reign Q. Eliz.* (Parker Soc. 1847) 572 Their speaking..is not softly and whisperingly. *a* **1586** SIDNEY *Arcadia* III. vii. (1912) 385 Bold onely in busie whisperings, and even in that whisperingnes rather indeed confident in his cunning, that it should not be bewraied. *a* **1603** T. CARTWRIGHT *Confut. Rhem. N.T.* (1618) 247 A man is bound to discharge all his sinnes..whisperingly or secretly into the eare of a Priest. **1747** RICHARDSON *Clarissa* (1748) I. 308 Thus she ran on,..but whisperingly, that my aunt might not hear her. **1872** GEO. ELIOT *Middlem.* xii, The pool..where the..trees leaned whisperingly. **1874** LISLE CARR *Jud. Gwynne* I. vi. 174 As the last words fell whisperingly from her lips. **1915** KIPLING *New Army* ii, Squad after squad..gathered up their target cards, and whisperingly compared them.

whisperless to **whispery**: see after WHISPER *sb.*

whispy, variant of WISPY.

whisquy-beath: see WHISKYBAE.

† **whiss**, *v.* *Obs.* Also 5 quysse, 6 **whisse, whyss(e, wiss(e,** *Sc.* **quheiss.** [Echoic. Cf. Icel. *hvissa* to whizz.]

1. *intr.* To make a sibilant sound of some kind; to whistle, hiss, whizz, or wheeze; *trans.* to whistle to. Hence † **ˈwhissing** *vbl. sb.* and *ppl. a.*

a **1400** *Parlt. 3 Ages* 234 He [*sc.* falconer] quysses thaym [*sc.* hawks] and quotes thaym, quyppeys full lowde. **1555** EDEN *Decades* (Arb.) 385 The whyssinge of a burninge forge. **1565** COOPER *Thesaurus* s.v. *Auster*, *Sibilus Austri*, the whissynge of the winde. **1583** MELBANCKE *Philotimus* T iij b, Like the sea which sodenlye with whissing noyse dooth moue, when with a little blast of winde it is but toucht. **1606** SHAKS. *Tr. & Cr.* V. i. 24 (Qo. 1) Whissing lungs. **1649** G. DANIEL *Trinarch., Hen. V*, ccliii, Their fled Troops, met whissing in the Bound, Gave their owne Terror, in a Treble Sound. **1654** GAYTON *Pleas. Notes* II. iv. 49 Such a Nose is worth a double tost in a pot of Ale, and will make it whisse as well as a hot steele. **1847** HALLIWELL, *Whiss*, to whistle.

2. *trans.* ? To strike with something pliant, to flog: cf. quot. *c* 1590 in sb. below.

c **1540** J. HEYWOOD *Wit & Folly* (Percy Soc.) 2 Some whysse hym, some whype hym.

Hence † **whiss** *sb.*, a blow with something pliant, a lash.

c **1590** J. STEWART *Poems* (S.T.S.) II. 235 Tak thair ane quheiss ȝit vith my skoullon clout.

whiss, whisshe, obs. ff. WISH.

whissall, -el(l, -il(l, obs. ff. WHISTLE.

whisse, obs. pa. t. of WASH *v.*

whissle: see WHISTLE, WISSEL.

Whisson, dial. f. WHITSUN.

† **whist**, *sb.*[1] *Obs. rare*[−1]. [Imitative.] A whistling sound, a whistle.

1579 TOMSON *Calvin's Serm. Tim.* 268/2 If a sheepeheard ..giue a whist with his mouthe to gather his sheepe together.

whist (hwɪst), *sb.*[2] [f. WHIST *int.*[1] or *v.*[1]]

†**1.** An utterance of the interjection 'whist!' as a command for silence. *Obs.*

1601 W. PERCY *Cuckqueanes & Cuckolds Errants* I. iii. (Roxb.) 15 With a whist and with a Hush Hast wee both Two to the Bush.

2. Silence: in phr. ***to hold one's whist***, to keep silence. *Irish.* (Cf. WHISHT *sb.* 2.)

c **1874** D. BOUCICAULT *Shaughraun* (*c* 1884), I. iii. 7/2 Hould your whist now! Wipe your mouth, an' give me a kiss! **1897** BARRÈRE & LELAND *Dict. Slang* s.v., 'Hold your whist,' *i.e.*, hold your tongue, is an Irishism which has passed into English slang. **1898** MACDONAGH *Irish Life* 237 'Tis yer brother that's spakin' to yez, and askin' yez to hould yer whist!

whist, *sb.*[3] [Altered f. WHISK *sb.*[2] explained as in quot. 1680.] **a.** A game of cards played (ordinarily) by four persons, of whom each two sitting opposite each other are partners, with a pack of 52 cards, which are dealt face downwards to the players in rotation, so that each has a *hand* of 13 cards; one of the suits (usually determined by the last card dealt, which is then turned face upwards) is *trumps* (see TRUMP *sb.*[2] 1); the players play in rotation, each four successive cards so played constituting a *trick* (TRICK *sb.* 12), in which each player after the leader must follow suit if he holds a card of the suit led, otherwise may either discard or trump; the winner of a trick becomes the leader of the next trick; points are scored according to the number of tricks won, and in some forms of the game also by the *honours* or highest trumps (HONOUR *sb.* 8 a) held by each pair of partners.

dummy whist: see DUMMY *sb.* 2. ***duplicate whist***, a form of the game in which the hands played are preserved and played again by the opposing partners. ***long whist***, a form of the game in which the score is ten points with honours counting. ***short whist***, the form now usual in England, in which the score is five points with honours counting.

1663 (spurious ed.) BUTLER *Hud.* II. i. 105 But what was this? A Game at Whist, Unto our Plowden-Canonist. **1680** COTTON *Compl. Gamester* (ed. 2) 83 Whist is a Game not much differing from [Ruff and Honours], only they put out the Deuces and take in no stock; and is called Whist from the silence that is to be observed in the play; they deal as before, playing four, two of a side, (some play at two handed, or three handed Whist). **1742** WALPOLE *Corr.* (1820) I. 225 Whist has spread an universal opium over the whole nation. **1758** JOHNSON *Idler* No. 33 ¶22 We sat late at whist. **1827** LYTTON *Pelham* iii, Elderly ladies, who..liked long whist. **1829** E. M. ARNAUD *Epitome Whist* 29 The game is won by the party whose score first amounts to ten points in Long Whist, or five in Short Whist. **1842** LEVER *J. Hinton* ix, My little gains at short-whist. **1861** E. DUTTON COOK *Paul Foster's Dau.* viii, I should like..a good rubber of long whist. **1885** R. A. PROCTOR *Whist* Introd. 1 Whist, properly played, is the finest of all card games. **1891** J. T. MITCHELL (*title*) Duplicate-Whist.

b. *attrib.* and *Comb.*, as ***whist club***, ***-like*** adj., ***memory***, ***party***, ***-play***, ***-player***, ***-playing*** sb. and adj., ***-table***; **whist-drive**, a party of progressive whist (see PROGRESSIVE *a.* 2 b) played for prizes, now often as a means of raising funds for charities.

1799 E. D. CLARKE in *Life* (1824) 349, I shall..ask him, if he will..belong to our *whist club. **1903** 'JAR' *Progr. Whist* 6 A *Whist Drive is a modification of Progressive Whist. **1915** T. BURKE *Nights in Town* 179 When I received the invitation to the whist-drive at Surbiton my first thought was, 'Not likely!' **1924** [see INSTITUTE *sb.*[1] 4]. **1959** [see *community centre* s.v. COMMUNITY 11]. **1977** *Lancs. Life* Nov. 73/1 They raised the money themselves (with hot pot suppers, whist drives, amateur drama and dances). **1981** G. MARKSTEIN *Ultimate Issue* 196 In the lobby of the officers' club the wives were having a whist drive. **1837** DICKENS *Pickw.* xxxv, Two other ladies of an ancient and *whist-like appearance. **1886** CAVENDISH *Whist* 136 With practice, you will acquire what may be termed '*whist memory'. **1744** S. FIELDING *Adv. David Simple* I. II. i. 144 One of the Ladies, who was of the *Whist-Party the Night before. **1828** SIR R. PEEL *Priv. Lett.* (1920) 109 A whist party consisting of the Duke of Wellington, Mrs. Arbuthnot, Lord Westmorland, Lady A. Beckett. **1861** LEVER *One of them* xxvii, His notion is, that life, like a whist-party, requires an accomplice. **1888** *Encycl. Brit.* XXIV. 544/2 All rules of *whist-play depend upon..general principles. **1744** S. FIELDING *Adv. David Simple* I. II. i. 147 Your Curiosity seems to be fully satisfied with what you have seen of the *whist-players. **1770** in *Alex. Carlyle's Autobiog.* (1910) 560 He makes a very good livelihood..by betting on the whist-players. **1824** MISS MITFORD *Village* Ser. I. *Country Cricket-Match*, Feeling what a whist-player feels when he takes up four honors, seven trumps! **1837** DICKENS *Pickw.* vi, The whist-players were Mr. Pickwick and the old lady; Mr. Miller and the fat gentleman. **1837** LOCKHART *Scott* IV. i. 7 A few *whist-playing brother officers, that met for an evening rubber at Fortune's tavern. **1842** DICKENS *Amer. Notes* ii, There was less whist-playing than might have been expected. **1753** *Scots Mag.* XV. 36/1 Her absence rendered one *whist-table useless. **1877** MRS. FORRESTER *Mignon* i, There were whist tables in the library if any one cared to play.

Hence (*nonce-wds.*) **whist** *v.* (*a*) *trans.* to play *out* (a card) at whist; (*b*) *intr.* to play whist; **ˈwhister**, a whist-player; **ˈwhisthood**, age or state of ability to play whist; **ˈwhisty** *a.*, addicted to whist.

1810 *Splendid Follies* III. 6 She generally whisted out kings before aces, and revoked every deal. **1827** LADY GRANVILLE *Lett.* (1894) I. 433 Talking, singing, whisting. **1854** *Chamb. Jrnl.* 2 Dec. 353/2 Young ladies, nearly arrived at whisthood. **1860** *All Year Round* No. 47. 482/2 Your erring mortal, your whister,..rash with his aces, and a niggard of some beggarly small trump. **1884** JEAN MIDDLEMASS *Pois. Arrows* ix, The whisty old colonel. **1890** 'R. BOLDREWOOD' *Col. Reformer* xxii, Bankers..in great force.., musical bankers, and bankers that danced, bankers that billiarded and whisted.

whist (hwɪst), *a.*[1] *arch.* and *dial.* Also 6 **whyst(e, whiste.** [f. WHIST *int.*[1] Cf. HUST, WHISHT, WHUSHT *adjs.*] Silent, quiet, still, hushed; making no sound; free from noise or disturbance. (Usually *predicative.*)

Also *advb.* = silently, quietly, without noise.

14.. *Chaucer's Boeth.* II. met. v (MS. B. Mus.) þo weren þe cruel clariouns ful whist [*MS. Camb.* hust] and ful stille. **1513** *Lydgate's Chron. Troy* I. viii. E j b, Than Pelleus whan al was whyste [*MSS.* huscht, hust, husshte] and styll, Began ryght thus. **1528** ROY *Rede me* (Arb.) 65 Kepe thou silence and be whyst..For a lytell season. **1588** GREENE *Pandosto* C 1 b, The Noblemen seeing the King in choler, were all whist. **1590** —— *Never Too Late* Wks. (Grosart) VIII. 228 The blythe and wanton windes are whist & still. **1610** SHAKS. *Temp.* I. ii. 379 Curtsied when you haue, and kist the wilde waues whist. **1615** G. SANDYS *Trav.* 307 In nights whist calme. **1629** MILTON *Hymn Nativ.* v, The Windes, with wonder whist, Smoothly the waters kist. **1682** FLATMAN *Heraclitus Ridens* No. 70 (1713) II. 179 Some few Relations..stand whist and silent, expecting the minute when she should depart. **1700** J. BROME *Trav. Eng., Scot.* ii. (1707) 83 All was very whist and still. **1819** J. R. DRAKE *Culprit Fay* ii, The winds are whist, and the owl is still. **1890** BRIDGES *Shorter Poems* IV. XXVIII. v, The huge unclouded sun, Surprising the world whist, Is all uprisen thereon. **1907** *Daily Chron.* 8 Apr. 4/6 The word 'whist' has still its ..signification of silence in Kent, though it is pronounced 'wist.' This writer, not long ago, was threatening to come in late..to a country cottage lodging. 'You'll come in wist?' said the lady of the house.

b. Keeping silence in relation to something; saying nothing about the matter.

1577 STANYHURST *Descr. Irel.* 6/1 in *Holinshed*, If he heard them, thinke you that he would haue beene whist, in hearing God so farre blasphemed? **1609** J. DAVIES *Holy Rood* Wks. (Grosart) I. 8/1 The heau'ns are whist, whiles hell reuiles their Lord. *c* **1650** in *12th Rep. Hist. MSS. Comm.* App. IX. 140 Yet they can silent be, though, when they list, On Charles his Martyrdome they are all whist. **1880** MRS. WHITNEY *Odd or Even?* vii. 59 The Heybrooks were whist folks about their concerns.

c. *transf.* Attentive. *nonce-use.*

[**1580** LYLY *Euphues* (Arb.) 283 All were whist to heare my iudgement.] **1890** BRIDGES *Shorter Poems* IV. II. iv, My jealous ears grew whist.

whist, *a.*[2] (*dial.*): see WISHT.

whist, *v.*[1] Also 6 **whyst.** Pa. t. and pple. **whisted, whist.** [f. WHIST *int.*[1]]

1. *intr.* To become or be silent, cease or refrain from speaking, hold one's peace, keep silence. *arch.* and *dial.*

In the imperative coinciding with WHIST *int.*[1], q.v.

a **1547** SURREY *Æneis* II. 1 They whisted all with fixed face attent. **1593** G. HARVEY *Pierce's Super.* Wks. (Grosart) II. 79 Whist sory pen, and be aduised how thou presume aboue the highest pitch of thy possibility. **1856** P. KENNEDY *Banks of Boro* xli. (1867) 336 Can't you whist? *a* **1859** L. HUNT *Shewe faire Seeming* x, They whist, and still'd their joyous crowd.

†**b.** *trans.* To be silent about, pass over in silence, keep secret. *Obs.*

1570 T. WILSON *Demosthenes* 35 All these matters are now whist and kept in. **1573–80** TUSSER *Husb.* (1878) 150 What ere he doth none ought dare say, but whist. **1594** O. B. *Quest. Profit. Concern.* 31 b, It seemed better vnto him to let fall his revenge, and to whist the matter.

†**2.** *trans.* To put to silence, to hush. Hence **whisted** *ppl. a.*, hushed, silent. *Obs.*

a **1541** WYATT *Poems, Compl. upon Love to Reason* 145 Dere Lady: now we waite thyne onely sentence. She smiling, at the whisted audience: It liketh me (quod she) [etc.] **1596** SPENSER *F.Q.* VII. vii. 59 So was the Titaness put downe and whist. **1602** MARSTON *Ant. & Mel.* I. B 2 b, The breath of darknesse, fatall when 'tis whist In greatnes stomacke; this same smoake, call'd pride.

†**whist,** *v.*[2] *Obs. rare.* [Imitative. (Perh. error for WHISTER.)] *intr.* To whisper, murmur.

a **1555** BRADFORD in Coverdale *Cert. Godly Lett.* (1564) 478 No man may be admitted once to whist agaynste them.

whist (hwɪst), *int.*[1] Now *dial.* Also 6 **whyst, whuist, quist,** 9 *Sc.* **wheest.** [A natural utterance enjoining silence: cf. HIST, HUST, IST, ST, also HUSHT, WHISHT.] An exclamation to command silence: Hush! (Coinciding with the imperative of WHIST *v.*[1] 1.)

1382 WYCLIF *Judges* xviii. 19 Thei answerden, Whist [*v.rr.* Whisht, Whischt; 1388 Be thou stille], and put fynger vpon thi mouth. **1575** A. F. *Virg. Bucol.* v. 14 Leaue of, whyst, say no more. **1593** G. HARVEY *Pierce's Super.* Wks. (Grosart) II. 89 If..your tongue [be] soe laxatiue,..whuist a while. **1598** R. BERNARD tr. *Terence, Adelphos* III. ii, Quist, quist, what man, art thou well in thy wits? **1611** J. DAVIES *Worthy Persons* Wks. (Grosart) II. 58/2 Whist, and me attend. **1611** COTGR., *Houische*,..husht, whist, ist, not a word for your life. **1762** STERNE *Tr. Shandy* V. i, Whist! —cried one—st, st,—said a second—hush, quoth a third— poo, poo, replied a fourth—gramercy! cried the Lady Carnavallette. **1834** MARRYAT *Peter Simple* xiii, Whist— hold your tongue—you've not heard the end of it. **1859** H. KINGSLEY *G. Hamlyn* xxxix, When I came to the door Donovan took me by the arm, and saying 'whist', led me into the sitting-room. **1891** ALEX. GORDON *Folks o' Carglen* 54 'Whist, whist,' cried Francie. **1894** LYTTLE *Betsy Gray* iii, Wheest, man, or ye'll wauken up the waen!

whist, *int.*[2] Imitation of the sound of a whistle.

1861 LD. HADDO in *Mem.* xv. (1873) 212 It was puff, puff, —whist, whist;—and we were under weigh. *a* **1896** in *Life & Lett. Millais* (1899) II. 408, I said to a beautiful young person in the bar, 'I want a bedroom with a fire in it.' Off she went to a pipe, and said, 'Whist! No. 238 and a fire.'

whiste, obs. f. *wist*, pa. t. of WIT *v.*, to know.

whistel, obs. form of WHISTLE.

ˈwhister, *v. Obs.* exc. *dial.* Also 5–6 **whyster.** [app. identical with OE. *hwǽstrian* 'susurrare', 'murmurare', with root-vowel raised (from **whester*), partly by assimilation to *whisper.*] = WHISPER *v.* Hence **ˈwhistering** *vbl. sb.* and *ppl. a.*; **ˈwhisterer** = WHISPERER.

1382 WYCLIF *Ecclus.* xii. 19 Grucchendeli whistrende. *Ibid.* xxviii. 15 The whistrende gruccħere. **14..** *Chaucer's Troylus* II. 1753 (Harl. MS. 3943) Was Troilus not in a kankerdorte, þat lay & myght the whistryng [*v.r.* whysprynge] of hem here. *c* **1500** MEDWALL *Nature* (Brandl) I. 1087 Reason wyll whyster hym in the ere. **1519** HORMAN *Vulg.* 162, I hate whisterars. **1562** J. HEYWOOD *Prov. & Epigr.* (1867) 97 Vnto them this lesson he whisters. **1565** T. STAPLETON *Fortr. Faith* 93 Peter Martyr..whistered to him in the eare that he should plainly denie that any laying on of handes..was required. **1586** W. WEBBE *Engl. Poetrie* (Arb.) 75 Oft fine whistring noise, shall bring sweete sleepe to thy sences. **1610** HOLLAND *Camden's Brit.* II. 147 She.. whistereth a certain odde praier with a Pater Noster into his eare. **1746** *Exmoor Courtship* (E.D.S.) 624 Chell tell tha sometheng—Zart! whistery! **1888** DOUGHTY *Trav. Arabia Deserta* I. 556 Whistling—a surprising sound in the Arabic countries! where it would be taken for one's whistering to the jan.

ˈwhister-clister. *dial.* or *slang.* A smart blow or cuff on the ear or the side of the head. So (in same sense) **ˈwhisterpoop, ˈwhistersniff,** †**ˈwhistersnivet, ˈwhister-twister.**

1787 GROSE *Prov. Gloss.*, **Whisterclister*, a stroke or blow under the ear. **1866** THORNBURY *Greatheart* ii, I thought.. he was going to give me a 'whister-clister' (Devonshire for a blow on the ear). **1605** *London Prodigal* II. i. 68 Chee would a giuen thee zutch a *whisterpoope vnder the eare. **1778** *Exmoor Scolding* Gloss., *A Whisterpoop*, a Sort of whistling, or rather whispering Pop,—a Blow on the Ear. **1818** SCOTT *Hrt. Midl.* xxxii, Keep hand off her, or I'se lend thee a whister-poop. **1883** *Hampsh. Gloss.*, **Whister-sniff*, a heavy blow. **1540** PALSGR. *Acolastus* IV. v. V ij b, You shall beare me oone *whystersniuet, or gerte on the bare buttoke. **1542** UDALL *Erasm. Apoph.* 99 b, A good whistersnefet truely paied on his eare. **1825** JENNINGS *Obs. Dial. W. Eng.*, **Whister-twister*, a smart blow on the side of the head.

whistle (ˈhwɪs(ə)l), *sb.* Forms: 1–2 **hwistle, wistle,** 4–7 **whistel(l,** etc. (see the vb.), 4– **whistle;** also 4 *Sc.* **quyschile,** 5 **whystyl,** *Sc.* **qwistle, quhissle,** 6 **whisstill,** *Sc.* **qwystelle, qwissel, vhissell,** 7 *Sc.* **whissille, whissall, whisle,** (8 *Sc. dial.* **fusle**), 9 *Sc.* and *north.* **whustle, whussel.** [OE. *hwistle* (also *wuduhwistle*), with a variant *wistle*, related to *hwistlian*, *wistlian* (see next). Sense 3 is prob. a new formation on the vb.]

1. a. A tubular wind instrument of wood, metal or other hard substance, having a more or less shrill tone, which is produced by impact of air upon a sharp edge; a shrill-toned pipe. Formerly also = pipe or flute.

Used in various forms and sizes for many different purposes: esp. (blown by the mouth) by boatswains, policemen, etc., for calling dogs or horses, or the like, or (blown by steam) on railway engines, steam-ships, etc., for giving a signal or alarm; also as a musical toy, usually of tin and pierced with six holes (commonly called ***penny whistle, tin whistle***). †***Almain*** or ***German whistle***, a fife.

c **950** *Lindisf. Gosp.* Luke vii. 32 We ȝesungun iuh mið hwistlum. *c* **1000** *Voc.*, in Wr.-Wülcker 311/22, 27 *Musa*, pipe, oððe hwistle... *Fistula*, hwistle. **11..** *Ibid.* 539/24 *Musa*, pipe, *uel* hwistle. *a* **1340** HAMPOLE *Psalter* cl. 4 Orgyns þat is made as a toure of sere whistils. *c* **1375** *Sc. Leg. Saints* vi. (*Thomas*) 60 A madyne com..hafand a quyschile in-to hand. **1387–8** T. USK *Test. Love* II. iii. (Skeat) l. 55 The bird is begyled with the mery voice of the foulers whistel. *c* **1400** *Destr. Troy* 6051 With qwistlis, & qwes, & other qwaint gere. **1427** *For. Acc.* 61 (P.R.O.), vj par' corn' voc' whisteles. **1463** *Bury Wills* (Camden) 41 My whistel of silvir. **1513** in *Lett. & Papers War France* (1913) 148 The boy..sawe hym [*sc.* the Admiral] take his whistill from aboute his neck,..and hurlid [*sic*] it in to the see. **1532–3** *Act 24 Hen. VIII* c. 13 §1 It shalbe lefull for..maisters of the Shipps..and maryners to weare whistells of Silver. **1576** GASCOIGNE *Steele Glas* Epil. 19 The yonger sorte, come pyping..In whistles made of fine enticing wood. **1585** JAS. I *Ess. Poesie* (Arb.) 56 O Mercure,..efter Pan had found the quhissill, syne Thou did perfyte, that quhilk he bot espyit. *a* **1610** HEYWOOD & ROWLEY *Fortune by Land & Sea* IV. i. (1655) 36 Boatswain with your whistle command the Saylors to the upper deck. **1661** BOYLE *Style Script.* 190 A Child, with a Whistle; a Trifle that onely pleases with a transient and empty sound. **1670–1** JAS. TURNER *Pallas Armata* III. xi. (1683) 219 The Bag-pipe..is not so good as the Almain Whistle. *c* **1770** BEATTIE *To Alex. Ross* ix, Where..shepherd lads on sunny knows Blaw the blythe fusle. **1819** SCOTT *Leg. Montrose* iii, They havena sae mickle as a German whistle, or a drum, to beat a march, an alarm,..or any other point of war. **1836** MAYNE *Siller Gun* I. xxxix, Dangling like a baby's whustle, The Siller Gun..Gleam'd in the sun! **1840** R. H. DANA *Bef. Mast* xxvii, Everything man-of-war fashion, except that there was no boatswain's whistle. **1898** FLOR. MONTGOMERY *Tony* i, The whistle sounded, and the train began slowly to glide out of the station.

b. Phrases, etc. †(*a*) ***box*** or (Sc.) ***kist of whistles***, a contemptuous appellation for a church organ. (Cf. *a* 1340 above.) (*b*) In comparisons, e.g. ***as clean, clear, dry as a whistle*** (often with play on other senses of the adjs.: see quots.). (*c*) ***to pay (too dear) for one's whistle*** (and similar phrases), to pay much more for something than it is worth: in allusion to a story of Benjamin Franklin (*Wks.* 1840 II. 182). (*d*) ***to blow the whistle on*** (a person or thing): to bring an activity to a sharp conclusion, as if by the blast of a whistle; now usu. by informing on (a person) or exposing (an irregularity or crime). Also without *on.*

(*a*) **1678** ALSOP *Melius Inq.* I. ii. 99 Pope Vitalian..first..taught Mankind the Art of Worshipping God with a Box of Whistles. **1866** [see KIST *sb.*[1] 1].

(*b*) **1786** BURNS *Author's Earnest Cry* vii, Her mutchkin stowp as toom's a whissle. **1828** *Craven Gloss.* s.v., 'As clean as a whistle', a proverbial simile, signifying completely, entirely. **1842** J. WILSON *Chr. North* I. 84 By the time we reach the manse we are as dry as a whistle. **1849** W. S. MAYO *Kaloolah* v. (1850) 41 A first rate shot;..head taken off as clean as a whistle. **1865** DICKENS *Mut. Fr.* I. xv, You're as clean as a whistle. **1880** A. GRAY *Lett.* (1893) II. 710 My throat was as clear as a whistle.

(*c*) **1851** TICKNOR *Life, Lett. & Jrnls.* (1876) II. xiii. 271 Too much, he thought, for the price of such a whistle. **1854** R. S. SURTEES *Handley Cr.* vii, I should not like to pay too dear for my whistle. **1876** GEO. ELIOT *Dan. Der.* xxxv, If a man likes to do it he must pay for his whistle.

(*d*) **1934** WODEHOUSE *Right Ho, Jeeves* xvii. 222 Now that the whistle had been blown on his speech, it seemed to me that there was no longer any need for the strategic retreat which I had been planning. **1953** R. CHANDLER *Long Good-Bye* vi. 38 Come on, Marlowe. I'm blowing the whistle on you. **1965** *Midnight* 12 July 20/1 More and more frequently though, a whistle is being blown on the more exuberant borrowers. **1978** S. WILSON *Dealer's Move* v. 98 So Arnie and Alfie blew the whistle on you all. What are you going to do about it? **1984** *Gainesville* (Florida) *Sun* 29 Mar. 5A/4 Jim Kirkland, the man who first blew the whistle on Gainesville's deteriorating financial condition, has resigned after less than three months on the job.

†**c.** *fig.* A person who speaks on behalf of another, an 'instrument', 'mouth-piece'; one who gives a secret signal (cf. WHISTLE *v.* 10). *Obs.*

c **1380** WYCLIF *Sel. Wks.* II. 2 Crist criede in desert, bi Baptist þat was his whistle. *Ibid.* 240 Poul whom God haþ made his whistil. **1633** MASSINGER *Guardian* III. vi. (1655) 51 Your neighbour, Your whistle, agent, parasite..Should be within Call, when you hem.

d. ***whistle and flute***: rhyming slang for 'suit' (SUIT *sb.* 19). Chiefly *ellipt.* as *whistle.*

1931 BROPHY & PARTRIDGE *Songs & Slang of Brit. Soldier, 1914–18* (ed. 3) 375 *Whistle and flute*, a suit (of clothes). **1941** G. KERSH *They die with their Boots Clean* I. 27 He is the one permanent type of Londoner..the..Cockney... To Barker..a suit is a Whistle, or Whistle-an'-Flute. **1960** A. PRIOR in *Pick of Today's Short Stories* XI. 180 Half-Nelson lives for clothes... He never keeps a whistle more than a month. **1970** A. DRAPER *Swansong for Rare Bird* vii. 51 My best whistle was in a big heap on the floor. **1980** 'J. GASH' *Spend Game* ix. 97 'Him with the fancy whistle.' Whistle-and-flute, suit.

2. *colloq.* A jocular name for the mouth or throat as used in speaking or singing; chiefly in phr. ***to wet*** (erron. ***whet***) ***one's whistle***, to take a drink.

c **1386** CHAUCER *Reeve's T.* 235 So was hir ioly whistle wel y-wet. **1530** PALSGR. 780, I wete my whystell, as good drinkers do, *je crocque la pie.* **1612** BEAUM. & FL. *Coxcomb* II. ii, Let's have no pitty, for if you do, here's that shall cut your whistle. **1653** WALTON *Angler* iii. 75 Lets..drink the other cup to wet our whistles, and so sing away all sad thoughts. **1674** [see WHET *v.* 6]. *a* **1680** BUTLER *Rem.* (1759) I. 216 He, that laugh'd, until he choak'd his Whistle. **1715** tr. *Pancirollus' Mem. Things* I. I. xi. 28 They did not only moisten their Pates, but their Whistles too. **1787** WOLCOT (P. Pindar) *Ode upon Ode* Wks. 1812 I. 447 Nor damn thy precious soul to wet thy whistle. **1836** [HOOTON] *Bilberry Thurland* II. 8 Let's have another drop to keep my whistle wet. **1840** MARRYAT *Poor Jack* xiii, Whet your whistle, Jim.

3. a. An act of whistling; a clear shrill sound produced by forcing the breath through the narrow opening made by contracting the lips; esp. as a call or signal to a person or animal; also as an expression of surprise or astonishment; *rarely*, the action of whistling a tune. Also, the act of sounding, or the sound made by, a whistle or pipe.

1447 BOKENHAM *Seyntys* (Roxb.) 151 Whan Marcuryis whystyl hym dede streyne To hys deed slepe. **1586** [? J. CASE] *Praise Mus.* iii. 43 The ploughman & carter, are..compelled to frame their breath into a whistle. **1607** TOPSELL *Four-f. Beasts* 608 He requireth of a skilfull shepheard a voyce or whisell intelligable to the sheepe, whereby to call them together. **1634** MILTON *Comus* 346 The..sound of pastoral reed.., Or whistle from the Lodge. **1671** TRENCHFIELD *Cap Gray Hairs* (1688) 53 When Dogs or Horses shew their ready motion at our Whistle or Chirrup. **1749** FIELDING *Tom Jones* VI. ii, She took an Opportunity..to interrupt one of his Whistles in the following Manner. **1823** SCOTT *Quentin D.* xviii, Lucky that Klepper knows my whistle, and follows me as truly as a hound. **1848** DICKENS *Dombey* xxiii, There was nothing but a whistle emphatic enough for the conclusion of the sentence. **1856** *Amy Carlton* 13 The engine gave its warning yell, as Amy called the whistle. **1896** CONAN DOYLE *Exploits Brig. Gerard* vi, The dry rattle of the drums and the shrill whistle of the fifes.

b. *fig.* or in figurative phrases: Call, summons.

Formerly often in phr. ***not worth a whistle***: hence as a type of something worthless. Rarely with other implications: †A moment, instant (in phr. ***in a whistle***): a 'whisper', slight mention (cf. WHISTLE *v.* 10).

a **1529** SKELTON *Col. Cloute* 238 They..woteth neuer what thei rede, Paternoster, Ave, nor Crede; Construe not worth a whystle Nether Gospell nor Pystle. *a* **1553** UDALL *Royster D.* I. iv. (Arb.) 26 Kocks nownes what meanest thou man, tut a whistle. *c* **1580** *Bugbears* III. ii, He red me a pistle and told a long round about not worth a whistle. **1583** STOCKER *Civ. Warres Lowe C.* II. 67 That hee shoulde be brought to the whistle, or daunce after their pipe. **1605** SHAKS. *Lear* IV. ii. 29, I haue beene worth the whistle. **1639** J. CLARKE *Paræm.* 232 Ready to run at every mans whistle. **1641** MILTON *Animadv.* 57 Those drossy spirits that need the lure and whistle of earthly preferment. **1643** TRAPP *Comm. Gen.* vi. 3 It bloweth where it listeth, and will not be at your whistle. **1784** BAGE *Barham Downs* II. 273 He could do it in a whistle. **1855** MACAULAY *Hist. Eng.* xiii. III. 337 All his followers..were ready at his whistle to array themselves round him. **1886** STEVENSON *Kidnapped* i, Can you forget..old friends at the mere whistle of a name?

c. The clear shrill voice or note of a bird, or of certain other animals.

1784 COWPER *Death of Mrs. Throckmorton's Bulfinch* 10 With a whistle blest, Well-taught, he all the sounds express'd Of flagelet or flute. **1816** SCOTT *Antiq.* xxxvii, A miserable linnet..began to greet them with his whistle. **1839** *Penny Cycl.* XV. 517/1 They [*sc.* Marmots]..when angry or before a storm pierce the ear with their shrill whistle. **1860** TYNDALL *Glac.* I. xv. 103 To its [*sc.* a chamois'] whistle our guide whistled in reply. **1881** JEFFERIES *Toilers of Field* (1892) 297 The blackbird's whistle is very human, like a human being playing the flute.

d. Any similar sound, as of wind blowing through trees or rigging, of a missile flying through the air, etc.

a **1648** LD. HERBERT *Occas. Poems, Ode whether Love shd. continue for ever*, Soft whistles of the wind, And warbling murmurs of a brook. **1826** J. F. COOPER *Last of Mohicans* xx, We..are already nearly out of whistle of a bullet. **1867** MORRIS *Jason* xv. 435 Therewithal must I..writhe beneath the whistle of the whip. **1888** BOTTONE *Electr. Instr. Making* (ed. 2) 30 To a practised ear the peculiar whistle tells when the glass is being cut, and when only scratched.

4. *attrib.* and *Comb.*, as *whistle-call*; **whistle-belly-vengeance** (*slang*), bad liquor, such as causes rumbling in the bowels (cf. *whip-belly-vengeance* under WHIP- 2 a); **whistle-blower** chiefly *U.S.*, one who 'blows the whistle' on a person or activity (see sense 1 b (d) above), esp. from within an organization; also **whistle-blowing** *vbl. sb.* and *ppl. a.* (lit. and *fig.*); **whistle-fish** [see quot. 1836], a name for different species of rockling or sea-loach; **whistle-grinder**, a contemptuous appellation for a church organist (cf. 1 b (*a*)); **whistle-insect** (see quot.); **whistle-kist**, *Sc.*: see 1 b (*a*); **whistle-language** = *whistle-speech* below; **whistle-line, -pull**, a line or cord by pulling which the whistle of a steamer is sounded; †**whistle-pipe**, a whistle for decoying birds; **whistle punk** *N. Amer. Logging*, a workman who sends signals by means of a whistle to those operating a donkey-engine; **whistle-ring**, a ring constructed to be sounded as a whistle; **whistle-speech**, a system of communication by whistling based on the spoken language, found esp. among peoples of mountainous districts and used to communicate over long distances; †**whistle-stalk**, a stalk made into a whistle or pipe, a 'reed'; **whistle-tankard**, a drinking-vessel fitted with a whistle, which sounds when it is emptied; **whistle-wing**, a name for the golden-eyed duck (GOLDEN-EYE 1 a), from the shrill sound made by its wings in flying; **whistle-wood**, a name for various trees whose bark is easily peeled off, used by boys to make whistles, as the alder, bass-wood, mountain-ash, and various species of maple.

1861 HUGHES *Tom Brown at Oxf.* xli, I thought you wouldn't appreciate the widow's tap..Regular *whistle-belly vengeance, and no mistake. **1970** *N.Y. Times* 23 Mar. 40 When they reflect more fully on how well the majority leader handled a *whistle-blower and protected their interests. **1983** *New Scientist* 23 June 838/1 A whistleblower who tries to alert his own organisation to a problem and fails will, if he feels strongly enough about the matter, go outside. **1971** *Ibid.* 9 Dec. 69 The Code [of Good Conduct of The British Computer Society] contains secrecy clauses that effectively prohibit Nader style *whistle-blowing. **1978** *Monitor* (McAllen, Texas) 21 May 16A/6 He has introduced legislation to protect 'whistleblowing' federal employees from reprisals if they reveal wasteful, illegal or improper government activities. **1980** *Times* 1 Apr. 3/4 The growth in Britain of 'whistle-blowing' journalism (blowing the whistle on the secret parts of the state and its servants by disclosing their activities) would seem to have sealed the fate of the D-notice system. **1983** D. DUNNETT *Dolly & Bird of Paradise* vii. 80 Whistle-blowing guys in white helmets. **1746** W. ELLIS *Agric. Improv'd* May xvi. 100 In a certain Park, where Pheasants and Partridges come at the *Whistle-call. **1830** SCOTT *Demonol.* x. 393 Mariners conceive they hear the whistle-call. *a* **1672** WILLUGHBY *Hist. Pisc.* (1686) 121 Mustela vulgaris Rondeletii..A Sea Loche Cestriæ. *Whistle-fish in Cornubia. **1769** PENNANT *Brit. Zool.* III. 128 The Irish have their song at the taking of the razor shell; and the Cornish theirs, at the taking of the whistle fish. **1836** YARRELL *Brit. Fishes* II. 188, I believe..that..the term has been changed,..and that for Whistle-fish we ought to read Weasel-fish. Both the Three and Five Bearded Rocklings were called *mustela* from the days of Pliny..to the present time. **1843** BALLANTINE *Gaberlunzie's Wallet* 237 Doors were shut against the '*whistle-grinder'. **1760** G. EDWARDS *Glean. Nat. Hist.* II. 161 The head is made like that of a locust: the..thorax is surrounded with many sharp points;..I have called it the *Whistle-Insect, because it very nearly agrees with another insect found in Africa, of which the natives make whistles to call their cattle together: these whistles consist of the whole outer cover of the insect. **1843** BALLANTINE *Gaberlunzie's Wallet* 139 Grinding muckle *whistle-kists, Sic abomination. **1956** J. WHATMOUGH *Language* iii. 48 In this book we are not concerned with such departures from true speech as the so-called *whistle 'languages' of Mazateco..and of the Canary Islands. **1957** *Amer. Anthropologist* LIX. 487 My direct interest in the subject stems from a brief encounter with a whistle-'language' and a slit-gong xylophone..among the Northern Chins of Burma. **1978** *Maledicta* II. 254 Whistle-Languages: Who knows whether there are insults or other abuses in whistled languages of the Canary Islands, Kuskoy/Turkey, etc.? **1898** 'H. S. MERRIMAN' *Roden's Corner* v. 46 The second mate, with his hand on the *whistle-line, blared out his warning note every half-minute. **1570** *Henry's Wallace* VIII. 1423 Ane *quhissil pype. **1587** A. DAY *Daphnis & Chloe* (1890) 14 Vpon what occasion to vse the Whistle-Pipe, and how at another time to call with their voice alone. **1892** 'H. S. MERRIMAN' *Slave of Lamp* xxvi, Her captain swearing on the bridge, with the *whistle-pull in his hand. **1925** *Amer. Speech* I. 136 The '*whistle-punk', who handles the signal wire that runs from the timber to the whistle of the donkey-engine. **1945** B. MACDONALD *Egg & I* xiv. 184 Sharp and clear came the whistle punk's signals for a skidder. **1965** M. MCINTYRE *Place of Quiet Waters* ix. 172 He might get a job as a whistle punk in a logging camp. **1877** W. JONES *Finger-ring* 534 *Whistle-rings, puzzle-rings, squirt-rings, &c. **1948** *Language* XXIV. 280 (*heading*) Mazateco *whistle speech. **1972** HARTMANN & STORK *Dict. Lang. & Linguistics* 255/2 Young English children often use whistle speech as a game. **1979** L. CAMPBELL in Campbell & Mithun *Lang. Native Amer.* 958 Whistle speech is shared by Amuzgo, Mazatec,..some Nahua dialects, and Mexican Kickapoo. *a* **1653** G. DANIEL *Idyll.* iv. 74 A *whistle-Stalke. **1909** *Daily Chron.* 12 July 4/7 In the possession of the Corporation of Hull..is a *whistle tankard which belonged to Anthony Lambert, Mayor of Hull in 1669. **1872** COUES *Key N. Amer. Birds* 361 *Whistle-wing = Golden-eye. **1825** BROCKETT *N.C. Gloss.*, **Whussel-wood*, the alder and plane-tree; used by boys in making whistles.

whistle ('hwɪs(ə)l), *v.* Forms: 1 **hwistlian, hwys(t)lian, huislian, wistlian,** 4 **wystel, whysle,** 4–5 *Sc.* **quhistle,** 4–6 **whistil(l, whissil(l,** 4–7 **whistel(l,** 5 **whistyll(e,** 5–6 **whystel(l, whystle,** *Sc.* **quhissil(l, quhisle,** 5–7 **wistle,** 6 **wyssel,** 6–7 **whissel(l,** *Sc.* **quhissel(l,** 8 *Sc.* **whissle,** 9 *Sc.* **whussle,** 4– **whistle.** [OE. *hwis(t)lian*, also *wistlian*, f. an echoic root + -LE 3. Cf. ON. *hvísla* to whisper, MSw. *hvisla*, Sw. *vissla* to whistle, Da. *hvisle* to hiss.]

I. Literal senses.

1. *intr.* To utter a clear, more or less shrill sound or note by forcing the breath through the narrow opening formed by contracting the lips (the tone being produced merely by the resonance of the mouth-cavity, without vibration of the vocal cords): esp. as a call or signal to a person or animal, also as an expression of derision, contempt, etc., later more usually of surprise or astonishment; also, to utter a melody or tune consisting of a succession of such notes, esp. by way of idle diversion.

The common superstitious practice among sailors to whistle for a wind during a calm, and to refrain from whistling during a gale, is referred to in quots. *c.* 1515, etc.

c **1000** *Gloss. Prudentius* in *Germania* (N.S.) XI. 398/176 Hwyslaþ, *exsibilat.* *c* **1000** *Sax. Leechd.* II. 258 Wistlað of þam dæle þe þæt sar bið. **1382** WYCLIF *Isa.* v. 26 He shall whistle [1388 hisse] to hym fro the coestes of the erthe; and lo! hastid he shal come swiftli. *a* **1400** *Octouian* 1436 Clement nere the stede stapte, He whyslede and hys hondys clapte. *c* **1400** *Beryn* 3418 Geffrey..was evir wistlyng att euery pase comyng. **1423** JAS. I *Kingis Q.* cxxxv, The foulere quhistlith in his throte Diuersely. *c* **1515** *Cocke Lorell's B.* (Percy Soc.) 12 Some stered at the helme behynde Some whysteled after the wynde. ? **1549** CRANMER *Serm.* Wks. (Parker Soc. 1846) 198 If we take it for a Canterbury tale,..why do we not laugh it out of place, and whistle at it? **1570** *Satir. Poems Reform.* xvi. 83 Thay say he can baith quhissill and cloik, And his mouth full of meill. **1581** A. HALL *Iliad* x. 186 He whistled to him in his fiste. **1592** SHAKS. *Rom. & Jul.* v. iii. 7 Whistle then to me, As signall that thou hearest some thing approach. **1623** in Ellis *Orig. Lett.* Ser. I. III. 140 That ye showlde quhissell and sing one to another like Jakke and Tom for faulte of bettir musike. **1632** MILTON *L'Allegro* 64 The Plowman..Whistles ore the Furrow'd Land. **1700** DRYDEN *Cymon & Iph.* 85 He trudg'd along..And whistled as he went, for want of Thought. **1742** BLAIR *Grave* 59 The Schoolboy..Whistling aloud to bear his Courage up. **1801** SCOTT *Eve St. John* vii, He whistled thrice for his little foot-page. **1827** in Hone *Every-day Bk.* II. 255 Our sailors..whistle for a wind. **1844** HOOD *Captain's Cow* vii, The more we whistled for the wind The more it did not blow. **1882** BESANT *All Sorts* xxiii, Another discovery..at sight of which he whistled and then shook his head. **1905** F. YOUNG *Sands of Pleasure* I. iii, Richard, whistling to the dog, led the way.

2. a. To utter a clear shrill sound, note, or song, as various birds and certain other animals; to pipe; †also formerly, to hiss, as a serpent.

*a*1100 *Aldhelm Gloss* I. 4703 (Napier 121/2) *Sibilans*, hwistliende. 13.. *K. Alis.* 5348 (Laud MS.) Dragouns..þat grisely whistleden & blasten, And of her mouþe fyre out casten. 1398 TREVISA *Barth. De P.R.* v. xxxvii. (Bodl. MS.), An adder..þat whisteleþ and blowith and corrumpith þe aier. 1484 CAXTON *Fables of Æsop* I. x, [The serpent] whystled about the hows. 1549 *Compl. Scot.* vi. 39 The chekyns began to peu quhen the gled quhissillit. 1599 ALEX. HUME *Poems* (S.T.S.) *Hymnes* iii. 190 The Maveis and the Philomeen, The Stirling whissilles lowd. 1663 BUTLER *Hud.* I. i. 54 Latine was no more difficile, Than to a Black-bird 'tis to whistle. 1766 J. COLLIER (Tim Bobbin) *Wks.* (1862) 344 They [*sc.* magpies] can whistle also! 1810 E. D. CLARKE *Trav. Russia* xii. 249 The Suroke, which is seen in all parts of the steppes, sitting erect, near its burrow, on the slightest alarm whistling very loud. 1820 KEATS *Autumn* iii, The redbreast whistles from a garden-croft. 1853 KANE *Grinnell Exp.* xxxix. (1856) 359 The white whale..whistled while submerged. 1900 *Blackw. Mag.* July 60/1 It [*sc.* a buck] turned and crashed away into the forest, 'whistling' as it went.

b. Of a broken-winded horse: cf. WHISTLER 2 d, WHISTLING *vbl. sb.* 2 b.

1898 *Encycl. Sport* Mar. 183/1 Whether his most promising two-year-old..did or did not whistle—or worse —as she passed him.

3. a. To produce a shrill sound of this kind in any way, esp. by rapid movement, as the wind, a missile, the lash of a whip, etc.

*c*1480 HENRYSON *Test. Cress.* 20 The blastis bitterly Fra Pole Artick come quhisling loud and schill. 1513 DOUGLAS *Æneis* IV. viii. 73 The souchand bir quisland amang the granis. 1581 A. HALL *Iliad* II. 25 Making such noise as doth the sea, when..It makes the shoare whistle along, with beating on eche crag. 1697 DRYDEN *Æneis* XII. 404 The winged Weapon, whistling in the Wind. *a*1718 PRIOR *Henry & Emma* 392 When the Winds whistle, and the Tempests roar. 1748 *Anson's Voy.* II. vi. 192 The first shot passed extremely near.., whistling just over the heads of the crew. 1853 DICKENS *Bleak Ho.* viii, The place became dilapidated, the wind whistled through the cracked walls. 1896 CONAN DOYLE *Rodney Stone* xxii, A whip whistled in the darkness. 1901 W. PETT RIDGE *Lond. only* i. 26 Mrs. Bell..turned up the gas until it whistled madly.

b. To rustle shrilly, as silk or other stiff fabric. *Obs.* or *dial.*

1633 G. HERBERT *Temple, Quip* iv, Then came brave Glorie puffing by In silks that whistled. 1669 FLAVEL *Husb. Spir.* etc. 240 Under poor garments more true worth may be, Than under silks that whistle. 1858 A. MAYHEW *Paved with Gold* II. vii, Making his nether garments 'whistle', as the noise produced by the friction of corduroy is musically styled by the vulgar.

4. To blow or sound a whistle; to sound, as a whistle.

1530 PALSGR. 781/1, I whystell in a whystell, or in my hande, *je ciffle.* 1549 *Compl. Scot.* vi. 40 The maister quhislit, and bald the marynalis lay the cabil to the cabil-stok. 1608 SHAKS. *Per.* IV. i. 64 The Boatswaine whistles,.. the Maister calles. 1668 [see 7 a]. 1818 SCOTT *Br. Lamm.* iv, She whistled on a small silver call..which..was sometimes used to summon domestics. 1849 THACKERAY *Contrib. Punch, Paris Revisited* ¶5 The engine whistled—the train set forth. 1896 *Law Times Rep.* LXXIII. 614/2 The engine driver began to whistle about ten seconds before the train passed over the crossing.

5. *trans.* To produce or utter by whistling (in sense 1, 2, or 4), as a tune or melody; to express by whistling.

1530 LYNDESAY *Test. Papyngo* 88 To play platfute, and quhissill fute before. 1575 A. F. *Virg. Bucol.* x. 31 If that your pipe would whistle vp my loue, which boyles in brest [L. *Vestra meos olim si fistula dicat amores*]. 1597 SHAKS. *2 Hen. IV*, III. ii. 342 (Qo.) Those tunes..that he heard the Car-men whistle. 1709 T. ROBINSON *Vind. Mosaick Syst.* 89 They [*sc.* God's creatures] have all their several ways of Pleasure and Diversion, some by dancing around in the open Air,..others by singing, or whistling out their chearful Notes. 1774 GOLDSM. *Nat. Hist.* (1776) V. 345 The linnet and bull-finch may be taught..to whistle a long and regular tune. 1837 DICKENS *Pickw.* ii, The officer whistled a lively air. 1853 MRS. GASKELL *Ruth* xi, Miss Benson had some masculine tricks, and one was whistling a long, low whistle when surprised or displeased.

6. a. To shoot or drive with a whistling sound.

1697 DAMPIER *Voy. round World* (1699) 116 The Spaniards..began to whistle now and then a shot among them. 1829 SCOTT *Anne of G.* xiii, Sturdy young giants as ever climbed cliff, or carried bolt to whistle at a chamois. 1853 FERRIS *Mormons at Home* xv. (1856) 278 The wind.. whistled the dust around us in clouds.

b. With *down*, *off*: To put on, or take off (the brakes of a railway engine).

1869 BRET HARTE *What Engines said* iii. Wks. (1872) 491 Said the Engine from the East:..S'pose you whistle down your brakes. 1891 C. ROBERTS *Adrift Amer.* 172 The engineer whistled the brakes off.

c. To make (one's way) with whistling.

1853 MRS. GORE *Dean's Dau.* xxxvi, The steamer thumped and whistled its way athwart Cowes Roads. 1866 BLACKMORE *Cradock Nowell* xvi, He..whistled his way to the main front-door.

II. Extended, allusive, and figurative senses.

7. *trans.* **a.** To call, summon, bring, or get by or as by whistling; †*fig.* to entice, allure.

1486 *Bk. St. Albans* b iv b, Stonde styll and cherke hir, and whistyll hir. 1580 LYLY *Euphues* Wks. 1902 II. 197 If Argus with his hundred eyes went prying to vndermine Iupiter, yet met he with Mercurie, who whiselled all his eyes out. 1589 R. HARVEY *Pl. Perc.* (1590) 22 When I lead a horse to the water, if he will not drinke, what can I doo, but whistle him. 1623 SANDERSON *Serm., Job xxix. 14–17* (1674) I. 98 Whether it be through his own cowardise or inconstancy, that he keepeth off; or that a fair word whistleth him off. 1623 MIDDLETON & ROWLEY *Sp. Gipsy* IV. (1653) H 3, If you can whistle her To come to Fist, make tryall, play the young Falconer. 1665 GLANVILL *Def. Van. Dogm.* 4 Whistling their dependants into apparent precipices. 1668 H. MORE *Div. Dial.* II. xxvi. 338 *Hyl.* If you fall a-drinking, I may well fall a-whistling on my Flagellet. *Cuph.* What, do you mean to make us all Horses, to whistle us while we are a-drinking? *Ibid.* xxix. 349 No Hags of Thessaly could ever whistle the celestial Dog out of the Sky. 1716 ADDISON *Freeholder* No. 22 ¶2 He..chanced to miss his dog... We stood still till he had whistled him up. 1759 STERNE *Tr. Shandy* I. xvi, Had he been whistled up to London, upon a Tom Fool's errand. 1774 GOLDSM. *Retal.* 108 He cast off his friends, as a huntsman his pack, For he knew when he pleased he could whistle them back. 1836 [HOOTON] *Bilberry Thurland* III. 3 A young man..came..and whistled her out through the palisadings of the area. 1876 *Field* 12 Feb. 156/2 The driver's whistle, as he tried to whistle the opposing signal down, would soon show to the man in the signal-box what was amiss. 1889 MRS. ALEXANDER *Crooked Path* iv, The polite man..whistled up a hansom for the two gentlemen.

b. (With *away*, *off*, etc.) To send or dismiss by whistling (esp. as a term of falconry); also *fig.* to dismiss, cast off, or abandon lightly: so ***to whistle down the wind*** (the hawk being usually cast off against the wind in pursuit of prey, but with the wind when turned loose).

*c*1555 HARPSFIELD *Divorce Hen. VIII* (Camden) 121 The which John Bacon was whistled and clapped out of Rome. 1604 SHAKS. *Oth.* III. iii. 262 If I do proue her Haggard, Though that her Iesses were my deere heart-strings, I'ld whistle her off, and let her downe the winde To prey at Fortune. *a*1616 BEAUM. & FL. *Bonduca* IV. iii, This is he.. that basely Whistled his honour off to th' wind. 1621 BURTON *Anat. Mel.* II. ii. III. 317 As a long-winged Hawke when he is first whistled off the fist, mounts aloft. *a*1721 SHEFFIELD (Dk. Buckhm.) *Jul. C.* I. ii, Those lofty Thoughts ..now are whistled off With every Pageant Pomp, and gawdy Show. 1759 FRANKLIN *Ess.* Wks. 1840 III. 269 He first acknowledges that right, and then whistles it away. 1775 JOHNSON *Tax. no Tyr.* 83 The Dean of Gloucester has proposed..that we should..release our claims, declare them masters of themselves, and whistle them down the wind. 1792 HOLCROFT *Road to Ruin* I. 14 Poverty is a trifle; we can whistle it off. 1840 MARRYAT *Poor Jack* xlvi, To the winds have I whistled her long ago! 1860 TROLLOPE *Cas. Richmond* xiv, Having accepted my love, you cannot whistle me down the wind as though I were of no account. 1871 MEREDITH *H. Richmond* liii, You're going, are you?.. Then I whistle you off my fingers!

8. a. *intr.* To issue a call or summons, to call; ***whistle for***, to summon. Now *rare* or *Obs.* (exc. as implied in sense 1 or 4).

1560 PILKINGTON *Aggeus* (1562) 158 Drought, hunger, plage, sworde, do tarye..for God's callinge and as soone as he whystles, they come straighte. *a*1626 BACON *Adv. King Sutton's Est.* Wks. 1826 V. 381 The greatness of the reward doth whistle for the ablest men..to supply the chair.

b. ***whistle off***: to go off, go away (suddenly or lightly). *colloq.* ? *Obs.*

1689 SHADWELL *Bury F.* II. 22 *Wild.* So, Madam, you have my Heart... *Gert.* 'Tis a light one, and always ready to whistle off at any Game. 1796 MME. D'ARBLAY *Camilla* VII. viii, [He] whistled off to his appointed chamber.

9. a. ***to go whistle***: to go and do what one will, to occupy oneself idly or to no purpose (esp. in phrases expressing unceremonious or contemptuous dismissal or refusal, as ***to bid one go whistle***; also without *go*). ***to whistle for***: to seek, await, or expect in vain, to fail to get, to go without (cf. note under sense 1). *colloq.*

1453–4 PECOCK *Folewer to Donet* 106 If eny man pretende so greet a curiosite anentis þe persoon of crist þat he lackid þe passioun of angir, he may go whistle til he leerne bettir. 1513 MORE in Hall *Chron., Edw. V.* (1548) 9 b, There they spende and byd their creditours goo whystle. 1605 *Lond. Prodigal* II. iv. 173 The Deuen-shyre man shall whistle for a wife. 1611 SHAKS. *Wint. T.* IV. iv. 715 This being done, let the Law goe whistle. 1642 PRYNNE *Pleas. Purge* 157 There is no Altar, Table in the Text. You may goe whistle then. 1677 *Govt. Venice* 271 Men are apt to promise any thing in danger, and to perform nothing when out of it, according to the Proverb of their Countrey:..When the danger's past, the Saint may go whistle. 1741 SHENSTONE *Poet & Dun* 24 Your fame is secure—bid the critics go whistle. 1760 C. JOHNSTON *Chrysal* II. II. xiv, 'Do not you desire to be free?' ..'aye! that I do! but I may whistle for that wind long enough, before it will blow.' 1812 COLMAN *Br. Grins, &c., Low Ambit.* ii, You may as well go whistle as go think Of mending the confusion. 1818 SCOTT *Hrt. Midl.* xviii, And sae we'll leave Mr. Sharpitlaw to whistle on his thumb. 1882 LADY G. BLOOMFIELD *Remin.* I. i. 14 She..rode off, telling him he might whistle for his money.

b. ***to whistle in the dark***: to put on a brave front; to make a pretence of confidence. *colloq.*

1939 [implied in WHISTLING *vbl. sb.* 1 d]. 1958 *Spectator* 8 Aug. 185/3 At his press conference, Mr. Dulles was whistling bravely in the dark. 1971 'L. EGAN' *Malicious Mischief* (1972) ii. 29 That fellow's whistling in the dark. And I think he knows it. 1983 S. HILL *Woman in Black* 92 'I am finding the whole thing rather a challenge.' 'Mr Kipps ..you are whistling in the dark.'

10. *intr.* and *trans.* To speak, tell, or utter secretly, to 'whisper'; to give secret information, turn informer. ? *Obs.*

1599 SIR J. HAYWARD *Hen. IV*, I. 27 Some of the secrete counsailers, or corrupters rather, and abusers of the King, whistled him in the eare, that his going to Westminster was neither seemly nor safe. 1611 SHAKS. *Wint. T.* IV. iv. 248 Is there not milking-time? When you are going to bed? Or kill-hole? To whistle of these secrets? 1627 J. TAYLOR (Water P.) *Armado* B 5, They dare speake fellony, whistle treason. 1681 FLAVEL *Right. Man's Ref.* 195 The bird of the air that carries tidings, and whistles deeds of darkness. 1815 SCOTT *Guy M.* xxxiii, I kept ay between him and her, for fear she had whistled. *Ibid.* l, I wadna like..to gang about whistling and raising the rent on my neighbours. 1917 H. A. VACHELL *Fishpingle* xii. 236 He hurried on, now doubly assured that Joyce had 'whistled'.

11. To smell unpleasantly or strongly. *slang. rare.*

1935 AUDEN & ISHERWOOD *Dog beneath Skin* II. v. 113 Wot wouldn't I give fer a bath? Cor! I don't 'alf whistle!

whistle, change, exchange: see WISSEL.

whistleable ('hwɪs(ə)ləb(ə)l), *a.* [f. WHISTLE *v.* + -ABLE.] Of a tune, etc.: capable of being whistled; suitable for whistling.

1962 *Guardian* 9 Oct. 7/1 This movement contains no fewer than four very singable and whistleable tunes. 1973 *Daily Tel.* 19 Apr. 10/4, I want to sit light to the glorious fantasy, to let it ride through my mind like a whistleable tune.

whistle-ation: see -ATION.

whistled ('hwɪs(ə)ld), *ppl. a.* [f. WHISTLE *v.* + -ED[1].]

1. a. Uttered by whistling.

1816 J. HECKLEWELDER *Let.* 24 July in *Trans. Hist. & Lit. Comm. Amer. Philos. Soc.* (1819) I. 396 Where *w* in this language is placed before a vowel, it sounds the same as in English; before a consonant, it represents a whistled sound. 1864 J. C. ATKINSON *Stanton Grange* 195 In obedience to his whistled signal. 1918 *Pall Mall Gaz.* 29 June 5/3 A shrill whistled chorus of 'Jack's the Boy'.

b. ***whistled language*** or ***speech***: = *whistle-language, -speech* s.v. WHISTLE *sb.* 4.

1948 *Langauge* XXIV. 283 Many words and phrases in Mazateco have identical tonal patterns. In the spoken language segmental phonemes usually distinguish tonally identical words and phrases. In the whistled language the absence of the segmental features gives opportunity for ambiguities. 1957 *Archivum Linguisticum* IX. 44 The Silbo Gomero is not the only whistled language in the world..but ..is unique in being based not on prosodic but on purely articulatory features. 1978 *Verbatim* Sept. 13/1 Such systems of communication by whistling, based on the language of the user, are conventionally referred to as 'whistled languages' or 'whistled speech'.

2. Summoned by whistling.

1912 *World* 7 May 692/2 As they waited for the whistled cab to come.

3. Drunk, (mildly) intoxicated. *slang* (orig. *Mil.*).

The relationship, if any, to *whistled drunk* is obscure.

1938 G. MARCH-PHILLIPPS *Ace High* II. iv. 216 They would be drunk as lords, tight as owls, screwed, canned, whistled. 1942 H. E. BATES *Greatest People in World* 8 He bounced in very late..and then began to eat as if he had returned from a hunting expedition. 'Pretty whistled last night, boys,' he would say. 'Rather off my feed.' 1968 'O. MILLS' *Sundry Fell Designs* viii. 83 He'd taken a skinful aboard, somewhere. He sounded more than a bit whistled. 1979 *Private Eye* 6 July 15/1 We all sidled off to a very nice little snug at the Golden Goose, where..all of us got faintly whistled.

¶ ***whistled drunk***: see quot.

1749 FIELDING *Tom Jones* XII. ii, He was indeed, according to the vulgar Phrase, whistled drunk.

whistler ('hwɪs(ə)lə(r)). Forms: see WHISTLE *v.*; also 6 *Sc.* **quhuslar**, 7 **whisler**. [OE. *hwistlere*, f. *hwistlian*, WHISTLE *v.*: see -ER[1].] A person, animal, or thing that whistles.

1. a. One who sounds, or plays upon, a whistle or pipe; a flute-player, piper, or fifer. Now *rare*.

*c*1000 *Ags. Gosp.* Matt. ix. 23 Þa se hælend com into þæs ealdres healle, & ȝeseah hwistleras. 1377 LANGL. *P. Pl.* B. xv. 475 With wederes and with wondres, he warneth vs with a whistlere. 1538 *Acc. Ld. High Treas. Scot.* VI. 399 In primis to iiij trumpetouris, iiij tabernouris, and iij quhislaris. 1538 in Pitcairn *Crim. Trials* I. 292* Debursat upoun þe Trumpetouris Tabernaris Quhuslaris and vtheris. 1638 SIR T. HERBERT *Trav.* (ed. 2) 30 The whistler with his iron Pipe encouraging the Marriners. 1844 MRS. BROWNING *Pain in Pleas.* 5, I desired the art Of the Greek whistler, who ..Could lure those insect swarms from orange-trees.

b. One who whistles with the lips.

*c*1440 *Promp. Parv.* 525/1 Whystelare, *ossinus, ossinator.* 1542 [see BENCH-WHISTLER]. 1652 BENLOWES *Theoph.* XIII. lxxxii, But, hark, 'tis late; the Whislers knock from Plough. 1711 STEELE *Spect.* No. 145 ¶4 Whistlers, Singers and common Orators. 1850 JAMES *Old Oak Chest* xxxviii, He was a great whistler, even when his thoughts were busiest. 1879 *All Year Round* 4 Jan. 184/1 He was a good whistler, and knew it.

c. *slang.* A keeper of a 'whistling-shop'; an unlicensed spirit-seller.

1821 W. T. MONCRIEFF *Tom & Jerry* III. v, The whistler, otherwise the spirit-merchant. 1837 DICKENS *Pickw.* xlv, 'Are these rooms never searched..?' said Mr. Pickwick. 'Cert'nly they are, sir,' replied Sam; 'but the turnkey knows beforehand, and gives the word to the wistlers, and you may wistle for it wen you go to look.'

2. a. A bird that whistles.

Applied locally to various species, as the golden-eye or whistle-wing (see WHISTLE *sb.* 4; also ***whistler-duck***), the widgeon, the ring-ouzel, the lapwing. Also *spec.* used of some nocturnal bird having a whistling note believed to be of ill omen: when flying in a flock, called ***the seven whistlers***.

1590 SPENSER *F.Q.* II. xii. 36 The Whistler shrill, that who so heares, doth dy. 1623 WEBSTER *Duchess Malfi* IV. ii, Hearke, now euery thing is still, The Schritch-Owle, and the whistler shrill, Call vpon our Dame, aloud, And bid her quickly don her shrowd. 1782 PENNANT *Gen. Syn. Birds* I. II. 443 Whistler O[riole]... Inhabits St. Domingo, where it is called *Siffleur.* 1848 THOREAU *Maine W.* (1894) 19 The note of a whistler-duck. 1874 J. W. LONG *Amer. Wildfowl* xxix. 281 Local names: butter-box, butter-ball, and little whistler. 1883 *Leisure Hour* Dec. 733/1 Immense flocks of birds were flying about uttering a doleful shrill whistling..

they were what were called the 'Seven Whistlers', and.. considered a sign of some great calamity. **1884** COUES *Key N. Amer. Birds* (ed. 2) 704 *Clangula glaucium.* Golden-eye. Whistler. Garrot.

b. [tr. Canadian Fr. *siffleur.*] A large species of marmot (*Marmota caligata*) found in mountainous parts of N. America; = SIFFLEUR.

1703 tr. *Lahontan's New Voy. N.-Amer.* I. 110 [We saw] little beasts called Siffleurs or Whistlers. **1820** HARMON *Jrnl.* 427 A small animal, found only on the Rocky Mountain, denominated, by the Natives, Quis-qui-su, or whistlers, from the noise which they frequently make, and always when surprised. **1829** J. RICHARDSON etc. *Fauna Boreali-Amer.* I. 150 The Whistler inhabits the Rocky Mountains from latitude 45° to 62°. **1866** J. K. LORD *Naturalist in Vancouver Island* II. 195 The Redskin is the whistler's most implacable enemy; he never tires of hunting and trapping the little animal. **1912** *Canad. Alpine Jrnl.* (Special No.) 28 The big hoary marmots are well named 'whistlers' by all mountain climbing people of the Canadian Rockies. **1973** *Islander* (Victoria, B.C.) 4 Feb. 4/3 Here we saw ptarmigan and heard the marmots, or whistlers.

c. = *whistle-fish*: see WHISTLE *sb.* 4.

1864 COUCH *Brit. Fishes* III. 105 Three-bearded Rockling. Whistler. Whistle-fish.. *Motella vulgaris.*

d. A broken-winded horse that breathes hard with a shrill sound.

1824 PERCIVALL *Vet. Art* xxxiv. II. 243 We hear of pipers, wheezers, whistlers, high-blowers, and grunters: a cant in common use among our horse-dealers and horse-men, of the vulgar meaning of which no professional man should show ignorance. **1829** *Sporting Mag.* (N.S.) XXIII. 214 It is very common to hear a person say 'my horse is a bit of a whistler', when he means to imply he is not an absolute roarer. **1845** W. C. SPOONER *Vet. Art* (1851) 46 We have the names, whistlers, wheezers, and high-blowers, given by horse-dealers to horses that roar.

3. a. Something that makes a whistling sound.

1812 J. H. VAUX *Flash Dict.*, *Browns* and *Whistlers*, bad halfpence and farthings; (a term used by coiners). **1822** R. G. WALLACE *Fifteen Yrs. India* 118 The quarter-master will transport with the corps forty thousand rounds of spare ammunition, after completing each pouch with sixty whistlers. **1896** *Daily News* 7 Feb. 5/5 A breezy norther from the frozen steppes—a real Arctic whistler which makes one's face tingle.

b. An atmospheric heard as a whistle that falls in pitch, caused by radio waves generated by lightning and guided by the lines of force of the earth's magnetic field.

1928 *Nature* 17 Nov. 768/1 These observations refer to a peculiar class of atmospheric, which from their musical nature are appropriately termed 'whistlers'. **1963** G. M. B. DOBSON *Exploring Atmosphere* viii. 141 It is also possible to get some information about the ionization at very great heights above the earth from the curious phenomenon of 'whistlers' or 'whistling atmospherics'. **1974** [see MAGNETOSPHERIC *a.*]. **1979** [see WAVE GUIDE].

Whistlerian (hwɪ'slɪərɪən), *a.* [f. the name *Whistler* + -IAN.] Of, pertaining to, or characteristic of the American painter and wit James Abbott McNeill Whistler (1834–1903) or his work; after the style of Whistler.

1891 E. DOWSON *Let.* 2 Feb. (1967) 183 Oscar arrived late looking more like his Whistlerian name, in his voluminous dress clothes, than I have ever seen him. **1905** W. J. LOCKE *Morals of Marcus Ordeyne* ii. 19 A sort of Whistlerian nocturne of golden fog! **1927** CHESTERTON *Robert Louis Stevenson* iv. 92 We talk of some Whistlerian satire as a squib; but satire can only shine in the dark. **1956** D. JONES *Let.* 24 Aug. in R. Hague *Dai Greatcoat* (1980) III. 170 I'm glad to have found one surviving little oil study from this almost Whistlerian world. **1960** *Times* 15 Nov. 16/5 This is all very well in an aesthetic and Whistlerian sense. **1979** S. WEINTRAUB *London Yankees* vi. 180 His [*sc.* Sargent's] icily elegant and Whistlerian portrait.. of Madame Judith Gautreau.

Also **Whistlerism** ('hwɪslərɪz(ə)m), the style or æsthetic theory of Whistler; '**Whistlerish** *a.*

1912 C. ROWLEY *50 Yrs. Work without Wages* 147 We discussed the prevailing fashions of Whistlerism, Impressionism, and.. post-Impressionism. **1918** G. B. SHAW *Pen Portraits* (1932) 40 They are art for art's sake: the political variety of Whistlerism. **1979** *Times Lit. Suppl.* 23 Nov. 10/4 The subject of the Thames.. her Whistlerish visual evocations.

'**whistle-stop**, *sb.* orig. *U.S.* Also **whistle stop.** [WHISTLE *sb.*]

1. A small station or town at which trains do not stop unless requested by a signal given on a whistle.

1934 M. H. WESEEN *Dict. Amer. Slang* 418 *Whistle Stop*, a small town. **1944** *Sat. Rev.* (U.S.) 2 Sept. 2/4 The frank.. and.. challenging story of the men of the U.S. Foreign Service who represent America in the whistle-stops of the world. **1948** *N.Y. Times* 7 Sept. 18/8 President Truman told a railroad station crowd here tonight that 'before this campaign is over I expect to visit every whistle stop in the United States'. **1949** *Time* 9 May 29/3 To protest making Electra a whistle stop for express trains, he had thousands of plastic whistles molded in the shape of locomotives. **1949** 'H. ROBBINS' *Dream Merchants* (1950) 290 He thought Rock had been acting strangely yesterday when they had been married at that whistle stop just inside the California border. **1957** B. HUTCHISON *Canada* 217 The railway traveler sees only the dismal villages of the main line, the whistle stops around a wooden grain elevator.. and a garage. **1965** S. G. LAWRENCE *40 Yrs. on Yukon Telegraph* xvii. 102 The railway company only recognized the town as a whistle stop.

2. One of a series of rapid, superficial visits.

1952 *Manch. Guardian Weekly* 7 Aug. 3 Truman opens his trap at the first whistle-stop. *Ibid.* 9 Oct. 3 As for Mr Truman's contribution by whistle-stop, his speeches have been.. violently abusive. **1959** *Observer* 2 Aug. 9/4 We have gone on the marathon round of the dress shows (making whistle stops at breakfast and lunchtime at the smaller houses). **1976** *Courier-Jrnl.* (Louisville, Kentucky) 17 Sept. A2/1 President Ford is making a three-day tour.. that will include a series of 'whistlestops' aboard a Mississippi riverboat.

3. Used *attrib.* to designate a journey with a lot of brief halts; *spec.* one by a campaigning politician that takes in many undistinguished places in this way. Also *fig.*

1949 *Time* 6 June 22/1 Louis Johnson.. raised enough money.. to pay for Harry Truman's whistle-stop campaign. **1952** *Manch. Guardian Weekly* 18 Sept. 3/1 On the whistle-stop tour down California's Central Valley. **1959** *Manch. Guardian* 23 July 1/3 The Queen and the Duke of Edinburgh.. continued their 'whistle stop' journey to Moose Jaw. **1972** G. DURRELL *Catch me a Colobus* v. 94 Our whistle-stop tours of the villages round about had paid dividends and when we went to visit them again we rarely came away empty handed. **1973** M. TRUMAN *Harry S. Truman* i. 1 We had left Independence, Missouri, earlier in the day, and made a whistle-stop visit to Junction City, Kansas, at 11:05 p.m. **1976** *Times Lit. Suppl.* 23 July 904/4 She goes on to a whistle-stop history of attitudes to female inversion from Ancient Greece to the present day. **1978** *Broadcast* 17 July 15/1 BBC Radio 1's Roadshow set off again this week with a seven-week whistle stop tour of Britain's holiday resorts. **1981** *N. & Q.* Dec. 556/1 The result is an unremitting whistle-stop tour through barren regions.

Hence '**whistle-stop** *v.*, (*a*) *trans.*, to travel through (a region) on a whistle-stop tour (*rare*); (*b*) *intr.*, to make a whistle-stop tour; also '**whistle-stopping** *vbl. sb.*

1952 *News* (Birmingham, Ala.) 26 July 1/3 In a sort of swan song to the Democratic Party as its leader, he offered to whistle-stop the country for his successor. *Ibid.* 23 Sept. 14/5 Ike Eisenhower had settled down to whistle-stopping. **1952** *Time* 13 Oct. 23/3 In Michigan last week, nearly 100,000 people turned out to see Eisenhower as he whistlestopped across the state. **1957** *Ann. Reg. 1956* 183 Most of the 'whistle-stopping' was left to the assiduous Mr. Nixon. **1959** *Observer* 12 July 4/7 The Queen and the Duke of Edinburgh have been whistle-stopping their way across British Columbia. **1964** J. RESTON in M. McLuhan *Understanding Media* xxxii. 339 Everybody's now whistle-stopping through somebody else's country, usually ours. **1972** *Observer* 23 Apr. 6/4 Italian politicians are whistle-stopping around the country this weekend in.. the.. election campaign. **1978** *Guardian* 14 Dec. 15/4 Howard Jarvis.. the Messiah of taxpayers.. has whistle-stopped across the United States with.. 226 events every 10 days.

whistling ('hwɪs(ə)lɪŋ), *vbl. sb.* Forms: see WHISTLE *v.*; also 5 *Sc.* **quhestlyng**, 6 *Sc.* **quhisling**, 7 **whisling.** [OE. (*h*)*wistlung*, f. (*h*)*wistlian*, WHISTLE *v.*: see -ING[1].] The action of the verb WHISTLE, in various senses.

1. a. The action of producing a shrill note or notes by forcing the breath through the lips; the utterance of a tune, etc. in this way; †hissing: see WHISTLE *v.* 1, 5.

c **897** ÆLFRED *Gregory's Past. C.* xxiii. 173 Sua sua mid liðre wisðlunga mon hors ȝestilleð, sua eac mid ð ære illcan wistlunga mon mæȝ hund astyriȝean. *c* **1100** *Voc.* in Wr.-Wülcker 162/44 *Sibilatio*, hwistlung. **1377** LANGL. *P. Pl.* B. xv. 456 Foules þat.. folwed his whistellynge. **1382** WYCLIF *2 Chron.* xxix. 8 He toke hem in to distourblynge, and into deth, and in to whistlyng [Vulg. *sibilum*]. **1398** TREVISA *Barth. De P.R.* XVIII. xiv. (Bodl. MS.) lf. 255 b/2 An oxe heerde.. plesеþ ham [*sc.* the oxen] wiþ whistelinge and wiþ songe. **1577** GRANGE *Golden Aphrod.* K iij b, Vnmanned Haukes forsake the lure, all whistlyng brings them not to fiste. **1663** COWLEY *Ess., Agric.* Wks. (1674) 106 Some swell up their sleight Sails with pop'lar fame, Charm'd with the foolish whistlings of a Name. **1787** GROSE *Prov. Gloss.*, *Superst.* etc. 66 Whistling at sea is supposed to cause an increase of wind, if not a storm. **1845** FORD *Handbk. Spain* I. 45 The same absence of thought which is shewn in England by whistling is displayed in Spain by singing. **1892** KIPLING *Lett. Trav.* (1920) 65 He continued an interrupted whistling of 'I owe ten dollars to O'Grady'.

b. The action of sounding a whistle or pipe; piping.

c **950** *Lindisf. Gosp.* Luke xv. 25 Wæs ða sunu his ældra on lond & miððy ȝecuome & ȝeneolecde to huse ȝeherde huislung [L. *simphoniam*] & pæt song. **1576** CURTEYS *Two Serm.* B iv b, The Shephearde needeth a Whistle, and.. a Dog and an hooke, that suche Sheep as wil not come in with whistling may be either baited in with a Dogge, or drawen in with a Hook. **1679** OATES *Myst. Iniq.* 14 The Master of a Galley.. with once whistling makes all the Galley Slaves fall to their Oars. **1884** *Manch. Exam.* 6 Oct. 5/6 The occasional whistling of an engine.

c. In phrases alluding to the act of whistling by way of a call or summons, as ***for the whistling*** (= quite easily, without any trouble), ***worth the whistling.***

1546 J. HEYWOOD *Prov.* I. xi. (1867) 35 It is.. a poore dogge, that is not woorth the whystlyng. **1601** W. CORNWALLIS *Ess.* II. lii. (1631) 334 Magnanimitie, state, absolutenes are qualities worth the whistling. **1610** J. ROBINSON *Justif. Sep.* 152 In England a man may haue a Priest for the whisteling. **1655** *Nicholas Papers* (Camden) II. 287 He may be had for whistlinge.

d. In *fig. phr.* ***whistling in the dark***: see WHISTLE *v.* 9 b.

1939 *Time* 18 Dec. 21/3 Since precious little German trade can be sailed, submarined or flown overseas, writing about 'new possibilities'.. sounded like official whistling in the dark. **1968** J. M. WHITE *Nightclimber* xix. 132 He, like me, hated and feared being carried in this ship, for all his whistling in the dark. **1977** *Listener* 10 Feb. 169/3 Lenin and his wife.. were not above a little whistling in the dark to keep up their spirits.

2. a. The utterance of a clear shrill note or notes, as the natural call of a bird or other animal; †also formerly, the hissing of serpents.

In quots. 1375 app. an error for *questing* = baying (of dogs).

c **950** *Guthlac* (Prose) viii. (1909) 139 Mislice fuȝela hwistlunge. **13..** *K. Alis.* 5247 (Laud MS.) Grete Addren comen flynge And scorpions wiþ vile whistlynge. **1375** BARBOUR *Bruce* VI. 87 He herd.. A hundis quhistlyng [*ed. Hart* whissilling, *MS. Edinb.* questionyng] apon fer. *Ibid.* 94 A hundis quhestlyng. **1426** LYDG. *De Guil. Pilgr.* 14140 Whan I here ther.. whystlynges, For verray Ioy I hoppe and daunce. **1728** POPE *Dunc.* III. 156 Each Cygnet sweet,.. Whose tuneful whistling makes the waters pass. **1847** LEICHHARDT *Jrnl.* xiii. 461 The leatherhead with its constantly changing call and whistling. **1855** C. E. NORTON *Let. to Lowell* 6 Apr., There is scarcely a sound but the whistling of the frogs.

b. A form of broken wind in horses: cf. WHISTLER 2 d.

1856 'STONEHENGE' *Brit. Sports* II. III. ii. § 1. 403 Roaring, whistling, and all defects of the wind, are easily discovered on the first smart gallop.

3. The production of any shrill sound of this kind, as by the wind, a missile, etc.

1513 DOUGLAS *Æneis* I. ii. 6 Quhair Eolus.. the wyndis lowde quhisling.. by his power refrenis. **1596** SHAKS. *1 Hen. IV*, v. i. 5 The Southerne winde.. by his hollow whistling in the Leaues, Fortels a Tempest. **1608** SYLVESTER *Du Bartas* II. iv. *Schism* 932 Sea's angry noise, loud bellowing of the Winde,.. the tackles whisteling. **1609** *Bible* (Douay) 1 Kings xix. 12 And after the fire a wistling of a gentle winde. **1681–6** J. SCOTT *Chr. Life* (1747) III. 9 We regard what he saith no more than we do the Whistling of the Wind. **1801** STRUTT *Sports & Past.* II. i. 58 The arrows made a loud whistling in their flight. **1841** J. F. COOPER *Deerslayer* iii, At the report of the rifle and the whistling of the bullet. **1844** DUFTON *Deafness* 77 If there is mucus, then various kinds of gurgling and whistling will be evident. **1899** J. G. MILLAIS *Breath fr. Veldt* 337 Swishing their white tails.. with such violence that the whistling caused by this movement can be heard nearly a quarter of a mile away.

4. *attrib.*, as ***whistling match***, ***pipe***; **whistling-post**, a post beside a railway-line, on passing which the engine-whistle is sounded; **whistling-shop** *slang*, a room in a prison in which spirits were secretly sold without a licence (a signal being given by whistling to escape detection).

1837 D. WALKER *Sports & Games* 344 *Whistling Match. A match of this kind is recorded in a paper of Addison's. **1586** [? J. CASE] *Praise Mus.* i. 18 The *whistling pipes which were made for the most part, of reedes. **1898** HAMBLEN *Gen. Manager's Story* x. 140, I managed to see most of the *whistling-posts,.. and.. I blew the crossing signal anyway. **1796** GROSE *Dict. Vulgar T.* (ed. 3), **Whistling shop*, rooms in the King's Bench prison where drams are privately sold. **1821** W. T. MONCRIEFF *Tom & Jerry* III. v, Scene V.—Interior of Whistling Shop. **1837** DICKENS *Pickw.* xlv, A whistling-shop, sir, is where they sell spirits.

'**whistling**, *ppl. a.* Forms: see WHISTLE *v.*; also 6 **whislyng.** [f. as prec. + -ING[2].] That whistles, in various senses.

1. a. Of inanimate things: see WHISTLE *v.* 3.

whistling arrow, a toy arrow formerly in use, with a hollow head so constructed as to make a whistling sound in flying. ***whistling buoy***, a buoy fitted with a whistle which is automatically sounded by the movement of the waves. ***whistling kettle***, a kettle fitted with a device that emits a whistle as the water boils.

c **1386** CHAUCER *Prol.* 170 Men myghte his brydel heere Gynglen in a whistlynge wynd. *a* **1547** SURREY *Æneis* IV. 586 The whistlyng ayre among the braunches rores. **1590** SHAKS. *Mids. N.* II. i. 86 To dance our ringlets to the whistling Winde. *a* **1593** MARLOWE *Lucan* I. 240 Shrill cornets, whistling fifes. **1667** FLAVEL *Saint Indeed* (1673) 71 To a guilty Conscience, the whistling leaves are Drums and Trumpets. *a* **1718** PRIOR *Henry & Emma* 333 Winged Deaths in whistling Arrows fly. **1784** COWPER *Task* III. 802 The whistling ball Sent through the trav'ller's temples! *Ibid.* VI. 941 The.. haughty world.. sweeps him with her whistling silks. **1842** TENNYSON *Sir Galahad* 59 Blessed forms in whistling storms Fly o'er waste fens. **1880** *Cassell's Fam. Mag.* 124/2 The Courtenay automatic whistling buoy. **1891** FARRAR *Darkn. & Dawn* xviii, The whistling strokes of the scourge. **1897** KIPLING *Capt. Cour.* viii, The *We're Here* crawled in on half-flood, and the whistling-buoy moaned and mourned behind her. **1928–9** *Army & Navy Stores Catal.* 173/4 *The Whistling kettle.* When the water boils the kettle whistles. **1961** J. STROUD *Touch & Go* iv. 43 The whistling kettle.. burst into an unnerving shriek. **1974** R. INGHAM *Yoris* xx. 63 She put a small whistling kettle on the gas ring.

b. *transf.* of a time or place: Characterized by or full of whistling.

1623 WODROEPHE *Marrow Fr. Tongue* 475/2 A Whistling March, that makes the Plough Man blithe. **1638** SIR T. HERBERT *Trav.* (ed. 2) 167 Our.. journey.. through whistling dales; in.. which we were.. weather-beaten with a raging storme. **1805** FORSYTH *Beauties Scot.* III. 227 The English Chapel [in Glasgow].. the common people,.. on account of its organ, stigmatize it with the contemptuous epithet of the whistling kirk.

c. *Mil.* Designating a missile which makes a whistling sound in flight, or a gun from which such missiles are fired. Freq. in the nicknames of these.

1864 J. BROBST *Let.* 28 May in M. B. Roth *Well, Mary: Civil War Lett. Wisconsin Volunteer* (1960) iv. 67 We dare not show our heads unless we want them to send one of their whistling jimmies at us. **1902** J. MILNE *Epistles of Atkins* iv. 67 At Ladysmith 'Sighing Sarah' and 'Whistling Willie' proclaim their own shots from Umbalwana. **1926** T. E. LAWRENCE *Seven Pillars* xcv. 507 The aeroplanes circled round in their cold-blooded way, to drop whistling bombs into its trenches. **1948** W. White *Man called White* 256 Three heavy German guns which the Americans nicknamed 'The Anzio Express' and 'Whistling Willies'.

2. a. Of a sound: Of the nature of a whistle; such as is produced by a whistle or shrill pipe.

1662 Boyle *Exam. Hobbes* iii. 16 The external Air rushing in with a whistling noise at the.. Orifice. **1668** Wilkins *Real Char.* 363 The u Gallicum, or whistling u,..cannot be denied to be a distinct simple vowel. **1750** G. Hughes *Barbados* iv. 119 The Wind, blowing into the Cavities of these Husks, makes a very sonorous whistling Noise. **1831** Scott *Ct. Rob.* ii, They..beheld the barbarian..brandish high his formidable weapon, the whistling sound of which made the old arch ring. **1851** W. H. Walshe *Dis. Lungs* 97 Sibilant rhonchus..two varieties, the short and the prolonged, or the clicking and the whistling.

b. ***whistling atmospheric***: = whistler 3 b.

1953 *Phil. Trans. R. Soc.* A. CCXLVI. 128 The main facts of observation concerning the whistling atmospherics..are summarized above. **1959** Davies & Palmer *Radio Stud. Universe* ix. 174 Storey at Cambridge in 1952..was investigating a phenomenon known as whistling atmospherics or simply 'whistlers' which are groups of radio waves at audio frequencies (15 kc/s). **1963** [see whistler 3 b].

3. a. Of a person: see whistle *v.* 1, 4.

1630 B. Jonson *New Inn* i. i, I must ha'..whistling boyes to bring my haruest home. **1721** Kelly *Sc. Prov.* 33 A crooning Cow, a crowing Hen, and a whistling Maid boded never luck to a House. **1741** Richardson *Pamela* (1824) I. xii. 250 Jackey..was the most thoughtless, whistling, sauntering fellow. **1802** Wordsw. *Poems, To Toussaint l'Ouverture* 2 Whether the whistling Rustic tend his plough Within thy hearing. **1850** *N. & Q.* 1st Ser. II. 164/1 A whistling woman and a crowing hen Is neither fit for God nor men.

b. That keeps a 'whistling-shop' (see prec. 4).

1837 Dickens *Pickw.* xlv, 'Any more?' said the whistling gentleman.

4. a. Of a bird or other animal: see whistle *v.* 2.

Chiefly as a descriptive epithet of particular species, as in **whistling dick**, a name for various species of thrush, esp. of the Australian genus *Colluricincla*; **whistling duck**, various species of duck, as the golden-eye and the widgeon (cf. whistler 2 a); **whistling eagle** or **hawk**, a small eagle or large hawk (*Haliastur sphenurus*) of Australia and New Caledonia; **whistling field bird** or **w. f. plover**, the grey plover (*Squatarola helvetica*); **whistling fish**, = *whistle-fish* (see whistle *sb.* 4); **whistling marmot** = whistler 2 b; **whistling moth** (see quot.); **whistling plover**, **swan** (see plover 2, swan *sb.* 1); **whistling thrush**, a local name for the song-thrush.

1848 Gould *Birds Australia* II. pl. 77 *Colluricincla Selbii*, ..*Whistling Dick, of the Colonists of Van Diemen's Land. **1699** Dampier *Voy.* II. ii. 69 *Whistling Ducks are somewhat less than our Common Duck... In flying, their Wings make a pretty sort of loud whistling Noise. **1863** Bates *Nat. Amazons* vii. (1864) 165 Flocks of whistling ducks (*Anas Autumnalis*), parrots, and..macaws..flew over. **1819** Stephens in Shaw's *Gen. Zool.* XI. ii. 467 [The Alwargrim Plover] is called in America the Large *Whistling Field Bird, from its note, which is very shrill. **1872** Coues *Key N. Amer. Birds* 243 Whistling Field Plover. Bull-head. Ox-eye. **1763** in Pennant *Brit. Zool.* (1776) I. 143 The seals.. are seen searching for their prey near shore, where the *whistling fish, wraws, and polacks resort. **1907** *Nature* 19 Sept. 516/1 The '*whistling (stridulating) moths' of the genus Hecatesia..emit sounds like the call of a Cicada. **1668** Charleton *Onomast.* 109 *Pluvialis Flavovirescens*, the green Plover, & *whistling Plover. **1725** De Foe *Voy. round World* (1840) 145 We..found..a great many of the whistling plover, the same with ours. **1785** Pennant *Arctic Zool.* II. 542 The *Whistling Swan carries its neck quite erect. **1802** Bingley *Anim. Biog.* (1813) II. 319 The hooper, or whistling swan..is an inhabitant of the northern regions. **1896** R. B. Sharpe *Handbk. Birds Gt. Brit.* II. 246 The Trumpeter Swan (*Cygnus buccinator*) and the Whistling Swan (*C. americanus*). **1668** Charleton *Onomast.* 100 *Boscas*, aliis *Anas Fistularis*,..the Whewer, or *Whistling Widgeon.

b. whistling thorn, a small prickly tree, *Acacia drepanolobium* or *A. zanzibarica*, found in East Africa.

1949 R. O. Williams *Useful & Ornamental Plants in Zanzibar* 102 *Acacia zanzibarica*..Coast Whistling Thorn. A thorny tree..bearing balls of bright yellow flowers. **1966** C. A. W. Guggisberg *S.O.S. Rhino* iii. 53 The rapid spread of the whistling thorn over vast areas..is probably a result of the reduction..of this animal! **1976** K. Thackeray *Crownbird* i. 9 The cab was full of whistling thorn, and swarming with red ants.

Hence **'whistlingly** *adv.*, with a whistle or whistling.

1851 H. Melville *Whale* II. xlii. 285 Stubb whistlingly gathers up the coil of the warp. **1891** *Illustr. Sporting & Dram. News* Christmas No., 36/2 A wind got up, suddenly, whistlingly.

whistly ('hwɪs(ə)lɪ), *a. rare.* [f. whistle *sb.* or *v.* + -y[1].] Resembling a whistle.

1907 'Q' *Merry Garden*, etc. 146 Makes a whistly noise in his speech—do he—like a slit bellows?

whistly ('hwɪstlɪ), *adv. arch.* [f. whist *a.*[1] + -ly[2].] Silently, quietly, softly, without noise.

a **1400–50** *Wars Alex.* 1851 Off þe whele of forton & þe whene þat whistely chaungez. **1592** *Arden of Feversham* iii. iii. 9, I vppon a little rysing hill Stoode whistely watching for the herds approch. **1854** S. Dobell *Balder* xxviii. 192 'Whistly, whistly,' said she:..'He must not wake.'

†whistness. *Obs.* [f. whist *a.*[1] + -ness.] Silence, stillness.

1609 W. M. *Man in Moone* (1849) 2 Whistnesse had taken possession of the woods. **1624** Heywood *Hist. Women* 116 This universall whistnesse; where none come But Taciturnitie and Silence dombe.

whit (hwɪt), *sb.*[1] Now *arch.* or *literary.* Also 5–6 **whyt**, 6 **whytt(e**, **wyt**, *Sc.* **quhit**, **quheet**, **quheit**, **vheet**, 6–7 **whitte**, 6–8 **whitt**, 7–8 **wit**. [Early mod.E. *whyt*, *wyt*, *whit(t*, app. an alteration of *wight*, *wite*, in *any wight*, *no wight*, *little wight* (see wight *sb.*).]

1. A very small, or the least, portion or amount; a particle, jot, 'bit'. **a.** without negative: esp. in ***every whit*** = the whole.

c **1520** Skelton *Magnyf.* 1271 What he sayth and she sayth to lay good ere, And tell to his sufferayne euery whyt. **1539** *Bible* (Great) 1 Sam. iii. 18 Samuel tolde him euery whitt, & hidd nothing from him. *c* **1590** J. Stewart *Poems* (S.T.S.) II. 198 His maist prencelie Spreit,..vill appaise thy hoip in euerie quheit. **1665** Bunyan *Holy Citie* (1669) 182 Thou must enter in by every whit of Christ, or thou shalt enter in by never a whit of him.

b. with negative expressed or implied: esp. in ***never a whit***, ***not a whit***, no whit = none at all.

1480 *Robt. Devyll* (1798) 10 The devyll have the whyt that he was soreye therfore. **1528** Roy *Rede me* (Arb.) 65, I trowe thou arte a syngynge man?.. The devil of the whit that I can. **1530**, etc. [see no whit]. **1533** J. Heywood *Johan, Tyb, & Syr Jhan* A j, Thynke ye that she wyll amende yet? Nay by our lady the deuyll spede whyt. **1538** Starkey *England* i. iii. (1878) 92 Some haue to much, some to lytyl, and some neuer a wyt. **1610** Holland *Camden's Brit.* i. 713 It can shew scarce any whit of the ancient state it had. **1631** [Mabbe] *Celestina* xviii. 183 The divell awhit shall I be able to tell them. **1635** R. N. tr. *Camden's Hist. Eliz.* iii. 284 Having sacked the Towne, they found not a whit of gold. **1678** R. Barclay *Apol. Quakers* iv. §2. 97 We do not ascribe any whit of Adam's Guilt to Men. **1830** Tennyson *Owl* ii. ii, Not a whit of thy tuwhoo, Thee to woo to thy tuwhit. **1870** Freeman *Norm. Conq.* (ed. 2) I. App. B. 545 It was not their policy to destroy or to change one whit more than was absolutely necessary. **1874** C. E. Norton *Let. to Ruskin* 10 Jan., No whit of faith in the good as good..has vanished from my soul.

2. Most commonly in phrases used adverbially: **a.** without negative: ***a whit*** = to a very small extent, a very little; ***any whit, one whit*** = to the least amount, in the least degree, at all; ***every (†each) whit*** = to the full amount, completely, altogether, thoroughly, quite (in later use almost always with *as* in comparisons of equality).

1526 Tindale *John* vii. 23 Disdayne ye at me: because I made a man every whit whoale on the saboth daye? *Ibid.* xiii. 10 He that is wesshed nedeth not but to wesshe his fete, but is clene every whit. *a* **1529** Skelton *E. Rummyng* 411 Elynour made the pryce For good ale eche whyt. **1555** in Strype *Eccl. Mem.* (1721) III. App. l. 161 Every Child..that can any whit speak. **1568** *Hist. Jacob & Esau* ii. iv, He eate it vp euery whit. **1574** Whitgift *Def. Aunsw.* ii. 104 Master Zuinglius (who woulde haue beene lothe one whit to strengthen the Papistes). **1618** in Foster *Engl. Factories Ind.* (1906) 49 Yf they be suffred but a whit longer, they will make claime to the whole Indies. **1672** Villiers (Dk. Buckhm.) *Rehearsal* ii. ii, I have written..a whole cart-load of things, every whit as good as this. *a* **1715** Burnet *Own Time* (1766) I. 384 Every whit as wild and extravagant. **1823** Scott *Quentin D.* xxiii, Were my situation one whit less perilous. **1869** Freeman *Norm. Conq.* III. xii. 231 The narrative of this campaign..is every whit as puzzling. **1903** Zangwill *Grey Wig*, etc. vi. 110 Mrs. Drabdump felt a whit uneasy.

b. with negative expressed or implied: ***never, not*** (etc.) ***a whit*** (***†awhit, a-whit***), ***any whit, one whit***; also ***no whit*** = not in the least, not at all.

1523 Ld. Berners *Froiss.* I. cccxliv. 219 b/2 He loued hym nat one whyt the better. **1558** Warde tr. *Alexis' Secr.* (1568) 7 Leaue the water vpon the fournesse, without mouing it any whit. **1564** *Brief Exam.* ****iij, You helpe your selues neuer awhyt. **1567** *Gude & Godlie B.* (S.T.S.) 203 Be na quhit of thame agast. **1594** Hooker *Eccl. Pol.* i. ii. §6 Nor is the freedom of the wil of God any whit abated..by meanes of this. **1596** Shaks. *1 Hen. IV*, ii. iv. 408 *Falst.* Art not thou horrible afraid?..*Prin.* Not a whit. **1607** *Puritan* i. i. 33 Shee cryed nere a whitte at all. **1634** Milton *Comus* 774 Natures full blessings would be well dispenc't.., And she no whit encomber'd with her store. **1642** D. Rogers *Naaman* 871 It never troubles you awhit! **1773** *Cook's Voy.* ii. ix. in Hawkesworth III, Not a whit behind them in cheerfulness and vivacity. **1775** Sheridan *Rivals* iv. iii, You don't seem one whit the happier at this. **1809–10** Coleridge *Friend* (1865) 175 He..is not a whit the better Christian for being a bad patriot. **1873** Symonds *Grk. Poets* v. 135 Grief will profit us no whit. **1893** Max Pemberton *Iron Pirate* ii, The novelty..did not surprise me one whit.

†3. As a term of contempt or abuse. *Obs. rare*[−1].

1610 B. Jonson *Alch.* iv. vii, Then you are an Otter, and a Shad, a Whit, A very Tim.

whit, *int.* (*adv.*), *sb.*[2], *v.* [Imitative. Cf. tuwhit.] A word expressing a shrill abrupt sound, as of a bird's chirp, a bullet striking something hard, etc.; also as *vb.* (Also repeated.)

1833 M. Scott *Tom Cringle* viii, The musket-balls were ..plumping into the timber whit-whit. **1854** R. S. Surtees *Handley Cr.* v, 'Whit' cries the coachman to his horses, off they go. **1859** Tennyson *Grandmother* x, And whit, whit, whit, in the bush beside me chirrupt the nightingale. **1888** Kipling *Ball. Boh Da Thone* 134 Where the *whit* of the bullet, the wounded man's scream Are mixed. **1900** *Longman's Mag.* Jan. 230 The whit-whit of the scraping knives. **1902** *Words of Eye-witness* 97 A storm of bullets.. whit viciously upon the woodwork.

Whit (hwɪt), *sb.*[3] [The first element of Whitsun, Whit Sunday, etc.] = Whitsun 1, Whitsuntide. **Whit walk**, a Whitsuntide event in which church congregations walk in procession through the streets.

For *Whit Monday*, etc., and *Whit-week* see s.v. Whit Sunday, Whitsunday.

1959 I. & P. Opie *Lore & Lang. Schoolch.* xii. 232 Well-dressing,..and the children's great Whit walks in Manchester and elsewhere, are undoubtedly exciting occasions in the lives of local youngsters. **1963** *Times* 5 June 7/1 (*heading*) Whit road toll down by 19. **1976** Nichols & Armstrong *Workers Divided* 108 This morning our foreman told us that we've got to work Whit Bank Holiday. **1978** P. Bailey *Leisure & Class in Victorian Eng.* ii. 46 The popular holiday ritual of the Whit walks—street processions of witness complete with flags and decorations and marching bands. **1979** *Guardian* 30 May 10/8 In Lancashire... Whit Walks in most towns and many villages.

whit, obs. f. quite, white, wight, with.

†whitage. *Obs.* (?)

1543 *Will of R. Elyot* (Somerset Ho.), The whitage of their kyne that was dewe unto me at Ester. **1618** Dalton *Countrey Justice* 282 The Master, or Mariners, transporting corne, Beere, Herring, Whitage, or Wood without license.

whitawer, whitawyer: see whittawer.

whitbed ('hwɪtbɛd). Also 9 **white bed.** [f. white *a.* + bed *sb.*] One of the upper beds of Portland Stone, lying next below the roach; stone from this, valued as a clean freestone for building.

1829 T. Webster in *Trans. Geol. Soc.* II. 38, I obtained from the quarrymen the thickness of the several beds, and the names by which they distinguished them from each other: but..these local appellations are not used by London architects and builders, the whole together passing here under the name of Purbeck stone only. The following is a list of the strata of limestone... 13. White bed, excellent. **1860** R. Damon *Handbk. Geol. Weymouth* 78 Whit Bed or Upper Tier.—This bed, the best stone that the island produces in point of quality, is of a whitish brown colour when first raised, but becomes paler on parting with its quarry water. **1911** *Encycl. Brit.* XXII. 122/1 The Portland limestones have been much in demand for building purposes; at Portland the 'Top Roach', the 'Whit Bed' or top freestone, and the 'Best Bed' (or Base Bed) are the best known. **1925** J. Bone *London Perambulator* ii. 32 You can see shell imprints on the freshly cut whitbed stone on the top of the new Bush Building. **1934** *Archit. Rev.* LXXV. 27 (*caption*) A 'close up' of the polished Portland stone wall sheathing—a new compact crystalline limestone, with a lovely fossil formation, discovered under the tiers of whitbed at the Portland quarries. **1936** [see curf]. **1980** *Univ. Coll. London Bull.* Mar. 2/2 The thickest and most sought after unit in the local sequence is the Whitbed, noted for its homogeneity stemming from its lack of fossils or flint masses which may blemish other horizons above or below in the succession.

whitblow(e, obs. forms of whitlow.

whitbre(a)d: see white bread.

†whitch. *Obs.* or *dial.* Forms: 1 **hwicce**, 4 **whichche**, 4–5 **whicche**, **whucche**, 4–6 **whiche**, **wyche**, 5 **whyche**, **wheche**, **whoche**, **wucche**, 6 **whytch(e**, **whitche**, (9 *dial.* **wytch**). [OE. *hwicce* (also in *cornhwycce*), cognate with the synonymous *hwæcce*.] A chest, coffer, ark; = hutch *sb.* 1, 1 b; a coffin.

a **1100** *Aldhelm Gloss* xviii[b]. 11 (Napier 186/1) *Clustella*, hwicce. **13..** *Metr. Hom.* (Vernon MS.) in *Archiv Stud. neu. Spr.* LVII. 254/1 Whon þis corn to þis kniht was solde He dude hit in a whucche to holde. **13..** *E.E. Allit. P.* B. 362 Alle woned in þe whichche [*sc.* Noah's ark] þe wylde & þe tame. **1387–8** T. Usk *Test. Love* ii. ii. (Skeat) l. 29 Pannes mouled in a whicche [*v.r.* wyche]. **1415** *Somerset Med. Wills* (1901) 401 And nether wheche, ne leede to be layde in, bote a grete clothe to hely my foule caryin. *c* **1430** *Hymns Virgin* (1867) 11 A table..Vnder þat auter In a whucche is done. **1541** *Will of John Hoper of Keynsham* 19 Jan. (MS.), ij coffers & ij whytchys. **1596** *Unton Inv.* (1841) 2, j olde whitche, and one musterd mill. [**1856** Morton *Cycl. Agric.* II. 727 *Wytch*, (Herefords.), same as *hutch* [= body of a waggon].]

whitch, variant of witch, flat fish.

whitche, whitchen, obs. ff. witch, witchen.

whitchet, var. wichert.

white (hwaɪt), *sb.*[1] Forms: see white *a.* [Various absolute uses of white *a.* Cf. L. *album*, F. *blanc* blank *sb.*]

1. The translucent viscous fluid surrounding the yolk of an egg, which becomes white when coagulated; = albumen 1. Usually in full, ***the white of an egg*** (or, as a substance, ***white*** or ***the white of egg***), pl. ***whites of eggs***.

c **1000** *Sax. Leechd.* II. 342 Ðedo æᵹes hwit to. *c* **1000** Ælfric *Hom.* I. 40 On anum æᵹe..þæt hwite ne bið ᵹemenged to ðam ᵹeolcan. *a* **1300** *Fragm. Pop. Sci.* (Wright) 240 As the white goth aboute the ᵹolke. **14..** *Stockholm Med. MS.* i. 432 in *Anglia* XVIII. 306 With eyes qwytys do cleryn es clene. *c* **1420** *Liber Cocorum* (1862) 24 Take whyᵹte of eyren harde soþun. *a* **1425** tr. *Arderne's Treat. Fistula*, etc. 30 Putte þerto als miche of whites of eiren, wele y-bette and scomed. **1528** Paynell *Salerne's Regim.* (1540) 20 b, The yolke is temperately hotte; The whyte is colde and clammye. **1535** Coverdale *Job* vi. 6 What taist hath yᵉ whyte within the yoke an egg? **1605** Shaks. *Lear* iii. vii. 106 (Qo.) Ile fetch some flaxe and whites of egges to apply to his bleeding face. **1629** Z. Boyd *Last Battell* 701 Like a squissed egge, whose yolke is mingled with its white. **1774** Goldsm. *Nat. Hist.* (1862) II. i. vi. 462 A mucus..like the white of an egg. **1883**

Hardwich's Photogr. Chem. (ed. 9) 31 The white of egg, which is a very pure form of Albumen.

2. The white part (sclerotic coat) of the eyeball, surrounding the coloured iris. Usually in full, ***the white of the eye***, pl. ***the whites of the eyes***.

Often in ***to turn up the whites of one's eyes*** and similar phrases (usually, in affected devotion, but also in death, in astonishment, horror, etc.).

c **1400** *Lanfranc's Cirurg.* 19 A watir þat comeþ bitwene þe white of þe iȝen & þe appil. *c* **1425** *Voc.* in Wr.-Wülcker 634/5 *Hec albugo*, wyte of the hee. **1448–9** METHAM *Amoryus & Cl.* 1739 Amoryus vpward had turnyd the qwyght Off hys eyn:..qwan sche sey hym ded Her chekys sche gan tere. *c* **1480** HENRYSON *Fox, Wolf, & Cadger* 103 (Harl. MS.) The quhite he turnit vp of his ene tway. **1523** FITZHERB. *Husb.* §55 If he [*sc.* a sheep]..haue reed stryndes in the white of the eye, than he is sounde. **1594** NASHE *Terrors Nt.* Wks. (Grosart) III. 280 Enthronizing graue zeale and religion on the eleuated whites of their eyes. *a* **1600** *Grim the Collier of Croydon* III, He, poor Heart, no sooner heard my news, But turns me up his Whites, and falls flat down. **1601** HOLLAND *Pliny* XI. xxxvii. I. 334 The ball or apple in the middest [of the eye] is ordinarily of another colour than the white about it. **1657** HEYLIN *Ecclesia Vind.* 349 Lifting up both his hands, and whites to heaven. **1725** *Bradley's Fam. Dict.* s.v. *Signs of Sickness*, When a Sick Horse turns up the Whites of his Eyes above, you may conclude that he is in Pain. **1771** SMOLLETT *Humphry Cl.* 10 June, Mrs. Tabitha..threw up the whites of her eyes, as if in the act of ejaculation. **1796** WOLCOT (P. Pindar) *Sat.* Wks. 1812 III. 409 Flimsy logic to surprise And raise the whites of Country Members' eyes. **1858** O. W. HOLMES *Aut. Breakf.-t.* xi. 108 The Professor showed the whites of his eyes devoutly. **1889** KIPLING *Ball. East & West* 28 And when he could spy the white of her [*sc.* the mare's] eye, he made the pistol crack.

Phr. [Cf. BLACK *a.* 12.] **1796** *Grose's Dict. Vulgar T.* (ed. 3) s.v. *Black Eye*, He cannot say black is the white of my eye; he cannot point out a blot in my character. **182.** G. SMEATON *Doings in London* 85 As Mother Cole said.., 'no one could say black was the white of her Eye'.

3. The white or light-coloured part of some substance or structure, as flesh, wood, etc.

c **1430** *Two Cookery-bks.* 14 Take þe Whyte of the lekys. *c* **1475** *Pict. Voc.* in Wr.-Wülcker 793/11 *Hoc mulsum*, the wyte of botyr. **1552** HULOET s.v. *Oister*, The white vnder the fysh cleauynge to the shell. **1665** *Phil. Trans.* I. 118 White ..like the white of a Custard. *a* **1756** ELIZA HAYWOOD *New Present* (1771) 159 Mince..the white of a chicken. **1815** J. SMITH *Panorama Sci. & Art* I. 95 The wood next the bark of a tree, called the white, or alburnum. **1854** MISS BAKER *Northampt. Gloss.*, *White*, a name given by butchers to that piece of beef which joins the round: i.e. the flank.

†**4.** A white spot or mark. *Obs.*

1551 *Knaresb. Wills* (Surtees) I. 59 One oxe stirke with a whitte in his forehede. **1585** HIGINS *Junius' Nomencl.* 38/1 *Exortus*,..the white growing in the naile. **1623** COCKERAM III, *Selenite*, a stone wherein is a white, that decreaseth and encreaseth as the Moone groweth. **1687** *Lond. Gaz.* No. 2280 A bay Nag..a white in one of his Eyes.

5. *Archery.* **a.** The white target usually placed on the butt. *arch.* or *Hist.*

[**1456**, *a* **1533**: see 6.] **1577** HELLOWES *Gueuara's Chron.* 467 They behaued themselues no more nor no lesse with the Germaines, then an archer with a white at a Butt. **1583** GREENE *Mamillia* 16 b, When the string is broken, it is hard to hit the white. **1618** BOLTON *Florus* III. viii. (1636) 195 A Boy gets no morsell at his Mothers hands, but that of which she makes a white, and which himselfe must hit. **1654** GATAKER *Disc. Apol.* 39 An Archer,..when he hath hit the white or cloven the peg. **1714** E. WARD *Field-Spy* 13, I turn'd my Head to see the doughty Knight Stand ready drawn to hit the distant White. **1831** SCOTT *Cast. Dang.* viii, A good archer..who..seldom missed a handsbreadth of the white. **1843** LYTTON *Last Bar.* I. i, No marksman had hit the white.

b. In modern practice, a circular band of white on the target, or each of two such bands (***inner*** and ***outer white***); hence, a shot that hits this white.

1687 in *Gent. Mag.* (1832) CII. I. 600/2 The third circumference, being usually knowne..by the name of the inner white... The fifth circle, being white, and usually called..the outer-white. **1865** *Archer's Reg.* 25 Ladies' Prizes... Miss Betham (less 113 for blacks and whites), 558.

6. *fig.* (or in fig. context). Now *rare* or *Obs.*

1456 SIR G. HAYE *Gov. Princes* Wks. (S.T.S.) II. 149 He that tuichis nerest the quhite and best gais nere the merche. *a* **1533** LD. BERNERS *Gold. Bk. M. Aurel.* (1546) D ii, The life of the prince is but a whyte, for al other to shote at. **1580** LYLY *Euphues* (Arb.) 407 If the eye of man be the arrow, and beautie the white. **1596** SHAKS. *Tam. Shr.* v. ii. 186 'Twas I wonne the wager, though you hit the white. **1597** BRETON *Auspicante Iehoua* Wks. (Grosart) II. 11/1 Bee Thou..the note of my comfort, the white of my loue, and the light of my lyfe. **1656** COWLEY *Pindar. Odes, 2nd Olympique* x, Let Agrigentum be the But, And Theron be the White. **1698** NORRIS *Pract. Disc.* (1707) IV. 166 So the subject of the following Discourse may be the more distinct, and we may have a clearer White for our mark. **1862** B. TAYLOR *At Home & Abr.* Ser. II. 411 His [*sc.* Browning's] faculty of hitting the target of expression full in the white, by a single arrowy word. **1864** LOWELL *Fireside Trav.* 294 Byron hit the white, which he often shot very wide of.., when he called Rome 'my country'.

7. a. *Printing.* The blank space in certain letters or types; a space left blank between words or lines (= WHITE LINE 2).

1594 PLAT *Jewell-ho.* III. 42 If the whites of certaine letters bee made of one equall bignesse with the o. **1683** MOXON *Mech. Exerc., Printing* xxii. ¶4 In Marginal Notes..the White between Words is often..greater than between Line and Line. **1808** STOWE *Printers' Gram.* 163 To a solid page, two leads make the usual white after the head. **1885** LOCK *Workshop Rec.* IV. 213/1 (Electro-typing) It will be found that the 'whites' have been almost sufficiently raised.

b. *Drawing*, etc. *pl.* White or blank parts.

1892 *Photogr. Ann.* II. 421 If a plate is over-exposed the image will come up quickly, the whites will be muddy, and the blacks lacking in richness. **1894** *Daily News* 26 June 6/5 The Horses of Rhesus..an ambitious picture of large size painted by Mr. Harington Bird, A.R.C.A.,..the scheme of whites appears to be well managed.

8. White cloth or textile fabric: applied *spec.*, with or without defining word, to various particular kinds; often in *pl.*

1297 R. GLOUC. (Rolls) 11923 Cope & oþer cloþes, hii lete make of wit. **1466** *Paston Lett.* II. 266 For xxiiii. yerdes of brod wythtys for gowns. **1503** *Privy Purse Exp. Eliz. York* (1830) 104 For v yerdes of Streyt white. **1594** NORDEN *Spec. Brit., Essex* (Camden) 9 Coghsull, wher are made the best whites in Englande. **1621** *Reg. Mag. Sig. Scot.* 45/1 Exceptis mantelliis lie plaidis et lie Galloway quhyte. **1742** *De Foe's Tour Gt. Brit.* (ed. 3) III. 134 Cloth in Imitation of Gloucester Whites. **1754** POCOCKE *Trav.* (Camden) II. 135 They..make..cloths called Salisbury whites for the Turkey trade.

9. a. White clothing, apparel, or array: usually in phr. ***in white***.

[*c* **1000** *Sax. Leechd.* III. 198 Hwite oððe beorhte hine ȝescrydan wynsumnysse ȝetacnað.] *a* **1300** *Cursor M.* 18772 Bi-side þam stode tua men in quite. **1387** TREVISA *Higden* (Rolls) IV. 321 Whan Pilatus sente Iesus i-cloþed in white to Herodes. *c* **1425** *Cast. Persev.* in *Macro Plays* 76 þe iiij dowteris schul be clad in mentelys; Merci in wyth, Rythwysnesse in red [etc.]. *a* **1548** HALL *Chron., Hen. VIII* 228 On the Assencion day folowyng, the kyng ware whyte for mournyng. **1680** C. NESSE *Ch. Hist.* 272 Having decked her self with the White of Simplicity. **1768** GOLDSM. *Goodn. Man* IV, It's the worst luck in the world [to be married] in anything but white. **1815** *Ann. Reg., Chron.* 49/2 The pall was supported by six young females attired in white. **1859** TENNYSON *Elaine* 1152 She herself in white.

b. *pl.* White garments or vestments: chiefly in specific uses, *esp.* (*a*) surplices worn by clergymen, choristers, etc. (now chiefly *Hist.*); (*b*) white trousers or breeches; (*c*) white clothes worn for sport (esp. Cricket and Lawn Tennis).

1622 S. WARD *Life of Faith in Death* 124 If we throughly beleeued..this to bee the state of our..dead friends,.. could we..mourne for them in blacks, whiles they are in whites? **1633** CHAS. I in *Bibliotheca Regia* (1659) 122 That the Dean of our Chapel..come..thither to Prayers upon Sundaies..in his Whites. **1780** A. YOUNG *Tour Irel.* I. 283 The girls..in their striped linens and whites. **1818** LADY MORGAN *Autobiogr.* (1859) 184 His tight whites and tight silk stockings showed his colossal legs..to great advantage. **1828** JOLLY *Sunday Services* (1848) 220 [The newly baptized] appeared at church..in their whites. **1840** THACKERAY *Barber Cox* Sept., I felt myself suddenly jerked by the waistband of my whites. **1840** J. T. J. HEWLETT *P. Priggins* xiv, Having his immaculate whites spotted and splashed by the spirts of Stephen, who..pulled stroke. **1882** 'EDNA LYALL' *Donovan* vi, They say the [choir-]boys in their whites is very attractive. **1922** E. RAYMOND *Tell England* II. iv. 207 All honest boys, we know, fancy themselves in their whites. **1974** K. MILLETT *Flying* (1975) I. 101 Rich playing championship tennis..in his whites. **1978** G. MCDONALD *Fletch's Fortune* (1979) xiv. 96 Stop at the pro shop... We'll fix you up with a racket and balls... Have whites?

†**c.** A white badge. *Obs.*

1647 in *Clarendon's State Papers* (1773) II. App. p. xlii, Perceiving Lilburne's regiment..to appear..with Whites in their hats. **1651** *Lanc. Tracts Civil War* (Chetham Soc.) 307 The enemies word was 'Iesu', and their signal a White about their Arme.

d. *pl.* White articles of washing.

1962 *Which?* Aug. 231/2 The programme you choose for the washing you want to do ('whites', for example, or 'delicate fabrics' are possible settings on both machines) automatically determines washing and spin drying times. **1979** A. PRICE *Tomorrow's Ghost* xiii. 229 It used to be right dirty rain... Woman couldn't put her whites out..when it was raining.

10. a. †Silver money, 'silver' collectively, as distinguished from *red* or *yellow* = gold (*obs.*); also (with *pl.*) a silver coin (*slang*). Also (*sing.*) in general sense, money (*slang*).

c **1374** CHAUCER *Troylus* III. 1384 They shul for-go þe white and eke þe rede. **1390** [see RED *sb.* 3 a]. *c* **1676** *Roxb. Ball.* (1889) VI. 15 A sawcy fellow! Come to me without his white and yellow. **1823** 'JON BEE' *Dict. Turf* 194 *Whites*, in the language of smashers, 'small whites' are shillings, 'large whites' half-crowns. **1903** A. M. BINSTEAD *Pitcher in Paradise* viii. 204 Again and again the needy one implored his obdurate chum to shake out at least a deuce of whites. **1960** [see CABBAGE *sb.*[1] 1 e].

b. = BLANK *sb.* 1. *Hist.*

1716 M. DAVIES *Athen. Brit.* III. 79 'Twas made Felony ..to pay or receive a certain base Coyn, call'd Blank or Whites. **1877** STEVENSON *New Arab. Nts.*, *Lodging for Nt.*, Two of the small coins that went by the name of whites.

11. = WHITE WINE.

c **1386** [see RED *sb.* 3 b]. **1610** T. COCKS *Diary* (1901) 95 A quarte of white, to make my skurvye-grasse drincke. *c* **1640** *Capt. Underwit* IV. i. in Bullen *O. Pl.* II. 375 The Stillyards Reanish wine and Divells white. **1720** E. WARD *Delights of Bottle* 37 Where ev'ry one that's low in Spirits, May be reliev'd by Whites or Clarets. **1842** [see RED *sb.* 3 b]. **1961** [see RED *sb.*[1] 5 b]. **1972** 'W. HAGGARD' *Protectors* ix. 111 He ..had drunk most of a bottle of wine. He had discovered the local whites with pleasure. **1978** T. L. SMITH *Money War* III. 182 He would have the filet of sole amandine... He couldn't quite make up his mind which of the wonderful whites to choose to go with it.

12. An animal of a species, breed, or variety distinguished by white colour; a white horse (*obs.*), butterfly, pigeon, pig, dog, cat, etc. (Chiefly as a fanciers' abbreviation.)

1530 PALSGR. 288/2 White, a horse of white colour, *cheual blanc, liart.* **1834** *Proc. Berw. Nat. Club* I. No. 2. 51 This fish I consider to be the *S. albus* of Fleming, the Herling..of the Scotch side of the Solway Frith,..the *White* or *Phinnock* of Pennant. **1857** GOSSE *Omphalos* xi. 307 We never find the egg of the Peacock Butterfly adhering to the leaf of a cabbage, nor that of the Garden White to the leaf of a nettle. **1879** L. WRIGHT *Pigeon Keeper* 96 Whites are..usually bred together. **1898** *Daily News* 5 Dec. 8/5 Pigs.., middle whites and large whites. **1907** *R. Leighton's New Bk. Dog* 429 The litter will consist of some whole-coloured blacks, and some whole-coloured whites.

13. A white man; a person of a race distinguished by light complexion: see WHITE *a.* 4.

poor whites = 'poor white folks' (see WHITE *a.* 4); also *sing.* and *fig.*

1671 CHARANTE *Let. conc. Customs Tafiletta* 10 After him raigned his Brother Muley Elwaly, who was a White, his Mother a Spanish Moor. **1726** *Adv. Capt. R. Boyle* (1744) 155 There may be about 20000 Whites (or I should say Portuguese, for they are none of the whitest,) and about treble that Number of Slaves. **1819** W. FAUX *Jrnl.* 28 July in *Memorable Days in Amer.* (1823) 118 The poor white, or white poor, in Maryland,..scarcely ever work. **1826** J. F. COOPER *Last of Mohicans* xiv, Red-skins and whites. **1833** in *Maryland Hist. Mag.* (1918) XIII. 338 The poor whites at the South are not as well off in their physical condition as the slaves, and hardly as respectable. **1879** SIR G. CAMPBELL *White & Black* 163 A large number of very inferior whites, known as 'mean whites', 'white trash', and so on. **1886** J. A. FROUDE *Oceana* xviii. 326 When he dies, the Maori and the poor whites in New Zealand will have lost their truest friend. **1888** CHURCHWARD *Blackbirding* 7 Having been longer in Samoa than any live white in the place. **1896** R. WALLACE *Farming Industries of Cape Colony* 406 The so-called 'poor whites' are chiefly the descendants of French protestant refugees, and, in some districts, of early Dutch settlers. **1934** A. N. J. DEN HOLLANDER in W. T. Couch *Culture in South* xx. 414 In discriminating southern speech, it was not used to include all white persons who were poor. .. The 'poor-whites' were those who were both poor and conspicuously lacking in the common social virtues and especially fell short of the standard in certain economic qualities. **1958** L. VAN DER POST *Lost World Kalahari* iii. 56 All who worked for my grandfather no matter whether Griqua, Hottentot,..Cape-coloured or poor white, were ultimately held in equal affection. **1974** 'J. LE CARRÉ' *Tinker Tailor* i. 9 Jim Prideaux was a poor white of the teaching community.

14. †(*a*) A white square on a chessboard. (*b*) with *the*: Either of the white balls in billiards; also, the white ball in pool.

c **1440** *Gesta Rom.* xxi, þe quene, that goth fro blak to blak, or fro white to white. **1562** ROWBOTHUM *Cheasts* A v b, Because of his [*sc.* the knight's] marching forth, whiche is made from three into three places, to witte, from whyte into blacke, and from black into whyte. **1614** SAUL *Chesse-play* To Rdr., The Bishop blacke in blacke must march..For in the white he may not come. **1750** 'PHILIDOR' *Chess Anal.* (1773) 7 *note*, When your Bishop runs upon White, you must strive to put your Pawn always upon Black. **1856** 'CRAWLEY' *Billiards* (1858) 29, I attempted a difficult cannon off the white. **1873** BENNETT & 'CAVENDISH' *Billiards* 213 The white will travel slowly on to the spot-white. **1981** P. QUINN *Tackle Pool* ii. 25 If the white is at point A it must be played into the black almost full ball.

15. a. (*a*) Applied variously to any white body or substance: see quots.

1540 PALSGR. *Acolastus* II. iii. L iij b, That..thou mayste haue a place worthy for the in our whyte... (Lyke as the pretours of Rome dyd set those mens names in a table hyghest, whose causes shulde first be pleaded,..whiche table was called *Album prætoris* .i. the whyte or table of the pretour). **1578** LYTE *Dodoens* III. lxxi. 413 Hauing at their extremities..certayne whites fashioned like gripes, or clawes. **1608** TOPSELL *Serpents* 237 Like as the windes driue whites from top of thistle Cardus. **1896** KIPLING *Seven Seas, Rhyme Three Sealers*, They groped through the whirling white [*i.e.* mist].

†(*b*) ***to spit white***: to eject frothy-white sputum from a dry mouth. (Cf. *to spit sixpences* s.v. SIXPENCE 2 d.) *Obs.*

[**1594** LYLY *Mother Bombie* III. ii, *Ri.*...We dyd but a little parboile our liuers, they haue sod theyrs in sacke these fortie yeeres. *Hal.* That makes them spit white broth as they doo.] **1597** SHAKS. *2 Hen. IV*, I. ii. 237 If it bee a hot day, if I brandish any thing but my Bottle, would I might neuer spit white againe. **1622** MASSINGER & DEKKER *Virg. Mart.* III. iii, Had I bin a Pagan stil, I could not haue spit white for want of drinke.

b. As a specific name (chiefly in *pl.*) for various manufactured articles and products of a white colour; e.g. pins, sugar, flour, etc.

?**1690** *Pinmakers' Case in oppos. to Killigrew's Bill* (Broadside, Brit. Mus.), Double long whites *alias* Calkins. **1826** *Haberdasher's Guide* 19 Short Whites, a smaller pin. **1844** H. STEPHENS *Bk. Farm* II. 14 The same rule of storing a quantity..is followed in regard to them as with the whites [*sc.* turnips]. **1883** N. D. DAVIS *Cavaliers & Roundh. in Barbados* 34 Not only were muscovadoes made, but the manufacture of 'whites' was accomplished. **1896** *Daily News* 8 Dec. 11/5 At a meeting of the London Flour Millers' Association,..the following prices were fixed:—Town households, 28s.; whites, 31s.

c. A white diamond.

1878 [see OFF COLOUR, OFF-COLOUR *phr.* and *a.* 2]. **1895** [see BYWATER]. **1928** [see BYE *sb.* 3]. **1972** V. CANNING *Rainbird Pattern* xi. 227 The diamonds were genuine,..blue whites, fine whites and whites. **1973** *Times* 25 Aug. 17/3 The (more or less) accepted English classes run thus in descending order: (1) finest fine white or river *alias* blue-white; (2) fine white; (3) commercial white.

d. A white ostrich-feather.

1881 A. DOUGLASS *Ostrich Farming S. Afr.* xiii. 81 The cocks' quill feathers..he will..sort first... Prime whites, first whites, second whites, tipped whites. **1890** A. MARTIN *Home Life on Ostrich Farm* vi. 103 A large and magnificent bunch of *wing*-feathers, the finest and longest of 'prime whites'.

e. *slang*. Morphine. Cf. *white stuff* s.v. WHITE *a*. 11 e.

1914 JACKSON & HELLYER *Vocab. Criminal Slang* 87 *White, noun*, current amongst morphine habitues. Morphine. Example: 'How many times a day are you shooting the white?' **1977** N. ADAM *Triplehip Cracksman* iii. 32 By 1965 they were growing poppies for half the world's white.

f. White bread; a white loaf. *colloq.*

1960 WENTWORTH & FLEXNER *Dict. Amer. Slang* 576/1 *White*, white bread. **1974** 'A. GILBERT' *Nice Little Killing* iv. 55 Last of all came the baker... Leave a small white to be on the safe side. **1977** D. E. WESTLAKE *Nobody's Perfect* 45 A luncheon-loaf sandwich on white with mayo in his left hand. **1978** R. WESTALL *Devil on Road* vi. 35, I got thick-sliced white and corned-beef.

g. An amphetamine tablet. *slang.*

1967 [see PILL *sb.*^{2} 1 d]. **1969** *Observer* 21 Dec. 1/1 The street pusher with his 'wanna score some whites (Benzedrine)? Dollar a roll.' **1972** H. C. RAE *Shooting Gallery* I. 19 He had anticipated a rash of arrests for possession of brown drugs and amphetamines—but not this, not a straight leap into the lethal whites.

16. *pl.* A popular name for leucorrhœa or 'white flux' (WHITE *a*. 11 e).

1572 J. JONES *Bathes Buckstones* 4 b, Such as haue their whites too abundant. **1579** LANGHAM *Gard. Health* 147 Barren women, and such as are troubled with the whites. **1683** DIGBY *Chym. Secr.* II. 264 It cures..the Whites in Women. **1758** J. S. tr. *Le Dran's Observ. Surg.* (1771) Dict. Cc 2, *Leucorhæ*, the Fluor Albus, or Whites in Women. **1822–9** GOOD *Study Med.* V. 68 Among novices there is some difficulty in distinguishing the discharge of whites from that of blenorrhœa.

17. a. White colour or hue; white coloration or appearance; whiteness. Sometimes semi-concr.

c **1000** in *Anglia* I. 285 Hwit asolað, *nitor squalescit*. *a* **1225** [see BLACK *sb.* 1]. *c* **1315** SHOREHAM VII. 544 Swyþe fayr þyng hys þat wyte, And þer by-syde blak..; þe wyte hyt þe uayrer makeþ. **1390** GOWER *Conf.* II. 46 In kertles and in Copes riche Thei weren clothed, alle liche, Departed evene of whyt and blew. *c* **1400** *Destr. Troy* 10970 All þaire colouris..were of cleane white. *a* **1461** *Pol. Poems* (Rolls) II. 241 Wyghte is wyghte, ȝyf yt [ys] leyd to blake. *a* **1548** HALL *Chron., Hen. VI* 138 So depe a Snowe, that all the ground was covered with white. **1592** SHAKS. *Ven. & Ad.* 398 Teaching the sheets a whiter hew then white. **1592** G. HARVEY *Four Lett.* Sonn. xi. Wks. (Grosart) I. 244 That whitest white on Earth. **1704** NEWTON *Optics* (1721) 133 Before I told him what the Colours were... I asked him, Which of the two Whites were the best? **1734** *Poor Robin* Feb. A 6, It fills the Ditch with either black or white [= rain or snow]. **1777** ROBERTSON *Hist. Amer.* IV. I. 301 Their skin is covered with a fine hairy down of a chalky white. **1821** CRAIG *Lect. Drawing*, etc. iii. 175 We must take black and white into our list, as colours with the painter though not with the optician. **1847** W. C. L. MARTIN *Ox* 61/1 A broad line of white along the back. **1859** TENNYSON *Vivien* 141 The curl'd white of the coming wave. **1868** W. B. MARRIOTT *Vest. Christ.* Introd. p. xvii, In the ancient world..white was regarded as the colour.. appropriate to things divine.

b. Whiteness or fairness of complexion.

In first quot. perh. confused with WLITE.

a **1225** *Ancr. R.* 56 Nu cumeð forð a feble mon,..& wule iseon ȝunge ancren, & loken..hu hire hwite like him, þet naueð nout hire leor uorbernd iðe sunne. *Ibid.* 98 'Þi stefne is me swete, & ti hwite schene.'.. 'vox tua dulcis, & facies tua decora.' **14..** *Voc.* in Wr.-Wülcker 626 White of þe face, *albucies*. **1578** H. WOTTON *Courtlie Controv.* 225 The princesse blushing with roseall shame whyche beautified hir naturall white. **1697** DRYDEN *Æneis* XII. 102 Varying her Cheeks by Turns, with white and red. **1816** BYRON *Parisina* x, The smoothest white That e'er did softest kiss invite.

c. *fig.* (or in fig. context) as a symbol of purity, goodness, truth, joy, etc.

[*c* **1394** *P. Pl. Crede* 694 Whijt..bytokneþ clennes in soule.] **1637** RUTHERFORD *Let. to Ld. Craighall* 10 Aug., Some few years will bring us all out in our black's and white's before our Judge. **1649** T. FORD *Lusus Fort.* 46 Our life is chequerd with the whites of pleasure and delight, and the blacks of sorrow and pain. **1680** C. NESSE *Ch. Hist.* 110 God Chequered his Providences..with the Black of Misery, and with the White of Mercy. **1818** KEATS *Endym.* III. 402, I loved her to the very white of truth.

d. Proverbial phr. ***to call white black, to turn white into black*** (and vice versa). Cf. WHITE *a*. 1 d.

1534 MORE *Comf. agst. Trib.* I. x. (1553) B viij b, More coumfort may he haue in his heart, that where whyte is called blacke..abydeth by the trueth. **1672** W. WALKER *Parœm.* 33 They turn black into white, and white into black. *Nigra in candida vertunt*, Juv. **1829** SOUTHEY *All for Love* IX. xxix, To prove..That right is wrong, and wrong is right, And white is black, and black is white.

e. Phr. ***white-on-white***, used *attrib.* to designate articles made of white cloth with a white woven-in design; also *fig.*

1955 W. GADDIS *Recognitions* II. vii. 572 A bow tie of propeller proportions stood out over extra-length collar bills on a white-on-white shirt. **1958** J. BLISH *Case of Conscience* xi. 113 'Why don't you give *me* a chance?' Michelis said raggedly. Then he turned white-on-white. **1976** A. GOLDMAN in D. Villiers *Next Year in Jerusalem* 221 Perhaps it was radio..that forced American humor in the thirties to enter a phase of white-on-white neutrality. **1978** *Detroit Free Press* 5 Mar. D9/2 The Smithsonian Institution has several white-on-white quilts done in this manner.

18. a. A white pigment; often with defining word denoting a particular kind, as *Chinese, flake, Paris, pearl, Spanish, Venice white*, etc.: see these words.

1546 [see SPANISH *a*. 7]. **1650** NORGATE *Miniatura* (1919) 93 Whyte lead ground with Nutt oyle maketh a perfect Whyte. **1731** *Art of Drawing & Paint.* 20 These Colours.. to shade the Whites. **1847** SMEATON *Builder's Man.* 139 The first white that was discovered..was extracted from the calx of lead. **1859** GULLICK & TIMBS *Painting* 293 The terrene whites, from their alkaline nature, are injurious to many colours in water.

b. *Her.* Used by some modern writers for a white tincture reckoned among the furs, as distinct from *argent*.

1777 PORNY *Her.* (ed. 3) 25 White, the natural colour of a little beast called Ermine,..is only to be termed so, when it is used for the doubling of Mantles.

19. a. A designation for a member of any one of certain political parties (from the colour of the badge worn, cf. WHITE *a*. 6 b); *esp.* a member of one of the two factions into which the Guelphs split (see BLACK *sb*. 8 a), or a Spanish Legitimist. Now usu., a member of any of various counter-revolutionary or strongly conservative parties.

1680 C. NESSE *Ch. Hist.* 428 The Guelphs.. and the Gibellines,..the Black and the White (as those Two Factions were called). **1802**, etc. [see BLACK *sb.* 8]. **1849** J. A. CARLYLE tr. *Dante's Inf.* 64 *note*, Florence was divided by two factions, the *Neri* and *Bianchi*, or Blacks and Whites. **1889** *Daily News* 4 Oct. 5/1 A true white—which is..of an infinitely more intense shade of Conservatism than the truest blue. **1892** *Nation* (N.Y.) 8 Sept. 177/1 The party of the Whites of Spain had been thrown into disorder. **1918** *Times* 9 Apr., Germany promised..to supply the Whites [of Finland] with arms and food. **1942** 'A. BRIDGE' *Frontier Passage* i. 6 There were a few Whites in Madrid..and..they had a pretty thin time of it. **1954** B. & R. NORTH tr. *M. Duverger's Pol. Parties* II. i. 216 In small French villages public opinion spontaneously distinguishes between 'Whites' and 'Reds', 'clerical' and 'anti-clerical'. **1965** M. MICHAEL tr. *Myrdal's Rep. from Chinese Village* (1967) IV. 186, I joined the Young Pioneers. There we had classes about which districts were red and liberated and which were held by the Whites or the Japanese.

b. *spec.* An opponent of the Bolsheviks during the Russian Civil War (1918–21).

1921 F. MCCULLAGH *Prisoner of Reds* iii. 26 A few miles off, on the west, was a large force of whites, which intended to advance on Krasnoyarsk that night. **1924** E. G. JELLICOE *Playing the Game* xiii. 224 Expeditionary Armies of Britain and the United States, invaded Northern Russia..in order to link up with Russian Whites against Russian Bolsheviks. **1944** M. LASKI *Love on Supertax* ix. 86 She *is* Russian... Her parents were Whites who fled to Paris just before the October Revolution. **1950** E. H. CARR *Bolshevik Revolution* I. 325 In all these regions the ultimate effect of the civil war waged by the 'whites' with foreign backing had been to consolidate the prestige..of the Russian Soviet Government. **1964** L. DEIGHTON *Funeral in Berlin* 318 Chekist operators... Originally these were an anti-sabotage, anti-revolutionary force..during the civil war..empowered to..execute Whites, or Reds who were getting a little bleached. **1976** [see RED *sb.*^{1} 6 b].

20. Short for *white squadron*: see WHITE *a*. 11 e.

[**16..** in Macgeorge *Flags* (1881) 69 The Lord Harvey was Rear Admirall..bearing..a white flag in the maine topp, and was Admirall of ye squadron of white colours.]

1704 J. CHAMBERLAYNE *St. Gt. Brit.* (ed. 21) 572 Admirals of the Fleet..White, Sir Cloudesly Shovel, Admiral. James Wishart, Esq. Vice-Admiral. **1751** *Crt. & City Reg.* 168 A List of the Admirals of the Royal Navy of Great-Britain... Admirals of the White. *c* **1815** JANE AUSTEN *Persuasion* iii, He is rear admiral of the white.

21. The player who holds the white pieces at chess or any similar game.

1750 'PHILIDOR' *Chess Analysed* (1773) 59, I have no need to go further in this Game, since it is evident that the White must win. **1808** *Hoyle's Game of Chess* 32 White has the best of the game. **1867** *Bohn's Hand-bk. Games* 460 (*Draughts*) White to move and win.

22. Phrases. ***in black and white***: see BLACK *a*. 15 b, c. ***in the white***: said of cloth in an undyed state; hence of manufactured articles generally in an unfinished state. (Cf. quot. 1846 in WHITE *a*. 2.) †***white and black***, name of some game.

1555 *Act 2 & 3 Phil. & Mary* c. 9 Bowlyng Tenyse Dysyng White & Blacke Making & Marryng, & other unlaufull Games. **1810** *Risdon's Surv. Devon* p. xxv, The articles..are merely manufactured here, and sent in the white to London, where they are dyed. **1876** F. S. WILLIAMS *Midl. Railw.* 636 Furniture, made in London, but unfinished,—'in the white' it is called. **1957** *N.Z. Timber Jrnl.* Aug. 59/2 *In the white*, applied to finished furniture ready for polishing or other treatment. **1965** *Wireless World* July 9 (Advt.), This range includes..ready-assembled cabinets in the white for finish to own requirements. **1968** J. ARNOLD *Shell Bk. Country Crafts* 130 Factory-made chairs are often dispatched for later finishing, 'in the white' they call it. **1971** *Country Life* 10 June 1416/2 James Giles ..bought consignments of Worcester porcelain in the white for decorating to commission. **1981** *Sci. Amer.* Oct. 134/3 Violinmakers often say that a violin sounds better in the white than it does after it is varnished.

23. *Comb.* **white-exceeding** *a.* (*poet.*), exceeding or surpassing white, 'whiter than white'; **white(s)-only** *a.*, reserved for white people.

a **1618** SYLVESTER *Ode to Astræa* Wks. (Grosart) II. 50/2 The white-exceeding skin Of thy neck and dimpled chin. **1968** *Listener* 18 July 86/3 In 1958, the Court of Appeal supported the Musicians' Union in their boycott of a whites-only dance-hall in dear old Wolverhampton. **1971** *Sunday Times* (Johannesburg) 28 Mar. 1/3 It was a Whites-only compartment. **1971** *Guardian* 29 Sept. 19/2 In Salisbury [Rhodesia], there are perhaps half a dozen 'Whites Only' signs—mainly on public lavatories. **1980** *English World-Wide* I. 1. 55 In the 1950's Nassau's whites-only schools, cinemas, and restaurants were desegregated.

White (hwaɪt), *sb.*^{2} The name of Gilbert *White* (1720–93), English naturalist, used in the possessive, in **White's thrush**, to designate *Zoothera dauma*, a yellowish-brown and white thrush with black markings native to Asia, eastern Europe, and Australia, and orig. named *T. whitei* in his honour by T. Eyton (1836).

1836 T. EYTON *Hist. Rarer Brit. Birds* 93 The general colour of White's Thrush, on the upper surface, is ochraceous yellow. **1893** *Ibis* 371 (*heading*) On the occurrence of White's thrush in European Russia. **1954** D. A. BANNERMAN *Birds Brit. Isles* III. 165 In its plumage White's thrush is characterized by the very prominent black crescentic markings.

white (hwaɪt), *a*. Forms: 1–3 **hwit**, (1 **huit**, 3 **ȝwit, ȝwijȝt**), 3– 4 **wit, wyt**, 3–6 (7–9 *dial.*) **whit**, (4 **whijt, whiȝt(e, huyt, with, wythe, wyht, quiht, quitte**), 4–5 **wyte, quyt(e, quite, (wyth)**, 4–6 **qwyt(e**, *Sc.* **quhit**, 4, 5–7 *Sc.* **quhite**, 4–6, 7 *Sc.* **whyt, whyte**, 4–8 *Sc.* **quhyt**, (5 **hwyte, whiyt, whyȝte, why(g)th(e, wyghte, wytht, wytte, qwhyt(t)e, qwhite, qwhyet, qwyght**, *Sc.* **qwhit**), 5–6 **whitt(e, (whight, whyght(e**, *Sc.* **quhytt**), 5–7 *Sc.* **quhyte**, 6 **whytt(e, (whith, whyth, whiet, wyet, wyȝht, wight, whait, weit, weyte**, *Sc.* **vhyt, quhet**), 6–7 **wheat**, 3– **white**. Comp. **whiter** ('hwaɪtə(r)), sup. **whitest** ('hwaɪtɪst); also, with shortened vowel, 3 **hwittere, -ore, -ure**, 4–5 **quitter**, 4–6 **whitter**, (4 **queþer**, 5 **qwhittar**); 5 **whyttest**. [OE. *hwít* = OFris., OS. *hwît*, OHG. (*h*)*wîz* (MHG. *wîz*, G. *weiss*), ON. *hvítr* (Sw. *vit*, Da. *hvid*), Goth. *hweits*:—OTeut. **χwītaz*.

The shortened form *whit* (now dial.) was presumably generalized from the comp. *whitter* or from compounds like *whitbred, whitporn*, where shortening is normal.

The grade *χwit-* is represented by OFris. *hwitt*, (M)Du., (M)LG. *wit* (*-tt-*):—**χwittaz*, prob.:—Indo-eur. **kwidnos*, **kwitnos*, the root of which is found also in Skr. **çvid* (perf. *çiçvinde*) to be white, Lith. *szvidùs* bright, Lett. *svīst* to dawn, and Skr. **çvit* to be bright or white, *çvitrá-* whitish, white, Zend *spaeta* white, Lith. *szvintù* to be bright, OSl. *světŭ* light, *svitati* to dawn.]

1. Of the colour of snow or milk; having that colour produced by reflection, transmission, or emission of all kinds of light in the proportion in which they exist in the complete visible spectrum, without sensible absorption, being thus fully luminous and devoid of any distinctive hue.

c **950** *Lindisf. Gosp.* John xx. 12 Tuoeᵹe engles in huitum ᵹeᵹerelum. *c* **1000** *Ags. Gosp.* Matt. v. 36 Þu ne miht ænne locc ᵹedon hwitne oððe blacne. *c* **1200** *Trin. Coll. Hom.* 57 Sume bereð clene cloð to watere to blechen him, þat hit beo wit. *Ibid.* 163 Hire chemise is smal and hwit. *c* **1250** *Gen. & Ex.* 2810 In hise bosum he dede his hond, Quit and al unfer he it fond. **1297** R. GLOUC. (Rolls) 2786 Tueye grete dragons..þe on was red þe oþer wyt. *a* **1300** *Cursor M.* 17288 + 216 Two aungels..Cled in white clothez. *c* **1300** *Havelok* 1144 An hold with couel. **13..** *E.E. Allit. P.* A. 220 Bornyste quyte was hyr uesture. **1340–70** *Alex. & Dind.* 719 A swan swiþe whit. *c* **1380** WYCLIF *Wks.* (1880) 357 Þe oost sacrid, whijt & round. **1423** JAS. I *Kingis Q.* xlvi, Hir goldin haire and rich atyre..couchit were with perllis quhite. **1471** CAXTON *Recuyell* (Sommer) 701 Myn eyen [are] dimmed with ouermoche lokyng on the whit paper. **1514** *Rec. St. Mary at Hill* (1904) 20 Oon hole sute of vestymenttes, Whight or Blake. **1541** *Test. Ebor.* (Surtees) VI. 135 A gowne..the one side blake and the other side whitt. **1556** J. HEYWOOD *Spider & F.* lx. 5 With wheat tuskes fo[r]mde like a bore. *a* **1586** MONTGOMERIE *Misc. Poems* XXV. 1 The tender snow, of granis soft & quhyt [*rime* delyte]. **1590** SPENSER *F.Q.* II. iii. 26 She..was yclad..All in a silken Camus lylly whight. *a* **1650** NORGATE *Miniatura* (1919) 52 Insteed of abortive parchment, by some called Gilding Vellum, make use of your pure white velim. **1733** BUDGELL *Bee* II. 924 It proving a Maiden Assizes, the Sheriffs, according to Custom, presented the Judges with white Gloves. **1806** SCOTT *Palmer* i, The glen is white with the drifted snow. **1833** TENNYSON *Miller's Dau.* 130 The lanes..were white with may. **1860** TYNDALL *Glac.* II. i. 227 White light..is made up of an infinite number of coloured rays. **1912** C. N. & A. M. WILLIAMSON *Guests of Hercules* xvii, A round white moon that flooded the night with silver.

b. Of the colour of the hair or beard in old age; also *transf.* of the person, white-haired, hoary.

c **1290** *S. Eng. Leg.* 265/145 Hire her was hor and swiþe ȝwijȝt, as þei it were wolle. **1390** GOWER *Conf.* I. 111 Here berdes weren hore and whyte. *c* **1440** *Partonope* 155 A knyghte, þe wyche hyte Nestor, Wyche for age was whyte and hore. **1448–9** METHAM *Amoryus & Cl.* 1027 The qwyght herys Off sapyens. **1596** SHAKS. *1 Hen. IV*, II. iv. 514 That hee is olde..his white hayres doe witnesse it. **1684** BUNYAN *Pilgr.* II. Introd., Old Honest,..With his white hairs treading the Pilgrim's ground. **1724** RAMSAY *Vision* v, His quhyt heid. **1887** F. M. CRAWFORD *Saracinesca* iii, His white hair and beard bristled about his dark face.

c. In comparisons usually hyperbolical.

esp. ***as white as*** (or ***whiter than***) ***snow, milk*** (cf. SNOW-WHITE, MILK-WHITE); ***as white as lily flower, glass, a swan*** (cf. SWAN-WHITE), ***whales bone, flour, a neap, wool, curds***, and (in sense 5) ***a cloth, sheet, ghost***.

c **1000** *Ags. Gosp.* Matt. xvii. 2 Hys reaf wæron swa hwite swa snaw. *c* **1200** *Vices & Virtues* 83 Ðanne wurð ic iclansed of alle mine sennes, and hwittere ðane ani snaw. *c* **1290** *S. Eng. Leg.* 85/80 A coluere..so ȝwijt so milk. *a* **1300** *Cursor M.* 10380 Ten lambes, quitte als milk. *a* **1300** *K. Horn* 15 (Camb.), He was whit so þe flur [*Harl.* So whit so eny lylye flour]. *a* **1330** *Syr Degarre* 15 The kynge had..A doughter as whight as whales bone. *c* **1330** R. BRUNNE *Chron. Wace* (Rolls) 2081 Scheo hadde a mayden childe: Sabren hit highte, as whit as glas. **13..** *Seuyn Sages* (W.) 78 Faire of chere and white as swan. **1375** BARBOUR *Bruce* VIII. 232 Hawbrekis, that war quhit as flour. *c* **1480** HENRYSON *Fox, Wolf & Husb.* 165 Quhyte as ane Neip, and round als as ane schell. **1508** DUNBAR *Gold. Targe* 51 A saill, als quhite as blossum vpon spray. **1533** Gau *Richt Vay* 63 Giff thay be reid as purpur neuertheles yai sal be quhit as wow. **1590** Spenser *F.Q.* I. i. 4 Vpon a lowly Asse more white then snow, Yet she much whiter. *a* **1732** Gay *Songs, New Song of New Similes* xiii, As smooth as glass, as white as curds. **1885** 'Mrs. Alexander' *At Bay* iv, I am as white as driven snow compared to some blackguards.

d. In allusive or proverbial phr., chiefly in collocation with *black*: cf. WHITE *sb.* 17 d.

1377 Langl. *P. Pl.* B. x. 436 And wherby wote men whiche is whyte if alle þinge blake were? *c* **1403** Lydg. *Temple of Glas* 1250 White is whitter, if it be set bi blak. **1546** J. Heywood *Prov.* (1867) 56 Were not you as good than to say, the crow is whight. **1581**, **1604** [see Blackamoor 1]. **1662** Stillingfl. *Orig. Sacræ* I. v. §5, I think they have striven if not to make an Ethiopian white, yet an Ægyptian to speak truth concerning his own Country.

e. ***whiter than white***: extremely white; freq. *fig.*

In mod. use popularized as an advertising slogan for Persil soap-powder.

[**1592**: see WHITE *sb.* 17 a.] *a* **1924** *N.E.D.* s.v. *White* sb. 23, Exceeding or surpassing white, 'whiter than white'. **1949** D. Smith *I capture Castle* vii. 95 The strangeness of her face: that look she has of belonging to a whiter-than-white race. **1962** *Daily Tel.* 28 June 1/3 He is said to have said that the report made out the BBC to be 'whiter than white'. **1974** 'A. Garve' *File on Lester* vii. 31 Where their leaders are concerned, the masses are puritan—they expect standards of personal behaviour whiter than white. **1979** K. Bonfiglioli *After you with Pistol* xxii. 180 My knuckles were now Whiter-Than-White.

f. *Sci.* and *techn.* Applied to (non-optical) radiation, esp. sound and X-rays, having approximately equal intensities at all the frequencies of its range; esp. ***white noise*** (also *fig.*).

This use arises by analogy with the spectral composition of white light.

1922 *Nature* 1 Apr. 414/2 Just as the spectrum of a hot body normally consists of a continuous spectrum of white light, together with certain spectrum lines the wave-lengths of which are characteristic of the radiating material, so an element emitting X-rays not only gives out 'white' radiation, but superposes its characteristic lines on the general spectrum. **1943** *Jrnl. Aeronaut. Sci.* X. 129/1 Inside the plane it is different; there all frequencies added together at once are heard, producing a noise which is to sound what white light is to light... That white noise is annoying needs little argument. **1948** *Bell Syst. Technical Jrnl.* XXVII. 642 If the noise is itself white.. the result reduces to the formula proved previously. **1959** *Lancet* 12 Sept. 342/2 'White-sound' generators, which blind out extraneous noises, are unsatisfactory [for use in perceptual isolation experiments]. **1976** *Jrnl. R. Soc. Arts* CXXIV. 588/2 The proportion of power converted into the more penetrating 'bremsstrahlung'—or 'white' radiation—is approximately proportional to the atomic number of the target material. **1977** P. B. & J. S. Medawar *Life Science* i. 14 When the noise signals are so subdued, random and heterogeneous that their pretensions to conveying information are negligible, we may speak of 'white noise', e.g. the sound—as of innumerable mice eating Rice Crispies—that sometimes accompanies long-distance telephone calls. **1980** P. Way *Icarus* ix. 57 Maybe they *could* listen in, even through the white noise of the running water. **1984** *Mail on Sunday* (Colour Suppl.) 2 Dec. 6/2 (Advt.), At standard or even very low listening levels, you will never be harassed by hum or white noise.

2. In looser or wider senses. **a.** Of a light or pale colour: applied to things of various indefinite hues approaching white, esp. dull or pale shades of yellow. (See also following senses, and WHITE BREAD, WINE, etc.)

c **950** *Lindisf. Gosp.* John iv. 35 *Uidete regiones quia albæ sunt.. ad messem*, ȝeseað ða lond forðon huito sint ȝee.. to hrippe. *c* **1300** *Havelok* 1729 Win hwit and red, ful god plente. *a* **1400–50** *Bk. Curtasye* 701 in *Babees Bk.*, A qwyte cuppe of tre. *c* **1430** *Two Cookery-bks.* 29 Hwyte Hony or Sugre. **1523–34** Fitzherb. *Husb.* §13 Sprot-barley hath a flat eare.. and the cornes be very great and white. **1626** Bacon *Sylva* §874 Water of the Sea.. looketh Blacker when it is moued, and Whiter when it resteth. **1664** Evelyn *Sylva* xix. 42 Such [osiers] as are for White-work (as they call it). *a* **1700** —— *Diary* 22 Oct. 1685, The canal and fish ponds, the one fed with a white, the other with a black running water. **1769** Falconer *Dict. Marine* (1780), *Cordage blanc*, white, or untarred cordage. **1846** Dodd *Brit. Manuf.* VI. 196 When a rope is to be used in the open air, but under cover, it is left in the 'white' state; that is, it is not coated with tar or any other substance.

(*b*) *spec.* applied to crops of corn or grain, formerly called ***white corn*** (cf. CORN *sb.*[1] 3), which turn 'white' or light-coloured in ripening, as distinguished from *black* and *green* crops: see CROP *sb.* 9. Hence *transf.* of land or soil adapted for such crops.

1523–34 Fitzherb. *Husb.* §27 The sherers of all maner of whyte corne. **1677** Plot *Oxfordsh.* 240 If it be of that poorest sort they call white-land, nothing is so proper as ray-grass mixt with Non-such, or Melilot Trefoil. **1780** Young *Tour Irel.* I. 197 Pease esteemed a refreshment, and enables them to have one or two crops of white corn. **1799** J. Robertson *Agric. Perth* 451 By the alternate changes of white and green crops. **1805** Forsyth *Beauties Scot.* II. 66 The soils under tillage are commonly arranged into two kinds;.. light and clayey. The former is called turnip or green soil; and the latter, white soil, because it is best adapted for growing oats, wheat, and other white grains. *c* **1830** *Glouc. Farm Rep.* 4 in *Libr. Usef. Knowl., Husb.* III, No white or corn crop should be repeated in too rapid succession.

b. Of metal, or objects made of metal, of a light grey colour and lustrous appearance. †Frequent in early use as an epithet of silver; hence = made or consisting of silver; also (of iron or steel armour) burnished and shining, without colouring or stain. See also *white metal*, *money* (in 11 c), *rent* (in 11 e), WHITE IRON.

Also technically applied to silver ware chased or roughened with the tool, as distinguished from burnished silver.

c **1000** Ælfric *Josh.* vii. 21 Twahund entsena hwites seolfres. *a* **1225** *Ancr. R.* 152 Read gold & hwit seoluer. *a* **1400–50** *Wars Alex.* 129 Quadrentis coruen all of quyte siluyre. **1419** *Mem. Ripon* (Surtees) III. 145 Et in D. de quytnayles empt. eod. temp. **1506** *Lincoln Wills* (1914) I. 44 A whytepece with a coveryng. **1530** Palsgr. 288/2 White harnesse, *blanche armure*. **1542** *Inv. Royal Wardr.* (1815) 72 Quhyt Werk. Item ane greit bassing for feit wesching. *a* **1627** Middleton, etc. *Widow* IV. ii, A white thimble that I found i' moon light. **1667** Dryden & Dk. Newc. *Sir M. Mar-all* v, Hang your white pelf. **1761** *Ann. Reg., Chron.* 232 One of his majesty's best suits of white armour. **1816** Scott *Antiq.* xi, Four white shillings and saxpence. **1856** Miller *Elem. Chem., Inorg.* xv. §674 Tin is a white metal with a tinge of yellow.

c. Colourless, uncoloured, as glass or other transparent substance.

c **888** Ælfred *Boeth.* xxxii. §3 Æȝðer ȝe hwite ȝimmas ȝe reade. **1398** Trevisa *Barth. De P.R.* XVI. cii. (1495) M iv b/2 Those [*sc.* Zineth stones] that ben whyttest.. ben not so precyous. *a* **1425** tr. *Arderne's Treat. Fistula*, etc. 54 Poudre of white glasse. **1662** Merrett tr. *Neri's Art of Glass* 147 The pots wherein Enamels are made must be glased with white glass and bear the fire. **1738** Deering *Catal. Stirp.* 128 Thousands of little white Bubbles filled with Water. **1890** C. H. Moore *Gothic Archit.* x. 303 White glass is introduced here and there [in a stained-glass window] to heighten the effect.

d. Blank, not written or printed upon; †(of a document) unendorsed (cf. *white-backed* in 12 c).

1466 *Stonor Papers* (Camden) I. 87 Ye seye þat ye have paid þe money: þer for y sende yowe the writte white. ? *a* **1550** *Faine wald I* 33 in *Dunbar's Poems* (S.T.S.) 311 Gif lytil rewarde be in wryting, Bettir war leif my paper quhyte. *a* **1600** *Flodden Field* lviii, Sweet sonne Edward, white bookes thou make, And euer haue pittye on the pore cominaltye. **1680**, **1772**, **1859** [see *white paper* (*b*) in 11 e]. **1683**, **1770** [see WHITE LINE 2].

e. [tr. It. *voce bianca* white voice.] Of a singing voice or its sound: lacking any emotional coloration (such as may be imparted by vibrato). Also *transf.* Cf. *voix blanche* s.v. VOIX.

1884 F. Niecks *Dict. Mus. Terms* 257 *Voce bianca* (It.), lit. 'white voice'. The female and children's voices, and also some bright-sounding instruments, are thus called. **1904** S. Joyce *Dublin Diary* (1962) 39, I called McCormack's voice 'a white voice'—it is a male contralto. **1921** L. Tetrazzini *My Life of Song* xix. 316 Be careful not to simulate too broad a smile. Too wide a smile often accompanies what is called 'the white voice'. This is a voice production where a head resonance alone is employed, without sufficient of the appoggio or enough of the mouth resonance to give the tone a vital quality. This 'white voice' should be thoroughly understood, and is one of the many shades of tone a singer can use at times.. to produce certain atmospheric effects. For instance, in the mad scene in *Lucia*, the use of the 'white voice' suggests the babbling of the mad woman, as the same voice.. in the last act of *La Boheme* suggests utter physical exhaustion, and the approach of death. An entire voice production on this colourless line, however, would always lack the brilliancy and the vitality which inspires enthusiasm. **1951** W. Morum *Gabriel* I. iv. 56 That vibrato .. [is] no use for symphony work. In the big orchestras the trumpeter employs what we call a *white* tone. A pure tone. **1957** V. Nabokov *Pnin* 182 'I want a last piece of advice from you,' said Liza in what the French call a 'white' voice. **1961** *Times* 28 Sept. 16/1 An attractive, brightly ringing voice, rather white at the top but pleasantly dark below. **1975** *Gramophone* Dec. 1075/1 The soprano, Emma Kirkby, produces a 'white tone' which is scarcely distinguishable from that of a choir boy in some items, and this makes for a commendable purity of intonation. **1976** *Times* 8 Nov. 8/6 Where another team might produce a remote, 'white' sound, without vibrato.. the Amadeus [Quartet] permitted a more human, warm tone. **1981** Ld. Harewood *Tongs & Bones* xiii. 209 He contented himself for the first act with accurate, small-scale singing in a rather small, white voice.

f. Of a drink of coffee: with milk or cream added.

[**1900** G. Bell *Let.* 25 May (1927) I. 113 Besides the bitter black coffee, we were handed cups of what they [*sc.* Hasineh Arabs] called 'white coffee'—hot water, much sweetened and flavoured with almonds.] **1925** X. M. Boulestin *Conduct of Kitchen* 10 It is somewhat distressing.. to have to stop at the coffee-stall on the way home for an honest sandwich and a cup of 'white' coffee. **1940** *Punch* 6 May (Summer No., unpaginated) (*caption*), Please don't hesitate to say if you prefer your coffee white. **1982** H. Shaw *Death of Don* i. 3 'Black or white, Master?' 'White, please.'.. They took their coffee and brandy and sat down.

3. Of or in reference to the skin or complexion: Light in colour, fair. (Often as a poetic term of commendation.) Now *rare* or *Obs.* exc. as in 4.

a **900** Cynewulf *Elene* 73 Wlitescyne.. hwit & hiwbeorht hæleða nathwylc. *a* **1225** *Ancr. R.* 116 Hire sulf biholden hire owune honden hwite. **1297** R. Glouc. (Rolls) 566 In þe worlde her pere nas, So ȝwit ne of suich color. *a* **1300** *Cursor M.* 28010 Yee leuedis, wit your quite hals. *c* **1374** Chaucer *Troylus* II. 1062 þow Mynerua þe white, Yef þow me wit my lettre to deuyse. **1422** Yonge tr. *Secr. Secr.* 225 Pyteous and merciabill man tokenyth whitte coloure and cleene. *c* **1480** Henryson *Thre Deid Pollis* 25 O ladeis quhyt, in claithis corruscant. **15..** Dunbar *Poems* lxxxviii. 46 Fair be their wives, right lovesom, white and small. **1598** Marston *Pigmal., Reactio* 35 Ye Granta's white Nymphs come. **1689** N. Lee *Princess of Cleve* II. ii, He has.. a Skin so white—and soft as Sattin with the Grain.

4. Applied to those of ethnic types (chiefly European or of European extraction) characterized by light complexion, as distinguished from *black*, *red*, *yellow*, etc. Also *transf.* See also *whitefellow*, *white slave*, etc. in 11 e, and WHITE MAN.

poor white folk*(*s*)** or ***trash : a contemptuous name given in America by Blacks to white people of no substance (1836, etc. in Thornton *Amer. Gloss.*); hence ***poor-white-folksy***, ***-trashy*** adjs.; cf. TRASH *sb.*[1] 4, WHITE *sb.* 13. So ***poor white***, ***poor-white*** as compound adj. (not always contemptuous, and in wider use, esp. in *S. Afr.*); also *fig.*

1604 E. G[rimstone] tr. *D'Acosta's Hist. Indies* II. xi. 106 Under the same line.. lies a part of Peru, and of the new kingdome of Grenado, which.. are very temperate Countries,.. and the inhabitants are white. **1680** C. Nesse *Ch. Hist.* 27 The White Line, (the Posterity of Seth,).. the black Line the Cursed brood of Cain. **1777** *Summary Acc. Tobago* 29 The white inhabitants.. do not exceed seven hundred. The negroes, amounting to about twelve thousand, are kept in awe by an active militia. **1821** *Austin Papers* (1924) I. 446 My friend could probably take with him about twenty negroes and perhaps a poor white family consisting of a man and his wife. **1833** [see TRASH *sb.*[1] 4]. **1836** J. K. Paulding *Slavery in U.S.* 205 The slave of a gentleman universally considers himself a superior being to 'poor white folks'. **1856** Olmsted *Slave States* 84, I have been.. told that the poor white people, meaning those, I suppose, who bring nothing to market to exchange for money but their labor,.. are worse off in almost all respects than the slaves. **1864** *Harper's Mag.* Aug. 412/2, I wouldn't do my hair in a three strand braid on no account; it is too poor-white-folksy for me. **1865** Whittier *Lesson & our Duty* Prose Wks. 1889 III. 151 The negro is to be left powerless in the hands of the 'White trash', who hate him with a bitter hatred. **1911** *Chambers's Jrnl.* Jan. 6/1 An effort has also been made to enrol men of the 'poor white' class in the police force, for which they appear well adapted. **1949** *Race Relations in S. Afr.* 413 It was not until 1898 that the first organized effort at their rehabilitation was made. In that year the Dutch Reformed Church in the Cape Colony established the Kakamas Labour Settlement for 'Poor White' families. **1951** H. Giles *Harbin's Ridge* 63 He never had been much account. Always content just to make out, which we considered poor-white-trashy in our parts. **1958** *New Statesman* 1 Feb. 143/1 In *The Hamlet* Faulkner describes the infiltration out of nowhere into.. that sequestered poor-white corner of Yoknapatawpha County, Mississippi, of the Snopes family. **1958** *Times Lit. Suppl.* 13 June 328/5 Mr. Chase's thesis allows us to see them [*sc.* many popular American novels] as, so to say, poor-white relations of incomparably more distinguished works, relations that all the same show, in however degenerate a way, similar fundamental responses to the nature of American experience. **1958** A. Jackson *Trader on Veld* 43 As a matter of course, every property was divided equally among the owner's sons upon his death... Few things contributed more effectively to the creation of a Poor White class than did this usage. **1979** J. Drummond *Patriots* xv. 77 He'd been poor, the son of a poor-white farmer.

b. *slang* or *colloq.* (by extension from WHITE MAN 2 b; orig. *U.S.*) Honourable; square-dealing. Also as *adv.*

1877 Besant & Rice *Golden Butterfly* xviii, A good fellow is Rayner; as white a man as I ever knew. **1890** *Century Mag.* Feb. 523/2 There ain't a whiter man than Laramie Jack from the Wind River Mountains down to Santa Fe. **1913** Edith Wharton *Cust. Country* ix, Well—this is white of you. *Ibid.* xviii, I meant to act white by you.

c. Of or pertaining to white people.

1852 Mrs. Stowe *Uncle Tom's C.* xxiii, He had white blood in his veins. **1868** *N.Y. Herald* 4 July 5/2 The registered white vote has been very greatly increased. **1870** Kingsley *At Last* xvi, Exclusive sugar cultivation had put a premium on unskilled slave-labour, to the disadvantage of skilled white-labour. **1896** Baden-Powell *Matabele Campaign* xviii, The white power of South Africa. **1933**, etc. [see *white jazz*, sense 11 e below]. **1937** L. & E. Dowling tr. *H. Panassié's Hot Jazz* ii. 28 White musicians were playing .. a so-called 'white' hot style intended to compete with the other style. **1944** *Living off Land* iv. 64 Natives are always hunting the coast for food. Also, there will be cattle stations, or white camps along the coast. **1959** 'F. Newton' *Jazz Scene* iv. 70 The most characteristically 'white' style in the history of jazz. **1965** F. Symington *Tuktu* 59 Most missionaries tried to teach their charges how to cope with the 'white' culture and economy. **1968** P. Oliver *Screening Blues* vi. 181 There appears to have been no relaxing of the strict segregation of record catalogues, nor any apparent attempt to secure a white market for Negro records of this [*sc.* pornographic] character. **1977** *Times of Swaziland* 25 Feb. 12 (Advt.), Farming estate... Strategically situated in centre of largest white area of popular Natal Midlands. **1984** J. McClure *Artful Egg* xi. 156 A couple.. who affected sophisticated white manners and even spoke English with an almost white accent.

5. †**a.** In early use app. applied to illness marked by pallor. *Obs.* **b.** Pale, pallid, esp. from fear or other emotion. (Often in hyperbolical phr. ***as white as a sheet***.) Also in allusive phrases expressing cowardice (cf. WHITE-LIVER, -LIVERED), and *transf.* (as in ***white rage***, ***terror***).

Phr. ***to bleed white***: (*a*) *intr.* (hyperbolically) to shed colourless blood (*rare*); (*b*) *trans.* to drain completely of resources.

c **1403** Clanvowe *Cuckow & Night.* 41, I am so shaken with the fevers whyte, Of al this May yet slepte I but a lyte. **1412–20** Lydg. *Chron. Troy* IV. 2369 While he laie þus in his þrowes white. *a* **1508** Dunbar *Tua Mariit Wemen* 426 Than lay I furtgh my bright buke on breid on my knee.. And drawis my clok forthwart our my face quhit. **1592** Shaks. *Ven. & Ad.* 643 Didst thou not marke my face, was it not white? Sawest thou not signes of feare lurke in mine eye? **1596** —— *Merch. V.* III. ii. 86 How manie cowards.. weare .. The beards of Hercules and frowning Mars, Who inward searcht, haue lyuers white as milke. **1605** —— *Macb.* II. ii. 65, I shame To weare a Heart so white. **1626** Bp. Hall *Contempl.* XIII. *David & Gol.*, Now wee see.. those, which haue giuen good proofes of magnanimitie, at other times, haue bewrayed white liuers. **1753** Jane Collier *Art Torment.* I. ii. 46 She.. looks as white as a cloth. **1799** Southey *Bp. Hatto* 35 He had a countenance white with alarm. **1841** S. WARREN *Ten Thou.* I. x, He hurried down.. white with rage. **1854** DICKENS *Hard T.* I. ii, His skin was so unwholesomely deficient in the natural tinge, that he looked as though, if he were cut, he would bleed white. **1860** SHIRLEY BROOKS *Gordian Knot* ii, The most gentlemanly millionaire of them all has since been transported, and another is in white terror of a similar destiny. **1866** G. MACDONALD *Ann. Q. Neighb.* xxxii, She is as white as a sheet. **1885** 'F. ANSTEY' *Tinted Venus* vi, He was in a white rage. **1897** HALL CAINE *Christian* III. xii, The man.. turned white as a ghost. **1935** *Sabbath School Worker* Nov. 6/1 'There are too many appeals for money', the people are 'bled white', and 'we can't give another penny'. **1945** R. CHANDLER in *R. Chandler Speaking* (1966) 113 It is the writers' own weakness as craftsmen that permits the superior egos to bleed them white of initiative, imagination, and integrity. **1982** 'W. HAGGARD' *Mischief-Makers* i. 16 Her husband had been a wealthy man, the lady's solicitors sharp and ruthless, and her husband had been bled white to get rid of her.

6. a. Clothed or arrayed in white; *spec.* belonging to an ecclesiastical order distinguished by wearing a white habit (see also *white canons* s.v. CANON *sb.* 1, and WHITE FRIAR, WHITE MONK).

white ball: a ball at which all the ladies are dressed in white. ***white nun***, a Cistercian nun (cf. WHITE MONK).

a **1225** *Leg. Kath.* 1576 Ha seh sitten þis meiden mid monie hwite wurðliche men. *a* **1400** *Prymer* (1891) 22 The white [L. *candidatus*] oost of martires. *c* **1400** *Brut* 314 þere aros anoþer cumpanye of diuers nacions þat was called 'þe white companye,' þe whiche, in þe parties & cuntre of Lumbardye, dede myche sorwe. *c* **1420** *Sir Amadace* (Camden) xxxviii, Quod the quite knyȝte 'Quat mon is this?' *c* **1450** HOLLAND *Howlat* 178 The Se Mawis war monkis, the blak and the quhyte. **1470–85** MALORY *Arthur* XIII. ix. 623 He came to a whyte Abbay. **1598** SHAKS. *Merry W.* V. v. 41 Fairies blacke, gray, greene, and white. **1895** *Pall Mall Mag.* Sept. 140 A month after Mamie's arrival Lidian gave a 'white ball' in her honour. **1877** J. PENDEREL-BRODHURST *Guide to Boscobel* v. 20 Whiteladies... The name is derived from the circumstance that the house was once a Priory of Cistercian or White Nuns. **1903** CHANDLERY *Pilgr. Walks Rome* (1908) 128 The Olivetans or white Benedictines. **1954** A. SETON *Katherine* xxxii. 536 Katherine.. surveyed the two nuns... White nuns, Cistercians, shrouded in snowy wimples and habits.

b. From the 17th century white has been specially associated with royalist and legitimist causes (e.g. the white flag of the Bourbons), and hence in recent times *white* has been applied to certain constitutional or anti-revolutionary parties and the policy for which they stand. In recent use applied to the Kuomintang in China and to the Christian Democrats in Italy. (See WHITE *sb.* 19, and cf. RED *a.* and *sb.*[1] 9 b.)

1749 J. RAY *Compl. Hist. Reb.* 331 She got together all her Clan, and marched at their Head (with a white Cockade, &c.) and presented them to the Mock Prince. *Ibid.* 341 The Rebel Army were assembled with their White Flags displayed. *a* **1784** JOHNSON in *Boswell* an. 1763 *note*, Boswell, in the year 1745,..wore a white cockade, and prayed for King James. **1848** REDHEAD *Fr. Rev.* II. 302 Suppressing the tricolour, and substituting in its stead the white flag. **1849** W. C. TAYLOR *House of Orleans* III. 222 He had been one of the first to raise the White Flag in 1814; he had levied a regiment of Royalists during the hundred days. *a* **1879** J. MACDONELL *France since 1st Empire* 117 The French ministers could show clemency at Paris, but they were not so well able to keep down the fury of the Royalists in the provinces. Thus was the Red Terror succeeded by the White. **1903** *Daily Chron.* 20 June 3/2 His position is that known in Italy as 'White', or constitutional, as compared with the clerical 'Blacks' and the republican 'Reds'. **1918** *Times* 9 Apr. 6/4 (Finland) Germany has secured a strong hold of the gratitude of 'White' public opinion. **1937** E. SNOW *Red Star over China* I. i. 21 To get in touch with Communists in the 'White' areas [of China] was extremely difficult. **1952** [see KUOMINTANG]. **1965** C. D. EBY *Seige of Alcázar* (1966) iii. 63 In less than forty-eight hours the Alcázar had become a solitary White island in the middle of a raging Red sea. **1965** M. MICHAEL tr. *Myrdal's Rep. from Chinese Village* (1967) III. 131 My father was taken by the white bandits and beheaded. **1967** C. SETON-WATSON *Italy from Liberalism to Fascism* xii. 514 A left wing, led by Miglioli, the pacifist and 'white' trade unionist, called for a Christian proletarian party that would make capitalism its main enemy. **1973** P. A. ALLUM *Politics & Society in Post-War Naples* 326 The DC and PCI are heirs to particular Italian subcultures, the Catholic and the marxist. Both.. ensure.. the electoral strengths of both parties in North and Centre, and above all in those regions (e.g. the 'white' provinces of the NE and 'red' provinces of the Centre, etc.) where they organise specific populations.

7. *fig.* Morally or spiritually pure or stainless; spotless, unstained, innocent.

971 *Blickl. Hom.* 147 Hwylc is of us Drihten þæt hæbbe swa hwite saule swa þeos halige Marie? *a* **1225** *Ancr. R.* 324 Vor euere so heo [*sc.* the soul] is hwitture, so þe fulðe is schenre. *c* **1450** CAPGRAVE *Life St. Aug.* xv, Whech seruauntis our Lord God had brout fro þe grete blaknesse of synne on-to þe fair white vertuous lyuyng. **1603** SHAKS. *Meas. for M.* III. ii. 198 Back wounding calumnie The whitest vertue strikes. **1608** BP. HALL *Char.* I. 21 Hee hath white hands, and a cleane soule. **1616** B. JONSON *Epigr.* xciii, I doe not know a whiter soule. **1645** G. DANIEL *Scattered Fancies* xxxiii, But Danger onlie gvilt attends; I bring White Thoughts. **1737** POPE *Hor. Epist.* II. i. 216 In our own [days].. No whiter page than Addison remains. **1859** HAWTHORNE *Marble Faun* xxiii, There can be no harm to my white Hilda in one parting kiss. **1862** TROLLOPE *Orley F.* xxxvi, It is I whose duty it is to see that your name be made white again.

b. Free from malignity or evil intent; beneficent, innocent, harmless, esp. as opposed to something characterized as *black* (cf. BLACK *a.* 8, 9): chiefly in phr. *white lie* (see LIE *sb.*[1] 1 b), ***white magic*** (MAGIC *sb.* 1 b; cf. BLACK ART); see also *white paternoster* s.v. PATERNOSTER 2, and WHITE WITCH.

1651 C. CARTWRIGHT *Cert. Relig.* III. 36 He did not know whether his admonisher were black or white.. an evill or a good spirit. **1655** FULLER *Ch. Hist.* II. v. §12 He made his Harp.. make musick of it self; which no White Art could perform. **1718** BP. HUTCHINSON *Witchcraft* ii. 26 A Teacher of the White Magic, that pretends to deal only with Good Angels. **1749–50** RICHARDSON in Mrs. Barbauld *Corr.* (1804) IV. 316 Don't you think.. that I have reason to exclaim against white fibs? **1828** MISS MITFORD *Village* Ser. III. *Admiral on Shore*, Julia.. asserted her female privilege of white-lying, and declared [etc.]. **1855** KINGSLEY *Westw. Ho!* iv, They be mortal feared of witches,.. and mortal hard on 'em, even on a pure body like me, that doth a bit in the white way. **1914** SIR E. SHACKLETON in *Scotsman* 29 Oct. 3/8, I send you my last cable as we start for the Antarctic. We are leaving now to carry on our white warfare.

c. Of propaganda: truthful.

1965 B. SWEET-ESCOTT *Baker Street Irregular* i. 29 The Ministry of Information.. confined itself to straight or 'white' propaganda in neutral and friendly countries. **1976** [see PROPAGANDA 3].

8. (Chiefly of times and seasons). Propitious, favourable; auspicious, fortunate, happy. Now *rare*.

1629 SHIRLEY *Grateful Serv.* II. i, Till this white houre, these walles were neuer proud, T'inclose a guest. **1638–56** COWLEY *Davideis* II. 830 Thy Fate's all white. **1660** DRYDEN *Astræa Redux* 292 And now times whiter Series is begun. **1728** RAMSAY *Bonny Christy* iv, He wisely this white Minute took, And flang his Arms about her. **1749** FIELDING *Tom Jones* VIII. xi, What is called by Schoolboys Black Monday, was to me the whitest in the whole Year. **1830** LYTTON *P. Clifford* xxix, I will not even press you to appoint that day, which to me will be the whitest of my life. **1855** MACAULAY *Hist. Eng.* xvii. IV. 2 That was one of the few white days of a life, beneficent indeed.. but far from happy.

†**9.** Highly prized, precious; dear, beloved, favourite, 'pet', 'darling'. Often as a vague term of endearment. (See also *white son* in 11 e, and WHITE BOY.) *Obs.*

c **1425** *Non-Cycle Myst. Plays* (1909) 33 Take vp Isaac, þi son so whyte. *c* **1537** in Ellis *Orig. Lett.* Ser. III. III. 126 Master Pole.. entred secretly in to a Monasterye.. called Seynt Justyns, wheras he is ther wyte God and they his blacke angells. **1602** *2nd Pt. Return fr. Parnass.* II. vi, I shall bee his little roague, and his white villaine for a whole weeke after. **1634** HEYWOOD *Lanc. Witches* I. i. Wks. 1874 IV. 184 A merry song now mother, and thou shalt be my white girle. **1646** *Extr. Kirk-Session Rec. Dunfermline* (1865) 17 Jonet Wely.. had slandered grissell walwood spouse to Jo[n] alisone, wright, calling hir white bird. **1647** TRAPP *Comm. Matt.* xiv. 3 If Iohn touch Herods white sin.. Iohn must to prison.

†**10.** Fair-seeming, specious, plausible. *Obs.*

c **1374** CHAUCER *Troylus* III. 901, I.. feffe hym with a fewe wordes whyte. *Ibid.* 1567 For alle youre wordes whyte. **1412–20** LYDG. *Chron. Troy* III. 4272 Hir wordis white, softe, & blaundyshynge, Wer meynt with feynyng & with flaterie. *c* **1480** HENRYSON *Cock & Fox* 205 Flatteraris with plesand wordis quhyte. **1513** DOUGLAS *Æneis* I. xi. 34 The schyning vissage of the god Cupyte, And his dissemelit slekit wordis quhyte. **1612** SIR J. DAVIES *Why Ireland.* etc. 93 The faire and white promises of Lewes the 11. **1613** CHAPMAN *Rev. Bussy d' Ambois* v. i, This bloud I shed, is to saue the bloud Of many thousands. *Guise.* That's your white pretext. **1721** KELLY *Sc. Prov.* 158 The Scots call Flatteries Whitings, and Flatterers white People. **1825** JAMIESON, *White-Wind*, flattery, wheedling; a cant term.

11. Special collocations. **a.** In names of species or varieties of animals distinguished by their white colour or colouring: as ***white bear, fox, heron, herring, pelican, perch, shark, stork, trout, wagtail***, for which see the sbs.; also **white †admirable, admiral** [ADMIRAL *sb.* 6], a dark-coloured butterfly, *Limenitis camilla*, with white markings; **white baker** (see e below); **white-bird**, (*a*) a name for the spotted flycatcher; (*b*) see quot. 1875; (*c*) (without hyphen) in Irish folklore, a bird of fairyland; **white egret** = *white heron* (*a*) below; **white-fly**, a small bug of the family Aleyrodidæ, usually covered with pale, powdery wax, esp. *Trialeurodes vaporariorum*, which is a pest of greenhouse plants; **white fox**, a small fox, *Alopex lagopus*, native to northern Canada, Greenland, and Iceland, which has white fur in winter; also, the fur of this animal; **white game** [GAME *sb.* 11] = *white partridge*; **white goat** = *Rocky Mountain goat* s.v. ROCKY *a.*[1] 1 c; **white grouse** = *white partridge*; **white grub**, the larva of the cockchafer or other scarabæid; **white heron** (usu. qualified by *great*), (*a*) the common egret, *Egretta alba*, a large white bird with a yellow bill and dark legs found in parts of Europe, Asia, North Africa, the Americas, and Australasia; (*b*) a white subspecies of the great blue heron, *Ardea herodias*, found in Florida; **white mouse** (see e below); **white owl**: see OWL *sb.* 1 b; **white partridge** ? *Obs.*, the ptarmigan; **white perch** *U.S.*: see PERCH *sb.*[1] 2; **white pointer**: see POINTER 12; **white rhino(ceros)**, a large, wide-mouthed rhinoceros, *Ceratotherium simum*, native to parts of Sudan, Uganda, and South Africa; **white slipper (limpet), snail** (see quots.); **white steenbras**, a large marine food fish, *Lithognathus lithognathus*, found in coastal regions of South Africa; **white whale** = BELUGA 2; **white worm** = *white grub*; see also WHITEBAIT, WHITEFISH, etc. **b.** In names of plants distinguished by white flowers or other parts, light-coloured bark, wood, root, fruit, seed, etc.; also applied to such flowers, wood, etc.: as ***white beech, beet, bind, bine, broom, currant, dead-nettle, grape, hellebore, honeysuckle, horehound, jasmine, lilac, mustard, oats, peas, pepper, pine, raspberry, rye, sanders, willow*** (see the sbs.); also **white ash**, (*a*) a species or variety of ash with light-coloured wood; *esp.* a North American ash, *Fraxinus americana*; hence (*colloq.*) an oar; also *attrib.* (jocular) as ***white-ash breeze***, the impetus of the oar; (*b*) a S. African ornamental tree with white flowers, *Platylophus trifoliatus*, the white alder (ALDER *sb.*[1] 3); **white-bark pine**, a pine with pale, flaky bark, *Pinus albicaulis*, native to northwestern North America; **white bath** (see e below); **white birch**: see BIRCH *sb.* 1 b; **white box**, either of two Australian trees, the evergreen *Bursaria spinosa*, which bears clusters of fragrant white flowers, or a box eucalypt, *Eucalyptus albens*, which has pale leaves; †**white-bush** = WHITETHORN; **white campion**: see CAMPION[2]; **white cedar**, (*a*) any of several North American conifers, esp. one of the genus *Chamæcyparis*; (*b*) *Austral.*, a name used for species of *Melia*, deciduous trees native to the East Indies and Australia; **white clover**: see CLOVER 1 b; **white corn** (see 2 a (b)); **white elm**, the American elm, *Ulmus americana*; also, the European elm, *Ulmus lævis*, which resembles it closely; **white fir**, any of several North American firs, esp. *Abies concolor*, native to the south-western United States; **white grass**, (*a*) *Holcus lanatus*; (*b*) American species of *Leersia*, esp. *L. virginica*; **white mangrove**: see MANGROVE[1] 2; **white maple**, any of several maples with pale bark, esp. the silver maple, *Acer saccharinum*, or the mountain maple, *A. spicatum*; **white mulberry**, a round-topped mulberry, *Morus alba*, or its white or pink fruit; **white oak**, any of several species of North American oak, esp. *Quercus alba*, which is native to the eastern part of the continent; also, the wood of this tree; †**white plum**, (*a*) = WHEAT-PLUM; (*b*) a plum of Barbados having whitish bark; **white poplar**, (*a*) (see POPLAR 1 b); (*b*) *N. Amer.*, the aspen, *Populus tremuloides*; (*c*) *N. Amer.*, the tulip-tree, *Liriodendron tulipifera*; **white-rot**: see ROT *sb.*[1] 2 c and sense 11 e below; **white spruce**, a spruce with bluish foliage, *Picea glauca*, native to North America; **white-tree**, a name for different trees having light-coloured wood; esp. *Melaleuca leucodendron* of Australia and the Malay archipelago; **white vine**, (*a*) the common bryony, *Bryonia dioica*; (*b*) traveller's-joy, *Clematis vitalba*; **white walnut** = BUTTERNUT 1; **white wheat**, wheat with white or light-coloured grain; **white wood**, (*a*) the alburnum, or lighter-coloured outer wood of a tree; (*b*) any non-resinous wood. **c.** In names of minerals, and of chemical or other products, of a white colour: as ***white amber, antimony, arsenic, clay, copper, dammar, enamel, feldspar, (iron) pyrites, precipitate, salt, schorl, soap, tellurium, tin, tombac, vitriol, wax***, for which see the sbs.; also **white ash**, refined soda-ash as distinct from the crude *black ash* (ASH *sb.*[2] 2); **white brass**, an alloy of copper and zinc, containing a large proportion of the latter; **white brick**, (*a*) app. Bath brick; (*b*) a hard, durable variety of brick made from gault; **white bronze**, any light-coloured bronze; **white cast iron** = WHITE IRON b; cf. *grey (cast) iron* s.v. GREY, GRAY *a.* 8 c; **white damp** [DAMP *sb.*[1] 1 b], carbonic oxide as occurring in coal-mines; **white earth**, earth material (as clay) that is light-coloured; *spec.* in *Painting*, white earth-colour; **white leather** (see LEATHER *sb.* 1 and WHITLEATHER); **white lights** *Obs.* exc. *dial.*, candles; **white metal**, a name for various alloys of a light grey colour (also *attrib.*); **white money**, silver money, silver coins; **white nickel**, a name for CHLOANTHITE or other native nickel arsenide; **white oil**, (*a*) crude oil that is pale in colour; (*b*) a colourless petroleum distillate; *spec.* a highly refined heavy distillate used medicinally and in the food and plastics industries; **white phosphorus**, (*a*) the white opaque incrustation that forms on phosphorus when it is kept under water (? *obs.*); (*b*) the ordinary allotrope of phosphorus, a translucent waxy whitish or yellowish solid which unlike red phosphorus is poisonous and very reactive; † **white powder**, a supposed kind of gunpowder exploding without noise; **white precipitate**, either of two mercuric amidochlorides obtained by treating mercuric chloride with ammonia: ***fusible white precipitate***, $HgCl_2(NH_3)_2$, and ***infusible white precipitate***, $HgClNH_2$ (ammoniated mercury), obtained when there is excess ammonia and used in ointments against worm infection; **white rock**, a name applied to intrusive basaltic rocks, altered to a light colour, occurring in coal-measures; **white-row** (see quot.); **white rubber**, (*a*) caoutchouc whitened by admixture of a pigment; (*b*) the light-coloured caoutchouc obtained from the ***white-rubber vine*** (*Landolphia owariensis*); **white rust** (see sense 11 e below); **white sapphire**, a variety of corundum that is colourless owing to the absence of the impurities responsible for the blue colour of ordinary sapphire; **white spirit**, a volatile colourless liquid distillate of petroleum that boils between about 150°C and 200°C and is widely used as a paint thinner and solvent; † **white straits** (see quots. and STRAIT *sb.* 9); **white tin**, (*a*) refined metallic tin, in contrast to black tin; (*b*) the ordinary allotrope of tin, in contrast to grey tin; **white trap** = *white rock*; † **white wire**, iron wire coated with tin. **d.** In names of bodily parts or structures, and of diseases or abnormal bodily conditions, characterized by white colour: as **white blood**, blood with an excess of white corpuscles, as in leuchæmia; † **white bone**, app. the costal cartilages; **white cell, corpuscle**, a colourless blood-corpuscle, a leucocyte; **white finger(s)** = *Raynaud's phenomenon* s.v. RAYNAUD; also *attrib.*; **white flood**, leucorrhœa; **white flux** (see e below); **white gangrene**, a form of gangrene in which the affected parts become whitish; **white haw**, an affection of the eye (see HAW *sb.*[3]); **white jaundice** (see JAUNDICE *sb.* 1 b); **white matter**, the fibrous matter of the brain and spinal cord, as distinct from the *grey matter*; **white scour**, a disease of calves, freq. due to infection with *E. coli*, causing severe diarrhœa, dehydration, and often death; **white softening**, a variety of softening of the brain (see quot. 1873); **white swelling** (see SWELLING *vbl. sb.* 2); **white (fibrous) tissue**, white connective tissue, as distinct from *yellow tissue* (YELLOW *a.* C. 1 e).

1798 E. DONOVAN *Nat. Hist. Brit. Insects* VII. 75 The *White Admirable Butterfly feeds upon the common honey suckle or woodbine. **1906** R. SOUTH *Butterflies Brit. Isles* II. 59 The White Admiral (*Limenitis sibylla*). The 'White Admirable Butterfly', as it was called by some of the older English entomologists, needs only to be seen to be at once recognized. **1717** J. PETIVER *Papilionum Britanniæ Icones* 1/2 in *Opera* (1764) II. VII, *White Admiral. Found about Dullidge and Wickham near Croyden, as also at Henly upon Thames. **1826** J. CURTIS *Brit. Entomol.* III. 124 (*heading*) Limenitis camilla. The White Admiral. **1857** H. T. STAINTON *Man. Brit. Butterflies & Moths* I. 33 White Admiral.. Blackish brown, with a broad white band crossing the centre of the wings. **1922** V. WOOLF *Jacob's Room* ii. 36 He had seen a white admiral circling higher and higher round an oak tree, but he had never caught it. **1968** *Oxf. Bk. Insects* 46/2 White Admiral.. belongs to the same family as the Fritillaries. **1801** SHAW *Gen. Zool.* II. 315 The Leucoryx or *White Antelope. **1683** *Coll. New Hampshire Hist. Soc.* (1866) VIII. 146 [They] did feloniously.. use about one cord of *white ash. **1784** [see *red ash* s.v. RED *a.* 17 d]. **1820** T. GREEN *Univ. Herbal* II. 856/2 *Fraxinus Americana*, American Ash-tree.—There are several varieties of this, White Ash, Red Ash, Black Ash, &c. **1851** H. MELVILLE *Whale* lxxxi, This clumsy lubber was striving to free his white ash. **1881** RAYMOND *Mining Gloss.*, *White-ash* (Penn.). See *Coal.* **1882** *Garden* 23 Sept. 273/1 The white Ash of the United States may be taken as the type of most of the American kinds. **1892** *Labour Commission Gloss.*, *White Ash Finishers*, men in the chemical industry.. engaged upon the manufacture of soda ash.. from salts derived from black ash. **1950** *Chicago Tribune* 27 Apr. III. 10/1 Under each cutting spindle is placed a block of white ash. **1851** H. MELVILLE *Moby Dick* II. xxxix. 262 There she slides, now! Hurrah for the *white-ash breeze! **1906** KIPLING *Puck of Pook's Hill* 101 We must wake the white-ash breeze,.. A long pull for Stavanger! **1908** N. L. BRITTON *N. Amer. Trees* 12 *White Bark Pine.. a rather small tree of alpine habitat. **1949** *Sierra Club Bull.* Dec. 24, I knew I could not get any sleep just by crawling under the low branches of a white-bark pine. **1974** *Blackw. Mag.* Oct. 307/1 Stands of whitebark pine mingled with spruce.. provide welcome shade. **1613** PURCHAS *Pilgrimage* VIII. iii. 620 There were *white Beares, and stagges farre greater then ours. **1852** SEIDEL *Organ* 169 The levers by which the tongues are kept upon the beaks are generally made of *white beech. **1805** R. W. DICKSON *Pract. Agric.* II. 744 There is only one species of this plant [*sc.* hop] in cultivation, but which has several varieties, as the red-bind, the green-bind, the *white-bind, etc. **1789** J. MORSE *Amer. Geogr.* 197 On the high lands are .. beech and *white birch. **1961** H. MACLENNAN *Rivers of Canada* 48 Otherwise nothing but the immense low forest of spruce with the occasional splash of white birch. **1980** *Family Handyman* Sept. 63/2 Because hardwoods are more dense, there is more energy in a cord of oak, say, than a cord of white birch or white pine. **1875** MELLISS *St. Helena* 98 *Gygis candida*, Wagl.—*White-bird. One of the most abundant sea-birds in the Island. **1892** W. B. YEATS *Countess Kathleen* 106 (*title*) The white birds. **1894** —— *Land of Heart's Desire* 41 The Child (*from the door*): White bird, white bird, come with me, little bird! Maire Bruin: She calls my soul! **1940** E. POUND *Cantos* lvi. 60 May the white birds remember this warrior. **1843** R. J. GRAVES *Syst. Clin. Med.* vii. 85 Abstracting [by blister] a considerable portion of *white blood from the system. **1863** AITKEN *Sci. & Pract. Med.* (ed. 2) II. 270 White-cell blood, or White blood—*Leucocythæmia*. **1511** *Mem. Ripon* (Surtees) I. 314 Quendam N. Wallez felonice percussit cum uno *le dager* in pectore super *le *wythbone*. **1909** A. E. MACK *Bush Calendar* 67 Flowers blooming [in January]. *Bursaria spinosa.* *White box or black thorn. **1923** *Census of Plants of Victoria* (Field Naturalists Club of Victoria) 46 *Eucalyptus albens* Miquel White Box. **1936** F. CLUNE *Roaming round Darling* xvii. 161 White box is a good burning wood, sheds a brown bark in springtime, then has a white surface. **1946** K. TENNANT *Lost Haven* (1947) xvii. 289 'What are those trees down there?' .. 'Blueberry ash, white box, whipwood.' **1965** *Austral. Encycl.* III. 406/2 White box.. having pallid glaucescent foliage. **1538** *Bury Wills* (Camden) 136 One lytle pot of *whyte brasse. **1875** KNIGHT *Dict. Mech.* **1538** ELYOT *Dict.*, *Leucantha*, *white bryer. *a* **1756** ELIZA HAYWOOD *New Present* (1771) 252 Rubbing.. with scouring paper, rotten-stone, or *white-brick. **1845** J. H. PARKER *Gloss. Terms Archit.* (ed. 4) I. 72 In colour they are paler than ordinary red bricks, but are redder than the common white brick of Suffolk. **1969** R. BLYTHE *Akenfield* ix. 140 The school at Akenfield.. is a stark, knife-edged building constructed of Suffolk white-brick, [etc.]. **1979** *Guardian* 10 July 19/7 The famous Suffolk whitebrick which Georgian architects favoured for the region's grander houses. **1884** LOCK *Workshop Rec.* Ser. III. 28/1 This new kind of '*white bronze' is not to be confounded with the alloy used in America under the same name.. which consists principally of zinc. **1882** *Garden* 3 June 384/1 The *white Broom and a sulphur-coloured Cytisus. **1676** M. COOK *Forest-Trees* xxxii. 97 If you would make a Fence of one particular sort of Wood, the very best is your *White-bush, or White-thorn. **1795** *White cast iron [see IRON *sb.*[1] 2]. **1967** A. H. COTTRELL *Introd. Metall.* xxv. 518 In white cast irons, which are usually made by limiting the content of graphite-forming elements such as silicon to low levels.., all the carbon exists as cementite and the name white refers to the bright fracture produced by this brittle constituent. **1674** J. JOSSELYN *Acct. Two Voy. New England* 67 The *white Cedar is a stately Tree. **1709** [see PITCH PINE]. **1781–2** T. JEFFERSON *Notes Virginia* (1787) 62 White cedar, *Cupressus Thyoides*. **1847** LEICHHARDT *Jrnl.* iii. 60 The white cedar (*Melia Azedarach*). **1856** [see CEDAR 3]. **1884** A. NILSON *Timber Trees New South Wales* 97 White Cedar.—An elegant tree. **1908** E. J. BANFIELD *Confessions of Beachcomber* I. i. 20 The white cedar.. is a welcome and not unworthy substitute in appearance and perfume for English lilac. **1941** *Sun* (Baltimore) 12 Aug. 15/2 The hulls will be of two thicknesses, mahogany over white cedar. **1980** P. MOYES *Angel of Death* xi. 148 A fallen tree—a biggish white cedar with a trunk about a foot in diameter. **1861** *Q. Jrnl. Microsc. Sci.* I. 167 Colourless corpuscles, or *white cells, exist in the blood in a comparatively small number. **1885**, **1968** White cell [see RED CELL 1]. **1480** *White clay [see CLAY *sb.* 1 a]. **1686** PLOT *Staffordsh.* 122 White-clay, so called it seems though of a blewish colour, and used for making yellow-colour'd ware. **1783** J. WEDGWOOD *Let.* 13 Oct. (1965) 272 Having seen a specimen of fine white clay.. and being told it came from the Apalachian moutains.. I was so delighted with the appearance of this beautiful raw material.. that.. I determined upon sending an agent to the spot. **1852** in *Proc. Amer. Antiquarian Soc.* (1933) XLIII. 373 Mr Nichols.. has in contemplation the purchase of a tract of land containing a mine of white or China Clay. **1790** S. DEANE *New-England Farmer* 58/2 Red and *white clover are the only sorts known and esteemed in this country. **1884** F. J. LLOYD *Science of Agriculture* xv. 268 White or Dutch clover .. is a well-known variety of good feeding quality. **1977** J. L. HARPER *Population Biol. Plants* i. 25 The useful measure is the number of leaves, for example in.. white clover. **1875** KNIGHT *Dict. Mech.*, **White Copper*, an alloy forming an imitation of silver. **1866**, **1898** *White corpuscles [see LEUCOCYTOSIS, LEUCOCYTE]. **1578** LYTE *Dodoens* I. lxxi. 107 The fifth.. may be.. called.. *white Crowfoote, & water Crowfoote. *Ibid.* II. xxviii. 180 [see WATER-LILY]. **1866** *Treas. Bot.*, *White dammer. **1881** RAYMOND *Mining Gloss.*, **White-damp*, a poisonous gas sometimes (more rarely than fire-damp or choke-damp, etc.), encountered in coal mines. **1832** W. A. FERRIS *Diary* 8 May in *Life in Rocky Mts.* (1940) xxv. 143 It is sometimes found in various parts of the country, and is sometimes called '*white earth'. **1910** A. P. LAURIE *Materials of Painter's Craft* iv. 42 Then among the whites we have a large number of white earths, of which chalk is of course the most important. **1969** R. MAYER *Dict. Art Terms & Techniques* 430/1 Because of its clarity and high absorbency, white earth is well suited for, and in limited use as, a base for certain lakes. **1835** J. J. AUDUBON *Ornith. Biogr.* III. 137 [The Louisiana Heron] is at all seasons a social bird, moving about in company with the Blue Heron or the *White Egret. **1872** E. COUES *Key to N. Amer. Birds* 267 Genus *Ardea* Linnæus... Great White Egret, White Heron... *Egretta*... Little White Egret, Snowy Heron... *Candidissima.* **1939** *Florida* (Federal Writers' Project) I. 26 The handsome white egret, once nearly extinct, is now protected. **1957** D. A. BANNERMAN *Birds Brit. Isles* VI. 68 The great white egret, though included in the genus *Egretta*, is in habit more like the grey heron and the purple heron and less like the egrets. **1770** J. R. FORSTER tr. *Kalm's Trav. N. Amer.* I. 67 *Ulmus Americana*, the *white elm. **1860** *Trans. Illinois Agric. Soc.* IV. 451 The White Elm.. is not good timber—is hard to split. **1948** *N.W. Ohio Q.* Winter 10 It was made of a strip of white elm bark about one foot wide. **1981** *Sci. Amer.* Aug. 40/3 Most European elms, including the European white elm (*U. laevis*), the Englsh elm (*U. procera*) and the varioius cultivars of the species *U. carpinifolia* are also susceptible. **1800** tr. *Lagrange's Chem.* II. 67 To make *white enamel, a hundred parts of lead and thirty of tin are generally calcined .. and.. mixed with a hundred parts of sand and twenty of potash:.. the result is a milky white opake glass, called White Enamel. **1839** DE LA BECHE *Rep. Geol. Cornwall*, etc. vi. 180 Plates of black mica and crystals of *white felspar. **1939** STEDMAN *Med. Dict.* (ed. 14) 1231/2 **White fingers*, an occupational disease occurring in operators of pneumatic hammers who are exposed to cold, affecting usually the fingers of the left hand. **1947** [see PNEUMATIC *a.* (*sb.*) 1 a]. **1971** *New Scientist* 15 Apr. 154/3 Researchers have found bone softening in chain saw operators and there is also the 'white fingers' complaint, with fingers going cold and numb. **1973** [see RAYNAUD]. **1978** *Kingston* (Ontario) *Whig-Standard* 18 July 15/2 Regular users of chain saws, grinders, and pneumatic hammers, drills and chisels often develop a condition called 'white finger' disease. **1850** A. J. ALLEN *Ten Years in Oregon* v. 52 They found the red and *white fir, spoken of by Clark and Lewis. **1897**, **1913** [see *grand fir* s.v. GRAND *a.* 12]. **1948** *Pacific Discovery* Mar. 7/2 Sequoias become established most easily.. on cool north and east slopes with sugar pine and white fir. **1900** *Technical Ser. Div. Entomol., U.S. Dept. Agric.* No. 8 10 The minute '*white-flies'.. may be flying around. **1925** A. D. IMMS *Gen. Textbk. Entomol.* 360 The 'white flies' are a much neglected group. **1946** *Nature* 14 Dec. 852/1 A few [gall midges] are carnivorous, preying upon.. white-flies, other gall midges and the like. **1981** *Farmstead Mag.* Winter 35/3 Mites, aphids and whiteflies sometimes bother green-house cukes, but don't let this panic you into using a chemical spray. **1578** LYTE *Dodoens* I. lix. 86 Wilde Tansie.. preuayleth.. agaynst the *white floud, or issue of floures. **1696** in H. Kelsey *Papers* (1929) 54 They [*sc.* Indians] brought nothing but 2 *white fox skins. **1774** GOLDSM. *Nat. Hist.* (1776) III. 333 The fur of the white fox is held in no great estimation. **1862** *Canad. Naturalist* May 138 White foxes have been killed on the south shore of Great Slave Lake. **1926** *Daily Colonist* (Victoria, B.C.) 22 July 19/6 The average price for white fox was $34.85. **1930** R. W. SERVICE *Coll. Verse* 269 Fur had they, white fox, marten, mink, to trade. **1969** *Beaver* (Winnipeg) Summer 10/2 The white fox is the principal source of fur income at Rankin [Inlet] as elsewhere. **1678** RAY *Willughby's Ornith.* 176 The *white Game, erroneously called the white Partridge, *Lagopus avis*. **1886** *Buck's Handbk. Med. Sci.* III. 300/2 '*White' Gangrene seems to be simply a moist gangrene.. in which there is a serous exudate. **1877** C. HALLOCK *Sportman's Gazetteer* 40 The *White Goat is confined to the loftiest peaks of the Rocky Mountains. **1936** D. MCCOWAN *Animals Canad. Rockies* xiv. 122 A full grown male White goat has a body length of about five feet, stands approximately forty inches high at the shoulder and is from two hundred to two hundred and fifty pounds in weight. **1846–7** THOREAU *Walden* (1957) 114 The red pine and the black ash, the *white grape and the yellow violet. **1780** YOUNG *Tour Irel.* I. 382 Rye grass (*lolium perenne*) and *white grass (*holcus lanatus*) do well. **1891** *Cent. Dict.* s.v. *Leersia*, Three species occur in the United States, and are known as white-grass, especially *L. Virginica.* **1797** BEWICK *British Birds* I. 303 *White Grouse. *a* **1817** T. DWIGHT *Trav. New Eng.*, etc. (1821) I. 77 The *white-grub has.. extensively injured meadows and pastures. **1551** TURNER *Herbal* I. I v, The leues also broken in oyle are good for the *whyte hawe, or the perle in the eye. **1624**, etc. *White heron [see HERON, HERN 1 b]. **1813** A. WILSON *Amer. Ornithol.* VII. 106 The opportunities which I have.. had, of observing them with the train.. from its first appearance to its full growth, satisfies me that the Great White Heron with, and that without the long plumes are one and the same species, in different periods of age. **1846**, etc. [see KOTUKU]. **1917** *Auk* XXXIV. 86 The Great White Heron is of more social habits than the Blue Heron. **1939** *Florida* (Federal Writers' Project) I. 26 The great white heron, a Florida native, nests on the keys. **1957** D. A. BANNERMAN *Birds Brit. Isles* VI. 71 The great white heron is.. very rare in North Africa in winter west of Egyptian territory. **1964** A. L. THOMSON *New Dict. Birds* 367/2 The Great White Heron *A*[*rdea*] '*occidentalis*' of Florida.. may be no more than a local population of a colour phase. **1966** *Encycl. N.Z.* I. 209/1 Swamp and lake-edge birds include the rare white heron ..(*Egretta alba*). **1966** P. SHERLOCK *West Indian Folk-Tales* 57 A flock of white herons flew across the river. **1857** MILLER *Elem. Chem., Org.* (1862) i. §3. 61 Blue indigo, under the combined action of protoxide of iron and alkalies, becomes converted into *white indigo. **1896** CHESTER *Dict. Names Min.*, **White iron ore*, an early name for siderite. *Ibid.*, **White iron pyrites*, a popular name for marcasite. **1526** in *Househ. Ord.* (1790) 162 One torch, one pricket, two sises, one pound of *white lights, ten talshides, eight faggotts. **1610** *Ibid.* 335 Halfe a pounde of white lightes.. per diem. **1731** MILLER *Gard. Dict.* 5 A b, The *White Lilac, or Pipe-Tree. **1882** *Garden* 6 May 317/2 A large bunch of white Lilac. **1774** in *Rep. Bd. Trustees Publ. Archives Nova Scotia* (1945) 34 This town.. affords a great store of fine timber.. white and black ash; *white mapple; rock mapple. **1832** D. J. BROWNE *Sylva Amer.* 101 The white maple puts forth green and yellow flowers early in the spring. **1916** E. T. SETON *Woodcraft Man.* 291 Silver Maple, White or Soft Maple.. usually a little smaller than the Sugar Maple. **1981** *Publ. Amer. Dial. Soc.* LXVII. 37 Sugar maple... All of the Iron Range respondents [in Minnesota] use the generic *maple*... On the Mesabi single instances of *soft maple*, *sugar maple*, and *white maple* are recorded. *c* **1440** *Promp. Parv.* 525/2 *Whyte marbulle, *carnium*. **1849** BURKE *Landed Gentry* III. 27/2 The splendid mausoleum.. was magnificently sculptured in white marble. **1839–47** *Todd's Cycl. Anat.* III. 695 A convolution [of the brain] consists of a fold of grey matter, enclosing a process of *white or fibrous matter. **1869** HUXLEY *Elem. Physiol.* (ed. 3) vi. 299 In the medulla oblongata,.. [as] in the spinal cord.. the white matter is external, and the grey internal. But, in the cerebellum and cerebral hemispheres, the grey matter is external and the white internal. **1613** in *Papers rel. Scots in Poland* (1915) 71 A *white metal cup. **1710** N. BLUNDELL *Diary* (1895) 86 We went to see y^m make White-Mettle Muggs. **1879** H. PHILLIPS *Addit. Notes upon Coins* 8 A number of medals in white metal and copper. **1884** LOCK *Workshop Rec.* Ser. III. 40/2 The term 'white metal' is applied to all alloys in which zinc, tin, or lead is in sufficient proportion to impart a white colour. **1482** *Cely Papers* (Camden) 116 The goldys and *whyte mony.. as they were corrant. **1593** GREENE *3rd Pt. Art Cony Catching* C 3, There was seuen pound in Golde, beside thirty shillings and odde white money. **1611** COTGR. s.v. *Blanc*, *Monnoye blanche*, white money; coyne of brasse, or copper, siluered ouer. **1696** *Lond. Gaz.* No. 3162/4 Where all Persons may be Accommodated with any of their sorts for white Money, either Half-Crowns, Shillings, or Sixpences. *a* **1700** EVELYN *Diary* 9 Mar. 1664, The fine new mill'd coin both of white money and guineas. **1809** BAWDWEN *Domesday Bk.* 405

Rutland pays to the King one hundred and fifty pounds white money. **1820** *Blackw. Mag.* May 158 My hand has nae been crossed with white money but ance these seven blessed days. **1610** *True Decl. Estate of Virginia* 55 There are innumerable *White Mulberry trees. **1737** J. WESLEY *Jrnl.* 2 Dec. (1910) I. 402 The white mulberry is not good to eat. **1850** [see MULBERRY 1]. **1957** M. HADFIELD *Brit. Trees* 248 The white mulberry..(so called from its white or pinkish, insipid fruit), is cultivated as the principal food plant of the caterpillar of the silkworm moth. **1975** E. WIGGINTON *Foxfire 3* 276 Dried white mulberries were used as a substitute for raisins or figs. **1868** DANA *Min.* (ed. 5) 70 Chloanthite;..*White Nickel. **1896** CHESTER *Dict. Names Min.* 287 *White nickel.* A syn. of both rammelsbergite and chloanthite. **1634** *White oak [see *red oak* s.v. RED *a.* 17d]. **1770** J. R. FORSTER tr. *Kalm's Trav. N. Amer.* I. 65 *Quercus alba*, the white oak. **1873** 'MARK TWAIN' & WARNER *Gilded Age* xvii. 163 You kin git all the rails you want outen my white-oak timber over thar. **1883** J. MACAULAY *Grey Hawk* iii. 44 The banks on both sides are covered with poplar and white oak and other trees, which grow to a considerable size. **1930** W. FAULKNER *As I lay Dying* 132 Tull take and cut them two big whiteoaks. **1941** *Sun* (Baltimore) 12 Aug. 17/2 They had in storage enough Dorchester county white oak to construct keels and frames. **1975** White oak [see *pin oak* s.v. PIN *sb.*[1] 18]. **1721** BAILEY, **White oakham*, a sort of Tow or Flax to drive into the Seams of Ships. **1913** V. B. LEWES *Oil Fuel* 38 In some parts of the world small deposits of what are called '*white oil' are..found. **1919** *Electric Jrnl.* XVI. 336/2 Lectroseal transformer oil and white oil of paraffin have marked absorption. **1925** A. B. THOMPSON *Oil-Field Explor. & Development* I. xi. 504 The so-called 'white' oils occasionally encountered in oil-fields are usually transparent and amber or sherry tinted, and are evidently filtration products of darker varieties commonly found in the neighbourhood. **1938** F. M. ARCHIBALD in A. E. Dunstan et al. *Sci. of Petroleum* IV. 2838/1 Petrolatum liquidum is the highest grade of white oil. **1977** *Lubricants Business* (Shell Internat. Petroleum Co.) 4 Technical and medicinal white oils are also important. **1674** tr. *Scheffer's Lapland* 138 No bird abounds there more then the *white Partridge. **1678** White partridge [see *white game* above]. **1747** G. EDWARDS *Nat. Hist. Birds* II. 72. **1775** A. BURNABY *Trav. N. Amer.* 15 These waters are stored with incredible quantities of fish, such as sheeps-heads, rock-fish, drums, *white perch. **1844** *Amer. Jrnl. Sci.* XLVII. 58 *Labrax mucronatus*, Cuv., White Perch. **1851** T. A. BURKE *Polly Peablossom's Wedding* 129 The trout and white perch bit beautifully. **1949** *Sat. Even. Post* 12 Mar. 46/4 About the best fun was going out to the pond after white perch. **1849** H. WATTS tr. *Gmelin's Hand-bk. Chem.* II. v. 107 Phosphorus, kept under water...gradually becomes covered with an opaque crust which..afterwards turns white... This *white phosphorus retains its original appearance when dried over oil of vitriol. **1865** *Chem. News* 24 Nov. 251/1 He establishes that white phosphorus is neither a hydrate nor an allotropic state of ordinary phosphorus...but that it is, in fact, merely ordinary phosphorus irregularly corroded on the surface by the action of air dissolved in the water. **1884** FRANKLAND & JAPP *Inorg. Chem.* xxx. 371 Amorphous phosphorus, prepared by any of the above methods, invariably contains a small quantity of white phosphorus, the presence of which renders the product dangerously inflammable. **1976** *New Yorker* 15 Mar. 80/3 Two white-phosphorus rounds were exploded over the landing zone to indicate the 'all clear'. **1530** PALSGR. 288/2 *White plome, *prune blanche.* **1696** PLUKENET *Almagestum* Opera 1769 II. 306 Prunus Sylvestris cortice albicante,..White Plumme Barbadensibus dicta. **1774** in J. L. Peyton *Adventures my Grandfather* (1867) 127 The forest of Kentucky consists of yellow and *white poplar, walnut, [etc.]. **1814** F. PURSH *Flora Americæ Septentrionalis* II. 383 *Liriodendron..* generally known by the name of Tulip-tree, or White and Yellow Poplar. **1908** C. MAIR *Through Mackenzie Basin* 81 It was well timbered..with the finest white poplar I had yet seen. **1954** H. EVANS *Mist on River* 19 The wide and sunny freedom of his valley, with birches and white poplars between the belts of jackpine. **1613** BEAUM. & FL. *Honest Man's Fort.* II. i, That you were kil'd with a Pistoll charg'd with *white Powder. **1689** N. LEE *Princess of Cleve* II. ii, A Secret Lover's like a Gun charg'd with White Powder, does Execution but makes no noise. **1825** *Phil. Mag.* LXV. 227 With common salt I obtained the same results, mercury remaining, and *white precipitate being thrown down from the solutions, by liquid ammonia. **1887** *Buck's Handbk. Med. Sci.* IV. 743/2 Mercurammonic Chloride, NH_2HgCl. This salt, commonly known as white precipitate, is officinal in the U.S. **1923** J. W. MELLOR *Comprehensive Treat. Inorg. & Theoret. Chem.* IV. xxxi. 786 Conversely, infusible white precipitate is converted back to fusible white precipitate by the action of a soln. of ammonium chloride in liquid ammonia. **1956** J. S. ANDERSON tr. *Remy's Treat. Inorg. Chem.* II. ix. 474 The most important example of an ammonia addition compound is the 'fusible white precipitate', and important examples of mercury-substituted ammonia or ammonium derivatives are the 'infusible white precipitate' and 'Millon's base'. **1769** MRS. RAFFALD *Engl. Housekpr.* (1778) 213 To make *White Raspberry Jam. **1838** W. C. HARRIS *Narr. Exped. S. Afr.* xix. 184 A pair of *white Rhinoceroses opposed our descent. **1941** J. S. HUXLEY *Uniqueness of Man* viii. 184 The numerous creatures which would have become extinct but for vigorous protection..such as the..white rhinoceros. **1972** *Islander* (Victoria, B.C.) 9 July 2/3 In South Africa the white rhino has increased from 20 to 2,000. **1981** P. TURNBULL *Deep & Crisp & Even* vii. 125 He stuck out like a white rhino at a tea party. **1885** GEIKIE *Text-bk. Geol.* IV. viii. §2. 560 Microscopical examination shows that this '*white-rock' or 'white-trap' is merely an altered form of some diabasic or basaltic rock. **1712** *Phil. Trans.* XXVII. 542 A blewish Bat, in which the following Iron-Stone lyes, called the *White-Row. *Ibid.*, A hard blackish Iron Oar, lying in small Nodules, having between them a White Substance; and from thence by the Miners called the White-Row-Grains. **1875** KNIGHT *Dict. Mech.*, **White-rubber*, caoutchouc mixed with..any white pigment [so] as to give a dead white color to it. **1887** MOLONEY *Forestry W. Afr.* 90 The white-rubber vine..grows in profusion in this part of the country. [**1668** *White sapphire: see SAPPHIRE 1 b.] **1884** E. W. STREETER *Precious Stones & Gems* (ed. 4) III. ii. 160 The varieties of Precious Corundum ascertained to exist in the Burmese dominions are the Oriental Sapphire..the Oriental Ruby..the Opalescent Ruby, the Star Ruby, the Green, the Yellow, and the White Sapphires, and the Oriental Amethyst. **1904** L. J. SPENCER tr. *Bauer's Precious Stones* III. 566 Zircon and corundum ('white sapphire'). **1942** B. W. ANDERSON *Gem Testing for Jewellers* ix. 88 Perfectly colourless corundum, usually referred to as 'White Sapphire', is not common in nature... Synthetic corundum ..is, however, manufactured on a large scale. **1744** W. ELLIS *Mod. Husbandman* Jan. xii. 79 He lost several of his Flock by the Gripes and the *White-scour. **1897** W. HOUSMAN *Cattle* viii. 251 Inflammation of the stomach and bowels [of calves] ..is also commonly spoken of as 'white scour'. **1963** *Times* 17 May 5/7 (Advt.), Today the vet can control mortality from diseases like white scours. **1859** P. P. CARPENTER in *Rep. Smithsonian Inst.* (1860) 203 The *White Slipper [limpet] is known..by its shaggy light-green skin. **1523–34** FITZHERB. *Husb.* §54 *White snailes be yll for shepe in pastures. **1881** E. INGERSOLL *Oyster-Industry* 250 *White-snails*, small species of mollusks noxious to the oyster-beds, particularly Urosalpinx and Natica. **1854** *White softening [see SOFTENING *vbl. sb.* 1 b]. **1873** T. H. GREEN *Introd. Pathol.* 41 White Softening..is [mostly] a chronic condition, dependent upon disease of the capillaries and small arteries, which interferes with the circulation... There is no hyperæmia, and the colour either resembles that of healthy brain-tissue, or is an opaque dirty white. **1920** *Chem. Abstr.* XIV. 3786 Eight samples of light, medium and heavy types of petroleum distillate (*white spirit) were examd. and compared with turpentine as to boiling range. **1977** *Reader's Digest Bk. Do-It-Yourself Skills & Techniques* 11/2 For cleaning out oil-based paints, wash the brush in white spirit. **1770** G. CARTWRIGHT *Jrnl.* 27 Aug. (1792) I. 30 About four miles above, are several small low islands, on which grow many fine *white, and black spruces. **1832** [see SPRUCE *sb.* 4 b]. **1949** *Sat. Even. Post* 12 Mar. 50/3 Banks.. were covered with a growth of fir and white spruce. **1968** R. KROETSCH *Alberta* IV. 164 Heavy stands of white spruce grow on the islands in Astotin Lake—the kind of spruce that covered much of the vicinity perhaps five hundred years ago. **1977** *New Yorker* 9 May 95/1 He thought that white spruce and other species could live farther north. **1801** *White steenbras [see STEENBRAS]. **1905** [see *mussel-cracker* s.v. MUSSEL *sb.* 4]. **1959** [see *foul-hooked* s.v. FOUL *adv.* 6]. **1974** *Stand. Encycl. S. Afr.* X. 263/2 White steenbras... One of the best-known angling-fishes in Southern Africa. **1792** PENNANT *Arctic Zool.* II. 157 *White Stork... primaries black: the rest of the plumage white. **1513** *Act 5 Hen. VIII* c. 2 Where..Clothes called *White Straytes be.. made within the seid Countie [of Devon]. **1672** MANLEY *Cowel's Interpr.*, *White Straits*, a kind of course Cloth made in Devonshire, about a yard and half a quarter broad, raw. *c* **1430** *Two Cookery-bks.* 7 Take *whyte sugre an caste þer-to. **1562** TURNER *Herbal* II. 106 Take the water & put white sugar vnto it. **1772** D. MACBRIDE *Meth. Introd. Physic* 194 Watery tumour of a joint, usually termed *White-swelling. **1610** HOLLAND *Camden's Brit.* I. 185 *White tinne, that is molten into mettall. **1706** [see TIN *sb.* 1 b]. **1902** A. FINDLAY tr. *Ostwald's Princ. Inorg. Chem.* xli. 720 Besides the ordinary white tin, a grey form is also known which has a much smaller density. **1944** C. PALACHE et al. *Dana's Syst. Min.* (ed. 7) I. 127 Solid white tin (β-tin) by contact with gray tin (α-tin), alters to a gray powder ('tin plague'). **1950**, **1965** [see *grey tin* s.v. GREY, GRAY *a.* 8 c]. **1973** J. J. LAGOWKSI *Mod. Inorg. Chem.* xi. 334 (*caption*) Each atom in white tin is surrounded by six other atoms arranged in a distorted octahedral structure. **1843** R. J. GRAVES *Syst. Clin. Med.* xxviii. 361 The vitality of the *white tissues is low. **1863** BATES *Nat. Amazons* ii. (1864) 38 Other grand forest-trees.. were the Moira-tinga (the *White or King tree)—probably the same as, or allied to, the Mora Excelsa..in British Guiana [etc.]. **1866** *Treas. Bot.*, White-tree, *Melaleuca Leucadendron.* *c* **1640** J. SMYTH *Hund. Berkeley* (1885) 319 The Salmon, *wheat trout or suen. **1542** ELYOT *Dict.*, *Amomum*,..the leaues be lyke to the leaues of Withwynde or *whyte vyne. **1598** [see BRYONY 1]. **1607** TOPSELL *Four-f. Beasts* 188 Burne them with twigs of white vines. **1866** *Treas. Bot.* 1217/1 Vine, White, *Clematis Vitalba.* **1743** J. CLAYTON *Flora Virginia* 190 *Juglans alba...* *White Walnuts. **1822** J. WOODS *Two Years' Residence Eng. Prairie* 228 White-walnut, or butter-nut, and black-walnut, are not so good as the English walnut. **1916** E. T. SETON *Woodcraft Man.* 275 White Walnut, Oil Nut, or Butternut..rarely 100 feet high. **1958** G. A. PETRIDES *Field Guide Trees & Shrubs* 86 Butternut..also known as White Walnut, wood lighter in colour than that of its more valuable relative. **1545** *White wax [see WAX *sb.*[1] 2 c]. **1567** *Gude & Godlie B.* (S.T.S.) 176 With bullis of leid, quhyte wax and reid, And vther quhylis with grene. **1815** KIRBY & SP. *Entomol.* x. (1818) I. 329 The wax (called *Pe-la*, white wax, because so by nature) begins to appear about the middle of June. **1697** H. KELSEY *Jrnl.* 6–7 July in *Papers* (1929) 88, 2 hands..brought news of a *white whale drove a shore. **1834** DEWHURST *Cetacea* 190 *Delphinapterus Beluga*, or the White Whale. **1923** *Beaver* June 340/2 Indian reports were received that porpoises, or white whales, were..making excursions..up a certain creek. **1978** *Weekend Mag.* (Toronto) 22 July 16/1 White whales or belugas..become progressively lighter with age. **1985** *Times* 6 Mar. 8/4 Soviet seaman trying to save a large pod of white whales..trapped in the ice. **1523–34** FITZHERB. *Husb.* §34 *Whyte wheate is lyke polerde wheate..but it hath anis, and..wyll make white breed; and in Essex they call flaxen wheate whyte wheate. **1805** R. W. DICKSON *Pract. Agric.* I. 540 Among the numerous varieties of.. wheat, the white and the red are the most esteemed in general. **1463–4** *Rolls Parlt.* V. 507/1 Cardes for Wolle, or *Whitewyre. **1587** MASCALL *Cattle, Hogges* (1596) 274 Some doe ring them [*sc.* hogs] with red wyar..Others doe put rings of yron, some with horse nailes or strong white wyar, in the groine of their snoutes. **1678** *Lond. Gaz.* No. 1302/1 It is Enacted..That no Iron Threed (commonly called White Wyer) nor Cards for Wooll, nor Card-Wyer, nor Iron-Wyer for making of Wooll-Cards, shall be Imported. **1765** *Newton* (Lincs.) *Enclosure Act* 13 Ash or other *white wood rails. **1812** P. GRAHAM *Agric. Surv. Stirling.* 40 The oaks are almost entire; the white wood, as it is called, or the outermost circles of the tree, only are decayed. **1825** J. NICHOLSON *Oper. Mech.* 348 The workman breaks these pieces of pots on his anvil, and mixes the pieces with charcoal of white wood. **1883** J. G. WOOD in *Longman's Mag.* Dec. 169 The terrible larva of the cockchafer, called, *par excellence, the* Grub, and sometimes known as the *White Worm.

e. Miscellaneous: **White Africa**, the white inhabitants of Africa; the parts of Africa ruled by white people; **white ale**, a Devonshire drink made of ale with flour, milk, and other ingredients (see *Eng. Dial. Dict.*); **White Army**, any of the armies which opposed the Bolsheviks during the Russian Civil War (1918–21); also, a group which opposed the Red Guards in Finland in 1918; **White Australia**, used *attrib.* and *absol.* to designate a policy of restricting immigration into Australia to white people; **white backlash**, resentment felt by white people against demands made by, or concessions made to, Black people; hence **white backlasher**; **white baker**, † (*a*) a baker of white bread (also as one word); (*b*) a name for the spotted flycatcher; **white bath**, (*a*) an emulsion of oil and alkaline carbonates used in dyeing; (*b*) a name for white-flowered species of *Trillium*; **white bonnet** [BONNET *sb.* 8], a fictitious bidder at an auction; **white book** [tr. med.L. *liber albus*; cf. ALBUM], a book of official records or reports bound in white; *spec.* (with capital initials) the book first published in 1882 as *Annual Chancery Practice* and now entitled *Supreme Court Practice*; † **white broth**, some kind of broth of a white or light colour (see also BROTH *sb.* 3); **white cane** = WHITE STICK 3; **white chauvinism** orig. *U.S.*, a white person's excessively high regard for his own race; so **white chauvinist**; **white Christmas**, a snowy Christmas; **white coal** (see quot. 1913); more commonly, flowing water as a source of energy; also, electricity; cf. *white fuel* (a) below; † **white colours** = *white flag* (a); **white cooper** (see COOPER *sb.*[1] 1); **white death** [after *black death*], a name for tuberculosis (? as specially a disease of white men); **white dominion**, a dominion (sense 2 b) in which the majority of the inhabitants are white; **white dwarf** *Astr.*, a small, faint, very dense star (usu. but not necessarily white in colour) lying below the main sequence, and representing the stable phase assumed by stars having less than 1·4 solar masses when their nuclear reactions cease; (not regarded as a type of dwarf: see quot. 1978 and cf. DWARF *sb.* 2 b); **white elephant**: see ELEPHANT 2; **white embroidery**, white-thread embroidery on a white ground; = *white work* below; **White English**, term occas. used in contrast to Black English, in the sense 'the English of white speakers'; **white ensign** (see ENSIGN *sb.* 5); **White Father**, (*a*) a white man regarded as protecting or controlling people of another race; (*b*) [tr. F. *Père Blanc*], a member of the Society of Missionaries of Africa, a Roman Catholic order founded in Algiers in 1868; **whitefellow**, applied by Australian natives to a white man, in contradistinction to *blackfellow*; **white flag**, (*a*) a flag of a white colour displayed in token of peaceful or friendly intention, desire for parley (= *flag of truce*, FLAG *sb.*[4] 1 b), or surrender; (*b*) the national flag of France before the Revolution (see 6 b); (*c*) used *attrib.* (with capital initials) to designate a communist group active in Burma since 1946; **white flight** chiefly *U.S.*, the migration of white people from inner-city areas (esp. those with a large black population) to the suburbs; **white flux**, (*a*) leucorrhœa; (*b*) see FLUX *sb.* 11, quot. 1826; † **white-folding**, some kind of cloth; **white folk(s)**, **white-folk(s)**, applied by U.S. Blacks to white people; **white frost**, hoar-frost; **white fuel**, (*a*) flowing water as a source of power; cf. *white coal* above; (*b*) lead-free petrol; **white goods**, (*a*) domestic linens, as sheets, towels, etc. (now not necessarily white); (*b*) electrical goods that are conventionally white, such as washing machines and refrigerators; **White Guard, Guardist**, (*a*) a member of a force which fought for the Finnish government against left-wing insurgents in the civil war of 1918; (*b*) a member of a counter-revolutionary force in Russia during the civil war of 1918–21; also *transf.*; **white hass, hawse**, *Sc.* = *white pudding* (a); **white hen**, *fig.* in proverbial phr. ***a white hen's chick***, etc. applied to a fortunate person or thing (cf. sense 8); **White Highlands**, an area in western Kenya formerly (1904–59) reserved for Europeans; hence **White Highlander**; **white hole** *Astr.* [opp. *black hole*], a celestial object which expands outwards from a space-time singularity emitting energy, in the manner of a time-reversed black hole; **white hope**, orig., a white boxer who might beat Jack Johnson, the first Black to be world heavyweight champion

(1908–15); hence, a person who, or a thing which, it is hoped will achieve much or on whom or which hopes are centred; **White Hun**, a member of a nomadic people of uncertain origin, also called Ephthalites or Hephtalites, who lived in Bactria in the fifth and sixth centuries A.D.; **white hunter**, a white man who hunts big game professionally; **white jazz**, jazz as played by white musicians; **white joint** (see quot.); † **white joke**, name of some dance; **white knight**, (*a*) (with allusion to a character in *Through the Looking-Glass*), an enthusiastic but ineffectual person; (*b*) a hero or champion; *spec.* (*Stock Exchange slang*) a company that comes to the aid of one facing an unwelcome take-over bid; **White Lady**, (*a*) a cocktail made of two parts of dry gin, one of orange liqueur, and one of lemon juice; (*b*) *Austral. slang*, a drink of methylated spirits, sometimes mixed with another ingredient; **white land** *slang*, open land that is not designated for development or change of use, or on which development is not allowed (so called from its being uncoloured on planning maps); **white leach** (see LEACH *sb.*[1] 2); **white letter** *Printing* [LETTER *sb.*[1] 2b], an occasional name for the (now) ordinary or 'roman' style of type, as distinct from BLACK-LETTER; **white level** *Television*, the signal level corresponding to the maximum brightness in transmitted pictures; **white lie**, (*a*) see 7b and LIE *sb.*[1] 1b; (*b*) see quot.; **white lightning** *slang* (orig. *U.S.*), (*a*) inferior or illicitly distilled whisky; (*b*) a kind of LSD; **white list** *colloq.* [after BLACK LIST], a list of people or things considered acceptable; **white-loose** (see quot.); † **white mark** = WHITE *sb.* 6; **white market** [after BLACK MARKET], authorized dealing in things that are rationed or of which the supply is otherwise restricted; **white mass** (see quot.); **white meter**, a meter that registers off-peak consumption of electricity; † **White Moors**, a nickname for the Genoese; **white mouse**, (*a*) an albino variety or fancy breed of the common house mouse; (*b*) a name for the collared lemming, *Cuniculus torquatus*, also called *snow-mouse*; (*c*) *fig.* applied to a person of mean or despicable character; **white mule** *U.S. slang*, a potent colourless alcoholic drink; *spec.* illicitly distilled whisky; **white Negro**, (*a*) a Negro, or a person with Negro ancestry, who has a pale or albino complexion; (*b*) a white person who defends the rights or interests of Negroes, or identifies with them; (*c*) *nonce-use* (see quot. 1949); **white nigger** *slang* (chiefly *U.S.*), (*a*) a derogatory term for a white person who does menial labour; (*b*) a Negro who is regarded as deferring to white people or accepting a role prescribed by them; (*c*) (see quot. 1970); **white night**, (*a*) (tr. F. *nuit blanche*), a sleepless night; (*b*) a night when it is never properly dark, as in high latitudes in summer; **white note** *Mus.*, (*a*) a note with an open head, as a semibreve or minim (opp. to *black note*); (*b*) a note corresponding to a white key on a keyboard; = NATURAL *sb.* 7a; **white paper**, (*a*) paper of a white colour (also *fig.*); (*b*) *techn.* blank paper, not written or printed upon; (*c*) an official document printed on white paper; *spec.* (with capital initials) before 1940, an Order Paper of the House of Commons which was a corrected and revised version of one issued earlier the same day (a Blue Paper); (*d*) (with capital initials) a government publication presented to Parliament and having white covers rather than blue ones (usu. less bulky than those with blue covers); *esp.* one outlining proposed legislation or stating policy; also *transf.*; ***White Paper candidate*** Naval slang (see quot. 1962); **white plague**, tuberculosis; cf. *white death*, *scourge*; **white port**, port wine made from white grapes; **white post** (*Paper-making*), see POST *sb.*[5] 1; **whitepox** [see quot. 1972], epithet of a pox-virus isolated from monkeys that is very similar to the smallpox virus; **white-print**, a document printed in white on a dark ground; **white pudding**, (*a*) a kind of sausage made of oatmeal and suet (cf. BLACK PUDDING and PUDDING *sb.* 1); (*b*) 'a pudding made of milk, eggs, flour, and butter' (*Cent. Dict.*); **white rabbit**, **White Rabbit**, used with allusion to the White Rabbit in Lewis Carroll's *Alice's Adventures in Wonderland* (1865), who was running because he was in danger of being late; also as *adj.* and *adv. phr.*; **white racism**, belief in the superiority of the white race, leading to antagonism towards people of other races; hence **white racist** *a.* and *sb.*; **White Rajah**, any of the three Rajahs belonging to the English family of Brooke who ruled Sarawak between 1841 and 1941; also *transf.*; **white rent** (*obs.* exc. *Hist.*), rent payable in silver money (see sense 2b, and cf. BLACK MAIL *sb.* 3); *spec.* in Devon and Cornwall, a rent or duty of eight pence a year payable by every tinner to the Duke of Cornwall; **white ribboner**, one who wears a white ribbon as a badge of temperance; a teetotaller; **white rod** = WHITE STAFF; **white room**, a clean and dust-free room used for the assembly, repair, or storage of spacecraft or delicate mechanisms; **white rose**, the emblem, and hence (with capitals) a designation, of the House of York in the Wars of the Roses (see ROSE *sb.* 6); also adopted by the Jacobites in the 18th c.; **white rot**, any of several fungal diseases of wood or living plants indicated by white patches of decay or mould (see also ROT *sb.*[1] 2c); **white rum**, a colourless variety of rum; **white rust**, (*a*) a fungus disease of certain plants indicated by white blisters on leaves or stems, esp. one caused by *Albugo candida* affecting cruciferous plants or one caused by *Puccinia horiana* affecting chrysanthemums; (*b*) a white coating that forms on zinc in air, consisting of some or all of the oxide, hydroxide, and carbonate; **white sale**, a shop sale of white goods and household linen; **white scourge**, tuberculosis (cf. *white death* above); **white settler**, (*a*) a white inhabitant of a non-white territory; (*b*) *transf.* (see quot. 1976); **white-sewing** = *white-seam* (SEAM *sb.*[1] 9); **white sheet** (see SHEET *sb.*[1] 1c); **White Sister**, a nun wearing a white habit; *spec.* a member of the Congregation of the Missionary Sisters of Our Lady of Africa, founded in 1869 to assist the White Fathers, or of the Congregation of the Daughters of the Holy Ghost, founded in 1706 in Brittany; **white slave**, a white person (sense 4) who is, or is treated like, a slave (cf. SLAVE *sb.*[1] 3); *spec.* a prostitute, esp. one trapped into prostitution by others; also (with hyphen) as *v. trans.*, to sell or trap (a girl) into enforced prostitution, esp. abroad; so **white slaver**, **white slavery** (*spec.* in reference to prostitution); **white-slaving** *vbl. sb.*; † **white son**, a beloved or favourite son; a boy or man who is specially favoured or petted (see 9); **white soup**, soup made with white stock; **white squadron**, one of the three squadrons into which the Royal Navy was formerly divided; **white squall** (see SQUALL *sb.*[3] 1c); **white steep**, a process, or liquor, used in bleaching (see STEEP *sb.*[1] 1, 4, and cf. *grey steep* s.v. GREY *a.* 8); **white stock**, stock made with chicken, veal, or pork; **white stone**, **whitestone**, (*a*) in prov. phr. ***to mark with a white stone***, to reckon as specially fortunate or happy (in allusion to the use of a white stone among the ancients as a memorial of a fortunate event); (*b*) a colourless gemstone; (*c*) a form of rendering; **whitestone** *v. trans.*, to whiten with stone (cf. HEARTHSTONE *sb.* and *v.*); **white stuff** *slang* (chiefly *U.S.*), morphine, heroin, or cocaine (cf. WHITE *sb.* 15e); **White Sunday**, an etymologizing modification of WHIT SUNDAY; **white supremacism**, a doctrine or the practice of white supremacy; hence **white supremacist** *sb.* and *a.*; **white supremacy**, domination by white races over non-white, esp. Black, races; **white suprematist** *rare* = *white supremacist* sb. above; **White Terror** (see TERROR *sb.* 4); also *spec.* a similar period in Hungary in 1919–20 and in China in the years following 1927; **white tie**, *spec.* a man's white bow-tie worn with a black tailcoat; also *ellipt.*, a man's formal evening dress including a white tie; freq. *attrib.*; **white trash**: see TRASH *sb.*[1] 4; **white war**, war without bloodshed; economic warfare; **white ware**, white goods or stuff, *esp.* white earthenware; **white way** *U.S.* (usu. with capital initials), a brilliantly lit city street; *spec.* (usu. ***Great White Way***), the part of Broadway either side of Times Square, the heart of New York's theatre district, or a similar street in any other town; **whitewear** = *white goods* (*a*) above; **white wedding**, a wedding at which the bride wears a formal white dress; **white whisky**, colourless whisky; *spec.* (*N. Amer.*) home-made or illicit whisky; **white window**, a stained-glass window in grisaille (see GRISAILLE); **white wings** *fig.*, sails; † **white woman**, name for a 'female' ingredient in alchemy; **white work**, embroidery worked in white thread on a white ground.

1910 J. BUCHAN *Prester John* xxii. 353 The amnesty came ..and *white Africa drew breath again. **1974** A. WILLIAMS *Gentleman Traitor* i. 16 The armies and police forces of White Africa. **1743** *London & Country Brewer* III. 195 Devonshire *White-Ale. About 60 years ago this Drink was invented at or near..Plymouth. It is brewed from pale Malt. **1806** WOLCOT (P. Pindar) *Tristia* Wks. 1812 V. 341 Your birthplace Dodbrook deign'd to bless Famed for white ale. **1813** VANCOUVER *Agric. Devon* 390 The brewing of a liquor called white ale, is almost exclusively confined to the neighbourhood of Kingsbridge. **1879** *N. & Q.* 5th Ser. XI. 193/2. **1918** *Times* 9 Apr. 6/4, The *White Army..is overwhelmingly pro-German. **1960** O. MANNING *Great Fortune* II. 109 It makes you look like a White Army officer. **1977** J. CLEARY *High Road* iii. 95 He had come out of Russia, a cavalry commander in one of the White Armies. **1921** *Round Table* Mar. 314 The *White Australia policy—the determination to keep Australia white, a home for European races. **1930** W. K. HANCOCK *Australia* iv. 77 The policy of White Australia is the indispensable condition of every other Australian policy. **1979** *Guardian* 5 Jan. 7/2 Mr Gough Whitlam's Labour Government abolished the 'white Australia' policy five years ago. **1964** *Courier-Mail* (Brisbane) 29 July 2 Goldwater is no racist, but there's little doubt that his supporters hope to win votes from the '*white backlash', the so-far unmeasured resentment among many whites to some of the negro demonstrations and riots. **1974** *Spartanburg* (S. Carolina) *Herald* 25 Apr. C2/1 He said a serious white backlash had developed against aboriginal advancement programs. **1966** *Economist* 17 Sept. 1130/2 The result leaves '*white backlashers' little choice in November: Mr Peabody, a staunch liberal.., will oppose a Negro, Mr Edward Brooke, who has won the Republican senatorial nomination. **1968** *Listener* 7 Nov. 625/1 The spies converge on Shaefer, and the homely white-backlashers adroitly lay them flat. **1568** in W. H. Turner *Select. Rec. Oxford* (1880) 325 No baker, be he *white baker or browne baker. **1633** *Stow's Surv.* 624 The Company of White-Bakers..were a Company of this City in the first yeere of Edward the second. **1725** *Lond. Gaz.* No. 6379/5 Samuel Fryer,..Whitebaker. **1862** JOHNS *Brit. Birds* 625 White Baker, the Spotted Flycatcher. **1857** MILLER *Elem. Chem., Org.* (1862) xi. §2. 775 In this condition it [*sc.* the skin] is ready for the operation of tawing, or passing through the *white bath. **1891** *Cent. Dict.* s.v. *Trillium*, The white species [are known] as *wake-robin, white bath, birthroot.* **1735** in R. Bell *Treat. Conveyance Land* (1815) 168 This too common practice of employing *white-bonnets at roups was a manifest cheat. **1815** *Ibid.*, What is commonly called a white bonnet, that is, a person employed by the seller to raise the price, without any intention of buying for himself. **1866** CARLYLE *Remin.* (1881) I. 205 Hazlitt..was at the Fonthill Abbey sale..'hired to attend as a white bonnet there', said he with a laugh. **1437** *Cal. Anc. Rec. Dublin* (1889) 294 The *Whit Boke. **1891** *Times* 4 Feb. 5/3 Another Whitebook on East African affairs has been presented to the Reichstag. **1895** *Law Times* C. 3/1 The judge and Master Macdonell hunted through the White Book, and unearthed a rule sufficiently elastic. **1911** B. NIGHTINGALE *Ejected of 1662* II. 1027 The White Book of Preston gives the following. **1965** J. DEDHAM *Young Man's Guide to Law* xiii. 150 Great industry has to be employed in really absorbing the procedure of the courts both from the 'White Book' (the High Court practice) and the 'Green Book' (the County Court practice). **1982** I. H. JACOB *Supreme Court Pract.* I. p. vii, It may fairly be claimed that the year 1982 is the hundredth anniversary of the White Book. **1606** DEKKER *Seven Deadly Sins* D, Heere and there (like a Prune in *White-broth) is stucke a spruice, but a meere prating vnpractised Lawyers Clarke all in blacke. **1691** MRS. D'ANVERS *Academia* 8 So she..In White-broath, and Canary steeps him. **1973** *Times* 8 June 7/7 (Advt.), Nowadays it takes more than a *white cane to help blind people. **1980** D. MACKENZIE *Raven & Paperhangers* vi. 85 There's a special place for blind men. *And* you get a white cane. **1946** *Political Affairs* XXV. 935/2 The corrupting influence of *white chauvinism has operated to maintain the most harmful division in the ranks of American labor. **1951** W. Z. FOSTER *Outl. Polit. Hist. U.S.* xxxiv. 563 White chauvinism—race hatred—has been, and still is, a question of hard cash to the big capitalists and landowners of the United States. **1984** *Washington Post* 26 Feb. 10/1 White chauvinism in jazz writing has in large part replaced the tentative thrust toward 'ethnomusical' and socially aware analysis that were evident in the 60's and 70's. **1951** W. Z. FOSTER *Outl. Polit. Hist. U.S.* xxxiv. 563 Much of the race prejudice that does exist among the Latin American peoples ..is due to the corrupting attitudes of *white chauvinists (diplomats, tourists, and businessmen) from the United States. **1857** C. KINGSLEY *Two Years Ago* III. x. 305 We shall have a *white Christmas, I expect. Snow's coming. **1913** *Collier's* 13 Dec. 8 (*heading*) A white Christmas. **1942** I. BERLIN (*song-title*) White Christmas. **1976** *Weekend Echo* (Liverpool) 4–5 Dec. 1/2 The weather men say the big shiver could bring our first white Christmas for years. **1885** *Neepawa* (Manitoba) *Star* 21 Aug. 2/1 Nor should those intrusted with the people's money..embezzle..the least portion of that money, under colour of black coal or *white coal, ditch contracts, or any other pretext. **1913** WESTON & CREW *Pitman's Dict. Econ. & Banking Terms* 149 *White Coal*, a fanciful name given to a glacier in so far as it is a reservoir of force. **1916** *Edin. Rev.* Oct. 397 Envying the Italians the clear atmosphere their towns..enjoy through the use of 'white coal' in place of black. **1963** *Daily Tel.* 18 Sept. 14 All may not think electricity the best heating or cooking or even lighting agent. But it is the cleanest and simplest and deserves its title of 'white coal'. **1971** *Nat. Geographic* July 25/2 Many former waterfalls now slip submissively through penstocks and turbines, and this abundant 'white coal' has drastically altered the country's age-old fish-forest-and-farm economy. **1676** *North's Plutarch, Add. Lives* 84 Sebastian..commanded one of his Souldiers to hold up the *white colours at his Spears-end, in token of his surrendring. **1688** HOLME *Armoury* III. vii. 317/2 The *White Cooper and Barrel Cooper..are two distinct Trades. **1837** WHITTOCK, etc. *Bk. Trades* (1842) 162 (*Cooper*) The White-cooper makes all the wooden vessels required in household concerns, dairies, or private breweries. **1901** *Munsey's Mag.* XXV. 643/2 The '*white death', as this most fatal disease is called, does not seem to horrify us as it should. **1966** *Guardian* 6 Sept. 8/4 Assuming that the crumbling process would continue, Britain would be left with the '*white dominions'. **1973** C. CARRINGTON in

Kipling *Compl. Barrack-Room Ballads* 23 After..1871, there were no British regular troops in the new 'White Dominions'. **1977** A. Wilson *Strange Ride R. Kipling* v. 253 Canada was the white dominion that Kipling had known longest. **1924** *Monthly Notices R. Astron. Soc.* LXXXIV. 322 The *white dwarfs Sirius (*comes*) and O_2 Eridani. **1925** *Nature* 5 Dec. 834/1 Invoked to decide the truth of a suspicion of transcendently high density in the 'white dwarf' stars, it [*sc.* Einstein's theory of gravitation] has decided that in the companion of Sirius matter is compressed to the almost incredible density of a ton to the cubic inch. **1935** B. Russell *Relig. & Sci.* viii. 217 If none of these things happen first, we shall in any case be all destroyed when the sun explodes and becomes a cold white dwarf. **1969** *Listener* 2 Jan. 10/3 White dwarfs are stars like the Sun which have collapsed into a sphere the size of a planet. **1978** Pasachoff & Kutner *University Astron.* x. 283 Do not confuse the term 'white dwarf' with the term 'dwarf'. The former refers to the dead hulks of stars.., while the latter refers to normal stars on the main sequence. **1876** Geo. Eliot *Dan. Der.* II. iv. xxix. 223 Gwendolen..held a piece of *white embroidery which on examination would have shown many false stitches. **1931** A. K. Arthur *Embroidery Bk.* viii. 83 Bullion knots are frequently used in white embroidery. **1971** S. Levey *Discovering Embroidery of Nineteenth Cent.* 9 White embroidery flourished throughout the century. **1974** *Florida FL Reporter* XIII. 3/3 *Black English* origins are almost entirely, if not entirely, rooted in *White English* dialect usage. **1974** *Newslet. Amer. Dial. Soc.* Nov. 44 Intonation patterns of Black English were studied and compared with those occurring in White English and formal Black English. **1879** *Queen's Reg. H.M. Naval Service* 19 All Her Majesty's Ships of War in Commission shall bear a *White Ensign. **1835** C. F. Hoffman *Winter in West* I. 251 The unfortunate agent..was shot in the act of appealing to the Indians as their friend and 'father',—the reply being ..'We have no longer any *white father.' **1889** R. F. Clarke *Cardinal Lavigerie* I. iv. 100 The White Fathers—a name given to the Algerian missioners on account of their wearing the long white robe of the Arab. **1894** *Harper's Mag.* Sept. 516/2 The White Father has sent me. **1969** *Telegraph* (Brisbane) 18 Sept. 2/2 The people we detest are the 'White Fathers'—those who control our destiny. **1977** B. Lucas tr. *De Foucauld's Lett. from Desert* vii. 130 The Apostolic Prefect will probably tell him to spend a few days at Maison-Carrée, near Algiers, the mother-house of the White Fathers. **1832** *Whitefellow [see budgeree *a.*]. **1853** C. B. Hall in T. F. Bride *Lett. Vict. Pioneers* (1898) 218 My black boy..showed me three or four bodies, partially concealed by logs. There were numerous tracks of horses round about. He explained the occurrence in his way—'I believe blackfellow bimbulalee sheep all about. Then whitefellow gilbert and put 'em along o' fire.' **1870** J. O. Tucker *Mute* 52 The natives, believing him to be the Spirit of their deceased King, welcomed him with every demonstration of joy; hence the well-known expression 'Go down blackfellow, come up whitefellow'. **1600** Holland *Livy* xxx. 765 There met him a ship of the Carthaginians, garnished with..*white flags of peace. **1695** *Lond. Gaz.* No. 3101/2 The Enemy hung out a White Flag, and desired a Parley. **1815** *Ann. Reg., Gen. Hist.* 129 A white flag was hung out as a signal that the troops..had surrendered. **1949** *New Statesman* 12 Feb. 147/1 The story begins last March. Then the Communists (White and Red Flag), who had already gone underground, began guerilla warfare on Government treasuries. **1959** *Listener* 18 June 1051/1 The so-called White Flag Communists who followed the Stalinist line. **1974** White Flag [see red flag 3 a]. **1967** *New Republic* 22 July 19/2 School quality is a far more important factor than racial feeling..in this *white flight from desegregated schools. **1975** *Political Sci. Q.* XC. 675 White flight from cities has been a much discussed phenomenon in the last decade. **1978** *Sci. News* 23 Sept. 216 Previous studies of this so-called 'white flight' phenomenon have been criticized for not taking into account the type of desegregation involved and for ignoring other factors that might have induced white families to leave the central city anyway. **1607** Topsell *Four-f. Beasts* 83 If a woman be troubled with the *white fluxe. **1827** Faraday *Chem. Manip.* xiii. (1842) 301 White flux is made by deflagrating a mixture of equal parts of nitre and cream of tartar. *c* **1423** in Raine *Ch. Yk. & Abps.* (Rolls) III. 307 Pro xij. virgis de panno vocato *whytefalddyng. **1929** W. Faulkner *Sound & Fury* 101 If it hadn't been for my grandfather, he'd have to work like *whitefolks. **1932** E. Caldwell *Tobacco Road* xv. 179 What's the matter with your automobile, white-folks? **1973** *Black World* May 20/1 In his essays on whitefolk, Du Bois invokes two specific historical occurrences which reflect the paradoxes, lies and hypocrisy of white civilization. **1981** A. Mackay *Death on River* (1983) 120 She dressed conservatively. White folks' clothes, she thought wryly. **1382, 1563, 1739** *White frost [see frost *sb.* 2]. **1780** W. Fleming *Jrnl* 14 Mar. in N. D. Mereness *Trav. Amer. Colonies* (1916) 634 Monday night there was a smart white frost. **1835** J. Martin *Comprehensive Descr. Virginia* 66 Our white frost is generally harmless, it being simple dew slightly congealed. **1967** White frost [see hoar-frost *a*]. **1913** F. Soddy *Matter & Energy* v. 135 The '*white fuel' of the Norwegian hill-sides. **1928** *Daily Tel.* 27 Mar. 10/7 Italy has..greater advantages for the development of 'white fuel', for Egypt has but one single river. **1958** *New Scientist* 6 Feb. 19 When the calalyst is used with 'white' or unleaded fuel (as on motorised trucks for indoor use in factories) this difficulty does not arise. **1900** *T. Eaton & Co. Catal.* White Goods & Midwinter Sale 12 These prices for Shirt Waists and Wrappers are special for the *White Goods Sale only. **1943** L. I. Wilder *These Happy Golden Years* xxxi. 276 Busily working with the white goods, Ma and Laura discussed Laura's dresses. **1960** *Economist* 8 Oct. 158/1 Refrigerators, deep freezers, washing machines, clothes dryers and other so-called 'white goods'. **1976** *Which?* Mar. 61/1 Electrical equipment..includes things like washing machines and fridges (what the trade calls white goods) as well as TVs and audio (which the trade calls brown goods). Specialist TV and audio shops don't normally sell white goods. **1981** *Times* 9 Mar. 19/6 An abiding problem for the white goods manufacturers is the high level of imports. **1922** *White Guard [see Red Guard 1 b]. **1970** G. Huizer in I. L. Horowitz *Masses in Lat. Amer.* xiii. 454 Tapia continued to have meetings with peasants in their houses although the soldiers or 'white guards' sent by the Cantabria hacienda tried several times to capture him. *Ibid.* 497 'White guards' ..were groups of armed men hired by the landowners [in Mexico] to fight against those peasants who petitioned for land. **1971** H. Trevelyan *Worlds Apart* xxiii. 267 The house was lucky to escape destruction during the Revolution, when it was said to have been for a time in the front line as a White Guard post opposite the Kremlin. **1974** J. White tr. *Poulantzas's Fascism & Dictatorship* iv. iii. 210 The fascist phenomenon was constantly identified with the Russian White Guards, as a strong reaction to a revolutionary situation. **1951** in J. Degras *Soviet Documents on Foreign Policy* I. 131 A White Terror eclipsing the atrocities of the Finnish *White Guardists. **1964** V. Nabokov *Defence* xiii. 211 Yes, yes, I know he's a chess player... But what is he? A reactionary? A White Guardist? **1971** S. Talbott tr. *Khrushchev Remembers* i. 15 Our army won many important victories against our White-Guardist class enemies in the first years of the Revolution. **1818** Scott *Br. Lamm.* xii, There is black pudding and *white-hass—try whilk ye like best. **1824** Mactaggart *Gallovid. Encycl., White Hawse*, a favourite pudding. **1540** Palsgr. *Acolastus* ii. iii. L ij b, May not I..be estemed the sonne of a *whyte henne .i. maye not men..thinke, that I was borne in a good howre. **1630** B. Jonson *New Inn* i. iii, All..are not sonnes o' the white Hen. **1716** *Poor Robin* Feb. A 6, Money is a Chick of the white Hen, he that hath it, hath Fortune by the forelock. **1976** P. Driscoll *Barboza Credentials* i. i. 24, I had seen Kenya..prosper in spite of the *White Highlanders sneering. **1935** E. Huxley *White Man's Country* I. ix. 208 In East Africa the settlers' principal anxiety was that Indians would permeate the relatively small area of land suitable for colonisation—the '*white highlands'. **1957** W. M. Hailey *Afr. Survey* (rev. ed.) xi. 719 The reservation of the White Highlands for Europeans prevented the process of expansion by which the more populous tribes would normally have found relief from congestion. **1978** S. Naipaul *North of South* i. iv. 114 Soil erosion had been one of the great settler obsessions. The battle against it had become part and parcel of the battle for civilisation, providing a powerful argument for the preservation of the status quo in the 'White' Highlands. **1971** *Nature Physical Sci.* 3 May 20/1 Black holes..are related in a genitive manner to '*white holes', defined to be singularities from which matter and energy emerge. **1977** *N.Y. Rev. Bks.* 29 Sept. 22/2 There is speculation..that every black hole is joined to a 'white hole'—a hole that gushes energy instead of absorbing it. **1911** *Daily Colonist* (Victoria, B.C.) 28 Apr. 11/4 A New York promoter has succeeded in arranging for a match between Albert Palzer, New York's most prominent *white hope, and Carl Morris, the giant locomotive engineer. **1912** I. S. Cobb *Back Home* 233 Judge Priest was a celebrity, holding the limelight to the virtual exclusion of grand opera stars, favourite sons, white hopes, [and] debutantes. **1919** *Observer* 16 Nov. 12/6 In the south, based on the Black Sea and liberally furnished with British material, Denikin and his Cossacks were the 'white hope' of the anti-Bolshevists. **1941** Ld. Berners *Far from Madding War* iii. 50 He was a composer: the white hope (thus a critic had described him) of English music. **1948** *Time* 5 July 40/2 Idol of the Negro race, and so popular with the whites that the old cry for a 'white hope' never came up, Joe Louis..was a champion the whole U.S. was proud of. **1952** M. Allingham *Tiger in Smoke* iv. 81 Detective Coleman had been one of Luke's white hopes. He had liked the boy for his eagerness. **1969** *Daily Tel.* 6 Oct. 12 In the immediate post-war years cheap and almost limitless atomic power was the white hope of a small island sadly short of raw materials. **1979** *Nature* 23 Aug. 638/1 Interferon is the great white hope of cancer therapy. **1781** Gibbon *Decl. & F.* II. xxvi. 584 The *white Huns, a name which they derived from the change of their complexions. **1866** H. Yule *Cathay & Way Thither* I. p. liv, The Yueichi..who became known in the West as Indoscythians, and at a later date as White Huns. **1965** G. Wheeler *Soviet Central Asia* i. 5 In the fifth century southern Turkestan was conquered by the Ephthalites or White Huns. **1945** N. Mitford *Pursuit of Love* xi. 90 She's happy now, isn't she, with her *white hunter? **1964** D. Varaday *Gara-Yaka* xiv. 124 Two white hunters lay in wait, and each shot one of the pride. **1980** G. M. Fraser *Mr American* xxvi. 546 He's an elephant hunter to trade—what they call a white hunter. **1933** (*record-title*) *White jazz. **1946** R. Blesh *Shining Trumpets* i. 23 No heterophony in white jazz except a chaotic sort in Chicago-style jazz. **1950** [see schmaltz 2]. **1976** J. Berendt *Jazz Bk.* 11 There seem to have been white bands almost from the start. 'Papa' Jack Laine led bands in New Orleans from 1891. He is known as the 'father' of white jazz. **1882** W. J. Christy *Joints* 32 *White Joint.—One formed with ordinary mortar as distinguished from blue mortar. Or it is made by pointing with white putty. **1744** Fielding *Tumble-Down Dick* Wks. 1766 IV. 250 Tho' all the earth was one continued smoke, 'Twould not prevent my dancing the *White Joke. **1895** M. Kingsley *Jrnl.* 23 May in *Trav.* (1897) vi. 110 The chief..bows with a jerk that causes the pantaloons to faint in coils, like the *White Knight in 'Alice in Wonderland'. **1956** N. Marsh *Off with his Head* (1957) ii. 41 'I believe I have made a really significant discovery..' cried Dr. Otterly with the infatuated glee of a White Knight. **1970** *Times* 23 Apr. 7 The Italian Communist Party..will take its members into the regional election campaign next month as white knights dealing with the joint evils of corruption and reaction. **1976** J. Philips *Backlash* (1977) iii. ii. 130 Woody would like nothing better than to play the white knight to my damsel in distress. **1979** *N.Y. Times Mag.* 30 Sept. 24/4 The Rangers' problems stemmed from the habit that..the team's general manager..had of hiring ineffectual cronies to coach the club, and then replacing them with himself when they failed—a kind of 'white knight' compulsion. **1981** *Guardian* 30 Oct. 15/1 Thomas Tilling.. emerged yesterday as the white knight appointed by Berec to save the Ever Ready battery maker from the clutches of Hanson Trust. **1930** H. Craddock *Savoy Cocktail Bk.* i. 175 **White Lady Cocktail.* ¼ Lemon Juice, ¼ Cointreau, ½ Dry Gin. **1935** K. Tennant *Tiburon* 19 Two old men in the corner lying stupefied over a mixture of 'white lady'—boiled methylated spirit with a dash of boot polish and iodine. **1952** B. Hamilton *So Sad, so Fresh* xviii. 117 He indicated a cocktail cabinet..and proceeded to mix two 'White Ladies'. **1964** *Telegraph* (Brisbane) 24 Sept. 5/2 Aborigines..used to swill cheap wines and other concoctions like 'White Lady' —a fiendish brew of methylated spirit and powdered milk. **1975** R. Beilby *Brown Land Crying* 225 'Ya was on the White Lady at the finish, mixin' it with Coke.'..'But jees, meths'n Coca Cola.' **1978** White lady [see sidecar 2]. **1960** *Guardian* 14 July 8/5 How much '*white land' the planning authorities have left between the limits of development shown on the town map and the beginning or inner edge of the green belt. **1971** P. Gresswell *Environment* 270 Open country and villages, both of which may be included in 'white land', have suffered. **1974** *Times* 19 Feb. 2/1 Mr. Rippon, Secretary of State for the Environment, should be challenged in the courts if he allows more 'white land' in the Worcestershire county structure plan to be used for development, a report by the county planning committee states. *c* **1450** *Brut* 447 A leyche called '*white leyche'. **1573, 1750** [see leach *sb.*[1] 2]. *c* **1700** Pepys in Rollins *Pepysian Garl.* (1922) Pref. p. vii, The Form..of the Black Letter with Picturs, seems (for cheapness sake) wholly laid aside, for that of the *White Letter without Pictures. **1717** Hearne *Collect.* (O.H.S.) VI. 95 It is printing..in the white Letter, contrary to Mr. Urry's mind, who was resolved upon the black Letter and would not hear of the white. **1879** Chappell *Roxb. Ball.* II. 450 Two of the copies were issued by Whitwood.., one by Norris in white letter. **1940** W. T. Cocking *Television Receiving Equipment* 298/2 (Index), *White level. **1950** Rabinoff & Wolbrecht *Questions & Answers Television Engin.* x. 233 The maximum white level shall be 15 per cent or less of the peak carrier amplitude. **1953** Amos & Birkinshaw *Television Engin.* I. i. 17 White level may be positive or negative with respect to black level. **1982** J. Goldberg *Fund. Television Servicing* i. 5 Television standards identify a white level and a black level of picture information. **1899** J. Hutchinson in *Archives Surg.* X. 146 The nail..exhibits white spots in consequence [of injury] —'*white lies'. **1921** *Double Dealer* July 20/1 The men lean or sit on the counter and talk politics, hard times..and more enthusiastically, the devastating and withering qualities of the current '*white lightning', 'white mule', or just plain 'corn', as the local moonshine whiskey is called. **1940** C. McCullers *Heart is Lonely Hunter* ii. iv. 119 He had a pint of bootleg white lightning. **1969** *Times* 9 Dec. (Taiwan Suppl.) p. ii/3 The distillery's main product is kaoliang, a potent liquor made out of Quemoy-grown sorghum and known as White Lightning. **1972** *Village Voice* (N.Y.) 1 June 77/3 Ellen..unfolded some tinfoil which she said contained three tabs of Owsley's original 'white lightning', the Mouton-Rothschild of LSD. **1975** B. Garfield *Hopscotch* xii. 128 It was white lightning country and the backhill bootleggers were numerous. **1979** R. L. Simon *Peking Duck* vi. 50 Mao tai, the Chinese version of White Lightning. **1900** G. B. Shaw *Let.* 31 Aug. (1972) II. 182 The Labor Leader's '*white list' is the final stroke—the white flag held up to Liberalism at the moment when we are on the verge of victory over it. **1939** *Country Life* 11 Feb. p. xxi/1 (Advt.), Furs.—Avoid those tortured to death. Buy only those named on the Fur Crusade White List. **1977** *Lancet* 30 Apr. 963/1 One idea is a 'white list' of preferred drugs or a list of excluded drugs for which the N.H.S. would not expect to pay. **1857** J. Scoffern etc. *Usef. Metals* 344 Parts which were unsound, occasioned, apparently, by a white powder embedded in the steel: to distinguish this from the effects of imperfect welding, it was called *white-loose. *Ibid.*, The files were without white-loose. **1603** J. Davies *Microcosmos* Wks. (Grosart) I. 9 Thou blessed Ile, *white Marke for Envie's aime. **1943** *New Yorker* 25 Dec. 36/2 Britons buying legally and mournfully on the *white market. **1973** *Times* 28 Dec. 1/4 A feature of the system would be a 'white market' in which unused coupons could be sold freely or bartered. **1895** *Atlantic Monthly* Mar. 333 His *white mass,—the first mass of a young priest. **1972** *Times* 2 Oct. 9/3 It is connected to a separate wiring circuit and an offpeak or *white meter. **1974** *Ecologist* Oct. 299/2 Measures such as low-tariff electricity ('White Meter') in off-peak periods only, have already made consumers prepared to group their demand for an intermittent supply. **1642** Howell *For. Trav.* (Arb.) 41 As it is proverbially said, there are in Genoa, Mountaines without wood, Sea without fish, Women without shame, and Men without conscience, which makes them to be termed the *white Moores. **1850** H. Melville *White Jacket* II. xxvi. 167 A set of sly, knavish foxes among the crew... In man-of-war parlance, they [are called] fancy-men and *white-mice. **1900** *Daily News* 10 Mar. 6/5 The miserable, anaemic, shifty, human white-mice. **1889** H. H. McConnell *Five Years a Cavalryman* 60 About this time I first became acquainted with a..drink known as 'pine-top' or '*white-mule' whiskey. **1928** *Collier's* 29 Dec. 8/1 What do you think about a bunch of boys and girls..stealin' a keg of white mule from a dealer? **1942** W. Faulkner *Go down, Moses* 156 Gets himself a whole gallon of bust-skull white-mule whisky. **1973** *Globe & Mail* (Toronto) 23 Feb. 37/8 At other times..the stuff would..lash out with its hind hooves at the little old wine-maker like the white mule once so respected in the Ozarks. **1765** *Phil. Trans. R. Soc.* LV. 45 (*heading*) An account of the *White Negro shewn before the Royal Society. **1790** W. Wilberforce *Jrnl.* 5 Apr. in R. I. & S. Wilberforce *Life W. Wilberforce* (1838) I. vii. 264 Hard at work on Slave Trade evidence all day with 'white negroes', two Clarksons and Dickson. **1824** J. Doddridge *Notes Settlement & Indian Wars W. Parts Virginia & Pennsylvania* 52 Mulattoes..are denominated white negroes. **1838** R. I. & S. Wilberforce *Life W. Wilberforce* I. vii. 255 Messrs. Clarkson, Dickson, &c. jocosely named by Mr. Pitt, his 'white negroes'. **1850** 'M. Tensas' *Odd Leaves Life Louisiana 'Swamp Doctor'* 76 He was one of that peculiar class called Albinoes, or white negroes. **1949** Koestler *Promise & Fulfilment* i. vii. 69 The Jewish Defence organization became another white negro, which changed its colour according to the political situation. **1957** N. Mailer in *Dissent* IV. 279 The hipster had absorbed the existentialist synapses of the Negro, and for practical purposes could be considered a white Negro. **1980** E. G. Wilson *John Clarkson* iv. 51 Both Clarksons were counted among the activists whom Pitt in a rare jest called the 'white Negroes'. **1837** R. M. Bird *Nick of Woods* I. 170 Hanging too good for him, *white niggah t'ief, hah! **1871** E. Eggleston *Hoosier Schoolmaster* 52 'Ole Miss Meanses' white nigger', as some of them called her, in allusion to her slavish life. **1934** *Esquire* Feb. 96 Art Hickman and other purveyors of sweet rose to meteoric fame while white men who continued to play hot received the chauvinistic appellation of 'white niggers'. **1965** *Listener* 15 Apr. 545/2 The intellectual West Indian is being told to stand up and be counted. Will he commit himself to his people or remain what our radical Negroes in the Southern United States would call a 'white nigger'? **1970** R. D. Abrahams *Positively Black* vi. 135 Hippies and other recent Bohemian groups have openly proclaimed themselves 'white niggers' by which they seem to mean that, like blacks, they represent an alternative to the life style of majority-group American culture. **1975** *Times Lit. Suppl.* 7 Nov. 1320/4 Dr Marcus Foster, a black,..suggested that the children be equipped with identity passes... The unfortunate Foster was widely accused of being an Uncle Tom and a white nigger. **1872** BROWNING *Fifine* xxxiii, O the knotty point—*white night's work to revolve. **1908** MISS BROUGHTON *Mamma* vii, The almost entirely white night she had just passed. **1960** G. BLANCHET *Search in North* ii. 28 There was a brief pause while the sun was just below the horizon—the 'white night' as it is called. **1981** *Times* 6 June 14/3 If you go to Leningrad at this time of year you catch the celebrated 'white nights', when there is only a brief twilight around midnight. **1959** D. COOKE *Lang. of Music* ii. 44 The *white-note scales on C (Ionian mode) and A (Aeolian mode) were already our C major and A minor scales. **1983** *Listener* 14 July 35/3 With its use of the traditional plainchant melody of the Psalm, its 'white-note' counter-melodies and harmonisations..it struck a fresh note after the highly-wrought complexity and chromaticism of most of Goehr's earlier works. **1569** *Aldeburgh Rec.* in *N. & Q.* 12th Ser. VII. 184/2, ij quares of *whyte paper. **1680** *Debates in Parl.* (1681) 166 These Bills will.. make your Banishing Bill, and Association-Bill too, as ineffectual as White Paper. **1683** MOXON *Mech. Exerc., Printing* 394 Although the first Form be Printed off, yet Press-men..call that Heap White-Paper, till the Reteration be Printed. **1687** *Lond. Gaz.* No. 2125/4 Linen Rags, and other Materials for making of White Paper. **1772** *Gentl. Mag.* Apr. 192/1 She's fair White Paper, an unsully'd sheet. **1859** *Stationers' Handbk.* 27 Printing papers, sometimes spoken of in a trade sense, as 'White papers'. **1899** *Daily News* 13 Mar. 5/1 An interesting White Paper has been published..giving reports from our Ambassadors and Consular officers abroad on the telephone services in the countries to which they are attached. **1906** *Minutes Evidence Sel. Comm. Official Publ.* 15/1 in *Parl. Papers* (Cd. 279) XI. 95 With regard to the White Paper, which is printed, and which is handed to Members with the notices of the day, that is printed from the same type, I presume, as the Blue Paper, which is sent to us in the morning? **1920** [see *white terror* below]. **1922** C. E. MONTAGUE *Disenchantment* viii. 115 Our rulers have continued to issue to the Press, at our cost as Blue Books and White Papers, long passages of argument and suggestion. **1924** H. B. LEES-SMITH *Guide to Parl. & Official Papers* ii. 19 Corrections in the Blue Paper, such as putting amendments to Bills in their right order, are made during the morning and sent to the printer in time for the White Paper. **1950** KERR & JAMES *Wavy Navy* 255 These ratings had been earmarked as suitable 'White Paper' candidates by their Commanding Officers and recommended to the Admiralty. **1955** *Times* 16 June 8/5 The text of the two agreements would be published in the next few days and laid before Parliament as White Papers. **1962** GRANVILLE *Dict. Sailors' Slang* 132/2 *White Paper candidate*, candidate for a temporary (wartime) commission in the RNVR. The White Paper was passed in Parliament for a scheme of promotion for suitable ratings who had served on the lower deck for at least three months in a ship at sea in time of war. **1967** *Listener* 8 June 739/2, I first hastened to read President Nyerere's 'White Paper' on education. **1971** H. WILSON *Labour Govt.* xiii. 201 Some of our major commitments..had been worked out only to White Paper stage. **1978** *Dædalus* Fall 3 He would have been ..the venerable statesman who delivered the White Paper on Defense in the postwar period. **1906** *Daily Colonist* (Victoria, B.C.) 10 Jan. 2/2 To Fight *White Plague... The tuberculosis convention..has been a great success. **1926** H. V. MORTON *Spell of London* 68 The peril of youth, the horrible white plague. **1961** L. MUMFORD *City in Hist.* xvii. 547 As early as the eighteenth century Mercier had observed this metropolitan form of the White Plague. **1723** J. NOTT *Cook's & Confectioner's Dict.* sig. Pp. 7ᵛ, Two Gallons of *White-port Wine. **1892** MEW & ASHTON *Drinks of World* 100 Of white Ports the best are *Muscatel de Jesus*, [etc.]. **1920** G. SAINTSBURY *Notes on Cellar-bk.* vi. 88 White Port.. I think nearly deserving of the curse above pronounced on sparkling claret. **1978** M. WALKER *Infiltrator* xiii. 144, I was given a glass of white port. [**1972** GISPEN & BRAND-SAATHOF in *Bull. World Health Org.* XLVI. 591/1 The parental Copenhagen virus..continually gives rise to a few white-pock forming virus particles by mutation. *Ibid.*, The occurrence of wild white poxvirus in healthy monkeys cannot be explained by the instability noted above.] **1977** *Brit. Med. Jrnl.* 26 Feb. 530/2 Viruses as yet indistinguishable from variola virus were isolated from the kidneys of six healthy monkeys and two rodents; these have been termed '*whitepox viruses'. **1979** *Nature* 24 May 295/2 Vaccinia, cowpox and camelpox viruses lack continuous transmissibility in man, but the situation with monkeypox virus and whitepox virus deserves further comment. **1919** H. LEVERAGE *White Cipher* 84 He memorized the details like a draughtsman reading a *white-print. **1967** White-print [see OZALID]. **17..** '*Get up and bar the door*' vii. in Herd *Scot. Songs* (1776) II. 159 And first they ate the *white puddings, And then they ate the black. **1930** R. LEHMANN *Note in Music* iv. 154 'I must hurry, I must hurry,' she said... Like the *white rabbit, he thought. **1979** S. BRETT *Comedian Dies* v. 52 Her pretty little face looked anxious... 'Oh, um. If you'll excuse me...' And she scuttled out, all White Rabbit. **1982** J. ELLIOTT *Country of her Dreams* xii. 144 Off he went, scuttling.., White Rabbit late for a date. **1970** *Rep. 20th Ann. Round Table Meeting Linguistics & Lang. Stud.* 221 Because such quasi-militants feel that Negro dialect is inherently 'bad' (as did conservative Negroes before them), they regard it as a product of *white racism. *Ibid.*, They see any attempt to describe and scientifically record Negro dialect as nothing more than a *white-racist exploitation of Negroes. **1973** *Black Panther* 17 Mar. 6/3 No charges were pressed against any of the club-wielding, epithet-sputtering white racists clearly because the Navy felt that only 'they' (Blacks) had been in the wrong. **1977** M. WALKER *National Front* 9, I despise nationalism, whether it be British, White Racist or Martian. **1909** BARING-GOULD & BAMPFYLDE (*title*) A history of Sarawak under its two *White Rajahs, 1839–1908. **1966** *New Statesman* 1 July 21/1 Her role is somewhere between a White Rajah and a VSO. **1974** *Radio Times* 19 Mar. 37/3 The story of the last White Rajah of Sarawak. **1463** *Bury Wills* (Camden) 24, xijs. of *white rente. **1630** DODRIDGE *Dvtchy of Cornewall* 99 White rent.. is a dutie payable yeerely by euery Tynner in the County of Deuon,..that is, of euery Tynner 8.d. **1664** SPELMAN *Gloss., Quietus redditus*..Vulgo Quit rente, qui & alias White rente nuncupatur, quod in denariis & argento penditur. **1717** *Northumbrian Docts.* (Surtees) 61 A white-rent of 13s. 6d. from two or three freeholds in Woodburne. **1887** *Voice* (N.Y.) 15 Dec. 2/2 Brother Finch endeared himself to all *White Ribboners. **1970** 'O. HENRY' *Trimmed Lamp* 32 The 'demon rum'—as the white ribboners miscall whiskey. **1974** *Daily Tel.* 3 July 17/7 The National British Women's Total Abstinence Union, which has 6,000 members, still issues a white ribbon bow in the form of a badge to its followers, who are known as the 'white ribboners'. **17..** *Song* in Farquhar *Beaux-Strat.* III. iii, *White rods are no trifles, I'm sure, Whatever their bearers may be. **1876** BANCROFT *Hist. U.S.* I. x. 347 A chancery court and a court-leet, sergeants and white rods. **1961** *Aeroplane & Astronautics* CI. 684/1 The new factory incorporates the latest production methods and in view of its development of special-purpose connectors—particularly in the micro-miniature field—a '*white room' is being fitted out so as to give the cleanest manufacturing conditions for this type of component. **1965** *Life* 5 Nov. 111/4 The capsule itself will be stored in the pristine solitude of a 'white room' near Cape Kennedy until Schirra and Stafford are ready to fly again. **1970** N. ARMSTRONG et al. *First on Moon* iii. 66 The other five members of the close-out crew were in the 'white room' on swing arm No. 9. **1558** G. CAVENDISH *Poems*, etc. (1825) II. 99 Adewe, my sonne Edward! sprong of the royall race Of the *wight rose and the red. **1622** BACON *Hen. VII* 4 The People, who..had beene fully made capable of the clearnesse of the Title of the White-Rose or House of Yorke. **1716** HEARNE *Collect.* (O.H.S.) V. 237 Divers were destroyed by the Georgian Party, only for having white Roses, a way by which..the Cavaliers distinguished themselves. **1887** F. M. CRAWFORD *Saracinesca* i, Men flocked to the standards of the White Rose of York. **1906** M. C. COOKE *Fungoid Pests of Cultivated Plants* 155 *White rot of Grapes..occurs on the fruit, leaves, and rarely on twigs. **1946** CARTWRIGHT & FINDLAY *Decay of Timber* iv. 48 Decompositions of wood by fungi is of two main types, which have been described as brown rots and white rots respectively... In a white rot all the components of the wood, including the lignin, are decomposed. **1951** *Dict. Gardening* (R. Hort. Soc.) III. 1426/1 White Rot of onions due to the fungus *Sclerotium cepivorum* shows when..affected plants are seen to have rotten roots while the base of the bulb is covered with a very white, fluffy mycelium. **1969** G. BECKER in Krishna & Weesner *Biol. Termites* I. xi. 356 A large number of mold fungi, white-rot fungi, and bacteria can produce toxic substances. **1962** S. WYNTER *Hills of Hebron* xvi. 198 With the money he bought bags of rice..and even a few bottles of *white rum. **1972** *Times* 19 Aug. 10/1 White rum promises to be the spirit of the 1970s. **1848** M. J. BERKELEY in *Jrnl. R. Hort. Soc.* III. 266 Nothing can have been more general than the *white rust..which is so common on cruciferous plants. **1932** *Iron Age* Jan. 232/1 A common corrosion found on the surface of zinc-coated products has been called by the industry 'White Rust'. **1937** F. D. HEALD *Introd. Plant Path.* vii. 97 The greatest development of the white rusts is during the cool periods of early spring. **1976** A. R. L. CHIVERS in L. L. Schrier *Corrosion* (ed. 2) I. iv. 156 Zinc which has been properly aged..is safe against white-rust formation. **1981** *Daily Tel.* 16 May 19/2 Several cases of white rust..have been found in imported plants [*sc.* chrysanthemums]. **1914** *Photo-Era* XXXIII. 168 (*caption*) A spring *white-sale. **1970** *New Yorker* 10 Oct. 158/2 The season of White Sales. **1909** OSLER in Klebs *Tuberculosis* 7 Throughout the world the most intense interest has been stimulated in the fight against the *white scourge. **1937** K. BLIXEN *Out of Afr.* iv. 298 Kitosch was a young Native in the service of a young *white settler of Molo. **1969** J. MANDER *Statis Society* vi. 154 A White Settler minority, as in South Africa, can usually keep power if it is sufficiently determined and has a monopoly of arms. **1972** [see *holiday home* s.v. HOLIDAY *sb.* 4a]. **1974** *Daily News* (Tanzania) 13 Sept. 1/2 The three-day occupation of the main radio station here by the criminals (white settlers) protesting at the independence settlement, and the subsequent fighting and looting in the city's African suburbs, have shattered Portuguese hopes of a peaceful and amicable transfer of power in the colony. **1976** *Listener* 3 June 716/2 'White settlers' is a phrase now in common currency in the Highlands to describe refugees from that well-known rat race who buy any old wreck of a cottage, spend a lot of money on it and live there, many of them, for a month or so in the summer. **1922** CHRISTINE ORR *Kate Curlew* ii, She learned *white-sewing from an aunt. **1594** *Zepheria* xxxvi. F2b, Thy face being vayld, this pennance I award, Clad in *white sheet thou stand in Paules Churchyard. **1659** in Morris *Troubles Cath. Foref.* (1872) I. vi. 316 Seventy-two..were Nuns of the Choir, the rest *White Sisters and Lay-sisters. **1890** E. H. BARKER *Wayfaring in France* vi. 305 It was a White Sister kneeling and praying. **1901** RHYS *Celtic Folklore* I. v. 351 Old people still living remember men and women clad in white sheets doing penance publicly in the churches of Man. **1908** *Catholic Times* 6 Mar. 11/2 We have in the Katanga many missions..and everywhere are White Fathers, religious women (White Sisters). **1957** G. D. KITTLER *White Fathers* vii. 81 The answer, Lavigerie realized, would be in establishing the White Sisters. **1789** *Deb. Congress U.S.* 13 May (1834) 350 He hoped it would comprehend the *white slaves as well as black, who were imported from all the jails of Europe. **1807** SOUTHEY *Lett. from England* II. xxxviii. 150 Let us leave to England..the distinction..of being the white slaves of the rest of the world, and doing for it all its dirty work. *c* **1833** M. T. SADLER in *Mem.* (1842) 405 Their tender hearts were sighing As negro wrongs were told, While the white slave lay dying Who gained their father's gold! **1840** T. GORDON tr. *W. Menzel's Ger. Lit.* IV. 87 Seume..like many thousands of 'white slaves', that is, German subjects, who were then sold by their princes to the Dutch or English, had been shipped for the colonies. **1889** [see SLAVE *sb.*[1] 3]. **1913** C. PANKHURST *Great Scourge* p. viii, Regulation of vice and enforced medical inspection of the White Slaves. **1917** A. HUXLEY *Let.* May (1969) 125, I am safe from these body-snatchers, kidnappers, baby killers and white slave traffickers, the Recruiters. **1970** 'J. QUARTERMAIN' *Diamond Hook* xvi. 99 If you stop me.., I'll white-slave Jessie to South America. **1977** D. WHEATLEY *Young Man Said* x. 147 Was she white-slaved—a fate which befell more than a few girls of her type and class in those days? **1922** *Times Lit. Suppl.* 27 Apr. 278/2 The villain of the piece..is a *white slaver [= procurer]. **182.** G. SMEATON *Doings in London* 83 Here is, indeed, the British *white slavery [*viz.* of dressmakers]; only, with this difference, that their more fortunate sufferers [*sic*] in the West Indies have regular food and appointed hours of work. **1835** *Edin. Rev.* July 463 These representations of the ruinous effects of what has been called white slavery..were..embodied in Mr. Sadler's famous Factory Report. **1857** W. ACTON *Prostitution* 94 The natural question, 'Why does not this woman escape from this white slavery?' is best answered by other queries—Whither can she fly? What can she do? **1960** D. LESSING *In Pursuit of English* i. 16 A father-figure..with a [*sic*] strong *white-slaving propensities. **1541** COVERDALE *Confut. Standish* (1547) l ij b, Maruaill not..though (whan I se you folowe your vnholy mother..) I call you..her owne *whyte sonne. *a* **1553** UDALL *Royster D.* I. i, Be his nowne white sonne. **1601** YARINGTON *Two Lament. Trag.* IV. vi. G4b, Young Allenso your white honnie sonne. *a* **1613** OVERBURY *A Wife* etc. (1630) P8b, The Deuill cals him his white sonne. **1723** J. NOTT *Cook's & Confectioner's Dict.* sig. L8ᵛ, To make White Cullis... Use this with *White Soops and Ragoos. **1813** JANE AUSTEN *Pride & Prejudice* I. xi. 123 As for the ball..as soon as Nicholls has made white soup enough I shall send round my cards. **1977** J. AIKEN *Five-Minute Marriage* vi. 95 Next week Mrs. Andrews really must start making white soup; and I must write..to Gunter's about the ices. **1666** *Lond. Gaz.* No. 85/4 To steer after the Enemy, with the *White Squadron in the Van, and the Blew in the Rear. **1840** [see BLUE *a.* 5b]. **1891** [see RED *a.* 16d]. **1815** J. SMITH *Panorama Sci. & Art* 546 *The *White Steep.* This part of the process is precisely the same with the last [*sc.* grey steep], except that the sheep's dung is omitted in the composition of the steep. **1853** R. RIDDELL *Indian Domestic Econ.* 63 Take three quarts of good *white stock. **1905** *Tasty Dishes* (new ed.) 10, 3 pints of white stock. **1960** *Good Housek. Cookery Bk.* (rev. ed.) 196/1 Vegetable water or stock made from bones should be used for gravies and brown sauces; milk, or milk and white stock for white sauces. *c* **1645** HOWELL *Lett.* I. I. xiii. (1890) 38 You are one ..whose Name I have mark'd with the *whitest Stone. **1748** SMOLLETT *Rod. Random* lii, 'God be praised! a white stone!' ..he alluded to the *Dies fasti* of the Romans, *albo lapide notati.* **1861** H. W. BRISTOW *Gloss. Mineral.* 320/2 When cut for jewelry, it [*sc.* rock crystal] is called by lapidaries, 'white stone'. **1885** HORNADAY *Two Yrs. in Jungle* xxvii. 318, I have marked that day with a white stone as being the one on which I ate my first durian. **1937** *Burlington Mag.* Nov. p. xix/2 A gold ring with a telling portrait carved in whitestone. **1941** F. THOMPSON *Over to Candleford* vi. 98 She kept the whole of the fair-sized house cleaned and polished and whitestoned. **1963** *Times* 11 June 15/4 The whitestone and glass frontage gives the impression of verticality. **1978** R. DOLINER *On the Edge* (1979) iv. 62 A whitestone Italian Renaissance mansion on Sixty-third Street. **1908** J. M. SULLIVAN *Criminal Slang* 27 **White stuff*, morphine. **1915** G. BRONSON-HOWARD *God's Man* I. iv. 39 There's quite a trade in laudanum... The 'White Stuff's' on the up-and-up too. **1953** W. BURROUGHS *Junkie* (1972) xiii. 129, I had never been able to drink before when I was on the junk, or junk-sick. But eating hop is different from shooting the white stuff. You can mix hop and lush. **1967** N. LUCAS *C.I.D.* x. 135 Luckier still not to have graduated from pep pills to ..'The White Stuff'..heroin. **1655** VAUGHAN *Silex Scint.* II. (*title*) *White Sunday. **1958** *Listener* 12 June 967/1 The steady propulsion towards *white supremacism. **1979** *Daily Tel.* 5 Sept. 6 He [*sc.* Ian Smith] is well aware that the noisy and active minority who regard him as the totem of white supremacism will call for his blood. **1959** *New Statesman* 30 May 751, I have wondered..whether there was any link between the demagogues of Notting Hill and *white supremacists elsewhere. **1961** *Spectator* 20 Jan. 65 A way of life..that is white-supremacist. **1964** L. NKOSI *Rhythm of Violence* II. i. 26 The White Supremacists will not get away so easily! **1977** *Times* 30 Aug. 10/3 Mr John Tyndall, the National Front's founder and chairman..describes himself as 'an unashamed white supremacist' and regards whites as intellectually..superior to blacks. **1981** *Times* 17 Mar. 12/3 The real contest in next month's general election will be between the ruling National Party and the white supremacist parties to the right of it. **1902** A. TOURGÉE *Let.* 15 May in T. L. Gross *Albion W. Tourgée* (1963) viii. 143 It is the very highest form of blasphemy to claim that the idea of '*white supremacy' and the later barbarism which demands race-subjection or extermination is pleasing to God or conformable to the religion of the Man of Nazareth. **1931** W. S. CHURCHILL in J. C. Squire *If it had happened Otherwise* 179 Upon the rebound from this there must inevitably have been a strong reassertion of local white supremacy. **1981** *Times* 18 Mar. 8/6 The Rustenburg constituency..represents some of its most far-right votes for white supremacy. **1958** *Times Lit. Suppl.* 11 July 386/3 They imply that, had the Supreme Court said 'desegregate by the so-and-so of this year', and had President Eisenhower backed the Courts to the limit, the Southern *white suprematists would not have 'fought back', or would only have done so unsuccessfully. **1971** J. BISHOP *Days of Martin Luther King, Jr.* iv. 332 A few White Suprematists said that there was no doubt that the bombing was the work of..a militant black who wanted to incite his people to riot. **1920** *Glasgow Herald* 7 May 9 A report on the alleged existence of a '*White Terror' in Hungary has been issued in the form of a White Paper. **1965** J. CH'ÊN *Mao & Chinese Revolution* (1967) I. v. 125 The less hesitant Wuhan declared the CCP [*sc.* Chinese Communist Party] outlawed on that fateful day of 13 July 1927. The so-called White Terror thus began and chaos ensued. **1970** G. HUIZER in I. L. Horowitz *Masses in Lat. Amer.* xiii. 480 The secretary-general..noted the continuous struggle of the CNC [*sc.* National Confederation of Peasants] against the 'white terror' of landowners and caciques. **1977** *Time* 21 Mar. 26/2 In the 1930s leftists lived in constant fear of the so-called White Terror imposed by the [Chinese] Nationalist secret police. **1980** *Times Lit. Suppl.* 25 Apr. 471/2 After the collapse of [Béla] Kun's regime, the White Terror raged, but Korda somehow survived unharmed. **1853** 'C. BEDE' *Adventures Verdant Green* vii. 65 You are going to wine with Smalls this evening. .. I suppose you would go properly dressed,—*white tie, kids, and that sort of thing, eh? **1930** M. KENNEDY *Fool of Family* xx. 208 'Is it a grand party?' asked Caryl nervously. .. 'I mean is it white tie?' explained Caryl. 'Oh yes, of course it's white tie.' 'Then it is grand.' **1936** [see *black tie* s.v. BLACK *a.* 19]. **1942** D. POWELL *Time to be Born* iv. 83, I will give a white-tie dinner for eighteen. **1981** LD. HAREWOOD *Tongs & Bones* i. 29 The glamour of the occasion impressed me greatly—I was probably the only person in the boxes not in a white tie. **1932** H. G. WELLS *Work, Wealth &*

Happiness xii. 607 Tariff obstruction at this higher level is, for all practical ends, *war at the frontier*, *White War, the chronic as distinguished from that acute form in which invasion, bomb, bayonet and poison gas play leading parts, which more emphatic sort of warfare we may call Red War. **1939** *New Statesman* 3 June 878/2 Armament firms will boom more conspicuously, but the promised Government limitation of earnings or special taxations of 'whitewar' profits must deprive the armament or semi-armament equities of their usual attraction. **1577** in Ellis *Orig. Lett.* Ser. III. IV. 26 Theire canvas and *whiteware. **1776** J. WEDGWOOD *Let.* 14 Jan. (1965) 189 But for *Usefull China*, or such a *white-ware* as you mention, I must beg a longer time. **1843** *Ecclesiologist* II. 31 A mean and unecclesiastical composition Font, containing a white-ware hand basin. **1909** *Sat. Even. Post* 20 Feb. 8/1 Start at Fifty-ninth Street and walk down what the Manhattanese call the 'Great *White Way'. **1920** S. LEWIS *Main Street* 416 Then, glory of glories, the town put in a White Way. **1933** E. CALDWELL *God's Little Acre* xi. 170 Out of the grey darkness of the building the girl suddenly appeared in the glow of the whiteway lights. **1939** *Florida* (Federal Writers' Project) II. 259 Central Avenue [in St. Petersburg], the city's 'White Way', extends rulerlike for 7 miles across the peninsula. **1977** *Washington Post* 30 Jan. E-1/1 When dancer-choreographer Merce Cunningham..appeared..at New York's Minskoff Theater recently..one might have supposed..that the Great White Way had suddenly gone avant-garde. **1980** *N.Y. Times* 10 Dec. A-14/2 'Welcome to Boston's Great White Way,' the sign on a theater marquee pridefully proclaimed. **1905** H. G. WELLS *Kipps* I. ii. 40 Cretonnes, chintzes, and the like; serviettes, and all the bright hard *whitewear of a well-ordered house. **1949** N. MITFORD *Love in Cold Climate* I. xvi. 170 She was awfully old for a *white wedding, thirty or something terrible. **1962** *Daily Herald* 8 Jan. 6/8, I had a lovely white wedding... Given my time again I would cheerfully splash everything on one. **1976** *Listener* 29 July 105/1 Young black girls [in Soweto] now demand white weddings with lots of bridesmaids and floating veils. **1901** G. PARKER *Right of Way* 23 Rouge Gosselin flung off his glass of *white whisky, and threw after it another glass of cold water. **1957** W. FAULKNER *Town* xxiv. 357 Ratliff..took a pint bottle of white whiskey from inside his shirt. **1968** 'N. BLAKE' *Private Wound* i. 17 Padraig, another Jamieson for Mr. Eyre. The white whiskey, mind, this time. Did y'ever try Jamieson's white? **1913** EDEN *Anc. Glass* 45 A small *white window, made up of quarries (panes) decorated in brown enamel let in a white and coloured border. **1813** BYRON *Corsair* I. iii, How gloriously her gallant course she [*sc.* the ship] goes! Her *white wings flying. **1880** BLACK (*title*) White Wings: a Yachting Romance. **1610** B. JONSON *Alch.* II. iii, Your red man, and your *white woman, With all your broths, your menstrues, and materialls. **1863** MRS. GASKELL *Sylvia's Lovers* III. i. 2 Sitting in the dark parlour..and doing '*white work', was..wearying to her. **1936**, etc. [see MOUNTMELLICK]. **1967**, **1975** White work [see RICHELIEU].

12. Combinations.

a. with other adjs. (or sbs.) of colour (= whitish, light), as ***white-blue***, ***-brown***, ***-fiery***, ***-green***, ***-grey***, †***-hoar***, ***-lyard*** (q.v.), ***-red***, ***-russet***, ***-yellow***. Also with other adjs., as WHITE-HOT, q.v.; **white-sick** (see quot.).

1608 SYLVESTER *Du Bartas* II. iv. *Schism* 935 The Eastern winde drives on the roaring train Of *white-blew billows. **1643** BAKER *Chron., James* (1653) 615 Course paper, commonly called *white brown paper. **1825** T. HOOK *Sayings* Ser. II. *Passion & Princ.* v, A small packet of white-brown paper. **1876** G. M. HOPKINS *Wreck of Deutschland* xiii, in *Poems* (1967) 55 Wiry and *white-fiery and whirlwind-swivellèd snow. **1578** LYTE *Dodoens* v. xii. 561 The white garden Succorie..hath..*whitegreene leaues. *c* **1533** in Ellis *Orig. Lett.* Ser. I. II. 32 Some faire white, or *white gray palfreies. **1556** *Chron. Grey Friars* (Camden) 28 The gray freeres chaungyd their habbetts from London rossette unto whytt gray. **1812** J. SMYTH *Pract. Customs* (1821) 218 The hair of the wild Cat is very long, and of a fine white grey. **14..** *Guy Warw.* (Camb.) 4775 Hys fadur ys olde and *whyte-hore. **1577** GOOGE *Heresbach's Husb.* 116 The best colours [for a horse]..the rone, the *white lyard, the bay, the sorell. **1607** [see LYARD]. *a* **1618** SYLVESTER *Woodman's Bear* xlv, Red-white hils, and *white-red plaines. **1601** HOLLAND *Pliny* XXXII. x. II. 446 A peece of cloth of a *white russet colour. **1797** *Encycl. Brit.* (ed. 3) XIII. 538/2 The female [oyster] *white-sick (as they term it), having a milky substance in the fin. **1922** JOYCE *Ulysses* 179 He.. felt a slack fold of his belly. But I know it's *whiteyellow.

b. with vbs. and pples., usually in instrumental sense = 'with white', 'in white (clothing or covering)', or with complemental force = 'so as to be, become, or appear white': as ***white-paint*** vb.; ***white-bordered***, ***-churned***, ***-clad***, ***-clothed***, ***-enamelled***, ***-flattened***, ***-flecked***, ***-heaped***, ***-marked***, ***-painted***, ***-pointed***, ***-quartered***, ***-salted*** (see HERRING 1 b), ***-set*** (SET *ppl. a.* 6 a), ***-spotted***, ***-spread***, ***-tinned***; ***white-flowing***, ***-glittering***, ***-looking***, ***-shining***, ***-steaming***, ***-waving*** adjs.; **white-burning** *a.*, applied to clay that gives a white product when fired; **white-dominated** *a.*, dominated by white people.

1830 *Withering's Brit. Pl.* (ed. 7) IV. 303 *White-bordered Cupping Peziza. **1965** G. J. WILLIAMS *Econ. Geol. N.Z.* xx. 359/2 The clays so formed are plastic, refractory and *white-burning. **1967** M. CHANDLER *Ceramics in Mod. World* ii. 49 A small proportion of more plastic white-burning clay is sometimes included. **1823** *Coll. Poems* (ed. Joanna Baillie) 259 The *white-churn'd waters. **1886** *Cornh. Mag.* Sept. 249 *White-clad Arabs. **1896** A. HOPE *Phroso* ii, Groups of *white-clothed women. **1960** *White-dominated [see QUESTION MARK 2]. **1981** *Listener* 31 Dec. 810/1 Blacks tend to regard journalists as part of the white-dominated, Establishment-prone media. **1915** 'BARTIMEUS' *Tall Ship* iii. 51 Forward, the *white-enamelled bulkhead was pierced by two entrances. **1918** D. H. LAWRENCE *New Poems* 47 Oh, masquerader, With a hard face white-enamelled. **1922** JOYCE *Ulysses* 86 Nose *whiteflattened against the pane. **1900** MARY E. WILKINS *Parson Lord, One Good Time* 196 Her black..gown was..*white-flecked..with..winged seeds of passed flowers. **1827** G. DARLEY *Sylvia* 5 Beautiful Glen of the *white-flowing torrent! **1729** SAVAGE *Wanderer* I. 75 *White-glittering ice, chang'd like the topaz, gleams, Reflecting saffron lustre from his beams. **1922** JOYCE *Ulysses* 39 Belly without blemish, bulging big, a buckler of taut vellum, no, *whiteheaped corn. **1870** P. M. DUNCAN *Blanchard's Transf. Insects* 121 A flabby,..*white-looking grub. **1887** *Amer. Naturalist* XXI. 581 The *white-marked tussock-moth. **1897** *Mag. of Art* Sept. 268 He whitewashed and *white-painted what was coloured. **1828** P. CUNNINGHAM *N.S. Wales* (ed. 3) II. 157 Four *white-painted tarpaulings. **1948** D. BALLANTYNE *Cunninghams* 165 The dark blue sea, *white-pointed by the wave tops. **1962** *White-quartered [see *pink-scrolled* s.v. PINK *a.*[1] C. b]. **1889** CONAN DOYLE *Micah Clarke* xxviii, The pile of bodies..with their twisted limbs and *white-set faces. **1851** J. G. WHITTIER *Benedicite* in *Nat. Era* 16 Oct. 166/5 God's love—unchanging, pure, and true—The Paraclete *white-shining through His peace. *a* **1973** J. R. R. TOLKIEN *Silmarillion* (1977) 262 A city white-shining on a distant shore. **1776** WITHERING *Bot. Arrangem.* 606 *White spotted Willow Lady-cow. **1903** CONRAD & HUEFFER *Romance* I. iv, A red, white-spotted handkerchief. **1918** D. H. LAWRENCE *New Poems* 26 Daisies that waken all mistaken *white-spread in expectancy. **1921** R. GRAVES *Pier-Glass* 26 And a *white-steaming mist Obscures desire. **1521–2** *Rec. St. Mary at Hill* (1904) 313 A brase of iron for the sacryng bell that was *whight tynned. **1822** CAMPBELL *Song of Greeks* 47 Our maidens shall dance with their *white-waving arms.

c. Parasynthetic Combinations, chiefly adjectives in -ED[2], unlimited in number (many occurring in specific designations of animals or plants), as ***white-aproned***, ***-armed***, ***-barked***, ***-barred***, ***-beaked***, ***-bellied***, ***-billed***, ***-bloomed***, ***-blossomed***, ***-bodied***, ***-bosomed***, ***-breasted***, ***-cheeked***, ***-coated***, ***-coned***, ***-crested***, ***-curtained***, ***-faced***, ***-fanged***, ***-flannelled***, ***-flowered***, ***-frilled***, ***-frocked***, ***-fronted***, ***-gaitered***, ***-glanced***, ***-gloved***, ***-handed***, ***-hatted***, ***-hooded***, ***-hoofed*** (***-hooved***), ***-horned***, ***-jacketed***, ***-leaved***, ***-legged***, ***-lipped***, ***-listed*** (LIST *sb.*[3] 5), ***-maned***, ***-mantled***, ***-naped***, ***-necked***, ***-plumed***, ***-polled***, ***-railed***, ***ribbed***, ***-ribboned***, ***-rinded***, ***-robed***, ***-roofed***, ***-rumped***, ***-shafted*** (SHAFT *sb.*[2] 4 b (*a*)), ***-sheeted***, ***-shouldered***, ***-sided***, ***-skinned***, ***-sleeved***, ***-smocked***, ***-souled***, ***-spatted***, ***-stockinged***, ***-stoled***, ***-strawed***, ***-throated***, ***-tied***, ***-tiled***, ***-tilted*** [TILT *sb.*[1]], ***-tipped***, ***-tongued*** (cf. 10), ***-toothed***, ***-topped***, ***-tufted***, ***-tusked***, ***-veiled***, ***-veined***, ***-waistcoated***, ***-walled***, ***-wanded***, ***-whiskered***, ***-wristed***, etc., etc.; **white-arsed** *slang*, a term of abuse; **white-backed**, having a white back; †in early use (of a document), blank on the back, unendorsed; **white-backed vulture**, an African vulture of the genus *Pseudogyps*; **white-blooded**, having light-coloured or colourless blood, without red corpuscles, as most invertebrate animals; **white-breasted nuthatch**, a North American nuthatch, *Sitta carolinensis*; **white-crossed**, bearing the figure of a white cross; **white-crowned**, having a white crown; ***white-crowned sparrow***, a North American sparrow, *Zonotrichia leucophrys*; **white-eyed**, having white eyes; having the iris of the eye white, or having white plumage around the eyes; **white-favoured**, wearing white favours (FAVOUR *sb.* 7 b); **white-floured**, with the face whitened by flour; **white-hearted**, (*a*) faint-hearted, timid, cowardly (cf. sense 5 and WHITE-LIVERED); (*b*) pure-hearted, saintly (cf. sense 7); **white-horsed**, (*a*) bearing the figure of a white horse; (*b*) having or driving a white horse or horses; **white-looked**, having a white or pale look or aspect; **white-mouthed**, (*a*) having the mouth white with foam, foaming; (*b*) having a white mouth or lip, as a shell; †**white-rigged** (*whyt reged*), white-backed (see RIGGED *a.*[1]); **white-throated sparrow** = PEABODY; see also WHITE-EARED, etc.; also **white-elephantine**, of the nature of a white elephant; uselessly splendid; **white-flesher**, a name for the ruffed grouse, from its light-coloured flesh or meat.

1868 J. G. WHITTIER in *Atlantic Monthly* 3 Jan. 1 Bare-armed..she came, *White-aproned, from her dairy. **1977** J. GILLIS *Killers of Starfish* x. 76 A white-aproned waiter appeared..bearing little plates of cheese squares. **1718** POPE *Iliad* xv. 98 The *white-arm'd Goddess. **1922** JOYCE *Ulysses* 587 He's a *whitearsed bugger. **1975** *Daily Colonist* (Victoria, B.C.) 18 May 1/1 Delegates..sat in shocked silence when an Indian leader accused them of being 'white-arsed Liberals'. **1466** *Stonor Papers* (Camden) I. 87 Ye must gete lenger day of his parte, and þer for y sende yow þe writte *white backed. **1783** LATHAM *Gen. Syn. Birds* II. I. 82 White-backed Thrush. **1884** R. B. SHARPE *Layard's Birds S. Afr.* (ed. 2) 794 African *White-backed Vulture... General colour deep brown. **1964** D. VARADAY *Gara-Yaka* ix. 78 The sitters were white-backed vultures, the most common in this area [by the Limpopo]. They were so dark brown in parts that they looked dirty, but their lighter parts appeared immaculate in contrast. **1779** *U.S. Mag.* (Philadelphia) Feb. 85 The lowly man-grove fond of wat'ry soil; The *white barked gregory rising high in air. **1948** White-barked [see ENGELMANN]. **1869** NEWMAN *Brit. Moths* 16 The *White-barred Clearwing (*Sesia Sphegiformis*). **1811** SHAW *Gen. Zool.* VIII. 13 *White-beaked Hornbill. **1611** COTGR., *Carpion*, a kind of.. *white-bellied Trout. **1774** *Phil. Trans.* LXV. 271 The *hirundo melba*, or great white-bellied Swift of Gibraltar. **1872** COUES *Key N. Amer. Birds* 82 White-bellied Nuthatch. **1782** LATHAM *Gen. Syn. Birds* I. II. 553 *White-billed Woodpecker. **1802** *White-blooded [see *red-blooded*, RED *a.* and *sb.*[1] 14 a]. **1835–6** *Todd's Cycl. Anat.* I. 165/1 The natural position of the white-blooded worms is by the side of those with red blood. **1922** BLUNDEN *Shepherd* 43 From *white-bloomed plum. **1911** J. MASEFIELD *Everlasting Mercy* 79 That *white-blossomed pond. **1904** W. B. YEATS *King's Threshold* 55 It was praise of that great race That would be haughty, mirthful, and *white-bodied. **1793** COLERIDGE *Compl. Ninathoma* 8 They blessed the *white-bosom'd Maid. **1756** P. BROWNE *Jamaica* (1789) 470 The *white-breasted Guinea-Hen. **1808** A. WILSON *Amer. Ornithol.* I. 41 The White-breasted Nuthatch is common almost everywhere in the woods of North America. **1946** G. STIMPSON *Bk. about Thousand Things* 491 The white-breasted cormorant is largely responsible for the production of the vast guano deposits on the islands off the coast of Peru. **1972** L. HANCOCK *There's a Seal in my Sleeping Bag* i. 14 Searching for the white-breasted sea eagle. **1980** *Northeast Woods & Waters* Dec. 23/2 Hairy and downy woodpeckers, white-breasted nuthatches..attack the suet on the old pear tree. *a* **1593** MARLOWE *Ovid's Elegies* II. xviii, *White-cheekt Penelope knewe Vlisses signe. **1781** PENNANT *Hist. Quadrup.* 331 White-cheeked Weesel. **1838** DICKENS *O. Twist* xv, A *white-coated, red-eyed dog. **1866** HOWELLS *Venetian Life* xii. 168 The white-coated sentinels. **1920** BLUNDEN *Waggoner* 40 Smoke's light blue pennants coil From *white-coned oasts. **1678** RAY *Willughby's Ornith.* 112 *White crested Parrot. **1848** C. C. CLIFFORD tr. *Frogs of Aristophanes* 34 Whitecrested morions. **1856** LEVER *Martins of Cro' M.* lviii, The wind-shaken foliage and the white-crested waves. **1632** LITHGOW *Trav.* VII. 329 *White cross'd. **1836** R. KING *Narrative of Journey* II. 196 The *fringilla leucophrys*, or *white-crowned finch..perched on the topmost branch. **1839** W. B. O. PEABODY *Rep. Ornithol. Mass.* 32 The *White-crowned sparrow..is one of the finest of this family of birds. **1894** B. TORREY *Florida Sketch-bk.* 235, I discovered..perched at the top of the oak, tossing back his head and warbling—a white-crowned sparrow. **1975** *Nature* 18 Sept. 182/1 The Californian scrub habitat is occasionally devastated by fire, so that the white-crowned sparrow population is reduced to a few birds living in isolated patches of surviving scrub. **1977** *New Yorker* 19 Sept. 123/1 The twisted fig tree, the almond, not yet white-crowned, the slow tendrils of grape reaching into the sky are companions for a time. **1914** D. H. LAWRENCE *Widowing of Mrs. Holroyd* I. i. 3 At the back is a *white-curtained window. **1959** *Economist* 28 Mar. 1152/1 The *white elephantine palace by the lake at Geneva may be good enough for the foreign ministers. **1971** A. SAMPSON *New Anat. of Britain* xvii. 335 Sir John Hill..had applied quite drastic economies to its white-elephantine operations [*sc.* those of the Atomic Energy Authority]. **1783** LATHAM *Gen. Syn. Birds* II. II. 475 *White-eyed Warbler. **1831** AUDUBON *Ornith. Biogr.* I. 328 The White-eyed Flycatcher,.. *Vireo Noveboracensis*. **1833** TENNYSON *Palace Art* lx, White-eyed phantasms weeping tears of blood. **1595** SHAKS. *John* II. i. 23 That *white-fac'd shore. **1781** PENNANT *Hist. Quadrup.* 82 White-faced Antelope. **1856** STANLEY *Sinai & Pal.* vi. 255 The white-faced hill..is the 'Blanche Garde' of the Crusading chroniclers. **1898** 'H. S. MERRIMAN' *Roden's Corner* i, The children, white-faced and melancholy. **1952** C. DAY LEWIS tr. *Virgil's Aeneid* XI. 254 His head was helmeted in a wolf's mask Whose gaping mouth with its *white-fanged jaws served for a visor. **1850** TENNYSON *In Mem.* Concl. 90 The time draws on, And those *white-favour'd horses wait. **1884** *Harper's Mag.* July 230/1 *White-flannelled cricketers. **1831** SIR J. RICHARDSON *Fauna Bor.-Amer.* II. 342 *Tetrao umbellus*... Ruffed Grouse... *White Flesher. **1925** E. SITWELL *Troy Park* 21, I saw the *white-floured zanies go. **1634** T. JOHNSON *Merc. Bot.* 40 *White flowred Rush-grasse. **1842** TENNYSON *Godiva* 63 The white-flower'd elder-thicket. **1837** CARLYLE *Fr. Rev.* I. IV. iv, Gilt-edged *white-frilled individuals. **1891** HARDY *Tess* ii, The *white-frocked maids. **1768** PENNANT *Brit. Zool.* II. 450 *White Fronted Wild Goose. **1908** E. J. BANFIELD *Confessions of Beachcomber* I. iii. 98 White-fronted Heron, *Notophoyx novæ-hollandiæ*. **1909** A. E. MACK *Bush Calendar* 23 Birds breeding in September... *Ephthianura albifrons*. White-fronted chat. **1955** E. POUND *Classic Anthol.* I. 60 Chariots, rank on rank With white-fronted horses. **1971** *Country Life* 27 May 1292/3 The famous Wexford Slobs, main winter headquarters of the Greenland race of white-fronted geese. **1922** JOYCE *Ulysses* 558 His nag, stumbling on *whitegaitered feet, jogs along the rocky road. **1930** BLUNDEN *Poems* 290 Those *white-glanced pools. **1712–14** POPE *Rape Lock* v. 13 Why round our coaches croud the *white-glov'd Beaux? **1897** FLANDRAU *Harvard Episodes* 318 The big, white-gloved policeman at the door. **1588** SHAKS. *L.L.L.* v. ii. 230 *White handed Mistris, one sweet word with thee. **1634** MILTON *Comus* 213 O welcom pure-ey'd Faith, white-handed Hope. **1828** STARK *Elem. Nat. Hist.* I. 60 White-handed Lemur.—Inhabits Madagascar. **1835** DICKENS *Sk. Boz, Last Cab-driver*, A brown-whiskered, *white-hatted, no-coated cab-man. *a* **1617** BAYNE *On Eph.* i. (1643) 8 Such *white-hearted Christians, who are ashamed of their Master. **1865** BURRITT *Walk to Land's End* 407 If the painter were a devout, white-hearted man. **1900** W. S. CHURCHILL in *Morning Post* 17 Feb. 8/1 *White-hooded, red-crossed ambulance waggons. **1927** A. CLARKE *Son of Learning* II. 38 The Abbot said There is a barrel of white-hooded ale Here. **1832** TENNYSON *Œnone* 50 A jet-black goat *white-horn'd, *white-hooved. **1832** J. BREE *St. Herbert's Isle* 5 War..her *white-horsed banner furls. **1872** CALVERLEY *Fly Leaves, Morning* i, The hour when white-horsed Day Chases Night her mares away. **1910** W. J. LOCKE *Simon the Jester* xxiii. 323 *White-jacketed waiters darting to and fro. **1980** H. R. F. KEATING *Murder of Maharajah* xiii. 156 White-jacketed Goan bearers. **1822** *Hortus Anglicus* II. 465 Chinese *White-leaved Nettle. **1716** GAY *Ep. to Earl Burlington* 16 Brentford,..For dirty streets and *white-legg'd chickens known. **1848** DICKENS *Dombey* xxxvii, As he rode away upon his white-legged horse. **1841** *Florist's Jrnl.* (1846) II. 78 *Oncidium leucochilum*, (*white-lipped). **1920** W. J. LOCKE *House of Baltazar* xxii, She replied, white-lipped: 'I'll never forgive you till I'm dead!' **1859** TENNYSON *Merlin & V.* 788 The tree that shone *white-listed thro' the gloom. **1690** *Lond. Gaz.* No. 2596/4 He is a short thin-faced *white-look'd Man. **1642** in J. Wilson *Ann. Hawick* (1850) 53 Ane foir meir, *quhyt mainet and quhyt taillet. **1883** W. WHITMAN *Daybks. & Notebks.* (1978) II. 319 The sea-beach and surf—its myriad ranks like furious white-maned racers, urged by demoniac emulation to the goal, the shore. **1955** E. POUND *Classic Anthol.* IV. 212 White-maned black stallions Pull with due order. **1825** SCOTT *Betrothed* iv, The *white-mantled Welshmen. **1629** QUARLES *Argalus & P.* III. Wks. (Grosart) III. 283/1 Whereat the angry Knight..forsooke His *white-mouth'd Steed. **1639** G. DANIEL *Ecclus.* xliii. 64 The white-mouth'd Billowes of yᵉ vnsounded Deepe. **1815** BURROW *Elem. Conchol.* 200 *Voluta Æthiopica*, white-mouth'd Melon. **1932** *Discovery* July 232/2 The *white-naped ravens and the mountain buzzards swing overhead. **1975** *New Yorker* 24 Mar. 34/2 The white-naped crane, fifteen hundred left, fifty in zoos. **1912** J. STEVENSON-HAMILTON *Animal Life Afr.* xvii. 299 The ravens are represented by the *white-necked raven (*Corvultur albicollis*) in the south..of the Ethiopian region. **1965** G. B. SCHALLER *Year of Gorilla* vii. 161 The most regular visitors to our meadow were a pair of white-necked ravens, lovely birds with iridescent black plumage and a striking white collar around the neck. **1968** *Sunday Mail Mag.* (Brisbane) 8 Sept. 6/1 Only two species of seals now live on the southern Australian coast-line, namely the white-necked hair-seal [etc.]. **1627** P. FLETCHER *Locusts* II. iv, As when the angry winds with seas conspire, The *white-plum'd hilles marching in set array Invade the earth. **1915** S. LEE *Life Shakesp.* xii. 225 A white-plumed helmet. **1922** JOYCE *Ulysses* 537 Staggering Bob, a *whitepolled calf, thrusts a ruminating head..through the foliage. **1909** H. BEGBIE *Cage* iv, *White-railed cattle-pens. *c* **1711** PETIVER *Gazophyl.* viii. 80 Small *white rib'd Barbadoes Limpet. **1885–94** R. BRIDGES *Eros & Psyche* Nov. xi, Taking his fair *white-ribbon'd herald's wand. **1568** *Wills & Inv. N.C.* (Surtees 1835) 293 One *whyt reged cowe. **1874** M. COLLINS *Frances* I. 214 Under a *white-rinded birch. **1625** MILTON *Death Fair Infant* 54 That crown'd Matron sage *white-robed Truth. **1816** WORDSW. *Ode, 'Imagination—ne'er before content'* 76 The white-robed choir. **1893** W. SHARP in *Mem.* (1910) 214 A white-robed Bedouin herding goats. **1863** MISS BRADDON *Eleanor's Vict.* i, The fruitful orchards and *white-roofed cottages. **1782** LATHAM *Gen. Syn. Birds* I. II. 544 *White-Rumped Black Cuckow. **1832** RENNIE *Butterfl. & M.* 230 The *White Shafted Plume [Moth] (*Pt[erophorus] tetradactylus*). **1881** E. F. POYNTER *Among the Hills* II. 317 The still, *white-sheeted meadows. **1892** E. REEVES *Homeward Bound* 209 We found the street.. blocked up with white-sheeted figures. These were Arab.. ladies escorting an intending bride..to the bath. **1781** LATHAM *Gen. Syn. Birds* I. I. 190 *White-Shouldered Shrike. **1870** BRYANT *Homer* I. I. 32 Juno the white-shouldered smiled. **1588** *Wills & Inv. Durh.* (Surtees) II. 33 One *white sided why. **1864–5** WOOD *Homes without H.* xiii. 234 That [nest] which is made by the White-sided Hill Star. **1523–34** FITZHERB. *Husb.* §68 A white horse, so that he be not al *white-skynned aboute the mouthe. **1579–80** NORTH *Plutarch, Agesilaus* (1595) 656 They scorned their bodies, because they saw them white skinned, soft, and delicate. **1851** SCHOOLCRAFT *Amer. Indians* 164 Their white-skinned, auburn-haired, and blue-eyed progeny. **1802** WORDSW. *Valley near Dover* 4 Boys..In *white-sleeved shirts. **1922** JOYCE *Ulysses* 102 The *whitesmocked priest came after him tidying his stole with one hand. **1973** M. AMIS *Rachel Papers* 186 There—round-eyed, white-smocked and spotless—was Rachel. **1874** J. G. WHITTIER *Sumner* in *Memorial to Charles Sumner* 100 He never brought His conscience to the public mart; But lived himself the truth he taught, *White-souled, clean-handed, pure of heart. **1902** G. W. E. RUSSELL *Londoner's Log-Book* iii. 40 Sir William Harcourt as the white-souled champion of spiritual religion. **1922** *White-spatted [see SLEW-FOOT]. **1934** DYLAN THOMAS *Let.* 14 Jan. (1966) 93 The white-spatted representatives of a social system that has, for too many years, used its bowler hat for the one purpose of keeping its ears apart. **1916** E. POUND *Lustra* 48 Her *white-stockinged feet. **1957** J. AGEE *Death in Family* III. xvii. 284 Catherine stood..looking at the skirt and at her white-stockinged feet. **1790** WOLCOT (P. Pindar) *Rowland for Oliver* etc. 30 To clasp with kisses sweet his *white-stol'd Maid. **1805** R. W. DICKSON *Pract. Agric.* I. 539 The *white-strawed wheat takes its name..from the colour of its ear. **1776** PENNANT *Brit. Zool.* II. pl. xcviii, *White throated duck. **1859** GEO. ELIOT *Adam Bede* xviii, A white-throated stoat..had run across the path. **1811** A. WILSON *Amer. Ornithol.* III. 51 *White-Throated Sparrow ..[winters] in most of the states south of New England. **1865**, etc. White-throated sparrow [see PEABODY]. **1977** *New Yorker* 5 Sept. 23/3 Dozens of white-throated sparrows.. have appeared among the cattails. **1848** A. H. CLOUGH *Bothie of Tober-na-Vuolich* i. 5 The Tutor..*White-tied, clerical. **1972** A. ROUDYBUSH *Sybaritic Death* (1974) ii. 5 Tail-coated, white-tied and silk-hatted men. **1924** G. B. STERN *Tents of Israel* xiii. 182 I've wanted things, too... Hundreds of baths; baths in *white-tiled rooms, and not skimping the hot water. **1978** T. GIFFORD *Glendower Legacy* (1979) 53 An ancient wino was mopping one corner of the long, narrow, white-tiled floor. **1939** F. THOMPSON *Lark Rise* i. 2 The baker's little old *white-tilted van. **1872** COUES *Key N. Amer. Birds* 184 The outer feathers *white-tipped. **1637** RUTHERFORD *Let. to Parishioners* 13 July, A heavie doom is for the liar and *white tongued flatterer. **1609** DEKKER *Gull's Horn-bk.* Proem. 5 The *whitest-toothd Blackamoore in all Asia. **1870** BRYANT *Homer* I. XI. 345 As when a hunter cheers His white-toothed dogs against some lioness. **1805** R. W. DICKSON *Pract. Agric.* II. 639 The ..*white topped,..and the Dutch turnip. **1867** MORRIS *Jason* II. 624 The white-topped billows. **1650** W. HOW *Phytol. Brit.* 1 *White Tuffted Wormwood. **1872** COUES *Key N. Amer. Birds* 302 White-tufted Cormorant. **1820** SHELLEY *Hymn Merc.* xcvi, The wild *White-tusked boars. **1856** MRS. BROWNING *Aur. Leigh* I. 81 The *white-veiled, rose-crowned maidens. *c* **1711** PETIVER *Gazophyl.* vii. 61 Common *white-veined Butterfly. **1828** MISS MITFORD *Village* Ser. III. *Lost & Found*, A rich trail of the white-veined ivy, which crept..over the ground. **1838** DICKENS *O. Twist* ii, The *white-waistcoated gentleman. **1816** BYRON *Pris. Chillon* 339, I saw the *white-wall'd distant town. **1958** *Punch* 21 May 670/3 Dunlop white-walled tyres, white pedals, and white pump. **1985** A. MCCANDLESS *Burke Foundation* i. 4 White-walled houses with red-tiled roofs. **1812** L. HUNT in *Examiner* 25 May 321/2 Any *white-wanded Lord at a levee. **1819** STEPHENS in Shaw's *Gen. Zool.* XI. 56 *White-whiskered Pigeon. **1916** CULLUM *Men who wrought* x, The white-whiskered face of his host. *c* **1611** CHAPMAN *Iliad* XX. 110 *White-wristed Iuno.

d. with sbs., forming adjs. (or phrases used attrib.) in senses (*a*) 'of, pertaining to, or consisting of (a) white ——', as ***white-brick, -duck, -flower, -linen***; (*b*) 'resembling (a) white ——', as ***white-dough, -loaf, -rag, -sand, -satin***; (*c*) 'having or characterized by (a) white ——' (equivalent to parasynthetic adjs. in *-ed*: see c), as ***white-berry, -eyelid, -nose, -underwing*** (see UNDERWING 2); **white-bead bandstring**, name for a species of coral resembling a string of white beads; **white-blood disease** (cf. *white blood* in 11 d) = LEUKÆMIA; **white hart silver** (see quot. 1658); **white-leaf**, applied to a species of frog with white spots; **white-shoe** *slang* (chiefly *U.S.*), effeminate, immature; **white telephone**, (of a film) telling an unrealistic story set in elegant surroundings; **white-wall**, (of a tyre) having white sidewalls. See also WHITE-EAR, -LINE, -SKIN *adjs.*

1696 PLUKENET *Almagestum Bot.* Wks. 1769 II. 118 *Corallina fistulosa Jamaicensis,..Nostratibus* *White Bead Bandstring *dicta*. **1814** LEWIS & CLARK *Trav. Missouri* xxvi. (1815) III. 124 *Whiteberry honeysuckle. **1866** AITKEN *Pract. Med.* II. 69 That the '*white-blood' disease proceeded from a primary affection of the spleen and lymphatic glands. **1909** H. BEGBIE *Cage* v, A little *white-brick cottage. **1886** *Buck's Handbk. Med. Sci.* III. 275/2 *Agaricus castus*, *White dough mushroom. **1849** *White duck [see DUCK *sb.*³ 3]. **1925** H. CRANE *Let.* 19 Aug. (1965) 214 White undershirt and loose white duck pants. **1966** in *Islands* (N.Z.) (1978) Aug. 93 White-duck curtains..Hang at the windows. **1781** PENNANT *Hist. Quadrup.* I. 189 *White-Eyelid Monkey.. The upper eyelids of a pure white. **1818** KEATS *Endym.* I. 669 Honey cells, Made delicate from all *white-flower bells. **1594** CAMDEN *Britannia* (ed. 4) 150 Ipsa prædia quæ illi tenuerunt ad hanc usque diem quotannis mulctæ nomine pecuniam in fiscum regium persoluunt, quæ **White hart Syluer*..appellatur. **1658** PHILLIPS, *Blacklow Forrest*, Called The Forrest of Whitehart from a very beautifull Whitehart, which King Henry the third..taking great care to spare, was killed by T. de la Linde, which so incensed the King, that he set a perpetual Fine upon the Land, which at this day is called Whitehart silver. **1802** SHAW *Gen. Zool.* III. 127 *White-leaf Frog... Its colour is rufous above, variegated..with milk-white spots. **1756** F. HOME *Exper. Bleaching* 26 Lye which has been used to white linen, called *white-linen lye. **1813** VANCOUVER *Agric. Devon* 161 The land sown..with the tankard and early *white loaf turnip. **1781** PENNANT *Hist. Quadrup.* I. 190 *White Nose Monkey. **1882** *White-rag Worm [see LURG]. **1822–7** GOOD *Study Med.* (1829) I. 326 Earthy or *white sand calculi. **1749** B. WILKES *Eng. Moths* etc. 21 The *white-satin moth. **1957** J. D. SALINGER *Zooey* in *New Yorker* 4 May 62/2 Phooey, I say, on all *white-shoe college boys who edit their campus literary magazines. Give me an honest con man any day. **1974** G. JENKINS *Bridge of Magpies* vi. 85 What sort of white-shoe captain are you? **1975** *N.Y. Times* 22 Sept. 33/1 Covert operations can be stripped from the CIA... So can such monkey business as dropping simulated poison cannisters in the New York subways—the games of white-shoe boys who never grew up. **1958** *Oxf. Mag.* 22 May 462/2 Then from Italy, which had hitherto only produced '*white telephone' films, came this simple, humble and extremely moving story. **1975** *New Yorker* 5 May 24/3 This is an icy high-minded white-telephone movie. [**1749** B. WILKES *Eng. Moths* etc. 23 The spotted red and *white under-wing moth.] **1909** *Westm. Gaz.* 9 Dec. 4/2 The common 'white underwing' moths. **1953** L. Z. HOBSON *Celebrity* viii. 116 A Buick Roadmaster... Fully equipped, radio, heater, *white wall tyres. **1965** *Punch* 20 Oct. 567/2 Then I shall buy this year's model, too, my beloved,..with whitewall tyres and a cigar-lighter. **1978** *Listener* 2 Feb. 158/2 When film makers go 'period', as they did for *Chinatown*, the bulky Buicks and Oldsmobiles have to be lovingly rebuilt, white-wall tyres, teeth-like radiator grills and bonnet 'ventiports', almost from scratch.

e. sbs. in which the second element denotes a distinctive part or attribute of that which is denoted by the whole word: **white-back**, local name for (*a*) the canvas-back duck; (*b*) the white poplar (from the colour of the under side of the leaves); (*c*) collectors' name for a species of moth (see quot. 1832); **white-bark**, local name for various trees with white bark (see quots.); **white-breech**, tr. L. *pygargus*, PYGARG 1; † **white-choker** *slang*, a clergyman (cf. CHOKER 2); so *whitechokerism*; † **white-cloak**, ? = WHITE MONK; **white-comb**, a form of favus attacking the combs of fowls; **white-eye**, name for various birds, either having a white iris, as the white-eyed pochard (*Nyroca ferruginea*) and the white-eyed fly-catcher (*Vireo noveboracensis*), or having white plumage around the eyes, as the species of the genus *Zosterops*, also called *silver-eye*; **white-front**, the white-fronted goose, *Anser albifrons*; **white-hat**, (*a*) one who wears a white hat (in quot. 1693, as *quasi*-proper name); (*b*) *U.S. Naval slang*, an enlisted man; (*c*) *slang* (orig. *U.S.*), a good man; a hero; **white-hood**, a regent member of the senate of the University of Cambridge (*obs.* exc. *Hist.*); **white-leg**, the disease *phlegmasia dolens* (see PHLEGMASIA); **white-nose** = *white-nose monkey*: see 12 d (*c*); **white point**, collectors' name for a moth (*Leucania albipuncta*) having a white dot on each of the fore wings; **white-root**, the herb Solomon's seal, from its white creeping rootstock; **white-rump**, (*a*) the wheatear, *Saxicola œnanthe*; (*b*) the Hudsonian godwit, *Limosa hæmastica*; **white-sides, white-spot**, collectors' names for species of moths (see quots.); **white-spur**, title of a class of esquires who wore silvered spurs; **white-stocking**, one who wears white stockings; in quot. applied to a horse with white legs; **white-straw**, name for a variety of wheat; **white-tip**, an artificial fly; **white-top**, (*a*) a N. American species of bentgrass, *Agrostis alba* (cf. RED-TOP 2); (*b*) an Australian tree, the Flintwood (*Eucalyptus pilularis*); **whitewall**, a white-wall tyre (see sense 12 d above); **white-wig**, one who wears a white wig. See also WHITEBEARD, -FEATHER, etc.

1814 ALEX. WILSON *Amer. Ornith.* (1832) III. 128 Canvass-back duck..on the Potowmac [they are called] *white-backs. *a* **1825** FORBY *Voc. E. Anglia*, *White-back*, the white poplar, *Populus alba*. So called from the whiteness of the under side of the leaves. **1832** RENNIE *Butterfl. & M.* 199 The White-back (*Y[ponomeuta] pruniella*). **1700** PLUKENET *Mantissa* Opera 1769 III. 113 Lappula Althæoides Americana..*White-Barke, Barbadensibus vulgo. **1889** MAIDEN *Useful Pl. Australia* 411 *Cupania semiglauca*,..White Bark. *Ibid.* 421 *Elæocarpus cyaneus*,.. White Bark. *a* **1661** HOLYDAY *Juvenal* (1673) 216 Trypherus ..Carves..th' Hare, Boar, the *White-Breech too, The Scythian Phesant,..And the Getulian Goat. **1903** A. H. LEWIS *Boss* xxi. 292 It's that same Reverend Bronson who gives Melting Moses th' office to dog me. I'll put Mr. *Whitechoker onto my opinion of th' racket. **1912** A. BENNETT *Matador of Five Towns* 100 You belong to that Methody lot... I seed you talking to them white-chokers. **1866** J. R. LOWELL *Let.* 10 Apr. (1894) I. 361, I don't understand your English taste for what you call 'respectability' (I should call it '*whitechokerism'), thinking, as I do, that the one thing worth striving for in this world is a state founded on pure manhood. **1621** LODGE *Summary of Du Bartas* II. 22 The *white Cloakes, the Carmes, The Augustines, the Bernardines, the Iacobins, the Cordeliers. **1854** *Poultry Chron.* II. 40 A list of diseases.. Apoplexy, *white comb, cramp, [etc.]. **1848** GOULD *Birds Australia* IV. 81 *Zosterops Dorsalis*,..Grey-backed Zosterops; *White-eye. **1862** JOHNS *Brit. Birds* 625 White-eye, the Nyroca Pochard. **1912** E. T. SETON *Arctic Prairies* 277 Honkers, *White-fronts and Ducks. **1693** C. MATHER in G. L. Burr *Narr. Witchcraft Cases* (1914) 284 That spirit by them [*sc.* the Newfoundlanders] called *White-Hat, who ordinarily appears on the Shore, in a White-hat..a little before some dangerous Tempest. **1956** E. N. ROGERS *Queenie's Brood* 241 There's a white hat out here who has gone crazy. **1975** *Courier-Mail* (Brisbane) 28 Feb. 5/2 Laver's the last of the white hats (the good guys who wear the white hats in cowboy movies). **1975** W. SAFIRE *Before the Fall* III. vii. 191 Nixon and Haldeman clung to the original game plan..against the urging of..Garment, and other 'white hats'. **1978** *Guardian Weekly* 15 Jan. 18/2 His judgments of the men he dealt with... The white hats are Truman [etc.]. A prime villain is Britain's postwar foreign secretary. **1764** *Ann. Reg., Chron.* 58 [Cambridge] There appeared among the black-hoods..placet, 103... Among the *white hoods the proctors accounts differed. **1811** R. HOOPER *Lexicon-Medicum* (new ed.) 615/2 *Phlegmasia dolens*... By the Germans it is called Œdema lacteum, and by the English the *white leg. **1860** MAYNE *Expos. Lex.*, *Phlegmatia Dolens*..the disease white-leg. **1899** [see *milk leg* s.v. MILK *sb.* 10 a]. **1939** M. SPRING-RICE *Working-Class Wives* v. 122 She is very anæmic, has 'whiteleg', constipation and piles. **1976** *Lancet* 27 Nov. 1197/2 Iliac-vein thrombosis or 'white leg' affects the left side more commonly than the right. **1982** P. BARKER *Union Street* 250 After our May was born she never walked properly again. She had what they called the white leg. **1774** GOLDSM. *Nat. Hist.* (1824) II. ix. 157 The seventh [monkey] is the Moustoc, or *White Nose. **1869** NEWMAN *Brit. Moths* 475 The *White-point (*Leucania Albipuncta*). **1578** LYTE *Dodoens* I. lxix. 102 *White roote or Salomons seale is of two sortes. **1797** BEWICK *Brit. Birds* I. 229 The *White-rump. Wheatear. **1817** SHAW *Gen. Zool.* X. 568 The White-rump has a very pretty song. **1888** G. TRUMBULL *Names of Birds* 209 *Limosa hæmastica*..[called] at West Barnstable, White-rump. **1832** RENNIE *Butterfl. & M.* 177 The *White Sides (*P[eronea] albicostana*). *Ibid.* 56 The *White Spot (*Gr[aphiphora] albimacula*). *Ibid.* 144 The White Spot (*M[acaria] unipunctata*). *Ibid.* 148 Ennychia..The White Spot (*E. octomaculata*). **1600** CAMDEN *Britannia* (ed. 5) 140 Rex..armigeros creat collum torque S.S. vel sigmatico argenteo, & candidis, & argentatis calcaribus exornans, vnde hodie in occidentalibus regni partibus vocantur **Whitespurres* ad discrimen Equitum auratorum qui auratis calcaribus vti solent. **1706** *Lond. Gaz.* No. 4219/4 A Plate to be run for,..by Galloways, not exceeding 13 hands and half high, (the Guilford *White-Stockings excepted). **1697** *Rector's Bk. Clayworth* (1910) 121 *White-straw & Joysting. **1805** R. W. DICKSON *Pract. Agric.* I. 539 The white-strawed wheat.. in other counties bears the appellation of the Kentish white-straw. **1867** F. FRANCIS *Bk. Angling* xii. 379 The *White Tip..is a standard Tweed pattern. **1819** WARDEN *United States* II. 8 The grasses are: White clover, *white top and red top. **1889** MAIDEN *Useful Pl. Australia* 502 *Eucalyptus pilularis*,..a Mountain Ash of Illawarra.., Willow, or White Top..(New South Wales). **1958** *Autocar* 31 Oct. 675 (*caption*) Bentley Flying Spur, sans fins, sans *whitewalls, sans tinsel. **1968** *Globe & Mail* (Toronto) 5 Feb. 26/5 (Advt.). Hardtop, big 6 with automatic, radio and whitewalls. **1978** *Detroit Free Press* 5 Mar. C7/2 (Advt.), A built-in Scuff Bar that helps keep whitewalls white. **1673** DRYDEN *Marr. à la Mode* Prol., *White-Wig and Vizard make no longer jar.

f. with sbs., forming vbs. (chiefly *nonce-wds.*): ***white-breast***; **white-ball**, to clean with a ball of whiting; **white-mail**, to seize or appropriate like *blackmail*, but for a good purpose; **white-tooth**, to show one's white teeth at. See also WHITE-LINE *v.*

1780 *Mirror* No. 93 ¶12 The servants had their liveries new *white-ball'd. *a* **1930** D. H. LAWRENCE *Mod. Lover* (1934) 11 The fallow flickered over with pink gleams of birds *white-breasting the sunset. **1861** READE *Cloister & H.* lii, He spent much of his gains..in..choice drugs, and would have so invested them all, but Margaret *white-mailed a part. **1876** A. J. EVANS *Through Bosnia* iii. 89 A dusky Ethiopian maiden *white-toothing us in the most coquettish fashion.

g. white-like *a.*, whitish; somewhat pale.

1608 *Phil. Trans.* XX. 379 The Petroleum which is found in Italy is a white-like Spirit of Turpentine. **1893** STEVENSON *Catriona* xxii, She looked white-like as she beheld the bursting of the sprays.

white, *v.*[1] (Also 4–6 whitt-, whytt-.) [OE. *hwītian*, f. *hwīt* WHITE *a.* Cf. OHG., MHG. *wīzen*, (G. *weissen*), Goth. *hweitjan*.]

1. a. *intr.* To become white: = WHITEN *v.* 2. *Obs.*

c **1000** ÆLFRIC *Saints' Lives* xxxiv. 113 Hwæs blod readaþ on rosan ʒelicnysse, and hwæs lichama hwitaõ on lilian fæʒernysse. *a* **1225** *Ancr. R.* 150 Þe bouh, hwon he adeadeð, he hwiteð wiðuten. *c* **1374** CHAUCER *Troylus* v. 276 Ful pale y-woxen was þe moone And whiten gan the Orisonte shene Al Estward. **1398** TREVISA *Barth. De P.R.* XVIII. xl. (Bodl. MS.), In wynter..alle þinge whiteþ bi colde and bi froste. **1471** RIPLEY *Comp. Alch.* VI. viii. in Ashmole (1652) 163 Drynes procedyth as Whytyth the matter.

b. Const. *out.* Of vision: to become impaired by exposure to a sudden bright light (see also quot. 1981). Also *trans.*, to 'blind' (an audience in a theatre) by such means.

1978 'A. STUART' *Vicious Circles* 22 At once my eyes whited out—as disoriented by the brilliant evening sun as a bat caught by a searchlight. **1981** *Times Lit. Suppl.* 30 Jan. 112/1 As the women lie down to sleep in the hot summer morning, the stage lights white out to mime the atomic fireball. **1983** *Listener* 3 Feb. 32/3 In Bristol the Little Theatre performs the stage play, using lasers and whiting-out audiences.

2. †**a.** *trans.* To make white: = WHITEN *v.* 1. *Obs.*

a **1000** *Rhyming Poem* ii. 62 (Grein III. I. 162) Flan man hwiteð. *c* **1325** *Pol. Songs* (Camden) 336 Be the hond i-whited, it shal go god i-nouh. **1340** *Ayenb.* 178 Ase þet line cloþ þet is y-huyted be ofte wessinge. **1398** TREVISA *Barth. De P.R.* XIX. xxiii. (Bodl. MS.), Colde..blakkeþ dry substaunce & whiteþ moiste substaunce. **1538** FITZHERB. *Just. Peas* 118 b, Euerie person that vsith the occupacyon of making of tyles, shall make them good and able and throughly whyted. **1561** DAUS tr. *Bullinger on Apoc.* 230 They haue washed and whited their garmentes in the bloud of the Lambe. **1568** HACKET tr. *Thevet's New found World* vii. 10 b, Milke..is but bloud whitted in ye dug. **1599** B. JONSON *Cynthia's Rev.* III. v, Your Passion hath sufficiently whited your Face. **1649** *Lanc. Tracts Civil War* (Chetham Soc.) 234 Who can white a Blackmore? **1721** E. WARD *Merry Trav.* I. (1729) 16 No yellow Fowl, or stale one, green, Can ever in his Shop be seen, Because he puts in use a strange Device, to white 'em when they change.

b. *spec.* To cover or coat with white; to whitewash; also *fig.*: = WHITEN *v.* 1 b, d. Now *rare.*

c **1200** *Vices & Virtues* 15 Mannes þruh, þe is wiðuten ihwited, and wiðinne stinkende. **1377** LANGL. *P. Pl.* B. III. 61, I shal keure ȝowre kirke..Wowes do whitten. *c* **1430** *Pilgr. Lyf Manhode* II. cxxii. (1869) 121 As the snow embelisheth and whiteth a dong hep with oute. **1534–5** *MS. Rawl. D.* 777 lf. 72 b, Pargyttyng and whyttyng the Stayers. **1572** *Ludlow Churchw. Acc.* (Camden) 149 For lyme, to make an end of whittinge the churche. **1599** NASHE *Lenten Stuffe* 23 A farthing worth of flower to white him ouer and wamble him in. *a* **1625** FLETCHER *Bloody Brother* IV. i, Thou ..Whit'st over all his vices. **1631** WIDDOWES *Nat. Philos.* 25 As it were Lead whited with silver. **1777** BRAND *Pop. Antiq.* 270 *note*, At Oxford, at this Time, the little Crosses cut in the Stones of Buildings, to denote the Division of the Parishes, are whited with Chalk. **1823** SCOTT *Quentin D.* xxviii, When he had thus cleared his conscience, or rather whited it over like a sepulchre. **1833** LOUDON *Encycl. Archit.* §235 The ceilings.., as well as the pediment in front of the house, to be lath laid, set, and whited.

Proverb. **1596** DALRYMPLE tr. *Leslie's Hist. Scot.* II. 373 That at anes, as vses to be said, tha wil quhite tua walis. **1629** H. BURTON *Babel no Bethel* Pref. Ep. 19, I doe in this Booke ..as the Proverbe is, white two walls with one brush.

c. To bleach; to blanch: = WHITEN *v.* 1 c.

1530 PALSGR. 457/1, I bleche, I whyte clothe. **1541** *Act 33 Hen. VIII* c. 15 §1 The said lynnen yarne must lye w^t^oute.. for..one half yere to be whyted. **1611** *Bible* Mark ix. 3 His raiment became..exceeding white as snow: so as no Fuller on earth can white them. **1658** EVELYN *Fr. Gard.* (1675) 208 The manner of whiting it [*sc.* lettuce] under earthen pots. **1714** *Fr. Bk. of Rates* 128 Wax, bleached or whited in Foreign Parts, and imported. **1972** E. WIGGINTON *Foxfire Bk.* 181 And it was the sulfur that whited the apples, and they had a little sulfur flavor.

d. *pa. pple.* Of a horse: see quot. 1737.

1737 BRACKEN *Farriery Impr.* (1757) II. 5 He is..called well Whited if his Hinder Feet be both White. **1760** HEBER *Horse Matches* ix. 147 He is a compleat strong horse, well whited. **1870** *Daily News* 6 June, Mr. Robson's His Majesty, in addition to being badly 'whited', had unpleasing action.

e. *Printing.* To space *out* (matter) with 'white'.

1892 A. OLDFIELD *Man. Typogr.* i. 15 Reglets for whiting out bills and placards are made of wood.

f. *to white out*: to obscure or cover with something white, esp. a white fluid used by typists. Also *fig.*

1975 J. BUTCHER *Copy-Editing* iii. 25 If you want to cancel an underlining for italic, white it out, or put two or three short lines through it, not a wavy line. **1978** M. DUFFY *Housespy* vi. 141 Its long shop window was whited out. **1982** R. LEIGH *Girl with Bright Head* xi. 74 There's also a couple of places where she has had to white out mistakes and type over them. **1983** 'J. LE CARRÉ' *Little Drummer Girl* xiii. 224 She drove with her mind whited out and her thoughts deliberately foreshortened. **1984** *Times Lit. Suppl.* 13 July 771/3 The embarrassed printer explained that he'd whited the little dot out, thinking that it was a dust spot.

g. To make *up* (an actor) to look white.

1977 R. BARNARD *Death on High C's* xv. 148 He was already 'whited up' for the part of the Duke of Mantua... He must look odd, with his deadly white colouring and negroid lips.

white, *v.*[2] *Sc.* and *n. dial.* Also 6 *Sc.* quhite, 7 whyt, 9 *dial.* whit. [north. variant of THWITE. Cf. WHANG.] *trans.* To cut slices off (a stick, etc.) with a knife or other sharp instrument; to pare; to whittle.

1567 *Gude & Godlie B.* (S.T.S.) 72 Stock and stane.. Quhilk men may carfe or quhite. **1662** in W. Hunter *Biggar & Ho. Fleming* (1862) 4 Elf-boyis, wha whyttis and dyghtis thame [*sc.* arrow-heads] with a sharp thing lyke a paking neidle. **1799** J. ROBERTSON *Agric. Perth* 267 Boys, who white a stick..until it be so worn down that it become useless. **1890** SERVICE *Notandums* ix. 62 Ye can be whitin' a stick.

white: see QUIT, WEIGHT, WIGHT, WIT, WITE.

white acre. Also whit(t)aker, witacre.

†**1.** *Law.* An arbitrary name for a particular parcel of ground, distinguished from another called BLACK ACRE, q.v. *Obs.*

1642 tr. *Perkins' Prof. Bk.* viii. §561 If a man seised in fee of white acre and black acre devisable, and deviseth white acre unto I.S. [etc.]. **1698** [see BLACK ACRE].

2. A local name for white quartz.

1796 MARSHALL *Rural Econ. W. Eng.* I. 16 A species of crystal, or quartz—provincially 'whittaker'; which, in colour, is mostly white, sometimes tinged with red. **1839** DE LA BECHE *Rep. Geol. Cornw.*, etc. xv. 473 *note*, Quartz is commonly known..as whiteacre in eastern Cornwall and part of Devon.

white ant, *sb.* [f. WHITE *a.* + ANT.]

1. A very destructive social insect of the Neuropterous order, also called Termite.

[*c.* **1328**, **1713**: see ANT 3.] **1684** LOCKE *Jrnl.* 17 Nov. in K. Dewhurst *Locke* (1963) 265 Told me of a sort of white ants that there mightily infests them. **1699** DAMPIER *Voy.* 127 Abundance of Ants of several sorts, and Woodlice, called by the English in the East Indies White Ants. **1729**, etc. [see ANT 3]. **1849** EASTWICK *Dry Leaves* 86 The never-to-be-sufficiently execrated white ants, who, if they had their will, would reduce all created things to impalpable dust. **1908** E. J. BANFIELD *Confessions of Beachcomber* I. vii. 227 The 'white ant' (which is not an ant)..would literally eat us out of house and home. **1928** R. CAMPBELL *Wayzgoose* i. 20 White-ants and borers, turning boards to dust. **1938** X. HERBERT *Capricornia* (1939) viii. 102 The white-ants have eaten the wheels of my buck-board. **1974** D. STUART *Prince of my Country* v. 40 The wind and the rain and the white ants will level the camps.

2. In *pl.* With allusion to the supposed destruction of the brain by white ants, implying loss of sanity, sense, or intelligence. *Austral. slang.*

1908 H. FLETCHER *Dads & Dan: between Smokes* 64 It wants a fool or a very sane cove indeed ter live in ther lonely bush an' keep ther white ants out o' his napper. **1926** L. G. E. GEE *Bushtracks & Goldfields* 65 And so he rambles on.. and in the unsteady glance of his honest, old eyes and his disconnected speech, I read the mark of the Australian solitudes—'white ants' they call it up north. **1938** H. DRAKE-BROCKMAN *Men without Wives* 27 '"Get the white ants?" What do you mean?' 'Go ratty. Mad.' **1948** V. PALMER *Golconda* vii. 49 They had a definite respect for Christy. He might have a few kinks..but there was something dinkum about him, and if there were white ants behind his forehead they had a lot of work ahead of them. *a* **1951** E. HILL in Murdock & Drake-Brockman *Austral. Short Stories* (1951) 292 My brownie days are over... I reckon I've got white ants.

white-'ant, *v.* Chiefly *Austral.* [f. prec.] *trans.* To destroy in the manner of termites or white ants; to undermine, eat away, or sabotage.

1925 *Glasgow Herald* 14 Nov. 9/6 The extremists..have deliberately 'white-anted' the Labour movement..and squandered the funds of the wealthy unions. **1952** L. OVERACKER *Austral. Party System* vi. 182 The Communists have 'white anted' the unions, elected their members to offices in the Miners' Federation, the waterside workers' and ironworkers' unions, and developed 'shop committees' as basic units in the factories. **1962** R. WALLIS *Point of Origin* 96 After hearing..about me..he decided he'd have to do his duty as a gentleman and tell Rockdale he was being white-anted. **1968** D. IRELAND *Chantic Bird* xi. 102 Television had white-anted their audiences, and they had to use the place for other things besides films.

Hence **white-'anted** *ppl. a.*, **white-'anting** *vbl. sb.*

1936 F. CLUNE *Roaming round Darling* xx. 205 The piece of the boat is five feet long and is made of soft wood, badly white-anted. **1945** BAKER *Austral. Lang.* xiv. 245 White-anting. **1950** D. CUSACK *Comets Soon Pass* in *Three Austral. Three-Act Plays* II. ii. 55 *Dr. John.* Each man must find his own pole to swing to. I have found mine. *Mrs. Ellington-Brown.* I think that's too wonderful, so mystic. *Talbot.* White-anting society! *Jack Smith.* Too mystic for my taste, Doc. I think you've got to get out and fight for things. **1973** *Sydney Morning Herald* 30 Aug. 6/4 We are promised largesse in the form of harbour-side parks in the same breath as the white-anting of a remote scenic gorge is sanctioned.

whitebait ('hwaɪtbeɪt). Formerly **white bait, white-bait.** [f. WHITE *a.* + BAIT *sb.*; so called from its former use as bait.] A small silvery-white fish, caught in large numbers in the estuary of the Thames and elsewhere, and esteemed as a delicacy.

Formerly reckoned by some as a distinct species, but now proved to consist of the fry of various fishes, chiefly the herring and sprat.

1758 *Descr. Thames* 227 A young Herring is by some termed a Yaulin, or a White Bait. **1763** in *Priv. Lett. Ld. Malmesbury* (1870) I. 93 We got back to Greenwich to dine. We had the smallest fish I ever saw, called whitebait; they are only to be eat at Greenwich, and are held in high estimation by the epicures. **1831** PEACOCK *Crotchet Castle* vii, As delicate as whitebait in July. **1836** MOLLARD *Cookery* 38 To dress White Bait. This is a fish peculiar to Greenwich and Blackwall. **1862** MISS BRADDON *Lady Audley* xxxiv, There are people who dislike salmon, and whitebait, and spring ducklings, and all manner of old-established delicacies.

b. *attrib.*

whitebait dinner: a dinner at which whitebait was eaten, held annually at Greenwich and attended by cabinet ministers from early in the 19th century till 1894. For the origin of the dinner see *Encycl. Brit.* (ed. 11) XII. 554.

1836 DISRAELI *Let. to Ld. Glenelg* 12 Mar., His Majesty's Ministers may then hold Cabinet Councils to arrange a white-bait dinner at Blackwall. **1840** MARRYAT *Poor Jack* viii, Whitebait parties at the Ship. [**1859** LEVER *Dav. Dunn* xxxvi, The Irishman that has soared to the realm of white-bait with a Minister.] **1902** C. J. CORNISH *Natur. in Thames* 201 White-bait shoals swarmed in the Lower Thames and the Medway.

c. Applied to other small fishes in different parts of the world resembling this and used as food.

e.g. The Chinese and Japanese fishes of the family *Salangidæ*, various N. American species of silversides, and various fishes of Australia and New Zealand (see quots.).

1882 TENISON-WOODS *Fish N.S.W.* 85 Count Castelnau states that it [*sc. Engraulis antarcticus*] is very common in the Melbourne market..and goes by the name of 'White-bait'. **1883** *Royal Comm. on Fisheries of Tasmania* p. iv, Retropinna Richardsonii, whitebait or smelt. Captured in great abundance in the river Tamar, in the prawn nets. **1886** SHERRIN *Handbk. Fishes N.Z.* 141 Together with the young of *Retropinna Richardsoni*, they [*sc. Galaxias attenuatus*] are called whitebait.

whitebeam ('hwaɪtbiːm). Also **white beam, white-beam.** [Of uncertain origin. Perhaps an alteration of WHITTEN on the analogy of *quicken* and *quickbeam*.] A small tree, *Pyrus Aria*, having large leaves with white silky hairs on the under side. Also ***whitebeam-tree*** (incorrectly *white beam-tree*: see BEAM-TREE).

1705 S. DALE *Pharmacol.* Suppl., Index, The White-Beam-Tree, Aria. **1770** *Phil. Trans.* LXI. 388 Of all soils this is the most favourable to beech, white-beam, [etc.]. **1800** [see BEAM-TREE]. **1902** C. J. CORNISH *Natur. in Thames* 152 The hawfinch is seen..picking up white-beam kernels.

white bear. Chiefly *N. Amer.* **a.** = *polar bear* s.v. POLAR *a.* b.

1600 HAKLUYT *Princ. Navigations* III. 6 The soile is barren in some places,..but it is full of white beares. **1823** *Canad. Mag.* I. 394 The great white bear takes refuge in the most icy climates. **1860** P. H. GOSSE *Romance Nat. Hist.* 62 The white bear, seated on a solitary iceberg in the Polar Sea. **1953** W. B. MOWERY *Tales of Mounted Police* 149 [He had] several livid weals across his left cheek where a white bear had once clawed him.

b. A grizzly bear (*Ursus horribilis*) in a light-coloured phase.

1791 J. LONG *Voy. Indian Interpreter* 95 The large white bear, commonly called the grizly bear, is a very dangerous animal. **1852** J. REYNOLDS *Hist. Illinois* 172 He was destroyed there [in the Rocky Mountains] by a white bear. **1952** J. JENNINGS *Strange Brigade* (1954) 105 There were also red deer or *biche*, and white bears and white partridges.

whitebeard ('hwaɪtbɪəd).

1. An old man with a white beard.

†Also as *quasi*-proper name: in quot. 1450 probably in allusion to the representation of God the Father as an aged man.

1450 SIR J. FASTOLF in *Paston Lett.* I. 131 They shall be quyt by Blackberd or Whyteberd; that ys to sey, by God or the Devyll. **1593** SHAKS. *Rich. II*, III. ii. 112 Whitebeards [*mispr.* White Beares] haue arm'd their thin and hairelesse Scalps Against thy Maiestie. **1829** SCOTT *Anne of G.* xii, 'If she were worth twenty crowns,'..said the old whitebeard.

2. Name in Australia for the plant *Styphelia ericoides*, from the white hairs on the corolla.

1898 MORRIS *Austral Engl.*

white-'bearded, *a.* [WHITE *a.* 12 c.] Having a white beard. **a.** Of a man.

1596 SHAKS. *1 Hen. IV*, II. iv. 509 Falstaffe, that old white-bearded Sathan. **1914** D. H. LAWRENCE *Widowing of Mrs. Holroyd* III. 81 A little stout, white-bearded man.

b. Of wheat.

1788 G. WASHINGTON *Diary* 8 Sept. (1925) III. 417 Also sowing..one bushel of the White bearded Wheat sent me by Beale Boardly. **1850** *Rep. U.S. Comm. Patents 1849*: *Agric.* 132 The white-bearded wheat, a valuable kind less liable to total failure than any other; not very popular with millers.

c. *fig.*

1920 E. SITWELL *Wooden Pegasus* 100 And, mourners too, white-bearded seas Walk slowly by them as they come. **1960** *Farmer & Stockbreeder* 19 Jan. (Suppl.) 1/1 Waves came solid green and white-bearded, like frost giants racing.

whiteblowe, obs. var. WHITLOW.

whiteboard ('hwaɪtbɔəd). [f. WHITE *a.* after *blackboard*.] A white surface for use like a blackboard but accepting felt-tipped pens and wax crayons.

1966 'W. COOPER' *Mem. New Man* II. v. 160 He.. went to the blackboard. (Actually it was an up-to-date plastic white-board, on which one wrote with a coloured wax crayon.) **1977** *Times Educ. Suppl.* 21 Oct. 28/1 (Advt.), They are whiteboards that stay white, year after year. **1978** J. MCNEIL *Consultant* ix. 106 They came to a meeting room... The walls were bare except for a white-board. **1985** *Times Educ. Suppl.* 19 July 20/5 We should also bear in mind that partially-sighted pupils often fare better if a white-board is used rather than a blackboard.

white-bottle. *Obs.* exc. *dial.* [See BOTTLE *sb.*[4]] †**a.** The ox-eye daisy, *Chrysanthemum Leucanthemum*. **b.** The bladder campion, *Silene inflata* (Treas. Bot.).

a **1400** *Alphita* (Anecd. Oxon.) 45 *Consolida media*,.. habet.. florem album latum et durum, similem camomille sed maiorem..a^ce. whit-bothel uel seynt Mary maythe. **1651** FRENCH *Distill.* ii. 56 Take.. White-bottles, Scabius, Dandelyon,.. of each one handfull.

white boy, 'whiteboy. Also 7 **white-boy.**

1. A favourite, pet, or darling boy: a term of endearment for a boy or (usually) man.

Cf. WHITE *a.* 9, and *white son* (WHITE *a.* 11 e).

1599 PORTER *Angry Wom. Abingt.* (Percy Soc.) 69 Whose white boy is that same? *c* **1600** *Timon* I. iii. (1842) 10 *Gelas.* .. What speake the virgines of me?.. *Pæd.* They terme you delight of men, white boye, Noble without comparison. **1639** FULLER *Holy War* I. xiii. 20 The Pope was loth to adventure his darlings into danger; those white-boyes were to stay at home with his Holinesse their tender father. **1690** C. NESSE *O. & N. Test.* I. 377 Joseph.. was not only his earthly fathers white-boy, but his heavenly's also. **1821** SCOTT *Kenilw.* xvi, Were war at the gates, I should be one of her [*sc.* Q. Elizabeth's] white boys. **1919** T. S. ELIOT *Let.* 9 July in *Waste Land Drafts* (1971) p. xvii, The small public which *I* could bring to it [*sc.* the *Egoist*] now reads the *Athenaeum* every week. There I am a sort of white boy; I have a longish critical review about three weeks out of four.

†**2.** A surpliced choir-boy. *Obs. nonce-use.*

1691 MRS. D'ANVERS *Academia* 32 The Organs set up with a ding, The White-men roar, and White-Boys sing.

3. (usually with capital.) A name adopted by or applied to the members of various illegal, rebellious, or riotous associations. **a.** *Eng. Hist.*

1644 (*title*) The Devills White Boyes: or, A mixture of malicious Malignants. **1684** DRYDEN tr. *Maimbourg's Hist. League* Postscr. 47 When a Body of white Boys was already appearing in the West. [*Footnote by Sir W. Scott*, White was the dress affected by those who crowded to see Monmouth in his western tour.]

b. *Irish Hist.* A member of a secret agrarian association formed in 1761: for the reason of the name see quot. 1762. Also *attrib.*

1762 *Ann. Reg., Chron.* 84 Rioters.. called Levellers.. likewise called White Boys, from their wearing shirts over their other cloaths, the better to distinguish each other by night. **1808-** [see RIGHT BOYS]. **1842** MADDEN *United Irishmen* I. 25 The Whiteboy disturbances.. had no more connection with religious controversy than with the disputes between the Scotists and Thomists. Whiteboyism was an association against high rents and tithes. **1842** S. C. HALL *Ireland* II. 79 Ambrose Power Esq., was murdered on his own hearth by a party of Whiteboys. **1881** DILLON in *Standard* 25 Jan., It was.. a relic of the Whiteboy days.

c. *transf.*

1768 H. WALPOLE *Let. to Strafford* 25 June, Those black dogs, the whiteboys or coal-heavers, are dispersed or taken. **1825** J. NEAL *Bro. Jonathan* III. 290 Who knows but you are one o' the tories yourself; or one o' the whiteboys—or cow boys—or skinners.

Hence **whiteboyism**, the principles or practices of the Irish Whiteboys (see 3 b).

1778 *Phil. Surv. S. Irel.* 313 Till some step is taken in favour of tillage and the poor Whiteboyism will probably remain. **1842** [see 3 b]. **1893** *Times* 2 Oct. 3/6 Five men who had been sentenced at the Kerry Assizes in 1888,—for moonlighting and whiteboyism.

white bread. [Cf. MHG. *wîzbrot*, G. *weissbrot*, LG. *witbrôd*, Du. *wittebrood*.] Bread of a light colour, made from fine wheaten flour, as distinguished from BROWN BREAD.

13.. in *Engl. Gilds* (1870) 354 Euerych bakere of þe town ..sholde make whitbred. *c* **1450** *Customs of Malton* in *Engl. Misc.* (Surtees) 62 No bakar y^t bakys qwhytte brede schall bake brown brede.. nor he y^t bakys brown brede schall bake no qwhyte brede. **1523-34** FITZHERB. *Husb.* §34 Polerde wheate.. is greatter corne, and wyll make whyte breed. **1598** *Epulario* D j b, Putting vnto it crums of Whitebread. **1605** SYLVESTER *Du Bartas* II. iii. *Law* 836 Thou, that from Heav'n thy daily White-bread hast. **1794** STEDMAN *Surinam* (1813) II. xxv. 248 The white bread, fruit, and Spanish wines.. I received as a present.

whitecap, white-cap ('hwaɪtkæp), *sb.* [CAP *sb.*[1]]

1. Name for several birds having a white or light-coloured patch on the head (see quots.).

1668 CHARLETON *Onomast.* 78 *Passeres*.. *Montanus*.. the White-Cap. **1874** T. BELT *Nat. Nicaragua* 138 The white-cap (*Microchera parvirostris*, Lawr.), the smallest of thirteen different kinds of humming-birds that I noticed around Santo Domingo. **1885** SWAINSON *Prov. Names Birds* 13 Redstart... The male is called 'whitecap' in Shropshire, from its white forehead. *Ibid.* 22 Whitethroat.. (from its grey head).. Whitecap.

2. *pl.* Local name for species of mushroom.

1818 *Withering's Brit. Pl.* (ed. 6) IV. 282 *Ag[aricus] Georgii*... Gathered in abundance for the London markets, where they are sold as Mushrooms, but by the more discriminating country people called White caps. **1866** *Treas. Bot.*, *White-caps*,.. *Agaricus arvensis*.. Horse Mushroom.

3. A white-capped or crested wave; a breaker.

1773 *Phil. Trans.* LXIV. 458 None, or very few white-caps (or waves whose tops turn over in foam) appeared. **1838** ASA GRAY *Lett.* (1893) I. 71 We had a strong head wind..: the surface of the lake was covered with white-caps. **1883** *Harper's Mag.* Aug. 375/1 Numerous reefs.. marked by white-caps where the ebb tide rushed over them.

4. A person wearing a white cap; *spec.* one of a self-constituted body in the United States who commit outrages upon persons under the pretence of regulating public morals.

1891 *Tablet* 13 June 941 The Lynchers in such cases are usually called white-caps, regulators, &c. **1894** *Westm. Gaz.* 23 May 2/3 A White Cap.. disguises himself and performs his errands at night.

So **'white-capped** (-kæpt) *a.*, wearing a white cap or caps; capped with foam, covered with white-crested waves.

1880 'OUIDA' *Moths* iii, White-capped old women looked on. **1895** *Outing* (U.S.) XXVI. 447/2 A white-capped sea. **1899** *Scribner's Mag.* XXV. 75 The whitecapped cavalry were caught unawares by French's brigade.

'whitecap, *v.* *U.S.* [f. the sb., sense 4.] *trans.* To commit an outrage upon (a person) in the style of the whitecaps. Chiefly as **'white-capping** *vbl. sb.* Also **'whitecapper.**

1895 T. ROOSEVELT in *Century Mag.* Nov. 72/2 The law-breaker, whether he be lyncher or whitecapper, or merely the liquor-seller who desires to drive an illegal business. **1900** M. NICHOLSON *Hoosiers* 45 The milder form of outlawry, known as 'white-capping', has also been practised in Indiana occasionally. **1904** *N.Y. Even. Post* 28 Jan. 9 The Mississippi has voted Gov. Vardaman a special appropriation to enable him to suppress the 'white cappers'. **1908** D. G. PHILLIPS *Old Wives for New* iv. 68 If he wasn't such a wonderful doctor he'd have been white-capped long ago—tarred and feathered and railed out of town. **1943** A. G. POWELL *I can go Home Again* 167 During the short time I served as county judge, a series of 'whitecappings', directed against Negroes, occurred in the lower part of the county. **1970** [see KU-KLUX 1 a].

'whitecapping, *a.* *rare*[−1]. [f. as WHITECAP *sb.* + -ING[2].] Covering with or as with a white cap.

1912 J. LONDON *Son of Sun* v. ii. 175 Their long slopes.. were broken by systems of smaller whitecapping waves.

Whitechapel ('hwaɪt,tʃæp(ə)l). [Name of a district in the East End of London, traditionally one of the poorer parts of the capital.]

1. a. In various slang uses, mostly *attrib.* (see quots.).

a **1700** B. E. *Dict. Cant. Crew*, *White-chappel-portion*, two torn Smocks, and what Nature gave. **1785** GROSE *Dict. Vulgar T.*, *Whitechapel breed*, fat, ragged, and saucy. *Whitechapel beau*, who dresses with a needle and thread, and undresses with a knife. **1860** *Slang Dict.*, *Whitechapel*, or Westminster Brougham, a costermonger's donkey-barrow. **1863** DICKENS *Uncomm. Trav.* xxv[ii], What is termed in Albion a 'Whitechapel shave' (and which is, in fact, whitening, judiciously applied to the jaws with the palm of the hand). **1865** *Slang Dict.*, *Whitechapel fortune*, a clean gown and a pair of pattens.

b. *attrib.* or *absol.* Applied to certain irregular or unskilful methods of play in whist and billiards: see quots. *colloq.*

1755 *Connoisseur* No. 60 ¶5 They know no more of the game [*sc.* whist] than what is called White-Chapel play. **1847** HALLIWELL, *Whitechapel-play* [= *Bungay-play*, a simple straightforward way of playing the game of whist, by leading all the winning cards in succession, without endeavouring to make the best of the hand.] **1866** *N. & Q.* 3rd Ser. IX. 372/2 The Saying at Whist, when you play ace and king of a suit—'That is Whitechapel play'. *Ibid.* 440 All billiard players know, that when an adversary 'pockets' your ball, it is called 'Whitechapel play', the act of doing so being considered anything but etiquette. **1899** A. MAINWARING *Cut Cavendish* 12 Avoid the hateful 'White-chapel', *i.e.* the lead from a single card.

2. ***Whitechapel needle***: some particular make of needle; in quot. 1828 allusively. *U.S.*

1774 *Pennsylv. Gaz.* 10 Aug. Suppl. 2/2 Whitechapel and Glovers needles. **1828** *Lights & Shades* II. 188 He had pricked his fingers with 'Gammer Gurton's needle', in buying a Whitechapel one. *Note*, A cant phrase for a counterfeited copy of this old play.

3. In full ***Whitechapel cart***, a kind of light two-wheeled spring cart.

1842 J. AITON *Dom. Econ.* (1857) 129 For a minister with a family, a whitechapel is, upon the whole, the best of the open conveyances... It carries six. **1859** *Carriage Builders' Art Jrnl.* I. 26/2 A light Whitechapel Cart, suitable to the use of a country gentleman. **1875** *Hints to Yng. Tandem Drivers* 6 Whitechapels (from the fact that the passengers sit *inside* them instead of *outside*) are dangerous to get out of in any emergency. **1900** GUNTON *Patent Specif.* No. 1332 Improved seat-shifting fittings for Dogcarts, Whitechapels or any other vehicles.

4. as *adj.* Low, vulgar.

1901 *Scotsman* 11 Mar. 7/5 The humiliation of the party by the Whitechapel scene of Tuesday.

white cliffs, *sb. pl.* [f. WHITE *a.* + CLIFF.]

1. Chalk cliffs; *spec.* those of Dover, regarded as a symbol of Great Britain.

1879 [see CLIFF 1 b]. **1902** KIPLING *Just-So-Stories* 7 Take me to my natal-shore and the white-cliffs-of-Albion. **1940** N. BURTON (*song*) There'll be blue-birds over the white cliffs of Dover. **1940** R. S. LAMBERT *Ariel & All his Quality* iii. 84 Full of a mystic vision of Empire.. inspired by the sight of the white cliffs of Dover. **1978** M. KENYON *Deep Pocket* xiv. 181 You'll be deported, you'll never see the White Cliffs again.

2. (With capital initials.) The name of a town in New South Wales, used *attrib.* to designate opals mined there.

1911 C. E. W. BEAN *'Dreadnought' of Darling* xxv. 222 The Wilcannia banks live on the White Cliffs opal. **1936** H. P. WHITLOCK *Story of Gems* x. 127 The White Cliffs opals are not unlike those from Hungary, but they show broader flashes of colour. **1975** R. WEBSTER *Gems in Jewellery* xi. 57 The White Cliffs opal is cream in colour and found in seams in sandstone.

whitecoat ('hwaɪtkəʊt). Also **white-coat, white coat.**

1. a. A soldier wearing a white or light-coloured coat: cf. BUFF-COAT 2. (Also *attrib.*) *Obs.* exc. *Hist.*

1555 in Arb. *Garner* VIII. 60 A certain Band of White Coats.. sent unto them from London. **1562** in *Archaeologia* XLVII. 221 Yt apeareth a greate differens.. betwene the excercised souldior and the rawe white coat. **1571** R. BANNATYNE *Mem.* (Bann. Club) 91 Thare began flyting, ..'Away blewcoate!' 'I defy the whytcoite!' **1605** HEYWOOD *If you know not me* C 2, Enter three white-cote soldiers. **1631** —— *Engl. Eliz.* 113 For her guard two hundred Northern White Coates were appointed.. to watch about her lodging. **1644** in Rushw. *Hist. Coll.* III. II. 634 The Marquess of Newcastle's Regiment of White Coats were almost wholly cut off for they scorned to fly. **1662** A. COOPER *Stratologia* VI. 115 In the main battail do our white Coats stand. **1840** HOR. SMITH *Oliver Cromwell* II. 159 Newcastle with all his whitecoats.

b. In modern times, an Austrian soldier.

1861 MEREDITH *Let. to Mrs. J. Ross* 19 Nov., Verona.. is now less a City than a fortress. You see nothing but white coats—who form the majority of the inhabitants.

2. A young seal, having a coat of white fur; also the fur itself.

1792 G. CARTWRIGHT *Jrnl. Labrador* III. p. x, *Whitecoat*, a young seal, before it has cast its first coat, which is white and furry. **1892** *Daily News* 28 Mar. 6/2 The skin of the small pup seal.. is of small value, being known as 'White-coat'.

3. A doctor or hospital attendant who wears a white coat.

1911 [see SCHMERZ]. **1932** 'JOCK' *Dartmoor from Within* vi. 134 He makes straight for the tub, and 'White Coat' alters his course to cut him off. **1980** *Brit. Med. Jrnl.* 29 Mar. 934/2 We roar into the hospital. White coats run out.

white-collar, *sb.* and *a.* orig. *U.S.*

A. *sb.* **a.** (As two words.) A white collar regarded as characteristic of a man engaged in non-manual work.

1919 U. SINCLAIR *Brass Check* xiii. 78 It is a fact with which every union workingman is familiar, that his most bitter despisers are the petty underlings of the business world, the poor office-clerks.. who, because they are allowed to wear a white collar.., regard themselves as members of the capitalist class. **1976** M. HINXMAN *End of Good Woman* i. 9 Tom emigrated to Canada. Dick put on a white collar and became a bank clerk.

b. A person engaged in non-manual work.

1930 A. P. HERBERT *Water Gipsies* iv. 39 That family over there.. come here every Thursday of their lives for a little family reunion, and white collars, too, all of them. **1938** W. SMITTER *F.O.B. Detroit* 32 It wasn't long before the white-collars up front began taking notice of what was going on on the floor. **1954** E. PANGBORN *Mirror for Observers* (1955) I. i. 19 A residential backwater for factory workers, white-collars, transients. **1962** 'K. ORVIS' *Damned & Destroyed* i. 12 A pair of white-collars from a near-by St. James Street brokerage office pounded the bar for fresh drinks. **1971** W. J. BURLEY *Guilt Edged* i. 5 [The] passenger ferry.. had made only two return trips, one for the workers at seven-thirty and one for the white-collars at eight-thirty.

B. *adj.* **a.** Of a person: engaged in non-manual, esp. clerical, work.

1921 *Ladies' Home Jrnl.* May 98/4 Urban chain restaurants have accustomed white-collar boys and girls to tasty viands, albeit in limited amounts. **1924** W. MCDOUGALL *Ethics & Some Mod. World Probl.* iv. 125 The strata of brain-workers made up the white-collar class or middle classes. **1937** *Atlantic Monthly* Dec. 750/1 Proletarian literature.. has been accompanied by books on the white-collar worker, the storekeeper.. the scientist, and the millionnaire in situations equally disastrous or degrading. **1948** *Chicago Tribune* 3 Apr. II. 1/4 The modern white collar girl wants a job which not only offers opportunities but advances as well. **1959** [see *blue-collar* s.v. BLUE *a.* 13]. **1969** *Times* 30 Apr. 26/6 The first strike action by manual workers against the British Steel Corporation's new policy of white collar union recognition broke out yesterday. **1982** D. GORHAM *Victorian Girl* ii. 29 Teachers and nurses.. were of less importance numerically than [female] 'white collar' workers.

b. Of work or an occupation: not manual or industrial; *spec.* clerical.

1926 *Amer. Speech* II. 96/2 The uneducated and uneducable found a new field opening to them, and rushed in, to take advantage of the 'white-collar' work. **1937** 'G. ORWELL' *Road to Wigan Pier* xi. 205 The typical Socialist.. is either a youthful snob-Bolshevik.. or, still more typically, a prim little man with a white-collar job. **1962** AUDEN *Dyer's Hand* (1963) 123 He has a dingy white-collar job. **1979** T. BENN *Arguments for Socialism* i. 41 The definition of a worker is extended to include all wage and salary earners and paves the way for the extension of trade unionism into the realms of clerical white collar, scientific and technical and managerial work.

c. (See quot. 1937.) *U.S.*

1932 [see *dirt farmer* s.v. DIRT *sb.* 7 d]. **1937** *Amer. Speech* XII. 105 The adjectives *suitcase* and *bonanza* and *whitecollar* are applied in recently developed wheat-farming areas to large owner-farmers who live outside the community and appear during the sowing and harvesting seasons.

d. Applied to a person who takes advantage of the special knowledge or responsibility of his position to commit non-violent, often financial, crimes; also to the crime itself.

[**1932** E. H. SUTHERLAND in *Publ. Amer. Sociol. Soc.* Aug. 60 The financial crimes of the white-collar classes.] **1934** —— *Princ. Criminol.* ii. 32 These white-collar criminaloids ..are by far the most dangerous to society..from the point of view of effects on private property and social institutions. **1964** M. ARGYLE *Psychol. & Social Probl.* v. 65 Older middle-class people are tempted to commit offences other than theft or violence, and the various kinds of 'white collar crime' are hard to detect—income-tax avoidance, bogus expense claims and complex business illegalities. **1977** *Wandsworth Borough News* 7 Oct. 5/3 Dangerous drivers and white-collar criminals are far more likely to receive lenient treatment than the petty habitual thief. **1984** *Daily Tel.* 12 Nov. 20/2 White-collar crime like fraud is..on the increase.., and the computer has opened enormous vistas of extra opportunity.

white-'collared, *a.* [-ED².] **1.** Wearing a white collar; also *fig.*

1932 H. G. WELLS *Work, Wealth & Happiness of Mankind* vii. 237 The black-coated, white-collared clerk. **1947** J. MULGAN *Report on Experience* 18 Ten millions of the rest, bowler-hatted, white-collared, moved in monotonous rhythm. **1951** D. GLOVER *Sings Harry* 41 It's plain hard hazardous work To work with the white-collared wave.

2. = WHITE COLLAR *a.* a.

1933 *Sun* (Baltimore) 14 Apr. 4/6 Hands blistered and backs sore from hard physical labor, so-called 'white-collared men' of West Virginia are calling for more and yet more work. **1947** *Hist. 'The Times'* III. v. 117 That public was the great and growing, vigorous 'white-collared' lower-middle class. **1959, 1967** [see *blue-collared* adj. s.v. BLUE *a.* 13]. **1977** M. GREEN *Children of Sun* (rev. ed.) x. 460 *Lucky Jim*..described a new class on the British scene, the white-collared proletariat, trained technicians but not educated gentlemen.

whited ('hwaɪtɪd), *ppl. a.* Now *rare* or *arch.*

I. [f. WHITE *v.*¹ + -ED¹.]

1. Covered or coated with white; *spec.* (*a*) plastered over with white, whitewashed, as a wall, building, etc.; now chiefly in the biblical phr. ***whited sepulchre*** (Matt. xxiii. 27) used allusively; † (*b*) of metal, tinned or silvered; also occas. *gen.*, e.g. of land covered with snow.

1340 *Ayenb.* 228 Huo þet is yhol of bodie and uoul ine herte is ase þe berieles yhuited. **1388** WYCLIF *Acts* xxiii. 3 Thanne Poul seide to hym, Thou whitid wal, God smyte thee. **1552** HULOET, Whyghted or paynted with white leade, *cerustatus*. **1645** MILTON *Hor. Ep.* I. *xvi.* 40 in *Tetrach.* 39 But his owne house, and the whole neighbourhood Sees his foule inside through his whited skin. **1669** STURMY *Mariner's Mag., Penalties & Forfeit.* 2 Iron Wyre, or whited Wyre, are forfeited if any such be Imported. **1733** POPE *Donne's Sat.* IV. 151 He tells..What Lady's face is not a whited wall. **1764** DODSLEY *Leasowes* in *Shenstone's Wks.* (1777) II. 305 A whited village among trees. **1835** J. E. ALEXANDER *Sketches in Portugal* i. 13 What a whited sepulchre we found the city to be! **1850** KINGSLEY *Alton Locke* iv, This old whited sepulchre, society. **1867** EMERSON *May-day* 104 The whited desert knew me not, Snow-ridges masked each darling spot.

2. Whitened by deprivation of colour; *spec.* bleached, as cloth; also, peeled so as to expose the white interior.

1529 *Dunmow Churchw. MS.* lf. 10 b, xxv. ells of whytyd normvndy at vi d the ell. **1692** *Lond. Gaz.* No. 2814/4 A considerable quantity of Whited Linen. **1794** *Trans. Soc. Arts* XII. 139 About a load and a half whited osiers. **1897** P. WARUNG *Tales Old Regime* 205 John Donnell,..brown complexion,..whited raised spot on lower part of right eye.

†**3.** ***whited brown*** (of paper); whitish brown, whity-brown. *Obs.*

1720 *Lett. Lond. Jrnl.* (1721) 11 Having put up my Books [etc.] in a Sheet of whited-brown Paper. **1846** DODD *Brit. Manuf.* Ser. VI. 18.

II. [f. WHITE *sb.* 1 + -ED².]

4. Of an egg: Having white or albumen (of a specified kind). *rare*⁻¹.

1599 T. M[OUFET] *Silkwormes* 66 Whited alike, and yellow yolked all.

white-ear, *sb.* and *a.* [EAR *sb.*¹] **a.** *sb.* A gastropod resembling, or having some part resembling, a white ear; e.g. one of the family *Vanicoridæ*, having a white-ribbed shell with a wide opening. **b.** *adj.* White-eared.

1815 BURROW *Elem. Conchol.* 204 *Helix Halitoidea*, White-ear Snail; Venus's Ear. **1826** STEPHENS in Shaw's *Gen. Zool.* XIII. II. 57 White-Ear Owl. **1854** A. ADAMS etc. *Man. Nat. Hist.* 133 White-Ears (*Vanicoridæ*).

So '**white-eared** (-ɪəd) *a.*, having white ears; (of a bird) having white feathers around the ears; ***white-eared flycatcher***, a monarch flycatcher, *Monarcha leucotis*, found in Australia; ***white-eared pheasant***, an eared pheasant, *Crossoptilon crossoptilon*, found in forest regions of eastern Tibet and neighbouring China.

1783 LATHAM *Gen. Syn. Birds* II. I. 84 White-Eared Thr[ush]. **1869** J. GOULD *Birds Austral. Suppl.* 12 (*heading*) White-eared Flycatcher. [**1918** W. BEEBE *Monogr. Pheasants* I. 187 Once only was a glimpse permitted to us of the wonderful White Eared-pheasants.] **1976** G. DURRELL *Stationary Ark* iv. 78 Our chances of establishing the White-eared pheasant in captivity seemed..slim. **1980** G. PIZZEY *Field Guide Birds Austral.* 258 White-eared Monarch Flycatcher..has been likened to a miniature Magpie Lark.

'**white-face**, *sb.* and *a.* Also **whiteface**, †**white face**. **A.** *sb.* †**1.** The widgeon. *Obs. rare.*

1709 [see BALD-FACE 1].

2. One of a Hereford herd of cattle. Now chiefly *N. Amer.*

1860 W. WHITE *Wrekin* xi. 93, I journeyed down..into the fertile champaign of the whitefaces. **1965** E. MCCOURT *Road across Canada* 152 Herds of white-faces dot the slopes .., grazing knee-deep in the lush grass of the wide valley-bottoms. **1970** M. G. EBERHART *El Rancho Rio* (1971) viii. 85 I've been breeding white-faces—pure-bred Herefords.

3. White or light-coloured make-up, esp. as worn by a clown, or by a Black actor playing a white character. orig. *U.S.*

1895 *N.Y. Dramatic News* 9 Nov. 14/4 Lew Dockstader, in his new white-face act,..will be seen at Keith's, November 18. **1947** *Partisan Rev.* Jan.–Feb. 65 The selection of Canada Lee, a negro in white-face, to play Bosola. **1948** M. WINTER in P. Magriel *Chron. Amer. Dance* 53/1 English clowns..returned to whiteface, but kept certain characteristics of blackface performers. **1981** *Times* 11 Apr. 7/1 We find him grovelling on the floor like a mock Othello in whiteface.

B. *adj.* Of an animal: having a white face.

1785 T. JEFFERSON *Notes Virginia* vi. 126 White face teal. **1961** R. P. HOBSON *Rancher takes Wife* xvii. 217 There's a herd of top whiteface cows. **1978** *Detroit Free Press* 5 Mar. C20/5 (Advt.), Whiteface Capuchin male, 2 years old. **1984** *Properties Open in 1984* (National Trust) 40 A Country Park surrounds the property and contains a flock of Whiteface Woodland sheep.

white feather. In phr. *to show the white feather*, etc.: see FEATHER *sb.* 1 b. Hence **white-feather**, one who 'shows the white feather', a coward; **white-feathered** *a.*, *lit.* having white feathers; *fig.* 'showing the white feather', cowardly; **white-featherism** (*nonce-wd.*), cowardice.

1785 GROSE *Dict. Vulgar T.*, **White feather*, he has a white feather, he is a coward, an allusion to a game cock, where having a white feather, is a proof he is not of the true game breed. **1805** *Sporting Mag.* XXVI. 56 According to the boxing phrase, shewed the white feather. **1816** SCOTT *Bl. Dwarf* ix, 'He has a white feather in his wing',..said Simon, ..somewhat scandalized by his ready surrender. **1825–** [see FEATHER *sb.* 1 b]. **1857** BORROW *Rom. Rye* xliii, Jack is a gentleman,..whilst t'other, though bred a lord, is a screw, and a *whitefeather. **1816** *Sporting Mag.* XLVIII. 4 He was one of the *white-feathered sort. **1854** *Poultry Chron.* I. 49 All white-feathered poultry are tender, save Aylesbury ducks. **1843** [JAMES] *Commissioner* iv. 39 That he might show as little *white featherism as possible.

Whitefieldian, Whitfieldian ('hwaɪt-, 'hwɪtfiːldɪən), *sb.* and *a.* [f. proper name *Whitefield* or *Whitfield* + -IAN.] **a.** *sb.* A follower of George Whitefield; a Calvinistic Methodist. **b.** *adj.* Of or belonging to George Whitefield or the Whitefieldians. So **Whit(e)'fieldianism**, '**Whit(e)fieldism**, the system or doctrines of the Whitefieldians; '**Whit(e)fieldite**, a Whitefieldian.

1744 in G. T. S. Farquhar *Three Bps. Dunkeld* (1915) I. xi. 94 He is looked upon by Lyon at Perth..as a Whitefieldian. **1748** *St. James' Even. Post* Oct., Hamburg... A new set of Methodists (much like our Whitefieldites). **1786** TOLD *Life* 87, I treated him with ridicule and contempt, he being a Whitfieldite. **1879** GLADSTONE *Glean.* VII. 224 Whitefieldism on the one hand, and the clericalism of the eighteenth century on the other. **1885** *Scribner's Mag.* XXX. 390/1 Puritanism, quakerism, and what may be comprehensively called Whitefieldism. **1915** G. T. S. FARQUHAR *Three Bps. Dunkeld* I. xi. 94 A..discourse.. upon the Christian doctrine of Justification (evidently intended to test his Whitefieldianism).

whitefish ('hwaɪtfɪʃ). Also **white-fish**, **white fish**. [Cf. Du. *witvisch* bleak, LG. *witfisk*, med.L. *albus piscis*.]

1. A general name for fishes of a white or light colour (esp. those having silvery scales without spots or ornamental colours), as cod, haddock, whiting, etc.

1461–2 in *10th Rep. Hist. MSS. Comm.* App. v. 301 Samon, heringe, hake, whitfishe. **1536** BELLENDEN *Cron. Scot.* (1821) I. p. xxxvii, This firth is richt plentuus of coclis, osteris [etc.]..with gret plente of quhit fische. **1612** DRAYTON *Poly-olb.* ix. 131 Those White-fish that in her [*sc.* Lin] doe wondrously abound, Are neuer seene in him [*sc.* Dee]; nor are his Salmons found At any time in her. **1701** [W. PATERSON] *Counc. Trade* (1751) 28 The vast numbers of herring and white-fish in all our channels, inletts and lakes. **1787** BEST *Angling* (ed. 2) 133 Carshalton-river, abounding with trouts and other white fishes. **1865** KINGSLEY *Herew.* xxxi, The great pike..sending the whitefish flying in shoals.

2. The Great Sturgeon (= BELUGA 1); the White Whale (= BELUGA 2).

1662 J. DAVIES tr. *Olearius' Voy. Ambass.* 165 A Fisherman..took a *Bieluga* or white-fish, which was above eight foot long, and above four broad. **1698** A. BRAND *Emb. fr. Muscovy* 31 The Oby..abounds in..Sturgeon, Whitefish or Belluja's, and others. **1743** *Phil. Trans.* XLII. 611 The White-fish are likewise in these Seas, like a Whale, but without Fins on the Back. **1792** G. CARTWRIGHT *Jrnl. Labrador* III. p. x, *Whitefish*, a fish of the Porpoise kind.

3. A common name for the fishes of the genus *Coregonus*, of the family *Salmonidæ*, found in the lakes of North America, and valued as food.

1748 [see TITTYMEG]. **1778** T. HUTCHINS *Top. Descr. Virginia* 47 Lake Erie has a great variety of fine fish, such as Sturgeon, Eel, White Fish. **1873** T. GILL *Catal. Fishes E. Coast N. Amer.* 29 *Pomatomus saltatrix*... Blue-fish..; white-fish and snap-mackerel (young). *Ibid.* 33 *Brevoortia menhaden*..white-fish (Saybrook to Milford, Connecticut). **1883** *Fisheries Exhib. Catal.* (ed. 4) 160 A The famous *Corregonus albus*, or White Fish, of Canadian lakes.

Hence **white fisher**, one who catches white fish (sense 1); **white fishery**, **fishing**, the occupation of catching white fish.

1528 *Extr. Aberd. Reg.* (1844) I. 121 All the *quhit fischaris..consentit to gif to thair chaplane..xii d. in the yeir. **1601** *Ibid.* (1848) II. 217 Willeame Brabner, Patrik Huchoun, and James Symsoun, quhytfischeris in Futtie. **1772** *Newspaper Cutting* (Douce Prints S. 9. 109) Died at Montrose,..Thomas Milne, white-fisher, aged 100 years. **1892** *Daily News* 26 Mar. 3/3 The Committee have devised a *modus vivendi* by which the rights of the salmon fishers have been protected, and at the same time the rights of the white fishers have been established. **1791** NEWTE *Tour Eng. & Scot.* 168 Small vessels [employed] in the *White Fisheries. **1840** BLAINE *Encycl. Rur. Sports* VIII. ii. 955 The British fisheries, which, besides the herring, embrace the cod, the ling, haddock, skate, halibut, turbot, &c. are collectively termed the white fishery. **1600** *Reg. Mag. Sig. Scot.* 341/1 Cum *lie stelyair*, halecum et salmonum piscationibus et *lie *quhite-fischingis*. **1703** J. BRAND *Descr. Orkney*, etc. 79 Excelling any other place of the King of Brittan's Dominions for Herring, White and Grey Fishing. **1892** *Rep. Solway White Fish. Comm.*, The white-fishing industry..on the Scottish shores of the Solway Firth.

whiteflaw, obs. var. WHITLOW.

whitefoot ('hwaɪtfʊt), *sb.* and *a.* [Cf. OE. *hwītfōt* adj.]

A. *sb.* **1.** *Farriery.* A white marking on a horse's foot (see quot.); also, a horse with such a mark.

1753 *Chambers' Cycl. Supp.*, *White-Foot*..called in French *Balzane*, is a white mark that happens in the feet of a great many horses, both before and behind, from the fetlock to the coffin.

2. Collectors' name for a species of moth.

1832 RENNIE *Butterfl. & M.* 161 The Whitefoot (*S[pilonota] fœnella*..). Wings..dusky brown,..with a large medial hook-shaped white band.

3. *Hist.* A member of a secret society in Ireland who committed murders and outrages about 1832. Pl. **whitefeet** (also irreg. used *attrib.*).

1832 in G. C. Lewis *Local Disturb. Irel.* (1836) 107, I find that the Whiteboy system has for the last sixty years continued under different names; as, Peep-o'-day-boys,.. Ribbon-men, the Lady Clares, the Terry Alts... Now we have the Whitefeet and Blackfeet. **1832** *Boston Herald* 6 Mar. 2 An armed party of Whitefeet paid the third visit to the house of the long-threatened Jeremiah Farrell. **1833** *Ibid.* 12 Mar. 3/6 James Jackman, a Whitefoot, for attacking the house of one Roche, and killing him, is to be hanged on Monday. **1886** *Irish Eccles. Gaz.* 4 Sept., The massacre of whitefeet men in the last days of that unfortunate secret society in the Queen's County.

B. *adj.* White-footed. *poet.*

1867 MORRIS *Jason* II. 359 White-foot Ino smiling, sat alone.

So '**white-,footed** *a.*, having white feet; ***white-footed mouse***, any of several species of North American mice of the genus *Peromyscus*, esp. *P. maniculatus* or *P. leucopus*; '**whitefootism**, the practices of Irish whitefeet.

14.. *Voc.* in Wr.-Wülcker 602/32 *Petulus*,..whyt foted *et dicitur de equo.* **1753** *Chambers' Cycl. Supp.* s.v. *Chausse trop-haut*, A white-footed horse. **1757** in *Eliz. Carter's Lett.* 29 July (1809) II. 251 One of the prettiest little white-footed black cats..you ever saw. **1781** PENNANT *Hist. Quadrup.* 91 The white-footed Antelope or Nil-ghau. **1821** SCOTT *Kenilw.* x, His white-footed nag. **1832** in G. C. Lewis *Local Disturb. Irel.* (1836) 77 If they continue suffering under hardships,..Whitefootism will revive again. **1857** *Rep. Comm. Patents 1856: Agric.* (U.S.) 86 The food of [the Northern shrike]..consists almost wholly of arvicolae and a few white-footed prairie mice. **1869** *Amer. Naturalist* III. 120 When the axe-man struck the tree, a Whitefooted Mouse..rushed from the nest. **1936** D. MCCOWAN *Animals Canad. Rockies* viii. 68 The White-footed mouse is of medium size and has a silky coat that is dark brown above and light on the underparts. **1977** J. L. HARPER *Population Biol. Plants* xv. 465 The seed was collected and buried mainly by white-footed mice.

white friar. [WHITE *a.* 6 a.]

1. A Carmelite friar (whose habit is distinguished by a white cloak and scapular). Also, loosely, a Premonstratensian or White Canon.

1412 in *Laing Charters* (1899) 24 Willyam Cokar, than beande prouincial of the Quite Freris of Scotlande. **1474** CAXTON *Chesse* III. ii. (1883) 88, I haue my self ben conuersant in a religious hous of white freris at gaunt which haue all thynge in comyn. **a 1550** *Lynn Chron.* in *Six Town Chron.* (1911) 198 In this yere one william chysborow and a whyght ffryere was hanged drawen and quartered. **1603** STOW *Surv.* 312 The white Fryers church in Fleet-street. **1762** BP. FORBES *Jrnl.* (1886) 170 An Abbacy of *Præmonstratenses*, or White Friars. **1766** [see CARMELITE].

2. *pl.* The Carmelite convent in Fleet Street, London; hence, the district or neighbourhood in which it was.

'Having been formerly a sanctuary, it long retained the privilege of protecting persons liable to arrest, and thus became the resort of debtors..and profligates' (Nares). Hence *attrib.*

1561 AWDELAY *Frat. Vocab.* (1869) 51 There came..a Counterfet Cranke vnder my lodgynge at the whyte Fryares. **1609** B. JONSON *Silent Wom.* Prol., Cates..fit for Ladies;.. Some for your waiting wench, and city-wires; Some for your men, and daughters of White-Fryars. **1620** MELTON *Astrologaster* 36 Some of his White-Fryer Mistresses.

3. *colloq.* or *dial.* A flake or particle of white scum or froth floating on liquid.

1729 SWIFT *Direct. Serv.* i. (1745) 22 If the Cork be musty, or White Fryers in your Liquor. **1856** P. KENNEDY *Banks Boro* xxv. 191 The white-friars came at last on the potatoes in the big pot: they then proceeded to boil.

white gold. 1. † a. Platinum. *Obs.*

1764 *Gentl. Mag.* XXXIV. 128/1 (*heading*) A farther Account of a Metal, called Platina, or White Gold. **1798** NEMNICH *Polygl.-Lex.* II. 936 White gold. The platina.

b. A name applied to various silvery-coloured alloys of gold with nickel, palladium, platinum, or silver.

1893 *Funk's Stand. Dict.* s.v. *Gold, White gold*, an alloy of about five parts of silver to one of gold. **1921** *Daily Colonist* (Victoria, B.C.) 12 Mar. 2/1 Modern Wedding Rings... White Gold Rings, $10. **1940** *Chambers's Techn. Dict.* 382/1 *White gold* is usually an alloy with nickel, but as used in dentistry this alloy contains platinum or palladium. **1946** G. STIMPSON *Bk. about Thousand Things* 242 White gold jewelry nowadays differs from regulation gold, not in the quality or the quantity of gold used, but in the kind of alloy. **1956** J. N. ANDERSON *Appl. Dental Materials* vii. 78 Casting alloys [of gold] containing a large amount of palladium together with silver are called white golds. **1971** *Nature* 18 June 443/1 Two basically gold-silver alloys were known to the Greeks and Romans: (1) 'white gold'—a haphazard mixture derived from grains of weathered auriferous ore; and (2) 'electrum'—an alloy of controlled quality. **1974** *Country Life* 26 Dec. 2002/3 Platinum has largely been superseded by white gold as a jewellery metal. **1980** 'E. MCBAIN' *Ghosts* ii. 28 One rope choker of eighteen-karat yellow and white gold.

2. Any white substance regarded as valuable.

1966 *Times* 28 Feb. (Canada Suppl.) p. xi/1 Most of the subterranean 'white gold' [*sc.* potash] lies beneath Saskatchewan. **1974** G. JENKINS *Bridge of Magpies* ii. 27 My job was to police the Sperregebiet from the sea... There is .. on this God-forsaken shore: a string of rocky little inshore islands coated in bird guano—white gold, they call it.

white-gum[1]. [after RED GUM[1], q.v.] An eruption of whitish spots with a red border (*Strophulus albidus*) incident to young children.

1799 UNDERWOOD *Dis. Childhood* (ed. 4) I. 81 Another species [of Red-gum]..often of a pearl colour and opake, which has generally been accounted a kind of red gum, but it has of late been suggested might..be termed the white-gum.

white-gum[2]. [GUM *sb.*[2] 5.] Any species of *Eucalyptus* with white or light-coloured bark. Also **white gum-tree**.

1827 P. CUNNINGHAM *Two Years in N.S. Wales* I. xii. 200 The red and white gums [so named] from their wood. **1827** *Trans. Linnæan Soc.* XV. 278 [The ground-parrot] chiefly breeds in a stump of a small White Gum-tree. **1891** *Argus* (Melbourne) 13 May, On the lower slopes [of the ranges] the bluegum trees become first commingled with trees locally designated whitegum and black butt.

white-haired, *a.* [Cf. ON. *hvíthárr, -hærðr.*]

1. Having white or hoary hair, esp. from age. Also, covered with white hairs or down, as a plant.

c **1400** [see HAIRED]. *c* **1440** *Alphabet of Tales* 519 Now I am olde & white-harid. **1530** PALSGR. 329/1 Whyte heared, *chennu.* **1726** *Papers rel. Scots in Poland* (S.H.S. 1915) 210 To two white-haired people..f. 24. **1796** WITHERING *Brit. Plants* (ed. 3) III. 825 *Bryum canescens*..leaves..white haired at the ends. **1848** DICKENS *Dombey* lxii, The white-haired gentleman's affection for the girl. **1885** 'MRS. ALEXANDER' *At Bay* vii, A sweet gravity about her..as charming in her white-haired age as in her fair youth!

2. ***white-haired boy***, a favourite. *colloq.* Cf. WHITE-HEADED *a.* 2 b.

1910 *Nat. Police Gaz.* (U.S.) 29 Jan. 3 (*heading*) The white haired boy. *Ibid.* 3/4 He, this white-haired Willie-boy, really wanted her to become his wife. **1923** H. C. BAILEY *Mr. Fortune's Practice* ii. 38 His mother's white-haired boy, he is. Not 'alf. **1936** J. DOS PASSOS *Big Money* 496 You're the whitehaired boy around here. **1977** I. SHAW *Beggarman, Thief* II. iii. 147 Rudy..was the white-haired boy of the family.

Whitehall[1] ('hwaɪthɔːl).

1. The name of a street in London, used to designate the government offices situated there, or the civil service in general.

1827 *Morning Post* 24 Mar. 3/2 In consequence of that accommodation, an equal amount of Exchequer Bills before locked up at Whitehall are afterwards to be locked up in Threadneedle-street. **1850** *Daily News* 13 Mar. 5/2 The infection of..'Christian Socialism' is spreading to Whitehall. **1910** *Times Educ. Suppl.* 6 Sept. 13/2 The introductory remarks..breathe a very different spirit from that of earlier official utterances of Whitehall. **1946** C. S. FORESTER *Lord Hornblower* ix. 79 Heaven only knew what Whitehall and Downing Street would say. **1958** *Radio Times* 23 Feb. 6/1 This is a tense story of sea warfare... The mess-room talk is most authentic..and Mr. White is obviously familiar with his 'Whitehall types'. **1977** *Listener* 7 Apr. 442/1 British Leyland..is almost entirely a Whitehall creation.

2. Special Combs.: **Whitehall farce**, any of a series of bedroom farces produced at the Whitehall Theatre, London, esp. those presented between 1950 and 1967 by Brian Rix; **Whitehall Warrior** *slang*, a civil servant; an officer in the armed forces employed in administration rather than on active service.

1966 N. MARSH *Black Beech & Honeydew* x. 233 My uncle ..was like a Professor in a Whitehall farce. **1966** *Guardian* 20 Aug. 4/4 Blackpool..fulfils a social need. Like a Whitehall farce, it dictates its own terms and makes general criticism futile. **1976** M. GILBERT *Night of Twelfth* v. 42 The play [sc. *Twelfth Night*]..[is] a love story mixed up with a Whitehall farce. **1973** K. GILES *File on Death* vii. 174 I'm Quarles, a battered old Whitehall Warrior. **1976** W. WHITE *Long Silence* vii. 57, I didn't want anybody to think I was a chairbound officer, a Whitehall Warrior. **1978** P. O'DONNELL *Dragon's Claw* v. 81 Roger was a Whitehall Warrior until he retired.

Hence **Whiteha'llese**, jargon regarded as typical of the civil service; **White'hallism**, attitudes or personnel regarded as typical of the civil service.

1915 LD. ESHER *Let.* 21 Oct. in M. Gilbert *Winston S. Churchill* (1972) III. Compan. II. 1232 In the Navy..there seems to be a trifle too much of 'Whitehallism'. **1940** *Manch. Guardian Weekly* 15 Mar. 216 Shortage of paper may now prompt economy of speech, and if it sloughs away some of the pomposities of business English and Whitehallese, which is slightly more correct in its heavy Latinity but just as lacking in sense and suppleness, the war may be said to have done us a little good. **1958** *Times* 15 Nov. 8/3 At the time he said the Government were snubbing Wales and there was no prospect of 'Whitehallism' ever understanding Welsh aspirations. **1975** *Economist* 15 Feb. 115/2 In spite of long exposure to Whitehallese, she writes in English. He lapses far too often into gobbledygook. **1984** *Guardian* 1 Jan. 4 Phrases that take two words to say what one used to—'check out', 'meet with', 'consult with' (although Mrs Thatcher may shortly ban the last one from Whitehallese).

† **White'hall**[2]. *U.S. Obs.* The name of a district of New York, used *attrib.* to designate a type of rowing-boat. So † **White'haller**, one who uses a Whitehall boat.

1828 J. F. COOPER *Notions of Americans* I. 40 The latter [*sc.* New York boatmen], it appears, are of a class of watermen, that are renowned in this country, under the name of Whitehallers. **1835** C. J. LATROBE *Rambler in N. Amer.* i. 25 The light skilfully managed wherry of the Whitehaller. **1849** H. MELVILLE *Redburn* II. xxix. 289 The Whitehall boats were around us. **1890** N. P. LANGFORD *Vigilante Days* II. 129 To attempt the passage..in a whitehall boat would be madness.

whitehead ('hwaɪthɛd), *a.* and *sb.*[1] (In earlier use as a personal name, e.g. *Jon Hwitheaved* (1332 in *Lit. Cantuar.*, Rolls, I. 458).)

A. *adj.* 1. = WHITE-HEADED. *rare.*

1577 WOLTON *Cast. Christians* E viij, Graue and whyte-headde Fathers. **1870** MORRIS *Earthly Par.* III. IV. 162 White-head waves.

B. *sb.* † 1. app. A white head-dress. *Obs.*

1587 *Acc. Mary Q. Scots* (Camden) 31 Parys heades... Whiteheades for gentlewomen attendaunte uppon the mourners.

2. A name for various species of birds having the head (wholly or partly) white: see quots.

1686 BLOME *Gentl. Recreat.* II. 37/1 Partridges; the first, when newly hatched, are called White-heads. **1885** *Encycl. Brit.* XVIII. 52/2 Two other small birds from New Zealand, where they are known as the 'Whitehead' and 'Yellowhead', were referred to the genus, under the names of *O[rthonyx] albic[ap]illa* and *O. ochrocephala.*

3. A West Indian feverfew, *Parthenium Hysterophorus.*

1864 GRISEBACH *Flora W. Ind. Isl.* 788.

4. Also **white head. a.** A disorder in which the scalp is covered with white spots or crusts. **b.** [After BLACKHEAD 4.] A white or white-topped pustule.

1911 *Trans. S. Afr. Med. Congr.: 12th Meeting* 165 The so-called 'white head', so often seen in Bechuanaland..is a pustular syphilide affecting the scalp. The pustules..tend to coalesce, forming thick whitish crusts... In some cases the head becomes covered, giving the appearance of a solid white cap. **1922** *Brit. Jrnl. Dermatol. & Syphilis* XXXIV. 267 The scalp condition we are about to discuss is known to the natives..by the name of wit kop, dikwakwadi, or white head. **1940** BECKER & OBERMAYER *Mod. Dermatol. & Syphilol.* xxix. 521 Milium or 'white head' is the name for a tiny, pearly-white globular lesion..with a shiny, translucent surface. **1978** PARSONS & SOMMERS *Gynecology* (ed. 2) xx. 308/1 Closed comedones ('whiteheads') are the precursors of the inflammatory papules and pustules that commonly occur. **1982** P. M. MARGOLIN *Last Innocent Man* I. vii. 70 The boy's right hand raised slowly and began to pick at a whitehead on his cheek.

Whitehead, *sb.*[2] A kind of torpedo, invented by Robert Whitehead. Also *attrib.*

1877 *Sci. Amer.* 2 June 337/2 The Whitehead torpedo can be made to go at the rate of 20 knots for 1,000 yards, and at any depth that is desired from 1 foot to 30 feet. **1884** *Pall Mall Gaz.* 13 Nov. 5/2 A blow with even an ordinary Whitehead, let alone the improved Whitehead of the German navy, would practically rip the bottom out of the strongest ship afloat. **1898** KIPLING *Fleet in Being* v. 54 Fancy a Whitehead smitten on the nose by one little shell. You'd go up.

white-headed ('hwaɪtˌhɛdɪd), *a.*

1. Of an animal: Having the head (wholly or partly) white; having white hair, plumage, etc. on the head.

(Freq. in specific designations of various birds.)

1525 in *Test. Ebor.* (Surtees) VI. 11 On whie whiteheded. **1547** *Knaresb. Wills* (Surtees) I. 53 One whittheaded calff. **1785** PENNANT *Arctic Zool.* II. 196. **1872** COUES *Key N. Amer. Birds* 192 White-headed Woodpecker.

2. a. Of a person: White-haired, esp. from age; also, having very light or fair hair, flaxen-haired.

1815 SCOTT *Guy M.* i, A great white-headed, bare-legged, lubberly boy of twelve years old. **1840** DICKENS *Old C. Shop* xxv, A small white-headed boy with a sunburnt face. **1886** TENNYSON *Locksley Hall 60 Yrs. after* 38 This old white-headed dreamer.

b. In colloq. use, with *boy*: Favourite, darling: cf. WHITE *a.* 9 and WHITE BOY 1.

1820 MATURIN *Melmoth* i, He was always her 'white-headed boy', she said,—(*imprimis*, his hair was as black as jet). **1894** HALL CAINE *Manxman* II. xi, He was always my white-headed boy, and I stuck to him with life. **1933** A. CHRISTIE *Lord Edgware Dies* xxii. 186 You're positively convinced now that Ronald Marsh is a white-headed boy who can do no wrong. **1954** T. S. ELIOT *Confidential Clerk* II. 60 Perhaps you think it would be bad for your prospects Now that you're Claude's white-headed boy.

3. Of a wave: White-capped, white-crested; also of a sea covered with such waves.

1897 KIPLING *Capt. Cour.* viii, An angry, white-headed sea. **1909** E. PHILLPOTTS in *R.P.A. Ann.* (1910) 10 The riotous march of mad, white-headed waves.

Whiteheadian (hwaɪt'hɛdɪən), *a.* [f. the name *Whitehead* + -IAN.] Of, pertaining to, or characteristic of the English mathematician and philosopher A. N. Whitehead (1861–1947) or his ideas.

1943 *Mind* LII. 68 The Whiteheadian attempt to reconcile permanence and flux, time and eternity. **1977** *Church Times* 25 Feb. 6/5 Process theology has taken over the Whiteheadian scheme and used it as a means of expounding the Christian faith. **1978** *Christian* IV. IV. 328 The last point..follows if it is true—as the Whiteheadian conceptuality to which I happen to subscribe would say—that 'a thing *is* what a thing *does*'.

'white-heart, *sb.* and *a.*

A. *sb.* 1. In full ***white-heart cherry*** (for *white heart-cherry*; cf. *black-heart* s.v. BLACK *a.* 19): A light-coloured variety of cultivated cherry.

1707 [see *black heart* s.v. BLACK *a.* 19]. **1733** W. ELLIS *Chiltern & Vale Farm.* 143 The May-duke, White-hart, Black-Orleance and the Morella. **1869** BLACKMORE *Lorna D.* xxvi, The blackbirds eating our white-heart cherries.

2. *Metallurgy.* Malleable cast iron made by keeping white iron at a high temperature for several days in an oxidizing environment, so as to remove the carbon from the surface layers and increase the ductility and strength. Freq. *attrib.*

1925 *Jrnl. Iron & Steel Inst.* CXII. 433 The material examined consisted of metal from the open-hearth furnace only, corresponding to that used for whiteheart castings and blackheart castings in Europe and America. **1949** [see RÉAUMUR b]. **1960** [see GRAPHITIZE *v.* 1 b]. **1968** A. H. COTTRELL *Introd. Metallurgy* xxv. 519 Whiteheart malleable iron is made by heating the casting in an oxidizing environment.

B. *adj.* Having a white or light-coloured 'heart'.

1747 H. GLASSE *Art of Cookery* iv. 57 Take a fine White-heart Cabbage. **1900** *Daily Express* 25 Apr. 6/4 Fine white-heart lettuces.

white heat. [HEAT *sb.* 1 c.] That degree of heat or temperature (higher than *red heat*) at which metals and some other bodies radiate white light; the state of being white-hot.

1710 J. HARRIS *Lex. Techn.* II, *White* or *Flame Heat*; is a Degree of Heat given by Smiths to their Iron..: This is a less Heat than a Welding Heat. **1815** J. SMITH *Panorama Sci. & Art* II. 357 If a bar of iron or steel, at a white heat, be rubbed with a roll of sulphur, the two bodies combine,.. forming sulphuret of iron. *c* **1865** LETHEBY in *Circ. Sci.* I. 89/2, 2000° (or an incipient white-heat).

b. *fig.* A state of intense or extreme emotion.

1839 SYD. SMITH *Ballot* 8 There are politicians always at a white heat. **1870** LOWELL *Study Wind.* 148 Carlyle is one of the natures, rare in these latter centuries, capable of rising to a white heat. **1883** W. H. BISHOP *Ho. Merch. Pr.* xix. (1885) 292 There was a vixenish quality in her anger when at white heat.

white horse.

1. The figure of a white horse: see HORSE *sb.* 24. Also as the sign, and hence the name, of an inn.

1647 in Nightingale *Ejected of 1662* (1911) II. 909 Send one of Yor servants to the White horse wthout Creeple gate.

2. A crested wave: see HORSE *sb.* 24 b.

1849 KINGSLEY *Let.* in *Life* vii. (1879) I. 168 The bay is now curling and writhing in white horses under a smoking south-wester. **1888** RIDER HAGGARD *Mr. Meeson's Will* v, Looking at the 'white horses' chasing each other across the watery plain.

3. Local name for a species of ray (fish).

1710 SIBBALD *Hist. Fife* 51 *Raia aspera*, the White Horse.

4. The West Indian shrub *Portlandia grandiflora* (N.O. *Rubiaceæ*), with large white flowers, cultivated in hot-houses.

1866 *Treas. Bot.* 1232/1.

5. A tough sinewy substance lying between the upper jaw and junk of a sperm-whale.

1846 J. R. BROWNE *Etchings of Whaling Cruise* 130 The white, hard blocks, containing but little oil, and which are found near the small, and at the flukes, are called 'white horse'. **1851** H. MELVILLE *Moby Dick* II. xcix. 173 White-horse,..obtained from the tapering part of the fish, and also from the thicker portions of his flukes. **1874** C. M. SCAMMON *Marine Mammals* 312.

6. *Mining.* (*local.*) See quot. and HORSE *sb.* 11.

1886 J. BARROWMAN *Sc. Mining Terms* 72 *White horse*, intruded white trap in a coal seam.

white-hot, *a.* Also **white hot** (now *rare*). Heated to such a degree as to radiate white light; at white heat.

1820 SHELLEY *Œd. Tyr.* II. i. 172 Innocent Queens o'er white-hot ploughshares tread Unsinged. **1827** FARADAY *Chem. Manip.* xiii. (1842) 299 Even bright red hot fuel will cool a white hot crucible. **1871** TYNDALL *Fragm. Sci.* (1879) I. ii. 30 To display all these colours at the same time the.. wire must be white-hot.

b. *transf.* (rhetorically): Very bright and hot.

1858 HAWTHORNE *Fr. & It. Note-bks.* (1871) II. 38 Cool and dim, after the white-hot sunshine.

c. *fig.*: cf. WHITE HEAT b and RED-HOT 2.

1885 *Harper's Mag.* Mar. 552/1 You occasionally turn white-hot. **1890** LE GALLIENNE *G. Meredith* 73 Not Carlyle himself had a more white-hot hatred of 'simulacra'.

white house. [HOUSE *sb.*[1]] **1.** (With capital initials.) **a.** The popular name for the official residence of the President of the United States at Washington; hence, the President or his office.

1811 F. J. JACKSON *Let.* 24 Apr. in H. Adams *Documents New-Eng. Federalism* (1877) 385 [Foster] goes.. to act as a sort of political conductor to attract the lightning that may issue from the clouds round the Capitol and the White House at Washington. **1812** A. BIGELOW *Let.* 18 Mar. in *Proc. Amer. Antiquarian Soc.* (1930) XL. 331 There is much trouble at the white house, as we call it, I mean the President's. **1833** T. HAMILTON *Men & Manners Amer.* (1843) 300 The President.. having politely intimated that he received company every evening, I ventured.. to present myself.. at the 'White House'. **1884** *Century Mag.* Apr. 803/1 There is no building quite as satisfying to my eye as the White House. **1927** S. BENT *Ballyhoo* iii. 80 Conversationally they referred to the 'White House Spokesman', when he existed, as the Executive Larynx or the Presidential Ghost. **1950** *Daily Ardmoreite* (Ardmore, Okla.) 14 Feb. 1/7 The White House said no further action on its part is contemplated at this time. **1958** *New Statesman* 11 Jan. 30/1 He has no influence in the White House, and in recent months the requests for his advice have been little more than perfunctory. **1977** M. EDELMAN *Political Lang.* vi. 111 The White House tapes exemplify this common form of public language.

b. *transf.* Applied to other buildings serving as official residences.

1860 *Southern Enterprise* 3 Oct. 2/5 He announces himself, in the event of Lincoln's election, as candidate for '*the White House*' of the independent State of Georgia! **1878** *Trans. Illinois Dept. Agric.* XIV. 146 Tecumseh had his thousands of braves encamped above and below Vincennes, Indiana, where Gen. Harrison occupied the 'White House' of this great Northwest. **1947** F. D. DOWNEY *Our Lusty Forefathers* 101 George Washington had been elected President, inaugurated in New York, and had established his 'White House' at No. 3 Cherry Street. **1974** *Encycl. Brit. Micropædia* VIII. 844/1 It [*sc.* San Clemente] gained national prominence in 1969 when Pres. Richard M. Nixon purchased property there for use as a summer White House. **1975** *Caribbean Contact* Feb. 16/1 Speaking with Mr. Ebenezer Joshua at his 'white house' home overlooking the prison compound—as I did during my visit to St. Vincent to cover the recent election—one immediately appreciates the feelings of St. Vincent's radical and disenchanted youth.

2. *Sc.* In north-western Scotland and the Hebrides, a house built of mortared stone; *spec.* one having single-thickness walls cemented with lime mortar. Cf. BLACK HOUSE 2. *Obs.* exc. *Hist.*

1824 J. MACCULLOCH *Highlands & Western Isles* I. 112 The true white house consists of masonry and slate.. but the heteroclite, 'kind of white house', is covered with thatch, and, what is much more essential, possesses a chimney. **1870** *Proc. Soc. Antiq. Scotland* VII. 154 The distinctive terms for a house built with lime-mortar, or without it, remain the same.... In the northern islands it is still a White-house, and in the Western Highlands it is Tigh-gal. **1955** A. GEDDES *Isle of Lewis & Harris* i. 27 Here and there new houses stand out, the 'white houses' (*tighean geala*).. are usually grey... These dwellings have generally been stone-built and were often slate-roofed. **1974** *Northern Stud.* IV. 22 The 1924 [Crofters] Act afforded an opportunity to improve housing and in the next decade the 'white house' began to replace the traditional 'black house' or 'taigh dubh'.

white iron. [= med.L. *album ferrum*, F. *fer-blanc* tin-plate.] **a.** Tinned iron, tin-plate. **b.** Cast iron of a silvery colour containing most or all of its carbon in combination.

1532 *Acc. Ld. High Treas. Scot.* VI. 155, vj mesouris of quhite irne for the hagbutis charge. **1632, 1745, 1881** [see IRON *sb.*[1] 2]. **1839** URE *Dict. Arts* 1252 The only alloy of iron interesting to the arts, is that with tin, in the formation of tin-plate, or white iron.

c. *attrib.* †**white-iron man, smith,** a tin-smith.

1731 in *Rec. Convent. Burghs Scot.* (1885) V. 528 Spurriers, gunsmyths, whiteiron smyths. **1765** WATT in Muirhead *Invent. Watt.* (1854) I. 13 My old white-iron man [*footn., Anglicé,* tin-man] is dead. **1785** BOSWELL *Hebrides* 19 Aug., James Hood, White Iron Smith. **1814** SCOTT *Wav.* lxiii, Deacon Clank, the white-iron smith.

white lead, *sb.* [LEAD *sb.*[1] Cf. L. *plumbum album* (in class. L. = tin), OF. *blanc plomb.*] A compound of lead carbonate and hydrated oxide of lead, much used as a white pigment; also called CERUSE.

c **1440** *Promp. Parv.* 525/2 Whyte led, or blanke plumbe. *c* **1450–1844** [see LEAD *sb.*[1] 2]. **1634** PEACHAM *Compl. Gent.* xiii. (1906) 131 Your flesh-colour is commonly compounded of white lead, lake, and vermilion. **1823** P. NICHOLSON *Pract. Builder* 410 White Lead, is the principal ingredient used in house-painting. **1827** FARADAY *Chem. Manip.* xviii. (1842) 487 White lead ground up with oil, when spread upon slips of cloth, is very useful for making joints tight.

b. *attrib.*: **white lead ore,** native carbonate of lead, cerussite.

1706 *Lond. Gaz.* No. 4216/4 The White Lead-House at Rotherhith. **1796** KIRWAN *Elem. Min.* (ed. 2) II. 203 White Lead ore. **1849** NOAD *Electricity* (ed. 3) 179 The box.. is put together with white-lead joints, as these are perfectly water-tight.

Hence **white-lead** *v.*, *trans.* to cover or impregnate with white lead.

1863 W. C. BALDWIN *Afr. Hunting* i. 12 White-leaded and varnished the boat. **1881** NEISON & KEMP *Pract. Boat Bldg.* I. 55 A piece of Stockholm tarred or white-leaded paper.

†**whitelewe,** *a. Obs. rare.* [f. WHITE *a.* + -LEWE.] = WHITELY *a.*

1495, etc. [see quot. 1398[2] s.v. WHITELY *a.*].

white lime, white-lime, *sb.* Now *rare* or *Obs.* [LIME *sb.*[1]] Lime mixed with water as a coating for walls, etc.; whitewash. Also *attrib.*

1528 PAYNELL *Salerne's Regim.* cj b, A playster made of Auripigmentum, Brymstoone, whyte lyme, and Sope, myngled to gether. *a* **1658** CLEVELAND *Plat. Love* iv. Wks. (1687) 212 Pictures might court each other and exchange Their white-lime Looks. **1824** SOUTHEY *Sir T. More* I. 173 The old cottages.. Substantially built of the native stone.. dirtied with no white-lime.

So **'white-lime** *v. Obs.* or *dial.*, *trans.* to coat or cover with white lime; to whitewash; hence **white-limed** (-laɪmd) *ppl. a.*, **white-liming** *vbl. sb.*; also **white-limer,** one who white-limes, a whitewasher.

13.. *Life of Jesus* (Horstm.) 422 þe roues þat beoth with-oute *ȝwitlimede and iplanede faire,.. And withInne fulle of caroyne. **1377** LANGL. *P. Pl.* B. xv. 111 Ypocrysie.. is lykned.. to a wal þat were whitlymed and were foule wyth-inne. **1398** TREVISA *Barth. De P.R.* XVI. xxiv. (Bodl. MS.), Suche medleynge is.. nedeful.. to pargette and whitelyme walles. **1556** *Chron. Grey Friars* (Camden) 54 Alle churches new whytte-lymed, with the commandmenttes wryttyne on the walles. **1583** GOLDING *Calvin on Deut.* xxvii. 2 The Iewes are commanded, To gather great stones, & to white-lime them ouer. **1602** *Balliol Coll. Oxf. Acc.* (MS.) Item for lyme, and the laborers woork, to whytlym the Hall, xvi[d]. **1634** BRERETON *Trav.* (Chetham Soc.) 13 The great church.. most daintily.. white-limed. **1588** SHAKS. *Tit. A.* IV. ii. 98 Ye.. shallow harted Boyes, Ye *white-limb'd [*sic*] walls. **1624** DONNE *Serm., Matt. iii. 17* (1640) 426 If we be not onely *Dealbati Christiani*, (as S. Augustine speaks) White-lim'd Christians, Christians on the out-side. **1655** FULLER *Ch. Hist.* I. i. §13 As white-limed houses exceed those which are only rough-cast. **1611** COTGR., *Pinceau*,.. a *Whitelimers Brush. **1622** R. HAWKINS *Voy. S. Sea* (1847) 121 Hayre, such as the whitelymers use. *c* **1440** *Promp. Parv.* 525/2 *Whytlymynge, *calcificacio*. **1547–8** in Swayne *Churchw. Acc. Sarum* (1896) 275 To Lytchefeelde for whitelymynge of the same. **1611** COTGR., *Blanche*,.. whiting or whiteliming.

white line, white-line, *sb.*

1. *Anat.* **a.** (tr. L. *linea alba.*) A longitudinal band of tendinous tissue extending from the sternum to the pubis. **b.** A whitish band in the pelvic fascia extending from the symphysis pubis to the spine of the ischium.

1598 FLORIO, *Linéa abba* [*sic*], the line or hollow tying from the nauell, the white line, the vmbelicall veine. *c* **1720** W. GIBSON *Farrier's Guide* I. ii. (1722) 6 The white Line.. is.. a tendinous Substance, form'd by the Endings of such of those Muscles as meet.. in it. **1874** HEATH *Anat.* (ed. 3) 286 'White line' of pelvic fascia.

2. a. *Printing.* A line left blank between two lines of type.

1683 MOXON *Mech. Exerc., Printing* xxiv. ¶7 That no Letters or Spaces lye in the White-lines of the Form. **1770** LUCKOMBE *Hist. Printing* 250 Open matter, with leads and white-lines between. **1863** [see EM]. **1960** G. A. GLAISTER *Gloss. Bk.* 28/2 *Blank line*, a line which is filled with quads, leads, or blank slugs; a white line in which no letters or other type characters appear.

b. *Engraving.* An engraved line which prints white; the art or technique of using such lines.

1884 H. A. DOBSON *Thos. Bewick & his Pupils* 145 The other difference, of which Bewick is said to be the inventor, consisted in the employment of what is known technically as 'whiteline'. **1906** A. HAYDEN *Chats on Old Prints* iii. 86 He [*sc.* Bewick] was not the inventor of the white line, but he used it freely and adapted his designs accordingly. **1924** H. FURST *Modern Woodcut* i. 10 The black line method keeps the woodprint.. in a servile reproductive state, the onus of design falling.. on the original designer.... The problem of the designer in white line is an entirely different one, requiring.. more forethought. **1938** F. WEITENKAMPF *Illustrated Bk.* ii. 52 For the woodcutter the white line was assuredly an easier method of producing tonal effect than elaborate cross-hatching in black. **1973** *Times* 31 July 10/6 His first two prints were from wood blocks, the wood-engraver's 'white line' being used with decision in the silhouetted *Reclining Nude* of 1931.

3. a. = BOBBIN *sb.*[1] 2. **b.** An untarred 'line' or rope (cf. WHITE *a.* 2 a, quots. 1769, 1846).

1824 J. F. COOPER *Pilot* xxvi. III. 35 'Bobbin, or white-line; they are the same thing,' added the young trader. **1867** SMYTH *Sailor's Word-bk.* s.v. *Line, White-line*, that which has not been tarred.

4. Alcohol as a drink; also, one who drinks alcohol. *U.S. slang.*

1908 J. M. SULLIVAN *Criminal Slang* 27 *White-line*, an alcohol drinker. **1914** JACKSON & HELLYER *Vocab. Criminal Slang* 88 *White line, white lime.* Current amongst yeggs and hoboes. Alcohol. Example: 'You'll have to go to the croker and get a stiff for the white line.' **1926** J. BLACK *You can't Win* vi. 66 'A four-bit micky, a fifty-cent bottle of alcohol—Dr. Hall, white line,' he translated in disgust. **1926** *Flynn's* 16 Jan. 640/1 All we could glom was a shot of white line.

5. A narrow white strip painted on the road surface to guide or direct motorists; *esp.* one that separates adjacent traffic lanes.

1924 *Oxford Times* 29 Aug. 9/4 The experiment of the white line, which has proved so successful in encouraging the careful driving of motors round corners in Worcestershire, might with advantage be tried in this district. **1930** *Motor* 10 June 892/2 We do think that observations might be directed at white line offences where they occur in really dangerous places. **1971** *Daily Tel.* (Colour Suppl.) 22 Oct. 25/3 White lines broken but close together can mean a corner or hillcrest is coming. **1976** *Evening Chron.* (Newcastle) 26 Nov., Mr. Cook ruled that the council was guilty of maladministration because it could have speeded up the painting of white line markings.

6. *attrib.* or as *adj.* (with hyphen) = *white-lined* (see below); **white-line dart (moth),** *Euxoa tritici*.

1840 J. & M. LOUDON tr. *Köllar's Treat. Insects* II. 102 The White-line Dart Moth... A moth injurious to buck-wheat and autumn-sown grain. **1869** NEWMAN *Brit. Moths* 330 The White-line Dart (*Agrotis Tritici*)... There is generally a sinuous line or interrupted series of linear spots parallel with the hind margin. **1948** W. J. STOKOE *Caterpillars Brit. Moths* I. 178 The White-line Dart.. is widely distributed.

So **white-line** *v.*, *trans.* to mark with white lines; so **white-lined** *a.*

1832 RENNIE *Butterfl. & M.* Index 285/1 White-lined Black. **1916** *Blackw. Mag.* Oct. 478/1 Rolled and white-lined for the game [of tennis].

'white-,liver. ? *Obs.* [WHITE *a.* 5.] A 'white-livered' person, coward, dastard; 'a flatterer' (Jam. 1825).

1615 BP. HALL *Contempl.* IX. *Gideon's Prep.* 103 Oh thou white liuer! doth but a foule word, or a frowne scarre thee from Christ? **1673** HICKERINGILL *Greg. Fr. Greyb.* 207 Milk-sops, dastards and white-livers.

white-livered (-əd), *a.* Having (according to an old notion, still surviving locally) a light-coloured liver, supposed to be due to a deficiency of bile or 'choler', and hence of vigour, spirit, or courage; feeble-spirited, cowardly, dastardly.

1549 CHEKE *Hurt Sedit.* (1569) F j b, What white lyuered Cities hath not only not withstande them, but also with shame fauoured them. **1599** SHAKS. *Hen. V*, III. ii. 34 For Bardolph, hee is white-liuer'd, and red-fac'd: by the means whereof a' faces it out, but fights not. **1640** HARSNET *Gods Summons* 154 Assurance of victory puts courage.. into the most white-livered, and fearful souldier. **1710** HEARNE *Collect.* (O.H.S.) III. 21 A white liver'd, sneaking, mean-spirited.. Fellow. **1840** DICKENS *Old C. Shop* li, A double-faced, white-livered, sneaking spy. **1888** MRS. H. WARD *Robt. Elsmere* xviii, No need to be white-livered, but every need.. to take no hasty needless offence.

whitelow, obs. form of WHITLOW.

whitely ('hwaɪtlɪ), *a.* Now only *Sc.* Forms: 4 **whitliche,** 4, 7 **whitley,** 6 **whitlie, whytley, whytely,** 5– **whitely;** *Sc.* 5 **quhitlie,** 6 **quhitly, quhytly, quhittlie.** [f. WHITE *a.* + -LY[1].] Whitish; pale; light-complexioned, 'fair'.

1398 TREVISA *Barth. De P.R.* IV. ix. (Tollem. MS.), [A phlegmatic man is] whitly in face, ferful of herte. *Ibid.* XI. vi, Rauene briddes while þey ben whitliche [*ed.* 1495 whitlew, 1535 whitelewe, 1582 whitlewe] in feþeris, or þey ben blake. *c* **1410** *Master of Game* (MS. Digby 182) iii, A Bucke is a diuerse beste; he hath nought his heer as an hert, for he is more whitely. *c* **1480** HENRYSON *Test. Cress.* 214 Four ȝokkit steidis full different of hew,.. The secund steid.. Quhitlie and paill. **1548** RECORDE *Urin. Physick* x. (1651) 82 If.. the colour of the garland [of the urine] be white, or whitely, it is a token full of good hope. *a* **1578** LINDESAY (Pitscottie) *Chron. Scot.* (S.T.S.) II. 17 He was fair and quhittlie. **1588** SHAKS. *L.L.L.* III. i. 198 A whitly wanton, with a veluet brow, With two pitch bals.. for eyes. *c* **1645** HOWELL *Lett.* II. xxii. (1890) 414 Those whitely Stars.. Which make the Milky-Way. **1684** BUNYAN *Pilgr.* II. 141 You have his whitely Look. **1737** RAMSAY *Sc. Prov.* (1750) 112 Whitely things are ay tender. **1833** *New Monthly Mag.* May 65, I know him by his whitely eyes.

Comb. **1528** PAYNELL *Salerne's Regim.* (1541) e iij, A flematike person is whytly coloured: the colerike is browne and tawny. **1588** *Cert. Advert. out of Irel.* B 3, The Prince of Ascule was a slender made man.. whitely faced. **1656** *Mercurius Politicus* No. 330 Flaxen haired, whitely faced.

whitely ('hwaɪtlɪ), *adv.* [f. WHITE *a.* + -LY[2].] So as to be or appear white; with a white colour or aspect.

1398 TREVISA *Barth. De P.R.* VIII. xxvi. (Tollem. MS.), Amonge all sterres Venus schineþ most comfortabely and whitly. **1611** COTGR., *Candidement*, whitely, fairely, in white. **1818** KEATS *Endym.* I. 626 See her hovering feet, More bluely vein'd,.. more whitely sweet Than those of sea-born Venus. **1844** BROWNING *Laboratory* i, These faint smokes curling whitely. **1876** HARDY *Ethelberta* i, A whitely shining oval of still water.

whitely, var. QUITELY *adv.*

white man. Also †**white-man, whiteman.**

†**1.** A man clothed in white: cf. WHITE *a.* 6. In quot. 1691, a surpliced chorister. *Obs. rare.*

1691 [see WHITE BOY 2]. **1693** *D' Emilianne's Hist. Monast. Orders* xix. 216 Of the Order of the White Men. In the year 1399,.. a certain Priest, came down from the Alpes into Italy,.. Cloathed all in White,.. great crouds both of Men and Women..followed him, and took White Cloaths likewise on their Backs.

2. a. A man belonging to a race having naturally light-coloured skin or complexion: chiefly applied to those of European extraction: see WHITE *a.* 4. ***the white man's burden***: see BURDEN *sb.* 2 a; ***the white man's grave***, equatorial West Africa considered particularly unhealthy for white people.

1695 MOTTEUX tr. *St.-Olon's Morocco* 12 [The Moors of Tetuan] are White-men, pretty well Civiliz'd. **1791** W. BARTRAM *Carolina* 96 The centinels..perceiving that I was a whiteman, ventured to hail me. **1835** C. F. HOFFMAN *Winter in West* I. 164 We white men have been spoiled by education; we have been taught to think many things necessary that you red men can do well without. **1836** F. H. RANKIN *White Man's Grave* I. p. viii, [Sierra Leone] bears the terrific and poetic title of the 'White Man's Grave'. **1897** M. H. KINGSLEY *Trav. W. Afr.* 2 My friends..said, 'Oh, you can't possibly go there; that's where Sierra Leone is, the white man's grave, you know.' **1904** HAZZLEDINE (*title*) The White Man in Nigeria. **1924** MAURICE & ARTHUR *Life Ld. Wolseley* iv. 65 The Gold Coast had well earned the name of 'The White Man's Grave'. **1938** X. HERBERT *Capricornia* (1939) iii. 24 The whitemen left the hunting to the [Australian] natives. **1944** F. CLUNE *Red Heart* 19, I dug up his body, souvenired his false teeth and diaries, and reburied him in whiteman fashion. **1952** P. ATKEY *Juniper Rock* xiv. 127, I was a bride at eighteen... I went out to the white man's grave. **1956** A. SAMPSON *Drum* xi. 156 As whites regard Africans as natives or boys, not people or men so Africans never describe whitemen (which they spell, significantly, in one word), as *abantu*, or people. **1970** G. F. NEWMAN *Sir, You Bastard* ii. 67 The street in Hammersmith where Whitmarsh lodged was so overrun with immigrants that an English-speaking whiteman was a latterday Livingstone.

b. orig. *U.S. slang.* A man of honourable character (such as was conventionally associated with one of European extraction): see WHITE *a.* 4 b.

1883 *Century Mag.* XXVI. 913/1 You've behaved to me like a white man from the start. **1887** *Pall Mall Gaz.* 22 June 5 Tricoupis the President is a white man—an extremely white man.

white meat, whitemeat. (Also with hyphen.) [WHITE *a.* 2, MEAT *sb.* 2. Cf. MSw. *hvitmater* pl. (Sw. *vitmat*).]

1. a. *collect. sing.* or *pl.* Foods prepared from milk; dairy produce (occas. including eggs). *Obs.* exc. *dial.*

c **1425** *Voc.* in Wr.-Wülcker 661/11 *Hoc lacticinium*, wyttemet. *c* **1450** *Mirk's Festial* 84 ȝe most fast from all maner flesch mete and whyt-mete. **1483** CAXTON *Gold. Leg.* 129/1 Without etyng fysshe ne mylke egges or whyte mete. **1538** FITZWARREN in *Lett. Suppr. Monast.* (Camden) 216 Concernyng forbyddyng of whytmeates in Lente. **1577** GOOGE *Heresbach's Husb.* III. 148 The olde wryters doo teache the making of a kinde of white meate, not much vnlike to Welcurdes. **1584** COGAN *Haven Health* cxciii. 150 A thirde kinde of meats, which is neither fishe nor fleshe, commonly called white meates, as egges, milke, butter, cheese. **1617** MORYSON *Itin.* III. 148 The Cowes..with large vdders, yeelding plenty of whitmeates. **1620** BRENT tr. *Sarpi's Counc. Trent* I. 4 Giuing..power to eate egges and whitmeats on fasting dayes. **1796** BP. G. HAY in *Ushaw Mag.* Dec. (1913) 286 In those countries where people have nothing else to eat with their bread but whitemeats; these are more or less permitted in Lent itself: and in some places Eggs also. **1886** ELWORTHY *W. Som. Gloss.*

b. Certain white or light-coloured flesh foods (see quot. 1877).

1752 CHESTERF. *Lett.* (1774) II. 233 Pray leave off..your ..pastry, fat creams, and..dumplings; and then you need not confine yourself to white meats, which I do not take to be one jot wholesomer than beef, mutton, and partridge. **1877** *N.W. Linc. Gloss.*, *White meats*, the flesh of lamb, veal, and rabbits,..chickens, pheasants, and partridges. **1973** *Guardian* 19 Mar. 7/5 People in Britain ate less red meat last year, but more 'white' meat such as pork and poultry. **1975** P. V. PRICE *Taste of Wine* vii. 134/1 White meat is generally taken to include pork, veal, chicken and turkey, while the 'reds' are beef, lamb, duck and goose. **1985** *Which?* Feb. 54/2 In general, nutritionists recommend that the average British diet should contain less fat and more fibre... They say a good way to achieve this change is to eat more white meat (especially poultry) and fish in place of red meat.

†**c.** *attrib.*

1721 N. BLUNDELL *Diary* (1895) 175 April 25th. It being a White-Meat day I dined at a Table by myself at the Swan.

†**d.** as *adj.* (*fig.*) Mean, pusillanimous. *Obs.*

?*a* **1611** BEAUM. & FL. *Four Plays* (1647) 33/1 Sirha, sirha, this whitmeat-spirit's not yours.

2. *slang* (chiefly *U.S.*). White women considered as sexual partners or conquests. Cf. MEAT *sb.* 3 e.

[**1937** *Printers' Ink Monthly* May 45/3 *White meat*, an actress.] **1940** 'J. CRAD' *Traders in Women* v. 134 The..liner took me to Shanghai, and here once again I met the European procurer and salesman of 'white meat'. **1972** [see HOME *sb.*[1] 14]. **1976** M. MAGUIRE *Scratchproof* x. 152 I'm off white meat. I have a good thing going with a negro film editor. **1982** J. PHILIPS *Target for Tragedy* (1983) I. iii. 52 Some stranger who sees a piece of white meat he thinks might come his way.

white monk. [WHITE *a.* 6 a: cf. WHITE FRIAR.] A Cistercian monk: so called from the colour of the habit of undyed wool.

1387 TREVISA *Higden* (Rolls) VIII. 31 He made Baldewyn þe whiȝte monk archbisshop of Caunterbury. *c* **1400** *Rom. Rose* 6695 These chanouns regulers Or white monkes or these blake. **1517** TORKINGTON *Pilgr.* (1884) 7 Seynt Elyn.. lith in a ffayer place of religion of whith monks. *c* **1630** RISDON *Surv. Devon* §136. (1810) 152 Duke Alfred erected a fair abbey for white monks of the order of Cistercians. **1799** J. ROBERTSON *Agric. Perth* 566.

whiten ('hwaɪt(ə)n), *v.* Also 5 qwhittyn, 5, 9 *dial.* whitten, 6 whyten, whyghten. [f. WHITE *a.* + -EN[5]. Cf. ON. *hvítna* to become white.]

1. *trans.* To make or render white; to impart a white colour or appearance to. **a.** *gen.*

a **1300** *E.E. Psalter* I. 9 [li. 7] Þou..salt wasche me,..And ouer snawe sal I whitened be. **1552** HULOET, Whyghten, *albo,..candefacio.* **1814** SCOTT *Ld. of Isles* III. xv, Whiten'd with foam a thousand streams Leap from the mountain's crown. **1853** DICKENS *Bleak Ho.* xxxiv, Take care, while you are young, that you can think in those days, '*I* never whitened a hair of her dear head.' **1873** BLACK *Pr. Thule* i, The sea whitened by the rushing of the wind.

b. To cover, coat, or overspread with something white; *spec.* to whitewash; to coat (metal) with tin, to tin.

Also said (chiefly *poet.* or *rhet.*) of a white substance or a number of white objects covering or spread over a surface.

1435 MISYN *Fire of Love* II. ix. 95 Of qwhome sum þer fowlnes to hyde or þer bewte þa study to increse with payntynge of begillynge avotre þer faces þa color & qwhittyn. **1664** in W. O. Blunt *Ch. Chester-le-Street* (1884) 96 For whitening the church four pound ten shillings. **1687** A. LOVELL tr. *Thevenot's Trav.* II. 88 In this Countrey of Persia,..they whiten, or if you will, tinn, brass and copper otherwise than with us. **1776** ADAM SMITH *W.N.* I. i. I. 6 To put it [*sc.* a pin-head] on, is a peculiar business, to whiten the pins is another. **1874** J. BIRCH *Country Archit.* 44 Lath, plaster, float, set and twice whiten all ceilings through-out. **1891** HARDY *Tess* li, I shall get the house swept out and whitened to-morrow morning.

1703 POPE *Thebais* 391 Where..human bones yet whiten all the ground. **1719** YOUNG *Busiris* I. i, Sails unnumber'd whiten all the stream. **1823** SCOTT *Quentin D.* xxv, Meadows ..whitened with the numerous tents of the Duke of Burgundy's army. **1854** J. S. C. ABBOTT *Napoleon* (1855) I. xxi. 335 The mountains, whitened with snow, were swept by the bleak winds of winter.

c. To make white by depriving of the natural colour; to blanch; to bleach; to make pale.

1693 EVELYN *De La Quint. Compl. Gard.* II. 148 To tie up ..the tops of the Leaves of Long Lettuce..to make them Cabbage, or at least to whiten them. **1726–31** WALDRON *Descr. Isle of Man* (1865) 15 A good air to whiten cloth. **1791** COWPER *Iliad* VIII. 90 Fear whiten'd every cheek. **1791** HAMILTON *Berthollet's Dyeing* I. I. I. iii. 51 Oxygen is capable of whitening..the colouring matter. **1839** URE *Dict. Arts* 767 (*Leather*) The effects of the paste are to whiten the skins, to soften them, and to protect them from the hardening influence of the atmosphere. **1860** GEO. ELIOT *Mill on Fl.* VI. xii, I've got cloth as has never been whittened.

d. *fig.* To free or clear from evil, guilt, or the like; also, to cause to seem right, good, pure, etc.; to give a specious appearance to.

c **1440** *Alphabet of Tales* 123 He went & shrafe hym of all his synys... And onone as he come in, þis man..said; 'A! welcom, frend! com ner, for þou hase wele whittend þe.' [**1667** *Observ. Burning Lond.* 10 And which are never true but by a supposition that if they do not happen in our Countrey, they may happen in another, which is called to Whiten Black.] **1679** BURNET *Hist. Ref.* I. Pref. (c) 2 b, Such remarkable blemishes, that..no man..can go about the whitening them. **1687** DRYDEN *Hind & P.* I. 44 The bristl'd Baptist Boar, impure as He, (But whitn'd with the foam of sanctity). **1873** H. SPENCER *Study Sociol.* ix. (1877) 220 By selecting the evidence any society may be relatively blackened, and any other society relatively whitened.

2. *intr.* To become or turn white; to assume a white colour or aspect; *vaguely*, to appear white.

a **1633** G. HERBERT *Jacula Prudentum* 943 Thornes whiten yet doe nothing. **1707** MORTIMER *Husb.* 451 They [*sc.* Cardons Spanish] whiten in about three Weeks and are fit to eat. **1720** POPE *Iliad* XXI. 382 A Foam whitens on the purple Waves. **1725** —— *Odyss.* IX. 160 The sea whitens with the rising gale. **1796** KIRWAN *Elem. Min.* (ed. 2) I. 152 When heated, it hardens and whitens. **1831** JAMES *Philip Aug.* xvi, Let his corpse remain unburied, and his bones whiten in the wind! **1833** TENNYSON *Lady of Shalott* I. ii, Willows whiten, aspens quiver,..By the island in the river. **1853** LONGF. tr. *Dante, Purgat.* XVI. 143 Behold the dawn,..Already whitening. **1914** 'IAN HAY' *Knt. on Wheels* xiv, His hair was whitening.

b. To turn pale, esp. from fear or other emotion. (Cf. REDDEN *v.* 2 b.)

1783 JUSTAMOND tr. *Raynal's Hist. Indies* V. 192 All the human species, in general, whitens in the snow, and is tanned in the sun. **1821** SHELLEY *Ginevra* 66 The cheek that whitens. **1880** RHODA BROUGHTON *Second Thts.* III. iv, 'I am very glad to hear it,' he says almost inaudibly, and whitening.

c. *fig.*: cf. 1 d.

1758 H. WALPOLE *Catal. Roy. Authors* (1759) I. 172 What character that he has censured, has whitened by examination. **1801** S. & HT. LEE *Cant. T.* V. 90 It..bids us whiten by a comparison with the imperfections of others.

Hence **whitened** ('hwaɪt(ə)nd), *ppl. a.*

a **1711** KEN *Hymns Evang.* Poet. Wks. 1721 I. 4 Patin and Chalice were of whiten'd Clay. **1860** FROUDE *Hist. Eng.* xxiv. V. 37 The sunlight stared in white and stainless upon the whitened aisles; the churches were new whitelimed. **1879** JEFFERIES *Wild Life in S. Co.* ii. (1889) 18 That peculiar whitened appearance left when water has passed over vegetation. **1881** —— *Wood Magic* II. iv. 99 In his rage and fear, with whitened face.

whiten, obs. or dial. f. WHITING *sb.* and *vbl. sb.*

whitener ('hwaɪt(ə)nə(r)). [f. WHITEN *v.* + -ER[1].]

1. One who whitens, in any sense; *spec.* a person employed in bleaching or other whitening process.

1611 COTGR., *Blanchisseur*,..a whitener of clothes. **1637** *Crompton's Jurisd.* 179 No tawer or whitener of skins shall remain in the forests. *c* **1700** KENNETT *MS. Lansd.* 1033 *Bleacher*, a whitener or whitester of linnen. **1748** RICHARDSON *Clarissa* (1768) VII. lxxxiv. 291 A partial whitener of his own cause, or blackener of another's. **1881** *Instr. Census Clerks* (1885) 45 Pin Maker..Whitener. **1895** *Daily News* 15 Nov. 7/1 Walter Wells, a silver-plater, in the employment of Messrs. Elkington,..Frank Naylor, whitener and repairer, employed by Messrs. Elkington.

2. A thing that whitens; *spec.* a substance or agent used for whitening, bleaching, etc.

1686 GOAD *Celest. Bodies* I. ii. 6 Wind is a Dryer,..Frost a Cooler, Dryer, a Whitener. **1971** D. POTTER *Brit. Eliz. Stamps* ii. 22 Optical whitener is used in the making of the paper.

whiteness ('hwaɪtnɪs). Also (with shortened root-vowel) 5 whitt-, whytnesse, 5–6 whitnesse. [OE. *hwítnes*: see WHITE *a.* and -NESS.] The quality or condition of being white; white colour or appearance.

971 *Blickl. Hom.* 7 Seo readnes þære rosan lixeþ on þe, & seo hwitnes þære lilian scineþ on þe. *c* **1400** *Pilgr. Sowle* (Caxton 1483) IV. iv. 60 The fayre blosme..whos whytenes passyd the snowe. *a* **1425** tr. *Arderne's Treat. Fistula* etc. 47 þe wondes haþ hardnes wiþ whitenes and redenes. **1483** *Cath. Angl.* 416/2 Whittnesse, *albedo.* **1577** GOOGE tr. *Heresbach's Husb.* 39 The webbe is layde out in the hotte Sunne,..whereby it is brought to a passing whitenesse. **1592** GREENE *Greene's Vis.* Wks. (Grosart) XII. 209 The whitenesse of their haires bewrayed the number of their dayes. **1613** PURCHAS *Pilgrimage* VIII. iii. 623 The brightnesse of the Starres and whitenesse of the snow, not suffering them to be quite forlorne in darkenesse. *a* **1650** NORGATE *Miniatura* (1919) 98 Temper them with white lead to what whytnes you please. **1756** C. LUCAS *Ess. Waters* II. 52 Salts of different degrees of purity and whiteness. **1827** FARADAY *Chem. Manip.* xxiv. (1842) 648 Heat a little chloride of silver..to whiteness. **1887** F. M. CRAWFORD *Saracinesca* iii, His very dark eyes and complexion made more noticeable by the dazzling whiteness of his hair.

b. Of the human skin or face: †(*a*) Lightness or fairness of complexion, (*b*) Paleness, pallor.

1398 TREVISA *Barth. De P.R.* XV. lxvi. (Bodl. MS.), Gallia ..haþ þat name..of whitenes of men for Gallia is grewe and is to menynge mylke. **1585** T. WASHINGTON tr. *Nicholay's Voy.* IV. viii. 119 Their beautie, whitenesse,..and shamefast grace. **1597** SHAKS. *2 Hen. IV*, I. i. 68 The whitenesse in thy Cheeke Is apter then thy Tongue, to tell thy Errand. **1794** S. WILLIAMS *Vermont* 389 The white men..lose their whiteness and become brown or red. **1821** LAMB *Elia* Ser. I. *Old Benchers*, His cheeks were colourless, even to whiteness. **1857** G. A. LAWRENCE *Guy Liv.* vii, It was no blush now, but a dead waxen whiteness, that came over the beautiful face.

c. quasi-*concr.* A white substance or part of something.

1560 *Bible* (Geneva) Tobit ii. 10 A whitenes came in mine eies, & I went to the phisicians who helped me not. **1592** SHAKS. *Ven. & Ad.* 1170 A purple floure..checkred with white, Resembling well his pale cheekes, and the blood, Which..vpon their whitenesse stood. **1650** JER. TAYLOR *Holy Living* iv. §10. 360 Those Creatures that live amongst the snowes..turne white with their..conversation with such perpetual whitenesses. **1651** FRENCH *Distill.* i. 34 These Rinds must be fresh, and (the inward whiteness being separated) be bruised. **1885** 'F. ANSTEY' *Tinted Venus* v, [To a barber] Do you not swathe them in the garb of humiliation, and daub their countenances with whiteness? **1905** R. BAGOT *Passport* ix. 79 The water-lilies lifted their pure whiteness to the..sunbeams.

d. *fig.* Purity, stainless character or quality.

1555 BRADFORD in Coverdale *Lett. Martyrs* (1564) 285 Sope, though it be blacke, soileth not the clothe,..so doth the blacke crosse helpe vs to more whitenes. **1645** MILTON *Tetrach.* Wks. 1851 IV. 181 To vindicat the whitenes and the innocence of this divine Law, from the calumny it findes. **1663** COWLEY *Verses & Ess.*, *Horace* III. i. 3 To Virgin Minds, which yet their Native whiteness hold,..these truths I tell. **1816** BYRON *Ch. Har.* III. lvii, He had kept The whiteness of his soul. **1884** HARROP *Bolingbroke* i. 44 Such ..was the whiteness of his record in this respect.

whitening ('hwaɪt(ə)nɪŋ), *vbl. sb.* [f. WHITEN *v.* + -ING[1].]

1. The action, or a process, of making white; bleaching, whitewashing, tinning, etc.; also *fig.* Also, the fact or process of becoming white.

1601 HOLLAND *Pliny* XXXI. xi. II. 423 An artificiall devise to make spunges looke white;..if the softest..be..bathed.. in the fome of salt: after which they ought to be laid abroad in the moon-shine,..that thereby they may take their whitening. **1705** ADDISON *Italy*, etc. 489 They have..great Commodities for Whitening [= bleaching]. **1713** *Guardian* No. 109 ¶6 Our Faces debar us from all artificial Whitenings. **1839** URE *Dict. Arts* 956 Pin manufacture... 9. Whitening or tinning. **1854** R. H. PATTERSON *Ess. Hist. & Art* (1862) 34 Whitening of the seams—a disagreeable vestiarian phenomenon produced by the surface..of the cloth being rubbed off. **1857** MILLER *Elem. Chem.*, *Org.* (1862) xi. §2. 773 After another scraping on the flesh side, or whitening, it [*sc.* the skin] is ready to be stored away. **1877** *Paper hanger* etc. 69 If the ceiling is a new one, prime with water, soft soap, and a little lime before whitening. **1878** SEELEY *Stein* II. 401 That popular agitation, that first whitening of the waves for the storm of the Anti-Napoleonic Revolution. **1891** *Athenæum* 26 Dec. 870/2 It goes too far in its blackening of Macbeth and in its whitening of Lady Macbeth.

2. *concr.* = WHITING *vbl. sb.* 4.

1710 LADY G. BAILLIE *Househ. Bk.* (S.H.S. 1911) 84 For whittining to the wals 1s. 3d. **1823** J. BADCOCK *Dom. Amusem.* 29 Derbyshire stone, whitening and plaister of Paris. **1906** 'G. TRAVERS' *Growth* i. 5 The smell of moisture and bathbrick and whitening.

3. *attrib.* and *Comb.*

1797 MME. D'ARBLAY *Diary*, *Let. to Mrs. Francis* 16 Nov., The silver of our plated [spoons] having feloniously made off under cover of the whitening-brush. **1800** *Hull Advertiser* 7 June 2/3 The warehouses, whitening-house,.. whitening and painting mills. **1826** GALT *Last of Lairds* xxxiv. 304 Jenny..was..whitewashing the lintels of the lower windows with an old hearth-brush; her whitening-pot was a handless and cripple tureen. **1875** KNIGHT *Dict. Mech.*, *Whitening-machine*, a machine for removing the red skin or cuticle from the grain of rice.

'whitening, *ppl. a.* [f. as prec. + -ING².] That whitens; making or becoming white.

1641 J. JACKSON *True Evang. T.* II. 143 The bleaching, whitening,..cleansing quality of Christs blood. **1648** J. BEAUMONT *Psyche* VII. lv, Made not by scorching but by whitening light. **1704** POPE *Spring* 19 Two Swains..Pour'd o'er the whitening vale their fleecy care. **1821** SCOTT *Pirate* xxxvii, My whitening bones will swing in the gibbet-irons. **1859** HAWTHORNE *Fr. & It. Note-bks.* (1871) II. 274 Marks of..coming age in many a whitening hair. **1902** BUCHAN *Watcher by Threshold*, etc. 88 My whitening face must have told them a tale.

white-out ('hwaɪtaʊt). Also **whiteout.** [f. phr. *to white out* (cf. WHITE *v.*¹), by analogy with BLACK-OUT.] **1. a.** *N. Amer.* A heavy snow-storm, a blizzard.

1942 *Sun* (Baltimore) 30 Mar. 8 (*caption*) Whiteout. **1980** *Sat. Rev.* (U.S.) May 66 Blizzards—white-outs they call them here [*sc.* in Labrador]—bring snow that whirls and thrashes and blinds, stinging noses, and cabins disappear in the whiteness.

b. A condition in which neither shadows nor the horizon can be seen and physical features are lost in the background, caused by an evenness of lighting such as sometimes occurs in cloud or in snow- or ice-covered regions.

1946 *Sun* (Baltimore) 20 Apr. 7/2 Hedine, of the United States Weather Bureau at Winnemucca, Nevada, described the 'Arctic whiteout' today, defining it as a condition of the snow country wherein all land features are camouflaged, 'blending earth and sky so that the horizon and all landmarks are indistinguishable'. **1955** *Sci. Amer.* Apr. 54/3 Lieutenant John P. Moore, a Navy pilot, was killed when his helicopter crashed during a 'white-out'. This condition, one of the chief hazards of Antarctic travel, occurs when sunlight diffuses through a solid overcast. **1959** V. FUCHS *Antarctic Adv.* vii. 96 A whiteout is something like a blackout in reverse... No surface irregularities in the snow are visible in the diffused, opaque light, but a dark object like a man or a vehicle may be clearly seen. **1966** F. HOYLE *October 1st* viii. 95 It was impossible to know whether you were looking ten yards..or even a hundred miles. The effect ..was far more weird than the kind of white-out you sometimes get on a snowfield in the mountains. **1976** M. MACHLIN *Pipeline* i. 7 White-out had set in just after Takolik had seen The-Man-Who-Hides. **1980** *Daily Tel.* 30 July 16 Bad weather, including white-outs caused by low cloud, hampered the early stages and Bonington is reported as saying he can well understand why the peak has never been climbed before. **1984** *Times* 5 Jan. 9/4 When whiteout exists, by the interaction of sunlight, snow, cloud and reflection, it induces the belief in a pilot that he is flying over flat terrain with unlimited forward visibility.

2. A white liquid that can be brushed on to paper to obliterate marks and provide a white surface on which to type or write afresh.

1977 L. O'DONNELL *Aftershock* xiii. 180 You changed the date... Did you cover the original entries with a strip of paper, or did you use white-out? **1984** *New Yorker* 23 Jan. 44/2 A Chinese version of typists' white-out.

white pine. [WHITE *a.* 11 b.]

1. *N. Amer.* Any of several North American pines, esp. *Pinus strobus*, which is native to eastern and central parts of the continent; also, the pale soft wood of such a tree. Cf. WEYMOUTH.

1682 *Early Rec. Providence, Rhode Island* (1899) XIV. 113 From yᵉ said heape of stones to range north..to a great white pine. **1767** *Quebec Gaz.* 8 Dec. 3/1 They are hereby forbid to cut down..White Pine..on the lands above described. **1785** MARTYN *Rousseau's Bot.* xxviii. (1794) 445 Weymouth Pine... In North America it is called White Pine, and is excellent for masts. **1893** *Scribner's Mag.* June 697/1 The white-pine supply of this country stands in the States of Michigan, Wisconsin, and Minnesota. **1901** *J. Black's Carp. & Build.*, *Home Handicr.* ix. 78 The material for a drawing-board that is..most satisfactory in use, is white pine. **1948** *Reader's Digest* Jan. 68/2 Of all American woods none has been more significant than white pine. **1961** H. MACLENNAN *Rivers of Canada* 97 When Wright surveyed the Ottawa forests he found an abundance of white pine standing two hundred feet tall. **1973** A. H. WHITEFORD *North Amer. Indian Arts* 107 White pine bark canoes were made by the Kutenai. **1974** M. BRAITHWAITE *Ontario* ix. 134 All about him..were great stands of white pines, tall trees stretching as straight as a ruler.

2. *Austral.* A tree belonging to any of several species of *Podocarpus* or *Callitris*. Cf. KAHIKATEA, PODOCARP.

1855 R. TAYLOR *Te Ika a Maui* 439 (*Podocarpus excelsus.*) This tree is generally called the white pine, from the color of its wood. **1888** *Cassell's Picturesque Australasia* III. 210 (Morris). **1898** MORRIS *Austral Eng.* s.v., White P[ine]—(In Australia) *Frenela robusta*,..*Podocarpus elata*. (In New Zealand) *P. dacryoides*. **1975** D. BAGLEY *Snow Tiger* ii. 33 Gone were the stands of tall white pine and cedar, of kahikatea and kohekohe.

3. Special Combs.: **white pine blister (rust)**, a rust disease of certain pines, caused by the fungus *Cronartium ribicola*, which spends part of its life cycle on gooseberry or currant bushes; **white pine weevil**, the larva of a brown beetle, *Pissodes strobi*, which tunnels in new shoots of certain pines.

1911 *Bull. U.S. Bureau Plant Industry* No. 206. 9 The white-pine blister rust now imported into this country from Germany is caused by a heterœcious fungus. **1974** M. HOYT *Thirty Miles* vi. 66 We had currant bushes..before anybody knew they were an intermediate host to..white-pine blister. **1905** *Bull. Forestry Bureau* (U.S. Dept. Agric.) No. 63. 14 The white pine weevil..is a reddish-brown snout beetle. **1976** *Columbus* (Montana) *News* 27 May (Joliet Suppl.) 4/5 Whitepine weevil..can kill twigs and branches of some evergreens.

'white-pot, 'whitepot. Also 6-7 whitpot. [POT *sb.*¹ 1 b.] A dish made (chiefly in Devonshire) of milk or cream boiled with various ingredients, as eggs, flour, raisins, sugar, spices, etc.; a kind of custard or milk-pudding. Also *attrib.*

1577 BATMAN *Golden Bk. Leaden Gods* 30 Hee is caried on the Backes of foure Deacons, after the maner of carying Whytepot Queenes, in Westerne Maygames. **1578** LYTE *Dodoens* IV. xiv. 468 The meale of Bockewheate is vsed..to make pappe, whitpottes and..cakes of light digestion. **1589** R. HARVEY *Pl. Perc.* (1590) A ij b, Some auncient familiaritie betweene a western fellow, and a whitpot. **1630** J. TAYLOR (Water P.) *Gt. Eater Kent* Wks. I. 146 The Norfolk Dumplin, and the Deuonshire White-pot. **1632** BROME *Northern Lasse* V. viii, Ha' you any Whitpots? **1653** URQUHART *Rabelais* II. iv. 19 They served in this whitepot-meat to him in a huge great Bell. **1708** W. KING *Cookery* (1709) 75 Cornwal Squab-Pye, and Devon White-Pot brings, And Lei'ster Beans and Bacon. **1747** MRS. GLASSE *Cookery* ix. 79 A Rice White-Pot. **1880** HARDY *Trumpet-Major* xvi, Seventy rings of black-pot, a dozen of white-pot, and twenty-five knots of tender..chitterlings.

whiteret, var. WHITRET, weasel.

White Russian, *sb.* and *a.* [f. WHITE *a.* + RUSSIAN *sb.* and *a.*; cf. BELORUSSIAN *a.* and *sb.*]

A. *sb.* **1. a.** The East Slavonic language spoken in Belorussia, a district in the western part of Russia which is now one of the constituent republics of the Soviet Union.

1850 'TALVI' *Hist. View Lang. & Lit. Slavic Nations* II. i. 51 The White-Russian is the dialect spoken in Lithuania and a portion of White Russia, especially Volhynia. **1932** C. A. PHILLIPS tr. *H. von Eckardt's Russia* VI. ii. 475 Up to the sixteenth century the Lithuanian Grand Princes and boyars regarded White Russian as their language. **1949** ENTWISTLE & MORISON *Russian & Slavonic Lang.* i. 30 White Russian became a chancery language, not a literary tongue. **1960** W. K. MATTHEWS *Russian Hist. Gram.* I. ii. 34 There are seven groups of Slavonic languages, viz. the East Slavonic (Russian, White Russian, and Ukrainian) [etc.].

b. A native or inhabitant of Belorussia.

1886 [see RUSSIAN *sb.* 1 a]. **1912** D. M. WALLACE *Russia* xxxix. 726 [The first Duma] was composed of many nationalities clustering round the dominant race. The chief ethnographical groups were the Great-Russians (265), the Little-Russians (62), the White-Russians (12), the Poles (51), the Lithuanians (10),..and the Bashkirs (4). **1918** R. WILTON *Russia's Agony* i. 9 The White Russians, a comparatively small section of the Northern Slav people, inhabiting Smolensk and the upper reaches of the Dnieper. **1960** W. K. MATTHEWS *Russian Hist. Gram.* III. ii. 309 The grammatical treatises of the time..are mainly the work of non-Russian scholars—White Russians and Ukrainians.

2. = WHITE *sb.* 19 b.

1927 *Daily Tel.* 29 Mar. 11/6 The White Russians in the Northern Army..were purely soldiers, while the Reds were carrying on propaganda. **1930** *Times* 17 Mar. 12/6 Yesterday afternoon 'White' Russians, most of them women, made a demonstration at the offices of Amtorg Trading Corporation, the Soviet's American commercial agency. **1943** tr. *N. Basseches's Unknown Army* iv. 59 If they were in the territory of the Soviets, they either broke through in time to join the White Russians or they were caught by the Red mobilization. **1973** 'D. HALLIDAY' *Dolly & Starry Bird* xii. 184 Innes was sitting looking at the Director like a White Russian receiving word of Biological Ajax. **1976** *New Yorker* 15 Nov. 39/1, I was surrounded by ..some of those privileged White Russians who abandoned their first-adopted countries of Europe to come to the States at the onset of the Second World War.

B. *adj.* **1.** Of or pertaining to Belorussia or its people.

1886 *Encycl. Brit.* XXI. 71/1 In 1879 in European Russia, —exclusive of six Lithuanian and White Russian governments,—42,530 persons were tried before the courts. **1918** TROFIMOV & SCOTT *Handbk. Russian* I. i. 4 The White Russian dialect covers the smallest area of all the Russian dialects. **1926** L. H. GUEST *New Russia* i. 21 The following are Independent Republics: The Ukrainian Socialist Soviet Republic..The White Russian Socialist Soviet Republic. **1944** [see BELORUSSIAN *a.* and *sb.*]. **1960** W. K. MATTHEWS *Russian Hist. Gram.* II. xii. 276 In the latter part of the seventeenth century the influence of the White Russian and Ukrainian scholars and writers began to be felt.

2. Of or pertaining to the Whites in the Russian Civil War.

1929 W. S. CHURCHILL *World Crisis* V. xii. 247 We have seen them [*sc.* the Czechs] already in October 1918.. exasperated by White Russian mismanagement. **1957** P. KEMP *Mine were of Trouble* iii. 39 The Requetés were raising two squadrons in Seville, under a White Russian colonel named Alkon. **1964** R. PERRY *World of Tiger* ii. 24 The White Russian hunter Yankovsky. **1974** *Encycl. Brit. Macropædia* XVI. 70/2 The Red Army..drove him [*sc.* Wrangel] and his army into exile. There remained only the Japanese and White Russian forces in eastern Siberia.

'white-skin, *a.* and *sb.*

A. *adj.* ? Having or resembling a white skin.

1634 QUARLES *Mildreiados* xv, The coorsegrain'd Lockrom, and the white-skin Lawne Are both subjected to the selfe-same Fate. **1823** JAS. KENNEDY *Poems* 85 (E.D.D.), Wauking some wife's white skin blankets, Or some flannel for her douf.

B. *sb.* A white-skinned man, a white man. (Cf. *redskin.*)

1826 J. F. COOPER *Last of Mohicans* xiv, 'Twould have been..an inhuman act for a white-skin; but 'tis the..natur' of an Indian. **1874** BLEEK in *Folklore* (1919) XXX. 155 The red Bushman looks down upon the black-man quite as much as any orthodox white skin does.

whitesmith¹ ('hwaɪtsmɪθ). [Cf. WHITE *a.* 2 b, and BLACKSMITH.] **a.** A worker in 'white iron'; a tinsmith. **b.** One who polishes or finishes metal goods, as distinguished from one who forges them; also, more widely, a worker in metals.

1302 in *Cal. Pat. Rolls* 50 John son of John le Whytesmith. **1682** *Lond. Gaz.* No. 1735/4 Joseph Carles of Birmingham in the County of Warwick White-Smith, having..received several Edge-Tools to be mended. *a* **1708** T. WARD *Eng. Ref.* III. (1710) 2 For not a White-Smith nor a Black, Could frame such things as he would lack. **1778** *Eng. Gazetteer* (ed. 2), *Swindon, Staff*...is one of those places which have blade-mills, where scythes, axes, reaping-hooks, &c. after being prepared for it by the white-smiths, are ground to a fine edge. **1826** SCOTT *Prov. Antiq.* 104 He was a white-smith, and published various lucubrations under the title of the Tinclarian Doctor. **1833** [see below]. **1866** ROGERS *Agric. & Prices* I. xxiii. 603 The brass was sometimes served out to the whitesmith to be manufactured. **1886** FENN *Patience Wins* xii, I arn't a blacksmith, I'm a whitesmith, and work in steel.

Hence **'white,smithery,** the occupation of a whitesmith.

1812 *Niles' Weekly Reg.* 25 Jan. 390/2 Emery..is an article of the first consequence in the cotton and woolen manufactories, and in white smithery. **1833** J. HOLLAND *Manuf. Metal* II. 124 A modern whitesmithery establishment generally comprises the..conveniences requisite for the production of every description of work, from what is called blacksmithing..to..machine-making or engineering... A first-rate whitesmith is not only required to understand generally the qualities of common iron and steel, and the methods of..working them; he must likewise have a competent knowledge of the principles of mechanical science.

'whitesmith². [f. WHITE *a.* + the surname of Sir William Sidney *Smith* (1764–1840).] A variety of gooseberry with white fruit.

1860 R. HOGG *Fruit Man.* 89 Whitesmith (Woodward's). .. Skin white, and downy. **1900** *Daily Express* 24 July 5/6 The coster..at Covent Garden exchanging his sixpences for 28lb baskets of 'White-smiths' or common reds according to the prevailing taste of his 'walk'.

whitesmithing ('hwaɪtsmɪθɪŋ), *vbl. sb.* [f. WHITESMITH¹ + -ING¹.] = WHITESMITHERY.

1835 *Lexington* (Kentucky) *Observer* 10 June, White-smithing. Frederick Klaiber lately from Germany..has just commenced the above business. **1900** *Daily Chron.* 2 Jan. 3/1 Part of the bench at which the missionary-explorer learnt whitesmithing is exhibited.

white staff. Pl. -staves. [STAFF *sb.*¹ 7.]

1. A white rod or wand carried as a symbol of office by certain officials, e.g. the steward of the king's household and the lord high treasurer; hence, the office held by these.

1581 J. HAMILTON *Cath. Traict.* in *Cath. Tract.* (S.T.S.) 90 Sa thair men be certane constitute vith thair quhyt staffas as sergeantis. **1640** [see STAFF *sb.*¹ 7]. **1647** CLARENDON *Hist. Reb.* I. §101 Sir Richard Weston had been advanced to the White-staff, into the office of Lord high Treasurer of England. **1678** *Jrnl. Ho. Comm.* IX. 554/1 The Lords..have appointed the Lords of the White Staves to attend his Majesty. *a* **1700** EVELYN *Diary* 27 Nov. 1666, Sir Hugh Pollard, Comptroller of the Household, died at White-hall, and his Majesty conferr'd the white staffe on my brother Commissioner for sick and wounded. **1714** DE FOE (*title*) The Secret History of the White-Staff, being An Account of Affairs under the Conduct of some late Ministers, and of what might probably have happened if Her Majesty had not Died. *a* **1715** BURNET *Own Time* II. (1724) I. 161 He [*sc.* Earl of Southampton] said, he would not..see the ruin of his countrey begun, and be silent: A white staff should not bribe him. **1827** [see STAFF *sb.*¹ 7].

2. An official who carries a white staff (see 1).

1601 in *Househ. Ord.* (1790) 282 These two [*sc.* Clerkes Comptrollers] (under the white staves) bee comptrollers of all household affaires. *Ibid.* 293 That so the Lord Steward, the whitestaves, and officers, might have their diettes served orderly. **1674** *Essex Papers* (Camden 1890) 256 The Seals being signed the white staffe is to be changed. **1675** *Ibid.* (1913) 25 Ye House of Lords..order their black Rod to apprehend ye Sergeant of ye House of Commons, and addresse to his Maᵗⁱᵉ by word of ye white-staves that another Sergeant might be appoynted.

3. *attrib.* **white staff officer** = 2.

1671 E. CHAMBERLAYNE *Pres. St. Eng.* I. (ed. 5) 162 The Lord Steward is a White-staff Officer; for he in the Kings Presence, carrieth a White-staff... This White-staff is taken for a Commission; at the death of the King, over the Herse made for the Kings Body, he breaketh this Staff, and thereby dischargeth all the Officers. *a* **1700** EVELYN *Diary* 17 Jan. 1687, Much discourse that all the White Staff Officers ..should be dismiss'd for adhering to their Religion. **1708** *Lond. Gaz.* No. 4488/2 Garter King of Arms proclaimed his Royal Highness's Stile, and the white Staff Officers broke their Staves, and threw them into the Vault.

white stick. [STICK *sb.*¹]

†**1.** A piece of white wood used as a tally. *Obs.*

c **1380** WYCLIF *Wks.* (1880) 233 Lordis many tymes.. taken pore mennus goodis & paien not þerfore but white stickis. *c* **1400** *Pilgr. Sowle* IV. xxxviii. (1859) 64 The kyng hath nought wherof to paye for his mete, but of white stikkes that no thyng auailen.

2. = WHITE STAFF 1, 2.

1777 EARL MARCH in Jesse *Selwyn & Contemp.* (1844) III. 256 Lord Onslow [as Comptroller of the Household] has Sir W. Meredith's White Stick. **1792** WOLCOT (P. Pindar) *Odes of Condol.* I. vi. Wks. 1812 III. 86 Then would they ponder on the white-stick row Of Uxbridge, Grey de Wilton, Leeds, and Co. **1812** BYRON *Waltz* xiii, New white-sticks, gold-sticks, broom-sticks, all new sticks! **1861** HUGHES *Tom Brown at Oxf.* iii, Lords and ladies in waiting, white sticks or black rods.

3. A white walking-stick carried by a blind person both as a distinguishing feature and to locate obstacles. Cf *white cane* s.v. WHITE *a.* 11 e.

1961 *A.A. Handbk.* 20 Responsible blind welfare organizations strongly recommend all blind persons to carry a white stick. **1967** S. BECKETT *Stories & Texts for Nothing* VIII. 110 But what is this I see, and how, a white stick and an ear-trumpet. **1974** *Times* 21 Feb. 10 His first perilous adventures with the white stick. **1978** 'H. CARMICHAEL' *Life Cycle* xiv. 150 The man who doesn't admire you shouldn't be allowed out in the street without a white stick.

white-tail ('hwaɪtteɪl). Also 7 whittaile. [TAIL *sb.*[1]]

1. = WHEATEAR[2] (q.v. for foreign equivalents). *Obs.* or *dial.*

1611 COTGR., *Cul blanc*, the bird called a Whittaile. **1666** MERRETT *Pinax* 178 *Oenanthe*, the Wheat ear, or White tail ..*in agro Warwicensi* Fallow Smiters. *a* **1705** RAY *Syn. Avium* (1713) 76 *Oenanthe*... Alibi ab Uropygii colore White Tail dicitur ut Italis *Culo bianco*.

2. The white-tailed deer (*Odocoileus virginianus*), a common N. American species, having the under side of the tail white. Also ***white-tail deer***.

1872 R. G. MCCLELLAN *Golden State* 241 There are several varieties: the mule-deer, black-tail, antelope, and white-tail. **1888** LEES & CLUTTERBUCK *B.C. 1887* xxix. (1892) 323 Mule-deer and cariboo were numerous here, but the white-tail.. was conspicuous by its absence. **1895** *Outing* (U.S.) XXVII. 43 The white-tail deer is especially prized as food. **1936** D. MCCOWAN *Animals Canad. Rockies* vii. 59 The hoofs of the wapiti and whitetail deer are too small to propel these animals through the water with any great speed. **1968** R. KROETSCH *Alberta* I. 12 White-tails and mule deer and mallards and grouse tumble before the unerring aim. **1980** *Hunting Ann. 1981* 29/1 My mountain-hunting buddy.. came down out of his renowned mule deer country .. to join me in a search of a big Colorado whitetail.

white-tailed ('hwaɪtteɪld), *a.* [WHITE *a.* 12 c.] Having a white tail; ***white-tailed deer*** = WHITE-TAIL 2; ***white-tailed eagle***, the European sea eagle (see EAGLE *sb.* 1 a); ***white-tailed gnu***, the common (as distinct from the brindled) gnu, *Connochætes gnou*; ***white-tailed ptarmigan***, a ptarmigan, *Lagopus leucurus*, found in western North America.

1642 Quhyt taillet [see *white-maned* s.v. WHITE *a.* 12 c]. **1678** J. RAY tr. *Willughby's Ornithol.* II. 61 Of the Pygarg or white-tail'd Eagle. **1832** W. A. FERRIS *Jrnl.* 27 Aug. in *Life in Rocky Mts.* (1940) 131 In the afternoon.. we killed a white-tailed fawn. **1887** I. R. *Lady's Ranche Life* 45 This is the first wild animal I've seen, except antelope and white-tailed deer. **1889** *Cent. Dict.*, (caption s.v. *Gnu*) Common or White-tailed Gnu. *Ibid.*, White-tailed ptarmigan. **1912** J. STEVENSON-HAMILTON *Animal Life Afr.* vii. 106 There is no more remarkable beast, either in appearance or manners,.. than the white-tailed gnu. **1926** F. C. R. JOURDAIN in J. J. Walker *Nat. Hist. Oxford Distr.* 146 White-tailed Eagle.. has occurred on Wantage Downs. **1941** J. S. HUXLEY *Uniqueness of Man* viii. 184 Other species now exist only in captivity. Such are the beautiful and fantastic white-tailed gnus. **1948** A. L. RAND *Mammals Eastern Rockies* 208 When the alarmed white-tailed deer goes bounding away, its tail usually stands straight up, and it is a great snowy banner that leaves no doubt of identity. **1968** R. KROETSCH *Alberta* II. 59 Soon after, we saw two white-tailed deer, just on the timberline. **1973** *Islander* (Victoria, B.C.) 1 Apr. 2/2, I have found myself staring at a whitetailed ptarmigan in the high mountains believing that he was snow. **1981** *Birds* Autumn 55/3 (*caption*) White-tailed eagle—last bred in Britain in 1916... A scheme to reintroduce these birds to Scotland is now underway.

white-tawer: see WHITTAWER.

whitethorn ('hwaɪtθɔːn). Also with hyphen, or (now rarely) as two words. [WHITE *a.* and THORN *sb.*, after L. *alba spina* (whence F. *aubépine*); so MHG. *wîzdorn* (G. *weissdorn*).] The common hawthorn, *Cratægus Oxyacantha*: so called from the lighter colour of its bark as compared with that of the BLACKTHORN.

In U.S. applied to *C. coccinea*, a species or variety with scarlet fruit.

c **1265** *Voc. Plants* in Wr.-Wülcker 559/25 *Bedagrage, i. spina alba, i.* witþorn. **1382** WYCLIF *Baruch* vi. 70 A whijt thorn, vpon whiche eche bridde sittith. **1398** TREVISA *Barth. De P.R.* XVII. clxvi. (Bodl. MS.), þese treen.. haue prickes as a white þorne. **1523–34** FITZHERB. *Husb.* §124 Gette thy quyckesettes in the woode-countreye, and let theym be of whyte-thorne and crabtree. **1637** MILTON *Lycidas* 48 When first the White thorn blows. **1733** W. ELLIS *Chiltern & Vale Farm.* 150 To be more sure of a strong Fence, White-thorn may be made every second Plant. **1870** MORRIS *Earthly Par.* III. II. 168 While round about the white-thorn shed Sweet fragrance. **1870** KINGSLEY *At Last* v, The Bauhinias, like tall and ancient white-thorns, which shade the road.

attrib. **1562** TURNER *Herbal* II. 73 Matthiolus holdeth y[t] our haw tre or whyte thorne tre is Oxyacantha. **1733** TULL *Horse-hoeing Husb.* xvi. 243 White-Thorns will not prosper set in the Gaps of a White-Thorn Hedge. **1813** *Ann. Reg., Chron.* 74 He struck her so violently with a white-thorn stick .. that she fell to the ground. **1827** CLARE *Sheph. Cal.* 45 Or short note of the changing thrush Above him in the white-thorn bush. **1842** LOUDON *Suburban Hort.* 105 The caterpillars of the white-thorn butterfly (*Papilio cratægi*).. had.. stripped all the hedges. **1885** PATER *Marius* I. xiv. 248 The torch of white-thorn-wood.

whitethroat ('hwaɪtθrəʊt), *sb.* (*a.*) (Also with hyphen, and formerly as two words.)

A. *sb.* Name of several birds characterized by a white throat.

1. Any one of several species of warbler (*Sylvia*), esp. the common whitethroat, *S. cinerea*, and the lesser whitethroat, *S. curruca*.

1676 GREW *Musæum, Anat. Stomach & Guts* viii. 38 The White-Throat hath no small Gut. **1688** HOLME *Armoury* II. 247/1 The White Throat.. hath.. the upper surface of the Body red. **1774** G. WHITE *Selborne, To Pennant* 2 Sept., The note of the whitethroat, which is continually repeated, and often attended with odd gesticulations on the wing, is harsh and displeasing... In July and August they.. make great havoc among the summer fruits. **1825** W. COBBETT *Rur. Rides* (1885) II. 320 The sweet and soft voice of the white-throat. **1839** MACGILLIVRAY *Brit. Birds* II. 345 *Sylvia hortensis*. The Garden Warbler or Pettychaps... Billy Whitethroat. *Ibid.* 357 *Sylvia garrula*. The White-breasted Warbler. Lesser White-throat. **1845** BROWNING *Home-thoughts from Abr.* ii, And after April, when May follows, And the whitethroat builds, and all the swallows!

2. The white-throated sparrow of N. America, *Zonotrichia albicollis*.

a **1862** THOREAU *Maine Woods* (1864) 198 We heard the white throats along the shore. **1889** *Science-Gossip* XXV. 146 White-throated sparrows sing magnificently all winter long... Here.. concerted action makes the charm. A single white-throat would prove a trifle monotonous. **1902** S. E. WHITE *Blazed Trail* xviii, The notes of the white-throat—the nightingale of the North. **1916** D. C. SCOTT *Poems* (1927) 47 A rocky islet followed With one lone poplar and a single nest Of white-throat-sparrows that took no rest. **1939** [see PEABODY]. **1978** A. LAMPMAN *Lyrics of Earth* 32 The white-throat's distant descant with slow stress Note after note upon the noonday falls.

B. *adj.* White-throated. ***whitethroat warbler*** = sense 1 above.

1876 *Rep. & Trans. Devonsh. Assoc.* VIII. 265 The White-throat Warbler... Common everywhere. **1884** W. C. SMITH *Kildrostan* 61 O white-throat swallow flicking The loch with long wing-tips.

whitewash ('hwaɪtwɒʃ), *sb.* [prob. f. the verb; cf. WASH *sb.* 4 d.]

†**1.** A cosmetic wash formerly used for imparting a light colour to the skin. *Obs.*

1689 *Several Disc. Vanities Modish Women* 175 Her Bottles of White washes, or Cosmeticks. **1713** ADDISON *Guardian* No. 116 ¶1, I have heard a whole Sermon against a White-wash. **1764** GRAY *Jemmy Twitcher* 2 When sly Jemmy Twitcher had smugg'd up his face, With a lick of court whitewash,.. A wooing he went.

2. A liquid composition of lime and water, or of whiting, size, and water, for whitening walls, ceilings, etc.

1697 VANBRUGH *Relapse* v. iii, A little Glasing, Painting, Whitewash, and Playster, will make it [*sc.* the house] last thy time. **1751** JOHNSON *Rambler* No. 161 ¶4 The Plaisterer having.. obliterated, by his White-wash, all the smoky Memorials which former Tenants had left upon the Cieling. **1776** G. SEMPLE *Building in Water* 81 A Peck of Roach-lime was slacked into White-wash. **1853** MRS. GASKELL *Cranford* xv, A wholesome smell of plaster and whitewash pervaded the apartment. **1858** HAWTHORNE *Fr. & It. Note-bks.* (1872) I. 48 Before the whitewash of Cromwell's time had overlaid their marble pillars.

attrib. and *Comb.* **1814** *Austin Papers* (1924) I. 240, 1 White Wash Brush. **1848** D. G. ROSSETTI *Let.* 20 Jan. (1965) I. 34 All my traps have been moved up into an attic, to make room for ladders, whitewash-pails, and such-like gear. **1881** *Century Mag.* XXIII. 128/2 With whitewash brush in hand. **1887** HISSEY *Holiday on Road* 26 Art-ignoring, whitewash-loving churchwardens.

3. *fig.* Something that conceals faults or gives a fair appearance: cf. next, 2.

1865 W. G. PALGRAVE *Arabia* II. 21 Such liberal semblance is merely a surface whitewash. **1883** *Fortn. Rev.* Feb. 284 Washed white with the whitewash of diplomacy. **1898** 'H. S. MERRIMAN' *Rodens's Corner* xi. 116 You know your uncle's reputation—the past one, I mean, not the whitewash.

4. An act of 'whitewashing', as of a bankrupt; also (*colloq.*, orig. *U.S.*) a victory at baseball or other game in which the opponents fail to score; also, a victory in a series of games of which the opponents fail to win any.

1851 J. HENDERSON *Excurs. N.S. Wales* I. 64 When once in a twelvemonth your agent goes smash, And bolts to New Zealand, or gets a whitewash. **1867** *N.Y. Clipper* 31 Aug. 164/2 The first 'whitewash' of the [baseball] game was drawn by the Mutuals. **1874** *State Jrnl.* (Lincoln, Nebraska) 26 June 4/1 The second match game of croquet took place yesterday morning, and resulted in a second whitewash for the latter named gentleman. **1884** *Boston* (Mass.) *Jrnl.* 13 Sept., The Bostons Give the Lawrence Team a White-wash Bath. **1920** *Westm. Gaz.* 22 May 2/2 The Report is a fairly comprehensive whitewash of everybody concerned. **1961** *Times* 4 May 4/6 Miss Truman who yesterday allowed Mrs. Cawthorn but 23 points in what the players of darts would term a 'whitewash'. **1962** *Times* 26 May 3/5 England nearly scored a whitewash over France.. only the victory of G. Mourgue d'Algue standing between them and a 12-0 lead on the first day. **1977** *Evening Gaz.* (Middlesbrough) 11 Jan. 14/1 Only one whitewash this week in the Friendly League. **1978** *Rugby World* Apr. 4/1 Scotland must be bitterly disappointed that they have suffered their first whitewash for ten years.

†**5.** *slang.* (See quot. 1864.) Cf. WHITEWASHER 3. *Obs.*

1864 HOTTEN *Slang Dict.* 270 *Whitewash*, a glass of sherry as a finale, after drinking port and claret. **1879** TROLLOPE *John Caldigate* III. x. 142 'Take another glass of port, old boy.' Bagwax did take another glass, finishing the bottle... 'Take a drop of whitewash to wind up, and then we'll join the ladies.'

6. *Comb.*: **whitewash gum**, either of two eucalypts with powdery white bark, *Eucalyptus apodophylla* and *E. terminalis*, found in northern and central Australia.

[**1926** J. M. BLACK *Flora S. Austral.* III. 420 *E*[*ucalyptus*] *terminalis*... Whitewashed gum; bloodwood.] **1934** *Bulletin* (Sydney) 2 May 21/2 The whitewash gum.. forms a striking feature of the landscape about Alice Springs. **1965** *Austral. Encycl.* III. 406/2 Whitebark or 'whitewash gum'.. of Arnhem Land has perfectly smooth trunks covered with a white mealy 'bloom' that rubs off when touched.

'**whitewash**, *v.* [f. WHITE *sb.* 18 + WASH *v.* 9 b.]

1. a. *trans.* To plaster over (a wall, etc.) with a white composition; to cover or coat with whitewash. Also *absol.*

1591 PERCIVALL *Sp. Dict.*, *Enxalvegar*, to white washe a house. **1707** J. STEVENS tr. *Quevedo's Com. Wks.* (1709) 329 She that White-washes her House, has a Mind to lett it. **1780** COXE *Russ. Discov.* 216 The houses are.. plaistered and white-washed. **1818** SCOTT *Hrt. Midl.* xliii, There were workmen.. altering, repairing, scrubbing, painting, and white-washing. **1834** L. RITCHIE *Wand. Seine* 104 To whitewash a church is, in our eyes, a profanity. **1877** C. GEIKIE *Christ* xxix. I. 485 The other [tomb].. whitewashed, to warn passers by not to defile themselves by too near an approach to the dead.

b. To apply a cosmetic 'whitewash' to.

1912 C. N. & A. M. WILLIAMSON *Guests of Hercules* xvii, She whitewashed her face and had strange eyes.

c. *intr.* To become coated with a white efflorescence: see WHITEWASHING *vbl. sb.* 1 b.

1889 C. T. DAVIS *Bricks, Tiles*, etc. (ed. 2) 90 The bricks made from them [*sc.* clays on the Hudson River] usually 'whitewash' or 'saltpetre' upon exposure to the weather.

2. *fig.* **a.** *trans.* To give a fair appearance to; to free, or attempt to free, from blame or taint; to cover up, conceal, or gloss over the faults or blemishes of.

With various shades of meaning; now usually somewhat contemptuous, and implying a false appearance of good.

1762 COLMAN *Prose Sev. Occas.* (1787) II. 34 Such as are blackened in the *North Briton* are.. white-washed in the *Auditor*. **1764** HOR. WALPOLE *Mem. Reign Geo. III* (1845) II. 35 A poet and an author will go as far in whitewashing a munificent tyrant. **1809** SIR G. JACKSON *Diaries & Lett.* (1873) I. 36 To be entirely exonerated from all blame, or —in the familiar language of the day—to be whitewashed. **1833** MARRYAT *Peter Simple* xxxi, A quadroon and white make the *mustee* or one-eighth black, and the mustee and white the mustafina, or one-sixteenth black. After that, they are whitewashed, and considered as Europeans. *a* **1845** BARHAM *Ingol. Leg.* Ser. III. *House-Warm.* x, Snore Hill (which we have since whitewash'd to Snow). **1856** *N. Brit. Rev.* XXVI. 87 Mr. Froude.. makes no attempt.. to white-wash Henry: all that he does is, to remove as far as he can, the modern layers of 'black-wash'. **1867** TROLLOPE *Chron. Barset* I. vii. 51 She would have given a finger to white-wash Mr. Crawley in the major's estimation. **1904** STUBBS *Lect. Eur. Hist.* II. viii. 229 Charles.. had.. whitewashed the cruel persecutions of Philip himself.

b. *spec.* To clear (a bankrupt or insolvent) by judicial process from liability for his debts. Also with the debts, etc. as obj., and *intr.* for *pass.* to go through the bankruptcy court.

1762 *Boston Evg. Post* 2 Aug. (Thornton *Amer. Gloss.*). **1773** FOOTE *Bankrupt* II. (1776) 37 Pass'd a few necessary notes to get him number and value, white-wash'd him, and sent him home. **1819** *Sporting Mag.* (N.S.) IV. 30 Two baronets' sons pleading to be white-washed, but remanded for fraud towards their creditors. **1832** *Egan's Bk. Sports* 99/2 The unthinking dashing sparks whitewash their long accounts for twist, tape, and buckram. **1837** THACKERAY *Ravenswing* i, If I'm dunned, I whitewash. **1881** E. J. WORBOISE *Sissie* xxvii, I am by no means sure that your father would not prefer to be made a bankrupt!.. he would be 'whitewashed', in vulgar parlance.

3. In *Baseball* and other games: To beat (the opponents) so that they fail to score. Also *loosely*, to beat by a large margin. *colloq.* (orig. *U.S.*)

1867 *Chicago Republican* 6 July 2/6 The Unions were whitewashed 3 times, and the Forest Citys 5 times. **1884** *Boston* (Mass.) *Jrnl.* 2 Oct. 4 Buffalo Whitewashes Providence, and Philadelphia Detroit. **1972** *Korea Times* 19 Nov. 1/5 Husky south Korean girls white-washed Thailand 106–17.. in the second game. **1981** R. LEWIS *Seek for Justice* vi. 193 He took the first game [of darts]... He all but whitewashed Freddy in the second.

whitewashed ('hwaɪtwɒʃt), *ppl. a.* [f. prec. + -ED[1].]

1. Covered, coated, or marked with whitewash.

1770 GOLDSM. *Des. Vill.* 227 The white-washed wall, the nicely sanded floor. **1850** THACKERAY *Pendennis* I[i], A flaring new whitewashed mansion. **1882** HOWELLS in *Longman's Mag.* I. 56 To.. chase the flying tennis-ball on the whitewashed lawn.

2. *fig.* Freed from blame or taint; glossed over with a fair appearance: see prec. 2.

1797 D. SIMPSON *Plea Relig.* (1808) 155 The white washed officer will.. declare.. that he trusts he is moved by the Holy Ghost. **1818** SCOTT *Rob Roy* vii, A white-washed Jacobite; that is, one who having been long a nonjuror,.. had lately qualified himself to act as a justice, by taking the oaths to government. **1859** HELPS *Friends in C.* Ser. II. II. x. 239 The whitewashed triumphs of despotism.

3. ***whitewashed American, Yank,*** or ***Yankee***, a person who affects American manners, or who has spent a short time in America; also *transf.*

1855 in *Occas. Papers Univ. Sydney Austral. Lang. Res. Centre* (1966) No. 10. 26 'I have heard people say they would like to see us clear altogether of British rule.'..'Have you heard that said here?'—'Yes, by a few of those disaffected persons; very few; they are generally what are termed "white-washed Yankees".' **1898** A. J. Boyd *Shellback* 73 He was not one of the low, bullying, half-Irish, half-American sort of men who are called 'whitewashed Yankees'. **1926** W. S. Dill *Long Day* 147 This particular story concerns a 'white-washed American', *i.e.* a native of Canada who had been naturalized in the United States and then secured repatriation in his own country. **1938** F. A. Worsley *First Voy. in Square-Rigged Ship* 82 Whitewashed Yanks (Europeans who had served a voyage in American ships or spent a short period in the States) were numerous. **1970** J. F. Leavitt *Wake of Coasters* 62/2 Some of the schooners in later years were 'white-washed yankees': American built vessels kept under U.S. registry but with the controlling interest actually owned across the border in New Brunswick or Nova Scotia.

whitewasher (ˈhwaɪtˌwɒʃə(r)). [f. as prec. + -ER¹.] One who or that which whitewashes.

1. One who lays on a coat of whitewash.

In quot. 1752 contemptuously for a clumsy artist.

1733 *S. Carolina Gaz.* 24 Feb., He's a Bricklayer, Plaisterer and White-washer. **1752** Foote *Taste* I, Thou Dauber, thou execrable White-washer. **1866** Mrs. Gaskell *Wives & Dau.* xxv, The ladders of whitewashers and painters were sadly in the way of the ladies.

2. *fig.* One who (or something that) frees from blame, conceals faults, or imparts a fair appearance.

1820 M. Wilmot *Let.* 27 Sept. (1935) 84 On recollection his cause is too *good* to be successful in such clever hands as her [*sc.* Queen Caroline's] whitewashers. **1862** M. Napier *Visct. Dundee* II. 228 *note*, A devoted and skilful whitewasher of Scotch fanatics. **1889** Mona Caird *Wing of Azrael* xxxi, Death is..the great whitewasher.

3. *slang* or *colloq.* A final glass of white wine taken after dinner.

1881 J. Grant *Cameronians* iii, The General..insisted..on one more glass of dry sherry, 'just as a white-washer'.

whitewashing (ˈhwaɪtˌwɒʃɪŋ), *vbl. sb.* [f. WHITEWASH *v.* + -ING¹.]

1. The action or process of coating with whitewash.

1663 Gerbier *Counsel* 80 White-washing and stopping, at three pence a yard. **1732** *Phil. Trans.* XXXVII. 234 They use Glue made very thin..instead of Size, for White-washing. **1834** Dickens *Sk. Boz, Boarding-ho.* i, The area and the area steps, and the street-door and the street-door steps..were all as clean..as indefatigable white-washing, and hearth-stoning, and scrubbing and rubbing, could make them.

b. The production of a white efflorescence (saltpetre rot: see SALTPETRE 2) on a brick wall.

1889 C. T. Davis *Bricks, Tiles*, etc. (ed. 2) 97 In damp positions..brick walls are often covered with a crystalline substance of a white fleecy appearance, suggestive of hoar-frost,..which..absorbs the humidity of the atmosphere..and carries off the paint in large patches, and the process is called by the English workmen 'saltpetring', and sometimes in this country it is termed 'whitewashing'.

2. *fig.*: see WHITEWASH *v.* 2, 2 b.

1801 *Marvellous Love-Story* II. 320 To set at defiance the wholesome restrictions imposed upon society, by countenancing Mrs. Smeddy's white-washing [by marriage after an immoral connexion]. **1823** *Blackw. Mag.* XIV. 101, I have been white-washed by the Insolvent Court.., let all my sins go with that white-washing. **1855** Kingsley *Misc.* (1859) I. 7, I think the book an altogether foolish..book,..having but one object, the whitewashing of James.

3. *attrib.* (in *lit.* or *fig.* sense).

1817 W. T. Moncrieff *Giovanni in Lond.* I. iv, With your tailor debts contract, In the Bench for three months pack'd. Get out by the white-washing act, And be as clean as ever. **1875** Knight *Dict. Mech.*, *White-washing-apparatus*..for whitening walls and ceilings. **1890** *Daily News* 28 Feb. 7/2 (Court of Bankruptcy) We allege that no assets have been recovered, and that this is a whitewashing case.

So **ˈwhitewashing** *ppl. a.*

1883 *Harper's Mag.* Nov. 829/2 The reaction..against whitewashing churchwardens and..other Goths and Vandals.

white water, *sb.* (Also with hyphen.)

1. Shallow or shoal water; water with breakers or foam, as in shallows or rapids on the sea or a river. Also *attrib.*

1586 Harrison *England* I. xi. 47 in *Holinshed*, The more that this riuer is put by of hir right course, the more the water must of necessitie swell with the white waters which run downe from the land. **1727** E. Laurence *Duty of Steward* 19 The..advantages which the Meadows near Rivers might receive by being flooded with Freshes and White-water. **1803** *Naval Chron.* IX. 440 The Bahama pilots make a distinction of *white water* and *ocean water*, applying the former term to the shallow banks contiguous to many of the islands. **1861** Hulme tr. *Moquin-Tandon* II. III. iii. 92 The water by its [*sc.* the whale's] progress being somewhat disturbed, is known by the whalers under the name of 'White water'. **1884** 'H. Collingwood' *Under Meteor Flag* xi, Keep a cool head, for it seems to me that you've white water all round you, whichever way you shape a course. **1902** S. E. White *Blazed Trail* xlvii, Men with a reputation as 'white-water birlers'—men afraid of nothing. **1911** —— *Rules of Game* I. xiii, 'Why won't he make a good riverman?'..'A good whitewater man has to start younger.'

2. Water mixed with oatmeal or bran, as a medicinal drink for horses.

1737 Bracken *Farriery Impr.* (1757) II. 202 Let him drink warm Water with Oat-meal, or what we term White-water.

3. A name for dropsy in sheep.

1801 *Farmer's Mag.* Nov. 372 The disorder..which in some places is called the blood or white water.

Hence **white-water** *v. intr.* (*Naut. colloq.*), of a whale, to splash with the flukes so as to make the water white with foam.

1891 *Cent. Dict.* s.v., There she white-waters!

whiteweed (ˈhwaɪtwiːd). Name in N. America for the Ox-eye Daisy (*Chrysanthemum Leucanthemum*).

1803 in *Mass. Hist. Soc. Coll.* (1804) IX. 200 On the upland and meadows grow burdens grass, ribwort, white weed, [etc.]. **1846–50** A. Wood *Class-bk. Bot.* 343 *L*[*eucanthemum*] *Vulgare*... White-weed. Ox-eye Daisy. **1869** B. Taylor in *Life & Lett.* (1884) II. 512 Thick as the white-weeds in my strawberry-patch.

white wine. [WHITE *a.* 2 a. Cf. L. *vinum album*, F. *vin blanc*, G. *weisswein*.] Any light-coloured transparent wine: a general designation for wines of various colours from pale yellow to amber, in contradistinction to *red wine*.

[*a* **1300**: see RED *a.* and *sb.*¹ 16.] **1377** Langl. *P. Pl.* B. Prol. 228 White wyn of Oseye and red wyn of Gascoigne. *c* **1430** *Two Cookery-bks.* 35 Draw vppe þorw a straynoure with a lytyl whyte Wyne & Sugre. *c* **1435** *Torr. Portugale* 292 Sche byrlyd whyt wyne and Rede. **1528** Paynell *Salerne's Regim.* F iij, White wyne enflameth or heteth leest of all wynes. **1617** Moryson *Itin.* III. 133 France..yeelds great plenty of red and white wines. **1749** R. James *Diss. Fevers* (ed. 2) 31 She set forward for London, and upon the Road drank near a Bottle of White-Wine. **1818** Scott *Hrt. Midl.* xlvi, Even white wine and claret were got for nothing, since the Duke's..rights of admiralty gave him a title to all the wine in cask which is drifted ashore. **1857** Miller *Elem. Chem., Org.* (1862) iii. §1. 160 Red grapes may be made to yield a 'white' wine.

b. *attrib.*, as ***white wine cask***; **white wine vinegar**, vinegar made from white wine; **white wine whey**, a medicinal drink consisting of white wine and whey (cf. WHEY *sb.* 1 b).

1567–8 in Swayne *Churchw. Acc. Sarum* (1896) 113 A *whyte wyne caske. **1620** Venner *Via Recta* vi. 97 *White wine Vinegar is generally to be preferred. **1769** Mrs. Raffald *Engl. Housekpr.* (1778) 27 Add to it a spoonful of white wine vinegar. **1749** Lady Luxborough *Let. to Shenstone* 8 Sept., Since blankets and *white-wine-whey have not cured you. **1824** Miss Mitford *Village* Ser. I. *Old Bach.*, Andrews,..regular as 'the chimes at midnight', prepared his white-wine whey. **1890** R. C. Lehmann *Harry Fludyer* 6 Blathers is..giving him some white wine whey cook has just sent up.

whitewing (ˈhwaɪtwɪŋ). Local name for birds having white (or partly white) wings. **a.** The chaffinch. **b.** *U.S.* The white-winged scoter or surf-duck, *Œdemia fusca deglandi*. **c.** ***whitewing dove***, a dove of the genus *Melopelia*.

1854 Miss Baker *Northampt. Gloss.*, *White-wing*, the chaffinch. **1884** Coues *Key N. Amer. Birds* (ed. 2) 569 *Melopelia leucoptera*. White-wing Dove. **1901** *Shooting Times* 22 June 21/2 In Ireland, the chaffinch is commonly called the 'whitewing', owing..to the white patches..conspicuous on the wings of the male bird when in flight.

white-winged (ˈhwaɪtwɪŋd, also *poet.* -ˌwɪŋɪd), *a.* Having white wings: often in specific names of birds which have the wings wholly or partly white; also *fig.*

1594 *Selimus* K 1, White-wing'd victorie sits on our swordes. **1728** Thomson *Spring* 645 Around the Head Of Traveller, the white-wing'd Plover wheels Her sounding Flight. **1757** Dyer *Fleece* I. 157 White-winged snow, and cloud, and pearly rain. **1821** Latham *Gen. Hist. Birds* I. 8 Vulture..White-winged..; some of the larger wing coverts,..white, with black ends. **1821** Campbell *Lover to Mistr.* I If any white-winged power above My joys and griefs survey. **1872** Coues *Key N. Amer. Birds* (ed. 2) 294 Velvet Scoter. White-winged Surf-duck.

white witch, *sb.* (Also with hyphen.) [WHITE *a.* 7 b.] A witch (or wizard) of a good disposition; one who uses witchcraft for beneficent purposes; one who practises 'white magic'.

1621 Burton *Anat. Mel.* II. i. I. i. 289 Sorcerers are too common, Cunning men, Wisards, & white-witches, as they call them, in every village. **1689** C. Mather *Mem. Provid.* (1691) 95 Creatures that they call White Witches, which do only Good-Turns for their Neighbours. **1715** Addison *Drummer* II. i, The common people call him a wizard, a white-witch. **1746** *Exmoor Courtship* (E.D.S.) 440 Tha Whit Witch. **1806** J. Carr *Stranger in Irel.* 265 The white witch..at Exeter,..who has female agents to whom she has imparted a portion of her magic, in almost every village, who have the property of discovering pilferers and stopping blood. **1855** Kingsley *Westw. Ho!* i, When he had warts or burns, he went to the white witch at Northam to charm them away.

Hence **white-witch** *v.* (*nonce-wd.*), *trans.* to bewitch by 'white magic', or in a beneficent way.

1917 *Contemp. Rev.* Nov. 585 The cows were white-witched. Milk came in such abundance as no memory records.

whitewood (ˈhwaɪtwʊd). (Also with hyphen; formerly sometimes as two words.) Name of various trees with white or light-coloured wood; also, the wood of any of these. (Also *attrib.*)

Among these are the N. American tulip-tree (*Liriodendron Tulipifera*) and bass-wood (*Tilia americana*); the W. Indian wild cinnamon (*Canella alba*, which furnishes white cinnamon or **whitewood bark**), *Tecoma* or *Tabebuia Leucoxylon* (**whitewood cedar**) and *T. pentaphylla*, loblolly sweetwood (*Oreodaphne* or *Ocotea Leucoxylon*) and white sweetwood (*Nectandra leucantha* or *Antilliana*); the Australian cheesewood (*Pittosporum bicolor*), *Lagunaria Patersoni*, and *Panax elegans* (**mowbulan whitewood**). Also locally applied in England to the lime-tree (*Tilia europæa*) and the wayfaring-tree (*Viburnum Lantana*); in quot. 1733, ? the white poplar (*Populus alba*). See also *white wood* s.v. WHITE *a.* 11 b.

1683 Poyntz *Tobago* 29 The White-wood is a Tree of that singular vertue, the worm will seldom touch it. **1696** Plukenet *Almagestum* Opera 1769 II. 215 Leucoxylon..Barbadensibus ostratibus White-wood, Tulip-flower & aliquando Trumpet-flower nuncupatur. **1733** W. Ellis *Chiltern & Vale Farm.* 183 On the level Ground of this Farm..grows several of these White-wood Trees [*viz.* poplars, etc.]. *Ibid.* 184 The low Country-men sometimes call it Dutch Arbel, but the common Name among them is White-wood. **1750** G. Hughes *Nat. Hist. Barbados* v. 124 Where-ever a Manchaneel-tree grows, there is found a White-wood, or a Fig-tree, near it. **1778** J. Carver *Trav. N. Amer.* xix. 499 The Bass or White Wood is a tree of a middling size, and the whitest and softest wood that grows. **1847** Halliwell, *White-wood*, the lime-tree. **1858** O. W. Holmes *Deacon's Masterpiece* v, The panels of white-wood, that cuts like cheese. **1864** Grisebach *Flora W. Ind.* 789 White-wood, *Oreodaphne Leucoxylon*, *Nectandra leucantha*, *Tecoma Leucoxylon* and *pentaphylla*. *Ibid.*, White-wood-bark, *Canella alba*. Whitewood-cedar, *Tecoma Leucoxylon*. **1884** Miller *Plant-n.*, *Lagunaria Patersoni*, White-wood, of Australia, Cow-itch-tree, or White Oak, of Norfolk Island. **1908** Kipling *Lett. Trav.* (1920) 133 The lard, the apples, the butter, and the cheese, in beautiful whitewood barrels.

whitewort. *rare.* ? *Obs.* [f. WHITE *a.* + WORT *sb.*, after Du. *witwortel* (G. *weisswurz*).] A name for several plants with white flowers or roots: **a.** Feverfew; **b.** Solomon's seal; **c.** a species of camomile.

1578 Lyte *Dodoens* I. xi. 19 It [*sc.* Parthenium] is called..in English, Feuerfew, & of some Whitewurte. *Ibid.* I. lxix. 103 Salomons seale is called..in English..White roote, or white wurte. **1866** *Treas. Bot.*, Whitewort, *Matricaria Chamomilla*.

whitey (ˈhwaɪtɪ), *sb.* Also **whity, whitie.** [f. WHITE *a.* + -Y⁶.]

1. A white man or woman; white people collectively; in quot. 1828 as a *quasi*-proper name: cf. BLACKY *sb.* 1. (Also with capital initial.) Freq. derog. *slang* (chiefly *Blacks'*).

1828 P. Cunningham *N.S. Wales* (ed. 3) II. 9 The instant *blacky* perceives *whity* beating a retreat, he vociferates after him—'Go along, you dam rascal'. **1942** Berrey & Van den Bark *Amer. Thes. Slang* §385/2 *White person*,..whitie. **1952** S. Selvon *Brighter Sun* iv. 61 A white-skinned girl..was called 'Whitey cockroach!' **1964** *Time* 31 July 12/3 Harlem..is where the white man is no longer the 'ofay' but 'Mr. Charlie' or 'the man', and mostly 'whitey', derived from the Black Nationalist talk of 'the blue-eyed white devil'. **1967** C. Drummond *Death at Furlong Post* xi. 138 Get to hell away from me! You Whities stink! **1968** *Times Lit. Suppl.* 4 Apr. 329/2 The world of 'Whitey' into which these Negroes no longer want to be integrated. **1971** A. King *One Love* 19 There's a Whitey in every Black man that has to come out, or die, before he's ever himself. **1972** R. K. Smith *Ransom* I. 24 We're gonna hit Whitey and hit him again. **1976** *Listener* 15 Apr. 462/1 There is a pub in south London where black intellectuals meet, and if you happen to be a white man, the landlord—who is of West Indian origin—delights in calling you 'whitie'. As far as he is concerned, it's all in fun. **1977** *New Yorker* 26 Sept. 131/1 He's no more than a trivial whitey to be squished. **1980** *Amer. Speech* LV. 211 It encompassed a protest of whitey's 'theft' of yet another style of jazz—swing.

2. = WHITING *sb.* 1 b (*a*).

1912 A. McCormick *Words fr. Wild-Wood* vi. 82, I had thrashed the stream..in the hope of getting a 'whitey'.

Whitfieldian, etc.: see WHITEFIELDIAN.

whitflaw, -flow, obs. var. WHITLOW.

Whitgiftian (hwɪtˈgɪftɪən), *sb.* and *a.* [f. *Whitgift* + -IAN.] **A.** *sb.* A pupil or former pupil of Whitgift School, Croydon. **B.** *adj.* Of, pertaining to, or characteristic of John Whitgift (*c* 1530–1604), Archbishop of Canterbury and founder of Whitgift School.

1880 *Whitgift Mag.* Jan. 13/2 We were glad to notice among the Chorus several 'Old Whitgiftians'. **1905** (*title*) The Whitgiftian. [*Previously* The Whitgift Magazine.] **1962** *Hist. Mag. Protestant Episcopal Church U.S.* XXXI. 128 The picturesquely rhetorical phrase of F. W. Maitland has been considered the most decent dismissal of the whole Whitgiftian flavour: 'a remorseless pre-destinarian'. **1967** P. Collison *Elizabethan Puritan Movem.* v. i. 245 Of this generation of clergy, few with minds of their own would subscribe to the Whitgiftian formula without a qualm. **1977** P. Clark *Eng. Provincial Soc. from Reformation to Revolution* v. 184 In the county [of Kent]..the Whitgiftian reaction caused a marked polarisation between moderate Puritans and conformist Presbyterians on the one hand, and less respectable radicals and separatists on the other.

whith, obs. form of WHITE, WITH.

whither (ˈhwɪðə(r)), *sb.*¹ *Sc.* and *dial.* Forms: see the vb. [f. WHITHER *v.*] A violent or impetuous movement, a rush; an attack, onset; a smart blow or stroke; a blast or gust of wind; a quivering movement, a tremble; a rushing or whizzing sound; *fig.* an access or attack of illness.

c **1480** HENRYSON *Pract. Medecyne* 55 þat ȝe tak sevin sobbis of ane selche, the quhidder of ane quhaill. **1513** DOUGLAS *Æneis* v. x. 62 Than ran thai sammyn in paris with a quhiddir. *Ibid.* VI. v. 85 Quham.. Saland from Troy.. The deidlie storm ourquhelmit with a quhiddir. **1791** LEARMONT *Poems* 82 (E.D.D.) His dart Hits ane a whuther. **1808** JAMIESON s.v. *Quhidder*, A quhither of the cauld, a slight cold. **1825** BROCKETT *N.C. Gloss.* s.v. *Whidder*, A whither of cold, a shivering cold. 'All in a whither',—all in a tremble. **1853** C. BRONTE *Villette* xvi, The 'wuther' of wind amongst trees. **1887** JESSIE M. E. SAXBY *Lads of Lunda, Running Free* vii, 'Tak' pace till the whidders dill awa'' (be patient till the gusts of wind quiet down).

whither, *sb.*[2]: see WHITHER *adv.* 6.

'whither, *v. Sc.* and *dial.* Forms: 5 **quhedir-, -thir, qwedyr,** 5–6 **quhidder,** 6 **-ir;** 6–7, 9 **whidder,** 8–9 **whedder, whuther,** 9 **whudder, wuther,** 8– **whither.** [a. ON. **hviðra* (cf. Norw. *kvidra* to go to and fro with short quick movements), related to *hviða* squall of wind (see WHID *sb.*[2]), fit (of coughing), OE. *hwiþa, hwiþu* (*hweoþu*) 'aura': see WHYȜT.]

1. *intr.* To move with force or impetus, to rush; to make a rushing sound, to whizz; to bluster or rage, as the wind.

1375 BARBOUR *Bruce* XVII. 684 The stane.. flaw out quhedirand [*MS. Edin.* quhethirand, *ed.* 1616 whiddering]. **1513** DOUGLAS *Æneis* v. vi. 65 Diores, quhidderand at his bak fute hate. *Ibid.* XII. xiv. 86 Neuer sa swiftly quhidderand the stane flaw. **15..** *Outlaw Murray* xvi. in Child *Ballads* (1894) IX. 191/2 He heard the.. arrows whidderand near him by. *a* **1736** WHITTELL *Sawney Ogilby's Duel* iv. Poet. Wks. (1815) 170 She whither'd about, and dang down all the gear. **1825** JAMIESON, To *Whither*, to whirl rapidly with a booming sound. *Ibid.*, To *Whudder*, to make a whizzing or rushing sort of noise. **1877** JESSIE FOTHERGILL *First Violin* VI. i, The wind wuthered wearily.

2. To tremble, shake, quiver.

c **1450** *Cov. Myst.* (Shaks. Soc.) 122 For joy I qwedyr and qwake. **1790** GROSE *Prov. Gloss.* (ed. 2), *Whedder*, to tremble. *Ibid.*, *Whither*, to quake or shake.

3. *trans.* To strike or beat forcibly; to throw violently.

1825 JAMIESON, To *Whither*, to beat, to belabour, Roxb. **1828** *Craven Gloss.*, *Whither*, to throw with violence.

Hence **'whitherer**, a vigorous person or thing (cf. *thumper, whopper*); **'whithering** *vbl. sb.*, a rushing, whizzing, blustering; **'whithering** *ppl. a.*, rushing, whizzing, etc.; also, very large or vigorous (cf. *thumping, whopping*).

1513 DOUGLAS *Æneis* v. ix. 29 Ȝoung Hippocaon.. A quhidderand arrow leit spang fra the string. **1585** JAS. I. *Ess. Poesie* (Arb.) 15 They heare the whiddering Boreas bolde. **1787** GROSE *Prov. Gloss.*, *Whithering*, a sudden great sound. **1790** *Ibid.* (ed. 2), *Whitherer*, a lusty, strong, or stout person, or thing. **1828** *Craven Gloss.* s.v., He's a girt withering tike. **1847** E. BRONTE *Wuthering Heights* i, Wuthering Heights is the name of Mr. Heathcliff's dwelling. 'Wuthering' being a significant provincial adjective, descriptive of the atmospheric tumult to which its station is exposed, in stormy weather. **1879** G. M. HOPKINS *Poems* (1967) 80 If a wuthering of his palmy snow-pinions scatter a colossal smile Off him, but meaning motion fans fresh our wits with wonder. **1951** J. STRACHEY *Man on Pier* 20 The routine hours that are without inspiration in a day—those spent in buying stamps for letters, in filing receipts, in the dreary wuthering of machineries, in the changings from place to place.

whither ('hwɪðə(r)), *adv.* (*sb.*[2]) Forms: see below. [OE. *hwider*, earlier (Northumb.) *huidir*, later *hwyder*, f. Teut. *χwi-* (cf. WHICH); the synonymous Goth. *hwadrē* is f. Teut. *χwa-* (see WHO). Late and occasional OE. *hwæder* (see A. γ) is prob. due to the analogy of *þæder* THITHER.]

A. Illustration of Forms.

α. 1–3 **hwider,** (1 **hw-, huid(d)ir, hwidder, huid(d)er,** 3 *Orm.* **whiderr),** 3–4 **wider, quider,** 4–6 **whider, whyder,** (4 **huider, huyder, whidur, whydre, wydur, wyddere, quidder,** 4–5 **whidere, whidir, wyder,** 5 **whidyr, whydyr, widir, wydyr, whiddir, whydder, -ur, whidre, widere),** 5–6 *Sc.* **quhidder,** (6 **-ir);** 4 **whithir, quiþer,** 5 **whiþer, whythyr,** 5–6 **whyther,** *Sc.* **quhither,** 6–7 **wither,** 6– **whither.**

c **825** *Vesp. Psalter* cxxxviii[i]. 7 From onsiene ðinre hwider fleom ic? *a* **900** *Leiden Gloss.* in *O.E. Texts* 115 *Cujatis*, huidirryne. **9..** ÆLFRED *Boeth.* xxii. (MS. Cott.) Ac þær ðu ongeate hwider ic ðe nu tiohiȝe to lædenne. *c* **1000** *Rituale Dunelm.* (Surtees) 55 Svæ hvidder. *c* **1000** ÆLFRIC *Gen.* xvi. 8 (MS. Laud Misc. 509, lf. 12) Hu færst þu oþþe hwider wylt þu? *c* **1250** *Gen. & Ex.* 2600 To loken quider it sulde ben went. *a* **1300** *Cursor M.* 64 Wydur [13.. *Gött.* quiþer, *c* 1375 *Fairf.* quidder] to wende ne wat he noght. *c* **1300** *Harrow. Hell* (L) 118 Y ne recche whyder y go. *c* **1320** *Sir Tristr.* 586 He no wist whider to go. *c* **1400** *26 Pol. Poems* 22 Gostly blynd goþ, and not neuere whidre. *c* **1450** *Mirk's Festial* 211 Whydyr þat þay ledyn þe wayne. *a* **1483** Whythyr [see WHITHERSOMEVER]. *a* **1500** *Cov. Corp. Christi Pl.* i. 230 Then forto goo wyst I nott whyddur. **1513** DOUGLAS *Æneis* VI. iii. 80 Behaldand.. quhat singnis thai schaw, Or quhiddir thai mark. **1523** Whyder [see B. 4]. **1556** OLDE *Antichrist* 128 No whider elles. **1588** PARKE tr. *Mendoza's Hist. China* 254 They let their ship saile.. whither as fortune did cary them. *a* **1700** EVELYN *Diary* 29 Jan. 1645, The towne Aversa, wither came 3 or 4 coaches.

β. 1 **hwyder,** 3 **hwuder, whuder(e, wuder.**

971 *Blickl. Hom.* 99 Hwyder ȝewiton.. þa idlan blissa? *c* **1205** LAY. 1202 Wise mi.. whuder ich mæi liðan. *Ibid.* 12169 Liðen wuder swa þu wult.

γ. 1 **hwæder,** 4 **whader** (?).

c **1000** ÆLFRIC *Gen.* xxxii. 17 (MS. Laud Misc. 509, lf. 23) Ȝif.. he eow axie, hwæs ȝe sin[d] oððe hwæder [*v.r.* hwyder] ȝe willon. *Ibid.* xxxvii. 30 (ib. lf. 25 b) Nys se cnapa her; hwæder ga ic? *c* **1000** *Ags. Gosp.* Matt. viii. 19 Ic fyliȝe þe, swa hwæder [*v.r.* hwyder] swa þu færst. *c* **1400** *Rom. Rose* 1874 (Glasgow MS.), I rought of deth ne of lyf Whader that loue wolde me dryf.

δ. 3 **weder,** 4–5 **wheder, -yr, queder,** 5 **whedir, -ire, -ur, -yre, whedder, qweder, quedire, -ur,** *Sc.* **qwhedyr;** 4 **whethir, queþer, -ir,** 4–5 **wheþer,** 5 **whethyr, wheither,** *Sc.* **quhether, qw(h)eþir,** 5–6 **wether,** 5–8 **whether,** 6 *Sc.* **quhethire,** 7 **wheather.**

a **1300** *Harrow. Hell* (O.) 110, I ne recche weder I go. *a* **1300** Queder [see WHITHERSUM]. **13..** *Northern Passion* (Harl.) 750 He spird.. Wheder þai war went. *a* **1400–50** *Wars Alex.* 3499 Pas quedire as him plese. *c* **1440** *Gesta Rom.* xxiii. 81, I wote not.. whether to go. **1471** MARG. PASTON in *P. Lett.* III. 24 We wut not qweder to fle. *c* **1480** HENRYSON *Fox, Wolf, & Husb.* 29 The Uolf said, 'quhether dryuis thow this, Pray?' **1589** NASHE *Anat. Absurd.* Wks. (Grosart) I. 70 Whether euery way leadeth. **1639** in *Verney Mem.* (1907) I. 95, I am newly come out of Scottland, wheather I am instantly returning again. **1697** DRYDEN *Æneis* x. 514 Whether wou'd you run? **1722** DE FOE *Plague* (1754) 202 In Heaven, whether, I hope we may come.

ε. 3 **ȝwodere,** 3–5 **woder,** 4–5 **whoder, -ir, -ur,** 5 **whodere, -yr, wheoder, hoder(e,** 6 **whother.**

c **1275** Woder [see B. 4]. *c* **1290** *St. Christopher* 38 in *S. Eng. Leg.* 272 Ȝwodere þenxt þou gon? *c* **1300** *Beket* 1648 Ynot whoder thu wolt go. *c* **1420** *Chron. Vilod.* 1560 Whethen he come & hodere he went, knewe nomone. *c* **1425** Whodyr [see WHITHERSO]. *c* **1440** *Gesta Rom.* xii. 38 Whens art þou, and whodir art þou boun? *c* **1475** *Partenay* 2764 Of your wif enquere.. at no day.. To what place she torn ne hoder wyll go. **1535** Whother [see B. 3 a].

B. Signification.

Now, in all senses, only archaic or literary; replaced in ordinary use by *where*, or colloq. *where ... to*: see WHERE 3, 1 c. (Cf. WHENCE I.)

I. Interrogative uses.

1. To what place? **a.** in direct questions.

c **1000** ÆLFRIC *Deut.* i. 28 Hwider fare we? *c* **1200** *Trin. Coll. Hom.* 147 Ac wider ȝeden hie? **13..** *Bonaventura's Medit.* 995 Whedyr shulde y wende, to frende, ouþer kyn? **1470–85** MALORY *Arthur* VII. v. 219 Ther came a man fleynge.. whether wolt thou sayd Beaumayns. **1591** SHAKS. *Two Gent.* IV. i. 16 Whither trauell you? **1649** C. WASE *Sophocles, Electra* 15 Whither away? **1697** DRYDEN *Æneis* x. 945 Whence am I forc'd, and whether am I born? **1722** DE FOE *Plague* (1754) 143 Whither will you go? and what can you do? **1836** DICKENS *Sk. Boz, Gt. Winglebury Duel*, 'Whither are we going?' inquired the lady tragically. **1848** THACKERAY *Van. Fair* lxiii, What was the use of cavalry in a time of profound peace?—and whither the deuce should the hussars ride? **1884** GILMOUR *Mongols* xvii. 202 If souls do not transmigrate, where do they come from at birth, whither do they go at death?

†*Humorous phr.* (as *sb.*). **1678** RAY *Prov.* (ed. 2) 346 How doth your whither goe you? (*your wife*). **1721** E. WARD *Northern Cuckold* 7 Not that our Northern Cuckold's *Whither D'ye go*, is such a Doxy neither. **1725** *New Cant. Dict.*, *Whither-D'ye-go*, an insolent prescribing Wife.

b. in dependent questions and similar clauses.

971 *Blickl. Hom.* 151 Hie.. nystan hwyder hie eodan. *Ibid.* 229 Hie sendon hlot him betweonum hwider hyra ȝehwylc faran scolde to læranne. *c* **1200** *Vices & Virtues* 17 Þe inreste þesternesse is in ðare hierte ðe ne wile forsceawin hwider he scal ðanne he henen farð. *c* **1200** *Trin. Coll. Hom.* 159 Lusteð nu.. hwo hire ledde, and wu and hwider. *c* **1290** *St. Matthew* 140 in *S. Eng. Leg.* 81 Nou god it wot and seint Matheu ȝwodere is soule wende. **1297** R. GLOUC. (Rolls) 2144 Hii nuste wuder drawe. *c* **1350** *Will. Palerne* 701 It is a selcouþe, me þinkes, whider þat lady is went. *c* **1420** *Avow. Arth.* xxv, The blonke him a-boute bore, Wiste he neuyr quedur! **1509** HAWES *Past. Pleas.* XXXIV. (Percy Soc.) 170 She.. did aske me whether That I so rode, and what I would have? **1589** NASHE *Anat. Absurd.* Wks. (Grosart) I. 70 Wee duely consider, whether euery way leadeth. **1660** *Nicholas Papers* (Camden) IV. 216 Intimating that Alison was now gonne hee knew not whither. **1722** DE FOE *Plague* (1754) 65 If he knew whether to go. **1840** DICKENS *Old C. Shop* xii, Wandering they knew not whither. **1882** BESANT *All Sorts* xxiii, What he did, whither he went, where he died, might be left to conjecture.

2. a. *gen.* or *fig.* with various shades of meaning: To what result, condition, action, subject, cause, etc.? †to what extent, how far?

9.. ÆLFRED *Boeth.* xl. (MS. Cott.), Hwæðer ðu nu onȝite hwider þios spræce wille? *a* **1225** *Leg. Kath.* 1299 Hwider is ower wit & ower wisdom iwent? *c* **1440** *Jacob's Well* 236 Whedir schal þi soule in þin ende, to peyne or ioye? *c* **1491** *Chast. Goddes Chyld.* 12 Wheder is all this become? **1538** STARKEY *England* II. iii. (1878) 215 Wel, Master Lvpset, I perceyue wether you go [= 'what you are driving at']. **1611** B. JONSON *Catiline* IV. ii. I 3, Whither at length wilt thou abuse our patience? [*Quousque tandem*..]. **1625** BURGES *Pers. Tithes* 31 Suspecting whether he may be drawne by yeelding that to be a Due. **1652** BP. HALL *Invis. World* I. §4 If there fall out.. any direful prodigies.. whither should they be imputed but to these mighty angels? *a* **1674** CLARENDON *Surv. Leviath.* (1676) 153 If they had known whether to have addressed their complaints. **1746** FRANCIS tr. *Hor.*, *Sat.* II. vii. 29 Thou tedious varlet, whither tends This putrid stuff? **1820** SHELLEY *Prometh. Unb.* III. iv. 122 Whither has wandered now my partial tongue? **1851** KINGSLEY *Yeast* x, Oh, Lancelot, Lancelot, whither are you forcing me?

b. Followed by a single word or short phrase.

1982 *English Studies* LXV. 90 The recently recycled interrogative adverb *whither* (as in *Whither Democracy?*).

II. Relative uses.

3. a. as compound relative: To the place to (or in) which. Also with correlative *thither*. Also *fig.*

c **950** *Lindisf. Gosp.* John xxi. 18 *Ambulabas ubi uolebas*, Ðu waldes ȝeonga huidir ðu waldes. **1382** WYCLIF *John* viii. 21 Whidur I go, ȝe mown not come. **1471** CAXTON *Recuyell* 683 To goo whyther the goddes wold consente that they shold dwelle. **1526** *Pilgr. Perf.* (W. de W. 1531) 26 Prouyde suche money y[t] may brynge hym whether he entendeth. **1535** JOYE *Apol. Tindale* (Arb.) 18 And whother the head went thither must the bodye folow. **1561** DAUS tr. *Bullinger on Apoc.* xxxvii. 237 Away with them and their sophistrie, whither they are worthie. **1682** N. O. *Boileau's Lutrin* II. 19 Then whether Honour calls thee, bravely follow. **1836** J. GILBERT *Chr. Atonem.* (1852) 343, I must go whither truth conducts me.

b. as simple relative: To which place; after a noun of place = to which; also with ellipsis = a place to which.

a **1400** *Morte Arth.* 3231, I ne wiste no waye whedire þat I scholde. *c* **1400** *Apol. Loll.* 31 He assignid seuenty and two disciplis, and sent hem.. in to ilk place and cite widir he was to com. **1549** *Bk. Com. Prayer, Coll. Sun. after Ascension*, Exalte us unto the same place whither our sauiour Christe is gone before. **1609** *Bible* (Douay) Deut. xix. 3 He which.. is a fugitive, may have.. whither to escape. **1617** MORYSON *Itin.* I. 42 Wee landed.. in Freesland, at the Village Anion, .. whether wee hired a sledge.. and were drawne thither ouer the yce and snow. **1664** POWER *Exp. Philos.* I. 68 The sense and motion of that part whither that Nerve was propagated. **1722** DE FOE *Plague* (1754) 1 The Plague.. had been very violent.. at Amsterdam and Roterdam, .. whether they say, it was brought, some said from Italy, others from the Levant. **1821** SHELLEY *Hellas* 862, I come Thence whither thou must go! **1825** SCOTT *Jrnl.* 28 Nov., Dined at Melville Castle, whither I went through a snow-storm. **1893** MAX PEMBERTON *Iron Pirate* i, At Cowes, whither I had taken my yacht.. for the Regatta Week.

4. In generalized or indef. sense: To (or in) any place to which; to whatever place; whithersoever.

Esp. with addition of †*as*, †*that*, †*ever*, *so*(*ever*): see also WHITHERSO, -SOEVER.

c **1275** LAY. 12169 Ich wolle.. wende woder þat þou wolt. *a* **1300** *Cursor M.* 10812 Forto help hir in hir nede, Quider þat [*Laud* Whethir so, *Gött.* Queþer-sua, *Trin.* Whoder so] sco rade or yede. **13..** tr. *Ælred* in *Engl. Stud.* VII. 324 Ȝif þu folwe þis blessed mayde whider-þat-euer sche goþ. **1340** *Ayenb.* 235 Uor to uolȝy þe lamb of mildenesse huyder hit geþ to huam hi byeþ y-spoused. *c* **1380** WYCLIF *Sel. Wks.* II. 17 Þe Holi Gost ledde Jesus whidir ever he wente, and what dedis evere he dide. *c* **1440** *Alphabet of Tales* 53 Whider as euer he went, or what thyng som evur he did, he was evur sayand Ave Maria. *c* **1450** *Two Cookery-bks.* 101 Cary him wheþer euer þou wolt. **1523** LD. BERNERS *Froiss.* I. ccccxlvi. 318 b/2, I haue hyred this shyppe.. to sayle whyder as me lyst. **1596** SHAKS. *1 Hen. IV*, v. iii. 22 Go with thy soule whether it goes. **1648** J. BEAUMONT *Psyche* VII. cxxi, Whether as he mounts, his News in every sphere He to th' inquisitive Spirits poureth forth. *a* **1672** WILKINS *Nat. Relig.* I. xvii. (1675) 241 We should.. follow whither ever he shall lead us. **1722** DE FOE *Plague* (1754) 170 They were at Liberty to travel whither they pleased. **1873** BROWNING *Red Cott. Nt.-cap* III. 192 A spark From Paris, answered by a snap at Caen Or whither reached the telegraphic wire.

III. Indefinite and substantival uses.

5. With preceding qualifying words, forming compounds: see ANYWHITHER, EVERYWHITHER, NOWHITHER, OWHITHER, SOMEWHITHER.

6. as *sb.* (*nonce-use.*) Place or state to which a person or thing moves or tends. (Cf. WHENCE 5.)

1875 [see WHENCE 5]. **1896** A. AUSTIN *England's Darling* I. i, He roams abroad.. Spying the where and whither of his foes.

whither, obs. form of WHETHER.

†whither-out, *adv. Obs. rare.* [f. prec. + OUT *adv.*; cf. WHEREOUT.] **a.** *interrog.* (*irreg.*) Out of what, from what source, whence. **b.** *rel.* In the direction in which; nearly = whereabouts.

1377 LANGL. *P. Pl.* B. XVI. 12 If any wiȝte wyte whider-oute it groweth? **1393** *Ibid.* C. VIII. 178 Couthest þow wissen ous þe way whoder out treuthe wonyeþ? *c* **1425** *Seven Sag.* (P.) 1929 [They] seten redy markys there Wydyr-out the coffyns were.

'whitherso, *adv. arch.* [ME. *hwiderse*, repr. OE. *swá hwider swá*: see SO *adv.* 17 d.] = next.

c **950** *Lindisf. Gosp.* Matt. viii. 19 *Quocumque ieris*, sua huider ðu færes [*Rushw.* hwider swa]. *c* **1205** LAY. 18969 Faren þu scalt bi ræde wuder swa ich þe læde. *c* **1230** *Hali Meid.* 31 Ha gað euer nest godd, hwiderse he turneð. **1297** R. GLOUC. (Rolls) 4163 Hii ne miȝte noȝt aȝen hym do no weþer so hii wende. *c* **1375** *Cursor M.* 6359 (Fairf.) Quidder-sa he welk here or þare þe wandis euer wiþ him he bare. *c* **1425** *Engl. Conq. Irel.* 40 Al the englysshe-men.. shold ben .. frely let goo whodyrso they wold. *c* **1475** *Rauf Coilȝear* 381 That I haue hecht I sall hald,.. Quhidder sa it gang to greif or to gawin.

a **1850** ROSSETTI *Dante & Circle* I. (1874) 118 Whereso I be or whitherso I turn. **1880** W. WATSON *Prince's Quest* IX. 31 Going whitherso the wild path went.

whithersoever (ˌhwɪðəsəʊ'ɛvə(r)), *adv.* Forms: see WHITHER *adv.*, SO, and EVER *adv.*; also 4 *contr.* **whidur-sever.** (In early use as two or as three words.) [f. prec. + EVER *adv.* 8 e; cf. SOEVER.] To whatever place. **a.** To (or in) any place to which: = WHEREVER 3.

c **1230** *Hali Meid.* 25 Folhen godd almihti.. hwider se he eauer wendeð. *c* **1320** *Cast. Love* (ed. Hall.) 1785 Thei shull be so lyȝht and swyft, That whidur-sever they thenk they may be lyft. **1464** *Rolls of Parlt.* V. 567/2 Over the See, or whether soo ever it please theym. **1535** COVERDALE *2 Sam.* viii. 6 Y[e] Lorde helped Dauid whither so euer he wente. **1622** R. HAWKINS *Voy. S. Sea* §45. 111 The Marchant having bought the goods, hee might presently transport them whethersoever he would. **1748** RICHARDSON *Clarissa* (1768) VI. 277, I will.. attend you whithersoever you please. **1863** HAWTHORNE *Our Old Home, Leam. Spa*, He has a right to go whithersoever they lead him. **1885** *Spectator* 30 May 704/2 With Victor Hugo inspiration is..to be followed blindly whithersoever it may lead.

b. Whether to one place or another; no matter to what place: cf. WHEREVER 4.

1583 MELBANCKE *Philotimus* Fiv, I remit thy crime howsoeuer or whithersoeuer thou wentest. **1749** FIELDING *Tom Jones* VIII. x, Whoever you are, or whithersoever you are going,..I have Obligations to you which I can never return. **1837** CARLYLE *Fr. Rev.* I. IV. iv, So walks Father Gérard; solid in his thick shoes, whithersoever bound. **1913** *Athenæum* 23 Aug. 183/3 Whatsoever you may be doing, or whithersoever you may turn.

So † **'whithersum**, † **,whitherso'mever** *advbs.* [see SUM *rel. adv.* 2, SOMEVER], in same senses.

a **1300** *Cursor M.* 6359 Queder-sum he welk her or þare, þis wandes euer he wit him bare. *Ibid.* 6666 Til ilk sted Quider-sum he þat folk ledd. *a* **1483** *Liber Niger* in *Househ. Ord.* (1790) 19 Clerkes and yeomen..to precede the King.. whythyr somever the King go. **1485** CAXTON *St. Wenefryde* 16 Euery man myght go..peasybly whyder someuer he wold. **1526** TINDALE *Matt.* viii. 19 Whythersumever thou goest.

whitherto (hwɪðə'tu:, 'hwɪðətu:), *adv.* Now *rare* or *Obs.* [f. WHITHER *adv.* + TO *prep.*; cf. HITHERTO.] To what place, state, result, etc.? to what? whither? whereto?

1549 COVERDALE, etc. *Erasm. Par. Heb.* xii. 1–6 Whitherto came he? By despisyng of this lyfe, he attained immortalitie. **1592** BRETON *C'tess Pembroke's Love* Wks. (Grosart) I. 27/2 All the world may see, From whence we came, and whetherto we must. **1624** BP. HALL *Art Medit.*, *Medit. Death* Wks. (1625) 129 Whitherto haue tended all thy serious meditations? **1658** W. BURTON *Itin. Anton.* 125 Whitherto shall we refer that verb? **1751** R. PALTOCK *P. Wilkins* (1884) II. 252 Fearing whitherto it might grow.

whitherward ('hwɪðəwəd), *adv.* (*sb.*) *arch.* [f. WHITHER *adv.* + -WARD.]

1. *interrog.* Towards or to what place? in what direction? whither? †Also with reference to situation (nearly = whereabouts?). Also *fig.* or *gen.* Towards what?

c **1200** ORMIN 17295 þu ne mahht nohht..sen..Fra wheþennwarrd..he comm..ne whiderrwarrd he wendeþþ. *c* **1200** *Trin. Coll. Hom.* 161 Ðan þe safarinde men seð þe sa sterre, hie wuten sone wuderward hie sullen weie holden. **1297** R. GLOUC. (Rolls) 307 Heo wende fram al hire kun,..& nuste an erþe ȝwderward, bote as þe wind blew. *a* **1300** *Cursor M.* 1246 'þou most now ga To paradis...' 'Yai, sir, wist i wyderward þat tat vncuth contre ware.' **1303** R. BRUNNE *Handl. Synne* 5916 Ȝeueþ gode tent, Whederward þat Pers ys went. *c* **1386** CHAUCER *Frankl. T.* 782 He..asked of hire whiderward she wente. *c* **1425** WYNTOUN *Cron.* VI. xviii. 2008 For til wit..qweþirwart þe thayne of Fiff þat tyme past. **1470–85** MALORY *Arthur* VII. xiii. 232 Whether ward ar ye way ledyng this knyghte? **1540** PALSGR. *Acolastus* V. v. Aaiv b, Whytherwarde take I my iourneye? or whyther warde am I goynge? **1614** W. BROWNE *Sheph. Pipe* I. 510 Forth of auenture his way is went, But whither-ward he draw, he conceitlesse Was. **1801** SOUTHEY *Thalaba* V. xiii, Unknowing whitherward to bend his way. **1851** CARLYLE *Sterling* I. xi, Whitherward to turn for a good course of life, was by no means too apparent. **1860** TROLLOPE *Framley P.* xlii, As one goes on pleasantly running down the path—whitherward?

2. *rel.* **a.** as compound relative: Towards the place that; usually in generalized or indefinite sense: Towards any place that, whithersoever.

c **1205** LAY. 9994 Whudereward þa ferde heore flæm makeden, þe eorles heom siȝen to. *a* **1225** *Ancr. R.* 168 Uorte ..uoluwen þe hwuderward so þu euer wendest. *a* **1300** *Cursor M.* 21228 O sant mathu þe gospel-bok Quider-ward sumeuer he scok..wit him he bar. *c* **1350** *Will. Palerne* 2830 Whiderward as þei went al wast þei it founde. *c* **1375** *Cursor M.* 23523 (Fairf.) Quidder-wart [*Trin.* Whiderward so] an wil loke þai loke al. **1398** TREVISA *Barth. De P.R.* XIX. cxxix. (1495) nn ij b/1 A way by the whyche a man maye goo whytherwarde that he woll. **1845** CARLYLE *Cromwell* I. 294 Shall he..conduct the King whitherward his Majesty wishes?

b. as simple relative: Towards which.

1398 TREVISA *Barth. De P.R.* XIII. iii. (Bodl. MS.), þe wel springe and þe finalle ende whederward hit [*sc.* the river] renneþ. **1582** ALLEN *Martyrdom Campion* (1908) 7 Whitherwarde by longe and great travail he came, going about by Rome..and by Remes. **1597** BEARD *Theatre God's Judgem.* xix. (1612) 353 Bombadilla..was called home againe into Spaine: whitherward..as hee imbarked himselfe ..there arose..a horrible..tempest. **1895** *Sat. Rev.* 21 Sept. 374/1 Four guns are sent..to advanced posts up the nullah, whitherward they make their way by forest routes.

3. *sb.* (*nonce-use*). Place towards which one goes.

1877 BLACKIE *Wise Men* 325 Athens hath no clew To track his whitherward.

So **'whitherwards** *adv.*

13.. *K. Alis.* 955 (Laud MS.), Who so wolde, he miȝth ryde..Whiderwardes so he wolde. *c* **1320** *Sir Beues* (A.) 2037 At þe kniȝt he askede þo 'Whider-wardes is Mombraunt?' **1909–10** SIR W. BUTLER *Autobiog.* xii. (1911) 186 Signs..indicating the whitherwards of coming events.

whiting ('hwaɪtɪŋ), *sb.* Forms: 5–6 **whytynge, whitynge,** (5 **wytenge, -yng**), 6 **whyting, -yng, whityng, -inge,** 7 **whytting,** *Sc.* **quhiting, quhittine,** 8 **whitting,** *Sc.* **whyten,** 8–9 *Sc.* **whiten,** 6– **whiting.** [ad. (M)Du. *wijting*, also †*wittingh*, MLG. *wîtink* 'aculeja', 'amia', 'asellus'; app. f. WHITE *a.* + -ING³. (The formal analogue ON. *hvítingr* = a kind of whale, etc.) Cf. WHITEFISH.]

1. a. A gadoid fish of the genus *Merlangus*, esp. *M. vulgaris*, a small fish with pearly white flesh, abundant off the coast of Great Britain, and highly esteemed as food.

14.. *Nom.* in Wr.-Wülcker 705/23 *Hic glaucus*, a whytynge. *c* **1425** *Voc.* ibid. 642/8 *Hic clamitus*, wytyng. **1433** *Stonor Papers* (Camden) I. 49 In xij podryd [= powdered] wytyng, viij d. *a* **1548** HALL *Chron.*, *Hen. VIII.* 23 b, He robbed certein poore Fisshermen of Whitynges. **1620** VENNER *Via Recta* iv. 76 The Whiting, notwithstanding that it is vnsauourie, and nourisheth very litle, is of some greatly..commended. **1664** in *Maitl. Club Misc.* (1840) II. 505 For a dishe of quhitingis 001 16 00. *Ibid.* 506 For a dishe of dryed quhittines 003 00 00. **1721** in W. Macfarlane *Geogr. Collect.* (S.H.S.) I. 39 The seas abound with..Turbet, Scate, Mackrel, Haddocks, whittings. **1724** RAMSAY *Tea-t. Misc.* (1733) I. 91 And there will be partans and buckies And whytens and speldings enew. **1769** PENNANT *Brit. Zool.* III. 155 Whitings appear in vast shoals on our seas in the spring. **1843** *Penny Cycl.* XXVII. 347/1 Whiting..is easily distinguished from the cod, haddock, and bib by the absence of the barbule on the chin.

b. Locally applied to fishes of other genera.

(*a*) Some fresh-water fish found in Wales; also, a name on the Solway Firth and in the south of Scotland for a small fish of the salmon family, of uncertain identity, perhaps the young of the salmon-trout, *Salmo trutta* (cf. WHITLING). (*b*) In U.S., A fish of the genus *Menticirrhus*; also applied to the silver hake, and to the menhaden. (*c*) In Australia, A fish of the genus *Sillago*: see quot. 1882. (*d*) ***blue whiting***, an oceanic fish of the cod family, *Micromesistius poutassou*, found in north-western Europe and the Mediterranean; = POUTASSOU.

1587 CHURCHYARD *Worthines of Wales* N, A Poole there is, through which this Cloyd doth passe, Where is a Fish, that some a Whiting call. **1774** *Ann. Reg.*, *Misc. Ess.* 163 [Bala] lake produces very fine trout, and a fish called whiting, peculiar to itself. **1795** *Statist. Acc. Scot.* XIV. 410 There is abundance of fish,..in Esk,..such as salmon, grilse, sea trout, and whitens. **1873** T. GILL *Catal. Fishes E. Coast N. Amer.* 18 *Merlucius bilinearis*..American hake; silver hake (Maine); whiting (Mass.). *Ibid.* 27 *Menticirrus alburnus*.. Carolina whiting. *Ibid.*, *Menticirrus nebulosus*..King-fish; whiting. **1882** TENISON-WOODS *Fish N.S.W.* 65 The 'whitings' are not like those of Europe. There are..four Australian species—the common sand whiting (*Sillago maculata*),..the trumpeter whiting (*Sillago bassensis*),.. *Sillago punctata*, the whiting of Melbourne..and *Sillago ciliata*. **1888** GOODE *Amer. Fishes* 81 The Norfolk Hog-fish *Pomodasys fulvomaculatus*..is the..'Pork-fish' and 'Whiting' at Key West. **1959** A. C. HARDY *Open Sea* II. xi. 229 The blue whiting..lives over the deep water off the edge of the continental shelf. **1974** *Guardian* 20 Mar. 11/1 The blue whiting..cod-like in taste and texture, slender in shape, about a foot long. **1977** *Grimsby Even. Tel.* 5 May 8/4 Certainly its size makes it an easier fish to process than the more publicised blue whiting.

2. Allusive uses of sense 1. **a.** In proverbial phr.

With quot. 1721 cf. WHITE *a.* 10.

1562 J. HEYWOOD *Prov. & Epigr.* (1867) 64 There lepte a whityng (quoth she) and lept in streite. **1570** *Marr. Wit. & Sci.* IV. i, But he that takes not such time while he maye, Shal leape at a whyting when time is a waye. **1670** RAY *Prov.* 199 To let leap a whiting. i.e. To let slip an opportunity. **1721** KELLY *Sc. Prov.* 158 He gave me Whitings, but Bones. That is, he gave me fair Words. The Scots call Flatteries Whitings, and Flatterers white People. **1808** JAMIESON s.v. *Quhyte*, A proverbial phrase, still used to denote flattery: 'He kens how to butter a whiting.'

†**b.** As a term of endearment: cf. *whiting-mop* (see 5). Also *whiting's eye*, an amorous look, a leer.

a **1529** SKELTON *E. Rummyng* 223 He callyth me his whytyng. **1673** WYCHERLEY *Gent. Dancing-Master* IV. i, I saw her..give him the languishing Eye,..the Whitings Eye, of old called the Sheeps Eye.

†**3.** = *white pudding*: see WHITE *a.* 11 e. *Obs.*

1674 N. FAIRFAX *Bulk & Selv.* 159 As the Darbyshire huswife [sorts out] her puddings when she makes whitings and blackings, and liverings and hackings.

4. (See quot.)

1792 G. CARTWRIGHT *Jrnl. Labrador* III. p. x, *Whitings*, trees which have been barked, and left standing.

5. *attrib.* and *Comb.* (in sense 1), as ***whiting-ground*** [GROUND *sb.* 12], ***-monger, -season***; † **whiting-mop**, a young whiting; also as a term of endearment for a girl (see MOP *sb.*⁴). Also in names of fishes resembling the whiting, as **whiting perch**, POLLACK, POUT (*sb.*¹), **salmon** (see quots.).

1891 *Daily News* 31 Oct. 6/5 About two hundred fishing boats were lying at anchor off the edge of the *whiting grounds about three miles outside Plymouth breakwater. **1599** NASHE *Lenten Stuff* 29 Colchester oystermen, or *whiting-mungers and sprot-catchers. **1803** SHAW *Gen. Zool.* IV. 548 *Whiting Perch. *Perca Alburnus*. **1686** RAY *Willughby's Hist. Pisc.* IV. ii. 167 *Asellus Huitingo-Pollachius*: ..A *Whiting Pollack. **1758** *Descr. Thames* 222 The Whiting-Pollack..has this Name given it here, from its Likeness to a Whiting. **1862** ANSTED *Channel Isl.* II. ix. 211 Next..in abundance are the whiting pollack..and the gar-fish or green bone. *a* **1672** WILLUGHBY *Hist. Pisc.* (1686) Tab. L. membr. i. n. 4 *Asellus mollis latus*. *Whiting Poutes *Londinensibus*. **1758** *Descr. Thames* 222 The Whiting-Pout is remarkably broad, in Proportion to its Length. **1804** SHAW *Gen. Zool.* V. 54 *Whiting Salmon, *Salmo Phinoc*. **1791** W. GILPIN *Forest Scenery* II. 190 In the *whiting-season..fleets of twenty or thirty boats are often seen lying at anchor on the banks.

whiting ('hwaɪtɪŋ), *vbl. sb.* Forms: 1 **hwiting,** 5 **whytyng(e, wytyng, whittyng,** 5–6 **whityng,** 6 **whyghtynge, whighting, whitting(e,** 6–7 **whitinge,** 7 **whiteing, whyting, whytting,** 8 **whiten,** 6– **whiting.** [f. WHITE *v.*¹ + -ING¹.] **I.** The action of the verb.

† **1.** The action or process of making white; whitening. *Obs.* **a.** by covering or coating with white: Whitewashing. Also *fig.*

c **1440** *Pallad. on Husb.* I. 413 For whytyng that lyme is conuenyent. **1495–6** *Rec. St. Mary at Hill* (1904) 220 Payd to Symon dawber for whittyng of the chyrch, v days iij s. **1540** *Dunmow Churchw. Acc.* lf. 31 (MS) For whyghtynge of the porche. **1605** *Shuttleworths' Acc.* (Chetham Soc.) 169 A plasterer, viij days and halfe whytting of the dyning chamber roffe..iiij^s iij^d. **1663** GERBIER *Counsel* 81 Whiting and Stopping of fret seelings.

fig. **1628** A. LEIGHTON *Appeal to Parlt.* 186 In this case, the whiting, daubing, or palliating will not serve.

b. by depriving of colour: Bleaching.

1477 *Act 17 Edw. IV.* c. 4 Whityng & anelyng de tewle appellez pleintile. **1594** PLAT *Jewell-ho.* I. 58 For the speedier whiting of yarne. **1620** in Foster *Engl. Factories India* (1906) 192 The whitster..detaynes them in whitinge and starchinge about three mounthes. **1683** *Lond. Gaz.* No. 1801/4 A convenient piece of Ground..for whiting of Linnen Cloth.

2. *Printing.* The use of 'white' (cf. WHITE *sb.* 7 a and *a.* 2 d).

1884 *Athenæum* 24 May 658 The variety of type and the liberal whiting are quite luxurious.

II. *concr.* **3.** A preparation of finely powdered chalk, used for whitewashing, cleaning plate, and various other purposes.

In OE. only in Comb. *hwitingmelu* 'whiting meal'.

c **1440** *Promp. Parv.* 525/2 Whytynge, or mater to make whyghte of.., *albatura, candidacium*. **1633–4** *Althorp MS.* in Simpkinson *Washingtons* (1860) App. p. lxiii, 12 balls of whiteing to scowre the plate. **1690** SIR J. FOULIS *Acc. Bk.* (S.H.S.) 129 To meg for whyting for teeth, 2 18 0. **1799** G. SMITH *Laboratory* I. 143 Take some whiten,..lay your foils upon it, and..polish your foils. **1844** *Civil Eng. & Arch. Jrnl.* VII. 150/1 Anoint the segments..with thin putty, made with fine whiting and some of the linseed oil. **1880** BARING-GOULD *Mehalah* viii, You cannot clean a deck with whiting, you must take holystone.

III. 4. *attrib.* and *Comb.*, as (in sense 1 a) ***whiting brush, work***; (in sense 1 b) ***whiting ground, time***; (in sense 3) ***whiting-manufacturer***.

1611 COTGR., *Escouëtte*,..*whiting brush. **1692** *Specif. Patent* No. 256 (Patent Office) Erected a bucking house, fitted and prepared a *whiteing ground. **1813** *Examiner* 22 Mar. 183/2 M. Price,..*whiting-manufacturer. **1598** SHAKS. *Merry W.* III. iii. 140 It is *whiting time, send him by your two men to Datchet-Meade. *c* **1440** *Pallad. on Husb.* I. 407 Eek *whyting werk is thyng of gret delyte.

whiting, obs. form of WHITTEN.

whitish ('hwaɪtɪʃ), *a.* (*sb.*) [f. WHITE *a.* + -ISH¹.]

1. Somewhat white; of a colour inclining to or approaching white.

1398 TREVISA *Barth. De P.R.* XVII. cl. (1495) T vj b/1 The leuys [of the trees of Sechym] ben rough and whitysshe. **1530** PALSGR. 329/1 Whytysshe, *blanchastre*. **1545** RAYNALDE *Byrth Mankynde* 122 Yf the wheles seme whytysshe. **1575** TURBERV. *Faulconrie* 17 Of the lesse Vulture, whiche is the browne or whitish Vulture. **1586** W. WEBBE *Eng. Poetrie* (Arb.) 74 When haires from my beard did ginne to be whitish. **1684** BOYLE *Exper. Poros. Bod.* II. vi. 105 A multitude of little cracks..which destroyed its former transparency, and made it [*sc.* a crystal] look whitish. **1790** *Cook's 1st Voy.* I. 17 A species of the Medusa..which ..emitted a whitish light. **1797** T. MORTON *Cure for Heartache* I. i. 6 How whitish and deadly bad he do look. **1815** SCOTT *Guy M.* x, A small swamp, the clay of which was whitish. **1897** *Allbutt's Syst. Med.* III. 333 The mucous membrane will..appear whitish from the presence of partially shed epithelium.

b. as *sb.* A colour approaching white.

1815 STEPHENS in *Shaw's Gen. Zool.* IX. I. 49 The shafts spotted with whitish, the feathers alternately banded with black and rufous.

2. a. Qualifying other adjs. (or sbs.) of colour, indicating a pale or light tint of the colour specified.

1653 R. SANDERS *Physiogn.* 166 A whitish-red colour. **1667** *Phil. Trans.* II. 430 Turquois..of the New [Rock] are of an ill whitish Blew. **1712** STEELE *Spect.* No. 436 ⁋1 A whitish brown Paper. **1869** MRS. STOWE *Oldtown Folks* iii, Her..whitish-blue eyes. **1883** D. C. MURRAY *Hearts* xvi, His swarthy face had taken an ugly tint of whitish-green.

b. In parasynthetic combinations.

1753 *Chambers' Cycl.* Suppl. s.v. *Cassida*, The whitish-flowered cassida. **1800** SHAW *Gen. Zool.* I. 538 Whitish-tailed Shrew.

Hence **'whitishness**, the quality of being whitish; whitish colour or tint.

1544 PHAER *Bk. Childr.* (1553) T vij b, Yelownes or whittishnes of the eyes. **1660** BOYLE *New Exp. Phys. Mech.* xxxvii. 307 They were wont..by their whiteishness, to emulate in some measure the apparition of Light. *a* **1722** LISLE *Husb.* (1757) 155 The best sort of barley..is of a pale lively yellow colour, with a bright whitishness in it. **1806** HERSCHEL in *Phil. Trans.* XCVI. 465 The north [polar regions of Saturn] retain..some whitishness. **1929** S. LESLIE *Anglo-Catholic* xii. 158 In the lamplight he noticed her deathliness of hue, the whitishness of lead-poisoning.

whitleather ('hwɪt,lɛðə(r)). Forms: 4 **witleȝtr'**, 5 **whittlether,** 5–7 **whit(-)lether,** 7–9 **whit-leather,** 6– **whitleather.** [WHITE *a.* 2 (with normal shortening in comb.) and LEATHER *sb.* For illustration of white leather see 1 *β*.]

1. a. Leather of a white or light colour and soft pliant consistence, prepared by tawing, i.e.

dressing with alum and salt, so as to retain the natural colour. Also *attrib.*

1366–7 *Priory of Finchale* (Surtees) p. lxxii, Cum ferrura, cingulis, capestris, witleȝtr', scutels [etc.]. **1487–8** *Durham Acc. Rolls* (Surtees) 417 Pro whitlether pro lez bawdrikez, vj d. **1573–80** TUSSER *Husb.* (1878) 36 Hole bridle and saddle, whit lether and nall. **1623** tr. *Favine's Theat. Hon.* I. vi. 58 A large strong thong or strap of whit-leather. **1784** TWAMLEY *Dairying Exempl.* 40, I have seen one part of a Skin of a well coloured sound nature, another Part that had somewhat the look of rough Parchment, or hard Whit-leather. **1877** *N.W. Linc. Gloss.*, *Whitleather*, sheep's-skins, prepared for thongs of flails, repairing harness, &c. Formerly used for baldricks of church-bells. **1960** G. E. EVANS *Horse in Furrow* xvii. 213 Sidney Austin, the harness-maker, still uses strips of whitleather to repair..the collars of farm-horses.

β. *c* **1440**, **1519** [see LEATHER *sb.* 1]. **1500** *Louth Church Acc.* in *N.W. Linc. Gloss.* (1889) s.v., For j horskyn & di. skyn whiett ledder. **1556** *Churchw. Acc. Minchinhampton* in *Archaeologia* (1853) XXXV. 423 For wyet lether, and makyng off bawryxes, xviij d. **1565** COOPER *Thesaurus* s.v. *Bos.*, *Bubuli cortabi*,..thonges of white leather. **1885** A. WATT *Leather Manuf.* 39 When tawed, or prepared with alum and salt, they [*sc.* sheepskins] form what is termed white leather.

attrib. and *Comb.* ? *a* **1600** *MS. Lansd. 241* (Halliw.) Thy gerdill made of the whittlether whange. **1635** J. GOWER *Pyrgomachia* C 3, Then from thy flesh I'le draw thy hide, And have it throughly tann'd, and dry'd Whit-lether-like. **1854** MISS BAKER *Northampt. Gloss.*, Whit-leather thongs.

b. In comparisons, or as a type of toughness, elasticity, softness, etc.; hence *fig.* Also *attrib.*

1605 BRETON *I pray you be not angrie* B 4, I am thus handled..with this wicked olde peece of Whit-leather. **1610** BEAUM. & FL. *Scornf. Lady* v. i, Hast thou so much moisture in the Whitleather hide yet, that thou canst cry? **1622** MASSINGER & DEKKER *Virg. Mart.* IV. ii. 1 2, The guts of my conscience beginne to be of whit-leather. **1697** VANBRUGH *Relapse* v. iii, *Nurse.* I'll soon bring his Nose to the Grindstone. *C[oupler] aside.* Well said, old White-leather! *a* **1713** ELLWOOD *Hist. Life* (1714) 316 My Sides are not of Iron, neither Are my Lungs made of Whit-leather. **1830** JAMES *Darnley* v, Pray God to make all your bones as soft as whit-leather. **1839** MRS. KIRKLAND *New Home* xxxiv. 225 Her eyes grew preternaturally pale, and her lips wan as whit-leather. **1913** D. H. LAWRENCE *Love Poems & Others* 44 A widow o forty-five As has sludged like a horse all her life, Till 'er's tough as whit-leather.

2. The tough ligament in the neck of an ox or other grazing animal, also called *paxwax*.

1713 DERHAM *Phys.-Theol.* VI. iii. 362 That..Ligament—Called the Whitleather, Packwax, Taxwax, and Fixfax.

Whitley ('hwɪtlɪ). The name of J. H. *Whitley* (1866–1935), chairman of a committee set up in 1916 to consider relations between employers and employees, used *attrib.* with reference to the recommendations of this committee concerning good industrial relations, etc.

1917 in *State Service* (1969) Sept. 226/3 The application of the Whitley report should be extended to occupations of a purely commercial or clerical character. **1919** *Manch. Guardian* 11 Feb. 7/3 (*heading*) The Whitley councils. **1923** *Daily Mail* 29 Jan. 7 Mistress and maid should be their own Whitley Council. **1924** *Glasgow Herald* 20 Sept. 11 During the war and after the war Whitley bodies were set up in industries which up till then had nothing of the kind. *Ibid.*, The Whitley machinery could be used to discuss reduction in wages. **1928** *Britain's Industr. Future* (Liberal Industr. Inquiry) III. v. 174 It is important to understand the causes of the limited degree of success which has attended the Whitley scheme. **1976** *Star* (Sheffield) 3 Dec. 5/2 He recommends that a national forum be set up where Ministers can discuss policies with staff representatives, along with new regional Whitley Councils, and local committees.

Hence **'Whitleyism**, the use of Whitley Councils or similar methods for dealing with relations between employers and employees.

1919 *Manch. Guardian* 28 Feb. 14/4 Judge Parry..criticised the bureaucracy for its failure to apply the principles of 'Whitleyism' to departments of the Government service. **1928** *Daily Tel.* 14 Aug. 10/6 There has now followed a striking development, completing the destruction of Whitleyism in the Post Office. **1969** *State Service* Sept. 226/1 (*heading*) Whitleyism in the Civil Service.

whitling ('hwɪtlɪŋ). *Sc.* and *north.* Also 6 **whiddelynge**, 9 **whitlin.** [f. WHITE *a.* + -LING. Cf. G. *weissling* whiting.

Late OE. *hwitling* 'glaucus' is perh. the whiting.]

A fish of the salmon family, not certainly identified; app. the young of the bull-trout, *Salmo eriox.* Also ***whitling-trout.*** Cf. WHITING *sb.* 1 b (*a*).

1597–8 *Shuttleworths' Acc.* (Chetham Soc.) 111 For floukes and eght whiddelynges, xviij[d]. **1769** J. WALLIS *Nat. Hist. Northumbld.* I. 389 The Whitling-Trout..is taken in the Till and Tweed from ten to twenty inches. **1793** *Statist. Acc. Scot.* VIII. 488 In some parts of the Ern, there are..great numbers of sea trouts... The fishermen call them whitlings. **1830** in T. Doubleday *Coquet-Dale Fishing Songs* (1852) 84 The Tweed, he may brag o' his sawmon, An' blaw of his whitlins the Till. **1867** F. FRANCIS *Bk. Angling* ix. 297 There is a disputed point as regards the bull-trout, whether or no he is the veritable 'whitling'.

attrib. **1769** [see above]. **1834** JARDINE in *Proc. Berw. Nat. Club* I. No. 2. 52 They..are taken with whitling flies. **1847** STODDART *Angler's Comp.* 84 On rivers, like the Tweed or Tay, I recommend the use of a whitling hook.

whitlockite ('hwɪtləkaɪt). *Min.* [f. the name of Herbert P. *Whitlock* (1868–1948), U.S. mineralogist + -ITE[1].] A calcium hydrogen phosphate containing ferrous iron and magnesium, $Ca_9(Mg,Fe)H(PO_4)_7$, found as transparent or translucent rhombohedral crystals of various colours and often occurring in dental calculi.

1940 C. FRONDEL in *Program & Abstr. 21st Ann. Meeting Mineral. Soc. Amer.* 7 Whitlockite is anhydrous calcium triphosphate..with Ca substituted for by Mg..and Fe... The mineral is named after Herbert P. Whitlock,..at present Curator of Minerals and Gems in the American Museum of Natural History. **1971** *Nature* 3 Dec. 264/1 The rock contains relatively small amounts of the phases that we have found in other Apollo basalts (..whitlockite, baddeleyite). **1979** WILLIAMS & ELLIOTT *Dental Biochem.* xii. 226 Whitlockite is more common in subgingival compared with supragingival calculus.

whitlow ('hwɪtləʊ). Forms: α. 4–7 **whitflawe**, 5 **whytflowe**, 5–6 **whitflowe**, 6 **whyte flaw**, **white flaw**, 6–7 **whiteflaw(e**, 7–8 **whit(-)flaw**, **whit(-)flow**, (8 *dial.* **whick-**, 8–9 **quickflaw**). β. 5 **whytlowe**, **whyte low**, 6 **whitlowe**, 7 **whitelow**, (**whitloaf**), 7–9 **whitloe**, 6– **whitlow.** γ. 6 **whytblow**, **whitblowe**, (**whetblowe**), **whiteblowe**, 6–7 **whitblow.** [app. orig. *whitflaw*, *-flow* = WHITE *a.* + FLAW *sb.*[1] (q.v. sense 4); but the similarity of the first syllable to early mod.Du. *vijt*, *fijt*, LG. *fit* 'whitlow' is remarkable and suggests the possibility of alien origin. The alterations to *whitblow*, *whitlow* are difficult to account for. The supposition that the original form was *whick-flaw*, dial. var. of *quickflaw* (Skeat), is not supported by the evidence.] A suppurative inflammatory sore or swelling in a finger or thumb, usually in the terminal joint; = PARONYCHIA 1 (cf. PANARICIUM).

α. *a* **1400** *Alphita* (Anecd. Oxon.) 138 *Paniritula uel paranicium, i. apostema inter digitos, a*[e]. a whitflawe. *a* **1425** tr. *Arderne's Treat. Fistula*, etc. 42 þe fistule bredyng in þe extremite of þe fynger deceyueþ sonner þe pacient þan in oþer places; ffor vnkunnyng seiþ þat it is þe whit-flowe, whiche þou shalt knowe þus. **1556** WITHALS *Dict.* (1562) 77 A whiteflaw, *rediuia.* **1562** TURNER *Herbal* II. 25 b, The asshes [of wild grapes]..are good for medicines for the eyes, and wyth hony it healeth whit flawes, agnayles & goomes bledinge. **1648** HERRICK *Hesper.*, *Oberon's Palace* 59 The nails faln off by Whit-flawes. **1707** J. STEVENS tr. *Quevedo's Com. Wks.* (1709) 340 A gold Ring does not cure a Whitflaw. **1746** *Phil. Trans.* XLIV. 228 Much used..in Cataplasms for the Fellon, or worst Kind of Whitflow. *a* **1800** PEGGE *Suppl. Grose*, Whick-flaw.

β. *c* **1440** *Promp. Parv.* 525/2 Whytlowe (*P.* whytflowe sore), *panarucium.* **1603** BRETON *Mad World* (1635) B 8 b, Healing but a Whitloe on a Lords thumbe. **1658** ROWLAND tr. *Moufet's Theat. Ins.* 1049 A live Chislep laid to a whitloaf, cures it. **1669** W. SIMPSON *Hydrol. Chym.* 206 They are not certainly able to perform the cure of..so much..as a paronychia or whitlow. **1765** STERNE *Tr. Shandy* VII. xxi, A novice of the convent..had been troubled with a whitloe in her middle finger. **1813** J. THOMSON *Lect. Inflam.* 337 Where the matter is lodged, as in some cases of whitloe, in the sheaths of the tendons. **1843** R. J. GRAVES *Syst. Clin. Med.* xxix. 371 A suppurating tumor resembling a whitlow. **1899** *Allbutt's Syst. Med.* VI. 575 Painless whitlow affects the fingers of patients suffering from peripheral nerve disease of the upper extremities.

γ. **1547** BOORDE *Brev. Health* lvi. 17 A white blowe, or a whyte flaw, the whiche doth grow about the rote of the nayle. **1547** SALESBURY *Welsh Dict.*, *Ewinor*, a whetblowe. **1598** FLORIO, *Panariccio*, a fellon, a whitblowe, that comes on ones finger tops.

b. *attrib.*: **whitlow-grass**, book-name of two early-flowering plants with white blossoms, formerly reputed to cure whitlows (cf. NAILWORT): *Saxifraga tridactylites*, Rue-leaved Whitlow-grass, and *Draba* (*Erophila*) *verna* (hence in mod. use extended to the whole genus *Draba*); **whitlow-wort**, a plant of the genus *Paronychia*, formerly reputed to cure whitlows.

1597 GERARDE *Herbal* II. clxxxvi. 498 Of Whiteblowe, or Whitlowe grasse. *Ibid.* 499 Rewe leafed Whitlowe grasse. Jagged Whitlowe grasse. **1634** T. JOHNSON *Merc. Bot.* 57 Rue Whitlow-grasse. **1650** [W. HOWE] *Phytol. Brit.* 88 *Paronychia altera*,..Rue Whitlow-grasse. *Paronychia major*,..Whitlow-wort... *Paronychia vulgaris*,..Chickweed Whitlow-grasse. **1785** MARTYN *Lett. Bot.* ii. (1794) 31 Those whose seed vessel is a silicle..as whitlow-grass. **1822** *Hortus Anglicus* II. 143 D[raba] Verna. *Common Whitlow Grass...* D. Aizoides. *Sen Green, or Alpine Whitlow Grass...* D. Pyrenaica. *Pyrenean Whitlow Grass.*

Whitmanesque (hwɪtmə'nɛsk), *a.* [f. the name *Whitman* + -ESQUE.] Characteristic or suggestive of Walt Whitman (1819–92), U.S. poet, or of his poetry.

1882 *Good Lit.* Sept. 2 Clever persons can manufacture Whitmanesque verse quite equal to the average of the original. **1901** E. CROSBY *Edward Carpenter* 6 The long series of poems in Towards Democracy is with few exceptions written in the Whitmanesque meter, or lack of meter. **1913** W. DE LA MARE in *Edin. Rev.* Jan. 193 Eloquence and facility are the danger of Whitmanesque verse of this nature. **1934** C. LAMBERT *Music Ho!* v. 281 There is very little Whitmanesque acceptance of life about the artist of today. **1957** P. WILDEBLOOD *Main Chance* 152 They have a Whitmanesque simplicity that we've quite lost. **1977** *Time* 1 Aug. 50/2 Such a collage has an effect of Whitmanesque tenderness.

So (mostly somewhat *nonce*) **Whitma'nese**, the characteristic style or diction of Whitman; **Whit'mania**, (*a*) [-MANIA], (a punning word for) exaggerated admiration for Whitman; (*b*) [-IA[1]], writings pertaining to Whitman; **Whit'maniac**, a devotee of Whitman; **Whit'manian** *a.* = WHITMANESQUE *a.*; **Whit'manian** *sb.*, an admirer or imitator of Whitman; **'Whitmanish** *a.* = WHITMANESQUE *a.*; **'Whitmanism**, Whitman's metrical or poetical style; a feature of this; **'Whitmanist**, **'Whitmanite**, a Whitmanian; **'Whitmanize** *v. intr.*, to write in the manner of Whitman; **Whit'mannic** *a.* = WHITMANESQUE *a.*

1887 Whitmania [see BRONTËAN *a.*]. **1887** M. BERENSON *Let.* 6 Jan. in Strachey & Samuels *M. Berenson* (1983) ii. 36, I was a Whitmanite at Smith College. **1889** *Pall Mall Gaz.* 25 Jan. 3/2 Having thus to a certain degree settled upon what one might call the *technique* of Whitmanism, he began to brood upon the nature of that spirit that was to give life to the strange form. **1893** R. LE GALLIENNE *Retrosp. Rev.* (1896) I. 213 'I see twenty-two young men from Foster's watching me, and the trousers of the twenty-two young men' is irresistible Whitmanese. **1894** *Nation* 7 June 433/1 One of the worst of Whitmanisms, the interlarding of foreign words. **1902** *Academy* 16 Aug. 173/1 Mr. Moody does not Whitmanise on the one hand, or follow the outworn Tennysonian convention on the other. **1906** *Dial* (Chicago) 1 Mar. 144/2 Much of the conversation reported is trivial to all but ardent Whitmanites. **1918** *Cambr. Hist. Amer. Lit.* II. III. i. 267 Whitmanism..has already had the ironical fate of developing something not unlike a cult. *a* **1930** D. H. LAWRENCE *Phoenix* (1936) 269 Whitmanish 'adhesiveness' of the social creature. **1934** *Times Lit. Suppl.* 30 Aug. 586/3 Before Rossetti established himself publicly as the principal English Whitmanist, 'Leaves of Grass' had been the subject of several reviews. **1948** L. SPITZER *Linguistics & Lit. Hist.* 218 The first [*sc.* the old alexandrine], Claudel replaced by the Biblical and Whitmanian verset. **1953** A. ALPERS *Katherine Mansfield* 124 Thus reminded that she had a country of her own, Katherine addressed to Wyspiański another of her Whitmanish declamations. **1959** *Times Lit. Suppl.* 16 Oct. 594/4 A foreword by Mr. Charles E. Feinberg, the noted Whitmaniac of Detroit. *a* **1960** E. M. FORSTER *Maurice* (1971) 217 Edward Carpenter..was..a Whitmannic poet whose nobility exceeded his strength. **1964** *New Statesman* 13 Mar. 414/3 The presses groan with Whitmania. **1977** *Listener* 30 June 866/3 The Fabian Society..sprang from an idealistic society called the Fellowship of the New Life, much influenced by the Whitmanian, Edward Carpenter.

whitmeate, obs. form of WHITE MEAT.

Whit Monday: see after WHIT SUNDAY.

whitmoreite ('hwɪtmɒraɪt). *Min.* [f. the name of Robert W. *Whitmore* (b. 1936), U.S. mineral collector + -ITE[1].] A secondary hydrated basic phosphate of ferric and ferrous iron, $Fe^{2+}Fe^{3+}{}_2(PO_4)_2(OH)_2.4H_2O$, found as twinned monoclinic crystals of a brownish colour.

1974 P. B. MOORE et al. in *Amer. Mineralogist* LIX. 900/2 Whitmoreite occurs as thin acicular crystals five to ten times as long as they are thick, which range from 0·1 to 2 mm in length. **1979** *Mineral. Abstr.* XXX. 450/1 The occurrence and parageneses of the following newly recognized secondary phosphates in the pegmatite of Hagendorf, West Germany, are recorded: whitmoreite, schoonerite, [etc.].

whitner, obs. form of WHITENER.

whitnes, -nesse, obs. ff. WHITENESS, WITNESS.

Whitney, erron. spelling of WITNEY.

whitneyite ('hwɪtnɪaɪt). *Min.* [f. the name of J. D. *Whitney*, an American geologist: see -ITE[1].] A native arsenide of copper, of a reddish-white colour, found near Lake Superior and elsewhere in America.

1861 BRISTOW *Gloss. Min.*

whitour, obs. form of QUITTER *sb.*[1]

whitpot, obs. form of WHITE-POT.

whitret ('hwɪtrɪt), **whitterick** ('hwɪtərɪk). *Sc.* and *dial.* Forms: α. 5 **whytrate**, (**-ratche**), **whitratt**, **whytrat**, *Sc.* **quhitrat**, 5, 9 **whitrat**, 6 *Sc.* **quhittrat**, **quhitred**, **fittret**, **quhittret**, 7–8 **whitred**, 7, 9 **whittret**, 8–9 **whiteret**, 9 **whitteret**, **whittrit**, (**whutthroat**), 8– **whitret.** β. 8–9 **whitrick**, 9 **whitrack**, (**w(h)utterick**, **-ock**, **whuttorock**), **whittrick**, **whitterick.** (See also *Eng. Dial. Dict.*) [The earliest known forms suggest a compound of WHITE *a.* and RAT *sb.*; the types *whitret*, *whitred*, *whitrick* exemplify Sc. tendency to modify the sounds of final syllables.] A weasel; also, a stoat.

α. *c* **1440** *Promp. Parv.* 525/2 Whytrate (*K.* whitratt, *P.* whytratche). *c* **1480** HENRYSON *Trial of Fox* 116 (Harl. MS.) The quhuirand quhitret with the quhasill went. **1486** *Bk. St. Albans, Hunting* fiiij b, The Graye, the Fox, the Squyrell, the whitrat, the Sot, and the Pulcatte. **1536** BELLENDEN *Cron. Scot.* (1821) I. p. xxxiii, Martrikis, bevers, quhitredis, and toddis. **1590** BUREL in Watson *Coll. Sc. Poems* II. (1709) 21 The Fumart and the Fittret straue, The deip and howest hole to haue. *Ibid.* 22 Out come the Quhittret. **1639** SIR R. GORDON *Geneal. Hist. Earld. Sutherld.* (1813) 3 Brocks, skuyrrells, whittrets, weasels, otters. **1681** COLVIL *Whigs Supplic.* (1751) p. xi, As harmless as a whitred without teeth. **1684** SIBBALD *Scotia Illustr.* II. II. 11 Mustela vulgaris ea est, quæ Whitred nostratibus dicitur. **1790** ALEX. WILSON *Disconsolate Wren* Poet. Wks. (1846) 96 Ony whitret's direfu' jaws. **1815** SCOTT *Guy M.*

xxiii, We maun off like whittrets before the whole clanjamfray be doun upon us. **1824** MACTAGGART *Gallovid. Encycl.* 275 The whut-throat or weazle, and the hoodie, have often bloody wars with other. **1880** *Fraser's Mag.* May 646 When a whitret or a fox came prowling past.

β. *c* **1800** *R. Jamieson's Pop. Ball.* (1806) I. 294 Her minnie had hain'd the warl, And the whitrack-skin had routh. **1802** G. V. SAMPSON *Statist. Surv. Londonderry* 455 The weazle (provincially *whitrick*). **1861** QUINN *Heather Lintie* (1863) 145 He yokes him fairly wi' his teeth As Brush wad dune a whitterick.

whitsour (ˈhwɪtsaʊə(r)). [? f. WHITE *a.* + SOUR *a.*] A variety of apple.

1733 MILLER *Gard. Dict.* s.v. *Apple*, The Whitsour. **1786** ABERCROMBIE *Gardener's Daily Assist.* p. xi, Apples valued principally for Cyder. White sour.

Whitstable (ˈhwɪtstəb(ə)l). The name of a coastal town in Kent, used *attrib.* and *absol.* to designate oysters bred there.

1883 *Queen* 20 Oct. (Advt.), Any others that are advertised at a low price..*cannot possibly* be the *genuine* Medina or Whitstable Oysters. **1940** A. L. SIMON *Conc. Encycl. Gastron.* II. 69/2 Most Whitstable oysters to-day are.. relaid Brittanys or Belons. The oysters known as *Royal Whitstables* are, however, genuine natives, taken from a breeding ground the boundaries of which were settled by law about 1900. **1960** *Times* 2 Nov. 13/6 They may not be Whitstables, but they are oysters of a kind. **1971** *Vogue* 15 Sept. 43/1 One of London's best fishmongers. Ask for fresh sardines, Whitstable oysters, game. **1973** 'J. STURROCK' *Wicked Way to Die* x. 142 They've got as fine a barrel of Whitstables here as ever I've seen.

whitster (ˈhwɪtstə(r)). Now *local.* Forms: 5 **whytstar, wytstare, whystare, qwytstare, qwyster, quister,** 6 **whitstarre,** 6– **whitster.** [f. WHITE *v.* + -STER. Cf. Du. *witster* 'a Woman that whitens the walls' (Sewel).]

1. A bleacher.

c **1440** *Promp. Parv.* 39/1 Bleystare, or wytstare (*K.* bleyster, *H.* bleyestare or qwytstare, *P.* bleykester or whytster), *candidarius.* **1530** PALSGR. 288/2 Whitstarre, *blanchisseur de toylles.* **1594** PLAT *Jewell-ho.* II. 58 The whitsters, and dutch laundresses. **1598** SHAKS. *Merry W.* III. iii. 11 Take this basket..and carry it among the Whitsters in Dotchet Mead. **1667** PEPYS *Diary* 12 Aug., My wife and maids being gone over the water to the whitster's with their clothes. **1701** J. HOUGHTON *Collect. Improv. Husb.* No. 493 ¶5 The Whitsters do use these Pot-Ashes, in the whitening of their Yarn and Cloth. **1881** *Instr. Census Clerks* (1885) 72 Scourer, Bleacher:..French Cleaner, Whitster.

2. A whitesmith.

1823 E. MOOR *Suffolk Wds.*

Hence †ˈ**whitstered** (-əd) *a.*, bleached.

1767 *Specif. Thos. Long's Patent* No. 869 A 'machine for printing..whitstered linen'.

whitstone, obs. variant of WHETSTONE.

†**whitsull.** *Cornish dial.* [f. WHITE *a.* + ? SOWL.] = WHITE MEAT a.

1602 CAREW *Cornwall* 66 Their meat, Whitsull, as they call it, namely, milke, sowre milke, cheese, curds, butter, and such like as came from the cow and ewe.

Whitsun (ˈhwɪtsən). Forms: 3 **witsonen, witesone,** 4 **witsone,** 4–6 **Wytson,** 5 **Wyte-, Wytt-, White-, Whyght-,** (*Sc.* **Vit-**), 5–6 **Whyt-,** 5–7 **Wit-,** 5–8 **Whitson,** 6 **Whitsone, Wytsone, -sen, Witteson,** (*Sc.* **Vytson**), 7–8 **Whitsund, Whit-sun,** 7– **Whitsun.** *β.* 5 *Sc.* **quysson,** 5, 9 *dial.* **Whisson,** 7 **Whesen.** (See also following words.) [ME. *w(h)itsone(n,* the first two elements of WHIT SUNDAY, WHITSUNDAY, analysed as *Whitsun Day.* Cf. ON. *hvítasunna* Whitsunday, *hvítasunnuvika* Whitsun week, *hvítasunnuaptann* Whitsun eve.]

1. Used *attrib.* to denote something belonging to, connected with, or occurring at the season of Whit Sunday or Whitsuntide: as ***Whitsun air, contribution, fair, holiday, market, morn, morris-dance, pastoral***; **Whitsun ale** *Hist.* [ALE 3], a parish festival formerly held at Whitsuntide, marked by feasting, sports, and merry-making; †**Whitsun eve, even** [EVE *sb.*[1] 2, EVEN *sb.* 2], the day before Whit Sunday; †**Whitsun farthing** = PENTECOSTAL *sb.*; **Whitsun gillyflower,** local name for a double-flowered variety of rocket (*Hesperis matronalis*); †**Whitsun lady, lord,** titles of the leading or presiding personages at a *Whitsun ale*; **Whitsun week,** the week beginning with Whit Sunday, Whit-week. Also occas. in names of the days of Whit-week, as **Whitsun Sunday** (*obs.* or *dial.*) = WHIT SUNDAY, **Whitsun Monday,** etc. = Whit Monday, etc. (see after WHIT SUNDAY). See also WHITSUNTIDE.

1846 KEBLE *Lyra Innoc.* x. xi, Thy dread Hours, Thou awful Trinity, Are but the *Whitsun airs, new set on high. **1614** W. BROWNE *Sheph. Pipe* I. C 6, This is a Tale Would befit our *Whitson-ale. **1619** *Pasquils Palin.* B 3, Happy the age,..When euery village did a May-pole raise, And Whitson-ales, and May-games did abound. **1633** CHAS. I. *Decl. conc. Sports* 11 That after the end of Diuine Seruice, Our good people be not disturbed, letted, or discouraged from..hauing of May-Games, Whitson Ales, and Morris-dances. **1698** WALLIS in *Phil. Trans.* XX. 301 When they flock about a Ballad-Singer in a Fair, or the Morrice-Dancers at a Whitsund Ale. **1727** SOMERVILLE *Yeoman of Kent* 32 At Whitson-ales king of the May..He tript it on each holyday. **1842** J. AITON *Dom. Econ.* (1857) 95 Royal proclamations had failed to revive Whitsunales, and May games, and Morris dancers. People will not be merry by rule. **1695** KENNETT *Par. Antiq.* ix. 597 The Pentecostals or *Whitsun-contributions. **1297** R. GLOUC. (Rolls) 11855 A *witsonen eue hii come þer. ? **1475** *Paston Lett.* (1904) V. 232 Wretyn at Mawteby, on Wyteson eve. **1553–4** in Swayne *Churchw. Acc. Sarum* (1896) 99 Ryngyng' none on Whytson yeve, ij d. **1624** LAUD *Diary* 15 May, Saturday, Whitsun-eve, The Bill passed in Parliament. **1709** *First Publishers of Truth* (1907) 242 The day Called whitsoneve. *c* **1425** in *Rep. MSS. Ld. Middleton* (Hist. MSS. Comm. 1911) 107 On *Qwysson even everilke man breke his severyll gresse, os hym lykes. **1533** *Songs, Carols,* etc. (E.E.T.S.) 165 On Wytson evyne was a gret thonder at London. **1620** *Reg. Mag. Sig. Scot.* 26/1 Die Sabbati ante festum Pentecostes lie Witson-evin et 12 Nov. **1807** CRABBE *Par. Reg.* I. 427 Loitering at the *Whitsun-fair. **1656** in Urwick *Nonconf. Worc.* (1897) 56 Oblations commonly called by the name of *Whitson Farthings payable to the Dean and Chapter of W[orcester]. **1730** BAILEY (folio) s.v. *Quadragesimals,* Pentecostals or Whitsund Farthings. **1797** *Encycl. Brit.* (ed. 3) XVIII. 852/1 Whitsun-Farthings, otherwise called Smoke-farthings.., a composition for offerings..anciently made in Whitsun-week by every man in England, who occupied a house with a chimney, to the cathedral church of the diocese. **1656** W. COLES *Art of Simpling* xi. 33 May brings Roses, Pinks, *Whitsungilliflowers. **1886** BRITTEN & HOLLAND *Plant-n., Gilliflower, Whitsun.* The double-flowered variety of *Hesperis matronalis,..Som.* (Whitsun Gilawfers). **1533** *Songs, Carols, etc.* (E.E.T.S.) 163 Justis at Weste[m]ynster all þe *Wytson halydais. **1609** B. JONSON *Silent Wom.* III. i, Were you ever so much as look'd upon by a Lord,..but on the Easter, or Whitsonholydayes? **1715** *Lond. Gaz.* No. 5336/1 Their Majesties intend to go after the Whitsun-Holidays to Marienzell. **1656** HEYLIN *Surv. France* 47 A Kitchen-wench,..now so tricked up with scarfs, rings, and cross-garters, that you never saw a *Whitsun-Lady better rigged. **1611** *Melismata* F 2 b, Ich haue beene twise our *Whitson Lord. **1633** B. JONSON *Tale of Tub* Prol. 8 Old records Of antique proverbs, drawn from Whitson-lords. **1495** HALYBURTON *Ledger* (1867) 108 At the *Vitson merkat. **1501** *Plumpton Corr.* (Camden) 154 From Lyncolns Inne,..this *Whitsonemunday. **1622** in *Crt. & Times Jas. I.* (1848) II. 315 The new Venetian ambassador ..had his first audience on Whitsun-Monday. **1687** *MSS. Dk. Rutland* (Hist. MSS. Comm.) II. 113 Whesen Monday. **1778** *Eng. Gazetteer* (ed. 2), *Linton,*..10 miles from Cambridge..has a market on Thursday, and fairs on Whitsun-Monday, and August 4. **1535** STARKEY *Let.* in *England* (1871) p. xxii, Your letturys..were receyuyd apon *Wytson morn. **1599** SHAKS. *Hen. V,* II. iv. 25 Busied with a *Whitson Morris-dance. **1611** —— *Wint. T.* IV. iv. 134, I play as I haue seene them do In *Whitson-Pastorals. **1556** *Chron. Grey Friars* (Camden) 36 On *Wytsonsonday, which was the xxxj. of May, was the coronacion. **1825** BROCKETT *N.C. Gloss., Whisson-Sunday,* Whitsunday. **1612** HOPTON *Concord. Yeares* 173 *Whitsun-thursday. **1599** *Min. Archdeaconry of Colchester* lf. 248 (MS.) In the afternoone on Whitson monday and *Whitson tuasedaye all daye. **1662** *Bk. Com. Prayer* N 3, Whitsun Tuesday. **1839** *Penny Cycl.* XIII. 403/1. **1549** *Compl. Scot.* 168 *Vytson veddyinsday. **1297** R. GLOUC. (Rolls) 10542 þe þorsdai þe *witesonewouke to londone lowis com. *c* **1375** *Sc. Leg. Saints* xl. (*Ninian*) 734 Of witsone owke þe twysday. *c* **1400** MAUNDEV. (Roxb.) xxxii. 147 Apon a Seterday in Whisson woke. **1478** *Paston Lett.* III. 224 Wretyn at London, the Wednysdaye in Whyghtsonweke. **1551–2** *Act 5 & 6 Edw. VI* c. 3 Monday and Tewisdaye in Witteson weike. **1597** SHAKS. *2 Hen. IV,* II. i. 95 On Wednesday in Whitson week. **1634** *Bk. Com. Prayer* H 5, Munday in Whitsun weeke. **1848** MRS. GASKELL *Mary Barton* v, The great annual town-holiday of Whitsun-week.

2. *sb.* Short for WHITSUNTIDE. *rare.*

1849 DISRAELI in Monypenny & Buckle *Life* (1914) III. viii. 204 There will be a hot and perhaps eventful campaign between this and Whitsun. **1856** *Ibid.* (1916) IV. iii. 45 Between Easter and Whitsun.

Whit Sunday, Whitsunday (hwɪt ˈsʌndɪ, ˈhwɪtsəndeɪ). Forms (see also DAY and SUNDAY): 1 (*obl.*) **Hwitan Sunnandæȝ,** 2 **wit(te)-sunnedei,** 3 **White(n)sune(n)dæi, hwitesune-, Witeson(ne)-, wit-sune-, wit(e)sone-,** 4 **wit sonday, wijt sundai, Wittsunday, whytsonen-, wit(te)sone-,** 4–6 **Witsonday(e,** 5 **Whytesonday, witsonen, -on-, witsun-, wyt-, wyth-so(u)nday, wythsson-, Qwytsonn-, qwyteson(e)-,** 6 **Whit sonday, Whit(t)son-, Whytson-, Witsounday, whitson, Wittson daye,** *Sc.* **Witsounda, Vyt-, Vitso(u)nday,** 6– **Whitsunday,** 7– **Whit Sunday,** (**Whit-Sunday,** 9 **Whitsun-Day**). *β.* 4 *Sc.* **Qwhyssonday,** 4–5 **qvhissonday,** 5 **w(h)issonday, whysunday,** 9 *dial.* **Whussenday.** [late OE. *Hwíta Sunnandæȝ* lit. 'white Sunday' (found once only and in oblique form *Hwítan S.*); whence app. ON. *hvítasunnudagr* in the same sense, also *hvítasunnudagsaptann, -nátt, -vika* (ON. *hvítadagr* 'white day', *hvítadróttinsdagr* 'white Lord's-day', *hvítadagavika* Whitsun week, cannot be taken as evidence of an independent Norse origin; they are prob. due to Icelandic attempts to obliterate heathen traces from the name of the festival). The epithet 'white' is generally taken to refer to the ancient custom of the wearing of white baptismal robes by the newly-baptized at the feast of Pentecost (cf. *Dominica in albis,* the name of the First Sunday after Easter, Low Sunday, given for the same reason).

The formal analogues of *Whitsunday* current on the Continent in Low German and neighbouring areas are mostly applied to the First Sunday after Easter (cf. above), or the First Sunday in Lent (prob. from the white church-hangings then used; cf. OFris. *hwita tornsdey,* Du. *Witte Donderdag* Maundy Thursday), e.g. MLG. *witsondach,* MDu. *wittensondagh,* and (from LG.) MDa. *hvidesøndag,* MSw. *hvita sunnodaghur.* (No confirmation has been found of Kilian's '*witten-son-dagh,* vetus Fland. Dominica Pentecostes,' and Cotgrave's '*Dimenche de blanches,* Palmes-Sunday' and Hexham's '*Witten Sondagh,* Palme-Sunday' are prob. blunders.)

In earlier OE. the name of Whitsunday was *pentecosten* (gen. *-enes*), the Græco-Latin name (see PENTECOST and cf. Goth. *paintekusten* acc.), which was adopted in other Teut. languages, e.g. OS. (*te*) *pincostôn,* MDu. *pinxteren,* Du. *pinkster,* OHG. (*zi*) **pfinkustin* (*fimfchustim*), MHG. *pfingesten,* G. *Pfingsten,* (M)LG. *pinksten,* Sw. *Pingst,* Da. *Pinse(dag)*: see PINKSTER.

As the name of a Scottish term-day, *Whitsunday* (stressed on the final syllable) has been long dissociated from the church festival.

According to different apprehensions of the composition of the word (the origin of which was obscured by the shortening of the first syllable), it has been divided either as *Whitsun day* or as *Whit Sunday,* and the first elements of both of these have been used attributively in the same sense: see WHITSUN and *Whit Monday,* etc. below.]

1. The seventh Sunday after Easter, observed as a festival of the Christian Church in commemoration of the descent of the Holy Spirit on the day of Pentecost: = PENTECOST 2.

c **1100** *O.E. Chron.* an. 1067 (MS. D.) On þisan Eastron com se kyng to Wincestre, & þa wæron Eastra on x kal. April, & sona æfter þam com Mathild seo hlæfdie hider to lande, & Ealdred arcebiscop hiȝ ȝehalȝode to cwene..on Hwitan Sunnandæȝ. *c* **1175** *Lamb. Hom.* 45 Muneȝeing of þam hali gast þe he sende in his apostles on þon dei þe is icleped wit-sunne-dei. *c* **1205** LAY. 17481 Þat al his folc.. come to Amberes-buri..to White-sunedæie. *c* **1290** *St. Brendan* 151 in *S. Eng. Leg.* 224 Þer ȝe schulle þis ester beo & þis wit-sonedai also. **1387** TREVISA *Higden* (Rolls) V. 445 In a Witsonday þe mayde was i-cristened. **1398** *Munim. de Melros* (Bann.) 488 At þe fest of qvhissonday. *c* **1400** *Rom. Rose* 2278 Haue hatte of floures as fresh as may Chapelett of Roses of wissonday. *c* **1400** *Ywaine & Gaw.* 16 He made a feste, the soth to say, Opon the Witsononday, At Kerdyf, that es in Wales. **1482** *Monk of Evesham* (Arb.) 95 On ascensyon day and wythssonday he put no lyght to hym, the whiche yn these festis specialy were wonte to brenne. *a* **1533** LD. BERNERS *Huon* clxxxi. 731 On a witsonday themperour and themperesse helde estate royall at there palayes for yᵉ solempnyte of that day. **1634** BRERETON *Trav.* (Chetham Soc.) 4 The next morning early, being Whit Sunday, was discovered land. **1827** KEBLE *Chr. Year* (heading of poem) Whitsunday. **1868** J. H. BLUNT *Ref. Ch. Eng.* I. 188 The coronation took place at Westminster on Whitsun-Day.

†**b.** Used for the actual day of Pentecost on which the event took place: see PENTECOST 1. *Obs.*

a **1240** *Lofsong* in *O.E. Hom.* I. 209 þe ȝeoue of þe holi goste þet þu on hwite sune dai sendest þine deorewurðe deciples. *c* **1275** *Passion our Lord* 657 in *O.E. Misc.* 56 At þon heye vndarne, a wit-suneday..þe holy gost heom com vp-on in fury tunge. *c* **1375** *Sc. Leg. Saints* i. (*Petrus*) 40 Petir broucht to cristis fay Thre thowsand men on witsonday. **1387** TREVISA *Higden* (Rolls) IV. 351 Bytwene þe ascencioun, þat is holy þorsday, and Witsonday, Mathias was i-chose.

2. (In form *Whitsunday* or *Whitsun Day.*) One of the Scottish quarter-days or term-days (see TERM-DAY b), ordinarily May 15, but in certain cases May 26 (= May 15 Old Style) or May 28.

1450 *Reg. Mag. Sig. Scot.* 84/1 Full powar..my malis..to raise & ressave, my Witsondais to set and to halde. **1539** *Extr. Aberd. Reg.* (1844) I. 164 Mertimes and Vytsonday. **1541** *Ibid.* 174 Thre merkis, to be payit be the said maisteris of wark at Vitsounday and Mertimess be equall portionis. **1693** *Sc. Acts Will. & Mary* c. 40 (1822) IX. 304/2 Our Soveraigne Lord and Lady The King and Queens Majesties ..Declare that the Fifteenth day of May was since the date of the forsaid Act, and shall be in all time comeing in place of the former Terme of Whitsunday, to all effects whatsoever. **1905** *Glasgow Herald* 10 June 10.

3. *attrib.* in senses 1 and 2.

1451 *Churchw. Acc., Yatton* (Som. Rec. Soc.) 93 The Wendisdaye of Wytsondaye tyme. **1483** *Acta Audit.* in *Acta Dom. Conc.* II. Introd. 108 The malis of the samyn landis of the Witsonday terme last bipast. *c* **1489** CAXTON *Sonnes of Aymon* xxvi. 544 On wytsondaye evyn. **1503** *Acc. Ld. High Treas. Scot.* II. 297 To the thre wemen that rokkit and kepit the barnes, thair Witsonday fee, iij li. **1503** *Sc. Acts Jas. IV* (1814) II. 243/2 Apon thurisday in witsonday wolk. *c* **1557** *Wills & Inv. N.C.* (Surtees 1835) I. 153 Debtes..to my lorde of durh'm for whitson daye rent of thold p'ke xlˢ.

So **Whit Monday, Whit Tuesday,** the Monday and Tuesday following Whit Sunday; also †***Whit Wednesday, Thursday,*** formerly called *Whitsun Monday,* etc.: see WHITSUN 1. (***Whit Saturday*** is in occas. recent use for the day before Whit Sunday, formerly called *Whitsun eve.*) So **Whit-week,** the week beginning with Whit Sunday.

1557 Q. MARY in *15th Rep. Hist. MSS. Comm.* App. II. 31 Untill the viiith daye of this present moneth whiche shall be Whitmondaye. **1665** *Wonders if not Miracles V. Gertrux* 5, I went up thither..on White-munday. **1778** *Eng. Gazetteer* (ed. 2) s.v. *Eye,* The market is on Saturday, the fair on Whit-Monday. *Ibid., Linfield,*..with 3 fairs, on May 6, on Whit-Tuesday, and on October 28. *Ibid., Llanbeder,* Cardiganshire..has..fairs on Whit-Wednesday, July 10 [etc.]. **1839** *Penny Cycl.* XIII. 403/1 Whit-Thursday. **1867** tr. *C'tess Hahn-Hahn's Fathers of Desert* 365 In the night between Whitsunday and Whitmonday. **1869** BLACKMORE

Lorna D. lxxiv, It was now Whit-Tuesday, and the lilacs all in blossom. 1899 *Daily News* 18 May 7/1 Whit-week would be a very good time to close the schools.

Whitsuntide ('hwɪtsəntaɪd). Forms (see also TIDE *sb.*): 3 **White-sune tide, wit sonentid,** 3–4 **witeson(e)-,** 3–6 **Wytson-,** 4 **whitson(e)-, Witsun-,** 4–6 **Witson-, Witte-,** 5 **Qhythson-,** 5–6 **Whytson-, (Witsenstyde),** 5–8 **Whitson-,** 7– **Whitsuntide.** *β.* 4 **Wissen-,** 5 **whisson(e)-, Whysson(e-, Whyssen-,** 6 **Whyson-,** 9 *dial.* **Whissontide.** [f. WHITSUN + TIDE *sb.*] The season of Whit Sunday; Whit Sunday and the days immediately following.

c 1205 LAY. 31524 Hit ilomp an ane time to þan Whitesune tide [*later text* Witsontime] þat þe king hehte of londen. 1297 R. GLOUC. (Rolls) 3111 Aȝen þe feste of witesontyd. *a* 1330 *Rouland & V.* (Abbotsf. Club) 16 At Ester, at Wissentide, And at seyn Iames day.., And in Yole. *c* 1440 *Alphabet of Tales* 76 On a tyme when þe grete Emperour Henrie..held his whisson-tyde. 1448 *Paston Lett.* I. 70 Harry Goneld hath browth to me xls.,..and he seyth I xal have more or Qhythson tyd. 1484 CAXTON *Chivalry* v. 52 To make and adoube a knyȝt it apperteyneth the day of some grete feste as Crystemas, Eester, Whitsontyd. 1553 in Sir W. Parker *Hist. Long. Melford* (1873) 97 At Witsenstyde. 1600 MARSTON, etc. *Jack Drum's Entert.* I. (1601) A 3 b, Tis Whitson-tyde, and we must frolick it. 1710 STEELE *Tatler* No. 178 ¶3 We wish..all our Customers a merry Whitsuntide. 1859 TENNYSON *Marr. Geraint* 145 Arthur on the Whitsuntide before Held court at old Caerleon upon Usk. 1916 G. E. BUCKLE *Life of Disraeli* IV. i. 9 After Whitsuntide the general debate was resumed.

†**b.** Used in early versions of N.T. for PENTECOST 1. *Obs.* (Cf. WHIT SUNDAY 1 b.)

1382 WYCLIF *1 Cor.* xvi. 8, I schal dwelle at Effecy, til to Witsuntide [TINDALE, vntill witsontyde; 1551 wytsontyde].

c. *attrib.*

1609 B. JONSON *Silent Wom.* III. i, I would haue you get your Whitsontide-velvet-cap. 1611 CORYAT *Crudities* 9 A Whitsuntide foole..wearing a long coate, wherein there were many seuerall peeces of cloth of diuers colours. 1687 in *Jrnl. Friends' Hist. Soc.* (1915) Oct. 182 Shee is willinge to sett out..after whitsuntide weeke soe called is ouer. *c* 1755 in B. Ward *Hist. St. Edmund's Coll.* (1893) 303 On all working days in ye Xmas and Whitsuntide Vacations. 1916 G. E. BUCKLE *Life of Disraeli* IV. i. 7 The Whitsuntide recess [of Parliament] was approaching.

whitt, obs. dial. f. QUICK *a.*; obs. f. WHITE.

whittawer ('hwɪtɔːə(r)). Now only *Hist.* or *dial.* Forms: 4 **whitetawier, white-tawyer, whit(t)awyer,** 5 **whytetawyer,** 5–7 **white tawyer,** (7 **whiteaw**[r]), 5– **whittawer,** 6–8 **white tawer,** 7–8 **white-tawer,** 9 **whitawer,** *dial.* **w(h)ittor, whittaw,** etc. [f. WHITE *a.* + TAWER[1]. (Cf. the synonymous MDu. *witgaerwer*, MHG. *wizgerwer*, G. *weissgerber*.)] One who taws skins into WHITLEATHER: = TAWER[1]. In mod. dial., a saddler, harness-maker.

1284 *12 Edw. I. Stat. Wallie* c. 4 De Whitauwariis [*v.rr.* Whitawyariis, Whytawyariis], scilicet qui coria bovina & equina furata scienter albificant ut sic non agnoscantur. 13.. *Liber Albus* (Rolls) III. 432 Galfridus le Whitetawier. 1311 *Letter Bk. D. Lond.* lf. 127 Walterus le Whitawyer, Joh'es le Megucer. 1346 *Ibid. F.* lf. 126 b, Les bones gentz appellez Whittawyers. 1411 *Close Roll 12 Hen. IV*, dorso, Willielmus Pratte, White tawyer. 1474 *Cov. Leet Bk.* 401 The sise of a whittawer is that he make nor tawe no maner of lether but Shepis lether, Gettes lethir, deris ledur, horse-lethir, or houndes-lether. 1615 *Manch. Crt. Leet Rec.* (1885) II. 303 Robart Hilton, whiteaw[r]. 1615 MANWOOD *Lawes Forest* xxv. 250 b, If any white Tawyer doe dwell in the forest, he shall be remoued, and make fine: for they are the common dressers of skins of stolne Deere. 1660 SHARROCK *Vegetables* 88 Lime, which the Tanner and White-Tawer take out of their lime-pits. 1720 *Lond. Gaz.* No. 5882/8 William Welden,..Whittawer. *a* 1722 LISLE *Husb.* (1752) 45 Few Harness-makers, that are white tawers, understand how to dress their hides. 1854 MISS BAKER *Northampt. Gloss.*, *Whitawer*, a collar-maker, or maker of husbandry harness. 1859 GEO. ELIOT *Adam Bede* vi, Men are busy there mending the harness, under the superintendence of Mr. Goby the 'whittaw', otherwise saddler.

Hence †**whittawing** *vbl. sb.*, the practice of whittawers.

1581 KITCHIN *Le Crt. Leete* 13 Auxi si ascun per ascun voie corrupt les common ewes per whitawinge per lyme ou per line.

whitte, obs. form of WHIT, WHITE, WIT.

whitten ('hwɪt(ə)n). *dial.* Also 6 *Sc.* **veyton,** 7 **whitting, whiting,** 9 **witten.** [Usually *whitten-tree*, repr. OE. *hwítingtréow*, f. *hwíting* (of identical formation with WHITING *sb.*) + *tréow* TREE.] More fully, ***whitten-tree***. A name for the water elder or wild guelder-rose (*Viburnum Opulus*), and the wayfaring-tree (*V. Lantana*). Also (by confusion with *whicken*, QUICKEN *sb.*[1]), the mountain-ash or rowan (*Pyrus aucuparia*), and some allied plants.

whitten pear-tree, the service-tree (*Pyrus Sorbus*): see quot. 1833 s.v. WHITTY.

c 1100 *Ælfric's Voc.* in Wr.-Wülcker 139/1 *Uariculus*, hwitingtreow. [Identified by Cockayne as *Pyrus Aria*, White-Beam-tree.] 1549 *Compl. Scot.* vi. 67, I sau veyton, the decoctione of it is remeid for ane sair hede. 1578 LYTE *Dodoens* VI. lxxx. 761 Of Marris Elder, Ople, or Dwarffe Plane tree... I take this to be a shrub that is called in Englishe, Whittentree, whereof are two kindes. 1597 GERARDE *Herbal* III. lxxii. 1237 The water Elder is called.. in English Marish Elder, and Whitten tree, Ople tree, and Dwarffe Plane tree. 1636 JOHNSON *Gerarde's Herbal* Table Eng. Names, Whicken tree, i. wilde Ash... Whitten tree, i. water Elder, or wilde Ash. 1668 *Phil. Trans.* III. 857 The Whitting or Quicking-tree, (Lat. *Fraxinus Sylvestris*, and by some *Fraxinus Cambro-Britanica*). *a* 1697 AUBREY (Royal Soc. MS. lf. 137) in Britten & Holland *Plant-n.*, About Cranbourn chace growes..a tree with a white leafe..no bigger than a cherry tree; they call it Whiting or White-wood. 1847 HALLIWELL, *Whitten*, the wayfaring tree. *Kent.* 1868 *Archaeologia* XLII. 125 The Rowan or Quick-beam,.. popularly termed the Mountain Ash.., and, in some counties, the Whiten-tree and the Witty.

whitter ('hwɪtə(r)), *sb.*[1] *Sc.* Also 6–7 **qu(h)-, -our.** [Imitative.] **a.** A talkative person, a chatterer. **b.** Chatter, 'loquacity, prattle' (Jam.). So **whitter-whatter** in same senses.

a 1585 MONTGOMERIE *Flyting* 767 Rank ruittour, scurliquitour [*v. rr.* scurlie whittour, scurliquhittor], and Iuittour. 1805 A. SCOTT *Poems* 47 What need we heed sic whitter-whatter? 1825 JAMIESON s.v., A woman who is very garrulous is said to be 'a perfect whitter-whatter'. 1897 E. HAMILTON *Outlaws Marches* iii, I would counsel you..to haud your whitter the night.

whitter, *sb.*[2] *Sc.* [Cf. WHITTLE *v.*[1]] A draught of liquor, a drink.

1785 BURNS *1st Ep. J. L*****k* xix, We'll sit down an' tak our whitter, To chear our heart.

'**whitter,** *v. Sc.* [Later form of QUITTER *v.*[2]]

1. *intr.* To warble, twitter. *Sc.*

1513 [see QUITTER *v.*[2]]. *c* 1800 *Elfer Hill* 24 in R. Jamieson *Pop. Ball.* (1806) I. 226 The sma' fowls in the shaw began to whitter in the dale.

2. To move lightly and briskly; to quiver, flutter, scamper, etc. *Sc.*

1513 [see QUITTER *v.*[2]]. 1819 W. TENNANT *Papistry Storm'd* (1827) 7 The dows and daws..Out-whirr'd and whitter't. 1894 FLORA A. STEEL *Potter's Thumb* xiii, A '*whittering*' beast..'*Whitter! Whitter!*' under the bed; behind the boxes. That was the worst of a musk-rat; no one could possibly tell where it would '*whitter*' next.

whitter, var. QUITTER *sb.*[1] (sense 2).

1833 SIR C. BELL *Hand* (1834) 296 Sandcracks, whitters, inflammations, and other diseases of the horse's foot.

whitter, var. of WITTER *v.*[2]

whitteret, -ick, var. WHITRET.

whitterish ('hwɪtərɪʃ), *a. dial.* [? Variant of QUITTERISH.] Pale, faded.

1679 *Hist. Jetzer* 14 A pallid whitterish colour. 1854 MISS BAKER *Northampt. Gloss.*, *Whitterish*, faded. Applied to clothes which have lost their colour from the effect of the sun, or frequent washing.

whittie-whattie ('hwɪtɪhwɒtɪ), *sb. Sc.* and *north. dial.* Also 7 **whytie whatie,** 8 **whity-whaty,** 9 **whittee-whattee.** [Reduplicated ? on WHAT *int. pron.*] Vague or undecided talk or statement; indecision, shilly-shallying; a frivolous excuse. So **whittie-whattie** *v. intr.*, to be undecided, to shilly-shally; also, to speak low or secretly, to mutter, whisper.

c 1680 R. MACWARD *Contend.* (1723) 363 The sense and substance of all this whittie whattie..will be only, 'O be quiet' [etc.]. 1692 'J. CURATE' *Sc. Presbyt. Eloq.* 110 Criticks with their frim frams and whytie whaties, may imagine a hundred reasons. 1808 JAMIESON, *Whitie-whaties*, silly pretences;..frivolous excuses. 1821 SCOTT *Pirate* vi, 'What are ye whittie-whattieing about, ye gowk?' said his gentle sister, who suspected the tenor of his murmurs.

whitting, obs. var. WHITING.

whittle ('hwɪt(ə)l), *sb.*[1] Now *dial.* Forms: 1–3 **hwitel,** 4 **whitel, wytel,** 5 **wytele,** 6 **whittel,** 7– **whittle.** [OE. *hwítel*, corresp. to ON. *hvítill* white bed-cover (Norw. *kvitel* blanket); f. *hwít* WHITE *a.* + -EL[1], -LE.] †**a.** A cloak, mantle. †**b.** A blanket. **c.** A baby's woollen napkin or flannel petticoat. **d.** A shawl or wrap.

c 900 tr. *Bæda's Hist.* IV. xxxi, Ða eode þes broðor sume dæge þæt he wolde his reon & his hwitlas [*saga*]..in sæ wæscan. *c* 1000 ÆLFRIC *Gen.* ix. 23 Sem and Iafeth dydon anne hwitel [*pallium*] on hira sculdra. *a* 1225 *Ancr. R.* 214 Boðe schulen beon of wurmes his kurtel [*v.r.* hwitel] & his kuuertur. *a* 1300 *Walter of Henley's Husb.* (1890) 4 Wo þat strechet forþerre þan his wytel wyle reche in þe straue his fet he mot streche. 1393 LANGL. *P. Pl.* C. XVII. 76 When he streyneþ hym to strecche, þe straw is hus whitel. 1422 *Will of Olney* (Somerset Ho.), j wytele & j chete. 1565 COOPER *Thesaurus*, *Crepundia*,..the first apparayle of children, as, swathes, whittels, wastecoates, and such lyke. 1668 in Alice M. Earle *Costume Colon. Times* (1894) 257 A whittle that was fringed. 1697 in C. Worthy *Devon. Wills* (1896) 214 To sister, Rachel Tucker, my largest red whittle. 1700 J. BROME *Trav. Eng.* 234 The [Devonshire] Women have a peculiar sort of Garment, which they wear upon their Shoulders, called Whittles, they are like Mantles with fringes about the edges. 1755 *Connoisseur* No. 80. ¶7 As great a store of caps, clouts, biggens, belly-bands, whittles, and all kinds of childbed-linnen, as would set up a Lying-in Hospital. 1850 SMEDLEY *F. Fairlegh* xiv, I sought out the..old lady, whose shawl I had so unceremoniously made use of [to extinguish fire]... I believe..she considered Miss Saville's safety dearly purchased at the expense of her favourite whittle. 1871 MRS. H. WOOD *Dene Hollow* xxiv, In a coarse red shawl —or, as it was called then, 'whittle',..Emma Geash started.

whittle ('hwɪt(ə)l), *sb.*[2] Now *dial.* Forms: 4 **qwetyll,** 5 **whyttel,** 6 **whittell,** *Sc.* **quhittil,** 7 **whitle,** 6– **whittle.** [Variant of THWITTLE; cf. *whack*, *whang*.] A knife, esp. one of a large size, as a carving-knife, a butcher's knife, or one carried as a weapon; also, a clasp-knife.

1404 *Nottingham Rec.* II. 22, j. whyttel, j d. 14.. *Stockholm Med. MS.* I. 446 in *Anglia* XVIII. 306 Schrape of þe ouerest bark with a qwetyll. 1515 BARCLAY *Egloges* III. (1570) B vj/1 The scullians..Came some with whittels, some other with fleshhokes. 1570 [see quot. 1470 s.v. THWITTLE *sb.*]. *a* 1586 SIDNEY *Arcadia* III. (1912) 434 He thought best..with a great whittle he had..to cut his throate, which he had used so with Calves, as he had no small dexteritie in it. 1592 GREENE *Greene's Vis.* Wks. (Grosart) XII. 209 A whittell by his belt he beare. 1608 WINGFIELD *Disc. Virg.* in *Archæol. Amer.* IV. 99 No penny whitle was asked of me, but a kniffe, whereof I had none to spare. 1653 GATAKER *Vind. Annot. Jer.* 136 We shall not need to borrow great Alexanders whiniard to cut this Gordian knot asunder, any sory whittle will serve the turn. 1668 DRYDEN *Even. Love* IV. (1671) 70 Here's the sixpenny whittle you gave me, with the Mutton haft: I can spare it, for knives are of little use in Spain. 1724 RAMSAY *Tea-t. Misc.* (1733) II. 181 A rousty whittle to sheer the kail. 1806 *Gazetteer Scot.* (ed. 2) 294 The knives [of Kilmaurs] were so much famed, that a Kilmaur's [*sic*] whittle became proverbial. 1821 SCOTT *Kenilw.* xxvii, Beshrew me,..but thou art sharper than a Sheffield whittle! [Cf. quot. *c* 1386 s.v. THWITTLE *sb.*] 1841 T. PARKER *Crit. & Misc. Writ.* v. (1848) 117 He wears a beaver hat, and a coat of English cloth, and has a Birmingham whittle, and a watch in his pocket. 1853 G. J. CAYLEY *Las Alforjas* I. 61 In the fingers of his right [hand] was a crooked whittle, with which..as the basketfuls arrived, he would nick the score upon notch-sticks.

b. *Comb.*: **whittle-gait (-gate),** see quot. 1804; **whittle-knife,** a whittle.

1804 R. ANDERSON *Cumbld. Ball.* (1805) 144 In some parts of Cumberland..he not only receives quarter-pence, but is provided with victuals at the homes of his scholars, which he visits in succession. This *whittle-gait (as it is called) subjects him however to the toil of travelling. 1825 BROCKETT *N.C. Gloss.* s.v., 'An harden sark, a guse grassing, and a whittle gait', were all the salary of a clergyman, not many years ago, in Cumberland. 1735 *Phil. Trans.* XXXIX. 76 The *Whittle-Knife, with the Box-Handle. *a* 1811 LEYDEN *Malay Annals* (1821) 54 In his hand was a whittle knife without the haft.

whittle, *sb.*[3] *Sc.* and *north. dial.* Also 6–7 **whittell,** 9 *Sc.* **whuttle.** Reduced form of WHITLOW. Also †**whittle-flaw** = *whitflaw* (see WHITLOW); **whittle-grass,** melilot (cf. *whitlow-grass*).

1596 J. MELVILL *Autob. & Diary* (Wodrow Soc.) 366 We feill mair a whittell in our fingar nor the helthe of the haill body. 1756 C. LUCAS *Ess. Waters* II. 66 Sea-water..relieves whittle-flaws before they exulcerate. 1774 MACLAURIN *Argts. & Decis.* 94 A distemper incident to the thumb, vulgarly called the whittle. 1825 JAMIESON, *Whuttle-grass.*

†'**whittle,** *v.*[1] *Obs.* Also 6 **whittel, whyttel(l, whityll,** 6–7 **whitle.** [Usually taken to be a fig. use of next (cf. WHET *v.* 6), but evidence is wanting.] *trans.* To ply with drink, to make drunk, intoxicate; in *pa. pple.* excited by drink, drunk, intoxicated. Hence **whittled** *ppl. a.*, **whittling** *vbl. sb.*

1530 PALSGR. 500 Whan he is well whyttelled, he wyll crake goodly of his manhode, *quant il a bien beu* [etc.]. *Ibid.* 844 Well whytled, nere dronken. 1543 BECON *Invective agst. Swearing* 24 Whan they are once set vpon the ale benche, and well whytled in theyr braynes thorow the many cuppes that haue bene fylled in. *c* 1566 *Merie Tales of Skelton* in Wks. 1843 I. p. lxiii, Skelton did fill all the cuppes..and whitled the frere. 1593 G. HARVEY *Pierce's Super.* 44 What? gorge vpon gorge, egges vpon egges, & sack vpon sacke?.. Such egging and whitling may happen bring you acquainted with the triumphant chariot of rotten egges. 1601 HOLLAND *Pliny* XIV. xxii. I. 427 When they..be throughly whitled,.. then..the secrets of the heart are opened. 1652 URQUHART *Jewel* 126 Drinking healths,..whitling themselves with Septembral juyce. 1694 MOTTEUX *Rabelais* v. Prognost. v. 236 Whittled, Mellow, Cupshotten Swillers.

whittle, *v.*[2] Also 6–7 **whitle.** [f. WHITTLE *sb.*[2]]

I. 1. a. *trans.* To cut thin slices or shavings from the surface of (a stick, etc.); to dress or pare with a knife; to reduce or sharpen by doing this. Also with *down* (cf. sense 2).

1552 HULOET, Whitle a thinge small, or sharpe like a shafte, *inspico*. 1590 FENNE *Frutes* Ded., The Persians..use commonly to whittle small twigs of birch, to keepe themselves from..idle cogitations. 1614 PURCHAS *Pilgrimage* IV. iv. (ed. 2) 353 Cambyses..whitling a sticke to passe away the time. 1639 J. CLARKE *Paræm.* 262 He will whittle an oke to a butcher[s] pricke. 1658 OSBORN *Mem. King James* To Rdr., A huge blame is due to such as mannage their pens no lesse impertinently then clowns do their knives and hatchets, with which..they deface and whittle the sacred graves..of great persons. 1662 ATWELL *Faithf. Surveyor* 13 You must have ten sticks about a foot long apiece, whitled and sharpned at the great end. 1724 E. WARD *Dancing Devils* 32 As Lawyers Clerks,..Instead of minding Bonds or Leases, Sit whitt'ling useful Pens to pieces. 1842 DICKENS *Amer. Notes* xiv, The captain..seated himself astride of one of these barrels,..and pulling a great clasp-knife out of his pocket, began to 'whittle' it..by paring thin slices off the edges. 1913 JANE E. HARRISON *Anc. Art & Ritual* iv. 94 These wands..are whittled at the top into spiral shavings. 1972 D. BLOODWORTH *Any Number can Play* xii. 103 A young orang..tried poking it [*sc.* a hole in a log] with a twig that was too thick, then whittled down the twig. 1979 J. HARVEY *Plate Shop* xv. 72 Ted put his feet up on the tin waste-paper box..and started absorbedly hewing and whittling a pencil down to the stub.

b. *transf.* To wear away or reduce by a process analogous to paring: see quots.

1736 *Gentl. Mag.* Aug. 457/1, I am told they'll..whittle You down twenty or thirty Legs of Mutton into one sorry Dish. **1837** EMERSON *Addr., Amer. Schol.* Wks. (Bohn) II. 181 Like those Savoyards who getting their livelihood by carving shepherds [etc.]..went out one day to the mountain to find stock, and discovered that they had whittled up the last of their pine-trees. **1854** MISS BAKER *Northampt. Gloss.* s.v., A saddle which pinches a horse's shoulder whittles the skin. **1860** GOUGER *Impris. in Burmah* xix. 213 The operator succeeded in whittling out [of a wen] a something which..resembled..two or three inches of a large dew-worm. **1860** SALA *Badd. Peer.* I. xviii. 312 An American gentleman..who, having tried to dissipate the *ennui* of the evening by a succession of juleps, had resorted to whittling the 'Liverpool Albion' up into fine shreds.

c. *absol.* or *intr.*

1614 [see *whittling* vbl. sb., below]. **1825** J. NEAL *Bro. Jonathan* I. 144 A..fellow..who was whittling in the corner. **1839** MARRYAT *Diary Amer.* Ser. I. II. 175 She was the first and only lady in America that I observed to whittle. **1880** MARY FITZGIBBON *Trip to Manitoba* xi. 133 He whittled away at a stick.

2. *fig.* To reduce or make smaller by successive abstractions; to diminish the amount, force, or importance of; to 'cut *down*'; to take *away* by degrees, so as to reduce to nothing.

1746 WALPOLE *Lett. to Mann* (1834) II. 169 We have whittled down our loss extremely. **1780** M. MADAN tr. *Thelyphthora* I. 126 Not..whittling away the strong, noble, manly sense of scripture, into the ridiculous whims and fancies of visionaries. **1862** *Major Jack Downing* (1867) 74 You estemated the receipts from land sales, in July, at $3,000,000. You cut it down in December to $2,300,000; and now Congress, by passing the Homestead bill, will whittle it all off. **1884** *Times* (weekly ed.) 17 Oct. 4/1 If Parliament is whittled down so that nothing remains of it but the House of Commons. **1888** M. BURROWS *Cinque Ports* vii. 171 The Ports were annually reminded of the extent to which their ancient supremacy had been whittled away.

3. To make or shape by whittling; to carve. Also *fig.*

1848 LOWELL *Let. to S. H. Gay* 5 May, I have contrived to whittle out something..for you in time for the mail. **1865** *Lond. Rev.* 30 Dec. 686/1 Robinson Crusoe whittled a diary upon a stick. **1895** ELIZ. S. PHELPS *Chapters from Life* i. 14 She is whittling little wooden feet to stretch the children's stockings on.

II. 4. *intr.* To worry or fret. Occas. *trans. dial.*

1880 *N. & Q.* 6 Mar. 205/2 When I was a boy my mother daily used this word to express fidgetiness or uneasiness. 'What are you *whittling* about?' seems to ring in my ears at this moment. **1913** D. H. LAWRENCE *Sons & Lovers* viii. 202 'How do you think I'm going to manage?' 'Well, it won't make it any better to whittle about it.' **1984** *Daily Tel.* 23 Oct. 10/3 'I'm whittled to death about the future of the mining industry.' These, or words like these, are attributed to Mr. Michael Eaton, the new character in the long-runnning serial story of the mining dispute.

Hence **whittled** (-(ə)ld) *ppl. a.*; also *whittled-down*; **whittling** *vbl. sb.*, (*a*) the action of the verb (also *attrib.*); (*b*) *concr.* (in *pl.*) fragments cut off in whittling, shavings; also *fig.*; **whittling** *ppl. a.*, that whittles, addicted to whittling. Also **whittler**, one who whittles, or is addicted to whittling as an idle trick.

1792 G. CARTWRIGHT *Jrnl. Labrador* III. p. x, *Whittled-sticks, sticks from which beavers have eaten the bark. **1884** GILMOUR *Mongols* 244 The bow..was a bent and whittled branch of some shrub. **1961** A. BROWNJOHN in E. Lucie-Smith *Brit. Poetry since 1945* (1970) 266 Farmers call hillocks And ponds..By the first words to hand; a heavy, *whittled-down Simplicity meets the need. **1962** E. SNOW *Other Side of River* (1963) xxiv. 183 If any of these somewhat blind guesses are right, the whittled-down results still remain impressive. **1980** M. BOOTH *Bad Track* ii. 34 Long streets with a whittled-down green, a church..a pub. **1839** MARRYAT *Diary Amer.* Ser. I. I. 236 In some courts they put sticks before noted *whittlers to save the furniture. **1907** *Elem. School Teacher* Mar. 393 No one thinks of denying him the pocket-knife because of the fear that its use will result in his becoming a mere whittler. **1614** PURCHAS *Pilgrimage* IV. v. (ed. 2) 364 He spent the time in *whitling with a knife. **1839** MARRYAT *Diary Amer.* Ser. I. II. 4 Each knife having two pen-blades, one whittling blade. **1854** C. GREATREX (*title*) Whittlings from the West. **1875** HOWELLS *Foregone Conclus.* iii. 61 Litter of shavings and whittlings strewed the floor. **1885** PROCTOR *Whist* Pref. 10 The Whist Whittlings include Whist stories, maxims, notes. **1849** LEVER *Con Cregan* xx, I am no lazy,..*whittling, tobacco-chewing Texan!

whittle, *v.*³ (*slang*), var. WHIDDLE, to 'peach'.

1727 SWIFT *Clever Tom Clinch* 16 Tom..said, I must speak to the People a little, But I'll see you all damn'd before I will whittle. **1874** *Slang Dict., Whittle*, to nose or peach.

whittret, -it, -ick, var. WHITRET.

Whit Tuesday: see after WHIT SUNDAY.

whitty ('hwɪtɪ). *dial.* Also 9 witty. Usually *whitty-tree* = WHITTEN-*tree*.

a **1686** AUBREY *Nat. Hist. Wilts* (1847) 56 Whitty-tree, or wayfaring tree, is rare in this country. **1853** E. LEES *Affin. Plants* (1834) 63 The true-service or sorb-tree... This tree..is called the whitty or witten pear-tree, its fruit being exactly similar to very small pears. **1847** HALLIWELL, *Whitty-tree*, the mountain ash. *West. Ibid., Witty* (L), the mountain ash. *Salop.* **1868** Witty [see WHITTEN].

whitwall, var. WITWALL, woodpecker.

Whitworth ('hwɪtwəθ). [f. name of the inventor: see below.]

a. In full, ***Whitworth gun*** or ***rifle***: A form of rifle (either cannon or small arm) invented by Sir Joseph Whitworth of Manchester (1854), having a hexagonal bore with a rapid twist, and firing an elongated shot. Also *attrib.*

Whitworth metal or ***steel***, a specially strong make of steel cast under hydraulic pressure, used for ordnance and for other purposes.

1858 GREENER *Gunnery* 380 The Whitworth has also a greater range, but at a cost of 300 per cent. more friction... The production of the Whitworth rifle will always be looked upon as an experiment of very great interest. **1860** *All Year Round* No. 73. 549 The Armstrong gun..is a built gun..; the Whitworth is a casting of what is called 'homogeneous iron'. **1863** in *Harvard Mem. Biogr.* (1866) I. 251 One family had a Whitworth shot through their house yesterday. **1868** *Rep. Brit. Assoc. Adv. Sci.* Not. & Abstr. 195 No. 1 projectile is Whitworth steel. **1869** *Ibid.* (1870) 439 A projectile of 'Whitworth' metal. **1902** P. MARSHALL *Metal Working Tools* 63 For very small threads up to about ¼ in. diameter, the British Association thread is generally used, while beyond this size the Whitworth Standard is the best.

b. Used *attrib.* and †in the possessive to designate a series of screw threads proposed by Whitworth in 1841 (and later additions to it), fasteners having one of these threads, and tools for use with the fasteners.

[**1841** *Proc. Inst. Civil Engineers* I. 157 (*heading*) 'On an uniform system of screw threads.' By Joseph Whitworth.] **1877** *Calvert's Mechanics' Almanack* 4 The terms, 'Whitworth's Threads', 'Whitworth Taps'..have sprung from the lips of all concerned with the iron trade. **1916** *Proc. Inst. Automobile Engineers* XI. 176 We all imagined that the Whitworth system for the larger sizes of screws was so perfect that there would be no difficulty in making sure that Whitworth nuts would fit Whitworth bolts sufficiently well for all practical purposes. **1968** J. ARNOLD *Shell Bk. Country Crafts* 160 Until the advent of the Whitworth thread, which standardized threads all over the country, it was the practice for smiths to tap their own threads. **1970** *Kay & Co.* (Worcester) *Catal.* 1970–71 Autumn/Winter 770/2 Ring Spanners... Available in Whitworth, AF or Metric sizes. **1972** *Practical Motorist* Oct. 209/1 Whitworth fasteners are no longer in general use, although you will encounter them on older cars.

whity, whitey ('hwaɪtɪ), *a.* (*adv.*) Also 6 whitty. [f. WHITE *a.* + -Y¹ 2.] = WHITISH.

1593 Q. ELIZ. *Boeth.* II. met. iii. 26 Whan Φebus..the light to spred begins, The star dimed..Pales her whitty lookes. **1862** C. P. SMYTH *Three Cities in Russia* II. 139 Lofty rooms of a whity style of decoration. **1897** J. HOCKING *Birthright* xiii, She fixed her whitey, shining eyes upon me.

b. *esp.* (quasi-*adv.*) with other adjs. (or *adj.* with sbs.) of colour. See also WHITY-BROWN.

1856 DE QUINCEY *Confess.* Wks. 1862 I. 139 The insipid whity-grey bread of towns. **1879** E. O'DONOVAN *Merv Oasis* (1882) I. 311 The Shah's yacht..is painted of a dirty whity-yellow colour. **1897** MARY KINGSLEY *W. Africa* 575 A great sedum, with a grand head of whity-pink flower.

'whity-'brown, *a.* (*sb.*) [WHITY *a.* b.]

1. Of a brown colour inclining to white; whitish brown; pale brown: most commonly of paper. As *sb.* (properly two words) a whitish brown; *ellipt.* = whity-brown paper.

1777 THICKNESSE *Journ. France* (1789) II. 104 The frequent marriages of these men..with white women, and the succession of black, brown, and whity brown people, produced by these very unnatural..alliances. **1786** MME. D'ARBLAY *Diary* 2 Aug., She seized a piece of whity-brown paper. **1815** *Zeluca* II. 83 Detestable Creature, with her whity-brown hair. **1816** COLMAN *Broad Grins, Mr. Champernoune* vii, A paper coarse in grain; For England's monarchs then were fain To handle whitey-brown. **1862** THACKERAY *Philip* xix, Whitey-brown bread. **1876** HARDY *Ethelberta* (1890) 17 A little green leather sheath, worn at the edges to whitey-brown.

2. *fig.* Neither one thing nor another, neutral, undecided, half-and-half.

1892 *Spectator* 19 Mar. 391/1 Let us..have no whitey-brown men. **1895** *Westm. Gaz.* 28 Dec. 8/2 The whitey-brown men, a political tribe of undecided colour,..who side with any party.

whiver ('hwɪvə(r)), obs. or dial. f. QUIVER *v.*²

1581 J. BELL *Haddon's Answ. Osor.* 37 It is not a whivering voyce of a vow..that can..quench..those..flames of naturall corruption. **1606** BIRNIE *Kirk-Buriall* (1833) 10 Stately standerts and punicall pinsels, displayed for whivering in the winde. **1825** JENNINGS *Obs. Dial. W. Eng.*, To *Whiver*, to hover.

whizgig ('hwɪzgɪg). [f. WHIZ(Z + GIG *sb.*¹] An object that whizzes round, as a revolving humming toy: cf. WHIZZER a, FIZGIG 2. Also *attrib.* So **whiz-jig** [cf. JIG *sb.*¹ 6], in quot. applied (? allusively) to a pumping apparatus.

1821 M. EDGEWORTH *Let.* 22 Nov. (1971) 279 A Whizgig for Pakenham in my next. **1848** THACKERAY *Bk. Snobs* xxxv, A bed about the size of one of those whizgig temples in which the Genius appears in a pantomime. **1891** *Cent. Dict., Whizgig*, a mechanical toy. **1891** *Century Mag.* Dec. 248 A labor-saving whiz-jig was now devised.

whizz, whiz (hwɪz), *sb.*¹ [f. WHIZZ, WHIZ *v.*]

1. a. An act, or the action, of whizzing; a sibilant sound somewhat less shrill than a hiss, and having a trace of musical tone like a buzz; a swift movement producing such a sound.

1620 T. GRANGER *Div. Logike* 201* Through skies by night shee flingeth, and Her whizze earth's darknesse teares. **1682** BUNYAN *Holy War* 74 Their shot would go by their ears with a Whizz. **1713** *Guardian* No. 92 ⁋5 He never once Duck'd at the whizz of a Cannon Ball. **1798** COLERIDGE *Anc. Mar.* III. xvii, Like the whizz of my cross-bow. **1848** MRS. GASKELL *Mary Barton* xxvi, The..whiz and scream of the arriving trains. *c* **1850** 'Dow jr.' in Jerdan *Yankee Hum.* (1853) 78 Shall we lumber along the road, and allow other nations to pass us with a whiz? **1897** MEREDITH *Amazing Marr.* ix, Amid a whizz of scythe-blades.

b. The practice of picking pockets (chiefly in phr. ***on the whizz***); a pickpocket. *slang* (orig. and chiefly *U.S.*).

1925 E. JERVIS *25 Yrs. in Six Prisons* i. 17 Some of the boys are 'on the whiz' (pickpockets). **1931** *Amer. Speech* VII. 117 *Whiz*, n. A pick-pocket. **1936** 'J. CURTIS' *Gilt Kid* 245 They might pinch him for being on the whizz. **1963** T. TULLETT *Inside Interpol* xii. 162 The pickpocket, known in the underworld as the 'whiz'..is always a specialist.

2. *U.S. slang.* An agreement, 'bargain'.

The relation to sense 1 is not clear.

1869 'MARK TWAIN' *Innoc. Abr.* xl, They said, each to his fellow, Let us sleep here..And each..said, It is a whiz. **1876** —— *Tom Sawyer* xxxiv, 'If we don't find it, I'll agree to give you my drum and everything I've got.'..'All right—it's a whiz.' **1888** *New York Times* 30 Dec., 'You will have to play that you are a boy, that I am master..Is it a whizz?' he asked.

3. An act of urination. *slang.*

1971 D. CLARK *Sick to Death* i. 21 She could have left him alone..while she went for a whizz or changed her clothes.

4. *attrib.* and *Comb.*, as **whizz-boy, -man** *slang*, a pickpocket; **whizz-mob** *slang*, a gang of pickpockets.

1931 M. ALLINGHAM *Police at Funeral* vii. 95 How many murders do we get in this class... It's navvies, whizz-boys, car thieves..who run off the rails and commit murder. **1938** F. CHESTER *Shot Full* xxv. 285, I used to frequent a number of public-houses, used by 'the boys', as criminals are known among the English. There were screwsmen,..'whizz-men', ..and 'drag-men'. **1959** *Listener* 12 Mar. 485/1 The quick-fingered craft of those whom the Elizabethans called nips and we call whizz boys. **1932** 'S. WOOD' *Shades Prison House* xix. 278 There one may rub shoulders with..thieves of every type, whiz-men, burglars, car-bandits. **1929** G. DILNOT *Triumphs of Detection* iv. 47 A 'wizz mob' which operated, say, at Hammersmith Broadway, would immediately suspend business..if they saw a local detective in the vicinity. **1941** J. PHELAN *Murder by Numbers* v. 53 'Putting a smother they call it... Crowd cover up something...' 'I see. Like a whizz mob—pickpockets, I mean.' **1955** D. WEBB *Deadline for Crime* iii. 52 Provincial police forces looked to him for help when they wanted their towns cleared of the 'whiz mob', as English pickpockets are known in the underworld.

whizz, whiz (hwɪz), *sb.*² *slang* (orig. *U.S.*). Also wiz (wɪz). [Perh. identical with WHIZZ *sb.*¹, but in sense 1 b also regarded as f. WIZ(ARD *sb.*]

1. a. Something very remarkable.

1908 G. H. LORIMER *Jack Spurlock* vii. 157 It is not only a whiz, but a hummah! You are in on the ground flo' of King Solomon's Mines, Limited. **1920** F. SCOTT FITZGERALD *This Side of Paradise* I. ii. 45 'Wonderful night.' 'It's a whiz.' **1959** *Times* 7 Dec. 13/3 Here are some of the gifts I have given to children in recent years: a massive iron key that could surely unlock the deepest dungeon in Nottingham Castle and makes a whizz of a paper-weight.

b. A person who is wonderfully skilful or talented in some respect.

1914 'HIGH JINKS, JR.' *Choice Slang* 20 A person is designated as a 'Whizz' when he has exceptional ability along one or more lines. **1921** H. CRANE *Let.* 1 Oct. (1965) 66, I..have a strong notion that as a copy writer I will eventually make a 'whiz'. **1924** W. M. RAINE *Troubled Waters* xiii. 142 Millie done fixed my game laig up with that ointment good as new. I want to tell you-all that girl is a wiz. **1928** S. LEWIS *Man who knew Coolidge* i. 36 He thinks he's such a wiz at cars, but..he couldn't locate that squeak. **1948** A. HUXLEY *Ape & Essence* (1949) 69 He's an absolute whizz at Malicious Animal Magnetism. **1962** E. B. WHITE *Let.* 13 July (1976) 493 You chose a real whiz..when you picked me for your grammarian. **1978** S. BRILL *Teamsters* vi. 211 Malnik was well known..as an associate of long-time mob financial wiz Meyer Lansky. **1982** *Financial Times* 22 June 9/2 He has since become a whizz at ping pong. **1984** *New Yorker* 9 July 35/3 Little Nick Silver, a math whiz from Toughkenamon..was the youngest kid at camp. **1984** *Times* 18 Oct. 14/6, I have a whizz of an accountant who will probably arrange things.

2. *Comb.*: **whiz(z)-kid**, an exceptionally successful or brilliant young person, esp. in politics or business; hence **whiz(z)-kiddery**, the phenomenon of whizz-kids; the style or mode of work of a whizz-kid.

1960 *Time* 21 Nov. 100/1 The 'Whiz Kids'—as the team soon was known. **1962** *Economist* 22 Dec. 1202/1 Critics..regard President Kennedy as a quiz-kid surrounded by whiz-kids. **1966** OGILVY & ANDERSON *Excursions in Number Theory* ix. 103 Zerah Colburn was an early nineteenth-century mathematical whiz-kid. **1967** *Economist* 24 June 1353/3 The whole programme has been a curious hotch-potch of whiz-kidery, preconceived theory and painstaking trial-and-error pragmatism. **1976** *Observer* 26 Sept. 8/1 Many in the institutions—banks insurance companies, investment funds, Stock Exchange and so on—who swallowed whizz-kiddery in its myriad forms. **1976** *Time* 27 Dec. 13/1 The sin of Whiz Kid Shelepin was that he tried to build a political base from which to promote his own post-Brezhnev candidacy for the top post. **1977** M. DRABBLE *Ice Age* I. 27 Anthony was watching unedited film of an interview with Len the property whizz kid. **1977** *Times* 4 July 22/3 Whizz-kiddery is out; gravitas is in. **1980** *Times Lit. Suppl.* 3 Oct. 1079/5 Editors are a humble and obscure race; lacking the glamour of the whiz-kids and wheeler-dealers.., they are rarely seen in polite society, their names unknown to the columns of *The Bookseller*. **1981** *Sunday Express* 25 Jan. 17/1 Prime Minister Margaret Thatcher will meet Britain's latest whizz-kid inventor when she hosts a unique gathering of inventors and financiers at Downing Street tomorrow. **1985** *Times* 22 June 9/5 We have often been tempted to listen to the siren voices of those who would advise..the latest radical church services, guitars and steel bands and other forms of whizkiddery.

whizz, whiz, *v.* Also 6 **whize**, 7 **whizze**, 6, 9 *dial.* **whuz(z**. [Echoic. Cf. HIZZ.]

1. a. *intr.* To make a sound as of a body rushing through the air (see WHIZZ *sb.*[1]); (of trees) to rustle; (of a burning or hot object) to hiss, sizzle. Now *dial.*

a **1547** SURREY *Æneis* II. 535 As wrastling windes.. Befight themselves,.. The woods do whiz. **1582** STANYHURST *Æneis* II. (Arb.) 67 Thee flams surmounting tenements doo whize to the skyward. **1589** [see WHIZZING *ppl. a.*]. **1627** MAY *Lucan* VI. 199 The fire whizzes in burning eyes. **1675** DRYDEN *Aurengz.* v. (1676) 85 'Tis dry—'twill burn—Ha, ha! how my old Husband crackles there!.. I know him; he'll but whiz, and strait go out. **1711** SWIFT *Jrnl. to Stella* 10 Apr., Is Dilly gone to the Bath? His face will whiz in the water. **1763** COLMAN *Terræ-Filius* No. 1. ⁋4 Some queer old Gentleman may be alarmed at the Crackers bouncing about his Ears,.. or a Squib whizzing in his Periwig. **1787** GROSE *Prov. Gloss., Whiz*, to hiss like hot iron in water. **1841** S. WARREN *Ten Thou.* i, The sound of his tea-kettle, hissing, whizzing, sputtering in the agonies of boiling over.

†**b.** To wheeze. *Obs.*

1607 [see WHIZZING *vbl. sb.*]. **1611** COTGR. s.v. *Pigeonneau, Il a mangé les pigeonneaux*, said of a man that whizzes, or speakes hoarse. **1688** HOLME *Armoury* II. 134/2 A Baboon Whizeth, hath a Shrill Whizing. **1748** [see WHIZZING *ppl. a.* b].

2. a. To move swiftly with or as with such a sound.

1591 HARINGTON *Orl. Fur.* IX. lxix, The shot, gainst which no armour can suffice,.. Doth whiz, and sing. **1601** SHAKS. *Jul. C.* II. i. 44 The exhalations, whizzing in the ayre, Giue so much light, that I may reade by them. *c* **1611** CHAPMAN *Iliad* XXII. 123 The Hauke comes whizzing on. **1697** DRYDEN *Æneis* XI. 1169 When the Jav'lin whizz'd along the Skies. *a* **1721** SHEFFIELD (Dk. Buckhm.) *Wks.* (1723) II. 8 Both of us sitting together on the quarter-deck, heard a bullet whizzing over our heads. **1814** WORDSW. *Excurs.* VII. 741 How the quoit Whizzed from the Stripling's arm! **1853** HAWTHORNE *Eng. Note-bks.* (1883) I. 423 The small, black steamers, whizzing industriously along. **1914** 'IAN HAY' *Knt. on Wheels* xiii. §2 Watching for the motors that whizzed.. along the straight white road.

b. *fig.* To have a sensation of such a sound.

1797, 1854 [see WHIZZING *vbl. sb.*]. **1865** DARWIN in *Life & Lett.* (1887) III. 34 Reading makes my head whiz. **1898** [see WHIZZING *vbl. sb.*].

3. *trans.* To cause to whizz; to hurl, shoot, or convey swiftly with a whizz; *spec.* in technical use, to dry by centrifugal force in a rapidly revolving apparatus (cf. WHIZZER b).

1836 W. IRVING *Astoria* xlv, He was on the point of whizzing a bullet into the target. **1880** MEREDITH *Tragic Com.* vii, A Balearic slinger about to whizz the stone. **1882** CROOKES *Dyeing & Tissue-Printing* 228 Enter at 112° F., raise to a boil in three turns, wash well, whiz, and dry. **1884** W. S. B. MCLAREN *Spinning* (ed. 2) 39 Most of the wool is 'whizzed' after drying.

4. *intr.* To urinate. *slang.*

1929 D. H. LAWRENCE *Pansies* 24, I wish I was a gentleman As full of wet as a watering-can To whizz in the eye of a police-man. **1976** R. B. PARKER *Promised Land* vii. 37, I wondered if anyone had ever whizzed on Allan Pinkerton's shoe.

whizz, whiz, *int.* and *adv.* An exclamation imitating the sound described under WHIZZ *sb.*[1] and *v.*; as *adv.* = with a whizz. Cf. GEE WHIZ(Z *int.*, WHIZZ-BANG *int.*, *sb.* and *a.*

1812 H. & J. SMITH *Rej. Addr., Fire & Ale*, The water.. bubbled and simmer'd and started off, whizz! **1818** SCOTT *Br. Lamm.* xx, Whiz went the bolt. **1869** BROWNING *Ring & Bk.* XII. 347 When whiz and thump went axe.

whizz-bang ('hwɪzbæŋ), *int.*, *sb.*, and *a. slang.* Also **whiz-bang**, without hyphen, and as two words. [f. WHIZZ, WHIZ *v.* or *int.* + BANG *sb.*[1]]

A. *int.* Expressing a whizzing sound that ends with a thud or explosion, such as may be heard as a bullet or shell strikes a target.

1836 DICKENS *Pickw.* (1837) ii. 9 Fired a musket.. rushed into wine shop.. back again—whiz, bang. *c* **1838** C. MATHEWS in M. R. Booth *Eng. Plays of 19th Cent.* (1973) IV. 133 She called in a farmer.. Who loaded his blunderbuss.. Whizz, bang! Lord, I thought I was murdered outright. **1920** LIPSCOMB *Staff Tales* 59 Whizz-bang! Something grazes parapet.

B. *sb.* **1.** *colloq.* The shell of a small-calibre high-velocity German gun, so called from the noise it made.

1915 'IAN HAY' *1st Hund. Thous.* xviii, A whizz-bang is a particularly offensive form of shell which bursts two or three times over, like a Chinese cracker. **1918** W. OWEN *Poems* (1920) 16 What murk of air remained stank old, and sour With fumes of whizz-bangs. **1923** KIPLING *Irish Guards in Gt. War* I. 143 Three men killed in the line by a single whizz-bang. **1968** J. R. ACKERLEY *My Father & Myself* vi. 51 In 1918, just before the Armistice, he was killed by a whizz-bang. **1979** S. WILSON *Vampire* II. 56 Those guns. Those ever present guns. Eighty-eights. Whizz-bangs. None of us need to be reminded of the names.

2. A resounding success; a marvel.

1916 in *Amer. Speech 1972* (1975) XLVII. 116 Masson is a whizbang at getting up the kind of food that makes the troops want to fight. **1944** T. H. WISDOM *Triumph over Tunisia* 182 The raid was a whizz-bang, the R.A.F. expression denoting something highly successful. **1978** M. PUZO *Fools Die* xvi. 169 These were the sharpest kids in America, the future business giants, judges, show business whizbangs. **1983** *Listener* 14 July 37/1 George Stevens.. knew how to make box-office whizz-bangs but not very interesting movies.

3. A firework that jumps around making a whizzing noise and periodic bangs.

1960 J. LODWICK *Asparagus Trench* 53, I carried.. whizz-bang fireworks, harmless but disconcerting pyrotechnical trivia these, by reason of their strange gyrations. **1983** D. LAMBERT *Judas Code* iii. 55 He lit three more firecrackers—Whizz Bangs they were called.

C. *adj.* **a.** Excellent. **b.** Fast-paced, very lively; spectacular.

1959 I. & P. OPIE *Lore & Lang. Schoolch.* ix. 161 Other superlatives currently in favour are:.. swell, whizzing, whiz-bang, whizzo. **1963** *Economist* 5 Jan. 28/1 Americans are often the first to admit that sometimes a whiz-bang quality about their methods tends to upset their friends. **1965** *Listener* 16 Sept. 431/1 I'm not suggesting that programmes on the arts should be as whizz-bang as *The Dick Van Dyke Show*, but I do suspect that Drama and Light Entertainment could teach them a lot. **1967** *Spectator* 8 Dec. 725/2 A sculptor whose inventions.. are made for prolonged contemplation when much work is made for whizzbang impact. **1972** *National Observer* (U.S.) 27 May 20/5 Bernstein inclines to brisk tempos; it would be interesting to see a regiment actually try marching to his whiz-bang 'Stars and Stripes Forever'. **1984** *Listener* 5 Jan. 8/3 As for home-grown, whizzbang, laugh-a-line comedy—Channel 4, where are you?

Hence as *v. trans.*, to shoot whizz-bangs at; **whizz-banged** *ppl. a.*

1918 G. FRANKAU *One of Them* ix. 66 How oft, in some wild Western whizz-banged dug-out.. Has my soul flown from Staff-emitted paper To the glad days, when from my purse I'd lug out That last fat stake. **1919** *King's Royal Rifle Corps Chron. 1916* 139 This line was whizz-banged heartily. **1928** BLUNDEN *Undertones of War* iv. 35 Some of us were just in time, when next the enemy gunners whizzbanged here, to jump down from the fire-step into a dugout stairway.

whizzer ('hwɪzə(r)). [f. WHIZZ *v.* + -ER[1].]

1. Something that whizzes; *spec.* **a.** a toy that makes a whizzing noise when whirled round; **b.** a machine for drying various articles by the centrifugal force of rapid revolution; a hydro-extractor. Cf. SPIN-DRIER, -DRYER.

1881 TYLOR in *Academy* 9 Apr. 265 A toy mechanically curious and called in England a 'whizzer' or 'bull-roarer'. **1887** *Pall Mall Gaz.* 6 July 14/1 The whizzer.. dries clothes in 1,000 revolutions a minute. **188.** *Sci. Amer.* (N.S.) LVIII. 178 (Cent. Dict.) Ritchie's Steam Whizzer.—A machine for treating musty grain.

2. Something or someone extraordinary or wonderful; a 'stunner'. *slang.*

1888 E. L. DORSEY *Midshipman Bob* I. x. 93 'Fore-top-gallant studdingsail-boom-tricing-line-block strap-thimble.' Ain't that a whizzer? **1947** 'N. BLAKE' *Minute for Murder* v. 98, I must say she was a whizzer in those days. **1976** *Zigzag* Apr. 28/1 'She's long' features Bill's best guitar solo (despite many other whizzers). **1977** 'J. GASH' *Judas Pair* viii. 95 It's a whizzer... I've found a cased set.

3. A pickpocket. *slang.*

1925 N. LUCAS *Autobiogr. Crook* vii. 108 The stalls of theatres at matinees are sometimes patronized by 'whizzers'. **1941** V. DAVIS *Phenomena in Crime* xiv. 195 There are a score of girl 'whizzers' in London who can get a man's pocket wallet.. with conjuring skill. **1974** R. EDWARDS *Dixon of Dock Green* 17 It was also a right place for 'whizzers'—pick-pockets.

4. ***on a whizzer***: on a drinking spree. *N. Amer. slang.*

1910 B. EDWARDS *Best of Bob Edwards* (1975) v. 104 He was only off on a little bit of a whizzer. **1936** *Univ. Texas Stud. in Eng.* XVI. 51 A number of phrases with *go* refer to the act of 'getting drunk': one may *go on.. a whizzer*.

whizziness: see after WHIZZY *a.*

whizzing ('hwɪzɪŋ), *vbl. sb.* [f. WHIZZ *v.* + -ING[1].]

1. a. The action or sound denoted by WHIZZ.

1607 TOPSELL *Four-f. Beasts* 11 Of the Cynocephale or Baboun.. Their voyce is a shrill whizing. **1631** ANCHORAN *Comenius' Gate Tongues* 110 For feare the hinges should make some noyse (or whizzing). **1710** LUTTRELL *Brief Rel.* (1857) VI. 623 His horse, being frighted by the whizzing of a cannon ball, threw him. **1797** T. MORTON *Cure for Heartache* I. ii, Such a whizzing and spinning in my head. **1832** HT. MARTINEAU *Manch. Strike* vi. 65 The incessant whizzing and whirling of the wheels. **1854** MISS BAKER *Northampt. Gloss.*, She complain'd of such a whuzzing in her ears. **1884** W. S. B. MCLAREN *Spinning* (ed. 2) 49 The whizzing in the hydro-extractor is sufficient. **1898** *Allbutt's Syst. Med.* V. 818 Whizzings in the head.. are complained of.

b. *attrib.* **whizzing-stick** = WHIZZER a.

1890 *Amer. Anthrop.* III. 258 The 'whizzing-stick' or 'bull-roarer' on the West Coast of Africa.

2. Pick-pocketing. *slang.*

1925 N. LUCAS *Autobiogr. Crook* vii. 98 My pals went in for every known form of getting other people's property... 'Drumming', 'parlor jumping', 'whizzing'. **1941** V. DAVIS *Phenomena in Crime* xv. 209 Nearly all classes of 'whizzing' take place on the 'shove-up' principle.

'**whizzing**, *ppl. a.* [f. as prec. + -ING[2].]

1. a. That whizzes: see the verb.

1589 A. F. *Virg. Bucol.* vii. 1 Daphnis.. sat him downe vnder a whizzing holme. **1592** R. D. *Hypnerotomachia* (1890) 3 A stopping hinderance to their current and whuzing fall. **1622** DRAYTON *Poly-olb.* xx. 231 When the whizzing Bels the silent ayre doe cleaue. **1638** W. LISLE *Heliodorus* IX. 152 A whizzing cloud of arrowes dimd the Sun. *a* **1769** FALCONER *Shipwr.* III. 734 My stun'd ear tingles to the whizzing tide. **1812** H. & J. SMITH *Rej. Addr., Tale Drury Lane* 165 Still o'er his head, while Fate he braved, His whizzing water-pipe he waived. **1840** THACKERAY *Paris Sk.-bk.* xix. (1869) 284 A whizzing, screaming steam engine. **1870** THORNBURY *Tour rd. Eng.* I. ii. 27 [We] sweep on with whizzing wheels past broad nursery gardens.

b. Of a sound: Of the nature of a whizz.

1621 T. WILLIAMSON tr. *Goulart's Wise Vieillard* 183 The heauens shall passe away, with a whizzing tempestuous noyse. **1664** S. TAYLOR in *Evelyn's Pomona* 50 Which evaporates with a sparkling and whizzing noise. **1748** tr. *Vegetius Renatus' Distempers Horses* 183 He makes a whizzing Noise in his Breast. **1829** GOOD *Study Med.* (ed. 3) I. 563 Whizzing voice. The voice accompanied with a whizzing or hissing sound. **1835–6** *Todd's Cycl. Anat.* I. 232/2 A peculiar whizzing sound,.. perceptible on applying.. a stethoscope to the tumour. **1891** SMILES *Mem. J. Murray* xx. II. 3 A whizzing sound in his ears.

2. Excellent, 'smashing'. *slang.*

1953 [see KNOCK-OUT *sb.* 4]. **1959** [see WHIZZ-BANG *a.*].

Hence '**whizzingly** *adv.*

In recent Dicts.

'**whizzle**, *v. dial.* Also 6 **whizle, whyzle**. [f. WHIZZ *v.* + -LE.]

1. *intr.* To whizz or whistle.

1582 STANYHURST *Æneis* I. 93 Rush do the winds forward through perst chinck narrolye whizling. **1901** *Daily News* 1 Apr. 5/4 The nagaikas whizzled, and the students were falling to the ground row after row.

2. *trans.* To obtain slily.

1787 GROSE *Prov. Gloss., Whizzle*, to get any thing away slily. **1847** HALLIWELL, *Whizzle*, to obtain anything slily. **1894** BRIDGES *Nero* II. I. ii. 319, 'Twould be guessed whence I whizzled it.

whizzo, wizzo ('hwɪzəʊ, 'wɪzəʊ), *int.* and *a. slang.* [f. WHIZZ, WHIZ *sb.*[1] + -O[2].]

A. *int.* An exclamation expressing delight.

1905 in *Engl. Dial. Dict.* **1943** *Penguin New Writing* XVI. 28 Wizzoh! No night fighters! **1954** D. AMES *Crime, Gentlemen, Please* xxi. 123 'It's really a little surprise for the kiddies.' 'Whizzo!' cried Anna, grabbing it. **1959** J. VERNEY *Friday's Tunnel* xxviii. 269 Friday.. yelled, 'Oh, whizzo!'

B. *adj.* Excellent, wonderful.

1948 *R.A.F. Rev.* Jan. 20/2 I'ts whizzo when you get a fried egg sunny-side-up for tea. **1948** I. BROWN *No Idle Words* 97 A father who told his son that he had.. arranged for the boy to visit Norway received the following answer: 'Absolutely wizard, flash, whizz-o, grand, lovely to beetle up to Norway.' **1955** M. ALLINGHAM *Beckoning Lady* xiii. 185, I wanted to look at some wizzo lettering on.. the Tomb. **1968** *Listener* 19 Dec. 810/3 The Squadron-Leader and I decided to give a party—what the Squadron-Leader called a proper whizzo party with marks on the ceiling.

whizzo ('hwɪzəʊ), *sb. slang.* [f. WHIZZ, WHIZ *sb.*[2] + -O[2].] = WHIZZ, WHIZ *sb.*[2] 1.

1977 *Daily Express* 29 Mar. 20/3 Keyboard whizzo Keith Emerson uses his [side of an album] for a neo-classical piano concerto, accompanied by the London Philharmonic Orchestra. **1981** *Sydney Mirror* 2 July 8/4 Electronics whizzo Dick Smith.. aims to become the taxman's friend in another way.

whizzy ('hwɪzɪ), *a. rare.* [f. WHIZZ *sb.*[1] or *v.* + -Y[1].] Characterized by whizzing; *fig.* (*dial.*) dizzy, giddy. Hence '**whizziness**, quality or state of whizzing.

1839 THACKERAY *Leg. St. Sophia of Kioff* XVIII. 42 The swift arrow's whizziness causing a dizziness. **1866** THORNBURY *Greatheart* lviii, I felt all whizzy and sleepy like.

who (huː, *unemph.* hʊ), *pron.* (*sb.*) Forms: 1–3 **hwa**, (1 **hua**), 2–3 **hwo, hwoa**, 2–4 **wa**, (2 **wua**, 3 **whæ, wæ, wea, wah, hwoo, ȝwo**), 3–5 **hoo**, 3–6 **wo**, 3–5, 6– *Sc.* **wha**, (4 **huo**), 4–6 **ho, whoo**, 4, 9 *dial.* **whe**, 5 **woo**, (*Sc.* **vho**, 5–9 *dial.* **how**, 6 **hou**, *Sc.* **vha**), 6–7 **whoe**, (9 *Sc.* **whae**), 3– **who**; 3–5 **quo**, (3 **quuo**), 4 **qwo, qwa**, 4–5, 6 *Sc.* **qua**, 4–8 *Sc.* **quha**, 5–6 *Sc.* **quhay**, 5–7 *Sc.* **quho**, (6 *Sc.* **qwha, quhe**). [OE. *hwā* = OFris. *hwā*, OS. *hwe, hwie* (MDu., Du. *wie*), OHG. *hwer, wer* (MHG., G. *wer*), ODa. *hwa* (Da. *hvo*), Goth. *hwas*, fem. *hwo*:—OTeut. **χwaz*, **χwez*:—Indo-eur. **qʷos*, **qʷes*. For oblique forms see WHOM, WHOSE. For the vocalism cf. TWO.

Indo-eur. *qʷo-*, *qʷe-*, *qʷā-* are represented outside Germanic by Skr. *ka*, fem. *kā*, neut. *kad* (WHAT), Zend *kô, kâ, kat*, Lith. *kàs*, OSl. *kŭ-to* (Russ. *kto*), Gr. *πότερος*, Ionic *κότερος*, etc., L. *quī, quæ, quod*, Umbrian *poi* who, Oscan *pod* what, OIr. *cia, cé, cad, ca-ch* any one, *ca-te, co-te* what is, W. *pwy* who, *pa* what, *paup* any one, Gael. *co* who; the variant *qʷi-* is represented by Skr. *kis* (interrog. particle), *cid* (indef. particle), *kim* what, how, why, etc., Zend *čiš*, Gr. *τίς, τί* (:—**τίδ*), L. *quis, quid*, Umbrian *sve-pis* if any one, Oscan *pis, pid*, OSl. *čĭ-to* what (Russ. *chto*), Ir., Gael. *ciod*. For the stem-types as represented in derivative formations in English see WHEN, WHERE, WHETHER, WHICH, WHITHER, WHON, WHY, and HOW *adv.*]

I. Interrogative and allied uses.

1. a. As the ordinary interrogative pronoun, in the nominative singular or plural, used of a person or persons: corresponding to *what* of things (WHAT A. 1).

Formerly sometimes with partitive *of*, where *which* is ordinarily used (WHICH 3 b).

c **1000** ÆLFRIC *Gram.* xviii. (Z.) 113 *Quis hoc fecit?* hwa dyde ðis? *c* **1200** ORMIN 9755 Wha tahhte ȝuw To fleon & to forrbuȝhenn þatt irre þatt to cumenn iss? *c* **1250** *Gen. & Ex.* 359 Quo seide ðe ðat ðu wer naked? *c* **1300** *Harrow. Hell* (L) 63 Who ys þat ych here þore? *c* **1375** *Cursor M.* 3725 (Fairf.) His fader asked him qua art þou, And he onsquared þi sone esau. *c* **1375** *Sc. Leg. Saints* ix. (*Bertholomeus*) 40 Quha is þat, we pray þe. **1382** WYCLIF *Gen.* xlviii. 8 Who ben thes? .. My sones thei ben. *a* **1400–50** *Wars Alex.* 834* (Dubl. MS.) Whyne ert þou & who & what makys þou here? **1526** TINDALE *Matt.* xii. 48 Who is my mother? or who are my brethren? **1600** SHAKS. *A.Y.L.* III. ii. 198 Nay, but who is it? **1663** KILLIGREW *Parson's Wedd.* III. v, *Carel.* How can that be? *Joll.* It is the Scrivener at the Corner. **1667** MILTON

P.L. I. 33 Who first seduc'd them to that fowl revolt? Th' infernal Serpent. **1703** Rowe *Fair Penit.* IV. i. G 2 b, Who of my Servants wait there? *c* **1800** *Jock o' the Side* xvi. in Whitelaw *Bk. Sc. Ballads* (1857) 380/1 Whae's this kens my name sae weil..? **1863** Miss Braddon *Aurora Floyd* xxx, 'Who can it be, dear?'..'at such a time too'. **1865** Kingsley *Herew.* x, 'And he is killed?' 'Who? Hereward?' **1904** Weyman *Abb. Vlaye* iv, And who—who does she say dared to commit this outrage?

b. With intensive additions, as ***who the devil, who on earth***, etc.

c **1470** Henry *Wallace* v. 743 Quha dewill thaim maid so galy for to ryd? **1525** Ld. Berners *Froiss.* II. ii. A iij, Some therat dide murmure and..sayd: Who the deuyll hath sent for theym? **1749** Fielding *Tom Jones* xv. v, Why, who the Devil are you? *a* **1849** H. Coleridge *Ess.* (1851) I. 255 Who upon earth could ever paint the bare sea?

c. In pregnant or emphatic sense, referring to a person's origin, character, position, or the like; cf. what A. 2.

In rhetorical questions often approaching or merging with 2.

1382 Wyclif *Rom.* xiv. 4 Who art thou, that demest anothir [*v.r.* anothris] seruaunt? **1526** Tindale *Acts* xix. 15 Jesus I knowe, and Paul I knowe: but who are ye? **1548** Udall, etc. *Erasm. Par. Matt.* xv. 16 Who saye ye that I am? **1611** *Bible* Exod. v. 2 Who is the Lord that I should obey him? —— Isa. lxiii. 1 Who is this that commeth from Edom? **1840** Browning *Sordello* II. 635 Who were The Mantuans, after all, that he should care About their recognition? **1898** *Belgravia* Aug. 462 'Who is he?' 'Mr. Legge—Eustace Legge.' 'Yes. But *who* is he?' 'I don't know.'

d. Substituted for the name of a person in asking for explanation: cf. what A. 4 b.

1749 Fielding *Tom Jones* XVI. ii, 'I am come..by the Command of my Lord Fellamar.' 'My Lord who?' **1837** Dickens *Pickw.* xx, 'I heerd 'em laughing, and saying how they'd done old Fireworks.' 'Old who?' said Mr. Pickwick. **1841** S. Warren *Ten Thou.* I. ii, 'What's your names?' 'Mr. Tittlebat Titmouse,' answered that gentleman..'Mr. *who*?' exclaimed the old woman.

2. In a rhetorical question, suggesting or implying an emphatic contrary assertion.

e.g. ***who would..?*** = No one would..; ***who would not..?*** = Any one would..; ***who knows..?*** = No one knows..; ***who but..?*** = No one but, no else than..; etc. See also *who not* in 4 b. (Cf. what A. 3, where 4.)

a **1000** *Boeth. Metr.* xxviii. 5 Hwa is moncynnes þæt ne wundrie? *c* **1000** Ælfric *Gen.* xxi. 7 Hwa wolde ȝelyfan, þæt Sarra sceolde lecgan cild to hyre breoste..on ylde? *a* **1300** *Cursor M.* 454 Qua herd euer a warr auntur? **13..** *E.E. Allit. P.* A. 427 Þe croune fro hyr [*sc.* Mary] quo moȝt remwe, Bot ho hir passed in sum fauour? *c* **1386** Chaucer *Knt.'s T.* 601 Who koude ryme in englyssh proprely His martirdom? for sothe it am nat I. **1526** Tindale *Rom.* viii. 35 Who shall seperate vs from goddes loue? **1633** G. Herbert *Temple, Quip* iv, Then came brave Gloria puffing by, In silks that whistled, who but he! **1735** Pope *Ep. Arbuthnot* 213–14 Who but must laugh, if such a man there be? Who would not weep if Atticus were he? **1782** Cowper *Gilpin* 113 Away went Gilpin—who but he? **1840** Dickens *Old C. Shop* lxxiii, Of course he married, and who should be his wife but Barbara? **1855** Tennyson *Maud* I. XII. ii, Where was Maud? in our wood; And I, who else, was with her. **1914** Kipling *For all we have and are* 39 Who stands if freedom fall?

3. In a dependent question, or clause of similar meaning. †In early use also with *that* (that *conj.* 6).

For the distinction between the dependent interrogative and the relative, cf. note s.v. what A. I.**.

Beowulf 52 Men ne cunnon secgan..hwa þæm hlæste onfeng! *a* **1175** *Cott. Hom.* 231 To underȝeite wa an alle his cynerice him were frend oðer fend. *c* **1200** *Trin. Coll. Hom.* 159 Lusteð nu wich maiden þat is..and hware he was fet and hwo hire ledde and wu and hwider. *a* **1240** *Lofsong* in *O.E. Hom.* I. 211 Ich..nabbe hwoa me froure. *a* **1250** *Owl & Night.* 1195 Ic wot hwo sal beo anhonge. **1297** R. Glouc. (Rolls) 985 Wan a child were ibore & me in doute were Wo were þe fader. **13..** *Northern Passion* 803 (Camb. Gg. 5. 31), Tell vs now who smate þe. **1340** *Ayenb.* 264 Me him acseþ huo he ys. *c* **1350** *Will. Palerne* 2733 Þe werwolf went þer-to to wite ho were þere. *a* **1400** *R. Glouc. Chron.* (1724) 40 (MS. B.) Among hem..stryf me myȝte se, Wuche mest maistres were, & hoo schulde lord be. **1423** Jas. I *Kingis Q.* lvii, Maist thou noght se Quho commyth ȝond? *a* **1450** *Le Morte Arth.* 47 That ladyes..might se Who that beste were of dede. **1469** *Paston Lett.* Suppl. (1901) 129 If he happed to dye, how shuld come after hym ye wote never. **1563–7** Buchanan *Reform. St. Andros* Wks. (S.T.S.) 13 The examinatouris..sal declair to the rectour..quha ar worthy of promotion. **1595** Shaks. *John* II. i. 400 Shall we..lay this Angiers euen with the ground, Then after fight who shall be king of it? **1611** —— *Wint. T.* IV. iv. 612 They throng who should buy first. **1617** S. Collins *Epphata to F. T.* 374 It might put him in minde of who had beene there sometime. **1677** Ravenscroft *Wrangling Lovers* v. i. 67 Did he know who I was? *a* **1700** B. E. *Dict. Cant. Crew, Highjinks*, a Play at Dice who Drinks. **1800** Lathom *Dash of Day* v. i, Tell the young gentleman..a gentleman wishes to see him immediately; don't say who, but bring him hither directly. **1803** G. Rose *Diaries* (1860) II. 56 Not having a guess of who he was. **1822** Besant *All Sorts* xxiv. (1898) 167 What her obligations were, and who this lady was, belongs in no way to this history.

4. Phrases. **a.** ***who is who*** (chiefly in dependent clause): who is one and who is the other; who each of a number of persons is, or what position each holds. (Cf. what A. 8 a, which 4 b.)

† ***who and who are*** (or ***who's***) ***together***: who is allied with or engaged to whom. ***Who's Who***, the title of a reference manual of contemporary biography, issued first in 1849, and in a new and enlarged form in 1897, and now updated annually; also *transf.* and *fig.* ***you and who else?***: a contemptuous expression of incredulity, conveying scepticism about a person's ability to do some past or threatened deed, esp. of violence.

c **1386** Chaucer *Reeve's T.* 380 She saugh hem bothe two But sikerly she nyste who was who. *a* **1500** [see what A. 8 a]. **1700** T. Brown tr. *Fresny's Amusem.* 70 Let's take a Trip into the Land of Marriage, and see Who and Who are together. **1709** Steele *Tatler* No. 35 ¶3 A general Knowledge of who and who's together. **1712–13** Swift *Jrnl. to Stella* 4 Jan., I showed the Bishop..at Court, who was who. **1720** Mrs. Bradshaw in *C'tess Suffolk's Lett.* (1824) I. 50 Pray let me hear a little how your court goes, who and who are together. **1860** Emily Eden *Semi-attached Couple* ii, Though she could not distinguish who was who, yet she had a right to say she had seen 'the marquess'. **1902** Eliz. L. Banks *Newspaper Girl* 76 With the exception of those persons of art and letters who were celebrated in my own country as well as in England, I knew nothing of 'who was who' in London. **1917** *Wells Fargo Messenger* V. 183/2 The Messenger is no 'Who's who'. **1917** *National Police Gaz.* (U.S.) 18 Aug. 2/4 We don't believe that Ed W. Dunn's latest effusion would win a place for him in the poet's 'Who's who!' corner. **1918** *Nat. Geogr. Mag.* XXXIV. 64 Those whose names would be in history's 'Who's Who'. **1929** 'E. Queen' *Roman Hat Mystery* xviii. 260 'Forget, and I'll dip you into the East River.' 'You and who else?' breathed Djuna. **1929** *Times Lit. Suppl.* 18 Apr. 308/2 First he [*sc.* the biographer] gets out of the way the 'Who's Who' of Wallace Williamson's career in a terse opening chapter. **1951** P. Branch *Lion in Cellar* iii. 38 ''Oo creased 'im?' he asked... 'I did,' he said firmly... 'You an' 'oo else?' he jeered. **1962** W. Nowottny *Lang. Poets Use* ii. 34 Whilst using obituary or *Who's Who* language, it [*sc.* the diction] subtly detaches itself from the social attitudes such language is normally associated with. **1971** A. Morice *Murder in Married Life* xiii. 124 Julian: 'Then I'll throw you out.' Murderer: 'You and who else, ha ha.' **1974** *Advocate-News* (Barbados) 19 Feb. 12/1 The list of batsmen to come is straight out of the 'who's who' of attacking cricketers. **1981** *Country Life* 16 July 205/4 *Women in History*..is a sort of *Who's Who* and *Who Was Who* of women who..should be known.

b. Phrases used as sbs., etc.

I know not (mod. ***I don't know***) ***who, Lord knows who***, etc.: some person or persons unknown, or of unknown origin, status, etc. (cf. 1 c): so ***and I don't know who all*** (colloq. rare: cf. what A. 8 b), = 'and various other persons unspecified'; ***who-do-you-think*** (†***who-dost-think***), substituted for the name of a person to be guessed; ***who not*** (cf. 2 above and what-not 1): any one whatever, any one and every one, all kinds of people (now rare or obs.); ***who does what(?)***: which person will do which task; *esp.* (in a demarcation dispute) members of which trade union will do a certain job; ***who-say*** (now *dial.*): a vague report, a rumour; in quot. 1583, a pretended excuse; also ***who's-afraid*** adj. phr., defiant, swaggering.

1583 *Leg. Bp. St. Androis* 789 Half way hameward vp the calsay, [He] Said to his servandis for a quha say: 'Alace! the porter is foryett'. *a* **1586** Sidney *Apol. Poetrie* (1595) D 2, Innumerable examples,..as Brutus, Alphonsus.., and Who not. **1615** Brathwait *Strappado* (1878) 131 Heere stood I musing..Till Iockie wha dost thinke speard vp to me. **1691** Wood *Ath. Oxon.* I. 18 He was great with..Erasmus, Grocyn, Latimer, Tonstall, and who not. **1744** M. Bishop *Life* 99 To throw herself away upon the Lord knows who. **1823** Southey *Hist. Penins. War* I. v. 249 *note*, St. Antonio on one side, and St. I know not who on the other. **1825** Jennings *Obs. Dial. W. Eng.*, *Whosay*, or *Hoosay*, a wandering report; an observation of no weight. **1837** Dickens *Pickw.* xli, A vagabondish who's-afraid sort of bearing. **1844** Haliburton *Sam Slick in Eng.* xlviii. (1858) 304 And then he'd go over a whole string—Mason, Mickle, Burns, and I don't know who all. **1905** Elin. Glyn *Viciss. Evang.* 5 Mamma's father was a lord, and her mother I don't know who. **1922** H. S. Walpole *Cathedral* II. iii. 194 But who's going to decide who does what?..We're not much in the sewing line. **1960** *Guardian* 13 Sept. 3/2 A who-does-what dispute between the Amalgamated Engineering Union and the Electrical Trades Union. **1962** *Economist* 13 Oct. 118/1 The squabble over who-does-what. **1962** *Daily Tel.* 28 Nov. 1/1 The Trades Union Congress will seek to settle future 'Who does what?' demarcation disputes with quick and decisive action. **1979** *Now!* 21–27 Sept. 60/1 The £100 million complex has stood idle, paralysed by an inter-union 'who does what' row over 42 jobs.

¶ **5.** Used ungrammatically for the objective whom, in senses corresponding to any of the above.

Common in colloquial use as obj. of a verb, or of a preposition following at the end of the clause; formerly also of a preposition preceding (now only when substituted for a noun or pronoun as in 1 d).

1450 *Paston Lett.* I. 112, I rehersyd no name, but me thowt be hem that thei wost ho I ment. **1540** Cranmer *Remains* (Parker Soc.) 401 Who shall your grace trust hereafter, if you might not trust him? **1546** J. Heywood *Prov.* (1874) 52 At sight of me he asked, who have we there? **1588** Shaks. *L.L.L.* IV. i. 74 To whom came he?..What saw he?..Who ouercame he? **1591** —— *1 Hen. VI*, III. iii. 62 Who ioyn'st thou with? **1681** T. Flatman *Heraclitus Ridens* No. 39 (1713) I. 258 Who have we to thank..but the Whigs? **1753** Foote *Englishm. in Paris* II, *Buck.* Why, have you observ'd nothing? *Mrs. Sub.* About who? **1807** Southey *Espriella's Lett.* (1814) III. 68 This leads to a discussion..who the son married, whether the daughter died single [etc.]. **1874** Hardy *Far from Mad. Crowd* xxx, Who are you speaking of? **1881** Mallock *Rom. 19th Cent.* II. 154, I know..who it comes from. **1941** V. Woolf *Between Acts* 101 Who was she looking for? **1958** *Observer* 6 Apr. 3 (*heading*) Who do you want to save? **1966** I. Murdoch *Time of Angels* x. 106 Who, after all, could I possibly be in love with? **1969** *Listener* 13 Nov. 664/1 One of the policemen..went up to him and almost shouted: 'Who do you think you're talking to?' **1980** J. Gerson *Assassination Run* ii. 35 The days of Philby and Blake when no one knew who to trust.

II. Relative uses (formerly often with *that*, that *conj.* 6, rarely with *as*).

6. As compound relative in the nominative in general or indefinite sense: Any one that: = whoever 1. *arch.* or *literary.* **a.** with pronominal correlative in following clause.

c **1230** *Hali Meid.* 23/233 Hwa þat sehe þenne hu þe engles beoð isweamed..stani were his heorte ȝif ha ne mealte i teares. *c* **1315** Shoreham I. 195 Who þat entreþ þer He his sauff euere more. *c* **1325** *Poem temp. Edw. II* (Percy) lxiii, Who that is in such offys, Ne come he ner so pore, He fareth witin a while As he had selver in horde. *c* **1330** *King of Tars* 990 Ho that nolde do bi heore red, Cristen men tak of heore hed. *c* **1375** *Cursor M.* 6781 (Fairf.) Wha dose..Þat wriched pliȝt He salle be done to dede. *c* **1400** *Anturs of Arth.* xix, But ho his bidding brekes, bare þei bene of blys. *c* **1460** *Wisdom* 71 in *Macro Plays* 38 To yowur loue wo dothe repeyer, All felycyte yn þat creatur ys. **1470–85** Malory *Arthur* I. vii. 43 Who that holdeth ageynst it we wille slee hym. *c* **1489** Caxton *Sonnes of Aymon* xx. 453 Who that had be there than, he sholde have seen grete faytes of armes. *c* **1540** Lyndesay *Auld Man & Wife* 199 Wks. 1879 II. 337 Quha wald haif weir, God send thame littill rest. **1573–80** Tusser *Husb.* (1878) 47 Who soweth in raine, he shall reape it with teares. **1607** Bp. Hall *Ps.* i. 1 Who hath not walkt astray,..Oh, how that man Thrice blessed is! **1892** Kipling *Barrack-room Ball., East & West* 24 Who rides at the tail of a Border thief, he sits not long at his meat.

b. without correlative.

c **1350** *Will. Palerne* 2379 Ho wol winne his wareson, now wiȝtly him spede Forto saue my sone, or for sorwe i deye. *c* **1375** *Sc. Leg. Saints* i. (*Petrus*) 211 Þat, quha to hym ferme treutht gafe, He suld euire luf oure þe lafe. **1400** *26 Pol. Poems* i. 145 Who that takeþ fro pore to eke with his, ffor that wrong is worthy wo. *c* **1470** Henry *Wallace* I. 33 Quha likis till haif mar knawlage in that part, Go reid. **1543** tr. *Act 6 Edw. I*, c. 5 Who that is attaynted of wast, shal lese the thing wasted. **1600** W. Watson *Decacordon* (1602) 101 *marg*, Let who as list be blinded with these patches. *Ibid.* 186 To lie open to the spoile of who that first can catch it. **1600** Marston etc. *Jack Drum's Entert.* I. (1601) B, Let who will climbe ambitious glibbery rowndes. **1601** Shaks. *Jul. C.* I. iii. 80 *Cask.* 'Tis Cæsar that you meane: Is it not, Cassius? *Cassi.* Let it be who it is. **1604** —— *Oth.* III. iii. 156 Who steales my purse, steales trash. **1650** Earl Monm. tr. *Senault's Man bec. Guilty* 25 Visible to the Eyes of who shall consider them. **1797** Jane Austen *Sense & Sensib.* xxx, When a young man, be he who he will,..promises marriage, he has no business to fly off from his word. **1855** Kingsley *Westw. Ho!* v, Each shall slay his man, catch who catch can. **1856** —— *Poems, Farew.* 9 Be good, sweed maid, and let who can be clever. **1871** Browning *Balaust.* 22, I passionately cried to who would hear. **1896** A. Austin *England's Darling* II. iv, Who holds the sea, perforce doth hold the land, And who lose that must lose the other too.

†**c.** In a dependent qualifying clause with loose construction (without correlative) and with conditional force: If any one: = whoever 2. *Obs.*

1297 R. Glouc. (Rolls) 2235 Inolde noȝt abbe uorsake þat lond, wo me adde ibroȝt þerto. *a* **1300** *Cursor M.* 42 Þis fruit bitakens alle oure dedis, Both gode and ille qua rightly redis. *Ibid.* 1969 Qua þat slas or man or wijf, Þar gas na ransun bot liue for lijf. **1375** Barbour *Bruce* I. 391 Quha in battaill mycht him se, All othir contenance had he. *c* **1400** *Destr. Troy* 298 Hit is tolde..wo þat trawe lyst,..he highyt vnto helle yates. **1420–2** Lydg. *Thebes* 2117 And in despit, who that was lief or loth A sterne pas thorgh the halle he goth. *c* **1500** *Melusine* 285, I were not so joyous who that had gyuen me a C thousand besans of gold, as I am to haue fond the. *a* **1536** Wyatt *Poems, To cause accord or to aggrie* 16 Twixt lyff and deth say what who sayth There lyveth no lyff that draweth breth. **1556** Lauder *Tractate of Kyngis* 69 Christe..sched, also quha vnderstude, Als grett abundance of his blude For the pure sely nakit thyng As he sched for the Potent kyng.

†**d.** Introducing a clause expressing comparison, with idiomatic superlative. *Obs.*

c **1500** *Melusine* 170 Thenne was the oost gretly mevyd, & came to the port who best coude. **1600** W. Watson *Decacordon* (1602) 347, I euer detesting [heresy] as much as who can detest it most. **1658** Gurnall *Chr. in Arm.* II. verse 14. vii. §4 Elijah, who did as great wonders..by prayer, as who greatest? *Ibid.* 15. xviii. §2 There was a time..that Paul loved the world as well as who most.

7. a. as who (freq. followed by *would* or *should*): as or like one who; hence (with loss of relative force), as if one. *arch.*

c **1380** Wyclif *Sel. Wks.* II. 401 Al þis shal be bouȝt, as who bieþ an oxe or a cow. *Ibid.* III. 123 Þei sellen Gods worde, as who schulde selle an oxe. *a* **1400–50** *Wars Alex.* 4649 We erd noȝt in elementis as euirmare to duell, Bot as qua pas a pilgrymage fra Parysch to rome. **1483** Caxton *Gold. Leg.* 294 b/2 He..pressyd her..bytwene foure grete stones as who shold presse olyues. **1513** Douglas *Æneis* VI. vii. 60 Sic wys as quha throw cluddy skyis saw. **1606** [see as B. 12 a]. **1659** Fuller *Appeal Inj. Innoc.* I. ii. 2 The Tanner was the Worst of all Masters to his Cattle, as who would not onely load them soundly whilest living, but Tan their Hides when dead. *a* **1677** Barrow *Serm.* Wks. 1687 I. 305 Every man gladly would be neighbour to a quiet person, as who..doth afford all the pleasure of conversation, without any..trouble. **1873** Morley *Rousseau* I. vi. 210 Such speech..was probably..a mere freak of the tongue,..as who should go to a masked ball in guise of Mephistopheles. **1887** Morris *Odyss.* XI. 608 With his bow..in his hand and the arrow laid on the string, And peering round about him as who would loose at a thing.

b. Most commonly with the vb. *say*: (*a*) †***as who saith*** or ***say***, as they say, as is commonly said, as the saying is; also = next; (*b*) ***as who should say*** (arch.), †(*c*) ***as who would*** (occas. ***might***) ***say***, as if saying, as if one should say, as one may say, as much as to say.

(*a*) **1297** R. Glouc. (Rolls) 24 Severne & temese; homber is þet þridde; & þanne is, as ȝwo seiþ, þat pur lond amidde. **1303** R. Brunne *Handl. Synne* 7046 Alle þat spake of syre Troyle Was skraped awey, as who sey oyle. *a* **1340** Hampole *Psalter* cxliii. 6 Lorde helde þi heuens and descend..Aswhasay, we ere in feghtynge [etc.]. *c* **1380** Wyclif *Sel. Wks.* II. 127 Pilat answeride, Þat Y have writun, I have writun; as who seiþ, þis writing shal stonde. **1423** Jas. I *Kingis Q.* lxxvii, Sodaynly, as quho sais at a thoght, It opnyt. **1438** in *Wars Eng. in France* (Rolls) II. 438 His tarying here dothe..grete hurte, what for the wages of hym and his retenue, as who say lost. **1559** *Mirr. Mag., Sir Thomas of Woodstock* xiv, To bridle the prince of a realme, Is euen (as who sayeth) to striue with the streame. **1611** W. SCLATER *Key* (1629) 14 Papists hence inferre [that the Scriptures are] not to be permitted to lay-people, in their Mother-tongue: abusing to this purpose the saying of Christ, *Mat.* 7. 6. as who say all Gods people were Dogges.

(*b*) *c* **1375** *Cursor M.* 8611 (Fairf.) Ho turned hir ouer.. As qua sulde sai, I knaw na harme. **1527** TINDALE *Wicked Mammon* (1528) 36 If I preache (sayeth he) I haue nought to reioyse in, for necessyte is put vnto me, as who shulde say, god hathe made me so. **1596** SHAKS. *Merch. V.* I. ii. 50 He doth nothing but frowne (as who should say, and you will not haue me, choose). **1661** R. L'ESTRANGE *Interest Mistaken* 127 This is but another Alarm, as who should say; Look to your selves my Masters. **1717** MRS. CENTLIVRE *Bold Stroke for Wife* I. ii, They command Regard, as who should say, We are your Defenders. **1841** DICKENS *Barn. Rudge* xliv, Mr. Dennis coughed and shook his head, as who should say, 'A mystery indeed!' **1905** WELLS *Kipps* II. ix. §1 Sid beamed at Kipps, as who should say, 'You don't meet a character like *this* every dinner-time'.

(*c*) **1526** *Pilgr. Perf.* (W. de W. 1531) 8 It was (as who myght saye) the hynder parte of god that they sawe. **1532** TINDALE *Expos. Matt.* v. (*c* 1550) 32 b, They sayed to the Apostles: ye wolde bryng thys mans bloud vpon vs, as who wolde saye, we slue him not. **1664** J. WILSON *A. Comnenius* I. i, They all lookt wistly one on t'other, As who would say, 'twas true enough, but yet [etc.]. **1675** BURTHOGGE *Causa Dei* 19 He shall come.. in Divine Majesty, as who would say, that when he Judges.. He will show himself like God.

8. a. As compound relative in the nominative, of persons (less freq. a person): The persons (or person) that. *arch.* (Chiefly a latinism; esp. in 'There are who...' = L. *Sunt qui...*)

1596 DALRYMPLE tr. *Leslie's Hist. Scot.* VIII. (S.T.S.) II. 90 *marg.*, Quha pape was in thir days, allowit al at the kings requeist. **1605** SHAKS. *Macb.* I. iii. 109 *Macb.* The Thane of Cawdor liues; why doe you dresse me In borrowed Robes? *Ang.* Who was the Thane, liues yet. **1627** J. DOUGHTY *Disc. Div. Myst.* (1628) 20 There are who hold no art or science to be extant, which [etc.]. **1644** MILTON *Judgem. Bucer* To Parlt. B4b, If thir own works be not thought sufficient to defend them, there livs yet who will be ready.. to debate.. this matter. **1656** EARL MONM. tr. *Boccalini's Advts. fr. Parnass.* II. xxiv. 262 Through the ingratitude of who commands [It. *di chi domanda*]. **1713** TICKELL *Poems, To Addison, on Cato* 36 Who think like Romans, could like Romans fight. **1805** WORDSW. *Ode to Duty* ii, There are who ask not if thine eye Be on them. **1871** BROWNING *Pr. Hohenstiel-Schwangau* 1007 He should know, sitting on the throne, how tastes Life to who sweeps the doorway. **1903** F. W. MAITLAND in *Camb. Mod. Hist.* II. xvi. 569 There were who held that the Queen was Supreme Head *iure divino*.

†**b.** In the phrase ***but who*** = 'except (one, those) who', 'who.. not': now replaced by *but what* (WHAT C. 5).

1675 BURTHOGGE *Causa Dei* 158 Should none arrive at Heaven but who had first arrived to a State of Perfection.., Heaven would be empty. **1757** WARBURTON *Lett. to Hurd* (1809) 249, I don't meet with one but who singly says yes. **1774** KAMES *Sketches* I. i. 31 There is scarce a peasant but who has a chess-board and men.

9. a. As simple relative (of a person or persons), introducing a clause defining or restricting the antecedent and thus completing the sense: = THAT *rel. pron.* 1.

In modern printing usually distinguished from 10 by the absence of a comma before the relative: cf. WHICH B. 8.

1297 R. GLOUC. (Rolls) 1977 He nadde bote an doȝter wo miȝte is eir be. **13..** *Northern Passion* I. 154/382* Als men may here wha takes entent. **1375** BARBOUR *Bruce* I. 445 Lordingis quha likis for till her, The romanys now begynnys her. **1599** SHAKS. *Much Ado* III. iii. 68 A man who hath anie honestie in him. **1633** G. HERBERT *Temple, Ch. Porch* i, A verse may finde him, who a sermon flies. **1707** *Sel. Charters Trad. Comp.* (Selden Soc.) 257 All and every other person and persons who shall be a subscriber or subscribers to the fund. **1709** POPE *Ess. Crit.* 363 As those move easiest who have learn'd to dance. **1768** GOLDSM. *Goodn. Man* IV, I must disclaim his friendship who ceases to be a friend to himself. **1819** LINGARD *Hist. Eng.* I. i. 11 The first who exported this metal.. were certain Phenician adventurers from Cadiz. **1864** NEWMAN *Apol.* 329 The men who had driven me from Oxford were distinctly the Liberals. **1893** MAX PEMBERTON *Iron Pirate* i, One who.. can command and be obeyed in ten cities.

†**b.** Used as correlative to *such*, where *as* is now idiomatic: cf. WHICH B. 10 b. *Obs.*

1584 J. MELVILL *Autob. & Diary* (Wodrow Soc.) 174 To.. mak his eares patent to sic wha could alienat his mynd from the guid cause. **1662** [see SUCH B. 12]. **1713** *Guardian* No. 3 ¶1 And instruct such who are not as wise as himself.

10. As simple relative introducing an additional statement about the antecedent, the sense of the principal clause being complete without the relative clause; thus sometimes equivalent to 'and he (she, they)': cf. WHICH B. 7, 9 a.

Formerly often placed at a distance from the antecedent (one or more sbs. intervening), with consequent obscurity or ambiguity: see quots. 1534, 1655.

1466–7 in *Mann. & Househ. Exp.* (Roxb.) 172 Be the grase of God, ho amend ȝower desposysyon. **1533** MORE *Answ. Poys. Bk.* Wks. 1037/2 As for Tyndal.. who before he fel to these fransies, men had went had hadde some wyt. **1534** —— *Treat. Passion* ibid. 1292/1 And he sayd vnto theym, what will ye gyue me and I shall delyuer hym to you, whoe whan they heard hym, were well apaid. **1556** LAUDER *Tractate of Kyngis* 115 That kyng, that sitts all kyngis abone, Quha heiris, and seis all that is wrocht. **1601** SHAKS. *Jul. C.* III. ii. 129, I should do Brutus wrong, and Cassius wrong, Who (you all know) are Honourable men. **1611** *Bible* Ps. lxv. 5 O God of our saluation: who art the confidence of all the ends of the earth. —— Matt. x. 4 Iudas Iscariot, who also betrayed him. **1655** FULLER *Ch. Hist.* IX. vi. §40. 180 As for her Son the King of Scots, from whom they expected a settlement of Popery in that land, their hopes were lately turned into despairs, who had his education on contrary principles. **1711** ADDISON *Spect.* No. 119 ¶4 Honest Will Wimble, who I should have thought had been altogether uninfected with Ceremony. **1750** JOHNSON *Idler* No. 99 ¶3 How different.. is thy condition, who art doomed to the perpetual torments of unsatisfied desire. **1793** BURNS *Bruce's Addr.* i, Scots, wha hae wi' Wallace bled. **1882** BESANT *All Sorts* xxviii, A chap like my cousin Dick, who's a clever fellow and a devil for fireworks.

11. a. With antecedent denoting or connoting a number of persons collectively: usually with plural concord.

1593 SHAKS. *Rich. II*, I. ii. 7 Put we our quarrell to the will of heauen, Who when they see the houres ripe on earth, Will raigne hot vengeance on offenders heads. **1602** —— *Ham.* IV. iii. 5 Hee's loued of the distracted multitude, Who like not in their iudgement, but their eyes. **1609** SKENE *Reg. Maj., Stat. Alex. II*, 14 Except in Galloway, quha hes their awne speciall and proper Lawes. **1711** ADDISON *Spect.* No. 112 ¶4 This authority of the knight.. has a very good effect upon the parish, who are not polite enough to see any thing ridiculous in his behaviour. **1771** GOLDSM. *Hist. Eng.* II. 238 The Hanse-towns, who were then at war with both France and England. **1885** *Pall Mall G.* 6 Jan. 12/2 The Midland, who first introduced American railway notions in their Pullman cars.

b. Used in reference to an animal or animals: usually with implication of personality, but sometimes merely a substitute for *which*.

a **1585** MONTGOMERIE *Cherrie & Slae* 16, I sawe the Hurchone and the Haire, Quha fed amang the flowers faire. **1601** SHAKS. *Jul. C.* I. iii. 21 Against the Capitoll I met a Lyon Who glaz'd vpon me, and went surly by. **1607** —— *Cor.* IV. vii. 34 As is the Aspray to the Fish, who takes it By Soueraignty of Nature. **1748** THOMSON *Cast. Indol.* II. xl, Like wily fox who roosted cock doth spy. *a* **1774** GOLDSM. *Hist. Greece* II. 163 He.. lost his horse,.. who was killed with the thrust of a sword. **1860** DICKENS *Uncomm. Trav.* x, Two honest dogs.. who perform in Punch's shows. **1884** PHILLIPS BROOKS *New Starts in Life* xviii. 306 Even the lowest creature who floats on the pool's surface.. feels.. some.. half-conscious pleasure in the mere act of living.

c. Used instead of *which* in reference to an inanimate thing or things; chiefly with personification (also with suggestion of personality, *e.g.* of a life-like statue); sometimes, as of a ship, approaching sense a.

1588 [see 12]. **1600** G. ABBOT *Expos. Jonah* xix. 402 The snow and raine, who come downe from aboue. **1610** SHAKS. *Temp.* I. ii. 7 A braue vessell (Who had no doubt some noble creature in her) Dash'd all to peeces. **1633** G. HERBERT *Temple, Provid.* xxiii, The windes, who think they rule the mariner, Are rul'd by him. **1659** *Nicholas Papers* (Camden) IV. 95, 3 Spanish men of warre.. who.. came vp with vs and fired at vs. *a* **1774** GOLDSM. *Surv. Exp. Philos.* (1776) II. 263 The sun, who is the great fountain of both [light and heat]. **1812** J. WILSON *Isle of Palms* III. 8 Some wandering Ship who hath lost her way. **1917** MISS M. T. JACKSON *Museum* ii. 33 The Venus de Milo, who has stood for so many years.. in the Louvre.

¶ **12.** In irregular constructions: **a.** with pleonastic personal pronoun in the latter part of the relative clause, *who* thus becoming a mere link between the clauses (cf. WHICH 14); **b.** preceded by redundant *and* (cf. WHICH 16 b).

1523 LD. BERNERS *Froiss.* I. lxxxiv. 43 b/1 Now let vs returne to sir Loyes of Spayne, who whan he was at the porte of Guerand.., he and his company sayled forth. **1588** SHAKS. *Tit. A.* III. i. 37, I tell my sorrowes.. to the stones, Who though they cannot answere my distresse, Yet in some sort they are better than the Tribunes. **1619** NAUNTON in *Fortescue Papers* (Camden) 105 He is well knowen to.. divers others, who if they should see him about the Court, it would make him uncapable to do the service. **1831** SCOTT *Cast. Dang.* xix, The very same place in which Sir Aymer de Valence held an interview with the old sexton; and who now, drawing into a separate corner some of the straggling parties whom he had collected,.. kept on the alert.

¶ **13.** Used ungrammatically for the objective WHOM, in senses corresponding to those above.

Still common colloquially.

13.. *Cursor M.* 4007 (Gött.) Qua þat godd helpis wid-all, Traistli may be wend ouer-all. *c* **1400** *Destr. Troy* 5943 Mony [he] dange to the dede with dynt of his hond: Who happit hym to hitte harmyt nomo. **1523** LD. BERNERS *Froiss.* I. ccx. 103 b/1 The kynge of Englande.. had great prouision for his oost, by the meanes of John Alenson, who he founde at Flauigny. **1596** SPENSER *F.Q.* VI. i. 44 The sad Briana.. Who comming forth yet full of late affray, Sir Calidore vpcheard. **1641** EARL MONM. tr. *Biondi's Civil Wars* IV. 42 A great Prince who I forbeare to name. **1725** DE FOE *Voy. round World* II. 17 Our Surgeons, who we all call Doctors at Sea. *a* **1774** TUCKER *Lt. Nat.* (1834) II. 442 Persons who in his best judgment he sees reason to confide in. **1849** FROUDE *Nem. Faith* 134 He has a right.. to choose who he will have for a teacher. **1858** R. S. SURTEES *Ask Mamma* xxxi, Not being able to ask exactly who he liked. **1979** *Globe & Mail* (Toronto) 27 Aug. 14/5 They come to see Bowser, who they equate not only with The Fonz, but the Cookie Monster and Mork from Ork, too. **1984** *Times* 6 Feb. 12/3 Just over half.. of our sample who we assessed as working class concurred.

III. Substantival nonce-uses.

14. †**a.** *old who*: the right man. *Obs.*

1594 NASHE *Unfort. Trav.* F 2, He must haue exquisite courtship in him or else he is not old who.

b. A person, indefinitely or abstractly; a 'some one'.

1654 WHITLOCK *Zootomia* 149 We have seen the Pittifull who's, and.. the slender whats are against modest Learning. **1904** *Strand Mag.* May 516/1 'What ever made you think of it?' 'It wasn't a what; it was a who'.

c. with *the*: The question 'who?'

1771 GOLDSM. *Haunch of Venison* 26, I was puzzled again, With the how, and the who, and the where, and the when. **1955** *Bull. Atomic Sci.* June 228/3 The 'who' and 'why' of ethical judgments may lie in the realm of metaphysics; but the 'how' are phenomena in the natural world.

who (wəʊ), *int.* (*sb.*) Forms: 5 whoo, 5–7, 9 *dial.* who, 7 whoe, 8 whoh, 9 whoo. [Variant of HO *int.*[2] = stop!] Stop! esp. as a call to a horse: = WHOA 2 (cf. WO). †Also as *sb.*

c **1450** [see WHOOP *int.* b]. **1467** in S. Bentley *Excerpta Historica* (1831) 211 Then the Kyng perceyvyng the cruell assaile, cast his staff, and with high voice, cried, Whoo! **1562** J. HEYWOOD *Prov. & Epigr.* (1867) 152 Thou art one of them, to whom god bad who, God tooke the for a carte horse, when god bad so. **1599** CHAPMAN *Hum. dayes Myrth* Plays 1873 I. 107 Who loe you bird, how much you are deceiued. *c* **1603** HEYWOOD & ROWLEY *Fortune by Land* II. i, Come Ile go teach ye hayte and ree, gee and whoe, and which is to which hand. **1606** *Choice, Chance*, etc. (1881) 15 The ploughman.. with haye Ree, & Who to his horse. **1621** BURTON *Anat. Mel.* I. ii. III. xiv. 165 He is madd, madd, no whoe with him. **1797** T. MORTON *Cure for Heart-ache* I, Scene 1. A Farm Yard... The Bells of a Team jingling. *Frank* (*without*) Woyh! Whoh! Smiler! **1814** *Sporting Mag.* XLIV. 146 Come hither, who-o. **1841** *Punch* 17 July 5/2 *Coachman.*—Whoo up!—d——n you! **1859** GEO. ELIOT *Adam Bede* xii, There was a great deal of strong language, mingled with soothing 'who-ho's' while the leg was examined.

who, obs. f. HO *int.*[1], HOW *adv.*, WOE.

whoa (wəʊ), *int.* [Variant of WHO *int.*]

†**1.** ***whoa ho ho***, used to call attention from a distance. *Obs.*

1623 *Shaks. Merry W.* v. v. 187 Whoa hoe, hoe, Father Page. **1623** —— *Wint. T.* III. iii. 79 He hallow'd but euen now. Whoa-ho-hoa.

2. A word of command to a horse or other draught-animal to stop or stand still; also used otherwise in conjunction with other words, as ***come hither whoa, gee-whoa, hait-whoa, whoa back***. Hence used jocularly to a person as a command to stop or desist. (Cf. WOA.)

1843 [see HAW *int.*[2] and *sb.*[5]]. **1849** W. S. MAYO *Kaloolah* iii. (1850) 32 'Soh! whow!' to his restive horses. 'Whow! I tell you... Whoa! I tell you.' **1862** THOREAU *Ess., Walking* (1895) 22 Who but the Evil One has cried 'Whoa!' to mankind? **1865** EMILY DICKINSON *Lett.* (1894) II. 256 Life.. will run away, notwithstanding our sweetest whoa. **1887** W. S. S. TYRWHITT *New Chum* ix. 195 Men shouting..: 'Whoa back! Whoa back!' **1898** HAMBLEN *Gen. Manager's Story* ix. 123 We were four minutes late, and as I shouted 'whoa' to Jack [the engine-driver], I could see that he was mad [*i.e.* angry].

Hence **whoa** *v.*, *intr.* to shout 'whoa!'

1841 S. C. HALL *Ireland* I. i. 73 The Englishman.. after 'who-aing' to his horse, looks over the hedge.

who-all ('huːɔːl), *pron.* *U.S. dial.* Also **who all**. [f. WHO *pron.* + ALL *a.*] Used for WHO *pron.* in interrogative and relative functions (with sing. as well as pl. sense).

1899 B. W. GREEN *Word-bk. Virginia Folk-Speech* 424 Who-all *interrog.* Meaning all who: as '*Who all* were there.' **1905** A. V. CULBERTSON *Banjo Talks* 15, I ain' care who-all come dis way! **1916** R. FROST *Let.* 21 Mar. (1964) 27, I wish I could remember.. who-all I've baptized into my heresies. **1938** M. K. RAWLINGS *Yearling* vii. 67 Jody asked brashly, 'Who-all's your sweetheart?' **1938** J. STUART *Beyond Dark Hills* vii. 184 Will you get up and tell the student group just why you were out there.. and who all were with you? **1944** in *Amer. Speech* (1946) XXI. 52 We always said, as the town [*sc.* Hawley, Minnesota] still does, 'Who-all was there?' and 'What all did you do?' Many of the Irish also use 'who-all' and 'what-all'.

whoar, whoat, obs. ff. WHORE, HOT, VOTE *v.*

whoave, var. WHAUVE *v. dial.*

whobble, var. WOBBLE.

whobub, obs. f. HUBBUB.

whoch, whoche, obs. ff. WHICH.

whoche, var. WHITCH, chest, coffer.

whochesafe, obs. f. VOUCHSAFE.

whod(de, obs. ff. HOOD.

whode, obs. f. HOOD, WOOD.

whoder, -ir, -ur, -yre, obs. ff. WHITHER.

whodunit (huː'dʌnɪt). *colloq.* Also **whodunnit** and (*rare*) other varr. [repr. *who done* (= illiterate for *did*) *it?*] A story or other work of fiction about the solving of a mystery, esp. a murder; a detective or murder story. Occas. used for 'who did it' in other contexts.

1930 D. GORDON in *News of Bks.* (U.S.) July 10 *Half-Mast Murder*, by Milward Kennedy—A satisfactory *whodunit.* **1942** G. MITCHELL *Laurels are Poison* vi. 61 That was another case of Oo-dun-it. Or was it? **1943** *Britannia & Eve* Feb. 16/1 Clifton Fadiman.. moved in with an intellectual slap-stick show, which could be appreciated equally by professors and the public for 'who-dun-it?' books. **1951** M. McLUHAN *Mech. Bride* (1967) 104/2 Would the thriller fan be abashed to learn that the whodunit anticipated the techniques of modern science and art? **1959** 'A. GILBERT' *Death takes Wife* xiii. 173 The whodunnit writers have got us all educated. **1961** *Times* 26 July 15/5 A new 'whodunit'.. is to be produced at St. Martin's theatre. **1971** WODEHOUSE *Much Obliged, Jeeves* vii. 69, I.. go in mostly for who-dun-its and novels of suspense. For the who-dun-it Agatha Christie is always a safe bet. **1971** E.

LAMARCHAND *Death on Doomsday* xi. 169, I think sleeping dogs will be let lie, provided we can establish whodunit. **1975** *New Yorker* 21 Apr. 2/1 (Advt.), *Equus*—A brilliant psychological whodunit by Peter Shaffer. **1980** *Times Lit. Suppl.* 30 May 615/5 In the whodunnit, we are conditioned to look for not the most obvious but the *least likely* suspect.

Hence **who'dun(n)itry**, material or writing such as occurs in a 'whodunit'.

1961 *Daily Tel.* 18 Dec. 10/4 'The Judge and his Hangman' on BBC television last night. This is whodunitry with undertones. **1966** *Punch* 8 June 859/2 His *The Weekend Girls*.. settles for whodunitry rather than sociology. **1972** *Daily Tel.* 4 Apr. 9/8 There is no sexual element whatever, and.. it doesn't dabble in whodunnitry.

whoe: see HOW, WHO.

whoes, obs. f. WHOSE.

whoever (huːˈɛvə(r)), *pron.*; contr. (*poet.*) **whoe'er** (huːˈɛə(r)). [Orig. two words, WHO *pron.* and EVER *adv.* 8 e.]

I. 1. As compound relative, or with correlative in principal clause, which usually follows but occas. precedes; in generalized or indefinite sense: Whatever person or persons; any one who, or any who.

†Formerly also followed by *that* (THAT *conj.* 6).

c **1175** *Lamb. Hom.* 47 Hwa efre þenne ilokie wel þene sunne dei,.. beo heo dal neominde of heofene riches blisse. *c* **1380** WYCLIF *Wks.* (1880) 45 Who euere of freris.. wilen goon among sarasyns.., axe þei leue þerof of here mynystris prouyncyal. **1382** —— *Matt.* xii. 32 Who euere shal seie a word aȝeins mannys sone, it shal be forȝouen to hym. **1561** T. HOBY tr. *Castiglione's Courtyer* IV. (1577) S iv b, In case a graue Philosopher should come beefore anye of our Princes, or who euer beside, that woulde shewe tham plainlye [etc.]. **1596** SHAKS. *Tam. Shr.* III. ii. 235 Heere she stands, touch her who euer dare. *c* **1600** —— *Sonn.* cxxxiii. 11 Who ere keepes me, let my heart be his garde. **1655** *Theophania* 173 Whoever have opposed their proceedings, ..instead of punishment have been rewarded. **1732** BERKELEY *Alciphr.* I. § 16 Whoever acts with design, acts for some end. **1813** SCOTT *Rokeby* II. xxvi, Whoever finds him, shoot him dead! **1833** I. TAYLOR *Fanat.* i. 1 Mental disorders which.. demand, in whoever would relieve them, ..the very purest intentions. **1906** E. V. LUCAS *Wand. in Lond.* i. 14 Whoever lives there believes nobly in heat, for the chimney is immense.

2. Introducing a qualifying clause with conditional or disjunctive force: If any one at all; whether one person or another; no matter who. (Sometimes with verb in subjunctive.)

Often implying opposition: = 'notwithstanding any one who', or 'notwithstanding that any one': cf. WHATEVER 3.

1500-20 DUNBAR *Poems* xxix. 24 Fra it [*sc.* my purse] as fra the Feynd thay [*sc.* coins] fle, Quha evir tyne, quha evir win. **1591** SHAKS. *1 Hen. VI*, I. iii. 7 Who ere he be, you may not be let in. **1595** —— *John* v. v. 19 Who euer spoke it, it is true. **1605** —— *Macb.* IV. i. 47 Open Lockes, who euer knockes. **1667** MILTON *P.L.* x. 14 Not to taste that Fruit, Whoever tempted. **1711** ADDISON *Spect.* No. 92 ¶7, I.. must here take occasion to thank A. B. whoever it is that conceals himself under those two Letters. **1781** COWPER *Expost.* 701 If he guard thee.., Whoe'er assails thee, thy success is sure. **1794** PALEY *Evid.* II. vi. (1817) 126 The books, whoever were the authors of them, were composed [etc.]. **1848** DICKENS *Dombey* xxxiii, Whoever you may be, sir,.. I am deeply grateful to you. **1863** MISS BRADDON *Aurora Floyd* xxx, Whoever it is, I won't see them to-night.

¶ **3.** Used ungrammatically for the objective: Any one whom; whomsoever.

1592 SHAKS. *Rom. & Jul.* v. iii. 173 Who ere you find attach. **1613** —— *Hen. VIII*, II. i. 47 Who euer the King fauours, The Cardnall instantly will finde imployment. **1780** *Mirror* No. 95 ¶3 Whoever you marry.. will have no reason to complain of your temper.

II. 4. *interrog.* [EVER *adv.* 8 d.] An emphatic extension of *who*, implying perplexity or surprise. *colloq.*

Properly written as two words.

[**1875** DASENT *Vikings* lvi, Who ever would have thought it, a short hour ago?] **1881** R. G. WHITE *Eng. Without & Within* xvi. 385 *Ever* is frequently heard in composition thus: 'Whoever is it?' 'Whatever can it be?' This usage is mostly confined to ladies, and is not regarded as good English.

whoff, whoffle, var. WAFF, WAFFLE.

1873 RHODA BROUGHTON *Nancy* xiii, A little shrewish shrill bark, speedily changed into an apologetic.. whiffling and whoffling. **1922** *Chamb. Jrnl.* Aug. 492 Whoff! Whoff!

whofull, obs. form of WOEFUL.

whois, obs. form of WHOSE.

whole (həʊl), *a.*, *sb.*, *adv.*, (*int.*). Forms: α. 1 hal, 3- hale, etc.; see HALE *a.* β. 3-5 hol, (3 hoal, 4 ol, hoel), 4-6 holl, hool(e, 4-8 hole, 5-6 holle, hooll(e, hoyll(e, wholle, (5 oull), 6 (w)hoale, (houll, woll(e), *Sc.* hoill, 6-7 whol, wholl, (7 *Sc.* quholl), 6- whole. [OE. *hál* (also *ȝehál* YHOLE) = (O)Fris., OS. *hêl* (MDu. *heel*, usually *gheheel*, Du. *heel*, *geheel*, MLG., LG. *heel*), OHG. (MHG., G.) *heil* (MHG. *geheil*), ON. *heill* HAIL *a.* (Sw. *hel*, Da. *heel*):—OTeut. *(*ga*)*χailaz* :—Indo-Eur. **qoilos*. From the same stem are also OSl. *cělъ*, *cělostъ* complete, whole, OPruss. *kailūstiska-n* acc. health (f. **kailūstas*), Gr. *κοῖλυ· τὸ καλόν* (Hesychius), OS. *hêl* omen, OHG. (MHG., G.) *heil* health, (good or bad) fortune, ON. *heill* neut. omen, fem. good luck, happiness, Goth. *hails* health (also *gahails*). The gradation-variant **qeilo-* is represented by OIr. *cēl* omen.

On the spelling *whole* (the *wh* first appears in the 15th cent.) see the article WH. Pronunciations with initial (w) exist in modern dialects over an area extending from Somerset to north-east Yorkshire. For the northern form corresp. to midland and southern *hōl*, *whole*, see HALE *a.* For derivatives with mutated vowel see HAIL *sb.*[2], HEAL *sb.*, HEAL *v.*[1]

The Germanic adj. has the meanings (not all represented in every dialect) of 'uninjured, sound, healthy, entire complete'; the sense 'healthy' gave rise to its use in several languages in salutations, e.g. Goth. *hails* = *χαῖρε*, OS. *hêl wes*, OE. *hál wes þú*, ON. *ver heill*, *sit heill*: see WASSAIL and HAIL *int.*]

A. *adj.* **I.** In good condition, sound. In senses 1-4 often in collocation with *sound* (OE. *hál ond ȝesund*, ME. *hol and sound*, also *hol and fer*, *hail and hol*).

1. a. Of a person or an animal, the body, limbs, skin: Uninjured, unwounded, unhurt; (contextually) recovered from injury or a wound; †(of a wound) healed. † *to lick whole*: see LICK *v.* 1 e. *arch.*

Beowulf 1974 þæt ðær on worðiȝ wiȝendra hleo.. cwom heaðolaces hal to hofe gongan. **971** *Blickl. Hom.* 177 Hie þa hine on rode ahengan.. & he.. hine halne & ȝesundne ðy ðriddan dæȝe æteowde. *a* **1000** *Daniel* 271 Hyssas hale hwurfon in þam hatan ofne. *c* **1175** *Lamb. Hom.* 29 Ane wunde on his licome þet ne mei beon longe hwile hal. *c* **1250** *Gen. & Ex.* 2812 In hise bosum he dede his hond, Quit and al unfer he it fond; And sone he dede it eft agen, Al hol and fer he wiste it sen. *c* **1290** *S. Eng. Leg.* 33/131 His heued ȝut and is finguer al-so boþe huy beoth hole and sounde. *a* **1310** in Wright *Lyric P.* xxxvii. 102 Nou thou art sekest, ant nou holest. **1357** *Lay Folks Catech.* (L.) 449 Betyn with scorgys, þat no skyn held hool. *c* **1386** CHAUCER *Friar's T.* 72 In this world nys dogge.. That kan an hurt deer from an hool knowe. **1388** WYCLIF *Job* v. 18 He smytith, and hise hondis schulen make hool. *a* **1400** *Minor Poems fr. Vernon MS.* xxix. v. 67 Whon he a-wok, he groped his leg; He feled hit hol and sount. **1452** *Paston Lett.* I. 239 Wheche wownde was never hol to the daye of her deth. **1523** LD. BERNERS *Froiss.* I. ccii. 98/2 Sir Eustace Dambreticourt.. was as thanne hole of his hurtes. **1530** PALSGR. 836/2 Hole and safe, *sayn et sauf*. *c* **1550-1712** [see LICK *v.* 1 e]. **1581** J. BELL *Haddon's Answ. Osor.* 131 When the wounde is whoale, what neede any playster or further surgery? **1581** W. STAFFORD *Exam. Compl.* iii. (1876) 91 Wee shoulde lycke our selues hoale againe in short space. **1590** SPENSER *F.Q.* III. v. 43 As his wound did gather, and grow hole. **1593** SHAKS. *2 Hen. VI*, IV. vii. 11 He was thrust in the mouth with a Speare, and 'tis not whole yet. **1599** PORTER *Angry Wom. Abingt.* (Percy Soc.) 104 A man is not so soon whole as hurt. **1844** GLEIG *Lt. Dragoon* xvi, One whole man.. is enough to take care of a wounded one. **1847** TENNYSON *Princess* vi. 194 She.. Felt it [*sc.* the babe] sound and whole from head to foot. **1855** BROWNING *An Epistle* 86 The evil thing out-breaking all at once Left the man whole and sound of body indeed.

b. Phr. *as whole as a fish* (*a trout*).

[Cf. *a* **1400-50** *Wars Alex.* 4282 Bot ay as fresche & as fere as fisch quen he plays.]

a **1425** *Cursor M.* 11884 (Trin.) A noble baþ we shul þe make; Bi þat þou com þerof oute þou shal be hool as any troute [*Cott.* hale sum ani trute]. *c* **1450** *Mirk's Festial* 265 Anon þe lepur fel from hym and he was hole as a fysche. **1518** [see TROUT *sb.*[1] 1]. **1591** SHAKS. *Two Gent.* II. v. 20 They are both as whole as a fish. **1700** T. BROWN tr. *Fresny's Amusem.* 120 In four and twenty Hours he made 'em as whole as Fishes.

c. In allusive phrases ***whole skin*** (***whole limbs***), esp. ***in a whole skin*** = uninjured.

1547 BOORDE *Introd. Knowl.* xviii. (1870) 169 The people ..loue no warre, but louyth to rest in a hole skin. **1555**, etc. [see SKIN *sb.* 6 c]. **1598** SHAKS. *Merry W.* III. i. 79 Let them keepe their limbs whole, and hack our English. *Ibid.* 111 Your hearts are mighty, your skinnes are whole. **1648** BP. HALL *Breathings Devout Soul* xxvii. 41 A third with Lazarus wants bread, and a whole skin. **1748** RICHARDSON *Clarissa* (1768) V. 260 Honest Hickman may now sleep in a whole skin. **1841** THACKERAY *Gt. Hoggarty Diam.* xiii, If he wants to keep his place and his whole skin. **1877** SPURGEON *Metrop. Tab. Pulpit* XXIII. 563 Others think the Gospel is true: Erasmus feels sure that it is, but Erasmus wants to die in a whole skin.

2. a. Of inanimate objects: Free from damage or defect; uninjured, unimpaired, unbroken, untainted, intact. (Cf. 6, 8.)

[*c* **1000**: see YHOLE.] *c* **1250** *Compassio Mariæ* 37 So gleam glidis þurt þe glas, Of þi bodi born he was, And þurt þe hoale þurch he gload. *c* **1250** *Gen. & Ex.* 2776 Ðo saȝ moyses, at munt synay,.. Fier brennen on ðe grene leaf, And ðoȝ grene and hol bi-leaf. *a* **1300** *Floriz & Bl.* 364 Ber wiþ þe forti pund And þine cupe hol and sund. **13..** *K. Alis.* 7389 (Laud MS.), Her armes riche of mounde Weren ȝitt hole & sounde. *c* **1305** *St. Swithin* 66 in *E.E.P.* (1862) 45 Seint swythin.. blessede þe eiren to-broke and hi bicome hole anon And sound as hi euere were. **1340** *Ayenb.* 205 A roted eppel amang þe holen makeþ rotie þe yzounde. **1377** LANGL. *P. Pl.* B. XIV. 1, I Haue but one hool hatere. *c* **1420** *Chron. Vilod.* 3368 When he was take vp of þe vrthe, he was as wholle And as freysshe as he was ony tyme þat day byfore. *c* **1450** *Merlin* 117 Yet hadde he his spere hoill. **1476** *Stonor Papers* (Camden) II. 4, I haue ressayved your wollys as ffayer and as hole as any mannys. **1599** SHAKS. *Hen. V*, III. ii. 37 Pistoll ..hath a killing Tongue, and a quiet Sword; by the meanes whereof, a breakes Words, and keepes whole Weapons. **1611** tr. *Serlio's Archit.* III. 27 b, Traians Columne is the wholest. **1642** FULLER *Holy & Prof. St.* II. xix. 121 His corslet wholler then his clothes. **1674** R. GODFREY *Inj. & Ab. Physic* 205 This is worse than what Tinkers do, to make a Hole in a whole Vessel. *a* **1700** EVELYN *Diary* Sept. 1646, Clad.. in blew cloth, very whole and warme. **1718** RAE *Hist. Reb.* 287 Bringing.. the whole Boats they found in their Way. **1829** *Chapters Phys. Sci.* 185 When the pipe is quite whole and sound. **1839** DE LA BECHE *Rep. Geol. Cornwall*, etc. xiii. 405 Whole ground, as the tin-streamers term the stanniferous gravel and super-incumbent beds which have not been previously disturbed by the old men. **1858** HAWTHORNE *Fr. & It. Note-bks.* (1871) II. 9 She is just as whole as when she left the hands of the sculptor.

†**b.** Of immaterial things: Intact, unimpaired.

c **1450** *Brut* II. 327 It was ordeyned in þe parlement þat all Cathedrall cherches shold ioy and haue her eleccions hool; & þat þe King.. sholde not write aȝens hem þat were ychosen. *a* **1500** in *Arnolde's Chron.* (1811) 35 That the citezens.. haue alle her fraunchyses and free custumes holl and vnblemyshed as they before this tyme hadden hem. *a* **1533** LD. BERNERS *Gold. Bk. M. Aurel.* Prol. (1535) A j, There is nothynge so entier, but it diminisheth, nor nothyng so hole, but that is wery.

3. a. In good health; free from disease; healthy, 'well'; (contextually) restored to health, recovered from disease, 'well again'. *arch.*

c **888** ÆLFRED *Boeth.* x, Ðu eart nu ȝit swiðe ȝesæliȝ, nu ðu ȝit liofost & eart hal. *a* **1200** *Moral Ode* 114 in *O.E. Hom.* I. 167 Wa se seið þet he bo hal, him solf wat best his smirte. *c* **1290** *St. Barnabas* 61 in *S. Eng. Leg.* 28 He bi-cam anon hol and sound. *c* **1305** *Pilate* 142 in *E.E.P.* (1862) 115 Anon þo he þe ymage iseȝ he was ol anon. ? *a* **1366** CHAUCER *Rom. Rose* 1097 A stoon.. so.. vertuous, That hole a man it koude make Of palasie, and tothe ake. *c* **1450** *Merlin* 52 To axe.. yef this seke shall euer be hoill of this sekenesse. **1526** TINDALE *Mark* v. 34 Thy fayth hath saved the [**1611** made thee whole], goo in peace, and be whole off thy plage. **1530-1** *Act 22 Hen. VIII*, c. 12 § 3 Yf any person.. beyng hole & myghtie in body & able to laboure.. be taken in beggyng. *a* **1533** LD. BERNERS *Gold. Bk. M. Aurel.* xxix. (1535) 49, I repute it a very perillous thinge for a hole man to reste and be idell. **1584** R. SCOT *Discov. Witchcr.* XVI. ix. (1886) 485 Endued with a cleare, whole, subtill and sweet bloud. **1629** *Orkney Witch Trial* in *County Folk Lore* III. (1903) 103 Quha being quholl then deit within thrie dayes be your witchcraft. **1722** DE FOE *Plague* (1754) 162 We are all whole and sound People here, and we would not have you bring the Plague among us. **1814** CARY *Dante, Parad.* IV. 49 Him who made Tobias whole.

absol. *c* **1000** *Ags. Gosp.* Matt. ix. 12 Nys halum læces nan þearf ac seocum. *c* **1330** *Assump. Virg.* (B. M. MS.) 69 Seke and hole sche dide gode. *a* **1425** *Cursor M.* 20119 (Trin.) To hoole & seke dud she bote. **1548-9** (Mar.) *Bk. Com. Prayer, Ordering of Priests*, As well to the sicke as to the whole. **1676** GLANVILL *Ess. Philos. & Relig.* VII. 1 We had all things, both for our Whole and Sick, that belonged to Charity and Mercy.

†**b.** OE. and early ME. *hāl* in salutations.

c **1000** ÆLFRIC *Hom.* II. 252 Sy ðu hal, leof, Iudeiscre leode cyning. *c* **1205** LAY. 14936 Hal wrð þu lauerd king. [**1583** STOCKER *Civ. Warres Lowe C.* IV. 12 b, Thei cried with a lustie courage, All whole noble mates all whole.]

c. *fig.* in biblical translation of reminiscence of biblical uses.

c **1000** *Ags. Ps.* (Th.) lxi[i]. 8 Doð eowre heortan.. hale and clæne. **1382** WYCLIF *Jer.* xxxviii. 2 His lif shal ben hoel and lyuynge. **1523-34** FITZHERB. *Husb.* § 149 Hole in body, holer in soule, and rycher in goodes. **1535** COVERDALE *2 Sam.* i. 9 My life is yet whole within me. **1738** WESLEY *Ps.* VI. ii, O Lord,.. save my Soul, And for thy Mercy sake make whole. **1833** TENNYSON *Miller's Dau.* ii, A soul.. So healthy, sound, and clear and whole. **1866** WHITTIER *Our Master* xiv, We touch Him in life's throng and press, And we are whole again.

†**4.** In reference to the mental faculties: Sound, sane. *Obs.*

In the language of wills *whole* = L. *sanus*, as in *sanus mente*, *sanæ mentis*.

c **1000** *Ags. Gosp.* Mark v. 15 Hales modes. *c* **1380** WYCLIF *Wks.* (1880) 38 þouȝ eche man.. myȝtte lyue hool & sond in bodi & wittis. **1418** *E.E. Wills* (1882) 30, I, Iohn Chelmyswyk squier of Shropshire, hole of mynde & in my gode memorie beyng. **1483-4** *Act 1 Rich. III*, c. 1 § 1 Eny persone.. beyng of.. hoole mynde at large and not in duresse. **1506** *Linc. Wills* (1914) I. 32 Of a holle mynde and hoill memory. **1581** PETTIE tr. *Guazzo's Civ. Conv.* I. (1586) 4 If I flatter not my selfe, I haue a whole minde within my crasie bodie.

†**5.** As a rendering (direct or indirect) of L. *sānus* in the sense: Sound, wholesome. *Obs.*

a **1225** *Ancr. R.* 370 Ne nomen heo neuer ȝeme hwat was hol, hwat was unhol te eten ne to drincken. **1340** *Ayenb.* 251 Ase moche ase þe welle yuelþ lesse of þe erþe, zuo moche hi is þe holer and þe betere of to drinke. *c* **1380** WYCLIF *Wks.* (1880) 228 3if ony man.. accordiþ not to þe hoole wordis [*1 Tim.* vi. 3 sanis sermonibus] of oure lord ihū crist. *Ibid.* 408 He lediþ his sheep wel in hool pasture þat wole not rote. ? *a* **1400** *Little Red Bk. Bristol* (1900) I. 1 3he schal.. 3hif trewe and hole counsell.. to the Mair. *c* **1440** *Pallad. on Husb.* I. 23 First biholde aboute, and se thyn aier; If hit be cleer and hool, stond out of fere. **1502** *Ord. Crysten Men* (W. de W. 1506) IV. iv. P iv b, After the moost hole opynyon [orig. *selon la plus saine opinion*].

II. Complete, total (and allied senses).

6. a. Having all its parts or elements; having no part or element wanting; having its complete or entire extent or magnitude; full, perfect.

Chiefly of abstract things; when used of material objects, this sense is coincident with 2.

[*c* **890** WÆRFERTH tr. *Gregory's Dial.* II. x. (1890) 124/14 þære kicenan ȝetimbrung stod ȝehal & ȝesund. *c* **1000** ÆLFRIC *Gen.* Pref., Se tægl sceolde beon ȝehal.. on ðam nytene æt ðære offrungæ. *c* **1315** SHOREHAM I. 720 þer he hys, he hys al yhol.] **13..** *Bonaventura's Medit.* 182 A derwurþ ȝyfte he wulde with þe lete, Hym self al hole vn to þy mete. *c* **1386** CHAUCER *Sec. Nun's T.* 111 The cleernesse hool of sapience. **1390** GOWER *Conf.* I. 6 With hol trust and with hol believe. *c* **1400** MAUNDEV. xxvi. [xxii.] (1919) I. 158 The nombre schall euermore ben hool. **1457** HARDING *Chron.* in *Engl. Hist. Rev.* (1912) Oct. 748 His vertuse dygne so hole were and plenere. **1560** DAUS tr. *Sleidane's Comm.* 227 b, He permitteth.. the whole supper of the Lorde [i.e. in both kinds]. **1581** PETTIE tr. *Guazzo's Civ. Conv.* III. (1586)

143 b, Seeing these women will not be the whole mothers of their children, they ought at least to be carefull to chuse good Nursses. **1585** T. WASHINGTON tr. *Nicholay's Voy.* IV. xiii. 126 b, A fair Turkie horse decked with the whole skinne of a great Lion. **1654** GATAKER *Disc. Apol.* 46 Either place required a whole man. **1701** STANHOPE *Pious Breathings* IV. viii. (1704) 257 Thou art the Bread of Life, every day eaten, yet still whole and never consumed. **1743** BULKELEY & CUMMINS *Voy. S. Seas* 103 At whole Allowance. **1812** L. HUNT in *Examiner* 9 Nov. 716/1 The pit was but moderately filled at whole price. **1818** *Art Bk.-binding* 4 Quarto whole-sheets, consist of eight printed pages. **1818** SCOTT *Hrt. Midl.* xlix, He..from half thief became whole robber. **1850** TENNYSON *In Mem.* lxxi. 8 That so my pleasure may be whole. **1891** *Pall Mall Gaz.* 27 Nov. 5/2 There were four occasions on which the wind reached force 10, or what is known among sailors as a 'whole' gale.

†**b.** Of will, intention, affection: Full, complete, perfect. *Obs.*

c **1369** CHAUCER *Bk. Duchesse* 1224 With hool herte I gan hir beseche. *c* **1400** *Rom. Rose* 2339 He that.. Yaff hoole his herte in will and thought. *c* **1400** *Destr. Troy* 2195 With hardynes of hond, & with hole might. *c* **1430** *Hymns Virgin* (1867) 103 Y bileeue in hool mynde, þe holi goost schalle knytte aȝen þe soule to þe fleische. **1535** COVERDALE *2 Chron.* xv. 15 They soughte him with a whole wyll. —— *Ps.* cxviii[i]. 34, I shal kepe thy lawe, yee I shal kepe it with my whole herte.

c. Containing all its proper or essential constituents; of milk, unskimmed. See also *whole meal* in D. 1.

1794 WEDGE *Agric. Chester* 37 The common practice of churning the 'whole milk,' instead of setting up the milk for the cream to rise, and churning it alone. **1894** *Field* 9 June 846/2 It is less trouble to churn whole milk than to churn cream.

d. ***whole or part***: attrib. use of *in whole or in part* (see B. 3 c). *rare.*

1880 SWINBURNE *Stud. Shaks.* 292 The evidence for Shakespeare's whole or part authorship.

7. a. The full or total amount of; all, all of (as distinguished from *part of* or *some of*). The prevailing current sense; only in attributive use, and now always preceding the sb.

Formerly pleonastically with *all, entire,* etc.: also following its sb.

(*a*) *a, the, his,* etc. *whole* with sing. sb.

[*a* **900** *O.E. Martyrol.* 10 Jan. 16 Ond þa sona brohte him se hræfn ȝehalne hlaf. *c* **1325** *Chron. Eng.* 413 in Ritson *Metr. Rom.* II. 287 Al Englond yhol. **1340** *Ayenb.* 126 Yef we yzeȝe þet we miȝte more ine one daye profiti þanne hi ne moȝe ine one yere y-hol.] **1362** LANGL. *P. Pl.* A. II. 6 Seo wher he stondeþ!..and al his hole Meyne! *c* **1369** CHAUCER *Bk. Duchesse* 554 To make yow hool I wol do alle my power hool. **1390** GOWER *Conf.* II. 121 Ye knowen al min hole herte. *c* **1400** *Destr. Troy* 6852 Menelay the mighty, & the mayn Telamon, So sturnly withstod with þaire strenkyth holl. *Ibid.* 13492 To hit into havyn with his hoole flete. *c* **1400** MAUNDEV. xvi. (1919) I. 86 þei fasten an hool moneth. *c* **1449** PECOCK *Repr.* Prol. 2 The clergie of Goddis hool chirche in erthe. *c* **1449** The hool al werk [see ALL A. 10]. **1491–2** *Rec. St. Mary at Hill* (1904) 181 The clarkes wages for an oull yere iiij s iiij d. **1523** WOLSEY in *St. Papers Hen. VIII,* VI. 205 Either for the hoole wynter or at the lest for a season. *a* **1532** *Rem. Love* xliii. Chaucer's Wks. 368 Eche letter an hole worde dothe represent. **1553** (*title*) The true and lyuely historyke pvrtreatvres of the woll bible. **1556** OLDE *Antichrist* 8 Al hole Germany..euery where cruelly vexed. **1597** HOOKER *Eccl. Pol.* v. liv. 114 To be the peace of the whole world. **1610** SHAKS. *Temp.* II. i. 315 The roare Of a whole heard of Lyons. **1613** —— *Hen. VIII,* I. i. 12 All the whole time I was my Chambers Prisoner. **1616** R. C. *Times' Whistle* v. (1871) 66 The lease..For a whole hundred yeares is good in lawe. **1654** H. L'ESTRANGE *Chas. I* (1655) 186 That Parliament from which the hole Kingdome expected a Reformation. **1667** MILTON *P.L.* II. 353 An Oath, That shook Heav'ns whol circumference. **1678** MOXON *Mech. Exerc.* iv. 73 Should workmen hold the Blade of the Paring Chissel in their whole hand. **1709** STEELE *Tatler* No. 78 ¶8 Hippocrates, who visited me throughout my whole Illness. **1756** TOLDERVY *Hist. Two Orphans* I. 169 In all the whole enlightened system. **1784** COWPER *Tiroc.* 225 The stout tall captain,..upon whom they fix Their whole attention. **1845** M. PATTISON *Ess.* (1889) I. 2 The whole..manner of looking at things alters with every age. **1849** MACAULAY *Hist. Eng.* vii. (1858) II. 462 The whole Anglican priesthood, the whole Cavalier gentry, were against him. *c* **1850** *Arab. Nts.* (Rtldg.) 632 He related his whole adventure from beginning to end.

(*b*) with numeral, as ***the whole three*** (†***the three whole***), ***two whole*** (†***whole two***).

a **1375** *Joseph Arim.* 340 ȝif vchon haue a godhede I graunte, bi him-selue, I seie þat on is also good as þe þreo hole. *c* **1380** *Sir Ferumb.* 4631 Charlys þe Citee þo gan asayle, Two dawes hole. **1577** HANMER *Anc. Eccl. Hist.* 80 Lying whole six dayes vnburied. **1597** BEARD *Theatre God's Judgem.* x. (1612) 41 A..pestilence, which lasted whole tenne yeares. **1611** *Bible* Acts xxviii. 30 Paul dwelt two whole yeeres in his owne hired house. **1641** J. JACKSON *True Evang. T.* I. 32 The fourth Persecution..wherein the Church had no breathing for whole twenty yeares together. **1796** ELIZA HAMILTON *Lett. Hindoo Rajah* (1811) II. 311 He ..staid whole ten days. **1827** O. W. ROBERTS *Voy. Centr. Amer.* 228, I brought the whole three to the ground at one shot.

(*c*) with pl. sb. (*the, my,* etc. *whole*...): now chiefly *Sc.* (replaced ordinarily by *the whole of the*...or *all the*...); formerly also without article (now only as in c).

1516 in Leadam *Sel. Cases Star Chamb.* (Selden Soc.) II. 115 Theseid decrees..shalbe..obserued..by the hole Burgesses and inhabitauntes of the same Towne. **1521** LD. T. DACRE in Ellis *Orig. Lett.* Ser. II. I. 279 Not doubting.. but ye shalbe..recompensed of your hool dueties with th'arreragies. **1596** *Edw. III,* I. i, All the whole dominions of the realm. **1650** EARL MONM. tr. *Senault's Man bec. Guilty* 89 There be whole intire Nations which approve of Incest. **1680** in *Proc. Soc. Antiq. Scot.* (1911) XLV. 233 All the whole ministers are content to be ordered by the enemies of Christ. **1764** GOLDSM. *Hist. Eng. in Lett.* (1772) II. 203 The French..having reduced almost the whole Netherlands to their obedience. **1798** *Monthly Mag.* Dec. 436 My whole friends are against me; all my friends. **1808** JEFFERSON *Writ.* (1830) IV. 112 We shall get our whole sea-ports put into that state of defence. **1831** CARLYLE *Sartor Res.* i. 2 His whole other tissues are included. **1895** *Times* (weekly ed.) 26 Apr. 324/1 A third of the whole inhabitants of India.

†(*d*) with sing. sb., without article: All, the whole of. *Obs.*

1535 COVERDALE *1 Esdras* viii. 7 He taught whole Israel all righteousnes & iudgment. **1551** T. WILSON *Logic* (1552) 165 b, As though whole religion stoude in these pointes onely. **1591** SAVILE *Tacitus, Agricola* 242 The figure..of whole Britannie, by Liuy.., is likened to a long dish or two edged axe. **1657** W. RAND tr. *Gassendi's Life Peiresc.* Ep. Ded., Not only whole Europe, but Asia also..had their Eyes ..fixed upon this Province. **1826** SOUTHEY *Vind. Eccl. Angl.* x. 455 *note,* All creatures stand astonished, whole Nature is amazed.

†**b.** In phr. ***whole and some*** (cf. 'all and some', ALL A. 12 a), rarely ***full and whole,*** following a plural or collective noun or a plural pronoun: The whole number or amount, 'the whole lot', all; in all, altogether. *Obs.*

c **1374** CHAUCER *Anel. & Arc.* 26 For which the people blisfull hole and somme..crydon [etc.]. ? *a* **1400** *Arthur* 424 And all þeire power hooll & soom. *c* **1430** *Hymns Virgin* (1867) 49 Alle to-gidere, boþe hool & some, To teer him from þe top to þe toon. **1542** UDALL *Erasm. Apoph.* 243 b, He made all the people full and whole to gase on hym. *Ibid.* 281 b. *a* **1566** R. EDWARDS *Damon & Pithias* (1571) Fj b, Though I be not learned, yet cha mother witte enough whole & some.

c. With rhetorical emphasis, where there is implication of an unusually large quantity or number.

1628 EARLE *Microcosm., Herald* (Arb.) 71 He tels you of whole fields of gold and siluer, Or and Argent. **1664** BUTLER *Hud.* II. III. 147 Sitting..Whole days and nights. **1855** MACAULAY *Hist. Eng.* xii. III. 163 Whole towns..were left in ruins. **1911** G. E. SMITH *Anc. Egyptians* I. 2 Whole shelves of libraries are filled with the records of this quest.

8. a. Not divided into parts or particles; not ground, broken up, or cut in pieces; undivided, entire. (Of various things, material and immaterial.) Cf. 2.

c **888** ÆLFRED *Boeth.* xxxiv. §12 Hwæþer þu þonne ongite þæte ælc þara wuhta þe him beon þencð, þæt hit þencð ætgædere bion, ȝehal, untodæled? forðæm ȝif hit todæled bið, þonne ne bið hit no hal. [*c* **1000** [see YHOLE]. *a* **1240** *Sawles Warde* in *O.E. Hom.* I. 251 Iteilede draken grisliche ase deoflen þe forswolheð ham ihal.] **1375** BARBOUR *Bruce* VI. 78 He saw the brayis hye standand, The vattir holl throu slike rynand. **1382** WYCLIF *Prov.* i. 12 Swolewe wee hym.. hol as the descendende in to the lake. *c* **1430** *Two Cookery-bks.* 9 Take þe pertryche, an stuffe hym wyth hole pepir. **1484** CAXTON *Fables of Æsop* v. ix, Pulle the skynne fro the body..& kepe it hoole. **1513** *Bk. Keruynge* in *Babees Bk.* 279 The goos & swanne may be cut as ye do other fowles yᵗ haue hole fete. **1530** PALSGR. 833 By retayle, as men sell wares that they sell nat hole [*i.e.* wholesale: cf. B. 3 b] or by great. *a* **1533** LD. BERNERS *Gold. Bk. M. Aurel.* let. iii. (1535) 105 b, We ete dyuers thynges by morsels which if we shulde eate hole, wolde choke vs. **1597** HOOKER *Eccl. Pol.* v. lvi. 126 A deede must either not be imputed..or..they which haue it by imputation must haue it such as it is whole. **1617** MORYSON *Itin.* I. 14 The walles being all of whole trees as they come out of the wood. **1648** BP. HALL *Rem. Wks.* (1660) 198 For the paschal Lamb it must be set on all whole. **1677** MOXON *Mech. Exerc.* ii. 32 Which will neither way be so strong as the Worm cut out of the whole Iron. **1709** T. ROBINSON *Vind. Mos. Syst.* 32 Moses..makes Fish and Fowl Congenial..From their manner of feeding, being both Swollowers hole. *a* **1756** ELIZA HAYWOOD *New Present* (1771) 197 One pint of whole oatmeal. **1806** A. HUNTER *Culina* (ed. 3) 215 To a pint of strong gravy, put two small onions sliced, a little whole pepper. **1842** LOUDON *Suburban Hort.* 687 In the manner of gooseberries and apples..baked whole in a dish. **1859** TENNYSON *Marr. Geraint* 318 Here had fall'n a great part of a tower Whole, like a crag that tumbles from the cliff.

†**b.** Undivided in allegiance or devotion; loyal, faithful, steadfast. (Cf. *whole-hearted, -souled,* in D. 2 d.) *Obs.*

13.. *E.E. Allit. P.* B. 594 þere he fyndez al fayre a freke wyth-inne þat hert honest & hol. *c* **1374** CHAUCER *Troylus* III. 1001, I..shal..Ben to yow trewe and hol with al myn herte. **1451** *Paston Lett.* I. 208 The Sheriff is noght so hole as he was, for now he wille shewe but a part of his frendeshippe. **1535** COVERDALE *Ps.* lxxvii[i]. 37 Their herte was not whole [1611 right] with him, nether continued they in his couenaunt. **1553** BRADFORD in Coverdale *Godly Lett.* (1564) 344 Gods deare chyldren, whose hartes are whole wyth the Lorde.

†**c.** Not divided in opinion; united, unanimous.

1451 *Paston Lett.* I. 183 The Kyng, by the hole advyse of all the greet Councell of Ingland,..send hider his said Commission. **1540–1** ELYOT *Image Gov.* iii. 3 b, By the hole consent of the Senate and people. *a* **1548** HALL *Chron., Hen. VI* 185 To whome they, with a whole voyce, aunswered nay, nay.

d. *Math.* Of a number: Denoting a complete and undivided thing, or a set of such things (not a part of a thing); integral, not fractional.

†In first quot., Composed of three prime factors: = SOLID *a.* 2 b (*obs.*).

c **1430** *Art of Nombryng* ix. (1922) 46 Of nombres one is lyneal, anoþer superficialle, anoþer quadrat, anoþer cubike or hoole. **1557** RECORDE *Whetst.* A ij, Some are whole nombers..Other are broken nombers, and are commonly called fractions. **1608** R. NORTON *Stevin's Disme* A 3 b, A Whole number is either a vnitie, or a compounded multitude of vnities. **1842** GWILT *Archit.* 229 A product.. is generated by the multiplication of two or more numbers. .. All whole numbers cannot result from such a multiplication.

e. *Coal-mining.* Applied to a portion of a coal seam which has not yet been worked, or is in the earlier stage of working: see quots.

1860 *Engl. & For. Mining Gloss.* (ed. 2) 67 *Whole,* where the coal has not been previously worked. **1883** GRESLEY *Gloss. Coal-m., Whole* or *Whole Mine* (N[orth of England]), that portion of a coal seam being worked by driving *headings* into it only, or the state of the mine before *bringing back* the *pillars,* or what is called *working the broken,* commences... *Whole Stalls* (S[outh] W[ales]), two or more stalls having their faces in line or on a thread with one another.

9. Constituting the total amount, without admixture of anything different; full, unmixed, pure. In various connexions: often opposed to *half.* **a.** ***whole blood***: see BLOOD *sb.* 9. So ***whole brother*** or ***sister,*** a brother or sister of the whole blood, i.e. a son or daughter of both the same parents (as distinguished from a HALF-BROTHER or HALF-SISTER).

1377 LANGL. *P. Pl.* B. XVIII. 375 Ac alle þat beth myne hole bretheren in blode & in baptesme. *c* **1420** *Chron. Vilod.* 711 Twey sones he had..Edwyge and Edgar, his hole brother. **1444** *Rolls of Parlt.* V. 104/2 No maner Walssh man of hole blode, ne half blode on the fader side. **1544** tr. *Littleton's Tenures* 1 Hys next cosyn collaterall of the hole blode. **1697, 1810** [see BLOOD *sb.* 9]. **1826** J. F. COOPER *Last of Mohicans* viii, As for me, who am of the whole blood of the whites.

†**b.** Said of a person who has the whole of some possession, charge, or function, not sharing it with any one else: = SOLE *a.* 5 b. *Obs.*

c **1420** *Chron. Vilod.* 3281 Knoude was made hole kyng of alle Englonde. **1455** *Rolls of Parlt.* V. 312/2 Hole heire in the taylle to the said Thomas. **1530** RASTELL *Bk. Purgat.* I. xv, One hye hole ordener of al thyngs. **1540** BARNES in Foxe *A. & M.* (1583) 1199/2 His grace is made a whole kyng, and obeyed in his Realme as a kyng. **1628** in *Engl. Hist. Rev.* (1918) Jan. 35 My..Nephew Thomas..whom I make my whole and onelie Executor.

c. *Bookbinding.* Forming the whole of the cover: opp. to HALF- II. j.

1839 *J. R. Smith's Catal. Second-hand Bks.* Dec. 8/1 Whole calf. **1879** in *Cassell's Techn. Educ.* IV. 87 The whole-binding..means that the whole of the cover of the book is covered with the same leather.

d. ***whole holiday***: a day the whole of which is observed as a holiday (opp. to HALF-HOLIDAY 2 c).

1839 LD. HOUGHTON *Barren Hill* iii. Poet. Wks. 1876 II. 109 Whole-holidays of joy. **1895** K. GRAHAME *Golden Age* 8 With us it was a whole holiday; the occasion a birthday.

e. Of a team of horses: All of the same colour, 'whole-coloured'.

1892 *Daily News* 31 May 6/1 Sir John, who used always to have a whole team, has now got one brown horse as wheeler.

B. *sb.* **1. a.** The full, complete, or total amount; the assemblage of all the parts, elements, or individuals (*of*). With def. art. (rarely with possessive); ***the whole of*** = all.

†In early use occas. (as in A. 7) qualified by *all.*

1398 TREVISA *Barth. De P.R.* XVII. i. (Bodl. MS.), A tree ..haþ no meuynge of hit silfe, noþer al þe hole noþer parties þereof. *c* **1440** *Jacob's Well* 201 ȝyf þou ȝyue counseyl to takyn..wrongfully oþeres good,..& be þi counseyl þat wrong is don in-dede, þou art bounde to restore þe hole. **1582** *N.T.* (Rhem.) Matt. xiii. 33 Leauen, which a woman tooke and hid in three measures of meale, vntil the whole was leauened. *a* **1586** *Satir. Poems Reform.* xxxv. 9 Quhy sould the hoill, for thair desert, That faine wald haue that fact withstand,..beir the blame? **1593** SHAKS. *Lucr.* 1159 They that loose halfe with greater patience beare it, Then they whose whole is swallowed in confusion. *c* **1600** —— *Sonn.* cxxxiv. 14 He paies the whole, and yet am I not free. **1615** E. S. *Brit. Buss* in Arber *Engl. Garner* III. 636 The very First Year's herrings only, may bring in to the Adventurer or Owner; all his whole both of Stock and Charges of £934 5s. 8d. aforesaid. **1709–29** V. MANDEY *Syst. Math., Arith.* 6 A number that measures the whole, and that which is taken away, will also measure the remainder. **1759** JOHNSON *Rasselas* xxviii[i], The good of the whole, says Rasselas, is the same with the good of all its parts. **1823** COBBETT *Rur. Rides* (1885) I. 273 In the whole of my ride, I have not seen much finer fields of wheat. **1840** THACKERAY *Barber Cox* Mar., The whole of the gentlemen of the hunt. **1853** SOYER *Pantroph.* 185 Thicken with flour, and pour the whole on the deer when roasted. **1889** H. W. PICTON *Story of Chem.* 296 We now define a salt as an acid having the whole or part of its hydrogen replaced by a metal.

b. U.S. ***the Whole*** = the Whole House (see COMMITTEE 3).

1840 *Congressional Globe* 5 May 364/2 The House then resolved itself into Committee of the Whole.

c. In a charade, ***my whole*** denotes the complete word of which the syllables, called *my first* and *my second,* are the parts.

c **1789** *Encycl. Brit.* (1797) IV. 341/1 My *first* is equally friendly to the thief and the lover... My *second* is light's opposite... My *whole* is tempting to the touch, grateful to the sight, fatal to the taste. *Night-shade.* **1836** *Penny Cycl.* VI. 489/1 My first makes use of my second to eat my whole [French *chiendent*]. **1844** G. S. FABER *Eight Dissert.* (1845) II. 262 If in the process, the actual Dissyllable itself, in that species of amusement technically called *my whole,* should evaporate into thin air.

2. Something made up of parts in combination or mutual connexion; an assemblage of things united so as to constitute one greater thing; a complex unity or system. Usually with indef. art.; also in pl.

1697 tr. *Burgersdicius' Logic* I. xiv. 43 A Whole is that which consists in the Union of any things, or Parts. **1725** WATTS *Logic* I. vi. §7 All Parts have a Reference to some Whole. **1732** POPE *Ess. Man* I. 267 All are but parts of one stupendous whole. **1791** W. GILPIN *Forest Scenery* II. 62 All together the view is picturesque. It is what the painter properly calls a whole. There is a fore-ground, a middle-ground and distance—all harmoniously united. **1821** SHELLEY *Hellas* 776 This Whole Of suns, and worlds, and men, and beasts, and flowers,..Is but a vision. **1833** TENNYSON *Pal. of Art* 58 Full of great rooms and small.., All various, each a perfect whole. **1860** J. BROWN *Horæ Subs.* Ser. II. (1861) 229 A child begins by seeing bits of everything;..it makes up its wholes out of its own littles. **1865** TYLOR *Early Hist. Man.* i. 1 The complex whole which we call Civilization.

3. Phrases in senses 1 and 2. **a. as a whole** (sense 2): as a complete thing (not in separate parts); as a unity; in its entirety, all together. So, in reference to a pl. sb., *as wholes.*

1828 CARLYLE *Misc., Goethe* (1857) I. 192 The beauty of the Poem as a Whole. **1852** MRS. STOWE *Uncle Tom's C.* xix, I must sustain his administration as a whole, even if there are, now and then, things that are exceptional. **1865** LECKY *Ration.* (1878) II. vi. 210 How readily nations, considered as wholes, always yield to the spirit of the time. **1912** *Engl. Hist. Rev.* Oct. 697 A close division in the committee might be reversed on appeal to the cabinet as a whole.

†**b. by the whole**: = WHOLESALE 1. *Obs.*

1592 GREENE *Upstart Courtier* E iv b, If the Currier bought not Lether by the whole of the Tanner, the shomaker might haue it at a more reasonable price.

c. in (the) whole. (*a*) To the full amount, in full, entirely, completely, wholly. (Usually, now always, without *the*: opp. to *in part.*)

c **1440** *Jacob's Well* 202 þou art bounde to restore þat thefte in þe hole. **1553** BRADFORD *Serm. Repentance* (1574) C v, They..which..wil prate, our merites or workes to satisfy for our syns in part or in whole. **1802–12** BENTHAM *Ration. Judic. Evid.* (1827) II. 118 They may have been spurious in the whole, or incorrect in every part. **1826** SOUTHEY *Let. to H. Taylor* 31 Aug. in *Life* (1850) V. 266 Collecting my stray letters, and selecting such, in whole or in part, as may not unfitly be published. **1855** NEIL *Boyd's Zion's Flowers* Introd. 8 This Work ought to be printed in whole. **1913** *Act 3 & 4 Geo. V*, c. 20 §123 Any creditors whose claim he has rejected in whole or in part.

(*b*) In total amount, all together, all told, in all. (Almost always with *the.*) Now *rare.*

1551 SIR J. WILLIAMS *Accompte* (Abbotsf. Club 1836) 24 White plate, of course broken siluer.., ccc oz. amountinge in thole. **1552–3** in Feuillerat *Revels Edw. VI* (1914) 108 Mowldes for the feltmakers to mowlde hattes vpon at xvj^{d} the pece in the hole ij^{s} viij^{d}. **1600** *Southampton Crt. Leet Rec.* (1906) II. 336 The expence of powder..wch charge in the wholle cannott amount vnto lese then..fyfty pownds yerely. *c* **1720** DE FOE *Mem. Cavalier* (1840) 255 They were..twice our number in the whole. **1754** in *Nairne Peerage Evid.* (1874) 48 Making up in whole..the sum of nine thousand merks. **1815** COLERIDGE *Let. to Lady Beaumont* 3 Apr., Three poems, containing 500 lines in the whole. **1918** *Act 8 & 9 Geo. V*, c. 27 §1 Any..sums not exceeding in the whole the sum of one million pounds.

d. on or **upon the whole**: (*a*) on the basis of the affair as a whole; considering the whole of the facts or circumstances; all things considered; 'taking it all together'. Hence †(*b*) as the upshot, or summing up, of the whole matter; as a final result, ultimately, in conclusion, in fine, in sum; (*c*) in respect of the whole, notwithstanding exceptions in detail; in general, for the most part.

The construction with *of* (quot. 1771) is *rare* and *obs.*

1698 COLLIER *Immor. Stage* 126 Shakespear's Sr. John has some Advantage in his Character... But the Relapser's business, is to sink the Notion, and Murther the Character, and make the Function, despicable: So that upon the whole, Shakespear is by much the gentiler Enemy. **1771** GOLDSM. *Hist. Eng.* III. 392 Upon the whole of this treaty, it was considered as inglorious to the English. **1780** COWPER *Adjudged Case* 21 On the whole it appears..that the spectacles plainly were made for the Nose. **1852** DICKENS *Bleak Ho.* lx, Still, upon the whole, he is as well in his native mountains. **1887** RUSKIN *Præterita* II. v. 179 [I] determined that the Alps were, on the whole, best seen from below. (*b*) **1711** STEELE *Spect.* No. 4 ¶1 Upon the whole I resolved..to go on in my ordinary Way. **1719** DE FOE *Crusoe* II. (Globe) 328 We came up with them, and in a word, took them all in, being..sixty four Men, Women, and Children... Upon the whole, we found it was a French Merchant Ship. **1768** GOLDSM. *Goodn. Man* Pref., Upon the whole, the author returns his thanks to the public for the favourable reception which 'The Good-Natured Man' has met with. *a* **1774** —— *Hist. Greece* II. 246 Upon the whole he was unanimously sentenced to die. (*c*) **1797–1811** JANE AUSTEN *Sense & Sensib.* xlii, She liked him..upon the whole, much better than she had expected. **1849** MACAULAY *Hist. Eng.* iii. I. 327 The clergy were regarded as, on the whole, a plebeian class. **1878** HUTTON *Scott* iii. 34 She made on the whole a very good wife. **1920** *Times Lit. Suppl.* 29 Apr. 266/2 We only have [in *King John*] the text of the first folio of 1623, but that upon the whole is admitted to be good.

4. *Coal-mining.* A seam or portion of coal not yet worked, or in the earlier stage of working: see A. 8 e.

1747 HOOSON *Miner's Dict.* G 3, If the Wholes be too Soft, that we think it will let the Forks settle when they come to be weighted, we put a Sill under them. **1883** [see A. 8 e].

C. *adv.* **a.** Wholly, entirely, fully, perfectly. *Obs.* exc. in nonce-use in explicit or implied opposition to *half* (and, like that word, sometimes hyphened to the word it qualifies).

1338 R. BRUNNE *Chron.* (1810) 279 Now is Scotland hole at our kynges wille. *c* **1374** CHAUCER *Anel. & Arc.* 310, I myght als weele kepe Aueryll from Rayne As holde yow trewe and make yowe hoole stedfaste. **1390** GOWER *Conf.* I. 136 Al the world in Orient Was hol at his comandement. *c* **1400** *Rom. Rose* 2068 That ye haue me surprised so And hole myn herte taken me fro. *a* **1500** *Chaucer's Dreme* 5 With her mantle whole couert. *a* **1533** LD. BERNERS *Gold. Bk. M. Aurel.* xiii. (1535) G ij b, I am hole ignorant of this yonge mans lyuynge. **1535** COVERDALE *Jer.* xlii. 15 Yf ye be whole purposed to go in to Egipte. **1585** T. WASHINGTON tr. *Nicholay's Voy.* I. viii. 8 b, Mayden slaues..being commonly whole naked. *a* **1586** *Satir. Poems Reform.* xxxv. 26 Mortounis race To covatice wes hoill Inclynde. **1656** COWLEY *Mistr., Innoc. Ill* iii, The ills thou dost are whole thine own. **1784** COWPER *Task* I. 608 War and the chase engross the savage whole. **1815** SCOTT *Guy M.* xliv, Laying a half-dirty cloth upon a whole-dirty deal table. **1854** R. S. SURTEES *Handley Cr.* xxvii, The half-dressed groom would whole-dress the horse. **1905** F. T. BARTON *Sporting Dogs* 204 A black-and-tan sire and dam produce a whole-red puppy.

†**b.** Pleonastically emphasized by *all*; occas. = In all, altogether. *Obs.*

This may often be construed as adj.: cf. A. 7.

1390 GOWER *Conf.* II. 157 Ytaile al hol thei overcome. *c* **1400** *Rom. Rose* 2363, I..comaunde thee That in oo place thou sette all hoole Thyn herte withoute halfen doole. *c* **1450** *Merlin* 317, I putte me all hooll in youre ordenaunce. **1481** CAXTON *Godfrey* x. 33 Alle the peple hool fledde to fore hym. *Ibid.* lvi. 97 This bataylle endured wel an houre al hoole. **1509** HAWES *Past. Pleas.* VIII. (Percy Soc.) 31 As after this shall appere more openly, All hole exprest by dame Phylosophy.

†**c.** Qualifying a following adv., forming advb. phr. (in which *whole* may sometimes be construed as adj.), as ***whole out***, throughout; ***whole together***, all together (occas., altogether, entirely).

a **1425** *Cursor M.* 13303 (Trin.) Twelue were þei to telle in dole Whenne þei were to gider hole. *c* **1430** *Freemasonry* (1840) 15 Alle the masonus..Wol stonde togedur hol y-fere. **1535** COVERDALE *1 Esdras* vi. 28 Also, that they shall buylde the house of the Lorde whole vp. **1551** TURNER *Herbal* I. Kj, Some call it wylde succory: but it is hole together smaller. **1562** *Ibid.* II. 50 b, The bark, pill, or shell of the Citron, is dry and hote in the thyrde degre hole out. **1677–8** MARVELL *Corr.* Wks. (Grosart) II. 595 The Commons were yesterday taken up..in hearing the cause..which not having..heard whole out, they orderd for to-morrow.

D. Special Collocations and Combinations.

1. The adj. qualifying a sb., forming phrases used in special senses: **whole caboodle**: see CABOODLE; † **whole cannon**, † **whole culverin**, a cannon or culverin of the full size, as distinguished from a DEMI-CANNON or DEMI-CULVERIN (also *fig.* and *attrib.*); **wholefood**, unrefined food containing no artificial additives; an article or kind of such food; **whole hog**, in the slang phr. ***to go to the whole hog*** (see HOG *sb.*[1] 11 b): also (usu. with hyphen) *attrib.* as *adj.*, thorough-going, out-and-out; hence nonce-derivatives, as ***whole-hogger***, ***-hoggery***, ***-hoggism***, ***-hoggite***; ***whole-hogging*** adj. = *whole-hog* adj.; **whole kit and boiling**, etc.: see KIT *sb.*[1] 3; **whole meal**, meal or flour made from the whole grain of wheat, etc. (sometimes including the bran); also *attrib.*; also (*colloq.*), a wholemeal loaf; **whole milk**, milk from which no constituents have been removed; also *attrib.*; **whole-moulding** ***Ship-building***, name for an old method of forming the principal parts of a vessel, now used only for boats; cf. quot. *c* 1850 s.v. *whole-moulded* in 2 d; **whole nine yards** *U.S. colloq.*, everything, the whole lot; also as *adv.*, all the way; **whole note** *Mus.*, †(*a*) a whole tone or major second, as distinguished from a 'half note' or semitone; (*b*) a semibreve, as the longest note in ordinary use (now *U.S.*); **whole plate** *Photogr.*, see PLATE *sb.* 5 c; also *attrib.*; **whole shift**, in violin-playing (see SHIFT *sb.* 15); **whole silk** [tr. med.L. (*h*)*olosericum*, ad. Gr. ὁλοσηρικός, f. ὅλος whole + σηρικός of silk], stuff consisting entirely of silk; **whole-stitch** *Lace-making*, a stitch in which the threads are woven together as in cloth; **whole tone** *Mus.* = *whole note* (*a*); ***whole-tone scale*** (see quot. 1928); freq. with reference to compositions based on this scale, particularly those of Debussy; **whole wheat**, wheat which has not been deprived of some constituents by sifting; usu. *attrib.* (with hyphen or as one word), designating flour or foodstuffs made from this. See also WHOLE CLOTH, WHOLESALE.

1666 *Lond. Gaz.* No. 65/2 Designing the building of twelve new Ships,..intending they shall carry a hundred Brass Guns a piece, and the lower Tyre *whole Cannon. **1723** E. STONE tr. *Bion's Math. Instrum.* v. iv. (1758) 147 Ordnance..an Eight-Pounder, a Demi-Culverin, a Twelve-Pounder, a Whole-Culverin, a Twenty-four-Pounder, a Demi-Cannon, Bastard-Cannon, and a Whole-Cannon. **1598** MARSTON *Sco. Villanie* I. iv. D 3, With *whole culuering raging othes to teare The vault of heauen. **1647** WARD *Simple Cobler* (1843) 85 Ye talke one to another with whole Culvering and Canon. **1723** [see *whole cannon*]. **1960** *Mother Earth* Oct. 341 We should like to hear from further growers who may have available supplies of *wholefood, especially winter salads, parsnips [etc.]. **1971** *It* 2–16 June 23/3 (Advt.), The Country Bizarre is a little seasonal magazine on traditions, crafts..whole food culture, poetry, drawings. **1978** *Peace News* 25 Aug. 19/3 (Advt.), If you are interested in wholefoods, running a shop collectively and a political awareness of food please contact us. **1980** *Times* 21 Feb. 12/3 The longest lunch queues in London now are for wholefood... Vegetarian restaurants and health food shops are not new. What is changing is their style. **1829** *Virginia Herald* (Fredericksburg) 28 Mar. 2/3 Of late he has shown a disposition to become 'a *whole hog man'. **1830–1876** Whole hog [see HOG *sb.*[1] 11 b]. **1855** I. C. PRAY *Mem. J. G. Bennett* 141 James Gordon Bennett..is a thoroughgoing, 'whole-hog' Jackson man. **1935** *Planning* 23 Apr. 8 Once you start planning you cannot stop half-way, and whole-hog planning means tyranny. **1956** N. PEVSNER *Englishness of Eng. Art* iii. 61 In the architecture of about 1900 there is in England the fresh yet friendly and human style of Voysey, not the whole-hog throwing overboard of all traditions as in Frank Lloyd Wright in America. **1977** *Rolling Stone* 30 June 69/2 My guess is that few white Rhodesian soldiers out there in the bush are wholehog white supremacists anymore. **1903** *Daily Chron.* 14 Oct. 4/4 The Chamberlainite party of '*whole hoggers'. **1904** *Daily Chron.* 28 July 5/6 The country is sick of the whole-hoggers, the half-hoggers,..and the whole lot of them. **1907** E. NESBIT *Enchanted Castle* xi. 333 Your ancestors were whole-hoggers. They have done the thing as it should be done—every detail attended to. **1920** D. H. LAWRENCE *Women in Love* xxix. 438 He is such a whole-hogger. **1923** R. MACAULAY *Told by Idiot* I. xvii. 60 Stanley was like that—enthusiastic, headlong, a deep plunger, a whole-hogger. **1966** *Listener* 26 May 749/1 In the matter of theatre censorship, I am a whole-hogger. **1834** SOUTHEY *Doctor* Interch. xvi, The *Whole-hoggery in the House of Commons. **1934** C. LAMBERT *Music Ho!* v. 301 He [*sc.* Berg] cannot be described as a *wholehogging atonalist. **1943** WYNDHAM LEWIS *Let.* 24 Nov. (1963) 370 He is a whole-hogging Thomist. **1960** *Guardian* 27 June 7/2 Whole-hogging festival visitors. **1838** *Carlisle Patriot* 18 Aug. 2/5 The quaint version which the *Times* gave the other day of '*whole hoggism'. **1848** *Blackw. Mag.* July 54 Purge the land of moderatism and anti-whole-hog-ism. **1906** *Westm. Gaz.* 23 Jan. 7/2 A Balfourite with leanings towards 'whole-hoggism'. **1840** *Whole-hoggites [see HOG *sb.*[1] 11 b]. **1620** VENNER *Via Recta* i. 18 Bread is also wont to bee made of the *whole meale, from which the bran is not separated. **1828** KEIGHTLEY *Fairy Mythol.* II. 182 A nice half griddle of whole-meal bread. **1903** LD. W. B. N[EVILL] *Penal Serv.* xv. 211 Neat little brown wholemeal loaves. **1904–5** *Civil Service Supply Price-list* 60 Whole Meal..per 7 lb. bag, 1/4. *Ibid.* 128 Biscuits, Cabin, Navy, and Whole Meal. **1967** Wholemeal [see HOVIS]. **1983** A. T. ELLIS *Other Side of Fire* xvi. 102 Small white, small wholemeal and a couple of croissants. **1970** *Kenya Farmer* Feb. 9/2 We send 110 gallons *whole milk per day to Eldoret and separate all the rest for rearing stock. **1977** *Lancet* 19 Feb. 388/1 Sensitivity to cow's whole milk was investigated in six patients. **1982** P. RANCE *Great Brit. Cheese Bk.* I. v. 97 These wholemilk cheeses, traditional in this area, vary considerably. **1797** *Encycl. Brit.* (ed. 3) XVII. 405/1 Of the Method of *Whole-moulding..used by the ancients, and which still continues in use among those unacquainted with the more proper methods. *c* **1850** *Rudim. Navig.* (Weale) 159 By whole-moulding, no more is narrowed at the floor than at the main breadth. **1970** *Word Watching* Apr. 7/2 **Whole nine yards*, the entire thing. **1981** *Washington Post* 16 Jan. (Weekend sect.) 20/3 A Japanese disaster film, *Virus*, goes the whole nine yards, showing the city as a deserted freeway underpass. **1983** *Aviation Week* 7 Mar. 46/2 The Army came out and gave us the whole nine yards on how they use space systems. **1597** T. MORLEY *Introd. Mus.* Annot. ¶b, A *whole note is that which the Latines call *integer tonus*, and is that distance which is betwixt any two notes, except *mi* & *fa*. **1698** *Phil. Trans.* XX. 250 The Difference of [a Fourth and Fifth] they agreed to call a Tone; which we now call a Whole note. **1890** *Science-Gossip* XXVI. 18/2 Printing from *whole-plate negatives. **1876** ROCK *Text. Fabr.* 9 The first emperor who wore *whole silk for clothing. **1882** CAULFEILD & SAWARD *Dict. Needlework*, **Whole Stitch*, a name sometimes applied to the Cloth Stitch of Pillow Lace. **1897** J. S. SHEDLOCK tr. *Riemann's Dict. Mus.* 863/1 **Whole-tone*, the larger of the two progressions by tone within the fundamental scale. **1928** *Melody Maker* Feb. 209/3 The *Whole Tone Scale..is composed entirely of intervals of a Tone, thus having only *seven degrees* between its Tonic and its Octave. It has only come into use quite recently and is employed by the school devoting itself to..'futuristic' harmony. **1934** [see ELEVENTH *sb.* 2]. **1935** G. ABRAHAM *Stud. Russ. Mus.* iv. 77 Dargomïzhsky's fondness for the sharpened fifth of the scale, for the augmented triad which is, so to speak, the 'common chord' of the whole-tone scale. **1952** B. ULANOV *Hist. Jazz in Amer.* (1958) 284 The augmented chords and whole-tone melodies reveal their Debussyan source more clearly. **1977** *Time* 21 Mar. 62/3 His inclusion of Russian folk music, Turkish airs, even the whole-tone scale from the Orient (more than half a century before Debussy) suggests that he was exceptionally curious and openminded. **1903** *Wholewheat bread [see *peanut butter* s.v. PEANUT 3 a]. **1946** *Sun* (Baltimore) 14 Feb. 14/1 As everybody knows, whole-wheat bread is more nutritious than white bread. **1971** *Times* 11 Sept. 10/4 The distinction between *galettes* (made from buckwheat or wholewheat) and crêpes. **1980** *Sunday Times* (Colour Suppl.) 20 Jan. 57/1 The most basic, natural loaves of all, contain 100 per cent whole wheat flour.

2. a. Combinations formed of phrases like those in 1 used *attrib.* or as adjs., in sense 'Consisting of, made with, relating to, comprising, or occupying the or a whole...', as ***whole-arm***, ***-body***, ***-cane***, ***-day***, ***-fruit***, ***-grain***, ***-house***, ***-width***, ***-word***, ***-world***; (in sense A. 9) ***whole-leather***, ***-worsted***. (See also *whole-colour*, etc. in d.)

1410 *Rolls of Parlt.* III. 637/2 Lesquelles sount appellez an Hol-worsted bed. **1820** LAMB *Elia* Ser. I. *Christ's Hospital*, The haunting memory of those whole-day leaves. **1866** HOWELLS *Venet. Life* xvi. 246 A grand, whole-arm movement. **1903** *Westm. Gaz.* 9 Oct. 6/3 A whole-leather boot could not be honestly purchased under 7s. 11d. **1904-5** *Civil Service Supply Price-list* Index p. cii, Whole Fruit Jam. **1910** *Encycl. Brit.* II. 28/1 (*Angling*), A light whole-cane rod of stiff build. [Cf. *split-cane*, quot. 1890, s.v. SPLIT *ppl. a.* 2.] **1920** *Cornh. Mag.* Nov. 533 A whole-day tramp across country. **1947** *Radiology* XLIX. 283/1 To determine whether a daily dose of whole-body irradiation when given over a period of several hours produced the same injury as when given within minutes. **1952** *Archit. Rev.* CXI. 212/2 The Radiation 'whole-house' warming system. **1960** *Farmer & Stockbreeder* 15 Mar. (Suppl.) 10/1 Second-class protein ..is found in whole-grain cereals, nuts, lentils and soya beans. **1961** *Lancet* 7 Oct. 784/2 Modification..would require interference with the normal whole-body response to injury. **1964** P. A. D. MACCARTHY in D. Abercrombie et al. *Daniel Jones* 157 This in turn facilitates the recognition of whole-word patterns. **1983** P. NIESEWAND *Scimitar* xx. 566 Lyle and Ross were..subjected to everything from lumbar punctures and sperm tests to whole body scans. **1975** *Language for Life* (Dept. Educ. & Sci.) xxvi. 521 Word recognition is not merely a matter of learning unique whole-word forms. **1976** *National Observer* (U.S.) 19 June 8 (Advt.), Your Trane Comfort Corps consultant is a full-time specialist in whole-house air conditioning. **1976** *Woman's Day* (U.S.) Nov. 158/2 Unleavened whole-grain bread should be served generously to assure that your family fills up on fat- and cholesterol-free foods. **1977** *Times* 10 Sept. 2/1 Patients from several London hospitals are being sent to BUPA's medical centre to be X-rayed by their EMI whole-body scanner. **1980** *Redbook* Oct. 220/1 Most important, the teaching of beginning reading was dominated by the 'whole-word' or 'look-say' method, in which children learned to recognize entire words, rather than by the method of 'phonics' in which they learned to sound out letters and groups of letters. **1985** *N.Y. Times Mag.* 6 Jan. 6/4 Popular among runners of marathons who stuff themselves with whole-grain pasta before trotting off to the day's race.

b. Parasynthetic comb., in various senses of the adj., as ***whole-backed, -bodied, -headed, -maned, -skinned, -skirted*** adjs. (See also *whole-chested*, etc. in d.)

1607 TOPSELL *Four-f. Beasts* 288 The Istrian Horsses are of good able feete, very straight, *whole backt, and hollow. **1577** HARRISON *England* III. xii. 111/1 in *Holinshed*, Flies.. whether they be cut wasted, or *whole bodyed..are voyde of poyson. **1844** H. STEPHENS *Bk. Farm* II. 660 If the carts are whole-bodied, the steward proceeds after the back-board is removed, to hawk out the dung; but if they are tilt or *coup*-carts [etc.]. **1611** COTGR., *Ail masle*, the *Whole-headed Garlicke. **1776** WITHERING *Bot. Arrangem.* 503 *Whole-leaved Water hemp Agrimony. **1685** *Lond. Gaz.* No. 2069/4 A bright bay Gelding..*whole maned unless cut since. **1523-34** FITZHERB. *Husb.* §56 If thou bye kye or oxen to feede,..loke well..that he..be *hoole-mouthed, and want no tethe. **1776** DA COSTA *Elem. Conchol.* 209 (Jod.) The first genus, which he calls 'wholemouthed'..is my genus of 'turbo' among the..snails. **1624** FLETCHER *Rule a Wife* I. i, He is *whole skin'd, has no hurt yet. **1683** *Lond. Gaz.* No. 1910/4 A new *whole skirted Black Saddle having the Seat of Velvet and the Skirts of Hogs skin.

c. Advb. comb., as *whole-bred* (see d); see also C.

d. Special Combs.: **whole-bred** *a.* [cf. A. 9a], of pure breed (opp. to HALF-BRED 1); †**whole-chase boot** (see quot.); †**whole-chested** *a.*, having a sound chest or breast; *fig.* loyal-hearted; **whole-colour, -coloured** *adjs.* [A. 9], of the same colour throughout, concolor; **whole-eared** (-ɪəd) *a.*, (*a*) having the ears whole, i.e. not cut; (*b*) listening 'with all one's ears', i.e. intently; so **whole-eyed** (-aɪd) *a.*, gazing intently; **whole-earther** *colloq.*, somebody who is actively concerned about the protection and wise use of natural resources and wildlife; **whole-feather** [A. 9], a variety of pigeon having all the feathers of one colour; so **whole-feathered** (-əd) *a.*; **whole-hearted** *a.*, (of a person) having one's whole heart in something, completely devoted (orig. and chiefly *U.S.*); (of an action, etc.) done with one's whole heart, thoroughly earnest or sincere; hence ***whole-heartedly*** adv., ***whole-heartedness***; **whole-hoofed** (-hu:ft) *a.* [A. 8], having undivided hoofs, solidungulate; **whole-length** *a.*, (*a*) of a portrait, etc. representing the whole human figure, usually standing; also *ellipt.* as *sb.* a whole-length portrait or statue; (*b*) *gen.* extending through the whole length; exhibited at full length; **whole-life** *a.*, pertaining to or designating an insurance policy for which the premiums are payable until the death of the insured person; **whole-minded** *a.*, giving one's whole mind to something, completely interested; hence ***whole-mindedness***; **whole-moulded** *a. Ship-building*, see quot. *c* 1850, and cf. *whole moulding* in 1; **whole-number rule** *Physics*, the empirical law that the atomic weights of the elements are mostly close to being whole numbers; **whole-pull** *Change-ringing*, see quots. (opp. to *half-pull*, HALF- II. n); **whole rock** *a. Geol.*, designating the use of a complete rock sample in an analytical procedure, as distinct from the individual minerals composing it; **whole-sail** *a.*, said of a wind in which a ship (esp. a yacht) can carry full sail; **whole-seas** *humorous nonce-wd.*, quite drunk (after *half-seas*, short for HALF-SEAS-OVER 2); **whole-souled** (-səʊld) *a.* orig. *U.S.* = *whole-hearted*; †**whole-steal** *nonce-wd.*, 'wholesale' theft; †**whole-stone** *a.*, (of lime) unslaked; **whole-time** *a.*, occupying the whole of some particular time, esp. of the working time; (of a person) employed during the whole time; **whole-timer**, = FULL-TIMER; **whole-working** *Coal-mining*, see quot., and cf. A. 8e, B. 4.

1846 *J. Baxter's Libr. Pract. Agric.* (ed. 4) II. p. xxi, A *whole-bred Southdown fat wether. **1656** BLOUNT *Glossogr.*, **Whole-chase Boots*, are whole hunting, or large riding Boots. **1603** J. DAVIES *Microcosmos* 37 We are *whole-chested, and our Breastes doe hold A single Hart, that is as good, as great. **1633** MASSINGER *Guardian* IV. i, A well timbred youth..he's whole chested too. **1896** *Westm. Gaz.* 2 Dec. 1/2 The collection includes a series of *whole-colour porcelain and soft paste blue and white. **1857** T. MOORE *Handbk. Brit. Ferns* (ed. 3) 42 Scales *whole-coloured or indistinctly two-coloured. **1907** *R. Leighton's New Bk. Dog* 429 The litter will consist of some whole-coloured blacks, and some whole-coloured whites. **1681** *Lond. Gaz.* No. 1633/4 A large light Brindle Mastiff Dog, ..*whole-Ear'd. **1975** *Times* 5 Aug. 12/7 The 'amenity lobby'..includes a new wave of '*whole earthers': notably the Conservation Society founded in 1966..and Friends of the Earth. **1980** *Blair & Ketchum's Country Jrnl.* Oct. 67/1 It includes..neo-Jeffersonians, back-to-the-landers, whole-earthers, communists, and neopioneers seeking to revive old country ways. **1918** W. J. LOCKE *Rough Road* xv, The village turned out to listen to them in *whole-eyed and whole-eared wonder. **1879** L. WRIGHT *Pigeon Keeper* 118 A Splash..may often be mated to advantage with a *Whole-feather. **1683** *Lond. Gaz.* No. 1799/4 A large black Mayled, *whole Feathered, and thorough mewed Falcon. **1840** CHANNING *Let. to Miss Aikin* 18 July, What a *whole-hearted man! as we Yankees say. **1855** PUSEY *Doctr. Real Presence* Notes 366 The most perfect and whole-hearted repentance. **1901** *Scotsman* 14 Mar. 6/4 The whole-hearted support of British policy by the Canadians. **1893** in Barrows *World's Parl. Relig.* I. 534 Socially, we unite *whole-heartedly and without reservation with our non-Jewish fellow-citizens. **1854** FABER *Growth in Holiness* iv. 60 The great lesson of the Crucifix is *whole-heartedness with God. **1882** FARRAR *Early Chr.* IV. xxii. II. 43 A wavering disposition,..a want of whole-heartedness, a dualism of life and aim. **1601** HOLLAND *Pliny* VIII. xxi. I. 206 In India, there be found bœufes *whole hoofed, with single hornes. *Ibid.* XI. xlvi. 351 In some parts of Sclavonia, the Swine are not cloven-footed, but whole houfed. **1677** PLOT *Oxfordsh.* 187 The Quadrupeda, whereof some are μονώνυχα, whole-hooft, such as Asses, Mules, Horses. **1835** [see SOLIPED *a.*]. **1748** RICHARDSON *Clarissa* (1768) III. 259 Your drawings.. are all taken down; as is also your own *whole-length picture. **1752** CHESTERF. *Let. to Son* 28 Nov., Undoubted originals (whether heads, half-lengths, or whole-lengths, no matter) of Cardinals Richelieu, Marzarin, and Retz. **1817** T. F. DIBDIN *Bibliogr. Decam.* II. 434 *note*, A small whole length of Joseph with an angel above. **1818** HAZLITT *Engl. Poets* iv. 139 The faultless whole-length mirror that reflected his own person. **1856** FARIS EL-SHIDIAC *Pract. Gram. Arabic* 18 Swelling the grammar unnecessarily with a great number of whole-length conjugations. **1865** C. R. LESLIE & T. TAYLOR *Sir Joshua Reynolds* I. 104 The portrait which tended most to establish his reputation was a whole-length of Captain Keppel..on a sandy beach. **1845** *Williams's Directory of Leeds* 46 (Advt.), One-third of the '*Whole Life' Premium may remain unpaid..as a Debt upon the Policy. **1881** *Harper's Mag.* Jan. 79/1 Never take a whole-life policy to embarrass the declining and unproductive years of life. **1977** *National Observer* (U.S.) 15 Jan. 9/2 Whole life—also called cash-value, straight, permanent, ordinary and endowment life—combines insurance protection with a savings or endowment plan. **1906** *Lit. World* 15 Nov. 504/2 Whilst admitting..the great spirit and immense intellectuality of the woman, he cannot but feel..a lack of sincerity, of *whole-mindedness. **1797** *Encycl. Brit.* (ed. 3) XVII. 406/1 Fixing a point for the aftermost timber that is *whole moulded. *c* **1850** *Rudim. Navig.* (Weale) 159 *Whole-moulded*, a term applied to the bodies of those ships which are so constructed that one mould made to the midship bend, with the addition of a floor hollow, will mould all the timbers, below the main breadth, in the square body. [**1919** F. W. ASTON in *Nature* 18 Dec. 393/2 Of more than forty different values of atomic and molecular mass so far measured all, without a single exception, fall on whole numbers.] **1923** E. N. DA C. ANDRADE *Structure of Atom* vii. 111 The *whole number rule allows us to suppose that all nuclei are built up of the same mass elements, *i.e.* protons. **1967** OLDENBERG & HOLLADAY *Introd. Atomic & Nuclear Physics* (ed. 4) xvi. 238 The great simplification was finally introduced through the whole-number rule, which indicates a few fundamental particles as building blocks of all matter. **1668** [STEDMAN] *Tintinnalogia* (1671) 54 *Whole-pulls, is to Ring two Rounds in one change, that is, Fore-stroke and Back-stroke, ..so that every time you pull down the bells at Sally, you make a new change differing from that at the Back-stroke next before; this Whole-pulls was altogether practised in former time. **1872** ELLACOMBE *Bells of Ch.* in *Ch. Bells Devon* iii. 228 A 'whole pull' includes swinging the bell round twice, off from the balance, and round up to the balance again... In whole-pull ringing each bell makes a whole pull to every change. [**1955** *Bull. Geol. Soc. Amer.* LXVI. 1711 Approximate minimum ages have been determined for the Cranberry gneiss..and Henderson gneiss by measuring A^{40}/K^{40} ratios on samples of the whole rock.] **1964** *Geochem. Internat.* I. 739/2 It was decided to determine the age of the granites by the Rb-Sr method on *whole rock samples. **1979** A. W. HOFMANN in Jäger & Hunziker *Isotope Geol.* 215 The evidence for a Caledonian age of the pre-Hercynian gneisses rests in part on two whole-rock Rb-Sr isochrons. **1885** *Sat. Rev.* 3 Jan. 11/1 The heeling occurs only in strong *whole-sail winds. **1821** *Joseph the Book-man* 85 Some, half-seas, like fools do swagger, While other some, *whole-seas, do stagger. **1834** *Kentuckian in New York* I. 190 (Thornton) [The New-Yorkers] are a *whole-souled people. **1863** HAWTHORNE *Our Old Home, Haunts of Burns* II. 72 A bust of Burns..looking..not so warm and whole-souled as his pictures usually do. **1893** F. ADAMS *New Egypt* 209 A most vigorous and whole-souled resentment. **1649** LIGHTFOOT *Battle with Wasp's Nest* Wks. 1825 I. 423 Whom you have so unworthily used, as to steal his arguments by *whole-steal. **1703** *Churchw. Acc. Bucknall, Lincs.* (MS.), 3 Chalden of *wholestone Lime. **1906** *Athenæum* 13 Oct. 421/3 The Inspector of Colleges.. will be a *whole-time officer of the University. **1918** *Act 8 Geo. V.* c. 5 Sched. I. §4 Engaged in whole-time work..of national importance. **1869** *Daily News* 18 Dec., To see that all the children of a district attend some school either as *whole-timers or half-timers. **1881** RAYMOND *Mining Gloss.*, **Whole-working*, Newc., working where the ground is still whole, i.e., has not been penetrated as yet with breasts. Opposed to *pillar-work*, or the extraction of pillars left to support previous work.

†**whole**, *v. Obs.* Also 5 hoole, 5-6 hole. [f. WHOLE *a.*]

I. 1. *trans.* To make whole, heal, cure.

14.. *Stockholm Med. MS.* I. 233 in *Anglia* XVIII. 301 þe cold festre xal be holyd with hete. *c* **1440** CAPGRAVE *Life St. Kath.* v. 1952 With whiche oyle of soores alle grevauns Whiche men suffre, it wil be hooled anoon. *c* **1450** —— *Life St. Gilbert* xxxiv. 110 Summe wer holed fro certeyn seknesse be þe merites of þis Seynt.

2. *intr.* To become whole; to recover from sickness; to heal, as a wound.

14.. *Stockholm Med. MS.* I. 241 in *Anglia* XVIII. 301 Of cler hony and rye-flour late bake a kake,..And ley't to þe hole of þe festeryd sor,..And so it schal holyn. **1460-70** *Bk. Quinte Essence* 15 þe oolde feble man schal vse þis deuyn drynk..and wiþinne a fewe dayes he schal so hool þat he schal fele him silf of þe statt and þe strenkþe of xl ȝeer. **1690** W. WALKER *Idiomat. Anglo-Lat.* 517 The wounds whole not.

II. 3. *trans.* To make into a whole; to assemble or unite.

1443-9 PECOCK *Donet* xvii. (1921) 186 þese spechis hoolid and maad of þe ij seid maners. *a* **1577** SIR T. SMITH *Commw. Eng.* (1609) 18 The Captaine wholed a multitude of people gathered..of diuers Nations..and beginneth a Commonwealth after this maner.

†**whole** = *who will* (cf. ILE).

1606 MARSTON *Parasit.* v. H4, Whole kisse thee now? whole court thee now? whole ha thee now?

whole, obs. form of HOLE *sb.*

whole cloth. A piece of cloth of the full size as manufactured, as distinguished from a piece that may be cut off or out of it for a garment, etc.

1433 *Rolls of Parlt.* IV. 451/2 Hole Clothes, called brode Clothes. **1525** *Wydow Edyth* in Hazl. *Shaks. Jest-bks.* (1864) 58 Might I be so bolde as of your hole cloth To desire you for to deliuer vnto me As much as wyll suffyse..To make a large Gowne and a Kyrtell. **1724** *Act 11 Geo. I* c. 24 § 1 Every Woollen Broad Cloth,..whether..called an End or Half Cloth, or a Long or Whole Cloth.

b. *fig.* or in fig. context, esp. in phr. *cut* (etc.) ***out of (the) whole cloth***, used in various senses; now esp. (*U.S. colloq.* or *slang*) of a statement wholly fabricated or false.

1579 G. HARVEY *Letter-bk.* (Camden) 77, I shalbe contente..to lende you the choyce of as many gentle wordes and loovelye termes as we..use to deliver ower thankes in. Choose whether you will have them given or yeeldid,..kutt owte of the whole cloathe, or otherwise powrid owte. **1594** NASHE *Christ's T.* 46 Two or three thousand pound... When hee hath it all in his handes, for a month or two he reuels it, and cuts it out in the whole cloth. **1630** BRATHWAIT *Eng. Gent.* 333 They cut it out of the whole cloth, and divide their acres peece-meale into shreds. **1634** PEACHAM *Compl. Gentl.* i. (1906) 5 The valiant Souldier..measureth out of the whole cloath his Honour with his sword. **1639** FULLER *Holy War* IV. vi. 177 This rent (not in the seam but whole cloth) betwixt these Churches. **1677** HUBBARD *Pres. St. New-Eng.* II. 1 The List or Border here being known to be more worth then the whole Cloth; That whole Tract of Land, being of little worth, unless it were for the Borders thereof upon the Sea-coast. **1843** C. MATHEWS *Writ.* 68 (Thornton) Isn't this entire story..made out of whole cloth? **1897** *Fortn. Rev.* July 140 Absolutely untruthful telegrams were manufactured out of 'whole cloth'. **1905** VACHELL *Hill* xii, That Eton captain is cut out of whole cloth; no shoddy there.

whole-footed (-fʊtɪd), *a.*

†**1.** Having 'whole' or undivided feet, i.e. with the toes united; web-footed, as a bird; *rarely*, solid-hoofed, as a quadruped. *Obs.*

13.. *E.E. Allit. P.* B. 538 þe hole-foted fowle to þe flod hyȝez. **1513** *Bk. Keruynge* in *Babees Bk.* (1868) 279 All maner hole foted fowles that haue theyr lyuyng vpon the water. **1607** TOPSELL *Four-f. Beasts* 32 The Asses of India ..differ from all other whole-footed beasts. **1696** JN. EDWARDS *Demonstr. Exist. God* I. 193 [Water-fowl] are generally whole-footed. **1704** RAY *Creation* (ed. 4) 147 Such Creatures as are whole-footed or fin-toed.

2. Treading with the whole foot on the ground, not lightly or on tip-toe.

a **1825** FORBY *Voc. E. Anglia, Whole-footed.* 1. Treading flat and heavy, as if there were no joints in the feet. **1896** WHERRY *Alpine Notes* 119 It has often been noticed in mountaineering that a guide can go face forward and whole-footed up a slope.

3. *fig.* Unreserved, frank, free and easy. *colloq.* or *slang.*

a **1734** NORTH *Life Dr. J. North* (1744) 278 His chief Remissions were when some of his nearest Relations were with him,..and then, as they say, he was wholefooted. *a* **1825** FORBY *Voc. E. Anglia, Whole-footed*..2. Very intimate; closely confederate.

† ˈ**wholeful**, *a. Obs. rare.* In 5–6 hol(e)full. [f. WHOLE *a.* + -FUL.] Health-giving, wholesome. Hence † **wholefully** *adv.*

1495 *Trevisa's Barth. De P.R.* VII. lxviii. (W. de W.) siv b/2 Iuys of Caprifoli Oynions Rewe [etc.]..with vyneygre and hony ben holfully [*Bodl. MS.* heelefulliche] layed to suche bytynges. *a* **1513** FABYAN *Chron.* VII. (1811) 306 Drawe ye..holefull water of lore of my wellys.

† **wholehead.** *Obs. rare*⁻¹. In 5 holehede. [f. WHOLE *a.* + -HEAD.] Completeness.

c **1440** *Jacob's Well* 171 þe iij. spanne lengthe muste be holehede, þat þi sorwe be hole for alle þi synnes to-gedere.

wholely, obs. form of WHOLLY.

wholeness (ˈhəʊlnɪs). [f. WHOLE *a.* + -NESS.] The quality or condition of being whole.

1. Soundness, freedom from injury; unimpaired state, integrity. Now *rare* and associated with other senses.

c **1000** in *Archiv für das Stud. d. neu. Spr.* CXXI. 46 Willende & nellende, on ȝesundfulnysse & on þan halnesse. [**1340**: see YHOLNESSE.] *c* **1374** CHAUCER *Boeth.* V. pr. iv. 127 (Camb. MS.) þou weenyst þat it be diuerse fro the hoolnesse of science, þat any man sholde deme a thing to ben oother weys thanne it is it self. **1435** MISYN *Fire of Love* II. xii. 103 Holnes..of mynde, redynes of wyll,..in holy saules, suffyrs þame not dedly to synne. **1443–9** PECOCK *Donet* x. (1921) 154 þilk hool [3rd] comaundement in his ful hoolnes is reuokid, ȝhe, and forboden. **1450–1530** *Myrr. our Ladye* 229 Neyther the godhed was mynysshed in the sonne ne the holenesse of the maydenhod in the mother. *c* **1460** *Oseney Reg.* 30 To be holde and to be had,..with all the integrite or hoolenysse in the which William of Saynte John..all þe foresaide thynges had and holde.

1883 H. DRUMMOND *Nat. Law in Spir. W.* (1884) 336 Holiness, that is..*wholeness.* **1885** *American* IX. 229 Rossa has too much regard for the wholeness of his skin to run that kind of a risk.

2. The character of having nothing wanting, or of having all its parts in due connexion; completeness, perfection; unbroken or undivided state; the quality of constituting a complex unity.

(ME. *all hoolenesse* is f. *all hool* + *nesse.*)

1398 TREVISA *Barth. De P.R.* XIX. cxvi. (1495) mm j b/1 All hoolenesse [orig. *totalitas*] and perfightnesse longyth to one & vnite. **1432–50** tr. *Higden* (Rolls) V. 279 The thynges seide..be seyde by anticipation, that the hollenesse of the story may be conservede. **1550** VERON *Godly Sayings* D iij, He dydde both geue vnto vs an wholsom refection of his body, and of his bloud, and also did brieflie assoil that hard question of his wholnes. **1581** MARBECK *Bk. Notes* 95 The wholenesse and substaunce of Baptime doth consist in two things,..the Word and the Element. **1674** N. FAIRFAX *Bulk & Selv.* 108 Those bedightings or affections that belong to it, as having parts; of which the wholeness..was one. **1744** HARRIS *Three Treat.* II. ii. (1765) 64 *note*, As far as Perplexity and Confusion may be avoided, and the Wholeness of the Piece may be preserved clear and intelligible. **1830** W. TAYLOR *Hist. Surv. Germ. Poetry* I. 265 A book of tales,.. without drift or wholeness of design: all is episode. **1849** ROCK *Ch. Fathers* I. iii. 246 The unbroken wholeness of this stone was a symbol of the unbrokenness of the Church. **1877** TENNYSON *Harold* I. ii. 114 Peace-lover is our Harold for the sake Of England's wholeness. **1886** —— *Locksley Hall 60 Yrs. After* 101 Sweet St. Francis of Assisi..He that in his Catholic wholeness used to call the very flowers Sisters, brothers.

b. The totality or total amount *of* something (*obs.*); something complete or unified (*rare*): = WHOLE *sb.* 1, 2.

a **1340** HAMPOLE *Ps.* cxxxvi. 8 Of þe & in þe..is þe hoolnes of my ioy. **1678** CUDWORTH *Intell. Syst.* Pref. A 4, These Three..taken all together, make up the Wholeness and Entireness of..The True Intellectual System of the Universe. **1856** HAWTHORNE *Engl. Note-bks.* (1870) II. 191 What shapeless and ragged utterances Englishmen are content to put forth, without attempting anything like a wholeness.

wholer (ˈhəʊlə(r)). *local.* [f. WHOLE *a.* or *sb.* + -ER¹.] (See quot.)

1633 *Terrier of Swinton* in *N. & Q.* 6th Ser. (1885) XI. 366/1 The inhabitants of Swinton as likewise the Lands are partly Wholers and partly Halfers to the Churches or Parsonages of Wath and Mexborough. Wholers are they that paye their Tythes wholy, bothe predial and personal, to one of the foresaide Churches onely, vizᵗ. to Wath onely or Mexborough onely.

wholesale (ˈhəʊlseɪl), *sb.*, *a.*, *adv.*

I. 1. Orig. two words, WHOLE *a.* and SALE *sb.*², in phr. *by whole sale* (also † *by the* or † *in whole sale*), now usually ellipt. as adv., qualifying *sell*, *buy*, or words of similar meaning: In large quantities, in gross (as opposed to *by retail*).

a **1417** *York Memorandum Bk.* (Surtees) I. 183 To sell any girdeles by retaile or holesale. **1579** WILKINSON *Confut. Fam. Love* 41 Those men which sell by whole sale haue a quicker dispatch. **1593** NASHE *Christ's T.* 53 If seates of iustice were to be solde for money, wee haue them amongst vs that would buy them vp by the whole sale. **1617** MORYSON *Itin.* III. 95 Great Merchants disdaine to sell, otherwise then by whole sale. **1731–2** *Norwich Merc.* 19–26 Feb. 3/2 William Steele..selleth the following Goods either by Wholesale or Retail. **1824** SOUTHEY *Sir T. More* (1829) I. 135 Purchasing articles for the community in wholesale. **1866** *Chamb. Encycl.* VIII. 691/1 These pegged goods [*sc.* shoes] are disposed of wholesale in boxes. **1883** *Law Times Rep.* 9 Feb. 727/1 Inviting the public to come and buy, both wholesale and retail.

2. *fig.* (with construction as in 1). In a large way, in large numbers or amount, in abundance, profusely, extensively, indiscriminately.

1601 W. CORNWALLIS *Ess.* II. xxix. Q 7, We whose narrow roomes are not able to traffick with vertue by the whole-sale but by retayle. **1613** PURCHAS *Pilgrimage* VI. vi. 489 Africanus, from whose Store-house Eusebius tooke his Chronicle,..almost by wholesale. *a* **1677** BARROW *Serm.* Wks. 1716 I. 330 St. Cyprian who was liberal by wholesale, bestowing all at once, a fair estate on God and the poor. **1741** WATTS *Improv. Mind* I. v. (1786) 108 They despise a valuable book, and..throw contempt upon it by wholesale. **1837** *Blackw. Mag.* XLII. 112 The wild Bashkirs.. slaughtered them by wholesale. **1869** GLADSTONE *Juv. Mundi* iii. 104 Homer never allows distinguished Greeks to fall wholesale by the Trojan sword. **1871** FREEMAN *Norm. Conq.* IV. xx. 503 The Norman version makes him overthrow Welsh Kings by wholesale.

† **3.** Sale in gross; *fig.* dealing in a large way or in big quantities; indiscriminate or unlimited disposal (opp. to *retail*). *Obs.*

1622 MABBE tr. *Aleman's Guzman d'Alf.* II. 166 Take them out of their tracke, put them from their whole-sale, and turne them to retayle... I will not giue a button for the best of them. **1667** *Decay Chr. Piety* i. §6 To which his ταυτα παντα σοι δωσω all this will I give (could he make such a whole-sale) can bear no proportion. **1788** PICKEN *Poems* 57 Merchants shops, For halesale or retailin'.

II. *attrib.* or *adj.* **4. a.** Selling a commodity by wholesale.

c **1645** in *Archaeologia* LII. 135 A hosyer & whole saleman for narrow wares. **1711** ADDISON *Spect.* No. 64 ¶3 A wholesale Dealer in Silks and Ribbons. **1724** DE FOE *Tour Gt. Brit.* I. 124 It being frequent for the London Wholesale Men to carry back Orders from their Dealers. **1773** *Life N. Frowde* 5 Mr. John Neville, a Wholesale ironmonger. **1812** SIR J. SINCLAIR *Syst. Husb. Scot.* II. 22 The farmer at a distance from markets..may be compared..to a wholesale merchant. **1876** F. S. WILLIAMS *Midl. Railw.* 637 Drugs from the wholesale houses for country druggists.

b. Pertaining to sale in gross; used for a commodity sold by wholesale.

1724 DE FOE *Tour Gt. Brit.* I. 130 When the great Hurry of Wholesale Business begins to be over. **1848** DICKENS *Dombey* iv, Pickles..in great wholesale jars. **1867** J. LAING *Theory of Business* ii. 15 The retail price of '13', we take to mean that shopkeepers received this amount of money for their stocks; and the wholesale price of '11', shows that they pay to warehousemen '2' less than they received. **1896** L. L. PRICE *Money* vi. 174 Greater friction prevails in the retail than in the wholesale market. **1902** *Builder* 5 Apr. p. xix, Clerk and Traveller required for a Wholesale Country Business.

c. As *sb.*, a wholesale dealer or organization.

1851, 1884 [see RETAIL *sb.*¹ (and *a.*) 3]. **1928** *Daily Express* 29 May 7/4 The ability of the wholesales to adopt methods of mass production..must be lessened.

5. *fig.* Having an extensive application; unlimited or indiscriminate in range; doing something, or done, largely, profusely, or in great quantities.

1642 FULLER *Holy & Prof. St.* II. xvii. 116 But how long shall I be retailing out rules to this Merchant?.. Take our Saviours whole-sale rule, Whatsoever ye would have men do unto you, do you unto them. **1664** BUTLER *Hud.* II. iii. 809 Those whole-sale Criticks, that..cry down all Philosophy. **1838** LYTTON *Leila* I. v, The Moors had treated this unhappy people with a wholesale and relentless barbarity. **1842** LOVER *Handy Andy* xlvii, Slaughtering lions in a wholesale way like rabbits. **1842** DICKENS *Amer. Notes* iii, I am by no means a wholesale admirer of our legal solemnities. **1843** SCUDAMORE *Gräfenberg* 27 It is a sort of wholesale theory, and equally serves for all persons, and for every known disorder. **1863** H. COX *Instit.* I. vii. 73 A wholesale creation of peers for the purpose of obtaining a majority. **1880** MRS. LYNN LINTON *Rebel of Family* xxii, 'Would you go to the colonies with the man you loved?'.. 'I would go into the desert!' she answered in her passionate wholesale way.

Hence ˈ**wholesale** *v. trans.*, to sell wholesale (in quot. *intr.* for *pass.*); also *absol.*; hence ˈ**wholesaling** *vbl. sb.* and *ppl. a.*; ˈ**wholesalely** *adv.*, in a wholesale way, extensively, profusely; ˈ**wholesaler**, one who sells goods wholesale (to retailers), a wholesale dealer; ˈ**wholesaleness**, wholesale quality, profuseness, indiscriminateness.

1800 M. L. WEEMS *Let.* 17 Dec. in *M. L. Weems: Wks. & Ways* (1929) II. 152 But for this I wd instantly *wholesale my books & quit the business forever. **1837** DICKENS in *Bentley's Misc.* Oct. 413 We have been prevailed upon to allow this number of our Miscellany to be retailed to the public, or wholesaled to the trade, without any advance upon our usual price. **1881** *Oregon State Jrnl.* 1 Jan. 7 We are prepared to Wholesale and Retail Cheaper than any place in this city. **1885** *Harper's Mag.* Jan. 289/1 English ladies' shoes, wholesaling at $1.50 per pair. **1962** R. B. FULLER *Epic Poem on Industrialization* 134 'Science News Service' An industrial syndicate Wholesaling to publishers Reported thirty thousand technical innovations. **1972** *Vogue* Jan. 12/2 They wholesale to many shops. **1984** *Listener* 23 Feb. 9/2 There is the jobber, wholesaling shares and making money out of the margin. **1906** S. E. SPARLING *Introd. Business Organization* xi. 254 In the trade jobbing is virtually synonymous with *wholesaling. **1926** N. S. B. GRAS in Crump & Jacob *Legacy of Middle Ages* 440 Although many merchants might prefer the wholesale trade, they were not allowed to be exclusively wholesaling merchants. **1975** 'E. LATHEN' *By Hook or by Crook* xiv. 137 Gregory takes care of the wholesaling in this country. Paul runs the retail stores. **1982** *Electr. Wholesaler* Sept. 40/1 He started a general electrical wholesaling firm. **1887** J. D. HOOKER in *Life* (1918) II. 295 The supposed facts..are *wholesalely unreliable. **1892** *Graphic* 24 Dec. 758/2 The very *wholesaleness of the present charges of corruption. **1857** TOOKE & NEWMARCH *Hist. Prices* V. 375 Nor..is it necessary..that the whole quantity..should be in the hands, either of the *wholesalers or the retailers. **1888** E. BELLAMY *Looking Backward* 146 The manufacturer sold to the wholesaler. **1907** *Times* 2 Oct. 3/6 In the bakery trade.. between the wholesaler and retailer the expression 'bushel' ..was a measure of weight.

wholescale (ˈhəʊlskeɪl), *a.* [f. WHOLE *a.* + SCALE *sb.*³, influenced by WHOLESALE *sb.*, *a.*, *adv.*] = WHOLESALE *a.* 5. Cf. *full-scale.*

1960 B. BERGONZI in F. Kermode *Living Milton* x. 168 Leavis's case..is not a mere critical reappraisal of Milton, but a whole-scale demolition. **1983** M. EDWARDES *Back from Brink* v. 76 If we were going to run into this sort of problem over £22 million of investment in one factory, how could we contemplate a wholescale modernisation and new product programme across BL, running into hundreds of millions of pounds in dozens of locations? **1984** *Amer. Banker* 5 June 3/1 For middle-level executives, there will be some 'shifting, but not on a wholescale scale', he said.

† **wholeship.** *Obs.* In 3 hal-, holsc(h)ipe. [f. WHOLE *a.* + -SHIP 1.] = WHOLENESS 1.

c **1230** *Hali Meid.* 7 Ilich him in halschipe, vnwemmet as he is. *a* **1240** *Ureisun* in *O.E. Hom.* I. 189 O muchele menske to beon moder of swuche sone mid holscipe [*Cott. MS.* (p. 203) iholschipe: see YHOLSCHIPE] of maiden.

wholesome (ˈhəʊlsəm), *a.* (*sb.*) Forms: see WHOLE; also 4–6 (with normal shortening) **holsum, -som,** 6–8 **wholsom**(e. (For north. dial. and Sc. forms see HALESOME.) [OE. **hálsum*, corresp. to OS. **hêlsam* (implied in adv. *hêlsamo*), MLG. *heilsam*, Du. *heilzaam* salutary (dial. = healthy), OHG. (MHG., G.) *heilsam*, ON. *heilsamr*: see WHOLE *a.* and -SOME *suffix*¹. The northern form (reinforced from ON.) is represented by HALESOME.]

1. Conducive to well-being in general, esp. of mind or character; mentally or morally healthful; tending or calculated to do good; beneficial, salutary.

c **1200** *Vices & Virtues* 111 ȝif ðu luuest ðine aȝene wille alre mast, þanne is ðe swiðe holsum ðat ðu þis ofri ðine louerde god. *c* **1200** *Trin. Coll. Hom.* 103 þenne riseð ure helend on his heorte, and techeð him holsum lore. **1382** WYCLIF *1 Tim.* vi. 3 The..holsum wordis of oure Lord Jhesu Crist. **1430–40** LYDG. *Bochas* IV. xxiii. (MS. Bodl. 263) 252/2 It is nat holsum with goddis to pleie. **1535** STARKEY *Lett.* in *England* (1878) p. xvii, Holsome ceremonys of the church. **1566** STAPLETON *Ret. Untr. Jewel* I. 22 It is manifeste..that we..do celebrate the memoriall of that One and holsome Sacrifice. **1600** MARSTON, etc. *Jack Drum's Entert.* I. (1601) A 4 b, So great a masse of coyne might mount from wholsome thrift. **1607** SHAKS. *Cor.* II. iii. 66 You'l marre all..Pray you speake to em..In wholsome manner. **1610** HOLLAND *Camden's Brit.* I. 695 A good example of wholsome severity. **1632** BROME *North. Lasse* I. iv, They are wholsomer company. **1711** ADDISON *Spect.* No. 10 ¶5, I will daily instil into them such sound and wholsome Sentiments, as shall have a good Effect on their Conversation. **1749** FIELDING *Tom Jones* I. vi, Wholesome Admonition and Reproof. **1824** SOUTHEY *Let. to G. C. Bedford* 24 May, To enjoy better air, keep better hours, and employ herself in quieter and wholesomer pleasures. **1839** THIRLWALL *Greece* xlvii. VI. 117 Thebes was destroyed.. that the example of its fate might strike the rest of Greece with a wholesome awe. **1879** FROUDE *Cæsar* ii. 12 The sober and wholesome manners of life among the early Romans had given them vigorous minds in vigorous bodies. **1892** KIPLING *Lett. Trav.* (1920) 62 It is wholesome and tonic to realise the powerlessness of man in the face of these little accidents.

2. Promoting or conducive to health; favourable to or good for health; health-giving or health-preserving; salubrious.

c **1374** CHAUCER *Troylus* I. 940 þilke ground þat bereth þe wedys wykke, Bereth eke þese holsome herbes. **1398** TREVISA *Barth. De P.R.* IX. xi. (Bodl. MS.), Marche water is not full holsom to drinke. *c* **1400** *Beryn* 2877 It is holsom to breke our fast be-tyme. *c* **1400** *Pilgr. Sowle* (Caxton 1483) IV. ii. 58 No holsome, ne lusty fruyte, but bytter and vnsauoury. *c* **1430** LYDG. *Compl. Bl. Knt.* 14 To take the holsome lusty eyre. **1528** LYNDESAY *Dreme* 96 O fair Phebus, quhare is thy hoilsum heit? **1562** TURNER *Herbal* II. 48 b, Abrecockes.. are lesse then the other peches and are holsummer for the stomack. **1613** PURCHAS *Pilgrimage* V. xvii. 457 The Ayre is not very holesome, by reason of the situation vnder the Line, and the multitude of Lakes and Riuers. **1667** MILTON *P.L.* x. 847 The still Night, not now..Wholsom and cool, and mild. **1726** LEONI *Alberti's Archit.* I. 103/1 Flat ceilings are wholesomer. **1775** ADAIR *Amer. Ind.* 230 Wholsome weeds, that their rich fields abound with. **1819** KEATS *Eve of St. Mark* 5 The city streets were clean and fair From wholesome drench of April rains. **1849** CLARIDGE *Cold Water Cure* 203 By this means the stable was rendered wholesome, and the horses..continued healthy. **1891** *Leeds Merc.* 2 May 6/5 Old spirits are more wholesome than the new, which are far more irritating to the stomach.

† **b.** Having the property of restoring health; remedial, curative, medicinal. *Obs.* (or merged in prec. sense).

c **1380** WYCLIF *Sel. Wks.* III. 27 Resseyvynge holsum medicyns of her hevenly lechis. **1484** CAXTON *Fables of Æsop* v. ix, That fayr skynne which is so holsome, ye shalle make hit to be..bound vpon your bely, and..hit shalle rendre you in as good helthe as euer ye were. **1557** TURNER (*title*) A Booke of the Bath of Baeth..with diverse other bathes moste holsom and effectual. **1590** SHAKS. *Com. Err.* V. i. 104. **1651** HOBBES *Leviath.* III. xxxii. 195 Wholsome pills for the sick.

3. Sound in (physical or moral) condition or constitution; free from disease or taint; healthy. Now *rare*, or associated with other senses.

a **1533** LD. BERNERS *Gold. Bk. M. Aurel.* x. (1535) F j b, He hated delicate and gay nurses, and they that were laborous homely and holsome he loued. **1602** SHAKS. *Ham.* I. v. 70 It doth..curd..The thin and wholesome blood. *Ibid.* III. ii. 271. **1614** B. JONSON *Barth. Fair* II. v, *Vrs.* I, I, Gamesters, mocke a plaine plumpe soft wench..because she's iuicy and wholesome. **1653** JER. TAYLOR *Serm.* iii. (L.) It is not to be expected that a diseased father should beget wholesome children. **1820** SHELLEY *Œd. Tyr.* I. 85 He has not half an inch of wholesome fat Upon his carious ribs. **1848** DICKENS *Dombey* ii, A plump rosy-cheeked wholesome apple-faced young woman. **1851** HAWTHORNE *Ho. Seven Gables* ix, The purifying influence scattered..by the presence of one youthful, fresh, and thoroughly wholesome heart. **1896** HOUSMAN *Shropsh. Lad* xxiv, Ere the wholesome flesh decay.

Comb. **1905** SLADEN *Playing the Game* I. xi, An unusually wholesome-natured woman.

b. *transf.* of a quality, condition, place, etc. (often approaching sense 1).

1604 SHAKS. *Oth.* III. i. 49 In wholsome Wisedome He might not but refuse you. **1605** —— *Macb.* IV. iii. 105 O Nation miserable!.. When shalt thou see thy wholsome dayes againe? **1641** in Rogers *Protests of Lords* (1875) I. 5 Such as shall disturb wholesome order. **1871** R. H. HUTTON *Ess.* II. 63 A wholesome busy city like Manchester.

c. *Naut.* Of a ship (see quots.); *transf.* of the sea.

1627 CAPT. J. SMITH *Sea Gram.* xi. 52 A Ship that will try, hull, and ride well at Anchor, we call a wholsome Ship. *Ibid.*, This makes her wholsome in the Sea without rowling. **1669** STURMY *Mariner's Mag.* I. 17 The Top-mast being aloft the Ship is the holsomest, and maketh better way through the Sea. **1762** *Elsdale's Narr.* (MS.), The long continuance of the Gale had rais'd a most mountainous sea, but it was remarkably long and wholsome.

B. as *sb.* in *pl.* Wholesome things.

In first quot. in a canting use (? suggested by *fulsome*).

1731-8 SWIFT *Pol. Conversat.* 158 Bring me a Dram after my Goose; 'tis very good for the Wholsoms. **1858** *Brit. Q. Rev.* LVI. 358 To provide..tables of the wholesomes and unwholesomes. **1863** 'HOLME LEE' *A. Warleigh* III. iii, Steer clear of novels before Miss Austen and Scott; if you would like me to make you out a list of amusing wholesomes, I will do it.

wholesomely ('həʊlsəmlɪ), *adv.* [f. prec. + -LY².] In a wholesome manner.

1. In a way conducive to well-being in general; with good tendency or effect; beneficially, salutarily.

c **1200** *Trin. Coll. Hom.* 107 Þe giue of eche lif..he giueð mid þe holi husel, þanne man it understondeð rihtliche and holsumliche. **1549** COVERDALE, etc. *Erasm. Par. Rom.* vi. 1-7 This bodye of synne is then in vs effectually and holsomely slaine. **1622** A. COURT *Constancie* II. 109 Afflictions.. happen to vs wholsomely. **1650** S. CLARKE *Eccl. Hist.* I. (1654) 47 What was wholsomly advised..that he willingly assented to. **1797** *Burn's Eccl. Law* (ed. 6) I. 250 *note*, He was a good man, and wholesomely governed the church committed to him. **1879** M. ARNOLD *Mixed Ess., Democr.* 24 That which operates noxiously in the one, may operate wholesomely in the other.

2. So as to promote health; in a way favourable to health; †remedially, medicinally (*obs.*); healthily (*rare*).

1398 TREVISA *Barth. De P.R.* XVIII. xxviii. (Bodl. MS.), Auctours comaundeþ to take such whelpes holsomliche aȝens venemous bitinge of houndes. **1546** J. HEYWOOD *Prov.* (1867) 9 The meate good and holsome and holsomly drest. **1557** *Order of Hospitalls* G ij, That their Linnen be wholsomly and cleanly washed. **1611** SPEED *Theat. Gt. Brit.* I. 47 b, This Citty..standeth holsomly and sweetly, as it were vpon a hill. **1634** T. JOHNSON *Parey's Chirurg.* IX. x. (1678) 222 Those things which do wholsomly and moderately nourish. **1859** *All Year Round* No. 32. 127 Paraguay tea..adulterates the real souchong wholesomely. **1870** *Echo* 15 Nov., A sufficiency of wholesome, and.. wholesomely cooked food.

wholesomeness ('həʊlsəmnɪs). [f. as prec. + -NESS.] The quality or condition of being wholesome, in any sense.

c **1200** *Trin. Coll. Hom.* 103 On þat wise lið ure helende on his heorte, alse on sepulcre, and swiȝeð of holsumnesse lore toȝenes him, forte þat on þen þridde dai, þat is heorte be liht. *c* **1380** WYCLIF *Wks.* (1880) 239 ȝif þei loueden treuþe of god ..as moche as þei louen helþe of here body & holsumnesse of here bodily mete. **1398** TREVISA *Barth. De P.R.* VI. xxi. (Bodl. MS.), Water þat renneth..vpon cleere stones oþer grauel haþ secunde holsumnes. **1547-64** BAULDWIN *Mor. Philos.* (Palfr.) 94 b, In meats the wholsomenesse is as much to be required as the pleasantnesse. **1553** T. WILSON *Rhet.* 16 b, The holsomnesse of the ayer in other countries. **1616** PURCHAS *Pilgrimage* v. vii. (ed. 3) 588 This yeeldes not to any Indian Region, in goodlinesse and wholesomenesse. **1796** MORSE *Amer. Geog.* I. 375 Malt liquor is not so frequently used, as its wholesomeness deserves. **1807** SOUTHEY *Let. to G. C. Bedford* 4 Oct., The bitterness of the cup will have passed away, and you will then perceive its wholesomeness. **1857** TOULMIN SMITH *Parish* 333 Not only to the repair of the roads themselves, but to..the safety, wholesomeness, and comfort of the passage along them. **1906** *Lit. World* 15 Nov. 517/2 The general wholesomeness of Dr. Gladden's position is..beyond cavil.

wholewise ('həʊlwaɪz), *adv. nonce-wd.* [f. WHOLE *a.* or *sb.* + -WISE.] As a whole, completely, all at once. Also as quasi-*adj.*

1674 N. FAIRFAX *Bulk & Selv.* 107 If you ask,.. Whether it touches *secundum se totum* or not? Whether wholewise or piecewise? **1880** LANIER *Hymns of Marshes* I. 147 The..sea-rim sinks..wholewise. **1937** *Mind* XLVI. 252 The whole-wise working of the organism is further illustrated by the 'privileged postures' which we take up as a convenient background to various performances.

wholey, wholie, obs. forms of WHOLLY.

wholism ('həʊlɪz(ə)m). [Alteration of HOLISM, after WHOLE *sb.*] The doctrine or belief that wholes must be studied as such, and that the parts can only be understood in relation to the wholes to which they belong; the doctrine that evolutionary forces tend towards the forming of new and more complex wholes; = HOLISM.

1939 J. E. BOODIN *Social Mind.* p. vii, Two conceptions.. have recently been emphasized in philosophy and social theory, namely creative synthesis or emergence and wholism or gestaltism... Wholism means that..events can be understood only as figuring in a whole or gestalt. **1941** *Mind* L. 394 Boodin is fully justified in claiming both that he thought and wrote in the spirit of 'creative synthesis' and 'wholism', before these terms had been invented or had, at any rate, become popular. **1962** R. & H. HAUSER *Fraternal Soc.* 9 The keynote of their work is 'Wholism'. **1981** *Amer. Jrnl. Clin. Biofeedback* IV. 33 The biofeedback experience also highlights the concept of wholism.

Hence **'wholist** *a.* and *sb.*, **who'listic** *a.*, **who'listically** *adv.*

1941 *Mind* L. 397 As everyone knows who has studied the use of the concept of 'creative synthesis', and, in general, all 'wholistic' types of philosophy, thinkers of this school are not content to describe the Universe merely as making and unmaking wholes of various sorts. **1956** J. S. BRUNER et al. in J. S. Bruner *Beyond Information Given* (1974) ix. 163 We shall refer to the ideal strategy just described as the wholist strategy. **1962** R. & H. HAUSER *Fraternal Soc.* II. ii. 121 As wholists we ask, is not all this..activity..useless. *Ibid.* iv. 181 Our approach to the problems of violence is wholistic. **1964** F. H. BLUM in I. L. Horowitz *New Sociol.* 166 Being concerned with the totality of the human situation, he [sc. Mills] dealt with them [sc. key problems] wholistically. **1972** L. S. HEARNSAW in Cox & Dyson *20th-Cent. Mind* I. vii. 232 Between the wars a new brand of psychology was born, the psychology of personality, wholistic in its presuppositions. **1974** H. J. KLAUSMEIER et al. *Conceptual Learning & Devel.* iii. 67 We rarely receive information in a nice sequence of positive instances so that we may adopt a wholist strategy. **1980** R. HERINK *Psychotherapy Handbk.* 698 Wholistic therapy.

wholl, wholle, obs. forms of WHOLE.

whollop, var. WALLOP *sb.* and *v.*

wholly ('həʊllɪ, 'həʊlɪ), *adv.* Forms: α. see HALELY. β. 4-5 **hollich(e,** 4-6 **hoolly, holy, holly,** 5-6 **hooly,** 6-8 **wholy,** (4 **hoolliche, holiche, holyke, holilich, holi, hooli,** 5 **hoolich, holych, holli, holely, hoyly,** 6 **hol(l)ye, hoolye, holie, whol(l)ye, whol(l)ie,** 7 **wholelye, whollily),** 7-8 **wholey,** 7- **wholely,** 6- **wholly.** [ME. *hol(l)iche, iholliche*, repr. OE. type *(ȝe)hállíce: see WHOLE *a.* and -LY². For the northern form see HALELY.

The normal development of OE. (*ȝe)hállíce was (y)*hǭlliche* (14th-15th c.), giving ultimately *holly* ('hɒlɪ), which survives dialectally. But, by the influence of the adj. *hǭl* WHOLE, a type with a long root-vowel was differentiated, *hǭlliche*; this type, with *ll* retained or with simplification to *l* (which appears to have taken place as early as the 14th cent.), is represented by the modern pronunciations ('həʊllɪ) and ('həʊlɪ). The current spelling *wholly* descends from the ME. *holliche*, and has ultimately prevailed over the once common *wholely* and *wholy*, which would more normally denote the resultant standard pronunciations. (For the simplification of *ll* to *l* cf. early forms of FOULLY, *fuli, fouly, fowlye*, and SOLELY, *sooly, soly*.)]

In all senses formerly sometimes pleonastically joined with *all, full,* or *fully*: cf. WHOLE A. 7.

1. As a whole, in its entirety, in full, throughout, all of it; †formerly also (in ref. to a pl. or collect. sb.), all of them, all together, in a body. Now *rare.*

a **1300** [see HALELY]. *c* **1330** R. BRUNNE *Chron. Wace* (Rolls) 1737 Al holyke [*v.r.* All holy] com þer flote In Dertemuthe. *Ibid.* 14357 Þre ȝer holy was he kyng. **1338** —— *Chron.* (1810) 34 Alle þe regne holy was þat tyme in his hand. **1377** LANGL. *P. Pl.* B. XVII. 25 Abraham..seigh holy [*v.r.* hoolly] þe Trinite, Thre persones in parcelles departable fro other. **1395** *E.E. Wills* (1882) 8 To parfourne holelich and trewlich this..testament. ? *a* **1400** *Morte Arth.* 3368 They heldede to hir heste alle holly at ones. *c* **1450** tr. *De Imitatione* III. xxxv. 103 To restore all þinges, not only holy, but also abundantly & ouerhepid. **1512** *Act 4 Hen. VIII* c. 18 §1 As yf all the.. purporte of the same Commission ware in this present acte holly and particularly rehersed. **1597** HOOKER *Eccl. Pol.* v. lv. §7 That infinite word..could not in part but must needes be wholie incarnate. **1611** *Bible* Lev. vi. 23 Euery meat offering for the Priest shal be wholly burnt: it shall not be eaten. **1681** FLAVEL *Meth. Grace* xxxi. 536 *Non omnis moriar*, I shall not wholly die; there is a life I live, which death cannot touch. **1711** STEELE *Spect.* No. 158 ¶4, I would have a Spectator wholly writ upon Good-breeding. **1824** SCOTT *Redgauntlet* let. xi, He..took off the brandy wholely at twa draughts. **1856** RUSKIN *Mod. Paint.* III. IV. vii. §3 A man who can see truth at all, sees it wholly, and neither desires nor dares to mutilate it. **1915** D. H. LAWRENCE *Rainbow* xii. 327 Then, and then only..could he act wholely, without cynicism and unreality.

2. a. Completely, entirely, to the full extent (so that there is no deficiency); altogether, totally, thoroughly, quite.

[*a* **1300**, etc.: see HALELY. *c* **1315**, **1340**: see YHOLLICHE.] *a* **1325** *MS. Rawl. B.* 520 lf. 56 Ant ȝif ani his ipult out of suuche entre, sal he recoueren his seisine of him pleinliche ant holliche ase he þe oþere les? **13..** *E.E. Allit. P.* B. 104 Þat my hous may holly by halkes by fylled. *c* **1350** *Will. Palerne* 495 Nis he holly at my hest in hard & in nesche. **1390** GOWER *Conf.* II. 4 Sche..dede al holi what he wolde. *c* **1400** tr. *Secr. Secr., Gov. Lordsh.* 105 Y desire welfare, helth, strynght and goodnesse, all holely to come to vche man. *c* **1440** *York Myst.* viii. 22 Þai shall be..for-done hoyly, hyde and hewe. **1550** CROWLEY *Last Trumpet* 551 Do thy selfe wholly addres To walke in thy vocation. **1568** GRAFTON *Chron.* II. 270 The Archers of England shot so wholy together, that the Frenche men were faine to geue place. **1600** W. WATSON *Decacordon* (1602) 355 *Amor & dilectio* (both loue in English) were the words most, & all wholy in request. **1611** SHAKS. *Cymb.* II. ii. 10 Sleepe hath ceiz'd me wholly. **1630** PRYNNE *Anti-Armin.* 104 Mr. Bradford makes wholy for our present Tenet. *a* **1708** BEVERIDGE *Thes. Theol.* (1711) I. 8 As he [*sc.* God] is not divided..in Himself, so neither let him be in your Affections; but love Him wholly, and wholly Him. **1833** HT. MARTINEAU *Tale of Tyne* i. 5 We were wholly at a loss what to do. **1849** MACAULAY *Hist. Eng.* iii. I. 358 The great majority of the houses..have..been wholly, or in great part, rebuilt. **1918** *Cornhill Mag.* June 636 His words..were wholly admirable and true.

b. Entirely, so as to exclude everything else; hence practically equivalent to 'exclusively, solely, only, without exception'.

c **1425** *Cast. Persev.* 598 in *Macro Plays* 95 Goddys seruyse þou must forsake, & holy to þe werld þee take. **1551** UDALL *Erasm. Par. Luke* xxii. 24-30 Neither shall he take the laude and praise vnto himselfe, but referre the same entierly and whollye vnto God. **1603** G. OWEN *Pembrokeshire* (1891) 47 Inhabited wholelye by Welshmen. **1651** HOBBES *Leviath.* II. xxx. 180 The Instruction of the people, dependeth wholly, on the right teaching of Youth. *a* **1708** [see 2]. **1710** PRIDEAUX *Orig. Tithes* ii. 67 They shall give up themselves wholy hereto without entangling themselves with the World. **1847** C. BRONTË *Jane Eyre* xvii, My ear was wholly intent on analyzing the mingled sounds. **1859** TENNYSON *Marr. Geraint* 441 A creature wholly given to brawls and wine.

3. Comb.: **wholly-owned** *a.*, applied to a company all of whose shares are owned by another company.

1964 *Financial Times* 11 Feb. 12/1 The directors..have decided to give the holders of Ordinary shares the opportunity of acquiring an interest in the wholly-owned subsidiary. **1972** *Accountant* 21 Sept. 360/1 The UK company is a subsidiary—although not wholly-owned. **1976** *Scotsman* 20 Nov. 3/2 The plan is recommended by the boards of all the companies, who will become wholly-owned subsidiaries of the new Malaysian group.

wholve, *sb. dial.* Also 5 **wolve, whulve,** (7 **hulve, hull),** 8 **whoulve.** [Variant of WHA(U)VE.] A short arched or covered drain under a path.

1395 (4 June) *View of Frankpledge Gt. Waltham* (MS.), Johannes Hereward de jure reparat quemdam Wholue juxta Stonfeld. **1466** *Birchanger Court Roll*, Vnum wholve non scuratum apud Grouchemede. **1469** *Maldon, Essex, Liber B.* fol. 18 (MS.) Le whulve atte crosse. **1637** *Maldon, Essex, Docts.* Bundle 161. No. 3 (MS.) We present Abell Hawkes.. for..not laying of a hull against his gate for the passing of the watter. **1712** *Maldon, Essex, Borough Deeds*, Bundle 114, No. 17 (MS.) We present Mr. Kemp for not laying a whoulve at yᵉ great avingnilk-well mead. **1903** (Essex dial.) I've been opening a wolve.

†**wholve,** *v. Obs. rare.* [Variant of WHA(U)VE.] = WHELVE *v.* 1.

14.. *Voc.* in Wr.-Wülcker 614/42 *Supinus*, wholuyd [*printed* wholnyd].

Wholy, obs. form of HOOLEE.

1622 in Foster *Engl. Factories Ind.* (1908) II. 76 Eighteen rupp[ees] at once given in pane to certayne banyans at the feast of Wholy.

wholy, obs. form of HOLY, WHOLLY.

whom (huːm), *pron.* Forms: α. 1 **hwæm,** 1-3 **hwam,** 3-5 **wam,** 3-5, 8-9 *Sc.* **wham,** 4-5 **whame, whaym(e,** wom, 4-7 **whome,** (3 **ȝwam, whæm,** *Orm.* **whamm,** 4 **huam, whaam, whaime,** 5 **wome, hom(e, whem, waim,** 6 **hoom,** *Sc.* **vhom),** 3- **whom;** *north.* and *Sc.* 3-4 **quam,** 4-6 **quham,** 4-6, 8 **quhome,** 4-7 **quhom,** (3 **quuam,** 4 **quaym, quem, quhowm,** 5 **qwhom(e, qwom(e, qhom).** β. 1 **hwone, hwane, hwæne,** 2 **hwen,** 2-3 **hwan,** 3 **whæn, wan, ȝwan, wanne,** 3-4 **whan.** [*Whom* represents formally OE. *hwám*, later variant of *hwǽm* (:—*χwaimi), dat. of *hwá* WHO, *hwæt* WHAT, corresp. (with variation of inflexion) to OFris. *hwâm* (WFris. *wam, waam*, NFris. *hûm*), OS. *hwem(u)*, OHG. *(h)wemu, -o* (MHG., G. *wem*), ON. *hveim* (MSw. *hwem* used as dat. and acc., early Da. also *hwam*), Goth. *hwamma*. In its usage *whom* combines the functions of OE. *hwǽm* and OE. *hwone, hwane, hwæne*, acc. masc. of *hwá*, corresp. to OFris. *hwane, hwene*, OS. *hwena* (MDu., Du. *wien*), OHG. *(h)wenan, wen(en* (MHG., G. *wen*), ON. (eastern) *hwan*, Goth. *hwana*. The history of OE. *hwone*, ME. *(h)wan* is therefore illustrated under this heading in order to exhibit the merging of the original acc. and dat. under the forms of the latter. (The form-history is complicated in the 12th and 13th centuries by the fact that in weak positions *(h)wam* often became *(h)wan*, and the latter when neuter is indistinguishable from WHON¹.)

The earliest instance here recorded of the use of the dat. form as an acc. or direct object is in the indef. relative *swa hwam swa swa* = whomsoever (Laud Chron. an. 1123): see sense 6. By 1200 this shift had extended to the relative and dependent interrogative uses, but examples of the independent interrogative use are hardly earlier than 1300: see sense 1 b.] The objective case of WHO: no longer current in natural colloquial speech.

1. In an independent question. **a.** as indirect object (dative) or as object of a preposition (or after *than*).

c **1000** *Ags. Gosp.* John vi. 68 Drihten to hwam ga we? *a* **1300** *Cursor M.* 8353 O mi kingrike quat redes þou? Quam sal i giue it for to ledd? *a* **1400–50** *Wars Alex.* 463 To quam has þou þe tane till, tell me þe sothe. **1535** COVERDALE *Ezek.* xxxi. 2 Whom art thou like in thy greatnesse? —— *Isa.* xl. 18 To whom then will ye licken God? **1539** *Bible* (Great) Isa. xxviii. 9 Whom then shal such one teach knowlege? **1591** SHAKS. *Two Gent.* II. i. 153 *Speed.* To be a Spokes-man from Madam Siluia. *Val.* To whom? **1603** DEKKER & CHETTLE *Grissil* IV. i. (Shaks. Soc.) 52 Seek'st thou a better nurse? A better nurse than whom? **1780** WARNER in Jesse *Selwyn & Contemp.* (1844) IV. 369 For whom in the world do you think that I was kept so long kicking my heels? **1842** RUSKIN *Lett. to a College Friend* (1894) 129 To whom should I write if not to the only one of my friends whom I cannot see? **1866** LE FANU *All in Dark* viii, I played to-day..two rubbers of fives; with whom do you think?

b. as direct object (accusative).

971 *Blickl. Hom.* 45 Hwane manaþ God maran gafoles þonne þone biscop? *c* **1000** *Ags. Gosp.* John xviii. 4 Hwæne sece ȝe?

a **1300** *E.E. Psalter* xxvi[i]. 1 Wham sal I drede? *c* **1320** *Cast. Love* 206 Whom mai he to helpe crauen? **1382** WYCLIF *Matt.* xvi. 15 Whom seien ȝe me to be? *Ibid.* xxvii. 21 Whom of the two wolen ȝee to be left? *c* **1450** HOLLAND *Howlat* 69 Quhom sall I blame? **1513** DOUGLAS *Æneis* I. vi. 38 Bot, O thou virgine, quham sall I call the? **1535** COVERDALE *Isa.* vi. 8 Whom shall I sende, and who wilbe oure messaunger? **1539** *Bible* (Great) Ps. lxxiii. 25 Whom haue I in heauen but the? **1704** TAVERNER *Faithf. Bride* III. 27 Whom wou'dst thou injure with a Villains Name? **1855** TENNYSON *Maud* I. VI. ii, Whom but Maud should I meet? **1870** MORRIS *Earthly Par.* III. 489 Whom think you she has seen?

2. In a dependent question, or clause of similar meaning. **a.** as indirect object or as object of a preposition.

The prep. regularly precedes, but often followed in obs. Sc. use (cf. 10); in mod. use it occas. appears at the end of the clause, but in such cases in colloq. speech *who* is commonly substituted (see WHO 5).

α. *Beowulf* 1696 Swa wæs..ȝemearcod..hwam þæt sweord ȝeworht..ærest wære. *c* **825** *Vesp. Ps.* xxxviii[i]. 7 [6] *Thesaurizat et ignorat cui congregat ea*, goldhordað & nat hwæm ȝesomnað ða. *c* **1200** *Trin. Coll. Hom.* 145 þe holi gost þe him dide..to understonden þat ure drihten wolde man bicumen and ware and wanne and of wam ben boren. *c* **1200** ORMIN 12612, I sahh cumenn Godess Gast Inn aness cullfress like, & I sahh uppo whamm he comm. *c* **1205** LAY. 11404 þe king..bæd heom ræden him ræd whæm [*c* **1275** wan] he mihte bi-tæche al his kine-riche. **13..** *Cursor M.* 10718 (Gött) Thoru þis prophete sal ȝe se Til quham þe may sal spousid be. **1338** R. BRUNNE *Chron.* (1810) 93 Ne he ne wist to wham þat he mot mak his mone. **1362** LANGL. *P. Pl.* A. I. 43 Tel me to whom þat Tresour appendeþ? *Ibid.* 47 He asked..whom þe ymage was lyk. **1375** BARBOUR *Bruce* IV. 111, I wat nocht for quhat enchesoun, Na quham with he maid the cowyne. **1448** MARG. PASTON in *P. Lett.* I. 69, I fell hym so disposyd that he wold..asett to morgage all that he hath, he had nowth rowth to qhom. *c* **1470** *Gol. & Gaw.* 259 Quha is lord of yone land,..Or quham of is he haldand, Fayne wald I wit. **1504** C'TESS RICHMOND tr. *De Imitatione* IV. v. (1893) 267 Se from whom this mysterye is gyuen vnto the. **1513** DOUGLAS *Æneis* XI. xiii. 133 Thar sall thou knaw onone, Quhamto this wyndy glore, voust, or avantis, The honor, or, with pane, the loving grantis. *c* **1560** A. SCOTT *Poems* (S.T.S.) xxiii. 42 Tak heid Quhomefor thow suffer pane. **1600** FAIRFAX tr. *Tasso* VIII. liii, To spie at whom to aske we gazed round. **1671** MILTON *Samson* 1088, I..am come to see of whom such noise Hath walk'd about. **1748** RICHARDSON *Clarissa* (1768) VIII. 189 They let me go.. They little thought with whom. **1848** DICKENS *Dombey* vi, Not that he cared to whom his daughter turned, or from whom turned away. **1859** *Sporting Mag.* Feb. 77 When he found Gemmy knocked down to him (he knew not whom for). **1905** ELIN. GLYN *Viciss. Evang.* 203 Getting a note, she did not tell me whom it was from, or what it was about.

β. *c* **897** ÆLFRED *Gregory's Past. C.* xliv. 331 Ac ðu findst wið hwone ðu meaht flitan. *a* **1200** *Moral Ode* 326 in *O.E. Hom.* I. 179 We scolden..us bi-þenche..hwet we beð, and to wan we sculle and of wan we come. *a* **1250** *Owl & Night.* 1509 ȝef he biþencþ bi hwan [*v.r.* hwam] he lai, Al mai þe luue gan a-wai. **1393** LANGL. *P. Pl.* C. XIV. 158 Ich hadde wonder at wham [*v.r.* whan] and wher þat þe pye Lernede legge styckes þat leyen in here neste.

b. as direct object.

α. *c* **1205** LAY. 27487 þeo at þan laste nuste nan kempe Whæm [*MS.* whǣ] he sculde slæn on [*c* **1275** wam he solde smite] and wham [*MS.* whā; *c* 1275 wan] he sculde sparien. **1297** R. GLOUC. (Rolls) 6417 þo bed he þe court..riȝt vnderstonde Wat vorewarde þer were ymad..Bituene him & king edmund..& wan [*v.rr.* wam, wham] edmond made is eir. *a* **1352** MINOT *Poems* (ed. Hall) xi. 4 Haue minde of þi man, þou whote wham I mene. *c* **1380** WYCLIF *Sel. Wks.* I. 348 Crist axide his disciplis whom þei seiden him to be. **1526** TINDALE *Luke* xii. 5, I will shewe you whom ye shall feare. —— *John* xiii. 18, I knowe whom I have chosen. **1535** COVERDALE *Josh.* xxiv. 15 Chose you this daye whom ye wyll serue. **1582** N. LICHEFIELD tr. *Castanheda's Conq. E. Ind.* I. ix. 22 b, He..coulde not tell whom he might trust. **1610** SHAKS. *Temp.* I. i. 20 Remember whom thou hast aboord. **1693** CONGREVE *Old Bach.* V. xv, I suppose you know whom I have got—now. **1737** POPE *Hor., Epist.* I. vi. 102 Hire a Slave..To..Tell at your Levee..To whom to nod, whom take into your Coach. *Mod.* I don't know whom to ask.

β. *c* **1175** *Lamb. Hom.* 127 þe deofel..geð abutan.. sechinde hwen he maȝe fordon. *c* **1275** [see *c* 1205 in *α*].

¶ **3.** Used ungrammatically for the nominative WHO, esp. as predicate in a dependent clause (being erroneously taken as object of the verb in the principal clause; sometimes app. from confusion with the Latin acc. and inf.).

[*c* **1000** *Ags. Gosp.* Matt. xvi. 13 Hwæne secgeað menn þæt sy mannes sunu?] **1526** TINDALE *Matt.* xvi. 13 Whom do men saye that I the sonne of man am? *Ibid.* 15 But whom say ye that I am? [So **1611**; *R.V.* 1881 who.] *c* **1530** LD. BERNERS *Arth. Lyt. Brit.* x. (1814) 20, I cannot thinke whome it should be. **1592** SHAKS. *Rom. & Jul.* I. i. 205 (Qo. 1) Tel me in sadnes whome she is you loue. **1654–66** EARL ORRERY *Parthen.* (1676) 574 The Horse seem'd to know whom 'twas he carri'd. **1817** BELOE *Sexagenarian* II. 227 Whom is it you mean? **1861** MRS. H. WOOD *East Lynne* III. i, Not having the least idea of whom Afy might be.

II. Indefinite (non-relative) use.

†**4.** The indefinite use of OE. *hwá* (*hwǽm*, etc.) 'some one' did not survive, but, on the analogy of OTHERWHAT, SOMEWHAT, ME. has *sum oþer wham* = some one else. (Cf. SOMEWHO.)

1303 R. BRUNNE *Handl. Synne* 6694 þan preyde þe ryche man Abraham, þat he wlde sende Lazare, or sum oþer wham, To hys breþryn.

III. Relative uses.

Also formerly with *that* following (see THAT *conj.* 6).

5. As compound relative, or with ellipsis of antecedent (= he, him, those, etc. whom), of a person or persons: as direct object, or object of a preposition. *arch.* (Cf. WHO 8.) Often approaching the indefinite sense 6.

[*c* **950** *Lindisf. Gosp.* Luke x. 22 *Filius et cui uoluerit filius reuelare*, se sunu & huæm wælle se sunu ædeaua.] *c* **1200** ORMIN 12888 Ne þarrf ȝuw nohht nu follȝhenn me, Her iss whamm ȝuw birrþ follȝhenn. **13..** *Eufrosyne* 424 in Horstm. *Altengl. Leg.* (1878) 179/1 Whom he loueþ, he wol chastise. *c* **1400** *Apol. Loll.* 70 Wam þat ȝe þus bynd, schal be bound, and wam þat ȝe bring out of synne, þe peyn schal be forȝeuen hem. **1507** *Registr. Aberdon.* (Maitl. Cl.) I. 352 And shuld present nain therto bot quhom that pleiss the said Mr. Alexander. **1526** TINDALE *John* xvii. 3 That they myght knowe the that only very God; and whom thou hast sent Iesus Christ. **1579** FULKE *Heskins' Parl.* 347 There were there, to whom Christe sauoured better in their heart, then Manna in their mouth. *a* **1600** HOOKER *Eccl. Pol.* VI. iii. §1 We are by repentance to appease whom we offend by sinne. **1713** ADDISON *Cato* II. v, I've offer'd to..gain you whom you love at any price. **1810** CRABBE *Borough* iii, A common bounty may relieve distress, But whom the vulgar succour, they oppress. **1820** BYRON *Juan* IV. xii, 'Whom the gods love die young' was said of yore. **1842** TENNYSON *Sir Galahad* ii, How sweet are looks that ladies bend On whom their favours fall! **1876** SWINBURNE *Erechtheus* 1315 Shall the sea give death whom the land gave birth?

b. with correlative in following clause. Cf. WHO 6 a. *arch.*

c **1250** *Gen. & Ex.* 1768 Ðat is min red, Wið quam ðu is findes, ðat he be dead. *c* **1275** *Passion our Lord* 103 in *O.E. Misc.* 40 Hwam ich biteche þat bred..He me schal bitraye. **1382** WYCLIF *Matt.* xxi. 44 Vpon whom it shal falle, it shal togidre poune hym. ? *a* **1400** *Morte Arth.* 770 Whayme that he towchede he was tynt for euer! *c* **1400** [see 5 above]. **1526** TINDALE *Luke* vii. 47 To whom lesse is forgiuen, the same doeth lesse loue. **1539** *Bible* (Great) Rom. viii. 30 Whom he appoynted before, them also he called [**1611** Whom he did predestinate, them he also called]. **1883** WHITELAW *Sophocles, Oed. Col.* 1332 Unto whom..Thou shalt be friend, the victory is his.

6. In general or indefinite sense: Any one whom, whomsoever. Cf. WHO 6. *arch.* or *literary*.

†Also with the indefinite sense indicated by *ever* following: see also WHOMEVER.

a **1154** *O.E. Chron.* an. 1123 þæt hi mosten cesen of clerchades man swa hwam swaswa hi wolden to ercebiscop. *c* **1275** LAY. 9081 þe holi gost..hine dealeþ to wam him beoþ lofue. **1297** R. GLOUC. (Rolls) 4935 He ne sparde old ne ȝonge... þat he ne slou wanne [*v.r.* wham] he vond. *c* **1375** *Sc. Leg. Saints* xvi. (*Magdalena*) 601 God mychty is..al temporale thinge to gyf & tak to quham he wil. **1429** *Rolls of Parlt.* IV. 343/1 No persone..shal conceyve indignation.. azeins any other of the seide Counseill, for saiyng his advys ..to any request..that shal be spoken..in the seide Counseill, whome that ever it touche. **1449** *Reg. Mag. Sig. Scot.* 70/2 Payand thereof yerely..to me or quhom that I assign fourti markis. **1515** in Leadam *Sel. Cases Star Chamber* (Selden) II. 77 Your most honorable Counsaill or whome it shall please your highnes to..appoynte. **1535** COVERDALE *Dan.* v. 19 Whom he wolde, he set vp: & whom he list, he put downe. **1664** in *Extr. St. Papers rel. Friends* Ser. III. (1912) 215 To leaue order with Mr. Williamson, or whom elce you please, to minde my Lord Chansellour tomorrow of this letter. **1744** BERKELEY *Siris* §354 Atheism, be it of Hobbes, Spinosa, Collins, or whom you will. **1865** RUSKIN *Sesame* i. §6 We cannot know whom we would. **1866** MRS. WHITNEY *Leslie Goldthwaite* vii, By-and-by she would be making up her own excursions, and asking whom she would.

7. As simple relative introducing a defining or restrictive clause, completing the sense: cf. WHO 9.

†Also formerly as correlative to *such*: cf. WHO 9 b.

a. As object of a preposition (usually preceding, occas. following at end of clause). See also 10.

a **1175** *Cott. Hom.* 233 Al þat we habbeð of þese feder we habbeð, of wam we alle ur [?] sielþe habbeð. *c* **1200** *Vices & Virtues* 49 He ðurh hwam kinges rixit. *c* **1200** ORMIN 6995 Jesu Crist wass..þatt illke, off whamm profetess Haffdenn forrlannge cwiddedd ær, þatt [etc.]. **13..** *E.E. Allit. P.* A. 131 þe wyȝ, to wham her wylle ho waynez. *c* **1386** CHAUCER *Frankl. T.* 258, I wol been his to whom þat I am knyt. *a* **1400** *Relig. Pieces fr. Thornton MS.* (1914) 27 If þou will be of lange lyfe, it es reson þat þou honoure thaym of whaym þou hase þe lyfe. *c* **1400** *Rule St. Benet* (Prose) 17 Yef it fallis yu ani time, On waim þe for-getilnes es on-long [etc.]. **1428** *Munim. de Melros* (Bann.) 519 Til all & syndry to quham þe knawlage of þir present lettris sall to cum. **1452–3** *Paston Lett.* Suppl. (1901) 47 The personez quom thei laboryd fore. **1526** TINDALE *Luke* xiii. 4 Those xviij. apon whom the toure in siloe fell. **1539** *Bible* (Great) 1 Sam. ix. 17 This is the man, whom I spake to the of. **1600** SHAKS. *A.Y.L.* II. ii. 8 The roynish Clown, at whom so oft, Your Grace was wont to laugh. *c* **1730** RAMSAY *Eagle & Robin* 60 By sic with quhome they ar opprest. **1829** [see SUCH B. 12]. **1840** MARRYAT *Poor Jack* xix, The boy with whom I had fought. **1882** BESANT *All Sorts* xix, Here was a woman the like of whom he had never imagined.

b. As direct or indirect object.

c **1200** ORMIN 6521 He maȝȝ wel bitacnenn himm whamm he stod inn to follȝhenn. *c* **1400** *Apol. Loll.* 68 þe disciplis lowsid him liuing, wam dead þe maister had reisid. *c* **1420** *Prose Life Alex.* 46 He sall be my helpere, wham in dremez I sawe appere vn-to me. **1507** *Reg. Privy Seal Scot.* I. 227/2 ȝe and ilk ane of ȝow quham it efferis. **1582** N. LICHEFIELD tr. *Castanheda's Conq. E. Ind.* I. ix. 22 b, Those whom he gaue license to enter aboorde his ship. *a* **1600** MONTGOMERIE *Sonn.* lvii. 2 Vha wald behold him vhom a god so grievis? **1632** MILTON *L'Allegro* 124 To win her Grace, whom all commend. **1680** in *Proc. Soc. Antiq. Scot.* (1911) XLV. 233 These men quhom blesed King Jesus delighteth to honour. **1751** JOHNSON *Rambler* No. 178 ¶9 Knowledge is praised and desired by multitudes whom her charms could never rouse from the couch of sloth. **1850** GLADSTONE *Glean.* (1879) II. 65 He was one of the most extraordinary men whom this century has produced. **1871** 'MARK TWAIN' *Lett.* (1920) 112, I think I shall call it 'Reminiscences of Some Pleasant Characters Whom I Have Met,' (or should the 'whom' be left out?).

8. Introducing an additional statement; thus sometimes = 'and him (her, them)': cf. WHO 10. †Formerly occas. preceded by *the* (cf. *the which*, WHICH B. 13). **a.** As direct or indirect object.

a **1300** *Cursor M.* 10 Kyng arthour..Quam non in hys tim was like. **1382** WYCLIF *Gen.* xxii. 2 Tak thin oonli gotun sone, whom thow louest. *c* **1386** CHAUCER *Friar's T.* 103 Witnesse on Iob whom that we diden wo. *c* **1420** ? LYDG. *Assembly of Gods* 854 Grace was the guyde of all thys gret meyny. Whom folowyd Konnyng with hys genalogy. ? **1472** *Stonor Papers* (Camden) I. 125, I trust to alle myty Jhesu to know more to my hertes ese than I do now, hom I beseche to preserve [you]. **1526** TINDALE *1 John* iv. 20 Howe can he that loveth nott his brother whom he hath sene, love god whom he hath not sene? **1556** LAUDER *Tractate of Kyngis* 95 The kyng had..The rewle of hunders and thousandis, Quhome that he sufferit..To tyne and perysche. **1566** W. P. tr. *Curio's Pasquine in Traunce* 108 Peter Luis..whom all men say to be a moste filthy Sodomite. **1645** ROW *Hist. Kirk* (1842) p. xxx, Otheris had gon out befor, quhom we thocht now to be slain. **1667** MILTON *P.L.* I. 438 Astoreth, whom the Phœnicians call'd Astarte. **1681** DRYDEN *Abs. & Achit.* 580 The Rascal Rabble..Whom Kings no Titles gave, and God no Grace. **1781** COWPER *Retirement* 742 Grant me still a friend in my retreat, Whom I may whisper—solitude is sweet. **1793** BURNS *Scots! wha hae* 2 Scots! wham Bruce has aften led. *a* **1849** H. COLERIDGE *Ess.* (1851) II. 84 Warburton (whom I presume to have been the annotator).

b. As object of a preposition (usually preceding, occas. following after the verb); also after *than* (see THAN 2 b). See also 10.

As to details of construction see note s.v. WHICH B. 7 a.

c **1200** *Trin. Coll. Hom.* 179 For eues gulte to wan ure drihten sede. In dolore paries filios. *Ibid.* 181 For adames gulte, to hwam ure drihten seide:..On þine nebbes swote þu shalt þin bred noten. *c* **1200** ORMIN 1976 Allmahhtiȝ Godd, þurrh whamm ȝho wass wiþþ childe. **1297** R. GLOUC. (Rolls) 220 Ascayn biȝet silvi, of ȝwan þe brut com. *a* **1300** *Cursor M.* 736 A messager he send, Wit quam best to spede he wend. *Ibid.* 5342 Eue, o quam we al began. *Ibid.* 9530 Doghtres four..To quam ilkan he gaf sum-thing. *c* **1325** *Metr. Hom.* 17 This Symond, of quaym I spak are. *c* **1380** WYCLIF *Sel. Wks.* III. 99 þe Holy Gost, to wham is apropryed love. *c* **1400** *Rule St. Benet* (Prose) 19 To god, of whaim þat al þe gude cumis. *c* **1400** tr. *Secr. Secr., Gov. Lordsh.* 88 Oon god, ffro whem ilke merueylouse werk descendys. *c* **1460** METHAM *Wks.* (1916) 96 Yt sygnyfyith that..that persone schuld haue a frend vpon home he schuld trost, the qwyche schuld dysseyve hym qwan he hath most nede. **1537** LATIMER *Let. to Cromwell* in *Facs. Nat. MSS.* (1866) II. xxxi, The byrth of our prynce, hoom we hungurde for so longe. **1548–1876** [see THAN 2 b]. **1611** SHAKS. *Wint. T.* IV. iv. 539 Your Mistris; from the whom, I see There's no disiunction to be made. **1667** MILTON *P.L.* v. 468 His wary speech Thus to th' Empyreal Minister he [*sc.* Adam] fram'd. Inhabitant with God [etc.]..To whom the winged Hierarch repli'd. **1796** H. HUNTER tr. *St. Pierre's Study Nat.* (1799) I. 433 His neighbours, the number of whom is restricted to four or five, according to the extent and form of his domain. **1872** TENNYSON *Gareth & Lynette* 878 Haughtily she replied. 'I fly no more...' To whom Sir Gareth answer'd courteously, 'Say thou thy say, and I will do my deed.'

9. a. Used in reference to a thing or things: orig. dative of WHAT (sense C. 7), later as a general objective case of WHICH (sense B. 7 or 8). *Obs.* exc. with personification: cf. WHO 11 c.

With the examples in *β* cf. WHON[1].

α. *c* **1175** *Lamb. Hom.* 129 Ðis is sunfulla monna leddre þurh hwam ure drihtan teh to him al moncun. *Ibid.* 153 þis beoð þe fif ȝeten þurh hwam kimð in deðes wurhte. *c* **1250** *Gen. & Ex.* 696 Ydolatrie ðus was boren, For quuam mani man is for-loren. *c* **1320** *Cast. Love* 1086 Algate he haþ mis-don, þorw whom he is in my prison. **1390** GOWER *Conf.* III. 3 It is the cuppe whom he serueth, Which alle cares from him kerveth. *c* **1400** tr. *Secr. Secr., Gov. Lordsh.* 106 My lawe & my fayth, yn whom y am norshyd. **1432–50** tr. *Higden* (Rolls) I. 27, I haue studiede that hit schal be called *Policronicon* of the pluralite of tymes whom it dothe conteyne. **1448–9** METHAM *Amoryus & Cleopes* 1263 A ston ..The name off home serpentyne ys. **1513** DOUGLAS *Æneis* VII. vii. 89 The round top of tre,..Quham childer drivis byssy at thair play. **1535** STEWART *Cron. Scot.* (Rolls) II. 334 He..left the way in quhome he first began. **1551** TURNER *Herbal* I. K v, We haue no herbe in Englande that I knowe to whome all thes hole descriptions do agre. **1562** *Ibid.* II. 81 Peplis whome som call wild porcellayn. **1608** DEKKER *Dead Tearme* C 3, What a rare inuention..was pen and Incke, out of whom (as streames from a Fountaine) flow all these wonders. **1611** SPEED *Theat. Gt. Brit.* 11/1 Redrith and Frensham..betwixt whom are extended thirty foure miles. **1648** tr. *Senault's Paraphr. Job* 163 Those trees, whom the thunder hath beaten down. **1770** LUCKOMBE *Hist. Printing* 466 The vowels..are seventeen in number; five of whom are pronounced long.

β. *c* **1200** *Vices & Virtues* 127 Tach me godnesse ðurh wan ich god muȝe bien. *c* **1275** LAY. 7220 He makede þane kalender bi wan geoþ al þe ȝer. *Ibid.* 7633 þat ilke swerd ..þorh wan his bane he hadde. *c* **1290** *St. Brandan* 580 in *S. Eng. Leg.* 235 Fewe goddedes ich haue i-don of ȝwan ich nouþe may telle. *a* **1300** *Leg. Rood* (1871) 24/72 An vaire welle Of wan alle þe wateres þat beþ anerþe comeþ.

b. Used in reference to a number of persons collectively: cf. WHO 11 a.

c **1230** *Hali Meid.* 10 Al is nawt þet ti folc—of hwam i spec þruppe—biheten þe to ifinden. **1297** R. GLOUC. (Rolls) 1315 þe kunde blod of þis lond of wam we boþe come. **1592** KYD *Sp. Trag.* III. i, The world, With whome there nothing can prenaile but wrong. **1606** G. W[OODCOCKE] *Hist. Ivstine* xxx. 102 The very same Army whom he had there standing in battell arraye. **1608** SHAKS. *Per.* I. iv. 22 A Cittie on whom plentie held full hand. **1671** MILTON *Samson* 1100 The unforeskinn'd race, of whom thou bear'st The highest name for valiant Acts.

c. Used in reference to animals: cf. WHO 11 b.

1340–70 *Alex. & Dind.* 793 Tri-cerberus þe tenful of wham i tolde haue. **1456** SIR G. HAYE *Law Arms* (S.T.S.) 85 His gude hors, in quham he traistis sa mekle. **1667** MILTON *P.L.* IV. 184 A prowling Wolfe, Whom hunger drives to seek new haunt for prey. **1770** GOLDSM. *Des. Vill.* 93 A hare whom hounds and horns pursue. **1783** JOHNSON in *Boswell* (1904) II. 478, I have had cats whom I liked better than this. **1849–52** *Todd's Cycl. Anat.* IV. II. 833/2 In the Horse, in whom the supra-renal corpuscles are yet richer in nerves.

†**10.** With a preposition immediately following, the two being often written as one word, forming compounds like those with *where-* (WHERE 15 b), but used in reference to persons (occas. to things). *Obs.* (chiefly *Sc.*).

c **1375** *Sc. Leg. Saints* xxxi. (*Eugenia*) 300 þe abbot of þat abbay, Quham-of before ȝe herd me say. **1461** *Rolls of Parlt.* V. 477/1 William Lord Bonvile, and Sir Thomas Kiryell,.. whom to he made feith and assurans..to kepe and defend theym. **1508** DUNBAR *Gold. Targe* 85 May, of myrthfull monethis quene,..Quham of the foulis gladdith al bedene. **1526** in M. A. E. Green *Lett. Royal Ladies* (1846) II. 7 His grace's lieges..whom at the said earl..has displeasure. **1551** ROBINSON tr. *More's Utopia* II. (1895) 253 For them, whomewyth they be in wayges, they fyghte hardelye. **1583** *Rot. Scacc. Reg. Scot.* XXI. 560 Samekle thairof to ather of thame quhomunto it appertenis. **1660** *Nicholas Papers* (Camden) IV. 252 The saide Sir Rob. Walsh, whome concerning I haue giuen sufficient precautions.

¶**11.** Used ungrammatically for the nominative WHO, as subj. or pred. in the relative clause, esp. (in later use only) when erron. taken as obj. of a verb of which the whole clause is really the obj.: cf. 3.

1467 *Stonor Papers* (Camden) I. 96, I schall se..yow.. with Godes Grase, whome evyr preserve yow and yowrs for his mersy. *c* **1540** tr. *Pol. Verg. Engl. Hist.* (Camden 1846) 271 Certayne of them..(whome mie minde geeveth mee are to bee folowed). **1557** NORTH *Gueuara's Diall Pr.* IV. xix. (1568) 169 b, I counsel..all wise..men, that they doo not accompany wyth those whom they know are not secret. **1603** DEKKER & CHETTLE *Grissil* IV. ii. (Shaks. Soc.) 65 Let him be whom he will. **1653** WALTON *Angler* 30 Comparing the.. humble epistles of S. Peter, S. James and S. John, whom we know were Fishers, with the glorious language..of S. Paul, who we know was not. **1752** MRS. LENNOX *Female Quix.* VII. ii, Are they yonder Knights whom you suppose will attack us? **1837** DICKENS *Pickw.* xxix, A strange unearthly figure, whom Gabriel felt at once, was no being of this world. **1906** R. H. BENSON *Richard Raynal* 81 He saw the man whom he knew must be the King.

¶**12.** In irregular constructions. **a.** With pleonastic personal pronoun in the latter part of the relative clause; often also with anacoluthon, *whom* serving as apparent obj. to a verb whose real obj. is a dependent clause of which the pron. is subj. (cf. 11). **b.** Preceded by redundant *and*: cf. WHO 12 b.

1556 *Chron. Grey Friars* (Camden) 46 The erle of Angwyche..whome the kynge had kepte hym with his brother and dyvers other here in Ynglond. **1567** PAINTER *Pal. Pleas.* II. 92, [He] asked..what hee shoulde doe to a woman, whome hee suspected that she hadde falsified hir fayth. **1606** G. W[OODCOCKE] *Lives Emp.* in *Hist. Ivstine* K k 2, Otho the third..was crowned Emperour by Gregory the fifth, his kinsman,..and whom he had preferred to the papacy. **1608** TOPSELL *Serpents* 23 Cælius Rhod..termeth the great deuill Ophioneus, whom both holy Scripture, and auncient Heathen say, that hee fell out of Heauen.

¶**13.** with genitive inflexion: ***whomes*** = WHOSE. [Cf. (M)Du. *wiens*, WFris. *hwiens*.] *Obs. rare.*

c **1489** *Plumpton Corr.* (Camden) 83, I purpasse to persew the law against him in their names, whomes cattell he heretofore helped to stele.

whom, obs. form of HUM *sb.*[1]

a **1529** SKELTON *Bouge of Court* 191 Wyth whom and ha, and with a croked loke.

whom, whome, obs. forms of HOME *sb.*[1]

whomble, whomel, var. WHEMMEL.

whomever (huːmˈɛvə(r)), *pron. literary.* Also *poet.* **whome'er** (-ˈɛə(r)). [Orig. two words, WHOM and EVER *adv.* 8 e.] The objective case of WHOEVER; as direct obj., or obj. of prep. (Less frequent than WHOMSOEVER.) **a.** As compound relative, or with correlative in principal clause (with constructions as in WHOEVER 1): Any (one) whom.

c **1330** *Arth. & Merl.* 4811 Wom euer þat he hitt, þe heued to þe chinne he slitt. *c* **1375** *Sc. Leg. Saints* i. (*Petrus*) 17 To bind and louss quhowm-euer þou will. *c* **1470** HENRY *Wallace* VII. 825 Quhom euir he hyt to ground brymly thaim bar. **1596** DALRYMPLE tr. *Leslie's Hist. Scot.* I. 181 He maist cruellie murtherit quhomeuir he knew weil fauoured. **1750** CARTE *Hist. Eng.* II. 775 Fear of death made him accuse whomever they pleased of treason. **1830** PUSEY *Hist. Enq.* II. 270 Whomever these men once brand with this mark of shame, is regarded by the people as a denier of God. **1883** R. W. DIXON *Mano* II. v. 80 Will ye not to that man some pity give Whomever dark temptations do assail? **1920** MAX BEERBOHM *And Even Now* 189 To impose his will on whomever he sees comfortably settled.

¶Misused for *whoever* as subject of relative clause preceded by a preposition.

c **1380** WYCLIF *Sel. Wks.* III. 347 Cursing for sacrilegie in whomever þat reveþ þis rente. *c* **1449** PECOCK *Repr.* II. xi. 215 Y dare putte this into iugement of whom euer hath seen the pilgrimage doon.

b. Introducing a qualifying clause (cf. WHOEVER 2): No matter whom.

1762 in Tytler *Mem. H. Home* (1807) II. 7 They freely pursue the truth,..whomever she may oppose, whomever she may countenance. **1845** *Newman's Lives Eng. Saints, Stephen Langton* v. 69 John would have been glad to have been aided by the strong arm, to whomever it might belong.

whomp (hwɒmp), *sb. colloq.* (orig. and chiefly *U.S.*). [Echoic.] **a.** A heavy, low sound. **b.** A heavy blow; also *fig.*

1926 *Blackw. Mag.* May 595/2 Ever think of Piccadilly in the evening, and the 'whomp' of an orchestra starting up in some theatre? **1970** J. H. GRAY *Boy from Winnipeg* 145 We got some special whomps just in case we had sneaked anything. **1977** R. L. DUNCAN *Temple Dogs* I. iii. 104 Corbett realized that he had heard a sound, a kind of muted whomp and the Colonel had been shot. **1979** *Washington Post* 4 Oct. A15/2 Liberal and conservative journals are good at least once a year for a whomp at the fat, spoiled, arrogant and pricey world they believe the average bureaucrat to live in. **1983** *Ibid.* 16 Oct. G4/4 He recruited bassist Tony Butler and drummer Mark Brzezicki. The massive and dramatic rhythmic whomp they provide reflects their studio work.

whomp (hwɒmp), *v. colloq.* (orig. and chiefly *U.S.*). [f. the sb.] **1.** *trans.* **a.** To defeat decisively. **b.** To strike (a person) hard, to hit, thump.

1952 *Britannica Bk. of Year* 667/1 *Whomp*, to defeat decisively. **1973** 'D. SHANNON' *Spring of Violence* xi. 194 If you did something wrong at school you got whomped. **1979** D. ANTHONY *Long Hard Cure* ix. 79 He had a history of whomping women. **1984** *New Yorker* 1 Oct. 113/1 Tuggle keeps whomping us on the skull.

2. *trans.* With *up.* **a.** To produce quickly, with little preparation or planning.

1955 T. TAYLOR *Grand Inquest* ix. 241 This procedural paraphernalia was, to borrow Al Capp's apt expression, stricly 'whomped up'. **1957** *New Yorker* 23 Nov. 67/1, I remember the agreement very well. The two of you whomped it up the day after Bob got his overseas orders. **1961** J. STEINBECK *Winter of our Discontent* 190 Wives whomping up a last-ditch dinner. **1980** *Christian Sci. Monitor* 22 May B-16/3 When people ask questions about things I really don't know the answer to..the temptation is to put on my sage mantle and whomp up something.

b. To arouse or stir up (feeling, a disturbance, etc.).

1961 in WEBSTER. **1970** *Daily Colonist* (Victoria, B.C.) 5 May 1/3 Antiwar groups held rallies at dozens of colleges and universities..to whomp up student interest in a national student strike during the closing weeks of the academic year. **1975** M. AMIS *Dead Babies* xv. 74 To his hopelessness and grief, Philboyd could not act immediately; time was—when there'd have been enough tubby little rednecks like himself still living in Tara—they could have pitched right in there and whomped up a storm.

3. *intr.* To fall with a 'whomp'.

1960 *New Scientist* 14 Apr. 933/1 The Sunday edition of the *New York Times*..whomped to the floor outside my apartment door.

whomso (ˈhuːmsəʊ), *pron. arch.*, chiefly *poet.* (In early use as two words.) [Early ME. *swa hwam swa swa* (quot. *a* 1154 s.v. WHOM 6): see WHOM and SO *adv.* 17 d.] = next.

c **1200** *Vices & Virtues* 85 Hwam swo ðin wille was te senden ðis loc to ofrien, he was ȝeherd of his niede. *c* **1205** LAY. 18384 He mai wham swa he wule wurðcipe bitachen. *a* **1225** *Ancr. R.* 184 Ne bet he nenne mon bute hwamso he luueð. **13..** *Cursor M.* 8379 (Gött.) Giue it to quham-so ȝe will. *c* **1375** *Ibid.* 4007 (Fairf.) Quam so god helpis. **1596** SPENSER *F.Q.* V. xii. 36 Her cursed tongue..Appear'd like Aspis sting, that closely kils, Or cruelly does wound whom so she wils. **1632** LITHGOW *Trav.* IV. 169 His Daughters.. are giuen in marriage to any Bassa, whom so they affect. **1837** CARLYLE *Fr. Rev.* III. v. v, They say to whomso they meet, Do; and he must do it. *a* **1850** ROSSETTI *Dante & Circle* I. (1874) 61 Whomso thou meetest, say thou this to each.

whomsoever (huːmsəʊˈɛvə(r)), *pron. literary.* Also *poet.* **whomsoe'er** (-ˈɛə(r)). The objective case of WHOSOEVER. (More freq. than WHOMEVER.)

1. = WHOMEVER a (with or without correlative): cf. WHOSOEVER 1.

c **1450** *Godstow Reg.* 606 þ^e^ seyde Roger & hys wyfe & hys heyrys sholde haue power to..gyfe þe seyde londe to whom-so-euyr þey wolden. **1523** LD. BERNERS *Froiss.* I. cccxxv. 206/1 Whome so euer he hytte full, wente to the erthe. **1539** *Bible* (Great) Gen. xxxi. 32 With whome soeuer thou fyndest thy goddes, let hym dye. **1812** BYRON *Ch. Har.* I. l, Whomsoe'er along the path you meet Bears in his cap the badge of crimson hue. **1856** R. A. VAUGHAN *Mystics* (1860) I. VI. iii. 170 Whomsoever the electors choose they will have acknowledged rightful emperor. **1867** tr. *C'tess Hahn-Hahn's Fathers of Desert* 62 Whomsoever men serve, by him will they be guided.

2. = WHOMEVER b; cf. WHOSOEVER 2.

a **1631** DONNE *Serm.* lxxxviii. (1649) II. 64 Whomsoever he washed first of his Apostles, he washed them all. **1667** MILTON *P.L.* IX. 1068 O Eve, in evil hour thou didst give eare To that false Worm, of whomsoever taught To counterfet Mans voice. **1790** COWPER *Let. to S. Rose* 30 Nov., The zeal and firmness of your friendship to whomsoever professed. **1832** LEWIS *Use & Ab. Pol. Terms* x. 117 A national government is when the sovereign power, by whomsoever exercised, extends over the whole country.

3. With loss of relative force: Any one at all (now *rare* or *obs.*); also qualifying the preceding word (now usually replaced by *whatever*): cf. WHOSOEVER 3 a, b.

1584 in *Cath. Rec. Soc. Publ.* V. 87 To take parte with the Catholike Church against whomesoever. **1609** SIR E. HOBY *Let. to T. H.* 6 To answere you, or any Fugitiue Romified Renegado whomsoeuer. **1641** MILTON *Reform.* I. 33 He counts it lawfull in the bookes of whomsoever to reject that which hee finds otherwise then true. **1856** HAWTHORNE *Engl. Note-bks.* (1870) II. 114 Overjoyed at seeing anybody whomsoever. **1881** SPEDDING *Even. with Rev.* I. 130 A true soldier, prepared to defend his position against whomsoever, friend or enemy.

¶Used ungrammatically for WHOSOEVER, chiefly by attraction to the case of the unexpressed antecedent (*him*, etc.).

1560 WHITEHORNE tr. *Machiavelli's Art of War* 84 Thei.. punished with death, whom so euer obserued not the same order. **1621** BP. MOUNTAGU *Diatribæ* 98 In him, whomsoeuer he be, that shall abet, maintaine, or broach them. **1631** HEYLIN *St. George* 170 A man that saw as cleerely, as any whomsoever. **1768** TUCKER *Lt. Nat.* (1834) II. 437 The literal sense ought not to be countenanced,..in whomsoever is susceptible of the other. **1877** RUSKIN *Fors Clav.* lxxiv. VII. 37 They shall not be impeded by whomsoever it may be.

†ˈ**whomsome,** *pron. Obs. rare*$^{-1}$. In 4 **quam-sum.** [See -SOME.] The objective case of WHOSOME: = prec. So †**whomsoˈmever.**

a **1300** *Cursor M.* 8379 Giue it to quam-sum þou will. **1502** ARNOLDE *Chron.* M iv, The childe of whom sumeuer or husumeuer, wherof they knowen not who is fader nor moder.

†**whon**[1], *interrog.* and *rel. pron. Obs.* Forms: 1–3 **hwon, hwan,** 3 **whan, wan.** [OE. *hwon*, used as instrumental case of *hwæt* WHAT.] In dependence on a prep. = What, which; *esp.* in ***for whon*** = because of what or which, why, wherefore.

c **950** *Lindisf. Gosp.* Matt. vi. 31 *Quo operiemur*, of huon we biðon wrigen. *c* **1000** *Guthlac* 244 Bi hwon scealt ðu lifȝan? *a* **1122** *O.E. Chron.* (Laud MS.) an. 1104 He wið þone cyng ȝeworhte, for hwan hine se cyng ealles benæmde. *c* **1200** *Trin. Coll. Hom.* 191 þe ne hauen mid hwan hie hem werien. *c* **1205** LAY. 2679 Maidene castel he wes icleoped, nat ich for wan it was swa idon. *a* **1250** *Owl & Night.* 716 Wostu to hwan man wes ibore? To þare blissi of heue[n]ryche. *c* **1275** *Passion our Lord* 49 in *O.E. Misc.* 38 Mvchel volk hym vulede, wyte ye for hwon.

†**whon**[2], *sb.* and *a. Obs.* Forms: 1 **hwon, huon,** 3 **whon, wan,** 4 **qu(h)on(e,** 4–6 **quhoyn(e.** [OE. *hwón*, the instrumental case of which, *hwéne*, is represented by WHEEN. After *c* 1200 the word is exclusively northern.] Few, *a* few.

Construed in OE. (i) as a sb. or an adv. with dependent genitive, (ii) as an adj. (indeclinable), in ME. as an adj. and absol., (iii) as an adv. = a little, a little while (see b, c).

c **950** *Lindisf. Gosp.* Mark p. 3/18 *De septem panibus et paucis pisciculis*, of seofa hlafum & hwon lytle fiscas. *c* **1000** *Sax. Leechd.* II. 32 Ðenim pipor..& hwon sealt. *Ibid.*, Do huniȝes hwon to. *a* **1300** *Cursor M.* 17285 þaa quon þat heild wit þe þair-witt. *Ibid.* 19495 O quoner þan o thre, Mai na biscop sacrid be. **13..** *Ibid.* 19782 (Gött.) He bad þa men be all vte-done, þat in þat hus left bot a quone [*Cott.* a fon]. *c* **1375** *Sc. Leg. Saints* xxiv. (*Alexis*) 265 Certis, now are fundine quhon þat in þat manere wald haf done. **1375** BARBOUR *Bruce* XI. 49 We ar quhoyne agayne sa fele. **1513** DOUGLAS *Æneis* X. i. 38 A few wordis on this wys Jupiter said. Bot nocht in quhoyn wordis him answer maid The fresch goldyn Venus.

b. ***na whon*** (= OE. *náteshwón*, *ná tó þæs hwón*), not at all.

c **1205** LAY. 13203 Nusten þa Bruttes na whon whæt Vortiger hæfde idon.

c. ***a litel wan*** (= OE. *lýthwón*): a little while.

c **1200** *Trin. Coll. Hom.* 69 þole me louerd alitelwan þat ich bimurne mi sor, er ich wite to þe þestere wunienge.

whon, obs. form of WHEN, var. WONE.

whon, whone, obs. forms of ONE.

1482 *Cely Papers* (Camden) 103 He sent whon of hys clarkys. **1530** TINDALE *Lev.* xv. 18 Yf a woman lye with soche a whone.

whonde, var. WOND *v. Obs.*, to hesitate.

whone, whon(n)ene, var. WHENNE *Obs.*, whence.

whoness (ˈhuːnɪs). *rare.* [f. WHO *pron.* (*sb.*) + -NESS.] **a.** That which makes a person who he is. **b.** The state of being an isolated individual.

1922 [see WHENCENESS]. 1931 *Times Lit. Suppl.* 28 May 422/4 A crisis of spiritual rebirth in which the personal will submit only after long struggle to an ineluctable impersonal destiny.. thus escaping from the anguish of 'whoness'.. into the peace of 'wholeness'.

whonne, obs. pa. t. and pple. of WIN *v.*

whoo (hwu:), *v.* [Cf. next.]

†**1.** *trans.* and *intr.* To hoot. *Obs.*

1599 PORTER *Angry Wom. Abingt.* H 4, He is gone vp and downe, whoing like an Owle for thee. 1614 BRETON *I would & I would not* xx, All the Beggers in the streets would whoo me.

2. *intr.* To utter the sound denoted by *whoo.*

1872 DARWIN *Emotions* ix. 232 A booing or whooing noise. 1891 HARDY *Tess* ix, Pouting up that pretty red mouth to whistling shape, and whooing and whooing,.. and never being able to produce a note.

whoo (hwu:), *int.* Also **whooh, woo.** [Variant of HOO *int.*] An exclamation of surprise, grief, or other emotion; *occas.* an imitation of an owl's hoot (cf. TU-WHOO). Also repeated and in WHOO-WHOOP.

1608 MIDDLETON *Mad World* III. ii. E 2, *Wife.* Will you but heare a word from mee? *Curtiz.* Whooh. *a* 1658 CLEVELAND *Content* Poems, etc. (1742) 248 The chattring Sembriefs of her [*sc.* the owl's] Woo hoo, hoo. 1683 VILLIERS (Dk. Buckhm.) *Rehearsal* v. i. (ed. 4) 49 *Smi.* I had rather be bound to Fight your Battel, I assure you, Sir. *Bayes.* Whoo! there's it now: fight a Battel? there's the common error. 1770 J. COLLIER (Tim Bobbin) *Wks.* (1862) 365 On hearing the news of his landlord's death, [Abraham] only cried out, *Whoo-who, whoo-who, whoo*—. 1787 GROSE *Prov. Gloss., Whoo, whoo,* an interjection, marking great surprize. 1796 MME. D'ARBLAY *Camilla* III. v, 'Pray, can he really read?' 'Whoo!' says I, 'why he does nothing else.' 1908 WEYMAN *Wild Geese* xviii. 282 He heard.. the 'Whoo! hoo! hoo!' of owls beginning to mouse beside the lake. 1915 MRS. STRATTON-PORTER *M. O'Halloran* xv, Whoohoo it's so good, Mickey!

So **whoo** *sb.*, an utterance of this exclamation, or a similar sound, a hoot.

1845 C. WILKES *Narr. U.S. Expl. Exped.* II. 199 At the end of each dance they finished with a loud whoo, or screech. 1851 MAYNE REID *Scalp Hunters* xviii, An owl hovered around our heads uttering its doleful woo-hoo-a. 1863 READE *Hard Cash* I. vii. 217 Down came the gale with a whoo.

whoo, obs. dial. f. *hoo*, HEO, she.

1688 SHADWELL *Sqr. Alsatia* III. i, Whoo kisses daintily; And whoo has a Breath like a Caw.

whoo: see WHO *pron.*, WHO *int.* and *sb.*, WHOA, WOE.

whoobub, whood(e, whoof, obs. ff. HUBBUB, HOOD, WOOF.

whoof (hwu:f, hwʊf), *int.* (*sb.*, *v.*). Also 8 **whuph.**

1. Imitation of a gruff abrupt cry or noise. So **whoogh** (also as exclamation of exultation, etc.).

a 1766 MRS. F. SHERIDAN *Sidney Bidulph* IV. 75 Whuph! it is past two o'clock in the morning. 1785 PENNANT *Arctic Zool.* II. 543 Its [*sc.* a swan's] sound is, *whoogh, whoogh,* very loud and shrill, but not disagreeable. 1815 G. BEATTIE *John o' Arnha'* (1826) 58 At ilka thud and sough, They cried 'weel done!—hey!! hilloa!!! whoogh!!!' 1863 SPEKE *Discov. Nile* 60, I planted a ball in the larger one [*sc.* rhinoceros], and brought him round with a roar and whooh-whooh.

2. Also **woof** (wu:f, wʊf). (Expressing) a sound like that of a sudden expulsion of air (less sibilant than 'whoosh').

1921 A. S. M. HUTCHINSON *If Winter Comes* III. ii. §3 Whoof! He blew a cyclonic blast down the speaking tube. 1921 'K. MANSFIELD' *Scrapbk.* (1939) 182 The heavy baize door swung to with a 'woof'. 1936 WODEHOUSE *Laughing Gas* vii. 88 He came over to the arm-chair and sank into it with a luxurious whoof. 1945 *Penguin New Writing* XXIII. 10 Her great guns swing up... Then woof! with a sheet of flame that hides the ship she's hurled a packet of one-ton bricks at something out of sight. 1966 R. H. RIMMER *Harrad Experiment* (1967) 34 Woof! I'm pooped.

So as *vb.*, to utter a gruff or abrupt cry; to make a sound as of air being expelled. Also *fig.*

1863 SPEKE *Discov. Nile* 229 A large female [rhinoceros].. came straight down whoof-whoofing upon me. 1966 'L. LANE' *ABZ of Scouse* 117 *Whoof,* to pass wind. 1978 J. UPDIKE *Coup* (1979) vi. 248 He took up a hand mike.., *whoofed* into it experimentally. 1979 *Homes & Gardens* June 126/1 'I am getting seriously worried about prices. They are going to whoof, like this.' And his arm rose at a steep angle from his desk and pointed somewhere in the direction of the stratosphere.

whoofle ('hwu:f(ə)l, 'hwʊf(ə)l), *v.* [Echoic; cf. WHOOF *int.* (*sb.*, *v.*) and WHUFFLE *v.*] *intr.* To make a snorting, gurgling, or snuffling sound; (in quot. 1902 *trans.*, to take *up* with such a sound). Hence '**whoofling** *vbl. sb.*

1902 H. F. DAY *Pine Tree Ballads* 225 To have him fill his saucer and go whoofling up his tea. 1934 L. A. G. STRONG *Don Juan & Wheelbarrow* 156 A whoofling and puffing behind him announced Joey. 1944 'BRAHMS' & 'SIMON' *No Nightingales* vi. 27 Mr. Blount sighed his content and moved the ledger to one side. He moved it over the chessboard and upset all the pieces. General Burlap whoofled.

whook't, obs. north. pa. t. of QUAKE *v.*[1]

whool, dial. var. WEEVIL; obs. f. WOOL.

whoom (hwʊm), *v.* [Echoic.] *intr.* To make a resonant booming or rushing sound. Hence as *sb.*

1936 L. DURRELL *Spirit of Place* (1969) 41 Wild pigeon whoomed over. 1942 D. M. CROOK *Spitfire Pilot* 90 The deep 'whoom' of a bursting bomb could be heard. 1956 C. D. SIMAK *Strangers in Universe* (1958) 21 He heard another jet whoom upward from the field. 1956 B. HOLIDAY *Lady sings Blues* (1973) xi. 105 There was a whoom and this big tree crashed over with a wham and a bang.

whoompf (hwʊm(p)f), *int.* (*sb.*) Also **whoomph,** etc. [Echoic.] (Expressing) a sudden, violent rushing sound, as when a quantity of flammable material bursts into flame. Cf. the synonymous WOOMPH *int.* (*sb.*, *adv.*).

1958 'W. HENRY' *Seven Men at Mimbres Springs* xv. 170 Then *whoomff*! land on it with all fours. 1962 *John o' London's* 6 Dec. 527/2 The whole place goes up in flames.., *whoomph.* 1973 D. LEES *Rape of Quiet Town* vii. 122 A rending crash of metal and a whoompf of flame. 1983 J. MANN *No Man's Island* xi. 145 Check for gas leaks. Light a match and—whoomph.

whoop (hu:p, hwu:p), *sb.* Also 6 **whoope, whoup.** [f. WHOOP *int.*; cf. HOOP *sb.*[2]]

1. a. An act of whooping; a cry of 'whoop!', or a shout or call resembling this; *spec.* as used in hunting, esp. at the death of the game, or by N. American Indians, etc. as a signal or war-cry (see also WAR-WHOOP); *occas.* the hoot of an owl.

1600 W. WATSON *Decacordon* (1602) 3 All with one voyce, .. with whoopes, whowes and hoobubs, would thrust them out. 1620 QUARLES *Feast for Worms* §6 When all thy laughter shall be turn'd to Doole;.. Thy whoops of Ioy, to howles of sad lamenting. 1622 FLETCHER *Beggars' Bush* v. i, I'll use My wonted whoops, and hollows, as I were A hunting for 'em. 1672 VILLIERS (Dk. Buckhm.) *Rehearsal* v. i, Ere a Full-pot of good Ale you can swallow, He's here with a whoop, and gone with a holla. 1675 in I. Mather *K. Philip's War* (1862) 246 They signified their sense of his approach by their whoops or watchwords. *a* 1700 in W. King *Usef. Trans. Philos.* (1709) 44, I must acknowledge my Happiness, who in a Manuscript found the following Verses,.. Boys, Boys, come out to play, The Moon doth shine as bright as day; Come with a Whoop, come with a Call, Come with a good will or not at all. 1775 ADAIR *Amer. Ind.* 276, I put up the shrill whoop of friendship. *Ibid.* 277 Instead of sounding the usual whoop of defiance, I went on slowly. 1808 SKURRAY *Bidcombe Hill* 9 O'er hedge and ditch we fly, 'Till the loud whoop proclaims the ended chase. 1831 SCOTT *Cast. Dang.* xi, Something resembling the whoop of the night-owl. 1840 DICKENS *Old C. Shop* xxv, With a joyous whoop the whole cluster took to their heels.

b. The characteristic sonorous inspiration following a fit of coughing in whooping-cough. Also applied to similar sounds (see quot. 1899).

1873 A. FLINT *Princ. Med.* (ed. 4) 240 A long and labored inspiration then takes place, giving rise to a crowing sound evidently due to spasm of the glottis; this is the whoop which enters into the name of the affection. 1897 *Allbutt's Syst. Med.* II. 239 When the whoop appears his power of communicating the disease begins to decline. 1899 *Ibid.* VII. 452 Occasionally the impediment is aggravated by the occurrence of associated sounds with the stutter, the patient emitting unpleasant little whoops, grunts, or whimpering sounds during his efforts to speak.

c. Slang phrases (orig. and chiefly *U.S.*): ***a whoop and a holler*** (and varr.): a short distance; ***not to care a whoop*** (and varr.): not to care one bit; to be indifferent.

[1753 C. GIST *Jrnl.* 27 Dec. (1893) 85 We grew uneasy, and then he said two whoops might be heard to his cabin.] 1815 SCOTT *Let.* 19 Jan. in *Lockhart*, We are much nearer neighbours, and within a whoop and a holla. 1904 *Baltimore American* 30 Aug. 6 The voting public as a whole doesn't care a whoop about the question. 1908 J. LONDON *Let.* 27 Oct. (1966) 268, I don't care a whoop in high water whether you get married.. or not. 1920 E. H. JONES *Road to En-Dor* (ed. 2) xxvii. 313, I don't believe Enver Pasha cares two whoops whether I've had syphilis or not. 1924 WODEHOUSE *Bill the Conqueror* vii. 141 'It isn't as if she cared a hang about him.' 'Doesn't she?' 'Not a whoop.' 1936 E. B. WHITE *Let.* 24 Dec. (1976) 145, I don't give a whoop about dignity. 1951 L. CRAIG *Singing Hills* 155 They lived in a cabin which Miriam said was three whoops and two hollers away. 1957 J. AGEE *Death in Family* II. x. 157, I wouldn't give a whoop if you got blind drunk, best thing you could do. 1974 D. SEARS *Lark in Clear Air* i. 14 A string of hounds.. were only a whoop and a bellow behind father.

2. A form of the game of hide-and-seek. Also ***whoop-hide.*** (In first quot. *allusively*.)

1798 in *Windham Papers* (1913) II. 77 He will not now be dodging with the world and playing at whoop with all his friends. 1861 MISS YONGE *Stokesley Secr.* ii, I thought they were to have a great game at whoop-hide. 1869 *Latest News* 26 Sept. 16 He was playing at whoop.., and to avoid being discovered by a companion he got upon some new coping, which gave way.

whoop (hu:p, hwu:p), *v.* Forms: 4–7 **whope,** 5 **whowpe,** 5–6 **whoupe,** 6 **whoup, whooppe, whup,** 6–7 **whoope,** 6– **whoop.** [Parallel with WHOOP *int.*; cf. HOOP *v.*[2]]

1. a. *intr.* To utter a cry of 'whoop!' or a loud vocal sound resembling this; to shout, hollo (as in incitement, summons, exultation, defiance, intimidation, or mere excitement).

a 1400 *Parlt. 3 Ages* 233 (Text B) And [the falconer] whopis hem [*sc.* the hawks] to whirry... He wharris & whotes hem & whopes ful lowde. *c* 1450 *Merlin* xi. 168 Whan he com nygh the loges he shette a-nother bolte; and whowped to the kynge Arthur. 1530 PALSGR. 781/2, I whoope, I call, *je huppe. Ibid.*, Whooppe a lowde, and thou shalte here hym blowe his horne. 1577 GRANGE *Golden Aphrod.* G ij b, With lure I play the Faukner kinde, I hallowe, and I whoupe, I shake my fiste, I whistle shrill, but nought will make hir stoupe. 1583 MELBANCKE *Philotimus* R iij b, I so sadlie syt whuppinge all the day vnder a hill. 1601 R. JOHNSON *Kingd. & Commw.* (1603) 91 They go no round,.. but.. one sentinel whopeth vnto another. ?1605 DRAYTON *Poems Lyr. & Past.* Eglog iv. E 3, With that the shepheard whoop'd for ioy. 1655 CULPEPPER, etc. *Riverius* III. i. 96 Others cannot hear.. except the speakers whoop and hallow in their Ears. 1775 ADAIR *Amer. Ind.* 160 To whoop.. for the warriors to come and join him. 1802 WORDSW. '*The Cock is crowing*' 15 The Ploughboy is whooping. 1818 SCOTT *Br. Lamm.* ix, The hunters.. whooping and blowing a *mort,* or death-note. 1854 R. S. SURTEES *Handley Cr.* vii. (1901) I. 57 Then if they killed! —.. How they holloaed! How they whooped! 1883 *Good Words* Aug. 544/1 They are careful to whoop out before 'letting go' with their slop-pails or dust-baskets.

b. *trans.* with obj. of cognate meaning (either a sb. or the actual words), or indef. *it*: To utter with a whoop; to express by whooping.

1576 TURBERV. *Venerie* 127 When the harte is kylled, then all the huntesmen.. shall blowe a note and whoupe also a deade note. 1596 NASHE *Saffron Walden* F 2 b, I thought to haue cald in a Cooper.. and bid him hoope it about,.. but then I remembered mee the boyes had whoopt it sufficiently about the streetes. 1727 ARBUTHNOT *John Bull* III. viii. 62 The attornies and their clerks.. whooping [*ed.* 1712 hooping] and hollowing, Long live John Bull. 1775 ADAIR *Amer. Ind.* 144 Whooping their revengeful noise. 1840 THACKERAY *Bedford-Row Conspir.* ii, Six lawyers' clerks might whoop a tipsy song.. but beyond this all was silence. 1865 PARKMAN *Huguenots* iv. (1875) 44 An Indian chief.. ran to meet them, whooping and clamoring welcome.

c. *trans.* with adv. or advb. phr.: To bring, summon, or urge by or with whooping.

a 1400 [see 1]. 1582 STANYHURST *Æneis* II. (Arb.) 63 Iuno .. furth from the nauye the Greek foas Dooth whoup. 1610 A. COOKE *Pope Joan* 10 A boy.. who should haue whoopt him out of his bed. 1854 R. S. SURTEES *Handley Cr.* i, There he stood.. with his fox grinning in grim death in one hand .. whooping and halloaing.. the pack up to him. 1893 CONAN DOYLE *Refugees* xxviii, The English colonists were whooping on the demons who attacked them.

d. *trans.* To shout at, hoot (a person).

1690 DRYDEN *Don Sebastian* II. i, I shou'd be hiss'd And whoop'd in Hell for that Ingratitude. 1902 *Essex Weekly News* 24 Jan. 2/6 When we charged down on the Boers we shouted and whooped them like redskins.

e. ***whoop it up*** (*colloq.* (orig. *U.S.*)): to create a disturbance; to keep up an excitement or revel; to act or work in a stirring or rousing way; also, to stir up political enthusiasm; similarly ***whoop things up.***

1884 *Harper's Mag.* LXIX. 472 He whoops it up with the plain people. 1887 T. STEVENS *Around World on Bicycle* I. 11 They simply, in the language of the gold fields, 'turned themselves loose', 'made things hum', and 'whooped 'em up' around the bar-room of their village for.. three days. 1888 *Century Mag.* May 156 His rival is a prominent politician, with an abundance of party workers to 'whoop it up' for him. 1891 B. HARTE *First Family Tasajara* i. 8 What did we whoop things up here last spring to elect Kennedy to the legislation [*sic*] for? 1935 WODEHOUSE *Luck of Bodkins* iii. 37 You didn't by any chance.. whoop it up with those mysterious foreign adventuresses who haunt those parts? 1951 E. PAUL *Springtime in Paris* ii. 19, I supposed that elsewhere in France there might be as many young enthusiasts whooping it up for De Gaulle. 1954 B. HECHT *Child of Century* IV. 230 Sherwood [Anderson] would be able to whoop it up for me in a half-dozen periodicals which had come to consider his word as artistic law. 1956 'J. WYNDHAM' *Seeds of Time* 136 Thousands of trippers whooping it up with pandemonium for most of the night. 1959 'N. BLAKE' *Widow's Cruise* 93 Some premonition seemed to cast its shadow over the revellers, in spite of Mr. Bentinck-Jones's efforts to whoop things up. 1983 *Listener* 8 Sept. 24/2 The broadcasting moguls and their groupies whooped it up in Edinburgh and other select watering holes.

f. ***whoop up*** (trans.): to arouse enthusiasm for; to promote or praise with vigour; also, to give a boost to.

1885 *South Florida Sentinel* (Orlando) 5 Aug. 3/3 Whoop up Florida to those Yankees. 1893 [see STANDOFF *sb.* 3]. 1904 *Sun* (N.Y.) 8 Sept. 10 The bail was reduced to $10,000, but was whooped up to $15,000 when Larry was re-arrested. 1950 *Sun* (Baltimore) 6 Nov. 3/2 Spokesmen for each party whooped up interest in the outcome. 1970 *Globe & Mail* (Toronto) 26 Sept. 6/5 All human progress, even in morals, has been the work of men who have doubted the current moral values, not of men who have whooped them up and tried to enforce them. 1976 *Listener* 23 Sept. 375/1 If there was any temptation to whoop the original up into contemporary shape, he resisted it. 1983 *Listener* 14 July 19/2 It somehow won that year's Prix Italia,.. which so immensely whooped me up that I galloped down to Venice to collect.

2. *intr.* To hoot, as an owl. Also *trans.* as in 1 b, c, d.

1658 WILLSFORD *Natures Secr.* 134 Owls whooping after Sunset, and in the night, foreshews a fair day to ensue. 1677 TATE *Poems* 98 Madge has whoopt me twice from her Ivy-bound Oak. 1798 COLERIDGE *Anc. Mar.* VII. v, The owlet whoops to the wolf below. 1821 CLARE *Vill. Minstrel* II. 33 The owl.. whoop'd a 'good-night'. 1847 TENNYSON *Princess* Concl. 110 Bats wheel'd, and owls whoop'd. 1861 FANE & LYTTON *Tannhäuser* 52 Let the owl Whoop the high glories of the noon.

3. *intr.* To utter the 'whoop' in whooping-cough: see prec. sb. 1 b. Also *trans.* as in 1 c.

1887 R. N. CAREY *Uncle Max* xviii. 144 Whooping-cough, —why, he nearly whooped himself to death. 1897 *Allbutt's Syst. Med.* II. 242 Young infants whoop seldom.

whoop (hu:p, hwu:p), *int.* Also 5 **whoppe,** 5–6 **whope,** 6 **whoup, whup,** 6–7 **whop,** 7 **whoope.** [A natural exclamation consisting of a voiceless *w* followed by an *o* or *u* sound, concluded by closure of the lips. The phonetic significance of some early forms is uncertain.] An exclamation, or representation of a shout or cry, expressing excitement, surprise, derision, exultation, incitement, etc.

1568 *Hist. Jacob & Esau* I. i. A iij b, Whoup. Nowe a mischief on all mopying fooles for mee. **1589** *Marprel. Epit.* (1843) 53 Whope papist, say the puritans, is that become scripture with you? **1596** HARINGTON *Apol.* Bb 8 b, Sir Raph Horsey, nine. Sir Hugh Portman, ten. Whop, why howe nowe Master K. Shiriffes man? Here is but ten. **1599** CUTWODE *Caltha Poet.* clxxx. E 7, The scantlin won, the winners must cry whup, The goale is got, and now the game is vp. **1603** DEKKER & CHETTLE *Grissil* IV. ii. 2128 Whoope whether is my brother basket-maker gone? **1622** MASSINGER & DEKKER *Virg. Mart.* II. i, *Dor.* Whisper but to mine eare, and you shall furnish them. *Hir.* Whisper, nay, Lady, for my part Ile cry whoope. **1638** BRATHWAIT *Barnabees Jrnl.* III. (1876) F j, Whup (Faustulus) all draw ny thee That doe love thee. **1677** W. HUGHES *Man of Sin* III. iii. 94 Joceline tells, that St. Patrick did..fast..a whole Lent together... Whoop! but St. Aidan, (as Capgrave tells us,) fasted full fifty days. **1691** MRS. D'ANVERS *Academia* 22 Whop Sir, thought I, and what ado's here? **1810** SCOTT *Lady of L.* VI. v, Yet whoop, Jack! kiss Gillian the quicker. **1820** KEATS *Cap & Bells* lxxv, She clapped her hands three times and cried out 'Whoop'. **1848** DICKENS *Dombey* lv, 'Halloa! whoop! Halloa! Hi!' Away, at a gallop. **1896** H. G. WELLS *Wheels of Chance* iv, Whoop for Freedom and Adventure!

b. Coupled with another interjection or with a vocative in an allusive phrase.

c **1450** *Mankind* 600 in *Macro Plays* 22 Whope! who! Mercy hath brokyn hys neke-kycher a-vows. *Ibid.* 713. 26 Hay, doog! hay, whoppe! whoo! go yowur wey lyghtly! **1592** NASHE *Strange Newes* F 2 b, And cry kulleloo, kulleloo, with whup hoo, there goes the Ape of Tully. **1593** HARVEY *Pierce's Super.* 178 The whoop-hooe of good boyes in London streetes. **1596** NASHE *Saffron Walden* X 2 b, So would hee haue writte Harueys whoope diddle, or the nonsuting, or vncasing of the animaduertiser. **1598** R. BERNARD tr. *Terence, Andria* III. i, Whup, hoida: what, in all hast? **1605** SHAKS. *Lear* I. iv. 245 Whoop Iugge I loue thee. **1621** B. JONSON *Masque Gypsies* Wks. (1640) 68 The ballet of Whoope Barnibie. **1634** HEYWOOD & BROME *Lanc. Witches* IV. i. G 2, Whoope, whurre, heres a sturre. **1678** DRYDEN *Limberham* v. i, Whoop Holiday! our trusty and well-beloved Giles, most welcome! **1688** HOLME *Armoury* II. 176/1 *Whoop, Whopoo*, is the Shepherds call or cry, to call the Sheep together.

whoop(e: see HOOP *sb.*[1], *sb.*[3] Also in comb. †**whoopcat**, **whoophooper** [cf. *hoopoop* s.v. HOOPOE] = HOOP *sb.*[3] I.

1694 MOTTEUX *Rabelais* v. ix. 41 O' my word this is a filthy Whoophooper. Tush, speak softly, said Æditnus,..he has a pair of Ears,..What then, return'd Panurge, so hath a Whoopcat.

whoop-de-do (ˌhuːpdɪˈduː, hw-). *U.S. colloq.* Also **whoop-de-doo**, etc. [A fanciful extension of WHOOP *v.* or WHOOPS *int.*] A fuss, bustle, or commotion; a 'to-do'; *spec.* in *Motor-cycling*, a very bumpy stretch of road.

[**1895** S. CRANE *Red Badge of Courage* xvi. 160 'Whoop-a-dadee,' said a man, 'here we are! Everybody fightin'.'] **1929** W. FAULKNER *Sound & Fury* 321 But I cant have all this whoop-de-do and sulking at mealtimes. **1949** S. LEWIS *God Seeker* vi. 34 But what's the use of a loud-mouthed evangelical like your Reverend Chippler,..with his..general circus whoop-tee-do? **1962** J. STEINBECK *Trav. with Charlie* 186 This is not patriotic whoop-de-do; it is a carefully observed fact. **1976** B. KAYSING *Fell's Beginner's Guide to Motorcycling* 256 *Whoop-de-doo*, a road that goes up and down like a roller coaster track. **1980** *Dirt Bike* Oct. 15/1 Very soon we were all lying beside the road, for even though the road looked good at first, it was plagued with whoopdiedoos, and we came into them a little hot. **1981** *Verbatim* Spring 24/1 There was many an angry powwow and much whoop-de-do, but in the end, of course, the bigwigs won. **1985** *Dirt Bike* Mar. 27/1 Through whoopdedos it takes a full stroke without bottoming harshly and keeps giving you maximum ground contact.

whoopee (see below), *int.* and *sb.* [f. WHOOP *int.* + -EE[2].] **A.** *int.* (hw-, wʊˈpiː) An exclamation of exuberant joy. Cf. HOOP-EE *int.*

1862 *Harper's Mag.* July 282/1 He yelled at the top of his voice, 'Whoopee! Whiskey only twenty-five cents a gallon!' **1890** KIPLING *Barrack-Room Ballads* (1892) 32 Whoopee! Tear 'im, puppy! **1895** *Outing* XXVI. 428/2 John's 'whoopee' had caused a little ebon..to set open the gates. **1932** B. C. PLOWRIGHT *For Groupers Only* iii. 23 Whoopee!! this is great news! **1974** *Listener* 19 Sept. 355/3 You take your second MB..and once you've passed this—whoopee! You're virtually guaranteed to qualify.

B. *sb.* (hw-, ˈwʊpiː; hw-, ˈwuːpiː) Exuberant or boisterous merry-making; revelry; †a lively or rowdy party; phr. ***to make whoopee***, to indulge in such behaviour; (in quot. 1928, to behave amorously). Cf. WHOOP-UP. *colloq.*

1928 G. KAHN *Makin' Whoopee* (song), Another bride, another June, Another sunny honeymoon, Another season, another reason for making whoopee! **1929** *Punch* 24 July 86/2 A London hostess, writing to a gossip page, said—'I am giving a Whoopee. Do come to it.' **1930** *Sat. Even. Post* 13 Dec. 25/1 Novelists portray him as the gin-drinking patron saint of whoopee. **1930** E. WAUGH *Vile Bodies* iv. 51 Noel and Audrey are having a little whoopee on Saturday evening. **1933** DYLAN THOMAS *Poems* (1971) 84 Even heaven has a smell Of putrefying angels who Make deadly whoopee in the blue. **1938** F. D. SHARPE *Sharpe of Flying Squad* ii. 27 Boys and girls at the end of an evening's 'whoopee', would come out of a night club and take the first car they saw for a joy-ride. **1945** M. SOAMES *Let.* 24 July in *Clementine Churchill* (1979) xxiv. 385 The evening broke up about midnight, in a general atmosphere of whoopee and goodwill. **1949** F. SWINNERTON *Doctor's Wife comes to Stay* 109 'I thought you and Mother would make whoopee here—' 'Whoopee!' muttered the Doctor. 'Disgusting word for a disgusting occupation!' 'Oh, just noisy hopelessness,' explained Rex. 'Despair set to rhythm.' **1972** D. FRANCIS *Smokescreen* ii. 26 We had left the bright lights, the adulation, and the whoopee, and gone to live in the country. **1976** *Times Lit. Suppl.* 13 Aug. 1009/5 Frustrated laughers, dancers and makers of whoopee. **1984** Q. CRISP *Manners from Heaven* vii. 74 'It often happens that when we think we're making whoopee we're only making a *whoops*! instead,' I replied.

2. Comb.: **whoopee cushion**, a cushion which when sat upon emits a sound like that of the breaking of wind.

1960 *Spectator* 3 June 804 The comically battered face of a whoopee cushion. **1975** P. THEROUX *Great Railway Bazaar* viii. 98 These people..were as hard to silence as whoopee cushions. **1977** *Sunday Times* (Colour Suppl.) 6 June 42/3 Andrew..has..a taste for practical jokes..slipping whoopee-cushions where his father or mother was likely to sit.

whooper (ˈhuːpə(r), ˈhw-). Also 7 **whopper**. [f. WHOOP *v.* + -ER[1].] A person or animal that whoops. **a.** *gen.* (See also HOOPER[2] I.) Also **whooper-up**.

1826 SOUTHEY *Let. to N. White* 11 Feb., Two of my whoopers still favour us with a little kennel-music. **1904** *N.Y. Times* 4 July 1 The only candidate who has back of him a boom which is not characterized by 'whooper-up' methods. **1908** *Academy* 27 June 926/2 The whoopers and the screamers and the female stump-orators. **1909** J. R. WARE *Passing Eng.* 266/1 *Whooperups*.., inferior, noisy singers. **1932** H. CRANE *Let.* 12 Apr. (1965) 408 They're generally preferable to all the trained and professional strummers and whoopers-up I've ever heard.

b. *spec.* The wild or whistling swan, *Cygnus musicus* (*ferus*): also ***whooper swan***. (See also HOOPER[2] 2.) Also, = *whooping crane* s.v. WHOOPING *ppl. a.*

1660 MAY *Accompl. Cook* (1665) 217 Turkey, Swan, Goose, Bustard, Crane, Whopper, wilde Geese, Brand-Geese,..and many more. **1838** C. H. MATSCHAT *Suwannee River* 286 It is the favorite haunt of the gray whoopers. **1860** *Southern Cultivator* XVIII. 324 Here [in Florida] is found every grade, kind, size, and color..from the beautiful little morning Dove..to the tall Whooper, of 5 or 6 feet high. **1880** BARING-GOULD *Mehalah* i, Occasionally the whooper swan sounds his loud trumpet. **1889** *Blackw. Mag.* Dec. 828 The whooper is the largest of our wild swans. **1902** H. W. TOMPKINS *Highways Hertfordsh.* v. 104 A pair of whooper swans frequented Water End near Great Gaddesden. **1979** *Time* 2 Apr. 23/3 Whatever he felt about the whooper, Carter appreciated the award, which recognized his support for environmental protection and recreation.

whooping (ˈhuːpɪŋ, ˈhw-), *vbl. sb.* [f. WHOOP *v.* + -ING[1].] The action of the verb WHOOP. (Cf. HOOPING *vbl. sb.*[2])

? **1605** DRAYTON *Poems Lyr. & Past., Man in Moone* I 1, With guilty conscience..That oft they start at whooping of an owle. **1657** G. THORNLEY *Daphnis & Chloe* 139 The clattering of the Oars, the whooping of the Sea-men. **1842** TENNYSON *St. Sim. Styl.* 32 The whoopings of the owl. **1854** DICKENS *Hard T.* II. i, The whooping of boys, the barking of dogs.

ˈwhooping, *ppl. a.* [f. as prec. + -ING[2].] **a.** That whoops; esp. in **whooping crane**, the large white crane of N. America, *Grus americana*; **whooping swan** = WHOOPER b. **b.** Of a sound or cry: Of the nature of a whoop. (Cf. HOOPING *ppl. a.*[2])

1757 *Phil. Trans.* LI. 78 An hideous whooping noise, like that of a child in a chin-cough. **1775** ADAIR *Amer. Ind.* 293 Suspicion, that he was sent to shoot me..as soon as he heard the whooping death-signal. **1791** W. BARTRAM *Carolina* 433 The great and beautiful whooping crane. **1731, 1837** Whooping crane [see HOOPING *ppl. a.*[2]]. **1839** LONGF. *Wreck of Hesperus* xvii, A whooping billow swept the crew Like icicles from her deck. **1852** MACGILLIVRAY *Brit. Birds* IV. 659 *Cygnus musicus*. The Whooping Swan. **1879** N. H. BISHOP *Four Months in Sneak-Box* 108 Whooping-cranes..in little flocks, dotted the grassy prairies. **1895** JAS. PRIOR *Renie* xix, A band of whistling, whooping lads playing at stalky. **1938** M. K. RAWLINGS *Yearling* x. 94 He pointed. 'The whoopin' cranes is dancin'.' **1976** *Daily Colonist* (Victoria, B.C.) 7 May 10/6 A scraggly-looking whooping crane chick, hatched this week at the government wildlife centre here.

c. *fig.* Unusually large; whopping; also, very noisy, wild, uproarious. Also as quasi-*adv.*, hugely, immensely. *slang* (chiefly *U.S.*).

1866 'MARK TWAIN' *Let.* 30 July (1917) I. v. 115 The first few days we came at a whooping gait. **1906** E. DYSON *Fact'ry 'Ands* vii. 88 Odgson..was then lyin' in ther City cells, whoopin' delirious. **1939** G. ADE *Let.* 7 June (1973) 211 Let's make each one of these parties a whooping success. **1969** FABIAN & BYRNE *Groupie* (1970) xiii. 94 They unstrap me and shoot two whooping great penicillin injections into my backside.

whooping-cough, hooping-cough (ˈhuːpɪŋ kɒf, -ɔː-). A contagious disease chiefly affecting children, and characterized by short, violent, and convulsive coughs, followed by a long sonorous inspiration called the hoop (whoop); the chincough.

α. **1739** MRS. E. MONTAGU *Corr.* (1906) I. 37 One little boy had whooping cough. **1755** JOHNSON, *Hooping-cough*,..(or whooping cough, from *hoop*, to shout). **1873** SPENCER *Study Sociol.* iii. 55 Will it..be carried off by scarlet fever or whooping-cough? **1937** [see *immunotherapy* s.v. IMMUNO-].

β. **1747** WESLEY *Prim. Physic* (1762) 43 Chin-Cough or Hooping-Cough. **1758** MRS. DELANY in *Life & Corr.* 475 The Duchess of Portland's receipt for a hooping, or any nervous cough. **1802** *Med. Jrnl.* VIII. 426 Treatment to be adopted in the latter stages of the Hooping Cough. **1877** ROBERTS *Handbk. Med.* (ed. 3) I. 179 Hooping-Cough is generally regarded as an infectious disease, depending upon a specific poison.

whoops (hwuːps, hwʊps), *int.* [Var. of OOPS.] An exclamation of dismay or surprise, usu. upon stumbling, or realizing an obvious mistake. Also **'whoopsie(-daisy)** *int.* = UPSIDAISY.

1925 *New Yorker* 26 Sept. 8/2 (*caption*) Whoopsie Daisy! **1937** E. POUND *Let.* Jan. (1971) 287 Whoops! And do I *envy* you. I *do*. **1957** J. KEROUAC *On Road* (1958) II. viii. 159 Whoops, I thought I was on the wrong side of the road. **1969** C. ARMSTRONG *Seven Seats to Moon* xiii. 126 The woman said, 'Whoopsie', and her strong hand came under his armpit. **1973** G. TALBOT *Ten Seconds from Now* xii. 161, I was appalled at the tape playback to hear that I had punctuated my commentary by a 'whoops!' every minute or so. **1980** G. M. FRASER *Mr American* xviii. 328 'Whoops!' said Pip.. 'Claridge's, eh? That's what I like to hear!'

whoopubb, obs. form of HUBBUB.

whoop-up (ˈhuːpʌp, hw-). Chiefly *N. Amer.* [f. vbl. phr. *to whoop it up*: see WHOOP *v.* I e.] An instance of 'whooping it up'; a noisy celebration or party; revelry.

1913 I. COWIE *Company of Adventurers* 319 As soon as the general 'whoop-up' began, all the traders..packed up their outfits snugly and retired. **1927** *Daily Express* 5 Oct. 3/3 The Ward Room is—apart from the 'whoops up' natural to lonely men—noted for its air of sober responsibility. **1953** D. CUSHMAN *Stay away, Joe* 22 Ain't you going to have no dance, no rodeo, whoop-up? **1968** E. S. RUSSENHOLT *Heart of Continent* III. ix. 153 For 'whoop-up juice' they [*sc.* whisky traders] reclaim the rifles Indian hunters have just bought with a year's hunting. **1976** D. HEFFRON *Crusty Crossed* xiv. 101, I thought it quite..sensible of Big Point to have one great annual public whoop-up in which to give a little exercise to the witch and devil of one's soul.

whoor(e, whoorish: see WHORE, WHORR, WHORISH.

whoorlbat, var. WHIRLBAT *Obs.*

whoos, obs. f. WHOSE.

whoosh (hwuːʃ, hwʊʃ), *v.* Also **woosh**. [Imitative; the vowel expressing a duller sound than that of WHISH.] **1.** *intr.* To utter or emit a dull soft sibilant sound, like that of something rushing through the air; to move rapidly with a rushing sound.

1856 DICKENS *Let. to Wilkie Collins* 13 July, The boys..whooshing and crying (after tigerish cat No. 2): 'French!' 'Here she comes!' **1909** H. G. WELLS *Tono-Bungay* II. ii. 163 Make it all slick, and then make it woosh. **1917** *Blackw. Mag.* July 47/2 Huge projectiles whooshed noisily through the air. **1922** D. H. LAWRENCE *Aaron's Rod* xxi. 306 You want to whoosh off in a nice little love-whoosh and lose yourself. **1966** I. JEFFERIES *House-Surgeon* viii. 156 The blood was wooshing in and Bernard nodded.

2. *trans.* To cause to move rapidly with a rushing sound. Also *fig.* Const. *up*, to enliven.

1909 H. G. WELLS *Tono-Bungay* II. ii. 162 A Real Live Thing! Wooshing it up! Making it buzz and spin! **1920** D. H. LAWRENCE *Touch & Go* 7 A system of vacuum tubes for whooshing Bradburys about from one to the other. **1956** W. SANSOM *Loving Eye* 102 Cars wooshed water-spray on the wet macadam. **1968** B. HINES *Kestrel for Knave* 27 He whooshed the curtains open and switched the light off. **1971** *Sunday Express* (Johannesburg) 28 Mar. (Home Jrnl.) 2/2 (Advt.), Removable Fibre-fill padlets whoosh you into high young curves, naturally. **1982** *Nature* 13 May 91/1 Chrétien will be the first Western astronaut to be whooshed into space by a Soviet rocket.

So **whoosh** *sb.*, a sound of this nature (also reduplicated); also, an exclamation 'whoosh!'; a movement accompanied by a rushing sound; a gushing or 'whooshing' style.

1880 'MARK TWAIN' *Tramp Abroad* xx. 194 He fetched a prodigious '*Whoosh*!' to relieve his lungs. **1906** 'Q' *Mayor of Troy* vii, With a whoo-sh a rocket leapt into the air. **1915** —— *Nicky-Nan* ix, Whenever her brush intromitted its harsh whoosh-whoosh. **1909** H. G. WELLS *Tono-Bungay* III. iv. 391 Once or twice before you've stepped in—with that sort of Woosh of yours. **1934** —— *Exper. in Autobiogr.* I. i. 37 Just because of that constitutional apathy it will be characteristically free from individual Woosh. **1962** 'R. GORDON' *Doctor in Swim* i. 9 We sat for a moment listening to the woosh of the jets. **1976** *Globe & Mail* (Toronto) 8 Nov. 16/6 When I develop a mental picture of the person I'm affecting, my objectivity goes out the window in a woosh of sympathy. **1984** *Listener* 14 June 32/3 We may be used to the idea of pressing buttons on commercial synthesisers and summoning whooshes of space-age sound.

whoosh, *int.* Also **woosh**. [f. the vb.] An exclamation evocative of or accompanying a sudden explosive rushing sound or movement.

1899 S. R. CROCKETT *Kit Kennedy* xxxvii. 261 The cravin' wad juist bank up like a water ahint a dam—and then—*whoosh*, awa' she gaed. **1909** H. G. WELLS *Tono-Bungay* II. ii. 162 That's you, steady and long and piling-up,—then, wo-oo-oo-oo-osh. **1927** *Blackw. Mag.* Apr. 488/1 John said, 'Woosh! some armful. Look out for the eggs.' **1936** 'R. HYDE' *Check to your King* 69 The Princess..shouts 'Whoosh!' **1949** DYLAN THOMAS *Let.* 13 Oct. (1966) 328 Bills and demand notes, at me like badgers, whoosh! **1965** *Family Circle* Oct. 13/1 Plain lonesome? Whoosh, it's a friend. **1977** *Sounds* 9 July 19/2 Onstage we just go like, woosh!

whoosher, obs. var. *husher*: see after HUSH *v.*[1]

whoosht, obs. var. HUSHT: see WHOSHT.

whoosy, whoozy, varr. WOOZY *a.*

†**whoot.** Also 5 **whwte**, 6 **whought**. Obs. variant of HOOT *sb.* and *v.*

*c***1425** *Cast. Persev.* 1939 in *Macro Plays* 135, I here an hydowse whwtynge on hyt [*cf.* howte *l.* 1927]. **1542** UDALL *Erasm. Apoph.* 97 He..hearde all the whole citee whoughtyng and shoughtyng..with ioye and solace. *a***1610–1750** [see HOOT *sb.* and *v.*].

whoot(e, obs. forms of HOT *a.*

whoo-whoop, who-whoop (huːˈhuːp), *int.* and *sb.* Also 7 **whoo-whup**, 8–9 **whooup**, 9 **who-oop**, **who(o)-hoop**. The shout of huntsmen at the death of the game; hence allusively in phr. ***to be whoo-whoop with***, to be 'all up with'. Hence **whoo-whoop** *v.* (in quot. *trans.* to kill with a shout of 'whoo-whoop!').

1611 COTGR., *Forhu*, a whoo-whup; or, the call..or whooping of huntsmen at the death of their chace. **1677** N. COX *Gentl. Recr.* I. (ed. 2) 81 If a Buck a double, if a Stag a treble Mort blown by one, and then a whole Recheat in Consort by all that have Horns; and that finished, immediately a general Whoo whoop. *c***1746** J. COLLIER (Tim Bobbin) *View Lanc. Dial.* Wks. (1862) p. xxxv, Yoan be hong'd or some Mischief on then aw'll be whooup with o' efeath! **1798** *Sporting Mag.* XI. 3 At the very moment of 'Who! Whoop!' a view halloo was given by a third. **1812** *Ibid.* XXXIX. 56 They who-ooped him [*sc.* a fox] without a hound missing. **1825** *Ibid.* (N.S.) XV. 257 It will sooner or later be whoo-hoop with us all. **1886** *Fores's Sporting Notes* III. 155 A loud, clear 'Who-whoop!' from Jack, who has, as it were, dropped from the skies just in time to take the cub from the hounds.

whop (hwɒp), *sb.* *colloq.* or *vulgar.* Also 5 **whapp**, 9 **whap**, **wop**. [f. next. Cf. WAP *sb.*[1]] An act of whopping; a heavy blow or impact; a bump.

*c***1440** *York Myst.* xxxiii. 199 For a whapp so he whyned and whesid And ȝitt no lasshe to þe lurdan was lente. *a***1825** FORBY *Voc. E. Anglia, Whop, Whap*, a heavy blow. **1895** KIPLING in *Youth's Compan.* 19 Sept. 442/4 Then he ..drew up with a doleful *wop! wop! wop!* by the side of the great forty-five-ton, six-wheel coupled,..Number Twenty-five. **1899** W. S. CHURCHILL *River War* I. xiii. 423 The *wop!* of the distant explosion came back, like the echo of the report. **1905** H. G. WELLS *Kipps* I. iv. §1 'I was coming downhill,'..explained the bicyclist... 'I came rather a whop.'

whop (hwɒp), *v.* (*adv.*) Forms: 5 **whappe**, 6, 9 **whap**, 8– **whop**, (9 **wap**, **wop**). [Variant of WAP *v.*[1]: see WH.]

1. *trans.* To cast, pull out, etc. violently; to take or put suddenly. *dial.*

*c***1400** *Destr. Troy* 4743 The grekes..With alblasteris also amyt full streght, Whappet in wharles, whellit the pepull. **14..** *Sir Beues* (N.) 1899 [Beues is swerd anon] out whappid. **1721** RAMSAY *Ode to the Ph—* 55 Frae her fair Finger whop a Ring. **1725** —— *Gentle Sheph.* III. ii, He.. whops out a Book. **1829** BROCKETT *N.C. Gloss.* (ed. 2), *Whopt, Whupt*, put, placed—embracing the idea of whipped. 'He whopt his foot on't.' **1904** *Westm. Gaz.* 19 Nov. 5/2 He just whopped up the papers out of my han' an' away wi' him.

†**b.** *intr.* To beat, throb; = QUAP *v.* *Obs.*

*c***1440** *Partonope* 6446 (Univ. Coll. MS.) His hert so sore ganne whappe tho.

2. *trans.* To strike with heavy blows; to beat soundly, flog, thrash, belabour (a person or animal; *rarely*, an inanimate object). *colloq.* or *vulgar.*

1575 *Depos. Durham* (Surtees) 292 The said James contynewed in his raidge, bragging and swerynge, and said that he wold 'whapp his coott.' *a***1825** FORBY *Voc. E. Anglia, Whop, Whap*, to beat severely. **1837** DICKENS *Pickw.* xxxv, 'Ain't nobody to be whopped for takin' this here liberty, sir?' said Mr. Weller. **1842** LOVER *Handy Andy* xviii, Half a dozen strapping fellows carrying..tea-trays which they whopped after the manner of a Chinese gong. **1848** THACKERAY *Bk. Snobs* xxvii, 'If you'll come across,..and take your coat off, I'le give you such a wapping as you've never had since the last time I did it'..'Wap one of your own weight,' Mr. Snapper said. **1869** W. S. GILBERT *'Bab' Ball., Prince Agib* xv, I was fastened to the floor, While a mercenary wopped me with a will! **1890** HENTY *With Lee in Virg.* xviii, Mother would whop me if I came back without the basket.

b. *fig.* To overcome, vanquish, defeat utterly (with literal blows, or in a contest of any kind); hence, to surpass or excel greatly: = BEAT *v.*[1] 10. *colloq.* or *vulgar.*

1836 [HOOTON] *Bilberry Thurland* I. 342 He comed to be a reg'lar cock o' th' walk, for he whopped all th' cocks they could bring to him. **1851** KINGSLEY *Yeast* ix, Fourteen men ..as'll play the whole vale to cricket, and whap them. **1865** J. HATTON *Bitter Sweets* iii, Nelson, as was a British General and wopped the French.

3. The vb.-stem used as *adv.*: With a 'whop'; with a sudden movement or impact; 'bump', 'flop'. Also as *int.*

1812 W. TENNANT *Anster F.* IV. xxix, Whap! there sinks another! **1870** E. PEACOCK *Ralf Skirl.* xviii, In less time than you can think, wop comes a big black thing down..as big as the stone of a cheese-press. **1905** H. G. WELLS *Kipps* I. vi. §6 He sat on the edge of the bed in profound meditation, and his boots fell 'whop' and 'whop' upon the floor, with a long interval between each 'whop.'

whop(e, obs. ff. HOOP *sb.*[1] and *v.*[1], WHOOP.

whopper (ˈhwɒpə(r)). *colloq.* or *vulgar.* Also **w(h)apper**, **wopper**. [f. WHOP *v.* + -ER[1].]

1. Something uncommonly large of its kind; a very big thing, animal, or person. (Cf. THUMPER 3, WHACKER 2.)

1785 GROSE *Dict. Vulgar T., Whapper*, a large man or woman. **1787** —— *Prov. Gloss., Whapper*, any thing large, a thumper. **1834** MARRYAT *Peter Simple* xxxv, We had to pass some whoppers,..but nothing would suit Nelson but this four-decked ship. **1854** R. S. SURTEES *Handley Cr.* xv, We killed the fox—my eyes, such a wopper!

b. *spec.* A great lie, a monstrous falsehood.

1791 NAIRNE *Poems* 93 Some do affirm—sure 'tis a Whapper! Thou'rt silver plated upon copper. **1870** 'A. R. HOPE' *My Schoolboy Fr.* xiv, He thinks it's..better to get a licking than to tell a whopper.

2. One who whops. (In mod. Dicts.)

whopper-jawed, erron. spelling of *wapper-jawed* adj. (see WAPPER *a.*).

1860 T. PARKER in *Life & Corr.* (1863) II. 428 This sheet is ruled as whopper-jawed as some women cut their bread.

whopping (ˈhwɒpɪŋ), *vbl. sb.* *colloq.* or *vulgar.* [f. WHOP *v.* + -ING[1].] The action of the verb WHOP; a severe beating or flogging; hence, an overwhelming defeat. Also *attrib.*

1812 *Sporting Mag.* XXXIX. 139 An athletic Nottinghamshire man, who..gave very unfavourable specimens of wapping talent. **1818** *Ibid.* (N.S.) II. 189 He wanted a good wapping and he had got it. **1838** DICKENS *O. Twist* xlii, I should like to..have the whopping of 'em. **1885** MRS. C. PRAED *Head Stat.* xvii, Blue-eyed fair-haired little girls who never fell into tantrums or wanted whopping.

ˈwhopping, *ppl. a.* *colloq.* or *vulgar.* [f. as prec. + -ING[2].] That whops; almost always *fig.* that is a 'whopper'; abnormally large or great; 'whacking', 'thumping'.

Rarely *spec.* (*a*) monstrously false; (*b*) of surpassing excellence, uncommonly good, first-rate. Also quasi-*adv.* = hugely, immensely.

*a***1625** R. G. in *Stanley Papers* I. (Chetham Soc.) 50 Our Chroniclers..stowed their volumes with wapping Tales of my Lord Maiors Horse. **1706** E. WARD *Wooden World Diss.* (1708) 98 See him in bad Weather, in his Fur-Cap and whapping large Watch-Coat. **1818** SCOTT *Rob Roy* xxiii, A wapping weaver he was, and wrought my first pair o' hose. **1836** HALIBURTON *Clockm.* Ser. I. xvii. (1839) 61 What a wappin large place that would make. **1851** *Amer. Mag.* Nov. 113 A couple of 'whopping' pumpkin stories. **1869** *Punch* 31 July 34/1 That's a wopping majority against us. **1881** FREEMAN in Stephens *Life & Lett.* (1895) II. 224 The Turk comes down with a whopping bit of oppression now and then, but leaves you alone between whiles.

whopstraw (ˈhwɒpstrɔː). *dial.* [f. WHOP *v.* (*dial.* 'to make up straw into bundles' E.D.D.) + STRAW *sb.*] A country bumpkin.

1821 CLARE *Vill. Minstrel* lxvii, The bumptious serjeant struts before his men, And 'clear the road, young whopstraws!' will he say. **1850** 'H. HIEOVER' *Pract. Horsem.* iii. 42 'Here cooms a flyer'..cries some whapstraw.

whor, obs. form of WHERE.

whorage (ˈhɔərɪdʒ). *dial.* [f. WHORE *sb.* + -AGE.] A company of whores or low women.

1891 HARDY *Tess* x, If I had known you was of that sort, I wouldn't have so let myself down as to come with such a whorage as this is!

whorcop: see WHORECOP.

whord, obs. form of HOARD.

whore (hɔə(r)), *sb.* Forms: 1–6 **hore**, 2–3 **heore**, 4–6 **hoore**, **houre**, 5–6 **hour**, 6 **howr(e**, **howir**, **hoare**, 6–7 **whoor(e**, **whoar**, 6– **whore**; *Sc.* 4–6 **huir**, 4–7 (9 *arch.*) **hure**, (6 **hwr**, **huire**); in comb. 2–7 **hor-**, 5 **hoer-**, 6 **hoor-**, **whure-**, **wor-**, 6–7 **whor-**; *Sc.* 5–7 **hur-**, 6 **huyr-**, **hwyr-**. [Late OE. *hóre*, corresp. to (M)LG. *hóre*, MDu. *hoere* (Du. *hoer*), OHG. *huora* (MHG. *huere*, G. *hure*), ON. *hóra*:—OTeut. **χōrōn-*, f. root represented also by ON. *hórr*, Goth. *hôrs* adulterer, OFris. *hôr* (also *overhôr*, *urhôr*), OHG. *huor*, ON. *hór* adultery, MLG. *horre*, MDu. *huerre*, OHG. *huorra* adulterer (:—**χōrjon-*), and OFris. (*over*)-*hôra* to fornicate, MDu. *hoeren*, OHG. *huorôn* (G. *huren*), ON. *hóra*, Goth. *hôrinôn*; Indo-Eur. *qār-* appears in L. *cārus* dear, OIr. *cara* friend, *caraim* I love, Lettish *kārs* lascivious.

From the late occurrence of OE. *hóre*, it may be inferred that it was a. ON. *hóra*, together with *hór* adultery, *hórcwene* (ON. *hórkona*) adulteress, *hórdóm* WHOREDOM, *hóring* whoremonger being in that case an English formation from it with -ING[3].

The pronunciation (hʊə(r)), now dialectal, is the normal phonetic representative of OE. *hóre*; it was widespread in the 17th and 18th centuries, and continued into the 19th century; Smart states that it 'is by no means universal or even common, yet it is sanctioned by good authority, and may be adopted, as Walker says, when we wish to soften the coarse effect of a coarse word'. The variation of (hʊə(r)) and (hɔə(r)) is due to the presence of *r*; cf. *moor* (mʊə(r), mɔə(r)) and the modern tendency to substitute (ɔə) for (ʊə) in *pure*, *sure*, and the like.

For the spelling with *wh*, which became current in the 16th century, see WH.

Whore is now confined to coarse and abusive speech, except in occas. echoes of historical expressions, as *the whore of Babylon*. The compounds are for the most part obs. or arch.]

1. a. A woman who prostitutes herself for hire; a prostitute, harlot.

*a***1100** *Aldhelm Gloss* I. 2940 (Napier 79/2) *Prostituta pellax*, i. *meretrix quæ prostat*, i. *mendax*, leas fyrnhicge, hore. *Ibid.* 3329. 89/1 *Meretricum*, horena. *c***1175** *Lamb. Hom.* 103 He..maceð of cristes leoman heoranna leoman. [*Cf.* I Cor. vi. 15 *Tollens Christi membra, faciam membra meretricis?*] *c***1200** *Trin. Coll. Hom.* 29 Ȝef þu..best rumhanded to glewmen and to hores. *a***1300** *Cursor M.* 26855 Hore or okerer, or Iogolour, Bot þai þair mister wille forsak, For fals penantes men sal þam tak. *c***1380** WYCLIF *Sel. Wks.* III. 310 Whanne tweyne horis stryvede whos was þe child þat lyvede. **1382** —— *Luke* xv. 30 This thi sone, which deuouride his substaunce with hooris. **1483** *Cath. Angl.* 192/2 An Hure, *vbi* a common woman. **1546** J. HEYWOOD *Prov.* II. vii. (1867) 71 Hop hoore, pipe theefe. **1595** in *Maitl. Club Misc.* I. 73 Ane ressavear of huiris and harlottis in her hous. **1597** SHAKS. *2 Hen. IV*, III. ii. 338 (Qo.) The whores cald him mandrake. **1632** LITHGOW *Trav.* II. 68 Let men take heed of Lais, Corinths whoore. **1728** YOUNG *Love Fame* I. 67 The whore is proud her beauties are the dread Of peevish virtue, and the marriage-bed. **1894** KIPLING *Seven Seas, The 'Mary Gloster'* 76 Your rooms at college was beastly—more like a whore's than a man's.

b. More generally: An unchaste or lewd woman; a fornicatress or adulteress. ***to play the whore*** (of a woman), to commit fornication or adultery.

In early use often as a coarse term of abuse. Occas. (esp. with possessive) applied opprobriously to a concubine or kept mistress; also with distinguishing epithet to a catamite.

*c***1205** LAY. 7028 Nes nan swa god wif i þon londe þe he walde..þet he ne makede hore. *c***1250** *Gen. & Ex.* 4082 He sluȝ Zabri..Hise hore bi-neðe and him abuuen. **1297** R. GLOUC. (Rolls) 5661 A fol womman in spousbruche he huld vnder is wif. Sein dunston him sede wel þat it was a luþer lif. .. Wroþ was þe king & is hore þat he hor folie wiþsede. *c***1440** *Gesta Rom.* i. 2, I knowe well þat my wif is an hore. **1535** in *Lett. Suppr. Monast.* (Camden) 58 The pope..gave hym licens to kepe an hore. **1535** COVERDALE *Ezek.* xvi. 28 Thou hast played the whore also with the Assirians. **1547** *Burgh Rec. Stirling* (1887) I. 48 Marioun Ray amerciat for trubling of Agnes Hendersoun, calland hir huir and theiff. **1561** *Child-Marriages* 78 Beynge demaundid why she did,.. contrary to the Lawe of wedlocke, play the hoore. **1605** SHAKS. *Lear* I. iv. 137 Leaue thy drinke and thy whore. **1606** —— *Tr. & Cr.* V. i. 20 *Ther...* Thou art thought to be Achilles male Varlot. *Patro...* What's that? *Ther.* Why his masculine Whore. **1694** MOTTEUX *Rabelais* V. *Pantagr. Prognost.* 237 Ingles, Fricatrices, He-whores. **1727** GAY *Begg. Op.* I. iv, Gamesters and Highwaymen are generally very good to their Whores, but they are very Devils to their Wives. **1749** CHESTERF. *Let. to Son* 7 Feb., Achilles..had so little regard for his country, that he would not act in defence of it, because he had quarrelled with Agamemnon about a w——e. **1817** SELWYN *Law Nisi Prius* (ed. 4) II. 1160 Calling a married woman or a single one a whore is not actionable, because fornication and adultery are subjects of spiritual not temporal censures. [Referring to a case, an. 1703, in Raymond's *Rep.* (1743) 1004.]

transf. **1575** *Gammer Gurton* I. iii, Gyb, our cat, in the milke-pan she spied..'Ah, hore! out, thefe!' she cryed aloud. **1607** TOPSELL *Four-f. Beasts* 745 Their Epithites.. attributed vnto them [*sc.* wolves] among seueral Authors are ..demonstrations of their disposition; as sowre, wilde,.. fierce, bold, greedy, whoare, flesh-eater.

c. A male prostitute; any promiscuous or unprincipled person. (Esp. as a term of abuse.)

1633 [see WORM *sb.* 10b]. **1906** J. JOYCE *Let.* 19 Aug. (1966) II. 152 He began to shout..when the lazy whores of priests began to chant. **1957** P. KEMP *Mine were of Trouble* vi. 108 Lyall would interrupt with..'But surely you can't expect the Irish to be any use in Spain? There aren't any hedges here for them to shoot from behind.'.. Lawler would storm out, shouting: 'Ye great buckin' whore!' **1968** E. GAINES in A. Chapman *New Black Voices* (1972) 103 'You hear me whore?' 'I might be a whore, but I'm not a merciless killer,' he said. **1976** *New Yorker* 12 Jan. 73/2 Gig Young can play the top whore in 'The Killer Elite' because his sad eyes suggest that he has no expectations and no illusions left about anything.

2. *fig.*; *spec.* in biblical use, applied to a corrupt or idolatrous community (cf. WHOREDOM 2), and hence in controversial use, esp. in phr. ***the whore of Babylon***, to the Church of Rome (in allusion to Rev. xvii. 1, 5, etc.).

1382 WYCLIF *Nahum* iii. 4 The hoore fair and able [**1611** wel-fauoured harlot],..whiche solde folkis in her fornycaciouns. —— *Rev.* xvii. 1 The dampnacioun of the greet hoore [**1611** Whore; R.V. 1881 harlot],..with whiche kynges of erthe diden fornycacioun. **1530** TINDALE *Pract. Prelates* F v b, The greate baude the hore of babylon [*sc.* the Pope]. *c***1540** *Pilgr. T.* 342 in *Thynne's Animadv.* (1875) 86 Of antichristes fall I will..sum-thing tell; & of this howr, this leyder to hell. ?**1545** BRINKLOW *Compl.* xiii. (1874) 30 That abhomynable whore of Babylon (Rome I meane). **1632** LITHGOW *Trav.* IV. 139, I may say of Constantinople..; A painted Whoore. *c***1640** in Maidment *Sc. Pasquils* (1868) 132 So you to Christian Kings shall break the ground, To loath the scarlet whoor. *c***1646** MILTON *Sonn. Forcers Consc.* 3 Because you have thrown of your Prelate Lord,..To seise the widow'd whore Pluralitie. **1684** SOUTHERNE *Disappointm.* II. i, But if her thoughts run foul, her mind's a Whore. **1704** C. LESLIE *Wolf Stript* (ed. 4) 31 They call her Episcopacy a Ragg of the Whore. **1743** H. WALPOLE *Let. to Mann* 3 Oct., He would have piqued himself on calling the

Pope the w——e of Babylon. **1818** SCOTT *Rob Roy* xix, Image worship, and surplices, and sic like rags o' the muckle hure that sitteth on seven hills.

3. † *whore's son, son of a whore* = WHORESON. ***whore's bird*** (also as one word, and dial. *wosbird*): properly, the child [see BIRD *sb.* 1 c] of a whore, a bastard; but usually as a mere vulgar term of abuse or reprobation. So ***whore's kitling***.

c **1500** *Melusine* 300 He cryed with a hye voys,..'hourys sone & fals geaunt, comme speke with me!' **1673** J. W[ADE] *Vinegar & Mustard* (1873) 17 Thou was a base whore's bird. **1675** *Char. of Town-Gallant* 5 He admires the Eloquence of, Son of a Whore,..and therefor applyes it to every thing; So that if his Pipe be faulty,..Tis a Son of a Whore Pipe. **1694** ECHARD *Plautus* 9 They'd set some sturdy Whores-bird to.. beat out ha'f a dozen o' my Teeth. *a* **1700** B. E. *Dict. Cant. Crew*, *Whores-kitling*, a Bastard. **1700** T. BROWN tr. *Fresny's Amusem.* 21 Another Son of a Whore yells louder than Homer's Stentor. **1701** SEDLEY *Grumbler* I. i, I will first let you see how I am serv'd by this whoresbird. **1772** GRAVES *Spir. Quix.* IV. ix, D—mn you all together, for a pack of whores-birds as you are! **1857** HUGHES *Tom Brown* I. ii, 'Imp'dent old wosbird!' says he, 'I'll break the bald head on un.' **1891** HARDY *Tess* xxi, Jack Dollop, a 'hor's-bird of a fellow.

4. *Comb.*, as ***whore-call***, ***-haunter***; ***whore-like*** adj.; **whore-hunt** *v.*, *intr.* to go after whores, practise fornication: so ***whore-hunter***, ***-hunting*** (also *fig.*; in quot. 1714, spying after whores to extort hush-money); † **whore-keeper**, one who keeps company with whores, a fornicator; † **whore-man**, a fornicator; **whoremistress**, a brothel-keeper; † **whore-play** [PLAY *sb.* 6 c], intercourse with whores, fornication; **whore's egg** *N. Amer.* (chiefly *Newfoundland*) = SEA-URCHIN 1; **whore-shop** *slang*, a brothel; **whore-sty** (*nonce-wd.*), a brothel; † **whore-toll**, a payment made by way of compounding for fornication or concubinage.

a **1692** SHADWELL *Volunteers* V. i, These Fiddles are Fop-Calls, and *Whore-Calls. **1580** *Orders for Orphanes* A iv, If any manchilde be a Thiefe, or a Fellon, or a common *whore haunter. **1597** BEARD *Theatre God's Judgem.* II. xx. (1612) 358 He went apart into Auignion, and there staied of purpose to doe nothing but *whore-hunt. **1786** BURNS *Twa Dogs* 164 He..Whore-hunting amang groves o' myrtles. **1532** MORE *Confut. Tindale* Wks. 666/1 *Scortatores*, which signifieth in englishe *whoore hunters. **1600** W. WATSON *Decacordon* (1602) 81 A notorious drunkard, whorehunter, cousiner, vsurer, &c. **1532** FRITH *Mirror* (1533) A v b, Yf.. the watcheman be a slepe,..or gone..a *whorehuntinge. **1577** tr. *Bullinger's Decades* II. ii. 124 That is spirituall adulterie & whore-hunting, when men doe partly loue and worship God, and yet..giue reuerence to straunge..Gods. **1620** *Westward for Smelts* (Percy Soc.) 44 Her husband.. had used to goe on whore-hunting in the night. **1714** RAMSAY *Elegy on J. Cowper* iii, Of Whore-hunting he gat his Fill, And made be 't mony a Pint and Gill. **1931** R. CAMPBELL *Georgiad* i. 15 Lovelorn poets..troop whore-hunting down the country lanes. **1530** TINDALE *Pract. Prel.* B iij b, If any synne agenst yᵉ doctrine of Christ..so yᵗ he be a dronckarde & an *horekeper. **1621** T. WILLIAMSON tr. *Goulart's Wise Vieillard* 68 There shall not be a whore among the daughters of Israell, nor a whore-keeper among the sonnes of Israel. **1550** CROWLEY *Epigr.* 1288 Our wiues do passe their whoris in *whorelyke deckynge. **1974** H. J. PARKER *View from Boys* 213 'A right scrubber' is a girl who's rough-looking, whorelike. *c* **1250** *Gen. & Ex.* 4072 Ðo seide god to moysen, Ðe meistres of ðise *hore-men,..Ðe bidde ic hangen ðat he ben. **1922** JOYCE *Ulysses* 515 Bella Cohen, a massive *whoremistress enters. **1969** A. MARIN *Rise with Wind* xii. 154 Consejo..works for a whoremistress we call Tía Concha. *c* **1250** *Gen. & Ex.* 530 Caymes sunes wroȝten vn-laȝe, Wið breðere wifes *hore-plaȝe. **1829** T. C. HALIBURTON *Hist. & Statist. Acct. Nova Scotia* II. ix. 405 Shell fish. *Whore's egg. **1930** *Amer. Speech* V. 393 *Whore's egg*,..a small spring crustacean esteemed by the Italians as a delicacy. **1948** Z. N. HURSTON *Seraph on Suwanee* 296 That damn whore's egg! Ruin you if only one spine gets into your hand. **1972** E. STAEBLER *Cape Breton Harbour* ix. 85 You be careful when you's swimming that you don't step on a whore's egg, they sea urchins is full o' prickles will give you a fester. **1938** V. S. PRITCHETT *You make your own Life* 79 What a town like this wants is a couple of good *whore shops and a factory. **1972** A. MACVICAR *Golden Venus Affair* vi. 67, I hate The Golden Venus... It's just a whoreshop. **1621** BP. MOUNTAGU *Diatribæ* 196 [Churches] turne[d] to barnes, stables, hogsties, and that which is worse, *whore-sties. **1545** COVERDALE *Def. Chr. Man* E ij b, Romishe prestes.. take harlottes..whan they will,..and aske no question for conscience sake, so that they paye the bishope the *whore toll.

whore, *v.* [f. prec. sb.]

1. a. *intr.* To have to do with a whore or whores; to commit whoredom, fornicate; (of a woman) to play the whore. Also *fig.* (See also WHORING.)

1583 BABINGTON *Commandm.* (1590) 178 Wee drinke, wee eate, wee surfet, wee sweare, wee play, wee daunce, wee whore. **1615** GODDARD *Neaste of Waspes* G iv b, Sheel fight, whore, drinke, vntill shee cannot see. **1642** BRIDGE *Serm. Norwich Volunteers* 5 They thinke him a foole or a child that will not drink and be drunke, and whore. **1682** SHADWELL *Sat. to Muse* 238 Against the Court, and David's-self he Roard, How ill he Govern'd, and how worse he W——d. **1732** BERKELEY *Alciphr.* II. §13 To cheat, whore, betray, get drunk, do all these things decently, this is true wisdom, and elegance of taste. **1766** *Midnight Spy* v. 43 The gay courtezan with her pockets lined with gold, may whore with impunity. **1896** KIPLING *Seven Seas, Song Engl.* iii, Hold ye the Faith..; Whoring not with visions.

b. *trans.* To spend in whoring; (with adv.) to get or bring by whoring.

1681 COLVIL *Whig's Supplic.* (1710) 53 Their Officers.. Had dic'd and drunk, and whor'd their Pay. **1682** MRS. BEHN *City-Heiress* I. i, A man might whore his heart out.

c. *intr.* fig. To pursue or seek *after* (something false or unworthy). In allusion to Exod. xxxiv. 15. Cf. WHORING *vbl. sb.* (quot. 1535).

1913 E. POUND *Let.* 13 Aug. (1971) 21 The unspeakable vulgo will I suppose hear of him [*sc.* F. M. Hueffer] after our deaths. In the meantime they whore after their Bennetts and their Galsworthys and their unspeakable canaille. **1937** J. M. MURRY *Necessity of Pacificism* 24 The intelligence of Socialism went a-whoring after the strange gods of Russia. **1970** R. LONG in A. Chapman *New Black Voices* (1972) 421 The University was whoring after strange gods, they all seemed to say: technology, athletics, materialism. **1972** *Language* XLVIII. 425, I do not accept Chomsky's conception of social scientists as universally whoring after the surface features of other sciences, neglecting all fundamental problems, and taking refuge in spurious precision and trivialities.

2. *trans.* To make a whore of; to corrupt by illicit intercourse; to debauch (a woman). Also *fig.* Now *rare.*

1602 SHAKS. *Ham.* V. ii. 64 He that hath kil'd my King, and whor'd my Mother. **1682** DRYDEN *Medal* 258 The Pander of the Peoples hearts,..Whose blandishments a Loyal Land have whor'd, And broke the Bonds she plighted to her Lord. *a* **1692** SHADWELL *Volunteers* III. i. (1693) 32 Did you mean to whore my Daughter? **1740** RICHARDSON *Pamela* (1741) II. 224 She ask'd her,..if I was whor'd yet! There's a Word for a Lady's Mouth! **1969** A. HUNTER *Gently Coloured* iii. 33 Some friend squeezing you dry, whoring your sister.

whore, obs. form of HOAR, WHERE.

whor(e)cop, late forms of HORCOP, bastard.

a **1590** *Marr. Wit & Wisd.* (Shaks. Soc.) 51 What, where be these whorecops? **1599** *Sir Clyom.* F 2 b, Whorcop.

whoredom ('həʊdəm). *arch.* Forms: see WHORE *sb.*; also 4 **-dame**, 4–5 **-dam**, 4–7 **-dome**, 6 **-doome**, *Sc.* **-dum**. [prob. a. ON. *hórdómr* = OFris. *hôrdôm*, MLG. *hôrdom*: see WHORE *sb.* and -DOM.]

1. The practice of playing the whore, or of intercourse with whores; illicit sexual indulgence in general; fornication, harlotry.

c **1175** *Lamb. Hom.* 57 Ne beo þu nawiht monslaht, ne in hordom dei ne naht. **1297** R. GLOUC. (Rolls) 9857 He leuede muche in hordom, & huld vnder þe quene rosemounde. *a* **1300** *Floriz & Bl.* 654 Nis noȝt ȝore þat i ne com And fond hire wiþ hordom, Me to schame..In hire bedde on mi Tur. *c* **1380** WYCLIF *Sel. Wks.* III. 417 Þis privey horedame makes myche harme. *c* **1450** *St. Cuthbert* (Surtees) 334 Þat he be getyn..In hordome. **1535** COVERDALE *Gen.* xxxviii. 24 By whordome is she gotten with childe. **1561** WINȜET *Wks.* (S.T.S.) I. 128 The renunceing of the warld and plesouris of the body, nocht only fra vnlesum huirdum, bot fra mariage sumtyme to thame lesum. **1605** M. SUTCLIFFE *Brief Exam.* 102 They..set up bordell houses for maintenance of whoredom & baudry. **1784** COWPER *Tiroc.* 833 Now flush'd with drunk'ness, now with whoredom pale.

b. *pl.* Acts of sexual immorality.

c **1175** *Lamb. Hom.* 33 Ȝe nulleð forleten hordomes and ȝifernesse and druncnesse. **1539** *Bible* (Great) 2 Kings ix. 22 Yᵉ whordomes of thy mother Iezabel. **1575–85** SANDYS *Serm.* xiv. 249 Otherwise they are not mariages, but whoredomes. **1611** *Bible* Hosea i. 2 A wife of whoredomes, and children of whoredomes. **1716** HEARNE *Collect.* (O.H.S.) V. 234 Notwithstanding his Whoredoms. **1862** HOOK *Lives Abps.* II. ii. 114 He will never be converted from his whoredoms and ruinous follies.

2. *fig.*; *esp.* in biblical and religious use, applied to idolatry or other form of unfaithfulness to the true God.

c **1380** WYCLIF *Sel. Wks.* I. 58 Kynrede of hordom sekiþ siche signes. **1535** COVERDALE *Jer.* iii. 2 Thorow thy whordome and shamefull blasphemies, is the londe defyled. —— *Hosea* i. 2 The londe hath committed greate whordome agaynst the Lorde. **1593** J. NAPIER *Rev.* To Rdr. A 6, Their seuen hilled citie Rome, painted out..by Saint Iohn, as the mother of all spirituall whoredome. **1742** YOUNG *Nt. Th.* VIII. 549 Think you there's but one whoredom? whoredom, all, But when our reason licenses delight. **1860** PUSEY *Min. Proph.* 13 Whoredom is to have many other objects of sinful love.

Hence † **'whoredomer (hurdomare)** *Sc. Obs.*, one who practises whoredom, a fornicator.

1456 SIR G. HAYE *Bk. Knthd.* Wks. (S.T.S.) II. 40 Na common leare, na commone vicioușe hurdomare.

whore-house. [Cf. OS. *hôrhûs* (MLG. *hoerhuus*, Du. *hoerhuis*), OHG., MHG. *huorhûs* (G. *hurenhaus*).]

1. A house of whores, a brothel. *Obs.* after 17th cent. until revived in recent (chiefly *U.S.*) use.

13.. tr. *Ælred* in *Engl. Stud.* VII. 308 A blessed mayden þat turnde an hoore-hows in to an oratorie. *c* **1475** *Pict. Voc.* in Wr.-Wülcker 804/10 *Hoc lupaner*, *Hec fornix*, *Hoc prostibulum*, a horehowse. *a* **1599** SIR J. DAVIES *Epigr.* xxxix, Sometimes he comes not to the play, But falls into a whore house by the way. **1608** DEKKER *Lanth. & Candle Lt.* G 4 b, The plague that a Whore-house layes vpon a Citty. **1688** BUNYAN *Last Serm.* Wks. 1862 II. 757 A whore-house, it may be, is more sweet to him. **1909** in J. A. & A. Lomax *Amer. Ballads & Folk Songs* (1960) 104 Frankie went down to de whore-house, Rang de whore-house bell, Says 'Tell me, is my lovin' Albert here? Caze Frankie's gwine to raise some hell—Oh, he's my man, but he's a-doin' me wrong.' **1935** J. STEINBECK *Tortilla Flat* i. 25 'Pilon!..I am an heir! I own two houses.' 'Whore houses?' Pilon asked hopefully. **1951** J. MASTERS *Nightrunners Bengal* I. vi. 82 Every one knew her as the madam of a high-grade whore-house. **1978** G. GREENE *Human Factor* III. iii. 123 'If you want to fuck a black whore,' Captain Van Donck interrupted with impatience, 'why don't you go to a whore-house in Lesotho or Swaziland?' **1982** *Times* 22 May 8/1 Prospectors came by the thousand, saloons and whore-houses were erected.

2. *attrib.* and *Comb.* **a.** Simple attrib., as ***whore-house bell***, ***owner***, ***perfume***, ***scum***. **b.** Designating or pertaining to a style of music, esp. jazz, played in brothels, as ***whore-house music***, ***piano***. **c.** *Comb.*, as ***whore-house madam*** = MADAM 3 c (*d*).

1909 Whore-house bell [see sense 1 above]. **1938** D. BAKER *Young Man with Horn* III. i. 141 You certainly play whorehouse piano, fella, and nigger whorehouse at that. **1946** R. BLESH *Shining Trumpets* xiii. 295 This rich and earthy piano playing, called by extreme jazz purists with an ear for the picturesquely accurate, 'whore-house piano'. **1949** R. CHANDLER *Little Sister* xvii. 110 A very cheap grade of whore-house perfume. **1954** W. FAULKNER *Fable* 379 Shoot now, you whorehouse scum. **1956** B. HOLIDAY *Lady sings Blues* (1973) i. 8, I guess I'm not the only one who heard their first good jazz in a whorehouse... A lot of white people first heard jazz in places like Alice Dean's, and they helped label jazz 'whorehouse music'. **1975** G. V. HIGGINS *City on Hill* vi. 150 When you try to talk about something else, it's like trying to discuss cryogenics with a whorehouse madam.

whorelle, obs. form of WHORL.

whoremaster ('həʊə,mɑːstə(r)). [f. WHORE *sb.* + MASTER *sb.*]

1. = next.

a **1508** DUNBAR *Tua Mariit Wemen* 168 My husband wes a hur maister... He has bene waistit apon wemen..And in adultre. **1596** SHAKS. *1 Hen. IV*, II. iv. 516 That hee is (sauing your reuerence) a Whore-master, that I vtterly deny. **1610** HEALEY *St. Aug. Citie of God* 188 The stage-plaiers act..love for the veriest whore-maister in the world. **1712** ADDISON *Spect.* No. 446 ¶7 Our ordinary Poets cannot frame to themselves the Idea of a fine Man who is not a Whore-master. **1747** CHESTERF. *Let. to Son* 27 Mar., A Man of Pleasure, in the vulgar acceptation of that phrase, means only, a beastly drunkard, an abandoned whore-master, and a profligate swearer. **1769** BLACKSTONE *Comm.* IV. xviii. 253 A justice may bind over all night-walkers; eaves-droppers; ..common drunkards; whoremasters; the putative fathers of bastards;..and other persons, whose misbehaviour may reasonably bring them within the general words of the statute, as persons not of good fame.

attrib. *c* **1570** *Depos. Durham* (Surtees) 264 Cauling this examinate hooremaster preiste. **1605** SHAKS. *Lear* I. ii. 137 An admirable euasion of Whore-master-man, to lay his Goatish disposition to the charge of a Starre. **1614** B. JONSON *Barth. Fair* V. iv, You whore-master knaue. **1878** *Prodigal Son* VI. in Simpson *Sch. Shaks.* II. 119 Shall I..be merry because my whoremaster brother is come back?

2. *spec.* A procurer or pimp.

1864 in WEBSTER. **1922** E. E. CUMMINGS *Enormous Room* vii. 163 Now I must tell you what happened to the poor Spanish Whoremaster. **1964** in Hamblett & Deverson *Generation X* 94 Johnny knew just when to corrupt and when to give the old ego a boost. He's one of the great whoremasters of all time, working on the principle of the carrot and the stick. **1977** M. T. BLOOM *13th Man* (1978) vii. 133 The newcomers had little money and..they got tempted by the whoremasters.

Hence **'whore,masterly** *a.*, having the character of a whoremaster, lecherous; **'whore,mastery**, the practice of a whoremaster, fornication.

1606 SHAKS. *Tr. & Cr.* V. iv. 7 That Greekish *whore-masterly villaine. **1706** BAYNARD *Cold Baths* II. (ed. 2) 96 The vile and wicked whore-masterly Husband. **1618** N. FIELD *Amends for Ladies* V. i, A great hurt to the art of *whore-mastry.

whoremonger ('həʊ,mʌŋgə(r)). *arch.* [f. WHORE *sb.* + MONGER 2. Now familiar mainly from its occurrence in the English Bible.] One who has dealings with whores; one who practises whoredom; a fornicator, lecher.

1526 TINDALE *Eph.* v. 5 No whormonger, other vnclene person,..hath any inheritaunce in the kyngdom of Christ. **1528** ROY *Rede me* (Arb.) 53 Lycknest thou to whoarmongers A colage of clarckes and scolears? **1603** SHAKS. *Meas. for M.* III. ii. 37. **1632** LITHGOW *Trav.* IX. 408 What was Clement the 5. but an open Whore munger? **1899** *Allbutt's Syst. Med.* VIII. 250 If, by their self-indulgence, the glutton, the drunkard, the loafer,..the whoremonger forfeit a future benefit [etc.].

So **whoremonging** ('həʊ,mʌŋgɪŋ), the practice of a whoremonger, fornication.

1549 COVERDALE, etc. *Erasm. Par. 2 Pet.* ii. 13–16 Nether haue they mynde of any thing elles, than vpon whore-monging, and other kyndes of wikednes. **1563** *St. Andrews Kirk-sess. Reg.* (1889) 189 The delacionis gevyn in upon tham..for huyrmongyn inveterat. **1893** *Voice* (N.Y.) 10 Aug., We would dissociate liquor selling from low, corrupt politics, from gambling, from whoremonging and from all other forms of immoral pursuit!

† **whorer** ('həʊərə(r)). *Obs.* [f. WHORE *v.* + -ER¹. Cf. OS. *hôrâri*, OHG. *huorari* (MHG. *huorer*, G. *hurer*), etc.] = WHOREMONGER.

c **1640** H. BELL *Luther's Colloq. Mens.* (1652) 318 It shall bee free for Priests to marrie, or to forbear: Howsoever many Priests are, and will remain whorers. **1681** COLVIL *Whig's Supplic.* (1710) 97 All of them proved Drinkers, Whorers, By Preachers, Forgers, and Perjurers. **1727** P. WALKER *Cameron* in *Biogr. Presbyt.* (1827) I. 289 A great Swearer, a great Whorer, Blasphemer, Drunkard.

whoreship ('həʊʃɪp). [f. WHORE *sb.* + -SHIP.] The personality of a whore: used with poss. pron. as a humorous title.

1607 R. TURNER *Nosce Te* E 1 b, Bifronted Peter's head,.. Yet a loues her whoreshippe as he loues his life. **1624**

DAVENPORT *City Night-cap* III, I have a penance for your pure whoreship. **1711** E. WARD *Quix.* I. 67 To shew his Worship The curteous Temper of her Whoreship.

whoreson ('hɔəsən). Now *arch.* Forms: see WHORE *sb.*; also 5 **hoursen, horosonne,** 6 **horisson.** [f. WHORE *sb.* + SON *sb.*[1], after AF. *fiz a putain* (see FITZ).]

a. prop. The son of a whore, a bastard son; but commonly used as a coarse term of reprobation, abuse, dislike, or contempt; sometimes even of jocular familiarity. (Cf. BUGGER 2 b.) Also rarely applied to a thing.

13.. *K. Alis.* 880 (Laud MS.) Fy vyle ateynt hores sone! To mysdon was ay þi wone. **13..** *Sir Beues* (A.) 410 An houre sone for soþ ich wes. *c* **1380** *Sir Ferumb.* 2016 Þow gadelyng horesone, lecher, & stronge þef. *c* **1400** *Brut* I. 207 He despisede þe grettest lordes.., and callede Sir Robert Clare Erl of Gloucestre, 'Horessone'. *a* **1425** *Cursor M.* 11879 (Trin.) 'Hore sones [*Cott.* Fiȝ aputains]' he seide 'what are ȝe'? 'Leches' þei seide 'to leche þe'. **1481** CAXTON *Reynard* xxi. (Arb.) 53, I trusted.. so moche the fals horeson the foxe. *a* **1483** *Liber Niger* in *Househ. Ord.* (1790) 68 Of what estate soever he be,.. usyng to swere customably by Goddes body.. unreverently.. that they charge the Butler to geve him no wyne at the meles... There was a lyke motion to be made for the customable word of hoursen. **1523** LD. BERNERS *Froiss.* I. cccxxvii. 139b/1 Kyng Dampeter was greatly chafed and moche desyred to mete with the bastarde his brother, and sayd, where is yᵗ horeson, that calleth hym selfe kynge of Castell. **1553** T. WILSON *Rhet.* 79b, The mother merelye beynge disposed, wyll saye to her swete Sonne: Ah you little hore-son, wyll you serue me so? **1560** DAUS tr. *Sleidane's Comm.* 135 Do they not graunt them selues to be whore sonnes all the packe of them? [orig. *nonne meretricum sese filios esse fatentur?*]. **1592** SHAKS. *Rom. & Jul.* IV. iv. 19 Masse, and well said, a merrie horson, ha! **1613** —— *Hen. VIII,* I. iii. 39 The slye whorsons Haue got a speeding tricke to lay downe Ladies. **1659** GAYTON *Art Longevity* 83 Nuts are dry whorsons. **1679** *Roxb. Ball.* (1883) IV. 614 Beware of those that.. tamper with thy foolish whoreson, And by false arguments ensnare The youth to think he is thy heir. **1712** ARBUTHNOT *John Bull* I. v, Nic. Frog was a cunning sly Whoreson. **1821** SCOTT *Kenilw.* xxxviii, They.. bestowed.. some round dozen of curses on them, as lazy knaves and blind whoresons. **1826** SOUTHEY *Devil's Walk* liii, Whoever shall say that to Porson These best of all verses belong, He is an untruth-telling whoreson. **1926** [see INGLE *sb.*[2]]. **1975** *Weekend Mag.* (Montreal) 1 Nov. 21/1 If the whoreson who dropped his socks into the chamber pot and sold the results to a lantern jaws like you is not at a rope's end since this fortnight, there is no justice left on earth!

b. *attrib.*: commonly as a coarsely abusive epithet, applied to a person or thing: Vile, abominable, execrable, detestable, 'wretched', 'scurvy', 'bloody'; also sometimes expressing humorous familiarity or commendation.

c **1440** *York Myst.* xxx. 60 Why, go bette, horosonne boy, when I bidde þe. **1533** GAU *Richt Vay* 15 Scheyme happine the lowne hursone theiff. **1534** in *Suss. Star Chamber Proc.* (1913) 40 Thow horisson prist yff thow ons move thow shalt dye. **1577–82** BRETON *Toys of an Idle Head* Wks. (Grosart) I. 30/1 Faith, she will say, you whorson Page, Ile purchase you an heritage. **1597** SHAKS. *2 Hen. IV,* II. iv. 225 Ah, you whorson little valiant Villaine, you! *Ibid.* III. ii. 193 *Fal.* What disease hast thou? *Bul.* A whorson cold sir, a cough sir. **1611** BEAUM. & FL. *Philaster* I. i, Oh! this same whorson Conscience, how it jades us! **1646** TRAPP *Comm. John* x. 8 Ah whoreson-thieves, rob God of his glory! said D. Taylor. **1739** *Joe Miller's Jests* 37 Thou Whoreson Rascal. **1760** STERNE *Tr. Shandy* III. xx, Ambition, and pride, and envy, and lechery, and other whoreson passions. *a* **1763** SHENSTONE *Ess.* iv. Wks. 1777 II. 16 The Impromptu, for which I was utterly disqualified by a whoreson slowness of apprehension. **1816** KEATS *Lett.* Wks. 1889 III. 47 It was so whoreson a Night that I stopped there all the next day. **1821** SCOTT *Kenilw.* xvii, Some of his whoreson poetry (I crave your Grace's pardon for such a phrase) has rung in mine ears. **1909** E. POUND *Exultations* 14 You whoreson dog, Papiols, come!

whorey, variant of WHORY.

Whorfian ('hwɔːfiən), *a.* [f. the name of the American linguist Benjamin Lee *Whorf* (1897–1941) + -IAN.] Designating the views and theories of B. L. Whorf, esp. in ***Whorfian hypothesis***, the theory that one's perception of the world is influenced or determined by the structure of one's native language (also ***Whorf hypothesis***). Cf. SAPIR-WHORF HYPOTHESIS.

1957 R. K. MERTON *Social Theory* (rev. ed.) ii. 92 It is the extreme Whorfian position which Joshua Whatmough attacks. **1963** J. LYONS *Structural Semantics* iii. 40 The view expressed in this quotation from Sapir has been championed more recently by Whorf, and has come to be known within linguistics as the 'Whorfian hypothesis'. **1964** R. H. ROBINS *Gen. Linguistics* ii. 80 This is part of what has come to be known as the 'Whorf hypothesis'. **1968** M. BLACK *Labyrinth of Lang.* iv. 75 Some interesting attempts have been made to determine the validity of Whorfian ideas. **1978** *Language* LIV. 167 His chapter on personal context contains discussions of the Whorfian hypothesis.

Hence **'Whorfianism,** a Whorfian conception; Whorf's theories regarded *collect.*

1963 J. LYONS *Structural Semantics* iii. 40 For a strong and convincing attack on the more extreme aspects of 'Whorfianism', cf. M. Black, 'Linguistic relativity'. **1978** *Language* LIV. 267 Parry's notion that formulaic language imposes formulaic thought is a kind of Whorfianism run wild.

whoring ('hɔərɪŋ), *vbl. sb.* [f. WHORE *v.* + -ING[1].] The action of WHORE *v.*; fornication; also *fig.*: *spec.* in biblical use, applied to idolatry, as an act of unfaithfulness to the true God (cf. WHOREDOM 2): chiefly in phr. ***to go a whoring.***

1535 COVERDALE *Exod.* xxxiv. 15 Whan they go a whoringe after their goddes. —— *Ps.* cv[i]. 38 Thus were they stayned with their owne workes, and wente a whoringe with their owne invencions. **1604** SHAKS. *Oth.* V. i. 116 This is the fruits of whoring. **1619** in Foster *Engl. Factories India* (1906) 153 Their private whorings, drunkennesse and such like ryotts. *a* **1638** MEDE *Wks.* (1672) 582 All the Visions contemporating with Babylon's times must be expounded of such things only as belong to the times of Babylon's whoring. **1668** SOUTH *Serm., Luke xxi.* 15 Wks. 1727 V. 416 When with Whoring, and Gaming, and Revelling, they have disabled themselves from paying their Butchers. **1709** STEELE *Tatler* No. 60 ¶2 The common Diversions of Men of Fashion; that is to say, in Whoring, Drinking, and Gaming. **1855** [J. D. BURN] *Autobiog. Beggar Boy* (1859) 73 The whole of this man's conduct tended to.. fighting, whoring, and roguery!

So **whoring** *ppl. a.*

1677 W. HUGHES *Man of Sin* II. x. 185 That either we must have a Married or a Whoring Clergy.

whorish ('hɔərɪʃ), *a.* Now *arch.* [f. WHORE *sb.* + -ISH[1].]

1. a. Having the character of a whore; addicted to whoredom; lewd, unchaste (of a woman; rarely of a man).

1560 *Bible* (Geneva) Prov. vi. 26 Because of the whoorish woman a man is broght to a morsel of bread. —— Ezek. xvi. 30 Yᵉ worke of a presumpteous whorish woman. **1611** *Coryat's Crudities* Panegyr. Verses g 2 b, He knew and felt the whores, yet was not whorish. **1624** DAVENPORT *City Night-cap* I. i, What plague can transcend A whorish wife, and a perfidious friend! **1632** LITHGOW *Trav.* IX. 382 Whoorish boyes. **1675** SOUTH *Serm., Judges viii. 34, 35* (1697) I. 509 Joseph.. a poor.. Stranger, languishing in Durance upon the false accusations of a lying, insolent whorish Woman! **1948** D. WELCH *Brave & Cruel* 245 Mary .. had nothing to take her mind from the hideous picture of a breast pump, a whorish wife and an idiot baby. **1981** V. CANNING *Boy on Platform One* iv. 60 Whorish.. the word swam gently into his mind. Whore, too, she was.

b. Belonging to or characteristic of a whore; meretricious; lewd, unchaste (of action, etc.).

1552 HULOET, Hooryshe.., or perteynynge to a hoore, *meretricius.* **1556** OLDE *Antichrist* 203 Men geuen to their paunche and hoorishe lustes. **1606** SHAKS. *Tr. & Cr.* IV. i. 63 You like a letcher, out of whorish loynes, Are pleas'd to breede out your inheritors. **1761** *Rec. Elgin* (New Spald. Club 1903) I. 198 Barbara Reid for whorish practices expelled the burgh. **1942** D. WELCH *Jrnl.* 30 Aug. (1952) 7 When we had.. pushed back the whorish, dirty red satin curtain. **1967** A. LASKI *Seven Other Years* iv. 56 It was a charming dress.. virginal in colour, whorish in cut. **1980** A. E. FISHER *Midnight Men* iv. 45 Bathrooms should reflect.. the woman of the house... I'd like a sort of whorish pink.

2. *fig.*, esp. in religious and controversial use (often = idolatrous): cf. WHORE *sb.* 2.

1535 COVERDALE *Ezek.* vi. 9 That whorish and vnfaithfull herte of theirs, wherwith they runne awaye fro me. **1538** BALE *Thre Lawes* C ii b, Regarde not the pope, nor yet hys whorysh kyngedom. *c* **1586** C'TESS PEMBROKE *Ps.* LXXIII. vii, They all shall be undone, Who leaving thee to whoorish idolls run. **1680** R. L'ESTRANGE *Citt & Bumpkin* (ed. 3) 16 The Church of England.. is not altogether the Whore of Babylon, though a good deal Whorish. **1696** BROOKHOUSE *Temple Opened* 47 The Bride has a Husband.. sufficient to maintain her against all Whorish, Beastly or Satannical Usurpations. **1711** STEELE *Spect.* No. 82 ¶3 Jack has a whorish unresisting Good-nature, which makes him incapable of having a Property in any thing.

Hence **'whorishly** *adv.*; **'whorishness.**

1538 ELYOT *Dict., Meretricie,* *hoorishely. **1589** NASHE *Martin Marprelate* Wks. (Grosart) I. 108 Howe whorishlie Scriptures are alleaged by them, I will discouer.. in another new worke. **16..** MIDDLETON, etc. *Old Law* IV. ii, Are you so whorishly provided? **1755** JOHNSON, *Meretriciously,* whorishly; after the manner of whores. **1977** *Listener* 25 Aug. 246/3 The gratuitous violence, slotted whoreishly into the sequences. **1546** BALE *Engl. Votaries* I. 18 Marke how abhominable *whoryshnesse.. is auaunced of that whorysh Rome churche, to the great blemyshynge of Godly marryage. **1691** WOOD *Ath. Oxon.* II. 706 The said Anne was.. for her whorishness lawfully divorced. **1727** BAILEY vol. II, *Meretriciousness,* whorishness.

†**whorism.** *Obs. rare.* [f. WHORE *sb.* or *v.* + -ISM.] Whoredom, fornication.

1598 FLORIO, *Puttaneggio,* whorisme, whoredome. **1611** COTGR., *s'Appaillarder,* to.. giue himselfe wholly to whoorisme; to turne leacher.

whorl (hwɔːl, hwɜːl), *sb.* Forms: α. 5 **wharwyl,** 5–9 **wharle,** 8–9 **wharl.** β. 5 **whorwhil, (whorlwyl),** **qworle,** 5–9 **whorle,** 6 **whorlle, whorelle,** *Sc.* **quhorle,** 8– **whorl.** [late ME. *wharwyl, whorwhil,* app. variants of WHIRL (early forms disyllabic, e.g. *wherwille, qwherel*) influenced by WHARVE *sb.*; but with the β-forms cf. early mod.Du. *worvel,* var. of *wervel* (Kilian).]

1. A small fly-wheel fixed on the spindle of a spinning-wheel to maintain or regulate the speed; a small pulley by which the spindle is driven in a spinning-machine. Also locally applied to small wheels or pulleys for other purposes.

α. *c* **1460** *Promp. Parv.* 526/2 (Winch. MS.) Wharwyl of a spyndyl, *vertebrum.* **1483** *Cath. Angl.* 417/1 A Wharle, *giraculum, neopellum, vertibulum.* **1532** MORE *Confut. Tindale* Wks. 628/2 Take out thy spindle & bryng me hither the wharle. **1566** in Peacock *Engl. Ch. Furnit.* (1866) 170 One crwet defaced whearof was made wharles for spindels. **1589** *Shuttleworths' Acc.* (Chetham Soc.) 55 Spindles and wharles ijᵈ. **1828** *Craven Gloss.,* Wharle. **1884** W. S. B. McLAREN *Spinning* (ed. 2) 239 [They] drive this spindle by the friction of a very heavy collar on it against a large leather washer, which rests on the wharl.

β. *c* **1440** *Promp. Parv.* 526/1 Whorlwyl, of a spyndyl (*K.* whorwhil, *P.* whorle), *vertebrum.* **1483** *Cath. Angl.* 298 A Qworle of A roke. **1610** R. VAUGHAN *Water-Wks.* O 4 b, The Stanke-royall (running on a whorle, his sluce being taken vp) is receiued by a Bastard-sluce. **1773** EMERSON *Princ. Mech.* (ed. 3) 189 Let EG be a spinning wheel,.. whilst the rim makes 1 revolution, the twill makes 9, and the whorle and feathers 6. **1808** JAMIESON, *Whorle,* a very small wheel, as that in a child's cart. **1865** LUBBOCK *Preh. Times* v. 133 Spindle whorls of rude earthenware were abundant in some of the Lake-villages even of the Stone age. **1886** J. BARROWMAN *Sc. Mining Terms* 73 *Whorls,* pithead pulleys.

2. *Bot.* A set of members, as leaves, flowers, or parts of the flower, springing from the stem or axis at the same level and encircling it; a verticil. Also in *Zool.* a set of parts or structures, as scales or tentacles, similarly arranged.

[**1551** TURNER *Herbal* I. G vj, The stalke is foure square,.. where about doth grow in equal order,.. certayne knoppes, lyke whorlles. **1578** LYTE *Dodoens* II. lxv. 232 The floures [of Pennyroyal] growe.. about the stemmes like whorles or garlandes.] **1688** HOLME *Armoury* II. 98/2 Rosemary, hath Wharles or small slender leaves set at distances about the stalk. *Ibid.* 106/1 Flowers set together in a Whorle or Coronett. **1713** PETIVER in *Phil. Trans.* XXVIII. 43 Its Spikes of Flowers are thick set in striated hairy whorls. **1837** *Penny Cycl.* VII. 215/1 An orange.. consists of one whorl of carpels, which are consolidated into a round fruit. **1860** SALA *Lady Chesterf.* iv. 64 A flattened head,.. a forked tongue, a body of scaly whorls. **1861** BENTLEY *Man. Bot.* 358 A flower is said to be complete, when the four whorls,— calyx, corolla, stamens, and pistil are present. **1872** H. A. NICHOLSON *Palæont.* 75 The stem terminates in a single polypite, the mouth of which is surrounded by a single whorl of slender processes or 'tentacles'.

3. a. *Conch.* and *Anat.* Each of the turns, coils, or convolutions of a spiral shell, or of any spiral structure.

1828 STARK *Elem. Nat. Hist.* II. 52 Shell conoid, with the whorls rounded or convex. **1855** TENNYSON *Maud* II. ii. 6 See what a lovely shell, Small and pure as a pearl,.. With delicate spire and whorl. **1890** BILLINGS *Med. Dict., Whorl of heart,* vortex of heart. [*Ibid., Vortex of heart,* the close spiral arrangement of fibres which occurs at the apex.]

b. A configuration in finger-prints.

1880, etc. [see LOOP *sb.*[1] 4 h]. **1954** F. CHERRILL *Cherrill of Yard* vi. 62, I noticed particularly the patterns on the ends of the fingers, for they were of the whorl type. **1977** *Sci. Amer.* Dec. 141/1 The resulting patterns are known to the dermatologist respectively as loops, triradii and whorls.

4. *gen.* A convolution, coil, curl, 'wreath' (esp. of something whirling, or suggesting a whirling movement).

1592 R. D. *Hypnerotomachia* 51 The head of a Storke, with her beake against the open mouth of a Monster,.. and certaine Whorelles or Beades rysing vp betwixt his mouth and her beake. **1851** NICHOL *Archit. Heav.* (ed. 9) 99 Intervals between successive whorls of the starry stream. **1863** BARING-GOULD *Iceland* xii. 210 Vast clouds of steam.. roll in heavy whorls before the wind.

5. *Comb.,* as ***whorl-flowered, -leaved, -shaped*** adjs.; **whorl-flower,** a plant of the genus *Morina* (N.O. *Dipsacaceæ*), having the flowers in dense whorls; **whorl-grass,** a grass of the genus *Catabrosa.*

1822 *Hortus Angl.* II. 204 M[alva] Verticillata, Whorl-flowered Mallow. *Ibid.* 423 C[oreopsis] Verticillata, Whorl-leaved Coreopsis. **1850** DAUBENY *Atom. The.* xii. (ed. 2) 423 The parts of the pistils are disposed in a whorl-shaped manner around an.. axis. **1861** MISS PRATT *Flower. Pl.* (1900) IV. 69 Whorl-grass (*Catabrosa*). Water Whorl Grass (*C. aquatica*). Panicle with half whorls of spreading branches. **1884** MILLER *Plant-n.* 220 *Morina longifolia,* Long-leaved Whorl-flower.—*persica,* Persian Whorl-flower.

Hence **whorl** *v. trans.* (*a*) to draw up by means of a 'whorl' or pulley (*local*); (*b*) to arrange in whorls or convolutions.

1886 J. BARROWMAN *Sc. Mining Terms* 73 The cage is said to be whorled when it is drawn up to or over the pulleys. **1904** *Daily Chron.* 6 Aug. 4/5 The stars, braided and whorled in patterns too intricate for our eyes.

whorl(e: see WHIRL *v.*, WHURL.

whorlbat, -bone, etc.: see WHIRLBAT, etc.

whorle borle, whorlle-bourlle, obs. ff. HURLY-BURLY.

c **1440** J. SHIRLEY in *Scot. Hist. Rev.* (1904) Oct. 98 During the whorlle bourlle in Scotland the olde King Robert died.

whorled (hwɔːld, hwɜːld), *a.* [f. WHORL *sb.* + -ED[2].] Having, or arranged in, a whorl or whorls; (of leaves, flowers, etc.) verticillate; (of a shell, etc.) convoluted, turbinate.

1776 J. LEE *Introd. Bot.* Explan. Terms 392 *Verticill[at]us,* whorled, many Flowers growing round the Stalk in a Circle. **1828** J. E. SMITH *Engl. Flora* II. 59 *S[ium] verticillatum,* Whorled Water-parsnep. Leaflets in numerous, linear,.. whorled segments. **1861** BENTLEY *Man. Bot.* 572 The Galiaceæ are.. distinguished.. by their whorled exstipulate leaves. **1867** MURCHISON *Siluria* viii. (ed. 4) 164 The large Whorled Shell.. has proved.. to be a true Lower-Silurian Maclurea. **1873** RALFE *Phys. Chem.* 17 Crystals which arrange themselves in whorled groups.

So †**'whorling,** †**'whorlish** *adjs., rare,* forming or constituting a whorl.

1562 TURNER *Herbal* II. 55 Comen rede fish mynt.. with whorlish circles goyng about the stalck. **1578** LYTE *Dodoens*

II. lxxxi. 256 The floures..growing in whorling knoppes rounde aboute the stalkes.

whorlwyl, obs. form of WHORL.

†**whorr**, *v. Obs.* Also whoor(r)e. [Echoic.] *intr.* To coo, as a dove.
1598 FLORIO, *Gemere*..To whorr as doues do. *Gemire*..To whoore or cry as turtle doues.

whorrowe, var. WHARROW; cf. s.w. dial. *worra.*
1578 LYTE *Dodoens* II. lxxxviii. 267 The floures be of a light blewe, compassing the stalke by certaine spaces like to garlandes or whorrowes.

whorry, obs. form of HURRY *v.*
1613 DEKKER *Strange Horse-Race* B 1 b, A Race..after the Roman fashion:..in their thundring velocity, lightning-like violence, and earth-quaking whorrying. *Ibid.* 24 From his Caues..out he whorries.

†**whorster.** *Obs. rare*$^{-1}$. [f. WHORE *sb.* + -STER.] = WHORER.
1654 VILVAIN *Enchir. Epigr.* VI. lxxvi, No Murdrer be: Whorster: Theef: fals Testee.

whort (hwɜːt). *dial.* Also 6–7 **whorte**, 7 **whurt**, 9 wort. [South-western dial. form of HURT *sb.*^{2} (cf. *whoam* for *home*, *whole* for earlier *hole*, and WHORTLEBERRY).] = WHORTLEBERRY. Also *attrib.* Hence **whorting** *vbl. sb.*, gathering whortleberries.
1578 LYTE *Dodoens* VI. xi. 670 There be two sortes of Whortes, and Whortel berries, wherof the common sort are blacke, and the other are red. 1597 GERARDE *Herbal* III. lxix. 1231. 1657 W. COLES *Adam in Eden* cxvi, Black Whorts, or Bill-Berries. 1661 J. CHILDREY *Brit. Baconica* 12 For Fruits, they [in Cornwall] have a sort called Whurts. 1746 *Exmoor Scolding* (E.D.S.) 91 And why dest thee, than, tell me 'Isterday o' losing my Rewden Hat in the Rex-bush, out a whorting? 1773 *Encycl. Brit.* s.v. *Vaccinium*, The *myrtillus* [mispr. *-is*], or black whortleberries or bilberries;..the *cantabricum*, or Irish whorts; the *vitis idea*, or red whorts. 1802 COLERIDGE *The Picture* 4, I..now climb, and now descend O'er rocks, or bare or mossy, with wild foot Crushing the purple whorts. 1856 G. ROBERTS *Soc. Hist. Eng.* 561 During the Whort-season children used to assemble to partake of Whort-pies..made with a brown crust, and eaten with clouted cream,..a west country delicacy. 1917 *Contemp. Rev.* Nov. 582, I do mind the autumn when Mrs. Ann Pugsley did witch John Craw. 'Twur at the whort gathering.

whorthy, obs. form of WORTHY.

whortle ('hwɜːt(ə)l). Also 7 **wortle**: see also HURTLE *sb.*^{2} [Short for WHORTLEBERRY.] = WHORTLEBERRY.
1597 [see HURTLE *sb.*^{2}]. 1620 VENNER *Via Recta* vii. 131 The people vse to eat the Wortles in creame and milke. 1655 MOUFET & BENNET *Health's Improv.* 219 Fen-berries..are of like temper and faculty with our whortles, but somewhat more astringent. 1796 WITHERING *Brit. Plants* (ed. 3) II. 371 Great Bilberry Bush or Whortle. 1811 SHELLEY *St. Irvyne* VI. i, I see her swift foot dash the dew from the whortle. 1863 BARING-GOULD *Iceland* 190 The..bog-whortle.., whose white flowers, pink-tipped, stuff the ptarmigan's crop.
Comb. 1857 MISS PRATT *Flower. Pl.* V. 108 *S[alix] myrsinites* (Green Whortle-leaved Willow).

whortleberry ('hwɜːt(ə)lbɛrɪ). Also (8 **whirtle-**), 8–9 **wortleberry**. [South-western dial. form of HURTLEBERRY: cf. WHORT. Used by Lyte, a Somerset man, in his translation of Dodoens' Herbal, whence app. by later writers on plants, so as to have become at length the usual 'book-name'.] The blue-black fruit of the dwarf shrub *Vaccinium Myrtillus*, or the plant itself; otherwise called BILBERRY or BLAEBERRY. Also extended to the genus *Vaccinium* as a whole (excepting the species called CRANBERRY, *V. Oxycoccos* and *V. macrocarpon*).
bear's whortleberry, a name for the Bearberry, *Arctostaphylos Uva-ursi.* **bog whortleberry**, *Vaccinium uliginosum.* **red whortleberry**, *V. Vitis-Idæa.* **Victorian whortleberry**, *Wittsteinia vacciniacea*, a shrub allied to *Vaccinium* found in Victoria.
1578 [see WHORT]. 1671 SALMON *Syn. Med.* III. xxii. 438. 1702 C. MATHER *Magnalia* VI. ii. 11 Sometimes we liv'd on Wortle berries, sometimes on a kind of Wild Cherry. 1764 *Ann. Reg., Char.* 9 The hair..is dyed with the juice of the red wortleberry. 1778 J. CARVER *Trav. N. Amer.* xix. 504 The Whirtle Berry. 1816 SCOTT *Bl. Dwarf* xiii, A territory, which, since the days of Adam, had borne nothing but ling and whortle-berries. 1869 BLACKMORE *Lorna D.* v, [They] laid him softly on a bank of whortle-berries.
attrib. 1770 J. R. FORSTER tr. *Kalm's Trav. N. Amer.* I. 66 A species of whortleberry shrub. 1825 J. NEAL *Bro. Jonathan* II. 340 A..whortle-berry pudding. 1863 BARING-GOULD *Iceland* 178 Hot mutton flavored with whortleberry jam. 1884 MILLER *Plant-n.*, Whortle-berry-bush, Victorian, *Wittsteinia vacciniacea.*

whorwhil, obs. form of WHORL.

whory ('hɔərɪ), *a.* Formerly *rare.* Also -ey. [f. WHORE *sb.* + -Y^{1}.] = WHORISH. (In 2nd quot. with play upon *hoary.*)
1682 HICKERINGILL *Hist. Whiggism* 11 The Papists, and the whory, roary, swory, scory, Tories. 1682 'T. RATIONALIS' *New News from Bedlam* 88 And should it light upon Your whorey Head, The Whigs would say, You're sweetly brought to Bed. 1955 J. KEROUAC in *Paris Rev.* Winter 11 The whorey smell of a big city. 1967 K. GILES *Death & Mr. Prettyman* i. 18 London was as whorey then as now. 1976 *New Yorker* 15 Nov. 180/3 At twenty she was taking care not only of herself and her child but also of a tubercular half sister, also cast off by their whorey mother. 1980 N. FREELING *Castang's City* xxii. 148 It's not a whory setup; three of these dames live there and they're secretarial types.

whos, obs. form of WHOSE, WHOSO.

whose (huːz), *pron.* Forms: 1 **hwæs**, 2–3 **hwas**, 3 **hwos**, (**wuas**), **ȝwas**, **hwes**, 3–4 **whes**, 3–5 **whas**, **was**, **wos**, 4 **huas**, **wais**, **hoes**, **woise**, 4–5 **whoos**, **hos**, 4–6 **whos**, **whois**, 5 **whayse**, **whoys**, **hoys**, (**hosse**), **wose**, 5–9 *Sc.* and *north.* **whase**, 6 **whoes**, **woos**, **wois**, **hose**, *Sc.* **vhais**, **vhois**, 7–8 **who's**, 5– **whose**; 3–5 **quase**, 4 **quos**, **quose**, 4–5 **quas**, *Sc.* 4–8 **quhais**, (5 **qwhos**, **qwose**), 5–7 **quhois**, 6 **quhas**, (**qwhois**), 6–7 **quhose**, 6–8 **quhase**, 7 **quhaes**, **quhoise**. [ME. *hwās*, later *hwǭs*, *whǭs*, altered form of *hwas*, *hwes*, OE. *hwæs* (:—*χwasa) genitive of *hwá* and *hwæt*, through the influence of *hwā*, *hwǭ* WHO, *hwām*, *hwǭm* WHOM. (Later ME. *whas* prob. represents an unstressed variant.) Cf. OS. *hwes*, MLG., MDu., OHG., G. *wes*, ON. *hues(s*, MSw. *hwes*, *hwas*, (Da. *hvis*), Goth. *hwis*:—*χwesa, Indo-Eur. *q^{w}eso, represented also by Gr. (Homeric) *τέο* for *τέσο, OSl. *česo*.]

The genitive case of WHO (and in OE. of the neuter WHAT: cf. 3 below). Used, in all senses, either before a sb. as a possessive adj. (like *his*, *her*, *my*, etc.), or absolutely (like *his*, *hers*, *mine*, etc.): in the latter case chiefly in the interrogative sense as predicate.

I. Interrogative uses (direct and dependent).

1. Of whom; belonging to whom; what person's.
c897 ÆLFRED *Gregory's Past. C.* xlvii. 357 Ðæt hie ʒeðencen hwæs folʒeras hie sindon. a1000 *Colloq. Ælfric* in Wr.-Wülcker 92 Hunta ic eom. hwæs? c1000 *Ags. Gosp.* Matt. xxii. 42 Hwæt þincð eow be criste, hwæs sunu ys he? c1200 *Vices & Virtues* 99 Ʒif hie [*sc.* ðohtes] cumeð fram mannen, hie [*sc.* ȝepnesse] cann hwatliche underfinden, an hwos half he is icumen. c1205 LAY. 17111 Næs nan witie þat auere wuste here whes sune he weore. a1240 *Ureisun* in *O.E. Hom.* I. 189 Maiden moder, maiden: and hwas moder? his hwas dohter þu art. c1275 *Passion of our Lord* 447 in *O.E. Misc.* 50 Hi casten heore lot hwes he scolde beo. 13.. *Cursor M.* 12224 (Gött.) Quat wamb him bar.., And wid was pappis was he fedd? 1340 *Ayenb.* 38 þo þet ofhyealdeþ þe þinges þet hi vindeþ and wyteþ wel huas þet hi byeþ. 13.. *Guy Warw.* (A.) 6826 Telle þou me, þis feir castel wos it be. c1380 *Sir Ferumb.* 1726 Was men buth ȝe? c1386 CHAUCER *Man of Law's T.* 920 Whos is that faire child that stondeth yonder? c1440 *Alphabet of Tales* 265 He fand a dead mans head, and he had grete mervayll whose it was. 1566 LAUDER *Tractate* Contents, And, last of all, vnto quhose actionis.. suld Kyngis geue rathest actendence. 1592 SHAKS. *Ven. & Ad.* 1077 Whose tongue is musick now? 1607 DEKKER & WEBSTER *Northw. Hoe* I. ii. A 4 b, Arrest me? at whose sute? 1613 SHAKS. *Hen. VIII*, I. iv. 43 Whose fault is this? 1791 COWPER *Judgm. Poets* 4 A warm dispute..Whose temper was the best. 1883 D. C. MURRAY *Hearts* vii, 'I'm sure of the voice...' 'Whose is it?' 1896 HOUSMAN *Shropsh. Lad* xxvii, I cheer a dead man's sweetheart, Never ask me whose. 1908 R. BAGOT *A. Cuthbert* vi. 58 Your offensive abuse of his poor father, and forgetfulness of Whose minister he was.

II. Relative uses. * as simple relative.

2. In reference to a person or persons (or to an animal or animals): Of whom. **a.** Introducing a defining or restrictive clause completing the sense: cf. WHO 9.
c1200 *Trin. Coll. Hom.* 37 þe deuel..on ech of hise deden is iefned to þe deore wuas geres he forðteoð. a1240 [see 1]. a1300 *Cursor M.* 2155 Of him o quas sede Was he born þat beit our nede. a1325 *MS. Rawl. B.* 520 lf. 53 b, After þe wille of him hos þe werkes beȝ [= beð]. c1400 tr. *Secr. Secr., Gov. Lordsh.* 81 It ys meruail of a man how he may be syke or dye, whos mete ys breed of good whete. 1526 TINDALE *Luke* i. 27 A virgin spoused to a man, whose name was Ioseph. 1539 *Bible* (Great) Ps. xxxii. 1 Blessed is he, whose vnryghteousnesse is forgeuen. 1609 SKENE *Reg. Maj.* 37 Of heires of qvhais age their is ane doubt. 1611 *Bible* Gen. xxxviii. 25 The man whose these are. *Ibid.* xliv. 17 The man in whose hand the cup is found. 1690 tr. *J. Le Clerc's Five Lett. Inspir.* 56 The Apostles did not pass in their own time for Persons, whose every word was an Oracle. 1723 RAMSAY *Fair Assembly* viii, A wife..Whase charms can silence dumps. 1790 BURKE *Fr. Rev.* 70 Persons who..sanctified their ambition by advancing the dignity of the people whose peace they troubled. 1836 W. IRVING *Astoria* xli, To feast upon the horses whose blood they had so vaingloriously drunk. 1893 MAX PEMBERTON *Iron Pirate* ii, Men whose laugh was a horrid growl.

b. Introducing an additional statement: thus sometimes equivalent to 'and his (their, etc.)': cf. WHO 10.
In early use occas. preceded by *the*: cf. WHICH B. 13, WHOM 8.
Formerly also separated from the antecedent, sometimes with resulting ambiguity (cf. WHO 10): occas. preceded by superfluous *and* (cf. WHO 12 b).
c1175 *Lamb. Hom.* 151 þe lauerd N[athaniel] hwas dei hit is to dei. c1220 *Bestiary* 764 Ðis der, Wos kinde we hauen told ȝu her. 1297 R. GLOUC. (Rolls) 4195 Eleyne þat noble mayde..was norice ich was. a1300 *Cursor M.* 1490 Noe, In quas time þe flod gan be. c1375 *Sc. Leg. Saints* iv. (*Jacobus*) 210 In-to þe name of criste Ihesu, Fore quhais cause I am led now. 1390 GOWER *Conf.* II. 103 Morpheus, the whos nature Is forto take the figure Of what persone that him liketh. a1400 *Pauline Ep.* (1916) 42 Cryste in woise deþ we ar baptysyd. 1467 *Stonor Papers* (Camden) I. 95 To performe my Nonkilles wyll, hoys sowle God pardon. c1469 *Ibid.* 104 Ʒowr modyr, hosse sowle Gode haue mersy. 1484 CAXTON *Fables of Æsop* I. viii, A wulf..deuoured a sheep of whos bones he had one in his throte. 1526 TINDALE *Rom.* ix. 5 My brethren..the israhelites,..whose also are the fathers. —— *1 Pet.* ii. 24 Christ also suffered for oure sakes... By whose strypes ye were healed. 1621 BURTON *Anat. Mel.* III. ii. I. i. 533 The young man..at last married her, to whose wedding amongst other guests came Apollonius. 1750 T. COOKE *Plautus* I. p. xxv, This Comedy is called *Bacchides* from two Sisters, Courtesans, who are the chief Characters in the Play; both whose Names are *Bacchis.* a1774 GOLDSM. tr. *Scarron's Com. Rom.* (1775) II. 170 A hamlet, inhabited by fishermen, who's humanity he had occasion to remember. 1791 BURKE *App. Whigs* 88 It does not arise out of the inherent rights of the people, as the national assembly does in France, and whose name designates its original. 1820 KEATS *Lamia* II. 279 The Gods, whose dreadful images Here represent their shadowy presences. 1864 J. HUNT tr. *Vogt's Lect. Man* ii. 26 Vegetable feeders, such as ruminants, whose lower jaw acts like a millstone.

3. In reference to a thing or things (inanimate or abstract). Originally the genitive of the neuter WHAT (sense 7); in later use serving as the genitive of WHICH (senses 7 and 8), and usually replaced by *of which*, except where the latter would produce an intolerably clumsy form.
1382 WYCLIF *Deut.* viii. 9 The loond of oyle and of hony; ..whos stones ben yren, and of the hillis of it ben doluen metallys of brasse. 1442 BECKINGTON *Corr.* (Rolls) II. 213 He hath..taken the townes and castles and fortheresses whoos names be specified. 1482 *Monk of Evesham* lv. (Arb.) 107 A ful glorious walle of crystal hoys heythe no man might see. 1528 TINDALE *Obed. Chr. Man* 130 Loke yer thou lepe, whose literall sence is, doo nothinge sodenly or without avisemente. 1577 HARRISON *England* II. ii. [v.] (1877) I. 46 Bath, whose see was sometime at Welles. 1602 SHAKS. *Ham.* I. v. 15, I could a Tale vnfold, whose lightest word Would harrow vp thy soule. 1632 MILTON *L'Allegro* 73 Mountains on whose barren brest The labouring clouds do often rest. 1661 FELTHAM *Lusoria, Lett.* 65 A Disposition..whose affability may sweeten life. 1760–72 H. BROOKE *Fool of Qual.* (1809) I. 74 A maxim of whose impropriety not St. Anthony himself could persuade him. 1807 SOUTHEY *Espriella's Lett.* (1814) II. 10 The clock, whose huge bell.. may be heard five leagues over the plain. 1863 READE *Hard Cash* I. 100 The nerve man had prescribed..a medicine.. whose effect on the nerves was nil. 1896 POLLOCK *1st Bk. of Jurispr.* vii. 179 Processes extending over two or three centuries, and whose fundamental analogies are..disguised in almost every possible way. 1906 CONRAD *Mirror of Sea* vii. 33 A newspaper of sound principles, but whose staff *will* persist in 'casting' anchors. 1927 E. BOWEN *Hotel* vi. 57 She looked down..and saw a little house, with a blue door whose colour delighted her. 1958 I. MURDOCH *Bell* iv. 47 Toby.. marvelled at this light which is no light..and whose strength is seen only in the sharpness of cast shadows. 1968 J. LYONS *Introd. Theoretical Linguistics* 55 Whether there are, or could be, two languages whose vocabularies are to no degree whatsoever isomorphic with one another is a question with which we need not be concerned. 1981 I. MCEWAN *Comfort of Strangers* ix. 122 There were pictures whose context she understood immediately.

4. As objective genitive, in reference to a person (or animal) or a thing. Now *rare*: commonly replaced by *of whom* or *of which*. (Cf. note s.v. HIS *poss. pron.* 2.)
1382 WYCLIF *Lev.* xxii. 5 He..that shal touche..eny vnclene, whos touchynge is hoory [1388 foul]. c1449 PECOCK *Repr.* v. ii. 493 Deedis whos forberingis schulden make hem the more sureli kepen hem fro breking of Goddis lawe. 1513 DOUGLAS *Æneis* VI. vii. 4 Our the fludis bank ful swiftlie sprent, Quhais passage is vnreturnable went. 1551 CROWLEY *Pleas. & Pain* Ded., The pore of thys realme, whoes oppression doeth alredy crye vnto the Lorde for vengeance. 1601 DOLMAN *La Primaud. Fr. Acad.* III. lxxxvii. 391 The Hart or Stag, in whose chase great Lords take much pleasure. 1605 SHAKS. *Macb.* III. i. 105, I will put that Businesse in your Bosomes, Whose execution takes your Enemie off. 1730 *Chamberlayne's Relig. Philos.* (ed. 3) II. xvii. §1 Things, whose particular Discussion would.. exceed the Design of this Book. 1754 CAMBRIDGE in *World* No. 102 ¶2 Any thing whose loss they can so easily supply. 1821 SOUTHEY *Let. to John May* 7 Apr., This deplorable old man, whose sight..excited in me a mingled feeling of horror and disgust.

** **5.** As compound relative, or with ellipsis of antecedent = he (him, etc.) whose. Often in generalized sense = whosesoever. Now *rare* or *arch.*: cf. WHO 6, 8, WHOM 5, 6.
Sometimes with the generalized sense indicated by *so(ever)* or *so ever* following the sb. (Cf. WHOSESOEVER.)
13.. *E.E. Allit. P.* B. 1648 & quos deth so he dezyre he dreped als faste. a1400 in *Engl. Gilds* (1870) 352 Ʒif oþere chalouns beþ y-founde þat ne habbeþ þelke a-syse, in was hond hij beþ y-founde, be forfeted. c1420 ? LYDG. *Assembly of Gods* 1299 Blere whos ey ye woll..with your myst. 1432–50 [see WHRINNY]. 1460 *Rolls of Parlt.* V. 384/1 In whos handes so evere they bee. 1567 *Gude & Godlie B.* (S.T.S.) 7 Quhais Sinnis ȝe forgeue, ar forgeuin vnto thame. 1592 *Arden of Feversham* 1092 Speede to my wish, whose wil so ere sayes no. a1633 G. HERBERT *Jacula Prudentum* 196 Whose house is of glasse, must not throw stones at another. 1667 MILTON *P.L.* VIII. 647 Heavenly Guest,..Sent from whose sovran goodness I adore.

†**whose**, for *who's* = who is: see WHO.
1593 SHAKS. *2 Hen. VI*, I. iv. 50 (Qo.) Whose within there!

whose, obs. form of WHOSO.

†**whoself**, *pron. Obs. rare*$^{-1}$. [Cf. SELF A. 2.] Who himself.
1539 CROMWELL in Merriman *Life & Lett.* (1902) II. 174 The said Burgartus canne testifie of her proportion, countenaunce and beautie, Whoself hath seen her.

whose'n (hu:z(ə)n), *pron. dial.* [f. WHOSE: cf. HISN.] = WHOSE.
a **1701** SEDLEY *Virg. Past.* v. Wks. 1722 I. 289 Tell Dametas! whose'n Sheep these are?

whosere, obs. contr. f. WHOSOEVER.

whosesoever (hu:zsəʊ'ɛvə(r)), *pron. arch.* The genitive of WHOSOEVER: Whatever person's; of whomsoever.
1611 *Bible* John xx. 23 Whose soeuer sinnes yee remit, they are remitted vnto them, and whose soeuer sinnes yee retaine, they are retained. **1821** SCOTT *Kenilw.* xxxii, Whosesoever be the speech, it is the thought of ninety-nine out of an hundred. **1903** *Sat. Rev.* 27 June 798/1 Whose-soever the fault there has been no effective cooperation.

whosever (hu:z'ɛvə(r)), *pron. rare.* [f. WHOSE + EVER *adv.* 8e; for the spelling cf. WHEREVER.] The genitive of WHOEVER: = prec.
1739 'R. BULL' tr. *Dedekindus' Grobianus* 133 Whos'ever Knife upon the Table lies. **1865** W. G. PALGRAVE *Arabia* II. 19 Whoever the footprint may be, the story is gospel among Mahometans.

whosh, obs. var. HUSH *v.*[1]

whosht, (whoosht) obs. var. HUSHT *int.*[1], *a.*, *v.*
1598 FLORIO, *Quetare*, to quiet,..to whosht. *Ibid.*, *Zita*, an aduerbe to commaund..silence, as we say isse, whosht or st. **1611** *Ibid.*, *Quattare*..to whosht and lie close, to lurke. *Ibid.*, *Quatto quatto*, very squat, very whoosht.

whosis ('hu:zɪs). Also **whoosis**. [Colloq. contraction of 'who is this?' (WHO *pron.*); in quot. 1923, perh. repr. 'whose is this?'] 'What's-his-name', 'so-and-so'. Often following a title, as ***Mr. Whosis***.
1923 J. E. BAXTER *Locker Room Ballads* 8 That number one's a Big League Green As slick as Whoosis Vaseline. **1939** R. STOUT *Some buried Caesar* vi. 72 He..introduced himself as Mr. Whosis, Assistant District Attorney. **1953** G. W. BRACE *Spire* xxiii. 229, I suppose..you mean he should go and see your precious Dr. Whoosis? **1962** J. D. SALINGER *Franny & Zooey* 130 How was the script? Did it come? You said Whosis—Mr. LeSage or whatever his name is—was going to drop it off with the doorman. **1965** I. FLEMING *Man with Golden Gun* vi. 89 Don't forget one thing, Mister Whoosis. I rile mighty easy.

whosit ('hu:zɪt). Also **whoosit, whoozit, whozit**. [Colloq. contraction of 'who is it' (WHO *pron.*).] = prec.
1948 'P. QUENTIN' *Run to Death* xxi. 156 *Ye Old Antique Shoppe* with little leaded glass panes. *Mother Whosit's Chicken Kitchen.* **1951** *Blue Bk. Mag.* Jan. 24/3 Mr. Whoozit—please come quickly. **1951** 'J. TEY' *Daughter of Time* viii. 112 Someone, say, insists that Lady Whoosit never had a child. **1967** O. NORTON *Now lying Dead* i. 9 That's what I've got to work out... Like Angela Whoosit was telling us. **1977** J. FLEMING *Every Inch a Lady* I. i. 7 Arrival..of Mrs Whozit, the lady help.

whoso ('hu:səʊ), *pron. arch.* Forms: see WHO and SO: also 2–3 **hwa se, hwase,** (2 **wa se**), 3 **hw(a)o se,** *Orm.* **whas(e,** 3–5 **wo se,** 4 *Sc.* **quha se,** (**woys**), 4–6 **whos,** 4–6 **whose, hose,** 5 *Sc.* **quhais,** (9 *dial.* **whos'**). [ME. *wha swa, hwa se*, reduced form of OE. *swá hwá swá*, generalized form of *hwá* WHO: see SO *adv.* 17d.]
1. = WHOEVER 1: Any (one) who.
1154 *O.E. Chron.* (Laud MS.) an. 1135 Wua sua bare his byrthen gold & sylure, durste nan man sei to him naht bute god. *c* **1200** ORMIN 677 Whas itt iss þatt wæpnedd iss wiþþ fulle trowwþe o Criste. *c* **1205** LAY. 3657 Wha swa wulle libba, alde þas sibba. [*c* **1275** Wo so wole libbe holde þus sibbe]. *Ibid.* 22307 Wha swa [*c* **1275** wose] come gladliche he sculden wurðe riche. ? **12..** in Kemble *Cod. Dipl.* V. 236 Ho so hit beo ðæt ðis my dede in oðere wise hit buturne oðer ȝewanye. *a* **1225** *Ancr. R.* 46 Et uhtsonge schal siggen hwo se con Domine labia mea. **1297** R. GLOUC. (Rolls) 6253 Ofte wo so coueiteþ al, al leseþ. **13..** *Cursor M.* 5829 (Gött.) Qua sua wil noght trou þe first, To trow þe toder him es best. *c* **1330** *King of Tars* 894 And hose nil not cristned be Hong hem heighe uppon a tre. *c* **1400** MAUNDEV. (Roxb.) iii. 10 Wha so weddes ofter þan anes, þaire childer er bastardes. *c* **1400** *Destr. Troy* 5551 Wo so staris on þis story, or stodis þerin, Take hede on þe harmys & þe hard lures! **1498** in J. Bulloch *Pynours* (1887) 57 And quhais doys in the contrar.. salbe punist. **1522** MORE *De quat. Noviss.* Wks. 73/2 Now whoso seeth not, that his laughter is more madde than the laughter of the mad man, I hold him madder than they both. **1539** *Bible* (Great) John vi. 54 Whoso eateth my flesshe & dryncketh my bloude, hath eternall lyfe. **1607** SHAKS. *Timon* v. i. 212 Who so please To stop Affliction, let him take his haste. **1667** MILTON *P.L.* IX. 724 This Tree, That whoso eats thereof, forthwith attains Wisdom. **1727** POPE, etc. *Art of Sinking* 118 Whoso loseth his place..hath forfeited his share in publick praise. *a* **1825** FORBY *Voc. E. Anglia* s.v., Whos' wull may do that. **1859** WHITTIER *On a Prayer-Book* 12 Let whoso can before such praying-books Kneel on his velvet cushion. **1883** WHITELAW *Sophocles, Antigone* 35 Whoso does this deed, A public death by stoning is his doom. **1891** CONAN DOYLE *White Company* xxxvii, The last stern welcome to whoso should join with them.
2. = WHOEVER 2: No matter who; †in early use often with mere unemphatic conditional force: If any one, if one.
c **1300** *Beket* (Percy Soc.) 35 Woldestou,..ho so it wolde bede the, Tholie deth for thi Louerdes love? **13..** *E.E. Allit. P.* C. 5 For quo-so suffer cowþe syt, sele wolde folȝe. *c* **1475** *Rauf Coilȝear* 675 With Dosouris to the duris dicht, quha sa wald deme. **1876** MORRIS *Æneids* VIII. 122 'Come forth', he said, 'whoso ye be'.

whosoever (hu:səʊ'ɛvə(r)), *pron.* Forms: see prec.; also *poet.* **whosoe'er** (-'ɛə(r)) (5 **hosere, who-sere,** 7 **whosoere**). In early use often as three words, occas. as two. [f. WHOSO + EVER *adv.* 8e: cf. SOEVER.]
Formerly occas. with gen. *whosoever's* = WHOSESOEVER.
1. = WHOEVER 1.
a **1225** *Ancr. R.* 286 Hwo so euer on him sulf nimeð ouðer of þeos two, he robbeð God. *a* **1240** *Ureisun* in *O.E. Hom.* I. 187 Hwa se euer wule habbe lot wiþ þe of þi blisse, he mot deale wiþ þe of þine pine on eorþe. *c* **1375** *Sc. Leg. Saints* v. (*Johannes*) 593 þat quha-se-euire vald almus crafe For luf of sancte Iohne suld hafe. *c* **1400** MAUNDEV. xix. [xv.] (1919) 113 Hem semeth þat whosoeuere be meke & pacyent he is holy & profitable. *c* **1420** *Chron. Vilod.* 4685 For pore and ryche & also for hosere wolde come þedur. *c* **1450** *Mirk's Festial* 111 Whosoeuer ys of God, heryth Godys worde. **1526** TINDALE *John* xx. 23 Whosoevers synnes ye remyt, they are remitted vnto them. —— *Rev.* xxii. 17 Let whosoever wyll, take of the water of lyfe fre. **1593** SHAKS. *3 Hen. VI*, IV. vii. 74 And whosoe're gainsayes King Edwards right, By this I challenge him to single fight. **1611** *Bible* Rev. xxii. 17 Whosoeuer will, let him take the water of life freely. **1681** COTTON *Wond. Peak* 72 Whosoere shall happen to come there, Will not reprove what I've deliver'd here. **1827** SCOTT *Chron. Canongate* iii, Christie regarded me as..a.. predestinated child of perdition, who was sure to..drag downwards whosoever might attempt to afford me support. **1882** BESANT *All Sorts* ii, We shall present our Case to Parliament, or the Queen, or the House of Lords, or the Court of Chancery, or whosoever is the right person.
2. = WHOEVER 2; also formerly = 'if any one' (cf. prec. 2).
13.. *Cursor M.* 4275 (Gött.) For qua-sua euer es glad or blith, Priue loue at end wil kith. ? *a* **1500** *Chester Pl.* xiv. 71 This ilke Boyst might haue bene sould For three hundreth penyes tould, And dealt to poor men, who-sere would, And wo-sere had bene wyse. *c* **1520** NISBET *N.T.* Prol. (S.T.S.) I. 5 Quha saeuir thow be,..ȝif thow be diligent in the estait that God has callid the vnto,..than art thow surelie blist. **1526** TINDALE *Matt.* xxiii. 16 Ye saye; whosoever sweare by the temple, yt ys nothinge: but whosoever sweare by the golde of the temple, he is detter. **1591** SHAKS. *1 Hen. VI*, V. iii. 52 Margaret my name, and daughter to a King,..who so ere thou art. **1640** BP. H. KING *Serm.* 31 Whosoevers Midnight is interrupted by the newes, Ours can complaine of no disturbance. **1751** F. COVENTRY *Pompey the Little* I. v. 39 Let me admonish thee, my gentle Friend, whosoever thou art,..not to be too forward in making Applications.
3. With loss of relative force by ellipsis: Any one at all. Cf. WHATEVER 4b. Now *rare* or *Obs.*
1583 BABINGTON *Expos. Commandm.* (1590) 336 Liueries of Prince or subiectes, Noblemen, Gentlemen, or whosoeuer. *c* **1643** LD. HERBERT *Autobiog.* (1824) 88 Having as clear a Reputation for my Courage as whosoever of my time.
b. qualifying a preceding sb. or *any*: now usually replaced by WHATEVER 4a (*b*).
1586 *Marlowe's Tamburl.* To Rdr., Gentlemen, and curteous Readers whosoeuer. **1621** BP. MOUNTAGU *Diatribæ* 203 By the vniuersall consent of all Writers whosoever, except..perchance two. **1697** DRYDEN *Virg. Georg.* Ded., Being capable, as much as any whosoever, of defending your Country.
¶ Used for the objective WHOMSOEVER.
Also qualifying the prec. word, in which case the construction may be regarded as elliptical = 'whosoever he (they, etc.) be': see 3b, quot. 1621.
1523 LD. BERNERS *Froiss.* I. cccliii. 230/2 Whosoeuer they hyt he dyed of the stroke. **1526** TINDALE *Mark* xiv. 44 Whosoever I do kisse, he it is.

†**whosome**, *pron. Obs.* [WHO and SUM *rel. adv.*] = WHOEVER 1, 2, WHOSO 1, 2.
c **1200** ORMIN 5564 An rihht god reowwsunnge þatt Godess þeoww, whasumm itt iss, Her bereþþ inn hiss heorrte. *a* **1300** *Cursor M.* 1953 Qua-sum o fless wil grait þair fode, Lok þai cast a way þe blod. *Ibid.* 16265 Tru it qua-sum wil it tru. **13..** *Evang. Nicod.* 665 in Herrig's *Archiv* LIII. 403, I come, wha som takes hede, Als witnes and warand. *c* **1400** *Rule St. Benet* (prose) 10 Wha sam heris yu, þan heris me.

whosomever (hu:səm'ɛvə(r)), *pron. Obs.* or ? *dial.* (In early use often as three words, occas. as two.) [f. prec. + EVER *adv.* 8e.] = WHOEVER, WHOSOEVER.
c **1400** *Cato's Morals* in *Cursor M.* App. IV. 91 Qua-simeuer þou be þat wille þi-self safe se. *a* **1400–50** *Wars Alex.* 3362 Qua-sum-euire in þat ilk his ymage behaldis, þe face is to þe fold-ward, þe fete to þe firment. **1429** in *15th Rep. Hist. MSS. Comm.* App. VIII. 10 Tyll the for said lorde of Drumlanryge, or tyll hys assygneis or speciale deputis qwa sumewer. *c* **1460** METHAM *Wks.* (1916) 119 Ho-ssum-euer yt be that owyth this fygure, he be hys dysposycion ys a leccherus man. **1502** Husumeuer [see WHOMSOMEVER]. **1526** TINDALE *Matt.* xiii. 12 Whosumever hath to him shall hit be geven. *a* **1592** GREENE *Alphonsus* 133 Nere to vnfold the secrets of my heart To any man or woman, who some ere Dwels vnderneath the circle of the skie. **1606** SHAKS. *Tr. & Cr.* II. i. 70 Who some euer you take him to be, he is Aiax.

whosshe, obs. f. WASH *v.*

whost, var. WHUST *v. Obs.*

whot(e, whott(e, obs. ff. HOT.

whot(e: see WIT *v.*

whou, whough(e, whouh, whow(e, variants of HOW, HOWE *int.*[1]
[*c* **1425** Quhow: see WHEW *int.*] **1542** UDALL *Erasm. Apoph.* 314 Whough, saieth he, half my brothers bodye is more then the whole. **1598** R. BERNARD tr. *Terence, Phormio* III. iii, How much money need you? speake. But thirtie poundes. Thirtie! Whow. **1615** BRATHWAIT *Strappado* 129 Whou Billie whou, what faire has thou bin at? **1627** W. HAWKINS *Apollo Shroving* II. iv. 33 He answered me nothing but whough, pugh. **1815** SCOTT *Guy M.* xlv, 'Eh whow! Eh whow!' ejaculated the honest farmer, as he looked round upon his friend's miserable apartment.
So †**whowb(e** (in quots. as *sb.*; cf. *howbub*, HUBBUB).
1600 W. WATSON *Decacordon* VII. x. (1602) 217 They hissed him out with whoubs & hoo-bubs. *Ibid.* IX. viii. 327 [see HOW, HOWE *int.*[1]].

whou(3, whough, whow(e, obs. ff. HOW *adv.*

whoule, whowl(e, obs. ff. HOWL.

whourliburly, obs. f. HURLY-BURLY.

†**whowball**. *Obs.* [f. *who(w)*, variant of HO *int.*[2] + BALL *sb.*[2] 2, a typical proper name of a horse (see *Plowman's T.* 402 my hors Ball, and quot. *a* 1697 below), of a sheep (*Promp. Parv.* 22/1), of a dog (*Privy Purse Exp. Henry VIII* 43), and of a cow (see quot. 1785).
a **1697** AUBREY *Lives*, *Fleetwood* (1898) I. 253 [Highwaymen] brought him under the gallowes, fastned the rope about his neck and on the tree,..and then left him to the mercy of his horse, which he called *Ball*. So he cryed 'Ho, Ball! Ho, Ball!' and it pleased God that his horse stood still.]
(See quots.) ***John Whoball***: app. a typical name for a yokel.
1598 R. BERNARD tr. *Terence, Andria* 17 *Se deludi facile haud patitur*. You cannot easily make him a foole. He is none of Iohn whoballs children. *a* **1700** B. E. *Dict. Cant. Crew*, *Whow-ball*, a Milk-maid. **1785** GROSE *Dict. Vulgar T.*, *Whow-ball*, a milkmaid, from their frequent use of the word whow, to make the cow stand still in milking; Ball is the supposed name of the cow.

who-whoop: see WHOO-WHOOP.

†**whowse**, *v. Obs.* [Echoic. Cf. WHUSH *v.*] *intr.* To make a rushing noise.
1620 T. GRANGER *Div. Logike* 66 The sea roareth, the winds whowse.

whoys, obs. form of WHOSE.

whr-: see words in WR-.

†**whrine**, *v. Sc. Obs.* In 6 **quhryn(e, whryne.** [a. OScand. **hwrina* (ON. *hrína*, Norw. *rina*; ENorw. and Swed. dial. *vrina*; with normal disappearance of *w* in West and *h* in East Scand.).] *intr.* To whine; to squeak.
1508 DUNBAR *Testament* 87 War I a dog and he a swyne, ..I suld ger that lurdane quhryne. **1513** DOUGLAS *Æneis* v. Prol. 32 Thairon aucht na man irk, complene, nor quhryne. **1549** *Compl. Scot.* vi. 39 The suyne began to quhryne. **16..** *Montgomerie's Flyting* 440 (Harl. MS.) As they could they maid it whryne.
Hence †**whrine** *sb.*, whining, querulous cry.
1513 DOUGLAS *Æneis* VII. i. 36 The birsit baris and beris in thair styis Roring all wod with quhrynis and wyld cryis.

†**whrinny**, *v. Obs. rare.* [Imitative. But cf. prec.] *intr.* = WHINNY *v.*
1432–50 tr. *Higden* (Rolls) III. 179 Whose horse made noyce firste, or did whrynny, he scholde be electe in to theire kynge.

whucche, var. WHITCH, chest, coffer.

whuch(e, obs. ff. WHICH.

whudder, var. WHITHER *sb.*[1] and *v. dial.*

whuff (hwʌf), *v.* [Imitative; cf. *whuff*, dial. var. WHIFF (see *Eng. Dial. Dict.*).] *intr.* To make a sound as of a forcible blast of breath or wind; *trans.* to utter with such a sound. Also as *int.* imitating such a sound. Hence **whuffing** *vbl. sb.* So **whuffle** ('hwʌf(ə)l) *v.*, *intr.* in same sense; *trans.* to drive by blowing forcibly.
1896 H. G. WELLS *Wheels of Chance* xix, He whuffed a contemptuous laugh. **1906** 'JOHN OXENHAM' *Giant Circumstance* ii, One of the horses..woke up enough to whuffle the flies out of its nose. **1907** —— *Carette* xxxiii, The water began whuffling against the rock walls. **1919** J. J. BENNETT *Dover Patrol* 172 'Whing! Whuff!' and another muffled burst comes a minute or so later.

whuist, obs. f. WHIST *int.*[1]

whulc, whulch, obs. ff. WHICH.

whule, obs. f. WEEVIL, WHEWL, WHILE.

whum(m)el, whummle, var. WHEMMEL.

whump (hwʌmp), *v.* Also **wump**. [f. as next.]
1. *intr.* To make a dull thudding sound; to move with a 'whump'; to bang or thump; to strike (with a thud).
1897 E. TERRY *Let.* 5 Feb. in *Ellen Terry & Shaw* (1931) 126 Not a single speech do I know yet, and my head is thumping and wumping. **1928** *Blackw. Mag.* Jan. 5/1 The look-out sentry..whumped twice, briskly, on his hand-gong. **1939** *Life* 11 Dec. 26 Taft of Ohio sturdily whumped at the New Deal's 'insane deficit policy'. **1981** B. GRANGER *Schism* xi. 89 The windshield wipers whumped, whumped slowly across the streaky glass.
2. *trans.* To strike heavily or with a 'whump'.
1974 D. E. WESTLAKE *Help* (1975) iii. 20, I would then adjust the rubber stamp.., wump it onto the stamp pad,

wump it onto the envelope. **1976** *National Observer* (U.S.) 24 Jan. 19/3 What had been lost at Waterloo and Sedan could be won back by whumping mud forts in the Sahel.

Hence ˈ**whumping** *vbl. sb.* and *ppl. a.*

1928 *Blackw. Mag.* Jan. 2/2 The occasional whumping and booming of war-gongs. **1977** P. Dickinson *Walking Dead* II. viii. 206 There was a slow, wumping explosion.

whump (hwʌmp), *sb.* (and *int.*) Also **wump.** [Echoic: cf. *bump*, *thump*, etc.] A dull thudding sound, as of a body landing heavily. Also *int.* Cf. WHOMP.

1915 D. O. Barnett *Let.* 6 May (1915) 130 Then there was a wump over beyond, and a young howitzer shell went zip over my trench. **1922** *Chambers's Jrnl.* 7 Oct. 707/1 The globe suddenly swung in a long arc across some hidden gully in the bottom and fetched up with a stunning 'wump' on the slope of the other side. **1926** Galsworthy *Escape* I. ii. 32 Still—up on the ladder and down with a whump—it hits 'em [*sc.* gentlemen] harder than it does the others. **1930** C. R. Samson *Fights & Flights* II. iv. 181 '*Wump*' fell a second bomb. **1967** *Boston Herald* 1 Apr. 20/2 (*caption*) Whump! **1976** *New Yorker* 8 Mar. 106/2, I heard this funny sound: a kind of *whummpp*.

whun, -stane: see WHIN[1], [2], WHINSTONE.

whunk (hwʌnk), *sb.* (and *v.*) *rare.* Also **whonk.** [Echoic.] A dull hollow sound, as of a bullet striking something. Also as *v. intr.*, to strike with a 'whunk'.

App. only in the work of Hemingway.

1935 E. Hemingway *Green Hills Afr.* II. iii. 53 We had both heard the whunk of the bullet. *Ibid.* II. iv. 76, I heard the *whonk* of the bullet. **1936** —— in *Hearst's Internat.* Sept. 168/1 He heard a *whunk* that meant that the bullet was home. *Ibid.* 170/3 Hearing the bullets whunk into him.

whunt, obs. dial. f. QUAINT *a.*

c **1425** *Non-Cycle Myst. Plays* (1909) 23 She is both whunt and slee.

whup, whuph, whur: see WHOOP, WHOOF, WHIRR.

whup (hwʌp), *Sc.* and *U.S. colloq.* and *dial.* var. of WHIP *v.*

†**whurl,** *v. Obs.* Also 5–6 **whorle,** 6 **whyrle,** 7 **wherl.** [Imitative.] *intr.* To make a roaring or rumbling noise; to purr, as a cat; to snarl or growl, as a dog. (Cf. WHARL *v.*, WHIRR *v.* 3, 3 b.) Hence †**whurling** *vbl. sb.* and *ppl. a.*; also †**whurl** *sb.* = WHARL *sb.*

1495 *Trevisa's Barth. De P.R.* XI. ii. (W. de W.), In yͤ eeres wynde makith whystlyng and whorlinge [*Bodl. MS.* trongelinge] and ryngynge. **1530** Palsgr. 781/2 This wynde whorleth so I can nat here. **1553** Brende *Q. Curtius* v. 81 b, Yͤ vse of the eares could not serue for one to receiue counsel . . at an other, the wynd whyrlid so amonges the leaues. **1555** Eden *Decades* (Arb.) 112 The sea raged and rored . . with a horrible whurlinge. **1607** Tourneur *Rev. Trag.* IV. ii. G 3, He whurles and rotles in the throate. **1608** Topsell *Four-f. Beasts* 105 How [the cat] whurleth with her voyce. **1611** Cotgr., *Gronder*, to whurle, whurre, yarre, like a dog that is angrie. **1625** in Foster *Engl. Factories Ind.* (1909) III. 51 The flying shoot . . macking such a wherling noyse in the ayere. **1797** *Encycl. Brit.* (ed. 3) XIII. 112/1 The commonalty are . . distinguished by a kind of shibboleth or whurle, being a particular way of pronouncing the letter R, as if they hawked it up from the wind-pipe, like the cawing of rooks.

whurl(e, whurr, whurra, whurry: see WHIRL, WHIRR, HURRAH, WHIRRY.

whurt, obs. form of WHORT.

whush, *v.* Now *dial.* [Imitative: cf. WHISH *v.*[1]] *intr.* To make a soft rushing sound, as wind, flowing water, waves, etc.; to move with such a sound. (Cf. HUSH *v.*[3]) Chiefly in *vbl. sb.* and *ppl. a.*

1581 A. Hall *Iliad* II. 23 When as the westerne winde doth meete a field of graine, . . & cause the eares to whush. *Ibid.* IV. 72 As the waues within the sea . . yeelds whushing noise. **1856** Dickens *An Ordeal* vi. in *Househ. Wds.* 12 Apr. 299/2 A 'whushing' music, as of distant waves. **1861** 'Holme Lee' *Adv. Tuflongbo* i. 3 The whushing and whispering amongst the trees.

whush, Sc. var. HUSH *sb.*[3]

whush, obs. or n. dial. var. HUSH *a.* and *v.*[1]

1548 Udall, etc. *Erasm. Par. John* xxi. 12–15 The disciples sate downe, but all whusht and spake no wordes.

whusht, obs. var. HUSHT *int.*[1] and *a.* (cf. WHISHT); pa. t. and pple. of *whush*, obs. var. HUSH *v.*[1] (see under WHUSH).

1557 *Tottel's Misc.* (Arb.) 202 The audience ceased . . , and euery thing was whusht. **1581** A. Hall *Iliad* v. 101 All for dread are whusht. **1598** Florio, *Citto*, a word to bid children holde their peace, as we say whusht, husht.

whuss (hwʌs). U.S. (chiefly Black English) colloq. abbrev. of 'what is . . ?'

1935 Z. N. Hurston *Mules & Men* (1970) I. iii. 74 Whuss de matter, Jack? **1938** C. Himes *Pork Chop Paradise* in *Black on Black* (1973) 174 Whuss yo' name? **1977** *Rolling Stone* 16 June 11/2 Whuss happnin'?

whussle, whustle, Sc. and dial. ff. WHISTLE.

†**whust,** *sb.*, *a.*, *v.* (Also 7 **whost.**) Variant of WHIST *sb.*[2], *a.*[1], *v.*[1]

1555 Phaer *Æneid* II. (1558) C iij b, They whusted all, and fyxt with eyes ententiue did behold. **1556** *Ibid.* IV. (1558) L j, Than was it night . . Whan whust is euery felde. **1573** Twyne *Æneid* XI. (1584) R ij, When whust was once proclaimed, & men were bid not silence breake. **1582** Stanyhurst *Æneis* I. (Arb.) 29 Thee murther he whusted. *Ibid.* II. 51 Thee Greeks . . al softlye be whusted. **1583** Melbancke *Philotimus* E e iij b, It were good for me to bee whust in these matters. **1586** J. Hooker *Hist. Irel.* in *Holinshed* II. 81 All should be related, and nothing whusted. **1589** Nashe *Pasquill & Marf.* 26 Seeing Martins matters begin to be whust. **1611** Florio, *Quetare*, to quiet, to whost. **1614** Gorges *Lucan* v. 193 The whusted guards.

whut (hwʌt), U.S. dial and Black English var. of WHAT *pron.*

1909 *Dialect Notes* III. 387 *Whut*, what. A common pronunciation. **1929** W. Faulkner *Sanctuary* (1981) viii. 94, I couldn't tell and wouldn't even keer whut I was eatin. **1936** M. Mitchell *Gone with Wind* v. lix. 996 Miss Melly, you know whut he done? **1961** J. Jahn in A. Dundes *Mother Wit* (1973) 101/1 Whut makes yore head so red. **1973** *Black World* July 62/2 Well, so whut.

†**whute,** *v. Obs. rare.* [Imitative.] To whistle. Hence †**whuting** *ppl. a.* So †**whute** *sb.*

c **1600** in *W. Fowler's Wks.* (S.T.S.) I. 340 The Robin, Wraine, & whutinge quaill. *a* **1663** *Robin Hood & Curtal Friar* xxix. in Child *Ballads* (1888) v. 125 Give me leave to set my fist to my mouth And to whute whutes three. *Ibid.* xxx, xxxi.

whuther, var. WHITHER *sb.*[1] and *v. dial.*

whutter (ˈhwʌtə(r)), *sb.* [Imitative; cf. *flutter.*] The sound of the flapping of the wings of a large bird or a flight of birds. So ˈ**whutter** *v.*, whence ˈ**whuttering** *ppl. a.*

1831 J. Wilson in *Blackw. Mag.* XXIX. 4 A sound like the whutter of wild-fowl on the feed along a mud-bank. **1870** *Pall Mall Gaz.* 12 Aug. 10 The startling of the wary cock, whose whuttering pinions will summon out of reach pack after pack of birds.

whutterick, whutthroat, whuttorock, var. WHITRET.

whuz, obs. or dial. var. WHIZZ *v.*

†**whuzsh.** *Obs. rare*$^{-1}$. ? = HUSH *sb.*[2] 2.

1600 W. Watson *Decacordon* I. vi. (1602) 15 [The Jesuits] lull babies a sleepe with a blacke Sanctus in a whuzsh of whispering foolish noyse.

whwte, variant of WHOOT.

why (hwaɪ), *adv.* (*sb.*, *int.*) Forms: 1–3 **hwy,** (1 **hwiȝ, hwie),** 1–4 **hwi,** (3 **hwui, wee, ȝwi),** 3–4 **wi,** 3–6 **whi, wy,** (4 *Kent.* **hue,** 4–6 **whye,** 5 **whyghe,** 6–7 **whie),** 4– **why;** 3–5 **qui,** 4–5 **quy, qwy, quhi,** 5 **qwi,** *Sc.* **qwhy,** 5–6 (8 *arch.*) *Sc.* **quhy.** [OE. *hwí, hwý* instr. case of *hwæt* WHAT, governed by *to* or *for* (see FORWHY) or used simply as adv., corresp. to OS. *hwí* used with preps. (*bi hwí, te hwí*) and simply = why, wherefore, ON. *hví* used as dat. of *hvat*, and as adv. = why (MSw., Da. *hvi*):—OTeut. **χwī*:—Indo-Eur. **qᵘei*, locative f. **qᵘo-* WHO; cf. Gr. (Doric) *πεῖ* where.]

I. 1. a. In a direct question: For what reason? from what cause or motive? for what purpose? wherefore?

c **1000** *Ags. Gosp.* Matt. xvii. 19 Hwi ne mihte we hyne ut-adrifan? *c* **1000** *Apollonius* (1834) 2 Hwiȝ eart þu . . swa ȝedrefedes modes? *a* **1175** *Cott. Hom.* 221 Hwi wolde god . . him forwerne? *c* **1200** Ormin 2407 Whi ȝaff ȝho swillc anndswere onnȝæn, þa Godess enngell seȝȝde þatt ȝho wiþþ childe shollde ben? *c* **1250** *Kent. Serm.* in *O.E. Misc.* 33 Wee bie ye idel? **1297** R. Glouc. (Rolls) 2757 Sire king wi lete ȝe mi moder & me biuore þe lede? *a* **1300** *Cursor M.* 1128 Sir cayn, Wy has þou þi broiþer slain? *Ibid.* 16295 Qui smites þou me? **1340** *Ayenb.* 47 And hue is hit uoul dede zeþþe hit is kendelich? **1362** Langl. *P. Pl.* A. XI. 66 Whi wolde God . . suffre such a worm . . þe wommon to bigyle? *c* **1470** Henry *Wallace* III. 361 Quhi, Scot, dar thow nocht preiff? **1526** Tindale *Matt.* xxi. 25 He wyll saye vnto vs: why dyd ye not then beleve hym? **1606** Shaks. *Tr. & Cr.* II. iii. 71 Patroclus is a foole positiue. *Patr.* Why am I a foole? **1683** Prior *Pastoral to Dr. Turner* 3 Why dost thou sigh, why strike thy panting breast? **1776** *Trial of Nundocomar* 60/2 When you came from Patna, why did you bring this paper with you? **1837** Newman *Par. Serm.* III. iii. 37 Why was Saul thus marked for vengeance from the beginning? **1883** D. C. Murray *Hearts* ix, Why don't you learn Italian?

b. Implying or suggesting a negative assertion (= 'there is no reason why . .'); hence often expressing a protest or objection (esp. with *should*).

c **897** Ælfred *Gregory's Past. C.* xxxvi. 250 Ȝif he ðæm ȝehiersuman mannum næfde ȝetiohhad his eðel to sellanne, hwy [*v.r.* hwie] wolde he hie mid ænȝum unȝetæsan læran? *a* **1000** *Cædmon's Gen.* 282 Hwy sceal ic æfter his hyldo ðeowian? . . ic mæȝ wesan god swa he! *c* **1200** *Vices & Virtues* 13 Ic . . sæide: Hwi me scolde cumen swilche unȝelimpes? *c* **1200** *Trin. Coll. Hom.* 103 Wi list þu turnd on þe eorðe? aris þat is to seien hwi luuest þu þine fule sunnes? forlet hem. *a* **1225** *Leg. Kath.* 1390 Hwi ne hihe we for to beon ifulhet? *a* **1250** *Owl & Night.* 1234 þat eni man beo falle in odwite, Wi schal he me his sor atwite? *a* **1300** *Cursor M.* 461 Qui suld I him seruis yield? *a* **1400** *Pistill of Susan* 284 Whi spille ȝe Innocens blode? *c* **1420** *Avow. Arth.* xxxiii, Qwi schuld I layne? *c* **1470** Henry *Wallace* II. 108 Eternaile God, quhy suld I thus wayis de? **1562** Winȝet *Cert. Tractates* iii. Wks. (S.T.S.) I. 28 Quhi abolissis he not the Sonday, as he dois ȝule? **1608** *Yorksh. Trag.* iii. 5 Whie should our faults at home be spred abroad? **1766** Goldsm. *Vicar W.* iii, The poor live pleasantly without our help, why then should not we learn to live without theirs? **1839** Thackeray *Fatal Boots* Feb., I said nothing about it, as why should I? *Ibid.* Aug., Why, why was I born to undergo such unmerited misfortunes?

c. With ellipsis of the remainder of the sentence, or of all except the principal word or words (esp. when emphatic); also with simple inf. (= 'why should one . . ?'). See also 4 b.

a **1380** *St. Aug.* 7 in Horstm. *Altengl. Leg.* (1878) 61/1 Seint Austin was nempned þat name For þreo causus of gret fame: . . Whi? furst for excellence of dignite. *c* **1440** *Gesta Rom.* lxxxvi. 406 (Add. MS.) The kyng . . askid hym whethere he was shreuyn or not? he saide, 'nay.' 'why so?' saide the kyng. **1528** Roy *Rede me* (Arb.) 113 *Wat.* Surely we shulde be proclaymed For outragious heretykis. *Ief.* Why more we then the Cardinall? **1528** More *Dyaloge* II. Wks. 182/2, I haue euer herde it sayd, that we should not pray to any dead man but with this condicion, if thou be a saint, than pray for me. Whi so quod I? **1611** Shaks. *Wint. T.* I. ii. 231 *Cam.* [He] Stayes here longer. *Leo.* I, but why? *a* **1625** Fletcher *Nice Valour* IV. i, But why a Peel-crow here? **1697** Vanbrugh *Æsop* v. i, Why so Cold, and why so Coy? **1746** Francis tr. *Hor., Epist.* I. ii. 65 Blest with a competence, why wish for more? **1841** Browning *Pippa passes* Introd. 196 Say not 'a small event!' Why 'small'? **1843** Wordsw. *Grace Darling* 73 But why prolong the tale? **1848** Dickens *Dombey* xi, 'Berry's very fond of you, ain't she?' Paul once asked Mrs. Pipchin. . . 'Yes,' said Mrs. Pipchin. 'Why?' asked Paul. **1905** *Times Lit. Suppl.* 15 Sept. 293/1 Why books, why chapters, why titles, why any arrangement at all, they queried.

d. With the negative form of the simple present tense in formulating a positive suggestion, as 'why don't I (we, etc.) . . ?'

1949 D. Smith *I capture Castle* xii. 212 Why don't I drive you over to hear it now? **1974** G. Mitchell *Winking at Brim* vi. 54 Mummy brought a couple of thermos flasks. . . Why don't I go and collect one? **1982** R. Doyle *Havana Special* vii. 182 Why don't I stop by her compartment . . and see how she is?

¶ ***and why?*** is used in some early biblical versions, and hence in the Prayer-book Psalter, to render Heb. *kī* because, since, for: app. in imitation of *forwhy* after this was apprehended as interrogative (cf. FORWHY B. 2, A. 1 b).

1535 Coverdale *Ps.* xx[i]. 7 For thou shalt . . make him glad wᵗ the ioye of yͤ countenaunce. And why? because [*so* **1539** (Great); 1560 (Geneva), 1568 (Bishops') Because; 1611 For] the kinge putteth his trust in the Lorde. *Ibid.* xxxiv. [xxxv.] 20 O let them not triumphe ouer me. . . And why? [*so* **1539**; 1560 *and later vv.* For] their comonynge is not for peace.

2. In an indirect question or a dependent clause of similar meaning, with sense and const. as in 1.

Formerly sometimes followed by *that* (THAT *conj.* 6).

c **888** Ælfred *Boeth.* xxvi. §2 Ic nat hwi ȝe fultruwiað ðæm hreosendan welan. *c* **1055** *Byrhtferth's Handboc* in *Anglia* VIII. 308 Uton . . witan hwæt he [*sc.* the moon] sy . . oððe hwy he sy swa ȝehaten. *c* **1200** Ormin Ded. 111 ȝiff mann wile witenn whi Icc hafe don þiss dede. *a* **1250** *Owl & Night.* 474 þv ayssest me . . Hwi ich a wynter singe & grede. **1303** R. Brunne *Handl. Synne* 9265 Yn hys redyng, none wyst why, he logh a grete laghter an hy. **1393** Langl. *P. Pl.* C. XI. 245 Ac whi þe worlde was a-drent holy writ telleþ. *c* **1400** *Laud Troy Bk.* 14241 Durste no man aske whi he were wroth. *a* **1425** *Cursor M.* 1323 (Trin.) Seth bigon to þenke whye þat þis tre bicoom so drye. *a* **1474** *Stonor Papers* (Camden) I. 136 Wherof to me-werd he makith gret straungenesse: y merveile why. **1538** Starkey *England* I. iii. (1878) 74, I can not se wy we schold lay any grete faute in the lake of pepul. **1581** *Cal. Scott. Pap.* VIII. 19, I dare give him no counsell, and I will tell you why. **1611** *Bible* Esther iv. 5 To know what it was, and why it was. **1724** Ramsay *Vision* xvi, Say how, and quhair ye met, and quhy. **1836** Dickens *Sk. Boz, Visit to Newgate*, Buoyed up with some vague . . hope of reprieve, he knew not why. **1849** Macaulay *Hist. Eng.* vi. II. 7 It is easy to explain why the Roman Catholic was treated with less indulgence.

3. a. With intensive additions (in direct or dependent questions): see DEVIL *sb.* 20, DICKENS a, EARTH *sb.*[1] 9 c, NAME *sb.* 11 b, etc.

c **1475** *Rauf Coilȝear* 95 Quhy Deuill makis thow na dule for this euill day? **1762** J. Collier (Tim Bobbin) *Let.* 4 Nov., Wks. (1862) 326 There's scarce a boy, . . that commits a fault, but can find one excuse or another. Then why the dickens must Tim be without one? **1860** W. W. Reade *Liberty Hall* II. 20 Why in the name of all patience should you work so hard as this? **1887** Darwin *Life & Lett.* I. 488 Give [the English names] by all means, but why on earth not make them subordinate to the Latin. **1895** Kipling *Lett. Trav.* (1920) 115 Why, in the name of Reason, . . should we vex ourselves?

b. Duplicated in phr. ***why, oh why . . ?***, as an emphatic interrogative, expressing dismay, disapproval, or complete lack of comprehension of another's actions; 'why on earth . . ?'

1865 M. Arnold *Let.* 23 July (1895) I. 294 Why, oh, why do not you and Edward come to the Black Forest and join us? *a* **1884** T. H. Huxley *Let.* in *Henry Bristow Ltd. Catal.* (1981) No. 269. 14 My students . . cannot get copies of the second edition of the Biology book. Why oh why was it not ready by October. **1934** N. Marsh *Man lay Dead* xi. 194 Why, oh why, did the murderer sound the gong? **1961** 'E. Lathen' *Banking on Death* (1962) viii. 70 Why, oh why, had she been so bitchy to his wife? **1975** *Times* 8 Mar. 13/7 Why, Oh why does Rolls-Royce . . name its latest product after an area of French marsh-land?

4. With a negative particle immediately following. †**a.** ***why ne*** (usually as one word *whine*, *whyne*, also contr. *whyn*): why not: used in expressions of desire or longing (e.g. *hwi nam ich* . . . = 'why am I not . . ?' = 'O that I were . . !'), in OE. of emphatic protest (cf. 1 b). *Obs.*

971 *Blickl. Hom.* 67 Hwy nelt þu ʒeman þæt min sweostor me læt ane þeʒnian? *a* **1000** *Ags. Ps.* (Th.) xi[i]. 4 Hwi ne synt we muðfreo? *c* **1200** *Vices & Virtues* 87 Hwi ne mai ich none wuneȝenge habben mid ðe? *a* **1240** *Ureisun* in *O.E. Hom.* I. 185 Hwi ne bi-hold ich hu þu strahtest þe for me on rode? *Ibid.*, A ihesu..hwi nam ich in þin earmes? **1340** HAMPOLE *Pr. Consc.* 1207 'O þou world', he says, 'unclene, Whyn mught þou swa unclen be, þat suld never mare neghe me' [L. *utinam esses ita immundus, ut me non tangeres*]. ? *a* **1400** *Morte Arth.* 703 Whyne myghte I, dere lufe, dye in ȝour armes! *Ibid.* 4157 Qwythene [app. = why then ne] hade Dryghttyne destaynede at his dere wille, þat he hade demyd me to-daye to dy for ȝow alle.

b. ***why not*** is used elliptically as in 1 c. (Hence as *sb.*: see WHY-NOT.)

a **1380** *St. Aug.* 920 in Horstm. *Altengl. Leg.* (1878) 77 And eny tyme ȝif hit schal beo, Whi not nou? *c* **1412** HOCCLEVE *De Reg. Princ.* 4883 Why naght, my gode lorde? what shuld yow eyle? But men do naght so; where-of I merueyle. **1552** HULOET, Whye not? *quid ni.* **1746** FRANCIS tr. *Hor., Epist.* I. i. 44 Yet why not cure the gout's decrepit pain? **1821** SCOTT *Kenilw.* xxxvi, Yet wherefore, if guilty, should she have perilled herself by coming hither? Why not rather have fled to her father's or elsewhere? **1882** BESANT *All Sorts* xxx, You can't marry me? Why not? When I offer you a fortune? *Ibid.* xxxvii, They say, 'Here is the Fourth Commandment. All the rest you continue to observe. Why not this?' *Mod.* I can't tell you why not.

II. 5. a. As relative: On account of which, because of which, for which. Usually, now almost always, after *reason* (formerly also *cause*, etc.). Also *ellipt.* (See also CAUSE *sb.* 3 c.)

Formerly also with *that* (THAT *conj.* 6).

a **1225** *Ancr. R.* 312 Monie oðre reisuns beoð hwui mon mei beon bitterliche sori uor his sunnen. *a* **1300** *Cursor M.* 17288 + 161 þis aungel..neuend peter by name, a skill I tel yow qwy. *a* **1380** *St. Aug.* 137 in Horstm. *Altengl. Leg.* (1878) 64/1 Heo..asked hire þe cause whi þat heo was so sori. **1390** GOWER *Conf.* I. 148 Sche sih hire fader sorwe and sike, And wiste noght the cause why. **1483** *Acta Audit.* in *Acta Dom. Conc.* II. Introd. 133 Quhill the said William.. schew uther lauchfull cause quhy scho suld nocht have the said thrid. **1521** *Acts Parlt. Scot.* (1875) XII. 39/1 We se nane appearance quhy ȝoure grace suld belieff [etc.]. **1548** UDALL *Erasm. Par. Luke* xxiii. 13–25 What hath this man committed or offended why he should dye? **1581** PARSONS (*title*) Reasons why Catholiques refuse to go to Church. **1599** SHAKS. *Hen. V*, v. ii. 34 If I demand..what Impediment there is, Why that the naked, poore, and mangled Peace..Should not..put vp her louely Visage? **1606** —— *Ant. & Cl.* IV. xiv. 89 *Eros.* My sword is drawne. *Ant.* Then let it do at once The thing why thou hast drawne it. *a* **1721** PRIOR *Female Phaeton* vi, I'll have my Earl, as well as She, Or know the Reason why. **1846** GREENER *Sci. Gunnery* 26 We can perceive the reason why a small proportion of carbonic oxide is always formed during the decomposition of nitre by charcoal. **1908** R. BAGOT *A. Cuthbert* xxviii. 372 It would be useless to deny that your life is in grave danger... But that is no reason why you should surrender it without a struggle.

†**b.** For which reason, wherefore. *Obs. rare*⁻¹.

a **1500** in *Arnolde's Chron.* (1811) 22 Also we haue grauntyd for vs and for our eyers to our citezens yᵗ they..be quyt for euer of pauage pontage and murage..Why we wyll and stedfastly byd for vs and for our eyers, yᵗ yᵉ same citezens..haue all her fraunches..and fre custumes aforesayd.

†**c.** *to do* (one) ***why***: to recompense (= *to do wherefore*: see WHEREFORE 3). *Obs. rare*⁻¹.

c **1400** LOVE *Bonavent. Mirr.* xxxviii. (1908) 195 So that they wolde mede hym and done hym why.

d. Introducing a subject or predicate clause: = 'the reason why'.

Closely allied to the indirect interrogative use (sense 2); e.g. 'Why this should be so is not clear' = 'It is not clear why this should be so.' (Cf. WHERE 6.)

1605 SHAKS. *Lear* IV. vi. 33 Why I do trifle thus with his dispaire, Is done to cure it. **1820** KEATS *La Belle Dame Sans Merci* xii, And this is why I sojourn here. **1882** BESANT *All Sorts* xv, At first I thought it must be a joke. That was why I went away. *Mod.* Why I mentioned that was because [etc.].

III. 6. as *sb.* (pl. *whys*). **a.** Reason, cause.

(Formerly as a general synonym for these words; now only in reference to something mentioned, and with conscious allusion to the interrogative use.)

1303 R. BRUNNE *Handl. Synne* 3758 ȝyf þou art wunt.. For to curse for lytyl why. **1377** LANGL. *P. Pl.* B. XII. 217 So I sey by þe þat sekest after þe whyes [*MS. C.* whaies; *MS. B.* wyes] And aresonedest resoun. **1393** *Ibid.* C. XIX. 147 [He] wepte water with hus eyen, the whi witen fewe. **1423** JAS. I. *Kingis Q.* lxxxvii, Vnkyndenes without a quhy. *c* **1500** *Lancelot* 123 Well he knowith of al my vo the quhy. **1560** ROLLAND *Seven Sages* (Bann. Club) 35 As may perchance be done for sum gude quhy. *a* **1644** QUARLES *Sol. Recant.* ch. vii. 10. 33 Where heav'n declares a Will, no wise mans eye Should search a Cause, or lips enquire a why. **1740** CHEYNE *Regimen* Pref. p. iii, But the Why? the final Causes, the moral Consequences, and the particular Detail, is only here conjectured about. **1768** TUCKER *Lt. Nat.* (1834) II. 521 Never to act upon mere impulse, but to have a why for all their proceedings. **1828** SOUTHEY *Ess.* (1832) II. 415 The reader who may not be..acquainted with the when, and the how, and the why of the surrender. **1907** ILLINGWORTH *Doctr. Trin.* xii. 250 The region not of life's how, but of life's why.

b. A question beginning with (or consisting of) the word 'why?'; a question as to the reason of something; hence, a problem, an enigma.

1532 MORE *Confut. Tindale* Wks. 427/1 But I aske of Tyndall no such farre fet whyes, but a why of hys owne dede... I aske hym thys why: Why dydde he translate the same by thys englyshe woorde elder? *a* **1592** GREENE *Alphonsus* I, Make you a why of that? **1637** WHITING *Albino & Bellama* 6 The testy Father with a furrow'd brow Comes to Bellama with demanding why? **1654** WHITLOCK *Zootomia* 31 Each Day brings forth its why. *a* **1754** FIELDING *Fathers* II. i, Why should you think he has my affections? *Valence.* Again at your why's! **1780** HARRIS *Philol. Enq.* II. i. (1781) 48 Till this Why is well answered, all is Darkness. **1866** A. STEINMETZ *Weathercasts* 20 She could supply the ready 'because' to many of the old philosopher's 'whys'.

c. Conjoined with *wherefore* similarly used.

1590, 1624 [see WHEREFORE 6]. **1634** SANDERSON *Serm.* (1674) I. iv. 65 Requiring a why for every wherefore. **1799** *Spirit Public Jrnls.* (1805) III. 329 By this they shall form assignations, with the *when* and the *where*—they shall break them off, with the *why* and the *wherefore*, and express a disappointment without a tear or a sigh. **1829** CARLYLE *Misc., Signs of Times* (1857) II. 113 For every Why we must have a Wherefore. **1833** HT. MARTINEAU *Brooke Farm* viii. 103 If I were to tell you all the whys and wherefores on that question. **1911** MARETT *Anthropol.* viii. 227 The savage is no authority on the why and wherefore of his customs.

IV. 7. Used interjectionally, before a sentence or clause. **a.** As an expression of surprise (sometimes only momentary or slight; sometimes involving protest), either in reply to a remark or question, or on perceiving something unexpected.

1519 *Interl. Four Elem.* B vij, Than I perceyue ye wyll make gode chere. *Hu.* Why, what shulde I els do? **1581** *Confer. with Campion* (1583) C iij, Why, is not Saint Iames Epistle called the Catholike Epistle of Saint Iames. How do you then denie it to be Canonicall? **1599** SHAKS. *Much Ado* IV. ii. 44 Why this is flat periurie, to call a Princes brother villaine. *Ibid.* v. iv. 73 *Bene.* Doo not you loue me? *Beat.* Why no, no more then reason. **1611** *Bible* Matt. xxvii. 23 They all sayde vnto him, Let him be crucified. And the Gouernour said, Why, what euil hath he done? **1712** STEELE *Spect.* No. 533 ¶1 What do I think? why, I think she cannot be above six foot two inches high. **1799** WARNER in Jesse *Selwyn & Contemp.* (1844) IV. 274 What was I to do in this more than Egyptian darkness? Why, go to bed. Very true. **1837** DICKENS *Pickw.* xxxix, 'Goodness gracious!' said Mary,.. 'Why, it's that very house.' **1847** DE QUINCEY *Secret Soc.* Wks. 1890 VII. 217 Were there no such people as the Essenes? Why, no; not as Josephus described them. **1863** KINGSLEY *Water-Bab.* iii, And, as he spoke, he turned quite pale, and then quite white. 'Why, you're ill!' said Tom. **1893** MAX PEMBERTON *Iron Pirate* i, Mary looked up suddenly..and said,..'Why, I believe I've been asleep!'

b. Emphasizing or calling more or less abrupt attention to the statement following (as in the apodosis of a sentence), in opposition to a possible or vaguely apprehended doubt or objection.

1545 RAYNALDE *Byrth Mankynde* 90 When she feleth greate ache in the inner parte of the eyes.., yᵉ reste of the body taken as it were with a werynesse without any outwarde apparent cause: why these thynges portende.. aborcement to be at hande. **1590** LODGE *Rosalind* (1592) N 2 b, And to conceale it, why it doubled her griefe. **1591** SHAKS. *Two Gent.* I. i. 33 If hap'ly won, perhaps a haplesse gaine, If lost, why then a grieuous labour won. **1594** *1st Pt. Contention* II. i, Why let me see, I thinke thou canst not see yet. *a* **1596** *Sir T. More* I. i. 122 Take an honest woman from her husband! why, it is intollerable. **1602** SHAKS. *Ham.* I. ii. 121 *Ham.* I shall in all my best Obey you Madam. *King.* Why 'tis a louing, and a faire Reply. *Ibid.* III. ii. 282 Why let the strucken Deere go weepe, The Hart vngalled play. **1647** COWLEY *Mistr., Request* iii, If her chill heart I cannot move, Why, I'le enjoy the very Love. **1724** SWIFT *Quiet Life* 27 Why, Dick, thy wife has devilish whims. **1769** GOLDSM. *Rom. Hist.* (1786) I. 439 If you will have Caesar for your master, why have him. **1840** DICKENS *Old C. Shop* i, 'A long way, wasn't it, Kit?'.. 'Why then, it was a goodish stretch, master,' returned Kit. **1863** KINGSLEY *Water-Bab.* iii, If she chooses to come, why she may; and if not, why I go without her. **1869** WHYTE-MELVILLE *Songs & Verses* 93 So he made for the gate,..And the chain being round it, why—over he flew! **1882** BESANT *All Sorts* xxiii, 'Not a doubt', added the Professor. 'Why, it stands to reason.'

†**c.** As an emphasized call or summons, expressing some degree of impatience. *Obs.*

1592 SHAKS. *Rom. & Jul.* IV. v. 2, 3 Mistris, what Mistris? Iuliet?.. Why Lambe, why Lady, fie you sluggabed, Why Loue I say?..why Bride? **1596** —— *Merch. V.* II. v. 6 What Iessica?.. Why Iessica I say. **1597** —— *2 Hen. IV*, v. i. 8 What Dauy, I say... Why Dauie.

†**d.** ***why, so!*** an expression of content, acquiescence, or relief. *Obs.* or *arch.*

1593 SHAKS. *Rich. II*, II. ii. 87 *Ser.* My Lord, your sonne was gone before I came. *Yor.* He was: why so: go all which way it will. **1596** —— *Tam. Shr.* IV. iii. 198 *Pet.*.. It shall be what a clock I say it is. *Hor.* Why so this gallant will command the sunne. **1605** —— *Macb.* III. iv. 107 Hence, horrible shadow..[*Ghost vanishes.*] Why, so, being gone, I am a man againe. **1826** SCOTT *Woodst.* iii, If you will have the things rendered even now—why so; and if not, hold me blameless.

V. 8. for why: a. *interrog.* For what reason, why (= 1, 2). **b.** *rel.* For which reason, wherefore; for which (= 5, 5 b). **c.** *conj.* For the reason that, because, for. *Obs.*, *arch.*, or *dial.* (See FORWHY and cf. WHY-FOR.)

In later use commonly apprehended as the adverb *why* with a redundant *for* prefixed (cf. *from whence*).

c **1000–1502** [see FORWHY]. **1596** SHAKS. *Tam. Shr.* III. ii. 169 [She] Trembled and shooke: for why, he stamp'd and swore. **1604** —— *Oth.* I. iii. 259 The Rites for why I loue him, are bereft me. **1782** COWPER *Gilpin* 212 Away Went Gilpin's hat and wig! He lost them sooner than at first—For why?—they were too big! **1819** *Metropolis* II. 207 We do not like him, I do not precisely know for why. **1821** SCOTT *Kenilw.* xi, 'Why, Dame,' said the hostler,..'as for what he was like I cannot tell,..for why I never saw un.' **1896** E. F. BENSON *The Babe B. A.* i, For why? I am dining with the Babe to-night.

VI. 9. *Comb.* **why-question**, a question inquiring after the reason for something; one which is introduced by the word 'why'. Cf. WH 2.

1973 A. DUNDES *Mother Wit* 568 'Why' questions are always difficult to answer. **1978** *Language* LIV. 71 A *that*-clause can be the basis of a *why*-question when it is assigned the semantic status of the volunteered stance of the subject of the verb whose complement it is.

Hence as *v. intr.*, to ask the question 'why?' (chiefly as *pres. ppl.*); also **'whying** *vbl. sb.*

1926 H. PEARSON *Whispering Gallery* ii. 19, I made the mistake of doing or dying, but at the same time why-ing. **1928** D. H. LAWRENCE *Phoenix II* (1968) 520 Why indeed? But once you start whying, there's no end to it. **1932** E. M. BRENT-DYER *Chalet Girls in Camp* i. 24 'Why?'.. 'For goodness' sake don't start why-ing, Rix!' **1959** *Times Lit. Suppl.* 2 Jan. 7/1 (*heading*) Howing and whying.

why(e, northern ff. QUEY, heifer.

whybeler, ? obs. form of QUIBBLER.

c **1425** *Engl. Conq. Irel.* 148 Ianglers & bosters,..and stronge lyers, foderes, whybelers.

whych(e, whyck, whydah, whyder, -yr, whydyrewyn, whyell, whyer: see WHICH, WHITCH, QUICK, WHIDAH, WHETHER, WITHERWIN, WHILE, CHOIR.

whydunit (hwaɪˈdʌnɪt). *slang.* Also **whydunnit**. [f. WHY *adv.* + WHO)DUNIT.] A story, play, or film in which the main interest lies in the detection of the motive for some crime or other action.

1968 *Guardian* 1 May 7/2 Patricia Highsmith..writes why-dunnits rather than who-dunnits, psychological thrillers. **1970** *Homes & Gardens* Feb. 122/2 This novel isn't so much a whodunit as a whydunit, with a revolver doing the deed. **1984** *Listener* 17 May 35/3 It is a terrific whodunnit, constantly hinting at whydunnit, at the ethical squalor of all the participants.

whyever (hwaɪˈɛvə(r)), *adv.* [f. WHY + EVER *adv.* 8 d, e.] **a.** *rel.* For whatever reason. **b.** *interrog.* An emphatic extension of *why*, implying perplexity or surprise (*colloq.*; more properly as two words).

1891 *Voice* (N.Y.) 20 Aug., Whatever it is and whyever it is. *Mod.* Whyever [*or* Why ever] did you do that?

why-for, why for, *advb.* and *conj. phr.*

†**1.** *rel. adv.*: = FORWHY A. 3, WHEREFORE 4, WHY 5. *Obs.*

In quot. with peculiar construction, thus = 'of which'.

a **1450** *Knt. de la Tour* (1868) 67 An aungelle shewed hym the payne..that she was made to suffre.., the cause why for he sawe perfitly, how a deuelle helde her bi..the here of her hede.

†**2.** *conj.* = FOR B. 2, FORWHY B. 2. *Obs.*

c **1450** *Cov. Myst.* (Shaks. Soc.) 254 Many of ȝow be dome; why? for ȝe wole not redresse, Be mowthe ȝour dedys mortal. *c* **1489** CAXTON *Sonnes of Aymon* xxvi. 545 Ye have lerned a fowle crafte, that ys, that ye can speke shrewdly wythoute a cause lawfull. Why for I have herde that ye have called me & my broder the sones of a traytour.

3. as *dependent interrog. adv.*: = FORWHY A. 2, WHEREFORE 2, WHY 2. *dial.*

1787 GROSE *Prov. Gloss.*, *Why-vore*, or *For why-vore*, wherefore. **1801** *Marvellous Love-Story* II. 232 Some folks call's't Crazy Castle, but I never could larn whyfore.

whyg, whyghe, whyght(e, whygth(e, whyht, Whyghtson, obs. ff. WHIG *sb.*[1], WHY, WHITE, WIGHT, WHITSUN.

†**whyȝt.** *Obs. rare.* [for *whith, OE. *hwiþa* = ON. *hviða.*] A wind, breeze.

c **1300** *K. Horn* 784 (Laud), þe whyȝt [*MS. L.* wynd] him gan stonde And drof tyl hirelonde.

whyk, whykyn, obs. dial. ff. QUICK *a.*, *v.*[1]

whyl, whylghe, obs. ff. WHILE.

whyle, whyles, -is, whylest, obs. ff. WHEEL, WHILE, WILE, WHILES, WHILST.

whylk(e, whyll(e, whyllys, obs. ff. WHICH, WEEL[2], WHEEL, WHILE, WHILES.

whylom(e, -on, -um, whyls(e, whylst, whylyst, obs. ff. WHILOM, WHILES, WHILST.

whylte, obs. f. *wilt*: see WILL *v.*

whyly, obs. f. WILY.

whym, whympel, whympernell, obs. ff. WHIM, WIMPLE, WHIMBREL.

whyn, whynde, obs. ff. WHIN, WIN, WIND.

whyn(e = why not: see WHY 4 a.

†**whyne,** *adv. Sc.* and *north. dial. Obs.* Forms: 4 quein, quheyne, qwyne, quhene, 4–5 wheyn, 4–6 quhyne, 5 whyne, 6 quhyn. [Contraction of WHETHEN; cf. SYNE.] = WHENCE.

a **1300** *Cursor M.* 7796 Quein cums þou? **13..** *Seuyn Sages* (W.) 3271 The erl said,..'Wheym [*read* Wheyn] es this faire lady?' The knight said, 'Sir,...Sho es cumen from myne awyn cuntre'. **1375** BARBOUR *Bruce* VII. 240 Scho askit hym..quhat he wes, And quhyne he com, and quhar he gais. ? *a* **1400** *Morte Arth.* 3503 'Fro qwyne come þou',.. quod þe kynge thane, 'That knawes kynge Arthure, and his knyghttes also?' *c* **1440** *Alphabet of Tales* 196 He askid hym whyne he was, & who was his fadur & his moder. *c* **1520**

NISBET *John* vii. 27 Quhen Crist sal cum, na man wate of quhyn he is.

whyne, obs. form of WHIN, WHINE, WINE.

whyness (ˈhwaɪnɪs). [f. WHY *adv.* + -NESS.] That which causes a thing to be as it is; the essential reason for something. Cf. WHATNESS.

1896 R. FRY *Lett.* (1972) I. 116 You who..care nothing about the *whyness* of the *what*. **1932** *Times Lit. Suppl.* 20 Oct. 765/3 But it is the whatness not the whyness of things that matters. **1950** *Mind* LIX. 405 Logical empiricism indicates the 'howness' of the world, but not the 'whyness'. **1962** *Time* 11 May 70 Teacher Foote reports that *-ness* added to nouns, pronouns, verbs, and phrases—a custom thought until now to be mostly whimsical, as in *whyness*, and *everydayness*—has become popular among distinctly unjocose people.

whyng(e, obs. forms of WING.

why-not (ˈhwaɪnɒt). [The phrase *why not?* (WHY 4 b) used as a sb.] **a.** An argument of the form 'Why not?', which attempts to leave the opponent without a reply. **b.** In *Backgammon*: see quot. 1680; hence allusively, esp. in phr. ***to take*** (***have***, etc.) ***at a why-not***, i.e. at an advantage or in a dilemma.

1611 W. SCLATER *Key* 123 That is answere sufficient to all such plausible why-nots. *a* **1612** HARINGTON in *Nugæ Antiq.* (1804) II. 144 This game..by certaine bootie play betweene a Protector and a Bishop, (I suppose it was at Tick-take), was like to have been lost with a *why not?* **1664** BUTLER *Hud.* II. ii. 530 O'er-reach'd your Rabbins of the Synod And snap'd their Cannons with a Why-not. **1680** COTTON *Compl. Gamester* 113 This is the plain Game of Tick-Tack, which is called so from *Touch*, and *take*, for if you touch a man you must play him though to your loss; and if you hit your Adversary and neglect the advantage, you are taken with a Why-not, which is the loss of one. *c* **1680** in *Verney Mem.* (1904) II. 335 You catch me with a why-not still: Indeed my memory growes bad.., and things go out as fast as they come into my head now. **1720** MRS. MANLEY *Power of Love* (1741) 285 He took me at a why not! naked, without Cloaths and Weapons. **1753** RICHARDSON *Grandison* (1754) VI. 142 Now, Dame Selby, I have you at a why-not.

whyou, variant of WHEW *int.*

1848 THACKERAY *Van. Fair* xiv, He knew the old gentleman's character well; and a more unscrupulous old —whyou—he did not conclude the sentence.

whyp, whype, whyppe: see WHIP, WIPE.

†**whyr**, *int. Obs. rare*⁻¹. A call used in driving sheep.

c **1460** [see TYR].

whyre, whyr(r)ie, etc., obs. ff. WHERRY *sb.*¹

whyrl(e, obs. f. WHIRL; var. WHURL *v. Obs.*

whysh, whyshly, whysht(e, Whys(s)ontyd(e, whysshe, whysshyne, -ssyne, obs. ff. WHISH *v.*², WISTLY, WHISHT *a.*¹, WHITSUNTIDE, WHISH *v.*¹, WISH, CUSHION.

whyst(e, whystare, whystel(l, -tle, -tyl(le, whystelare, -er: see WHIST, WHITSTER, WHISTLE, WISSEL, WHISTLER, WISSELER.

whyt, obs. f. QUICK *a.*, WHIT, WHITE, WIGHT, WITH.

whytch(e, var. WHITCH.

whyte, obs. f. QUIT, WHITE, WIT.

whyten, obs. f. WHITEN *v.*, WHITING *sb.*

whyth(e, whythene, whythy: see WHITE, WITH, WHETHEN, WITHY.

whytowre, whytrat, -ratche, -rate, whyt rent, whytsafe, obs. ff. QUITTER, WHITRET, QUIT-RENT, VOUCHSAFE.

whytt(e, whytting, obs. ff. QUIT *v.*, WHITE, WIT, WHITING.

whyver, whywer, obs. ff. QUIVER *sb.*¹

†**wi**, *sb. Obs.* Forms: 1 wiᵹ, 3 wiȝ, wyȝ, wi. [OE. *wiᵹ* str. n. = OFris. *wîch*, OS. *wîg* (MLG. *wîch*), OHG., MHG. *wîc*, ON. *víg*:—OTeut. **wīgom*, f. pre-Teut. *weig-* (:*waig-*: *wig-*) to fight:—Indo-Eur. *wĭk-* to be strong.

The form *weig-* is represented by OE. *wiᵹan* to fight, OS., OFris. *wîgand*, OHG. *wîgant* pr. pple. used as sb. warrior, ON. *vígr* brave in war, neut. *vígt* WIGHT *a.*; *waig-* by OE. *wǽᵹan*, OHG. *weigen* (:**waigjan*) to afflict, ON. *veig* strength, strong drink, drinking glass (cf. OS. *wêgi*, OE. *wǽᵹe* cup); *wig-* by OE. *wiga* warrior, WY, Goth. *wigana* dat. sing., *waihjô* battle. The Indo-Eur. *wīk-* is represented by L. *vincere*, perf. t. *vīcī* to conquer, OIr. *fichim* to fight.]

Battle, conflict; *transf.* a military force or troop. Also *attrib.* as in *wi-ax*, a battle-axe.

Beowulf 1080 Wiᵹ ealle fornam Finnes þeᵹnas nemne feaum anum. *c* **897** ÆLFRED *Gregory's Past. C.* 3 Hu him ða speow æᵹðer ᵹe mid wiᵹe ᵹe mid wisdome. *c* **1205** LAY. 1567 þe bearn..igrap..ana wiæx swiðe stronge. *Ibid.* 25365 þer com mid muchle wiȝe [*c* **1275** wyȝe] Irtac king of Turckie. *c* **1250** *Gen. & Ex.* 1854 Emor his fader,..And his burȝe-folc fellen in wi.

†**wi**, *int. Obs.* [Cf. WE *int.*] An exclamation used to introduce an anxious question or a statement of something regrettable.

a **1200** *Moral Ode* 90 He þurþ-sicheþ uches monnes þonc: wi hwat scal us to rede? *Ibid.* 106 Wi hwi weren ho biȝeten to hwon weren ho iborene þet sculen bon to deþe idemet? *c* **1200** *Ibid.* 104 (Trin. Coll. MS.), Wi swo fele beð icleped, swo fewe beð icorene. *a* **1300** *Cursor M.* 3752 'Consail me, fader, how to liue.' 'Wi, quatkin consail mai i þe giue?' *Ibid.* 5013 'Him sal deliuer your yongeist child.' 'Wi how sal beniamin come þare?' *Ibid.* 23845 Wi qui þan mak we us sa kene?

wi, obs. form of WHY.

wi' (wɪ), Sc. and dial. abbrev. f. WITH *prep.*

wiage, wiar, obs. ff. VOYAGE, WIRE.

wibble-wobble (ˈwɪb(ə)lˈwɒb(ə)l), *colloq.*, reduplication of WOBBLE (with vowel-variation symbolizing alternation of movement: cf. *zigzag*); hence **wibble** as a simple word (conjoined with *wobble*). So **ˈwibbly-ˈwobbly** (also simply **wibbly**), **wibblety-wobblety** *adjs.*, characterized by 'wibbling and wobbling', unsteady; also **ˈwibbly-ˈwobbly** *sb.*, in phr. ***all of a wibbly-wobbly*** (*nonce-use*).

1847 HALLIWELL, *Wibble-wobble*, unsteadily. **1871** L. W. M. LOCKHART *Fair to see* ii, The ample round red face, which wibbled and wobbled in its billowy fatness. **1877** *Holderness Gloss.*, *Wibblety-wobblety*, shaky; tottering; insecure. *Wibble-wobble*, to vibrate; to quiver; to oscillate. **1901** *B'ham Daily Post* 16 Dec. (E.D.D.) His wibblely-wobblely speeches. **1905** *Motor-Car Jrnl.* 23 Sept. 630/1 The gait [of a motor-car] was ungainly by reason of the wibbly-wobbly nature of a rear wheel. **1914** *Daily News* 5 June 6, I..hauled myself up again, and with wibbly knees crossed to the bushes south of the track. **1922** JOYCE *Ulysses* 399 Bless me,..I'm all of a wibbly-wobbly.

wibel, -ill, obs. forms of WEEVIL.

wic, obs. f. WICK *sb.*² and *a.*

wicar, -age, obs. Sc. ff. VICAR, -AGE.

Wiccamical: see WYKEHAMICAL.

wicche, obs. form of WITCH.

Wicclifize: see WYCLIFFIZE.

wice, obs. Sc. f. VICE *sb.*¹ and ⁴; obs. f. WISE *sb.*

wich, wych (wɪtʃ, locally waɪtʃ). *local.* Also 7 wietch. [app. a differentiated variant of WICK *sb.*²; cf. *ditch* and *dike* (OE. *dīc*), *lich* and *lyke* (OE. *līc*). The orig. meaning may have been the group of buildings connected with a salt-pit. The chief names of salt-making towns in which the word occurs are *Droitwich* (formerly *Wich*) in Worcestershire, *Middlewich*, *Nantwich*, and *Northwich* in Cheshire.] A salt-works, salt-pit, or brine-spring, in the salt-manufacturing district of Cheshire and neighbouring parts; *pl.* the salt-making towns of these parts.

716–17 in Birch *Cartul. Sax.* I. 203 Aliquam agelli partem in qua sal confici solet ad meridianam plagam fluminis quod dicunt Saluuerpe, in loco qui dicitur Lootwic et Coolbeorg. **1086** *Domesday Bk.*, *Cheshire* 268 In eodem Mildestvic Hvndredo erat tercium Wich quod uocatur Norvvich,.. Ipsæ leges & consuetudines erant ibi quæ erant in alijs Wiches... Cætera omnia in his Wichis sunt similia. **11..** (spurious charter) in Birch *Cartul. Sax.* I. 203 Wich... Unam portionem mansionis in Wico emptorio salis quem nos Saltwich vocamus. *c* **1250** MATTH. PARIS *Chron. Majora* an. 1245 (Rolls) IV. 486 Rex insuper puteos fecerat salinarum de Witz obturari et everti. **1601** HOLLAND *Pliny* xxxi. vii. II. 415 In Chaonia there be certaine springs of saltish water, which the people of that country doe boile, and when it is cooled againe, it turneth into salt. *margin*, This is the order of salt with us in our Wiches here in England. **1610** —— *Camden's Brit.* I. 607 These are verie famous Salt-wiches [Camden *salinæ*],.. where brine or salt water is drawne out of pittes. *Ibid.* 608 The Britans call it *Hellath wen*, that is, The white Wich or Salt pitte. **1612** DRAYTON *Poly-olb.* iii. 265 But that which vext her most, was, that..th' Wyches for their Salts such state on them should take. **1613** A. STANDISH *New Direct.* 15 In Cheshire neere vnto the Wietches (where Salt is made..). **1682** J. COLLINS *Salt & Fish.* 2 At Namptwich they have one Pit within the Town, and two without,..the Bryne being..of a weaker kind than those of the other Wyches. **1810** LYSONS *Magna Brit.* II. 699. **1860** W. WHITE *All round Wrekin* 88 There lies the region of salt-mines, and of the wyches or brine springs which began to flow long before Henry III stopped the works at Nantwich.

b. *Comb.*: **wich-(wych-)house**, a building in which brine is evaporated for making salt; **wich-man**, a man employed in salt-making; **wich-waller**, a salt-boiler; †**wich-work** = *wich-house*.

1534 (12 May) *Ancient Deeds* C. 7583 (P.R.O.) Rauff Maynwaryng of Mydlewiche sendeth gretyng..that where Richard Leftwiche the younger and Margret his wyff have giffen..all their meses *wiche houses landes..to Richard Maynwaryng [etc.]. **1559** *Lanc. Wills* (Chetham Soc. 1861) 125 My hole estate of halffe a wyche house in the Northewyche wᵗⁱⁿ the countye of Chester. **1610** HOLLAND *Camden's Brit.* I. 608 Troughes..by which it [*sc.* brine] is carried into the wichhouses. **1756** C. LUCAS *Ess. Waters* II. 35 The houses in which the salt works are carried on are called also wich-houses. **1818** J. W. PLATT *Hist. Nantwich* 78 Earl Edwin had a wych-house upon his estate at Aughton. **1688** HOLME *Armoury* III. 161/2 A Salter, or Salt-Man, or *Wich-Man. **1670** RAY *Prov.* 208 To scold like a *wych-waller. **1298** in Rogers *Agric. & Prices* (1866) I. xix. 456 [The saltern in which the brine was evaporated is called a] *wychwerke.

wich, wiche, obs. ff. WHICH, WITCH.

wichauf, wich(e)safe, -saif, -sauf, obs. ff. VOUCHSAFE.

wichert (ˈwɪtʃət). *dial.* Also **whitchet, witchert**, etc. [Orig. uncertain; perh. repr. a local pronunc. of 'white earth'.] A variety of chalk marl subsoil found near the Chilterns in Buckinghamshire, which is mixed with chopped straw and used locally for walling.

1912 *R. Comm. Hist. Monuments*: *Buckinghamshire, South* 342 *Wichert* or *Whitchet* (white earth).—A local term for a kind of white marl or mud found at Haddenham, Dinton, and in the district, and used unburnt mixed with chopped straw for walling. **1916** C. F. INNOCENT *Devel. Eng. Building Construction* x. 136 In Buckinghamshire, where the walls were built of a kind of white clay called 'witchit', about eighteen inches below the surface of the ground. **1929** H. HARMAN *Bucks. Dial.* 165 The wichert (or whitchet), which is a kind of white marl found locally, is laid in heaps beside the line of the intended wall and well soaked with water. When the stonework is in position, the wichert is turned and short straw is trodden into it; the purpose of this is merely to keep it fairly compact whilst it is wet. **1942** W. ROSE *Good Neighbours* iv. 42 He also made the curious three-pronged forks, with flat tines, with which the masoners built the wichert walls of the village. **1951** P. OYLER *Feeding Ourselves* iii. 32 Hand-made bricks and tiles, stone and thatch, cob or wichert cannot be out of place in the scenery from which they come. **1958** *Records of Buckinghamshire* XVI. III. 136 It is considered most probable that the main walls were built of the local chalk mud charged with chopped straw, known in these parts as *witchert*. **1977** *Oxford Times* (S.E. ed.) 4 Mar. 1 The cottage was built of Witchert, a sophisticated sort of mud, of which there are many examples in Haddenham. The material crumbles when demolished.

wichetty, var. WITCHETTY.

Wichita (ˈwɪtʃətɔː). Also 9 Wichataw. [f. the name of *Wichita*, in Kansas.] **a.** (A member of) a Caddoan Indian people of southern central N. America (now Oklahoma, formerly also Kansas and Texas). **b.** Their language. Also *attrib.*

1841 H. S. FOOTE *Texas & Texans* I. xiv. 299 There are several other remnants of tribes in Texas..the *Wichataws*, who live far North, on the Brassos. **1883** W. F. CODY in B. A. Botkin *Treas. Amer. Folklore* (1944) Music. Enter a group of Wichita Indians. **1960** R. W. MARKS *Dymaxion World of B. Fuller* 37/1 When the first Wichita house finally was opened to the public, many were struck by its spaciousness and air of luxury. **1965** *Language* XLI. 84 The consonantal opposition nasal/oral occurs in all the languages of the world except Wichita. **1978** *Ibid.* LIV. 503 Of the three American Indian linguistic groupings discussed here, those of the Cadoan family, spoken in the Southern Plains, are perhaps the least described; of the surviving languages —Caddo, Wichita, and Pawnee—none is being learned by children.

wicht, obs. Sc. form of WIGHT.

wichuraiana (wɪˌtʃʊraɪˈɑːnə). [A specific epithet of *Rosa wichuraiana* (F. Crépin 1886, in *Bull. Soc. Bot. Belgique* XXV. 189), f. the name of Max Ernst *Wichura* (1817–66), German botanist + -IANA.] A climbing, almost evergreen, rose belonging to the species *Rosa wichuraiana*, which is native to eastern Asia and bears white flowers, or one of many cultivars developed from it, usually distinguished by small glossy leaves and flowers in clusters. Freq. *attrib.*

1907 [see PENZANCE]. **1913** [see DOROTHY PERKINS]. **1923** *Daily Mail* 10 Mar. 15 The top growth of roses, excepting ..wichuraianas, should be severely pruned in the first season. **1945** G. M. TAYLOR *Roses* xv. 76 Some of the Wichuraianas..will cover a wall very quickly. **1960** *News Chrons.* 6 Aug. 6/1 The wichuraiana ramblers are a case in point. **1962** R. PAGE *Education of Gardener* vi. 199 Among rambler roses I like to use the wichuraiana varieties.

wick (wɪk), *sb.*¹ Forms: α. 1 weoce, 3 wueke, 4–6 **weke, weyke, wyke**, 5–7 **wike, weeke**, (–9 *dial.*) **week**, 6 **weyk**, (**weack**), 6–7 **weik, wieke**, (6, 8 **weak**), 7 **wiek, wieck**. β. 4–7 **wicke**, 5 **wyk**, 6 **wycke**, 7– **wick**. [OE. *wéoce* wk. fem., also *wéoc* str. fem. (in *candelwéoc*), corresp. to MDu. *wiecke* (Du. *wiek*), MLG. *wêke*, *weike* (LG. *weke*) lint (whence Sw. *veke*, Da. *væge*, Norw. dial. *veik*), OHG. *wioh* str. m. or n. 'lucubrum' (MHG., G. *wieche* wick-yarn), MG. *wieke*, *wîke*, *wicke* (G. *wieke* lint, dial. *wicke*). For the phonology cf. SICK *a.*

No certain cognates are known. It has been suggested that the base is an Indo-Eur. *weg-*, represented by OIr. *figim* to weave, spin, L. *vēlum* VEIL, Skr. *vâgurâ*. There is no evidence for the alleged OE. *wice*.]

1. a. The bundle of fibre, now usually loosely twisted or woven cotton (formerly rushes, tow, flax, etc.) in a lamp, candle, or taper (formerly also in a torch), immersed or inclosed except at one end in the oil or grease, which it absorbs and draws up on being kindled at the free end, so as to maintain the flame.

α. c **1000** in *Techmer's Internat. Zeitschrift* (1885) II. 126 Wæt mid þinum scytefingre on midden, swylce þu weocan settan wylle. c **1200** *Trin. Coll. Hom.* 47 On ure helendes lichame wiðuten sene, þe holie saule wiðinne unsene, and te michele wisdom on eiðer: Alse wex on þe candele sene, þe wueke wiðinnen unsene, and þe fur on boðe. **1377** LANGL. *P. Pl.* B. XVII. 204 As wex and a weke were twyned togideres. **1393** *Ibid.* C. xx. 178 Of a torche þe blase beo blowen out ȝut brenneþ þe weke. c **1440** *Promp. Parv.* 520/2 Weyke, of a candel, *lichinius.* c **1450** LYDG. *Life Our Lady* lxxxii. (1484) M ij b, The waxe bytokeneth his manhede, The weke [*MS. Ashm.* 39 wyke] his sowle, the fyre his godhede. c **1485** *Digby Myst.* I. 490 In yone tapir therbe thing iij[e], wax, week and light. **1513** *State Papers Hen. VIII* No. 4101 (P.R.O.) Item in torche weke and taper weke iiij[xx] v li. **1570** LEVINS *Manip.* 206/45 Y[e] Weak of a candle, *lichnus.* **1590** SPENSER *F.Q.* II. x. 30 When the oyle is spent, The light goes out, and weeke is throwne away. **1604** E. G[RIMSTONE] tr. *D'Acosta's Hist. Indies* II. vii. 99 In candles of tallow or waxe, if the wike be great, it melts the tallow or the waxe. **1626** BACON *Sylva* §370 Triall was..made of seuerall Wiekes; As of Ordinary Cotton; Sowing Thred. a **1691** BOYLE *Hist. Air* (1692) 247 The Smoak that issues out of the Weik of a Candle newly blown out. **1707** N. BLUNDELL *Diary* (1895) 54 Mr. Plumb tryed his Lamp with two Weaks. a **1728** WOODWARD *Nat. Hist. Fossils* (1729) I. I. 76 A small Piece of [English talc].. serves very well for a Wiek to a Lamp. **1875** *Lanc. Gloss.*, *Week*..the wick of a candle or lamp.

β. **1393** LANGL. *P. Pl.* C. xx. 205 As þe wicke and þe warme fuyr wol make a fayr flamme. c **1450** *Alphita* (Anecd. Oxon.) 99 *Licinum*,..mecche uel wyk. **1555** EDEN *Decades* (Arb.) 230 The wycke or twyste of hempe. **1583** STUBBES *Anat. Abus.* II. (1882) 50 As for the wickes within them [*sc.* the candles], they are of hurds, rope ends, and such other good stuffe. **1784** COWPER *Task* III. 164 The little wick of life's poor shallow lamp. **1815** J. SMITH *Panorama Sci. & Art* II. 316 The candle or lamp used with the blowpipe should have a thick wick, which should be snuffed clean. **1840** THACKERAY *Catherine* iii, The candles were burning dim, with great long wicks. **1903** THURSTON *Circle* I. xv, She.. raised the wick of the lamp.

b. Collectively, without article, as the name of a substance: = WICKING.

1391 *Earl Derby's Exp.* (Camden) 67 Clerico speciarie.. pro wyke per ipsum empto..pro torches faciendis..xxxj s. **1404** *Durham Acc. Rolls* (Surtees) 395, vj libri de weke pro torgis. **1529** *Burgh Rec. Edin.* (1871) 6 That thai mak thair candill..of gud and sufficient stuff baith weyk and tallone. **1571** *S'hampton Crt. Leet Rec.* (1905) 76 The Channdel[rs].. doo mak their candels wth grat torch weack and yll tallowe. **1602** SHAKS. *Ham.* IV. vii. 116 (Qo. 2) There liues within the very flame of loue A kind of weeke or snufe that will abate it. **1883** *Century Mag.* Feb. 585/2 He carried too much wick for his candle.

c. Used as a tent or dressing in surgery. (Cf. G. *wieke*, etc.)

1658 A. FOX *Würtz' Surg.* I. iii. 9 Some..take grosse strong weeks, and thrust them to the bottom of the wounds. *Ibid.* vii. 27 Of the abuses which are committed with wicks, tents, lints, mullipuffs, &c. **1906** *Brit. Med. Jrnl.* 13 Jan. 72 A..glass drainage tube was placed in the pelvis, another in the right loin..and gauze wicks were placed in the tubes.

d. In fig. phr. ***to turn the wick up*** (or ***down***), to open (or close) the throttle of an engine; to accelerate (or decelerate). *colloq.*

1948 [see THROTTLE *sb.* 4b]. **1965** PRIESTLEY & WISDOM *Good Driving* iii. 28 The gas pedal can be likened to the wick of an oil lamp. Turn it up and you get more light... Indeed it is a simile much used by motor cyclists who talk of 'turning the wick up' as a more graphic and descriptive way of saying 'I accelerated'.

2. a. to ***get on*** (one's) ***wick***, to irritate or annoy (a person); to exasperate; to get on one's nerves (NERVE *sb.* 8e). *colloq.*

It is sometimes suggested that both this and the next sense derive from (Hampton) *Wick*, rhyming slang for PRICK *sb.* 17. See Partridge and WICK *sb.*[2] 2.

1945 *Penguin New Writing* XXVI. 56 Parades and bullshit get on his wick. **1958** K. AMIS *I like it Here* 32 But I wish he wouldn't think he'd got the right to knock the English. That's what really gets on my wick. **1961** 'B. WELLS' *Day Earth caught Fire* iv. 54 'Strewth, these licensing laws get on your wick, don't they,' they grumbled. **1977** K. BENTON *Red Hen Conspiracy* iii. 22 The way you talk about Pat gets on my wick. **1984** B. FRANCIS *AA Car Duffer's Guide* 6/2 Gets on my wick, she do.

b. *to dip* (one's) *wick*: of a man, to engage in sexual intercourse. *slang.*

1958 J. CAREW *Black Midas* vi. 96 'Come on!' Santos bellowed. 'If every time you dip your wick you going to fall in love, then God help you!' Belle jumped out of bed and pulled on her dress. **1969** D. NILAND *Dead Men Running* iv. 159 When you're starved for a woman dip your wick, and the starvation's gone. **1971** B. W. ALDISS *Soldier Erect* 111 Di asked, 'You don't feel like a bit of a bunk-up this evening, Stubby, by any chance?' 'A bit of what?' 'Dipping your wick, man!' **1981** R. BARNARD *Sheer Torture* xiii. 137 None of your barmaids or local peasant wenches for Pete. He's very calculating where he dips his wick.

3. *attrib.* and *Comb.*, as ***wick-holder***, ***-screw***, ***-spout***, ***-trimmer***, ***-yarn***.

1498 in *Compotus Rolls Obedientiaries St. Swithun's Winch.* (1892) 388 In xij lb. Wekeyorne,..iij s. **1756** *W. Owen's Bk. Fairs* (1788) 54 Bridgenorth..horned cattle, horses, sheep, hops, cheese, wick-yarn. **1840** *Civil Eng. & Arch. Jrnl.* III. 175/2 A sudden blaze as if the wick-screw had been raised a turn. c **1865** J. WYLDE in *Circ. Sci.* I. 304/1 A cap..fits over the wick-holder. **1875** KNIGHT *Dict. Mech.*, *Wick-trimmer*, a shears for trimming wicks. **1911** J. WARD *Roman Era in Brit.* xii. 210 The typical Roman lamp..has.. a covered wick-spout or nozzle (*nasus*, *rostrum*).

wick (wɪk), *sb.*[2] Now only *local.* Forms: 1–3 **wic**, 3–4, 7 **wike**, 4 **wik**, 4–5 **wyk**, 4–5, 8–9 **wyke**, 6–7 **wicke**, 7 **week**, 7– **wick**. [OE. *wíc* m., f. = OFris. *wîk* f., OS. *wîc* m. dwelling-place, house, MLG. *wîk* f., n. town, place, MDu. *wijc* m. district, (Du. *wijk* f. quarter, district, ward, WFris. *wyk*), OHG. *wîch* str. m. dwelling-place, town, MHG. *wîch* in *wîkbilethe* civic rights, *wichbilde* (G. *weichbild*) precinct and jurisdiction of a town, *wîchgrave* recorder; app. ad. L. *vīcus* row of houses, quarter of a city, street, village (cognate with Gr. οἶκος house, etc., Goth. *weihs* village).]

†**1.** An abode, dwelling, dwelling-place (in general). *Obs.*

Beowulf 1125 Ƀewiton him ða wiȝend wica neosian. c **900** tr. *Bæda's Hist.* IV. iii, Þa ȝelomp sume dæȝe, þæt he wæs in þæm forespрecenan wicum mid ane breðer wuniende, þæs noma wæs Owine. a **1000** *Cædmon's Gen.* 1812 Ðær ræsbora þraȝe siððan wicum wunode & wilna breac. c **1200** ORMIN 8512 Josæp..bærenn ure Laferrd Crist..Fra land to land, fra tun to tun, Fra wic to wic i tune. c **1205** LAY. 7786 In to France he wende & sette his wike. a **1250** *Owl & Night.* 604 Ich can loki monne wike & mine wike beoþ wel gode. a **1300** *Cursor M.* 2090 Asie to sem, to cham affrik, To Iaphet europ, þat wil-ful wike. c **1300** *Harrow. Hell* 177 Louerd god, ȝef vs leue,..To faren of þis loþe wyke To þe blisse of heueneryke.

2. A town, village, or hamlet. *Obs.* or *dial.* (Survives as an element of place-names in both forms, *-wich* and *-wick*, the local distribution of which presents difficulties.)

971 *Blickl. Hom.* 77 He cwæþ: 'Gaþ on þa wic þe beforan inc stondeð.' c **1000** *Ags. Gosp.* Mark viii. 23 & þa æthran he þæs blindan hand & lædde hine butan þa wic. c **1205** LAY. 31960 His biweddede wif weore on þere ilke wike. a **1300** *Cursor M.* 7917 Þar was wonand wit-in a wike, Tua men a pouer and a rike. c **1350** in *Rel. Ant.* II. 93 The toun Off Cauntyrbery, that noble wyke.

1600 HOLLAND *Livy* xxxiv. xxii. 866 The rest abandoned the warre, and slipt..into their owne wickes and villages. [**1885** E. LAW *Hampton Crt. Pal.* 12 *note*, As a popular equivalent for the word village, the expressions 'going to the Wick' [*i.e.* Hampton Wick], and 'living at the Wick', being constantly heard among the older inhabitants.]

3. A farm; *spec.* a dairy farm. Now *local.*

1086 *Domesday Bk.*, *Berks.* 58b, Wica de .x. pensis caseorum ualentes .xxxii. sol. & .IIII. den. **1467–8** *Rolls of Parlt.* V. 585/1 A dayery, otherwise called a Wyk, called Dangebrigge. **1594** [see DAIRY *sb.* 3]. **1598** STOW *Surv.* 171 In diuers countries, Dayrie houses or cottages, wherein they make butter and cheese, are vsually called Wickes. **1607** CAMDEN *Brit.* 318 Caseos ouillos conficere in casearijs illis tuguriolis quæ ibi [i.e. in Essex] *Wiches* [sic] vocant, vidimus. **1628** COKE *On Litt.* 5 A fearme in the North parts is called a Tacke, in Lancashire a Fermeholt, in Essex a Wike. **1641** *Surv. Plesheybury Manor, Essex* fol. a[v] (MS.) Berwick *quasi* Berrywick, for it is supposed that auntiently it was a dairy wick or ferme to High Ester Bury. **1701** KENNETT *Cowel's Interpr.*, *Wica*, a Country House or Farm, of which many a one is now call'd the Wike, and the Wick. a **1825** FORBY *Voc. E. Anglia*, *Wick*... A few instances may be produced in which it means a farm. There is one at a short distance from the town of Watton, commonly called Watton-wick, but by the inhabitants, simply the *Wick.* **1879** JEFFERIES *Wild Life in S. Co.* 126 Wick Farm—almost every village has its outlying wick—stands alone in the fields.

†**4.** An enclosed piece of ground, a close. *local.*

1301 *Rolls of Parlt.* I. 259/2 Apud Lex[eden] in Wyka que vocatur Arnodynes Wyk. ? a **1461** *Stonor Papers* (Camden) I. 55 Ȝe have yn Bysschopyston the iij part of a close callyd Bondmannys Wyke, and yn on othere callyd Hanketes Wyke. **1631** *Terrier of Masworth Rectory* (MS.) A close of pasture ground called y[e] Parsonidge Wick. **1635** *Survey of Masworth Parish* (MS.) The close called Three Wicks. **1680** *Terrier of Masworth Vicarage* (MS.) One other close or wick ..called Blockwicks..a wick called Pound Wick. **1811** *Masworth Parish Enclosure Award* (MS.) An old enclosure called Meadow Wick.

†**5.** *Comb.*: **wick-master**, ? a mayor or burgomaster; **wic-reeve**, modernization of OE. *wícȝerefa*, a town-reeve.

1587 FLEMING *Contn. Holinshed* III. 1337/2 Behind them went the bodie of the citie, that is to wit, the *wickemasters, the wardens, the ancient magistrate, the masters of the wardes, the boroughmasters [etc.]. **1853** J. STEVENSON *Ch. Hist. Eng.* I. 233 Beornulf, *wic-reeve of Winchester.

wick, wike, *sb.*[3] Now only *dial.* Forms: 4–5, 7 **wyke**, 6, 8–9 **wike**, 7 **weeke**, 8– **week**, 9 **wick**, *Sc.* **weik**. [a. ON. *vik*, as in *munnvik* (Da. *mundvig*) corner of the mouth; f. *wĭk-* to bend (cf. WEEK *sb.*, WICK *sb.*[4], WOKE).]

1. A corner of the mouth or eye.

13.. *Gaw. & Gr. Knt.* 1572 Þe froþe femed at his mouth vnfayre bi þe wykez. **13..** *E.E. Allit. P.* B. 1690 Faxe fyltered, & felt flosed hym vmbe, þat schad fro his schulderes to his schyre wykes. **1483** *Cath. Angl.* 417/2 A Wyke of ye eghe.., *hirquus.* **1570** LEVINS *Manip.* 122/24 Y[e] Wike of the eye, *hirquus.* **1607** MARKHAM *Cavel.* I. 82 To make some expert Horse farrier, to slit vp the weekes of your Horses mouth, equallie on both sides..with a sharpe raysor. **1641** BEST *Farm. Bks.* (Surtees) 14 A greate parte of theire meat, whiles that they are chewinge of it, workes forth of the wykes of their mouthe. **1709** M. BRUCE *Soul-Confirm.* 18 (Jam.) We will let them ken that we will hing by the wicks of the mouth for the least point of truth. **1721** W. GIBSON *Dieting Horses* viii. (1726) 128 If the Bit be too long or too short, it will injure the Horse's Mouth, and cut his Weeks. c **1730** RAMSAY *Fables* xviii. 14 To weed out ilka sable hair.. Frae crown of head to weeks of mouth. **1787** GROSE *Prov. Gloss.*, *Wikes* or *Wikers* (of the mouth), corners of the mouth. a **1835** HOGG *Tales, Hunt of Eildon* (1837) III. 14 [He] now and then cast a sly look-out at the wick of his eye.

2. In full *wick-tooth*: see quot. 1726.

1726 A. MONRO *Anat. Bones* 171 The Two inferior [*Canini*] are named angular or Wike-teeth, because they support the Angles of the Mouth. **1759** H. WALPOLE *Let. to Earl of Strafford* 13 Sept., This noble summer is not yet over with us—it seems to have cut a colt's week [cf. COLT *sb.* 8b].

Hence **wicking** (**wyking**), corner of the mouth.

1604 *Mem.* in *N. & Q.* 3rd Ser. III. 445/2 Her eyes stod in the wykinges of her mouth. **1886** *S.-W. Linc. Gloss.*, *Weekin*, s., the corner of the mouth.

wick, *sb.*[4] *Sc.* and *dial.* Forms: 7 **weeke**, 8 **wike**, 9 **wick**, **wik**, **wyck**, **wyke**. [a. ON. *vík* fem. (occurring in place-names, but not usually distinguishable in form from WICK *sb.*[2]), whence app. also MLG. *wîk* (LG. *wiek*, *wicke*), MDu. *wijck*, Fris. *wik* bay; f. OTeut. *wĭk-* to bend, as if = a bend.] A creek, inlet, or small bay.

[**1610** CAMDEN *Brit.* I. 326 From hence the Tamis goeth to Green-wich, that is, the Green Creeke, for the creeke of a river in the old English tongue was called *Wic*, a place in times past famous for the Danish Fleet that lay there often at Rode.] **1664–5** *Patent Roll 16 Chas. II*, Pt. 8 (MS.) (Charter of the Royal Fishing Company) The greate Plentie of Fish wherewith the Seas Estuaries or Inletts Creekes Armes of the Sea Publick Rivers Weekes and Lakes of Our Dominions..doe abound. **1753** *Scots Mag.* Aug. 417/1 We have as many [herrings] come into our wike as would fill 300 barrels. **1821** SCOTT *Pirate* xix, By beach and by cave,—.. By air and by wick. **1846** BROCKETT *N.C. Gloss.* (ed. 3), *Wik*, *Wyck*, or *Wyke*, a crook or corner, as in a river or the sea shore. **1878** R. DICK *Geol. & Bot.* viii. 85 Between this and Rough Head is a wick or bay.

wick, *sb.*[5] *Sc. Curling* and *Bowls.* [f. WICK *v.*[2]]

1. An act of wicking: see WICK *v.*[2], and cf. INWICK *sb.*

1823 JAS. KENNEDY *Poems* 29 (E.D.D.). **1842** *Chambers's Inform. People* No. 84. 539 A player stepping aside to take a brittle (or wick), or other shot, shall forfeit his stone for that end.

2. = PORT *sb.*[3] 3b.

1824 [see INWICK *v.*].

wick, *sb.*[6] ? *dial.* [Related to WICKER.] Wicker; a wicker basket or creel.

1802 C. JAMES *Milit. Dict.* s.v. *Calote*, Calotes are usually made of iron, wick, or dressed leather. **1821** CLARE *Vill. Minstrel* II. 102 A captive fish still fills the anxious eyes, And willow-wicks lie ready for the prize.

wick, *a.*[1] *Obs.* exc. *dial.* Forms: [2 **wicci**], 3–5 **wicke**, **wikke**, **wik**, 4 **wic**, **wyc**, 4–5 **wycke**, **wykke**, **wyk**, 5 **wyke**, (**wekke**), 4–5, 8–9 *dial.* **wick**. [orig. *wicke*, *wikke*, app. adj. use of OE. *wicca* wizard (of which the fem. is *wicce* WITCH); but perhaps an alteration of early ME. *wicci* (?:—**wicciȝ*, f. *wicca*), of which the following is the only known instance:—

1154 *O.E. Chron.* (Laud MS.) an. 1140 Þe king him sithen nam in Hamtun þurhc wicci ræd.]

1. = WICKED *a.*[1] 1 a, b.

c **1200** ORMIN 6185 Ȝiff þatt iss þatt ȝho iss all wittlæs, & wac, & wicke. c **1220** *Bestiary* 593 He speken god-cunhede, and wikke is here dede. c **1290** *S. Eng. Leg.* I. 203/119 Þe feondes luþere and wicke. c **1325** *Metr. Hom.* 28 Thair wike dedes. *Ibid.* 51 Sin and wik dedis. **13..** *Cursor M.* 2777 (Gött.) Þe foule feluns wid wic entent. c **1386** CHAUCER *Pars. T.* ¶ 355 (Egerton 2726), The fende seith I woll chace and pursue man by wyk suggestion. c **1460** *Towneley Myst.* xxi. 262 Was ther neuer man so wyk bot he myght amende. a **1500** *Hist. K. Boccus & Sydracke* (? 1510) Ij, A..sowle synful and wycke Is also blacke as eny pycke.

1901 SUTCLIFFE *Mistr. Barbara Cunliffe* i, She's just her maister ower again—same wick' look o' th' devil about her.

2. a. = WICKED *a.*[1] 2 a, b, c.

a **1225** *Ancr. R.* 104 (MS. T.) Of swati hattre oðer of wikke air. a **1300** *Cursor M.* 27877 O glotori and o drunkenhede Fele wick branches se we sprede. **1340–70** *Alex. & Dind.* 537 Tricerberus þe helle-hound..Boþe wakrong & wikke. a **1350** *S. Stephen* 421 in Horstm. *Altengl. Leg.* (1881) 33 Þai raysed þe wynd with weders wik. c **1374** CHAUCER *Troylus* I. 946 For þilke ground þat bereth þe wedys wykke Bereth eke þese holsome herbes. c **1374** —— *Boeth.* III. met. i. (1868) 64 Hony is þe more swete yif mouþes han firste tastid sauoures þat ben wikke. c **1380** *Sir Ferumb.* 4721 In helle habbe he þynes wycke. c **1385** CHAUCER *L.G.W.* 1242 *Dido* (Gg. 4. 27) The wikke fame a-ros..How Enias hath with the queen I-gon. c **1386** —— *Knt.'s T.* 229 Som wikke aspect or disposicioun Of Saturne. c **1400** *Laud Troy Bk.* 15306 That he be sclayn..That he no wyse passe quyk, For that were then to vs ful wik. *Ibid.* 15733 The fyght was sterne and wyk. c **1440** *Pallad. on Husb.* I. 973 Al the lond that thou hast goon aboute Fro cloudis wicke is saaf. a **1450** *Le Morte Arth.* 3365 Arthur of batayle neuyr blanne To dele woundys wykke and wyde. **1756** in *N. & Q.* 12th Ser. XI. 390/2 For the warding off of all things whatsoever from the dead—be they imps, wraithspells, wick things & the like ket.

†**b.** = WICKED *a.*[1] 2d; in quot. 1297, feeble, lacking in force. Also as the equivalent of a negative prefix = *un-*, *dis-* (e.g. *wiklose* = dispraise). *Obs.*

c **1200** ORMIN 16515 Jesu Crist wel unnderrstod all þeȝȝre wicke trowwþe. a **1225** *Ancr. R.* 358 Nis he a kang [*MS. T* wicke] knit þet secheð reste iðe uihte? c **1250** *Hymn* in *Trin. Coll. Hom.* App. 259 Wicke is here ure fare & ure wuniȝinge. **1297** R. GLOUC. (Rolls) 4228 Þe scolle [was so] hard & þikke, Þeruore, þei it ne come noȝt þoru, þe dunt nas noȝt wikke. c **1300** *Havelok* 2457 With poure mete, and feble drink, And with swiþe wikke cloþes. a **1340** HAMPOLE *Psalter* lxvii. 33 And swa it bifalles þat þai out close þaim fra þaire wiklose þat ere proued in syluere [L. *ut excludant eos, qui probati sunt argento*]. c **1398** CHAUCER *Fortune* 55 Wikke appetyt comth ay before sykenesse. c **1400** *Leg. Rood* (1871) 153 My wonynge is wel wykke. a **1500** *Hist. K. Boccus & Sydracke* (? 1510) Q ij b, As foly among wys-men is wyke Wysdome among folys is lyke.

†**c.** = WICKED *a.*[1] 2f. *Obs.*

c **1320** *Sir Tristr.* 775 Morgan is wick to slow. **1340–70** *Alex. & Dind.* 938 þanne wol he [*sc.* man]..wexe wilde of his wil & wikke to staunche.

†**3.** *absol.* or as *sb.* **a.** = WICKED *a.*[1] 4 a, b.

1297 R. GLOUC. (Rolls) 4650 So þat here nas no3t bileued bote heþene & wikke. *a* **1300** *Cursor M.* 2752 It semes not to be þi will For þe wik þe dughti spill. *Ibid.* 8631 'þou wik,' sco said, 'ai be þe waa, Qui has þou me bi-suiken sua?' *c* **1375** *Sc. Leg. Saints* ii. (*Paulus*) 177 Ger do þis wik away, And hed hym but mare delay. **1390** GOWER *Conf.* II. 325 O werste of alle wicke..lo, what thou hast do!

†**b.** In abstract sense: Evil, ill; wickedness.

c **1330** R. BRUNNE *Chron. Wace* (Rolls) 2432 Fro wycke vntil wors y nam. *c* **1374** CHAUCER *Troylus* III. 1074 Now is wykke I-turned vn-to worse. **1393** LANGL. *P. Pl.* C. XII. 272 No wyght Wot ho is worthi for wele oþer for wicke. **1447** BOKENHAM *Seyntys* (Roxb.) 85 Lyk smal infauntys wych kun no wykke.

†**4.** as *adv.* = WICKED *a.*[1] 5. *Obs.*

c **1330** R. BRUNNE *Chron. Wace* (Rolls) 10004 For..ageyns þer lord do so wyk. *c* **1380** *Sir Ferumb.* 882 þan laid he on þe Sarsyns wykke. **1393** LANGL. *P. Pl.* C. XVII. 177 At my lykynge chese, To do wel oþer wikke.

Hence †**wickdom**, †**wickhede**, †**wickness**, wickedness, iniquity; †**wickly** *adv.*, wickedly.

c **1440** *R. Glouc. Chron.* (Rolls) 2390 Princes oueral.. Speke him vuel & hated him vor is suikedom [*MS.* δ *wyckedome]. *Ibid.* 4822, 7278. *c* **1305** *11,000 Virg.* 34 in *E.E.P.* (1862) 66 To cheose þe ten maidenes wiþoute enie *wikhede. **1338** R. BRUNNE *Chron.* (1725) 124 Tresore *wikly wonnen. *a* **1300** *E.E. Psalter* v. 7 [6] þou hated al þat wirkes *wiknesse. **1382** WYCLIF *Prov.* v. 22 His wickenesses taken the vnpitouse.

wick, *a.*[2] Also **whick**. *North.* var. of QUICK *a.*

c **1760** W. HUTTON *Dialogue in Vulg. Lang. Storth & Arnside* (*c* 1900) 4 Was It whick, says Ta? **1790** [see QUICK *a.* 2]. **1848** MRS. GASKELL *Mary Barton* I. viii. 127 In th' Infirmary..there be good chaps there to a man, while he's wick, whate'er they may be about cutting him up at after. **1879–** Whick [see *Eng. Dial. Dict.*]. **1911** F. H. BURNETT *Secret Garden* xi. 105 'It's as wick as you or me,' he said;.. Martha had told her that 'wick' meant 'alive' or 'lively'. **1970** 'J. HERRIOT' *If only they could Talk* ix. 69 This 'oss is as wick as an eel. **1972** *Observer* 23 Apr. 23/4 Knott is, to use a Yorkshire expression, 'wick', but wick cricketers are rare these days. **1978** *Lancashire Life* Oct. 99/1 Granny Martha Mosscropp, approaching her century and as wick as a flea, had known in girlhood the enclosed life of Victorian Ramstwistle.

†**wick, wike**, *v.*[1] *Obs.* Forms: 1 **wician, wikian**, 3 **wikie(n**, 3–4 **wick**, 4 **wike, wyk.** [OE. *wician*, f. *wíc* WICK *sb.*[2]] *intr.* To take up one's abode; to encamp; to lodge, dwell.

c **897** ÆLFRED *Gregory's Past. C.* xli. 304 Ðu cans eal ðis westen, & wasð hwær we wician [L. *castra ponere*] magon. *a* **1000** *Colloq. Ælfric* in Wr.-Wülcker 99 Eallum us leofre ys wikian [L. *hospitari*] mid þe yrþlincge þonne mid þe. *c* **1205** LAY. 18102 Wikien 3e scullen here. *a* **1300** *Cursor M.* 25232 þat in þis wreche werld we wike.

b. *trans.* To pitch (a tent).

c **1330** R. BRUNNE *Chron. Wace* (Rolls) 12512 His pauilons, his penceles, þykke Nought fer fro þenne had þey don wyk.

Hence †**wicking** *vbl. sb.*[1], lodging, dwelling.

c **1205** LAY. 30453 He underfeng Cadwadlan:..and 3af him wickinge [*c* 1275 wikeninge] 3eond Irlonde. *Ibid.* 31861 He..nom þe wickinge mid Alaine þan kinge.

wick, *v.*[2] *Curling.* [Origin unknown.] **a.** *intr.* = INWICK *v.* **b.** *trans.* in phr. *to wick a bore*, 'to drive a stone dexterously through an opening between two guards' (Jam.). Cf. WICK *sb.*[5] Hence **wicking** *vbl. sb.*[2]

1786 [see GUARD *v.* 9]. **1811** *Acc. Game Curling* 9 It then becomes necessary..to strike another stone lying at the side, in an oblique direction. This is called wicking. *Ibid.* 10 Whether they have to draw, strike, wick, or enter a port, they will seldom deviate an inch from their aim. **1831** [see INRINGING]. **1898** [see INWICK *v.*].

wick, Sc. and north. f. QUICK *sb.*[2], *v.*[3]; obs. and dial. f. WEEK.

-wick, *suffix*, shortened form of WIKE (OE. *wíce*) office, function of an official, as in BAILIFFWICK, BAILIWICK, SHERIFFWICK. A secondary sense of 'jurisdiction of the official', passing into 'district over which the official's jurisdiction extends', is found with some words containing this suffix, the development of the latter sense being no doubt furthered by the sense 'district' of WICK *sb.*[2] An example of a compound in occasional or local use is †*warden-wick*:—

1499 *Pilton Churchw. Acc.* (Somerset Rec. Soc.) 67 Yn hys yer of ye wardeyn wyke.

In HERDWICK (first in *Domesday Book*), *-wick* appears to be WICK *sb.*[2]

wickaby, var. WICOPY.

wickar, obs. Sc. form of VICAR.

wicked ('wɪkɪd), *a.*[1] (*sb.*, *adv.*) Forms: 3– wicked; also 4–6 wyck-, wikk-, wykk-, (chiefly *Sc.* vick-, vikk-); 3–5 -ed(e, (4 -ud), 4–5 -id(e, -yd(e, 4–6 *Sc.* -it, -yt; (4 wikcud, wekked, wikket, 5 weckid, 5–6, 9 *Sc.* wicket, 6 *Sc.* weckit); 4 wikid(e, (-ud, vikede, *Sc.* vikit, -yt), 4–5 wiked, *Sc.* wikyt, wykit, 4–6 *Sc.* wikit, 5 wyked, -yd; 4 *Sc.* wekit, (vekyt), 4–5 wekyd, 4–6 weked, 5 -ede, -id, 6 *Sc.* weikit. [ME. (13th cent.) *wicked*, *wikked*, app. f. WICK *a.*, as *wretched* from *wrecche* WRETCH. The later *wiked* appears to be merely a graphic variant; forms with the lowered stem-vowel are of both types, *wekked*, *weked*.]

I. *adj.* **1.** Bad in moral character, disposition, or conduct; inclined or addicted to wilful wrong-doing; practising or disposed to practise evil; morally depraved. (A term of wide application, but always of strong reprobation, implying a high degree of evil quality.) **a.** of a person (or a community of persons).

the Wicked One, the Devil, Satan.

c **1275** LAY. 14983 Hercne ou 3eo tock an, þes wickede [*earlier text* swicfulle] wifman. **1340** *Ayenb.* 1 Ich bidde þe hit by my sseld auoreye þe wycked uend. **13..** *Cursor M.* 170 (Gött.) Iesu wan he longe hade fast Was temped wid þe wicked [*v.r.* wikket] gast. *c* **1375** *Sc. Leg. Saints* x. (*Mathou*) 73 Mare reuerens Is gewine..To vekyt men fore dred ..þane to gudmen for luf. *c* **1380** WYCLIF *Wks.* (1880) 76 Of siche vikede men seiþ god bi his prophete [etc.]. *c* **1380** *Sir Ferumb.* 2187 In al heþenis ys no Sarsyn wikkeder þan is he. *a* **1400–50** *Wars Alex.* 2425 3e at wickid ere within ay wickidly 3e thinke. *c* **1450** *Mirk's Festial* 222 All wekyd spyrytys schall for ferd fle away from þe. **1456** SIR G. HAYE *Law Arms* (S.T.S.) 32 Wikkit tyrane Emperouris. **1508** DUNBAR *Tua Mariit Wemen* 214 My weckit kyn, that me away cast. **1533** GAU *Richt Vay* (S.T.S.) 60 Thow vikkit seruand I forgaiff ye al thy det. **1535** COVERDALE *Gen.* xiii. 13 Y[e] men of Sodome were wicked, and synned exceadingly agaynst the Lorde. **1562** WIN3 ET *Cert. Tractatis* Wks. (S.T.S.) I. 5 Wes not the sacramentis..prophanit be ignorantis and wikit persones? **1567** *Satir. Poems Reform.* iv. 109 O wickit wemen, vennomus of nature! **1582** N. T. (Rhem.) *Matt.* xiii. 19 There cometh the wicked one, and catcheth away that which was sowen in his hart. —— 1 John ii. 13 You haue ouercome the wicked one. **1610** SHAKS. *Temp.* v. i. 130 You (most wicked Sir) whom to call brother Would euen infect my mouth. **1670** MILTON *Hist. Eng.* III. Wks. 1851 V. 130 Looking on the poor Christian with.. Contempt; but fawning on the wickedest rich men. **1696** WHISTON *The. Earth* III. iv. 207 This Deluge..was a signal Instance of the Divine Vengeance on a Wicked World. **1727** DE FOE *Syst. Magic* I. ii. 58 'Tis very strange Men should be so fond of being thought wickeder than they are. **1732** BERKELEY *Alciphr.* v. §7 Vice increases, and men grow daily more and more wicked. **1818** SCOTT *Hrt. Midl.* xv, 'Then you are the wicked cause of my sister's ruin?' said Jeanie, with a natural touch of indignation. **1820** COLERIDGE in *Lit. Rem.* (1838) III. 399 Bunyan was never, in our received sense of the word, wicked. He was chaste, sober, honest; but he was a bitter blackguard..and was fond of a row. **1873** LELAND *Egypt. Sketch-Bk.* 155 However wicked a man may be, he is sure to find a wickeder.

b. of action, speech, thought, or other personal attribute; also *transf.* of a thing connected in some way with such action, etc.

a **1300** *Cursor M.* 1227 þai him warryd wit wickud dedis. *Ibid.* 12991 Na langer Mai i nu þi wicked wordes ber. **13..** *Northern Passion* (A) 506 [Satan] wyl the dryfe in wekyd þoughte. **1362** LANGL. *P. Pl.* A. v. 217 þenne was he a-schomed,..And gon..gret deol to make For his wikkede lyf þat he I-liued hedde. *c* **1375** *Sc. Leg. Saints* i. (*Petrus*) 474 Throw his wekit sorcery. *Ibid.* viii. (*Philepus*) 66 Wikit heresy. *c* **1380** WYCLIF *Wks.* (1880) 37 Wickid lawis & wrong execucions of hem. *c* **1400** *Rom. Rose* 7424 They to Wicked Tonge comen That at his gate was syttyng. **1535** COVERDALE *Ezek.* viii. 9 What wicked abhominacions that they do. **1539** *Bible* (Great) 2 Chron. vii. 14 Yf they..do humble them selues..and turne from their wycked wayes. **1567** *Satir. Poems Reform.* iii. 176 Doggis could hir wickit bainis gnaw. **1602** SHAKS. *Ham.* III. iii. 59 Offences gilded hand may shoue by Iustice, And oft 'tis seene, the wicked prize it selfe Buyes out the Law. **1667** MILTON *P.L.* v. 890 Yet not for thy advise or threats I fly These wicked Tents devoted. **1727** DE FOE *Syst. Magic* I. ii. 48 All the wicked things, which have ..given a black Character to the very Name of a Magician; for under the shelter of Religion, the worst and most Diabolical things were practis'd. **1848** THACKERAY *Van. Fair* viii, 'Yes, hang it' (said Sir Pitt, only, he used, dear, a much wickeder word). **1878** H. STEVENS *Bibles Caxton Exhib.* 114 In 1855 Mr. Henry Stevens exhibited..a..copy of this long-lost..Bible [of 1631], and..nick-named it 'The Wicked Bible,' from the fact that the negative had been left out of the Seventh Commandment by a typographical error. **1905** R. BAGOT *Passport* iii. 23 The mysterious old professor ..who wrote wicked books.

c. Designating a stock evil character in a fairy-tale, as ***Wicked Fairy***, ***Stepmother***, ***Uncle***, etc. Freq. *transf.*

1897 KIPLING *Stalky & Co.* (1899) 39 He owned a soft, slow smile which well suited the part of the Wicked Uncle. **1906** *Sleeping Beauty* ('Tales for Little People' ed.) 8/2 'That looks like the wicked fairy, I'm sure,' said his majesty to himself. **1946** A. HUXLEY *Let.* 26 May (1969) 544 That blessing and curse of cleverness, with which the Fairy Godmother, who is also the Wicked Fairy, endowed me. **1978** M. BABSON *Tightrope for Three* xv. 78 He could not see Lillian in the classic 'wicked stepmother' situation. **1982** 'J. MELVILLE' *Painted Castle* i. 21 If you left Tad out of consideration, uncomfortable things were apt to happen. He had a touch of the Wicked Fairy about him.

2. Bad, in various senses (not always clearly distinguishable). Frequent in ME. use; later chiefly *dial.*, or in colloq. use as a conscious metaphor (now often jocular) from sense 1, and implying 'very or excessively bad', 'horrid', 'beastly'. **a.** In reference to character or action: Cruel, severe, fierce. Of animals: Savage, vicious.

13.. *Cursor M.* 5571 (Gött.) Quat he was wicked and wode Again þat folk sua mild of mode! **1375** *Creation* 980 in Horstm. *Altengl. Leg.* (1878) 136 Who so were..venympd wiþ eny wikked beste. ?*a* **1400** *Morte Arth.* 3232 Woluez, and whilde swynne, and wykkyde bestez. **1513** DOUGLAS *Æneis* I. x. 23 Quhat wise thi brothir Eneas..Is blawin and warpit euery coist abowt, Of wickit Juno throw the cruell invy [L. *odiis Iunonis acerbæ*]. **1607** TOPSELL *Four-f. Beasts* 308 As they [*sc.* horses] are wilde and fierce, so are they wicked and harmefull. **1725** RAMSAY *Gentle Sheph.* I. ii, If canker'd Madge, our aunt, Come up the burn, she'll gie 's a wicked rant. **1819** W. TENNANT *Papistry Storm'd* (1827) 7 Sae wud and wicket was their wraith [= wrath] Gainst Papish trash and idol-graith. **1829** HOGG *Sheph. Cal.* i. 8 It's hard to gar a wicked cout leave off flinging. **1895** MILLAIS *Breath from Veldt* (1899) 228 The Cape buffalo..has ample power to carry out his evil intentions when he means to be wicked.

b. Actually or potentially harmful, destructive, disastrous, or pernicious; baleful; when applied to air, odour, taste, etc. passing into: Offensive, foul.

1340 *Ayenb.* 124 Aye þe wykkede hetes..aye þe wyckede cheles..aye þe wyckede raynes. **1375** BARBOUR *Bruce* v. 12 To vyn the heling of thar hevede, That vikkit vyntir had thame revede. **1379** *Glouc. Cath. MS.* 19 No. I. i. iii. lf. 6 b, Wicked ayr or grevaunce, or cold takyng. *c* **1386** CHAUCER *Monk's T.* 626 Thurgh his body wikked wormes crepte. *c* **1391** —— *Astrol.* II. §4 A fortunat assendent clepen they whan þat no wykkid planete, as saturne or Mars,..is in þe hows of the assendent. **1398** TREVISA *Barth. De P.R.* IV. xi. (1495) f v b/2 Flyes shunne & voyde the wycked & horryble sauour therof. *c* **1400** MAUNDEV. xv. [xi]. (1919) 83 The perilous watres & wykkede mareys. *c* **1400** *Song Roland* 857 The wekid wedur lastid full long. *c* **1400** *Rom. Rose* 6511 If that wikkid deth hym haue I wole go with hym to his graue. *c* **1400** *Laud Troy Bk.* 5638 A wicked strok he him hit. *c* **1440** *Alphabet of Tales* 59 When þe wikkid fyre was in howsis nere-hand hur. *c* **1460** *Play Sacram.* 267 in *Non-Cycle Myst. Plays* 65 Alle wykkyd metys yt wylle degest. *c* **1480** HENRYSON *Test. Cress.* 412 Fell is thy Fortoun, wickit is thy weird. **1578** LYTE *Dodoens* II. lxxxix. 270 Fenell.. is good agaynst..the bitings of..wicked & venimous beastes. **1590** SPENSER *F.Q.* III. xi. 24 Faire Amoret must dwell in wicked chaines. **1600** BRETON *Pasquil's Foole's Cappe* Wks. (Grosart) I. 26/1 Who loues to feede vpon a Sallet dish, Among his Herbes some wicked weede may haue. **1610** SHAKS. *Temp.* I. ii. 321 As wicked dewe, as ere my mother brush'd With Rauens feather from vnwholesome Fen, Drop on you both. *a* **1627** MIDDLETON, etc. *Widow* IV. i, What's good, Sir, for a wicked tooth? **1639** J. TAYLOR (Water P.) *Part Summers Trav.* 41 It is too well known what a wicked number of followers he hath had. **1697** DRYDEN *Virg. Georg.* I. 103 Lest wicked Weeds the Corn shou'd over-run. **1725** MANDEVILLE *Fab. Bees* (ed. 4) I. 268 There comes a wicked Cold through that Door,..pray shut it. **1894** G. A. SMITH *Hist. Geog. Holy Land* 69 Tents may be carried away by wicked gusts. **1894** *Times* 27 Oct. 7/2 The 'Milo' was not a particularly 'wicked' engine with regard to giving off sparks. **1895** MILLAIS *Breath from Veldt* (1899) 133 It was a wicked country for fever. **1903** *Brit. Med. Jrnl.* 25 Apr. 967 A proprietary..form of chloride of ethyl and inferior to it on account of its wicked smell.

†**c.** Of wounds, disease: Severe; malignant.

c **1400** *Lanfranc's Cirurg.* 221 þo he was in dispeir of hir lijf, I was sent after & foond hir in wickide staat. *Ibid.* 338 To make a wickid enpostym maturatif. **14..** *Pol. Rel. & L. Poems* (1903) 245 A wycked wound hath me walled. **1576** BAKER *Gesner's Jewell of Health* 102 b, A water agaynst long continuing ulcers, yea how peryllous or wycked so euer they bee.

d. Of bad quality; poor, vile, 'sorry'; *occas.* perverted, abnormal; †in early use sometimes merely negative = *un-*, *dis-*.

13.. *Spec. S. Edm.* in *Hampole's Wks.* (1895) I. 225 þare-of commes tresones,..wykked reste [L. *inquietudo*], Malice and hardnes of herte. **1375** BARBOUR *Bruce* IX. 75 Ane of thame sall be vorth thre Of thame that vikkid chiftane has. *c* **1384** CHAUCER *H. Fame* III. 530 Ye shal haue..wikkyd loos and wors name. [Cf. quot. *a* 1340 s.v. WICK *a.* 2 b.] *a* **1425** tr. *Arderne's Treat. Fistula*, etc. 68 A Rial þing expert, þat.. amendeþ þe errour als wele of þe first digestion as of þe seconde, and doþ away wicked colour & vnnatural. *c* **1440** *Jacob's Well* 78 Of good sede he repyth wycked corn.

1663 *Lauderdale Papers* (Camden) I. 145 It will be hard to billet me for this wicked inke, for this place affords no better for fine paper. [*Cf. ante* p. 136 If you write not upon better paper and with better pens, wee will have yow billetted again.] *a* **1704** T. BROWN *Dial. Dead, Reas. Oaths* Wks. 1711 IV. 76 Retailer of wicked Bottle Ale and Brandy. **1764** H. WALPOLE *Let. to G. Montagu* 16 July, They talk wicked French.

†**e.** Difficult or dangerous; *esp.* of roads, passing into: In bad condition, out of repair (cf. d).

c **1350** *Will. Palerne* 3507 Ouer mires & muntaynes & oþer wicked wei3es. **1377** LANGL. *P. Pl.* B. VII. 27 þey shulde.. amende mesondieux þere-myde and myseyse folke helpe, And wikked wayes wi3tlich hem amende. *c* **1430** *Pilgr. Lyf Manhode* I. xci. (1869) 50 Bi ful wikkede pases þou shalt go, and wikkede herberwes þou shalt fynde. **1513** DOUGLAS *Æneis* V. iv. 86 Ontill a wickit place his schip did steir. *Ibid.* XII. xi. 160 Lyke till a wykkit hill of huge wecht [L. *mons improbus*]. **1533** BELLENDEN *Livy* IV. xviii. (S.T.S.) II. 115 þe battell was fochtin in ane wikkit place [L. *loco iniquo*]. *Ibid.* v. xxii. 222 Quhare ony strait or wikkit passage was. **1600** HAKLUYT *Voy.* III. 375 It is most wicked way,.. because they are inaccessible mountaines.

†**f.** Difficult *to* do something with. *Obs.*

a **1352** MINOT *Poems* (ed. Hall) xi. 8 þat woning was wikked for to win. *c* **1400** *Brut* I. 55 þat lande was strong and wikkede to wynne. *c* **1440** *Pallad. on Husb.* II. 155 This lond is ful wikked to be wrought, To hard in hete and ouer softe in wete.

3. a. In weakened or lighter sense (from 1), usually more or less jocular: Malicious; mischievous, sly.

1600 SHAKS. *A.Y.L.* IV. i. 216 That same wicked Bastard of Venus,..that blinde rascally boy. **1750** GRAY *Long Story* 44 A wicked Imp they call a Poet. **1781** JOHNSON 1 Apr. in *Boswell*, She [*sc.* Mrs. Thrale] is the first woman in the world, could she but restrain that wicked tongue of hers. **1809** MALKIN *Gil Blas* x. x. (Rtldg.) 369 Rubicund in the jowl, efflorescent on the nose, with a wicked eye at a bumper or a girl. **1829** LYTTON *Devereux* IV. v, You are the wickedest witty person I know. **1857** B. TAYLOR *Northern Trav.* xxx. (1858) 312 He had..wicked black eyes, and a mouth which laughed even when his face was at rest. **1868** LOUISA M. ALCOTT *Little Women* v, 'You are not afraid of anything, you know,' returned the boy, looking wicked.

b. Excellent, splendid; remarkable. *slang* (orig. *U.S.*).

1920 F. SCOTT FITZGERALD *This Side of Paradise* I. iii. 119 'Tell 'em to play 'Admiration'!' shouted Sloane... 'Phoebe and I are going to shake a wicked calf.' **1977** *Western Mail* (Cardiff) 5 Mar. 8/2 He could, as I say, sidestep off either foot, but what sped him on was a wicked acceleration over 20 yards.

II. *absol.* or as *sb.*

4. In sense 1 a: chiefly in biblical and religious use; often opp. to RIGHTEOUS 1 b. **a.** *absol.* in *pl.* sense: Wicked persons. (Usually, now always, with *the*.) Also in phrs. ***no peace for the wicked***: see PEACE *sb.* 16; ***no rest for the wicked***.

13.. *Cursor M.* 22999 (Edinb.) Þe wikid þat dred noht his aw, Her doun þai sal be demed law. **1393** LANGL. *P. Pl.* C. XXI. 430 Ther þat dom to þe deoþ dampneþ alle wyckede. *c* **1400** *Pety Job* 271 in *26 Pol. Poems* 129 Wycked and worse, good and bette, I wote well thow considerest alle. *a* **1425** *Cursor M.* 18279 (Trin.) Mony wickede & mis dedy Hastou lost. **1535** COVERDALE *Job* iii. 17 There must the wicked ceasse from their tyranny. —— *2 Macc.* i. 17 God be praysed, which hath delyuered the wicked in to oure hondes. **1539** *Bible* (Great) Gen. xviii. 23 Wylt thou also destroy the rightwes wyth the wicked? **1596** SHAKS. *1 Hen. IV*, II. iv. 517 If Sacke and Sugar bee a fault, Heauen helpe the Wicked. **1781** COWPER *Charity* 280 Prisons expect the wicked, and were built To bind the lawless. **1935** MARSH & JELLETT *Nursing-Home Murder* iv. 57 The throat specialist.. remarked: 'No rest for the wicked, nurse.' **1958** A. SILLITOE *Sat. Night & Sunday Morning* i. 20 'No rest for the wicked,' she laughed. **1965** T. CAPOTE *In Cold Blood* iv. 321, I wish you'd send me earplugs. Only they wouldn't allow me to have them. No rest for the wicked, I guess. **1979** M. BABSON *So soon done For* vii. 54 'I wish *I* could take some time and get away. But there's no rest for the weary.' 'Or the wicked.'

b. *absol.* or as *sb.* in *sing.* sense: A wicked person. *Obs.* or *rare arch.*: also in *nonce-use* with *pl.* in *-s*.

1484 CAXTON *Fables of Æsop* III. xii, Ne none wycked may hurte another wycked. **1526** TINDALE *Eph.* vi. 16 The shelde off Fayth, wherwith ye maye quenche all the fyrie dartes of the wicked [so **1611**: *R.V.* of the evil one]. —— *2 Thess.* ii. 8 That wicked..whom the lorde shall consume with the sprete off hys mouth. **1560** *Bible* (Geneva) Isa. lv. 7 Let the wicked forsake his waies, and the vnrighteous his owne imaginations. **1853** in *Friendsh. Miss Mitford* (1882) II. 115 Falling upon the tender mercies of two such wickeds as papa and she.

†**c.** genitive in *-s* (sing. or pl.). *Obs.*

1587 T. HUGHES *Misfort. Arthur* v. i. (1900) 57 The wickeds death is safety to the iust. **1597** BRETON *Arbor Amorous Deuices* Wks. (Grosart) I. 10/2 What is the world but wickeds way to hel? **1607** BP. HALL *Ps.* vii, Let mee the wicked's malice see Brought to an end.

III. 5. as *adv.* Wickedly; fiercely, savagely, furiously; 'cruelly', 'terribly'.

a **1425** *Cursor M.* 15840 (Trin.) Whil þei þus him handeled wicked as þei mou3t. **1663** T. PORTER *Witty Combat* IV. i, Yesterday was..a wicked hot day. **1829** HOGG *Sheph. Cal.* i. 8 A hungry louse bites wicked sair. **1849** W. S. MAYO *Kaloolah* v. (1850) 45 He came towards me with his hatchet in his hand. I saw that he was determined to act wicked. **1902** 'VIOLET JACOB' *Sheep-Stealers* ix, They was fightin' very wicked an' nasty.

IV. 6. *Comb.*, as ***wicked-like*** [LIKE *adv.* 7, -LIKE *suffix* 2 a], ***-looking***, ***-tongued*** adjs.; †**wicked-doer, -doing** = EVIL-DOER, -DOING; †**wicked-walking**, that 'walks wickedly' (cf. *Ps.* xxvi. 1); **wicked-worded** *nonce-wd.* as *pa. pple.*, euphem. for 'damned'.

a **1380** *St. Aug.* 945 in Horstm. *Altengl. Leg.* (1878) 77 Wikked-tonged men Wolde speke vuel of hem. *c* **1450** *Mirk's Festial* 1 Forto deme all wikytdoers ynto þe pyt of hell. **1535** COVERDALE *Ezek.* xxxvii. 23 With their..Idols and all their wicked-doinges. *c* **1550** ROLLAND *Crt. Venus* II. 297 So wickit like, and als so venemois. **1608** SYLVESTER *Du Bartas* II. iv. *Decay* 236 The traytor Manahem's wicked-walking Son. **1823** BYRON *Island* II. xxi, She seem'd a wicked-looking craft. **1865** H. KINGSLEY *Hillyars & Burtons* xxxii, He..wished he might be wicked-worded if he didn't. *a* **1871** DE MORGAN *Budget Parad.* (1872) 100 It made a book look wicked-like to have a feigned place of printing.

Hence †**wickedfully** *adv.*, wickedly; **wickedish** *a.* [-ISH[1] 3], somewhat wicked; †**wickedlek** [-LAIK], †**wickedrede** [-RED], wickedness.

c **1375** *Sc. Leg. Saints* iii. (*Andreas*) 104 Wikit women, þou ..has consawit giltfully, And consalite þe fend *wikitfully. **1853** READE *Chr. Johnstone* i, His master replied with..a quiet, but *wickedish look. *a* **1400** *Minor Poems fr. Vernon MS.* 478 3if we haue wille to *wikkedlek. *c* **1375** *Cursor M.* 1227 (Fairf.) Þai wraþet him wiþ *wikked rede.

wicked (wɪkt), *a.*[2] [f. WICK *sb.*[1] + -ED[1].] Furnished with or having a wick or wicks; usually in comb., as ***broad-wicked***, ***two-wicked***.

1507 *Extr. Aberd. Reg.* (1844) I. 437 That ale candil makaris has candile reddy to sele.., small weikit and dry. **1797** *Encycl. Brit.* (ed. 3) IX. 518/1 The broad-wicked lamp seems to have the advantage. **1899** H. G. GRAHAM *Soc. Life Scot. 18th C.* iv. I. 143 Their fathers had..sold dried herring or 'wicked candles'.

†**wickedhed(e.** *Obs.* [f. WICKED *a.*[1] + -HEAD.] Wickedness, iniquity; *pl.* wicked acts or doings.

a **1300** *Cursor M.* 841 Strang wickedhed Broght adam to suilk a ded. *Ibid.* 23142 Sa duked in þair wicked hedis. **1340** *Ayenb.* 114 He þet..heþ ine his herte hate, wreþe, oþer wyckedhede. **1370–80** *Vis. St. Paul* 46 in *O.E. Misc.* 224 Sore hit is to drede þe places of helle for wikked-hede.

wickedly ('wɪkɪdlɪ), *adv.* [f. as prec. + -LY[2].] In a wicked manner, in various senses of the adj.

1. In the way of wilful wrong-doing; iniquitously, immorally.

a **1300** *Cursor M.* 4376 Leuer es me be pour and lele þan wikudli at win catell. **1303** R. BRUNNE *Handl. Synne* 1203 Wykkedlyche al þat gode he dyspendyþ. *c* **1375** *Sc. Leg. Saints* xxxiii. (*George*) 414 Þu dois nocht anerly Wrang til ws, bot als wykitly Callis oure godis al dewilis. *c* **1385** CHAUCER *L.G.W.* 1918 *Ariadne*, But wikkedely he quitte hire kyndenesse. *c* **1386** —— *Clerk's T.* 667 He wikkedly.. Hath mordred bothe his children. *a* **1400–50** *Wars Alex.* 2425 3e at wickid ere within ay wickidly 3e thinke. **1535** COVERDALE *Gen.* xix. 7 O brethren, do not so wickedly. —— *Prov.* x. 2 Treasures that are wickedly gotten, profit nothinge. **1542** UDALL *Erasm. Apoph.* 338 b, Scipio Africane the seconde..was wekedly slaine in his bedde. **1562** WINȜET *Cert. Tractates* §66. Wks. (S.T.S.) I. 116 An hæretik denyand wickitlie the Father, the Sone, and the Haly Gaist. **1593** SHAKS. *Lucr.* 365 Into the chamber wickedlie he stalkes. **1611** B. JONSON *Catiline* IV. K 2, No man Could be so wickedly, or fondly stupide. **1734** POPE *Ess. Man* IV. 231 Who wickedly is wise, or madly brave, Is but the more a fool, the more a knave. **1808** MRS. M. T. KEMBLE *Day after Wedding* 31 Somebody has deceived you, wickedly deceived you.

2. Harmfully, injuriously; fiercely, savagely, severely, cruelly; terribly, disastrously; in later use (chiefly jocular), very badly, abominably, execrably, vilely, 'horridly'.

13.. *Cursor M.* 15840 (Gött.) Quilis þai him war þus handland wikidli als þai moght. *c* **1350** *Will. Palerne* 1218 Þey wiþ fyn force for-barred his strokes, & woundede him wikkedly. *c* **1400** *Laud Troy Bk.* 13149 Him and euery another prince That haue died here thus wickedly. *a* **1425** tr. *Arderne's Treat. Fistula* etc. 86 Þis puluis bigileþ neuer þe paciente ne þe cirurgene, for it doþ not wickedly. *c* **1440** *Engl. Conq. Irel.* 53 Some thay vndide and bettyn vickydly. **1556** in W. H. Turner *Select. Rec. Oxford* (1880) 245 A great number..did run to see him go so wickedly to his death. **1589** R. HARVEY *Pl. Perc.* (1860) 32 A Iewes letter scrible scrable ouer the Copurtenaunce of a mans countenaunce will dash a body wickedly. **1662** J. DAVIES tr. *Olearius' Voy. Ambass.* 54 Ladies..most wickedly be-painted. **1762** STERNE *Tr. Shandy* V. xv, Do you know whether my fiddle's in tune or no?..'Tis wickedly strung. **1858** HAWTHORNE *Fr. & It. Note-bks.* (1871) I. 4 The night was now setting in, wickedly black and dreary.

3. Mischievously, maliciously, roguishly.

1848 DICKENS *Dombey* xxiii, A glowering visage, with its thin lips parted wickedly. **1853** —— *Bleak Ho.* v, His cat looked so wickedly at me, as if I were a blood-relation of the birds upstairs. **1880** MRS. FORRESTER *Roy & V.* iii, 'I thought you would be tremendously obliged to me', whispered Netta wickedly.

wickedness ('wɪkɪdnɪs). [f. as prec. + -NESS.]

1. The quality of being wicked; wicked character or disposition; depravity, iniquity, immorality.

a **1340** HAMPOLE *Psalter* xxx. 13 Luf kelis and wickidnes brennys. *c* **1400** MAUNDEV. (Roxb.) ix. 33 Þai er..full of all maner of wickedness and malice. **1599** SHAKS. *Much Ado* III. ii. 113 *Clau.* Disloyall? *Bast.* The word is too good to paint out her wickednesse. **1625** BACON *Ess., Truth* (Arb.) 501 The Wickednesse of Falshood, and Breach of Faith. **1703** DE FOE *More Reform.* 12 What tho' the Baudy runs thro' all he Writ, The more the Wickedness, the more the Wit. *a* **1768** SECKER *Serm.* (1770) I. ix. 211 As all this arose from Infirmity, not Wickedness, they met with an easy Pardon. **1834** DICKENS *Sk. Boz, Steam Excurs.*, The unfortunate little victim..receiving sundry thumps..for having the wickedness to tell a story. **1873** 'OUIDA' *Pascarèl* II. i, So I reasoned in the wickedness of my heart.

2. Wicked action or conduct; iniquity as committed or perpetrated; *occas.* wicked speech or statement.

a **1300** *Cursor M.* 1090 Mistrauing þan had he son, þat he sum wikcudnes hade don. *c* **1375** *Sc. Leg. Saints* iii. (*Andreas*) 179 Þat I sic vikitnes Wald with hyr do and foulnes. *c* **1393** CHAUCER *Mariage* 7, I dar not writen of hyt noo wikkednesse. *c* **1470** HENRY *Wallace* III. 344 Causer of wer, wyrkar of wykitnes. **1560** DAUS tr. *Sleidane's Comm.* 23 Conteinyng bothe the Heresies already condemned, and also newe errours, and great wickednes. **1567** *Gude & Godlie B.* (S.T.S.) 72 That we suld leif our wickitnes, And fle vaine warldlie appetyte. **1605** SHAKS. *Lear* III. vii. 98 (Qo. I) Ile neuer care what wickednes I doe, If this man come to good. **1651** HOBBES *Leviath.* I. vi. 27 For Calamity arriving [*sic*] from great wickedness, the best men have the least Pitty. **1827** SOUTHEY *Hist. Penins. War* II. 65 The scene of an action..infamous to the French for the enormous wickedness with which they abused their victory. **1855** MACAULAY *Hist. Eng.* xiii. III. 367 Persons who think that there is no excess of wickedness for which courage and ability do not atone. **1901** BESANT *London in 18th Cent.* 237 The greatest wickedness that any man could commit, in his eyes, was not to pay his debts.

b. (with *a* and *pl.*) A piece of wickedness; a wicked act or proceeding.

a **1325** *Prose Psalter* lxxxviii[i]. 32 Y shal uisite in chasteing her wickednesses. *c* **1430** LYDG. *Min. Poems, De Prof.* 99 Ther wikkednessis yif thow do Observe, Tabyde thy doom yt were to hard a schour. **1535** COVERDALE *Amos* i. 13 For thre and foure wickednesses of Edom I wil not spare him. **1641** J. JACKSON *True Evang. T.* I. 26 He fed his eyes by being a spectator of those wickednesses, which Nero only commanded to be done. **1748** RICHARDSON *Clarissa* (1768) III. 47 So premeditated and elaborate a wickedness. **1817** SOUTHEY *Let. to Editor of Courier* 17 Mar., That it might be published surreptitiously at any future time, was a wickedness of which I never dreamt. **1859** GEO. ELIOT *Adam Bede* xli, I'd sooner do a wickedness as I could suffer for by myself, than ha' brought her to do wickedness.

†**3.** Poorness of spirit: cf. WICKED *a.*[1] 2 d. *Obs.*

1375 BARBOUR *Bruce* XII. 280 Gif 3he let cowardis And vikkidnes 3our hertis suppris.

†**4.** In physical sense: Malignancy, corruption: cf. WICKED *a.*[1] 2 c. *Obs. rare.*

c **1400** *Lanfranc's Cirurg.* 18 Whanne þe bodi is purgid fro wickide humouris, þe wickidnes of þe mater renneþ fro þe wounde.

wicken, variant of QUICKEN *sb.*[1], *sb.*[2]

wicker ('wɪkə(r)), *sb.* Forms: 4–5 **wyker**, 4–6 **wekir**, 6–7 **wycker**, (5 **wikre**, **wikir**, **wykyr**, **qwykyr**, **wekker**, 6 **wycre**, **wykir**, **-ur**, **wiker**, **wikker**, **wykkyr**, **wickar**, **-ir**, 7 **wykker**), 5– **wicker**. [East Scandinavian (MSw. and Sw. dial. *viker*, early Da. *viger*, Da. dial. *vigger* willow, osier, branch of willow); f. root of Sw. *vika* to bend (cf. OE. *wican* to give way, collapse, and WEAK *a.*, WOKE).]

1. A pliant twig or small rod, usually of willow, esp. as used for making baskets and various other objects; an osier; a withe. Chiefly in *pl.* (= sense 2).

1398 TREVISA *Barth. De P.R.* XIX. cxxviii. (1495), Suche vessels were fyrste made of tree and of wykers: as panyers, baskettes. **1426** LYDG. *De Guil. Pilgr.* 23385 Whan the smale wikres brak, The hopes wenten al to wrak. **14..** *Nom.* in Wr.-Wülcker 717/25 *Hoc vimen, -nis*, qwykyr. **1508** DUNBAR *Poems* vi. 45 My hert that neuer wes sickir,..Thought I wald bynd it with a wickir. **1551** ROBINSON tr. *More's Utopia* I. (1895) 31 The sayles were made of greate russhes, or of wyckers, and in some places of lether. **1586** HOLINSHED *Chron.* III. 861/2 Great images of wickers..made like great men of diuerse strange nations. **1657** S. PURCHAS *Pol. Flying-Ins.* 58 In our Country, the Hives principally in use, are either made of wickers, or of straw. **1807** CRABBE *Sir Eustace Grey* 247 And stones erect their shadows shed On humble graves, with wickers bound. **1811** COL. HAWKER *Diary* (1893) I. 33 The wickers of the [lobster] pots. **1899** KROPOTKIN *Mem. Rev.* IV. ix. II. 70 To ply the wickers and to shape them into an elegant basket.

b. Such a twig or small branch, as part of the living plant. ? *Obs.*

1508 DUNBAR *Lament for Makaris* 14 As with the wynd wavis the wickir. **1591** PERCIVALL *Sp. Dict.*, *Esparto*, wicker, a kinde of tree whereof they make frailes. **1796** BURNS *Poem on Life* iii, Flickering, feeble, and unsicker.., Aye wavering like the willow-wicker.

c. A twig or small branch used as a mark. *local.*

1825 BROCKETT *N.C. Gloss.*, *Wike*, *Wicker*, a mark used in setting out tithes; generally a small branch of a tree.

2. (without *pl.*) Wickers collectively, or as plaited together; wickerwork.

1336 *Cal. Docum. Scot.* (1887) III. 356 Et stramen, 'wekirr' et 'tempil' pro coopertura domorum. *Ibid.*, In empcione..de 'wekir' et 'tempil' per vices xij d. **1491** CAXTON *Vitas Patr.* (W. de W. 1495) II. 227/1 His vessell wherin he weted his wekker & roddes for to make withall panyers maundes & baskettes. **1552–3** in Feuillerat *Revels Edw. VI* (1914) 112, iiij^or hampers of wicker to put in thapparrell. **1660** *Act 12 Chas. II* c. 4 Sched. s.v. *Bottles*, Bottles of Glass covered wth Wicker. **1791** COWPER *Iliad* XVIII. 709 Youths and maidens blithe In frails of wicker bore the luscious fruit. **1838** THIRLWALL *Greece* xxxi. IV. 203 Shields of wood or wicker, whitened over, were substituted by some for metal armour.

3. A basket, cradle, chair, etc. of wicker.

1646 CODRINGTON *Earl of Essex* 2 To omit the presages.. of the promising Madams who rocked his Cradle, I will not say, that in that moving wicker (like another Hercules) hee strangled in each hand the two invading Dragons of transcending Prerogative and Superstition. **1699** MEAGER *New Art Garden.* 40 The Orange-trees..are so tender, that they must be planted in Pots, Wickers, or Wooden Troughs. **1740** SOMERVILLE *Hobbinol.* II. 329 By that illustrious Wicker, where they sate In comely Pride. **1818** KEATS *Endym.* I. 137 Each having a white wicker over brimm'd With April's tender younglings. **1861** S. THOMSON *Wild Fl.* III. (ed. 4) 137 Huge wickers of eggs.

4. *attrib.* Made or consisting of wicker, as a basket, chair, etc.; also, covered with or encased in wicker, as a bottle. See also WICKERWORK.

1502 *Privy Purse Exp. Eliz. York* (1830) 84 Two wycre bottelles. **1523–4** *Rec. St. Mary at Hill* (1904) 322, ij yerdys of wykur matt. **1576** FLEMING *Panopl. Epist.* 358 The.. valliaunt warriour, was once wrapped in swathling clowtes, and lay crying in a wicker cradle. **1587** A. FLEMING *Contn. Holinshed* III. 1315/2 Pendents made of wicker rods. **1596** SPENSER *Prothal.* ii, A Flocke of Nymphes..And each one had a little wicker basket, Made of fine twigs. **1603** *Reg. Mag. Sig. Scot.* 515/2 Ilk hundreth wykker sparris..2 penneis. **1611** MIDDLETON & DEKKER *Roaring Girl* K 2, A wicker cage tames a nightingale. **1619** *Depos. Bk. Archdeac. Essex & Colch.* lf. 98 (MS.) We found the said Testatrix sitting in a wicker chayer by the fyer side. **1676** SAMMES *Brit. Antiq. Illustr.* I. 105 In sacrificing of Men to their Idols, in a Wicker Image. **1707** MORTIMER *Husb.* 203 Wicker-hives made of Privet, Willow, or Harl. **1719** DE FOE *Crusoe* I. (Globe) 74 Twigs that would bend to make Wicker Ware. **1822** GOOD *Study Med.* (1829) V. 338 A wicker basket of palm twigs. **1837** DICKENS *Pickw.* xxix, Gabriel Grub..drew forth his wicker bottle. **1891** HARDY *Tess* lii, The wicker-cradle they had all been rocked in.

b. ***wicker wings***, attributed to various sinister creatures.

The source of the allusion is unascertained; connexion with the passage translated in quot. 1837 in c below is improbable.

1637 B. JONSON *Sad Shepherd* I. v, Harke, harke, harke the foule Bird [*viz.* the screech-owl]..how shee flutters with her wicker wings! **1697** DRYDEN *Æneis* VII. 478 The Fury..on her wicker Wings, sublime through Night, She to the Latian Palace took her Flight. *a* **1729** CONGREVE *Imposs. Thing* 84 The Goblin plys his wicker wings.

c. *Comb.*, as ***wicker-bottomed, -cased, -covered, -weaving, -winged, -woven*** adjs.; ***wicker-wise*** adv.
1859 Geo. Eliot *Adam Bede* xiv, In the large *wicker-bottomed arm-chair..sat old Martin Poyser. **1870** Dickens *Edwin Drood* xii, A goodly *wicker-cased bottle. **1848** Thackeray *Van. Fair* xxx, A *wicker-covered flask. **1920** *Chamb. Jrnl.* 28 Feb. 205/1 A *wicker-weaving loom. **1837** Wheelwright tr. *Aristoph., Birds* I. 248 *Wicker-wing'd Diitrephes [Διτρέφης γε πυτιναῖα μόνον ἔχων πτερά]. **1601** Holland *Pliny* xii. xiv. I. 367 A quilt or mat made of Datetree twigs, plaited and wound one within another *wicker-wise. **1859** Boyd *Recreat. Country Parson* v. 168 The *wicker-woven box.

'wicker, *v.* [f. prec. sb.] *trans.* To furnish, fit, cover, or inclose with wicker. (Chiefly in pa. pple.: see also WICKERED.)
1599 B. Jonson *Ev. Man out of Hum.* i. ii, A mustie bottle, new wickerd. **1670** Milton *Hist. Eng.* ii. 49 Thir Ships of light timber wickerd with Oysier betweene, and coverd over with Leather. **1838** *Civil Engin. & Arch. Jrnl.* I. 275/2 Upon this [*sc.* a surface of dry moss], hurdles..wickered with heath, were laid. **1882** F. M. Crawford *Mr. Isaacs* xii, High frames made by planting four bamboos in a square and wickering the top.

wicker, variant of WHICKER *v.*, to whinny.

wickered ('wɪkəd), *a.* [f. WICKER *sb.* or *v.* + -ED.]
1. Encased in wicker; inclosed or surrounded by wickerwork.
1725 De Foe *Voy. round World* 6 French Wine in Wicker'd Bottles. **1755** *Connoisseur* No. 73 ¶4 A painted board..stuck up at the end of his wicker'd turf. **1860** *All Year Round* No. 53. 60 Near which you always find some sherbet-seller, resting his wickered bottles.
2. Made of wicker: = WICKER *sb.* 4 a.
1751 Deering *Nottingham* 73 An old wickered Chair. **1838** *Civil Engin. & Arch. Jrnl.* I. 275/2 The hurdles, or wickered foundation. **1919** *Chamb. Jrnl.* 25 Oct. 743/1 Wickered furniture predominated.

wickerwork ('wɪkəwɜːk). [f. WICKER *sb.* + WORK *sb.*] Work consisting of wickers; a structure of flexible twigs, osiers, or the like plaited together; basket-work.
1719 De Foe *Crusoe* i. (Globe) 252 We fell to work to make more Wicker Work. **1780** Cowper *A Fable* 3 A raven..on her wicker-work high mounted Her chickens prematurely counted. **1836** Thirlwall *Greece* xiv. II. 214 The houses of Sardis were chiefly of wicker-work. **1842** Dickens *Amer. Notes* ii, Every plank and timber creaked, as if the ship were made of wicker-work. **1855** Macaulay *Hist. Eng.* xvi. III. 622 Those rude coracles of wickerwork covered with the skins of horses, in which the Celtic peasantry fished for trout and salmon.
attrib. **1846** Sharpe *Hist. Egypt* xi. 376 Ceylon..had often been reached from Africa..in wickerwork boats made of papyrus. **1871** L. Stephen *Playgr. Eur.* (1894) xiii. 305 A house with open wickerwork sides.
Hence **'wickerworked** (-wɜːkt) *a.*, made of or inclosed in wickerwork; **'wickerworker**, one who makes wickerwork.
1881 *Instr. Census Clerks* (1885) 80 Basket maker... Wicker Worker. **1900** 'H. Lawson' *Over Sliprails* 66 A big old wicker-worked demijohn.

wicket ('wɪkɪt). Forms: [3 wicat], 3–5 **wykett(e**, 3–6 **wyket, wiket**, 4–5 **wikett, wekett**, 4–6 **wykket(t, wycket, wickett**, 5 **wickette, wekyt, (wigate)**, 5–6 **weket**, 6 **weiket**, 5– **wicket**. [a. AF. = ONF. *wiket* (Norman *viquet*, Walloon *wichet*) = OF. (mod.F.) *guichet*; usually referred to the Teut. root appearing in ON. *víkja* to move, turn (Sw. *vika*, Da. *vige*); but the forms OF. *guischet*, *wisket*, Pr. *guisquet* indicate the possibility of another source.]
1. a. A small door or gate made in, or placed beside, a large one, for ingress and egress when the large one is closed; also, any small gate for foot-passengers, as at the entrance of a field or other enclosure.
[**12..** in E. M. Thompson *Cust. St. Aug. Cant.* (1904) II. 256 Servientes sacristiæ tenentur esse intro ad 'Covrefou';.. tunc deferentur claves ad sacristam, tam 'wicat' quam magnæ portæ cimiterii.] *a* **1300** *K. Horn* 1074 (Camb. MS.) Horn gan to þe ȝate turne & þat wiket vnspurne. *a* **1366** Chaucer *Rom. Rose* 528, I fonde a wiket small, So shett that I ne myght In gon. *a* **1400–50** *Wars Alex.* 5545 In at a wicket he went. *a* **1483** *Engl. Gilds* (1870) 320, ij. keyys for þe wekett. **1485** in *Comp. Rolls Obed. St. Swithun's, Winch.* (1892) 384 Super magnam portam et *le Wigate* ejusdem portæ. *c* **1489** Caxton *Sonnes of Aymon* xxi. 462 Mawgys cam nere to the wycket of the gate. *a* **1533** Ld. Berners *Huon* cxlvi. 546 He came to the abbey gate & callyd yᵉ porter,..he openyd the weket & beheld Huon,..& sayd 'pylgryme, enter when you plese'. Then Huon enterid in at the weket. **1578** H. Wotton *Courtlie Controv.* 295 He tooke his leaue of hir, and went out at a little wicket into a narrowe by lane. **1667** Milton *P.L.* iii. 484 Now Saint Peter at Heav'ns Wicket seems To wait them with his Keys. **1766** Goldsm. *Hermit* xi, The wicket, opening with a latch, Received the harmless pair. **1818** Hazlitt *Engl. Poets* ii. 70 You see a little..old man by a wood-side opening a wicket. **1823** Scott *Quentin D.* x, He who would thrive at Court must know the private wickets and concealed staircases. **1853** Dickens *Bleak Ho.* xv, A..boy came out of a sort of office, and looked at us over a spiked wicket. **1899** Gosse *Donne* I. 92 The gates of the house were shut upon the dignified envoys, but, after some stay,..they were let in by the wicket.
b. *fig.* or in fig. context.
a **1400** *Prymer* (1895) 12 Thou art wiket of þe hiȝ king, & þe greet ȝate of liȝt þat schyneþ briȝt. *c* **1400** *26 Pol. Poems* xxii. 4 þou..wan in at þe wyket of synne. **1526** *Pilgr. Perf.* (W. de W. 1531) 117 b, Stryue to entre by the strayte wycket. **1573–80** Tusser *Husb.* (1878) 169 With hir that will clicket make daunger to cope, Least quickly hir wicket [*i.e.* mouth] seeme easie to ope. **1663** G. Mackenzie *Relig. Stoici* xii. (1665) 96 Seeing nothing is roomed in our judgement and apprehension, but what first entred by the wicket of sense. **1693** Congreve *Old Bach.* iii. ii. 22 Thou art the Wicket to thy Mistresses Gate, to be opened for all Comers. *a* **1870** Rossetti *Poems, Love's Nocturn* v, At death's wicket.
†**2.** A small opening, esp. one through which to look out or communicate with the outside; a loophole, grill, or the like. *Obs.*
1296 *Acc. Exch. K.R.* 5/20 m. 4 *dorso* (P.R.O.) In .xxv. anulis ad Hecch', tribus paribus gemell ad Wykett' Bargie, xij Keuillis ferri ad Castrum .vij. d. *c* **1430** *Syr Gener.* (Roxb.) 4362 Ayenst the toure A postern ther is,.. There is right A privey wiket; Draw we thidre..That our frendes may se vs within. *c* **1440** *Promp. Parv.* 527/2 Wykett, or lytylle wyndowe, *fenestra*. ? **1449** *Paston Lett.* I. 83 They have made wykets on every quarter of the hwse to schote owte atte. **1489** Caxton *Faytes of A.* ii. xxii. 136 Eche of them shal haue a litel wiket open for to shete a gonne. **1616** *Extr. Aberd. Reg.* (1848) II. 341 With ane litill wicket..to luik in to the paissis. **1676** Coles *Dict.*, *Wicket*, a casement. **1677** *Lond. Gaz.* No. 1181/4 Having seized the Wicket or Sally-port, they got on the Ramparts. **1785** Grose *Dict. Vulgar T.*, *Wicket*, a casement, also, a little door. **1797** *Encycl. Brit.* (ed. 3) XVIII. 853/2 *Wicket*, a small door in the gate of a fortified place, &c. or a hole in a door through which to view what passes without.
3. *Cricket.* **a.** A set of three sticks called *stumps*, fixed upright in the ground, and surmounted by two small pieces of wood called *bails* (BAIL *sb.*[4] 2), forming the structure (27 × 8 in.) at which the bowler aims the ball, and at which (in front and a little to one side of it) the batsman stands to defend it with the bat. (The wicket formerly consisted of two stumps and one long bail, forming a structure one foot high by two feet wide.)
single wicket, a form of the game in which there is only one wicket, and therefore only one batsman 'in' at a time. (Also *attrib.*) *double wicket*, the ordinary form, in which there are two wickets placed 22 yards apart, between which the two batsmen run. ***to keep wicket***, to act as WICKET-KEEPER.
1733 in Waghorn *Cricket Scores* (1899) 6 The wickets are to be pitched by twelve o'clock. *c* **1750** in 'Bat' *Crick. Man.* (1850) 30 [Cricket] is performed by a person who, with a clumsy wooden bat, defends a wicket raised of two slender sticks, with one across. **1773** J. Burnby *Kentish Cricketers* 14 Davis, who loves a Game of Cricket, And shines whene'er he keeps the Wicket. **1778** *Coventry Mercury* 6 July 3/4 On Tuesday last..a Cricket Match, (full set at double wicket) was played between the Wappenbury and Coventry players. **1801** J. Strutt *Sports & Pastimes Eng.* II. iii. 83 Cricket... This game which is played with the bat and ball, consists of single and double wicket. **1803** *Laws of Cricket* 6 The Bowler..shall bowl four balls before he changes wickets. **1837** Dickens *Pickw.* vii, Played a match once—single wicket. **1849** *Laws of Cricket* in 'Bat' *Crick. Man.* (1850) 60 The bowler is subject to the same laws as at double wicket. **1850** 'Bat' *Crick. Man.* 98 A single wicket player. **1859** *All Year Round* No. 13. 306 Serjeant-Major McJug,..one of our best bats, went to the wicket first with Winterburn. **1884** *Lillywhite's Crick. Ann.* 10 Tylecote kept wicket well. **1888** *Pall Mall Gaz.* 22 May 11/1 When the wickets were drawn Gloucestershire had made 361.
b. In various expressions referring to a batsman's tenure of the wicket, or that part of an innings during which some particular batsman is (or might be) 'in', i.e. at the wicket:
e.g. *to take four wickets* (said of a bowler), to put four batsmen 'out'; *three wickets* (or *third wicket*) *down*, three men having been put out; *the sixth wicket fell for 75* = the sixth batsman was put out after 75 runs had been made in the innings; *to win by eight wickets*, i.e. by exceeding the opponents' full score of runs, with eight wickets yet to 'fall' (= with two men 'not out' and seven not having been 'in' in the innings).
1738 in Waghorn *Cricket Scores* (1899) 21 Battle..left Eastbourne 43 to get, which they did with ease, leaving four wickets to be put up when Battle was beat. **1749** *Ibid.* 42 They..had two wickets to go down. **1877** Blackmore *Cripps* lv, [They] had beaten the dalesmen by ten wickets. **1881** *Standard* 28 June 3/1 Another wicket now fell,.. —six for 76. **1883** *Daily Tel.* 15 May 2/7 Full score, six wickets for 72 runs. **1900** *Daily Chron.* 16 Dec. 8/1 The first-wicket partnership of MacLaren and Hayward. **1902** *Ibid.* 4 June 6/7 Jackson took four wickets with five consecutive balls.
c. *transf.* The ground between and about the wickets, esp. in respect of its condition; the pitch.
1862 *Sporting Life* 14 June, Nottinghamshire..sent C. Daft and Brampton to two as fine wickets as the Surrey 'or any other ground' in England could furnish. **1881** *Standard* 14 June 3/8 The condition of the wicket, on which the fast bowling bumped and the slows popped about. **1881** *Daily News* 9 July 2 The wicket did not seem to play particularly well. **1884** *Lillywhite's Crick. Ann.* 3 The English eleven commenced batting on a perfect wicket. **1889** *Pall Mall Gaz.* 17 Apr. 6/1 The wickets were all matting,..there being not a single turf wicket in the [Cape] colony.
d. Fig. phrs.: ***to be on a good wicket***, to be in an advantageous or favourable position; ***to bat*** (or ***be***) ***on a sticky wicket***: see STICKY *a.*[2] 1 c.
1941 *Punch* 24 Dec. 551/1, I wondered why I was so anxious to conceal my age; for the old *are on a good wicket*. **1961** *Listener* 2 Nov. 737/2 Perhaps the most satisfactory contributions are those of Lord Birkett, who is on a good wicket in describing the change in legal attitudes to obscenity, and Dr. Robert Gosling. **1977** *Verbatim* Dec. 3/2 To *be on a good wicket* is, like *being on a good pitch*, to 'be in a good spot'. To *be on a good wicket* with someone is to 'be in favor' with him.
4. *U.S. Croquet.* A hoop.
1868 Louisa M. Alcott *Little Women* xii, Jo was through the last wicket, and had missed the stroke... Fred..gave a stroke, his ball hit the wicket, and stopped an inch on the wrong side. **1890** *Century Dict.* s.v. *Croquet*, Each person in turn strikes his own ball once; if his ball passes through a wicket..he is allowed another stroke.
5. In various technical senses.
a. A small gate or valve for emptying the chamber of a canal-lock, or in the chute of a water-wheel for regulating the passage of water. **b.** *Coal-mining.* A very wide heading or stall, usually with two road-ways, in a variety of pillar-and-stall work (called ***wicket-work***) in use in North Wales. **c.** One of a set of gratings in the form of which the lead is made up in the manufacture of white lead.
1875 Knight *Dict. Mech.*, *Wicket*, a gate formed like a butterfly-valve, in the chute of a water-wheel, to graduate the amount of water passing to the wheel. **1881** Raymond *Mining Gloss.* **1893** *Times* 16 Dec. 9/5 The dangers to health begin with the second process, the conversion of the 'wickets' by the corrosion of an acid into white lead.
6. *attrib.* and *Comb.*, as ***wicket-door*** (= sense 1), ***-grate, -window***; (sense 3) ***wicket-bag, -taker***. See also WICKET-GATE, -KEEPER.
1813 Scott *Trierm.* iii. xix, An arch'd portal door, In whose broad folding leaves..Was framed a wicket window-grate,..The gallant Knight took earnest view The grated wicket-window through. **1814** —— *Wav.* ix, A little oaken wicket-door. **1842** Borrow *Bible in Spain* xxxix, A dusky passage, at the end of which was a wicket door. **1916** Joyce *Portrait of Artist* (1969) 90 A team of cricketers passed,.. one of them carrying the long green wicketbag. **1962** *Times* 20 June 4/1 In the second Test match..Coldwell wins his [cap] as the season's premier wicket-taker. **1976** J. Snow *Cricket Rebel* 76 Barry Knight had been the main wicket-taker in the West Indies first innings with four.

wicket, obs. form of WICKED.

'wicket-gate. [GATE *sb.*[1]] = WICKET 1.
1362 Langl. *P. Pl.* A. vi. 92 To wynne vp þe wiket-ȝat þat þe wey schutte. **1678** Bunyan *Pilgr.* i. 10 That side of the Slough, that was..next to the Wicket-gate. **1833** Loudon *Encycl. Archit.* §316 A wicket gate, separating the yard from the passage. **1838** Dickens *O. Twist* xxxiv, A garden, whence a wicket-gate opened into a small paddock. **1881** Besant & Rice *Chapl. Fleet* i. i, She opened the little wicket-gate which led to the vicarage garden, and passed in.
fig. **1891** Farrar *Darkn. & Dawn* xxii, So Nero deliberately chose the evil and refused the good, and the narrow wicket-gate of repentance was closed behind him.

wicket-keep, colloq. abbrev. of next.
1867 *J. Lillywhite's Cricketer's Compan.* 107 [He] promises very well as a wicket-keep. **1904** *Westm. Gaz.* 7 July 3/1 One of these days [he] will be as good a batsman as he is a wicket-keep. **1912** *Sat. Rev.* 15 June 739/1 Reid was a first-rate wicket-keep.

'wicket-ˌkeeper. *Cricket.* A player stationed behind the wicket to stop the ball if it passes it, and if possible to put the batsman 'out' by 'stumping' or 'catching' (see STUMP *v.*[1] 8, CATCH *v.* 24 c).
17.. *Laws of Cricket* in Grace *Cricket* (1891) 15 The Wicket Keeper shall stand at a reasonable distance behind ye Wicket, and shall not move till ye Ball is out of ye Bowler's Hands. **1875** 'Stonehenge' *Brit. Sports* iii. i. i. §4. 671 The office of Wicket-keeper is second only to that of the bowler. **1910** *Times* 5 Feb. 6/3 David Hunter..is retiring after having been 21 years wicketkeeper for Yorkshire.

wicket-keeping. The occupation of a wicket-keeper (also *attrib.*).
1826 F. Reynolds *Life & Times* II. xiv. 170 No man could..surpass..Hammond in wicket keeping. **1833** *Sporting Mag.* LXXXII. 353/2 The wicket-keeping of Wenman. **1836** Jesse *Angler's Rambles* 297 One or two prided themselves on their wicket-keeping. **1851** Lillywhite *Guide Cricketers* 62 Box has..improved very much upon the wicket-keeping glove. **1861** Dickens *Gt. Expect.* xxvii, It demanded..a constant attention, and a quickness of eye and hand, very like that exacted by wicket-keeping.
Hence (as a back-formation) **'wicket-keep** *v. intr.*, to keep wicket; **'wicket-keeping** *ppl. a.*
1891 W. G. Grace *Cricket* v. 138 Lillywhite was bowling and I was wicket-keeping. **1955** I. Peebles *Ashes* i. 13 Two wicket-keeping batsmen. **1976** *Milton Keynes Express* 25 June 49/5 In his nine games for the club so far this season the wicket keeping batsman has claimed 19 victims.

wickeyberry, wickey-up: see WICKY, WICKYIUP.

†**wickhals.** *Obs.* [app. f. WICK *a.* + HALSE *sb.*[1], neck.] app. A gallows-bird, rogue.
1338 R. Brunne *Chron.* (1725) 267 To while þise cardinals trauaild for þe pes, Here of a wikhals how he bigan a res. *c* **1400** *Laud Troy Bk.* 10086 Let him neuere dye of no wykhals!

Wickham ('wɪkəm). *Angling.* Colloq. shortening of ***Wickham's fancy***, an artificial trout-fly.
1876 F. Francis *Bk. Angling* vi. (ed. 4) 241 The Wickham's Fancy..enjoys a wide reputation. **1911** *Corner of Harley Street* i. 9 Snatching his joy as one of your own parr will take a Wickham on a clear pool.

Wickhamick: see WYKEHAMIC.

wickid, obs. form of WICKED.

wicking ('wɪkɪŋ), *sb.* [f. WICK *sb.*[1] + -ING[1] 1 g.] Material for making wicks; cord or tape of cotton or other fibre, to be cut into lengths for wicks.

1847 *Rep. Comm. Patents 1846* (U.S.) 220 This is combined with a small tube within it, through which the wicking is introduced, to cause the tallow to unite around the wicking. **1873** J. Richards *Operator's Handbk.* 95 The wicks should be of wire wound round with textile material, ordinary wicking for instance. **1902** S. E. White *Blazed Trail* xi, Torches, which were often merely catsup jugs with wicking in the necks.

wicking, *vbl. sb.*[1], [2]: see WICK *v.*[1], [2].

Wicking, var. VIKING; see also s.v. WICK *sb.*[3]

wickir, obs. form of WICKER.

wickit, obs. Sc. form of WICKED.

wickiup ('wɪkɪʌp). *U.S.* Also **wick(e)yup, wickie-up, wi(c)kiup; wakiup, wackie-up.** [American Indian (Menominee *wikiop*, Saki *wekeab*; cf. Cree *mekewap*, Montagnais *mitshiuap*); perh. a variant of *wikiwam*, WIGWAM.] A rude hut consisting of a frame covered with brushwood or the like, used by nomadic peoples in the west and south-west. Hence extended to any small hut or shanty.

1857 *Jrnl. Discourses* (1858) V. 80 After feeding to our guide some bread and water..we asked which was the way to Jacob's 'Wickyup'. **1872** C. King *Mountain. Sierra Nev.* xiii. 273 An Indian ranchero where several willow wickyups were built upon the bank of a cold brook. **1874** T. B. Aldrich *Prud. Palfrey* vii, A city of tents, pine-huts, and rude brush wakiups. **1876** *Sun* (N.Y.) 10 May 2/6 Come up and see me at my wickiup in Montana. **1905** *Pearson's Mag.* XIX. 359 The American Indian uses his 'wackie-up' as a mere stopping place for a night or two while trekking across country. **1930** E. Ferber *Cimarron* i. 11 He was raised in a tepee; a wickiup had been his bedroom, a blanket his robe. **1959** E. Tunis *Indians* 110/1 In winter the Diggers put their wickiups over pits for additional warmth, just as the Basketmakers did. **1973** 'P. Buchanan' *Requiem of Sharks* xi. 111 In the slang of the Pascagoula Indians, she was built like a brick wickiup.

'wickless, *a.* [f. WICK *sb.*[1] + -LESS.] That burns without a wick; not fitted with a wick.

1899 *T. Eaton & Co. Catal.* 'Summer Needs' 13 (*heading*) Wickless blue flame oil stoves. **1924** *Chambers's Jrnl.* Sept. 638/1 In all wickless stoves and lamps particles of carbon are deposited in the vaporiser. **1950** [see *gun-flash* sv. GUN *sb.* 16 a].

Wicklif- (-lef-, -lev-, -liv-): see WYCLIF-.

wickmanite ('wɪkmənaɪt). *Min.* [f. the name of F.-E. *Wickman* (b. 1915), Swedish mineralogist + -ITE[1].] A cubic hydroxide of manganese and tin, $MnSn(OH)_6$, found as small yellowish or colourless octahedral crystals.

1967 Moore & Smith in *Arkiv för Mineral. och Geol.* IV. 398 Wickmanite..is of interest since it is the first tin mineral reported from Långban. **1977** *Canad. Mineralogist* XV. 437/1, Wickmanite, $MnSn(OH)_6$, schoenfliesite, $MgSn(OH)_6$, and manganoan schoenfliesite occur in separate low-temperature parageneses in hydrothermally mineralized skarns at Pitkäranta, Karelia.

wickner. *Obs.* exc. *local.* Forms: 1–2 **wicnere,** 3 **wikenere, -are,** 5–6 **wig(e)ner,** 6– **wickner.** [OE. *wícnere*, f. *wícnian*, f. *wíce* WIKE *sb.*] An official; in spec. use (see quots. 1574).

c **1000** *Ags. Gloss.* in *Haupt's Zeitschrift* (1853) IX. 453 *Dispensator*,..wicnere. **1155** *Charter* in *Anglia* (1884) VII. 220 Swa ful & swa ford swa mine aȝene Wicneres hit sechan scolden. *c* **1205** Lay. 6704 He sende word bi his beste wikeneren. *Ibid.* 18175 Imong þat he king wæs: & his wikenares chæs. **1391-2** *Duchy of Lancaster Ministers' Acc.* 288/4734 (P.R.O.) In alloc[acione] j p[re]pos[iti] j. messor[is] j. collector[is] et iiij Wik[enariorum] videl[ice]t de Gymynham Southreppes Trunch et Monesle. **1485** in C. M. Hoare *Hist. E. Angl. Soke* (1918) 180 Wegenarius. **15..** *Ibid.* 132 Yᵉ wigners of Gymi[n]ghm, Trunche, Southrepps, Monisley, & Trymi[n]ghm. **1574** in *Orig. Papers Norf. & Norwich Archæol. Soc.* (1923) XXI. III. 386 Agnes Swan widdow..payeth to yᵉ Wicknʳ of Sydestrond 2ˢ 9ᵈ for & in consideracon of rent of Assize, common helpe, moueable rents & other Customes and services. *Ibid.* 387 There is a wicknerʳ Chosen eu'ry yeare in eu'ry towne through yᵉ Soken & during his yeare his duty is to warne yᵉ Courte & Leete for yᵉ towne where he is chosen wicknʳ & to warne yᵉ Tennants upon warneing given to him by yᵉ Hayward to doe their workes. *Ibid.* 388 And further the said wicknᵉʳˢ office is to distreyne within the towne where he is wicknʳ. [*Ibid.*, The duties of the modern wickners of the several parishes within the Soke of Gimingham are limited to the periodical collection and payment of certain small rents and fines due to the lord of the manor.] **1614** in C. M. Hoare *E. Angl. Soke* 132 To goe Wykner for this yere to come. **1633** *Ibid.* 343, I doe also put the sayd Tho: Playford in authoryty to serve as wickner for my howse Southwood in Northrepes. **1719** *Ibid.* 132 We chuse Mary Calk widdow to serve yᵉ office of wickner for yᵉ yeare ensuing.

wickopick, -opy, -up, var. WICOPY.

wickud, -yd, obs. forms of WICKED.

wicky ('wɪkɪ). *local.* [? dial. alteration of QUICKEN.] **a.** The mountain-ash or rowan-tree: = QUICKEN *sb.*[1] 1 a. Also **wickeyberry tree. b.** *U.S.* The sheep-laurel, *Kalmia angustifolia*, and an allied species, *K. hirsuta*.

1681 T. Langford *Instr. Fruit-trees* 118 Graff the Service on the Wickeyberry-tree, or the White-thorn. **1804** A. F. M. Willich *Domestic Encycl.* I. 53/1 The plant [*sc.* Andromeda] is there [*sc.* in the southern states] called 'wickie'. **1847** Halliwell, *Wicky*, same as *Wicken-tree*. **1901** C. T. Mohr *Plant Life Alabama* 654 Wicky.. Louisianian area..Low sandy pine barrens.

wickyup, var. WICKIUP.

Wiclif- (-lef-, -lev-, -liv-): see WYCLIF-.

wicopy ('wɪkəpɪ). Also 8 **wickopick,** 9 **wickopy, wickaby, wickup, wikop, wicup.** [American Indian (Cree *wikupiy*, etc.).] **a.** The leatherwood or moosewood of N. America, *Dirca palustris*; also, the basswood or American linden, *Tilia americana*. **b.** An American name for species of willow-herb (*Epilobium*): distinctively ***Indian*** or ***herb wicopy***.

1778 J. Carver *Trav. N. Amer.* xix. 499 The Wickopick or Suckwick appears to be a species of the white wood,.. distinguished..by a peculiar quality in the bark, which when pounded and moistened..becomes..of the consistence..of size. **1837** P. H. Gosse in *Life* (1890) 106 The tall wickup plants with which the ground was.. covered. [*note*, Or 'wickaby', the leather-plant (*Dirca palustris*), a shrub common in the Canadian woods.] **1888** *Cornh. Mag.* Oct. 373 He will be attracted by the whahoo and the wicopy.

wictaill, -ale, -ayle, -ayll, obs. ff. VICTUAL.

wicth, wictor(e, -orag, -ori(e, -ory, -our(e: see WIGHT *a.*, VICTOR *sb.*[1] and [2], VICTORAGE, VICTORY.

wid (wɪd), repr. colloq. and dial. pronunc. of WITH *prep.*

[See WITH *prep.* for pre-16th cent. examples.] **1869** S. H. Bradford *Scenes in Life Harriet Tubman* 26 Jesus will go wid you. **1884** D. Boucicault *Shaugraun* I. i. 3 Never fear, I'll be even wid your honour yet. **1895** Baines & Smiley in A. Dundes *Mother Wit* (1973) 256/2 You an' I was sittin' at de table wid but one dish ob soup. **1897** Kipling *Capt. Cour.* iii. 77 We do be condescending to honour the second half wid our presence. **1935** [see Jack *sb.*[1] 2 e]. **1953** K. Tennant *Joyful Condemned* xi. 106 What's up wid yuh now? **1978** J. Irving *World according to Garp* xix. 432 She didda lot for people wid *complicated* lives.

wid: see WADE *v.*, WED *v.*, WIDE, WIGHT, WITH, WOOD *sb.* and *a.*

Widal (vɪ-, wɪ'dɑːl). *Path.* The name of G. F. *Widal* (1862–1929), French physician, used *attrib.* and in the possessive to designate an agglutination test for typhoid and other *Salmonella* infections described by him in 1896.

1899 H. M. Biggs in *Typhoid Fever* (N.Y. State Med. Assoc.) 272 A negative result from the Widal test cannot be regarded as having much significance. *Ibid.*, While the Widal reaction may be very late in its appearance,..when present it is of the greatest possible value in the diagnosis. **1908** *Practitioner* Sept. 423 The absence of spots, Widal's reaction,..and the presence of a marked leucocytosis and of localised pain, will settle any doubt. **1974** R. M. Kirk et al. *Surgery* ii. 35/2 This is the basis of Widal's reaction..for the diagnosis of typhoid, and it can also be used to detect dysenteric infection. **1976** *Lancet* 20 Nov. 1143/2 Stool microscopy, stool culture (including viral culture), and a Widal test failed to establish a diagnosis.

widbin, dial. var. WOODBINE.

widda(h, vulgar pronunciation of WIDOW.

†**'widdendream, 'widdrim.** *Sc. Obs.* Also **wudden dream, widdrum, -dreme, windrem, woo-, wuddrum.** [OE. *wódendréam* 'furor animi' and *wóddréam* 'demonium' (also phr. *on wódum dréame* in delirium, lit. in mad joy: see WOOD *a.*, DREAM *sb.*[1]). For its survival in Sc. cf. WEDENONFA'. For the phonology of the first syllable cf. Sc. *widcok* woodcock, *widbin* woodbine, and for the survival of the medial syllable, southern Sc. *Munonday* (OE. *mónandæg*) Monday.] A state of mental disturbance or confusion; a wild fit. Chiefly in phr. ***in a widdendream*** or ***widdrim***, usu. = in a 'furious' hurry, all of a sudden.

[*c* **893** Ælfred *Oros.* III. vi. 108 On swelcum wodan dreame, þæt hie woldon ælcne mon,..mid atre acwellan, & hit on mete oþþe on drynce to ȝepicgenne ȝesellan. *a* **1000** *Voc.* in Wr.-Wülcker 245/10 *Furor enim animi cito finitur, uel grauius est quam ira*, reþnes, wodendream. *c* **1000** Ælfric *Hom.* II. 110 Seo dohtor, þe on wodum dreame læȝ dweliȝende.]

1755 R. Forbes *Ajax's Sp.* etc. 31 At last we, like fierdy follows, flew to't flaught-bred, thinkin to raise it in a widden-dream. **1805** Jamieson *Water Kelpie* xix, The trout, the par, now here, now thare, As in a widdrim bang. **1819** W. Tennant *Papistry Storm'd* (1827) 45 Sae fiercelins had his wid-dreme stirr'd him. **1871** W. Alexander *Johnny Gibb* xxxix, [He] should, in a sort of reckless 'wudden dream', determine that [etc.].

widder, obs. f. WETHER, WITHER; dial. or vulgar f. WIDOW.

widderschins, -shins, -sins, etc., Sc. var. WITHERSHINS.

widdiful ('wɪdɪfʊl), *sb.* (*a.*) *Sc.* Forms: 6 **widdi-, -e-, -iefow, widdy fow, viddeful(l,** 8 **widdy-fou', 8–9 widdiefu',** 9 **wuddiefu', (widi-, woodiefu), widdiful (-fu').** [f. WIDDY + -FUL 2: = one who would fill a 'widdy' or halter.] One who deserves hanging, a gallows-bird; a scamp, rascal. (Cf. HEMPY.) Also *attrib.* or *adj.* Fit for a halter, deserving to be hanged; scampish, rascally.

1508 Dunbar *Flyting* 101 Wan wisaged widdefow, out of thy wit gane wyld. **1535** Lyndesay *Satyre* 3676 My Lords, for Gods saik let not hang me, Howbeit that widdiefows wald wrange me. *Ibid.* 3986 The widdifow wairdanis tuke my geir. **1549** *Compl. Scot.* vi. 41 Viddefullis al, viddefuls al grit and smal. **1737** Ramsay *Sc. Prov.* (1750) 123 Ye're a widdy-fou' against hanging time. **1793** Burns *Meg o' the Mill* ii, The Laird was a widdiefu', bleerit knurl. **1882** *Jamieson's Sc. Dict.*, *Widdifow*.., a cantankerous, spiteful person, of small stature. **1916** G. Abel *Wylins fae my Wallet* 15 The baillie loon, that widdiefu' Files sets me at the kye.

widdle ('wɪd(ə)l), *sb.*[1] *Sc.* and *north. dial.* Also **widdil, wuddle.** [app. f. WIDDLE *v.*[1]] Commotion, bustle; disturbance, trouble; strife, contention.

1786 Burns *Ep. to Major Logan* iii, To cheer you through the weary widdle O' this wild warl'. **1825** Jamieson s.v., They had a widdil thegither. **1847** J. Halliday *Rustic Bard* 326 This wearifu' world's a wuddle o' care.

widdle ('wɪd(ə)l), *sb.*[2] *colloq.* [Echoic: cf. PIDDLE *sb.*, WEE *sb.*[2], and WIDDLE *v.*[3]] An act of urination.

1954 J. Pudney *Smallest Room* 36 The *wee-wee*, the *widdle*, the *pee-pee*, and the *piddle*. **1969** D. Clarke *Nobody's Perfect* iii. 77, I hardly ever saw him unless I..wanted a widdle. **1977** A. Coren *Lady from Stalingrad Mansions* 63 Love is..mekkin' sure yer betrothed 'as a pensionable position wi' luncheon vouchers an' gets out of 'is bath when he wants a widdle.

†**widdle,** *v.*[1] *Sc. Obs.* Forms: 6 **wid(d)ill, widle,** 7 **widdle.** [Origin obscure.]

1. *trans.* To invoke or inflict a curse upon: = CURSE *v.* 2, 5.

1552 Abp. Hamilton *Catech.* (1884) 63 Quha brekis the secund command?..thai that..wariis, bannis and widdillis thair saule..for ony vaine mater. *Ibid.*, Thai that will nocht chasteis..thair barnis fra lesingis, sweiring, banning and widling. *a* **1568** in *Bannatyne MS.* (Hunter. Club) 385/29 The hennis of Hadingtoun sensyne wald nocht lay, For this wyld wilroun wich thame widlit sa and wareit. *a* **1585** Montgomerie *Cherrie & Slae* 250 Like Dido, Cupido I widill and warye.

2. To beguile, to lead astray.

1697 Cleland *Poems* 80 It's Antichrist his Pipes and Fidles, And other Tools, wherewith he Widdles Poor Caitiffs into dark delusions.

widdle, *v.*[2] *Sc.* and *north. dial.* Also 9 **wuddle.** [Parallel to WADDLE.] *intr.* To move slowly and irregularly; to waddle; to wriggle; *fig.* to work slowly and laboriously; to get ***through*** something in spite of difficulties or hindrances. Also **widdle-waddle** *v.*, and †*adv.*, with a waddling or unsteady movement.

1660 in W. W. Wilkins *Pol. Ball.* (1860) I. 160 But Noll, a rank rider, gets first in the saddle,..She quickly perceiv'd that he rode widdle-waddle. **1808** in Jamieson. **1844** *Whitelaw's Bk. Sc. Song* 268/2 We hope to wuddle through Life's linked and ravelled clew. **1864** Latto *Tam. Bodkin* xiii, Her mind was..engrossed wi' thochts o' her bit laddie, an' hoo he wad widdle through the warl'. **1886** Cunliffe *Gloss. Rochdale*, *Widdle-waddle*, to walk from side to side, as a duck. **1890** Service *Notandums* xix. 124, I aye like to be waunerin' aboot and widdlin' amang the beasts.

widdle ('wɪd(ə)l), *v.*[3] *colloq.* [f. as WIDDLE *sb.*[2]: cf. PIDDLE *v.* 2.] *intr.* To make water, to urinate. Hence '**widdling** *ppl. a.*

[**1956** G. Durrell *My Family & Other Animals* xi. 143 Larry's suggestion that [the puppies]..be called Widdle and the Puke was greeted with disgust by Mother.] **1968** *Listener* 13 June 785/2 *Work is a Four-Letter Word*, with its short-term expedients (including some inferior pop music and a widdling dog), is grimly unrisible. **1970** 'R. Gordon' *Doctor on Boil* ii. 15 From some of the receptacles you physicians produce, you seem to imagine a camel could widdle through the eye of a needle. **1974** 'D. Meiring' *President Plan* xii. 95 Martinez was practically widdling with excitement. **1983** W. Harriss *Bay Psalm Bk. Murder* ix. 82 He headed straight for me... I damn near widdled.

widdle, variant of WHIDDLE, to peach.

widdow, -ed, -er: see WIDOW, WIDOWED, WIDOWHEAD, WIDOWER.

widdrawte, var. WITHDRAUGHT *Obs.*

widdrim: see WIDDENDREAM.

widdy ('wɪdɪ). Chiefly *Sc.* Forms: 5 **widde, wedde,** *pl.* **wedeis, -ys, wyddis,** 6 **wedy, viddy, -ie, woddie,** *pl.* **widdeis, weddeis, veddeis,** 6–9 **widdie,** 7 **wyddie,** 8–9 **woodie, woody,** 9 **widdey, wuddy -ie,** 5– **widdy.** [Sc. and north. dial. variant of WITHY.]

1. A band or rope, properly one made of intertwined osiers or the like.

c **1470** Henry *Wallace* III. 215 Thai band thaim fast with wedeis [*ed.* **1570** widdeis] sad and sar. **1501** Douglas *Pal. Hon.* I. xii, Out throw the wod come rydand catiues twane, Ane on ane asse, a widdie about his mone. **1513** *Rec. Burgh Prestwick* (Maitland Club) 45 For..cuttyn of the vyddyis of þe dur. *a* **1578** Lindesay (Pitscottie) *Chron. Scot.* (S.T.S.) II. 90 Witht widdieis [*v.r.* windassis] and towis. *c* **1730** Burt *Lett. N. Scot.* (1754) I. 87 Instead of Ropes for Halters and Harness, they generally make use of Sticks of Birch twisted and knotted together; these are called *Woodies*. **1789** Burns *To Dr. Blacklock* vi, I hae a wife and twa wee laddies, They maun hae brose and brats o' duddies;..But I'll sned besoms —thraw saugh woodies Before they want. **1824** Carr *Craven*

Gloss., *Widdy*, twigs of willows or hazles dried partially in the fire, and then twisted into wreaths for many agricultural purposes.

2. A rope for hanging, a halter; used (like *halter* and *gallows*) in various allusive expressions referring to hanging.

In later use sometimes app. understood as = gallows (in forms *wuddy*, *woodie* perh. by association with *wood*).

c **1450** HOLLAND *Howlat* 823 Callit him thryss thevisnek, to thrawe in a widdy. **1500–20** DUNBAR *Poems* xxxiii. 48 He had purgatioun to mak a theif To dee withowt a widdy. **1508** KENNEDIE *Flyting w. Dunbar* 367 Thou has a wedy teuch.. about thy crag to rax. *c* **1536** LYNDESAY *Compl. Bagsche* 151 This Prouerb, it is of verite,.. Hiest in Court, nixt the weddie. *a* **1568** in *Bannatyne MS.* (Hunter. Club) 299/40 All tymes in thair legasie, Fyre, sword, watter and woddie, Or ane of thir infirmeteis. **1717** WODROW *Corr.* (1843) II. 221 In short, I think what the wooddie leaves the water gets. **1762** BP. FORBES *Jrnl.* (1886) 213 God sin the Liars girn i' the Widdy. **1785** BURNS *Twa Herds* xvi, Then Orthodoxy yet may prance, And Learning in a woody dance. **1818** SCOTT *Rob Roy* xxxiv, There is as much between the craig and the woodie as there is between the cup and the lip. **1893** STEVENSON *Catriona* iii, There's the shadow of the wuddy.. that lies braid across your path.

†**3.** A certain quantity of iron: perh. orig. a bundle bound with a 'widdy'. *Obs.*

1482 in *Charters*, etc. *Edin.* (1871) 168 The hundreth widde of Oismond irne..cumand to Leith. **1483** *Acta Audit.* in *Acta Dom. Conc.* II. Introd. 124, iij^xx xv wedeis of irne, price of the wedde ij s. **1484** *Exch. Rolls Scot.* IX. 239, xx wethyis ferri..xx wyddis ferri. **1527** in Sir W. Fraser *Sutherland Bk.* (1892) III. 79 Fowrtein xx of veddeis of irne. **1603** *Reg. Mag. Sig. Scot.* 516/1 Ilk hundreth wyddie of Oismond iryn of unfremen cumand to Leith.

4. *attrib.* and *Comb.* (in sense 2): †**widdy-neck**, one deserving or destined to be hanged. (See also WIDDIFUL.)

c **1480** HENRYSON *Fox & Wolf* 653 In dreid and schame our dayis we indure; Syne widdienek and crakraip callit als, And till oure hire hangit vp be the hals. *a* **1583** MONTGOMERIE *Flyting* 765 Spew bleck, widdie neck!

widdy, dial. or vulgar var. WIDOW.

widdy-widdy-way (ˌwɪdɪˌwɪdɪˈweɪ). *dial.* Also widdy(-way), etc. [A rhyme used during the game: see also in *Eng. Dial. Dict.* and quot. 1969 source below.] A children's game of tag.

1846 J. R. PLANCHÉ *Invisible Prince* I. ii. 9 And hail the scenes where I was wont to play At marbles, hopscotch, hoop, and widdy way. **1859** *Games & Sports for Young Boys* 1 *Widdy.* This is a very spirited game, and is peculiarly adapted for wintry weather. **1893–4** R. O. HESLOP *Northumb. Words* II. 788 *Widdy-widdy-way*,..a boys' game. Two boys start hand in hand from a 'bay', and endeavour to touch their opponents. Anyone touched must return with them to the bay and join hands with the first to make a fresh sally... If the chain of hands be broken, the sally has proved a failure, and each outsider endeavours to capture and ride in triumph on the back of one of his quondam pursuers. **1897** H. G. WELLS *Plattner Story* 250 Figures kept moving from one line to another, like children playing at Widdy, Widdy Way. **1969** I. & P. OPIE *Children's Games in Street & Playground* ii. 94 In Peckham Rye the game is known as 'Chain Widdy'.

wide (waɪd), *sb.* [absol. use of WIDE *a.* (OE. *wíde* did not survive.) Cf. ON. *vídd* width, widening, *víðir* the wide sea, the main, f. *víðr* WIDE *a.*]

†**1. a.** Width, breadth. *Obs.*

a **1300** *Cursor M.* 1646 Couetys, hordan, envie, and pride Has spred þis werld on lenth and wide. *Ibid.* 1676 A schippe ..Seuen score ellen lang and ten, Thrys aght on wyde, on heght fiueten.

†**b.** *on wide*: abroad, all around. *Obs.*

13.. *E.E. Allit. P.* B. 1423 He waytez onwyde, his wenches he byholdes.

2. †**a.** The open sea. **b.** A wide, extensive, or open space. Now only *poet.*

[Cf. *c* **1000** *Ags. Ps.* (Th.) xcii[i]. 4 Fram wæterstefnum widra manigra; Vulg. *a vocibus aquarum multarum.*]

c **1320** *Sir Tristr.* 1013 Þai seylden in to þe wide. **1833** TENNYSON *Two Voices* xl, The waste wide Of that abyss.

3. *Cricket.* [Short for *wide ball*, WIDE *a.* 10 a.] A ball bowled wide of the wicket, counting one against the bowler's side.

1846 W. DENISON *Cricket* 5 The parties deliver beyond their natural powers; control of the ball is thus lost, and a 'wide' is the consequence. **1850** 'BAT' *Crick. Man.* 46 Rule the [scoring] sheet..with three additional [lines] for wides, byes, and no-balls.

4. *to the wide*: to the extreme; entirely, utterly. Used in various slang phrs., as ***blind*** (***broke***, ***dead***, ***out***, etc.) ***to the wide***; ***done to the wide***: see DO *v.* 11 e.

1915 G. FRANKAU *Tid'apa* iii. 19 'Blind, blind to the wide.' It *was* shaky, his hand on the dipper-bar, As the water slopped over, gurgling, from its Ali-baba jar. **1920** WODEHOUSE *Jill the Reckless* xiv. 208 Here was a girl who seemed to like him although under the impression that he was broke to the wide. *a* **1936** KIPLING *Something of Myself* (1937) vi. 155, I have seen a Horse Battery 'dead to the wide' come in at midnight in raging rain. **1946** *Coast to Coast 1945* 29 Now yer broke to the wide—I'd rather yer died. **1958** F. C. AVIS *Boxing Dict.* 96 *Out to the wide*, completely unconscious. **1959** L. LEE *Cider with Rosie* 90 Wake up, lamb... He's wacked to the wide. Let's try and carry him up. **1963** M. DUGGAN in C. K. Stead *N.Z. Short Stories* (1966) 97 Honest, simple and broke to the wide.

wide (waɪd), *a.* Forms: 1–4 **wid**, 4–5 (6 *Sc.*) **wyd**, 4–6 **wyde** (4 *Sc.* **vyde**, 5 **wyyd**, **wijd**, 7 **weede**), 3– **wide**. Comp. **wider** (ˈwaɪdə(r)), also, with shortened vowel, 1 **widdra**, 4 **wydder**, 4–6 **widder** (5 -ir, -ur); sup. **widest** (ˈwaɪdɪst). [Com. Teut. (wanting in Gothic): OE. *wíd* = OFris., OS. *wíd* (MLG. *wîd*, MDu. *wijt*, Du. *wijd*, etc.), OHG., MHG. *wît* (G. *weit*), ON. *víðr* (Sw., Da. *vid*):—OTeut. **wīdaz*; further relations obscure.]

I. 1. a. Having great extent (esp. horizontally); vast, spacious, ample, extensive, roomy. *Obs.* exc. as generalized use of sense 5.

Beowulf 1859 Þenden ic wealde widan rices. *a* **900** CYNEWULF *Juliana* 9 Wæs his rice brad, wid & weorðlic. *c* **1386** CHAUCER *Prol.* 28 The chambres and the stables weren wyde. *Ibid.* 491 Wyd was his parisshe and houses fer a sonder. **1387** TREVISA *Higden* (Rolls) VI. 15 Cristendom was nyh wydder þan þe empere of Rome. *c* **1400** *Destr. Troy* 9481 He woundit þat worthy in his wide þrote. **1535** COVERDALE *Prov.* xxi. 9 It is better to dwell in a corner vnder yᵉ house toppe, then with a braulinge woman in a wyde house. **1600** SHAKS. *A.Y.L.* II. vii. 137 This wide and vniuersall Theater Presents more wofull Pageants then the Sceane Wherein we play in. **1600** *1st Pt. Sir J. Oldcastle* v. viii, The wide horrison. **1698** FRYER *Acc. E. India & P.* 263 The wide open Places under the Chief Cupuloes of their Buzzars. **1724** RAMSAY *Vision* xvii, A wyde and splendit hall. **1847** YEOWELL *Anc. Brit. Ch.* viii. 84 At Iona, or Icolm-kill, in the midst of wide waters. **1871** G. MACDONALD *Wks. Fancy & Imag.*, *Longing* iii, O all wide places, far from feverous towns!.. Room! give me room!

b. as a conventional epithet of words denoting an extensive area, esp. the earth and the sea (*poet.* and *rhet.*); as an epithet of *world*, in later use sometimes implying contrast to the privacy or security of one's own home or country. Also (*Austral.*) ***the wide brown land***, Australia; ***wide open spaces***: see OPEN *a.* 8 a.

a **1000** *Cædmon's Gen.* 104 Ac þes wida grund stod deop & dim. *c* **1000** ÆLFRIC *Hom.* I. 542 Sume hi wæron..on widdre sæ besencte. *c* **1200** ORMIN 12117 Off all þiss wide middellærd þe kinedomess alle. *c* **1205** LAY. 112 Eneas þe duc mid his driht folcke Widen iwalken ȝend þᵗ wide water. *c* **1250** *Gen. & Ex.* 60 Ðat was ðe firme morȝen tid, Ðat euere sprong in werld[e] wid. *a* **1300** *Cursor M.* 13702 Þair lagh wald man suld hir stan, In to midward þis temple wide. **13..** *K. Horn* 643 (Harl.) Þe kyng rod on hontynge to þe wode wyde. **1340** HAMPOLE *Pr. Consc.* II. 934 Alle þe world so wyde and brade, Our Lord speciali for man made. **1390** GOWER *Conf.* I. 179 Al the wide worldes fame Spak worschipe of hire goode name. *c* **1475** *Rauf Coilȝear* 2 Within thay fellis wyde. **1535** COVERDALE *Ps.* ciii[i]. 25 Yee the earth is full of thy riches. So is this greate and wyde see also. **1591** SPENSER *M. Hubberd* 135 As we bee sonnes of the world so wide. **1598** R. BERNARD tr. *Terence, Hecyra* IV. iv, Shall we rather..leaue him to the wide world? **1622** PEACHAM *Compl. Gentl.* iv. 35 Turne them out into the wide world with a little money in their purses. **1652** NEDHAM *Selden's Mare Cl.* 27 The wide Ocean. **1658** in *Verney Mem.* (1907) II. 69 The world being wyde she would not venture her conscience upon a disputable point. **1662** STILLINGFL. *Orig. Sacræ* I. i. §3 These were so fully known to him..that he needed not to go to School to the wide world. **1722** DE FOE *Plague* (1756) 141, I shall be turn'd a drift to the wide World. **1842** DICKENS *Amer. Notes* vi, The coarse and bloated faces..have counterparts..all the wide world over. **1844** KINGLAKE *Eothen* xv, A shout that tore the wide air into tatters. **1847** BUCKSTONE *Flowers of Forest* III. vii, No, no —not for the wide wide world. **1863** KINGSLEY *Water-Babies* iii, Tom thought nothing about what the river was like. All his fancy was, to get down to the wide wide sea. **1914** D. MACKELLAR *Witch Maid* 29 Her beauty and her terror—The wide brown land for me. **1934** J. & G. MACKANESS (*title*) The wide brown land. **1973** *Australian* 4 May 11 Migrants are staying away in droves from the widest and brownest part of this wide, brown land.

c. Of a garment or piece of dress: Capacious; large and loose. *Obs.* as a specific sense, exc. *dial.* in ***wide coat***, a great-coat, overcoat.

a **1225** *Ancr. R.* 56 Nu cumeð forð a feble mon, & halt him þauh heihliche, ȝif he haueð enne widne hod & one ilokene cope. *c* **1386** CHAUCER *Monk's Prol.* 61 Why werestow so wyd a Cope? **1393** LANGL. *P. Pl.* C. XIX. 271 Thenne hadde ich wonder of hus wordes and of hus wide cloþes. *c* **1450** *Mirk's Festial* 196 His cloþes were lompurt, and scho wold haue amende hom, but scho myght not, for þay wern so wyde. **1511** *Acc. Ld. High. Treas. Scot.* IV. 197 To be the King ane wyd doublete fra Maistir Johne of Murray. **1590** SHAKS. *Mids. N.* II. i. 256 And there the snake throwes her enammel'd skinne, Weed wide enough to rap a Fairy in. **1609** J. DAVIES *Humour's Heaven* I. iv, Poliphagus a sute of Satten ware, Made wide and side. **1825** BROCKETT *N.C. Gloss.*, *Wide-coat*, an upper or great coat.

2. *transf.* Extending over or affecting a large space or region; far-reaching, extensive. Chiefly *poet.*

a **1000** *Cædmon's Satan* 189 Þæs ðe ic ȝeþohte adrifan drihten of selde,..sceal [ic] nu wreclastas settan sorhȝcearig siðas wide. *a* **1300** *Cursor M.* 24991 He es tald alsua o sight sa wide, þat fra his sight mai naman hide. **1596** SPENSER *F.Q.* IV. ix. 23 They [*sc.* the winds]..tosse the deepes, and teare the firmament, And all the world confound with wide vprore. **1697** DRYDEN *Virg. Georg.* III. 660 He [*sc.* a snake] rages in the Fields, and wide Destruction threats. **1818** KEATS *Endym.* II. 307 O woodland Queen,..Where dost thou listen to the wide halloos Of thy disparted nymphs? **1841** JAMES *Corse de Leon* i, A turn where they could obtaine a wider view. **1859** HAWTHORNE *Marble Faun* xxxiii, After wide wanderings through the valley [etc.].

b. *Coal-mining.* (See quot. 1883, and cf. WIDE *adv.* 1 c.)

1883 GRESLEY *Gloss. Coal-mining*, *Wide Work.* A South Yorkshire system (now nearly obsolete) of working coal. Sets of short *stalls* or *banks*, 7 or 8 yards in width, forming a line of *faces* about 60 yards, were carried to the *rise*, about 3 or 4 feet of coal being left between each *bank*, the main road pillars being subsequently extracted. **1904** *Times* 23 May 7/6 Men engaged on 'wide' work were paid yardage to which they were not entitled.

†**3.** Great (in various non-physical senses). *Obs.*

a **1300** *Cursor M.* 2200 Þis nembrot wit his mikel pride Wend to wyrk wondres wide. *Ibid.* 20030 For ai þe mar i soght to sai, þe widder suld i find þe wai. *Ibid.* 23104 Wreches stad in wa ful wide. **1393** LANGL. *P. Pl.* C. XXI. 403 Now by-gynneþ..my grace to growe ay wydder and wydder. *a* **1400–50** *Wars Alex.* 1970 For wella wide ware þe wele,.. Bathe þi glorie & þi grace, þi gladnes in erthe, Miȝt þou þe marches of Messedoyne mayntene þi-selfe. *c* **1560** A. SCOTT *Poems* xxxvi. 62 Lowse thow my lippis, that tyme and tyd I may gif to the lovingis wyd.

4. *fig.* Having a large range; comprising, affecting, applying or relating to a great number or variety of persons, cases, subjects, points, etc.; extensive, largely inclusive; (of a word or term) having a large extent of meaning: = BROAD *a.* 10.

Common since 1800.

1534 WHITINTON *Tullyes Offices* I. D 4, Therfore ryseth the large and wyde prayse by rhetoriciens of Marathon [orig. *Hinc rhetorum campus de Marathone*]. *a* **1600** MONTGOMERIE *Misc. Poems* xliii. 35 So wyd thy word does waxe That the immortall maks. **1670** MILTON *Hist. Eng.* II. 77 These perpetual exploits abroad won him wide fame. **1782** MISS BURNEY *Cecilia* III. iv, I fear the misfortunes of Mr. Belfield have spread a ruin wider than his own. **1797** MALONE *Sir J. Reynolds' Wks.* I. p. xxxv, In the historical department [of pictures], he took a wider range. **1815** J. SMITH *Panorama Sci. & Art* II. 106 There is yet a wide field for useful experiment. **1843** RUSKIN *Mod. Paint.* I. I. I. ii, I want a definition of art wide enough to include all its varieties of aim. **1856** MISS MULOCK *John Halifax* xxxvi, The boy—to whose destination we had no clue but the wide word, America. **1858** MRS. PAUL *Uncle Ralph* xxii, 'Never is a wide word, Miriam,' said Ailie. **1865** TYLOR *Early Hist. Man.* i. 13 *note*, His wide knowledge of ethnography. **1868** NETTLESHIP *Ess. Browning* i. 54 How to use each his own and his mistresses' attributes for the widest good. **1868** M. PATTISON *Academ. Org.* 2 The ideas of the wider public. **1895** *Bookman* Oct. 15/1 [His] wide experience as a teacher ..and an inspector of schools.

b. Of views or opinions, or *transf.* of the person holding them: = BROAD *a.* 11.

1824 MACAULAY *Athen. Orators* ¶22 States have always been best governed by men who have taken a wide view of public affairs. **1833** TENNYSON *Two Voices* xlii, When, wide in soul and bold of tongue, Among the tents I paused and sung. **1884** *Spectator* 19 Apr. 513/2 Both the High Churchman and the Wide Churchman. *Ibid.*, The Wide Church or High-Church circles.

†**c.** Vague. *Obs. rare.*

1698 FRYER *Acc. E. India & P.* 288 Though his Verses are most Elegant,..yet the description is very wide.

II. 5. a. Having great extent from side to side; large across, or in transverse measurement. (Opp. to *narrow.*)

Now distinguished from *broad* in so far as it tends to be restricted to applications in which actual mensuration from point to point is possible or contemplated, and in which there is no implication of superficial extent; hence in certain technical uses (see quots.).

c **1000** *Ags. Gosp.* Matt. vii. 13 Þæt ȝeat is swyþe wid, & se weȝ is swiþe rum, þe to forspillednesse ȝelæt. **11..** in Birch *Cartul.* (1887) II. 207 Ðonon to widan ȝeate; ðonon to eadulfes mære. *a* **1300** *Cursor M.* 1682 Þu sal..Mak a dor wit mesur wide. *Ibid.* 8081 Þair muthes wide, þair eien brade, Vn-freli was þair face made. **1375** BARBOUR *Bruce* III. 23 Till sum gaiff thai woundis wid. *c* **1375** *Sc. Leg. Saints* iv. (*Jacobus*) 302 On a bryge, as þai can ryd Our a wattyr, depe and wyd. *c* **1384** CHAUCER *H. Fame* II. 289 Euery sercle causynge othir Wydder than hym self was. *c* **1440** *Promp. Parv.* 526/1 Wyyd, large yn brede. **1567** *Gude & Godlie B.* (S.T.S.) 22 Christis woundis wyde. **1632** MILTON *L'Allegro* 76 Shallow Brooks, and Rivers wide. **1642** TASMAN *Jrnl.* in *Acc. Sev. Late Voy.* I. (1694) 135 Those Men when they walked made very wide paces. **1667** MILTON *P.L.* VIII. 467 Wide was the wound, But suddenly with flesh fill'd up & heal'd. **1725** POPE *Odyss.* I. 173 A purple carpet spread the pavement wide. **1841** *Penny Cycl.* XIX. 256/2 One of the great recommendations of a wide gauge. **1868** *Rep. U.S. Comm. Agric.* (1869) 416 Making experiments in the cultivation of wheat in wide drilling and thin seeding. **1884** KNIGHT *Dict. Mech.* Suppl., *Wide Spade* (Whaling), used to cut the blubber in the rough, before mincing. **1888** JACOBI *Printers' Voc.*, *Wide measures*, long and wide measures of type, distinct from narrow or short ones.

b. *transf.* of the lateral boundaries: Having a wide space between, far apart. (Cf. 7 and 8.)

1840 DICKENS *Old Cur. Shop* i, It runs between green banks which grow wider and wider until at last it joins the broad vast sea.

c. As the final element in comb. with sbs. which denote regions, organizations, etc., as WORLD-WIDE, and *country-wide*, *nation-wide*, *state-wide* (see at first element), in the sense 'as wide as the——' or 'extending throughout the whole——'.

6. Having a specified or particular transverse measurement indicated by a numerical quantity or by a comparison; (so much) across.

971 *Blickl. Hom.* 127 Hwene widdre þonne bydenfæt. *a* **1000** *Cædmon's Gen.* 1307 Fær ȝewyrc fiftiȝes wid, ðrittiȝes heah, þreohund lang elnȝemeta. *c* **1250** *Gen. & Ex.* 565 Ðat arche was..l.ᵗⁱ elne wid, and .xxx.ᵗⁱ heȝ. *c* **1330** R. BRUNNE *Chron. Wace* (Rolls) 7503 Graunte me..Namore lond, wyd ne syd, þan y may sprede a boles hyd. *c* **1400** *Pilgr. Sowle* (Caxton 1483) IV. xxxvi. 84 A traylyng gowne of twelue yerdes wyde. *a* **1400–50** *Wars Alex.* 1324 Þurȝe þaim he rynnes, And makis a wai wyde enoȝe waynes to mete. *c* **1449** PECOCK *Repr.* III. xi. 347 That these schoon be notabli widdir than the meetenes of hem wolde aske. *Ibid.*, These schoon to be no wijdir than euen meete to hise sones feet.

1579 SPENSER *Sheph. Cal.* Sept. 210 Had his wesand bene a little widder, He would haue deuoured both hidder and shidder. **1592** SHAKS. *Rom. & Jul.* III. i. 100 'Tis not so deepe as a well, nor so wide as a Church doore. **1663** GERBIER *Counsel* 11 A Bed-chamber..Thirty foot wide. *Ibid.* 19 Windowes..must be higher then wide. **1842** LOUDON *Suburban Hort.* 637 Take half-inch and two-inch wide rods or laths. **1918** *Times Lit. Suppl.* 28 Mar. 152/1 The island is small..and at its widest part about a mile and a half in width.

7. a. (*a*) Opened widely, expanded; of the arms, stretched widely apart. Now superseded in general use by *wide open* (see WIDE *adv.* 3).

1508 DUNBAR *Tua Mariit Wemen* 335 3it tuk I neuir the wosp clene out of my wyde throte. **1560** DAUS tr. *Sleidane's Comm.* 449b, That a wyder entrie be not set open to yᵉ Turkes to inuade us. **1607** *Puritan* I. iv. 96 Speake lowe, George; Prison Rattes haue wider eares then those in Malt-lofts. **1611** *Bible* Isa. lvii. 4 Against whom make ye a wide mouth, and draw out the tongue? **1667** MILTON *P.L.* I. 762 All access was throng'd, the Gates And Porches wide. **1697** DRYDEN *Virg. Georg.* III. 431 The Mares..with wide Nostrils snuff the Western Air. **1707** E. SMITH *Phædra & Hipp.* I. i She from his wide, deceiv'd, desiring Arms Flew tastless. **1820** KEATS *St. Agnes* iv, Many a door was wide. **1822** GALT *Provost* xxxvi. With wide and wild arms, like a witch in a whirlwind. **1867** MORRIS *Jason* xv. 839 The three ..gazed at him with wide eyes wondering.

(*b*) *sup.* as quasi-*sb.* in phr. ***at widest.***

1610 SHAKS. *Temp.* I. i. 63 Though euery drop of water sweare against it, And gape at widst to glut him.

b. *Phonetics.* Of a vowel-sound: Pronounced with the tongue relaxed, or with a wider opening between it and some other part of the mouth than the corresponding *narrow* vowel.

1867 A. M. BELL *Visible Speech* 72 The vowels—whether 'Primary', 'Wide', or 'Rounded'—are divided into three classes of palato-lingual formations. **1890** [see NARROW *a.* 1 d].

III. 8. Extending far between limits; existing between two things which are far apart, literally or figuratively, as a distance or interval, a distinction or difference.

to give a wide berth to: see BERTH *sb.* 1.

1589 PUTTENHAM *Engl. Poesie* II. ix. (Arb.) 96 Bycause your concordes containe the chief part of Musicke in your meetre, their distaunces may not be too wide or farre a sunder. **1611** SHAKS. *Cymb.* v. v. 194 The wide difference 'Twixt Amorous, and Villanous. **1746** FRANCIS tr. *Hor., Epist.* II. ii. 293 The wide Distinction..Between an open, hospitable Man, And Prodigal; the Frugalist secure, And Miser, pinch'd with Penury. **1857** MILLER *Elem. Chem., Org.* (1862) i. §2. 49 The wider is the interval between the respective places in the series. **1865** RUSKIN *Sesame* ii. §75 There is a wide difference between elementary knowledge and superficial knowledge. **1912** *Daily Tel.* 19 Dec. 2/3 Among foreign railways,..after some wide fluctuations San Paulo finished at a substantial improvement.

†9. a. Situated a great way off, distant, far; in quot. 1590, held at a distance, not close. Also, situated at a specified distance (const. *of* = from). *Obs.*

Only predicative, or following the sb.; thus nearly approaching WIDE *adv.* 5.

?*a* **1400** *Arthur* 552 [He] strenghthed hym on eche syde Wyth Men of contreys ferre & wyde. **1535** COVERDALE *Ps.* cii[i]. 12 Look how wyde the east is from the west, so farre hath he set oure synnes from vs. **1590** SPENSER *F.Q.* II. viii. 36 His poinant speare he thrust..At proud Cymochles, whiles his shield was wyde. **1597** J. DEE *Diary* (Camden) 59 Calcot in Chesshyre, abowt six myles wide of Chester. **1682** O. HEYWOOD *Diaries* (1885) IV. 76 A place..4 miles wide of St. Albans. **1729** SWIFT *Hist. 2nd Solomon* Wks. 1841 II. 320 He was to set out..to another part of the kingdom, thirty miles wide of the place appointed. **1854** R. S. SURTEES *Handley Cr.* xxxvi, Shortstubble put him on a line as wide of his own wheat as he could.

b. *fig.* Far, far apart (in nature, character, views, statements, etc.); not in accordance, disagreeing, different; foreign, alien; far *from* (doing something). Const. *from, of.* (Often approaching or coinciding with 10b.) Now *rare.*

1542 UDALL *Erasm. Apoph.* Pref. **v b, Valerius Maximus and Plinius, in the reportyng of a certain alter[c]acion yᵗ was betwene Cn. Domitius & Lucius Crassus.., how wyde been thei the one from the other. ?**1545** BRINKLOW *Compl.* 11 What a cruell lawe is this! how farre wyde from the Gospel, yea from the lawe of nature also. **1561** T. HOBY tr. *Castiglione's Courtyer* II. (1577) G iij b, It seemeth a matter very wide from reason. **1566** W. P. tr. *Curio's Pasquine in Traunce* 9b, The which things..were al farre wide..from that true & most pure virgin the Lords mother. **1600** MARSTON, etc. *Jack Drum's Entert.* I. (1601) C 3b, Those that are farre more yong and wittie, Are wide from singing such a Dittie. **1630** HAKEWILL *Apol.* (ed. 2) Advts. Zz 2b, How farre wide the foure most noted doctours of the Westerne Church.. were in the exposition of many passages of holy Scripture. *a* **1700** EVELYN *Diary* 7 Nov. 1691, The relation he gave..was very wide from what we fancied. **1754** HUME *Hist. Eng.* I. *Chas. I* iii. 199 That rustic contempt of the fair sex, which James affected..was very wide of the disposition of this monarch. **1807** BENTHAM *Mem. & Corr.* Wks. 1843 X. 423 My own notions..were too wide of the notions prevalent among lawyers. **1812** CARY *Dante, Parad.* VIII. 136 Hence befals That Esau is so wide of Jacob. **1871** EARLE *Philol. Engl. Tongue* 244 Languages whose development has been wide of ours, as the Hebrew.

c. Situated far apart in a series: *spec.* in *Cards* (see quot.).

1897 R. F. FOSTER *Complete Hoyle* 414 Cards which are likely to form parts of sequences are called close cards, and those which are too widely separated to do so are called wide cards.

10. Deviating from the aim, or from the direct or proper course; missing the mark or the way; going astray. Also const. *of* (†*from*). (Most commonly predicative, approaching or coinciding with WIDE *adv.* 6.) **a.** *lit.*; *spec.* in *Cricket*, of a ball bowled too far aside from the wicket for the batsman to strike it (now usually *ellipt.*: see WIDE *sb.* 3).

1588 SHAKS. *L.L.L.* IV. i. 135 Wide a' th bow hand, yfaith your hand is out. **1669** STURMY *Mariner's Mag.* v. xii. 70 If the Shot be both wide and too low. *a* **1700** B. E. *Dict. Cant. Crew, Wide*, when the Biass of the Bowl holds not enough. **1851** LILLYWHITE *Guide Crick.* 13 The Umpire must take especial care to call..'Wide Ball' as soon as it shall pass the Striker. **1853** 'C. BEDE' *Verdant Green* I. xi, The first ball was 'wide'. **1854** LEVER *Sir Jasper Carew* xl, His guards were all wide, and his eyes unsteady.

b. *fig.* (*a*) without prep. (now *rare*): in early use often = Astray in opinion or belief, mistaken (now expressed by the full phr. *wide of the mark*). In quot. 1605, perh. Wandering in mind, delirious.

1561 T. HOBY tr. *Castiglione's Courtyer* I. (1577) E v b, Whoso heareth him, may.. thinke yᵗ he also with very little a do, might attaine to yᵗ perfection, but when he commeth to yᵗ proofe, shall finde himselfe farre wide. **1579** TOMSON *Calvin's Serm. Tim.* 140/2 Let vs see if this be well practised, alas, the matter is farre wide [orig. *Helas il s'en faut beaucoup*]. **1592** KYD *Sp. Trag.* III. xi, Tis neither as you thinke, nor as you thinke, Nor as you thinke; you'r wide all. **1605** SHAKS. *Lear* IV. vii. 50 *Lear.* You are a spirit I know, when did you dye? *Cor.* Still, still, farre wide. **1621** T. WILLIAMSON tr. *Goulart's Wise Vieillard* 107 To them that are wide, and strangers to the true light. **1632** MASSINGER *Maid Hon.* II. ii, You are wide, the whole field wide. I in my understanding Pitty your ignorance. *a* **1652** BROME *City Wit* v. i, *Py.* I know your purpose..; you come after the Marriage to forbid the banes... *Lin.* Good Mrs. Sneakup, you are wide. I come to wish joy to the match. **1687** SETTLE *Refl. Dryden* 83 He was a little wide there.

(*b*) Const. *from* (now rare or obs.), *of*: esp. in phr. ***wide of the mark.***

Sometimes scarcely distinguishable from 9b.

1566 W. P. tr. *Curio's Pasquine in Traunce* 34b, They are so farre wyde from the institution of Christ, & from the truth. **1587** *Mirr. Mag., Stater* i, Of wit and of reason recklesse and wide, That tooke so vppon vs to rule all the land. **1597** MORLEY *Introd. Mus.* 115 Though I should talke of halfe as manie more, I should not be farre wide of the truth. **1646** SIR. T. BROWNE *Pseud. Ep.* I. vii. 28 How wide he is from truth. **1672** W. WALKER *Parœm.* 29 You are quite out of the way; wide of the mark; clearly mistaken;.. *Tota erras via.* **1681** W. ROBERTSON *Phraseol. Gen.* (1693) 1321 He is wide of the cushion; *errat longè.* **1711** in *10th Rep. Hist. MSS. Comm.* App. v. 112 A lasting happiness, of which they are wide..thro' want of religion. **1735** BERKELEY *Def. Free-thinking* §46 Your Comment must be wide of the Author's meaning. **1747** *Mem. Nutrebian Crt.* II. 25 Sentiments.. you think so wide from the duty I should..pay. **1813** T. BUSBY *Lucretius* II. IV. *Comm.* p. xv, In his solar images he is not quite so wide from the fact. **1836** G. S. FABER *Prim. Doctr. Election* II. vi. (1842) 339 Most wide, then, from the mark..is the modern Calvinist. **1846** DICKENS *Cricket on Hearth* iii, You had best not interrupt me..till you understand me; and you're wide of doing so. **1848** —— *Dombey* xl, These questions..are all wide of the purpose. **1892** *Sat. Rev.* 15 Oct. 442/2 This belief of the French critic is not so very wide of the mark.

†c. Amiss. *Obs. rare.*

1614 BP. HALL *Contempl., Aaron & Miriam*, It were wide for vs, if our suites should be euer heard. *Ibid., Rahab*, It would bee wide with the best of vs, if the eye of God should looke backward to our former estate.

11. a. Going beyond bounds of restraint, propriety, or virtue; †unrestrained, violent (*obs.*); lax, loose, immoral (now *colloq.* or *slang*). Cf. BROAD *a.* 6, 8.)

1574 *Satir. Poems Reform.* xlii. 395 The Courteour, with wordis wyde, Said 'I hear nathing bot prouyde, And get now that, and get now this.' **1656** G. COLLIER *Answ. 15 Quest.* Pref., Any man that hath not a weak head and a wide conscience. **1902** WISTER *Virginian* xiii, Wide females in pink. **1904** *Daily Chron.* 29 Nov. 3/4 Madrid was full of 'wide' characters.

b. Going beyond bounds of moderation; excessive, immoderate. (Cf. slang *tall, steep.*)

1858 GREENER *Gunnery* Advts. 2 Producing..guns equal, if not superior, to anything yet produced by any maker whatever. This may be considered a wide assertion, but to prove he does not make it rashly he is prepared to test the fact by a competiton with any maker. **1895** *Daily News* 3 Sept. 7/5 Prices asked are very wide, and are beyond the values that merchants are disposed to give.

c. *slang.* Wide-awake, cute; shrewd, sharp-witted; (dishonestly) cunning or knowledge-able; skilled in sharp practice; engaging in shady dealings. See also *wide boy*, sense 12c below.

1879 *Macmillan's Mag.* Oct. 502/1, I got in company with some of the widest (cleverest) people in London. **1891** *Daily News* 24 Feb. 2/1 Well, she was tipsy; but she was very 'wide'. **1928** E. WALLACE *Gunner* xxviii. 226 You can handle these swells, Danty, and you're wide enough to keep yourself out of trouble. **1938** F. D. SHARPE *Sharpe of Flying Squad* i. 13 Underworld men and women..refer to themselves as 'wide people' or 'one of us'. They're a colourful, rascally lot these 'wide 'uns'. **1956** T. HUDDLESTON *Naught for your Comfort* ii. 28 He must become a 'tsotsi', a cosh-boy, a wide-guy—because at least there's excitement that way, while it lasts. **1981** *Event* 16 Oct. 101/3 They've never struck me as a bunch of wide-persons.

IV. 12. *Comb.* **a.** Parasynthetic, forming adjs. in -ED[2] (unlimited in number), as ***wide-arched, -armed, -banked, -beaked, -bellied, -branched, -brimmed, -chapped*** († ***chopt***), ***-handed, -hearted, -jointed, -lapped, -legged, -lipped, -margined, -minded, -necked, -realmed, -shouldered, -skirted, -sleeved, -spaced, -spanned, -streeted, -throated, -waked, -wayed, -windowed***, etc. **b.** Rarely with simple sbs., forming adjs. in sense 'having, involving, pertaining or relating to a (or the) wide ——', as ***wide-head, -row, -world.*** **c.** Special Combs.: **wide-angle** *a.*, applied to a lens of short focus, the field of which extends through a wide angle, used for photographing at short range; also in extended use and as *sb.*; **wide-aperture** *a.*, applied to (an instrument having) an objective lens of large diameter; **wide-band** *a.*, capable of transmitting or handling signals in a wide frequency band; **wide-bodied** *a.*, of a large jet aeroplane: having a wide fuselage (cf. JUMBO 1 b); also **wide-body** (usu. *attrib.*); **wide boy** *slang*, one who lives by his wits, often dishonestly; one who engages in petty-criminal activities, a 'spiv'; cf. sense 11 c; **wide-cut** *a. Oil Industry*, involving or produced by fractional distillation over a wide temperature range, or the fraction so obtained (see quots. 1958, 1966); **wide-eared** *a.*, having wide ears; also in sense 7, having the ears wide open, listening intently; **wide-eyed** *a.*, having wide eyes; usually in sense 7, having the eyes wide open, gazing intently; also *fig.*; **wide-gab**, local Sc. name for the fishing-frog or frog-fish; **wide gauge** *Railways* = BROAD GAUGE; **wide-leafed, -leaved** *a.*, having a wide leaf or leaves; *transf.* of a hat, broad-brimmed; **wide-meshed** *a.*, of a net: having wide meshes or interstices; (in quots., *fig.* of a survey); **wide receiver** *Amer. Football*, a pass receiver who stands several yards to the side of an offensive formation; cf. FLANKER *sb.*[1] 3 d, RECEIVER[1] 1 c (*a*); **wide-scale** *a.*, that occurs on a wide scale; extensive; cf. *large-scale* adj. s.v. LARGE *a.* 15 c; **wide screen**, a cinema screen which presents a wide field of vision in proportion to its height (see quot. 1957); freq. *attrib.*; † **wide-side** *a.* [SIDE *a.*[1]], wide and long, capacious; **wide-spectrum** *a.*, (*a*) *fig.*, effective against a wide range of organisms; = *broad-spectrum* s.v. BROAD *a.* D. 2; (*b*) *lit.*, characterized by light of a wide range of wavelengths; **wide-wale** a., of fabrics, esp. corduroy: broad-ribbed; **wide-winged** *a.*, having wide wings; flying through a wide space or region (chiefly *poet.*). See also WIDE-MOUTHED, -WATERED.

1878 ABNEY *Photogr.* (1881) 204 The next lens..is what is known as a '*wide angle' doublet, in which the separation between the lenses is very small, and their foci considerably shorter... Some of these combinations are made so as to cover a circle whose diameter subtends an angle of 90° from the optical centre. **1897** C. M. HEPWORTH *Animated Photogr.* xiii. 97 The use of a wide-angle lens..is.. abominable in connection with the production of a living photograph. **1947** H. LEWIS *Photogr. Today* 53 On analysing my shots..I usually find that 70 per cent. have been taken with a 5 cm. lens, 2 per cent. with a long-focus lens, and the rest with a 3.5 cm. wide-angle lens. **1955** *Mademoiselle* Mar. 113 *Oklahoma!* is made in 'fabulous new Todd-AO wide-angle, large-screen process'. **1965** C. FORSYTE *Double Death* iii. 22 He kept most of his attention on the special wide-angle driving mirror that raked the traffic on his tail. **1974** J. IRVING *158-Pound Marriage* i. 11 Forget the wide-angle. (I see Edith and Severin Winter only in close-ups.) **1983** *Which?* Sept. 388/3 A zoom lens lets you move in from a wide-angle view to a closer shot. **1958** *Amateur Photographer* 31 Dec. 914/2 For colour work a *wide-aperture lens is invaluable. **1966** D. G. BRANDON *Mod. Techniques Metallogr.* i. 57 With a wide-aperture telescope..there is no loss of brightness on magnification. **1820** KEATS *Lamia* II. 121 The glowing banquet-room shone with *wide-arched grace. **1869** J. R. LOWELL *Poet. Works* (1912) 415 The friend of all the winds, *wide-armed he towers. **1898** G. MEREDITH *Odes Fr. Hist.* 27 With view of wide-armed heaven. **1935** *Wireless Engineer* XII. 251/1 A means of examining the behaviour of *wide-band amplifiers when supplied with transient input waves. **1967** E. CHAMBERS *Photolitho-Offset* iv. 42 Although this ideal is not fully realised the fact remains that very acceptable results can be obtained using either wide-band (trichromatic) or narrow-cut filters. **1982** *Economist* 6 Mar. 25/2 The government wants Britain's cities to be cabled quickly with wideband cable. **1903** KIPLING *5 Nations* 73 Beside *wide-banked Ouse. **1807** J. BARLOW *Columbiad* III. 131 The *wide-beak'd hawk, that now beholds me die, soon with his cowering train my flesh shall tear. **1921** D. H. LAWRENCE *Birds, Beasts & Flowers* 30 An enormously wide-beaked mouth. **1921** W. DE LA MARE *Veil* 6 Dipped the *wide-bellied boat. **1980** *Jrnl. R. Soc. Med.* LXXIII. 7 A wide-bellied, ungainly but functional ambulance. **1970** *Times* 4 Sept. (Aviation Suppl.) p. i/4 About £200m. is being requested to get the proposed BAC 3-11 *wide-bodied, 250-seater subsonic airliner off the ground. **1983** *Times* 12 Feb. 20/8 Western airlines..were not allowed to fly wide-bodied jets such as the Airbus into Moscow until the Russians had developed their own Il 86. **1968** *Flight Internat.* 14 Nov. 777/1 BAC foresees a demand for standards matching the high-capacity *wide-body aircraft of the long-haul routes on short/medium-haul routes. **1979** T. GIFFORD *Hollywood Gothic* (1980) xxx. 308 The wide-bodies slid down..into the bustle of Los Angeles International Airport. **1983** *Listener* 9 June 6/2 Only two companies are now producing wide-body airliners. **1937** R.

WESTERBY *Wide Boys never Work* 232 Jim was turning, or had already turned, into a Smart Aleck, a *Wide Boy, a despiser of the Mugs who worked. **1947** *People* 22 June 5/3 It seems the wide boys are trying to muscle in and buy these dogs to put against one another in private fights. **1952** 'J. TEY' *Singing Sands* iv. 57 He was a wide boy. Wide boys don't want trouble. **1960** V. GIELGUD *To Bed at Noon* III. i. 159 Blackmailed—for the murder? Not even the widest of the local wide-boys could have got on to it. **1976** J. O'CONNOR *Eleventh Commandment* iii. 38 All the wide boys thought I had gone mad when they saw me in khaki. **1819** SCOTT *Ivanhoe* i, Short-stemmed, *wide-branched oaks. **1918** J. W. GERARD *Face to face with Kaiserism* xv. 180 An actress who wore a *wide-brimmed hat. **1610** SHAKS. *Temp.* I. i. 60 This *wide-chopt-rascall. **1958** *Chambers's Techn. Dict.* 1027/2 **Wide-cut fuel*.., low octane petrol (gasoline) obtained from wide-cut distillation used in turbojets in order to conserve kerosene. **1966** *McGraw-Hill Encycl. Sci. & Technol.* X. 54/2 Petroleum is separated by distillation into fractions designated as (1) straight-run gasoline..; (2) middle distillate..; (3) wide-cut gas oil, which boils at about 345–540°C,..and (4) residual oil. **1982** *Fuelling Aviation* (Shell Internat. Petroleum Co. Ltd.) 5/2 The military wide-cut fuel is called JP-4 and this is the major fuel for the airforces of the world. **1684** *Lond. Gaz.* No. 1976/4 A black Coach Mare.., a little *wide Eared. **1865** KINGSLEY *Herew.* iv, The boys listened, wide-eyed and wide-eared. **1788** COWPER *Gratitude* 11 This wheel-footed studying chair, ..*Wide-elbow'd, and wadded with hair. **1853** TENNYSON in Ld. T. *Mem.* (1897) I. 369 The *wide-eyed wonder of a babe has a grandeur in it. **1855** KINGSLEY *Heroes, Argon.* I. 80 The boy listened wide-eyed. **1894** *Forum* (N.Y.) Feb. 717 Madison's..wide-eyed prudence in counsel. **1923** D. H. LAWRENCE *Birds, Beasts & Flowers* 109 The human soul is fated to wide-eyed responsibility In life. **1983** L. DEIGHTON *Berlin Game* ix. 95 You ask him all those wide-eyed innocent questions about making profits from cheap labour. **1808** NEILL in *Mem. Wernerian Nat. Hist. Soc.* (1811) I. 548 *L[ophius] piscatorius*... Frog-fish... In the North Isles of Scotland, it is..termed the *Wide-gab, the mouth being hideously large. **1836** YARRELL *Brit. Fishes* I. 269 The Fishing Frog. Angler. Sea Devil. Wide Gab. Scotland. **1841** *Wide gauge [see WIDE *a.* 5 a]. **1982** S. G. DUFF *Parting of Ways* iv. 43 We all boarded the train for Moscow, changing onto the wide-gauge railway at the Soviet frontier. **1600** BRETON *Pasquil's Foole's-cappe* Wks. (Grosart) I. 20/2 In the aime of Wisdomes eye, *Wide handed Wits will euer shoote awry. **1870** MORRIS *Earthly Par.* III. IV. 371 The *wide-head oaks. **1855** KINGSLEY *Westw. Ho!* viii, The old Anglo-Norman teachableness and *wide-heartedness. **1917** *Blackw. Mag.* Nov. 677/1 Ladies..narrow in their interests, ..but wide-hearted. **1874** J. H. PARKER *Introd. Gothic Archit.* I. i. (ed. 4) 11 *Wide-jointed masonry is a usual characteristic of the eleventh century in England and Normandy. **1680** *Lond. Gaz.* No. 1527/4 Open *wide-kneed Breeches. **1856** J. G. WHITTIER *Poet. Works* (1898) 353/1 Pacific rolls his waves a-land, From many a *wide-lapped port and land-locked bay. **1928** BLUNDEN *Japanese Garland* 19 Fine fields, wide-lapped, whose loveliest-born Day's first bright cohort finds. **1779** P. FRENEAU *House of Night* in *U.S. Mag.* Aug. 356 A *wide-leaf'd table stood on either side. **1855** MOTLEY *Dutch Rep.* VI. vii. (1866) 894 He wore a wide-leaved..hat of dark felt. **1894** WEYMAN *Man in Black* ix, A dark, sallow man,..with a wide-leafed hat. **1938** R. GRAVES *Coll. Poems* 28 The *wide-legged robin with his breast aglow. **1837** DICKENS *Pickw.* xxxviii, Those *wide-lipped crystal vessels..in which chemists..measure out their liquid drugs. **1889** O. WILDE in *Fortn. Rev.* Jan. 43 Book-bindings, and early editions, and *wide-margined proofs. **1938** *Dialect Notes* VI. 626 Professor A. H. Marckwardt.. has begun a *wide-meshed survey of the Great Lakes region and the Ohio River valley. **1980** *English World-Wide* I. I. 28 Unfortunately..his survey is even more wide-meshed than Orton's. **1883** *A. Barratt's Phys. Metemp.* Pref. p. xx, In politics his sympathies were liberal and *wide-minded. **1914** TOLLINTON *Clement of Alex.* II. xx. 273 Wide-minded teachers, who have the power to discern affinities and to greet the ally in disguise. **1880** J. DUNBAR *Pract. Papermaker* 69 A *wide-necked glass-stoppered bottle. **1725** POPE *Odyss.* XIII. 506 At his side a wretched scrip was hung, *Wide-patch'd, and knotted to a twisted thong. **1838** MRS. BROWNING *Island* ix, *Wide-petalled plants. **1968** *Redskins* 17 Nov. 77/3 Depth at *wide receiver is strong, too, in rookie Dennis Homan. **1981** *Washington Post* 8 Apr. D 1 We will have to take the best athlete available... That could be an offensive lineman, a running back or a wide receiver. **1821** COBBETT *Rur. Rides* 9 Nov. (1885) I. 28 The advantages of the *wide-row culture. **1958** G. LIENHARDT in Middleton & Tait *Tribes without Rulers* 108 There was little *wide-scale co-operation against the common enemies. **1980** *Daily Tel.* 26 May 6/7 By confining the emergency arrangements as far as possible to the Bristol line, BR has avoided widescale timetable changes. **1931** *Ann. Reg. 1930* II. 48 The *Wide Screen is still only a matter for experiment, as standardisation has not yet been achieved. **1932** *Ibid. 1931* 47 The 'Wide Screen' invention, though perfected, was not offered to the public by the big producing concerns, seeing that it would involve the studios in huge expenditure. **1953** *Manch. Guardian* 13 Aug. 4/7 Hollywood..had decided to coast for the present on a compromise between 3-D and Cinemascope—namely on the less spectacular development known as Wide Screen. **1957** *Encycl. Brit.* XV. 862/1 Basically 'wide screen' means any departure from the screen proportions fixed by Edison and his contemporaries at 4 to 3 (or 1·33 to 1); *i.e.*, three units high for every four wide... If the aspect ratio were to be changed there was only one practical way—screens would have to be wider. **1967** H. HARRISON *Technicolor Time Machine* (1968) iii. 27 An accurate, full-length, wide-screen, realistic, low-budget, high-quality historical. **1976** *National Observer* (U.S.) 16 Oct., Imagine, right before your eyes on the wide screen, the stern of the Titanic..comes shooting out of the water as if the projector had been reversed. **1935** KIPLING *Two Forewords* 19 But *thou*, O Nakhoda, art young and *wide-shouldered. **1973** T. PYNCHON *Gravity's Rainbow* I. 127 A few women in clinking boots and wide-shouldered swagger coats, but no children. **1606** SYLVESTER *Du Bartas* II. iv. II. *Magnificence* 266 Glory..Her *wide-side Robes.. All Story-wrought with bloudy Victories. **1605** SHAKS. *Lear* I. i. 66 Champains rich'd With plenteous Riuers, and *wide-skirted Meades. **1838** DICKENS *O. Twist* xxxvii, The coat was wide-skirted. *c* **1590** GREENE *Fr. Bacon* xi. 129 A *wide sleeued gowne. **1926** D. H. LAWRENCE *David* viii. 63 Takes off striped coat, or wide-sleeved tunic. **1980** *Catal. Fine Chinese Ceramics* (Sotheby, Hong Kong) 214 A Jade Carving of a lady wearing a wide-sleeved robe. **1665** BRATHWAIT *Comm. Two Tales* (1901) 62 She was gap-tooth'd, or *wide-spaced. **1889** *Pall Mall Gaz.* 30 Aug. 3/2 Wide-spaced houses, beautiful gardens. *a* **1878** SIR G. SCOTT *Lect. Archit.* (1879) I. 65 *Wide-spanned arches. **1959** S. DUKE-ELDER *Parsons' Dis. Eye* (ed. 13) xv. 175 One of the *wide-spectrum antibiotic drugs such as the tetracyclines. **1972** *Country Life* 25 May 1351/1 The farmer uses..a wide-spectrum weedkiller, which is a mixture of chemicals designed to control a whole range of weeds. **1977** J. L. HARPER *Population Biol. Plants* x. 321 They inserted wide-spectrum fluorescent tubes between the rows of a close canopied crop of soyabeans. **1982** *Sci. Amer.* Mar. 98 Snakes of two families can detect and localize sources of infrared radiation. Infrared and visible-light information are integrated in the brain to yield a unique wide-spectrum picture of the world. **1868** M. COLLINS *Sweet Anne Page* III. 187 *Wide-streeted Troy. **1591** PERCIVALL *Sp. Dict.*, *Papado*, *wide throated. *a* **1627** MIDDLETON *Mayor of Quinb.* I. i, Will that wide-throated Beast, the multitude, Never leave bellowing? **1791** COWPER *Iliad* x. 8 Wide-throated war calamitous. **1856** J. G. WHITTIER *Poet. Works* (1898) 52/2 With steeds of fire and steam, *Wide waked Today leaves Yesterday behind him like a dream. **1957** M. R. PICKEN *Fashion Dict.* 374/2 **Wide-wale serge*, serge with broad diagonal weave. **1980** L. BIRNBACH et al. *Official Preppy Handbk.* 98 Wide wale corduroy pants. **1848** BUCKLEY *Iliad* 23 The *wide-wayed city of the Trojans. **1869** J. R. LOWELL *Poet. Works* (1917) A life *wide-windowed, shining all abroad, Or curtains drawn to shield from sight profane. **1970** *Daily Tel.* 30 Apr. 17 A wide-windowed bar parlour. **1818** SHELLEY *Hom. Moon* 3 Muses ..Sing the *wide-winged Moon! **1848** BAILEY *Festus* (ed. 3) 250 The wide-winged wind. **1871** TENNYSON *Last Tourn.* 423 The wide-wing'd sunset of the misty marsh. **1884** J. G. WOOD in *Sunday Mag.* May 307/2 Wide-winged as they are, the Locusts are very feeble in the air. **1851** RUSKIN *Stones of Venice* I. App. xv. 385 He [*sc.* Rubens] has neither cloister breeding nor boudoir breeding,..but he has an open sky and *wide-world breeding in him.

wide, *adv.* Forms: 1– **wide**, (3 **weide**), 3–4 **wid**, 4–6 **wyde**, (4 *Sc.* **vyde**), 5 (6 *Sc.*) **wyd**. [OE. *wíde* = OS. *wîdo* (MLG., MDu. *wîde*, Du. *wijd*), OHG. *wîto* (MHG. *wîte*, *wît*, G. *weit*), ON. *víða* (Sw., Norw. *vida*): advb. f. OE. *wíd*, etc. WIDE *a.*] = WIDELY, in various senses.

In modern texts freq. illogically hyphened to a pple.

1. a. Over or through a large space or region; so as to reach or affect many or various places or persons; far abroad. Chiefly *poet.* (superseded in prose by *far and wide*: see b).

Beowulf 1403 Lastas wæron æfter waldswaþum wide ȝesyne. *c* **1000** *Ags. Gosp.* Matt. xxiv. 7 Mann-cwealmas beoð & hungras wide ȝeond land. *c* **1200** *Trin. Coll. Hom.* 87 He wandrede wide, weruende longe, sechende him oðer stede. *c* **1205** LAY. 25662 Þet lond he weste wide. **1297** R. GLOUC. (Rolls) 921 We beþ men wide idriue aboute Fram contreie to contreie. **13..** *K. Alis.* 7118 (Laud MS.), His Marshal Tholomeu þat many Prince wyde kneu. **1377** LANGL. *P. Pl.* B. XIV. 98, I wiste neuere.. Man þat with hym spake, as wyde as I haue passed! **1387** TREVISA *Higden* (Rolls) VI. 399 He..sprad þe endes of his kyngdom wydder þan dede his fader. *c* **1400** *Parce Michi* 183 in *26 Pol. Poems* 148 In salt see I sayled well wyde. **1596** DALRYMPLE tr. *Leslie's Hist. Scot.* (S.T.S.) I. 45/16 Quhair ance it fixis the rute it spredis the selfe sa braid and wyde, that [etc.]. **1670** MILTON *Hist. Eng.* VI. 247 Thence horsing thir Foot, diffus'd far wider thir outragious incursions. **1726–46** THOMSON *Winter* 801 There..Wide roams the Russian exile. **1740** AKENSIDE *Ode, On Winter-Solstice* v, Each hov'ring tempest..Which now wide-threat'ning loads the sky. **1831** WORDSW. *Yarrow Revisited* 9 Grave thoughts ruled wide on that sweet day. **1889** SWINBURNE *Poems & Ball.* Ser. III. *Jacobite's Exile* xiv, On Keilder-side the wind blaws wide.

b. in phr. ***far and wide*** (rarely ***wide and far***); † ***wide and side*** (see SIDE *adv.*[1] 1).

a **900** *O.E. Martyrol.* 10 June 94 He..ferde..feorr ond wide ȝeond middanȝeard. *c* **900** tr. *Bæda's Hist.* III. x, Wæron þas wundor feorr & wide ȝemæred. *a* **1000** *Andreas* 1637 þa ȝesamnodon..weras..wide & side. *c* **1200**– [see SIDE *adv.*[1] 1]. *a* **1250** *Owl & Night.* 710 (Jesus MS.) þu axest me..[I]f ich con eny oþer dede Bute syngen in sume tyde & bringe blisse veor & wyde. *c* **1250** *Gen. & Ex.* 1256 Fro ðe riche flod eufrate, Wid and fer to ðe rede se. *c* **1400** *St. Alexius* 161 (Cotton MS.) Hys Fader send bothe fer and vyde Messengers on euery syde. **1560** DAUS tr. *Sleidane's Comm.* 196 b, They distroye the countrie with fyre farre & wyde. **1592** SHAKS. *Rom. & Jul.* II. iv. 91 That word, broad, ..added to the Goose, proues thee farre and wide, a broad Goose. **1667** MILTON *P.L.* II. 133 Thir Legions..Scout farr and wide into the Realm of night. **1761** GRAY *Fatal Sisters* 60 Far and wide the notes prolong. **1813** SCOTT *Rokeby* v. x, Their vassals wander wide and far [:war]. **1828** SOUTHEY *Ess.* (1832) II. 434 Multitudes..assemble, coming from far and wide. **1862** H. KINGSLEY *Ravenshoe* xix, Though they scoured the country far and wide.

c. *Coal-mining.* (See WIDE *a.* 2 b.)

1904 *Times* 23 May 7/6 Payment was by tonnage raised when working 'wide'—*i.e.*, on the face of the seam.

2. a. With a large space or spaces between; at a wide interval or intervals; far apart or asunder; in quot. 1481, with 'wide' or long steps. (Cf. 5.)

a **1000** *Wife's Compl.* 13 þæt hy todælden unc þæt wit ȝewidost in woruldrice lifdon. *a* **1122** *O.E. Chron.* (Laud) an. 1012 þa to ferde se here wide swa he ær ȝegaderod wæs. *a* **1240** *Ureisun* in *O.E. Hom.* I. 201 Hwi ne worþe ich me bi-tweonen þeo ilke ermes so swiðe wide to-spredde and i-opened? **1481** CAXTON *Reynard* xxxix. (Arb.) 105 The wulf stode wyder than reynard dyde and ofte ouertoke hym. **1684** BURNET tr. *More's Utopia* II. 68 Where the Towns lie wider, they have much more Ground. **1727** A. HAMILTON *New Acc. E. Ind.* I. xii. 136 The Churches being built wide from one another. **1820** KEATS *Lamia* II. 178 A sacred tripod.. Whose slender feet wide-swerv'd upon the soft..carpets. **1861** READE *Cloister & H.* i, But when Elias whispered 'Sit wider!' says she, 'Ay! the table will soon be too big for the children.' **1885** *Manch. Exam.* 22 June 5/3 Their fields of activity are so wide apart.

b. Of a horse: With the legs apart: opp. to NEAR *adv.*[2] 11.

1680 *Lond. Gaz.* No. 1557/4 A Bright Bay Gelding.. Walks and Gallops wide behind. **1737** BRACKEN *Farriery Impr.* (1757) II. 40 A Horse that goes wide before, and near behind. *Ibid.* 63 He should stand pretty wide behind, and near before.

c. Loosely asunder; so as not to remain close or in contact.

1784 COWPER *Task* I. 567 The sportive wind blows wide Their flutt'ring rags, and shows a tawny skin. **1819** SHELLEY *Cyclops* 66 Shaking wide thy yellow hair. **1833** TENNYSON *Lady of Shalott* III. v, Out flew the web and floated wide.

3. With a wide or broad opening; esp. with *open* vb. or adj. = fully; to the full extent; with *fling*, *fly*, *set*, etc. (in ref. to a door, gate, or the like) = *wide open* (coinciding with the predicative use of WIDE *a.* 7).

With *wide open* cf. Du. *wijd open*, G. *weit offen*, ON. *víðopnir* name of the hall of Hel.

c **1000** *Ags. Ps.* (Th.) cxviii[i]. 131 Muð ic ontynde minne wide. *c* **1220** *Bestiary* 506 Ðanne him hungreð he gapeð wide. *a* **1400–50** *Wars Alex.* 2142 Werpis þam vp..& wyde open settis. *c* **1400** *Siege Jerus.* (E.E.T.S.) 22/389 A dragoun ..Wydegapande,..gomes to swelwe. *c* **1450** *Cursor M.* 18125 (Laud MS.) Opyn your yates ye prynces wyde. **1535** COVERDALE *Ps.* lxxx[i]. 10 Open thy mouth wyde, & I shal fyll it. **1610** SHAKS. *Temp.* II. i. 214 This is a strange repose, to be asleepe With eyes wide open. **1718** POPE *Iliad* XV. 813 The Scene wide-opening to the Blaze of Light. **1727–46** THOMSON *Summer* 1145 Wide-rent, the clouds Pour a whole flood. **1798** COLERIDGE *Anc. Mar.* I. ii, The Bridegroom's doors are opened wide. **1824** BYRON *Juan* XVI. cxvii, The door flew wide. **1854** PATMORE *Angel in Ho., Betrothal* 18 The windows, all wide open thrown. **1895** RIDER HAGGARD *Heart of World* xvi, The doors were flung wide. **1909** STACPOOLE *Pools of Silence* xix, [Elephants] with trunks swung up, ears spread wide.

4. ***wide open***. † **a.** (Of a person): Stretched at full length, esp. on the back. *Obs.*

13.. *Northern Passion* (1913) I. 187/1604 A token ihesu.. And leiden him wid opene on þe rod. *a* **1440** *Sir Degrev.* 335 He laf slawe..Forty score..Wyd opene one here bake. **14..** *Voc.* in Wr.-Wülcker 607/43 *Resupinus*, wyde ope. **1526** *Pilgr. Perf.* (W. de W. 1531) 254 He thus lyenge wyde open, & they goynge ouer hym & bestrydynge hym. **1551** T. WILSON *Logic* D vj b, Whan a mans body is in any wyse placed, as to lie a syde, to stande vpright, to sitte, to leane, to lye grouelyng, to lye wyde open.

b. *Boxing*, etc. Fully exposed to assault; unprotected, off one's guard. Freq. *fig.*, esp. in phr. ***to leave*** (***lay***, etc.) (oneself) ***wide open***.

1915 E. CORRI *30 Yrs. Boxing Referee* 150 Johnny Summers..in an unguarded moment, left himself wide open and encountered one of the most decisive knock-out punches I ever saw. **1941** B. SCHULBERG *What makes Sammy Run?* i. 14 You never find me going in for favors... It leaves you wide open. **1948** 'N. SHUTE' *No Highway* vi. 148 Honey lays himself wide open to that sort of thing. **1966** 'A. HALL' *9th Directive* iv. 42 One fine day he would catch me wide open and slam me down.

c. *transf.* Of an issue, case: not circumscribed or prejudiced by conditions; unrestricted (in its implications, effects, etc.); not resolved or decided; *spec.* of a police investigation.

1963 'J. MELVILLE' *Burning is Substitute* iii. 51 Charmian suddenly had the feeling that this affair..was wide open, could reach anywhere. **1970** *Daily Tel.* 10 July 19 The fate of Penguin Publishing Company is still wide open. **1973** J. THOMSON *Death Cap* iii. 41 They're the only people who so far have entered the case... As far as I'm concerned, it's still wide open. **1982** C. AIRD *Last Respects* xiii. 137 It's [*sc.* a murder enquiry] what you might call wide open still... You'll have to look on it as a challenge.

5. At (to, from) a (great, or specified) distance; far, far away, far off; (so far) away or off. Now only *dial.*

Beowulf 1588 Hra wide sprong. *a* **1250** *Owl & Night.* 288 Ich wende from heom wide. **1387** TREVISA *Higden* (Rolls) II. 5 White rokkes aboute þe clyues of þe see þat were i-seie wide [L. *a longe apparentibus*]. **1572** *Satir. Poems Reform.* xxxi. 176 Wandering wyde fra this countrie Amang all vther Natiounis. **1590** SPENSER *F.Q.* I. i. 34 A little wyde There was an holy Chappell edifyde. **1623** J. TAYLOR (Water P.) *New Discov.* B 1, A Towne call'd Goreing, stood neare two miles wide. **1690** TEMPLE *Misc.* II. ii. 57 The Chineses: a People, whose way of thinking, seems to lie as wide of ours in Europe as their Country does. **1693** PLOT in *Miscell. Cur. Subj.* (1714) 44 His Ships..lying above a Mile and half wide off the Town of Sandwich. **1756** WASHINGTON *Lett.* Writ. 1889 I. 391 Fort Cumberland lying..wide of all other forts. **1857** HAWTHORNE *Engl. Note-bks.* (1870) II. 197 Not only in this district, but wide away. **1859** MEREDITH *Juggling Jerry* iv, I was a lad not wide from here.

6. At a distance to one side; aside from the aim, or from the direct or proper course; so as to miss the mark or the way; astray. Also const. *of* (†*from*). Cf. WIDE *a.* 10. **a.** in physical sense. *spec.* in *Cricket*, out of reach of the batsman.

1545 ASCHAM *Toxoph.* I. (Arb.) 101 To shoote wyde and far of the marke. *Ibid.* 102 Than..those be wiser men, which couete to shoote wyde than those whiche couete to hit the prycke. **1590** SPENSER *F.Q.* I. xi. 5 Then bad the knight his Lady..to an hill her selfe with draw aside,..She him obayd, and turnd a little wyde. **1602** SHAKS. *Ham.* II. ii. 494 Pyrrhus at Priam driues, in Rage strikes wide. **1639** FULLER *Holy War* I. xvii. 27 In bowling they must needs throw wide, which know not the green or alley whereon they play. **1687** A. LOVELL tr. *Thevenot's Trav.* I. 97 A little wide of the way to the Right Hand, I saw the Church. **1799** E. DU BOIS *Piece Fam. Biog.* II. 3 The doctor..had escaped by going a little wide of the ass. **1833** NYREN *Yng. Crick. Tutor* 24 A..ball ..pitched a little wide of the off stump. **1857** HUGHES *Tom Brown* II. viii, Johnson the young bowler is getting wild, and bowls a ball almost wide to the off. **1859** LEVER *Dav. Dunn* xlix, He shot with the pistol, he fenced, he whipped the trout stream... He only hit the bull's-eye once in three shots—he fenced wide—a pike carried off his tackle. **1876** *Coursing Calendar* 27 Well Park,..raced past Skedaddle for first turn, and went wide. **1899** RIDER HAGGARD *Swallow* xviii, [He] fired at him, but the ball went wide.

b. *fig.* (or in fig. context); †in early use often = so as to err, mistakenly (cf. WIDE *a.* 10 b).

1534 MORE *Comf. agst. Trib.* I. 1151/2 Nay Cosyn,..there walke you somewhat wide, for ther you defende your owne righte for your temporal auayle. **1535** COVERDALE *Bible* Prol., Many wryters..seldome made mencyon of yᵉ scripture of the Byble: & though they some tyme aleged it, yet was it done..so wyde from yᵉ purpose, that a man maye well perceaue, how that they neuer sawe the oryginall. **1542** UDALL *Erasm. Apoph.* 269 Cæsar auouched hym to had dooen ferre wyde. *c* **1586** C'TESS PEMBROKE *Ps.* LXVII. ii, Thou their guide Go'st never wide From truth and righteousnes. **1586** DAY *Engl. Secretorie* I. (1625) 80 You reckon too wide;..you are too much deceived. **1599** SHAKS. *Much Ado* IV. i. 63 Is my Lord well, that he doth speake so wide? **1610** HOLLAND *Camden's Brit.* 486 If I should fetch it from *Gron* a Saxon word that signifieth a fenny place, I might perhaps goe wide. *a* **1625** FLETCHER *Captain* II. ii, You hurt not me, Your anger flies so wide. **1677** OTWAY *Titus & Berenice* I. ii, Thou answerst wide of my desire. **1705** tr. *Bosman's Guinea* 242 This carries me wide from my Subject. **1710** STEELE *Tatler* No. 234 ¶4 To compare our Practice with their Precepts, and find where it was that we came short, or went wide. **1784** COWPER *Task* II. 810 Vice parries wide Th' undreaded volley [of rusted arrows] with a sword of straw.

7. *Comb.* with pres. or pa. pples., less commonly with adjs., forming adjs. (unlimited in number), as ***wide-branching***, ***-circling***, ***-climbing***, ***-consuming***, ***-echoing***, ***-expanding***, ***-extending***, ***-gaping***, ***-ranging***, ***-reaching***, ***-resounding***, ***-rolling***, ***-straddling***, ***-stretching***, ***-sweeping***, ***-wasting***, ***-winding***, ***-yawning***; ***wide-expanded***, ***-extended***, ***-flung***, ***-opened***, ***-stretched***; ***wide-apart***, ***-distant***, ***-imperial***; **wide-open** *a.*, (*a*) *lit.* (see also senses 3, 4); (*b*) *U.S.* Of a town: not oppressed by laws or law enforcement. See also WIDE-AWAKE, -SPREAD, -SPREADING *adjs.*; WIDE-WHERE *adv.*

1941 E. BOWEN *Look at all those Roses* 39 The *wide-apart birch-trees. **1983** T. HUGHES in *Listener* 21 Apr. 27/1 They have a chirruppy, chicken-sweet expression With goo-goo starlet wide-apart eyes. **1708** J. PHILIPS *Cyder* I. 481 Her *wide-branching Arms. **1873** HOWELLS *Chance Acquaintance* ii. (1883) 45 An audacious, wide-branching moustache. *a* **1700** CONGREVE *Poems, To the King* iii. Wks. 1730 III. 213 Thro' Seas, Earth, Air, and the *wide circling Sky. **1872** BLACKIE *Lays Highl.* 164 There's room in God's wide-circling arm For all that swear by all the creeds. **1887** MOLONEY *Forestry W. Afr.* 301 A *wide-climbing shrub. **1742** YOUNG *Nt. Th.* III. 223 Smoke betrays the *wide-consuming fire. **1750** SHENSTONE *Rural Elegance* 124 Fame's *wide-echoing trumpet. **1860** PUSEY *Min. Proph.* 321 A *wide-expanding knowledge of the enlargement of mankind. **1695** CONGREVE *Mourn. Muse* 178 Lord of these Woods, and *wide extended Plains. **1708** J. PHILIPS *Cyder* II. 588 His wide-extended Wings. **1765** *Museum Rust.* IV. 375 With numerous, wide-extended branches. **1831** JAMES *Philip Aug.* xxxviii, Gazing over the wide-extended view. **1889** F. COWPER *Captain of Wight* 34 The *wide-extending view, over broad pasture and swelling down. **1860** LONGF. *Wayside Inn* I. *K. Olaf* v. ii, The *wide-flung door. *a* **1721** SHEFFIELD (Dk. Buckhm.) *Wks.* (1753) I. 71 The *wide-gaping gulph. **1728–46** THOMSON *Spring* 56 Such themes as these the rural Maro sung To *wide-imperial Rome. **1865** TYLOR *Early Hist. Man.* ix. 258 The common notion..has strong and *wide-lying evidence in its favour. **1852** TENNYSON in Ld. T. *Mem.* (1897) I. 357 Looking at me with such apparently earnest, *wide-open eyes. **1877** BLACK *Green Past.* i. 9 They..drew up in front of the wide-open door. **1892** *Harper's Mag.* June 103/1 It is what they call in Montana 'a wide-open town'. **1975** J. GORES *Hammett* xi. 79 He has been elected three times because the citizens *want* a wide-open town. **1864** SKEAT tr. *Uhland's Songs*, etc. 269 From Heav'n's *wide-opened portals. **1876** 'OUIDA' *Winter City* xii, She could only look at him with wide-opened eyes. **1816** *Edin. Rev.* Sept. 182 This *wide-ranging Intellect was illuminated by the brightest Fancy. **1958** *Times Lit. Suppl.* 7 Feb. 76/4 A representative anthology, which is so wide-ranging in its material..that its final effect is rather of confusion than of enlightenment. **1980** B. HILL in *Beautiful Brit. Columbia* Summer 39 The wide-ranging sheep that are one of the island's main farm products provide the source of wool for local weavers. **1856** GROTE *Greece* II. xciv. XII. 346 The..powerful, and *wide-reaching impression. **1726–46** THOMSON *Winter* 996 The *wide-resounding plain. **1785** T. DWIGHT *Conquest of Canäan* XI. 295 *Wide-rolling dust the neighbouring concave fills. **1805** MONTGOMERY *Ocean* i, Thou wide-rolling Ocean, all hail! **1605** SYLVESTER *Du Bartas* II. iii. IV. *Captains* 945 As..the Grass..Fals at the Foot of the *wide-straddling Mower. **1599** SHAKS. *Hen. V*, II. iv. 82 All *wide-stretched Honors, that pertaine..Vnto the Crowne of France. **1742** YOUNG *Nt. Th.* VII. 747 The wide stretcht realm of intellectual woe. **1726–46** THOMSON *Winter* 951 *Wide-stretching from these shores... A huge neglected empire. **1876** GEO. ELIOT *Dan. Der.* lxix, Wide-stretching purposes. **1924** *Motor* 14 Oct. 491 (*caption*) One of the two *wide-sweeping bankings on the new speedway at Montlhery, near Paris. **1979** *Jrnl. R. Soc. Arts* CXXVII. 409/2 Wessex..will therefore not be subjected to wide-sweeping environmental problems. **1674** MILTON *P.L.* (ed. 2) XI. 487 *Wide wasting Pestilence. **1814** WORDSW. *Ode, 'When the soft hand of sleep'* 145 Wide-wasting Time. **1816** SHELLEY *There is no work* 28 The *wide-winding caves. *a* **1876** M. COLLINS *Pen Sketches* (1879) II. 231 O'er earth's wide-winding ways. **1591** SYLVESTER *Du Bartas* I. v. 241 His yet *wide-yawning lips. **1598** *Ibid.* II. ii. IV. 591 Wide-yawning Gulfs.

†**wide**, *v. Obs.* [f. WIDE *a.*; cf. ON. *víða*; OE. *wídian* app. did not survive.] *trans.* To make wide or wider: = WIDEN *v.* 2; in 2nd quot. to set widely apart.

a **1300** *Cursor M.* 8232 Þan dide þe king tilward þat side þat orchiard al for to wide. *c* **1440** *Pallad. on Husb.* III. 923 And wide hem so that, though the winde him shake, No drope of oon vntil another take. *c* **1440** *Promp. Parv.* 526/2 Wydyn, or make wyde, *dilato.*

wide, Sc. f. WADE *v.*; var. WEDE *v. Obs.*; obs. f. WEED.

'wide a'wake, *adj. phr.*, **'wide-awake**, *a.* and *sb.* [WIDE *adv.* + AWAKE *pred. a.*; predicatively, (usually) as two words; attributively, as one, with hyphen, or occas. without, esp. in senses A. 3, B. 1, 2.]

A. *adj.* (or *adj. phr.*) **1.** Awake with the eyes wide open; fully awake. (Usually *pred.*)

1818 SHELLEY *Julian* 392, I..Will lie and watch ye from my winding-sheet—Thus..wide awake tho' dead [etc.]. **1820** [see AWAKE *pred. a.* 1]. **1840** DICKENS *Old Cur. Shop* xxxix, The baby, who was dreadfully wide awake. **1888** BURGON *Lives 12 Gd. Men* I. iii. 355 He always knew what the Sermon had been about,—better than many who boasted that they had kept wide awake.

2. *fig.* Thoroughly vigilant or on the alert; fully aware of what is going on, or of what it is best to do; intellectually keen, sharp-witted, knowing. *colloq.* (orig. *slang*).

Rarely const. *to* (cf. AWAKE *pred. a.* 2 b).

1833 *Q. Rev.* July 413 In the language of the turf, his grace was 'wide awake'. **1835** DICKENS *Sk. Boz, Mr. Watkins Tottle* ii, Our governor's wide awake, he is... He knows what's o'clock. **1857** TROLLOPE *Barchester T.* xxxviii, Mr. Slope..was wide awake to what he hoped was his coming opportunity. **1906** *Spectator* 18 Aug. 222/2 Foreign capitalists will not advance it..still less would the very wideawake Chinese merchant.

3. Applied jocularly to a soft felt hat with broad brim and low crown: said to have been punningly so named as not having a 'nap'. Now usually *absol.* as *sb.* (B. 1).

1841 [W. J. NEALE] *Paul Periwinkle* I. viii, Jonathan replied, that his hat was like himself—wide awake. **1861** *Illustr. Lond. News* 23 Feb. 168/2 Mr. Hubbard..wears a 'wide awake' hat, which is a novelty in the House. **1891** F. W. MAUDE *Merciful Divorce* iii. 25 Half a dozen young men in long covert coats, loose breeches and gaiters, and wideawake hats.

B. *sb.* **1.** A 'wide-awake' hat: see A. 3.

1837 HOWITT *Rur. Life* II. iii. (1862) 117 Such is the farm-servant, whether you see him in..his straw-hat, or his wide-awake. **1849** J. FORBES *Phys. Hol.* i. (1850) 9 No covering for the head can compete with the thin small-crowned broad-brimmed beavers now known by the name of *wide-awakes*. **1894** CONAN DOYLE *Mem. Sherlock Holmes* 35 He..carried a brown wide-awake in his hand.

2. A sailors' name for the Sooty Tern (*Sterna fuliginosa* and allied species), from its cry. Also *attrib.* in ***wide-awake fair***, a name for the assemblage of these birds on the island of Ascension at the breeding season.

1877 R. L. PRICE *Two Americas* iv. 57 Sea-gulls and wide-awakes hovered in hundreds over the water. **1881** *Standard* 12 Aug. 5/2 It [*sc.* Ascension] nurtures nothing save turtle and wideawakes. **1896** NEWTON *Dict. Birds* 1039 These crowd at certain seasons in innumerable multitude to certain suitable islands, where they breed, and the wonderful assemblage at present known as 'Wide-awake fair' on the island of Ascension has been..described from very ancient times.

3. A 'wide-awake' person (see A. 2). *nonce-use.*

1865 DICKENS *Mut. Fr.* II. ii. xii. 111 You have been told that he might pull through it.., Wide-Awake; have you? **1890** C. MARTYN *W. Phillips, Agitator* 122 A circle of wide-awakes meeting at irregular intervals under the name of 'The Friends'.

Hence **wide-a'wakeness**, the state, or character, of being wide awake (usually in sense A. 2). Also (bad formations, due to association with other words) **wide-awakeativeness**, **-awakedness**, **-awakefulness**, in same sense.

1859 S. BROOKS *Gordian Knot* xvii, Work that requires.. great *wideawakeativeness, and great industry. **1882** BESANT *All Sorts* viii, He felt inclined..to slap himself on the back for *wide-awakedness of the rarest kind. **1851** *Fraser's Mag.* XLIV. 140 An expression of unutterable self-conceit and conscious *wide-awakefulness. **1887** MISS BETHAM-EDWARDS *Next of Kin Wanted* v, They sharpen each other's wits, and worry each other into a proper state of wideawakefulness. **1865** LOWELL *Ess., Scotch the Snake* Wks. 1890 V. 245 *Wide-awakeness of temperament. **1886** STUBBS *Lect. Med. & Mod. Hist.* vi. 123 There was something..besides the literary wideawakeness of Henry.. that made England..a centre of literary activity.

widely ('waɪdlɪ), *adv.* [f. WIDE *a.* + -LY².]

Commonly hyphened to a following ppl. or other adj. when preceding its sb.: cf. DEEPLY *adv.* 7, HIGHLY *adv.* 6.

1. Over or through a wide space or region; in or to various places; extensively.

1697 DRYDEN *Æneis* I. 559 Her..dishevel'd Hair,.. widely spread Ambrosial Scents around. **1697** —— *Virg. Georgic* IV. 768 Where he leap'd, the Waves in Circles widely spread. **1748** THOMSON *Cast. Indol.* I. xxxi, All the widely-silent places round. **1802** R. WARNER *Tour Northern Counties* II. 289 Ornamenting the widely-extended carpet of green with occasional spots of the most brilliant white. **1855** *Orr's Circ. Sci., Inorg. Nat.* 83 The coal measures..are widely distributed in England, Wales, Scotland, and Ireland; in Belgium, France, and Spain; in many parts of Western Germany [etc.]. **1883** KEANE in *Nature* 1 Mar. 410/1 This widely-ramifying family.

2. Over a wide range; among a large number or variety of persons; in relation to many or various things, subjects, cases, etc.; extensively.

1695 LD. PRESTON *Boeth.* II. 85 For though his Fame doth widely fly,.. At last the mighty thing must die. *a* **1718** PRIOR *Ode to Queen* ii, When bright Eliza rul'd Britannia's State, Widely distributing Her high Commands. **1834** LYTE *Hymn, 'Praise, my soul, the King of heaven'* iii, Praise Him, praise Him, Widely as His mercy flows. **1836** DICKENS *Sk. Boz, First of May*, The widely-spread taste for register-stoves. **1849** MACAULAY *Hist. Eng.* vi. II. 33 Viscount Mordaunt, widely renowned, many years later, as Earl of Peterborough. *Ibid.* 122 One tract..was widely circulated in manuscript. **1862** BURTON *Bk. Hunter* (1863) 12 The drunken laird and the widely tolerant wife. **1915** W. C. ALLEN *Gosp. St. Mark* 67 The Semitic word..is used very widely of seas, lakes, and even rivers.

3. With (at, by) a wide interval or intervals (of space or time); far, far apart; to a great or considerable width.

1663 PATRICK *Parab. Pilgr.* xxiii. (1687) 240 Two Hills.. which were..very widely distant the one from the other. **1697** DRYDEN *Æneis* III. 927 We..widely shun the Lilybæan Strand, Unsafe, for secret Rocks, and moving Sand. **1779** *Mirror* No. 13 ¶7 The poetical productions of widely-distant periods of society. **1838** DICKENS *O. Twist* xlviii, Those widely staring eyes..appeared in the midst of the darkness. **1860** WRAXALL *Life in Sea* i. 24 Widely-extended jaws. **1875** WHITNEY *Life Lang.* ix. 157 Widely-sundered castes and classes. **1879** SWEET in *Trans. Philol. Soc.* 465 In loud declamation..the mouth is naturally opened widelier. **1890** 'R. BOLDREWOOD' *Col. Reformer* xviii, Through the widely-opened gateways.

4. *fig.* To a large extent, greatly, very much, extremely, 'far'; *esp.* † (*a*) so as to be 'wide of the mark', with large deviation from accuracy, as in ***widely mistaken***; (*b*) so as to be far apart in nature, character, amount, etc., as in ***widely different, to differ widely***.

1688 BUNYAN *Heavenly Footman* (1886) 154 Alas, thou art widely mistaken! **1705** BERKELEY *Commonpl. Bk.* Wks. 1871 IV. 459 Malbranch..differs widely from me. **1802** MARIA EDGEWORTH *Moral T., Forester* viii, Negligence and inhumanity are widely different. **1821** SCOTT *Kenilw.* viii, She must indeed be widely changed from what she once was. **1880** GEIKIE *Phys. Geog.* iv. 242 The proportion of mineral matter..differs widely in different springs.

†**5.** With 'latitude' of conduct, beyond the bounds of propriety, uncivilly: cf. WIDE *a.* 11 a. *Obs. rare*⁻¹.

1666 PEPYS *Diary* 6 Aug., My Lord..did treat her..very widely and ungenteely.

wide-mouth ('waɪdmaʊθ), *a.* and *sb. rare.*

A. *adj.* = next.

1596 SIR J. DAVIES *Epigr.* xl, The wide-mouth slave Will eate as fast as he will utter lies. **1822** *Auction Catal. Fonthill Abbey* 74 A fine wide-mouth Jar.

B. *sb.* One who speaks loudly, boastfully, or without restraint. Cf. *big mouth* s.v. BIG *a.* B. 2.

1959 I. & P. OPIE *Lore & Lang. Schoolch.* x. 189 The tell tale is christened..a tout, traitor, quisling, or wide-mouth. **1978** *Times Lit. Suppl.* 28 Apr. 462/2 You feel, frequently, like booing him for a bighead and a wide-mouth.

wide-mouthed ('waɪdmaʊðd, -maʊθt), *a.*

1. a. Of a person or animal: Having a wide mouth.

1611 COTGR., *Diable de mer*,..the ouglie wide-mouthed fish, called, the sea Frog. *Ibid.*, s.v. *Fendu, Bien fendu de gueule*, wide-mouthed, sparrow-mouthed. **1843** TENNYSON *Godiva* 56 The little wide-mouth'd heads upon the spout. **1854** A. ADAMS etc. *Man. Nat. Hist.* 86 Wide-mouthed Fishes (Plagiostomi).

b. Of a vessel or receptacle: Having a wide mouth or opening.

1611 COTGR., *Mortier*, the short, and wide-mouthed peece of Ordnance called a Morter. *a* **1711** KEN *Preparatives* Poet. Wks. 1721 IV. 92 Two wide-mouth'd Quivers fill'd with Store, Of deadly Darts. **1769** MRS. RAFFALD *Engl. Housekpr.* (1778) 363 Put your gooseberries into wide-mouthed bottles. **1847** LONGF. *Ev.* I. II. 52 The wide-mouthed fireplace. **1886** WINCHELL *Geol. Talks* 61 Another of these sea-bottom fishes hangs like an open wide-mouthed meal-bag.

2. Having the mouth wide open, or opening the mouth wide: **a.** for utterance, etc.; also *transf.* of the utterance; also *fig.* speaking, or spoken, loudly or without restraint.

1593 CHUTE in *G. Harvey's Pierces Super.* Gg 2 b, Thy wydemouth'd..phrase..Aptly hath knowne thine Armory to blase In termes peculiar vnto none but thee. **1594** NASHE *Unfort. Trav.* L 4 b, Murder is wide-mouthd, and will not let God rest till he grant reuenge. **1648** J. BEAUMONT *Psyche* XIII. xcv, His wide-mouth'd Blasphemies. **1664** BUTLER *Hud.* II. iii. 384 His Sonnets charm'd th' attentive Crowd, By wide-mouth'd Mortal troul'd aloud. **1667** *Phil. Trans.* II. 603 Those wide-mouthed Languages, which do remarkably expose to the Eye the Motions of the Tongue, Lips, Throat, &c. **1745** CIBBER in Ayre *Mem. Pope* II. 85 This..is a Scent, that those wide-mouth'd Hounds the Daily-Paper Criticks could never hit off! **1903** *M.A.P.* XI. 137/1 His face wide-eyed and wide-mouthed in a voiceless panic.

b. for swallowing: Voracious, devouring, destructive.

1596 R. L[INCHE] *Diella* etc. F 1 b, That wide-mouth'd time..shall shut his iawes, & ne're deuoure thy name. **1648** J. BEAUMONT *Psyche* IV. lv, Here wide-mouth'd Luxury Might gormandize her fill. **1887** MEREDITH *Phaethon* in *Ballads & P.* 156 The rage of the havoc wide-mouthed.

widen ('waɪd(ə)n), *v.* [f. WIDE *a.* + -EN[5].]

†**1.** *trans.* To open wide, set wide open. (Cf. WIDE *a.* 7.) *Obs. rare.*

1607 SHAKS. *Cor.* I. iv. 44 So, now the gates are ope:..'Tis for the followers Fortune widens them, Not for the flyers. **1627** DRAYTON *Agincourt* cxi, The gates thus widen'd.. Their ample entrance to the English gaue.

2. To make wide or wider: = BROADEN 2. **a.** *lit.* To increase the width or spatial extent of.

1669 STAYNRED *Fortif.* 8 You may..widen the Necks of the Gorges. **1694** tr. *Marten's Voy. Spitzbergen* in *Acc. Sev. Late Voy.* II. 127 A piece of Board, whereon the Dyers widen or stretch their Stockins. **1785** J. PHILLIPS *Treat. Inland Nav.* 45, I would cleanse, widen, and deepen the river Stort. **1818** [S. WESTON] *La Scava* 3 Under the pavement..we found foundations of a house that had been probably thrown down to widen the road. **1856** KANE *Arctic Expl.* II. xiv. 148 These split-off lines of ice were evidently in motion.. widening their fissures. **1919** *Engl. Rev.* July 26 An outsweep of the left flanking hedge, widening the path for a few feet.

b. *fig.* To increase the magnitude or range of; to extend.

1671 STILLINGFL. *Serm. Matt.* xxi. 43 Wks. 1710 I. 119, I speak not these things to widen our differences, or increase our animosities. **1675** *Essex Papers* (Camden 1913) 22 Parliament is like to sitt longer..for ye differences between ye houses are so widened. **1748** RICHARDSON *Clarissa* (1768) III. 45 Ought I to widen my error by obstinacy and resentment? **1812** LANDOR *Ct. Julian* I. i, To..Widen the solitude of lonely sighs. **1842** TENNYSON *Locksley Hall* 138 The thoughts of men are widen'd with the process of the suns. **1870** ROCK *Text. Fabr.* iv. (1876) 33 The word diaper became widened in its meaning. **1885** *Manch. Exam.* 13 July 5/5 The society is widening its scheme of operations.

3. *intr.* To become wide or wider: = BROADEN *v.* 1. **a.** *lit.*

1709 STEELE *Tatler* No. 118 ¶10 An Extinguisher, with a little Knob at the upper End, and widening downward. **1802** PLAYFAIR *Illustr. Hutton. The.* 404 Of a very uniform breadth except that at each end it widens considerably. **1853** KANE *Grinnell Exp.* xii. (1856) 89 The aperture, at first a mere crack, widened to a couple of feet. **1877** HUXLEY *Physiogr.* xi. 174 The current widens, and its speed is slackened. **1920** *Sat. Westm. Gaz.* 22 May 9/1 The streamlet widens into a pond.

b. *fig.*

1650 E. WILLIAMS *Virgo Triumphans* B 2 b, A reall quarrell widening. **1690** LOCKE *Hum. Und.* II. xi. §11 That .. difference [between brutes and men]..which at last widens to so vast a distance. **1760–2** GOLDSM. *Cit. W.* xcii, His wishes now rise one step above his station;..his prospects widen as he ascends. **1848** DICKENS *Dombey* xliii, Florence..observed the estrangement between her father and Edith, and saw it widen more and more. **1866** J. MARTINEAU *Ess.* I. 169 These questions deepen and widen under our hand.

Hence **widened** (-d(ə)nd) *ppl. a.*, **widening** *vbl. sb.* (also *concr.*) and *ppl. a.*; also **widener**, one who or that which widens; an apparatus for widening something, *spec.* a drill constructed to bore a hole of greater diameter than its own.

1759 R. SMITH *Harmonics* (ed. 2) 181 If any slider be drawn back again, which the *widened holes will permit. **1892** *Daily News* 6 Apr. 7/3 Good dividends and a widened market for the shares. **1901** *Westm. Gaz.* 7 Oct. 5/1 When we have our widened line system completed, it will be possible..to run express electric trains to and from Brighton. **1683** SNAPE *Anat. Horse* IV. xiv. (1686) 172 The *Wideners or Dilaters of the Chest [*sc.* muscles]. **1908** *Daily Chron.* 21 Oct. 7/5 Then..it [*sc.* the glove] is ready for the dresser, who puts it into shape by means of sticks and wideners. **1569** in *Surrey & Kent Sewers Comm.* (1909) 22 To the *wydnynge of the Mouth of the brydge there one foote and a halfe. **1659** *Burton's Diary* (1828) IV. 281 If your body politic be mishapen at the making, the widening or straightening of it will not help it. **1677** GILPIN *Demonol.* (1867) 149 The widening of their capacities. **1782** A. MONRO *Compar. Anat.* (ed. 3) 22 Respiration being chiefly performed..by the widening of the chest. **1884** *Manch. Exam.* 29 Sept. 5/3 The deepening, widening, and straightening of the rivers Mersey and Irwell. **1897** MARY KINGSLEY *W. Africa* 562 We..pass by a widening in the path. **1791** MACKINTOSH *Vind. Gallicæ* Wks. 1846 III. 93 *Widening prospects of happiness. **1859** JEPHSON *Brittany* x. 169 Making a series of widening rings on the surface [of the water]. **1884** CHURCH *Bacon* ix. 212 New ideas and widening thoughts. **1913** W. M. RAMSAY *Teaching of Paul* xxiii. 133 The widening gap that intervenes.

†**widen**, *adv.* *Obs.* Also 3 widene, 4 wydene. [OE. *widan*, f. *wid* WIDE *a.* Cf. OHG. *wîteno*, MHG. *wîten(e*, also *wîtenan.*] In OE., from far; in ME., widely, far and wide.

932, *c* **1205** [see SIDEN]. *c* **1000** in Kemble *Cod. Dipl.* (1845) III. 315 He his witan widan ȝesomnod hæfde. *c* **1205** LAY. 112 Eneas þe duc mid his driht folcke widen iwalken ȝend þ[e] wide water. *Ibid.* 161 þ word..þ was widene cuð. **1362** LANGL. *P. Pl.* A. Prol. 4 In Habite of an Hermite..Wende I wydene in þis world wondres to here.

wideness ('waɪdnɪs). Forms: see WIDE *a.*; also (with normal shortening of the stem-vowel) 6–7 **widnesse**, 7 (9 *dial.*) **widness**. [OE. *widnes*, f. WIDE *a.* + -NESS.] The quality or state of being wide, in various senses: and derived uses. Now generally replaced by WIDTH.

1. Large extension, vastness, spaciousness.

In late use only as transf. from 3.

a **1225** *St. Marher.* 17 þe widnesse of þe world. *c* **1320** *Cast. Love* (ed. Halliw.) 1764 Of hevyn he may i-se þe wydnes, The feyreshepe & þe heynes. **1398** TREVISA *Barth. De P.R.* XIV. lv. (1495) F iij, By cause of wydnesse therof it [*sc.* a cave] is an able place to abyde in. **1596** SPENSER *State Irel.* 93 Though otherwise the widenes of the mountaine pasturage doe recompence the badnes of the soyle. **1740** CIBBER *Apol.* (1756) I. 243 The immoderate wideness of their house. **1862** [see 5]. **1883** *American* VII. 55 He will probably..muse on the wideness of this world.

†**2.** Extent from side to side, transverse measurement (of any amount); diameter, breadth; *occas.* extent of opening, distance apart. *Obs.* exc. *dial.* (replaced by WIDTH 1).

c **1000** in *Anglia* XI. 9/27 þæs temples længc wæs syxtiȝ fæðma, & seo widnes wæs twentiȝ fæþma, & his heahnys wæs þrityȝ fæþma. *c* **1000** ÆLFRIC *Hom.* II. 578 þæt tempel wæs..on widnysse twentiȝ fæðma. **1340** HAMPOLE *Pr. Consc.* 7576 þat clerkes calles cristallyne, þat next oboven þe sterned heven es, And es mare þan þat of wydenes. *c* **1380** WYCLIF *Sel. Wks.* II. 62 þei maken þer abitis myche boþe in widnesse and sidnesse. **1463** *Bury Wills* (Camden) 39 The seid dore to me maad as large of wydnesse as may be. **1535** COVERDALE *Ezek.* xl. 11 He measured the wydenesse of the dore: which was x cubites, & the heyth of the dore xiij cubites. **1551** RECORDE *Pathw. Knowl.* I. v, Open your compasse to the wydenes of those ij. new prickes. **1618** M. BARET *Hippon.* 20 His legges must carry such an equidistance in widenesse that they may describe two parallel lines in their motions. **1667** *Phil. Trans.* II. 604 To every Vowel belongs a peculiar dimension of Wideness in the Mouth. **1669** STURMY *Mariner's Mag.* V. xii. 59 The difference..is the just wideness of the Chamber. **1688** HOLME *Armoury* III. vii. 309/1 They are of severall widenesses. **1726** SWIFT *Gulliver* III. i, A small creek about three times the wideness of my canoe. **1748** *Anson's Voy.* III. viii. 379 By the great wideness of his ports he could traverse almost all his guns upon the enemy. **1756** MRS. CALDERWOOD in *Coltness Collect.* (Maitland Club) 132 A long-bodied narrow cart, that just holds two to sit in the wideness. **1765** A. DICKSON *Treat. Agric.* (ed. 2) 195 The furrow that the plough makes, will be, below, equal in wideness to B C, and, above, to N D.

†**b.** Size or amount generally (of spatial measurement, or of time). *Obs. rare.*

1657 W. RAND tr. *Gassendi's Life Peiresc* I. 134 The Romans..ordained that their Congius (or Gallon) should be in widnesse half a Cubick foot. **1699** BENTLEY *Phal.* 211 It still leaves his Age undetermined, within the wideness of xxxx years.

3. Great extent from side to side; large transverse measurement: opp. to *narrowness*.

a **1548** HALL *Chron., Hen. VIII* 48 b, Therfore was erected an Arche of widnes at the tournelles besyde the strete. **1596** DALRYMPLE tr. *Leslie's Hist. Scot.* (S.T.S.) I. 46 Quhais Wydnes of his banes and gretnes teiches that he was xiiii. fute lang. **1622** CALLIS *Stat. Sewers* (1647) 82 Wideness and shallowness of the..Streams. *a* **1700** EVELYN *Diary* 10 July 1656, The stair-case of extraordinary widnesse. **1794** G. ADAMS *Nat. & Exp. Philos.* III. xxxv. 436 The wideness or narrowness of the pump. **1828** *Craven Gloss.*, *Widness*, width. **1841** *Civil Engin. & Arch. Jrnl.* IV. 195/1 The wideness of their mouths gives them a firm seat in the gallery.

4. In *quasi*-concrete uses. **a.** (from 1.) A wide space or region; (large) extent, (vast) expanse: = WIDTH 3.

1535 COVERDALE *Isa.* viii. 8 He shal fyl also the wydenesse of thy londe with his brode wynges. **1585** FETHERSTONE tr. *Calvin on Acts* xvi. 6 In that confused widenesse God beckened vnto him..how far he would haue him goe, or whither. *c* **1586** C'TESS PEMBROKE *Ps.* XCVI. vi, Sea and all thy widenesse yieldeth. **1681** *Whole Duty of Nations* 14 A Nation..is a part of Mankind canton'd..from the whole world, and the wideness of that. **1844** KINGLAKE *Eothen* xvii, To stand thus alone in the wideness of Asia. **1849** LYTTON *K. Arthur* XI. cxxxii, Lost in the wideness of the weltering Sea. **1918** A. MENZIES *Study of Calvin* 88 To get a view far out over the 'wideness of the sea'.

†**b.** (from 2 or 3.) Opening, aperture. *Obs.*

1585 HIGINS *Junius' Nomencl.* 213/2 *Hypothyrum*,..the wide opening or open widenes of the doore. *Ibid.* 443/1 *Vulneris os*,..the mouth, opening, or widenesse of a wound. **1612** DRAYTON *Poly-olb.* xiii. 215 To close the wideness of a wound.

5. *fig.* Largeness of range, extensiveness; relation to a great number of persons, things, cases, etc.: wide reach or applicability. In quot. 1551, Extent of meaning, 'extension'.

1551 T. WILSON *Logike* E iij b, The diuision..ought to be made with twoo contrary differences, fully containyng in them self the whole cumpasse or widenes of the generall worde. **1649** E. REYNOLDS *Hosea* ii. 87 The puritie, spiritualnesse, and widenesse of that Law which they have sworne unto. *c* **1801** J. FOSTER in *Life & Corr.* (1846) I. 225 A wideness of compass without solidity and exactness. **1862** FABER *Hymn, 'Souls of men! why will ye scatter'* iv, There's a wideness in God's mercy, Like the wideness of the sea. **1865** KINGSLEY *Herew.* xii, The merest varnish of Roman culture had given..a wideness of range to their thoughts.

wider, comp. of WIDE *a.* and *adv.*; obs. f. WHITHER, WITHER.

wide-spread ('waɪd'sprɛd: stress var.), *a.* (Also as one word, without hyphen.) [f. WIDE *adv.* + *spread*, pa. pple. of SPREAD *v.*] Spread widely (*lit.* and *fig.*).

1. Extended over or occupying a wide space; broad in spatial extent.

1735 SOMERVILLE *Chase* I. 250 Strait Hams, and wide-spread Thighs. **1816** WORDSW. *Ode, 'Who rises on the banks of Seine'* 4 How sweet to rest her wide-spread wings beneath! **1863** A. C. RAMSAY *Phys. Geog.* 124 On the western parts of the Weald,..there are some very wide-spread heaths. **1878** HARDY *Ret. Native* I. iii, A wide-spread woman whose stays creaked like shoes whenever she stooped or turned.

2. Distributed over a wide region; occurring in many places or among many persons; extensively or generally diffused.

1705 BERKELEY *Commonpl. Bk.* Wks. 1871 IV. 434 The vast, wide-spread, universal cause of our mistakes. **1837** CARLYLE *Fr. Rev.* I. I. ii, The cardinal symptom of the whole wide-spread malady. **1849** MACAULAY *Hist. Eng.* i. I. 11 The Danish and Saxon tongues, both dialects of one widespread language, were blended together. **1880** WALLACE *Isl. Life* 29 The relics of once widespread types. **1913** R. LUCAS *Ld. North* II. 112 The demand for economical reform was.. widespread.

So (irreg.) **wide-spreaded** *a. rare.*

1821 KEATS *Lamia* I. 354 The wide-spreaded night above her towers.

wide-spreading ('waɪd'sprɛdɪŋ: stress var.), *a.* [f. WIDE *adv.* + SPREADING *ppl. a.*] Spreading widely (*lit.* and *fig.*).

1. Extending over or occupying a wide space; nearly = prec. 1.

1591 SYLVESTER *Du Bartas* I. iii. 222 Wide-spreading Plains, open and spacious Fields. **1743** FRANCIS tr. *Hor., Odes* I. xvii. 5 The vales, wide-spreading round The sloping hills. **1809–11** COMBE *Syntax* XVII. 184 Beneath an oak's wide-spreading shade. **1850** R. G. CUMMING *Hunter's Life S. Afr.* (1902) 57/2 A number of cattle..came to drink at the pit. Some of these carried enormous wide-spreading horns. **1862** SPENCER *First Princ.* II. xvi. §131 (1875) 367 Wide-spreading marine currents. **1909** E. H. BURTON *Bp. Challoner* II. 278 One old wide-spreading cedar.

2. Extending to, reaching, or affecting many places or persons; extensive in effect; far-reaching; nearly = prec. 2.

1766 *Complete Farmer* s.v. *Thistle* 7 K 4/1 To prevent the wide-spreading mischiefs occasioned by the seeding of this pernicious weed. **1833** NEWMAN *Arians* III. i. (1876) 241 That wide-spreading Association, of which the faith of the Gospel was the uniting and animating principle. **1842** in *Westm. Gaz.* (1903) 1 July 2/3 The wide-spreading distress of the working-classes. **1902** *Words of Eyewitness* 336 Kindliness, not little but vast, wide-spreading.

wide-watered ('waɪd'wɔːtəd: stress var.), *a.* [Parasynthetic f. *wide water* (WIDE *a.* + WATER *sb.*) + -ED[2], or f. WIDE *adv.* + WATERED *ppl. a.*] Having a wide expanse of water; watered over a wide extent; bordered or traversed by wide waters.

1632 MILTON *Penseroso* 75, I hear the far-off Curfeu sound, Over som wide-water'd shoar. **1718** POPE *Iliad* xv. 761 Amidst the Plain of some wide-water'd Fen. **1749** G. WEST tr. *Pindar, Pythian Odes* I. xvii, On fair Himera's wide-water'd shores, Thy sons, Dinomenes, my lyre demand. **1904** RICKERT *Reaper* ix, Low-lying, wide-watered Balta.

widewe, widewer, obs. ff. WIDOW, WIDOWER.

†**wide-where.** *adv.* Also as two words. *Obs.* or *rare arch.* Also 4 **wyden where.** [f. WIDE (WIDEN) *adv.* + WHERE *adv.* Cf. ON. *víðast hvar* in most places, mostly.] In or to various places, over a wide region, widely, far and wide; in or to a distant place, far away.

1122 *O.E. Chron.* (Laud MS.), þæræfter comen feale tacne widehwear on Englaland. *c* **1200** ORMIN 8943 Witt hafenn sohht te widewhar icc & ti faderr baþe. **13..** *Northern Passion* (1913) I. 1242 *b* As pilate stod be him thore His þouht was ful wide whore. **1362** LANGL. *P. Pl.* A. IX. 53 þus I wente wyden where [*v.rr.* wyde where, wide whare] Dowel to seche. *c* **1375** *Sc. Leg. Saints* viii. (*Philepus*) 5 Quhene he had..goddis worde prechit wyd-quhare. *c* **1386** CHAUCER *Man of Law's T.* 38 In Surrye whilom dwelte a compaignye Of chapmen..That wyde where senten hir spicerye. *c* **1450** *Mirour Saluacioun* (Roxb.) 98 The feith of oure lord crist spredde wydewhere day be day. **1470–85** MALORY *Arthur* IV. ii. 340 My name is sir kay the seneschal that wyde where is knowen. **1513** DOUGLAS *Æneis* VII. iii. 5 The fame thairof walkis full couth Our all the citeis of Italy wydequhair. **16..** *Sir Lambewell* 6 in *Percy Folio MS.* (1867) I. 144 With him he had many an heire As he had else many a whide where; Of his round table they were Knights all. **1906** C. M. DOUGHTY in *Academy* 5 May 425/2 Fair champaign Which flower of broom gilds widewhere.

†**widge.** *dial. Obs.* Also 3 irreg. **wig.** [OE. *wicg* = OS. *wigg*, ON. *vigg*:—OTeut. **wegjom*, f. *weg-* to carry (see WAY *sb.*, WEIGH, etc.).] In OE. (poetical) a steed; later, a beast of burden; in quot. 1553, a mare.

For the specialization of meaning, cf. F. *jument* mare, from L. *jumentum* beast of burden.

Beowulf 234 Ȝewat him þa to waroðe wicge ridan þeȝn Hroðgares. *c* **1200** *Trin. Coll. Hom.* 89 [He] bed hem bringen a wig one to riden, noðer stede, ne palefrei, ne fair mule..he sende after þe alre unwurþeste wig one to riden, and þat is asse. **1553** *Respublica* IV. iii. 1023 That tyme chad a widge, and hir vole.

widgeon, wigeon ('wɪdʒən), *sb.* Forms: 6 **wegyon, -ion, wygeon, wigion, 6–7 wigen, widgen, -in, 7 -ine, widg(e)ing, widgion, 6– wigeon, 7– widgeon.** [Of difficult etymology.

The form suggests a French origin (cf. *pigeon*), but no appropriate Fr. forms are evidenced as early as the English word or with the required meaning; cf. *vigeon* a West Indian duck (1667 Du Tertre, *Hist. Gén. des Antilles* II. 277), of which there is a nasalized form *vingeon* (1) widgeon in Eastern dial., (2) a duck of Madagascar (1771 *Dict. de Trévoux*); beside which there are *gingeon* 'sorte de canard qu'on trouve dans les grandes Antilles' (1832 Raymond *Dict. Gén.*), and Angevin dial. *digeon* widgeon.

F. *vigeon* and It. *bibbio* wild duck have been referred to L. *vipio* kind of crane, but this derivation is very dubious. The various extant forms suggest the possibility of a series of formations with suffix *-io(nem)* on parallel onomatopœic bases, *piu-, biu-, viu-, diu-, giu-* (cf. WHEW, WHEWER).]

1. A wild duck of the genus *Mareca*, esp. *M. penelope* of Europe and northern Asia; other species are *M. americana* of N. America and *M. sibilatrix* of southern S. America. (Collective pl. in later use usually *widgeon*: cf. *teal*.)

1513 *Bk. Keruynge* in *Babees Bk.* 279 In the second course ..chekyns, pygyons, teeles, wegyons, mallardes. **1544** TURNER *Avium Præcip.* C 5, Quum multæ sint aues aquaticæ anati similes, sed minores, ut sunt, telæ uocatæ ab Anglis Vuigene & pochardæ. **1591** HARINGTON *Orl. Fur.* Pref., At my Lord Maiors dinner they say he would put vp a widgen for his supper. **1604** E. G[RIMSTONE] tr. *D'Acosta's Hist. Indies* III. xvi. 170 Great numbers of wilde-duckes and wigens. **1655** MOUFET & BENNET *Health's Improv.* xii. 107 Teals and Widgins..commonly..are very fat and sweet of taste. **1703** DAMPIER *Voy.* III. 75 Wigeon and Teal also are said to be in great plenty here. **1774** GOLDSM. *Nat. Hist.* (1776) VI. 139 The Lincolnshire decoys..principally contribute to supply the markets of London with wild-fowl. The number of ducks, wigeon, and teal, that are sent thither is amazing. **1788** *Encycl. Brit.* I. 662/1 The American wigeon..is rather bigger than our wigeon. **1877** BLACK *Green Past.* xl, In this bountiful and beneficent land, flowing over with broiled bluefish, Carolina widgeon, [etc.]. **1886** PAYNE-GALLWEY *Bk. Duck Decoys* 17 A Decoy..by means of which wildfowl, such as Wigeon, Mallard, and Teal, are caught alive. **1901** *Shooting Times* 22 June 21/2 On Lough Neagh, the wigeon is known as the 'grass-wigeon' or the 'grass-duck'. This may be due to its habit of feeding on the grassy sward along the shores.

b. Locally applied to various wild ducks of other genera: see quots.

1668 CHARLETON *Onomast.* 99 *Anas Fusca*..the Red-headed Widgeon. **1676** RAY *Willughby's Ornith.* III. 288 The Pochard or great red-headed Wigeon. **1885** SWAINSON *Prov. Names Birds* 155 In Shropshire every species of wild duck, with the exception of *Anas boscas*, is called wigeon. **1898** MORRIS *Austral Engl.*, *Widgeon*, the common English name for a Duck of the genus *Mareca*, extended generally by sportsmen to any wild duck. **1901** *Shooting Times* 22 June 21/2 The pochard is distinguished by the name of the 'red-headed wigeon' or 'stone wigeon'.

†**2.** Applied to a person, in allusion to the supposed stupidity of the bird: A fool, simpleton, ninny. (Cf. *goose*, *gull*, etc.) *Obs.*

1612 CHAPMAN *Widow's T.* II. i. E3b, Come y'are a widgine. **1639** [J. TAYLOR (Water-P.)] *Divers Crabtree Lect.* 122, I [said the Poulterer's wife] call him Goose, and Widging, and Dotrell, and Woodcock. **1647** LILLY *Chr. Astrol.* cxxviii. 584 The Native will prove a very Asse or Widgion. **1693** *Humours Town* 93 'Till the Widgeon is Caught, and his Pocket empty. **1741** LAVAL *Hist. Ref.* IV. VIII. 985 Those poor silly Widgeons, which they could convert.

3. *attrib.* and *Comb.*, as †***widgeon-lord*** (see 2); **widgeon-grass, -weed**, local names for the grasswrack, *Zostera marina*.

1621 BRATHWAIT *Time's Curtain drawn* G 3 b, Here lies a Widgin-lord, a foot-cloth Asse. **1878** BRITTEN & HOLLAND *Plant-n.*, Widgeon-grass. *Zostera marina*, L. **1912** 'GUY THORNE' *Gt. Acceptance* x, The 'mud' was covered with the marsh zostera, or widgeon-weed.

Hence † **widgeon** *v. trans.* to make a 'widgeon' of, befool, cheat.

a **1596** *Sir T. More* I. ii. (Malone Soc.) 256 Let them gull me, widgen me, rooke me, foppe me.

widger ('wɪdʒə(r)). Also *erron.* **wigger**. [See quot. 1956.] A gardening tool consisting of a small strip of metal with a shallow furrow down the centre, used as a miniature trowel to move seedlings, cultivate pot plants, etc.

1956 *Dict. Gardening* (R. Hort. Soc.) Suppl. 333/1 The original widger..is the shape of a small spatula... The name 'Widger' was transferred to this horticultural tool by Mr. Clarence Elliott; it comes from one of a series of nonsense definitions used to test the memorizing ability of British Naval Cadets. **1962** *Listener* 22 Nov. 887/3 A stainless steel 'wigger' is a very useful little gadget for pricking out seedlings. **1973** *Country Life* 5 Apr. 940/1 Seedlings..I move..with a widger—an invaluable narrow-bladed, long trowel-like hand tool.

widget ('wɪdʒɪt). orig. *U.S.* [Perh. alteration of GADGET.] An indefinite name for a gadget or mechanical contrivance, esp. a small manufactured item.

1931 *Amer. Speech* VI. 259 Widget. **1937** E. LYONS *Assignment in Utopia* (1938) III. iii. 299 Every time the percentage of widgets turned out by her factory rose her features shone. **1961** *N.Y. Times Mag.* 26 Nov. 109 Widgets by wire... Suppose something goes wrong with your Westinghouse appliance. What then? Your Westinghouse dealer can get you any new part faster than anyone around. He orders it by special telegraph line. **1966** 'E. LATHEN' *Murder makes Wheels go Round* i. 5 The corporation would ..go about its business of producing bigger and better widgets. **1973** S. ALSOP *Stay of Execution* (1974) II. 193, I asked Joe if the widget could be protected by patent. Joe said..it couldn't... A few weeks ago,..IBM began to make its own widget, cheaper and better serviced than the Intercomp widget. **1982** BARR & YORK *Official Sloane Ranger Handbk.* 11/1 You never have to see the industry ('widget factories') and commerce ('selling brushes') that make the money.

widgie ('wɪdʒɪ). *Austral.* and *N.Z.* Also **weegie**. [Origin uncertain.] An Australasian teddy-girl, the female counterpart of a BODGIE.

1950 *Sun* (Austral.) 5 July 19 There'll be..prizes for the most colorfully dressed 'bodgy' and 'weegie'. **1956** S. HOPE *Diggers' Paradise* 86 A popular district with bodgies and widgies is 'the Cross'. **1965** E. BROWN *Big Man* xix. 168 A mob of bodgies and widgies on a camping holiday. **1977** *Times* 13 May 14/1 Gang delinquency..has made its mark around the world..in Australia the bodgies and widgies.

widifu: see WIDDIFUL.

widir, obs. f. WHITHER.

widish ('waɪdɪʃ), *a.* [f. WIDE *a.* + -ISH[1].] Somewhat wide (*lit.* and *fig.*).

In first two quots. used *advb.*

c **1780** DUCH. DEVONSHIRE in *Daily News* 27 Oct. 6/5 His hair..flattish at top—frizzed out widish on each side. **1828** *Trial of W. & J. Dyon* 20 The man walked widish and turned his toes out. **1845** FORD *Handbk. Spain* II. 931 A widish interpretation of the laws of non-intervention. **1849** R. CURZON, JR. *Vis. Monast.* 298 The..rock..is separated from the end of a projecting line of mountains by a widish chasm. **1864** CARLYLE *Fredk. Gt.* XVI. x. (1872) VI. 254 Kind of Manuscript Newspaper..which seems to have had a widish circulation.

widle: see WIDDLE *v.*[1]

Widmanstätten ('vɪt-, 'wɪdmənʃteɪtən, -st-). Also **-staetten, -statten.** The name of A. J. *Widmanstätten* (1754–1849), Austrian scientist, used *attrib.* with reference to an orderly pattern of intersecting bands seen in some meteorites and steels when a polished section is etched, attributed to the crystallization or precipitation of a new solid phase along the crystal planes of a parent solid phase.

1861 *Q. Jrnl. Geol. Soc.* XVII. II. 9 The plane of the cutting shows strings of whitish colour indicative of crystalline structure ('Widmannstetten's figures'). **1881** L. FLETCHER *Guide Meteorites Brit. Museum* 16 The want of homogeneity in meteoric iron is beautifully shown by the 'Widmanstätten' figures. **1927** *Jrnl. Iron & Steel Inst.* CXVI. 584 He points out the difference between the needle-like structure of the ferrite and the Widmanstätten structure. **1971** I. G. GASS et al. *Understanding Earth* viii. 116/2 Those irons..usually show the Widmanstaetten structure.

Hence † **Widman'stättian** *a.*

1842 *Amer. Jrnl. Sci.* XLIII. 359 The powder arranged itself in directions coinciding with the Widmanstättian figures. **1883** *Phil. Trans. R. Soc.* CLXXIII. 889 It is the constituent of nickel-iron which forms the fine lines constituting the Wiedmannstättian figures, and not schreibersite, as usually stated in writings on the etched figures of meteoric iron. **1886** [see NEUMANN].

widness, obs. or dial. f. WIDENESS; Sc. var. WOODNESS *Obs.*

widou, -ed: see WIDOW, WIDOWHEAD.

widow ('wɪdəʊ), *sb.*[1] Forms: *α.* 1 widuwe, 1–5 widewe, wydewe, 1, 4 widwe, 3 (*Orm.*) widdwe, 3–6 widue, 4 widu (*pl.* widuen, -uus, -us), wydw, *pl.* widos, 4–5 wydue, wydwe, 4–6 wydow(e, *Sc.* widou, 4–7 widowe, 5 wydew, wyddo, widw, 5–6 wydo, 5 (6 *Sc.*) vidue, 6 wyddow(e, (vidoy), *Sc.* vidow, -ou(e, 6–7 widdowe, 7–8 widdow, 9 *dial.* or *vulgar* widda, widder, widdy, 4– widow. *β.* 1 weodewe, 4 *Sc.* wedoue, vedo, 4–5 wedewe, wedu, 4–6 wedew, wedow, wedou, 5 wedw(e, wedue, *Sc.* wedeu, wedaw, 5 (6 *Sc.*) wedo, 5–6 wedowe, weddow(e, (6 wedoo, *Sc.* vedou, weido, *gen.* wedvis). *γ.* 1 wudewe, -uwe, 4 wodow, 4–5 wodewe (4 *pl.* -en, -on). [OE. *widewe, widuwe, wuduwe* wk. fem. = OFris. *widwe* (Fris. *weduwe, widewia, wudu*), OS. *widowa* (MLG., LG. *wedewe, -uwe*, MDu. *weduwe, -ewe*, Du. *weduw(e, weeuw*), OHG. *wituwa, -awa*, (MHG. *witewe*, G. *wittwe*), Goth. *widuwô*: orig. an Indo-European adj. formation **widhewo-, -wā* on the base *widh-* to be empty, be separated (Skr. *vidh* to be destitute, lack, cf. L. *dī-videre* to divide); cf. Skr. *vidhavā* widow, Pers. *bēva*, Gr. *ἠίθεος* unmarried man, L. *viduus* bereft, void, widowed (fem. *vidua* widow, whence F. *veuve*, It. *vedova*, Sp. *viuda*, Pg. *viuva*), OPruss. *widdewu*, OSl. *vĭdova* (Russ. *vdova*), W. *gweddw*, OIr. *fedb*, Cornish *guedeu*.]

1. a. A woman whose husband is dead (and who has not married again); a wife bereaved of her husband.

hempen widow: see HEMPEN *a.* 1 b.

α. *c* **825** *Vesp. Ps.* cviii[i]. 9 Sien bearn his asteapte & wif his widwe. *c* **1100** *O.E. Chron.* (MS. D) an. 975 [Hi] wydewan bestryþtan oft & ȝelome. *c* **1175** *Lamb. Hom.* 115 He scal biwerian widewan and steopbern. *c* **1200** ORMIN 7998 An weppmann & an widdwe. *a* **1225** *Ancr. R.* 10 To helpen widewen & federlease children. *c* **1290** *S. Eng. Leg.* 329/222 Ane holie wydewe. *a* **1300** *Cursor M.* 6787 Widues [*Gött.* Wydw; *Fairf.* widow; *Trin.* widewe] ne barns faderles Do yee na wrang. *Ibid.* 6793 Widus sall i mak your wifes. **1323** *Rec. St. Mary at Hill* (1904) I, I, Rose Wrytell, wydue, sumtyme the wyf of William ffayrstede, Clerk. *c* **1380** *Sir Ferumb.* 5521 Many a wydewe þar was mad, And many child faderles. *c* **1386** CHAUCER *Knt.'s T.* 313 Al be she mayde or wydwe or elles wyf. *c* **1440** *York Myst.* xli. 61, I haue beyn a wyddo this threscore yere. *c* **1450** *Mirk's Festial* 32 A wydow þat het Drusyan, lay ded on bere. **1519–29** *Lincoln Wills* (1914) I. 81, I Jane scheffelde of Croxby vidoy. **1526** TINDALE *Matt.* xxiii. 14 Ye devoure widdowes houses. —— *Mark* xii. 43 This povre widowe hath cast moare in, then all they which have caste into the treasury. **1533** GAU *Richt Vay* (S.T.S.) 68 Christ rasit wp ane vidous sone. **1540** *Test. Ebor.* (Surtees) VI. 127 If she kepe her widue..or if she forton to marie. **1596** DALRYMPLE tr. *Leslie's Hist. Scot.* (S.T.S.) I. 222 Nathir soulde a Vidue be compelled a thousand pace ouer her awne dores to ansuer to the Lawes. *Ibid.* II. 240 Marie..vidow to the duik of Longouaile. **1602** SHAKS. *Ham.* III. ii. 233 Both heere, and hence, pursue me lasting strife, If once a Widdow, euer I be Wife. **1607** —— *Cor.* II. i. 196 The Widowes..And Mothers that lacke Sonnes. **1684** BUNYAN *Pilgr.* II. 168 The Cake that the Widdow gave to the Prophet. **1781** GIBBON *Decl. & F.* xviii. II. 79 Constantia.. remained the widow of the vanquished Licinius. **1837** DICKENS *Pickw.* xx, Take example by your father, my boy, and be wery careful o' widders. **1877** GILBERT *Sorcerer* II, No saucy minx and giddy..But a clean and tidy widdy. **1897** MARY KINGSLEY *W. Africa* 466 In Calabar..all the widows of a dead man are subjected to ordeal.

β. *c* **1000** *Ags. Ps.* (Th.) cxlv[i]. 8 [9] þa elðeodiȝan ealle Drihten lustum healdeð, and lif ȝeofeð weodewum wencelum, he hiom wel onfehð. *c* **1375** *Sc. Leg. Saints* v. (*Johannes*) 226 þat vedo can hym mene. *Ibid.* xxi. (*Clement*) 112 þis wedou. *c* **1380** WYCLIF *Wks.* (1880) 433 Wedewis & nedy men. *c* **1400** *Destr. Troy* 3481 Wyues made wedowys, & wayling for euer. *a* **1450** *Knt. de la Tour* lxx, Maydenes and wedues. **1476** *Exch. Rolls Scot.* VIII. 344 *note*, Till oure pure wedeu and beidwoman Marioun of Corry. **1500–20** DUNBAR *Poems* xxxv. 34 Jonet the weido. *a* **1533** LD. BERNERS *Huon* lx. 210 He dystroyeth..wedous & orphelyns. **1562** WINȜET *Cert. Tractates* §57 Wks. (S.T.S.) I. 112 ȝoung wedowis quha had wowit continence. **1583** *Leg. Bp. St. Androis* 281 The sillie wedew.

γ. *c* **1000** *Ags. Gosp.* Luke ii. 37 Heo wæs wudewe oð feower & hundeahtatiȝ ȝeara. *Ibid.* iv. 25 Maneȝa wudewan wæron on helias daȝum. **1340** *Ayenb.* 48 þe þridde [kind of adultery] is of man sengle mid wodewe oþer aye-ward. *Ibid.* 225 Wodewehod..is a stat þet zaynte paul prayzeþ moche þet zayþ to wodewon [etc.]. *c* **1440** *Gesta Rom.* xliv. 172 (Harl. MS.), iij. wodewis wer I-left bihinde.

b. Law. ***king's widow***: see quot. 1607.

1540 *Act 32 Hen. VIII* c. 46. §25 The said maister.. shalhave auctoritie by this acte to survey all the Kinges widowes..that have maried them selfis without the Kinges licence..for their reasonable fynes to be made to the Kinges use. **1607** COWELL *Interpr.* s.v., The widow of the King, or the Kings widow..is that widow, which after her husbands death being the Kings tenent *in capite*, is driuen to recouer her Dower by a writ *De dote assignanda*... It appeareth that other common Lords haue the same power ouer their widowes, touching their consent, in their mariage, that the King hath.

c. Prefixed as a title to the name. Now chiefly *dial.* or *vulgar*.

1576 FOXE *A. & M.* (ed. 3) 1981/1 Widowe Swayne. **1610** SHAKS. *Temp.* II. i. 76 Not since widdow Dido's time. **1636** in *Parish Bks. St. Julian's, Shrewsbury* I. 20 (MS.) Received for a Restall of Widdow Crosse 6/8. **1818** SCOTT *Hrt. Midl.* viii, The Laird..was ashamed to tax too highly the miserable means of support which remained to the widow Butler. **1835** J. POOLE *Sk. & Recoll.* I. 82 The cold and hot baths kept by Widow Sniggerston, No. 14, Market Square. **1882** MRS. RIDDELL *Pr. Wales's Gard.-Party* ii, Once, when overtaken by a thunder-storm, she sought refuge in widow Harting's cottage.

d. In extended sense: A wife separated from or deserted by her husband; esp. in colloq. or dial. phr. ***a widow bewitched***. Also in other allusive uses: see quot. 1908, *college widow* s.v. COLLEGE *sb.* 9 b, GRASS WIDOW.

1461 *Paston Lett.* Suppl. (1901) 74, I pray you socour my wif, for she is wedow yet for me. **1725** BAILEY *Erasm. Colloq.* (1878) I. 259 Divorc'd from your Husband; a Widow, nay, to live, a Widow bewitcht, worse than a Widow. **1863** MRS. GASKELL *Sylvia's Lovers* xxxix, Who'd ha' thought of yo'r husband, him as was so slow and sure,..making a moonlight flitting, and leaving yo' to be a widow bewitched! **1901** 'ZACK' *Dunstable Weir* 283 Martha Barnaby..was a widdy by will, her man bein' friendly to furren parts. **1908** *Westm. Gaz.* 29 June 2/2 Has Mr. Balfour never heard of the Golf Widow? The husband who goes away for a weekend to play golf may improve his health, but conceivably the wife..may feel it rather dull and lonely. **1952** W. M. MILLER in *Galaxy* Nov. 153/1 It was different if the business-widow called on a couple. Then the lone male could retire. **1965** *Guardian* 30 July 10/5 One Scottish TA unit, aware of the dangers of creating 'TA widows' opens its bar on drill nights to wives and girl-friends. **1973** R. BUSBY *Pattern of Violence* ii. 32 You tell her to come and see me. We police widows have got to stick together. **1980** *Financial Rev.* (Austral.) 14 Jan. 8/2 Dick Smith's resident computer expert..said the keyboards, screens, printers and central processors are giving birth to a new social problem, 'computer widows'.

e. *Eccl.* One of a class or order of devout or consecrated widows in the Early Church (see *Acts* ix. 39, 41).

Cf. *Nonna*, arwurþe wydwe (*MS. Bodl. 730* lf. 146 b, *c* 1200).

1572 T. CARTWRIGHT *Repl. Whitgift* 153 Although there is not so great vse of these widowes with vs, as there was in those places where the churches were first founded,..yet.. I conclude that (if such may be gotten) we ought also to kepe that order of widowes in the church still. **1587** [see WIDOWER[1] 2]. **1708** BINGHAM *Orig. Eccles.* II. xxii. 315 The Council of Laodicea in the Eastern Church had forbidden them [*sc.* deaconesses] under the Name of ancient Widows or Governesses. **1709** J. JOHNSON *Clergy-Man's Vade M.* II. 241 A Widow or Deaconess, must, according to St. Paul, be Sixty. **1862** BP. WORDSWORTH *Hymn*, '*Hark the sound of holy voices*' ii, Saintly Maiden, godly Matron, Widows who have watch'd to prayer. **1884** *Catholic Dict.* 611/2 The Church recognised..several classes of pious women, such as widows, deaconesses, hospitallers, Canonesses.

f. *transf.* A female animal, esp. a hen bird, that has lost its mate.

c **1220** *Bestiary* 706 If hire make were ded, and ȝe widue wore. **1821–2** [see *widow bird* in 4 a]. **1878** *Daily News* 16 Sept. 3/1 'Widows', alias old hens, are to be bought at a shilling each.

g. *fig.*

c **1380** WYCLIF *Sel. Wks.* II. 187 þe Chirche, þat is wydowe for þis tyme. *c* **1480** HENRYSON *Orpheus & Eurydice* 455 For than gois bakwart to the syn agayn Oure appetite,.. And makis reson wedow for to be. **1594** SYLVESTER *Elegies*,

Monodia Wks. (Grosart) II. 330/1 Soon as ever the bright season-stinter Hath left her widow of his wonted raies. **1867** LEWES *Hist. Philos.* (ed. 3) II. iii. 98 Bruno wittily called Oxford the widow of sound learning—'la vedova di buone lettere'.

h. ***the Widow*** (*of* or ***at Windsor***): a familiar epithet for Queen Victoria, whose husband predeceased her by forty years. orig. chiefly *Services*'.

1888 KIPLING *Private Learoyd's Story* in *Soldiers Three* 14 They tell me t' Widdy herself is fond of a good dog. **1890** —— *The Widow at Windsor* in *Barrack-Room Ballads* (1892) 39 Then 'ere's to the Widow at Windsor, An' 'ere's to the stores an' the guns, The men an' the 'orses what makes up the forces O' Missis Victorier's sons. **1900** *Captain* III. 235/1 The design..shows the Queen as a widow—the 'Widow of Windsor'. **1932** *Times* 12 Feb. 14/2 'The Widow' (as we subalterns had irreverently nicknamed the Empress of India). **1964** E. LONGFORD *Victoria R.I.* xxxvi. 562 She died just after half-past six... The famous 'hush' which had always surrounded 'The Widow at Windsor' was shattered. **1980** R. HALL *Lovers on Nile* xiv. 216 The 'Widow of Windsor' would feel herself justified in having ostracized Sam and Florence.

2. a. A bird of the subfamily *Viduinæ*: = WIDOW-BIRD. ***mourning widow***, a bird of the genus *Coliopasser* belonging to this subfamily. **b.** Collectors' name for a geometrid moth, *Cidaria luctuata*: also ***mourning widow***. **c.** ***mournful*** or ***mourning widow***, popular names of certain plants with dusky flowers: see MOURNFUL 5, MOURNING *ppl. a.* 3.

1747 EDWARDS *Nat. Hist. Birds* II. 86 The Red-Breasted Long-Tailed Finch..from Angola in Africa... A Gentleman, who lately arrived from Lisbon, tells me the Portuguese call this Bird the Widow, from its Colour, and long Train. **1796** H. HUNTER tr. *St. Pierre's Study Nat.* (1799) I. 287 In the feathery race, the widow, the cardinal, &c...exhibit much more brilliant colouring, when the Sun approaches the Line. **1869–73** T. R. JONES *Cassell's Bk. Birds* I. 179 The Mourning Widows (*Coliuspasser*).

3. Miscellaneous colloq. or slang uses. **a.** (See quot. 1710, and cf. *widow's fire* in 5.) **b.** An extra hand dealt to the table in certain card-games. **c.** ***the widow***: champagne. [From 'Veuve Cliquot', the name of a firm of wine merchants.] **d.** *Typogr.* A short line at the end of a paragraph, esp. one which is set at the top of a page or column, or which contains only (part of) one word, and is therefore considered unsightly. **e.** ***five-fingered*** (also ***dry-mouthed***) ***widow***, in phrs. alluding to the act of masturbation. *slang* (chiefly *Services*').

1710 *Brit. Apollo* III. No. 91. 3/1 Fire expiring's call'd a Widow. **1781** BOSWELL *Jrnl.* 28 Apr. (1977) 333 He [*sc.* Lord Townshend] had called Sir Joshua, 'Will you give us one cool bottle of claret?' They were taking away the former. 'No,' said Lord Townshend, 'Let us first take the widow.' **1891** *Hoffmann's Cycl. Card Games* 204 Whiskey Poker... Five cards are..dealt to each player, with an extra hand, known as 'the widow'. The elder hand may either play his own hand, pass, or take the widow. **1899** GUY BOOTHBY *Red Rat's Dau.* xvii, A good luncheon and a pint of the Widow to wash it down. [**1904** *Man. Rules Compositors S.S. McClure Co.* 25 All running heads are to be set one nonpareil from the body, unless otherwise instructed. Care must be taken to overcome 'rivers', and to this end indiscriminate division of words is allowed. Care should also be exercised to overcome 'widdies' at the top of pages.] **1925** [see SLUG *sb.*[2] 4 f]. **1932** P. VAN D. STERN *Introd. Typogr.* ii. 15 When a single word runs over, it is often desirable to alter the copy ..so that the words can be run back. Single words standing in a line are called 'widows'. **1948** *Bull. N.Y. Public Library* Jan. 3 Early in 1936, H. M. Lydenberg..began a quiet, and not quite humorless, investigation into the origin and identity of the typographical 'widow', that awful slattern of the printed page. **1954** M. LASKI in *Author* Winter 30/2 It is a common experience, when working for *Vogue*, to be asked to add a few words to a paragraph so as to avoid unsightly 'widows' or single-word lines. **1963** D. OGILVY *Confessions Advertising Man* vii. 124 It has been discovered that 'widows' increase readership, except at the bottom of a column. **1971** B. W. ALDISS *Soldier Erect* 44 In there [*sc.* the 'shithouse'], behind the stable-like door of one compartment or another, I went to a regular evening rendezvous with my dry-mouthed widow. **1975** C. ALLEN *Plain Tales from Raj* xv. 159 Many turned, as a last resort, to the 'five-fingered widow'. **1980** B. CRUTCHLEY *To be Printer* 55 Our best customers were those who looked to us ..to..print well, which meant avoiding 'widows'.

4. Combinations. **a.** appositive (= that is a widow), as ***widow child***, ***duchess***, ***lady***, ***mother***, ***queen***, ***woman*** (the last now usually arch. or dial.); (in sense 1 f) ***widow bird***, ***turtle***. **b.** attrib. Of or pertaining to a widow or widowhood, as ***widow bed***, ***comfort***, ***dolour***, ***life***, ***night***, ***state***; consisting of widows, as ***widow-club***. **c.** objective, instrumental, etc., as ***widow-burning*** (= SUTTEE 2), ***-hunter***, ***-hunting***, ***-making***; ***widow-cursed*** adj.; ***widow-like*** adj. and adv. **d.** Special Combs.: **widow church**, a church without a bishop or pastor; **widow-duck**, a species of tree-duck, *Dendrocygna viduata*; **widow-finch** = WIDOW-BIRD; **widow flower** = *mourning widow* (*b*) (MOURNING *ppl. a.* 3): cf. 2 c; **widow-maker**, a killer or potential killer of men, *spec.* (*a*) *N. Amer. slang*, a dead branch caught high in a tree which may fall on someone below; (*b*) *slang* [tr. G. *witwemacher*], a nickname for the Lockheed F-104 Starfighter strike and reconnaissance aircraft (see quot. 1975); also (*U.S. Mil.*), a grenade launcher; **widow-man** *dial.* = WIDOWER[1] 1 a; **widow moth** = 2 b; **widow right**, that part of a deceased husband's estate to which a widow has a right. See also WIDOW-BIRD, -WAIL.

1650 HOWELL *Giraffi's Rev. Naples* I. 119 He commanded ..the House of a *widow-Baker to be burnt. **1602** MARSTON *Antonio's Rev.* III. iv, O thou cold *widdowe bed, sometime thrice blest, By the warme pressure of my sleeping lord. **1821–2** SHELLEY *Chas. I*, v. 4 A *widow bird sat mourning Upon a wintry bough. **1856** MAX MÜLLER *Chips* (1868) II. 34 The custom of *widow-burning. **1856** AYTOUN *Bothwell* I. x, To claim the hand of Scotland's Queen, The *widow-child of France. *a* **1759** A. BUTLER *Lives of Saints* (1836) I. 179 He..recommends himself and his *widow-church of Antioch to their prayers. **1714** ADDISON *Spect.* No. 561 ⁋1 A certain Female Cabal..who call themselves the *Widow-Club. **1595** SHAKS. *John* III. iv. 105 My faire sonne,..My *widow-comfort, and my sorrowes cure. **1614** SYLVESTER *Parl. Vertues Royall* 767 Hundred Laurels never *widow-curst. **1594** SHAKS. *Rich. III*, II. ii. 65 Our fatherlesse distresse was left vnmoan'd, Your *widdow-dolour, likewise be vnwept. **1711** SWIFT *Jrnl. to Stella* 8 Nov., The *widow Duchess will not stand to the will. **1885** *Riverside Nat. Hist.* (1888) IV. 542 The vida-finches, often called *widow-finches. **1882** *Garden* 11 Mar. 155/3 The purple Scabious.. is known in some places by the name of the *Widow Flower. **1714** ADDISON *Spect.* No. 561 ⁋1 These unhappy gentlemen, who are commonly distinguished by the name of *widow-hunters. **1853** R. S. SURTEES *Sponge's Sp. Tour* i. (1893) 8 With this popular sport he combined the diversion of *widow-hunting. **1595** SHAKS. *John* II. i. 548 How may we content This *widdow Lady? **1863** D. G. MITCHELL *Sev. Stor., My Farm of Edgewood* 17 Another letter, from a widow lady. **1625** in Halliw. *Lett. Kings Eng.* (1846) II. 236, I had rather live banished..with you, than live a sorrowful *widow-life without you. **1590** SPENSER *F.Q.* I. xii. 22 She had layd her mournefull stole aside, And *widow-like sad wimple throwne away. **1706** GARDINER tr. *Rapin's Gardens* I. 351 Or Widowlike beneath a sable Veil, Her purest Lawn may artfully conceal. **1747** RICHARDSON *Clarissa* IV. 120 She wrote such a widow-like refusal. **1839–52** BAILEY *Festus* 439 This bosom..is burning for thee, though thy love be dead, Widow-like, on her lord's death-bier. **1595** SHAKS. *John* V. ii. 17 It grieues my soule, That I must draw this mettle from my side To be a *widdow-maker. **1906** KIPLING *Puck of Pook's Hill* 67 What is a woman that you forsake her, ..To go with the old grey Widow-maker [*i.e.* the sea]? **1945** M. H. ALLEE *Smoke Jumper* iv. 47 He remembered the Kid's caution about widow-makers, limbs falling from high overhead. **1965** M. MCINTYRE *Place of Quiet Waters* ix. 163 Now's the time to look out for widow-makers... Don't you go walking about in the woods when she's blowing like this. **1975** *Times* 26 Sept. 7/2 The loss of 178 aircraft in Germany earned it [*sc.* the Starfighter] the title of 'Witwemacher', or widow-maker. **1976** *Courier-Mail* (Brisbane) 13 Feb. 4/4 They opened up with automatic rifle fire, a Browning machine-gun, and 66 anti-tank rockets, and a 'widow-maker'—a grenade launcher. **1657** TOMLINSON *Renou's Disp.* 267 Mezereon is as much as viduifical, or *widow-making Plant. **1876** G. M. HOPKINS *Wreck of Deutschland* xiii, in *Poems* (1967) 55 The widow-making unchilding unfathering deeps. **1887** T. E. BROWN *Doctor & Other Poems* 35 Sir John, it appears, Was a *widda man. **1946** C. MCCULLERS *Member of Wedding* II. 43 He was a widowman, for her mother had died the very day that she was born—and, as a widowman, set in his ways. **1819** SAMOUELLE *Entomol. Compend.* 363 *Widow moth. *a* **1711** KEN *Hymns Evang.* Poet. Wks. 1721 I. 99 The Son for whom his *Widow-Mother groan'd. **1821** R. POLLOK in D. Pollok *Life* iv. (1843) 87 A small house, inhabited by a widow-mother and an only daughter. **1937** C. DAY LEWIS *Starting Point* 36 Theo's getting as fussy as a widow-mother. *a* **1586** SIDNEY *Arcadia* III. v. (1912) 379 O *widow-nights, beare witnes with me of the difference. **1690** LOCKE *Govt.* §123 Who has the paternal power whilst the *widow-queen is with child? **1569** *N. Country Wills* (Surtees 1912) II. 55 After the *widowright of my wief. **1617–18** *Knaresb. Wills* (Surtees) II. 49 One third of my goodes, which is her widdow right. **1755** JOHNSON, *To Widow, v. a.*.. 2. To endow with a widow-right. **1591–5** C'TESS PEMBROKE *Astrophel* II. 27 All the fields do waile their *widow state. **1615** SYLVESTER *Bethulia's Rescue* IV. 318 So, on the wither'd Spray The *Widow-Turtle sighes her mournfull Lay. **1649** LOVELACE *Lucasta* etc. 99 Peason, Chickens, sawces high, Pig and the *Widdow-Venson-pye. **1382** WYCLIF *2 Sam.* xiv. 5 A womman widowe I am [**1611** a widow woman; Vulg. *mulier vidua*]. —— *1 Kings* vii. 14 Yram, the sone of the *widowe womman [1611 a widowes sonne; Vulg. *mulieris viduae*]. *Ibid.* xvii. 9 A womman widowe [*Douay* **1609** a wydow woman]. **1711** ADDISON *Spect.* No. 101 ⁋7 He lived as a Lodger at the House of a Widow-Woman. **1891** HARDY *Tess* xxix, 'Not he, sir. Never meant to,' replied the dairyman. 'As I say, 'tis a widow-woman, and she had money, it seems —fifty poun' a year or so.' **1889** 'J. S. WINTER' *Mrs. Bob* iii. (1891) 41 Gay little widow woman that she was.

5. Special collocations with the genitive: **widow's bench** = FREE BENCH; **widow's chamber**, the furniture of the bed-chamber, to which the widow of a freeman of the city of London was formerly entitled; **widow's cross**, a name for a purple-flowered N. American species of stonecrop, *Sedum pulchellum*; **widow's cruse** *fig.* (with allusion to I Kings xvii. 12–16) [see CRUSE], a supply which, though apparently meagre, is, or seems to be, inexhaustible; **widow's fire** (see quot., and cf. 3 a); **widow's lock**, a lock or tuft of hair growing apart from the rest, supposed to presage early widowhood; **widow's man**, (*a*) a man such as to attract widows; (*b*) *Naut.* one of a number of fictitious seamen whose names were formerly entered in the books of a ship's company, their pay being set apart for pensions; **widow's mite**, a small money contribution (in allusion to Mark xii. 43; see MITE[2] 1 c); **widow's peak** (see PEAK *sb.*[2] 1 f, and cf. *widow's lock*); **widow's terce** (see TERCE 2); **widow's walk** chiefly *N. Amer.*, a rectangular balustraded platform (characteristic of New England architectural styles in the 18th and 19th cent.) built on top of the roof of a house, esp. for providing an unimpeded view of the sea (see quot. 1978); **widow's weeds**, the mourning apparel of a widow (see WEED *sb.*[2] 6 b).

1694 N. H. *Ladies Dict.* 468 **Widdows-bench* [mispr. *-benob*]..Ss. [= Sussex] a share of their Husbands Estate, which they enjoy beside their joynture. **1766** BLACKSTONE *Comm.* II. xxxii. 518 Deducting the widow's apparel and furniture of her bed-chamber, which in London is called the *widow's chamber. **1816** SCOTT *Old Mortality* in *Tales my Landlord* 1st Ser. IV. xii. 268 'Can you lodge a stranger for a night?' 'I can, sir, if he will be pleased with the widow's cake and the *widow's cruize.' **1915** D. H. LAWRENCE *Phoenix II* (1968) 382 Wherein..is the immortality, in the constant occupation of the nest, the widow's cruse, or in the surpassing of the phoenix? **1977** *Jrnl. R. Soc. Arts* CXXV. 463/1 Information is infinitely reproducible without diminishing it: it is a veritable widow's cruse. **1919** *19th Cent.* Dec. 1049 '*Widow's fire'—a fire on one side of the grate only. *a* **1540** J. LONDON in Ellis *Orig. Lett.* Ser. III. III. 132 Suche as..hadde any slottiche *wydowes lockes, viz. here growen to gether in a tufte. **1896** NORTHALL *Warw. Word-bk.*, *Widow's-lock*, a small lock or fringe growing apart from the hair above the forehead. Credulous persons believe that a girl so distinguished will become a widow soon after marriage. **1749** FIELDING *Tom Jones* III. vi, As to Square, who was..what is called a jolly Fellow, or a *Widow's Man, he easily reconciled his Choice to the eternal Fitness of Things. **1790** *Jackson's Oxf. Jrnl.* 2 Oct., Fictitious Seamen called Widow's Men. **1867** SMYTH *Sailor's Word-bk.*, *Widows' men*, imaginary sailors, formerly borne on the books as A. B.'s for wages in every ship in commission; they ceased with the consolidated pay at the close of the war. **1595** GOODWINE *Blanchardine* Ded., Crauing your acceptance of this pore *widowes mite. **1849** *Widow's peak [see PEAK *sb.*[2] 1 f]. **1838** BELL *Dict. Law Scot.* 985 Where a husband has disponed property in which he stands infeft, but dies before the disponee has taken infeftment, the *widow's terce will form a burden on the property so disponed. **1715**, **1836** *Widow's weeds [see WEED *sb.*[2] 6 b]. **1939** S. CHAMBERLAIN *Nantucket* 25 Variously termed a 'Captain's Walk', or the '*Widow's Walk', it is just 'The Walk' in Nantucket. **1961** J. STEINBECK *Winter of our Discontent* i. 14 The fine old house,..his great-grandfather's,..with..Adam decorations and a widow's walk on the roof. **1978** J. A. MICHENER *Chesapeake* 463 The name *widow's walk* derived from romantic tales of those loyal women who continued to keep watch for a ship that had long since gone to the bottom of some coral sea.

Hence †ˈ**widowess** (*Obs. rare*[-1]), a widow (sense 1); ˈ**widowish** *a.* = *widowly* adj.; †ˈ**widowist** [-IST used irreg.] = sense 1 e; †ˈ**widowity** *Obs.* [hybrid alteration of VIDUITY], widowhood; ˈ**widowly** *a.* [-LY[1]], pertaining to, characteristic of, or befitting a widow (in quot. 1884, widowed, or having the character of a widow); ˈ**widowly** *adv.* [-LY[2]], in a way befitting a widow, like a widow; ˈ**widow-wise** *adv.* (*nonce-wd.*), in the manner of a widow, like a widow; ˈ**widowy** (†**-ie**) *a.* = *widowly* adj.

1596 CLAPHAM *Briefe Bible* II. 126 [She] had bene 84 yeares *Widowesse. **1567** TURBERV. *Ovid's Ep.* 60 b, My *widowish couch. **1578** H. WOTTON *Courtlie Controv.* 280 Turning and tossing..in hir widowishe bed. **1593** BANCROFT *Surv.* 221 There is a second sorte of Disciplinary *Widdowistes, that are very farre growen past Cartwright's *lfs.* [Cf. sense 1 e, quot. 1572.] **1609** SKENE *Reg. Maj.* I. 39 Suppose his mother in her *widowetie committed huredome. **1664** in Jervise *Mem. Angus* (1885) II. 15 Earl George..left her 'the use of all his moveables in all his houses duering her widowity'. **1750–1** MACFARLANE *Geneal. Coll.* (S.H.S. 1900) II. 465 She calls her Self when in her widowity Relicta Normani de Lessly. **1753** *Stewart's Trial* 53 The poor disconsolate lady, who now weeps over her own widowity. **1532** MORE *Confut. Tindale* Wks. 494/1 Virginitie, & *widoly chastitie. **1632** J. HAYWARD tr. *Biondi's Eromena* 158 The Princesse..had now converted her widdowly meane into fresh teares of conjugall affection. **1884** *Century Mag.* XXVIII. 541 This charming young person,..the daughter of a widowly exile of France. **1909** RICKERT *Beggar Heart* 285 She conducted herself most *widowly. **1904** MARSON *Folk Songs fr. Som.* Introd. p. xvi, Song is not won *widow-wise, 'by brisk assault and putting on',..but rather must be wooed by slow approaches, like a maid. **1656** EARL MONM. tr. *Boccalini's Advts. fr. Parnass.* I. iii. (1674) 4 The very Muses..did..assist at the Obsequies in *widowie apparel.

widow, *sb.*[2] *Obs.* exc. *dial.* [OE. *widewa*, masc. corresp. to *widewe* WIDOW *sb.*[1]] = WIDOWER[1] 1. †Also of common gender.

c **1000** *Instit. Polity* xxii. in Thorpe *Laws* (1840) II. 332 þæt he þanan-forð wydewa þurhwunige. **1340** *Ayenb.* 193 And alneway me ssel ham bleþeliche yeue, and nameliche to þe poure ssamueste, and to þe uaderlease, an to wyfmen wodewen, and to oþre nieduolle. *Ibid.* 225 þe stat of wodewehod..þet zaynte paul prayzeþ moche, þet zayþ to wodewon, 'hou þet guod is, he him hyealde ine þet stat'. *c* **1480** HENRYSON *Orpheus & Eurydice* 297 A wofull wedow [*v.r.* wedaw] hamewart is he went. **1518** H. WATSON *Hist. Oliver of Castile* (Roxb.) B 4, Seynge that bothe partyes were wydowes,..it were moost conuenyent that he came theder for to wedde her. **1579** TOMSON *Calvin's Serm. Tim.* 257/2 He abstened from marriage: whether hee neuer had a wife, or was a widowe, and kepte himself without one. **1633** RUTHERFORD *Lett.* (1765) II. xv. 341 Our Bridegroom cannot want a wife: can he live a widow? **1789** CHARLOTTE SMITH *Ethelinde* (1814) IV. 93 He still lived a widow, on his estate in Jamaica. **1894** CROCKETT *Raiders* xxii, I had been a widow three years when I began to gang aboot Parton Hoose to see her.

attrib. c **1560** A. SCOTT *Poems* (S.T.S.) iv. 35 Wedow men þat wantis To steill a pair of swyvis. c **1700** *Directions for Distrib. Estate T. Rawlins of Barrow-on-Soar* (MS.), Those poor Widdow men and Widdow women that have a charge of children to keep. **1841** S. C. HALL *Ireland* I. 30 Her father came here soon after she was born, a widow-man with only her.

ˈwidow, *v.* [f. WIDOW *sb.*[1] or [2].]

1. *trans.* To make a widow (or, *rarely*, widower) of; to reduce to widowhood; to bereave of one's husband (or wife). Most commonly in *pa. pple.*: see also WIDOWED *ppl. a.*

13.. *Cursor M.* 24197 (Edinb.) Ik am nu widuit of mi spus. **1607** SHAKS. *Cor.* v. vi. 153 In this City hee Hath widdowed and vnchilded many a one. **1748** RICHARDSON *Clarissa* IV. 84 The Royal butchers, who..widow ten thousand at a brush, and make twice as many fatherless. **1814** SOUTHEY *Roderick* III. 290 One hour hath orphaned me and widowed me. **1884** ANNIE S. SWAN *Dorothea Kirke* x, Be careful of yourself—for Dorothea's sake. I would not like to see her early widowed. **1887** HATTON *Gay World* xv, When he widowed her, as he must do, being so much her senior.

b. *fig.* To deprive *of* a valuable or highly prized possession (person, thing, or quality); to bereave. Usually in *pa. pple.* Deprived, bereft.

1595 MARKHAM *Trag. Sir R. Grinuile* cxv, Beeing.. widow'd of her comly shape. **1649** C. WASE *Sophocles, Electra* 53 The House Widow'd of Friends, and seiz'd upon by Fiends! **1677** BAKER in Rigaud *Corr. Sci. Men* (1841) II. 18 The second equation is widowed of its geometrical construction. **1742** YOUNG *Nt. Th.* VIII. 1264 Wit, widow'd of good-sense, is worse than nought. **1791** COWPER *Iliad* v. 763 He..Lay'd Troy in dust, and widow'd all her streets. **1847** LE FANU *T. O'Brien* 303 Odd niches and nooks—widowed of the clocks and presses. **1874** MOTLEY *John of Barneveld* I. Pref. 8 France, widowed of Henry and waiting for Richelieu.

†**2.** To survive as a widow, become the widow of. *Obs. rare*[−1].

1606 SHAKS. *Ant. & Cl.* I. ii. 26 Let mee be married to three Kings in a forenoone, and Widdow them all.

†**3.** To endow with a widow's right. *Obs. rare*[−1].

1603 SHAKS. *Meas. for M.* v. i. 429 For his Possessions,.. We doe en-state, and widow you with all, To buy you a better husband.

Hence **ˈwidowing** *vbl. sb.* and *ppl. a.* (in first quot. app. vaguely used for 'funereal').

? **1605** DRAYTON *Poems Lyr. & Pastoral* Eglog vi. 105 Nor mournefull Cipresse nor sad widowing yew. **1906** *Athenæum* 17 Nov. 614/3 The widowing of the hero is a valueless shadow upon a vigorously improbable..story. **1921** *Public Opin.* 18 Feb. 157/2 She had earned her widowing by eight years' happiness.

ˈwidow-bird. [Representing L. generic name *Vidua*, F. *veuve* (Brisson *Ornithol.* 1760) widow. (Altered to WHIDAH-*bird*.)] A bird of the genus *Vidua* or subfamily *Viduinæ* of the family *Ploceidæ* (Weaver-birds), found in various parts of Africa: so called from the prevailingly black plumage of the males, which are also distinguished by an immensely elongated train of tail-feathers.

[**1747**: see WIDOW *sb.*[1] 2 a.] **1772** BARRINGTON in *Phil. Trans.* LXII. 282 *note*, These long feathers would be very inconvenient to the hen during incubation; and they are likewise confined to the cock widow-bird. **1783** LATHAM *Gen. Syn. Birds* II. I. 179 Whidah B[unting]... This is pretty common at Angola, and other parts of Africa; and is called la Veuve, or Widow Bird, from the colour. **1807** [MRS. DORSET] *Peacock 'at Home'* (1838) 10 The Widow-Bird came, though she still wore her weeds. **1869–73** T. R. JONES *Cassell's Bk. Birds* I. 179 The Long-tailed Widow Bird (*Chera caffra*) the largest of all the South African species. *Ibid.* 180 The Cock-tailed Widow Birds (*Steganura*) are found throughout the whole of Central Africa. *Ibid.*, The Paradise Widow Bird (*Vidua paradisea*)..found principally in the thinly-wooded forests of Africa. **1871** DARWIN *Desc. Man* II. viii. 269 The male widow-bird, remarkable for his caudal plumes. **1896** NEWTON *Dict. Birds* 1030 The females of all the Widow-birds differ greatly in appearance from the males, and are generally clothed in a plumage of mottled brown.

widowed (ˈwɪdəʊd), *ppl. a.* [f. WIDOW *sb.*[1] or [2] or *v.* + -ED.]

1. Made or become a widow (or widower); bereaved of one's husband (or wife). Also of an animal, esp. a bird: Bereaved of its mate.

1606 WARNER *Alb. Eng.* XIV. lxxxvi. 355 A pitious Storie of King Eugens widowed wife. a **1718** PRIOR *Solomon* III. 193 A widow'd Daughter. **1730–46** THOMSON *Autumn* 974 Some widowed songster pours his plaint. **1813** SCOTT *Trierm.* I. i, Constant and true as the widow'd dove. **1823** —— *Quentin D.* Introd., He was a widowed husband and childless father. **1855** MACAULAY *Hist. Eng.* xvii. IV. 5 He was a child at his widowed mother's knee. **1885** *Mistletoe Bough* 28/1 An acquaintance of mine—a twice widowed wife. **1893** TOUT *Edw. I* xi. (1896) 182 There was..talk of a marriage between the widowed Edward and the French king's sister.

b. *transf.*

c **1600** SHAKS. *Sonn.* xcvii. 8 The teeming Autumne big with ritch increase..Like widdowed wombes after their Lords decease. **1627** MAY *Lucan* v. 928 Sleepelesse she spent in her now widow'd bed..the night that followed. **1634** HEYWOOD *Maidenh. well lost* I. i, What is't to me? If being a Bride, you haue a widdowed fortune. **1725** POPE *Odyss.* I. 455 Your widow'd hours,..with female toil And various labours of the loom, beguile. **1768** C. SHAW *Monody* xiv. (1769) 12 How shall I find repose on a sad widow'd bed? **1780** COWPER *Doves* 36 Denied th' endearments of thine eye, This widow'd heart would break. **1825** T. HOOK *Sayings* Ser. II. *Pass. & Princ.* iii, For..six and twenty years had the veteran lover..solaced himself in widowed singleness. **1828** P. CUNNINGHAM *N.S. Wales* (ed. 3) II. 279 She tripped out of doors to solace her widowed heart with the joys of a second husband. **1894** DYAN *Man's Keeping* xviii, He could only hold the poor widowed hand tenderly in his while he told her the tiny details of those last few days.

2. *fig.* Deprived of a partner, friend, companion, or mate; bereaved; hence, deserted, desolate, solitary.

1633 P. FLETCHER *Purple Isl.* II. iv, Straight from the ashes ..A new-born Phœnix flies, & widow'd place resumes. **1687** NORRIS *Coll. Misc.* 17 No Second Friendship can be found To match my mourning Widow'd Love. a **1763** SHENSTONE *Elegies* viii. 33 From Twitnam's widow'd bow'r. **1763** CHURCHILL *Proph. Famine* 498 What if we seiz'd, like a destroying flood, Their widow'd plains. **1820** SHELLEY *Naples* 108 Widowed Genoa wan By moonlight spells ancestral epitaphs. **1850** TENNYSON *In Mem.* lxxxv. 113 My heart, tho' widow'd, may not rest Quite on the love of what is gone. **1908** E. V. LUCAS *Over Bemerton's* x, He sees far more with his widowed orb than the ordinary observer does with two.

b. Of an elm: Not 'mated' with a vine; conversely of the vine; also of a branch. (After L. *ulmus* and *vitis vidua, ramus viduus.*)

1743 FRANCIS tr. *Hor. Odes* IV. v. 44 The hind Weds to the widow'd elm his vine. **1756** MASON *Ode to Indep.* vii, When pining Care,..sees thee, like the weak, and widow'd Vine, Winding thy blasted tendrills o'er the plain. **1763** MILLS *Pract. Husb.* IV. 357 No shoots should be suffered to grow out of the firm wood, unless they are wanted in order to marry them to a widowed branch.

widower[1] (ˈwɪdəʊə(r)). Forms: 4 **wid(e)wer, wydewer,** 4–5 **wedewer,** 5 **wyduare,** 5–6 **wydower, (wydward),** 6 **wedower, wydoer,** 7 **widdower,** 9 *dial.* **widver,** 7– **widower.** [A new formation with -ER[1] on WIDOW *sb.*[1], appearing in late ME. and substituted as an unequivocal form for WIDOW *sb.*[2] Cf. MHG. *witewære*, G. *wittwer*, MDu. *wedewâre.*]

1. a. A man whose wife is dead (and who has not married again); a husband bereaved of his wife.

1362 LANGL. *P. Pl.* A. x. 194 Widewers and widewes [**1377** B. IX. 174 Widwes and widwers]. **1393** *Ibid.* C. XI. 282 Wydewers and wydewes weddeth ayther othere. **1477** *Paston Lett.* III. 178 Sir T. Greye..is a wydower now late. c **1482** *Monk of Evesham* (Arb.) 75 His wyfe dide afore him ..after hoys dethe he leuyd continent and chaste, in a wydwardys lyfe. c **1500** *Melusine* 187 That pucelle reffused hym bycause he had be wedded tofore, & of late he was wydower. **1601** SHAKS. *All's Well* v. iii. 70 Heere wee'l stay To see our widdowers second marriage day. **1635** J. TAYLOR (Water P.) *Old, Old Man* B 3 b, She dead, he ten yeares did a Widdower stay. **1694** *Act 6 & 7 Will. & Mary* c. 6. §46 The several duties..upon Batchelors and Widdowers by this Act granted. **1778** JOHNSON in Boswell *Life* (1904) II. 184 He was not content as a widower; for he married again. **1856** KANE *Arctic Expl.* II. xi. 119 The mourners came together to weep and howl, while the widower recited his sorrows and her praise. **1905** *Daily Chron.* 14 Apr. 4/6 Mr. Otto Goldschmidt, widower of the late Jenny Lind.

b. ***widower bewitched***: a husband separated from or deserted by his wife. *colloq.* (Cf. WIDOW *sb.*[1] 1 d.)

1705 DUNTON *Life & Err.* (1818) I. 405 If my marrying a fortune has made me a scoundrel,..it is but while I continue a Widower bewitched.

c. The counterpart of WIDOW *sb.*[1] 1 d in allusive use, as ***football widower***, etc. *colloq.*

1969 *Listener* 17 Apr. 534/3 He's a football widower because I'm the one who's always trooping away to football matches. **1971** A. NIXON *Attack on Vienna* xi. 109 Mr Fletcher had had a quiet drink with another bridge widower. **1973** *Guardian* 25 May 11/2 The age of golf widowers is developing.

†**2.** One of an ecclesiastical class or order of men corresponding to the order of 'widows'. *Obs.*

1587 D. FENNER *Def. Ministers* 141 As they had their Leuiticall dispensors, or orderers of the holy Treasurie,.. So we haue as members of the Church, as set of God as helpers, the Deacons, Church-seruauntes, Widowers and widowes. **1610** BP. HALL *Apol. Brownists* §19 Let there be Widdowers (which you call relieuers) appointed euery where to the Church-seruice. Let certaine discreete and able men which are not Ministers be appointed to preach the Gospell.

Hence **ˈwidowered** (-əd) *a. rare* [after WIDOWED], made or become a widower, bereaved of one's wife; **ˈwidowerˌhood** [after WIDOWHOOD], the condition of a widower, or the time during which a man is a widower; so **ˈwidowerˌship, ˈwidowery** (*rare*) in same sense; in quot. 1886 *transf.* the condition of being absent from one's wife.

1852 ROCK *Ch. Fathers* III. I. viii. 31 The splendid signet of gold..which a weeping husband had drawn from off his *widowered finger. **1880** M. BETHAM-EDWARDS *Forestalled* II. xviii, Norland..felt more than ever widowered, orphaned, and forlorn. a **1796** BURNS *Let.* (*Pearson's 76th Catal.* (1894) 7) Bred a zealous Antiburger; but during his *widowerhood, he has found their strictness incompatible with certain compromises he is often obliged to make. **1834** *Blackw. Mag.* XXXV. 829 She makes an attempt..on the widowerhood of the Centenarian. **1883** MRS. LYNN LINTON *Ione* xv, Pledged to eternal widowerhood and constancy. **1889** —— *Thro' Long Night* III. xv, This first year of his widowerhood. **1641** EARL MONM. tr. *Biondi's Civil Wars* I. 29 As if Fortune had conspired to make all the Princes of the bloud, accompany the King in his *widowership. **1886** STEVENSON *Let.* 13 Feb., My wife is at Bath with my father and mother* and the interval of *widowery explains my writing.

ˈwidower[2]. *rare.* [f. WIDOW *v.* + -ER[1].] One who or that which widows, or bereaves (a woman) of her husband.

1818 MILMAN *Samor* XI. 360 Hengist begirt with that fam'd falchion call'd The 'Widower of Women'.

†**ˈwidowhead.** *Obs.* Forms: see WIDOW *sb.*[1]: 4–5 **-hede,** 4–6 **-hed,** 6 **-heade,** *Sc.* **-heid(e,** 6–7 **-head;** also 4 **viduid, widoued,** 5 **weddewede, wydewede, wedowed, wedoet,** 6 **wydowed, widuede,** 7 **widdowed.** [f. WIDOW *sb.*[1] or [2] + -HEAD.]

a. = next, 1 a.

a **1300** *Cursor M.* 11346 Anna,..þat liued had foursith tuenti yeier In viduid [*Gött.* widowhede, *Trin.* wodewehode]. c **1385** CHAUCER *L.G.W.* Prol. 295 Alle kepid they here maydynhed Or ellis wedlek or here widewehed. **1447** in *Reg. Mag. Sig. Scot. 1451* 106/1 Cristiane has set and to ferm latyn in her pur wedowhed to the said Alex...hir landis of Stratoune. **1563** *Cal. Anc. Rec. Dublin* (1891) II. 29 That mistres Margarete Handcoke..shalbe free of all.. taxis,..during her widuede and living sole. **1591** SPENSER *Teares Muses* 240 During the time of that her widowhead. c **1610** *Women Saints* 28 As true widdowed..is of rare dignitie and power,..so false widdowed,..which liueth so more freelie to take her pleasure..is likewise more dishonorable. **1662** HICKERINGILL *Apol. Distressed Innoc.* Wks. 1716 I. 298 Tamar after she had plaid her wicked prank, resumed the garment of her Widowhead.

attrib. a **1586** SIDNEY *Arcadia* II. iii. (1912) 160 The comfort of her widowhead life.

b. *gen.* = next, 1 b.

c **1375** *Sc. Leg. Saints* xxiv. (*Alexis*) 41 Symeone, þat in wedoue-hed þat lang tyme þat his lyf can led. c **1460** *Emare* 77 Aftur, when hys wyf was dede, And ledde hys lyf yn weddewede. **1530** TINDALE *Answ. More* III. xiii. Wks. (1575) 313/2 Virginitie, wedlocke and widowed are none better then other to be saued by. **1552** ABP. HAMILTON *Catech.* (1884) 10 Of the chastitie of mariage wydohed & virginitie. **1601** HOLLAND *Pliny* X. xxxiv. I. 290 They [*sc.* doves] abandon not their owne nests, unlesse they be in state of single life or widdowhead by the death of their fellow. **1612** T. TAYLOR *Comm. Titus* i. 6 Where the Apostle affirmeth it to be good to abide single, either in virginitie or widowhead..shall no time afford lawfulnes for some sort of men to marie?

c. *fig.* = next, 1 c.

1624 DONNE *Lett.* (1651) 10 Upon you, who are a member of the spouse of Christ the Church, there can fall no widow-head. **1697** G. KEITH *2nd Narr. Proc. Turner's Hall* 31 The words of G. W. and W. Penn about the Souls of the Deceased Saints being in a state of Purgatory or Widow-head, if they look for the Resurrection of their bodies.

widowhood (ˈwɪdəʊhʊd). Forms: see WIDOW *sb.*[1] and -HOOD; also 5 **wydewood;** 3 (*Orm.*) **widdwesshad.** [OE. *widewanhád*, f. gen. of WIDOW *sb.*[1] or [2] + *-hád* -HOOD.]

1. The state or condition of a widow or widower, or (contextually) the time during which one is a widow or widower; the condition of a wife bereaved of her husband, or of a husband bereaved of his wife. **a.** of a woman.

c **1000** *Ags. Hom.* (Assmann) 114 Iudith..þurhwunode on hire wudewanhade. c **1175** *Lamb. Hom.* 85 Meiden þet hire meiden-hat wit and haldeþ..and widewe of hire widewe-had. c **1450** *Godstow Reg.* 320 Anneys, þat was þe wyfe of henry sclatter of Eynysham, in her pur weduhod & lauful power beynge, gaf, grauntyd, & confirmyd [etc.]. c **1450** *Knt. de la Tour* cxix. 163 Them that worshipfully and perfitly kepe thaire wedwhode. **1513** BRADSHAW *St. Werburge* I. 2139 The quene for her husbande..Remayned in wydohode and mournynge vesture. **1535** COVERDALE *Judith* x. 3 She..put of the garmentes of hir wyddowhode. **1653** VAUX tr. *Godeau's St. Paul* 184 He exhorts Widows to continue in their widow-hood. **1753** *Scots Mag.* XV. 54/1 In the 96th year of her age, and 71st of her widowhood. **1827** JARMAN *Powell's Devises* II. 283 An annuity during widowhood..is good. **1841** JAMES *Corse de Leon* iv, I little dreamed that my mother, in her widowhood, would willingly wed a stranger. **1846** LYTTON *Lucretia* II. xviii, Lucretia..was in the deep weeds of widowhood. **1882** MISS BRADDON *Mt. Royal* i, Mrs. Tregonell had never been to London since her widowhood.

b. of either sex, or of a man (= WIDOWERHOOD). Also *transf.* of an animal, esp. a bird.

c **1000** *Ags. Hom.* (Assmann) 20 Wudewanhad is, þæt man wuniȝe on clænnysse for godes lufon..æfter his ȝemacan ..æȝðer ȝe weras ȝe wif. c **1200** *Trin. Coll. Hom.* 45 Þre hodes of bilefulle men, on is meidhod, þat oðer spushod, þe þridde widewehod. c **1200** ORMIN 4624 Forr maȝȝdennhad & widdwesshad & weddlac birrþ ben clene. **1340** *Ayenb.* 48 Of man oþer of wyfman þet ne habbeþ nenne bend ne of wodewehod ne of spoushod. c **1386** CHAUCER *Pars. T.* ¶842 Chastitee in mariage and chastitee of widwehode. **1528** *Test. Ebor.* (Surtees) V. 250 In my wedowhode, afore I maried this gentilwoman. **1539** *Act 31 Hen. VIII* c. 14 §1 Vowes of Chastitye or Wydowhood, by Man or Woman made to God advisedly ought to be observed. a **1652** BROME *Queenes Exch.* I. ii, What have I done at home, since my Wife died? No Turtle ever kept a widowhood, More strict then I have done. **1768** BOSWELL *Corsica* iii. 222 Signor Clemente, being in a state of widowhood. **1866** MRS. H. WOOD *St. Martin's Eve* vii, During Mr. St. John's widowhood.

c. *fig.*

c **897** ÆLFRED *Gregory's Past. C.* xxxi. 207, & ðæs bismeres ðines wuduwanhades [Isa. liv. 4 *viduitatis*] ðu ne ȝemansð, forðæm ðæt is ðin Waldend ðe ðe ȝeworhte.
1818 BYRON *Ch. Harold* IV. xi, The spouseless Adriatic mourns her lord;.. The Bucentaur lies rotting unrestored, Neglected garment of her widowhood! **1821** —— *Sardanap.* IV. i. 227 Which I have worn in widowhood of heart. **1853** RUSKIN *Stones Venice* II. ii. §2 Mother and daughter, you behold them both in their widowhood,—Torcello, and Venice. **1867** FREEMAN *Norm. Conq.* I. vi. 565 *note*, The canons of Durham are met to choose a Bishop after the three years' widowhood of the see.

†**2.** An estate settled on a widow, a widow's right. *Obs. rare*−1.

1596 SHAKS. *Tam. Shr.* II. i. 125 And for that dowrie, Ile assure her of Her widdow-hood.

widowie: see *widowy*, after WIDOW *sb.*[1]

widowish to **widowship:** see after WIDOW *sb.*[1]

widow-wail. [See quot. 1597.] **a.** A name for the shrub Mezereon (*Daphne Mezereum*) or other species of *Daphne*. **b.** A shrub of the genus *Cneorum* (N.O. *Simarubaceæ*), esp. *C. tricoccum*, a dwarf shrub with evergreen leaves and pink sweet-scented flowers, found in Spain and the south of France.

1597 GERARDE *Herbal* III. lviii. 1215 *Chamelæa Arabum Tricoccos.* Widow Wayle... It is also named of diuers *Oliuella*, as *Mathæus Syluaticus* saith: it is called in English Widow Wayle. *quia facit viduas. Ibid.* lx. 1217 *Thymelea.* Spurge Flaxe, or mountaine Widow Wayle. **1601** HOLLAND *Pliny* XXIV. xv. II. 198 Chamelæa [*marg.*] otherwise called Mezereon, Widow-waile. **1697** *Phil. Trans.* XIX. 396 Tricoccos Shrubs called Widdow-Wayles. **1760** J. LEE *Introd. Bot.* App. 331 Widow Wail, *Cneorum.* **1846** KEIGHTLEY *Notes Virgil* Flora 380 Spurge-flax or Mountain Widow-wail.

widraught, widre: see WITHDRAUGHT, WITHER.

width (wɪdθ). [A literary formation of the 17th century, taking the place of *wīdness* WIDENESS (which is the usual word in modern dialects), the short vowel of *breadth* (6–7 *bredth*) providing an analogy. Johnson 1755 calls it 'a low word'.]

1. Extent across, or from side to side; transverse dimension: = BREADTH 1; *occas.* extent of opening, distance apart (of the two parts of something, as a pair of compasses).

†In first quot. quasi-*concr.* Opening: = WIDENESS 4 b.

1627 DRAYTON *Agincourt* cxlii, Whence from the wydth of many a gaping wound, There's many a soule into the Ayre must flye. **1678** MOXON *Mech. Exerc.* v. 82 For the width of the Mortess Gage this side,.. then for the Tennant, Gage on that end of the Quarter you intend the Tennant shall be made. **1731** W. HALFPENNY *Perspective* 22 The Perspective Widths of the Squares, parallel to EF. **1835** DICKENS *Sk. Boz, Astley's*, A child.. with very large round eyes, opened to their utmost width. **1836** W. IRVING *Astoria* xliv, The river was here a rapid stream four hundred yards in width. **1859** TENNYSON *Geraint & Enid* 264 The two remain'd Apart by all the chamber's width. **1871** A. MEADOWS *Man. Midwifery* (ed. 2) 186 The power of the forceps increases with the length of its blades,.. the compressing power.. is dependent first upon the character of the lock.. and secondly upon the width or divergence of the blades. **1902** S. E. WHITE *Blazed Trail* xviii, Thin, flexible cedar strips of certain arbitrary lengths and widths.

2. Large extent across, or in general: = WIDENESS 1, 2. Also *fig.* (cf. BREADTH 1, WIDENESS 5).

1697 DRYDEN *Virg. Georg.* II. 388 Let thy Vines in Intervals be set,.. Indulge their Width, and add a roomy Space, That their extreamest Lines may scarce embrace. **1832** L. HUNT *Sir R. Esher* (1850) 349 The general width of his manner, if I may so call it. **1841** —— *Seer* (1864) 54 Milton.. was never weak in his creed..; he forced it into width enough to embrace all place and time.

3. quasi-*concr.* A wide region or expanse: cf. BREADTH 2 b.

1866 LYTTON *Lost Tales Miletus, Secret Way* 29 'Mid funeral earth-mounds, skirting widths of plain.

4. *concr.* **a.** = BREADTH 2.

1872 D. G. ROSSETTI *Let.* 26 Sept. (1967) III. 1076 It would be quite enough to make four curtains.. 6 ft ½ wide (or under would do if more convenient with the widths of the velvet). **1876** 'OUIDA' *Winter City* iii, In the back widths of her skirt. **1882** CAULFEILD & SAWARD *Dict. Needlework*, *Width*, a term employed in dressmaking, synonymously with that of Breadth; meaning the several lengths of material employed in making a skirt, which—according to the fashion of the day—is composed of a cetain number, gored or otherwise. The term Breadth is more generally in use. **1892** E. REEVES *Homeward Bound* 242 She mounted the steps, and I watched her go on her knees right up to the altar.. I am sure she would need a new width in the front of her dress.

b. The width of a swimming-bath taken as a measure of the distance swum. Cf. LENGTH *sb.* 4 d.

1930 *Swimming Instruction* (Amateur Swimming Assoc.) 55 From this stage the class should proceed to swim.. several widths, legs only, using supports or 'Dog Paddle'. **1971** *Daily Tel.* 17 Nov. 3/6 Mrs Annie Oakley, 86,.. has been presented with a certificate for swimming two widths at Soundwell Swimming Club. **1981** H. ENGEL *Ransom Game* (1982) xxx. 198 She went off the board again... She did two lengths to each of my widths.

Hence '**widthless** *a.*, having no (great) width, narrow; '**widthways, -wise** *adv.*, in the direction of the width, transversely.

1852 *Meanderings of Mem.* I. 98 The *widthless road. **1794** S. WILLIAMS *Vermont* 316 When applied to uses which require plaiting *widthways. **1890** W. J. GORDON *Foundry* 63 If they are to be curved lengthways or widthways. **1882** BLADES *Caxton* 105 The mould.. was capable of a sliding adjustment, *widthwise to the width of the various letters. **1900** O. ONIONS *Compl. Bach.* xv, [She] looked me up, down, widthwise, and through, and found no speech.

widu(e, widual, widuede: see WIDOW, VIDUAL, WIDOWHEAD.

wid-uten (-yn), var. WITHOUTEN *Obs.*

widw(e, widwer, obs. ff. WIDOW, WIDOWER.

wie, obs. f. WEIGH; var. WY *Obs.*, man.

wiech, wieck, wiek(e, wied, wief(f, obs. ff. WITCH *sb.*[2], WICK, WEED *sb.*[1], WIFE.

Wiedemann-Franz ('viːdəman fraːnts). *Physics.* [The names of G. H. *Wiedemann* (1826–99) and R. *Franz* (1827–1902), German physicists, who published the law in 1853 (*Ann. d. Physik* LXXXIX. 497).] ***Wiedemann-Franz law***: the law that at any given temperature the ratio of the thermal to the electrical conductivity has approximately the same value for all metallic elements; ***Wiedemann-Franz ratio***: this ratio or the Lorenz ratio (see LORENZ).

1924 J. R. PARTINGTON in H. S. Taylor *Treat. Physical Chem.* I. xi. 490 The Wiedemann-Franz law is only approximate. **1966** PHILLIPS & WILLIAMS *Inorg. Chem.* II. xix. 23 The transition metals are also good conductors of heat. On the free-electron theory it is predicted that there should be a direct relation between the thermal, k, and electrical, σ, conductivities, the Wiedemann-Franz ratio. **1975** D. G. FINK *Electronics Engineers' Handbk.* VI. 10 The Wiedemann-Frantz [*sic*] ratio L is defined as $L = \lambda/\sigma T$. **1975** *Jrnl. Low Temperature Physics* XX. 691 The Lorenz numbers.. are very close to the theoretical value.. predicted by the Wiedemann-Franz law for pure electronic heat conduction limited by impurities.

wiederkom ('viːdəkɒm). Also **wiederkomm** and with capital initial. [ad. F. *vidrecome* goblet (Robert, 1752), ult. ad. G. *wiederkommen* to return, come again (see quots.).] A tall, cylindrical, German drinking-vessel, made of (usu. coloured or painted) glass.

The Eng. form reflects the original Ger. derivation. F. *vidrecome* is sometimes understood as a fanciful corruption of G. *willkomm* loving-cup, but this suggestion appears to be unsubstantiated.

1878 A. NESBITT *Descr. Catal. Glass Vessels S. Kensington Museum* p. cxxiii, The cylindrical drinking vessels, generally called wiederkoms.. are sometimes very large, some being as much as 20 in. in height. **1881** C. C. HARRISON *Woman's Handiwork* III. 229 For side-board decoration, the Wiederkom or 'come again' drinking-cups in emerald-hued [Bohemian] glass, have always been popular. **1897** A. HARTSHORNE *Old Eng. Glass* xv. 82 A glass called a 'Wiederkom' was one which was filled, passed round the table.. and 'came again' empty. **1907** E. DILLON *Glass* xvi. 266 The term *wiederkomm* given by so many English.. writers to the large broad forms [of drinking-glasses], is unknown in Germany, so that I think the expression may be definitely abandoned and replaced by the word *humpen* or *willkomm humpen*. **1926** N. H. MOORE *Old Glass* I. 81 The huge glasses known as 'Willkommen'.. were originally used by a host to welcome his newly arrived guest... The term 'Wiederkom' by which these glasses are known in England is a misnomer. **1946** W. B. HONEY *Glass* vi. 75 The *Stangenglas*.. became popular in a modified form as the *Willkomm*, or 'greeting-glass' (sometimes mistakenly called a *Wiederkom*), in thin metal. **1977** H. NEWMAN *Illustr. Dict. Glass* 342 *Wiederkomm* (*humpen*),.. literally, come again beaker. A term used by A. Nesbit [*sic*].. in referring to *Willkomm* (*humpen*) and many other types of enamelled *Humpen*... It is a term not used by German museums.

†**wiel.** *Obs.* Forms: 1 **wiȝ(e)l-, wiȝul-, wil-,** 3 **wiȝel, wihel, wiel.** [OE. *wiȝ(e)l* str. n. (also in *steorwiȝl* astrology), whence *wiȝlian* vb. (cf. ME. *biwiȝelien*), *wiȝlere* agent-n., *wiȝlung* n. of action, corresp. to MLG., (M)Du. *wichelen*, †*wîgelen*, MDu. *wijchelâre*, *wich-*, MLG. *wicheler*; of obscure origin.] Sorcery, magic; a piece of magic; a deceit, delusion.

a **1100** *Aldhelm Gloss.* vii. 165 (Napier 159/2), *Diuinationis*, wiȝles. —— in *Anglia* XIII. 33/162 *Ceremonias*, wiȝlum. *c* **1200** *Trin. Coll. Hom.* 11 He [*sc.* a devil] makeð þe unbilefulle man to leuen swilche wiȝeles, swo ich ar embe spac. *c* **1205** LAY. 19250 Ygærne wes mid childe:.. al þurh Merlines wiȝel. *a* **1225** *Ancr. R.* 92 Þurh þet sihðe ȝe schulen iseon alle þes deofles wieles. *Ibid.* 300 His [*sc.* the devil's] wiȝeles & his wrenches. *a* **1225** *St. Marher.* 13/9 Wið sume of mine wiheles ich wrenchte ham adun hwen ha lest wenden.

So †**wielare**, a sorcerer, magician; a deceiver; †**wiele (wyle)** [OE. type **wiȝela*], a sorcerer, wizard; †**wiȝelful** *a.*, magical; deceitful; †**wiȝeling**, sorcery, magic.

c **1000** ÆLFRIC *Hom.* II. 330 Drymen.. and.. wiccan and oðre *wiȝeleras, beoð to helle bescofene. **11..** *Fragm. Ælfric's Gram.* (1838) 2 *Augur*, wielare. *a* **1225** *Ancr. R.* 106 Þe wielare, of sum derne þing.. makeð a swote smel cumen. *a* **1310** in Wright *Lyric P.* x. 38 Nes y never wycche ne *wyle. *c* **1205** LAY. 2880 Mid *wiȝeful his fluhte. *Ibid.* 21140 His sweorð.. wes iworht.. mið wiȝele-fulle craften. *Ibid.* 31659 Heo weore wiȝel-fulle. *a* **1000** *Kent. Gloss.* in Wr-Wülcker 71/3 *Diuinatio*, *wilung. *c* **1000** ÆLFRIC *Hom.* I. 102 Nu ȝe cepað daȝas and monðas mid ydelum wiȝlungum. *c* **1175** *Lamb. Hom.* 115 He scal wicche creft aleggan and wiȝelunge ne ȝeman. *c* **1205** LAY. 15791 Monies godes monnes child heo bicharreð þurh wiȝeling.

wiel, var. WEEL[1]; obs. f. WELL *adv.*

†**wield,** *sb. Obs.* Forms: α. 1–3 **weald,** 1 **-wild, -wyld,** *North.* **wæld,** 3–4 **weld,** 4 **weilde,** 4–5 **welde, weild,** 5 **weelde, wielde, wylde.** β. 2–5 (6 *Sc.*) **wald,** 3–5 **walde,** 5 *Sc.* **wauld.** γ. 3–5 **wold,** 3–6 **wolde.** [(1) OE. *weald* (rare), usually *ȝeweald*, Anglian *ȝewald* = OS. *giwald*, OHG. *gawalt* (MHG., G. *gewalt*); (2) OE. *(*ȝe*)-*wield*, *-wild*, *-wyld*, *-*weld*: see Y- and WIELD *v.*]

1. Command, control; possession, keeping; *occas.* hold, grasp: chiefly in phr. ***at, in, on*** (one's) ***w.***; ***to have in w.***, to have command or control of, to possess, have; ***to w.***, in or into one's possession. (See also 4 a.)

α. *c* **893** ÆLFRED *Oros.* II. iv. § 10 Hie.. þæt win drincende wæron oð hi heora selfra lytel ȝeweald hæfdon. *Ibid.* III. ix. §10 Æfter þæm þe Alexander hæfde ealle Indie him to ȝewildon ȝedon. *Ibid.* IV. xi. §4 Þa bæd he Scipian friþes, & him his sunu ham onsende, se wæs on his ȝewealde [*Cott. MS.* wealde]. *a* **1300** *Cursor M.* 462 Qui suld I him seruis yeild? Al sal be at myn auen weild. *Ibid.* 788 Sone quen sco þis frutte biheild, Sco desirred it to haue in weild. *Ibid.* 25445 Þou þat has þis werld to weld. **1338** R. BRUNNE *Chron.* (1810) 160 Vitaile inouh at weld. ? *a* **1366** CHAUCER *Rom. Rose* 395 The tyme, that hath al in welde To elden folk, had maad hir elde. *c* **1380** *Sir Ferumb.* 3716 Þat y mote þe seo, On crysten mannes welde. *a* **1400–50** *Wars Alex.* 2994 An ymage.. Of Sexeres þat sum-quyle þat cite had to welde. *c* **1400** *Roland & Otuel* 828 Thaire saules went alle to lucyfere, þat hade þam alle to welde. *c* **1440** *York Myst.* i. 67 All welth in my weelde es. *a* **1500** *Hist. K. Boccus & Sydracke* (? 1510) *G* ij b, Whan the colers haue al in welde A great keelth in man they yelde. **1567** *Gude & Godlie B.* (S.T.S.) 166 All this warld to weild thow had.

β. **971** *Blickl. Hom.* 47 Hi habbaþ maneȝa saula on heora ȝewaldum. *c* **1175** *Lamb. Hom.* 147 Ne mei na Mon me folȝen, bute he forlete al þet he iwald ach. *c* **1200** ORMIN Ded. 204 To lesenn mannkinn þurrh his dæþ Ut off þe defless walde. *a* **1300** *Cursor M.* 9482 (Cott.) Nu has him sathanas in wald. **13..** *Ibid.* 21917 (Edin.) Alle sal we die bath ginge and alde Es [= as] nau havis of him selvin walde. *c* **1375** *Sc. Leg. Saints* xxi. (*Clement*) 10 Wedyr & wynd he has in wald. *c* **1470** HENRY *Wallace* x. 579 God, that has the warld in wauld.

γ. *c* **1250** *Gen. & Ex.* 1958 Ȝet wast bettre he ðus was sold, Ðan he ðor storue in here wold. *Ibid.* 3116 'Wold', quod god, 'wile ðor-of crauen'. **13..** *K. Alis.* 6716 (Laud MS.) Þou shalt habbe.. my londe al to wolde. *c* **1330** R. BRUNNE *Chron. Wace* (Rolls) 3215 Þou hast namo breþere in wold; þy fader ys ded, þy moder ys old. *c* **1440** *York Myst.* xxxii. 273 We wille it noght welde with-in oure wolde. *a* **1450** *Le Morte Arth.* 3233 Goo thow, syr lucan de boteler, That wyse wordys haste in wolde. *c* **1460** *Towneley Myst.* vii. 32 God that has alle in wold. *Ibid.* xxviii. 137 When I gaf myself to wold to you in fourme of bred. *a* **1500** *Hist. K. Boccus & Sydracke* (? 1510) *I* ij b, The payne that he had fyrst in wold Shal than be encresed thre fold.

b. In gen. case in advb. phr. ***willes and waldes***: intentionally and purposely.

c **980–1060** *Laws of Æthelred* VI. lii, Ȝif hit ȝeweorþeð þæt man unwilles oþþe unȝewealdes æniȝ þing misdeð, na bið þæt na ȝelic þam þe willes & ȝewealdes sylfwilles misdeð. *a* **1225** *Ancr. R.* 6 Heo.. suneȝeð deadliche iðe bruche, ȝif heo hit brekeð willes & woldes. *c* **1230** *Hali Meid.* 37 Þat forschuppes te self willes & waldes into hare cunde.

2. Power, might, force, strength.

c **1250** *Gen. & Ex.* 2000 To don swilc dede adde he no wold. *a* **1300** *Cursor M.* 3564 Til vnwelth windes al his wald. ? *a* **1400** *Morte Arth.* 2689 Þoffe my schouldire be schrede, and my schelde thyrllede, And the wielde of myne arme werkkes a littille. *a* **1510** DOUGLAS *K. Hart* II. 220 All thing ȝe haue wrocht With help of Wisdome, and his willis wald.

3. Meaning, significance (cf. 4 c).

c **1250** *Gen. & Ex.* 2122 If he can rechen ðis dremes wold.

4. In phr. ***aȝen*** (***owen***) ***awold***, also ***aȝen*** or ***haven wold*** (***wald, weld***), representing OE. *on* (*ȝe-*)*wealde habban*, and *ȝeweald áȝan* or *habban* with genitive (cf. A *prep.*[1], O *prep.*[1], OWE *v.* B. 1):

a. To have in control or possession, possess.

[*Beowulf* 1727 He ah ealra ȝeweald. *c* **1000** *Dream of the Rood* 107 On domdæȝe dryhten.. ah domes ȝeweald.] *c* **1000** in *Anglia* I. 31 Hine.. þet alle þing haueð on wealde. *c* **1200** *Trin. Coll. Hom.* 79 Swo holie mihte is þoleburdnesse þat he þe hit kið, þer þurh haueð his soule weald. *Ibid.*, He .. þermide ouercumeð þe unfele and his soule lokeð, and haueð swo wald. *Ibid.* 205 Bute he forsake alle þe woreld winne þat he weld ahȝ. *c* **1250** *Gen. & Ex.* 3412 Al bi ðhusenz ðis folc was told, Ilc ðhusent adde a meister wold. *a* **1275** *Prov. Ælfred* 181 in *O.E. Misc.* 113 Ȝif þu hauest welþe a wold. *a* **1300** *Harrow. Hell* 232 (Digby MS.) Ich am moises.. Ich dude þe lawen þat þou astolde Wor to ben owin [*MS.* oþin] on wolde.

b. To be the cause of, be responsible for: = WIELD *v.* B. 3 a.

c **1200** ORMIN 11815, I me sellf all ah itt wald þatt deofell maȝȝ me screnkenn. *c* **1250** *Gen. & Ex.* 2054 He herde hem murnen.. Harde dremes oȝen awold ðat.

c. To mean, signify, denote, imply.

c **1250** *Gen. & Ex.* 324 Quat oȝet nu ðat for-bode o-wold, Ðat a tre ȝu forboden is..? *Ibid.* 1671 Luue wel michil it aȝte a wold, Swilc seruise and so longe told. *Ibid.* 1944 Quat-so his dremes owen a-wold. *a* **1300** *Havelok* 1932 Betere is.. i se Wat þis baret haueth on wold [*MS.* þat þis baret on hwat is wold].

†**wield,** *a. Obs.* Forms: 1 **wielde, wylde,** 2–3 **welde,** 3 **wilde.** [OE. *wielde*, also *ȝewielde*, f. root of WIELD *sb.*] Strong, powerful, mighty.

c **890** WÆRFERTH tr. *Gregory's Dial.* IV. xxxvii. 320 Ac þæt is bedeohlod us.. hweþer þa wyldre wære in Stephane & þone siȝor ahte. *c* **893** ÆLFRED *Oros.* IV. i. 156 Hit næs þeaw on þæm tidum þæt mon æniȝ wæl on þa healfe rimde þe þonne wieldre wæs. *c* **1000** ÆLFRIC *Saints' Lives* XVI. 336 Þæt se mann beo ȝeðyldiȝ,.. and læte æfre his ȝewitt ȝe-wyldre þonne his yrre. [*c* **1175** *Lamb. Hom.* 105 Weldre þene his wreððe.] *a* **1272** *Luue Ron* 94 in *O.E. Misc.* 96 He is . . freo of heorte, of wisdom wilde. *c* **1275** LAY. 3197 Þo we[n]de þe welde-king þat hit were for gyle.

wield (wiːld), *v.* Forms: see below. [Two OE. verbs are here represented: (1) a Com. Teut. reduplicating strong verb, OE. (WS.) *wealdan*, (Anglian) *waldan*, pa. t. *wéold*, pa. pple. *ʒewealden* (see WALDIN) = OFris. *walda*, OS. *giwaldan*, pa. t. *giwêld*, OHG. *waltan*, pa. t. *wialt* (MHG. *walten*, pa. t. *wielt*, G. *walten* wk.), ON. *valda*, pres. *væld*, pa. t. (wk.) *olla*, pa. pple. neut. *valdet* (Sw. *vålla*, Da. *volde* to cause, occasion), Goth. *waldan*; (2) a weak verb, OE. (WS.) *ʒe*wieldan*, *wildan*, *wyldan*, (Anglian) *wældan*, containing a mutated form of the same stem *wald-* (see also WIELD *sb.* and *a.*), = Balto-Slavic *wald-* (:*weld-*) in OSl. *vlado* to rule, *vlastĭ* power, Lith. *veldu* to rule, possess, iterative *valdaũ*, OPrussian *weldīsnan* acc., inheritance, *wāldnikans* acc. pl., kings; another grade is in Goth. *wulþus* glory.

The above forms are generally held to contain an extended form of the root of L. *valēre* to be strong, *validus* strong, Celtic *walo-* in many proper names, and in **walatros* (whence MWelsh *gwaladr* chief), ON. pa. t. *olla* (:—**wul-þō*).

The current form *wield* descends from ME. *wēlde(n* (see A. 1 ϵ) as representing OE. (non-WS.) **weldan*, variant of WS. *wieldan*, not as representing WS. *wealdan*, the Anglian form of which gave ME. *wālde*, *wǫlde* (A. 1 β, γ). The pa. t. and pa. pple. in *-ed* are new formations dating from the 14th century. (The OE. and early ME. contracted forms of the 2nd and 3rd pres. indic. sing. of OE. *wealdan* and *wieldan* (A. 1 η) are identical.)]

A. Illustration of Forms.

1. *Infin. and Present Stem.* α. 1 **wealdan, 2–3 wealden.**

c **888** ÆLFRED *Boeth.* xxxix. §8 Sume . . secgað þ sio wyrd wealde æʒþer ʒe ʒesælða ʒe unʒesælða. *c* **1000** *Beowulf* 2038 Þenden hie ðam wæpnum wealdan moston. *c* **1200** *Trin. Coll. Hom.* 79 On ȝiwer þoleburdnesse ȝe shulen wealden ȝiwer saule. *c* **1230** *Hali Meid.* 577 Wið him þu schalt wealden, . . heouenliche wunnen.

β. 1 **waldan, wældan, 3–4 walde(n (3 wælden), 4** *Sc.* **valde, 4–5** *Sc.* **wauld(e, 4–5 (9** *Sc.*) **wald.**

c **825** *Vesp. Ps.* lxxxviii[i]. 10 [9] Ðu waldes maehte sæs. *c* **950** *Lindisf. Gosp.* Mark x. 42 Wutas ʒie forðon ðas ðaðe ʒesene sint þæt hia aldordom [*sic*] hædnum ʒe-wældes ðæm. *a* **1000** *Boeth. Metr.* xxiv. 35 Se ðe waldeð . . ealra oðra eorðan cyninga. *c* **1205** LAY. 1250, & scal þin mære kun wælden þus londes. *Ibid.* 2966 Hu mochel worȝ leste þu me to walden kineriche? **12..** *Moral Ode* 2 (Egerton MS.), Ic wælde more þanne ic dude. *a* **1300** *Cursor M.* 9958 Þan was þar neuer suilk a hald, Ne nan welier in werld to wald. *c* **1375** *Sc. Leg. Saints* xl. (*Ninian*) 1178 To wauld ȝoure lymmys at ȝour wil. *c* **1425** waulde [see B. 5]. *a* **1500** *Bernard. de cura rei fam.* I. 351 Quham god of mycht bade wald and virke. **1825** JAMIESON, *Wald*, *walde*, to wield, to manage, to govern, to possess. **1915** wald [see B. 1 b].

γ. 3–5 **wolde, 4 wold.**

c **1260** *K. Horn* 308 (Camb. MS.) Me to spuse holde, & ich þe lord to wolde. *c* **1425** *Cursor M.* 22874 (Trin.) Miȝty god þat al woldeþ. *c* **1460** *Towneley Myst.* xxvi. 1 Peasse, I warne you, woldys in wytt!

δ. 1 **wildan, wyldan, 4–5 wilde, wylde, 6–7 wild.**

c **960** ÆTHELWOLD *Rule St. Benet* (1885) 11 He sceal mid twyfealdre lare þa wyldan and tyn, þe him underþeodde synt. **13..** *Cursor M.* 6741 (Gött.) And na keping did him in wilde, Ox for ox þan sal he ȝelde. **1387** wilde [see B. 3 a]. *c* **1480** wilde [see B. 2]. *c* **1485** wyldyng [see WIELDING *ppl. a.*]. **1563, 1603** wild [see B. 5].

ϵ. 2–4 **welden (5 -on), 3–4 weld(e, 4** *Sc.* **velde; 4–8 weild, 5–6 weilde, 6 weyld,** *Sc.* **veild; 4–6 weelde, 5–7 weeld; 6–7 weald; 6 wielde, wyelde, 6– wield.**

c **1175** *Lamb. Hom.* 153 Þa awariede gastes þet weldeð þosternesse [*rectores tenebrarum*]. *a* **1200** *Moral Ode* 2 (Lamb. MS.) Ich welde mare þene ich dede. *c* **1205** LAY. 1140 Þe wrse hit hafde to welden. *a* **1300** *Cursor M.* 22813 Al mai he do he þat al weldes. *c* **1380** WYCLIF *Wks.* (1880) 369 Þes goodis þat þei welden now. *c* **1400** *Destr. Troy* 1881 For to wirke with my wille, & weld as myn owne.

a **1300** *Cursor M.* 586 Adam was mad of mans eild, Als he moght welle him self weild. *c* **1400** *Sc. Trojan War* (Horstm.) II. 1625 Gevin . . To king Teuteus, to kepe and weild. **1500–20** DUNBAR *Poems* xxi. 61 O! quha sall weild the wrang possessioun. **1579** weyld [see B. 2 b]. **1581** W. STAFFORD *Exam. Compl.* iii. (1876) 77 Hauinge much land in their hand, and not being able to weilde all. **1696** PHILLIPS (ed. 5), To *weild*, to manage, to govern: Thus we say to weild a Scepter. **1742** weild [see B. 4].

c **1380** WYCLIF *Sel. Wks.* III. 22 Þei ben endurid in her unskilful errour til eendelees deeþ weelde hem. *c* **1425** weeld [see B. 5]. *c* **1449** PECOCK *Repr.* III. i. 276 Ȝe schulen not weelde eny thing in the lond of hem. **1603** DRAYTON *Odes* i. 49 That sturdy Glebes, And massie Oakes could weeld. **1633** weeld [see B. 4].

1593 CHURCHYARD *Challenge* 22 Why doe wee wish, to weald a world at will? **1629** weald [see B. 5].

1559 *Mirr. Mag., Dk. Suffolk* ix, They were more then we might easely wyelde. **1586** MARLOWE *1st Pt. Tamburl.* II. i, What stature wields he, and what personage? **1590** SPENSER *F.Q.* II. i. 18 Vnder him a gray steede did he wield.

ζ. (with short vowel) 6–7 **weld(e, (7 welld).**

1530 welde [see B. 4]. *c* **1550** *Disc. Common Weal Eng.* (1893) 100 Havinge muche landes in theire handes, and not being able to welde all. **1591** SPENSER *Ruines of Time* 14 A broken rod she held, Which towards heauen shee seemd on high to weld. **1594** WILLOBIE *Avisa* XXV. iii, You see the sore, whence springs my griefe, You weld the sterne of my reliefe. *a* **1628** F. GREVIL *Mustapha* I. i, Strength knowes what strength can weld. **1647** welld [see B. 4 b].

η. *2nd and 3rd sing. pres. contr.* 1 **weltst, wylst, wylt, wilt, 1–3 wealt, 1–4 welt, 3–5 walt.**

c **888** weltst, welt [see B. 1, 4]. *c* **897** wilt [see B. 3 a]. *c* **1000** *Ags. Ps.* (Th.) ii. 9 Þu heora wylst. *c* **1000** wealt [see B. 3 a]. *c* **1200** *Trin. Coll. Hom.* 181 We one awlencð alle þe hundlimen, and welt þe sowle. *c* **1205** LAY. 32049 Ure drihten þe walt alle deden. *a* **1225** *Leg. Kath.* 1798 He . . wisseð & wealt—þe heouene & te eorðe. *c* **1250** *Gen. & Ex.* 54 Hali froure welt oc ðat miȝt. *c* **1275** *Moral Ode* 83 in *O.E. Misc.* 61 He wit and wald [*v.rr.* waldeð, walt, wealdeð] alle þing. **13..** *Guy Warw.* (A.) 3892 Lord þat woneþ an heye, Þat al þing walt fer & neye. **1377** LANGL. *P. Pl.* B. x. 83 Þe more he wynneth and welt welthes & ricchesse, . . þe lasse good he deleth. *c* **1425** *Cursor M.* 23105 (Trin.) Þe lord of myȝt þat al walt.

2. *Pa. t.* α. 1 **weold, wieold, 3 wield, 3–5 weld(e.**

Beowulf 465 weold [see B. 1]. *c* **897** ÆLFRED *Gregory's Past. C.* l. 391 Maniʒra folca ʒestreones hie wieoldon. *c* **1100** *O.E. Chron.* (MS. D) an. 1036, Þæt ne ʒeþafodon þa þe micel weoldon on þisan lande. *c* **1200** *Trin. Coll. Hom.* 169 On alle þe winne þe he erur wield. *c* **1205** LAY. 183 He wes king & heo quen & kinelond heo welden. **1432–50** tr. *Higden* (Rolls) I. 7 Riches þat þey welde [*Caxton* welded] while þey were alyue.

β. 1 **wylde, 2 (ȝe)wellde, -welt, 3–4 welt(e, welde.**

a **1000** *Voc.* in Wr.-Wülcker 225/1 *Domuit, i. uicit, mitigauit*, wylde. *c* **1175** *E.E.* (*Vesp.*) *Hom.* 106 Ic ȝewellde & ȝewann feola þeodan. *Ibid.* 107 Ne mid his scelde heo ne ȝewelt. *c* **1250** *Gen. & Ex.* 532 Wimmen welten weres mester. *c* **1350** welt [see B. 2].

γ. 3 **wald(e, wælde, 4–5 walt; 3–5 wolde, 4 wolt.**

c **1205** LAY. 8976 Androgeus walde [*later text* welde] al þat he wolde. *Ibid.* 24134 Na lengere þat lond he ne walde [*later text* wolde]. *a* **1250** *Prov. Ælfred* 389 in *O.E. Misc.* 126 Þeyh o mon wolde al þe worlde. **13..** *Gaw. & Gr. Knt.* 231 He stemmed & con studie, Quo walt þer most renoun. *Ibid.* 485 Wyth wele walt þay þat day. *c* **1350** *Will. Palerne* 3887 Was neuer man vpon mold þat swiche miȝt walt. *a* **1425** *Cursor M.* 10181 (Trin.) Þe secounde party þat he walt Was among þe prestes dalt.

δ. 4–7 **welded (4 -id), 5–6** *Sc.* **weildit, 6 weelded, 7 weilded, 7– wielded.**

1338 weldid [see B. 5]. **1382** WYCLIF *Isa.* lxiii. 18 As noȝt thei weldeden thin hoeli puple. *c* **1475** *Rauf Coilȝear* 578 The wy that weildit the wane. **1601** welded [see B. 5 d]. **1838** JAMES *Louis XIV*, III. iii. 89 Boileau too wielded his satirical pen.

3. *Pa. pple.* 1 **ʒewealden, 3 iwealde, iwald, wold, 5 welde(n, weld; 1 wyld(d; 4 weldid, 7 (9** *dial.*) **welded, 7– wielded.**

Beowulf 1732 [He] ʒedeð him . . ʒewealdene worolde dælas. *c* **1000** *Ags. Ps.* (Spelman) xviii. 14 [xix. 13] Ʒif min hine beoþ wyldde. *c* **1200** [see B. 3]. *a* **1225** *Leg. Kath.* 189 Al þe world is iwald þurh his wissunge. *c* **1250** wold [see B. 1 c]. *a* **1340** HAMPOLE *Psalter* xv. 7 Thurgh þe whilke þe heritage of heuen may be sene and weldid. *a* **1425** *Cursor M.* 13821 (Trin.) Eiȝte & þritty ȝeer in bonde Haue I not welden foot ny honde. *c* **1470** HARDING *Chron.* CCIX. iii, The which the duke of Bargoyn wold haue weld. *Ibid.* CCXXXII. iii, So was the lande wᵗ Frenchmen wonne & welde. **1688** HOLME *Armoury* III. vii. 321/2 The Hand Hammer . . may be welded . . with one hand. **1750** JOHNSON *Rambler* No. 82 ¶10 A Scymitar once wielded by a Soldier. **1891** welded [see B. 4].

B. Signification.

†**1.** *trans.* To rule or reign over, govern, rule, command. *Obs.* exc. as merged in 5.

Beowulf 465 Ic . . weold folce Deniʒa. *c* **888** ÆLFRED *Boeth.* xxxiii. §5 Dryhten . . þu ðe ealle . . ʒesceafta . . ʒesceope & . . heora weltst. *c* **1175** *Lamb. Hom.* 153 To fihten . . to-ȝeines þa awariede gastes þet weldeð þosternesse [*rectores tenebrarum*]. *c* **1250** *Gen. & Ex.* 840 Ðe kinges welten burȝes ðoa. **1303** R. BRUNNE *Handl. Synne* 9891 God almyȝty, þat al þyng weldes. ? *a* **1400** *Morte Arth.* 650, I make the kepare, sir knyghte, of kyngrykes manye, . . to weilde al my landes. *c* **1420** *Prose Life Alex.* 37 So sall ȝe wele & peysably welde ȝour empire. *a* **1513** FABYAN *Chron.* I. cxcix. (1811) 206 Weldynge yᵉ countre at his wyll. **1575** GASCOIGNE *Kenelworth* Wks. 1910 II. 115 Though she finde the skil A kingdome for to weelde. **1633** BP. HALL *Hard Texts* Neh. v. 14, I, and my familie have not taken that allowance which was appointed for the governour, so as, though I weilded the place, yet I forbore to take the maintenance allotted unto it.

b. *intr.* To rule, have the command; *fig.* to prevail. *Obs.* exc. *Sc. dial.*

a **1450** *Ratis Raving* 2270 Vilfulnes and mysknawleg Ay wodly weildand. ? *a* **1500** *Chester Pl.* (Shaks. Soc.) vi. 112 As was from the begininge, And never shall have endinge, From worlde to worlde aye weildinge, Amen! God of mighte moste. **1915** G. SINCLAIR *Poems* 63 May . . love an' friendship freely wald Around her ingle.

†**c.** *trans.* To overcome, subdue. *Obs.*

a **1000** [see A. 2 β]. *c* **1250** *Gen. & Ex.* 421 Abel an hundred ȝer was hold, Ðan he was of is broðer wold. *Ibid.* 526 Ðor is writen quat aȝte awold, Ðat ðis werld was [of ?] water wold.

†**2.** To have at command or disposal, have as one's own or in one's keeping, hold, own, possess; to have the advantage of, enjoy; sometimes (contextually), to get possession of, gain, win, obtain.

Beowulf 2051 Hi weoldon wælstowe. *a* **1000** *Guthlac* 239 Oft we oferseʒon . . þeoda þeawas, þræce modiʒra, þara þe in ʒelimpe life weoldon. **11..** in Kemble *Cod. Dipl.* IV. 200 And ic cyðe eow ðæt Ordric abbud and eal ðæt hired on Abbendunes mynstre be minre unne and ʒife friʒelice habban and wealdan Hornemeres hunred on hyre aʒenre andwealde. *c* **1220** *Bestiary* 176 If ðu hauest is broken, Al ðu forbreðes, forwurðes and forgelues, Eche lif to wolden. *a* **1225** *Ancr. R.* 388 [Christ] wrot mid his owune blode saluz to his leofmon, of luue gretunge . . forte welden hire luue. *a* **1300** *Cursor M.* 10328 Oft sith lates he be lett Man wit womman child to gett, Bituix and þair forþer eild, And þan þam sendes child to weild. *Ibid.* 24188 Moght i þe ans weld in arm, Hale me think of all mi harm. **13..** [see A. 2 γ]. **13..** *Gaw. & Gr. Knt.* 835 Ȝe ar welcum to welde as yow lykez þat here is; al is yowre awen, to haue at yowre wylle. *c* **1350** *Will. Palerne* 76 Þai seide þe child schuld weld al here godis. *Ibid.* 144 He wex to a wer-wolf . . ac his witt welt he after as wel as to-fore. *Ibid.* 2946, I not where he schal ȝou to wiue welde. *c* **1386** CHAUCER *Monk's T.* 20 Adam . . welte all Paradys sauynge o tree. **1470–85** MALORY *Arthur* V. vii. 172 Ye be worthy to welde all your honour and worship. *c* **1480** *Childe of Bristowe* 542 in Horstmann *Altengl. Leg.* (1881) 321, Y haue no childe, Myn heritage for to wilde. **1513** DOUGLAS *Æneis* VII. vi. 127 Lat nevir his feris weild Ane fut braid of Italiane ground nor feyld. **1586** [see A. 1 ϵ]. **1593** CHURCHYARD *Challenge* 116 What cunning heads and hands can catch in hold, That covetous mindes, doth seek to weld alone. **1603** HOLLAND *Plutarch's Mor.* 510 They . . would never be able with wisdom and moderation to weld any great prosperitie [τὰς εὐπραγίας . . φέρειν].

†**b.** To have in oneself, experience, feel; to have as one's lot or fate, suffer, undergo; to suffer patiently, endure, tolerate. *Obs.*

c **1350** *Will. Palerne* 2990 So gret wonder walt þe quen of þe worþ bestes. *a* **1400** *Leg. Rood* viii. (1871) 143 Weopyng and wo I walt. *a* **1400** *Relig. Pieces fr. Thornton MS.* xi. (1914) 88 Wele or wa, ane of þase twa, To welde with-owtten ende. **1532** MORE *Confut. Tindale* Wks. 594/2 God . . maketh with the temptacion a way out also, that ye may well weild it. **1579** LYLY *Euphues* N ij, At the first the Oxe weyldeth not the yoke, nor the Colt the snaffle, . . yet time causeth the one to bend his neck [etc.].

†**3. a.** To decide, determine, ordain; to be the author or cause of; to bring about; to carry out, execute, perform. *Obs.*

In OE. chiefly const. gen. In later use prob. transf. from 4.

Beowulf 2574 Ðær he þy fyrste forman doʒore wealdan moste. *c* **897** ÆLFRED tr. *Gregory's Past. C.* 377 Ʒif hwelc folc bið mid hungre ʒeswenced, & hwa his hwæte ʒehyt & oðhielt, hu ne wilt he . . hiera deaðes? *a* **900** CYNEWULF *Elene* 760 Þæs ðu . . wealdest. *c* **1000** *Instit. Pol.* xxv. in Thorpe *Anc. Laws* II. 340/14 Syndon . . cyrcan . . wace ʒegriðode . . wa þam þe þæs wealt. *c* **1200** *Trin. Coll. Hom.* 45 Þurh mannes gemeleste . . and naht bi his aȝene wille . . deað him wes iwealde. *c* **1275** in *O.E. Misc.* 101 Bidde we alle þen heye kyng þat welde schal þe laste dom. **13..** *E.E. Allit. P.* A. 811 For synne he set hymself in vayn, That neuer hade non hymself to wolde. **1387** TREVISA *Higden* (Rolls) I. 419 He may no werk soche wilde. **1513** DOUGLAS *Æneis* VIII. Prol. 22 All is wele done, God wait, weild he his will.

†**b.** *intr.* (for *refl.*) To occupy oneself, be doing; to act, do, fare (well, etc.); to 'manage'.

This use does not seem to be continuous with the intr. sense of OE. *wealdan* 'to contrive or manage to do something expressed or implied'.

c **1400** *Beryn* 1803 Howe shuld o sely lombe, a-mong wolvis weld, And scapen vn-I-harmyd? *c* **1470** HENRY *Wallace* IV. 339 Now lycht, now sadd; now blisful, now in baill; . . Nowe weildand weyle; now calde weddyr, now hett. *a* **1500** *Bernard. de cura rei fam.* I. 351 Quham god of mycht bade wald and virke & leffe In wytnes of adame and of eue. **1565** *Satir. Poems Reform.* I. 407 Rather given whollie to weld wᵗʰ the sworde, Then worke that wisdome have firmelie affied. **1581** A. HALL *Iliad* v. 93 Although he weelded wel in fight. **1613** P. FORBES *Comm. Rev.* Ep. Ded., The inexpert student, in search of letters weilding amidst infinite variety, is cast in such doubt of choise.

†**4.** *trans.* To direct the movement or action of, to control; to use, have the use of, as a bodily member or a faculty; to lead, guide, direct; *occas.* to hold in check; *gen.* to deal with, have to do with; to deal with successfully, manage. *Obs.* or *dial.* exc. as in 5.

Here are included various shades of meaning, *lit.* and *fig.*: see also below. In quot. 1530, to inflect grammatically. In OE. const. gen.

c **888** ÆLFRED *Boeth.* xxxix. §8 Sio eax welt ealles þæs wænes. **1297** R. GLOUC. (Rolls) 3093 Hii ne ssolleþ abbe þe leste ston þe wule ich may weld [*v.r.* wolde] min hond. *c* **1386** CHAUCER *Sompn. T.* 239 In our Chapitre praye we . . To crist þat he thee sende heele and myght Thy body for to weelden. *c* **1450** *Mirk's Festial* 196 Then callyd þe norys to þe modyr, and bade hur . . helpe hur forto folde þe chyldys cloþis; for scho was to woke, and myght not welde hom. *c* **1470** *Gol. & Gaw.* 450 Quhill I may my wit wald, I think my fredome to hald. **1508** DUNBAR *Tua Mariit Wemen* 77 Than suld I waill ane . . That suld my womanheid weild. **1513** DOUGLAS *Æneis* XII. xii. 129 The wond tarreis Enee sum deyll . . To weild hys kne maid sum impedyment. **1530** PALSGR. Ded. A ii b, How to welde hym [*sc.* a frenche worde], in his cases, gendre, nombres, modes, tenses, and persons. **1555** PHAER *Æneid* II. 529 So sayd she, and gan to welde Hym aged man, and in the sacred seat hym set and helde. **1581** T. HOWELL *Deuises* G iii b, Let wisedome welde your wit. **1595** SPENSER *Col. Clout* 130 Loue will not be drawne, but must be ledde, And Bregog did so well her fancie weld, That her good will he got her first to wedde. **1596** —— *State Irel.* Wks. (Globe) 663/2 According to the quantitye of such land, as euerye man . . shalbe founde able to weelde. **1601** HOLLAND *Pliny* X. iii. I. 272 The very Ægles, not able to weld the prey that they have seazed upon, are together with it drawne under the water. **1612** DRAYTON *Poly-olb.* ii. 131 Her new-beginning banke her water scarcely weelds. **1633** P. FLETCHER *Purple Isl.* VII. xli, Her daughters . . Much pain'd themselves her stumbling feet to weeld. **1650** FULLER *Pisgah* III. v. 326 It is no shame for one to admit a partner in that weighty work, which he cannot weild by himself. **1742** YOUNG *Nt. Th.* II. 449 Whose mind was . . strong to weild all science. **1891** *Sheffield Gloss.*, Suppl., A farmer living at Ashover, in Derbyshire, said to me, 'There's no farm I could ha' liked better if I could only ha' welded it'.

†**b.** *refl.* in various senses (see above); *occas.* to conduct oneself, behave. *Obs.*

c **1200** *Vices & Virtues* (1888) 51 He lai alswa ðat child ðe nan god ne cann, ne speken ne mai, ne isien, ne him seluen wealden. **13..** *Sir Beues* (A.) 368 Whan þow ert of swich elde, Þat þow miȝt þe self wilde, And ert of age. *c* **1375**

Cursor M. 24358 (Fairf.) þorou mi hert I felde hit stange My-self I mu3t no3t welde. *c* **1400** *Destr. Troy* 8655 His sheld on his shulders shot was behynd, And his brest left bare,.. To weld hym more winly þat worthy to lede. **1426** LYDG. *De Guil. Pilgr.* 20587 Somme be lame, and feble.. And somme strong, and gon vp-ryht, And many welde hem sylff ryht wel. *c* **1430** *How Good Wife taught Dau.* in *Babees Bk.* (1868) 46 So wysely thee welde That þy frendys haue Ioy of thee. **1545** RAYNALDE *Byrth Mankynde* II. ii. (1552) 60 b, Nether can it welde, or helpe it selfe to come forthe. **1647** HARVEY *Sch. of Heart* VI. iii, The limbs unable are themselves to welld [*rime* swell'd].

†**c.** To carry (something heavy or requiring effort). *Obs.*

c **1205** LAY. 1131 þa Troinisce men.. duden of þan wilden al heora iwilla, to þan scipen wælden [*later text* to þe sipes ladden so moche so iwolden]. *Ibid.* 21874 Heo.. heore uæx fæire wælden to volde [*later text* hire her faire al hii totere]. *c* **1386** CHAUCER *Monk's T.* 272 She wolde kille Leons leopardes and Beres.. And in hir Armes weelde hem at hir wille. *a* **1400–50** *Wars Alex.* 838 þan Alexander.. Wynnes him vp a wardrere he walt in his handis. **1592** KYD *Sp. Trag.* I. iv, I tooke him up, and wound him in mine armes; And welding him unto my priuate tent, There laid him downe.

†**d.** To express, utter. *Obs. rare.*

1581 A. HALL *Iliad* v. 77 To the Gods.. he wold not weeld his thought. **1587** A. DAY *Daphnis & Chloe* (1890) 121 The best are mute, And may not weld the greatnes of her praise. **1605** SHAKS. *Lear* I. i. 56 Sir, I loue you more then word can weild ye matter. *a* **1635** CORBET *Poems* (1672) 95 Out-went the Townsmen all in Starch,.. into the Field, Where one a Speech could hardly wield.

5. To use or handle with skill and effect; to manage, actuate, ply (a weapon, tool, or instrument, now always one held or carried in the hand). (The current sense.)

In OE. const. gen., dat., or instrumental.

Beowulf 2038 þenden hie ðam wæpnum wealdan moston. *a* **1000** *Battle of Maldon* 83 þa hwile þe hi wæpna wealdan moston. *c* **1300** *Havelok* 1436 Nou ich am up to þat helde Cumen, that ich may wepne welde. **1338** R. BRUNNE *Chron.* (1810) 23 Sex 3ere was he kyng, with werre weldid þe scheld. **1375** BARBOUR *Bruce* XI. 97 He left nane mycht vapnys velde. *c* **1385** CHAUCER *L.G.W.* 2000 *Ariadne*, He.. hath Rovme.. To welde an axe or swerde or staffe or knyffe. *a* **1400–50** *Wars Alex.* 651 Wele & wi3tly in were to welden a spere. *c* **1425** WYNTOUN *Cron.* VII. vii. 1304 A childe.. þat wapynnys mycht noucht wichtly waulde. *c* **1425** *Non-Cycle Myst. Plays* (1909) 22/82 Worklooms for to work and weeld. **1470–85** MALORY *Arthur* IX. ii. 340 Is there ony of you here that wille take vpon hym to welde this shelde? **1563** P. WHITEHORNE *Onosandro Platon.* 74 Muche lesse the slingers can wild their slinges..: being hindered of the Souldiers. **1598** SHAKS. *Merry W.* I. iii. 24 O base hungarian wight: wilt y^u^ the spigot wield? **1603** G. OWEN *Pembrokeshire* (1892) 275 Monstrouse cudgells.. as bigge as the partie is well able to wild. **1629** H. BURTON *Truth's Tri.* 251 We can tell better how to weald our owne weapons. **1736** GRAY *Statius* i. 1 Whoe'er the quoit can wield, And furthest send its weight. **1784** COWPER *Task* III. 636 Strength may wield the pond'rous spade. **1798** WORDSW. *Peter Bell* Prol. xxx, A potent wand doth Sorrow wield. **1860** TYNDALL *Glac.* I. xxii. 159 Never wielding my hatchet until my balance was secured.

b. *to wield a* or *the sceptre* (and similar phrases): to exercise supreme authority, to reign or rule (also *fig.*). Cf. SWAY *v.* 8.

1593 SHAKS. *3 Hen. VI.* IV. vi. 73 His Head by nature fram'd to weare a Crowne, His Hand to wield a Scepter. **1595** DANIEL *Civ. Wars* I. xxix, Edward the third being dead, had left this child.. The crowne and Scepter of this Realme to wield. **1635** J. TAYLOR (Water P.) *Old, Old Man* C 4, How he and 's son th' eighth Henry, here did wield The Scepter. **1809** SYD. SMITH *Serm.* I. 64 Providence.. gives to many a man a soul far better than his birth, compelling him to dig with a spade, who had better have wielded a sceptre. **1821** SCOTT *Kenilw.* vii, The late prime favourite of England, who wielded her general's staff and controlled her parliaments. **1858** MAX MÜLLER *Chips* (1880) III. i. 28 The intellectual sceptre of Germany was wielded by a new nobility.

c. To exercise (power, authority, influence).

1612 T. TAYLOR *Comm. Titus* ii. 9 He forbiddeth them not to exercise rule.. ouer their seruants, but only teacheth them after what manner to weild their authoritie. *a* **1677** BARROW *Serm.* III. xxii. (R.) To wield power innocently,.. for the maintenance of right,.. for the suppression of injury,.. is a matter of no small skill. **1836** J. GILBERT *Chr. Atonem.* iv. (1852) 97 Physical power wielded by an omnipotent Being.. must overcome every possible obstacle. **1861** BUCKLE *Civiliz.* II. vi. 412 Over the inferior order of minds, they still wield great influence. **1868** J. H. BLUNT *Ref. Ch. Eng.* I. 100 Wielding.. an authority which he had no just right to wield. **1874** GREEN *Short Hist.* i. §6. 53 Dunstan.. wielded for sixteen years.. the secular and ecclesiastical powers of the realm.

d. To use after the fashion of a tool or weapon for the performance of something.

1601 W. CORNWALLIS *Ess.* II. xlix. Nn 3 b, I am the veriest bungler.. that euer welded tongue. **1849** MACAULAY *Hist. Eng.* iii. I. 354 Wielding the strength and representing the dignity of the city of London. **1857** MAURICE *Mor. & Met. Philos.* IV. vii. §13. 343 Wielding the learning of the old times with incomparable facility. **1871** T. R. JONES *Anim. Kingd.* (ed. 4) 725 The dorsal ribs [of serpents] wielded.. by.. powerful muscles.. perform the office of internal legs. **1882** PEBODY *Engl. Journalism* xxiii. 183 A trained soldier wielding a graphic and powerful pen. **1886** A. WEIR *Hist. Basis Mod. Europe* (1889) 588 [The] increasing importance of the middle classes, as they wielded more efficiently capital and machinery. **1918** A. MENZIES *Calvin* 396 Who could wield such scathing invective?

Hence **'wielded** *ppl. a.*; also (*nonce-wds.*) **'wieldable** *a.*, capable of being wielded; †**'wieldance**, the action of wielding.

1800 SOUTHEY in Robberds *Mem. W. Taylor* I. 325 As easy and as *wieldable as blank verse. *c* **1625** BP. HALL *St. Paul's Combat* II. Wks. 1634 II. 451 This spirituall edge shall either turne againe, or (through our weake *weildance) not enter the stubburne and thick hide of obdured hearts. **1842** TENNYSON *Talking Oak* lxvi, May never saw dismember thee, Nor *wielded axe disjoint.

wielder ('wiːldə(r)). Forms: see WIELD *v.*; 4 -ere, 5 -are, -ire, 5–6 -ar, 5– -er. [f. WIELD *v.* + -ER[1].] One who wields, in various senses.

†**1.** A ruler, governor, master; sometimes applied to God; *locally*, a manager (?). *Obs.*

13.. *E.E. Allit. P.* C. 129 þe welder of wyt, þat wot alle þynges. **1382** WYCLIF *Isa.* i. 3 The oxe kne3 his weldere, and the asse the cracche of his lord. *a* **1400–50** *Wars Alex.* 1608 þe lege Emperoure, þe wildire [*v.r.* welder] of all þe werde. **1402** in *Pol. Poems* (Rolls) II. 78 As that we were welders and lordes of alle. **1593** Q. ELIZ. *Boeth.* I. met. v. 44 O weldar, apeace the Roring floudes. **1600** BRETON *Melancholike Humours* Wks. (Grosart) I. 9/1 They, like the wielders of the world, command, and haue their will. **1723** SWIFT *Argts. Power Bps.* Wks. 1841 II. 219/1 Such.. tenants, generally speaking, have others under them, and so a third and fourth in subordination, till it comes to the wielder (as they call him), who sits at a rack-rent. **1823–49** LINGARD *Hist. Eng.* (1855) I. ii. 52/1 The title.. of Bretwalda, the wielder or sovereign of Britain.

†**2.** The author or cause *of* something. *Obs. rare.*

1570 *Satir. Poems Reform.* xvii. 53 The veildars of yis greif.

3. One who uses or actuates skilfully: const. *of* (a weapon, instrument, etc.); also *fig.*

1760–72 H. BROOKE *Fool of Qual.* (1809) III. 57 He is the free wielder of all the powers of a free.. people. **1855** BRIMLEY *Ess., Westw. Ho!* (1858) 303 These are the high aims of fiction in the hands of its master wielders. **1862** R. W. PROCTER *Our Turf, Stage & Ring* 81 The rough-hewn wielders of the spade. **1866** WHITTIER *Snow-bound* 438 Brisk wielder of the birch and rule, The master of the district school. **1884** R. F. BURTON *Bk. Sword* viii. 166 The Zanzibari's Sword is.. dangerous to the wielder. **1908** *Spectator* 11 Apr. 564/2 Some able wielder of autocratic power.

wielding ('wiːldɪŋ), *vbl. sb.* [f. WIELD *v.* + -ING[1].] The action of the verb WIELD, in various senses.

†**1.** Government, power, command; possession, keeping: see WIELD *v.* B. 1, 2. *Obs.*

c **1205** LAY. 19011 þa hædden heo.. Vðer þene king wið inne heore walding [*c* **1275** weldyng]. *c* **1325** *Metr. Hom.* 1 Al es loken in thi welding. Thou ert Lauerd.. That al op-haldes. *c* **1386** CHAUCER *Melib.* ¶ 644 Ye haue hem in youre myght and in youre weeldynge. *c* **1440** *York Myst.* i. 39 And haue al welth in 3oure weledyng. *c* **1460** *Play Sacram.* 35 In þe dukedom of Oryon moche have I in weldyng. *c* **1485** *Digby Myst.* III. 59 Thys castell.. is at my wylddyng.

2. Control, (power of) using, management, etc.: see WIELD *v.* B. 4, 5.

a **1425** *Cursor M.* 13781 (Trin.) His lymmes had he so forgone þat of hem weldyng had he none. **1551** ROBINSON tr. *More's Utopia* II. iv. (1895) 140 Their garmentes.. [are] no let to the mouynge and weldynge of the bodie. **1581** A. HALL *Iliad* VII. 125 Areithous that bare the great and massie club, And.. got such praise by force and weelding good. **1820** LAMB *Elia* Ser. I. *South-sea House*, He was.. equal to the wielding of any of the most intricate accounts. **1836** KEBLE in *Lyra Apost.* (1849) 223 Behold your armoury!—sword and lightning shaft,.. And in your wielding left! **1880** TENNYSON *Brunanburh* xi, The wielding of weapons.

'wielding, *ppl. a.* (*sb.*) [f. as prec. + -ING[2].] That wields; †ruling, governing; as *sb.* a ruler, governor (see WALDEND); in quot. 1622, ? faring, 'doing' (well). (See also ALL-WIELDING.)

a **900** CYNEWULF *Crist* 1011 Mihti3 god,.. waldende god. *c* **1000** ÆLFRIC *Hom.* I. 328 Se Wealdenda Drihten. *a* **1300** *Cursor M.* 5206 Of egypti.. Es he liuand and maister weldand. *c* **1485** *Digby Myst.* III. 1832, I be-leve In þe father, þat is of all wyldyng. **1622** WITHER *Faire-Virtue* B 2, A faire weilding-tree.

†**'wieldless,** *a. Obs.* [f. WIELD *v.* + -LESS.] That cannot be wielded; unmanageable, uncontrollable, unwieldy.

1560 PHAER *Æneid.* IX. 740 Down sinks the weldlesse weight. **1593** G. FLETCHER *Licia* (1876) 36 The warlike Mars, can weildles weapons guide. **1596** SPENSER *F.Q.* IV. iii. 19 With the weight of his owne weeldlesse might, He falleth nigh to ground.

†**wieldly,** *a. Obs. rare.* In 5 weldely. [f. WIELD *v.* + -LY[1]. Cf. *unwieldly*.] = WIELDY 2 (quot. *c* 1440).

†**'wieldness.** *Obs.* In 4 weld-, weildnes. [f. WIELD *a.* + -NESS. Cf. OE. *waldnis* 'dominatio'.] Command, control, possession.

a **1300** *Cursor M.* 13781 Sua herd him was his limes þan þat he o þaim had weldnes nan. *Ibid.* 23641 [þe gode] þir sal haf weldnes of all wale, [þe wicked] þai sal vnweldid be wit bale.

†**'wieldsome,** *a. Obs. rare.* [f. WIELD *v.* + -SOME.] = WIELDY 3.

1565 GOLDING *Cæsar* 99 b, The Galleyes wherof the facion was more straunge to the sauage Britons, and the mouing more redy and wieldsome [*et motus ad usum expeditior*].

wieldy ('wiːldɪ), *a.* Forms: 4–6 weldy (6 -ie), 5 weeldy, 6 wyldy, 7 wieldie, weildy, 7– wieldy. [f. WIELD *v.* + -Y[1]. Cf. MLG. *weldich* etc., and UNWIELDY.]

1. Capable of easily 'wielding' one's body or limbs, or a weapon, etc.; vigorous, active, agile, nimble. *Obs.* exc. *dial.*

c **1374** CHAUCER *Troylus* II. 636 So fressh so yong so weldy semed he. **1422** YONGE *Secr. Secr.* xxiii. 154 Where ben the Weldy Werriours? *c* **1450** LOVELICH *Grail* xii. 57 Eche man.. That weren weldy Armes to bere. **1528** MORE *Dyaloge* I. Wks. 153 The hole body is the more wyldy and lusty by some kynde of exercise. **1592** WYRLEY *Armorie, Ld. Chandos* 75 Armd like youthfull Troyilus And fresh as he.., As stirring, weldie, and as cheualrous As Chaucer makes him. **1677** GILPIN *Dæmonol.* (1867) 79 By reason of our burden we are less wieldy and more unapt to make any resistance.

†**2.** ? Requiring strength to wield, heavy or bulky; wielded with force, powerful. *Obs.*

c **1440** *Partonope* 3876 (Univ. Coll. MS.) A-boute hys nekk heng a sheelde.. And hit was full weeldy [*v.r.* weldely]. **1592** WYRLEY *Armorie, Ld. Chandos* 57 [He] did stand To his defence, when slaine was euerie mate With weldie axe.

3. Easily wielded, controlled, or handled; manageable; handy. [In later use a back-formation from *unwieldy*.]

1583 MELBANCKE *Philotimus* H iv, When you breake a colte, you firste beate him for his wildnes, and afterward being weldy do cherish your hobby. **1656** HEYLIN *Surv. France* 183 The boat.. wieldie and fit for speed. **1678** R. L'ESTRANGE *Seneca's Mor.* III. v. 28 In the Choice of a Sword, we take care that it be weildy. **1795** SOUTHEY *Joan of Arc* x. 286 Their javelins lessen'd to a wieldy length. **1839** J. ROGERS *Antipopopr.* v. §2. 192 One mighty league, in one body wieldy, tractable, governable. **1903** *Times Lit. Suppl.* 19 June 189/1 For its bulk it is admirably wieldy and light in hand.

¶ Erroneously used for *unwieldy*.

1687 WOOD *Life* (O.H.S.) III. 227 [He] being fat and weildy, could not ride or walk as the others could.

wiele, wier, wierangel, -gle, wierd, wiery, wiese, wiesshe, wiet, wietch, wieth, obs. ff. WILE, WEIR, WIRE, WARIANGLE, WEIRD, WIRY, WISE, WISH *v.*, WIT *v.*, WICH, WITHE.

Wien[1] (viːn). *Physics.* The name of Wilhelm *Wien* (1864–1928), German physicist, used *attrib.* and in the possessive to denote (*a*) an approximation to Planck's law that holds at short wavelengths, according to which the flux of radiant energy of wavelength λ emitted by a black body at temperature T is proportional to $1/\lambda^5 \exp(hc/\lambda kT)$; (*b*) the displacement law (sense (i) s.v. DISPLACEMENT 2 e).

1899 *Astrophysical Jrnl.* X. 40 My observations.. make it seem possible that the law derived by W. Wien represents the emission of 'the absolutely black body'. In Wien's formula, J = [etc.]. **1900** *Sci. Abstr.* III. 383 Wien's laws, according to which the wave-length of the maximum radiation is inversely proportional to the absolute temperature, and the corresponding maximum energy proportional to the fifth power of the absolute temperature, were confirmed. **1904** Wien's displacement law [see DISPLACEMENT 2 e]. **1948** [see RAYLEIGH-JEANS]. **1963** G. L. PICKARD *Descriptive Physical Oceanogr.* v. 52 According to Wien's Law this energy is concentrated round a wavelength of 0.5μ. **1978** PASACHOFF & KUTNER *University Astron.* ii. 24 From Wien's displacement law, we can see that the colors of stars in the sky are telling us something about their temperatures.

Wien[2] (viːn). [The name of M. C. *Wien* (1866–1938), German physicist.] **a.** *Electr.* ***Wien bridge***: an alternating-current bridge circuit devised by Wien which is used to measure capacitance (or frequency) in terms of resistance and frequency (or capacitance); ***Wien bridge oscillator***: an oscillator based on this circuit.

1922 GLAZEBROOK *Dict. Appl. Physics* II. 1029/1 *Wien bridge*, for the measurement of the capacity and power factor of a condenser. **1957** *Practical Wireless* XXXIII. 709/2 In Fig. 2 a simple bridge for capacitor testing is given. This is known as a Wien bridge. **1967** *Electronics* 6 Mar. 63/3 (Advt.), Here, the RA-240 is used in the design of a highly stable, uncompensated Wien bridge oscillator. **1979** R. HAMILTON *Electronics for Technicians* vii. 157 The other type of *R-C* oscillator to be considered is known as a Wien bridge oscillator. (The name derives from a type of bridge circuit used in measurements, the feedback network of the oscillator being part of a balanced Wien bridge.)

b. *Physical Chem.* ***Wien effect***: the increase in the electrical conductivity of an electrolytic solution as the field strength is increased.

1934 R. P. BELL *Electrolytes* v. 90 The increase in conductivity [with frequency] is.. of the same order of magnitude as the Wien effect. **1978** P. W. ATKINS *Physical Chem.* xxv. 832 The Wien effect is the observation of higher mobilities [of ions] at higher electric fields. (There are two Wien effects. The first Wien effect is the one just described; the second Wien effect is the enhancement of the degree of ionization of an ionogen, or weak electrolyte, by the applied field.)

wiener ('viːnə(r)), *a.* and *sb.* Also erron. weiner. [a. Ger., of Vienna.]

A. *adj.* **1.** ***wiener schnitzel***: see SCHNITZEL.

2. ***wienerwurst*** [G. *wurst* sausage]: = *Vienna sausage* s.v. VIENNA 1 a. *U.S.*

1889 *Gallup* (New Mexico) *Gleaner* 27 Mar. 3/3 We.. are willing to bet our unpaid debts, against a weiner-wurst [*sic*] that the modest local of the *Democrat* blushed more than the bride when he saw her in the diaphanous costume he describes. **1899** F. NORRIS *McTeague* v. 75 The lunch baskets were emptied... There were wienerwurst and frankfurter sausages. **1949** *Los Angeles Times* 15 May II. 5/2 I've never lamped a crooked dime, not e'en a wienerwurst.

‖**3.** ***Wiener Kreis*** [G. *kreis* circle]: = *Vienna Circle* s.v. VIENNA 1 a.

[**1929** (title) *Wissenschaftliche Weltauffassung. Der Wiener Kreis* (E. Mach Verein).] **1932** *Jrnl. Philos.* XXIX. 122 The philosophy of the 'Wiener Kreis' is unique in that it was formulated for the first time in a concise joint manifesto. **1950** B. RUSSELL *Logic & Knowl.* (1956) 370 Wittgenstein's *Tractatus Logico-Philosophicus*..provided a stimulus which helped in the formation of the 'Wiener Kreis', where logical positivism first took the form of a definite school. **1964** *New Statesman* 10 Apr. 574/2 The early chapters are full of perception theory, Chicago School aesthetics, *Wienerkreis* linguistics,..Platonic misconceptions and all stations to the Hochschule at Ulm.

B. *sb.* **a.** = *wiener wurst* above. Cf. WEINER. *N. Amer.*

1904 H. R. MARTIN *Tillie* iii. 34 I'm havin' fried smashed potatoes and wieners. **1935** *Motion Picture* Nov. 79/1 Hot dogs are just wiener sausages! **1970** S. J. PERELMAN *Baby, it's Cold Inside* 81 Platters of smoking hot wieners flanked by creamed spinach.

b. *Comb.* **wiener roast** *N. Amer.*, a barbecue at which wieners are cooked and served.

1920 *Outing* July-Aug. 245/1 All over France they introduced the women war workers to American hikes, wiener roasts, camping in the open, and games of all sorts. **1970** J. H. GRAY *Boy from Winnipeg* 53 Snow-shoeing clubs ..given to walking for miles after every snow, usually stopping for a wiener roast somewhere along the way.

wienie ('wiːniː). *N. Amer. slang.* Also erron. **weinie.** [f. WIENER *a.* and *sb.*: see -IE.] = WIENER *sb.* a. Cf. WEENY *sb.*[2], WINNY.

1911 *Daily Colonist* (Victoria, B.C.) 26 Apr. 7/3 Weinies, pretzels and coffee were served and German relishes. **1919** U. SINCLAIR *Jimmie Higgins* xx. 195 Mocking soldier-boys, who made merry..over sauerkraut and..'wienies', otherwise known as 'hot dogs'. **1940** R. CHANDLER *Farewell, my Lovely* xxxiv. 161, I spotted him [*sc.* the hot dog man] in a white barbecue stand tickling wienies with a long fork. **1959** E. AMBLER *Passage of Arms* iv. 103 The barman opened up a can of weinies. **1977** *Time* 4 July 37/1 One man's meat is another man's corndog (a wienie impaled on a stick and dunked in a bubbling cornbread batter).

wife (waɪf), *sb.* Pl. **wives** (waɪvz). Forms: *Sing. α.* 1–5 (6 *Sc.*) **wif**, 3–5 **wijf**, 3–6 **wyf**, 4–6 **wyff(e, wyfe**, (chiefly *Sc.*) **vif, vyf(e**, 5–6 **wiff(e**, 6 *Sc.* **vyff**, (1, 4 **wiif**, 4 **vijfe, whife, wieffe, wyefe, weyffe**, 4–5 **weife, wiue, wyue**, 5 **wyif, wyyfe, wyȝffe, whyf(f)e**, 5–7 **wiefe**, 6 **wieff**, 6–7 **wief**), 4– **wife**. *Gen.* 1–7 **wifes**, 3–7 **wiues**, (4 **wiuis, wyuys**), 4–5 **wijfes, wyues**, 4–6 **wyfes**, 5–6 *Sc.* **wyf(f)is**, 7 **wives**, 8 **wive's**, 8– **wife's**; *uninflected* 4 **wijf**, 4–5 **wife**. *Pl.* 1–3 **wif**; 2–7 **wifes**, 3–7 **wiues**, 4–5 *Sc.* **wyffis**, 4–6 **wyfes, wyues, wifis**, *Sc.* **wiffis**, 5–6 *Sc.* **wyfis**, (4 **wijf(e)s, vijfes, wiuis, wiuus, wiwes, vyuez**, *Sc.* **vifis**, 5 **wifs, wifys, wyuys**, 5–6 **-is**, 6 *Sc.* **vyffis, vyfues, vyuis**, 7 **wiefs**), 7– **wives**. *Gen.* 1 **wi(i)fa**, 3 **wife, wiue**; 3 **wiuene**; 4–7 **wives**, 8– **wives'**. [OE. *wíf* str. n. = OFris., OS. *wîf*, (LG. *wief*, Du. *wijf*), OHG., MHG. *wîp* (G. *weib*), ON. *víf* (Sw. *vif*, Da. *viv*); not in Gothic (which uses *qinô* 'mulier' QUEAN and *qêns* 'uxor' QUEEN *sb.*); of obscure origin.]

1. a. A woman: formerly in general sense; in later use restricted to a woman of humble rank or 'of low employment' (J.), esp. one engaged in the sale of some commodity. Now *dial.*, exc. with prefixed descriptive word, esp. in compounds such as ALE-WIFE[1], APPLE-*wife*, FISHWIFE, OLD WIFE, OYSTER-*wife*, etc.

c **725** *Corpus Gloss.* A 646 *Anus*, alduuif. *c* **900** tr. *Bæda's Hist.* IV. xxiii, Seo ærest wiifa [L. *feminarum*]. *c* **950** *Lindisf. Gosp.* John iv. 7 Cuom uif of ðær byriȝ to ladanne uæter. **971** *Blickl. Hom.* 5 For þære synne þæs ærestan wifes. *c* **1175** *Lamb. Hom.* 111 Wisdom biriseð weran and clenesse birisað wifan. *c* **1205** LAY. 1507 þa scipen todraȝen & þa wif drenchen. *a* **1225** *Ancr. R.* 158 Seint Johan baptiste, bi hwam ure Louerd seið, þet among wiuene sunes ne aros neuer betere. *a* **1300** *Cursor M.* 12904 Amang all wiue [**13..** *Gött.* wiues] suns,..A heier barn was neuer nan. *c* **1300** *Havelok* 1713 Hw god helpen kan O mani wise wif and man. *c* **1375** *Sc. Leg. Saints* xviii. (*Egipciane*) 1067, I coniure þe, þat it, þat þu has hard of me,..þat þu tel nothyre to man na vyf. *c* **1386** CHAUCER *Miller's T.* 155 The wyues of the parisshe. —— *Doctor's T.* 71 Whan she woxen is a wyf. *c* **1425** WYNTOUN *Cron.* VI. xviii. 2235 þat man is noucht born of wiff Off powar to reff me my lif. *c* **1470** HENRY *Wallace* I. 94 Eduuard..gert sla..Off man and wiff, vij thousand and fyfty. **1488** *Acc. Ld. High Treas. Scot.* I. 91 The wyfis of Dunbar. **1526** TINDALE *Rev.* xvii. 6, I sawe the wyfe dronke with the bloud of saynctes. *c* **1563** *Jack Juggler* C iij, Then came I by a wife that did costerds sell. **1570** *Satir. Poems Reform.* xii. 118 The wyfis that fostred ȝow. **1625** BACON *Apophthegms* §54 [19] Strawberrie wiues, that laid two or three great strawberries at the mouth of their pot, and all the rest were little ones. **1635** in *Daily Chron.* (1908) 11 Mar. 6/7 Oyster wives, herb wives, tripe wives. **1818** KEATS *Dawlish Fair* 3 Where ginger-bread wives have a scanty sale. **1825** BROCKETT *N.C. Gloss.*, *Wife*, a woman, whether married or not. 'An apple wife',—'a fish wife',—'A tripe wife'. **1859** TENNYSON *Guinev.* 55 She..shuddered, as the village wife who cries 'I shudder, some one steps across my grave.'

b. Qualified by *old*, esp. in the phr. ***old wives' fable, story, tale***: see OLD WIFE 1.

c **725** [see above]. **1340**, etc. [see OLD WIFE 1]. **1561** T. NORTON *Calvin's Inst.* III. 220 An old wiues request. **1656** MENNIS & J. SMITH *Mus. Delic.* (ed. 2) 2 An old wifes-Tale.

c. ***Wife of Bath***, one of the pilgrims in Chaucer's *Canterbury Tales*; used allusively (usu. *attrib.*), chiefly with reference to sexual appetite and outspokenness.

1926 A. HUXLEY *Essays New & Old* 178 Her comments on the connubial state were so very Juliet's Nurse, so positively Wife-of-Bath, that we were made to feel quite early Victorian. **1946** 'J. TEY' *Miss Pym Disposes* xviii. 185 The wide flat hat planked slightly to the back of her head on top of her wimple—Wife of Bath fashion—gave her an air of innocent astonishment. **1974** K. MILLETT *Flying* (1975) II. 183 Alison sings, a great lusty Wife of Bath woman. **1978** R. RENDELL *Sleeping Life* iii. 23 Horrifyingly, she added, with a Wife of Bath look, remembering the old dance, 'Wouldn't be for sex, not so likely.'

2. a. A woman joined to a man by marriage; a married woman. Correlative of HUSBAND *sb.* 2. (The ordinary current sense.)

c **888** ÆLFRED *Boeth.* x, Hu ne liofað þin wif eac, þæs ilcan Simaches dohtor? *c* **975** *Rushw. Gosp.* Matt. i. 24 *Accepit coniugem suam*, feng wiue his. *c* **1000** *Ags. Gosp.* Matt. xviii. 25 Hyne het hys hlaford ȝesyllan, & hys wif & hys cild. *a* **1175** *Cott. Hom.* 225 Sem cham iafet and hare þreo wif. *c* **1175** *Lamb. Hom.* 49 Riche men..þe habbeð..feire wifes and feire children. *Ibid.* 129 He forseh his scuppend þurh his wifes red. *c* **1205** LAY. 25 Noe & Sem Japhet & Cham & heore four wiues [*c* **1275** wifes]. *Ibid.* 14142 Ich wulle.. senden after mine wiue. *c* **1250** *Gen. & Ex.* 1219 God him bad is wiues tale Listen. *c* **1290** *S. Eng. Leg.* 30/26 To take is broþer wijf. *a* **1300** *Cursor M.* 918 þou, man,..has vndertaken þi wijf red [*Gött.* þi wiues rede]. **13..** *E.E. Allit. P.* A. 785 þe lambes vyuez in blysse we bene. *c* **1350** *Will. Palerne* 242 My menskful moder is his meke wiue. **1422** YONGE tr. *Secr. Secr.* xxxvi. 192 The loue that a vif shold haue to hir spous. *c* **1460** FORTESCUE *Abs. & Lim. Mon.* iii. (1885) 114 Thair wyfes and childeren. **1483** *Cath. Angl.* 417/1 A Wife modir, *socrus*. **1549** *Compl. Scot.* ii. 24 Thou sal spouse ane vyfe, bot ane vthir sal tak hyr fra the. **1562** J. HEYWOOD *Prov. & Epigr.* (1867) 72 A good wife makth a good husbande, (they saie). **1580** in *Cath. Tractates* (S.T.S.) 58 Ane of Jacobs vyfues. **1603** HOLLAND *Plutarch's Mor.* 16 Slaves unto their wives goods. **1628** COKE *On. Litt.* I. 112 A man may not grant nor giue his tenements to his Wife during the couerture, for that his Wife and hee bee but one person in the Law. **1628** in *Cath. Tractates* (S.T.S.) 273 Their wifes and bairnes. *c* **1635** SIR W. POLE *Descr. Devon* III. (1791) 166 S^r. Thomas Beamont..maried 2 wiefs. **1637** *Sc. Prayer Bk.*, *Vis. Sick*, Visit him, O Lord, as thou didst Peters wives mother. **1722** HEARNE *Collect.* (O.H.S.) VII. 382 His Wive's first Husband. **1749** FIELDING *Tom Jones* IX. vii, She passed for that Gentleman's Wife,..and yet..there were some Doubts concerning the Reality of their Marriage. **1834** DICKENS *Sk. Boz, Boarding-ho.* i, He had never been married; but he was still on the look-out for a wife with money.

b. Phrases. (*a*) ***to wife*** (TO *prep.* 11 b), for a wife, to be one's wife: in such phrases as ***to take to wife***, to marry (somewhat *arch.*); † ***to give (grant) to wife***, to bestow in marriage; † ***to have (hold) to wife***, to have as one's wife, be the husband of; † ***to will to wife***, to desire to marry. †(*b*) ***wife's light***, a light (in a church) maintained by married women (cf. *maiden's light*, MAIDEN *sb.* 10). (*c*) ***all the world and his wife*** (humorous colloq.), all men and women, everybody: usually hyperbolically for a large and miscellaneous body or company of people of both sexes. (*d*) ***wife and mother***, a conventional epithet describing a woman who shows a zealous devotion to her family (now also somewhat *joc.*). (*e*) preceded by an adj. or sb. denoting the husband's occupation (freq. of a Mil. character, as ***navy, service wife***), and esp. connoting a wife who fulfils official expectations of this role.

Also in various other phrases, as ***bachelor's wife*** (BACHELOR 4 b), ***wife of one's bosom*** (BOSOM *sb.* 1 c), ***wife of the left hand*** (LEFT HAND 2), ***man and wife*** (MAN *sb.*[1] 8).

(*a*) *c* **1000** *Ags. Gosp.* Matt. xiv. 4 Nys þe alyfed hi to wife to hæbbenne. *c* **1250** *Gen. & Ex.* 2147 Iosep to wiue his dowter nam. **1297** R. GLOUC. (Rolls) 8926 þe emperour of alimayne willede to wiue [*v.rr.* to his wyfe, to his wyff] Mold þe kinges doȝter. *a* **1300** *Cursor M.* 7482, I suld..giue mi doghter him to wijf. **1362** LANGL. *P. Pl.* A. III. 106 ȝif he wilne þe to wyf, wolt þou him haue? *c* **1385** CHAUCER *L.G.W.* 1304 *Dido*, Haue ȝe nat sworn to wyue me to take? **1390** GOWER *Conf.* II. 217 This Steward..A lusti ladi hath to wyve. ? *a* **1400** *Morte Arth.* 3575 He has weddyde Waynore, and hyr to wyefe holdes. **1415** in *Reg. Mag. Sig. Scot. 1430*, 39/1 Huchon Fraser..God grantand, sal lede into wyf Jonet of Fentoun the systir. **1513** DOUGLAS *Æneis* VII. viii. 61 Bot he the grant to wyf his child Lavine. **1526** TINDALE *Mark* xii. 23 In the resurrecion then..whose wyfe shall she be of them? For seven had her to wyfe. **1588** GREENE *Pandosto* Wks. (Grosart) IV. 234 This Pandosto had to Wife a Ladie called Bellaria. **1711** STEELE *Spect.* No. 80 ¶3 She..was taken to Wife by a Gentleman. **1726** POPE *Odyss.* XXI. 73 If I the prize, if me you seek to wife. **1849** MACAULAY *Hist. Eng.* ii. I. 231 James had..taken to wife the princess Mary of Modena. **1907** C. HILL-TOUT *Brit. N. Amer., Far West* x. 182 Early marriages were..the custom, the girls being often barely pubescent when taken to wife.

(*b*) **1547–8** in Swayne *Churchw. Acc. Sarum* (1896) 275, x li. of wex for the wyfes Light.

(*c*) **1731–8** SWIFT *Pol. Conversat.* III. 192 *Miss.* Pray, Madam, who were the Company? *Lady Smart.* Why, there was all the World, and his Wife. **1822** BYRON *Let. to Sir W. Scott*, 'All the world and his wife', as the proverb goes, were trying to trample upon me. **1865** DICKENS *Mut. Fr.* I. xvii, All the world and his wife and daughter leave cards. **1912** *World* 7 May 701/1 So much has been heard of Hardelot lately..that its name must be familiar to all the world and his wife.

(*d*) **1798** MRS. INCHBALD *Lovers' Vows* (ed. 3) II. iii. 31 Go to Amelia—explain to her the duties of a wife and of a mother. **1850** MRS. GASKELL *Let.* Apr. (1966) 108 One of my mes is..a true Christian..another of my mes is a wife and mother, and highly delighted at the delight of everyone else in the house. **1911** G. B. SHAW *Getting Married* 196 She's a born wife and mother, maam. Thats why my children all ran away from home. **1930** A. CHRISTIE *Murder at Vicarage* xxxii. 252 I'm going to be a real 'wife and mother' (as they say in books). **1974** M. CECIL *Heroines in Love* v. 128 They could remain devoted wives and mothers *and* do their bit for the Cause.

(*e*) **1951** 'J. TEY' *Daughter of Time* i. 9 The present Valerie or Angela or Cecile..must be a naval wife. **1975** 'J. BELL' *Victim* i. 17 All the vulgar arrogance of an overseas army wife between the wars. **1981** P. MCCUTCHAN *Shard calls Tune* ii. 18 Beth had been a police wife..and a Foreign Office Security wife... She knew she mustn't ask where Simon was going.

c. (*a*) *euphem.* A kept mistress, concubine.

c **1425** WYNTOUN *Cron.* VI. x. 880 Bot scho wes blamyt in hir live, The bischop of Dunkeldynnis wif.

(*b*) ***a wife in every port***, a licence or indulgence (jocularly) said to be enjoyed by sailors.

1761 I. BICKERSTAFFE *Thomas & Sally* I. iii. 5 'Tis pretty sport, for one that gets a wife at ev'ry port. **1907** *Punch* 22 May 365/2 (*caption*) *Admiral.* And what made *you* wish to become a sailor, my boy? *Navy Candidate* (*in perfect good faith*). Because he's got a wife in every port, sir. **1933** SOMERVILLE & 'ROSS' *Smile & Tear* xi. 132 'The wife in every port', supposed to be the perquisite of sailors, is no more than the constant aspiration of every self-respecting dog.

†**d.** Applied as a term of affection to a female friend. *Obs.*

1592 *Wills & Inv. Durh.* (Surtees 1860) 205 To Mrs. Clopton one old ryall, to hir daughter, my wiffe, Alice, one angell. **1601** in *Blackw. Mag.* (1898) Nov. 654/2, I came lately thence..about a match for my wife, which is since dispatcht with younge Gifford.

e. *transf.* The female of a pair of the lower animals; the mate of a male animal.

c **1386** CHAUCER *Nun's Priest's T.* 63 As Chauntecleer among hise wyues alle Sat on his perche. *c* **1440** *Pallad. on Husb.* I. 669 Fesauntis..first in Marche vppon they go Theyr wyuys. **1513** DOUGLAS *Æneis* XII. Prol. 159 Phebus red fowle..Pykland his meyt..Hys wifis, Toppa and Pertelok, hym by. **1657** G. THORNLEY *Daphnis & Chloe* 125 The he-goats..every one had his own wives. **1838** *Lett. fr. Madras* (1843) 194 The monkeys were in a rage... The old father hunted his wife and children up the tree. **1870** P. M. DUNCAN *Blanchard's Transf. Insects* 436 Wives appear to be at a premium amongst these spiders. **1887** G. W. CABLE in *Century Mag.* Mar. 677/1 The song-birds..making the.. wood merry with their carolings to the wives and younglings in the nests.

f. *fig.* of a thing: see quots. See also *Dutch wife* s.v. DUTCH A. 4.

1813 in Brighton *Adm. Wallis* (1892) 45 [His] wooden wife [as he sometimes called his ship]. **1823** EGAN *Grose's Dict. Vulgar T.* (ed. 3), *Wife*, a fetter fixed to one leg. **1859** *Habits Gd. Society* vii. (new ed.) 254 The pipe is the bachelor's wife.

g. The passive member of a homosexual partnership. *slang.*

1883 W. A. HAMMOND *Sexual Impotence in Male* i. 57 The one who was in this disgusting arrangement to act the part of 'husband' came to his 'wife's' bed and remained there during the night. **1957** DANFORTH & HORAN *D.A.'s Man* (1958) i. 3 He's got a new girl. His 'wife' went home last week. **1978** J. HYAMS *Pool* xiii. 199 The group's leader [a homosexual]..made his 'wife' head of production.

3. The mistress of a household; the hostess or landlady of an inn. In quot. *c* 1430 = housewife, economist. *Obs.* exc. as surviving in GOODWIFE 1, HOUSEWIFE 1.

c **1386** CHAUCER *Can. Yeom. Prol. & T.* 462 A preest.. Which was so plesaunt and so seruysable Vn-to the wyf where as he was at table That she wolde suffre hym no thyng for to paye. *c* **1430** *How Good Wife taught Dau.* 168 in Hazl. *E.P.P.* I. 191 Be thou wise wif of thin owen. **1485** in *Yorks. Archæol. Soc., Record Ser.* XLI. 5 The wiff of this hous is your doughter..and it is most metlye for you to tarye here. **1535** COVERDALE *1 Kings* xvii. 17 The sonne of the wife of ye house was sicke. **1560** MACHYN *Diary* (Camden) 238 The wyff of the Bell in Gracyous-strett. **1577** GOOGE *Heresbach's Husb.* II. (1586) 48 b, The olde husbandes..vsed..to iudge, that where they founde the garden out of order, the wyfe of the house..was no good huswyfe. **1620** *Frier Rush* 14 He called the wife of the house and said: Mistresse, I pray you fill a pottle of wine.

4. Collectors' name for a moth, *Catocala nupta*, also called Willow Red Underwing.

1832 RENNIE *Butterfl. & Moths* 99 The Wife..appears among willows the beginning of August.

5. *attrib.* and *Comb.* **a.** *attrib.* (*a*) of or pertaining to a wife or wives, as WIFEKIN, WIFTHING; (*b*) appositive = 'that is a wife', as ***wife-slave, -whore*** (†***-houre***). **b.** *obj.* (*a*) with agent-n., as ***wife-basher, -beater, -broker, -hunter, -seeker***; (*b*) with n. of action, as ***wife-bashing, -battering, -beating, -murder, -purchase, -slaughter***; (*c*) with pr. pple., as ***wife-beating, -hunting*** adjs. **c.** *instr.* = 'with or by a wife', as ***wife-awed, -worn*** adjs. **d.** Special Combs.: **wife-bound** *a.*, bound or united to a wife, married; **wife-carl** *Sc.*, a man who occupies himself with a woman's or housewife's work, a 'cotquean'; **wife-old** *a.*, *Sc.*, old enough to be a wife, of marriageable age; **wife-ridden** *a.*, tyrannized over by one's wife, 'hen-pecked'; **wife-swapping**, the interchange of marital partners for sexual purposes within a social group; hence **wife-swap** *sb.* (occas. as *v. intr.*); **wife-swapper**; **wife-widow** (*nonce-wd.*), a wife living apart from her husband.

1615 Chapman *Odyss.* xi. 370 She brought her *wife-awd husband, Neleus. **1909** *Practitioner* Dec. 828 Poisoning conducted on these lines . . resembles the action of the *wife-basher, who attacks his victim with a poker. . . The wife-basher, however, is aware of the obviousness of his crime. **1979** J. Wainwright *Tension* 98 She walked to the home of the 'wife-basher' . . and . . went into action. **1978** —— *Thief of Time* 221 'Why should some wandering female run to the nearest doctor?' . . '*Wife-bashing. Unwanted pregnancy. A score of reasons.' **1978** *Times* 16 Feb. 4/7 *Wife-battering is most likely to occur among couples with a family history of violence. **1892** *Boston* (Mass.) *Jrnl.* 21 Nov. 4/1 If the whipping-post has a mission, it is for the punishment of *wife-beaters. **1830** Miss Mitford *Village* Ser. iv. *Walks, Shaw*, An assurance of tenderness and protection such as no *wife-beating tyrant . . ever could inspire. **1856** Geo. Eliot *Let.* 18 Jan. (1954) II. 225 A Petition . . that married women may have a legal right to their own earnings, as a counteractive to wife-beating and other evils. **1882** L. Oliphant *Land of Khemi* iv. 199, I asked whether there was much wife-beating among the natives of Egypt. *a* **1547** Surrey *Æneis* iv. 343 A *wifebound man. **1820** Keats *Let.* 28 Jan. (1958) II. 247 Henry is wife-bound in Cambden Town there is no getting him out. **1700** T. Brown tr. *Fresny's Amusem.* vii. (1709) 63 These Marriage-Hucksters, or *Wife-brokers. **1508** Dunbar *Tua Mariit Wemen* 351, I maid that *wif carll to werk all womenis werkis. **1816** Scott *Antiq.* xiv, An ye will be a wife-carle, and buy fish at your ain hands. **1826** Cobbett *Rur. Rides* (1885) II. 171 Young *wife-hunters, in search of rich and ugly old women. **1864** Tennyson *Aylmer's F.* 212 *Wife-hunting, as the rumour ran, was he. **1907** E. V. Lucas *Swan & Friends* 90 Having loved in vain a lady whom he met at Shaftesbury while on a wife-hunting expedition. **1871** C. Kingsley *At Last* x, *Wife-murder is but too common among these Hindoos. **1901** Eden Phillpotts *Striking Hours* 31, I was *wife-auld, an' a peart gal very interested in men-folk. **1891** Westermarck *Hist. Hum. Marr.* (ed. 2) 382 *Wife-purchase and husband-purchase still persist . ., though in disguised forms. **1694** Congreve *Double Dealer* v. xiii, By Heav'n I'll not be *Wife-ridden. **1859** Cornwallis *New World* I. 231 The profession of the *wife-seeker was greatly in his favor. **1609** *Bible* (Douay) Num. v. *comm.*, God ordained this law . . to avoid *wiveslaughter. **1902** *Westm. Gaz.* 6 Aug. 1/3 He retires from work . . and purchases *wife-slaves to maintain him in idleness. **1976** *Private Eye* 24 Dec. 8/2 M. Phillipe Dannat . . told the magistrates of Nice that he had assaulted M. Georges David at a *wife-swap rendezvous in the hills above St. Tropez. **1978** F. Weldon *Praxis* xx. 184 They played strip poker; they *wife-swapped. **1969** C. Himes *Blind Man with Pistol* x. 111 *Wife swappers, gang fuckers, seekers of depravity. **1959** M. Pugh *Chancer* xiv. 170 He began to discuss the *wife-swapping parties held locally. . . 'But how do they get away with it here?. . . The town's so small. I would have thought that after six months . . they'd have to convene a mass divorce trial.' **1967** W. & J. Breedlove *Swinging Set* x. 119 They brought up the subject of 'wife-swapping' with four other couples. **1976** 'W. Trevor' *Children of Dynmouth* iii. 77 There was wife-swapping every Saturday night at parties on the new estate. **13..** *Sir Beues* (A.) 310 Alle *wif houren . . þe deuel of helle ich hii be-take. **1875** Tennyson *Q. Mary* iii. i, If this Philip . . Left Mary a *wife-widow here alone. **1647** Ward *Simple Cobler* 27 Our considerate, I dare not say *wife-worne Commons.

Hence **wifekin**, **wifelet**, **wifeling**, **wifelkin** (*dial.*), as terms of endearment = little wife; **wifeship**, the position or relation of a wife; **wifeward** *adv.*, towards or to one's wife. (All *nonce-wds.*)

1829 Carlyle in *Love Lett. T. C.* (1909) II. App. 355 *Wifekin waits and coffee simmers. **1890** *Daily News* 14 Oct. 5/6 With *wifelet and chubby children. **1868** Farrar *Seekers* ii. iv. 226 If . . some *wifeling or childling be granted you. **1851** Borrow *Lavengro* v, Leave him to me, *wifelkin. **1891** T. K. Cheyne *Orig. Psalter* vii. 315 The figures of sonship and *wifeship were no longer adequate to express Israel's relation to its Lord. **1886** Kipling *Departm. Ditties* etc. (1888) 48 [He] travelled *wifeward.

† **wife**, *v. Obs. rare.* [f. prec. sb.]

1. *intr.* To take a wife, to marry: = WIVE *v.* 1.

1387 Trevisa *Higden* (Rolls) I. 263 þey . . kepeþ besiliche here children, and suffreth hem nouȝt to wyfe wiþ ynne foure and twenty ȝere. *c* **1460** *Towneley Myst.* xii. 97 It is sayde full ryfe, 'a man may not wyfe And also thryfe, And all in a yere.' **1725** Bailey *Erasm. Colloq.* (1878) I. 348 *Eu.* An't you weary of wifeing? *Po.* . . If this Eighth should die to Day I would marry the Ninth to-Morrow.

2. *wife it*: to play the wife, act as a wife.

1599 Porter *Angry Wom. Abingt.* C 3, I should Wife it as fine as any woman could.

wifedom ('waɪfdəm). [f. WIFE *sb.* + -DOM.]

1. The position or condition of a wife, married state (of a woman); the character or qualities of a wife: = WIFEHOOD 1, 2.

1848 *Tait's Mag.* XV. 114 Joy and merriness are not for me, . . nor wedded wifedom. **1887** *Contemp. Rev.* Jan. 114 This essential for good wifedom is also an essential for good womanhood. **1898** *Daily Tel.* 15 Aug. 7/6 Unfettered by the cares of wifedom and motherhood.

2. Wives collectively, married women as a class.

1891 Ebsworth *Roxb. Ball.* VII. 489 The new race of Wifedom is sadly degenerating. **1894** Hall Caine *Manxman* iii. ii, A circle of official wifedom.

† **wifehead.** *Obs. rare.* [f. WIFE *sb.* + -HEAD.] = next.

14.. *Chaucer's L.G.W.* Prol. 253 (Selden MS.), Pennolope and Marcia Catoun, Make of ȝour wyfhede no comparison. *Ibid.* 545, 691, 1687.

wifehood ('waɪfhʊd). Forms: see WIFE *sb.* and -HOOD; also 6 **wiue-**, 7 **wivehood.** [f. WIFE *sb.* + -HOOD. (OE. had *wífhád* womanhood.)]

1. The position or condition of a wife; married state (of a woman).

1390 Gower *Conf.* III. 51 Fro ferst that sche wifhode tok. *c* **1440** *Promp. Parv.* 526/2 Wyyfhood, *uxoratus.* **1748** Richardson *Clarissa* (1768) IV. 305 To restore her to her Virgin State by my confession, after her Wifehood had been reported to her Uncle. **1856** Mrs. Browning *Aur. Leigh* ii. 356, I ask for love . . For wifehood. **1884** *Leeds Mercury* 30 Apr. 4/5 Her daughter has now grown to womanhood, and to-day enters upon the sacred duties of wifehood.

2. The character of, or befitting, a wife; 'behaviour becoming to a wife' (J.); wifeliness.

c **1385** Chaucer *L.G.W.* Prol. 253 Penolope & Marcia catoun Mak of ȝoure wyfhod no comparisoun. **1390** Gower *Conf.* I. 74 Wifhode is lore In me, which whilom was honeste. **1596** Spenser *F.Q.* iv. v. 3 The vertue of chast loue, And wiuehood true. **1616** B. Jonson *Devil an Ass* i. vi, Thou, onely art to heare, not speake a word, . . on your wiue-hood, wife. *a* **1625** Fletcher *Woman's Prize* iv. iv, She hath neither manners, honesty, behaviour, Wife-hood, nor woman-hood. **1830** Tennyson *Isabel* 12 The stately flower . . Of perfect wifehood. **1873** Symonds *Grk. Poets* iv. 107 Plutarch's Life of Cleomenes contains two historical pictures of heroic wifehood.

wifekin: see after WIFE *sb.*

wifeless ('waɪflɪs), *a.* Forms: see WIFE *sb.*; also 5–6 **wyue-**, 5–7 **wiue-**, **wiveles**, **-less(e.** [OE. *wífléas*, f. *wíf* WIFE *sb.* + *léas* -LESS.] Having no wife; unmarried, celibate; *rarely*, deprived or bereaved of, or not accompanied by, one's wife.

a. of a man.

a **1000** in Thorpe *Laws* II. 190 Wuniȝe he a syððan wifleas. *a* **1300** *Cursor M.* 26281 He þat slas his aun wijf, He agh be wijfeles al his lijf. *c* **1380** Wyclif *Sel. Wks.* I. 364 þei ben dowid and wyflees aȝens Goddis autorite. *c* **1386** Chaucer *Merch. T.* 4 Sixty yeer a wyflees man was hee. *c* **1400** *Beryn* 1090 Agea was enterid, And ffawnus lyvid wyfles. **1480** *Robt. Devyll* 25 in Hazl. *E.P.P.* I. 219 Wyueles longe . . haue I taryed, And lyued sole, withoute any mate. **1574** T. Newton *Health Mag.* V iij b, Wiuelesse Bachelers and husbandlesse maydens. **1613** Purchas *Pilgrimage* v. vii. 410 They liue on almes, . . They are wiuelesse. *a* **1623** H. Swinburne *Spousals* (1686) 169 He was then Wifeless. **1842** C. Whitehead *R. Savage* xviii, Many of the married fellows do not appear to be a whit happier than your wifeless men. *a* **1849** J. C. Mangan *Poems* (1859) 459 Wifeless, friendless, flaggonless, . . Not quite bookless, though. **1859** Tennyson *Elaine* 1362 A lonely man Wifeless and heirless.

b. of life, state, etc.

1546 Bale *Engl. Votaries* Pref. 4 Their vowed wyuelesse and husbandelesse chastyte. **1548** Crowley *Confut. Shaxton* H vj b, The gyft of wyueles lyfe. **1563** *Homilies* ii. *Matrimonie* Tttt ij, They in theyr wiuelesse state run into open abhominations. **1840** Hood *Our Lady's Chapel* 13 Whose mouldy, wifeless husbandry but yields Beans, peas, potatoes, mangel-wurzel, rye.

¶ Catachrestically used of a woman: That is not a wife; unmarried.

1824 Scott *St. Ronan's* xxxii, A wifeless mother.

Hence '**wifelessness**, wifeless condition.

1886 'M. Gray' *Silence of Dean Maitland* iii. ii, His six years' wifelessness had weighed sorely upon him.

wifelet, wifeling: see after WIFE *sb.*

wifelike ('waɪflaɪk), *a.* and *adv.* [f. WIFE *sb.* + -LIKE.]

A. *adj.* Resembling, or having the character of, a wife; characteristic of or befitting a wife.

1613 Shaks. *Hen. VIII*, ii. iv. 138 Thy rare qualities, . . Thy meeknesse Saint-like, Wife-like Gouernment. **1796** *Plain Sense* (ed. 2) II. 190 With a kind of bitter raillery he treated her wife-like fears. **1856** Merivale *Rom. Emp.* xlii. V. 37 Her heart swelling with wifelike pride.

B. *adv.* In the manner of a wife.

1598 Chapman *Iliad* iv. [viii.] 138 Nor canst thou skale our turrets tops nor leade the wiues to Fleete Of valiant men; that wifelike fear'st my aduerse charge to meete. **1611** Shaks. *Cymb.* iii. ii. 8 She . . vndergoes More Goddesse-like, then Wife-like; such Assaults As would take in some Vertue. **1864** Tennyson *Aylmer's F.* 808 When she laid, Wifelike, her hand in one of his.

wifely ('waɪflɪ), *a.* Forms: see WIFE *sb.*; also 6 **wyue-**, 6–7 **wiue-**, 7–8 **wively.** [OE. *wíflíc*: see WIFE *sb.* and -LY[1]. Cf. OHG. *wîblich* (MHG. *wîplich*, G. *weiblich*), Du. *wijflijk*.]

† **1.** Of or pertaining to a woman or women; womanly, feminine. *Obs. rare* (exc. OE.).

c **893** Ælfred *Oros.* i. ii. §2 Ac hio mid wiflice niðe wæs feohtende on þæt underiende folc Æthiopiam. *c* **900** tr. *Bæda's Hist.* ii. xx. §2 þæt he ne furþum wiiflice hade . . arede. **1513** Douglas *Æneis* vii. vii. 7 All inflambit in ire and wyfly thochtis [L. *jemineæ curæque iræque*]. **1533** Bellenden *Livy* i. xxii. (S.T.S.) I. 123 The victorie . . of þis wyfelie contencioun [L. *muliebris certaminis*] was gevin to lucres.

2. Pertaining to, characteristic of, or befitting a wife.

c **1000** *Gloss.* in *Haupt's Zeitschrift* IX. 505 *Matronalis*, wiflicre. *c* **1385** Chaucer *L.G.W.* 1737 *Lucrece*, Hire wifly chastite. *Ibid.* 1843 Hir hert was so wyfely and so trewe. **1549** Coverdale, etc. *Erasm. Par. 1 Cor.* vii. 12–16 Howe knowest thou . . whether thou shalt . . by wyuely loue, cause thy husbande to amende? **1591** Harington *Orl. Fur.* xxi. xiii, Against all wiuely care . . she lets her raging loue to raunge. **1739** G. Ogle *Gualth. & Gris.* 1313 Wively Patience. **1844** Mrs. Browning *Duchess May* lxv, Wifely prayer meets deathly need! **1863** Miss Yonge *Chr. Names* II. iv. 142 A picture of wifely patience. **1872** Jeaffreson *Brides & Bridals* I. ii. 21 The duty of wifely submissiveness to marital authority was impressively inculcated.

3. Having the character befitting a wife; such as a wife should be.

1633 P. Fletcher *Purple Isl.* x. xl, Where she a maiden wife might live, and wifely maid. **1853** Reade *Chr. Johnstone* xvii, A wifely wife, a motherly mother, and above all, a lady. **1871** H. B. Forman *Living Poets* 231 Lest our wives and daughters should lose delicacy or refinement, become less wifely and daughterly.

Hence † **wifelihead** (**wive-**), **wifeliness**, wifely character or quality.

1557 *Tottel's Misc.* (Arb.) 204 Whose perfect vertues . . So did adorne that humble *wiuelyhed. **1868** Browning *Ring & Bk.* v. 604 With a wife I look to find all *wifeliness. **1896** Mrs. Caffyn *Quaker Grandmother* xxii, Mossy beamed with gentle wifeliness. . . 'You needn't tell me how to appreciate my husband, Mr. Royds.'

† '**wifely**, *adv. Obs. rare.* In 5 **wyuly.** [f. WIFE *sb.* + -LY[2]. (OE. had *wíflíce* 'muliebriter'.)] As a wife.

c **1400** *Destr. Troy* 3359 Thou shalt haue . . me . . wyuly to weld; & I the wed shall.

wifeship, wifeward: see after WIFE *sb.*

wiff(e, obs. forms of WIFE.

wiffin, obs. Sc. pa. pple. of WEAVE *v.*

Wiffle ('wɪf(ə)l). *U.S.* Also **wiffle.** [f. WHIFF *sb.*[1] 1 d + -LE.] A proprietary term used *attrib.* to designate a hollow perforated ball used for playing a variety of baseball, esp. as ***Wiffle ball*** (also a game played with such a ball); ***Wiffle bat***, a bat designed for use with a Wiffle ball. Cf. *whiffle-ball* s.v. WHIFFLE *sb.* 4.

1957 *Official Gaz.* (U.S. Patent Office) 22 Jan. TM138/1 *Wiffle.* For simulated or auxiliary pliable plastic baseball and a game played therewith. First use Feb. 5, 1954. **1965** *Ibid.* 16 Nov. TM123/1 *Wiffle.* . . For bats and a device for tossing a ball. First use 1959. **1970** *Time* 25 May 43 [David Eisenhower] passing the afternoon playing wiffle ball on the south lawn of his father-in-law's White House. **1985** *Yankee* Oct. 172/2 The first Wiffle bats were broomstick handles taped at one end—the plastic Wiffle Bat didn't come along until later. *Ibid.*, Some people use the term *Wiffleball* for *any* plastic ball. **1987** *N.Y. Times* 1 July B-1/1 Five Sports Mobiles, equipped with Ping-Pong tables, wiffle balls and bats, a pool table [etc.].

wifie ('waɪfɪ). Also **wifey, wify.** [f. WIFE *sb.* + -IE, -Y[6].] Little wife: used as a term of endearment for a wife.

1786 Burns *Poems, chiefly in Scottish Dial.* 126 His clean hearth-stone, his thrifty Wifie's smile. **1819** Keats *Let.* 18 Sept. (1931) II. 439, I intend to write a letter to you[r] Wifie. **1825** Jamieson, *Wiffie*, a diminutive from *wife*; generally expressive of smallness of size, but sometimes merely a fondling term, S. *wifie.* [The accompanying quot. for *wiffie* is dubious.] **1841** Tupper *Twins* vi, Turn bachelor again . ., leave wifey at home. **1862** E. B. Ramsay *Remin.* i. i. 13 Whaur's the auld wifie? **1888** Mrs. H. Ward *Robt. Elsmere* xix, I know you have worries of your own, wifie.

wifing ('waɪfɪŋ). *rare.* [f. WIFE *sb.* + -ING[1].] The activity or condition of being a wife or housewife.

1905 G. B. Shaw *Let.* 3 Jan. (1972) II. 499 As to ordinary domestic mothering and wifing she [*sc.* Shaw's mother] was utterly unfitted for the sentiment of it. **1952** S. Kauffmann *Philanderer* (1953) ii. 28 If there was one kind of wife he didn't want . . it was one who made a career of 'wifing'.

wifish ('waɪfɪʃ), *a.* Forms: 6 **wyuysh, -ish,** 7 **wiuish, wivish,** 8– **wifish,** (9 *erron.* **wifeish**). [f. WIFE *sb.* + -ISH[1]. Earlier *wivish*; cf. *thievish* from *thief*.]

† **1.** Belonging to or characteristic of a woman; womanly; in depreciatory sense, womanish. *Obs.*

1535 Coverdale *2 Macc.* vii. 21 She exorted . . them . . boldly and stedfastly, . . wakynge vp hir wyuysh thought with a manly stomacke. ? **1560** —— *Treat. Death* iii. v. 264 To wayte stil till heauinesse forget itselfe, is a wyuish thinge: . . to brydle it by times, beseemeth the . . sobernesse of a man.

2. Belonging to or characteristic of, or having the character of, a wife. (Usually in more or less depreciatory sense: see -ISH[1] 2.) †In quot. 1616, Too devoted or submissive to one's wife.

1616 T. Scott *Christs Pol.* 17 The Prophet would not haue any wise man to be so wiuish, and so wedded to the loue of his wife. **1664** N. B. *St. Athanasius* 213 [She] by her wivish and womanish solicitations . . hampered Valentinian. **1773** in *Early Diary Fr. Burney* (1889) I. 192 We used to wonder at Hetty's being so wifish. **1797** in C. K. Paul *W. Godwin* (1876) I. 245 With a true wifish submission to your judgment. **1895** Meredith *Amazing Marr.* xxvii, The mother's wifeish lines would, perhaps, have been tested in a furnace.

† **wifkin.** *Obs.* [OE. *wífcyn(n*: see WIFE *sb.* and KIN *sb.*[1]] Womankind, women collectively.

c **900** tr. *Bæda's Hist.* i. i, þæt hi . . of þam wifcynne him cyning curan. **971** *Blickl. Hom.* 143 þu eart ȝebletsod betuh ealle wifcyn. *c* **1250** *Gen. & Ex.* 656 Wið-uten wifkin and childre smale. *Ibid.* 1177 Noȝt wif-kinnes non birðe ne nam.

† **wifle.** *Obs.* Also 4 **wefle,** 4–5 **wyfle,** 5 **wyfele.** [OE. *wifel*, f. OTeut. stem *wiƀ-* (cf. ON. *vifr* sword):—Indo-eur. *wip-* to wave, swing, shake

(cf. Skr. *vip* switch, rod, shaft of an arrow): see WAIVE *v.*²

Parallels to the formation with the suffix *-il-* are found in MDu., MLG. *weifelen* to sway, wobble, waver, early mod.G. *weibeln*, OHG. *weibil* (MHG. *weibel*) apparitor, summoner, ON. *vifl* cudgel, bat.]

A dart, javelin, spear; a battle-axe.

c **1000** *Gloss.* in *Haupt's Zeitschrift* IX. 432 *Spiculo*, gare *vel* wifele. *c* **1330** R. BRUNNE *Chron. Wace* (Rolls) 4383 Wyþ wyfles strike, wyþ axes hewe. *c* **1365** in Hudson & Tingey *Rec. Norwich* (1906) I. 396 Roger servant of William de... sword, coutel, wefle. *c* **1400** *Sowdone* 2650 With Wifles, Fauchons, Gauylokes and Dartes. *c* **1440** *Promp. Parv.* 526/2 Wyfle, wepene.., *bipennis*. **1449** *Paston Lett.* Suppl. (1901) 24 That she shuld make here men to leue here wyfeles and here jackes. *c* **1460** *Invent. Sir J. Fastolfe* in *Archæologia* XXI. 272 Item, j Borespere. Item, vj Wifles.

wifman(n, -mon, obs. ff. WOMAN.

wift, variant of WHIFT *sb.*

wift, *v. Obs.* or *dial.* Also 6 **wyfft.** [Onomatopœic.] *intr.* †**a.** To turn aside or go astray (*obs.*). **b.** To move lightly to and fro, or along; to waver; to drift.

1554-8 in *Songs & Ball. Phil. & Mary* (Roxb.) 4 To walke the wurthy wayes, and frame them not to wyfft. **1609** HOLLAND *Amm. Marcell.* XVI. v. 63 Dragons, wrought with woufe of purple thred,..leaving their winding tailes to wift in the wind. **1864** *Harland's Lanc. Lyrics* (1866) 234 An' tell me, while thae 'rt wiftin' on, Heaw things are deawn i' Howden Dale.

†**wifthing.** *Obs.* [OE. *wifþing*, f. WIFE *sb.* + THING *sb.*] An affair connected with a woman or wife. **a.** Sexual intercourse. **b.** A wedding, nuptial ceremony.

c **1000** *Sax. Leechd.* I. 340 þæt þis sy to wif þingum on bysmær [*irritamentum ad coitum*]. *c* **1000** in Thorpe *Laws* II. 180 Be þam men þe ȝelomlice wif-þing begæð [*de homine qui crebras nuptias conciliat*]. *c* **1205** LAY. 4444 Belin ihærde..of his broðer wifðinge. *Ibid.* 31128 þe wes wif-ðing riche.

wig (wɪg), *sb.*¹ Now *dial.* Forms: 4-6 **wygge**, 5-8 **wigg**, 6-7 **wigge**, (8 **whigg**, 8-9 **whig**), 7- **wig.** [a. MLG., MDu. *wigge* (Westphalian *wigge*, Du. *wig*) wedge, wedge-shaped cake, by-form of MLG. etc. *wegge* (see WEDGE *sb.*).] A kind of bun or small cake made of fine flour.

1376 *Munim. Gildh. Lond.* (Rolls) III. 424 Cum uno pane de obolo, vocato 'wygge'. **1413** *Maldon, Essex, Crt.-rolls* Bundle 8 No. 1 (MS.) Ponderatores panis presentant quod ..panis wastell pistoris de Writle in defectu xs; item, le wigg ejusdem in defectu, xs. *c* **1440** *Promp. Parv.* 526/2 Wygge, brede (*P.* or bunne brede). **1528** MORE *Dyaloge* II. xi. (1529) 63 b/2 Some wax dronk in lent of wygges & craknels. **1600** SURFLET *Country Farm* v. xx. 710 The workers in pastrie do vse the rising of beere to make their wigs withall. **1620** J. TAYLOR (Water P.) *Jack a Lent* C j b, His round halfe-penny loaues are transformd into sq[u]are wiggs, (which wigges like drunkards are drownd in their Ale). **1664** PEPYS *Diary* 8 Apr., Home to the only Lenten supper I have had of wiggs and ale. **1688** HOLME *Armoury* III. vi. 293/2 A..Wigg is White Bread moulded long ways, and thick in the middle. **1769** MRS. RAFFALD *Engl. Housekpr.* (1778) 285 Toast a light wig. **1810** A. BOSWELL *Edin.* 163 Rich Whigs and Cookies smoke upon the board. **1888** MRS. H. WARD *Robt. Elsmere* ii, An exasperating belief in the sufficiency of buttered 'whigs' and home-made marmalade for all requirements.

wig, *sb.*² *Sc.* and *north.* Also 7 **wigge**, 9 **wyg.** [a. ON. *veggr* wall (cf. RIG *sb.*² = ON. *hregg*). Cf. WIG-LOUSE.] Only in phr. ***from wig to wall***, backwards and forwards, from pillar to post.

1600 W. WATSON *Decacordon* (1602) 239 Tossed from poste to piller, from wigge to wall, by a restles course of miseries. **1768** ROSS *Helenore* II. 99 Mind what this lass has suffer'd now for you,..How she is catcht for you frae wigg to wa. **1808** JAMIESON s.v., A thing is said to gang frae wyg to waw, when it is moved backwards and forwards from the one wall of a house to the other.

wig, *sb.*³ Also 8 **wigg.** [Shortened form of PERIWIG, as *winkle* of *periwinkle*.]

1. a. An artificial covering of hair for the head, worn to conceal baldness or to cover the inadequacy of the natural hair, as a part of professional, ceremonial, or formerly of fashionable, costume (as still by judges and barristers, formerly also by bishops and other clergymen), or as a disguise (as by actors on the stage): = PERIWIG 1, PERUKE 2. (See also BAG-WIG, *bob-wig* (BOB *sb.*¹ 4 b), FULL-BOTTOMED *wig*, TIE-WIG.)

1675 *Char. Town-Gallant* 4 He..looks down with Contempt on every body, whose Wig is not right Flaxen. *a* **1700** B. E. *Dict. Cant. Crew*, *Bar-wig*, between a bob and a long one. **1710** SWIFT *City-Shower* 42 Triumphant Tories, and desponding Whigs, Forget their feuds, and join to save their wigs. **1716** GAY *Trivia* III. 55 Nor is thy Flaxen Wigg with Safety worn. **1782** COWPER *John Gilpin* 98 Away went Gilpin, neck or nought, Away went hat and wig! **1835** GLADSTONE in Morley *Life* (1903) I. 127 The disappearance of the bishops' wigs, which he said had done more harm to the church than anything else! **1845** J. T. SMITH *Bk. for Rainy Day* 93 He was a spare man, and wore a powdered club-wig, similar to that worn by Tom Davies, the bookseller and biographer of Garrick. **1853** DICKENS *Bleak Ho.* i, There is the registrar below the Judge, in wig and gown. **1879** BROWNING *Ned Bratts* 44 Serjeant Postlethwayte—Dashing the wig oblique as he mopped his oily pate.

b. Phrases. ***dash my wig(s*** (colloq.), a mild imprecation (see DASH *v.*¹ 11). ***my wig(s!*** (colloq.) a meaningless expression of surprise, etc. ***wigs on the green***, a colloquial expression (orig. Irish) for coming to blows or sharp altercation (wigs being liable to fall or be pulled off in a fray).

1797 MRS. M. ROBINSON *Walsingham* IV. 75 Dash my wig, if Ainsforth is not as well-looking as your finical Welsh baronet. **1812** Dash my wigs [see DASH *v.*¹ 11]. **1856** *Chamb. Jrnl.* 1 Mar. 139/1 If a quarrel is foreseen as a probable contingency, it is predicted that 'there'll be wigs on the green'. **1871** HOPPE *Engl.-Deutsch. Suppl. Lex.*, *Wig*, s. my wigs! **1891** MORRIS in Mackail *Life* (1899) II. 257, I am writing a short narrative poem. My wig! but it is garrulous. **1903** M. G. GERARD *Leaves fr. Diaries* i. 22 Whenever they saw them advancing, they felt there would be wigs on the green.

c. Jocularly applied to a (natural) head of hair, esp. of a child; hence ***curly-wig***, a jocular appellation for a child with curly hair.

d. *transf.*

1823 COBBETT *Rur. Rides* (1885) I. 226 Those white, curled clouds, that we call Judges' Wigs. **1843** *Tait's Edin. Mag.* X. 444 Plunging his nose amidst such an enormous wig of yeast as o'ertopped his cannikin.

e. *Austral. Sheepshearing.* The wool of a sheep growing around the eyes and on top of the head, removed during shearing. Cf. TOPKNOT 1 b.

a **1964** H. P. TRITTON in R. Ward *Penguin Bk. Austral. Ballads* (1964) 228 Two blows to chip away the wig. **1972** J. S. GUNN in G. W. Turner *Good Austral. Eng.* iii. 61 One thing I did notice about shearing was..two terms for the one idea..for example *rouseabout/shedhand..topknot/wig.*

2. *transf.* A person who wears a wig (professionally); a dignitary. *colloq.* (Cf. BIGWIG.)

1828 *Sporting Mag.* (N.S.) XXI. 323 The horrid systematic opposition to hunting, which has justly raised so great odium against the Wigs. **1828** SCOTT *Jrnl.* 18 Apr. (1891) 576 Dined with the Dean of Chester..There were the amiable Bishop of London,..Bishop of Llandaff, the Dean of St. Paul's, and other dignitaries... It was a very pleasant day—the wigs against the wits for a guinea in point of conversation. **1858** CARLYLE *Fredk. Gt.* IX. iv. II. 436 So the heirship fell to us, as the biggest wig in the most benighted Chancery would have to grant.

3. Technical name for the coarse hair on the shoulders of a full-grown male fur-seal, and hence for the seal itself when bearing this.

1830 N. DANA *Mariner's Sk.* 145 (Thornton) These old wigs are more than twice as large as the female seal. **1832** C. M. GOODRIDGE *Voy. S. Seas* 29 The dog seals are named by South Seamen Wigs. **1883** *Q. Rev.* Oct. 449 At five years.. what is called the 'wig'—a mass of coarse hair on the shoulders—appears,..so that it does not pay to kill an animal of this age. **1910** *Encycl. Brit.* XI. 352/2 The largest skins, known in the trade as 'wigs', which range up to 8 ft. in length, are uneven and weak in the fur.

4. [Cf. WIG *v.*² 2.] A severe rebuke or scolding, ? orig. from a 'bigwig'; an act of WIGGING. *slang* or *colloq.*

1789 J. WOODFORDE *Diary* 1 Feb. (1927) III. 81 Thomas Carr dined with our Folks in Kitchen. Gave him a tolerable good Wigg. **1804** SIR J. MALCOLM in *Life* (1856) I. 267 If you got a private wig about Gwalior, I shall get a dozen. **1813** MOORE *Twopenny Post Bag* ii. 52 Else, though the Pr——e be long in rigging, 'Twould take, at least, a fortnight's wigging—Two wigs to every paragraph—Before he well could get through half. **1852** DOVETON *Burmese War* iii. 76 At the risk of a wig in G. O., or even a court-martial. **1903** *Daily Chron.* 21 Nov. 3/3 As often as not a 'wig' ended by the offer of a cheroot.

5. *attrib.* and *Comb.*, as ***wig-box***, ***-dresser***, ***-maker***, ***-making***, ***-puffer***, ***-tie***, ***-wearer***, ***-wearing***, ***-weaver***, ***-weaving***; ***wig-like*** adj.; **wig-block**, a rounded block for placing a wig upon when being made or not in use; **wig-picker** *U.S. slang*, a psychiatrist; **wig-stand**, a support, usu. of wood or porcelain, comprising a base and rounded stem upon which a wig may rest when not in use (cf. *wig-block*); **wig-tail**, (*a*) a name for a tropic-bird, from its long tail-feathers; (*b*) the tail of a wig; **wig-sumach, -tree**, a name for the Venetian sumach (*Rhus Cotinus*), from its hairy inflorescence.

a **1745** SWIFT *Country Life* 123 Nim lost his *wig-block, Dan his jordan. **1828** MISS MITFORD *Village* Ser. III. *Country Barber*, He..lived alone..with no other companions than his wig-blocks and a tame starling. **1713** ADDISON *Guardian* No. 145 ¶4, I take the Liberty of enclosing it to you in my *Wig-Box. **1751** *Affecting Narr. H.M.S. Wager* 118 These odd Creatures [*sc.* armadillos] are cased with a covering in Shape somewhat..resembling that of a travelling Wig Box. **1850** THACKERAY *Pendennis* lii[i], Scarce anything told of the lawyer but the wig-box beside the Venus upon the middle shelf of the bookcase. **1828** MISS MITFORD *Village* Ser. III. *Country Barber*, Appointed his shaver, *wig-dresser, and wig-maker. **1853** HUMPHREYS *Coin-coll. Man.* I. xii. 141 Rows of stiff *wiglike curls. **1755** JOHNSON, *Perukemaker*,..a *wigmaker. **1828** [see *wig-dresser*]. **1961** *Amer. Speech* XXXVI. 147 **Wig picker*,..a psychiatrist. **1971** M. MCCARTHY *Birds of Amer.* 153 Was I afraid of what a wig-picker might say? **1742** RICHARDSON *Pamela* (1785) IV. 247 [He] should keep no Company, but that of Tailors, *Wig-puffers, and Milleners. **1883** R. W. PROCTER *Barber's Shop* (rev. ed.) xix. 189 Here is the lost one's original epitaph (with the *wig-stand and block to match)..*The Barber's Epitaph.* **1911** O. ONIONS *Widdershins* i. 18 A couple of mushroom-shaped old wooden wig-stands. **1970** *Country Life* 17-24 Dec. 1245/2 Hand-painted wig stands from Dodo Designs. **1867** *Chambers' Encycl.* IX. 203/2 Venetian S[umach]..known also as *Wig S[umach] or Wig Tree. **1888** *Amer. Natur.* Oct. 862 The *wig-tail, a white bird about the size of a pigeon, having two long, flexible, streamer-like tail feathers. **1905** A. T. SHEPPARD *Red Cravat* III. ii. 242 The powdered wig-tail poked out truculently above the red collar. **1878** BROWNING *Poets of Croisic* cxxxviii, Flounce Of *wig-ties and of coat-tails. **1867** *Wig tree [see *wig sumach* above]. **1852** S. R. MAITLAND *Eight Ess.* 236 The cap was only such an one as *wig-wearers were wont to use. **1784** COWPER *Task* IV. 543 Her head..Indebted to some smart *wig-weaver's hand For more than half the tresses it sustains. **1828** MISS MITFORD *Village* Ser. III. *Country Barber*, His dexterity in *wig-weaving.

Hence (chiefly *nonce-wds.*) **'wigdom**, judges or lawyers as a body; **'wigful**, as much as fills a wig; **'wiggish** *a.*, having the character of a wig (whence **'wiggishness**); **'wiggism**, the practice of wearing wigs; **'wigless** *a.*, destitute of a wig, not wearing a wig; **'wiglet**, a little wig; **wiglome'ration** [after *conglomeration*], humorously for 'ceremonious fuss' (in legal proceedings).

1886 *Illustr. Lond. News* 27 Nov. 588/3 '*Wigdom', preparing for its most dignified exhibition on the Bench of the High Court of Justice. **1836** E. HOWARD *R. Reefer* vii, I was told to..get a *wigful of potatoes.., the..pedagogue coolly taking off his wig. **1866** TROLLOPE *Claverings* iii, An effort..to hide the *wiggishness of his wigs. **1821** *New Monthly Mag.* I. 573 The history of *wiggism in this country..from its origin down to its decline and fall. **1825** *Ibid.* XIV. 256. **1799** E. DU BOIS *Piece Fam. Biog.* I. 224 Thrusting his *wigless head out of the window. **1813** COLMAN *Br. Grins, Vagaries Vind.* xlix, Wigless, with his cassock torn. **1906** CALTHROP *Engl. Costume* III. 133 In the days when to be wigless was to be undressed. **1831** *Examiner* 660/1 Disarray'd and bare Of cassock, shovel-hat, and *wiglet fair. **1964** *Sun-Herald* (Brisbane) 21 June 56/3 Wiglets, or half wigs start from 11 gns and full wigs are from 32 gns. **1979** L. KALLEN *Introducing C. B. Greenfield* xi. 131 A stand bearing wigs and wiglets. **1853** DICKENS *Bleak Ho.* viii, He is a ward in Chancery..The whole thing will be vastly ceremonious, wordy, unsatisfactory, and expensive, and I call it, in general, *Wiglomeration.

wig (wɪg), *v.*¹ *dial.* Also 6 **wygge.** [See WIGGLE *v.*] *intr.* and *trans.* To move lightly from side to side; to wag, waggle.

a **1529** SKELTON *E. Rummyng* 137 It wygges and it wagges, Lyke tawny saffron bagges. **1865** *Slang Dict.* (ed. 3), *Wig*, move off, go away. **1882** *Jamieson's Scott. Dict.*, *Wig, wigg*, *v.* 1. To move, shake, wag. Shetl.

wig, *v.*²

1. [f. WIG *sb.*³ 1, or back-formation on WIGGED.] *trans.* To supply with a wig; to put a wig upon; *spec.* to provide with wigs in preparation for a theatrical performance (with the actors or the performance as obj.).

1826 *Examiner* 119/2 Cooper performed the husband, and had to wig himself into age for the purpose. **1872** E. YATES *Castaway* I. i, It was Mr. Samuel's boast that he had 'wigged and painted' more 'stars' than any other man out of London. **1889** *Pall Mall Gaz.* 3 July 4/2, I..have the pleasure of congratulating Mr. Clarkson on having 'wigged' three operas in one evening.

2. [f. WIG *sb.*³ 4, or back-formation on WIGGING.] To rebuke or censure severely, scold, rate. Also rarely *intr.* with *at.* *slang* or *colloq.*

1829 *Examiner* 595/1 The *Chronicle* discovers too much disposition to what is vulgarly but expressively called, wigging us. **1831** CAPT. B. HALL *Voy. & Trav.* I. iii. 73, I had..from the first day I went afloat—a great horror at being reproached, or 'wigged', as we called it. **1908** W. DE MORGAN *Somehow Good* xxv, What are you wigging at her for? **1911** *Times* 13 Apr. 9/4 A subordinate..who presumably has been severely 'wigged' by his chief.

3. [perh. f. prec. or WIG *sb.*³ 1.] *intr.* With *out.* To be overcome by extreme emotion; to be stimulated to the point of imbalance; to go mad, 'freak out'. *U.S. slang.*

1955 *Amer. Speech* XXX. 305 He wigged out at the prof's gag. **1968** P. WELLES *Babyhip* xx. 139 'The Boss Pornographers,' he said, 'it's LSD Music, to wig-out by.' **1975** *Time* 27 Oct. 70/3 Some in the startled crowd recall him saying, 'The company is now in God's hands.' One executive wondered if Goshorn had 'wigged out'. **1978** J. GORES *Gone, no Forwarding* (1979) xi. 69 Kearney was going to wig out when the expense voucher for $100 worth of cocaine came in.

Hence **wigged-out** *ppl. a.*

1977 *New Yorker* 24 Oct. 152/2 The lunacies..just function as part of a normally wigged-out mode of existence. **1980** *San Francisco Bay Guardian* 16-23 Oct. 21/2 It's a barbed, wigged-out satire on hypocrisy and authoritarian therapy via the problem of alcoholism.

wig, var. WHIG *sb.*¹; obs. f. WHIG *sb.*²; var. WIDGE *dial.*, beast of burden.

Wigan ('wɪgən). A stout make of calico, originally manufactured at Wigan in Lancashire.

1875 KNIGHT *Dict. Mech.* **1882** CAULFEILD & SAWARD *Dict. Needlework.*

wigen, wigeon: see WIDGEON.

wigg, obs. f. WHIG, WIG.

wigged (wɪgd), *a.* [f. WIG *sb.*³ + -ED².] Furnished with or wearing a wig.

1777 MME. D'ARBLAY *Early Diary* (1889) II. 192 Dr. Wall was so differently wigged, that I really did not know him. **1822** SYD. SMITH *Prisons* Wks. 1859 I. 362/2 The judge, wigged and robed as he is, is often very inferior in acuteness to either of the persons who are pleading under him. **1883** D. C. MURRAY *Hearts* xxviii. (1885) 235 Wigged heads went together in the well of the court, and papers were rustled to and fro on the table.

wiggen, -in, dial. var. QUICKEN *sb.*[1]

wigger, obs. dial. form of WICKER; var. WIDGER.

wiggery, (ˈwɪgərɪ). [f. WIG *sb.*[3] + -ERY.]

1. Wigs or false hair collectively; the practice of wearing a wig.

1775 STURGES in *Lett. J. Granger* (1805) 168 Dr Loveday shewed me your waggery upon wiggery. **1800** in *Spirit Publ. Jrnls.* IV. 59 When I contemplate the Female wiggery, whether it be Roman or Athenian. **1866** TROLLOPE *Claverings* iii, He had lost the hair from the crown of his head, and had preferred wiggery to baldness.

2. Used by Carlyle for: Empty formality (in legal proceedings), 'red tape'.

1843 CARLYLE *Past & Pr.* II. xvii, There is yet in venerable wigged Justice some wisdom amid such mountains of wiggeries and folly. **1858** —— *Fredk. Gt.* VI. ix. II. 131 Long lawsuit,..lengthy law-pleadings, and much parchment and wiggery.

wigging (ˈwɪgɪŋ), *vbl. sb. slang* or *colloq.* [f. WIG *sb.*[3] 4 + -ING[1].] A severe rebuke, reproof, or reprimand; a scolding.

1813 [see WIG *sb.*[3] 4]. **1834** MARRYAT *Peter Simple* I. iv, It was her idea, that I should have a confounded wigging and be sent on board. **1895** *Times Law Rep.* XI. 204 The clerk of the board gave these religious people a fine wigging, pointing out that in spite of their religious professions they were deliberate liars.

wiggish, wiggism: see after WIG *sb.*[3]

wiggle (ˈwɪg(ə)l), *v.* Now *colloq.* or *dial.* Forms: 3–4 **wigel(en, 4 wygle, -el, 7 wigle, 9 wiggle,** (*Sc.* **weegle**). [Cognate with or a. (M)LG. *wiggelen*, MDu. *wighelen* (Du. *wiggelen*), frequentative f. *wig-* (cf. LG. *wiggen*, Norw. dial. *vigge*, WIG *v.*[1]). Cf. the parallel WAG *v.*, WAGGLE *v.*

Some compare OE. *wiccliende* (Haupt's *Zeitschrift* IX. 459/6) glossing *nutabundum*, but this is prob. an error for *cwiccliende* (Napier *O.E. Glosses* I. 2234).]

1. *intr.* To move to and fro or from side to side irregularly and lightly, to waggle; to walk with such a movement, to stagger, reel, also to waddle (now *dial.*); to go or move sinuously, to wriggle. Also *fig.*

a **1225** *Ancr. R.* 214 þe ȝiure glutun..wigeleð [*Corpus MS.* wigleð] ase uordrunken mon. **1398** TREVISA *Barth. De P.R.* XVIII. ix. (Add. MS. 27944) Centris is a serpente þat bendiþ noughte nouþer wigeleþ but holdeþ alway forþ right. **1611** [see *wiggling* ppl. adj. below]. **1839** in F. W. Maitland *Leslie Stephen* (1906) 25 He wished I would not read that kind of book that went wiggling from one subject to another. **1839** LONGF. *Hyperion* IV. ii, To pass the morning, to use his own quaint language, 'in making dodging calls, and wiggling round among the ladies!' **1864** LATTO *Tam. Bodkin* xiv. 133, I warselled an' weegled, an' kickit, an' flang. **1901** *Munsey's Mag.* XXV. 340/1 He wiggled over the grass towards the concealed marksman. **1913** MRS. STRATTON-PORTER *Laddie* vii. (1917) 122 Father..pulled his lower lip until his ears almost wiggled. **1927** H. A. VACHELL *Dew of Sea* 260, I must wiggle out of the mess.

2. *trans.* To move (something) in this way; *refl.* = 1. Also *fig.*

1685 in *Buccleuch MSS.* (Hist. MSS. Comm.) I. 343 A bare shift or pretence to wigle myself out of danger. *c* **1850** 'Dow jr.' in Jerdan *Yankee Hum.* (1853) 86 Wiggle yourselves..among the three, and make headway the best way you can. **1897** VIOLET HUNT *Unkist, Unkind!* xii, He unhooked a Malay kris..and wiggled it about in the crack of the door.

Hence **ˈwiggling** *vbl. sb.* and *ppl. a.*; also **ˈwiggletail**, name for the larva of a gnat or mosquito.

1855 *Chicago Times* 9 Aug. 4/6 The mosquito proceeds from the animalcule commonly termed the *wiggle-tail. **1884** J. C. HARRIS *Nts. Uncle Remus* 172 Water too full of wiggletails. **1398** TREVISA *Barth. De P.R.* XVIII. ix. (Bodl. MS.), Serpentes swymmeþ in water bi *wiglinge and foldinge of þe bodie [orig. *per corporis inflexionem*]. **1894** *Educator* (Philad.) Mar., The ceaseless motion—the wiggling of the child. **1611** COTGR., *Serpentant*.., wrigling, *wigling, crooking, winding. **1849** ALB. SMITH *Pottleton Legacy* (repr.) 51 One of those little wiggling dogs. **1895** *Century Mag.* Aug. 541/2 A small, wiggling fish.

wiggle (ˈwɪg(ə)l), *sb.* and *a.* [f. the vb.]

A. *sb.* **1.** An act of 'wiggling', a light wagging or wriggling movement. ***to get a wiggle on*** (U.S. slang), to hurry, bustle.

1816 J. K. PAULDING *Lett. from South* I. 235 They suffered their hair to grow into a mighty bunch behind, and walked with the genuine *Rutland wiggle*; that is to say, on tiptoe, and with a most portentous extension of the hinder-parts. **1869** L. M. ALCOTT *Little Women* II. xxiv. 355 Rob's footstool had a wiggle in its uneven legs. **1896** *Inlander* Jan. 147 *Get a wiggle on you*, hurry up; bestir yourself. **1894** *Educator* (Philad.) Feb. 279 Every fleeting expression of their faces or wiggle of their bodies. **1903** A. ADAMS *Log Cowboy* iv, Hasn't the boss got a wiggle on himself to-day! **1904** E. ROBINS *Magnetic North* xvii. 298 You can bunk early and get a four a.m. wiggle on.

2. = WIGGLER 1.

1831 T. BUTTRICK *Voy., Trav., & Discoveries* 78 The water was very bad... After straining it would still exhibit live insects, which they call wiggles.

3. A wavy line drawn by a pen, pencil, etc.

1942 *Punch* 12 Aug. 127/1 An old envelope bearing the regimental Paymaster's stamp, partly obliterated by adhesive tape, and the word 'Confidential' crossed out with a wiggle in pencil. **1967** R. D. MATTUCK *Guide to Feynman Diagrams in Many-Body Problem* iv. 63 The majority of writers draw the above interaction with a dashed line... However, we shall always use the wiggle.

B. *adj.* 'Wiggling', wagging swiftly and lightly.

1888 DOUGHTY *Trav. Arabia Deserta* I. 324 Butting under the mothers' teats with their *wiggle tails.

ˈwiggler. [f. WIGGLE *v.* + -ER[1].] **1.** Something that 'wiggles'; applied esp. to the larva of a mosquito.

1859 J. R. BARTLETT *Dict. Americanisms* (ed. 2) 492 *Waggletail*, the larva of the mosquito, etc.; also called a wiggler. **1895** *Outing* (U.S.) XXVI. 375/2 We..took..a box of worms,..for without one squirming wiggler the Madame would not have secured her bass. **1938** J. STEINBECK *Long Valley* 186 The mosquito wigglers tumbling up and down, end over end, in the water. **1969** K. M. WELLS *Owl Pen Reader* IV. 365 In a month or two this bog hole will be full of wigglers.

2. *Physics.* A magnet designed to make a beam of particles in an accelerator describe a sinusoidal path in order to increase the amount of radiation they produce. Freq. *attrib.*

1974 *IEEE Trans. Nucl. Sci.* XX. 984/1 This proposal projects the installation of many additional beam runs and 'wiggler' magnets. **1981** *Science* 16 Oct. 316/2 A wiggler is a special magnet that fits into one of the straight sections of a storage ring between the bending magnets. The wiggler bends the electrons into a sine wave-shaped path whose local radius of curvature is smaller than that of the smooth circular arc of the bending magnets.

wiggle-waggle (ˈwɪg(ə)lˌwæg(ə)l), *v. colloq.* Reduplicated form combining WIGGLE *v.* and WAGGLE *v.* (cf. LG. *wigel-wageln* vb.), emphasizing the alternation of movement: used *intr.* or *trans.* So **wiggle-waggle** *sb.*, (*a*) the act of 'wiggle-waggling'; also, a children's game in which the players waggle their thumbs at a word of command; (*b*) (also ***wiggle-woggle***) = CAKE-WALK *sb.* 2; **wiggle-waggle** *a.*, that 'wiggle-waggles'; *fig.* vacillating.

1825 BROCKETT *N.C. Gloss.*, **Wiggle-waggle*, a tremulous undulating motion. **1895** *Outing* (U.S.) XXVI. 42/2 Brisk holding up of fingers and turning down of thumbs, like the children's game of 'wiggle-waggle'. **1910** *Penny Guide Japan-British Exhib.* 25 Fun on the Wiggle Waggle. **1923** R. MACAULAY *Told by Idiot* III. xxi. 256 The establishment of the White City at Shepherd's Bush, with the Franco-British Exhibition..and flip-flaps, switchbacks, wiggle-woggles, and scenic railways. **1938** 'G. ORWELL' *Homage to Catalonia* xii. 254 A dreadful thing called the Wiggle-Woggle at the White City Exhibition. **1778** JOHNSON in *Mme. D'Arblay's Diary* Sept., Poll is a stupid slut;..she was *wiggle-waggle, and I could never persuade her to be categorical. **1828** *Craven Gloss.*, *Wiggle-waggle*, quivering, vibrating. **1887** *Good Words* 673 Wiggle-waggle dress-improvers. **18..** *Scotch Haggis* 95 (E.D.D.) *Wiggle-waggling his walking-stick ower his left elbow. **1847** HALLIWELL, *Wiggle-waggle*, to wriggle. *East.* **1848** *Punch* XV. 14 The parachute..would ..have wiggle-waggled itself into annihilation. **1897** *Outing* (U.S.) XXX. 224/1 It [*sc.* a fish] is gently removed from the hook, and suffered to go wiggle-waggling back to its green retreats.

wiggly (ˈwɪglɪ), *a. colloq.* [f. WIGGLE *v.* or *sb.* + -Y[1]: cf. WAGGLY.] Characterized by or suggestive of 'wiggling'; (in reference to form) having small irregular undulations. Also in reduplicated forms **wiggly-waggly** (cf. WIGGLE-WAGGLE *sb.*, *a.*), **-woggly**.

1903 G. H. LORIMER *Lett. Self-made Merch.* vii. 84 A mule..with..droopy, wiggly-woggly ears that swung in a circle as easy as if they ran on ball-bearings. **1907** *Westm. Gaz.* 29 Oct. 2/3 His [*sc.* a dog's] legs are wiggly. **1907** *Blackw. Mag.* Apr. 459/1 Black 'Arscot' tie with a white wiggly bacterial pattern. **1913** *Daily News* 12 Nov. 8 The wiggly-waggly movement of the seal's body. **1919** CHRISTINE ORR *Glorious Thing* iv, That wiggly seam down the front.

wiggy (ˈwɪgɪ), *a.* **1.** [f. WIG *sb.*[3] + -Y[1].] Wearing, or distinguished by, a wig, bewigged; sometimes implying 'extremely grave, formal, or ceremonious'.

1817 MARIA EDGEWORTH *Harrington* vi, And there's our old apothecary..has taken such a fancy to her! But he's too old and wiggy. **1822** *Blackw. Mag.* XII. 198 Those of the wisest and wig-iest members of the fraternity. **1840** MRS. GORE in *New Monthly Mag.* LX. 51 Powdered footmen and wiggy body-coachmen. **1884** *Athenæum* 21 Oct. 473/3 Mr. Kendal, though his get-up is a little 'wiggy', remains excellent as Philippe Derblay.

2. [f. WIG *v.*[2] 3.] Mad, crazy, 'freaky'. *U.S. slang.*

1963 L. DEIGHTON *Horse under Water* xxii. 96, I just got some new jazz records from the States, Ace. Pretty wiggy. **1972** *Last Whole Earth Catalog* (Portola Inst.) 31/1 Traditionally considerations such as his—economics, organizations, the future—turn a prophet's soul terrible and dark or at least partially wiggy. **1978** *Amer. Poetry Rev.* Nov./Dec. 26/2 'Poor devil,' she added, 'he blew the star's fuse when we went wiggy for the Thin Man on a cross.'

wighee, wigh-hie, wighie, -y, var. WEHEE.

wiȝel, var. WIEL *Obs.*, sorcery, etc.

wigher, var. *wicker*, WHICKER *v.*, to neigh.

1660 *Faithf. Friends* III. ii, I cut it [*sc.* a tail] from a dead horse that can now Neither wigher nor wag tail.

wight (waɪt), *sb. arch.* Forms: 1–5 **wiht**, 1, 3–5 **wyht**, (1 **wuht**), 3 (*Orm.*) **wihht**, (**wiþt, wid**), 3–4 **whit, wiȝt(e**, 4 **wyȝt, wyghte, whiȝt, whyȝte, whyt**, (**wiȝth, wijȝt, wieth, wihct, with, weiht, weith**), 4–6 **wyght, wighte, wite**, *Sc.* **wycht**, (8 *arch.*) **wicht**, 5 **whyȝt, whiht, whyht, wyt**, (**whith, wyth(e, wythte**), 5–6 **wyte**, (5–7 **weight**, 6 **white**, *Sc.* **weycht**), 4– **wight**. [OE. *wiht* m., f., n. = OS. *wiht* m. thing, pl. demons (MLG. *wicht* m., n. thing, being, creature, demon, LG. *wicht* n. girl, MDu., Du. *wicht* little child), OHG., MHG. *wiht* m., n. creature, being, thing, esp. of elves and dwarfs, (G. *wicht* m. creature, being, infant), ON. *vættr, véttr, vitr* f. living creature, thing (also in idiomatic uses and phr. *ekki vætta, vættki, vættr* not a whit, naught, not, *vettugi* nothing, *hvatvetna* anything whatever), Goth. *waiht* n. (only in *ni..waiht* nothing), *waihts* f. εἶδος, πρᾶγμα (*ni...waihtais* or *waihts* nothing); ulterior connexions uncertain. For compounds in English see AUGHT *sb.*[2], NAUGHT, NOUGHT, UNWIGHT.]

†**1.** A living being in general; a creature. *Obs.*

Beowulf 120 Wiht unhælo, grim and grædiȝ. *c* **888** ÆLFRED *Boeth.* xvi. §2 Nanre wuht lichoma ne beoð þonne tederra þonne þæs monnes. *c* **1000** *Sax. Leechd.* I. 224 Swa lange swa ðu hy mid þe byrst, nan wiht yfeles þe onȝean cymeð. *c* **1200** ORMIN Ded. 273 Þatt nan wihht, nan enngell, nan mann,..Ne mihhte þurrh himm sellfenn þa Seffne godnessess shæwenn O mannkinn. *c* **1200** *Moral Ode* 78 (Trin. Coll. MS.) He wot hwat þencheð and hwat doð alle quike wihte. *c* **1205** LAY. 25869 Whæt ært þu fære whit? eært þu angel? eært cnih? *c* **1250** *Owl & Night.* 87 Snailes mus & fule wiȝte [*v.r.* wihte]. **13..** *Northern Passion* (1913) I. 151 A neddir rampande, a lothely wyghte. **14..** *Pol. Rel. & L. Poems* (1903) 43/20 God saue þis place fro alle oþer wykked wytes Boþe be dayes & be nytes! *c* **1450** *St. Cuthbert* (Surtees) 2416 Bestes of þe se and othir wyght. **1559** W. CUNINGHAM *Cosmogr. Glasse* 142 Vnto man, beast & euerye liuinge wite. **1586** B. YOUNG *Guazzo's Civ. Conv.* IV. 177 Man is the onelie white whereat infinit..infortunes doe ayme at. **1587** GOLDING *De Mornay* ii. 15 We reduce..All men vnder the terme of Wight; all wights vnder the terme of liuing things.

b. orig. and chiefly with (good or bad) epithet, applied to supernatural, preternatural, or unearthly beings. *Obs.* or *rare arch.*

In the 17th c. *esp.* of the four beasts of the Apocalypse.

c **950** *Lindisf. Gosp.* Mark vi. 49 *Phantasma*, yfel wiht. **971** *Blickl. Hom.* 31 Þæt manfulle wuht wolde þæt he hine weorþode. *c* **1000** *Prayer* iv. 57 (Gr.) Ȝeluȝon hy him æt þam ȝeleafan, forþon hy longe sculon Werȝe wihta wræce þrowian. *c* **1100** *Gloss.* in Wr.-Wülcker 108/23 *Satiri, uel fauni,..uel fauni ficarii*, unfæle men, wudewasan, unfæle wihtu. *c* **1200** *Moral Ode* 285 (Trin. Coll. MS.) Þat beð ateliche fiend and Eiseliche wihten þo sulle þe wreche sowle isien þe sineȝeden þurh sihte. **1297** R. GLOUC. (Rolls) 2750 Þer beþ in þe eyr an hey,..As a maner gostes, wiȝtes as it be. *c* **1386** CHAUCER *Miller's T.* 293, I crouche thee from Elues and fro wightes. *c* **1400** *Pilgr. Sowle* (Caxton 1483) I. iii. 4 The angel vpon my right syde and the fowle wyght vppon the other syde. **1610** HOLLAND *Camden's Brit.* I. 13 The gods above And heavenly wights. *a* **1638** MEDE *Wks.* (1672) 92 The Wights, the Elders, and every creature in Heaven. **1679** C. NESSE *Antichrist* 196 Those 4 living wights and 24 elders. **1826** W. IRVING *Babylon* II. VI. 124 Those four wights upon the white, red, black, and pale horses. **1830** SCOTT *Demonol.* v. 147 That these were the good wights (fairies) dwelling in the court of Elfland. **1894** MORRIS *Wood beyond World* xxx. 230 Our protection against uncouth wights.

c. A local name for the shrew-mouse.

1795 *Statist. Acc. Scot.* XIV. 317 A small species of mice, commonly called here [*sc.* Orkney] wights.

2. A human being, man or woman, person. Now *arch.* or *dial.* (often implying some contempt or commiseration).

c **1200** ORMIN 1761 Unnseȝȝenndlike mare inoh þann aniȝ wihht maȝȝ þennkenn. *a* **1275** *Prov. Ælfred* 633 Wel worþe þe wid, þad þe first taite. *a* **1300** *K. Horn* 397 (Laud) Of þat fayre wihcte Al þe halle gan licte. **13..** *Gaw. & Gr. Knt.* 1792 'Þat is a worde', quod þat wyȝt, 'þat worst is of alle'. **1340–70** *Alex. & Dind.* 39 Neuere werrede we wiþ wiȝth upon erþe. **1362** LANGL. *P. Pl.* A. IX. 4 Ȝif any wiȝt wiste, where do-wel was at Inne. *c* **1386** CHAUCER *Prol.* 71 He neuere yet no vileynye ne sayde In al his lyf vn to no maner wight. *c* **1425** *Cast. Persev.* 978 in *Macro Plays* 106 In wo & in wrake, wyckyd wytis schal wepe. *c* **1470** HENRY *Wallace* XI. 395 Gret syn it war yon saikless wicht to sla. **1500–20** DUNBAR *Poems* lxxv. 17, I nevir wowit weycht bot ȝow. **1550** CROWLEY *Last Trumpet* 614 Thou learned man, do not disdayne, To learne at me, a symple wyght. **1567** TURBERV. *Epit.*, etc. 34 Away shee went a wofull wretched Wight. **1579** SPENSER *Sheph. Cal.* Apr. 47 Of fayre Elisa be your siluer song, that blessed wight. **1604** SHAKS. *Oth.* II. i. 159 She was a wight, (if euer such wightes were)..To suckle Fooles, and chronicle small Beere. **1609** HOLLAND *Amm. Marcell.* 361 The heavenly gift of God granted unto blessed and happie weights. **1667** MILTON *P.L.* II. 613 And of it self the water flies All taste of living wight, as once it fled The lip of Tantalus. **1724** RAMSAY *Vision* ii, Boreas branglit..like a drunken wicht. **1735** POPE *Prol. Sat.* 165 The Wight who reads not, and but scans and spells. **1805** SCOTT *Last Minstr.* I. i, No living wight, save the Ladye alone, Had dared to cross the threshold stone. **1867** JEAN INGELOW *Dreams that came true* xxiv, She is a broken-down, poor, friendless wight. **1869** TOZER *Highl. Turkey* II. 308 The unlucky wight..is doomed to speedy death.

b. Applied to a thing personified. *rare. arch.*

c **1399** CHAUCER *Purse* 1 To yow, my purse, and to noon other wight Complayn I, for ye be my lady dere. **1579** LYLY *Euphues* (Arb.) 77 Canst thou then be so vnwise to swallowe the bayte which will breede thy bane?.. To desire the wight that will worke thy death? **1802** WORDSW. *To the Daisy* I. ii, Autumn, melancholy Wight! **1859** KINGSLEY *Glaucus* (ed. 4) 72 His [*sc.* the worm's] place has been occupied by one Sipunculus Bernhardi; a wight of low degree.

†**3.** In advb. phrases, qualified by *no*, *any* (OE. *æniȝ wiht*, *nán wiht*), *a little*, or the like: (A certain) amount; for (any, a little, etc.) time or distance. (See WHIT *sb.*[1] 1, 2.) *Obs.*

c **888** ÆLFRED *Boeth.* xxvii. §3 Þær hi æniȝe wuht aȝnes oðőe ȝecyndelices godes an heora anwealde hæfdon. **971** *Blickl. Hom.* 235 Andreas, ne ȝefyrenodest þu nan wuht. *c* **1220** *Bestiary* 657 [The elephant] Fikeð and fondeð al his miȝt, ne mai he it forðen no wiȝt. *a* **1225** *Ancr. R.* 72 Hwon ȝe nede moten speken a lutewiht. *a* **1300** *St. Gregory* 703 in Herrig's *Archiv* LVII. 66 A litel wiȝt after þe none. *Ibid.* 1152 Ich wene on lyue nys he no wiȝt. *a* **1300** *K. Horn* 503 (Camb.) He smot him a litel wiȝt & bed him beon a god kniȝt. *c* **1320** *Cast. Love* 638 Þat monnes kuynde hedde al ariht, þat hi neore to luite ne to muche wiht. **1340–70** *Alex. & Dind.* 354 Þat we no wante no wite of worldliche fode. **13..** *Seuyn Sages* (W.) 293 Yif thou me lovest ani wight, Let me of him han a sight! *c* **1374** CHAUCER *Boeth.* III. pr. i. (1868) 63 Whan they ben resseyuyd with-inne a whyht than ben they swete. *c* **1386** —— *Reeve's T.* 363 She was falle aslepe a lite wight. *c* **1420** *Chron. Vilod.* 4701 Þo he leyde hurre doune þere to slepe a litulle whyȝt. *a* **1450** *Le Morte Arth.* 472 Ector ne liked that no wight. *c* **1470** HENRY *Wallace* IV. 154 Thai wyst no wyt quhar that thai suld him get.

†**b.** *a little wight* (adj. phr.): a small. *Obs.*

c **1205** LAY. 21991 Þer þis water wendeð, is an lutel wiht mære.

wight (waɪt), *a.* (*adv.*) *arch.* and *dial.* Forms: 3–4 **wiht**, 3–5 **wiȝt**, (4 **wicth**, **with**, **wiȝth**, **wit**, *Sc.* **vicht**, **vycht**), 4–5 **wyht(e**, **wyȝt(e**, (**vight**), 4–6 **wyght(e**, **wighte**, *Sc.* **wycht**, 5 **whight**, **whyght**, **wyt(e**, **whyt**, **white**, (**wygth**, **wyth**, **wythȝ**, **wyþtȝ**, **weight**), 5–6 *Sc.* **wichte**, 4– **wight**, *Sc.* **wicht**. [a. ON. *vígt* used in phrase = in self-defence; neut. of *vígr* of fighting age, skilled in arms; f. OTeut. *wīg-* (*waig-*, *wig-*), for other derivatives of which see WI *sb.* Other adoptions of ON. adjs. in the neuter form are *quert*, *scant*, *thwart*, *want*.]

1. Strong and courageous, esp. in warfare; having or showing prowess; valiant, doughty, brave, bold, 'stout'.

a. of a person, esp. a warrior.

c **1205** LAY. 777 Wihte wal-kempen on heora wiðer-winnan. *Ibid.* 20575 Seoue þusen monnen, ohte men and wihte. *Ibid.* 21359 Fif and twenti þusend whitere monnen. **1297** R. GLOUC. (Rolls) 456 Mid six þousend wiȝtemen. *a* **1300** *Cursor M.* 6409 'Cheues þe', he said, 'wit man an freck And ga fight a-pon amalec'. *c* **1350** *Will. Palerne* 3293 He wist him wiȝht of dede. *c* **1375** *Sc. Leg. Saints* v. (*Johannes*) 610 In Ingland þat tym ves a knycht, In ded of armys þat ves vycht. *c* **1425** WYNTOUN *Cron.* III. ii. 269 Thre thousande wicht men of Iuda. *c* **1470** HENRY *Wallace* v. 1057 Schyr Jhon the Grayme, with Wallace that was wycht. *c* **1510** *Lytell Geste Robyn Hode* III. 17 Say me now wyght yonge man What is now thy name? **1596** DALRYMPLE tr. *Leslie's Hist. Scot.* I. 131 Of ane inuincible mynd, and a wichte weiriour. **1601** MUNDAY & CHETTLE *Death Robt. Earl of Huntington* I. i, Where is Robin Hood, And yᵉ wight Scarlet? **1775** *Hobie Noble* xxiii. in Child *Ballads* VII. 3/1 Had he been as wight as Wallace was. **1808** SCOTT *Marm.* VI. xx, O for one hour of Wallace wight. **1858** MORRIS *Def. Guenev.* etc. 108 They ought to sing of him who was as wight As Launcelot or Wade.

b. of actions or personal attributes.

c **1330** R. BRUNNE *Chron. Wace* (Rolls) 10516 Knyght þat losed was of dedes wyght. *c* **1375** *Sc. Leg. Saints* iii. (*Andreas*) 542 For warldis wa oþir is licht, And may be tholit with hart wycht. *c* **1400** *Destr. Troy* 1098 The worde of your werkes & your wight dedis .. passes o fer! **1500–20** DUNBAR *Poems* viii. 12 That many ane fo in feild hes put to flycht, In weiris wicht. **1596** DALRYMPLE tr. *Leslie's Hist. Scot.* I. 248 Quhen Eugenie had won sa wicht a victorie.

2. Strong, vigorous, robust, stalwart, mighty; exercising strength, energetic (passing into 3).

a **1300** *Cursor M.* 9003 Sampson þat wightest was in lijf. *c* **1300** *Havelok* 344 He was fayr man, and wicth. **1377** LANGL. *P. Pl.* B. IX. 21 Sire worche-wel-wyth-þine-hande, a wiȝte man of strengthe. *a* **1400** *Relig. Pieces fr. Thornton MS.* (1914) 57 In þe fermory of this religyon are moo seke þan hole, mo febyll þan wighte. *c* **1440** *York Myst.* xviii. 219 Are was I wayke, nowe am I wight. *c* **1440** *York Myst.* xviii. 219 Are was I wayke, nowe am I wight. **1486** *Bk. St. Albans* c j b, It is goode to make her to mewe, bot specialli it shall make her wight after hir soore aage. *c* **1560** A. SCOTT *Poems* (S.T.S.) ii. 33 William wichttar wes of corss Nor Sym, and bettir knittin. *a* **1600** *Floddan F.* vii. (1664) 62 And of thy hands hardy and wight. **1726** *Fleming's Fulfilling Script.* (ed. 5) Table Scots Phr., *Wight*, strong or clever.

†**b.** Powerful, forcible, violent; powerful in effect, strong. (Also *absol.*) *Obs.*

13.. *Gaw. & Gr. Knt.* 1591 In þe wyȝt-est of þe water, þe worre hade þat oþer. *c* **1470** HENRY *Wallace* VI. 659 The Scottis all as swyne lyis droukyn thar, Off our wycht wyne. *c* **1475** *Rauf Coilȝear* 36 In wickit wedderis and wicht. **1583** *Leg. Bp. St. Androis* 786 Wachting the wyne, for it was wicht.

†**c.** Strong to resist force; strongly built or constructed; stout. *Obs.*

c **1320** *Sir Tristr.* 1029 Swiche meting was neuer non made Wiþ worþli wepen wiȝt. *c* **1425** WYNTOUN *Cron.* clxxiii. 5404 The wardane has þat castell tane, And saw it wycht of lyme and stane. *c* **1440** *Generydes* 3634, I must haue A shippe bothe good and wight, And that it be right swift vnder a saile. **1509** BARCLAY *Shyp of Folys* (1874) II. 318 Though the braunches be stronge and wyght. *a* **1533** LD. BERNERS *Huon* xxxii. 96 He toke fro me yᵉ toure and a wyght harnes. **1583** *Leg. Bp. St. Androis* 930 Sayand, he wald ride furth a whyle, To seay a bow that was sumthing wicht. *a* **1600** MONTGOMERIE *Misc. Poems* xli. 42 The freikis on feildis That wight wapins weildis.

3. Moving briskly or rapidly; active, agile, nimble, quick; swift, fleet.

1375 BARBOUR *Bruce* II. 120 Thar na horss is in this land Sa wycht, na ȝeit sa weill at hand. *c* **1386** CHAUCER *Reeve's T.* 166, I is ful wight god waat as is a raa. **1390** GOWER *Conf.* III. 298 Hem that ben delivere and wyhte. *c* **1430** *How Good Wife taught Dau.* 120 in *Babees Bk.* (1868) 41 Manye handis & wight Make an heuy worke light. *c* **1440** *Promp. Parv.* 527/1 Wyte, or delyvyr, or swyfte. *c* **1440** *Gesta Rom.* xxxii. 121 Sche was so wyght of fote, that no man myght Rynne with hire by a grete space. *c* **1480** HENRYSON *Fox, Wolf & Cadger* 233 The wolf was wicht, and wan away. **1548** PATTEN *Exped. Scot.* C vij, If Carres horse had not ben exceding good & wight his lordship had surely run him thrugh. **1586** WHITNEY *Choice Emblems* 107 Since fame is wighte of winge. **1703** THORESBY *Let. to Ray* Gloss. (E.D.S.), *Wight*, swift. **1805** SCOTT *Last Minstr.* I. xxii, Mount thee on the wightest steed.

B. *adv.* **1.** Actively, nimbly, energetically; quickly, rapidly, swiftly. *Obs.* or *dial.*

13.. *Cursor M.* 3836 (Gött.) Iacob lifted vp þat ston ful wight. **13..** *E.E. Allit. P.* C. 103 Cables þay fasten, Wiȝt at þe wyndas weȝen her ankres. **13..** *Gaw. & Gr. Knt.* 1762 Wiȝt wallande Ioye warmed his hert. *c* **1460** *Towneley Myst.* xxii. 264 Sithen we fled away full wight. *a* **1578** LINDESAY (Pitscottie) *Chron. Scot.* (S.T.S.) I. 341 The rest of airchouris schott far and wight. **1787** W. TAYLOR *Scots Poems* 65 Down the brae I gaed fu' wight.

†**2.** Quickly, without delay, directly, immediately. *Obs.*

13.. *E.E. Allit. P.* B. 617, I schal wynne yow wyȝt of water a lyttel. *c* **1430** *Hymns Virgin* (1867) 49 Euerlastynge ȝatis, openeþ wight! *c* **1485** *Digby Myst.* III. 227 My lord, it xall be done ful wygth. **1606** SYLVESTER *Du Bartas* II. iv. *Magnificence* 726 Their winged words th' effect ensues as wight.

C. *Comb.* †**wight-rider**, a stout and active horseman; a mounted raider; so †**wight-riding** *a.* (see also quot. 1894); **wight-wapping** *a.* [WAP *v.*[1]], moving rapidly, or characterized by such movement.

1569 in Strype *Ann. Ref.* (1709) I. lv. 556 'About the Queen', say good-fellows, *Wight-riders and Robbers in the Borders of the two Realms. **1580** HOLLYBAND *Treas. Fr. Tong*, *Vn rodeur ou coureur*, a roder or wigh[t]rider. **1575** LANEHAM *Lett.* (1871) 22 Too the number of a sixteen *wight riding men. **1894** *Northumb. Gloss.*, *Wight-riding*, of the upper class. (Obs.) **1830** SCOTT *Ayrshire Trag.* I. 1, The weaver shall find room At the *wight-wapping loom.

Hence †**wightlayke** *a.* [? -LIKE influenced by -LAIK], quick, immediate (cf. B. 2 above); †**wightling** [-LING[1] 1], a valiant man, a brave warrior; †**wightship**, valour, bravery.

c **1450** *Mirour Saluacioun* (1888) 144 *Wightlayke delyvrenesse with out ony tarditee. *c* **1330** *Arth. & Merl.* 8093 Galathin com swiþe flinge Wiþ þre þousand *wiȝtling. *Ibid.* 7653 Of *wiȝtschippe & cheualrie.

wight, obs. f. WEIGHT, WHITE, WITH; var. WITE *Obs.*, blame; pa. t. of WECCHE *Obs.*

wightly (ˈwaɪtlɪ), *adv. arch.* and *dial.* Forms: see WIGHT *a.* [f. WIGHT *a.* + -LY[2].]

1. Bravely, boldly, valiantly, 'stoutly'; strongly, vigorously, forcibly, powerfully, energetically.

a **1300** *Cursor M.* 7642 Wit þat vnled son dauid mete, And wightli wan o þam his dete. *a* **1340** HAMPOLE *Psalter* vi. 10 Thai ga noght whidere thai thoght: and shame thaim ful wightly. *a* **1400–50** *Wars Alex.* 1405 Þai within on þe wall wightly withstondyn. *a* **1450** *Le Morte Arth.* 2822 Wightly hys swerd A-bowte he wavyd. *a* **1450** *Ratis Raving* etc. 2 How wychtly þai sustenyt al tormentis .. done to thaim. **1513** DOUGLAS *Æneis* XI. Prol. 64 To stand wichtly, and fecht in the forfront. *a* **1813** in W. S. Crockett *Minstrelsy* (1893) 101 Wightly can he wield a rung. **1819** GALL *Poems* 49 You .. wightly wag the skelping whang.

2. Actively, briskly, nimbly, with agility or alacrity; swiftly, rapidly; quickly, without delay.

c **1330** R. BRUNNE *Chron. Wace* (Rolls) 10131 Lyghtly to go, wightly to fle, þey leften al, & fledde to þe se. **13..** *Gaw. & Gr. Knt.* 688 He made non abode, Bot wyȝtly went hys way. *c* **1425** *Cast. Persev.* 3226 in *Macro Plays* 173 Now go we hens wyztly to þe Trinite. *c* **1500** *Smith & Dame* (Copland) A iij b, Croked I was truely Now may I walke wyghtly. **1579** SPENSER *Sheph. Cal.* Sept. 5 Day, that was, is wightly past. **1583** tr. *Maison Neuve's Gerileon* I. 8 The good king Floridamant .. wightly forsaking the Saddle, set foote on ground. *a* **1650** *Sir Cawline* x. in Child *Ballads* III. 58 But rise vp wightlye, man, for shame! Neuer lye here soe cowardlye. **1757** W. THOMPSON *Poems, Nativity* i, Wightly his Senses all were rapt into a Dream. **1884** D. GRANT *Lays* 75 Wichtly Dobbin reached the Kirkton.

ˈwightness. *Obs.* or *arch.* [f. WIGHT *a.* + -NESS.] The quality of being 'wight'; valour, courage, bravery; strength, might, force, vigour, energy; activity, agility, alacrity.

13.. *K. Alis.* 5495 (Laud MS.), Wiþ suerd & shelde in batayle To proue his wiȝtnesse. **1377** LANGL. *P. Pl.* B. XIX. 240 He wissed hem wynne it aȝeyne þorw wightnesse of handes. **1393** *Ibid.* C. XII. 284 That noþer wit ne wyghtnesse wan neuere þe maistrie With-oute þe grete gyfte of god. *c* **1440** *York Myst.* x. 58 Now .. fra me is all wightnes wente. **1483** *Cath. Angl.* 417/2 Wightnesse, *alacritas*, .. *celeritas factorum*, *velocitas pedum est & corporum.* **1596** DALRYMPLE tr. *Leslie's Hist. Scot.* I. 105 Gretlie thay take plesure in the wichtnes of thair bodie. *Ibid.* 334 His strang defence of the Clergie of Scotland, and his wichtnes contrare the aduersar. **1742** R. FORBES *Ajax's Sp.* (1755) 8 Gin my wightness doubted war, I wat my gentle bleed .. Right sickerly does plead.

wighty (ˈwaɪtɪ), *a.* *Obs.* exc. *dial.* [f. WIGHT *a.* + -Y[1] 2.] = WIGHT *a.*

14.. LANGL. *P. Pl.* C. xvi. 172 (MS. E) Al þe wytt of þis worlde ne wyȝty mennes strengþe Can noȝt performe a pes of þe pope. *c* **1475** *Partenay* 4704 Gaffray tombled there. Anon releuing in wighty manere. **16..** *Adam O Gordon* 124 in Pinkerton *Scot. Trag. Ball.* (1781) 48 Put on, put on, my wichty men, Sae fast as ye can drie. **1825** BROCKETT *N.C. Gloss.*, *Wighty*, strong and active.

Hence †**wightily** *adv.* = WIGHTLY.

c **1480** HENRYSON *Cock & Fox* xxiii, Full wichtilie [*v.r.* wichtlie] thay throw wod and watteris went.

wighy, var. WEHEE.

wigion, **wigle**, obs. ff. WIDGEON, WIGGLE.

wigless, **wiglet**, **wiglomeration**: see after WIG *sb.*[3]

†**wiglouse.** *Obs.* Pl. wiglice. [a. ON. *veggjalús*, f. *veggr* WIG *sb.*[2] + *lús* LOUSE *sb.*] The bed-bug: = *wall-louse* (*a*) (WALL *sb.*[2] 25 b).

1658 ROWLAND tr. *Moufet's Theat. Ins.* 1046 They are enemies to Wiglice, that are most stinking creatures. **1660** R. READ *Wecker's Secr. Art & Nat.* 129 For Wiglice, Make a smoke with Ox dung and it will drive away Wall-lice.

wigsby (ˈwɪgzbɪ). *slang* or *colloq.* ? *Obs.* [f. WIG *sb.*[3]: see -BY 2.] A jocular appellation for a person wearing a wig. So **ˈwigster** in same sense.

1785 GROSE *Dict. Vulgar T.*, *Mr. Wigsby*, a man wearing a wig. **1797** MRS. M. ROBINSON *Walsingham* III. 337 Tip old wigsby a twitch of the heart, in return for his golden padlock. **1821** *Sporting Mag.* (N.S.) VII. 267 He was answered by the aforesaid wigsters, that it was '*Impossible separer les deux*'. **1830** H. INGELO *Remin.* II. 119, I left these two wigsbys, puffed up with pride and self-confidence. **1842** LOVER *Handy Andy* xxi, The .. forms .. were borrowed from the chapel: the old wigsby, who had the care of them .. doubted the propriety.

wig-wag (ˈwɪgwæg), *v.* *colloq.* or *techn.* [Reduplicated formation combining WIG *v.*[1] and WAG *v.*, the vowel-change symbolizing the alternation of movement: cf. *wiggle-waggle*, *zig-zag*.] To move lightly to and fro, to wag; *esp.* to wave a flag or other object to and fro in signalling; to signal in this way (*intr.*, or *trans.* with the flag, etc. or the signal as obj.). Also as *adv.* = with a to-and-fro movement. So **ˈwig-wag** *sb.*, (*a*) an act of 'wig-wagging'; also *attrib.* (in quot. 1582 expressing a tortuous or writhing movement); (*b*) in *Watch-making*, a polishing instrument to which a reciprocating motion is imparted by a crank attached to a wheel of the lathe. Hence **ˈwig-ˌwagger**, one who 'wig-wags'; **ˈwig-ˌwaggy** *a.*, characterized by 'wig-wagging', or by a form suggestive of this; tortuous, winding.

1582 STANYHURST *Æneis* II. (Arb.) 50 His midil embracing with wig wag circuled hooping. **1846** *Congress. Globe* 16 Jan. 208/1 Wig-wag went her tail. **1875** KNIGHT *Dict. Mech.*, *Wigwag* (Watch-making), a rubbing-instrument .. driven by the lathe. **1884** BRITTEN *Watch & Clockm.* 203 Where pinions are made in large quantities the polisher is actuated by a 'Wig Wag'. **1886** *Sci. Amer.* 9 Jan. 16/2 In the army wig-wag system, a flag moved to right and left [etc.]. **1892** *Lippincott's Mag.* Dec. 764, I requested Lieutenant Marix to 'wigwag to signal' to Captain Whiting. **1893** C. KING *Foes in Ambush* 10 It's ten minutes since I got the last wig-wag of the signal-flag. **1899** R. H. DAVIS *Cuban & Porto Rican Campaigns* 3 Wig-waggers beat the air from the bridges. **1903** A. ADAMS *Log Cowboy* xx. 313 Some one in the lead wig-wagged his lantern. **1914** *Blackw. Mag.* July 96/2 The path is beastly wig-waggy.

wigwam (ˈwɪgwɒm, -wæm), *sb.* Also 7 **wigg-wamme**, 8 **wigwang**, **wigg-wham**, **whigwham**, **wigwaum**, 9 **weekwam**. [a. Ojibwa *wigwaum*, *wigiwam*, var. of Algonkin *weekuwom*, *wikiwam* (Delaware *wiquoam*) lit. their house (cf. *neek* my house, *keek* thy house, *week* his house).] **a.** A lodge, cabin, tent, or hut of the North American Indian peoples of the region of the Great Lakes and eastward, formed of bark, matting, or hides stretched over a frame of poles converging at the top: corresponding to the TEPEE of other peoples.

1628 C. LEVETT *Voy. N. Eng.* i. in *Collect. Mass. Hist. Soc.* Ser. III. VIII. 166 We built us our wigwam, or house, in one hour's space. **1659** GORGES *America Painted to the Life* 38 This Sachem passing from one Wigwam to another, was shot through the arm with an arrow. **1722** BEVERLEY *Hist. Virginia* (ed. 2) 148 When they would erect a Wig-wang, .. they stick Saplins into the Ground. **1821** DWIGHT *Trav.* I. 117 They called a house *weekwam*, pronounced by their successors *wigwam*. **1855** LONGF. *Hiaw.* Introd. 5 The curling smoke of wigwams. **1865** LUBBOCK *Preh. Times* xii. 421 The huts or wigwams are .. of two kinds, one for summer, and the other for winter. **1893** CONAN DOYLE *Refugees* xxix, The great plains where the wooden wigwam gave place to the hide tee-pee.

b. Extended to similar structures among primitive societies in other parts of the world.

1743 BULKELEY & CUMMINS *Voy. S. Seas* 37 They hawl'd their Canoes up, and built four Wigg-whams. **1793** W. HODGES *Trav. India* 66 The wigwams of the torpid, wretched, unsettled Pecherais on the frozen coast of Terra del Fuego. **1814** SCOTT *Wav.* viii, A miserable wigwam, compiled of earth, loose stones, and turf. **1865** LUBBOCK *Preh. Times* viii. 228 The wigwam of the recent Mandan consisted of an outer layer of earth supported on a wooden framework.

c. Humorously applied to a house or dwelling in general; in *U.S. slang* to a large building (formerly often a temporary structure) used for political gatherings.

1818 SCOTT *Rob Roy* xxxiv, They..bore me..towards Mrs. MacAlpine's. On arrival before her hospitable wigwam I found [etc.]. **1884** HALLIWELL-PHILLIPPS *Handlist Drawings Shaks.* title-p., Preserved at Hollingbury Copse, near Brighton. That quaint wigwam on the Sussex Downs.

d. A pyramidal frame-work of bamboo and similar poles used to support beans, sweet peas, etc.

1971 H. EVANS *How to cheat at Gardening* viii. 120 If you must have sticks, tie them in threes, wigwam fashion. *Ibid.* 121 (*caption*) Easiest way of arranging bean-poles—the wigwam. **1978** A. HUXLEY *Illustr. Hist. Gardening* v. 150/2 We continue to grow beans and the like..on wigwams formed of bamboo canes.

Hence ˈ**wigwam** *v.* (*nonce-wd.*), *intr.* to erect wigwams or huts.

1906 *Harper's Mag.* Apr. 770 Having seen..that the fur traders were really wigwamming on the bay.

wihe, wihee, -ie, -y, wihel, wiht: see WYE, WEHEE, WIEL, WIGHT, WITH.

wiif, wiis, obs. ff. WIFE, WISE.

wijf, wijnd, wijs, wijt, wijte: see WIFE, WIND, VICE *sb.*³, WIS *v.*, WISE, WIT, WITE.

wik, obs. form of WICK.

†**wike.** *Obs.* Also 4 **wyke.** [OE. *wíce* wk. fem.:—OTeut. **wīkōn-*, f. *wīk-*: *waik-* to soften, to bend, turn, change, represented also in ON. *vík* WICK *sb.*⁴, OE. *wicu* WEEK *sb.*, OE. *wác*, ON. *veikr* WOKE, WEAK; cf. L. *vicēs* change, turn, office, duty, Gr. εἴκειν to yield, f. Indo-Eur. *weiq-*. (See also -WICK *suffix*.)] An office, duty, function.

c **1000** ÆLFRIC *Hom.* II. 592 Hu dear ænig læwede man him to ȝeteon þurh riccetere Cristes wican? *c* **1175** *Lamb. Hom.* 137 Oðer don scal wiken and cherres. *c* **1200** *Trin. Coll. Hom.* 91 Betfage..bitocneð holie chirche þat men noten ine here muðes wike þanne hie seien here sinnes. *c* **1205** LAY. 29752 Austin..haueð his cantel-cape on of Gregorie þan pape, and mid wurðscipe mucle haldeð his wike. *a* **1225** *Juliana* 24 He me walde warpen ut of mine wike ant demen me to deaðe. *a* **1250** *Owl & Night.* 605 Mine wike boþ wel gode. *Ibid.* 1179 Wat, quaþ ho, hartu ihoded?.. For prestes wike ich wat þu dest. *c* **1275** *Prov. Ælfred* 316 in *O.E. Misc.* 121 Wlanc on werȝe, and unwurþ on wike [*Jesus MS.* wlonk bi þe glede, and vuel at þare neode]. **13..** *K. Alis* 4592 (Laud MS.), Þerfore ne shulde no gentil kniȝth..beggers blood brynge in heiȝe wyke. *c* **1315** SHOREHAM I. 660 Ase þe ryȝte bodyes lemes Habbeþ dyuerse wyke, So habbeþ ryȝt membrys eke Of þe body ine mystyke.

b. *Comb.* **wike-tun,** ? a place for divine service.

a **1250** *Owl & Night.* 730 Clerekes Munekes & canunes, Þar beoþ þos gode wike tunes, Ariseþ vp to middelnyhte.

wike, wiked, obs. ff. WEEK, WICK, WICKED.

†**wiken.** *Obs.* [Peculiar to Ormin. ? Back-formation f. WICKNER or OE. *wícnian*.] = WIKE.

c **1200** ORMIN 7217 Forrþi þatt teȝȝre wikenn wass To writenn laȝhebokess. *Ibid.* 10168.

wikenare, obs. form of WICKNER.

wiker, -ir, wiket(t, wikid, -it, Wiking, obs. ff. WICKER, WICKET, WICKED, VIKING.

wikke, wikked, -et, -it, -yd, -yt, wikker, obs. ff. WICK *a.*, WICKED, WICKER.

wikop, variant of WICOPY.

wikre, wikut, -yt, obs. ff. WICKER, WICKED.

†**wil.** *Obs. rare.* [? a. ON. *víl.*] Misery, ill.

c **1400** *Rule St. Benet* (prose) 28 Þat nane be costiue, ne nane oþir wil, þurȝ surfait o mete. *Ibid.*, Þat we alle wils o bodi & saul mai fle.

wil, obs. f. VILE, WHILE, WILE, WILL.

wil-, attrib. use of WILL *sb.*¹ (as in OE. *wilcuma*, WELCOME); only in OE. and early ME. compounds = (*a*) pleasant, welcome, (*b*) voluntary: **wil-daȝe,** a welcome day; **wil-ȝeoue** [GIVE *sb.*¹], a voluntary or free gift; **wil-ȝomen** [GAME *sb.*], pleasant sport; **wil-shrift,** voluntary confession; **wil-spell, wil-tidende** [TIDING], welcome news.

a **900** CYNEWULF *Crist* 459 Hy þæs lareowes on þam *wildæȝe word ne ȝehyrwdon hyra sincȝiefan. *c* **1205** LAY. 1798 Þat heo heora wil-daȝes wælden weoren. *a* **1225** *Ancr. R.* 368 'Me Sire,' þu onswerest me, 'sulleð God his grace? Nis grace *wil-ȝeoue?' *a* **1225** *St. Marher.* 16 Hwet so ich am þurh godes grace ich hit do ant am wilȝeoue unofseruet. *c* **1205** LAY. 20944 Castles biwinnen & *wilgomen wurchen. *a* **1225** *Ancr. R.* 340 Wel seið he, 'is iflured': vorte bitochen *wilschrift. *a* **900** CYNEWULF *Elene* 993 Wæs him frofra mæst ȝeworden in worlde æt ðam *willspelle. *c* **1205** LAY. 1350 A steores-man ham talde wil-spel. *Ibid.* 17090 Komen to þan kinge *wil-tidende.

wilani(e, obs. ff. VILLAINY.

wilayet, variant of VILAYET.

wilbe, -bie: see WILL *v.*¹

wilc, wilch, obs. ff. WHICH.

wilcat, Sc. f. WILD CAT.

wilch (wɪltʃ, wɪlʃ). *Suffolk dial.* Now *Hist.* Also **wilsh.** [Origin unknown.] A bottle-shaped wicker strainer formerly used in brewing to strain the liquid from grains of steeped malt. Cf. THEAD.

1823 E. MOOR *Suffolk Words & Phrases* 484 *Wilch*, the sediment or lees of beer, home-made wine,..also a brewing utensil. **1830** R. FORBY *Vocab. East Anglia* II. 375 *Wilch*,.. the wicker strainer set upright in the mash-tub, to prevent the grains from running off with the wirt. **1956** G. E. EVANS *Ask Fellows who cut Hay* v. 61 The utensils used in the brewing were..*a wilch* (or wilsh), a bottle-shaped appliance made of wicker. (The wilsh was a filter used when straining off the liquid or *wort* from the *mash* of steeped malt.) **1962** A. JOBSON *Window in Suffolk* i. 28 The brewing tackle would be housed in a large shed or outhouse set apart for that purpose, and would include the tubs or keelers, the wilches, mash sticks,..mallets, spigots and taps.

wilco (ˈwɪlkəʊ), *int.* orig. *Mil. slang.* Also **willco.** Abbrev. of '*will comply*', used to express acceptance of instructions, esp. those received by radio or telephone. Cf. *will do* s.v. WILL *v.*¹ 11 c.

1946 F. HAMANN *Air Words* 56 *Willco*, will comply; will do. **1948** A. M. TAYLOR *Lang. World War II* (ed. 2) 221 *Wilco*, radio term for 'will comply'. Used throughout the services and also taken up by civilians. **1961** H. WAUGH *Road Block* i. 12 'Roger, wilco, and out,' the staticky voice sang. **1972** D. HART-DAVIS *Spider in Morning* ii. 28 'If it happens again, hold your breath.' 'Wilco.' **1977** D. BEATY *Excellency* xvii. 190 'Please clear the runway quickly for the President's Starjet!'..'Wilco,' he said.

wild (waɪld), *a.* and *sb.* Forms: 1–7 **wilde,** (3 **wuilde**), 3–6 **wylde,** 4–7 **wyld,** (4 **wiylde, wijlde, whilde, wyled,** 4–6 **wield(e,** 4–7 *Sc.* **vylde,** 5 **wiilde, wyelde, wyyld(e,** *Sc.* **wulde,** 6 **wylld,** *Sc.* **vild, vyld, vyild, wyild,** 7 **weild),** 3– **wild.** [Com. Teut.: OE. *wilde* = OFris. *wilde*, MDu. *wilde, wilt*, (LG., Du. *wild*), OHG. *wildi* (MHG. *wilde, wild*, G. *wild*), ON. *villr* bewildered, astray, whence WILL *a.* (Norw. *vill* wild, Sw. *vill* confused, giddy, Sw., Da. *vild* wild), Goth. *wilþeis*:—OTeut. **wilþijaz*. The sb., OE. **wild*, **wildor* (cf. *wildorlic* adj.), pl. *wildru* (later *wildéor, wildedéor* WILD DEER), OHG. *wild*, pl. *wildir* wild beast, is app. a derivative (**wilþaz-, -iz-*) with *s*-stem from the same root (cf. *lamb*).

The problem of the ulterior relations of this word is complicated by uncertainty as to its primary meaning. The possible analogy of sense-development in L. *silvestris, silvāticus* (whence F. *sauvage* wild, etc.), f. *silva* wood, has sugggested connexion with OTeut. **walþus* forest (OE. *weald, wald* WOLD). But it is more probable that OTeut. **wilþijaz* represents a pre-Teut. **ghweltijos*, the root of which is found in Welsh *gwyllt*, Ir. *geilt* wild, and may have a parallel form in *ghwēr-*, the base of L. *ferus*, Gr. θήρ, Lith. *zvèris*, OSl. *zvěrь* wild beast (for a similar phonological development of *ghw-* cf. WARM *a.*).]

A. *adj.*

I. 1. Of an animal: Living in a state of nature; not tame, not domesticated: opp. to TAME *a.* 1.

Freq. in names of particular species or varieties, for which see the sbs.: see also Special Collocations (16), and WILD CAT, FOWL, GOOSE in the main series.

In later use often hyphened to the following sb., esp. in names of particular species, or in verse to indicate rhythmic stress on the adj.

c **725** *Corpus Gloss.* (Hessels) I. 427 *Indomitus*, wilde. *c* **825** *Vesp. Psalter* ciii[i]. 11 Drencað ða alle wilddeor wuda; bidað wilde assan in ðurs[t] heara. *c* **893** ÆLFRED *Oros.* I. i. §17 Ða beoð swyðe dyre mid Finnum, for ðæm hy foð þa wildan hranas mid. *c* **1000** *Sax. Leechd.* III. 180 On .xv. nihte monan hys god to fixianne & huntum heortas to secanne & wilde swin. *c* **1050** [see WILD GOOSE 1]. *c* **1205** LAY. 1781 Wind stod on willen, ploȝede þe wilde fisc. *c* **1386** CHAUCER *Monk's T.* 267 To wode she went And many a wilde hertes blood she shedde With arwes brode. ? *a* **1400** *Morte Arth.* 3232 Woluez, and whilde swynne, and wykkyde bestez. **1529** *Burgh Rec. Edin.* (1871) II. 9 Ony maner of wyld foule or tayme. **1606** SHAKS. *Ant. & Cl.* II. ii. 183 Eight Wilde-Boares rosted whole. **1778** PENNANT *Brit. Zool.* II. 447 The goose, in its wild state always retains the same marks. **1793** COLERIDGE *Songs of Pixies* iv, The murmuring throng Of wild-bees hum their drowsy song. **1808** SCOTT *Marm.* II. Introd., And mark the wild swans [*later edd.* wild-swans] mount the gale. **1827** P. CUNNINGHAM *N.S. Wales* xvii. I. 321 Our wild turkeys..consist of two varieties, the dusky and the blue-feathered. **1847** TENNYSON *Princess* IV. 414 The leader wildswan. **1849** MACAULAY *Hist. Eng.* iii. I. 312 Wild animals of large size were then far more numerous than at present.

fig. *c* **1645** HOWELL *Lett.* I. v. xxvii, Twas a tough task believe it, thus to tame A wilde and wealthy language.

absol. *c* **1205** LAY. 1112 Heo wenden vt i wide sæ, þa wilde wurðen itemede. *c* **1375** *Sc. Leg. Saints* xviii. (*Egipciane*) 1037 To þis day saw I nane,..Of vylde, na tame, na kind beste. *c* **1480** HENRYSON *Lion & Mouse* 192 He..slew baith tayme and wyld.

2. Of a plant (or flower): Growing in a state of nature; not cultivated.

Freq. in names (unlimited in number) of particular species or varieties, for which see the sbs. *to sow one's wild oats* (fig.): see OAT *sb.* 4.

Often hyphened as in 1 (and regularly in phrases used attrib.) or (chiefly in early use) combined with the following sb. as one word.

c **725** *Corpus Gloss.* A 396 *Agre[s]tis*, wilde. *c* **1000** *Sax. Leechd.* II. 90 *Oleastrum* þæt is wilde elebeam. **1382** WYCLIF *Rom.* xi. 24 The kyndely wylde [*later vers.* wielde] olyue tre. **14..** *Voc.* in Wr.-Wülcker 569/2 *Brionia*, wylde-nepe. *c* **1440** *Promp. Parv.* 528/1 Wyylde malowe, or holy-hokke. *c* **1489** CAXTON *Sonnes of Aymon* xviii. 401 Suche wylde herbes as grewe in the woode. **1549** *Compl. Scot.* i. 20 Al the grond..is ouergane vitht gyrse ande vild scroggis. **1590** SHAKS. *Mids. N.* II. i. 249, I know a banke where the wilde time blowes. **1665** BOYLE *Occas. Refl.* I. 63 The Husbandman uses onely to prune the Trees of his Garden, not those that grow wild in his Woods. **1781** COWPER *Retirem.* 420 Her hedge-row shrubs..With woodbine and wild roses mantled o'er. **1810** SCOTT *Lady of L.* I. viii, Cold dews and wild flowers [*later edd.* wild-flowers] on his head. **1842** LOUDON *Suburban Hort.* 444 Plants in a wild state. **1855** TENNYSON *Maud* II. I. 3 Plucking the harmless wild-flower on the hill.

1797 SCOTT *To a Lady* ii, Wild-flower wreaths for Beauty's hair. **1810** —— *Lady of L.* IV. ii, The wild-rose spray. **1890** 'R. BOLDREWOOD' *Col. Reformer* xxii, A young lady with a wild-rose complexion.

3. a. Produced or yielded by wild animals or plants; produced naturally without cultivation; sometimes, having the characteristic (usually inferior) quality of such productions (cf. b). ***wild silk***, silk produced by wild silkworms or an imitation of this made from short silk fibres.

With 'wild meat' cf. OS. *wildflêsc*, etc.; with 'wild leather' cf. MSw. *wilskin*.

c **1200** ORMIN 3213 Hiss drinnch wass waterr..Hiss mete wilde rotess. *c* **1200** [see HONEY *sb.* 1 b]. **1519** *Registr. Aberdon.* (Maitland) II. 177 The kiching witht..ij pair of raxis. Item iij spyttis ane grit ane less and ane for wild met. **1528** *Burgh Rec. Edin.* (1871) 3 All maner of persouns that takis wylde meitt. **1528** PAYNELL *Salerne's Regim.* (1541) R iv b, There be also prunes called wylde prunes, yᵉ whiche growe in the woddes. **1560** *Bible* (Geneva) Isa. v. 2 He loked yᵗ it shulde bring forthe grapes: but it broght forthe wilde grapes. **1582** N. LICHEFIELD tr. *Castanheda's Conq. E. Ind.* 75 These ships..are sowed together with ropes made of Cairo, & pitched ouer with wild incense. **1600** J. PORY tr. *Leo's Africa* IX. 340 Their flesh is hot and vnsauorie, and hath a wilde tast. **1612** *Sc. Bk. Rates* in *Halyburton's Ledger* (1867) 338 Leather called wyld lether the daker, xxs. **1614** in *10th Rep. Hist. MSS. Comm.* App. I. 43 Lett not my leadie our mother trubll hirself in bying much vylde meitt to your sons bapttisme. **1777** ANBUREY *Trav.* (1789) I. 214 A dinner entirely of wild-meats. **1866** ROGERS *Agric. & Prices* I. xviii. 418 It is very rare in the present day that honey is found wild. **1876** [see TUSSER 1 a]. **1883** R. HALDANE *Workshop Rec.* Ser. II. 40/1 The wild or Tussah silk. **1896** [see TUSSER 1 b]. **1911** *Daily Colonist* (Victoria, B.C.) 28 Apr. 14/2 The cargo was made up as follows: Raw silk, 960 bales; wild silk, 49 bales. **1963** R. HIMMEL *It's Murder, Maguire* vii. 46, I always suspected him of wearing wild silk underwear. **1972** J. AIKEN *Butterfly Picnic* ix. 162 Her white wild-silk bikini.

b. *Mining.* Applied to impure or inferior minerals or ores. (Cf. G. *wilderz*.)

1778 PRYCE *Min. Cornub.* 93 A Black-jack or Mock-lead Lode... This Wild-lead is commonly found with Stones of Copper and Lead intermixed with it. **1883** GRESLEY *Gloss. Coal-m.*, Wild Ground, Wild Measures, Wild Stuff. **1886** J. BARROWMAN *Sc. Mining Terms*, *Wild-coal*, a thin seam of inferior coal.

4. a. Of a place or region: Uncultivated or uninhabited; hence, waste, desert, desolate. (Often with special reference to the character or aspect of such places.)

c **893** ÆLFRED *Oros.* I. i. §18 Licgað wilde moras.. emnlange þæm bynum lande. *a* **1122** *O.E. Chron.* (Laud MS.) an. 1010 On þa wildan fennas. *c* **1200** ORMIN 17408 A wilde wesste. **1297** R. GLOUC. (Rolls) 2751 Me may hem ofte an erþe in wilde studes yse. *c* **1375** *Sc. Leg. Saints* xl. (*Ninian*) 430 Quhare now þe corne is beste, þat tyme wes wilde foreste. *c* **1385** CHAUCER *L.G.W.* 2163 *Ariadne*, In an yle amyd the wilde se. *a* **1533** LD. BERNERS *Gold. Bk. M. Aurel.* (1546) K vj b, The erthe that is vntylled, and waxen wyld. **1593** SHAKS. *Rich. II*, II. iii. 4 These high wilde hilles, and rough vneeuen waies. **1617** MORYSON *Itin.* I. 36 Fenny and woody wild grounds. **1644** MANWAYRING *Sea-mans Dict.* 85 A wild Roade, is a Roade where there is little Land on any side, but lies all open to the sea. **1703** ROWE *Ulysses* II. i, Some fair field..That..left unheeded, like a barren Moor, Lies fenceless, wild, uncultivate, and waste. **1817** BRADBURY *Trav. Amer.* 297 They are well aware that, by undertaking to bring wild land into a state of cultivation, they must undergo some hardships. **1849** LEVER *Con Cregan* xxv, The scenery was wild without being grand. **1883** *Eng. Illustr. Mag.* Nov. 72/1 The wild beauty of Wicken Fen is in striking contrast with the cultivated land lying around it. **1885** W. H. WHITE *M. Rutherford's Deliv.* iii, The garden was large and half-wild.

b. *transf.* Belonging to or characteristic of a wild region; of or in a wilderness.

1690 C. NESSE *O. & N. Test.* I. 298 Neither God nor good men take any pleasure in a..wild retiredness. **1817** MOORE *Lalla Rookh* 131 The glories of Nature and her wild, fragrant airs, playing freshly over the current of youthful spirits.

5. Of persons (or their attributes): Uncivilized, savage; uncultured, rude; also, not accepting, or resisting, the constituted government; rebellious. (Sometimes with implication of sense 8.) See also *wild Irish* in 16.

a **1300** *Cursor M.* 24747 For þof mi [*MS.* in] wijt war neuer sa wild..þat giues me lust of hir to rede. *a* **1352** MINOT *Poems* (ed. Hall) i. 60 Þare was crakked many a crowne Of wild Scottes and alls of tame. *c* **1450** HOLLAND *Howlat* 616 The rouch Wodwyss wyld. **1471** CAXTON *Recuyell* (Sommer) 59 She was euyl clothid and half wilde and sauage. **1500–20** DUNBAR *Poems* l. 25 Was never vyld Robeine wnder bewch,..So bauld a bairne as he. *a* **1548** HALL *Chron.*, *Hen. IV* 23 The prince..had tamed..the furious rage of the wild and sauage Welshemen. **1561** HOBY tr. *Castiglione's Courtyer* II. M iij b, A man at armes in fourm of a wield shepehearde. **1586** HOLINSHED *Chron.* I. *Hist. Scot.* 358/2 After the example of one..Robert Hood a wild or vplandish man. **1670** DRYDEN *1st Pt. Conq. Granada* I. (1672) 7 When wild in woods the noble Savage ran. **1700** PRIOR *Carmen Sec.* xxxvii, Nations yet wild by Precept to reclaim, And teach 'em Arms, and Arts. **1709** MRS. MANLEY *Secret Mem.* (1720) 303 A Party of the Goths and wild Russes. **1822** SCOTT *Nigel* v, It's ill taking the breeks aff a wild Highlandman. **1850** TENNYSON *In Mem.* xxxvi. 15 Those wild eyes that watch the wave In roarings round the coral reef. **1901** *Scotsman* 29 Nov. 6/1 These men..are up to all the 'slim' ways of the wild Boer.

II. 6. Not under, or not submitting to, control or restraint; taking, or disposed to take, one's own way; uncontrolled. Primarily of animals (cf. 1), and hence of persons (see also 7) and things, with various shades of meaning.

a. Acting or moving freely without restraint; going at one's own will; unconfined, unrestricted.

a **1000** *Cædmon's Gen.* 1465 Ða wæs culufre eft of cofan sended..wilde seo wide fleah. *c* **1000** *Sax. Leechd.* III. 202 Hors wilde yrnan. *a* **1310** in Wright *Lyric P.* xv. 48 Thar er wes wilde ase the ro, Nou y swyke. **1596** SHAKS. *Merch. V.* V. i. 71 A wilde and wanton heard..of youthful and vnhandled colts. **1599** SHAKS., etc. *Pass. Pilgr.* xii. 8 Youth is wild, and Age is tame. **1671** MILTON *Samson* 974 In his wild aerie flight. **1761** COLMAN *Jealous Wife* III, That the wild little Thing shou'd take Wing, and fly away the Lord knows whither! **1817** BYRON *Manfred* III. iv, I have found our thoughts take wildest flight Even at the moment when they should array Themselves in pensive order. **1820** SHELLEY *Prometh. Unb.* III. iii. 136 The dark linked ivy tangling wild. **1836** DICKENS *Sk. Boz, Medit. Monmouth-St.*, The children wild in the streets, the mother a destitute widow. **1865** P'CESS ALICE *Mem.* (1884) 101 Victoria is very wild, and speaks more German than English.

b. Resisting control or restraint, unruly, restive; flighty, thoughtless; reckless, careless; *fig.* not according to rule, irregular; erratic; unsteady. (Cf. 15.)

c **1350** *Libeaus Desc.* (Kaluza) 188 A child þat is witles and wilde. **1450** *Paston Lett.* I. 159 But if the day of the oyer and termyner stonde, it wole be full harde, by cause the peple is so wylde. **1594** NASHE *Unfort. Trav.* I 3 b, Like the trauaile wherein smithes put wilde horses when they shoo them. **1597** MORLEY *Introd. Mus.* 81 Your fift, sixt, and seuenth notes be wilde and vnformall. **1628** SHIRLEY *Witty Fair One* II. ii, You are too wild and aery to be constant to that affection. **1748** H. WALPOLE *Lett.* (1846) II. 256, I meant nothing in the world by wild, but the thoughtlessness of a boy of nineteen. **1831** SCOTT *Ct. Rob* xviii, Depriving Cupid's wing of some wild feathers. **1857** HUGHES *Tom Brown* II. viii, Johnson the young bowler is getting wild, and bowls a ball almost wide to the off. **1867** SMYTH *Sailor's Word-bk.*, *Wild*, a ship's motion when she steers badly, or is badly steered. **1879** HARLAN *Eyesight* ii. 25 The new lashes sometimes take a wrong direction, and turn their points against the eyeball. They are then popularly called wild hairs.

c. Shy; *esp.* of game, afraid of or avoiding the pursuer (opp. to TAME *a.* 3); *transf.* having a timid expression like a wild animal.

1594 WILLOBIE *Avisa* xlvii, Though copy at first she seeme and wielde. **1599** SHAKS. *Much Ado* III. i. 35 She is too disdainfull, I know her spirits are as coy and wilde, As Haggerds of the rocke. **1813** COL. HAWKER *Diary* (1893) I. 76 The birds were so extremely wild that it was almost impossible to get near them. **1877** MARCH. DUFFERIN *Canad. Jrnl.* (1891) 362 They did not bring back a great deal—the birds were so wild. **1887** RIDER HAGGARD *Allan Quatermain* xi, The woman had a sweet face, wild and shy.

d. Phr. ***to run wild***: (*a*) of an animal or plant (combining senses 1 or 2 and 6), to live in, or revert to, a state of nature, not under domestication or cultivation; (*b*) of a person (or thing personified), with various shades of meaning (see above), sometimes passing into other senses (e.g. 7, 11, 12).

1549-62 [see RUN *v.* 2 b]. **1774** GOLDSM. *Nat. Hist.* (1776) II. 347 Of all countries..where the horse runs wild, Arabia produces the most beautiful breed. **1799** WORDSW. *Matthew* 3 That every hour thy heart runs wild, Yet never once doth go astray. **1838** [see RUN *v.* 2 b]. **1853** DICKENS *Bleak Ho.* lv, He had a bold spirit, and he ran a little wild, and went for a soldier. **1892** *Longman's Mag.* XIX. 614 The boy had run wild since his young mother's death.

(*c*) of an oil-well, to release uncontrollable quantities of fluid or gas. Also ***to blow wild***.

1925 [see *relief well* s.v. RELIEF[2] 9 b]. **1931** *Times* 18 Feb. 15/6 When the wells 'blow wild' the city is enveloped in a dark spray of oil. **1975** L. CROOK *Oil Terms* 35 *Blow out*, a situation where a well becomes out of control due to the fluids from the formation 'blowing wild' at the surface.

7. *spec.* **a.** Not submitting to moral control; taking one's own way in defiance of moral obligation or authority; unruly, insubordinate; wayward, self-willed.

Often scarcely distinguishable from 6 a or b, but implying blame or reproach.

c **1000** *Sal. & Sat.* 377 He ʒeong færeð, hafað wilde mod. *c* **1175** *Lamb. Hom.* 5 Ne beo þu þereuore prud ne wilde ne sterc. *c* **1200** ORMIN 6191 ȝiff þatt ȝho iss gætelæs, & eȝȝelæs & wilde. *c* **1205** LAY. 785 þat nan ne beo so wilde nan swa unwitti, þat word talie..ær he ihere minne horn. *a* **1300** *Cursor M.* 9307 Quarfor er yee o will sa wild? *c* **1380** WYCLIF *Sel. Wks.* III. 431 Somme men ben beterid bi bynding to þise chargis, þat ellis wolden be wylde. *c* **1450** *Mirk's Festial* 67 Mannys flesche ys so wyld and lusty to synne. **1535** COVERDALE *2 Macc.* xi. 4 Not consideringe the power of God, but was wylde in his mynde. **1567** *Gude & Godlie B.* (S.T.S.) 151 Man was sa wylde and nyce, And rageing in all vyce. **1579** LYLY *Euphues* R iv b, The wildest child is as soone corrected with a word as with a weapon. **1700** PRIOR *Carmen Sec.* 66 Valour grown wild by Pride, and Pow'r by Rage. **1797-1812** JANE AUSTEN *Pride & Prej.* xliii, 'He is now gone into the army', she added, 'but I am afraid he has turned out very wild.' **1836** MARRYAT *Japhet* xxvii, When a curate, he had had an only son, very wild, who would go to sea in spite of his remonstrances. **1898** 'H. S. MERRIMAN' *Roden's Corner* xii. 128 It was about that time..that I took seriously to my work. Before, I had been a little wild.

b. Giving way to sexual passion; also, more widely, licentious, dissolute, loose.

c **1250** *Gen. & Ex.* 2013 His wif wurð wilde, and nam in ðoȝt Vn-riȝt-wis luue. **13..** *St. Paula* 87 in Horstm. *Altengl. Leg.* (1878) 5 Whon þe ȝonge in hote blood Bigonne to waxe wylde of mod. **13..** *St. Theodora* 221 ibid. 38 His monk was waxen to wyld þat hedde igeten him such a child. **13..** *Gaw. & Gr. Knt.* 2367 Bot þat was for no wylyde werke, ne wowyng nauþer. *c* **1460** *Towneley Myst.* xix. 167 Ther was neuer man neghyd hyr nere, In word ne wark she was neuer wylde. **1522** *World & Child* A ij, Dalyaunce,..It is a name that is ryght wylde. **1550** CROWLEY *Last Trumpet* 1505 If thou se hir wanton and wilde. **1598** SHAKS. *Merry W.* III. ii. 74 Hee kept companie with the wilde Prince, and Pointz. **1614** D. DYKE *Myst. Self-Deceiv.* 328 Wild and wanton widowes. **1778** (13 May) JOHNSON in *Boswell*, If a young man is wild, and must run after women and bad company. **1849** MACAULAY *Hist. Eng.* vi. II. 50 The wildest of libertines.

8. Fierce, savage, ferocious; furious, violent, destructive, cruel. (In later use passing into other senses: cf. 5, 9, 11. See also *wild beast*, *wild horse*, in 16.)

1297 R. GLOUC. (Rolls) 1322 þe prinse..þat in time of worre as a lomb is boþe mek & milde & in time of pes as leon boþe cruel & wilde. **13..** *K. Horn* 1045 (Harl. MS.), Y come ..from brudale wylde of maide remenylde. *c* **1330** R. BRUNNE *Chron. Wace* (Rolls) 13796 Was neuere..wilde wolf ne dragoun, þat was so wod, beste to byte, As Wawayn was Romayns to smyte. *c* **1385** CHAUCER *L.G.W.* 805 *Thisbe*, Allas there comyth a wilde lyones. *c* **1400** *Destr. Troy* 1463 A man witty & wise, wight, wildist in Armes. *c* **1425** WYNUTON *Cron.* v. xiii. 4384 Wolwis wulde þan weryit men. *c* **1435** *Chron. London* (Kingsford 1905) 52 He wole be as wilde a Tyraunte to holy Cherche as euer was eny. **1526** *Pilgr. Perf.* (W. de W. 1531) 38 b, Brynge to me ye wyldest bull that is. **1530** PALSGR. 329/2 Wylde or sharpe prickyng as a nettyll is, *griasche*. **1595** SHAKS. *John* IV. iii. 48 This is the bloodiest shame, The wildest Sauagery.

9. a. Of the sea, a stream, the weather, etc.: Violently agitated, rough, stormy, tempestuous, 'raging'; hence *fig.* or *gen.* Full of disturbance or confusion, tumultuous, turbulent, disorderly.

c **1205** LAY. 6226 We habbeð ihaued..moni walc moni wind bi wilde þisse watere. *a* **1250** *Owl & Night.* 946 Wraþþe meynþ þe heorte blod þat hit floweþ so wilde flod. **1381** in *Knighton's Chron.* (Rolls) II. 139 Synne fareth as wilde flode. *c* **1420** *Sir Amadace* (Camden) xli, Thay were drounet on the see, With wild waturs slone. **1590** SHAKS. *Com. Err.* II. i. 21 Man..Lord of the wide world, and wilde watry seas. **1597** —— *2 Hen. IV*, I. i. 9 The Times are wilde: Contention..madly hath broke loose. **1605** —— *Lear* II. iv. 311 'Tis a wild night..come out oth' storme. **1610** HOLLAND *Camden's Brit.* I. 566 Wilde Brookes meeting together make a broad poole. **1629** MILTON *Hymn Nativ.* i, It was the Winter wilde, While the Heav'n-born-childe, All meanly wrapt in the rude manger lies. **1673** [R. LEIGH] *Transp. Reh.* 112 Your state of conscience leads to a wilder anarchy. **1697** DRYDEN *Virg. Georg.* III. 386 The..Bear..In Woods and Fields a wild destruction makes. —— *Past.* IX. 59 Let the wild Surges vainly beat the Shore. **1713** ADDISON *Cato* III. ii, His passions and his virtues..mixt together in so wild a tumult, That [etc.]. **1769** GRAY *Installat. Ode* 89 Thro' the wild waves as they roar. **1818** BYRON *Mazeppa* xiv, The wild horse swims the wilder stream! **1842** DICKENS *Amer. Notes* ii, On a bad winter's night in the wild Atlantic. **1864** LOWELL *Study Wind.* (1886) 110 He is still in wild water. **1883** 'OUIDA' *Wanda* i, 'I think we shall have wild weather', said the Princess.

†**b.** In imprecations or intensive expressions.

a **1352** MINOT *Poems* (ed. Hall) v. 30 In þe wilde waniand was þaire hertes light. *c* **1440** *York Myst.* xxx. 545 Now in þe wilde vengeaunce ye walke with þat wight. *a* **1530** HEYWOOD *Wether* 430 (Brandl) A myschyefe vpon them and a wylde thunder. *c* **1580** *Bugbears* IV. iv. 11 Now a wild wannion on it.

c. Of vocal sounds: Loud and unrestrained.

1549 *Compl. Scot.* vi. 39 The herrons gaif ane vyild skrech. **1667** MILTON *P.L.* III. 710 Confusion heard his voice, and wilde uproar Stood rul'd. **1742** GRAY *Adversity* 19 Wild Laughter, Noise, and thoughtless Joy. **1831** JAMES *Philip Aug.* iii, Filling the air with his long wild neighings. **1891** FARRAR *Darkn. & Dawn* xxxix, Those who should be left dead..indifferent for ever to those wild shouts.

10. Of feelings or their expression: Highly excited or agitated; passionately vehement or impetuous.

1594 SHAKS. *Rich. III*, IV. iv. 229 But that still vse of greefe, makes wilde greefe tame, My tongue should to thy eares not name my Boyes, Till that my Nayles were anchor'd in thine eyes. **1718** POPE *Iliad* III. 512 Too deep my anguish, and too wild my woe. **1730** —— *Ode St. Cecilia* Addit. Stanza, Amphion thus bade wild dissension cease. **1813** SCOTT *Rokeby* IV. x, The child Renew'd again his moaning wild. **1828** CARLYLE *Ess.*, *Burns* (1840) I. 370 Wild Desires and wild Repentance alternately oppress him. **1885** 'MRS. ALEXANDER' *At Bay* x, She clung to him and burst into a fit of wild weeping. **1890** HALL CAINE *Bondman* III. i, 'The sweep!' 'the thief!' 'the wastrel!' 'the gomer-stang!' they called him, with wilder names beside.

11. Of persons: Violently excited.

a. Extremely irritated or vexed; angry, 'furious'.

1653 HOLCROFT *Procopius* III. *Goth. Wars* 103 Artabanes was wild at this misfortune [*orig.* Quam rem cum calamitatis loco Artabanes duceret, & ægerrime ferret]. *a* **1839** PRAED *County Ball* xviii, He makes a College Fellow wild By asking for his wife and child. **1873** MARCH. DUFFERIN *Canad. Jrnl.* (1891) 79 Dent, my precious maid, wild about her boxes, and giving warning on the spot. **1889** JEROME *Three Men in Boat* xi, It made me awfully wild, especially as George burst out laughing.

b. Passionately or excitedly desirous *to do* something. Also const. *for*.

1797 JANE AUSTEN *Sense & Sens.* xxvi, Mrs. Palmer..was wild to buy all, could determine on none. **1797-1812** —— *Pride & Prej.* xlvi, She was wild to be at home. *a* **1817** —— *Persuasion* (1818) III. vi. 107 The girls were wild for dancing. **1847** TENNYSON *Princess* I. 149 All wild to found an University For maidens. **1894** FENN *Real Gold* ii, He is wild to go. **1937** J. T. FARRELL *Fellow Countrymen* 184 He imagined that she was his woman... She was saying she was crazy about him... She was wild for him.

c. Elated, enthusiastic, 'raving'. Also † const. *after*.

a **1817** JANE AUSTEN *Persuasion* (1818) IV. vii. 134 The men are all wild after Miss Elliot. **1865** R. HENNING *Let.* 21 Oct. (1966) 214 The whole family are wild after music. **1868** WHYTE-MELVILLE *White Rose* xxviii, He was wild about.. the town, and the castle, and the Black Forest. **1889** 'J. S. WINTER' *Mrs. Bob* xi, She was quite wild about it, when I went to tell her the news. **1891** C. JAMES *Rom. Rigmarole* 180 She had accepted me, and I was wild with joy.

d. ***like wild***: with passionate eagerness, with great excitement. Cf. *like mad* s.v. MAD *a.* 1 c.

1674 C. STEWKELEY *Let.* 4 May in M. M. Verney *Mem.* (1899) IV. vii. 225 Ursula..hath bin at all the Salsbury rasis, dancing like wild with Mr Clarks. **1962** *Radio Times* 17 May 43 Should he [*sc.* a jazz musician] 'blow' with feeling, or great excitement ('like wild') [etc.].

12. a. Not having control of one's mental faculties; demented, out of one's wits; distracted; hence in weakened sense, Extremely foolish or unreasonable; holding absurd or fantastic views (cf. 13).

c **1300** *K. Horn* 252 (Camb.) Heo louede so horn child þat neȝ heo gan wexe wild. *Ibid.* 296 Anon upon Aþulf child Rymenhild gan wexe wild. **13..** in Horstm. *Alt. Leg.* (1881) 14 Furth scho went als woman wilde, To se þe lordes, and left hir childe. *c* **1400** *Ywaine & Gaw.* 1650 For wa he wex al wilde and wode. **1630** RANDOLPH *Aristippus* 7, I am the Wilde-man, and I will be wilde: is that an age to be in a mans right wits? **1769** BURKE *Late St. Nat.* 25 Is this writer wild enough to imagine [etc.]? **1796** MRS. M. ROBINSON *Angelina* II. 291, I am really almost wild with affliction! **1835** DICKENS *Sk. Boz, Parish* v, Her misery had actually drove her wild. **1841** HELPS *Ess.*, *Man of Business* (1842) 82 Else he may be driven wild by any great pressure of business. **1849** MACAULAY *Hist. Eng.* vi. II. 6 When the fictions of Oates had driven the nation wild.

advb. **1613** SHAKS. *Hen. VIII*, I. iv. 26 If I chance to talke a little wilde, forgiue me: I had it from my Father. *An. Bul.* Was he mad Sir?

b. Of the eyes or look: Having an expression of distraction.

1592 SHAKS. *Rom. & Jul.* V. i. 28 Your lookes are pale and wild, and do import Some misaduenture. *a* **1658** CLEVELAND *Ruins of St. Pauls* 28 Now its Face appears like whither'd Care, Or wilder than the Looks of Fevers are. **1843** R. J. GRAVES *Syst. Clin. Med.* xiv. 158 His face being flushed, eyes wild, and head aching. **1878** J. P. HOPPS *Jesus* IV. 17 Poor mad people..recovered their senses when he looked into their wild eyes.

†**c.** Bewildered, perplexed; = WILL *a.* 2 b, 3 b.

c **1440** *Bone Flor.* 35 Whan the emperys was dedd, The emperowre was wylde of redd. **1456** SIR G. HAYE *Law Arms* (S.T.S.) 33 All the warld is in a wylde thocht, un-stedefast.

13. a. Of undertakings, actions, notions, statements, etc.: Going beyond prudent or reasonable limits; rashly or inconsiderately venturesome; going to extremes of extravagance or absurdity; fantastically unreasonable. Also in phr. ***in*** or ***beyond one's wildest dreams***, in or beyond one's most fantastic or unrestrained imaginings or expectations.

1515 *Burgh Rec. Edin.* (1869) I. 158 Gif it sall happin the toun to hald the commoun mylnis and proffeittis thairof and the wild aventouris into thair awin handis. **1591** SHAKS. *1 Hen. VI*, IV. iv. 7 This vnheedfull, desperate, wilde aduenture. **1602** —— *Ham.* I. v. 133 (Qo. 1) These are but wild and wherling words, my Lord. **1604** —— *Oth.* II. i. 62 He hath atchieu'd a Maid That paragons description, and wilde Fame. **1654** WHITLOCK *Zootomia* 509 A wild Reformation; to reforme Hierarchy by Anarchy, a Remedy worse then the Disease. **1667** MILTON *P.L.* V. 112 Mimic Fansie..misjoyning shapes, Wilde work produces oft. **1699** BENTLEY *Phal.* 427 The wild Question that the Examiner puts to me. *a* **1728** WOODWARD *Nat. Hist. Fossils* (1729) I. I. 84 'Twas not a very wild Name, Ludus, to be given, to a Dye, or Talus lusorius; considering how humourous a Writer Paracelsus was. **1732** BERKELEY *Alciphr.* IV. § 16 How came you to entertain so wild a Notion? **1829** SCOTT *Anne of G.* xi, I should make wild work were I to attempt a description of such an animal. **1849** MACAULAY *Hist. Eng.* iv. I. 442 We cannot..wonder that wild stories..were.. believed by the common people. *Ibid.* viii. II. 308 To cherish a wild hope. **1887** SAINTSBURY *Hist. Elizab. Lit.* 247 Serious arguments are mixed up with the wildest buffoonery. **1894** HALL CAINE *Manxman* V. ii, Two long weeks he spent in this wild quest. **1961** C. MCCULLERS *Clock without Hands* x. 203 In his wildest dreams he could not associate Johnny with danger. **1969** *Listener* 24 July 123/3 The programme has succeeded beyond its instigators' wildest dreams. **1984** *Tampa* (Florida) *Tribune* 5 Apr. 6C/2 You know, it's hard to believe I'm really here. It's beyond my wildest dreams that I'd be managing a team that I once played for.

†**b.** Used as a nickname for the extreme Evangelical party in the Church of Scotland, as opp. to *moderate*: see MODERATE B. b. *Obs.*

1778 D. Loch *Tour Scotl.* 49 The people here are very wild with regard to religious principles, there being no less than three large seceding meeting-houses, and but one small kirk of the established religion. **1820** Alex. Stewart in *Mem.* 352 [I] am settled minister of what is called the First Charge of Canongate Parish (where seldom has wild man been placed before). *a* **1830** H. Cockburn *Mem.* (1856) 234 Except Sir Harry Moncrieff, the Wild (as the Evangelical party is called) have never had an established head.

14. a. Artless, free, unconventional, fanciful, or romantic in style; having a somewhat barbaric character (usually in good sense, as a pleasing quality).

1632 Milton *L'Allegro* 134 If..sweetest Shakespear fancies childe, Warble his native Wood-notes wilde. *a* **1700** Evelyn *Diary* 27 Feb. 1644, We then saw a large and very rare grotto of shell-worke, in the shape of satyres and other wild fancys. **1802** Leyden *Mermaid* xxv, Say, heard'st thou not these wild notes swell? **1813** Byron *Corsair* II. ii, While dance the Almas to wild minstrelsy. **1859** Jephson *Brittany* xvii. 284 A wild ballad, still sung in Cornouaille, to an equally wild tune. *a* **1864** Bryant *Sella* 4 When man to man gave willing faith, and loved A tale the better that 'twas wild and strange. **1891** Rider Haggard *Nada* Pref., The setting out of a wild tale of savage life.

b. Of strange aspect; fantastic in appearance.

1605 Shaks. *Macb.* I. iii. 40 These,..so wilde in their attyre, That looke not like th' Inhabitants o' th' Earth. **1784** Cowper *Task* v. 118 There, embossed and fretted wild, The growing wonder takes a thousand shapes Capricious. **1844** Mrs. Browning *Lay of Brown Rosary* I. iv, To dilate and assume a wild shape in the mist.

c. *U.S. slang.* Remarkable, unusual, exciting. Used as a general term of approbation.

1955 L. Feather *Encycl. Jazz* x. 347/2 *Wild*, adj., remarkable, exciting. **1960** [see lay *v.*[1] 55 l]. **1968** *Listener* 22 Aug. 236/3 Los Angeles is so wild they should just let it swing and see what happens. **1978** *Hot Car* June 103/5 Naugahyde..has long been the favourite amongst Stateside rodders because of its stretchy qualities, amazing range of colours (including some wild marble-like effects).

15. a. (*fig.* from 6.) Aimed wide of the mark, or at random; random: usually *advb.* at random, astray.

a **1810** Shelley *M. Nicholson Fragm.* 14 Wild flew the meteors o'er the maddened main. **1831** James *Phil. Aug.* xxvii, The soldier who fronted him, struck wild, reeled, staggered. **1890** W. Camp in *St. Nicholas* Aug. 831/1 The catcher..must begin by a resolution..to consider no ball beyond his reach, no matter how wild. **1895** *Edin. Rev.* July 149 The Chinese shells found in the abandoned forts 'went wild' when the Japanese gunners tried to fire them.

b. Of a playing card: having any rank chosen by the player holding it. Also *fig.* See also *wild card*, sense 16 below.

1927 *Auction Bridge Mag.* May 26/1 These are played with all the twos as jokers and usually known as 'Deuces Wild'. **1940** O. Jacoby *On Poker* x. 139 Any card or cards may be counted as wild, in which case they have the same rights as jokers. **1963** E. Linington *Death of Busybody* vi. 72 Don't tell me, a tie-up. Look, Luis, let's not call every card in the deck wild, for God's sake. **1973** M. Catto *Sam Casanova* vi. 109 Think of the amazing variations of the game [*sc.* poker]! Five-Card stud. Seven-Card Draw with Joker wild.

III. 16. Special Collocations (sometimes hyphened as in 1 and 2, esp. in verse to indicate stress, and regularly in attrib. use); **wild beast**, orig. in sense 1, now always with mixture of sense 8 (see beast *sb.* 2 c); also *fig.* (cf. beast *sb.* 1 c, 5); **wild berry**, the berry of a wild plant; app. applied locally to particular kinds; **wild boar** (in early use also as one word): see boar *sb.* 1 c; **wild card**, (*a*) (see sense 15 b above); also *fig.*; (*b*) *Sport* (orig. *U.S.*), a player or team chosen for a tournament at the discretion of the organizers after the regular places have been taken up; freq. *attrib.*; (*c*) *Computers*, a character that will match any character or combination of characters in a file name, etc.; **wild cherry**: see cherry *sb.* 3 a; **wild dog**, any wild species of dog, or of the dog tribe, as the hyena-dog of S. Africa (hunting-dog 2 a), the Dhole of India (hunting-dog 2 b), the Dingo of Australia, etc.; **wild duck**, a duck belonging to any of numerous undomesticated species; **wild garden**, a group of hardy plants, exotic or native, in an informal setting, designed to look as natural as possible; hence **wild gardener, gardening**; **wild geranium** *S. Afr.* = geranium 2; **wild ginger**, in North America, any of several plants of the genus *Asarum*, esp. *A. canadense*, or, in India, a wild plant of the genus *Zingiber*; **wild goat**, any wild species of goat, as the ibex, or (*loosely*) a goat-like antelope, as the chamois; **wild grape**, a wild species of *Vitis* or its fruit; **wild horse**, a horse not domesticated or broken in; esp. in phrases referring to a mode of punishment or torture (cf. quots. s.v. draw *v.* 5), and hence humorously with negative (see quots.); in quot. 1834 (with hyphen) rendering Du. *wildepaard* as a name for the zebra; **Wild Huntsman**, a phantom huntsman of Teutonic legend, fabled to ride at night through the fields and woods with shouts and baying of hounds; **wild Irish** (see Irish B. 1 a); **wild Irishman** (see Irishman b); also a name for a spiny rhamnaceous shrub of New Zealand and Australia, of the genus *Discaria*; **wild lime**: see lime *sb.*[2] b; **wild mare**: see mare[1] 2 b; also *attrib.* in *wild mare hunch* (*hinch, hitch*), a name for string-halt; **wild orange**: see orange *sb.*[1] 3; also, in Australia, any of several species of *Capparis* or *Canthium*; in South Africa = *Kaffir orange* s.v. Kaffir 4; **wild parsnip**: see parsnip 2; also, = cow-parsnip; also, a poisonous plant of the family Umbelliferæ, esp., in North America, the water hemlock, *Cicuta maculata*, or, in Australia, *Trachymene glaucifolia*; **wild party**, a boisterous, unchecked, or dissolute party; **wild pig** = Captain Cooker; **wild pitch** *Baseball*, a pitch which is not hit by the batter and cannot be stopped by the catcher, enabling a base-runner to advance; hence as *v. trans.*, to enable (a runner) to advance in this way; **wild plum**: see plum *sb.* 3; **wild rice**, an aquatic grass, *Zizania aquatica*, native to North America, having seeds resembling rice and used as food; **wild rye**: see rye *sb.*[1] 2 c; a North American grass of the genus *Elymus*; **wild talent**, any of various psychic powers such as extrasensory perception, telepathy, telekinesis, etc.; **wild track** *Cinematogr.* (see quot. 1940); **wild well**, an oil well which is out of control and blowing oil or gas from the borehole (cf. sense 6 d (*c*) above); **wild wind**, a violent wind, whirlwind, hurricane (*obs.* or *dial.*); † **wild worm**, a fantastic notion, whim. See also wild cat, wild-fire, etc.

1297–1833 *Wild beast [see beast *sb.* 2 c]. **1855** Leifchild *Cornwall* 67 For fruits you have only furze and *wild-berries. **1918** H. Bindloss *Agatha's Fortune* xxi, She liked the acid wild-berries he brought on a bark tray. *c* **1205–1863** *Wild boar [see boar *sb.* 1 c]. **1484** Caxton *Fables of Æsop* I. xvi, A wyldbore..with his teeth rent..a grete pyece of his body. **1813** Scott *Rokeby* IV. xii, How the grim wild-boar fought and fell. **1940** O. Jacoby *On Poker* x. 138 The Bug, three sixes and a ten merely count as three sixes since the Bug is not strictly a *wild card. **1971** *Guardian* 17 June 12/6 Kennedy is the wild card in the 1972 Deck, as the Nixon men see it. **1976** M. Nelson *Crusoe Test* iii. 35 The joker. The wild card. The card the holder can use as he pleases. **1976** *Sunday Mail* (Brisbane) 15 Aug. 3/11 Renee was not ranked high enough to be accepted on her standard of play, but she could be nominated as the 'wild card'—a crowd pleaser. **1977** *Hongkong Standard* 14 Apr. 11/2 Fifteen-year-old Betty Newfield of the US reached the second round by defeating Marlie Buehler of Australia 4–6, 6–0, 7–5 after getting into the draw as a wild card. **1984** *Times* 21 Sept. 19/6 The wild card in the BPCC pack is Mr Maxwell's dual role as head of both BPCC and Mirror Group Newspapers. **1984** K. Buckner et al. *Using UCSD p-System* vi. 56 The wildcard '?' should be used to remove several files from a disk. **1985** *Personal Computer World* Feb. 244/1 (Advt.), Powerful wild cards permit editing of categories of file name in one instruction. **1666** *Brief Descr. Province Carolina* 4 There are many sorts of fruit Trees, as Vines, Medlars, Peach, *Wild Cherries. **1784** W. Walton *Narr. Captivity B. Gilbert* 81 They were under the Necessity of eating wild Cherries. **1972** G. Chadbund *Flowering Cherries* 11 Wild cherries occur naturally on chalky soil. **1786** tr. *Sparrman's Voy.* I. 157 These *wild dogs are some of the most pernicious beasts of prey. **1816** Byron *Siege of Corinth* xvi, The scalps were in the wild dog's maw. **1844** E. Warburton *Crescent & Cross* v, A beggar devouring his crust, but religiously leaving a portion of it in some clean spot for the wild dogs. **1877** *Encycl. Brit.* VII. 324/2 The wild dog of the Falkland Islands (*Canis antarcticus*). **1538** *Nottingham Rec.* III. 378 He kyllyd ij. *wyld duckes with a crosbow. **1676** Grew *Musæum, Anat. Stomach & Guts* viii. 33 The Wild-Duck and Teal also, I suppose all of this kind, and most other Birds, are without a Crop. **1723** J. Nott *Cook's & Confectioner's Dict.* sig. M6, Draw and truss your Wild Ducks, parboil them, and half roast them. **1881** O. Wilde *Poems* 115 The water-rat..Made for the wild-duck's nest. **1852** C. M. Yonge *Two Guardians* iii. 29 Strangers would.. think her *wild garden a collection of weeds. **1925** J. Buchan *John Macnab* xiii. 268 An expert from Kew..had made a wonderful wild garden. **1980** A. Wilson *Setting World on Fire* II. vi. 170 It's your garden parties that are ridiculous... And Rosemary's famous wild garden. **1966** 'J. Berrisford' *Wild Garden* x. 117 The *wild gardener who is also a plantsman..may grow the meconopses. **1870** W. Robinson *Wild Garden* I. 19 It [*sc.* Caucasian comfrey] will soon run about, exterminate the weeds, and prove quite a lesson in *wild and natural gardening. **1911** *Daily Colonist* (Victoria, B.C.) 30 Apr. (Mag. Section) 3/4 The cult of wild gardening is apt to run into the same kind of excesses as the pursuit of the simple life. **1978** A. J. Huxley *Illustr. Hist. Gardening* ix. 309 William Robinson and Gertrude Jekyll.. preached a return to more naturalistic and even 'wild' gardening. **1840** *Wild geranium [see ivy-berry b]. **1966** E. Palmer *Plains of Camdeboo* xvii. 281 Here and there are Pelargoniums—wild geraniums to us. **1804** M. Lewis *Jrnl.* 1 June in *Orig. Jrnls. Lewis & Clark Exped.* (1905) VI. iv. 154 *Wild ginger grows in rich bottom land. **1866** [see ginger *sb.* 2 b]. **1964** R. Perry *World of Tiger* xi. 160 The Great Indian rhino..feeding on the succulent shoots of marsh reeds and especially the wild ginger. **1973** M. Crowell *Greener Pastures* 187 We recognize the wild ginger. **1398** Trevisa *Barth. De P.R.* XVIII. xxii. (1495) bb iiij, The *wylde gote hyghte Caprea. **1530** Palsgr. 289/1 Wylde goote, *cheuereul*. **1688** Holme *Armoury* II. 162/1 The Aspian wild Goat..some term..a Shamois. **1744** Mason *Musæus* 253 Nor did the wild goat bronze the shrubby rocks. **1813** Scott *Rokeby* II. xiv, Now, like the wild goat, must he dare An unsupported leap in air. **1763** G. Milligen-Johnston *Short Descr. Prov. S. Carolina* (1770) 9 *Wild Grapes grow on this Land. **1843** [see guarri]. **1929** M. de la Roche *Whiteoaks* xvi. 202 The jewelled leaves of the wild grape..scarcely dried before another dew. **1958** G. A. Petrides *Field Guide to Trees & Shrubs* 114 The number of cultivated varieties have been developed from wild grapes. *c* **897** Ælfred *Gregory's Past. C.* xli. 303 Swa swa *wildu hors, ðonne we hie æresð ȝefangnu habbað, we hie ðacciað straciað. *c* **995** in Kemble *Cod. Dipl.* VI. 133 Hio becwið Cynelufe hyre dæl ðera wildera horsa ðe mid Eadmere synt. *a* **1250** *Owl & Night.* 1062 Þu naddest non oþer dom ne laȝe, Bute mid wilde horse were todraȝe. *c* **1375** *Sc. Leg. Saints* xxix. (*Placidas*) 318 Wyld hors & tayme. *a* **1400–50** [see horse *sb.* 1 e]. *c* **1400** *Melayne* 57 He sall be hangede or oþer morne And with wylde horse be drawen. **1424** in *Wills & Inv. N.C.* (Surtees 1835) 71, iiij Wildehorsez, ad tunc nuper tractros vel in stabulo. *c* **1546** in *Suss. Star Chamber Proc.* (1913) 36 Or ells they wolde draw hym fourth with wylde horses. **1834** Pringle *Afr. Sk.* 14 The buffalo bendeth to my yoke, The wild-horse to my rein. **1883** D. C. Murray *Hearts* xii, After that wild horses would not have drawn him to an exculpation of himself. **1890** [see horse *sb.* 1 e]. **1796** Scott (*title of poem*) The *Wild Huntsman. **1829** —— *Anne. of G.* xxii, Sailed to the mountains of the Brockenberg, where witches hold their sabbath, or gone on a hunting-party with the Wild Huntsman. **1399** Langl. *Rich. Redeles* Prol. 10 Whyle he werrid be west on þe *wilde yrisshe. **1547** Boorde *Introd. Knowl.* iii. (1870) 132 Irland..is deuyded in ii. partes, one is the Englysh pale, & the other, the wyld Irysh. **1622** Bacon *Hen. VII* 138 The Wild-Irish fled into the Woods and Bogges. **1684** Bunyan *Pilgr.* II. Introd., Highlanders, and Wild-Irish can agree My Pilgrim should familiar with them be. **1857** G. A. Lawrence *Guy Liv.* iv, The low-browed rooms where the wild Irish sat howling and wrangling over their liquor. **1401** *Close Roll 2 Hen. IV*, II. m. 6 (P.R.O.) Si Nicholaus Hogonona capellanus per suggestionem quod ipse fuit *Wildehirissheman Hibernicus et inimicus noster in prisona..detentus existat. *c* **1450** *Brut* II. 357 þese rebellis of Ireland bith callid 'wilde Irisch men'. **1608** Dekker *Lanth. & Candle-light* iii. D, No wild-Irishman could out-runne him. **1862** J. Von Haast *Geol. Westland* 25 (Morris) *Discaria toumatoo*, the Wild Irishman of the settlers. **1597** Shaks. *2 Hen. IV*, II. iv. 268 Hee playes at Quoits well,..and rides the *wilde-Mare with the Boyes. **1622** Wither *Faire-Virtue*, etc. O 4 b, The Boyes are come to catch the Owles, The Wild-mare in is bringing. **1661** M. Stevenson *Twelve Moneths* 4 And the ventrous youth show their agility in shooing the Wild-Mare. **1802** J. Drayton *View S. Carolina* 8 Small rising grounds sometimes present themselves, on which grow..*wild orange. **1858** J. A. Warder *Hedges & Evergreens* 44 Our beautiful Wild Orange..is much planted about Southern residences, for hedges. **1932** [see klapper]. **1936** F. Clune *Roaming round Darling* xvii. 165 The wild orange, ten feet high, dark green brittle leaves, large yellow-stemmed flowers, and bearing fruit as big as tennis-balls, with pomegranate seeds inside. **1969** T. H. Everett *Living Trees of World* xx. 172/1 Known as wild-orange and mock-orange, it [*sc. Prunus carolina*] has creamy white flowers and glossy black fruits. **1790** *Trans. Amer. Philos. Soc.* III. 234, I have heard this poisonous herb, called by the names of Wild-Carrot, *Wild-Parsnep, ..and Mock-Eel-Root. **1807** [see *musquash-root* s.v. musquash 3]. **1889** J. H. Maiden *Useful Native Plants Austral.* 142 The sudden death of numbers of cattle in the vicinity of Dandenong..was attributed to their having eaten a plant known as the wild parsnip. **1932** J. W. Winson *Weather & Wings* 51 The poison is described further as being 'wild-parsnip', 'cowbane', [etc.]. **1955** *Arctic Terms* 88/1 *Wild parsnip*. The cow parsnip. **1965** *Austral. Encycl.* VIII. 546/2 The wild parsnip of inland plains, does seem to be responsible for stock losses. **1925** F. Scott Fitzgerald *Lett.* (1964) 295 It is true I saved McAlmon from a beating he probably deserved and that we went on some *wild parties in London with a certain Marchioness of Milford Haven. **1970** 'D. Halliday' *Dolly & Cookie Bird* iii. 35 He was probably just afraid of the talk. It was rather a wild party. **1840** W. Deans *Let.* 30 Oct. in J. Deans *Pioneers of Canterbury* (1937) i. 29, I will visit it [*sc.* Palliser Bay] in company with 50 or 60 natives who are going to hunt *wild pigs. **1930** L. G. D. Acland *Early Canterbury Runs* 1st Ser. x. 237 Stonyhurst has always been a great place for wild pigs. **1977** C. McCullough *Thorn Birds* iv. 75 Wild pigs frightened of nothing, savage and flesh-eating, black hairy things the size of fully grown cows. **1867** *Ball Players' Chron.* 4 July 1/2 Zeller,..getting round on a passed ball and *wild pitch, came home on another passed ball. **1970** *Washington Post* 30 Sept. D1/8 In the first game, young Bob Grich led off the home 10th with a single and Coleman wild-pitched him to second base. **1979** *Arizona Daily Star* 1 Apr. c6/4 Greg Laing walked in the bottom of the eighth and scored on a wild pitch. **1748** H. Ellis *Voy. Hudson's-Bay* 170 By the Sides of Lakes and Rivers there is abundance of *wild Rice. **1778** J. Carver *Trav. N.-Amer.* 522 Wild Rice ..grows in the greatest plenty throughout the interior parts of North America. **1911** G. S. Porter *Harvester* vi. 94 Wild rice..he had planted for the birds. **1934** H. Miller *Tropic of Cancer* 47 They were eating too. A young chicken with wild rice. **1980** *Times Lit. Suppl.* 26 Sept. 1064/5 The paper ..was full of reports of discontent around Ompah at overcropping of wildrice. **1984** *Times* 13 June 9/4 Wild rice is not really rice at all but the seeds of a grass that grows wild along the waters-edge of lakes in Minnesota, Wisconsin and southern Canada. **1751** C. Gist *Jrnl.* 27 Jan. (1893) 43 The *wild Rye appeared very green and flourishing. **1968** F. W. Gould *Grass Systematics* 181 Widespread and variable in the United States are *Elymus canadensis* L., Canada wildrye, and *E. virginicus* L., Virginia wildrye. **1944** A. Huxley *Let.* 28 July (1969) 510 The fact of what Charles Fort calls '*wild talents' is admitted by all open-minded people. **1960** K. Amis *New Maps of Hell* (1961) iv. 98 A new type of human being, sometimes outré in appearance, more often gifted with the 'wild talent' which has become a science fiction catch-phrase and convention. **1940** *Chambers's Techn. Dict.* 908/2 **Wild track*, a soundtrack which is recorded independently of any photographic track or mute, but is destined to be used in editing a sound-film. **1980** 'P. Loraine' *Lions' Ransom* I. iii. 51 Fox was..making a 'wild-track' of Busai's morning birdsong. **1915** Redwood & Eastlake *Petroleum Technologist's Pocket-bk.* iv. 244 '**Wild' well.* This term is used to denote a well which produces such quantities of oil or gas, or both, under such high pressure that it is either impossible to bring it under control or it is only controlled when a very considerable time has elapsed after the oil or gas has been met with. **1977** *Sunday Times* 24 Apr. 1/2 If the wild well..is not brought under control within the next 24 hours, the fight could last for weeks, months even. *a* **1661** FULLER *Worthies, Essex* (1662) I. 319 In the year of our Lord 1639 in November here happened an Hirecano or *wild wind. **1821** CLARE *Vill. Minstrel* (1823) I. 79 The frighted wild-wind trembles to a breeze. *a* **1548** HALL *Chron., Rich. III* 42 The *wilde worme of vengaunce wauerynge in his hed. *Ibid., Hen. V* 44 Some priuate Scorpion in your heartes, or some wild worme in your heades.

attrib. **1801** *Marvellous Love-Story* II. 198 Raree-shows, and wild-beast exhibitions. **1834** LYTTON *Pompeii* I. iii, When is our next wild-beast fight? **1879** BROWNING *Halbert & Hob* 10 The genuine wild-beast breed. *a* **1850** MRS. BROWNING *Confessions* ix, Then, at least, have the Human shared with thee their wild berry-wine? **1918** H. BINDLOSS *Agatha's Fortune* xxvii, He..fell among a clump of wild-berry canes. **1776** MICKLE tr. *Camoens' Lusiad* III. 89 Dextrous in the wild-boar chace. **1818** KEATS *Teignmouth* ii, No wild-boar tushes and no Mermaid's toes. **1842** *Dumfries Herald* Oct., That fine flavour..in the wild-boar ham. **1866** *Treas. Bot., Wild-boar's tree*, a San Domingo name for *Hedwigia balsamifera*. **1970** *New Yorker* 3 Oct. 34/3 The other thirteen games..will be 'wild-card' encounters, to be played on alternate Monday nights. **1981** *Washington Post* 18 Mar. D3 The conference championship games are now played on the home field of the competitor that has the best season record, unless it's a wild-card team. **1984** K. BUCKNER et al. *Using UCSD p-System* xv. 156 the WILD unit makes available wild card pattern matching on string variables. **1899** S. O. JEWETT *Queen's Twin* 81 She had a sprig of wild-cherry blossom in her dress. *a* **1916** 'SAKI' *Toys of Peace* (1919) 82 By the time they had arrived at the wild duck course it was beginning to be a rather expensive lunch. **1703** *Lond. Gaz.* No. 3966/4 Stolen or strayed.., two Mares, one a white-grey,..has the Wild Mare Hunch with the far hind Leg. **1824** CARR *Craven Gloss., Wild-mare-hinch* or *hitch*, string-halt. **1964** HALL & WHANNELL *Popular Arts* ix. 258 The..combined use of wild-track voices with counter-pointing visual images.

fig. **1847** TENNYSON *Princess* v. 256, I.., when first I heard War-music, felt the blind wildbeast of force.. Stir in me. **1886** GILLMORE *Hunter's Arcadia* p. vii, Some bastard descendants of Europeans..this weapon is better than argument with such wild beasts.

17. Combinations. **a.** with pples., in adverbial relation (= 'wildly') as ***wild-billowing***, ***-booming***, ***-flying***, ***-fought***, ***-made***, ***-staring***, ***-warring***, ***-woven*** adjs.; or in complemental relation, as ***wild-born***, ***-bred***, ***-caught***, ***-grown***, ***looking*** adjs. **b.** parasynthetic, as ***wild-blooded***, ***-brained***, ***-coloured***, ***-eyed***, ***-haired***, ***-headed***, ***-hearted***, ***-spirited***, ***-winged***, ***-witted*** adjs. **c.** with sbs., forming descriptive appellations corresponding to the adjs. in b, as ***wild-blood*** (a wild-blooded person), ***-brain***, ***-head*** (a wild-brained or wild-headed person, a hare-brain).

1837 CARLYLE *Fr. Rev.* III. VII. viii, One red sea of Fire, *wild-billowing, enwraps the World. **1820** SCOTT *Abbot* xix, Even in the Castle of Avenel thou wert a *wild-blood enough. **1837** CARLYLE *Fr. Rev.* III. v. ii, So..whirls and spins this immeasurable *tormentum* of a Revolution; *wild-booming. **1816** BYRON *Ch. Har.* III. xv, A *wild-born falcon with clipt wing. **1580** HOLLYBAND *Treas. Fr. Tong, Testu*, a headstrong fellow, a *wildebrayne. **1608** MIDDLETON *Mad World* I. i, I must..turn wilde-braine, lay my wits vpo' th' Tenters. **1894** 'MARK TWAIN' in *Harper's Mag.* Oct. (1914) 675/2 *Wild-brained martyrdom was succeeded by uprising and organization. **1885** RIDER HAGGARD *K. Sol. Mines* vi, We knew what a wonderful instinct these *wild-bred men possess. **1888** *Pall Mall Gaz.* 20 Sept. 3/1 Wild-bred pheasants appear to have done fairly well. **1949** *Amer. Speech* XXIV. 98 American mink..may be either *wild-caught or ranch-raised. **1970** SAUNDERS & PHELPS in H. W. Mulligan *Afr. Trypanosomiases* xiv. 329 The ovaries of wild-caught females..can be used. **1954** M. K. WILSON tr. *K. Z. Lorenz's Man meets Dog* (1964) xix. 176 The striped markings in the face of the '*wild-coloured' cat enhance the least movements of the facial skin. **1817** SHELLEY *Rev. Islam* IV. xx, The *wild-eyed women. **1890** 'R. BOLDREWOOD' *Col. Reformer* xx, The fierce and wild-eyed bullocks. **1617** FLETCHER *Valentinian* I. ii, His *wild flying courses. **1902** S. PHILLIPS *Ulysses* I. ii, The wild-flying cloud. **1795** FAWCETT *Art of War* 18 Their *wild-fought field. **1885** W. K. PARKER *Mammal. Desc.* vi. 153 The peri-chondrial..bone..takes on a very remarkable form; it becomes *wild-grown so to speak. **1872** J. G. WHITTIER in *Atlantic Monthly* Apr. 474 The *wild-haired Bacchant's yell. **1896** HOWELLS *Impr. & Exper.* 24 The wildest-haired Comeouter. **1583** STUBBES *Anat. Abus.* I. (1879) 147 All the *wilde-heds of the Parish, conuenting togither. *c* **1590** *Trag. Rich. II* (1870) 13 A wild-head, yett a kingly gentleman. *a* **1400–50** *Wars Alex.* 12 Sum..þat ere *wild-hedid. **1583** GOLDING *Calvin on Deut.* iv. 1 If they that neuer were taught Gods trueth bee wildeheaded. **1617** MORYSON *Itin.* I. 259 A wild-headed Turke tooke my hat from my head. **1702** CALAMY *Abridgm. Baxter's Life* vi. 108 Wild-headed Sectaries. **1904** W. DE LA MARE *Henry Brocken* viii. 83 Beasts of a long-sharpened sagacity, *wild-hearted, rebellious. **1916** JOYCE *Portrait of Artist* (1969) iv. 171 He was alone and young and wilful and wild-hearted. **1814** SCOTT *Diary* 16 Aug. in *Lockhart*, The hogs are..queer *wild-looking creatures. **15..** *Sir Andrew Barton* xvii. in *Surtees Misc.* (1890) 69 Before Ile leave off my serving God, My *wild maide oeth may brooken be. **1856** MISS YONGE *Daisy Chain* I. xxvii, His warm-hearted, *wild-spirited son. **1608** SYLVESTER *Du Bartas* II. iv. III. *Schism* 863 *Wilde-staring Hag. **1727** SOMERVILLE *Occas. Poems, Offic. Messenger* 261 Wild-staring, thunder-struck, and dumb. **1748** THOMSON *Cast. Indol.* I. xli, *Wild-warbling nature. **1777** POTTER *Æschylus* 64 With vollied thunders and *wild warring winds. *c* **1611** CHAPMAN *Iliad* xv. 637 Floods that nourish *wild-wing'd fowles. **1906** HARDY *Dynasts* II. I. v. 161 A straggler merely he... But they decide, At last, to post his news, wild-winged or no. **1936** L. B. LYON *Bright Feather Fading* 45 The wild-winged bliss. **1614** J. COOKE *Greene's Tu Quoque* D I b, *Wilde witted sister, I haue preuented you. **1839** DARLEY *Beaum. & Fl. Wks.* I. Introd. p. xlix, A wild-witted, mercurial comedy. **1800** CAMPBELL *Exile of Erin* ii, The *wild-woven flowers.

d. in nonce *poet.* uses, as ***wild-worst***, ***-worth***.

1876 G. M. HOPKINS *Poems* (1967) 59 The cross to her she calls Christ to her, christens her wild-worst Best. *c* **1878** *Ibid.* 75 Only the breathing temple and fleet Life, this wildworth blown so sweet.

B. *sb.*

†**1.** A wild animal, or wild animals collectively; *spec.* a beast, or beasts, of the chase; a hunted animal or animals; game. *Obs.*

OE. *wild (see etym. above) is recorded only in gen. sing. *wildres*, nom. pl. *wildru*, gen. *wildra*, dat. *wildrum*.

c **1205** LAY. 1129 þa Troinisce men tuhten to þon deoren & duden of þan wilden al heora iwilla. **13..** *Gaw. & Gr. Knt.* 1150 At þe fyrst quethe of þe quest quaked þe wylde. *a* **1340** HAMPOLE *Psalter* xlix. [l.] 11 All þe wilde of wodis. ? *a* **1400** *Morte Arth.* 657 That nane werreye my wylde, botte Way-nour hir seluene. *c* **1465** *Chevy Chase* vi, Then the wyld thorowe the woodes went, on euery syde shear. *c* **1480** HENRYSON *Lion & Mouse* xxviii, The lioun..slew baith tayme and wyld. **1599** ALEX. HUME *Poems* (S.T.S.) *Hymn* ii. 181 All venneson, an vther wilde they serue him at his neid.

†**2.** Phr. *at wild, on wild*: ? bewildered, distracted. *Obs. rare.*

c **1430** *Syr Tryam.* 801 Some were wery and on wylde. **1477** *Paston Lett.* III. 179 Trust hym never the more for the bylle that I sent yow by hym, but as a man at wylde, for every thyng that he told me is not trewe.

3. a. (*a*) A wild or waste place; a region or tract of uncultivated and uninhabited land; a waste, a wilderness. Now mostly *rhet.* or *poet.*

1637 HEYLIN *Answ. Burton* 191 As if wee lived in the wild of Africke. **1667** MILTON *P.L.* I. 407 The wild Of South-most Abarim. **1709** PRIOR *Henry & Emma* 395 Nor Wild, nor Deep our common Way divide. **1722** TICKELL *Kens. Garden* I A snow of blossoms, and a wilde of flowers. **1732** POPE *Ess. Man* I. 7 A wild, where weeds and flow'rs promiscuous shoot. **1847** TENNYSON *Princess* III. 230 You young savage of the Northern wild! **1849** MACAULAY *Hist. Eng.* iii. I. 313 Turned from a wild into a garden. **1905** D. WALLACE *Labrador Wild* iv. 55 The plunge into the wild.

(*b*) *pl.* (Chiefly in ***the wilds of*** a specified region.)

1596 SHAKS. *Merch. V.* II. vii. 41 The Hircanion deserts, and the vaste wildes Of wide Arabia. **1612** DRAYTON *Polyolb.* v. 312 The sandie Wyldes of spicefull Barbarie. **1634** MILTON *Comus* 424 Huge Forests..and sandy perilous wildes. **1726–31** WALDRON *Descr. Isle of Man* (1744) 53 They call them the good People, and say they live in Wilds and Forests. **1827** J. F. COOPER *Prairie* i, The..resolute forester who first penetrated the wilds. **1842** DICKENS *Amer. Notes* viii, Among the wilds and forests of the west. **1868** NETTLESHIP *Ess. Browning* ii. 63 A northern principality.. which kept its rough simple traditions in its own wilds.

b. *transf.* of air, water, etc.

1712 POPE *Rape Lock* I. 107 The crystal wilds of air. **1795** WOLCOT (P. Pindar) *Frogmore Fête* Wks. 1812 III. 308 As soon might lift old Ocean from his bed And dash his wild of waters to the skies. **1813** SHELLEY *Q. Mab* VIII. 57 A lighthouse o'er the wild of dreary waves.

c. *fig.*

1596 SHAKS. *Merch. V.* III. ii. 184 Where euery something being blent together, Turnes to a wilde of nothing, saue of ioy Exprest, and not exprest. **1599** NASHE *Lenten Stuff* 66 To this wild of sorrowes and excruciament she was confined. **1651** BIGGS *New Disp.* ⁋73 [To] confine themselves to a mediocrity in opinioning, and not ramble over the whole wild of Fancy. *a* **1704** T. BROWN *1st Sat. Persius imit.* Wks. 1730 I. 52 His tagg'd nonsense, t'other's wilds of wit. *a* **1832** BENTHAM *Princ. Legisl.* xviii. §27 *note* Striving to cut a new road through the wilds of jurisprudence. **1855** TENNYSON *Maud* I. XVI. i, To save My yet young life in the wilds of Time.

4. Phr. ***to play the wild***: to behave in a careless or reckless manner; to play havoc *with*. *U.S.*

1849 J. B. JONES *Wild Western Scenes* i. 10 But love can play the 'wild' with any young man. **1911** R. D. SAUNDERS *Col. Todhunter* ix. 143 I'm shorely glad to get home. I been playin' the wild in St. Louis.

wild (waɪld), *v. rare.* [f. WILD *a.* Cf. AWILDEN (OE. *áwildian*), MHG. *wilden*.]

1. *intr.* Of an animal or plant: To be or become wild; to run wild, grow wild.

a **1225** *Ancr. R.* 136 Vet kelf & to wilde is þet fleschs þet awilgeð [*MS. T.* wildes] so sone hit euer uetteð. **1387–8** T. USK *Test. Love* I. iii. (Skeat) l. 45 Heerdes gonne to wilde. **1880** EARLE *Engl. Plant Names* 80 This is held by botanists to be an old garden-plant escaped and wilded.

2. *trans.* To make wild, in various senses; †*esp.* to affect with frenzy, to madden (*obs.*).

1421 HOCCLEVE *Compl.* 235 This grevous venyme that had enfectyd and wildyd my brayne. **1628** FELTHAM *Resolves* II. [I.] xxii. 71 The Mad worme hath wilded all Humanitie. **1655** VAUGHAN *Silex Scint.* I. *Misery* 81 Thus wilded by a peevish heart..I storm at thee.

wild(e, obs. ff. WEALD, WIELD *v.*; obs. pa. t. of WILL *v.*

wildbore. *local.* [?] A stout and closely woven unglazed tammy.

1784 *Salem Gaz.* in Alice M. Earle *Costume Colonial Times* (1894) 257 Marone Ribb'd Wildbores. **1788** *Massachusetts Spy* 23 Oct. 3/4 Wildbore Camblets. **1798** *Times* 28 June 4/4 Durants, Callimancoes, Wildbores, &c. **1852** in A. Holroyd *Collect. Bradf.* (1873) 179 About 1813, Messrs. James Akroyd and Son, of Halifax,..produced the articles known by the names of wildbores and plainbacks, from which sprung the single-twilled merinos. **1857** J. JAMES *Worsted Manuf.* 374 A dobby piece was..nothing more than a figured wildbore. *Ibid.* 627 About the year 1783, their use [*sc.* Leeds camblets]..began to decline, and the stuff makers at Leeds commenced making wildbores. **1876** CUDWORTH *Round about Bradford* 330 The worsted business,..the principal make being shalloons and wildbores.

†**wild bred.** *Obs. rare.* [ad. ON. *villibráð*, corresp. to MLG. *viltbrêde*, *-brêt*, also *-brât* (LG. *wil(d)brat*, *-prät*), MHG. *wildbræte*, *-brât* (G. *wildbret*), etc.: see WILD *a.* and BREDE *sb.*[1]] Game, venison.

c **1375** *Cursor M.* 13373 (Fairfax) þat folk..was fed Wiþ soiþen & roste & wilde bred [*Cott.* O bred and flexs bath soþen and bredd].

wild cat. (Also with hyphen, or, esp. in early use, as one word.) Forms: see WILD *a.* and CAT *sb.*[1]; also *β.* (*Sc.*) 6 **wilkatt**, 8 **wilcat**, **wil'-cat**, 9 **wull-cat**. [Cf. MLG. *wildkatte*, MHG. *wilde katze* (G. *wildkatze*), Sw. *vildkatt*, Da. *-kat*.]

1. The European wild species of cat, *Felis catus* (see CAT *sb.*[1] 1 c); also applied to other wild animals of the cat tribe, esp. in U.S. to species of lynx. †Also *pl.*, the skins of these used as fur.

1418 *E.E. Wills* (1882) 37 A gowne of gray russet furred wit Ionetis and wylde Catis. **14..** *Voc.* in Wr.-Wülcker 591/26 *Laero, -ronis, est quoddam animal pilosum ut cuniculus secundum alios*, a wylde cat. *c* **1480** HENRYSON *Wolf & Wether* viii, Nouther wolf, wyld-cat, nor ȝit tod. **1566** *Act 8 Eliz.* c. 15 §2 For the Heade of everie Fitchewe Polcatte or Wilde Catte, one peny. **1596** SHAKS. *Merch. V.* II. v. 48 He sleepes by day More then the wilde-cat. **1682** T. A. *Carolina* 20 The Tyger, Wolf, and wild Cat. **1805** SCOTT *Let.* in *Lockhart* (1837) II. ii. 51 We have a curious breed of wild-cats who have eaten all Charlotte's chickens. **1843** MACAULAY *Horatius* xlv, Then, like a wild cat mad with wounds, Sprang right at Astur's face. **1884** *Marcus Clarke Mem. Vol.* 127 How many nights..have I listened to the skirr of the wild cats. **1904** *Daily Chron.* 31 Mar. 7/3 A terrible struggle between a man and a monstrous wildcat.

β. **1596** DALRYMPLE tr. *Leslie's Hist. Scot.* (S.T.S.) I. 7 To hunte the hair and the fox,..the Wolfe, or the Wilkatt. *c* **1730** RAMSAY *Fables* XIX. 44 The tyger, bair, and ev'ry powerfu' fur, Down to the wilcat and the snarling cur. **1818** SCOTT *Hrt. Midl.* x, I never ask what brings the Laird of Dumbiedikes glowering here like a wull-cat..day after day. **1887** P. MCNEILL *Blawearie* 153 Still haudin' on till its tail wi' the determination of a wull-cat.

2. *fig.* Applied to a savage, ill-tempered, or spiteful person, esp. a woman: cf. CAT *sb.*[1] 2.

†*to run wild-cat* (quot. *a* 1652): to 'run mad', become demented: cf. WILD *a.* 12, and the *attrib.* use in 4 b below.

1573–80 TUSSER *Husb.* (1878) 168 Where window is open, cat maketh a fray, Yet wilde cat with two legs is worse by my fay. **1596** SHAKS. *Tam. Shr.* I. ii. 197 But will you woo this Wilde-cat? **1612** N. FIELD *Woman is a Weathercock* I. ii, Like a Wilde-Cat of Pickt-hatch. *a* **1652** BROME *Damoiselle* I. i, The care of Children's such a startle-braine, That had I more then one, I should run Wild-cat. **1771** SMOLLETT *Humphry Cl.* 17 Apr. (1815) 14 That wild-cat my sister Tabby. **1894** CROCKETT *Raiders* xiii, 'Come back to your post, ye wull cat,' I shouted.

3. *fig.* **a.** One who forms a rash project, or engages in a risky or unsafe enterprise. **b.** An unsound business undertaking, as a 'wild-cat bank' (see 4 b); also, a note, or notes collectively, of a 'wild-cat bank'. (Orig. and chiefly *U.S. colloq.*)

1812 *Columbian Centinel* 6 June 2/5 Some of the Wild-cats of Congress. **1839** MRS. KIRKLAND *New Home* xxxi. 204 The celebrated term 'Wild Cat,' justified fully by the course of these cunning and stealthy bloodsuckers. **1861** 'MARK TWAIN' *Lett.* (1917) I. iii. 54 'Wild cat' isn't worth ten cents. **1883** F. M. CRAWFORD *Dr. Claudius* x, Complacent holders of preferred, and scatter-brained speculators in wild-cat. **1896** *Nation* (N.Y.) 3 Dec. 417/2 Whether this feature of our banking system can be amended without giving the field to wildcats. **1902** *Westm. Gaz.* 7 Aug. 9/1 The market has been crowded with 'wild cats'.

c. An exploratory oil-well, drilled where there is only a possibility of success. Cf. WILD *a.* 6 d, *wild well* s.v. WILD *a.* 16.

1877 *Sci. Amer.* 22 Dec. 387/3 A large number of 'wildcats', or test wells, have gone down off the eastern edge of the defined line, but with very few exceptions they have proved to be dusters. **1943** *Jrnl. Sedimentary Petrol.* XIII. 111/2 Both deep, off-structure wildcats and field wells are important. **1977** *Offshore Engineer* May 39/1 Esso is drilling in the deepest water off Egypt's Mediterranean coast with a second wildcat in 470m of water 100km off Alexandria.

d. Illicitly distilled whisky. Cf. *wild-cat whisky*, sense 4 b.

1887 A. A. BROWN *Lumbering on Cumberland* vii. 80 Mr. Kearney alighted and tendered us a drink from his bottle of 'wild cat'. **1945** M. LYON *Fresh from Hills* iv. 47 You can keep on a-makin' wildcat till hell freezes over.

e. *ellipt.* for *wildcat strike*, sense 4 c below.

1959 *Daily Mail* 28 Oct. 1 (*heading*) War on the wild-cats. **1969** *Guardian* 22 Aug. 9/1 The TUC made their 'solemn and binding declaration' to the Prime Minister about dealing with wildcats. **1978** J. WAINWRIGHT *Ripple of Murders* 43 They'd thought he was bluffing... So there's been wildcats and pickets, and lock-ins.

4. *attrib.* (usually with hyphen). **a.** *lit.* in sense 1: Of a wild cat.

1624 CAPT. J. SMITH *Virginia* I. 17 Some..wilde Catte skinnes. **1863** W. C. BALDWIN *Afr. Hunting* ix. 421 Jackal and wild-cat skins.

b. *fig.* Applied to banks in the western United States which, before the passing of the National Bank Act of 1863, fraudulently issued notes with little or no capital, or to their notes or transactions; hence extended to unsound or risky business enterprises generally; also to illicit businesses or their products (e.g. ***wild-cat whisky***); and more widely to reckless, rash, or extravagant undertakings, statements, etc. (cf.

WILD *a.* 13), and (*colloq.*) with reference to wildcat strikes (see sense 4 c below).

This application is said to have arisen from the fact that the notes of a bank in Michigan bore the device of a panther, locally known by the name 'wild cat'.

1838 *The Jeffersonian* (Albany) 14 Apr. 72/3 About 400 Irishmen working on the canal, took offence at being paid in 'Wild Cat' money, instead of Illinois. **1839** Mrs. Kirkland *New Home* xxxi. 205 Once in the grasp of a 'wild cat bank,' his struggles were unavailing. *a* **1854** W. North *Slave of Lamp* 38 (Bartlett) Much bogus coin and wild-cat, red dog bills are in circulation. **1881** Hughes *Rugby, Tennessee* ii. v, Wild-cat whisky—or 'moonshine' as the favourite illicit beverage of the mountains is called. **1890** *Daily News* 12 Nov. 6/2 In no way did I undertake to uphold Major Barttelot in any wild-cat expedition. **1959** *Daily Tel.* 31 Dec. 11/2 'Wildcat' risk in bank staffs. **1973** *Black Panther* 29 Sept. 3/3 A majority of the Black workers..voted..to reject the union proposal, upholding the original wildcat demand. **1976** M. Machlin *Pipeline* xix. 241 Some people think it was some wildcat members of 798 that set them after the company laid off about a hundred of them.

c. Special Comb.: **wildcat drilling**, the drilling of a wildcat well; **wildcat strike**, a sudden and unofficial strike; hence **wildcat striker**; similarly ***wildcat stoppage***, ***walkout***; **wildcat train** *U.S.*, an extra train running in addition to those on the timetable (see quot. 1885); occas. *ellipt.*; similarly ***wildcat engine***; **wildcat well** = sense 3 c above.

1937 *Bull. Amer. Assoc. Petroleum Geologists* XXI. 1079 A study of wildcat drilling in the Gulf Coast Plains during 1935 and 1936 indicates that between 7 and 11 per cent of all such holes opened new oil or gas pools, the remaining 93–89 per cent having been dry. These figures speak eloquently of the risk involved in wildcat drilling. **1976** *Offshore Platforms & Pipelining* 60/1 The time span from hard freeze in late autumn to the melt in the late spring leaves an opportunity for no more than about 6,000 ft of wildcat drilling. **1888** *Missouri Republican* 23 Feb., The Montreal night express was thrown from the track..by a wild-cat engine that had been turned loose..by an evil-disposed person. **1891** E. S. Ellis *Check No. 2134* xiii. 88 There was just one chance in a hundred of a wild-cat engine approaching. **1974** *Telegraph* (Brisbane) 5 Feb. 16/1 Freelance truckers entered the fifth day of their wildcat stoppage. **1937** *Sun* (Baltimore) 16 Nov. 3/1 A clause.. conceding to the corporation the right to discipline persons responsible for 'wildcat' strikes. **1954** *Encounter* June 7/2 [The workers'] behaviour itself becomes a judgement... It ..takes the form of slow-downs, a silent war against production standards, and most spectacularly in the violent eruptions of wildcat strikes against 'speed-ups' or changes in the timing of jobs. **1978** S. Brill *Teamsters* v. 179 Carey led a militant wildcat strike over a symbolic issue. **1945** *Chicago Daily News* 10 Dec. 1/9 (*caption*) Would fire or fine wildcat strikers. **1981** M. Nabb *Death of Englishman* ii. iii. 89 He wasn't going to stand by and see his country insulted, disrupted..by wildcat strikers. **1870** *Daily Territorial Enterprise* (Virginia City, Nevada) 22 Oct. 3/1 In company with four or five others, he had gone out on the road upon a hand car, when a 'wild cat train' (an extra train running on no regular time) overtook them. **1885** *Good Words* July 452/1 Every now and then the newspapers allude to 'wild-cat' trains... The 'wild-cat' is the slowest of all trains. It is only used for freight, and reaches its destination when it can, running whenever the line is clear, and shunting when a passenger train is due on the same track. **1942** *Sun* (Baltimore) 26 Sept. 9/6 Our estimated 400 were out in what both union and management termed a 'wildcat' walkout. **1977** *Time* 28 Mar. 46/2 The month-long wildcat walkout by 3,000 precision toolmakers at British Leyland. **1883** *Century Mag.* July 331/2 When he begins to put down a wild-cat well, he usually leases all the land in the vicinity. **1907** *Bull. U.S. Geol. Survey* No. 318. 25 In making maps of subsurface strata in areas that have not been productive, most of the records used for making a convergence sheet must be taken from 'wild-cat wells'. **1975** W. G. Roberts *Quest for Oil* (rev. ed.) iii. 35 It is nowadays extremely rare to hear of anyone sinking a true 'wildcat' well—that is, one drilled simply because someone has a hunch that his patch of ground has oil beneath.

wild-catter. [f. WILD CAT + -ER[1].] **a.** A prospector who sinks wildcat wells. **b.** A wildcat striker.

1883 *Century Mag.* July 327/2 The 'wild-catters,' as the prospectors are called who take the risks of sinking wells in unknown territory. **1925** A. B. Thompson *Oil-Fields Explor. & Devel.* I. vii. 314 The speculative spirit aroused by the gusher has had much to do with..inspiring the wild-catter to pursue his quest for extended areas of development. **1947** R. Bedichek *Adv. with Texas Naturalist* x. 116, I left the highway, following an old road which led me to the site of some wildcatters' dream and disillusionment. **1966** *Punch* 23 Mar. 404/3 That union refusing membership to a one-armed labourer may have had a point. Just as you don't hit a boy with glasses, even the wildest wildcatter might jib at intimidating this man. **1973** [see SHOOT-'EM-UP]. **1980** A. Coppel *Hastings Conspiracy* iv. 31 The militant wildcatters or the British air traffic controllers' union. **1981** *Sci. Digest* Aug. 118/3 Like wildcatters bringing in a gusher, a few of the students develop products with gilt-edged possibilities.

wild-catting, *vbl. sb.* [f. WILD CAT + -ING[1].] The action of engaging in a 'wild-cat' business or enterprise; *spec.* (*a*) the drilling of a wildcat well; (*b*) participation in a wildcat strike; occas. also as *ppl. a.*

1883 *Century Mag.* July 331/1 'Wild-catting' is the name applied to the venturesome business of drilling [oil] wells on territory not known to contain oil. **1893** *Nation* (N.Y.) 2 Feb. 76/3 The kind of wild-catting and red-dogging that was rife before the war. **1909** W. S. Tower *Story of Oil* v. 66 Many of the most valuable oil deposits..have been revealed by the more or less random process of 'wild-catting'. **1967** *Economist* 18 Mar. 1014/2 Just like wild-catting shop stewards, they [*sc.* demonstrators] brought into disrepute the cause that they affected to support. **1969** *Guardian* 22 Sept. 15/1 The West Berlin workers decided that anything their Ruhr brothers can do in the way of wildcatting the Berliners can do better. **1972** L. M. Harris *Introd. Deepwater Floating Drilling Operations* xv. 159 Nearly always, a floating drilling operation is a wildcatting venture in an area previously undrilled. **1976** M. Machlin *Pipeline* xxxii. 370 The way things are going these days, I think I might just go back to the wildcatting in East Texas.

wild deer. [In sense 1, OE. *wil(d)déor, wildedéor*, alteration (after *wilde* adj. WILD and *déor* DEER) of **wildor*, pl. *wildru*: see WILD *a.* etym. (Cf. ON. *villidýr*, OSw. *vil(li)diur*, Da. *vildtdyr*.) In sense 2, f. WILD *a.* + DEER.]

†**1.** A wild animal. Chiefly *collect. Obs.*

c **825** [see WILD *a.* 1]. *c* **888** Ælfred *Boeth.* xxxix. §1 Swa swa wilde deor willnað oðer to acwellenne. **971** *Blickl. Hom.* 95 Ac biþ þonne reþra & þearlwisra þonne ænig wilde deor. *c* **1175**, *c* **1200** [see DEER 1 β]. *c* **1205** Lay. 1125 Ah swa monie þar waren wilde deor. *c* **1250** *Gen. & Ex.* 169 De sexte dais li3t, So made god..Al erue, and wrim, and wilde der. **1338** R. Brunne *Chron.* (1810) 110 Þe kyng no man suld deme in courte for wilde dere.

2. Deer in a wild state.

1748 Thomson *Cast. Indol.* ii. xvii, The wild-deer bouncing thro' the glade. **1817** Shelley *Rev. Islam* x. iv, The roaring Of fire, whose floods the wild deer circumvent In the scorched pastures of the South. **1896** Visct. Ebrington in *Red Deer* 245 Wild deer in their extremity do get into as curious places as carted ones.

wilde: see WIELD, WILD, WILL *v.*

Wildean ('waɪldɪən), *a.* [f. the name of Oscar *Wilde* (see below) + -AN.] Of, pertaining to, or characteristic of the Irish writer Oscar Fingal O'Flahertie Wills Wilde (1854–1900), or his works.

1924 *Nation* 26 Mar. 352/1 Epigrams are his undoing. The Wildean nineties are in his blood. **1937** *Scrutiny* V. 386 Ravel is Wildean, 'witty' in the nineteenth century salon. **1958** R. Williams *Culture & Society* ii. ii. 171 A good example of the Wildean paradox. **1967** *Listener* 6 July 15/1 Social morality is turned on its head with a Wildean comment on one of the film's less violent fatalities: 'Marie's tragic death restored my faith in suicide.' **1977** *Time* 21 Feb. 28/3 They are cold, loveless creatures, incapable of responding to one another except by lobbing epigrams, Wildean in rhythm but not in wit, back and forth.

‖**wildebeest** ('vɪldəbeːst, -biːst, 'wɪ-). Also wildebees. [S. African Du., f. *wild* WILD *a.* + *beest* BEAST *sb.*] The gnu, *Connochætes taurinus* or *C. gnou*.

[**1801** J. Barrow *Acct. Trav. S. Afr.* I. iv. 259 The *gnoo* or *wild beast*, as it is called by the Dutch.] **1824** W. J. Burchell *Trav. S. Afr.* II. 109 Wild animals; among which were.. many *wilde-beests* or *gnues*. **1838** W. C. Harris *Narr. Exped. S. Africa* 380 *Catoblepas Gnoo*. The Gnoo. Wilde Beest of the Cape Colonists. **1850** R. G. Cumming *Hunter's Life S. Afr.* iv. 84 Having inspected the wildebeest bull, which was a noble specimen. **1889** Rider Haggard *Allan's Wife* iii, Here to the right might be a herd of vilderbeeste that could not number less than two thousand. **1895** Millais *Breath from Veldt* x. 218 The white-tailed gnu or black wildebeest. **1929** D. Reitz *Commando* 129 Great herds of zebra, wildebeest, and sable, stood fearlessly gazing at us. **1958** *Cape Times* 13 Aug. 3/4 For the rest it was impala, wildebeest and koodoo. **1970** *Life* Jan. 50 Their faces covered with grotesque tufts of hair, the wildebeest..are the oddest and fiercest-looking antelopes.

wilder ('wɪldə(r)), *v. arch.* (now chiefly *poet.*) [Of uncertain origin: prob. (by an unusual process) extracted from WILDERNESS on the analogy of the form of *wander*; but cf. MDu. *verwilderen*, frequent. of *verwilden* (f. *ver-* FOR-*prefix*[1] + *wilde, wilt* WILD *a.*), and G. *wildern*. It has been frequently apprehended as an aphetic f. BEWILDER (which is later in appearance), and occas. spelt '*wilder*.]

1. *trans.* To cause to lose one's way, as in a wild or unknown place; to lead or drive astray; *refl.* to lose one's way, go astray.

1613 Purchas *Pilgrimage* viii. ix. 653 Unknowne Lands, where we have wildered our selves. *a* **1620** J. Dyke *Sel. Serm.* (1640) 138 They had been in danger of being wilderd, of losing their way. **1687** Dryden *Hind & P.* ii. 682 This she desir'd her to accept and stay, For fear she might be wilder'd in her way. **1717** Addison tr. *Ovid's Met.* iii. 236 Young Actæon, wilder'd in the wood. **1796** Southey *Hymn to the Penates* 96 O ye whom Youth has wilder'd on your way. **1819** Shelley *New Nat. Anthem* iv, 'Wilder her enemies In their own dark disguise.

b. *fig.*; *esp.* to render at a loss how to act, or what to think; to perplex, bewilder.

1642 D. Rogers *Naaman* 55 Having himselfe sent for him to his house, when he was wildred. **1648–9** *Eikon Bas.* xv. 131 Extravagances wherewith some men have now even wildred..both Church and State. **1654** E. Johnson *Wonder-wkg. Provid.* ii. 4 You shall be left wildred and strange Revelations. **1701** Collier *M. Aurel.* 259 His Understanding, being misty and misled, he was willdred in the Qualities of Things, and mistook the Nature of Good and Evil. **1811** Shelley *St. Irvyne* Pr. Wks. 1888 I. 218 Wolfstein,..wildered by the suscitated energies of his soul almost to madness. **1816** —— *Alastor* 139 To her cold home Wildered, and wan, and panting, she returned. **1887** Bowen *Virg. Æneid* iv. 69 Over the city she wanders, the sad Queen, wildered of thought.

2. *intr.* To lose one's way, go astray, stray, wander; to be bewildered; to move or extend in a confused way.

1658 Gurnall *Chr. in Arm.* ii. 39 A heavy curse, did we rightly judge of it, to wander and wilder in a maze of errour. *a* **1734** North *Life Dudley North* (1744) 200 He used the Room above to wilder in his Accounts. **1805** Scott *Last Minstr.* i. Introd. iv, And scenes long past of joy and pain, Came wildering o'er his aged brain. **1838** S. Bellamy *Betrayal* v. 166 A fornix vast, that rangeless from the eye Ran wildering. **1854** Lowell *Cambr. 30 Yrs. Ago* Writ. 1890 I. 96 The fierce snow-storm wildering without.

b. *trans.* with adv. To spend or waste in 'wildering'.

1668 Owen *Expos. 130th Ps.* 131 So he wilders away all his dayes in uncertainties.

†**3.** *trans.* and *intr.* To render, or become, wild or uncivilized. *Obs. rare.*

1798 W. Taylor in *Monthly Mag.* VI. 550 The yoke of the Egyptians had degraded the Hebrews into the rudest and worst of nations, wildered by three hundred years of neglect. **1804** —— in *Crit. Rev.* I. 20 Her dole-lands..will again be suffered to wilder into sheep walks. **1806** —— in *Ann. Rev.* IV. 111 European families transported to Canada must wilder in a generation or two.

wildered ('wɪldəd), *ppl. a.* Also 7 wildred. [f. prec. + -ED[1].]

1. That has lost one's way; straying, 'lost'.

1656 in Clarendon *Hist. Reb.* xv. §112 Like poor wilder'd Travellers, perceiving that We have lost our way. **1742** Young *Nt. Th.* ix. 1703 Ye, who guide the wilder'd in the waves. **1818** Keats *Endym.* iii. 219 The wilder'd stranger. **1870** Morris *Earthly Par.* III. iv. 46 A sound as of a wildered wind, Half moan, half sigh.

b. *fig.* At a loss, perplexed, bewildered.

1642 D. Rogers *Naaman* 149 See Naaman here, in what a wildred case he is! **1689** J. O. tr. *Cowley's Plants* i. *Scurvy Grass* 31 Nor does it to your wilder'd Sense appear, Where their Pain is, 'cause it is every where. **1789** W. Blake *Songs Innoc., Dream* 5 Troubl'd, wilder'd, and forlorn. **1813** Scott *Rokeby* iv. xxix, In secret, doubtless, to pursue The schemes his wilder'd fancy drew. **1881** Kipling *Departm. Ditties, Simla Dancers* iv, And murmurs of past merriment pursue Your 'wildered clerks that they indite in vain.

2. Of a place or region: In which one may lose one's way; pathless, wild.

a **1810** Shelley *M. Nicholson Fragm.* 26 Our ghosts, whilst raves the maddened storm, Will sweep at midnight o'er the wildered wave. **1821** Clare *Vill. Minstrel* I. 203 Brushing through the wilder'd dell. **1860** Patmore *Faithf. for Ever* i. i, A long, green slip of wilder'd land.

b. Confused, disordered; mingled confusedly.

1853 C. Bronte *Villette* xlii, Certain..feelings..when reviewed must strike us as things wildered and whirling. **1909** Stopf. Brooke in *Life & Lett.* (1917) II. 613 The sun set among the trees in a wildered glory of gold and crimson.

wildering ('wɪldərɪŋ), *ppl. a.* [f. as prec. + -ING[2].] That 'wilders', in various senses.

1. Leading or driving one astray; *esp.* of a place: in which one loses or may lose one's way.

1749 Shenstone *Irreg. Ode* 83 And some had bent the wild'ring maze. **1793** Coleridge *Lines Autumnal Even.* 77 Toss'd by storms along Life's wild'ring way. **1804** W. L. Bowles *Spir. Discov.* iv. 64 Safe in the wildering storm. **1867** H. Macmillan *Bible Teach.* vi. (1870) 126 Their wildering mazes of exquisite flowers.

b. *fig.* Producing mental confusion or aberration; perplexing, bewildering.

1742 Collins *Ecl.* iv. 8 Where wild'ring fear and desperate sorrow led. **1812** J. Wilson *Isle of Palms* i. 223 In waking thoughts she still retains The memory of these wildering pains. *a* **1850** Rossetti *Dante & Circle* i. (1874) 74 These 'wildering phantasies Then carried me to see my Lady dead. **1870** Morris *Earthly Par.* III. iv. 370 The clash Of rain-beat boughs and wildering lightning-flash.

2. Going astray, straying, wandering.

1827 Keble *Chr. Y., Sexagesima Sunday* ii, Ruin below and wrath above Are all that now the wildering fancy meets. *Ibid., 5th Sunday in Lent* iv, Ye too, who tend Christ's wildering flock. **1871** B. Taylor *Faust* (1875) II. i. iii, Lamps are gleaming, Through the festal's wildering train.

wilderment ('wɪldəmənt). *poet. rare.* [f. as prec. + -MENT.] Bewilderment.

1830 *Fraser's Mag.* I. 144 Music's gush, With all its moving wilderment. **1844** Mrs. Browning *Lost Bower* lvii, So, in wilderment of gazing, I looked up and I looked down.

†**wildern,** *a.* and *sb. Obs.* Forms: 1 wilddeoren, 3–5 wilderne, (3 wulderne), 4 wildern, 5 wylderne; 3–4 wildren, 4 wildrin, wyldren. [OE. *wilddéoren*, f. *wilddéor* WILD DEER + -EN[4].]

A. *adj.* Wild, savage, desert.

a **1050** *Liber Scintill.* xxv. (1889) 99 *Cum feralibus dentibus*, mid wilddeorenum toþum. *a* **1300** *Cursor M.* 3081 [Ysmael] wond als a wildren man. *Ibid.* 4080 His breþer in þe wildrin land. *Ibid.* 5734, 10293. **13..** *E.E. Allit. P.* C. 297 Ande euer walteres þis whal bi wyldren depe.

B. *sb.* = WILDERNESS.

The genitive of this word is indistinguishable in form from next.

c **1200** *Vices & Virtues* 137 Þo þe he faste fowerti daiȝes on ða wilderne. *c* **1200** *Trin. Coll. Hom.* 127 He makede his wuniende in þe wilderne. *a* **1225** *Ancr. R.* 160 He..wende into onliche stude iðe wildernesse [*MS. C.* wilderne]. **13..** *Cursor M.* 5852 (Gött.) To worschip god in wildrenes land. *c* **1375** *Ibid.* 5734 (Fairf.) His flok he ledde a-pon a tide Bi a wildernes side. *a* **1400** *Sir Orfeo* 212 (MS. Ashm. 61, lf. 153) To wylderne I wyll gone..And lyve þer in holtys hore.

wilderness ('wɪldənɪs). Forms: 3–6 wyldernesse, 3–7 wildernesse, 4–6 wil-, wyl-, -der-, -dir-, -dre-, (-dur-), -dyr-, -nes, -ness(e,

(-nys), (4 *Sc.* vildirnes, 5 wyyldernesse), 4- wilderness. [OE. **wild(d)éornes* (Sweet's A.-S. Dict.) = MLG., MDu. *wildernisse* (Du. *wildernis*, G. *wildernis*); f. *wilder*, *wil(d)déor* (see WILD *a.*, WILD DEER) or, perh. more probably, *wilddéoren* WILDERN *a.* + *-nes* -NESS (for the concrete sense cf. *héahnes* summit, *smépnes* 'planities').

The other types of derivatives of *wild* meaning 'wilderness' in the Teutonic languages are represented by (1) MHG., G. *wilde* fem. (cf. WILD *sb.*), (2) MLG., MHG. *wilt(e)nisse*, G. *wildnis* (cf. WILDNESS 2), (3) G. (now dial.) *wilden(e*, *wildin*, (4) ME. WILDERN.]

1. a. (without article) Wild or uncultivated land.

Distinguished from *desert*, in that the latter denotes an uninhabitable and uncultivable region, and implies entire lack of vegetation.

c **1200** *Trin. Coll. Hom.* 161 Weste is cleped þat londe, þat is longe tilðe atleien, and wildernesse, ȝef þare manie rotes onne wacseð. *c* **1205** LAY. 30335 He scal habben paþes weste and wildernesse inoȝe. *a* **1300** *Cursor M.* 2617 In wildernes al bi a well. **13..** *Sir Beues* (A.) 3867 Þe geaunt.. In a castel hire hadde to ward, In wildernesse al be selue. *c* **1375** *Sc. Leg. Saints* xviii. 52 Als he trewyt na man was In abay, na in vildirnes, þat mocht do mare þane he had done. *c* **1400** MAUNDEV. (Roxb.) xxi. 98 A grete party of þis cuntree es waste and wilderness and noȝt inhabitid. *c* **1450** CAPGRAVE *Life St. Aug.* xiv. 20 Holy heremites whech dwelled in wildyrnesse. **1590** SPENSER *F.Q.* II. vii. 2 He traueild through wide wastfull ground, That nought but desert wildernesse shew'd all around. **1596** DALRYMPLE tr. *Leslie's Hist. Scot.* II. (S.T.S.) I. 164 Twyse he compelled him to take his refuge in wod and wildirnes. **1613** PURCHAS *Pilgrimage* v. v. 404 The Countrey of Gouren, where we found but few villages, and almost all wildernesse. **1835** W. IRVING *Tour Prairies* 143 Passing through tracts of wilderness which they have never before traversed. **1847** TENNYSON *Princess* I. 110 By tilth and grange,..and blowing bosks of wilderness.

b. (with article or other defining word) A wild or uncultivated region or tract of land, uninhabited, or inhabited only by wild animals; 'a tract of solitude and savageness' (J.).

a **1225** *Ancr. R.* 160 He..feste þer as he was one iðe wildernesse [*v.r.* wilderne]. *Ibid.* 196 Iðe wildernesse [*v.r.* wildene] heo aspieden us to slean. *a* **1300** *Cursor M.* 11110 (Cott.) He..liued wit rotes and wit gress, Wit honi o þe wildernes. **1303** R. BRUNNE *Handl. Synne* 172 Hyt was onys a munke, and had a celle In a wyldernes for to dwelle. **13..** *Gaw. & Gr. Knt.* 701 In þe wyldrenesse of Wyrale. *c* **1475** *Pict. Voc.* in Wr.-Wülcker 798/7 *Hec solitudo*, a wyldernys. **1535** COVERDALE *Job* xxxix. 6 Vnto whom I haue geuen the wyldernes to be their house, & the vntilled londe to be their dwellinge place. **1597** SHAKS. *2 Hen. IV*, IV. v. 137 O my poore Kingdome..thou wilt be a Wildernesse againe, Peopled with Wolues (thy old Inhabitants). **1645** MILTON *Tetrach.* 10 By forcing that upon us as the remedy of solitude, which wraps us in a misery worse then any wildernes. **1784** COWPER *Task* II. 1 Oh for a lodge in some vast wilderness. **1831** SCOTT *Cast. Dang.* xv, Finding only boundless wildernesses, and varied combinations of tangled woodland scenery. **1855** MACAULAY *Hist. Eng.* xix. IV. 368 Temple had made a retreat for himself at a place called Moor Park... The country round his dwelling was almost a wilderness.

c. A piece of ground in a large garden or park, planted with trees, and laid out in an ornamental or fantastic style, often in the form of a maze or labyrinth.

a **1644** QUARLES *Sol. Recant.* ch. ii. 6, I cut me Aquiducts, whose current flees And waters all my wildernesse of trees. **1668** DRYDEN *Even. Love* v, Disperse your selves, some into the Wilderness, some into the Allies, and some into the Parterre. **1770** H. CHAMBERLAIN *Hist. & Surv. London* 641/2 In one part of it [*sc.* the park] is a pretty wilderness laid out in walks, and planted with a variety of ever-green trees. **1784** COWPER *Task* I. 351. **1839** E. JESSE *Summer's Day Hampton Crt.* 77 On the opposite side of the palace there is a large space of ground called the Wilderness, planted and laid out by William III. **1885** MISS BRADDON *Wyllard's Weird* i, Manifold as were the cares of the hot-houses and ferneries and wildernesses.

2. *transf.* or *gen.* A waste or desolate region of any kind, e.g. of open sea, of air.

1588 SHAKS. *Tit. A.* III. i. 94, I stand as one vpon a Rocke, Inuiron'd with a wildernesse of Sea. **1629** *Drayner Conf.* (1647) B 2, The difference between a Wildernesse of water and a goodly green Meadow. **1665** WALLER *Instr. Painter* 78 But who can always on the Billows ly? The watry Wilderness yields no supply. **1821** BYRON *Cain* II. i, This blue wilderness of interminable Air. **1865** PARKMAN *Huguenots* iii. (1875) 30 They..saw the long, low line where the wilderness of waves met the wilderness of woods.

3. *fig.* **a.** Something figured as a region of a wild or desolate character, or in which one wanders or loses one's way; in religious use applied to the present world or life as contrasted with heaven or the future life (cf. 6 b).

a **1340** HAMPOLE *Psalter* cxlvii. 4 He forsakis vs noght in þis wildirenes. *c* **1390** CHAUCER *Truth* 17 Here is non home, here nys but wyldernesse. *c* **1480** HENRYSON *Trial of Fox* 317 The Meir is Men of gude conditioun, As Pilgrymes walkand in this wildernes. **1640** BROME *Antipodes* I. iii, But sure his mind Is in a wildernesse: For there he sayes Are Geese that have two heads a peece. **1664** POWER *Exp. Philos.* I. 52 Thus discursive Argumentation and Rational probabilities mislead men in the Wilderness of Enquiry. **1678** BUNYAN *Pilgr.* I. 1 As I walk'd through the wilderness of this world. *a* **1708** T. WARD *Eng. Ref.* II. (1710) 46 All they can do's to bid you pore On Bibles till your Eyes are sore, And in that Wilderness of Letter Hunt for your Faiths. **1813** BYRON *Giaour* 939 The vacant bosom's wilderness. **1868** LOUISA M. ALCOTT *Little Women* iv, The cosy chairs, the globes, and best of all, the wilderness of books, in which she could wander where she liked.

b. Rhetorically applied to a place (e.g. a building or town) which one finds 'desolate', or in which one is lonely or 'lost'.

1842 DICKENS *Amer. Notes* vi, Passing this wilderness of an hotel with stores about its base. **1848** —— *Dombey* xxiii, So Florence lived in her wilderness of a home. **1891** KIPLING *Light that Failed* 118 Meantime Maisie was alone in London... And the packed wilderness was very full of danger.

c. *in the wilderness* (in allusion to *Numbers* xiv. 33), (*a*) of a politician, political party, etc.: out of office; (*b*) *gen.*, unrecognized, out of favour.

1930 *Economist* 2 Aug. 220/1 For Charles X represented a Restoration of the *Ancien Régime*..which had 'learnt nothing and forgotten nothing' during a quarter of a century in the wilderness. **1958** *Spectator* 6 June 719/3 Parties should liquidate their failures and frustrations in the wilderness, not in power. **1966** *Listener* 5 May 661/2 Richard Baker asked Bernard Keeffe why Mahler, so long in the wilderness as far as England was concerned, is now a box-office success. **1969** *Ibid.* 3 July 12/3 Carmichael has now accepted a junior post in the Panther hierarchy and Rap Brown and Jim Foreman have been driven into the wilderness. **1976** *Southern Even. Echo* (Southampton) 17 Nov. 22/3 If he fails to gain the title he lost to Cain on a cut eye decision, it could mean months in the wilderness and set him back even further. **1984** *Times* 1 Aug. 17/2 After months in the wilderness, which has seen the price slip from a high of 95¼p to a low of 65½p shares of Marley..is [*sic*] back in favour with the institutions.

4. A mingled, confused, or vast assemblage or collection *of* persons or things. (Usually coloured by other senses; in reference to a growth of plants, nearly coinciding with 1 b; in reference to buildings, etc., often approaching 3 b.)

1588 SHAKS. *Tit. A.* III. i. 54 Dost thou not perceiue That Rome is but a wildernes of Tigers? **1596** —— *Merch. V.* III. i. 128, I would not haue giuen it for a wildernesse of Monkies. **1613** PURCHAS *Pilgrimage* VII. xii. 598 It was called Madera, of the wildernesses of Trees there growing. *a* **1616** BEAUM. & FL. *Bonduca* v. i, The Land thou hast left a wilderness of wretches. **1667** MILTON *P.L.* v. 294 Through Groves of Myrrhe, And flouring Odours, Cassia, Nard, and Balme; A Wilderness of sweets. **1678** E. HOWARD *Man of Newmarket* I. i. 1 This Metropolitan Wilderness of Houses, call'd London. **1775** SHERIDAN *Duenna* I. ii, A wilderness of faults and follies. **1824** BYRON *Juan* XVI. iii, This epic will contain A wilderness of the most rare conceits. **1857** DICKENS *Dorrit* I. ix, The wilderness of masts on the river, and the wilderness of steeples on the shore.

†**5. a.** Wildness, uncultivated condition. *Obs.*

c **1449** PECOCK *Repr.* III. xiv. 370 The tenementis..which the clergie..holden..is better..kept fro falling into nouȝt and into wildirnes, than if tho same tenementis..weren in the hondis of grete lordis. **1667** MILTON *P.L.* IX. 245 These paths and Bowers doubt not but our joynt hands Will keep from Wilderness with ease.

b. *fig.* Wildness of character, licentiousness. *Obs. nonce-use.*

1603 SHAKS. *Meas. for M.* III. i. 142 For such a warped slip of wildernesse Nere issu'd from his blood.

6. *attrib.* **a.** *lit.* (in quot. 1670 in sense 1 c).

a **1586** SIDNEY *Arcadia* I. xvii. (1912) 112 Being one of that little wildernesse-company. **1670** MEAGER *English Gardener* Title-p., The ordering of the Garden of Pleasure, with variety of Knots, and Wilderness-work. **1801** *Farmer's Mag.* Aug. 297, 14 acres of wilderness land converted into grass. *c* **1875** E. THRING in Skrine *Mem.* (1889) 218 The poor beggars had tightish work with all that wilderness life before them.

b. *fig.*; *esp.* in former religious use, belonging to the present world or life (cf. 3).

1651 BAXTER *Saints' Rest* II. ix. §1 (ed. 2) 290 If they had not felt their Wildernes-necessities, God should not have exercised his Wildernes-providences and mercies. **1675** T. BROOKS *Gold. Key* Wks. 1867 V. 473 A wilderness-condition is..a condition of straits, wants, deep distresses, and most deadly dangers. **1679** C. NESSE *Antichrist* 208 Tainted both with Egypts idolatry, and wilderness-sins. **1719** J. T. PHILLIPS tr. *Thirty-four Confer.* 79 The Progress thro' this Wilderness-World, towards a better..Life. **1898** MEREDITH *Odes Fr. Hist.* 16 Her soul On eddies of wild water cast, In wilderness division.

wild-fire, wildfire ('waɪldfaɪə(r)). [Cf. G. *wildfeuer* lightning, will-o'-the-wisp, erysipelas, etc.]

†**1.** Furious or destructive fire; a conflagration (in early quots. app. one caused by lightning: cf. 2 d). *Obs.* (as a specific use).

a **1122** *O.E. Chron.* (Laud MS.) an. 1032 On þissum ȝeare atywde þæt wildefyr, ðe nan mann æror nan swylc ne ȝemunde. *c* **1366** *Chronicon Brevius* an. 1047 in *Eulogium Hist.* (Rolls) III. 294 Mortalitas in Anglia et ignis aereus, quæ dicitur wildfire, blada combussit in pago Derebiæ. ?*a* **1400** *Morte Arth.* 797 He hade weryede the worme by wyghtnesse of strenghte, Ne ware it fore the wylde fyre that he hyme wyth defendez. *c* **1450** *St. Cuthbert* (Surtees) 1870 How wild fyre was sloken sall be sene. **1538** BALE *God's Promises* III. B iv, Wylde fyre and brymstone shall lyght vpon them all. **1634** S. R. *Noble Soldier* II. i. C 4 b, You to quench a wild fire, Cast oyle upon it.

2. In various specific uses (*wild* often implying 'natural, not artificially produced', or 'out of doors, not domestic': cf. WILD *a.* 1-4). †**a.** The flames of spirituous liquor burning on some dishes, as plum-pudding, when served up. *Obs. rare*$^{-1}$.

c **1386** CHAUCER *Pars. T.* ¶ 371 Swiche manere bake metes and dissh metes brennynge of wilde fir.

†**b.** A fire kindled out of doors for warmth. *Obs. rare*$^{-1}$.

a **1400** *Sir Perc.* 855 Than wist Percyvelle by thatt, It servede hym of somwhatt The wylde fyre that he gatt.

c. Will-o'-the-wisp, *ignis fatuus*; also *fig.*

Also dialectally applied to other phosphorescent appearances: see *Eng. Dial. Dict.*

1663 G. WHARTON *Cal. Carol.* A 3 b, [They] wonder by what Wild fires they were led To feed on Thistles 'stead of wholsome Bread. **1683** [see 2 e]. **1727** P. WALKER *Life R. Cameron* in *Biogr. Presbyt.* (1827) I. 243 Some Willies with the Wisps, or Spunkies of Wild-fire, seen mostly in boguish myrish Ground. **1814** SCOTT *Ld. of Isles* VI. xxii, As springs the wild-fire from the moss. **1847** TENNYSON *Princess* v. 431 Tho' yourself Be dazzled by the wildfire Love to sloughs That swallow common sense. **1873** C. M. DAVIES *Unorth. Lond.* (1876) 405 He taught..that intellectual culture without moral practice is a wildfire, and that conscience is the voice of God. **1885** J. PAYN *Talk of Town* vii, Led by wildfire of this sort to the brink of disappointment.

d. Lightning; *esp.* sheet lightning without audible thunder, 'summer lightning'.

1795 BURNS *Verses Destr. Woods Drumlanrig* v, Or was 't the wil'fire scorch'd their boughs? **1888** TAIT in *Encycl. Brit.* XXIII. 330/1 What is called 'summer lightning' or 'wild-fire' is sometimes a rather puzzling phenomenon.

e. †Volcanic fire (*obs.*); fire-damp in coal-mines.

1683 G. SINCLAIR *Nat. Philos., Misc. Observ.* 293 In some Coals,..there is a certain Fire,..and I judge, that from its resemblance to *Ignis fatuus*, which the Vulgar termeth Wild-fire, it hath the same name. **1692** RAY *Disc.* I. iii. (1693) 12 If such Hills..may be, and have been elevated by subterraneous Wild-fire, Flatus or Earthquakes. **1883** GRESLEY *Gloss. Coal-mining*, *Wild-fire*, an old term used by colliers for *fire-damp*.

3. A composition of highly inflammable substances, readily ignited and very difficult to extinguish, used in warfare, etc.

1297 R. GLOUC. (Rolls) 8485 Hii asailede þe toun mid þis tour wel uaste, & wilde fur wiþ pich & grece. **13..** *Coer de L.* 5229 With trepeiettes they slungen alsoo,..And blewe wylde-fyr in trumpes of gynne. *c* **1386** CHAUCER *Wife's Prol.* 373 Thou liknest wommenes loue..to wilde fyr The moore it brenneth the moore it hath desir. **1471** *Pol. Poems* (Rolls) II. 278 At Londone brige anodyr sawte thay made agayne, Wyth gunpowdir and wildefire and straw eke. *a* **1490** BOTONER *Itin.* (Nasmith, 1778) 279 Destruxit per obcidionem civitatem per passeres cum wyldfyre ad eorum caudas ligata, volando ad civitatem. *a* **1548** HALL *Chron.*, *Hen. V*, 56 Some set skalyng ladders to the wal, and other cast in wylde fyre. **1629** MALTHUS *Fireworks* in Hodgkin *Rariora* (1902) III. III. 16 Hand-granades, fiery Wheeles, a Shippe of wilde Fire, and a Petard. *a* **1642** SIR W. MONSON *Naval Tracts* III. (1704) 344/2 Pikes of Wild-fire to stick burning into a Ship's side. *a* **1674** MILTON *Hist. Moscovia* i. Wks. 1851 VIII. 479 Then out of Mortar-pieces they shoot Wild-fire into the Air. **1742** WESLEY *Jrnl.* 26 Jan., The exceeding thick smoke, which was occasion'd by the wild fire and things of that kind, continually thrown into the room. **1783** JUSTAMOND tr. *Raynal's Hist. Indies* (new ed.) I. 61 Chymistry was know'n; and wildfire had been invented. **1871** *Fireworks & How to make them* 58 Port or Wildfires. Saltpetre 4 parts, mealpowder 6 parts, and sulphur 3 parts.

4. a. A name for erysipelas and various inflammatory eruptive diseases, esp. those in which the eruption spreads from one part to another.

c **1000** ÆLFRIC *Gloss.* in Wr.-Wülcker 114 *Erysipila*, wilde fyr. *a* **1425** tr. *Arderne's Treat. Fistula*, etc. 40 It quenchiþ wele herisiplam, þat is wilde fire or few sawage. **1562** TURNER *Herbal* II. 33 Lentilles..are good for..the wylde-fire and for the kybes. **1601** HOLLAND *Pliny* XXIII. Proeme II. 146 Shingles, ringworms, and such like wild-fires. **1614** MARKHAM *Cheap Husb.*, *Sheep* ix. 72 This disease which is called the wildfire is a very infectious sicknesse, and will indanger the whole flocke. **1818–20** E. THOMPSON tr. *Cullen's Nosol. Method.* (ed. 3) 331 Herpes; Ringworm; Shingles; Wildefire. **1841** DICK *Man. Vet. Sci.* (1862) 175 Erysipelas in sheep appears in various slight modifications. .. Wildfire..generally shews itself at the beginning of winter... The skin inflames and rises into blisters. **1907** 'Q' *Merry-Garden* etc., *Black Joke* i, Wounds showing signs of inflammation and threatening to set up wildfire.

b. A leaf-spot disease of tobacco, caused by the bacterium *Pseudomonas tabaci*. Also *attrib.*

1918 *Jrnl. Agric. Res.* XII. 451 The disease appeared so quietly, spread so rapidly, and affected the leaves so seriously that it was commonly given the appropriate designation 'wildfire'. **1955** *Sci. News Let.* 29 Jan. 73/2 Immunity to wildfire..was first transferred..from a wild tobacco species. **1971** *Nature* 15 Jan. 174/1 Wildfire disease of tobacco is perhaps the most thoroughly studied of all toxin-mediated plant diseases.

5. a. *fig.* or in fig. allusions (usually from sense 3, sometimes 4), in reference to a destructive agency, or to excited, violent, or fervid feeling or utterance.

a **1300** *Cursor M.* 4314 Thoru þine ei þe sal be sent A flan, wit wild fire al brent, First to brin þin hert wit-in. *c* **1425** *Cast. Persev.* 2116 in *Macro Plays* 140 Belsabub..Bad me brenne þee with wyld fere. **1581** J. BELL *Haddon's Answ. Osor.* 271 b, What thunderboltes and wildefire he [*sc.* the Pope] threw out of his bloudy turrettes agaynst Luther's life. **1593** NASHE *Christ's T.* To Rdr., Neuer more let him looke to quench wilde fire with milke. **1612** J. DAVIES *Muse's Sacrifice* Wks. (Grosart) II. 18/1 The wilde-fire of my Passions burnèd me. **1646** J. HALL *Poems* 34 Admit no wildfire in Poetick rage. *a* **1653** G. DANIEL *Idyll.* IV. 106 Caesar..Is but a Wild-fire to wast Senate Raggs, And silence Cato. **1736** NEAL *Hist. Purit.* III. 539 It was impossible to stop the impetuous wildfire of the army. **1765** *Ann. Reg.*, *Char.* 1 The wild-fire of applause or reproach is let off at the authors, in an undistinguishing blaze. **1825** SCOTT *Betrothed* iii, That which will but warm your Flemish hearts, will put wildfire into Norman brains. **1888** DOUGHTY

Trav. Arabia Deserta II. 148 There is a wild-fire in my heart which cannot be appeased till I be avenged.

†**b.** In imprecations (in sense 3 or 4). *Obs.*

c **1350** *Will. Palerne* 1188 Ho-so faileþ for feyntyce wild fur him for-brenne. *c* **1386** CHAUCER *Reeve's T.* 252 A wilde fyr vp on thair bodyes falle. *c* **1407** LYDG. *Reson & Sens.* 3802 That she wolde, in her entent, In wilde fire that he were brent. **1520** *Calisto & Melib.* (1536) Bj, That a wyld fyre bren the, Celestena. *c* **1622** ROWLEY, etc. *Birth of Merlin* III. vi, Wilde-fire and Brimstone eat thee! *c* **1705** POPE *Jan. & May* 641 So may some wildfire on your bodies fall.

c. Phr. ***like wildfire***: with immense rapidity and effect; very swiftly and forcibly: usually with *run*, *spread*, etc.; hence occas. *gen.* forcibly, vigorously. (The commonest current use.)

[**1593** SHAKS. *Lucr.* 1523 Whose words like wild fire burnt the shining glorie Of rich-built Illion.] **1699** DAMPIER *Voy.* II. ii. 58 We set fire to it [*sc.* sedgy grass], which runs like Wild-fire. **1762** GOLDSM. *Cit. W.* xxx, Though I was at that time rich in fame—for my book ran like wild-fire—yet I was very short in money. **1837** DISRAELI *Venetia* I. xvi, The report . . spread like wild-fire through the town. **1857** READE *Course of True Love, Clouds & Sun.* i, She would . . go . . and flirt like wild-fire for a fortnight. **1886** *19th Cent.* Dec. 883 With such thoughts running like wild-fire through her mind.

6. *attrib.*: in sense 3, as ***wildfire arrow***, ***ball***, ***plot***; *fig.* (cf. 5), as ***wildfire blood***, ***zeal***; **wildfire rash**, a disease of infants, a form of strophulus with a wandering eruption (cf. 4).

1706 PHILLIPS (ed. Kersey), **Wild-Fire Arrows*, such as are trimmed with Wild-Fire. **1614** GORGES *Lucan* VI. 222 Shoures of *wildefire balls. **1824** SCOTT *Redgauntlet* ch. xviii, The *wildfire blood of Redgauntlet. **1641** (*title*) A *Wild-fire Plot found out in Ireland, shewing how the Rebels would have consumed the City of Dublin with Wild-fire. **1822–7** GOOD *Study Med.* (1829) V. 566 Children . . liable to the *strophulus volaticus*, or *wild-fire rash. **1601** BP. W. BARLOW *Defence* Ep. Ded., A *wilde-fire zeale.

‖**Wildflysch** (ˈvɪltflɪʃ). *Geol.* Also **wildflysch**. [Ger. (F. J. Kaufmann 1871, in B. Studer *Index der Petrogr.* (1872) 258): see FLYSCH.] Flysch containing large, irregularly distributed blocks and occupying beds that are distorted.

1929 P. G. H. BOSWELL tr. *Heritsch's Nappe Theory Alps* iv. 47 A great part of the sheared Flysch has the character of the Wildflysch: dark, puckered and highly micaceous marls with interbedded seams of sandstone, quartzite, limestones, breccias, conglomerates and exotic blocks. **1960** *Bull. Geol. Soc. Amer.* LXXI. 878/2 The general aspect of Wildflysch forcibly suggests submarine slumping and sliding on a large scale. **1963** [see FAMENNIAN *a.*]. **1981** A. HALLAM *Facies Interpretation* iv. 82 A thick series of shallow-water carbonate platform deposits . . are overlain by a wildflysch unit with a chaotic jumble of limestone blocks in a shaly matrix.

wild-fowl. (Also as one word, or as two.) Forms: see WILD *a.* and FOWL; also 6 **wyelfoyle**. [Cf. MLG., G. *wildvogel*, ON. *villifygli* (Sw. *vildfågel*, early Da. *vildfugi*).] A wild bird, or (usually) wild birds collectively; chiefly applied to those caught for food, game birds (now esp. of the duck and goose kinds).

a **1000** *Bi Manna Wyrdum* 85 (Gr.) Sum sceal wildne fuȝel wloncne atemian, heafoc on honda. **1377** LANGL. *P. Pl.* B. x. 363 Delyte in wyn and wylde foule. *a* **1417** *York Memo. Bk.* (Surtees) I. 223 Pultre wyldefoule and other vytayll. **1439** *Maldon, Essex, Court-roll* Bundle 25. No. 1, Johannes Yutte est communis foristallator volucrum vocat. Wyldefoule. **1500–20** DUNBAR *Poems* xxxix. 19 Vennesoun, wyld fowill, wyne and spyce. **1532–3** *Durham Househ. Bk.* (Surtees) 215 Et de magistro de Fayrne 6 dd. wyelfoyle et 4 puffyngs. **1601** SHAKS. *Twel. N.* IV. ii. 55 What is the opinion of Pythagoras concerning Wildefowle? **1784** COWPER *Task* IV. 612 Whoso seeks an audit here Propitious, pays his tribute, game or fish, Wild-fowl or ven'son. **1817** SCOTT *Harold* V. xvi, As the scared wild-fowl scream and fly.

b. Humorously misapplied in the first quot. to a wild beast; hence *allusively*; also *fig.* of persons.

1590 SHAKS. *Mids. N.* III. i. 33 There is not a more fearefull wilde foule then your Lyon liuing. **1610** B. JONSON *Alch.* V. iii, What's your med'cine, To draw so many seuerall sorts of wild-fowle? **1905** *Times Lit. Suppl.* 3 Feb. 38/1 One has to drag in fundamental principles of art and other fearful wildfowl.

c. *attrib.*

1825 HOOD *To Mrs. Fry* x, To tame the wild-fowl-ways of Jenny Diver! **1870** N. F. HELE *Aldeburgh* ii. 8 Very few wild-fowl shooters frequent this part of the river. **1886** C. E. PASCOE *Lond. of To-day* xli. (ed. 3) 360 Wild fowl guns.

Hence **wild-ˈfowler**, a sportsman who shoots or catches wild-fowl; **wild-ˈfowling**, the pursuit or capture of wild-fowl.

1859 FOLKARD (*title*) The Wild-Fowler: a Treatise on Ancient and Modern Wild-Fowling. **1874** J. W. LONG *Amer. Wild-fowl* xv. 193 In no other branch of wild-fowling is a breech-loader of more advantage than in teal-shooting.

wild goose. (Also with hyphen.) Forms: see WILD *a.* and GOOSE; also 7 **wilgosse**. [Cf. (M)HG. *wildgans*, Sw. *vildgås*, Da. *vildgaas*.]

1. Any wild bird of the goose kind; an undomesticated goose; in Britain usually the greylag (*Anser ferus* or *cinereus*), in N. America the Canada goose (*Bernicla canadensis*).

c **1050** *Voc.* in Wr.-Wülcker 364/1 *Cente*, wilde gos. *c* **1325** *Gloss. W. de Bibbesw.* in Wright *Voc.* 165 Jo voy là une owe rossée [*gloss* a wilde-gos]. *c* **1440** LYDG. *Hors, Shepe & G.* 171 Whan wilde gees hihe in the ayer vp fleen. **1513** BRADSHAW *St. Werburge* I. 2619 A great multytude somtyme of wylde gees, Comunely called Gauntes. **1597** SHAKS. *2 Hen. IV*, V. i. 79 They flocke together in consent, like so many Wilde-Geese. **1600** —— *A.Y.L.* II. vii. 86 If he be free, Why then my taxing like a wild-goose flies Vnclaim'd of any man. **1752** HILL *Hist. Anim.* 421 We have the wild goose flying over our heads, in the fens of Lincolnshire, in vast flocks. **1845** WHITTIER *Lumbermen* ii, O'er us, to the southland heading, Screams the gray wild-goose.

2. *fig.* **a.** Used of or in reference to a flighty or foolish person: cf. GOOSE *sb.* 1 f. **b.** *Eng. Hist.* (*pl.*) A nickname for the Irish Jacobites who went over to the Continent on the abdication of James II and later.

1592 [see WILD GOOSE CHASE 2]. **1843** M. J. BARRY in *Spirit of the Nation* (Dublin 1845) 230 The wild geese—the wild geese,—'tis long since they flew, O'er the billowy ocean's bright bosom of blue. **1845** *Ibid.* 231 *note*, The recruits for the Irish Brigade . . were entered on the ship's books as 'wild geese'. **1845** M. O'CONOR *Milit. Hist. Irish Nation* 367 *note*, Clare, it may be added, was a great recruiting county for the Brigade. On its stern coast the French used to land smuggled claret, brandy, &c., and take away wool, and, what was more precious, 'Wild Geese,' for such was the name usually given to the recruits for 'The bold Brigade.' **1872** TENNYSON *Gareth & Lynette* 36 Thou art but a wild-goose to question it. **1881** FROUDE *Eng. in Irel.* II. iii. I. 405 In 1715 . . Tens of thousands of young Irishmen were in the French service, and thousands more were continually recruited under the name of Wild Geese. **1902** in Emily Lawless *With the Wild Geese* Pref. p. viii, The 'Wild Geese' was the name given . . to the exiles who, like the wild birds . . migrated to the Continent before and after the Battle of Aughrim, and the Surrender of Limerick in 1691.

3. *attrib.* **a.** [after WILD GOOSE CHASE 2, as apprehended in later use.] Wild, fantastic, very foolish or risky.

1770 CUMBERLAND *West Indian* II. xi, To fit him out upon some wild-goose expedition to the coast of Africa. **1781** COWPER *Anti-Thelyphthora* 53 She tutor'd some in Dædalus's art, And promis'd they would act his wildgoose part. **1833** T. HOOK *Parson's Dau.* III. vi, 'All mad, wild-goose nonsense,' said MacGopus. **1841** DICKENS *Barn. Rudge* iv, He'll . . have gone away upon some wild-goose errand, seeking his fortune.

b. wild-goose plum, **rye**, names for N. American varieties of those plants raised from seeds found in the crops of wild geese; **wild-goose race** = next.

1909 *Month* Dec. 599 A well-known American plum is called the '*wild-goose' plum, because a plum-stone from which the whole race has been raised was found in the stomach of such a bird. **1594** WILLOBIE *Avisa* (1880) 83 As weary of this *wild-goose race That led askance, I know not where. **1624** GATAKER *Transubst.* 145 As one running the wild goose race, he windeth backe to a passage in the former argument. **1884** *Lisbon* (Dakota) *Star* 15 Aug., The introduction of *wild goose rye into Dakota.

wild goose chase.

†**1.** A kind of horse-race or sport in which the second or any succeeding horse had to follow accurately the course of the leader (at a definite interval), like a flight of wild geese. *Obs.*

[**1592**: see 2.] **1602** BRETON *Mother's Blessing* Wks. (Grosart) I. 6/2 Esteeme a horse, according to his pace, But loose no wagers on a wilde goose chase. **1604** H. SPURWAY in *Trevelyan Papers* (Camden) 60 The King hath beene latelye at Royston, at a wilgosse chase. **1621** BURTON *Anat. Mel.* II. ii. IV. 342 Horse-races, wilde-goose chases, which are the disports of greater men. **1685** N. COX *Gentl. Recreat.*, *Hunting-horse* vii. (1697) 65.

2. *fig.* An erratic course taken or *led* by one person (or thing) and followed (or that may be followed) by another (or taken by a person in following his own inclinations or impulses); in later use (the origin being forgotten) apprehended as 'a pursuit of something as unlikely to be caught as the wild goose' (J.); a foolish, fruitless, or hopeless quest.

1592 SHAKS. *Rom. & Jul.* II. iv. 75 Nay, if our wits run the Wild-Goose chase, I am done: For thou hast more of the Wild-Goose in one of thy wits, then I am sure I haue in my whole fiue. **1623–4** MIDDLETON & ROWLEY *Sp. Gipsy* I. v, I have had a fine fegary, The rarest wildgoose chase! **1646** G. DANIEL *Poems, An Addresse* 48 We pursue A Wild-goose-Chase, to what none ever knew. **1656** R. FLETCHER tr. *Martial* 202 No hints of truth on foot? no sparks of grace? No late sprung light? to dance the wild-goose chase? **1662** in *Engl. Hist. Rev.* (1920) Apr. 257 If you cannot reason him to what may bee for his good . . let him goe the wild goosechase. **1673** *Ess. Educ. Gentlewom.* 37 If we should dance that wild-Goose-chase usually led, it would require longer time. **1754** H. WALPOLE *Let. to Bentley* 20 Nov., Don't let me think, that if you return, you will set out upon every wild-goose chase, sticking to nothing. **1876** F. E. TROLLOPE *Charming Fellow* xii, His journey to London on such slender encouragement is a wild-goose chase! **1885** 'MRS. ALEXANDER' *At Bay* vii, 'I see you have found nothing,' exclaimed Lady Gethin. . . 'It was a wild goose chase,' he replied with a weary look.

†**wildgrave.** *Obs.* [ad. G. *wildgraf* (MHG. *wiltgrâve*): see WILD *a.* and GRAVE *sb.*[4]] In Germany, formerly the chief magistrate of an uncultivated or forest region; *spec.* the title of a hereditary race of rulers in parts of the Rhineland (cf. RHINEGRAVE, WALDGRAVE). So **wildgravess** (tr. G. *wildgräfin*).

1762 tr. *Busching's Syst. Geog.* V. 504 Juliana, . . Wild-gravess and Rhinegravess of Grumbach. **1796** SCOTT *Wild Huntsman* i, The Wildgrave winds his bugle horn. **1798** tr. *Bürger's Wild Huntsm.* 2 Shrill sounds the haughty Wildgrave's horn.

†**wildhede.** *Obs. rare.* [f. WILD *a.* + *-hede*, -HEAD.] Wildness of character or conduct.

1421–2 HOCCLEVE *Min. Poems* xxi. 52 That for myne honore showlde I by no weye Any thinge mynge or towche of my wildhede.

wilding (ˈwaɪldɪŋ), *sb.* and *a.* Forms: 6 **wyldyng**, **-ynge**, **-ing(e**, **wildinge**, 7 **wilden**, 6– **wilding**. [f. WILD *a.* + -ING[3].] **A.** *sb.*

The meaning in the following quot. has not been ascertained:—

1296 *Acc. Exch. K.R.* 5/20 m. 1 (P.R.O.) In .ij. petris de Burre emptis . . et quatuor petris de Wyldyng emptis de vxore Andree Skaket.

1. A wild apple or apple-tree; a crab-apple or crab-tree.

1525 *Grete Herbal* cclxxxiii. (1529) Q ij, De macianis pomis. Wood crabbes, or wyldynges. **1530** PALSGR. 289/1 Wyldyng a sower apple, *pomme de boys*. **1621** T. GRANGER *Expos. Eccles.* xii. 13. 342 The wilding maketh a fairer shew then many a good apple, but by the taste. **1651** R. CHILD in *Hartlib's Legacy* (1655) 16, I never saw . . any Apples or Pears thrive in an Hedge, unless Crab, or a Wilden, or some Sweeting of little worth. **1697** DRYDEN *Virg. Past.* III. 107 Ten ruddy Wildings in the Wood I found. **1776** BOLTON in A. Young *Tour Irel.* (1780) II. 202 Do not press wildings till Candlemas. **1786** ABERCROMBIE *Arr.* in *Gard. Assist.* p. xi, Apples valued principally for Cyder. Royal wilding. **1842** LOUDON *Suburban Hort.* 535 Wildings or seedling apple stocks.

2. *gen.* A wild plant, flower, or fruit.

1577 B. GOOGE *Heresbach's Husb.* II. (1586) 73 b, The Filbert will onely be graffed in the Wilding. **1586** WARNER *Alb. Eng.* IV. xx. (1612) 95 Wildings, or the Seasons-fruit he did in scrip bestow. **1590** SPENSER *F.Q.* III. vii. 17 Oft from the forrest wildings he did bring. *a* **1700** SEDLEY *4th Bk. Virg. Georg.* Wks. 1778 I. 33 Among the wildings . . they [*sc.* bees] feed. **1791** W. GILPIN *Forest Scenery* II. 37 The wildings of the forest. **1813** SCOTT *Rokeby* II. ix, Nor wilding green, nor woodland flower, Arose within its baleful bower. **1826** CAMPBELL *Field Flowers* i, Ye field flowers! . . wildings of Nature, I doat upon you. **1840** *Cottager's Man.* 14 in *Libr. Usef. Knowl., Husb.* III, The principle is to form the hedge of a double row of wildings. **1884** BROWNING *Ferishtah, Mihrab Shah* 74 The wilding, . . Ruffled outside at pleasure of the blast. **1892** C. E. NORTON *Dante's Paradise* xxvii. 178 Well blossoms the will in men, but the continual rain converts the true plums into wildings.

3. A wild animal. *rare.*

1897 *Advance* (Chicago) 23 Sept. 409/3 Not a specimen of these wildings [*sc.* deer, turkey, and otter] can be seen now.

4. *fig.* (applied to a person or thing).

1621 T. GRANGER *Expos. Eccles.* vii. 7. 165 These are Sathans wildings, whom he hath blinded, and so rideth them at his pleasure. **1866** LAWRENCE *Sans Merci* xiv, He made professional acquaintance with two or three wildings of gentle birth. **1881** STEVENSON *Virg. Puerisque* 6 The air of the fireside withers out all the fine wildings of the husband's heart. **1906** *Athenæum* 29 Dec. 822/1 He was swayed by the wildings of his imagination and his affections. **1908** EDITH WHARTON *Hermit* I. iii. 17 You are not a heathen wilding, but a child of Christ.

B. *attrib.* or *adj.*

1. Applied to a crab-apple or crab-tree: cf. A. 1.

1538 ELYOT, *Arbutus*, a wyldyng tree. **1552** HULOET, Wildinge aple, or crabbe, *arbutum*. **1575** A. F. *Virg. Bucol.* III. 9, From a wylding tree, Ten Apples rype I sent. **1632** BROME *Crt. Beggar* II. i, He lookes so like a wilding crab, good neither for drink nor sauce. **1650** [W. HOWE] *Phytol. Brit.* 73 Crab-tree, or Wilden-tree. **1665** LOVELL *Herball* (ed. 2) 469.

2. a. Of a plant (or its flower or fruit): Growing wild: = WILD *a.* 2. Chiefly *poet.*

1697 DRYDEN *Virg. Georg.* IV. 269 Wilding Blooms. **1810** SCOTT *Lady of L.* IV. i, O wilding rose. **1824** LOUDON *Green-house Comp.* I. 227 Grafted on the crab and wilding pear. **1827** CLARE *Sheph. Cal.* 84 Wilding fruit that shines upon the trees. **1895** CROCKETT *Bog-Myrtle & Peat* V. iv, Lo the wilding treasure Glows . . in my sweetheart's gardens.

b. Of an animal: = WILD *a.* 1. *poet. rare.*

1856 BRYANT *Gladness of Nature* ii, The wilding bee hums merrily by.

3. *fig.* Developed without culture or training, like a wild plant; natural, native.

1884 SYMONDS *Shaks. Predec.* vii. (1900) 199 It was too late now for critics . . to resist that growth of wilding art.

wildish (ˈwaɪldɪʃ), *a.* [f. WILD *a.* + -ISH[1].] Somewhat wild; inclining to wildness.

1714 *Lond. Gaz.* No. 5218/3 A Young Man about 22 Years of Age, . . a wildish Look. **1740** RICHARDSON *Pamela* (1824) I. i. 18 He was once thought to be wildish; but he is now the best of gentlemen, I think. **1796** *Plain Sense* (ed. 2) III. 102 A wildish heath, which was skirted by a thick wood. **1803** WORDSW. *Stepping Westward* 2 'Twould be a *wildish* destiny If we, who thus together roam In a strange Land, and far from home, Were in this place the guests of Chance. **1858** CARLYLE *Fredk. Gt.* VIII. v. (1872) III. 39 Prince answers as wildish young fellows will, quizzing my grave self. **1888** 'R. BOLDREWOOD' *Robbery under Arms* vii, She could frighten a wildish cow.

wild life. Also **wildlife**, **wild-life**. [f. WILD *a.* 1 and 2 + LIFE *sb.* 1.] **1.** The native fauna and flora of a particular region.

1879 R. JEFFERIES (*title*) Wild life in a southern county. **1912** A. R. DUGMORE (*title*) Wild life and the camera. **1958** *Times Lit. Suppl.* 21 Nov. p. xxii/2 The chance to live among country things and indulge a native passion for wild life (for if you scratch an Englishman you are likely to find a naturalist *manqué*). **1982** *Times* 18 Oct. 20/8 Ancient woods . . are especially important for wildlife.

2. a. *attrib.*

1936 *Discovery* June 190 His description of the patient progress of the wild-life photographer has authority behind it. *Ibid.* 191/2 (*heading*) The wild-life film. **1943** J. S. HUXLEY *TVA* 12 The total range of activities covered by the TVA..includes..wild life conservation. *Ibid.* 54, I spoke earlier of the wild life survey of the region. **1958** *Times Lit. Suppl.* 10 Jan. 24/1 A well-illustrated anthology based on the B.B.C.'s wild-life and naturalist programmes. **1982** G. HAMMOND *Fair Game* v. 47 The shooting man..needs a rich wildlife scene. **1984** *Guardian* 22 Oct. 3/2 The Liberals estimate that annual compensation to farmers who are preserving scenic land or important wildlife habitats..is running at the rate of £1 million.

b. *Comb.*, as **wildlife park**, a park in which wild animals are kept and displayed to the public in conditions as close as possible to their natural ones; **wildlife sanctuary**, an area of land in which hunting, collecting, or any other disturbance of the native fauna and flora is forbidden.

1965 P. WAYRE *Wind in Reeds* xvi. 234 We became officially known as the Norfolk Wildlife Park. Britain's first wildlife park was away to a flying start. **1976** P. R. WHITE *Planning for Public Transport* viii. 157 Coach operators' inclusive prices for visits to stately homes and wild-life parks. **1936** D. MCCOWAN *Animals Canad. Rockies* i. 12 A warning to poachers in a wild life sanctuary. **1973** V. CANNING *Flight of Wild Goose* iv. 57 The whole of that area was kept as a wild life sanctuary.

Hence **'wildlifer**, a person interested in the study and conservation of wild plants and animals.

1963 *Spectator* 8 Feb. 177/3 Children either drop the whole thing or become wildlifers of the intrepid, modern, TV-inspired kind. **1982** G. HAMMOND *Fair Game* v. 49, I can just picture a bunch of slightly hostile wild-lifers.. running the estate.

wildling ('waɪldlɪŋ). [f. WILD *a.* + -LING[1] 1. Cf. Du. *wildeling*, G. *wildling*.]

1. A wild plant or flower: = WILDING A. 2.

1840 F. D. BENNETT *Whaling Voy.* I. 345 The turmeric, *hena*,..considered too valuable..to remain a wildling. **1861** S. THOMSON *Wild Fl.* III. (ed. 4) 153 His dried garden of wildlings. **1907** *Daily Chron.* 10 July 3/3 Notes as to the growing of woodland and hedgerow 'wildlings' in a garden.

2. A wild creature or animal: = WILDING A. 3.

1841 S. BAMFORD *Passages in Life of Radical* I. xi. 72 All said he was killed... The doctor..approached along an avenue made through those wildlings. **1884** *St. James's Gaz.* 4 Apr. 6/1, I am one of her [*sc.* nature's] 'wildlings'. [Cf. WILDING A. 2, quot. 1826.] **1907** J. H. CRAWFORD *From Fox's Earth* i. 13 The wildling of the breezy heights is quite as interesting as the wildling of the cool water.

wildly ('waɪldlɪ), *adv.* [f. WILD *a.* + -LY[2].] In a wild manner, in various senses.

†**1.** Without order, irregularly; in disorder or confusion; at random, 'anyhow'; aimlessly, heedlessly. *Obs.* exc. as implied in other senses.

c **1369** CHAUCER *Dethe Blaunche* 875 Were she neuer so glad, Hyr lokynge was nat foly sprad Ne wildely, thogh that she pleyde. **1450** *Paston Lett.* I. 159 How the cuntre of N. and S. [= Norfolk and Suffolk] stonde right wildely, withowt a mene may be that justice be hadde. *a* **1548** HALL *Chron., Hen. VIII* 46 The kynge lyke a louynge broother woulde not sende hys syster wyldely withoute a dowar assured. **1595** SHAKS. *John* IV. ii. 128 How wildely then walkes my Estate in France? **1611** —— *Wint. T.* IV. iv. 550 As th'vnthought-on accident is guiltie To what we wildely do, so we professe Our selues to be the slaues of chance. *a* **1633** G. HERBERT *Country Parson* xxii. (1652) 92 The Questions must be propounded loosely and wildely, and then the Answerer will discover what hee is. **1638** JUNIUS *Paint. Ancients* 193 There is more copiousness in things wildely scattered, than in things well and orderly digested. [**1727–46** THOMSON *Summer* 80 The wildly-devious morning-walk. **1808** SCOTT *Marm.* VI. Introd. 19 Wildly-loose their red locks fly. **1820** CAROLINE A. SOUTHEY *Ellen Fitzarthur* 80 Fancy's wildly-roving eye. **1848** DICKENS *Dombey* vi, A hundred thousand shapes and substances of incompleteness, wildly mingled out of their places.]

2. Without restraint (in various shades of meaning). **a.** Beyond limits of reason; extravagantly, fantastically; distractedly, as if out of one's wits.

c **1449** PECOCK *Repr.* I. xiii. 72 A greet licence han writers and spekers..forto write and speke more wijldeli than thei schulden be suffrid forto write and speke. **1593** SHAKS. *Lucr.* 1150 As the poore frighted Deare that stands at gaze, Wildly determining which way to flie. **1598** —— *Merry W.* III. iii. 94 Sweating, and blowing, and looking wildely. **1675** M. CLIFFORD *Hum. Reason* 68 This opinion is so wildly uncharitable, that it strikes out ten thousand Millions out of the book of Life, for each single Name that it leaves in it. **1697** DRYDEN *Virg. Past.* VIII. 22 Damon..wildly staring upwards, thus inveigh'd Against the conscious Gods. **1726** SWIFT *Gulliver* II. viii, Some of them, upon hearing me talk so wildly, thought I was mad. **1802** MARIA EDGEWORTH *Moral T., Forester* xii, Enthusiasm frequently..injures those whom it wildly attempts to serve. **1816** BYRON *Ch. Har.* III. vii, Yet must I think less wildly:—I *have* thought Too long and darkly, till my brain became..A whirling gulf of phantasy and flame. **1849** MACAULAY *Hist. Eng.* x. II. 663 How many times should we have rushed wildly from extreme to extreme! **1913** *Daily Graphic* 26 Mar. 9/1 'The Great Adventure'..is wildly extravagant and yet it is very simple and human.

b. Without moral restraint; dissolutely, licentiously; in freedom from control, at one's own will.

1561 tr. *Calvin's Four Serm.* iii. I. vij, Thei might haue liued in other places wildly & wantonly. **1611** SHAKS. *Wint. T.* V. i. 129 That I should..speake of something wildly By vs perform'd before. **1653** J. TAYLOR (Water P.) *Cert. Trav. Uncert. Journey* 8 Some few do travell in the wayes Divine, Some wander wildly with the Muses nine. **1794** MRS. RADCLIFFE *Myst. Udolpho* li, That M. Valancourt had comported himself wildly at Paris, and had spent a great deal of money.

c. With unrestrained or violent movement, feeling, or utterance; vehemently; excitedly; 'frantically', 'like mad'.

1592 SHAKS. *Ven. & Ad.* 874 Some [bushes] twin'd about her thigh to make her stay, She wildly breaketh from their strict imbrace. **1599** SANDYS *Europæ Spec.* (1632) 187 Those septentrionall inundations,..have..wildly deluviated over all the South. **1656** COWLEY *Pindar. Odes, Nemeæan Ode Pindar* vii, Some wildly fled About the room, some into corners crept. **1754** GRAY *Pleasure* 29 Their raptures now that wildly flow. **1781** COWPER *Hope* 517 The wretch, who once sang wildly, danc'd and laugh'd,..Is sober, meek, benevolent. **1828** SCOTT *F.M. Perth* xxvii, A shout.. terminating in a cadence so wildly prolonged, that..the deer started from their glens. **1855** MACAULAY *Hist. Eng.* xii. III. 173 The villagers danced wildly to the music. **1860** TYNDALL *Glac.* I. xxvii. 212 The flakes sped wildly in their oblique course. **1909** STACPOOLE *Pools of Silence* xix, The whole..herd [of elephants] wheeled, trumpeted wildly.

3. a. Without cultivation, naturally, like a wild plant. *rare.*

1611 SHAKS. *Cymb.* IV. ii. 180 Valour That wildely growes in them, but yeelds a crop As if it had beene sow'd. **1653** H. MORE *Antid. Ath.* II. vii. §5 That which grows wildly of it self is worth nothing.

b. Without the refinement or orderliness of culture or training; rudely, roughly, savagely. Also (now *esp.*) in good sense: In a free, natural, or unconventional style; with the romantic aspect of uncultivated country.

1590 SHAKS. *Com. Err.* V. i. 88 When he demean'd himselfe, rough, rude, and wildly. **1599** —— *Hen. V*, V. ii. 43 Her Hedges.., Like Prisoners wildly ouer-growne with hayre, Put forth disorder'd Twigs. **1730–46** THOMSON *Autumn* 1225 The toil-strung youth, By the quick sense of music taught alone, Leaps wildly graceful in the lively dance. **1789** G. WHITE *Selborne, Invitation* 3 The mountain ground, Wildly majestic. **1799** J. ROBERTSON *Agric. Perth* 483 The wildly wooded banks of the Ardoch. **1842** BORROW *Bible in Spain* vii. 44 Here the view became wildly interesting.

wild man. (Also formerly with hyphen, or as one word.) [Cf. Du. *wilde mann* cannibal, G. *wildemann*, *wildmann*, *wilder mann*, ON. *villumaðr*.]

1. A man who is wild, in various senses of the adj. **a.** A man of savage, fierce, uncultured, or unruly nature or character (cf. WILD *a.* 6, 7).

c **1290** *S. Eng. Leg.* 47/17 Wylde Men ne louede he nouȝt, þat rechelese weren of þouȝte. **13..** *R. Glouc. Chron.* (Rolls) App. H. 136 A wuilde men [*read* man] fol bolde þe king sende in to þe court to þe heiȝe men of þe londe. *c* **1375** *Sc. Leg. Saints* x. (*Mathou*) 402 þare-for be ȝe of stedfast wil, þocht wyld men wil ȝov do Il. **1513** *St. Papers Hen. VIII* No. 4101. lf. 5 (P.R.O.) A Seler and a tester of Redsay and therein a wilde man Ryding on a horse. **1630** [see WILD *a.* 12]. *a* **1639** WHATELEY *Prototypes* I. xvi. (1640) 161 A wild man lives as he lists himselfe.

b. (WILD *a.* 5.) A man of an uncivilized race or tribe; a savage, or one reverted to a savage state.

13.. *Cursor M.* 3081 (Gött.) [Ishmael] wonid þar as a wild man, In þat desert þat hight pharan. **1530** in *Ancestor* (1904) Oct. 181 Wolton beryth to his crest a woodwous a wylld man in his kynde vert. **1568** HACKET tr. *Thevet's Newfound World* xxiv. 31 b, We were well received of the Indians or wilde men of the Countrey. **1575** in Brydges *Brit. Bibliogr.* (1810) I. 541 To make waye in the streetes, there are certayne men apparelled lyke devells, and wylde men, with skybbs and certayne beadells. **1611** W. ADAMS *Let.* in Rundall *Mem. Japon* (Hakl. Soc.) 37 Eight of our men..ranne from vs with the pinnesse, and (as we suppose) were eaten of the wild men. **1767** *Ann. Reg., Chron.* 47/1 Peter the wild man, who was taken in the Hartz Forest in Hanover. **1825** J. NEAL *Bro. Jonathan* II. 2 The wild man of North America is exceedingly unlike the wild man of every other country.

c. An extremist in a political party, a profession, etc. Usu. in *pl.*

1905 D. G. PHILLIPS *Plum Tree* 266 And I wished for a 'wild man' as the candidate for governor. **1910** BELLOC *Pongo & Bull* xix. 287 The Wild Men on the Opposition side might cheer. **1923** *Weekly Dispatch* 13 May 2 The wild men pin their faith to the Capital Levy as a vote-catcher. **1923** *Daily Mail* 23 July 14 All the 'wild men' of European music, such as Schönberg, Bartok, Prokoviev, Stravinsky, Alois Haba.., Milhaud, and Poulenc.

2. (WILD *a.* 1.) A name for the orang-outang: also ***wild man of the woods*** (see WOOD *sb.*).

[**1769** E. BANCROFT *Guiana* 131 These animals [*sc.* Orang-Outang], in all the different languages of the natives, are called by names signifying a Wild Man.] **1791** SMELLIE tr. *Buffon's Nat. Hist.* VIII. 97 As there is a greater similarity between this animal and man than between those creatures which resemble him most, as the Barbary ape [etc.], the Indians are to be excused for associating him with the human species, under the denomination of *orang-outang*, or *wild man*. **1881** J. HATTON *New Ceylon* iii. 72 The Bornean 'wild man' is quite harmless.

wildness ('waɪldnɪs). Forms: see WILD *a.* [f. WILD *a.* + -NESS. Cf. MHG. *wiltnisse*, G. *wildnis*.] The quality or condition of being wild, in various senses.

1. a. Undomesticated state (of an animal); the untamed disposition characteristic of such state; fierceness, savageness, ferocity; also, shyness.

c **1440** *Promp. Parv.* 528 Wyldnesse, *indomitas, ferocitas.* **1509** HAWES *Past. Pleas.* XI. (Percy Soc.) 40 Mylyzyus.. Dyd fyrst attame and breke the wyldenes Of the riall stedes. **1593** SHAKS. *Lucr.* 980 And let milde women to him loose their mildnesse, Wilder to him then Tygers in their wildnesse. **1596** DALRYMPLE tr. *Leslie's Hist. Scot.* (S.T.S.) I. 31 Lyke wylde hartes,..throuch a certane wyldnes of nature, flie the..syght of man. **1611** [see BEAUTY 8]. **1774** GOLDSM. *Nat. Hist.* V. 125 His necessities, and the privation of light, make him lose all idea of liberty, and bring down his natural wildness. **1859** DARWIN *Orig. Spec.* vii. 212 The greater wildness of all our large birds than of our small birds.

b. Uncultivated state (of a plant).

1599 SHAKS. *Hen. V*, V. ii. 55 Our Vineyards, Fallowes, Meades, and Hedges, Defectiue in their natures, grow to wildnesse. **1697** DRYDEN *Virg. Georg.* II. 73 These [trees].. change their salvage Mind: Their Wildness lose. **1892** KATH. TYNAN in *Speaker* 3 Sept. 290/1 The roses..will deteriorate year after year, returning gradually to wildness.

2. Uncultivated state (of a place or region); the character or aspect of such a place or its scenery. Also *concr.* a wild place, a wilderness (now *rare* or *obs.*).

c **1374** CHAUCER *Former Age* 34 Thyse tyrauntz put hem gladly nat in pres No places wyldnesse ne no busshes for to wynne. *a* **1513** FABYAN *Chron.* clxxxv. (1516) oiv b/2 Nat ferre from warwyke in a wyldenesse [*later edd.* wyldernes(se)]. **1615** W. LAWSON *Country Housew. Garden* (1626) 3 The wildnesse of the earth and weeds..is killed by frosts and drought. **1625** BACON *Ess., Gardens* (Arb.) 562 The Heath..I wish..to be framed, as much as may be, to a Naturall wildnesse. **1709** PRIOR *Henry & Emma* 420 The Wildness of the Wood. **1801** COXE *Tour in Monmouthshire* I. 67 The scenery..is a pleasing intermixture of wildness and cultivation. **1815** SCOTT *Guy M.* xvii, All the wildness of Salvator here, and there the fairy scenes of Claude. **1832** R. & J. LANDER *Exped. Niger* I. xi. 78 The gloomy fastnesses and wildnesses of nature.

3. Uncivilized or uncultured state or character (of persons); savagery, barbarity; †rudeness, roughness of manners (*obs.*).

1639 N. N. tr. *Du Bosq's Compl. Woman* I. 62 The wildnesse of the one, prevailes more then the faire perswasion of the other. **1680** OTWAY *Orphan* I. iv, I'd rather..grow wrinckled and deform'd As wildness and most rude neglect could make me. **1869** TOZER *Highl. Turkey* II. 174 The wildness of the tribes by which it was inhabited. **1871** BURR *Ad Fidem* iv. 63 There is a native wildness in every man.

4. Unrestrained condition or quality; want of, resistance to, or freedom from restraint or control (with various shades of meaning).

a. Disposition to take one's own way; unruliness, insubordination; disorderly or riotous conduct; dissolute character, looseness of morals, licentiousness, wantonness; excessive liveliness or frolicsomeness.

c **1400** *Rom. Rose* 4894 The tyme of yougth forto pace Withoute ony deth or distresse, It is so full of wyldenesse. *Ibid.* 4939 Folkes forto lede Into disporte and wyldenesse. *c* **1440** *Promp. Parv.* 528 Wyldnesse, or wantonhede, *insolencia, dissolucio.* **1523** LD. BERNERS *Froiss.* I. cccxciii. fff v/2 Somtyme ryot dothe good. We haue well aduaunsed forthe our payment with a lytell wyldnesse. *a* **1548** HALL *Chron., Hen. V* 33 Turnyng insolencie and wildnes into grauitie and sobernes. **1601** SHAKS. *Jul. C.* II. i. 189 He is giuen To sports, to wildenesse, and much company. **1605** *Lond. Prodigal* III. iii, Impute his wildnesse, syr, vnto his youth. **1692** DRYDEN *St. Euremont's Ess.* 28 The Roman people had something of wildness in them; afterwards this Humour turned into Austerity, and became a rigid Vertue. **1710** R. WARD *Life H. More* 51 Ye are running into strange Wildnesses and Excesses. **1748** RICHARDSON *Clarissa* (1810) III. ii. 23 To be sure Mr. Lovelace was a wild gentleman, but wildness was a distemper which would cure itself. **1801** MARIA EDGEWORTH *Contrast* i, She hoped his wildness was only the effect of good spirits, and that he would soon settle to some business. **1827** COLERIDGE *Table-t.* 23 July, Genius may co-exist with wildness, idleness, folly, even with crime. **1879** D. J. HILL *Life Irving* 152 Moore, full of troubles from want of means and the wildness of his son.

b. Frenzy, distraction; distracted air or aspect; extreme folly or unreasonableness, irrational or fantastic character, extravagance; violence, vehemence, passionateness (of a feeling, etc.); excitedness, extreme eagerness.

c **1400** *Destr. Troy* 9197 What wildnes, or worship, waknet my hert, For to hap her in hert? **1602** SHAKS. *Ham.* III. i. 40, I do wish That your good Beauties be the happy cause Of Hamlets wildenesse. **1621** FLETCHER *Pilgrim* V. v, Though he be rash, and suddain (which is all his wildness) Take heed ye wrong him not. **1725** WATTS *Logic* II. iii. §3 A Delirium is but a short Wildness of the Imagination. **1785** SARAH FIELDING *Ophelia* II. vi, I enquired for Lord Dorchester with an eager wildness. **1808** SCOTT *Marm.* VI. v, Joy unwonted, and surprise, Gave their strange wildness to his eyes. **1883** D. C. MURRAY *Hearts* xix, Alarmed by his aspect and the wildness of his words. **1884** PENNINGTON *Wiclif* viii. 269 There is no fanaticism, no wildness in his statements.

5. In reference to style or aspect, with various implications: cf. prec. senses and WILD *a.* 14, 14 b.

1762 WARTON *Observ. Spenser's F.Q.* (ed. 2) I. v. 197 His [*sc.* Chaucer's] romantic arguments, his wildness of painting, his simplicity and antiquity of expression. **1797** MRS. RADCLIFFE *Italian* xiii, The simplicity of their appearance, approached to wildness, was tempered by an hospitable spirit. **1860** TYNDALL *Glac.* I. xxv. 184 There was a wildness in the sky like that of anger. **1887** MISS BRADDON *Like & Unlike* ix, Your wildness was your charm... You were a beautiful, ignorant creature, knowing nothing of the world.

wildred, wildren, -in, wildrenes(**se**: see WILDERED, WILDERN, WILDERNESS.

†**wildship.** *Obs. rare.* In 3 **wildscipe** (**-sipe**). [f. WILD *a.* + -SHIP 1.] Wildness.

c **1205** LAY. 20845 [The fox] for wildscipe [*c* **1275** wildsipe] climbið, and cluden isecheð.

wildsome: see WILSOME *a.*[1]

Wild Turkey. The proprietary name of a brand of whisky; a drink or glassful of this.
1949 *Official Gaz.* (U.S. Patent Office) 26 Apr. 1007 Austin Nichols & Co., Incorporated, Brooklyn, N.Y... Wild Turkey... For Whiskey. Claims use since May 29, 1942. **1968** *Trade Marks Jrnl.* 20 Mar. 448/1 Wild Turkey 917,193. Wines, spirits (beverages) and liqueurs. Five Mills Limited, 37 Grafton Way.. London W.1; Merchants. **1975** *New Yorker* 20 Jan. 30/1, I know—it took me seven weeks to do a page and a half the last time, but I was into the Wild Turkey then, and you'd be amazed how fast I can write when my pencil can actually form legible letters. **1979** J. CROSBY *Party of Year* (1980) viii. 48 He poured Cassidy another Wild Turkey. **1980** J. KRANTZ *Princess Daisy* xvi. 258 Two bottles of Soave Bolla and one of Wild Turkey bourbon.

wild type. *Genetics.* The type of strain, gene, or characteristic that prevails among individuals in natural conditions, as opposed to an atypical mutant type. Freq. *attrib.* or as *adj.*
[**1913** C. B. BRIDGES in *Jrnl. Exper. Zool.* XV. 587 When a female [Drosophila] with white eyes is mated to a wild male with red eyes, the daughters have red, and the sons, white eyes.] **1914** —— in *Science* 17 July 107/2 Half of the wild-type daughters.. when out-crossed to barred males.. gave exceptions as follows:.. Exceptions. 5% of both sexes. Wild type ♀; barred ♂. **1932** [see SUPPRESSOR 2]. **1946** *Nature* 19 Oct. 558/1 These include wild-type strains [of *E. coli*] with no growth-factor deficiencies, and single mutant types requiring only thiamin or phenylalanine. **1970** *Sci. Amer.* Mar. 103/1 Most mutant genes are nonfunctional or do something very different from wild-type genes, so that they can be easily distinguished. **1970** *Nature* 22 Aug. 806/1 Albinism is monofactorial and is recessive to wild type pigmentation. **1976** *Ann. Rev. Microbiol.* XXX. 90 A number of compounds produce phenocopies of morphological mutants when added to the growth medium of wild type.

wilducke, wildurnes, obs. ff. *wild duck* (see WILD *a.* 1), WILDERNESS.

†**wildware.** *Obs.* [a. MLG. *wildware* (whence early Da. *vild(t)vare*), f. *wild* WILD *a.* + *ware* WARE *sb.*[3]] Fur of wild animals.
1393 *Close Roll 17 Rich. II* m. 3 (P.R.O.) De uno vate de wyldeware videlicet de Cristygrey fyngrey pople Bys Ermyn et letuse. *Ibid.* 24 Sex kipp de wildware. *c* **1400** *Brut* ccxxv. 293 Ne non wyldware in Furreure of beȝonde see. **1402** *Nottingham Rec.* II. 20 Appretiatores de wyldware, videlicet, v. pellium de ermyn, ijs. **1433** *Will of Fitz-John* (Somerset Ho.), Togam penulatam cum Wyeldeware.

Wild West. Also wild west, wild West. **1.** The western part of the U.S. during its lawless frontier period.
1849 C. BRONTË *Shirley* III. xiii. 272 What suggested the wild West to your mind? **1851** MAYNE REID *Scalp Hunters* i. (1852) 7 The Wild West. **1898** H. JAMES in *Literature* 30 Apr. 512/1 Has he [*sc.* Bret Harte] continued to distil and dilute the Wild West because the public would only take him as wild and Western? **1903** CHESTERTON *Robert Browning* v. 111 A gambling hell in the Wild West. **1937** PHILLIPS & NIVEN *Colour in Canad. Rockies* ix. 61 On my first visit there were many marked qualities of the 'wild west' there. **1977** *Times* 20 Sept. 12/1 The Rio Grande.. has been oversold in the legends and songs of the old Wild West.
2. *transf.* and *fig.*
1889 G. B. SHAW *London Music in 1888–89* (1937) 170 Somewhere in the wild west of the Old Brompton Road. **1944** F. CLUNE *Red Heart* 69 Australia's Wild West, as picturesque as Texas, was buzzing with rumours of raids, hold-ups. **1975** J. O'FAOLAIN *Women in Wall* 11 My setting is the Wild West of an age often called 'Dark'.
3. a. *attrib.*
1922 E. E. CUMMINGS *Let.* 26 Feb. (1969) 82 Attacks by Bedoins, wild-west style, shooting at Dos with rifles. **1922** E. M. FORSTER *Life to Come* (1972) 100 They passed through the village, on their way back past a cinema, which was giving a Wild West stunt. **1940** 'G. ORWELL' in *Horizon* Mar. 193 The Wild West story.. with its cattle-rustlers. **1965** A. NICOL *Truly Married Woman* 5 She removed the Wild West novels and romance magazines. **1971** *Advocate-News* (Barbados) 17 Sept. (Guyana Suppl.) p. iv/2 There it will link up at the 'wild west' border town of Lethem with a similar road the Brazilian army engineers are building to connect with Manaus and the Pan-American Highway.
b. Special Comb.: **Wild West show**, a circus or fairground entertainment depicting cowboys and Indians with exhibitions of riding, shooting, etc.; also *fig.*; similarly ***Wild West exhibition***.
1885 in B. A. Botkin *Treas. Amer. Folklore* (1944) I. 150 Buffalo Bill's 'Wild West' Prairie exhibition and Rocky Mountain show. **1895** 'MARK TWAIN' in *N. Amer. Rev.* July 8 A man who could hunt flies with a rifle and command a ducal salary in a Wild West show. **1914** A. BENNETT *Price of Love* vii. 133 Skating-rinks, Wild West exhibitions, Dutch auctions. **1937** N. MARSH *Vintage Murder* xxiv. 268 'Shut up. This isn't a Wild West show.' 'You give me the lie!' 'Oh, for God's sake don't go native.' **1976** *Billings* (Montana) *Gaz.* 20 June 8-c/2 Later, the way it worked in the 'wild west' shows of the day, the U.S. cavalry came along, rescued the passengers and drove off the Indians. **1979** J. WAINWRIGHT *Duty Elsewhere* vii. 29 'Y'mean—illegal methods?.. Something of a wild west show.' 'That's one way of putting it.'
Hence **wild 'western** (also with initial capitals) *a.*, characteristic of or resembling the Wild West; as *sb.*, a film about the Wild West; = WESTERN B. 4; **Wild 'Westerner**.
1864 M. B. CHESNUT *Diary* 2 Dec. in C. W. Woodward *M. Chesnut's Civil War* (1981) 682 He had come to take Serena—alone. That is his wild western fashion. **1934** *Cinema Q.* III. IV. 198 'Wild Western' was, almost from the inception of the film, one of its most popular subjects. **1963** I. FLEMING *On Her Majesty's Secret Service* xvii. 192 A group of harlequins, Wild Westerners and pirates. **1967** D. FRANCIS *Blood Sport* viii. 95 Jackson preserved its own wild western flavour to the extent of a small authentic stage coach waiting in front of the drug store. **1981** A. LURIE *Lang. of Clothes* iv. 112 At any national convention the Wild Westerners will be the easiest to identify. **1982** W. MANKOWITZ *Mazeppa* vii. 118 The Menken enjoyed the Washoe wild western atmosphere.

wildwood ('waɪldwʊd). [Orig. two words, WILD *a.* 4 and WOOD *sb.*] A forest of natural growth, or allowed to grow naturally; an uncultivated or unfrequented wood. (In later use chiefly *poet.*)
a **1122** *O.E. Chron.* (Laud MS.) an. 963 Syððon com se biscop Aðelwold to þære mynstre þe wæs ȝehaten Medeshamstede.. ne fand þær nan þing buton ealde weallas & wilde wuda. *c* **1205** LAY. 25905 þer þe eotend unc ifeng forð mid him seoluen fiftene mile into þisse wilde wude. **1382** WYCLIF *Isa* x. 18 The glorie of his wilde wode. —— *Zech.* xi. 2 Ʒoule, ȝe ookis of Basan, for the stronge wijlde wod is kitt doun. **1814** SCOTT *Mass. of Glencoe* ii, Those for whom I pour the lay, Not wild-wood deep, nor mountain grey.. Could screen from treach'rous cruelty. *a* **1864** HAWTHORNE *Amer. Note-bks.* (1879) II. 102 Whether in garden or wild-wood. **1884** RUSKIN in *Pall Mall Gaz.* 10 Dec. 11/2 Such a piece of mountain wildwood.
attrib. *a* **1568** in *Bannatyne MS.* (Hunter. Club) 291/73 Ane heklit hud maid of the wyld wode sege. **1611** SHAKS. *Cymb.* IV. ii. 390 When With wild wood-leaues & weeds, I ha' strew'd his graue. **1776** MICKLE tr. *Camoens' Lusiad* 40 The turf his bed, the wild-wood boughs his shade. **1794** S. T. COLERIDGE in J. D. Campbell *Life* ii. (1894) 34, I had been wandering among the wildwood scenery and terrible graces of the Welsh mountains. **1814** WORDSW. *Yarrow Visited* 66 How sweet, on this autumnal day, The wild-wood fruits to gather. **1856** WHITTIER *Mayflowers* ii, The wild-wood flowers.

wile (waɪl), *sb.* Forms: 2–5 wil, 4–8 wyle, (4 wylle, *Sc.* quhile, 5 whyle, wyhylle, wele, *Sc.* wyill), 5–6 wyll, (while, vyle, 6 wyell, 7 wiele), 4– wile. [Origin and early history obscure. The earliest examples are from regions subjected to strong Scandinavian influence. Early ME. *wil* may therefore perhaps represent prehistoric Scand. *wīhl-, whence ON. *vél* craft, artifice, contrivance, engine (cf. the several compounds of this, and *véla* to defraud).
The current derivation of *wile* from an AF. var. of OF. *guile* GUILE *sb.* with initial *w* is open to the objection that no such variant is known. Through similarity of sense *wile* prob. became associated with WIEL, q.v.; cf. the parallelism of *bywyle* (which occurs beside *bygyle* in Shoreham's poems) and *biwiȝelien* (Layamon), *biwihelin* (St. Juliana). The relation of *wile* to the synonymous *wilt* is obscure.]
1. A crafty, cunning, or deceitful trick; a sly, insidious, or underhand artifice; a stratagem, ruse. Formerly sometimes in somewhat wider sense: A piece of deception, a deceit, a delusion. Chiefly *pl.* (in *sing.* now *arch.* or *poet.*).
1154 *O.E. Chron.* (Laud MS.) an. 1128 He hit dide forði þæt he wolde þurh his micele wiles ðær beon wær it tweolf monð oððe mare. *c* **1200** ORMIN 6635 All þatt badd he þurrh swikedom & all þurrh ille wiless. *c* **1220** *Bestiary* 385 A wilde der is ðat is ful of fele wiles, fox is hire to name. *Ibid.* 541 Ðis deuel is mikel wið wil and maȝt. **1303** R. BRUNNE *Handl. Synne* 361 Manyon trowyn on here wylys, And many tymes þe pye hem gylys. *c* **1330** —— *Chron. Wace* (Rolls) 539 Hereþ now of a quynte wyle, How eche of þo þoughte oþer gyle. **1340** HAMPOLE *Pr. Consc.* 1360 þe world.. ledes a man with wrenkes and wyles. *c* **1350** *Ipomadon* 6674 Imayne hathe an while fonde And thought hym to haue begyld. **1390** GOWER *Conf.* I. 129 With suche wiles as thei caste. *Ibid.* 130 Thei schope among hem such a wyle, The king was ded withinne a whyle. *c* **1400** *Rom. Rose* 4293 She knewe eche wrenche and euery gise Of love and euery wile. **1456** SIR G. HAYE *Law Arms* (S.T.S.) 189 To conquest landis and heritagis fra Cristin folk, with wylis and falshede. *c* **1485** *Digby Myst.* III. 377 With wrath or wyhylles we xal hyrre wynne. **1558** G. CAVENDISH *Poems* (1825) II. 13 Whilest I was workyng witty whiles in Fraunce, I was at home supplanted. **1573** *Satir. Poems Reform.* xl. 50 Bot sum, perchance, that winks mair wylelie, Will say thay wait ane wyle that I na wist. **1590** SHAKS. *Com. Err.* IV. iii. 10 Sure these are but imaginarie wiles, And lapland Sorcerers inhabite here. **1651** HOBBES *Leviathan* I. xiii. 61 By force, or wiles, to master the persons of all men he can. **1654** GATAKER *Disc. Apol.* 36 He by a wile drew me to Preach one Afternoon on the Week Lecture day there. **1781** COWPER *Hope* 649 This.. Rejects all treaty; penetrates all wiles. **1825** SCOTT *Talism.* xix, That Richard would burst through the flimsy wiles you spread for him. **1876** SWINBURNE *Erechtheus* 216 By the fraud of a two-fold wile. **1888** BRYCE *Amer. Commw.* lxx. II. 549 The wiles by which its members are lured or driven to their goal.
b. Without implication of deceit: A subtle contrivance; a skilful device or scheme; an artifice, 'dodge'. *Obs.* or merged in prec. sense.
a **1300** *Cursor M.* 4153 Bot sin he algat sal be ded Do it þan wit suilk a wile þat yee youre handes ne þer-wit file. *c* **1400** MAUNDEV. (Roxb.) xxxiii. 149 þai vse anoþer wyle for to get þis gold with. *a* **1400–50** *Wars Alex.* 1148 For wele wist þai þam nane to wyn to þe cite. *c* **1470** HENRY *Wallace* IX. 1176 Wattir fra thaim forsuth can nocht be set; Sum wthyr wyill ws worthis for to get. **1508** DUNBAR *Gold. Targe* 224, I coud eschew hir presence be no wyle. *a* **1628** PRESTON *New Covt.* (1634) 21 We think God not able to doe it, except we help him with wyles and tricks..of our own. **1830** A. CUNNINGHAM *Brit. Painters* (ed. 2) I. 235 He became acquainted with all the wiles and stratagems of position and light and shade.
c. In lighter sense: An amorous or playful trick; a piece of sportive cunning or artfulness.
c **1600** J. LANE in *Shaks. Cent. Praise* (1879) 32 Venus straight courted him with many a wile. **1632** MILTON *L'Allegro* 27 Haste thee nymph, and bring with thee.. Quips and Cranks, and wanton Wiles, Nods, and Becks, and Wreathed Smiles. *a* **1721** PRIOR *Songs* xiii, Victoria shews me all her wiles, Which yet I dare not shun. **1770** GOLDSM. *Des. Vill.* 183 E'en children followed with endearing wile. *a* **1839** PRAED *Charades* ix, And telling of Love's wiles To ears that listen. **1847** EMERSON *Repr. Men, Shakesp.* Wks. (Bohn) I. 362 He read the hearts of men and women,.. and their second thought, and wiles; the wiles of innocence. **1865** DICKENS *Mut. Fr.* I. ii, Lady Tippins's winning wiles are contagious. **1880** MORRIS *Ode of Life* 17, I treasure up each baby wile.
d. *spec.* A cunning turn or other trick of the hare to escape the hunters.
1691 RAY *Creation* I. (1692) 128 The wiles and ruses, which these timid Creatures make use of to save themselves. **1735** SOMERVILLE *Chase* II. 202 The puzling Pack unravel Wile by Wile, Maze within Maze. **1781** W. BLANE *Ess. Hunting* (1788) 210 The wiles of the Hare have been all along the study of my leisure hours.
2. Deceit or deceitfulness; craft, cunning, subtlety, guile. Now *rare.*
c **1374** CHAUCER *Troylus* I. 719 þow wost I do it for no wyle. *c* **1375** *Sc. Leg. Saints* Prol. 8 Gret foly, quhile, & vantones. *c* **1400** *Beryn* 2239 Falshode, wrong & while. **1426** LYDG. *De Guil. Pilgr.* 1815 Sleythe, falshed, or any whyle. **15..** DUNBAR *Poems* lxxxii. 41 That ȝe haue nether witt nor wyll To win ȝour selff ane bettir name! **1634** MILTON *Comus* 906 Through the force, and through the wile Of unblest inchanter vile. **1814** CARY *Dante, Inf.* xx. 114 Michael Scot, Practised in every slight of magic wile. **1848** LYTTON *Harold* v. iii, This Godwin is a man of treachery and wile. **1904** *Sat. Rev.* 7 May 576/1 The humour but not the wile of the publisher stopped at this point.
3. a. Applied to particular mechanical contrivances: see quots. **b.** (*nonce-use.*) An ingenious or fanciful figure or device.
1674 N. COX *Gentl. Recreat.* I. (1677) 18 Engines that we take Deer withal, are called Wiles. **1824** MACTAGGART *Gallovid. Encycl.* 446 Throok the wyle, the thawcrook, the twister. **1825** JAMIESON, *Wile, wylie*, an instrument for twisting straw ropes. Dumfr. **1849** NEALE *Seaton. Poems, Edom* xxvi, Ivory, carved in thousand curious wiles.

wile, *v.* [f. WILE *sb.*, or aphetic f. BIWILE.]
†**1.** *trans.* To deceive by a wile; to beguile, delude. *Obs. rare* (exc. as implied in other senses).
c **1375** *Sc. Leg. Saints* xxx (*Theodera*) 311 Quhat, wenys þu I wald þe wile, Gud douchtir?
2. To bring, draw, or get by a wile (a person or animal to or from a place, course of action, etc., or a thing from a person); to lead, induce, or obtain by craft or cunning.
a **1400** *Pistill of Susan* 213 Wylyliche heo wyled hir wenches a-way. *c* **1400** *Beryn* 2691 Ʒit som ageyn hym wyled A grete part of his pepill. *c* **1460** *Towneley Myst.* viii. 233 Whence is yond warlow with his wand that thus wold wyle oure folk away? *c* **1475** *Rauf Coilȝear* 709 Allace, that I was hidder wylit. *a* **1500** *Coventry Corpus Chr. Pl.* ii. 840 From vs no man wyll hym wyle. *c* **1560** A. SCOTT *Poems* (S.T.S.) xxxiv. 26 The wysest woman þairout W^t wirdis may be wyllit To do þe deid. **1572** *Satir. Poems Reform.* xxxviii. 36 As the fals fowler.. Deuoiris the pure volatill he wylis to the net. **1590** GREENE *Orl. Fur.* (1599) 54 When Iuno wil'd the trull. **1599** T. CUTWODE *Caltha Poet.* (Roxb.) xxiii, Wyelling fond louers sometime from their wits. *a* **1600** MONTGOMERIE *Misc. Poems* xl. 13 My wofull hairt auay with thee thou wyld, Fra me to be exyld. **1789** BURNS *Blue-Eyed Lassie* 9 She talk'd, she smil'd, my heart she wil'd. **1818** SCOTT *Hrt. Midl.* xxii, He could wile the very flounders out o' the Firth. **1853** MRS. GASKELL *Ruth* xviii, He's such winning ways he wiles one over to anything. **1879** STEVENSON *Lay Morals*, etc. (1911) 297 She could neither be driven nor wiled into the parish kirk.
fig. **1847** TENNYSON *Princess* VII. 48 To wile the length from languorous hours, and draw The sting from pain.
†**b.** *refl.* To get *away* by stealth, steal *away*.
? *a* **1400** *Morte Arth.* 3908 Whills he myghte wile hyme awaye, and wyne to hir speche.
3. (as a substitute for WHILE *v.* 3) To divert attention pleasantly from (something painful or tedious); to charm *away*; *esp.* to cause (time) to pass *away* pleasantly or insensibly: = BEGUILE *v.* 5.
Cf. L. *decipere tempus*, F. *tromper le temps*.
1796 MME. D'ARBLAY *Camilla* III. x, He persuaded his sisters, therefore, to walk out with him, to wile away at once expectation and retrospection. **1810** SCOTT *Lady of L.* II. x, Her smile.. Wiled the old harper's mood away. **1817** KIRBY & SP. *Entomol.* xxiv. II. 379 Happy industry, that wiles the toils of labour with a song. **1838** DICKENS *O. Twist* xlvi, I was reading a book to-night, to wile the time away. **1840** E. E. NAPIER *Scenes & Sports For. Lands* II. v. 172 We.. used to wile away the day with all manner of fun. **1880** 'VERNON LEE' *Italy* II. iii. 59 Foreigners who came to study art or to wile away a lazy existence.
Hence **wiling** *vbl. sb.*
1583 *Leg. Bp. St. Androis* 971 The vther.. Concludit schortlie for to slea him, For vyling of his syluer fra him.

wile, obs. f. VILE *a.*, WALE *sb.*[2] and *v.*[1], WEEL[2], WHILE, WILL.

wileare, pseudo-archaic f. WHILERE.
1616 J. LANE *Contn. Sqr.'s T.* v. 585 Whence they whoe woold Algarsife killd wileare.

wilecoit, obs. form of WYLIECOAT *Sc.*

wilele, obs. form of WILILY.

†**wilely**, *a. Obs.* [f. WILE *sb.* + -LY[1].] = WILY. (Also in comb.)

1556 J. HEYWOOD *Spider & F.* xxiv. 10 The faughter herin, so wilely witted, To saue his lyfe, apealth to be repride. **1572** in D. Digges *Complete Ambass.* (1655) 219 Your Mr. Worseley, whom I found wilely and wilful. **1675** H. MORE in R. Ward *Life* (1710) 276 'Twill find a Million of Tergiversations and wilely Reasonings to excuse a Man from his Duty. **1709** SACHEVERELL *Serm. 5 Nov.* 21 The Crafty Insidiousness of such wilely Volpones. **1793** W. ROBERTS *Looker-on* No. 79 (1794) III. 248 Son of Henry Waldron, .. under the wilely alias of George Barrington.

wilen, obs. form of WHILOM.

wilesome, var. WILSOME *a.*[1]

wiley, obs. form of WILY.

Wilfridian (wɪl'frɪdɪən). *Eccl. Hist.* [f. St. *Wilfrid* (634–709) + -IAN.] A member of a religious fraternity founded by Father F. W. Faber (1814–63) for his fellow-converts to Roman Catholicism; later united with the oratory of St. Philip Neri, Birmingham.

1847 F. W. FABER *Let.* 23 Sept. in J. W. Bowden *Life & Lett. Frederick William Faber* (1869) viii. 329 The Wilfridians are allowed to work their double work, against ignorance and brutal sin. **1848** J. H. NEWMAN *Let.* 2 Jan. (1962) XII. 144 What seems to me best is .. for .. St John and you to go to Cotton to take charge of the Wilfridians. **1869** J. W. BOWDEN *Life & Lett. Frederick William Faber* viii. 295 From the name of the latter Saint they were commonly called Wilfridians. **1928** *St. Wilfrid* xvii. 231 Father Faber did much to make him known and loved... In his first year as a Catholic priest, he and his forty Wilfridians converted a whole parish in Staffordshire. **1981** S. CHITTY *Gwen John* ix. 134 Frederick Faber .. became a Catholic and founded the order of Wilfridians at Elton.

wilful ('wɪlfʊl), *a.*[1] (*adv.*, *sb.*) Compared wilfuller, wilfullest (both *rare*). Also 3–4 **wil(le)uol, wyl(le)fol**, 3–7 **wilfull**, 3–5, 7–8 (9 *U.S.*) **willful**, 4 **wyluolle, (weleful)**, 4–5 **willef(f)ul**, 4–6 *Sc.* **vilful(l**, also various forms with *y*, *ll*, *ff*, with or without final *e*. [f. WILL *sb.*[1] + -FUL: not recorded in OE. (but see WILFULLY): cf. WILLESFUL.]

A. *adj.* **1. a.** Asserting or disposed to assert one's own will against persuasion, instruction, or command; governed by will without regard to reason; determined to take one's own way; obstinately self-willed or perverse. (Of persons or personal attributes, or *transf.* of actions: see also 5.)

c **1200** *Trin. Coll. Hom.* 75 *Pertinaces in malo eliminat ecclesia* holie chirche deleð fro cristendom, þo þe wilfulle ben here sinnes to luuen. *c* **1250** in *O.E. Misc.* 184 Hwan þu sixst on leode King þat is wilful. *c* **1374** CHAUCER *Troylus* III. 935 For verray sloupe and oþere wilful tacches. *c* **1400** *Rule St. Benet* (verse) 280 Men or wemen of wilful mode, þat order of religion takes. **1529** in Leadam *Sel. Cases Star Chamber* (Selden Soc.) II. 34 The seid Henry is sklanderus and a wylfull person and wyll not be ordered but after his owne wyll. **1570–6** LAMBARDE *Peramb. Kent* 256 Some blinde and wilfull worshipper. **1579** LYLY *Euphues* 43 He that to day is not willyng, will to morrow bee more wilful. **1605** SHAKS. *Lear* II. iv. 305 To wilfull men, The iniuries that they themselues procure, Must be their Schoole-Masters. **1773** MRS. CHAPONE *Improv. Mind* (1774) II. vi. 24 The smallest disappointment .. will put wilful young people out of temper. **1821** SHELLEY *Adonais* xi, One .. in her wilful grief would break Her bow and winged reeds. **1867** SWINBURNE *Blake* (1868) 190 These opinions, and stranger than these, he put forth in the cloudiest style, the wilfullest humour, and the stormiest excitement.

Comb. **1632** LITHGOW *Trav.* I. 34 What wilfull-hearted man can be so apt to belieue, that our blessed Lady had such estimation of morter and stones?

†**b.** In good sense: Strong-willed, strongly persistent. *Obs. rare.*

c **1330** R. BRUNNE *Chron. Wace* (Rolls) 5663 A myghtful [*v.r.* wilfull] man was Maryus, Of fair speche merueillous. **1633** T. JAMES *Voy.* 92 Being now become wilfull in our indeauours.

c. In nonce Comb. with *wavy*.

1877 [see *meal-drift* s.v. MEAL *sb.*[1] 3 a].

†**2.** Having the will *to do* something; purposing, intending; wishful, desirous. Also said of the purpose or desire: Eager, earnest. *Obs.*

1340 *Ayenb.* 162 Nou yziȝ ane yongne boryeis and ane newe kniȝt. Mochel habbeþ þos of uele þoȝtes newe diuerses and wyluolle. Þe borgeys wylneþ to chapfari .. þe knyȝt .. wilneþ corteysyes to done an largeliche yeue. **1375** BARBOUR *Bruce* II. 345 Arayit rycht awisely, Willful to do chewalry. **1390** GOWER *Conf.* I. 361 Whan that he .. hadde his wilful pourpos wonne Of al this Erthe under the Sonne. *c* **1400** *Destr. Troy* 725 [She] Wan þe thy worship & wilfull desire. *a* **1500** *Ratis Raving* 2919 Wysmen ar wylfull to do grace, & mercyable in petwous cas. **1513** DOUGLAS *Æneis* XII. Prol. 270 On fut I sprent into my bayr sark, Wilfull for till compleyt my langsum wark. **1573–80** TUSSER *Husb.* (1878) 77 Be wilfull to kill and vnskilfull to store, And looke for no foison.

†**3.** Willing; consenting; ready to comply with a request, desire, or requirement. *Obs.*

1375 BARBOUR *Bruce* XI. 266 The worthy kyng, quhen he has seyn His host .. wilfull to fulfill His liking, with gud hert and will. **1456** SIR G. HAYE *Law Arms* (S.T.S.) 207 Gif thai lordis .. defendis maliciously the ref, and is nocht wilfull to mak reformacioun and redress. *c* **1460** *Oseney Reg.* 39 With þe wilfull consent of þe Kyng and of the Aduocates of the same church. *c* **1475** *Partenay* 1641 With A wilfull hert full gentilly resceyuyng .. thys souerayn. **1590** SHAKS. *Mids. N.* V. i. 211 When Wals are so wilfull, to heare without warning. **1598** —— *Merry W.* III. ii. 44, I will .. divulge Page .. for a secure and wilfull Acteon.

†**4. a.** Proceeding from the will; done, undertaken, assumed, or undergone of one's own free will or choice; not compulsory or enforced: = VOLUNTARY A. 1 b, 3. *Obs.*

c **1374** CHAUCER *Boeth.* III. pr. xi. (1868) 98, I ne trete nat heere now of weleful moeuynges of the sowle. *c* **1380** WYCLIF *Wks.* (1880) 14 Men þat haue .. taken cristis mekenesse and gret pouert bi wilful profession. *c* **1400** *Rule St. Benet* (prose) 142 The secunde is, þat þe behouis liue in wilfull powerte. *c* **1470** HENRY *Wallace* x. 218 The gret debait in Wallace wit can waid, Betwix kyndnes and wyllfull wow he maid. *c* **1480** HENRYSON *Fox & Wolf* xxvi. (Bann.), Do wil-full pennance here, and ȝe sall wend .. to ioy withouttin end. **1531** TINDALE *Expos. 1 John* (1538) 37 b, By wylfull kepynge of the commaundement we be sure that we loue God. **1613** PURCHAS *Pilgrimage* II. ix. 131 He there died .. through his wilfull want of bread and water. **1667** MILTON *P.L.* X. 1042 No more be mention'd then of violence Against our selves, and wilful barrenness, That cuts us off from hope. **1687** DRYDEN *Hind & P.* II. 715 The silent stranger stood amazed to see Contempt of wealth, and wilful poverty.

b. Involving unfettered exercise of will; arbitrary; ***wilful empire***, absolute sovereignty, autocracy. *Obs.*

1533 BELLENDEN *Livy* III. xviii. (S.T.S.) II. 24 Thus sall It be clerely schewin .. quhidder wilfull empire or public liberte be erast establist be þir lawis.

5. Done on purpose or wittingly; purposed, deliberate, intentional; not accidental or casual. Chiefly, now always, in bad sense, of an action either evil in itself or blameworthy in the particular case; often (with colour of sense 1) implying 'perverse, obstinate'. Also *transf.* of the agent, as ***wilful murderer***, one who commits wilful murder.

a **1300** *Cursor M.* 9633 It was his aun .. wilful sin þat did vs all fra him to tuin. **1526** *Pilgr. Perf.* (W. de W. 1531), Mortall synnes, & carnall consentes to the same, and wyllfull delectacyons in synne. *a* **1548** HALL *Chron.*, *Edw. V* 9 b, Wylfull murtherers, whom God commaundeth to be taken from the aulter. **1583** STUBBES *Anat. Abus.* II. (1882) 13 Although it be wilfull and purposed murther. **1591** SHAKS. *1 Hen. VI*, IV. i. 142 How will their grudging stomackes be prouok'd To wilfull Disobedience, and Rebell? *a* **1625** FLETCHER *Nice Valour* v. ii, Can there be wilfuller destruction? **1736** BAILEY (fol.) s.v. *Waste*, Wilful Waste makes woful Want. **1781** COWPER *Truth* 20 Charge not .. Your wilful suicide on God's decree. **1844** THIRLWALL *Greece* lxvi. VIII. 387 Though his character has .. been misrepresented through hostile prejudices and wilful calumny. **1883** D. C. MURRAY *Hearts* xxviii, On a charge of wilful and corrupt perjury.

B. as *adv.* †**1.** = WILFULLY 4, 5. *Obs.*

a **1300** *Cursor M.* 16429 To þaa wilful wod he taght þe lauerd es al-weldand. *c* **1381** CHAUCER *Parl. Foules* 429 Dishobeysaunt or wilful necligent. ? **1541** COVERDALE *Confut. Standish* (1547) d vij, Forgetfull what ye sayd afore, or els wilfull blind. **1592** KYD *Sp. Trag.* I. iii, Could she [Fortune] heare, yet is she wilfull mad. **1595** SHAKS. *John* V. ii. 124 The Dolphin is too wilfull opposite And will not temporize with my intreaties. **1596** [see BLAME *v.* 6]. *c* **1600** SHAKS. *Sonn.* li. 13 Since from thee going, he went wilfull slow. **1611** —— *Wint. T.* I. ii. 255 If euer I were wilfull-negligent.

†**2.** Voluntarily, of free will: = WILFULLY 2.

c **1380** WYCLIF *Wks.* (1880) 87 So þat whanne þei schulden ben most wilful pore & preche þe gospel of cristis pouert & his apostlis. **1450–1530** *Myrr. our Ladye* II. 161 The sete of dome where the wylfull powre shall sytte and deme wyth cryste.

C. as *sb.* A wilful person; *rarely*, a wilful act.

1819 SCOTT *Ivanhoe* xxxi, Nay, then, if wilful will to water, wilful must drench. **1829** —— *Anne of G.* xvi, That is as much as to say, wilful will to it. **1875** TENNYSON *Q. Mary* III. v, One of those wicked wilfuls that men make, Nor shame to call it nature. **1885** *Academy* 14 Nov. 322/1 The unfortunates or the wilfuls who are under restraint.

Hence †**wilfulhead** (whence irreg. †**wilful-headness** in same sense), †**wilfulship**, wilfulness; †**wilfulling** *nonce-wd.* [irreg. f. *wilful* + -ING[1]], a wilful act.

c **1385** CHAUCER *L.G.W.* Prol. 355 Lyk tyrauntis of lumbardye That vsyn *wilfulhed & tyrannye. *c* **1400** *Pilgr. Sowle* (Caxton 1483) IV. xii. 63 Only that thyng euery wyght may which he may by ryght and nought of wilful-hede. **1485** *Coventry Leet Bk.* 523 Yf any personne of obstinacie or *wilful-hednesse will withstand .. the said .. Rules. **1605** SYLVESTER *Du Bartas* II. iii. III. *Law* 610 No more bay with thy *wilfullings His wrath's dread Torrent. *c* **1200** *Trin. Coll. Hom.* 205 þat oðer is *wilfulshipe and lichamliche lustes. *c* **1280** *MS. Douce 139* lf. 157 þe idel mon .. þat þurstes of wilfulscipe and drinket sorwenesse.

†**wilful**, *a.*[2] *Obs. rare.* [f. *wil*, WILE *sb.* + -FUL.] Crafty, wily.

c **1425** *Cursor M.* 11807 (Trin.) Heroude .. þat wilful [*Cott.* wili] wolf þat ferde so fals Aȝeynes fremde & frendes als.

wilfully ('wɪlfʊlɪ), *adv.* Forms: see WILFUL *a.*[1] [Late OE. *wilfullice*, f. **wilfull* WILFUL *a.*[1] (cf. OE. *carfull* careful, *carfullice* carefully): see -LY[2].]

†**1.** Willingly, readily, without reluctance; patiently, submissively (with *suffer*, etc.); gladly, 'fain' (with *will* vb. expressing desire: cf. 3). *Obs.*

a **1100** *Gloss. Ælfric's Colloq.* 146 (Napier 225/1) *Uolenter*, wilful[lice]. *a* **1240** *Wohunge* in *O.E. Hom.* I. 279 Alle þat clenli for þi luue mesaise and pouerte wilfulliche þolien. **1357** *Lay Folks' Catech.* (L.) 1100 Men schuld wilfully fede pore hungry men and þrusty. **1375** BARBOUR *Bruce* II. 172 He serwyt ay lelely; And the tothir full wilfully, .. Rewardyt him weile his seruice. **1382** WYCLIF *Acts* xxi. 17 Whanne we camen to Jerusalem, bretheren resceyueden vs wilfulli. *c* **1460** *Godstow Reg.* 132 Mansel .. willid & acceptid wilfulli þe gifte þat Raph bloet made to þe church. **1493** *Festivall* (W. de W. 1515) 9 He must .. suffre trybulacyon mekely, and do almes dedes wylfully. **1513** DOUGLAS *Æneis* VIII. iii. 89 Wilfully I obey thair command.

†**b.** With good will, heartily; 'with a will'.

1375 BARBOUR *Bruce* II. 386 And with that word sa wilfully He dang on. *Ibid.* VIII. 462 Thai .. prikit furth sa vilfully To vyn the ladis at thai saw pass. *c* **1430** LYDG. *Min. Poems* (Percy Soc.) 7 First understond, and willfully procede.

†**2.** Of one's own free will, of one's own accord, voluntarily. Rarely in reference to an inanimate thing: Spontaneously, 'of itself'. *Obs.*

c **1000** in Haupt's *Zeitschr. f. deutsches Alt.* IX. 435/2 *Sponte*, wilful[l]ice. **1357** *Lay Folks' Catech.* (L.) 1163 How moche more be þei cursyd of god; þat bynde hem-self wilfully. **1377** LANGL. *P. Pl.* B. xx. 48 Syth he þat wrouȝte al þe worlde was wilfullich nedy. *c* **1400** MAUNDEV. xvi. (1839) 176 Hem that sleen hem self wilfully, for love of here Ydole. *a* **1425** tr. *Arderne's Treat. Fistula* etc. 87 If þe puluis putte in go willfully out with þe dede flesch þi nedez is wele sped. *c* **1440** *Gesta Rom.* lxiv. 277 (Add. MS.) Do of thi clothes wilfully, or thou shalt agayn thi wille. *a* **1536** TINDALE *Exam. W. Thorpe* in Foxe *A. & M.* (1563) 155/1 The night before y[t] Christ Jesu wold suffer wilfullye passion for mankinde. **1590** SPENSER *F.Q.* II. i. 15 She wilfully her sorrow did augment. **1642** FULLER *Holy & Prof. St.* v. xi. 403 Martyrs are to die willingly but not wilfully. **1705** CLARKE *Disc. Nat. Relig.* (1706) 103 A Man is obliged not to depart wilfully out of this Life, which is the general Station that God has appointed him.

†**b.** According to one's own will; at will, freely. *Obs.*

1340–70 *Alex. & Dind.* 604 But ȝe, folliche folk ȝour fals godus alle Wil-fully worschipen wiþ wordliche godus. *c* **1350** *Will. Palerne* 1782 To me tended þei nouȝt bot tok forþ here wey wilfulli to sum wildernesse. *c* **1475** *Partenay* 327 Ouer all thys hors so went wylfully here and there ouer all where at hys lust wold. *c* **1600** SHAKS. *Sonn.* lxxx. 8 But since your worth (wide as the Ocean is) The humble as the proudest saile doth beare, My sawsie barke (inferior farre to his) On your broad maine doth wilfully appeare.

†**3.** With desire, longingly. *Obs. rare.*

c **1350** *Will. Palerne* 3300 þat quen & hire douȝter & meliors þe schene wayteden out at a windowe wilfulli infere. *c* **1611** CHAPMAN *Iliad* VIII. 497 And all did wilfully expect, the siluer-throned morne.

4. Purposely, on purpose, by design, intentionally, deliberately. Chiefly, now always, in bad sense (cf. WILFUL *a.*[1] 5); often with admixture of, or passing into, sense 5; occas. implying 'maliciously'.

c **1374** CHAUCER *Troylus* II. 284 Yf þat he wole take of it no cure, Whan þan it cometh, but wylfully it weyuen. **1377** LANGL. *P. Pl.* B. XVII. 285 How myȝt he axe mercy, or any mercy hym helpe, þat wykkedlich & willefullich wolde mercy anynte? *c* **1400** *Pilgr. Sowle* (Caxton) II. li. (1859) 54 He that wylfully deceyued hym self, who may hym releue of myschyef? **1477** *Rolls of Parlt.* VI. 184/2 Money so molten, beten or wilfully broken. **1526** R. WHYTFORD *Martiloge* 67 b, The feest also of saynt Dace bysshop of mylen, y[t] in his journey toward constantynople was wylfully lodged in a hous y[t] was occupyed w[t] wycked spirytes. **1617** J. TAYLOR (Water P.) *Three Weekes Observ.* C 3, For those that set houses on fire wilfully, they are smoked to death. **1726** SHELVOCKE *Voy. round World* (1757) 242 Deaf to all I could say, and so wilfully insensible of the impendant destruction. **1819** SCOTT *Ivanhoe* xliv, His administration was wilfully careless, now too indulgent, and now allied to despotism. **1849** MACAULAY *Hist. Eng.* v. I. 545 Instead of the money came excuses .. which ought to have opened the eyes of all who were not wilfully blind. **1879** *Cassell's Techn. Educ.* VIII. 107 A mill containing 500 of his looms was wilfully burnt down. **1911** *Ac. 1 & 2 Geo. V* c. 6 §1 If any person lawfully sworn as a witness .. wilfully makes a statement .. which he knows to be false.

5. In a self-willed manner, perversely, obstinately, stubbornly.

a **1586** SIDNEY *Arcadia* I. v. (1912) 33 The mother .. beyng determinately (least I shoulde say of a great Lady, wilfully) bent to marrie her to Demagoras. *Ibid.* II. xiii. 232 Now so evill could she conceale her fire, and so wilfully persevered she in it, that [etc.]. **1595** SHAKS. *John* III. i. 142, I .. demand Why thou against the Church, our holy Mother, So wilfully dost spurne. **1596** SPENSER *State Irel.* Wks. (Globe) 654/1 Surely of such desperat persons as will willfully followe the course of theyr owne follye, there is noe compassion to be had. *a* **1694** TILLOTSON *Serm.*, *Luke xii. 47, 48* Wks. 1717 I. 425 He that first acknowledgeth him for his Prince, and then affronts him, deserves to be prosecuted with the utmost severity, because he did it wilfully, and in meer contempt. **1726**– [see 4].

wilfulness ('wɪlfʊlnɪs). [f. WILFUL *a.*[1] + -NESS.]

1. The quality or character of being wilful; disposition to assert one's own will against reason, persuasion, etc.; determination to take one's own way; self-will, perversity, obstinacy, stubbornness.

c **1200** *Trin. Coll. Hom.* 75 Willfulnesse letteð þe mannes shrift, þat þincheð uuel þat man him wile neden his sinnes to forleten and fro þe deuel to gode turnen. **1375** BARBOUR *Bruce* XVIII. 176 On this wiss war thai nobill men Throu wilfulness all losit then. *c* **1386** CHAUCER *Knt.'s T.* 2199 The contrarie of al this is wilfulnesse. **1412–20** LYDG. *Chron. Troy* I. 3661 Sith sche wrouȝt only of wilfulnes, With-oute conseil or avysenes. **1547** *Act 1 Edw. VI* c. 3 §11 Yf theie refuse of wilfulnes and stubbernes to worke. **1583** WHITGIFT in Strype *Life* (1718) App. 67 Your Lordship further semith to burthen me with Wyllfulness... There ys a Difference betwixt Willfullness and Constancie. **1674**

OWEN *Holy Spirit* (1693) 238 A Child-like state, accompanied with, (1) Weakness. (2) Instability. And, (3) Wilfulness. **1729** BUTLER *Serm.* Wks. 1874 II. 76 That obstinacy and wilfulness, which renders men so insensible to the motives of religion. **1838** LYTTON *Alice* II. vi, She could..contradict, with a pretty wilfulness, his most favourite dogmas. **1870** LOWELL *Study Wind., Carlyle* (1871) 98 To confound it [*sc.* Will] with its irritable and purposeless counterfeit Wilfulness.

b. (with *pl.*) An instance of this, a wilful act.

1833 COLERIDGE *Table-t.* 23 Oct., Whole volumes of Wordsworth's poems were formerly neglected..solely because of some few wilfulnesses, if I may so call them, of that great man. **1883** SPURGEON *Illustr. & Medit.* 221 The rebellions and wilfulnesses of mankind.

2. †**a.** Purpose, determination, resolution. *Obs.*

c **1386** CHAUCER *Melib.* ¶416 Thou shalt considere if thy myght and thy power may consenten and suffise to thy wilfulnesse and to thy conseillours. **1606** G. W[OODCOCKE] *Hist. Ivstine* XII. 53 He..had slaine himselfe, had he not beene preuented by his friendes... He continued certaine daies after in this wilfulnesse to die. **1633** T. JAMES *Voy.* 18 In this wilfulnesse we continued till the 21.

b. Intentional character (of an act); the fact of being done on purpose.

1876 MOZLEY & WHITELEY *Law Dict.* s.v. *Murder*, The deliberateness and wilfulness, or, as we prefer to call it, the intention, which constitutes the crime of murder.

†**3.** Readiness of will, willingness, inclination.

1398 TREVISA *Barth. De P.R.* XVIII. xxxix. (1495) cc v b/1 The wylfulnesse [of a horse] is know yf he is bolde of herte. **1408–9** tr. *Vegetius' De Re Milit.* (MS. Digby 233) lf. 185/1 Newe knyȝtes ben chosen not onlich by strengþe & myȝt of body bote also by lusti wilfulnesse to werre.

†**4.** Liberty to do what one will; free will or choice; voluntary action. *Obs.*

c **1460** SIR R. ROS *La Belle Dame* 628 Falshode is so full of cursydnesse, That highe worschip may never haue enterprise Where hit rayneth, and hath the wylfulnysse. **1501** in *10th Rep. Hist. MSS. Comm.* App. I. 68 [The lands should be redeemable] be dissent or wilfulnes of the said Ihonne or William his fader. **1530** PALSGR. 289/1 Wylfulnesse, *uoluntairete*. **1553** BRADFORD *Serm. Repentance* (1574) C ij b, Such workes as they neede not to do, but of their own voluntarines & wylfulnes (wylfulnes in deede).

wilga (ˈwɪlgə). [Native name in New South Wales.] An Australian tree of the genus *Geijera* (N.O. *Rutaceæ*), esp. *G. parviflora*. Also *attrib.*

1889 MAIDEN *Usef. Plants Australia* 130 *Geijera parviflora*, Wilga, Sheep-bush, Dogwood and Willow. **1891** 'R. BOLDREWOOD' *Sydney-side Sax.* vii, We rode..through a wilga scrub.

wilger (ˈwɪlgə(r)). *local.* Also 6, 9 **willger,** 7 **welger,** 9 **-ar, wolgar.** [Obscurely f. *wilghe*, WILLOW *sb.*]

1. = WILLOW *sb.* 1.

1682–3 in *Hartland Gloss.* (E.D.S.) s.v., Pd. for welgers 1*s.* 6*d.* **1867** ROCK *Jim an' Nell* xxxiv, Nor welgars, no, nor withy-bans 'll vix ther herts ner bin' ther hans.

attrib. **1853** in *Rep. & Trans. Devonsh. Assoc.* XXVII. 60 Let Berry the wolgar plot, 1 s. a bundle next year. **1882** *Ibid.* XIV. 150 Down by the wilger plot.

2. = WILLOW *sb.* 3, WILLY *sb.*[1] 2.

1542 *Admir. Crt. Warrant Bk.* 1, 19 Aug. (MS.), Septem duodenas excipularum anglice vij dosen of shrympe leapes vulgariter voc' willgers.

3. = WILLOW *sb.* 4, WILLY *sb.*[1] 3.

1871 *Daily News* 26 Aug. (Leicester), A recommendation that more care should be exercised in the use of 'willgers' or 'devils'.

†**wilgern,** *a. Obs. rare.* [f. WILL *sb.*[1] + north. ME. *gern*, a. ON. *gjarn* YERN *a.*

This word or a corresp. *wilȝern survived in 17th c. north. dial. *willern* (Ray).]

Wilful, perverse.

c **1325** *Metr. Hom.* 61 Godd..gert them lef thair wilgern werk.

wilghe, obs. form of WILLOW.

wilgosse, obs. form of WILD GOOSE.

†**wilhede.** *Obs. rare.* In 4 **wyl-.** [f. WILL *sb.*[1] + -HEAD.] Will.

1340 *Ayenb.* 164 Magnanimité is heynesse gratnesse and noblesse of wylhede [orig. *corage*].

Wilhelmine (ˈvɪlhɛlmaɪn), *a.* [f. the Ger. name *Wilhelm* William (see below) + -INE[1].] Of or pertaining to (the reign of) William II, emperor of Germany 1888–1918. Also **Wil'helmian, Wilhel'minian** [cf. G. *wilhelminisch*] adjs.

1931 C. R. TURNER tr. *G. Schultze-Pfaelzer's Hindenburg* xii. 279 A swaggering general of the later Wilhelminian period. **1948** A. HUXLEY *Ape & Essence* (1949) 21 Floating products of Wilhelmine wealth and culture. **1956** S. BEDFORD *Legacy* IV. v. 282 The events..shed a queer light on the Wilhelminian era. **1957** *Cassell's German & Eng. Dict.* I. 614/2 *Wilhelminisch, adj.*, of William II, Wilhelmian (*of Germany*). **1962** *Times* 14 Nov. 16/2 The Wilhelmian empire. **1973** *Times Lit. Suppl.* 5 Oct. 1183/1 Like so many intellectuals in Wilhelminian Germany. **1975** *Historical Jrnl.* XVIII. 821 It was in this situation that the role of the Centre party in Wilhelmine politics became decisive. **1979** *Observer* 18 Nov. 35 The mood of fatalism that overtook the Wilhelmine Empire of Germany before the advent of the First World War.

Wilhelmstrasse (ˈvɪlhɛlmˌʃtrɑːsə). [Ger.] The name of a street in Berlin, the site of the German foreign office until 1945; hence used for the pre-war German foreign office and its policies.

1914 in *Conc. Oxf. Dict.* Addenda. **1919** LD. F. HAMILTON *Vanished Pomps of Yesterday* i. 28 The Ambassador took the hint, and that was the last note in Russian that reached the Wilhelmstrasse. **1923** G. BUCHANAN *My Mission to Russia* I. iv. 45 The reception, however, accorded to this tentative proposal by the Wilhelmstrasse was not encouraging. **1938** H. NICOLSON *Diary* 21 Sept. (1966) I. 363 What remains of Czechoslovakia..must subordinate her foreign policy to that of the Wilhelmstrasse. **1956** S. BEDFORD *Legacy* III. iv. 143, I can't think what they made of him at the Wilhelmstrasse. **1979** G. ST. AUBYN *Edward VII* vii. 316 Chamberlain was resolved to seek partnership with France ..should discussions with the Wilhelmstrasse break down.

‖**wili, willi** (ˈvɪlɪ). *Slavonic Mythol.* [Ger. or Fr. *wili, willi*, ad. Serbo-Croat *vila* nymph, fay. Cf. VILA.] (See quot. 1949). Chiefly used in connection with the ballet *Giselle*.

[**1841** VERNOY DE SAINT-GEORGES et al. *Giselle ou Les Wilis* 14 C'est l'heure lugubre où, selon la chronique du pays, les Wilis se rendent à leur salle de bal.] **1949** A. CHUJOY *Dance Encycl.* 511/1 *Wilis* (or *Willis*), in Western-Slavic and Eastern-German legends, the spirits of betrothed girls who have died as a result of being jilted by faithless lovers. They came out to dance at night and led the faithless ones to their death by making them dance until they fell dead of exhaustion. **1961** *Times* 2 Oct. 16/6 Miss Jill Bathurst.. danced Odette and the wili Giselle. **1963** P. HANSFORD JOHNSON *Night & Silence* xx. 138 The cat continued to dance, star of the snowy ballet, with a million Wilis whirling behind him. **1977** *N.Y. Rev. Bks.* 13 Oct. 44/2 She gazes out of the fascinating portrait that Henri Lehmann painted of her in 1843 like some supernatural being, a willi, a peri, or a refined succubus.

wili, wilie, obs. forms of WILY.

wilik, obs. form of VILELY.

wilily (ˈwaɪlɪlɪ), *adv.* Forms: see WILY; also 5 **wilele,** 6 **wylely, -ie, wilely.** [f. WILY *a.* + -LY[2].] In a wily manner; craftily, cunningly, by stratagem.

a **1400** *Pistill of Susan* 213 Wylyliche heo wyled hir wenches away. *c* **1400** *Anturs of Arth.* 575 (Douce MS.) Wilele þes wighte mene þaire wepenes þey welde. *a* **1425** tr. *Arderne's Treat. Fistula* etc. 15 If peraunture þe pacient haue wilyly broȝt in with hym any leche for to aspye. **1531** TINDALE *Expos. 1 John* (1538) 44 Antichrist disgysed hymselfe..& preached Christ wylyly, bryngyng in now thys tradicion, and now that. **1596** DALRYMPLE tr. *Leslie's Hist. Scot.* (S.T.S.) I. 268 Wittilie and wylelie tuecheng the king. **1611** *Bible* Josh. ix. 4 They did worke wilily, and went and made as if they had beene embassadours. **1682** BUNYAN *Holy War* 243 'Tis you Mr. Carnal Security that have wilily stripped Mansoul, and driven her glory from her. **1724** RAMSAY *Tea-t. Misc.* (1733) I. 85 And wylily they shot the lock. **1847** GOSSE *Birds Jamaica* 412 A flock of swimming Pelicans, wilily endeavouring to approach some unwary one. **1885** W. ROSS *Aberdour & Inchcolme* i. 23 He wilily succeeded to his title and estates.

wiliness (ˈwaɪlɪnɪs). Forms: see WILY. [f. as prec. + -NESS.] The quality or character of being wily; craftiness, cunning, guile.

c **1450** tr. *De Imitatione* I. vii. 8 Truste not in þin ovne konnyng, ner in þe wilynes of eny man livyng. *c* **1460** METHAM *Wks.* (1916) 133 A mowght þe qwyche ys smal off qwantyte with thynne lyppys sygnyffyith onmyghtynes, ferffulnes, and wylynes. **1556** OLDE *Antichrist* 162 b, So (with certain foxlike wylynesse) they clooke the bloody meanyng. **1601** R. JOHNSON *Kingd. & Commw.* (1603) 2 Neither let any man suppose that from wilines without force, nor force without iudgement, can preceed any proiect of worthy consideration. **1698** FRYER *Acc. E. India & P.* 181 To defend them from all Assaults and Wiliness of the Devil. **1818** MRS. SHELLEY *Frankenstein* xix. (1823) II. 126, I will watch with the wiliness of a snake, that I may sting with its venom. **1878** BAYNE *Purit. Rev.* iii. 81 He had the wariness and wiliness of the cat.

wiling, *vbl. sb.*: see WILE *v.*

wilis, obs. form of WHILES.

wiliwili (ˈwiːlɪwiːlɪ). [Hawaiian.] A coral tree, *Erythrina sandwicensis*, of the family Leguminosæ, native to Hawaii and Tahiti and bearing clusters of orange flowers.

1888 W. F. HILLEBRAND *Flora Hawaiian Islands* 100 'Wiliwili'..loses its leaves in late summer. **1913** J. F. ROCK *Indigenous Trees Hawaiian Islands* 191 The very soft, white wood of the Wiliwili..is still used by the natives for outriggers on their fishing canoes. **1917** *Nature* 20 Sept. 57/2 In the arid regions is found the wiliwili.., a deciduous tree with gnarly growth. **1965** *N.Z. Listener* 17 Dec. 4/2 The Hawaiian chiefs..riding the lighter, balsa-like wili-wili boards.

wilk, wilke, obs. forms of WHELK, WHICH.

wilkatt, obs. form of WILD CAT.

wilkeite (ˈwɪlkiːaɪt). *Min.* [f. the name of R. M. *Wilke*, 20th-c. U.S. mineral collector + -ITE[1].] A silicate and sulphate mineral of the apatite group occurring as translucent pink or yellow hexagonal crystals (see quot. 1982).

1914 EAKLE & ROGERS in *Amer. Jrnl. Sci.* CLXXXVII. 263 The writers take pleasure in naming it wilkeite in honor of R. M. Wilke, who as a mineral collector and dealer has done much to advance the science of mineralogy. **1937** *Amer. Mineralogist* XXII. 977 It has become necessary to investigate the substitutions of the sort found in wilkeite. **1975** *Nature* 27 Feb. 722/1 Among the minerals described to have any significant degree of P(V)–Si(IV) partial substitution are viseite, nagatelite and wilkeite, an apatite with partial SiO_4 + SO_4 substitution for PO_4. **1982** *Amer. Mineralogist* LXVII. 90 Wilkeite is not a valid mineral species, since it is only one of many solid solutions involving the six end-members fluorapatite, hydroxyapatite, chlorapatite, fluorellestadite, hydroxyellestadite, and chlorellestadite.

†**wilkin.** *Obs.* Also 5 **wylkyn, wilken,** 6 **wellkyn,** 7 **welkyn, wilking.** [? orig. a proper name, perh. of Du. or LG. origin.] A ram; a pile-driving engine.

1495 *Naval Acc. Hen. VII* (1896) 156 Rammes of Yron called Wylkyns..j. **1497** *Ibid.* 91 Wilken Rammers of Iren ..ij. *Ibid.* 94 Wilken ramme of iren..j. **1580** in P. Thompson *Hist. Boston* (1856) 310 Lord Clynton to borrow the wellkyn of brasse of this Corporation for his necessarie, according to his desire. **1657** *Ibid.*, A great brasse welkyn belonging to the borough, being now no longer useful to this borough, to be sold. **1694** *Ibid.*, 10*l.* paid to John Sherlock to buy a wilking with at Nottingham. [**1804** *Ibid. note*, applied to a pile-driving apparatus.]

Wilkism (ˈwɪlkɪz(ə)m). [Irreg. f. the name of John *Wilkes* (1727–97), English radical politician + -ISM.] The principles or policies associated with John Wilkes.

1769 MRS. HARRIS *Let.* 24 Mar. in Earl of Malmesbury *Lett.* (1870) I. 177 The Wilkism, and obscenity of the woman proved the greatest attraction. **1778** J. WITHERSPOON *Address to Natives Scotl. residing in Amer.* 5 What effect this *Wilkism* (If I may so speak) of many Americans may be supposed to have had upon the minds of gentlemen from Scotland, it is not difficult to explain. **1930** R. POSTGATE '*That Devil Wilkes*' xiv. 248 (*heading*) The end of Wilkism.

Also **'Wilkite,** a follower of John Wilkes or his ideas.

a **1797** J. WILKES in Lincoln & McEwen *Lord Eldon's Anecdote Bk.* (1960) 15, I have nothing to do with such a Man. He was a Wilkite, which I never was. **1917** H. BLEACKLEY *Life Wilkes* xiv. 251 The zeal of hundreds of sturdy Wilkites had oozed away. **1930** R. POSTGATE '*That Devil Wilkes*' xiv. 258 They knew only that he had shot down Wilkites.

wilkume, obs. form of WELCOME.

will (wɪl), *sb.*[1] Forms: 1–2 **willa,** (1 **-o**), 1–7 **wil,** 2–4 **wile,** 2–7 **wille,** 3–6 **wylle,** 4–6 **wyll, wyl** (2 **welle,** 4 **wele,** *Sc.* **vil,** 5 **wel, well, wulle, wyle,** 6 *Sc.* **vill,** 9 *Sc. dial.* **wull),** 1– **will.** [OE. *willa* wk. masc. = OFris. *willa* (EFris. *wel*, WFris. *wille*), OS. *willio*, MDu. *wille*, Du. *wil*, OHG. *willo, willjo* (MHG., G. *wille, willen*), ON. *vili, vilja-* (Sw. *vilja*, Da. *vilje*), Goth. *wilja*:—OTeut. **wiljon-*:—pre-Teut. **weljon-*; also OE. *wil(l* str. n. (chiefly in gen.: see sense 10), = ON. *vil*, and OE. *ȝewil, -wile* str. n. I-WILL; see WILL *v.*[1]]

I. 1. a. Desire, wish, longing; liking, inclination, disposition (*to do* something). In mod. use coloured by or merged in sense 5.

Beowulf 635 þæt ic anunga eowra leoda willan ȝeworhte. *a* **900** CYNEWULF *Juliana* 50 Ic beo ȝearo sona..willan þines. *c* **1000** *Ags. Gosp.* John i. 13 Ða ne synt acennede..of flæsces willan, ne of weres willan; ac hiȝ synt of gode acennede. *a* **1225** *Ancr. R.* 60 Wilnen, & habe wille uorte beon iwilned. **12..** *Moral Ode* 172 (Egerton MS.) þe brode stret is vre iwil ðe is us lod for to lete. þe ðe al folewed his wil, fared bi þusse strete. *c* **1300** *Beket* 121 So gret wille him com to To wende eft to the holi lond, that he nuste what do. *c* **1315** SHOREHAM I. 421 Ac nou þat wil þat is to gode His al iset bi-hinde. **1340** *Ayenb.* 9 Wyþoute greate wille an willinge uor to harmi oþren. **1375** BARBOUR *Bruce* xv. 79, I trow that he Sall haf no gret will for to ficht. *c* **1450** *Knt. de la Tour* 14 Fastinge.. refrainithe the flesshe of euelle willes. **1485** CAXTON *Paris & V.* (1868) 69 He had grete wylle to goo to Iherusalem. **1568** GRAFTON *Chron.* I. 91 As he and his Souldiours had no will to marrie the daughters of the Frenchmen. **1591** SHAKS. *Two Gent.* I. iii. 63 My will is something sorted with his wish. **1601** —— *Jul. C.* III. iii. 3, I haue no will to wander foorth of doores, Yet something leads me foorth.

1837 DICKENS *Pickw.* xvii, Don't stop him, Maria,..if he has the will to strike me, let him. **1844** KINGLAKE *Eothen* vii, There was a will, and a longing, more imperious than mere curiosity. **1896** HOUSMAN *Shropsh. Lad* xxxiii, This long and sure-set liking, This boundless will to please.

b. An inclination *to do* something, as contrasted with power or opportunity.

1594 KYD *Cornelia* III. iii, Shee hath not onely power and will T'abuse the vulgar wanting skill. **1647** W. BROWNE *Polexander* III. IV. 113 The Queene..is perswaded I have serv'd her because I had a will to it. **1667** EARL ORRERY *St. Lett.* (1742) 308 They desired the power, and want not the will, to do us an ill turn. **1697** DRYDEN *Æneis* VII. 279 Not forc'd to Goodness, but by Will inclin'd. **1751** JOHNSON *Rambler* No. 178 ¶14 Great Numbers who quarrel with their Condition have wanted not the Power but the Will to obtain a better State. **1818** SCOTT *Br. Lamm.* xxv, Your lordship..will experience that the faculty of the present proprietor to entertain his friends is greatly abridged,..the will, I need hardly say, remains the same. **1832** LANDER *Exped. Niger* xxi. III. 263 Mr. Lake had certainly a will or inclination to enter into arrangements with him. **1879** FROUDE *Cæsar* x. 111 No one questioned that it could be done if there was a will to do it.

†**2.** *spec.* Carnal desire or appetite: = DESIRE *sb.* 2.

971 *Blickl. Hom.* 91 þa flæsclican willan & þa unȝereclican uncysta. *c* **1000** *Sax. Leechd.* I. 358 Weres wylla to ȝefremmanne nime bares ȝeallan. *c* **1400** *Rule St. Benet* (verse) 37 All fleschly wyll for to for-sak. **1593** SHAKS. *Lucr.* 247 Thus..holds he disputation, Tweene frozen conscience and hot burning will. **1603** —— *Meas. for M.* II. iv. 164.

3. a. *transf.* (chiefly as obj. of *have*): That which one desires, (one's) 'desire'. Now *arch.* or *poet.*

c **950** *Lindisf. Gosp.* John v. 30 Ne soeco ic uillo min ah uillo his seðe mec asende. *a* **1122** *O.E. Chron.* (Laud MS.) an. 1097 Se cyng ȝeseah þæt he nan þingc his willes þær ȝeforðian ne mihte. *a* **1300** *Cursor M.* 26880 Þe warlau sal noght in þis man Haue sa mikel of his will, Als if he desseli did ill. *a* **1310** in Wright *Lyric P.* x. 37 Have ȝe or wyl, ȝe waxeth unwraste. **1390** GOWER *Conf.* I. 73 He..With blinde tales so hire ladde, That all his wille of hire he hadde. *c* **1420** ? LYDG. *Assembly of Gods* 1309 Bettyr were a chylde to be vnbore, Then let hyt haue the wyll & for euer be lore. *a* **1508** DUNBAR *Tua Mariit Wemen* 336 Quhill I oucht wantit of my will, or quhat I wald desir. **1593** SHAKS. *3 Hen. VI*, I. iv. 144 Would'st haue me weepe? why now thou hast thy will. **1593** —— *Lucr.* 128 The sundrie dangers of his wils obtaining. **1611** W. ADAMS *Let.* in Rundall *Mem. Japon* (Hakl. Soc.) 25 God..would not suffer them to haue their willes of vs. **1693** LOCKE *Educ.* §35 He had the Will of his Maid before he could Speak or Go. **1798** COLERIDGE *Anc. Mar.* I. iv, The Wedding-Guest..listens like a three-years' child: The Mariner hath his will. **1865** SWINBURNE *Atalanta* 929 Have all thy will of words; talk out thine heart. **1896** HOUSMAN *Shropsh. Lad* xxv, A lad that lives and has his will Is worth a dozen dead.

b. A desire or wish as expressed in a request; hence (contextually) the expression of a wish, a request, petition (sometimes passing into the sense 'a command': see 7). *arch.* or *dial.*

what's your will? (now *arch.* or *dial.*, esp. *Sc.*): What do you want? What do you wish me to do?

1340 *Ayenb.* 138 Þanne zayþ he..þet he y-herþ þe benes and þe wylles of þe poure. *c* **1400** *Destr. Troy* 1918 When Castor hade clanly consayuit his wille, He onswared hym honestly with ornyng a litill. *a* **1510** DOUGLAS *K. Hart* II. 21 May thow nocht heir? Langar how I culd schout! What war ȝour will? I will cum in but dout. **1591** SHAKS. *Two Gent.* IV. ii. 92 *Sil.* What's your will? *Pro.* That I may compasse yours. *Sil.* You haue your wish: my will is euen this, That you hie you home to bed. **1606** —— *Ant. & Cl.* I. ii. 7 *Alex.* Soothsayer. *Sooth.* Your will? *Char.* Is this the Man? Is't you sir that know things? **1775** SHERIDAN *Rivals* v. iii, Tell me now, Mr. Acres, in case of an accident, is there any little will or commission I could execute for you? **1808** JAMIESON s.v., *What's your will?* a common Scotticism for, 'What did you say?' It is also given as a reply to one who calls. **1826** GALT *Last of Lairds* i. 5 When..one of the lasses looks from behind it, and says, 'What's your wull and pleasure?'

c. ***to take one's will***: to do as one pleases (in respect *of*). Chiefly *Sc.*

1825 JAMIESON s.v., *To tak one's will o'*. 1. To treat or use as one pleases. 2. To take as much of any thing as one pleases. **1882** G. MACDONALD *Castle Warlock* vi, He..jist loot the maister tak his wull o' 'im! **1890** *Good Words* Aug. 565/2 Carr let his own horse take his will.

4. †**a.** Pleasure, delight, joy. *Obs.*

Beowulf 824 Denum eallum wearð æfter þam wælræse willa ȝelumpen. *a* **1000** *Andreas* 356 Forȝife þe dryhten domweorðunga willan in worulde & in wuldre blæd. *a* **1240** *Ureisun* 46 in *O.E. Hom.* I. 193 Mid englene wille. *Ibid.* 62 Inouh liues wil and eche pleie. [*a* **1250**: see 12 a.] *a* **1310** in Wright *Lyric P.* iv. 23 This wilde wille went a-wai, with mone and mournyng muchel un-mete.

b. ***to have no will of*** (Sc.), †***in***: to take no pleasure in, have no liking for.

1609 *Bible* (Douay) Mal. i. 10, I have no wil in you. *c* **1626** in W. K. Tweedie *Sel. Biogr.* (Wodrow Soc.) I. 353, I have na will of strangers. **1871** W. ALEXANDER *Johnny Gibb* xxii, Na, man; I hinna will o't.

II. 5. a. The action of willing or choosing to do something; the movement or attitude of the mind which is directed with conscious intention to (and, normally, issues immediately in) some action, physical or mental; volition.

971 *Blickl. Hom.* 35 We..agyltaþ þurh feower þing, þurh ȝeþoht, & þurh word, & þurh weorc, & þurh willan. *c* **1230** *Hali Meid.* (Titus MS.) 123 Ga ut þrof wið wil of þin heorte. *a* **1300** *Cursor M.* 13759 He said noght allan, 'namar þou sin,' Bot 'lok þi will bi noght þar-in.' *c* **1386** CHAUCER *Sqr.'s Prol.* 5, I wol seye as I kan With hertly wyl. *c* **1475** *Stonor Papers* (Camden) I. 160 Yff..he wull geve hys dowttyr hys part of Snowys well..I wold with the glader wyll dele with hym. *a* **1619** FLETCHER, etc. *Q. Corinth* III. ii, You know well Even actual sins committed without will, Are neither sins nor shame. **1742** YOUNG *Nt. Th.* IV. 615 But since the naked will obtains thy smile, Beneath this monument of praise unpaid. **1831** JAMES *Philip Aug.* xxviii, He strove to speak, but no voice answered his will. **1861** MILL *Utilitar.* iv. 59 Will, the active phenomenon, is a different thing from desire, the state of passive sensibility.

b. Intention, intent, purpose, determination. ? *Obs.*

a **1300** *Cursor M.* 23552 If it sett þam in to will To mak anoiþer erth or heuen. *c* **1375** *Sc. Leg. Saints* xxxiii. (*George*) 1 Ȝete of sancte george is my wil,..To translat þe haly story. **1390** GOWER *Conf.* VIII. 3037* With al the wil that I mai yive. *c* **1400** *Destr. Troy* 4222 Þai wetyn full wele þe wyllys of vs here, That we purpos a pouer to put in hor lond. **1450–1530** *Myrr. our Ladye* II. 267 Hou we oughte..to say that salutacion wyth wylle to leue synne and to do good dedes. **1471** CAXTON *Recuyell* (Sommer) 547 By one wylle and volente. **1477** EARL RIVERS (Caxton) *Dictes* (1877) 1, I rested in that wyll & purpose. **1483** *Cath. Angl.* 418/2 Of an [= one] Wille, *vnanimis.* **1523** LD. BERNERS *Froiss.* I. xxxix. 22/2 Whan the flemynges..sawe the fierse wylles of them within. **1619** J. TAYLOR (Water P.) *Kicksey Winsey* B 2, Your wills are good, and whilst I keepe your bills Instead of paiment I accept good wills. **1712** ARBUTHNOT *John Bull* IV. iii, My Will at present is to have Dinner.

c. ***will to*** with sb. or inf. (after G. *wille zu*). Chiefly used in the names (often hyphenated) of supposed natural instincts or drives, as ***will to art*** [tr. G. *wille zur kunst*]; ***will to be, believe, live*** (also *transf.*); ***will to*** (or †***unto***) ***power*** [tr. G. *wille zur macht*], in Nietzsche's philosophy and, later, in analytic psychology (esp. A. Adler's individual psychology): the driving force behind all human behaviour which should lead to self-mastery but when frustrated can become the will to dominate others; cf. POWER-DRIVE *sb.* 2.

Cf. *Der Wille zum Leben* in the title of Schopenhauer's *Welt als Wille und Vorstellung* IV., 1819.

1823 J. C. ROBERTSON *Percy Anecdotes* XI. *Imagination* 87 (*heading*) The Will to be Well. **1889** G. B. SHAW *How to become a Musical Critic* (1960) 147 Vegetarianism, the higher Buddhism..negation of the Will-to-Live..all these are but samples of what Wagnerism involves nowadays. **1891** —— *Let.* 29 July (1965) I. 301 John Robertson seeks for facts that support his will-to-believe that Materialist-Rationalists are the only honest Secularists. **1896** TILLE tr. *Nietzsche's Thus Spake Zarathustra* 163 Wherever I found living matter I found will unto power. **1903** CHESTERTON *R. Browning* vi. 139 That really boisterous will to live which may be found in *Martin Chuzzlewit.* **1907** ZIMMERN tr. *Nietzsche's Beyond Good & Evil* 20 Life itself is Will to Power. **1908** R. BAGOT *A. Cuthbert* xxviii. 370 The triumph of the will to live over the threatening assaults of death. **1923** J. VAN TESLAAR tr. *Stekel's Psychoanal.* II. 61 That 'will to power' means, 'Above all, I want to be loved.'.. Will to power is will to be loved. **1926** GALSWORTHY *Silver Spoon* I. xiv. 110 Humanity has got to save itself! To save itself—what was that, after all, but expression of 'the will to live'? **1929** H. READ *Staffordshire Pottery Figures* 21 The 'folk' spirit which makes the early salt-glaze..figures so precious as evidences of an innate 'will-to-art'. **1930** D. H. LAWRENCE *Virgin & Gipsy* ii. 35 Yvette suddenly saw the stony, implacable will-to-power in the old..Granny. **1931** J. S. HUXLEY *What dare I Think?* iv. 143 Only by banishing the driving force of emotion and the false certitude of the will-to-believe..does she [*sc.* Science] arrive at greater power. **1945** W. DE LA MARE *Burning-Glass* 12 And naught but his marooned precarious self For questing consciousness and will-to-be. **1948** R. STAGNER *Psychol. of Personality* (ed. 2) xv. 288 Adler believed..that the will to power was a fundamental drive, and that it was thwarted by some inferiority. **1963** N. FRYE *Romanticism Reconsidered* 14 The tremendous will-to-power finales of Beethoven. **1972** D. V. TANSLEY *Radionics* iv. 33 The ancient seers of India..observed that the base chakra was responsible for..providing a channel for the will-to-be to express itself. **1976** J. GOODE in Mitchell & Oakley *Rights & Wrongs of Women* vii. 232 Partly this is based on a will to power, the demand for a totally submissive love. **1977** *Times* 2 Dec. 21/3 The [Crown] agents' 'remarkable will to live' pushed them into critical change in their financial operation in 1966. **1979** E. H. GOMBRICH *Sense of Order* vii. 193 That 'will to art', which Riegl had conceived as an alternative to the mechanistic explanations of individual motifs, developed into a vitalistic principle underlying the whole history of art. **1985** E. GELLNER *Psychoanalytic Movement* i. 27 The Will to Power is a far, far more disturbing, more corrosive idea for human optimism than is the domination of the human psyche by sexuality.

6. a. The power or capacity of willing; that faculty or function which is directed to conscious and intentional action; power of choice in regard to action. (See also FREE WILL.)

c **888** ÆLFRED *Boeth.* xiv. §2 Andȝit & ȝemynd, & se ȝesceadwislica willa þæt hine þara tweȝa lyste. *c* **1000** ÆLFRIC *Hom.* I. 288 Of ðam willan cumað ȝeðohtas, and word, and weorc. *a* **1175** *Cott. Hom.* 219 Se fader and his wisdom..hare beire wille þat is se hali gast. *c* **1200** ORMIN 11509 Wille iss hire þridde mahht þurrh whatt menn immess ȝeornenn. *a* **1300** *Cursor M.* 664 He þam gaf þer will alfre; þe gode to do, to leue þe ill. **1390** GOWER *Conf.* I. 322 Thi will is thi principal, And hath the lordschipe of thi witt. *c* **1460** *Wisdom* 213 in *Macro Plays* 42 And I of þe soull am þe wyll. **1538** STARKEY *England* (1878) 29 Euer the wyl chesyth the yl, and leuyth the gud. **1590** SHAKS. *Mids. N.* II. ii. 115 The will of man is by his reason sway'd. **1594** HOOKER *Eccl. Pol.* I. vii. §3 Appetite is the wills sollicitor, and the will is appetites controller; what we couet according to the one, by the other we often reiect. **1597** *Ibid.* v. xlviii. §9 Will, whether it be in God or man, belongeth to the essence and nature of both. **1601** SHAKS. *Jul. C.* II. ii. 71 The cause is in my Will, I will not come. **1635** A. STAFFORD *Fem. Glory* 63 Whose Wils and Vnderstandings have a combat before they can be brought to a consent. **1667** MILTON *P.L.* I. 106 All is not lost; the unconquerable Will,..And courage never to submit or yield. **1738** POPE *Universal Prayer* iii, Who..binding Nature fast in Fate, Left free the Human Will. **1848** R. I. WILBERFORCE *Doctr. Incarnation* iv. (1852) 80 In our Lord, first of all descendants of Adam, was will exhibited in that complete freedom, which was its normal condition and perfect state. **1880** GOLDW. SMITH in *Atlantic Monthly* Feb. 203 The spring of all existence, and so of evil, is will, which Schopenhauer erects into a universal substance, apart from intelligence and consciousness.

b. With qualification, in reference to individual character; idiomatically in ***a will of one's own***, implying a strong or self-assertive will, and hence used as a euphemism for 'wilfulness'.

c **1470** *Gol. & Gaw.* 100 Schir Kay wes haisty and hate, and of ane hie will. **1752** MRS. LENNOX *Female Quix.* I. xi, Since I am not allowed any will of my own,..it matters not whether I am pleased or displeased. **1760** FOOTE *Minor* I. i, Was Charlotte to set up a will of her own,..she must expect to share the fate of her sister. **1798** S. & HT. LEE *Cant. T.*, *Young Lady's T.* II. 341 If once she could be brought to assert a will of her own. **1907** *Verney Mem.* I. 422 A girl of high spirit and strong will.

7. a. Intention or determination that something shall be done by another or others, or shall happen to take place; (contextually) an expression or embodiment of such intention or determination, an order, command, injunction (cf. 3 b). Also *fig.*

Formerly freq. in the ejaculations (*by*) *God's will*, occas. *'ods my will* (Shaks. *A.Y.L.* IV. iii. 17): see GOD *sb.* 14 a.

Beowulf 1739 Him eal worold wendeð on willan. **835** in Birch *Cartul. Sax.* (1885) I. 575 Ic Abba ȝeroefa Cyðe & writan hate hu min willa is þæt mon ymb min ærfe ȝedoe æfter minum dæȝe. *c* **1000** *Ags. Gosp.* Matt. vi. 10 Ȝewurþe ðin willa on eorðan, swa swa on heofonum. *c* **1175** *Lamb. Hom.* 21 We suneȝiet on-ȝein drihtenes welle ofter þene we scolde. *c* **1200** ORMIN 2381 All ȝho leȝȝde þatt o Godd & onn hiss lefe wille. *a* **1250** *Prov. Alfred* 399 in *O.E. Misc.* 126 Bute if we wurcheþ wyllen cristes. *a* **1300** *Cursor M.* 12322 Sco..duted noght, þat godds wil ne suld be wroght. *c* **1380** WYCLIF *Sel. Wks.* II. 55 Al þing þat shal come moot nedis come bi Goddis wille. **1390** GOWER *Conf.* I. 48 Mi will is ferst that thou be schrive. *c* **1450** HOLLAND *Howlat* 874, I wait ȝour will, and quhat way ȝe wald that I wrocht. **1464–5** in *Acts Parlt. Scot.* (1874) XII. 31/1 Thai..sall..entire þe kingis ward and there abide Enduring þe kingis will. **1543–4** *Act 35 Hen. VIII*, c. 1. §1 It is the onlye pleasure and will of Almightie God howe longe his Highnes..shall lyve. **1558** in J. M. Stone *Hist. Mary I* (1901) App. 518 My mynd and will ys, that the said Codicell shall be accepted. **1601** SHAKS. *All's Well* II. iv. 56 In euery thing I waite vpon his will. **1603** —— *Meas. for M.* II. ii. 7 Is it your will Claudio shall die to morrow? **1667** MILTON *P.L.* II. 1025 Such was the will of Heav'n. **1711** STEELE *Spect.* No. 96. ¶2 It was the Will of Providence that Master Harry was taken very ill of a Fever. **1756** C. LUCAS *Ess. Waters* II. 144 They are all..dependent on the will of the magistrate. **1833** TENNYSON *Dream Fair Wom.* lix, It comforts me in this one thought to dwell, That I subdued me to my father's will. **1841** MYERS *Cath. Th.* III. §1 The Books commonly called The Bible contain special Revelations of the Will of God. **1842** TENNYSON *Dora* 43 My will is law. **1888** BRYCE *Amer. Commw.* xcvii. III. 360 This method of consulting the popular will.

†**b.** Consent, acquiescence, permission, favour, good will. *Obs.*

a **1300** *Cursor M.* 199 Wit crist will þan sal I telle How he siþen hared helle. *c* **1440** *Gesta Rom.* xxxviii. 154 In so moche þat he wanne ther by the wille & the love of Eueri man. *c* **1450** *Godstow Reg.* 362 With the wille and graunte of Raaf his sone and heire. **1535** COVERDALE *Jer.* xliv. 19 Did we..poure vnto her drinkofferinges, to do her seruyce, without oure huszbondes wylles?

c. Intent, purport (of a document; cf. 23); also, in *Sc. Law*, a clause in a summons expressing a royal command (see quot. 1684).

1439 in *Ancestor* (1904) July 18 After that the will of my testament be fulfilled and my dettes paid. **1684** SIR G. MACKENZIE *Inst. Law Scot.* IV. i. (1694) 236 The King in his Summons says, Our will is, &c. that ye cite such and such Persons, &c. which is called the Will of the Summons, and which Will of the Summons does comprehend a Command to the Messengers to cite the Defenders. **1743** KAMES *Decis. Crt. Sess.* 1730–52 (1799) 67 It was necessary for the suspender to follow out the will of the letters.

8. Qualified by possessive, esp. in such phr. as †***if his will be, if it be his will*** (= if it be his good pleasure) and as obj. of *do, work*, or the like: That which one wills should be done; (one's) 'pleasure'.

c **825** *Vesp. Ps.* xxxix. 9 [xl. 8] Ðæt ic doe willan ðinne, god. **971** *Blickl. Hom.* 205 To secenne hwæt þæs willa sie. *a* **1000** *Menologium* 201 Sancta symbel þara þe sið oððe ær worhtan in worulde willan drihtnes. *a* **1122** *O.E. Chron.* (Laud MS.) an. 1085 Ȝebete hit God elmihtiȝa þonne his willa sy. *c* **1175** *Lamb. Hom.* 121 Ȝif hit hys willa nere, ne mahte him nan deð ne nan pine derian. *c* **1205** LAY. 2793 & euer ælc wilde mon hefde al his wil to don. *c* **1220** *Bestiary* 41 Ðo ure driȝten ded was, And doluen, also his wille was. *a* **1300** *Cursor M.* 407 Þe sex dais he wroght þat was his will. *Ibid.* 1229 To wrik þare wik[ke] wil þai thoght. **13..** *K. Horn* 201 (Harl. MS.) Ah ȝef hit is þi wille Help vs þat we ne spille. *c* **1400** *Rule St. Benet* (prose) 10 Ye sal leue yure ahen propir will, and do oþir mens. *c* **1420** *Avow. Arth.* xxxiii, Bothe my dethe and my lyfe, Is inne the wille of thi wife. *c* **1420** *Anturs of Arth.* 197 One þing wold I wite, if þi wil ware. **1535** COVERDALE *Ps.* xxvi[i]. 12 Delyuer me not in to the wylles of myne aduersaries. **1542** UDALL *Erasm. Apoph.* 295 The stronger must bee obeyed & haue his wille. **1590** LODGE *Rosalynde* (1592) O 2 b, Shall I then haue..no comfort, but bee posted off to the will of time? **1607** SHAKS. *Cor.* IV. iv. 7 Direct me, if it be your will, where great Auffidius lies: Is he in Antium? **1765** GRAY *Shakespeare* 13 If then he wreak on me his wicked will. **1818** SCOTT *Br. Lamm.* xii, If it's your wull, I'll just tak a step as far as Dunse. **1865** RUSKIN *Sesame* ii. §90 Leaving misrule and violence to work their will among men.

†**9. a.** Undue assertion of one's own will; wilfulness, self-will. *Obs.*

c **1175** *Lamb. Hom.* 9 Ȝif hwa is swa sunful..þet nulle..for his fule heorte wil his scrift ihalden. *c* **1325** *Spec. Gy Warw.* 169 Þat þurw here pride and here wil þeih fallen ofte in gret peril. **1362** LANGL. *P. Pl.* A. VI. 77 Alle þe walles beþ of wit to holde wil þeroute. **1401** *26 Pol. Poems* iii. 38 By witles wille þey gedre pres. *a* **1500** *Ratis Raving* 1562 With will and ȝouthed duellis hee. **1546** J. HEYWOOD *Prov.* I. xi. (1867) 28 Wyll wyll haue wyll, though will wo wyn. *a* **1568** ASCHAM *Scholem.* I. (Arb.) 48 Lyinge, pickinge, slouthe, will, stubburnnesse. **1615** J. TAYLOR (Water P.) *Urania* xli. B 8, When hare-braind Will, o're Wit doth rule & raigne.

b. A piece of wilfulness, a whim. *Obs. rare.*

1619 PURCHAS *Microcosmus* lxii. 623 Shall Christians lose ..the Hopes of Heauen..for a Will, for a Humour, for malicious Spight.

III. Special uses and phrases.

* †**10.** gen. sing. **willes**, etc., as adv. (or in advb. phr.) or predicative adj. *Obs.* **a.** simply (also in phr. ***willes and woldes***: see WIELD *sb.* 1 b), or with poss. pron.: Of one's own will; voluntarily; intentionally, purposely. (Cf. SELFWILLES.)

c **960** ÆTHELWOLD *St. Benet* 28 Ȝeneadod to anre mile gange, gang willes twa. *c* **1000** in Thorpe *Laws* (1840) II. 180 Be þam men ðe willes man ofslihð. *c* **1380** *Sir Ferumb.* 221 Wilt þ[u] silf willes lete þe slen þy purpos ne preyse y noȝt. *c* **1386** CHAUCER *Wife's Prol.* 272 (Harl. MS.) Thing þat no man wol, his willes, holde. *c* **1450** *Mirk's Festial* 174, I am a fende of helle and wold not knele on noþyr kne my wylles, but I am made to do so aȝen my wylle.

b. with poss. pron.: According to one's choice or desire, as one will: used pred. with impers. vb. *to be*, in such phrases as ***if your willes is*** = if you will, if you please, if you wish.

a **1300** *Cursor M.* 1406 Inogh now liued haue .i., þou tak mi saul out of þe flexs And do it ware þi wils [*Gött.* willes] es. *Ibid.* 10094 He moght do quat his wils [*Gött.* willis] was. **1375** Barbour *Bruce* I. 618 Giff that ȝour willis wer, Ic ask ȝow respyt for to se This lettir. *c* **1450** Holland *Howlat* 312 Ȝe sall heir in schort space Quhat worthy lordis thar was, Gif ȝour willis war. *c* **1475** *Rauf Coilȝear* 502, I wait not quhat his willis be.

c. as predicative adj.: Voluntary.

a **1225** *Ancr. R.* 302 Schrift schal beon..dredful, & hopeful, wis, soð & willes.

** with qualifying adjs.

11. a. ***good will, ill will*** (with various shades of meaning: cf. 1, 5–7): see goodwill, ill will. So with the comparative, †***better will*** = 'more goodwill'; †***evil will*** = ill will.

1338 R. Brunne *Chron.* (1810) 237 To Leulyn forgaf he alle his euelle wille. **1357** *Lay Folks' Catech.* (T.) 565 To gif yhou better will for to kun tham. **1461** *Paston Lett.* II. 48 Because of such tales, your tenaunts owe hym the bettir will. *c* **1482** *Cely Papers* (Camden) 131, I wrote not so unto yow for no spyte nedor for no hewell well that I have to yow. **1560** Daus tr. *Sleidane's Comm.* 35 b, He dyd so, of no euill wyll or contempte. **1621** Bp. Mountagu *Diatribæ* 388 All such as haue an euil will to Sion.

b. ***with the best will*** (***in the world***).

1857 B. Taylor *Northern Trav.* xxxii. (1858) 333 With the best will we found it impossible to eat anything. *Ibid.* xxxiii. 344 All that the old woman, with the best will in the world, was able to furnish, was milk, butter, [etc.].

c. See free will.

*** with prepositions.

†**12. a will** [A *prep.*[1] or [2]]. **a.** To (one's) pleasure or satisfaction. *Obs.*

a **1250** *Owl & Night.* 1722 Heo [*sc.* the wren] hadde gode þrote & schille & fale monne song a wille [*v.r.* awille].

†**b.** At command or disposal. *Obs.*

c **1430** *Chev. Assigne* 79 Bothe howndes & men haue hadde þe a wylle.

†**13. after** (*one's*) **will** [after *prep.* 13, 15]: according to one's choice or intention, as one will; according to one's wish or liking, as one desires.

c **1205** Lay. 31650 And longe hit walden after heore willen. *c* **1290** *St. Brendan* 109 in *S. Eng. Leg.* 223 Þe see drof here schip after wil. *a* **1300** *Cursor M.* 15793 O þe forel a suerd he drogh, þe ere he smat of an; For had it ben efter his wil, he wald him fain ha slan.

14. against (†**again**) *one's* **will** [against 10, again B. 7]: in opposition to (one's own) inclination or liking, unwillingly (*rarely*, against one's purpose, unintentionally); in opposition to (another's) choice, intention, or desire.

c **1400** Maundev. (Roxb.) xviii. 85 He schall noȝt be brynt with hir agayne his will. *c* **1400** *Pilgr. Sowle* (Caxton 1483) iv. xx. 68 Thou hast byreued me Ageyne my wyll, no thyng with myn assent. *c* **1450** [see 10 a]. **1512** *Act 4 Hen. VIII.* c. 20 *Preamble*, The said John..fortuned to be slayn..ayenst the will and mynde of your seid Besecher. **1559** *Mirr. Mag., Dk. Suffolk* xxii, King and queene were forst against their willes. **1605** Shaks. *Lear* i. iv. 116 This fellow ha's banish'd two on's Daughters, and did the third a blessing against his will. **1639** J. Clarke *Parœm.* 29 He is willing sore against his will. **1678** Butler *Hud.* iii. iii. 547 He that complies against his Will, Is of his own Opinion still. **1784** Cowper *Task* vi. 520 His steed Declined the death, and wheeling swiftly round,..Baffled his rider, saved against his will. **1845** McCulloch *Taxation* i. (1852) 38 The Grand Seignior cannot do a more absolute act than to order a man to be dragged away from his family, and, against his will, run his head against the mouth of a cannon.

15. at (*one's*) **will. a.** According to one's volition or choice; as (when, where) one will. †occas., Of one's own free will, voluntarily.

(*a*) with possessive: ***at his, your, God's*** (etc.) ***will.***

a **1300** *Cursor M.* 6136 Ma sacrifice your lauerd vntill, Quar yee wil at your aun will. *c* **1325** *Spec. Gy Warw.* 19 Al at his wille he wole þe lede. **1389** in *Engl. Gilds* (1870) 30 Qwo-so schal ben escused for any oyer schyl, it schal ben at ye aldermannes wyl. *c* **1430** *Syr Tryam.* 257 At Goddys wylle muste hyt bene. **1570** T. Norton tr. *Nowel's Catech.* 67 b, God alone is able at his owne will to geue what soeuer he hath appointed. **1601** Shaks. *Jul. C.* ii. i. 17 We put a Sting in him, That at his will he may doe danger with. *a* **1721** Prior *Songs* xiii. 4 Enjoying sweetest liberty, And roving at my will. **1802**, **1873** [see sweet *a.* 8 d].

(*b*) simply: ***at will.***

13.. *Cursor M.* 19324 (Gött.) Na strinth did þai þaim till, For þai come wid þaim all at will. *c* **1400** *26 Pol. Poems* x. 4 For pride hem þenkeþ goddis pere, þat welde þis worldis wele at wylle. *c* **1470** *Gol. & Gaw.* 253 Al thai that ar wrocht vndir the hie hevin Micht nocht warne thame at wil to ische nor entre. **1579** Spenser *Sheph. Cal.* Sept. 144 They wander at will, and stray at pleasure. **1607** Shaks. *Cor.* i. vi. 39 Holding Corioles in the name of Rome, Euen like a fawning Grey-hound in the Leash, To let him slip at will. **1615** R. Cocks *Diary* (Hakl. Soc.) I. 42 [He] geveth out that he is not the Companies servant, but at will. **1667** Milton *P.L.* v. 295 Nature here Wantond as in her prime, and plaid at will Her Virgin Fancies. **1671** —— *P.R.* iv. 269 The famous Orators..whose resistless eloquence Wielded at will that fierce Democratie. **1825** Wordsw. *To a Skylark* 5 Thy nest which thou canst drop into at will. **1871** R. H. Hutton *Ess.* I. 47 The only test we have of the truth of scientific hypothesis is the degree of aid it gives us in representing to ourselves at will the facts of the universe. **1888** F. H. Bradley in *Mind* Jan. 27 And if we think of various sensations in parts of our bodies we can produce them at will.

b. In readiness to be dealt with as one will; at one's command or disposal.

13.. *Gaw. & Gr. Knt.* 836 Al is yowre awen, to haue at yowre wylle & welde. **1387–8** T. Usk *Test. Love* iii. viii. (Skeat) l. 5 Sithen her restinge-place is now so nygh at my wil. *c* **1400** *Parce Michi* 165 in *26 Pol. Poems* 147 Whyle I had my streyngth at wyll, ffull many a man I dyd vnreste. *c* **1440** *Generydes* 33 Whenne he lyste she was all atte his wille. **1577** Googe *Heresbach's Husb.* i. 7 With wealth yenough and pastures wyde at wyll. **1604** Shaks. *Oth.* ii. i. 150 She that was euer faire, and neuer proud, Had Tongue at will, and yet was neuer loud. **1611** —— *Cymb.* iv. iii. 13 Sir, my life is yours, I humbly set it at your will. **1667** Milton *P.L.* v. 377 These mid-hours, till Eevning rise I have at will. **1784** Cowper *Task* ii. 202 What is his creation less Than a capacious reservoir of means Formed for his use, and ready at his will? **1913** M. Roberts *Salt of Sea* ix. 218 At sunset the wind failed and left me at the will of the tides.

†**c.** According to one's desire, as one wishes or likes; *esp.* (*pred.* or *compl.*) of wind or weather, Favourable. *Obs.*

a **1300** *Cursor M.* 2243 Quen þai at wil had festend grund þe wark þai raised in a stund. **1340–70** *Alex. & Dind.* 1 Whan þis weith at his wil weduring hadde. *c* **1400** *Rule St. Benet* (verse) 492 All þat nedes ȝou vntill Sal ȝe haue at ȝour awne wyll. *c* **1425** Wyntoun *Cron.* ii. viii. 710 Þai tuk wp sayl and past in hy Withe wynde at wil to Brigancy. *a* **1533** Ld. Berners *Gold. Bk. M. Aurel.* (1546) E vj b, Thus haue ye had the goddes at wyl. **1579** T. Stevens in Hakluyt *Voy.* (1589) 161 Our Pilot..thinking himselfe to haue wind at will. **1825** Jamieson s.v., *At a' will*, to the utmost extent of one's inclination or desire.

d. In reference to an estate held during the owner's or lessor's pleasure, from which the tenant may be ousted at any time: chiefly in phr. ***estate, tenant,*** etc. ***at will.***

1451 *Rolls of Parlt.* V. 217/2 Grauntes of..annuitees, made by you of estate of enheritaunce, for terme of lif, or terme of yeris, or at Will. **1589** in *Trans. Cumbld. & Westmld. Antiq. Soc.* (N.S.) XX. 222 Which castell..John glaisters balyfe there occupyethe at will and ought to pay yerely the said rents. **1603** G. Owen *Pembrokeshire* (1892) 191 They were not tenantes at will at the Comon lawe. **1663** Butler *Hud.* i. ii. 1022 For we are their true Landlords still, And they our Tenants but at will. **1766** Blackstone *Comm.* II. ix. 145 An estate at will is where lands and tenements are let by one man to another, to have and to hold at the will of the lessor. **1794** Vancouver *Agric. Cambr.* 52 The largest farm is held at will. **1868** Rogers *Pol. Econ.* xiii. (1876) 178 The customary occupation was reduced to a tenancy at will.

†**16. by** *one's* **will**: with one's consent, or of one's own free will, willingly; according to one's desire, if one had one's wish. (Cf. goodwill 3 b.)

c **1393** Chaucer *Mariage* 12, I dar seyn, were he oute of his peyne, As by his wille, he wolde be bounde nevere. *c* **1400** *Rom. Rose* 5728 For by her wille withoute lees Eueriche man shulde be seke. **1599** Shaks. *Much Ado* iii. iii. 67 *Ver.* You haue bin alwaies cal'd a merciful man partner. *Dog.* Truely I would not hang a dog by my will. **1601** —— *Twel. N.* iii. iii. 1.

17. in will. †**a.** With the will or intention, intending, purposing (*to do* something); ***to be*** (also ***have***) ***in will***, to intend, purpose. (Also ***in a will.***)

a **1300** *Cursor M.* 4125 All he sagh þam in a wil þair broþer sacles for to spil. *Ibid.* 11525 þai had in wil þat ilk night To torn be herods. **1303** R. Brunne *Handl. Synne* 6985, Y was yn wyl for þe feste þat euery hadde a peny. *c* **1375** *Sc. Leg. Saints* xxxiv. (*Pelagia*) 8 Of his mysdide hafand hert sare, In wil to mysdo nomare. *c* **1400** *Gamelyn* 173 Gamelyn was in wille to wende þerto. **1513** Douglas *Æneis* ix. xii. 27 His broderis slauchtyr to revenge in wyll.

†**b.** ***to put*** oneself ***in***, or ***to come in*** (a person's) ***will***, also ***to come in will to*** (a person): to submit oneself to his will, surrender at discretion. *Sc. Obs.*

c **1430** *Syr Tryam.* 1009 He wylle put hym yn yowre wylle. *c* **1470** Henry *Wallace* ix. 984 Quhill tha, for hungyr sor, Cum in his will. **1560** *Rec. Inverness* (New Spalding Club) I. 46 The said Thom Stuert is cumin in the townis wyll, and dome gyffin thairapon. **1596** Dalrymple tr. *Leslie's Hist. Scot.* (S.T.S.) II. 218 Al the rest with Sinklar cam in wil to thame of Orknay. *a* **1670** Spalding *Troub. Chas. I* (Bannatyne Club) I. 3 The honest men..was forced to come in the earle's will, whilk was not for their weill. **1690** *Rec. Burgh Lanark* (1893) 237 All quhich [offences] Nathaneell acknowledged and came in will. **1756** *Pennecuik's Coll. Sc. Poems* 108 Come in his will; Lay down the talents, or be debtor By band or bill.

18. of (*one's*) **will. a.** Of one's own accord, spontaneously, voluntarily. Now only with poss. and *own*, e.g. 'He did it of his own (free) will'.

c **1374** Chaucer *Boeth.* iii. pr. iv. (1868) 74 Yif þat dignites wexen foule of hir wille by þe filþe of shrewes. *c* **1375** *Sc. Leg. Saints* iii. (*Andreas*) 685 And to þe tormentoris of will He gafe þame. *c* **1400** *Rom. Rose* 7441 He knewe nat that she was constrayned,..But wende she come of wyl al free. *c* **1475** *Rauf Coilȝear* 541 For that I hecht of my will, And na man threit me thair till, That I am haldin to fulfill. **1825** Jamieson s.v., *O' will*, spontaneously.

†**b.** ***of will***: with the intention, on purpose (*to do* something). *Obs.*

c **1375** *Sc. Leg. Saints* xxxvi. (*Baptista*) 479 Nocht of resone, bot of wil A wyfis ȝarnyng til fulfil.

†**19. on will**: = ***at will*** (15 c). *Obs. rare.*

c **1205** Lay. 1102 Heo wunden up seiles, wind ston [= stod] an willen. *Ibid.* 7845 Weder heom stod on wille.

†**20. to** (*one's*) **will**: as one will, as one chooses; at one's disposal; to one's liking: = ***at will***, 15 a, b, c. *Obs.*

a **1300** *Cursor M.* 3647 It sal him sauur al to will. *Ibid.* 23432 O welthes mar mai na man tell, þan haf to will o welth þe well. *a* **1400–50** *Wars Alex.* 301 And wild ȝour self to will, nyll he so will he. *c* **1400** *Rule St. Benet* (prose) 7 May þai ler at serue him to will. *c* **1430** *Chev. Assigne* 181 Thenne hadde I þis londe hollye to myne wylle.

21. with (*one's*) **will.** †**a.** Intentionally; willingly; voluntarily: = 16, 18. *Obs.*

c **1230** [see 5]. *a* **1300** *Cursor M.* 6673 Qua slas animan wit will. *c* **1325** *Poem Times Edw. II* 431 in *Pol. Songs* (Camden) 343 So the fend hem prokede uch man to mourdren other wid wille. *c* **1400** *Rule St. Benet* (verse) 1971 When we þam resaue with wil Crist resaue vs vntil. **1485** Caxton *Paris & V.* (1868) 6 They ansuerd to them ye shal now come to hym other wyth your wylle or by force. **1513** in Ellis *Orig. Lett.* Ser. iii. I. 156, I see veray few..that with their wills wold go agayne to the trade.

b. ***with a will***: with determination, resolutely, vigorously, energetically.

1848 Dickens *Dombey* l, He turned to (as he himself said) with a will. **1866** Ruskin *Crown of Wild Olive* i. 44 Work is only done well when it is done with a will. **1896** Housman *Shropsh. Lad* vii, I picked a stone and aimed it And threw it with a will.

**** **22.** In allusive or proverbial phrases, e.g. in contrast with *deed*, esp. in ***to take the will for the deed***; †***will is no skill*** (skill *sb.*[1] 3); ***where there's a will there's a way*** (way *sb.*[1] 13).

13.. *Pol. Rel. & L. Poems* (1903) 251–2 Wil is wo..Wil is Red. *c* **1460** *Wisdom* 221 in *Macro Plays* 43 Wyll for dede oft ys take. *c* **1520** Skelton *Magnyf.* 148 But haue ye not herde say that Wyll is no Skyll? **1597** Hooker *Eccl. Pol.* v. lx. §6 Where we cannot doe what is inioyned vs [God] accepteth our will to doe instead of the deede itself. **1661** Morgan *Sph. Gentry* To Rdr. b 2, The reasonable will accept the will for the deed. **1801** Lamb *Let. to Godwin* 9 Sept., In this little scrawl you must take the will for the deed. **1842** Car. Ward *Nat. Prov.* 152 Where there's a will there's a way. **1853** Lytton *My Novel* i. iii, Oh, sir, it is not the deed—it is the will. *a* **1865** Mrs. Gaskell *Wives & Dau.* xiv. (1867) 147 We will take the will for the deed, as the common people express it. **1880** Meredith *Tragic Com.* vi, 'Two wishes make a will,' you say.

IV. 23. a. A person's formal declaration of his intention as to the disposal of his property or other matters to be performed after his death, most usually made in writing (but see nuncupative 1, parol *a.* 1, quot. 1706); commonly *transf.* the document in which such intention is expressed.

Formerly properly used only in reference to the disposal of real property, thus distinguished from a *testament* relating to personal property; whence the phrase (now tautological, but still in formal use) *last will and testament*: see testament *sb.* 1.

(*a*) qualified by *last* (†*latter* obs. rare).

1387 Trevisa *Higden* (Rolls) IV. 11 þanne Alisaundre loste his speche, and wroot his laste wille. **1424**, **1464**, **1590**, **1637** [see testament *sb.* 1, 1 c]. **1467** *Stonor Papers* (Camden) I. 94 The last wulle of the seyd Thomas Sakevyle. **1575–6** *Reg. Privy Council Scot.* Ser. i. II. 497 In his testament and latter will. **1768** Sterne *Sent. Journ., Fragment, Paris*, He disposed every thing to make the gentleman's last will and testament.

(*b*) simply.

c **1380** Wyclif *Wks.* (1880) 48 þis testament is riȝtful wille of dede fraunseis. **1439** *E.E. Wills* (1882) 128 If ther be eny clause or matier in his olde will. **1463** [see testament *sb.* 1]. **1549** *Bk. Com. Prayer, Visit. Sick* rubric, If he haue not afore disposed his goods, let him then make his will. **1595** Shaks. *John* i. i. 109 Vpon his death-bed he by will bequeath'd His lands to me. **1758** Johnson *Idler* No. 29. ¶9 She threw her will into the fire. **1766** Blackstone *Comm.* II. xxxii. 496 Every person hath full power and liberty to make a will, that is not under some special prohibition by law or custom. **1818** Cruise *Digest* (ed. 2) VI. 61 Where a will is written on several sheets of paper, it is the usual practice for the testator to sign each of them. **1827** Jarman *Powell's Devises* (ed. 3) II. 11 A will of real estate, wherever it be made, or in whatever language it be written. **1858** Bright *Sp., Reform* 27 Oct. (1868) II. 10 If it [*sc.* landed property] were left to him by will,..it paid no legacy duty.

fig. **1719** De Foe *Crusoe* (Globe) 180 A most monstrous..He-goat,..making his Will, as we say, and gasping for Life, and dying indeed of meer old Age.

b. = testament *sb.* 5 a. ? *nonce-use.*

[*c* **1570** *Latimer's Protest.* in Strype *Eccl. Mem.* (1721) III. App. xxxiv. 91 If God wolde have had a newe kynde of sacrificynge preste..then he, or some of his Apostles, wolde have made some mention therof in their master Christ's will.] *a* **1893** J. Paul in Ford *Harp Perthsh.* 364 A tawny tattered leaf atween the Auld Will an' the New.

V. 24. *attrib.* and *Comb.* **a.** Simple attrib., as ***will-force, -power, -spirit, -web.*** **b.** Objective, instrumental, and locative, as ***will-commanding*** adj., (in sense 23) ***-maker, -making***; ***will-fraught, -strong*** adjs. **c.** Special Combs.: **will-fire** (see quot.); **will-form**, a form on which a will may be made out; †**will government**, arbitrary or autocratic government; **will-office**, an office in which wills of deceased persons are kept; †**will-wisdom**, wisdom depending on one's will or fancy without divine influence; †**will-work**, a work performed by the human will, without divine grace (cf. will-worship).

a **1644** Quarles *Sol. Recant.* solil. vi. 62 This *will-commanding Saint. **1826** *Monthly Rev.* 24 June 399/2 The fuel was ignited by *will-fire, that is, fire obtained by friction. **1886** W. Wallace in *Encycl. Brit.* XXI. 451/1 The *will-force operating in all is the same. **1924** D. H. Lawrence *England, my England* 150 Say I want to see Mr. Whittle as soon as he can, and will he bring a *will-form. **1948** 'J. Tey' *Franchise Affair* vi. 56 An old woman.. wanted to alter her will... So Robert had taken some new will-forms. **1649** Howel *Pre-em. Parlt.* 5 Tyrannical Rule, and unbounded *Wil government. **1880** Disraeli *Endym.* vi, Events..which alike consigned the will and the *will-maker to oblivion. **1828** Lytton *Pelham* xxvii, A thing of state and solemnity—long faces—early rising—and *will-making. **1672** Wood *Life* (O.H.S.) II. 243 This journey was taken to London by A. W. purposely to peruse the *Will-Office then in or neare Exeter-house. **1874** Hopps *Relig. Moral.* xiv. 44 The drunkard..whose *will-power and whose moral force have been conquered by degraded appetite. **1899** *Allbutt's Syst. Med.* VIII. 315 Insanity of doubt, due to loss of will-power. *a* **1761** Law *Comf. Weary Pilgr.* (1809) 11 Whilst your *will-spirit is good..the changes of creaturely fervour lessen not your union with God. **1654** Gataker *Disc. Apol.* 73 His *Will-strong Objector. **1866** Whipple *Char.* 322 No opinionated, will-strong, untamable passion. **1904** Hardy *Dynasts* I. I. 6 As key-scene to the whole, I first lay bare The *Will-webs of thy fearful questioning. **1647** Trapp *Comm. Rev.* xiii. 18 Humane inventions and *will-wisdome. **1538** Bale *God's Promises* vii. E iv, In hys onlye deathe was mannys lyfe alwayes restynge, And not in *wyll workes. **1580** Vautroullier *Luther on Ep. Gal.* 85 They take from him ye power both to iustifie and saue, and geue ye same to their owne wilworks.

†**will**, *sb.*² *Obs. rare.* Forms: 3 wil, 4 wille. [f. will *a.*] Bewilderment, distraction.

c **1250** *Gen. & Ex.* 1079 Wil siðen cam on euerilc on. [*a* **1400** *Morte Arth.* 3836 And for wondsome and wille alle his wit failede. (See for *prep.* 10.)]

Will, *sb.*³ Abbreviated pet-form of the Christian name *William* (cf. *Piers Plowman* B. xiv. 148, Shaks. *Sonn.* cxxxvi, etc.). **b.** *dial.* = will-o'-the-wisp.

a **1718** Parnell *Fairy Tale* 157 Will, who bears the wispy fire To trail the swains among the mire. **1750** Collins *Ode Superstit. Highlands* 91 Let not dank Will mislead you to the heath. **1888** Fenn *Dick o' the Fens* viii, You may go right into the bog and be smothered, and that's what the wills like.

will, *sb.*⁴ [f. will *v.*¹] **a.** An utterance of the auxiliary verb 'will'; a determination expressed by this. **b.** The auxiliary verb 'will' as used in contradistinction to 'shall'.

1677, **1837–1891** [see shall *sb.* 1, 2].

will, *a.* (*adv.*) Now only *Sc.* and *dial.* Forms: 3–5 wil, wille, (4 *Sc.* vill), 4–5 wyl(le, 5–6 wyll, 4–6, 8–9 *Sc.* and *dial.* will, (9 *Sc.* wull). [a. ON. *villr* bewildered, erring, astray: see wild *a.*]

1. Going or gone astray; that has lost his way, or has nowhere to go for rest or shelter; straying, wandering, 'lost'.

c **1250** *Gen. & Ex.* 975 Ðo fleȝ agar fro sarray,.. In ðe diserd, wil and weri. **13..** *Cursor M.* 23091 (Edin.) Quen I was wil and out of rest, Godli tok ye me to rest. *c* **1400** *Destr. Troy* 2369 All wery I wex and wyll of my gate. *c* **1425** Wyntoun *Cron.* vi. xvi. 1614 He trawalit al day, qwhil þe nycht Hym partit fra his company. Þan was he wil of herbery. *c* **1460** *Towneley Myst.* xxx. 450 When I was will and weriest ye harberd me full esely. *c* **1475** *Rauf Coilȝear* 35 In thay Montanis, I-wis, he wox all will. **1806** [see waif *sb.*¹ B. 2]. **1815** G. Beattie *John O' Arnha'* (1826) 62 His will and weary ghost. **1871** W. Alexander *Johnny Gibb* xxvii, Gyaun awa' to Aiberdeen like a wull chucken.

2. *fig.* †**a.** Going astray in thought, belief, or conduct; going wrong, erring; wayward, 'wild'.

a **1300** *Cursor M.* 7310 Noght yow allan, bot your ox-spring, Sal reu ful sare your will ȝerning. **13..** *E.E. Allit. P.* B. 76 More to wyte is her wrange, þen any wylle gentyl. *Ibid.* C. 473 Þen wakened þe wyȝe of his wyl dremes. *c* **1375** *Sc. Leg. Saints* xxviii. (*Margaret*) 360 Ȝoure consal is wikit & wil.

b. Not knowing what to do or how to proceed; at a loss, at one's wit's end, uncertain, perplexed.

c **1300** *Havelok* 863 Hwan he kam þer, he was ful wil, Ne hauede he no frend to gangen til. *Ibid.* 1042 Of puttingge he was ful wil, For neuere yete ne saw he or Putten the stone, or þanne, þor. *c* **1330** R. Brunne *Chron. Wace* (Rolls) 12208 Arthur was al wyl On whilk hil þe geaunt was. *c* **1440** *York Myst.* xviii. 208 Allas! Joseph for woo Was neuer wight in worde [= world] so will! **1456** Sir G. Haye *Law Arms* (S.T.S.) 53 [They] had sik drede that thai war will quhat to do. *c* **1475** *Rauf Coilȝear* 138 Ȝit was I mekle willar than. **1721** Kelly *Sc. Prov.* 375 You are so will of your wooing, you wat not where to wed. *Note*, You have such Choice of Mistresses.

3. Phrases. †**a.** *will of wane* (*wone*) [wane *sb.*², wone *sb.*²: *lit.* wandering without a dwelling-place, homeless] = 1; also *fig.* = 2b. *Obs.*

a **1300** *Cursor M.* 980 Adam went out ful will o wan. **1375** Barbour *Bruce* ii. 471 And he wes als sa will off wane, That he trowit in nane sekyrly. *Ibid.* vii. 2 The kyng toward the vod is gane, Wery for-swat and vill of vayn. *c* **1440** *York Myst.* xix. 217 Was neuere so wofull a wyffe, Ne halffe so wille of wone! *c* **1480** Henryson *Test. Cress.* 543 Wrappit in wo, ane wretch full will of wane. **1535** Stewart *Cron. Scot.* (Rolls) II. 343 So will of wane [*printed* wand], and weipand for greit wo.

†**b.** *will of rede* [rede *sb.*¹ 2: *lit.* at a loss for a plan or scheme] = 2b. Also *will of good rede.*

1375 Barbour *Bruce* iii. 494 He wes alsua will off red, That he durst rest in-to na place. *c* **1400** *Ywaine & Gaw.* 379 That weder made me so will of rede, I hopid sone to have my dede. *c* **1425** Wyntoun *Cron.* vi. xvi. 1652 His lemman was wil of gud rede. **1513** Douglas *Æneis* ii. xi. 6 The top of litle Ascanius heid, Amang the dulefull armes, will of red Of his parentis.

c. *will gate* (Sc.), †*gate will* [gate *sb.*²]: going astray.

c **1440** *Alphabet of Tales* 90 Þan sho went in & tolde hym þe cauce of hur gate will. *c* **1440** *Promp. Parv.* 527/2 Wylgate, or wronge gate, *deviacio.* **1825** Jamieson, *Will-gate, wull-gate sb.* 1. An erroneous course, literally used. S. 2. In a moral sense, any course that is improper.

4. *compl.* or as *adv.* (chiefly with *go*): Astray, out of the way (*lit.* and *fig.*); *to go will*, to go astray, lose one's way, wander, err.

c **1220** *Bestiary* 52 Silden he us wille, If we heren to his word Ðat we ne gon nowor wille. *a* **1300** *Cursor M.* 4100 Bot ar he till his breþer wan, Will he yode, and mett a man. *c* **1375** *Sc. Leg. Saints* xxiii. (*vii Sleperis*) 255 Wenand þat he had gane wil, Ane vthyre ȝet þane ȝed he til. *c* **1425** Wyntoun *Cron.* iv. xxi. 1987 Welth and riches wont was ay In wantones mare wil to draw þan hawyngе fayr and mesoure haw. *c* **1440** *Alphabet of Tales* 453 He gaff vnto ane honeste womman in wyldrenes, goand wyll, iij c penys. *c* **1475** *Rauf Coilȝear* 73 Walkand will of his way. **1500–20** Dunbar *Poems* lxvi. 74 It is so lang in cuming me till, I dreid that it be quyt gane will. **1567** *Gude & Godlie B.* (S.T.S.) 92 Thocht I wauer, or ga wyll, Or am in danger for to die. **1724** Ramsay *Vision* iii, I deimt dame Nature was gane will To rare with rackless reil. **1855** *N. & Q.* 1st Ser. XII. 489/1 Each time she attempted to cross this place she was irresistibly, and against her will, prevented by some invisible power; or, as she said, was 'Will led'.

†**5.** Of a place: Out-of-the-way, unfrequented, desolate. *Obs.*

13.. *Gaw. & Gr. Knt.* 2084 Wela wylle was þe way, þer þay bi wod schulden. *c* **1425** *Engl. Conq. Irel.* li. 129 Hit was wille londe and woddy. **1513** Douglas *Æneis* iv. vi. 61 To nane wncouth landis,.. Nother to fremmyt place, nor steddis will. *Ibid.* xi. x. 64 Him self ascendis the hie band of the hyll By wentis strait and passage scharp and wyll.

Hence †**willness** (**whylenes**), wildness, madness.

c **1400** *Destr. Troy* 9327 What whylenes or wanspede wryxles our mynd?

will (wɪl), *v.*¹ *Pa. t.* **would** (wʊd). Forms: see below. [OE. **willan*, pres.t. *wille*, *willaþ*, pa. t. *wolde*, Anglian *walde*, = OFris. *willa*, *wille*, *wilde*, *wolde*, OS. *willian*, *williu*, *williad*, *wolda*, (M)LG. *willen*, (M)Du. *willen*, *wilde*, ON. *vilja*, *vil*, *vilda*, *viljat* (Sw. *vilja*, *ville*, Da. *ville*, *vilde*), Goth. *wiljan*, *wiljau*, *wilda*:—OTeut. **wel(l)jan*, parallel with OTeut. **wal(l)jan*, whence OFris. *wella*, *welde*, OS. *wellian*, *welda*, MLG. *wellen*, OHG. *wellen*, *well*, *wellemes*, etc., *welta*, *wolta* (MHG. *wellen*, *wollen*, *wöllen*, *welte*, *wolte*, *gewellt*, G. *wollen*, *will*, *wollen*, *wollte*, *gewollt*), ON. *velja*, *vel*, *valði*, *valiðr* (Sw. *välja*, Da. *vælge*) to choose, (see wele *v.*), Goth. *waljan* to choose; for other Teut. derivatives see will *sb.*¹, will *v.*², wale *sb.*² choice, well *adv.*: f. Indo-Eur. *wel-*: *wol-*: *wl-*, represented by L. *velle*, *volo*, (*velim*, *voluī*), Lith. *vēlyju*, *vēlyti* to wish, *pa-velmi* to allow, *viltis* hope, OSl. *velěti* to command, *voliti* to will, choose, *volja* will, W. *gwell* better, Skr. *várati* chooses, wishes, prefers, *vára-* wish, choice, *váram* better, *vṛṇati* wishes, prefers.

The most remarkable feature of this vb., besides its many idiomatic and phrasal uses, is its employment as a regular auxiliary of the future tense, which goes back to the OE. period, and may be paralleled in other Germanic languages, e.g. MHG.

In some uses it is not always possible to distinguish this vb. from will *v.*²]

A. Inflexional Forms.

1. *Infinitive.* 1 wyllan, 3–5 willen, (3 *Orm.* wilenn), 5 wylen, 5–7 wille, (7 wil), 4– will.

c **1000** Ælfric *Gram.* xxxii. (Z.) 200 Uelle, wyllan. *c* **1200** Ormin 5297, & te birrþ wilenn swelltenn. *c* **1400** *Rom. Rose* 2482 Thou shalt not willen to passen away. *c* **1400** *Apol. Loll.* 49 To wylen to mak God felow of þis violence. **14..** in *Babees Bk.* (1868) 331 Strangers,.. the whiche they knowen you to wille for to admitte and receyue. **1621** Burton *Anat. Mel.* i. i. i. xi. 44 *Velle*, and *Nolle*, will and nill. **1654** Vilvain *Theorem. Theol.* ii. 50 Man, at Creation, had to wil or nil naturaly.

2. *Present Tense.* *1st* and *3rd pers. sing.* α. 1–4 wile, wyle, 1–6 wille, wylle (1 *North.* willo, uillo), 4–6 wyl, wyll, 1 *North.*, 4–7 wil, (1 uil, 6 *Sc.* vil), 1 *North.*, 4– will. β. 2–3 wulle, 3–5 wule, 5–6 wul, (7–9 *dial.*) wull, 9 *dial.* ull. γ. 3–5 wole, 3–6 wolle, 4–6 wol(l (3 uole, 5 vol); 5–7 wooll (5 -lle, whowl), *dial.* 8–9 wool, woul, 9 ool. δ. 1 *Anglian*, 3 welle, 3–5 wele, well, 4 wel, 8–9 *dial.* el.

α. *c* **888** (MS. *c* **1100**) Ælfred *Boeth.* iii. §4 Ic nu wille ȝeornlice to Gode cleopian. *c* **950** *Lindisf. Gosp.* Matt. xvi. 24 Ðif hua wil [*Rushw.* wille, *Ags. Gosp.* wylle, *Hatton* wile] æfter meh ȝecyme. —— Luke xiii. 31 Herodes will [*Ags. Gosp.* wyle] ðec ofslaa. *c* **1000** *Ags. Gosp.* Matt. xx. 15 Oþþe ne mot ic don þæt ic wylle? *c* **1030** *Rule St. Benet* xlviii. 81 Se ðe wyle him sylfan rædan. *a* **1122** *O.E. Chron.* (Laud MS.) an. 656, Ic þe wile finden þær to gold & siluer, land & ahte. *c* **1200** *Trin. Coll. Hom.* 57 Gif man beð forwunded, he wile anon sechen after leches. *a* **1300** *Cursor M.* 9018 To will als sott sco will him lede. **1340** *Ayenb.* 57 Huo þet wyle conne and weȝe þe zennes of þe tonge. *a* **1352** Minot *Poems* (ed. Hall) xi. 7 Of Gynes ful gladly now will I bigin. **1357** *Lay Folks' Catech.* (L.) 922 A lyte wyl of þe herte þat he wyl not ȝeve to hys god. **13..** *Guy Warw.* (A.) 535 Ȝif ich it hir schewe, sche wil telle Hir fader. *c* **1375** *Sc. Leg. Saints* iii. (*Andreas*) 1049, I wyll Ane vthyre questione send hym till. *c* **1430** *Chev. Assigne* 128, I wylle soone aske hym. **1526** *Pilgr. Perf.* (W. de W. 1531) 1 Yf man wyll put to his good wyll to brynge hym safe to the ende of his said iourney. **1548** Hutten *Sum of Div.* K viij, God wylle all men to be saued. **1549** *Compl. Scot.* Ep. 3 Ther is na prudent man that vil iuge [etc.]. **1611** *Bible* Zech. xiv. 2, I wil gather all nations against Ierusalem to battell.

β. *c* **1175** *Lamb. Hom.* 123 Þu helle ic wulle beon þin bite. *c* **1205** Lay. 3658 Wha swa wulle libba [*c* **1275** wole libbe]. *a* **1225** *Ancr. R.* 156 Hwo se wule wel don. *c* **1430** *Pilgr. Lyf Manhode* ii. liii. (1869) 96 Wule he other noon. **1448–9** Metham *Amoryus & Cl.* 163 As myn autor dothe wryte, ryght so wul I. **1616** B. Jonson *Forest, To World* 31 What bird, or beast, is knowne so dull, That fled his cage,.. wull Render his head in there agaìne? **1836** [Hooton] *Bilberry Thurland* I. xviii. 307 To be sure, sartinly, that I wull. **1869** A. Macdonald *Love, Law & Theol.* xxiv. 542 'Oh, never mind Mrs. McCreesh.' 'Oh, but a wull mind.'

γ. *a* **1275** *Prov. Alfred* 688 in *O.E. Misc.* 137 He uole brinhin on and tuenti to nout. *c* **1290** *Beket* 121 in *S. Eng. Leg.* 110 Þat þing þat god helpe wole. **1297** R. Glouc. (Rolls) 669 Ich wolle telle þat cas. **1390** Gower *Conf.* I. 7 The werre wol no pes purchace. *a* **1436** *Domesday Ipswich* v. in *Black Bk. Admir.* (Rolls) II. 31 Ȝif that he wooll done his lawe. **1471** Caxton *Recuyell* (Sommer) 29 Wole y or wole y not. **1505** in *Mem. Hen. VII* (Rolls) 261 And so wolle the kynge my lorde do. **1557** Lds. Wharton & Eure in Lodge *Illustr. Brit. Hist.* (1791) I. 267 We know yor Lordship's noble wysdome woll consyder thes. **1652** *Hermeticall Banquet* 82 Then drink't I wooll. **1718** J. Fox *Wanderer* 118 Write me down,.. what wool please you. **1788** Vallancey *Voc. Bargie* in *Trans. R. Irish Acad.* II. 34 *Woul*, to wish. *a* **1801** Bloomfield *Richard & Kate* vii. in *Rural Tales* (1806) 3 Ay, Kate, I wool. **1875** 'S. Beauchamp' *N. Hamilton* II. 17 'A thinks a ool,' says she.

δ. [*c* **825** *Vesp. Ps.* v. 5 [4] Forðon ne wellende god unrehtwisnisse ðu earð.] *c* **950** *Lindisf. Gosp.* Matt. x. 39 Seðe welle losiȝe sawel his. *a* **1275** *Prov. Alfred* 140 in *O.E. Misc.* 111 God may giuen wanne he wele goed after yuil. *Ibid.* 631. 136 Þanne welle he sawin sone one his worde. **13..** *Cursor M.* 11524 (Gött.) Ful wele he wele þaim quite þar mede. *Ibid.* 18462 And ȝe sal be, sua well iesu, All dumb of speche. **1474** *Cov. Leet Bk.* 397 If he well nott be war by iij warnynges. **1790** Mrs. Wheeler *Westmld. Dial.* ii. 50, Th reek el blaw ea yer feace.

3. *2nd pers. sing.* **a.** α. 1– wilt; also 1, 4, 6 wylt, 3 *Orm.* willt, 5 wilte, 6 wylte. β. 2–6 wult, 3 wlt. γ. 3, 5, 7 wolt, 5–6 -e. δ. 7 woo't, w'oot, wot, wut, 7, (9 *dial.*) woot.

α. *c* **950** *Lindisf. Gosp.* Matt. xxvi. 39 Nallas sua ic wille ah sua ðu wilt. *c* **1000** *Ags. Gosp.* Matt. xx. 21 Þa cwæð he hwæt wylt-tu? *c* **1200** Ormin 2039, & ȝiff þatt tu willt tælenn me. **1303** R. Brunne *Handl. Synne* 3730 Ȝyf þou yn yre a man hate, And þat wraþþe wylt nat late. *c* **1450** *Merlin* ii. 34 Yeve us counseile how thow wilte we shall sey. **1531** Elyot *Gov.* i. xiii, If thou wylte eshewe bytter aduenture. **1563** Whitehorne *Onosandro Platon.* 123 If thou wylt that speadelye some woorke be..doone. **1849** M. Arnold *Sick King in Bokhara* 131 Wilt thou they straightway bring him in?

β. *c* **1175** *Lamb. Hom.* 25 Þu wult bi-haten god almihtin ..þet þu wult forleten þine misdede. *c* **1205** Lay. 694 Ȝif þu wlt [*c* 1275 wolt] þu miht wel. *c* **1430** *Pilgr. Lyf Manhode* ii. liii. (1869) 96 If thou wult,.. thou shalt make him chek and maat. **1557** Phaer *Æneid.* vi. (1558) Sj, Wult see the Tarquin kings?

γ. *c* **1205** Lay. 1577 Goffar mid þire ferde, wi wolt þu fleam makian? **1390** Gower *Conf.* I. 118 If thou wolt live In vertu, thou most vice eschuie. *c* **1400** Love *Bonaventura's Mirr.* x. (Gibbs MS.), Ȝyfe þow wolte seen ensaumple hier of Jhū. *c* **1430** *Hymns Virgin* (1867) 17 Bringe, if þou wolt, þo soulis to blis. **1540** Palsgr. *Acolastus* ii. iii. Mij, Wolte thou not take vs in to the nomber of thy clientes? **1602** Marston *Ant. & Mel.* i. C 2, Wolt doe me a favour?

δ. **1602** Shaks. *Ham.* v. i. 297 Woo't weepe? Woo't fight? Woo't teare thy selfe? **1602** Middleton *Blurt* ii. ii. C 4 b, Wut open doore? **1607** —— *Fam. Love* i. ii, Wo't thou forsake me then? **1620** I. C. *Two Merry Milk-maids* iv. i. L 1 b, Wut thou be iust to me? **1639** Shirley *Ball* iv. i, Thou wot stop a breach in a mudde wall.

b. 4 wille, wile, wel, 4–5 will, wolle, 4, 6 wil, woll, 5 wole, 6 wyll.

a **1300** *Cursor M.* 5632 Wil þou i ga.. To fot a womman o þat lede? *Ibid.* 20657 It sal be al als tu it wille. **1393** Langl. *P. Pl.* C. ix. 153 Wolle þow, ne wolle þow, we wolleþ habbe oure wil. *c* **1400** *Rule St. Benet* (prose) 2 Yef þu will haue þat ioy. **1513** Douglas *Æneis* v. iv. 15 Quhare, dismale, wil thow now? gan Gyas cry. **1526** *Pilgr. Perf.* (W. de W. 1531) 6 b, Wyll thou or nyll thou, thou mayst lese thy goodes. **1534** Whitinton *Tullyes Office* i. A 2, Thou shalt lerne as longe as thou woll.

4. *Plural.* α. 1 willaþ, wyllaþ, 3–4 willeþ, 4 wylleþ, 5 -yth; 1 (*Subj.*) willen, -on, -an, 3 wilen, 4 willen, 4–5 wylen, -yn, wiln, 5 wyllen, willyn; 5 wyn; (1), 2–6 wille, 3–4 wile, 4–5 wil, 4–6 wyll, 5 wylle, *Sc.* vyll, 4– will. β. 2 wuleþ, 2–4 wulleþ, (3 -et, wlleð, -et); 5 wull(e, 5–6 wul. γ. 3–4 wolleþ, 5 woleth; 4–5 wol(l)en; 4–5 wol(l)e, 4–6 wol(l. δ. 1 *North.* welle, 4 welen, -yn; 5 wel, 4–5 wele, well(e. ε. 1 *North.* wallað, -as, 5 wal.

α. *c* **825** *Vesp. Psalter* xxxiv. [xxxv.] 27 Ðefiað & blissiað ða willað rehtwisnisse mine. *c* **1000** Ælfric *Gram.* xxxii. (Z.) 199 *Uolumus*, we wyllað. *c* **1175** *Lamb. Hom.* 13 Þenne wille ȝe hit bireusian. *c* **1250** *Kent. Serm.* in *O.E. Misc.* 33 Yef we uilleth don his seruise. *c* **1250** *Gen. & Ex.* 191 Leunes and beres him wile to-draȝen. *Ibid.* 2304 If ȝe wilen ȝu wið treweiðe leden. *a* **1300** *Cursor M.* 14951 Þai wil me neuer luue. **1303** R. Brunne *Handl. Synne* 16 Fyrst we wylyn [*v.r.* welyn] of hem be shreuyn. **1340** *Ayenb.* 16 Huanne hi wylleþ by aboue oþren. **13..** *Cursor M.* 4118 (Gött.) Nou þai wil him noght spar. *c* **1380** Wyclif *Wks.* (1880) 249 Ydel schaueldouris willen loke to be festid of siche curatis. **1382** —— *Isa.* xiii. 17 That siluer sechen not, ne gold wiln. *c* **1400** *Rule St. Benet* (prose) 11 Yef ȝe wille cume to þe ioy of heuin. **1411** *E.E. Wills* (1882) 21 Os ȝe wylle answere a-fore god. *c* **1420** *Anturs of Arth.* xx, Sethyn charitè is chefe to those that wyn be chast. *c* **1425** *Stonor Papers* (Camden) I. 42, I beseche ȝow þat ȝe willyn speke to John Martyn. **14..** in *Babees Bk.* (1868) 331 They wyllen to do that ye wylle to do. **1466** in *Bull. Inst. Hist. Research* I. 72 *note*, Rather then we wyll suffre hytt ther shall xx personys dye in j day. **1491** *Acta Dom. Conc.* (1839) 177/2 Sic richtis as þai vyll vse in þe said mater. ?**1545** BRINKLOW *Compl.* xxiv. (1874) 70 It is euydent thei wil no wyues. **1562** WINȜET *Cert. Tractatis* i. Wks. (S.T.S.) I. 7 Quhat wyll ye geve me?

β. *c* **1175** *Lamb. Hom.* 7 Nu we wulleð seggen mare wet þis godspel itacnet. *Ibid.* 41 Ȝef ȝe lusten wuleð. *c* **1205** LAY. 3056 Men þe wllet luuien. *a* **1225** *Ancr. R.* 168 We wulleð foluwen þe; we wulleð don al so. *c* **1400** *Destr. Troy* 11419 We wull treate of a trew. **1482** *Monk of Evesham* (Arb.) 66 They wulle haue be to me as enemyes. **1490** wul [see B. 6]. **1581** A. HALL *Iliad* I. 3 Although conceale they wul A crosse receivde of simple wight.

γ. *c* **1205** LAY. 479 Þat heo moten wonien wer swa heo wolleð. **1297** R. GLOUC. (Rolls) 3261 Hii wolleþ yswyke by daye. **1340–70** *Alex. & Dind.* 1026 Þanne we wollen of þe watur wilfully drinke. **1362** LANGL. *P. Pl.* A. VI. 44 Ȝif ȝe wolleþ I-wite wher þat he dwelleþ. *c* **1386** CHAUCER *Sompn. T.* 129 What wol ye dyne? *a* **1400** *Pistill of Susan* 123 We wol wassche us. *c* **1400** LOVE *Bonavent. Mirr.* xiii. (Gibbs MS.) lf. 30 Ȝyfe we woleth hier take good entent. *c* **1440** *Generydes* 4403 They wolle shende oure purpose euery dele. *c* **1449** PECOCK *Repr.* II. vi. 171 Perauenture summen wolen in other wise seie. *a* **1450** MYRC 150 A-nother tyme gyf hem folghthe As the fader & þe moder wolþe. **1534** in *Lett. Suppr. Monast.* (Camden) 46 We wol not be so bolde. **1534** in Leadam *Sel. Cases Crt. Requests* (Selden Soc.) 43 We.. desire you that.. ye woll groundely examyne the said witnesses.

δ. *c* **950** *Lindisf. Gosp.* Matt. vii. 12 *Quaecunque uultis*, sua huæt ȝie welle. *a* **1300** *Cursor M.* 16327, I wat and seis þai wel noght fine. **13..** welyn [see *a* 1303]. *c* **1380** WYCLIF *Wks.* (1880) 23 Þes coueitous symonyentis welen be þe firste to lette hem. **14..** *Gosp. Nicod.* (S.) 100 We welle lay our lyfe to wedde. *c* **1450** wele [see B. 48].

ε. *c* **950** *Lindisf. Gosp.* Matt. xx. 32 *Quid uultis*, huæt wallað ȝie? **1436** in *Rep. Hist. MSS. Comm., Var. Coll.* (1907) IV. 199 Prayngе yow.. that ye wal tenderly consider.. the thynges afore rehersed. **1452** *Ibid.* 201 Suche men as wal have ther service accordyng to the statutes thereof made.

5. Reduced forms: **a.** 1st sing. pres. combined with pron. *ich*, I: 3 **icholle, (ich chulle), ychulle,** 3–4 **ichulle,** 5 **y chull,** 6 **chil, chyll,** 6–7 **chill,** 7 **'chill,** 8 **chell.**

a **1225** *Ancr. R.* 126 Forȝif, & ichulle forȝiue þe. *a* **1240** *Lofsong* in *O.E. Hom.* I. 213 Forto þe one ich chulle trusten. **13..** *K. Horn* 3 (Harl.) A song ychulle ou singe. *c* **1420** *Chron. Vilod.* 908 Sone, he sayde, y chulle ȝow telle. [For other evidence see CH, 'CH, I *pron.* β^2, β^3.]

b. Contracted 'll (since the 17th cent.), esp. after prons.: **I'll** (aɪl), 6–7 **Ile,** 7 **I'le,** 8 **I'il; he'll** (hiːl), 8 **hee'l; she'll** (ʃiːl), 6–7 **sheele,** 7 **shele; it'll** ('ɪt(ə)l); **we'll** (wiːl), 6–7 **weele,** (6 **wyll**), 7 **wee'l(e, wee'll; you'll** (juːl), 6–7 **youle,** 7 **you'le; ye'll** (jiːl), 8 **yeil; they'll** (ðeɪl), 7 **theile,** 7–8 **they'l; who'll** (huːl), 7 **whole.**

?**15..** *King Estmere* xii. in Child *Ballads* II. 52, I doubt sheele do you the same. **1578** WHETSTONE *Promos & Cass.* II. III. ii, And for this faulte, wyll passe it ore in ieaste. *c* **1590** *Sir T. More* II. iv. 166 Yf youle stand our freind. **1591** LYLY *Endym.* I. iii, Next time weele haue some prettie Gentle-women with vs to walke. **1591** SHAKS. *Two Gent.* II. vi. 29 And Valentine Ile hold an Enemie. **1602** MARSTON *Antonio's Rev.* IV. ii, They'l wriggle in and in. **1606** SHAKS. *Ant. & Cl.* III. vii. 60 Wee'l to our Ship. **1607** DEKKER & WEBSTER *Westw. Hoe* V. i, Theile scrape themselues into your company. **1608** SHAKS. *Lear* V. i. 34 (Qo. 1) Sister you'l [*Qo. 2* youle; *Folio* you'le] goe with vs? **1610** HEYWOOD *Gold. Age* I. i, I'le not kill my part. **1623** *Shaks. Two Gent.* II. ii. 6 Wee'll make exchange. **1676** HOBBES *Iliad* To Rdr. (1686) A 3 b, How is it possible (you'll say) to please them all? *Ibid.*, I'll name as many as shall come into my mind. *c* **1730** RAMSAY *Wyfe of Auchtermuchty* iii, Yeil ken what drinkers drie. **17..** *Johnie Armstrang* in *Ever-Green* (1761) II. 192 I'il gie thee all these Milk whyt Steids. **1785** BURNS *Holy Fair* v, Gin ye'll go there, yon runkl'd pair. **1833** TENNYSON *May Queen* II. xii, She'll find my garden-tools upon the granary floor. **1842** BROWNING *Caval. Tunes, Give a Rouse* i, Who'll do him right now? **1859** H. KINGSLEY *G. Hamlyn* xiv, It'll be known all over the country. **1859** RUSKIN *Two Paths* i. §21 To see if they'll bear shaking. **1904** WEYMAN *Abb. Vlaye* ix, You'll laugh on the other side of your faces. *Mod.* (*colloq.*) There, that'll do! That dog'll bite you. These chimneys'll fall down soon.

c. 2nd sing. pres. ind.: **thou'lt,** (†**thou't**).

1588 SHAKS. *Tit. A.* IV. i. 117 Come, come, thou'lt do thy message, wilt thou not? **1607** —— *Timon* I. i. 195 That's a deed thou't dye for. *a* **1849** BEDDOES *Wolfram's Dirge*, And there alone.. thou'lt meet her.

6. a. With prons. affixed: *1st pers. sing.* 1 *North.* **willic,** 3–4 **willy,** 4 **wyly, wol(l)y,** 5 **whilli;** *2nd pers. sing.* 1, 8 *Sc.* **wiltu,** 3 **wultu,** 3–5 **woltou,** 4 **weltu, wilte,** 4–5 **wil(l)tou, -ow,** 5 **woltowe, wyltowe, whylte.**

c **950** *Lindisf. Gosp.* Matt. xv. 32 *Misereor turbae*, willic milsa ðreatas. *c* **975** *Rushw. Gosp.* Matt. xiii. 28 Wiltu we gæn & ȝesomniȝe hiæ? *a* **1225** *Leg. Kath.* 2064 Hwerto wultu wreastlin wið þe worldes wealdent? **1297** R. GLOUC. (Rolls) 6375 Hou woltou it ȝelde me. *a* **1300** *Harrow. Hell* (O.) 75 Wiþ reisoun willy tellen þe. *c* **1300** *Havelok* 528 Wilte don mi wille al [etc.]. *c* **1330** R. BRUNNE *Chron. Wace* (Rolls) 4595 Ȝit wyly make assay. *a* **1352** MINOT *Poems* (ed. Hall) ii. 21 Whider wiltou fare? *c* **1400** LOVE *Bonavent. Mirr.* xii. (Gibbs MS.) lf. 30 Sone wyltowe not gone home aȝayne wyt vs. *Ibid.* xxxiv. 65 Howe longe woltowe make vs in suspens? **14..** *Northern Passion* II. 174/401 For þe þanne whilli take þat deþ. *c* **1489** CAXTON *Sonnes of Aymon* i. 28 Lorde god.. whylte deffende me this daye from shamefull dethe. **1721** RAMSAY *Elegy on Patie Birnie* 23 O wiltu, wiltu do't again! *a* **1776** in Herd *Scot. Songs* II. 98 O sleepy body, And drowsy body, O wiltuna waken and turn thee?

b. With negative *not* (*na*) affixed: α. 5 **wynnot,** 6–9 **wonnot,** 7 **woonnot,** 7–8 **wo'not,** 7–9 **wonot,** (9 **winnot, wunnet**); 7– **won't** (7–8 **wont**); 8 **we'n't,** 9 **willn't, willot.** (*Won't* alone survives in gen. colloq. use; the rest are obs. or dial.) β. *Sc.* and *north. dial.* 8– **winna** (9 **wunna**).

c **1420** *Liber Cocorum* (1862) 45 Ȝif þay ben harde and wynnot alye. **1584** R. WILSON *Three Ladies Lond.* D, Sirra Ile tell thee, I wonnot tell thee, and yet Ile tell thee, nowe I member me too. **1631** SHIRLEY *Sch. Compl.* IV. i. 56, I.. can worke, and woonnot. **1633** ROWLEY *Match at Midn.* IV. i. H 3 b, You wonnot pull off your bootes too will you? **1666** *Char. Province of Mary-Land* (1869) 44 In relieving at a distance the proud poverty of those that wont be seen they want. **1667** PEPYS *Diary* 10 June, People that have been used to be deceived by us as to money, won't believe us. **1670** DRYDEN *1st Pt. Conq. Granada* IV. ii. (1672) 49 But what I cannot grant, I will not hear. *Almanz.* You wonnot hear! **1686** tr. *Agiatis or Civ. Wars Lacedemonians* 101 Wo' not you pardon me? **1708** *Caldwell Papers* (Maitland Club) I. 213 Nanse has a good steady heart that wont soon break. **1721** RAMSAY *Richy & Sandy* 5 Na, na, It winna do! **1754** SHEBBEARE *Matrimony* (1766) II. 53 That we'n't bring thee a great Income. **1802** R. ANDERSON *Cumbld. Ball.* 32, I fear His word he wunnet keep! **1820** SCOTT *Abbot* xvii, To leave the place while the lad is in jeopardy, that I wonot. **1824** CARR *Craven Gloss.*, Willot, Winnot. **1824** SCOTT *Redgauntlet* let. x, He wunna budge. **1849** C. BRONTE *Shirley* xviii, That willn't wash, Miss. **1897** MARY KINGSLEY *W. Africa* 240 They don't, and I fancy won't.

c. Written continuously with the inf. *be*.

c **1440** *Generydes* 6516 And so to leve in rest and it wilbe. **1475** *Bk. Noblesse* (Roxb.) 30 A noble.. cheveteyn, whiche wolbe a leder of a felowship in werre. **1573** in *Cath. Tractates* (S.T.S.) 18 It wilbie verray hard to me.

7. *Imper.* 1 *pl.* **willaþ,** *North.* **wællað, -as, wallað,** 4 **wile,** 5 **wylleth, wyl.**

c **950** *Lindisf. Gosp.* Mark xvi. 6 *Nolite expauescere*, ne wællas ȝefrohtiȝa. **1382**, *c* **1400** [see B. 12 b].

8. *Past Tense. 1st and 3rd sing.* (*and pl.*) α. 1–6 **wolde,** 4–7 **wold** (1, 3 **wuolde,** 3 **weolde,** (*Orm.*) **wollde;** 4 **wolld, woled,** 5 **volde, wholde,** 6 **woold(e, wolt,** 7 **vold);** 3–5 **wulde,** 5 **wuld, wude,** 7 **wud, wu'd;** (5 **whowl(l)de, whowllyd;**) 6– **would** (6 **woulde, owld);** 5 **whowde,** 6 **wood,** 7 **woo'd, wo'd,** *pl.* (*dial.*) **wouden,** 7–8 **wou'd;** 5– (now *dial.*) **wod.**

c **888** (MS. *c* **960**) ÆLFRED *Boeth.* xvi. §2 Hu wunderlic wolde eow ðæt þincan; hwelce cehhettunge ȝe woldan þæs habban, & mid hwelce hleahtre ȝe woldon beon astered. *c* **1200** ORMIN 150 Forr þatt he wollde himm frofrenn. *c* **1205** LAY. 4052 Þat heo wuolden al þis lond dælen heom bi-twenen. *Ibid.* 8453 An of þon he weolden him don. **13..** *Cursor M.* 13701 (Gött.) Þair lau wold men suld hir stane. **1390** GOWER *Conf.* III. 247 Be so that thei him helpe wolde. **1399** LANGL. *Rich. Redeles* IV. 87 Somme dede rith so, and wolld go no fforþer. **1473** WARKW. *Chron.* (Camden) 11 Alle tho that wolde holde with hym. **1480** *Cely Papers* (Camden) 34 The woll.. whos not so good as I wholde hyt had bene. ?**15..** *Love Songe* in Ritson *Anc. Songs* (1792) 115 Chryst wolt the ffuger of hur swete face Were pyctored wher euer I be. **1530** CROMWELL in Merriman *Life & Lett.* (1902) I. 330, I woolde haue sene your grace long er this. **1551** in Feuillerat *Revels Edw. VI.* (1914) 59 We wolde you sholde send vs convenient apparell. **1557** *Tottel's Misc.* (Arb.) 175 Whom if the perfect vertues wolden daine To be set forth with foile of worldly grace. **1693** *Col. Rec. Pennsylv.* I. 390 And yt he wold promote it as much as he can.

c **1205** LAY. 7964 Þæt Cesar wulde þe ȝet wunnien þar. *c* **1250** *Gen. & Ex.* 1071 Oc he ne wulden his doȝtres noȝt. *c* **1440** *Generydes* 374 Of his labour wuld he neuer sese. **1620** I. C. *Two Merry Milk-maids* II. ii. F 2 b, Wud I were i' the Countrey againe. **1650** HEATH *Clarastella* 19 What mortal wu'd Believe?

c **1469** *Stonor Papers* (Camden) I. 104, I woll hertely pray ȝow.. that ȝe wod do make astate wnto me. **1480** *Cely Papers* (Camden) 55 (MS.), I whowlde a wyse yow brynge houer aulle yowr trottynge hors. **1481** *Ibid.* 76, I whowllyd fayn heyr some good tydyngys of yowr matter. **1487** *Ibid.* 158, I whowde awysse my syster & yow to com agayne into Essex. *a* **1500** *Flower & Leaf* 216 As it would seme. *a* **1533** LD. BERNERS *Gold. Bk. M. Aurel.* (1559) Hh viij, What is that realme that sleeth theim that wold their wealth, and are angry with them that woulde helpe their yll. **1587** in Ellis *Orig. Lett.* Ser. I. III. 23 Yf I had bid ought I owld have bid by yt. *c* **1620** GOFFE *Careless Shepherdess* III. i, You had better have been hang'd at first, as I wo'd had you. **1658** J. JONES *Ovid's Ibis* 86 Or like Admetus father-law that would, Return to youthful years when he was old. **1665** FLECKNOE *Erminia* III. iii. 49, I wod not force what I might obtain by gentleness. *Er.* You wod not? you cannot Sir. **1688** SHADWELL *Sqr. Alsatia* I. i. 4 Yeow wouden ha leen a Bed aw th' morn. **1697** DRYDEN *Æneis* XI. 189 Wou'd I your Justice or your Force express. **1711** SHAFTESB. *Charac.* II. 227 Wou'd you then appeal..? Most certainly I shou'd appeal, said I. **1787** INCHBALD *Such things are* I. i, Why, you wou'd not inform against me sure! **1790** MRS. WHEELER *Westmld. Dial.* 5, I wod fain hev hed him tae hed a Docter. **1828** CARR *Craven Gloss.*, *Wod*, *Wold*, would.

β. Chiefly *north.* and *Sc.* 1–6 **walde** (1, 3 **wælde, ualde),** 3–8 **wald,** (4 **walld,** 4, 6 **vald,** 5 **wallde, wauld);** 8– **wad** (6 **waude, wawd**).

c **825** *Vesp. Ps.* xxxix. 9 *Volui*, ic walde. *c* **897** ÆLFRED *Gregory's Past. C.* lviii. 443 He walde.. ðæt hi wæren ȝedrefde. *c* **950** *Lindisf. Gosp.* John vii. 44 Sumo.. of ðæm ualdon ȝegrioppa hine. *c* **1175** *Lamb. Hom.* 7 Walden heo naldden heo. *c* **1205** LAY. 1416 Wheþer heo walden hælden grið. *a* **1352** MINOT *Poems* (ed. Hall) iv. 56 Þat king Edward in feld walld dwell. **1375** BARBOUR *Bruce* v. 126 To se quha frend or fa vald be. *c* **1440** *York Myst.* xv. 70 What it was fayne witte walde I. *c* **1470** HENRY *Wallace* XI. 1400 Quhill thai till him had done all at thai wauld. **1487** *Cely Papers* (Camden) 69 The pope hollynes.. wallde a sente me home agayn. **1581** J. HAMILTON in *Cath. Tract.* (S.T.S.) 76 All thame, quha vald not be reformit. **1596** DALRYMPLE tr. *Leslie's Hist. Scot.* (S.T.S.) I. 2 Gif quha walde knawe the name of Britannie monie referris it vnto Brutus. *c* **1620** A. HUME *Brit. Tongue* (1865) 10 Heer I wald commend to our men quhae confoundes these the imitation of the south. **1674** G. FOX in *Jrnl. Friends' Hist. Soc.* (1914) July 100 Be cas I wald not be a capting aganst the king. **1724** RAMSAY *Vision* ix, The hardy wald, with hairty wills, Upon dyre vengeance fall. **1825** JAMIESON, *Wald*.. 1. Would.. 2. Should, or ought to be.

1564–78 BULLEIN *Dial. agst. Pest.* (E.E.T.S.) 5 God.. sende you comfort of all thynges that you waude haue gud of. **1581** N. WOODES *Confl. Consc.* III. iv. in *Five Old Plays* (Roxb.) 32 It wawd theam all deceue. **1720** RAMSAY *Edinb. Salut. to Ld. Carnarvon* ii, My auld grey-head I yet wad rear. **1816** SCOTT *Old Mort.* xxxviii, I wad kill him a chicken in an instant. **1825** BROCKETT *N.C. Words* s.v. *Wad*, He wad, at wad he.

γ. 4–5 **wyld,** 4–5, 7 **wild** (4 **weld, wijld,** 4, 6 **wylde, wilde,** 5 **whelde),** 6 **willed.**

Orig. northern, from ON. *vilda*; late examples may belong to WILL *v.*[2]

a **1300** *Cursor M.* 8446 His fader biding wel he heild, And did al þat his moder weld. *Ibid.* 21773 Sco delt it wiseli als sco wild. **1303** R. BRUNNE *Handl. Synne* 6933 And he myȝt helpe, ȝyf he wylde. **1476** *Stonor Papers* (Camden) II. 14 My cosyn.. askyde me whenne ye wyld cum hyddyr. **1481** *Cely Papers* (Camden) 74 Sche [*sc.* a bitch] whelde newyr hett mette and so sche ys Deyd. **1546** BALE *Engl. Votaries* I. 31 b, Least wanton youthe wolde brynge them togyther wylde they nylde they. **1583** tr. *Maison Neuve's Gerileon* I. 52 b, Willed or nilled his Maister. **1610** HOLLAND *Camden's Brit.* I. 270 Constantine.. they forced wild he, nild he, to usurpe the empire.

9. *2nd pers. sing.* α. 1–5 **woldest,** (1 **waldes,** 1, 3 **ualdes,** 3 **wældest, waldest, wuldes),** 3–4 **wost,** 4 **wldest,** 4–5 **woldist** (4 **-ez,** 5 **-es, -ust, -yst,** 6 **-ys),** 6– **wouldest, wouldst** (6 **woldst,** 7 **wudst,** 9 **would'st).**

c **825** *Vesp. Psalter* xl. 12 *Voluisti*, ðu waldes. **971** *Blickl. Hom.* 85 Þu woldest symle þone besmitan þe þu nan wiht yfles on nystest. *c* **1175** *Lamb. Hom.* 93 Hwi woldest þu swikian on þine aȝene þinge. *c* **1205** LAY. 7376 Þu waldest beon min hærrn. *Ibid.* 18815 Þat þu wældest. *c* **1220** *Bestiary* 501 Ðat tu wuldes seien ȝet ȝef [etc.]. *c* **1275** LAY. 16035 Ȝef þou were so wis man.. þanne þou wost axi of þine mochele care. **1303** wldest [see WIN *v.*[1] 9 b]. **13..** *Gaw. & Gr. Knt.* 2128 Þat lelly me layne, I leue wel þou woldez! *c* **1320** *Sir Tristr.* 2076 Þat þou wost hir se Wiþ siȝt. **1382** WYCLIF *Matt.* xxiii. 37 And thou woldist nat. **1426** AUDELAY *Poems* 11 And do as thou woldust me dud by the. *c* **1449** PECOCK *Repr.* I. xx. 123 Loke how thou woldist in this case answere to me. **1471** CAXTON *Recuyell* (Sommer) 13 What woldest thou that I shold do. **1518** *Sel. Pleas Star Chamber* (Selden) II. 134 Thow woldys nott delyuer one of my bullockes. **1550** CROWLEY *Last Trumpet* 308 Lest, when thou wouldst, it be to late. **1620** I. C. *Two Merry Milk-maids* III. i. I 1, What wudst thou doe? **1810** CRABBE *Borough* ii. 53 And would'st thou, artist, with thy tints and brush, Form shades like these? **1839** LANE *Arab. Nts.* I. 97 Thou wouldest nothing but my destruction.

β. (orig. *Subj.*). 1, 5 **walde,** 3 **wld,** 4 **wild,** 4–6 **wald,** 5 **wold,** 7 **vold, would.**

c **825** *Vesp. Psalter* l. 18 *Si voluisses*, ȝif ðu walde. *a* **1275** *Prov. Alfred* 681 in *O.E. Misc.* 138 Ȝif [*MS.* þif] þu wld don after mi red. *a* **1300** *Cursor M.* 6233 Qui wald þou ledd vs o þat land? *Ibid.* 9641 Þat sua þou wald his sorus slak. **13..** *Ibid.* 901 (Gött.) Þou þu wild euer haue hat stede, In cald sal euer be þi bede. *a* **1400–50** *Wars Alex.* 690 Þat I couet to ken, if þou me kythe wald. *c* **1400** *Anturs Arth.* lii, The wurschip of Wales to weld, and thou wold. **1562** A. SCOTT *Poems* (S.T.S.) i. 37 Wald thow be servit, and thy cuntre sure. **1588** SHAKS. *Tit. A.* III. i. 209 What would thou kneele with me? **1602** COLVILLE *Parænese* 163 Vold thou then knou the incertenty of thy speculatyue knouleg. **1670** J. STUBBS in *Jrnl. Friends' Hist. Soc.* (1914) Oct. 154 If thou would Order me soe to doe.

10. Reduced forms: **a.** with pron. *ich* (cf. 5 a): 4–5 **ycholde. b.** Contracted **'ld** (formerly **-ld**), **'d** (**'ud**), as **I'd** (†**I'ld**), **he'd** (†**held, he'ld**), **we'd, you'd, they'd, who'd. c.** *2nd pers.* 7 **thoud'st,** 8 **thou'dst.**

a **1327** [see I *pron.* A. β^2]. *c* **1420** *Chron. Vilod.* 1223 W[t] as gode wylle y cholde hym seruy. **1591** SHAKS. *Two Gent.* IV. iii. 3 Ther's some great matter she'ld employ me in. **1607** —— *Timon* I. i. 208 *Ape*... I eate not Lords. *Tim.* And thou should'st, thoud'st anger Ladies. **1610** —— *Temp.* I. ii. 198 Sometime I'ld diuide And burne in many places. **1676** HOBBES *Iliad* II. 261 To Sea they'ld go. **1712** STEELE *Spect.* No. 326 ¶5 My Request to you is, that.. you'd speedily afford us your Assistance. **1737** *Gentl. Mag.* VII. 50 He swore fra thence he'd ne'er remove. **1835** DICKENS *Sk. Boz, Mistaken Milliner*, They all agreed that it ''ud serve 'em quite right'. **1862** CALVERLEY *Verses & Transl.*, *Voices of the Night* v, Albert.. Whom almost any lady'd Have given her eyes to get. **1883** *Harper's Mag.* Aug. 457/2 Anybody 'd say you were a Bull of Bashan.

11. a. With pron. affixed: *1st pers. sing.* 5 **woldy;** *2nd pers. sing.* 3 **wostou,** 3–5 **woldestou,** 4 **-ustow, -estow,** 9 *dial.* **wodto.**

1297 R. GLOUC. (Rolls) 1339 Wat wostou more of him bote þat he truage þe bere? *c* **1300** *Beket* 35 Woldestou.. Tholie deth for thi Louerdes love? **1362** LANGL. *P. Pl.* A. III. 50 Woldustow Glase þe Gable and graue þerinne þi nome. *a* **1425** *Cursor M.* 17622 (Trin.) Woldestou þe seme To com wiþ vs to speke & mele. **14..** *Pol. Rel. & L. Poems* (1903) 253 Ne woldy ȝeue a pese iwis.

b. With negative affixed: 9 **wouldn't** (*north.* **wad-n't, waddent);** *Sc.*, etc. 8 **wadna,** 9 **wudna, wunna, wanna, oodna.**

1785 BURNS *Halloween* viii, Wha 'twas, she wadna tell. **1828** CARR *Craven Gloss.*, *Wad-n't*, would not. **1836** DICKENS *Sk. Boz, Gt. Winglebury Duel*, You wouldn't have me.. run away with an old one, I presume? **1863** *Tyneside Songs* 92 An he waddent let yen doon belaw tyest a bit. **1871** W. ALEXANDER *Johnny Gibb* iii, I wudna advise you to dee that. **1879** MISS JACKSON *Shropsh. Word Bk.* s.v. *Sick*, I oodna let 'im.

12. *Pres. pple.*: see WILLING *ppl. a.*

13. *Pa. pple.* 4–6 **wold(e,** 5 **i-wollyd,** 6–7 **would.**

In form *i-wollyd*, formed as a regular pa. pple. from the form *woll* of the pres.

c **1380–1633** [see B. 49].

B. Signification and uses.

I. The present tense **will**.

* Transitive uses, with simple obj. or obj. clause; occas. intr.

†**1.** *trans.* with simple obj.: Desire, wish for, have a mind to, 'want' (something); sometimes implying also 'intend, purpose'. *Obs.*

c **825** *Vesp. Ps.* lxvii[i]. 31 [30] Tostenc ðiode ða ȝefeht willað. *c* **1000** *Ags. Gosp.* Luke v. 39 Ne drincð nan man eald win, & wylle sona þæt niwe. *c* **1205** Lay. 3570 Wenne þu wult more suluer, sæche hit at me suluen. *a* **1225** *Ancr. R.* 398 Wultu kastles and kinedomes? *a* **1300** *Cursor M.* 20657 [see A. 3 b]. **1382** [see A. 4 *a*]. **1423** Jas. I *Kingis Q.* cvi, This will my son Cupide, and so will I. *a* **1450** Myrc *Par. Pr.* 962 þou dost syngen ylle, þy neghbores wyf for to wylle. **1470–85** Malory *Arthur* iii. iii. 102 Wylt thow ony thynge with hym? **1483** Caxton *G. de la Tour* viii. a vij, Ye ar moche beholden to serue god, whan he wylle youre saluacion. **1545** Taverner *Erasm. Prov.* 48 Whan that thynge can not be done that thou woldest, woll that thou cannest. **1560** *Bible* (Geneva) Judges i. 14 And Caleb said vnto her, What wilt thou? **1577** Grange *Golden Aphrod.* I iij b, Who wil the curnell of the nut must breake the shell. **1601** Shaks. (*title*) Twelfe Night, Or what you will. **1654** Whitlock *Zootomia* 44 Will what befalleth, and befall what will. **1734** tr. *Rollin's Anc. Hist.* V. 31 He that can do what ever he will is in great danger of willing what he ought not.

b. *intr.* with *well* or *ill*, or *trans.* with sbs. of similar meaning (e.g. *good, health*), usually with dat. of person: Wish (or intend) *well* or *ill* (to some one), feel or cherish good-will or ill-will. *Obs.* (cf. will *v.*[2] 1 b). See also well-willing *a.*

c **1000** Ælfric *Saints' Lives* xvi. 254 þæt is seo soðe lufv, þæt man his scyppend lufiȝe..and ða menn þe wel willað. *c* **1000**, etc. [see well-willing *a.*]. **1414** Brampton *Penit. Ps.* (Percy Soc.) 46 Myn enemyes that wole me ille. *c* **1450** *Godstow Reg.* 88 Gregory,..willyng helth and his blissyng to his welbeloued children. **1450–1530** *Myrr. our Ladye* iii. 313 In that he ys father, he muste nedes wylle all good to hys chyldren. **1513** Douglas *Æneis* Direction 99, I will weill otheris can say mair curyusly. Bot I haue said eftir my fantasy. *a* **1592** Greene *Jas. IV*, iv. ii, Frolic huntsmen of the game Will you well and give you greeting.

c. *trans.* with negative (*will no ..., will none of*, etc.) = have no desire for, do not wish for, 'don't want': often implying 'refuse, decline'.

c **1325** *Metr. Hom.* 148 Yef he wil noht of glotounye. *c* **1374** Chaucer *Anel. & Arc.* 244, I wolle noon oþer medecyne ne lore. **1393** Langl. *P. Pl.* C. ii. 8 þei willen no betere. *c* **1400** *Rule St. Benet* (verse) 207, I wil not þe dede of sinful man, Bot þat he turn hym & lif þan. **1542** Udall *Erasm. Apoph.* 128 The oxe eateth heigh, the lyon woll none of it. **1597** Shaks. *2 Hen. IV*, ii. iv. 81 Ile no Swaggerers:.. shut the doore, there comes no Swaggerers heere. **1606** —— *Tr. & Cr.* v. v. 47 Hector, wher's Hector? I will none but Hector.

d. *to will well that*: to be willing that (cf. 17 d).

1483 Caxton *Gold. Leg.* 166/1, I wyl wel that thou say, and yf thou say ony good, thou shalt be pesybly herde.

†**2.** *trans.* with obj. clause (with vb. in pres. subj., or in periphrastic form with *should*), or acc. and inf.: Desire, wish; sometimes implying also 'intend, purpose' (that something be done or happen). *Obs.* or *arch.*

971 *Blickl. Hom.* 61 Deme ȝe nu swa swa ȝe willon þæt eow sy eft ȝedemed. *c* **1175** *Lamb. Hom.* 13 Uwilc mon scal beoden oðre alswa he wile þet me him beode. *a* **1225** *Ancr. R.* 72 Ichulle þet ȝe speken selde. *a* **1300** [see A. 3 b]. *c* **1350** *Will. Palerne* 281 þat y am þat ilk weiȝh i wol wel þou wite. *c* **1386** Chaucer *Pars. T.* ¶ 1 Owre swete lord..þat no man wil perisshe, but wil þat we commen all to the knowlecch of hym. **1470–85** Malory *Arthur* vii. xxi. 246, I wil syster that ye wete he is a ful noble knyȝt. **1548** Hutten *Sum of Diuinitie* K viij, God wylle all men to be saued. **1561** Hoby tr. *Castiglione's Courtyer* i. (1577) E vij, Will you (quoth he) custome shoulde be more apprised in the vulgar tong, than in the Latin? **1646** Sir T. Browne *Pseud. Ep.* i. viii. 34 Thus have we made a briefe enumeration of these learned men, not willing any to decline their Workes,..but to apply themselves with caution thereunto. *a* **1761** Law *Comf. Weary Pilgr.* (1809) 54 This is not willing Christ to be thy Saviour. **1849** [see A. 3 a. *a*].

†**3.** Denoting expression (usually authoritative) of a wish or intention: Determine, decree, ordain, enjoin, give order (*that* something be done). *Obs.*

a **1325** *MS. Rawl. B.* 520 lf. 32 b, Ant te King wole þat in his oune demeine wodes..te weies ben i largist. *a* **1431** *Stonor Papers* (Camden) I. 47, Y..wole and hertely prey you..that ye seale the deedes. *c* **1470** *Gol. & Gaw.* 145, I will na vittale be sauld your senyeour vntill. **1528** Cromwell in Merriman *Life & Lett.* (1902) I. 320 His grace then wille that thellection of a new Dean shalbe emonges them of the colledge. **1560** in Feuillerat *Revels Q. Eliz.* (1908) 112 We woll and commaunde that Imediatly vppon the sight hereof ye delyuer..vnto Sir Thomas Benger [etc.]. **1682** [see 23].

b. *spec.* in a direction or instruction in one's will or testament; hence, to direct by will (*that* something be done). Cf. will *v.*[2] 3 a.

871–89 *Charter* in *O.E. Texts* 452 Ic ælfred willio & wille þæt hio sion soðfestlice forðweard ȝetrymed me & minum erfeweardum. **1430–31** [see 23]. **1504** *Bury Wills* (Camden) 99, I wyll that Rose Plandon shall haue x marc. **1557** in *Lanc. Wills* (Chetham Soc. 1884) 58 My bodye I wyll be buryed in the Parysshe Churche of Manchester. **1820** *Gifford's Compl. Engl. Lawyer* 672, I..do hereby will and direct that my executrix..do excuse and release the said sum of 100*l.* to him.

†**c.** *fig.* of an abstract thing (e.g. reason, law): Demands, requires. *Obs.* (See also 17 c.)

a **1300** *Cursor M.* 11663 'Ioseph,' sco said, 'fain wald i rest.'..'Gladli,' said he, 'þat wil resun.' **1377** Langl. *P. Pl.* B. xix. 392 That is my conseille,..þat vche man forȝyue other, and þat wyl þe paternoster. **1556** *Aurelio & Isab.* N 4, The perputall feithe geuen amonge hus will [orig. *veult*] that whan I shall be in my liberte that I followe thy. **1597** Shaks. *2 Hen. IV*, iv. i. 157 Our Battaile is more full of Names then yours... Then Reason will, our hearts should be as good.

†**4.** *transf.* (from 2). Intends to express, means; affirms, maintains. (Cf. 10 c.) *Obs.*

1534 Tindale *James* Prol., When he sayth that a man is iustified by dedes & not of fayth onlye, he will no more then that fayth dothe not so iustifie euery where, that nothinge iustifieth saue fayth. **1602** Dolman *La Primaud. Fr. Acad.* (1618) III. 662 Hee will that this authority should be for a principle of demonstration.

** With dependent infinitive (normally without *to*).

5. Desire to, wish to, have a mind to (do something); often also implying intention (cf. 7, 11, 13). *Obs.* or *arch.*, or merged in other senses.

Beowulf 2864 Se ðe wyle soð specan. **971** *Blickl. Hom.* 233 Ȝif þu þonne wille mildheortnesse us don, sæȝe us þæt hrædlice. *a* **1000** *Guthlac* 5 Ȝif we haliȝ bebodu healdan willað. *c* **1175** *Lamb. Hom.* 37 Ȝif þu wult habben bone to drihten, þu most beon on ward þine sunnen. *a* **1225** *Ancr. R.* 398 Wultu welden al þene world? **1377** Langl. *P. Pl.* B. v. 40 þe Englich of þis latyn is, who-so wil it knowe, Who-so spareth þe sprynge, spilleth his children. *c* **1380** Wyclif *Sel. Wks.* II. 56 Wolt þou be hool? seide Crist to him. *c* **1440** *Generydes* 4432 'Yet woll I wete,' quod he,..'From whense she came, and what she is'. **1527** *St. Papers Hen. VIII.* IV. 471 Meanes thowe to strive with me? woll thowe wynne any thing at my handes? **1562** Winȝet *Cert. Tractatis* iii. Wks. (S.T.S.) I. 24 Sen now al men wilbe theologis. **1697** *C'tess D'Aunoy's Trav.* (1706) 149, I will not write to you often, because I will always have a stock of News to tell you, which ..is pretty long in picking up. *a* **1704** Locke *Hum. Und.* i. iv. §8 The great Encomiasts of the Chineses, do all to a man agree and will convince us that the Sect of the *Literati*..are ..Atheists. **1862** Thackeray *Philip* iii, He..examines the dinner-card..; points..to the dishes which he will have served.

6. In relation to another's desire or requirement, or to an obligation of some kind: Am (is, are) disposed or willing to, consent to; †in early use sometimes = deign or condescend to.

With the (rare and obs.) imper. use, as in quot. 1490, cf. b and the corresponding negative use in 12 b.

832 *Charter* in *O.E. Texts* 447 Se man se ðis healdan wille & lestan ðet ic beboden hebbe..se him seald & ȝehealden sia hiabenlice bledsung. *a* **1000** *Cædmon's Genesis* 559 Ȝif þu þeah minum wilt, wif, willende wordum hyran. *c* **1200** Ormin 5297 & te birrþ wilenn swelltenn Forr Cristess þeowwess. *c* **1205** Lay. 13063 Ȝif þu wult me swærie aðes, ich wulle don of þe þas clađes. **1297** R. Glouc. (Rolls) 701 Ich þe wole marie wel..To þe nobloste bacheler þat þin herte wile to stonde. **1362** Langl. *P. Pl.* A. iii. 106 Ȝif he wilne þe to wyf, wolt þou him haue? **1470–85** Malory *Arthur* ix. xxxix. 402 Fayre lordes said he wille ye preue ony aduenture in the forest of Morris..? Syr said sir kay I wille preue hit. **1490** Caxton *Eneydos* xix. 72 O goddes celestial,..gyue socours to me,..and wul permute rigoure to equyte. **1508** Kennedie *Flyting w. Dunbar* 470 Thair is na schip that wil the now ressaue. **1605** Shaks. *Lear* ii. iv. 207 If..You will returne and soiourne with my Sister,..come then to me. **1791** Cowper *Iliad* xiii. 450, I will confess, That thou art more than mortal, if thou yield To ancient Priam all thy promis'd aid. **1800** Wordsw. *Hart-Leap Well* 134 There's neither dog nor heifer, horse nor sheep, Will wet his lips within that cup of stone. **1865** Ruskin *Sesame* ii. 192 Will you never..fence them in their shuddering from the fierce wind? **1921** *Times Lit. Suppl.* 10 Feb. 88/3 Literature thrives where people will read what they do not agree with, if it is good.

b. In 2nd person, interrog., or in a dependent clause after *beg* or the like, expressing a request (usually courteous; with emphasis, impatient).

a **1300** *Vox & Wolf* 186 in Hazl. *E.P.P.* I. 64 Thou hauest ben ofte min i-fere, Woltou nou mi srift i-here? *a* **1400** *Pistill of Susan* 135 Wolt þou, ladi, for loue, on vre lay lerne? **1470–85** Malory *Arthur* i. vi. 42 Sir said Ector vnto Arthur woll ye be my good and gracious lord when ye are kyng? **1592** Greene *Philomela* To Rdr., I..craue that you will beare with this fault. **1599** Shaks. *Hen. V*, ii. i. 47 Will you shogge off? **1605** [see beg *v.* 2 d]. **1721** Ramsay *Yng. Laird & Edin. Katy* 9 O Katy, wiltu gang wi' me, And leave the dinsome Town a while? **1824** Scott *St. Ronan's* xxx, I desire you will found nothing on an expression hastily used. **1878** Hardy *Ret. Native* v. iii, O, O, O,..O, will you have done!

7. Expressing voluntary action, or conscious intention directed to the doing of what is expressed by the principal verb (without temporal reference as in 11, and without emphasis as in 10): = choose to (choose *v.* B. 3 a).

The proper word for this idea, which cannot be so precisely expressed by any other.

971 *Blickl. Hom.* 23 Nu eft sceolan [we] oþerne eþel secan, swa wite, swa wuldor, swe we nu ȝeearnian willaþ. *a* **1300** *Cursor M.* 5987 Gas þan, sin yee wil þider ga. *c* **1386** Chaucer *Melib.* Prol. 8 Why so? quod I, why wiltow lette me Moore of my tale than another man? **1398** Trevisa *Barth. De P.R.* i. i. (1495) A iij b/2 [God] may do euery thyng that he woll doo, but he wyll not do euery thyng that he may doo. *c* **1420** *Avow. Arth.* xxxiii, Bothe my dethe and my lyfe, Is inne the wille of thi wife, Quethur ho wulle stynte me of my strife, Or putte me to payne! *c* **1470** Henry *Wallace* v. 124, I bott rahers as my autour will say. **1528** in Leadam *Sel. Cases Star Chamber* (Selden Soc.) II. 19 Mulso ..sayeth..that your sayed besechar shall..pay hym suche a Fyne..as he woll demaund at hys pleasure. **1578** Whetstone *Promos & Cass.* iv. vii, Dalia, arte thou gone? what wolt serue me soe? **1685** Baxter *Paraphr. N.T.* Matt. ix. 25 When God will tell us we shall know. **1746** Francis tr. *Horace, Ep.* i. i. 42 You cannot hope for Lynceus' piercing eyes: But will you then a strengthening salve despise?

8. Expressing natural disposition to do something, and hence habitual action: Has the habit, or 'a way', of ——ing; is addicted or accustomed to ——ing; habitually does; sometimes connoting 'may be expected to' (cf. 15).

c **893** Ælfred *Oros.* v. vii. 230 Elpendes hyd wile drincan wætan ȝelice & spynge deþ. **13..** *Eufrosyne* 424 in Horstm. *Altengl. Leg.* (1878) 179 Whom he loueþ, he wol chastise. *c* **1366** Chaucer *Rom. Rose* 1683 Brode Roses and open also Ben passed in a day or two, But knoppes will fresh be Two dayes atte leest or thre. *c* **1400** Maundev. (Roxb.) xxii. 100 þai er rowgh and will clymbe in to treesse als lightly as þai ware apes. *a* **1450** *Knt. de la Tour* xxiv. 34 Women that wol goo to see iustinge..and also wol go on pilgrimage more for sporte than for deuocion. *c* **1489** Caxton *Sonnes of Aymon* vii. 174, I have bounde this horse thus by cause he wyll fyghte. *c* **1520** Skelton *Garl. Laurel* 32 Humors superflue, that often wyll crepe Into the brayne. **1539** *Bible* (Great) Ecclus. xxi. 24 A foole will pepe in at the window into the house, but he that is wel nourtured, wyll stande without. **1599** Shaks. *Much Ado* ii. iii. 206 The man doth fear God, howsoeuer it seemes not in him, by some large ieasts hee will make. **1646** Sir T. Browne *Pseud. Ep.* iii. xv. 142 Crabs move sideling, Lobsters will swim swiftly backward. **1780** *Mirror* No. 93 Of those trifles, the nature will commonly mark the man. **1865** Ruskin *Sesame* ii. §91 Men, by their nature, are prone to fight; they will fight for any cause, or for none. **1884** *Times* (weekly ed.) 26 Sept. 13/3 Should they make a good haul on Monday, they will lounge away the rest of the week.

9. Expressing potentiality, capacity, or sufficiency: Can, may, is able to, is capable of ——ing; is (large) enough or sufficient to.

†*it will not be*: it cannot be done or brought to pass; it is all in vain. So, †*will it not be?*

c **1374** Chaucer *Boeth.* v. pr. ii. (1868) 153 In spiritz Iugement is more clere and wil nat be corumped. *c* **1430** *Two Cookery-bks.* 31 Ley þe quarterys v. or vj. in a dysshe, as it wole come a-bowte. *c* **1440** *Generydes* 6516 That ye speke with hir that she may haue hir pece, And so to leve in rest and it wilbe. *c* **1537** De Benese *Measurynge Lande* Cont., To knowe howe many foote of borde or stone wyll borde or paue it. **1538** Elyot *Dict.*, *Trochum*, a certayne stoole or chaire, whiche wyll be tourned aboute. **1592** Shaks. *Ven. & Ad.* 607 But all in vaine, good Queene, it will not bee. **1592** —— *Rom. & Jul.* iv. v. 11, I must needs wake her: Madam, Madam, Madam... Will it not be? **1690** Locke *Hum. Und.* iii. i. §1 Parrots..will be taught to make articulate Sounds. **1710** S. Palmer *Proverbs* 47 The Hazard of being Ridiculous won't Ballance the Inclination to be talk'd on. **1728** E. S[mith] *Compleat Housew.* (ed. 2) 98 When the Oven is ready, pour in your Stuff... Half an hour will bake it. **1750–1848** [see do *v.* 20]. **1790** Cowper *Let.* 21 Mar., My periwig is arrived,..my head will only go into the first half of it. **1833** N. Arnott *Physics* (ed. 5) I. 597 The heart will beat after removal from the body. **1866** R. Simpson *Life Campion* ix. (1907) 279 [His] words, though they will bear, yet do not warrant, such a translation.

10. As a strengthening of sense 7, expressing determination, persistence, and the like (without temporal reference as in 11).

†**a.** Purposes to, is determined to. *Obs.*

c **1489** Caxton *Blanchardyn* xli. 155 Men sayen comynly, that he whome god wyll haue kept, may not be peryshed. **1490** —— *Eneydos* xv. 55 Iuno the goddesse, wyllynge accomplysshe the maryge of Eneas to dydo. **1539** *Bible* (Great) Isa. lxvi. 6, I heare yᵉ voyce of the Lorde, that wyll rewarde, & recompence his enemyes.

b. *emphatically.* Is fully determined to; insists on or persists in ——ing: sometimes with mixture of sense 8. (In 1st pers. with implication of futurity, as a strengthening of sense 11 a.) Also *fig.* = must inevitably, is sure to.

c **1611** Chapman *Iliad* vi. 498 Fate's such a shrewish thing, She will be mistris. **1633** Ford *'Tis Pity* v. iii, *Vas.* Dare come? *Gio.* So I said, and tell him more, I *will* come. **1673** Dryden *Marr. à la Mode* i. i. 5, I know not that; but obey I will and must. **1794** Mrs. Radcliffe *Myst. Udolpho* xxxi, If he will lock the door,..and take away the key, how am I to get out? **1802** Wordsw. *To the small Celandine* 51 Buttercups, that will be seen, Whether we will see or no. **1817** T. L. Peacock *Nightmare Abbey* xiii, There is a girl concealed in this tower, and find her I will. **1845** M. Pattison *Ess.* (1889) I. 9 An impulse which will vent itself in some form or other. **1892** E. Reeves *Homeward Bound* viii. 239, I have spent 6,000 francs to come here..and I *will* see it!

c. In phr. of ironical or critical force referring to another's assertion or opinion. Now *arch.* except in *will have it* (see have *v.* B. 13 b).

1591 Shaks. *1 Hen. VI*, ii. iii. 58 This is a Riddling Merchant for the nonce, He will be here, and yet he is not here. **1605** Verstegan *Dec. Intell.* ii. 25 Some, not contented to haue them [*sc.* the Saxons] a people of German race, wil needs bring them from elswhere. **1664** Butler *Hud.* ii. iii. 652 The Rosie-cross Philosophers, Whom you will have to be but Sorcerers. **1728** Chambers *Cycl.* s.v. *Honey*, Some naturalists will have honey to be of a different quality, according to the difference of the flowers..the bees suck it from.

11. As auxiliary of the future tense with implication of intention or volition (thus distinguished from shall *v.* B. 8, where see note).

a. In 1st person: sometimes in slightly stronger sense = intend to, mean to.

971 *Blickl. Hom.* 191 Hwyder wilt þu gangan? Min Drihten, ic wille gangan to Rome. *a* **1000** *Cædmon's Genesis* 1296 Ic wille mid flode folc æcwellan. *c* **1175** *Lamb. Hom.* 13 Ic eou wille ȝeuan wela..inoȝe. *a* **1225** *Leg. Kath.* 485

Ichulle fordon þe wisdom of þeos wise worldmen. *c* **1320** *Sir Tristr.* 140 Mi rede is taken þer tille, Þat fare y wille wiþ þe. ? **1476** *Paston Lett.* III. 159, I wyll and shall at all seasons be redy. **1539** *Bible* (Great) John xii. 28, I haue both glorified it, and will glorify it agayne. **1600** Shaks. *A.Y.L.* v. iii. 2 To morrow will we be married. **1607** —— *Cor.* v. iii. 127 Ile run away Till I am bigger, but then Ile fight. **1777** Clara Reeve *Champion of Virtue* 55 Never fear it.. I will speak to Joseph about it. **1820** Keats *Isabella* xxvi, Good bye! I'll soon be back. **1842** Tennyson *Morte d'Arthur* 43 Yet I thy hest will all perform at full.

b. In 2nd and 3rd pers., in questions or indirect statements.

971 [see a]. *a* **1300** *Cursor M.* 5671 Wil þou sla me als þou has slain þis endir dai þe egypcian? **1450–80** tr. *Secr. Secr.* xi. 11 That eche mane se.. that he dredith god, and that he wolle governe him aftir goddis plesaunce. **1610** Shaks. *Temp.* iv. i. 100 Her waspish headed sonne.. Swears he will shoote no more. **1635** Shirley *Lady Pleas.* v. (1637) I 4 b, I know you.. wonot ruine What you have built to honour you. **1795** Burns *Heron Election Ball.* i. i, Whom will ye send to London town, To Parliament and a' that? **1839** Lane *Arab. Nts.* I. ii. 85, I will cure thee without giving thee to drink any potion... When King Yoonán heard his words, he.. said.., How wilt thou do this?

c. ***will do*** (with omission of *I*): an expression of willingness to carry out a request. Cf. wilco. *colloq.*

1955 W. Tucker *Wild Talent* xvi. 217 'Paul! Bring my gate pass.'.. 'Will do.' **1967** L. White *Crimshaw Memorandum* v. 91 'And find out where the bastard was.'.. 'Will do,' Jim said. **1971** J. Wainwright *Last Buccaneer* ii. 220 'Make sure he comes.' 'Will do,' said the D.D.I. **1981** A. M. Stein *Body for Buddy* ix. 176 'Let me know.' 'Will do,' I said.

12. With negative, expressing the contrary of senses 6, 7, 10, 11: thus commonly = refuse or decline to; *emph.* insist on or persist in not ——ing. Also *fig.* of a thing. (See also 9, 13.)

a **1000** *Cædmon's Gen.* 2388 Ne wile Sarran soð ʒelyfan wordum minum. **1303** R. Brunne *Handl. Synne* 3728 3 yf þou for wraþþe wylt nat abyde. *c* **1386** Chaucer *Wife's Prol.* 347, I wol nat wirche as muche as a gnat. *c* **1440** *Partonope* 900 Partanope wole no lenger byde. **1526** Tindale *John* v. 40 And yett will ye nott come to me that ye myght have lyfe. **1606** Shaks. *Ant. & Cl.* v. ii. 234 Heere is a rurall Fellow, That will not be deny'de your Highnesse presence. **1670** Dryden *2nd Pt. Conq. Granada* iii. i, I wonnot lift an arm in his defence. **1710** S. Palmer *Proverbs* 351 Love and Tenderness won't permit a Good Man always to make a strict Computation. **1742** Richardson *Pamela* II. 290, I cannot, I wo'not sit down at Table with her. **1857** Ruskin *Pol. Econ. Art* ii. §90 All copies are bad; because no painter who is worth a straw ever *will* copy. **1885** Stevenson in *Contemp. Rev.* Apr. 557 Those blindest of the blind who will not see. **1891** *19th Cent.* Dec. 859 The Court cannot and will not stand.. journalistic personalities about its members.

†**b.** Rendering L. *noli*, *nolite* as auxiliaries of the negative imper. *Obs.*

a **1000** *Cædmon's Exod.* 266 Ne willað eow andrædan deade feðan. *c* **1000** *Ags. Ps.* (Th.) cii[i]. 2 Ne wylt þu oferʒeottul æfre weorðan ealra goda. **1382** Wyclif *Ecclus.* vii. 1 Wile thou not don eueles. *c* **1400** *26 Pol. Poems* xxiv. 37, Y shal saye to god.. Wyl noȝt dampne me fro blisse. **1450–1530** *Myrr. Our Ladye* 151 Wylleth not geue place to the fende.

13. In 1st pers., expressing immediate intention: ***I will*** = 'I am now going to', 'I proceed at once to'. With negative, used idiomatically with *say* or the like: ***I will not*** = 'I do not venture so far as to'.

12.. *Moral Ode* 155 in *O.E. Hom.* I. 169 I wule nu comen eft to þe dome þat ich er ow of sede. *c* **1250** *Gen. & Ex.* 277 'Min fliȝt,' he seide, 'ic wile up-taken.' *c* **1300** *Havelok* 3 Herknet to me.. Of a tale þat ich you wile telle. *c* **1386** Chaucer *Prol.* 42 And at a knyght than wol I first bigynne. *c* **1449** Pecock *Repr.* ii. v. 167 That this conclusioun is trewe, y wole proue thus. **1582** Allen *Martyrdom Campion* (1908) 83 Sledd that Notorious varlet, and infamous Iudas (I will not say wickid homicid). **1591** Shaks. *Two Gent.* iii. i. 381. **1655** Fuller *Ch. Hist.* ii. vi. §38 I'le onely adde this short Story and then proceed. **1684** Bunyan *Pilgr.* ii. 134, I will not call them Cheaters. **1719** De Foe *Crusoe* i. (Globe) 122 In the Morning I had three very good, I will not say handsome, Pipkins. **1848** Thackeray *Van. Fair* xxix, 'I will go in and pay my respects to your wife', said he. **1856** Olmsted *Slave States* 78 My host (whom I will call Mr. Newman) observed [etc.]. **1885** 'Mrs. Alexander' *At Bay* iii, Very well; I will wish you good-evening.

b. In 1st pers. pl., expressing a proposal: ***we will*** (†***wule we***) = 'let us'.

c **1200** *Trin. Coll. Hom.* 3 Here cumeð ure king; wule we fare toȝenes him. *c* **1420** *Chron. Vilod.* 3021 Sore þey wepton & sayden, 'wollen go henne, For we se welle þat hit is goddes owen wylle'. **1591** Shaks. *Two Gent.* iv. i. 9 Peace: we'll heare him. **1610** —— *Temp.* i. ii. 308 Come on, Wee'll visit Caliban. **1798** Coleridge *Nightingale* 4 Come, we will rest on this old mossy bridge! **1824** Scott *St. Ronan's* xii, We will forget Mistress Dods for the present, if you please.

†**c.** *fig.* (in 3rd pers.) of a thing: Is ready to, is on the point of ——ing. *Obs. rare.*

a **1225** *Ancr. R.* 254 A treou þet wule uallen, me underset hit mid on oðer treou.

14. In 2nd and 3rd pers., as auxiliary expressing mere futurity, forming (with pres. inf.) the future, and (with pf. inf.) the future pf. tense: corresponding to *shall* in the 1st pers. (see note s.v. shall *v.* B. 8).

c **1000** *Ags. Ps.* (Th.) lxxiii. 20 [lxxiv. 21] He wyle naman þinne neode herian. *c* **1000** Ælfric *Gram.* xli. (Z.) 247 *Loquuturus*, se ðe wyle oððe sceal sprecan. *c* **1375** *Cursor M.* 12919 (Fairf.) Bot or he wille him ffully shaw, Bot ȝet a quile he wille a-bide. *c* **1400** *Pilgr. Sowle* (Caxton 1483) iv. xxx. 80 No doute he wol be redy anon to the deth to kepe the countre and defende it fro his enemyes. *a* **1425** *Cursor M.* 12436 (Trin.), I drede men wol [*other texts* sal] þis childe forfare. **1459** Marg. Paston in *P. Lett.* I. 438, I hope he wyl be well demenyd to plese yow heraftyrward. **1529** in *Lett. Suppr. Monast.* (Camden) 4, I.. have showed unto hym my full myende therin, the which I doubte not he wull declare unto your grace. **1592** *Arden of Feversham* v. i. 145 Mosbie will be there, whose very looks Will add unwonted courage to my thought. **1613** Shaks. *Hen. VIII*, i. ii. 86 If we shall stand still, In feare our motion will be mock'd, or carp'd at. **1697** Dryden *Virg. Georg.* iii. 448 Time is lost, which never will renew. **1788** Cowper *Let. to J. Newton* 9 Dec., They will probably return this day fortnight. **1847** Tennyson *Princess* iii. 12 Rest, rest, on mother's breast, Father will come to thee soon. **1858** Lytton (*title*) What will he do with it? **1872** Morley *Voltaire* i. 12 His pigmy hope that life will one day become somewhat better. **1872** Hardy *Under Greenw. Tree* ii. iii, The sooner begun, the sooner over; for come it will.

b. As auxiliary of future substituted for the imper. in mild injunctions or requests.

1824 Scott *St. Ronan's* xii, You will permit me to say [etc.]. **1831** —— *Ct. Rob.* vii, In your intercourse with their chiefs,.. you will take care to give no offence to their natural presumption. **1876** Ruskin *St. Mark's Rest.* i. §7 That they should use their own balances, weights, and measures; (not by any means false ones, you will please to observe).

15. As auxiliary of future expressing a contingent event, or a result to be expected, in a supposed case or under particular conditions (with the condition expressed by a conditional, temporal, or imper. clause, or otherwise implied).

c **888** Ælfred *Boeth.* xxxvi. §3 Ȝif þu æfre cymst.. to þære stowe,.. þonne wilt ðu cweþan [etc.]. *c* **897** —— *Gregory's Past. C.* xi. 71 Ȝif hiere ne bið sona ʒestiered, hio wile weahsan mid unʒemete. *a* **1240** *Lofsong* in *O.E. Hom.* I. 215 Vnwrih him þene wei þet is þi wilnunge, and he wule hit forðen. *a* **1400–50** *Wars Alex.* 297 For, bow he fra þe bataill, .. þen will he wed anoþire wife, & wayfe me for euer. *c* **1440** *Pallad. on Husb.* xii. 112 Yef hem this drynke, anoon they wole be sounde. **1563** W. Fulke *Meteors* (1640) 50 b, If a darke cloud be at the sunne rising, in which the Sunne soone after is hidde,.. rayne will followe. **1573** Tusser *Husb.* (1878) 109 Let Iuie be killed, else tree will be spilled. **1602** Shaks. *Ham.* iv. v. 3 *Qu.* I will not speake with her. *Hor.* She is importunate, indeed distract, her moode will needs be pittied. **1605** —— *Lear* iii. vi. 85, I do not like the fashion of your garments. You will say they are Persian; but let them bee chang'd. **1664** *Marvell's Corr.* Wks. (Grosart) II. 98, I think it wilbee very vnseemely for you or them to endeavour the destruction of the others charter. **1661** Morgan *Sph. Gentry* To Rdr. b 2, The reasonable will accept the will for the deed. **1715** De Foe *Fam. Instruct.* i. i. (1841) I. 10 Won't God be angry with me if I should love him? **1738** Bolingbroke *Patriot King* Introd., He who abandons or betrays his country, will abandon or betray his friend. **1782** Miss Burney *Cecilia* x. iv, If I am never happy till then,.. sad, indeed, will be my life! **1842** Browning *Cristina* viii, And then, come next life quickly! This world's use will have been ended. **1861** M. Pattison *Ess.* (1889) I. 46 The lover of the Elizabethan drama will readily recal many such allusions. **1882** Besant *All Sorts* xxx, You'll be surprised when you find how easy it is, and yet how you can't do it.

b. With pers. subject (usually 1st pers. sing.), expressing a voluntary act or choice in a supposed case, or a conditional promise or undertaking: esp. in asseverations (e.g. ***I will die sooner than ...***, ***I'll be hanged if ...***, etc.).

1393 Langl. *P. Pl.* C. xxi. 266 And ȝut ich, book, wol beo brent, bote he arise to lyue. **1596** Shaks. *Merch. V.* i. ii. 75 He hath neither Latine, French, nor Italian, and you will come into the Court & sweare that I haue a poore pennieworth in the English. **1599** —— *Much Ado* i. i. 235 [That] is the opinion that fire cannot melt out of me. I will die in it at the stake. **1610** —— *Temp.* i. i. 49 Ile warrant him for drowning. **1769** Johnson 26 Oct. in *Boswell* (1904) I. 399 I'll take you five children from London, who shall cuff five Highland children. **1852** Thackeray *Esmond* i. vi, I will rather die than let you see this wardrobe. **1898** 'H. S. Merriman' *Roden's Corner* xiii. 138 But I will be hanged if I see what it all means, now.

c. Expressing a determinate or necessary consequence (without the notion of futurity).

1387 Trevisa *Higden* (Rolls) II. 235 Þe comoun cubite.. conteyneþ but a foot and an half.. But a cubite of gemetrie conteyneþ sixe comoun cubites, þat wil be nyne foot long. *c* **1425** *Craft Nombrynge* (E.E.T.S.) 15 Doubull 2. þat wel be 4... þan doubul 5. þat wel be 10... þen draw downe 1 to 4 & þat woll be 5. **1592** Hues *Treat. Globes* iv. x, That Starre will set Heliacaly. **1709** J. Ward *Yng. Math. Guide* iii. ii. (1734) 293 Then ioyn the Points *A* and *f* with a Right-line, and it will form the Angle requir'd. **1838** De Morgan *Ess. Probab.* 140 That the mean risk of error will, in the long run, be $\frac{10}{17}$ of that error which is as often exceeded as not. **1887** Fowler *Deductive Logic* (ed. 9) 47 From what has been said it will be seen that I do not agree with Mr. Mill. *Mod.* If, in a syllogism, the middle term be not distributed in either premiss, there will be no conclusion.

d. With the notion of futurity obscured or lost: = will prove or turn out to, will be found on inquiry to; may be supposed to, presumably does. Hence (chiefly *Sc.* and *north. dial.*) in estimates of amount, or in uncertain or approximate statements, the future becoming equivalent to a present with qualification: e.g. ***it will be ...*** = 'I think it is ...' or 'it is about ...'; ***what will that be?*** = 'what do you think that is?'

c **1450** *Cov. Myst.*, *Assumption* 349, I am aferd there wylle be sumthyng amys. **1584** *Hornby Priory* in *Craven Gloss.* (1828), Where on 40 Acres there will be xiij.s. iv.d. per acre yerely for rent. **1641** in Cochran-Patrick *Rec. Coinage Scot.* (1876) I. Introd. 31 The kings haill tale vpoun the bullioun will not be 3000 li by yeir. *a* **1791** Grose *Olio* (1792) 106, I believe he will be an Irishman. *Ibid.* 107 *C.* How far is it to Dumfries? *W.* It will be twenty miles. **1812** Brackenridge *Views Louisiana* (1814) 156 The agriculture of this territory will be very similar to that of Kentucky. **1818** Scott *Hrt. Midl.* xiii, I think.. ye will be the same lad that was for in to see her yestreen? **1852** M. Arnold *Tristram & Iseult* i. 5 What lights will those out to the northward be? **1859** *Habits of Gd. Society* v. (new ed.) 219 An untravelled man is always at some disadvantage in *good* English society, where almost every one but himself will have crossed the channel. **1876** *Whitby Gloss.* s.v. *Biddels*, This word we have only once heard, and that will be twenty years ago.

¶**16.** Used where *shall* is now the normal auxiliary, chiefly in expressing mere futurity: since 17th c. almost exclusively in Scottish, Irish, provincial, or extra-British use (see shall *v.* B. 7, 8, 10).

c **888** Ælfred *Boeth.* x, Hwæt wille we cweðan be þinum twam sunum? **14..** in *Anglia* XXVII. 287 Blyþ will I be For to worschip þat wight. **1464** *Stonor Papers* (Camden) I. 67 Nothyng.. attemptyng to the contrarie therof, as they woll answere at theyr parell. **1561** Hoby tr. *Castiglione's Courtyer* (1577) Author's Ep. B iv, If the booke shall generally please, I wyll count him good. **1590** Shaks. *Com. Err.* iv. i. 39 Perchance I will be there as soone as you. *a* **1600** in Ramsay *Ever-Green* (1761) II. 224 Allace! that Day I'll neir forzet. **1602** Shaks. *Ham.* v. ii. 184, I will win for him if I can: if not, Ile gaine nothing but my shame, and the odde hits. **1733** W. Crawford *Infidelity* xiv. (1748) 107 Then we will be pleased with the Exertments of his Authority. *a* **1774** Goldsm. *Surv. Exp. Philos.* (1776) II. ii. 27 If I draw a cat-gut or any other cord to a great length between my fingers, I will make it smaller than it was before. **1793** Burns *Thou hast left me ever, Jamie* i, I maun see thee never, Jamie, I'll see thee never! **1822** Scott *Let.* 12 May (in Davey's *Catal.* (1895) 30), I will be happy to contribute anything in my power. **1825** —— in Lockhart *Ballantyne-humbug* (1839) 99, I expect we will have some good singing. **1875** E. H. Dering *Sherborne* xxxix, 'Will I start, sir?' asked the Irish groom. **1892** Gunter *Miss Dividends* ii, Perhaps you are right,.. However, I will know all about it myself in a few weeks. **1923** S. Kaye-Smith *House of Alard* i. §21 But I'll be all right.. if I go away.

*** Elliptical and quasi-elliptical uses.

17. In absol. use, or with ellipsis of obj. clause as in 2: in meaning corresponding to senses 5–7.

if you will is sometimes used parenthetically to qualify a word or phrase: = 'if you wish it to be so called', 'if you choose or prefer to call it so'.

c **950** *Lindisf. Gosp.* Matt. xxvi. 39 Nallas sua ic wille, ah sua ðu wilt. *c* **1175** *Lamb. Hom.* 15 Al hit mei us rede and to lare ȝif we wulleð. **1340** *Ayenb.* 101 Ich wile þe zigge yef þou wylt. **1362** Langl. *P. Pl.* A. ix. 44 Euer is þi soule saaf Bote ȝif þi-self wolle. *c* **1400** Maundev. vii. [x]. (1919) I. 52 Whan god alle myghty wole, right als the londes weren lost,.. so schulle þei ben wonnen. **1470–85** Malory *Arthur* i. iii. 38 Ye must puruey yow for the nourisshyng of your child. As thou wolt said the kyng be it. **1526** *Pilgr. Perf.* (W. de W. 1531) 6 It neuer.. leueth vs except we wyll. **1586** A. Day *Engl. Secretorie* i. (1625) 47 Let us consider if you will in generall. **1595** Spenser *Epithal.* 252 Poure not by cups, but by the belly full, Poure out to all that wull. **1696** Whiston *The. Earth* iv. i. §2. 218 Gravity.. depends entirely on the constant and efficacious, and, if you will, the supernatural and miraculous Influence of Almighty God. **1821** Scott *Kenilw.* vii, The sober russet shall be donned to-morrow, if you will. **1876** Ruskin *St. Mark's Rest* vii. §78 Very savage! monstrous! if you will.

b. In parenthetic phr. ***if God will*** (†also ***will God***, rarely ***God will***), ***God willing***: if it be the will of God, 'D.V.'

In OE. ***Gode williʒende*** (will *v.*[2]) = L. *Deo volente*.

a **1300** *Cursor M.* 18462 And yee sal be, sua wil iesu, Als dumb o speche wit ilk man. **13..** *Ibid.* 199 (Coll. of Arms MS.) ȝif god wole þenne shal I telle How he.. harrewede helle. **1438** in Fraser *Lennox* (1874) II. 67 Jhone Stewart,.. God wylland, sall haff to wyff.. Margaret off Mongomry. *c* **1470** Henry *Wallace* ix. 179 For thar, God will, is our purpos to be. **1520** in Ellis *Orig. Lett.* Ser. iii. I. 234 At my comynge thedyr God wyllynge I shale cawse the sayd Hanggyns to be made. **1544** *St. Papers Hen. VIII*, V. 396 We sall tak voyage, wilGod, with all diligence. *a* **1578** Lindesay (Pitscottie) *Chron. Scot.* (S.T.S.) I. 5, I sall do bettir will god ane vthir day. **1605** Erondelle *Fr. Gard.* H 5 b, I shall see (God willing) how you will profit. **1716** Strype in *Thoresby's Lett.* (1832) II. 368 Next week, God willing, I take my journey to my Rectory in Sussex.

†**c.** *fig.* Demands, requires (*absol.* or *ellipt.* use of 3 c). *Obs.*

1297 R. Glouc. (Rolls) 6979 Ich mot nede be milde, As kunde of moder wole & blod, aȝen my childe. **1362** Langl. *P. Pl.* A. x. 128 Folk þat ben I-weddet, And libbeþ as heore lawe wole. **1417** *York Memorandum Bk.* (Surtees) I. 184 To redresse it.. als ryght wyll for the profit of the kinges poeple. *c* **1440** tr. *Pallad. on Husb.* i. 13 Plesaunce and fruyt the tilman forto bringe As seeson wol. *a* **1450** Myrc *Par. Pr.* (1868) 714 Oþer þan þe lawe of þe lond woll. **1511** *Reg. Privy Seal Scot.* I. 345/1 That na seculare personis have intrometting with thaim uther wais than law will.

†**d.** Phr. ***I will well***: I assent, 'I should think so indeed'. *Obs.* (Cf. F. *je veux bien.*)

1470–85 Malory *Arthur* i. xvi. 59, I truste in god myn eure is not suche but some of them may sore repente thys, I wol wel said Arthur, for I see your dedes full actual. *Ibid.* iv. xxi. 146 Yonder is a knyht.., lete vs put it bothe vpon hym, and as he demeth so shall it be. I wylle wel said the knyght.

18. With ellipsis of a vb. of motion. *arch.*

Beowulf 318 Ic to sæ wille. *c* **1000** *Ags. Ps.* (Th.) c. 1 [ci. 2] Hwænne þu me wylle to [*quando venies ad me*]. *a* **1225** *Ancr. R.* 60 (MS. T.) Hund wile in at open dure, þer man him ne wernes. **13..** *Gaw. & Gr. Knt.* 2132 Bot I wyl to þe chapel. **13..** *Cursor M.* 20356 (B. M. Add. MS.) Furst my lord was brouȝt to dede,.. And now my ladi wil me fro! *c* **1386** Chaucer *Friar's T.* 89 Wher rydestow..? Seyde this yeman wiltow fer to day? *c* **1400** *Lanfranc's Cirurg.* 163 If a candel þat brenneþ.. be putt al in oile.. þe fier þerof wole out. *c* **1430** *How Good Wife taught Dau.* 165 in Hazl. *E.P.P.* I. 191 Borowed thinge wole home. **1532** Tindale *Expos. Matt.* v. (*c* 1550) 16 Who so euer will to heauen. *c* **1550** Lloyd *Treas. Health* X vj b, Geue ther of to the woundyd partye asmuche therof.. as wil into an egges shell. **1598** Shaks. *Merry W.* iii. iii. 145 Ile in, Ile in. **1610** —— *Temp.*

III. i. 94 Ile to my booke. **1647** TRAPP *Comm. 2 Cor.* xii. 20 They will on in sinne to their utter ruine. **1718** *Entertainer* No. 25. 167 Nothing will down with these Zealots but a preaching Ministry. **1822** BYRON *Werner* I. i. (1823) 36 Sir, you will with me? **1825** SCOTT *Betrothed* xxx, 'Thither will I then,' said the Constable. **1885–94** BRIDGES *Eros & Psyche* Aug. xviii, I will to thee o'er the stream afloat.

19. With ellipsis of active inf. to be supplied from the context.

c **888** ÆLFRED *Boeth.* v. §3 Cunna swa þu wille. *c* **1175** *Lamb. Hom.* 77 [We] habbeð ou iseið twa uers and wule nuþe þet þridde. *c* **1205** LAY. 3320 Lete we sum þis mochele folc fare wher ha wulleð. *a* **1300** *Cursor M.* 4095 'Fader', he said, 'i will ful fayn, þi bod i aght noght to stand agayn.' *c* **1400** MAUNDEV. xx. [xxiv.] (1919) I. 145 Whoso þat wole, may leve me ȝif he wille. **1470–85** MALORY *Arthur* I. xxiii. 70 Who is greued with my custome, lete hym amende hit that wol. I wil amende it said Arthur. **1548–9** *Bk. Com. Prayer, Matrimony*, Wilt thou haue thys woman to thy wedded wyfe ..? I will. **1599** T. CUTWODE *Caltha Poet.* (Roxb.) xlii, That which will, will bee. *a* **1633** HERBERT *Jacula Prudentum* Wks. (1857) 306 Marry your son when you will; your daughter when you can. **1692** DRYDEN *Cleomenes* III. iii, *Crat*... Think not on us. *Cleom.* I wonnot. **1818** KEATS *Isabella* v, I may not speak. And yet I will, and tell my love all plain. **1836** DICKENS *Sk. Boz, Steam Excurs.*, 'Will you go on deck?' 'No, I will not.' This was said with a most determined air. **1853** —— *Bleak Ho.* lii, I can't believe it. It's not that I don't or I won't. I can't! **1866** RUSKIN *Let.* 10 May, I hope it may do you some good, as it won't me. **1870** MORRIS *Earthly Par.* (1890) 241/2 And so mid varied talk the day went by, As such days will, not quite unhappily. **1885** 'MRS. ALEXANDER' *Valerie's Fate* vi, 'Do you know that all the people in the house will think it very shocking of me to walk with you?'.. 'The deuce they will!'

b. With generalized ellipsis, esp. in proverbial saying (now usually as in quot. 1562, with *will* for *would*).

14.. *Lat. & Eng. Prov.* (MS. Douce 52, lf. 31), Who so wylle not when he may he shall not when he wylle. **1560** BECON *New Catech.* VI. Wks. 1564 I. 495 Therfore ought suche as be godly learned to trauaile with heretikes & to conuince them, not with fire & fagot, with swerde & halter, or with lawe will I. **1562** J. HEYWOOD *Prov. & Epigr.* (1867) 130 He that will not when he may, When he would he shall haue nay. **1639** J. CLARKE *Parœm.* 237 He that may and will not, when he would he shall not. **1736** A. HILL *Zara* Epil., A Woman Will, or Won't—depend on 't.

c. With *so* or *that* substituted for the omitted inf. phr.: now usually placed at the beginning of the sentence.

c **1430** *Chev. Assigne* 260 'A, boy,' quod she, 'wylt þou so, þou shalt sone myskarye.' **1548–9** *Bk. Com. Prayer, Catechism, Question.* Doest thou not thinke that thou art bound to beleue, and to doe as they haue promised for thee? *Aunswere.* Yes verely. And by Gods helpe so I will. **1596** SHAKS. *Tam. Shr.* I. ii. 215 *Hor.* I promist we would.. beare his charge of wooing... *Gremio.* And so we wil. **1607** [see SO B. 2b]. **1900** [see THAT *dem. pron.* 2b].

d. Idiomatically used in a qualifying phr. with relative, equivalent to a phr. with indef. relative in *-ever*; often with a thing as subj., becoming a mere synonym of *may*: e.g. ***shout as loud as you will*** = 'however loud you (choose to) shout'; ***come what will*** = 'whatever may come'; ***be that as it will*** = 'however that may be'.

1439 *Cases bef. King's Council* (Selden) 105 Complaine as yo wole y defie thi manasing. **1592** SHAKS. *Rom. & Jul.* I. v. 38 'Tis since the Nuptiall of Lucentio, Come Pentycost as quickely as it will, Some fiue and twenty yeares. **1596** —— *1 Hen. IV*, I. ii. 162 Well, come what will, Ile tarry at home. **1602** —— *Ham.* v. ii. 10. **1633** EARL MANCH. *Al Mondo* (1636) 186 Let his condition here civilly bee what it will, it will not content him. **1732** POPE *Mor. Ess.* III. 153 The ruling Passion, be it what it will, The ruling Passion conquers Reason still. **1827** SCOTT *Two Drovers* i, The drovers usually sleep along with their cattle, let the weather be what it will. **1860** RUSKIN *Unto this Last* iv. §61 Think what you will of it,.. the value of the thing itself is neither greater nor less.

†**20.** With ellipsis of pass. inf. *Obs. rare.*

a **1774** GOLDSM. *Surv. Exp. Philos.* (1776) II. 145 The air's force is compounded of its swiftness and density, and as these are encreased, so will the force of the wind.

21. In const. where the ellipsis may be either of an obj. clause (as in 17) or of an inf. (as in 19).

a. In a disjunctive qualifying clause or phr. (usually parenthetic), as ***whether he will or no***, ***will he or not***, †(with pron. omitted) ***will or no***, (with *or* omitted) ***will he will he not***, ***will he nill he*** (see VI. below and WILLY-NILLY), etc.

In quot. 1592 *vaguely* = 'one way or another', 'in any case'.

a **1425** tr. *Arderne's Treat. Fistula*, etc. 101 He schal slepe alsone, wille he wil he noȝt. **1568** HACKET tr. *Thevet's New found World* xiv. 21 b, They floote aboue water, will they or not, and by this meanes they are taken. **1581** A. HALL *Iliad* I. 12 They Bryseis fetche away, whether she wil or no Out of my Tent. **1592** BRETON *C'tess Pembroke's Love* Wks. (Grosart) I. 21/1 Fortune? shee skornde: friendes? who durst be a foe? Seruants? a worlde would serue her will or no.

II. The past tense **would** with temporal function.

* With simple obj. or obj. clause: corresponding to the pres. tense in I.*

†**22.** (with simple obj.) Desired, wished for; sometimes implying or passing into the sense 'intended'; with negative, often implying 'refused': cf. 1, 1 b, 1 c. *Obs.*

c **900** tr. *Bæda's Hist.* III. viii, [Heo] cwæð.. þæt heo þa hy fruȝne, hwæt heo sohten oððe hwæt heo þider wolden. *c* **1000** ÆLFRIC *Saints' Lives* xx. 13 Se ealdor-man ȝewat þa ða hit wolde god. *c* **1250** *Gen. & Ex.* 3620 Ðis folc.. Offreden him siluer and golde, And oðer metal swilc he wolde. *a* **1300** *Cursor M.* 16 Wit sarazins wald þai na saght. *c* **1380** *Antecrist* in Todd *Three Treat. Wyclif* (1851) p. cxxvi, Crist forsoke worldly glorie... Crist wold not worldly lordschip. *c* **1450** *Merlin* xiii. 192 Thei seide thei wolde the londe.. for her oncle. **1470–85** MALORY *Arthur* IV. xv. 138 He.. asked yf she wold any thing vnto kynge Arthur. **1523** LD. BERNERS *Froiss.* I. viii. 3/2 He wolde nothyng to her but all loue and good faith. **1629** GAULE *Pract. Theories Christ* 158 God and the Iewes, both would the Passion and Death of Christ. **1643** [ANGIER] *Lanc. Vall. Achor* 18 When we would no Pardon they laboured to punish us. **1692** WASHINGTON tr. *Milton's Def. People* xii. 238 To perform, not what he himself would, but what the People.. requir'd of him.

23. (with obj. cl., or acc. and inf.: cf. 2, 3.) Desired, wished; often implying 'intended'; determined, ordained; *fig.* demanded, required (that something should be done). *Obs.* or *rare arch.*

c **888** ÆLFRED *Boeth.* iv, Hwy þu la Drihten æfre woldest þæt seo wyrd swa hwyrfan sceolde? *c* **897** —— *Gregory's Past. C.* xvi. 101 Hu he wolde ðæt mon him miltsode. **1154** *O.E. Chron.* (Laud MS.) an. 1132 Þa uuolde he ðat his nefe sculde ben abbot. *c* **1200** ORMIN 7708, & tatt te Laferrd Jesu Crist þa wollde þatt hiss moderr Swa shollde to þe kirrke gan. *a* **1300** *Cursor M.* 1590 Wald he noght it war sua fordon. *Ibid.* 11212 Maria barn ber in chastite, Sin godd wald þat it sua suld be. *Ibid.* 13701 Þair lagh wald man suld hir stan. *c* **1380** WYCLIF *Sel. Wks.* I. 107 Crist axide him, what he wolde þat Crist did to him. **1430–31** *Rolls of Parlt.* IV. 370/2 He wolde and bequath be the said Testament, yat [etc.]. *c* **1489** CAXTON *Sonnes of Aymon* xii. 301 Ye shall see that Rowlande wold he had not gon there. **1513** DOUGLAS *Æneis* VIII. vi. 26 He.. wald also this regioun euery steid War callit Latium. **1535** COVERDALE *1 Macc.* iv. 27 Because Israel had not gotten soch mysfortune as he wolde they shulde. **1542** UDALL *Erasm. Apoph.* 327 He would his richesse to bee a cloke of goodnesse. **1600** SHAKS. *A.Y.L.* III. ii. 161 Heauen would that shee these gifts should haue. **1682** BUNYAN *Holy War* (1905) 263 He would that Captain Credence should join himself with them. **1868** TENNYSON *Lucretius* 68 Because I would not one of thine own doves, Not ev'n a rose, were offer'd to thee.

†**24.** *transf.* (cf. 4.) Maintained, 'wanted to make out'. *Obs.*

a **1500** *Bernard. de cura rei fam.*, etc. 25/82 He walde þat A watter, or a well, hayd wecht it away. **1545** WRIOTHESLEY *Chron.* (Camden) I. 152 Fayninge and counterfeyting a miracle that he woulde had done whilest he was at masse. **1567** *Satir. Poems Reform.* vii. 5, I vnderstuid thair sentence quhat thay wald.

** With dependent infinitive (as in I.**).

25. (Cf. 5.) Wished to; often with implication 'intended to'. *Obs.* or *arch.* except in dependence on a principal vb. in past time.

c **888** ÆLFRED *Boeth.* vii. §3 Wast þu hu ic ȝewand ymb Croeses.. þa þa hine Cirus.. ȝefangen hæfde, & hine forbærnan wolde? **900–30** *O.E. Chron.* (Parker MS.) an. 755, Ymb .xxxi. wintra þæs þe he rice hæfde, he wolde adræfan anne æþeling se was Cyneheard haten. *Ibid.* 877 Swa fela swa he habban wolde. *c* **1000** *Ags. Gosp.* Luke x. 29 Ða cwæþ he to þam hælende, & wolde hine sylfne ȝerihtwisian. *a* **1154** *O.E. Chron.* (Laud MS.) an. 1132, He uuolde underþeden ðat mynstre to Clunie. *a* **1300** *Havelok* 354 Deth him tok þan he best wolde Liuen. *c* **1386** CHAUCER *Friar's T.* 80 (Petw.) Feynyng a cause for he wold haue a bribe. **1470–85** MALORY *Arthur* II. ii. 77 He.. sawe this aduenture.. and wolde assaye it as other knyghtes dyd. **1526** TINDALE *John* xvi. 19 Jesus perceaved that they wolde axe hym. **15..** *Christ's Kirk* 26 in *Bannatyne MS.* (Hunter. Club) 283 Scho of lufe wes sillie;.. Scho wald haif bot sweit Willie. **1611** *Bible* Transl. Pref. ¶2 Certaine, which would be counted pillars of the State. **1697** DAMPIER *Voy.* I. 302 To assist us in getting as many dry Coco-nuts as we would have. **1705** DE FOE *True Relation* in *Early Wks.* (1889) 443 Mrs. Bargrave asked her whether she would drink some tea. **1808** SCOTT *Marm.* IV. i, Till one, who would seem wisest, cried, 'What else but evil could betide..?' **1810** CRABBE *Borough* xiv. 108 He now would build—and lofty seat he built. **1871** G. MACDONALD *Sonn. conc. Jesus* xvi. 11 Thou of the truth not less than all wouldst make. **1876** MARCHIONESS DUFFERIN *Canad. Jrnl.* (1891) 291 They asked us if we would have tea, and as we 'would', they took us into an adjoining room.

†**b.** in direct statement: Was about to. *rare.*

a **950** *Guthlac* v. (Prose) 135/270 Ða hit þa on merȝen daȝian wolde [*imminente aurora*]. *c* **1450** *Merlin* 463 As the queene hem saugh she wiste well she was be-traied, and wolde crye as she that was sore affraied, and thei seide [etc.].

26. (Cf. 6, 7.) Was (were) willing to, consented to; †deigned to; chose to; †also in weakened sense (nearly = did). Now only in dependence on a principal vb. in past time.

c **888** ÆLFRED *Boeth.* iii. §4 Sint þis nu þa god.. þe þu .. ȝehete þam monnum þe þe heorsumian woldan? *a* **1300** *Cursor M.* 6233 Qui wald [*Gött.* wild, *Trin.* woldes] þou ledd vs o þat land? **13..** *Bonaventura's Medit.* 25 Of a mayden he wulde be bore. *c* **1400** MAUNDEV. (Roxb.) Pref. 1 In þat land he wald lede his lyf and suffer hard passion. *c* **1450** *Merlin* i. 2 For to saue man he wolde come down in to erthe to be born of a woman. **1574** in *Maitl. Club Misc.* I. 99 Thair wes tyme and place grantit, to all that wald appone thame thairto. **1611** BP. HALL *Imprese of God* i. Wks. (1625) 444 In the Creation hee could haue made all at once, but hee would take dayes for it. *a* **1629** HINDE *J. Bruen* xlvii. (1641) 149 He shewed himselfe to be of that extraordinary strength, that if he would fold his hands together, no man could pull them asunder. **1680** OTWAY *Orphan* III. iv, Why would you delay so long to give it? **1753** CHALLONER *Cath. Chr. Instr.* 183 St. Francis would have his Religious for Humility called Friars Minors. **1884** WALFORD *Baby's Grandm.* xii, I said you would be all right in a few days if you would only hold on.

b. (Cf. 6 b.) In a dependent clause after an expression of request, command, or the like, where the principal vb. is in past time. Now *rare.*

a **1325** *MS. Rawl. B. 520* lf. 54 b, [They] habbez bi souȝt us that we hit [*sc.* the maletolt] wolden relessen. **1526** TINDALE *Acts* ix. 38 They sent vnto hym, desyrynge him that he wolde not be greued to come vnto them. **1535** COVERDALE *1 Esdras* ix. 40 They spake vnto Eszdras.. yᵗ he wolde brynge yᵉ lawe of Moses. **1745** A. BUTLER *Lives Saints, St. Jane Frances de Chantal*, It was her.. prayer.. that he would conduct her to a truly holy spiritual guide. **1813** SOUTHEY *Nelson* I. ii. 84 He requested the admiralty that they would not leave him to rust in indolence. **1855** MACAULAY *Hist. Eng.* xx. IV. 532 She.. faltered out her commands that he would sit down.

27. (Cf. 8.) Was (were) accustomed to; used to.

c **888** ÆLFRED *Boeth.* xxxv. §7 Wildu dior ðær woldon to irnan & stondan swilce hi tamu wæren. *c* **1000** ÆLFRIC *Saints' Lives* xxvi. 114 He wolde æfter uhtsange oftost hine ȝebiddan. *c* **1290** *Beket* 26 in *S. Eng. Leg.* I. 107 Ofte-siþe heo wolde speke with him. **1387** TREVISA *Higden* (Rolls) VIII. 33 Sche wolde selden come at cherche. **1470–85** MALORY *Arthur* IX. xxxvii. 399 Euery day syr Palomydes wold repreue sir Tristram of old hate betwixe them. **1573** L. LLOYD *Marrow of Hist.* (1653) 40 The Athenians at any victory, would crown the Conqueror with a Garland made of Oken leaves. **1587** UNDERDOWNE tr. *Heliodorus* VII. (1895) 184 So lay shee all that night.. sometime would she rise up: .. sometime would shee cast her cloathes almoste all from her. **1622** BACON *Hen. VII* 210 They would also ruffle with Iurors. **1750** GRAY *Elegy* 103 There at the foot of yonder nodding beech.. His listless length at noontide would he stretch. **1805** SCOTT *Last Minstr.* III. xvii, He never counted him a man, Would strike below the knee. **1848** THACKERAY *Van. Fair* xxi, The girls would ask her.. for a little music, and she would sing her three songs. **1915** WIN. HOLT *Beacon for Blind* xxx. 307 He would often return home exhausted from his work, and when Mrs. Fawcett read to him he would frequently fall fast asleep.

28. (Cf. 9.) Was capable of ——ing; could.

Usually in a relative clause.

c **1386** CHAUCER *Prol.* 631 Ther nas.. Ne oynement that wolde clense and byte That hym myghte helpen. *a* **1440** *Sir Eglam.* 491 Ther was no knyfe that wolde hym byte, So harde of hyde was hee. **1470–85** MALORY *Arthur* IV. xiv. 138 Thenne he loked for the scaubard, but it wold not be founde. **1601** HOLLAND *Pliny* XXXV. x. II. 542 As often, he had wiped out that which was done, and all to see if he could hit upon it: but it would not be, for yet it was not to his fansie. **1663** BUTLER *Hud.* I. I. 351 With Basket-hilt, that wou'd hold broth, And serve for Fight, and Dinner both.

29. (Cf. 10 b.) Was determined to; insisted on or persisted in ——ing. Also (*colloq.*), could naturally or inevitably be expected to, esp. in the light of one's known character or tendencies.

1706 FARQUHAR *Recruiting Officer* Ep. Ded., Be it known .. that it was my Act and Deed, or rather Mr. Durfey's; for he *wou'd* play his Third Night against the First of mine. **1794** MRS. RADCLIFFE *Myst. Udolpho* xxv, The signor was cruel enough, but he would be obeyed. **1835** DICKENS *Sk. Boz, Parish* ii, Then he took to breeding silkworms, which he *would* bring in.. to show the old lady. **1884** *Manch. Exam.* 20 May 5/2 The fussiness of Thiers, who would have a finger in every pie that was being made. **1919** 'C. DANE' *Legend* 43 One never knew what Madala would do next, and yet when she'd done it, one said—'Of course! Just what Madala *would* do!' **1926** C. MACKENZIE *Rogues & Vagabonds* 268 'He always pushes me out.' 'He would.' **1930** E. WAUGH *Vile Bodies* ix. 150 There's our Lily now. You know how she would go in for being a manicurist. **1932** M. H. RINEHART *Miss Pinkerton* xvi. 164 'We're interested in Monday night, and that's all.'.. 'You would be!' **1946** H. J. MASSINGHAM *Where Man Belongs* iii. 96 He, Ireson told me, 'is the most promising boy of the lot.' He would be. **1963** *Times* 1 July 6/6 Mr. Burge asked: Do you know Lord Astor has made a statement to the police saying that these allegations of yours are absolutely untrue? Miss Rice-Davies: He would, wouldn't he? **1980** 'T. HINDE' *Daymare* i. 8 'Well, he would, wouldn't he,' she says. 'It's what you'd expect of a born capitalist.'

30. (Cf. 11, 13.) In indirect reports, usually in 3rd pers., of past utterances, etc. in the 1st pers. (now) implying intention.

971 *Blickl. Hom.* 183 Ic wæs heafde becorfen, & nu on þyssum þriddan dæȝe aras, swa ic ær beforan þe sæȝde & ȝeheht þæt ic don wolde. *c* **1100** *O.E. Chron.* (MS. D.) an. 1066 Hi.. sworon aðas, þat hi æfre woldon fryð & freondscype into þisan lande haldan. **1340–70** *Alex. & Dind.* 45 He sikurede hem alle, þat he wolde fare wiþ his folk in a faire wise. *c* **1400** *Sowdone Bab.* 2060 He.. made a vowe to Mahounde of myght, He wolde that Cite wynne. *a* **1533** LD. BERNERS *Huon* lxxxviii. 278 He commaundyd them to assamble as myche people as they coude, by cause he sayde that he wolde goo to his vncle themperour of Almayne. **1639** *Hamilton Papers* (Camden) 69 Thay all answered me that they wold keepe the castell. **1719** DE FOE *Crusoe* II. (Globe) 497 He would go, he said. **1837** DICKENS *Pickw.* i, Was it some vain.. man—he would not say haberdasher—who [etc.]. **1871** M. COLLINS *Marq. & Merch.* xxxiii, Adrian.. resolved that they would have a jolly rough honeymoon.. with everything simple and rustical. **1908** R. BAGOT *A. Cuthbert* xxvi. 339 Anthony suggested to her that she and his sister should slip away unobserved. He himself would remain half-an-hour longer, and would then follow their example.

31. (Cf. 12.) With negative, commonly denoting refusal.

c **1250** *Gen. & Ex.* 969 And sarrai wuldet noȝt ðolen Ðat agar wore ðus to-bolen. **1340** HAMPOLE *Pr. Consc.* 6193, I thrested, and of drynk had nede, And yhe wald na drynk me bede. *c* **1420** ? LYDG. *Assembly of Gods* 941 Vertu wold nat tary, but hyghyd hym thydyr blyue. **1526** TINDALE *Luke* xviii. 13 The publican stode afarre of, and wolde not lifte vp his eyes to heven. **1610** SHAKS. *Temp.* I. ii. 267 This damn'd Witch Sycorax.. was banish'd: for one thing she did They wold not take her life. *c* **1720** DE FOE *Mem. Cavalier* (1840) 269 He would not stir. **1802** WORDSW. *Alice Fell* 52 She wept, nor would be pacified. **1880** TENNYSON *Def. Lucknow* vi. 12 Cholera, scurvy, and fever, the wound that *would* not be heal'd. **1918** *Times Lit. Suppl.* 21 Mar., Editors and publishers.. would have none of it.

32. (Cf. 14, 15.) Forming (with pres. inf.) the auxiliary of the 'anterior future' or 'future in the past', and (with pf. inf.) of the 'anterior future perfect', in the 2nd and 3rd pers.: cf. SHALL *v.* B. 14 b, e. **a.** in dependent clause (or virtual reported speech or thought).

c **893** ÆLFRED *Oros.* III. ix. 128 þa Darius ȝeseah þæt he oferwunnen beon wolde, þa wolde he hiene selfne on ðæm ȝefeohte forspillan. *c* **1200** ORMIN 689 þatt seȝȝde he.. forrþi þatt ta wass cumenn time þatt Drihhtin wollde lesenn ut hiss follc off deofless walde. **1297** R. GLOUC. (Rolls) 7087 þis child wax so wel & þeu as iseie fremde & sibbe þat he wolde be a noble mon. **1470–85** MALORY *Arthur* XX. vii. 809, I.. told my bretheren.. afore hand what wold falle in the ende. **1496** *Acta Dom. Conc.* II. 10 Chargeing thame to do justice to baith the saidis partiis as thai wald ansuer to God. **1582** ALLEN *Martyrdom Campion* (1908) 3 This he protested to be true, as he would answer before God. **1586** in *Engl. Hist. Rev.* (1920) Jan. 113 The lorde chauncellor aunswered that diverse of the lordes had byn and woulde be.. suitors unto her maiestie. **1663** in *Extr. St. Papers rel. Friends* Ser. II. (1911) 183 Saying.. that the time would come he should be found as good a subiect as myselfe. **1794** MRS. RADCLIFFE *Myst. Udolpho* xxv, The planet.. was not yet risen; but.. she kept her eyes fixed on that part of the hemisphere where it would rise. **1841** MACAULAY *Ess., L. Hunt* (1853) III. 38 He promised.. to furnish them with a play every year, if his health would permit. **1872** MORLEY *Voltaire* i. 2 It disclosed to them a gracious.. being, who would one day redress all wrongs. **1918** *Cornh. Mag.* June 569 The Elizabethan's chief concern was that the present would soon merge in the past and be gone.

b. (Cf. 15 d.) without notion of futurity: Probably or presumably did.

1857 MRS. GASKELL *C. Brontë* I. iv. 79 'Of the two younger ones.. I have very slight recollections, save that one .. was quite the pet nursling of the school.' This last would be Emily. **1906** R. H. BENSON *Richard Raynal* v. 91 It would be about half an hour before the King's dinner-time.. that Master Richard came again to the hall. **1909** E. H. BURTON *Life Bp. Challoner* I. ii. 12 The last of the Douay martyrs.. had suffered but one year previously. Some of the priests living at Douay would have known this martyr personally.

¶**33.** (Cf. 16.) Used where *should* is now the normal auxiliary.

1760–72 H. BROOKE *Fool of Qual.* (1809) III. 90 The captain fearing that I would die of grief. **1870** DASENT *Annals* xiv, Of course my Aunt did not expect that I would be plucked in any examination. **1901** *Empire Rev.* I. 380, I .. rejoiced in the fact that to get there I would have to travel to New York.

*** **34.** Elliptical and quasi-elliptical uses as in I.***, 17–21. Now *rare* or *Obs.* except with ellipsis of active inf. to be supplied from the context, or in disjunctive qualifying clauses (e.g. *whether he would or no*).

†In quot. *c* 1400 (*Beryn*) *wold nat* = was of no avail.

c **897** ÆLFRED *Gregory's Past. C.* iii. 35 & ða he him from wolde, ða ȝefeng he hine. **971** *Blickl. Hom.* 79 [Hi] þæt land ȝesetton swa hie sylfe woldon. *c* **1205** LAY. 18815 Wi naldest þu me suggen þurh nanes cunnes þinge þat þu wældest to þan kinge? *c* **1290** *S. Eng. Leg.* I. 273/79 Ȝwane any man wolde ouer þat watur. **1377** LANGL. *P. Pl.* B. x. 127 Al was as þow wolde [*v.r.* woldest] lorde, yworschiped be þow. *c* **1385** CHAUCER *L.G.W.* 952 *Dido*, He.. saylyth forth al his cumpanyne Toward ytayle as wolde his desten. *c* **1400** *Beryn* 1082 Ffawnus saw it wold nat. *c* **1400** *Pilgr. Sowle* (Caxton) II. lx. (1859) 57, I was nought but abyl for to suffre, whether I wold or no. **1431** *Munim. de Melros* (Bann.) 522 þe qwilk brefe of Inqueste as law wald I gert procede. *c* **1450** *Merlin* 204 Thei.. wente to the courte euen and morowe whan thei wolden. **1530** TINDALE *Pract. Prelates* H ij, After that the Emperoure wolde in to Spayne. **1568** GRAFTON *Chron.* II. 28 Anselme might not.. correct his clergie but as the king would. **1593** DRAYTON *Ecl.* viii, Would she ought or would she nought, This lad would neuer from her thought. **1603** KNOLLES *Hist. Turks* (1621) 174 Would he, would he not, they made choice for him themselues. **16..** in Percy *Relig., Baffled Knight* xiv, He that wold not when he might, He shall not when he wold-a. **1624** *Capt. J. Smith's Virginia* III. vi. (Arb.) II. 432 They cryed to vs to doe no more, all should be as we would. **1719** DE FOE *Crusoe* II. (Globe) 497 The Captain told me, he would go and help his Men, let what would come. *Ibid.* 555 He told me he would do just as I would. **1837** DICKENS *Pickw.* xxxv, Look where you would, some exquisite form glided gracefully through the throng. **1849** MACAULAY *Hist. Eng.* vi. II. 102 It was determined that the elector should have a chapel in the city whether he would or not. **1867** MORRIS *Jason* v. 47 When on the morn they would away. **1882** 'LESLIE KEITH' *Alasnam's Lady* xxvii, I wanted Mr. Meyers to come with us, but he wouldn't. **1920** *Discovery* Nov. 331/1 The bulbs were then sealed up again and set aside to ferment if they would.

III. The past tense **would** with modal function.

* With simple obj. (or equivalent), or obj. clause.

†**35.** *trans.* with simple obj. (also *intr.* with *well* or *ill* and dat. of person), as a qualification, becoming a virtual equivalent, of the present tense *will* in 1, 1 b: Could or might desire; 'should like'; desire, wish for, 'want' (sometimes implying 'intend'). Cf. 40. *Obs.* or *rare arch.*

1470–85 MALORY *Arthur* I. xix. 65 What wold ye with the best? *c* **1530** LD. BERNERS *Arth. Lyt. Bryt.* (1814) 356, I am in certayne yt he would you more honour than ony persone lyuynge. **1532** MORE *Confut. Tindale* Wks. 408/1 Wherin euery mannes eares that woulde hym well, glowe for very shame. **1588** SHAKS. *L.L.L.* v. ii. 174 What would these strangers? **1596** —— *Merch. V.* I. iii. 66 Is he yet possest How much ye would? *Shy.* I, I, three thousand ducats. **1599** A. HUME *Hymnes* ii. 70 What sa the fantasie wald. **1611** *Bible* Josh. xv. 18 Caleb said vnto her, What wouldest thou? **1820** BYRON *Mar. Fal.* II. i, *Doge.* Come hither, child, I would a word with you. **1822** —— *Werner* I. i. (1823) 35 But, in a word, what would you with me?

36. Similarly with const. as in 2: viz. with obj. clause, with vb. in past subj. (*arch.* except in ***would rather*** or ***sooner*** = 'should prefer'), †rarely in pres. subj., or with acc. and inf. Hence (*arch.*) with ellipsis of 1st pers. pron. as an expression of longing = 'I wish', 'O that'; also, by confusion with 37, in the form (*I*) ***would to God*** (or ***heaven***).

a **1225** *Ancr. R.* 64 Sum is so wel ilered,.. þet heo wolde þet he wuste hit. *c* **1325** in *E.E.P.* (1862) 133 But in heore hertes .i. wolde þei hade.. Hou sone þat god hem may degrade. *c* **1400** *Rule St. Benet* (prose) 8 Do til na man bot als tu walde man did to þe. *c* **1400** *Destr. Troy* 472, I wold yonder worthy weddit me hadde. **1440** [see RATHER *adv.* 9]. *c* **1449** PECOCK *Repr.* I. xiv. 73 Wherfore it myȝte seme that God wolde not him to be oure reule in deedis of oure seruice to God. *c* **1485** *Digby Myst.* III. 522 So wold to god ȝe wold my loue fele. *a* **1529** SKELTON *Bowge of Courte* 481 And so I wolde it were, so God me spede. *c* **1530** REDFORDE *Wyt & Sci.* (1848) 6 My hed akth sore, I wold wee returne. **1539** *Bible* (Great) Exod. xvi. 3 Wolde to God [1535 COVERDALE, Wolde God] we had dyed by the hand of the Lorde in the lande of Egypt. **1590** SHAKS. *Mids. N.* v. i. 255, I am wearie of this Moone; would he would change. **1595** —— *John* III. iv. 48, I am not mad, I would to heauen I were. **1597** J. PAYNE *Royal Exch.* 33 Wch I would yee ever to remember. **1599** B. JONSON *Cynthia's Rev.* To Rdr. A 4 b, I would thou hadst some Sugar Candyed, to sweeten thy Mouth. **1675** [see RATHER *adv.* 9 e]. **1777** MISS M. TOWNSHEND in Jesse *Selwyn & Contemp.* (1844) III. 260 This news I picked up at Bet's door. Would to God that we had peace! **1816** J. WILSON *City of Plague* II. i, At a sad hour the sailor hath return'd; Would he were yet at sea! **1831** SCOTT *Ct. Rob.* xix, I would to God I had more. **1865** WHITTIER *Kallundborg Church* 48 Would I might die now in thy stead! **1882** TENNYSON *Charge of the Heavy Brigade* Epil. 10–11, I would that wars should cease, I would the globe from end to end Might sow and reap in peace.

37. Used optatively in the phr. ***would God*** (also † ***God would***, † ***Christ would***) = 'O that God would', 'O that it were God's will', as an expression of earnest desire or longing. *Obs.* or *rare arch.*

?*c* **1375** in Horstm. *Altengl. Leg.* (1878) 125/1 Wolde god ded y wore! *c* **1385** CHAUCER *L.G.W.* 1726 *Lucretia*, God wolde the wal were falle adoun! *c* **1450** CAPGRAVE *Life St. Aug.* xxix, Wold God ȝe were swech as I fynde hem. ?**15..** *Love Songe* in Ritson *Ancient Songs* (1792) 115 Chryst wolt the ffuger of hur swete face Were pyctored wher euer I be. **1529** RASTELL *Pastyme* A iv, Wold good it were so vsyd at this day. **1535** Wolde God [see 36, quot. 1539]. *c* **1600** *Hymn, 'Hierusalem my happie home'* xi, Ah my sweete home Hierusaleme Would god I were in thee.

†**38.** *fig.* as a qualification or equivalent of 3 c.

c **1460** *Towneley Myst.* xxvi. 9 And sesse your cry till I haue told What that my worship wold. *c* **1460** SIR R. ROS *La Belle Dame* 272 Yet reson wolde it were in remembraunce.

†**39.** *transf.* as a qualification or equivalent of 4.

1559 in Strype *Ann. Ref.* (1709) I. App. xi. 34 The fantasticall opynion, that woulde every man should be saved by his own faithe.

** With dependent infinitive (as in I.** and II.**).

As with *should*, the notion of past time is usually expressed by the pf. inf.: see note s.v. SHALL *v.* B. II.***

40. The past subj. used with potential or conditional force as a softening of the pres. ind. in sense 5, and hence virtually equivalent to it: Could or should wish to; should like to; wish, desire, or 'want' to (sometimes implying 'intend'). *arch.* or *dial.* exc. in ***would have*** (with obj. and inf. or compl.) = 'should like, wish (a person or thing) to be or to do something': see HAVE *v.* 18 b.

The notion of desire (in later use often passing into that of consent or willingness) is often emphasized by *fain, gladly, willingly*, or the like. The use then becomes scarcely distinguishable from the strictly conditional use in 41.

c **888** ÆLFRED *Boeth.* xx, Mid hu micelan feo woldest þu þa habban ȝeboht? *Ibid.* xl. §7 Ic wolde acsian hwæðer we æniȝne freodom hæbben.. hwæt we don. **1297** R. GLOUC. (Rolls) 580 & þou wost now vorsake Mi doȝter þat ssolde be þi wif. *a* **1300** *Cursor M.* 4227, I wald sinc in-til helle depe Wit mi sun þar for to wepe. *Ibid.* 24560 þai wald ha berid him ful fain, Bot i him held wit al mi main. **13..** *E.E. Allit. P.* A. 772 Quat-kyn þyng may be þat lambe þat þe wolde wedde vnto hys vyf? **13..** *Gosp. Nicodemus* (A.) 292 Be what skille walde þai haue hym dede? *c* **1350** *Will. Palerne* 1851 þe werwolf.. went to him euene, Wiþ a rude roring, as he him rende wold. *c* **1375** *Sc. Leg. Saints* Prol. 97 Ȝet vald I, & I mycht, Na var eld & falt of sycht, Of þe twelf apostolis spek now. *Ibid.* ii. (*Paulus*) 164 þe folk of rowme.. wald have brokyn his palace done. *c* **1400** *Brut* lxxx. 82 þe Britons wolde haue slayne þe messagers, but Arthure wolde nouȝt soffre hit. *c* **1420** ? LYDG. *Assembly of Gods* 1953 For feere I lookyd as blak as a coole, I wold haue cropyn in a mouse hoole. **1539** *Bible* (Great) Ps. cvii. 30 And so he bryngeth them vnto the hauen where they wolde be [1611 their desired hauen]. **1550** CROWLEY *Last Trumpet* 765 Thus haue I tolde the, as I woulde Be tolde, if I were in thy place. **1579–80** HARVEY *Lett.* Wks. (Grosart) I. 76, I would gladly be acquainted with M. Drants Prosodye. **1591** SHAKS. *Two Gent.* III. i. 80 What would your Grace haue me to do in this? **1599** —— *Much Ado* II. iii. 6, I know that, but I would haue thee hence, and heere againe. **1682** DRYDEN *Medal* Ep. Whigs, If you were the Patriots you would seem, you would not at this rate incense the Multitude to assume it. **1727** POPE, etc. *Art of Sinking* 120 Be sure they are qualities, which your patron would be thought to have. **1742** in *Johnson's Debates* (1787) II. 162 What is to be understood by this last sentence, I would willingly be informed. **1869** FREEMAN *Norm. Conq.* III. xii. 77 *note*, I would not.. be thought to share Mr. St. John's extreme scepticism. **1895** *Bookman* Oct. 17/2 The Duc d'Aumale's great work, 'L'Histoire des Princes de Condé', for which some of us would gladly give all the novels ever written. **1896** HOUSMAN *Shropsh. Lad* lvi, Far I hear the bugle blow To call me where I would not go. **1905** *Athenæum* 11 Feb. 172/3 Second-rate 'romantism', as Mr. Marion Crawford would have us call it.

¶with omission of *have* in pf. inf.

1508 DUNBAR *Gold. Targe* 146 First of all,.. Come dame Beautee, rycht as scho wald me schent. **1560** ROLLAND *Seven Sages* 93 Ȝe say he wald deforcit ȝour Dame. **1654** GATAKER *Disc. Apol.* 38 Sir R. Owen would gladlie had me seated in Shropshire.

b. In lighter shades of meaning: Am (is, are) disposed or inclined to; often (in 1st pers. sing.) in hesitating or deferential statement = 'wish to ... if I may'. (Cf. 13.) ***would say*** = 'intend to say, mean'. ***would have*** = 'is inclined to believe or assert (something *to be* so-and-so)': cf. 10 c.

c **1386** CHAUCER *Sompn. T.* 106 Of your grete goodnesse, by your leve, I wolde prey yow that ye nat yow greve. **1467** *Stonor Papers* (Camden) I. 96, I wold pray yow.. that ye woll se my pore howse for yowr logyng. *a* **1547** SURREY *Æneis* II. 654 Percase you would ask what was Priam's fate? **1564** HARDING *Answ. Jewel* 215 What you would saye M. Iuell, I wote not, what you saye, well I wote. **1633** G. HERBERT *Temple, Love-unknown* 52 When I thought to sleep out all these faults.. I found that some had stuff'd the bed with thoughts, I would say thorns. **1709** T. ROBINSON *Vind. Mosaick Syst.* 19 Dr. H. M. would have Light to be the Platonick *Anima Mundi.* **1779** *Mirror* No. 3 ¶7, I would, nevertheless, humbly propose to the ladies, to be good-humoured. **1800** WORDSW. *Hart-Leap Well* I. 96 But there is matter for a second rhyme, And I to this would add another tale. **1919** *Engl. Hist. Rev.* July 440 Working-men's colleges and institutes.. are, the author would hope, built on a surer basis.

†**c.** *fig.* of a thing: Needs or requires to, ought to, should. *Obs.*

c **1440** *Paston Lett.* I. 39 The goune nedyth for to be had; and of colour it wolde be a godely blew, or erlys a bryghte sangueyn. **1523** FITZHERB. *Husb.* §122 There is a bee called a drone,.. and they wyll eate the honny, and gather nothynge: and therfore they wolde be kylde. **1598** *Epulario* G j, All fish would be very wel sodden, and with leisure. **1601** HOLLAND *Pliny* XVI. xxxix. I. 488 To have good and profitable timber, the trees would bee cut downe that are of a middle age. **1602** SHAKS. *Ham.* III. iii. 75 That would be scann'd. **1626** BACON *Sylva* §625 The Conseruation of Fruit would be also tried in Vessells, filled with fine Sand. **1682** EVELYN *Let. to Pepys* 19 Sept., Besides all this, the nature of Prescription would be enquir'd into as well when it makes against us, as for us.

41. In the apodosis of a conditional sentence (expressed or implied), with pers. subject, forming the auxiliary of the periphrastic past subj. or so-called 'conditional mood' with implication of intention or volition: = 'should choose or be willing to': cf. 6, 7, 11.

a **1240** *Sawles Warde* in *O.E. Hom.* I. 253 Ich walde ȝef hit mahte beon þolien a þusent deaðes to a rudden him ut þrof. *a* **1352** MINOT *Poems* (ed. Hall) v. 5 War mi sorow slaked sune wald I sing. **1470–85** MALORY *Arthur* VIII. ii. 276 She wold haue slayne the with that poyson and she myghte haue hadde her wille. **1526** TINDALE *Matt.* xxiii. 37 Howe often wolde I haue gaddered thy children to gedder, as the henne gaddreth her chickens vnder her wynges? but ye wolde not. **1598** SHAKS. *Merry W.* II. i. 189 If hee should intend this voyage toward my wife, I would turne her loose to him. **1610** —— *Temp.* v. i. 230 If I did thinke, Sir, I were well awake, I'ld striue to tell you. **1662** in *Extr. St. Papers rel. Friends* Ser. II. (1911) 151 Let me by no meanes be continued sheriff .. I would rather endure a Fine than be kept on another yeare. **1738** JOHNSON *London* 9 Who would leave, unbrib'd, Hibernia's Land? **1832** WORDSW. in *Mem.* (1851) II. 257 If .. I should be asked how I would myself vote, if it had been my fortune to have a seat in the House of Lords. **1848** DICKENS *Dombey* xlii, I wouldn't do such a thing here, sir,.. upon my word and honour, I wouldn't, sir. **1920** *Times Lit. Suppl.* 29 Apr. 264/4 The main object of writers on Bolshevism, whether they would admit it or not, has been to justify or condemn Lenin's great experiment.

b. ***I would*** (sc. 'if I were you') is often used colloq. as = 'I advise or recommend you to' (= *I should*, SHALL *v.* B. 19 f.) So ***I wouldn't*** = 'I advise you not to'.

1591 SHAKS. *Two Gent.* III. i. 110, I would resort to her by night. **1835** ARNOLD *Let.* 18 May in Stanley *Life* (1898) I. vii. 360 If possible, I would take a Strabo with me, and an Herodotus. *Mod.* I wouldn't go skating to-day; the ice isn't safe.

c. Interrog. in 2nd pers.: †***wouldst thou ...?*** = 'art thou willing to ...?'; hence as a softened form of request: ***would you ...?*** = 'will you, please ...?: cf. 6 b.

c **1420** *Sir Amadace* (Camden) xl, Quod the quite knyȝte, 'Wold thou luffe him aure alle thing?' **1607** DEKKER & WEBSTER *Northw. Hoe* I. i, *Bell...* Was this her ring? *Green.* Her ring Sir. *May.* A pretty idle toy, would you take mony for 't? **1876** MRS. EWING *Six to Sixteen* ii, Would you say the Lord's Prayer for me, old fellow?

42. In the apodosis of a conditional sentence (expressed or implied), in the 2nd or 3rd pers., forming the auxiliary of the simple 'conditional mood', expressing merely a possibility or contingency in the supposed case: cf. 14.

For the distinction between *should* and *would* see note s.v. SHALL *v.* B. 19 b.

c **888** ÆLFRED *Boeth.* xvi. §2 Ȝif we nu ȝesawan hwelce mus þæt wære hlaford ofer oðre mys, & sette him domas.. hu wunderlic wolde eow ðæt þincan. *c* **1200** *Trin. Coll. Hom.* 31 Ȝef he þat hielde synne, he wolde þe hede wiðtien. **1297** R. GLOUC. (Rolls) 5521 Ȝif ichadde him bisuike, þe wors þou wost leue me. *c* **1374** CHAUCER *Troylus* III. 502 þere was som

Epistel hem by-twene, That wolde as seyth myn Auctor wel contene Neigh half þis bok. **1484** *Acta Audit.* (1839) *147/1 Pay to him samekle malis.. & vþeris deweteis as he may preif þe said landis walde have gevin him. **1538** Starkey *England* iii. (1878) 73 Yf hyt were dylygently laburyd, hyt wold bryng forth frute. **1579** Lyly *Euphues* (Arb.) 93 If thou haddest learned the first point of hauking, thou wouldst haue learned to haue held fast. **1592** Shaks. *Rom. & Jul.* ii. ii. 44 (Qo. 1) That which we call a Rose, By any other name would smell as sweet. **1670** in *12th Rep. Hist. MSS. Comm.* App. v. 22, I am suere you would bee with us if wishes could bring you. **1754** Huxham in *Phil. Trans.* XLVIII. 849 Perhaps some other salino-sulphureous medium would do as well. **1757** Mrs. Griffith *Lett. Henry & Frances* (1767) II. 44 There is a butterfly in my study, which would be dead some time past, but that I watched it. **1845** M. Pattison *Ess.* (1889) I. 19 They would have refused their co-operation if they dared. **1859** Ruskin *Two Paths* iii. §96 Your stuffs need not be such as would catch the eye of a duchess. **1902** Violet Jacob *Sheep-Stealers* xiv, Had it been possible to teach him the rudiments of good manners, [he] would have been a really valuable member of the household. **1920** *Act 10 & 11 Geo. V* c. 50 §22 (1) Any documents..such as would be subject to production in a court of law.

¶ with omission of *have* in pf. inf.

1523 Ld. Berners *Froiss.* I. ccxi. 105/1 If..his cosyn had nat counsayled hym to haue peace, he wolde nat agreed thervnto. **1813** Picken *Poems* II. 135 That wad been milkin' his cow in a sieve.

b. With the hypothetical notion obscured or weakened, the 'conditional mood' becoming a qualification of the pres. ind. expressing some degree of hesitation or uncertainty: in such phr. as ***it would seem*** (= 'it almost or somewhat seems'), ***one would think*** (= 'one is inclined to think'). So †***would be*** = 'probably is'. Cf. 15 d, and similar use of *should* s.v. shall *v.* B. 19 d.

c **1449** Pecock *Repr.* iii. viii. 322 The first premisse of this argument muste needis be grauntid, as it wolde seeme. *a* **1500** *Flower & Leaf* 247 Every bosse of brydel and peitrel ..was worth, as I would wene, A thousand pound. **1533** More *Apol.* 255 Men wolde haue went soneste to haue founde them. **1560** *Bible* (Geneva) Job xli. 32 He [*sc.* the Leviathan] maketh a path to shine after him; one wolde thinke the depth as an hore head. **1600** *Essex Reb. Exams.* in *Shaks. Cent. Praise* (1879) 35 The play wold be of harry the iiij^th. **1786** Burns *Twa Dogs* 81 An' when they meet wi' sair disasters,.. Ye maist wad think, a wee touch langer, An' they maun starve o' cauld and hunger. **1853** Miss Pratt *Wild Flowers* II. 75 This plant is not, as one would suppose from its name, a native of woods and meadows. **1882** Besant *All Sorts* iv, If it was only to see her own vats, you'd think she'd get off of her luxurious pillows for once. **1918** *Pall Mall Gaz.* 29 June 4/3 The standard suits..are steadily rising in price, and it would seem that by the time they are on the market they will come under the proposed luxury tax.

¶ **c.** Used in the 1st pers. instead of the normal auxiliary *should*.

Still freq. with such vbs. as *like*, *wish* (cf. shall *v.* B. 19 c), prob. by association with 40; otherwise now restricted in usage like the similar use of *will*: see 16 and 33.

1448 [see 48]. *c* **1477** *Stonor Papers* (Camden) II. 29 Y wolde be ago and ȝe werre y-comme, fore we may nat go yn-tylle ȝe comme. **1561** Hoby tr. *Castiglione's Courtyer* i. (1577) Ej, He that shoulde wryte, I woulde thinke he committed an errour in not vsing them. **1599** Shaks. *Much Ado* ii. iii. 119, I would haue thought her spirit had beene inuincible against all assaults of affection. **1603** —— *Meas. for M.* iv. ii. 18, I would bee glad to receiue some instruction. **1662** *Extr. State Papers rel. Friends* Ser. ii. (1911) 150 Wee would be glad that all our Subjects could be brought to agree in an uniforme Worship of God. **1733** W. Crawford *Infidelity* (1836) 189 The more we view them, the more would we be satisfied of their reality. **1780** Johnson *Let. to Mrs. Thrale* 24 Aug., I would be glad to know when we are to meet. **1794** Hutton *Philos. Light* 15 The more..that we should reason upon such a mistaken principle, the more we would proceed in error. **1817** Coleridge *Biog. Lit.* (1847) II. 223 He makes everything turn out exactly as we would wish it. **1887** Moloney *Forestry W. Afr.* 43, I would be disposed to question the accuracy of this information. **1921** *Oxford Mag.* 4 Feb. 180/2 We feel that we would recognize them if we met them.

d. ***I wouldn't know***: see know *v.* 11 g.

43. In a question or indirect statement in the 2nd or 3rd pers., where *should* would be used in the corresponding direct statement in the 1st.

In categorical questions and reported utterances varying with *should*, as *will* with *shall*: cf. note s.v. shall *v.* B. 8. But in rhetorical questions implying emphatic assertion (e.g. 'Would you believe it?' 'Who would have thought it?') *should* is never substituted.

1387–8 T. Usk *Test. Love* iii. v. (Skeat) l. 119 What woldest thou demen if a man wold yeve three quarters of nobles of golde? **1582** Bentley *Mon. Matrones* iii. 291 Who would not haue beene confounded, & haue gotten him awaie at these thy words? **1598** Shaks. *Merry W.* ii. i. 10 You loue sacke, and so do I: would you desire better simpathie? **1654** Dorothy Osborne *Lett.* (1888) 229 What think you, have I not done fair for once, would you wish a longer letter? **1775** Johnson *Let. to Mrs. Thrale* 1 June, Tell me what you would be most willing to spare. **1779** *Mirror* No. 12 ¶8 Would you believe it, Sir, my daughter Elizabeth..said it was fanatical to find fault with card-playing on Sunday. **1785** [see shall *v.* B. 19 c]. **1861** T. L. Peacock *Gryll Grange* xxix, Do you think..you would find many examples of love that is one and once for all? **1863** [see mind *v.* 8]. **1868** Thirlwall *Lett.* (1881) I. 299 If you would like to see it I could send it you. **1886** Story *Fiammetta* vii, Would you like to see it?

44. In a conditional (or equivalent) clause with pers. subject, with implication of intention or volition: = 'chose to', 'were willing to': cf. 41.

a **900** Cynewulf *Crist* 1107 Ðeseoð him to bealwe þæt him betst bicwom, þær hy hit to gode onȝietan woldan. *c* **1205** Lay. 6230 Ȝif hit weoren þin iwille and þu hit don woldest To ȝifuen us an ende i þine kinne-londe, We wulleð þine men beon. *a* **1352** Minot *Poems* (ed. Hall) v. 4 Wald he salue vs sone, mi sorow suld slake. *a* **1375** *Joseph Arim.* 640 'Woldestou leeue vppon him,' he seis 'I wolde' [etc.]. *a* **1400–50** *Wars Alex.* 311, I be-seke þe,..if þou me say wald, Quatkyn fygour on fold or fourme at he beris. *c* **1475** *Rauf Coilȝear* 70 With thy thow wald be payit of sic as thow fand, Forsuith thow suld be wel-cum to pas hame with me. **1594** in *Cath. Rec. Soc. Publ.* V. 293 He converted 5 or 6 felons in the short tyme he was in Newgate, whereof 2 or 3 might have beene reprieved from the gallows, if they would have denied what they had professed there. **1649** Bp. Hall *Cases Consc.* To Rdr., In the handling of all which, would I have affected that course..I could easily [etc.]. **1714** in *Jrnl. Friends Hist. Soc.* (1918) 30 Several Expressing their love to me—telling me would I stay I need not fear a congregation. **1865** Ruskin *Sesame* ii. §92 She knows, in her heart, if she would only look for its knowledge, that [etc.]. **1873** Browning *Red Cott. Nt.-cap* iv. 587 Would Providence.. make me certain of the same, That I survive you..certainly I would accept Your bounty.

b. With inversion of subj., expressing desire or longing. (But cf. 37.)

1593 Shaks. *3 Hen. VI*, ii. i. 75 Now my Soules Pallace is become a Prison: Ah, would she breake from hence. **1786** Burns *To a Louse* 43 O wad some Pow'r the giftie gie us To see oursels as others see us!

†**c.** *fig.* of a thing: Could, might: cf. 9. *Obs.*

c **1440** *Generydes* 214 And furthe he rideth..With his knyghtes to mete and it wold be. *c* **1450** *Godstow Reg.* 21 Sacred Cipriane, ȝif hit wold be gete, With Cosme and damiane wold I dyne.

†**45.** In a hypothetical clause merely expressing a condition or supposition: = 'should', 'were to'.

c **1374** Chaucer *Troylus* ii. 1147 To dethe mote I smete be with þonder If..Wold I a lettre vn-to yow brynge or take, To harm of yow. *c* **1400** *Pety Job* 500 in *26 Pol. Poems* 137 That bed shall I neuer lese, Though I wolde for angor raue. *c* **1480** Henryson *Sheep & Dog* 163 Seis thow not, Lord, this warld ouerturnit is, As quha wald change gude gold in leid or tyn. **1527** Andrew *Brunswyke's Distyll. Waters* b iij b, Than make fyre vnder it that it may droppe tretably as yf yᵉ wolde tell yᵉ clocke i. ii. yᵗ than there fall a drop. *c* **1550** Rolland *Crt. Venus* ii. 5 Wald Venus court retreit, cast or conuert, Or in sum part thairin mak resistence.

†**b.** After *as if* (or *as* in same sense): = 'were about to' (= *should*, shall *v.* B. 20 a, b). *Obs.*

a **1550** *Dunbar's Poems* (S.T.S.) 308/18 Sum drowpis down as he wold die. **1719** De Foe *Crusoe* i. (Globe) 210 At this I..made as if I would vomit at the thoughts of it.

46. In a noun-clause expressing the object of desire, advice, or request.

Usually with a person as subj., implying voluntary action as the desired end: thus distinguished from *should*, which may be used when the person's will is not in view. Also (almost always after *wish*) with a thing as subject, in which case *should* can never be substituted because it would suggest the idea of command or compulsion instead of mere desire. Cf. shall *v.* B. 22 a.

1555 Pole in *Engl. Hist. Rev.* (1913) July 530, I wold my syster wold ataryed a littell longer. **1590** Shaks. *Mids. N.* i. i. 195 O that your frownes would teach my smiles such skil. **1611** —— *Cymb.* ii. iv. 6 Quake in the present winters state, and wish That warmer dayes would come. **1685** in *Engl. Hist. Rev.* (1920) Jan. 116 His Lordship desires you would present his most humble duty to my Lord Duke. **1736** Sheridan *Let. to Swift* 15 Sept., Indeed if you pleased,..I would rather that you would, I mean should, charge only five per cent. **1775** —— *Rivals* iv. ii, I wish the lady would favour us with something more than a side-front. **1833** Tennyson *May Queen, New Year's Eve* iv, I wish the snow would melt. **1849** Macaulay *Hist. Eng.* iv. I. 465 The general wish of Europe was that James would govern in conformity with law and with public opinion. **1912** *Engl. Hist. Rev.* Oct. 754 It is much to be wished that some one would clear up the tangled web of these peace negotiations.

¶ **b.** Used irreg. for *should* (shall *v.* B. 22): with restriction of usage as in 16. ? *Obs.*

1760–72 H. Brooke *Fool of Qual.* (1809) IV. 7, I should be sorry..that the wretch would die in his present state of reprobacy. **1766** Mrs. S. Pennington *Lett.* II. 197, I choose rather you would carry it yourself. **1771** Goldsm. *Hist. Eng.* III. 312 It was intended that this would encrease the severity of his punishment.

*** **47.** Elliptical and quasi-elliptical uses, as in I.***, 17–21.

c **1230** *Hali Meid.* (1922) 44 Hwa-se lið i leifen deope bisuncken,..he ne schal nawt up acouerin hwen he walde. *c* **1374** Chaucer *Troylus* iii. 115 And Pandare wep as he to watre wolde. **1390** Gower *Conf.* I. 84 Thogh I wolde, I myhte noght Obeie unto my ladi heste. **1393** Langl. *P. Pl.* C. viii. 285 Wist ich þe soþe, Ich wolde no forþer a fot for no freres prechinge. **14..** Hoccleve *Min. Poems* xvi. 10 Tho men..Fayn wolden þat they and I euene were: And so wolde I. **1423** Jas. I *Kingis Q.* clxvii, It stant noght with the as thou wald, perchance? **1484** Caxton *Fables of Auian* ii, Who so mounteth hyher than he shold he falleth lower than he wold. **1548** Udall, etc. *Erasm. Par. John* x. 15–18 Yet could thei not kyll me vnlesse I would my selfe. **1556** Olde *Antichrist* 120 b, Is it the proprétie of a shepehearde, to renne madde upon his flocke, worse than a wolfe wolde? **1591** Shaks. *Two Gent.* iv. iii. 22, I would to Valentine To Mantua, where I heare, he makes aboad. **1605** —— *Macb.* i. vii. 44 Letting I dare not, wait vpon I would. **1610** —— *Temp.* ii. i. 185 You would lift the Moone out of her spheare, if she would continue in it five weekes without changing. *Seb.* We would so, and then go a Bat-fowling. *Ibid.* iii. i. 61 *Fer.* I am, in my condition A Prince (Miranda) I do thinke a King (I would not so). **1777** [see so B. 2 b]. **1848** Dickens *Dombey* xlii, I wouldn't do such a thing here, Sir,..upon my word and honour, I wouldn't, Sir, I wish I may die if I would, Sir. **1865** Ruskin *Sesame* i. §21 Never think Milton uses those three words to fill up his verse, as a loose writer would.

b. ***wouldn't it?*** (ellipt. for *wouldn't it rock you?*, *wouldn't it root you?*, and similar catch-phrases): an exclamation of annoyance and disgust or (less usually) amusement. *Austral.* and *N.Z. slang.*

1940 *Telegraph* (Sydney) 13 Jan. 4/7 Favorite expression with the troops is, of course, '*Wouldn't it?*'—Short for 'Wouldn't it make you sick?' **1941** *2nd N.Z.E.F. Times* 3 Nov. 6 Well, *wouldn't* it? **1951** Cusack & James *Come in Spinner* 382 Guinea kicked a hassock across the room. 'Wouldn't it!' she muttered furiously, 'wouldn't it?' **1954** J. Cleary *Climate of Courage* xii. 185 'Asking your wife if you can write to her. Wouldn't it?'

IV. 48. Followed by *to* with inf., esp. after an intervening word or words (cf. to *prep.* B. 19); now the regular const. only with pres. pple. *willing*.

(Not always distinguishable from will *v.*²)

c **1320** *Sir Tristr.* 303 Tristrem herd it say, On his playing he wold Tuentischilling to lay. **1382** Wyclif *Matt.* xiv. 5 And he willynge to slea hym, drede the peple. **1448** Shillingford *Lett. & Papers* (Camden) 55 Elles we wolde truely to have had tyme. *c* **1450** *Merlin* iii. 54 Thei haue assembled a grete power, and wele to conquere this londe be force. **1450–60** *Bp. Grossetest's Househ. Stat.* in *Babees Bk.* 331 And they wyllen to do that ye wylle to do. **1453** Marg. Paston in *P. Lett.* I. 251 It semyth..that she wold never so fayn to have be delyveryd of her as she woll now. *c* **1460** *Play Sacram.* 288, I wollnot for an hundder pownd to stond in fere my lord to tene. **1548** Hall *Chron., Edw. IV* 213 Not willyng if he might, to displease any of bothe the parties. **1568** Grafton *Chron.* II. 764 He could not get away, and to keepe himselfe close he would not. **1610** Shaks. *Temp.* iii. i. 61, I..would no more endure This wodden slauerie, then to suffer The flesh-flie blow my mouth. **1632** Lithgow *Trav.* iii. 101 The which I willing to see. **1633** [see rather *adv.* 9 c]. **1648** Kem *Let. to Ld. Denbigh* 19 Nov. (MS.), Nor is it thoght he will to stay onely to get yᵉ saylers aboard.

V. †**49.** Pa. pple. **would**, *wold(e* (mostly with ellipsis): chiefly in sense 7, = chosen. *Obs.*

c **1380** Wyclif *Sel. Wks.* II. 293 He myȝt, ȝif he hadde wolde, have take greet veniaunce of hem. *c* **1385** Chaucer *L.G.W.* 1209 *Dido*, The fomy brydil..Gouernyth he, ryght as hym self hath wold. *c* **1412** Hoccleve *De Reg. Princ.* 1075 Crist himself,..To loue and teche and prechen it hath wold. *c* **1450** *Oseney Reg.* 164 Where I haue i-wollyd me to be i-beried. **1470–85** Malory *Arthur* vii. xiii. 232 Many tymes he myghte haue had her and he had wold. **1583** Golding *Calvin on Deut.* clxxxiv. 1145 Not that hee was vnable to let them, or withstande them, if hee had would. **1633** J. Done *Hist. Septuagint* 216 If hee had would, hee might easily.. occupied the Monarchy.

VI. Conjoined with nill *v.*, etc.

In later use also with 3rd pers. sing. *willeth* or *wills*, pa. t. *willed*, and thus blending with will *v.*²

50. *absol.* or *intr.* **a.** In disjunctive qualifying phr. such as ***whether he*** (etc.) ***will or nill***, also ***who(ever will or nill*** (in senses 2, 5–7): whether (one) will or not; willingly or unwillingly; voluntarily or compulsorily. *Obs.* or *rare arch.*: replaced by the inverted form in b.

c **888** Ælfred *Boeth.* xxxiv. §12 We sceolon beon nede ȝeþafan, sam we willan sam we nyllan, þæt he sie se hehsta hrof eallra goda. *c* **900** tr. *Bæda's Hist.* v. ix, Saȝa him, swa he wille swa he nelle, he sceall to Columban mynstre cuman. **1411** *26 Pol. Poems* x. 8 Hym þat is loþ, good to lere, He shal, wheþer he wole or nylle. *c* **1449** Pecock *Repr.* iv. iii. 428 And ȝit, who euere wole or nyle, Holi Scripture wole that preesthode and dekenhode be had and vsid. **1470–85** Malory *Arthur* xiii. xx. 641 Thow shalte knowe hym whether thow wilt or nylt. *c* **1550** Rolland *Crt. Venus* iv. 345 Now sall he sit..Quha will, quha Nill, intill ane deip dungeoun. **1565** Harding *Confut.* 275 Truth is truth, and God is God, whether any Councell will or nill. **1651** N. Bacon *Disc. Govt. Eng.* ii. xxx. 239 They do what they list, let the Plebeian Presbyter wil or nill. **1873** T. Cooper *Parad. Martyrs* (1877) 355 Each thing.., whether it will or nill, The eternal purpose..Doth..fulfil.

pa. t. *c* **1470** Harding *Chron.* clxiii. ii, [He] theim compelled..To become his men..whether they wold or nolde. **1470–85** Malory *Arthur* xvii. xi. 705 Els had there ben mortal werre vpon the morne not withstandyng she wold none other whether they wold or nold.

b. esp. with inversion of subj. (usually a pron.), as ***will I*** (or) ***nill I*** (*he, they*, etc.), or †abbreviated, as ***will*** (or) ***nill, willing*** (or) ***nilling*** (see willing *ppl. a.*); occas. vaguely = 'one way or another, in any case, anyhow'. Now chiefly in the reduced form willy-nilly, q.v.

c **1000** Ælfric *Saints' Lives* xvi. 121 Forðan þe we synd synfulle and sceolan beon eadmode, wille we, nelle we. *c* **1230** *Hali Meid.* (1922) 41 Wullen ha nullen ha. *a* **1300** *XV Signa* 173 in *E.E.P.* (1862) 12 For wolny nulni hi sul fle. ? *a* **1300** *Salomon & Sat.* (1848) 271 Mote hit al habben is wille, Woltou, nultou, hit wol spille. **1340** *Ayenb.* 164 þet is al þet he may lyese, wylle him nolle him. **1362** Langl. *P. Pl.* A. vii. 144 Wol þou so nulle þou. **1377** *Ibid.* B. vi. 158 Wiltow or neltow. *Ibid.* xx. 29 Wolhe, nolhe. *c* **1400** *Laud Troy Bk.* 17560 Wil thow, nele thow—the pees schal be! **1548** Udall, etc. *Erasm. Par. Matt.* v. 14–16 Yᵉ hyll..that beareth it [*sc.* the city], willeth it, nilleth it, maketh it sene of al men. **1550** Bale *Image Both Ch.* ii. xvi. R v b, Will she nyll shee, neede must shee abyde his..sentence. *a* **1555** Latimer in Foxe *A. & M.* (1563) 1324/2 If my Lorde wyll needes..inuade my inwarde manne, wyll I nyll I. **1565** Harding *Confut.* 117 Well, how so euer it be, will ye nill ye ..ye be dryuen to confesse the same to be no newe thing. *a* **1566** R. Edwardes *Damon & Pithias* (1571) G iv, Wyl I or nil I, it must be done. **1567** Jewel *Def. Apol.* 715 God is able (..wil the Councelles, nil the Councelles) to maintaine..his owne Kingedome. **1590** Spenser *F.Q.* i. iii. 43 And will or nill, Beares her away. **1596** Shaks. *Tam. Shr.* ii. i. 273 Will you, nill you, I will marry you. **1599** Sylvester *Sonn. Mirac. Peace* xii, A sacred rage..Will-nill-I, raps mee boldly to rehearse Great Henrie's Tropheis. **1600** Holland *Livy* iii. xxx, The Nobles were so neere driven and to such streights, that will they, nill they, yeeld they must thereto. **1614** Gorges *Lucan* v. 187 For will, or nill, powre them constraines. **1647** J. Booker in Lilly *Chr. Astrol.*, Be you for or against, or will ye, nill ye; I'm for the Art, and th' Author William Lilly. **1750** Gray *Long Story* xxii, Will he, nill he, to the Great-house He went, as if the Devil drove him. **1818**

KEATS *Let.* Wks. 1889 III. 134 In hopes of cheering you.. I was determined, will he nill he, to send you some lines. **1822** BYRON *Juan* VI. cxviii, But go they must at once, and will I—nill I. **1852** JERDAN *Autobiogr.* I. xvi. 116, I was obliged, will-i-nill-i, to take a sailor's advice. **1870** LOWELL *Among my Bks., New Eng. 2 Cent. ago* 230 Land for all who would till it, and reading and writing, will ye nill ye, instead. **1899** SIR G. DOUGLAS *James Hogg* iii. 68 The galloping movement of the metre hurries us, will-we nill-we, on.

(*b*) in pa. t. (***would...nould...***, also ***willed... nilled...***). *Obs.* or *rare arch.*, the pres. form being ordinarily used even when the principal vb. is in pa. t. (see quots. 1600, 1750, 1852 above).

c **1000** ÆLFRIC *Hom.* (Th.) II. 388 Se brym..hine bær, wolde he, nolde he. *c* **1175** *Lamb. Hom.* 7 Summe hit sungen þurh þene halie gast, walden heo naldden heo. **1297** R. GLOUC. (Rolls) 10463 Wolde he so nolde. *c* **1330** R. BRUNNE *Chron. Wace* (Rolls) 10772 Wold he, nold he, forþ he mote. *Ibid.* 13755 Þe Romains, wold ho, ne wolde, Flede. *c* **1400** *Brut* I. 79 He knelede to þe grounde, wolde he nolde he. **1549** LATIMER *1st Serm. bef. Edw. VI* (Arb.) 28 For would they, nyl they, theyr kinge shold be of his chosynge. **1596** DANETT in *Burton's Diary* (1828) III. 127 So that, would I, nould I, to the presse the booke must go. **1889** WRATISLAW tr. *Sixty Folk-Tales* 65 The good prince—would he, nould he—was obliged to put some of the leaden dumplings into his pocket.

1548 PATTEN *Exped. Scot.* L vij b, Which whither he did for the doubt he had that we woold haue releaced him wild he nild he [etc.]. **1577** HOLINSHED *Chron.* I. 233/1 Shee ruled them (willed they nilled they). **1610** HOLLAND *Camden's Brit.* I. 549 That will'd hee nill'd hee, at length he yeelded up unto him this Castle.

51. (Always inflected *willeth* (*wills*), *willed*; thus properly belonging to WILL *v.*²). **a.** *trans.* To desire, have a mind to (= 1), choose (as opp. to *nill* = 'refuse'); to exercise the will with intent to effect (something), to determine by the will (as opp. to *nill* = 'negative, prevent').

1585 FETHERSTONE tr. *Calvin on Acts* iv. 32. 101 All of them do both will and nill one thing. **1596** SPENSER *F.Q.* IV. vii. 16 But whether willed or nilled friend or foe, I me resolu'd the vtmost end to proue. **1612** T. TAYLOR *Comm. Titus* iii. 3. 613 A facultie of willing, or nilling that which is first understood and iudged of in the minde. **1616** B. JONSON *Epigr.* xlii, To will, and nill The selfe-same things. **1645** PAGITT *Heresiogr.* (1661) 143 The will may..of her self, will or nill, choose or refuse any kind of good. **1722** WOLLASTON *Relig. Nat.* v. 76 *note*, He is both cause and effect; He both willes and nilles,..loves and hates the same thing at the same time. **1775** FLETCHER *Scrip. Scales* II. §21. Wks. 1795 V. 335 The will..cannot be forced to will or nill anything against its own dictates. **1860** [see NILL *v.* 2].

b. *absol.* or *intr.*

1577 tr. *Bullinger's Decades* 588 Will chooseth, for in it dooth lye bothe to will and to nill. *a* **1610** BABINGTON *Expos. Cath. Faith* Wks. 1622 II. 192 Whatsoeuer is done, is done either God willing, God nilling, or God not regarding. **1611** B. JONSON *Catiline* I. v. C1b, To will, or nill, to thinke things good, or bad. **1642** D. ROGERS *Naaman* 12 From the different dispositions, and free-will of him that nilleth or willeth. *a* **1680** CHARNOCK *Attrib. God* (1682) 190 How had he the power of willing and nilling without a Being? Nothing cannot will or nill.

52. So **wilto shalto** *dial.* [= *wilt thou, shalt thou*], whether voluntarily or by compulsion (cf. SHALL *v.* B. 3, 6a); willy-nilly.

1824 CARR *Craven Gloss.* **1857** WAUGH *Lanc. Life* 203 There is at'll believe naught at o', iv it isn't fair druvven into um, wilto, shalto.

VII. 53. *Comb.* (nonce-wds.): **will-be**, *sb.* a person or thing that will be but is not yet; one whose career or efficiency belongs to the future (cf. HAS-BEEN, *have-been* s.v. HAVE *v.* 27); *adj.* that will be; that aims at being, or is ready to be (cf. WOULD-BE); †**will-do-all**, money (cf. Eccl. x. 19).

1748 RICHARDSON *Clarissa* (1768) I. 232, I have looked backward to the *have-been's*, and forward to the **will-be's*. **1801** in *Spirit Publ. Jrnls.* V. 377 Our will-be Squires. **1900** T. R. WILLIAMS *Greenfield Pulpit* No. 72 (title of sermon) Jesus and will-be disciples; Luke ix. 57-62. **1583** STUBBES *Anat. Abus.* II. (1882) 13 It commeth to passe by reason of (*will doe all) otherwise called mony.

will (wɪl), *v.*² Pres. t. 2 sing. **willest**, 3 sing. **willeth** (*arch.*), **wills**; pa. t. and pple. **willed** (wɪld). Forms: 1 **willian**, 3-4 **willi**, 3-6 **wyll**, 5-6 **wille**, 5-7 **wil**, 5- **will**. *Pa. t.* 1 **willode**, **-ade**, 3 **will-**, **wyllede**, 3-6 **wylled**, 4 **willyd**, 5 **-ied**, *Sc.* **-it**, 5-6 **-id**, 3- **willed**; 4 **wijld**, 4-6 **wilde**, 6 **wild**. *Pa. pple.* 5 **willid**, **-yd**, 5-6 **wylled**, 6 **willet**, 6- **willed**; 6 **willd(e**, 6-7 **wild**. [OE. *willian* wk. vb. = OHG. *willôn* (MHG., G. *willen*, pa. pple. *gewillt*): f. WILL *sb.*¹]

1. *trans.* To wish, desire; sometimes with implication of intention: = WILL *v.*¹ 1, 2, 5. *Obs.* or *rare arch.*

c **825** *Vesp. Psalter* xxxiii[i]. 13 [12] Hwelc is mon se wile lif & willað ȝesian dæȝas gode? *c* **1100** *Ælfred's Boeth.* xl. §3 Ðy ne sceolde nan wis man willian [*Cott. MS.* wilnian] seftes lifes. *c* **1205** LAY. 879 ȝif ȝe hit willed [= willeð; *c* 1275 wolleþ], ich hine wlle spillen. **1297** R. GLOUC. (1724) 12 Þat he wilnede [*v.rr.* wyllede, willed] mest of alle þing to him eliance. **1340** *Ayenb.* 142 Herte þet þis heþ a-sayd naȝt ne willeþ more þanne uor to by..uoryete to þe wordle. **1377** LANGL. *P. Pl.* B. XII. 221 [þu þat] willest of briddes and of bestes and of hire bredyng to knowe. **14..** *Lat. & Eng. Prov.* (MS. Douce 52) lf. 13 He þ[t] a lytul me ȝeuyth to me wyllyth [*optat*] longe lyffe. **1471** CAXTON *Recuyell* (Sommer) 218 So had he well willyd that the monstre had deuoured perseus. **1548** UDALL, etc. *Erasm. Par. Matt.* v. 21-24 Who so euer hath gotten to hymselfe the charitie of the gospell, whyche wylleth wel to them that wylleth yll. **1581** A. HALL *Iliad* v. 87 By Mineruas helpe, who willes you all the ill she may. *a* **1677** BARROW *Serm. Luke xxii. 42* Wks. 1686 III. 45 Two things he willeth, that we should be good, and that we should be happy. **1875** TENNYSON *Q. Mary* I. iv, A great party in the state Wills me to wed her.

†**b.** ? To assert, affirm: = WILL *v.*¹ B. 4. *rare.*

1614 SELDEN *Titles Hon.* 134 None of this excludes Vnction before, but only wils him the first annointed by the Pope.

c. Conjoined with NILL: see WILL *v.*¹ B. VI.

2. a. To direct by one's will or testament (*that* something be done, or something *to be* done).

871-89 [see WILL *v.*¹ B. 3b]. **1338** R. BRUNNE *Chron.* (1810) 34 At Wynchestre he lies, so himself willed. *a* **1513** FABYAN *Chron.* (1811) 613 Robert Chycheley,..the which wylled in his testament, that vpon his mynde day a good.. dyner shuld be ordeyned for .xxiiii. C. poore men. **1590** SPENSER *F.Q.* II. x. 32 So to his crowne she him restor'd againe, In which he dyde, made ripe for death by eld, And after wild, it should to her remaine. **1634** PEACHAM *Compl. Gentl.* xv. (1906) 199 Willing his body to be buried in the Cathedrall Church of Rochester. **1642** tr. *Perkins' Prof. Bk.* viii. §547. 237 If a man willeth that his lands shall be sold for payment of his debts. **1881** LADY HERBERT *Edith* vii, It was a simple walking funeral, as he had wished and willed it should be.

b. To dispose of by will; to bequeath or devise.

c **1460** *Oseney Reg.* 7 Willyng and grauntyng my lorde Robert Doylly, all my londe. **1521** *Test. Ebor.* (Surtees) VI. 6 First I will my saull to God Almyghtie. **1524** *Lincoln Wills* (Lincoln Rec. Soc.) V. 132 The resydue of all my goodes not willet nor bequethed. **1546** *Yks. Chantry Surv.* (Surtees) II. 462, iij[s]. iiij[d]...willed and bestowed of one obit. **1691** E. TAYLOR *Behmen's Theos. Phil.* 74 The Will of every of them willeth its Property. **1865** DICKENS *Mut. Fr.* II. xiii, Was it not enough that I should have been willed away, like a horse? **1883** *Law Times* 20 Oct., The statute of Henry VIII did something to restore the power of willing land. **1908** MRS. H. WARD *Diana Mallory* iii, The vast bulk of Henry Marsham's fortune, had been willed to Lady Lucy.

3. To determine by the will; to attempt to cause, aim at effecting by exercise of will; to set the mind with conscious intention to the performance or occurrence of something; to choose or decide to do something, or that something shall be done or happen.

Const. with simple obj., acc. and inf., simple inf. (now always with *to*), or obj. clause; also *absol.* or *intr.* (with *as* or *so*).

Nearly coinciding in meaning with WILL *v.*¹ 7, but with more explicit reference to the mental process of volition.

a **950** *Guthlac* xx. (Prose) 161 Æfter þon fiftyne ȝear þe he gode williȝende lædde his life. *a* **1340** HAMPOLE *Psalter* vii. 17 He willyd noght flee synn. *c* **1440** *Alphabet of Tales* 263 Lady, þow hase willid me..to suffre suche a turmentrie, at þou sufferd þe instrument of þine offes for to be þus cut off. **1556** *Aurelio & Isab.* (1608) A vij, When..I have willed experiment it, I have founde it trewe and certaine. **1581** A. HALL *Iliad* v. 95 Fate had not willd that Vlysses Sarpadons death should be. **1594** HOOKER *Eccl. Pol.* I. vii. §2 To choose is to will one thing before another. **1615** R. COCKS *Diary* (Hakl. Soc.) I. 9 He willed to take it all, for that he had need to use money heare. **1630** PRYNNE *Anti-Armin.* 119 He had onely a power, not to fall into sinne vnlesse he willed it. **1667** MILTON *P.L.* VIII. 549 So absolute she seems..that what she wills to do or say, Seems wisest. **1710** J. CLARKE tr. *Rohault's Nat. Philos.* (1729) I. 11 If I *will* to move my Arm, it is presently moved. **1712** BERKELEY *Pass. Obed.* §11 He that willeth the end, doth will the necessary means conducive to that end. **1837** CARLYLE *Fr. Rev.* I. v. v, All shall be as God wills. **1880** MEREDITH *Tragic Com.* vi, So great,..heroical, giant-like, that what he wills must be. **1891** FARRAR *Darkn. & Dawn* liv, Who..were ready, if God so willed, to die for their faith. **1896** HOUSMAN *Shropsh. Lad* xxx, Others, I am not the first, Have willed more mischief than they durst.

b. *intr.* To exercise the will; to perform the mental act of volition.

1582 *N. T.* (Rhem.) Phil. ii. 13 It is God which worketh in you, both to will and to accomplish. **1594** HOOKER *Eccl. Pol.* I. vii. §2 To will, is to bend our soules to the hauing or doing of that which they see to be good. **1635** QUARLES *Embl.* IV. viii, See how my Sin-bemangled body lies, Not having pow'r, to will; nor will, to rise! **1690** LOCKE *Hum. Und.* II. xxi. §30 He, that shall turn his thoughts inwards upon what passes in his mind when he wills. **1830** MACKINTOSH *Eth. Philos.* Wks. 1846 I. 85 But what could induce such a being to will or to act? **1867** A. P. FORBES *Explan. 39 Art.* i. 12 Is this infinitely powerful and intelligent Being free? wills He? loves He?

c. *trans.* To bring or get (*into*, *out of*, etc.) by exercise of will.

1850 L. HUNT *Table-t.* (1882) 184 Victims of opium have been known to be unable to will themselves out of the chair in which they were sitting. **1874** H. R. REYNOLDS *John Bapt.* iii. §2. 156 The great powers of nature..were willed into being by the word of Jehovah.

d. To control (another person), or induce (another) *to do* something, by the mere exercise of one's will, as in hypnotism.

1882 *Proc. Soc. Psych. Research* I. 57 *note*, The one to be 'willed' would go to the other end of the house, if desired, whilst we agreed upon the thing to be done. **1886** *19th Cent.* Dec. 883 They are what is called 'willed' to do certain things desired by the ladies or gentlemen who have hold of them. **1897** A. LANG *Dreams & Ghosts* iii. 59 A young lady, who believed that she could play the 'willing game' successfully without touching the person 'willed'.

4. To express or communicate one's will or wish with regard to something: with various shades of meaning. (Cf. WILL *v.*¹ 3.)

a. To enjoin, order; to decree, ordain. *Obs.* or *arch.*

(*a*) with personal obj., usually with inf. or clause.

a **1300** *Cursor M.* 11293 Þe lai of moyses..wijld Womman þat had a knaue child, At hir formast birth suld sco It offer þe hali temple to. **1481** *Cov. Leet Bk.* 496 We desire and also will you that vnto oure seid seruaunt..ye yeue your aid. **1547** EDW. VI in Rymer *Foedera* (1719) XV. 192 We Wyll and Commaunde yowe to Procede in the seid Matters. **1568** GRAFTON *Chron.* II. 659 Their sute was smally regarded, and shortly after they were willed to silence. **1588** LAMBARDE *Eiren.* II. vii. 272 If a man do lie in awaite to rob me, and (drawing his sword upon me) he willeth me to deliver my money. **1591** SHAKS. *1 Hen. VI*, I. iii. 10 We doe no otherwise then wee are will'd. **1596** NASHE *Saffron Walden* P4, Vp he was had and..willed to deliuer vp his weapon. *a* **1656** HALES *Gold. Rem.* (1673) I. 31 The King in the Gospel, that made a Feast, and..willed his servants to go out to the high-ways side. **1799** NELSON in Nicolas *Disp.* (1845) III. 397 Willing and requiring all Officers and men to obey you.

(*b*) with thing as obj., either sb. (alone or with inf. pass.) or obj. clause; also *absol.* in clause with *as*. (See also 2a.)

c **1400** *Destr. Troy* 13261 At þat orribill I asket angardly myche, Of dethe, & of deire, as destyny willes. **1412** in *15th Rep. Hist. MSS. Comm.* App. VIII. 10 We..wil for the mare sekernes this oure confirmacioune be..selit with oure grete sele. **1526** *Pilgr. Perf.* (W. de W. 1531) 224b, Where scripture wylleth the contrary. **1565** COOPER *Thesaurus* s.v. *Classicum*, By sounde of trumpet to wyll scilence. **1585** in *Engl. Hist. Rev.* (1914) Jan. 115 Th'act..was ones red..and was willed to be ingrosed to the third reading. **1612** BACON *Ess., Of Empire* (Arb.) 300 It is common with Princes (saith Tacitus) to will contradictories. **1697** DRYDEN *Æneis* I. 112 'Tis yours, O Queen! to will The Work, which Duty binds me to fulfil. **1877** TENNYSON *Harold* VI. i, Get thou into thy cloister as the king Will'd it.

†**b.** To pray, request, entreat; = DESIRE *v.* 6.

1454 *Paston Lett.* Suppl. (1901) 54 As for the questyon that ye wylled me to aske my lord, I fond hym yet at no good leyser. **1564** HAWARD tr. *Eutropius* III. 26b, The Romaines sent ambassadoures to him, to wyll him to cease from battayle. **1581** A. HALL *Iliad* II. 19 His errand done, as he was willde, he toke his flight from thence. **1631** [MABBE] *Celestina* xiii. 150 Did I not will you I should not be wakened? **1690** DRYDEN *Amphitryon* I. i, He has sent me to will and require you to make a swinging long Night for him.

†**c.** *fig.* of a thing: To require, demand (cf. WILL *v.*¹ B. 3c); also, to induce, persuade (a person to do something). *Obs.*

1445 in *Anglia* XXVIII. 267 Constaunce willeth also That thou doo nouȝte with weyke corage. **1563** GOOGE *Eglogs* Ded. (Arb.) 24 These..mischiefes vtterly diswaded me from the folowynge of my frendes perswasions, and wylled me rather to condem them. **1579** LYLY *Euphues* (Arb.) 88 Wisedome willeth me to pawse. **1607** SHAKS. *Cor.* II. iii. 125 What Custome wills in all things, should we doo't? The Dust on antique Time would lye vnswept. **1667** MILTON *P.L.* IV. 633 Mean while, as Nature wills, Night bids us rest.

will, *v.*³ Now only *Shetland dial.* Pa. t. and pple. **willed**, **wilt** (also 4 **wylt**, 5 **welt**). [a. ON. *villask*, refl. of *villa* to lead astray, f. *villr* WILL *a.*] *intr.* To go astray, lose one's way; to stray; *pa. pple.* gone astray, 'lost' (= WILL *a.* 1).

13.. *Metr. Hom.* (Vernon MS.) in Herrig's *Archiv* LVII. 277 So fer forþ þis foul him tilled þat atte last in wode he willed. **13..** *Gaw. & Gr. Knt.* 1711 He..Stelez out ful stilly ..Went haf wylt of þe wode with wylez fro þe houndes. ?*a* **1400** *Morte Arth.* 3230 Me thoughte I was in a wode willed myne one. *c* **1440** *York Myst.* xxviii. 17 Qwat way is he willed In þis worlde wyde?

1887 JESSIE M. E. SAXBY *Lads of Lunda, Helyers* v, 'To will', in Shetlandic parlance, means to lose your way. **1899** J. SPENCE *Shetl. Folk-Lore* 227 'They're wilt that wales' has reference to the difficulty often experienced in choosing among many things.

will, obs. f. VILE, WELL *sb.*¹, *v.*¹, *adv.*

willable ('wɪləb(ə)l), *a. rare.* [f. WILL *v.*¹ or ² + -ABLE.] †**a.** That is to be willed or desired. *Obs.*

14.. *Cloude of Onknowing* MS. Univ. Coll. 14. a3b, Þe hyȝest wyllabyll þing [L. *vellibile*], þe whych is god.

b. Capable of being willed.

1880 CAIRD *Introd. Philos. Relig.* ix. 292 All truth is knowable as *my* knowledge, all good willable as *my* will.

willage, -aige, willane, willans, willany, obs. Sc. ff. VILLAGE, VILLAIN, VILLAINS, VILLAINY.

will-a-wisp: see WILL-O'-THE-WISP.

†**wille, wil**, *a.* and *adv. Obs.* [Partly developed from predicative use of ME. *wille*, WILL *sb.*¹ (cf. UNWILLE); partly aphetic f. IWIL *a.* (OE. *ȝewill in *unȝewill*); cf. WIL-.]

A. *adj.* Pleasing, pleasant, acceptable, agreeable.

c **1200** *Trin. Coll. Hom.* 213 Unriht heo doð ec toȝenes his emcristene, þenne he hine laðeð to drinken more, noht þe him beo wille oðer queme, ac þenne him ned were. *c* **1205** LAY. 20816 ȝif hit þe weore wille an heorte þat we mosten ouer sæ. *a* **1225** *Leg. Kath.* 571 ȝef ow is wilre for to wunien wið me. *c* **1375** *Cursor M.* 3647 (Fairf.) Hit salle him sauour wonder wil [*Cott.* It sal him sauur al to will, *Gött.*..to his wille, *Trin.*..al at wille].

B. *adv.* Voluntarily, willingly.

a **1300** *Cursor M.* 22387 All þat will [*Fairf.* wille] him sal witstand Sal coround be to liif lastand. *c* **1450** *Ibid.* 9645 (Laud) To eche man she yevyþ wille Right to haue good and ille.

wille, obs. Sc. f. VILE; obs. f. WELL, WILL.

willed (wɪld), *a.* [f. WILL *sb.*¹ + -ED².]

1. Having a will of a specified kind: chiefly in comb., as EVIL-*willed*, ILL-WILLED, SELF-WILLED.
14.. in *Harrow. Hell* p. xxv, Witted [as] a wodkok; Wylled as a wedercoke.
2. Having the will directed to some (specified) action; minded, disposed, inclined (*to do* something). Cf. WELL-WILLED (comp. †*better-willed*).
1398, etc. [see WELL-WILLED]. **1465** MARG. PASTON in *P. Lett.* II. 202 That shall cause hym to be the beter wyllyd. **1563** GOOGE *Eglogs* (Arb.) 125 A Souldier stoute of Reasons bande, is wylled there to ryde. **1580** LYLY *Euphues* (Arb.) 468, I, taking my leaue departed, being willed to visite the Ladie Flauia. **1831** JAMES *Philip Aug.* xxxvii, The peers of France could hardly have refused to assist at the trial.. even had they been so willed.

willed (wɪld), *ppl. a.* [f. WILL *v.*[2] + -ED[1].]
1. Disposed of by will or testament.
1865 DICKENS *Mut. Fr.* III. ix, I am the willed-away girl.
2. Determined or effected by the will; voluntary.
1871 G. MACDONALD *Rest* iii. 11 A mighty, conscious, willed repose. **1899** *Allbutt's Syst. Med.* VI. 514 The prolonged natural discharges of neurons underlying willed and natural movements. **1905** RICKABY *God & His Creatures* I. lxxii. 56 Understood good, as such, must be willed good.
b. Controlled by another's will, as in hypnotism.
1886 GURNEY, etc. *Phantasms of Living* I. 14 The 'willed' performer after various.. indications of a tendency to move in.. [a] wrong direction at last hits on the right one.

willeful, obs. form of WILFUL.

willeliche, variant of WILLY *adv.*

†**willemin.** *Obs. rare.* = GUILLEMIN.
*c*1483 CAXTON *Dialogues* 24 Wyllemyns and frere menours.

willemite ('wɪləmaɪt). *Min.* [ad. Du. *Willemit* (A. Levy, 1829), f. *Willem* William I of the Netherlands.] Native silicate of zinc, abundant in New Jersey, found in masses or crystals of various colours from light greenish-yellow to flesh-red.
1850 ANSTED *Elem. Geol., Min.* etc. §472. **1907** *Times* 25 Mar. 15/3 To detect them [*sc.* certain rays] he used the luminiscence produced by them as they fell on willemite, which was the most sensitive substance he [*sc.* Professor Thomson] had discovered for the purpose.

willer ('wɪlə(r)). [f. WILL *v.*[2] + -ER[1].] One who wills, in various senses.
1. One who desires; a wisher. Chiefly, now only, in obj. or advb. comb., as EVIL-WILLER, GOOD-WILLER, ILL-WILLER, WELL-WILLER, q.v. So †*cursed willer*, after *evil-willer*.
*c*1395 *Plowman's T.* 228 Such willers of worship must evil fele. *Ibid.* 780 Such willers wit is nat worth a neld. *c*1586 C'TESS PEMBROKE *Ps.* LXXXIX. viii, Not closly under-min'd by cursed willer, Nor overthrown by foe in open fight.
2. One who exercises his will; one who sets himself with conscious intention to do something; a voluntary agent.
1435 MISYN *Fire of Love* II. x. 96 Qwho-euer wyll to it myght cum, & ȝit it is not of ylk rynnar ne willar, bot of criste lufand, lyftand & takand [cf. *Rom.* ix. 16]. **1534** *Act 26 Hen. VIII*, c. 13 §1 Willers and wurkars of the same. **1549** COVERDALE, etc. *Erasm. Par. James* iv. 1–6 There is nothynge harde to the louing willer. *a*1677 BARROW *Serm. Luke xxii. 42* Wks. 1686 III. 45 Who the willer is to whom we must submit. **1678** NORRIS *Coll. Misc.* (1699) 289 Every Dependence of an irregular Act upon the Will, is not such as derives Guilt upon the Willer. **1850** KINGSLEY *Alton Locke* xvi, Nature was spoken of as the willer and producer of all the marvels which he describes. **1872** *Dublin Rev.* Apr. 368 The Fathers.. fixing their eyes upon the oneness of the thing willed and the oneness of the willer.
b. *spec.* One who influences another by mere exercise of will, as in hypnotism.
1882 *19th Cent.* June 892 A much larger percentage of successful results.. occurred when a near relative of the guesser was the 'willer'.

†**willerdom.** *Obs. rare.* Also 4 (? erron.) **willardis dom.** [? f. prec. + -DOM.] Wilfulness, self-will.
*c*1380 WYCLIF *Sel. Wks.* III. 295 Worldly coveitouse prestis tradicions, maad of here owene willardis dom for here pride and coveitise. *a*1450 *Pol. Poems* (Rolls) II. 247 Than willerdome with old envy Can none other way but wronge.

willern: see WILGERN.

willes, *adv.*: see WILL *sb.*[1] 10.

Willesden ('wɪlzdən). The name of a suburb of north-west London, used *attrib.* to denote forms of paper or canvas that have been toughened and waterproofed by being treated with cuprammonium solution.
1895 C. F. CROSS et al. *Cellulose* I. 13 Vegetable textile fabrics passed through a bath of the cuprammonium hydroxide are 'surfaced' by the film of gelatinized cellulose. .. These fabrics are sold under the style or description of 'Willesden' goods; the manufacture being in the hands of a company whose works are situated at Willesden. The company's processes are based on the patents of Drs. J. Scoffern and C. R. A. Wright. **1907** *Yesterday's Shopping* (1969) 283/1 Patent Sleeping Valise... No. 3. Willesden Kharki cotton canvas throughout. No. 4. In Willesden flax canvas. **1911** *Encycl. Brit.* XXIII. 705/1 'Willesden paper' ..is cardboard chemically treated to render it tough, waterproof and fire-resisting. **1912** R. A. FREEMAN *Singing Bone* I. ii. 30 Boscovitch continued to stare up at the little square case covered with Willesden canvas... Thorndyke good-naturedly lifted it down and unlocked it. As a matter of fact he was rather proud of his 'portable laboratory'. **1926–7** *Army & Navy Stores Catal.* 219/3 Willesden Canvas. Suitable for.. awnings, shelters, etc. **1964** J. S. SCOTT *Dict. Building* 358 *Willesden paper*, a building paper made of cardboard treated with cuprammonium hydroxide to rotproof it. **1982** J. SHERWOOD *Shot in Arm* xiv. 141 A second-hand Willesden canvas cabin trunk with leather corners.

†**willesful,** *a. Obs.* [f. *willes*, gen. of WILL *sb.*[1] + -FUL.]
1. Strong-willed; obstinate: = WILFUL *a.*[1] 1.
*a*1240 *Sawles Warde* in *O.E. Hom.* I. 257 þe willesfule husewif halt hire al stille. *c*1290 *Beket* 1291 in *S. Eng. Leg.* I. 143 þe Erchebischop is willesful [*v.r.* wilful] and ȝwane he is alles i-brouȝt In ani wille þat is luytel wuyrth he nele bi-leue it nouȝt. *Ibid.* I. 319 Sone old and nouȝt willesfol. **1297** R. GLOUC. (Rolls) 7402 He ne let noȝt clupie al is folc so willesfol he was. **1340** *Ayenb.* 263 Huych mayne to moche slac and wylles uol ssel by, bote yef þe ilke uaderes stefhede hise strayny and ordayny.
2. Desirous: = WILFUL *a.*[1] 2.
*a*1225 *Ancr. R.* 56 ȝif eni is onwil [*MS. T.* ful willes ful] uorte iseon ou. *c*1290 *S. Eng. Leg.* I. 435 þis Maidenes þat beoþ willesfole folie forto do.
Hence †**wilsfully** *adv.*, wilfully; eagerly.
13.. *E.E. Allit. P.* B. 268 þay.. controeued agayn kynde contrare werkez, & vsed hem.. wylsfully, vpon a wrange wyse. **1340–70** *Alisaunder* 590 þat worthlych too þis wight wilsfully saide: 'Fro what kith bee yee comme?'

willet ('wɪlɪt). [So called from its cry, *pill-will-willet*.] A North American bird of the snipe family, *Symphemia semipalmata*.
1862 COUES & PRENTISS in *Rep. Smithsonian Inst.* 1861, 416. **1893** *Outing* (U.S.) XXII. 94/1 Curlew, willet, plover and other beach birds swarm upon the flats in the spring, summer and fall months.

willeuol, obs. form of WILFUL *a.*[1]

willey: see WILLY *sb.*[1]

will-gill, -jill ('wɪl'dʒɪl). *dial.* [f. WILL *sb.*[3] + GILL *sb.*[4]] A hermaphrodite; an effeminate man. Also in comb.
1678 LITTLETON *Lat. Dict.* II, *Androgynos*,.. an Hermophradite or Scrat; a Will-jill. **1845** S. JUDD *Margaret* I. vi, One or two ragged will-gill-looking men.

will-he, nill-he: see WILL *v.*[1] 50b.

willi, var. WILI.

William ('wɪljəm). 1. A common masculine personal name, used in the names of certain species of pinks and other flowers: now only in SWEET-WILLIAM. †*wild Williams*, the Ragged Robin (*Lychnis Flos-cuculi*).
1597 GERARDE *Herbal* II. clxxv. 481 The Crow flower is called.. wilde Williams, marsh Gilloflowers, and Cockowe Gilloflowers. **1650** [W. HOWE] *Phytol. Brit.* 10 *Armerius sylvestris*... Crowflower and Wild Williams. *Armeria flore simplici*, William with single flower in a Wood beyond Redding. **1785** MARTYN *Lett. Bot.* xix. (1794) 276 Ragged-Robin, Meadow-Pinks, Wild-Williams.
2. An obsolete Dutch coin (see quot. 1893).
1844 T. B. MACAULAY *Let.* 9 Oct. (1977) IV. 218 While he was changing me a gold William I got away from the old villain. **1893** R. BITHELL *Counting-Ho. Dict.* (rev. ed.) 317 *William*, a gold coin formerly used in Holland, and valued at 10 guilders. Its metallic value was about 16s. 2d. sterling.
3. *slang.* [With a pun on BILL *sb.*[3]] a. An account for payment, a bill.
1859 H. J. BYRON *Maid & Magpie* ii. 18 When de farmers around are behind in their rent I does little Villiams, at sixty per shent. **1903** FARMER & HENLEY *Slang* VII. 353/2 *To meet sweet William*, to meet a bill on presentation.
b. A dollar note. (See also quot. 1869.) *U.S.* Sometimes without a capital initial.
1865 *Republican Banner* (Nashville, Tenn.) 5 Oct. 3/1 Will. had to remember the Workhouse in his will to the tune of a 'ten dollar William'. **1869** *Overland Monthly* III. 128 $100 bills were there [*sc.* in Texas] called 'Williams', and $50 bills 'Blue Williams'. **1887** in Wentworth & Flexner *Dict. Amer. Slang* (1960) 580/1 [He] lost his five dollar William. **1927** C. A. SIRINGO *Riata & Spurs* i. 10 Mr. Myers wrote me.. to buy a suit of clothes with the twenty-dollar 'william'.
4. Used *attrib.* to designate the style of architecture, furniture, etc., associated with the reign of monarchs of this name; esp. **William and Mary** (freq. hyphenated), with reference to William III and Mary, joint King and Queen of Great Britain, 1689–94; **William IV**, with reference to William IV, King of Great Britain, 1830–7.
1905 FENN & WYLLIE *Old Eng. Furnit.* vii. 74 The low-backed armchair.. was.. subsequently displaced by the more dignified and far more comfortable high-backed kind known to us as the 'Stuart' and the 'William and Mary' chair. **1927** *Daily Tel.* 29 Nov. 7/1 Jacobean and William and Mary chests. **1948** D. WELCH *Jrnl.* 31 Aug. (1952) 266 Our chairs were William and Mary with high caned backs. **1955** 'W. MOLE' *Hammersmith Maggot* iii. 41 A fine set of William IV chairs. **1977** *New Scientist* 3 Mar. 512/1 A William-and-Mary country house in the depths of Somerset. **1982** 'J. GASH' *Firefly Gadroon* i. 13 A blazing row over a William IV davenport desk.
¶ ***Wiliam pear***: see WILLIAMS[1].

Williamite ('wɪljəmaɪt), *sb.* and *a.* [f. the name *William* + -ITE[1]. In sense 1 = mod.L. *Guil-, Wilhelmita*, F. *Guillemite*, etc.]
A. *sb.* †1. A member of an order of Augustinian hermits: = GUILLEMIN. *Obs.*
[**1549** CHALONER *Erasm. on Folly* N j b, Those Augustines, these Guilhelmites, those Iacobites.] **1668** J. WILSON tr. *Erasmus' Praise of Folly* 109 These Williamites, and those Jacobines. **1693** tr. *d'Emiliane's Mon. Orders* vii. 49 Heremitical Congregations, which were spread.. under different names, and especially of the Williamites, and Zambonites.
2. A supporter of William of Orange (King William III): opp. to JACOBITE *sb.*[4] Also *attrib.*
1689 [see JACOBITE *sb.*[4]]. **1706** HEARNE *Collect.* (O.H.S.) I. 193 Upon y[e] Revolution he grew a mighty Williamite. **1854** J. C. O'CALLAGHAN *Hist. Irish Brigades* I. 209 To oppose the Williamite invasion under the Marshal Duke of Schonberg. **1855** MACAULAY *Hist. Eng.* xvi. III. 697 The infamous triumvirs who had been, in the short space of a year, violent Williamites and violent Jacobits, became Williamites again. **1901** *Athenæum* 16 Nov. 654/3 [Fitzgerald Molloy] is as much a Jacobite in his sympathies as Macaulay was a Williamite.
B. *adj.* Of glass: bearing portraits or emblems of William III, as an indication of anti-Jacobite feelings.
1905 P. BATE *Eng. Table Glass* xii. 105 No. 213 is a Williamite glass bearing the inscription—'*The immortal memory*'; others read, '*To the glorious memory of King William*'. **1936** *Burlington Mag.* Oct. p. xxiii/1 Many specimens of engraved glasses including Jacobite specimens ..and Williamite, Volunteer and other inscribed glasses. **1973** *Country Life* 22 Mar. Suppl. 72/2 A rare Williamite glass.

William Morris. = MORRIS *sb.*[4]
1944 D. WELCH *Jrnl.* 26 Oct. (1952) 135 We had tea at Pitt's Cottage, on a William Morris, mortifying sofa. **1962** I. MURDOCH *Unofficial Rose* xiv. 128 The bright blue bird-woven William Morris tiles. **1969** S. SITWELL *Gothic Europe* xiii. 155 They are Brussels tapestries.. too 'flowered' in the foreground and therefore too 'William Morris' in style. **1981** M. E. ATKINS *Palimpsest* ii. 18 You'll splash the wallpaper, it's William Morris.
Hence '**William** '**Morrisy** *a.*, resembling, or in the style of, William Morris.
1960 *Times* 29 July 13/5 A William Morrisy life of craftsmanship close to the soil. **1968** 'O. MILLS' *Sundry Fell Designs* viii. 88 She's a William Morrisy person; and all she was after was the simple, creative life. **1977** R. BARNARD *Blood Brotherhood* x. 113 A William Morrisy stained-glass window.

william-nilliam ('wɪljəm 'nɪljəm), *adv.* Humorously extended form of WILLY-NILLY *adv.*
1907 G. S. GORDON *Let.* 9 Sept. (1943) 23, I have called you sweet girl. But I will not.. retract; and so sweet girl you must remain william nilliam. **1917** A. HUXLEY *Let.* 18 Apr. (1969) 123, I.. found myself pushed—almost william-william [*sic*]—into a very nasty and ill-paid job. **1959** P. BULL *I know Face, But*... x. 188 A splendid change from ordinary digs where the plate is plonked in front of you william-nilliam.

Williams[1] ('wɪljəmz). In full, *Williams'*, *Williams's* (erron. *William*) *Bon Chrétien*: A very juicy variety of the Bon Chrétien pear (see BON *a.*), ripening in September, so called from the name of its first distributor in England.
Called also *Bartlett* from the name of its importer into U.S.
1814 AITON *Epit. Hortus Kewensis* 151 Bishop's-thumb Pear. Bonchrétien winter... Williams's. **1852** G. W. JOHNSON *Cottage Gard. Dict.* 690 Useful and profitable orchard Pears... Williams's Bon Chretien. **1860** HOGG *Fruit Man.* 220 Williams' Bon Crêtien (Bartlett; De Lavault; Williams'). **1884** *Pall Mall Budget* 22 Aug. 11/1 The.. juicy flavour of the famous William Bon Chrétien. **1895** C. W. DALMON *Song Favours* 34 Luscious Harvest plums and William pears.

Williams[2] ('wɪljəmz). *Computers.* [The name of F. C. *Williams* (1911–77), English electrical engineer, who with T. Kilburn described such a tube in 1948.] ***Williams tube***: a cathode-ray tube used in some early computers to store and display an array of spots representing bits; so ***Williams memory***.
1950 W. W. STIFLER et al. *High-Speed Computing Devices* x. 202 The proposed machine will have an electrostatic storage system consisting of a bank of Williams tubes. **1970** O. DOPPING *Computers & Data Processing* x. 150 The Williams memory had many weaknesses but until the middle fifties it was the only available memory in the microsecond class apart from the expensive flip-flop registers. **1982** D. P. SIEWIOREK et al. *Computer Structures* vii. 107/2 The Williams Tube which implemented the control register was also used to hold the present instruction ..itself subsequent to its being read out of main store.

Williamsite ('wɪljəmzaɪt). [f. the surname *Williams* + ITE[1].]
1. A follower of Roger Williams, an American colonist of the 17th century.
1833 WHITTIER *Pr. Wks.* (1889) I. 269 I'm afraid you have become a Williamsite.

2. *Min.* An impure variety of serpentine, named after L. W. Williams, an American mineralogist.

1848 SHEPARD in *Amer. Jrnl. Sci.* Ser. II. VI. 249.

williche: see WILLY *adv.*

willick, variant of WILLOCK.

willie: see WILLY *sb.*[2]

willies (ˈwɪlɪz), *sb. pl. slang* (orig. *U.S.*). [Etym. unknown.] ***the willies***: a fit of nervous apprehension. Chiefly in phrs. ***to give*** (someone) ***the willies***, ***to get the willies***.

1896 *Dialect Notes* I. 427 *To have the willies*, to be nervous. **1900** G. BONNER *Hard Pan* 99 It just gives me the willies to think of your being down on your luck. **1913** J. LONDON *Valley of Moon* 105 Bert gives me the willies the way he's always lookin' for trouble. **1927** H. A. VACHELL *Dew of Sea* 261, I sure got the willies at the thought of meeting you. **1942** G. KERSH *Nine Lives Bill Nelson* ix. 57 It *can* give you the willies when, in broad daylight, you hear a rifle go off. **1953** F. SWINNERTON *Month in Gordon Square* 202 Gosh! She was getting the willies. It was awful. **1962** J. HELLER *Catch-22* xii. 127 Chief White Halfoat shuddered. 'That guy gives me the willies,' he confessed. **1975** FELTON & FOWLER *Best, Worst* 277 You can now visit Winchester House. But we wouldn't advise it if you suffer from the willies. **1984** A CARTER *Nights at Circus* III. i. 199 Not that the 'wagon salon' isn't very pleasant, if it don't give you the willies.

willily, -ness: see after WILLY *a.*

willing (ˈwɪlɪŋ), *vbl. sb.* [OE. *willung*, f. *willian* WILL *v.*[2]: see -ING[1].]

1. Wishing, desire, inclination. *Obs.*, or *arch.* in conjunction with *nilling* (with mixture of sense 2). †***good willing***, the action of wishing well to some one, favourable disposition, GOODWILL.

c **900** tr. *Bæda's Hist.* IV. v. (1890) 278 þætte nænig biscopa hine oðrum forbære þurh unrehte willunge [orig. *per ambitionem*]. *c* **1374** CHAUCER *Boeth.* v. pr. ii. (1868) 152 In hem also is libertee of willyng and of nillynge. *c* **1386** —— *Clerk's T.* 263 My willynge Is as ye wole ne ayeyns youre likynge. *c* **1400** *Rom. Rose* 5952 Whanne she assentith to my willyng. **1418–20** J. PAGE *Siege of Rouen* in *Hist. Coll. Cit. Lond.* (Camden) 23 He sayde, 'What ys youre wyllynge?' **1556** *Aurelio & Isab.* (1608) N vj, All the wyseste desires their favour and goode willinge. **1690** NORRIS *Beatitudes* (1694) I. 105 By impotent willing meaning that natural Inclination..we have to every Good. **1710** —— *Chr. Prud.* v. 218 Our willing of Evil is always with a mixture of nilling. **1865** NEALE *Hymns on Paradise* 10 One in willing, one in nilling, Unity their spirits show.

2. The action or an act of exercising the will, volition; voluntary choice or determination, intention.

1340 *Ayenb.* 9 Wyþoute greate wille an willinge uor to harmi oþren. **1390** GOWER *Conf.* II. 319 Thou soffrest many a wrong doinge, And yit it is noght thi willinge. *c* **1425** *Lucidarie* (Schmitt 1909) 4 Aungels & men, her þewis, willynges, seiynges. **1587** GOLDING *De Mornay* ii. 22 What haue we then to thinke of him, whose willings are powers, and whose thoughts are deedes? **1663–70** SOUTH *Serm., Col. ii. 2* (1715) IV. 296 One and the same Mind is both Being, Understanding, and Willing. **1754** EDWARDS *Freed. Will* I. iv. 27 The very willing is the doing. **1865** BUSHNELL *Vicar. Sacr.* II. ii. (1868) 159 All the senses and sentiments, and willings, and wishes of their lives. **1892** *Daily News* 2 Feb. 6/6 The two first are of human willing; the last is purely.. necessary, inevitable.

b. The action of influencing another by mere exercise of will, as in hypnotism. Also *attrib.*

1883 *Fortn. Rev.* 1 Aug. 263 The well-known drawing-room game of 'Willing' (where one finds out a hidden object by means of more or less subtle muscular indications from another). **1883** *Chamb. Jrnl.* 82 The first division corresponds to the 'willing-game' described by Dr. Carpenter.

†3. Command; injunction. *Obs.*

c **1400** *Rom. Rose* 5879 My modir..Nis not all at my willyng Ne doth not all my desiryng. *c* **1450–60** *Bp. Grossetest's Househ. Stat.* in *Babees Bk.* (1868) 328 The wyllyng of god to be performed and fulfyllydde.

4. The action of bequeathing by will.

1847 GROTE *Greece* II. xi. III. 183 Throughout most rude states of society the power of willing is unknown.

ˈ**willing**, *ppl. a.* Comp. **willinger**, sup. **willingest** (now *rare*). [OE. *willende* (WILL *v.*[1], -ING[2]) appears in *selfwillende* SELF-WILLING, *unwillende* UNWILLING, *welwillende* WELL-WILLING *a.*, *yfel-willende* EVIL-WILLING, and *willendlice* WILLINGLY. But there is no evidence in the simplex or the compounds of continuity of use from OE.]

†1. Wishing, wishful, desirous; inclined, disposed. *Obs.*

1450–1530 *Myrr. our Ladye* II. 69 Yt were not spedefull to hym..to study in bokes of heuynes & of drede though he felte hymselfe wyllyng therto. **1553** T. WILSON *Rhet.* 111 He was not receiued of his woman,..when he was moste willyng to se her. **1587** HOLINSHED *Chron.* II. 435/2, I haue ..beene the willinger to set downe the same..for that I would not suffer so worthie a man..to be buried in obliuion. **1594** T. BEDINGFIELD tr. *Machiavelli's Florentine Hist.* (1595) 191 The Pope and the King became more willing one of the others friendship. **1622** WOTTON *Lett.* (1907) II. 230 The willinger to increase his haste. **1697** tr. *C'tess D'Aunoy's Trav.* (1706) 168 They alledge that the Heat is so excessive, that they are willing to hinder the Sun from coming in, as much as they can. **1825** HONE *Every-day Bk.* I. 403 Some little 'peep-o'-day boy', willing to take the 'top of the morning' before the rest of his compeers.

2. Having a ready will; disposed to consent or comply; ready to do (what is specified or implied) without reluctance, having no objection, 'not disposed to refuse' (J.); *spec.* disposed to do what is required, ready to be of use or service.

a. in attrib. use, preceding the sb.

a **1300** *Cursor M.* 18359 Lauerd..þi wiling merci [þou] beris wit-in, And sua þou slockens al vr sin. **1509** HAWES *Past. Pleas.* I. (Percy Soc.) 7 To a willyng harte is nought impossible. **1526** TINDALE *2 Cor.* viii. 12 If there be fyrst a willynge mynde, it is accepted accordynge to thatt a man hath. **1605** SHAKS. *Macb.* IV. iii. 73 We haue willing Dames enough. **1667** MILTON *P.L.* III. 73 Satan..ready now To stoop with wearied wings, and willing feet On the bare outside of this World. **1671** —— *P.R.* I. 222 By winning words to conquer willing hearts. **1697** DRYDEN *Æneis* VIII. 541 Eager of her Charms, He snatch'd the willing Goddess to his Arms. *a* **1721** PRIOR *Colin's Mistakes* iii, The willing Steed receiv'd her soft Command. **1797** GODWIN *Enquirer* I. ix. 82 A willing temper makes every burthen light. **1843** CARLYLE *Past & Pres.* I. i, Fifteen millions of workers, understood to be the..cunningest and the willingest our Earth ever had. **1858** FROUDE *Hist. Eng.* III. xiii. 133 Work is done rapidly by willing hands, in the midst of a willing people. **1893** SELOUS *Trav. S.E. Africa* xiv. 270 Our men were a good-tempered, willing lot, and gave us no trouble.

absol. **1852** *Blackw. Mag.* Mar. 365 For the willing there is ever a way. **1868** RUSKIN *Arrows of Chace* (1880) II. 195 Aid the willing.

b. in predicative use, or following the sb.: const. *to* and inf., with clause, or absol.; †also formerly *to* with sb.

In quot. 1647 with *with* = agreeing with, consenting to.

a **1540** BARNES *Supplic. Hen. VIII* c iv b, Bycause the king and his lordes shulde bee the wyllynger to take this battaile on them, he sent a commaundement to the byshops, to rayse ..a taxe, for to paye the souldyours with. **1559** W. CUNINGHAM *Cosmogr. Glasse* Pref. 1 The Souldiors allured with the commodities of the Countries, were made the willinger to the thinge. **1599** SHAKS. *Much Ado* III. iii. 86 He may staie him, marrie not without the prince be willing. **1601** —— *Twel. N.* IV. iii. 29 He shall conceale it Whiles [= until] you are willing it shall come to note. **1647** WARD *Simple Cobler* 21, I am perswaded the Devill himselfe was never willing with their proceedings. **1685** BAXTER *Paraphr. N.T.* Matt. x. 11 Enquire who is a godly person, willingest to entertain the Gospel. *c* **1720** DE FOE *Mem. Cavalier* (1840) 257 The king was willinger to comply with anything than this. **1754** SHEBBEARE *Matrimony* (1766) I. 144 Mr. Trueman..[fancied] that Mr. Sharply would be very willing to this Union between his Son and his Ward. **1759** GOLDSM. *Bee* No. 8 They..grew willing to be burnt or hanged out of a world which was no other to them than a scene of persecution and anguish. **1850** DICKENS *Dav. Copp.* v, Barkis is willin'. **1874** GREEN *Short Hist.* viii. §3. 480 The nation was willing to take his obstinacy for firmness.

c. ***willing horse*** (in proverbial phrases), applied to one who is willing to work or to take trouble.

c **1580** J. COOKE *Narr.* in *World Encomp. by Sir F. Drake* (Hakluyt Soc.) App. iv. 207 There nedyd no spure to a willing horsse. **1616** DRAXE *Bibl. Scholast.* 93 All lay load on a willing horse. **1881** *Daily News* 29 Dec. 5/2 It was probably on the well-known principle of working a willing horse that he was left to labour as an ordinary Judge for fifteen years.

d. *transf.* Given, rendered, offered, performed, assumed, borne, or undergone willingly.

1568 GRAFTON *Chron.* II. 757 The people..in a willyng and louyng obedience among themselues. **1599** SHAKS. *Hen. V*, III. v. 63 We send, To know what willing Ransome he will giue. *c* **1600** —— *Sonn.* vi. 6 That vse is not forbidden vsery, Which happies those that pay the willing lone. **1628** MILTON *Vac. Ex.* 52 Held with his melodious harmonie In willing chains and sweet captivitie. **1697** DRYDEN *Æneis* II. 965 Haste, my dear Father,..And load my Shoulders with a willing Fraight. **1715** DE FOE *Fam. Instruct.* I. v. (1841) I. 104 Here, Madam, is the willingest sacrifice I ever made in my life. **1814** BYRON *Lara* II. iii, With eye, though calm, determined not to spare, Did Lara too his willing weapon bare. **1849** MACAULAY *Hist. Eng.* ii. I. 230 The affection and willing obedience of his subjects.

e. *fig.* of things: Compliant, yielding; (of the wind) favourable.

1500–20 DUNBAR *Poems* lv. 22 Sum, thocht tham selffis stark,..Ar now maid waek lyk, willing wandis. **1688** PRIOR *Ode Exod. iii. 14* v, Why does He wake the correspondent Moon, and fill her willing Lamp with liquid Light? **1697** DRYDEN *Æneis* III. 253 And leaving few behind, We spread our sails before the willing Wind. **1749** SHENSTONE *Irreg. Ode* 85 And some entwin'd the willing sprays, To shield th' illustrious dame's repose. **1791** E. DARWIN *Bot. Gard.* I. 54 Down the steep slopes He led with modest skill The willing pathway, and the truant rill. **1844** KINGLAKE *Eothen* i. 9 The willing fume [of the tchibouque] came up, and answered my slightest sigh.

f. *advb.* Willingly, consentingly, without reluctance. (Now *rare* or *Obs.*) ***willing*** (*or*) ***nilling*** (arch.), with or against one's will, willy-nilly.

1585 SIDNEY *Lett.* Misc. Wks. (1829) 323 Which I the willinger do becaws I think him a good honest gentleman. **1607** SHAKS. *Timon* III. vi. 32. **1667** MILTON *P.L.* IX. 382 With thy permission then, and thus forewarnd,..The willinger I goe. **1697** DRYDEN *Æneis* VII. 294 Willing we sought your Shores.

1578 H. WOTTON *Courtlie Controv.* 148 [These] conquered in such sorte the hearts of euery one vnto hym, as willing, nilling, it behoued enuy to hang the heade. **1626** T. H[AWKINS] *Caussin's Holy Crt.* 488 Arcadius willing, nilling, was constrayned..to signe the petition. **1798** W. TAYLOR in *Monthly Mag.* IV. 197 And willing or nilling thou'lt come. **1874** SAYCE *Compar. Philol.* iii. 100 Every idiom, ancient or modern, has to be brought willing, nilling, under some 'family'.

†3. That is so, or is done or borne, of one's own will; voluntary, intentional, deliberate, wilful.

1550 CROWLEY *Epigr.* 33 To the willinge wicked no prophete shall be sente. *a* **1586** SIDNEY *Arcadia* II. xxi. (1912) 286 But so by Lelius willing-missing was the odds of the Iberian side. **1607** SHAKS. *Timon* IV. iii. 242 Willing misery Out-liues incertaine pompe. **1613** —— *Hen. VIII*, III. i. 49 The willing'st sinne I euer yet committed.

4. Exercising or capable of exercising the will, volitional; conveying impulses of the will.

1875 E. WHITE *Life in Christ* I. i. 8 We know nothing of the *post-mortem* existence of the thinking willing energy of man. **1896** HOUSMAN *Shropsh. Lad* xxiv, Ere the wholesome flesh decay, And the willing nerve be numb.

5. *Comb.*, as ***willing-hearted***, ***-minded*** adjs.

1539 *Bible* (Great) Exod. xxxv. 22 And they came..(euen as manye as were willynge harted) & brought bracelettes, & earynges, rynges & cheynes. **1648** HEXHAM II, *Willemoedigh*, willing-minded. **1830** COLERIDGE *Lett., to T. H. Green* (1895) 751 Our Harriet, whose love and willing-mindedness to me-ward [etc.].

willinghood (ˈwɪlɪŋhʊd). *rare.* [f. prec. + -HOOD.] Willingness, readiness of mind (esp. as a personal quality or disposition).

1880 W. M. TAYLOR *Gosp. Mirac.* 225 Everything is made to depend on the willinghood of the individual to be blessed. **1890** SPENCER *Plea for Liberty* Introd. 7 Suppose now that this industrial *régime* of willinghood..is replaced by a *régime* of industrial obedience. **1892** *Independent* 29 Apr. 285/2 Surely the spread of Christ's kingdom is not to be hindered simply for want of willinghood on the part of those who profess His name.

willingly (ˈwɪlɪŋlɪ), *adv.* (Also 5 **welyngly**, 7 **wollinglie**.) [OE. *willendlice*: see WILLING *ppl. a.* and -LY[2].] In a willing manner (in various senses of the adj.).

†1. a. Intentionally, deliberately, wilfully. *Obs.*

c **1386** CHAUCER *Clerk's T.* 306 Heere I swere that neuere willyngly In werk ne thoght I nyl yow disobeye. **1402** HOCCLEVE *Let. Cupid* lvi, Sauf willyngly the feende deceyued Eve. **1531** TINDALE *Expos. 1 John* ii. (1538) 17 b, God is lyghte, and therfore..no man which wyllinglye walketh in the vnfrutefull workes of darknesse, hath ony fellowshyp wyth that lyght. **1550** CROWLEY *Way to Wealth* 521 Wittinglye and willinglye..ye haue..disobeied youre kinge. **1590** SHAKS. *Mids. N.* III. ii. 346 Still thou mistak'st, Or else committ'st thy knaueries willingly [*Qo's* wilfully]. **1622** in Foster *Engl. Factories Ind.* (1908) II. 132 That nyght, wee carryinge the lighte, the Dutch (as wee suppose) lost us willinglye. **1727** DE FOE *Syst. Magic* I. iii. (1840) 78 Men that do not willingly deceive the people, or that at least have not a wicked design to deceive. **1748** in *10th Rep. Hist. MSS. Comm.* App. I. 302, I will not willingly stand in any body's way.

†b. Of one's own will, voluntarily. *Obs.*

1552 ABP. HAMILTON *Catech.* (1884) 43 Thai ar content to do it willingly without ony compulsioun. **1596** SHAKS. *1 Hen. IV*, V. iii. 61. **1617** MORYSON *Itin.* I. 205, I had no remedie but to pay those Crownes for him,..if I had not rather chosen willingly to doe it. **1695** LD. PRESTON *Beeth.* I. 12 *note*, For this he was banished his Country, or rather willingly left it.

2. With a ready will, consentingly, without reluctance: with various shades of meaning from 'with acquiescence, submissively' to 'with pleasure, cheerfully, gladly' or 'wishfully, eagerly'.

Often with *would*: ***would willingly*** = should like to; ***would not willingly*** = would rather not, should be loth to.

a **1000** in Wr.-Wülcker *Voc.* 222/20 *Diligenter*, willendlice.

1538 ELYOT, *Libenter*, wyllyngely, gladly. **1549** CHEKE *Hurt Sedit.* K j b, And so be contented to byde the ende willingly, which set on the beginning wilfully. **1559** AYLMER *Harborowe* M 2, Thou maist the rather, the willinglier, and gladlier do it. **1560** PILKINGTON *Expos. Aggeus* (1562) 159 They would not willingly serue hym, whiche woulde not willingly serue and obey their God and kinge. *a* **1586** SIDNEY *Arcadia* II. xx. (1912) 279 To bring us (as willingly-caught fishes) to bite at her baite. **1592–3** in Ellis *Orig. Lett.* Ser. III. iv. 109, I may neither dispose of my owne..as others usuallie doe, and I willingliest would. **1600** SHAKS. *A.Y.L.* II. iv. 95, I like this place, and willingly could Waste my time in it. **1603** —— *Meas. for M.* v. i. 481, I craue death more willingly then mercy. **1649** in *Spalding Club Misc.* (1852) V. 380, I sall werey wollinglie concwre withe them. **1653** WALTON *Angler* iv. 115, I would willingly fish on the Lee-shore. **1711** STEELE *Spect.* No. 254 ¶3, I would willingly give you a little good Advice. **1835** in Cornwallis *New World* (1859) I. 364 Their cheerful and willingly-offered services. **1859** TENNYSON *Geraint & Enid* 1056 'Friend, let her eat; the damsel is so faint.' 'Yea, willingly,' replied the youth. **1881** BESANT & RICE *Chapl. Fleet* I. vi, Often have I observed one..of the sisters willingly go without her dinner..in order that her portion might be reserved for Mr. Stallabras.

†b. *fig.* Readily, easily. *Obs.*

1600 SURFLET *Country Farm* III. lxv. 581 The vttermost pilling of common walnuts, whether it shale willingly or no. **1615** CROOKE *Body of Man* VII. x. 456 If the braine had been one entire massie substance, it would not so willingly and gladly as we say, haue risen and falne in the *Systole* and *Diastole*.

willingness (ˈwɪlɪŋnɪs). [f. as prec. + -NESS.] The quality or state of being willing; readiness of will; freedom from reluctance; disposition to consent or comply; *spec.* disposition to do what is required, readiness to be of service.

1561 tr. *Calvin's 4 Godly Serm.* ii. D vij b, [This] maye bring vs..to that willingnes, that we shall not refuce to suffer death for Goddes name. **1592** GREENE *Conny Catch.* III. 11 What dissembled willingnesse of departure hee vsed. **1630** PRESTON *Breastpl. Faith* 93 God requires no more but a willingnesse to come. **1654** tr. *Scudery's Curia Pol.* 96 Though she discovered her willingnesse to my Succession, to make me King of England. **1711** in T. W. Marsh *Early Friends* (1886) 9 To signifie..our willingnesse yt a Preparitive Meeting should be setled. **1873** MOZLEY *Univ. Serm.* viii. (1876) 168 The willingness of the Sacrifice. **1877** FROUDE *Short Stud.* (1883) IV. I. ii. 23 The pope..professed a willingness and an anxiety to be of corresponding service to Henry.

will-i-nill-i: see WILL *v.*[1] 50 b.

will i(n) the wisp: see WILL-O'-THE-WISP.

williwa(e: see WELLAWAY.

williwaw ('wɪlɪwɔː). Also **willy-, -ie-, wulli(e)-, wully-wa.** [?] A sailor's (whaler's, etc.) name for a sudden violent squall, orig. in the Straits of Magellan.

1842 J. D. HOOKER in *Life* (1918) I. vi. 137 A squall or Williewaw, as they are called [round Cape Horn]. **1863** FITZROY *Weather Bk.* 125 *note*, Those whirlwind squalls, formerly called by the sealers in Tierra del Fuego, 'williwaws'. **1901** KIPLING *Kim* xiii, Where storm and wandering wullie-wa got up to dance.

will-jill: see WILL-GILL.

will-less ('wɪllɪs), *a.* Also 8 **wil-less**, 9 **willess**. [f. WILL *sb.*[1] + -LESS.]

1. Not having 'a will of one's own'; not exercising, or not involving exercise of, the will.

1747 RICHARDSON *Clarissa* (1811) I. xv. 99 Your blind duty and wil-less resignation. **1823** GALT *R. Gilhaize* II. 283, I walked in a willess manner. **1892** MRS. H. WARD *David Grieve* III. x, The last year's leaves..whirled helpless and will-less in the dust-storm of the road!

2. Having no will; destitute of the faculty of volition.

1804 ANNA SEWARD *Mem. Darwin* 89 Reasonless, will-less instinct, limited but undeviating. **1871** MACMILLAN *True Vine* vi. 240 A mindless, will-less, impersonal solitude.

Hence **'will-lessly** *adv.*, **'will-lessness**.

1871 MACMILLAN *True Vine* vi. 245 He is to do consciously and willingly—what the plant does unconsciously and will-lessly. **1902** *Academy* 8 Nov. 509 Among the many signs of that hysteria, what is called *abulia* or 'willessness' is one of the most common.

willo, obs. form of WILLOW.

willock ('wɪlək). *local.* Also **-ick**. [f. WILL *sb.*[3] + -OCK. Cf. etym. of *guillem, guillemot*.] The GUILLEMOT; also, the puffin and the razor-bill.

1631 PELHAM *Gods Power* 31 We found abundance of Willocks egges; (which is a Fowle about the bignesse of a Ducke). **1635** *Voy. Foxe & James to N.W.* (Hakluyt Soc.) I. 168 Going to kill willicks. **1802** MONTAGU *Ornith. Dict.* s.v. *Puffin*, At Dover, this, as well as the Razorbill, is indiscriminately called Willock. **1855** KINGSLEY *Glaucus* 2 Your boys..endanger your personal safety, by blazing away at innocent gulls and willocks. **1859** [see GUILLEMOT].

†**willok.** *Obs.* [? an error.] *pl.* ? Garments.

c **1400** *Beryn* 1295 Then toke he suche willokis as he fond there.

will-o'-the-wisp ('wɪləðə'wɪsp), *sb.* Forms: see below. Pl. **will-o'-the-wisps**, also **wills-o'-the-wisp**. [orig. *Will with the wisp*: see WILL *sb.*[3] and WISP *sb.* Cf. JACK-O'-LANTERN, and, for the second element, G. *irrwisch*.]

1. = IGNIS FATUUS; *fig.* a thing (rarely a person) that deludes or misleads by means of fugitive appearances.

α. 7–9 **Will with the** or **a wisp (whisp)**; 7 **-with-wispe, with th' wisp**, 9 **wit** or **wi' t' wisp**; also 7 **Will the Wispe**.

1608 DAY *Law Trickes* v. H 2 b, I haue playd Will with the wispe with my brother, and haue led him vp and downe the maze of good fellowship. **1623** 'JACK DAWE' *Vox Graculi* 45 When you are mis-led with lust (that Will-with-wispe). **16..** in *Mad Pranks Robin Goodfellow* (Percy Soc.) p. xviii, Some call him Robin Goodfellow,..some againe doe tearme him oft by name of Will the Wispe. **1654** WHITLOCK *Zootomia* 159 *Ignes fatui*, Fooles fires, wills with a wisp. **1729** *Phil. Trans.* XXXVI. 211 Thus far, what I could learn concerning the Will with a Whisp, as it hath been observed in the Plains. **1832** J. HODGSON in Raine *Mem.* (1858) II. 291 *Ignis Fatuus* or Will-with-the-wisp. **1839** LONGF. *Hyperion* IV. ii, His imagination is continually lantern-led by some will-with-a-whisp in the shape of a lady's stomacher.

β. 7–9 **will of the wisp, o' the wisp** (8 **o' th'**, 9 **o-the-**); also with hyphens and one or two capitals.

1661 BLOUNT *Glossogr.* (ed. 2), *Ignis Fatuus*, foolish fire, or (as the Country people call it) Will of the Wisp. **1748** RICHARDSON *Clarissa* (1768) V. 115 Knowledge by theory only is a vague uncertain light: a Will o' the Wisp. **1760** STERNE *Tr. Shandy* III. xxxi, All the polemical writings in divinity are not as clear and demonstrative as those upon a Will o' the Wisp, or any other sound part of philosophy. **1806–7** J. BERESFORD *Miseries Hum. Life* (1826) XVII. i, Those Wills-o-the-wisp, the Reviewers. **1831** SCOTT *Cast. Dang.* xi, Through what extraordinary labyrinths this Love, this Will-of-the-Wisp, guides his votaries. **1840** DICKENS *Old C. Shop* l, I'll be a Will o' the Wisp, now here, now there. **1840** THACKERAY *Paris Sk.-bk.* (1869) 190 No light except that of..the wicked..wills-o'-the'wisp, as they gambol among the marshes. **1858** GREENER *Gunnery* 208 Proof positive, that we have been on the wrong scent, and running after a 'Will o' the Wisp.' **1879** HUXLEY *Sensation* Sci. & Cult. (1881) 247 The metaphysical Will-o'-the-wisps generated in the marshes of literature and theology. **1918** INGE *Philos. Plotinus* I. 188 The utterly unscientific notion of an automatic 'law of progress', that strange Will-o'-the-wisp of nineteenth-century thought.

γ. 7 **will-a-wisp**, 8 **will o' whisp**, 9 **will-o-wisp** (or **o'**); also with one or two capitals.

1679 OLDHAM *Sat. Jesuits* III. 331 White Sheets for Ghosts, and Will-a-wisps have past For Souls in Purgatory unreleast. **1738** MRS. E. MONTAGU *Corr.* (1906) I. 29 Will o' Whisp never led the bewildered traveller over hedge and ditch as a moon does us country folk. **1829** A. CUNNINGHAM *Magic Bridle* 363 in *Anniversary* 149 Dank will-o'-wisp sank midst the mire. **1863** MEREDITH *Lett.* (1912) I. 114 Young Cupid was he called of old: That Will o' Wisp incorporate.

δ. 7–8 **Will in the Wisp** (8 **i'the whisp**).

1689 *Irish Hudibras* To Rdr. 1 b, [They] made him skip the Bogs like a Will in the Wisp. **1706** VANBRUGH *Mistake* I. (1734) 16 What a Shame they should be allow'd to play Will in the Wisp with Men of Honour. **1762** FOOTE *Orator* I. i, A Will in the Wisp, to confound, perplex, and bewilder you. **1768** TUCKER *Lt. Nat.* II. I. 132 We should see them dance about like so many Will i'the whisps.

ε. 7–9 **Willy-wisp** (7 **Wispe**), 8 **Willy wi'** (**Willie with**) or **and the wisp, Willy's wisp**.

1628 *Mad Pranks Robin Goodfellow* (Percy Soc.) 21 Wenches, that doe smile and lispe Use to call me Willy Wispe. **1679** JAS. GORDON *Reformed Bp.* 250, I do firmly believe, That..He would have chosen rather to have sent down some English Doctors to have govern'd us..than have permitted any of those Willy-wisps to jump into these empty Chairs. **1727** Willies with the Wisps [see SPUNKIE 1]. **1756** *Collect. Sc. Poems by Pennecuik* etc. 23 Travelling of late in fogs and thro' thick mist, Without a guide, save Willy wi' the wisp. *a* **1761** [S. HALIBURTON & HEPBURN] *Mem. Magopico* xiii. (ed. 2) 39 Plumbino is Willie-with-the-wisp; Magopico a flash of wild-fire. **1790** MORISON *Poems* 38 Willy's wisp wi' whirlin' cant Their blazes ca', That's nought but vapours frae a stank. **1828** *Craven Gloss., Willy-wit-wisp*, called also a Willy-wisp; an ignis fatuus, or Jack with a lantern.

b. *attrib.*

1860 W. W. READE *Liberty Hall* II. 44 A fluttering, shadowy, will-o-the-wisp style. **1873** *All Year Round* 5 July 226/1 Strange will-o'-the-wisp lights begin to flutter about the cordage. **1883** BLACK *Shandon Bells* xxi, Kitty's will-o'-the-wisp flashes of petulance.

2. An alga, *Nostoc commune*, so called from the inexplicable suddenness of its appearance.

1866 in *Treas. Bot.*

Hence **will-o'-the-wisp** *v. trans.*, to lead astray like a will-o'-the-wisp; **will-o'-the-wispish, -wispy** *adjs.*, of the nature of a will-o'-the-wisp.

1660 R. WILD *Iter Boreale* ix, Dark-Lanthorn Language, and his peep-boe play, Will-E-Wispt Lambert's New-Lights out o' th' way. **1698** FRYER *Acc. E. India & P.* 375 But to return to our Men of Learning, from whence we have been Will-ith-whisped. **1866** CARLYLE *Remin.* (1881) II. 177 His Mrs. Taylor too, a very will-o'-wispish 'iridescence' of a creature. *a* **1873** LYTTON *Ken. Chillingley* II. ii, The boy..became impish and Will-of-the-Wisp-ish. **1886** MISS BROUGHTON *Dr. Cupid* xxxi, The Will-of-the-wispy laughter of his eyes. **1926** J. B. PRIESTLEY *G. Meredith* v. 129 Woman..is far less likely than man to be Will-o'-the-Wisped away by sheer unreason masquerading as reason. **1954** L. MACNEICE *Autumn Sequel* xxvi. 159 Words may will-o'-the-wisp him.

willow ('wɪləʊ), *sb.* Forms: α. 1 **weliȝ**, 5 **weleygh**; 5 *Sc. pl.* **willeis**, 4–5 **wilghe, wylghe**, 6 **wylly(e, -ie**, 6, 9 *dial.* **willie, willy**, 8 **willi-** (9 **-ey, wullie, -y**); 7 **wilfe**, 8- *dial.* **wilf**. β. 4 **welew**, 5 **welogh**, 5–6 **welowe**; 4 **wilewe**, 4–5 **wilw(e, wylw(e, wyl(o)ugh, (whilwh), wil(l)ou, wylo, wyllo, wilowe**, 5–6 **wylow(e, (whylowe)**, 6 **willo, wyllow(e, -ough**, 7 **willough**, 5- **willow**. [OE. *weliȝ* f., corresp. to Fris. *wylch, wil(l)ig*, OLG. *wilgia* (LG. *wilge*), MDu. *wilge* (Du. *wilg*), MHG. *wilge*; f. Teut. *walg-, welg-*, whence also OE. *wiliȝe* WILLY *sb.*[1]

The form-history is obscure, partly from the fact that examples of the word are not forthcoming for the period between late OE. and the 14th century, when the immediate precursor of the present form, viz. *wilwe*, is already established, instead of the normal representative of OE. *weliȝ*, which would be **welly*. The change in the root-syllable may be due to WILLY *sb.*[1] (OE. *wiliȝe*), or an OE. **wiliȝ* may have existed; for the terminal syllable cf. *bellows* beside *belly* (OE. *beliȝ*), *fellow* beside *felly* (OE. *feliȝ*). The type *willy* survives dial.]

I. 1. a. Any plant of the genus *Salix*, which consists of trees and shrubs of various sizes, widely distributed in temperate and cold regions, growing for the most part by the side of watercourses, characterized by very pliant branches and long narrow drooping leaves, and valued economically as furnishing osiers, a light smooth and soft wood, or a medicinal astringent bark, or grown ornamentally by the side of water.

α. *a* **750** *Blickl. Glosses* in *O.E. Texts* 123 *In salicibus*, on welȝum. *c* **1000** *Sax. Leechd.* II. 156 Weliȝes leaf wylle on wætere. *a* **1340** HAMPOLE *Psalter* cxxxvi[i]. 2 In þe wylghes in þe myddis of hit. *c* **1400** tr. *Secr. Secr., Gov. Lordsh.* 81 þat he haue weleyghes and myrt. **14..** *Liber pauperum* in *MS. Lincoln A. i.* 17, lf. 295 (Hall.) Tak the bark of wilghe that is bitwene the tre and the utter barke. **1473** *Rental Bk. Cupar-Angus* (1879) I. 178 Plantation of willeis. **1483** *Cath. Angl.* 418/1 A Wylght [sic], *salix*. **1535** COVERDALE *Lev.* xxiii. 40 Wyllies of the broke. —— *Isa.* xliv. 4 The Willies by the waters side. [**1641** wilfe: see WILLOW-TREE.]

β. *c* **1325** *Gloss. W. de Bibbesw.* in Wright *Voc.* 163 Sauz [*glossed* wytie; *Camb. MS.* wilwe; *All Souls MS.* withe or wilghe]. *c* **1340** *Nominale* (Skeat) 659 *Sauce*..Welew. *c* **1386** CHAUCER *Knt.'s T.* 2064 Wylugh [*v.rr.* Wylow, Wylw, Willow]. **1387** TREVISA *Higden* (Rolls) I. 365 At Glyndalkan ..wilewys bereþ apples as it were appel treen. **14..** *Nom.* in Wr.-Wülcker 716/19 *Hec salix*, a welogh. **1426** LYDG. *De Guil. Pilgr.* 15178 Som whilwh ful off levys grene. *c* **1450** *Cokwolds Daunce* x. in Hartshorne *Anc. Metr. T.* (1829) 212 Garland of wylos sculd be fette, And sett vpon his hed. **1546** *Supplic. Poore Commons* (1871) 78 A christalline ryuer garnished with wyllouse. **1634** MILTON *Comus* 891 By the rushy-fringed bank, Where grows the Willow and the Osier dank. **1727–46** THOMSON *Summer* 1275 Plaintive breeze, that play'd Among the bending willows. **1784** COWPER *Task* I. 268 The willows dip Their pendent boughs, stooping as if to drink. **1818** KEATS *Endym.* I. 43 While the willow trails Its delicate amber. **1859** H. KINGSLEY *G. Hamlyn* ii, The old willows by the river.

b. The wood or osiers of any tree of this genus.

c **1489** CAXTON *Sonnes of Aymon* xxiv. 517 He..toke the balke..as lightly as it had be som pece of welowe. **1610** HOLLAND *Camden's Brit.* I. 491 Willowes..Whereof..there be Baskets made. **1815** J. SMITH *Panorama Sci. & Art* II. 15 The pressure of the external air will then force the mercury through the pores of the hazel or willow.

c. in allusive use with reference to pliability.

1832 MACAULAY *Ess., Burleigh* ¶4 Burleigh, like the old Marquess of Winchester, who preceded him in the custody of the White Staff, was of the willow, and not of the oak. **1847** EMERSON *Poems, Musketaquid* 70, I am a willow of the wilderness, Loving the wind that bent me. **1910** J. D. MOFFAT *Paul & Paulinism* 24 Barnabas was of the willow rather than of the oak order.

d. Taken as a symbol of grief for unrequited love or the loss of a mate; esp. in phr. ***to wear (the) willow, the willow garland*** (see 6 d), or ***the green willow***: to grieve for the loss of a loved one.

1584 LYLY *Sappho* II. iv, Peace miserable wretch, enioy thy care in couert, weare willow in thy hatte, and baies in thy hart. **1596** SHAKS. *Merch. V.* v. i. 10 In such a night Stood Dido with a Willow in her hand Vpon the wilde sea bankes. **1597** BRETON *Wit's Trenchmour* Wks. (Grosart) II. 20 Some dolefull Ballad, to the tune of all a greene willow. **1603** DEKKER & CHETTLE *Grissil* v. ii, Bring me a crown of gold to crown my loue; A wreath of willow for dispised Grissill. **1604** SHAKS. *Oth.* IV. iii. 51 Sing all a greene Willough must be my Garland. **1625** FLETCHER & SHIRLEY *Nt. Walker* I. i, We see you'r willow and are sorry for't. **1632** MASSINGER *Maid of Hon.* v. i, You may cry willow, willow for your brother. **1668** DRYDEN *Secret Love* v. i, If you had not forsaken me, I had you: so the Willows may flourish for any branches I shall rob 'em of. **1678** D'URFEY *Fool turn'd Critick* II. ii. 19 *Lady A*...so that for his sake I quitted all the rest. *Pen.* And left them Willowes. **1714** GAY *Sheph. Week* Thurs. 134 Nor shall she crown'd with willow die a maid. **1825** HONE *Every-day Bk.* I. 1080 'She is in her willows'.. implies the mourning of a female for her lost mate. **1885** KATH. S. MACQUOID *At Red Glove* VI. i, There's..Marie.. wearing the willow because..Engemann is away courting Madam Carouge.

2. a. With qualification denoting a particular species or variety of the genus *Salix*: see quots. and *almond w.* (ALMOND 10), CRACK-WILLOW, *goat w.* (GOAT *sb.* 4 b), *ground w.* (GROUND *sb.* 18 c), *rose w.* (ROSE *sb.* 23 b), *sage w.* (SAGE *sb.*[1] 6 b), *sallow w.* (SALLOW *sb.* 4), †*stake w.* (STAKE *sb.*[1] 7), *swamp w.* (SWAMP *sb.* 3 c), *sweet w.* (SWEET C. 1 b), WEEPING WILLOW, *whipcord w.* (WHIPCORD *sb.* 3). Cf. OSIER and SALLOW *sb.*

1868 *Rep. U.S. Comm. Agric.* (1869) 202 Weeping and drooping trees... *Babylonian willow (*Salix Babylonica*). **1847** DARLINGTON *Amer. Weeds* etc. (1860) 328 S[alix] viminalis..Osier. *Basket Willow. **1731** MILLER *Gard. Dict.* s.v. *Salix*, The *Bay-leav'd Sweet Willow. **1841** *Penny Cycl.* XX. 360/1 *Salix Russelliana*, Russell or *Bedford willow. **1845–50** MRS. LINCOLN *Lect. Bot.* App. 161 *Salix discolor* (*bog willow). **1650** [W. HOWE] *Phytol. Brit.* 107 *Salix angustifolia pumila; In uliginosis.* *Dwarf-Willow. **1857** MISS PRATT *Flower. Pl.* V. 111 This species is sometimes called the *Golden Willow (*Salix chrysantha*), on account of the beautiful golden catkins which in May and June ornament its boughs. **1868** *Rep. U.S. Comm. Agric.* (1869) 202 *Kilmarnock willow (*Salix caprea*, var. *pendula*). **1841** *Penny Cycl.* XX. 360/2 *Salix purpurea*, *purple willow. **1842** *Proc. Berw. Nat. Club* II. No. 10. 7 The *tree willow (*Salix caprea*). **1597** GERARDE *Herbal* III. li. 1203 *Salix aquatica*. The Oziar, or *water Willow. **1640** PARKINSON *Theat. Bot.* 1430 *Salix arborea angustifolia alba vulgaris*... Our ordinary *white Willow groweth quickely to be a great and tall tree. **1882** *Garden* 9 Sept. 227/3 The wood of the white Willow..is always in request. **1796** WITHERING *Brit. Plants* (ed. 3) II. 48 *Salix myrsinites*..*Whortle leaved Willow. **1841** *Penny Cycl.* XX. 360/2 *Salix vitellina*, the *yellow willow.

b. Extended, with qualification, to plants of other genera having some resemblance to the willow: see quots.

1548 TURNER *Names Herbes* (E.D.S.) 41 Halimus..may be called in englishe sea wyllowe or prickwylowe because it hath the leaues of a wylowe and prickes lyke a thorne. **1597** GERARDE *Herbal* III. lxviii. 1228 Gaule, sweete Willow, or Dutch Myrtle tree. **1760** J. LEE *Introd. Bot.* App. 331 Willow, Spiked, of Theophrastus, *Spiræa*. **1866** BROGDEN *Prov. Wds. Lincs., Roman Willow*, a garden plant, *Syringa cœruleo flore*. **1866** *Treas. Bot.*, Willow... Golden. A Madeira name for *Genista scoparia*...—, Primrose. A West Indian name for *Œnothera*. **1875** *Ibid.* Suppl., Willow, Australian. *Geijera parviflora*. —, Water, of the United

States. *Dianthera americana*. **1889** MAIDEN *Useful Plants Australia* 306 *Acacia calamifolia*, Willow, or Broom Wattle.

c. With qualification *bay*, *flowering*, *French*, *Persian*: the WILLOW-HERB, *Epilobium angustifolium*.

1633 JOHNSON *Gerarde's Herbal* II. cxxix. 479 *Chamænerium* is called of Gesner, *Epilobion*: in English, Bay Willow. **1741** *Compl. Fam.-Piece* II. iii. 386 French Willow. **1857** MISS PRATT *Flower. Pl.* II. 280 *E[pilobium] angustifolium* (Rose Bay, or Flowering Willow). **1866** *Treas. Bot.*, Willow.. Persian, *Epilobium angustifolium*.

II. †3. = WILLY *sb.*¹ 2. *Obs.*

1385–6 *City of London Rec., Pleas & Mem. Rolls* Roll 27 A m. 28 (MS.) Grant destruccion de pesson par engyns appeles Wilwes. **1495** *Trevisa's Barth. De P.R.* XVIII. i. (W. de W.) Y iij, For flesshe rostyd crabbes come in to wylowes [*Add. MS.* wyles] & pytches. *a* **1555** PHILPOT tr. *Curio's Def. Christ's Ch.* Wks. (Parker Soc. 1842) 385 Many unclean and damnable persons is contained in this church, which we behold as it were fishes of all sorts in a fisher's trunk or willo.

4. = WILLY *sb.*¹ 3.

1835 URE *Philos. Manuf.* 164 Blowing and lapping machines.. are universally employed for cleaning and opening cotton after it has passed through the willow. **1877–80** *Gt. Industr. Gt. Brit.* I. 229 The conical self-acting willow, invented by Mr. Lillie, of Manchester. **1891** MARSDEN *Cotton Spinning* (ed. 4) 85 The spikes on the cylinder and casing of the willow.

5. A cricket-bat (made of willow-wood). Similarly, the bat at baseball. Cf. *King Willow* s.v. KING *sb.* 6 b.

1846 J. MARTIN in *Frederick Lillywhite's Cricket Scores & Biographies* (1863) III. 442 And now the 'willow' see them wield. **1866** LE FANU *All in Dark* xxxiv, He handles the willow pretty well. **1869** *Routledge's Ev. Boy's Ann.* 639, I had my turn at the 'willow'. **1876** in Box *Engl. Game Cricket* (1877) 414 Willow the King is a monarch grand, Three in a row his courtiers stand.

III. 6. *attrib.* and *Comb.* **a.** Simple attrib., as ***willow band***, ***bark***, ***bed***, ***bottom***, ***bush***, ***dust***, ***gall*** (GALL *sb.*³), ***garth***, ***ground***, ***grove***, ***head***, ***hedge***, ***holt***, ***hoop***, ***island***, ***rind***, ***row***, ***shadow***, ***swamp***, ***top***, ***tribe***, ***twig***, ***walk***, ***wand***, ***withe***, ***wood***; made of willow-wood, as ***willow-cylinder***, ***polisher***. **b.** Instrumental, parasynthetic, objective, and similative, as ***willow-bordered***, ***-coloured***, ***-fringed***, ***-grown***, ***-leaved***, ***-like***, ***-lined***, ***-shaded***, ***-tufted***, ***-veiled*** adjs.; ***willow-peeler***. **c.** Special Combs.: **willow bay**, *Salix pentandra*; **willow-branch**, a branch of a willow-tree; also allusively as in 1 d; **willow curtain** (see quot.); **willow-earth**, compost made of rotten willow-branches; **†willow-flower** = WILLOW-HERB 2; **willow gentian**, a herbaceous perennial, *Gentiana asclepiadea*, native to Europe and bearing deep blue or white flowers in axils along its curving stems; **willow-green**, a variety of green resembling the colour of willow-leaves; **willow grouse**, (*a*) the common ptarmigan of North America, *Lagopus albus*; (*b*) the ruffed grouse, *Bonasa umbellus*, called thus chiefly in British Columbia; **willow-lark**, the sedge-warbler; **willow leaf**, a leaf of the willow-tree, or a figure resembling this; *pl.* the luminous filaments of the sun's surface; also as *adj.* = *willow-leaved* adj., sense 6 b; **willow-leaved pear(-tree)**, a tree, *Pyrus salicifolia*, that is related to the pear and is native to S.E. Europe and Asia Minor, bearing long narrow leaves and small fruit and often thorny; **willow myrtle**, a myrtaceous willow-leaved tree (*Agonis flexuosa*) of Western Australia; **willow-nightingale** *local*, the reed-sparrow; **willow oak**, a North American oak, *Quercus Phellos*, having narrow entire leaves like those of the willow; also, the laurel oak, *Q. laurifolia*; **willow partridge**, = *willow-grouse*; **willow pattern**, a pattern of domestic crockery in blue, orig. designed by Thomas Turner in the late 18th century, having willow-trees as a prominent feature; hence **willow-patterned** *a.*; **willow ptarmigan** = *willow-grouse*; **willow-sparrow** = *willow-warbler*; **willow sheets**, **squares**, pieces of plaited willow for hat-making; **willow-thorn**, sea-buckthorn, *Hippophaë rhamnoides*; **willow tit (mouse)**, a black-headed, buff-coloured European tit, *Parus montanus* (formerly *P. atricapillus*); **willow-warbler**, a small bird, *Sylvia trochilus*; **willow-ware**, (*a*) crockery-ware of a willow pattern; (*b*) articles woven from osiers; **willow weapon**, a cricket-bat; **willow weed** = WILLOW-HERB 2, 3; also, various species of *Polygonum*, knotweed; **willow-wielder**, a batsman at cricket; **willow-wort**, = WILLOW-HERB 1, 3; also pl., Lindley's name for the willow family; **willow-wren**, = *willow-warbler*. Also in several names of insects or their larvæ which infest willows, as **willow-beauty** (*Boarmia rhomboidaria*), **-bee** (*Megachile willughbeia*); **-beetle** (spec. *Phyllodecta vitellinæ*), **-butterfly**, **-caterpillar**, **-cimbex**, **†-cricket**, **-fly** (any insect of the family *Perlidæ*), **-moth** (*Caradrina quadripunctata*), **-sawfly**, **-slug** (larva of the sawfly), **-worm**.

1819 SHELLEY *Cyclops* 203 My young lambs coupled two by two With *willow bands. **1836** J. M. GULLY *Magendie's Formul.* (ed. 2) 193 *Willow-bark having been frequently employed against intermittent fevers. **1650** [W. HOWE] *Phytol. Brit.* 108 *Salix folio laureo*,.. *Willow-bay. **1832** RENNIE *Butterfl. & Moths* 111 The *Willow Beauty.. appears the beginning of July, in woody places and gardens. **1591** PERCIVALL *Sp. Dict.*, *Bimbrera*, a *willow bed. **1897** WATTS-DUNTON *Aylwin* VII. i, A winding, *willow-bordered river. **1807** P. GASS *Jrnl.* 51 Passed a *willow bottom on the south side, and a creek on the north. **1962** W. STEGNER *Wolf Willow* I. i. 12, I see a black iron bridge, new, that evidently leads some new road off into the willow bottoms. **1611** BEAUM. & FL. *Maid's Trag.* II. i. *Song*, Maidens, *Willow branches bear; say I died true. **1830** TENNYSON *Dying Swan* 37 The willow-branches hoar and dank. **1860** TROLLOPE *Framley P.* xxx, I have been overwhelmed with presents of willow branches. **1876** GEO. ELIOT *Dan. Der.* xvii, It was bordered by a line of *willow-bushes. **1773** B. WILKES *Engl. Moths* 58 The *Willow-Butterfly. *c* **1633** in *Verney Mem.* (1907) I. 68 The *willow colored satten suite. **1799** G. SMITH *Laboratory* II. 300 *Willow-cricket, or small peacock fly. **1884** KNIGHT *Dict. Mech.* Suppl., **Willow Curtain*,.. a device to curb the rapidity of streams and induce deposit of sediment. **1731** MILLER *Gard. Dict.* s.v. *Layers*, Mould, mix'd with a little rotten *Willow-dust. **1683** J. REID *Scots Gard'ner* (1907) 69 *Willow-earth or rotten willow-sticks at the bottom of the pot, helps to retain the moisture. **1799** G. SMITH *Laboratory* II. 143 A little willow-earth is very proper to mix with the above compost. **1633** JOHNSON *Gerarde's Herbal* II. cxxix. 477 *Chamænerion alterum angustifolium*. Narrow leaued *Willow-floure. **1787** BEST *Angling* (ed. 2) 119 The *Willow-Fly comes on about the beginning of September. **1749** WARTON *Tri. Isis* 6 O'er Isis' *willow-fringed banks I stray'd. **1870** KINGSLEY *At Last* xiii, Certain alder and willow-fringed reaches of the Thames. **1812** *Sporting Mag.* XXXIX. 231 Trotting on to the small *willow garth near Clifford [Yorkshire]. **1857** MISS PRATT *Flower. Pl.* V. 93 Osier-holts or Willow-garths, as such grounds are called in Yorkshire. **1883** W. ROBINSON *Eng. Flower Garden* 136/1 *Willow Gentian prefers a sheltered position. **1935** C. ELLIOTT *Rock Garden Plants* 123 The Willow Gentian of sub-alpine woods, grows two feet high, with arched wiry stems, strung along their upper half with fine blue trumpet-flowers. **1962** R. PAGE *Education of Gardener* xiii. 357, I may choose *Gentiana asclepiadea*, the willow gentian. **1672** W. HUGHES *Amer. Physitian* 28 A more blewish green colour, much like the colour called a *Willow-green. **1703** *Lond. Gaz.* No. 3906/4 A Piece Ditto, striped with Willow-green and small Orange or Philamot. **1832** T. BROWN *Bk. Butterfl. & M.* (1834) I. 172 Of a pale willow-green above. **1608** *Merry Devil Edmonton* III. ii, Heere in the walke neere to the *willow ground. **1849** D. J. BROWNE *Amer. Poultry Yd.* (1855) 311 The *willow grouse on the rock crows his challenge aloud. **1907** J. G. MILLAIS *Newfoundland* 274 The Newfoundland willow grouse.. fly in large bodies from one district to another. **1960** *Gulf Islander* (Galiano, B.C.) 23 July 1/1 We listened to the resonant call of the willow grouse. **1961** W. P. KELLER *Canada's Wild Glory* II. 93 The grouse came back, too. These were the willow grouse, or as the same bird is known in the east, 'the drummer' or ruffed grouse. **1552** HULOET, *Willow groue, *salicetum*. **1577** GOOGE *Heresbach's Husb.* I. 17 Meddowe, Wood Lande, and Wyllowe Groues. **1855** SINGLETON *Virgil, Georgics* II. 575 The wild willow-grove. **1871** MORRIS in Mackail *Life* (1899) I. 265 A sandy plain somewhat *willow-grown. **1798** *Act 38 Geo. III* c. v. §2 Any *Willow Heads, Loppings of Pollard or Doddard Trees. **1805** DICKSON *Pract. Agric.* I. Plate xxxi, A protection of *willow-hedge, raised by setting the stakes. **1832** *Boston, Linc.* etc. *Herald* 13 Nov. 4/3 Secreted in a *willow holt.. in Holland Fen. **1697** J. PUCKLE *New Dial.* 18 Nor do We in England (as you [the Dutch]) want *Willow Hoops from Hamburgh. **1814** BRACKENRIDGE *Jrnl.* in *Views Louisiana* 204 Having passed a small *willow island. **1769** G. WHITE *Selborne, To Pennant* 29 May, A new salicaria, which at first I suspected might have proved your *willow-lark. **1562** TURNER *Herbal* II. 43 b, Of Lysimachia.. The leues.. are thinne and in fasshon lyke *wylow leues. *c* **1711** PETIVER *Gazophyl.* Dec. vii. Tab. 63 This has plain Willow Leaves. **1818** A. EATON *Man. Bot.* (ed. 2) 447 Willow-leaf golden-rod. **1829** SHELLEY *Summer* 9 The willow leaves that glanced in the light breeze. **1860** NASMYTH in *Monthly Not. Royal Astron. Soc.* (1864) XXIV. 67 What I claim to be the first to discover.. in reference to the structure of his entire luminous surface, as well as the precise form of the structural details, which, from their general similitude in respect to form, I at once compared with willow-leaves. *Ibid.*, These luminous filaments or willow-leaf-shaped objects. **1975** *Country Life* 20 Mar. 699/3 Willow-leaf pears .. form charming leafy tapestries. **1731** MILLER *Gard. Dict.* s.v. *Adhatoda*, The *Willow-leav'd Malabar Nut. **1789** W. AITON *Hortus Kewensis* II. 176 Willow leav'd Crab Tree. Nat[ive] of the Levant. **1820** *Bot. Reg.* VI. 514 (*heading*) Willow-leaved pear-tree. **1864** LOCKYER in *Reader* 16 Jan. 79/2 Mr. Nasmyth's discovery of the willow-leaved things .. covering like so many scales the whole surface of the sun. **1914** W. J. BEAN *Trees & Shrubs Hardy in Brit. Isles* II. 292 Willow-leaved Pear... Branchlets covered with down which is quite white when young. **1980** V. CANNING *Fall from Grace* ix. 155 A carpet of silvery *Cineraria maritima* spread under a group of willow-leaved pears. **1712** PETIVER in *Phil. Trans.* XXVII. 422 Its Leaves below are long *Willow-like. **1897** MARY KINGSLEY *W. Africa* 186 A long-branched willow-like shrub. **1946** J. W. DAY *Harvest Adventure* x. 159 Half-way between Yarmouth and Acle on that dead straight, *willow-lined road. **1845** G. E. DAY tr. *Simon's Anim. Chem.* I. 101 The caterpillar of the *willow-moth. **1898** MORRIS *Austral Engl.*, **Willow Myrtle*,.. with willow-like leaves and pendent branches. **1773** *Phil. Trans.* LXIII. 281 *note*, In the neighbourhood of Shrewsbury, the [reedsparrow] hath obtained the name of the *willow-nightingale. **1717** *Petiveriana* III. 208 *Willow Oak. From the Likeness of its Leaf. **1813** Willow oak [see *grey oak* s.v. GREY *a.* 8]. **1897** [see *peach oak* s.v. PEACH *sb.*¹ 6]. **1949** *Amer. Forests* Sept. 18/3 A tall willow oak drips slender verdant fingers. **1975** *Country Life* 2 Jan. 38/3 More native trees were also planted, notably.. the willow oak. **1772** FORSTER in *Phil. Trans.* LXII. 390 *Willow-partridges. **1829** S. SHAW *Staffordsh. Potteries* ix. 214 The Pattern Mr. Turner used was the *willow, designed by him from two oriental Plates, still preserved. **1848** NEWMAN *Loss & Gain* I. x. 68, I myself found half a willow-pattern saucer in the crater of Vesuvius. **1878** LONGF. *Kéramos* 326 The willow pattern, that we knew In childhood, with its bridge of blue Leading to unknown thoroughfares. **1857** MISS YONGE *Dynevor Terr.* ii, The homely black tea-pot and *willow-patterned plates. **1875** KNIGHT *Dict. Mech.*, **Willow-peeler*, a device or a machine for stripping the bark from the willow wands. **1884** F. J. BRITTEN *Watch & Clockm.* 214 Plates for carriage and other small clocks.. are polished with a *willow polisher. **1872** COUES *Key N. Amer. Birds* 235 *Lagopus albus*. *Willow Ptarmigan. *c* **1500** *World & Child* (1522) A iij, I can wystell you a fytte Syres in a *whylowe ryne. **1806** GRAHAME *Birds Scot.* 5 He sits And warps the skep with willow rind. **1586** W. WEBBE *Engl. Poetrie* (Arb.) 75 Greene *willow rowes which Hiblæ bees doo reioice in. **1845** *Florist Jrnl.* 193 Over the margin of the *willow-shaded pond. **1827** CLARE *Sheph. Cal.* 56 To wash-pools, where the *willow shadows lean. **1819** *P.O. Lond. Direct.* 364 Patentee.. of Beaver, Silk and Willow Hats, and *Willow-squares. **1834** *1st Rep. Poor Law Comm.* (1885) 199, I formerly carried on the business of a willow-square maker. **1901** SEEBOHM *Birds of Siberia* xiv. 125 This never-ending, almost impenetrable *willow-swamp. **1857** MISS PRATT *Flower. Pl.* V. 49 Sea Buckthorn, Sallow-thorn, or *Willow-thorn. **1907** *Brit. Birds* I. 44 The *Willow Tit varies a good deal geographically. **1979** C. M. PERRINS *Brit. Tits* vii. 60 The Willow Tit was the last British species to be recognized. **1958** *Spectator* 22 Aug. 244/1, I discovered a rare bird, then almost unknown,.. at Beckenham—a *willow titmouse. **1693** CONGREVE in *Dryden's Juvenal* xi. (1697) 285 No bitter *Willow-tops have been its Food. **1805** DICKSON *Pract. Agric.* I. 119 The farmer may have recourse to plants of the *willow tribe for the forming of his hedges. **1764** GOLDSM. *Trav.* 294 The *willow-tufted bank. **1653** WALTON *Angler* ii. 62 Oh it is a great logger-headed Chub: Come, hang him upon that *Willow twig. **1819** SCOTT *Ivanhoe* xxxi, It shore asunder, as it had been a willow twig, the tough and plaited handle of the mace. **1833** TENNYSON *Lady of Shalott* I. iii, By the margin, *willow-veil'd. **1803** J. PALMER *World as it Goes* II. 14 The carriage entered a *willow-walk, terminated by a small antique building. **1816** SCOTT *Old Mort.* xxxviii, When you want me for breakfast, I will be found in the willow-walk by the river. *a* **1585** MONTGOMERIE *Flyting* 82 With a *willie wand thy skin was well scourged. *c* **1650** *Robin Hood & Q. Kath.* xxii. in Child *Ballads* v. 201 I'le cleave the willow wand. **1715** RAMSAY *Christ's Kirk Gr.* II. v, Clever houghs like willi-wands. **1748** THOMSON *Cast. Indol.* I. xxiii, As lithe they grow as any willow wand. **1810** SCOTT *Lady of L.* v. ix, The rushes and the willow-wand Are bristling into axe and brand. **1954** J. R. R. TOLKIEN *Fellowship of Ring* iii. 80, I shall be as thin as a willow-wand. **1846** JENYNS *Nat. Hist.* 133 We found to-day the nest of a *willow-warbler. **1882** *Proc. Berw. Nat. Club* IX. No. 3. 429 The willow-warbler (*Sylvia trochilus*). **1851** C. CIST *Cincinnati* 172 Baskets, cradles, wagons and other *willow-ware. **1880** *Harper's Mag.* June 30/1 We find women employed in making.. willow-ware and cane chairs. *c* **1885** R. COLLYER in J. H. Holmes *Life & Lett.* (1917) I. ii. 24 A great rack for the pewter dishes and willow ware. **1850** 'BAT' *Crick. Man.* 45 The way to use the *willow weapon. **1741** *Compl. Fam.-Piece* II. iii. 379 *Willow Weed or French Willow. **1855** TENNYSON *Brook* 46 And many a fairy foreland set With willow-weed and mallow. **1866** *Treas. Bot.*, Willow-weed, *Lythrum Salicaria*; also *Polygonum lapathifolium*. **1903** *Times* 13 July 11/6 Wily *willow-wielders. **1870** MORRIS *Earthly Par.* II. III. 292 The goodman.. from a corner nigh Took up some *willow-withes. **1799** G. SMITH *Laboratory* I. 4 The charcoal of *willow-wood is preferred, by many, for the manufacture of gunpowder. **1845** G. DODD *Brit. Manuf.* IV. 61 Wheels.. made of.. willow-wood. **1896** LODEMAN *Spray. Plants* 373 *Willow-worm; Antiopa Butterfly (*Vanessa Antiopa*). **1591** SYLVESTER *Du Bartas* I. iii. 753 As Betonie breakes friendship's ancient bands, So *Willo-wort makes wonted hate shake hands. **1698** FRYER *Acc. E. India & P.* 307 In an Hollow made by the falling of the Water in the Rains, grows Willow-wort. **1731** MILLER *Gard. Dict.* s.v. *Salicaria*, Willow-wort or spiked Lose-strife. **1846** LINDLEY *Veg. Kingd.* 254 *Salicaceæ*. Willow-worts. **1805** SCOTT *Last Minstr.* II. xi, And changed the *willow-wreaths to stone. **1768** PENNANT *Brit. Zool.* II. 266 The *willow-wren frequents large moist woods. **1882** *Proc. Berw. Nat. Club* IX. No. 3. 556 Aug. 16th, Willow-wrens had deserted the furze bushes and hedges. **1870** *John Wisden's Cricketers' Almanack* 91 With *willow wielders like these, it is no wonder Notts holds the high position it does as a batting shire.

d. In uses containing an allusion to the willow as a symbol of mourning or of being lovelorn.

1585 in Chappell *Old Engl. Pop. Mus.* (1893) 110, I wylbe the turtle most stedfast [still] to the: & paciently were this grene wyllow garland. **1593** SHAKS. *3 Hen. VI*, III. iii. 228 Tell him, in hope hee'l proue a widower shortly, I weare the Willow Garland for his sake. **1632** LITHGOW *Trav.* III. 112 Still for to weare the Willow wreath. **1638** FORD *Fancies* III. iii, A knot of Willow Ribbands. **1648** HERRICK *Hesper.*, *To Willow-tree* 7 When once the Lovers Rose is dead,.. Then Willow-garlands, 'bout the head, Bedew'd with teares, are worne. **1825** T. HOOK *Sayings* Ser. II. *Sutherl.* 36 This willow-wearing fair one. **1833** —— *Parson's Dau.* I. xii, The .. willow-wearers at Ullsford.

e. quasi-*adj.* = WILLOWY *a.* 2. See also quot. *a* 1700.

1634 S. R. *Noble Soldier* IV. i. F i b, I yeelded With willow-bendings to commanding breaths. *a* **1700** B. E. *Dict. Cant. Crew*, *Willow*, Poor, and of no Reputation. **1875** MISS BRADDON *Strange World* ii, Tall, slim, and willow-waisted.

f. Short for *willow pattern* (sense 6 c above), as ***willow cup***, ***plate***, ***pottery***. See also *willow ware* (*a*).

1926 R. MACAULAY *Crewe Train* II. x. 179 It would look jolly with blue willow cups and plates on it. **1928** T. S. ELIOT in E. Pound *Sel. Poems* p. xvii, People who like Willow pottery and Chinesische-Turms in Munich and Kew. **1961** M. BEADLE *These Ruins are Inhabited* (1963) xi. 142 In contrast, the laburnums.. curved earthward with willow-plate grace.

willow, *v.* [f. WILLOW *sb.* 4.] *trans.* To put (cotton, etc.) through a willow.
1835 URE *Philos. Manuf.* 330 It must be willowed..in an appropriate manner, by machines differing in structure and adjustment for different qualities of goods.

willowed ('wɪləʊd), *a.* [f. WILLOW *sb.* + -ED[2].] Bordered or grown with willows.
1745 WARTON *Ode to Morning* 14 The willow'd marge of murmuring brook. **1747** COLLINS *Ode to Liberty* 56 Willow'd Meads. **1805** SCOTT *Last Minstr.* IV. i, No longer steel-clad warriors ride Along thy wild and willow'd shore. **1891** E. R. PENNELL *Stream Pleas.* 44 All the elm-lined roads and willowed backwaters lead to pretty villages.

willowed ('wɪləʊd), *ppl. a.* [f. WILLOW *v.* + -ED[1].] Separated by means of a willow.
1880 J. DUNBAR *Pract. Papermaker* 26 Fine stuff, such as willowed rope.

willower ('wɪləʊə(r)). [f. WILLOW *sb.* 4 or *v.* + -ER[1].] One who tends a willow.
1881 *Instr. Census Clerks* (1885) 65 Woollen Cloth Manufacture... Willower, Willyer, or Woolleyer. *Ibid.* 82 Paper Making... Willower (Paper Mill).

'willow-herb. [So named from the resemblance of the leaves to the willow's. Cf. the earlier *herb willow* (HERB *sb.* 7 b).
All the plants so named were formerly included under the name *Lysimachia*.]
1. Yellow loosestrife, *Lysimachia vulgaris*.
1578 LYTE *Dodoens* I. li. 74 The first [Lysimachion] which we may call Golden or yellow Lysimachus, Willow herbe, and Louse strife. **1597** GERARDE *Herbal* II. cxxii. 386 *Lysimachia lutea*. Yellow Willow herbe. **1755** B. STILLINGFL. *Cal. Flora* 2 Sept. **1857** MISS PRATT *Flower. Pl.* IV. 236 (Great Yellow Loosestrife)..is sometimes called Yellow Willow-herb.
2. Any plant of the extensive genus *Epilobium*, esp. *E. angustifolium* and *hirsutum*.
1578 LYTE *Dodoens* I. li. 73 *Lysimachium purpureum primum*. The first purple red, willow herbe. **1597** GERARDE *Herbal* II. cxxii. 386 *Lysimachia siliquosa*. Codded Willow herbe... *Chamænerion*. Rose bay Willow herbe. **1697** LHWYD in *Phil. Trans.* XXVII. 50 The Common French Willow-Herb. **1785** MARTYN *Lett. Bot.* xix. (1794) 257 Our European Willow Herbs. **1802** COLERIDGE *Picture* 89 Lychnis, and willow-herb, and fox-glove bells. **1861** S. THOMSON *Wild Fl.* III. (ed. 4) 224 The willow-herb, or *Epilobium* genus. **1899** CROCKETT *Kit Kennedy* xxxvii, A little ten-yard square island all overgrown with red purple willow herb.
3. *spiked* or *purple-spiked willow-herb*: purple loosestrife, *Lythrum Salicaria*.
1578 LYTE *Dodoens* I. li. 75 Poynted willow Herbe with the purple floure. **1597** GERARDE *Herbal* II. cxxii. 386 *Lysimachia purpurea spicata*. Spiked Willow herbe. **1755** B. STILLINGFL. *Cal. Flora* 1 July.
4. In full *hooded willow-herb*: *Scutellaria galericulata* or *S. minor*.
1597 GERARDE *Herbal* II. cxxii. 387 *Lysimachia galericulata*, or hoodded Willowe herbe. **1777** LIGHTFOOT *Flora Scotica* I. 320 *Scutellaria minor*... Little red Scull cap, or Willow-herb. **1785** MARTYN *Lett. Bot.* iv. (1794) 46 Some plants only having little or no smell as..hooded willow herb. **1866** in *Treas. Bot.*

willowing ('wɪləʊɪŋ), *vbl. sb.* [f. WILLOW *sb.* 4 or *v.* + -ING[1].] = WILLYING (after WILLY *sb.*[1]).
1851 L. D. B. GORDON in *Art Jrnl. Illustr. Catal.* p. iv**/1 A scutching machine, so arranged that the preliminary process of willowing is performed within it. **1875** KNIGHT *Dict. Mech.*, *Willowing-machine*... 2. (Cotton.).. Called also *twilly, shake-willy, willow, willy, willey, devil, opening-machine*. **1879** *Cassell's Techn. Educ.* IV. 339/2 The willowing or willying process, which opens and disentangles the locks of wool. **1891** R. MARSDEN *Cotton Spinning* (ed. 4) 82.

willowish ('wɪləʊɪʃ), *a.* [f. WILLOW *sb.* + -ISH[1].]
1. Somewhat resembling that of a willow, esp. in reference to the colour of willow-leaves.
1653 WALTON *Angler* v. 105 First for a May-fly: you may make his body with greenish-coloured crewel, or willowish colour. **1656** BEALE *Heref. Orchards* (1657) 19 A fady willowish broad leaf. **1676** J. SMITH *Art of Painting* ii. 21 It's Willowish colour must be corrected with Yellows.
2. Like a willow; *fig.* of a pliant character. *rare.*
1919 SAINTSBURY *Hist. Fr. Novel* II. 12 *note*, It is intended to bring before the reader's mind the utterly *willowish* character of Oswald, Lord Nelvil.

willow-tree. = WILLOW *sb.* 1; cf. also 1 d, 6 d.
c **1425** *Voc.* in Wr.-Wülcker 646/33 *Hec silex*, wyllotre. **1495** *Trevisa's Barth. De P.R.* XVII. cxliii. (W. de W.) T iiij/2 A wylowe tree..hath noo fruyte but oonly sede or floure. **1535** COVERDALE *Ps.* cxxxvi[i]. 2 As for oure harpes, we hanged them vp vpon the trees [fo. dlxxxij Vpon the trees, *rede*, Vpon the wyllye trees]. **1548** TURNER *Names Herbes* (E.D.S.) 70 *Particalis salix* is the greate Wylowe tree whyche hath longe roddes..growynge in it. **1563** GOOGE *Eglogs* vi. (Arb.) 51 This mournynge looke, this Vesture sad, this wrethe of Wyllow tree. **1599** SHAKS. *Much Ado* II. i. 225. **16..** R. BARNSLEY in *Wit Restor'd* (1658) 35 That I may goe free From the sad branches of the willowe tree. **1610** R. JONES *Muses Gard.* xii. (1901) 18 For once thou wert where thou wouldst be Though now thou wear'st the willow-tree. **1641** BEST *Farm. Bks.* (Surtees) 41 A wilfe tree that groweth in the hedge of the Bramble hill bottomes. **1860** PIESSE *Lab. Chem. Wonders* 3 Willow-trees are allowed to grow here and there.

willowy ('wɪləʊɪ), *a.* [f. WILLOW *sb.* + -Y[1].]
1. Bordered, shaded, or clad with willows.
1766 [ANSTEY] *Bath Guide* 121 Where the languid old Cam rolls his willowy flood. **1769** GRAY *Install. Ode* 29 Where willowy Camus lingers with delight. **1816** SHELLEY *Lett.* Pr. Wks. 1888 I. 339 The willowy plain of the Rhone. **1833** TENNYSON *Lady of Shalott* IV. iii, The willowy hills and fields among. **1840** LOUISA S. COSTELLO *Summer amgst. Bocages* II. 97 We had been sitting on a willowy ait, such as our own beautiful Thames presents.
2. Resembling a willow in its flexible or drooping gracefulness.
1791 WOLCOT (P. Pindar) *Rights of Kings* IV. ii. Wks. 1816 II. 188 Unceasing bends the willowy neck to ground. *a* **1835** MRS. HEMANS *Shepherd-Poet of the Alps* 165 A fragile form, With a willowy droop. **1864** G. A. LAWRENCE *Maurice Dering* II. 32 He, who always raved about willowy waists. **1883** HOWELLS *Register* ii, Slender, willowy party, with a lot of blonde hair.
3. Suggesting the sound of willows agitated by the wind.
1895 MEREDITH *Amazing Marr.* ix, The willowy swish of silken dresses.
4. *Comb.*
1890 'R. BOLDREWOOD' *Miner's Right* xliv, Certain delicate-featured willowy-figured Sydney demoiselles.
Hence **'willowily** *adv.*; **'willowiness.**
1932 A. HUXLEY *Brave New World* xi. 192 He put his arm round the Head Mistress's waist. It yielded, willowily. **1972** *Daily Tel.* 13 Mar. 11 Virile shoulders, tapering downward to a more traditional willowiness, are the hallmark of the 1972 Cardin man.

will-pit: see WEEL[1].

'will-,worship. [f. WILL *sb.*[1] + WORSHIP *sb.*, rendering Gr. ἐθελοθρησκεία (Col. ii. 23).] Worship according to one's own will or fancy, or imposed by human will, without divine authority.
1549 CHEKE *Hurt Sedit.* (1641) 59 Seeing..true worship taught, and wil-worship refused. **1565** CALFHILL *Answ. Martiall* To Rdr. 6 b, A wilworship, a naughty seruice, hauing no ground of the worde of God. **1611** *Bible* Col. ii. 23 Which things haue in deed a shew of wisedome in will-worship [Vulg. *superstitione*; TINDALE chosen holynes, COVERDALE chosen spiritualtie, *Geneva* volontarie worshipping]. *a* **1629** HINDE *J. Bruen* xxx. (1641) 93 That such service unto Saints, is but witt-worship, will-worship, and Idol-service. **1641** SANDERSON *Serm., Matt. xv.* 9 (1681) II. 4 Those Pharisees..intending by those superstitious Will-worships to honour God. **1730** BERKELEY *Serm.* Wks. 1871 IV. 641 Not lip-worship, nor will-worship, but inward and evangelical. **1827** G. S. FABER *Sacr. Cal. Prophecy* (1844) II. 106 A declension from evangelical soundness to unwarrantable superstition and will-worship. **1846** TRENCH *Mirac.* Introd. (1862) 5 The will-worship of Jeroboam.
So **will-worshipper**, one who practises will-worship; † **will-worshipping**, will-worship.
1571 GOLDING *Calvin on Ps.* ix. 12. 28 The wil woorshippinges which superstitious persones have forged too themselves of theyr owne heades. **1660** JER. TAYLOR *Ductor Dubit.* II. iii. rule 13. §9 He that sayes God is rightly worshipped by an act or ceremony concerning which himself hath no way express'd his pleasure, is superstitious, or a will-worshipper.

willy, willey ('wɪlɪ), *sb.*[1] Forms: 1 wiliȝe, wyliȝe, -ie, 7, 9 weely, 8–9 willey, 9 willy. [OE. *wiliȝe*: see WILLOW *sb.* Cf. *wyle, wile*, WEEL[2].]
1. A basket: see quots. *dial.*
c **1000** ÆLFRIC *Gram.* ix. (Z.) 55 *Corbis*, wyliȝe oððe windel. *c* **1000** *Ags. Gosp.* Mark vi. 43 Hi namon þara hlafa & fixa lafe twelf wilian fulle. *a* **1100** *Voc.* in Wr.-Wülcker 336/7 *Corbis uel cofinus*, wyliȝe oððe meoxbearwe. [**1256**, etc.: see WEEL[2]. **1398** TREVISA *Barth. De P.R.* XVII. cxxvi. (Add. MS. 27944), Of russhes beþ ymade panyers: Wiles, cupes and casis.] **1825** JENNINGS *Obs. Dial. W. Eng.*, *Willy*, a term applied to baskets of various sizes, but generally to those holding about a bushel..: sometimes called also *willy-basket*. **1886** *W. Som. Word-bk.*, *Willy*, a large basket—of a shape deep rather than flat... A willy has two small handles at the upper edge, one opposite the other.
2. A fish-trap. *local.*
[**1398** TREVISA *Barth. De P.R.* XVIII. i. (Add. MS. 27944), For fleissh yrosted crabbes comeþ in to wyles and pyches.] **1602** CAREW *Cornwall* I. 28 The Trowte..are mostly taken with a hooke-net, made like the Easterne Weelyes, which is placed in the stickellest part of the stream..and kept abroad with certaine hoopes. **1813** VANCOUVER *Agric. Devon* 320 Below the lower flood-hatch, a trap (or *willey*, as in this neighbourhood it is called) is made for the catching of smaller fish. **1880** *W. Cornw. Gloss.*, *Weelys*, wicker pots or traps for catching crabs.
3. A revolving machine of a conical or cylindrical shape armed internally with spikes for opening and cleaning wool, cotton, flax. Called also *twilly*.
[**1780**: see WILLY *v.* quot. 1864]. **1835** URE *Philos. Manuf.* 160 The wool-mill or willy (called willow, in the cotton manufacture..) is the first machine to which clothing-wool is subjected. **1870** *Engl. Mech.* 31 Dec. 610/1 The machine ..is called a willow, or willey, vulgarly a devil; it is used principally for opening raw cotton. **1894** C. VICKERMAN *Woollen Spinning* 122 A 'Fearnought' or tenter-hook willey.
Hence **'will(e)y** *v.*, to treat with the willy or willowing-machine; **'will(e)yer**, one who tends a willy; **'will(e)ying** *vbl. sb.* (also *attrib.*).
1835 URE *Philos. Manuf.* 204 Wool-sorters, pickers, willyers (winnowers). **1844** G. DODD *Textile Manuf.* iii. 98 Some kinds of wool require willying more than once. **1864** A. JEFFREY *Hist. Roxb.* IV. 115 In 1780, when a small hand 'willy', for oiling and teazing the wool, was put up in the garret of John Roberts. It was a joint stock adventure, and willied for the whole town. **1871** *Daily News* 18 Aug., Cloth finishers, dressers, fettlers, and willeyers. *Ibid.*, The cotton willeying-room. **1884** W. S. B. MᶜLAREN *Spinning* (ed. 2) 185 The wool must be freed from all dirt, etc., by willeying and thorough washing, it must then be oiled and again willeyed to spread the oil over all the fibres. **1907** CLAPHAM *Woollen & Worsted Ind.* 188 The willeying machine must also have an efficient exhaust draft.

willy, willie ('wɪlɪ), *sb.*[2] [Pet-form of the name WILLIAM.] 1. Applied locally to various animals; e.g. the guillemot, = WILLOCK; also *attrib.*, as in **willy-goat**, a he-goat (= BILLY-GOAT); **willy-wagtail**, (*a*) the water wagtail; (*b*) in Australia, = WAGTAIL *sb.* 2 b. (See also WILL-O'-THE-WISP 1 e.)
1849 *Zoologist* VII. 2393 The common guillemot is a 'willy'. **1883** *Sunday Mag.* Aug. 528/1 Some birds flying.. over the vessel..called willies.
1852 W. WICKENDEN *Hunchback's Chest* 82 You might have broken the leg of the *willy-goat. **1824** MACTAGGART *Gallovid. Encycl.*, *Wullie-Wagtail. **1885** MRS. C. PRAED *Head Station* (new ed.) 156 A brisk little willy-wagtail hopping about on the gravel.
2. *slang.* An infantile name for the penis. Also *Comb.*, as *willy-warmer*.
1905 *Eng. Dial. Dict.* Suppl. 178/2 *Willy*, the male organ; a slang name for a child's penis. Cum., Wm. **1972** *Listener* 22 June 841/3 The gallant soldier-boys are afflicted with 'syph, darling' ('their willies rot away'). **1975** *Observer* 7 Dec. 27/3 Joky gifts are speechlessly embarrassing; this season's dud is a woolly willy-warmer. **1977** J. WILSON *Making Hate* ix. 113 A younger male [baboon]..fingered its crimson penis... 'It's playing with its *willie*!' Nicky squealed. **1985** P. ANGADI *Governess* x. 93 We used to hold each other's willies... We didn't know about sex then.

willy ('wɪlɪ), *sb.*[3] [Prob. related to WILLIWAW: cf. WILLY-WILLY.] In the South Atlantic (Tristan da Cunha): (see quots.).
1832 A. EARLE *Narr. Residence N.Z.* (1966) 204 These sudden squalls are called '*Willies*', at least, such is the name given them by the sailors who frequent the island [*sc.* Tristan da Cunha]. **1941** A. B. CRAWFORD *I went to Tristan* xi. 158 A shower is a 'light squall' and 'willies' are eddies of spray above the surface of the sea caused by small whirlwinds. *Ibid.* 268 *Willie*, whirlwind of spray over the sea.

† **'willy**, *a. Obs.* Forms: 4–5 willi, wylly, (5 wille, wyle, wyly, 6 wylle), 4– willy. [f. WILL *sb.*[1] + -Y[1], prob. after ON. *viljugr* (MSw. *viliogher*, Sw., Da. *villig*), corresp. to OS., (M)Du. *willig*, OHG. *willîg* (MHG. *willec*, G. *willig*). But an OE. **willic* may have existed; cf. next.]
1. Willing, eager.
a **1300** *Cursor M.* 23073 Þai..willi war to do, and gladd, Þat men of hali kirc þam badd. *Ibid.* 26351 Propre, stedfast, Ernexst, willi, buxum, sothfast. **13..** *Gosp. Nicod.* (G.) 161 Þe men þat wight and willy ware said: 'to þi steuin we stand'. *c* **1440** *Destr. Troy* 1775 Wisest of wordes and wille þerto. *c* **1449** PECOCK *Repr.* v. iii. 496 Forto make hem the redier and the willier forto counceyle with leerned men. **1489** CAXTON *Faytes of A.* I. vi. A vij b, A prynce ought not be byleued that therin shold be ouer wylly & courageous.
2. Well-disposed, benevolent.
With first quot. cf. Chaucer's 'welwilli planet' (*Troylus* III. 1208).
c **1403** LYDG. *Temple of Glas* 1348 Willi planet, O Esperus so briȝt, þat woful hertes can appese. **1449** *Paston Lett.* I. 88, I fonde her never so wylly to noon as sche is to hym. **1483** *Cath. Angl.* 418/2 Willy, *beneuolus*.
3. ? Of the will.
c **1400** tr. *Secr. Secr., Gov. Lordsh.* 96 And þanne fallys to hym a reale willy [orig. *uoluntaria*] vertu.
b. in parasynthetic compounds, EVIL-WILLY, GOODWILLY, ILL-WILLY, WELL-WILLY.
Hence † **'willily** *adv.*, voluntarily, willingly.
a **1300** *Cursor M.* 26942 Willili lok þat þou be scriuen, Noght wit strength þar-to be driuen. *c* **1400** *Abbey Holy Ghost* in *Hampole's Wks.* (Horstman) I. 334 Make þame arely to ryse and go þe wyllylyere to þaire seruysse.

† **willy**, *adv. Obs.* Forms: 1 willice, 2–3 willeliche, 4 williche. [Late OE. *willíce* = OHG. *willíco* (MHG. *williche*): see WILL *sb.*[1], -LY[2]. With the quadrisyllabic forms cf. ON. *viljanliga*.] Willingly, voluntarily.
c **1000** in *Anglia* XIII. 375/138 Ofre ȝehwylce ða wyllice we onfengon. *c* **1175** *Lamb. Hom.* 41 Ȝef ȝe lusten wuleð, and ȝe willeliche hit understonden. *a* **1225** *Ancr. R.* 338 Schrift ouh to beon willes, þet is willeliche iureined and nout idrawen of þe. *Ibid.* 396 Auh ure Louerd willeliche totweamde his soule urom his bodie vorto ueien ure boðe togederes. *a* **1300** in Horstmann *Altengl. Leg.* (1875) 8 Þo dronk Marie al hire fulle Swiþe williche of þat welle.

willy, dial. f. WILLOW; obs. form of WILY.

willya ('wɪljə). Repr. colloq. pronunc. of 'will you..?', esp. as a tag after an imperative.
1941 B. SCHULBERG *What makes Sammy Run?* ix. 241 Willya find out who rang for a messenger boy? **1956** 'E. MCBAIN' *Cop Hater* (1958) iv. 38 Hey, shut up, will-ya? **1968** C. BURKE *Elephant across Border* i. 28 Now go away, willya? **1981** G. MCDONALD *Fletch & Widow Bradley* viii. 28 Write a new story... Only get the competition to print it this time, willya, Fletch?

willyamite (wɪlɪ'ɑːmaɪt). *Min.* [See quot. 1893 and -ITE[1].] A sulphide and antimonide of cobalt and nickel, (Co,Ni)SbS, in which Co exceeds Ni, found as white or grey pseudo-cubic crystals having a metallic lustre.
1893 E. F. PITTMAN in *Jrnl. & Proc. R. Soc. New S. Wales* XXVII. 366, I propose to name the mineral Willyamite (pronounced Willy-ah'-mite) after Willyama the official name of the Broken Hill township, and the aboriginal word meaning a hill with a broken contour. **1976** *Norsk. Geol. Tidsskr.* LVI. 449 Ullmannite, cobaltian ullmannite and

willyamite occur as blebs and laths in galena from Espeland mine, Aust-Agder, Norway.

'willyart, *a. Sc.* and *n. dial.* Also 6 **wilȝart**, 8 **wylart**, 9 **willyard**, **williard**, **willward**. [Obscurely f. WILL *a.*²; associated later with WILL *sb.*¹]

1. Wild; shy.

1590 BUREL in Watson *Coll. Sc. Poems* II. (1709) 19 Quhiles wandring, quhiles dandring, Like royd and wilzart rais. **1786** BURNS *On Dining with Lord Daer* iv, But O for Hogarth's magic pow'r To show Sir Bardy's willyart glowr!

2. Self-willed, obstinate.

1791 LEARMONT *Poems* 26 Had ye Byng'd some wylart bairns, It wad hae gien the laive mair harns. **1818** SCOTT *Hrt. Midl.* xiii, Uh! uh! it's a hard-set willyard beast this o' mine. **1876** *Whitby Gloss.*, *Willward*, self-willed. **1880** *Antrim & Down Gloss.*, *Williard*, obstinate; self-willed.

willy-coat, var. WYLIECOAT *Sc.*

willy-nilly ('wɪlɪ 'nɪlɪ), *adv.* and *a.* Also 7 **wille nille**, 8 **willi nilhi**. [= *will I*, *nill I* (*he*, *ye*) 'be I (he, ye) willing, be I (he, ye) unwilling': see WILL *v.*¹ VI, NILL *v.*]

A. *adv.* Whether it be with or against the will of the person or persons concerned; whether one likes it or not; willingly or unwillingly, *nolens volens*.

1608 MIDDLETON *Trick to catch Old One* I. ii, Thou shalt trust me spite of thy teeth, furnish me with some money wille nille. **1797** MRS. BERKELEY *Poems of G. M. Berkeley* Pref. p. ccxxix, But her Ladyship would, *willi nilhi*, constantly join the one who drank the waters every morning, and converse with her. **1807** W. IRVING *Salmag.* ix. (1824) 145 He was sure, willy nilly, to be drenched with a deluge of decoctions. **1818** J. BROWN *Psyche* 121 From whence it follows, will y' nill y', The thought of your's is mighty silly. **1884** A. GRIFFITHS *Chron. Newgate* II. vii. 306 He.. conceived an idea of carrying her off and marrying her willy nilly at Gretna Green. **1898** L. STEPHEN *Stud. Biogr.* II. vii. 272 You are engaged in the game willy-nilly, and cannot be a mere looker-on.

B. *adj.* **1.** That is such, or that takes place, whether one will or no.

1877 TENNYSON *Harold* v. i, And someone saw thy willy-nilly nun Vying a tress against our golden fern. **1880** *Cornhill Mag.* Feb. 182 All willy-nilly spinsters went to the canine race to be consoled. **1882** TENNYSON *Promise of May* II. 119 If man be only A willy-nilly current of sensations.

¶ **2.** *erron.* Undecided, shilly-shally.

1883 GALTON *Hum. Faculty* 57 The willy-nilly disposition of the female in matters of love is as apparent in the butterfly as in the man. **1898** BESANT *Orange Girl* II. vi, Let us have no more shilly shally, willy nilly talk.

willy wet-leg: see *wet-leg* s.v. WET *a.* 21.

willy-willy ('wɪlɪ,wɪlɪ). Also **willi-willi**. [Native name.] In north-west Australia, a cyclonic storm or tornado. Also *attrib.*

1894 *Age* (Melbourne) 20 Jan. 13/4 A.. report of a 'Willy Willy' in the north-west portion of West Australia. **1902** *Blackw. Mag.* May 664/2 The pools formed by the willy-willy shower had evaporated.

Wilms (vɪlmz). *Path.* [The name of M. *Wilms* (1867–1918), German pathologist.] ***Wilms('s)*** or (erron.) ***Wilm's tumour***: a malignant tumour of the kidney that occurs in infants and children.

1910 E. L. KEYES *Dis. Genito-Urinary Organs* 974/2 (Index), Wilms tumor of kidney. **1928** EISENDRATH & ROLNICK *Text-bk. Urol.* xlviii. 753 These tumors in their pure state have been termed mixed cell or Wilms tumors and are composed of.. muscle fibres, blood vessels, cartilage, [etc.]. **1948** R. A. WILLIS *Path. of Tumours* lx. 925 Many names have been applied to the embryonic renal tumours—'adenosarcoma',.. 'Wilms's tumour'.. and 'nephroblastoma'... It is now clear that there is but one entity, embryonic renal tumour. **1961** R. D. BAKER *Essent. Path.* xiii. 307 Embryonal and mixed tumors are most frequently mixed salivary gland tumors, Wilm's tumor of the kidney, and testicular and teratomatous tumors. **1971** *Brit. Med. Bull.* XXVII. 68/1 Retino-blastomata and Wilms' tumours were found to have shorter latent periods. **1980** *Jrnl. R. Soc. Arts* Jan. 99/1 In rhabdomyosarcoma, Ewing's sarcoma and Wilm's tumour considerably increased survival has been obtained.

† **wilne**, *sb. Obs. rare.* [f. next.] Desire.

c **1400** *Destr. Troy* 13768 All the pure Troiens.. Were deliuert yche lede, & lause at hor willne.

† **wilne**, *v. Obs.* Also 3 **welne**, 4–6 **wylne**, 5 **willne**, **wol(l)ne**. [OE. *wilnian*, f. *wil-*, stem of WILL *sb.*¹, WILL *v.*¹ + *-n-* formative + *-ian* -Y². Cf. ON. *vilna* to favour, refl. to hope (cf. *örvilnask* to despair).] To desire. **a.** *trans.* with simple obj. (in OE. gen. or acc.).

Beowulf 188 Drihten secean, and to fæder fæþmum freoðo wilnian. *c* **888** ÆLFRED *Boeth.* xxxvi. §4 Ʒif ðu æniȝne mon ȝesihst wilnian ðæs ðe he næfð. *c* **1175** *Lamb. Hom.* 13 Ne wilne þu oðres monnes wif. *c* **1205** LAY. 1073 Ʒef us þat we wilniað. **1297** R. GLOUC. (Rolls) 6301 Ichabbe quaþ knout ywilned þi kinedom ar þis, & nou wel more þan þi lond þi sulue ich wilni ywis. *a* **1300** *Leg. Rood* ii. (1871) 20 Ich wilny muche my deþ. *c* **1386** CHAUCER *Pars. T.* ¶443 Thy neighebore artow holden for to loue and wilne hym alle goodnesse. *c* **1400** *Destr. Troy* 3996 Of wemen werkes wilnet ho none. ? **1464** *Paston Lett.* II. 171 To.. wilne yow goode wylle and trewe hert.

(*b*) with clause or acc. and inf.

c **897** ÆLFRED *Gregory's Past. C.* xix. 141 Se bið.. Godes ȝewinna se se ðe wilnað ðæt he hæbbe ða weorðunga.. ðe God habban sceolde. *c* **1050** *O.E. Chron.* (MS. C) an. 977 He wilnode þæt his lic ræst sceolde beon æt Cridiantune, æt his bisceop stole. *c* **1374** CHAUCER *Troylus* III. 121, I not nat what ȝe wilne þat I seye. *c* **1384** —— *H. Fame* III. 4 Nat that I wilne, for maistrye, Here Art poetical be shewed. *c* **1449** PECOCK *Repr.* II. ix. 196 Wherbi is excludid and wilned of Crist to be removed, that eny man schulde worschipe God bi eny outward ymagis. *c* **1475** *Partenay* 3178 Wilnyng you to come hastly thys instaunce. *c* **1540** *Pilgryms T.* 108 in *Thynne's Animadv.* (1875) 80 What rekis them, the sayng of paull, Which wylnith 'to men we shall not call'?

(*c*) with inf. (with or without *to*).

c **888** ÆLFRED *Boeth.* xxiv. §2 Ælc mod wilnað soðes godes to beȝitanne. *c* **1000** *Ags. Gosp.* Luke xxiii. 8 He wilnode hine ȝeseon. *c* **1205** LAY. 1892 Heora eiþer wilnada oðer [*c* **1275** aiþer wilnede oþer] to wælden. *a* **1300** *Leg. Rood* ii. (1871) 20 Of is lif he was anuyd, he wilnede be of dawe. **1377** LANGL. *P. Pl.* B. XVIII. 4 Tyl I wex wery of þe worlde, and wylned eft to slepe. *c* **1430** *Hymns Virgin* (1867) 99 In good praiers þou muste wake, And neuere wilne to do a-mys. **1447** *Bekynton Corr.* (Rolls) II. 341, I.. suppose that.. ye wold.. wilne exhorte.. al tho to whom [etc.]. *c* **1450** *Mirk's Festial* 285 Ʒif ȝe wollnoth to haue mercy of God.

b. *intr.*; simply or const. *after*, *for*, *to*; also with ellipsis of inf.

a **1000** *Andreas* 283 (Gr.) þu wilnast nu ofer widne mere. *c* **1200** *Moral Ode* 319 (Trin. Coll. MS.), We wilnieð after wereldes wele. *c* **1200** *Trin. Coll. Hom.* 213 Hire beoð wo þat hie sal þer-inne wunien, and þere-fore wilneð ut. *c* **1205** LAY. 2626 Heo wilneden [*c* **1275** welnede] after worre. *c* **1230** *Hali Meid.* (Titus) 125 Ne þarf þe bute wilnen, & lete godd wurchen. *c* **1350** *Will. Palerne* 3563 As redili araiȝed as any rink þort wilne. **1393** LANGL. *P. Pl.* C. IV. 387 þei wilnen and wolde as best were for hem-selue. ? *a* **1400** *Morte Arth.* 2224, I watte be thi wauerynge thow willnez aftyre sorowe. *Ibid.* 3479 Whedire wilnez thowe, wye, walkand thyne onne? *c* **1449** PECOCK *Repr.* III. iv. 295 That Crist schulde wilne and bidde in lijk maner to eny other man.

† **wilnesful**, *a. Obs. rare.* [f. gen. of WILNE *sb.* + -FUL. Cf. *willesful*.] Phr. ***for wilnesful*** (see FOR *pref.*¹ 10): because of obstinacy or perversity.

13.. *E.E. Allit. P.* B. 231 Ne neuer wolde, for wylnesful, his worþy god knawe.

† **'wilning**, *vbl. sb. Obs.* Also 4 **willenyng**. [OE. *wilnung*, f. *wilnian*: see above and -ING¹ I.] Desire.

c **888** ÆLFRED *Boeth.* xxxiii. §5 Twa þara ȝecynda habbað netenu swa same swa men; oðer þara is wilnung, oðer is irsung. *a* **1225** *Ancr. R.* 278 Prude is wilnunge of wurðschipe. **13..** *Gaw. & Gr. Knt.* 1546, I wolde yowre wylnyng worche at my myȝt. *c* **1350** *Will. Palerne* 3983 To willne swiche willenyng þat wol nouȝt a-sente. **1357** *Lay Folks' Catech.* (T.) 506 A wrangwise wilnyng Or yernyng to hafe any kyns gode that us augh noght. *c* **1449** PECOCK *Repr.* v. ix. 533 With the lasse good kunnyng, the lasse gode wilnyngis, and purposis.

So † **wilning** *ppl. a.*, voluntary; also quasi-advb.; whence † **wilningly** *adv.*, willingly.

The survival of the vb. *wilne* in *wilningly*, if genuine, is remarkable.

a **1225** *Ancr. R.* 182 Vorte beon martirs efning, þuruh a wilninde wo. **1382** WYCLIF *Num.* xxxv. 15 To hem, the which not wilnynge [1388 wilfuli; Vulg. *nolens*] shedith blood. —— *Eccl.* xiv. 7 Vnwitendely, and not wilnende [1388 not wilfuli; Vulg. *ignoranter et non volens*] he doth. **1597** *Return fr. Parnass.* II. i. 618 (MS. Rawl. D. 398, lf. 211 b) We haue yelded to her conqueringe hande And wilninglie goe captiues in her bande.

wilowe, rare obs. var. WALLOW *v.*², to fade.

a **1340** HAMPOLE *Psalter* lxxii. 17 When þair flour welkes [*v.r.* wilowes] & wytes awaye.

† **wilrone**. *Sc. Obs.* Also **wolroun**, **-ron(n)**. [? f. ON. *vilr* WILL *a.* + *runi* boar.] A wild boar.

Used chiefly as a term of abuse.

1508 DUNBAR *Tua Mariit Wemen* 90 A waistit wolroun. **1508** KENNEDIE *Flyting w. Dunbar* 432 Wnhonest wayis all, wolronn, that thou wirkis. *c* **1560** A. SCOTT *Poems* (S.T.S) xxxiv. 106 The bich the curtyk fannis; The wolf the wilrone vsis. *a* **1568** *Bannatyne MS.* (Hunter. Club) 385 This wyld wilroun wich thame widlit sa and wareit. *a* **1851** in R. Chambers *Pop. Rhymes Scot.* (1870) 70 In place o' her ain bonny bairn, she fand a withered wolron.

wilsfully: see after WILLESFUL.

wilsh, var. WILCH.

wilsome ('wɪlsəm), *a.*¹ *Obs.* exc. *Sc.* Forms: 4–5 **wilsom**, **wylsom(e**, **-sum**, 4–7 **wilsome**, **-sum**, 5 **wyld-**, **wel(d)som(e**, **whylsum**, 6 **weilsum**, **wildsome**, **wolsome**, **volsum**, (6–7 **wilesome**), 9 **wullsome**, **wullsum**. [a. ON. *villusamr* erroneous, false (Sw. *villsam* perplexing, embarrassing, in MSw. also, gone astray, Da. *vildsom* perplexed, intricate), f. *villr* wild, WILL *a.* + *-samr* -SOME. Sometimes assimilated in spelling to *wild*.]

1. Chiefly of a way or path: Leading astray as through wild and desolate regions; hence, desert, lonely and wild; dreary. (A conventional epithet of ME. poetry.)

13.. *Evang. Nicod.* 1604 in Herrig's *Archiv* LIII. 421þai wend no wilsom way. **13..** *Gaw. & Gr. Knt.* 689 Mony wylsum way he rode. *a* **1400–50** *Wars Alex.* 5565 A wilsom wast & a wild. **1470–85** MALORY *Arthur* VII. xxii. 247 Lynet the damoysel that had ryden wyth hym many wylsome wayes. *c* **1480** HENRYSON *Two Mice* 143 Till hir hart straike mony wilsome stound. *c* **1480** —— *Orpheus* 128 To seke his wyf.. our mony wilsum wane Wyth outyn gyde. **1513** DOUGLAS *Æneis* XI. xi. 26 He.. socht onto the wilsum holtis hair. **1562** WINȜET *Cert. Tractatis* i. Wks. (S.T.S.) I. 9 In the wyldsum way of this daingerous lyfe. **1578** H. WOTTON *Courtlie Controv.* 129 Nor wildsome wood or deserts. **1584–7** GREENE *Carde of Fancie* Wks. (Grosart) IV. 139 The wildsome woods were his wished walkes. **1632** LITHGOW *Trav.* VI. 294 We imbraced our wilsome and fastidious Way. **1806** R. JAMIESON *Pop. Ballads* I. 244 He blew, till a' the wullsome waste Rebellowin' echoed round.

2. Erring, wandering, straying; bewildered, perplexed; doubtful, uncertain (*of*).

Phr. *wilsome of wane* = WILL *a.* 3 a.

c **1350** *Will. Palerne* 5394 þus was þe kowherd out of kare kindeli holpen, He & his wilsum wif wel to liuen for euer. **1387** TREVISA *Higden* (Rolls) VII. 95 Hym self in þe mene tyme ful wilsom [orig. *naviter oberrans*] at þe Ile of Wight halowede Cristemasse. *a* **1440** *Sir Eglam.* 867 They namyd the chylde syr Degrabelle, That welsome was of wone [*read* wane]. *c* **1440** *York Myst.* xxvii. 92 So wilsom wightis as we, Was neuere in worlde walkand in wede. *c* **1440** *Promp. Parv.* 528/2 Wylsome, or dowtefulle, *dubius*, *fluctuans*. *c* **1450** HOLLAND *Howlat* 43 Wa is me, wretche in this warld, wilsome of wane! *c* **1460** *Towneley Myst.* xxvii. 204 Wilsom of hart, ye ar vnabyll, And outt of the right way. **1500–20** DUNBAR *Poems* ix. 29 To hungre meit, nor drynk to thristy gaif,.. Harbreit the wolsome, nor naikit cled att all. **1513** DOUGLAS *Æneis* III. iii. 105 Wncertanlie we went Thre dais wilsum throu the mysty streme. **1535** STEWART *Cron. Scot.* (Rolls) III. 44 Werie forwrocht, and richt weilsum of wane. *c* **1550** ROLLAND *Crt. Venus* III. 526 Wilsum of ane gude reid. **1554** KNOX *Let.* in *Answ. Jesuit Tyrie* F iv b, God shall guyde the footesteppes of him that is wilsome. *c* **1590** J. STEWART *Poems* (S.T.S.) II. 35 Vandring as ane volsum vagabound. **1614** LITHGOW *Trav.* L 2, If it had not been for a Christian Amaronite, who accidently encountred with vs, in our wilsum [**1632**, 190 wilesome] wandring, wee had beene miserably lost. **1808** JAMIESON, *Wilsum*, in a wandering state, implying the ideas of dreariness, and of ignorance of one's course, S. pron. *wullsum*.

Hence **'wilsomely** *adv.*¹, erringly, perversely; wanderingly, at random; **'wilsomeness**¹, error, perverseness; doubt, uncertainty.

13.. *Evang. Nicod.* 1365 in Herrig's *Archiv* LIII. 417 Fro wayes of wilsomnes.. he has þam taken. *c* **1420** *Sir Amadace* (Camden) xxxv, To somun alle tho, That wilsumly ar wente me fro. *c* **1440** *Promp. Parv.* 528/2 Wylsomenesse, or dowtefulnesse. *c* **1460** J. RUSSELL *Bk. Nurture* 17 As y wandered weldsomly in-to þe lawnd þat was so grene.

wilsome, **willsome**, *a.*² *Obs.* exc. *dial.* [? orig. a use of WILSOME *a.*¹, later associated with WILL *sb.*¹ There appears to be no connexion with OE. *wilsum*, *wilsumlic* 'desiderabilis', 'voluntarius', 'devotus', *wilsumlice* 'sponte', 'voluntarie'.] Wilful, obstinate, stubborn.

13.. *Cursor M.* 9633 (Gött.) It was his aun wilsum [*Cott.* wilful] sinne, þat did vs all fra him to tuynne. *c* **1440** *Promp. Parv.* 528/2 Wylsome, or folwynge only hys owne wylle, *effrenus*. **1590** *Cobler Canterb.* 3 He was wide and wildsome in the brest. **1818** TODD, *Wilsome*, obstinate; stubborn. A forgotten old word, but as proper as *humoursome*, and the like. **1826** HOR. SMITH *Tor Hill* I. 26 Within stone walls he is ever willsome and upon the fret. *a* **1835** HOGG *Poems*, *Spirit of the Glen* xxvii, Marjorie smiled a willsome smile.

Hence **'wilsomely** *adv.*², wilfully; **'wilsomeness**², wilfulness, frowardness.

1382 WYCLIF *Ecclus.* xxxi. 40 The wilsumnesse [Vulg. *animositas*] of drunkenhed. *c* **1440** *Promp. Parv.* 528/2 Wylsomenesse, or froward wylle, *effrenitas*, *vel proprie voluntatis sequela*. *a* **1835** HOGG *Poems*, *Connel of Dee* xvi, His sins were like crimson—all bent and uneven, The path he hed wilesomely trod.

Wilson¹ ('wɪlsən). *Path.* [The name of S. A. Kinnier *Wilson* (1878–1937), English neurologist.] ***Wilson's disease***: = *hepato-lenticular degeneration* s.v. HEPATO-.

1915 STEDMAN *Med. Dict.* (ed. 3) 1032/2 *Wilson's disease*, progressive degeneration of the lenticular nucleus, occurring as a familial disease associated with cirrhosis of the liver. **1919** *Arch. Internal Med.* XXIV. 497 (*heading*) Progressive lenticular degeneration associated with cirrhosis of the liver (Wilson's disease). **1978** *Brit. Med. Jrnl.* 18 Nov. 1384/2 Though originally described as a neurological disorder with associated cirrhosis, we now recognise hepatolenticular degeneration (Wilson's disease) as a copper storage disorder in which other tissues become affected as the excess copper is released from the liver.

Wilson² ('wɪlsən). *Physics.* The name of C. T. R. *Wilson* (1869–1959), Scottish physicist, used *attrib.* and in the possessive to designate the cloud chamber (see CLOUD *sb.* 12) invented by him.

1917 *Sci. Abstr.* A. XX. 337 Wilson's condensation chamber.. was still smaller than the author's small sphere. **1931** *Ann. Reg. 1930* 59 Harkins and Smith took 39,000 photographs of the tracks of 390,000 α-particles in a Wilson cloud chamber containing nitrogen. **1961** *New Scientist* 23 Feb. 474/2 The Wilson cloud chamber had done heroic work for many years in the examination of the tracks of particles, but its limitations in speed and scope were becoming increasingly apparent.

Wilsonian (wɪl'səʊnɪən), *a.* (and *sb.*) [See -IAN.] Pertaining to or characteristic of Woodrow *Wilson* (1856–1924), president of the United States 1913–21, noted for his uncompromising idealism. Also as *sb.*, a follower of Woodrow Wilson.

1921 *Labour Monthly* Sept. 285 In whatever shades or purgatory await our public men after the completion of their labours, a special circle should be reserved for the Old Wilsonians. **1924** *Amer. Mercury* Jan. 53/1 It was at this precise moment in his career that the Wilsonian storming of Valhalla began. **1934** H. G. WELLS *Exper. Autobiogr.* II. ix. 694 The Wilsonian notion of a League. **1962** *Listener* 22 Mar. 524/1 Mr. Tillman remains a starry-eyed Wilsonian. **1980** J. LEES-MILNE *Harold Nicolson* I. vii. 116 The French bitterly opposed the very idea of the covenant as Wilsonian idealistic nonsense.

Also **'Wilsonism**, the policies of Woodrow Wilson.

1920 *Harvey's Weekly* 16 Oct. 13/1 No more time need be lost in following the slush-fund herring trail away from the vital issue of Wilsonism. **1945** KOESTLER *Yogi & Commissar* III. i. 125 Movement followed Movement and withered away. Jacobinism,.. Wilsonism, the League of Nations.. they were all branches of the same tree rooted in the Age of Enlightenment. **1977** *N.Y. Rev. Bks.* 12 May 16/4 But they were fighting to save Wilsonism, if need be from Wilson himself.

† **wilt**, *sb.*[1] *Obs.* [Origin obscure.] = WILE *sb.* Hence † **wiltful** *a.*, wily.

a **1230** *St. Kath.* 891 Þe wrenchfule feont, þurh onden, wið his wiles [*MS. Royal* wiltes] weorp him ut. *a* **1250** *Ancr. R.* MS. C.C.C.C. 402, lf. 61 Hu ȝe schulen witen ow wið þes deofles wiltes. *Ibid.* 73 b, Hit bringeð to noht al þes deofles wiheles nawt ane his strengðes & his stronge turnes ah deð his wiltfule [*so also MS. Caius 234, lf. 156 b; MS. Cott. Nero* wihtful, *Titus* wilfule] crokes & his wrenchfule wicche-creftes.

wilt (wɪlt), *sb.*[2] [f. next.] The action or an act of wilting; *spec.* (also ***wilt disease***) any fungous disease of plants which is characterized by wilting.

1855 AINSLIE *Land of Burns* (1892) 315 To stiffen the wilt that this wilderness Has brought on this bosom and brain. **1916** *Q. Rev.* Oct. 357 Rusts, smuts, wilts, and insect-attacks were calamities to be patiently endured. **1918** [see PSYLLA]. **1946** *Nature* 13 July 56/1, I came across what is apparently a hitherto undescribed wilt disease of the oil palm. **1961** A. SCHOENFELD tr. *Stapp's Bact. Plant Pathogens* I. 103 This wilt disease [of beans] can be said with certainty not to occur in Germany. **1981** BUCZACKI & HARRIS *Collins Guide to Pests of Garden Plants* 306 Most wilts are caused by Deuteromycete fungi.

wilt (wɪlt), *v.* [Of dial. origin (in early 19th c. largely U.S.), having a widespread variant *welt* (WELT *v.*[3]); perh. alteration of *wilk*, WELK *v.*]

1. a. *intr.* Of plants or their parts: To become limp or flaccid, through heat or drought.

1691 RAY *N.C. Words* (ed. 2) 80 To *Wilt*, for wither, spoken of green Herbs or Flowers, is a general word. **1779** *Projects* in *Ann. Reg.* 108/1 Let it remain exposed to the sun throughout the day, or until the leaves are entirely wilted, as it is termed in America. *Ibid.* 108/2 If the sun does not appear for several days,.. they [*sc.* leaves of the tobacco-plant] must remain to wilt. **1790** GROSE *Prov. Gloss.* (ed. 2) s.v., These flowers are all wilted. **1807** W. IRVING *Salmag.* xvii. (1824) 315 A Cabbage leaf wilting before a hot fire. **1825** [see b]. *a* **1864** GESNER *Coal, Petrol.*, etc. (1865) 36 [They] wilted down like leaves when the forest is on fire. **1867** LOWELL *Lett.* (1894) I. 378 Some flowers will not bear to be handled without wilting. **1887** *Amer. Naturalist* XXI. 506 The tissues of the flower begin to soften and wilt very soon after separation from the plant. **1897** T. H. WARREN *By Severn Sea* 27 Magic bowers never wilting.

b. *transf.* and *gen.* To become limp; to lose energy or vigour; to become dispirited or nerveless.

1787 ABIGAIL ADAMS *Lett.* (1848) 333 Mrs. Cranch.. is wilted just enough to last to perpetuity. **1825** J. NEAL *Bro. Jonathan* xvii. II. 109 Look o' the major!.. pale as death; and wiltin' away, like a cabbage leaf, in the hot sun. **1857** in *Harper's Mag.* Dec. (1883) 165 My.. ruffles wilted to the consistency.. of an after-dinner napkin. **1862** LOWELL *Biglow P.* II. iii. 200 Poems 1890 II. 291 They.. wilt right down ez debtors will thet stumble on a dun. **1890** HENTY *With Lee in Virg.* xv, The man is as hard as a rock... He wilted a little when you were telling your story, but [etc.]. **1920** *Times Lit. Suppl.* 22 Jan. 1/2 The old aristocracy seemed as if it was going to wilt before this new commonwealth of wits.

2. a. *trans.* To cause to become limp; to deprive of stiffness, energy, vigour, or spirit.

1809 T. DWIGHT *Theol.* (1819) IV. 165 Despots.. have wilted the human race into sloth and imbecility. **1854** J. S. C. ABBOTT *Napoleon* (1855) II. xix. 349 They had secured for his cause no monarchical friends, but had wilted the enthusiasm of the people. **1888** DELAND *John Ward* 233 The full blaze of sunshine.. was wilting the dish of violets.

b. *Agric.* To leave (mown grass, etc.) to dry partially in the open before putting it in a silo.

1971 *Power Farming* Mar. 9/1 'But,' said Mr. Whitton, 'the loader must be used as part of a system, and it is most essential that the silage be wilted and chopped.' **1974** *BSI News* May 8/3 The process of wilting the crop [of grass] from 75%–85% moisture content down to 55%–65%. **1980** *Daily Tel.* 28 Jan. 10/4 New techniques such as wilting the crop in the field before it is ensiled.

Hence **'wilted** *ppl. a.*; **'wilting** *ppl. a.* and *vbl. sb.*; *spec.* ***wilting coefficient***, the moisture content of the soil (expressed as a percentage of its dry weight) when a plant begins to wilt.

1809 W. IRVING *Knickerb.* III. vii. (1812) I. 185 Fanciful festoons of wilted peaches and dried apples. **1830** *Examiner* 35/1 A wilted, sinew-shrunk old hunks. **1883** G. ALLEN in *Knowledge* 3 Aug. 65/1 It is a tall wilted-looking thing, this broomrape. **1884** *Century Mag.* Jan. 356/2 Wilting flowers are hardly appropriate to a steamship. **1912** BRIGGS & SHANTZ in *Bull. U.S. Bureau Plant Industry* No. 230. 9 It appears advisable to use a more specific term for the moisture content of the soil corresponding to the wilting point of a plant, and we have employed the term 'wilting coefficient' in this sense in the present paper. **1980** *Communications Soil Sci. & Plant Analysis* XI. 843 Studies were performed to determine the wilting coefficient of various selected light tropical soils collected at different locations in.. Venezuela.

wilt: see WILL *v.*

wilt, obs. f. QUILT *sb.*

wilter ('wɪltə(r)), *v. dial.* [f. WILT *v.* + -ER[5].] = WILT *v.*

1790 GROSE *Prov. Gloss.* (ed. 2), To *wilt*, or *wilter*, to wither. **1888** LEES & CLUTTERBUCK *B.C. 1887* xxxiii, 'He just wiltered'.. What is wiltering? How did he do it? **1916** CULLUM *Men who Wrought* ix, The tide of the Prince's anger was too swift for the youthful Prussian's armour of official effrontery. He came near to wiltering before it.

wiltful: see WILT *sb.*[1]

Wilton[1] ('wɪltən). Name of a town in the south of Wiltshire, noted since the reign of Queen Elizabeth I for the manufacture of carpets: applied to †(*a*) a kind of cloth, (*b*) a carpet of which the manufacture resembles that of Brussels carpet but differing in having the rib cut so as to produce a velvet pile.

1773 *Pennsylv. Gaz.* 21 Apr. 1/1 Fine broadcloths, cassimers, saggathies, and Wiltons. **1774** *Ibid.* 10 Aug. Suppl. 2/2 Wilton and Scotch carpets. **1776** *Pennsylv. Even. Post* 21 May 256/2 A brick coloured Wilton coattee. **1889** CONAN DOYLE *Micah Clarke* xxiii, As soft and velvety as a Wilton carpet. **1904** BRADBURY *Carpet Manuf.* i. 43 The difference in shade was greatest in Wilton and Velvet pile structures. *Ibid.* iv. 127 The wire used for Wilton is usually deeper and therefore produces a loftier pile than Brussels.

Wilton[2] ('wɪltən). The name of a farm near Grahamstown, Cape Province, South Africa; used *attrib.* to denote a later Stone Age culture of southern Africa.

1928 A. J. H. GOODWIN in *Ann. S. Afr. Mus.* (1929) XXVII. x. 251 Our first knowledge of the Wilton Industry comes from the Cape Peninsula, various crescents, thumbnail scrapers, and the like appearing from a number of kitchen middens and sand-dune sites in this district. **1936** L. S. B. LEAKEY *Stone Age Afr.* v. 96 In the Wilton culture the most typical tools are,.. crescents and other small geometric microliths, together with small double-end and thumb-nail scrapers. **1959** J. D. CLARK *Prehist. S. Afr.* ii. 41 The Wilton [culture] is named from the rock-shelter on the farm of that name west of Grahamstown. Its distribution is very wide. **1980** *Cambr. Encycl. Archaeol.* 174/1 The microlithic industries (known as Wilton in eastern and southern Africa) of the early to mid-Holocene.

Wiltshire ('wɪltʃə(r)). Name of an English county, applied to (*a*) a breed of sheep; ***Wiltshire Horn(ed)***, (a sheep of) a recently revived breed, distinguished by its very light short wool; (*b*) a kind of 'smoked' bacon; (*c*) a kind of cheese (also ***Wilts***), ***North Wiltshire***.

1794 T. DAVIS *Agric. Wilts* 22 The Wiltshire Horned Sheep. *Ibid.*, A flock of Wiltshire ewes. *Ibid.* 29 The old Wiltshire bacon. **1805** LUCCOCK *Wool* 279 The sheep most commonly met with [in Buckinghamshire] are derived from the blood of the Dorset, the Wiltshire, and from a mongrel kind. **1816** JANE AUSTEN *Emma* I. x. 188 She was come in herself for the Stilton cheese, the north Wiltshire, the butter, the cellery, [etc.]. **1823** J. BADCOCK *Dom. Amusem.* 17 A smoky taste.. such as that we find in Wiltshire bacon. **1837** YOUATT *Sheep* 245 These Wiltshires have now passed quite away. **1863** H. JONES *Jrnl.* 20 Aug. in F. W. Lindsay *Cariboo Dream* (1971) 38, 1 case Gloucester Cheese $75.72 Wiltshire do. $97.35. **1881** SHELDON *Dairy Farming* 246 Different-sized cheeses, from flat Wilts to 'truckles' and Cheddars. **1894** OLIVER *Milk, Cheese*, etc. 255 The small cylindrical cheeses known as 'Wiltshire loaves'. **1912** *Times* 19 Dec. 20/4 Bacon... Canadian was steadier, with Wiltshires 1s. dearer. **1945** J. F. H. THOMAS *Sheep* ii. 34 The Wiltshire Horned.. is no longer to be found in Wiltshire..; the main area of distribution is now Northamptonshire and Buckinghamshire. **1970** *Observer* 26 Apr. (Colour Suppl.) 36/1 Wiltshire Horn.. has no wool but, instead, a thick matted coat. **1977** *Jrnl. R. Soc. Arts* CXXV. 708/1 Supposing, for example, that wool became a nuisance and that it was far better to keep sheep that were wool-less and just had hair. It so happens that we have got such a breed, the Wiltshire Horn, that has a rather hairy coat, and so we can use that.

wiluol, obs. form of WILFUL.

wily ('waɪlɪ), *a.* (*sb.*, *adv.*) Forms: 4 **wili, wyli,** 4–5 **wyle,** 4–6 **wyly,** (4, 6 **wely**), 5 **wilye,** (**whily,** 5–6 **wylly,** 5, 7 **willy**), 5–7 (8 *Sc.*) **wylie,** 6 **wylye,** (**whyly,** *Sc.* **vylie**), 6–7 **wilie,** 8 **wiley,** 4– **wily.** [f. WILE *sb.* + -Y[1].]

1. Full of or characterized by wiles; crafty, cunning, sly, artful. **a.** Of a person or animal (or *fig.* of a thing personified).

Rarely in a good sense: Astute, clever.

a **1300** *Cursor M.* 11807 Þis herods.. þat wili [*Fairf.* wely] wolf. *c* **1330** R. BRUNNE *Chron. Wace* (Rolls) 9849 He was boþe wyly & sley. **13..** *Gaw. & Gr. Knt.* 1728 So reniarde was wyle. *c* **1386** CHAUCER *Monk's Prol.* 52 No poure cloystrer ne no Novys Bot a gouernour wily and wys. —— *Pars. T.* ⁋ 252 The serpent that was moost wily of alle othere beestes. **1470–85** MALORY *Arthur* IV. xxvi. 155 And there he was in grete peryl, for the gyant was a wyly fyghter. **1489** CAXTON *Faytes of A.* I. vii. Bj b, Be he.. wyly to deffende hym fro theym, & wysely to assaille them. **1526** *Pilgr. Perf.* (W. de W. 1531) 60 Lyke as yᵉ sparowe the wyly byrde escheweth all panters & snares. **1581** A. HALL *Iliad* II. 23 To finde the wilie Vlysses straight downe she tooke hir walke. **1639** J. CLARKE *Parœm.* 285 As willy as a foxe. **1662** R. MATHEW *Unl. Alch.* 177 The wily spirits of the Armoniack. **1729** SAVAGE *Wanderer* I. 95 Mark! wiley Fowlers meditate their Doom. **1807** CRABBE *Library* 243 Here wily Jesuits simple Quakers meet. **1878** BAYNE *Purit. Rev.* ii. 49 The brilliant wily Welshman found himself sharply repelled. **1905** TREVES *Other Side of Lantern* III. viii. (1906) 225 In the.. night the wily tide will glide a shoal across the fairway.

b. Of personal attributes, actions, etc.

c **1400** *Beryn* 444 Tapsters, & oþer such, þat hath wyly wittis To pik mennys pursis. *c* **1407** LYDG. *Reson & Sens.* 2758 Hercules.. by his whily sleyght Bar away the ryche fruyt. **1509** HAWES *Past. Pleas.* XXIX. (Percy Soc.) 139 She had him caught in suche a wyly snare. **1551** T. WILSON *Logic* C iv b, The wily vsyng of wordes that in sence haue double meanyng. **1613** PURCHAS *Pilgrimage* IV. iii. 298 Ventidius.. by a wily Stratageme, counterfeiting flight and feare. **1641** MILTON *Ch. Govt.* II. E 4, The wily suttleties and refluxes of mans thoughts. **1721** RAMSAY *Prospect of Plenty* 33 Artfu' Nets, and Fishers' wylie Skill. **1850** KINGSLEY *Alton Locke* xxxvii, Judas's averted and wily face. **1905** *Times Lit. Suppl.* 11 Feb. 45/3 An imaginary line.. offered no real obstacle to a determined and wily advance.

†**2.** *ellipt.* as *sb.* A wily person or animal; in quot. *c* 1460 as proper name (cf. 4). *Obs.*

13.. *Gaw. & Gr. Knt.* 1905 Þay fel on hym alle, & woried me þis wyly wyth a wroth noyse. *c* **1460** *Wisdom* 607 in *Macro Plays* 55 Yt ys clepyde wysdom: 'ware þat!' quod Wyly.

†**3.** as *adv.* Craftily, cunningly: = WILILY. *Obs.*

13.. *E.E. Allit. P.* B. 1452 Aþel vessel, þat wyth so curious a crafte coruen was wyly. **1567** HARMAN *Caveat* A ij, All these.. rabblement of rakehelles, that.. do.. gayne great almes in all places where they wyly wander. **1574** *Satir. Poems Reform.* xlii. 59 Thocht for thair tyme sum wylie winkit. **1623** COCKERAM, *Wily*, craftily.

4. Special Collocations and Combinations.

†**a.** **wily-man, wily-pie** [PIE *sb.*[1]], **wily-wat** [WAT[1]], appellations for a crafty or cunning fellow (the first as a proper name). *Obs.*

1393 LANGL. *P. Pl.* C. v. 27 Then waryn wysman and wyly-man his felawe Fayn were to folwen hem. *c* **1450** *Chance of Dice* 147 in *Engl. Studien* LIX. 9 Lorde verrely ye ben a wyly pye. **1542–79** [see PIE *sb.*[1] 2]. **1550** BALE *Apol.* 73 Ye are a wyly watte in the kyngdome of crafte and generacion of falshede. *c* **1550** —— *K. Johan* (Camden) 3 Ye are a wyly wat, & wander here full warelye. **1581** J. BELL *Haddon's Answ. Osor.* 244 b, Osorius is a wylypye, and will not be destitute of a starting hoale. [**1587** HARRISON *England* II. iii. 149/1 Oh madam (saith he) the wiliest pie of all, these are no pies but soules in purgatorie that craue releefe.]

†**b.** **wily beguile**, also freq. in jingling form **wily beguily** (and similar expressions): orig. in phr. ***to play wily beguile oneself*** (also later in various corrupt forms), to act wilily in such a way as to be oneself beguiled, to be entrapped by one's own craftiness; hence ***wily beguily*** (rarely ***wily beguile, gilie, guile***) as sb. phr. (*a*) a person who acts thus, or (simply) who acts wilily or craftily; (*b*) an act of this kind, or (simply) a wily act or action, a crafty trick, cunning trickery; rarely as adj., an emphatic extension of *wily*. *Obs.*

1555 LATIMER in Strype *Eccl. Mem.* (1721) III. App. xxxvi. 103 Let men beware that they play not *wylye begile themselves*, as I feare me they do that go to masse. *Ibid.*, Thus they play *wyly, beguylyng them selves*. **1562** J. HEYWOOD *Prov. & Epigr.* (1867) 103 To whiche smart mocke, and wyly begylyng, He.. saide [etc.]. **1570** FOXE *A. & M.* (ed. 2) 193/2 While they thinke to deceaue the simple, these wylye begely most of all deceaue them selues. **1581** J. BELL *Haddon's Answ. Osor.* 303 b Sufficiently instructed in those your wyly beguilye and.. to well acquainted with your ambitious hawtynes. **1589** [? NASHE] *Almond for Parrat* 17 b, The wicked.. being so full of their wilie gilies. **1606** SYLVESTER *Du Bartas* II. iv. *Magnificence* 684 Smiles, Wylie-Guiles, queint witty-pretty Toyes. **1618** BRETON *Courtier & Countryman* C 4 b, What is the end of all wily beguily? seeking to deceiue other, deceiu'd himselfe most of all. **1621** BP. MOUNTAGU *Diatribæ* 137 It shall go hard, but our wily-beguily Wits, will one way or other finde an euasion. **1625** J. ROBINSON *Observ.* xv. 102 Such wily-beguilies may for a time.. get the opinion of prudent, and politick persons. **1639** J. CLARKE *Parœm.* 101 Wilie beguilie deceives himself.

c. *Comb.* (of the adj. or adv.), as ***wily-headed, wily-witty*** adjs.

1596 SPENSER *State Irel.* Wks. (Globe) 619/1 They are.. soe cautelous and wylye-headed. **1624** GEE *Foot out of Snare* App. 108, I shall begin to recant my opinion of his wily-witty worth.

wim, *v. s.w. dial.* Forms: 5 (?)–6 **wym,** 7 **wimme,** 7, 9 **wimb,** 7– **wim** (9 **whim**). [Of obscure origin; cf. WIMBLE *v.*[2]] To winnow.

Form and meaning in first quot. are doubtful.

1455 *Churchw. Acc., Yatton* (Som. Rec. Soc.) 98 For j man to helpe to wymmynge the malte to the mylle.. ijᵈ. **1681** *Oates Well Thresht* 2 They are thresh't, and wimb'd. **1691** RAY *S. & E.C. Words* (ed. 2), To *Wimme*; *Suss.* Dial. i.e. Winnow. **1886** *W. Som. Word-bk.* s.v., Our volks be all busy wimin o' barley.

b. *Comb.*: † **wimsheet**, a winnowing-sheet. Also **'wimming** *vbl. sb.* in Comb. ***wimming-dust, -sheet.***

1532 in Weaver *Wells Wills* (1890) 111 One whit wymshete. **1535** *Ibid.* 116 To Pascowe Lethall, a wymeshit and bushell of rye. **1681** WORLIDGE *Syst. Agric.* 61 Some have strain'd a Wimsheet athwart a Barns Floor about the middle thereof, and with a Scoop or Shovel cast their Wheat against the upper part of the Sheet. **1825** JENNINGS *Observ. Dial. W. Eng.*, *Wim-sheet*, *Wimmin-sheet*, a sheet upon which corn is winnowed. *Wimmin-dust*, chaff.

wim, var. WHIM *sb.*[1] in sense 4.

1802 MAWE *Min. Derbysh.* Gloss., *Wim*, an engine or machine to draw ore, worked by horses.

wiman, obs. form of WOMAN.

wimbeame, var. WIND-BEAM[1] *Obs.*

wimble (ˈwɪmb(ə)l), *sb.* Now *dial.* or *techn.* Forms: 3–7 **wymble**, 4–5 **wymbul**, **-il** (5 **-el**, **-ulle**), 5–6 **-yl(l**, **-lle**, **wymel(l** (5 **-ulle**, 6 **wyemblye**), 5–7 **womell** (5 **-yll**), **womble**, (5 **wommil**, 6 **-ill**, **womyl**, **-lle**, **wombill**, **wembel**, **whymble**), 8 **wimple**, 8–9 **whimble**, 4– **wimble** (9 *Sc.* and *north.* **wum(m)il**, **wummle**, **wimmel**, etc.). [a. AF. **wimble* (var. of **guimble*, represented by rare 13th c. *gymble*, and the dim. GIMLET), ad. MLG. *wiemel*, (also Flem.) *wemel* (whence OSw. *wimla*, Da. *vimmel*), MDu. *wimpel*.]

1. a. A gimlet.

1295 *Acc. Exch. K.R.* 5/8 m. 4 (P.R.O.) Et iiij. d. ob. in Wymbles emptis. [**1296** *Ibid.* 5/20 m. 5 In tribus Gymblis ferri emptis..vj. d.] *c* **1325** *Gloss. W. de Bibbesw.* in Wright *Voc.* 170 Terere [*gloss* wymble (nauger)]. **1411** *Nottingham Rec.* II. 86, j. parvum wymble, j d. *c* **1440** *Pallad. on Husb.* XI. 85 Vnto the pith a ffrensh wymbul inbore. *c* **1440** *Promp. Parv.* 528/2 Wymbyl, or persowre, *terebellum*. **1555** EDEN *Decades* (Arb.) 154 So eaten with woormes, as though they had byn bored through with wimbles. **1577** GOOGE *Heresbach's Husb.* II. 107 b, The haftes and handles of Wymbles and Augurs. **1636** FEATLY *Clavis Myst.* xxix. 377 As the wimble bores a hole for the auger. **1662** GURNALL *Chr. in Arm.* III. xxvi. § I. 222 The little Wimble once entred, the Workman can then drive a great Nail. *c* **1781** G. WHITE *Selborne, To Barrington* (1789) 275 The second [field-mouse] nibbles a hole with his teeth, so regular as if drilled with a wimble.

b. *transf.* and *fig.*

a **1633** G. HERBERT *Jacula Prudentum* 955 Gifts enter every where without a wimble. **1719** D'URFEY *Pills* IV. 81 Joan 's a Piece for a Man to bore, With his Wimble. **1781** BARBUT *Gen. Insect.* 287 The Gad-fly... From the hinder part of their body, issues a whimble of wonderful structure. **1805** PRISC. WAKEFIELD *Dom. Recreat.* iv. 62 The whimble is of an admirable structure, and consists of three pieces:.. It is the most easily seen in the long whimbled fly.

2. An auger; also, a brace.

?**1362** *Durham Acc. Rolls* (Surtees) 565 Willo Couper ad reparacionem duorum Wymbles, quia fracta in opere Prioris, xij *d.* **1489** CAXTON *Faytes of A.* II. xxxix. L ij, Men ..with grete wymellis and awgours shal perce the ship undreneth. **1502** ARNOLDE *Chron.* (1811) 165 Perce yᵉ tree thorugh wyth a percer crosse wyse or wyth a wymble. **1573** TUSSER *Husb.* xvii. (1878) 36 Cart ladder and wimble, with percer and pod. **1583** JEWEL *Serm. Paul's Crosse* D j b, That part of the Carpenters wimble, which turneth about, goeth rounde, and by litle and litle draweth in the iron, or steele bit. **1621** *Shuttleworths' Acc.* (Chetham Soc.) 248 P'd for layinge 3 wimbles, vjᵈ. **1625** MARKHAM *Farew. Husb.* II. vi. (1638) 32 A great Augure or wimble of Iron made to receive many bits one longer than another. **1677** MOXON *Mech. Exerc.* iii. 53 The other end of the Shank must be fitted into the square Socket of the Wimble. **1789** *Trans. Soc. Arts* I. 38 Hinges, Wimble, and Jack for Ship-Builders. **1824** CARR *Craven Gloss.*, *Wummle*, an auger, a wimble.

3. An instrument for boring in soft ground, or for extracting rubbish from a bore-hole in mining.

1692 RAY *Disc.* (1693) 41 They bore this Earth or Soil with a long Wimble. **1708** J. C. *Compl. Collier* (1845) 12 [He] puts or screws on the Wimble, or Scoop which takes up the cut stuff. **1789** BRAND *Hist. Newc.* II. 678 The chisel is screwed off [the boring rod], and the wimple or scoop put on. **1881** RAYMOND *Mining Gloss.*, *Wimble*, a shell-auger used for boring in soft ground.

4. Also **wimbel**, *dial.* **wimbrel**. An implement for twisting together strands (esp. of straw) to make rope for tying up hay-trusses, fleeces, etc.

1863 J. R. WISE *New Forest* 288/1 *Wimble*, an instrument with which to take up faggots or trusses of hay. **1874** HARDY *Far fr. Madding Crowd* I. xxii. 243 Gathering up the fleeces and twisting ropes of wool with a wimble for tying them round. **1886** —— *Mayor Casterbr.* I. i. 2 A rush basket, from which protruded at one end the crutch of a hay-knife, a wimble for hay-bonds being also visible. **1939** D. HARTLEY *Made in England* ii. 76 There are other types [of implement], such as the wimbrel, rather like the spindle of a spinning wheel in principle. **1969** E. H. PINTO *Treen* 97 Wimbels are essentially cranked devices for twisting ropes out of straw, formerly required for binding corn stooks... Other country names for them include wimbrels, straw twisters, [etc.].

5. *attrib.* and *Comb.*, as ***wimble-bit***, ***-bore***, ***-hole***, ***-like*** adj., ***-stock***; †**wimble-cock**, a wimble-bit.

1583 *Shuttleworths' Acc.* (Chetham Soc.) 9 For towe broste *wyemblye bittes and a nale percell bitte, ijᵈ. **1628** *Toke* (Kent) *Estate Acc.* (MS.) lf. 118 For 5 wimble bitts. [**13..** *Childh. Jesus* 411 in *Archiv neu. Spr.* LXXIV. 332 With his fyngere he plukede hym owte Att a full littille *wymbilles bore.] **1808** JAMIESON, *Wimblebore*, a hole in the throat, which prevents one from speaking distinctly, S. in allusion to a hole bored by a wimble. **1607** B. BARNES *Divils Charter* III. v. F 3, If I lye, call me thy *Wimble-cock. **1585** HIGINS *Junius' Nomencl.* 215/1 *Foramen rotundum*,..a *wimble hole. **1613** MARKHAM *Eng. Husbandman* I. iv. 14 Take a board..which shalbe bored full of large wimble holes. **1683** J. REID *Scots Gard'ner* (1907) 88 Bore them [*sc.* wooden cases] full of auger or wimble-holes. **1845** S. JUDD *Margaret* II. viii. (1871) 288 Margaret pressed herself into the porch; *wimble-like, she pierced the stacks of men and women that filled the hall. **1601** HOLLAND *Pliny* XVI. xliii. I. 493 [Wood] excellent good for awgre-handles and *wimble-stocks. **1648–9** in Swayne *Churchw. Acc. Sarum* (1896) 219 A wymble stock and Nayles 1s. 4d.

wimble (ˈwɪmb(ə)l), *a. dial.* (and *obs. arch.*) Also 6 **wymble**. [app. a northern word taken up by Spenser; recorded in mod. dial. use from Yorkshire and Lancashire. The immediate source is unknown. (Scand. words of appropriate form, e.g. Norw. *vimmel* giddy, confused, have not the required sense.)] Active, nimble.

1579 SPENSER *Sheph. Cal.* Mar. 91 He was so wimble, and so wight [*gloss* Quicke and deliuer]. **1579** HAKE *Newes out of Powles* (1872) Bj, I spyde a pretie wymble lad. **1602** MARSTON *Ant. & Mel.* III. Wks. 1856 I. 40 Buckle thy spirits up, put all thy wits In wimble action. **1614** J. DAVIES (Heref.) *Sheph. Pipe, Ecl.* G 5, Then nought can be atchieu'd with witty shewes, Sith griefe of Elde accloyen wimble wit. **1748–58** MENDEZ *Sqr. Dames* I. I. xxvii, Man throws the wimble bait, and greedy woman bites.

Hence †ˈ**wimbly** *adv.*, nimbly.

1594 W. PERCY *Coelia* (1877) 9 Upon my foot, her tender foot alighted, With that she pluckt it off full wimbely.

ˈ**wimble**, *v.*[1] *Obs.* exc. *dial.* [f. WIMBLE *sb.*]

1. a. *trans.* To pierce with or as with a wimble; to make (a hole) with a wimble.

c **1440** *Promp. Parv.* 528/2 Wymbelyn, or wymmelyn, *terebro*. **1642** FULLER *Holy & Prof. St.* IV. ix. 279 To use force first before people are fairly taught the truth, is to knock a nail into a board, without wimbling a hole for it. **1663** SIR T. HERBERT *Mem. Chas. I* (1702) 142 A Foot-Soldier..wimbled a hole into the Coffin that was largest. **1713** C'TESS WINCHILSEA *Misc. Poems* 127 A Nutshell, wimbl'd by a Worm. **1791** COWPER *Odyss.* XXIII. 232, I wimbled, next, The frame throughout.

b. *transf.* (Cf. WIMBLE *sb.* 1 b, quot. 1719.)

1656 R. FLETCHER tr. *Martial* VII. lxxiv, Wouldst thou be wimbled *gratis* when thou art A wrinkled wretch deformed in every part? *c* **1670** *Roxb. Ball.* (1891) VII. 486 And well he could dissemble, when wenches he would wimble.

2. *intr.* To bore *into*; chiefly *fig.* (*intr.* and *refl.*), to penetrate or insinuate oneself *into*.

1601 W. LEIGH *Christians Watch* (1605) 17 How this spirit hath entred and wimbled into your soules..I know not. *a* **1641** SPELMAN *Dial. Coin* Reliq. S. (1698) 210 In this latter age we have wimbl'd even into the bowels of Plutus's Treasury. **1671** COSIN in *Northumbrian Docts.* (Surtees) 240 Hee would fain wimble himselfe into some employment under mee. **1830** GALT *Lawrie T.* III. ii. 189 Charley..felt something like a man's finger wimbling in under his neck. **1839** *New Monthly Mag.* LVI. 61 Wimbling deeper and deeper still, till he has shattered the remains of your nerves to atoms.

3. *trans.* To make (a rope) using a wimble (sense 4).

1874 HARDY *Far fr. Madding Crowd* I. x. 131 'What have you been doing?' 'Tending thrashing-machine, and wimbling haybonds.'

Hence ˈ**wimbler**, one who makes ropes with a wimble; ˈ**wimbling** *vbl. sb.* and *ppl. a.*

1623 COCKERAM, *Terebration*, a wimbling. **1637** WHITING *Albino & Bellama* 59 We men..in our silent beds of earth will court The slender-wasted wormes, and with them sport,..and vow their wimbling busse Is full as sweet as womens was to us. **1648** HERRICK *Hesp.*, *Kisses Loathsome*, Those lips please me which are plac't Close, but not too strictly lac't: Yeilding I wo'd have them; yet Not a wimbling Tongue admit. **1964** *Courier-Mail* (Brisbane) 21 Dec., The policeman asked Godfrey Booth: 'Your occupation, sir?' Mr. Booth..replied 'Cag handed straw wimbler.' Mr. Booth lives in Bobbington, Staffordshire. *Ibid.*, Mr. Booth said: 'When I left school I took up farming, and wimbling took second place.'

†**wimble**, *v.*[2] *Obs. rare.* [f. WIM *v.* Cf. WIND *v.*[3], WINDLE *v.*[2]] To winnow.

1556 WITHALS *Dict.* (1562) 20/2 A trey or shawlde to wynowe or wymble corne with.

ˈ**wimbled**, *ppl. a.* [f. WIMBLE *v.*[1] or *sb.* + -ED.]

1. Pierced, bored.

1582 STANYHURST *Æneis* II. (Arb.) 58 Warding long wymbled entryes.

2. Furnished with a 'wimble'.

1805 [see WIMBLE *sb.* 1 b].

Wimbledon (ˈwɪmb(ə)ldən). The name of a district of South London, used *colloq.* to designate the Lawn Tennis Championships on Grass played annually at the All-England Lawn Tennis and Croquet Club there. Also *transf.* and *attrib.*

1907 F. W. PAYN *Tennis Topics & Tactics* xvi. 157 The presence of nearly 30,000 spectators in all at the Wimbledon Championships. **1919** *Country Life* 5 July 29/1 Mr. Gore, the former champion, whose twenty-eighth Wimbledon this is. *Ibid.* 12 July 54/2 Whether the 'Victory' Championships will go down to history as 'The Wet Wimbledon' or 'The Wonderful Wimbledon' time alone can tell. **1930** A. P. HERBERT *Water Gipsies* xxv. 381 Fay's *livid*—Says she wouldn't marry him now if he gave her free seats for Wimbledon. **1935** *Encycl. Sports* 385/2 No record of the Wimbledon championships would be complete without mention of a few of the winners of the men's and women's doubles championships. **1965** V. CANNING *Whip Hand* xii. 134 He's..Wimbledon standard tennis, Olympic standard swimming. **1971** *Guardian* 17 Nov. 10/3 Alun Owen is an old hand at the ding-dong, the ping-pong, the Wimbledon of sex. **1979** D. ANTHONY *Long Hard Cure* v. 42 Was that the year you won Wimbledon?

†**wimblet**. *Obs.* Also 7 **wimlet**. [f. WIMBLE *sb.* after GIMLET.] A gimlet or auger.

1670 *Short Relat. Suff. Quakers* 62 They got a Wimlet, and bored a hole in the Mault-Floor. *a* **1711** KEN *Anodynes* Poet. Wks. 1721 III. 440 Saw, Bodkin, Fish-hook, Wimblet, Dart, To stab, tear, jag, or gore each part.

wimble-wamble (ˈwɪmb(ə)lˈwɒmb(ə)l), *adv.* and *sb. dial.* or *arch.* [Redupl. f. WAMBLE *sb.* and *v.*] **a.** *adv.* (See quot.) **b.** *sb.* ? The 'general run', the ordinary crowd.

1890 J. D. ROBERTSON *Gloss. Dial. & Archaic Wds. Glos.* 179 *Wimble-wamble, to go sort of*, *vb.* to roll about in walking. **1937** H. G. WELLS *Star Begotten* viii. 142 They will observe how they resemble each other and how they differ from the wimble-wamble of the common world.

wimbly-wambly (ˈwɪmblɪˈwɒmblɪ), *a. dial.* Also **wimley-wamley**. [Redupl. f. WAMBLY *a.*] Shaky, unsteady; feeble, effeminate.

1881 *Leeds Loiners' Comic Olmenac* 24, I went all wimley-wamley e me head. **1882** F. W. P. JAGO *Ancient Lang. & Dial. Cornwall* 312 I'm all wimbly-wambly. **1929** D. H. LAWRENCE *Pansies* 113 Flat-chested, crop-headed, chemicalised women, of indeterminate sex, And wimbly-wambly young men, of sex still more indeterminate.

†**wimbrekin**. [Alteration of OF. *vibrequin*, *vil(e)-*, *virebrequin*, after WIMBLE *sb.*] A wimble.

1489 CAXTON *Faytes of A.* I. xiv. C iij, Sawis, axes, nayles, wymbrekyns [orig. *tarrieres*] and..al other ferrementis.

wimbrel[1], var. WHIMBREL.

wimbrel[2], dial. var. WIMBLE *sb.* 4.

wimman, **-en**, **-on**, obs. ff. WOMAN.

Wimmera (ˈwɪmərə). The name of a river and the region surrounding it in northwestern Victoria, Australia, used *attrib.* in **Wimmera rye-grass** to designate a grass belonging to a drought-resistant variety of *Lolium rigidum* first identified in the area about 1900.

1920 *Proc. R. Soc. Victoria* XXXII. 199 Wimmera Rye Grass. **1928** R. G. STAPLEDON *Tour Austral. & N.Z.* ix. 74 The so-called Wimmera rye-grass..first appeared in Victoria, presumably as a stowaway, about thirty years ago. **1934** *Bulletin* (Sydney) 4 Apr. 28/1 Next sow (in N.S.W. anyway) 5 lb. Wimmera rye grass. **1973** TOTHILL & HACKER *Grasses Southeast Queensland* 197 Wimmera ryegrass..is grown widely in southern Australia. **1977** *Weekly Times* (Melbourne) 19 Jan. 10/5 Wimmera rye grass is regarded as a curse.

wim(m)ick, *v. dial.* [Imitative.] (See quots.)

1850 DICKENS *David Copp.* li, 'Wen Mrs. Gummidge takes to wimicking',—our old county word for crying,—'she's liable to be considered to be..peevish-like.' **1865** H. KINGSLEY *Hillyars & Burtons* xxi, Three times had that child wimmicked at its aunt as she knelt there.

wimmin (ˈwɪmɪn). A semi-phonetic spelling of 'women', recently adopted by some feminists as a form not containing the ending *-men*. Also, at an earlier date, occasionally used ironically in other contexts.

1910 H. G. WELLS *Hist. Mr Polly* vi. 201 'Wimmin's a toss up,' said Uncle Penstemon. 'Prize packets they are, and you can't tell what's in 'em till you took 'em 'ome and undone 'em. Never was a bachelor married yet that didn't buy a pig in a poke.' **1938** *Snow White & Seven Dwarfs* 31 'Didn't I tell you?' sniffed Grumpy. 'She's crazy. Wimmin! Pah!' **1983** *Observer* 13 Mar. 16/4 Another woman was writing the words of a song... 'We coil and spring we grow and sing we dance with the tree of life we are the serpents of healing and rebirth wimmin have reclaimed the earth'... 'Why 'wimmin'?' I asked... 'We want to spell women in a way that does not spell men.' **1983** *Sunday Times* 10 Apr. 36/3 Return to Greenham Common, view the wool webs, the papier mâché masks, the eccentric re-spelling of words like 'wimmin', the improbable cosiness of the little tents in a landscape of wire fencing and policemen. **1983** *Listener* 14 Apr. 4/1 Meanwhile, what of the Peace Women ('wimmin' in feminist placards) camped outside Greenham Common? **1983** *Private Eye* 22 Apr. 5/2 (*heading*) Wimmin. **1985** *Sunday Tel.* 11 Aug. 13/8 The Greenham women—God bless 'em! (Sorry—I should write 'wimmin', since the word 'women' contains the horrid inclusion of 'men'. Their little eccentricity!)

†**wimount**. *Obs.* [perh. the personal name *Wimound*, OE. *Wigmund*.] A name of the hare.

c **1280** *Names of Hare* in *Rel. Ant.* I. 133 The wimount, the babbart.

wimp[1] (wɪmp). *slang.* [Origin uncertain; perh. an abbreviated corruption of *women*.] A woman or girl.

'*Wimp* was also used as a verb at Oxford *c.* 1917, e.g. *to go wimping*' (M. Marples, *University Slang* (1950), p. 98).

1923 J. MANCHON *Le Slang* 338 *Wimp*, femme, fille, donzelle. **1937** PARTRIDGE *Dict. Slang* 959/1 *Wimp*, a (young) woman, a girl: from ca. 1920. **1940** [see *Skinny Liz* s.v. SKINNY *a.* 6].

wimp[2] (wɪmp). *slang* (orig. *U.S.*). [Origin uncertain; perh. f. WHIMPER (cf. Eng. dial. *wimp* (of a dog) to whine.] A feeble or ineffectual person; one who is spineless or 'wet'. (Used only as a term of abuse or contempt.)

1920 ADE *Hand-made Fables* 97 Next day he sought out the dejected Wimp. **1964** *Amer. Speech* XXXIX. 119 A *baff* is 'a person who does silly things deliberately'; but *wimp* is still mysterious and undefined in my notes. **1966** *Current Slang* Winter 8 *Wimp*, a backward person... He's a real *wimp* on a date. **1970** *New York* 16 Nov. 10/2 That Goodell, he's nothing but a wimp. And this Ottinger, it got so I couldn't stand the sight of him. **1976** *New Mus. Express* 31 July 8/2 Although he's best known here as a fairly muscular MOR wimp,..he has a big reputation as a prodigiously talented multi-media whizz in the States. **1979** T. GIFFORD *Hollywood Gothic* (1980) xxii. 220 Solly Roth and his wimp of a son..what a wet bunch that family was. **1981** P. THEROUX *Mosquito Coast* vi. 48, I can afford to be robbed... But what about the poor wimps who can't afford it? **1984** *Sunday Tel.* 30 Dec. 15/6 In daily life Ronnie Lee is a wimp.

Put him in a balaclava and he thinks he's a he-man. **1985** *She* July 140/2 Masseur! Huh! He sounds a right little wimp.

WIMP[3] (wɪmp). *Computing.* Also **Wimp, wimp; WIMPS.** [Acronym f. *w*indows, *i*cons, *m*ouse and a fourth word variously given: see quots.] A set of software features and hardware devices (such as windows, icons, mice, pull-down menus, etc.) that are designed to simplify or demystify computing operations for the user. Freq. *attrib.* or in *Comb.*

1984 *Daily Tel.* 9 July 11/3 WIMP is an acronym for Windowing Icon Mouse Products; in short the state-of-the-art in software technology. *Ibid.* 11/5 What *Silicon Office* doesn't have is WIMPs; since all the operations can be controlled with the same 18 commands, it doesn't need them. **1985** *Pract. Computing* May 116 Wimps in the Accounts Department. Chris Bidmead looks at how the coming generation of window, icon and mouse programs are set to change the face of accounting software. **1985** *Which Computer?* July 35/1 An intriguing WIMPS (Windows, Icons, Mouse and Pointer-based System) implementation that does a creditable job of imitating the workings of the Apple Macintosh. **1986** *Internat. Conf. on Speech Input/Output* (IEE Conf. Ser. CCLVIII) 154/1 This paper ..summarizes the design for an interface which is intended to make Wimp-type programs accessible to visually disabled users. **1987** *Daily Tel.* 13 Apr. 24/4 Another name is WIMP. This is an acronym for Windows, Icons and Mouse Program ...The windows in WIMP refer to ability to open up separate areas on the screen. **1987** *Guardian* 18 June 15/7 The so-called Wimp interface (windows, icons, mice, pull-down menus) available on the Macintosh and other computers, has changed all that.

Wimpey, var. WIMPY *sb.* 2.

wimpish (ˈwɪmpɪʃ), *a. slang* (orig. *U.S.*). [f. WIMP[2] + -ISH[1].] Characteristic of a 'wimp'; feeble, ineffectual; snivelling. Freq. of persons.

1925 S. Lewis *Arrowsmith* xxvi. 288 They looked like lunching grocers: brisk featureless young men;..wimpish little men with spectacles, men whose collars did not meet. **1977** *Sounds* 9 July 30/6 The ever so slightly wimpish 'Give Me Some Time'. **1978** J. Irving *World according to Garp* xiii. 255 You call that wimpish asshole and say good-bye. **1982** *Mail on Sunday* 2 May 13/3 The wimpish young schoolmaster. **1983** *Times* 28 May Suppl. 1/5 The only motive for reading it may be to swank about it at literary cocktail parties, which is a wet and wimpish reason. **1985** *Times* 11 Feb. 14/1 The Duke of Edinburgh had adopted a new 'limp' handshake... Expecting something flabby and wimpish, the men got royal bonecrushers.

Hence ˈ**wimpishness**, ineffectual character or behaviour; feebleness.

1978 *Oxford Times* 6 Jan. 13/4 *Renaissance: Novella* (Warner Bros. K 56422)—It's fashionable to sneer at the 'wimpishness' of delicate music like this but.. I like it. **1983** *Times* 9 Mar. 10/1 If Michael Straight is a wimp (weakling or 'wet') as some people allege, the wimpishness is not immediately apparent. **1984** *Daily Express* 17 July 8/1 Now he has raised a coast-to-coast horselaugh by his best ever display of wimpishness. Having sacked the party's incompetent national chairman, he promptly reinstated him in the face of protests.

wimple (ˈwɪmp(ə)l), *sb.* Forms: 1, 3–6 **wimpel**, 3–5 **wympel**, 4–6 **wymple** (1, 3 **winpel**, 3 **wempel**, 4 **whympel**, 5 **wim-, wym-, win-, wyn-, -pil, -pill, -pul, -pulle, -pyl, -pylle,** *Sc.* **wompyll,** 6 **wympyll,** *Sc.* **womple,** 7 **wimpell,** 9 **whimple**), 4– **wimple.** [Late OE. *wimpel* = (M)LG., (M)Du. *wimpel*, OHG. *wimpal* veil, banner (MHG., G. *wimpel* streamer, pennon), ON. *vimpill* (Sw., Da. *vimpel* from LG.), whence OF. *guimple* (mod. F. *guimpe*), of which the variant *wimple* coincided with the native form. Ultimate origin uncertain.

It is doubtful whether the senses provisionally placed together here and under the vb. belong all to the same word. In branch II there may be an onomatopœic element; for formation and meaning cf. *dimple, rimple, rumple, wrimple.*]

I. 1. A garment of linen or silk formerly worn by women, so folded as to envelop the head, chin, sides of the face, and neck: now retained in the dress of nuns. Also *gen.* a veil.

Used loosely in early glossaries as a rendering of L. *anabola, cyclas, peplum, ricinum.*

a **1100** *Aldhelm Gloss.* i. 4296 (Napier 112) *Cyclade, .i. ueste,* wimple. *a* **1100** *Gloss.* in Wr.-Wülcker 107/37 *Ricinum,* winpel *uel* orl. *Ibid.* 125/8 *Anabola,* winpel. *c* **1200** *Trin. Coll. Hom.* 163 Hire winpel wit oðer maked ȝeleu mid saffran. *c* **1240** *Ancr. R.* 420 (MS. C), Sum seið þæt hit limpeð to ene wummon cundeliche forte were wimpel. *c* **1250** *Meid. Maregrete* xlvii, Ðoru þe mitte of ihū christ, wid her wempel ho hin bond. **1297** R. Glouc. (Rolls) 6941 Hire bodi wiþ a mantel, a wimpel [*v.r.* whympel] aboute hire heued. *c* **1374** Chaucer *Troylus* ii. 110 Do a-woy ȝoure wimpil & schew ȝoure face bare. *c* **1386** —— *Prol.* 151 Ful semyly hir wympul pynched was. **14..** *Voc.* in Wr.-Wülcker 601/43 *Peplum,* a wynpul. *c* **1425** Wyntoun *Cron.* ix. xxv. 2992 Hyre hayre in wompyll arayande. *c* **1440** *Gesta Rom.* lxix. 317 The emperesse hydde hire face with a wympill, for she wolde not ben y-knowe. **1513** Douglas *Æneis* i. vii. 115 To ask supple, with thaim ane womple bair thai, With handis betand ther breistis by the way. *c* **1530** *Crt. Love* 1102 And eke the nonnes, with vaile and wimple plight. **1560** *Bible* (Genev.) Isa. iii. 22 The costelie apparel and the vailes, and the wimpels, and the crisping pinnes. **1805** Scott *Last Minstr.* v. xvii, White was her whimple, and her veil. **1819** —— *Ivanhoe* xlii, Her flowing wimple of black cypress. **1879** Walford *Londoniana* II. 247 Three nuns with veils and whimples.

transf. **1615** Crooke *Body of Man* 123 A certaine smooth and slippery veyle or wimple is substrated. **1861** A. Austin in *Temple Bar* III. 472 Graves are the sheltering wimples Against Life's rain.

¶ **2.** A flag, streamer. [An alien sense.]

1656 Blount *Glossogr., Wimple*..a Streamer or Flag.

II. 3. A fold or wrinkle; a turn, winding, or twist; a ripple or rippling in a stream.

1513 Douglas *Æneis* ii. iv. 30 Bot thai about him lowpit in wympillis [orig. *spiris*] threw. **1593** Nashe *Christ's T.* 74 b, Be not more curious of a wimple or spot in thy vesture, then thou art of spotting and thorow-stayning thy deere bought Spyrit. **1818** Hogg *Brownie of Bodsbeck* xii. I. 225 A shepherd.. hates the wimples, as he calls them, of a turnpike. *Ibid.* xiv. II. 22 He had as mony links an' wimples in his tail as an eel. **1845** Eliza Cook *Waters* i, Waters, bright Waters,..your wimple just lulleth the minnow to sleep! **1878** Stevenson *Will o' Mill, Parson's Marj.*, The river ran between the stepping-stones with a pretty wimple.

4. A crafty turn or twist; a wile. *Sc.*

1638 Sir A. Johnston *Diary* (S.H.S.) 320 Notwithstanding al wyles, wimples, offers, motions, and uther letts. **1755** R. Forbes *Ajax's Sp.* 24 The gouden helmet will sae glance, An blink wi' skyrin brinns, That a' his wimples they'll find out Fan i' the mark he sheens. **1818** Scott *Hrt. Midl.* xxiv, There is aye a wimple in a lawyer's clew.

Hence **wimple-less** *a.*, not wearing a wimple.

a **1225** *Ancr. R.* 420 Ȝif ȝe muwen beon wimpel-leas, beoð bi warme keppen.

ˈ**wimple,** *v.* Forms: see prec.; also *Sc.* 6 **wumpil,** 7 **wo(o)mple.** [f. WIMPLE *sb.*; cf. LG. *wimpelen.*]

I. 1. *trans.* To envelop in a wimple; loosely, to veil (†occas. *pass.* to take the veil).

c **1240** *Ancr. R.* 420 (MS. C) Wrihen, he seið, naut wimplin. *Ibid.*, Al beo þu i-wimplet. *c* **1374** Chaucer *Boeth.* ii. pr. i. (1868) 31 She þat ȝit couereþ hir and wympleþ [orig. *velat*] hir to oþer folk haþ shewed hir euerydel to þe. *c* **1386** —— *Prol.* 470 Ywympled wel, and on hir heed an hat. *c* **1407** Lydg. *Reson & Sens.* 2837 Wympled but in symple guyse. **1430–40** —— *Bochas* ii. xxviii. (1554) 64 Rhea.. Entered into religion, For to be wympled in that holy house, Sacred to Uesta. *c* **1430** *Syr Gener.* (Roxb.) 9938 Wympled she was both cheke and chin. **1470–85** Malory *Arthur* x. lxviii. 531 Al wayes she was wympeld that no man myȝt see her vysage. **1592** Lyly *Midas* i. i, Iustice her selfe, that sitteth wimpled about the eyes. **1615** W. Hull *Mirr. Majestie* 82 They wimpled those eyes. **1616** J. Lane *Contin. Sqr.'s T.* vii. 91 *note,* Ne Titan on woold putt his golden flize, But wimpled fast his melancholie eies. **1822** Scott *Nigel* Introd. Ep., His figure was so closely veiled and wimpled, either with a mantle, morning-gown or some such loose garb. **1870** Rock *Text. Fabr.* i. 30 A female, crowned and wimpled.

†**b.** *intr.* for *pass.* To be veiled. *Obs. rare.*

1591 Percivall *Sp. Dict., Reboçar,* to wimple, to go with the face hidden, *caput inuoluere.*

2. *fig.* To veil, cover.

1387–8 T. Usk *Test. Love* ii. xiv. (Skeat) l. 25 With fayre honyed wordes heretykes and mis-meninge people skleren and wimplen their errours. *Ibid.* iii. ix. l. 76 In this boke be many privy thinges wimpled and folde. **1620** *Hist. Reynard the Fox* xviii, He that cannot wimple falshood in truths kerchiffe, hath neither Art nor cunning. **1898** *Atlantic Monthly* Apr. 503/2 He will gaze tenderly into the white faces of his cauliflowers, as with pinned leaves he wimples them from the sun.

†**3.** *transf.* and *fig.* To enfold, enwrap, wrap up.

1513 Douglas *Æneis* vi. iv. 93 Wymplit and buskit [orig. *innexa*] in a bludy bend. *Ibid.* vii. xii. 61 His body wymplit [orig. *impexum*] in A felloun bustuus and gret lyoun skyn. *Ibid.* x. xiii. 134 The fatale sisteris tho in deyd Had wymplyt vp [orig. *legunt*] this Lawsus lattyr threid. *a* **1578** Lindesay (Pitscottie) *Chron. Scot.* (S.T.S.) I. 61 Ane body of ane zoung chyld..wumpillit wpoun sandell. **1594** R. Carew *Tasso* (1881) 80 Her sparing looke a coy regard doth beare, And loues treasures, and hers vp wympelled. *a* **1600** Montgomerie *Misc. Poems* v. 2 No wonder thoght I waill and weip, That womplit am in woes. **1607** B. Barnes *Divils Charter* iv. iii. H 1, I perceiue a little riueling Aboue my forhead but I wimple it Either with iewels or a lock of haire. **1616** *Rollock's Lect. Passion* Ep. Ded. ¶ 2 b, He will thirst to be woompled in the wounds of Iesus. *a* **1670** Spalding *Troub. Chas. I* (Bannatyne Club) I. 208 Whilk charge so wrytten was wompled about ane arrow head, syne shott up over the castle walls, wher Ruthven might find the same.

4. *pass.* and *intr.* To fall in folds.

1590 Spenser *F.Q.* i. i. 4 A vele, that wimpled was full low. **1751** R. Lloyd *Progr. Envy* viii. Poems (1762) 210 Her mantle wimpled low. **1859–60** Jas. Hamilton *Moses* xviii. (1871) 283 Curtains of delicate texture, all wimpling with the golden wings of cherubim.

5. *pass.* To be stretched like a wimple or veil.

1868 E. R. Sill *Poems, Evening* i, The Sun is gone: those glorious chariot-wheels Have..left Thin rosy films wimpled across the West.

II. 6. *intr.* Of a stream: To meander, twist and turn; also, to ripple. Chiefly *Sc.*

1721 Ramsay *Poet's Wish* i, Tay and Tweed's smooth Streams..quietly..wimple to the Seas. **1785** Burns *Halloween* ii, Amang the bonie, winding banks, Where Doon rins, wimplin, clear. **1848** Eliza Cook *Bonnie green bough* iv, Streamlets, ye are pleasant things, Whimpling as ye glide. **1849** Aytoun *Poems, Refusal of Charon* iii, Or near some sparkling fountain, Where the waters wimple down! **1879** Stevenson *Trav. Cevennes* 19 You may hear it wimpling over the stones, an amiable stripling of a river.

transf. **1896** Crockett *Grey Man* i, A dark train of horsemen..Their line wimpled like a serpent.

7. To move shiftily or unsteadily.

1819 J. R. Drake *Culprit Fay* xix, They struck her keel with jerk and blow,..She wimpled about, in the pale moonbeam, like a feather. **1886** Kipling *Departm. Ditties* etc. (1888) 73 When comes the licht That wimples on his face?

wimple, occas. var. WIMBLE.

wimpled (ˈwɪmp(ə)ld), *ppl. a.* Also 9 *Sc.* **whumplet.** [f. WIMPLE *v.* or *sb.* + -ED.]

1. Enveloped in or wearing a wimple; hence, veiled, *occas.* blindfolded.

1579 Hake *Newes out of Powles* (1872) G ij, Which all doth spring from wimpled B: and old deceitfull Bawde. **1588** Shaks. *L.L.L.* iii. i. 181 This wimpled, whyning, purblinde waiward Boy. **1839** Longf. *Hyperion* iii. iii, Neither wimpled nun nor cowled monk. **1874** L. Morris *Gilbert Beckett* xix, The wimpled maid, demurely shy.

2. Arranged or falling in folds like a wimple; hence, wrinkled; rippled.

1599 T. Storer *Life & D. Wolsey* E 1, A wimpled scarfe bedew'd with hearers teares. **1812** Cary *Dante, Purg.* viii. 74 Since she has changed the white and wimpled folds. **1909** 'Q' *True Tilda* xv, She..could read nothing of his faith in the wimpled surface [of the stream].

3. *fig.* Involved, intricate. *Sc.*

a **1722** Fountainhall in M. P. Brown *Suppl. Dict. Decis.* (1826) III. 329 This was thought an odd and wimpled interlocutor. **1725** Ramsay *Gentle Sheph.* iii. ii, The wimpled Meaning of your unco Tale. **1768** Ross *Helenore* Introd., Sick wimpl'd wark would crack a pow like thine. **1823** Galt *R. Gilhaize* lxvii, There was no difficulty in reading the whumplet meaning of this couthiness anent the reeking o' the chamber.

ˈ**wimpler**[1]. *Obs.* exc. *Hist.* [f. WIMPLE *sb.* + -ER[1].] A maker of wimples.

1260 *Husting Roll City of London* 2 (169) (MS.) Isabella uxor Thome le Wimpler. **1284** *Ibid.* 15 (34) Alicia la Wymplere relicta quondam Henrici le Wympler. **1342** *Ibid.* 69 (106–7) Avicia filia Henrici le Wimpler. **1887** Gilliat *Forest Outlaws* 295 The booths of the vintners, the fletchers, the plumiers, and wymplers.

So †ˈ**wimplester,** a female wimpler.

1379 in Bardsley *Surnames,* Crystiana, Wympylster.

ˈ**wimpler**[2]. *rare.* [f. WIMPLE *v.* + -ER[1].] 'A waving lock of hair' (Jam.).

1724 Ramsay *Vision* v, Doun his braid back, frae his quhyt heid, The silver wympler's grew.

ˈ**wimpling,** *vbl. sb.* In 3 **wimlunge.** [f. WIMPLE *v.* + -ING[1].]

†**1.** The wearing of a wimple. *Obs.*

c **1240** *Ancr. R.* 420 (MS. C) Ancren, sume sungið in hare wimlunge na lesse þene lefdi.

2. The winding or meandering of a stream; also, rippling.

1729 Ramsay *2nd Answ. Somerville* 30 Its wimplings [*Wks.* 1851 III. 94 whimplings] led by Nature's hand. **1863** Le Fanu *House by Churchy.* lxxix, Those..pleasant dimples, like the wimpling of a well. **1893** Jos. Thomson in *Biogr.* (1896) 288 The wimpling of the burns over stony beds.

ˈ**wimpling,** *ppl. a.* [f. WIMPLE *v.* + -ING[2].]

1. Veiling, concealing.

1747 Ridley *Psyche* xi, That wimpling Slough shall fall like Filth away. **1817** Scott *Harold* ii. ii, Where wimpling tissue from the gaze The form half hides.

2. Winding, meandering (esp. of streams); also, rippling. Also *transf.* in *poet.* use.

1721 Ramsay *Richy & Sandy* 28 Wimpling Waters which in Latium flow. **1785** Burns *Scotch Drink* ii, Guid auld Scotch Drink! Whether thro' wimplin' worms thou jink, Or, richly brown, ream owre the brink. **1827** W. G. S. *Excurs. Village Curate* 50 The old brook with its whimpling current. **1847** Longf. *Ev.* ii. ii. 18 Along the wimpling waves of their margin,..flocks of pelicans waded. **1861** Smiles *Engineers* II. viii. i. 294 The solitude..is only broken by the wimpling sound of the burns. **1877** G. M. Hopkins *Poems* (1967) 69 How he rung upon the rein of a wimpling wing In his ecstasy. **1894** Crockett *Lilac Sunbonnet* i, The wimpling lane.

Wimpy (ˈwɪmpɪ), *sb.* [The name of the cartoon character J. Wellington *Wimpy* in the 'Popeye' cartoon strip, who was often portrayed eating a hamburger.] **1. a.** A proprietary name for a variety of hamburger. Also (*rarely*) in slang use.

1935 *Official Gaz.* (U.S. Patent Office) 21 May 557 Wimpy Grills, Inc., Chicago, Ill... *Wimpy*..For sandwiches, roasted and toasted meats... Claims use since Sept. 12, 1934. **1935** J. Hargan *Gloss. Prison Lang.* 8 *Wimpy,* hamburger. **1943** *American Mercury* Nov. 553/2 Other chow terms in popular use..*wimpies* for hamburgers. **1954** *Trade Marks Jrnl.* 20 Jan. 63/2 Wimpy...B720, 112. Bread rolls containing cooked foods. Edward Vale Gold, 140, North Dearborn, Chicago, Illinois, United States.. Manufacturer and Merchant. **1959** *Observer* 8 Nov. 3/1 The bright glossy bars where Wimpies are served are the most striking example of Britain's changing eating habits. **1967** T. Harknett *Two-Way Frame* x. 77, I had a sterile Wimpy and cup of insipid black coffee. **1981** C. Storr *Vicky* vii. 56, I can always go out and get a Wimpy or something.

b. Shortened form of ***Wimpy bar***, sense 3 below.

1966 M. Waddell *Otley* xix. 171 We wound up in the Wimpy by the Broadway. **1968** *Listener* 13 June 763/1 Two years of success by any standard and then a break-up. Mecca had opened a dance hall... A Wimpy came and a bowling alley.

2. Usu. in form ***Wimpey.*** A Wellington bomber aeroplane. *slang.*

1942 *Tee Emm* (Air Ministry) II. 81 You have the mad sort of chauffeur who tries to roll a Wimpey. **1944** 'N. Shute' *Pastoral* i. 1 There was a Wimpey running up one engine, somewhere away out in the middle distance of the aerodrome. **1954** [see *map reference* s.v. MAP *sb.*[1] 5].

3. *attrib.* and *Comb.*, as ***Wimpyburger, Wimpy culture, -eating; Wimpy Bar,*** an establishment where Wimpy hamburgers are sold.

1959 *Observer* 8 Nov. 3/1 At least once a week a 'Wimpy Bar' is being opened somewhere in England. **1966** 'K. A. SADDLER' *Gilt Edge* xiii. 180 That night in the Wimpy Bar.. Len had summed him up at a glance. He had only agreed to take part in the job to get out of the Wimpy Bar. **1982** M. GILBERT *Final Throw* v. 35 'Let's find somewhere to eat.'.. They found a Wimpy Bar that was open. **1939** *Amer. Speech* XIV. 154/2 *Wimpyburger*, a specially large hamburger sandwich. **1971** LAVER & COLLINS *Education of Tennis Player* xvi. 209 A tea garden.. is located outside of Centre Court [at Wimbledon] where the famous strawberries and cream are sold.., along with a concession to the present day: Wimpyburgers. **1971** 'J. QUARTERMAIN' *Man who walked on Diamonds* i. 7 A London throbbing with traffic and Wimpy culture. **1959** *Observer* 8 Nov. 3/1 Behind this wave of Wimpy-eating lies a simple commercial formula.

wimpy ('wɪmpɪ), *a. slang* (orig. *U.S.*). [f. WIMP[2] + -Y[1].] = WIMPISH *a.*

1967 *Current Slang* Spring 5, [1964] *Wimpy*, stupid or sluggish. **1969** *Publ. Amer. Dial. Soc.* LI. 16 *Wimpy*, spineless. **1977** D. LINZEE *Discretion* (1981) i. 16 'It is exquisite.' 'I think it's kind of a wimpy little picture, personally. **1977** *Sounds* 9 July 31/1, I vaguely anticipated something wimpy and limpy prattling about San Francisco and love and peace man. **1980** *High Fidelity* June 106/2 The Seventies witnessed macho rock & rollers sneering at singer/songwriters as 'wimpy'. **1984** *Nutshell* (Gainesville ed.) Spring 52/2, I *was* this little wimpy kid in elementary school and high school. **1984** *Melody Maker* 6 Oct. 15/4 Dennis had a brilliant artist last summer, really strong drawings, but now it's gone back to being a bit wimpy.

Hence **'wimpiness** = WIMPISHNESS.

1982 *Chicago Sun-Times* 1 Sept. 54 (*caption*) Wanna be a political activist? Are you held back by wimpiness?

Wimshurst ('wɪmzhɜːst). *Physics.* [The name of James *Wimshurst* (1832–1903), English engineer.] ***Wimshurst machine***: an electrostatic generator consisting of two or more counterrotating discs of insulating material mounted close together on a common axle and having a ring of metal sectors around their periphery; each disc has a stationary pair of brushes at diametrically opposite positions which are electrically connected, so that successive sectors become inductively charged as they come into contact with a brush and give up their charge later in the turn as they pass a fixed set of needle points connected to one or other electrode.

1886 R. WORMELL *A. von Urbanitzky's Electricity in Service of Man* I. 63 The Wimshurst machine and that of Carré.. are the least subject to these defects of any that we are acquainted with. **1978** *Sci. Amer.* Apr. 159/1, I placed my candle between the oppositely charged poles of a Wimshurst machine, the ancient hand-crank generator of high-voltage static electricity.

win (wɪn), *sb.*[1] Forms: 1–3 winn, (3 *pl.* wunnen), 4–5 winne, wynne, wyn(e, 3– win. [OE. *win(n)* labour, strife, conflict (cf. MG. *win*), more frequently *ȝewinn*: see I-WIN *sb.* The modern senses are from WIN *v.*[1]]

I. †**1.** Strife, contention, conflict; tumult, disturbance, agitation. *Obs.*

a **1000** *Cædmon's Gen.* 259 He..ongan him winn up ahebban wið þone hehstan heofnes wealdend. *c* **1200** *Trin. Coll. Hom.* 161 Hwile lat te deuel hem..& weccheð among hem flite & win. *a* **1250** *Owl & Night.* 670 He mot gon to al mid gynne Hwan þe horte beoþ on winne. *c* **1250** *Gen. & Ex.* 598 Ðo ðe tende moneð cam in, So wurð draȝen ðe watres win. *c* **1275** LAY. 9044 Þat heold fiht and win [*earlier text* iwin].

†**2.** Gain, acquisition, profit; also, advantage, benefit. *Obs.*

c **1200** ORMIN 6118 Þe birrþ þin rihhte swinnkess winn Upponn ȝuw alle nittenn. *a* **1300** *Floriz & Bl.* 805 (Camb. MS.) Ac floriz nolde for no winne; Leuere him were wiþ his kinne. *c* **1440** *Pallad. on Husb.* III. 5 Ek newer, gretter wynne Is to the gresse. **1495** *Acta Dom. Conc.* (1839) 409/1 Þe said tend penny of all wynnis pertenyn to our souerane lord. *a* **1500** *Bernard. de cura rei fam.* 1. 180 Eftyr þi wyne with worschipe, clethyng wer. *a* **1500** *Thrie Priests Peblis* 619 Quhan thay ar full of sic wrang win. **1500–20** DUNBAR *Poems* xvii. 16 Thir merchantis takis vnlesum win. **1535** LYNDESAY *Satyre* 3507 In pryde, invy, in ire, and lecherie, In covetice, or ony extreme win.

†**b.** Possessions, riches, wealth. *Obs.*

For the phr. ***worldes win(ne*** see WIN *sb.*[2] 2.

c **1205** LAY. 3099 Ic hem ȝeue al þa winne þe ich æm walding ouer. *Ibid.* 22668 Wif & mine weden and alle mine wunnen. *a* **1300** *Cursor M.* 7879 Bot oft þe weliest o win Riue-liest þai fal in sin. *c* **1460** *Towneley Myst.* i. 185 To walk here in this worthely wone, In all this welthly wyn.

II. 3. A victory in a game or contest. *colloq.*

1862 *Illustr. Lond. News* 10 May 492/3 The opposition.. gathered strength after this slovenly win. **1866** *Daily Tel.* 3 Nov., Pineapple..won the first race, it being his eighth win since he was sold. **1894** ASTLEY *Fifty Yrs. Life* II. 78, I was real pleased with the win, for lots of my pals had backed Actea.

4. A gain; *pl.* gains, winnings. *colloq.*

1891 NAT GOULD *Double Event* ii, His gambling wins would have been enough for that. **1893** *Kennel Gaz.* Aug., Although the Shows might not be affected, their wins would be. **1897** T. R. WILLIAMS *Serm. on 'Just as I am'* 3 Every mental win on your part is a draw upon universal truth.

†**win**, *sb.*[2] *Obs.* Forms: 1 wynn, (1 wunn, wenn), 3 wnne, wonne, (also 7) wun, 3–4 winne, (also 7) wunne, 3–5, 7 win, 4–5 wyn, wenne, 4–6 wynne, 5 wyne. [OE. *wyn(n*, corresp. to OS. *wunnia*, OHG. *wunnja*, *wunna* str. f., *wunnî* f. and *wunno* wk. masc. (MHG. *wünne*, *wunne*, G. *wonne*); f. Teut. *wun-*, found also in OE. *ȝewun*, *wunian* (see WONT), *wýscan* (:—**wunskjan*) to WISH, and related to *wen-* (see WEEN *sb.* and *v.*) and WINE *sb.*[2], friend. Cf. WINSOME.]

1. Joy, pleasure, delight, bliss; a source of joy, a delight.

Beowulf 2262 Hearpan wyn, gomen gleobeames. *c* **1205** LAY. 9071 Jesu Crist..alre worulde wunne. *Ibid.* 22732 Ne mihte nauere mon cunne nan swa muchel wunne. *a* **1225** *Ancr. R.* 192 Alle þeo ilke uondunges..puncheð wouh, & nout wunne, auh heo wendeð efterward to weole and to eche blisse. *a* **1240** *Ureisun* in *O.E. Hom.* I. 183 Ihesu mi weole, mi wunne. *c* **1275** LAY. 25569 Louerd drihtene crist.. middilerþes win. *a* **1310** in Wright *Lyric P.* xv. 47 Away is al my wunne. *c* **1330** R. BRUNNE *Chron. Wace* (Rolls) 14908 Fair folk ys þere-inne! Þer faces to se, hit ys gret wynne! *c* **1386** CHAUCER *Frankl. T.* 54 Wyn, wo, or chaungynge of complexion. *c* **1425** *Cast. Persev.* 204 in *Macro Plays* 83 *Belyal.* In woo is al my wenne. *c* **1700** KENNETT *Lansd. MS. 1033* lf. 430b, *Wunsome*, pleasant..a *wunne* gaudium, whence a *wun to see*, a pleasure or satisfaction to see.

b. In vague commendatory sense, and often in phr. ***with*** (or ***mid***) ***win***, which, orig. intensive, freq. becomes a mere tag.

c **1300** *Havelok* 660 Slep sone, with michel winne. *Ibid.* 2965 Hauelok bi-lefte wit ioie and gamen In engelond, and was þer-inne Sixti winter king with winne. **13..** *Gaw. & Gr. Knt.* 15 On mony bonkkes ful brode Bretayn he settez, wyth wynne. *c* **1330** R. BRUNNE *Chron. Wace* (Rolls) 9617 Þer com þey to þe toun wyþ wyn. *a* **1400** *Sqr. lowe Degre* 263 Wyth welth and wynne to were the crowne. *c* **1400** *Destr. Troy* 13346 Penolope,..Þat had keppit hir full cloise as a cleane lady, With myche worship & wyn. **14..** *Poem to Virgin* in *Rel. Ant.* II. 213 Swete lady, full of wynne, Full of grace and gode within. *c* **1440** *Syr Gowghter* 51 in Utterson *E.P.P.* I. 163 The worthi duk and ducheese They levid togeder with wenne. *c* **1460** *Towneley Myst.* xxiv. 153 For I may swere with mekill wyn I am the most shrew in all myn kyn. *c* **1475** *Rauf Coilȝear* 925 Wed ane worthie to wyfe, and weild her with win.

c. In benedictory phrases.

c **1400** *Ywaine & Gaw.* 1113 Sho said smertly, Do lat me her, Cumes he sone, als have thou wyn. *Ibid.* 2219 So have i wyn, Mi lyoun and i sal noght twyn. *c* **1425** *Seven Sag.* (P.) 1373 So God almyghty gyf me wyne, Thou ne schalt to come hyre-ine. *a* **1500** *Sir Beues* (Pynson) 2453 There was a wel, so haue I wynne, And Beuys stumbled ryght therin. **1553** BRADFORD *Serm. Repentance* F viij b, Thoughe a great whyle he laye a slepe (as many do now a dayes, god geue them wynne waking) [*ed.* 1574 G ij *by a misunderstanding reads* good waking]. **1640** M. PARKER *King & poore North. Man* lxxx, Man, with thy money God give thee win.

2. ***worldes winne*** (earlier *woreld winne*, OE. *worolde wynn*), also ***worldly winne***: worldly delight or pleasure; later, by association with WIN *sb.*[1], worldly wealth or possessions.

Beowulf 1080 Þær heo ær mæste heold worolde wynne. *c* **1175** *Lamb. Hom.* 147 On twa wise Mon mei forlete world winne. *c* **1200** *Trin. Coll. Hom.* 195 Erest he strepte of him his shep, þe waren his woreld winne. *a* **1225** *Ancr. R.* 196 Worldes weole, & wunne, & wurschipe. *c* **1230** *Hali Meid.* (MS. Titus) 90 For worldliche wunne þat tu wendes to biȝeten. *c* **1325** *Metr. Hom.* 15 For rifli gers werldes win Thir fair wimmen fal in sin. *c* **1375** *Sc. Leg. Saints* xvi. (*Magdalena*) 56 Þat mychty ware & of gret kyne, & mykil had of warldis wyne. *a* **1400** *Minor Poems fr. Vernon MS.* 337/341 Alle worldes winne He sendeþ, whon he wile. **1535** LYNDESAY *Satyre* 3535 Covetice of warldlie win.

win, *sb.*[3] *slang.* Also 6–7 wyn, 9 whinn, winn, wing. [Origin obscure; quot. 1812 suggests that it may be short for *Winchester*.] A penny.

1567 HARMAN *Caveat* 85 A flagge, a wyn, and a make. **1608** DEKKER *Lanth. & Candle Lt.* i. C 2b, If we..nip a boung that has but a win. **1618** [see MAKE *sb.*[3]]. *a* **1693** *Urquhart's Rabelais* III. xli. 341 They had not a Win in their Fab. **1812** J. H. VAUX *Flash Dict.*, *Win* or *Winchester*, a penny. **1823** 'JON BEE' *Dict. Turf*, *Scuddick*,..'not a scuddick'—not any brads, not a whinn, empty clies. **1859** *Slang Dict.*, *Winn*, a penny. **1900** FLYNT *Tramping* 241 Just go and get a shave now, Jim. I'll give you a wing (penny), if you will, for the doin' o' 't.

†**win**, *a. Obs.* Forms: 3 wn-, 4 wunne, wynne, 5 wyn. [Only in ME. alliterative verse; adj. use of WIN *sb.*[2], derived from OE. poetical compounds such as *wynbéam* tree of joy, *wynland* pleasant land.] Delightful, pleasant; goodly, fine; good.

c **1205** LAY. 1385 Þer he mihte þurh-wunian mid his wnfolke [*later text* gode folke]. *a* **1310** *Lenten ys come* 35 This wunne weole y wole forgon, Ant wyht in wode be fleme. **13..** *Gaw. & Gr. Knt.* 1032 Þere he draȝez hym on-dryȝe, & derely hym þonkkez, Of þe wynne worschip þat [*MS.* &] he hym wayued hade. *Ibid.* 2430 Þat wyl I welde wyth good wylle, not for þe wynne golde. **13..** *E.E. Allit. P.* A. 154 Euer me þoȝt I schulde not wonde For wo, þer welez so wynne wore. *c* **1400** *Destr. Troy* 4265 A faire temple..With wallis vp wroght, wyn to beholde.

win (wɪn), *v.*[1] Pa. t. and pple. won (wʌn). Forms: *Inf.* α. 1–2 winnan, (1 wynnan), 3 winnen, (*Orm.*) -enn, 3–6 wynne, (3–5 -en), 3–7 winne, 3–8 winn, (4 whyn, *Sc.* vyn(e), 4–6 wine, wyne, wynn, wyn, (5 wenne), 4– win. β. (chiefly *Sc.*) 5, 7–8 wone, 6–9 won, 7 wonne, 9 wun. *Pa. t.* α. 1, 4 wann, 1–7 (8–9 *dial.* and *arch.*) wan, (4–5 whan(ne), 4–6 wane, (*Sc.* van), 4–7 wanne, (6 *Sc.* vane). β. 1. *2nd pers. sing.* wunne; *pl.* 1 wunnon, 1, 5 wunnun, 3 (*Orm.*) -enn, 3–5 wonne(n, 4–5 -yn, 5 wonen, -yn; 4–6 wunne, 6–7 wun. γ. 1 wonn, 4–7 wonne, (5 whonne), 6–7 woon, 1– won. δ. 6 winned, 7 wined. *Pa. pple.* α. 3–4 wunnen, (3 *Orm.* -enn), 4–5 wunne, 4 (6 *Sc.*) wun, (5 *north.* vun, 6 *Sc.* wvne); 4 (5 *Sc.*) woun, 5 *Sc.* wown, (woung). β.[1]. 4 wonnun, (*Sc.* wonone, vonnyn, vonyng), 4–5 wonnin, -ene, -yn(e, wonen(e, -yn(e, 4–6 wonnen, 5 wonun, (*Sc.* wonnyng). β.[2]. 3–4 iwonne, 3–5 ywonne, 4 ywon, 5 ywone, ywonnen, e-wonne. β.[3]. 4–7 wonne, (8 *Sc.*) wone, 5–7 wonn, 4– won; 6–7 woon(e, (6 woonne). γ. 4–7 wan, 6 wanne. δ. *Sc.* 5 winin, (wyn(n)ynge); 6 winn, wyn, wyne, 6–8 win, 7 winne, wynn. (Cf. WIN *ppl. a.*) ϵ. 7 wind. [Com. Teut. str. vb.: OE. *winnan*, (*wann*, *wunnen*), also *ȝewinnan* I-WIN *v.* = OFris. *winna* to obtain, OS. *winnan* to suffer, win, *giwinnan* to obtain, (MLG., MDu. *winnen* to till the ground, obtain, acquire), OHG. *winnan* (MHG. *winnen*) to be excited, rage, contend, exert oneself, also *gawinnan* to gain as by labour or exertion (MHG., G. *gewinnen*), ON. *vinna* to labour, bring about, gain (Sw. *vinna*, Da. *vinde*), Goth. *(ga)winnan* to suffer: ulterior relations are uncertain; forms of cognate meaning are Goth. *winno*, *winna*, *wunns* suffering, OHG. *winna* conflict, MHG. *winne* pain, ON. *vinna* labour; see also WITHERWIN (OE. *wiþerwinna*, OHG. *widarwinno*).

The senses run parallel to a considerable extent with those of GAIN *v.*[2] and GET *v.*]

†**1.** *intr.* To work, labour (OE.); to strive, contend, fight. *Obs.*

Beowulf 506 Eart þu se Beowulf, se þe wið Brecan wunne? *c* **888** ÆLFRED *Boeth.* xxxv. §4 Nis nan ȝesceaft þe tiohhie þæt hio scyle winnan wið hire scippendes willan. *c* **900** tr. *Baeda's Hist.* IV. iii. (1890) 264 He þy ma mid his hondum wonn & worhte þa þing, þe nydþearfleco wæron. *a* **1000** in Wr.-Wülcker 202/41 *Pugnaui*, ic wan. *a* **1122** *O.E. Chron.* (Laud MS.) an. 685 Her ongan Ceadwala winnan æfter rice. *c* **1200** ORMIN 3488 Forr þatt menn sholldenn..winnenn swa to cumenn upp till heofennrichess blisse. *c* **1200** *Trin. Coll. Hom.* 51 Ierusalem and babilonie beð two burȝes, and fliteð eure, and winneð bitwinen hem. *Ibid.* 187 Iob..wan wið þe þurse. *c* **1220** *Bestiary* 521 Til it cumeð ðe time Ðat storm stireð al ðe se, Ðanne sumer and winter winnen.

†**2.** *trans.* To conquer, subdue, overcome, defeat, vanquish, 'beat'. *Obs.*

1297 R. GLOUC. (Rolls) 136 Alle þes kinges were þo, ac bote on nov þer nis; Vor þe king of westsex alle þe oþere wan iwis. *a* **1300** *Cursor M.* 14832 He has vs wonnen [*c* **1375** *Fairf. MS.* wonnin] wit maistri. **13..** *Guy Warw.* (A.) 889 Wel mani kniȝtes Gij wan þat day. **1375** BARBOUR *Bruce* XII. 47 He thoucht that he suld weill lichtly Vyn hym, and haf hym at his will. *c* **1375** *Sc. Leg. Saints* vii. (*Jacobus Minor*) 752 Quhene þat tytus Ierusalem had wonone. *c* **1400** *Ragman Roll* 168 in Hazl. *E.P.P.* I. 76 Or that ye be conqueryd and e-wonne. *c* **1420** *Avow. Arth.* xxii, Thus hase he wonun Kay on werre. *c* **1470** *Gol. & Gaw.* 1198 Wourschipful Wavane had wonnin him on weir. **1470–85** MALORY *Arthur* VII. xxiii. 250 He wanne me in playne bataille hande for hand. **1513** *Life Hen. V.* (1911) 108 He deliberated by proces of time to wynn them by hunger and thirst. **1535** STEWART *Cron. Scot.* (Rolls) I. 84 How that Reuthar..faucht with Cecelus..and wan him. **1577** T. KENDALL *Flowers Epigr.* 38b, Here sensuall pleasure doeth assault to winne me by her might. **1610** HEYWOOD *Gold. Age* V. i, Creet thou hast wonne My thirty thousand Souldiers, and my Sonne.

fig. **1567** MAPLET *Gr. Forest* 1 But whiles it [*sc.* the adamant] is inuincible or can not be woonne that way [*sc.* by fire]: yet..with the..freshe bloud of the Goate, it breaketh ..in sunder. **1575** A. F. *Virg. Bucol.* vii. 22 Phillis loues the Hazils well,..The Myrtle shall them neuer wynne, nor Phoebus Bay trees tall.

3. a. To be victorious in (a contest of any kind, as a battle, game, race, action at law, etc.). Also ***to win the day***, ***the field***. (Cf. *to win the victory*, 6 b.)

Formerly used with a wider range of obj. (e.g. *conquest*, *exploit*).

a **1300** *Cursor M.* 7793 Dauid had gin him batail kene; Wit godds grace þe feild he wan. **1338** R. BRUNNE *Chron.* (1810) 24 Tuo & tuenty batailes he wanne þe first ȝere. *c* **1400** *Beryn* 1747 The meyne [viz. chessmen] were I-set vp; they gon to pleye fast: Beryn wan the first, þe second, & þe þird. **1474** CAXTON *Chesse* II. iii. (1883) 38 The tonges of aduocates.. must be had yf thou wylt wynne thy cause. **1489** *Barbour's Bruce* XI. *title*, The battale of Bannokburne, strykyne & vonyng be gud kyng Robert the Bruce. *a* **1533** LD. BERNERS *Huon* liii. 177 How kynge Iuoryn caused his doughter play at the chesse with Huon,..and how Huon wan the game. *c* **1590** MARLOWE *Faustus* 1029 Wks. (1910) 180 Howe they had wonne by prowesse such exploits. **1591** SHAKS. *1 Hen. VI*, I. vi. 17 'Tis Ioane, not we, by whom the day is wonne. **1594** R. CAREW *Tasso* (1881) 15 Conquests he winned. **1600** HOLLAND *Livy* I. ii. 3 The Aborigines and Trojanes wan indeed the field, but lost their Captaine Latinus. *a* **1650** CALDERWOOD *Hist. Kirk* (1843) II. 263 'Prove that, and wonne the plea!' said Lethington. **1653** HOLCROFT *Procopius, Pers. Wars* I. 22 He wanne this battell. **1728** RAMSAY *Monk & Miller's Wife* 233 His courage wan the day. **1781** [see RACE *sb.*[1] 10]. **1837** DICKENS *Pickw.* vii, Won the toss—first innings—seven o'clock a.m. **1878** H. GIBBS *Ombre* (ed. 2) 26 If either of the adversaries win the game. **1908** [ELIZ. FOWLER] *Betw. Trent & Ancholme* 380 About that time, Waterloo was won.

(*b*) *transf.* in catch-phr. ***to win the peace***, to bring about the successful reconstruction of a country defeated in or severely damaged by a war; hence ***win-the-peace*** attrib.

1942 H. A. WALLACE *Century of Common Man* (1944) 10 As part of the effort to win the peace, I am hoping that what might be called the 'ever normal granary principle' can be established for a number of commodities on a world-wide scale. **1945** *Daily Herald* 31 Aug. 2/1 The nation, girding itself for a supreme win-the-peace endeavour, will derive high encouragement from this enterprise by the mining community. **1950** A. HUXLEY *Themes & Variations* 243 That the Russians have been 'winning the peace' is due.. to the fact that they profess and teach, as absolutely true, a clear-cut philosophy of man and nature. **1962** *Listener* 8 Mar. 402/2 They have also tried to agree that nobody was going to win the peace, but nobody was going to lose it either.

b. Phrs. ***you can't win them all***; ***you win some, you lose some***, etc.

1954 R. CHANDLER *Long Goodbye* xxiv. 122 Take it easy, Doc. You can't win them all. **1966** P. O'CONNELL *Sabre-Tooth* xiv. 189 You win a few, you lose a few, and it's no good getting sore. **1976** *Times* 23 Nov. 14/1 You look like being saddled with the uninspiring Willy... On the other hand, you seem to have got your way over Mrs. Thatcher's nominee... You win some, you lose some. **1979** K. M. PEYTON *Marion's Angels* ix. 151 'It'll be all right,' she said. 'I daresay. You can't win them all.' **1984** *Listener* 1 Nov. 24/3 Academic friends.. have found just one definite factual error... Ah, well; win some, lose some.

4. a. *absol.* or *intr.* To overcome one's adversary, opponent, or competitor; to be victorious, gain the victory (now chiefly in sports or games of skill); *fig.* to prevail.

1297 R. GLOUC. (Rolls) 4688 Hii worrede norþward & wonne ver & ner. **13..** *Cursor M.* 20004 (Edin.) Werande on þe wrang þai wan. **1375** BARBOUR *Bruce* XII. 373 In punȝeis is oft hapnyne Quhill for to vyne, and quhill to tyne. *c* **1400** *26 Pol. Poems* xxiv. 288 Haue mercie on me, let mercie wyn! **14..** AUDELAY *Poems* (Percy Soc.) Introd. p. ix, Oure faders in Frawns had won beforne. *c* **1440** *Alphabet of Tales* cxviii. 83 How.. ij men played at þe dyce, and when þe tane of þaim began to lose, he began to.. flite with God for þat he wan nott. **1546** J. HEYWOOD *Prov.* (1867) 10 He laughth that wynth. **1551** EDW. VI *Jrnl.* in *Lit. Rem.* (Roxb.) II. 312, I lost.. at roundes, and wane at rovers. **1597** SHAKS. *2 Hen. IV*, I. i. 132 The summe of all, Is, that the King hath wonne. **1607** MARKHAM *Cavel.* VI. iv. 15 Nor haue I seene anye horse winne, but I haue seene many Horses loose, which haue beene kept with such dyett. **1697** DRYDEN *Virg. Georg.* IV. 127 Obstinately bent to win or dye. **1818** BYRON *Ch. Har.* IV. cxl, He is gone, Ere ceased the inhuman shout which hail'd the wretch who won. **1837** DICKENS *Pickw.* ii, That [advice] which bystanders invariably give to the smallest boy in a street fight, namely, 'Go in and win'. **1842** TENNYSON *Godiva* 35 The passions of her mind.. Made war upon each other for an hour, Till pity won. **1871** FARRAR *Witn. Hist.* iii. 100 Yet, unaided by any, opposed by all, Christianity won. **1880** W. DAY *Racehorse in Training* xviii. 169 If an owner runs two horses in a race, he has a right to declare with which of the two he will win. **1884** *Manch. Exam.* 21 May 4/7 The M.C.C. winning by an innings and four runs.

b. Phrs. ***you can't win***, said (often in exasperation) to emphasize that whatever one does, it will be judged wrong or insufficient; ***you win***, used to concede defeat in argument, etc.

1926 J. BLACK (*title*) You can't win. **1943** N. MARSH *Colour Scheme* vi. 99 All right... You win. I apologize. **1962** *Redbook* Mar. 44/2 She says I should always be dignified in front of him. Next she hands me the garbage pail and says, 'Take this out.' You can't win, no matter which way you turn! **1976** P. LIVELY *Stitch in Time* v. 55 'You can't win,' said Martin with sudden gloom, 'when you're the eldest. Whatever you do, you shouldn't have because you're old enough to know better.' **1982** 'S. WOODS' *Enter a Gentlewoman* II. iii. 113 'It's hardly fair to judge other people by one's own principles.' 'All right, you win.'

5. a. *trans.* To subdue and take possession of; to seize, capture, take (a place). *arch.* (now associated with 6).

ME. phr. ***to win to*** or ***into one's hand*** or ***will***.

a **1122** *O.E. Chron.* an. 1070 (Laud MS.), Hi wendon þæt hi sceoldon winnon eall þæt land. *c* **1200** *Trin. Coll. Hom.* 51 þe king.. bilai þe burh forte þat hit [= he it] wan. **1297** R. GLOUC. (Rolls) 1033 Engelond aþ ibe mid strengþe iwonne. *Ibid.* 3859 King howel wiþ is poer wan sone peyto Al to king arthures wille. *Ibid.* 7878 Ar is fader wonne engelond. *a* **1300** *Leg. Rood* ii. 219 He ouercom is fon And.. al is lond won. *a* **1300** *Cursor M.* 9202 In his time was þe Iuen land Wonnen [*Fairf.* wonnyn] into þe sarzins hand. **13..** *E.E. Allit. P.* B. 1305 Nov he þe kyng has conquest & þe kyth wunnen. **13..** *Coer de L.* 1348 The toun of Acres he has wunne. **1387** TREVISA *Higden* (Rolls) IV. 9 Whanne Alisaundre hadde i-wonne alle þe est londes. *c* **1425** WYNTOUN *Cron.* XX. 36 Sic assawtis þare he maid That neire þe tovne he wonyn [*v.r.* wonnynge] hade. *Ibid.* clxx. 4816 Quhen þe wardane.. of þat land Had wonnyn gret part till his hand. *c* **1425** *Engl. Conq. Irel.* lvii. 136 He come ynto Irland, & whan the lond. **1430–40** LYDG. *Bochas* IX. 2134 Whan the saide cite was first wonne. *c* **1440** *Gesta Rom.* lvii. 240 (Harl. MS.) þey entrid into þe citee, & whonne hit. *c* **1470** HENRY *Wallace* VII. 1007 Ramsay and Graym the turat ȝet has wown. *Ibid.* x. 959 Schynnoun thai tuk, at Wallace fyrst had woun [*ed.* **1570** winin]. **1470–85** MALORY *Arthur* I. vii. 44 Arthur wan alle the north scotland. *a* **1548** HALL *Chron., Hen. V* 39 b, He that will Fraunce wynne must with Scotlande firste begyn. **1556** *Chron. Grey Friars* (Camden) 21 Thys yere the towne dech was new cast... And the towne of Barwyke wanne. **1578** H. WOTTON *Courtlie Controv.* 145 As men say, the Towne wonne, the Castell yeeldeth. **1603** G. OWEN *Pembrokeshire* (1892) 47 A greate parte thereof was woon from them by the Englishmen. **1613** J. SARIS *Voy. Japan* (Hakl. Soc.) 34 There land, which they had wone with there swordes. **1697** DRYDEN *Æneis* x. 493 On either Hand, These fight to keep, and those to win the Land. **1791** COWPER *Iliad* IV. 495 Should the Greeks.. win imperial Troy, The glory shall be his. **1836** THIRLWALL *Greece* xxv. III. 387 He advised that they should.. endeavour first to win Messana. **1871** FREEMAN *Norm. Conq.* IV. xviii. 155 In the eyes of William it was a means by which Exeter might be won.

b. To seize, capture, take as spoil; to catch (fish, a bird); to capture, take captive (a person). *Obs.* exc. in euphemistic slang, to steal.

a **1300** *K. Horn* 1144 (Harl.) ȝef eny fyssh is þer inne þer of þou shalt wynne. **1375** BARBOUR *Bruce* VII. 88 Schir Thomas Randale than.. the kyngis baner van. *c* **1400** *Destr. Troy* 4803 The souerain.. deuidet Tho godes to his gomes .. þat hom wan with woundes before And put hom in perell. **1481** CAXTON *Reynard* iii. (Arb.) 6 That pudyng was myne ffor I hadde wonne it by nyghte in a mylle. *a* **1533** LD. BERNERS *Huon* cxlii. 527 A ryche shyp, the whiche was wonne vpon the sowdans men. **1560** ROLLAND *Seven Sages* (Bann. Club) 1 Thay war sa repleit of all riches Win into weiris be martiall besynes. **1567** *Gude & Godlie B.* (S.T.S.) 112 Lyke to ane bird taine in ane net,.. Sa is our lyfe weill win away. **1596** DALRYMPLE tr. *Leslie's Hist. Scot.* (S.T.S.) I. 42 Nocht sa mekle fishe thay with nettis, as with skepis, or long kreilis, win with wickeris in the forme of a hose sa round wouen. **1628** FELTHAM *Resolves* II. [I.] lxxi. 205 The Spoyles he wanne from Cowards. *a* **1700** B. E. *Dict. Cant. Crew*, *To Win*, to Steal. **1785** GROSE *Dict. Vulgar T.* **1919** *Athenæum* 8 Aug. 727/2 Everyone will have heard of 'strafing' and also 'souvenir', the latter usually meaning anything stolen, or 'won'.

†**c.** *fig.* To reclaim (land) as for cultivation.

1531–2 *Act 23 Hen. VIII* c. 5 §1 Marsshe groundes.. wonne and made profitable for the greate common welthe of this Realme. **1541** *Reg. Mag. Sig. Scot.* 554/1 To win and rife out the saidis landis with the Eisly hillis of the samin. **1573–80** TUSSER *Husb.* (1878) 114 The fen and the quamire, so marrish be kind, And are to be drained, now wine [*later edd.* win] to thy mind.

†**d.** Of the sea: To gain on (the land): cf. 10 a.

1639 G. PLATTES *Discov. Subterr. Treas.* xi. 52 The sea.. perpetually winning land in one place, and losing in another.

e. *Cards.* (*a*) (*fig.* from 2) To be of higher value than, to 'beat' (another card, hand, or suit); also *intr.* with *of* (cf. 10 a); (*b*) to gain possession of, take (a trick).

1680 COTTON *Compl. Gamester* vii. 71 He that can win five Tricks of the nine hath a sure Game. *Ibid.* x. 83 A Ten wins a Nine if not Trumps. **1778** *Hoyle's Games Impr.* 63 A.. wins two Tricks... The first Hand wins of the second. **1892** 'CAVENDISH' *Bézique* 4 The highest card of the suit led wins the trick... Trumps win other suits. **1910** DALTON '*Saturday*' *Bridge* 41 This is an undoubted No Trump call for the dealer, although in itself it will not win many tricks.

6. To get, obtain, acquire; *esp.* to get as something profitable or desired; to gain, procure. **a.** with concrete (material) obj. *Obs.* or *arch.* exc. in specific uses: see 7.

c **1200** ORMIN 6111, & tuss þu mihht te weorelldþing Wiþþ Godess lefe winnenn. *Ibid.* 7890, & ȝiff ȝho wass summ wædle wif þatt lamb ne mihhte winnenn. *c* **1220** *Bestiary* 411 Ðe rauen is swiðe redi, Weneð ðat ȝe rotieð, And oðre fules hire fallen bi For to winnen fode. *c* **1290** *Beket* 1439 in *S. Eng. Leg.* 147 His men he broȝte In seruise heore mete to wynne þere. **13..** *Cursor M.* 4376 (Gött.) And leuere me es be pouer and lele, þan falsli to winne catele. **1362** LANGL. *P. Pl.* A. v. 237 Al þat I wikkedliche won seþþe I wit hade. *c* **1400** *Gamelyn* 283 (Corpus MS.) Thus wan Gamely þe Ram and þe Ryng. **1430** *Reg. Mag. Sig. Scot.* 38/2 The tanehalf of the sayd to be wonnyn fra the sayd Andro be the law. *c* **1449** PECOCK *Repr.* III. xix. 409 If ẏe riche and haue wunne more good than is necessarie to me. **1526** TINDALE *Luke* ix. 25 For what shall itt avauntage a man, to wyn the whole worlde yff he loose hym silfe? **1549** *Compl. Scot.* xx. 172 The inglis men van neuyr na thing at ȝour handis. **1553** BECON *Reliques of Rome* (1563) 247 b, Euery winning lefully wonnen in merchaundise. **1563** *Homilies* II. *Matrimony* ⁋ 13 He tylleth it [*sc.* the ground], and so wynneth fruite thereof. **1616** T. SCOT *Philomythie* I 3 b, Till th'one his topsaile fairely doth aduance To win the winde. **1670** W. WALKER *Idiomat. Anglo-Lat.* 549, I will win the horse, or lose the saddle. **1813** SCOTT *Rokeby* I. xii, Right English all, they rush'd to blows, With nought to win, and all to lose. **1868** MORRIS *Earthly Par.* (1870) I. II. 556 A certain man Who from being poor great riches wan.

b. with abstract (immaterial) obj., or *gen.*

Still in regular current use in reference to something gained by merit or the like, as *confidence, esteem, fame, favour, honour, love, praise, respect*, etc.; also with *consent, obedience*, etc.; ***to win the*** (or ***a***) ***victory***, to be victorious (cf. 3); ***to win one's way***, to make or find one's way, 'get along', succeed in getting somewhere (also *fig.*). In other connexions ordinarily replaced by *gain* or *obtain*.

c **1000** *Passio S. Marg.* in Cockayne *Narratiunculæ* (1861) 49 Eadiȝ eart þu.. for þon þe þu wunne reste a oþ ende mid halȝum fæmnum. *c* **1200** ORMIN Ded. 313 To winnenn.. Att Crist soþ sawle berrhless. *a* **1300** *Cursor M.* 17497 If we ne soth said, quat suld we win? For-soth nanoþer thing bot sin. *Ibid.* 20056 þair beniscun þan bes not wan. **13..** *Coer de L.* 1884 The galyes came unto the cite, And had nigh won entrie. **1340** HAMPOLE *Pr. Consc.* 2769 Na mede in heven to wyn. *c* **1375** *Sc. Leg. Saints* iii. (*Andreas*) 560 þat þu mycht ..of þi cristis lawis blyne, þat þu mycht oure frendschepe vyne. ? *a* **1400** *Morte Arth.* 22 How they whanne.. wyrchippis many. *c* **1400** *Rom. Rose* 2316 In armes also if thou konne, Pursue to thou a name hast wonne. **1470–85** MALORY *Arthur* x. lix. 513 Whanne they wend best to haue wonne worship they loste hit. ? *a* **1500** *Chester Pl.* XII. 91 But ever he wynnes the victory. *a* **1548** HALL *Chron., Edw. IV* 203 b, To destroy the Realme, and wynne the hatred & malice of all the nacion. **1567** *Gude & Godlie B.* (S.T.S.) 59 He.. spolȝeit Sathan, hell and sin, And heuinlie gloir to vs hes win. **1570** DEE *Math. Pref.* ☛ iv b, To wyn due and common credit. *a* **1586** SIDNEY *Ps.* XXXI. v, O Lord, of thee, lett me still mercy wynne. **1617** MORYSON *Itin.* II. 166 In defending this fort [they] woon great reputation by their valour. *c* **1620** A. HUME *Brit. Tongue* (1865) 18 He snapped me on this hand and he on that, that the doctour had mikle a doe to win me room for a syllogisme. **1754** GRAY *Progr. Poesy* 39 In gliding state she wins her easy way. *a* **1796** BURNS '*As I stood by yon roofless tower*', Like fortune's favours, tint as win. **1853** DICKENS *Bleak Ho.* xiii, I am glad to have won your confidence. **1866** GEO. ELIOT *F. Holt* i, Winning small triumphs in bargains and personal economies. **1888** BRYCE *Amer. Commw.* lxxiii. II. 596 They failed to win obedience. **1910** A. LANG in *Encycl. Brit.* X. 135/1 Fairies naturally won their way into the poetry of the middle ages.

†**c.** *absol.* or *intr.*: in early use *esp.* to get gain, make profit; *spec.* in Sc. legal use, in such phrases as ***able to tine or win***, i.e. having means sufficient to aim at profit or risk loss. *Obs.*

a **1300** *Cursor M.* 19574 To win wit-all he wend it bij. **1340** HAMPOLE *Pr. Consc.* 1457 Now we wyn, now we tyn. **1362** LANGL. *P. Pl.* A. I. 153 þauȝ ȝe ben trewe of tonge and treweliche winne, And eke as chast as a child. *c* **1386** CHAUCER *Pard. T.* 133 A moral tale yet I yow telle kan Which I am wont to preche for to wynne. **1414** *26 Pol. Poems* xiii. 155 Wiþ fiȝt ȝe wynne, wiþ trete ȝe lese. **1421** *Ibid.* xviii. 138 Byȝe no thyng to selle and wynne. *c* **1450** *Godstow Reg.* 159 To wyn or to lese. **1476** *Acta Audit.* (1839) 47/1 To defend þe said causs of Erroür.. with ful powere to tyne and wynne. **1609** SKENE *Reg. Maj.* 53 Be his procuratour constitute be him, in his place, to tine or to wone in the cause. **1699** in *Rec. Convent. Burghs Scot.* (1880) IV. 281 Ane person that.. can tin and win in all ther affairs.

7. In various specific uses. †**a.** To beget: = GET *v.* 26. *Obs.*

13.. *E.E. Allit. P.* B. 112 Hit weren not alle on wyuez sunez, wonen with on fader. *a* **1400–50** *Wars Alex.* 587 þe twa þat I wan on myne oþire wyfe þat I wedd first.

†**b.** To get for immediate use, procure; hence, contextually, to fetch, bring (cf. 14 c). *Obs.*

c **1350** *Will. Palerne* 2852 þe werwolf went wiȝtly & whan hem mete & drink. **13..** *E.E. Allit. P.* B. 617, I schal wynne yow, wyȝt, of water a lyttel. *c* **1470** HENRY *Wallace* v. 865 The Scottis wan hors, becaus thair awne couth faill.

c. To obtain (a woman) as a wife or 'lady' by action or effort of some kind: usually with implication of gaining her affection and consent (cf. 9).

to win and wear: see WEAR *v.*[1] 8 b.

c **1320** *Sir Tristr.* 1913 Wiþ þine harp þou wonne hir þat tide. *c* **1374** CHAUCER *Anel. & Arc.* 100 Ful mychell besynesse had he or þat he myght his lady wynne. **1470–85** MALORY *Arthur* VIII. xxvi. 312 Sythen I am ladyles I wil wyn thy lady. **1579** LYLY *Euphues* (Arb.) 91 After al his strife hee [*sc.* Menelaus] wan but a strumpet. **1639** J. CLARKE *Parœm.* 40 Faint heart never won faire lady. **1668** SEDLEY *Mulberry Gard.* IV. i. 49 There had been More hope of winning a Widow at her Husbands Funeral, then of any favour for her now. **1789** BURNS *To Dr. Blacklock* viii, And let us mind, faint heart ne'er wan A lady fair. **1847** TENNYSON *Princess* Prol. 220 Take Lilia, then, for heroine.. and be you The Prince to win her! **1885** 'MRS. ALEXANDER' *Valerie's Fate* v, Valerie, will you let me try to win you?

d. To gain by effort or competition, as a prize or reward, or in gaming or betting, as a wager, etc. Also *absol.*

to win one's †***shoes, spurs***: see SHOE *sb.* 2 i, SPUR *sb.*[1] 3 a.

c **1320** *Sir Tristr.* 340 Tristrem wan þat day Of him an hundred pounde. *c* **1330** R. BRUNNE *Chron. Wace* (Rolls) 449 Iasan.. Whan þe Ram wyþ gilden flees. *c* **1400** *Destr. Troy* 172 And wo this wethur shuld wyn bude wirke as I say. *a* **1400–50** *Wars Alex.* 818 þis renke & his rounsy, þai reche vp a croune, As gome at has þe garland.. Wonn. *c* **1489** CAXTON *Sonnes of Aymon* vii. 169 For to assaye our horses for to wynne the pryce that the kyng hath set vpon. *a* **1533** [see WAGER *sb.*[2] 2]. **1549** *Compl. Scot.* vi. 64 Iason van the goldin fleice. **1610** B. JONSON *Alch.* I. i, He would haue.. a familiar To rifle with, at horses, and winne cups. **1621** T. GRANGER *Expos. Eccles.* vii. 7. 166 Our first Parents for an apple lost Paradise, and woon hell. **1645** VANE *Lost Sheepe* 35 Haueing woone the prize in the Pythian games. **1704** NORRIS *Ideal World* II. xii. 484 A man would be ridiculous that should go to prove by mere reason, that such a one won the plate at a horse-race. **1835** DICKENS *Sk. Boz, Mr. Watkins Tottle* i, Frank took dummy; and I won sixpence. **1848** THACKERAY *Van. Fair* lxiv, The Rev. Mr. Muff,.. of whom she won large sums at *écarté*. **1885** *Law Rep.* Weekly Notes 145/2 The defendant.. having won on those bets received the winnings from the persons with whom he had betted.

e. To get by labour, to earn (now *dial.*); †to get as profit, to gain (*obs.*). Also *absol.*

c **1200** ORMIN 10175 þeȝȝ [*sc.* publicans].. wunnenn mikell to þe king, & mare till hemm sellfenn. **1340–70** *Alex. & Dind.* 450 Wiþ us schineþ euery schalk in schippus for to saile, For to winne on þe watur wordliche fode. *c* **1386** CHAUCER *Prol.* 715 He moste preche and wel affile his tonge To wynne siluer. **1429** *Rolls of Parlt.* IV. 360/2 Yai wil.. receive for paiement.. nobles,.. ye which.. yai leede.. into oyer straunge Cuntrees, where hit is chaunged to yair encresce, and forged into oyer coygnes, so yat yai wynne in ye alay of ech noble xx d. *a* **1500** *Ratis Raving* 520 The gudis þat he has with his trew labore wynynge. **1530** in *Maitl. Club Misc.* II. 103 Honest and laborius personis abill to wyne thar liffing. **1531** *Dial. on Laws of Eng.* II. xxxix. 79 If a preest haue wonne moche by sayenge of masse. *c* **1620** Z. BOYD *Zion's Flowers* (1855) 54 Win little and win oft.. Makes merchands rich. **1623** J. TAYLOR (Water P.) *New Discov.* A 5, I am a Fisherman Who many yeares my liuing thus haue wan. **1724** RAMSAY *Tea-t. Misc.* (1733) I. 87 Wi' cauk and keel I'll win your bread. **1819** SCOTT *Noble Moringer* xxii, Of him I held the little mill which wins me living free. **1823** —— *Quentin D.* xiv, Every one wins his bread in this country. **1893** SNOWDEN *Tales Yorksh. Wolds* 188 Then Aw can win summat, cannot Aw?

f. To get, gather (crops or other produce); to gather in, harvest. Now *dial.*

1375 BARBOUR *Bruce* x. 189 Syndri cornys that thai bair Woxe rype to wyn to mannys fude. *Ibid.* 193 Thai of the peill had vonnyn hay. *Ibid.* 219 To vyn thair harvist. **1491** *Acta Dom. Conc.* (1839) 205/2 The cornez.. sall be led and wonnyne.. and stakkit. **15..** *Battle of Otterburn* i, Yt fell abowght the Lamasse tyde, Whan husbondes wynnes ther haye. **1549** D. MONRO *Descr. W. Isles* (1773) 46 The place quhar he winnes his peitts this zier, ther he sawis his corne the next zeire. **1565** *Reg. Privy Council Scot.* I. 402 The cornis.. ar nocht sa weill win as neid wer. *a* **1578** LINDESAY (Pitscottie) *Chron. Scot.* (S.T.S.) I. 30 [They] micht nocht saw nor wine thair cornis. **1683** J. REID *Scots Gard'ner*

(1907) 137 Peas..When ripe, you may easily win some for seed. *a* **1791** GROSE *Olio* (1792) 110 *W.* He is gone to the field to his workmen. *C.* Hey. *W.* Just so; to try to win his hay. **1834** SOUTHEY *Doctor* vi. (1848) 20 If they had fine weather for winning their hay or shearing their corn, they thanked God for it. **1891** A. LANG *Angling Sk.* 101 On a hillside..the countryfolk were winning their hay.

g. To get or extract (coal, stone, or other mineral) from the mine, pit, or quarry; also, to sink a shaft or make an excavation so as to reach (a seam of coal or vein of ore) and prepare it for working, as by drainage, etc. (cf. 11). See also WINNING *vbl. sb.* 5 a, 5 b.

1447 in *Reg. Mag. Sig. Scot. 1451* 106/1 With lefe..for to wyn colis and stanis within the saide landis. **1456–70** in *Acts Parlt. Scot.* (1875) XII. 27/2 Becaus of his colys and fuell..to be woung in tyme of ȝeir. **1497** *Acc. Ld. High Treas. Scot.* I. 380 The man that ȝeid to vesy to se gif he could wyn sclait. **1509** *Reg. Privy Seal Scot.* I. 284/1 Fredome to wyn and fyne lede ure within the ilis. **1614** in Cochran-Patrick *Early Rec. Mining Scot.* (1878) 163 The minerallis..to be wroght and wynn at the saidis mynes. **1630** *Burgh Rec. Glasgow* (1876) I. 374 To won alsmony lymstanes in the lyme craig at the Channown mos as he can. **1648** *Ibid.* II. 132 Alsmanie stones to be..win as may serve the building of the midwall. *Ibid.* 151 To the end alse manie staines may be wind furthe therof as [etc.]. **1708** J. C. *Compl. Collier* (1845) 10 You tell me you have hopes to win a Colliery in my grounds. **1725** *Rep. MSS. Dk. Portland* VI. (Hist. MSS. Comm. 1901) 106 When they have sunk it [*sc.* the pit] till they come at the bed of coals, they are then said to have won the colliery. **1789** J. WILLIAMS *Min. Kingd.* I. 168 Coals are so far wasted near water carriage in the neighbourhood of Newcastle, that they are become already very difficult and expensive to winn. **1839** URE *Dict. Arts* 968 Of fitting or winning a coal-field. **1869** *Law Rep., Ch. App.* V. 111, I conceive that coal is won when it is put in a state in which continuous working can go forward in the ordinary way. **1885** *Law Times* LXXIX. 153/2 The trustees..had power to win the minerals lying under their land. **1886** J. BARROWMAN *Sc. Mining Terms* 73 A seam is said to be won when a pit is sunk, or a mine driven to it, and the pit or mine is said to win all to the rise of the level.

†**h.** To gain (ground) *upon* (*of*); to gain (time).

c **1400** *Beryn* 2384 Beryn..gan to turn a-side, on-to þe see stronde, And the cripill aftir, & wan oppon hym londe. *c* **1435** *Torr. Portugal* 656 Thus erthe on hym he wane. **1471** CAXTON *Recuyell* (Sommer) 230 We muste nedes wynne vpon Amphitrion on this way a nyght and a day. **1577** HOLINSHED *Chron.* I. 131/1 They dayly wanne grounde vpon the Brytons. **1606** SHAKS. *Ant. & Cl.* II. iv. 9 Your way is shorter,..you'le win two dayes vpon me. **1611** —— *Cymb.* III. iv. 112. **1717** POPE *Iliad* x. 409 Yet let him pass, and win a little Space.

†**8.** To regain, recover (something lost); hence, to make up for (loss, waste); to rescue, deliver; in religious use, to redeem: often with *again*. *Obs.*

c **1220** *Bestiary* 768 Ful wel he taunede his luue to man Wan he ðurȝ holi spel him wan. **1362** LANGL. *P. Pl.* A. v. 25 He bad wastors go worche what þei best couþe, And wynne þat þei wasteden [**1377** B. v. 25 wynnen his wastyng]. **1375** BARBOUR *Bruce* II. 111 Throw hym I trow my land to wyn, Magre the Clyffurd and his kyn. *c* **1380** in *Pol. Poems* (Rolls) I. 264 By God, that al this world wan. *c* **1400** *Rule St. Benet* (verse) 1306 How a hird-man A febil schepe warest & wane. *c* **1440** *York Myst.* xi. 405 Now ar we wonne fra waa, and saued oute of þe see. **1450–1530** *Myrr. our Ladye* II. 253 Saye we endelesse thankes to god that hathe wonne vs ageyne. *a* **1533** LD. BERNERS *Gold. Bk. M. Aurel.* (1546) F vij, The losse of the father by euyll children, is wonne by vertuouse sonnes in lawe. **1562** *Child-Marriages* 14 To wyne all the tenement together againe. **1567** *Gude & Godlie B.* (S.T.S.) 18 Giue thow thy self thy saull culd win, In vaine I deit for thy sin. *Ibid.* 39 He was loste, and now is win. **1633** P. FLETCHER *Purple Isl.* v. lxi, Thus Orpheus wanne his lost Eurydice.

9. a. To overcome the unwillingness or indifference of; with various shades of meaning: to attract, allure, entice; to prevail upon, persuade, induce; to gain the affection or allegiance of; to bring over to one's side, party, or cause, to convert. Also *absol.* or *intr.* (see also WINNING *ppl. a.* 3).

Some of the applications are now more usual with the constructions illustrated in b.

a **1340** HAMPOLE *Psalter* vii. 2 þe deuel þat sekis how he myght wynn mennys saule. *c* **1400** *Cursor M.* 28000 (Cott. Galba) If þou..wowid hir with wordes sleghe,..And þarthurgh so has won hir will. **1474** CAXTON *Chesse* II. iv. (1883) 51 They wynne wyth yeftes the hertes of the goddes and of men. **1535** COVERDALE *Prov.* xi. 30 A wyse man also wynneth mens soules. **1555** EDEN *Decades* (Arb.) 141 Meanyng hereby too woonne the myndes of the other kynges. **1567** JEWEL *Def. Apol.* 417 The Embassadoure of so Noble a Common Wealthe, was soone, and easily, and willingly woonne. **1576** T. FORTESCUE *Forest of Hist.* (ed. 2) 141 He wun the harts of the Citisens. *a* **1589** in Puttenham *Engl. Poesie* III. xix. (Arb.) 217 His wealth wan many friends. **1591** SHAKS. *Two Gent.* III. i. 89 Win her with gifts, if she respect not words. **1629** SIR W. MURE *True Crucif.* 592 Hee..With this soft speech..Doth wound, not wonne, the traytor's heart of stone. **1653** AUSTEN *Fruit Trees* I. (1657) 31 The worst temper of minds are wonne. **1698** FRYER *Acc. E. India & P.* 269 How far..a Graceful Mein, and Innocent Discourse, wins among more refined Christians. **1784** COWPER *Task* IV. 694 Slighted as it is,..the country wins me still. **1871** TENNYSON *Last Tourn.* 703 For courtesy wins woman all as well As valour may. **1874** LONGF. *Hanging of Crane* iii, The ways that win, the arts that please. **1914** TOLLINTON *Clem. Alex.* I. vii. 236 The missionary goes to win and to save souls.

b. with adv. or prep. (*away, over; from, to*, etc.).

1303 R. BRUNNE *Handl. Synne* 6606 ȝyf þou to drunkenes wldest hym wynne. *c* **1375** *Sc. Leg. Saints* xv. (*Barnabas*) 128 Paule to þe treutht wonnyn was. *c* **1386** CHAUCER *Doctor's T.* 132 þat he by slyghte The mayden to his purpos wynne myghte. *c* **1450** in Aungier *Syon* (1840) 269 The presidente..in as moche as in her is..owethe to wynne al to God. **1542** UDALL in *Lett. Lit. Men* (Camden) 5 Thei have thereby woonne to goodnes innumerable persons. **1594** in *Maitl. Club Misc.* I. 67 That the said ladie may be winn to God. **1603** DANIEL *Def. Ryme* Pref. A 2, To hold him from being wonne from vs. **1632** SANDERSON *Serm., Ad Pop.* iv. 407 If our Inclinations cannot be wonne over to that course. **1637** GILLESPIE *Engl. Pop. Cerem.* III. viii. 187 He is already winne to repentance. **1646** SIR T. BROWNE *Pseud. Ep.* I. iii. 11 The Priests of Elder time..winning their credulities unto the literall and downe-right adorement of Cats, Lizards, and Beetles. **1662** *Extr. St. Papers rel. Friends* Ser. II. (1911) 151 All the Acts of a most gracious Prince..can not winne them..from these..rebellious Courses. **1761** MRS. F. SHERIDAN *Sidney Bidulph* II. 336 She has won me to her party. **1796–7** JANE AUSTEN *Pride & Prej.* xi, She could not win him, however, to any conversation. **1821** SCOTT *Kenilw.* xxiv, She can sing and play o' the lute, would win the fish out o' the stream. **1882** J. H. BLUNT *Ref. Ch. Eng.* II. 205 To win her over to an ultramontane policy.

c. with *to* and inf. *arch.*

1540 PALSGR. *Acolastus* II. ii. I iv b, How moch Philautus..hath wonne me holely..to be his. **1591** SHAKS. *Two Gent.* III. i. 67. **1596** DALRYMPLE tr. *Leslie's Hist. Scot.* (S.T.S.) I. 323 Thay conspyre, and winnis him with money quyetlie to putt doune the king. **1640** T. CAREW *Poems, Disdain returned* iii, No teares, Celia, now shall win, My resolv'd heart, to returne. **1664** in *Verney Mem.* (1907) II. 210 So much fre kindnes as wold winn any creture to admier it. **1725** POPE *Odyss.* XII. 53 Unblest the man, whom music wins to stay Nigh the curst shore. **1812** J. WILSON *Isle of Palms* II. 17 Gleam'st thou, as if delighted with the strain, And won by it the pious bark to keep In joy for ever?

10. *intr.* with *upon, on*, †*of*. †**a.** To gain an advantage over, get the better of; to gain or encroach upon; *rarely*, to overcome, subdue. *Obs.*

c **1440** *Pallad. on Husb.* III. 4 As Luna gynneth wexe & wynne Vppon the nyght. **1590** in *Rep. Hist. MSS. Comm., Var. Coll.* IV. 284 Where the sea dailie wynnethe of the land againste this Towne. *c* **1600** SHAKS. *Sonn.* lxiv. 7 When I haue seene the hungry Ocean gaine Aduantage on the Kingdome of the shoare, And the firme soile win of the watry maine. **1607** —— *Cor.* I. i. 223 The rabble..will in time Win vpon power. **1611** —— *Cymb.* I. i. 121 So in our trifles I still winne of you. **1613** J. HAYWARD *Lives 3 Normans* 21 Henry..did many other times..inuade his Countrey; sometimes with purpose to winne vpon him, and sometimes to keepe him from winning vpon others. **1685** DRYDEN *Thren. Aug.* iv, Thus, at half Ebb, a rowling Sea Returns, and wins upon the shoar. **1754** SHEBBEARE *Matrimony* (1766) II. 33 This young Gentleman used every Art..to win on the Resentment which the Baronet had entertained against him. **1791** MRS. RADCLIFFE *Rom. Forest* (1820) I. 121 So much did passion win upon her judgement, by time and indulgence.

b. To gain influence over, to prevail with (often implying 'to gain increasing influence over, to prevail more and more with'); to gain the favour or engage the affections of (esp. gradually or increasingly). Also with *affection, esteem, regard*, or the like as obj.

1601 B. JONSON *Poetaster* To Rdr. 87, I at last..Thought, I would try, if shame could winne vpon 'hem. *a* **1616** BEAUM. & FLETCHER *Cust. Country* II. i, The courage they exprest..And their contempt of death wan more upon me Than all they did. *a* **1665** DIGBY *Priv. Mem.* (1827) 205 Her excessive beauty and gracefulness did so win upon his senses. **1749** FIELDING *Tom Jones* XIV. viii, By the Force of the true Catholic Faith, St. Anthony won upon the Fishes. **1755** J. SHEBBEARE *Lydia* (1769) I. 438 The pleasing countenance of Lydia won on this woman's opinion. **1796** COLERIDGE *Let. to T. Poole* 24 Sept., Charles Lloyd wins upon me hourly. **1842** DICKENS *Amer. Notes* xviii, I never was so won upon, as by this class. **1884** CHURCH *Bacon* vi. 124 He had won greatly on the confidence of the King.

†**c.** To prevail upon (*to do* something). *Obs.*

1674 N. FAIRFAX *Bulk & Selv.* 183 As some of the uppermost seat of Philosophers..have themselves thought, and wonne upon others to think so too. **1698** FRYER *Acc. E. India & P.* 217, I was easily won upon to embark on the Scipio African. **1802** H. MARTIN *Helen of Glenross* II. 217 Who shall I win upon to aid me in my future views?

11. a. *trans.* To reach, attain, arrive at: = GAIN *v.*[2] 7; *occas.* to get at, get hold of (an object); to overtake (a person); to be in time for, 'catch'. *arch.*

1471 CAXTON *Recuyell* (Sommer) 211 Yf he had not wonne a roche vpon whiche he gate vp with grete payne. *c* **1480** HENRYSON *Fox, Wolf & Cadger* 137 Bot all for nocht, he wan his hoill that day. **1517** TORKINGTON *Pilgr.* (1884) 61 The wynde enforcyd So myche.., that our governor Saw it was not possible for to wyne the porte. **1596** SPENSER *F.Q.* VI. i. 23 But Calidore did follow him so fast, That euen in the Porch he him did win. **1697** DRYDEN *Virg. Past.* VIII. 56 Then scarce the bending Branches I cou'd win [orig. *Iam fragilis poteram ab terra contingere ramos*]. **1768** ROSS *Helenore* I. 58 Yet wi' what pith she had, she takes the gate, An' wan the burn. **1808** SCOTT *Marm.* III. i, The stony path..By which the naked peak they wan. **1821** HODGSON in Raine *Mem.* (1857) I. 339 Having got your letter late in the day, I am compelled to be brief to win the post. **1842** MACAULAY *Lays, Horatius* xxvi, And if they once may win the bridge, What hope to save the town? **1848** ROSSETTI *Poems, Last Confess.* 253 As when a bird flies low Between the water and the willow-leaves, And the shade quivers till he wins the light. **1892** RIDER HAGGARD *Nada* xxv, The Halakazi were worsted in the field, but many lived to win the great cave.

†**b.** To get across, to cross; to get through, accomplish. *Obs. rare.*

1426 LYDG. *De Guil. Pilgr.* 903 To chyldre that be yonge of age, And offter han thys ryver wonne Than folk that ben on age ronne. **1573–80** TUSSER *Husb.* (1878) 124 Thry fallowing won, Get compassing don. *a* **1585** MONTGOMERIE *Cherrie & Slae* 645 Fra we get our voyage wun.

12. a. (*a*) *intr.* To make or find one's way; also in weakened sense, to arrive at or come to some place, etc.; in early use often a mere synonym of 'come' or 'go': = GET *v.* 31. With various preps. and advs., sometimes in specialized senses: cf. corresponding uses of *get* s.v. GET *v.* VI, VII. Formerly chiefly *Sc.* and *n. dial.*

This use depends on that of ON. *vinna*.

a **1300** *Cursor M.* 996 A firin wall þar es a-bute, Mai nan win in þat es wit-oute. *Ibid.* 2499 þe fiue gaue bak to wine a-way. *Ibid.* 10592 Quils þai locked þam biside, Sco was won to þe heist stride. *c* **1330** R. BRUNNE *Chron. Wace* (Rolls) 8457 Vneþes to Glouecestre y wan. **13..** *E.E. Allit. P.* B. 1777 þay..Lyfte laddres..& vpon lofte wonen. **13..** *Gaw. & Gr. Knt.* 461 Neuermore þen þay wyste fram queþen he was wonnen. **1375** BARBOUR *Bruce* XV. 221 [Thai] slow all that thai mycht to vyn. *a* **1400–50** *Wars Alex.* 3438 Sen I wan in-to þe werld. *c* **1400** *Destr. Troy* 649 Bes wakond and warly; wyn to my chamber. *c* **1420** *Liber Cocorum* (1862) 19 And cover hit þat no hete oute wynne. *c* **1450** *Cov. Myst., Purification* 43 To jherusalem ffast now wynne. *c* **1475** *Rauf Coilȝear* 625 Say thow art not worthy to Wymond to win. **1508** KENNEDIE *Flyting w. Dunbar* 433 Thou may not pas Mount Barnard for wild bestis, Nor wyn throw Mount Scarpre for the snawe. **1541** WYATT *Declar.* Wks. 1816 II. 281 This, me-thought, was so gladsome unto me to win to the King..that all my policy..was clean forgotten with me. **1585** *Reg. Privy Council Scot.* Ser. I. III. 743 He at last wan to his said hous. **1643** in Boyd *Zion's Flowers* (1855) App. 41/2 That none win to the Sessions loft till the Sessioners be placed. **1652** EARL MONM. tr. *Bentivoglio's Hist. Relat.* 10 Full of channels and rivers, and very hard to be wonn into. **1717** WODROW *Corr.* (1843) II. 262, I hope to win off beginning of next week. **1724** E. ERSKINE *Serm.* Wks. (1791) 120 Christ is in heaven, how shall I win at him? **1813** BYRON *Bride Abydos* II. xxv, Had Selim won..To where the strand and billows met. **1816** SCOTT *Antiq.* xv, And how am I to win hame? **1816** —— *Old Mort.* xl, Whiles the tear wan into my e'e. *c* **1830** HOGG *Tales & Sk.* (1837) III. 205, I canna won sae weel through the snaw. **1865** G. MACDONALD *Alec Forbes* xii, Whan I was na bigger than you, Annie, I could win oot at a less hole than that. **1892** KIPLING *Barrack-room Ballads, East & West* 23 The Colonel's son to the Fort has won. **1893** STEVENSON *Catriona* xv, When we won in by the pier. **1923** EDITH THOMPSON *Hist. Eng.* xlvi. 437 The Germans never won through to the Channel ports.

(*b*) ***to win up***: to get up; to get up on one's feet, to rise; to get on horseback, mount. So ***to win upon***.

a **1300** *Cursor M.* 15760 þai fell þaim don vn-to þe grund,..all vp þai siþen wan. **1375** BARBOUR *Bruce* X. 435 His menȝhe all War wonnyn vp apon the wall. *c* **1400** *Destr. Troy* 1165 Iason..and Ioly knightes moo,..Wonen vp wynly vppon wale horses. *Ibid.* 13938 Whan he wackont of wo, he wan vpo fote. *c* **1460** *Towneley Myst.* xxiii. 114 And wyn apon youre palfray sone. *c* **1802** *Jellen Grame* in Child *Ballads* II. 303/2 'Win up, my bonny boy,' he says, 'As quick as e'er you may.' **1868** MORRIS *Earthly Par.* (1870) I. I. 41 And now we set ourselves in haste to win Up to that mountain's top. **1893** STEVENSON *Catriona* xxx, Just let me win upon my horse!

b. *absol.* without prep. or adv.: To get to the place implied (*Sc.* and *dial.*); to come, go.

c **1430** *Syr Tryam.* 216 Bettyr hyt ys..Owt of yowre londe sche be flemyd..And faste ye schalle hur comawnde to wynne. *a* **1670** SPALDING *Troub. Chas. I* (Bann. Club) I. 99 The marquess wrote back his excuse, saying, he could not win. **1894** P. H. HUNTER *James Inwick* v. 70 There was a by-ordinar congregation that day; a'body that could win was there.

†**c.** In static sense: To 'come', reach. *Obs.*

a **1578** LINDESAY (Pitscottie) *Chron. Scot.* (S.T.S.) I. 258 Reid ȝallow hair..quhilk wan doune to his schoulderis.

d. In reference to a desired end, a condition, experience, proceeding, etc.: with various preps. and advs., often in specialized senses: = GET *v.* 31 b and various uses in VI and VII (see also below). Formerly chiefly *Sc.* and *n. dial.*

win by... (BY *prep.* 16 b), to escape, avoid. †***win of eld***, to 'come of age'. ***win out***, to come out successfully, succeed in attaining one's end; (without *of*, orig. *U.S.*; cf. *to lose out* s.v. LOSE *v.*[1] 4 d). ***win through***, to come out successfully. ***win to***, to begin eating, 'set to', 'fall to' (= GET *v.* 77).

a **1300** *Cursor M.* 25363 Oft þe men þat er rightwis Thoru faanding win þai to þair pris. *c* **1300** *Havelok* 174 Til þat she mowe winan of helde. **13..** *Northern Passion* (1913) I. 153/330* He hopid forto win fra wogh. *c* **1400** *Destr. Troy* 9212 He his wit cast, For to wyn to his will. *a* **1400–50** *Wars Alex.* 3986 Quen he wan to wax.., Thre cubettis fra þe croune doun his cors had a lenghte. *c* **1440** *Pallad. on Husb.* v. 67 The growyng of hem into oon heed wole wynne. *a* **1585** MONTGOMERIE *Cherrie & Slae* 280 Ay houping, throu louping, To win to liberty. *c* **1635** RUTHERFORD *Lett., to Marion McKnaught* III. xxiv. (1675) 190, I look not to win away to my home, without wounds and blood. **1644** BAILLIE *Lett.* (1841) II. 211 There is so much matter yet before us, as we cannot winn through for a long time after our common pace. **1709** M. BRUCE *Soul Confirm.* 15 Soul-confirmation..is not easilie wonne at,..you that keeps only your old Job-troot,..you will not wone at Soul-confirmation. **1721** RAMSAY *Horace to Virgil* 21 The Man wha cou'd sic Rubs win o'er. **1816** SCOTT *Old Mort.* xiv, We got some water-broo and bannocks; and mony a weary grace they said,..or they wad let me win to. *Ibid.* xxxv, The job is how we are to win by hanging. *a* **1850** ROSSETTI *Dante & Circle* I. (1874) 94 The anguish..that we must bow Beneath, until we win out of this life. **1868** J. C. ATKINSON *Gloss. Cleveland Dial.* 575 He's sair an' badly. But t'doctor thinks he'll *win thruff*. **1896** *Voice* 9 Apr. 4/5 McKinley will lead on the first ballot, but 'who will win out' is a different question. **1902** KIPLING *Traffics & Discoveries* (1904) 7 But on delusions—as to their winning out next Tuesday week at 9 a.m.—they are—if I may say so—quite British. **1919** MAX BEERBOHM *Seven Men* 103, I wish he could have won out, as I did, into a great and lasting felicity. **1924** GALSWORTHY *Forest* III. 78 You,

Lockyer—a soldier! One spurt and we'll win out. Come! **1927** *Daily Express* 14 Dec. 13/5 It is good to know that Wodehouse's clever humour has won through. **1931** A. L. ROWSE *Politics & Younger Generation* i. 262 If the League can manage to win through the divisions of the post-war world,..it will have established itself. **1947** 'G. ORWELL' *Eng. People* 38 The American tendency is to burden every verb with a preposition that adds nothing to its meaning (*win out, lose out, face up to*, etc.). **1959** *Listener* 28 May 958/1 He made many enemies, but finally won through opposition to become one of the most controversial commanders of the last war. **1969** A. J. MEADOWS *High Firmament* vii. 160 Eventually, the uniformitarian concept won out in both astronomy and geology. **1974** 'M. INNES' *Appleby's Other Story* i. 7 Victorian bankers who won out when all the little local concerns began to be bundled up together. **1977** 'E. CRISPIN' *Glimpses of Moon* ii. 28, I won through, though... I survived. **1984** *Times Educ. Suppl.* 30 Nov. 28/1 The book has a brisk story and impeccable moral attitudes: gypsies, orphans, teachers and policemen are all good, ordinary people who win out in the end.

e. with adj. as compl.: = GET *v.* 33.

1886 R. F. BURTON *Arab. Nts.* (abr. ed.) I. 82 *note*, He labours to win free from every form and observance. **1902** *London Mag.* June 452/2 Smiling to see him struggle when he thought he could win clear.

13. *intr.* with *to* and inf.: To succeed in doing (what is denoted by the vb.); to contrive, manage *to do* something. Now only *Sc.* and *dial.*

a **1300** *Cursor M.* 26816 For mai naman wit quem to winn To serue at ans lauerds tuin. *c* **1300** *K. Horn* 1112 (Laud) Myȝte he nowt wynne For to come þer inne. *c* **1400** *Destr. Troy* 3145 O nowise may we wyn þat woman to gete. **1483** CAXTON *Gold. Leg.* 121 b/2 That yͧ mayst..wynne to spare the tormentes that ben yet to come. *a* **1600** MONTGOMERIE *Misc. Poems* xxvii. 32 Thee to imbrace once, God! if I micht win! *c* **1655** *Roxb. Ball.* (1886) VI. 209 The Repulsive Maid, Who Once took a young-man, but now cannot win To open the door, and let him come in. **1730** T. BOSTON in Morrison *Mem.* (1899) 137, I am habitually cast down, and cannot win to get my heart lifted up in the ways of the Lord. **1893** STEVENSON *Catriona* xv, As sune as I can win to stand on my twa feet we'll be aff this craig o' Sawtan.

14. *trans.* with prep. or adv. of place: **a.** To succeed in bringing, putting, etc.: = GET *v.* 27 a. *Obs.* or *arch.*

a **1300** *Cursor M.* 8219 Sua depe þair rote þai samen kest, þat moght þam naman þeþen win. *c* **1350** *Will. Palerne* 94 þere walked he a-boute þe walles to winne in siȝt. *c* **1374** CHAUCER *Anel. & Arc.* 20 And do that I my shippe to haven wynne. *c* **1400** *Destr. Troy* XI. 4772 þai..Robbit the Riches ..And wonnyn it wightly the wallis withoute. *c* **1400** *Ywaine & Gaw.* 1803 Bot yit his clathes on he wan. **14..** *Tundale's Vis.* 939 Whan the vermyn wold have owt crepon At the holys that thei made opon Thei myght not wyn owt hor taylys. **1604** E. G[RIMSTONE] tr. *D'Acosta's Hist. Indies* III. x. 152 They gave over the enterprize to win the red sea into Nile. *a* **1636** MARMION *Antiquary* III. i, That I should owe my life to her! which way, I wonder? something depends on this, I must win out. **1825** SCOTT *Betrothed* ix, Her kind attendant..tried softly to win the spear from her lady's grasp. **1904** *Daily Chron.* 3 Nov. 3/3 His sweet and level-headed wife wins him through his difficulties.

†**b.** To put, set, take (expressing merely the act, without implication, as in sense a, of overcoming difficulty or hindrance). ***win out***, to take or draw out, extract. ***win up***, (*a*) to open (a door or gate); (*b*) to take up, pick up, lift. *Obs.*

13.. *Sir Beues* (A.) 4364 In haste þe dore he gan vp winne. **1362** LANGL. *P. Pl.* A. VI. 92 To wynne vp þe wiket-ȝat þat þe wey schutte. *a* **1400-50** *Wars Alex.* 837 þan Alexander at þis knyȝt angirs vnfaire, Wynnes him vp a wardrere. *c* **1400** *Rowland & O.* 463 Rowlande owte his swerde wanne. **1515** *Acc. Ld. High Treas. Scot.* V. 24 To ane masone of the lard of Sefeildis quhilk wan the alloring to the said place of Inchegarvy, xxs.

†**c.** To bring, take, move (a person somewhere).

13.. *Gaw. & Gr. Knt.* 831 Alle hasped in his heȝ wede to halle þay hym wonnen. *c* **1420** *Avow. Arth.* xxxviii, ȝe wynnun him noȝte owte of his way.

†**d.** *refl.* To betake oneself: = 12. (Cf. GET *v.* 27 b.) *Obs.*

13.. *Gaw. & Gr. Knt.* 402, I schal ware alle my wyt to wynne me þeder. *c* **1400** *Destr. Troy* 1138 [We] Wyn vs to the wallis, wacche þere vndur.

15. *Comb.* in sense 'one who or that which wins...', as *win-all*, *win-penny*.

1580 HOLLYBAND *Treas. Fr. Tong, Gaigne-denier*, a porter, a winne-penny. **1639** FULLER *Holy War* II. xlvi. 107 One the winne-all, another the lose-all.

†**win**, *v.*² *Sc.* and *north. dial. Obs.* Forms: 4 vyn, wine, 5–6 wynn(e, 6 wyn(e, winne, 6–9 win, 8 winn. [Variant of *won*, *wonn(e*: see WON *v.*] *intr.* To dwell, reside.

c **1375** *Sc. Leg. Saints* i. (*Petrus*) 690 þat I ma ga To ihesu criste,..With hym to wine in-to his blise. *Ibid.* xvi. (*Magdalena*) 816 Fra þe place, Quhare þe magdelane vynnand vas. *c* **1425** WYNTOUN *Cron.* xxvii. 789 þe Yrischery, That wynnis in Irland to þis day. *c* **1480** HENRYSON *Two Mice* 4 The eldest dwelt in ane Borrous toun, The vther wynnit Upon-land [*v. rr.* vp on land, apon land]. **1513** DOUGLAS *Æneis* VII. xii. 138 Thai that in Flavynia feyldis duell, Or that wynnis besyd the laik or well Of Cymynus. **1560** ROLLAND *Seven Sages* (Bann. Club) 52 Into ane Realme thair wynnit ane vailȝeant knicht. **1721** RAMSAY *Prospect of Plenty* 81 Alake we winn o'er far free King and Court! *a* **1824** G. BEATTIE *John o' Arnha'* etc. (1826) 88 An ancient town..where, tradition says, A housekeeper winned in other days. **1846** BROCKETT *N.C. Gloss.* (ed. 3).

win, *v.*³ *Sc.* and *north. dial.* Also 6 wyn, 7 wind, 8 winn, (9 won). Pa. pple. 8 winned, *Sc.* win(n), 6, 9 won, 8 wun. [? WIN *v.*¹ with specialized development from sense 7 f, but associated also with WIND *v.*² 2.] *trans.* To dry (hay, seed, turf, wood, etc.) by exposure to the air, or to the heat of the sun or a fire. Also *intr.* for *pass.*

1557 *Reg. Mag. Sig. Scot.* 271/2 Tertiam partem 24 dietarum feni lie won hay. **1588** *Exch. Rolls Scot.* XXI. 412 For making of 36 dawarkis of hay..and for wynning and putting of the samyn in tramp ruckis. **1641** *Peebles Burgh Charters* (1872) 107 To cast and wind peites, turres, fewall [etc.]. **1733** P. LINDSAY *Interest Scot.* 154 So much of his Lint as he intends for his best Seed, he builds up in a Stack like Corn, after it is thoroughly win. **1765** *Museum Rust.* IV. cvi. 455 Scots seed, when well winned and kept. **1794** *Statist. Acc. Scot.* XI. 268 Cutting, winning, and carrying home their peats, however, consumes a great deal of time. **1812** SIR J. SINCLAIR *Syst. Husb. Scot.* I. 396 The sun and air gradually win it [*sc.* hay]. **1844** H. STEPHENS *Bk. Farm* II. 259 Feathers may be hung up in bags against the wall behind the fire, and there they will soon win. *Ibid.* III. 909 [The skin for rennet] is then hung stretched over a stick near the fire to dry and won. *Ibid.* 978 By the afternoon the hay is so dry and won as to be fit to be stacked. **1884** *Whitby Gaz.* 9 Aug. 1/2 A Stack of well won Hay.

†**win**, *ppl. a. Sc. Obs.* Also 5 wyn, **wynnynge**. [Sc. pa. pple. of WIN *v.*¹, q.v. (Forms, pa. pple. δ.)] = WON *ppl. a.*; ***evil win***, ill-gotten. Of stone, etc.: Worked, quarried.

c **1425** WYNTOUN *Cron.* IV. xviii. 1712 Eftyr..syndry wynnynge wictoryis. *c* **1475** *Rauf Coilȝear* 921 That is full euill wyn land To haue quhill thow ar leuand, Sine at thine end hell. **1583** *Leg. Bp. St. Androis* 372 Ane carling of the Quene of Phareis, That ewill win geir to elphyne careis. **1609** *Burgh Rec. Glasgow* (1876) I. 307 That the tirrit quarrell and craig thairof and the win werk lyand in the same can nocht be wrocht.

win, obs. f. WEEN *v.*, WHIN¹, WINE.

winability: see WINNABILITY.

winable, obs. form of WINNABLE.

†**winage.** *Obs. rare.* [ad. F. *vinage* (f. *vin* wine + *-age*; cf. med.L. *vinagium*), assimilated to WINE *sb.*¹] A seignorial due derived from vineyards.

1523 LD. BERNERS *Froiss.* I. xxix. 18 He leuyed the rentes, wynages [orig. *vinages*], and rightes, that pertayned to therle through out all Flanders.

winam, winare, winberi, winberry: see VENOM, WINER, WINEBERRY, WHIMBERRY.

†**winbrow.** *Obs.* Also 5 wyn-. [ad. MLG. *winbrâ*, corresp. to OHG. *wintbrâwa* (MHG. *wintbrâwe*, *-brâ*, G. *wimper* eyelash), f. *wint* WIND *sb.*¹ + BROW *sb.*] An eyebrow.

1471 CAXTON *Recuyell* (Sommer) 542 Neptolonyus was grete, black heer and grete eyen,..his wynbrowes Ioyned. **1485** —— *Chas. Gt.* 26 He had the eyen like a lyon..his wynbrowes grete. **1609** HEYWOOD *Brit. Troy* x. xl, His hairy win-browes meet. [Cf. quot. 1471.]

wince (wɪns), *sb.*¹ [f. WINCE *v.*¹] An act of wincing.

1. A kick. Now *dial.*

1612 SHELTON *Quix.* I. II. i. (1620) 66 [The Mule] within two or three winces, ouerthrew him to the ground. **1638** J. TAYLOR (Water P.) *Bull, Beare & Horse* E 1 b, And as I fell, his hoofe bestow'd a wince, Upon my pate. **1840** THACKERAY *Cox's Diary* Jan., Our respective patients gave a wince out.

2. An involuntary shrinking movement (see WINCE *v.*¹ 2).

1865 DICKENS *Mut. Fr.* III. xii, She looked up with a wince. **1891** CONAN DOYLE *White Company* ix, The villein took the cruel blow without wince or cry.

wince (wɪns), *sb.*² [Variant of WINCH *sb.*¹ But cf. LG. *win(n)s* small capstan, Du. *wins* winch.]

1. = WINCH *sb.*¹ 1, 3.

1688 HOLME *Armoury* III. v. 272/1 When the Spinner hath drawn out his Rope Yarn.., then it is taken from the Wheele Spindle, and Wound upon the Wince. **1829** *Good's Study Med.* (ed. 3) IV. 52 The human frame is, hence, a barrel-organ..and life is the music... So long as either the vital or the mechanical instrument is duly wound up by a regular supply of food or of the wince, so long the music will continue. **1837** KIRKBRIDE *Northern Angler* 66 The wince of the reel.

2. *Dyeing.* A reel or roller placed over the division between two vats so that a fabric spread upon it may be let down into one or the other. Also *attrib.*

1839 URE *Dict. Arts* 227 After 48 hours suspension [the calico] is to be washed in water at 170° containing some chalk, by the wince apparatus. **1852** *Abridgm. Specif. Patents, Bleaching*, etc. (1859) 374 The fabric may be caused to pass several times round these winces before it leaves the cistern. **1875** KNIGHT *Dict. Mech.* 2777/1 The tanks are wince-pots.

wince (wɪns), *v.*¹ Forms: 3 wynci, 4–5 wynse, (5 wynce, wyncy, 6 wins, 6–7 winze), 6–7 winse, 5– wince. [a. AF. **wencir* or **wencier*, = OF. *guencir* or *-ier*, dial. variants of *guenchir* or *-ier* WINCH *v.*¹]

I. *intr.* To kick restlessly from impatience or pain. Now *dial.*

[*c* **1290**: see b.] *c* **1380** WYCLIF *Sel. Wks.* III. 231 A horce unrubbed, þat haves a sore back, wynses when he is oght touched or rubbed on his rugge. **1382** —— *2 Sam.* vi. 6 Oza strauȝte out the hoond to the arke of God, and heelde it, for the oxen wynseden, and boweden it. *c* **1386** CHAUCER *Miller's T.* 77 Wynsynge she was as is a ioly colt. **1493** [H. PARKER] *Dives & Pauper* (W. de W. 1496) x. v. 376/2 Whan he begynneth to wexe proude & wynsynge & kykyng ayenst his mayster. ? *a* **1550** *Schole-house Wom.* 1014 in Hazl. *E.P.P.* IV. 145 Rub a scald horse vpon the gall, And he wil bite, wins and went. **1598** FLORIO, *Recalcitrare*, to kicke or strike or winze with ones heeles agaíne. **1600** J. PORY tr. *Leo's Africa* IX. 340 They bray out a loude, kicking and wincing with their heeles. **1663** BUTLER *Hud.* I. ii. 847 The angry Beast..Begun to kick, and fling, and wince. **1717** PRIOR *Alma* I. 275 Before the child can crawl, He learns to kick, and wince, and sprawl. *c* **1750** JOHNSON in *Boswell* (1793) I. 236 *note*, A fly, Sir, may sting a stately horse and make him wince. **1782** WOLCOT (P. Pindar) *Odes* iv. Wks. 1812 I. 22 As for poor St. Leger and Prince, Had I their places I should wince, Thus to be gibbeted for weeks on high. **1890** *Glouc. Gloss.*, *Wincing*, used of a horse kicking out behind.

b. In fig. and allusive phr., e.g. ***to wince against the prick*** (cf. KICK *v.*¹ 1 c and PRICK *sb.* 13); hence *gen.* to be recalcitrant or impatient.

c **1290** *St. Paul* 23 in *S. Eng. Leg.* 190 To wynci aȝein þe pricke swiþe strong it is þe. **1388** WYCLIF *Acts* Prol., Poul.., whom the Lord hadde chosun, that long tyme wynside aȝen the pricke. **1393** LANGL. *P. Pl.* C. v. 22 It is þe wone of wil to wynse and to kyke. **1426** LYDG. *De Guil. Pilgr.* 14196 Off verray surquedy and pryde, I smyte and wynse on euery syde. *Ibid.* 14531 For to wynse and dysobeye, And to tourne A-nother weye. *c* **1449** PECOCK *Repr.* II. xvii. 254 Thouȝ ȝe wolde wyncy and repugne aȝens the clergie. **1560** BECON *New Catech.* Wks. 1564 I. 508 Not to winse, kick & spurn against their sayinges. **1603** SHAKS. *Ham.* III. ii. 255 (Qo. 1) Let the galld iade wince [*other edd.* winch]. **1642** FULLER *Holy & Prof. St.* II. ix. 81, I should suspect his preaching had no salt in it, if no gald horse did winse. *a* **1677** BARROW *Serm.* Wks. 1716 III. 65 What boots it to winse and kick against fortune? *a* **1764** LLOYD *Poet* 21 The fancies of our rambling wits, Who wince and kick at all oppression. **1814** CARY *Dante, Parad.* XVII. 124 Let them wince, who have their withers wrung.

†**c.** *transf.* To dart *from place to place.* (*rare.*)

c **1400** *Laud Troy Bk.* 6115 Fro stide to stide aboute he wynces, He slees kynges, dukes, & princes.

2. To start or make an involuntary shrinking movement in consequence of or in order to avoid pain, or when alarmed or suddenly affected.

a **1748** WATTS *Improv. Mind* II. v, Perhaps the gamester shrugs and winces, turns and twists the argument every way, but he cannot fairly answer it. **1781** COWPER *Conversat.* 325 Some fretful tempers wince at ev'ry touch. **1831** LYTTON *Godolphin* xix, Why, man, you wince at the word 'marry!' **1842** TENNYSON *Walking to Mail* 63 You should have seen him wince As from a venomous thing. **1890** BESANT *Demoniac* vi, In your strong frame already beats the heart of a coward... When I told you this once before, you winced: now you laugh.

wince, *v.*² *Dyeing.* [f. WINCE *sb.*²] *trans.* To immerse in or pass through a vat by means of a wince. Also *absol.* Hence **wincing** *vbl. sb.*²; *attrib.* in ***wincing-machine*** = WINCE *sb.*² 2.

1839 URE *Dict. Arts* 224 They are winced for a few minutes in a weak solution of chloride of lime. *Ibid.* 1300 *Wincing-machine*, is the English name of the dyer's reel, which he suspends horizontally,..over the edge of his vat. **1875** *Ure's Dict. Arts*, etc. (ed. 7) I. 660 Wince again five times. *Ibid.*, 2 pieces of 30 yards of velvet are put in and winced backwards and forwards five times.

wince, obs. form of QUINCE.

wincer¹ ('wɪnsə(r)). Now *rare.* [f. WINCE *v.*¹ + -ER¹.] A kicker. In quot. 1642 *fig.*

c **1440** *Promp. Parv.* 530/1 Wynsare, *calcitrator, calcit[r]atrix.* **1580** HOLLYBAND *Treas. Fr. Tong, Regimbeur*, a winser. **1611** COTGR., *Rueur*, a kicker, striker, winser. **1642** MILTON *Apol. Smect.* 19 Is it blasphemy..for me to answer a slovenly wincer of a confutation, that [etc.]?

'**wincer**². *Dyeing.* [f. WINCE *sb.*² + -ER¹.] One who tends a wince.

1881 *Instr. Census Clerks* (1885) 69 Cotton, Calico, Printer... Hooker. Wincer. Steamer.

wincey ('wɪnsɪ). Also **winsey, -ie.** Pl. **-eys**, occas. **-ies.** [orig. Sc.; app. alteration of *woolsey* in LINSEY-WOOLSEY, through the medium of the assimilated form **linsey-winsey*.] A very durable cloth having a linen warp and a woollen weft. (*occas.* A garment made of this.) Also *attrib.*

1808 JAMIESON, *Winsey*, adj. Of or belonging to wool... *Cotton-winsey* denotes what is made of cotton and wool; *Linen-winsey*, of linen and wool, linsey-woolsey. **1810** JAS. DUFF *Poems* (1816) 2 Her winsies war made by sweet Modesty's rule. **1858** E. B. RAMSAY *Remin.* v. (1859) 161 A striped wincey apron. **1862** *Cornh. Mag.* Nov. 695 Some wincey and a number of pieces of coburg. **1862** *Catal. Internat. Exhib., Brit.* II. No. 4032, Dress wincies. **1893** MRS. C. PRAED *Outlaw & Lawmaker* xi, All varieties, from the honest brown and grey wincey to the Park turn-out. **1907** MRS. C. KERNAHAN *Fraud* iv. 29 She..wore a brown winsey dress.

winceyette (wɪnsɪ'ɛt). [f. WINCEY + -ETTE; cf. FLANNELETTE.] A lightweight napped cotton fabric used for nightclothes, etc. (see quot. 1955).

1922 *Daily Mail* 14 Nov. 1 (Advt.), Ponting's offer of shirtings and winceyette. **1955** *Textile Terms & Definitions* in *Jrnl. Textile Inst.* (*Standardisation*) XLVI. 544 *Winceyette*, a light-weight fabric, originally and usually of cotton, raised on both sides, the weave usually being plain or twill. **1962** *Economist* 20 Jan. 253/2 The Nelson [cotton] factory was to begin production of denim, winceyette, cotton wool and surgical dressings in May. **1979** D. Cook *Winter Doves* II. v. 87 She applied the paste with two fingers, wiping them clean on her Winceyette nightdress.

winch (wɪnʃ), *sb.*[1] Forms: 1 **wince**, 4–7 (9) **wynch**, (3–5 **wenche**, 4–6 **wynche**, 6 **winche**, 7 **wintch**, 9 **winsh**), 7– **winch**. [Late OE. *wince*:—OTeut. **wiŋkjo-*:—**weŋkjo-*, f. Indo-Eur. root *weŋg-*, repr. also by WINK *v.*[1] (Cf. WINK *sb.*[2])]

1. a. A reel, roller, or pulley.

c **1050** *Voc.* in Wr.-Wülcker 416/6 *Gigrillus* [= *girgillus*], wince. **1295** *Acc. Exch. K.R.* 5/7 (P.R.O.) In vno velamine empto .vj. li. iiij. d. In Wenches emptis ad idem. iiij s. vj. d. **1384** *For. Acc.* 20 C *dorso* (P.R.O.), j wynche ferri pro vna petra vertibili. *Ibid.*, j gross[a] wynche ferri pro factura cordarum. **1511–12** *Act 3 Hen. VIII*, c. 6 §1 That the byer of Wollen clothes..shall not..cause to be drawen in lenght ..the same clothes..by teyntoʳ or wynche or by eny other meane. **1563** Golding *Cæsar* VII. (1565) 232 With slinges that went wyth wynches [orig. *fundis librilibus*]..& wyth pellets, they put the Galles in feare. **1611** Cotgr., *Tournoir*, ..the vice, or winch of a Presse.

b. *spec.* An angler's reel.

1662 R. Venables *Exper. Angler* iv. 44 You may buy your Trowle ready made,..onely let it have a winch to wind it up withall. **1760** Sir J. Hawkins *Walton's Angler* 139 *note*, The winch must be screwed on to the butt of your rod. **1867** F. Francis *Bk. Angling* i. 13 Your winch should hold forty or fifty yards of fine line.

c. *Naut.* A small machine used for making ropes and spun-yarn; † the quantity of yarn so made.

1640 in Birch *Charters of London* (1887) 220 For a winch of cable yarn..0*s.* 4*d.* **1772–84**, etc. [see SPUN-YARN 2]. **1794** *Rigging & Seamanship* I. 90 *Winch*, to make or twist spun-yarn with is made of 8 spokes, 4 at each end, and 4 wooden pins 15 inches long driven through the end of them.

†**2.** A well-wheel (turned by a crank); hence, a well. *Obs.* (Cf. dial. *winch-well* a deep well, and WINK *sb.*[2], quot. 1886.)

c **1440** *Pallad. on Husb.* I. 426 In stede of welle or wenche [orig. *fons..aut puteus*] haue a sisterne. *Ibid.* III. 894 The water cleer Of cisterne or of wynche. *Ibid.* IX. 120 The wynchis when we delue [orig. *in fodiendis puteis*]. **1556** Withals *Dict.* (1562) 47 b/1 The wynch or wheele of the well. **1580** Hollyband *Treas. Fr. Tong*, *La trieule*,..the beame or rounde wood whereabout the cord of a well is winded, some do call it a winch. **1632** J. Hayward tr. *Biondi's Eromena* 195 An old well or deepe wintch..boild all the night long.

3. The cranked handle by means of which the axis of a revolving machine is turned.

1660 R. D'Acres *Water-drawing* 11 Winches or Cranks of Wood or Iron are..fitted to mens hands, thereby to make a round motion. **1683** Moxon *Mech. Exerc.*, *Printing* xi. ¶16 On the Square Pin is fitted a Winch somewhat in form like a Jack-winch. **1774** *Phil. Trans.* LXIV. 390 After about ninety or an hundred turns of the winch. **1787** Imison *Treat. Mech. Powers* 46 The wheel is turned by means of a winch fix'd on the axle of a trundle. **1801** Strutt *Sports & Past.* III. v. 209 One of them turned the winch of an organ which he carried at his back. **1834** Fearnside *Tombleson's Thames* 31 By Pinkle Lock and Weir,..it is necessary for the aquatic tourist to be provided with a winch to open the gates. **1843** *Penny Cycl.* XXVII. 436/1 Winch and axle is a machine constituting a small windlass. **1874** Hardy *Far fr. Mad. Crowd* xx, I'll turn the winch of the grindstone.

4. a. A hoisting or hauling apparatus consisting essentially of a horizontal drum round which a rope passes and a crank by which it is turned.

1577 Googe tr. *Heresbach's Husb.* 11 b, The smaller sort [of husbandry necessaries]..Hammers, Chippe Axes, Winches, Pulleys, Wheeles [etc.]. **1674** Blount *Glossogr.* (ed. 4), *Winch*, a pulling or skrewing Engin. **1688** Holme *Armoury* III. xviii. (Roxb.) 139/2 A Hand screw, or screw engine: or Ghynne or Wynch. **1706** Phillips (ed. Kersey), *Winches*, a kind of Engine to draw Barges, &c. up a River against the Stream. **1769** Falconer *Dict. Marine* (1776), *Winch*, a cylindrical piece of timber, furnished with an axis, ..turned about by means of an handle resembling that of a draw-well. **1820** Scoresby *Acc. Arctic Reg.* II. 233 An apparatus called a 'winch',..for heaving the lines into the boat after the fish is..killed. **1838** *J. M. Wilson's Tales Borders* IV. 253/2 By the assistance of the wynch, the jib again rose to its former place. **1905** *Times Lit. Suppl.* 25 Aug. 268/1 The value of steam applied to winches and capstans.

b. In the navigation of the river Thames, a revolving apparatus at the river-side, round which a rope was wound to haul craft through difficult places; a toll levied for the use of this (abolished by the Thames Conservancy Act of 1866).

1623 *Act 21 Jas. I*, c. 32 §5 For that the sayd passage from Bircot aforesayd, to the sayd Citie of Oxford, is against the streame, the Barges..must..bee haled vp by strength of men, horses, winches [etc.]. **1694** *Act 6 & 7 Will. & Mary* c. 16 *Preamble*, For the..convenience of the Navigation [of the Thames and Isis] there..are diverse Lockes Weares, Buckes Winches..and other Engines. **1754** *Extr. Navig. Rolls Thames* (1772) 19 The Owner of every Winch, belonging to every Lock below Reading. **1795** *Jrnls. Ho. Comm.* L. 125/1 Tolls..payable at the Old Locks, Weirs, and Winches. **1864** *Thames Navig., Tables of Tolls* July 1 Tables of Tolls (Including Old Lock Dues and Winches), which will be taken on and from July 1, 1864.

5. *Dyeing.* = WINCE *sb.*[2] 2.

1791 Hamilton *Berthollet's Dyeing* I. I. II. ii. 159 For the pieces of stuff, a winch or reel is used. **1799** G. Smith *Laboratory* I. 385 Stir it well about, and..put in your stuffs: ..turn it on a winch, till you see the colour is to your mind. **1822** *Imison's Sci. & Art* II. 185 The stuffs..are drawn through them [*sc.* the baths] by a winch, or reel. **1876** *Encycl. Brit.* IV. 688/1 Mounted on a strong frame-work over the trough [of the dye vat] is the winch.., which by its revolutions..keeps the cloth moving down and up continuously into and out of the trough.

6. *attrib.* as ***winch-bit***, ***-gear***, ***-handle***, etc.; **winchman**, (*a*) a man who operates a winch; (*b*) a man lowered by a winch from a helicopter, esp. to rescue people from shipwrecks, etc.

1867 Smyth *Sailor's Word-bk.*, **Winch-bitts*, the supports near their ends. **1893** *Westm. Gaz.* 28 Feb. 10/3 Kemp was standing against the winch-bit. **1875** Knight *Dict. Mech.*, **Winch-capstan*, a combination in which winch-heads are arranged on top of the capstan. **1881** E. Matheson *Aid Bk.* II. 362 The lifting power in a crane is generally obtained by ordinary *winch-gear. **1825** J. Nicholson *Oper. Mech.* 229 So that the power must act in like manner as if it were applied at a *winch-handle. **1894** Bottone *Electr. Instr.* 171 It is mounted upon an iron spindle..at one end of which is a winch-handle. **1847** T. T. Stoddart *Angler's Comp.* 44 The triple gut casting-line..is intended..to be appended immediately to the *winch-line, by the trout-fisher. **1824** R. Stevenson *Bell Rock Lighthouse* vi. 329 A *winch-machine, with wheel, pinion and barrel, round which last the chain was wound. **1946** A. J. Hall *Stand. Handbk. Textiles* iv. 169 The winch machine is essentially a vat..above which is mounted a horizontal winch. **1882** *Standard* 26 Aug. 3/7 A man should have watched the case and given orders to the gangwayman, who, in turn, ought to have given orders to the *winchman. **1894** *Times* 5 Feb. 3/3 The winchman and the bullrope man..in assisting to unload the vessel. **1958** *Times* 23 June 6/1 The girls..were brought up into the helicopter by winchman Sergeant Jim Gilpin. **1977** *R.A.F. News* 27 Apr.–10 May 1/4 Along with winchman FS Roger Lynn he airlifted a two-ton cabin into the garden of a Durham man so that a kidney machine could be installed. **1979** *Globe & Mail* (Toronto) 15 Aug. 1/2 (*caption*) Winchman on a rescue helicopter hangs over a crew member from yacht Ariadne. **1883** W. C. Russell *Sea Queen* II. ii. 30 The tiny clink of *winch-pawls. **1902** *How to make useful things* 10/1 A few inches from the lower end of the butt a recess is made sufficiently large to take the *winch-plate. **1831–3** *Encycl. Metrop.* (1845) VIII. 528/2 When one or more pieces of goods are to be dyed the *winch-reel is employed.

†**winch**, *sb.*[2] *Obs. rare.* [f. WINCH *v.*[1]]

1. A 'turn' or 'twist' in argument.

1549 Gardiner in Foxe *A. & M.* (1563) 804/1, I thinke there was neuer man had more playne euident matter to alledge, then I haue, without winches or arguments or deuises of wit.

2. = WINCE *sb.*[1] 2.

c **1738** J. Skinner *Christmas Ba'ing* xix, Poor Petrie gae a weary winch.

winch (wɪnʃ), *v.*[1] *Obs.* exc. *dial.* Forms: 3 **wenche**, 4–6 **wynche**, 6 **winche**, (7 **whinch**, 9 *dial.* **winsh**), 6– **winch**. [a. AF. **wenchier*, **wenchir* = OF. *guenchier*, *-ir* intr. to turn aside, trans. to avoid, a. Teut. **weŋkjan* (OHG., MHG. *wenken*, OS. *wenkean*):—**waŋkjan*, f. *waŋk-* (whence OHG. *wank* side movement, return, OHG., G. *wanken*, ON. *vakka*, OE. *wancol* WANKLE *a.*): *weŋk-* (whence WINCH *sb.*[1], WINK).]

1. *intr.* To start back or away, recoil, flinch; to wince.

a **1225** *Ancr. R.* 98 Auh for alle onsweres, wendeð ou ant wencheð frommard him. ?*a* **1400** *Morte Arth.* 2104 Qwarelles qwayntly swappez thorowe knyghtez With iryne so wekyrly, that wynche they neuer. ?*a* **1500** *Peblis to the Play* xiii, He stert till ane broggit stauf, Wincheand as he war woode. **1540** Palsgr. *Acolastus* Prol. B iv, Thou begynnest to wynche or to startle on this facion. **1553** *Respublica* I. iii. 284 He that ones wincheth shall fele the waite of my fiste. **1595** Shaks. *John* IV. i. 81, I will not stirre, nor winch, nor speake a word. **1628** *Robin Goodfellow* (1841) 41 Sluts and slovens I doe pinch, And make them in their beds to winch. **1634** W. Wood *New Eng. Prosp.* II. viii, Beate them, whip them, pinch them, punch them, if they resolve not to whinch for it, they will not. **1687** Dryden *Hind & P.* III. 133 Yet seem'd she not to winch, though shrewdly pain'd. **1718** Cibber *Non-juror* v, You must not winch nor stir too soon, at any Freedom you observe me take with him. **1878** *Cumbld. Gloss.*, *Winsh*, wince.

†**b.** *fig.* To recoil in fear or disgust (*at*). *Obs.*

1605 Marston *Dutch Courtezan* III. i, He must nere winch, that would or thriue, or saue, To be cald Nigard, cuckold, Cut-throat, Knaue. **1637** Heylin *Antid. Lincoln.* Pref. A 6 b, A long studied discourse in maintenance of sitting at the holy Sacrament, which good Master Burton never winched at. **1680** H. More *Apocal. Apoc.* 23 They shall..severely rule them, so that they shall not be able to whinch but at their own peril. **1709** Steele *Tatler* No. 76 ¶8 A general Representation of an Action, either ridiculous or enormous, may make those winch who find too much Similitude in the Character with themselves to plead Not Guilty.

†**2.** Of a horse: To kick restlessly or impatiently; = WINCE *v.*[1] 1. *Obs.*

1483 *Cath. Angl.* 420/1 To Wynche, *calcitrare.* **1510** Stanbridge *Vocabula* (W. de W.) C v, *Recalcitro*, to wynche agayne, or kyke. *a* **1529** Skelton *Col. Cloute* 182 Let se who that dare Sho the mockysshe mare; They make her wynche and keke. **1575** Gascoigne *Weedes*, *Green Knt.* 87 He winched still alwayes, and whisked with his taile. **1591** Greene *Farew. Folly* B 3 b, Sylenus asse neuer sawe a wine bottle but he would winch. **1706** Phillips (ed. Kersey), To *Wince* or *Winch*,..properly to throw out the hinder Feet, as a Horse does.

b. In allusive and proverbial phr., esp. with reference to the 'wincing' of a 'galled' horse.

1493 *Festivall* (W. de W. 1515) 173 b, As a galled horse whiche is touched on the sore he wyncheth & wryeth. *c* **1520** Skelton *Magnyf.* 2023 Remembre the tourne of Fortunes whele, That wantonly can wynke, and wynche with her hele. **1548** Udall *Erasm. Par.* Ep. Ded. ℂ2, Who so wyncheth and kicketh at the ghospell. *a* **1566** R. Edwards *Damon & Pithias* (1571) B iv b, I know the galde horse will soonest winche. **1566** Drant *Horace*, *Sat.* v. D 2 b, Synce you agaynst these churchly rites so longe and sore dyd wynche. **1615** Brathwait *Strappado* (1878) 109 Yet do not winch (good iade) when thou art gall'd. **1626** W. Fenner *Hid. Manna* Ep. Ded., The will of it self, the more reason it hath to be turned, the more it is wilful, it hinches and winches, and snuffes against it. **1693** Congreve *Old Bach.* v. xiii, *Aram.* Bless me! What have you done to him? *Belin.* Only touch'd a gall'd beast till he winch'd. **1718** Cibber *Non-juror* II. i, Sir, you cannot conceive the wonderful use of Clamour, 'tis so teizing to a Ministry, it makes them winch and fret.

†**c.** *trans.* To kick (a person) *out of*. *rare.*

1623 Fletcher & Rowley *Maid in Mill* II. i, A galled Jennet that will winch him out o' the Saddle.

Hence **'winching** *vbl. sb.*[1] and *ppl. a.*[1]

1525 *Stanbridge's Vocabula* (W. de W.) C v b, *Sternax*, a wynchynge horse. **1577** Hanmer *Anc. Eccl. Hist.* 205 A certaine shamefull winching & repining. **1593** G. Harvey *Pierce's Super.* Wks. (Grosart) II. 246 Not such a powting waspe in Ramme-ally, or such a winching iade in Smithfield. **1631** [Mabbe] *Celestina* III. 40 [Women] are all of them ticklish, and skittish; the whole generation of them is given to winching and flinging. **1664** H. More *Myst. Iniq.* 101 That they might, without any ones whinching, decree.. what-ever would tend to the encrease of their own honour and wealth.

winch, *v.*[2] [f. WINCH *sb.*[1]]

1. *trans.* To hoist or draw *up*, etc. with or as with a winch.

1529 *Dunmow Churchw. Acc.* lf. 10 (MS.) To fett a gabull to wynche up the tymber. **1530** Palsgr. 408 b/2, I wynche or wynde vp with a wyndlasse or a crane... You shall neuer get this stryng in to the nocke but you wynche it vp. **1599** Hakluyt *Voy.* II. I. 128 He..was winched vp in that chaire, and fastened vnto the maineyard of a galley. **1633** J. Fisher *Fuimus Troes* II. ii, I'le winch vp thy estate. **1909** *E. Suffolk Gaz.* 12 Jan. 3/7 All slack line must be winched in. **1913** Conrad *Within the Tides*, etc. (1915) 219 It was she who winched up that infernal machine, and it was she too who lowered it that night.

2. *Dyeing.* = WINCE *v.*[2]

1831–3 *Encycl. Metrop.* (1845) VIII. 514 The silk should be winched through a copper of water at the heat of 160°. **1855** *Abridgm. Specif. Patents, Bleaching*, etc. (1859) 565, I ..keep the liquor to the boiling point for about one hour and twenty minutes, during which time the cloth should be winched as before. **1883** R. Haldane *Workshop Rec.* II. 40/1 For ungumming, the piece is simply winched backwards and forwards.

Hence **'winching** *vbl. sb.*[2] and *ppl. a.*[2]

1875 H. R. Robertson *Life Upper Thames* 19 The tightening of the bolts before tying them is called winching ..: two stout pieces of wood are used which are called the levers, and are connected by a strong cord passed round the bolt. **1902** *Daily Record & Mail* 6 Aug. 3 The winching-away men and sweepers and screwers.

Winchester ('wɪntʃɪstə(r)). [Proper name.]

I. The name of a city in Hampshire, the capital of Wessex and later of the Anglo-Saxon kingdom: used *attrib.* in specific designations.

1. a. (*a*) ***Winchester measure***: dry and liquid measures the standards of which were orig. deposited at Winchester. Also *fig.* So (*b*) ***Winchester bushel***, ***gallon***, for which (*c*) *Winchester* is used for short (in druggists' use = *Winchester quart*); in mod. use (see quots. 1959, 1972); also ***Winchester bottle***.

(*a*) *c* **1550** *Skelton's Ghost* 23 in *S.'s Wks.* (1843) II. 154 Full Winchester gage We had in that age. **1670** *Act 22 Chas. II*, c. 8 §1 The Standard marked in his Majestyes Exchequer commonly called the Winchester Measure containing Eight Gallons to the Bushell. **1680** Alsop *Misch. Impos.* xiii. 94 The Advice to those in Communion with the Church, was short and sweet, but the Dissenters shall now have it by Winchester measure. **1682** Warburton *Hist. Guernsey* (1822) 114 The Guernsey bushel, great measure, contains about 6 gallons, Winchester measure. **1688** Holme *Armoury* III. 337/2 An Halfe Peck, of old it contained 5 Quarts, but by Winchester Measure to which by the Statute of the Land all others now conforme, is but 4 Quarts and a Pint. **1846** McCulloch *Acc. Brit. Empire* (1854) I. 215 An acre has been known to yield 300 bushels (Winchester measure) of early potatoes for the first crop. **1860** *All Year Round* No. 70. 479 A runlet (two gallons, Winchester measure).

(*b*) [**1603** G. Owen *Pembrokeshire* vii. (1891) 55 Theire bushell beinge more then doble winchester.] **1702** *Act 1 Anne* Stat. 2. c. 3 §6 A Bushel according to the Standards remaining in the Custody of the Chamberlains of Her Majesties Exchequer commonly called..by the Name of the Winchester Bushel. **1737** *Act 10 Geo. II*, c. 30 §2 All Oysters which shall..be imported from France.., shall..be rated at seven Pence per Bushel strike Measure, according to the Winchester Corn Bushel. **1768** *Ann. Reg.*, *Chron.* 92 The lords of the manor of Tetbury..were convicted..for not using in the public market a brass Winchester bushel. *c* **1790** *Encycl. Brit.* (ed. 3) V. 102/2, 268·8 cubic inches to the Winchester gallon. **1835** *Act 5 & 6 Will. IV*, c. 63 §6 Be it enacted, That from and after the passing of this Act the Measure called the Winchester Bushel, and the Lineal Measure called the Scotch Ell,..shall be abolished.

(*c*) **1702** T. Brown *Lett. fr. Dead* II. (1707) 68 Seal'd Winchesters of Three-penny Guzzle. **1722** E. Ward *Wand. Spy* II. 67 [They] Call'd for full Winchester's of Stout. **1758** Borlase *Nat. Hist. Cornw.* 87 Bay-salt..is sold to the husbandman from four-pence to six-pence a winchester. *Ibid.* 88 Each bushel three winchesters, or twenty-four gallons. **1862** *Chemist & Druggist* 15 Feb. (Advt. sect.) 37/1 Druggists' Bottles... Winchester, 100 oz. **1880** J. Dunbar *Pract. Papermaker* 66 The 'Winchester' is duly labelled. **1905** Wastell & Bayley *Hand Camera* 145 *note*, A 'Winchester', or 'Winchester Quart', is a bottle holding eighty ounces. **1959** *Gloss. Packaging Terms (B.S.I.)* 28 *Winchester*, a term applied to round, narrow or wide-mouth bottles usually used for the distribution of chemicals or pharmaceutical products. **1963** *Pharm. Jrnl.* CXCI. 59 The author suggests that the Winchester bottle was thus named by the druggists who utilised it for supplying the [Winchester] hospital's drug orders. **1972** *Bottlers' Year Bk. 1972–73* 423 *Winchester*, a large bottle of variable capacity used for soluble essences, etc., usually containing from about 6 to 10 lb. of the product.

b. ***Winchester quart***: (*a*) a quart (2 pints) in Winchester measure; (*b*) *Pharm.*, 4 Imperial pints, i.e. 80 fluid ounces (in quot. 1870, 100 fl. oz.); also, a bottle holding 4 pints.

See *Pharm. Jrnl.* (1963) CXCI. 59 for an argument that in sense (*b*) it is properly 85 fl. oz., a quarter of the new barn gallon of 2⅛ Imperial gallons.

1742 W. Ellis *Mod. Husbandman* July x. 61 At our Country Towns, they sell a Winchester Quart of Milk.. for a Penny. **1758** *Rep. Comm. House of Commons Weights & Measures* 39 Standard weights and measures in the possession of the Hall-keeper of the Guild-Hall... 1 corn half peck marked 1601. 1 Winchester quart ditto. 1 ditto pint ditto. **1816** P. Kelly *Metrology* 89 The Coal Bushel holds one Winchester quart more than the Winchester bushel [*sc.* 2150.42 cubic inches]; it therefore contains 2217.62 cubic inches. **1870** *Pharm. Jrnl.* XI. 650 Omagh is said to take about 400 Winchester quarts (equal to 250 gallons) [of methylated ether] yearly. **1874** *Ibid.* 2nd Ser. V. 442/1 A Winchester quart (four pints) is first half filled with infusion. **1880** J. Dunbar *Pract. Papermaker* 65 Fill a 'Winchester quart' bottle with this test acid. **1897** *Chemist & Druggist* 5 June 891/1 The questions on which we should like information are—What is a Winchester quart the fourth of, or how it came to designate a half-gallon? and whether it and the Winchester pint were ever recognised measures? **1963** *Pharm. Jrnl.* CXCI. 60/1 The Winchester quart's success was due, one suspects, to the fact that it is the largest bottle which can conveniently be held in one hand.

†**2.** ***Winchester goose***: see goose *sb.* 3.

3. ***Winchester school***, a southern English style of manuscript illumination of the 10th and 11th cent., originating at Winchester. Also ***Winchester manner, style.***

1892 J. H. Middleton *Illuminated MSS. Classical & Mediaeval Times* vii. 101 Another very fine example of the Winchester school of illumination is the manuscript Charter which King Edgar granted to the new minster at Winchester in 966. *Ibid.*, In artistic power this tenth century Winchester school of illuminators appears, for a while at least, to have been foremost in the world. **1910** G. F. Warner in Warner & Wilson *Benedictional of Saint Æthelwold* p. xl, It is an example of Canterbury modification of Winchester style. **1928** E. G. Millar *Eng. Illuminated MSS XIVth & XVth Cent.* ii. 14 The Anglo-Saxon outline draughtsmen of the Winchester and related schools. **1954** M. Rickert *Painting in Britain: Middle Ages* ii. 42 But it is not until the second half of the tenth century that the full force of Carolingian art under Æthelwold's sponsorship of the production of manuscripts resulted in the development at Winchester of the famous Winchester style. **1970** *Oxf. Compan. Art* 559/1 *Winchester School*... Though some splendid manuscripts came from Winchester, books decorated in the 'Winchester' manner were certainly made in other southern English monasteries.

II. 4. a. The name of Oliver F. *Winchester* (1810–80), an American manufacturer, used as the designation of a breech-loading rifle having a tubular magazine under the barrel and a horizontal bolt operated by a lever on the underside of the stock.

1871 *Standard* 1 Feb., The arms.. being the Remington and the Chassepot, with some few Winchesters. **1891** C. Roberts *Adrift Amer.* 163 He rushed over to his house and brought out a 17-shot Winchester. **1897** Hinde *Congo Arabs* xi. 185 About fifteen Winchester expresses, and the same number of ordinary Winchesters.

b. *Computers.* Used *attrib.* and *absol.* with reference to a hermetically sealed storage device incorporating one or more high-capacity hard discs with heads and sometimes also a drive unit. [So called because the original device was intended to contain two 30 megabyte discs and its IBM number would have been 3030, the same as that of a famous Winchester rifle (which used a 0·30 calibre cartridge containing 0·30 grains of powder).]

1973 *Modern Data* July 60/1 The 'Winchester' Disk... The product of the so-called 'Winchester' project, the eventual nature of the 3340 has been the subject of rumors reported in the trade press. **1976** *Computer Weekly* 26 Aug. 16/6 There are also special cabinets for the Winchester type of disc module—a recording medium that is expensive in itself irrespective of the data stored on it, and that requires extremely careful handling. **1978** *IEEE Trans. Magnetics* XIV. 201/1 An example of the current state of the art in fixed head designs utilizing Winchester technology are the fixed heads used in IBM's 3340 and 3350 disc drives. **1980** *Sci. Amer.* Aug. 117/2 It is now known generically as Winchester technology, that being the code name under which the device was developed at IBM. A Winchester disk memory has one or more rigid disks, either eight or 14 inches in diameter. **1985** *Which Computer?* Apr. 61/2 One machine has twin floppies, the other has a 10MB Winchester.

Hence †**Win'chestrian** *a.* (see sense 2).

a **1637** B. Jonson *Underwoods, Execr. Vulcan* 142 And this a Sparkle of that fire let loose That was lock'd up in the Winchestrian Goose.

winchite ('wɪntʃaɪt). *Min.* [f. the name of H. J. *Winch* + -ite¹.] A blue or violet monoclinic mineral of the amphibole group, approximately $NaCa(Mg,Fe^{2+})_4(Al,Fe^{3+})Si_8O_{22}(OH)_3$.

1906 L. L. Fermor in *Trans. Mining & Geol. Inst. India* I. 79 *Winchite*.. is the name which has been bestowed.. upon the blue amphibole... An analysis of this mineral shows it to be closely allied to tremolite in chemical composition. **1980** *Canad. Mineralogist* XVIII. 101/1 In composition, this asbestos probably ranges from a potassian richterite to a potassian winchite.

wincing ('wɪnsɪŋ), *vbl. sb.*¹ [f. wince *v.*¹ + -ing¹.] The action of wince *v.*¹; kicking; flinching or recoiling as from pain.

1426 Lydg. *De Guil. Pilgr.* 12002 So that no mater off wynsyng Ys ffounde in hym in fflessh nor bon,.. Gruchchyng, nor rebellioun, Nor no contradiccioun. *c* **1449** Pecock *Repr.* I. xx. 129 Thei schulden be aschamed.. of her wyncing in witt, and of her hopping bisidis witt. **1530** Palsgr. 75/2 Wynsyng of an horse, *regibement*. **1598** Marston *Sco. Villanie* iii. x, The Asse must be kindly whipped for winsing. **1841** Livingstone in Blaikie *Life* iii. (1881) 51 They are excellent patients too besides. There is no wincing; everything prescribed is done *instanter*. **1858** O. W. Holmes *Aut. Breakf.-t.* ii. (1859) 32 There is not a clerk who could raise the money to hire a saddle with an old hack under it that can sit down on his office-stool the next day without wincing. **1872** Black *Adv. Phaeton* xxviii. 382 He bade goodbye to both of them without wincing.

wincing, *vbl. sb.*²: see wince *v.*²

'**wincing**, *ppl. a.* [f. wince *v.*¹ + -ing².] That winces; †restive (*lit.* and *fig.*); recoiling, flinching.

1603 Holland *Plutarch's Mor.* 12 Winsing asse, Kicking colt, and such like nick-names. **1659** Torriano, *Cavallina-donna*, a skittish, or winzing woman. **1756** Mrs. Calderwood in *Coltness Collect.* (Maitland Club) 234 The Franciscans.. were a set of poor whinsing-like bodies. **1842** Dickens *Amer. Notes* xiv, The scruples of such wincing landlords. **1876** *Daily News* 27 Oct. 3/5 Outsiders are sure to conclude that the wincing jade is galled. **1918** *Blackw. Mag.* Jan. 84/2 He dug his.. spurred boot-heel against the wincing flank of the sweating.. mare.

Hence '**wincingly** *adv.*

1883 Miss Broughton *Belinda* I. x, Belinda.. shrinks wincingly away. **1891** Meredith *One of our Conq.* I. viii. 131 She remembered it.. wincingly, insurgently.

winck(e, obs. forms of wink.

Winco: see Wingco.

wincopipe, obs. form of wink-a-peep.

wind (wɪnd, *poet.* also waɪnd), *sb.*¹ Forms: 1– **wind**, 3–6 **wynd**, (4 **wint, wynt, whynde, wend**, *Sc.* **vend**), 4–6 **wynde**, *Sc.* **vynd**, 4–7 **winde**, (5 **wende, wyind, wijnd, wyynd**; *Sc.* 6–7 **wound**, 6–8 **win**, 9 **win'**, **wun**). [OE. *wind* = OFris., OS., (M)LG., (M)Du. *wind*, OHG., MHG. *wint, wind-* (G. *wind*), ON. *vindr* (Sw., Da. *vind*), Goth. *winds*:—OTeut. **windo-z*:—pre-Teut. **wentos*, cognate with L. *ventus*, W. *gwynt*, Breton *guent*; orig. a pres. ppl. formation (**wēnto-*) f. root *wē-* of OE. *wāwan* (see wowe), OHG. *wājan* (G. *wehen*), Goth. *waian* to blow, waft, Lith. *vėjas* wind, OSl. *vějati* blows, *větrŭ* wind, OIr. *feth* air, Gr. ἄησι (:—*ἄϝησι) blows, ἀήτης wind, Skr. *vāti* blows, *vāta* wind.

The normal pronunciation would be (waɪnd), as in *behind, bind, find, grind, hind, mind, rind*, etc., and this pronunciation remains dialectally and in ordinary poetical usage. The pronunciation (wɪnd) became current in polite speech during the 18th c.; it has been used occas. by poets, but the paucity of appropriate rhyming words (such as *sinned, thinned, dinned*) and the 'thinness' of the sound have been against its general use in verse. The short vowel of (wɪnd) is presumably due to the influence of the derivatives *windmill, windy*, in which (ɪ) is normal.

1747 Johnson *Plan of Engl. Dict.* 12 To fix the pronunciation of monosyllables, by placing with them words of correspondent sound.. so that the words *wound* and *wind*, as they are now frequently pronounced, will not rhyme to *sound*, and *mind*.

The following quots. contain examples of the pronunciation (wɪnd) in modern poets:—

1855 Lynch *Rivulet* lxxxi. (*Jerusalem*) iii, She hath sinned; Like ashes now her scattered sons Fly on the wind. **1866** Swinburne *Poems, A Litany* 17 As the tresses and wings of the wind Are scattered and shaken, I will scatter all them that have sinned. **1885** Tennyson *Wreck* vii, When her orphan wail came borne in the shriek of a growing wind, And a voice rang out in the thunders of Ocean and Heaven 'Thou hast sinn'd'. **1913** Bridges *La Gloire de Voltaire* 94 When sickening France adulterously sinned With Virtue, and went mad conceiving wind.]

I. The literal sense, in various applications.

1. Air in motion; a state of movement in the air; a current of air, of any degree of force perceptible to the senses, occurring naturally in the atmosphere, usually parallel to the surface of the ground.

a. In general or collective sense.

In the collective sense now always with the definite article.

(*a*) *sing. Beowulf* 1132 Holm storme weol, won wið winde. *c* **897** Ælfred *Gregory's Past. C.* xxxix. 285 Se ðe him ealneȝ wind ondræt, he sæwð to seldon. *a* **900** Cynewulf *Elene* 1272 Winde ȝeliccost, þonne he.. hlud astiȝeð. **971** *Blickl. Hom.* 65 Ne biþ þær hungor, ne þurst, ne wind, ne ȝewenn. *c* **1200** *Vices & Virtues* 47 Se ðe gadereð mihtes wiðuten eadmodnesse,.. he is ilich ðo manne ðe berð dust amidewarde ðe winde. *a* **1300** *Cursor M.* 23667 Hat and cald and rain and wind. *c* **1320** *Sir Tristr.* 372 Þe wawes were so wode Wiþ winde. **1340–70** *Alex. & Dind.* 92 Whan þe wind on þe watur þe wawus arereþ. *c* **1380** Wyclif *Sel. Wks.* I. 72 A reede wawinge wiþ þe wynde. *c* **1400** Maundev. iii. (1919) I. 10 The eyr so cleer þat men may fynde no wynd þere. **1471** Caxton *Recuyell* (Sommer) 381 On a night whan hit was paisible of wynd & of storme. **1535** Coverdale *Ps.* xvii[i]. 42, I will beate them as small as the dust before the wynde. —— *Amos* iv. 13 He maketh the mountaynes, he ordeneth the wynde. **1594** *Selimus* C 2, Let our winged coursers tread the winde. **1609** Dekker *Ravens Alm.* G, He seemed so chary ouer her, that it grieued him the winde should blowe on her. **1624** Quarles *Job Milit.* ix. 4 A storme of wind. **1667** Milton *P.L.* I. 231 As when the force Of subterranean wind transports a Hill Torn from Pelorus. **1697** Dryden *Æneis* I. 438 Bare were her Knees, and knots her Garments bind; Loose was her Hair, and wanton'd in the Wind. **1794** Vancouver *Agric. Cambridge* 177 Water engines that go by wind. **1849** James *Woodman* viii, Not a breath of wind crossed the heavens. **1887** *Field* 10 Dec. 897 [He] kicked off.. against both wind and sun. **1893** *Law Times* XCV. 104/2 A gust of wind blew the plaintiff's mackintosh coat against the fence.

(*b*) *pl. c* **825** *Vesp. Psalter* xvii[i]. 11 [10] *Volavit super pinnas ventorum*, fleȝ ofer fiðru winda. **971** *Blickl. Hom.* 51 Þas windas & þas reȝnas syndon ealle his. *a* **1300** *Cursor M.* 22630 Windes on ilk side sal rise. **1390** Gower *Conf.* I. 34 Right now the hyhe wyndes blowe. *c* **1460** Metham *Wks.* (1916) 157 [I]ff Crystemes day falle vp-on Moneday, yt schuld be a gret wyntyr, and fulle off wyindys. *a* **1593** Marlowe *Ovid's Elegies* II. xi, Hither the winds blow, here the spring-tide roar. *a* **1614** J. Melvill *Autob. & Diary* (Wodrow Soc.) 261 The Lord of Armies, wha ryddes upon the winges of the woundes. **1638–56** Cowley *Davideis* I. Notes, Wks. 1710 I. 357 The Matter of Winds is an Exhalation arising out of the Concavities of the Earth. **1748** Gray *Alliance* 43 Command the Winds, and tame th' unwilling Deep. **1830** Tennyson *Ode to Mem.* 14 The dew-impearled winds of dawn. **1860** Tyndall *Glac.* II. viii. 263 The lighter débris is scattered by the winds far and wide over the glacier.

b. In particularized use (see also 2).

c **1000** *Sax. Leechd.* III. 56 Bærn eal to somne on ða healfe ðe se wind sy. *c* **1250** *Gen. & Ex.* 3087 Ðis wind hem broȝte ðe skipperes. **13..** *Cursor M.* 18919 (Gött.) Þar come a sune vte of þe air.. Wid a wend at come wid-all And.. fild all þat hall. *c* **1400** tr. *Secr. Secr., Gov. Lordsh.* 52 An hote wende. *a* **1533** Ld. Berners *Huon* xiv. 39 A small rayne abatyth a grete wynd. **1682** Dryden *Medal* 252 The Climate, vex't with various Winds. **1798** Coleridge *Anc. Mar.* v. v, And soon I heard a roaring wind. **1837** Dickens *Pickw.* xxviii, There was just such a wind and just such a fall of snow, a good many years back. **1880** Sutherland *Tales of Goldfields* 1 Hot winds and floods destroyed the crops. **1895** Stopf. Brooke in Jacks *Life & Lett.* (1917) II. 520 A low wind wandered about like a fairy.

c. A symbolical representation of the wind. (Cf. F. *têtes de vents*.)

1848 Dickens *Dombey* xxxi, A cherub on a monument, with cheeks like a young Wind.

d. *fig.* (sometimes = 'rage'): cf. whirlwind 2.

c **1485** *Digby Myst.* I. 45 Sle them all either for ffoo or ffrende: thus he commaundid in his furious wynde. **1787** Beckford *Italy* (1834) II. 248 The wind is up in the archbishop's brain just at this moment, and by the least contradiction more would become a hurricane. **1876** Hardy *Ethelberta* xi, Lady Petherwin crashed out of the room in a wind of indignation.

2. a. With specific reference to the direction from which it blows; usually qualified by the name of a point of the compass, or in *pl.* by a numeral, esp. *four* (hence sometimes *transf.* = points of the compass, directions).

c **725-** [see south *a.* 3]. *c* **888** Ælfred *Boeth.* vi. § 1 Se suðerna wind hwilum mid miclum storme ȝedrefeð þa sæ. *a* **1000** *Boeth. Metr.* xii. 14 Ȝif hine lytle ær stormas ȝestondað & se stearca wind, norðan & eastan. *c* **1000** *Sax. Leechd.* III. 274 Ðas feower heafodwindas habbað betweox him on ymbhwyrfte oðre eahta windas. *c* **1340-** [see north *a.* 3]. **1362** Langl. *P. Pl.* A. v. 14 Þis souþ-Westerne wynt. *c* **1374** Chaucer *Boeth.* I. met. iii. (1868) 9 þe wynde þat hyȝt borias. **1377-** [see south-west C. 1]. **1379** *Glouc. Cath. MS.* 19. No. I. lib. I. c. 4 lf. 12 b, The four wyndes, & thayre 8 wyndes. **1382** Wyclif *Ezek.* xxxvii. 9 Fro four wyndys cum, thou spirit. *c* **1425** *MS. Digby 233* lf. 224 b/2 Est wynde.. hath tweyne syde wyndes oþer quarter wyndes. **1549** *Compl. Scot.* vi. 61 The marynalis.. hes.. discriuit thretty tua sortis of vyndis. **1602** Shaks. *Ham.* II. ii. 397 When the Winde is Southerly. **1610** —— *Temp.* I. ii. 254 To run vpon the sharpe winde of the North. **1625** N. Carpenter *Geog. Del.* I. vi. (1635) 151 One Rhumbe answers to two coasts or windes. **1651** T. Barker *Art of Angling* (1820) 2 The Winde in the South, then that blows the Flie in the Trouts mouth. **1659** Twysden *S. Foster's Miscell.* xiv. v. 27 Project these Azimuths or winds into the horizontal line. **1667** Milton *P.L.* II. 516 Toward the four winds four speedy Cherubim Put to thir mouths the sounding Alchymie. **1819** Shelley *Ode to West Wind* I. 1 O, wild West Wind, thou breath of Autumn's being. **1849** Lever *Con Cregan* xviii, The wind was a nor'-wester. **1853** Dickens *Bleak Ho.* xxviii, The cousins disperse to the four winds of heaven.

b. *Mah Jong.* Any of the four compass-positions about the wall of tiles taken up by a player; the player who occupies this place. Also, any of sixteen tiles (four of each sort) representing one of the four winds used in the game.

1922 M. S. Rosenblatt *Majong* 2 There are 4 'Winds'.. and there are 4 pieces of each 'Wind'. **1925** [see pung *v.*², *sb.*², and *int.*]. **1938** V. L. Cecil *Maajh* 2 Each player took the position of one of the four Winds. **1960** R. C. Bell *Board & Table Games* vi. 152 The tiles are grouped into: Cardinal tiles... Winds... Honour tiles... Minor tiles. *Ibid.* 156 Each wind in turn becomes the wind of the round. The first round is East Wind's. **1979** M. Hammer *Learn to play Mah Jongg* ii. 35 The next step is to evaluate which tiles are more prevalent—odds, evens, winds, singles, pairs.

3. a. In reference to navigation, as the means of propulsion of a sailing vessel.

Beowulf 217 Ȝewat þa ofer wæȝholm winde ȝefysed flota famiheals. *c* **900** tr. *Bæda's Hist.* v. i, To þon ðætte ..ȝesyndȝe windas..usic æt lande ȝebrohte. *c* **1205** LAY. 236 He þonene iuatte forð aȝein mid þan winde. **1297** R. GLOUC. (Rolls) 6827 þe wind hom paide wel & to þe se hii come. **13..** *Propr. Sanct.* in Herrig's *Archiv* LXXXI. 112/83 þe wynt wox þo contrarious. *c* **1375** *Sc. Leg. Saints* vi. (*Thomas*) 44 þan vent þai to þe se.. &..gud vend þai had. *c* **1425** *Engl. Conq. Irel.* xxxiii. 80 As thay wer wynd abydynge. **1543-4** *Acc. Ld. High Treas. Scot.* VIII. 249 The saidis boittis witht artalȝe, quhilkis war seperat be ane gret wound. **1549** *Compl. Scot.* vi. 40 Afoir the vynd. **1617** MORYSON *Itin.* I. 209 We sayled commonly with a fore wind, the winds being more constant in that sea. *a* **1625** MANWARYNG *Seaman's Dict.* (1644) s.v. *Ride*, To *Ride betwixt wind and tide*, is when the wind and tyde have equall power. **1633** G. HERBERT *Temple, Provid.* xxiii, The windes, who think they rule the mariner, Are rul'd by him, and taught to serve his trade. **1691** *Sir J. Ashby's Acc. Engagem.* 15 If the Wind had stood, we should have had more fighting. **1726** SWIFT *Gulliver* III. i, I set up my sail, the wind being fair. **1792** MRS. P. L. POWYS *Passages fr. Diaries* (1899) 268 [We] set off in our vessel for Ryde, with wind and tide both against us. **1879** [see FAIR *a.* 13].

b. *Naut.* in various expressions referring to the direction or position of the wind in relation to the ship: hence also allusively.

e.g. *to gain, get,* or *take the wind of*, to get to windward of (another ship) so as to intercept the wind, to get the weather gage of: so to *give, have the wind of*. *to keep one's (the, a good) wind*, to keep close to the wind without falling away to leeward. *to take the wind out of the sails of* (fig.), to deprive of one's means of progress, put a check upon the action of, put at a disadvantage. *to turn (the) wind*, to turn so as to get on the other side of the wind. (For other phrases, as *to haul one's wind, to hold a good wind*, etc. see the verbs.)

14.. *Sailing Directions* (Hakl. Soc.) 13 By turnyng wynde at an est south of the moone. **1563** GRESHAM in Burgon *Life* (1839) II. 41 They did all they colde to tacke the wynde of us. **1600** HAKLUYT *Voy.* III. 198 All the three Biskainers made toward our ship, which was not carelesse to get the winde of them all. **1600** DALLAM in *Early Voy. Levant* (Hakl. Soc.) 97 We havinge the wynde of the Spanishe ships. **1629** WADSWORTH *Pilgr.* ii. 7 We..made all haste possible to gaine the winde of him. **1666** *Lond. Gaz.* No. 74/2 The Zealand Admiral kept his wind, the Admiral of the Blew, with eight or ten more standing after him. *a* **1687** PETTY *Treat. Naval Philos.* I. iii, What makes her [*sc.* a ship] Leeward or keep a good Wind. **1696** tr. *Du Mont's Voy. Levant* xxvi. 350 They are oblig'd to take the Wind of us. **1704** *Lond. Gaz.* No. 4054/1 The Wind shifted..to the Westward, which gave the Enemy the Wind of us. **1805** NELSON 6 Oct. in Nicolas *Disp.* (1846) VII. 82 To keep the wind under three topsails and foresail for the night. **1822** SCOTT *Nigel* ix, He would take the wind out of the sail of every gallant. *a* **1828** *Young Allan* vi. in Child *Ballads* VIII. 379 My master has a coal-carrier Will take the wind frae thee. She will gae out under the leaf, Come in under the lee, And nine times in a winter night She'll turn the wind wi thee. **1849** *Blackw. Mag.* LXV. 333, I felt the ship bring her wind a-quarter. **1883** *Harper's Mag.* Feb. 339/2 A young upstart of a rival, Llanelly..which has taken a great deal of the wind out of the sails of its older neighbor.

4. As conveying scent, esp. the scent of a person or animal in hunting, etc.: in various phr., *lit.* and *fig.*

to take, have, get, gain the wind of, to scent or detect by or as by the wind; hence occas. to keep under observation. Conversely, *to give* (an animal) *one's wind*. *to keep the wind*, to keep the game on the windward side so as to scent it, or so that it does not scent one. † *on one's wind*, on one's trail or track. † *to the wind*, to windward. *within wind of*, near enough to be detected by.

c **1330** *Arth. & Merl.* 7956 þis seiȝen þe sexten þousinde & comen swiþe on our winde. *c* **1470** HENRY *Wallace* VII. 469 The stynk scalyt off ded bodyis.., The Scottis abhord ner hand for to byd; ȝeid to the wynd. **1530** PALSGR. 751/1, I take the wynde, as a dere dothe of a person... Let hym take good hede that they take nat the wynde of him. **1588** SHAKS. *Tit. A.* IV. ii. 133 My sonne and I will haue the winde of you. **1593** —— *3 Hen. VI*, III. ii. 14 Hee knowes the Game, how true hee keepes the winde? **1601** —— *All's Well* v. ii. 10 *Clo.* Truely, Fortunes displeasure is but sluttish if it smell so strongly as thou speak'st of.. Prethee alow the winde. *Par.* Nay you neede not to stop your nose sir: I spake but by a Metaphor. **1602** —— *Ham.* III. ii. 362 Why do you go about to recouer the winde of mee, as if you would driue me into a toyle? **1606** MARSTON *Parasit.* II. D 1, Peace the woolfes eare takes the winde of vs. *Ibid.* III. F 1 b, We can take the winde, And smell you out. **1697** DAMPIER *Voy.* I. 391 We could smell them out in the thick Woods if we had but the wind of them. **1850** R. G. CUMMING *Hunter's Life S. Afr.* xviii, I gave the large herd my wind, upon which they instantly tossed their trunks aloft. **1865** CARLYLE *Fredk. Gt.* XVIII. ii. V. 36 For here are the Prussians within wind of us! **1883** STEVENSON *Treas. Isl.* x, We had run up the trades to get the wind of the island we were after. **1887** *Field* 19 Feb. 251/3 A small troop of four rhebok, which had..got our wind shortly before. **1890** S. W. BAKER *Wild Beasts* II. 92, I have myself been hunted out of the jungle by two rhinoceroses which thus gained our wind.

5. In alliterative conjunction with *weather*: most freq., now always, *wind and weather*; formerly also *weather and wind*, also with *the*, or with one or both sbs. in pl.

†(*a*) orig. connoting stormy inclement weather (cf. WEATHER *sb.* 1 g, h); (*b*) later, in neutral sense, atmospheric conditions as favourable or unfavourable for travelling; (*c*) now chiefly with reference to exposure to weathering influences.

a **1225** *Juliana* 72 Buldeð ower boldes uppon treowe staðele þat ne dredeð na wind ne na weder nowðer. **13..** *E.E. Allit. P.* B. 444 Where þe wynde & þe weder warpen hit wolde, Hit saȝtled. *c* **1375** *Sc. Leg. Saints* xvi. (*Magdalen*) 220 Bo[t] tholyt al þat haly rowte In wynd & wedyre ly þare-owt Of þare tempil. **1377** LANGL. *P. Pl.* B. VIII. 41 Like to þe grete wawes, þat as wyndes and wederes walweth aboute. *a* **1400** *Octouian* 1237 Good wynd and wedyr þay hadde at wylle. **1455** *Rolls of Parlt.* V. 335/1 At the next Wynde and Wedder that wille serve theym. **1513** SIR E. HOWARD in Ellis *Orig. Lett.* Ser. III. I. 150 If wynde and wedour will serve. **1587** *Maitland Club Misc.* (1840) II. 356 That he sould keip his hour wind and weddar servand. **1601** SHAKS. *Twel. N.* I. v. 255 Tis in graine sir, 'twill endure winde and weather. *c* **1630** RISDON *Surv. Devon* §330 (1810) 341 Wind and weather were ever against him, a proverb applied to the unfortunate. **1654** BRAMHALL *Just Vind.* iv. (1661) 56 With what art..the Papacy..was tacked into the Church contrary to wind and weather. **1667** WELLSHURE in Earl Orrery *St. Lett.* (1742) 293 If it should be my fortune to meet with prizes, I shall bring them here, if wind and weather will permit me. **1712** SWIFT *Jrnl. to Stella* 17 June, If it did not come in due time, can I help wind and weather? **1848** DICKENS *Dombey* lix, It is a great house still, proof against wind and weather.

6. As a thing devoid of sense or perception, or that is unaffected by what one does to it: in phrases usually expressing futile action or effort, as *to beat the wind* (see BEAT *v.*[1] 1 c), *to speak to the wind, to spit against* (or *into*) *the wind*.

c **1330** *Arth. & Merl.* 7072, xii hundred ogain fourti þousinde Ferd, so smoke ogain þe winde. **1526** *Pilgr. Perf.* (W. de W. 1531) 90 b, In so doynge, it may not be sayd that we bete the wynde. **1569** BLAGUE *Sch. Conceytes* 261 He spake to the winde. **1577** GRANGE *Golden Aphrod.* G iij, I see I swimme agaynst the streame, I kicke against a gode, I caste a stone against the winde. **1578** H. WOTTON tr. *Yver's Courtlie Controversie* II. 109 Thou shalte be like him that spitteth againste the winde, whose slaver fleeth in his owne face. **1599** PEELE *David & Bethsabe* B iij b, He..makes their weapons wound the sencelesse winds. **1612** WEBSTER *White Divel* sig. E4, For your names, of Whoore and Murdresse they proceed from you, As if a man should spit against the wind, The filth returne's in's face. **1614** J. COOKE *Greene's Tu Quoque* G 3, To strike Ayres, or buffet with the Winde, That playes vpon vs. **1622** J. TAYLOR (Water P.) *Shilling* C 4, Like throwing feathers 'gainst the winde. **1697** DRYDEN *Æneis* v. 595 Entellus wasts his Forces on the Wind. **1713** SWIFT *Jrnl. to Stella* 10 Apr., This I tell her, but talk to the winds. **1860** MISS YONGE *Hopes & Fears* I. 201 'Have you spoken to her?' 'As well speak to the wind.' **1968** *Guardian* 1 Oct. 8/5 The decision to withdraw our forces..was inevitable, and Mr Heath is spitting into the wind when he tells Australian audiences that a Conservative Government would go back. **1975** *Times* 10 Nov. 12/4 To adopt a vivid barrack-room expression, it is no good spitting against the wind or shouting against thunder.

7. In comparisons, as a type of violence or fury (†phr. *wroth as (the) wind*), swiftness, freedom or unrestrainable character, mutability or fickleness, lightness or emptiness (cf. 15).

13.. *E.E. Allit. P.* C. 410 He wex as wroth as þe wynde towarde oure lorde. **1377** LANGL. *P. Pl.* B. XVII. 350, 'I may no lenger lette', quod he,..And went away as wynde. *c* **1470** *Gol. & Gaw.* 770 Schir Gologrnetworthy fe greif his gray ene brynt, Wod wraith as the wynd. **1500-20** DUNBAR *Poems* lxvi. 27 Purpois dois change as wynd or rane. **1526** *Pilgr. Perf.* (W. de W. 1531) 7 b, All dependeth of a thynge that is more lyght than is the wynde. *c* **1585** [R. BROWNE] *Answ. Cartwright* 83 A man of the winde, and false fellowe. **1590** SHAKS. *Mids. N.* III. ii. 94 About the wood, goe swifter then the winde. **1592** —— *Rom. & Jul.* I. iv. 100 Vaine phantasie ..more inconstant then the wind. **1606** —— *Tr. & Cr.* I. iii. 253 Speake frankely as the winde. **1610** —— *Temp.* I. ii. 499 Thou shalt be as free As mountaine windes. **1785** C. WILKINS tr. *Bhagvat-Geeta* vi. 66, I esteem it as difficult to restrain as the wind. **1855** LONGF. *My lost Youth* i, A verse of a Lapland song..'A boy's will is the wind's will'.

II. Transferred senses. (See also 1 c, 2.)

†**8. a.** Air in general, as a substance or 'element'. *Obs.* exc. as in b.

to take wind: to become tainted or corrupted by exposure to or access of air; also *fig.*

c **1250** *Hymn* in *Trin. Coll. Hom.* App. 258 þu sscope eld & wind & water, þe molde is þet feorþe. **1393** LANGL. *P. Pl.* C. x. 56 Witt and water, wynd and fuyr. *c* **1400** *26 Pol. Poems* 101/19 In heuene, wiþ angels, aboue þe wynde. *c* **1420** *Liber Cocorum* (1862) 34 Do hit in a barel þenne;..Stop wele þo hede for wynde. **1562** J. HEYWOOD *Prov. & Epigr.* (1867) 183 It hath tane to much wynde in the poudryng tubbe. *c* **1586** C'TESS PEMBROKE *Ps.* LV. ii, Then say I, O might I but cutt the wind Borne on the wings the fearfull dove doth beare. **1605** SHAKS. *Macb.* I. iii. 82 Whither are they vanish'd? *Macb.* Into the Ayre: and what seem'd corporall, Melted, as breath into the Winde. *a* **1610** HEALEY *Theophrastus* To Rdr. (1616) I 2, By powring it out of the Latin into the vulgar..it cannot but (by my vnskilfulnesse) it hath taken some wind. **1626** BACON *Sylva* §998 The Sword it selfe must be Wrapped vp Close, as farre as the Ointment goeth, that it taketh no Wind. **1685** J. CHAMBERLAYNE *Coffee, Tea*, etc. 44 If it [*sc.* tea] takes wind, 'tis spoiled, and has no more strength then dead leven. **1712** J. JAMES tr. *Le Blond's Gardening* 180 Settle the Ground about the Plants, lest the Roots take Wind.

b. *wind and water.* (*a*) in phr. *between* (or *betwixt*) *wind and water* (Naut.), referring to that part of a ship's side which is sometimes above water and sometimes submerged, in which part a shot is peculiarly dangerous; hence in fig. phr. expressing serious injury or attack. (*b*) attrib. and comb., as *wind and water line*, the part of a ship's side between wind and water; also *transf.* (see quot. 1876[1]); †*wind and water tight* adj., proof against wind and rain or flood.

a **1550** *Hye Way to Spittel Hous* 615 in Hazl. *E.P.P.* IV. 52 Landlordes that do no reparacyons, But leue..Theyr housyng vnkept wynd and water tyght. **1588** *Cert. Advert. Losses Sp. Navie Irel.* B 2, One of the shot was betweene the winde and the water, whereof they thought she would haue sonke. **1614** T. HERODE in W. Foster *Lett. E. Ind. Co.* (1897) II. 94 His ship had been long out and very much eaten between wind and water. *a* **1652** A. WILSON *Inconstant Ladie* III. iv, Now they haue crackt mee betwixt wind and water A'most past cure. Stay, let me feele my selfe. **1655** FULLER *Ch. Hist.* x. ii. §10 The good old man was shot between Wind and Water, and his consent was assaulted in a dangerous joincture of time to give any deniall. **1691** *Satyr agst. French* 27 These Female Frigats did more Mischiefs scatter, By their low tire of Guns 'twixt wind and water. **1726** *Adv. Capt. R. Boyle* (1768) 260 They..had receiv'd a Shot between Wind and Water, and the Ship leak'd very much. **1823** J. BRIC *Let.* 22 Feb. in *Corresp. D. O'Connell* (1972) II. 447 You have hit the thing between wind and water and whilst you have justly elevated your own name you have done much for your country. **1876** PREECE *Telegraphy* 161 The ground line, or, as it is more frequently termed, the wind and water line. **1876** BANCROFT *Hist. U.S.* V. ix. 426 The 'Congress'..was hulled twelve times, and hit seven times between wind and water. **1967** M. GILBERT *Dust & Heat* III. 239 Mallinson *must* have guessed what was coming. Nevertheless, it hit him between wind and water.

9. Compressed or confined air; air that inflates or is contained within some body. Now *rare* (and superseded by *air*) exc. as in 10, 12(*b*). (With quot. 1689 cf. WINDAGE 1.)

a **1225** *Ancr. R.* 282 A bleddre ibollen ful of winde. *Ibid.*, A nelde prikiunge worðe al ut þene wind. **1450-1530** *Myrr. our Ladye* I. v. 17 As a blather full of wynde. **1560** B. GOOGE tr. *Palingenius' Zodiac* I. (1561) A vij, A blather full implete wyth wynde. **1615** MARKHAM *Country Contentm.* I. viii. 109 A great ball of double leather fild with winde. **1689** BINNING *Light to Art of Gunnery* xiii. 42 How to Extract the Wind from the Bore of a Peece Geometrically, and thereby to know a fit Ball for the same.

10. a. 'Air' or gas in the stomach or intestines (or, according to early notions, in other parts of the body); flatus. †Also *pl.*

to break wind, to discharge flatus from the stomach or bowels (see BREAK *v.* 47); †of a remedy, to cure or dispel flatulence.

c **1000** *Sax. Leechd.* II. 224 Ȝif sio wamb biþ windes full, þonne cymð þæt of wlacre wætan. **1398** TREVISA *Barth. De P.R.* v. xxxvii. (Bodl. MS.) Grete ventosite and winde þat stoppith þe weye of þe breeþ. *a* **1400-50** *Stockholm Med. MS.* 151 For wynd in þe hed. *c* **1400** *Secr. Secr., Gov. Lordsh.* 70 It sterys hete to þe body, and destroyes wyndes. **1542** BOORDE *Dyetary* xxix. (1870) 292 Make no restryctyon of wynde and water, nor seege that nature wolde expelle. **1552-** [see BREAK *v.* 47]. **1611** SPEED *Hist. Gt. Brit.* IX. xxi. §76 An ouer-much quantity of a confection to breake winde from off his stomacke. **1620** VENNER *Via Recta* v. 89 The vse of milke is very hurtfull vnto them that are subiect to winde. **1637** MILTON *Lycidas* 126 The hungry Sheep..swoln with wind. **1661** PEPYS *Diary* 14 Aug., His pain (which was wind got into the muscles of his right side). **1702** J. PURCELL *Cholick* (1714) 65 When the Pain spreads itself all over the Belly, 'tis occasion'd for the most part by Winds. **1707** FLOYER *Physic. Pulse-Watch* 378 That the Liver produces a Wind in the Heart that is, the Rarifaction of Humours. **1851** MAYHEW *Lond. Labour* I. 206/1, I can dispel wind in two minutes. **1855** LEECH *Pict. Life & Char.* i, *Domestic Bliss.* [speaking of a baby] That is not taking notice; it's only the wind. **1897** *Allbutt's Syst. Med.* II. 911 Even respectable people take the ether.., pretending that it is useful for 'the wind in the stomach'.

b. *to get the wind up* (slang): to get into a state of alarm or 'funk'. So *to put the wind up* (a person).

1916 P. GIBBS *Battles of Somme* xxii. 172 It was obvious that the blinking Boche had got the wind up. **1918** W. OWEN *Let.* 11 Oct. (1967) 584 Shells so close that they thoroughly put the wind up a Life Guardsman in the trench with me. **1922** C. ALINGTON *Strained Relations* viii. 118, I tell you you've absolutely put the wind up Uncle Bob and Peter! They're scared to death of your finding them out.

11. a. Air inhaled and exhaled by the lungs: = BREATH *sb.* 3. *Obs.* exc. as coloured by d below.

a **1000** *Riddles* xv. 14 Ic [*sc.* a horn] winde sceal sincfaȝ swelȝan of sumes bosme. **13..** *K. Alis.* 6415 (Laud MS.), A litel hole in her chyn Where her wynde gooþ out & in. **13..** *Cursor M.* 531 (Gött.) þis wind [*Cott.* aand] þat men draus oft Bitakins wind þat blauis on loft. *c* **1400** MAUNDEV. (Roxb.) xxii. 99 þe preste..castez a clath on his mouth and stoppez his wynde. **1535** *Goodly Primer* O ij b, I begynne to waxe faynte, and scarcely able to drawe my wynde. **1601** HOLLAND *Pliny* XIV. xxii. I. 427 His wind he never tooke while the cup was at his mouth, but justly observed the rule of drinking with one breath. **1606** SHAKS. *Tr. & Cr.* III. ii. 33 She does so blush, & fetches her winde so short, as if she were fraid with a sprite. **1611** *Bible* Ecclus. xxxi. 19 And he fetcheth not his wind short vpon his bed [*marg.* Or, and lieth not puffing and blowing]. **1865** *Field* 4 Mar. 151/2 Which seemed to knock all the wind out of him. **1918** H. LAUDER *Minstrel in France* xv. 174, I had precious little wind left to breathe with.

b. Breath as used in speaking; hence *transf.* speech, talk (esp. in such phr. as *to waste one's wind*). *Obs.* or *arch.* (exc. as implied in LONG-WINDED 2).

a **1330** *Otuel* 216 þat wind þou hauest i-lore. *c* **1400** *Destr. Troy* 9788 All þaire wordis þai wast, & þaire wynd alse. *c* **1430** *Hymns Virgin* (1867) 97 Do way, mercy, þou spillist myche winde. *c* **1460** SIR R. ROS *La Belle Dame* 795 Ye noye me sore, in wastyng all þis wynde. *c* **1520** SKELTON *Garl. Laurel* 565, Let vs wast no wynde For ydle iangelers haue but lytill braine. **1590** SHAKS. *Com. Err.* I. ii. 53 Stop in your winde sir, tell me this I pray. **1602** —— *Ham.* IV. vii. 67 For his death no winde of blame shall breath. **1616** WITHALS *Dict.* 573 *Os opprime*, keepe your wind to coole your pottage. **1722** W. HAMILTON *Wallace* 216 The Earl Buchan, tender but, and Young He did obtain for the wind of his Tongue.

c. Breathing as a vital process; hence *transf.* life: = BREATH *sb.* 5. So *to slip one's wind*, to die. *Obs.* exc. in low slang.

c **1450** *Cov. Myst.* (Shaks. Soc.) 226 My wynde is stoppyd, gon is my brethe. *c* **1530** *Songs, Carols*, etc. (E.E.T.S.) 92 Now deth is vnkynd; For he seyth: 'Man! stop thy wynde'. **1658** SIR T. BROWNE *Hydriot.* i. 8 The Scythians..swore by winde and sword, that is, by life and death. **1812** J. H. VAUX *Flash Dict.*, *Wind*, a man transported for his natural life, is said to be *lag'd for his wind*. **1860** *Slang Dict.* (ed. 2) 247 *To slip one's wind*, coarse expression meaning to die. **1883** *Gringo & Greaser* 1 Sept. 2/2 He had entirely slipped his wind—for want of which he was buried the 11th ult. **1896** H. LAWSON *While Billy Boils* 233 He laid the longest strip [of bark] by the side of the corpse... 'Come on, Brummy,.. yer ain't as bad as yer might be, considerin' as it must be three good months since yer slipped yer wind. I spect it was the rum as preserved yer.'

d. (*a*) Easy or regular breathing; power or capacity of breathing; condition with regard to respiration: = BREATH *sb.* 7. Now only in sporting phrases.

second wind, a condition of regular breathing regained after breathlessness during long-continued exertion; also *transf.* and *fig.* ***wind and limb, limb and wind***: see LIMB *sb.*[1] 2 d.

c **1330** *Arth. & Merl.* 8456 What for sorwe & eke for paine, Sche les winde & ek alaine. *Ibid.* 9226 Þer whiles Merlin.. Dede his out wende, to take þe winde. *c* **1440** *York Myst.* xxxv. 204 Þis bargayne will noght bee, For certis me wantis wynde. *c* **1440** CAPGRAVE *Life St. Kath.* II. 1465 She was lyfted vp and comforted newe a-gayn. And at the laste, whan she had caute wynde, 'Allas,' she seyde. ? **1529–30** WOLSEY in Ellis *Orig. Lett.* Ser. II. II. 27 My brethe and wynde by sything was so short that [etc.]. **1579** E. K. *Gloss* in *Spenser's Sheph. Cal.* Apr. 50 He was almost out of wind [*other edd.* winds]. **1596** SHAKS. *1 Hen. IV*, II. ii. 14 If I trauell but foure foot by the squire further a foote, I shall breake my winde. **1606** CHAPMAN *Gentl. Usher* II. i. 27, I never was more sound of winde and limbe. **1607** MARKHAM *Cavel.* III. 8 By the many stops and stayes which are made therein, the horse recouers his winde. **1610** SHAKS. *Temp.* I. i. 9 Blow till thou burst thy winde. **1650** B. *Discolliminium* 39 Reformation of Religion has come.. in such post-haste, that it hath broke its owne winde. **1686** JEVON *Devil of a Wife* I. 6 Ay and he holds out the Note of one Verse till the Clark begins to sing the next, he has a pure Wind. **1735** SOMERVILLE *Chase* I. 252 His round Cat Foot, strait Hams, and wide-spread Thighs, And his low-dropping Chest, confess his Speed, His Strength, his Wind. **1812** *Sporting Mag.* XXXIX. 18 After sparring for wind in which the Black was deficient. **1830** HOOD *Epping Hunt* Advt. to 2nd ed., I am much gratified to learn from you, that the Epping Hunt has had *such a run*, that it is *quite exhausted*, and that you intend therefore to give the work what may be called '*second wind*', by a new impression. **1838** DICKENS *Nich. Nick.* xxii, You had better get your wind now, and change your clothes. **1842** J. WILSON *Chr. North* I. 19 Schoolboys are generally in prime wind. **1857** HUGHES *Tom Brown* I. v, Three-quarters of an hour are gone; first winds are failing, and weight and numbers are beginning to tell. *Ibid.* II. v, Tom.. hits two heavy body blows, and gets away again before the Slogger can catch his wind. **1893** LYDEKKER *Horns & Hoofs* 147 A bull.. if allowed to get its 'second wind'.. will go on almost for ever. **1824** *Sporting Mag.* XIV. 166/2 Langan shewed a faint glimpse of second wind, and came up boldly. **1907** W. JAMES *Mem. & Stud.* (1911) x. 229 Everybody knows what it is to 'warm up' to his job. The process of warming up gets particularly striking in the phenomenon known as 'second wind'. **1948** 'J. TEY' *Franchise Affair* i. 15 Perhaps it was the presence of an ally that had heartened her; or perhaps she had just got her second wind. **1963** MRS. L. B. JOHNSON *White House Diary* 21 Dec. (1970) 18, I believe I am about to catch my second wind.

(*b*) in reference to diseased or disordered breathing in horses: see BROKEN WIND.

[**1523–**: implied in BROKEN-WINDED]. **1615** J. TAYLOR (Water P.) *Urania* xlix. C 2, When hee's [i.e. the horse is] broken in his winde. **1746** FRANCIS tr. *Hor., Epist.* I. i. 14 Loose from the rapid Car your aged Horse, Lest in the Race ..He drag his jaded Limbs, and burst his Wind. **1777** THICKNESSE *Journ. France* (1789) I. 18 A very handsome English coach-horse (a little touched in the wind). **1918** *Act 8 & 9 Geo. V* c. 13 §3 On the ground only of the stallion being affected in its wind.

e. *transf.* (*Pugilistic slang*). That part of the body in front of the stomach a blow upon which takes away the breath by checking the action of the diaphragm.

1823 in H. D. Miles *Pugilistica* (1906) II. 206 Ward made play—whack on the head at both sides, then at the wind. **1853** DICKENS *Bleak Ho.* xxvi, Judy.. pokes him.. particularly in that part which the science of self-defence would call his wind. **1898** *Daily News* 24 Nov. 7/3 Sharkey came back with his right, delivering several smashes on Corbett's wind.

12. a. Air as used for 'blowing' or sounding a musical instrument (***wind-instrument***) such as a horn, trumpet, flute, etc., or an organ-pipe: either (*a*) the blast or stream of air thus used, furnished by the breath of the player or by bellows; (*b*) the supply of air from which this is obtained, usually under compression (cf. 9), as in the ***wind-chest*** of an organ; or (*c*) the body of air within the instrument, whose vibration produces the sound.

spec. in *Hunting*, A blast or series of blasts on a horn blown at one breath.

c **1374** CHAUCER *Troylus* v. 443 Þer is noon Instrument Delicious þorugh wynd or touche or corde [etc.]. *c* **1500** in *Antiq. Rep.* (1809) IV. 407 Immoderate wyndes in a Clarion causith it for to rage. **1596** GRYNDALL *Hawking* etc. G iij b, When you goe into the field, blow with one wind one short, one long, and a longer. **1667** MILTON *P.L.* I. 708 As in an Organ from one blast of wind To many a row of Pipes the sound-board breaths. **1700** DRYDEN *Flower & Leaf* 357 Their Instruments were various in their kind, Some for the Bow, and some for breathing Wind. **1788** CROWE *Levesdon Hill* 27 Instruments of wind and string. **1873** HAMERTON *Intell. Life* I. iii. 21 The wind in the pipes of an organ. **1915** G. B. SHAW *Androcles* Prol. *stage dir.*, Heaving a long sigh, like wind in a trombone, he goes to sleep.

b. *transf.* The wind instruments of an orchestra (or their players) collectively, as distinguished from the 'strings' and 'percussion'. Also *pl.*, wind instruments.

1876 STAINER & BARRETT *Dict. Mus. Terms*, *Wood wind, or Wood wind-band*, the flutes, oboes, clarinets, bassoons, and instruments of their nature, in an orchestra. **1880** ROCKSTRO in Grove *Dict. Mus.* II. 561/2 An Orchestra consisting of thirty Stringed Instruments, with a full complement of Wind. **1904** *Daily News* 25 Feb. 8/5 The wind and percussion are prominent members of London orchestras. **1976** *Early Music* July 293/1 The author seems not to differentiate sufficiently between 'folk' and 'art' instruments of the Middle Ages, and especially when he deals with winds. **1978** P. GRIFFITHS *Conc. Hist. Mod. Music* vii. 102 His [*sc.* Berg's] atonal chamber concerto for piano, violin and thirteen winds.. is full of triple formations.

13. A blast of air artificially produced, *e.g.* by bellows (see also 12); the rush of air caused by a rapidly moving body. Const. *of*.

1556 WITHALS *Dict.* (1562) 48 The wynde of the belowes. **1594** MARLOWE & NASHE *Dido* II. i, He.. whiskt his sword about, And with the wind thereof the King fell downe. **1602** SHAKS. *Ham.* II. ii. 495 With the whiffe and winde of his fell Sword, Th' vnnerued Father fals. **1626** PEEKE *Three to One* B 1 b, The last Shotte flying so close by Captaine Portar, that with the winde of the Bullet his very Hands had almost lost the Sence of feeling. **1804** *Naval Chron.* XII. 247 He was knocked down by the wind of the shell. **1888** 'R. BOLDREWOOD' *Robbery under Arms* III. v. 75 The bullet went so close that the wind of it half turned him round.

14. The solar wind (see SOLAR *a.* 7), or a similar stream of particles emanating uniformly from any other star.

1966 *McGraw-Hill Encycl. Sci. & Technol.* III. 500/2 Presumably the wind is stronger when solar activity is high, but direct observations cannot be made before the next maximum. **1968** *Times* 5 Dec. 8/7 The fascinating region of space where the earth's magnetic field interacts with the 'wind' of atomic particles streaming out from the sun. **1982** *Sci. Amer.* July 83/1 Most stars, including the sun, are known to be losing mass in the form of a stellar wind.

III. Figurative and allusive uses. (See also 1 d, 3 b, 4, 8 a, 8 b, 10 b, and phrases in IV.)

15. Applied to something empty, vain, trifling, or unsubstantial. **a.** Empty talk, vain or ineffectual speech, mere 'breath' (cf. 11 b); †*occas.* empty fame (*obs.*).

c **1290** *S. Eng. Leg.* I. 289 Word nis aȝein hire bote wind. **1412–20** LYDG. *Chron. Troy* IV. 240 It [*sc.* what you say] is but wynde, no þinge for to leue. **1413** *26 Pol. Poems* 52/50 For word of wynd lityl trespase; Non harm nys don, þouȝ word be spoken. *c* **1480** HENRYSON *Cock & Jewel* 159 (Makculloch MS.) Of þis mater to speik it wair bot wynd. **1564** BECON *Wks.* I. Pref. ☛ C iv, When such as are yet weake in knowledge of Christ.. see nothyng in the Preachers but wynde & words. **1667** MILTON *P.L.* VI. 282 Nor think thou with wind Of airie threats to aw whom yet with deeds Thou canst not. **1798** COLERIDGE *Three Graves* 194 A curse is wind. **1823** SCOTT *Quentin D.* xix, Hard words, or kind ones,.. are but wind.

b. Vain imagination or conceit (with which one is 'puffed up': cf. 9); also ***wind in the head*** (with allusion to 10).

1484 CAXTON *Chivalry* 86 A knyght that.. byleueth in deuynacyes.. hath gretter fayth and hope in the wynde of his hede.. and the deuynours than in god. **1526** *Pilgr. Perf.* (W. de W. 1531) 103 Pryde.. bloweth & fylleth a man or woman full of wynde & vayne glory. **1591** SAVILE *Tacitus, Hist.* IV. xxxix. 198 When Mutianus had filled with these windes of hope and desire his empty vainglorious minde. **1603** HOLLAND *Plutarch's Mor.* 311 Many.. puffe up their owne conceits with nothing els but winde. **1634** S. R. *Noble Soldier* III. i. E 1, Fellowes which swell bigge with the wind of praise. **1779** J. BROWN in R. Mackenzie *Life* (1918) 146, I hope the Lord has let some of the wind out of you, that I thought was in you when first I knew you. **1918** *Blackw. Mag.* Dec. 765/1 He has probably got wind in the head through living in that gorgeous Gothic pagoda.

c. *gen.*

1382 WYCLIF *Job* vii. 7 Haue mynde, for wind is my lif [COVERDALE, my life is but a wynde]. **1539** *Bible* (Great) Isa. xxvi. 18 Wee haue bene wt chylde,.. as though we had brought forth winde. **1560** —— (Genev.) Hosea xii. 1 Ephraim is fed with the winde. **1687** P. AYRES *Lyric Poems* (1906) 306 Plough water, sow on rocks, and reap the wind. **1697** DRYDEN *Virg. Georg.* IV. 575 Then all his Frauds will vanish into Wind. **1831** JAMES *Philip Aug.* xxi, But, in the mean time, we are disputing about wind. **1850** CARLYLE *Latter-Day Pamph.* v. 25 Is Society become wholly a bag of wind, then, ballasted by guineas?

16. a. In various proverbial and other expressions, figuring or denoting a force, agency, or influence that drives or carries one (or something) along, or that strikes upon one (or something), or to which one (or something) is exposed. Also freq. in formula ***wind(s) of...*** Cf. sense c below.

esp. in phrases (with variations: see quots.) ***what wind blows you here?***; † ***all this wind shakes no corn*** (*obs.*); ***it's an ill wind that blows nobody good*** (orig. † *to good*: cf. 3). ***to raise the wind***: see RAISE *v.* 7. ***to sow the wind and reap the whirlwind***: see WHIRLWIND 2.

(*a*) in neutral or favourable sense.

c **1374** CHAUCER *Troylus* II. 1104 What maner wyndes gydeth yow now here? **1546** J. HEYWOOD *Prov.* (1867) 20 What wynde blowth ye hyther? *Ibid.* 30 To take wynde and tyde with me, and spede therby. **1579–80** NORTH *Plutarch* (1595) 996 (*Antonius*) To tell him what wind brought him thither. **1599** SHAKS. *Hen. V*, III. iii. 30. **1639** MAYNE *City Match* I. iii, All this is possible, And in the starres and windes. **1663** PATRICK *Parab. Pilgr.* xxvii. (1687) 309 When we have the Wind and Tyde of these pleasures to help us forward. **1859** MEREDITH *R. Feverel* xxii, A good wind of laughter had relieved him of much of the blight of self-deception, and oddness, and extravagance. **1877** DOWDEN *Shaks. Prim.* v. 54 Shakspere is not yet caught up in the passionate wind of his own imagination.

(*b*) in unfavourable sense. Also *fig.* (***wind of doctrine***: in allusion to *Eph.* iv. 14).

c **897** ÆLFRED *Gregory's Past. C.* xlii. 306 Ne læte ȝe eow ælcre lare wind aweccgan. [*Eph.* iv. 14.] *a* **1300** *Cursor M.* 26995 Quat es mans lijf bot.. a rek þat.. skailles wit a windes blast? **1393** LANGL. *P. Pl.* C. XIX. 32 The worlde is a wykkede wynde to hem þat wolde treuthe. *c* **1450** *Cast. Persev.* 2542 It is good, whon-so þe wynde blowe, A man to haue sum-what of his owe. *c* **1480** HENRYSON *Cock & Fox* 211 This wikkit wind of adulatioun. **1526** TINDALE *Eph.* iv. 14 Waveryinge and caryed with every wynde of doctryne. **1546** J. HEYWOOD *Prov.* (1867) 30 All this winde shakis no corne. *Ibid.* 77 An yll wynde that blowth no man to good, men say. **1573–80** TUSSER *Husb.* (1878) 29 It is an ill winde turnes none to good. **1589** R. HARVEY *Pl. Perc.* (1590) 1 All this wind shakes none of my Corne. **1633** G. HERBERT *Temple, Affliction* (1st), Thus thinne and lean without a fence or friend, I was blown through with ev'ry storm and winde. *c* **1665** MRS. HUTCHINSON *Mem. Col. Hutchinson* (1846) 19 They.. may let loose the winds of passion to bring in a flood of sorrow. **1693** CONGREVE *Old Bach.* II. i, 'Tis an ill Wind that blows no body good. **1768** [see TEMPER *v.* 2]. **1776** HUME *Hist. Eng., Life* (1778) I. p. xiii, This variety of winds and seasons to which my writings had been exposed. **1815** WORDSW. *Sonn.*, '*Weak is the will of Man*', Wreaths that endure affliction's heaviest shower, And do not shrink from sorrow's keenest wind. **1833** MRS. BROWNING *Prometh. Bound* 1152 Such a wind of pride Impelled thee of yore full sail upon these rocks. **1907** W. RALEIGH *Shakespeare* iv. 108 If once we are foolishly persuaded to go behind the authority of Heminge and Condell.. we.. are afloat upon a wild and violent sea, subject to every wind of doctrine. **1913** G. SANTAYANA *Winds of Doctrine* ii. 25 Prevalent winds of doctrine must needs penetrate at last into the cloister. **1926** R. H. TAWNEY *Relig. & Rise of Capitalism* iii. 179 With such a wind of doctrine in their sails men were not far from the days of complete freedom of contract. **1953** H. WEISINGER *Tragedy & Paradox of Fortunate Fall* vi. 267 The winds of new doctrine swept through the streets of Athens and London and left the old and conventional modes of religious thought bare. **1953** E. COXHEAD *Midlanders* vii. 158 The winds of want still blew about the world. **1962** *Listener* 26 Apr. 717/1 Ideas.. become ossified if they are not exposed to the wind of criticism. **1968** *Globe & Mail* (Toronto) 3 Feb. 10/5 To protect their own lives and those of their children, they will bend with the winds of war.

b. In expressions referring to a tendency, turn, or condition of affairs:

e.g. ***to know which way the wind blows***; ***the wind has changed***; † ***is the wind in that corner*** or ***door?*** (see CORNER *sb.*[1] 8, DOOR 6 b); ***to sail with every*** (***shift of***) ***wind***, to turn every change of circumstance to one's advantage; † ***to have the wind at will***, to have circumstances or conditions favourable for one's purpose.

c **1400** *Gamelyn* 703 To telle him tydynges how the wind was went. **1470–1668** [see DOOR 6 b]. **1546** J. HEYWOOD *Prov.* (1867) 75, I.. knew, which waie the winde blewe. **1560** DAUS tr. *Sleidane's Comm.* 334 b, The Byshoppes of Germany hauynge the wynde at wyll, restore the same. **1562** BULLINGHAM in Foxe *A. & M.* (1563) 1541/1 Wel Palmer (sayd I) is the wind in that corner with you? I warrant you it wyl blow you to litle ease at thend. **1615** SWETNAM *Arraignm. Wom.* To Rdr. A 3, You may perceiue the winde is changed into another dore. **1672** W. WALKER *Parœm.* 9 To have the wind with one. **1695** CONGREVE *Love for L.* IV. xiii, The Wind's chang'd? **1710** R. G. *Sacheverell's Def.* 7 We see the Dissenters can Sail with every Wind. **1818** SCOTT *Br. Lamm.* xxv, 'Have I heard!!!' said Caleb (who now found how the wind set). **1859** FARRAR *J. Home* iv, Miss Sprong.., seeing how the wind lay, had tried to drop little malicious hints against the favourite nephew. **1914** T. DREISER *Titan* xiii. 103, I know all about this. I've seen which way the wind is blowing. **1929** 'E. QUEEN' *Roman Hat Mystery* xxii. 301 Ellery got his first indication of which way the wind blew during the meeting at the Ives-Pope house. **1957** N. MITFORD *Voltaire in Love* x. 115 Thieriot.. seeing.. that the wind was now blowing in Voltaire's direction, consented.. to give the required evidence. **1976** LD. HOME (*title*) The way the wind blows.

c. *spec.* in phr. ***wind*** (also ***winds***) ***of change***. Harold Macmillan (Lord Stockton) delivered his celebrated 'wind of change' address to the South African parliament in Cape Town on 3 Feb. 1960 (see quot.). Our records show a marked increase in the frequency of the phrase after this date.

1905 S. NAIDU *Golden Threshold* 97 The wind of change for ever blows Across the tumult of our way. **1927** D. H. LAWRENCE *Mornings in Mexico* 154 The place of after-life and before-life, where house the winds of change. **1932** J. CLAPHAM *Econ. Hist. Mod. Britain* II. iii. 107 The [gas] companies or municipal works with their comfortable monopoly areas.. began to find a little wind of change blowing among their retorts and coke heaps. **1954** J. MASTERS *Bhowani Junction* xxxix. 345 Then the great changes swept across India and the world, and she had searched, not by deliberate plan but because the wind of change blew through her too, for ways of escape. **1960** H. MACMILLAN in *Times* 4 Feb. 15/3 The wind of change is blowing through the continent. **1960** *Economist* 15 Oct. 275/2 This is but one way in which the mining complex of De Beers, Anglo American and Rhodesian Anglo American is adapting itself to the winds of change in Africa. **1965** D. FRANCIS *Odds Against* vi. 86 'Is this your own show.. or whose?' 'I suppose—mine.' 'Uh-huh... The wind of change, if I read it right?' **1971** *Nature* 26 Nov. 179/1 The universities are also likely to feel some eddies from the winds of change that are swirling around the White House. **1976** 'J. CHARLTON' *Remington Set* xiv. 69 The winds of change are beginning to blow.. and your purpose in life isn't quite as defensible.. as it used to be.

17. a. ***to get*** or ***take wind***: to be revealed or divulged, become known, transpire. Now *rare*.

1667 DRYDEN & DK. NEWC. *Sir M. Mar-all* iv. i, Keep this Wooing secret; if it takes the least wind, old Moody will be sure to hinder it. **1682** *News fr. France* 15 So the thing got wind, and was look'd on as a great impiety. **1711** SWIFT *Jrnl. to Stella* 30 Dec., Masham's being a lord begins to take wind: nothing at Court can be kept a secret. **1808** SCOTT *Let. to Ellis* 23 Dec. in *Lockhart*, Do you know the Review begins to get wind here? **1855** PRESCOTT *Philip II*, I. II. vi. 401 Long before that time, the project had taken wind, and created a general sensation through the country.

b. *to get wind of*: to receive information or a hint of, to come to know (cf. 4). Also with clause. Hence, in recent use, *wind* = a hint or slight intimation (*of*). (Cf. F. *avoir le vent de*, Cotgr.)

1809 Malkin *Gil Blas* vii. vii. ¶3 The corregidor..got wind of our correspondence. **1866** P'cess Alice *Mem.* (1884) 133 They retreated again, when they got wind that troops were assembling. **1888** Stevenson *Black Arrow* iv. iv, Some wind of the disaster seemed to find its way..even to the chamber where the ringers were leaping on their ropes. **1917** T. R. Glover *From Pericles to Philip* xii. 378 It may be that the Spartan government had some wind of this.

c. *to sniff the wind*: to try the atmosphere; to examine the prevailing state of affairs before taking action (cf. sense 4).

1972 'R. Crawford' *Whip Hand* i. v. 22 Schuyler sniffed the wind and took his time about it. **1974** 'D. Kyle' *Raft of Swords* viii. 78 'I have no *reason*... I just know.' 'You sniff the wind. Very sensible. What do you smell?' **1977** *Time* 22 Aug. 5/2 Certainly the Labor government and the nation's judiciary system are sniffing the wind.

IV. Phrases with prepositions.

before the wind: see before B. 1 b.

18. by the (†a) wind (*Naut.*): as near as possible to the direction from which the wind is blowing (see by *prep.* 9).

1585 T. Washington tr. *Nicholay's Voy.* i. xvii. 19 Hauing stroke our sayles, we did nothing but lie by the winde. *a* **1612** J. Melville *Celeusma Naut.* (MS.), With chearfull schowt and mirrie plesant sounde Scho saild fast be ye winde. **1627** J. Smith *Sea Gram.* ix. 42 All your Sheats, Brases, and Tackes are trimmed by a Winde. **1697** *Lond. Gaz.* No. 3315/1 The best Sailer I ever met with by a Wind. **1794** *Rigging & Seamanship* 247*. **1806** Moore *Steersman's Song* ii, When by the wind close-hauled we go.

19. down (the) wind. a. In the direction in which the wind is blowing; along the course of the wind. Also ***down-wind*** (attrib.), situated in this direction, 'lee'.

1604 Shaks. *Oth.* iii. iii. 262 I'ld whistle her off, and let her downe the winde, To prey at Fortune. **1674** N. Cox *Gentl. Recreat.* i. (1677) 93 The Hare..will..run upon a side or down the Wind. **1780** Cowper *Progr. Err.* 333 Down the wind she swims, and sails away. **1834** Medwin *Angler in Wales* I. 235, I have had a hundred trimmers floating down the wind. **1855** Kingsley *Westw. Ho.* xxxii, The Spaniard fell off again, and went away dead down wind. **1885** Ld. Walsingham *Shooting* 141 (Badm. Libr.) It is best to 'give the dogs the wind' at the beginning of the day—that is, to start down wind and gradually to work the ground in the direction from which it blows. **1895** C. J. Cornish *Wild England* 184 We..found that..the birds had all run to the edge. Here we made the mistake of working the down-wind side first.

†**b.** *fig.* Towards decay or ruin; into or (commonly) in a depressed or unfortunate condition, in evil plight; *to go down the wind*, to 'go down', decline. *Obs.*

1600 Holland *Livy* xxxiv. xxiii, When they saw him downe the wind and fortune to frowne upon him. **1671** tr. *Machiavelli's Marr. Belphegor* 141 Though [he] was of one of the noblest Families.., yet he was look'd upon as down the winde [orig. *poverissimo*]. **1673** Cave *Prim. Chr.* ii. vi. 147 In the time of Constantine when Paganism began to go down the wind. **1683** —— *Ecclesiastici* Introd. p. lxvi, The Gentile-Temples, with all their Pomp and Retinue, went down the wind apace. **1827** Scott *Jrnl.* 25 Apr., The old Tory party is down the wind.

†**20. in wind** (*fig.* from 11 d): ready or fit for action of some kind. *Obs.*

1768 Earl Carlisle in Jesse *Selwyn & Contemp.* (1843) II. 356 The shops are all as fine as if they expected you, and the people belonging to them all in wind to answer your questions. **1777** Burke *Let. to Sheriffs of Bristol* Wks. 1842 I. 217 In order to keep power in wind, it was necessary..to exert it in those very points in which it was most likely to be resisted.

21. in the wind. a. In (or into) the direction from which the wind is blowing; to windward: (*a*) in reference to something which can be scented or perceived by means of the wind blowing from where it is (cf. 4, and see also b below); (*b*) in nautical use; also ***all in the wind*** (see quot. 1769).

c **1410** [see 27]. **1580** in Hakluyt *Voy.* (1589) 474 Wee had a ledge of rockes in the winde of vs. **1582** N. Lichefield tr. *Castanheda's Conq. E. Ind.* i. lxiv. 130 He cut and made his course into the Sea, to bring himselfe in the winde of those Sayles. **1634** Massinger *Very Woman* iii. v, Oh! how she holds her nose up, like a jennet In the wind of a grass-mare! **1678** Dryden *All for Love* Pref., The tyrants were suspicious, as they had reason, that their subjects had 'em in the wind. **1697** *Lond. Gaz.* No. 3262/3 It blowing fresh, and they bringing their Ship in the Wind, carried away their Foretop-mast. **1700** T. Brown tr. *Fresny's Amusem.* 3 Like a heated Stallion that had a Mare in the Wind. **1769** Falconer *Dict. Marine* (1780), *All in the Wind*, the state of a ship's sails when they are parallel to the direction of the wind, so as to shake and shiver. **1834** Marryat *P. Simple* xvi, We threw up in the wind, and raked them. **1818** 'A. Burton' *Johnny Newcome* iii. 175, I did not think..I was so much in drink! But now by th'holy smut I find That cursedly I'm in the wind.

b. *fig.* So as to be 'scented' or perceived (or so as to 'scent' or perceive something); ***to have in the wind***, to 'scent', to detect or discover the presence of; sometimes, to be on the scent or trail of, be in search of.

1540 Palsgr. *Acolastus* ii. iii. Lj, Where we can get any meate in the wynde, thyther wylle we resorte. **1599** Nashe *Lenten Stuffe* Wks. (Grosart) V. 230 Of him and none but him who in valuation is woorth 18 huge Argosees..haue I took sent or come in the wind of. **1601** Shaks. *All's Well* iii. vi. 122, I sent to her By this same Coxcombe that we haue i'th winde Tokens and Letters, which she did resend. **1624** Sanderson *Serm., 1 Tim. iv. 4* (1674) I. 248 The Courtiers and Officers lie in the wind for them. **1771** Smollett *Humphry Cl.* II. 10 June Let. i, The first was noted for having a seaman's eye, when a bailiff was in the wind. **1826** J. F. Cooper *Last of Mohicans* xiii, The Mohicans hear an enemy!..They scent danger in the wind! **1844** Dickens *Mart. Chuzz.* xxv, Mrs. Gamp..scenting no more rum in the wind (for the bottle was locked up again) rose to take her departure.

c. predicatively: Happening or ready to happen; astir, afoot, 'up'; (of a person or thing) as the subject of what is going on, 'in the business': usually with implication of being suspected or indistinctly apprehended (cf. b).

c **1535** Sir F. Bygod *Treat. Impropriations* D j, A thynge there is in the wynde..which I trust in God wyl one day come to lyght. *a* **1566** R. Edwards *Damon & Pithias* (1571) B iij b, There is sumwhat in the winde: His lookes bewrayes his inwarde troubled mynde. **1681** Dryden *Span. Friar* iii. i. 32 Where are you, Gentlewoman? there's something in the wind I'm sure. **1748** Richardson *Clarissa* II. xliv. 304 She thought something was in the wind, when my Brother came into my dining here so readily. **1826** Disraeli *Viv. Grey* v. xiv, There must be something in the wind, perhaps a war. **1855** Kingsley *Westw. Ho!* iv, There's a woman in the wind... I'll lay my life on it. **1891** Kipling *Light that Failed* vi, He'd have told us if there was a horse in the wind. It's a girl.

d. *to hang in the wind*: to remain in suspense or indecision.

c **1536** Starkey *Let. to Cromwell* in *England* (1878) p. xxxix, You schal fynd me..to be no sterter, wauerar, nor hengar in the wynd. **1555** J. Proctor *Hist. Wyat's Rebell.* 42 b, Such of those partes as honge in the wind, as neuters. **1640** J. D. *Knave in Grain* ii. i. D 2 b, Hang not ith' winde, (delay does torture). **1881** [see hang *v.* 17].

†**e.** *to cast in the wind*: to 'fling to the winds'.

1652 H. Bell *Luther's Colloq.* iii. 66 Otherwise, wee had cast in the winde, and scorned to..consider of that which now wee have plainly expressed in the Scriptures. *Ibid.* xi. 178 It regarded them not, but casteth them in the winde.

f. *Horsemanship.* (See quot.)

1805 C. James *Milit. Dict.* (ed. 2) s.v., A horse that carries in the wind, is one that tosses his nose as high as his ears, and does not carry handsomely.

g. *Naut. slang* (predicatively). Intoxicated; the worse for liquor: usually with qualification, esp. ***three sheets in the wind***. (Cf. *all in the wind* in a (*b*) above.)

1821–1883 [see sheet *sb.*[2] 2]. **1835** *Court Mag.* VI. 197/2 The anger of those who were what is termed 'a little in the wind', was now roused. **1840** Marryat *Poor Jack* xlvii, I'm not in the wind, at all events, for you see I'm perfectly sober.

22. into the wind: into or towards the direction from which the wind is blowing; so as to face the wind.

1918 *Blackw. Mag.* Mar. 294/2 You [in an aeroplane] are tempted to turn into the wind and land.

23. near the wind: nearly in the direction from which the wind is blowing; hence *fig.* nearly up to the possible or permissible limit; about as far as is safe, justifiable, or decent.

1560 W. Honnyng in Wright *Q. Eliz.* (1838) I. 44, I went so near the winde with the keper, that I told hym your Lordshippe knewe I wolde in reason respecte the game as fully as he. *a* **1700** B. E. *Dict. Cant. Crew*, *He'll go as near the Wind as another*, live as thrifty and wary as any one. **1837** Wellington in *Davey's Catal.* (1895) 35 It is impossible for me to attempt to go too near the Wind. **1883** [see sail *v.*[1] 1 c].

24. off the (†a) wind (*Naut.*): away from the wind; the opposite of *on* or *near the wind*.

1813 *Examiner* 4 Jan. 6/1 The enemy keeping two points off the wind. **1836** Marryat *Pirate* xiv, The Enterprise was again steered more off the wind. **1846** Raikes *Life of Brenton* 332 The Spartan was off the wind. **1862** 'Vanderdecken' *Yacht Sailor* 144 Running off the wind with a quarterly sea will test your powers to the utmost.

25. on a (less commonly the) wind (*Naut.*): towards or close to the direction from which the wind is blowing; (of the ship) sailing or heading in this direction.

1697 *Lond. Gaz.* No. 3315/1, I crouded Sail to Leeward to him, trimming my Sails on a Wind tho' I went before it, that he should not discover my square Yards. **1748** *Anson's Voy.* iii. v. 342 The proas..sailing most excellently on a wind. **1798** in Nicolas *Disp. Nelson* (1846) VII. p. cliv, The Swiftsure and Alexander standing towards us with all sail on a wind. **1840** R. H. Dana *Bef. Mast* iv, Clippers are fastest on the wind. **1897** F. T. Bullen *Cruise of 'Cachalot'* 377 We, being 'on the wind, close hauled', were bound by the 'rule of the road at sea' to keep our course when meeting a ship running free.

26. to the wind. a. *Naut.* Towards the direction from which the wind is blowing; so as to be *on the wind* (see 25). ***close to the wind***, very nearly in this direction: also *fig.* (see sail *v.*[1] 1 c, and cf. 23).

1795 Nelson 14 Mar. in Nicolas *Disp.* (1845) II. 15 Signal for the Fleet to come to the wind on the larboard tack. **1836** Marryat *Midsh. Easy* xviii, Gascoigne went to the helm, [and] brought the boat up to the wind.

b. ***to fling, give, throw***, etc. ***to the winds*** (fig.): to cast away, reject utterly. So ***to go to the winds***: to be cast away or aside, to vanish utterly.

1667 Milton *P.L.* ix. 989 And fear of Death deliver to the Windes. **1739** J. Wesley *Hymn, 'Commit thou all thy Griefs'* (tr. P. Gerhardt 'Befiehl' du deine Wege') ix, Give to the Winds thy Fears. **1801** *Marvellous Love-Story* II. 319 The specious cant of subtilty and self-interest she always..'gave to the winds'. **1884** 'Edna Lyall' *We Two* iii, Science went to the winds. **1885** 'Mrs. Alexander' *At Bay* ii, You must throw your fears to the winds.

27. under the wind: on the side away from the wind; on one's lee, to leeward; *spec.* in a position of shelter from the wind; under the lee of something. Chiefly *Naut.* and *dial.*

c **1410** *Master of Game* xxvi. (1904) 83 If þei may se hym and þei be in þe wynde þei ought to wiþdrawe hym in þe softest maner..and þan go preuyli to þei be vndir þe wynde. **1598** Florio, *Sottouento*, vnder the lee or winde. **1603** Lodge *Treat. Plague* iv. (Hunter. Cl.) 23 The healthfull ought to keepe themselues vnder, not ouer the winde. **1698** Froger *Voy.* 42 They kept their word, so that the Portugueses conveyed the vessel under the wind into a creek. **1787** Best *Angling* (ed. 2) 131 Always pitch your boat under the wind. **1826** Samouelle *Direct. Collect. Insects & Crust.* 46 The most successful places for mothing are the skirts of woods under the wind. **1893** Selous *Trav. S.E. Africa* 92 As he had come up under the wind, the dogs had not scented him.

28. up (the) wind: in the direction contrary to that in which the wind is blowing; against the wind: the opposite of *down (the) wind*, 19 a.

1611– [see up *prep.*[2] 4]. **1709** *Brit. Apollo* II. No. 51. 2/2 Rabits when they go a grazing in the Night go up the Wind. **1719** D'Urfey *Pills* III. 269 The Fox has broke Covert,..she runs up the Wind. **1838** [see up-wind *adv.*]. **1859** *Sporting Mag.* Jan. 5 Passing over the earths, he came away directly, with his head up wind. **1874** *Kennel Club Stud Bk.* 128 Rake and Romp went off merrily, but flushed some birds up wind.

29. upon a wind (*Naut.*) = 25.

a **1687** Petty *Treat. Naval Philos.* i. ii, The line unto which she stoops upon a Wind of either side. **1708** *Lond. Gaz.* No. 4422/7 They clapp'd again upon a Wind and left us. **1810** Scott *Let.* in *Lockhart* (1837) II. vii. 276, I would ..endeavour to go, as the sailors express it, *upon* a wind, and make use of it to carry me my own way. **1846** Raikes *Mem. Brenton* 328 Every ship..made all the sail she could carry upon a wind.

30. with the wind: in the direction in which the wind is blowing. Now esp. in *fig.* phr. ***gone with the wind***: gone completely (as if blown away by the wind), disappeared without trace.

1577 Googe tr. *Heresbach's Husb.* 41 b, In reapyng, you must regarde to goe with the wynde. **1607** Topsell *Four-f. Beasts* 136 He betaketh himselfe to his heeles againe, running still with the wind. **1616** W. Browne *Brit. Past.* ii. ii. 48 A gallant Stag..Came running with the winde. **1722** De Foe *Col. Jack* (1840) 298 We went spooning away large with the wind for one of the islands. **1896** E. Dowson *Verses* 17, I have forgot much, Cynara! gone with the wind. **1918** Galsworthy *First & Last* ix, in *Five Tales* 61 A man, when he drowns, remembers his past. Like the lost poet he had 'gone with the wind'. Now it was for him to be true in his fashion. **1936** M. Mitchell (*title*) Gone with the wind. **1948** W. S. Churchill *Gathering Storm* xix. 271 The services of thirty-five Czech divisions..[were] cast away,..all gone with the wind.

V. 31. Obvious combinations. **a.** attrib. Of, pertaining to, consisting of, produced or effected by (the) wind, as ***wind-action, -blast, -current, -dispersal, effect, -erosion, -flaw*** (flaw *sb.*[2]), ***-force, -gust, -movement, -power*** (power *sb.*[1] 13), ***-pressure, -puff, resistance, -rush, -shift, -song, -speed, -storm, -streak, -supply*** (sense 12), ***-torrent, -walk, -wave, -well***; serving for the passage of wind, as ***wind-passage***; for defence against the wind, as ***wind-guard, -shelter***.

1883 *Science* II. 142/2 This in combination with the *wind-action..has added nearly one hundred square miles of low-land. **1582** Stanyhurst *Æneis* i. (Arb.) 19 A great hurly burlye the *wyndblasts. **1902** F. Thompson *Cecil Rhodes* 82 Like to a smouldering fire by wind-blasts swirled. **1866** A. Steinmetz *Weathercasts* 53 Two constant principal *wind-currents—North-east and South-west. **1911** J. A. Thomson *Biology of Seasons* iii. 277 Any structural peculiarity that increases area without increasing weight will aid in *wind-dispersal. **1937** *Wind effect [see *air position* s.v. air *sb.*[1] III. 1]. **1941** B. Hellström in *Ingeniörsvetenskapsakad. Handl.* No. 158. 8 A denivellation of the water surface takes place, by which the level of the lake is lowered at the windward and raised at the leeward shore. This denivellation is called the Wind Effect. **1901** *Athenæum* 7 Dec. 778/2 The study of *wind-erosion of snow. **1913** J. Masefield *Daffodil Fields* 110 Flicking *windflaws fill the air with brine. **1931** E. Linklater *Juan in Amer.* i. 15 A frown on that bland forehead was like the wind-flaw on a saucer of milk that some petulant child has blown across. **1935** *Geogr. Jrnl.* LXXXVI. 533 The most remarkable feature was the great variation in *wind-force and direction. **1976** *Islander* (Victoria, B.C.) 14 Nov. 7/2 The seas began to look greyer—but we hadn't had anything more than windforce seven—so far. **1862** *Catal. Internat. Exhib.* II. x. 12 The following designs in terra cotta chimney tops have proved themselves the most efficient *wind guards introduced. **1820** Clare *Poems, Crazy Nell* x, A *wind-gust blew high. **1853** Kane *Grinnell Exp.* xxxv. (1856) 319 The apparent *wind-movements of our exhibitions [of aurora] in Lancaster Sound. **1900** *Jrnl. Sch. Geog.* (U.S.) Apr. 155 The average monthly wind movement at Denver is two thousand miles less than at New York. **1844** H. Stephens *Bk. Farm* II. 303 In the *wind-passage of the fanners. **1903** *Daily Chron.* 14 Jan. 5/2 *Wind-power, water-power, and solar-power are running to waste. **1892** *Chambers's Encycl.* X. 677/2 The British Association Committee on *Wind-pressure have reported cases of 80 and 90 lb. to the square foot. **1582** Stanyhurst *Æneis* iv. (Arb.) 121 Foorth with her heat fading, her liefe too *windpuf auoyded. **1881** G. M. Hopkins *Poems* (1967) 89 A windpuff-bonnet of fawn-froth Turns and twindles. **1934** *Discovery* Dec. 344/2 At a high speed, *wind resistance becomes an important factor. *a* **1945** E. R. EDDISON *Mezentian Gate* (1958) xxxix. 218 Their pure eyes.. turned.. to that thunder-laced *windrush of darkness which is the heat and unpicturable secret centre of light's and beauty's self. **1976** 'A. HALL' *Kobra Manifesto* xv. 201 The faint scream of the windrush [under an aeroplane at take-off] in the roaring background. **1930** E. POUND *XXX Cantos* viii. 30 With the road leading under the cliff, in the *wind-shelter into Tuscany. **1968** G. MAXWELL *Raven seek thy Brother* ix. 127 Windshelters.. of stone or turf and furnished with artificial nesting sites, are usually colonized immediately [by eider ducks]. **1914** J. MASEFIELD *Philip the King* 53 A sudden *windshift snatched us from our graves And drove us north. **1963** *Times* 30 May 14/7 A windshift.. brought the nauseating smell of the penguin rookery straight over the camp. **1946** J. W. DAY *Harvest Adventure* vi. 83 Rigging drummed and whistled a raw *wind-song. **1934** *Discovery* June 150/2 High *wind-speeds in relation to aircraft. **1977** J. L. HARPER *Population Biol. Plants* x. 323 Turbulence falls off rapidly down through a canopy but is a function of wind speed, even deep in a corn crop. **1398** TREVISA *Barth. De P.R.* XVII. cxvii. (Bodl. MS.), þe vine.. wiþstondeþ bi helpe þerof *winde stormes. **1883** G. C. DAVIES *Norfolk Broads* xxxiv. (1884) 263 In a country as open as the sea, wind-storms are frequent and heavy. **1930** E. POUND *XXX Cantos* xxvii. 127 Twig where but *wind-streak had been. **1973** C. SAGAN *Cosmic Connection* (1975) viii. 62 The Mariner 9 photography of the Martian volcanoes, windstreaks, moons, and polar icecaps. **1879** *Organ Voicing* 6 If the holes in the upper-board.. pinch the *wind-supply. **1929** BLUNDEN *Near & Far* 57 Dim stars like snowflakes are fluttering in heaven, Down the cloud-mountains by *wind-torrents riven. **1877** G. M. HOPKINS *Poems* (1967) 70 Summer ends now; now, barbarous in beauty, the stooks rise Around; up above, what *wind-walks! **1900** G. K. CHESTERTON *Wild Knight* 7 Meadows where the *wind-waves pass. **1946** L. D. STAMP *Britain's Struct. & Scenery* vi. 51 The waves of the sea are primarily wind-waves. **1984** A. C. & A. DUXBURY *Introd. World's Oceans* viii. 249 Most waves observed at sea are progressive wind waves.. generated by the wind. **1936** DYLAN THOMAS *25 Poems* 23 Why east wind chills and south wind cools Shall not be known till *windwell dries.

b. objective, as ***wind-gatherer***, ***-seller***; ***wind-cheating***, ***-making***, ***-spilling*** (SPILL *v.* 13b); ***wind-obeying***, ***-outspeeding***, ***-raising*** (RAISE *v.* 7) adjs.; indirect objective = to (the) wind, as ***wind-exposed***, ***-like*** adj. and adv.; = from or against (the) wind, as ***wind-screening*** adj.

1963 BIRD & HUTTON-STOTT *Veteran Motor Car* 246 Both had their engines placed.. very low down so as to allow the use of flat *wind-cheating bodies. **1977** *Lancashire Life* Jan. 81/1 Because of their wind cheating shape and fairly high overall gearing, the Citroen CXs are very economical on long motorway journeys. *c* **1611** CHAPMAN *Iliad* III. 323 *Winde-exposed Ilion. **1621** T. GRANGER *Eccles.* vi. 16. 130 The *wind-gatherer feeleth the winde, but graspeth naught. **1638** COWLEY *Love's Riddle* IV. i, I am not satisfied with *wind-like promises Which only touch the lips. **1820** SHELLEY *Prometh. Unb.* III. ii. 45 Behold the Nereids under the green sea, Their wavering limbs borne on the wind-like stream. **1590** SHAKS. *Com. Err.* I. i. 64 The alwaies *winde-obeying deepe. **1820** SHELLEY *Hymn Merc.* xciv, Their *wind-outspeeding wings. **1850** THACKERAY *Pendennis* v, The *wind-raising conspiracies in which he engages with heroes as unfortunate as himself. **1923** KIPLING *Land & Sea Tales* 214 She hovers On the summits of *wind-screening seas. **1600** S. NICHOLSON *Acolastus* (1876) 28 Idle words,.. *wind-wasting arbitrators.

c. instrumental, locative, etc. By, in, or with (the) wind, as ***wind-aided***, ***-beat***, ***-beaten***, ***-bit***, ***-bitten***, ***-borne***, ***-broken***, ***-buffeted***, ***-built***, ***-chapped***, ***-chilled***, ***-clipped***, ***-curled***, ***-dappled***, ***-dispersed***, ***-driven***, ***-fanned***, ***-fertilized***, ***-flawed***, ***-flown***, ***-flushed***, ***fluted***, ***-formed***, †***-grown***, ***-hardened***, ***-heeled***, ***-laced***, ***-laden***, ***-laid***, ***-lifted***, ***-loved***, ***-mastered***, ***-milled***, ***-parted***, ***-perplexed***, ***-pollinated***, ***-powered***, ***-puffed***, ***-rent***, ***-rinsed***, ***-ripped***, ***-scarred***, ***-scattered***, ***-scoured***, ***-scourged***, ***-shorn***, ***-snatched***, ***-sown***, ***-spun***, ***-stirred***, ***-stormed***, ***-struck***, ***-stuffed***, ***-sucked***, ***-swept***, ***-swung***, ***-thrashed***, ***-torn***, ***-tossed***, ***-transported***, ***-turned***, ***-washed***, ***-waved***, ***-whipped***, ***-worn***, ***-wrinkled***, ***-writhen*** adjs.; ***wind-flowing***, ***-wandering***, etc. adjs.; ***wind-waving*** sb. and adj.; ***wind-winnow*** vb.

1959 *Times* 12 Mar. 3/3 Langton kicked another long *wind-aided penalty goal. **1978** *Detroit Free Press* 16 Apr. E 3/2 He won the 100-yard dash with a wind-aided performance of 9.5 seconds. **1877** G. M. HOPKINS *Poems* (1967) 66 *Wind-beat whitebeam! airy abeles set on a flare! **1582** STANYHURST *Æneis* III. (Arb.) 89 A *windbeaten hard shrimp. **1622** BACON *Hen. VII*, 188 The Casuall and Wind-beaten Discouerie.. of a Spanish Pilot. **1800** CAMPBELL *Exile of Erin* 4 To wander alone by the wind-beaten hill. **1900** W. B. YEATS *Shadowy Waters* 45 These waste waters and wind-beaten sails. **1973** *Canadian Antiques Collector* Jan.–Feb. 59/1 Inland, behind wind-beaten villages and red capes. **1892** KIPLING *Other Verses* 161 In the heel of the *wind-bit pier. **1919** J. MASEFIELD *Reynard the Fox* II. 61 Blown Hilcote Copse, *Wind-bitten beech. **1965** F. SARGESON *Memoirs of Peon* ix. 270 The trees.. had redeemed a windbitten waste from its native barbarism. **1646** QUARLES *Sheph. Oracles* v. 52 *Wind-blazing Tapours hurry to and fro. **1842** EMERSON *Saadi* in *Poems* (1914) 133 To northern lakes fly *wind-borne ducks. **1969** BENNISON & WRIGHT *Geol. Hist. Brit. Isles* xvi. 368 The brickearths may, however, have been not solely laid down in expanses of water but be in part wind-borne. **1914** J. MASEFIELD *Philip the King* 44 They have died, Far from *wind-broken Biscay, far from home. **1901** 'L. MALET' *Hist. R. Calmady* v. i. 383 Heavily-cloaked figures tacking, *wind-buffeted, across the grey-black street. **1820** SHELLEY *Cloud* 55 When I widen the rent in my *wind-built tent. **1629** QUARLES *Argalus & P.* III. 3 Aprills gentle show'rs are slidden downe To close the *wind-chapt earth. **1921** D. H. LAWRENCE *Tortoises* 25 The autumn, *wind-chilled sun-shine. **1855** KINGSLEY *Westw. Ho!* xxviii, The row of *wind-clipt trees. **1952** L. MACNEICE *Ten Burnt Offerings* 51 *Wind-curled fountain, tigerish weir, garrulous rain. **1883** R. BRIDGES *Prometheus the Firegiver* in *Poet. Works* (1912) 25 Piloting over the *wind-dappled blue Of the summer-soothed Aegean. **1920** J. MASEFIELD *Enslaved* 109 The grey sea.. cloud-coloured, flat, Wind-dappled from the glen. **1865** DICKENS *Mut. Fr.* II. xiii, The water of the kennels, *wind-dispersed, flew about in drops like rain. **1882** W. D. HAY *Brighter Britain!* I. iii. 89 The sun shining on the *wind-driven sand that covers them [*sc.* hilltops]. **1967** *Oceanogr. & Marine Biol.* V. 102 The Strait of Dover may accept a wind-driven residual current averaging 3½ miles and occasionally reaching 20 miles per lunar day. **1612** *Two Noble K.* v. i. 146 Pure As *windefand Snow. **1879** LUBBOCK *Sci. Lect.* i. 9 *Wind-fertilised flowers produce much more pollen than those which are fertilised by insects. **1971** G. M. BROWN *Fishermen with Ploughs* 95 A huge *wind-flawed mirror. **1820** SHELLEY *Prometh. Unb.* IV. 222 The *wind-flowing folds Of its white robe. **1938** C. DAY LEWIS *Overtures to Death* 30 The *wind-flown tower. *Ibid.* 55 To reproach you we rise *Wind-flushed and early. **1943** —— *Word over All* 15 Wherein the shores Foam-fringed, *wind-fluted of the strange earth dwell. **1911** F. O. BOWER *Plant-Life* 124 The *wind-formed dune takes a very definite crescentic shape styled a Barchan. **1660** T. GENTLEMAN *Best Way* 11 In distresse of *wind-grown Sea. **1926** D. H. LAWRENCE *Sun* iv. 17 He was powerless against her rosy, *wind-hardened nakedness. **1939** DYLAN THOMAS *Map of Love* 20 *Wind-heeled foot in the hole of a fireball. **1887** G. M. HOPKINS *Poems* (1967) 104 Curls Wag or crossbridle, in a wind lifted, *windlaced—See his wind- lilylocks -laced. **1928** C. DAY LEWIS *Country Comets* 9 The unconscious dignity Of hills and *wind-laden grass. **1965** G. J. WILLIAMS *Econ. Geol. N.Z.* ix. 132/2 Both water- and *wind-laid blacksand sediments formed. **1924** 'L. MALET' *Dogs of Want* iv. 112 The soft green blur and flickering flames resolved themselves into gently *wind-lifted leaves and distant sparkling water. **1936** AUDEN *Look, Stranger!* 11 Upon *wind-loved Rowley. **1945** P. A. LARKIN *North Ship* 27 Two tall ships, *wind-mastered, wet with light. **1947** DYLAN THOMAS *In Country Sleep* in *Horizon* Dec. 303 The dew falls on the *wind-Milled dust of the apple tree. **1827** HOOD *Hero & Leander* x, Like trees, *wind-parted, that embrace anon. **1864** G. M. HOPKINS *Poems* (1967) 128 His body sway'd upon tiptoes Like a *wind-perplexed rose. **1911** F. O. BOWER *Plant-Life* 96 As for instance in the Rue (Thalictrum), which has become *wind-pollinated. **1968** F. W. GOULD *Grass Systematics* i. 7 Grasses.. are wind-pollinated. **1976** *Jrnl. R. Soc. Arts* CXXIV. 732/1 It is very logical to feed *wind-powered energy in the form of either electricity or direct heat directly into a buffer system and thence to direct use. **1592** NASHE *P. Penilesse* 40 Those *wind puft bladders. **1592–6** GREENE *Groatsw. Wit* Wks. (Grosart) XII. 145 Wind-puft wrath. **1788** COLERIDGE *Sonn. to Autumnal Moon* 7 The *wind-rent cloud. **1948** L. MACNEICE *Holes in Sky* 20 *Wind-rinsed plumage of oat-field. **1960** S. PLATH *Colossus* (1967) 33 The spindrift Ravelled *wind-ripped from the crest of the wave. **1939** S. SPENDER *Still Centre* 41 Beyond the *wind-scarred hill. **1833** TENNYSON *Dream Fair Women* viii, White surf *wind-scatter'd over sails and masts. **1896** KIPLING *Seven Seas* 73 Bone-bleached my decks, *wind-scoured to the graining. **1980** D. K. CAMERON *Willie Gavin* vi. 54 There was hardly a year when the winter ploughs did not turn up an old hunter of that wind-scoured plain. **1898** J. G. WHITTIER *M. Martin* in *Poet. Works* 67/2 You *wind-scourged sand-dunes, cold and bleak. **1924** 'L. MALET' *Dogs of Want* ii. 29 Bare, wind-scourged, rock-strewn slopes. **1867** J. G. WHITTIER *Poet. Works* (1898) 280/2 Lonely and *wind-shorn, wood-forsaken.. Lieth the island of Manisees. **1933** W. DE LA MARE *Lord Fish* 61 Gnarled, wind-shorn trees. **1980** R. MABEY *Common Ground* II. i. 70 At no more than 590 feet.. above sea level some of its windshorn oaks are reduced to a metre or so in height. **1925** C. DAY LEWIS *Beechen Vigil* 32 The *wind-snatched rumour. **1902** W. STEVENS *Jrnl.* 18 Aug. in *Lett.* (1967) 59, I lay under a group of dark cedars near that strange *wind-sown cactus with its red blossom. **1922** BLUNDEN *Shepherd* (ed. 2) 74 *Windspun leaves burn silver-grey. **1843** J. G. WHITTIER *Poet. Works* (1898) 388/1 And down again through *wind-stirred trees He saw the quivering sunlight play. **1946** R. MACAULAY in E. Brontë *Wuthering Heights* p. vi, The lonely, *wind-stormed old farmhouse that stood on the heights above Haworth's grey streets. **1880** SWINBURNE *Songs bef. Sunrise, Christmas Antiphones* III. 64 Though man's vain desire Hang faith's *wind-struck lyre Out in tuneless air. **1627** MAY *Lucan* III. 1 Now had the *wind-stuffde sailes brought out the Fleet. **1946** R. S. THOMAS *Stones of Field* 26 The *wind-sucked bone shows blue. **1812** TENNANT *Anster Fair* II. lxix, From Cellardyke to *wind-swept Pittenweem. **1877** BLACK *Green Past.* xxxiv, The wind-swept waters. **1805** SCOTT *Last Minstr.* I. xiv, The groan of the *wind-swung oak. **1933** SOMERVILLE & 'ROSS' *Smile & Tear* ix. 98 A few miserable *wind-thrashed ash-trees. **1910** KIPLING *Rewards & Fairies* 244 The *wind-torn breaker-tops. **1957** T. GUNN *Sense of Movement* 58 Not like the fighting boys and wind-torn rooks. **1838** J. R. LOWELL *Class Poem* 20 Flapping his raven pinions in the west, The thunder brooding o'er his *wind-tost crest. **1860** MISS YONGE *Hopes & Fears* I. 240 Lucilla.. before the glass, arranging her wind-tossed hair. **1887** BOWEN *Virg. Æneid* VI. 335 Over the wind-tossed waters. **1946** F. E. ZEUNER *Dating Past* iii. 56 Minute grains of *wind-transported pollen caught on the wet surface of the bog. **1935** DYLAN THOMAS in *Life & Lett. To-day* Dec. 75 Doom on deniers at the *wind-turned statement. **1971** *Country Life* 8 July 84/1 The raw elements of Millet's compositions, granite walls, dirty-legged cattle,.. wind-turned trees. **1820** SHELLEY *Witch Atl.* l. 6 Some *wind-wandering Fragment of inky thunder-stroke. **1912** C. MACKENZIE *Carnival* xvi. 186 At such an hour.. even Piccadilly Circus stands.. *wind-washed and noble. **1919** J. MASEFIELD *Reynard the Fox* 92 The wind-washed steeple stood serene. **1809** R. KERR *Agric. Surv. Berwick* 233 In years of peculiarly windy weather, the stem, where it enters the earth, is often blown about, in a whirling manner... This is provincially called *wind-waved. **1928** BLUNDEN *Retreat* 18 The wind-waved bough betrayed the wild sylph glancing. **1799** W. NICOL *Pract. Planter* i. 13 *Wind-waving.. by loosening the old, and.. breaking the new fibres, contributes to stint the whole tree in growth. *c* **1300** *Metr. Hom.* (Small) 36 To se a *wind waiuande rede. **1848** BUCKLEY *Iliad* 406 The wind-waving fig-tree. **1873** B. HARTE *Fiddletown* 28 There was a fierce unrest in the *wind-whipped streets. **1710** HILMAN *Tusser Rediv.* Sept. (1744) 116 A Cart Nave I suppose is to stand up upon when they *Wind-winnow. **1816** BYRON *Ch. Har.* III. xxxii, The ruin'd wall Stands when its *wind-worn battlements are gone. **1925** V. WOOLF *Mrs Dalloway* 242 Suddenly she shoots to the surface and sports on the *wind-wrinkled waves. **1921** F. B. YOUNG *Black Diamond* ix. 116 They crossed a zone of huge, *wind-writhen hawthorns. **1954** J. R. R. TOLKIEN *Fellowship of Ring* 401 High ridges crowned with wind-writhen firs.

d. similative and parasynthetic, in epithets (chiefly poetic) expressing swiftness, as ***wind-foot***, ***-footed***, ***-grey***, ***-hard***, ***-long***, ***-raw***, ***-smooth***, ***-swift***, ***-wild***, ***-winged*** adjs.

1598 CHAPMAN *Iliad* VII. [XI.] 178 The *wind-foote swift Thaumantia obayde. **1848** BUCKLEY *Iliad* 272 *Wind-footed, swift Iris. *c* **1944** A. POWER *From Old Waterford House* xi. 95, I had seen it under so many moods, from *wind-grey to sun-yellow. **1954** W. FAULKNER *Fable* 184 Like the *wind-hard banner of the old Norman earl. *a* **1890** G. M. HOPKINS *Poems* (1967) 180 Or *wind-long fleeces on the flock A day off shearing day. **1922** JOYCE *Ulysses* 48 About her *windraw face her hair trailed. **1929** E. SITWELL *Gold Coast Customs* 38 *Wind-smooth fruits. *c* **1280** *Names of Hare* in *Rel. Ant.* I. 133 þe *wint swifft. **1592** SHAKS. *Rom. & Jul.* II. v. 8 Therefore hath the wind-swift Cupid wings. **1883** BRIDGES *Prometh.* 530 Meteors.. ever on their windswift course. **1936** C. DAY LEWIS *Noah & Waters* 50 Under the *wind-wild sky. *c* **1595** J. DICKENSON *Sheph. Compl.* (1878) 11 The *wind-wing'd Naiads. **1817** SHELLEY *Rev. Islam* IX. xxii, O Spring, of.. love, and youth, and gladness Wind-winged emblem.

32. Special combinations: **wind axis** *Aeronaut.*, each of a set of rectangular coordinate axes having their origin in the aircraft and the *x*-axis in the opposite direction to the relative wind; usu. *pl.*; **wind-balanced** *a.*, applied to rotary gun mountings on aircraft having a device which automatically compensates for the turning moment caused by air pressure on the guns; also **wind-balancing** *vbl. sb.*; †**wind-balk**, (*a*) = WIND-BEAM[1] (see BALK *sb.*[1] 11); (*b*) = WINDROW *sb.* (cf. BALK *sb.*[1] II); **wind-bar**, the back of the wind-chest of an organ; †**wind-barge**, a slab placed along the edge of a roof as a protection from the wind (cf. WATER-BARGE); †**wind-bed**, an air-bed; **wind-bells** *sb. pl.*, slips of glass or porcelain suspended from a frame so as to tinkle against one another in the wind; **wind-belt**, a belt of trees planted for protection from the wind; **wind-bill** *Sc.* (cf. sense 15), an accommodation-bill; †**wind-bladder**, (*a*) an inflated bladder; (*b*) the air-bladder of a fish; **wind-blow**, (*a*) a stretch of land eroded by wind; (*b*) (see quot. 1955); (*c*) = *windthrow* below; **wind-blown** *a.*, blown up or inflated; blown along or about; blown upon by (the) wind; **windblown bob** [BOB *sb.*[1] 5b], a bobbed hairstyle popular among women in the 1930s (see quot. 1975); **wind-bore**, the suction-pipe of a pump, or the lower end of this; **wind-box** = *wind-chest*; **wind-brace**, a diagonal brace (BRACE *sb.*[2] 17) connecting the rafters of a roof; **wind-bracing**, connecting members designed to stiffen a building or other structure against the wind; the provision of such members; **windbreaker**, †(*a*) (cf. 10), a drug that expels flatulence, a carminative; (*b*) *U.S.* = WIND-BREAK 1; (*c*) *U.S.* (with capital initial) the proprietary name of a kind of shirt or leather blouse; *gen.* (chiefly *N. Amer.*) = *windcheater* (b) below; †**wind-breaking** *a.*, carminative; †**wind-broach** [cf. BROACH *sb.*[1] 12], a name for a hurdy-gurdy; **windburn** [after *sunburn*, etc.], (usu. superficial) inflammation or discoloration of the skin caused by exposure to wind; hence **wind-burned**, **-burnt** *a.*; †**wind-cane** = WIND-GUN; **windcap** *Mus.* [tr. G. *windkapsel*] = *reed cap* s.v. REED *sb.*[1] 13a; freq. *attrib.*; †**wind-catch**, a squall of wind; **wind-changing** *a.*, changing like the wind, inconstant; **wind-channel** = *wind tunnel* below; **windcharger**, a small windmill which generates electricity for a farm, dwelling, etc.; **windcheater**, (*a*) *Golf*, a ball driven low into the wind, *spec.* one played with strong backspin (see quot. 1909); (*b*) a kind of wind-resistant jacket or blouson; **wind-chest**, an air-tight chest or box in an organ or similar instrument, which is filled with wind from the bellows, and from which the wind is admitted to the pipes or reeds; **wind chill**, the cooling effect of moving air on a body; also, = *wind-chill factor*; **wind-chill factor**, **index**, a measure or scale of the combined effect of low temperature and wind-speed on body temperature (see quot. 1939); **wind chimes** *sb. pl.* = *wind-bells* above; **wind-cistern** = prec.; **wind-cock**, †(*a*) = *wind-mow*; (*b*) a weathercock; **wind-colic**, colic caused by flatulence; **wind cone** *Aeronaut.* =

wind sock below; **wind-contusion**, an internal injury without any external mark of violence, formerly supposed to be caused by the 'wind' (see 13) of a cannon-ball, shell, or other projectile; **windcrust** *Mountaineering*, a crust formed on the surface of soft snow by the wind (see quot. 1936); **wind-dial**, a dial showing the direction of the wind by means of a pointer connected with a wind-vane; also *fig.* (cf. 16 b); † **wind-discusser** = *wind-breaker*; **wind-dog** [DOG *sb.* 10 a], name for a fragment of rainbow, supposed to presage wind; † **wind-dropsy** = TYMPANITES, TYMPANY 1; **wind energy**, energy obtained from harnessing the wind; cf. SOLAR *a.* 4 a; **wind-engine**, a machine driven by the wind, as a windmill; † **wind-fan**, a winnowing-fan; **wind-fanner (-vanner)** *local*, the kestrel; **wind farm**, a group of energy-producing windmills or wind turbines; **wind-fast** *a.* = WIND-TIGHT 1; † **wind-fill** *v. trans.*, to fill up gaps or cavities in (a wall, etc.) so as to keep the wind out (cf. FILLING *vbl. sb.* 2); † **wind-flaucht** *a.* or *adv. Sc.* [FLAUGHT *adv.*], sprawling, as if overthrown by the wind; **wind-furnace**, a furnace in which the draught is obtained by means of a (high or narrow) chimney without the aid of bellows or other mechanical blower as in a *blast-furnace*; **wind-firm** *a.*, of a tree: firmly rooted so as to be able to withstand strong winds; hence **wind-firmness**; **wind-flag**, a flag on a shooting-range designed to indicate the direction and force of the wind; **wind-gap** (see GAP *sb.*[1] 5 b); *spec.* (see quot. 1939); † **wind-glass** (see quot.); **wind-god**, a deity presiding over the winds; † **wind-gout**, gout supposed to be caused by 'wind' (see 10); **wind-grass**, a name for *Agrostis Spica-venti*; † **wind-hand**, the side towards the wind; **wind-harp**, an Æolian harp (also *allusively*); **wind-hole**, †(*a*) the opening at the top of the windpipe, the glottis; (*b*) an opening in brickwork for the passage of air; (*c*) the hole in the lower board of a pair of bellows; (*d*) a ventilating shaft in a mine; (*e*) each of the openings in the sound-board of an organ, through which wind is admitted to the pipes; **wind-jacket** = *windcheater* (b) above; **wind-jammer** *slang*, (*a*) *U.S.* a bugler, bandsman; (*b*) a sailing-vessel (*obs.* exc. *Hist.*); (*c*) *U.S.* a rumour-monger, a loquacious person; (*d*) = *windcheater* (b) above; hence **wind-jamming**, (*a*) sailing a windjammer; (*b*) talking, gossiping; (*c*) playing a wind instrument; **wind-knot**, a knot tied on a rope, supposed magically to ensure a favourable wind; **wind-lane**, a current on the surface of a body of water, caused by the wind; † **wind-lap**, the tongue or reed of a wind-instrument; **wind-lipper** *Naut.* [LIPPER *sb.*[1]], a rippling or ruffling of the surface of the water caused by the first rising of a breeze; **wind-list** [LIST *sb.*[3] 4] (see quot.); **wind load** *Engin.*, the force on a structure arising from the impact of wind on it; also **wind loading**; **wind-logged** *a.* [cf. WATER-LOGGED] (see quot.); † **wind-loft** *Naut.*, ? = *wind-taut* sb.; **wind-lop** *Canad.* [LOP *sb.*[6]], a choppy surface on the sea, caused by wind; **wind-machine**, a machine driven by the wind, or one for producing a 'wind' or blast of air; (*a*) *spec.* one that blows out relatively warm air for protecting crops against frost (see quot. 1976[2]); (*b*) in theatrical and other productions, a machine for simulating the sound or other effects of wind; also *fig.*; **wind-motor** [MOTOR 3], a machine deriving its motive power from the force of the wind; esp. of the form of a windmill; **wind-mow** *dial.* [MOW *sb.*[1]], one of a number of small ricks in which hay or corn is temporarily stacked in showery weather to be dried by exposure to the wind; † **wind-music**, music played on wind-instruments; also such instruments themselves, or a company of players on them (cf. MUSIC *sb.* 5, 6); † **wind-musket** = WIND-GUN; **wind noise**, the sound of the wind against a motor vehicle moving at speed, as heard within the vehicle; **wind-pinning** [cf. PIN *v.*[1] 3 c, PINNING 1 a, 2 a], the filling up of interstices in masonry to keep out the wind; **wind-pole** [POLE *sb.*[2]], each of two opposite points of the compass taken as the standard ones in relation to the direction of the wind; **wind-porch**, a chamber constructed on the inner side of a doorway to keep the wind out; **wind-pox**, chicken-pox (Billings *Med. Dict.* 1890); **windproof** *a.*, impervious or resistant to wind; used esp. of outer garments; hence *ellipt.* as *sb.*, a windproof garment; **wind-pump**, †(*a*) an air-pump; (*b*) a pump driven by a wind-wheel (Knight *Dict. Mech.* 1875); † **wind-ræs** [RESE *sb.*], a storm of wind; † **wind-rake**, ? the raking up of windfalls, or the right to do this; **wind-reef** *U.S.*, the semblance of a reef on the surface of a river, caused by the wind; **wind-road**, (*a*) a track or course habitually taken by the wind (*nonce-use*); (*b*) a passage for ventilation in a mine (Gresley *Gloss.* 1883); **windrock**, damage to the roots of young plants, caused by the movement of the stem in the wind; also as *v. trans.*; so **wind-rocking**; **wind-rode**, also † **-road** (see RIDE *v.* A. 3 *γ*), *a.*, *Naut.*, swung by the wind, as a ship riding at anchor (opp. to *tide-rode*: see TIDE *sb.* 16 b); also as *sb.*, the position of a ship so riding; **wind-scorpion** = SOLPUGID; **windscreen**, a screen for protection from the wind, now esp. in front of the driver's seat on a motor-car; **windscreen washer** = *screen-washer* s.v. SCREEN *sb.*[1] 9 a; **windscreen wiper**, a device (usu. one of a pair) on a motor vehicle for automatic wiping of the outside of the windscreen during rain, snow, etc., usu. consisting of a mechanically or electrically operated moving rubber blade; also one on an aircraft; **wind shadow**, (*a*) *nonce-use*, a ripple caused by the wind on water and having the appearance of a shadow running over it; (*b*) an area behind a moving object where the air is disturbed and its pressure reduced; **wind-shaft**, the shaft that carries the sails in a windmill; **wind shear**, a variation in wind velocity along a direction (usu. vertical or horizontal) at right angles to the wind's direction; **windship**, a wind-powered ship; a sailing-ship; **wind-sight**, a special arrangement of the back-sight of a rifle capable of adjustment to compensate for the effect of wind on the bullet; **wind-slab** *Mountaineering*, a thick wind-crust, of a kind liable to slip and create an avalanche; cf. *slab avalanche* s.v. SLAB *sb.*[1] 6; **wind-slash**, slash resulting from windthrow; **wind sleeve** *Aeronaut.* = *wind sock*; **wind sock**, a cloth cone flown from a mast, esp. on an airfield, to indicate the direction of the wind; = DROGUE 3 (*c*); **wind-spider** = *wind-scorpion* above; **wind-splitter** *colloq.* (chiefly *U.S.*), something so sharply drawn or so swift as to suggest the notion of splitting the wind; cf. WIND-CUTTER; so **wind-splitting** *a.*; **wind sprint** *Athletics* (see quot. 1948); **wind-stocking** = *wind sock* above; **wind-stream**, an air-stream, esp. the disturbed air in the wake of an aircraft; **wind stress**, stress or force due to wind; **wind-stroke**, a stroke or injury caused or supposed to be caused by the wind (see quots.); **wind-swell**, a form of swell in an organ operated by a valve in the wind-trunk; **wind-swept** *a.*, (*a*) (see sense 31 c); (*b*) *spec.* of a hair-style, designed to give the appearance of having been blown by the wind (cf. *windblown bob* above); **wind-taut** *a.*, *Naut.* [from phr. *to hold wind taut*]: see quots.; also as sb. = condition of being wind-taut; **wind-throstle** = *wind-thrush*; **windthrow**, the uprooting and blowing down of trees by the wind; also (usu. *attrib.*) of timber so uprooted; **wind-thrush**, the redwing; **wind-tie** = *wind-brace*; **wind-trunk**, a large tube (usually of wood) in an organ or similar instrument, through which the wind passes from the bellows to the wind-chest; **wind tunnel**, a tunnel-like apparatus for producing an air-stream of known velocity past models of aircraft, buildings, etc., in order to investigate flow or the effect of wind on the full-size object; also *attrib.*, *transf.*, and *fig.*; **wind turbine**, a turbine driven by wind; an apparatus designed to generate electricity when a large vaned wheel is rotated by the wind; **wind-vane**, (*a*) the sail of a windmill (= VANE 3 a); (*b*) a weathercock (= VANE 1); **wind-vanner**: see *wind-fanner* above; † **wind-vent** = SUSPIRAL 2; **wind-way**, (*a*) a ventilating passage in a mine, an air-way; (*b*) the narrow slit in an organ-pipe through which the wind strikes upon the lip so as to make the pipe speak; also in a woodwind instrument; (*c*) access of the wind to a sailing vessel so as to give her freedom of passage (cf. WAY *sb.*[1] 6); **wind-wheel**, a wheel turned by the wind to drive some mechanism, as in a windmill or wind-pump; **wind wing** *U.S.*, †an adjustable glass ventilation panel attached to the side of the windscreen of a motor vehicle (*obs.*); a small ventilation window or quarterlight on a motor vehicle; † **wind-work** (cf. 11), the process or function of respiration.

1932 *Jrnl. R. Aeronaut. Soc.* Mar. 194 Calculations..of a complete model rotated about the *wind axis..give a fair approximation to the spinning characteristics of the aeroplane. **1984** F. J. HALE *Introd. Aircraft Performance* i. 4 The wind axes are not body axes; that is, they are not fixed to the aircraft other than at the cg. A change in the direction of flight can change *x* without changing the attitude of the aircraft. **1928** *Daily Tel.* 6 Mar. 6/3 Royalties not exceeding £7,500 to Messrs. Vickers, Ltd., for *wind-balanced ring mountings. **1928** G. F. S. GAMBLE *Story N. Sea Air Station* xiii. 219 A wind-balancing gear was provided which relieved the observer of much fatigue at high altitudes. **1532–3** *Durham Acc. Rolls* (Surtees) 173 Pro sarracione $1\frac{3}{4}$ rod in *wyndbalks, stoys, pouynchys, 4s. 8d. **1611** COTGR. s.v. *Rouë, Mettre le foin en rouë*, viz. in wind-baulkes, or wind-rowes. **1894** *Northumbld. Gloss.*, *Wind-balk*, a wind-beam or collar-beam; a beam stretching across the upper part of two roof principals. (Obs.) **1881** W. E. DICKSON *Organ-Build.* v. 60 The back of the chest, called the '*wind-bar',..should be of strong and sound stuff. **1603** G. OWEN *Pembrokeshire* (1892) 79 Arches, Coinestones, waterberges, and *wynd berges or any other hewen worke. **1576** TURBERV. *Venerie* 194 Some vse to carrie a *Windbed which is made of leather strongly sowed on all foure sides, and hauing a pype at one of the corners to blow it,..and when it is blowen full of wind, to stoppe it vp and lie vpon it on the grounde. **1901** 'L. MALET' *Hist. R. Calmady* II. ii. 105 They pressed him back and back against the base of a seven-storied pagoda, the *wind-bells of which jangled far above him from the angles of its tiers of fluted roofs. **1983** *Daily Tel.* 21 Oct. 16/1 Windbells tinkled from the eaves of temples, spreading the Holy Word of Buddha, keeping demons away. **1903** C. BALD *Indian Tea* x. (1917) 128 This characteristic [*sc.* evergreen foliage] makes the several varieties of *Dalbergia* very suitable for planting as *windbelts. **1813** HEADRICK *Agric. Surv. Forfarshire* 589 If they [*sc.* bank notes] be not convertible into specie at the option of the holder, there is a strong temptation to issue them on what are called *wind bills, where there is no corresponding value of commodities in existence. **1821** SCOTT *Pirate* iv, He would have got a bank-credit, manœuvred with wind-bills. **1594** NASHE *Terrors Nt.* To Rdr., If they chance but on a moate or a *wind bladder, they neuer haue done with it, till they haue cleane..tost it out of sight. **1692** RAY *Creation* I. (ed. 2) 141 As for Fishes ..The Wind-bladder, wherewith most of them are furnished, serves to poise their Bodies. **1921** H. GUTHRIE-SMITH *Tutira* xx. 180 The sheep..are returfing the naked *windblows. **1944** W. STEVENS in *Q. Rev. Lit.* Spring 157 The drivers in the wind-blows cracking whips. **1955** *Britannica Bk. of Year* 489/2 *Wind-blow*, a destructive gale of wind. **1961** *New Scientist* 16 Mar. 662/2 Comparisons have been made of trees on sites where wind-blow has occurred and those where similar trees are stable. **1979** *National Trust* Spring 18/3 Marram grass..holds the sand together and reduces the effects of wind blow. **1593** NASHE *Christ's T.* 72 What is beauty more then a *wind-blowne bladder? **1600** ROWLANDS *Letting of Humours Blood* Sat. vii. 83 More light and toyish than the wind-blown chaffe. **1638** BRATHWAIT *Barnabees Jrnl.* I. (1818) 17 A wind-blowne house. **1876** M. COLLINS in F. Collins *Lett. & Friendsh.* (1877) II. 158 Wind-blown daffodils. **1888** F. COWPER *Cædwalla* i. 6 A low island, covered with bushes and a few wind-blown trees. **1933** N. WALN *House of Exile* III. i. 187 She had her hair cut in a new fashion which, she told me, was called a windblown bob. **1975** *Fairchild's Dict. Fashion* 262/2 *Wind-blown bob*, popular 1930's woman's hairstyle, cut short and shingled,..so that hair fell softly about the face as if blown by the wind. **1797** CURR *Coal Viewer* 58 The *Wind Bores..May be cast 8 feet long with a plain or egg bottom. **1838** *Civil Eng. & Arch. Jrnl.* I. 189/1. **1852** SEIDEL *Organ* 38 A square box, called the *wind-box. **1889** *Cath. Household* 30 Nov. 4 Traceried *windbraces. **1890** W. J. GORDON *Foundry* 51 The *wind-bracing was fitted in its long diamonds of lattice. **1911** HUSBAND & HARBY *Structural Engin.* ix. 278 Wind bracing in roofs is employed to counteract the overturning moment of the wind acting on the ends. **1961** *Listener* 28 Sept. 464/1 An enormous funnel of unoccupied space goes from top to bottom of it [*sc.* a skyscraper] in order to provide mere wind bracing for the rest of it. **1974** *Sci. Amer.* Feb. 98/2 The statue [of Liberty] posed a special problem in wind bracing. **1694** SALMON *Bate's Dispens.* (1713) 620/1 The sugared oily Carminative, or *Wind-breaker. **1873** J. H. BEADLE *Undevel. West* xxxiv. 730 If there is any wind-breaker northwest, between there and Alaska, I had no evidence of it. **1918** *Official Gaz.* (U.S. Patent Office) 5 Nov. 214/2 The Hilker-Wiechers Manufacturing Co., Racine, Wis. *Windbreaker*... Men's shirts for outer wear. **1925** *Ibid.* 13 Jan. 256/2 Gufterman Bros., Inc., St. Paul, Minn... *Windbreaker*... Leather blouses, shirts, [etc.]. **1934** *Beaver* (Winnipeg) June 6/2 The wind-breakers and coats are shown by a series of photographs. **1964** 'R. MACDONALD' in H. Q. Masur *Murder most Foul* (1973) 109 A man with a bulky shoulder harness under his brown suede windbreaker. **1985** *Times* 9 Feb. 36/4 The terminal was full of muscular young men in windbreakers and running shoes. **1609** ROWLEY *Search for Money* (Percy Soc.) 17 Good holsome *windebreaking pippins. **1653** URQUHART *Rabelais* II. xxx. 198 A..player on that instrument which is called a *windbroach. **1702** T. BROWN *Lett. fr. Dead* Wks. 1730 II. 234 To fumble out a fine sonata upon a wind-broach. **1939** C. MORLEY *Kitty Foyle* xxx. 313 It was comical to see the dames..worrying about *windburn and sunsquint and brittle nails. **1977** *Birds* Spring 40 All night my skin is hot with windburn, and between my teeth..the salt-sharp flavour of the rain. **1942** J. STEINBECK *Moon is Down* vi. 137 They were *windburned and strong..Will Anders and Tom Anders, the fishermen. **1954** 'BRYHER' *Fourteenth of October* ii. 17 His eyes were the same blue in his windburnt face. **1981** 'E. LATHEN' *Going for Gold* iv. 40 Practicing for the Swiss women's slalom team had left her with windburned cheeks. **1723** E. STONE tr. *Bion's Math. Instrum.* III. ii. (1758) 95 The Construction of the *Wind-Cane. **1940** C. SACHS *Hist. Musical Instr.* (1942) xv. 320 *Wind-cap instruments were first introduced to art music in the fifteenth century. The cromorne was the oldest European instrument with a wind cap. **1970** W. APEL *Harvard Dict. Music* 588/2 More important are the *crumhorns*... Their tube was nearly cylindrical,..and a pierced cap (wind cap) covered the reed so that the player could not touch it. **1980** *Early Music Gaz.* Apr. 13/3 There will be a weekend for players of the recorder, gemshorn, windcap instruments, cornetti and for renaissance dancers in Hutton Hall, near Carlisle. **1610** FOLKINGHAM *Feudigraphia* 10 Sweeping or floating Waters, which flit and fleete to and fro with *wind-catches. **1665** W. DODSON *Designe Draining Gt. Level Fens* 13 Those Banks I did not make for Sea Banks,..but laid them near to avoid a Winde-catch. **1593** SHAKS. *3 Hen. VI*, v. i. 57 *Wind-changing Warwicke now can change no more. **1918** COWLEY & LEVY *Aeronautics* iv. 98 A series of experiments are conducted in the *wind channel to test the lift and drag for different forms of sections. **1972** *Nature* 18 Aug. 375/1 The secrecy..was lifted in 1919 to reveal..developments in techniques for scale model testing in wind 'channels' (tunnels). **1946** E. W. MANNING *Igloo for Night* 156 We could hear the wind tearing past, and the high screaming whine as it met the wires of the radio masts and the *wind-charger. **1949** *Farmer's Weekly* (S. Afr.) 13 July 69/5, I have an old car generator. Can this be converted into a windcharger? **1976** *Sci. Amer.* June 94/3 The introduction of the windcharger in the 1930's brought to remote farms and ranches enough electricity to power radios and a few light bulbs and appliances. **1909** P. A. VAILE *Mod. Golf* xii. 180 The *wind-cheater, the ball that skims away over the daisies and then rises gracefully at the end of its flight, to fall sometimes almost dead. **1940** [see *crew neck* s.v. CREW *sb.*[1] 7]. **1956** L. MCINTOSH *Oxford Folly* 53 Incongruous in his neat suit and tidy hair among the tousled undergraduates in windcheaters or polo-necked sweaters. **1977** G. PEPER *Scrambling Golf* ix. 162 One of those low, delayed-rising 'wind-cheaters'. **1982** C. THOMAS *Jade Tiger* 195 The first chill of the night, seeping through his thin windcheater, alerted and refreshed him. **1797** *Encycl. Brit.* (ed. 3) XIII. 487/2 (*Organ*) IKKK is the *wind-chest, which is a square box fitted close to the under side of the lower board. **1852** SEIDEL *Organ* 52 The length of the wind-chest depends on the compass of the key-board. **1939** P. A. SIPLE *Adaptations of Explorer to Climate of Antarctica* (Ph.D. diss., Clark University) 166, I therefore propose in this discussion to multiply temperatures in degrees Centigrade below freezing by wind velocity in meters per second, the product of which I shall call the **wind-chill index*. *Ibid.* 177 July exhibited a mean wind-chill of 462·8. **1949** *Jrnl. R. Aeronaut. Soc.* LIII. 1/2 'Wind Chill'... This is the worst form of cold weather to encounter, as not only does it cause exhaustion, low morale, pain and frustration, but in some cases the lack of the will to live when the wind chill factor is unusually high. **1959** R. E. HUSCHKE *Gloss. Meteorol.* 629 *Wind-chill index*—(Also called *wind-chill factor*), the cooling effect of any combination of temperature and wind, expressed as the loss of body heat in kilogram calories per hour per square meter of skin surface. **1963** *New Scientist* 7 Feb. 276/1 Wind chill, which is actually another name for the dry convective cooling power of the atmosphere, is a term descriptive of the cooling effect of air movement and low temperature. **1977** J. F. FIXX *Compl. Bk. Running* xiii. 151 Because of the wind-chill factor, a given temperature feels colder than in still weather. **1985** *Times* 8 Jan. 26/4 Francis Wilson, the BBC weatherman, yesterday introduced *Breakfast Time* viewers to a new and chilly forecasting feature: the 'wind chill factor'. **1958** T. WILLIAMS *Orpheus Descending* III. iii. 85 Someone has entered the confectionery door, out of sight, and the draught of air has set the *windchimes tinkling wildly. **1976** M. MILLAR *Ask for Me Tomorrow* (1977) iii. 18 Go..to the glass door and shake the wind chimes good and hard. She's in Marco's room. **1880** E. J. HOPKINS in Grove *Dict. Mus.* II. 605/1 The *wind-cisterns or wind-chests. **1610** R. VAUGHAN *Water-Workes* M 4 b, You mow one day, you ted an other, you spend one in gathering it into *winde-cockes. **1920** MASEFIELD *Right Royal* 5 Spires of churches Gleaming with swinging wind-cocks on their perches. **1593** NASHE *Christ's T.* 45 b, Euery part of thee [shall] be wrunge as with the *wind-chollick. **1654** GATAKER *Disc. Apol.* 57, I came home, arrested with a sharp fit of the Wind-Colick. **1731** FIELDING *Tom Thumb* I. iii, I feel a sudden Pain within my Breast, Nor know I whether it arise from Love, Or only the Wind-Cholick. **1822–7** GOOD *Study Med.* (1829) I. 239 The oppressive distention of wind-colic. **1918** *Flight* 2 May 496/1 A *wind cone set up in..fields..near aerodromes, would enable cross-country fliers to know..where to land and in what direction. **1857** DUNGLISON *Med. Lex.*, *Wind of a ball*, a term applied to the compression of air, supposed to be produced by the passage of a ball near a part of the body, so as to occasion what has been called a **wind contusion*. **1877** LONGMORE *Gunshot Injuries* 95 The true explanation of the phenomena observed in cases of so-called 'wind contusions' is to be found in the peculiar direction, the degree of obliquity, with which the missile has happened to impinge against the elastic skin. **1936** E. A. M. WEDDERBURN *Alpine Climbing* iv. 50 Wind both causes the snow to drift and forms a crust on the powder snow; this is the chief kind of crust found in winter. It is most important to distinguish between sun crust and *wind crust. **1955** E. HILLARY *High Adventure* 69 The surface here was most unpleasant—a thick wind-crust over deep unstable snow. **1706** in Ashton *Soc. Life Reign Q. Anne* (1882) II. 56 The *Wind Dial, lately set up at Grigsby's Coffee..House,..being of Constant use to those that are in any wise Concerned in Navigation. **1761** LD. HARDWICKE in *Life* (1847) III. xiv. 257 A great change was made in the political wind-dial before you left us. **1676** J. COOKE *Mellif. Chirurg.* Alph. Table, *Wind-discussers. **1860** FITZ-ROY in *Merc. Marine Mag.* VII. 344 '*Wind dogs', and the rainbow, are more or less significant of increasing wind. **1607** TOPSELL *Four-f. Beasts* 386 The Timpany, which..may be called in English the *wind dropsie. **1822–7** GOOD *Study Med.* (1829) V. 451 Making an artificial opening into the cavity of the abdomen in the case of wind-dropsy, as well as in that of water-dropsy. **1976** *Jrnl. R. Soc. Arts* CXXIV. 731/2 At present the main bar to developing and using *wind energy in this country is very high capital costs of equipment. **1669** WORLIDGE *Syst. Agric.* (1681) 21 *note*, *Wind-Engines for the raising of Water. *c* **975** *Rushw. Gosp.* Luke iii. 17 His..*wind fone in honda his. **1761** *Descr. S. Carolina* 7 Afterwards it is.. winnowed, which was formerly a very tedious Operation, but it is now performed..by a very simple Machine, a Wind-Fan. **1668** CHARLETON *Onomast.* 64 *Accipiter Tinnunculus*,..the *Wind-vanner. *a* **1836** JOHNES in Mrs. Bray *Tamar & Tavy* (1879) I. 301 The kestrel, called here the 'wind-fanner' and 'windhover', from its motion when hovering over the same spot in search of its quarry. **1980** *Sunday Times* 24 Aug. 4/4 The plan is to set up one (windmill) of medium size as soon as possible to gain experience, and then to establish a '*wind farm', of about ten windmills, each capable of generating a megawatt of electricity. **1982** *Energy Spectrum* (Shell Internat. Petroleum Co. Ltd.) 8/1 Larger systems of more than 1 MW are also envisaged either singly or in 'wind farms' for integration into utility grids. **1648** in J. Davidson *Inverurie* (1878) 302 To keep the kirk *wind-fast and water-tight. **1601** *Stanford Churchw. Acc.* in *Antiquary* (1888) May 213 To John Rayner for *wind-fillinge the Church wall ij[s]. **1895** W. R. FISHER *Schlich's Man. Forestry* IV. IV. iii. 469 The westerly border-trees..have now become so *wind-firm that the severance-felling might be widened. **1927** *Forestry* I. 21 To keep plantations wind-firm..initial spacings of the order of six feet..are necessary. **1981** *Southern Horticulture* (N.Z.) Spring 31/2 Containerisation of such material without this evening-out treatment produces trees that are neither wind-firm in the container, nor on the planting site. **1962** *Times* 1 Jan. 6/4 It [*sc.* a tree] was there to increase the *wind-firmness of the woodland. **1923** KIPLING *Land & Sea Tales* 181 He pointed towards the stiff-tailed *wind-flags that stuck out at all sorts of angles as the eddy round the shoulder of the Down caught them. **1513** DOUGLAS *Æneis* v. vi. 86 He..Maid hym lycht *windflaucht [orig. *revolutus*] on the ground vnclene. **1651** FRENCH *Distill.* vi. 190 Put those cakes..into a *Winde Furnace. **1683** *K. Digby's Chym. Secr.* 132 Put them in a Wind-Furnace to Calcine. **1704** J. HARRIS *Lex. Techn.* I. s.v. *Furnace*, A Wind Furnace, or Furnace for Fusions, which is so called, because the Wind comes forcibly to blow the Coals, in order to Melt or Fuse the Matter in the Crucible or Coppel. **1763** W. LEWIS *Comm. Philos.-Techn.* 11 A Wind-Furnace, for the fusion of metals. **1869** ROSCOE *Elem. Chem.* (1871) 240 The oldest method of manufacturing wrought iron was to reduce it at once from the ore by heating in a wind-furnace with charcoal or coal. **1875** KNIGHT *Dict. Mech.*, *Wind-furnace*, a furnace in which a strong heat is obtained..by means of a powerful draft, depending on a narrow flue or chimney of considerable elevation. **1884** *Ibid.* Suppl. 948/2 *Wind Furnace* (*Metallurgy*), one depending upon the draft of a chimney, as distinguished from a blast furnace. **1889** *Wind-gap [see GAP *sb.*[1] 5 b]. **1895** *Geogr. Jrnl.* V. 144 If the land should be raised a few hundred feet, these head-waters would soon be gained by the Trent; and the divide between the successful and defeated systems would be pushed to the notch in the hard Oölite, which would then be a 'wind-gap', instead of a 'water-gap', as the Pennsylvanians say. **1939** *Bull. Geol. Soc. Amer.* L. 1343 The term 'wind gap' is now more commonly restricted to abandoned water gaps, while those gaps not believed to have been former water gaps are designated as 'cols'. **1977** Wind gap [see *river capture* s.v. RIVER *sb.*[1] 5 d]. **1585** HIGINS *Junius' Nomencl.* 262/1 *Cucurbitula*,..a *wind glasse, cupping glasse, or boxing glasse. **1594** MARLOWE & NASHE *Dido* I. i, The *Wind-god warring now with Fate. **1803** H. K. WHITE *Rem.*, *To Herb Rosemary* iii, The wind-god, as he flies, Moans hollow in the Forest trees. **1930** BLUNDEN *Summer's Fancy* 31 They stole away, and heard the windgod trill Winging the corn that to the bright west rolled. **1940** F. SMYTHE *Adventures of Mountaineer* xi. 201 It was all we could do..to pull off our *wind jackets. **1955** G. BAND *Road to Rakaposhi* vii. 87 David and I, who were wearing bright red windjackets,.. slipped carefully past. **1662** R. MATHEW *Unl. Alch.* 144 A man near fourteen years, afflicted..with the *Wind-Gout in his hands. **1847** LEICHHARDT *Jrnl.* xi. 339 The dry *wind-grass of the plains north of the Staaten. **1884** MILLER *Plant-n.*, *Apera* (*Agrostis*) *Spica-venti*, Corn-grass, Wind-grass. **1670** NYE *Gunnery* II. 12 When you come to your Peece, set your Boudge barrel on the *wind-hand thereof. **1813** HOGG *Queen's Wake* (1814) 109 When..*wind-harp at thy window swells. **1841–4** EMERSON *Ess.*, *Nature* Wks. (Bohn) I. 225 The musical steaming odorous south wind, which converts all trees to wind-harps. **13..** *Gaw. & Gr. Knt.* 1336 þay..graypely departed þe wesaunt fro þe *wynt-hole. **1683** MOXON *Mech. Exerc.*, *Printing* xviii. ¶ 2 Lay the ends of each Brick about three Inches off each other, to serve for Wind-holes. **1688** HOLME *Armoury* III. xiv. (Roxb.) 7/1 The wind hole, a square hole in the middle of the under board [of a pair of bellows]. **1802** MAWE *Min. Derbysh.* Gloss., *Wind-holes*, shafts or sumps sunk to convey wind or air. **1881** W. E. DICKSON *Organ-Build.* ix. 122 Let us be sure that the flow of wind to that pipe is not interrupted..by a chip in the wind-hole. **1880** *United Service* Oct. 458 [The adjutant] watched the roll-call of his '*wind-jammers'. **1892** *Rudder* Sept. 217/1 The deck-hands on the liners contemptuously refer to [sailing vessels] as 'wind-jammers'. **1893** *Columbus* (Ohio) *Disp.* 7 Aug., The few workers present are effectually playing the part of windjammers and many rumors are afloat. **1899** *Harmsworth's Mag.* Mar. 102 A large three-masted wind-jammer was caught by the gale and disabled. **1909** *Athenæum* 31 July 121/3 It deals with the homeward passage of a big steel 'windjammer' from Calcutta—a typical chapter from the life of merchant-service Jack. **1917** S. LEWIS *Job* 209 We do our work and don't howl about like all these socialists and radicals and other wind-jammers. **1930** *Even. Standard* 20 Aug. 2 (Advt.), Thousands of golfers wear the Barker 'Windjammer' and report it to be a splendid garment. **1931** *Amer. Mercury* XXIV. 354/2 [Circus Words.] *Windjammer*, a band musician. **1932** AUDEN in *Rev. Eng. Stud.* (1978) Aug. 282 My hand was wrung By one bareheaded in a windjammer jacket. **1942** M. HARGROVE *See here, Private Hargrove* xlii. 119 *Wind-jammer*, the bugler. **1976** *Milton Keynes Express* 25 June 4/4 The very popular zip-fronted cotton velour wind-jammer..is also great weekend gear with jeans. **1886** D. KEMP *Man. Yacht & Boat Sailing* (ed. 5) 658/1 *Wind jamming. A new-fashioned slang term for sailing by the wind. **1893** *Columbus* (Ohio) *Dispatch* Oct. 5 Could this power of wind-jamming have been saved there would have been some good accruing from the extra session. **1894** *Nautical Mag.* Feb. 102 People would begin to understand the meaning of seamanship as apart from the so-called and much-despised 'wind-jamming'. **1919** S. LEWIS *Free Air* 182 You're the worst wind-jamming liar I ever met. **1946** *Seafarers' Log* 18 Jan. 4/1 He really fooled the entire crew, and the Chief Mate was so impressed with his windjamming that he wanted to make him Bosun. **1868–9** *Routledge's Ev. Boy's Ann.* 367 The witches of Lapland sold '*wind-knots' tied on a rope to their sea-faring customers. **1943** T. DUDLEY-GORDON *Coastal Command at War* 22 He knows its direction by the '*wind-lanes' on the sea. **1979** *Fisherman's Weekly* 21 June 6/1 Thousands of tiny shucks from the freshly opened beech leaves, blown onto the surface, had collected in floating rafts, and were marking the wind lanes. **1570** LEVINS *Manip.* 27/29 Ye *Wynd-lappe, *lingula*. **1789** *Trans. Soc. Arts* II. 210 We can do nothing with the guns when there is any swell, or *wind lipper. **1815** W. SCORESBY in *Mem. Wernerian Soc.* II. 324 *note*, The first effects of a breeze of wind on smooth water is by seamen called wind-lipper. **1898** MISS YONGE *J. Keble's Parishes* 173 **Windlist*, white streak of faint cloud across a blue sky, showing the direction of the wind. **1911** HUSBAND & HARBY *Structural Engin.* ii. 36 (*heading*) *Wind load. **1961** *B.S.I. News* Dec. 16/2 Stability requirements for cranes (including consideration of wind loads). **1970** *New Scientist* 17 Sept. 584/2 The BRS project will improve wind-tunnel techniques, as well as increasing knowledge of windloads—which means better, safer, and perhaps more economic building. **1924** P. A. FRANKLIN in Hool & Kinne *Movable & Long-Span Steel Bridges* I. 47 Design machinery for *wind loadings as set forth in chapter of design of operating machinery. **1985** *Times* 19 July 13/4 In windy winter conditions the windloading presses the door up against the weatherstrip. *a* **1687** PETTY *Treat. Naval Philos.* I. ii, The next enquiry must be, what extent of Sail our Vessel must carry,..and from thence the *Wind-loft. **1829** R. STUART *Anecd. Steam Eng.* I. 149 Air remained in the cylinder, and prevented..the fall of the piston..: from this cause alone, (and which was afterwards known by the term of *wind-logged) this engine must have soon ceased its motion. **1908** N. DUNCAN *Every Man for Himself* i. 18 An' the sea was runnin' high—a fussy *wind-lop over a swell that broke in big whitecaps. **1974** F. MOWAT *Boat who wouldn't Float* xix. 234 The combination of wind-lop and heavy swell produced a motion that was indescribable. **1745** in *6th Rep. Dep. Kpr.* App. II. 122 A self-regulating *Wind Machine. **1799** *Hull Advertiser* 7 Sept. 4/2 These wind machines.. species of gigantic bellows. **1812** SIR J. SINCLAIR *Syst. Husb. Scot.* I. 341 The annual expence of repairs..will not much exceed that of a wind machine. **1906** R. A. STREATFEILD *Mod. Music & Musicians* xix. 338 The fantastic pieces of musical extravagance that are a special feature of 'Don Quixote', such as the wind machine and the bleating sheep, are thoroughly in keeping with..Strauss's real methods. **1928** D. H. LAWRENCE *Lady Chatterley's Lover* xvi. 282 So many people, like your famous wind-machine, have only got minds tacked on to their physical corpses. **1928** A. ROSE *Stage Effects* 9 Fig. 4 shows a wind machine, as used in many theatres. It is built up in the form of a paddle-wheel. **1962** A. NISBETT *Technique Sound Studio* x. 181 A wind machine consists of a weighted piece of heavy canvas hung over a rotating, slatted drum... A wind machine produces just one sound: wind. And the same goes for thunder sheets. **1976** *Gramophone* Apr. 1611/2 Calling as it does for no fewer than twenty horns.., quadruple woodwind, six trumpets and trombones.., not to mention the windmachine, thunder-machine and numerous other percussion instruments, it is impractical to mount nowadays. **1976** *Upper Valley Progress* (Mission, Texas) 6 Oct. 10/1 (Advt.), With thermal inversion, created by our Tropic Breeze wind machine, crop level temperatures are raised as much as 10 degrees. **1881** SIR W. THOMSON in *Nature* 8 Sept. 434/2 It is most probable that windmills or *wind-motors in some form will again be in the ascendant. **1813** T. DAVIS *Agric. Wilts.* 265 **Wind Mows*, cocks of a waggon-load or more, into which hay is sometimes put previous to ricking in catching weather. **1650** BULWER *Anthropomet.* (1653) 274 *Wind-Musique doth not deform the Visage. **1661** [see MUSIC *sb.* 6]. *a* **1700** EVELYN *Diary* 21 Dec. 1662, Instead of the..solemn wind musiq accompanying the organ, was introduced a concert of 24 violins. **1700** J. BROME *Trav.* 127 The Statues of two Men playing on Wind-Musick. **1795** *Life John Metcalf* 109 There being at that time no music in the army except Colonel Howard's, (the Old Buffs) and which being wind music were unaccustomed to country dances. **1661** [T. POWELL] *Hum. Industry* 34 *Wind-muskets that some have devised to shoot bullets withal. **1936** *Wind-noise [see FAIRING *vbl. sb.*[2]]. **1984** *Buses* Aug. 346/2 Only the wind noise through the roof light..gave any indication of our speed. **1833** LOUDON *Encycl. Archit.* §234 To do all the *wind-pinnings (filling in the angle between the wall-plate and the roof). **1863** FITZROY *Weather Bk.* 173 Taking, with Dové, north-east and south-west (*true*) as the '*wind-poles'. **1899** *Committee's Appeal for Hexham Abbey* 6 The old internal *wind porch, now used as a press in the vestry. **1616** CHAPMAN *Odyss.* VI. 341 A shore, *wind-proofe, and full of shade. **1856** KANE *Arctic Expl.* I. xxvii. 355, I have some eight sledge-loads more to collect before our little home can be called wind-proof. **1923** F. WILD *Shackleton's Last Voyage* v. 76 Each man was provided with a fur-lined leather cap, heavy pea-jacket, light windproof jacket, a stout pair of trousers. **1937** F. SMYTHE *Camp Six* xiv. 150 Too tired..to remove our ice-caked wind-proofs. **1975** E. HILLARY *Nothing venture, Nothing Win* viii. 120 We..crawled out of our tents, dressed in all our warm clothing and windproofs. **1977** *Navy News* July 16/3 Availability of the windproof jacket will lead to the progressive phasing out of personal greatcoats and over-coats. **1660** BOYLE *New Exp. Phys.-Mech.* Proem 6 The *Wind-Pump..is so contriv'd, that to evacuate the Vessel there is requir'd the..labor of two.. men. *c* **950** *Lindisf. Gosp.* Mark iv. 37 *Wind-ræs..michelo windes. *c* **1205** LAY. 9244 Mid þan wind-ræsen al heo gunnen to-reosen. **1622** *N. Riding Rec.* (N.S.) II. 4 Every Towen or lorshipp that of reighte haith any *winderake for there goodes in the forrest. **1875** 'MARK TWAIN' in *Atlantic Monthly* Mar. 288/1 It wasn't a bluff reef... It wasn't anything but a *wind reef. The wind does that. **1860** MAURY *Phys. Geog. Sea* xii. §551 There are two '*wind-roads', crossing this sea. **1902** *Daily Chron.* 10 Sept. 5/7 Being in the wind road we got a little air. **1969** *Gloss. for Landscape Work* (*B.S.I.*) v. 19 *Wind rock. The loosening of the root ball of a tree or plant through the oscillation of the stem by wind. **1972** S. EMBERTON *Year in Shrub Garden* III. 151 Any plants which have..been wind-rocked..must be staked upright. *Ibid.* 181 Roses, bush types—shorten to prevent wind-rocking. **1981** BUCZACKI & HARRIS *Collins Guide to Pests of Garden Plants* 486 Windrock very commonly occurs on young trees, shrubs and herbaceous plants with a large top in relation to their root system. *c* **1635** CAPT. N. BOTELER *Dial. Sea Services* (1685) 136 To Ride *Wind-rode, is when the Wind hath more power over her in her Riding than the Tide hath. **1635** *Voy. Foxe & James to N.W.* (Hakl. Soc.) II. 379 The Ship came not to wind-road. **1794** *Rigging & Seamanship* II. 302 The ship becomes windroad. **1841** R. H. DANA *Seaman's Man.* 89 To get under Way wind-rode, with a Weather Tide; that is, a tide setting to windward. **1912** J. H. COMSTOCK *Spider Bk.* 35 The solpugids are exceedingly agile; on this account they have been called '*wind-scorpions. **1959** *Southwest Rev.* Spring 137/1 An arachnid frequently, and naturally, confused with the true vinegarone is the solpugid—or wind-scorpion, wind-spider, or sun-spider. **1858** J. A. WARDER *Hedges & Evergreens* 240 The common Cedar is.. much used.. where a quick, permanent, and effective *wind-screen is wanted. **1887** *Cent. Mag.* Mar. 740/2 That department.. was nearly surrounded by a wind-screen of hemlock boughs and odd pieces of canvas. **1903** *Cornhill Mag.* Oct. 574 Peering over the canvas wind-screen of the bridge [of a yacht]. **1905** *Westm. Gaz.* 18 Nov. 9/1 With its hood and wind-screen, [the car] is well fitted for the use of the general practitioner. **1908** *Animal Managem.* 150 Wind screens may be.. made of turf walls or tall, wattled hurdles, placed to windward of the lines. **1948** *Autocar* 5 Nov. 1093/1 Trico-Folberth's *windscreen washer drives home the lesson..'None so blind as those who can't see.' **1973** *Country Life* 22 Feb. 468/2 Windscreen washers and wipers are operated by a right-hand steering column stalk. **1984** B. FRANCIS *AA Car Duffer's Guide* 18 I've been fiddling about for ages trying to get the windscreen washers to work properly. **1922** *Motor* 21 Nov. 831/3 (*heading*) An automatic *windscreen wiper. **1975** *Daily Tel.* (Colour Suppl.) 4 Apr. 18/2 Peter Wallace, the Flight Engineer, began his safety check, examining everything from the windscreen wipers to the radar. **1985** *Computing* 15 Aug. 25/2 We still have to make do with dreadful windscreen wipers in cars. **1909** D. H. LAWRENCE in *English Rev.* No. 565, I wait for the baby to wander hither to me, Like a *wind-shadow wandering over the water. **1931** *Flight* 25 Dec. 1269/2 He had found that behind the wings of an aeroplane 'wind shadows' existed covering a region of reduced pressure. **1977** J. F. FIXX *Compl. Bk. Running* xvii. 202 It also makes sense to vary your speed in order to take advantage of an opponent's wind shadow. **1825** J. NICHOLSON *Oper. Mech.* 123 The other method of bringing the *wind-shaft and sails into a position proper for receiving the impression of the wind. **1951** *Gloss. Aeronaut. Terms* (*B.S.I.*) III. 36 *Wind shear. **1976** *Sci. Amer.* Nov. 32 For a typical wind shear of one mile per hour per mile of height and an average wind speed of 20 miles per hour, the pattern of fallout 100 miles downwind from ground zero would be about 25 miles wide. **1977** *Time* 18 Apr. 37/3 'Wind shear', created by colliding air masses, was listed as the probable cause of an Eastern 727's crash while landing. **1934** A. J. VILLIERS (*title*) Last of the *wind ships. **1980** *Times* 7 Nov. 21/4 Will the rising price of oil bring back the sailing ship—or windship as it is now called—to the trade routes of the world from which it was largely banished a century ago? **1985** *Tel. Sunday Mag.* 18 Aug. 9/1 At 75 he [sc. Jacques Cousteau] is as lean and as trim as his revolutionary new 'wind ship', Alcyone, which he has just sailed successfully—and using less fuel—across the Atlantic. *c* **1400** *Sege Jerus.* (E.E.T.S.) 40 Suþ went to þe walle on þe *wynde syde, & alle abrod on þe burwe blewen þe powder. **1601** HOLLAND *Pliny* XVII. xxviii. I. 547 Some content themselves to perfume Vines onely with the smoke of this composition, so as it bee done on the wind-side, that it may carie the fume directly to them. **1727** *Bradley's Family Dict.* s.v. *Blight*, To provide large Heaps of Weeds, Chaff, and other combustible Matter on the Wind-side of their Orchards. **1923** KIPLING *Land & Sea Tales* 182 Give your *wind-sight another three degrees, Walters. **1920** *Wind slab [see SLAB *sb.*[1] 6]. **1936** E. A. M. WEDDERBURN *Alpine Climbing* iv. 51 A form of wind crust is wind slab. As this causes the worst kind of avalanche it is important to detect it. Its surface is smooth and unfortunately often little wind marked and its colour is matt white or yellowish. Wind slab is often found alternating with patches of softer wind marked snow. **1975** E. HILLARY *Nothing venture, Nothing Win* xviii. 286, I had.. noticed the debris of two large windslab avalanches nearby. **1978** Y. CHOUINARD *Climbing Ice* ii. 40 The wind will also scour ridges and deposit some snow on the lee side; this then becomes an unstable mass called wind slab. **1866** *N.Y. Times* 13 Apr., All persons having occasion to.. start a fire in any old chopping, *wind-slash.. [etc.] shall give five days' notice. **1905** *Forestry Bureau Bull.* No. 61. 53 An area upon which the trees have been thrown by the wind... blow down, wind slash. **1971** F. C. FORD-ROBERTSON *Terminol. Forest Science* 244/1 All such material [*sc.* slash] blown down by wind is termed wind slash. **1920** *Flight* 29 Apr. 470/1 Three *wind sleeves have been installed at Lyons (Bron) aerodrome... Two of these 'sleeves' are red, and are situated on the western side of the landing-ground. **1939** *Air Ann. Brit. Empire* 371 Pilots of those days mistrusted a wind sleeve, which was difficult to see. **1929** E. W. DICKMAN *This Aviation Business* 139 It requires more work than to stake out a cow pasture, put up a hangar and *wind sock, and announce the opening. **1958** *Woman* 9 Aug. 31/4 Briony walked.. along the sands as far as the wind-sock up on the golf-course. **1979** J. LEASOR *Love & Land Beyond* vi. 88 A wind sock hung limply on a mast. **1959** *Wind-spider [see *wind-scorpion* above]. **1966** C. SWEENEY *Scurrying Bush* vi. 88 A large solipugid, a very hairy, fast running arachnid that in Africa is often called a 'hunting spider' or sometimes a 'wind spider'. **1893** M. A. OWEN *Voodoo Tales* 28, I seed dem ole *win'splittehs [*sc.* long lean hogs]. **1900** *Daily Express* 13 July 6/6 The wind-splitter.. keeps up a wonderful pace. **1941** I. L. IDRIESS *Great Boomerang* vii. 51 No 'wind-splitters' nearly as wide across the hips as the forehead. **1890** *Harper's Mag.* Dec. 58/2 A tall thinnish man, with.. a white *wind-splitting face. **1900** *Daily Express* 13 July 6/6 The 'wind-splitting train' was tested over the line between Baltimore and Washington recently. **1948** DUNCAN & BONE *Oxf. Pocket Bk. Athletic Training* 35 '*Wind-sprints'.. consist of covering one or two laps of the track, and in so doing moving up very gradually from walking or slow running into faster running and then reversing the process, which will be repeated several times. **1981** *Northeast Woods & Waters* Jan. 19/1 My last $\frac{1}{8}$ of a mile was done doing wind sprints to help my lungs and heart to weather the beating of what was to come. **1932** D. GARNETT *Rabbit in Air* II. 60 It seemed to me several points different if judged by the factory smoke than if judged by the *wind stocking. **1983** P. DEVLIN *All of Us There* vii. 78 The wind-stocking fluttering to show pilots which way the wind is blowing. **1929** *Oxford Poetry* 1 Let's pick the petals of all joy apart, And launch them uncontrolled on the *wind-stream. **1934** *Discovery* June 155/1 The wind-stream is so powerful that a man could not possibly stand against it. **1954** FISHER & LOCKLEY *Sea-Birds* v. 127 The oceanic travellers.. spend their time making ground by.. excursions (by gravitational falls) into the sheltered trough between the crests of the waves, out of the main wind-stream. **1976** A. WHITE *Long Silence* vii. 59 You don't go out at right angles to the plane or the windstream can spin you. **1884** *Engineering* 5 Sept. 225/1 The position and character of the floor between the girders also materially affect the *wind stresses. **1953** *Jrnl. Marine Res.* XII. 249 (*heading*) Wind stress on an artificial pond. **1984** A. C. & A. DUXBURY *Introd. World's Oceans* viii. 272 The sea surface slopes, as happens.. under wind stress. **1656** BEALE *Heref. Orchards* (1657) 47 The clay-land binds the tree faster from *wind-strokes, the sandy-land hasteneth the growth more. **1890** BILLINGS *Med. Dict.*, *Wind-stroke*, acute spinal paralysis in the horse. **1913** D. BRAY *Life-Hist. Brahui* v. 109 Men well stricken in years often suffer from wind-stroke,.. a woman sometimes quits her bed after childbirth lamed by the wind in one leg. **1852** SEIDEL *Organ* 27 The *Wind swell. Here the trunk is provided with a valve of velvet. **1932** *Daily Tel.* 2 Mar. 9/5 Curls have ousted points of straight hair, and the old *windswept hair is dead. **1940** GRAVES & HODGE *Long Week-End* xvi. 280 The 'windswept' coiffure came over from Paris in 1931... The hair was cut short, brushed forward with a swirling movement. **1963** WODEHOUSE *Stiff Upper Lip, Jeeves* iii. 29 She is.. as loony a young shrimp as ever wore a wind-swept hair-do. **1985** *Hair* Summer 64 (*caption*) Windswept layered hair requires mousse. *a* **1625** MANWAYRING *Sea-man's Dict.* (1644) s.v., Any thing that holds wind aloft, which may prejudice the ship saileing or riding, is said to be *wind-taught (as too much rigging high roapes, and the like;) Also when we ride in any great stresse, we bring our yards alongst ships, strike downe our top-masts and the like: because they hold wind taught, that is, they hold wind stiffely. **1674** PETTY *Disc. Dupl. Proportion* 31 Where the Masts, Yards, Sails, and Rigging are great, the Wind-taught of the Ship will correspond, and will require proportionable Cables. **1704** J. HARRIS *Lex. Techn.* I. s.v., Too much Rigging,.. or any thing catching or holding Wind aloft, is said to hold a Ship Wind-taught. **1826** *Sporting Mag.* (U.S.) XVII. 199 The *wind-throstle or whindle.. travels out of the North with the fel-fare. **1939** H. J. LUTZ in *Amer. Jrnl. Science* CCXXXVII. 392 This investigation was devoted particularly to the influence of tree *windthrow on soil morphology. **1953** *Brit. Commonw. Forest Terminol.* I. 147 *Windthrow*, uprooted by wind; a tree or trees so uprooted. Syn. *Windblow*. **1966** *Brit. Columbia Logging* 3/1 They also can sell in their local areas wind-throw timber and stands threatened with destruction by disease or insects. **1981** *N.Z. Jrnl. Forestry* XXVI. 96 Line transects recording soil depth and percentage windthrow were made through single-aged stands of trees where definite patterns of windthrow occurred. **1668** CHARLETON *Onomast.* 83 *Turdus Illas*.. the *Wind-Thrush. **1706** PHILLIPS (ed. Kersey) s.v. *Thrush, Wind-Thrush*, a Bird so call'd because it comes in high Winds into England, in the beginning of Winter. **1873** T. CARGILL *Strains Bridge Girders* 186 Roofs, if they be thoroughly well secured by *wind-ties. **1858** J. BARON *Scudamore Organs* 61 The essential parts of an organ are a set of keys,.. a bellows, a *windtrunk, a windchest with its soundboard, and the pipes. **1911** *Aeronaut. Jrnl.* Oct. 53 The planes were tested in a 'wind tunnel'. *Ibid.* 62 Wind tunnel experiments. **1933** *Jrnl. R. Aeronaut. Soc.* XXXVII. 36 The aerodynamic characteristics were observed on a model of the airship in a wind tunnel. **1961** L. MUMFORD *City in History* (1966) x. 355 Not by accident did the medieval townsman, seeking protection against winter wind, avoid creating such cruel wind-tunnels as the broad, straight street. **1970** *New Scientist* 23 July 194/2 Wind-tunnel tests.. establish airflow patterns over ships. **1974** *Times Lit. Suppl.* 13 Dec. 1410/5 The Weimar Republic was above all a testing time, part of that great German wind tunnel in which ideas and principles, standards and personalities were subjected to the gale of history. **1983** *Aviation News* 8 Sept. 339/1 To compare inflight data with wind tunnel data for the same aircraft. **1985** *Times* 1 Mar. 3/3 The ultimate aim was C15, in every way a family car, using a very streamlined body already being tested in a wind tunnel. **1909** *Chambers's Jrnl.* Mar. 203/1 A small petrol or oil engine as a standby to be used when there is insufficient wind to drive the *wind-turbine. **1946** A. HUXLEY *Let.* 5 Nov. (1969) 557, I gather that the experimental wind turbine which has been producing fifteen hundred kilowatts in Maine has proved entirely satisfactory. **1982** *Daily Tel.* 17 Nov. 1/6 A £650,000 wind turbine machine.. was switched on yesterday by Sir Walter Marshall, chairman of the Central Electricity Generating Board. **1725** *Bradley's Fam. Dict.* s.v. *Wind-mil*, That it may, swivel-like, turn any way, as you turn your *wind Vanes. **1858** FROUDE *Hist. Eng.* IV. xx. 228 The imbecile Arran could play no part but that of the wind-vane marking the changes in the air-currents. *c* **1450** in *Archæologia* (1902) LVIII. 302 The firste *wynde went closid in ston. **1562** [see SUSPIRAL 2]. **1875** KNIGHT *Dict. Mech.*, **Wind-way* (*Mining*), a passage for air. **1876** HILES *Catech. Organ* iv. (1878) 24 Between the language and the lips [of an organ-pipe] is a narrow slit or wind-way for the current of air to pass from the foot to the body of the pipe. **1887** *Daily News* 28 Sept. 3/1 Leaving the water very choppy for the Thistle and stopping her wind-way. **1959** Wind-way [see FLÛTE-À-BEC]. **1979** *Early Music* July 365/1 It is also possible to wash the windway with water and washing-up liquid... This is recommended for very dirty or mouldy windways. **1867** A. BARRY *Sir C. Barry* iii. 76 A horizontal *wind-wheel for raising water. **1908** HARDY *Dynasts* III. III. iii, A fire is lit Near to the Thonberg wind-wheel. [**1933** *Automobile Trade Jrnl.* Nov. 52/1 Such items as windshield wings, either as a part of or separate from front door windows [etc.].] **1934** *Wind wing [see STICKER[1] 5 a]. **1951** R. CHANDLER in Gardiner & Walker *R. Chandler Speaking* (1962) 110 It sounded like old Simpson's Chevvy. .. He could tell by the broken windwing. **1581** MULCASTER *Positions* x. (1888) 56 The exercise of the voice.. aideth.. and comforteth the lunges in his *windworke.

wind (waɪnd), *sb.*[2] [Partly a. MDu., MLG. *winde* windlass, convolvulus, etc. = OHG. *wintâ* (MHG., G. *winde*), ON. *vinda* hank of yarn (Sw. *vinda* bindweed, Da. *vinde* pulley, windlass, from LG.); cf. OE. *ȝewind* spiral, tendril, winding path, *-winde* in *ȝearnwinde* reel, *wiþowinde* bindweed, ON. *vindr* winding: f. *windan* WIND *v.*[1] Partly a direct formation on the vb.]

1. An apparatus for winding (see WIND *v.*[1] 19), a winch or windlass. *Obs.* exc. *dial.*

1399 *Acc. Exch. K.R.* 473/11 m. 2 *dorso* (P.R.O.) Reddit compotum de vna Machina vocata Wynde [etc.]. **1538–9** in *Archaeologia* (1871) XLIII. 211, j olde wynde for stone. **1568** in *Coventry Corpus Chr. Pl.* App. II. 101 Payd for a cord for the wynde ij s. vj d. **1651** T. BARKER *Art of Angling* (1653) 9 Within two foot of the bottome of the Rod there was a hole made, for to put in a winde, to turne with a barrell, to gather up his Line, and loose at his pleasure. **1790** W. H. MARSHALL *Rural Econ. Midl. Co.* (1796) II. Gloss. (E.D.S.) *Wind*.., a winch, or wince. **1851** STERNBERG *Dial. Northampt.*, *Wynd*, a winch. **1883** GRESLEY *Gloss. Coal-mining*, *Wind*. 1. A hand-windlass or jack-roll... 4. A steam-engine used purposely for lowering and raising men in an engine pit or pumping-shaft.

†**2.** A twining plant, e.g. convolvulus. *Obs.*

1538 TURNER *Libellus, Conuoluulus, dioscoridæ clematis, altera, est aliquibus liliastrum, anglis autem*, The comon bynde, *aut* The lytell wynde. **1562** —— *Herbal* II. 141 Of the smooth Smilax or great arbor wynde. *Ibid.*, I neuer sawe anye kinde of wynde, or wyth winde, or arbor winde, haue anye suche cod. **1576** LOBEL *Plant. Hist.* 340.

3. An act or instance of winding; curved or twisted form; *techn.* bend or twist (cf. WIND *v.*[1] 5 b), esp. in phr. ***out of wind***, not twisted.

1825 J. NICHOLSON *Oper. Mech.* 586 If the two edges and his eye be not in one plane, the upper parts are planed down until the piece is said to be out of wind. **1859** CAPERN *Ball. & Songs* 137 The vermeil-beaded bryony, In many a graceful wind. **1875** KNIGHT *Dict. Mech.*, *Twist*.., the wind of the bed-joint of each course of voussoirs in a skew arch. **1883** *Hampshire Gloss.* s.v. *Wynd, On the wynd* = warped or twisted. Applied to boards or planks. **1896** *Archaeol. Jrnl.* LIII. 52 There is never any trace of wind on them [*sc.* Danish knife-blades], although occasionally they may not lie quite flat.

wind (waɪnd), *v.*[1] Pa. t. and pple. **wound** (waʊnd). Forms: 1 **windan**, 3 **winden**, 3–7 **winde**, 4–7 **wynde**, 4–9 **wynd**, (4 **vynd(e**, 5 **wy(y)ndyn**, 6 *Sc.* **veynd(e)**, 4– **wind**; *3rd sing. contr.* 1–3 **wint**, (1 **wient**), 4 **wynt**. *Pa. t.* 1–5 **wond**, 1–6 (–9 *dial.*) **wand**, 4–6 **wonde**, **wounde**, (5 **woonde**, 7 **woon'd**), 6– **wound**; *pl.* 1 **wundon**, **-an**, 3 **wunden**; also *wk.* 6 *Sc.* **vindit**, 6–9 **winded**, 8 *Sc.* **win't**. *Pa. pple.* 1–3 **wunden**, (3 *Orm.* **wundenn**), 4 **wondin**, **-yn**, **-ene**, (**wnden**), 4–5 **wonden**, **woundyn**, 4–6 **wounden**, (5 **wonddyn**, 6 **windin**); 4–6 **wounde**, 5–7 **wonde**, **woond**, (5 **won**, 7 **wown**), 6– **wound**; 2 **iwunde(n**, 4 **ywonde(n**, **ywounde(n**, **iwounde**; also *wk.* 5 *Sc.* **woundit**, 6 **wynded**, *Sc.* **-it**, 6–9 **winded**. [OE. *windan* str. vb. = OFris. *winda*, OS. *windan*, OHG. *wintan*, *windan*, (M)LG., (M)Du., (M)HG. *winden*, ON. *vinda*, (Sw. *vinda*, Da. *vinde*), Goth. **windan* in *biwindan*, *dugawindan*, *uswindan*:—OTeut. **wendan*, related to *wand-* in WANDER *v.*, WEND *v.*, WONDE *v.*

In many senses coupled with *turn* vb.

In ME. often graphically confused with WEND *v.*, q.v. etym. γ-forms.]

I. †**1.** *intr.* Used to express various kinds of rapid or forcible motion, as of water flowing, missiles flying through the air, sparks flying upwards, and the like; hence *gen.* to pass. Also with *about*, *adown*, *away*. *Obs.*

Beowulf 212 Streamas wundon, sund wið sande. *Ibid.* 1119 Wand to wolcnum wælfyra mæst. *c* **897** ÆLFRED *Gregory's Past. C.* xxi. 167 Sio æcs wient of ðæm hielfe. **993** *Battle of Maldon* 322 Oft he gar forlet wælspere windan on þa wicingas. *a* **1000** *Judith* 110 Sloh ða eornoste ides ellenrof oþre siðe þone hæðenan hund, þæt him þæt heafod wand forð on ða flore. *c* **1205** LAY. 27461 Stanes heo letten seoððen sturnliche winden. *Ibid.* 28049 [Ich] smæt of Modred is hafd þat hit wond a þene ueld. *a* **1225** *Ancr. R.* 296 þe sparke þet wint up ne bringeð nout anonriht þet hus al o fure, auh lið & keccheð more fur. **13..** *Guy Warw.* (A.) 3096 Boþe bifore & eke bihinde, þe blod gan out fast winde. *c* **1330** *Arth. & Merl.* 6320 þe launce.. ran þurch þe hors bihinde; King & hors adoun gan winde. **13..** *Gaw. & Gr. Knt.* 530, & þus ȝirnez þe ȝere in ȝisterdayez mony, & wynter wyndez aȝayn, as þe worlde askez. *c* **1375** *Cursor M.* 8968 (Fairf.) Prophecy.. ho talde.. of domys-day How al þis werlde sal winde a-way.

†**2. a.** Of living things: To go on one's way, take oneself; to proceed, go. Also *fig.* *Obs.*

a **1000** *Boeth. Metr.* xxiv. 10 Meahtes ofer rodorum ȝereclice feðerum lacan, feor up ofer wolcnu windan. *c* **1205** LAY. 20818 þat we mosten ouer sæ winden [*later text* wende] mid seile. *Ibid.* 25541 Ankeres heo up droȝen.. Wunden into widen sæ. *c* **1250** *Gen. & Ex.* 4136 His bodi was biried wið angeles hond, Ðer non man siðen it ne fond, In to lef reste his sowle wond. *c* **1330** *Arth. & Merl.* 9152 Hors wel gode chepe þai founde & anon in þe sadel wounde. *a* **1400–50** *Wars Alex.* 3325 (Ashm. MS.) Vp to þe souerayne sege with Septour he wyndis. *c* **1400** *Rom. Rose* 2056 For thee so sore I wole now bynde, That thou away ne shalt not wynde. *a* **1500** *Coventry Corpus Chr. Pl.* i. 168 Now to Bedlem must I wynde. **1519** *Interl. Four Elem.* B ij b, With huffa galand synge tyrll on the bery, And let the wyde worlde wynde. **1555** BRADFORD in Foxe *A. & M.* (1570) 1813/2 Such as walke in theyr wickednes and wind on with the world. **1579** HAKE *Newes out of Powles* (1872) A vij, And boughing Curs that barck and winde away. **1587** A. DAY *Daphnis & Chloe* (1890) 123 Phœbe being by this Time wounde into the highest Skies. **1600** SHAKS. *A.Y.L.* III. iii. 104 But winde away, bee gone I say. **1608** TOPSELL *Serpents* 266 Least she [*sc.* the spider] should wind downe in vaine.

b. *refl.* in same sense; also *fig.* *Obs.*

c **1330** R. Brunne *Chron. Wace* (Rolls) 15843 He..So queyntely aboute hym wond, þe kynges court at ȝork he fond. *c* **1430** *Syr Gener.* (Roxb.) 3645 Into the tent he him wond. *c* **1520** Skelton *Magnyf.* 2340 Wynde you from Wanhope and aquaynte you with me. *c* **1580** *Bugbears* iv. iv. in *Archiv Stud. neu. Spr.* (1897) XCIX. 39 Then best I stand not thus..and tel a tale to the wynd, but wynd me streight about it.

c. *intr.* Of a way: To 'go' somewhere. *Obs.*

1555 Bradford in Foxe *A. & M.* (1570) 1816/2 The multitude goeth the wideway which windeth to woe.

3. *trans.* **a.** To wield (a weapon, an implement). *Obs.* or *dial.*

993 *Battle of Maldon* 43 Byrhtnoð..bord hafenode, wand wacne æsc. *c* **1480** Henryson *Swall. & other Birds* xv, Sum the pleuch can wynd. **1607** J. Carpenter *Plaine Mans Plough* xx. 138 The Handle..on the which the Plough-man holding his hand by winding and wilding the same, turneth the Soole. **1627** W. Hawkins *Apollo Shroving* iii. i. 38 How to winde it [*sc.* a rapier] about when I salute. **1632** G. Hughes *Saints Losse* 46 Thou canst not hand before the enemy, nor wind a weapon for thy defence. **1845** J. Keegan *Leg. & Poems* (1907) 250 Raising aloft the heavy iron spade, I wound it with all my strength.

†**b.** To haul, hoist, lift. *Obs.*

c **1400** *Sege Jerus.* (1891) 281 Fresch water & wyn wounden þu faste & stof of alle maner store. **1577** Hanmer *Anc. Eccl. Hist., Socr.* i. xvi. 241 By the deuine prouidence of God the pilloure is winded vp in the ayer, ouer the foundacion. **1633** C. Farewell *E.-India Colation* 45 [The Elephant] taking his meat with the end thereof, and winding it vp, (or vnder rather) to his mouth, so eates it. **1681** Grew *Musæum* Pref., The Proboscis of an Elephant, whereby he..winds the Grass in great quantities..into his Mouth.

4. *intr.* To turn this way and that; to writhe, wriggle. *Obs.* exc. *dial.*

In OE. app. only contextual use of 1.

c **1000** Ælfric *Hom.* I. 414 He wand þa swa swa wurm. *c* **1205** Lay. 5715 Doð [heom] up and [= on] waritreo, þer on heo scullen winden. *c* **1386** Chaucer *Wife's T.* 246 Thou art so loothly and so oold also..That litel wonder is thogh I walwe and wynde. **1421** Hoccleve *Lerne to Dye* 509 In peynes sharpe y walwe & wynde. **1666** Bunyan *Grace Abound.* §165 Thus did I wind and twine and shrink under the burthen. **1887** *Kentish Gloss.* s.v., I had a terrible poor night surely, I did turn and wind so.

5. †**a.** *trans.* To put into a curved or twisted form or state; to bend; to twist; to wring. *Obs.*

For earlier quots. see wounden *ppl. a.*

1398 Trevisa *Barth. De P.R.* iii. xviii. (1495) d v b/1 A gristylbone set in yᵉ eere [*i.e.* the cochlea],..wounde [orig. *tortuosum*] & wrapped as a wyspe. *Ibid.* v. xxv. (Bodl. MS.), Beestes þᵗ foldeþ and windeþ ham silfe rounde as a ryng haue none necke distingued frame þe body. **1422** Yonge tr. *Secr. Secr.* xxvii. 161 Whyle an hooke [= oak] is a yonge Spyre, hit may be wonde into a wyth. **1538** Elyot *Dict.* s.v. *Topiarium*, Lyke trees or thornes that be flexible, or wyll be wounden. **1578** Lyte *Dodoens* 330 Growing vpon small stalkes that are winded or turned two or three tymes. **1581** Pettie tr. *Guazzo's Civ. Conv.* iii. (1586) 126 They would winde her neck behinde her, like a chicken [orig. *le torcerebbono il collo*]. **1610** Guillim *Heraldry* vi. v. 269 An ancient ornament of the head, [called] a Torce..: *Nempe quia torquetur*, because it is wound [*ed.* **1632** woond] or twisted. **1624** Wotton *Archit.* ii. 111 The figure of a sturdie woman, washing and winding of linnen clothes.

b. *intr.* To take or have a bent form; now only *dial.* or *techn.* of a board, door, etc., to be twisted.

c **1374** Chaucer *Troylus* i. 257 The yerde is bet þat bowen wole and wynde þan þat þat brest. **1538** Elyot *Dict.*, *Vimen*, roddes, which wyll wynde lyghtly, wherof baskettes are made. **1711** W. Sutherland *Shipbuild. Assist.* 165 *Winding*, when the Plank or Timber's Side or Edge is not upon a direct Plan, but seemingly twists. **1736** Pegge *Kenticisms* (E.D.S.) s.v. *Wind*, A board shrunk or swell'd, so as to be uneven, is said to wind; and when it is brought straight again, it is said to be out of winding. **1875** Sir T. Seaton *Fret Cutting* 82 A board is said to wind or wynd, when the two opposite corners..are lower than the other two.

6. a. *refl.* = 7 a, b. *arch.*

a **1300**, etc. [see turn v. 64 a]. *a* **1400–50** *Wars Alex.* 3631 (Ashm. MS.) Þai [*sc.* elephants] wend þai ware wees & wyndis þaim agayn. **1569** Blague *Sch. Conceytes* 26 When the Ele [= eel] had led the Dolphin into shallow places she wound hir selfe into the mudde. **1601** Holland *Pliny* xxxv. x. II. 541 A little infant winding it selfe and making prettie means to creepe unto the mothers pap. **1665** Hooke *Microgr.* 206 It posted away with such speed, and turn'd and winded it self so quick, that I should presently lose sight of it. **1690** C. Nesse *O. & N. Test.* I. 42 The serpent is a slippery creature, soon winding himself in and out. **1700** J. Brome *Trav.* 104 Abington, to which the River Isis, after it hath winded it self a long way about in a crooked Channel, makes its near approaches. **1723** Waterland *2nd Vind. Christ's Div.* Pref. 14 He endeavors to wind and turn Himself every way to evade its Force. **1821** Clare *Vill. Minstrel* I. 110 Glad I wind me down the lane.

b. *trans.* To turn; to cause to move in a curve. Also *absol. arch.*

13.. *Somer Soneday* v. in *Rel. Ant.* II. 8 With a wonderful whel that worthi wyth wond. *c* **1440** *Promp. Parv.* 529/1 Wyndyn', or turnyn' a-bowte, *giro, verto.* **1483** Caxton *G. de la Tour* a viij b, The tortuse [and] the crane..which..wynde their hede here and there as a vane. **1596** Shaks. *1 Hen. IV*, iv. i. 109 As if an Angell dropt downe from the Clouds, To turne and winde a fierie Pegasus. **1614** D. Dyke *Myst. Self-Deceiv.* (1630) 187 Let the Serpent but wind in his head. **1638** W. Lisle *Heliodorus* x. 177 As Camell..Doth eu'rie way his small head nimbly winde. **1665** Hooke *Microgr.* 199 Having so small..a body..upon such long leggs, it is quickly able so to wind, and turn it, as to see any thing distinct. **1757** Dyer *Fleece* ii. 462 Or where the Lune or Coker wind their streams. **1760–72** H. Brooke *Fool of Qual.* (1809) III. 92 The young nobles..turning and winding their fiery horses.

7. a. *intr.* To move in a curve; to turn, esp. in a specified direction. *Obs.* exc. as implied in b, c.

c **1385** Chaucer *L.G.W.* 818 *Thisbe*, Whan that this lyonesse hath dronke hire fille, A-boute the welle gan sche for to wynde. **1398** Trevisa *Barth. De P.R.* ii. v. (1495) b iij b/1 As a whele wyndeth abowte [orig. *in se volvitur et revolvitur*] and mouyth alwaye abowte in compaas, Soo angels..moeue abowte yᵉ thynge that longyth to god. **1601** Shaks. *Jul. C.* iv. i. 32 It is a Creature that I teach to fight, To winde, to stop, to run directly on. **1607** Topsell *Four-f. Beasts* 174 To..gallop and amble, to run a race, to wind in compasse, and so foorth. **1654** Earl Monm. tr. *Bentivoglio's Wars Flanders* 326 Winding about [orig. *torcendo*] on the left hand towards the gates Cantimper and Selle, he came before them. **1725** De Foe *Voy. round World* (1840) 260 We went winding now from the south-east to the left, till our course looked east by north.

b. To move along in a sinuous course; to go or travel *along, up, down*, etc. a path or road which turns this way and that.

a **1682** Sir T. Browne *Tracts* x. (1683) 165 How the Jordan passed or winded,..is a point too old for Geography to determine. **1697** Dryden *Virg. Past.* vii. 15 Here wanton Mincius windes along the Meads, And shades his happy Banks with bending Reeds. **1715** Desaguliers *Fires Impr.* 102 The External Air..will go winding thro' the Cavities. **1750** Gray *Elegy* i, The lowing herd wind slowly o'er the lea. **1789** Mme. D'Arblay *Diary* 15 Sept., It made me..tired to wind up the flight of stairs. **1859** Green *Oxford Studies* (O.H.S.) 24 Long processions of pilgrims wound past the Jewry to the shrine of Saint Frideswide. **1863** Reade *Hard Cash* xxx, Making a sudden turn, [he] dived into a street, then into a passage, and so winded and doubled till he got to a small public-house. **1905** Sir F. Treves *Other Side of Lantern* ii. ii. (1906) 36 A train of donkeys winding along among the hansoms.

c. *transf.* Of a line, road, or the like: To have a curved (esp. a sinuous) course; to lie or extend in a curve or succession of curves. †Formerly also of an object: To have a curved or sinuous form.

1555 in Feuillerat *Revels Q. Mary* (1914) 184 Garded with a gard of oken leaves gold and greene sylke wyndinge lyke a wrethe embrodred vpon redd silke. **1585** Higins *Junius' Nomencl.* 345/2 *Lituus*,..a writhen or crooked trumpet winding in and out. **1613** Purchas *Pilgrimage* i. xi. (ed. 2) 58 The passage to mount vp was very wide and great, winding about on the outside. **1635** Jackson *Creed* viii. xxviii. §4 The crooked paths which winde to cursednesse and malediction. **1667** Milton *P.L.* iv. 545 A Rock Of Alabaster, pil'd up to the Clouds,..winding with one ascent Accessible from Earth. **1748** Thomson *Cast. Indol.* i. v, Where this valley winded out, below, The murmuring main was heard..to flow. **1850** Tennyson *In Mem.* xxvi, Still onward winds the dreary way. **1896** Baring-Gould *Broom-Squire* xvii, The path winded in and out among the grave-stones.

d. with advb. acc., or *trans.* with obj. (*one's* or *its*) *way*, etc.

1667 Milton *P.L.* iii. 563 He..windes..his oblique way Amongst innumerable Starrs. **1794** Mrs. Radcliffe *Myst. Udolpho* i, A rivulet that..wound its silent way beneath the shades it reflected. **1823** Scott *Quentin D.* xxxii, The mole ..winds not his dark subterraneous path beneath our feet the less certainly. **1857** Livingstone *Trav.* v. 101 The slow pace at which we wound our way through the colony. **1887** L. Oliphant *Episodes* 281 A funeral procession, winding its solemn way to the cemetery. **1922** Housman *Last Poems* xli, Content..to wind the measures [= dances].

e. *trans.* To traverse in a curved or sinuous course; also *transf.* of a path, as in c. *arch.*

1648 Gage *West Ind.* 90 We had not winded the mountain upwards much above a mile. **1697** Dryden *Æneis* ix. 533 He winds the Wood. **1743** Francis tr. *Hor., Odes* i. xxxiii. 22 Though fiercer she than waves that roar, Winding the rough Calabrian shore. **1821** Clare *Vill. Minstrel* I. 202 Sweet it is to wind the rill, Sweet with thee to climb the hill. **1906** *Daily Chron.* 20 Aug. 4/4 Wherever a river winds a valley.

8. *Naut.* **a.** *intr.* Of a ship: To turn in some direction; *e.g.* to swing round when at anchor; to lie with her head towards a particular point of the compass (esp. in phr. ***how wind you? how does the ship wind?***). **b.** *trans.* To turn (a vessel) about (about A. 6 b) or in some particular direction. See also 19 b (*b*), 24 g.

App. a substitution for wend *v.*, q.v. (1 d, 6 c).

1613 J. Saris *Voy. Japan* (Hakl. Soc.) 44 She came to an anckor so neare ahead of vs as we could scarse wynd cleare one of the other. **1623** (Sept. 10) *Admiralty Crt. Exam.* 44 (MS.) She was not quicke of steeridge nor easye to be turned or winded. *a* **1625** Manwayring *Sea-mans Dict.* (1644) 115 When they are under saile, they use to aske, how winds the ship, that is, vpon what point of the Compasse doth she lie with her head. **1627** J. Smith *Sea Gram.* vi. 27 Winde the Boat is to bring her head the other way. *a* **1668** Davenant *Song, Winter Storms* ii. Wks. (1673) 292 Alee, or we sink! Does no man know to wind her! **1669** Sturmy *Mariner's Mag.* i. ii. 18 How Wind you? N.N.E. thus werr no more; no near, keep her full. **1769** Falconer *Dict. Marine* (1776) *French Sea-Terms* s.v. *Cap*, *Où est le Cap?* how is the head? how does the ship wind? **1798** P. Revere in *Collect. Massachusetts Hist. Soc.* (1816) V. 107 It was then young flood, the ship was winding, and the moon was rising. **1830** Marryat *King's Own* xxxi, One of the cutters has winded ..; she's stretching out for the shore. **1836** —— *Midsh. Easy* xiii, Mr. Sawbridge..winded the boats with their heads the same way. **1856** Olmsted *Slave States* 607 We backed out, winded round head up.

9. *trans.* and *intr.* In the management of horses in the yoke: To turn to the left, or towards the driver: opp. to hap *v.*⁴, hup *v. Sc.*

a **1745**, **1794** [see hap *v.*⁴]. **1816** Scott *Old Mort.* xxiii, A feckless loon..had catched twa dragoon naigs and he could neither gar them hup nor wind. **1851** *Jrnl. R. Agric. Soc.* XII. i. 125 To plough three 12-yard ridges by winding, or turning to the left hand. *Ibid.*, By laying two ridges (24 yards) together at each of these, marking and winding out the intermediate spaces, there will only be one open furrow every 60 yards.

†**10.** To draw or pull *out* with a twisting movement. Also *intr. Obs.*

c **1400** *Rom. Rose* 1810 But euere the heed was left bihynde For ought I couthe pulle or wynde. *a* **1513** Fabyan *Chron.* ccix. (1542) 257 By cruell deathe, as windynge theyr guttes out of theyr bodyes. **1600** Fairfax *Tasso* xi. lxviii, He stroue in haste the weapon out to winde, And broke the reed, but left the head behinde.

11. a. In immaterial sense: To turn or deflect in a certain direction; *esp.* to turn or lead (a person) according to one's will; also ***to turn and wind*** (see turn *v.* 64 b). Now *rare* or *Obs.*

† ***to wind up and down***: to revolve in the mind. † ***to wind off***: to turn aside. ***to wind about***: to use circumlocution with (cf. 12).

c **1374** Chaucer *Troylus* ii. 601 Criseyde..euery word gan vp and down to wynde That he hadde seyd as it come here to mynde. *c* **1385** —— *L.G.W.* Prol. 85 She is the clerenesse and the verray lyght That in this derke worlde me wynt and ledyth. **1586** A. Day *Engl. Secretorie* i. (1625) 136 That by your timely looking to those matters, you may winde him from that. **1605** Bacon *Adv. Learn.* i. iii. §7 To be speculatiue into another man, to the end to know how to worke him, or winde him, or gouerne him. **1606**, **1673** [see *turn and wind*, turn v. 64 b]. **1677** Gale *Crt. Gentiles* iv. 298 Socrates windes off his Audience from the curiose prying into the Nature. **1708** Mrs. Centlivre *Busie Body* ii. i, These flattering fops imagine they can wind, Turn and decoy to love all woman-kind. **1713** Tickell *Prol. Univ. Oxford* 34 To wind the Passions, and command the Heart. **1753** Richardson *Grandison* I. xxxvi. 258 He winds one about, and about, yet seems not to have more curiosity than one would wish him to have. **1777** Johnson *Let. to Mrs. Thrale* 29 Sept., There was not time for many questions, and no opportunity of winding and winding them, as Mr. Richardson has it, so as to get truth without questions. **1821** Scott *Kenilw.* vii, He can wind the proud Earl to his will. **1827** Carlyle *Germ. Rom.* I. 235 Love, which had once for all taken root in her heart, now dexterously winded and turned the matter.

†**b.** To draw, bring, or involve (a person) *in*, attract *into*, by alluring or enticing methods. *Obs.*

1538 Elyot *Dict.* Addit., *Lacio*.., to brynge into a snare, or to wynde one in to deceyue him. **1571** Golding *Calvin on Ps.* xxxvi. 4 Hee doth not simply fynd fault with the vngodly for winding in other folkes with their wyles and fetches. **1577** Holinshed *Chron.* II. 1847/1 A subtile practise (as was thought) intended to wynde him wythin daunger. *a* **1586** Sidney *Arcadia* iii. xxvi. (1912) 504 Which winded her againe into the former maze of perplexitie. **1608** Topsell *Serpents* 48 A certaine man.., being trecherously wound in and intrapped, by the craftie wilines of a certaine woman. **1635** Quarles *Embl.* ii. Epigr. iv. 79 If ev'r it winds thee Into a loosenesse once, take heed. **1653** H. More *Antid. Ath.* i. iv. §2 You will be wound into the most notorious absurdities. **1655** R. Younge *Agst. Drunkards* 7 It is admirable how they will winde men in, and draw men on by drinking first a health to such a man.

†**c.** To bring (a thing) *in* by insinuating methods. *Obs.*

1570 Drant *Serm.* C vij, This is the fine force of Sanders most fine witte, in finding out fetches, and winding in stuffe to strengthen and fortifye Antichristianisme. *c* **1650** Bradford *Plymouth Plant.* (1856) 301 He with his former dealings had wound in what money he had in yᵉ partnership into his owne hands. **1674** *Govt. Tongue* ix. 160 Tis pleasant to see what little Arts and dexterities they have to wind in such things into discourse.

†**d.** With *out*: To draw out, extricate, disentangle. *Obs.*

c **1535** W. Roper *Life Sir T. More* vi. (1729) 40 To wynde suche quarrells out of the Cardinall's head. **1577** tr. *Bullinger's Decades* 309 Iacob and Ioseph being wrapped in sundrie tribulations, were by their merciful God woond out and rid from all [orig. *explicantur*]. **1577** *S. Aug. Manual* T v b, Wynde me out [orig. *evolve*], & unloade me, that the pit shut not his mouth upon me. **1601** F. Godwin *Bps. of Eng.* 121 By and by he ouertopped the Archbishop, and quickly wound him out of all authority. **1607** Tourneur *Rev. Trag.* iii. i. (1608) E 3, Weele haue some trick and wile, To winde our yonger brother out of prison.

†**e.** To circulate, put in circulation (money or merchandise): usually in phr. ***turn and wind***. *Obs.*

1598, **1686** [see turn *v.* 64 c]. **1624** Capt. Smith *Virginia* iv. 157 Tobacco..passes there as current Siluer, and by the oft turning and winding it, some grow rich, but many poore. *c* **1645** Howell *Lett.* i. xli, There is no state that winds the penny more nimbly and makes quicker returns. **1678** Butler *Hud.* iii. ii. 1450 Whence turning of Religion's made The means to turn and wind a Trade.

12. *intr.* (also †*refl.*, and with *it.*) To pursue a devious, circuitous, or intricate course in argument, statement, or conduct; (†esp. with *about* adv. or prep.) to use circumlocution or subtle terms of argument (*arch.*).

c **1386** Chaucer *Can. Yeom. Prol. & T.* 427 For in hise termes, so he wolde hym wynde And speke hise wordes in so sly a kynde. Whanne he commune shal with any wight, That he wol make hym doten anon right. **1528** More *Dyaloge* i. Wks. 173/1 Truly quod he ye wynde it well about. **1596** Shaks. *Merch. V.* i. i. 154 You know me well, and herein spend but time To winde about my loue with circumstance. **1607** Beaum. & Fl. *Woman Hater* ii. i, You must not talk to him as you doe to an ordinary man, honest plain sence, but you must wind about him. **1680** Aubrey in *Lett. Eminent Persons* (1813) III. 612 He turned, and winded, and compounded in philosophy, politiques etc. as if he had been at mathematicall work. **1686** Jevon *Devil of a Wife* i. 14 He has a mind to wind about, but this shan't serve his turn. **1753** Richardson *Grandison* I. xxxvi. 258, I have winded and winded about him, as he has done about me; but all to no purpose. **1800** Maria Edgeworth *The Will* ii, I winded and winded, . . till, at the last, out comes the truth. **1838** LYTTON *Leila* IV. v, Why dost thou wind and turn, good Ximen? . . thou knowest well what my words drive at. **1850** ROBERTSON *Serm.* Ser. III. vii. 93 He did not adroitly wind through the dangerous forms of evil. **1881** JOWETT *Thucyd.* I. Introd. p. xii, In winding through the long notes . . we have sometimes a difficulty in separating his own view from that of others whom he is confuting.

†13. *intr.* and *refl.* **a.** With *out*: To extricate or disentangle oneself from a state of confinement or embarrassment. *Obs.*

1412-20 LYDG. *Chron. Troy* I. 2207 Love in his lawes often schulde erre, And wynden out of honestees cheyne. *a* **1569** KINGESMYLL *Man's Est.* vi. (1580) 34 As the birde taken in the nette, we lie fast fettered, our owne eyes not servyng us to espie any waie to winde out. **1599** HAYWARD *1st Pt. Hen. IV*, 83 To wind out of these intricate troubles. **1608** P. GOLDING *Sleidane's Epit. Frossard* 168 Not able . . to winde out of the linnen which entangled him. **1667** MILTON *P.L.* VI. 659 Long strugling underneath, ere they could wind Out of such prison.

1530 PALSGR. 782/1, I am tangled in busynesse, and can nat tell howe I may wynde me out. **1538** ELYOT *Dict.* Addit., *Euoluere se turba*, to wynde hym selfe oute of trouble. **1561** HOBY tr. *Castiglione's Courtyer* Z ij b, He . . struggled the more to winde himself out of their handes. **1597** HOOKER *Eccl. Pol.* v. lxviii. §8 They make it . . more easie for such kinde of persons to winde themselues out of the law. **1635** JACKSON *Creed* VIII. vii. §2 Hee could not wound himselfe out of those bonds of servitude wherein his lusts had insnared him. **1647** tr. *Wishart's Hist. Kings Affairs Scotl. under Montrose* iii. 25 Assoon as he had wound himself out of that present danger. **1653** H. MORE *Antid. Ath.* I. i. *heading*, To wind themselves from under the Awe of Superstition. [**1865** CARLYLE *Fredk. Gt.* XIX. ii. (1872) VIII. 121 Soltikof . . winded himself out of Posen one day, veiled by Cossacks. (Cf. G. *sich auswinden.*)]

b. With *in*, *into*: To insinuate oneself.

1548 UDALL, etc. *Erasm. Par. John* i. 1 That being so knowen by the wonderfulnes of his moste fayre workemanship, he mighte wind himself into our inwarde mocions. **1607** SHAKS. *Cor.* III. iii. 64 To winde Yourselfe into a power tyrannicall. **1640** RUTHERFORD *Let. to Lady Fingask* 27 Mar., If ye can wynd-in in his love . . what a second heaven's paradise . . is it, to be . . burned with fevers of love sickness for him. **1646** SALTMARSHE *Some Drops* ii. 57 This is the old way to winde in under the wing of Authority. **1690** C. NESSE *O. & N. Test.* I. 15 The old serpent easily winded himself into his heart. **1848** DICKENS *Dombey* xxix, Of your having basked at my brother's fireside, like a serpent, and wound yourself, through me, almost into his confidence. **1886** C. BIGG *Chr. Platonists Alex.* iv. 130 Origen does not wind himself into the heart. He has not the blithe geniality of Clement.

14. a. *trans.* To turn or pass (something) around something else so as to encircle or enclose it and be in contact with it; to twine, twist, fold, or wrap (something) *about*, *round*, or *upon* something else.

Also occas. to put around something so as to encircle it without contact.

1303 R. BRUNNE *Handl. Synne* 8055 Aboute þe body a rope þey wonde. **1390** GOWER *Conf.* II. 359 He, which hadde of nothing doute, Hire wympel wond aboute his cheke. *c* **1450** *Mirk's Festial* 126 Hur lady, his modyr, wonde hyr kerchef about hym. *c* **1460** *Towneley Myst.* xxi. 391 When it is well won knyt a knot fast. **1593** SHAKS. *3 Hen. VI*, v. i. 54 This Hand, fast wound about thy coale-black hayre. **1618** GAINSFORD *Glory Eng.* I. xvii. 151 They weare linnen rowles about their heads . . in Vlster carelesly wonde about. **1655** tr. *Sorel's Com. Hist. Francion* v. 8 Instead of a Night Cap he had winded the Linings of his Breeches about his head. **1667** MILTON *P.L.* IX. 215 Whether to wind The Woodbine round this Arbour, or direct The clasping Ivie where to climb. **1680** MOXON *Mech. Exerc.* x. 189 Upon the thin end of the Pole is wound a considerable Bundle of String. **1819** SHELLEY *Faust* II. 320 When she winds them [*sc.* her locks] round a young man's neck. **1842** BROWNING *Count Gismond* x, Wind the penance-sheet About her! **1866** LYTTON *Lost Tales Miletus, Secret Way* 25 As hunters round the wild beasts in their lair Marked for the javelin, wind a belt of fire. **1870** ROCK *Text. Fabr.* Introd. i. p. xxii, [A] bandage to be winded and kept about the patient's arm. **1896** HOUSMAN *Shropsh. Lad* v, Suppose I wound my arm right round. **1916** J. J. BELL *Little Grey Ships, Patrol* 18 [He] began to wind about his neck a dark blue muffler.

b. *fig.*: esp. in phr. ***to wind*** (a person, etc.) ***round one's little finger*** (cf. FINGER *sb.* 3, and sense 11 above).

1698 COLLIER *Immor. Stage* 279 To play People out of their Senses, . . and wind their Passions about their Fingers as they list. **1818** SCOTT *Br. Lamm.* xxi, I am told the mother can wind them both round her little finger. **1854** MILMAN *Lat. Christ.* IV. viii. (1864) II. 396 Irene wound her toils with consummate skill around her ill fated victim. **1865** SWINBURNE *Chastelard* III. i. 96 My life being wound about you as it is.

15. a. To put (thread, tape, or the like) in coils or convolutions around something, as a reel, or upon itself (either by passing the thread, etc. round and round, or by turning the reel or other object round and round), so as to form it into a compact mass (hank, skein, ball, etc.). (Also in *fig.* phrases: cf. PIRN *sb.*[2] 1 b.) Also with *from* or *off*, to undo the coils of (thread, etc.) by rotating the object on which they are wound; to unwind. (See also *wind up*, 24 c.)

c **1325** *Gloss. W. de Bibbesw.* in Wright *Voc.* 157 E vostre filoe là wudez [*gloss* wynde thi yarn]. **1377** LANGL. *P. Pl.* B. v. 525 He bare a burdoun ybounde with a brode liste, In a withewyndes wise ywounden aboute. *c* **1440** *Alphabet of Tales* 359 Þe iuge axkid ather of þaim whar-of þe bothom at þe clew was won on was. **1483** *Cath. Angl.* 419/1 To Wynde spules, *deuoluere*. **1530** PALSGR. 782/1 This yerne is so tangled that I can nat wynde it. **1577** GRANGE *Golden Aphrod.* D iv b, If she wanted a bottome whereon to winde hyr silke. **1590** BARROUGH *Meth. Phisick* III. xviii. (1639) 131 It seemeth wounden together like a string. **1601** SHAKS. *All's Well* I. iii. 188 If it be so, you haue wound a goodly clewe. **1767** BICKERSTAFFE *Love in the City* I. i. stage-dir., One seated and holding a skain of silk, while the other winds it off on a ball. **1787** MME. D'ARBLAY *Diary* Mar., Miss Planta left the room while I was winding some silk. **1827** CARLYLE *Germ. Rom.* I. 21 The long threads which . . she winded daily from her spindle. **1860** *Slang Dict.* (ed. 2) 247 I'll wind your cotton, i.e. I will give you some trouble. **1889** F. C. BEACH in *Harper's Mag.* Jan. 292/2 To operate the instrument it is only necessary to snap the shutter and wind off the paper.

absol. **1377** LANGL. *P. Pl.* B. v. 555, I weue an I wynde and do what treuthe hoteth. **1581** A. HALL *Iliad* VI. 119 Do passe the time to winde and reele, & with your maids to spinne. **1785** BURNS *Halloween* xii, An' aye she win't, an' ay she swat. **1818** *Min. Evid. Committee Ribbon Weavers* 154 Just according to how many looms they wind for. **1870** *Inquiry Yorksh. Deaf & Dumb* 18 She . . winds for journeymen weavers.

†b. To roll or fold up. *Obs.*

1523 FITZHERB. *Husb.* §52 Let the wol be well folden or wounden with a woll-wynder. **1549** COVERDALE, etc. *Erasm. Par. Heb.* i. 10-14 As a vesture shalt thou winde them aboute.

16. a. To encircle *with* or enclose in something passed round and in contact; †to wrap up; †to embrace, enfold in the arms; now, in ordinary prose use, only of binding a thing *round* with tape, wire, or the like.

c **1175** *Lamb. Hom.* 83 He wes iwunde mid wine and smirede mid oli. *Ibid.* 127 He wes imacad to monne ilicnesse and iwunden mid flesce al swa mon. *c* **1200** ORMIN 3320 & tær ȝho barr Allmahhtiȝ Godd . . & wand himm sone i winndeclut. *c* **1250** *Gen. & Ex.* 2597 In an fetles, . . Ðis child wunden ȝhe wulde don. *c* **1290** *Mary Magdalene* 383 in *S. Eng. Leg.* 473 Huy nomen þe Quiene and hire child and wounden in a mantel. *a* **1300** *Cursor M.* 1672 First bind it wele wit balk and band, And wind it siþen well wit wand. *c* **1300** *Havelok* 546 Hwan grim him hauede faste bounden, And siþen in an eld cloth wnden. **13..** *Gaw. & Gr. Knt.* 215 Þe stele of a stif staf . . þat was wounden wyth yrn. *c* **1374** CHAUCER *Troylus* III. 1232 Gan eche of hem in armes oþer wynde. **1471** *Paston Lett.* Suppl. 140 Sche byd that yt schuld be woond in a canivasse for brochyng of the caryars. **1483** CAXTON *Gold. Leg.* 229 b/2 A yong child that lay wounden in smale clowtes in hys moders lappe. ? *c* **1500** *Clariodus* v. 1917 Glaider war never Sir Troylus . . , When he had Cressed in his arms windin. **1535** COVERDALE *Isa.* xxviii. 20 The coueringe to small, that a man maye not wynde him self therin. *a* **1548** HALL *Chron., Hen. VIII*, 8 b, Their scaberdes wounde about with satyne. *a* **1578** LINDESAY (Pitscottie) *Chron. Scot.* (S.T.S.) I. 197 This hielandman . . tuik the samyn [crown] and wand it in his playd. **1593** *Rites of Durham* (Surtees 1903) 51 And so to wynde hime in his cowle and habett. **1610** SHAKS. *Temp.* II. ii. 13 Sometime am I All wound with Adders, who with clouen tongues Doe hisse me into madnesse. **1611** BEAUM. & FL. *Maid's Trag.* II, Let me wind thee in these arms, Till I have banisht sickness. **1662** ATWELL *Faithf. Surveyour* 106 If they . . winde their hurdles on two sides with broome. *a* **1722** LISLE *Husb.* (1757) 294 Drench the beast, and then wind him up warm in hay. **1851** MEREDITH *Love in Valley* xiv, Jasmine winds the porch with stars two and three. **1853** DICKENS *Bleak Ho.* xxi, Such is Judy. And her twin-brother couldn't wind up a top for his life. **1859** SALA *Gaslight & D.* xxi, There, are tops wound, and marbles gambled for. **1885** TENNYSON *Ancient Sage* 97 And wind the front of youth with flowers. **1918** *Blackw. Mag.* Apr. 491/1 The corner-posts were padded and wound with many layers of red and blue bunting.

b. (*a*) *spec.* To wrap (a corpse) in a shroud or *winding-sheet*; to shroud. *Obs.* exc. *dial.*

c **1250** *Gen. & Ex.* 2448 First .ix. niȝt [men] ðe liches beðen, And smeren, and winden, and bi-queðen. **13..** *Cursor M.* 17288 + 118 (Cott.) Þe clothez þat iesus was wonden in. *c* **1375** *Sc. Leg. Saints* xxii. (*Laurentius*) 503 Ypolyt tuk þe cors away, & wand It in clathis fyne. *c* **1425** WYNTOUN *Cron.* v. xcv. 4003 (MS. W.) To se þe quyk þe dede dispulȝe Quhen he is woundit in his schete. **1526** TINDALE *John* xix. 39 Then toke they the body of Jesu and wonde it in lynnen clothes. **1605** *London Prodigal* I. i. 170 Yes, truly, syr, your father is dead, these hands of mine holpe to winde him. **1660** RUTHERFORD *Let. to Mrs. Craig* 4 Aug., The mother . . possibly, cannot get leave to wind the son, nor to weep over his grave. **1719** D'URFEY *Pills* III. 335 Vowing he'll not conform, before The Old-Wives wind their dead in Wollen. **1860** W. COLLINS *Wom. in White* II. Narr. i. II. 349 That she had winded a many of them in her time.

†(*b*) *nonce-use.* To carry *out* in a winding-sheet.

1604 *Meeting of Gallants* B 1 b, Tenne wound out of one house, must for shame carry fiue payre of sheetes with them.

c. Chiefly in pa. pple. and *fig.*: To involve, entangle; †occas. to wrap up (in fair words).

c **1315** SHOREHAM *Poems* I. 913 Ne wynd þou naut þy senne ine selke Ac telle out al þat rouȝe. *a* **1400-50** *Wars Alex.* 2811 My warke, þat I am in wonden. *c* **1425** *Cast. Persev.* 703 in *Macro Plays* 98 Worthy World, in welthys wonde. *c* **1485** *Digby Myst.* III. 23, I am wonddyn in welth from all woo. **1833** MRS. BROWNING *Prometh. Bound* Poet. Wks. (1904) 160/2 In the great net of Até, whence none cometh out, Ye are wound and undone! **1863** COWDEN CLARKE *Shaks. Char.* i. 27 Then they wound him in their devil's web. **1883** R. W. DIXON *Mano* II. ii. 72 But, ere he reached, in death the babe was wound.

17. *intr.* To turn so as to encircle and lie in contact with something else; to twist or coil itself, or be or become twisted or coiled, *about*, *around*, or *upon* something. So *to wind off*, to become uncoiled from something, to unwind.

1575 GASCOIGNE *Kenelworth* Wks. 1910 II. 126 What tree soever it [*sc.* ivy] ryse by, it never leaveth to wynde about it. **1577** GOOGE *Heresbach's Husb.* I. 38 It wyndeth about, and killes his neighbours as the Iuie dooth. **1677** MOXON *Mech. Exerc.* ii. 35 If your spindle is to have three or four Worms winding about it. **1686** JEVON *Devil of a Wife* I. 2 Go home and Spin, or else my Strap will wind about thy Ribs. **1759** *Phil. Trans.* LI. 55 The single thread winded off the pod in the same manner as that of the common silk-worm. **1825** J. NICHOLSON *Oper. Mech.* 113 The leather shuttle winds upon it as it descends, or unwinds from it as it ascends.

†18. *trans.* **a.** (*a*) To form or construct by twining or plaiting; to plait, wreathe, weave. *Obs.*

971 *Blickl. Hom.* 23 Hie . . wundan beaȝ of þornum & him setton on heafod for cynehelme. *a* **1300** *Cursor M.* 1670 Quen þi timber es festend wele þou wind þe sides ilk dele. *c* **1330** *Assump. Virg.* (B.M. MS.) 795 A seynt . . Off silk and gold wounden in pal. **1495** *Trevisa's Barth. De P.R.* XVII. clii. (W. de W.) T vj b/2 Wrethes wouen & wounden of thornes & roddes. **1526** TINDALE *John* xix. 2 The soudiers wonde a croune off thornes. **1590** SPENSER *F.Q.* II. xii. 82 That same net so cunningly was wound, That neither guile nor force might it distraine. **1601** HOLLAND *Pliny* VI. xxii. I. 129 The boates . . were made and wound of papyr reeds.

†(*b*) *spec.* To make or repair (a wall) with 'windings' (see WINDING *vbl. sb.*[1] 10). *Obs.*

c **900** ÆLFRED *Solil.* Pref., þæt he . . ȝefeðriȝe hys wænas mid feȝrum ȝerdum, þat he maȝe windan maniȝne smicerne wah. **1474-5** [see WINDING *vbl. sb.*[1] 10]. **1550** *Ludlow Churchw. Acc.* (Camden) 70 Paid for 3 burthen of roodes to wynde the wals of the store howse. **1574** *Surrey & Kent Sewers Comm.* (L.C.C. 1909) 194 To wind with roddes & to fill vp the walle against his Mille banck. **1618** GAINSFORD *Glory Eng.* 147 Their houses wonde with rods and couered with turffs. **1649** *Order Bk. Hartlebury Gram. School* (1904) 72 To a man to studd and winde walls.

b. To twine or plait *together*, to intertwine; *fig.* to associate. *Obs.*

1387 TREVISA *Higden* (Rolls) II. 345 Þey . . wonede vnder bowes and twigges i-wounde to gidres. **1393** LANGL. *P. Pl.* C. xx. 169 As wexe and weke if þei were wounde to-gederes. **1523** FITZHERB. *Husb.* §127 Wrappe and wynde theym together. **1578** LYTE *Dodoens* III. lxxxvii. 440 Stringes, inter-laced, woven, and winded one in another. **1618** GAINSFORD *Glory Eng.* I. xvii. 144 And so intricately winde them, or lay them, that they shall be a strong barricado. **1646** A. HENDERSON in *Charles I's Wks.* (1662) 172, I wind together Diotrephes and the Mystery of Iniquity.

19. To haul or hoist by turning a winch, windlass, or the like, around which a rope or chain is passed. **a.** *gen.*

c **1440** *Promp. Parv.* 529/1 Wyndyn' wythe a wyndlas. **1900** *Law Rep., App. Cas.* 407 The head-line of the net is then wound in by means of the windlass.

b. *Naut.* †(*a*) To hoist (sail); (*b*) to move or warp (the ship), by hauling, as on a capstan or windlass. Also *absol.* or *intr.* (Cf. 8.) See also 24 g.

Cf. ON. *vinda segl* to hoist sail.

c **1205** [see 24 a]. **1379** *Mem. Ripon* (Surtees) III. 100 In potu dato diversis auxiliantibus pro ii[s]dem exaltand. et wyndand. 3*d.* *c* **1470** HENRY *Wallace* x. 872 He . . Bad wynd the saill in all the haist thai may. *c* **1515** *Cocke Lorell's B.* (Percy Soc.) 12 Some wounde at ye capstayne. **1535** STEWART *Cron. Scot.* (Rolls) II. 607 The Danis . . Wand saill to top. **1549** *Compl. Scot.* vi. 40 The maister . . bald the marynalis lay the cabil to the cabilstok, to veynde and veye. Than the marynalis began to veynd the cabil. **1570-1** (Feb. 17) *Admiralty Crt. Exam.* 18 (MS.) Layde an ancre right astern . . to winde her out of the dock. **1598** FLORIO *Dict.* To Rdr., I was but one to turne and winde the sailes, to vse the oare [etc.]. **1600** HAKLUYT *Voy.* III. 490 We cut our cables, wound off our ships, and presently fought with them. *Ibid.*, Cutting our cables in the halse, and winding off by our sternefast. **1633** (July 18) *Admiralty Crt. Exam.* 50 (MS.) The Delight was thwart the river and wynding down. **1729** CAPT. W. WRIGLESWORTH *MS. Log-bk. of the 'Lyell'* 17 Oct., Unmoared the Ship, and got all things in a readiness for Winding her head down. **1853** KANE *Arctic Expl.* (1856) I. vii. 71 We dropped our heaviest anchor with the desperate hope of winding the brig.

c. *Mining.* To hoist (coal, etc.) to the surface by means of a *winding-engine*.

1883 GRESLEY *Gloss. Coal-mining*, *Wind.* **1887** P. McNEILL *Blawearie* 186 To get their coals winded to the pithead.

20. *trans.* **†a.** To tighten the strings of a musical instrument by turning the pins or pegs around which they are passed. (With the pins or the strings as obj.) See also 24 e (*b*). *Obs.*

1607-12 BACON *Ess., Empire* (Arb.) 298 In gouernement sometymes he vsed to wynd the pynnes to highe, and sometymes to let them downe to lowe. *a* **1700** PRIOR *To C'tess of Exeter* 31 Your Lute may wind it's Strings but little higher, To tune their Notes to that immortal Quire.

b. To set (a watch, clock, or other mechanism) in order for going by turning an axis with a key or similar device so as to coil the spring tighter or draw up the weights.

Usually ***wind up*** (see 24 e); occas. ***wind down***, to cause to stop.

1601, etc. [see 24 e]. *a* **1648** *Ess. on Death* in *Bacon's Remaines* (1648) 10 Wooing the remorseless Sisters to wind down the watch of their life, and to break them off before the hour. **1760** WINTHROP in *Phil. Trans.* LII. 14 He was winding his watch at that time. **1880** HARDY *Trumpet-Major* iii, When he wound his clock on Sunday nights the whirr of that monitor reminded the widow to wind hers.

c. *fig.* To exalt or 'screw up' *to* a certain pitch. Now with *up* (see 24 f).

a **1635** SIBBES *Confer. Christ & Mary* (1656) 5 Like Jonah, . . when he rejoyces, his joy is wound to the highest pitch. **1823** SCOTT *Quentin D.* Introd., He at length wound himself to such a pitch of resolution, as to invite me to dine. **1827** KEBLE *Chr. Y., Morning* xiii, We need not . . strive to wind ourselves too high For sinful man beneath the sky.

II. In combination with advs. (See also prec. senses and the advs.)

21. wind down. a. *intr.* To draw gradually to a close.

1952 DYLAN THOMAS *Coll. Poems* p. ix, This day winding down now At God speeded summer's end. **1977** *Time* 19 Sept. 22/1 Instead of winding down, investigations were being stepped up. **1985** R. BARNARD *Disposal of Living* vi. 75 The fête was beginning to wind down then. I *think* Mary was still around.

b. *intr.* for *refl.* Of a person who has been 'screwed up' to a certain pitch or is in a state of tension: to relax, to unwind.

1958 *Observer* 7 Sept. 3/5 He is slowly 'winding down' after his exhausting television shows. **1970** *New Yorker* 24 Oct. 50/1 Even the West Indian was winding down. **1979** *Homes & Gardens* June 77/2 It takes him about two days to wind down. When your husband runs his own firm his stress is very great. **1985** R. HUNTER *Fourth Angel* viii. 137 An evening at the theatre and a chance to wind down and relax.

c. *trans.* To open (the window of a vehicle) downwards by rotating a handle. Cf. *wind up*, sense 24 e (*c*) below.

1961 I. MURDOCH *Severed Head* viii. 71 The windscreen was becoming opaque... I wound down the window on my side and the cold choking air came in. **1975** D. LODGE *Changing Places* v. 165 Philip stopped at a red light and wound down his window.

d. *fig.* To reduce in scale gradually; to bring (an activity) to an end.

1969 *Washington Post* 16 Apr. A22/2 Very little else is possible before the war is wound down. **1969** *Guardian* 5 Aug. 2/7 The enemy might prefer gradually to 'wind down' the level of combat step by step. **1977** *Rolling Stone* 16 June 56/3 Natalie is pregnant and will wind down her work schedule in anticipation of a fall delivery. **1981** *Daily Tel.* 26 Nov. 21 He might be able simply to wind the business down to a size which becomes manageable again.

22. wind off. a. See simple senses and OFF. †**b.** *intr.* and *trans.* To close, conclude, terminate: = *wind up*, 24 d (*b*), (*d*). *Obs. rare.*

1650 FULLER *Pisgah* II. i. 60 O that all differences between brethren might winde off, in so welcome a conclusion. **1675** TEMPLE *Lett.* (1701) III. 160 The Prince continues to say he talks to him no further than is necessary to wind off such Businesses as were left in his hands.

23. wind on. *Photogr.* To turn (the film in a camera) to the next position in readiness for taking another photograph. Also *absol.*

1947 A. RANSOME *Great Northern?* xxiii. 289 Dick wound on the film, closed the camera and put it in its case. **1964** 'F. CLIFFORD' *Hunting-Ground* vi. 67 Thirty-six on the film and I'm supposed not to have wound on once. **1982** C. THOMAS *Jade Tiger* iii. 66 He adjusted the focus... Click, wind on, click again.

24. wind up. a. *trans.* To draw up or hoist with a winch or the like: cf. 19.

c **1205** LAY. 30607 Heo wunden up seiles to coppe. **13..** *Coer de L.* 3955 The Sarezynes.. Her brygges wounden up in haste. *c* **1330** R. BRUNNE *Chron. Wace* (Rolls) 14564 Crosses, belles, men haue founden, In welles, in watres, vp haue wounden. *a* **1450** *Knt. de la Tour* viii. (1906) 11 Folke come to feche and wynde up water at that well. *c* **1477** CAXTON *Jason* 67 b, He.. went to the see and made to winde up the sayle. **1530** PALSGR. 782/2 Wynde up the crane faster. **1580** H. SMITH in *Hakluyt's Voy.* (1589) 470 We brought a cable vnder her sterne, and with our capstaine did winde vp her sterne. **1612** BEAUM. & FL. *Coxcomb* II. ii, Let me see thy hand, this was ne'er made to wash, or wind up water. **1793** [EARL DUNDONALD] *Descr. Estate of Culross* 55 The adoption of.. Steam Engines to wind up the Coals from the pits. **1825** J. NICHOLSON *Oper. Mech.* 124 A rope wrapped about it to wind up the sacks of corn.

absol. **1846** *Bentley's Misc.* Dec. 555 Walk down stream with him and wind up as fast as you can. He's a fine fish, and shows excellent sport.

b. (*a*) †To bind or wrap up (*obs.*); see also 16 (quot. 1853).

c **1532** DU WES *Introd. Fr.* in *Palsgr.* 948 To wynde up, *housser*. **1609** *Bible* (Douay) Ezek. xxx. 21 Behold it is not wound up, that health might be restored to it. **1611** *Bible* Acts v. 6. **1616** W. BROWNE *Brit. Past.* II. iii. 67 The Sea-Nimphes.. Learning of Fisher-men to knit a net, Wherein to wynde vp their disheuel'd hayres. **1627** J. SMITH *Sea Gram.* xiii. 61 Winde vp the slaine, with each a.. bullet at their heads and feet to make them sinke. **1657** J. WATTS *Dipper Sprinkled* 72 The spider doth winde up, and truss up the Fly, being come into its cobweb.

†(*b*) *fig.* To involve, implicate. Cf. 16 c. *Obs.*

In quot. 1651 app. = 'to have included in one's nature'; so in quot. 1674[2] *intr.* for *pass.* = 'to be included'.

1599 SHAKS. *Hen. V*, IV. i. 296 Winding vp Dayes with toyle, and Nights with sleepe. **1651** CLEVELAND *Poems, Rupertismus* 73 Whatever man winds up, that Rupert hath. **1674** N. FAIRFAX *Bulk & Selv.* 127 Well may one motion, of one sort, after sinking into its spring, or being wown up in it, be.. brought on again to a kind of quickness. *Ibid.* 187 So little of boundedness to winde up in. **1784** *New Spectator* No. 13 My happiness is wound up in thine. **1819** KEATS *Otho* I. ii, I am wound up in deep astonishment! **1819** W. S. ROSE *Lett. N. Italy* II. 96 [They] imagined that her life was wound up in his. **1841** ALISON *Hist. Eur.* lxix. IX. 138 His political existence was thenceforth wound up with the success of Russia in the German war.

c. †(*a*) To coil, roll, or fold up; to furl: cf. 15 b. *Obs.* exc. as in (*b*).

1590 SPENSER *F.Q.* I. xi. 11 His huge long tayle wound vp in hundred foldes. **1595** SHAKS. *John* v. v. 7 After such bloody toile, we.. woon'd our tott'ring colours clearly vp. **1659** RUSHW. *Hist. Coll.* (1721) IV. III. 269 He.. wound up his Hair with his Hands, and put on a White Cap. **1759** R. BROWN *Compl. Farmer* 35 See that the wool be well wound up.

(*b*) To coil (thread, etc.) into a compact mass (cf. 15): chiefly in phr. †*to wind up a bottom* or *one's bottoms* (BOTTOM *sb.* 15), usually *fig.* to sum up, conclude (cf. d).

1631 ANCHORAN *Comenius' Gate Tongues* 99 Off a reele clewes or bottomes of threads are winded vp and web is made. **1639** J. CLARKE *Parœm.* 46 Wind up your bottome. **1652** PEYTON *Catastr. Ho. Stuarts* (1731) 64, I have ravelled out the Pieces to wind up this Bottom. **1749** LAVINGTON *Enthus. Meth. & Papists* II. (1754) Pref. p. xxxii, But, to wind up my Bottoms [etc.]. *a* **1766** MRS. F. SHERIDAN *Sidney Bidulph* IV. 27 That would be tipping the spire and winding up her bottoms with a witness. **1770** DIBDIN *Deserter* I. i, I'll give you while I wind up this bottom and another, and you sha'n't find it out.

d. *fig.* †(*a*) To gather up the points of (a discourse) in a compact statement by way of conclusion; to sum up. *Obs.*

1583 MELBANCKE *Philotimus* X iij b, To winde vp all in a short conclusion, [etc.]. **1630** PRYNNE *Anti-Armin.* 137 To winde vp all in briefe. *c* **1645** HOWELL *Lett.* (1650) I. VI. iii. 186 Be pleas'd to dispense with the prolixity of this Discours, for I could not wind it up closer, nor on a lesser bottom. **1692** R. L'ESTRANGE *Fables* Pref. B 1 b, I shall now Wind up what I have to say. **1791** BURKE *Th. French Aff.* Wks. 1842 I. 580, I wind up all in a full conviction within my own breast,.. that [etc.].

(*b*) †To make up as the conclusion or final scene (*obs.*); to bring to a close or conclusion; to form the conclusion of, be the final event in.

1740 RICHARDSON *Pamela* II. 17, I shall be better directed in what manner to wind up the Catastrophe of the pretty Novel. **1759** STERNE *Tr. Shandy* I. xii, To wind up the last scene of thy tragedy, Cruelty and Cowardice.. shall strike together at all thy infirmities and mistakes. **1821** SCOTT *Dryden's Wks.* VIII. 454 The moral, by which the whole Masque is winded up, was sadly true. **1833** T. HOOK *Parson's Dau.* I. vii, Her ladyship was winding up the day with her accustomed bottle of soda-water. **1848** THACKERAY *Van. Fair* xliv, Sobs and tears wound up the sentence in a storm. **1912** *World* 7 May 685/1 An evening party on Saturday wound up the season's entertaining.

(*c*) To put in order and settle (an affair) with the view of bringing it to an end; to bring to a final settlement; *spec.* to arrange and adjust the affairs of (a company or business concern) on its dissolution; also *absol.*

1780 *Mirror* No. 97 ¶7 Some company concerns to be wound up, or some bottomry-accompt to be adjusted. **1794** GOVR. MORRIS in Sparks *Life & Writ.* (1832) II. 458, I have some affairs in London which I wish to wind up. **1848** DICKENS *Dombey* lviii, It was understood that the affairs of the House were to be wound up as they best could be. **1875** *Economist* 30 Jan. 131/2 The Master of the Rolls has made an order to wind-up, and has appointed Mr. John Smith.. official liquidator. **1893** SARAH O. JEWETT *Deephaven* 213 He was trading up to Parsonsfield, and business run down, so he wound up there, and thought he'd make a new start. **1924** MACKAIL in *Proc. Class. Assoc.* 13 The Association was never formally wound up and still technically existed.

(*d*) *absol.* or *intr.* To bring the proceeding to a close; to come to a close; to conclude *with* something.

1825 T. HOOK *Sayings* Ser. II. *Passion & Princ.* x. III. 185 And a dish of maccaroni to wind up with. **1835** DICKENS *Sk. Boz, Astley's*, One of the little boys wound up by expressing his opinion, that 'George began to think himself quite a man now'. **1855** —— *Lett.* (1880) I. 396, I want to wind up with that popular farce. **1882** E. O'DONOVAN *Merv Oasis* I. 329 An extreme amount of fever, winding up with delirium on the fifth day.

(*e*) *intr.* Of a person, etc.: to end up, to finish up (in a certain place or condition); to find oneself eventually. *colloq.*

1918 V. WOOLF *Diary* (1979) I. 115, I went to have my tooth finished, winding up for tea at the Club. **1921** E. O'NEILL *Emperor Jones* i. 155 When I gits a chance to use it I winds up Emperor in two years. **1942** W. STEVENS *Let.* 2 Oct. (1966) 421 The same reasons would prevent her from marrying as long as the war goes on, and.. she may wind up as an old maid. **1952** WODEHOUSE *Barmy in Wonderland* iii. 29 Men who own hotels always wind up in the breadline with holes in their socks. **1968** *Globe & Mail* (Toronto) 17 Feb. 3/1 Canada has made no written request that military equipment sent to the United States should not wind up in Vietnam. **1976** *National Observer* (U.S.) 13 Mar. 9/2 Somebody who wants to get away from it all is likely to wind up in a chalet in a Heidilike village on a mountain. **1980** L. BIRNBACH et al. *Official Preppy Handbk.* 111/1 Many of these forays.. wind up involving mayhem or destruction of property.

e. (*a*) In reference to a watch, etc.: see 20 b.

1601 SHAKS. *Twel. N.* II. v. 66, I frowne the while, and perchance winde vp my watch. **1639** *Crabtree Lect.* 41 Gladly he would have interrupted her,.. but the Jacke was woond up, and downe it must. **1648** WILKINS *Math. Magick* I. xix. (1707) 80 These Mathematical Engines cannot be so easily and speedily wound up, and so certainly levelled as the other may. **1674** N. FAIRFAX *Bulk & Selv.* 125 A Watch or a Jack, by being only wown up [etc.]. **1712** BUDGELL *Spect.* No. 277 ¶17 Another Puppet, which by the Help of several little Springs to be wound up within it, could move all its Limbs. **1762** CHURCHILL *Poems, Night* 83 Wound up at twelve at noon, his clock goes right, Mine better goes, wound up at twelve at night. **1883** RITCHIE *Bk. Sibyls* ii. 148 Climbing a ladder to wind up an old clock.

†(*b*) In reference to the strings of a musical instrument (see 20 a); *fig.* to put in tune.

1605 SHAKS. *Lear* IV. vii. 16 Th' vntun'd and iarring senses, O winde vp, Of this childe-changed Father. **1645** WALLER *Chloris & Hilas* i. Poems 157 Winde up the slack'ned strings of thy Lute.

(*c*) In reference to a motor vehicle: to close (the window) by rotating a handle. Cf. *wind down*, sense 21 c above.

1970 H. R. F. KEATING *Inspector Ghote breaks Egg* ii. 16 He slowly wound up the window of his big car. **1971** P. D. JAMES *Shroud for a Nightingale* i. 16 She wound up the car window and stepped on the accelerator.

f. *fig.* To set in readiness for action; to raise (feeling) to a high degree; now usually, to put into a state of tension or intensity of feeling, etc.; also, to annoy, to provoke deliberately (*colloq.*); to excite; to brace up; in *Racing slang*, to put (a race-horse) into fit condition for running.

1602 MARSTON *Antonio's Rev.* IV. iii, Straine all your wits, winde up invention Unto his highest bent. **1605** SHAKS. *Macb.* I. iii. 37 Peace, the Charme's wound vp. **1609** B. JONSON *Sil. Wom.* v. i, His knights reformadoes are wound up as high and insolent as ever they were. **1660** F. BROOKE tr. *Le Blanc's Trav.* 269 Having wound him up with good chear. **1665** J. SPENCER *Prodigies* ii. (ed. 2) 136 These blind.. Powers must be.. perpetually woond up by an Hand of Power and Counsel. **1748** RICHARDSON *Clarissa* (1768) VII. 20 My passions are so wound up, that I am obliged either to laugh or cry. **1759** GOLDSM. *Voltaire* Wks. (1889) 489/2 Voltaire seemed wound up to no other pursuit than that of poetry. *Ibid.* 500/1 Our poet was at last wound up to the height of expectation. **1822** HAZLITT *Table-t.* II. vii. 176 He had wound himself up to the last pitch of expectation. **1843** R. J. GRAVES *Syst. Clin. Med.* xxiii. 294 Ladies of fashion use it constantly to wind themselves up, when reduced to a little below par. **1864** NEWMAN *Apol.* iv. (1904) 126/2 It is not at all easy (humanly speaking) to wind up an Englishman to a dogmatic level. **1871** 'M. LEGRAND' *Cambr. Freshm.* 197 There's one that's what we call wound up: going to run next week in a big handicap. **1880** A. H. HUTH *Buckle* II. 257 Mr. Buckle's interjections come in very usefully to help Mr. Glennie along, and wind him up again, as it were, when he has run down. **1979** *Time Out* 30 Nov. 11/2 The kids are proud of the successful thieving they have done, and though they'll 'wind you up' (take the piss) as much as they can, the conversation becomes deadly serious on certain topics. **1984** *Sunday Times* 26 Feb. 10/5 They started winding her up, which is not difficult since she does not have a great sense of humour. **1985** *Times* 11 Jan. 3/6 When he heard the car horn sound and saw the car lights flash at his window he thought his neighbour was 'trying to wind me up'. **1987** *Match* 21 Mar. 5/1 All he kept saying was 'boss, you're kidding me, boss you're winding me up'.

†**g.** *Naut. intr.* and *trans.* See quots., and cf. 8, 19 b (*b*). *Obs.*

a **1625** MANWAYRING *Sea-mans Dict.* (1644) 115 The ship winds-up, that is, when she comes to ride by her Anchor. **1633** T. JAMES *Voy.* 10 This Anker had neuer bin able to winde vp the Ship. **1639** [see WINDING *vbl. sb.*[1] 1 b]. **1691** T. H[ALE] *Acc. New Invent.* p. lv, Ships.. have Water enough to wind up with the Tide of flood. **1711** *Milit. & Sea Dict.* (ed. 4).

wind (wɪnd, waɪnd), *v.*[2] Pa. t. and pple. **winded.** Forms: 5 **wynde**, 6–8 **winde**, 6– **wind.** *Pa. t.* and *pple.* 6– **winded**; 8–9 **wound** (see sense 3). [f. WIND *sb.*[1] In ordinary prose use the pronunciation is (wɪnd) except in sense 3, where it is (waɪnd).]

I. From WIND *sb.*[1] I.

1. a. *trans.* To get the wind of (WIND *sb.*[1] 4); to perceive (an animal, a person, or thing) by the scent conveyed by the wind.

†Occas. with obj. clause and absol. In quot. 1607, to perceive (a sound) conveyed by the wind, to hear.

c **1410** *Master of Game* (MS. Digby 182) vi, þe wolfe is so maliciouse, when he seeth hir comme withoute fedynge, þat he goth wynde at hir musel. And if he wynde þere she hath brought any thynge, he.. biteth her. *Ibid.*, Somme men seith þat she bateth.. hir heede, because þat the wolfe shulde wynde nothyng of hir fedynge whan she cometh agayne. **1580** LYLY *Euphues* (Arb.) 394 You might.. haue tourned the Hare you winded, and caught the game you coursed. **1583** GOLDING *Calvin on Deut.* xxiii. 6. 807/1 As a swyne when he hath once winded his meat, runnes on to swash himself in it. **1601** HOLLAND *Pliny* XII. xxii. I. 375 A man may wind the sent of it presently a great way off. **1602** *2nd Pt. Return fr. Parnass.* IV. ii, Any sensible snout may winde M. Amoretto and his Pomander. **1607** TOPSELL *Four-f. Beasts* 584 The greedy beast winding the voice of the Dogge. **1644** DIGBY *Nat. Bodies* xxvii. §7. 248 He could att a great distance wind by his nose, where whole-some fruites or rootes did grow. **1726** POPE *Odyss.* XVII. 385 His scent how true, To winde the vapour in the tainted dew. **1850** R. G. CUMMING *Hunter's Life S. Afr.* xxii. II. 126 Soon after fourteen buffaloes came; but.. they got an alarm.. They had winded two lions. **1880** CARNEGIE *Pract. Trap.* 32 A good terrier, one which will wind, and, if necessary, fight a fox. **1892** *Field* 7 May 695/1 Deuce dropped to birds that got up as we entered, and Dulcimer ran into a pair that she just winded before they rose.

b. *intr.* Of an animal: To sniff in order to scent or on scenting something.

c **1410** [see above]. **1607** TOPSELL *Four-f. Beasts* 125 When a hart pricketh vp his eares he windeth sharpe. **1842** J. W. CARLETON *Sporting Sk. Bk.* 29 Palatine.. suddenly raised his head, winded high in the air, sprung over the bushes, winded again, then leaped again.

c. *fig.* (*trans.*) To perceive by some subtle indication; to get wind of, to smell or nose *out*.

1583 MELBANCKE *Philotimus* Q iij, Philotimus winding Aurelia to haue munched on this carrion.. trotted to her lodging once or twise, where she would not be sene. **1596** SPENSER *F.Q.* v. ii. 25 Talus, that could like a limehound winde her. **1611** L. BARRY *Ram Alley* II. i, No nose to smell, and winde out all your tricks. **1640** C. HARVEY *Synagogue, Search* ii, My senses are too weake to wind him. *a* **1641** FINETT *Observ.* (1656) 13, I winding the cause to be some new buz, gotten into his Braine. **1779–81** JOHNSON *L.P., Pope* Wks. IV. 51 A cat, hunted for his musk, is, according to Pope's account, but the emblem of a wit winded by booksellers. **1829** LANDOR *Imag. Conv.* Ser. II. I. *Chaucer, Boccaccio, & Petrarca* 226, I never knew a priest at a fault, whatever he winded.

II. From WIND *sb.*[1] II.

2. a. *trans.* To expose to the wind or air; to dry by such exposure, to air.

c **1440** *Promp. Parv.* 529/1 Wyyndyd, *ventilatus, vel vento et aure expositus.* **1585** HIGINS *Junius' Nomencl.* 385/2 *Offringitur ager*,..the land is winded, fallowed, or twise laboured ouer. **1872** SMYTH *Mining Stat.* 64 As Mr. Spear says, 'he leaves the air to wind the ground the other 16 hours'.

b. *intr.* To 'take wind', become tainted by exposure to air; *trans.* to taint by such exposure. *dial.*

1842 J. AITON *Dom. Econ.* (1857) 222 A handful of salt shaken on the top of it, which keeps it from turning mouldy or winding. **1844** H. STEPHENS *Bk. Farm* III. 905 If the least cell of air be left in its mass...it will wind the butter.

3. a. *trans.* To sound by forcing the breath through, to blow (a wind-instrument, esp. a horn).

In this sense often with pa. t. and pple. *wound*, by confusion with WIND *v.*[1], perh. due to vague suggestion from the curved form of a horn or bugle.

1586 [? J. CASE] *Praise Mus.* i. 17 Minerua was delighted with her pipe, and vsed euen in the assemblie of the gods very much to winde it. **1602** MARSTON *Antonio's Rev.* I. iii, Boy, winde thy cornet. **1706** SWIFT *To Earl of Peterborough* 16 The Post-boy winds his Horn. **1746** COLLINS *Ode Evening* 11 Where the Beetle winds His small but sullen Horn. **1789** G. KEATE *Pelew Isl.* 33 The boatswain called all hands out to work by winding his pipe. **1790** PENNANT *London* 243 Hunters who wound their horns. **1810** SCOTT *Lady of L.* I. xvii, But scarce again his horn he wound. **1814** —— *Ld. of Isles* IV. xviii, That blast was winded by the King! **1859** TENNYSON *Pelleas & Ettarre* 371 Gawain..raised a bugle hanging from his neck, And winded it. **1859** —— *Elaine* 169 Thither he made and wound the gateway horn.

b. To blow (a blast, call, or note) on a horn, etc.

1599 SHAKS. *Much Ado* I. i. 243 But that I will haue a rechate winded in my forehead. **1735** SOMERVILLE *Chase* II. 292 With Cheeks full-blown they wind Her solemn Dirge. **1769** FALCONER *Dict. Marine* (1776), *Winding a Call*, the act of blowing or piping upon a boatswain's whistle. **1888** STEVENSON *Black Arrow* V. vi, He raised a little tucket to his mouth and wound a rousing call.

c. *absol.* or *intr.* To blow a blast on a wind-instrument.

1600 HOLLAND *Livy* II. lxiv. 86 Quintius..caused certaine cornetiers..to wind and sound before the trench.

d. *trans.* To supply (an organ-pipe) with wind at a particular pressure.

1879 *Organ Voicing* 28 They must be winded to match those below in strength.

†**4.** *trans.* To blow (a fire, etc.). *Obs. rare.*

1605 TIMME *Quersit.* II. vii, The fire..the which he had spread abroad, and winded or bellowsed in vaine. *a* **1660** *Contemp. Hist. Irel.* (Ir. Archæol. Soc.) I. 69 The freshe lime shaken and winded, filled the place with its smoke.

5. To deprive of 'wind' or breath, put out of breath, 'blow', 'puff'.

1811 *Sporting Mag.* XXXVII. 18 Parkes was very faint, and apparently quite winded. **1842** LOVER *Handy Andy* iii, 'Two to one on Dick—he's closing.' 'Done! Andy will wind him yet.' **1857** G. A. LAWRENCE *Guy Liv.* ii. 9 A country.. where there was no hill steep enough to wind a horse in good condition. **1888** 'R. BOLDREWOOD' *Robbery under Arms* xx, He can't hardly keep from barking till he's hoarse, and rushing through and over everything till he's winded and done up.

6. To cause (a baby) to bring up wind after feeding; to 'burp'.

1958 *Observer* 19 Oct. 10/6 My five-month-old son, though well fed, thoroughly winded and much loved, delights in yelling loud and long. **1961** *Guardian* 28 June 6/3 Two babies..to feed and wind and change. **1978** D. MURPHY *Place Apart* x. 211 Paddy's wife handed him their six-months-old daughter, to be 'winded' while she was undressing their two-year-old son... The baby burped dutifully.

wind, *v.*[3] *dial.* Also 5–6 **wynd**, 8 *Sc.* **winn.** [Perh. a use of WIND *v.*[2]; cf. OHG. *wintôn* (MHG., G. *winden*), Goth. *diswinþjan* to scatter like chaff (cf. *winþiskaurô* and OHG. *winta* winnowing-fan).

Late Northumb. *windung*, rare var. of *winnung*, *wynnung*, appears to be unconnected, and *winden* in *Ancr. R.* (ed. Morton) 270 is prob. an error for *windwen*.]

To winnow. Chiefly in *vbl. sb.* (*attrib.*).

a **1500** *Promp. Parv.* 529/1 Wynewynge, wythe wyynd (*K.*, *P.* wyndynge), *ventilacio.* **1538** *Aberd. Reg.* XVI. (Jam. 1825), And see the same bair wyndit & dycht. **1548**, etc. [see WINDING-CLOTH[2]]. **1578** *Reg. Mag. Sig. Scot.* 783/1 The beir granell, malt barne and windinhous. **1688** HOLME *Armoury* III. 74/1 Winnowing, Winding or Haveing. **1733** BUDGELL *Bee* No. 7. I. 293 Their Mother coming home presently after from winding of Corn, affrighted at this tragical Scene, threw the winding Cloth which she had in her Hand into the Cradle where the youngest Child was asleep, and smother'd it unawares. **1785** BURNS *Halloween* xxi, Meg fain wad to the barn gaen To winn three wechts o' naething. **1847** HALLIWELL, *Wind*..To winnow corn. *Devon.* **1869** PEACOCK *Lonsdale Gloss.* **1891** *Hartland Gloss.* s.v. *Wind*, Although winnin' or windin' by hand is nearly obsolete, some farms have still a Windin'-place, a spot of high ground where it was performed. **1919** CHOPE *Some Old Farm Impl.* 24 [Devonshire] the 'machine fan', or winding-van.

wind, obs. var. WEND *v.*; obs. pa. pple. of WIN *v.*[1]; var. WIN *v.*[2]; obs. Sc. f. WOUND *sb.*; var. WYND.

wind-[1], the stem of WIND *v.*[1] in combination, in a few obsolete compounds: †**wind-clout** (in Ormin *winndeclut*), a swaddling-band; †**wind-hatch** [HATCH *sb.*[1] 5 b], an opening to a mine, at which a winding apparatus is fixed; †**wind-lift**, a windlass (in quot. *fig.*); †**wind-rope**, a rope for winding or hoisting, used with a windlass.

c **1200** ORMIN 3320 & tær ȝho barr Allmahhtiȝ Godd..& wand himm sone i *winndeclut. **1671** *Phil. Trans.* VI. 2104 A Winder with two Keebles (great buckets made like a barrel with iron hoops, placed just over the then termed *Wind Hatch). *a* **1734** NORTH *Exam.* II. v. §64 (1740) 354 The Author intends no Good in all this, but brings it in as a *Wind-lift to heave up a gross Scandal. **1359** in *Pipe Roll 38 Edw. III* m. 47 (P.R.O.) In diuersis Cabulis, *Wyndropes, Caggyngcables. **1402** *Acc. Exch. K.R.* 43/6 m. 7 In ij hausers emptis pro j Wyndrope et j boltrope lix s. vj. d.

wind-[2], the stem of WIND *v.*[3] in combination = winnowing-, as in ***wind-cloth, -screen, -sheet.***

1500 *Ortus Vocab.* (W. de W.) PP vj, *Ventilabrum*,..a wynde clothe. **1565** *Inv.* in *Trans. Cumb. & West. Arch. Soc.* X. 32 Husbandre gere...vii steckes, one wyndcloythe. **1763** MILLS *Pract. Husb.* III. 125 After passing twice through the wind screen, that objection was entirely removed. **1891** *Hartland Gloss.*, *Win-shet*, a winnowing-sheet.

windabout (ˈwaɪndəbaʊt), *sb.* and *a. nonce-wd.* [f. WIND *v.*[1] + ABOUT *adv.*] †**a.** *sb.* Suggested name for a circumflex accent. **b.** *adj.* That winds about, meandering.

1589 PUTTENHAM *Engl. Poesie* II. vi. (Arb.) 92 We might very properly call him the (windabout) for so is the Greek word [περισπώμενον]. **1889** GRETTON *Memory's Harkback* 321 The erratic, windabout stream.

windage (ˈwɪndɪdʒ). [f. WIND *sb.*[1] + -AGE.]

1. An allowance of space (for expansion of gas in firing) between the inner wall of a fire-arm and the shot or shell with which it is charged: measured by the difference of the diameters of the bore and the shot.

1710 J. HARRIS *Lex. Techn.* II. **1778** HUTTON in *Phil. Trans.* LXVIII. 84 It would also be an improvement to diminish the windage; for by so doing, one third or more of the quantity of powder might be saved. **1860** ABP. THOMSON *Laws Th.* §117. 238 The windage of a loose ball in the barrel of the piece.

2. Allowance made (esp. in shooting) for deflection from the direct course by the wind; such deflection itself.

1867 *Morning Star* 30 July 6 At half-past nine the firing commenced..but with a breeze almost too strong for accurate aiming, and considerable 'windage' was required. **1891** CONAN DOYLE *White Company* iv, 'Seven yards windage, Hal,' said one.

3. = WIND *sb.*[1] 13.

1889 *Buck's Handbk. Med. Sci.* VIII. 11/1 To support the idea of injuries from the 'windage' of balls.

4. The (actual or potential) air resistance of a moving object, esp. a vessel or a rotating machine part; also, the force of the wind on a stationary object.

1897 PEMBERTON *Complete Cyclist* 78 This will..save a good deal of windage. **1898** *Westm. Gaz.* 26 May 4/1 [Yachts in which] an innovation is made..giving a maximum of head room with a minimum of windage. **1903** *Nature* 29 Oct. 635/1 The power wasted by the windage of fly-wheel and dynamo armatures. **1909** A WILLIAMS *Engin. Wonders of World* III. 42/2 The designer has to consider how to curve the [propeller] blades so as to give a maximum thrust for a minimum windage. **1948** *Times* 24 Nov. 2/2 A new type of anchor designed to prevent warships, particularly aircraft-carriers with their large windage area, from dragging their anchors. **1953** C. S. FORESTER *Hornblower & 'Atropos'* 60 Their twelve oars hardly sufficed to control their more than forty feet of length, and the windage of the huge cabin aft was enormous. **1958** *Engineering* 31 Jan. 157/3 The radar aerial..is of parabolic section and slatted to reduce windage. **1961** E. LIGHTFOOT *Moment Distribution* v. 123 Design against windage is important in skyscraper buildings. **1971** *Sci. Amer.* Dec. 7/1 If the time cycle between storage and retrieval is long, most of the stored energy [of the flywheel] is lost in windage and friction. **1977** *Mod. Boating* (Austral.) Jan. 98/1 There is a tremendous amount of windage in that topsides and cabin.

5. Special Comb.: **windage loss**, loss of power through the air resistance of rotating parts.

1922 *Encycl. Brit.* XXX. 35/2 In determining the useful H.P. of rotary engines, 'windage loss'..had first to be determined. **1966** *McGraw-Hill Encycl. Sci. & Technol.* IV. 449/1 Windage loss is relatively large in air-cooled high-speed machines.

windar, var. WINDER *sb.*[4], widgeon.

†**windas.** *Obs.* Forms: 3–6 **wyndas** (3–5 **-ase**, 4 **-az**, 4–6 **-ace**, 5 **-asse**, 5–6 **-es**, 6 **-esse**, **-ys**, **-ais**), 4–7 **windas**, (6 **-is**, **-ose**, **-eous**, *Sc.* **-ois**, 6–7 **-es**, 7 **-us**, **-owes**); 5 **weyndas**, 6 **wendess.** [a. AF. *windas* = OF. *guindas* (latinized *wind-*, *guindasium*, *-agium*), a. ON. *vindáss* (whence MLG., MDu., Du. *windas*), f. *vinda* WIND *v.*[1] + *áss* (= Goth. *ans*) pole.]

1. = WINDLASS *sb.*[1] 1.

[*c* **1180** in *Materials Hist. Thos. Becket* (Rolls) I. 300 Ligno quod nautæ windasium vocant caput rudentis circumposuere.] **1293** *Acc. Exch. K.R.* 5/2 m. 2 (P.R.O.), Maeremium..pro Wyndase et Wyndase Stockez. **1295** *Ibid.* 5/8 m. 13, xix. d. in quodam Wyndas empto..ad galeam. *c* **1330** R. BRUNNE *Chron. Wace* (Rolls) 12087 Somme aforced þe wyndas, Somme þe loof, somme þe bytas. **13..** *E.E. Allit. P.* C. 103 Wiȝt at þe wyndas weȝen her ankres. *c* **1386** CHAUCER *Sqr.'s T.* 184 Ther may no man out of the place it dryue For noon engyn of wyndas ne polyue. *c* **1440** *Partonope* 4604 Goo hye yow fast to the wyndase [*v.r.* wyndace] And pull the Ankre vp in hast. **1515** *Acc. Ld. High Treas. Scot.* V. 17 Making of crane and wyndais for fourtene pecis of artaȝery. **1578** *Harl. MS. 847*, lf. 53 b, Windoses for the defence of ordinaunce. **1609** in Cochran-Patrick *Early Rec. Mining Scot.* (1878) 149 Helping to mak and sett the windes over the somp and drawing the watter out of it. **1609** *Churchw. Acc. Pittington*, etc. (Surtees) 155 For bringinge the windowes and roopes from the Colledge. **1627** *Capt. J. Smith's Seaman's Gram.* ii. 8 A windas is a square peece of timber, like a Role before the fore Castle in small ships, and forced about with handspikes for the same vse as is the Capstaine.

b. A winch-like contrivance used for bending a cross-bow.

1443 *Bekynton's Corr.* (Rolls) II. 235 Ibi datus erat 1 arcus de Wyndas. ? **1449** *Paston Lett.* I. 82, I..prey ȝw to gete som crosse bowis, and wyndacs to bynd them with. **1506** *Acc. Ld. High Treas. Scot.* III. 204 For..grathing of the Kingis corsbow and windes. **1511–12** *Ibid.* IV. 327, vij pair wyndasis cordis. [**1888** STEVENSON *Black Arrow* I. iv, Richard had unslung his cross-bow, and held ready in one hand the windac, or grappling-iron that he used to bend it.]

2. *attrib.*, as ***windas cord*** [= OF. *corde a guindas*], ***man, rule***; **windas-stock**, a windlass-bitt.

1504 *Acc. Ld. High Treas. Scot.* II. 466, iij pair *wyndes cordis for corsbowis. **1608** in Cochran-Patrick *Early Rec. Mining Scot.* (1878) 149 To cover the *windes men fra the injurie of the wedder. **1641** *Sc. Acts Chas. I.* (1817) V. 509 Wattermen and windusmen. **15..** *Debate Carp. Tools* 163 in Hazl. *E.P.P.* I. 85 What, ser, seyd the *wyndas rewle, Me thinke thou arte bot a fole. **1293** *Wyndase Stockez [see 1]. **1404** *Customs Acc.* 180/1 (P.R.O.) 1 weyndas et weyndestok.

wind-bag, windbag (ˈwɪndbæg). [f. WIND *sb.*[1] + BAG *sb.*]

1. A bag containing 'wind' or air. **a.** The bellows of an organ (*obs.*) or bag of a bagpipe.

1470–3 *Rec. Andover* 15 For amendyng of the wyndbagge of the organys vi[s]. **1606** [implied in *wind-bagged*: see below]. **1838** G. F. GRAHAM *Mus. Comp.* App. 50 Possibly the anatomical structure of the sonorous organs of these *Cicadæ* did not exactly resemble the wind-bag, and reed, and pipe of our biped bagpipers.

b. The lungs (also *pl.*); the chest or body considered as a receptacle of breath. Now only *jocular.*

1552 HULOET, Wynde bagge of a man out of the which the winde passeth, and commeth forthe. **1565** COOPER *Thesaurus* II. s.v. *Anaxarchus*, He doubted these woordes worthy of remembraunce: Beate on, beate on Anaxarchus wynde bag: for Anaxarchus thou beatest not: accomptinge his body but a bagge full of wynde. **1860** W. W. READE *Liberty Hall* I. i. 10 The dubious condition of his wind-bags occasioned him considerable..distress.

c. An inflated bag used as a charm to ensure a favourable wind.

1870 MORRIS *Earthly Par.* III. IV. 202 From witch-wives have I bought ere now Wind-bags indeed, but yet did trow Nothing therein.

2. *fig.* (*contemptuous*). An empty pretender, or something pretentious but unsubstantial; *esp.* a voluble and senseless talker. (Cf. WIND *sb.*[1] 11 b, 14.)

1827 CARLYLE *Misc., Richter* (1869) 10 Consigned..to the Limbo appointed for all such windbags and deceptions. **1894** SALA *London up to date* II. xxii. 343 He is at best a noisy wind-bag and braggart.

3. *Naut. slang.* A sailing ship or 'windjammer'.

1924 R. CLEMENTS *Gipsy of Horn* 11 A sailing ship—an old wind-bag, as the young, up-to-date watchkeeper would call it. **1930** J. MASEFIELD *Wanderer of Liverpool* 47 A crowd of windbags moored fore and aft, to buoyed anchors. **1946** W. MCFEE *In First Watch* i. 15 He had been cook in a windbag and a sailor before the mast.

Hence **ˈwind-bagged** *a.*, furnished with a wind-bag (sense 1 a); **ˈwindˌbaggery**, inflated talk.

1606 J. REYNOLDS *Dolarnys Primerose* (1880) 118 There might be heard, the hollowe *wind bag'd droan's, with direfull roaring. **1859** SALA *Tw. round Clock* (1861) 396 Irremediably pin-perforated *windbaggery. **1920** *Sat. Westm. Gaz.* 21 May 4/2 The stunt press, which greatly prides itself on its inexhaustible windbaggery on this subject.

wind-ball (ˈwɪndbɔːl). [f. WIND *sb.*[1] + BALL *sb.*[1]] An inflated ball; a game played with such a ball by striking it with the fist.

1578 H. WOTTON *Courtlie Controv.* 264 Diuers sortes of pastimes, as the Windball, the barre, fencing [Cf. *Yver* (1599) 156 b, comme de Pallemaille, de barre, d'escrime]. **1585** HIGINS *Junius' Nomencl.* 296/1 *Follis*,..a wind ball beaten with the fists to and fro in play. **1601** W. PERCY *Cuckqueanes & Cuckolds Errants* v. iv. (Roxb.) 70 Els will wee make this thy Hed a wind Ball, to our fistes, straite.

†**wind-band**[1]. *Obs.* [f. WIND *v.*[1] + BAND *sb.*[1]] A band which is 'wound' or put around something, as the nave-band or tire of a wheel.

1313–14 *Durham Acc. Rolls* (Surtees) 512 In Hurtures, Windbandes, et Doules empt., ijs. **1350–1** *Ibid.* 551 Cum Wyndbandis factis de proprio ferro pro rotis molend. de Wystone. **1496** *Acc. Ld. High Treas. Scot.* I. 287 For iij[c] nalis to the wyndbandis. **1545** *Ibid.* VIII. 391 Ane wynd band of irne to ane of the quhelis. **1616** *Churchw. Acc. Pittington*, etc. (Surtees) 72 Thre gudgions and thre vrters and a windband. **1825** JAMIESON, *Wund-band.*

ˈwind-band[2]. [f. WIND *sb.*[1] + BAND *sb.*[3]] A band of wind-instruments, as a military band; the wind of an orchestra.

1876 [see WIND *sb.*[1] 12 b]. **1894** KAPPEY *Milit. Mus.* 87 The introduction of the clarinet into wind-bands. *Ibid.* 88 The event which had the greatest influence upon the progress of wind-bands was the French Revolution.

†**wind-beam**[1]. *Obs.* Forms: see WIND *sb.*[1] and BEAM *sb.*[1]; also 5 **wynbeme, 7 wimbeame.** [f. WIND *sb.*[1] + BEAM *sb.*[1] Cf. G. *windlatte, sturmlatte, sturmband.*] A cross-beam tying the rafters of a roof: = COLLAR-BEAM 1.

1374 in Willis & Clark *Cambridge* (1886) I. 238 Wyndbems suchlates Asthelers Corbels. *c* **1440** *Promp. Parv.* 529/1 Wyyndbeme, of a roof, *lacunar, vel laquear.* **1448** in Willis & Clark *Cambridge* (1886) II. 9 All the wynbemes shull conteyne in brede squar vj inches. **1579** *Ibid.* I. 310 Fyve windbeames to the principals eche windbeame xvij foote long ix vnche sqware. **1617** *Ibid.* 205 Principall sparrs, doble purlinges and wimbeames. **1615** CHAPMAN *Odyss.* XXII. 292 The wind-beame, that along did ron The smoaky roofe. **1703** T. N. *City & C. Purchaser* 286.

†**wind-beam**[2]. *Obs.* [f. WIND *v.*[1] + BEAM *sb.*[1]] A capstan; a windlass.

1585 HIGINS *Junius' Nomencl.* 300/1 *Ergata*,..a capstand, or windbeame, or drawbeame. **1611** COTGR. s.v. *Ergate.* **1659** HOOLE tr. *Comenius' Vis. World* (1672) 135 A Wind-Beam is a post which is turned by going about it.

wind-berry, obs. f. *winberry*, WHIMBERRY.

'**wind-bound**, *a.* [f. WIND *sb.*[1] + BOUND *ppl. a.*[2]] Detained by contrary or stormy winds.

1588 HUNSDON in *Archæologia* XXX. 169 Having been.. soe wind-bound, as he could by no meanes gett out of the haven. *c* **1645** HOWELL *Lett.* II. lx. (1890) 475 Being now wind-bound for Africk. *a* **1718** PRIOR *Mercury & Cupid* 46 No Matter tho' This Fleet be lost; Or That lie wind-bound on the Coast. **1854** H. MILLER *Sch. & Schm.* i. 9 Next morning the wind-bound vessels were crowding the harbour of refuge as before. **1875** *Zoologist* Ser. II. X. 4712 As to swallows or martins being wind-bound..I cannot entertain the idea. **1899** BRIDGES *New P., Summer-ho. Mound* 35 Brigs and barques that windbound ride At their taut cables heading to the tide.

†**b.** Stopped or rendered inaccessible by contrary winds. *Obs. rare.*

1614 GORGES *Lucan* v. 187 He findes the hauens mouth winde-bound [orig. *clausas ventis brumalibus undas*].

c. *fig.* or in fig. context.

1646 FULLER *Wounded Consc.* ix. 62 Though thou beest water-bound, be not wind-bound also. **1658–9** in *Burton's Diary* (1828) IV. 30 They, being now in possession, may be admitted, *de bene esse*; else you are wind-bound. You cannot do aught without them. **1675** COCKER *Morals* 66 Wind-bound in the port of Sorrow. **1711** ADDISON *Spect.* No. 211 ¶9 When I sit still without doing any thing, his Affairs forsooth are Wind-bound. **1779** in *Lett. Lit. Men* (Camden) 408 That the papers..he wants, lye wind-bound at Sir James Harris's. **1901** C. M. MASTERMAN *Folia Dispersa* 17 My Soul, windbound, in her dull haven lies!

'**wind-break**, *sb.* Also windbreak. [f. WIND *sb.*[1] + BREAK *sb.*[1]]

1. Something, esp. a row of trees, used to break the force of the wind, or serving as a protection against it. orig *U.S.*

1861 *Trans. Ill. Agric. Soc.* IV. 479 These trees, which are valuable as shade and wind-breaks, should be planted. **1868** *Rep. U.S. Comm. Agric.* (1869) 196 Among evergreen plants the Norway spruce (*Abies excelsa*) is the most valuable where a high, strong wind-break is necessary. **1883** W. H. BISHOP in *Harper's Mag.* Mar. 502/1 A young orchard.., sheltered by a wind-break of three rows of ash-trees. **1894** *Chamb. Jrnl.* 7 July 425 The margin of virgin hummock left standing to act as a wind-break. **1910** W. SCHLICH *Man. Forestry* (ed. 4) II. 123 Species with a thin crown are indifferently adapted for wind breaks. **1934** *Times Educ. Suppl.* 10 Feb. p. iv/3 Whether as ornament or to secure privacy, as a windbreak or to indicate a boundary, a hedge has its place in most gardens. **1950** *N.Z. Jrnl. Agric.* July 5/3 Such a wind-break is very valuable for sheltering dipped sheep. **1962** *Coast to Coast 1961–62* 138 An old limestone place, with a slate roof, and a windbreak of pepper-trees at one side. **1968** *Southerly* XXVIII. 172 The pine trees acted as a wind-break for the solitary house set a hundred yards lower down. **1970** J. H. B. PEEL *Country Folk* ii. 38 A hedge serves as a windbreak for crops and as a nesting-place for birds. **1975** *Toronto Star* 27 Dec. D4/1 So except in balmy weather, be sure to tote a plastic or canvas wind-break. **1981** *Farmstead Mag.* Winter 49/1 Some people prefer deciduous trees in all or part of the windbreak.

2. A rippling change of colour produced by the wind passing over foliage. *nonce-use.*

1892 STEVENSON *Across the Plains* 205 The silver wind-breaks run among the olives.

'**wind-break**, *v. rare.* [f. WIND *sb.*[1] 11 d + BREAK *v.* 12 b.] *trans.* To break the wind of, render broken-winded.

1638 FORD *Fancies* II. ii, 'Twould wind-breake a moyle, or a ring'd mare, to vie burthens with her.

So '**wind-,broken**, *a.* = BROKEN-WINDED.

1603 FLORIO *Montaigne* II. xvii. 373 A restie and wind-broken jade. **1667** *Phil. Trans.* II. 545 A wind-broken Dog or Horse. **1708** *Lond. Gaz.* No. 4453/4 Stoln.., one large black Mare,..Wind broken. **1805** C. JAMES *Milit. Dict.* (ed. 2). **1851** MAYNE REID *Scalp Hunters* xxiii, She [*sc.* the mare] was badly wind-broken.

wind-cutter ('wɪnd,kʌtə(r)). [f. WIND *sb.*[1] + CUTTER *sb.*[1]] One who or that which cuts the wind, in various senses.

†**a.** (See quot. 1611.) **b.** *slang.* A broad-brimmed hat. **c.** The lip of an organ-pipe, against which the wind strikes so as to make it sound (Knight *Dict. Mech.* 1875).

1611 COTGR., *Taille-vent*, a wind-cutter; an idle, or fond swaggerer. *c* **1823** SURTEES in *Mem.* (Surtees Soc.) 250 The ghost of a prebendary would be nothing without a wind-cutter and rose. **1886** DOWDEN *Shelley* I. i. 21 His face.. surmounted by the venerable 'wind-cutter', or cocked-hat.

wind-door, †wind-dore.

Pseudo-etymologizing of WINDOW *sb.* Cf. WINDORE.

1606 J. DAVIES (Heref.) *Bien Venu* ii, Ope those wind-dores. **1659** H. L'ESTRANGE *Alliance Div. Off.* 317 When so many wind-dores are open, the cold air..is ready to enter. [**1671** SKINNER *Etymol. Ling. Angl., Window*, Fenestra, melius efferunt Linc. agri incolæ *Windore*, q.d. Venti Janua, v. Wind & Dore.] **1828** *Craven Gloss., Winder*, a window. Our Craven corruption approaches much nearer the presumed etymology, *wind-door.* **1836** SMART *Dict.*, *Window*, a *wind door* or aperture to admit air into the building.

'**wind-down.** *colloq.* [f. vbl. phr. *to wind down*: see WIND *v.*[1] 21.] The process of bringing or coming to an end; a gradual reduction in scale.

1969 *Time* 21 Feb. 29 The campaign heralds the official wind-down of the Cultural Revolution, a finale that is to climax in 'all-round victory'. **1971** *New Scientist* 8 July 95/3 The reduction in the number of students.., the cutback in ..spending, the cancellation of the SST, the wind-down of space exploration, [etc.]. **1971** *Guardian Weekly* 25 Dec. 3 Even now, with the virtual completion of the wind-down begun in 1970, the military break with Indochina is not complete.

'**wind-drift.** *rare.* [f. WIND *sb.*[1] + DRIFT *sb.*]

a. A drift or current of wind.

1887 MORRIS *Odyssey* XI. 400 With the wind-drift stirred against thee, and the whirl-blast laden with woe. **1921** *Discovery* Apr. 89/2 The drifts of vessels in the ice..show.. a wind-drift which can be paralleled in all the other oceans.

b. The action of wind currents, esp. on water.

1898 *Geogr. Jrnl.* June 662 The sand so produced is rounded by wind-drift in an unmistakable manner, the grains being entirely different from those of sea-sand. **1964** *Oceanogr. & Marine Biol.* II. 257 This patch [of effluent] is subject to wind-drift and can be carried directly on to beaches. **1967** *Ibid.* V. 103 Since the cross sections of these two straits are much less than that of the throat of the Celtic Sea much surface wind drift water must return to the Atlantic some other way.

'**wind-,driven**, *ppl. a.* Also 4 -dryve, -drive. [f. WIND *sb.*[1] + DRIVEN.] Driven, carried, impelled, or propelled by the wind.

1387 TREVISA *Higden* (Rolls) VI. 137 Seyllynge in þe see he was wynd dryven into Affrica. **1390** GOWER *Conf.* III. 49 Wynddrive he was al soudeinly Upon the strondes of Cilly. *c* **1595** CAPT. WYATT *R. Dudley's Voy. W. Ind.* (Hakl. Soc.) 16 Huge mountaines of windedriven sandes. *a* **1604** HANMER *Chron. Irel.* (1809) 174 Certaine tall ships of theirs were wind-driven thither. **1629** H. BURTON *Truth's Tri.* 345 St. Iames compares the faithlesse man to the winde-driuen waue. *a* **1680** BUTLER *Rem., Refl. Milford-Haven* (1759) I. 412 That Enemy, that would invade it, and were wind-driven on the British Coast. **1787** BURNS *Extempore in Crt. Sess.* ii, Like wind-driv'n hail, it did assail. **1859** H. KINGSLEY *G. Hamlyn* xliv, The harbour was a sheet of wind-driven foam. **1900** H. SUTCLIFFE *Shameless Wayne* i, To brush away a cobweb, wind-driven against her cheek. **1906** CORNFORD *Defenceless Islands* 75 Ships, coal-driven instead of wind-driven.

winded ('wɪndɪd), *a.* [f. WIND *sb.*[1] + -ED[2].] Having wind, i.e. (usually) breath, of a specified kind or in a specified condition: chiefly in parasynthetic combinations, as BROKEN-WINDED, LONG-WINDED, SHORT-WINDED; also †**calm-winded** = in which the wind, i.e. the air, is calm.

c **1440** *Pallad. on Husb.* I. 49 The longis hool and wynded with the best. **1470–85** MALORY *Arthur* X. lviii. 512 The clenest myȝted man and the best wynded of his age that was on lyue. *Ibid.* lxii. 521 At the last sir Palomydes waxed bygge and better wynded. **1577** GRANGE *Golden Aphrod.* N j b, Making as heauenly a noyse as doth an arbor of Nightingales in a calme winded night. **1736** BRACKEN *Farriery* (1757) II. 15 A Sign of a good winded Horse.

winded, *ppl. a.*[1] [f. WIND *v.*[2] + -ED[1].]

1. ('wɪndɪd) Exposed to wind or air; *spec.* spoilt or tainted by exposure to air.

1595 [see WINDEDNESS]. **1824** CARR *Craven Gloss., Winded*, dry. **1840** *Civil Eng. & Arch. Jrnl.* III. 68/2 The same changes are sometimes produced by other causes, when the coal is said to be winded. **1847** HALLIWELL, *Winded*, said of meat hung up when it becomes puffed and rancid. **1887** *Jamieson's Sc. Dict.* Suppl.

2. ('waɪndɪd) Sounded with the breath, blown, as a wind-instrument.

1622 DRAYTON *Poly-olb.* xxvi. 320 His fellowes winded Horne not one of them but knew. **1805** SCOTT *Last Minstr.* IV. xii, Little care we for thy winded horn. **1820** —— *Abbot* iii, A winded bugle.

3. ('wɪndɪd) Put out of breath, breathless, 'blown', 'puffed'.

1883 'MARK TWAIN' *Life on Miss.* iii. 49 They couldn't keep that up very long without getting winded. **1897** *Outing* (U.S.) XXIX. 596/1 My pursuers..imparted a prodigious lashing to their winded mustangs. **1919** *Chamb. Jrnl.* Aug. 520/2 A ten-foot leap, easy enough on the flat, but with a difficult 'take off' for a winded man.

Hence '**windedness**, tainted condition (see 1).

1595 DUNCAN *App. Etym.* (E.D.S.) 73/1 *Rancor*, vitium carnis, windednes.

winded ('waɪndɪd), *ppl. a.*[2] *rare.* [wk. pa. pple. of WIND *v.*[1]] Wound *up*.

1642 H. MORE *Song of Soul* I. II. lv, My fairly winded up clew.

wind-egg ('wɪndɛg). [f. WIND *sb.*[1] + EGG *sb.* Cf. G., LG., Du. *windei.*] An imperfect or unproductive egg, esp. one with a soft shell, such as may be laid by hens and other domestic birds.

1398 TREVISA *Barth. De P.R.* XIX. lxxix. (Add. MS. 27944), Wynde eyren beþ litel and vnsauory... And suche eyren beþ yfounde in hennes & gees. **1577** GOOGE *Heresbach's Husb.* 169 The Hennes wyl treade one the others, but theyr Egges neuer come to good, but are wind Egges. **1611** COTGR., *Harde*,..an egge laied with a soft skin, or filme (about it) in stead of a shell; a soft-sheld egge; a wind egge. **1741** J. MARTYN *Virg. Georg.* III. 273 *note*, Varro affirms it as a certain truth, that about Lisbon some mares conceive by the wind, at a certain season, as hens conceive what is called a wind egg. **1844** H. STEPHENS *Bk. Farm* II. 721 Hens will lay what are called wind eggs, that is, eggs without a hardened shell. **1893** NEWTON *Dict. Birds* 198 Want of calcareous food may explain the soft-shelled or 'wind' eggs.

b. *fig.*

a **1616** BEAUM. & FL. *Wit without M.* I. i, Other men with all their delicates, and healthfull diets, can get but winde egges. **1645** MILTON *Colast.* 3 From such a wind-egg of definition as this, they who expect any of his other arguments to bee well hatcht [etc.]. **1661** STILLINGFL. *Irenicum* II. vi. §2. 237 The pretended division of Provinces so early among the Apostles, is only the wind-egge of a working fancy, that wants shell of reason to cover it. **1826** BEDDOES *Let. to T. F. Kelsall* 5 Oct., Here is a Dr. Raupach who lays a tragedy or two in the year—mostly windeggs.

windego, obs. var. WINDIGO.

windell, obs. form of WINDLE.

winder ('waɪndə(r)), *sb.*[1] [f. WIND *v.*[1] + -ER[1]. (14th c. AF. had *gyndour, gwynder* in senses 1 and 2. Later Fr. had *guindre* 'a reele, or wheel to wind silke on', Cotgr.)] A person or thing that winds, in various senses.

I. Senses denoting persons.

1. One who turns or manages a winch or windlass, esp. at a mine; a windlass-man.

1747 HOOSON *Miner's Dict.* K iij b, Upon the Stoblade which the Winder stands to draw at, there is a Hole bored through, just below the Spindle. **1809** *Ann. Reg.* (1821) 867 The miners in the work, and the winders at the mouth of the pit. **1899** *Edin. Rev.* Jan. 124 Coalowners cannot work their mines without hewers and winders.

2. An operative employed in winding wool, etc.

1552 HULOET, Wynder of thread or yarne. **1599** T. M[OUFET] *Silkwormes* 69 What neede I count how many winders liue, How many twisters eke, and weauers thriue Vppon this trade? **1662** *Act 14 Chas. II*, c. 15 §5 Whereas there is a necessity lying upon the Silke throwers to deliver to theire Winders or Doublers considerable quantities of silke. **1751** DEERING *Nottingham* 72 Almost every Seamer, Sizer, and Winder, will have her Tea. **1818** *Min. Evid. Committee Ribbon Weavers* 7 What can a common winder earn?—Three shillings. What a quill winder?—Four shillings. **1828** T. ALLEN *York* II. 312 If they take away their work from carders and spinners, they return it them back ten-fold as winders, warpers, weavers. **1879** *Cassell's Techn. Educ.* VIII. 128/2 The winders, who put the silk, cotton, or thread on the bobbins.

3. One who winds a clock or other mechanism.

1823 MRS. SMYTH in J. A. Heraud *Voy. & Mem. Midshipman* viii. (1837) 128 William aspired sometime ago to the honour of winding up the chronometers, when Mr. Graves, the regular winder, happened to be absent. **1881** *Instr. Census Clerks* (1885) 46 Jobber and Winder (Clock).

II. Senses denoting things.

†**4. a.** A tendril of a climbing plant. **b.** A twining plant. *Obs.*

1577 GOOGE tr. *Heresbach's Husb.* 33 b, The one sort [of Pease]..runneth vp vppon sticks, to whiche with little wynders he bindeth hym selfe. **1626** BACON *Sylva* §536 Winders, and Creepers; As Iuy, Briony, Hops, Woodbine. **1673–4** GREW *Anat. Pl.* (1682) 136 The Wood of all Convolvula's [*sic*] or Winders.

5. An apparatus (of various kinds) for winding something, or upon which something is wound or coiled; *e.g.* a winch or windlass, or the crank or handle of one; a reel or spool, or a stick or strip of something serving as a substitute.

1585 HIGINS *Junius' Nomencl.* 300/2 *Succula*,..a winder or rather the ouerthwart barrel turned with leauers. **1657** T. BARKER *Art of Angling* (1659) 25 You must have your winder within two foot of the bottom to goe on your [salmon-]rod made in this manner, with a spring. **1677** MOXON *Mech. Exerc.* iii. 37 The Winch, or Winder, or Handle, the Iron part is the Winder, the Wood the Handle. **1773** W. EMERSON *Princ. Mech.* (ed. 3) 284 *Winder*, a winch or handle to wind about. **1825** J. NICHOLSON *Oper. Mech.* 369 The reel or winder being now withdrawn, the coil of paper is cut on both sides. **1843** *Civil Eng. & Arch. Jrnl.* VI. 213/2 Attached to the heads of these posts are a number of winders for stretching the wires.

6. A key for winding a jack, clock, or other mechanism. Also *attrib.* in **winder-hole**, the hole through which the key is passed in winding.

1606 CHAPMAN *Gentl. Usher* III. ii. 25 Even as in that queint engine you have seene A little man in shreds stand at the winder. **1686** PLOT *Staffordsh.* 387 The coard *i*, that is wound round the wheel *k*, by a key or winder applyed to the Axis *l*. **1729** SWIFT *Direct. Serv.* ii. (1745) 41 Always leave the Winder sticking on the Jack. **1837** BARHAM *Ingol. Leg.* Ser. I. *Look at the Clock*, The two little winder-holes turned into eyes. **1884** BRITTEN *Watch & Clockm.* 293 Clock keys are often spoken of as winders.

7. A winding step in a staircase: usually in *pl.*, opp. to *flyers* (see FLYER 4 b).

1667 [see FLYER 4 b]. **1808** P. NICHOLSON *Carpenter's New Guide* (ed. 2) Pl. 53 A dogleg Stair Case with Winders. **1823** —— *Pract. Builder* 185 When the treads of the steps diminish in breadth toward the well-hole, the steps are called winders. **1838** LOUDON *Suburban Gard.* 45 The best staircases are those without winders.

III. 8. ***winder-up***: †(*a*) something that concludes an argument; (*b*) one who winds up a business.

1795 PAINE *Age of Reason* II. 78 The lying imposition of Isaiah to Ahaz..has been perverted, and made to serve as a winder-up. **1921** W. DE MORGAN *Old Man's Youth* xviii, I heard the expression 'men of straw' used more than once by winders-up, or victims.

'winder, *sb.*[2] [f. WIND *v.*[2] + -ER[1].]

1. ('waɪndə(r)) One who blows a wind-instrument.

1611 FLORIO, *Cornettáro*, a Cornet-maker or winder. **1818** KEATS *Endym.* I. 281 Winder of the horn, When snouted wild-boars routing tender corn Anger our hunts-men.

2. ('wɪndə(r)) a. Something that takes one's breath away; a blow that 'knocks the wind' out of one; a run, climb, or other exertion that puts one out of breath. *colloq.*

1825 C. M. WESTMACOTT *Engl. Spy* (1907) I. 158, I did give her [*sc.* a mare] a winder,..to be sure, only one day's hunting, though, a good hard run over Somerset range. **1828** *Blackw. Mag.* XXIV. 212 Do you put it [*sc.* your hand] across your breast in case of an unexpected winder from your apparently peaceable acquaintance? **1861** DICKENS *Gt. Expect.* v, It was a run indeed now, and what Joe called, in the only two words he spoke all the time, 'a Winder'. **1866** C. BROOKE *10 Yrs. Sarāwak* I. 246 We had to ascend a hill of 500 feet high... This was a winder.

b. *fig.* †*spec.* a sentence of transportation for life (*obs. slang*).

1812 J. H. VAUX *Vocab. Flash Lang.* in *Mem.* (1964) 279 A man transported for his natural life, is said..to have *knap'd a winder*. **1836** J. F. O'CONNELL *Residence in New Holland* 37 Previous convictions and character must have affected his sentence, as it was, in flash phraseology, a winder. **1913** D. H. LAWRENCE *Sons & Lovers* ix. 243 It's a winder when you have to pour your own tea out—an' nobody to grouse if you team it in your saucer and sup it up.

'winder, *sb.*[3] *rare.* [f. WIND *v.*[3] + -ER[1].] A winnower.

1570 DRANT *Serm.* D vij b, Mowers, threshers, winders and grinders.

winder ('wɪndə(r)), *sb.*[4] *dial.* Also 7 **whinder**, 9 **windar**. [a. early Flem. *winder*, *wender* 'anas mas' (Kilian).] A widgeon.

1542 in *Househ. Ord.* (1790) 223 Item, Winders, the doz. 2 s. 4 d. **1668** CHARLETON *Onomast.* 100 *Boscas*..the whinder. **1672** *Brasenose Coll. Oxf. Bills* 23. 130 (MS.), Pulitz, 3 whinder 2 s. 9 d. **1719** D'URFEY *Pills* III. 322 But George he cut the Dragon up, as 't had bin Duck or Winder. **1803-4** in Col. Hawker *Diary* (1893) II. 358 Windar (i.e. wigeon diver or dunbird). **1887** *Kentish Gloss.*

winder ('wɪndə(r)), *sb.*[5] Repr. dial. or slovenly pronunc. of WINDOW *sb.* Also in *Comb.*

1683 G. M[ERITON] *Yorks. Dial.* 8 Nan steeke'th winder-board, and mack it darke. **1838** DICKENS *Nickleby* (1839) viii. 69 We go upon the practical mode of teaching, Nickleby;..W-i-n, win, d-e-r, der, winder, a casement. **1877** J. HARTLEY *Halifax Clock Almanack* 43 Sam made a grab at it, an it flew to th' winder-bottom. **1901** M. FRANKLIN *My Brilliant Career* xxxii. 272 Lizer, shut the winder quick. **1935** D. L. SAYERS *Gaudy Night* xvii. 372 Winderpane, we called 'im, along of the eyeglass, but meanin' no disrespect. **1976** *Trans. Yorks. Dial. Soc.* XIV. 37 Ah've just been cleeanin' t'winders.

winder ('wɪndə(r)), *v. Obs.* exc. *dial.* Also 7 **whinder**. [Origin unknown. Cf. WINDLE *v.*[3]]

1. *intr.* To wither; to pine or waste *away*.

1600 HOLLAND *Livy* II. xxiii. 58 Until at length his bodie also began to winder away in a consumption. **1601** —— *Pliny* VII. ii. I. 155.

†2. *trans.* To crush into fragments. *Obs.*

1610 HOLLAND *Camden's Brit.* II. 154 By the fall of a towre [he] was crushed and whindred to death [orig. *compressus & comminutus*].

winder, winderous: see WONDER, WONDROUS.

†**'windermost**, *a. Obs.* [f. WIND *sb.*[1], after *hindermost*, *innermost*, etc.] Furthest to windward.

1622 R. HAWKINS *Voy. S. Sea* (1847) 202 For that the windermost shippe, by opening her sayle, may be upon the other before shee be looked for. **1702** *Lond. Gaz.* No. 3838/1 The Fire of the Cannon began at the Windermost Fort at Nevis. **1707** *Treas. Papers* CIII. 212 b (P.R.O.) This being the windermost, best, and Richest Island, tis most likely they will attack this first.

windes, windewe: see WINDAS, WINDOW.

windfall ('wɪndfɔːl). Forms: see WIND *sb.*[1] and FALL *sb.*[1]; also 5 **wynfall**, 6 **wyndefale**, **winde faulle**. [perh. of foreign origin; cf. MHG. *wintval* (G. *windfall*): see WIND *sb.*[1], FALL *sb.*[1]]

1. Something blown down by the wind, or the fall of something so blown down: a. a tree or branch, or a number of trees or branches; *spec.* (chiefly *U.S.*) a heap or tract of fallen trees blown down by a tornado. Also in fig. context.

1464 *Rolls of Parlt.* V. 540/2 Trees Boghes and Woode called Wyndfalles. *a* **1552** LELAND *Itin.* (1769) V. 91 How or when thes Trees cam doune other be Cutting or Wind Faulle no Manne ther can telle. **1582** STANYHURST *Æneis* II. (Arb.) 53 Downe tears yt wyndfals, and thick woods sturdelye tumbleth. **1602** in G. P. Scrope *Castle Combe* (1852) 334 Les mortuos arbores, Anglicè the starveling trees and wyndfalls. **1625** BACON *Ess.*, *Greatness Kingd.* (Arb.) 479 The Spartans..when they did spread, and their Boughs were becommen too great, for their Stem, they became a Windfall vpon the suddaine. **1664** EVELYN *Sylva* xxxii. 109 That no unnecessary Imbezelment be made by pretences of Repair of Paling, Lodges, Browse for Deer, &c., Wind-falls, Root-falls. **1772** FORSTER in *Phil. Trans.* LXII. 376 They do not burrow under ground, but live..under wind-falls and roots of trees. **1784** BELKNAP in *Belknap Papers* (1877) II. 177 We kept one man before, with an ax, to cut away windfalls. **1830** GALT *Lawrie T.* III. v, Through the windfalls and the openings of the settlement, the rising sun was beginning to silver the leaves. **1866** R. D. CRAIG *Trees & Woods* 123 If the windfall be of trees which are not timber in their nature. **1872** *Builder* 7 Dec. 964/2 The village constable..charged her with picking up a few rotten windfalls from the trees.

b. fruit from a tree or bush (*rarely* flowers).

a **1592** GREENE *Orpharion* (1599) 49 If Roses be not gathered in the bud, they either wither or proue windfalls. **1604** N. F. *Fruiterers Secr.* 12 They which fall before the time of gathering, as wind-falles. **1661** M. STEVENSON *Twelve Moneths* 42 The wind begins to bluster among the Apples,..and the wind-falls are gathered to fill the Pies for the houshold. **1705** E. WARD *Hud. Rediv.* II. 17 The grizly Boar is hunting round; To see what Windfals may be found. **1768** PENNANT *Brit. Zool.* I. 42 They will reject the fruit that has lain but a few hours on the ground, and continue on the watch..for a fresh wind-fall. **1802** W. FORSYTH *Fruit Trees* vii. 99 When the men numbered the Pears, there was near a barrowful of wind-falls at the bottom of the old tree. **1880** JEFFERIES *Gt. Estate* x. 197 Heaps of the windfalls collected there to wait for the cider-mill.

2. *fig.* A casual or unexpected acquisition or advantage.

1542 UDALL *Erasm. Apoph.* 321 b, After beeyng come to a good wyndefall of inheritaunce. **1603** HOLLAND *Plutarch's Mor.* 1237 This man..who otherwise before-time was but poore and needy, by these windfalles and unexpected cheats became very wealthy. **1647** N. BACON *Disc. Govt. Eng.* I. xvi. 50 Where ever neighbouring Princes of their own Nation watched for the windfals of Crowns. **1706** PHILLIPS (ed. Kersey), *Wind-fall*,..some Estate or Profit unexpectedly come to one. **1802** MARIA EDGEWORTH *Moral T.*, *Forester* xix, Where he..kept little windfalls, that came to him by the negligence of customers—..loose silver, odd gloves, &c. **1822** HAZLITT *Table-t.* Ser. II. iv. 70 These and many more wind-falls of character he gave us in thought, word, and action. **1897** MRS. OLIPHANT *Blackw. & Sons* xix. II. 256 Mr. Langford..was a most unusual windfall to drop thus casually into the new concern.

3. a. *attrib.* (from 1): That is a windfall; blown down by the wind: = next. Also *fig.* (from 2): Casual, 'chance'. Applied (*poet.*[−1]) to a flood of unexpected light.

1465 MARG. PASTON in *P. Lett.* II. 176 Ther is wynfall wod at the maner that is of noo gret valewe. **1589** *Shuttleworths' Acc.* (Chetham Soc.) 93 For barke of a wyndfolle trie at Smytheles vj[d]. **1594** MARLOWE & NASHE *Dido* I, You shall haue leaues and windfall bowes enow. **1762** in *Sixth Rep. Dep. Kpr.* App. II. 132 The Wood called Browsings, Windfall Wood, and Dead Wood. **1845** S. JUDD *Margaret* II. i, All wind-fall comers here seem to be without names. **1860** *All Year Round* No. 74. 560 The windfall fruit in his uncle's garden. **1882** BESANT *All Sorts* xii, Early August apples, and windfall pears. **1945** DYLAN THOMAS *Fern Hill* in *Horizon* Oct. 221 And once below a time I lordly had the trees and leaves Trail with daisies and barley Down the rivers of the windfall light.

b. Special Comb. **windfall profit** *Econ.*, unexpectedly large or unforeseen profit; similarly ***windfall gain, loss***, etc.

1936 J. M. KEYNES *Gen. Theory Employment* II. vi. 57 The change in the value of the equipment, due to unforeseen changes in market values, exceptional obsolescence or destruction..may be called the *windfall loss*. *Ibid.* v. xx. 288 The windfall gain will wholly accrue to those entrepreneurs who happen to possess products at a relatively advanced stage of production. **1951** SLOAN & ZURCHER *Dict. Economics* 266 *Windfall profit*, a profit in excess of that which can be considered normal. **1973** *Times* 21 Dec. 6/7 A proposal for Congress to impose 'an emergency windfall profits tax' on the oil company. Although President Nixon himself told the American consumer, 'there will be no windfall profits at their expense.' **1977** *N.Y. Rev. Bks.* 26 May 31/4 The shift to free market pricing would give the oil companies windfall profits.

'wind-fallen, *a.* [f. as prec. + FALLEN *ppl. a.*] Blown down by the wind.

1612 DRAYTON *Poly-olb.* xiii. 182 To gather wind-falne sticks. *a* **1678** in *Evelyn's Pomona* 406 That the Fruit be carefully gather'd, not windfall'n nor bruis'd. **1792** BELKNAP *Hist. New Hampsh.* III. 155 They take advantage of wind-fallen trees. **1836** MRS. C. P. TRAILL *Backw. Canada* 201 Some of the stumps of these wind-fallen trees.

fig. **1563** WINȜET tr. *Vincent. Lirin.* Ded., Wks. II. 10 Ane of our windfallin brethir, laitlie snapperit in the cummerance of Caluin. **1660** TATHAM *Rump* II. i. 18 *Lady Bertlam.* 'Twill get her nothing, She beats against the Wind. *Prissilla.* She's Wind fall'n.

'wind-flower. [Turner's rendering of L. *anemōnē*, Gr. ἀνεμώνη; see ANEMONE. Cf. MHG., G. *windblume*.] The wood-anemone (*Anemone nemorosa*), or any plant or flower of the genus *Anemone*.

1551 TURNER *Herbal* I. C v b, Anemone hath the name in Greke of wynde, because the floure neuer openeth it selfe, but when the wynde bloweth..: it may be called wynde floure. **1650** [W. HOWE] *Phytol. Brit.* 8 The wood Anemone or Windfloure. **1714** tr. *Joutel's Jrnl. Voy. Mexico* (1719) 66 A Sort of purple wind Flowers. **1820** SHELLEY *Sensit. Pl.* I. 17 The pied wind-flowers and the tulip tall. **1852** WHITTIER *April* 5 Where wind-flower and violet..On south-sloping brooksides should smile in the light. **1898** A. AUSTIN *Lamia's Winter Quarters* 69 The Apennine windflower.

b. A name for species of gentian. (Cf. *lung-flower*, LUNG 7.)

1866 in *Treas. Bot.*

†**windfucker.** *Obs.* [Cf. '*Fuckwind*, a species of hawk. *North*.' (Halliwell).]

1. A name for the kestrel: cf. WINDHOVER.

1599 NASHE *Lenten Stuffe* 49 The kistrilles or windfuckers that filling themselues with winde, fly against the winde euermore.

2. *fig.* as a term of opprobrium.

1602 *Narcissus* MS. Rawl. Poet. 212, lf. 80, I tell you, my little windfuckers, had not a certaine melancholye ingendred with a nippinge dolour overshadowed the sunne shine of my mirthe, I had beene I pre, sequor, one of your consorte. **1609** B. JONSON *Silent Wom.* I. iv. (1620) C 3 b, Did you euer heare such a Wind-fucker, as this? *c* **1611** CHAPMAN *Iliad* Pref. A 4, There is a certaine enuious Windfucker, that houers vp and downe, laboriously ingrossing al the air with his luxurious ambition. *a* **1616** BEAUM. & FL. *Wit without M.* IV. i, Husbands for Whores and Bawdes, away you wind-suckers [*sic ed.* 1639].

windgall[1] ('wɪndgɔːl). Forms: see WIND *sb.*[1] and GALL *sb.*[2]; also 7 **-gaul**. A soft tumour on either side of a horse's leg just above the fetlock, caused by distension of the synovial bursa.

1523-34 FITZHERB. *Husb.* §99 Wyndgalles is a lyghte sorance, and commeth of great labour. **1596** SHAKS. *Tam. Shr.* III. ii. 53 Full of Windegalls, sped with Spauins. **1607** MARKHAM *Cavel.* VII. 78 Windgalls are little blebs raisd vp by extreame trauel on each side the horses Fetlockes. **1690** DRYDEN *Don Sebastian* I. i, Feel his Legs, Master, neither Splint, Spavin, nor Wind gall. **1714** *Lond. Gaz.* No. 5195/4 Windgalls on both Heels of her hinder Feet. **1766** GOLDSM. *Vicar W.* xiv, A third perceived he had a windgall, and would bid no money. **1846** J. BAXTER *Libr. Pract. Agric.* (ed. 4) I. 448 Wind-galls of the knee-joint.

Hence **windgalled** (-gɔːld) *a.*, affected with a windgall or windgalls.

1665 BRATHWAIT *Comm. Two Tales* 36 The Love of his dear Alyson..quickens his wind-gall'd feet. **1674** *Lond. Gaz.* No. 926/4 Her off Leg before Wind-gaulled. **1705** *Ibid.* 4159/4 A black Gelding,..Wind-gall'd in all his Legs. **1805** C. JAMES *Milit. Dict.* (ed. 2) s.v. *Wind-gall*, Long-jointed horses are apt to be wind-galled.

'wind-gall[2]. [Cf. G. *windgalle*, *-gelle*, and WATER-GALL, WEATHER-GALL.] A fragment of a rainbow or of a prismatically-coloured halo, supposed to presage windy weather: = WEATHER-GALL.

1823 J. F. COOPER *Pilot* I. ii. 19 There be streaked wind-galls in the offing, that speak..plainly..to shorten sail. **1840** F. D. BENNETT *Whaling Voy.* I. 3 We noticed the phenomenon named by nautical men a 'wind-gall'..or 'sun-dog'. **1860** FITZ-ROY in *Merc. Marine Mag.* VII. 344.

'wind-gauge, -gage. [f. WIND *sb.*[1] + GAUGE.]

I. †1. = Weather-gage: see WEATHER *sb.* 8 and GAUGE *sb.* 5 a. *Obs. rare.*

1652 *French Occurrences* 29 Nov.–6 Dec. 214 They were got up neer the Ness-point, ours keeping still the wind-gage.

II. 2. = ANEMOMETER I.

1774 *Phil. Trans.* LXIV. 426 To which may be added, the rain-gage, wind-gage, &c. **1815** J. SMITH *Panorama Sci. & Art* II. 38 The Anemometer, or Wind-Gauge. **1883** GRESLEY *Gloss. Coal-m.*, *Wind-gauge*, an anemometer for testing the velocity of the wind in mines.

3. A graduated attachment to the sights of a gun, to enable allowance to be made for the effect of the wind on the projectile. Also *attrib.*

1862 *Catal. Internat. Exhib.* II. xi. 7 Small bore, ·451 rifle with wind gauge sight and movable shade. **1909** STACPOOLE *Pools of Silence* iv, His telescopic sights and wind-gauges are second to none in the world.

4. = ANEMOMETER 2.

1876 [see ANEMOMETER 2]. **1881** W. E. DICKSON *Organ-Build.* ix. 121.

†**'wind-gun.** *Obs.* [f. WIND *sb.*[1] + GUN *sb.*] A gun for shooting a missile by the force of compressed air: = AIR-GUN.

1644 DIGBY *Nat. Bodies* xii. §6. 104 The experience of windgunnes assureth vs that ayre duly applyed is able to giue greater motion vnto heauy bodies then vnto light ones. **1728** POPE *Dunc.* I. 181 As, forc'd from wind-guns, lead itself can fly. **1779** *Phil. Trans.* LXIX. 399 That air compressed to one tenth in a wind gun possesses a power not much short of gunpowder. **1800** *Sporting Mag.* XVI. 273 It will not be out of place here to add some remarks on wind-guns.

fig. **1663** COWLEY *Cutter Coleman St.* Prol., They [*sc.* critics] shoot, alas, with Wind-gunns, charg'd with Air. **1680** *Collect. Poems* 190, I am one of those that have been shot at by Wind-Guns, which have prejudiced my Reputation. **1781** COWPER *Conversat.* 274 His whisper'd theme, dilated and at large, Proves after all a wind-gun's airy charge.

windhover ('wɪnd,hɒvə(r), -,hʌvə(r)). Also 7 **windover**. [f. WIND *sb.*[1] + HOVER *v.*] A name for the kestrel, from its habit of hovering or hanging in the air with its head to the wind. Also *attrib.*

1674 RAY *Collect., Engl. Birds* 82 The Kestrell or Stannel, in some places the Windover. **1738** ALBIN *Nat. Hist. Birds* III. 5 The Windhover Cock. **1778** G. WHITE *Selborne, To Barrington* 7 Aug., The kestrel, or windhover, has a peculiar mode of hanging in the air in one place, his wings all the while being briskly agitated. **1864** TENNYSON *Aylmer's Field* 321 For about as long As the wind-hover hangs in balance.

1884 *19th Cent.* Aug. 331 The windhover hawk poising at mid-distance above his quarry.

†**windi**, *a. Obs.* Also **wundi**. [perh. related to the stem of WEND *v.*; cf. OHG. *wendig* (MHG. *wendic, -ec*) devoid (of), exempt (from).] Devoid *of*; quit *of*.

a **1225** *Leg. Kath.* 376 Ha beoð al witlese, & windi [*v.r.* wundi] of wisdom. *a* **1225** *Juliana* 10 ȝef þu wult leauen þe lahen þat tu list in..ichulle wel neomen þe; ȝef þu nult no, þu art wundi [*v.r.* windi] of me.

Windic, var. WENDIC.

Windies ('wɪndɪz), *sb. pl. colloq.* (orig. *Austral.*). [Contraction of *West Indies*.] West Indians, *spec.* the West Indian cricket team; also, immigrants from the West Indies.

1965 W. GROUT *My Country's Keeper* 69 The Australian public..took the Windies to their hearts from that moment. **1971** J. BRUNNER *Honky in Woodpile* ii. 15 Skinheads and others were out bashing Pakis and Windies. **1976** *Sunday Tel.* 4 Jan. 52 Windies roll with brutal pace beating. **1980** *Economist* 21 June 51/1 Would the West Indies beat England in the first Test match?.. In the cricket match, the 'Windies' scraped home in a nail-biting finish.

windigo ('wɪndɪgəʊ). Also 9 **weendego(ag, wendigo; wihtigo, witiko**, etc.; and with capital initial. [Ojibwa *wintiko*, pl. *wintikok*; some spellings reflect the Cree cognate *wihtikow*.] In the folklore of the northern Algonquian Indians: a cannibalistic giant, the transformation of a person who has eaten human flesh.

1714 J. KNIGHT *Jrnl.* 7 Oct. in W. Cowan *Papers of Seventh Algonquian Conference 1975* (1976) 21 Some Indians came from Fort Nelson who says they saw a Whitego wch is an Apparition. **1830** E. JAMES *Narr. John Tanner* 316 The Muskegoes, who inhabit the low and cheerless swamps on the borders of Hudson's Bay, and are themselves reproached by the other tribes as cannibals, are said to live in constant fear of the Weendegoag. **1847** J. B. NEVINS *Two Voyages* 115 When Windego saw him, he was very angry, and said, 'What do you mean, boy, by coming out and making that noise? I am going to eat you.' **1859** P. KANE *Wanderings of Artist among Indians N. Amer.* 60 The Weendigoes are looked upon with superstitious dread and horror by all Indians. **1924** *Chambers's Jrnl.* Mar. 170/1 At midnight they were wakened by what Jacques took to be a wendigo in the woods behind. **1933** J. M. COOPER in *Primitive Man* Jan. 20 The Cree Witiko Psychosis... This peculiar form of mental disturbance is characterized by (1) a craving for human flesh, and (2) a delusion of transformation into a Witiko who has a heart of ice or who vomits ice. **1934** *Jrnl. Abnormal & Social Psychol.* XXIX. 7 The repugnance to food is construed as positive evidence that the person is becoming a 'wihtigo', *i.e.*, a cannibal. **1960** T. STACEY *Brothers M.* II. xxxii. 361 Daudi..was still utterly subjected, as if by some unseen windigo that was withdrawing him to its own element. **1961** O. NASH *Coll. Verse* 425 The Wendigo, The Wendigo! Its eyes are ice and indigo! **1971** *Brit. Med. Bull.* XXVII. 78/1 States of excitement or panic may be so influenced by local conditions as to give the appearance of specific psychoses... The Windigo psychosis of the Chippewa, Ojibwa and Cree Indians illustrates the way in which such states can develop.

windill, obs. form of WINDLE *v.*^{1}

windily ('wɪndɪlɪ), *adv.* [f. WINDY *a.* + -LY^2.] In a windy manner; as if driven or agitated by the wind; also *fig.*

1866 R. BUCHANAN *Poems, In London* ii, For the world rolls on with air and ocean Wetly and windily round and round. **1880** W. CLARK RUSSELL *Sailor's Sweeth.* iv, The stars were glittering windily even before this crimson melted out of the east. **1890** —— *Marriage at Sea* iii, The Cape Gris Nez lantern windily flashing on high from its shoulder of land. **1901** *Athenæum* 21 Sept. 379/3 The young lady who writes stories and windily reviles the world that will not accept them.

windiness ('wɪndɪnɪs). [f. WINDY *a.* + -NESS.] The quality or condition of being windy.

1. Windy condition of the atmosphere; prevalence of windy weather.

a **1687** PETTY *Pol. Anat.* (1691) 51 The windiness of the same Month was at Dublin 20 and at London but 17. **1922** A. MACHEN *Far off Things* i. 10 Holborn has a certain vastness and windiness about it as the sky grows from black to grey. **1957** G. E. HUTCHINSON *Treat. Limnol.* I. vii. 446 (*heading*) Windiness and area. **1971** *Nature* 10 Dec. 345/1 The classic loess deposits in China..can probably only be explained in terms of greater windiness in the China/Gobi Desert area.

†**2.** Air as an 'element': = WIND *sb.*^{1} 8. *rare.*

1587 GOLDING *De Mornay* xv. 266 Neither is there any moysture, any wyndinesse [orig. *flabile*], or any firy matter in them.

3. a. Flatulence; *concr.* = WIND *sb.*^{1} 10. Now *rare.*

c **1450** BURGH *Secrees* 1932 Wyn moost Reed..Take out of mesure..reyseth wyndynesse. **1545** RAYNALDE *Byrth Mankynde* II. vii. (1552) 100 b, To discusse & vanquyshe ventosyte and wyndynesse. **1590** BARROUGH *Meth. Phisick* I. i. (1596) 2 Sometime it [*sc.* headache] commeth..through windinesse ingendred in some part of the head, being weake. **1725** *Fam. Dict.* s.v. *Honey* ⁋ 3, Raw Honey, by Reason of its Acrimony, loosens the Body, and causes Windiness. **1897** *Allbutt's Syst. Med.* III. 506 A temporary windiness.

b. Quality of causing or tendency to cause 'wind': = FLATULENCE 2 b. Now *rare.*

1576 [T. TWYNE] *Schoolemaster* III. xii. N ij, Beanes are naturally more windy then barly,..for that beanes are of a.. more..grosse substance then barly, which is light and houer, and is sooner discharged of the windines. **1664** TAYLOR in Evelyn *Pomona* 50 People labour to correct that windiness which they fancy to be in it [*sc.* cider]. **1707** MORTIMER *Husb.* 594 Ginger renders it [*sc.* cider] brisk, and corrects its Windiness.

4. Resemblance to, or admixture of, the sound of the wind.

1879 *Organ Voicing* 17 *Windiness.* If the conveyances and wind chest holes are sound, blame attaches solely to the pipe.

5. *fig.* 'Airiness', emptiness, want of substance; inflated or verbose style.

1614 BREREWOOD *Lang. & Relig.* Pref. ¶ b, His modest, and humble charity (vertues which rarely cohabite with the swelling windenesse of much knowledge). **1649** E. REYNOLDS *Hosea* v. 35 Full of vanity, windinesse, vexation, disappointment. **1866** *Sat. Rev.* 19 May 584/1 The feebleness and windiness of bad poets.

winding ('waɪndɪŋ), *vbl. sb.*^{1} [f. WIND *v.*^{1} + -ING^1.

OE. had *windung* only in concr. sense, 'plecta' = Du. *winding* coil, convolution, OHG., early MHG. *winting, winding* 'fascia', 'fasciola', stocking, ON. *vindingr* hose.]

I. The action of WIND *v.*^{1}, or the resulting condition. (See also 10.)

1. a. Motion in a curve; turning this way and that in one's course; sinuous progress or movement; †formerly also, revolution, rotation; undulating motion.

In first quot. of doubtful meaning; ? = TROPIC *sb.* 1 a.

1387–8 T. USK *Test. Love* I. iii. (Skeat) l. 39 To travayle and see the wynding of the erthe in that tyme of winter. **1398** TREVISA *Barth. De P.R.* IX. iii. (Add. MS. 27944), A ȝere is þe fulle cours and passinge and windinge aboute of þe sonne. **1530** PALSGR. 289/1 Wyndyng, *uolubilité.* **1552** LATIMER *Serm., Luke xxi.* (1562) 133 How he stretcheth out all his membres, what a winding is there, so that all his body commeth out of frame! **1573** BARET *Alv.* W 233 The windinges of serpentes. **1620** MELTON *Astrolog.* 70 Birds, and Fowles, with their Motions, Chatterings, Croakings, Winding. **1623** J. TAYLOR (Water P.) *New Discov.* C 2 b, For there hath he..vsed such a deale of intricate Setting, Grafting, Planting..turning, winding, and returning circular [etc.]. **1679** MOXON *Mech. Exerc.* ix. 151 These [stairs], because they sometimes wind, and sometimes fly off from that winding, take therefore the more room up in the Stair-Case. **1709** T. ROBINSON *Vind. Mos. Syst.* 101 These [Plants]..in their Windings, always follow the Motion of the Sun. **1760–72** H. BROOKE *Fool of Qual.* (1809) IV. 27 That graceful winding of person. **1770** W. GILPIN *Wye* (1782) 32 The winding of the river. **1834** NEWMAN *Par. Serm.* I. xviii. 274 They wish to arrive at the heights of Mount Zion without winding round its base. **1844** KINGLAKE *Eothen* xii, With very little of devious winding, it [*sc.* Jordan] carries the shining waters of Galilee..into the solitudes of the Dead Sea. **1869** FITZWYGRAM *Horses & Stables* §931 Winding of the fore-foot is also very objectionable.

b. *Naut.* (see WIND *v.*^{1} 8, 19 b, 24 g).

c **1635** CAPT. N. BOTELER *Dial. Sea Services* (1685), Winding of a Ship. **1639** (Oct. 18) *Admir. Crt. Exam.* 55 (P.R.O.) It being upon wyndeinge upp of the tide. [Cf. quot. 1691 s.v. WIND *v.*^{1} 22 g.]

2. *fig.* **a.** Turning this way and that in thought or conduct; nearly always *pl.* devious or intricate motions, tortuous or crooked ways or dealings.

1621 BURTON *Anat. Mel.* II. iii. III. 404 Hearts ease, I cannot compasse with all my carefull windings, & running in & out. *a* **1641** BP. MOUNTAGU *Acts & Mon.* v. (1642) 395 The boughts and windings of a deceitfull heart. **1658–9** *Burton's Diary* (1828) IV. 19 All this winding to me, in plainness, seems an aiming at no House. *a* **1677** BARROW *Serm. Eph. v. 4* Wks. 1687 I. 195 The numberless rovings of fancy and windings of language. **1818** SCOTT *Br. Lamm.* xx, The subtle lawyer, accustomed..to trace human nature through all her windings. *a* **1859** MACAULAY *Hist. Eng.* xxiii. V. 114 To trace all the windings of the negotiation would be tedious. **1870** DISRAELI *Lothair* l, We are friends and can speak without windings.

†**b.** *Mus.* A melodic alternation or variation.

1667 C. SIMPSON *Compend. Pract. Mus.* 85 These little windings and bindings with Discords and Imperfect Concords after them, do very much delight the Ear. **1667** PLAYFORD *Skill Mus.* I. 41 Those long windings and turnings of the Voyce are ill used. **1706** A. BEDFORD *Temple Mus.* iv. 75 Which he performs with various turnings and windings of the Voice. **1917** T. S. ELIOT *Prufrock & Other Observations* 18 Among the windings of the violins And the ariettes Of cracked cornets.

3. *Carpentry*, etc. Condition of being twisted; chiefly in phr. ***out of winding*** = *out of wind* (WIND *sb.*^{2} 3); ***in winding***, twisted.

1711 W. SUTHERLAND *Shipbuild. Assist.* 46 To make the side Lines and middle Lines of the Decks out of winding one with another. **1721** J. PERRY *Daggenham Breach* 60 Such Piles..could be brought by a straight Line..to meet in the middle of the Breach, and be out of winding,..in the same continued Line as first drove down. **1842** GWILT *Archit.* §1911 A stone is taken out of winding principally with points. **1880** J. LOMAS *Alkali Trade* 328 The tiles themselves must be of good quality—Dutch preferred—and of faultless 'winding'.

4. a. The action of twining a flexible object round another or itself, *esp.* the coiling or twining of thread, silk, etc.; wrapping in a shroud (now *dial.*).

With quot. *c* 1386 cf. sense 8.

c **1386** CHAUCER *Pars. T.* ⁋ 343 The cost of..barrynge, owndynge,..wyndynge or bendynge. *c* **1440** *Promp. Parv.* 530 (Winch. MS.) Wyn[d]yng, or twynynge of threde, *tortura,..uel torsura.* **1463–4** *Rolls of Parlt.* V. 503/2 Grete disceit, in wyndyng, foldyng, and makyng of Flecez of Wolle. **1552** HULOET, Wyndynge of sylke, or thread. **1579** *Aldeburgh Rec.* in *N. & Q.* 12th Ser. VII. 328/2 To myles harrisons wiffe and Ales gillion for wyndinge of mother Hue ..vi^d. **1619** in Foster *Engl. Factories India* (1906) I. 116 Bengala silke..in cleare windinge. *c* **1796** BURNS *The Cardin' o't* 6 The cardin' o't, the spinnin' o't; The warpin' o't, the winnin' o't. **1831–3** *Encycl. Metrop.* (1845) VIII. 716/2 The winding requires the unwearied attention of children to mend the threads that break. **1834** DICKENS *Sk. Boz, Steam Excurs.*, A vast deal of screwing, and tightening, and winding, and tuning, during which Mrs Briggs expatiated to those near her on the immense difficulty of playing a guitar. **1844** G. DODD *Textile Manuf.* i. 37 The process of 'winding' is that by which the weft is transferred from the bobbins to the shuttle. **1910** S. P. THOMPSON *Life Ld. Kelvin* II. 754 The zigzag winding for alternators.

b. With advs. *on, out, up*; also *attrib.*

1825 J. NICHOLSON *Oper. Mech.* 421 Each spinner..fixes the end of the piece that is spun to a winding-up reel. **1835** URE *Philos. Manuf.* 301 Till the stretch and winding-on were once more completed. **1839** —— *Dict. Arts*, etc. 1110 A winding-on bobbin. **1844** G. DODD *Textile Manuf.* ii. 63 The 'winding-on room' where the cloth is wound uniformly round a thick beam or roller preparatory to the printing. **1873** SPON *Workshop Rec.* Ser. I. 201/2 The spools for winding up and winding out should be of the same weight. **1883** *Yorksh. Textile Direct.* 58 Patent Crabbing or Winding-on Machine. **1898** P. MANSON *Trop. Diseases* xxxiii. 517 A system of managing guinea worm cases which bids fair to..obviate the serious risks of the old winding out system.

5. Hoisting or hauling by means of a winch, windlass, or the like. Also with *up*.

c **1440** *Promp. Parv.* 529 (Winch. MS.) Wyyndyng with wyndas, *obvolucio. Ibid.* 530 Wyndynge vp of thyngis þat bene heuy, *euolucio.* *c* **1575** *Ship Lawis* in *Balfour's Practicks* (1754) 620 Gif ane tun or pype be tint in the winding or heising, in fault of the cordis. **1881** RAYMOND *Mining Gloss.*, *Winding*, hoisting with a rope and drum. **1883** GRESLEY *Gloss. Coal-mining*, *Winding*, the operation of raising by means of a steam-engine, with ropes and cages, the produce of the mine.

6. Usually with *up*, of a clock or other mechanism: see WIND *v.*^{1} 20 b, 24 e. Also *fig.*

1630 J. TAYLOR (Water P.) *World runs on Wheels* Wks. II. 234/1 The new found Instrument that goes by winding vp like a Iacke. **1728** YOUNG *Love Fame* I. 282 Is there a tongue, like Delia's o'er her cup, That runs for ages without winding-up? **1737** *Gentl. Mag.* Feb. 68/1 So that no Time is lost in winding. **1832** BABBAGE *Econ. Manuf.* v. (ed. 3) 38 The half minute which we daily devote to the winding-up of our watches. **1884** *St. James's Gaz.* 28 Mar. 6/1 The unfortunate thing about spirit-drinking is..that the drinker requires more and more 'winding-up' as he goes on.

7. ***winding up***: conclusion, finish (see WIND *v.*^{1} 24 d); now usually, the bringing to an end the activities of a business concern; also *attrib.*

1560 DAUS tr. *Sleidane's Comm.* 64 b, How vnfortunate.. hath bene the successe and wyndyng vp of commotioners [orig. *seditiosorum exitus*]. **1570–6** LAMBARDE *Peramb. Kent* (1596) 481 Crafty counseiles..be hard in the handeling, and wofull in the winding vp [orig. *euentu tristia*]. **1576** FLEMING tr. *Caius' Dogs* (1880) 1 In the wynding vp of your Letter written and directed to Doctour Turner. *Ibid.* 44 The winding vp of this worke, called the Supplement, &c. **1678** CUDWORTH *Intell. Syst.* 879 If they would but expect the winding up of things, and stay till the last Close. **1705** R. CROMWELL *Let.* in *Engl. Hist. Rev.* (1898) XIII. 123 The winding up of your bottom will be more pleasing. **1782** in *Mme. D'Arblay's Diary* (1904) II. 97 My warm approbation of the whole work ['Cecilia'] together:..the winding up beyond all compare, more happy, [etc.]. **1809** MALKIN *Gil Blas* IV. vi. ⁋ 15 She..detailed the progress of the plot to the winding up of the catastrophe. **1824** LADY GRANVILLE *Lett.* (1894) I. 271 The Hague season is nearly over, and a ball on Thursday is almost the winding up. **1834** DE QUINCEY *Autob. Sk.* ix. Wks. 1853 I. 240 The year 1782 brought that war to its winding up. **1858** SIMMONDS *Dict. Trade*, Winding-up Act. **1875** *Economist* 30 Jan. 131/2 The shareholders are asked to oppose the projected winding-up. **1895** *Times* 19 Jan. 15/6 A winding-up order having recently been made against this company.

II. That which winds or is wound.

8. a. An object that winds or is wound round; a coil or coiled object; †a curved, circular, or twining pattern, ornament, piece of material, etc.

c **1050** *Voc.* in Wr.-Wülcker 505/24 *Plecta*, windonge. [Cf. 471/1 *Plectas*, ȝewind.] **1356** in *Pipe Roll 32 Edw. III*, m. 33/2 (P.R.O.), ij. Exeronges, xxiiij. Wyndynges, ij. naues, ij. lynces. **1382** WYCLIF *1 Kings* vii. 29 Betwix the litil crownes and wyndyngis, liouns, and oxen. **1486** *Nottingham Rec.* III. 244, iij. wyndynges of iren aboute a ledder. **1555** in Feuillerat *Revels Q. Mary* (1914) 183 Wroughte with white partye payned barwyse wyndinge which was taken owte of the borders of hanginges. **1612** T. TAYLOR *Comm. Titus* i. 7 (1619) 151 Those who are alreadie clasped in the windings of this sinne. *c* **1633** MILTON *Arcades* 47 To nurse the Saplings tall, and curl the grove With Ringlets quaint, and wanton windings wove. **1699** T. BAKER *Refl. Learn.* ix. 102 A Man must see the folds and windings of a knot before he can unty it. **1764** J. FERGUSON *Lect.* iii. 43 The winch..must turn the cylinder once round before the weight or resistance ..can be moved from one spiral winding to another. *a* **1825** FORBY *Voc. E. Anglia* s.v., In Suffolk the flannel, which is wound round a corpse, is called a winding.

b. *Electr.* An electric conductor that is wound round a magnetic material, esp. (*a*) a coil encircling part of the stator or rotor of an electric motor or generator, or an assembly of such coils connected to form one circuit; (*b*) one forming part of a transformer.

1888 S. P. THOMPSON *Dynamo-Electric Machinery* (ed. 2) xii. 259 If the successive sections are to be connected up consecutively, then they must be wound..alternately with right-handed and left-handed windings. **1947** R. LEE *Electronic Transformers & Circuits* v. 141 In step-down transformers the capacitance may be regarded as existing mainly across the primary winding; in step-up transformers, across the secondary winding. **1962** *Newnes Conc. Encycl.*

Electr. Engin. 894/1 The simplest type of winding is a field coil around a salient pole.., the coil comprising a number of turns (between one and several thousand) of wire or strip. **1979** NASAR & UNNEWEHR *Electromechanics & Electric Machines* iii. 67 Transformer windings are constructed of solid or stranded copper or aluminum conductors.

9. A curved, sinuous, or meandering line, path, passage, or the like; esp. *pl.* meanderings, twists and turns.

1387 TREVISA *Higden* (Rolls) I. 9 Þis matir, as laborintus, Dedalus hous, haþ many.. wyndynges and wrynkelynges. **1398** —— *Barth. De P.R.* XIII. vi. (1495) C v b/1 Tygris.. passith in to yᵉ redde see after many turnynges & wyndynges. **1552** HULOET, Wyndynges and turnynges, *amfractus*. **1601** HOLLAND *Pliny* V. v. I. 94 Berenice standeth upon the utmost winding and nouke of Syrtis. **1615** CHAPMAN *Odyss.* IV. 1084 The wards, or windings of the key. **1631** WIDDOWES *Nat. Philos.* 50 A little skin in the lowest winding, or turning of the eare. *a* **1700** EVELYN *Diary* 9 June 1654, The Mount, to which we ascended by windings for neere halfe a mile. **1725** DE FOE *Voy. round World* (1840) 192 Fetching several compasses and windings. **1788** COWPER *Dog & Water-Lily* 28, I..follow'd long The windings of the stream. **1801** SOUTHEY *Thalaba* V. xxv, A loud shriek, That shook along the windings of the cave. **1847** W. C. L. MARTIN *Ox* 134/2 That action by which the aliments are carried through the windings of the intestinal canal. **1873** MAXWELL *Electr. & Magn.* II. 277 The number of windings of the wire between any two small circles.

10. A flexible rod or withy (*obs.* or *dial.*); †*esp.* (*collect. sing.* or *pl.*) the rods or withies used in making or repairing walls; hence, the process involving their use.

1405–6 *Durham Acc. Rolls* (Surtees) 222 Cariantibus stramen ad tecturam, 2*s.* It. pro adquisicione de wyndyng, 15*d.* **1474–5** *Ibid.* 289 In le dalbyng et le wyndyng inter-close wallez, sydewallez, gawellez. **1523–34** FITZHERB. *Husb.* § 126 With the wyndynge of the edderynges thou doost leuse thy stakes. **1550** *Ludlow Churchw. Acc.* (Camden) 44 Item, to John James for wyndynge and dawbynge ther.. viij d. **1599** *Order Bk. Hartlebury Gram. School* (1904) 24 It'm.. for windinge and dawbinge of the church howse. **1601** HOLLAND *Pliny* XIII. iv. I. 387 To make windings to bind vines. *Ibid.* XXXV. xiv. II. 555 The manner of making walls, by dawbing windings and hurdles with mud and clay. **1649** *Order Bk. Hartlebury Gram. School* (1904) 72 For poules for studds ease poules and windings and carriadge of them o 6 o. **1674** RAY *S. & E.C. Words, Vrith*, Eththerings or windings of hedges. **1688** HOLME *Armoury* III. xiv. (Roxb.) 19/2 Thatchers Termes... Windings, twigs that will bend. **1852** *Jrnl. R. Agric. Soc.* XIII. II. 281 Farmers find posts and rails cheaper..than the old system of 'stake and rice'. *Note.* Called 'cock-guard' in some parts; in others 'winding'. **1887** *S. Chesh. Gloss., Weindins*, the boughs which are interwoven with the stakes used to shore up the bank of a stream.

III. 11. *attrib.* and *Comb.*, as (sense 4) ***winding*** †***blade*** (BLADE *sb.* 10 c), ***-loft, -machine, machinery, master, room,*** † ***stool*** (STOOL *sb.* 6); (sense 5, esp. in nautical and mining use) ***winding accident,*** † ***baly*** (app. = BAIL *sb.*⁵, bucket), ***engine*** (***-engineman***), ***-gear,*** † ***hawser, hour,*** † ***iron, pit,*** † ***-pulley, -rope, shaft, tackle, time, wheel***; (sense 6) ***winding button, hole, pinion, square, wheel***; †**winding band** [BAND *sb.*² 5], a bandage; **winding sticks, strips,** two equal pieces of wood with straight parallel edges used to determine whether a surface is true (cf. 3).

1895 *Cath. News* 14 Sept. 3 Two terrible *winding accidents occurred in mines in Rhondda Valley. **1336** *Acc. Exch. K.R.* 19/31 m. 5 (P.R.O.) In .ij. *Wyndi[n]gbalies emptis ad eandem [galeam]... Et in ij petris corde de canabo emptis pro Wyndyngrop. **1582** *N. T.* (Rhem.) John xi. 44 Bound feete and handes with *winding bandes. **1585** HIGINS *Junius' Nomencl.* 262/2 *Fascia*,..a swathing cloth or winding band to..tye vp wounds. **1530** PALSGR. 184 *Vnes tournettes*, a payre of *wyndynge blades to wynde yarne upon. **1881** BRITTEN *Watch & Clockm.* 71 A contrate wheel squared on to the stem of the *winding button. **1858** SIMMONDS *Dict. Trade*, **Winding-engine*, an engine for drawing up buckets, etc. from a well or shaft. **1875** KNIGHT *Dict. Mech., Winding-engine*,..a hoisting steam-engine. **1883** GRESLEY *Gloss. Coal-mining*, Winding Engine. **1904** *Daily Chron.* 23 Apr. 6/4 A terrible calamity was averted at the Navigation Colliery..by the heroism..of the *winding engineman. **1875** KNIGHT *Dict. Mech.*, **Winding-gear*, an English term for the winding-machine for mines. **1417** in *For. Acc. 8 Hen. V* D/2 (P.R.O.), j *Wyndyng hauncer. **1485** *Naval Acc. Hen. VII* (1896) 36 Smalle Warps,.. Hawsers,.. Wyndyng hausers. **1688** HOLME *Armoury* III. xx. (Roxb.) 240/1 On[e] thick gut string, which is played upon with a long Bow or Base Viol stick at the head of it a little below the *winding hole. **1893** *Daily News* 4 May 2/1 In South Wales the *winding hours were 9½ to 10 hours on four days in the week. **1420** in *For. Acc. 3 Hen. VI* F/2 *dorso* (P.R.O.), *Wyndyng [i]rone. **1846** G. DODD *Brit. Manuf.* Ser. VI. 197 The tarred haul then passes into the '*winding-loft', where it is wound..upon bobbins. **1825** J. NICHOLSON *Oper. Mech.* 422 The two *winding-machines may also be driven by the endless rope. **1855** *Orr's Circ. Sci., Inorg. Nat.* 248 Disarrangement of the *winding machinery. **1881** *Instr. Census Clerks* (1885) 68 Cotton Mill:..Winding Room... *Winding Master. **1885** C. G. W. LOCK *Workshop Rec.* Ser. IV. 337/1 Examine the *winding-pinion depth, to see that it is neither too deep nor shallow. **1417** in *For. Acc. 8 Hen. V* D/1 *dorso* (P.R.O.), j Ketille j Fane et *Wyndyngpoley. **1890** W. J. GORDON *Foundry* 165 The *winding room, where the women sit some twenty deep in rank after rank by the side of the benches. **1913** *Times* 7 Aug. 4/4 [He] denied that he ever smoked in the 'winding' or operating rooms. **1336** *Wyndyngrop [see *winding-baly*]. **1424** *For. Acc.* 59 m. 22 *dorso* (P.R.O.), j hausere pro wyndyngrope. **1883** GRESLEY *Gloss. Coal-mining, Winding Ropes*, the ropes by which a cage, chair,..&c., are raised and lowered in a pit-shaft. *Ibid.*, **Winding Shaft or Pit*, the pit-shaft used chiefly for winding purposes. **1884** BRITTEN *Watch & Clockm.* 35 During the going of the clock the shutter..stood in front of the *winding square. **1823** P. NICHOLSON *Pract. Builder* 255 *Winding Sticks are always used in pairs. **1530** PALSGR. 289/1 *Wyndyng stole, *tournette*. *a* **1625** MANWAYRING *Seaman's Dict.* s.v., The *winding tackle is thus fitted: a great double block with three shivers in it, which is fast seized to the end of a small cable, which is brought about the head of the mast and so serves for a pendant [etc.]. *c* **1635** CAPT. N. BOTELER *Dial. Sea Services* (1685) 116 *Winding Tackle blocks*. **1867** SMYTH *Sailor's Word-bk., Winding-tackle pendant*, a strong rope made fast to the lower mast-head, and forming the support of the winding-tackle. **1908** *Daily Chron.* 10 Dec. 5/7 Both *winding times are to be excluded from the calculation of eight hours. **1675** in Jeaffreson *Middx. County Rec.* (1892) IV. 61 Unam rotam Harpedon anglice vocatam a *winding wheele. **1884** BRITTEN *Watch & Clockm.* 240 The operation of throwing the winding wheels out of action.

winding ('wɪndɪŋ, 'waɪndɪŋ), *vbl. sb.*² [f. WIND *v.*² + -ING¹.] The action of blowing or making a blast, chiefly *of* horns.

c **1500** in Grose *Antiq. Rep.* (1809) IV. 407 To myche wyndinge of the pipis is not the best. **1605** TIMME *Quersit.* II. vii. 138 That renuing is to be attributed to the fire—the outward ventilation or winding comming between as the instrument. **1615** G. SANDYS *Trav.* 58 At the winding of a horne. **1670** *Caveat to Conventiclers* 2 This dreadful appearance..was ushered in by the winding of Hornes. **1732** BERKELEY *Alciphr.* v. § 1 A confused Noise of the opening of Hounds, the winding of Horns [etc.]. **1826** SCOTT *Woodst.* x, The winding of horns and the galloping of horse. **1940** W. DE LA MARE *Pleasures & Speculations* 48 The first windings of the Last Trump.

winding, *vbl. sb.*³: see WIND *v.*³

winding ('waɪndɪŋ), *ppl. a.*¹ [f. WIND *v.*¹ + -ING².] That winds, in various senses.

1. That follows a sinuous course, takes or has a curvilinear form, or is full of bends and turns.

a. Of a staircase: Spiral. Chiefly in ***winding stairs*** (sometimes hyphened).

1530 PALSGR. 158 *Vne vis*, a wyndingstayre. **1580** HOLLYBAND *Treas. Fr. Tong* s.v. *Noyau*, A paire of winding staires. **1653** H. COGAN tr. *Pinto's Trav.* xxxv. 141 A round Tribunal, whereunto one ascended by fifteen winding stairs. **1679** MOXON *Mech. Exerc.* ix. 153 These Winding steps are made about a solid Newel. **1687** A. LOVELL tr. *Thevenot's Trav.* I. 22 You may go up to the top by a winding staircase that is within it. *a* **1700** EVELYN *Diary* 20 July 1654, A paire of artificial winding-stayres of stone. **1823** P. NICHOLSON *Pract. Builder* 191 Having finished the first flight of steps, fix the top of the first bearer for the winding-tread. **1840** DICKENS *Old Cur. Shop* liii, She left the chapel,..and coming to a low door, which plainly led into the tower, opened it, and climbed the winding stair.

b. Of plants or their parts, lines or figures, etc.

1538 ELYOT, *Vimineus*, wyckers, wyndynge roddes, or osyars. **1545** ASCHAM *Toxoph.* (Arb.) 164 A payre of windynge prickes. **1552–3** in Feuillerat *Revels Edw. VI* (1914) 137 Wynding plate abowte hedd peces. **1577** GOOGE *Heresbach's Husb.* 34 The stalke is sclender, wyndyng, with claspes about such plantes as are next hym. **1607** TOPSELL *Four-f. Beasts* 78 If his necke be winding and weake (as if it were broken). **1622** BACON *Hen. VII*, 193 It was ordained, that this Winding-Iuie of a Plantagenet, should kill the true Tree it selfe. **1697** DRYDEN *Virg. Georg.* IV. 184 The winding Trail Of Bears-foot. **1726** LEONI *Alberti's Archit.* I. 9 Of involved winding Lines it is not necessary to speak. **1799** G. SMITH *Laboratory* I. 16 Thus you may mark a winding figure with a thread on a rocket. **1822** J. PARKINSON *Outl. Oryctol.* 163 The chambers separated by winding septa. **1836** *Penny Cycl.* V. 230/2 Many of the sheep have upright winding horns.

c. Of the course or outline of natural features, roads, passages, etc.

1555 EDEN *Decades* 303 b, Saylynge alonge by the coaste of a wyndynge and bendynge shore. **1591** SHAKS. *Two Gent.* II. vii. 31 And so by many winding nookes he straies. **1610** HOLLAND *Camden's Brit.* I. 618 Wy with a crooked and winding streame rolleth downe by Whitney. **1697** DRYDEN *Virg. Georg.* II. 691 A winding Vally. —— *Æneis* III. 905 Megara's winding Bay. **1791** COWPER *Four Ages* 8 Taking my lonely winding walk, I mus'd. **1794** MRS. RADCLIFFE *Myst. Udolpho* xxxi, The winding mountains at length shut Udolpho from her view. **1878** J. BULLER *40 Yrs. N.Z.* I. ii. 27 The river is winding in its course. **1890** 'R. BOLDREWOOD' *Col. Reformer* xiii, He could rattle five horses and a loaded coach in and out of the creeks and winding bush tracks.

d. Of animals or their movements.

1613 PURCHAS *Pilgrimage* I. v. 20 He windes himselfe into this winding Beast, disposing the Serpents tongue to speake to the woman. **1631** QUARLES *Samson* iv. 20 The suck-egge Weasell, and the Winding Swallow. **1697** DRYDEN *Æneis* II. 288 Twice round his waste their [*sc.* the serpents'] winding Volumes rowl'd. **1748** RICHARDSON *Clarissa* (1810) III. xii. 79 Thou..dost not know the joys of a chase, and in pursuing a winding game. **1820** CLARE *Poems Rural Life* 118 Swallows check their winding flight.

†**e.** Pliant, bending. *Obs. rare.*

1609 HOLLAND *Amm. Marcell.* 192 Feathers and delicat winding beds [orig. *pluma & flexiles lectuli*].

2. *fig.* †**a.** Tortuous, crooked, wily. *Obs.*

1594 CAREW *Huarte's Exam. Wits* 204 A man doubtlesse winding and craftie. **1629** H. BURTON *Truth's Tri.* 241 For all his winding wit and wrangling about this place. **1655** STANLEY *Hist. Philos.* III. 76 Old, winding, bragging, testy, crafty fox. **1693** J. EDWARDS *Author. O. & N. Test.* I. 245 Jupiter..was represented Horned, because of his Winding Oracles.

b. Of a narrative: Circuitous, rambling.

[*a* **1596** *Sir T. More* IV. v. 37 The winding laborinth of thy straunge discourse Will nere haue end.] **1887** BOWEN *Virg. Æneid* I. 341 The grief is a winding story and long. **1923** *Times Lit. Suppl.* 4 Jan. 9/2 The long and winding narrative.

Hence **'windingly** *adv.*, in a winding manner, circuitously, with twists and turns; **'windingness,** circuitous or meandering form.

1576 BAKER *Gesner's Jewell of Health* 215 b, The pype.. doth ascende right up, and not as in the others, *windingly. **1626** T. H[AWKINS] *Caussin's Holy Crt.* 47 A riuer, that windingly creepeth with many wauy turnings. **1817** BYRON *Beppo* xlii, Where the green alleys windingly allure. **1877** BLACKMORE *Erema* xiv, The long descent into the depth of winter is..taken..gently, and softly, and windingly, with a great many glimpses back at the summer. **1730** BAILEY (fol.), *Tortuousness*, *Windingness or the Turning in and out. **1861** *Macm. Mag.* IV. 134/1 There should be good in the stream's windingness.

winding ('wɪndɪŋ, *in sense* 1 'waɪndɪŋ), *ppl. a.*² [f. WIND *v.*² + -ING².]

1. Of a horn: That is winded.

1735 SOMERVILLE *Chase* III. 402 The winding Horn, and Huntsman's Voice, Let loose the gen'ral Chorus.

2. That 'winds' one; taking one's breath away.

1842 LOVER *Handy Andy* ix, The drunken man at least gave some tokens of returning consciousness by making several winding blows at his benefactors.

†**winding-cloth**¹. *Obs.* [f. WINDING *vbl. sb.*¹ + CLOTH *sb.*] = WINDING-SHEET 1.

a **1300** *Cursor M.* 14354 In windingclath als he was wonden, Bath fete and hand þar was he bunden. **1439** in *Ancestor* (1904) July 18, I gife my modir the best pece of lynnyn cloth that I have over that that beleveth over my wyndyng cloth. *c* **1440** *Alphabet of Tales* 43 Þis ffurst frend is werldly possessions, whilk þat when we dye giffis vs bod a wyndyng clothe to lap vs in.

†**winding-cloth**². *Obs.* [f. WINDING *vbl. sb.*³] = WINNOW-, WINNOWING-CLOTH.

1548 *Burgh Rec. Edin.* (1871) II. 136 Ane bathsket with windinclaith syf ryddill sek and peyk. **1588** *Lanc. Wills* (Chetham Soc. 1893) 150 Sacks windinge clothes pocks. **1733** [see WIND *v.*³].

winding-sheet ('waɪndɪŋʃiːt). [f. WINDING *vbl. sb.*¹ + SHEET *sb.*¹]

1. A sheet in which a corpse is wrapped for burial; a shroud.

c **1420** ? LYDG. *Assembly of Gods* 420 As he had bene a goste came in wyndyng shete. **1547** in Feuillerat *Revels Edw. VI* (1914) 21 One wyndyng shite of Incarnacion Lawnd strypide with crossis Crymson satten. **15..** *Doun by ane Rever* 54 in *Dunbar's Poems* (S.T.S.) 306 Thy windene scheit is nocht in weir. **1603** DEKKER *Wond. Year* C 3 b, A thousand Coarses, some standing bolt vpright in their knotted winding sheetes. **1624** CAPT. J. SMITH *Virginia* II. 35 They..rowle them in mats for their winding sheets. **1723–4** *Burgh Rec. Stirling* (1889) II. 357 A coffine..and a winning sheet. **1746** HERVEY *Medit.* (1767) I. 72 Your Nobility arrayed in a Winding-sheet; your Grandeur mouldering in an Urn. **1869** TOZER *Highl. Turkey* II. 92 The spectre had sworn by his winding-sheet..that he would do him no harm.

Comb. **1603** DEKKER *Wond. Year* D 2 b, These winding-sheete-weauers.

b. *transf.* and *fig.*

1593 SHAKS. *3 Hen. VI*, II. v. 114 These armes of mine shall be thy winding sheet: My heart (sweet Boy) shall be thy Sepulcher. **1625** BACON *Ess., Viciss. Things* (Arb.) 569 The great Winding-sheets, that burie all Things in Obliuion, are two; Deluges, and Earth-quakes. **1669** J. OWEN *Serm. 2 Sam. xxiii.* 5 Wks. 1851 IX. 414 Let us..be content to see all our comforts in their winding-sheet every day. **1757** GRAY *Bard* 50 Weave the warp, and weave the woof, The winding-sheet of Edward's race. **1817** SHELLEY *Rev. Islam* IX. xxii, Disturbing not the leaves which are her winding-sheet. **1864** LOWELL *Fireside Trav.* 147 Dead cedars, in winding-sheets of long gray moss. **1875** MANNING *Mission Holy Ghost* ii. 59 He raised you from death, and loosed you from your winding-sheet of habitual sin.

2. A mass of solidified drippings of grease clinging to the side of a candle, resembling a sheet folded in creases, and regarded in popular superstition as an omen of death or calamity.

1708 *Brit. Apollo* No. 17. 2/1 Letters, Winding Sheets, &c. in a Candle. **1819** KEATS *Party of Lovers* 16 There's a large cauliflower in each candle. A winding sheet. **1824** MISS MITFORD *Village* Ser. I. *Aunt Martha*, She..sees..gifts in her finger-nails, letters and winding-sheets in the candle. **1882** *Century Mag.* Nov. 113/1 The candles..burned dim, with long winding-sheets clinging to them.

'wind-,instrument. (Often as two words.)

1. A musical instrument played by means of 'wind' (WIND *sb.*¹ 12), supplied either by the breath of the player or by bellows: most commonly applied to portable instruments of this kind, such as those used in an orchestra.

Strictly, one whose sounds are produced by vibration of air in a pipe or tube (as the flute, trumpet, etc.) or in a number of pipes (as the organ); but usually also including those sounding by vibration of reeds (as the clarinet, harmonium, and concertina).

1582 N. LICHEFIELD tr. *Castanheda's Conq. E. Ind.* I. lxxvi. 155 He had also with him certeine wind instruments. **1628** FORD *Lover's Mel.* I. ii, *Cucul.* Was thy father a Piper, saist thou? *Grill.* A sounder of some such wind-instrument forsooth. **1777** THICKNESSE *Journ. France* (1789) II. 202 During the supper, a good band of music played; but it was all wind instruments. **1838** DICKENS *Nich. Nick.* ii, Two or three violins and a wind instrument from the Opera band. **1880** F. TAYLOR in Grove *Dict. Mus.* II. 5/2 The Harmonium..although played by wind, is not strictly a wind-instrument.

Comb. **1776** HAWKINS *Hist. Mus.* V. IV. vii. 364 The younger Stanesby, the wind-instrument-maker.

b. *fig.* or *allusively*.

1604 SHAKS. *Oth.* III. i. 10. **1634** S. R. *Noble Soldier* IV. i. F 3, *Bal.* What Instrument playd she upon? *Cor.* A wind instrument, she did nothing but sigh.

†**2.** A machine or contrivance driven by the wind, as a windmill. *Obs. rare.*

1601 HOLLAND *Pliny* VII. xxxvii. I. 175 Ctesibius also was much accounted of for devising wind-instruments: and by the meanes of certaine engines to draw and send water to any place.

Hence ˌ**wind-instruˈmental** *a.*; ˌ**wind-instruˈmentalist**.

1869 J. ELLA *Mus. Sk.* I. 344, I know of no other example of wind-instrumentalists acquiring an independance by orchestral employment in London. **1894** J. A. KAPPEY (*title*) Military Music. A history of wind-instrumental bands.

Windish, var. WENDISH.

windister, var. WINNOWSTER *Obs.*

windlass (ˈwɪndləs), *sb.*[1] Forms: 5 **wynlas(s)e, wyndelas**, 5–6 **wyndlas**, 6 **-lasse, wynlas**, 6–7 **windlesse, -lasse, wyndles(se**, (also 9) **windlace**, 6–8 **windlas, windles**, 7 **wyndeles**, 7–8 **windless, winlace**, 8 **winlass**, 7– **windlass**. [prob. alteration of WINDAS, of obscure origin.

The alleged Icel. *vindiláss* is not authentic.]

1. A mechanical contrivance working on the principle of the wheel and axle, on a horizontal axis (thus distinguished from a *capstan*); consisting of a roller or beam, resting on supports, round which a rope or chain is wound; used for various purposes, esp. on board ship for weighing the anchor or hauling upon a purchase, at the head of a mine-shaft for hoisting coal or other mineral, or for raising a bucket from a well.

Chinese or *differential windlass*: see CHINESE *a.* 2, and cf. DIFFERENTIAL *a.* 4 b. *Spanish windlass*: see SPANISH *a.* 7.

c **1400** *Laud Troy Bk.* 12652 The schippes were sone on a blase, Thei brende bothe mast & wynlase. *c* **1440** *Promp. Parv.* 529 Wyndynge, wythe wyndelas [*Winch. MS.* wyndas], *obvolucio*. **1526** *Dunmow Churchw. Acc.* lf. 5 b (MS.), Item to John Harvy and Wylyem barcar for a brayde to helpe to make the wynlas, iii.*d.* **1538** ELYOT, *Tractorium*, a windlas to drawe vp heuy thingis. **1552** in Glasscock *Rec. St. Michael's, Bp.'s Stortford* (1882) 137 A wyndles for the pix. **1585** *Shuttleworths' Acc.* (Chetham Soc.) 25 A grete roppe for the wyndlas in the slayhter housse. **1603** G. OWEN *Pembrokeshire* (1892) 89 With a wyndeles turned by fowre men they drawe vpp the coales. **1608** *Relat. Trav. W. Bush* B 2 b, She had twooe stronge Cables..strayned by wyndlesses. **1616** *Extr. Aberd. Reg.* (1848) II. 342 Ane wyndles for heising vp of stanes. **1670** COVEL in *Early Voy. Levant* (Hakluyt Soc.) 143 Carrying out an Anchor a sterne ..with the Winlace. **1743** WOODROOFE in Hanway *Trav.* (1762) I. II. xxiii. 101 A great sea obliged us to cut the cable at the windlass. **1789** *Trans. Soc. Arts* VII. 218 Anchor-stocks..supplying the place of the upper gudgeon; and in a merchant-ship the clamps of her windles. **1800** WEEMS *Washington* x. (1877) 129 Some seizing the ready handspikes, vault high upon the windlasses. **1822** *Imison's Sci. & Art* I. 56 If two men work at the end of a roller, or windlass, as in drawing up coals or ore from a mine, or water from a well. **1836** THIRLWALL *Greece* xxvi. III. 427 A great vessel of burthen..to cover the operations of a number of parties in boats, which..forced up the piles by means of cranes or windlaces.

¶ The form *windles* taken as pl. *Obs.*

1601 HOLLAND *Pliny* XXXVI. xv. II. 586 To force the water ..with devise of engines and windles up to the top of the hill. **1680** *Lond. Gaz.* No. 1526/4 The Adventure Pink,..two Decks, with a Fall where the Windles stand.

†**2.** Applied to various smaller contrivances of a similar kind: a winch used in discharging a cross-bow (= WINDAS 1 b) or a pistol ('dag'); a reel on an angler's rod, or for winding yarn (= WINDLE *sb.*[3]). *Obs.*

1481–90 *Howard Househ. Bks.* (Roxb.) 273, ix. cross-bowes, wyndlas. **1587** HOLINSHED *Chron.* III. 1099/2 With the windlace of his dag hanging thereon. **1588** *Lanc. Wills* (Chetham Soc. 1861) 12 My crosbowe with the windlesse. **1669** WORLIDGE *Syst. Agric.* (1681) 258 A very long Line wound up at the handle of your Rod on a small Winch or Windlace. **1737** OZELL *Rabelais* III. 236 *note*, A Reel or Yarn-Windless. **1819** SCOTT *Ivanhoe* xxviii, Two arblasts.. with windlaces and quarrells.

3. *attrib.*, as ***windlass axle, -end, -head, -pawl, rope***; **windlass-bar**, any of a set of bars inserted in holes in a ship's windlass, by which it is turned; **windlass-bitt, -chock**, each of the supports of a ship's windlass; **windlass-jack, windlass-lining** (see quots.); **windlass-man**, a man employed to turn a windlass.

1842 LOUDON *Suburban Hort.* 157 Two *windlass axles are supported on four props. **1867** SMYTH *Sailor's Word-bk.* s.v., The cables [of the windlass] have three turns round this main-piece..: holes are cut for the *windlass-bars in each eighth of the squared sides. **1846** A. YOUNG *Naut. Dict.* 369 Iron spindles working in collars or bushes inserted in the *Windlass-bitts. *Ibid.*, **Windlass-chocks*, fore-and-aft pieces of oak fitted on the deck and bolted to the beams immediately before the windlass. *Ibid.*, **Windlass-ends*..are two horizontal pieces forming a continuation of the windlass outside these bitts. **1867** SMYTH *Sailor's Word-bk.*, *Windlass* ..is composed of the carrick-heads or *windlass-heads. **1875** KNIGHT *Dict. Mech.*, **Windlass-jack*, a form of lifting-jack having a winch-handle for turning the pinion which gears into the crown-wheel. **1846** A. YOUNG *Naut. Dict.* 369 Pieces of hard wood, called the *Windlass-lining, fitted and bolted round it to preserve it from being chafed. **1851** CARLYLE *Sterling* III. iii, Both shouted vehemently to the coadjutor at the windlass, both sprang at the basket; the *windlass man could not move it with them both. **1867** SMYTH *Sailor's Word-bk.* s.v., Amidships it is supported by chocks, where it is also furnished with a course of *windlass-pawls. **1669** STURMY *Mariner's Mag.* v. xii. 81 By a *Windless Rope, and weight to sink it, he may first let down the weight.

†**windlass**, *sb.*[2] *Obs.* Forms: 6 **wynd(e)-, winlesse, windlas(se, (-laies ?), wyndlas(s)e, -lace**, 6–7 **windlace, -lesse**, 7 **-lass, winde-lase**, (8 **windlatch**). [Alteration of WANLACE, by association with WIND *v.*[1] and perh. with prec. sb.]

1. A circuit made to intercept the game in hunting (= WANLACE 1); *gen.* a circuit, circuitous movement: esp. in phr. ***to fetch a windlass***, to make a circuit, go round about, 'fetch a compass'.

1530 PALSGR. 231 Hewar that fetteth the wyndelesse in huntyng. **1563** GOLDING *Cæsar* VII. (1565) 206 Bidding them fetche a windlasse a great waye about, and to make al to-ward one place. **1567** —— *Ovid's Met.* VII. 93 b, He runnes not forth directly out, Nor makes a windlasse ouer all the champion fieldes about. **1580** LYLY *Euphues* (Arb.) 270, I now fetching a windlesse, that I myght better haue a shoote, was preuented with ready game. **1600** FAIRFAX *Tasso* XIV. xxxiv, The beauies faire of Shepheards daughters bold, With wanton winde laies ronne, turne, play and pas. **1602** R. CAREW *Cornwall* 75 Sometimes a foote-man..will carry the same quite backwards, and so, at last, get to the goale by a windlace.

2. *fig.* A circuitous course of action; a round-about proceeding; a crafty device (= WANLACE 3).

a **1569** KINGESMYLL *Man's Est., Godly Adv.* (1574) I vij, With suche winlesses some are dryuen into the net. **1575** LANEHAM *Let.* (1871) 55 And heer iz my windlesse, lyke yoor coorse as pleaz ye. **1575** *Mirr. Mag., Humfrey Dk. Glouc.* xlvi, Which by slye driftes, and wyndlaces aloofe, They brought about. **1602** SHAKS. *Ham.* II. i. 65. **1617** COLLINS *Def. Bp. Ely* II. viii. 317 These were the trances, and the windlaces of the first Iesuites. **1631** [MABBE] *Celestina* IV. 54 What a wind-lace hast thou fetcht, with what words hast thou come upon me? *a* **1734** NORTH *Exam.* II. iv. §143. (1740) 307 The former are brought forth, by a Windlatch of a Trial, to charge the latter with the foulest of Crimes.

†**windlass**, *v.*[1] *Obs.* [f. WINDLASS *sb.*[2]] **a.** *trans.* (*fig.*) To decoy or ensnare. **b.** *intr.* To 'fetch a windlass', make a circuit; *fig.* to act circuitously or craftily. Hence **windlassing** *vbl. sb.*[1]

a **1586** SIDNEY *Astr. & Stella* xxi, My young mind.., whom Loue doth windlas so; That mine owne writings.. show My wits quicke in vaine thoughts, in vertue lame. *a* **1660** HAMMOND *Serm., Ezek. xvi. 30* (1664) 12 She is not at so much leasure as to windlace, or use craft to satisfie them; she goes downright a woing. *Ibid., Luke xviii. 11* 131 A skilful woods-man, that by wind-lassing presently gets a shoot.

ˈ**windlass**, *v.*[2] [f. WINDLASS *sb.*[1]] *trans.* To hoist or haul with a windlass. Hence ˈ**windlassing** *vbl. sb.*[2]

1834 MARIA EDGEWORTH *Helen* xiv, None of our windlassing will ever bring her [*sc.* the truth] up. **1870** *Daily News* 20 Jan., He was hauled into the barn and windlassed clear of the floor. **1897** KIPLING *Capt. Cour.* ix. 203 As though the words were being windlassed out of him.

windle (ˈwɪnd(ə)l), *sb.*[1] Now *dial.* or *local.* Forms: 1–3 **windel**, (1 -il), 3–6 **wyndel**, 6 **wyndle, -dille, -dell**, 8–9 *dial.* **winnel**, 6– **windle**. [OE. *windel* str. m., 'cartellus', 'fiscella', 'canistrum', 'corbis', f. *windan* to plait, WIND *v.*[1]: see -LE 1.

Parallel in formation are OHG. *wintilâ* (MHG., G. *windel*) swaddling-clothes, ON. *vindill* wisp.]

1. A basket. Now only *dial.* (see quot. 1879): app. associated or confused with WINDLE *sb.*[2]

c **725** *Corpus Gloss.* (Hessels) C 10 *Cartellus*, windil. *c* **1000** ÆLFRIC *Gen.* xl. 16 Ic geseah swefn, þæt is, ðæt ic hæfde ðry windlas mid melewe ofer min heafod. *c* **1400** *Laud Troy Bk.* 17973 Thei did brynge the kiddis drye..And colis also In bollis & wyndel. **1879** *Norfolk Archæol.* VIII. 174 *Windle*, a basket used in winnowing corn.

2. A measure of corn and other commodities, varying in different localities; of wheat, usually about 3 bushels. *local* (*north.*).

[**1268, 1282** in Rogers *Agric. & Prices* I. xviii. 428 [Nuts] are purchased in Cumberland by the windle.] **1281–2** *Inq. post mortem Edw. I* 31/3 (P.R.O.), Et sciendum quod quelibet eskeppa continet sexdecim Windellos, et illi sexdecim Windelli faciunt quarterium Londiniense et dimidium. **1309** *Crt. Rolls Wakefield* (1906) II. 194 One wynd[el ?] of barley and a quarter of oats. **1521** *Pleadings Duchy Lancaster* (1896) 106 [Dealing of corn by] mettes and wyndilles. **1525** *Test. Ebor.* (Surtees) V. 216 To everichon of the same Orders a wyndle of wheate, or the price therof. **1566** in Picton *L'pool Munic. Rec.* (1883) I. 86 One wyndle containing 56 quarts of wine measure up heaped shall..be the right and just standard. **1636** *Farington Papers* (Chetham Soc. 1856) 13, 8 windles of wheat Lanc^r measure. **1729** P. WALKDEN *Diary* (1866) 62 Spent the day wholly at home in winnowing my barley, and I measured a windle and an awkendale for going to the malt-kilns. **1790** GROSE *Prov. Gloss.* (ed. 2), *Windle*, or *Winnel*, a bushel. **1849** *Jrnl. R. Agric. Soc.* X. I. 18 The cost [of limestone] at the kiln is 11 *d* a windle, and two windles are equal to 3 cwt. **1881** *Daily News* 17 Jan. 3/4 Preston. Jan. 15... Wheat 19 s. to 22 s. per windle.

3. A bundle or band (of straw or hay). *Sc.*

1825 JAMIESON, *Winnle*, the same with *Windlen*, a bottle of straw. **1893** MACKINTOSH *Around the Orkney Peat Fires* (1905) 207 [He] had the kegs tied up in windles of straw.

†ˈ**windle**, *sb.*[2] *Obs.* Forms: 3 (*Orm.*) **winndell**, 4 **wyndel**, 5 **-dylle, -dle**, 6 **windle**. [f. stem of OE. *windwian* WINNOW *v.* + -LE 1. Cf. WIND *v.*[3]] A winnowing-fan.

c **1200** ORMIN 10483 Himm shollde brinngenn inn hiss hannd Hiss winndell forr to winndwenn. *a* **1400** *N. T.* (Paues) Matt. iii. 12 Whos wyndel is in his honde, & he schal clense fully his korne. *c* **1425** *Voc.* in Wr.-Wülcker 664/7 *Hoc uentilabrum*, wyndylle. **1550** COVERDALE *Spir. Perle* vii. 65 When the corne is threshed, the kernel lyeth mixed among the chaf, and afterwarde are they disseuered a sonder wyth the fanne or wyndle.

windle (ˈwɪnd(ə)l), *sb.*[3] *Obs.* exc. *dial.* Forms: 8–9 *Sc.* **winnel, win(n)le**, 7– **windle**. [The second element of GARNWINDLE, YARNWINDLE, q.v. for earlier examples.] An appliance for winding yarn or thread.

1687 MIÈGE *Gt. Fr. Dict.* II, Windles, or Blades to wind Yarn on, *un Devidoir*. **17..** *Loving Lass* in *Ramsay's Tea-t. Misc.* (1762) 172 My hanks of yarn, my rock and reel, My winnels and my spinning-wheel. **1791** ALEX. WILSON in *Poems & Lit. Prose* (1876) II. 45 Jennock turn't the winles' blade An' waft in lapfu's left her. **1845** S. JUDD *Margaret* ii. (1871) 5 From a windle the thread is conducted to the quills.

ˈ**windle**, *sb.*[4] *local.* Also **whindle**. [? f. WIND *sb.*[1]] The redwing (*Turdus iliacus*), also called *wind-thrush, -throstle*.

1674 N. COX *Gentl. Recr.* III. (1677) 63 The Wind-throstle (or Whindle). *a* **1698** C. MORTON *Enquiry* in *Harl. Misc.* (1744) II. 558/2 The..Wind-Thrush (or the Redwing, Wheenerd, Whindle; for so many Names it has in divers Countries). **1772** RUTTY *Nat. Hist. Dublin* I. 342. **1885** SWAINSON *Prov. Names Birds* 5 Redwing.., Winnard (Cornwall). Windle (Devon).

ˈ**windle**, *v.*[1] Now *dial.* Forms: 4 *Sc. pr. pple.* **wyndland, vyndland**, 6 **windill**, 6– **windle**, (9 *dial.* **winnle**). [f. WIND *v.*[1] + -LE 3. With sense 2 cf. MDu., MHG., G. *windeln* to swathe, swaddle.]

1. *intr.* To move circularly or sinuously; to turn over and over, or round and round; to whirl; to meander: = WIND *v.*[1] 7 b. Hence ˈ**windling** *vbl. sb.* and *ppl. a.*[1]

1375 BARBOUR *Bruce* XVII. 721 Sum dede, sum dosnyt, come doun vyndland. **1623** LISLE *Ælfric on O. & N. Test.* To Rdr. p. xxviii, The one hoodwinked with his implicite faith, as with a bumble on his head, thinkes he goes forth-right, when he windles in a mill. **1802** MRS. RADCLIFFE *Gaston de Blondeville* IV. (1826) 140 Beside some windling brook. **1856** P. THOMPSON *Hist. Boston* 730 *Windling*, snow-drifting. **1905** *Engl. Dial. Dict.* s.v. (Lincolnsh.), The snow windles under the tiles.

2. *trans.* To wind (thread, etc.); also *absol.*: = WIND *v.*[1] 15. Also *Sc.* (see quot. 1808, and cf. WINDLE *sb.*[1] 3, WINDLING *sb.*).

1587 W. FOWLER *Wks.* (S.T.S.) I. 117/132 Than did I spye Chrysippus..with a large and brodest roll his threid & webbs to windill. **1599** T. M[OUFET] *Silkwormes* 1 These flocks as white as milke, That make, and spinne, and die, and windle silke. **1808** JAMIESON, *Windle*, to make up (straw or hay) into bottles. **1859** A. WHITEHEAD *Leg. Westmld.* 14 (E.D.D.) The servant lasses they'd begun To winnle, wind, and spin.

†ˈ**windle**, *v.*[2] *Obs. rare.* [f. as WINDLE *sb.*[2] + -LE 3. Cf. WIMBLE *v.*[2]] *trans.* To winnow.

14.. *Nom.* in Wr.-Wülcker 696/23 *Hoc ventilabrum*, a wyndyllynge. [The English gloss appears to be incomplete.] **1550** COVERDALE *Spir. Perle* vii. 65 When they are fanned or wyndled, and when the wynde of trouble and affl̄yccion begynneth once a litle to blowe. **1887** *Jamieson's Sc. Dict.* Suppl., *Winnel-claith*, v. *Windin-claith*.

windle, *v.*[3] *Obs.* exc. *dial.* Also 5 **winele**, 6 **windell**. [? Back-formation from WINDLESTRAW; but cf. WINDER *v.*] *intr.* To lose strength or vigour; to wither, waste away, dwindle. Hence **windling** *ppl. a.*[2]

c **1325** *Gloss. W. de Bibbesw.* in Wright *Voc.* 161 Jo ay la mayn si estomye [*gloss* so acomeled, *v.r.* wineled]. **1579** W. WILKINSON *Confut. Fam. Love* 31 b, The fruite thereof for want of moysture begynneth to windell. **1620** GATAKER *David's Instruct.* 6 Tender plants..are in danger else to windle and wither away. **1888** *Sheffield Gloss.*, *Windle*, v. to dwindle... *Windling*, adj., feeble, delicate.

windles, obs. form of WINDLASS *sb.*[1]

windless (ˈwɪndlɪs), *a.* [f. WIND *sb.*[1] + -LESS.]

1. Breathless, out of breath. Now *rare.*

a **1400–50** *Wars Alex.* 1271 Sa waike & so wyndles & wery for-foȝten. **1570** FOXE *A. & M.* (ed. 2) 2126/1 His accuser ..came..in such post speede, that in a maner he was wyndlesse entryng into the Bishops chamber. **1609** HOLLAND *Amm. Marcell.* 114 With all the speed I could make I returned all windlesse for hast. **1643** TRAPP *Comm. Gen.* xlix. 27 Panting and windless as a tired Woolf. **1894** J. A. STEUART *In Day of Battle* i, He was stupefied and windless before the smile of disdain had time to leave his face.

2. Free from wind; not exposed to or stirred by the wind, in or upon which no wind blows.

In first quot. applied to wind supposed to be pent underground and to cause earthquakes: = not causing any movement in the atmosphere.

1591 SYLVESTER *Du Bartas* I. iii. 480 When steeples stagger, and huge mountains tremble With wind-less wind [orig. *Le vent sans faire vent*]. **1802** MAWE *Min. Derbysh.* Gloss. (E.D.S.) s.v., A place in a mine where the air is bad or short..is then said to be windless. **1818** SHELLEY *Rosal. & Helen* 1106 The windless sky. **1843** RUSKIN *Mod. Paint.* II. III. iv. §35. 251 Colder and more quiet than a windless sea under the moon of midnight. **1855** M. ARNOLD *New Sirens* 146 In some windless valley.

†**3.** Not causing flatulence. *Obs. rare.*

1562 TURNER *Herbal* II. 85 b, Phasiolus..of Dioscorides is wyndy.., & yᵉ other ar *flatuum expertes* yᵗ is windlesse.

Hence ˈ**windlessly** *adv.*; ˈ**windlessness.**

1897 *Edin. Rev.* Oct. 387 The dawn broke windlessly over the dark mountain pass. **1916** E. F. BENSON *David Blaize* x, The sea slept in the windlessness of this August weather.

windlesse, obs. form of WINDLASS.

windlestraw (ˈwɪnd(ə)lstrɔː). *Sc.* and *dial.* Forms: 1 windelstreaw, -streow, 6 *Sc.* wynd-, windilstray, 7 windle-strawe, 8–9 *Sc.* winlestrae, 9 *dial.* windle-, winnelstrae, -stray, etc., 7– windlestraw. [OE. *windelstrēaw*, ? f. *windel* WINDLE *sb.*¹ + *strēaw* STRAW *sb.*]

1. A dry thin withered stalk of grass, such as is left standing after the flower or seed is shed.

In north. dial. shortened to *windle*.

a **1000** *Voc.* in Wr.-Wülcker 273/23 *Calmum*, windelstreow. **1513** DOUGLAS *Æneis* VII. Prol. 134 With hyrstis harsk of waggand wyndilstrays. *a* **1585** MONTGOMERIE *Cherrie & Slae* 303, I stakkerit at the windilstrayis. *a* **1598** D. FERGUSSON *Scot. Prov.* (1641) 328 He that is redd for windlestrawes, should not sleep in lees. **1641** BEST *Farm. Bks.* (Surtees) 76 If the weather bee harde and sharpe, and the hey shorte and good, they [*sc.* sheep] will not leave soe much as a pile of grasse or a windle-strawe. *a* **1722** in M. P. Brown *Suppl. Dict. Decis.* (1826) IV. 793 To restrict him to the fifth part of the rent, was to send him to lift the rest of his stipend from windlestraws and sandy laverocks. *c* **1730** RAMSAY *Fables* xix. 67 They'll start at winlestraes. **1815** SHELLEY *Alastor* 528 Tall spires of windlestrae Threw their thin shadows down the rugged slope. **1821** SCOTT *Pirate* iv, The air is close,..and the day so calm, that not a windlestraw moves on the heath. **1865** CARLYLE *Fredk. Gt.* XXI. ii. VI. 350 Think what a fine figure of rye and barley, instead of mere windlestraws, beggary and desolation, was realised by that act alone. **1872** BROWNING *Fifine* ix, Thistle fluffs and bearded windlestraws.

2. A name for various long-stalked species of grass, as *Cynosurus cristatus* (dog's-tail grass), *Lolium perenne* (rye-grass), and *Agrostis Spicaventi*. Also ***windlestraw-grass.***

c **1000** *Sax. Leechd.* II. 44 Wiþ earwicgan, genim þæt micle greate windel streaw twyecge. **1636** JOHNSON *Gerarde's Herbal* I. iii. 6 Reed-grasse..in Latine..*Spica venti agrorum*... Some.., much agreeable to the Latine name, call these, Windle-strawes. **1775** J. ANDERSON *Ess. Agric.* 418 The crested dogs-tail-grass, *Cynosurus crystatus*, commonly known in Scotland by the name of Windlestraw-grass. **1801** LEYDEN *Elfin-King* xiii, The windlestrae, so limber and grey [*note*, Rye-grass]. **1862** MRS. NORTON *Lady of La Garaye* Prol. 112 The pale tufts of the windle-strae grass Hang like locks of dry dead hair.

3. *fig.* **a.** Applied to something (material or immaterial) light, trifling, or flimsy; occas. contemptuously to a spear or lance.

1637 RUTHERFORD *Lett.* 6 Jan. (1671) 414 No windle-straws, no bits of clay, no temptations..will then be able to with-stand you. **1831** SCOTT *Ct. Rob.* xi, Not one has the courage to throw his windlestraw while he perceives that of another pointed against himself. **1895** CROCKETT *Men of Moss-Hags* xl, He grippit me with one hand and drew his windle-strae of a sword wi' the other. **1905** *Times Lit. Suppl.* 25 Aug. 267/3 Her..blank verse and other heavy..things..have none of the life and sweetness of her windlestraw.

b. Applied to a thin lanky person, or one of feeble health or character.

1818 MISS FERRIER *Marriage* xxxiv, A wheen puir feckless windlestraes. **1836** J. M. WILSON *Tales* II. 214/2 D'ye ken that this winnle-straw o' a lassie..has won the kirn? [**1845** CARLYLE *Schiller* I. 30 An honest man you may form of windle-straws; but, to make a rascal, you must have grist.] **1907** 'Q' *Poison Isl.* xxxi, A thin, windlestraw of a man.

windling (ˈwɪndlɪŋ), *sb.* Forms: 3–4 wynelynge, 5 wenelyng(e; 7 winling, 8 windlen, wonlyne, 9 winlin, windlin, windling. [? f. WIND *v.*¹ + -LING¹ 2. But perhaps two distinct words.

The word in sense 1 seems to be synonymous with *wyn(e)wes, wynwys* in **1304** *Acc. Exch. K.R.* 12/6 m. 3, **1336** *Ibid.* 19/31 m. 5, **1420** *For. Acc. 3 Hen. VI* G/2.]

†**1.** *collect. sing.* or *pl.* ? Small ropes or cords. *Obs.*

1295 *Acc. Exch. K.R.* 5/7 m. 1 (P.R.O.) In Wynelyngges emptis ad nauem ix.s. v.d. **1356** in *Pipe Roll 32 Edw. III* m. 33/1 (P.R.O.) In CCC. lb. de towe, vjˣˣ. fassibus straminis, xviij Millibus de Wynelynge emptis. **1402** *Acc. Exch. K.R.* 43/6 m. 4 In iiijˣˣ petris de Wenelyng..in factura dicte balengere expenditis. **1407** *Ibid.* 44/11 (1) m. 2 In iij. libris de Wenelynge emptis..iij. d.

2. A bundle of straw or hay. *Sc.*

1645 in J. Davidson *Inverurie* (1878) 206 Twa winlingis of stray. **1737** RAMSAY *Sc. Prov.* (1750) 41 He stumbles at a strae and lowps o'er a wonlyne. **1844** H. STEPHENS *Bk. Farm* II. 125 The cattle-man resumes his labours by bunching up windlings of straw, which are small bundles having a twisted form, of 10 lb. weight, or more each. **1845** *New Statist. Acc. Scot.* XV. *Caithness* 146 The tenants of each penny-land..had..to furnish a certain number of winlins to thatch the mains' stacks. **1862** HISLOP *Prov. Scot.* 88 He starts at straes, and lets windlins gae.

windling, *ppl. a.*: see WINDLE *v.*¹ and *v.*³

windmill (ˈwɪndmɪl, ˈwɪnmɪl), *sb.* (Formerly also as two words.) [f. WIND *sb.*¹ + MILL *sb.*¹; cf. MHG. *wintmül*, G. *windmühle*, LG., Du. *windmolen*, and F. *moulin à vent* (from 13th c.).]

1. A mill the machinery of which is driven by the wind acting upon sails, used (chiefly in flat districts) for grinding corn, pumping water, etc. The older and most characteristic European form consists of a conical mill-house with a dome or 'cap' carrying (usually) four sails; the modern American type consists of a disk of sails mounted on a framework of girders, and is used chiefly for pumping or sawing.

The *sails* (SAIL *sb.*¹ 5) are turned by the force of the wind around an axis or *wind-shaft*, usually nearly horizontal and having some contrivance (now often automatic) for turning it in any direction to enable the sails to catch the wind.

1297 R. GLOUC. (Rolls) 11383 þe king of alemaine was in a windmulle inome. *c* **1384** CHAUCER *H. Fame* III. 190, Y saugh him carien a wyndmelle Vnder a walsh note shale. *a* **1400** *Gloss* in *Rel. Ant.* I. 7 *Ventagile*, a wyndmylne. *c* **1450** *Godstow Reg.* 63 His winde-mille þat stondit vppon hoge wiþ-oute þe towne of doninton. **15..** *Ladye Bessie* (Percy Soc.) 77 He went up unto a wynde mylne, And stoode upon a hyll soe hye. **1546** *Yks. Chantry Surv.* (Surtees 1894) 11 The rente of a wynde mylle there, xxs. **1596** SHAKS. *1 Hen. IV*, III. i. 162, I had rather liue With Cheese and Garlick in a Windmill. **1630** *R. Johnson's Kingd. & Commw.* 644 At no time there bloweth so much wind as will move a windmill. **1759** SMEATON in *Phil. Trans.* LI. 159 Windmills, such as the different species for raising water for drainage, &c. **1774** GOLDSM. *Nat. Hist.* (1776) II. 21 If we look upon the sails of a windmill moving, at a distance, they appear to go very slow. **1841** T. A. TROLLOPE *Western France* I. xii. 212 Behind the town is a high bluff..entirely covered with windmills. **1885** *Law Rep. 10 App. Cas.* 411 Some spars and canvas were sacrificed in order to erect a windmill to assist in working the pumps. **1888** *Encycl. Brit.* XXIV. 599/2 American windmills generally have the sails arranged in an annulus or disk.

2. A figure of a windmill; a sign or character resembling this, as a cross or asterisk. Also *attrib.* Now *rare* or *Obs.*

1402 *Pol. Poems* (Rolls) II. 57, I know not an a from the wynd-mylne. **1581** CAMPION in *Confer.* II. (1583) I ij, A note is a marke that may be remoued, that teacheth to turne..by this crosse, or by that windmill or marke. **1898** MORRIS *Austral Engl.*, *Windmill J.P.*, expression formerly used in New South Wales for any J.P. who was ill-educated and supposed to sign his name with a cross x.

3. a. A model of a windmill. **b.** A toy consisting of a cross-shaped piece of card or other light substance fixed at the end of a stick so as to revolve like the sails of a windmill when moved through the air.

1557 *Will of E. Pettinger* (Somerset Ho.), I giue..to my vncle..my wyndmylle whych hangeth in my hall. **1598** FLORIO, *Ventarèllo*,..a piece of a card or paper cut like a crosse, and with a pin put in at the end of a sticke, which running against the wind doth twirle about, our English children call it a wind-mill. **1611** COTGR. s.v. *Virolet*. **1836** [HOOTON] *Bilberry Thurland* I. v. 113 Last week,..I sold windmills and lambs for children. **1853** DICKENS *Bleak Ho.* xiv, I so conciliated Peepy's affections by buying him a windmill and two flour-sacks, that [etc.].

c. *Cricket.* A style of bowling with a high overarm delivery. ? *Obs.*

1867 *Australasian* 19 Jan. 76/3 A change in bowling was tried, Wardill going on with his 'windmills', *vice* Conway. **1900** W. A. BETTESWORTH *Walkers of Southgate* 124 Taking his run up to the wicket, swinging his arm in what has been described as 'a windmill action'. **1920** in P. F. Warner *Cricket* 86 Spofforth's windmill deliveries.

4. *fig.* and *allusively.* †**a.** A fanciful notion, a crotchet; a visionary scheme or project. *Obs.*

1612 WEBSTER *White Devil* II. ii. 12 Others that raise up their confederate spirits, 'Bout windmils. **1622** MASSINGER & DEKKER *Virg. Mart.* II. ii, Thy head is full of Winde-mils. **1639** J. CLARKE *Parœm.* 158 He hath wind-milnes in 's head. **1648** JENKYN *Blind Guide* iii. 39 You have a windmill upon your pate. **1728** EARL OF AILESBURY *Mem.* (1890) 576 Frize, who had a windmill in her head like her husband. **1749** LAVINGTON *Enthus. Meth. & Papists* (1820) 18 The wind-mill is indeed in all their heads.

b. In allusions to the story of Don Quixote (see QUIXOTE) tilting at windmills under the delusion that they were giants.

1644 CLEVELAND *Char. Lond. Diurnall* 3 The Quixotes of this Age fight with the Wind-mills of their owne Heads. **1646** LLUELYN *Men-Miracles* etc. 84 No doubty Don Quixote, like those that fight, With Warlike Wind mill, and then rise up Knight. *a* **1656** R. COX *Actæon & Diana* 30 The Barber..vows to make you the windmill, whilest he plays Don Quixot against you furiously. *a* **1658** [see QUIXOTE]. **1782** MISS BURNEY *Cecilia* IX. iii, Our giants may indeed be only windmills. **1869** LE FANU *Wyvern Myst.* III. 105 What have I to do wi' other folk's windmills? **1894** FARRAR *Christ* 84 *note*, Dr. Edersheim is again—so far as I am concerned—fighting a windmill. **1898** [see TILTER *sb.*¹ 1]. **1937** A. CHRISTIE *Death on Nile* xxiv. 238 Rather eccentric..inclined to tilt at windmills. **1978** P. BRYERS *Cat Trapper* viii. 57 Mike was into the sort of thing I'd like to be doing...Tilting at windmills?

c. *to fling (throw) one's cap over the windmill* [= F. *jeter son bonnet par-dessus les moulins*]: to act recklessly and defiantly, fly in the face of convention.

1885 MRS. LYNN LINTON *Chr. Kirkland* xiii, A wild outward kind of young fellow, who had enjoyed his youth too freely and flung his cap too far over the windmill. **1920** LOCKE *House of Baltazar* xxii, You're going to make a bolt with Godfrey and throw your cap over the windmills. **1923** F. H. KITCHIN *Divers. Dawson* 305 Throwing their caps over the windmill under the stimulus of war patriotism.

†**5.** *fig.* (from WIND *sb.*¹ 10). A cause of 'wind'.

1616 DRAXE *Bibl. Scholast.* 80 A full stomacke is a windemill.

6. An airscrew, esp. one of the kind designed by Cierva for the autogiro. Now *Hist.*

1931 CIERVA Y CADORNIU *Wings of Tomorrow* 88, I designed the blades of the windmill. **1935** *Sun* (Baltimore) 31 Jan. 3/3 This new fast auto gyro will have no propeller. It will tilt its present windmill, gear it to the engine and so get its lift and forward drive. **1949** *Gloss. Aeronaut. Terms* (*B.S.I.*) II. 20 *Windmill*, an airscrew designed to produce power by axial transmission relative to the air.

7. *attrib.* and *Comb.* (See also 2.) **a.** attrib., as ***windmill country, hill, sail***; moving like windmill-sails, as ***windmill arms***; having a radiating form like windmill-sails, as †***windmill battle*** (see quot.); (sense 6 above) ***windmill aeroplane, (air)plane, rotor, wing***; **b.** Comb., as ***windmill-like, -studded*** adjs.; **windmill brake state** *Aeronaut.* (see quot. 1969); **windmill-cap,** the upper story of a windmill when made movable so as to turn the sails to the wind (Knight *Dict. Mech.* 1875); **windmill-grass,** an Australian grass, *Chloris truncata*, with long spreading flower-spikes; **windmill plant** = TELEGRAPH-*plant*; **windmill-pump,** a pump worked by a windmill, a wind-pump; †**windmillward,** = MILLWARD.

1931 *Statesman* (Calcutta) 5 Dec., The Autogiro or '*windmill' aeroplane has just been put on the public market in this country for the first time. **1928** *Daily Express* 10 Aug. 11/4 A '*windmill' airplane is to fly the channel. **1891** KIPLING *City Dreadf. Nt.* 88 The *windmill arms and the angry eyes fall. **1639** MARKHAM *Soldier's Gram.* II. 65 This ..forme of Battaile following, which is called by the name of the *Wind-Mill Battaile,..standeth every way ready prepared to entertaine fight. **1948** *Jrnl. R. Aeronaut. Soc.* 269/1 In the *windmill brake state, the rotor is again working in a regular slipstream. **1969** *Gloss. Aeronaut. & Astronaut. Terms* (*B.S.I.*) v. 19 *Windmill-brake state*, the operating condition of a rotor when the rotor thrust and the axial flow through and outside the rotor disc area are all in the same direction. **1887** HISSEY *Holiday on Road* 83 Approaching Mayfield, we entered upon the heart of a *windmill country. **1889** MAIDEN *Useful Pl. Australia* 80 *Chloris truncata*, *Windmill Grass. **1440** *Extr. Aberd. Reg.* (1844) I. 395 In quodam ludo de ly Haliblude ludendo apud ly *Wyndmylhill. **1568** GRAFTON *Chron.* II. 275 A little windemill hill heard by. **1577** LEIGH *Surv.* I ij b, The most notable knowen markes,..as..Marlepittes,..Brokes,..Windmill hilles, etc. **1587** *Engl. Misc.* (Surtees 1890) 91 The oulde walles of the toune from the castell-bridge alongeste the *wyndmylle hole. **1848** tr. *Hoffmeister's Trav. Ceylon*, etc. vii. 277 Their *wind-mill-like wings. **1927** *Times* 27 Apr. 16/3 It was agreed to use the word..aerodyne to designate all heavier-than-air craft, in which category the class name for the *windmill plane appears as gyro plane. **1891** C. ROBERTS *Adrift Amer.* 149 A kind of patent *windmill-pump. **1944** H. F. GREGORY *Anything Horse can Do* iv. 48 The stick [of the Autogiro] was connected to the hub of the *windmill rotor by push-pull tubes and cables. **1583** STUBBES *Anat. Abus.* I. (1879) 71 Sometimes they [*sc.* ruffs] are suffered to hang ouer their shoulders, like *windmil sayles fluttering in the winde. **1759** SMEATON in *Phil. Trans.* LI. 138 In trying experiments on windmill-sails, the wind itself is too uncertain to answer the purpose. **1864** KINGSLEY *Let. from Biarritz* in *Life* xxi. (1879) II. 169 The vulture [in the courtyard] has been..expanding concave wings as big as windmill sails. **1845** FORD *Handbk. Spain* II. 585/2 Corrales under its *windmill-studded hill. **1314–15** *Cal. Rotul. Chartarum* (1803) 241 Will'us *Wyndmilward. **1931** CIERVA Y CADORNIU *Wings of Tomorrow* 82 A flying machine with a *windmill wing.

†**c.** quasi-*adj.* (*fig.*): Variable, flighty. *Obs.*

a **1644** QUARLES *New Distemper* Wks. (Grosart) I. 151/1 Your windmill fancies. **1657** J. SERGEANT *Schism Dispach't* 134 Your vertible and wind-mill uncertainty.

Hence †**windmill** *v.*; ˈ**wind,miller** [cf. G. *windmüller*], the keeper of a windmill; ˈ**wind,milly** *a.*, abounding in windmills.

a **1530** J. HEYWOOD *Wether* (Brandl) 509, I am a *wynd myller as many mo be. **1654** VILVAIN *Theorem. Theol.* iii. 113 Like Wind-millers, they make every wind serv their turns. **1705** *Lond. Gaz.* No. 4170/4 John Childs,..a Wind-Miller by Trade. **1865** W. WHITE *East. Eng.* II. iii. 40 It 'blew hard enough to winner taters', as a windmiller in Warwickshire once said to a friend of mine. **1863** DICKENS *Uncomm. Trav.* xxvii, A *windmilly country this.

windmill, (ˈwɪndmɪl, ˈwɪnmɪl), *v.* [f. the *sb.*]

†**a.** *intr.* To turn or change direction like a windmill *obs. nonce-wd.*

1694 N. H. *Ladies Dict.* 230/2 Not many days had passed ere this extraordinary Passion Wind-mill'd about to the contrary point of the Compass.

b. *trans.* and *intr.* To move (one's arms or legs) in a manner suggestive of a windmill.

1927 W. E. COLLINSON *Contemp. Eng.* 18 At this school we had our first taste of fighting or rather windmilling with the arms. **1928** *Daily Express* 6 Nov. 8 They..set about their efforts again, windmilling his arms and legs until he gasped with unconscious exhaustion. **1959** R. COLLIER *City that wouldn't Die* v. 67 Windmilling your arms to keep the blood coursing. **1979** S. BRETT *Comedian Dies* v. 55 Lennie Barber ..seemed to lose his balance and sank back, arms windmilling, on to the side of his chair. **1982** W. BOYD *Ice-Cream War* 4 The colonel windmilled his arms and cracked his knuckles.

c. *intr.* *Aeronaut.* Of the propeller or rotor of an aircraft: to spin unpowered; *to windmill down*, to descend with the rotor spinning; also *fig.*

1934 *Jrnl. R. Aeronaut. Soc.* XXXVIII. 18 Captain Barnwell said..that it could be assumed that when an engine was fully throttled the airscrew was windmilling freely. **1942** *Flight* 26 Mar. 296/2 When an airscrew is windmilling..the effect is exactly opposite to its normal one. **1958** *Listener* 2 Jan. 10/1 The rotor windmilling freely as on an autogiro. **1963** SOBEY & SUGGS *Control of Aircraft & Missile Powerplants* vii. 181 The forward flight of the airframe will cause the engine to windmill and create sufficient airflow through the engine to minimize the probability of a hot start. **1976** *Shooting Times & Country*

Mag. 16–22 Dec. 29/2, I shot at another goose which peeled off, flew fluttering for a hundred yards, and then windmilled down stone dead. **1978** M. Babson *Tightrope for Three* xxvi. 152 Autorotation was a standard and perfectly safe manoeuvre, the helicopter windmilling down with the pilot still in complete control.

Hence '**windmilling** *ppl. a.* and *vbl. sb.*

1945 *Jrnl. R. Aeronaut. Soc.* XLIX. 716 With the windmilling propeller the changed air-flow over the aircraft does not impair the handling characteristics. **1959** C. A. Meyer in O. E. Lancaster *Jet Propulsion Engines* 149 A typical curve showing the drag of a turbo-jet engine during windmilling is shown in Fig. C, 11f. **1973** J. Wainwright *Touch of Malice* 98 The young man was obviously a nutter. .. His slobbing mouth. His windmilling arms. **1978** M. Farren *Feelies* 33 The other girl was spun, flat on her back with windmilling arms and legs.

Windmill Hill. The name of the site of a causeway camp near Avebury, Wilts., type site of the neolithic age in Britain, used to designate the type of culture, pottery, etc., characteristic of that period.

1930 E. C. Curwen in *Antiquity* IV. 26 The varieties of pottery.. have been collectively described as the Windmill Hill type. **1947** J. & C. Hawkes *Prehist. Britain* ii. 40 The mausoleum most fashionable among the Windmill Hill people was the long barrow. **1954** S. Piggott *Neolithic Cultures* ii. 18 The Windmill Hill culture was basically that of cattle-breeders. **1963** *Field Archaeol.* (Ordnance Survey) (ed. 4) 33 While 'Windmill Hill' pottery predominates, most other forms of Neolithic pottery are represented. **1971** *World Archaeol.* III. 239 The Q1 skeleton strongly suggested that a member of the Windmill Hill Culture was cut to pieces by this type of large metal weapon. **1983** P. A. Crowl *Intell. Traveller's Guide to Historic Britain* i. 15 Those large mounds of earth thrown up by people of the Windmill Hill culture to cover their dead.

windo(e, -dok, obs. ff. window, winnock.

†'**windolet.** *Obs.* [f. window *sb.* + -let.] A small window. Also *fig.*

1592 R. D. *Hypnerotomachia* 9 The same loopes or windolets in diverse places.. dispersed and set. **1596** R. L[inche] *Diella* (1877) 31 When leaden-harted sleepe had shut mine eyes, and close o'redrawn their windolets of light. **1597** Middleton *Wisd. Sol.* vii. 10 The heart-strong health is the soules brightest eye, The heart-sick body heal'd by beauties wealth, Two sunnie windolets of eithers skie.

†**windolf.** *Obs.* (*E. Anglia.*) In 5 wyndolff(e. [Obscure. The second syllable is prob. related to delf[1], delve *v.*; cf. E. Anglian *delf*, a drain, ditch.] ? A refuse pit.

14.. *Bk. Brome* (1886) 162 ȝe shall enquere ȝef ony mane make ony wyndolsse [*sic*], and ley oney dong in the comyne wey. **1440** *Crt.-roll Gt. Waltham* (Essex) *Manor* 19 May (MS.), Andreas Longe de Plecy fodit regiam viam.. et inde fecit unum wyndolff ad nocumentum.

windolite ('wɪndəʊlaɪt). Also **Windolite, windowlite.** [f. window *sb.* + *-lite* (alteration of light *sb.*).] The name of a transparent material serving as a substitute for glass.

A proprietary name in Australia.

1927 *Glasgow Herald* 1 Feb. 6/4 If the pullets are to be confined.. wide shelter boards and glass, or 'windolite', shutters must be fixed. **1935** *Times Educ. Suppl.* 16 Mar. p. iv/1 A sheet of glass or windolite or a small *cloche* will afford them [*sc.* plants] shelter. **1951** 'N. Shute' *Round Bend* 30 An upstairs window was broken and shut up with windowlite tacked over the frame.

'**wind-on,** *a. Photogr.* [f. vbl. phr. *to wind on*: see wind *v.*[1] 23.] Designating or pertaining to (part of) the mechanism for advancing a film to the next position.

1963 *Listener* 31 Jan. 198/2 As for the camera.. the wind-on mechanism jammed. **1976** J. McClure *Rogue Eagle* vi. 101 Oeloefse removed a sliver of film from behind the wind-on spool.

'**windore.** *Obs.* or *dial.* Also 6 wyndoor(e, 7–9 windoor, windor, 8 windeoor, vindore. [Altered form of window *sb.* by association with door *sb.*: cf. wind-door.] A window.

1542 Udall *Erasm. Apoph.* 245 b, The other without any more bones cast me the byrde.. out at the wyndoore. **1582** Stanyhurst *Æneis* iii. (Arb.) 75 At thee wyndoors, where moonshyne brimlye dyd enter. **1605** B. Jonson *Volpone* i. v, Neuer do's come abroad, neuer takes ayre, But at a windore. **1663** Butler *Hud.* i. ii. 214 Knowing they were of doubtful gender, And that they came in at a Windore. *a* **1687** Petty *Pol. Anat.* (1691) 14 Stone-wall Houses, with Chimneys, Doors, Windores, Gardens and Orchards. **1722** in *Rutland Gloss.* (1891), The North Weste windeoor. **1771** Smollett *Humphry Cl.* iii. 18 July, One Issabel, a painted harlot, that was thrown out of a vindore. **1825** Jennings *Obs. Dial. W. Eng.*, *Windor*, a window.

windostar, var. winnowster *Obs.*

window ('wɪndəʊ), *sb.* Forms: 3 windoȝe, -ohe, -ewe (?), wyndouwe, 3–4 windou, 4 wyndew, wondowe, wyntdouwe, *pl.* windos, *Sc.* vyndow, 4–6 wyndow(e, -ou, wyndo, 5–6 wyndoe, 6 -oo, wendo, windoe, *pl.* wyndose, wyendos, vynndovs, wendoyes, *Sc.* vindo, wondow, 6–7 windo, -owe, 4– window. [ME. *windoȝe*, a. ON. *vindauga*, f. *vindr* wind *sb.*[1] + *auga* eye *sb.*[1] (See also wind-door, windore, windown, winnock.) The Scand. word replaced and finally superseded OE. *éaȝþyrel* eyethurl, *éaȝduru*, but the French-derived fenester was in concurrent use down to the beginning of the modern period.]

1. a. An opening in a wall or side of a building, ship, or carriage, to admit light or air, or both, and to afford a view of what is outside or inside.

In ancient buildings it was either left entirely open, furnished with shutters or curtains, or (sometimes) glazed; in modern buildings or vehicles for human occupation, it is usually fitted with sheets of glass (horn, mica, etc.), a frame containing a pane or panes of glass, or glazed sashes, the whole framework being known as the window.

It has been suggested that *widewen* in Lay. 30822 is a miswriting for *wīdewen* = *windewen* 'windows'.

a **1225** *Ancr. R.* 50 þe leste þæt ȝe euer muwen luuieð our þurles, al beon heo lutle, þe parluris lest & nerewest [*Titus MS.* windohes, al beon ho lutle, þe parlure windohe beo least & narewest]. *c* **1250** *Gen. & Ex.* 602 Fowerti dais after ðis, Arches windoȝe undon it is. *c* **1290** *S. Eng. Leg.* I. 241/35 To a derne wyndouwe softeliche seint Nicholas gan gon. *a* **1300** *Cursor M.* 15035 O walles and windos als þair hefdes ouer þai hang. **13..** *K. Alis.* 6164 (Laud MS.), Wyndewes closed by on gynne. **1362** Langl. *P. Pl.* A. iii. 52 þer nis nouþur Wyndou ne Auter, þat I ne schulde maken oþur mende and my nome write. *c* **1375** *Sc. Leg. Saints* xxii. (*Laurentius*) 725 His vyndow opnyt he in hy. *c* **1380** *Sir Ferumb.* 1362 Atte wondowe sche lynede out. *c* **1450** *Merlin* x. 140 Merlin.. opened the two wyndowes towarde the gardyn, for he wolde that thei hadde lyght ther-ynne. **1530** Palsgr. 289/1 Wyndowes that be in a house toppe, *lucarne*. **1542** Boorde *Regyment* viii. Ej b, In the nyght let the wyndowes of your howse, specyallye of your chambre bee closed. **1549** *Compl. Scot.* xvii. 148 In ȝour glasyn vindois. **1566** in Peacock *Engl. Ch. Furniture* (1866) 98 The roode lofte—taken downe and sold.. to harrie walwyn.. wch he doth mynd to make windoes of. *a* **1578** Lindesay (Pitscottie) *Chron. Scot.* (S.T.S.) II. 177 The earle Bothwell.. come out at ane wondow [*v.r.* windok] be ane tow. **1592** Shaks. *Rom. & Jul.* ii. ii. 2 But soft, what light through yonder window breaks? **1632** Milton *Penseroso* 159 Storied Windows richly dight. **1667** —— *P.L.* iv. 191 As a Thief.. In at the window climbes. **1781** Cowper *Retirement* 498 Trees are to be seen From ev'ry window. **1837** Dickens *Pickw.* li, The windows were looked out of often enough to justify the imposition of an additional duty upon them. **1853** —— *Bleak Ho.* xx, Mr. Guppy has been lolling out of window all the morning. **1855** *Poultry Chron.* III. 507 A window.. of perforated zinc. **1860** Tyndall *Glac.* i. xxiii. 162 Against some of the windows.. the snow was also piled, obscuring more than half their light. **1864** Lewins *H.M. Mails* 201 [At the last stroke of] six, when all the windows fall like so many swords of Damocles.

b. With qualification denoting (*a*) the building, room, vehicle, etc. to which the window belongs, as ***carriage, church, door-, lobby, office, parlour, steeple, stove window***, shop-window, or (*b*) the form or material, as ***double-, drop-, French, wheel-window***, bay-, bow-, glass-, rose-window.

a **1225** [see above]. **1428** [see bay-window]. **1447–8** [see gable *sb.*[1] 4]. **1450** *Rolls of Parlt.* V. 182/2 A Gavill Wyndowe over a Cloyster. **1485** *Rec. St. Mary at Hill* 29 All the glass wyndowes in the saide place. ? *c* **1495** *Ibid.* 102 Church wyndowis, the vestry wyndowis. **1560, 1680** [see stove *sb.*[1] 6]. **1581** Burne in *Cath. Tractates* (S.T.S.) 110 At the tolbuith vindo. **1583** *Exchequer Rolls Scot.* XXI. 556 At the chekker hous windo. **1616** [see door *sb.* 8]. **1854** *Directory Bath, Wells, etc.* p. ix, When the Letter-box is closed for the despatch of any Mail,.. an extra box is opened in the Lobby Window. **1875** Knight *Dict. Mech.*, *Double-window*, one having two sets of sash, inclosing a body of air as a non-conductor of heat and to deaden noise.

2. *transf.* A window space or opening; *esp.* in phr. ***in the window***, now chiefly with reference to the exhibition of notices, advertisements, etc., or the display of goods (as in a shop-window).

to dress a window: cf. *window-dresser, -dressing* in 5 e.

a **1310** in Wright *Lyric P.* xxxi. 91 In a wyndou ther we stod, we custe us fyfty sythe. *c* **1375** *Sc. Leg. Saints* xlv. (*Cristine*) 19 Incense laid in a wyndo by. **1382** Wyclif *Acts* xx. 9 Sum ȝong man, Euticus bi name, sittinge on the wyndow [*Vulg.* super fenestram; ἐπὶ τῆς θυρίδος; **1526** Tindale in a wyndowe]. **1543** *Galway Arch.* in *10th Rep. Hist. MSS. Comm.* App. v. 410 No man.. shall have no kynd of merchandiz in ther houssis shopis or wyndous to be sold to strangers. **1601** Shaks. *Jul. C.* ii. i. 36 Searching the Window for a Flint, I found This Paper. **1648** Bp. Hall *Breathings Devout Soul* xix. 29 Whiles I have but a spider in my window, or a bee in my garden, or a worm under my feet. **1655** Fuller *Ch. Hist.* ix. vi. §46 At Fotheringhay-Castle I have read written by Her in a window, with a pointed Diamond [etc.]. **1757** *Hist. Two Mod. Adventurers* II. 195 The Sashes were thrown up, and they were all sitting in the Windows. **1823** Scott *Quentin D.* xix, An old *romaunt*.. which lay beside him in the window. **1835** Dickens *Sk. Boz, Pawnbroker's Shop*, The articles of stock which are displayed in some profusion in the window. **1861** *Brit. Postal Guide* 1 Jan. 26 A list of the addresses is fixed in the window of the Post Office to which they may have been sent. **1905** Wells *Kipps* i. ii. §2 Carshot, the window-dresser.. nagged persistently.. until the window was done.

b. ***goldsmith's window*** (*Gold-mining colloq.*): a rich working in which the gold shows abundantly.

1890 'R. Boldrewood' *Miner's Rt.* xiv, This.. was after we had worked out our 'goldsmith's window', as the adjacent diggers christened it.

3. a. Applied to openings resembling or likened to a window in shape or function.

e.g. †An opening in the side of a vessel, as a salt-cellar, a censer, and the like; †an opening or gap; †a blank space left in a writing; a shutter, valve, door, or similar opening; *pl.* a pattern of squares made with sugar on bread and butter; soap-bubbles blown between the finger and thumb.

c **1400** Maundev. (Roxb.) x. 38 þat tabernacle has na wyndowes. ? *a* **1400** *Morte Arth.* 911 The vesare, the aventaile, enarmede so faire, Voyde with-owttyne vice, with wyndowes of syluer. **1459** *Paston Lett.* I. 470, j saltsaler.. with many wyndowes. **1517** in *Archaeologia* LXI. 84 A tabernacle of golde with vij wyndowes of birell for the sacrament. *c* **1530** in Gutch *Coll. Cur.* (1781) II. 311 Oone Sensour parcell gilte withe Windowes gilte and thoppar Boolls. **1533** Cranmer *Let.* in *Misc. Writ.* (Parker Soc.) 249 That your said collation have a window expedient to set what name I will therein. **1549** Chaloner *Erasm. on Folly* N j, How many wyndowes [orig. *nodos*] they muste make to theyr shooes. **1576** Baker *Gesner's Jewell of Health* 162 An apt hole.. which may one whyles shutte, and another whyles open,.. through the helpe of a certayne plate or wyndowe of yron. **1632** Lithgow *Trav.* vii. 317 Euery House openeth their Cisterne window, and receiueth as much water, as is able to suffice them till the next Inundation. *a* **1700** Evelyn *Diary* 30 Sept. 1644, In the piers of the arches are windowes as it were, to receive the water when it is high and full. **1708** W. King *Cookery* (1709) 81 The Fav'rite Child.. makes great clutter, Till he has Windows on his Bread and Butter. **1832** L. Hunt *Lines written in May* 15 The merry sap has run up in the bowers, And burst the windows of the buds in flowers. **1859** H. Kingsley *G. Hamlyn* xxxii, Putting the fore-finger and thumb of each hand together, as if he was making 'windows' with soap-suds. **1892** *Photogr. Ann.* II. 476 A large, well-made lamp, having side windows. **1894** Bottone *Electr. Instr. Making* (ed. 6) 52 The.. finished fixed sheet, with its 'windows', central aperture, and side strips.

b. ***windows of heaven***: openings in the firmament through which rain was thought to pour.

A literalism from Heb. *'ărubbōth hashshāmayim*, which is rendered in the LXX by καταρράκται τοῦ οὐρανοῦ, in the Vulgate by *cataractæ cæli* = 'the floodgates of heaven' (Douay version); in the early Wycliffite version 'the goteris of heuene': cf. cataract 1.

1388 Wyclif *Gen.* vii. 11 The wyndowis of heuene weren opened, and reyn was maad on erthe. *c* **1420** *Prymer* 67 [Ps. xlii. 7] Deppe clepiþ deppe, in þe vois of þi wyndowis. **1611** Cotgr., *Ventailles du ciel*, the windowes, or floud-gates, of heauen. **1667** Milton *P.L.* xi. 849 The deep, who now had stopt His Sluces, as the Heav'n his windows shut. **1866** Macdonald *Ann. Q. Neighb.* xxx, The rain was worse than ever,.. the wind was not cold, but the windows of heaven were opened. **1869** Goulburn *Purs. Holiness* i. 1 [Elijah] shut up the windows of the sky by his prayers, and by his prayers re-opened them.

c. *Anat.* = fenestra 1.

1615 Crooke *Body of Man* 603 Betwixt these two windows aboue the lower hole is there a little knub or protuberation. **1683** Snape *Anat. Horse* iii. xiv. (1686) 139 The third is called the Stirrop,.. and is fixed.. round that passage that is called the oval window. **1718** J. Chamberlayne *Relig. Philos.* I. xiii. §7. 249 There are yet two Openings in.. the Drum [of the ear]: the first of 'em are called the Oval Window... The other is called the Round Window. **1879** Calderwood *Mind & Br.* 71.

d. *Geol.* = fenster.

1908 H. B. C. Sollas tr. *Suess's Face of Earth* III. viii. 350 This term 'window' has been brought into use by our fellow geologists in Switzerland, and we shall adopt it in this work for those cases in which a subjacent tectonic element is brought to light by erosion. **1927** L. W. Collet *Structure of Alps* ii. i. 26 Three windows occur in the Eastern Alps. **1939, 1954** [see fenster]. **1980** *Sci. Amer.* Oct. 131/2 The presence of sedimentary rocks in the windows of the Blue Ridge indicates that the crystalline rocks there overlie sedimentary material.

e. A transparent panel in a package, through which the contents can be seen; *spec.* on an envelope (see *window-envelope*, sense 5 e).

1914 [see *window-envelope*, sense 5 e below]. **1938** D. E. A. Charlton *Art of Packaging* 94 The latest.. improvement.. [paper] napkins visible through a cellophane window. **1952** E. J. Labarre *Dict. Paper & Paper-making* (ed. 2) 90 The use of.. envelopes.. with cellophane windows is prohibited by most continental postal administrations. **1977** C. McCarry *Secret Lovers* iii. 40 Wilson.. flipped the plastic windows to make certain that all the papers were still in the wallet.

f. Freq. with capital initial. Mil. code name: = chaff *sb.*[1] 6 b.

1942 Ld. Cherwell in *Oxf. Mag.* (1963) 9 May 283/1 If you go into the meeting and try to get 'Window' used, you'll find me and Tizard united against you. **1946** J. P. Baxter *Scientists against Time* vi. 93 The British used Window for the first time over Hamburg on the night of July 24–25, 1943. **1947** [see chaff *sb.*[1] 6 b]. **1962** A. P. Rowe *Let.* in R. V. Jones *Most Secret War* (1978) iv. 41 What I want to emphasize is that from no one at no time did I hear a breath of anything like window. **1963** D. Irving *Destruction of Dresden* iii. iii. 135 The crews of these new bomber formations had been cascading *Window* into the air in copious amounts. **1980** M. Middlebrook *Battle of Hamburg* viii. 125 It is not known which aircraft dropped the first bundle of Window.

g. *Computers.* (i) The screen of a VDU regarded as a means of displaying part of a drawing stored in a computer; the part of a drawing, program, etc., chosen for display.

1966 *Computer Jrnl.* IX. 21/1 The 10-inch square display screen.. is treated as a 'window' on to a very large drawing board. *Ibid.* 22/1 The display 'window' can be moved one grid space in any of four directions. **1968** *IBM Systems Jrnl.* VII. 163 A subsequent computation can determine the point at which any line crosses the edge of the window. **1982** J. E. Scott *Introd. Interactive Computer Graphics* vii. 124 The size and location of the window are expressed in user coordinates because the window is specified in relation to the drawing... The dimensions and center point of the viewport are expressed in normalized screen coordinates.

(ii) = viewport 2.

1974 *AFIPS Conf. Proc.* XLIII. 251/1 The display screen is divisible into rectangular, possibly overlapping 'windows'. **1980** W. Newman in C. E. Vandoni *Eurographics 80*, 4 NAN.. uses overlapping windows, in this case in colour but with contents restricted to text. **1983** *MicroComputer Printout* Sept. 57/2 A similar, but more flexible system allows you to split the screen into two windows for viewing different sections of the model at once. **1985** *Acorn User* Feb. 37/2 Windows can be created which can then be rearranged to provide any print format required.

4. a. *fig.* Applied to the senses or organs of sense, esp. the eyes, regarded as inlets or outlets to or from the mind or soul (also *transf.* in Shaks., applied to the eyelids).

a **1340** HAMPOLE *Psalter* cxviii. 37 We syn wiþ oure eghen when we couayte the þynge þat we see, and swa ded cummys in at þe wyndous of oure wittes. *c* **1386** CHAUCER *Melib.* ¶456 Thou hast suffred hem entre in to thyn herte wilfully by the wyndowes of thy body. **1481** CAXTON *Reynard* xl. (Arb.) 109 Whan ye here after slepe ye nede not to shette but one wyndowe where another muste shette two. **1544** PHAER *Regim. Lyfe* (1553) B viij, The eyes..are the windowes of the minde, for bothe ioye and anger..are seen..through them. **1588** SHAKS. *L.L.L.* v. ii. 848 Behold the window of my heart, mine eie. **1592** —— *Ven. & Ad.* 482 Her two blew windowes faintly she vpheaueth. **1594** —— *Rich. III*, v. iii. 116 Ere I let fall the windowes of mine eyes. **1652** BENLOWES *Theoph.* III. xxx, Those Lights, the radiant Windows of her Minde. **1860** *Slang Dict.* (ed. 2), *Windows*, the eyes, or 'peepers'. **1889** RIDER HAGGARD *Cleopatra* (II. iii.) in *Illustr. Lond. News* 23 Feb. 236/3 She..opened the windows of her eyes.

b. *fig.* and in allusive or proverbial expressions. *to go* (*be thrown*, etc.) *out of the window* (U.S. without *of*), to be abandoned, discarded, or made worthless; also (U.S.) *to be out the window*. *to open a window to*: to give an opportunity or occasion for (after Terence *Heaut.* III. i. 72 [481] quantam fenestram ad nequitiem patefeceris). *to throw the house out at* (*the*) *window* [= F. *jeter la maison par la fenêtre*]: to make a great commotion, turn everything topsy-turvy. *to come in by the window* [= F. *entrer par la fenêtre*], to come in stealthily.

c **1420** *Prymer* 12 þou art maad wyndowe of heuene, þat soreuful men entre as sterris. **14..** *Pol. Rel. & L. Poems* (1903) 187 Loke owt at the wyndows of kyndnesse. **1523** [COVERDALE] *Old God* (1534) G, Whan Pipine..sawe so great a wyndowe opened, and so great an occasyon gyuen to hym self, for to inuade the realme. **1551** CROWLEY *Pleas. & Payne* 350 And youe were gladde to take them in, Bycause you knewe that they dyd knowe That youe came in by the wyndowe. *c* **1586** C'TESS PEMBROKE *Ps.* CXXXIX. i, Yea closest closett of my thought Hath open windowes to thine eyes. **1589** NASHE *Countercuffe* Wks. (Grosart) I. 128 To open such a windowe to the deuill, as they were presently giuen ouer as a pray to the iawes of hell. **1603** HOLLAND *Plutarch's Mor.* 129 For such a fault as this, which of us here would not have cried out that the walles should have burst withall, and beene readie to have throwen the house out of window? **1611**, **1844** [see HOUSE *sb.*[1] 19]. **1621** T. WILLIAMSON tr. *Goulart's Wise Vieillard* 73 Sometimes shee is all for belly cheare and banquettings, and as we say, throwes the house out at the windowes. **1639** J. CLARKE *Parœm.* 28 Love creeps in at window, but goes out at doore. **1687** BOYLE *Martyrd. Theodora* vi. 110 The wounds that we quietly suffer to pierce our Breasts, would open you Windows into our hearts. **1809** MALKIN *Gil Blas* VII. xi. ¶6 The enraged marquis.. pounding Laura's fair face to a jelly with his fist, and turning her whole house out at window. **1879** FARRAR *St. Paul* II. 90 His Second Epistle to the Corinthians opens a window into the very emotions of his heart. **1939** H. L. ICKES *Secret Diary* (1954) III. 3 Steve Early..said that the 'brain trust was out of the window'. **1945** *Sun* (Baltimore) 1 Oct. 4-0/3 Production of specialty goods—such as birthday and wedding cakes—was 'out the window'. **1946** *Ibid.* 6 July 4/1 As a guide, past experience went out the window early this year when the number of retirements suddenly increased. **1964** S. M. MILLER in I. L. Horowitz *New Sociol.* 300 The concept of 'unemployables' was largely thrown out the window. **1968** F. LUNDBERG *Rich & Super-Rich* iv. 173 As FDR himself said, 'the New Deal is out the window.' **1969** G. DONALDSON *Fifteen Men* xi. 184 'The Uncle Louis kissing babies went out of the window this afternoon', said Green. **1977** *Chicago Tribune* 2 Oct. XIII. 24/3 The old rule-of-thumb of putting insulation with a resistance rating of 19 in your attic (R-19) is 'out the window'.

c. A continuous range of electromagnetic wavelengths for which the atmosphere (or some other medium) is relatively transparent.

1949 *Bull. Amer. Meteorol. Soc.* XXX. 233/1 Dr. Buettner indicated as one problem the measurement of solar radiation near 0·21μ, where absorption due to ozone decreases and that due to oxygen increases, forming a 'window' in the solar spectrum. **1969** *Guardian* 6 Feb. 9 The earth's infra-red 'windows' are at wavelengths of 1 to 2 and 8 to 14 microns. **1970** *Nature* 10 Oct. 158/1 This particular solvent is transparent in the region of the neodymium laser wavelength (1·06 μm) and..the absorption spectrum of the resulting solution exhibits a 'window' in this region. **1974** *Sci. Amer.* Apr. 71/3 The most recently opened window on the galactic center is at X-ray wavelengths.

d. = *launch window* s.v. LAUNCH *sb.*[1] 7; ***weather window***: see WEATHER *sb.* 7. Chiefly *U.S.*

1965 [see *launch window* s.v. LAUNCH *sb.*[1] 7]. **1967** *N.Y. Times* 18 Oct. 30/1 The Soviet and American vehicles flew to Venus close together because both were fired during one of the periodic 'windows' for such shots. **1968** *Sci. Jrnl.* Dec. 17/2 Between February and April next year the 'window' will be open for launchings to Mars. **1973** *Times* 15 May 1/5 There will be tomorrow only a 10-minute 'window'—the period in which the rocket must be launched to reach the appropriate orbit. **1977** A. PECCEI *Human Quality* ix. 190 This is therefore the time to act. The seventies offer what in space exploration is called a 'window', an opportunity, and probably one of the last ones, for us to launch such an undertaking.

e. Hence used more widely in sense 'a period of time', in phrases ***window of opportunity*** (or ***vulnerability***), esp. with reference to the arms race. orig. *U.S.*

1979 *Hearings U.S. Congr. Sen. Comm. Armed Services* I. 168 We are facing a window of ICBM vulnerability during the period of 1982 to 1986. **1980** *N.Y. Times* 22 Sept. A27/2 To intimidate the Americans with a Soviet 'window of opportunity' to knock out Minuteman missiles. **1981** *Ibid.* 3 Oct. 13/1 Mr. Reagan..enlarged upon the meaning of his oft-repeated theme about the 'window of vulnerability'... The term is generally used to mean the time period in which American land-based missiles are believed to be vulnerable to a surprise Soviet attack. Today, Mr. Reagan said it also applied to Soviet superiority at sea and in Europe. **1982** *Nature* 4 Mar. 5/1 Environmentalists and labour union groups are seizing this 'window of opportunity' between the failure of the last industry challenge and the eventual tightening up of administrative requirements to get as much information on existing pesticides..as they can. **1985** *Sunday Times* 16 June 60/8 Regional bank bosses know that ..they must rush to acquire their neighbours, to make the most of their window of opportunity.

5. *attrib.* and *Comb.* **a.** Simple attrib., as ***window-arch***, †***-band*** (BAND *sb.*[1] 3), ***-bay*** (cf. BAY-WINDOW), ***-blind*** (BLIND *sb.* 2), †***carpet*** (CARPET *sb.* 1), ***-casement***, ***-clasp***, ***-circle***, ***-curtain***, ***-cushion***, ***-flower***, ***-frame*** (FRAME *sb.* 11), ***-glass*** (GLASS *sb.*[1] 1, 7), ***-grate***, ***-hanging***(*s*, ***-head***, ***-hole***, ***-hook***, ***-jamb***, ***-leaves*** (pl.; LEAF *sb.*[1] 12 b), †***-nail***, ***-opening***, ***-pole***, ***-recess***, ***-sash*** (SASH *sb.*[2] 1), ***-shade***, ***-shaft***, ***-shelf***, †***slab***, ***-slit***, ***-square***, ***-sticker*** (STICKER 5 a), ***strap***, †***stuff***, ***-ticket***, ***-tracery***, ***-unit***, ***-void*** (VOID *sb.*[1] 3 a). **b.** Objective, as ***window-breaking*** (in quots. attrib.), ***-smashing***, ***-veiling***; ***window-breaker***, ***-mender***, ***-smasher***, ***-surveyor***. **c.** Adverbial, as ***window-broken*** adj.; †***window-gazer***. **d.** Appositive, 'that is a window', consisting chiefly of glass, as ***window door***, ***wall***.

1835 R. WILLIS *Archit. Mid. Ages* vi. 57 The..*window-arch side. **1419** *Mem. Ripon* (Surtees) III. 145 In iiij par. de dorbandes, j *wyndoband. **1551** *Acc. Ld. High Treas. Scot.* X. 34, xl pair of wyndo bandis. **1861** ROSSETTI *Let.* June (1965) II. 406, I offered to paint figures of some kind on the blank spaces of one of the gallery *window bays. **1920** D. H. LAWRENCE *Women in Love* i. 3 Ursula and Gudrun Brangwen sat..in the window-bay of their father's house.. working and talking. **1730** FIELDING *Tom Thumb* II. ii, Ha! the *Window-Blinds are gone, A Country Dance of Joys is in your Face. **1865** DICKENS *Mut. Fr.* III. ii, The yellow window-blind of Pubsey and Co. was drawn down upon the day's work. **1903** 'O. HENRY' IN *McClure's Mag.* July 333/1 We'll get that cannon..and fire some *window-breakers with it. **1944** BLUNDEN *Cricket Country* i. 14 Marbles, tops of various shape and various function—the window-breaker never was so bad as his name, the peg-top always looked more sinister. **1784** COWPER *Tiroc.* 228 His wild excursions, *window-breaking feats. **1861** AGNES STRICKLAND *Old Friends* Ser. II. 71 The notorious young outlaw..of window-breaking fame. **1859** HELPS *Friends in C.* Ser. II. I. 11 *Window-broken, rat-deserted..houses. **1575** in *Archaeologia* XXX. 10, v *windowe carpetts of Bramage. **1683** MOXON *Mech. Exerc.*, *Printing* x. ¶10 The Fore-end of the Tympan is made of Iron... This Iron is somewhat thinner and narrower than an ordinary *Window-Casement. **1865** G. M. HOPKINS *Poems* (1967) 34 The towers musical, the quiet-walled grove, The *window-circles. *a* **1865** MRS. GASKELL *Wives & Dau.* xxxiv. (1867) 339 The *window-clasp was unused and stiff. **1600** in W. F. SHAW *Mem. Eastry* (1870) 225 Three *window curtaines. **1713** BERKELEY *Guardian* No. 49 ¶8 My Couches, Beds, and Window-Curtains are of Irish Stuff. **1870** DICKENS *Edwin Drood* i, Through the ragged window-curtain, the light of early day steals in from a miserable court. **1617** in W. F. Shaw *Mem. Eastry* (1870) 227 Fowre *window cushens. **1926** D. H. LAWRENCE *Plumed Serpent* xi. 181 Ramón.. closed the *window-doors. **1818** KEATS *Endymion* II. 28 Juliet leaning Amid her *window-flowers. **1703** *Window-frame [see WINDOW-SILL]. **1804** W. L. BOWLES *Spir. Discov.* v. 51 When winds of winter shake the window-frame. **1837** DICKENS *Pickw.* xi, A tear trembled on his sentimental eyelid like a rain-drop on a window-frame. **1574** HELLOWES *Gueuara's Fam. Ep.* (1577) 304 Her sonnes gluttonous, her daughters *windowgazers. **1634-5** BRERETON *Trav.* (Chetham Soc.) 89 The glass-works, where is made *window-glass. **1709** *Lond. Gaz.* No. 4538/4, 60 Cases of White Normandy Window-Glass. **1844** DICKENS *Mart. Chuz.* xii, [He] let down the window-glass. **1847** MARY HOWITT *Ballads* 6 The ivy creeps o'er the window-glass. **1892** 'H. S. MERRIMAN' *Slave of Lamp* xvi, That super-innocent old man with the white hair who wears window-glass spectacles... They struck me as window-glass—quite flat. **1813** SCOTT *Trierm.* III. xix, A wicket *window-grate. **1840** DICKENS *Old Cur. Shop* lii, The tattered *window-hangings. **1730** T. BOSTON *Mem.* viii. (1899) 169, I espied above the *window-head two little old books. **1835** R. WILLIS *Archit. Mid. Ages* vi. 65 A row of small sunk pannels upon the space between the dripstone and the window head. **1884** 'MARK TWAIN' *Huck. Finn* xxxiv. 351 When we got to the cabin, we took a look..and on..the north side we found a square *window-hole. **1897** MARY KINGSLEY *W. Africa* 558 There are a mass of black heads sticking through the window hole. **1659** [Harvard] *College Book* 1, in *Publ. Colonial Soc. Mass.* (1925) XV. 10 It[em] for *window-hookes...—04[d.]. **1932** BLUNDEN *Face of England* 130 One bird came to the window-hook. **1727** E. LAURENCE *Duty of Steward* 158 Door-Jaumes and *Window-Jaumes. **1748** RICHARDSON *Clarissa* IV. li. 302 The slit-deal lining of the window-jambs. **1466** *Churchw. Acc., Yatton* (Som. Rec. Soc.) 104 For angyng of *wyndow-levys in the treser-howse vj[d]. **1547** *Inv. of Guarderobes* (MS. Harl. 1419, lf. 58), Twoo wyndowe leves. **1758** BORLASE *Nat. Hist. Cornw.* 57 In the Smith's shop the window-leaves shook, and the slating of the house cracked. **1350** in Riley *Mem. Lond.* (1868) 262, 2,600 de *wyndounail,..23,000 de rofnail. **1502-3** *Acc. Ld. High Treas. Scot.* II. 355 For xij[c] windo nales quhilk ȝeid to the wrichtis in Cambusnethane. *a* **1878** SIR G. SCOTT *Lect. Archit.* (1879) I. 136 The walls..are replaced by *window-openings decorated with stained glass. **1922** W. B. YEATS *Trembling of Veil* I. xix. 64 A fellow-theosophist once found him hanging from the *window-pole. **1984** *New Yorker* 24 Dec. 44/2 Dusk was gathering in the tall windows that needed a window pole to close. **1838** DICKENS *O. Twist* xxxvi, Oliver walked into the *window-recess. **1806** J. BERESFORD *Miseries Hum. Life* x. §61 The machinery of the *window-sash abruptly striking work. **1837** DICKENS *Pickw.* xxxvi, Throwing up the window-sash. **1810** *Hull Improv. Act* 55 Any..*window-shades, blinds, or other projections. **1921** *Daily Colonist* (Victoria, B.C.) 20 Oct. 7/4 If you want window shades for your home, we will be pleased to send our men and give you an estimate. **1978** S. BRILL *Teamsters* iv. 127 Though darkened by the drawn windowshade it was a comfortable room. **1918** D. H. LAWRENCE *New Poems* 54 Petals heaped between the *window-shafts In a drift die there. **1884** BLACK *Jud. Shakespeare* iii, Did I leave it on the *window-shelf? **1769-91** P. WHALLEY *Northamptonshire* II. 185/1 Chimney pieces and *window slabs of this stone. **1880** 'MARK TWAIN' *Tramp Abr.* xlii. 490 It [*sc.* the Castle of Chillon] has romantic *window-slits that let in generous bars of light. **1955** J. R. R. TOLKIEN *Return of King* VI. i. 184 A door on his left faced a window-slit looking out westward. **1909** *Daily Chron.* 15 Dec. 7/7 The police state that the *window smashers were not local men. **1907** *Westm. Gaz.* 12 Dec. 9/4 Much *window-smashing took place. **1699** J. WALLIS *Let.* 10 Oct. in *Private Corresp. Samuel Pepys* (1926) I. 189 The sun-shine does appear with the distinct figure of the *window-squares upon the ground within doors. **1956** D. GASCOYNE *Night Thoughts* 24 Behind the rows of window-squares. **1963** *Daily Tel.* 3 Dec 15/4 A new *window-sticker and poster campaign. **1888** BARRIE *When a Man's single* v, As he drew near his destination his hands fidgetted with the *window strap [of a carriage]. **1591** in *Archaeologia* LXIV. 369 Hewinge and woorckinge of ix foots of playne *windoe stuffe for the stayres. **1750** in *Jrnl. Friends Hist. Soc.* (1918) 23 The *Window Surveyor came. **1881** *Instr. Census Clerks* (1885) 20 *Window Ticket-Maker. *a* **1878** SIR G. SCOTT *Lect. Archit.* (1879) I. 276 The development and progressive changes in *window-tracery. **1962** *Listener* 11 Jan. 63/2 The endlessly repeated small *window-units of multi-storey buildings tend to be both boring and overpowering. **1828** MISS MITFORD *Village* Ser. III. *My Godmothers*, She seemed to consider this *window-veiling as a point of propriety. **1844** H. STEPHENS *Bk. Farm* I. 213 The sink..should be of polished free-stone, made to fit the *window-void. **1970** *Globe & Mail* (Toronto) 25 Sept. 34/7 (Advt.), Recreation room..with '*window wall' walkout to patio and garden. **1977** *Chicago Tribune* 2 Oct. XII. 10/2 Two large terraces which can be entered through window walls provide a breathtaking lake view.

e. Special combs.: **window-bar**, (*a*) any of a set of bars fitted in a window to prevent ingress and egress or accidental fall (in quot. 1607 *fig.* in reference to open work in a dress); (*b*) a bar to secure window-shutters when closed; (*c*) a mullion; **window bill**, a poster or advertisement for display in a window; **window-board**, (*a*) a shutter; (*b*) a wooden window-ledge; **window bottom** *dial.* = WINDOW-SILL; **window-box**, a box placed outside a window, in which ornamental plants are cultivated; **window-card**, a card to be displayed in a window; **window-case** [CASE *sb.*[2] 5], a window-frame; **window-cleaner** (see quot. 1858); **windowclerk**, = *window-man* (a); †**window-clothes**, window-curtains; **window display**, a display of goods in a shop-window; **window-dress** [back-formation f. *window-dresser*, etc.], (*a*) *intr.* to arrange and display goods to the best advantage in a shop-window; (*b*) *trans.* (in quots. *fig.*: see *window-dressing* (*c*)); **window-dresser**, one whose business it is to arrange and display goods to the best advantage in a shop-window; also *fig.* (see next, *c*); **window-dressing**, †(*a*) the fittings and ornaments of a window; (*b*) the dressing (DRESS *v.* 8) of a window with goods attractively displayed; (*c*) *fig.* a display made in such a manner as to give a falsely favourable impression of the facts; *esp.* the arrangement of a balance-sheet so as to suggest that the business concerned is more prosperous than it is; †**window-dropper**, one who drops (stealthily) from a window; **window-envelope**, an envelope with an opening or transparent 'panel' in the front through which the address is visible; †**window fine**, ? a fine exacted from non-burgesses for exposing goods for sale in their windows; **window gardening**, the cultivation of plants in window spaces or on window-sills; **window garden**, (a display of plants in) flower pots or boxes on a window-ledge or sill; **window-gazing**, staring at the displays in shop-windows, window shopping (see *window-gazer*, sense 5 c); hence (as back-formation) **window-gaze** *v. intr.*; **window guidance**, a form of credit rationing practised by Japanese banks; **window-jack**, 'a scaffold for carpenters, painters, or cleaners, enabling them to reach the outside of the window' (Knight *Dict. Mech.* 1875); **window-ledge**, = WINDOW-SILL; †**window-lid** [LID *sb.* 1 b], a window-shutter; **window-lights** *pl.* [LIGHT *sb.* 10], window-panes, esp. as the subject of tax; the tax itself; †**window-look**, a look or glance through a window; **window-man**, (*a*) a man formerly employed at a post-office to attend at the window to receive packets and answer inquiries; (*b*) a salesman who sells from the window (not from the counter); **window-martin**, = *window swallow*; **window-mirror**, a mirror fixed outside a window and adjustable so as to reflect the image of objects in the street

(Knight 1875); †**window-money**, = *window-tax*; **window-mount** *v.*, to fix in a mount in the manner of panes of glass in a window; **window operation** = *window guidance*; (see quot. 1965); **window-oyster**, an oyster of the family *Placunidæ*, so called from its translucent shell; **window-pane**, (*a*) see PANE *sb.*[1] 6; (*b*) *U.S.*, see quot. 1873; (*c*) *slang*, a monocle; (*d*) in full, ***window-pane check***: a kind of large check pattern on clothes; a single square of this; also ***window-pane checked*** *a.*; **window-peeper**, a surveyor whose duty it was to inspect the assessment of window-tax; **window plant**, (*a*) a plant grown indoors in the light of a window; (*b*) any of several succulent plants of the genera *Mesembryanthemum*, *Lithops*, or closely related genera, which grow almost buried in the ground, with only a transparent section of a leaf visible above it; †**window-post**, any of the vertical parts of a window architrave; **window-screen**, (*a*) an ornamental device of any kind for filling a window-opening, e.g. lattice-work or stained glass; (*b*) *U.S.*, a screen of mesh designed to be put across a window-opening to admit air whilst excluding insects, etc.; **window-seat**, a seat fixed under a window or windows, in a room usually in a recess or bay, often upholstered; also a seat by the window in a train, bus, aeroplane, etc.; †**window-set** *pa. pple.*, set or furnished with windows; **window-shell**, = *window-oyster*; **window-shop** *v. intr.*, to go from shop to shop to look at the goods displayed in shop-windows without buying; freq. as *pres. ppl.*; also in extended use and *fig.*; hence **window-shopper**; **window-shopping** *ppl. a.* and *vbl. sb.*; †**window-shut** = **window-shutter**, a shutter used to darken or secure a window-opening; †**window-song**, a serenade; **window-stone**, a stone window-sill; **window-stool** [STOOL *sb.* 9] = WINDOW-SILL; **window swallow**, the house martin; **window table**, a table (pleasantly situated) by the window in a restaurant, etc.; **window-tax**, a duty levied upon windows, imposed in 1695 and abolished in 1851; **window-trimmer** *U.S.* = *window-dresser*; **window-trimming** *U.S.* = *window-dressing*; also *fig.*; **window-washer** (chiefly U.S.), (*a*) = *screen-washer* s.v. SCREEN *sb.*[1] 9a, (*b*) one whose job is to wash windows, a window-cleaner; also **window-washing** *vbl. sb.*; **window winder**: in a motor vehicle, a mechanism for opening and shutting the (side-)windows; †**window work**, lattice-work used to screen window-openings (in quot. *fig.* of open lace-work); the structure of a window (in quot. *fig.* of that of the eye); †**window yeld** [YIELD *sb.*[1]], see quot.

1607 SHAKS. *Timon* IV. iii. 116 Those Milke pappes That through the *window Barne [*sic*] bore at mens eyes. **1677** MOXON *Mech. Exerc.* i. 14 Only fit for sleight uses, as Window-Bars, Brewers-Bars, Fire-Bars, &c. **1833** TENNYSON *May Queen* III. x. **1853** DICKENS *Bleak Ho.* lii, The massive iron window-bars and iron-bound door. **1868** *Era Almanack* p. xi, Theatrical posters, *window bills, show cards, portraits, &c. **1965** *Spectator* 29 Jan. 124/1 Window-bills went up in streets where they had never formerly been seen. **1628** *Maitl. Club Misc.* III. 372 The *window brodis hie and low to be layit over. [**1683**: see WINDER *sb.*[5]] **17..** *Dainty Davie* ii. in *Herd's Scott. Songs* (1776) II. 215 It was in and through the window-broads, And a' the tirlie wirlies o'd. **1805** R. W. DICKSON *Pract. Agric.* I. 91 Eight window-boards, and shelves and work to pantries. **1823** *Joanna Baillie's Coll. Poems* 295 The seam'd window-board betrays Interior light. [**1877** Window-bottom: see WINDER *sb.*[5]] **1914** D. H. LAWRENCE *Prussian Officer* 162 The daffodils in the white *window-bottoms shone across the room. **1960** *Times* 24 Oct. 12/6 Altar and every window-bottom would be bright with rosy apples. **1895** 'MARK TWAIN' in *Harper's Mag.* Dec. 144/1 A watering-pot in her hand and *window-boxes of red flowers under its spout. **1899** *Westm. Gaz.* 30 Aug. 1/3 You are worthy of a sort of window-box cultivation. **1905** *Window-card [see CUT-OUT *sb.* 2c]. **1965** F. SARGESON *Memoirs of Peon* v. 115 There was a window-card that advertised board and lodging. **1663** GERBIER *Counsel* 44 Well proportioned *window-cases. **1766** ENTICK *London* IV. 185 With window-cases, handsomely ornamented. **1807** W. IRVING *Salmag.* No. 5 (1811) I. 107 And can it be this book so base Is laid on every window-case? **1884** [see FACING *vbl. sb.* 6b]. **1858** SIMMONDS *Dict. Trade*, **Window-cleaner*, a frame for placing outside of a window, to sit or stand on when cleaning the window-panes; a person who contracts for cleaning windows. **1881** *Instr. Census Clerks* (1885) 52 Painter. Glazier... Window Cleaner. **1864** LEWINS *H.M. Mails* 239 In larger towns where one clerk is specially retained for these duties, he is known as the '*window clerk', as it devolves upon him to answer all.. inquiries. **1584–5** SIR R. SADLER *St. Papers* (1809) III. 247 Some dornix to make..*window clothes for her chambre. **1897** *Sears, Roebuck Catal.* 689/1 Store Lamp... Just the thing to throw light on a *window display. **1930** *Daily Express* 6 Oct. 9/2 A blaze of warm, glowing colours, elaborate window displays..usher in..the autumn shopping season. **1962** E. SNOW *Other Side of River* (1963) lxx. 538 One corner store nearby offered a neat window display of ready-made, well-tailored children's garments. **1913** J. M. KEYNES *Indian Currency & Finance* vii. 205 It is scarcely possible..that they should '*window-dress' their balance sheets. **1928** *Britain's Industr. Future* (Liberal Industr. Inquiry) 417 The common practice of 'window-dressing' the published statements by making them refer to the figures of specially selected days instead of the daily averages should be made illegal. **1957** A. C. L. DAY *Outl. Monetary Economics* xiii. 177 Each of the four of the Big Five banks which window-dressed its balance sheet made it up on a different day of the week from the others. **1971** D. CLARK *Sick to Death* iii. 56 Nobody will let us near a shop to window dress on Saturdays... But on Sundays we get a free run because the shops are shut. **1980** *Daily Tel.* 24 Sept. 17/8 The cheque was part of an elaborate fraud designed to 'window-dress' the balance sheet of a troubled banking company. **1865** *General Advertiser* (Dublin) 9 Dec., Wanted for the Drapery, a first-class, pushing Sales-woman; must be a good *window dresser. **1897** *Westm. Gaz.* 22 July 8/1 The London and Westminster Bank is not one of the window-dressers. **1790** *Act 30 Geo. III*, c. 53 §58 Copings, Cornices, Facies, Door, and *Window Dressings. **1862** *Catal. Internat. Exhib.* II. x. 13 These shutters may be fixed at small cost, and without interfering with the existent window dressings. **1895** *Daily News* 17 Oct. 5/4 Prizes are to be given to tradesmen for the best display of what is called window dressing. **1898** *Westm. Gaz.* 24 Sept. 6/1 [The finances of Chili] are..in a chaotic state despite all the elegant window-dressing. **1909** *Ibid.* 9 Mar. 2/1 The promise of high duties against other countries deceives nobody: it is only political window-dressing. **1753–4** RICHARDSON *Grandison* VI. 65 The hedge and ditch-leapers, the river-forders, the *window-droppers. **1914** *Maclean's Mag.* Dec. 124/1 Use B-E *window envelopes. **1923** *Glasgow Herald* 7 Apr. 14 The use of 'window' envelopes for the transmission of medical records. **1529** *Nottingham Rec.* III. 180, xiiij d. pro le *wyndow fyne. **1884** G. W. CABLE *Dr. Sevier* xii. 81 The asylumed window of 'St. Anna's' could glance down into it over their poor little *window-gardens. **1980** *News & Observer* (Raleigh, N. Carolina) 28 Oct. WA-2/7 Additions, solariums, greenhouses, window gardens, decks. **1824** LOUDON *Greenhouse Comp.* I. 256 Those who wish further details as to plants in rooms, or what the French and Germans call *window gardening. **1959** *Spectator* 21 Aug. 218/3 As you walk the busy streets and *window-gaze. **1968** *Daily Mirror* 20 Aug. 9/4 Take a look at the men's wear section in the chain stores; window-gaze in any man's shop. **1949** M. STEEN *Twilight on Floods* IV. vi. 614 Up the Haymarket to Regent Street for an orgy of *window-gazing. **1961** R. GRAVES *More Poems* 42 Window-gazing, at one time or another In the course of travel. **1964** *Econ. Picture of Japan* (Keidanren) IV. 53 For several years after the War, the financial policy of the Bank of Japan was characterized more or less by a qualitative control policy or a selective loans system or a so-called '*window guidance'. **1977** *Ann. Rep. Bank Internat. Settlements* 60 In Japan the authorities kept 'window guidance' ceilings on bank credit expansion in force as a precaution. **1836–7** DICKENS *Sk. Boz, Hospital Patient*, The miserable shadow of a man.. which crouches beneath a *window-ledge, to sleep where there is some shelter from the rain. *a* **1697** AUBREY in Thoms *Anecd.* (1839) 96 Whereas his former physitian shutt up his windows,..he did open his *window lids, and let in the light. **1711** *Lond. Gaz.* No. 4876/3 *Window Lights stopped up after Michaelmas last..are subject to the Duty on Window Lights. **1774** FOOTE *Cozeners* I. (1778) 10 The collector of the window-lights in Falkland's Island. **1801** T. PECK *Norwich Directory* 4 Surveyor of the Window-Lights, &c. for Yarmouth District. *a* **1586** SIDNEY *Eclogues* I. Wks. 1922 II. 217 These shepheards two..Whose mettall stiff he [*sc.* Cupid] knew he could not bende With hear-say, pictures or a *window looke. **1708** J. CHAMBERLAYNE *St. Gt. Brit.* II. III. (ed. 22) 714 Officers of the Inland-Office..*Window-Man, 60*l.* **1718** *Ibid.* (ed. 25) 165 A List of the Officers of the General-Post-Office in Lombard-Street... Window-Man for the By-Days. **1850** *Q. Rev.* June 113 The Postmaster-General, by printed 'Notices'..remonstrated with the public; his recommendations, however, were not only unheeded, but the window-men, who..repeated them, were ..insulted. **1887** *Daily News* 6 July 8/7 Cheesemongers.—Wanted, by Advertiser, Situation as Manager, Windowman, or Scalesman. **1860** TRISTRAM *Gt. Sahara* vi. 100 The swallow and the *window-martin thread the lanes. **1700** O. HEYWOOD *Diaries* (1885) IV. 228 Naylor Hopkin came for *window-mony, 5 sh. **1759** STERNE *Tr. Shandy* I. xxiii, If the fixture of Momus's glass in the human breast.. had taken place,..This foolish consequence would certainly have followed,—That the very wisest..of us all..must have paid window-money every day of our lives. **1900** *19th Century* Apr. 619 Many years later we had them [*sc.* drawings] *window-mounted with great care. **1961** *Monthly Econ. Rev.* (Bank of Japan) Sept. 9/1 The practice of the Bank of Japan in giving guidance to client commercial banks regarding their fund position and operation..has come to be ..known as '*window operation'. **1965** H. T. PATRICK in W. W. Lockwood *State & Econ. Enterprise in Japan* xii. 609 In 1954..and especially in 1957 and 1961–1962, the Bank of Japan had to resort to direct credit rationing... The term for this is *madoguchi shidō*. The Bank of Japan does not like to have this technique called credit rationing, referring to it instead as 'window operation', a more literal translation. **1854** A. ADAMS, etc. *Man. Nat. Hist.* 159 *Window-Oysters (Placunidæ). **1819** KEATS *Eve of St. Mark* 49 With forehead 'gainst the *window-pane. **1873** T. GILL *Catal. Fishes E. Coast N. Amer.* 17 *Lophopsetta maculata*... Spotted turbot; window-pane (New Jersey); sand flounder (New York). **1876** BRIDGES *Growth of Love* xlv, And hope behind the dusty window-pane Watches the days go by. **1923** J. MANCHON *Le Slang* 338 *Window-pane*,..un monocle. [**1935**: see WINDER *sb.*[5]] **1966** WODEHOUSE *Plum Pie* ix. 249 Freddie no longer wore the monocle... His father-in-law had happened to ask him one day would he please remove that damned window-pane from his eye. **1966** *Guardian* 28 Sept. 3/3 Trends towards large windowpane checks. **1969** 'O. BLEECK' *Brass Go-Between* (1970) v. 60, I had the chance to admire his fawn trousers with their burnt orange windowpanes. **1973** *Country Life* 10 May 1330/1 Window pane checked Voile shirt £10.50. **1978** L. BLOCK *Burglar in Closet* i. 4 My suit was a tropical worsted, a windowpane check in light and dark gray. *c* **1735** in J. D. Leader *Rec. Sheffield* (1897) 362 Paid Mr. John Smith for the presents of knives, &c., made to the *window peeper, 10*s.* 6*d.* **1828** *Craven Gloss.* **1863** MRS. GASKELL *Let.* 5 Dec. (1966) 720, I have been waiting..for my cousin Mr Holland to bring me in his list of subscriptions to Mr Parkes' 'booklet' on *window-plants. **1895** C. COLLINS (*title*) Greenhouse and window plants. [**1951** *Dict. Gardening* (R. Hort. Soc.) III. 1290/2 Some species..normally grow buried in the soil with only the upper surface of the leaves exposed; this upper surface is translucent..: such plants are known as 'windowed plants'.] **1971** *Stand. Encycl. S. Afr.* III. 652/2 The amazingly adapted 'window-plant',..almost entirely embedded in the ground, only the transparent apical part of the corpusculum being exposed to the air, allowing light to enter the body of the leaf. **1688** HOLME *Armoury* III. 450/1 *Window Posts, Prick Posts, the sides of the Window. **1745** WESLEY *Wks.* (1872) VIII. 211 They..broke the window-posts, and threw them into the house. **1850** INKERSLEY *Inq. Styles Archit. France* 338 Below the *window-screen extends a suite of projecting canopies. **1890** C. H. MOORE *Gothic Archit.* ix. 304 Chartres [cathedral]..singularly fortunate in retaining its magnificent jewel-like window-screens. **1892** *Vermont Agric. Rep.* XII. 135 Mills manufacturing..furniture and window screens. **1907** *St. Nicholas* May 614/1 We tried to buy wire netting—the sort we use for window screens at home. **1942** W. FAULKNER *Go down, Moses* 158 Walks out of the cell toting the door over his head like it was a gauze window-screen. **1778** MISS BURNEY *Evelina* (1791) II. xxxi. 194 Looking on the *window-seat, she presently found the books. **1853** DICKENS *Bleak Ho.* iii, We were sitting in the window-seat. **1926** KIPLING *Debits & Credits* 410 They entered the little train. .. 'Isn't it lucky we've got window-seats?' **1967** O. HESKY *Time for Treason* x. 77 He took a window-seat in the special bus. **1967** E. HUNT *Danger Game* viii. 142 In the plane Elaine was annoyed to find Mrs. Delf had the window seat allotted her. **1981** G. MARKSTEIN *Ultimate Issue* 289 The train came into the station, and Verago took a window seat. **1632** LITHGOW *Trav.* x. 443 This palatiat cloyster is quadrangled foure stories high, the vppermost whereof, is *window-set in the blew tecture. **1861** P. P. CARPENTER in *Rep. Smithsonian Inst. 1860*, 271 Family Placunidæ. (*Window-Shells.) **1922** S. LEWIS *Babbitt* ix. 122 They ate chocolates, went to the motion-pictures, went *window-shopping. **1936** B. & S. SPEWACK *Boy meets Girl* II. iii. 70 Is it true, Mrs. Seabrook, that you and Larry have been window shopping? **1945** G. ENDORE *Methinks the Lady* ii. 27 Sometimes I went window-shopping with that apartment in mind. **1951** *Landfall* V. 167 'Maybe we could window-shop then?' Wally said. 'Care for a diamond necklace like that one?' **1957** *Times* 12 Nov. (Canada Suppl.) p. xv/3 At weekends carloads of three-generation family groups visit suburban areas to 'window-shop' for somewhere to live. **1973** R. BUSBY *Pattern of Violence* vi. 96 The office girls came out..and..joined the phalanxes on the pavements to window-shop outside the big stores. **1934** WEBSTER, *Window-shopper. **1951** H. MACINNES *Neither Five nor Three* xxv. 341 A pavement filled with window-shoppers. **1972** P. MARKS *Collector's Choice* I. 23 Behind a window..stood a Boudin drawing... The window-shopper smiled. **1955** D. DAVIE *Brides of Reason* 32 And at our back His eye augments our *window-shopping greed. **1956** D. M. DAVIN *Sullen Bell* xi. 72 The old, innocent pleasure of window-shopping in Regent Street. **1978** *Lancashire Life* Nov. 140/2 (Advt.), Window-shopping may be fun. But instead of admiring from the outside we'd like to welcome you inside. **1649** J. ELLISTONE tr. *Behmen's Epist.* xxxv. 213 My Wife need not cause any *Window-shuts to be made. **1694** *Merton Reg.* II. 610 Quod Ly window-Shuts de opere tabulato in istis sociorum cameris, ubi deerunt, fabricentur. **1729** SWIFT *Direct. Serv.* viii. (1745) 78 When you bar the Window-shuts of your Lady's Bed-chamber. **1796** *Phil. Trans.* LXXXVI. 237 Placing a piece of paper round the hole in the window-shut. **1756–7** tr. *Keysler's Trav.* (1760) I. 171 A masterly piece of the sufferings of Christ..on two *window-shutters, done by Holbein. **1871** tr. *Schellen's Spectrum Anal.* §18. 60 If a ray of sun-shine be allowed to pass through a small hole in a window-shutter of a darkened room. **1633** G. HERBERT *Temple, Dulnesse* v, Where are my lines then? my approaches? views? Where are my *window-songs? **1822** W. IRVING *Braceb. Hall* I. *Stud. Salamanca* 259 Flowers standing on the *window-stone. *a* **1700** EVELYN *Diary* 27 Oct. 1664, Laying it on the *window-stool, he with his own hands design'd to me the plot for the future building of White-hall. **1867** LE FANU *Tenants of Malory* lxii, Cleve went on knocking and ringing, and the head of the Rev. Isaac Dixie appeared high in the air over the window-stool. **1797** BEWICK *Brit. Birds* I. 255 The Martin. Martlet, Martinet, or *Window-swallow. **1936** KIPLING *Something of Myself* v. 143, I..was elected to the Athenaeum... I managed to be taken to a delightful *window-table [for lunch]. **1957** M. KENNEDY *Heroes of Clone* I. v. 46 She and Roy shared a window table. Mundy sat..at the other end of the dining-room. **1979** *Tucson Mag.* Apr. 78/2 Ask for a window table or one on the patio. *a* **1735** ARBUTHNOT *Misc. Wks.* (1751) II. 160 Considering..that they are excused the Charges of House-Rent, House-keeping, and the *Window-Tax. **1850** MISS MARTINEAU *Hist. Peace* IV. xi. II. 147 The window-tax is a duty upon fresh air, sunshine, and health. **1910** *Chambers's Jrnl.* Aug. 512/1 Mr. W. W. Sawyer..was originally a *window-trimmer in the cities of Chicago, Milwaukee, and Portland. **1980** *Washington Post* 1 Feb. B4/3 Mr. Van Der Linden began working for Woodward & Lothrop in 1926 as a window trimmer. **1926** *Publishers' Weekly* 22 May 1676/1 *Window-trimming. **1984** *N.Y. Times* 21 Mar. D21/3 They even have an Association of Legal Administrators, which is not just window trimming but evidence of the increasing importance of business managers. **1968** *Globe & Mail* (Toronto) 17 Feb. 49/9 (Advt.). 65 Austin..new tires, *window washers. **1970** *Wall St. Jrnl.* 15 June 7/1 Mr. Welk arrived at his office building early and encountered a window-washer. **1977** *New Yorker* 27 June 84/2 One of the cops..had been sent out on a window-washer's platform to talk him into coming down. **1910** W. JAMES *Mem. & Stud.* (1911) xi. 291 To coal and iron mines,..to dishwashing, clothes-washing, and *window-washing..would our gilded youths be drafted off. **1950** S. F. PAGE *Body Engin.* iii. 59 Window pillars and *window winders should not be permitted to obstruct the view. **1971** *Sunday Times* (Johannesburg) (Business Sect.) 28 Mar. 4/6 The faults usually consisted of..faulty window winders, loose door handles and sticky locks. **1976** *Derbyshire Times* (Peak ed.) 3 Sept. 20/6 They'll be even more irritated by low-geared window winders. **1586** T. B. *La Primaud. Fr. Acad.* I. (1594) 487 When [women] make great *window-works before their dugs. **1619** PURCHAS *Microcosmus* viii. 89 Nor will I speake of..the Chrystalline, Glassie, and Waterie Humors; the Optike and Mouing

Nerues;..with other these curious Window-workes. **1348** *Cal. Inquis. Post Mortem Edw. III* IX. 44 [A custom called] 'Buchellyeld' [and] '*Wyndowe-yeld'.

† **'window**, *v. Obs. rare.* [f. prec.]

1. *trans.* To furnish with windows (see WINDOWED 1) or window-like openings.

a **1639** WOTTON *Panegyr. K. Charles* in *Reliq.* (1651) 133 If Nature her self (the first Architectress) had (to use an expression of Vitruvius) windowed your brest. **1728** POPE *Dunc.* II. 43 She form'd this image of well-body'd air; With pert flat eyes she window'd well its head.

2. To place in a window.

1606 SHAKS. *Ant. & Cl.* IV. xiv. 72 Would'st thou be window'd in great Rome, and see Thy Master thus..?

window, obs. or dial. var. WINNOW.

windowed ('wɪndəʊd), *ppl. a.* [f. WINDOW *sb.* + -ED², partly after OF. *fenestré.*]

1. Furnished with or having windows. Also with prefixed word in comb.

c **1483** CAXTON *Dialogues* 6 The hous well ordeyned Ought to be well wyndowed Of diverse wyndowes. **1611** COTGR., *Fenestré*, windowed, hauing windowes. **1624** WOTTON *Archit.* 76 The whole Roome was windowed round about. **1636** PEACHAM *Coach & Sedan* A iv b, Windowed before and behind with Isen-glasse. **1712** STEELE *Spect.* No. 276 ¶3 A strange windowed House,..which is so built that no one can look out of any of the Apartments. **1797** *Encycl. Brit.* (ed. 3) XVIII. 869/1 Some of the principal buildings we may reasonably suppose to have been windowed in a superior manner. **1816** BYRON *Ch. Har.* III. xxiii, Within a window'd niche of that high hall. **1819** CRABBE *T. of Hall* XVII. 131 She built a room all window'd to the west. **1866** GEO. ELIOT *F. Holt* iii, Tall-windowed brick houses. **1881** *World* 28 Dec., The disproportioned, ill-windowed, and pretentious palace at Kensington. **1883** *Standard* 3 Aug. 5/7 The windowed side of the new building.

2. Having decorative openings (see WINDOW *sb.* 3).

1483 CAXTON *Gold. Leg.* 366/1 A crowne of gold wyndowed. **1849** ROCK *Ch. Fathers* II. 246 They had, like Chaucer's layman parish-clerk, black windowed shoes, which let the scarlet stockings be seen from beneath. **1873** BROWNING *Red Cott. Nt.-cap* 69 Palace-panes Pinholed athwart their windowed filagree By twinklings sobered from the sun outside.

3. Full of holes. (In later use echoing Shaks.)

1605 SHAKS. *Lear* III. iv. 31 Your lop'd, and window'd raggednesse. **1755** HAY *Epigr. Martial* III. xxxviii, In window'd hose, and garments twice convey'd. **1894** *Westm. Gaz.* 6 Oct. 2/1 When we sat with sadly windowed clothes on the not very extensive summit of the Crystallino.

windowful ('wɪndəʊfʊl). [f. WINDOW *sb.* + -FUL.] As much as fills or will fill a window or the space which a window gives a view of.

1878 MRS. OLIPHANT *Primrose Path* iv, That windowfull of sky had darkened, it was almost night. **1886** ROSA MULHOLLAND *Marcella Grace* xxi, In poorer homes on the out-skirts of the city,..one sees windowfuls of flowers.

'windowing. [f. WINDOW *sb.* + -ING¹.]

† **1.** The fittings or furniture of a window. *Obs.*

1612 STURTEVANT *Metallica* 85 To make windowing of the pure mettle of Venice-glasse. *Ibid.* 95 Windowing and Monyons for windowes, which may be made and cast of white clay. **1659** TORRIANO, *Balconáta*, any windowing.

2. *Computers.* The process of selecting part of a stored image for display or enlargement.

1969 S. BIRD in Parslow & Prowse *Computer Graphics* I. 20 The display file is produced from the data structure by the display program package and the transformations such as expansion..and 'windowing' are carried out in the process. **1973** NEWMAN & SPROULL *Princ. Interactive Computer Graphics* viii. 154 In the case of the windowing routine, there are various ways in which the page-to-screen transformations may be defined: one obvious way is to specify window and viewport boundaries. **1981** *Internat. Jrnl. Numerical Methods Engin.* XVII. 1110 Only a segment of the first-level window may be delegated to second-level windowing; the rest should remain permanently in operational memory. **1985** *Personal Computer World* Feb. 165/1 It includes functions to deal with the more esoteric of the QL's facilities, such as windowing and general screen-handling.

windowless ('wɪndəʊlɪs), *a.* [f. WINDOW *sb.* + -LESS.] Not having or furnished with windows.

1760–72 H. BROOKE *Fool of Qual.* (1809) II. 125 Naked walls and windowless rooms. **1836** STERLING in Carlyle *Life* II. iv, One would think he had spent his whole life in the Younger Pliny's windowless study. **1863** KINGLAKE *Crimea* I. xiv. 249 The windowless vans which are used for the transport of felons. **1887** RIDER HAGGARD *Allan Quartermain* xvi, The moon..threw great..patches of light through the high windowless openings in the walls.

Hence **'windowlessness.**

1917 A. K. COOK *About Winchester Coll.* 228 The comparative windowlessness, and the positive ugliness, of the back of School.

† **windown.** *Obs.* Also 4–5 **wyndown**, 9 *dial.* **windon.** Obscure var. WINDOW *sb.*

c **1380** WYCLIF *Wks.* (1880) 8 ȝif þei drawen þe peple..by coryouste of gaye wyndownes. *c* **1450** CAPGRAVE *Life St. Aug.* xxiii. 32 As his moder and he stood lenyng out at a wyndown. **1477** *Paston Lett.* III. 211 The bordes had ben good for wyndownes and dores. *a* **1825** FORBY *Voc. E. Anglia*, *Windon*, a window. **1838** W. HOLLOWAY *Provinc.* 190 *Windon*, a window. *Norf.*

'window-sill. = SILL *sb.*¹ 2.

1703 T. N. *City & C. Purchaser* 241 Window-sells (sometimes call'd Window soils,) which are the bottom pieces in a Window-frame. **1814** SCOTT *Ld. of Isles* V. iii, Till on the mossy window-sill Their track effaced the green. **1819** CRABBE *T. of Hall* VII. 495 The curtains fell Half down, and rested on the window-sill. **1837** WHITTOCK, etc. *Bk. Trades* (1842) 325 (*Mason*), He also constructs and lays the window cells of all buildings. **1840** DICKENS *Old Cur. Shop* viii, The little flower-pots which always stood on the window-sill outside. **1850** INKERSLEY *Inq. Styles Archit. France* 311 The string-course below the window-cill. **1886** STEVENSON *Kidnapped* ii, I heard the blunderbuss rattle on the window-sill.

'window-sole. *dial.* [SOLE *sb.*¹ 4 a.] = prec.

1570–80 *Fabric Rolls York Minster* (Surtees) 118 For lyme for the masons to sett the wyndowe sole with, 16 d. **1591** in *Archaeologia* LXIV. 370, 111 midell peeces of windo sole. **1737** RAMSAY *Sc. Prov.* Ded., May never a window-sole..be without them. **1828** MOIR *Mansie Wauch* xxii. 326 Sharp frosty nights that left all the window-soles white-washed over with frost-rind in the mornings. **1847** H. MILLER *First Impr. Eng.* vi. 100 In fashioning the soft red sandstone into door-pieces, and window-soles.

'windowy, *a.* [f. WINDOW *sb.* + -Y¹.] † **1.** Full of 'windows' or openings. *Obs. rare.*

a **1631** DONNE *Bait* 20 Or treacherously poore fish beset, With strangling snare, or windowie net.

2. Having many or large windows.

1863 'G. HAMILTON' *Gala-Days* 353 The homes of the students, which seem to have been built..solely to furnish shelter,—angular, formal, stiff, windowy. **1888** *Harper's Mag.* June 130/2 Several large, ugly, windowy wooden bulks grew up for shoe shops.

windpipe ('wɪndpaɪp, 'waɪndpaɪp). [f. WIND *sb.*¹ + PIPE *sb.*¹ Cf. Du. †*windpijpe* (Kilian).]

1. The tube which leads from the throat and (dividing into the two bronchi) conveys air to and from the lungs in breathing: = TRACHEA 1 a. †Formerly also *pl.* = the trachea and bronchi collectively.

1530 PALSGR. 289/1 Wyndpype, *sifflet de gosier*. **1538** BALE *God's Promises* III. C ij, Stoppe not my wynde pypes, but geue them lyberte, To sounde to thy name. **1565** COOPER *Thesaurus* s.v. *Arteria*, *Aspera arteria*, the wine pipe [*sic*]. **1581** MULCASTER *Positions* xv. (1888) 70 The cowgh which commeth of some cold distemperature in the windepipes. **1662** J. BARGRAVE *Pope Alex. VII* (1867) 12 Their heads, with the livers and lungs hanging by the wine-pipes [*sic*]. **1791** BOSWELL *Johnson* 19 Sept. an. 1777, When one considers what variety of sounds can be uttered by the windpipe, in the compass of a very small aperture. **1866** BALLANTYNE *Shifting Winds* ii, There was only just sufficient opening in the wind-pipe to permit of her breath passing..through her..mouth. **1874** COUES *Birds N.-W.* 531 The Whooping Crane has a windpipe between four and five feet long—quite as long as the bird itself.

2. An artificial pipe or tube for conducting a blast of air. *rare.*

1688 HOLME *Armoury* III. v. 259/1 A Pair of Bellows..; the Wind Pipe erected. **1689** BURNET *Tracts* I. 94 A hole [let into a hill] which all the Summer long blows a fresh Air into the Cellar..but this Wind-pipe did not blow when I was there.

3. *attrib.* and *Comb.*: **windpipe-stretcher**, *jocular*, a hangman; **windpipe sweetbread**, the thyroid gland (of a calf) used as food.

1617 J. TAYLOR (Water P.) *Three Weekes Observ.* B 4 b, Our Wapping windpipe-stretcher. *a* **1756** ELIZA HAYWOOD *New Present* (1771) 19 The fore-quarter [of veal] contains the shoulder, neck, and breast, the throat sweet-bread, and the windpipe sweetbread.

Hence (*nonce-wds.*) **'windpipe** *v.*, *trans.* to utter through the windpipe, to 'pipe'; **'windpiped** (-paɪpt) *a.*, supplied with pipes figured as windpipes.

1860 HOLMES *Prof. Breakf.-t.* x, A city, water-veined and gas windpiped. **1895** MEREDITH *Amazing Marr.* xlv, The three guardian ladies..headed over the..town.. windpiping these and similar Solan notes.

† **'windress.** *Obs. rare.* Also -eresse. [f. WINDER + -ESS.] A woman who winds (silk, etc.).

1598 FLORIO, *Diuidatrice*, a silke winderesse. *Ibid.*, *Naspatrice*, a reeler, or windresse of thrid, silke or yarne.

† **'windring,** *ppl. a.* ? mispr. for WINDING *ppl. a.*

1610 SHAKS. *Temp.* IV. i. 128 You Nimphs cald Nayades of yᵉ windring brooks.

wind-rose ('wɪndrəʊz). [f. WIND *sb.*¹ + ROSE *sb.*; in sense 2 after G. *windrose* (cf. ROSE *sb.* 14 c).]

1. Name for several papaveraceous plants, or their flowers: **a.** the 'bastard wild poppy', *Argemone mexicana*, or the common wild poppy, *Papaver Rhœas*; **b.** the violet horned poppy, *Rœmeria hybrida*.

1597 GERARDE *Herbal* II. lxx. 301 The bastard wilde Poppie is called..in English winde Rose, and bastarde wilde Poppie. **1874** *Treas. Bot.* Suppl., Rose, Wind, *Römeria hybrida*.

2. *Meteorol.* A diagram indicating the relative frequency, force, etc. of (or the temperature, etc. accompanying) the winds from the various points of the compass at some given place.

1846 SABINE tr. *Humboldt's Cosmos* I. 310 Tables of atmospheric pressure accompanying different winds, which have received the name of barometric windroses. **1883** R. H. SCOTT *Elem. Meteorol.* ix. 166 The best mode of publishing the records for different stations is the construction of 'wind-roses'. *Ibid.* xiv. 278 Dr. Hann..has calculated the prevalent winds and the thermal windroses for a great number of stations.

windrow ('wɪndrəʊ), *sb.* Forms and etym.: see WIND *sb.*¹ and ROW *sb.*¹ (also 8–9 **winrow**).

a. A row in which mown grass or hay is laid before being made up into heaps or cocks, in which sods, peats, or sheaves of corn are set up to be dried by exposure to the wind, or in which dead branches, etc. are gathered to be burnt.

Also *collect.* or *abstr.* in phr. ***into*** or ***out of windrow***.

1523–34 FITZHERB. *Husb.* §25 On the nexte daye, tourne it agayne before none, and towarde nyght make it in wynd-rowes, and than in smal hey-cockes. **1641** BEST *Farm. Bks.* (Surtees) 54 Others,..when barley is loggery, and full of greenes, will sette it windrowe stooke. **1691** RAY *S. & E.C. Words*, *A Wind-row*, the Greens or Borders of a Field dug up, in order to the carrying the Earth on to the Land to mend it. It is called Windrow because it is laid in rows, and exposed to the Wind. **1726** [see UPGANGER]. **1764** *Museum Rust.* III. lxv. 297 A machine for raking hay-grass into wind-row, drawn by a horse. **1802** SIBBALD *Chron. Scot. Poetry* IV. Gloss., *Winraw*, hay or peats put together in long thin heaps for the purpose of being more easily dried. **1830** HODGSON in Raine *Mem.* (1858) II. 176 They are also leading much of their hay out of windrow. **1844** H. STEPHENS *Bk. Farm* III. 967 After the second 2 ridges have been thus cleared, the third ridge being in the middle, contains the grass of 5 ridges, which is called a windrow. **1882** HOWELLS *Modern Instance* xxxix, The farmers were.. heaping into vast winrows for burning the winter-worn stalks of the last year's crop.

b. *transf.* of similar rows of various things, *e.g.* of trees blown down (cf. WINDFALL 1) or of dust heaped up by the wind.

1868 *Rep. U.S. Comm. Agric.* (1869) 176 Logs of all sizes lie in winrows. **1881** *Scribner's Mag.* Aug. 529/2 The river [Hudson] is divided into long lanes and fields of smooth ice by windrows crossing in every direction. **1901** 'LUCAS MALET' *Sir Richard Calmady* I. x, The blue of the upper sky was crossed by curved winrows of flaky, opalescent cloud.

c. *fig.* Used of similar rows of various things not exposed to or caused by the wind.

1948 *Times* 13 Feb. 5/6 Bulldozers then level off the soil and uprooted bush, packing it aside to form banks known as 'windrows' between each contour. **1957** L. EISELEY *Immense Journey* 49 The slowly contracting circle of the water left little windrows of minnows. **1974** *Sci. Amer.* Aug. 21/1 The water soon turned cold again and the fish departed, leaving windrows of dead *Pleuroncodes* along the beaches. **1980** *Ibid.* Oct. 156/2 The soft rock is gathered into long windrows and transferred mechanically to conveyor belts that carry it away to the processing plant.

'windrow, *v.* Also **winrow.** [f. prec. sb.] *trans.* To lay or set in windrows.

1729 P. WALKDEN *Diary* (1866) 28 This afternoon, son Thomas went and winrowed our turf o' th' Black Moss. **1787** GROSE *Prov. Gloss.*, To *windrow*, to rake the mown grass into rows, called windrows. **1844** H. STEPHENS *Bk. Farm* III. 968 The grass which had been tedded in the forenoon is windrowed and put into grass-cocks. **1889** DOUGHTY *Friesland Meres* viii. 173 Women were windrowing hay, with rakes different to ours.

Hence **'windrowed** *ppl. a.* (in transf. sense); **'windrower**, a machine for cutting and raking crops into windrows; **'windrowing** *vbl. sb.*

1851 H. MELVILLE *Moby Dick* I. xli. 311 The desolate shiftings of the windrowed snows of prairies. **1946** R. CAMPBELL *Talking Bronco* 24 All round the snarled and windrowed sands Expressed the scandal of the waves. **1948** TURNER & JOHNSON *Machines for Farm, Ranch & Plantation* x. 316 Select side-delivery windrowers when cutting grass-seed crops such as alfalfa. **1955** 'P. JANVIER' in *Astounding Sci. Fiction* Nov. 68/1 Straggled clumps and windrowed hay ..were all that remained of the shrubbery and the lawn. **1970** K. C. WILLETT in H. W. Mulligan *African Trypanosomiases* xxx. 583 If 'windrowing' (clearing of the felled vegetation into wind-rows) is necessary the cost is greatly increased. **1976** *Columbus* (Montana) *News* 17 June 5 (Advt.), Hay Equipment... Windrowers... Balers.

winds, var. WINZE.

windsail ('wɪndseɪl). [f. WIND *sb.*¹ + SAIL *sb.*¹]

1. *Naut.* A long wide tube or funnel of sail-cloth used for ventilating a ship.

1741 *Phil. Trans.* XLII. 65 The Wind-Sails..are usually between 25 and 30 Foot long, according to the Size of the Ship. **1835** MARRYAT *Olla Podr.* iii, I trimmed my ear like a windsail in the tropics. **1842** DICKENS in Forster *Life* (1872) I. 321 From the roof, a couple of windsails dangled and drooped, limp and useless.

2. A sail of a windmill.

1725 DE FOE *Tour Gt. Brit.* II. 151 Here are some wonderful Engines for throwing up Water,..one..goes by Wind-Sails, 12 Wings or Sails to a Mill. **1843** *Penny Cycl.* XXVII. 450/2. **1883** MEREDITH *Poems, Sense & Spirit* 8 We go distraught, At best but circle-windsails of a mill.

wind-shake ('wɪndʃeɪk), *sb.* Also 9 *dial.* **-shack.** [f. WIND *sb.*¹ + SHAKE *sb.*¹ 9 a, 2.] **a.** A flaw or crack in timber, supposed to be due to a strain caused by the force of the wind.

1545 ASCHAM *Toxoph.* (Arb.) 114 Not marred with knot, gaule, wyndeshake, wem. **1824** CARR *Craven Gloss.*, *Wind-shacks*, cracks in wood, occasioned, it is supposed by the wind. **1866** *Treas. Bot.*, *Wind-shake.* See *Anemosis.*

b. A shaking (of something) in or by the wind. *poet. nonce-use.*

1939 DYLAN THOMAS *Map of Love* 12 After the funeral, mule praises, brays, Windshake of sailshaped ears.

† **'windshake,** *v. Obs. rare*⁻¹. [f. as prec. + SHAKE *v.*] *trans.* To shake as with a violent wind; to inflict a severe shock upon.

1614 BUDDEN tr. *Ærodius' Disc. Parents Hon.* 156 To windshake all that commerce and societie, which is between man & man, euen from the very ground plot, and foundation.

†**'wind-shaked,** *ppl. a. Obs. rare.* [f. WIND *sb.*[1] + *shaked*, wk. pa. pple. of SHAKE *v.*] = next, 1.

1604 SHAKS. *Oth.* II. i. 13 The winde-shak'd Surge. **1624** QUARLES *Job Milit.* medit. iv. 41, I quake, Like wind-shakt Reeds.

wind-shaken ('wɪndʃeɪk(ə)n), *ppl. a.* [f. WIND *sb.*[1] + *shaken*, str. pa. pple. of SHAKE *v.*]

1. Shaken or agitated by the wind.

c **1550** CHEKE *Matt.* xi. 7 A windschaken reed. **1553** *Respublica* (Brandl) v. x. 28 Baggs tottering looce abought me like windshaken rags. **1607** SHAKS. *Cor.* v. ii. 117 The Oake not to be winde-shaken. **1644** *Prerog. Anatomized* 7 All the trees were wind-shaken, and those that were not fast rooted, fell. **1856** LEVER *Martins of Cro' M.* lviii, The wind-shaken foliage. **1876** SWINBURNE *Poems & Ball.* Ser. II. *Forsaken Garden* iii, The weeds wind-shaken.

2. Of timber: Affected with wind-shake. Also *fig.*

1565 COOPER *Thesaurus* s.v. *Rima*, To be wyndeshaken as tymber is. **1571** GOLDING *Calvin on Ps.* xlv. 5 God doo oftentymes tumble them downe from their wyndshaken and rotten seeges. **1611** MIDDLETON & DEKKER *Roaring Girl* H, Some poore winde-shaken gallant. **1668** CLARENDON *Vind.* Tracts (1727) 33 The middle of every piece was wind-shaken and rotten. **1707** MORTIMER *Husb.* 387 The discharging Trees of unthrifty broken wind-shaken Boughs. **1866** *Treas. Bot.*, *Anemosis*, the condition known in timber by the name of wind shaken.

windshield ('wɪndʃi:ld). [f. WIND *sb.*[1] + SHIELD *sb.*] **a.** Any of various devices for shielding a person or thing from wind; *spec.* (chiefly *U.S.*) on a motor vehicle = *windscreen* s.v. WIND *sb.*[1] 32.

1902 *Encycl. Brit.* (ed. 10) XXVII. 327/1 A motor.. driven at a rate which the cyclist can follow with the protection of a wind-shield. **1907** *Yesterday's Shopping* (1969) 320D/1 [Coat] Fitted with wind shield and storm cuffs, for driving or motoring. **1911** *N.Y. Times* 16 Oct. 12/7 (Advt.), Speedwell 1911 four-passenger, semi-racer.. extraordinary equipment includes top, windshield, shock absorbers, [etc.]. **1924** P. C. MACFARLANE *Tongues of Flame* ii. 12 She steadied herself with one hand upon the wind-shield while the other waved to the enthusiastic group of welcomers. **1941** F. H. JOSEPH *Lett. Home from Britain at War* (1942) 6 We circled the airport three times to allow the captain to clear his windshield of ice by hand. **1946** B. MACDONALD *Egg & I* 110 A blast went off almost under the truck and the rocks broke my windshield. **1962** A. NISBETT *Technique Sound Studio* 277 *Windshield*.., shield which fits over microphone and protects diaphragm from 'rattling' by wind, and also contours the microphone for smoother airflow round it. **1978** W. F. BUCKLEY *Stained Glass* 230 Fifty cars, with special passes on their windshields, squatted around the tall, leafless elm trees.

b. *attrib.* and *Comb.* ***windshield cleaner, scraper, squirter***; **windshield wiper** = *windscreen wiper* s.v. WIND *sb.*[1] 32.

1921 *Daily Colonist* (Victoria, B.C.) 13 Mar. 10/6 The Folberth automatic windshield cleaner. **1927** *Sat. Even. Post* 24 Dec. 56/2 Each has extra wide windshield..and windshield wiper. **1955** W. TUCKER *Wild Talent* v. 62 Paul could see the rain falling, could see the madly swinging windshield wipers on the waiting cars. **1975** B. GARFIELD *Hopscotch* xxvi. 275 A combination windshield-scraper and brush. **1976** M. MACHLIN *Pipeline* ii. 31 The misty, sentimental look on Steele's face disappeared as though a giant windshield wiper had cleared its teary ambience. **1978** *Time* 10 Apr. 22/1 Johnson..once had to halt his automobile to solve the problem of turning on the windshield squirter.

wind-shock ('wɪndʃɒk). [f. WIND *sb.*[1] + SHOCK *sb.*[3]]

†**1.** = WIND-SHAKE *sb.* Also *attrib.* = prec. 2.

1664 EVELYN *Sylva* xxx. 94, I have seen Wind-shock-timber so exquisitely closed, as not to be discerned where the defects were. **1679** *Ibid.* xxvii. (ed. 3) 143 The Wind-shock is a bruise, and shiver throughout the Tree. **1797** *Encycl. Brit.* (ed. 3) XVIII. 868/2. **1805** PIKE *Sources Mississ.* (1810) 37 One of them [*sc.* canoes] sunk, in which was the ammunition and my baggage; this was occasioned by what is called a wind-shock.

2. A shock or disturbance of equilibrium caused by a violent gust of wind.

1913 *Daily News* 7 Mar. 1 England must have got a bad windshock, and the machine [an aeroplane] fell like a stone.

'wind-shook, *ppl. a. rare*[−1]. [f. WIND *sb.*[1] + *shook*, pa. pple. of SHAKE *v.*] = WIND-SHAKEN 2; in quot. *transf.* having internal cavities like wind-shaken timber.

1784 TWAMLEY *Dairying Exempl.* 51 The cause of jointing or wind-shook Cheese, is from a small quantity of Slip-Curd being much broke, so as not sufficient, to form Eyes in the Cheese.

Windsor ('wɪnzə(r)). Name of a town in Berkshire, on the right bank of the Thames, at which is Windsor Castle, a royal residence.

1. *attrib.* in names of various things now or originally obtained, made, cultivated, etc. at or near Windsor, or of persons connected with Windsor Castle. **Windsor bean,** the common broad bean; **Windsor blue** = *phthalocyanine blue* s.v. PHTHALOCYANINE c; **Windsor brick,** a kind of red fire-resisting brick formerly made at Hedgerley, near Windsor; **Windsor chair,** †(*a*) a kind of low-wheeled carriage (*obs.*); (*b*) a kind of wooden chair with the back formed of upright rod-like pieces surmounted by a cross-piece, and often with arms; **Windsor herald,** an officer whose duties are now performed by Garter King of Arms; **Windsor knight,** one of a body of military pensioners residing within the precincts of Windsor Castle; **Windsor knot,** a large, loose knot in a (neck)tie; so **Windsor-knotted** *a.*; **Windsor loam,** the earth from which *Windsor bricks* were made; **Windsor pear** (see quots.); **Windsor Red,** the name of a recently introduced type of English cheese containing red wine; **Windsor soap,** a kind of scented (usually brown) soap; **Windsor tick** (TICK *sb.*[1] 2), app. a small variety of Windsor bean; **Windsor tie** *U.S.*, a broad bias-cut necktie or scarf; **Windsor tub** (see quot.); **Windsor uniform,** a uniform introduced by King George III, consisting of a blue coat with red collar and cuffs, and a blue or white waistcoat, worn on certain occasions at Windsor Castle by members of the royal household, and by royal or other distinguished guests by permission of the sovereign.

1712 tr. *Pomet's Hist. Drugs* I. 133 Fruit in Pods, of the Size of our *Windsor Beans. **1848** JOHNS *Week at Lizard* 300 [The Buck-bean's] leaves closely resemble those of the Windsor Bean. **1912** R. RIDGWAY *Color Standards & Color Nomenclature* 40/1 *Windsor blue. **1938** H. NICOLSON *Let.* 17 Apr. (1966) 336 His Windsor blue eyes were wistful. **1970** Windsor blue [see MONASTRAL]. **1702** SAVERY *Miner's Friend* 26 The Furnace being made of Sturbridge or *Windsor-Brick. **1825** J. NICHOLSON *Oper. Mech.* 535 Red bricks..which will stand the greatest heat..called Windsor bricks. **1724** in Amherst *Gardening* (1895) 234 My wife was carry'd in a *Windsor chair like those at Versailles. **1740** C'TESS HARTFORD *Corr.* (1805) II. 4 A tolerably large circle, with Windsor chairs round it. **1766** *Jackson's Oxf. Jrnl.* 29 Nov., The Bodleian Library has most confessedly been very much improved by the Introduction of Windsor-Chairs, so admirably calculated for Ornament and Repose. **1867** TROLLOPE *Chron. Barset* iv, There was one arm-chair in the room,—a Windsor-chair, as such used to be called. **1473–4** *Acc. Ld. High Treas. Scot.* I. 53 For *Wyndissoris heraldis expensis quhen he come agane for the renewyne of his conduct. **1517–18** in *Archaeologia* XLVII. 310 Wyndesore Harald at Armes. **1631** WEEVER *Anc. Funeral Mon.* To Rdr., Augustine Vincent, Esquire, Windsor Herald, & keeper of the Records in the Tower. **1953** *Man about Town* Spring 117 (*caption*) How to tie the '*Windsor' knot. **1959** T. WILLIAMS *Sweet Bird of Youth* III. 111 He nods slightly, loosening the Windsor-knot of his knitted black silk tie. **1976** J. H. SPENCER *Surgenor Campaign* i. 18 The tie was a crisp silver, the sort normally worn only with morning dress and tied in a Windsor knot. **1953** K. AMIS *Lucky Jim* ix. 98 His *Windsor-knotted silk tie. **1747** *Phil. Trans.* XLIV. 458 Hedgerley, the Place where there is dug an Earth commonly call'd *Windsor Loam. **1827** FARADAY *Chem. Manip.* xviii. (1842) 484 Windsor loam: obtained at Hampstead, &c...is frequently used for the lining of furnaces. **1664** J. EVELYN *Kalendarium Hortense* 72 August..Pears. *Windsor, Soveraign, Orange, [etc.]. **1860** R. HOGG *Fruit Man.* 221 Windsor... A fine old pear for orchard culture. Ripe in August. It should be gathered before it becomes yellow. **1940** J. BETJEMAN *Old Lights for New Chancels* 17 Remaining orchards ripening Windsor pears. [**1969** *Vogue* 15 Mar. 65/2 *Red Windsor*, a new British cheese..basically an English cheddar, gets its pink tinge from an English wine.] **1969–70** *Wine & Food* Dec.–Jan. 11/2 More ideas for cheese gifts... *Windsor Red in plain jar, each 10/6. **1982** P. RANCE *Gt. British Cheese Bk.* I. ii. 50 These cheeses are made by breaking up Cheddar or Double Gloucester..and..in the case of Windsor Red, pouring wine over the re-milled curd. **1822** B. HAYDON *Jrnl.* 16–17 Sept. in *Mem.* (1926) I. 321 A barber who shaved me..so praised his *Windsor soap, that I..took six cakes. **1826** *MS. Accounts* (D. Dewar, St. Andrew's), To Windsor Soap, 3[d]. **1837** MORIER *Abel Allnutt* xxvii, A..lamb..which she..kept..washed with the best brown Windsor soap. **1895** *Montgomery Ward Catal.* 95/2 *Windsor Ties... Japanese Silk Windsors... Size $4\frac{1}{4}$ × 34 inches. **1912** J. LONDON *Smoke Bellew* 147 He went on dressing,..tying a Windsor tie in a bow-knot at the throat of his soft cotton shirt. **1968** J. IRONSIDE *Fashion Alphabet* 114 A bias-cut wide tie, usually black, tied in a loose bow in front of the neck—known in America as a Windsor tie. **1797** A. YOUNG *Agric. Suffolk* 58 The little common horse-bean, ticks, and *Windsor ticks, are the sorts generally cultivated. **1800** ALVES *Banks of Esk* 166 Old Port pipes or casks, laid open at one side with conical tops, and seats placed at the ordinary height from the bottom,—which turn round upon perpendicular axis, denominated *Windsor Tubs, from their having been first introduced there. **1781** *Gentl. Mag.* LI. 391/2 The birth-day of the Prince of Wales..was celebrated with extraordinary magnificence... The King, the Prince, the Duke of Cumberland, the great officers of state, and nobility, appeared in the *Windsor uniform on this occasion—blue and scarlet. **1805** *Ann. Reg.* (Rivington's ed.), *Chron.* 12* The gentlemen [at a fête at Windsor Castle] were dressed in the full Windsor uniform, except those who wore the military habit of their respective regiments. **1825** T. HOOK *Sayings* Ser. II. *Doubts & F.* i, The hotel..was a..red brick building, edging the blue wave of the ocean, as the collar of the Windsor uniform garnishes the coat.

2. Short for *Windsor bean, brick, chair, soap, tie.*

1786 ABERCROMBIE *Gard. Assist.* Feb. 32 A full crop of long-pods, Windsor's,..or other broad kinds. **1836** T. POWER *Impressions of America* I. 440 A bit of old brown Windsor to shave withal. **1840** THACKERAY *Barber Cox* Sept., My dearest girl now turned from red to be as pale as white Windsor. **1840** THACKERAY in *Comic Almanack* Nov. 45, I never..knew Naples from brown Windsor. **1841** *Civil Eng. & Arch. Jrnl.* IV. 342/1 The red sandy bricks called Windsors. **1859** *Habits of Gd. Society* ii. (new ed.) 124 The old brown Windsor being still..far the best for the skin. **1884** 'H. COLLINGWOOD' *Under Meteor Flag* xii, As thorough an ablution as was possible in the absence of my cake of old brown windsor. **1895** [see *Windsor tie*, sense 1 above]. **1901** [see *comb-back* s.v. COMB *sb.*[1] 9]. **1939** F. THOMPSON *Lark Rise* vi. 102 If the father had a special chair ..it would be but a rather larger replica of the hard windsors with wooden arms added. **1969** 'J. MORRIS' *Fever Grass* ii. 21 A small electric fan..and two more Windsors, were the room's only furnishings. **1976** J. PHILIPS *Backlash* (1977) I. ii. 27 Two armchairs, Windsors, for visitors.

windster ('waɪndstə(r)). ? *Obs.* Also 5 **wynstere.** [f. WIND *v.*[1] + -STER.] A person (orig. a woman) engaged in winding silk, etc.

14.. LANGL. *P. Pl.* A. v. 129 (MS. T) My wyf was a wynstere [*B. & C. texts* webbe] & Wollene cloþ made. *c* **1700** *Douce prints S.* 9 fol. 2 b, Comber. Dyer. Throwster. Windster. Spinster. **1723** *Lond. Gaz.* No. 6187/4 Eleanor Brown,..Silk-Windster. **1812** J. SMYTH *Pract. Customs* 185 Husks and Nubs are the refuse, which is thrown aside by the windster, during the process of winding the Silk from the cocoons. **1825** *New Monthly Mag.* XIV. 259 Your warpers, your windsters, your weavers.

wind-suck ('wɪndsʌk), *v.* [Back-formation from next (sense 2).] *intr.* Of a horse: To have the vice of noisily drawing in and swallowing air (often associated with crib-biting). Also **'wind-,sucking** *vbl. sb.* and *ppl. a.*

1844 H. STEPHENS *Bk. Farm* II. 228 Wind-sucking consists in swallowing air, without fixing the mouth. *Ibid.* 229 He continued to crib-bite or wind-suck. **1875** KNIGHT *Dict. Mech.*, *Crib-strap*, a neck-throttler for crib-biting and wind-sucking horses. **1908** *Animal Managem.* 81 Indigestion and colic..result from windsucking and crib-biting.

wind-sucker ('wɪnd,sʌkə(r)). [f. WIND *sb.*[1] + SUCKER.]

†**1.** The valve of a pair of bellows. *Obs.*

1688 HOLME *Armoury* III. xiv. (Roxb.) 7/2 The wind sucker, a flap of strong Leather set ouer the wind hole within the belly.

2. A horse addicted to wind-sucking.

1825 JAMIESON. **1853** R. S. SURTEES *Sponge's Sp. Tour* x, Whose horse had a cough, whose was a wind-sucker, whose was lame after hunting. **1908** *Animal Managem.* 127 Wind-suckers and crib-biters should..be fed apart from the rest.

wind-sucker: see WINDFUCKER 2.

1880 SWINBURNE *Study Shaks.* 54 The veriest wind-sucker among commentators.

windsurf ('wɪndsɜ:f), *v.* orig. *U.S.* [Back-formation f. WINDSURFER: see next.] *intr.* To ride a sailboard; to sailboard. Also **'windsurfing** *vbl. sb.*

1969 *Chr. Sci. Monitor* 17 Nov. 17/1 Depending on the wind and water conditions, older as well as young people can windsurf. *Ibid.*, Windsurfing is new, so new that it's been on the market only within the past month. **1972** *Islander* (Victoria, B.C.) 16 Jan. 3/1 Spreading up and down the west coast is a brand new water sport—windsurfing. **1976** *Southern Even. Echo* (Southampton) 11 Nov. 23/1 Windsurfing, a cross between sailing, surf-riding and high-wire walking, has one big attraction: your boat can be small enough to carry under your arm. **1977** *Austral. Sailing* Jan. 69/2 Young or old, guy or girl, thick or thin, we'll teach you to windsurf in a few short hours. **1980** C. MATTHEWS *Loosely Engaged* 9 Swam, sunbathed and wind-surfed the whole day. **1984** *U.S.A. Today* 6 Apr. 2C/1 But windsurfing—on the Windsurfer—is merely a demonstration sport in the 1984 Olympic Games. **1984** *Times* 25 Aug. 11/3 Earlier this year..an Oxford graduate, aged 25, spent 10 weeks windsurfing clockwise around the coast of Britain.

Windsurfer ('wɪndsɜ:fə(r)). orig. *U.S.* Also **windsurfer.** [f. WIND *sb.*[1] + SURFER.] **1.** The proprietary name in the U.S. of a kind of sailboard.

1969 *Chr. Sci. Monitor* 17 Nov. 17/2 The board segment of the Windsurfer is shaped, with 'slight changes', like a surfboard, though it is heavier, at 37 pounds and longer, at 12 feet. **1974** *Official Gaz.* (U.S. Patent Office) 20 Aug. TM 166/1 Windsurfer, Windsurfing International Inc., Santa Monica, Calif... For sailboats comprising a surf board type hull and a sail. **1981** *Daily Mail* 9 Apr. 39/3 He [*sc.* Hoyle Schweitzer] kept production of his Windsurfer down in order to monitor quality. **1983** *Reader's Dig.* Apr. 132 More Windsurfers..have been sold than any class of sailing boat ever. **1984** *Sunday Times* (Colour Suppl.) 28 Oct. 25/2, I wanted to learn more and get myself back on a windsurfer as soon as I could.

2. One who engages in the sport of windsurfing, a sailboarder.

1969 *Chr. Sci. Monitor* 17 Nov. 17/3 The lone windsurfer (one per board) stands near the middle, left foot just ahead of the mast and hands holding tightly to the 'wishbone'. **1977** *Austral. Sailing* Jan. 27/3 Clive Colonso is one of Britain's few expert windsurfers. **1982** *Times* 3 May 5/1 Twenty windsurfers were rescued from the North Sea yesterday. **1984** *Times* 25 Aug. 11/7 Windsurfers tend to be individualists, happy to sail alone.

wind-tight ('wɪndtaɪt), *a.* [f. WIND *sb.*[1] + TIGHT *a.*]

1. Solidly constructed so as to keep out wind: chiefly of a building; also of a vessel = AIR-TIGHT.

1507 [see TIGHT *a.* 2a]. **1514**, etc. [see WATERTIGHT 1]. **1623** *Extr. Aberd. Reg.* (1848) II. 383 The grammar schole ..is nather watterthicht nor wyndthicht to the great hinderance of the studentis within the same. **1647** N. WARD *Simple Cobler* 33 For England, however, the upper Stories are shroadly shattred; yet the foundations and frame being good or mendable by the Architectors now at worke, there is good hope, when peace is setled, people shall dwell more wind-tight and water-tight than formerly. **1718** CHAMBERLAYNE *Relig. Philos.* II. xvii. §10, I..took a Tin Tube..but found..that it was not compleatly Wind-tight. **1867** SMYTH *Sailor's Word-bk.*, *Wind-tight*, a cask or vessel to contain water is said to be wind-tight and water-tight.

†**2.** *Naut.* = Wind-taut (see WIND *sb.*¹ 32). *Obs.*

1642 SIR W. MONSON *Naval Tracts* II. (1704) 301/1 They ..cut down..Things over-head, which makes them wind Tite and Burthensome.

wind-up ('waɪnd'ʌp), *sb.*¹ and *a.* [f. the phr. *to wind up*, WIND *v.*¹ 24.]

A. *sb.* **1.** The action of 'winding up', or something that 'winds up' or concludes a course of action, story, etc.; close, conclusion, finish, *dénouement*; final settlement; closing act or proceeding. †Also formerly **wind-up-all**.

1573 G. HARVEY *Letter-bk.* (Camden) 47 Whitch was the Epiphonema and as it were the windupal of that meting. **1588** J. HARVEY *Disc. Probl.* 74 Doth not the diuel, I say, in the winde-vpall, and in fine, oftner play wilie beguile him selfe? **1665** BUNYAN *Holy Citie* (1669) 266 This New Jerusalem shall be the wind-up of the world. **1683** —— *Greatn. Soul* (1691) 56 So the wind-up of the whole will be this, They shall have like for like. **1816** JANE AUSTEN *Emma* xxii, That was the wind-up of the history. **1844** ALB. SMITH *Adv. Mr. Ledbury* xxiv. (1886) 75 Getting through a few.. quadrilles,..and Sir Roger de Coverley as a wind-up. **1853** DICKENS *Bleak Ho.* xviii, To take myself well to task, and have a regular wind-up of this business now. **1869** OUSELEY *Counterp. Canon & Fugue* xxiii. 181 The dominant pedal always announces the termination, or 'wind-up', of a fugue.

2. *Baseball.* The motions of a pitcher preparing to pitch the ball. Also *fig.* and in other sports.

1931 D. RUNYON in *Collier's* 25 Apr. 38/2, I take a good wind-up..but..the ball does not break as I expect. **1936** *Philadelphia Rec.* 30 July 19/1 Blanton is the sort of orator who cannot shorten his pitching motion... He is unable to make a simple motion without taking a full windup. **1951** [see STRETCH *sb.* 1 i]. **1974** MILLS & BUTLER *Tackle Badminton* v. 45 The great temptations to be avoided with drop shots are..making an exaggerated wind-up with over-emphasized power, [etc.]. **1976** *Webster's Sports Dict.* 483/2 The windup, which is usually accompanied by a rocking of the body, sets a rhythm which the pitcher follows until the ball is released.

3. a. Material that has become wound round something. **b.** The action of winding or coiling something round something else. **c.** The action of becoming twisted or stressed by the application of torque.

1964 *Gloss. Letterpress Rotary Printing Terms* (B.S.I.) 21 *Wind up*, paper accidentally wrapped round the impression cylinder, plate cylinder, or inking rollers. **1966** J. S. COX *Illustr. Dict. Hairdressing & Wigmaking* 165/2 *Wind-up*,.. the winding of the hair on curlers. **1969** W. R. R. PARK *Plastics Film Technol.* ii. 15 This technique..generates a greater percentage of scrap or recycle material than the use of a stationary windup. **1972** *Sci. Amer.* Dec. 51/1 The carriage was pushed back and forth by the spinner, one way during the drawing-twisting operation and the other way during windup. **1975** *Drilling Technol. & Collet Chuck* (Bristol Erikson Ltd.) 4 Since the forces created in any cutting action are never constant, it follows that the amount of torsional 'wind-up' will be continually varying. **1976** G. ROBSON *Land-Rover* vii. 117 To take care of transmission wind-up..the new car was to have a third, central differential with a limited-slip mechanism inside it. **1978** *Hot Car* July 89/4 Traction bars..are..bolted by way of U-bolts and brackets to the rear leaf springs of a car such that they prevent wind-up of the rear axle on full-power starts.

4. A deliberate attempt to 'wind up' or provoke someone by misleading or hoaxing; a trick or practical joke. Also *attrib.*, as ***wind-up artist***, etc. *colloq.*

1984 *Times* 10 May 1/3 My recollection of this is quite clear. I thought it was a wind-up to be honest with you. **1986** *Times* 18 Aug. 10/1 After being inundated with bogus small ads from constables trying to sell off their superiors' cars, Muil once said to me: 'Policemen are the biggest wind-up artists of all time.'

B. *adj.* **1.** Constructed to be wound up. Also of a window: made to be moved up (to shut) and down (to open) by means of a handle wound with a rotary motion.

1784 *Morn. Chron.* 21 Apr. 4/3 Advt., A wind up range. **1951** *Festival of Britain Catal.* 149/1 Wind-up plate glass window, weatherproof and draughtproof. **1962** E. O'BRIEN *Lonely Girl* v. 64 The last record lay on the green baize of the wind-up gramophone. **1968** 'E. MCBAIN' *Fuzz* ix. 155 The police in this city are like wind-up toys with keys sticking out of their backs. **1970** *Motoring Which?* July 98/1 A few of these modifications—wind-up windows..also appeared on the ordinary Mini. **1982** N. PAINTING *Reluctant Archer* vii. 105 There were other gramophones, too. Wind-up ones.

2. Forming the 'wind-up' or conclusion of something; concluding, closing.

1843 MOZLEY *Ess.* (1878) I. 25 Strafford determined not to be wanting to himself at the wind-up scene. **1900** 'MARK TWAIN' *Man that corrupted* etc. 153 We had a wind-up champagne supper.

wind-up ('wɪndʌp), *sb.*² *colloq.* [f. phr. *to get the wind up* s.v. WIND *sb.*¹ 10 b.] A state of nervous anxiety or fear; an occurrence of this.

1917 G. S. GORDON *Let.* 13 Feb. (1943) 69 By that time my runner was showing signs of 'wind-up'... He thought I was very unfeeling, not to go down to a cellar till the shower [of shelling] was over. **1922** *Encycl. Brit.* XXX. 64/1 Many other pilots..have been through the same stages of 'wind-up'. **1931** J. HILTON *Murder at School* x. 204 We were having a smoke... We got an awful wind-up, thinking somebody..might have smelt something. **1952** *Chambers's Jrnl.* Feb. 82/2 Putting on a bold face, but with a fair amount of wind-up, I walked..in the direction the hand pointed to. **1980** A. PRICE *Hour of Donkey* xiv. 220 Bit of nerves..the old wind-up.

windward ('wɪndwəd), quasi-*sb.* in *phr.*, *a.*, and *adv.* Also 6 *Sc.* **wyndwart, vynduart**, 7 **winward**, 9 **win'ard**. [f. WIND *sb.*¹ + -WARD. (In all senses the opposite of LEEWARD.)]

A. Phr. ***to (the) windward*** (also formerly with other preps.): to the windward side or direction.

1549 *Compl. Scot.* vi. 42 The said galiasse in schort tyme cam on vynduart of the tothir schip. **1562** WINȜET *Cert. Tractatis* i. Wks. (S.T.S.) I. 4 To lat down ane grete dele thair hie sailis, and hald to wyndwart. **1626** CAPT. J. SMITH *Accid. Yng. Seamen* 18 A sayle, how stands she, to windward or leyward. **1666** MONK *Let.* (in *Quaritch's Rough List, No. 202* (1900) Oct.) Sir William Berkeley kept his course, at which a gun was fired at winward of him. **1687** A. LOVELL tr. *Thevenot's Trav.* I. 281 About Noon he was got to the Windward. **1719** DE FOE *Crusoe* II. (Globe) 329 The Sound coming from the Windward. **1833** HT. MARTINEAU *Charmed Sea* iv. 53 The heavens were grey, and there was a very dark line to windward. **1876** MISS BRADDON *J. Haggard's Dau.* i. 27 Before Joshua could reach him, the first of those giant masses of water struck on the rock to windward of him.

b. In *fig.* phrases, such as ***to get to windward of***, to gain an advantage over (cf. WIND *sb.*¹ 3 b); ***to keep to windward of***, to keep out of the reach of (cf. WINDY 2 d); ***to cast an anchor to windward***, to adopt measures for security.

1783 COWPER *Let. to J. Newton* 7 Mar., That my vanity may not get too much to windward. **1882** DE WINDT *Equator* 12 His intention of 'getting to windward of those "Maylays"'. **1888** RIDER HAGGARD *Mr. Meeson's Will* vi, If I happen to have got to windward of the young woman, why, so much the better for me. **1890** [see LEEWARDLY]. **1919** *19th Cent.* Dec. 1152 This policy was based on a desire to keep an anchor to the windward, to secure the United States for a friend.

B. *adj.*

1. Having a direction towards, *i.e.* opposite to that of, the wind; moving against the wind.

1627 CAPT. J. SMITH *Sea Gram.* x. 47 You say..a windward Tide when the Tide runnes against the wind. **1739** (*title*) A description of the Windward Passage and Gulf of Florida. *c* **1850** *Rudim. Navig.* 56 Windward Great Circle Sailing.

b. Of or in reference to a sailing vessel, expressing ability to sail close to the wind: = WEATHERLY 2.

1895 *Outing* (U.S.) XXVI. 382/1 She is so slender and graceful that one is prone to wonder that such prettiness is consistent with windward power. **1901** *Daily Chron.* 27 Sept. 5/7 A better windward boat than the Columbia.

2. Situated towards the direction from which the wind blows; facing the wind.

a **1687** [see LEEWARD A. 2]. **1725** DE FOE *Engl. Tradesman* iii. (1732) I. 21 His windward leg being hurt by a bruise. **1731** MILLER *Gard. Dict.* s.v. *Blight*, On the Wind-ward Side of the Trees. **1783** JUSTAMOND tr. *Raynal's Hist. Indies* V. 5 Those that lie nearest the East, have been called the Windward Islands; the others the Leeward, on account of the wind's blowing generally from the eastern point in those quarters. **1858** FROUDE *Hist. Eng.* IV. xxii. 424 The vessel laying slightly over, the windward tier slipped across the deck.

C. *adv.* Towards the wind, to windward.

1690 in *14th Rep. Hist. MSS. Comm.* App. IV. 243 The fleet that came from Plymouth..were plying windward of that place. **1700** TYRRELL *Hist. Eng.* II. 833 Tacking about, and so getting Windward of them, they..gain'd a great Advantage.

Hence **'windwardly** *a.* = B. 1 b, 2; **'windwardmost** *a.*, furthest to windward; **'windwardness**, 'windward' or weatherly quality.

1657 R. LIGON *Barbadoes* (1673) 23 The most *windwardly Island of all the Caribbies. *a* **1734** NORTH *Lives* (1826) III. 92 The characters of the several vessels,.. some windwardly, some not stay well, some slugs. **1902** *Edin. Rev.* Oct. 422 The island is the most windwardly of the whole Caribbean Archipelago. *a* **1625** MANWAYRING *Seamans Dict.* (1644) s.v. *Weather Bow*, Any thing that is to the *wind-ward-most-side, we say, it is the weather-part, or a-weather. **1777** *Summary Acc. Tobago* 78 A mile from the windwardmost point of Minster-Bay. *a* **1618** RALEIGH *Invention of Shipping* (1650) 29 By reason of their ready staying and turning, by reason of their *windwardnesse.

windwards ('wɪndwədz). Also 7 **winwards**. [f. WIND *sb.*¹ + -WARDS.] = WINDWARD A.

1589 HAKLUYT *Voy.* 525 [He] appointed 24. of the lustiest rowers in the great boate, to rowe to windwards. **1622** R. HAWKINS *Voy. S. Sea* xxvi. 57 We saw a Shippe turning to Windwards. **1625** in Foster *Engl. Factories India* (1909) III. 100 Four Portugall galliones..though to winwards of them, came noe neerer then to descrye their cullours. **1631** PELLHAM *Gods Power* 8 Wee found the winde..so fiercely blowing, that we could not possibly row to Wind-wards.

†**'windweed.** *Obs. rare.* [f. WIND *v.*¹ + WEED *sb.*¹] = BINDWEED.

1578 LYTE *Dodoens* III. lv. 396 The leaues and fruite of sharpe Windeweede. *Ibid.* v. vii. 555 Amongst those kinds of plantes called Windweeds, or bindweedes.

windwen, obs. form of WINNOW *v.*

windy ('wɪndɪ), *a.* Forms: 1 **windiȝ**, 1, 4 **windi**, 4–5 **wyndi**, 4–6 **wyndy**, 6 **-die, -dye, windye**, *Sc.* **vyndie, wondie**, 6–7 **windie**, 5– **windy**. [OE. *windiȝ*: see WIND *sb.*¹ and -Y¹. Cf. MHG. *windic*, G. *windig*.]

I. Literal and directly connected senses.

1. a. Consisting of wind; of or pertaining to (the) wind; having the command of the winds, as a heathen deity; indicating or suggesting wind.

c **1000** *Ags. Gosp.* Luke viii. 23 Ða com windi yst. **1390** GOWER *Conf.* III. 313 The wyndy Storm began to skarse. **1590** SPENSER *F.Q.* II. viii. 48 As when a windy tempest bloweth hye. *a* **1593** MARLOWE *Ovid's Elegies* II. xvi, If stern Neptune's windy power prevail. **1602** W. BASSE *Three Past. Elegies* ii. (1893) 49 March, departed with his windy rage. **1617** J. TAYLOR (Water P.) *Three Weekes Observ.* Ep. Ded., All the watery, windy, earthly, and drinking Deities. **1781** COWPER *Retirement* 432 While morning kindles with a windy red. **1873** BLACK *Pr. Thule* vi. 89 The sea that lay beyond..was of a windy green.

b. Produced, or actuated, by 'wind' or compressed air: said of music played on wind-instruments, or of a wind-instrument.

1841 THACKERAY *Mem. Gormandising* Wks. 1900 XIII. 576 Music, whether windy or wiry. **1871** LONGF. *Wayside Inn* II. *Cobbler of Hagenau* 45 Two angels carved in wood, That by the windy organ stood.

2. a. Of places, etc.: Full of, exposed to, blown upon or through by the wind.

Beowulf 1358 Windiȝe næssas. *c* **1000** ÆLFRIC *Hom.* II. 322 Heora wyrtruma bið swa-swa windiȝe ysla. **1483** *Cath. Angl.* 419/1 Wyndy, *ventosus, ventuosus*. **1552** HULOET, Wyndy houses, or places. **1555** EDEN *Decades* (Arb.) 279 A coulde and wyndy clime. **1573** *Satir. Poems Reform.* xxxix. 350 Then wes he worsland our ane wondie swyre. *a* **1593** MARLOWE & NASHE *Dido* I. i, Iuno..Made Hebe to direct her ayrie wheeles Into the windie countrie of the clowdes. **1667** MILTON *P.L.* III. 440 On this windie Sea of Land, the Fiend Walk'd up and down. **1833** TENNYSON *May Queen, New Year's Eve* v, The building rook 'ill caw from the windy tall elm-tree. **1864** LOWELL *Fireside Trav.* 191 As he paces the windy deck. **1873** LONGF. *Wayside Inn, Monk of Casal-Maggiore* 84 My wretched lodging in a windy shed.

b. Of times, conditions, etc.: Characterized by wind, in which wind is frequent or prevalent; accompanied by (much) wind.

c **1000** *Sax. Leechd.* III. 162 Windiȝ lengten & reniȝ sumer. **1431** LYDG. *Min. Poems* (Percy Soc.) 2 Toward the ende of wyndy Februarie. **1579** J. DEE *Diary* (Camden) 5 A moyst Marche and not wyndy. **1600** SURFLET *Country Farm* v. viii. 671 Windie drouthes. **1685** in *Verney Mem.* (1904) II. 382 The wettest & the windiest day that I have seene. **1749** FIELDING *Tom Jones* I. iii, It is a good Night, only a little rainy and windy. **1877** HUXLEY *Physiogr.* 69 A windy day soon dries a wet pavement. **1904** W. E. HODGSON *Trout Fishing* 210 Meanwhile the rain goes on: no longer a slight windy spray.

c. Stirred by or wavering in the wind; moving so as to produce a wind or current of air.

c **1450** tr. *De Imitatione* II. vii. 47 Truste not ner leene not upon a windy rede. **1590** SPENSER *F.Q.* III. xii. 8 He..in his hand a windy fan did beare. **1826** DISRAELI *Viv. Grey* VI. i, Hans quivered like a windy reed.

d. Situated towards the wind, windward: in phr. ***on the windy side of*** (fig.), so as not to be 'scented' and attacked by (cf. WIND *sb.*¹ 4), out of the reach of; away from, clear of.

In modern use echoing Shaks.

1599 SHAKS. *Much Ado* II. i. 327 *Pedro.* Infaith Lady you haue a merry heart. *Beatr.* Yea my Lord I thanke it, poore foole it keepes on the windy side of Care. **1601** —— *Twel. N.* III. iv. 181 Still you keepe o'th windie side of the Law: good. **1814** SCOTT *Wav.* xii, He had just so much solidity as kept on the windy side of insanity. **1863** COWDEN CLARKE *Shaks. Char.* vii. 190 You cut off his resources; while you yourself keep on the windy side of assassination and murder.

3. Resembling the wind in storminess, quality of sound, swiftness, †changefulness, etc.

c **1000** ÆLFRIC *Hom.* II. 388 Þeah þeos woruld wede, and windiȝe ehtnysse astyriȝe onȝean Cristes ȝelaðunge. *c* **1374** CHAUCER *Boeth.* II. pr. viii. (1868) 6 The amyable fortune maysthow sen alwey wyndy [MS. wyndynge; *uentosam*] and flowynge and euere mysknowynge of hir self. **1592** SHAKS. *Ven. & Ad.* 51 Then with her windie sighes, and golden heares, To fan, and blow them drie againe she seekes. **1595** —— *John* II. i. 477 Zeale now melted by the windie breath Of soft petitions. **1614** PURCHAS *Pilgrimage* VIII. v. (ed. 2) 756 The windy inconstancy of some of the companie. **1670** DRYDEN *Tyr. Love* II. i, A fire which every windy passion blows. **1697** —— *Æneis* XII. 1227 Indu'd with windy Wings to flit in Air. **1869** MRS. STOWE *Oldtown Folks* xviii. (1870) 185 Polly gave a sudden windy dart from the room. **1883** R. RITCHIE *Bk. Sibyls* i. 5 The sweet windy drone of the organ. **1915** *Chamb. Jrnl.* 20 Mar. 245/1 Singing the lines in a high, windy voice.

4. a. Characterized by, arising from, or affected with 'wind' (WIND *sb.*¹ 10) in the stomach or bowels (†or other parts): = FLATULENT 4.

c **1000** *Sax. Leechd.* II. 214 Wiþ þa þing þe windiȝne æþm on men wyrcen. **1563** T. GALE *Antidot.* II. 30 In all cold and wyndye infirmities of the brayne. **1598** MARSTON *Pygmal., Sat.* iv. 151 The windie-chollicke striu'd to haue some vent. **1620** VENNER *Via Recta* viii. 185 Waterish and impure stomacks, by reason of windie crudities, wherewith they abound. **1799** UNDERWOOD *Dis. Childhood* (ed. 4) I. 56 A costive and windy state of the bowels. **1879** *St. George's Hosp. Rep.* IX. 348 After some windy eructations. **1889** in J. Hutchinson *Archives Surg.* (1898) IX. 121 When well I am generally very windy.

b. Of food or drink: Causing or liable to cause 'wind': = FLATULENT 3.

1398 TREVISA *Barth. De P.R.* XVII. clxxxvi. (Add. MS. 27944), Newe muste is ful wyndy & smoky. **1533** ELYOT *Cast. Helthe* (1541) 28 Nauews do not nouryshe so moche as rapes, but they be euen as wyndye. **1617** MORYSON *Itin.* III. 101 They..feede on bread very black, heauy and windy.

1698 Floyer *Asthma* ii. (1717) 25 When the Meat is crude, slimy, windy, acerb. **1897** *Allbutt's Syst. Med.* III. 494 If the food be poor and windy.

II. Figurative senses. (See also 2 d, 3.)

5. Having 'nothing in it', 'airy', intangible, empty, unsubstantial, flimsy, vain, frivolous, trifling, worthless. (Often passing into other senses; see below.) Similarly of persons (*rare*).

1593 G. Harvey *New Let.* B 1, A wan, or windy Hope, is a notable breake-necke vnto itselfe. **1598** Barret *Theor. Warres* v. v. 165 There is nothing more vniust then to make men to liue by windy words & ayre. **1601** [see 6 a]. **1650** Milton *Tenure of Kings* (ed. 2) 47 Neither is Cæsar to make Warr as head of Christ'ndom, Protector of the Church, Defender of the Faith; these Titles being fals and Windie. **1693** Dryden tr. *Juvenal* x. 219 Exchanging solid Quiet, to obtain The Windy satisfaction of the Brain. *a* **1700** B. E. *Dict. Cant. Crew*, *Windy-fellow*, without Sense or Reason. **1830** Carlyle *Ess.*, *Richter* (1840) II. 340 What a hollow, windy vacuity of internal character this indicates. **1854** De Quincey *War* Wks. 1862 IV. 271 The windiest of levities. **1861** Thackeray *Four Georges* iv. (1862) 193 The Prince of Wales had some windy projects of encouraging literature, science, and the arts. **1877** Carlyle in *Mrs. Carlyle's Lett.* II. 116 *note*, Sending windy gossip to the newspapers.

6. a. Of speech or discourse, with various shades of meaning: Verbose, long-winded; violent, vehement; empty and high-sounding, inflated, bombastic; exaggerated, extravagant.

1382 Wyclif *Job* xvi. 3 Whethir windi woordis [Vulg. *verba ventosa*] shul not han ende? **1590** J. Davidson in *Wodrow Soc. Misc.* (1844) 517 Notwithstanding all the windye volumes written by them. **1601** B. Jonson *Poetaster* v. iii. (1602) M 3 b, *Tibullus*. O, terrible, windy words! *Gallus*. A signe of a windy Braine. **1638** Junius *Paint. Ancients* 209 Windie and unmeasurable babbling was not long since brought to Athens out of Asia. **1660** Fuller *Mixt Contempl.* xii. 19 By such windy particulars [he] did blow up his losses to the summe by him nominated. **1810** Coleridge in *Lit. Rem.* (1839) IV. 379 To what purpose then this windy declamation about John Calvin? **1868** M. Pattison *Academ. Org.* v. 245 A vague and windy rhetoric has supplanted solid acquisition. **1886** *Illustr. Lond. News* 21 Aug. 194/1 The windy speeches made at public political meetings.

b. Of a speaker or writer: Full of talk or verbiage, talkative, loquacious, long-winded; violent or extravagant in utterance, 'blustering'; bragging, boastful (cf. 7 b).

1513 Douglas *Æneis* xi. viii. 33 Quhidder, gif thi marcial deidis, as thai war ay, Into thy wyndy clattryng toung sal be. **1581** J. Hamilton *Cath. Traict.* in *Cath. Tract.* (S.T.S.) 85 Ane vyndie sophist. **1594** Shaks. *Rich. III*, iv. iv. 127 Windy Attturnies to their Clients Woes. **1648** Milton *Observ. Art. Peace* Wks. 1851 IV. 566 There will not need more words to this Windy Railer, convicted..of all those Crimes which he..charges upon others. **1824** Scott *Redgauntlet* ch. x, He is a windy body when he gets on his..stories. **1825** Brockett *N.C. Gloss.*, *Windy*, noisy, verbose, marvellous in narration. **1855** Motley *Dutch Rep.* vi. ii. III. 450 The windy demagogue, who had filled half Flanders with his sound and fury.

7. a. That 'puffs one up'; inducing pride or vain-glory. *Obs.* or merged in other senses.

1590 Nashe *Pasquils Apol.* D 4 b, Let witte, which is windie obtaine the lesse, that Charitie which edifieth may gaine the more. [Cf. *1 Cor.* viii. 1.] **1597** J. Payne *Royal Exch.* 43 Puffed vp wth wynd[i]e knowledge. [**1693** Penn *Fruits Sol.* ii. cx. Wks. 1782 V. 181 We may be too easily swelled beyond our just proportion, by the windy compliments of men. **1784** Cowper *Task* v. 269 Inflated and astrut with self-conceit, He gulps the windy diet.]

b. 'Puffed up'; inflated with, or showing, pride or vain conceit; vain-glorious, proud. Now *Sc. colloq.* (const. *of*).

1603 [see *windy-headed* in 9]. **1625** T. Adams *Five Serm.*, *Job* xlii. 6 (1626) 10 After these blustring insolencies, and windie ostentations. **1695** Dryden tr. *Dufresnoy's Art Paint.* 63 He who has a windy Head, and flatters himself with the empty hope of deserving the praise of the common people. **1888** Barrie *Auld Licht Idylls* ix, I'm thinking he was windier of the cock.

8. a. Apt to 'get the wind up'; 'funky'. *slang.*

1916 Hankey *Student in Arms* vii. (1917) 130 The anticipation of danger makes many men 'windy'. **1918** C. J. Biddle *Fighting Airman* (1968) 147 He thought what made the men more 'windy' than anything else..was the thought of..having to lie there all day before being able to get to a doctor. *a* **1948** D. Welch *Voice through Cloud* (1950) iv. 39 He [*sc.* a patient facing an operation] laughed so much that the man with the bandaged ear became exasperated and said, 'Why do you make so much noise? That shows you're windy. If you didn't care, you wouldn't say anything.' **1960** J. R. Ackerley *We think World of You* 123 'E was windy, but I swore it was safe and that nothing could 'appen. **1985** D. Clark *Performance* ii. 40 'Are you feeling windy?' 'Do I look as if I am?'

b. Applied to a frightening or nerve-wracking place or situation. *Services'.*

1919 *Narrative Battery A, 101st Field Artillery* (U.S. Artillery) 118 It was a 'windy' place to be.., as the enemy raked it with machine gun and trench mortar fire all day and night. **1925** Fraser & Gibbons *Soldier & Sailor Words* 305 *Windy Corner*,..any place specially dangerous or trying to the nerves on account of enemy fire. **1927** A. M. Sullivan *Old Ireland* xi. 226 All the 'windy corners' of his front. **1928** T. E. Lawrence *Let.* 1 May (1938) 599 Such performances require a manner to carry them off... A windy business.

9. *advb.* and *Comb.*, as *windy-blowing*, *clear*, *-footed* (cf. 3), *-headed* (cf. 6, 7 b), *-looking* adjs.; *Windy City* (*U.S.*), a nickname for Chicago.

a **1629** Goffe *Orestes* ii. iii, With a North gale of *windy blowing sighs. **1887** *Courier-Jrnl.* (Louisville, Kentucky) 31 Jan. 5/1 An alleged anarchist dynamite plot from the *Windy City. **1908** K. McGaffey *Show Girl* 58 Chicago is surely rightly named when they call it the Windy City. **1948** *News-Dispatch* (Michigan) 3 Apr. 9/3 The handsome Windy City youngster has an enormous following. **1979** K. Bonfiglioli *After you with Pistol* xvi. 120 The scent of the Chicago River as it slides greasily under the nine bridges in the centre of the Windy City. **1899** T. S. Moore *Vinedresser*, *Duet* iii, Cloudless eyes, blue eyes so *windy clear. *c* **1611** Chapman *Iliad* xv. 163 The *windie-footed Dame. **1603** Knolles *Hist. Turks* (1621) 81 The great..applause of the *windie headed people. **1879** Stevenson *Trav. Cevennes* 26 The sun had gone down into a *windy-looking mist.

windy ('wɪndɪ), *sb.*[1] Repr. colloq. and dial. pronunc. of window *sb.* Cf. winder *sb.*[5]

1830 W. Carleton *Traits & Stories Irish Peasantry* I. 193 Will you hand me over that other clew out of the windy-stool [= window-sill] there? *c* **1883** D. Boucicault *Shaughraun* ii. i. 11 He got sight of my face agin the windy. **1921** V. Jacob *Bonnie Joann* 37 Lowse ye the windy-sneck a wheen. **1977** *Hot Car* Oct. 15/2 Another problem with fitting 'lectric windys to English cars is their narrow door design.

windy ('wɪndɪ), *sb.*[2] *N. Amer. local slang.* [f. windy *a.* 6 a.] A tall story; a piece of boasting or exaggeration.

1933 *Amer. Speech* VIII. i. 53/2 *Windy*,..a tall tale, a wildly unreasonable story. **1933** J. V. Allen *Cowboy Lore* iii. 60/2 *Telling a windy*, telling a boastful story. **1935** H. L. Davis *Honey in Horn* iii. 24 He could invent windies about his stand-in with the girls.

wine (waɪn), *sb.*[1] Forms: 1–4 win, (2–3 uin), 3–6 wyn, 4–6 (7 *Sc.*) wyne (4 wyin, vyn, 4–5 wiȝn(e, 4, 6 *Sc.* vyne, 5 wynne, wyen(e, wyyn(e, wiyn, whyne, whyene, 6 *Sc.* wynn, vine), 4– wine. [OE. *wīn* = OFris., OS., MLG., MDu. *wīn* (Du. *wijn*), OHG., MHG. *wīn* (G. *wein*), ON. *vín* (Sw., Da. *vin*), Goth. *wein*:—OTeut. **wīnom*, a. L. *vīnum*, the source also of the Balto-Slavic (OSl. *vino*, Lith. *vỹnas*) and Celtic words (Ir. *fín*, W. *gwin*).

L. *vīnum* is primitively related to Gr. ϝοῖνος, οἶνος wine, οἴνη vine, wine, Alb. *vēne*, Arm. *gini*, which according to some scholars are all derived from a common Mediterranean source, while according to others prim. Arm. **woiniyo* (Arm. *gini*) is the immediate origin of the Gr., Lat., and Alb. words; the nature of the connexion of the Indo-Eur. words with the Semitic (Arab., Ethiopic *wain*, Hebrew *yayin*, Assyrian *înu*) is disputed.]

1. a. The fermented juice of the grape used as a beverage.

It is essentially a dilute solution of alcohol, the proportion of which in its composition depend its stimulating and intoxicating properties. Wines are classed as red or white, dry or sweet, still or sparkling.

Beowulf 1162 Byrelas sealdon win of wunderfatum. **805–31** in Sweet *O.E. Texts* 444 Selle mon..mittan fulne huniȝes oððа tueȝen uuines. **971** *Blickl. Hom.* 165 Ne drincþ he win ne ealu. *a* **1122** *O.E. Chron.* (Laud MS.) an. 1012 Wæron hi eac swyðe druncene, forþam þær wæs ȝebroht win suðan. *a* **1175** *Cott. Hom.* 229 He awende water to uine. *c* **1205** Lay. 14299 Ane guldene bolle i-uulled mid wine. *a* **1300** *Cursor M.* 180 How þat haly drightin Turned watur in to vyn. *Ibid.* 12679 He dranc neuer cisar ne wine, Ne wered neuer clath o line. **13..** *Seuyn Sag.* (W.) 211 Other ich am of wine dronke, Other the firmament is i-sonke. *c* **1350** *Will. Palerne* 3259 þan asked þei þe win & went to bedde after. *c* **1380** Wyclif *Wks.* (1880) 13 Dilicious ale and spisid and heiȝe wynes. *c* **1386** Chaucer *Prol.* 334 Wel loued he by the morwe a sope in wyn. *c* **1440** *Gesta Rom.* xxi. 339 But man contrarious aunswereth, The wyne is over myghty, it is not good. *c* **1450** *Brut* ii. 422 The cite faste did encrese of bredde and wyn, fisshe and flesshe. **1535** Coverdale *Ps.* ciii[i]. 15 Wyne to make glad yᵉ herte of man. **1577** Googe *Heresbach's Husb.* 148 Old Cheese wyl become new in taste, yf you lay them in Time, Vineger, or in Wine. **1667** Milton *P.L.* i. 502 The Sons Of Belial, flown with insolence and wine. *a* **1718** Prior *Epitaph* 29 Their Beer was strong; Their Wine was Port. **1781** Cowper *Conversat.* 263 When wine has giv'n indecent language birth. **1837** Dickens *Pickw.* viii, 'It wasn't the wine,' murmured Mr. Snodgrass, ..'It was the salmon'. (Somehow or other, it never *is* the wine, in these cases.)

b. As one of the elements in the Eucharist.

c **1005** in Wright *Biogr. Brit. Lit., A.-S. Period* (1842) 498 Se Drihten..cwæþ þ se hlaf wære his aȝen lichama, & þ win wære witodlice his blod. *c* **1100** *Gloss.* in Wr.-Wülcker 128/22 *Infertum uinum*, messewin. *c* **1200** *Vices & Virtues* 51 Notieð ðat ȝe isieð bread and win wiðuten, and on ȝeure iþanke ilieueð ðat ȝe naht ne ȝesieð. *c* **1400** *26 Pol. Poems* xxiii. 37 So dede crist..By holy ordynaunce tauȝt vs to lere, Halwe bred and wyn. *a* **1450** Myrc *Par. Pr.* 251 In þe chalys ys but wyn & water. **1531** *Test. Ebor.* (Surtees) VI. 23 He to fynde the brede and wyne. **1552, 1886** [see bread *sb.* 2 d]. **1567** *Gude & Godlie B.* (S.T.S.) 17 His blude to drink, in forme of wyne. **1582** N. Lichefield tr. *Castanheda's Conq. E. Ind.* i. xxxix. 92 They consecrate wᵗ leuened bread and with wine made of raisons. **1781** Cowper *Expost.* 377 The Saviour's feast, his own blest bread and wine.

c. With qualifying word denoting colour, place of origin, etc., as alicant *wine*, claret *wine*, port-wine, *red wine* (red *a.* 16), sherry *wine*, white wine, *wine seck* (sack *sb.*[3]).

a **1300** *Cursor M.* 4678 Wines, quite and red. *c* **1430** *Two Cookery-bks.* 35 Take Datys, an do a-way þe stonys, & sethe in swete Wyne. **1436** *Libel Eng. Policy* 53 in *Pol. Poems* (Rolls) II. 160 Wyne bastarde. **1623** Markham *Engl. Housew.* i. 148 The Wines of the hie countries, and which is called Hie-country wine, are made some thirtie or fortie miles beyond Burdeaux. **1632** Lithgow *Trav.* iii. 78 Best Maluasy, Muscadine and Leaticke wines. **1746** Francis tr. *Hor.*, *Sat.* ii. viii. 12 The lees of Coan wine.

d. Regarded as the usual accompaniment of dessert; see also quot. 1843.

1824, 1833 [see walnut[1] 1 b]. **1843** Lytton *Last Bar.* i. vi, Madge appeared with the final refreshment called 'the Wines', consisting of spiced hippocras and confections. **1859** M. Thomson *Story of Cawnpore* ix. 151 In their wine-and-walnut arguments.

e. *fig.* or in fig. context.

a **1300** *Cursor M.* 21294 þe stile o matheu, water it was, And win þe letter o lucas. **1526** *Pilgr. Perf.* (W. de W. 1531) 154 Allegyng..the dignytees of theyr oyle & wyne of contemplacyon. *c* **1586** C'tess Pembroke *Ps.* cxix. L. ii, I like a smoked bottle am become, And yet the wine of thy commandments hold. **1605** Shaks. *Macb.* ii. iii. 100 The Wine of Life is drawne, and the meere Lees Is left this Vault, to brag of. **1808** Scott *Marm.* i. Introd. 181 The wine of life is on the lees. **1823** Byron *Island* i. iii, Unless he drain the wine of passion—rage. **1825** Carlyle in Froude *Life* (1882) I. xvi. 271 Literature is the *wine* of life. **1865** Kingsley *Herew.* I. Prel. 19 Cheered by the keen wine of that dry and bracing frost. **1875** Stevenson *Lett.* (1899) I. 94 The look of his face was a wine to me.

f. (*a*) Phrases.

† *to drink wine ape* (cf. F. *avoir vin de singe*), to be merry in one's cups. † *wine of height*: 'a former perquisite of seamen on getting safely through a particular navigation' (Smyth *Sailor's Word-bk.*). *wine of honour* (= F. *vin d'honneur*): wine presented by municipal officers to great personages on their entry into a town. *in wine* (see in *prep.* 10 b; cf. F. *dans le vin*): in a state of intoxication with wine; in one's cups. † *to give wine*: to draw blood (cf. claret *sb.*[2] 2). *to take wine*: to drink wine *with* another person in a ceremonial manner, esp. as a token of friendship or regard.

c **1386** Chaucer *Manciple's Prol.* 44 Me thynketh ye been wel yshape. I trowe that ye dronken han wyn Ape. **1518** *Sel. Pl. Star Chamb.* (Selden) II. 134 He seyd vyolently on to hym I shall gyve the a quart of Wyne. **1594** in *Capt. J. Smith's Virginia* (Arb.) 633 The Pilots..demanded of the Captaine their Wine of hight as out of all danger. **1600** Shaks. *A.Y.L.* iii. v. 73, I am falser then vowes made in wine. **1706** *Lond. Gaz.* No. 4276/3 The Magistrates waited on his Grace..and presented him with what they call the Wine of Honour. **1742** Richardson *Pamela* III. 190, I am not sure..whether I should not have Reason to wish you were brought home in Wine, rather than to come home so sober..as you do. **1837** Dickens *Pickw.* ii, 'Glass of wine, sir?' 'With pleasure,' said Mr. Pickwick; and the stranger took wine, first with him,..and then with the whole party together. **1856** Emerson *Engl. Traits*, *Relig.* Wks. (Bohn) II. 102 If a Bishop meets an intelligent gentleman, and reads fatal interrogations in his eyes, he has no resource but to take wine with him. **1904** Sir A. Geikie *Scott. Remin.* xi. 318 One still meets with old-fashioned gentlemen, especially at public dinners, who 'take wine with you'.

(*b*) Proverbs and proverbial phrases.

new wine in old bottles (see Matt. ix. 17). *to look on the wine when it is red* (see Prov. xxiii. 31). *good wine needs no* (*ivy*)*bush* (see also bush *sb.*[1] 5 c, ivy-bush). *when wine is in, wit* (*or truth*) *is out*. *wine and women* (Eccles. xix. heading, A.V.).

1420–22 Lydg. *Thebes* 1732 Wyn and wymmen ben ek set a-syde. *a* **1532** *Rem. Love* xxxvii. Chaucer's Wks. 367/1 Wyne and women in to apostasy Cause wyse men to fal. **1535** Coverdale *Prov.* xxiii. 31 Loke not thou vpon the wyne, how reed it is. **1546** J. Heywood *Prov.* (1867) 23 Ye praise the wyne, before ye tast of the grape. **1616** T. Windham *Commend. Poem* in J. Lane *Contin. Sqr.'s T.* 7 The ivie needes not, wheare theare is good wine. **1616** Drake *Bibl. Scholast.* 235 When the wine is in, the wit is out. **1621** Burton *Anat. Mel.* i. ii. iii. xiii. 160 Those two maine plagues and common dotages of humane kind, Wine & Women. **1727** Gay *Begg. Op.* ii. i, Women and Wine should Life employ. **1755** B. Franklin *Poor Richard* (1890) 241 When the Wine enters, out goes the Truth. **1819** Byron *Juan* ii. clxxviii, Let us have wine and women, mirth and laughter, Sermons and soda-water the day after. **1862** Thackeray *Philip* vii, As Doctor Luther sang, Who loves not wine, woman, and song, He is a fool his whole life long.

g. In collocation with other words, as *wine and water* (hence *wine-and-watery* adj.), *wine*(*s*) *and spirit*(*s*) (also attrib.), *wine and cheese* (*party*, etc.), *cake and wine*; see also d.

1819 Byron *Juan* ii. lvii, The same cause..Left him so drunk, he jump'd into the wave,..And so he found a wine-and-watery grave. **1828** *Wine & Spirit Adulterators Unmasked* 12 The spurious Brandy, which generally comprises the stock of the Advertising Wine and Spirit Merchant. **1843** *Penny Cycl.* XXVII. 467/1 Wine and Spirit Trade. **1867** H. Latham *Black & White* 111 Able to produce the cake and wine of hospitality. **1961** *Daily Tel.* 5 Dec. 9/2 To my mind, the ideal wine and cheese party is given around midday. **1969** *Times* 25 Sept. 27/2 All 550 members of the staff have been invited to a wine and cheese party on that day. **1976** M. Duke *Death at Wedding* xiii. 148 He's gone to the local Labour Party wine-and-cheese do. **1977** B. Pym *Quartet in Autumn* xvii. 155 She did not feel capable of guessing what kind of an evening party, for she could only think of 'wine and cheese' which seemed altogether unworthy of Mr Strong.

2. In wider use, usually with qualifying word: A fermented liquor made from the juice of other fruits, or from grain, flowers, the sap of various trees (e.g. birch and palm), etc.: sometimes called *made wine* (made *ppl. a.* 3).

the wine of the country (= F. *le vin de pays*): properly, the wine made in a particular locality for local consumption; usually *transf.* the alcoholic beverage most drunk in a particular country, or regarded as peculiar to it.

1398 Trevisa *Barth. De P.R.* xvii. clxxxvii. (Add. MS. 27944), Wyne ymade is ymade by crafte of good spicery & herbes. And it farep of þe wyn þat hatte Salinacum & of þe wyn þat hatte rosatum & Gariofilatum. **1542** Boorde *Dyetary* x. (1870) 254 All maner of wynes be made of grapes, excepte respyse, the whiche is made of a bery. **1613** [see palm *sb.*[1] 7]. **1694** Worlidge *Two Treatises* 102 Peaches also and Apricocks, by some are made to yield pleasant Wines. **1710** in *Swift's Lett.* (1767) III. 29, I spent the evening with Wortley Mountague and Mr. Addison, over a bottle of Irish wine. **1712** Addison *Spect.* No. 328 That detestable Catalogue of counterfeit Wines, which derive their Names from the Fruits, Herbs or Trees of whose Juices they are chiefly compounded. **1746** Warton *Progr. Discontent* 84 And tho' she boasts no charms divine, yet she can carve and make birch wine. **1750** (*title*) Οινος Κριθινος, a Dissertation concerning the Origin and Antiquity of Barley Wine. **1803** J. BURNEY *Discov. S. Sea* I. iii. 88 The wine of rice. **1817** H. MATTHEWS *Diary of an Invalid* (1820) ii. 39 As much of the wine of the country as you like. **1842** LOUDON *Suburban Hort.* 561 The gooseberry... Wines and brandies are made from the green fruit. **1865** A. TROLLOPE *Can you forgive Her?* II. xxxvi. 287 He had ordered a bottle of Sauterne; but the landlord had thought.. that a bottle of ordinary wine of the country would do as well. **1888** CHURCHWARD *Blackbirding* 102 What they called the wine of the country—square gin.

3. *Pharmacy.* A solution of a medicinal substance (denoted by a qualifying word) in wine; a medicated wine.

1652, 1900 [see STEEL *sb.*[1] 12]. **1728** CHAMBERS *Cycl.* II. s.v. *Wine, Chalybeate, or Steel Wine,* is prepared of steel filings. **1811** A. T. THOMSON *Lond. Disp.* (1815) 655 The solutions thus formed have been denominated Medicated Wines. *Ibid.* 656 Wine of Ipecacuanha. **1866** AITKEN *Pract. Med.* II. 51 The wine of the root of colchicum.

4. A wine-party, esp. of undergraduates.

1857 'C. BEDE' *Mr Verdant Green Married* xii. 101 Mr Bouncer.. gave his last wine (wherein he produced some 'very old port'). **1860** W. W. READE *Liberty Hall* I. viii. 130 When I go out to a wine I always bring my own straws. **1862** KINGSLEY *Alton Locke* xiii. (new ed.) 123 The interval being taken up.. in 'wines', and an hour of billiards. **1885** M. PATTISON *Mem.* 144 Oh the icy coldness, the dreary Egyptian blankness of that 'wine'.

5. ***spirit(s) of wine***, alcohol, rectified spirit; ***oil of wine***, œnanthic ester; also, a heavy oily liquid (***heavy oil of wine***) consisting of etherin, etherol, and ethyl sulphate, called also ***ethereal oil***. See also LOW-WINES.

[Cf. quot. 1626 s.v. ROSCID *a.*] **1646** SIR T. BROWNE *Pseud. Ep.* III. xxi. 161 An evaparation of spirits of wine and Camphir. *a* **1648** DIGBY *Chym. Secr.* (1682) 172 An excellent Spirit of Wine, fit to draw Tinctures. **1741** *Complete Fam.-Piece* I. iv. 246 Pour on it a Pint of the ordinary Spirit of Wine, that of twelve-pence a Quart. **1807** T. THOMSON *Chem.* (ed. 3) II. 411 A peculiar kind of oil known by the name of sweet oil of wine. **1839** URE *Dict. Arts* I. 43 Raymond Lully was acquainted with 'spirits of wine', which he called *aqua ardens*. **1882** WATTS *Dict. Chem.* II. 507 *Heavy oil of wine*,.. according to Liebig, an ethyl-sulphate of etherol.

6. A wine-glass. Usu. in *pl.*

1848 THACKERAY *Little Dinner at Timmins's* iii, It was calculated that.. a dozen or so tumblers, four or five dozen wines, eight water-bottles.. were requisite. **1935** W. A. THORPE *Eng. Glass* iv. 129 Mansell had three grades of 'wines' which in 1639 he described as follows.. 'Ordinary Drinking-Glasses—for Wine.' **1947** *Glass Notes* Dec. 16 *Problem for 1948*, to discover the following:.. a facet stem wine with a domed foot. **1974** *Habitat Catal.* 72/2 *Bistro.* Really good value for drinking anything from sherry to sweet stout. 3½ oz sherry 14p, 5 oz wine 15p 8 oz goblet 16p.

7. Passing into *adj.* A dark red colour.

1895 *Montgomery Ward Catal.* 3/1 Royal Serge, 22 inches wide, in plain, solid colors.. Colors: Cardinal, wine, brown. **1923** [see LAUREL *sb.*[1] 2 e]. **1950** B. PYM *Some Tame Gazelle* xv. 166 She had visions of herself.. in her brown velvet or wine crêpe de Chine. **1981** *Country Life* 22 Jan. 226/3 Feather-stitch grey and wine pullover.

8. *attrib.* and *Comb.* **a.** Simple attrib. (*a*) Of, made of or with, wine, as ***wine alcohol***, ***-breath***, ***-draff***, ***-drast***, ***-dregs***, ***-harvest*** (also attrib.), ***-marc***, ***-mother***, ***-must***, ***-offering***, ***-posset***, ***-sap***, ***-sauce***, †***-shench*** (also attrib.), ***-sillabub***, ***-stain***.

c **1000** *Ags. Ps.* (Th.) ciii. 14 [civ. 15] Heortan manna must and windrinc myclum blissað. *c* **1205** LAY. 3529 Heo iward reode on hire benche, swilche hit were of wine scenche. *c* **1400** *Lanfranc's Cirurg.* 186 þeron schulen be dissolued wijndrastis brent. *c* **1440** *Pallad. on Husb.* III. 162 Wyndraf is good also commyxt with donge. *c* **1440** *Promp. Parv.* 529/2 Wyne dreggys, or lye. **1580** HOLLYBAND *Treas. Fr. Tong, Grappage*, grape-gathering, wyne haruest. *Ibid.*, *Vendangeur*, a Wine-haruest man. **1597** A. M. tr. *Guillemeau's Fr. Chirurg.* 21 b/1 The wine mother or dregge. **1601** HOLLAND *Pliny* XXIII. i. II. 147 As many as have lien among wine-Marc. **1667** MILTON *P.L.* XII. 21 With large Wine-offerings pour'd. **1701** S. SEWALL *Diary* 2 June (1879) II. 36 Treated them with bread, Beer, wine Sillibub. **1794–6** E. DARWIN *Zoon.* (1801) IV. 424 He gradually takes more custard every day,.. and takes wine syllabub. **1809–12** MARIA EDGEWORTH *Absentee* vi, The wine-sauce for the hare was spilt by their collision. **1818** DK. SUSSEX in Lady Morgan *Autobiogr.* (1859) 19 You did not expect me to have stayed for the wine-posset? **1838** DICKENS *O. Twist* xlviii, Wine-stains, fruit-stains, beer-stains. **1853** URE *Dict. Arts* I. 155 The fermentation of wine-must. **1857** MILLER *Elem. Chem., Org.* (1862) i. §2. 29 Wood spirit and fousel oil.. are termed homologues of wine alcohol. **1917** D. H. LAWRENCE *Look! We have come Through!* 158, I want the fine, kindling wine-sap of spring. **1922** W. B. YEATS *Seven Poems* 1 Being sharpened by his death To drink from the wine-breath While our gross palates drink from the whole wine.

(*b*) Of, for, or connected with the production, sale, storing, or use of wine, as ***wine-barrel***, ***basket***, ***-bin***, ***-bottle***, ***-bowl***, ***box***, ***-butt***, ***-can***, ***-cask***, ***cistern***, ***-country***, ***-cup*** (also fig.), ***-decanter***, ***-district***, ***-flask***, ***funnel***, ***-gourd***, ***-horn*** (OE.), ***industry***, ***-jar***, ***jug***, ***-kitchen***, ***-land***, ***-merchant***, ***-office***, ***-pipe***, ***-shop***, ***-store***, ***table***, ***-tavern*** (hence †***-taverner***), ***-trade***, ***-trough***, ***-tun***, ***-vessel***.

c **950** *Lindisf. Gosp.* Matt. xxi. 33 Monn.. seðe ȝesette ðone winȝeard.. & dalf in ðær win-troȝ. *c* **1000** *Rule of Chrodegang* vi, ðif hwa on þam winlandum.. win wylle forgan. *c* **1000** in Thorpe *Anc. Laws* (1840) II. 354 Ne he ne drince æt wintunnum. *c* **1205** LAY. 30677 He hafde on his uore wintunnen inoȝe. **13..** *Sir Beues* (A.) 2673 Sextene fot a was a lingþe; His bodi ase a wintonne. **1382** WYCLIF *Josh.* ix. 4 Rent wyn botels. —— *Job* xxxii. 19 Must.. that breketh newe litle win vesselys. **1401** *Close Roll 2 Hen. IV*, II. m. 10 *dorso* (P.R.O.) Thomas Nightgale wyntaverner. *c* **1449** *Pol. Poems* (Rolls) II. 223 The Water-Bowge and the Wyne-Botelle. **1530** PALSGR. lf. 178, I Broche a wyne vessell. **1535** COVERDALE *Hos.* iii. 1 They.. loue the wyne kannes. **1538** ELYOT, *Oenopolium*, a wyne tauerne. **1580** HOLLYBAND *Treas. Fr. Tong, Vn verdun*, a wine troughe. **1597** A. M. tr. *Guillemeau's Fr. Chirurg.* 41 b/1 Ashes which are burned of the inveterate sydes of a wyne pipe. **1622** J. TAYLOR (Water P.) *Shilling* B 6, From thence vnto the Wine-Marchant I went. **1635** HEYWOOD *Philocoth.* 46 Flagons, Tankards, Beere-cups, Wine-bowles. **1636** BULKELEY *Gospel Covt.* IV. 306 The heart.. having beene as a Wine-vessell, which hath had no vent. **1684** *Invent.* in *Archaeol. Cambr., Orig. Doc.* (1877) 9 In the Sellar.. two wine casks. **1714** MANDEVILLE *Fab. Bees* (1723) I. 81 That multitude of Wine-Merchants, Vintners, Coopers. **1736** *Gentl. Mag.* VI. 340/1 Portugal, and other Wine-Countries. **1766** ENTICK *London* IV. 351 The freemen.. have the privilege of retailing wine without a licence from the Wine-office. **1780** T. DAVIES *Mem. Garrick* ii. (1781) 16 He engaged for some time in the wine trade. *a* **1800** *Fair Annie* xxvii. in Child *Ballads* (1885) III. 70/2 Has your wine barrels cast the girds? **1816** SCOTT *Old Mort.* xxxiv, Thou.. hast partaken of the wine-cup of fury. **1819** —— *Ivanhoe* I. xiv. 294 He raised.. the wine-cup to his lips. **1821** —— *Kenilw.* xviii, He.. took another long pull at the wine flask. **1825** COBBETT *Rur. Rides* (1885) I. 345 The 'Squire had many wine-decanters. **1833** MOORE *Mem.* (1853) I. 2 My father kept a small wine store in Johnson's Court. **1835** DICKENS *Sk. Boz.* (1836) 1st Ser. I. 291 Waiters with wine-baskets in their hands are placing decanters of Sherry down the tables. **1835** J. E. ALEXANDER *Sk. in Portugal* xi. 260 A considerable reach of the river was also seen to the east and west, and the wine-district in the far distance of Alto Douro. **1837** CARLYLE *Fr. Rev.* I. v. v, Fat are your larders; over-generous your wine-bins. *Ibid.* II. vi. viii, Wine-bottles were broken, wine-butts were staved in and drunk. **1838** J. G. FLÜGEL *Compl. Dict. Ger. & Eng. Languages* II. 833/2 *Wein*,.. *-trichter*, m. wine-funnel. **1839** POE in *Burton's Gentleman's Mag.* Oct. 212, I had indulged more freely than usual in the excesses of the wine-table. **1848** DICKENS *Dombey* lv, A troubled vision.. of wine-shops, water-carriers, great crowds of people. **1853** —— *Bleak Ho.* v, Pickle bottles, wine bottles, ink bottles. **1855** KINGSLEY *Heroes, Argon.* VI. 189 Heracles opened the fatal wine-jar. **1864** BURTON *Scot Abr.* I. v. 319 Wine-barrels would burst if the bung were not sometimes opened to give them air. **1875** *Ure's Dict. Arts* III. 1142 Hérault is the most important wine country in the south of France. **1881** W. J. CRIPPS *College & Corporation Plate* v. 132 (*caption*) *Wine Cistern*, circa 1701. **1910** S. W. BUSHELL *Chinese Art* II. 17 The poets of the time liken their wine cups to 'disks of thinnest ice'. **1922** JOYCE *Ulysses* 142 'Tis the hour, methinks, when the winejug, metaphorically speaking, is most grateful in Ye ancient hostelry. **1924** D. H. LAWRENCE in M. Magnus *Mem. Foreign Legion* 45 So we went into a little cave of a wine-kitchen to drink a glass of wine. **1935** *Burlington Mag.* May p. xli/2 A superb wine-table, also tripod, a pair of torchères, *circa* 1760. **1952** L. MACNEICE *Ten Burnt Offerings* 56 Did not these whitewashed rooms among wine-gourds, goat-skins, ikons, Include a letter or two with a foreign postmark. **1963** *Punch* 21 Aug. 280/2 The most northerly German winelands. **1966** P. V. PRICE *France* 132 More than three million Frenchmen are engaged in the wine industry and there are about a million and a half wine growers. **1966** P. V. PRICE *France* 133 The wine trade in Great Britain consider that the British wine drinker is protected.. by the laws of the country. **1971** *Country Life* 1 Apr. 766/1 His [*sc.* Thomas Heming's] earlier shallow sauce tureens.. were echoed in his own 1,457-ounce massive wine cistern for Belton House. **1971** *Sunday Times* (Johannesburg) 28 Mar. 25/1, (Advt.), On a southern mountain slope, in the heart of the Stellenbosch winelands, the skills of man and the secrets of nature combine to create five distinctive wines. **1974** *Habitat Catal.* 81/2 Wicker wine basket. For serving fine delicate wines, without disturbing the sediment. **1976** R. M. STERN *Will* iv. 24 Prohibition stifled the California wine industry. **1976** *Derbyshire Times* (Peak ed.) 3 Sept. 15/5 (Advt.), Two Walnut pie crust wine tables. **1976** *National Observer* (U.S.) 4 Dec. 8/3 A bureau spokesman says it could be the first step toward establishment of a national wine-district system similar to that of France. **1977** *Times* 14 May 13/3 Accommodation will be heavily booked at vintage time by the wine trade. **1980** *Catal. Fine Chinese Ceramics* (Sotheby, Hong Kong) 75 An incised white dragon Winecup of thinly potted bell shape. **1981** R. MANHEIM tr. *G. Grass's Meeting at Telgte* xv. 88 His busy treasure hunting seemed to leave him no free hand for the wine jug. **1981** *Times* 17 Oct. 12/7 A Dundee wine funnel of about 1820 by William Law sold for £680. **1982** *Daily Tel.* 8 Dec. 17/1 Wine boxes have made buying easier... Wine boxes are generally about £7.50 for three litres. **1984** *Which?* May 195/1 *Which? Wine Monthly* has been testing wine boxes again. A few this time were rather nice.. but many were still disappointing, particularly when they'd been opened for a week or so.

(*c*) With reference to the colour of wine, as ***wine colour*** sb., and predicatively as adj., ***tint***; ***wine-black***, ***-bright***, ***-coloured***, ***-red*** adjs., ***-yellow*** (after G. *weingelb*) adj., also as sb.; ***wine-tint*** vb.

1805 T. WEAVER *Werner's Ext. Charact. Fossils* 57 Wine-yellow is a pale reddish-yellow colour. **1831** BREWSTER *Optics* xliii. 369 All achromatic telescopes.. exhibit the secondary colours, viz. the wine-coloured and the green fringes. **1838** T. THOMSON *Chem. Org. Bodies* 402 The wine-red substance which remains in solution in the carbonate of ammonia. **1842** JOHNSTON in *Proc. Berw. Nat. Club* II. No. 10. 36 The foot of the snail is a wine-yellow. **1855** MILMAN *Lat. Christ.* XIV. x. VI. 606 In the East, the Christ is.. of delicate complexion, dark beard (it is sometimes called wine-coloured beard). **1857** MILLER *Elem. Chem., Org.* (1862) viii. 621 A wine-red amorphous precipitate. **1863** T. W. HIGGINSON *Army Life* (1870) 57 He is jet-black, or rather, I should say, wine-black. **1876** SWINBURNE *Erechtheus* 114 His wine-bright waves. **1876** *Encycl. Brit.* IV. 644/2 *Cairngorm*,.. a wine-yellow or brown variety of rock-crystal. **1893** *Daily News* 14 Feb. 2/3 Wine tints. **1895** S. CRANE *Red Badge* iii, A glaring fire wine-tinted the waters of the river. **1902** R. W. CHAMBERS *Maids Parad.* xxii. 381 The twigs on the peach-trees had turned wine-colour.

b. Objective, as ***wine-bottler***, ***conner***, †***-crier***, ***-drinker***, ***-importer***, ***-lover***, ***-maker***, ***-seller***, ***-shipper***, ***-spiller***, †***-sucker***, †***-supper***, †***-tapper***, †***-tunner***, ***-vendor***, ***-worshipper***; ***wine-drinking***, ***-loving***, ***-making***, ***-producing***, ***-selling***, ***-swilling***, ***-yielding***, vbl. sbs. and ppl. adjs.; also ***wine-like*** adj.

c **1000** *Ags. Gosp.* Matt. xi. 19 Her ys ettul mann & win-drincende. *a* **1100** *Aldhelm Gloss.* I. 2652 (Napier 72/1) *Cauponibus, i. negotiatoribus*, wintæpperum. **1382** WYCLIF *2 Kings* xxv. 12 Wyne makers, and erthtiliers. **1398** Wyne drinkinge [see UNTEMPERATELY *adv.*]. **14..** *Nom.* in Wr.-Wülcker 697/20 *Hic vinitor*, a wynmaker. *c* **1483** CAXTON *Dialogues* 35/23 Frederik the wyn criar. **1535** COVERDALE *Joel* i. 5 Mourne all ye wyne suppers, because of youre swete wyne. **1550** *Rental Bk. Cupar-Angus* (1880) II. 76 Wyne selling, or ony vther mercheandice. **1591** PERCIVALL *Sp. Dict.*, *Vendimiador*, a wine maker. **1598** STOW *Surv.* 192 The successors of those Uintners and wine Drawers.. were all incorporated by the name of wine tunners, in the 15. of Henry the sixt. **1601** DOLMAN *La Primaud. Fr. Acad.* III. 329 A wine-like iuyce. **1604** *Meeting of Gallants at Ordinarie* C 1 b, This strange Wine-sucker. **1607** G. WILKINS *Miseries Enforced Marr.* III. D 4, Scrape-trencher,.. Wine-spiller. **1611** [see CONNER[1]]. **1639** JUNIUS *Sinne Stigmatiz'd* 313 These wine-worshippers will be at it on their knees. **1676** WORLIDGE *Vinetum Brit.* 41 Wine-yielding-fruits. **1748** RICHARDSON *Clarissa* I. 267 My.. aunt Hervey had.. given us to apprehend much disagreeable evil.. from a wine-lover. **1814** P. P. CARNELL (*title*) A treatise on family winemaking. **1825** SCOTT *Talism.* xxi, Ye beef-devouring, wine-swilling English mastiffs. **1835** LYTTON *Rienzi* x. vii, An honest wine-vender. **1846** R. FORD *Gatherings from Spain* xiv. 150 The wine-producing districts. **1855** PUSEY *Doctr. Real Presence* Note S. 473 Some consecrated virgins pleaded for their wine-drinking that it was the element used in the Sacrament. **1875** *Ure's Dict. Arts* III. 1136 The great wine-producing district of Burgundy. **1881** V. LUSH *Jrnl.* 27 Aug. (1975) 245 If life and health be spared to us, wine-making will become hence-forth like jam making and fruit tinning, one of the fixed employments of the Autumn. **1895** *Cornh. Mag.* Nov. 506 As early as 1141 we hear of the wine criers.. being an organised body in France. **1900** J. HUTCHINSON *Archives Surg.* XI. 206 A robust-looking man, by occupation a wine-bottler. **1921** 'L. H. DAVISON' *Movements in European Hist.* iv. 43 The Romans of Latium were short, dark men of the wine-loving lands. **1935** A. G. MACDONELL *Visit to Amer.* x. 183 California could produce a vin ordinaire to sell at thirty or forty [cents]. If she did, she would gradually build up a great community of wine drinkers. **1949** C. GRAVES *Ireland Revisited* x. 151 The traditional story about James Lynch Fitzstephen is that he was a leading wine-shipper in Galway. **1959** E. H. CLEMENTS *High Tension* ii. 21 My family were wine-importers with offices in London, Edinburgh and Bordeaux. **1972** *Times* (Wines & Spirits Suppl.) 27 Nov. p. viii/5 With their large number of outlets they could go direct to wine growers on the Continent, by-passing the wine shippers. **1979** A. MALING *Koberg Link* (1980) xxv. 135 'We have vineyards.'.. 'Tough business, winemaking.' **1980** *Times* 27 Nov. 21/1 A wine-loving traveller. **1981** W. J. BURLEY *House of Care* i. 6 His job with a firm of London wine importers. **1983** *Listener* 14 July 18/3 Burgundy and Bordeaux are still the British wine-drinker's dream lands.

c. Instrumental, as ***winebig***, ***-crowned***, ***-drabbled***, ***-drenched***, ***-driven***, ***-ensanguined***, ***-fizzling***, ***-flushed***, †***-heat***, ***-heated***, ***-heavy***, ***-inspired***, ***-shaken***, ***-stained***, ***-stuffed***, ***-warm***; also ***wine-hardy***, ***-red***, ***-wise*** adjs.

a **1000** *Judith* 71 Weras winsade. *c* **1200** *Trin. Coll. Hom.* 213 Idele lehtres and winrede bruwes [at drinche]. *c* **1563** *Jack Juggler* (facs.) C 4, Wine shakin pilorye peepours. **1598** SYLVESTER *Du Bartas* II. ii. I. *Ark* 137 His wine-stuft stomack wrung with wind he feels. **1611** J. DAVIES *Commend. Poems* Wks. (Grosart) II. 15/1 Their wine-driv'n brains, involv'd in follie's cloud. **1612** BEAUM. & FL. *Coxcomb* I. i, The Gentleman is Wine-wise. **1615** CHAPMAN *Odyss.* III. 200 Their wine-heat bloud. *Ibid.* XVIII. 481 For feare can get no state In your wine-hardy stomacke. **1677** MRS. BEHN *Rover* II. i, The Wine Inspir'd Bullies of the Town. **1835** DICKENS *Sk. Boz, Parl. Sk.*, The playful exuberance of their wine-inspired fancies. **1852** THACKERAY *Esmond* I. Introd., Such a wine-drabbled divinity. **1859** TENNYSON *Geraint & Enid* 1200 Wine-heated from the feast. **1867** MORRIS *Jason* v. 217 A wine-crowned golden cup. **1897** W. B. YEATS *Secret Rose* 2 The old and foolish king.. snored fitfully in a wine-heavy sleep. **1899** —— *Wind among Reeds* 49 Dwelt among wine-stained wanderers in deep woods. **1912** E. POUND *Ripostes* 26 Wealthy and wine-flushed. **1914** W. B. YEATS *Responsibilities* 2 Those wine-drenched eyes. **1922** JOYCE *Ulysses* 249 John Henry Menton.. stared from winebig oyster eyes. *Ibid.* 420 Come on, you winefizzling.. existences! **1925** H. ACTON in *Oxf. Poetry* 4 And we had thought to fashion of our joy Round crackling pearls to pelt our wine-drenched loves. **1928** W. B. YEATS tr. *Sophocles' King Oedipus* 6 And Bacchus' wine-ensanguined face that all the Maenads sing. **1953** C. DAY LEWIS *Italian Visit* vi. 65 When cypresses jetted like fountains of wine-warm air. **1964** J. MICHIE tr. *Horace's Odes* I. vii. 33 Set on his wine-flushed brow brave garlands of poplar. **1983** J. MASTERS *Man of War* xxiii. 299 A Michelin map spread out on the wine-stained.. table.

9. a. Special combs.: **wine apple** [cf. G. *weinapfel*, Du. *wijnappel*], a large red apple with a winy flavour; †**wine ball** = *wine-stone*; **wine bar**, (*a*) a bar or counter in a club, shop, etc., where wine is kept or sold; (*b*) a licensed establishment specializing in the serving of wine (and food); †**wine-belly** *a.*, with a belly full of wine; **wine-biscuit**, a small light biscuit served with wine; **wine book**, (*a*) a book for keeping records of wines bought and consumed; (*b*) a book about wines; †**wine-brewer** (see quot.); **wine-buff**, a wine enthusiast; †**wine-bush** =

BUSH *sb.*[1] 5; **wine butler**, a servant who has charge of the wine-cellar and serves the wine (cf. BUTLER *sb.* 1 a); **wine-cake**, a cake of which wine was an ingredient; **wine-card** [= G. *weinkarte*] = *wine-list*; **wine-cart**, a cart in which wine is conveyed, esp. for sale; **wine-cave**, a cave in which wine is kept to mature; **wine coaster** = COASTER 6; **wine-cooler**, a vessel in which bottles of wine can be immersed in ice or iced liquid; also *fig.*; **wine-cooper** = COOPER *sb.*[1] 2; **wine-crust** (see CRUST *sb.* 5 b); **wine-dance**, a dance performed in celebration of wine; **wine-dark** *a.*, of the colour of deep-red wine; used esp. to render Gr. *οἴνοψ* as an epithet of the sea; occas. (*poet.*) as *sb.*; **wine-dot** [joc. f. WYANDOTTE] *Austral. slang*, an addict of cheap wine; † **wine-drawer**, (*a*) a carrier or seller of wine; (*b*) one who draws wine from the cask for customers; **wine farm** *S. Afr.*, a farm on which grapes are grown for winemaking and on which wine is frequently made; **wine-farmer**, a vine-grower; **wine-fly**, any fly (as of the genus *Piophila*), the larva of which lives in wine or other fermented liquor; **wine fountain**, a large vessel for holding and dispensing wine; **wine-gallon**, the standard gallon by which wine is measured (see quot. 1706); † **wine garland**, a tavern sign in the form of a garland or bush of ivy; † **wine-gnat**, app. = *wine-fly*; **wine-god**, a or the god of wine, esp. Bacchus, Dionysus; **wine-grower**, one who cultivates vines for the production of wine; so **wine-growing** *vbl. sb.* and *ppl. a.*; **wine gum** [GUM *sb.*[2] 1 g], a fruit-flavoured sweetmeat made with gelatine; † **wine-knight**, one who drinks valiantly; **wine label**, (*a*) a label hung round the neck of a decanter to indicate what wine it holds; (*b*) the paper label affixed to a bottle of wine, stating its name and provenance; **wine lake**, a stockpile or surplus of wine; † **wine law** [LAW *sb.*[2]; cf. LAWING *sb.*], payment for one's share of wine; **wine list**, a list of the wines that may be obtained at a restaurant; **wine lodge**, (*a*) = LODGE *sb.* 12 c; (*b*) a licensed establishment selling wine, beer, and soft drinks; **winemanship**, the display of real or pretended knowledge about wine; **wine-measure**, the standard of liquid measure used for wine; **wine-palm**, any palm from which palm-wine is obtained; **wine-party**, a party, esp. of undergraduates, the chief object of which is to drink wine; **wine-piercer** (see quot.); **wine-pint, -quart** (cf. *wine-gallon*); **wine-porter**, one whose business it is to carry wine, esp. to deposit it in cellars; **wine rack**, a frame with compartments for holding bottles of wine; **wine room**, a bar-room where wine is served; **wine-roping**, the development of ropiness in wine; † **wine-sack**, a sack used for straining wine; **wine-sap**, a large red American winter apple; **wine-shades** (see SHADE *sb.* 10); **wine-shed**, the 'shedding' or pouring out of wine (a facetious formation after *bloodshed*); **wine-skin**, a wine-vessel made of an animal's skin; *fig.* one who 'fills his skin' with wine, a tippler; also *transf.*; **wine snob** (see quot. 1951); hence **wine-snobbery**; **wine-sop**, † (*a*) a sop in wine; † (*b*) and (*c*) = SOPS-IN-WINE 1, 2; (*d*) ***winesop black***, a salmon fly; **winesour**, a small acid variety of plum; **wine-spirit**, spirit of wine; † **wine-sprung** *a.*, intoxicated; **wine steward**, a servant responsible for serving wine; **wine-stone**, the deposit of crude tartar or argol found in wine-casks (cf. G. *weinstein*); **wine-taster**, (*a*) one who judges the quality of wine by tasting; (*b*) an instrument for drawing a small sample of wine from a cask; **wine-tasting**, testing the quality of wine by tasting; an occasion when this is done; **wine-vault(s**, (*a*) a vault in which wine is stored (VAULT *sb.* 2 b); (*b*) a pretentious name for a public-house; **wine-vinegar** (cf. G. *weinessig*), vinegar made from wine, as opposed to *malt vinegar*; **wine-wagon**, (*a*) = *wine-cart*; (*b*) a carriage on which bottles of wine are brought into a room; **wine waiter**, a waiter responsible for serving wine; similarly **wine waitress**; **wine-warrant**, a warrant authorizing the delivery of wine from bond; † **wine-washing** *a.*, 'washing' or swilling as wine; **wine-whey**, whey made by curdling milk with wine (see WHEY *sb.* 1 b); **wine writer**, a person who writes about wine for publication.

1802 G. V. SAMPSON *Statist. Surv. Londonderry* 438 *Wine-apple; from its dark red colour. *c* **1440** *Promp. Parv.* 529/2 *Wyyne ballys.., *pilaterie, vel pile tartaree.* **1938** R. GRAVES *Count Belisarius* iii. 65, I was busy at some task behind the *wine-bar. **1940** M. SADLEIR *Fanny by Gaslight* I. 270 He offered her a job as barmaid... Her new place of business was a girlery as well as a wine-bar. **1976** *Amer. Speech 1974* XLIX. 117 *Wine bar*, counter in a liquor store, stocked with wines. **1981** B. KNOX *Killing in Antiques* iv. 87 Dunbar stopped the car in a side street.. just a stone's throw from the wine bar. **1983** *Which?* Dec. (Publications Suppl.), For an accurate description of over 200 wine bars across the country, this section of the book is unbeatable, with critical comments on the range of wines, and an assessment of the food and perceptive summing-up of the atmosphere. **1603** DEKKER & CHETTLE *Grissil* 2560 Dost thou not see our *wine-bellie drunkards reele? **1835** C. F. HOFFMAN *Winter in West* II. 100 A tray of *wine-biscuits and a fragrant Ohio cheese. **1947** L. G. GREEN *Tavern of Seas* vii. 59 Documents, *wine-books, casks and iron chests.. all make a picture of careful work and gay entertainment. **1975/76** *Listener* 25 Dec. & 1 Jan. 891/1 It is easy to mock the pretensions of wine writers... Writing a new wine book is as difficult as building a better mouse-trap. **1709** *Tatler* No. 131 ¶1 A.. fraternity of chymical operators, who.. can.. draw Champagne from an Apple... These adepts are known among one another by the name of *Wine-Brewers. **1976** *Listener* 5 Aug. 158/2 One area which beer connoisseurs will have to cultivate in order to approach the influence of *wine-buffs—the language of appreciation. **1638** BRATHWAIT *Barnabees Jrnl.* D d viij, The Poets *wine-bush, which they use to prate on. **1880** E. W. HAMILTON *Diary* 9 May (1972) I. 10, I have been offered and have undertaken the post of Chief *Wine Butler to Mr. G., which I hope will secure something rather less nasty in his cellars. **1973** *Times* 25 Aug. 12/6 Wine service is of such skill that it should make the average English wine butler blush. *a* **1661** HOLYDAY *Juvenal* (1673) 95 Why loose thy feast and *wine-cakes [orig. *mustacea*], when thy friends Half-cloy'd depart? **1837** WHEELWRIGHT tr. *Aristophanes* I. 58 The wine-cake [*οἰνοῦτταν*], honey, figs, whate'er 'tis right For Mercury to eat. **1851** MAYNE REID *Scalp Hunters* ii, Whenever I took up a *wine-card or a pencil, these articles were snatched out of my fingers. **1837** W. B. ADAMS *Carriages* i. 25 A *wine-cart, or rather waggon. **1908** *Daily Chron.* 20 Mar. 4/6 Wine-carts used to go round the streets of Edinburgh dispensing the 'lairds' drink' to jug-customers. **1845** DODD *Brit. Manuf.* 82 The *wine-caves of Epernay. **1956** G. TAYLOR *Silver* ix. 201 **Wine Coasters*, circular wooden base on baize, with silver sides. **1971** *Country Life* 15 July 183/1 The platform [of a cruet] was encircled with a deep gallery of wood.. in the manner of a giant wine coaster. **1815** SCOTT *Guy M.* xiii, Dominie, take the key of the *wine-cooler,.. the gentleman will surely take something. **1828** LYTTON *Disowned* xl, Borodaile's looks are the best wine coolers in the world. **1848** Wine-cooler [see *en permanence* s.v. EN *prep.*] **1977** W. M. SPACKMAN *Armful of Warm Girl* 29 The waiter had swooped in rolling a second wine-cooler to set beside the first. **1635** *Canterbury Marr. Licences* Ser. II. (1894) 1079/1 Edward Orlcocke of the city of London, *wine-cooper. **1765** TUCKER *Lt. Nat.* (1834) II. 528 Brewing poisonous liquors in a wine-cooper's vaults. **1837** [see COOPER *sb.*[1] 2]. **1872** SYMONDS *Dante* 213 Mildew is now where the *wine-crust used to be. **1920** D. H. LAWRENCE *Touch & Go* I. ii. 29 They begin to sing, dancing meanwhile, in a free little ballet-manner, a *wine-dance, dancing separate and then together. **1855** KINGSLEY *Westw. Ho!* vi, The *wine-dark depths of the crystal. **1865** MISS BRADDON *Sir Jasper's T.* xxvi, The.. Marquise, in her wine-dark violet dress. **1879** BUTCHER & LANG *Odyssey* 7 Sailing over the wine-dark sea. **1934** W. B. YEATS tr. *Sophocles' Oedipus at Colonus* in *Coll. Plays* 543 Come praise The wine-dark of the wood's intricacies. **1953** T. A. G. HUNGERFORD *Riverslake* 35 'Is he a *wine-dot?' 'Is he hell!.. He's never off it.' **1976** D. HEWETT *This Old Man comes rolling Home* 11 Gawd, you smell like an old wine-dot, Laurie. **1415** *York Myst.* Introd. p. xxvi, *Wyndrawers. **1468** *Mann. & Househ. Exp.* (Roxb.) 522 Of Reynold the wynedrawer vij. pipz. **1536** *Rem. Sedition* 18 b, If a tapster or a wyne drawer recken a peny or two more than his duetie. **1583** FOXE *A. & M.* 1690/2 He desired the wine drawer that he might haue a pinte of malmesy & a loafe. **1705** tr. *Bosman's Guinea* ix. 120 The Commonalty, such as Wine-Drawers, Fishermen, and such like. **1923** O. SCHREINER in *Cape Times* 18 Aug. 3/1 The sinking valley with its sprinkling of *wine-farms. **1970** *Cape Times* 28 Oct. 21/1 (Advt.), Choice Wine Farm in extent 40 morgen. **1984** *Times* 1 Nov. 27/7 He had invited Miss Budd to stay on his wine farm. **1792** A. YOUNG *Trav. France* I. 133 The greatest *wine-farmer in all Champagne. **1909** *Westm. Gaz.* 16 Aug. 5/1 The very wine-farmers appear to have agreed to drop.. their agitation for the repeal of the Excise. **1915** G. McC. THEAL *Hist. S. Afr. 1795–1872* ii. 36 The British government held out great inducements to South African winefarmers to increase the quantity of their produce. **1585** HIGINS *Junius' Nomencl.* 73/1 *Ephemera*,.. a day flie, liuing not aboue a dayes space, or *wineflies. **1658** ROWLAND tr. *Moufet's Theat. Ins.* 949 The Fly *Bibio*.. called .. in the English, Wine Fly. **1753** *Chambers' Cycl.* Suppl. s.v. *Wine*, *Wine-Fly*,.. a small black fly, found in empty Wine-casks, and about Wine-lees. **1889** *Cent. Dict.*, *Wine-fountain. **1931** E. WENHAM *Domestic Silver* ii. 17 Wine-fountains nearly 4 feet long and 3 feet wide. **1969** E. H. PINTO *Treen* 53/1 The lignum vitae wine fountain.. is part of the Burrell Bequest to Glasgow Museum and Art Gallery. **1657** PARTRIDGE *Double Scale Prop.* (1671) 68 So many *Wine-gallons are in that vessel. **1706** *Act 6 Anne* c. 27 §22 Any round Vessel.. having an even Bottom and being Seven Inches Diameter throughout and Six Inches deep from the Top of the Inside to the Bottom or any Vessel containing Two hundred thirty one cubical Inches and no more shall be deemed.. to be a lawful Wine Gallon. **1533** MORE *Answ. Poys. Bk.* Wks. 1138/1 Likening them to *wine garlandes and ale poles. **1668** CHARLETON *Onomast.* 43 *Vinacei* (*quia ex vini fæcibus gigni creduntur*) *Wine-gnats. **1634** SIR T. HERBERT *Trav.* 31 Agray, a City first built by *Wine-god Bacchus. **1640** J. GOWER *Ovid's Fest.* III. 759 The Wine-God laughs. **1891** MEREDITH *One of our Conq.* iv. (1892) 27 You shall not take the Winegod on board to entertain him as a simple passenger. **1844** MILL *Ess. Pol. Econ.* i. 45 The *wine-growers of France.. imagine that free trade would relieve their distress by raising the price of their wine. **1859** *Habits of Gd. Society* xi. 311 A famous wine-grower at Epernay. **1846** KEIGHTLEY *Notes Virg., Georg.* II. 89 The different kinds now cultivated in *wine-growing countries. **1953** *Winegum [see HUNDRED *sb.* and *a.* 7]. **1981** *Times* 1 May 19/3 Energy is stored in plastic pellets, like wine gums. **1601** HOLLAND *Pliny* XXI. xx. I. 105 Our *wine-knights [Fr. *yurongnes*] when they purpose to sit square at the taverne and carouse lustily, if they drinke Saffron, never feare surfeit. **1848** H. R. FORSTER *Stowe Catal.* 113 Seven *wine-labels. **1954** 'M. COST' *Invitation from Minerva* 209 On the wine label, above the sycamore.. is a coat of arms. **1980** N. FREELING *Castang's City* xxi. 139 People belonged to a multiplicity of little gatherings.. Wine-label collectors, neighbourhood betterment leagues. **1974** *Wine lake [see LAKE *sb.*[4] 1 b]. **1979** *Guardian* 14 Mar. 14/1 Wine-lakes and butter-mountains may be jokes, but they are sick ones. **1984** *Times* 4 Oct. 1/4 The table wines.. have.. fared reasonably well, to the distress no doubt of the European community, whose wine lake is already overflowing. *c* **1488** *Cely Papers* (Camden) 173 For your *wyene lawgh at tabull iiij[s] iiij[d]. **1898** G. B. SHAW *You never can Tell* II. 251 Crampton snatches the *wine list rudely from him and irresolutely pretends to read it. **1935** A. G. MACDONELL *Visit to America* x. 182, I waved the wine list.. and shouted for the wine waiter. **1972** P. V. PRICE *Eating & Drinking in France* 248 The Nicolas establishments are reliable and the wine lists especially attractive. **1880** *Wine lodge [see LODGE *sb.* 12 c]. **1922** JOYCE *Ulysses* 392 *Mort aux vaches*, says Frank then in the French language that had been indentured to a brandy shipper that has a winelodge in Bordeaux. **1962** *Guardian* 24 Dec. 4/3 There's the Wine Lodge. You can get a glass of small white Australian for ninepence. **1977** *Punch* 31 Aug.–6 Sept. 345/1 Huge and dingy, the saloon bar looked like a cross between the main hall in the old Euston railway station and one of Yates's less-glamorous Wine Lodges. **1958** *Observer* 11 May 16/4 (*heading*) *Wine-manship. **1977** T. HEALD *Just Desserts* v. 87 A passable imitation of genuine winemanship. **1728–51** CHAMBERS *Cycl.* s.v. *Measure*, That eight pounds troy of wheat, gathered from the middle of the ear, and well dried, should weigh a gallon of *wine measure. **1771** *Encycl. Brit.* (1773) I. 313/2, 80 English quarts, wine measure. **1681** GREW *Musæum* II. I. i. 184 The Country-People tap the *Wine-Palm about two feet above the ground. **1870** KINGSLEY *At Last* v, Leaves (as in the wine-palm) like Venus's hair fern. **1829** *Gownsman* 10 Dec. 37 **Wine party*, a meeting of individuals of an unlimited number, for the purpose of conversation, in which the topics are invariably the same, *viz.* the ladies, wine, proctors, and examinations. **1861** HUGHES *Tom Brown at Oxf.* iv, An Oxford undergraduate's room, set out for a wine-party. *c* **1828** BERRY *Encycl. Her.* I. Gloss., **Wine-Piercer*, an instrument to tap, or bore, holes in wine-casks. **1769** *Phil. Trans.* LIX. 220 One drop of tincture of galls gave a rosy purple colour to a *wine-pint of this water. **1580** HOLLYBAND *Treas. Fr. Tong*, *Avallage*, *wine porters wages when they do lay wine into the seller. **1622** J. TAYLOR (Water P.) *Shilling* B 4 b, When in the Celler it is laid, The Carmen, and Wine-Porters must be paid. **1669** E. CHAMBERLAYNE *Pres. St. Eng.* 261 [In the Royal Household] Wine-Porters, 8. **1831** *Lincoln Herald* 1 July 1/6 Mr. Hunt presented a petition from the wine-porters of Dublin, praying for the repeal of the union. **1660** BOYLE *New Exp. Phys. Mech.* Proem 9, 30 *Wine Quarts, each of them containing near two pound.. of water. *c* **1791** *Encycl. Brit.* (1797) VII. 684/1 A Paris pint is 48 cubical Paris inches, and is nearly equal to an English wine-quart. **1974** *Habitat Catal.* 82/1 *Wine rack. Wood and metal frame. **1981** 'J. STURROCK' *Suicide Most Foul* vii. 129 Wine racks, but.. not many bottles. **1865** *Leaves from Diary Celebrated Burglar & Pickpocket* xxxv. 116/1 Several ladies.. made their way to where we were sitting, and in the usual *wine-room style flung themselves into our lap! **1898** A. BENNETT *Man from North* xxvi. 224 Seated in a wine-room or lager-beer hall. **1965** O. ARUNDELL *Sadler's Wells* viii. 102 [In 1825] they made Rosoman's old private house at the New River Head end of the theatre into box-offices, wine-rooms and saloon. **1704** *Dict. Rust.* (1726), **Wine-Roping*: To alter this take a coarse Linen-Cloth [etc.]. **1625** T. GODWIN *Moses & Aaron* I. vii. 38 The *Winesacke, through which wine is so drained from the dregges. **1826** *Lond. Hort. Soc. Catal. Fruits* 151 [Apples] *Wine-Sap, American. **1892** AMÉLIE RIVES *Barbara Dering* xxv, Great crackling bites from a crisp, wine-sap apple. **1879** T. H. S. ESCOTT *England* I. 161 *Wine-shades, bodegas, and saloons. **1771** SMOLLETT *Humphry Cl.* II. 8 Aug., She is become a toast.., and has already been the occasion of much *wine shed. **1812** BYRON *Harold* II. xii. *note*, We had such ink-shed, and wine-shed, which almost ended in bloodshed! **1821** SCOTT *Kenilw.* xxix, This fellow can appear before him drunk as a *wineskin, and yet meet no rebuke. **1825** —— *Talism.* xi, You have been dining with the Teutonic wineskin. **1828** LYTTON *Pelham* xlviii, That persons who have been converting their 'solid flesh' into wine skins, cannot stick so close to one another as when they are sober. **1881** *N. T.* (R.V.) Mark ii. 22 No man putteth new wine into old wine-skins. **1923** D. H. LAWRENCE *Birds, Beasts & Flowers* 15 What is it, in the grape turning raisin, In the medlar, in the sorb-apple, Wineskins of brown morbidity. **1928** E. WAUGH *Decline & Fall* x. 113 Hullo, Prendy, old wine-skin! How are things with you? **1951** R. POSTGATE *Plain Man's Guide to Wine* i. 17 A *Wine Snob is a man.. who uses a knowledge of wine, often imperfect, to impress others with a sense of his superiority. **1977** Wine snob [see SNOB *sb.*[1] 3 d]. **1982** 'W. HAGGARD' *Mischief-Makers* i. 17 He bought it [*sc.* wine] at a multiple grocer but his excellency was not a wine snob. **1966** H. W. YOXALL *Fashion of Life* xxv. 241 There's been much talk recently about *wine snobbery, most of it rather stupid. **14..** *Nom.* in Wr.-Wülcker 742/5 *Hec vipa*, a *wynsope. **1582** STANYHURST *Æneis* III. (Arb.) 91 With chuffe chaffe wynesops lyke a gourd bourrachoe replennisht. **1586** W. WEBBE *English Poetrie* sig. I iv, Let vs haue the Wynesops, With the Cornation. **1826** *Lond. Hort. Soc. Catal. Fruits* 151 [Apples] Wine-Sop, Winter. **1880** F. FRANCIS *Bk. Angling* xii. (ed. 5) 450 The Winesop Black.—Mr. Ramsbottom says this is 'a real old Ribble favourite'. **1836** LOUDON *Encycl. Plants* 423 Several sorts of plums found wild,.. such as the bullace, damson, muscle, and *winesour. **1846** MRS. GORE *Engl. Char.* I. 320 Compôtes of wine-sours. **1753** *Chambers' Cycl.* Suppl. s.v. *Wine*, The phrase **Wine-spirit* is used to express a very clean and fine spirit, of the ordinary proof strength, and made in England from Wines of foreign growth. **1909** *Daily Chron.* 25 Mar. 3/3 Pure wine spirit brandies. **1633** G. HERBERT *Temple, Ch. Porch* vii, Shall I, to please anothers *wine-sprung minde, Lose all mine own? **1658** GURNALL *Chr. in Arm.* verse 14. x. §2. 113 Who when he is wine-sprung thinks (as they say he can skip over the Moone). **1898** A. M. BINSTEAD *Pink 'Un & Pelican* iii. 65 'Aha!' cried Swears.. 'here's a bit o' luck—the *wine-steward! Half a dollar is never thrown away on a wine-steward.' **1978** *Chicago* June 237/1 Freddy's the least intimidating and probably most knowledgeable wine steward in town. **1526** *Great Herbal* (1529) Table, *Tartarus*, wyne lyes or *wyne stone. **1839** URE *Dict. Arts* 1305. **1632** SHERWOOD, A *Winetaster, or Wine-broker (for Marchants). **1679** E. CHAMBERLAYNE *Pres. St. Eng.* II. (ed 12) 238 Mr. Henry Potkins, Wine-Taster. **1825** MACAULAY *Ess., Milton* ¶19 Johnson..was as ill qualified to judge between two Latin styles as a habitual drunkard to set up for a wine-taster. **1858** LARDNER *Handbk. Nat. Phil.* 193 Wine taster.—When it is desired to draw a small sample of wine from a cask, a little instrument..is used [etc.]. **1936** 'R. WEST' *Thinking Reed* vii. 216 He paused..to say in his thick, *wine-tasting voice: 'Your wife's looking very pretty!' **1945** E. WAUGH *Brideshead Revisited* I. iv. 75 Sebastian had found a book on wine-tasting, and we followed its instructions. **1958** [see PUT *v.*[1] 38 f (*a*)]. **1980** *Sunday Times Mag.* 14 Sept. 96 He or she might take a dozen trips abroad each year, attend five or six wine tastings in a week, sample 30 or so bottles of wine a day. **1791** J. WOODFORDE *Diary* 27 Sept. (1927) III. 301 Mr. J[n] Priest having the keys of his Father's *Wine Vaults, I went and tested some Port Wine. **1835** DICKENS *Sk. Boz, Making a Night of it*, They went into a wine-vaults, to get materials for assisting them in making a night. **1837** *Ibid.* 2nd Ser. 73 The old tottering public-house is converted into a spacious and lofty 'wine-vaults'. **1893** HODGES *Elem. Photogr.* (1907) 148 A wine-vault in the City. *a* **1617** BAYNE *Lect.* (1634) 300 Toasts sowred in *wine vineger. **1753** *Chambers' Cycl.* Suppl. s.v. *Vinegar*, Infuse this powder in the strongest wine-Vinegar. **1839** URE *Dict. Arts* 3 Genuine wine or raisin vinegar. **1837** *Wine waggon [see *wine-cart*]. **1848** H. R. FORSTER *Stowe Catal.* 112 A pair of double wine-wagons. **1906** *Blackw. Mag.* Nov. 660/2 We rattle past a wine-waggon. **1927** C. CONNOLLY *Let.* 11 Feb. in *Romantic Friendship* (1975) 251, I met the Spanish *wine waiter. **1969** I. DRUMMOND *Man with Tiny Head* i. 24 The *wine-waitress brought the wine-list. **1974** *Times* 9 Oct. 18/7 A race by wine waiters and waitresses..each carrying a tray bearing four glasses and an open bottle of wine. **1857** TROLLOPE *Barchester T.* xix, With *wine-warrants and orders for dozens of dressing-cases. **1592–6** GREENE *Groat's W. Wit* Wks. (Grosart) XII. 136 These honest men..whose wisedome..gaue light to the Iury what power *wine-washing poyson had. **1603** H. CROSSE *Vertue's Commw.* (1878) 141 This wine-washing licour giueth such..libertie to the tongue, as it rowleth vp and downe. **1975** *Wine writer [see *wine book* above].

¶ In OE. there are several compounds of *wín* in which the word is equivalent to 'vine' or 'grapes', as *wínbéam* vine-pole, *wínclyster* bunch of grapes, *wínléaf* vine-leaf, *wínȝeard* vineyard, WINYARD. From the 14th century onwards instances of *wine* = 'vine' occur in various texts in which *w* is not normally written for *v* (as in Scottish texts: see VINE *sb.* 1 b *β*).

1340–70 *Alex. & Dind.* 847 Ȝe telle vs þat ȝe tende nauht to tulye þe erþe,..no plaunte winus. *a* **1400–50** *Wars Alex.* 3667 Gilden wynes with grapis of gracious stanes. **1456** SIR G. HAYE *Law Arms* (S.T.S.) 114 Knychtis ar nouthir ordanyt to labour cornis, na grouve the wynis. *Ibid.*, A knycht aw nocht to by..wynis, croftis, na heretagis. **1471** CAXTON *Recuyell* (Sommer) 308 In suche wise as the yonge wyne..groweth in heighte. **1632** LITHGOW *Trav.* I. 14 Round about Rome, there are neither Cornes, nor Wines, nor Village.

b. *attrib.* and *Comb.* (*a*) ***wine-man***, a vine-dresser; (*b*) in reproduction of Ger. compounds, in Coverdale's version of the Bible, rendering Luther's language, as ***wine-garden***, ***-gardener***, ***gathering***, ***harvest***, ***kernel***, ***stock***, after G. *weingarten*, *-gärtner*, *-ernte*, *-kern*, *-stock*; (*c*) in mod. use, ***wineberg***, ***wine-hill***, after G. *weinberg*, *-hügel* vineyard.

1456 SIR G. HAYE *Law Arms* (S.T.S.) 239 Labouraris of the erde, as plewmen, harow men, wyne men. *c* **1483** CAXTON *Dialogues* 46/37 *Ysaac le vigneron*, Ysaac the wyneman. **1535** COVERDALE *Num.* vi. 4 From the wyne cornels vnto the hulle. —— *2 Chron.* xxvi. 10 He had..wynegardeners on the mountaynes. —— *Isa.* xxiv. 13 Like as when a man..seketh after grapes, when the wyne gatheringe is out. —— *Ezek.* xv. 2 What commeth of the vyne amonge all other trees? and of the wyne stocke, amonge all other tymbre of the groaue? **1870** *Daily News* 7 Dec., The Tirailleurs..scrambled up through the winebergs. **1885** tr. *Hehn's Wand. Plants & Anim.* 70 The Calydonian legend of the wine-man [orig. *Weinmann*] as given by Homer. **1906** *Academy* 6 Jan. 14/1 Matins, sung High in these wine-hills, wakened me.

†**wine**, *sb.*[2] *Obs.* [OE. *wine* = OFris. *winne*, MLG. *wine*, OS., OHG. *wini* (MHG. *wine*, *win*), ON. *vinr*.] A friend. Also *attrib.* **wine mai** [OE. *winemǣȝ*], a kinsman.

Beowulf 30 þenden wordum weold wine Scyldinga. *Ibid.* 65 þa wæs Hroðgare heresped ȝyfen,..þæt him his winemaȝas ȝeorne hyrdon. *a* **1122** *O.E. Chron.* (Laud MS.) an. 975, Eadgar..West-Seaxena wine. *c* **1200** *Moral Ode* 223 (Trin. Coll. MS.) Werse he doð his gode wines þan his fiendes. *c* **1205** LAY. 17601 Her wit scullen wel wreken unker wine-mæies. *c* **1220** *Bestiary* 374 Eurilc luuen oðer, Also he were his broder, Wurðen stedefast his wine. [**1481** CAXTON *Reynard* xxix. (Arb.) 74 He hath nether kyn ne wyn ne frende that wylle enterprise to helpe hym.]

wine (waɪn), *v.* [f. WINE *sb.*[1]]

†**1.** *trans.* (*nonce-uses.*) **a.** with *out*, to spend in drinking wine.

c **1624** [see WENCH *v.*].

b. To furnish (a cellar) with wine.

c **1645** HOWELL *Lett.* II. liv. (1890) 456 Tho' it be interdicted to wine the King's Cellar with it, in respect of the corrosiveness it carries with it.

2. *intr.* To take wine, formerly esp. at an undergraduates' wine-party. Freq. in collocation with *dine*: cf. sense 3. *colloq.*

1829 C. WORDSWORTH *Ann.* (1891) 70 Dined with Twisleton at Trin.: wined with Payne at Bal. **1875** *My First 'Wine'* 5 'Mr. Topthorne's compliments, and will you wine with him to-night?' Such were the words addressed to me by a scout in Hall. **1877** BLACKMORE *Cripps* xxxiii, He had dined and wined, once or twice, in a not ignoble college. **1937** L. HART in R. Rogers *Rodgers & Hart Songbk.* (1951) III. 166 I've wined and dined on mulligan stew, and never wished for turkey. **1961** *Guardian* 10 Nov. 7/1 Mr Delmer dined and wined with the enemies of democracy in Germany. **1981** *N.Z. Listener* 4 July 80/1 Impressive consultants (with many of whom I have wined and dined).

3. *trans.* To entertain to wine: usually in collation with *dine*. *colloq.*

1862 *Illustr. Lond. News* 5 July 18/2 An esteemed friend..who had just been admitted to the Bar..and..'wined' his friends on the night of his call. **1867** *Standard* 29 Apr., He has dined and wined everybody who has had anything to do with his success. **1916** *Times* 13 Oct. 4/3 He was motored and wined and dined through the conquered country under the watchful chaperonage of German officers.

wineberry ('waɪnbərɪ). Forms: 1 **winber(i)ȝe**, 3 **winberi**, *erron.* **wind-**, 6 **wynberry**. *β.* 6 **wyneber(r)y**, 7– **wineberry**. [OE. *winberiȝe* = OS. *wînberi*, OHG. *wînberi* (MHG. *-ber(e*, G. *weinbeere*), ON. *vínber* (cf. Goth. *weinabasi*): see WINE *sb.*[1], BERRY *sb.*[1] ME. *winberi* normally represents the OE. word; *wineberry* is a new formation.]

†**1.** A grape. *Obs.*

c **1000** *Ags. Gosp.* Matt. vii. 16 Cwyst þu, gaderað man winberian of þornum? *c* **1050** *Voc.* in Wr.-Wülcker 451/2 *Medus*, winberȝe te huniȝe awylled. *a* **1225** *Ancr. R.* 276 Of te druie sprintles bereð winberien? *Ibid.* 296 þet beoð þe erest prokunges þet sturieð þe winȝeardes, he seið, ure Louerd, þet beoð ure soulen, þet mot muche tilunge to uorte beren windberien. *a* **1300** *Cursor M.* 4468 Me-thoght i sagh a wintre,..O þis tre apon ilk bogh Me-thoght hang winberis inogh. **1562** TURNER *Herbal* II. 142 b, Smooth lyke a grape or wynberry.

β. **1535** COVERDALE *2 Esdras* ix. 21 A wynebery of the grapes. [**1783** LEMON *Engl. Etymol.* Pref. p. vi. note, Our Saxon ancestors had Grapes; but, having no name for them, they were obliged to call them Wine-berries.]

attrib. *c* **1265** *Voc. Plants* in Wr.-Wülcker 558/20 *Omfacium*, i. winberi stones.

2. Applied formerly or now locally to various berries.

e.g. †The bilberry or whortleberry; *dial.* the currant, the gooseberry; *Austral.* (*a*) = TOOT *sb.*[6], TUTU[1], (*b*) *Polyosma cunninghamii*; a raspberry of China and Japan, *Rubus phœnicolasius*; *N.Z.* = MAKOMAKO[2].

14.. *True Thomas* in R. Jamieson *Pop. Ballads* (1806) II. 20 The darte, and also the damsyn tre. The fygge, and also the wynne bery. **1597** GERARDE *Herbal* Suppl., Wyneberries is *Vaccinia*. **1612** *Shuttleworth's Acc.* (Chetham Soc.) 201 Wineberies ij[d]. **1622** in Burton *Hist. Scot.* lxvi. (1870) VI. 67 Gooseberries, Strawberries,..and a kind of red wineberrry. **1703** THORESBY *Let. to Ray* (E.D.S.), *Wine-berries*,..not grapes, but gooseberries. **1824** CARR *Craven Gloss.* **1866** *Treas. Bot.*, Wineberry...*Ribes rubrum.* ——, New Zealand, a name given by the colonists to *Coriaria sarmentosa*. **1889** MAIDEN *Useful Pl. Australia* 590 *Polyosma Cunninghamii*, Wineberry, and Feather-wood in Southern New South Wales. **1889** T. KIRK *Forest Flora N.Z.* 223 The makomako or 'wine-berry' of the settlers was discovered by Banks and Solander. **1900** *Westm. Gaz.* 14 Aug. 8/2, I have grown the Japanese wineberry for some years. **1910** L. COCKAYNE *N.Z. Plants & their Story* iii. 37 The wineberry ..has distinctly pleasing rosy-coloured flowers. **1966** [see MAKOMAKO[2]]. **1971** *N.Z. Listener* 6 Sept. 17/1 There were wineberry trees in the bit of bush.

wine-bibber ('waɪnˌbɪbə(r)). Also 6 **wyne bebber.** [f. WINE *sb.*[1] + BIBBER *sb.* Invented by Coverdale to render Luther's *säufer*, *weinsäufer*.]

1. A tippler, a drunkard. Now *literary* and *arch.*

1535 COVERDALE *Prov.* xxiii. 20 Kepe no company with wyne bebbers and ryotous eaters of flesh. —— *Matt.* xi. 19. **1609** DEKKER *Gull's Horn-bk.* Proem. B 2 b, An honest red-nosed wine bibber. *a* **1704** T. BROWN *Char. Jacobite Clergy* Wks. 1711 IV. 266 Look into their Conversation and you'll find them Wine-bibbers to the highest Excess. **1778** [W. MARSHALL] *Minutes Agric., Digest* 8 He commences wine-bibber at Fair and at Market. **1807** W. IRVING *Salmag.* xvi. (1824) 300 When the guzzlers, the gormandizers, and the wine-bibbers meet together. **1870** BRYANT *Iliad* I. I. 13 Wine-bibber, with the forehead of a dog And a deer's heart.

†**2.** A name for the African genet (*Genetta pardina*). *Obs.*

1705 tr. *Bosman's Guinea* xiv. 252 The Negroes call it Berbe, and the Europeans Wine-bibber, because 'tis very greedy of Palm-Wine. **1771** PENNANT *Syn. Quadr.* 237.

So **'wine-ˌbibbing** *vbl. sb.* (also *attrib.*) and *ppl. a.*; also **'wine-ˌbibbery**, wine-bibbing.

1549 COVERDALE, etc. *Erasm. Par. 1 Pet.* iv. 1–7 Nowe in stedde of outragious luste, chastitie is pleasaunte:..for wynnebybbyng, sobrietie. *a* **1593** MARLOWE *Ovid's Elegies* III. i, Wine-bibbing banquets. **1603** H. CROSSE *Vertue's Commw.* (1878) 140 O what lamentable Tragedies is by this Vice acted among wine-bibbing companions. **1816** SCOTT *Old Mort.* v, To..close your evening with wine-bibbing in public-houses and market-towns. **1832** J. WILSON *Noctes Ambros.* in *Blackw. Mag.* Sept. 398 The secret antiquities and private history of royal wine-bibbery. **1873** H. MORLEY *1st Sk. Engl. Lit.* ii. 25 Wine-bibbing monks.

Winebrennarian (waɪnbrə'nɛərɪən), *sb.* (and *a.*) *U.S.* Also **Winebrennerian.** [f. the name of John *Winebrenner* (1797–1860), founder member of the sect + -ARIAN.] A name given to a member of the Church of God, an evangelical sect founded in 1830 in Pennsylvania. Occas. also as *adj.*

1867 W. H. DIXON *New Amer.* II. xxix. 309 No sect escaped this rage for separation..[neither] River Brethren, nor Winebrennarians. **1889** *Cent. Dict.*, Winebrennerian ..*a.* and *n.* **1903** *Christian Advocate* 8 Jan. 7 Christian Scientists..Church of God (Winebrennarian). **1925** T. DREISER *Amer. Tragedy* (1926) II. II. xlvii. 65 It was the summer seat and gathering place of some small religious organization or group—the Winebrennarians of Pennsylvania. **1974** R. KERN *John Winebrenner* p. vii, It would be regrettable if only 'Winebrennerians' of all sorts read the book.

'wine-ˌcellar. Also 6 *erron.* **windseller.** [f. WINE *sb.*[1] + CELLAR *sb.* Cf. MLG. *wînkelder*, MHG. *winkeller*, ON. *vínkjallari*.] **a.** A cellar used for storing wine. Also *fig.*

1371 *Close Roll 45 Edw. III* m. 4 *dorso* (P.R.O.) Vnam magnam Cameram vocatam la Whit Chambre cum vno celario sub dicta camera vocata le Wyn celer. **1375** BARBOUR *Bruce* v. 399 All the vittale, outakin salt,..In the vyne-sellar gert he bryng. **14..** *Pallad. on Husb.* (Bodl. MS.) lf. 1, Cisterne celar for oyles, wyne celar, and columbary. **1538** ELYOT, *Canabus*, a wyne sellar. **1577** GOOGE tr. *Heresbach's Husb.* 11 b, I wyll shewe you..Pipes, Tonnels,..when you come to the Brewhouse, and Windseller. **1647** T. CALVERT *Heart Salve* To Rdr., The soule..is led into the Winecellar of Gods promises. **1756–7** tr. *Keysler's Trav.* IV. 189 The council's wine-cellar is so spacious, that a coach and six may turn about in it. **1839** URE *Dict. Arts* 1303 Wine-cellars ought to be dry at bottom.

b. The wine stored in a wine-cellar, esp. with reference to its quality.

1861 MRS BEETON *Bk. Househ. Managem.* 963 Nothing spreads more rapidly in society than the reputation of a good wine-cellar. **1976** J. ARCHER *Not a Penny More* viii. 87 James arrived carrying a bottle of Beaune Montée Rouge 1971—even his wine cellar was fast disappearing. **1976** P. G. WINSLOW *Witch Hill Murder* (1977) ii. 30 Her cook, her wine cellar and the service at her table were not to be matched.

wined (waɪnd), *ppl. a.* [f. WINE *sb.*[1] or *v.* + -ED.]

1. Mingled with wine; coloured or flavoured with wine.

1604 F. HERING *Mod. Defence* 24 Hee did [call] a cuppe of drinke mixed by his friend..wined water, and not watred wine. **1884** R. V. FRENCH *19 Cent. Drink* 288 Gin—spiced and wined.

2. That has taken wine, esp. in abundance. Also const. *up.*

1640 J. D. *Knave in Gr.* I. i. C 3 b, We'le pledge, we'le pledge: Victual'd and Win'd already. **1898** J. MCCABE *Life Mod. Monastery* vi. 153 He invariably returned..well wined and nourished. **1973** C. BONINGTON *Next Horizon* ii. 41 'We'll get them well wined up tonight, and persuade them that there's a good route round the back of the Tower,' said Barrie. **1982** *Newsweek* 11 Jan. 26/2, I think they were wined up and looking for a joy ride.

†**wine-drunk(en**, *a.* *Obs.* [OE. *wíndruncen* = Du. *wijndroncken* (Kilian), G. *weintrunken*, ON. *víndrukkinn*.] Drunk (with wine). Hence †**winedrunkenness.**

a **1000** *Daniel* 753 Windruncen ȝewit. *c* **1205** LAY. 8126 þa drihliche gumen weoren win drunken. *a* **1250** *Prov. Alfred* 270 in *O.E. Misc.* 118 Ne wurþ þu neuer so wod ne so wyn-drunke þat euere segge þine wife alle þine wille. **1387** TREVISA *Higden* (Rolls) III. 357 [Polemius] was wyn-dronke. *Ibid.* VI. 39 He hated wyn dronkenes. **1390** GOWER *Conf.* III. 19 That man mai wel noght longe stonde Which is wyndrunke of comun us. *c* **1440** *Promp. Parv.* 529/2 Wyyne drunkon. **1549** COVERDALE, etc. *Erasm. Par. 1 Thess.* v. 7 Those that are wynedrunken, are drunken in the night.

wine-fat: see WINE-VAT.

wineȝarde, obs. Sc. f. VINEYARD.

'wine-glass. [f. WINE *sb.*[1] + GLASS *sb.*[1] Cf. (M)LG., MHG. *winglas*, (Du. *wijnglas*, G. *weinglas*), etc.] **a.** A small drinking-glass for wine. Also = ***wineglassful***.

Wine-glasses, which are characterized by having a stem and a foot, vary in shape (and, in some cases, in colour) according to the wine for which they are intended, and are distinguished as *champagne glass*, *claret glass*, *port glass*, etc.

1709 *Lond. Gaz.* No. 4595/4 Wine and Water Tumblers, Beer and Wine Glasses with Covers. **1786** J. WOODFORDE *Diary* 18 Aug. (1926) II. 264 She is to take a Wine Glass of the Mixture..every six Hours. **1846** *Jewish Man., or Pract. Information Jewish & Mod. Cookery* i. 2 Pour in a wine-glass of port-wine. **1856** KANE *Arctic Expl.* II. ii. 37, I am dealing these out to them by the wine-glass. **1882** FLOYER *Unexpl. Baluch.* 331 We began with minute wine-glasses of raki, red wine, purple wine.

b. *attrib.* Resembling a wine-glass in shape. **c.** *Comb.*, as ***wineglass-cooler***, ***-shaped*** adj.

1851 REDDING *Wines* (ed. 3) 370 Wine-glass coolers.. should be laid on the table and the glasses reversed in them. **1884** HOWELLS *Silas Lapham* i, A smooth piece of interval, with half a dozen good-sized wine-glass elms in it. **1907** M. C. F. MORRIS *Nunburnholme* 78 The..smaller bell, which was long and wineglass-shaped. **1908** *Essex Rev.* XVII. 6 An old-fashioned wine-glass pulpit, with reading-desk below.

Hence **'wineglassful**, the contents of a full wine-glass; the amount that a wine-glass will hold, usually reckoned as 2 fluid ounces.

1824 SCOTT *St. Ronan's* vii, My venerated instructor.. took a wine-glassful of old rum..every day after his dinner. **1884** M. MACKENZIE *Dis. Throat & Nose* II. 352 A wineglassful of spirits of turpentine.

'wine-grape. [f. WINE *sb.*[1] + GRAPE *sb.*[1]]

†**1.** A cluster or bunch of grapes. *Obs.*

c **1250** *Gen. & Ex.* 3710 Ðes .xii. ðider hem hauen broȝt, .. An win-grape on an cuuel-staf.

2. A grape from which wine is made. orig. *U.S.*

1838 *Penny Cycl.* XI. 356/2 The fruit of several other species of vitis, natives of America, possess some merit as wine-grapes. **1845–50** Mrs. Lincoln *Lect. Bot.* 149 He has traced the northern limit of the wine-grape, where the mean annual temperature is about 50°. **1868** *Rep. U.S. Comm. Agric.* (1869) 212 What varieties are in highest repute as wine grapes? **1922** Joyce *Ulysses* 468 Mammoth roses murmur of scarlet winegrapes. **1981** *Times* 7 Feb. 13/4 They do not want any modification of traditional Dao style by the introduction of other European wine grapes.

'wine-house. [OE. *wínhús* = MLG., MDu., MHG. *wînhûs* (Du. *wijnhuis*, G. *weinhaus*), ON. *vínhús*.]

1. A public house where wine is drunk. Now chiefly *Hist.* or with particular local reference.

1607 Dekker & Webster *Westw. Hoe* II. i, From him come I, to intreate you.. to meet him this afternoon at the Rhenesh-wine-house ith Stillyard. **1621** in Foster *Engl. Factories Ind.* (1906) 355 Our warehowse roome, dyninge roome, and wyne howse. **1655** Vaughan *Silex Scint.*, *Agreement* 19 Thou [*sc.* the Bible] art the oyl and the wine-house. **1660** Pepys *Diary* 24 Nov., Creed and Shepley and I to the Rhenish winehouse, and there I did give them two quarts of Wormwood wine, and so we broke up. **1805** C. James *Milit. Dict.* (ed. 2), *Wine-houses*, certain places of resort in the garrison of Gibraltar, from which the governor has been accustomed to derive a pecuniary profit. **1816** Keatinge *Trav.* I. 50 [In Spain] It is disgraceful to be seen entering a wine-house. **1909** *Westm. Gaz.* 30 Apr. 5/3 The wine-house known as the White Hart in the Euston-road.

2. A house that deals in wine; a firm of wine-merchants.

1834 Dickens *Sk. Boz, Boarding-ho.* ii, A clerk in a wine-house. **1875** *Ure's Dict. Arts* III. 1140 No natural Sherry comes to this country; no wine house will send it.

'wine-lees. [f. wine *sb.*[1] + pl. of lee *sb.*[2]] The sediment deposited in a vessel containing wine. Also *fig.*

c **1400** *Lanfranc's Cirurg.* 60 Aischis of wiyn lies. **1483** *Cath. Angl.* 419/2 Wyne lees.., *tartarum, vinacium.* **1585** Higins *Junius' Nomencl.* 95/2 *Fex vini vsta*,.. wine leeze. **1642–4** Vicars *God in Mount* 40 The wine-lees of poysoning Popish fopperies. **1734** tr. *Rollin's Anc. Hist.* (1827) I. 103 Their faces smeared over with winelees. **1765** Sterne *Tr. Shandy* VII. xxi, The under-gardener dressed the muleteer's hat in hot wine-lees. **1859** Dickens *T. Two Cities* I. v, One tall joker.. scrawled upon a wall with his finger dipped in muddy wine lees—Blood.

attrib. **1843** R. J. Graves *Syst. Clin. Med.* xviii. 202 A matter of a wine lees colour.

wineless ('waɪnlɪs), *a.* [f. wine *sb.*[1] + -less.]

1. Lacking or destitute of wine.

1436 *Libel Engl. Pl.* in *Pol. Poems* (Rolls) II. 183 What nedeth a garlande, whyche is made of ivye, Shew a tavern wynelesse, also thryve I. **1891** *Daily News* 2 Feb. 5/6 Invitations to wineless dinners. **1910** *Expositor* Mar. 284 Altars at which only wineless offerings were made.

†**2.** Lacking the characteristic qualities of wine. *Obs. nonce-use.*

1603 Holland *Plutarch's Mor.* 684 A winelesse weake wine as one may say [ἀοίνῳ οἴνῳ].

'wine-pot. [f. wine *sb.*[1] + pot *sb.*[1] Cf. ON. *vínpottr.*] A 'pot' or flagon for holding wine.

14.. *Voc.* in Wr.-Wülcker 619/29 *Viniferum*, a wynpot. *c* **1450** *Mirk's Festial* 108 Why þer stondyth a wyne-potte and a lyly bytwyx our lady and Gabyrell at hur salutacyon. **1561** T. Norton *Calvin's Inst.* IV. 81 By the olde order it is vnlawfull to bryng winepots to the borde. **1585** Higins *Junius' Nomencl.* 235/1 *Epichysis*,.. a wine pot or wine vessel. **1831** Scott *Cast. Dang.* v, When the wine-pot.. hath brought thee on occasion into something of a scrape. **1848** Clough *Amours de Voy.* I. 39 Rome.. is.. Merely a marvellous mass of broken and castaway wine-pots.

b. *attrib.*: †**wine-pot herb**, the foxglove.

1552 Huloet, Wyne pot herb, other do call it oure ladies gloues, *asdrabacca.*

'wine-press. [f. wine *sb.*[1] + press *sb.*[1] 12. Cf. MLG. *wînperse*, MHG. *wînpresse* (G. *weinpresse*).] A press in which the juice is extracted from the grapes in the manufacture of wine. Also *fig.*, esp. with ref. to Isa. lxiii. 3, Rev. xiv. 19, 20, xix. 15.

1526 Tindale *Matt.* xxi. 33 [He] set a vyneyarde, and hedged it rounde about, and made a wynpresse in it. **1584** J. Melvill *Autob.* (Wodrow Soc.) 177 They haiff cast down the dyk, cutted the hedge, demolished the towre, brokin the wyne-pres. **1611** Donne *Ess. Div.* (1651) 24 To put him [*sc.* Moses] in a wine-presse, and squeeze out Philosophy and particular Christianitie, is a degree of that injustice, which all laws forbid. **1671** Milton *P.R.* IV. 16 As a swarm of flies .. About the wine-press where sweet moust is powr'd. **1712** Budgell *Spect.* No. 425 ¶3 The succeeding Month [*sc.* October] was all soiled with the Juice of Grapes, as if he had just come from the Wine-Press. **1813** Shelley *Q. Mab* VII. 218 Drunk from the winepress of the Almighty's wrath. **1849** Froude *Nem. Faith* 107 He must tread the wine-press alone, calling no God-fearing man his friend. **1875** *Ure's Dict. Arts* III. 1140 In the United States the wine-press is constructed much on the same principle as the ordinary screw cider-press. **1910** E. Barker in *Encycl. Brit.* VII. 524/2[The Crusader] might butcher all day,.. and then at nightfall kneel.. at the altar of the Sepulchre—for was he not red from the winepress of the Lord?

Hence †**'wine-presser.**

1632 Sherwood, A Wine-presser, *pressureur.*

winer ('waɪnə(r)). [f. wine *sb.*[1] or *v.* + -er[1].]

1. A vintner. ? *Obs.*

1532 More *Confut. Tindale* Wks. 395/2 God thanke you maister winer for your good wyne. **1548** *Aberd. Reg.* XX. (Jam.) The winaris of the same gat. **1886** *Boston* (Mass.) *Jrnl.* 1 Dec. 1/9 You gather a few tons of grapes and cast them to a winer and are told that it is a bad year for selling grapes.

2. One who drinks wine. *colloq.*

1906 Furnivall in *Lydgate's Chron. Troy* (1906) I. 309 *marg.*, A winer is an unreasonable beast. **1908** *Daily Chron.* 2 Oct. 4/4 The diners and the winers of those spacious days of conviviality.

winery ('waɪnərɪ). orig. *U.S.* [f. wine *sb.*[1] + -ery.] An establishment for making wine.

1882 *Harper's Mag.* Dec. 55/1 The road to the large substantial buildings of the winery was bordered by a deep orchard of oranges. **1885** *Advance* (Chicago) 8 Jan. 885 Wine grapes and wineries are on the rapid increase. **1912** *Times* 22 Apr. 24/4 As the result of this legislation the British wine-makers have not shut up their wineries.

'wine-tree. *Obs.* or *dial.* [OE. *wíntréow* = ON. *víntré*, Goth. *weinatriu*: see wine *sb.*[1] and tree *sb.*] A vine.

Also a local name for blackthorn and mountain ash.

c **950** *Lindisf. Gosp.* John xv. 5 Ic am þæt wintreo, ȝie ða tuiggo sint. *c* **1250** *Gen. & Ex.* 2059 Me drempte, ic stod at a win-tre, Ðat adde waxen buȝes ðre. **13..** *Cursor M.* 7159 (Gött.), þair olyues wid þair wyn tres [*Cott.* vintres]. **1637** Rutherford *Lett., to Lady Kilconquhair* 13 Sept. (1671) 151 A land of olives and wine-trees. **1857** Wright *Dict. Prov. Eng.*, *Wine-tree*, a vine. *Norf.*

'wine-vat. *arch.* -fat. [f. wine *sb.*[1] + vat, fat *sb.*[1] Cf. (M)LG. *wînfat*, MHG. *wînvaz* (G. *weinfass*), ON. *vínfat*, etc.] A vat in which the grapes are pressed in wine-making; a wine-press.

1526 Tindale *Rev.* xix. 15 He trode the wynefatt of fearsnes. **1596** Spenser *F.Q.* VII. vii. 39 The must, Which he was treading in the wine-fats see. **1605** B. Jonson *Volpone* v. iv, You should ha' some would swell, now, like a wine-fat, With such an Autumne. **1611** *Bible* Mark xii. 1 A certaine man planted a vineyard, and set an hedge about it, and digged a place for the wine fat. *a* **1746** Holdsworth *Rem. Virgil* (1768) 22 In this dance, he flung himself into different postures, as if he was gathering the bunches of grapes,.. flinging them into the wine-vat;.. and drinking the must. **1879** *Cassell's Techn. Educ.* IV. 214/2 The grapes are.. emptied into a tub with holes at the bottom... This tub is placed over another much larger, named the wine-vat. **1881** Christina Rossetti *Poems, Prodigal Son* iii, The purple wine-fat froths with foam.

winey, var. winy *a.*

†**winful**, *a.*[1] *Obs. rare.* [f. win *sb.*[1] + -ful.] Laborious.

1443–9 Pecock *Donet* II. vi. (1921) 128 Al seruile werk, þat is to seie, al worldly wynful werk.

†**winful**, *a.*[2] *Obs. rare.* [f. win *sb.*[2] + -ful.] Pleasant.

1438 *Bk. Alexander Gt.* (Bann.) 107 And burgeons of thare brancheis bredis, And woddis winnis thare winfull wedis.

wing (wɪŋ), *sb.* Forms: *Plural.* α. 2 wenge; β. 3 **wengen, winguene, wynguene, whingen, hwingen,** 4 **wingen, wyngen, -yn, -on;** γ. 3–5 **wenges,** (3 *Orm.* -ess), 4 **weengus,** 4–5 **wengis,** 4, 6 **weyngis,** 5 **wengys, -ez, weingis, wengges;** 4 **wyenges, wingges, whinges,** 4–6 **wyngis, -es,** 5 **-ys, whyngis, -ys,** 5–6 **whynges,** 5, 6–7 *Sc.* **wingis,** 6–7 **-es,** 6– **wings.** *Sing.* 4–5 **wenge,** 5 **weng, whenge, weynge,** 5–6 *Sc.* **weyng,** 6 *Sc.* **weing;** 4–6 **wynge,** 4–7 **winge,** 5–6 **wyng, whyng(e,** 6 **whing, wynke,** 6– **wing.** [ME., first in pl. forms *wenge, wengen, wenges*, a. ON. *vængir*, acc. *vængi*, pl. of *vængr* (Sw., Da. *vinge*) wing of a bird, aisle, etc.; replacing OE. *feþra* wings, pl. of *feþer*, and *fiþere* (see feather *sb.* 3).]

I. 1. a. Each of the organs of flight of any flying animal, as a bird, bat, or insect.

In birds the wings are specially modified fore-limbs; in bats (and the extinct pterodactyls, etc.), extensions of the skin attached to modified parts of the fore-limbs (see bat *sb.*[1] 1); in insects, membranous expansions attached to the thorax in addition to the limbs. In a few birds the wings are rudimentary, and either functionless (as in the *Apteryx*) or used only to assist in swimming or walking (as in Penguins).

Occas. loosely applied to the enlarged fins of flying-fishes and to the appendages of flying squirrels, etc. which serve for movements resembling flight.

bastard or ***false wing*** (Ornith.) = winglet 2 b.

c **1175** *Lamb. Hom.* 81 A vuhel com flon from houene into orðe; her he uette feþer-home and wenge. *c* **1205** Lay. 29263 þat alle heore [*sc.* sparrows'] whingen noht awemmed neoren. *a* **1225** *Ancr. R.* 130 Ase brid hwon hit wule vleon stureð his hwingen. *c* **1290** *S. Eng. Leg.* 64/356 He ȝifht eov .. wynguene for-to fleo, And feþerene to beren eov up-on heiȝ. *Ibid.* 230/388 þe drem of is winguene murie was. **13..** *K. Alis.* 485 Him thoughte a goshauk with gret flyght.. yenith and sprad abrod his wyngyn. **1390** Gower *Conf.* I. 173 The Scharnebudes kinde, Of whos nature this I finde, That in the hoteste of the dai,.. He sprat his wynge and up he fleth. *a* **1400** *Leg. Rood* 221 þe Egle is frikest fowle in flye, Ouer all fowles to wawe hys wenge. *c* **1425** *Seven Sag.* (P.) 2196 The byrde.. bylle undyr wynge layede. **1426** Lydg. *De Guil. Pilgr.* 18521 Wonder hygh ther sate a krowe, His whynges splayynge to and ffro. *c* **1440** *Promp. Parv.* 522/1 Wenge, of a fowle or bryde. *c* **1470** Henry *Wallace* III. 7 On fute and weynge ascendand to the hycht. **1513** *Bk. Keruynge* in *Babees Bk.* 278 That all maner of fowle that hath hole fete sholde be reysed vnder the wynge, and not aboue. **1578** Lyte *Dodoens* VI. lxxxi. 762 The fruite [of the maple tree] is long, flat, and thinne, almost lyke to a feather of a small birde, or lyke the whing of a grashopper. **1690** Locke *Hum. Und.* III. vi. §12 There are Fishes that have Wings. **1725**, **1807** [see bat *sb.*[1] 1]. **1857** Hughes *Tom Brown* I. iii, The beautiful little blue butterfly with golden spots on his wings. **1867** W. S. Dallas tr. *Nitzsch's Pterylogr.* 27 The false wing (*ala notha*) described by Möhring. **1888** Goode *Amer. Fishes* 304 The genus *Prionotus*.. resembles *Dactylopterus* in general form, but the wings are much smaller. **1912** S. E. White *Land of Footprints* xiv. 193 Spreading wide their wings at the last moment to check their speed.

b. The wing of a bird, used as food. Also, the shoulder of a hare or rabbit.

c **1470** *Noble Bk. Cookry* (1882) 64 Cony rost. A cony tak and drawe hym,.. rost hym and lard hym then raise his leggs and hys winges. *a* **1530** *Frere & Boye* (Ritson) 154 His fader toke a capons wynge,.. And badde hym ete apace. **1598** Bp. Hall *Sat.* IV. iv. 29 A pestle of a Larke, or Plouers wing. **1656** Osborn *Adv. Son* iv. (ed. 4) 124 A Carver at Court,.. who being laughed at.. for saying *The wing of a Rabbet*, maintained it as congruous, as the fore-legge of a Capon, a phrase used in Scotland. **1746** Francis tr. *Hor., Sat.* II. iv. 56 Wise palates choose the wings of pregnant hare. **1820** Byron *Blues* II. 42 Miss Lilac, permit me to help you;—a wing? **1840** Dickens *Old Cur. Shop* xlvi, Something light for supper—the wing of a roasted fowl. **1841** 'Nimrod' in *Sporting Oracle* 48 The most vulnerable part of the rabbit is about its neck and wings, as the shoulders of this animal are called.

c. The wing of a bird (usually of a hen, goose, or turkey) used as a brush: cf. next, 7.

1573–80 Tusser *Husb.* (1878) 35 Husbandlie furniture.. Wing, cartnaue and bushel. **1641** Best *Farm. Bks.* (Surtees) 67 Then are the two women to have each of them a cleane bowle to wringe the honey into, and the man is to stande ready with a winge in his hande. **1688** Holme *Armoury* III. 243/2 Broom, Wing, Winnow sheet, and Sack with a Band. **1710** Hilman *Tusser Rediv.* Sept. (1744) 116 A Straw-fork and Rake to turn the Straw off from the thresh'd Corn, a Fan and Wing to clean it.

d. A figure or imitation of a wing (e.g. on an image of a bird, etc., or on an angler's artificial fly).

1552–3 in Feuillerat *Revels Edw. VI* (1914) 94 Cupide a small boye.. with a payre of winges of gold. **1584** *Kenilw. Inv.* in Scott *Kenilw.* Note K, 6 rowlers and ij wings for the spreade eagle. **1633** G. Herbert *Temple, Easter Wings* [title of a poem in the form of two pairs of wings]. **1682** Dryden *Mac-Fl.* 207 Chuse for thy Command Some peaceful Province in Acrostick Land; There thou may'st Wings display, and Altars raise, And torture one poor Word ten thousand Ways. **1711** Addison *Spect.* No. 58 ¶4, 6. **1853** J. Jackson *Pract. Fly-Fisher* (1880) 10 To make a winged Fly. .. Wings; a piece of feather, stripped from a Snipe's quill.

†**e.** With qualification (*goose-wing, fly's wing*) used as a type of something of no value. *Obs.*

1377, **1549** [see goose-wing 1]. *c* **1450** *Mankind* 783 in *Macro Plays* 29 Tysche! a flyes weynge!

2. a. Attributed to supernatural beings, as angels, demons, etc., and to fabulous creatures, as dragons, griffins, etc.

c **1200** Ormin 8024 þatt all þatt hallȝhe genge, þatt borrȝhenn iss þurrh marrtirdom, Flæh upp wiþþ tweȝȝenn wengess. **13..** *Sir Beues* (A.) 2675 Whan hit schon þe briȝte sonne, His wingges schon so þe glas. **1382** Wyclif *Isa.* vi. 2. *c* **1385** Chaucer *L.G.W.* Prol. 236 And aungellych hyse wengis gan he sprede. *c* **1386** —— *Knt.'s T.* 1106 Biforn hire stood hir sone Cupido, Vp on his shuldres wynges hadde he two. **14..** *Sir Beues* (Pynson) 2527 Beuys.. hyt the dragon vnder the wynge. **1513** Douglas *Æneis* III. iv. 34 The Harpyes on ws fell, With huge faird of weingis and mony ȝell. **1671** Milton *P.R.* IV. 582 A fiery Globe Of Angels on full sail of wing flew nigh. **1815** Byron *Destr. Sennacherib* iii, The Angel of Death spread his wings on the blast. **1821** Wordsw. *Eccles. Sonn.* III. v. 4 The feather, whence the pen Was shaped that traced the lives of these good men, Dropped from an Angel's wing. **1885** Hardy *Changed Man, Mere Interlude* (1913) 269 Since my poor husband left me to wear his wings.

b. Attributed to inanimate or abstract things represented as flying, or as carrying one swiftly along (esp. in phr. ***on the wings of***).

1398 Trevisa *Barth. De P.R.* II. i. (Add. MS. 27944) In olde tyme poetes peyntide þe winde wiþ wynges. *c* **1510** More *Picus* E j b, Whynges of the loue of God. **1535** Coverdale *Ps.* ciii[i]. 3 Thou makest the cloudes thy charet, and goest vpon the wynges of the wynde. —— *Ps.* cxxxviii[i]. 9 Yf I take the wynges of the mornynge. —— *Prov.* xxiii. 5 Riches make them selues wynges. **1594** Shaks. *Rich. III*, v. iii. 106 When I should mount with wings of Victory. **1598** —— *Merry W.* II. ii. 209, I haue pursu'd her, as Loue hath pursued mee, which hath beene on the wing of all occasions. **1608** [Tofte] *Ariosto's Sat.* I. (1611) 11 With inke To giue his fame large wings. **1611** Sir W. Mure *Misc. Poems* iv. 8 Deceau'd by loues alluiring wingis. **1665** Boyle *Occas. Refl.* I. i. 7 When a pious Soul is once got upon the wing of Contemplation. **1704** Prior *Celia to Damon* 40 Upon the Wings of Time born swift away. **1709** Watts *Hymn*, Give me the Wings of Faith, to rise Within the Veil. **1829** Scott *Rob Roy* Introd. 2nd half, A cold north-east wind, with frost on its wing. **1837** W. Irving *Capt. Bonneville* II. xix. 35 Where the foe.. seems to come and go on the wings of the wind. **1873** Burton *Hist. Scot.* VI. lxxii. 307 [The Scots in 1640] seemed to be, indeed, carried forward on the wings of destiny.

3. *transf.* and *fig.* **a.** Power or means of flight, or of action figured as flight; action or manner of flying, flight. (*a*) in reference to literal flying.

1377 Langl. *P. Pl.* B. XII. 263 þe larke, þat is.. wel awey of wenge [*v. rr.* wynge, whenge] swifter þan þe pecok. **1390** Gower *Conf.* II. 328 A Swalwe swift of winge. **1667** Milton *P.L.* x. 316 The self same place where hee First lighted from his Wing. **1706** PRIOR *Ode to Queen* v, Upward the Noble Bird directs his Wing. **1709** T. ROBINSON *Nat. Hist. Westmld.* x. 60 As soon as the young Brood gets wing. **1877** CONDER *Basis of Faith* v. 225 The bird of strongest wing may be driven out to sea by the tempest.

(*b*) *fig.* in various connexions. (See also III.)

a **1225** *Ancr. R.* 132 Auh þe treowe ancren þet we efneð to briddes.. Heo spredeð hore hwingen, ant makieð a creoiz of ham suluen. *a* **1340** HAMPOLE *Psalter* cxxxviii. 7 Take twa wenges of charite. *c* **1380** WYCLIF *Wks.* (1880) 473 He ordeynede godis of vertu wyngis to men to fle to heuene. **1418** *26 Pol. Poems* xiv. 47 To fliȝe to hyȝe, treste not þy wyng. **1590** NASHE *Pasquil's Apologie* C 4, Other excellent points I could.. pinch him with to the like purpose, were I not contented to strike the winge, and come downe to his capacitie. **1593** SHAKS. *2 Hen. VI*, IV. vii. 79 Knowledge the Wing wherewith we flye to heauen. **1596** —— *1 Hen. IV*, III. ii. 30 Thy affections which doe hold a wing Quite from the flight of all thy ancestors. **1648** G. DANIEL *Eclog.* i. 120 You have a wing of Strength, might toure into The purest Region fancie breaths. **1670** DRYDEN *1st Pt. Conq. Granada* V. ii, Give wing to your desires, and let 'em fly. **1749** SMOLLETT *Gil Blas* X. x. (1816) 307/2 Every thing they said to me seemed to lend me wings to run away. **1830** SCOTT *Monast.* Introd., When the peculiar kind of folly keeps the wing no longer. **1849** J. HARE *Serm.* II. iv. 80 In old times,.. many stories got wing.

b. In biblical and derived expressions referring to a mother bird's use of her wings for the protection of her young (cf. esp. Matt. xxiii. 37); thus virtually = protecting care. (See also 16 a.)

a **1300** *E.E. Psalter* xvi[i]. 8 Hile me under schadou of þi wenges twa. **1535** COVERDALE *Ps.* lxiii. 7 Vnder the shadowe of thy wynges wil I reioyse. **1567** *Gude & Godlie B.* (S.T.S.) 107 His [*sc.* God's] wingis ar thy weirlie weid, His pennis ar thy strang defence. **1719** YOUNG *Revenge* IV. i, Why did I leave my tender father's wing, And venture into love? **1883** D. C. MURRAY *Hearts* xxxiii, Azubah, once more under the shelter of her aunt's wing.

4. *transf.* **a.** In phr. *of* (such-and-such) *wing*, used, like *feather* = kind or description of bird (usually *fig.*). *Obs.* exc. in echoes of Ezek. xvii. 23.

1598 R. BERNARD tr. *Terence, Phormio* I. v, All alike: all feathered of one wing [orig. *omnes congruont*]: knowe one, and know all. **1601** SHAKS. *Phœnix* iii, From this Session interdict Euery foule of tyrant wing, Saue the Eagle feath'red King. **1608** DEKKER *Belman of London* (ed. 2) D 2, Of all the mad Rascalls (that are of this wing) the Abraham-man is the most fantastick. **1608** D. T[UVILL] *Ess. Pol. & Mor.* 90b, A prying eye, a listning eare, and a prating tongue, are all birds of one wing. **1611** *Bible* Ezek. xvii. 23 All foule of euery wing. **1630** *Pathomachia* IV. iii. 35 Here is another Bird of the same Wing I beleeue.

b. Qualified by a restrictive word, or in technical phr., = bird or birds.

1601 SHAKS. *Phœnix* i, Let the bird of lowdest lay.. Herauld sad and trumpet be: To whose sound chaste wings obay. **1725** POPE *Odyss.* II. 188 The Prince of Augurs.. drew A sure presage from ev'ry wing that flew. **1840** BREMNER *Excurs. Denmark*, etc. I. 293 We did not wonder to see scarcely a single wing of game in a whole day's journey. **1874** *Kennel Club Stud Bk.* p. xii, He does not lose one [point] for each fault, providing it is simply not dropping to wing or shot.

c. A flock (of plover).

1805 A. MACKINTOSH *Driffield Angler* 294 Wing of plover.

II. 5. An appliance or appendage resembling or analogous to a wing in form or function. **a.** An artifical apparatus attached to the human arms or shoulders, (*a*) according to early accounts, for flying through the air, (*b*) for assistance in swimming. **b.** One of the floats of a water-wheel or sails of a windmill. **c.** Poetically or rhetorically applied to the sails of a ship. (See also *white wings* s.v. WHITE *a.* 11 e.) **d.** Various: see quots.: *spec.* (*a*) one of the planes of an aeroplane; (*b*) *transf.* (*pl.*) in the Royal Air Force, a certificate of ability to pilot an aeroplane, indicated by the addition to the uniform of a badge representing a pair of wings; (*c*) *slang*, an arm; also *transf.*

a. 1297 R. GLOUC. (Rolls) 671 Vor þat men ssolde is enchantement se, He let him makie wengen [*v. rr.* wyngon, wingen, wynges, whyngys] an hei vor to fle. *c* **1375** *Sc. Leg. Saints* i. (*Petrus*) 562 [Symon Magus] passit vpe, and his weyngis dycht,.. And flaw, as he a foule had bene. **1390** GOWER *Conf.* II. 37 This Dedalus.. Hath mad to fle diverse wynges For him and for his Sone also. **1742** POPE *Dunc.* IV. 452 The head that turns at super-lunar things, Pois'd with a tail, may steer on Wilkins' wings. **1908** *Daily Chron.* 29 July 5/6 Being unable to swim he had made use of a pair of swimming wings.

b. 1484 CAXTON *Fables of Æsop* v. x, For the swyftnesse of the water he must nedes passe vnder the whele of the mylle, And god wote yf the wynges of the mylle bete hym wel or not. **1585** T. WASHINGTON tr. *Nicholay's Voy.* II. x. 44 b, Windmilles, hauing euery one of them 10. wings. **1609** W. BIDDULPH in *Lavender's Trav.* 15 There are very many wind milles there, hauing ten wings a piece. **1681** OWEN *Inq. conc. Evang. Ch.* ii. 16 To render the Gospel-Church-State a Machin.. to be turned unto any Interest like the Wings of a Mill unto the Wind. *a* **1700** B. E. *Dict. Cant. Crew, Sails*,.. Windmill-wings. **1773** W. EMERSON *Princ. Mech.* (ed. 3) 284 *Wing*,.. as the hands in a water wheel; a part of a sail, &c. *a* **1866** C. W. HATFIELD *Hist. Notices Doncaster* Ser. I. 203 The wings of some of the these [wind-mills] describe a circuit of 100 feet diameter.

c. 1596 SHAKS. *Merch. V.* I. i. 14 Your Argosies with portly saile.. As they flye by them with their wouen wings. **1735** SOMERVILLE *Chase* II. 222 All their Canvass Wings. **1812** BYRON *Ch. Har.* I. xiii, While flew the vessel on her snowy wing. **1833** MRS. BROWNING *Prometh. Bound* 543 The sea-man's chariots, wandering on the brine With linen wings. **1878** JOAQUIM MILLER *Songs of Italy* 29 The yellow wide wings of a bark.

d. 1796 *Grose's Dict. Vulg. T.* (ed. 3), *Pair of Wings*, oars. *Cant.* **1799** G. SMITH *Laboratory* I. 17 There are rockets made without sticks. Fix to the small ones.. four wings, in the nature of arrow-feathers. **1815** J. SMITH *Panorama Sci. & Art* II. 159 The use of wings, rudders, oars,.. to direct the course of a balloon. **1823** EGAN *Grose's Dict. Vulgar T.* (ed. 3), *Wings*, arms. **1875** KNIGHT *Dict. Mech.*, *Wing*.. 2. A vane of a rotating fan... 10. (*Milling.*) A strip, commonly of leather, attached to the skirt of the runner to sweep the meal into the spout. **1883** W. AITKEN *Lays of Line* 65 Cam' an auld sodger yince wha was short o' a wing. **1904** O. & W. WRIGHT *Brit. Pat. 6732* 1 The superposed horizontal surfaces.. formed by stretching cloth upon frames of wood and wire, constitute the 'wings', or supporting part of the apparatus. **1910** R. FERRIS *How it Flies* 17 Aeroplanes are those forms of flying machines which depend for their support in the air upon the spread of surfaces which are variously called wings, sails, or planes. **1917** 'CONTACT' *Airman's Outings* i. 5 The pilots have passed their tests and been decorated with wings. **1918** J. T. B. MCCUDDEN *5 Yrs. R.F.C.* 1 Having qualified for his R.F.C. wings in July of 1912. **1947** *Sun* (Baltimore) 3 Apr. 20/1 He came up with a bad arm during the season, and had been troubled before with it. If the big man's wing behaves this year he should be of considerable value. **1964** J. CHEEVER *Wapshot Scandal* II. xxvii. 259 He.. began to pitch the eggs... He had a good wing and by heaving the eggs far away.. he was able to divert the.. crowd. **1967** *Boston Globe* 22 Mar. 11/1 Wins wings as stewardess for American Airlines. **1976** *Publishers Weekly* 19 Apr. 78/3 Mike Hagen earns his wings as a crop duster in rural Florida.

6. A lateral part or appendage: in various connexions. (See also senses 7–12.)

a. A lateral or outlying portion of a space or region. **b.** Something forming a lateral boundary, as the side wall of a dock, sluice, chimney, etc.; also, a lateral component, extension, or complement of a structure, etc., e.g. either of the retaining walls at the ends of a bridge; also *spec.* of jumps for horse-riding: see quot. 1953[1]. **c.** A side piece (usually projecting), a lateral projection or member (in various tools, pieces of mechanism, or other structures: see quots.); *spec.* the part of a ploughshare which extends sideways and cuts the bottom of the furrow. **d.** A projecting part of a fishing-net on one side of the main or central part. **e.** In a carriage, each of a pair of curved pieces extending over the wheels to provide protection from the splashing of mud; the mudguard of a motor vehicle. **f.** Each of two side pieces at the top of an arm-chair against which the head may be rested.

a. *a* **1400–50** *Wars Alex.* 1051 An-other wynge of þe werld. **1794** MORSE *Amer. Geog.* 491 On the north end it subsides gradually into extensive pasture grounds; while on the south it slopes more steeply in a shorter distance... On either wing is a thick grove of.. forest trees. **1864** CARLYLE *Fredk. Gt.* XI. ii. (1873) IV. 36 Königsberg, Preussen, the easternmost outlying wing of his long straggling Dominions. **1874** BLACKIE *Lett. to Wife* (1909) 228 The Hill of Howth, forming the north wing of the bay of Dublin. **1920** *Westm. Gaz.* 16 June 10/1 His fore-hand return across court off the service into the right-hand wing of his opponent's base line.

b. *c* **1482** J. KAY tr. *Caoursin's Siege of Rhodes* ¶ 10 (1870), A place.. by the weste banke of Rhodes: which maked with her walles and wynges a pleasaunt hauen.. and ys called the tour of Seynt Nycholas. **1531** *Lett. & Pap. Hen. VIII*, V. 180 Settyng the wynkes of the said slewse new made. **1663** CHARLETON *Chorea Gigantum* 24 The outward Circle or wing of stones [of Stonehenge]. **1703** T. N. *City & C. Purchaser* 107 An apt falling-back of the Back, and convenient gathering of the Wings, and Brest of the Chimney. **1715** DESAGULIERS *Fires Impr.* 128 You may on each side [of the chimney] raise a Wing of Plaister. **1721** LEONI *Palladio's Archit.* I. 67 The Wings (that is, the spaces between the Wall and the Columns, which is not comprehended in the breadth of the Atrium). **1726** —— *Alberti's Archit.* I. 14 All this Wing of Wall.. is exposed as a Butt to the.. Blasts of the North-East. **1821** RICH *Journ. Persepolis* 27 Aug., The mountains.. form a wing of stupendous perpendicular cliffs. **1850** PARKER *Gloss. Archit.* (ed. 5) I. 206 *Fillet*,.. a small flat face or band used principally between mouldings, to separate them from each other in classical architecture... When this appendage is.. attached to the sides [of the moulding, it is called] its wings. **1851** *B'ham & Midl. Gardeners' Mag.* Apr. 38 Many fine trees which have.. become unsightly.. by losing whole wings at a time. **1875** KNIGHT *Dict. Mech.*, *Wing*.. A lateral extension of an abutment... A leaf of a gate or double door... A side dam on a river shore to contract the channel. **1895** *Daily News* 14 Mar. 3/5 Tribune, the winner of the Beaudesert Steeplechase, was objected to for jumping the wing of one of the fences. **1953** G. BROOKE *Introd. Riding & Stablecraft* 12 *Wings to a fence*, something in the nature of hurdles placed on either side and at an angle to a fence to prevent a horse from running out to either hand. *Ibid.* iv. 39 It is advisable to start over a small fence with wings. **1960** *Times* 23 July 9/4 The moment to hit the pony is when it is well into the wings and about half a stride from the jump. **1977** J. KIDD *Horse & Pony Man.* iv. 56 When the fence is introduced always place wings or sloping poles on either side to discourage the horse from running out.

c. 1577 GOOGE tr. *Heresbach's Husb.* I. 21 They haue a litle wyng on the ryght syde of the Coulter, which wyng is to be remooued to whiche syde you list. **1597** A. M. tr. *Guillemeau's Fr. Chirurg.* 15 b/1 The winges of the Trepane, which delicatelye and easilye cut. **1688** HOLME *Armoury* III. 286/2 The Feathers or Fly, or Wing [of a spinning-wheel] is that which the crooked Wyres are set in. **1707** MORTIMER *Husb.* 42 Some place on the right side of the Coulter a small Wing or Finn. **1839** URE *Dict. Arts* etc. 346 The wings or vanes revolve from 120 to 150 times in the minute. **1842** J. AITON *Dom. Econ.* (1857) 166 This second spade is provided with an iron wing upon its shaft, by which the digger.. forces it with his foot into the ground. **1875** KNIGHT *Dict. Mech.*, *Sinker*.. (Knitting-machine). A wheel with thin plates or projections, called *wings*,.. used to depress (sink) the yarn between the needles. **1902** P. MARSHALL *Metal Working Tools* 13 The legs [of wing compasses].. when opened to the required width are secured by means of the thumb-screw which binds on to the projecting wing.

d. 1678 *Act 30 Chas. II* c. 9 § 1 Above Fifty yards in length and Six yards in breadth or depth in the wing of the Nett. **1883** *Fisheries Exhib. Catal.* 295 A Tench Weel without wings.. An Eel Weel, with loose pits and wings. **1884** KNIGHT *Dict. Mech.* Suppl. s.v. *Stake-net*, The salmon, swimming up the current, come in contact with the bar-net, and turning to pass around it, find themselves opposed by the wing.

e. 1783 *Morn. Chron.* 14 Mar. 4/2 Advt., A new roomy Gig, with head to take off, wings, and new harness. **1794** W. FELTON *Carriages* (1801) I. 204 Wings are fixed to the sides or elbows of the chaise bodies..; their use is to form a rest for the arm, and shelter the passenger from the dirt which splashes from the wheels. **1881** J. W. BURGESS *Coach-bldg.* v. 50 The wings.. sometimes still are of wood, in which case they are hooped to the perch by iron hoops. **1928** *Daily Mail* 25 July 9/3 The force of the impact threw the car temporarily out of control, but with its front wings crumpled it continued its dash towards London. **1955** *Times* 10 May 7/7 The visibility forward would be better if it took in the near side front wing, but the rearward view through the 3ft. 9in. wide window is excellent.

f. 1907 G. O. WHEELER *Old Engl. Furniture* 190 The wings formed by the arm enclosures were padded. **1911** F. M. CRAWFORD *Uncanny Tales, Deadly Smile* ii, A great old leathern arm-chair with wings.

7. a. Either of the two divisions (RIGHT WING, LEFT WING) on each side of the main body or *centre* of an army or fleet in battle array; also, each of the two divisions of a regiment or an air force.

c **1400** *Brut* ccxxiii. 283 þe Scottis comen ferseliche in iiij wengus. *Ibid.* 285 þo hade euery Englisshe bataile ij wenges of pris Archiers. *c* **1425** WYNTOUN *Cron.* VIII. xvi. 2520 A noþir weynge þai saw cum sone Off Inglis men. *c* **1500** *Melusine* 230 Anthony.. ordeyned archers & crosbowes to be vnder the wynges of hys batayll. **1523** LD. BERNERS *Froiss.* I. cxxx. 64/2 Therle of Northampton & therle of Arundell with the second batell were on a wyng in good order. **1535** [see LEFT WING 1 a]. **1622** MABBE tr. *Aleman's Guzman d'Alf.* II. 333 Wee did presently battell-wise cast our selues into a Wing, as if we had been the Turkish Gallies. **1667** MILTON *P.L.* I. 617 Their doubl'd Ranks they bend From Wing to Wing. *c* **1720** DE FOE *Mem. Cavalier* II. 294 The Armies coming close up, the Wings engaged first. **1769** FALCONER *Dict. Marine* (1776) s.v., Wings are also the skirts or extremities of a fleet when it is ranged into a line a-breast. **1844** [see LEFT WING 1 a]. **1868** *Queen's Reg. & Ord. Army* ¶ 300 When the Service Companies of a Regiment happen to be divided into Wings, the head Quarter wing will assign a due proportion of the Mess necessaries for the use of the other wing. **1915** C. G. GREY *Tales of Flying Services* 71 One of the chief duties of this 'wing'.. was to look out for Zeppelins.

b. In football and similar games: The position of the forwards on either side of the centre; a player or players occupying this position. Cf. LEFT WING, RIGHT WING.

1882, etc. [see LEFT WING 1 b]. **1898** J. GOODALL *Assoc. Football* 38 Suddenly there will be a swift clear side-kick to the other wing.

c. A section of a political or other party, holding views deviating in one direction or the other from those generally held (often distinguished as *left* or *right*).

[Cf. quot. 1670 s.v. LEFT WING 1 a.]

1879 FROUDE *Cæsar* xiii. 186 There is always a disreputable wing to the radical party. **1884** *Christian Commonw.* 21 Feb. 449/1 The democratic wing of the Tory party, of which Lord Randolph Churchill aspires to be the leader. **1898** [see LEFT WING 2].

8. a. One of a pair of lateral projecting pieces of a garment on or near the shoulder, as of a doublet; also, a side-flap of a cap, etc.; in military uniform, a kind of epaulette (now worn by bandsmen) which stands out from the seam at the top of the shoulder.

1412–20 LYDG. *Chron. Troy* III. 67 þer wer.. Vauntbras with wynges, & rerebras þer-to. **1557** in Dugdale *Orig. Jurid.* lxx. (1666) 310 That none of the Companions except Knights or Benchers.. wear.. Wings in their Gowns. **1604** DEKKER *Meeting of Gallants* B 2, There is as much perill betweene the wings and the skirts of one of their Doublets, as in all the liberties of London. **1688** HOLME *Armoury* III. 94/2 The Wings, are Welts or peeces set over the place on the top of the Shoulders, where the Body and Sleeves are set together. **1703** *Rules of Civility* 56 If short Sleeves be worn, she [who pushes fashion to an extreme] will have nothing but Wings. **1810** *Army Gen. Order* 19 Feb., Field Officers.. are to wear Wings in addition to their Epaulettes. **1834** L. RITCHIE *Wand. Seine* 139 A linen cap with large wings which concealed the face. **1844** *Queen's Regul. & Ord. Army* 152 The whole of the remaining Clothing (with the exception of the wings and fringe). **1869** BLACKIE *Lett. to Wife* (1909) 181 A sort of spencer open in the middle, with two wings, one on each breast.

†**b.** *pl.* The armpits. *nonce-use.* (Cf. L. *ala.*)

1586 T. B. *La Primaud. Fr. Acad.* I. 470 He tooke hir with both his armes by the wings [orig. *les aisselles*].

9. a. A subordinate part of a building on one side of the main or central part. Also in extended use, any more or less separate section of a building, esp. of a hospital or prison.

spec. in *Fortification*: see quot. 1704.

1523 WOLSEY in *St. Papers Hen. VIII*, VI. 209 Who with his armye was.. loged in the countrey in thre wardes and sundry winges. **1613–39** I. JONES in Leoni *Palladio's Archit.* (1742) II. 46 This Edifice.. has.. two Wings. *a* **1700** EVELYN *Diary* 10 Oct. 1683, The Court at entrie, and wings for officers seeme too neere the streete. **1704** J. HARRIS *Lex. Techn.* I, *Wings*, in Fortification, are the large Sides of Horn-works, Crown-works, Tenailles, and the like Out-works. **1767** G. WHITEFIELD *Let.* (1768) 12 Allowing another thousand for repairing the house, and building the two intended wings. **1820** W. IRVING *Sketch Bk.* II. 61 (*Christmas Eve*) It was an irregular building of some magnitude... One wing was evidently very ancient, with heavy stone-shafted bow windows. **1908** J. M. SULLIVAN *Criminal Slang* 27 *Wing*, a section of a prison. **1959** L. LEE *Cider with Rosie* 132 Hannah Brown was put to bed in the Woman's Wing, and Joseph lay in the Men's. **1967** *Listener* 1 June 718/3 Three weeks later he was back in C wing. **1981** C. PRIEST *Affirmation* iii. 19, I found a letter from the Governor of Durham Prison, saying that Uncle William had been admitted to the hospital wing.

b. *Naut.* (*a*) That part of the hold or space between decks which is next the ship's side. (*b*) In a steamer (see quot. 1846). (*c*) In a canal-boat or barge (see quot. 1906).

1730 WRIGLESWORTH *MS. Log-bk. of the 'Lyell'* 25 Sept., Levelled the Hold from the Fore-hatchway clear aft,..and picked out the large Stones to lay in the Wings. **1805** in *Naval Chron.* XV. 34 He..was carried down into one of the wings. **1846** A. YOUNG *Naut. Dict.* 370 The term wing is also applied to the projecting part of a steam-vessel's deck before and abaft each of the paddle-boxes; this is bounded by a thick plank called the sponsing-rim or wing-wale which extends from the extremity of the paddle-beam to the ship's side. **1906** *Daily Chron.* 19 Feb. 10/5 If the tunnel is too wide, boards projecting over the boat's side, termed 'wings', are brought into use for them [*sc.* 'leggers'] to lie on.

c. *Theatr.* Each of the side-scenes on the stage; also *pl.* (occas. *sing.*) the space at each side of the stage where these stand. Also in *fig.* phr. ***waiting in the wings*** and varr., ready to act or make an appearance; (for the moment) taking no part in the action.

1790 MALONE *Shaks. Wks.* I. II. Acc. Stage 83 The technical modern term, *wings*, or side scenes. **1807** *Director* II. 330 The turning of one single wheel effects at once..the simultaneous retreat of the entire assemblage of wings and drops and flat. **1835** DICKENS *Sk. Boz, Private Theatres*, The little space there is between the wings and the wall, and one wing and another. **1847** BRODERIP *Zool. Recr.* 320 The frantic stage-manager in the wing. **1876** H. JAMES in *Atlantic Monthly* Dec. 691/1 The author has given him a mother who..has been kept waiting in the wing, as it were, for many acts. **1885** MABEL COLLINS *Prettiest Woman* i, She had known her maintain that cold sternness to the very wings, and then bound on to the stage. **1946** P. BOTTOME *Lifeline* iii. 39 We've Churchill waiting in the wings, to take the helm when the storm breaks. **1963** V. NABOKOV *Gift* iv. 237 Already famous, he remained as it were in the wings of his busy, talkative thought. **1977** *Sat. Rev.* 3 Sept. 44/1 Despite vast expenditures on research and development.. the videodisc is still hovering diffidently in the wings. **1985** *Times* 19 Jan. 21/1 Yesterday's huge jump in the share price suggests there is a buyer in the wings.

10. *Anat.* A lateral part or projection (usually, one of a pair) of some organ or structure; *e.g.* each of the lateral cartilages of the nose, a lateral process of a bone (esp. of the sphenoid): = ALA 1.

1650 BULWER *Anthropomet.* vii. (1653) 118 That beauty which so manifestly appears in the wings of the Nose. **1663** BAYFIELD *Treat. De Morb. Capitis* 100 The Haw, nail, or little wing (as they term it) of the eye. **1693** tr. *Blancard's Phys. Dict.* (ed. 2), *Pinna Auris*, the upper and broader part of the Ear, called the Wing. **1758** J. S. tr. *Le Dran's Observ. Surg.* (1771) 31 The Wing of the right Nostril. **1831** R. KNOX *Cloquet's Anat.* 289 The great wing of the sphenoid bone. **1897** *Allbutt's Syst. Med.* III. 570 When one wing [of the diaphragm] is much raised, as by a collection of gas.

11. *Bot.*

†**a.** The axil of a leaf: = ALA 2a. *Obs.* †**b.** Each of the lateral divisions or leaflets of a pinnate leaf. (Cf WINGED *a.* 3a.) *Obs.* **c.** Each of the two lateral petals of a papilionaceous flower: = ALA 2b. **d.** A thin membranous appendage of a seed or fruit, serving for its dispersal by the wind; a thin lateral projection extending along a stem; any thin appendage, as on some part of a flower. (Cf. WINGED *a.* 3b.)

a. 1763 MILLS *Syst. Pract. Husb.* IV. 402 The flowers.. are produced.. from the wings of the leaves.

b. 1776 WITHERING *Brit. Plants* 651 Fern. *Filix mas*... Leaves doubly winged; wings blunt.

c. 1776 J. LEE *Introd. Bot.* Gloss., *Ala*, a Wing, the Side Petals of a papilionaceous Blossom, or a Membrane added to a Seed, Stalk, &c. **1796** WITHERING *Brit. Plants* (ed. 3) I. 307 Wings are 2 equal petals. **1870** HOOKER *Stud. Flora* 85 Genista..Wings oblong.

d. 1776 [see c]. **1787** *Linnæus' Fam. Plants* 183 Fruit egg'd, encompass'd with a wing striated on both sides. **1911** W. S. FURNEAUX *Field & Woodl. Plants* iii. 37 In the Narrow-leaved Everlasting Pea..the 'wings' of the stem and petioles.

12. *Physics.* A part of a spectral line where the intensity tails off to nothing at either side of it.

1959 *Canad. Jrnl. Physics* XXXVII. 1252 (*caption*) Graph illustrating the dispersion line form for the high-frequency wing of the S(1) line of normal hydrogen at 85° K. **1982** *Sci. Amer.* July 77/3 At positions in the cloud other than the position of the infrared source the broad velocity wings disappeared and the lines had the narrow widths we had originally expected.

III. Phrases. * with prepositions.

13. in (the) wing. †**a.** ***in wing of***: in course or process of, engaged in. *Obs. rare.*

c **1482** J. KAY tr. *Caoursin's Siege of Rhodes* ¶7 Whenne thay were in wyng of these werkys [*Dum hæc..agerentur*].

†**b.** ***in the wing of***: ? in the overshadowing presence of. *Obs. rare.*

1579 W. WILKINSON *Confut. Fam. Love* 39b, Our owne Newtralisme and Lukwarmenes shall in the wyng of Gods sonne vtterly condemne vs.

14. on or upon the wing or †**one's wing,** †**on wing;** also A-WING. **a.** *lit.* Flying, in flight.

1486 *Bk. St. Albans* djb, When she is on wyng and comyth low bi the grounde. **1616** FLETCHER *Hum. Lieut.* I. i, The roiall Eagle When she hath tri'd her young ones gainst the Sun,..next teacheth 'em to prey, How to command on wing. **1667** MILTON *P.L.* I. 332 They heard, and were abasht, and up they sprung Upon the wing. *Ibid.* 345 So numberless were those bad Angels seen Hovering on wing under the Cope of Hell. **1742** GRAY *Spring* 25 The insect youth are on the wing. **1831** AUDUBON *Ornith. Biog.* I. 137 It is seldom that one of these birds is on wing..without uttering its cry. **1857** HUGHES *Tom Brown* II. iv, The old birds were too strong on the wing for our young marksmen. **1859** E. FITZGERALD *Omar* vii, The Bird of Time has but a little way To fly—and Lo! the Bird is on the Wing. **1882** BLACKIE *Lett. to Wife* (1909) 299, I have been as happy as a bird on the wing.

b. *fig.* (*a*) Moving or travelling swiftly or briskly; astir, active, on the move.

1508 DUNBAR *Poems* vii. 50 Throw Scotland, Ingland, France, and Lumbardy, Fleys on weyng thi fame, and thi renoune. **1602** SHAKS. *Ham.* II. ii. 132 When I had seene this hot loue on the wing. **1616** FLETCHER *Hum. Lieut.* I. i, 'Tis time his fortune be a wing [*v. rr.* o' wing, o' th' wing], high time sir. **1642** D. ROGERS *Naaman* To Rdr. b3b, So long as we can keep sound Doctrine on wing, we shall hope to kill.. all three [evils]. **1655** LD. NORWICH in *Nicholas Papers* (Camden) III. 217 With what impatience his good subiects ..expect to heare yᵗ his Maᵗʸ were uppon his wing. **1759** JOHNSON *Rasselas* xiii, The prince, whose thoughts were always on the wing. **1839** LONGF. *Hyperion* I. iii, Nobody is on the wing; hardly a single traveller. **1871** MRS. H. WOOD *Dene Hollow* xxxix, Captain..Clanwaring was on the wing early.

(*b*) 'Taking flight', going off or away, starting, departing; ready to start or depart.

1622 MABBE tr. *Aleman's Guzman d'Alf.* II. To Rdr. **2 Hauing beene too prodigall in communicating my papers,.. they caught me when I was vpon my wings. **1668** DRYDEN *Even. Love* I. i, Look you, they are on the wing already. **1675** —— *Aurengz.* IV. (1676) 55 He's wild, and soon on wing, if watchful eyes come near. **1721–2** POPE *Let. to Atterbury* 8 Feb., When I went last to town, and was on wing for the Deanry. **1861** MRS. H. WOOD *East Lynne* III. xx, She fell on her knees..in prayer for the departing spirit, on its wing. **1898** *Punch* 20 Aug. 81/2 The Courts are up, and the members of the four Inns are supposed to be on the wing.

15. on wings: (going) with light steps as one in a joyously exalted mood.

1859 MEREDITH *R. Feverel* xx, Now the young gentleman was off and out every night, and seemed to be on wings. **1861** READE *Cloister & H.* vi, They sealed the promise with a long loving kiss, and Gerard went home on wings.

on the wings of...: see 2b.

16. under (..) wing. a. ***under the wing of, under ——'s wing*** (†***wings***): under the protection, care, or patronage of. (Cf. 3b.)

c **1230** *Hali Meid.* (1922) 66 ȝef þu wel wrist te under godes wengen. *a* **1300** *Cursor M.* 17638, I blisce þe, lauerd, þou me has gett And sauf vnder þi wenges sett. *a* **1400–50** *Wars Alex.* 1769 Turne þe, trechoure,..And drawe a-gayn to þi den vndire þi dam wingis [*v.r.* wengez]. **1455** *Rolls of Parlt.* V. 281/2 Such as abide and kepe theim self undre the wynge of your Mageste Roiall. **1503** HAWES *Examp. Virtue* VII. 87 And vnder the wynge of my proteccyon All rebels brought be to subieccyon. **1540** PALSGR. *Acolastus* II. i. Hiij b, I haue euer be brought vp at home i. vnder my mothers wynge. **1669** H. MORE *Exp. 7 Epist.* Ep. Ded. A3b, If I had not taken this opportunity..of doing that right to the Truth I here professe as to put it under the wings of so fit and able a Patron. **1765** FOOTE *Commissary* III. 47 There liv'd Miss Cicely..under the wing of an old maiden aunt. **1879** FROUDE *Cæsar* xxi. 353 They fled for their lives to find safety under Pompey's wing in Capua.

†**b.** ***to keep one's bill under wing***: to remain quiet or inactive (like a sleeping bird). *Obs. rare.*

[Cf. quot. *c* 1425 in 1.] *a* **1548** HALL *Chron., Hen. VI*, 174 After this..the duke of Yorke..thought it mete neither lenger to dissimule, nor farther to kepe his bill vnder wyng.

c. ***hit under the wing*** (slang): intoxicated.

1844 ALB. SMITH *Adv. Mr. Ledbury* iv, He being..'hit under the wing'.

** with verbs. (For other phrases, as ***clip the wings***, see the vbs.)

†**17.** ***to hang the wing*** (cf. HANG *v.* 4c): to hesitate, show timidity. *Obs.*

a **1601** NORTH *Plutarch, Epamin.* (1612) 1122 Afraid onely of the name and reputation of Epaminondas, and hanging the wing, as they say. *a* **1624** BP. SMYTH *Serm.* (1632) 40 If Saint Peter..had hanged the wing, as they speake, or let fall his Crest.

18. ***to make wing*** (cf. 3a and MAKE *v.*¹ 59): to make one's way by flying, to fly. ? *Obs.*

1605 SHAKS. *Macb.* III. ii. 51 Light thickens, And the Crow makes Wing to th' Rookie Wood. **1650** FULLER *Pisgah* II. xiii. 281 Hence he made wing, taking a long and strong flight to Mizpah. **1666** DRYDEN *Ann. Mirab.* lxxxvii, The dastard Crow that to the Wood made wing. **1856** BRYANT *Winds* 17 The weary fowls of heaven make wing in vain, To escape your wrath.

19. a. ***to take to wing*** (TAKE *v.* 74b): = b. ? *Obs.*

1693 J. DRYDEN, jun. *Juvenal* XIV. 99 Soon as e'er to Wing they take. **1870** N. F. HELE *Aldeburgh* vii. 84 It was within ten yards of me when it took to wing.

b. ***to take*** (†***its***, etc.) ***wing*** (TAKE *v.* 24c); (*a*) Of a bird, etc.: To take flight, begin flying.

1807 WORDSW. *Song at Feast of Brougham Castle* 130 He knew the rocks which Angels haunt..He hath kenned them taking wing. **1812** COL. HAWKER *Diary* (1893) I. 62 They will instantly take wing and give you a beautiful shot. **1890** C. DIXON *Stray Feathers* i. 6 The Ring Doves, startled at this, took wing.

(*b*) *fig.* To 'take flight', take one's departure, make off, flee.

1704 *Lond. Gaz.* No. 4056/5 Success, like Fame, has taken Wing. **1715** BENTLEY *Serm. Popery* 24 The weary Soul.. ready to leave the Carcase, and yet not suffer'd to take it's Wing. **1806–7** J. BERESFORD *Miseries Hum. Life* (1826) iv. Introd., I lately changed my lodgings... I took wing at a moment's warning. **1825** T. HOOK *Sayings* Ser. II. *Sutherl.* (Colburn) 32 As he touched the lock, they took wing like a covey of partridges. **1876** GEO. ELIOT *Dan. Der.* xxxvi, I found a fellow who..knew this Mrs Glasher before she took wing.

20. ***to spread*** (***stretch, try***) ***one's wings***: to test or develop one's powers; to lead a life of wider scope than hitherto.

1864 G. MEREDITH *Let.* 1 June (1970) I. 260 One thought my Marie merely trying her wings. **1872** GEO. ELIOT *Middlem* II. IV. xxxiv. 192 He is trying his wings. He is just the sort of young fellow to rise. **1876** TROLLOPE *Prime Minister* III. xx. 332 When I found myself the son-in-law of a very rich man I thought I might spread my wings a bit. **1926** R. H. TAWNEY *Relig. & Rise of Capitalism* ii. 67 It was in an age of political anarchy that the forces destined to dominate the future tried their wings. **1953** 'W. COOPER' *Ever-Interesting Topic* V. ii. 252 He decided to compose music as well as to play it: he began to try his wings as a creative artist, and he found they held him up. **1973** 'P. MALLOCH' *Kickback* xi. 69 'Hagan's stretching his wings a bit.' 'Beginning to feel his weight, is he?' **1978** S. RADLEY *Death & Maiden* xv. 145 She wanted to spread her wings a bit, meet new people.

*** **21. wing-and-wing** (*Naut.*): (of a ship) sailing directly before the wind, with the foresail hauled over on one side and the mainsail on the other.

1781 J. GREENWOOD in *Maryland Hist. Mag.* (1910) V. 129 We were now wing and wing, that is right before the wind. **1828** J. F. COOPER *Red Rover* I. iii. 84 That.. schooner would make more way going wing-and-wing than jammed up on a wind. **1841** R. H. DANA *Seaman's Man.* 135. **1893** KIPLING *Seven Seas, Coastwise Lights* 13 We greet the clippers, wing-and-wing, that race the Southern wool.

22. ***a wing and a prayer***, a joc. form of reference (after quot. 1943) to an emergency landing by an aircraft. Also *fig.* and as *attrib. phr.* in allusion to reliance on hope in desperate situations.

1943 H. ADAMSON *Comin' in on a Wing & a Prayer* (song), Tho' there's one motor gone, we can still carry on, Comin' In On A Wing And A Pray'r. **1967** *Economist* 3 June 998/2 The ITA's problem is to decide which applicants give most promise of maintaining an improvement over six years... This is largely a wing and a prayer decision. **1971** P. O'DONNELL *Impossible Virgin* xii. 250, I reckoned it was better to get kitted up for a proper job rather than come charging down 'ere on a wing and a prayer. **1977** W. MARSHALL *Thin Air* xii. 150 The co-pilot brought it in.. Wing and a prayer! **1980** T. BARLING *Goodbye Piccadilly* xvi. 334 The pilot spoke to him... 'This is real wing and a prayer weather.'

IV. Attributive uses and Combinations.

23. a. Simple attrib.: (*a*) in sense 1 (in reference to parts, structure, or function), as ***wing area, -beat, -bone, feather, flight, -length, membrane, neuration, patch, pattern, pinion, power, quill, ray, shoulder, -span, -spread, vein***; (*b*) in sense 5d; (of aeroplanes) ***wing-length, -skid, -span, -spread, -stay***; (*c*) in sense 6 or 9 (= side, lateral), as ***wing boiler, cabin, room, walk***; (*d*) in sense 7, as ***wing adjutant, -back, commander, officer***; in sense 7b, as ***wing forward, half, -man, player***; (*e*) = having wings or side appendages (6, 8), as ***wing bonnet, cap, chair, gudgeon, -nut***.

(*a*) **1582** STANYHURST *Æneis* IV. (Arb.) 101 Furth she quicklye galops, with wingflight swallolyke hastning. **1675** HANNAH WOOLLEY *Gentlew. Comp.* 114 Put under the wing-Pinions on each side the long slices of flesh which you did cut from the Breast-bone. **1704** PETIVER *Gazophyl.* iii. 23 Its Belly, Wing-shoulders, Collar, and about the Eyes white. **1752** J. HILL *Hist. Anim.* 343 The exterior wing-feathers are black. **1815** STEPHENS in Shaw's *Gen. Zool.* IX. I. 3 Interior wing-quills externally margined. **1826** SAMOUELLE *Direct. Collect. Insects & Crust.* 37 The Pterigostia or wing-bones, hairy. **1837** *Penny Cycl.* VII. 25/1 It [*sc.* a bat] hybernates.. snugly wrapped up in the wing-membranes. **1856** *Zoologist* Ser. I. XIV. 5157 The wing-veins of insects. *Ibid.* 5195 The Wing-rays of Insects. **1872** COUES *N. Amer. Birds* 100 Wing-patch resolved into two bars. *Ibid.* 174 When very young, the wing-markings more fulvous. **1893** NEWTON *Dict. Birds* 269 Those..which can soar are mostly large birds, with a relatively large wing-area. **1897** 'N. BLANCHAN' *Bird Neighbors* 143 Bank Swallow... About an inch shorter than the English sparrow, but apparently much larger because of its wide wing-spread. **1902** *Spectator* 26 July 112 The wing-power of the dragon-flies. **1909** *Westm. Gaz.* 2 Nov. 2/3 For wing-beats of great angels we would hear the herdsman's call. **1910** *Encycl. Brit.* XIII. 432/1 Orthopteroid wing-neuration. **1911** *Ibid.* XVI. 469/1 The darkening of wing-patterns in many species of Lepidoptera. **1922** JOYCE *Ulysses* 505 Head askew, arches his back and hunched wingshoulders. **1927** *Daily Express* 31 Aug. 8/3 It ..is shaped like the wing-bone of a chicken. **1943** A. CLARKE *Coll. Plays* (1963) 173 This big wind that filled My wingbones blew me into the trees. **1946** *Nature* 21 Dec. 904/1 The accompanying table shows..the weight in kgm. and wing-length in cm. of the female. **1949** *Brit. Birds* XLII. 187 The wing-span was found to measure nearly four feet, and the length was 21 inches. **1957** *New Yorker* 13 July 22/2 We got over six hundred bats, from insectivorous ones with an eight-inch wingspread to fruit eaters with a five-foot wingspread. **1971** *Sci. Amer.* Dec. 79/3 For aerodynamic reasons large birds have a slow wingbeat. **1977** P. WAY *Super-Celeste* 123 The skull and upper bones of the [eagle's] wingspan had.. driven like a cannon ball into the pilot's belly.

(*b*) **1897** LANCHESTER *Aerodonetics* (1908) 353 The reaction of the air on the upper and under wing surfaces. **1908** H. G. WELLS *War in Air* x. 317 It had taken only an hour or so to substitute wing stays from the second flying-machine and to replace the nuts he had himself removed. **1910** R. FERRIS *How it Flies* xx. 474 *Wing Plan*, the outline of the wing or main plane surface as viewed from above. *Ibid.*, *Wing skid*, a small skid, or runner, placed under the tip of the wings of an aeroplane. **1912** *Q. Rev.* July 231 If the

1000 lb. aeroplane is to travel slower, it must have a larger wing-spread. **1918** Pagé & Montariol *Gloss. Aviation Terms* 33/1 Wing span. **1920** *Flight* XII. 864/1 The Loughead S1 model, as it is called, is a single-seater biplane with a wing span of 28ft. **1975** *Farnborough 76* (Soc. Brit. Aerospace Companies) 30/2 The world's smallest jet aircraft, the Bede BD-5J..with a wing span of only 17ft. **1978** R. Jansson *News Caper* 9 There was the fighter again, flying parallel half a winglength away. **1978** *Sci. Amer.* Nov. 135/1 In 1899 the Wrights built a biplane kite with a five-foot wingspread that embodied their wing-twisting roll control.

(*c*) a **1697** Aubrey *Lives, Bacon* (1898) I. 79 In the middlemost three coaches may passe abreast: in the wing-walkes two may. **1838** *Civil Eng. & Arch. Jrnl.* I. 284/2 The furnaces in the wing boilers. **1877** L. Jewitt *Half-Hours Engl. Antiq.* 112 The sleeved surcoat; the ailettes or wing-pieces, behind the shoulders. **1883** Gresley *Gloss. Coal-mining* 291 *Wing-bore*..a side or flank bore-hole. **1889** *Pall Mall Gaz.* 20 Aug. 2/1 The wing cabin at the foot of the companion. **1893** T. N. Page *Ole Virginia* 194 The great chamber was given up to the baby, the Colonel going to the wing room. **1923** J. C. Rogers *Engl. Furnit.* 64 The back..fitted with forward wing-pieces.

(*d*) **1734** in *10th Rep. Hist. MSS. Comm.* App. I. 192, I sent a pinnace and brought the Velt Marshall's Wing Adjutant to me. **1876** Voyle & Stevenson *Milit. Dict.* (ed. 3) 470/2 *Wing Officer*, an officer of the Indian army attached to a wing of a native infantry regiment. **1882** *Cassell's Bk. Sports* 40 Wing players should be good dribblers. **1898** J. Goodall *Assoc. Football* 30 The wing game—that is to say, the two pairs playing together, leaving the centre-forward waiting for something to turn up. *Ibid.* 78 Wing-halves should keep their eyes on the wing-forwards. **1914** *Times* 22 Dec. 4/3 Royal Flying Corps..Wing Commander.—Brev. Maj. H. R. M. Brooke-Popham, Oxf. and Bucks. L.I. **1918** W. T. Blake *R.F.C. in War* vii. 42 The Wing Headquarters. **1933** *Time* 13 Nov. 57/1 A wing-back is..a halfback who takes position about a yard and a half behind the line of scrimmage and about the same distance outside his own end. **1942** *Sun* (Baltimore) 26 Jan. 4/1 Baltimore scored first on a pass from Charley Ernst, center forward, to Harry McAdams, newly acquired wingman. **1943** J. B. Priestley *Daylight on Saturday* xxviii. 217 And a real wing-commander came in yesterday and talked to me. **1974** Wingback [see rush *v.*² 6 g]. **1976** *Derbyshire Times* (Peak ed.) 3 Sept. 26/1 Matlock, in contrast, always looked dangerous with Peter Scott, the Fenoughty brothers, Mick and Nick, and wing-man Colin Oxley constantly troubling the Runcorn defence with their speedy breaks.

(*e*) **1775** Mme. D'Arblay *Early Diary* 28 Feb., She had on a large dirty wing cap, made of muslin. **1817** Maria Edgeworth *Harrington* xiii, Then at the top of the mount of hair and horsehair..there was sometimes a fly-cap, or a wing-cap, or a *pouf*. **1883** *Longman's Mag.* July 259 The wing bonnet like the tilt of a waggon. **1891** *Anthony's Photogr. Bull.* IV. 121 Put a ¼ inch bolt with a wing thumb nut, through. **1907** G. O. Wheeler *Old Engl. Furniture* 190 The ordinary English 'wing' or 'grandfather' chair. **1910** *Chambers's Jrnl.* May 349/1 The wing-nut on its shaft is released, the detachable rim-wheel placed on the shaft, and the nut replaced. **1971** *Flying* Apr. 26/2 The control and gust locks..are adjustable to fit virtually any light aircraft by means of easy-to-operate wing nuts.

b. Instrumental, adverbial, parasynthetic, etc., as ***wing-borne, -broken, -clipped, -flapping, -hoofed, -like, -limed, -shadowed, -shaped, -shattered, -stiff, -weary, -wide*** adjs.

1934 Webster, *Wing-borne. **1942** S. Smith *Mother, what is Man?* 67 Than earth-born engine-borne, heaven-born wing-borne is better? **1977** *Guardian Weekly* 5 June 3/2 About half the crashes happened when the aircraft was hovering, or in transition from normal wingborne flight. a **1793** G. White *Naturalist's Cal.* etc. (1795) 96 As a person was lately pursuing a pheasant that was *wing-broken. **1874** J. W. Long *Amer. Wild-fowl* iii. 71 Rather a cruel method, perhaps, but one attended with great success in wild-goose shooting, is, on securing a wing-broken one, to fasten it to a stake a short distance from the blind. **1892** *Pall Mall Gaz.* 24 Mar. 2/1 Some of the birds can fly,..but the *wing-clipped ones..are..shot down. **1915** E. Pound *Cathay* 10 He goes out to Hori, to look at the *wing-flapping storks. **1953** N. Tinbergen *Herring Gull's World* xxi. 183 A screaming, wing-flapping tangle. **1615** Chapman *Odyss.* xxiii. 377 Who th' extended night With-held in long date; nor would let the light Her *wing-hoou'd horse ioyne. **1795–1804** W. Blake *Vala* vi, in *Compl. Writings* (1972) 318 And the *wing-like tent of the Universe, beautiful, surrounding all. **1848** Dunglison *Med. Lex.*, *Alaria ossa*, the wing-like processes of the sphenoid bone. **1606** Sylvester *Du Bartas* ii. iv. ii. *Magnificence* 428 Why the wilde Fen-Goose..as *wing-lim'd, cannot fly. **1938** D. Gascoyne *Hölderlin's Madness* 28 The bewildered words which try to tell The tale of his bright night And his *wing-shadowed day. **1829** Loudon *Encycl. Plants* (1836) 598 Leaves..*wing-shaped. **1928** Blunden *Retreat* 60 But now the grey age passes by my faint senses And charm lies *wing-shattered or dead. **1945** P. A. Larkin *North Ship* 33 It was your severed image that grew sweeter, That floated, *wing-stiff, focussed in the sun. **1868** J. G. Whittier in *Atlantic Monthly* Jan. 1 The sky is hot and hazy, and the wind, *Wing-weary with its long flight from the south. **1946** J. W. Day *Harvest Adventure* x. 154 The woodcock come in wing-weary from their North Sea voyagings. **1818** Keats *Walking in Scot.* 19 Eagles may seem to sleep *wing-wide upon the air.

24. Special Combs.: **wing-back chair** = *wing chair*, sense 23 a (*e*)); also *ellipt.*; **wing-band** = *wing-bar* (*b*); **wing-bar**, (*a*) a lateral bar in a scuffling-plough; (*b*) a bar or band of colour on the feathers of a bird's wing, *spec.* one formed by distinctive coloration of the greater or median coverts or both; (*c*) in an aeroplane: see quot. 1910; **wing-bay**, a marking on a bird's wing formed by distinctive coloration of the secondaries, in certain game-cocks characteristically of a bay colour; **wing-bow**, a marking on the shoulder or bend of the wing formed by distinctive coloration of the lesser coverts; **wing-bud**, in insect larvæ, a histoblast from which the wings develop; **wing-case**, each of the structures (modified fore-wings) which cover the functional wings in certain insects, as the *elytra* of beetles and the *tegmina* of *Orthoptera*; **wing-chick**, a young chicken still under the protection of its mother's wing; **wing-clapping**, the production of a noise by a bird slapping its wings against its body; hence **wing-clap** *sb.* and *v. intr.*; †**wing-cleft** *a.*, *Bot.* = pinnatifid (cf. 11 b); **wing collar**, a high stiff shirt collar with the upper corners turned down; **wing-compass**, a compass having one leg fitted with an arc-shaped 'wing' or projecting piece which passes through the other leg and may be clamped in any required position (Knight *Dict. Mech.* 1875); **wing-cover** = *wing-case*; **wing-covert** [covert *sb.* 5], any one of the small feathers overlying the flight-feathers of a bird's wing; **wing-dam** *sb.*, a dam or barrier built into a stream to deflect the current; hence **wing-dam** *v. trans.*, to furnish with a wing-dam; **wing-deck** = sense 9 b (*b*); **wing-elm** = *winged elm* (see winged *a.* 3 c); †**wing-fashion** *a.* or *adv.*, in the form of wings; **wing-fish**, (*a*) = Pterichthys; (*b*) a flying-fish, esp. of the genus *Prionotus*; **wing-flap**: see flap *sb.* 5 e; **wing flutter** *Aeronaut.*, flutter (flutter *sb.* 1 d) of an aircraft wing; **wing-footed** *a.*, having winged feet, swiftly-moving; also *fig.*; **wing formula** (see quot. 1964); **wing-game**, game-birds collectively, as distinguished from *ground-game* (ground *sb.* 18); †**wing-laid** *a.*, ? = *wing-and-wing* (see 21); †**wing-leaved** *a.*, *Bot.* having pinnate leaves (cf. 11 b); **wing loading** *Aeronaut.*, the gross weight of an aircraft divided by the total wing area; (in quot. 1912 perh. used differently); cf. power loading *vbl. sb.* 1; **wing-man**, the pilot of an aircraft which is positioned behind and to one side of the leading aircraft, as in formation for combat; the aircraft itself; **wing mirror**, (*a*) a side mirror (freq. adjustable) on a dressing table; (*b*) a rear-view mirror projecting from the side of a motor vehicle; **wing-net**, (*a*) a 'wing' in a fishing-net (= 6 d), or a fishing-net with wings; (*b*) a net at the side of a tennis-court; **wing-over**, of an aircraft or hang-glider (see quot. 1959); **wing-passage**, a passage along the side of a ship's hold: see 9 b (*a*); also *attrib.*; **wing-poke (collar)** = *wing collar* above; †**wing-post**, *nonce-wd.* [post *sb.*² 2], a carrier pigeon; **wing-rail** = guard-rail 2 (Knight *Dict. Mech.* 1875); **wing rib**, the end rib of a loin of beef; **wing root** *Aeronaut.*, the part of a wing where it is attached to the fuselage; **wing-sail**, ? a sail abaft the main course; **wing-sheath** = *wing-case*; **wing-shell**, †(*a*) the wing-sheath of an insect; (*b*) any of several kinds of molluscs having the shell or some part of it resembling a wing, as the genus *Pinna* (= sea-wing 2); also, a wing-snail; **wing-shooting**, the practice of shooting birds 'on the wing', i.e. when flying; **wing-shot** *sb.*, (*a*) a shot aimed at a flying bird; (*b*) a person skilled in wing-shooting; *adj.* shot while flying, or in the wing; **wing-snail** = pteropod; **wing-stopper** [stopper *sb.* 9], a cable-stopper formerly used in the wings of a ship; **wing-tag** *v. trans.*, to attach a distinguishing marker to the wing of a bird; **wing-tip**, (*a*) the tip of the wing of a bird, bat, or insect; (*b*) the outer end of the 'wing' of an aeroplane; (*c*) chiefly *U.S.*, applied *attrib.* to shoes with a toecap having a backward extending point and curving sides, suggestive of the shape of a wing; also *absol.*; **wing-tipped** (-tɪpt) *ppl. a.*, (of a bird) having the tips of the wings clipped so as to prevent it from flying; **wing-transom**, the uppermost and longest of the transoms in the stern-frame of a ship; **wing-wader**, an Australian wading bird having a spur or claw on each wing; **wing-wale** (see quot. 1846 in 9 b); **wing-walking**, acrobatic stunts performed on the wings of an aircraft which is airborne, as a public entertainment; **wing-wall**, a lateral wall forming a support to an abutment and to the adjacent earth; **wing-warping**, in early powered flight, the bending or twisting of a wing by means of an attached wire as a method of stabilizing the aeroplane or turning it.

1933 J. Steinbeck *To God Unknown* i. 1 The *wing-back chair by the fireplace. **1973** 'D. Jordan' *Nile Green* xlvi. 247 She sat in her wingback chair flicking through one of the coffee table books. **1977** *Chicago Tribune Mag.* 2 Oct. 9/1 (Advt.), The chair that stands still in time—the Classic Wingback with Chippendale legs. **1872** Coues *N. Amer. Birds* 101 *Wing-bands generally fused into one large patch. **1844** H. Stephens *Bk. Farm* III. 959 The ends of the *wing-bars having a mortise formed to receive the quadrant, are moved upon this to any required width. **1855** *Poultry Chron.* III. 348/2 They are light blue on the coloured parts and have no wing bars. **1910** R. Ferris *How it Flies* 474 *Wing Bar*, the larger construction members of a wing, running from the body outward to the tips. The ribs are attached to the wing bars, usually at right angles. **1867** Tegetmeier *Poultry Bk.* 338 *Wing Bow.—Rich dark red. **1917** R. J. Tillyard *Biol. of Dragonflies* iii. 47 The *wing-bud is simply an ectodermal evagination, in the form of a small bag lined internally with hydoderm cells, and externally with the cuticle. **1969** R. F. Chapman *Insects* xxi. 407 A progressive development of the wing buds occurs at each moult. **1661** Lovell *Hist. Anim. & Min.*, *Isagoge* c 2 b, Some [Insects] have *wing-cases, as beetles, and cantharides. **1815** Kirby & Sp. *Entomol.* iii. (1818) I. 64 Two wings, and two wing-cases, ornamented with yellow bands. **1885** Meredith *Diana* xxviii, A young poet..is not the same kind of *wing-chick as a young actress. **1964** A. L. Thomson *New Dict. Birds* 631/2 More rattling or clattering *wing-claps may be made by pigeons suddenly taking wing when alarmed. **1976** *Country Life* 18 Mar. 672/2 The long-eared owl will wing-clap during its spring nuptial flight. **1941** H. F. Witherby et al. *Handbk. Brit. Birds* IV. 142 Performance [of display-flight by turtle-dove] may be accompanied by *wing-clapping. **1976** *Country Life* 18 Mar. 672/2 The mechanical production of snaps from the beak may be compared with wing-clapping by birds. **1796** Withering *Brit. Plants* (ed. 3) II. 294 Leaves winged; leafits *wing-cleft. **1822** *Hortus Anglicus* II. 120 More properly twice wing-cleft than twice pinnate. **1915** H. L. Wilson *Ruggles of Red Gap* (1917) ii. 33, I chose a shirt of white piqué, a *wing collar with small, square-cornered tabs, and a pearl ascot. **1975** *Times* 19 May 12/7 Saturday's guide was Charles E. Lee, a transport historian whose wing collar..enhanced the building's period atmosphere. **1816** Kirby & Sp. *Entomol.* xxiii. (1818) II. 350 In the next order (*Orthoptera*), the *Tegmina*, or *wing-covers..assist them in flying. **1888** Rolleston & Jackson *Anim. Life* 500 The fore wings may be converted into wing covers for the hind wings. **1815** Stephens in Shaw's *Gen. Zool.* IX. i. 3 Greater *wing-coverts tipped with crimson. **1809** T. G. Fessenden *Pills Poetical* 36 All his rhetorick was directed toward election districts, and *wingdam bills, and seconding motions. **1863** Wing dam [see paddock *v.* 2]. **1882** *Rep. Prec. Metals U.S.* 102 By sinking a shaft and drifting preparatory to building a wing-dam. **1857** J. D. Borthwick *Three Yrs. California* xvii. 265 A company of fifteen or twenty white men would have *wing-dammed this claim. **1889** *Century Mag.* July 374/1 (Steamboat Decoration) More of this glass gives a desirable touch of color in the lights above the *wing-decks at each end. **1547** in Feuillerat *Revels Edw. VI* (1914) 14, vij peyre of Sleves *wyng ffasshion. **1855** *Orr's Circ. Sci.*, *Inorg. Nat.* 80 The Pterichthys (*wing-fish). **1888** Goode *Amer. Fishes* 304 [Fishes of the genus *Prionotus*] are eaten..only in the vicinity of Hartford, Conn., where they are known as 'Wing-fish'. **1927** *Daily Tel.* 21 Jan. 10/7 The new theory..suggests that *wing-flutter may be more common than has been supposed. **1982** C. L. Ruhlin et al. *Transonic Flutter Study of Wind-Tunnel Model* (NASA Rep. 82-23239) viii. 5/2 Most of the winglet effect on the wing flutter speed was due to the winglet mass, not aerodynamics. **1591** Spenser *Ruins of Time* 666 *Wing footed Mercurie. **1612** Drayton *Poly-olb.* x. 322 Wing-footed Time. **1658** Rowland tr. *Moufet's Theat. Ins.* 923 Hail the daughters of the wing-footed steed. **1977** *Time* 22 Aug. 13/1 Wing-footed United Nations Ambassador Andrew Young has been exploring the politically and economically troubled waters of the Caribbean, and soon will attend an anti-apartheid conference in Lagos, Nigeria. **1936** *Brit. Birds* XXX. 226 This specimen..has..a *wing formula as follows. **1964** A. L. Thomson *New Dict. Birds* 892/2 Wing formula: a statement of, mainly, the relative lengths of the primary feathers. **1879** Jefferies *Wild Life in S. Co.* vii, The neighbouring squire takes the pick of the *wing-game. **1632** Lithgow *Trav.* x. 502 The *wing-layd Galley, with her factious oares. **1822** *Hortus Anglicus* II. 119 *Wing-leaved Fig Wort, or Dog's Rue. **1912** *Q. Rev.* July 246 A range of this amount is obtained entirely by proportioning the position of masses, the wing-curve and the *wing-loading. **1916** A. W. Judge *Design of Aeroplanes* iii. 29 In current practice the wing loading expressed in pounds per square foot for biplanes is about $0.005V^2$, ..where V is the maximum designed speed in feet per second. **1972** *Times* 19 May 17/4 It cannot be a glider, as it has far too high a wing-loading. **1946** *Sat. Even. Post* 6 Nov. 86/2, I looked to both sides of us. Our two *wing men were gone. **1981** S. Dunmore *Ace* i. i. 15 We will fly together... You will be my wingman..to protect my rear end. **1982** *Daily Tel.* 25 May 1/4 He hit two Mirages with Sidewinder missiles while his wingman hit the third in the formation. **1925–6** *T. Eaton & Co. Catal.* Fall & Winter 311/2 Dressing table..triple mirrors, centre one beveled..two plain *wing mirrors. **1948** *Motor* 3 Nov. 396/3 An assortment of wing mirrors. **1959** C. Williams *Man in Motion* vi. 62 The dressing-table with its wing mirrors. **1959** *Motor Manual* (ed. 36) viii. 217 Additional wing mirrors are..very useful, particularly on the off-side as traffic on the point of overtaking is then clearly visible. **1981** M. Nabb *Death of Englishman* iii. i. 143 He..had banged his head on a Carabiniere car wing-mirror. **1884** Knight *Dict. Mech.* Suppl. s.v. *Stake-net*, At from 30' to 40' down stream another row of stakes is set, each opposite a stake in the bar-net, and between these stakes a *wing-net is stretched. **1884** *Marshall's Tennis Cuts* 96 A gentleman,.. in a fit of passion at some *coup manqué*, flung his racket high in air, and it lodged on the ledge above the tambour, behind the wing-net. **1928** *Morning Post* 20 Oct. 9/3 One of the passengers..got panicky when the pilot executed a '*wing-over'. **1959** F. D. Adams *Aeronaut. Dict.* 183/2 *Wing-over*, *noun*, an airplane maneuver in which the airplane makes a steep zooming climb then banks and turns in the vertical plane into a dive or glide from which the recovery is made at approximately the original altitude and in a direction opposite to the original direction. **1978** A. Welch *Bk. Airsports* i. 9/2 They indulge in 'show-off' flying—fast dives and steep wing-overs—that the simple hang glider was never designed to take. **1869** E. J. Reed *Shipbuild.* vi. 101 The *wing passages of wooden ships of war. **1879** *Cassell's Techn. Educ.* IV. 364/1 The 'wing-passage-bulkhead' as a protection against under-water attacks such as ramming or torpedoes. **1905** H. G. Wells *Kipps* iii. i. 351 Kipps wears a grey suit, with a *wing poke collar. **1910** —— *Hist. Mr. Polly* i. 13 His collar was chosen from stock, and with projecting corners, technically a 'wing-poke'. *a* **1661** FULLER *Worthies, Northamptonshire* (1662) II. 279 Such practices, by these *Wing-posts, would spoil many a Foot-post. **1883** 'ANNIE THOMAS' *Mod. Housewife* iv. 48 A seven or eight pound piece of *wing rib or sirloin of beef. **1906** A. SAMUELSON *Flight-Velocity* I. 12 Near the *wing root an outrigger or boom..is fastened. **1966** M. WOODHOUSE *Tree Frog* xxvi. 195, I jumped down off the wing root..and started to think about search parties. **1794** *Rigging & Seamanship* I. 135 **Wingsail for Ketches*. This sail is quadrilateral, and similar to the mizen-course of a ship. It.. bends abaft the mainmast to hoops which encircle the mast. **1874** GARROD & BAXTER *Mat. Med.* 411 The elytra or *wing-sheaths are long. **1681** GREW *Musæum* I. §vii. ii. 164 The *Wing-shells almost square-knobed on each side before. *Ibid.*, The Long-Shell'd Goat-Chafer..is above an inch long, and the Wing-shells of them-selves an inch. **1835** KIRBY *Hab. & Inst. Anim.* I. viii. 252 The wing-shell belonging to the unimuscular section. **1854** WOODWARD *Mollusca* II. 260 The wing-shells, or pearl-oysters. **1881** GREENER *Gun* 58 These guns..were probably intended for *wing-shooting. **1875** *Fur, Fin & Feather* 118 Bogardus, champion *wing-shot of America, uses Orange Lightning [powder] for trap-shooting. **1878** C. HALLOCK *Hallock's Amer. Club List & Sportsman's Gloss.* p. xii, *Wing-shot*, a., hit in the wing. *Wing-shot*, n., a shot at birds on the wing; one who shoots at birds while flying. **1883** *Century Mag.* Aug. 493/2 Last season, I shot with the best wing-shot I ever hunted with. **1892** GREENER *Breech Loader* 253 The contest for the American Field Champion Wing-Shot Cup. **1895** G. J. MANSON *Sporting Dict.*, *Wing-shot*,..hit on the wing. **1794** *Rigging & Seamanship* I. 176 Dog-stoppers are used as additional securities..to ease the deck-stoppers. *Wing-stoppers are used for the same purpose. **1953** SCOTT & FISHER *Thousand Geese* 215 Five of the young were *wing-tagged. **1981** *Animal Behaviour* XXIX. 302/1 Three females and one male were wing-tagged. **1872** COUES *N. Amer. Birds* 175 The *wing-tip projects only about ½ an inch beyond the secondaries. **1890** DARWIN *Desc. Man* II. xi. (ed. 2) 322 The female of *Anthocharis cardamines* does not possess the beautiful orange wing-tips of the male. **1909** *Daily Chron.* 2 Feb. 5/6 He..hesitated a second to see that the man at the wing tip was ready. **1928** *World* (N.Y.) 23 May 4/6 (Advt.), Wing tip oxfords by Horsheim have unusually good style. **1971** *Weekend World* (Johannesburg) 9 May 14/5 (Advt.), Walk tall in the elegant clean lines of a Bostonian wing-tip or genuine handsewn moccasin. **1976** 'B. SHELBY' *Great Pebble Affair* 45 Get a pair of black wingtip shoes. **1980** M. GORDON *Company of Women* I. ii. 38 The hard, expensive shoes of John F. Kennedy, the shoe with pinholes in the leather, wing tips they were called. **1849** D. J. BROWNE *Amer. Poultry Yd.* (1855) 236 Being *wing-tipped and unable to fly, he caught it and brought it home alive. **1711** W. SUTHERLAND *Shipbuild. Assist.* 70 The *Wing Transom to have a long arm'd Knee. **1815** BURNEY *Falconer's Dict. Marine* s.v. *Transoms*, The arms of the transoms, being gradually closer in proportion to their distance from the wing transom downwards. **1867** PITT-RIVERS *Evol. Culture, Prim. Warfare* I. (1906) 71 The *wing-wader of Australia. **1927** C. A. LINDBERGH *We* i. 11 Exhibitions..in which I usually made a jump and did a little *wing-walking. **1979** *Sunset* Apr. 3/3 Also awesome is a wing-walking act in which specially trained gymnasts do headstands and other maneuvers on the wings of a W.W. II Stearman biplane as it loops, rolls, and lands. **1791** *Rep. Navig. Thames & Isis* Estimate 5 Taking down the Side-Walls of Godstow Lock, re-building them, strengthening the *Wing-Walls, and finishing, £450. **1842** *Civil Eng. & Arch. Jrnl.* V. 95/1 Retaining walls were generally introduced at the ends of bridges, to connect the abutments of the bridge with the natural ground; but in these cases they were called 'wing walls'. **1910** R. M. NEILSON *Aeroplane Patents* 27, 6732 of March 19, 1904.—O. and W. Wright. This is the famous *wing-warping patent. **1969** K. MUNSON *Pioneer Aircraft 1903–14* 7 Wing-warping was not, in itself, an invention of the Wrights; what was significant was their improvement of linking the warp-control cables with a single, hinged rudder.

wing, *v.* Forms: see prec.; also *pa. pple.* 5 **wyngged, y-whyngged**. [f. prec. sb.]

I. Senses derived from senses 1–5 of the sb.

† **1.** *trans.* To carve (a quail or partridge). *Obs.*

1486 *Bk. St. Albans* f vij b, A Quayle wyngged. *c* **1500** [see ELE *v.*[2]]. **1513** *Bk. Keruynge* in *Babees Bk.* 265. **1598** BP. HALL *Sat.* IV. ii. 44 Him list not spend his idle meales In quinting Plouers, or in winging [*printed* winning] Quailes. **1694** N. H. *Ladies Dict.* 415 (*bis*). *a* **1756** MRS. HEYWOOD *New Present* (1771) 269. **1804** FARLEY *London Art of Cookery* (ed. 10) 292 Partridges and quails. To wing either of these birds, nothing more is to be done than to raise the legs and wings.

2. a. *intr.* (†occas. *refl.*) To use one's wings, take flight, fly; occas. *transf.* to sail; *fig.* to 'fly', pass swiftly, speed; also (chiefly *U.S.*) with an aircraft as subject, or *transf.* of a passenger, to travel by aircraft. orig. *poet* or *rhetorical*.

1611 SHAKS. *Wint. T.* v. iii. 133, I (an old Turtle) Will wing me to some wither'd bough. **1623** 'JACK DAWE' *Vox Graculi* 51 It will be better going by Land..then to wing against winde and tide without a tilt-Cloath. **1628** FELTHAM *Resolves* II. [I.] xxxii. 101 Iuvenal does tell vs, how Life wings away! **1688** CROWNE *Darius* v. 62 He wings along the Air in Clouds of Dust, And does not march, but fly. **1726** *Adv. Capt. R. Boyle* (1768) 268, I had nothing else to do but to Wing to the Place where the Joy of my Life did once reside. **1801** W. HUTTON *Life* (1816) 238 The year winged away in feasting upon a pleasure to come. **1816** SCOTT *Antiq.* vii, Many of these wild tribes..were now winging towards their nests. **1844** HOOD *Haunted Ho.* III. v, In the upper gloom The bat—or something in its shape—was winging. **1879** 'E. GARRETT' *House by Works* xv, He was dead before the telegram, winging over sea and land, announced his danger to his son. **1938** *Sun* (Baltimore) 21 July 1/8 (*heading*) English plane wings swiftly over Atlantic. **1973** C. SAGAN *Cosmic Connection* (1974) xxviii. 197 A single bit of radio information, sent winging across space to the Earth, would cost far less than a penny. **1977** *Time* 30 May 25/2 As Air Force One winged toward Washington, one Californian was clearly relieved that Carter's visit had been so brief. **1983** *Fortune* 18 Apr. 137/1 Winging into New Hampshire from Los Angeles headquarters aboard an Arco jet one Sunday, Cooper began the next three days at 7:30. **1984** *Times* 4 Aug. 32 The Prince of Wales flies back from Monaco, only to wing off within hours for Papua New Guinea.

b. In pa. pple. = flying, on the wing. *Obs.* or *arch.*

1591 SHAKS. *1 Hen. VI*, IV. vii. 21 Thou antique Death,.. Two Talbots winged through the lither Skie, In thy despight shall scape Mortalitie. **1611** —— *Cymb.* IV. ii. 348, I saw Ioues Bird, The Roman Eagle, wing'd From the spungy South to this part of the West. **1737** H. BROOKE tr. *Tasso* III. (1738) 10 Far wing'd before his Squadron Tancred came. **1844** KINGLAKE *Eothen* vi, Brave thoughts winged on Grecian words gained their natural mastery over Terror.

3. *trans.* **a.** To fly through, upon, or across; to traverse by flying.

1605 SHAKS. *Lear* IV. vi. 13 The Crowes and Choughes, that wing the midway ayre. **1667** MILTON *P.L.* IV. 936, I alone first undertook To wing the desolate Abyss. **1733** POPE *Ess. Man* III. 120 All that roam the wood, Or wing the sky, or roll along the flood. **1760–72** H. BROOKE *Fool of Qual.* (1809) III. 26 Thoughts that wing infinity, apprehensions that reach through eternity. **1820** SHELLEY *Skylark* ii, The blue deep thou wingest, And singing still dost soar, and soaring ever singest. **1883** WHITELAW *Sophocles, Oedipus Colonus* 1081 Oh that I were a dove, that I might wing the wind With pinion swift and strong.

b. with cognate obj. (*flight, way*).

1697 DRYDEN *Virg. Georg.* III. 14 New ways I must attempt, my groveling Name To raise aloft, and wing my flight to Fame. **1698** CONGREVE *Semele* II. i. 2 From Samos have I wing'd my Way. **1790** ALEX. WILSON *To David Brodie* Poet. Wks. (1846) 7 The parting year prepares to wing its way. **1848** DICKENS *Dombey* xxx, The week fled faster. It had nearly winged its flight away. **1893** SIR R. BALL *Story of Sun* xvii. 320 If we were able to wing our way from this Earth into the depths of space.

4. a. To put wings upon, furnish or fit with wings for flying; to feather (an arrow); also *poet.* in ref. to the sails of a ship.

a **1616** B. JONSON *Barriers* 41 Marriage Loves obiect is;.. For her, he wings his shoulders. **1661** BOYLE *Style Script.* 90 The Feathers that wing our Arrows. **1725** POPE *Odyss.* IV. 785 With sails we wing the masts. **1757** DYER *Fleece* II. 296 Nimbly they wing'd the bark. **1867** F. FRANCIS *Bk. Angling* xiii. 399 The nicest operation of all,..that of winging the fly.

b. *fig.* (or in fig. context): To 'give wings to'; to enable to 'fly' or 'soar'; to give speed or swift motion to; to speed, hasten.

1599 PEELE *David & Bethsabe* C j b, Cast as was Eua from that glorious soile (Where al delights sat bating wingd with thoughts, Ready to nestle in her naked breasts). **16..** *Lust's Domin.* I. iii. (1657) B 8, Ambition wings his spirit, keep him down. *a* **1625** FLETCHER *Bloody Brother* III. i, *Gis.* Tyrant, twill haste thy owne death. *Rol.* Let it wing it. **1647** TRAPP *Comm. 1 Cor.* vii. 5 (1656) 673 Fasting-days are soul-fatting days: prayer is edged and winged thereby. **1667** MILTON *P.L.* I. 175 The Thunder, Wing'd with red Lightning and impetuous rage. **1781** COWPER *Catharina* 50 With her book, and her voice, and her lyre, To wing all her moments at home. **1814** CARY *Dante, Parad.* xx. 102 Lively hope, that wing'd The prayers [of St. Gregory] sent up to God for his release. **1818** SCOTT *Hrt. Midl.* xiv, The hours glided on,.. whether winged with joy or laden with affliction. **1835** LYTTON *Rienzi* VI. v, The Convent was at some distance, but ..fear would wing her steps. **1849** M. ARNOLD *Sonn. to G. Cruikshank*, Artist, whose hand, with horror wing'd, hath torn From the rank life of towns this leaf.

5. To convey by or as by means of wings; 'to transport by flight' (J.); to carry through the air as if flying, to waft (also *fig.*).

1628 FELTHAM *Resolves* II. [I.] xlvii. 139 It is these two only [*sc.* water and earth], that seeme to make the body, while the two purer, Fire and Ayre, are wing'd away. **1682** OTWAY *Venice Preserv'd* III. ii. 37 First, let's embrace, Heav'n knows who next shall thus Wing ye together. **1807** J. BARLOW *Columb.* II. 126 When future gales shall wing them o'er the tide. **1820** CLARE *Poems Rural Life* 174 Sad was the day when my Willy did leave me, Sad were the moments that wing'd him away. **1876** GEO. ELIOT *Dan. Der.* xiii, There was enough breeze..to wing the shadow of a cloud across the soft grey downs. **1976** C. EGLETON *State Visit* xiv. 123 The VC 10 winged him back to Heathrow.

6. To send flying, let fly (as a missile); to send off swiftly, to dart.

1718 POPE *Iliad* XIII. 832 With his full Strength he bent his angry Bow, And wing'd the feather'd Vengeance at the Foe. **1831** JAMES *Philip Aug.* iii, Whether any of his train could draw a good bow, and wing a shaft well home. **1880** MEREDITH *Tragic Com.* viii, The desire to wing a telegram to her he thought it wise to repress. **1887** MORRIS *Odyss.* XI. 396 And therewith I bespake him and winged a word for his ears [ἔπεα πτερόεντα προσηύδων].

7. To brush with a bird's wing: cf. prec. I c.

1669 STURMY *Mariner's Mag.* VII. xxxiv. 49 With Blew Smalts strew very thick the Border while it is wet; and when it is dry, wing that which is loose off. **1866** [see WINGED *ppl. a.* 2].

8. To shoot (a bird) in the wing, so as to disable it from flying without killing it; *transf.* to wound (a person) with a shot in the arm or shoulder, or some other not vital part; to injure or disable (something) by a shot. Also, to pluck off the wings of (an insect).

1802 G. COLMAN *Poor Gentl.* v. iii. 77 We are on the ground first..What are the odds now, that he doesn't wing me? **1803** W. TAYLOR in *Ann. Rev.* I. 365 Snatched at, like flies by children, to be winged and let go. **1826** F. REYNOLDS *Life & Times* I. 82 Though I regularly fired,..I never even winged a tomtit. **1837** DICKENS *Pickw.* ii, Be steady, and wing him. **1884** 'H. COLLINGWOOD' *Under Meteor Flag* v, Tompion was..bid do his best to 'wing' the Frenchman [*sc.* a ship]. **1914** *Times* 28 Oct. 9/6 One aeroplane was winged by the Russian soldiery.

II. Senses derived from senses 6–9 of the sb.

9. † **a.** *Mil.* To furnish (a force) *with* additional troops on the wings; also of such troops, to form the wings of. (occas. *absol.*) *Obs.*

1591 *Garrard's Art Warre* 202 This squadron is..flanked with Musket..and winged with horsemen. **1594** SHAKS. *Rich. III*, V. iii. 300 In the maine Battell, whose puissance on either side Shall be well-winged with our cheefest Horse. **1622** F. MARKHAM *Bk. War* III. i. 82 They [*sc.* cavalry armed with petronels] wing the Launces or Pistolleirs. **1647** CLARENDON *Hist. Reb.* VI. §248 Having winged his Foot with his Horse and Dragoons. **1677** W. HUBBARD *Pres. St. New-Eng.* 125 We asked him what they intended who promised to wing us. **1699** *Relat. Sir T. Morgan's Progr. France* 6 We were forced to march up in four Lines (for we had not room enough to Wing).

b. To furnish with side parts or projections, as a building, etc.

a **1700** EVELYN *Diary* 31 Aug. 1654, Two courts,..wing'd with cloisters. **1789** *Trans. Soc. Arts* VII. 56 A new pair of flood-gates, winged with stone-walls. *a* **1830** *Edin. Encycl.* XIV. 349/1 If the pillars are to be winged afterwards, they must be left of an extra strength. **1882** C. A. YOUNG *Sun* vi. 198 The hydrogen is in such a state that the lines of its spectrum are widened and 'winged'.

10. *Naut.* **a.** To carry *up* (ballast) in the wings of a ship.

1794 *Rigging & Seamanship* II. 286 The iron ballast..is winged up 3 or more pigs above the floor-heads. **1867** SMYTH *Sailor's Word-bk.* 735 To *Wing up ballast*, to carry the dead weight from the bottom as high as consistent with the stability of a ship.

b. *intr. to wing out*: to set a sail on a boom projecting sideways. Hence ***winged out*** or ***wung out***, = *wing-and-wing* s.v. WING *sb.* 21.

1867 G. E. CLARK *Seven Yrs. Sailor's Life* i. 14 Here was I, deep-loaded, winged out, and oft-times flying before the winter blast. **1890** WEBSTER, wung out. **1907** *Rudder* Nov. 827/2 On rounding, the schooners winged out; but..the wind came out of East of South, and they jibed their foresails and trimmed sheets a little. **1956** A. F. LOOMIS *Hotspur Story* 109 Thither we sailed, main-sail to starboard and staysail wung out. *Ibid.* 214 The wung-out schooner which we had noticed earlier in the afternoon lost the race. **1969** H. HORWOOD *Newfoundland* x. 71 Tearing down the outside passages with sails 'wung out' before a roaring nor'-wester.

11. *Theatrical slang. trans.* To study (a part) in or about the wings, having undertaken it at short notice; also *intr.* Hence in phr. ***to wing it***; now usu. in *slang* use (orig. and chiefly *U.S.*), to improvise; to speak or act without preparation, to make statements on unstudied matters (see also quot. 1950).

1885 *Stage* 21 Aug. 12/2 'To wing'..indicates the capacity to play a *rôle* without knowing the text, and the word itself came into use from the fact that the artiste frequently received the assistance of a special prompter, who..stood..screened..by a piece of the scenery or a wing. **1886** *Stage Gossip* 70 In the event of an artiste being suddenly called upon to play a part of which he knows nothing..he frequently has to 'wing' the part. **1933** P. GODFREY *Back-Stage* iii. 39 He must give a performance by 'winging it'—that is, by refreshing his memory for each scene in the wings before he goes on to play it. **1950** *Amer. Speech* XXV. 238/1 *Wing it, vb.*, to lay off an approximate 90° angle by eye. **1959** *Esquire* Nov. 70 *Wing*, to do something without preparation. **1970** *Time* 26 Jan. 12 *Cox*: The resistance put up against us dictates [our] strategy. *Bernstein*:..You mean you've got to wing it. **1971** *Publishers' Weekly* 6 Dec. 20/2 They can talk about the book, kind of winging it based on the ads, just like other people do with reviews. **1979** *Globe & Mail* (Toronto) 22 Jan. 8/2 Mr. Trudeau came without notes, choosing to wing it, and struggled..unsuccessfully to establish Mr. Leger's resemblance to an owl.

† **12.** *intr.* To incline to a particular wing, side, or party. *Obs. nonce-use.*

1617 R. FENTON *Treat. Ch. Rome* 52 This made the people wing on that side.

wing, var. WIN *sb.*[3] (*slang*), a penny.

Wingco ('wɪŋkəʊ). *R.A.F. slang.* Also Winco, Winko, and with small initial. Abbrev. of *Wing Commander*: see WING *sb.* 23 a (*d*).

1941 MICHIE & GRAEBNER *Lights of Freedom* iii. 45 A cockney member of the ground crew piped: 'Sir, I think the 'Winko' [wing commander] is after the Hun.' **1942** *R.A.F. Jrnl.* 3 Oct. 12 One of them was a Winco and the other two were Army officers. **1943** 'T. DUDLEY-GORDON' *Coastal Command at War* ix. 88 On another raid... The wingco, was leading. **1944** 'N. SHUTE' *Pastoral* iii. 54 Don't let Winco hear him, or he'll get us into trouble. **1957** J. BRAINE *Room at Top* xii. 120 I've sung that..with Wingcos and Group Captains joining in. **1974** T. ALLBEURY *Snowball* xxii. 135 Wing Commander Pallin from the Ministry of Defence... I'd like to ask the Wingco to keep himself free to check..on the state of the game in Moscow. **1982** F. PARRISH *Snare in Dark* ii. 25 There was a pub..taken over by a retired Wing Commander... The Winco, as he liked to be called, was a ready market.

wing-ding, wingding ('wɪŋdɪŋ). Also **whingding**. [Redupl. of WING *sb.*] **1.** *U.S. slang.* A fit or spasm, esp. as simulated by a drug addict; freq. in phr. ***to throw a wing-ding***. Also in weakened sense, a furious outburst.

1927 *Amer. Speech* II. 281/1 *Wingding*, a false illness or fit. **1933** *Ibid.* VIII. II. 28/1 When an addict who..cannot obtain dope..becomes desperate, he may throw a wing-ding (feign a highly realistic fit in public) in the hope that the doctor..will administer narcotics to quiet him; professional wing-dingers are addicts who make a practice of obtaining their narcotics in this manner. **1939** R. CHANDLER *Big Sleep* xxxii. 292 She threw a wingding. Looked like a mild epileptic fit. **1944** *Amer. Speech* XIX. 107 A wing-ding is a particularly explosive fit of rage or frustration (I'm telling you the mate will throw a wing-ding!). **1946** 'J. EVANS' *Halo in Blood* xiv. 166, I..watched her take deep unsteady breaths... Her hands were locked together in her lap but that didn't keep them from trembling. 'About a minute,' I said mildly, 'You're going to throw a wing-ding they'll hear in Detroit. You're wound up tighter than a dollar watch.' **1957** V. PACKARD *Hidden Persuaders* ix. 102 This venture back to the womb touched off a little wingding in advertising circles. **1965** P. TAMONY *Americanisms* (typescript) No. II. 3 It assigned..Winifred Sweet..to throw a wing-ding..in Market Street.

2. *slang* (orig. and chiefly *U.S.*). A wild party; a celebration or social gathering.

1949 *Sat. Even. Post* 5 Mar. 10/3 We are not sure just what the Festival is to be, but some sort of native whingding no doubt. **1955** R. BRADBURY *October Country* 18 We would have to arrive when the local Rotary's having its whingding. **1964** *Punch* 15 July 79/3 My invitation to a White House schnapps wingding. **1972** *Sunday Sun* (Brisbane) 6 Aug. 3/4 Last Tuesday was Pat's birthday, so there was a big wing-ding at Maroochydore's posh Surfair pub. **1975** *Listener* 18 Dec. 832/3 The funeral bak'd meats will serve the triple economy of a divorce wing-ding as well. **1979** A. HAILEY *Overload* III. xi. 243 How are you, Nim? Don't see you often at these Jewish wingdings.

Hence **wing-'dinger**, (*a*) (see quot. 1933); (*b*) a pretended fit; a wild outburst.

1933 [see sense 1 above]. **1949** V. J. MONTELEONE *Criminal Slang* (new ed.) 253 *Wing-dinger* (*n.*), a pretended fit or spasm; a forced faint. **1976** *Telegraph* (Brisbane) 5 Aug. 39/3 This leads to a wing-dinger of a brawl, when Bobbie's brother..sights the louts who have busted up his father and their truck on the bridge.

winge, var. WHINGE *v.*

winged ('wɪŋɪd, wɪŋd), *a.* Forms: see WING *sb.*; also 5 **venged(e**, 6 *Sc.* **vengit**. [f. WING *sb.* + -ED[2].]

1. a. Having wings, as a bird, bat, insect, supernatural or mythical being, etc.; represented or figured with wings.

Her. Having the wings of a specified tincture.

Also in numerous parasynthetic compounds, as *long-winged*, *strong-winged*, *swift-winged*, *white-winged*, etc., q.v. in their alphabetical places.

c **1386** CHAUCER *Knt.'s T.* 527 The wynged god Mercurie. **1426** LYDG. *De Guil. Pilgr.* 22816 Toward the heuene sche took hir fflyght; For..Sche was whynged, ffor to ffle. **1513** DOUGLAS *Æneis* I. x. 13 The vengit god of luif. **1572** BOSSEWELL *Armorie* II. 111 b, An Harpie, Vert, Wynged de Or. **1590** SHAKS. *Mids. N.* I. i. 235 Loue lookes not with the eyes, but with the minde, And therefore is wing'd Cupid painted blinde. **1599** —— *Hen. V*, II. Chorus 7 With winged heeles, as English Mercuries. **1667** MILTON *P.L.* v. 55 One shap'd and wing'd like one of those from Heav'n By us oft seen. **1708** PRIOR *Turtle & Sparrow* 172 Our winged Friends thro' all the Grove. **1819** KEATS *Hyperion* I. 197 His winged minions in close clusters stood. **1846** J. BAXTER *Libr. Pract. Agric.* (ed. 4) I. 66 This insect becomes winged in the month of August. **1854** TENNYSON *Marr. Geraint* 275 Tits, wrens, and all wing'd nothings peck him dead! **1873** E. BALFOUR *Cycl. India* (ed. 2) V, Winged Sea-horses. **1891** FARRAR *Darkn. & Dawn* xv, The stop which regulated the play of the water was formed into the winged figure of a child moulded in silver.

b. *poet.* Applied to a ship with sails set.

c **1586** C'TESS PEMBROKE *Ps.* CVII. viii, How many mounting winged tree For traffique leave retiring land. **1614** W. BROWNE *Inner Temple Masque* i. *Syrens' Song* 1 Steere hither, steere, your winged pines, All beaten mariners. **1634** RAINBOW *Labour* (1635) 34 Why..doe those winged vessels cut the water? **1725** POPE *Odyss.* VIII. 550 From the shores the winged navy flies. **1812** BYRON *Ch. Har.* II. xxviii, Sailors..Coop'd in their winged sea-girt citadel.

†**c.** Full of wings; crowded with flying birds. *poet. Obs.*

1634 MILTON *Comus* 730 Th' earth cumber'd, and the wing'd air dark't with plumes.

2. Furnished with or having a wing or wings, i.e. lateral part(s), appendage(s), or projection(s).

1597 A. M. tr. *Guillemeau's Fr. Chirurg.* 13/1 Ther forme, which we cal *Terrebellum alatum*, the winged trepane. **1613** T. GODWIN *Rom. Antiq.* IV. ii. 178 Sometimes they would make a winged army, so that the maine body thereof should be in the middle, & on each side a lesser company. **1620–55** I. JONES *Stone-Heng* 76 *Dipteros Hypæthros*, which is double winged about uncovered. **1780** A. YOUNG *Tour Irel.* II. 198 Mr. Wyse ploughed lightly with a winged plough. **1844** H. STEPHENS *Bk. Farm* II. 520 Winged grass-seed harrows. **1859** REEVE *Brittany* 176 A well-to-do peasant father and son with the embroidered gaiter, winged leather boot, many-buttoned waistcoat. **1862** *Catal. Internat. Exhib., Brit.* II. No. 5728, A winged wardrobe, with circular ends. **1881** J. EVANS *Anc. Bronze Implem.* 71 The winged celts may be generally described as those in which the flanges are short and have a great amount of lateral extension. **1923** J. C. ROGERS *Engl. Furnit.* fig. 33 A fine example of a winged armchair upholstered in damask.

3. In special scientific applications.

†**a.** *Bot.* = PINNATE 1 a. Also *winged clefts*, the divisions of a pinnatifid leaf (cf. *wing-cleft*, WING *sb.* 24). *Obs.* (An inexact rendering of L. *pinnatus*, in this case intended to mean 'feathered' or 'feather-shaped'.) **b.** *Bot.*, etc. Having wings, i.e. lateral processes or appendages, as a stem, seed, fruit, shell, etc. **c.** *Bot.* in names of plants distinguished by having pinnate leaves (*obs.*), or winged stems or other parts; **winged bean**, a tropical legume, *Psophocarpus tetragonolobus*, native to south-eastern Asia and cultivated for its edible leaves, winged pods, and tubers; cf. *Goa bean* s.v. GOA[1]; **winged elm**, a small N. American species of elm (*Ulmus alata*) with corky winged branches; **winged pea**, a plant of the S. European genus *Tetragonolobus* (now included in *Lotus*), having four-winged pods (see PEA[1] 3); **winged thistle** *N.Z.*, either of two thistles of the genus *Carduus*, *C. tenuiflorus* or *C. pycnocephalus*, which have winged stems.

a. 1668 WILKINS *Real Char.* 84 Winged leaves; like those of Tansy. **1721** MORTIMER *Husb.* (ed. 5) II. 214 Many winged Leaves like those of the Ash. **1776** WITHERING *Brit. Plants* Gloss., *Winged-Leaves*, when an undivided leaf-stalk hath many little leaves growing from each side; as in..Ash and Pea. *Ibid.*, Winged-Clefts. **1796** *Ibid.* (ed. 3) III. 772 Leaf triply-winged.

b. 1776 WITHERING *Brit. Plants* Gloss., *Winged-Leaf-stalk*: one that is not cylindrical, but flattish, with a thin leafy border at each edge. **1787** tr. *Linnæus' Fam. Plants* I. 383 The seeds pedicel'd pendulous three-side-winged. **1822** J. PARKINSON *Outl. Oryctol.* 203 Trigonal, with angular, winged, membranaceous processes. **1866** *Treas. Bot.* 1135/1 *Tetragonolobus*, a genus of leguminous plants allied to *Lotus*, from which they are well distinguished by their quadrangular winged pods.

c. 1650 [W. HOWE] *Phytol. Brit.* 31 Corallina pennata longior. Inter Scopulos. Winged Coralline. **1665** LOVELL *Herball* (ed. 2) 470 Winged wind weed. **1739** MILLER *Gard. Dict.* II, *Ochrus*, Winged Pea. **1832** *Veg. Subst. Food of Man* 168 The Winged Yam. **1858** A. GRAY *Man. Bot. U.S.* (1860) 396 *Ulmus alata*..(Winged Elm). **1910** H. F. MACMILLAN *Handbk. Trop. Gardening & Planting* 189 *Psophocarpus tetragonolobus.* Winged bean; Goa bean; Manilla bean. **1915** *N.Z. Jrnl. Agric.* 21 June 550 Winged thistle [seed]..About the same size as spear-thistle seed. **1966** *Encycl. N.Z.* III. 599/1 Noxious weeds..are here listed... Winged thistle. **1975** *Times* 30 Aug. 12/7 An international panel..[is] recommending a major development effort to turn..the winged bean into a main crop.

4. *fig.* (or in fig. context): Capable of or performing some movement or action figured as flight, 'flying'; flying or passing swiftly, swift, rapid.

1513 DOUGLAS *Æneis* IX. viii. 30 The weyngit messengeir, Fame. **1593** SHAKS. *2 Hen. VI*, III. iii. 16 Combe downe his haire; looke, looke, it stands vpright Like Lime-twigs set to catch my winged soule. **1596** —— *1 Hen. IV*, IV. iv. 2 Beare this sealed Briefe With winged haste to the Lord Marshall. **1600** —— *A.Y.L.* IV. i. 142 *Ros.*.. A Womans thought runs before her actions. *Orl.* So do all thoughts, they are wing'd. **16..** *Lust's Domin.* I. ii. (1657) B 5 b, Old time I'le..be a foot-boy to thy winged hours. **1638** P. VINCENT *True Relat.* in *Mass. Hist. Coll.* (1837) Ser. III. VI. 39 Divers loopholes, through which they let fly their winged messengers [*i.e.* arrows]. **1639** FULLER *Holy War* IV. vii. (1640) 180 Which race [*sc.* the Spanish gennet], for their winged speed, the Poets feigned to be begot of the wind. **1651** —— etc. *Abel Rediv.*, *Ramus* 327 He was belov'd of all that lov'd the fame of learning; for he had a winged name. [Cf. Cicero, *nomen nostrum volitare et vagari.*] **1697** DRYDEN *Virg. Georg.* I. 508 The winged Thunder takes his way From the cold North. **1709** PRIOR *Henry & Emma* 333 And winged Deaths in whistling Arrows fly. **1799** CAMPBELL *Pleas. Hope* II. 377 What though my winged hours of bliss have been, Like angel-visits, few and far between. **1821** CLARE *Vill. Minstrel* I. 175 With double speed the wing'd hour gallops by. **1824** MRS. GRANT *Mem. & Corr.* (1844) III. 65 The dear old friends with whom I passed that winged week. **1866** LOWELL *At Comm. Dinner*, A kind of winged prose that could fly if it would. **1877** MRS. FORRESTER *Mignon* viii, Oswald leaves her with winged heels to make his arrangements. **1877** TENNYSON *Harold* III. ii, Wing'd souls flying Beyond all change and in the eternal distance To settle on the Truth.

b. *esp.* of words or speech (rendering or imitating the Homeric phrase ἔπεα πτερόεντα).

1616 CHAPMAN *Odyss.* x. 488 Circe..Bowing her neare me, these wing'd words did vse. **1697** DRYDEN *Æneis* IV. 388 Then thus, with winged Words, the God began. **1791** COWPER *Iliad* XXII. 92 His mother..Then in wing'd accents, weeping, him bespake. **1813** BYRON *Br. Abydos* I. viii, Through her ears Those winged words like arrows sped. **1876** GEO. ELIOT *Dan. Der.* xxxvi, When our own winged words seem to be hovering around us.

5. *Comb.*, as (in sense 4) ***winged-footed***, ***-heeled***, †(in sense 3 a) ***-leaved*** adjs.

1869 RUSKIN *Q. of Air* i. §26 There..is born the shepherd of the clouds, *winged-footed, and deceiving. **1590** *Winged heeld [see WINGY *a.* 4, quot. 1596]. **1808** COBBETT *Weekly Reg.* 25 June 1001 If..such a winged-heeled gentleman..should be to be found in their country. **1824** LOUDON *Green-house Comp.* I. 88 *Lotus jacobæus*,..A..pea-flower, on a delicate *winged-leaved plant.

Hence **wingedly** ('wɪŋɪdlɪ) *adv.*; **wingedness** ('wɪŋɪdnɪs).

1651 DAVENANT *Gondibert* I. II. lxvii, (So *wingedly he wheeles) No one could catch, what all with trouble finde. **1710** R. WARD *Life H. More* 146 So lightly and wingedly did he pass through it. **1818** KEATS *Endym.* I. 813 Nor with aught else can our souls interknit So wingedly. **1787** BECKFORD *Italy* (1834) II. 325 Such a palpable manifestation of archangelic beauty and *wingedness. **1909** W. BATESON *Mendel's Princ. Heredity* I. x. 172 Here we see that the one 'dose' of wingedness—as we may call it—sufficed only to bring the wings to half the full size, and two 'doses' are needed to develop them properly.

winged (wɪŋd), *ppl. a.* [f. WING *v.* + -ED[1].]

1. Shot or wounded in the wing.

1789 *Ess. on Shooting* xiv. 223 He [*sc.* the dog] should be held in a string, ready to be slipped in case of need, after a winged partridge, or a wounded hare. **1810** *Sporting Mag.* XXXVI. 149 Winged, wounded, or dead birds. **1865** MEREDITH *Rhoda Fleming* xix, He like a winged eagle, striving to raise himself from time to time.

2. Brushed with a bird's wing (WING *v.* 7).

1866 WHITTIER *Snow-bound* 156 We sat the clean-winged hearth about.

wingeing, var. WHINGING *vbl. sb.* and *ppl. a.*

winger ('wɪŋə(r)). [f. WING *sb.* + -ER[1].]

1. *Naut.* A small cask or tank stowed in the wing of a ship's hold (WING *sb.* 9 b (*a*)).

1794 *Rigging & Seamanship* II. 286 The sides are filled-in with wingers of [? or] small casks. **1815** BURNEY *Falconer's Dict. Marine.*

2. In *Assoc. Football*, a player in the (right or left) wing; in *Rugby*, a forward whose place is on the 'wing' in the back row of the scrum. Also in *Hockey* and *Lacrosse*, a wing player.

1896 *Bootle Times* 18 Jan. 3/2 Dow making pretty headway and then passing to the left winger. **1903** P. TREVOR *R.U. Football* 44 The danger..is that a race of mere 'shovers' will succeed a race of 'wingers'. **1922** *Daily Mail* 15 Dec. 13 No right winger has more visibly impressed me than Sutcliffe this season. **1969** *West Australian* 5 July 32/3 Allowing winger Kaye Olsen to gain position and put Wembley into attack.

3. *Naut. slang.* **a.** A steward.

1929 F. C. BOWEN *Sea Slang* 152 *Winger*, a steward waiting at table, with the class prefixed. **1962** *Times* 26 Apr. 15/2 A winger is a steward on a passenger liner. **1962** [see BLOOD *sb.* 15 d].

b. A comrade or friend (see also quot. 1977).

1943 *Penguin New Writing* XVII. 46 He had seen his 'winger', his best friend, decapitated. **1948** PARTRIDGE *Dict. Forces' Slang* 208 *Winger*, an assistant or 'stooge'. The term has displaced 'raggie' as a name for a pal. (Navy.) **1957** R. WATSON-WATT *Three Steps to Victory* xl. 233 Bickell,..Max's *fidus Achates* and 'winger' in M.A.P. and in the wide circles which rippled..out from that most explosive of Ministries. **1977** G. MELLY *Rum, Bum & Concertina* v. 57 The expression 'winger' means, at its most innocent, a young seaman who is taken under the wing of a rating or Petty Officer older and more experienced than himself to be shown the ropes.

4. ***left-winger***, ***right-winger***: see LEFT WING, RIGHT WING.

Hence '**winging** *vbl. sb.* (*Rugby Football*).

1922 J. M. B. SCOTT *Rugby Football* 72 'Winging'..is the most scientific game a forward can play.

wingless ('wɪŋlɪs), *a.* [WING *sb.* + -LESS.] Having no wings; destitute of wings.

Also applied by extension to birds having rudimentary wings not used for flight.

1591 SYLVESTER *Du Bartas* I. v. 808 Mamuques..Food-less they live;..Wing-less they fly. **1668** CHARLETON *Onomast.* 50 *Anthrenus*,..the wingless Hornet. **1704** PETIVER *Gazophyl.* ii. 13, This wingless Wasp I have had from Virginia. **1830** LINDLEY *Nat. Syst. Bot.* 235 They differ from Bignoniaceæ in their wingless seeds. **1835** WORDSW. *Athens & Attica* xiv, The statue of Victory in this temple, was sculptured wingless. **1855** *Orr's Circ. Sci., Inorg. Nat.* 125 The apteryx..a New Zealand wingless bird. **1910** *Encycl. Brit.* II. 233/1 Many wingless insects—such as lice, fleas and certain earwigs and cockroaches.

fig. **1598** BASTARD *Chrestol.* IV. vi. 80 As if my thoughtes.. Winglesse & footelesse, now like snailes did creepe. **1742** YOUNG *Nt. Th.* II. 343 Our freedom chain'd; quite wingless our desire. **1820** SHELLEY *Prometh. Unb.* I. 48 The wingless, crawling hours. **1827** HOOD *Retrospective Rev.* v, My joys are wingless all and dead. **1873** C. E. NORTON *Lett.* (1913) I. 460, I have had to read of late some wingless verse, and it was a delightful refreshment to find in your sonnet poetry that soared.

Hence '**winglessness**.

1890 *Universal Rev.* Apr. 536 The winglessness of the Madeira beetles.

winglet ('wɪŋlɪt). [f. WING *sb.* + -LET.]

1. A little wing; also *transf.* something resembling a little wing, as a petal.

1611 [see 3]. **1800** MOORE *Anacreon* IV. 19 And flights of loves, in wanton ringlets, Flit around on golden winglets. **1851** MEREDITH *Poetry of Shelley* 1 See'st thou a Skylark whose glistening winglets ascending Quiver like pulses beneath the melodious dawn? **1855** ALLINGHAM *Day & Nt. Songs* Ser. II. *The Choice* iii, Pea-bloom winglets.

2. a. *Entom.* A small appendage at the base of each wing or wing-sheath, as in certain flies and beetles, or on each side of the rostrum in certain weevils. **b.** *Ornith.* A process on the terminal joint of a bird's wing, clothed with small and somewhat stiff feathers: also called ***bastard*** or ***false wing***.

1816 KIRBY & SP. *Entomol.* xxiii. (1818) II. 348 The winglets are small concavo-convex scales, of a stiff membranaceous substance. **1862** C. A. JOHNS *Brit. Birds* 263 The Jay..winglet and greater coverts barred with black, white, and bright blue.

3. A small wing-like appendage on some part of dress.

1611 FLORIO, *Talare*,..certaine shooes with winglets as Mercury is fained to weare on his feet. **1870** C. C. BLACK tr. *Demmin's Weapons of War* 43 The small winglets that were attached to the shoulder-pieces of the earlier coats of leather and..were sorts of escutcheons.

4. A small projecting part in a piece of mechanism: see quot.

1835 URE *Phil. Manuf.* 227 L is the winglet, which in turning along with the spindle, has the power of making it traverse and distribute the thread evenly over the surface of the bobbin.

wingmanship ('wɪŋmənʃɪp). [f. WING *sb.* after such words as *oarsmanship*, *penmanship* (see -SHIP 2 b), the meaning of the element *-man-* being lost sight of.] Skill in the use of the wings; flying regarded as an art or accomplishment.

1867 DK. ARGYLL *Reign of Law* 46 To stand still in the air is not..impossible to a flying bird,..but it is one of the most difficult feats of wingmanship. **1923** *Times Lit. Suppl.* 30 Aug. 564/4 In sheer wingmanship, the peregrine has no peer among British birds.

†**wing-thrush.** *Obs.* [? Arising from a misunderstanding of LG. **wîngaardsvogel*, *weingartdrossel*, f. *wîngaard* vineyard, WINYARD + *vogel* bird, *drossel* thrush. Perhaps never current; cf. WINNARD.] The redwing, *Turdus iliacus*.

1544 TURNER *Avium Præcip.* I 7, Tertium genus [Turdorum] ab Anglis a wyngthrushe, et à Germanis eyn weingaerdsuoegel nuncupatur. Hic turdus..maculas habet latiusculas rubras. **1580** HOLLYBAND *Treas. Fr. Tong*, *Litorne*, a birde of the bignesse of a blacke bird called a wing thrushe. **1611** COTGR. s.v. *Litorne*.

†'**wingwise,** *adv. Obs. rare.* [f. WING *sb.* + -WISE.] In the manner of wings: used in quots. in reference to opposite (as distinguished from alternate) leaves.

1551 TURNER *Herbal* I. K ij b, They [*sc.* leaves of Cicer] stand not wyngewyse, that is one ryght against another. **1568** *Ibid.* III. 33 Gratiola..The leaues growe wingwise by coples one against an other.

wingy ('wɪŋɪ), *a.* [f. WING *sb.* + -Y[1].]

†**1.** Of, pertaining to, or resembling a wing or wings; wing-like. *Obs.*

1658 SIR T. BROWNE *Gard. Cyrus* iv. 66 The lower leaf [of leguminous plants] closely involving the rudimental Cod, and the alary or wingy divisions embracing or hanging over it. **1694** ADDISON *Ovid's Met.* II. *Phaeton* 183 With wingy speed [they] outstrip the eastern wind.

2. Having wings, winged (*poet.*); having large or conspicuous wings (cf. *leggy*).

1596 [see 4]. **1718** ROWE tr. *Lucan* v. 1029 If some rushing Storm the Journey cross, The wingy Leaders all are at a loss. **1757** DYER *Fleece* I. 588 With tar Prevent the wingy swarm and scorching heat. **1892** 'MICHAEL FIELD' *Sight & Song* 1 The Indifférent. Watteau. The Louvre... He dances on; the world is his, The sunshine and his wingy hat. **1918** [A. G. GARDINER] *Leaves in Wind* 2 Those wingy, nippy, intrepid insects that we call, vaguely, mosquitoes.

3. *fig.* Capable of 'flight', soaring, aspiring; soaring out of reach, eluding grasp or comprehension.

1643 SIR T. BROWNE *Relig. Med.* I. §9 Those wingy mysteries in Divinity, and airy subtleties in Religion. *Ibid.* §32 The noble Soule..Whose wingy nature ever doth aspire, To reach a place whence first it tooke its fire. **1678** CUDWORTH *Intell. Syst.* I. v. 792 That this [etherial vehicle], being made Light, and Alate or Wingy, might no way hinder the Souls Ascent upward. **1760** BEATTIE *Ode to Hope* II. i, Youth's gallant trophies..invite His wingy nerves to climb. **1855** SINGLETON *Æn.* II. 1121 The phantom-form..a match For wanton winds, and likest wingy [orig. *volucri*] sleep.

4. *Comb.*, as **wingy-footed**, **-heeled** adjs. (cf. *wing-footed*, WING *sb.* 24).

1596 SPENSER *F.Q.* (ed. 2) III. xii. 12 [Fear] fast away did fly, As ashes pale of hew, and wingyheeld [1590 winged heeld]. **1716** ROWE *Ode for 1716* iii. 16 Wingy-footed was he Born. **1740** SOMERVILLE *Hobbinol.* I. 304 Thus on the slacken'd Rope The wingy-footed Artist..Stands tott'ring.

wingy ('wɪŋɪ), *sb. colloq.* [f. WING *sb.* + -Y[6].] A one-armed man; also (with capital initial) used as a nickname. Cf. WING *sb.* 5 d (*c*).

1880 D. W. BARRETT *Navvies* (ed. 2) II. iii. 49 If a poor fellow..is short of a leg or an arm, 'Peggy' or 'Wingy' is at once affixed to him. **1910** H. LAWSON *Stories* (1964) 2nd Ser. 296 Wingy..is a ratty little one-armed man whose case is usually described in the head-line as 'A 'Armless Case' by one of our great dailies. **1931** 'D. STIFF' *Milk & Honey Route* v. 58 Missions are very anxious to recruit the 'wingies' and 'armies', or the one-armed hobos. **1964** T. RONAN *Packhorse & Pearling Boat* 129 As Dad later referred to him as 'Wingy' Collins I presume that he had one arm amputated, or some similar disability.

†**wining,** *sb. Obs.* In *white-wining* [app. f. WHITE WINE + -ING[3]], a variety of apple.

1676 WORLIDGE *Vinetum Brit.* etc. 161 The White-Wining, is a small white Apple;..the fruit juicy and pleasant, but soon perishing.

wining ('waɪnɪŋ), *vbl. sb.* Also **wineing.** [f. WINE *v.* + -ING[1].] The drinking of wine in company. Also *attrib.*

1847 MRS. GORE *Castles* xiii. I. 287 Hampden's rooms [at Cambridge], where one of our so-called wining parties was prepared. **1891** *Daily News* 2 Oct. 5/1 At the wining, he finished his reply to the toast of the evening with a happy conceit. **1917** *Morning Post* 16 Feb. 4/2 Lunching, dining, and wineing with English members..made them the dupes of the Liberal party.

So '**wining** *ppl. a.*, wine-drinking.

?**1755** [E. THOMPSON] *Meretriciad* (1765) 13 When sep'rate you enjoy'd the wining man, What could resist a well-laid bedded plan?

wining(e, obs. forms of WINNING *vbl. sb.*

winish ('waɪnɪʃ), *a.* Now *rare.* Also 6 **wynyshe**, **-is(s)he.** [f. WINE *sb.*[1] + -ISH[1].] Having the quality or nature of wine; resembling wine.

1540 PALSGR. *Acolastus* III. iv. Q iij, I neuer that wot of, haue I dronk wyne more wynyshe, or purer from any water put vnto it. **1551** TURNER *Herbal* I. C v b, A wynisshe iuyce. **1665** HAVERS *P. della Valle's Trav. E. India* 70 *Ananas*..the whole Fruit is..held to be hot and good to promote digestion, having in my opinion, somewhat of a winish taste and strength. **1741** *Compl. Fam.-Piece* I. i. 43 Use no Wine, or winish Possets.

wink (wɪŋk), *sb.*[1] Forms: see WINK *v.*[1]; also 7 **whinke.** [f. WINK *v.*[1]]

1. A closing of the eyes for sleep; a (short) spell of sleep, a nap. *rare* exc. as in b, c.

In Shaks. in phr. referring to death.

1362 LANGL. *P. Pl.* A. v. 3 þenne Wakede I of my wink. *c* **1375** *Sc. Leg. Saints* xxvii. (*Machor*) 1204 Till þai þe seruice all had mad, þat to sic deide men suld parteyne, Or ony wink come in þar eyne. *c* **1450** *Cov. Myst.* (Shaks. Soc.) 343 Here I Aske To go to taske A wynke. **1610** SHAKS. *Temp.* II. i. 285 Whiles you doing thus, To the perpetuall winke for aye might put This ancient morsell. **1611** —— *Wint. T.* I. ii. 317 Thou..might'st be-spice a Cup, To giue mine Enemy a lasting Winke. **1869** MRS. A. WHITNEY *We Girls* vi, 'What is it, dear?' asked Mrs. Hobart, rousing from a little arm-chair wink.

b. Phr. (*not*) *to sleep a* or *one wink*, (*not*) *a wink of sleep*, etc.

1303 R. BRUNNE *Handl. Synne* 9146 þey..Ne mete ete, ne drank drynke, Ne slepte onely a-lepy wynke. *c* **1325** *Metr. Hom.* 79 That might he nouther ete ne drink, Ne have night rest, ne slepe no wynk. **1508** DUNBAR *Poems* vi. 14 This night I myght nocht sleip a wink. **1513** DOUGLAS *Æneis* IV. x. 15 For neuir mair may scho sleip a wynk. **1542** UDALL *Erasm. Apoph.* 316 *marg.*, Reuilus a vigilaunte consul, for ne neuer slept wynke in his consulship. **1611** SHAKS. *Cymb.* III. iv. 103 Since I receiu'd command to do this businesse, I haue not slept one winke. **1682** N. O. *Boileau's Lutrin* II. 22 My aking head can get no wink of Sleep! **1740** RICHARDSON *Pamela* II. 167, I will go to-bed; but not one Wink, I fear, shall I get this Night. **1840** DICKENS *Old C. Shop* v, Whether Mr. Quilp took any sleep by snatches of a few winks at a time. **1883** MISS BROUGHTON *Belinda* I. ix, He has slept no wink all night. **1891** KIPLING *Light that Failed* xiii, I can't sleep a wink with you at the window.

c. *forty winks*: a very brief sleep, a short nap. *colloq.*

1828 EGAN *Finish to Tom & Jerry* iii. (1871) 87 The uncommonly big gentleman, told out, taking forty winks. **1851** *Westm. Rev.* July 326 His quiet 'forty winks' after dinner. **1890** J. HATTON *By order of Czar* II. iv, 'Well, I declare, Dolly, you are going to sleep!' 'I am very tired; only forty winks. Is there time?'

2. a. A glance or significant movement of the eye (often accompanied by a nod) expressing command, assent, invitation, or the like. *Obs.* exc. in the proverb ***a nod's as good as a wink to a blind horse*** (see also NOD *sb.*[1] 1), and phr. ***to tip, give***, or ***get the wink*** (now apprehended as sense 5).

1500–20 DUNBAR *Poems* lxxxiv. 35 3itt women sould.. Thair vertewis all mak of na availlis, Be subtill winkis, and thair desaitfull talis. **1540** ELYOT *Image Gov.* xxxviii. (1541) 94 Of a mayster sturdy and fierce, a lyttell wynke to his seruant is a fearefull commaundement. **1583** MELBANCKE *Philotimus* S j b, I am not so blind, that thou canst make me beleue with a winke, it is midnight at noone day. **1591** SYLVESTER *Du Bartas* I. v. 24 Thou eternall Father, at whose wink The wrathfull Ocean's swelling pride doth sink. **1602** SHAKS. *Ham.* IV. v. 11. *a* **1631** DONNE *Poems, Sunne Rising* 13 Thy beames, so reverend and strong Why shouldst thou thinke? I could eclipse and cloud them with a winke. **1676** ETHEREDGE *Man of Mode* I. i, I only tip him the wink, he knows an Ale-house from a Hovel. **1710** S. PALMER *Proverbs* 100 A nod and a wink are very often treacherous and false. **1756–7** tr. *Keysler's Trav.* (1760) III. 313 At last..he gave him the wink. **1760–72** H. BROOKE *Fool of Qual.* (1809) III. 139 Harry, upon a wink, stepped out. *a* **1774** GOLDSM. tr. *Scarron's Com. Romance* (1775) II. 262 The surgeon, who had previously got the wink, confined him to his bed. **1809** MALKIN *Gil Blas* IV. v. ¶11 Don Felix thinks a wink as good as a nod. **1818** SCOTT *Hrt. Midl.* xvi, A wink's as gude as a nod to a blind horse. **1832** HT. MARTINEAU *Each & All* v. 69 On this, the wink went round, and the neighbours dropped off. **1872** C. GIBBON *For the King* xvii, He gave me the wink that the lady was a friend of his.

b. A glance or glimpse. (Cf. BLINK *sb.*[2] 2.)

[**1598–1868**: see EYE-WINK a.] **1848** DICKENS *Dombey* xii, A trifle of orthography, a glance at ancient history, a wink or two at modern ditto.

3. *transf.* **a.** A moment of time, as being that occupied by a glance of the eyes; phr. ***in a wink*** (†***with*** or ***at a wink***), in a trice. (Cf. EYE-WINK b.)

1585 MONTGOMERIE *Sonn.* xiii. 4 Bright Apollo..Quhais glorious glance 3it stoutly skaillis the skyis, Quhen with a wink we wonder vhair they war. **1596** DALRYMPLE tr. *Leslie's Hist. Scot.* (S.T.S.) II. 206 How..radie to do the king pleisour, at a wink quhen he wald charge. **1633** EARL MANCH. *Al Mondo* (1636) 31 Man is only a winke of life. **1658** J. ROBINSON *Endoxa* 33 The rest..were coexisting with their first Being; or, upon the least Wink of Opportunity, prest to be drawn forth. **1693** SOUTHERNE *Maid's last Prayer* III. ii, The company will be here in a wink, as a body may say. **1790** D. MORISON *Poems* 7 Then aff a' wallop in a wink. **1826** HOOD *I Remember* 5 He [*sc.* the sun] never came a wink too soon. **1859** TENNYSON *Vivien* 701 For in a wink the false love turns to hate. **1893** STEVENSON *Catriona* xxx. 362 The next wink of time their blades clashed together.

b. (*not*) ***a wink***: (not) the slightest amount; esp. in ***not to see a wink***.

1596 NASHE *Saffron Walden* S 3, Hath he..exprest in his countenaunce the least wincke of dislike of them? **1610** SHAKS. *Temp.* II. i. 242 Ambition cannot pierce a winke beyond. **1621** MOLLE *Camerar. Liv. Libr.* II. xiii. 117 He was shut into a hole where he saw not a whinke. **1706** ESTCOURT *Fair Example* v. i, *Whims.* Look up, I say... *Sym*... In Sincerity, Sir, I can't see a Wink. **1841** THACKERAY *Gt. Hoggarty Diamond* v, At least in my bed-room..I could not see a wink.

c. In *Work Study*, a unit of time equivalent to one two-thousandth of a minute. Also *Comb.*, as ***wink-counter***. orig. *U.S.*

1937 R. M. BARNES *Motion & Time Study* ix. 72 There are 100 equal divisions on the dial of the clock; therefore, time is indicated directly in 1/2000 of a minute by the large hand. This time interval of 1/2000 of a minute was called a 'wink' by Gilbreth. **1946** R. L. MORROW *Time Study & Motion Economy* ix. 90 The wink-counter..is a small motor driven device, originated by Professor David B. Porter..to be used for both motion and time studies. In appearance it resembles a 'speedometer'. **1961** *Engineering* 15 Sept. 352/1 A very early type of micromotion filming was used by the Gilbreths in the early days of motion study, and the unit of time which they employed, a two thousandth of a minute or a 'wink', is still often used for detailed motion analysis.

4. A nictitation of the eyelid; a blink.

1611 SHAKS. *Wint. T.* v. ii. 119 Euery winke of an Eye, some new Grace will be borne. **1825** SCOTT *Talism.* xvii, Mark me the smallest twitch of the features, or wink of the eyelid. **1848** THACKERAY *Van. Fair* xi, Sir Giles Wapshot had a particularly noisy manner of imbibing his soup, and her ladyship a wink of the left eye.

5. An act of winking (see WINK *v.*[1] 8).

1837 DICKENS *Pickw.* ix, Jingle..then..added, with a knowing wink, and a jerk of the thumb towards the interior of the chaise [etc.]. *Ibid.* lvi, He had been much struck with Mary's appearance; having, in fact, bestowed several very unfatherly winks upon her, already. **1848** THACKERAY *Van. Fair* xiv, 'That is, if you're not on duty to that pretty Miss Sedley,' Crawley said, with a knowing wink. **1851** D. JERROLD *St. Giles* vii. 60 [He] gave a saucy wink to the servant, and bounded..up stairs. **1891** EARL ROSEBERY *Pitt* xiii. 227 Facts of this kind can of course be always dismissed by a knowing wink or a sarcastic smile.

6. *attrib.* and *Comb.*

1708 CIBBER *Lady's Last Stake* I. i. 9 Tea!.. Heart-opening, Wink-tipping Cordial. **1775** S. J. PRATT *Liberal Opin.* lxxiv. (1783) III. 51 Upon mention of the wink money, he was driving off as fast as he could. **1902** MONKSHOOD & GAMBLE *Kipling* 191 One of Mr. Kipling's jaunty,..wink-tipping sketches. **1903** HARDY *Dynasts* I. VI. i, Should issues stand at pause But for a wink-while.

wink, *sb.*[2] *s.w. dial.* Var. WINCH *sb.*[1]

1847 HALLIWELL, *Wink*..(2) A winch, or crank. *West.* **1873** WILLIAMS & JONES *Gloss. Som.*, *Wink*, an excavated or sunken well. **1878** D. KEMP *Yacht & Boat Sailing* 380 *Wink*, a west country term for a kind of winch used in the bow of a boat by fishermen to raise the anchor. **1886** ELWORTHY *W. Som. Word-bk.*, *Wink*, a well from which the water is drawn by a winch, chain, and bucket. **1919** CHOPE *Some Old Farm Implem.* 23 The apparatus for spinning rope was known as a wink (winch) or spinner.

wink, *sb.*[3] *slang.* Short for WINKLE *sb.*

1851 MAYHEW *Lond. Labour* I. 76/1 The 'wink' men, as these periwinkle sellers are called. *Ibid.* 479/2 Salt (or fresh) herrings, winks, or shrimps.

wink, *sb.*[4] Shortening of TIDDLYWINK 2 c. orig. *U.S.*

1890 *Game of Tiddledy Winks* (McLoughlin Bros., New York) 1 Its great interest and success lies in the novel feature of jumping the Winks into the Wink-pot. **1957** *Times* 17 Dec. 9/4 Tiddlywinks does not yet qualify for a 'blue', or even half a one, but it is nice to know that the club has a tie, dark blue with a blue cup and a wink rampant. **1979** F. R. SHAPIRO *Encycl. Tiddlywinks* 8 The Silver Wink, donated by Prince Philip, is awarded to the winner of an annual elimination tournament for universities.

wink (wɪŋk), *v.*[1] Forms: 1 **wincian**, 3 **winken**, 4–6 **wynk(e**, 4–7 **winke**, **winck**, 6–7 **wincke**, (4 *Sc.* **vynk**, 5 **wynkyn**, *pa. t.* **wanke**, **wonk**, 6 **wynck(e**, 9 *pa. t.* and *pa. pple.* **wunk**), 4– **wink.** [OE. *wincian* wk. vb. = OS. *wincon* to nod, MLG., MDu. *winken*, related to OHG. *winchan* str. vb. (MHG., G. *winken*) to move sideways, stagger, nod; cf. OHG. *winch* (MHG. *winc*, G. *wink*) m. nod, OE. *wince* WINCH *sb.*[1]: f. Teut. *wiŋk-*, older *weŋk-*:—Indo-Eur. *weŋg-*.

Other formations on the base *wiŋk-* (*weŋk-*): *waŋk-*:—*weŋg-*: *woŋg-*, to move sideways or from side to side, are OHG. *wanc*, *wanch*, MHG. *wanc* turning, return, instability, OS., OHG. *wankôn* (MLG., MDu., MHG. *wanken*); OHG. *wenkan*, OS. *wenkean* to waver, vacillate (MLG., MDu., Du. *wenken* to nod), whence OF. *guenchir* WINCH *v.*[1]; Lith. *véngiu* to do unwillingly, avoid, *vangùs* inactive, *vingis* m. bend, curve, Albanian *vank* (*vang-*) felloe. See also WANKLE *a.*, WENCHEL.

Examples of a strong conjugation in English (pa. t. *wank*, *wonk*) are very rare. The modern pa. t. and pa. pple. *wunk* are jocular.]

†**1. a.** *intr.* To close one's eyes. (Also in fig. context: cf. 5, 6.) *Obs.*

c **897** ÆLFRED *Gregory's Past. C.* xxxix. 287 Se stæpð forð mid ðam fotum & wincaþ mid ðæm eaȝum [orig. *oculos claudit*]. *c* **1000** ÆLFRIC *Gram.* xxvi. (Z.) 156 Ic wincige, *connіveo*. *a* **1225** *Ancr. R.* 288 Hwon þe heorte draweð lust into hire, ase þing þet were amased, & foð on ase to winken & forte leten þene ueond iwurðen. *c* **1374** CHAUCER *Troylus* III. 1537 Al for nought he may wel lygge and wynke But slep ne may þere in his herte synke. *c* **1386** —— *Nun's Pr. T.* 486 He wolde so peyne hym, that with bothe hise eyen He moste wynke, so loude he wolde cryen. *Ibid.* 611 For he that wynketh whan he sholde see, Al wilfully god lat him neuere thee. **1390** GOWER *Conf.* I. 54 For ofte, who that hiede toke, Betre is to winke than to loke. *c* **1480** HENRYSON *Two Mice* 333 Quhylis wald he lat hir rin vnder the stra; Quylis wald he wink, and play with hir buk heid. *c* **1500** in *Rel. Ant.* I. 289 Sore me for-thinked, that I so moche wynked, For had I never more nede than nowe for to loke. *a* **1542** WYATT in *Tottel's Misc.* (Arb.) 57 For cause your self do wink, Ye iudge all other blinde. **1562** [see WINKING *ppl. a.* 1]. **1584** LYLY *Campaspe* IV. iv. 4 Though I winke, I sleepe not. **1611** SHAKS. *Cymb.* V. iv. 194 There are none want eyes, to direct them the way I am going, but such as winke, and will not vse them. **1621** in Kempe *Losely MSS.* (1836) 454 When you see y^m [*sc.* the nuns] they must winke and not speake to you. *a* **1631** DONNE *Serm.*, *John x. 10* (1640) 70 That man that is blinde, or that will winke, shall see no more sunne upon S. Barnabies day, then upon S. Lucies. **1633** G. HERBERT *Temple, Collar* 26 Good cable, to enforce and draw, And be thy law, While thou didst wink and wouldst not see. **1664** TILLOTSON *Wisdom of being religious* 44 Men are not blind, but they wink, and shut their eyes; they can understand, and will not. **1700** S. L. tr. *Fryke's Voy. E. Ind.* 236, I open'd my Eyes..and [they] said, it was high time for me to open 'em; for if I had winck'd but a little longer, over I had gone. **1784** COWPER *Tiroc.* 255 To follow foolish precedents, and wink With both our eyes, is easier than to think. **1816** SCOTT *Bl. Dwarf* v, I thought I saw him still, though I winked as close as ever I could.

winking *pr. pple.*: with the eyes shut (or blindfolded).

c **1375** *Cursor M.* 23462 (Fairf.) Als wele þen saltow se Wincande als wiþ opin eye. **1390** GOWER *Conf.* II. 189 Thoas..Whan Anthenor this Juel tok, Wynkende caste awei his lok. **1538** ELYOT *Dict.* Addit., *Andabatæ*, certayne men that faughte with swordes wynkynge. **1599** SHAKS. *Hen. V*, v. ii. 332 *Burg.* They are then excus'd, my Lord, when they see not what they doe. *King.* Then good my Lord, teach your Cousin to consent winking.

†**b.** Said of the eyes, occas. *transf.* of other things: To close. *Obs.* or *rare arch.*

In quots. 1598, 1898, said of the closing of the day.

1340 HAMPOLE *Pr. Consc.* 4970 In als short whyle als hert may thynk, Or mans eghe may open or wynk. **1576** GASCOIGNE *Steele Glas* 683 That one eye winks, as though it were but blynd. **1577** GRANGE *Golden Aphrod.* I ij, Yet coulde he not perswade himselfe whether he dreamed ..(although he knew of a certentie his eyes winked not). **1598** *Mucedorus* IV. i. 38 The christall eye of Heauen shall not thrise wincke,..Till we salute the Aragonian King. **1642** H. MORE *Song of Soul* II. I. II. i, While the Evening keen With sharper air doth make his pores to wink. **1649** DAVENANT *Love & Hon.* III. iv. 44 Where shadows vanish when the world's eye wincks Behind a cloud. **1898** MEREDITH *Odes Fr. Hist.* 69 The sister Hours..Are gone on flow with the day that winked, With the night that spanned at golden gates.

†**c.** In association with drinking off at a draught.

1548 ELYOT *Dict.*, *Amystis*, a..drynke, which the Thracians vsed to drynke vp at one draughte, wynkyng. **15..** *Wyf of Auchtirmwchty* 76 in *Bannatyne MS.* (Hunter. Club) 344 Ay scho winkit and scho drank. **1692** BENTLEY *Boyle Lect.* ii. 37 And yet these same cautious and quick-sighted Gentlemen can wink and swallow down this sottish Opinion about Percipient Atoms.

2. a. To open and shut one's eyes momentarily and involuntarily; to blink, nictitate.

a **1300** *Cursor M.* 341 All his comament was don, Suiftliker þen hee may wink. *c* **1440** *Promp. Parv.* 530/1 Wynkyn, idem quod twynkelyn. *a* **1450** *Knt. de la Tour* xii, She loked small and wynked ofte,..euer beting her eyelyddes togedre. *c* **1500** *Lancelot* 1058 When that he felt the vatter that vas cold, He wonk, and gan about hyme to behold. **1582** STANYHURST *Æneis* IV. (Arb.) 108 At my tears showring dyd he sigh? dyd he winck with his eyelyd? **1649** JER. TAYLOR *Gt. Exemp.* II. Disc. ix. 122 It is impossible to prevent them..any more than we can refuse to winke with our eye when a sudden blow is offered at it. **1703** *Lond. Gaz.* No. 3892/4 Robert Stephens,..Stammering Speech, winks on the left Eye. **1819** SHELLEY *Cyclops* 631 Dare not to breathe, Or spit, or e'en wink, lest ye wake the monster. **1842** DICKENS *Amer. Notes* iii, The white wooden houses (so white that it makes one wink to look at them). **1853** —— *Bleak Ho.* xxi, He..adjusts his skull-cap with such a rub, that the old man winks with both eyes for a minute afterwards. **1916** *Q. Rev.* July 227 When there is a loud report close at hand we instinctively wink.

b. Said of the eyes or eyelids: To blink. Also occas. of other things: To open and shut quickly. Now *rare*.

1661 LOVELL *Hist. Anim. & Min.* Isagoge b 3, Amongst Birds..The eyes, are as those of other creatures,..but they winke, a membrane passing from the angle. **1668** CULPEPPER & COLE *Barthol. Anat.* II. vii. 111 The trebble-pointed valves do not only wink, but they are close shut by the blood distending the Heart. **1710** J. CLARKE tr. *Rohault's Nat. Philos.* I. xxxv, When we look upon a lighted Candle at a little Distance with our Eyes winking. **1814** SCOTT *Ld. of Isles* VI. xv, The eye-lid scarce had time to wink. **1905** A. T. SHEPPARD *Red Cravat* I. ii. 24 The eyes winked-to again and closed for ever.

c. Of a light, a burning or glowing object, etc.: To emit quick intermittent flashes; to twinkle. (Now associated with sense 8.) Also with advbs.: to go *out* or *off* suddenly; to come *on* suddenly.

1591 SYLVESTER *Du Bartas* I. ii. 665 Like as a coal, that winkt [orig. *qui dort*] On a stick's end (and seemed quite extinct). *a* **1633** AUSTIN *Medit.* (1635) 81 [The Light of Nature] is no Starre indeed, but a Candle: and..it winkes in the Socket too. **1707** E. SMITH *Phædra & Hipp.* I. i. 5 Feed with new Oil the wasting Lamp of Life, That winks and trembles, now, just now expiring. **1802** WORDSW. *Sonn.*, '*Fair star of evening*', Thou..shouldst wink, Bright Star! with laughter on her banners. **1820** KEATS *To a Nightingale* ii, A beaker..With beaded bubbles winking at the brim. **1848** THACKERAY *Lett.* Nov., The candles are just winking out. **1851** MEREDITH *Love in Valley* xvii, A rill where on sand the minnows wink. **1876** MISS BRADDON *J. Haggard's Dau.* x, The polished grate winking and twinkling in the red light from a neat little fire. **1883** HARDY *Wessex Tales* (1888) I. 16 Beyond all this winked a few bleared lamplights through the beating drops. **1930** W. FAULKNER *As I lay Dying* 244 He locks the door. Dewey Dell is inside. Then the light winks out. **1972** *Sci. Amer.* Jan. 108/3 An observer who is a few miles away but within the shadow sees the star wink off and five minutes later reappear slightly west of the moon. **1979** *Tucson* (Arizona) *Citizen* 20 Sept. 7B/6 (*heading*) 'Buck Rogers' no supernova, but it won't wink out, either. **1982** *Washington Post* 21 Mar. 3/2 Bleuzinski perched on the pool table, leaned forward and looked directly into the camera. The red light winked on.

†**3.** To have the eyes closed in sleep; to sleep; sometimes, to doze, slumber. *Obs.*

1375 BARBOUR *Bruce* VII. 182 The kyng than vynkit a litill we. **1412–20** LYDG. *Chron. Troy* IV. 2384 Ofte he waketh whan he sholde winke. *c* **1430** *How Wise Man Tauȝt his Sonne* 72 in *Babees Bk.* 50 And go to bedde bi tymes, & wynke. *c* **1480** HENRYSON *Want of Wyse Men* 22 For warldly wyn sik walkis, quhen wysar wynkis. **1535** *Goodly Primer* L ij b (*Ps.* cxxi. 4), Loo, neyther wyll he slepe, nor yet ons wynke, that kepeth Israell. **1553** *Respublica* 1135 Repose yourselfe, Madame, a while & winke. **1602** FULBECKE *1st Pt. Parall.* 19 Yes, our law in this case hath not either slumbred or winked. **1610** SHAKS. *Temp.* II. i. 216 Thou let'st thy fortune sleepe: die rather: wink'st Whiles thou art waking. **1616** T. SCOT *Philomythie* B 6 b, When others soundly sleep, he must but winke. **1649** J. TAYLOR (Water P.) *Wand. Wonders West* 8 Wearinesse..began to inforce sleep upon me, so that..I began to winke.

†**4.** To close one eye, as in aiming at a target; hence, to aim: usually ***to wink with the one*** or ***the other eye***. *Obs.*

c **1340** *Nominale* (Skeat) 180 *Homme doile clune*, M[an] with ee wynkyth. *c* **1460** *Frere & Boye* (Ritson) 89 Yf thou shote and wynke, The prycke thow shalt hytte. *c* **1480** HENRYSON *Trial of Fox* 959 His Hude he drew laich attour his Ene, And, winkand with ane Eye, furth he wend. **1530** PALSGR. 782/2 He that wynketh with one eye and loketh with the tother, I wyll nat trust hym and he were my brother. **1538** ELYOT *Dict.*, *Collimare*, to wynke with one eye. **1594** BLUNDEVIL *Exerc.*, *Navig.* xxii. (1597) 329 Mooue the Transame..vntil you may see with the one eye (winking with yᵉ other) the one end of the transame to meete iust with the centre..of the Sun. **1638** SIR T. HERBERT *Trav.* (ed. 2) 20 The *Arimaspi* (who from wincking when they shoot are said to be *Monoculi*). *a* **1680** BUTLER *Rem.*, *Satyr Imperfect. Hum. Learn.* I. 55 As Men, that wink with one Eye, see more true, And take their Aim much better, than with two.

5. a. To 'shut one's eyes' to something faulty, wrong, or improper; to be complaisant. (Now *rare* exc. as in 6.)

c **1480** HENRYSON *Cock & Fox* 571, I wes vnwyse that winkit at thy will. **1562** COOPER *Answ. Def. Truth* 61 b, Some learned and holy men for the time did winke and beare with suche thinges. **1633** G. HERBERT *Temple, Miserie* xi, And yet as though he knew it not, His knowledge winks and lets his humours reigne. **1781** COWPER *Expost.* 256 Too just to wink, or speak the guilty clear. **1859** TENNYSON *Vivien* 630 Is he man at all, who knows and winks? **1861** READE *Cloister & H.* xlvi, Many is the time I have winked and wouldn't see too much.

b. Phr. ***to wink hard***. Now *rare* or *Obs.*

1620 QUARLES *Feast for Wormes* iii. Med. iii. 38 Hard must he winke, that shuts his eyes from heau'n. **1790** BURNS *Prol. Suthld.* 40 And aiblins when they winna stand the test, Wink hard and say, the folks hae done their best! **1831** SCOTT *Ct. Robt.* ii, The Emperor, who will rather wink hard than see disagreements. **1866** GEO. ELIOT *F. Holt* ii, Jermyn must be his [election-]agent; Harold must wink hard till he found himself safely returned.

6. a. ***to wink at***. (*a*) To 'shut one's eyes to' (an offence, fault, defect, impropriety, or irregularity); to connive at.

1537 CROMWELL in Merriman *Life & Lett.* (1902) II. 108 Persons that..by..wynkyng at his preparacions.. encouraged hym to be the bolder. **1540** ELYOT *Image Gov.* xxxiii. (1541) 76 b, Ye secretely winkyng at the sayd faultes. **1644** MILTON *Judgm. Bucer* xlvii. 24 When as all kind of unchastity is tolerated, fornications and adulteries winkt at. *a* **1708** T. WARD *Eng. Ref.* I. (1710) 112 If I this saucyness in you, Shou'd seem to wink-at or allow. **1775** SHERIDAN *Rivals* III. iii, Suppose you were to wink at her corresponding with him for a little time. **1815** SCOTT *Guy M.* xxxiv, You had the price of half a cargo for winking at our job. **1861** TROLLOPE *La Beata* I. ix. 250 A very evident tendency..to wink at the shortcomings of their friends.

(*b*) To disregard, overlook, pass unnoticed (a fact or occurrence). Now *rare* or *Obs.*

1535 JOYE *Apol. Tindale* (Arb.) 32 He stretched forth his penne agenst me as farre as he dirst,..at the whiche chaleng I winked. **1568** *Bible* (Bishops') Acts xvii. 30 And the tyme of this ignoraunce God wyncked at. *a* **1656** BP. HALL *Rem. Wks.* (1660) 371 We do willingly wink at the rest of the differences of like nature. **1691** *Weesils* Postscr. 13 Some, who,..either wink at, or absolutely forget her admirable, tho plain Principles. **1848** SCHOMBURGK *Ralegh's Discov. Guiana* (Hakl. Soc.) 172 It is..evident that they winked at consequences which they must have foreseen.

†(*c*) To be complaisant with (an offending or contumacious person); to connive at the doings of.

1567 *Reg. Privy Council Scot.* I. 516 Seing the saidis rebellis ourlukit and winkit at be sic as duellis maist ewest to thame. **1605** SHAKS. *Macb.* I. iv. 52 Let not Light see my black and deepe desires: The Eye winke at the Hand. **1674** *Jackson's Recantation* C 2, My other two Comerades [in thieving] lay in an Inn where they..were winkt at by the Master of the House. **1703** DE FOE *More Reform.* 37 Thou art blam'd for Winking at a L--d Whose Rapes and Vices stand upon Record.

†**b.** (*a*) ***to wink on, upon***: = a(*a*), above. *Obs.*

1546 J. HEYWOOD *Prov.* (1867) 19 She can wynke on the yew, and wery the lam. **1591** SHAKS. *Two Gent.* II. iv. 98 Vpon a homely obiect, Loue can winke. **1634** MILTON *Comus* 401 You may as well..bid me hope Danger will wink on Opportunity. **1824** LANDOR *Imag. Conv.* I. *Cromwell & Noble* 59, I acknowledge his weaknesses, and cannot wink upon his crimes. **1835** LYTTON *Rienzi* I. v, Justice must never wink upon great offenders.

†(*b*) ***to wink against***: = a(*b*), above. *Obs.*

1653 H. MORE *Antid. Ath.* III. xv. §4 He that denies this seems to me wilfully to wink against the light of Nature. **1741** WATTS *Improv. Mind* I. i. (1786) 21 Having asserted his former opinions in a most confident manner, he is tempted now to wink a little against the truth.

†**c.** *trans.* = a(*a*), above. *Obs. rare.*

1570 *Satir. Poems Reform.* xviii. 58 Trow ȝe..that God omnipotent Will wynk vnsene sic wickitnes and wrang? **1695** KENNETT *Par. Antiq.* ix. 301 This cheat was winkt in the times of ignorance.

†**7. a.** *intr.* To give a significant glance, as of command, direction, or invitation: usually const. *on, upon*, later *to, at*. *Obs.*

c **1100** *Gloss.* in Wr.-Wülcker 118/15 *Annicto uel annuto*, ic wincie. **13..** *Minor Poems of Vernon MS.* xxxvii. 680 Whon þei comen togedere, eiþer on oþer wynkeþ. **1377** LANGL. *P. Pl.* B. IV. 152, I seiȝe mede in the moot-halle on men of lawe wynke, And þei lawghyng lope to hire. *Ibid.* XIII. 85 Pacience perceyued what I thouȝt, and wynked on me to be stille. *c* **1386** CHAUCER *Sqr.'s T.* 340 The Norice of digestioun the sleepe Gan on hem wynke. *c* **1400** *Gamelyn* 453 Whan I wynke on the loke for to gone. **14..** *K. Edw. & Shepherd* in Hartshorne *Metr. T.* (1829) 79 Oure kyng on the schepherde wanke, Priuely with his eye. *c* **1520** SKELTON *Magnyf.* 2023 Syr, remembre the tourne of Fortunes whele, That wantonly can wynke, and wynche with her hele. **1530** PALSGR. 782/2 He hath wynked upon me thrise, what so ever he meaneth. **1552** HULOET, Wyncke at one, *adnicto*. **1599** SHAKS. *Hen. V*, v. ii. 333, I will winke on her to consent, my Lord. **1623** MIDDLETON *More Dissemblers* III. i, Then cast she up Her pretty eye and wink'd. **1640** tr. *Verdere's Rom. of Rom.* II. xxxiii. 124 She winked to him, whereupon he approaching with a great deal of respect unto the Queen [etc.]. **1671** CARYL *Sir Salomon* II. 30 Why could not you tell me on't? *Single.* I wincked, and wincked upon you, and did all that I could. **1711** ADDISON *Spect.* No. 57 ¶7, I winked upon my Friend to take his Leave. **1782** MME. D'ARBLAY *Diary* 4 Nov., Mrs. Thrale winked at him to give up the place. **1819** *Sporting Mag.* (N.S.) IV. 236 Davis winked to his friends that it was all right. **1821** MONCRIEFF *Tom & Jerry* II. iii. 43 Winking at me not to take any notice. **1835** DICKENS *Sk. Boz*, *Astley's*, Ma having first nodded and winked to the governess to pull the girls' frocks a little more off their shoulders.

†**b.** ? To 'give the tip'. *Obs. rare.*

c **1460** *Towneley Myst.* xii. 244 Haue good aylle of hely; bewar now, I wynk, For and thou drynk drely, in thy polle wylle it synk.

†**c.** *transf.* To make a sign. *Obs. rare.*

1738 [G. SMITH] *Curious Relat.* II. 337 The Image of *Sichæus* which stands on the Altar, winks with its Hand.

†**d.** *trans.* To bring into a specified state by a glance or nod. *Obs.*

1633 G. HERBERT *Temple, Home* vii, What is this woman-kinde, which I can winke Into a blacknesse and distaste? **1728** SWIFT *Jrnl. Mod. Lady* 193 They..Convey a Libel in a Frown, Or wink a Reputation down.

†**e.** phr. ***wink all hid*** [see HIDE *v.*[1] 1 e, and cf. OF. *clignemusset*]: hide-and-seek. *Obs.*

1609 J. DAVIES *Humour's Heaven* II. iv, So that he did Driue them from dancing vnto Winck-all-hid.

8. *intr.* To close one eye momentarily, in a flippant or frivolous manner, esp. to convey intimate information or to express good-humoured interest.

1837 DICKENS *Pickw.* xxxiii, Mr. Weller..winked so indefatigably..that Sam began to think he must have got the *tic doloureux* in his right eye-lid. **1838** —— *Nich. Nick.* xvi, He winked towards Nicholas with a degree of familiarity which he, no doubt, intended for a rather flattering compliment. **1886** KIPLING *Departm. Ditties* etc. (1888) 73 An' Jock he sniggered, an' Jock he smiled, An' ower the card-brim wunk. **1912** G. B. SHAW *Pygmalion* II. 142 He winks at Higgins.

9. a. *trans.* To close (an eye, the eyes) for a moment, either voluntarily (sense 8) or involuntarily (sense 3).

Colloq. phr. ***to wink the other eye***, to treat what has been said with flippant disregard.

1838 BUCKSTONE *Shocking Events* 11 Hollo! hollo! he's winking his eye at my maid. **1846** JAMES *Step-mother* liv. III. 8, I shouldn't have winked an eye all night if you hadn't been here. **1849** THACKERAY *Pendennis* xxv[i], Lady Clavering, giving the young gentleman a delighted tap with her fan, winked her black eyes at him. **1872** EARL PEMBROKE & G. H. KINGSLEY *S. Sea Bubbles* viii. 228 There was my princess.. winking winks that ought never to have been wunk. **1883** D. C. MURRAY *Hearts* xiv, Lording's eyes tingled with tears. He winked both eyes together and blew his nose with violence. **1898** 'H. S. MERRIMAN' *Roden's Corner* xxxii, The lighthouse winked a glaring eye that seemed to stare over their heads far out to sea.

b. ***to wink away***: to remove (tears) by blinking one's eyes.

1876 MISS BROUGHTON *Joan* II. i, Joan, trying to smile, and to wink away the two large tears that have rushed to her eyes. **1892** MRS. S. BATSON *Dark* I. v. 105 She winked away a few hot tears of shame that rose to her eyes.

c. To move swiftly, cause to flicker like an eyelid.

1883 BRIDGES *Prometheus* 1464 Like butterflies, that.. upon a wall Winking their idle fans at pleasure sit. **1897** S. CRANE *Third Violet* xxviii. 190 He told me you swore like a drill-sergeant if the model winked a finger.

d. To give (a signal), express (a message), etc. by means of flashlights.

1918 *Glasgow Herald* 22 Nov. 5 Their flagship's great.. eye of flame winking out a message. **1919** *Ibid.* 21 Apr. 7 H.M.S. Glory..winked us welcome from the mast-head.

†**wink**, *v.*[2] *Obs. rare.* [var. WINCH *v.*[1] Cf. WINK *sb.*[2]] *intr.* To shrink, wince.

1598 SYLVESTER *Du Bartas* II. i. I. *Eden* 145 That boistrous Adam's body did not shrink For Northren Windes, nor for the Southren wink. **1677** [see WINKING *vbl. sb.*[2]].

wink, *v.*[3] orig. *U.S.* [f. WINK *sb.*[4]] *intr.* To play tiddlywinks. Freq. as *vbl. sb.* Occas. *trans.* (in quot. *fig.*).

1955 V. NABOKOV *Lolita* I. v. 26 This is all very interesting, and I daresay you see me already frothing at the mouth in a fit; but no, I am not; I am just winking happy thoughts into a little tiddle cup. **1958** *Sunday Times* 2 Mar.

16/3 While practising secretly, I pulled an important muscle in the second or tiddly joint of my winking finger. **1962** *Boston Globe* 14 Oct. 81 The Crimson tiddlers winked their way to a 23 to 12 victory over a green Purple team. **1979** *Harvard Mag.* May–June 38 They went to many carpet stores to find the perfect surface for winking.

wink, obs. form of WINNOCK *Sc.*, window.

wink-a-peep ('wɪŋkəpiːp). Also 7 winkapipe, wincopipe. [f. WINK *v.*[1] + PEEP *sb.*]

†**1.** *pl.* The eyes. *Obs.*

Cf. Devon dial. *wink-a-peeps* 'drowsiness'.

1615 BRATHWAIT *Strappado* 4 Those wink-apipes of thine, those ferret eies. *Ibid.* 116 Awake for shame, open thy wink-a-peeps!

2. *dial.* The pimpernel, *Anagallis arvensis*.

1626 BACON *Sylva* §827 There is a Small Red Flower in the Stubble-Fields, which Country People call the Wincopipe. **1886** *Cheshire Gloss.* **1897** *Outing* (U.S.) Mar. 593/1 The wincopipes are opening, señor.

winked (wɪŋkt), *ppl. a.* [f. WINK *v.*[1] + -ED[1].] *winked-at, -on*, connived at, tolerated.

1632 BROME *Northern Lasse* v. viii, [He] has been a loose Liver,..at..most of the winkt at houses about the Town. **1810** CRABBE *Borough* iv. 352 Plays, Put out by heathens in the wink'd-on days. **1971** J. BRUNNER *Honky in Woodpile* iii. 24 Some winked-at gambling and smuggling. **1979** *Dædalus* Summer 107 Such genre paintings represent not a random clutter of whimsically winked-at transgressions but an array of symbols encoding quite specific moral instructions.

‖**winkel** ('vɪŋk(ə)l). Also winkle. [Du.] A store or general shop in South Africa. Hence '**winkler**, a store-keeper.

1827 G. THOMPSON *Trav. & Adv. S. Afr.* I. iii. 35 The village contains a couple of small retail shops, or *winkels*, as they are called. **1839** W. C. HARRIS *Wild Sports S. Afr.* xxxvii. 332 We lost not a moment in opening a *winkel*, or shop. **1853** W. R. KING *Campaign. Kaffirland* vi. 139 'Winkel waggons' had come out to the camp, and the 'winklers', or private traders, sold everything they had. **1902** *Blackw. Mag.* Feb. 169/1 Richmond Road is not a township. .. It boasts of one winkel adjoining the railway buildings.

winker[1] ('wɪŋkə(r)). [f. WINK *v.*[1] + -ER[1].]

1. One who winks (in various senses). *rare.*

1549 LATIMER *3rd Serm. bef. Edw. VI* (Arb.) 94 He was no gyfte taker, he was no wynker, he was no bywalker. **1550** BALE *Image Both Ch.* II. xiii. f vij, That franticke papist Iohn Eckius, and our wynchester the wynker of wyles. *c* **1590** in *Collect. B.L. Ballads* (1867) 254 Cat will after kind, All winkers are not blind. **1649** BULWER *Pathomyot.* II. iv. 164 True Cowards who are of the worse Sect of winkers are wont to shut their Eyes. **1715** POPE *Let. to Craggs* 15 July, A sett of nodders, winkers, and whisperers. **1820** J. CHAMBERS *Illustr. Worc.* 539 'Are you a gentleman and wink at whist?' This was too much for the winker. **1902** *Sat. Rev.* 19 July 77/1 Self-conscious winkers and gigglers over their own misconduct.

2. a. Chiefly *pl.* applied to the eyes or the eyelashes. Now *dial.* or *slang.*

1734 in Mrs. Delany *Autobiogr.* (1861) I. 519 As soon as my winkers are opened I am always blessed with one of your epistles. **1808** JAMIESON, *Winkers*, the eye-lashes. S. **1893** *Boy's Own Paper* Jan. 157/3 Here, youngster, clap your winker to this glass. **1894** CROCKETT *Raiders* xxvi. 226 Curling upward like the winkers of an old man's eye.

b. The nictitating membrane of a bird's eye.

1884 COUES *N. Amer. Birds* (ed. 2) 180.

3. a. *pl.* (rarely *sing.*) = BLINKER 2 b; also *attrib.* Also *fig.* or allusively.

1583 FULKE *Def., Confut. Papists* 32 He is the common packhorse of the Papistes,..he weareth a paire of winkers ouer his eyes like a milhorse. **1746–7** MRS. DELANY in *Autobiogr.* (1861) II. 449 Most people wear vast winkers to their heads. **1755** J. SHEBBEARE *Lydia* (1769) II. 29 Her cap standing beyond her eyes like a coach-horse's winkers. **1794** FELTON *Carriages* (1801) II. 136. **1859** *Carriage Builders' Art Jrnl.* I. 43/1 The winker-cheek is cut eight inches from buckle to buckle. **1882** J. PHILIPSON *Harness* 18 Hogskin is utilized for the pads, winkers, &c. of brown harness.

Comb. **1845** BROWNING in *Lett. R. B. & Eliz. B. Barrett* (1899) I. 79, I am set going with a hand, winker-wise, on each side of my head.

b. *transf.* Spectacles *rare.*

1816 'QUIZ' *Grand Master* I. 11 A patent pair of goggle winkers, Conceal'd from public view his blinkers.

4. A direction indicator on a motor vehicle in the form of a flashing light; = INDICATOR 3 g.

1951 *Autocar* 2 Nov. 1411/1 Another advantage of the 'winkers' is the fact that no mechanical fault can develop. **1960** *News Chron.* 21 July 6/4 On the M1..there are no curves to cancel the winkers. **1967** *Autocar* 28 Dec. 2/2 The main-beam and winker lights have little, pull-down 'eyelids'. **1970** A. SILLITOE *Start in Life* v. 255, I put on the winkers, swung out, and swept forward.

Hence (in sense 3) '**winkered** *a.*

1804 M. WILMOT *Let.* 5 July in *Russ. Jrnls.* (1934) I. 110 Women..dress'd in a sort of winker'd cap of *pearls* which showes the face very becomingly. **1907** J. M. SYNGE *Playboy of Western World* III. 61 That's the play-boy on the winkered mule.

winker[2]. Short for *tiddlywinker* (b) s.v. TIDDLYWINK. orig. *U.S.*

1958 *N.Y. Times* 9 May 28 Tomorrow..the Cantab Winkers play the Oxonian Tiddlers in Oxford. **1965** *Times* 5 Jan. 11b The nation's 'winkers' have two ambitions for 1965. **1979** *Harvard Mag.* May–June 39 Winkers lost interest in recruiting new winkers.

winkey, variant of WINKY.

winking ('wɪŋkɪŋ), *vbl. sb.*[1] [f. WINK *v.*[1] + -ING[1].] The action of WINK *v.*[1]

†**1.** Closing the eyes in sleep; dozing, slumbering; also, a doze, a nap. *Obs.*

c **1175** *Lamb. Hom.* 145 þer scal beon..lokinge wið-uten winkunge, song wið-uten lisse. **1377** LANGL. *P. Pl.* B. v. 3 þanne waked I of my wynkynge and wo was with-alle, þat I ne hadde sleped sadder. **1393** *Ibid.* C. XII. 167 In a wynkynge ich worth and wonderliche ich mette.

attrib. **1625** FLETCHER & SHIRLEY *Nt.-Walker* IV. i, So, so, he's fast; Fast as a fish ith' net, he has winking powder Shall worke upon him to our wish.

b. The taking of 'forty winks'.

1862 SMILES *Engineers* III. xii. 239 Stephenson..would occasionally refresh himself..by a short doze, which..he would never admit had exceeded the limits of 'winking', to use his own term.

2. The shutting of the eyes, as in blinking, as a gesture of aversion or connivance, and now esp. as a flippant indication of intimate knowledge or amused interest. †Also, a significant glance or movement of the eyes; with *at*, connivance.

c **1440** *Promp. Parv.* 530/1 Wynkkynge, of the eye (*S.* with the eye), *nictitacio,..nictus,..conquinicio,..connivencia.* *c* **1460** J. RUSSELL *Bk. Nurture* 282 Glowtynge ne twynkelynge with your yȝe..Watery wynkynge ne droppynge but of sight clere. **1538** ELYOT *Dict.*, *Nictus*, a wynkynge, as whan one doth sygnifie his mynde to an other by loking. **1564–78** BULLEIN *Dial. agst. Pest.* (1888) 20 What meaneth hee by winkyng like a Goose in the raine? **1572** *Instructions Earl Worc.* in Digges *Compl. Ambass.* (1655) 318 To suffer no permission or winking at of any other Religion then that which..our Realm hath always held. **1595** SHAKS. *John* IV. ii. 211 On the winking of Authoritie To vnderstand a Law. **1602** —— *Ham.* II. ii. 137 If I had..giuen my heart a winking, mute and dumbe. **1641** J. JACKSON *True Evang. T.* II. 152 Breaches of charity..by the wincking and scorning of our eyes. **1664** TILLOTSON *Wisdom of being religious* 33 If there be a God, a man cannot by an obstinate dis-belief of him make him cease to be, any more then a man can put out the Sun by winking. **1684** HOWE *Redeemer's Tears* Wks. 1724 II. 15 Men may indeed, by resolved, stiff, winking, create to themselves a darkness amidst the clearest Light. **1693** LOCKE *Educ.* §138 If..any one..should..make them think there is any difference between being in the dark and winking, you must get it out of their Minds. **1783** O'KEEFFE *Birth-Day* 28 Sly winking and blinking, As leering and jeering. **1824** MISS L. M. HAWKINS *Annaline* I. 206 What..is all this winking and smirking about? **1831** SCOTT *Ct. Robt.* xiv, It is the misfortune of the weaker on such occasions..to be obliged to take the petty part of winking hard, as if not able to see what they cannot avenge. **1837** DICKENS *Pickw.* xxviii, The fat boy swallowed a glass of liquor without so much as winking.

3. The rapid alternating motion of an object; the intermittent flashing of light.

1859 J. BROWN *Rab & F.* 16 The mobility..of that bud [of a tail],..its expressive twinklings and winkings..were of the oddest and swiftest. [**1899** F. T. BULLEN *Way Navy* 28 The flagship keeps breaking out into rapid winkings of lofty electric eyes.] **1908** C. W. WALLACE *Children Chapel Blackfriars* 11 The modern signal bell of the German theatre ..when an act is ready to begin;—a signal reduced in American theatres to the winking of the lights.

4. *like winking*: in a flash, in a twinkling, very rapidly or suddenly; also, with vigour or persistency, 'like one o'clock', 'like anything'. So, *as easy as winking*.

1827 HOOD *Sailor's Apol.* 71 Both my legs began to bend like winkin. **1841** MARRYAT *Poacher* xxii, He's a regular scholar, and can sum up like winkin. **1872** 'ALIPH CHEEM' (Yeldham) *Lays of Ind* (1876) 85 But [we] cry 'pray grow your opium!' Because it pays like winking. **1907** H. WYNDHAM *Flare of Footlights* xxxv, She'll..make a hundred and fifty a week as easy as winking.

†'**winking**, *vbl. sb.*[2] [See WINK *v.*[2]] Wincing.

1677 W. HUGHES *Man of Sin* II. i. 7 What a Desperate Cause is this;..Is not this meer winking to avoid a blow?

winking ('wɪŋkɪŋ), *ppl. a.* [f. WINK *v.*[1] + -ING[2].] That winks.

1. That shuts the eyes or one eye intermittently or for an instant; blinking; †slumbering, sleepy; in OE. as sb. = the blind.

Used to render the specific name *connivens* of certain birds.

a **1000** *Sal. & Sat.* 77 Lamena he is læce, leoht wincendra [*v.r.* winciendra]. **1377** LANGL. *P. Pl.* B. XI. 4 Þo wepte I for wo and wratth of her speche, And in a wynkyng wratth wex I aslepe. **1562** J. HEYWOOD *Prov. & Epigr.* (1867) 162 Smalle holes keepe small mise, from wily winkyng cats. **1611** SHAKS. *Cymb.* II. iv. 89 Her Andirons..were two winking Cupids Of Siluer. **1630** BP. HALL *Occas. Medit.* xxi. 53 Wee are wont to salute it [*sc.* the light] at the first comming in, with winking, or closed eyes. **1693** DRYDEN *Ovid's Met.* I. 990 The Keeper's winking Eyes began to fail. **1784** COWPER *Task* II. 773 Blame we most the nurslings or the nurse? The children,..deform'd, Through want of care; or her, whose winking eye And slumb'ring oscitancy mars the brood? **1801** LATHAM *Synopsis, Suppl.* II. 53 Winking Falcon [*Falco connivens*]. It has a wonderful faculty of contracting and dilating the iris. **1810** CRABBE *Borough* x. 243 And prosing topers rub their winking eyes. **1855** *Poultry Chron.* III. 381 The nictitating (winking) muscles. **1860** PATMORE *Faithful For Ever* II. 109 And I, contented,..idly stroke The winking cat, or watch the fire. **1870** DISRAELI *Lothair* liv, Starveling saints and winking madonnas.

†**b.** Characterized by shutting of the eyes or averted looks; conniving. *Obs.*

1577–82 BRETON *Floorish upon Fancie* Wks. (Grosart) I. 37/1 Some finely vse a winking kinde of wile, Some looke alofte, and some doo still looke downe. **1579** HAKE *Newes out of Powles* (1872) F viij b, See, see, what wyly winking shiftes, by cliffe browde beasts are made. **1605–6** EARL NORTHAMPTON in *Crt. & Times Jas. I* (1848) I. 55 The winking course which I am forced to take daily in the ports ..hath..tired me with struggling between both parts.

2. *transf.* That opens and shuts; often, by extension, applied to intermittent light, the flashing of lamps, the twinkling of a reflexion, or the like.

1595 SHAKS. *John* II. i. 215 All preparation for a bloody siedge, And merciles proceeding,..Confronts your Citties eies, your winking gates. **1611** —— *Cymb.* II. iii. 25 (Song) And winking Mary-buds begin to ope their Golden eyes. **1681** DRYDEN *Span. Friar* III. ii, A dim winking Lamp. **1789** WOLCOT (P. Pindar) *Subj. for Painters* Wks. 1812 II. 142 A winking Light of paltry Rush. **1840** DICKENS *Old C. Shop* xxviii, These [houses] had very little winking windows, and low-arched doors. **1904** HICHENS *Garden Allah* xx, The first glass of blithely winking champagne.

3. *Comb.*, as †**winking-eyed** *a.*, blind (*fig.*).

1621 *Eng. Prot. Plea for Eng. Preists & Papists* 60 The councell could not be so winking eyed, but they would haue found foorth some one or other culpable.

Hence '**winkingly** *adv.*, with winking eyes; †with a casual look; with a wink or winks.

1594 NASHE *Unfort. Trav.* I 3 b, Whose pleasing face he had scarce winkingly glanst on [etc.]. **1612** PEACHAM *Gentl. Exerc.* III. (1634) 138 If any one beholdeth..some very white object, he vieweth it winkingly. **1868** *N. Brit. Rev.* Dec. 429 The left eye of Raff..asks winkingly, 'What do you bring to-day?' **1897** BLACKMORE *Dariel* xlix. 437 Looking out winkingly in all directions,..I beheld a company of little rocks.

winkle ('wɪŋk(ə)l), *sb.* Also 6 wincle, 7 winckle.

1. Shortened f. PERIWINKLE[2] (cf. *wig* from *periwig*).

1585 HIGINS *Junius Nomencl.* 65/2 *Cochlea*,..a Wincle: a periwincle or cockle. **1601** HOLLAND *Pliny* VIII. xxxix. I. 218 Lisards, (deadly enemies to the Snailes or Winkles above named). **1610** —— *Camden's Brit.* (1637) 727 Stones like unto sea winkles or cockles and other sea fish. **1615** CROOKE *Body of Man* 601 It is called *Concha*..because it is like a Winkle or Periwinkle. **1844** DICKENS *Mart. Chuz.* xxi, The very winkle of your country in his shelly lair. **1899** WHITEING *No. 5 John St.* vii. 60 A typical family..lives before the public on a nutriment of winkles and gin.

attrib. **1845** COL. HAWKER *Diary* (1893) II. 256 The 'winklemen were on the mud all day. **1881** *Instr. Census Clerks* (1885) 39 Winkle Gatherer. **1903** *Times* 13 Aug. 13/2 A shilling used to be charged for a winkle license, which lasted during the winkle season.

2. *slang* (chiefly *juveniles'*). The penis (of a young boy).

1951 PARTRIDGE *Dict. Slang* Add. 1223/2 *Winkle, n.*, penis: children's, (young) schoolboys': late C. 19–20. **1970** *Guardian* 3 Feb. 8, I was mildly troubled by the insistence, especially of one headmaster, on the 'proper names for things'. Penis is right and winkle is wrong. **1970** T. HUGHES *Crow* 63 O do not chop his winkle off His Mammy cried. **1973** M. AMIS *Rachel Papers* 78 'Thanks,' he said to his (new) witch-like girlfriend as she handed him a joint so ill-made that it resembled a baby's winkle.

3. *Comb.*, as **winkle-picker** *slang*, a shoe with a long pointed toe; **winkle-pin** *Mil. slang* = BAYONET 2.

1960 *Spectator* 15 Apr. 553 The incredibly pointed custom-built shoes in which teenagers keep other teenagers at arm's length... The shoes, called winklepickers, look like something out of Grimm's fairy tales. **1960** *News Chron.* 13 Sept. 5/3 The 'winkle picker' high heels and the high spirits have gone. **1978** C. SYKES in R. Buckle *U & Non-U Revisited* 57 The mass-produced variety, popularly known as 'winkle-pickers', were very ugly. **1980** *Bulletin* (Sydney) 6 May 5/3, I had the hairdo, the lairy shirt, the winkle-picker shoes. **1924** KIPLING *Debits & Credits* (1926) 314 As his sergeant I had to check him for misusin' his winkle-pin on dirt. **1950** PARTRIDGE *Here, There & Everywhere* 62 The bayonet..has many names..[e.g.] *winkle-pin.*

Hence '**winkling** *gerund.*

1898 *Punch* 20 Aug. 77/2 D'year as 'ow old Bob Osborne 'ave give up Shrimpin' an took ter Winklin'?

winkle ('wɪŋk(ə)l), *v.*[1] *dial.* [f. WINK *v.*[1] + -LE 3.] *intr.* To emit light intermittently; to twinkle.

1791 LEARMONT *Poems* 37 In vain the starry winkling gleam. **1807** HOGG *Mountain Bard* 63 What though she has twa little winkling een? They're better than nane. **1905** MRS. BARNES-GRUNDY *Vacil. Hazel* 198 The stars and planets twinkled and winkled, and sparkled and glittered.

winkle, *v.*[2] *colloq.* (orig. *Mil. slang*). [f. WINKLE *sb.*] trans. *to winkle out*: to extract or eject (as a winkle from its shell with a pin); to draw forth, find out or elicit.

[**1925** FRASER & GIBBONS *Soldier & Sailor Words* 306 *Winkle, to*, to capture individual prisoners by stealth... Also,..to steal.] **1942** 'M. HOME' *House of Shade* ii. 20 What's winkled you out at this goddam hour? **1943** *People* 31 Oct. 1/7 Methodically winkling the Germans out of their strongpoints. **1951** 'M. INNES' *Operation Pax* v. vi. 220 Until we winkle out this young man..you and I make not a bad team. **1958** J. PRESS *Chequer'd Shade* 4 It is illegitimate to compare the far-fetched conjectures of Eliot's commentators with the inside information which we might have winkled out of Donne. **1966** *Listener* 20 Jan. 111/3 It's the cunning of the interviewer that counts most of all, and certainly Mr. Muggeridge manages to winkle out some interesting bits and pieces. **1970** *Sunday Mail Mag.* (Brisbane) 17 May 14/1 He could winkle out sin where no other man dreamed it existed. **1976** A. EDEN *Another World* vii. 79 Hart's skills were in a sense wasted upon us, and he was at length winkled out to the advantage of a base hospital.

winkler ('wɪŋklə(r)). [f. WINKLE *sb.* + -ER[1].]

1. One who gathers winkles; a boat used for this.

1889 A. T. PASK *Eyes Thames* 58 Eel-trawlers and 'winklers'.

2. *slang.* One who assists in the eviction of tenants (see quot. 1970). Cf. WINKLE *v.*[2]

1970 *Sunday Times* 15 Nov. 3/5 Plausible, highly-paid 'winklers' who are hired by property companies and landlords to persuade families to leave their rent-controlled tenancies so the homes can be sold at high prices. **1977** *Whig-Standard* (Kingston, Ontario) 29 Sept. 26/3 The tenants said the agents aided by middlemen called 'winklers', had bribed and harassed them to get them to move.

winkless ('wɪŋklɪs), *a.* [f. WINK *sb.*[1] + -LESS.] Without a wink, unwinking.

1861 WYNTER *Soc. Bees* 93 The upturned gaze of winkless scores [of artificial eyes]. **1867** F. H. LUDLOW *Brace of Boys* 255 Sat bolt upright in the pew, winkless as a deacon.

winkling ('wɪŋklɪŋ), *vbl. sb.* [f. WINKLE *v.*[2] + -ING[1].] The action of the vb., esp. with reference to the removal of tenants from rented accommodation. Also ***winkling-out***. Cf. WINKLER 2.

1970 *Guardian* 20 Nov. 7/1 'Winkling'—persuading private tenants to quit. **1973** *Daily Tel.* 24 May 11/2 He described the 'winkling' processes followed by certain developers to rid themselves of unwanted but protected tenants. **1974** E. AMBLER *Dr Frigo* III. 195 An army assault team had been called in. In their winkling-out of the defenders they had..made rather a mess of the Palace. **1975** *Listener* 18 Nov. 826/1 Mr Skeaping had been accused of 'winkling'; bribing his tenants to leave so that he could sell the property with vacant possession.

†**winklot.** *Sc. Obs.* [Obscure; for the ending cf. *giglot*, GIGLET.] A wench.

15.. *Peblis to Play* 73 in *Maitland Fol. MS.* (S.T.S.) 178 Ane winklot fell and hir taill vp. *Ibid.* 233, 182 Quhen the winklottis and the wawaris twynnit.

winks (wɪŋks). Shortening of *tiddlywinks*: see TIDDLYWINK 2 b. *U.S.*

1942 R. & L. FREEMAN *Cavalcade of Toys* xvi. 366 Back in 1903 'Battle Winks' was a popular game. **1962** *Harvard Crimson* 6 Nov. 3/2 (*heading*) Crimson winks squad downs two opponents. **1979** *Technology Rev.* Mar./Apr. B23 Unlike chess, which has limited predictable moves, winks is a game of chance as well as skill, says Mr. Lockwood.

winky ('wɪŋkɪ). Also **-ey, -ie.** [f. WINK *v.*[1] + -Y[6].] Only in slang phr. ***like winky***, 'like winking'.

1830 LYTTON *P. Clifford* xxxi[ii], The parson forks him out ten shiners, preaching all the while like winkey. **1838** MRS. SMYTHIES *Fitzherbert* ix, We'll be back like winky. **1846** W. CROSS *Disruption* vii. 61 Jimes and mee are going On with owre studdys already like winkie. **1901** M. FRANKLIN *My Brilliant Career* xix. 163 Every one has to obey him like winkie or they can take their beds up and trot off quick and lively. **1902** BEGBIE *Sir J. Sparrow* iii. 33 She kicks like winky. **1923** KIPLING *Land & Sea Tales* 115 This Baxter-man..SOS'ed like winkie.

winle, Sc. form of WINDLE *sb.*[3]

winless ('wɪnlɪs), *a. N. Amer.* [f. WIN *sb.*[1] + -LESS.] Characterized by an absence of victories in a series of sporting contests; also, designating a period of time during which no victory was won.

1966 *Daily Progress* (Charlottesville, Va.) 8 June 30/1 People keep telling VMI's Gary McPherson he has the very best winless basketball team in the country. **1970** *Globe & Mail* (Toronto) 25 Sept. 32/3 Winless in 14 previous starts this season, Miss Ella Cinders had little trouble with Sandy Hawley up last Saturday as she galloped to a 12-length win. **1972** J. MOSEDALE *Football* iii. 36 They..went through another winless season. **1977** *Arab Times* 3 Dec. 9/3 Bechtel now go into their final game against AG & P with both teams winless in what should be quite a battle to see which team makes it out of the cellar.

†**winly,** *a. Obs.* Forms: 1 wynlic, wenlic, 3 wunlic, wun-, wund-, wune-, wonliche, 4 wynly, -lich(e, -wynnelych, 5 wynlyche, winli. [OE. *wynlic*, f. *wyn(n* joy, WIN *sb.*[2] + *-lic*, -LY[1].] Pleasant, agreeable; goodly, splendid, beautiful. (Often merely a vague epithet of commendation.)

a **1000** *Phœnix* 34 Sunbearo lixeð, wuduholt wynlic. *c* **1000** *Ags. Hom.* (Assmann) ix. 205 Heo wæs swiðe wlitig and wenlices hiwes. *c* **1205** LAY. 8090 Wæs at foren þan wæfde imaked an wunlic fur. *Ibid.* 10000 Stod þe wundliche [*c* **1275** wonliche] wude amidden ane wælde. *a* **1300** *E.E. Psalter* xxiii[i]. 3 Wha sal stegh in hille of lauerd winli? **1303** R. BRUNNE *Handl. Synne* 1411 Some of þo wynly wones Were peynted with precyus stones. *a* **1400** *Pistill of Susan* 99 With wardons winlich and walshe notes newe. ?*a* **1400** *Morte Arth.* 181 Ther-to wylde to wale, and wynlyche bryddes.

†**winly,** *adv. Obs.* Forms: 1 wynlice, 3 wunliche, 4 wynli, -lyche, wynn-, wynnely, 4–5 wynly, 5 winly. [OE. *wynlice*, f. *wynlic*: see prec. and -LY[2].] Pleasantly, agreeably; finely, splendidly. (Often vague in alliterative verse.)

c **1000** *Ags. Ps.* (Th.) cvii[i]. 2 þæt ic wynlice on psalterio þe singan mote. *c* **1205** LAY. 3605 Sone werð þe alde king wunliche iæðeled. *c* **1350** *Will. Palerne* 749 A gardin euene, ..wynli wiþ heie wal was closed al a-boute. *c* **1400** *Sc. Trojan War* (Horstm.) I. 225 The stretis ware strautht & wynly maide. *a* **1400–50** *Wars Alex.* 5545 In at a wicket he went & wynly it speris. *c* **1440** *York Myst.* xlv. 103 What ayles yow women, for wo þus wynly to wepe? *c* **1450** HOLLAND *Howlat* 660 The Pape and the patriarkis.. Welcummit thaim wynly.

winn, obs. form of WIN.

winna. *Sc.* = 'will not': see WILL *v.*[1] A. 6 b *β*.

winnability (ˌwɪnə'bɪlɪtɪ). Also **winability.** [f. WINNABLE *a.*: see -ITY.] Capacity for winning or being won.

1972 *New Society* 16 Nov. 400/2 The penal cases committee seems to be heavily influenced by two considerations... The other is the 'winability' of the case; the penal cases committee refers chiefly open-and-shut cases to the disciplinary committee. **1975** W. SAFIRE *Before the Fall* I. iv. 43 'My biggest problem,' Nixon concluded, 'is "Nixon can't win".'.. We discussed ways to build 'winability'. **1979** *Guardian* 2 Nov. 13/6 Kennedy..has that overriding quality—winnability. **1983** *Times* 16 Apr. 2/5 The most detailed work on the winnability of the new seats has been done by a few academics.

winnable ('wɪnəb(ə)l), *a.* Also 6 wyn(n)able, 7 winneable, 8–9 (*erron.*) **winable.** [f. WIN *v.*[1] + -ABLE.] Capable of being won, in various senses.

1544 BETHAM *Precepts War* I. v. B iv b, All cyties..be more wynable on the one syde, then on the other. **1611** COTGR., *Gaignable*, gettable, winnable, gaineable. **1747** HOOSON *Miner's Dict.* L 3 b, When Work is Soft, Kind, and Winable enough without any Hardship. **1807** ANNA M. PORTER *Hungarian Bro.* xi. (1832) 131 The best proof I can have of her heart's being winable only by a brave and upright man. **1888** *Pall Mall Gaz.* 18 Feb. 8/1 All the rest are winnable exactly as Southwark was won.

winnackew, -acoe, obs. var. GUANACO.

1729 J. WOOD *Voy.* 86 Here is Plenty of Winnackews, or Spanish sheep.

winnaill, obs. Sc. form of VENNEL.

winnard ('wɪnəd). Also 7 **wheenerd.** [app. a. LG. *weingartdrossel, -vogel* (see WING-THRUSH), with the second element dropped.] A local name of the redwing, *Turdus iliacus*.

a **1698** [see WINDLE *sb.*[4]]. **1758** BORLASE *Nat. Hist. Cornw.* xxi. 245. **1880** *E. Cornwall Gloss.*

winne, obs. form of WIN.

Winnebago (wɪnə'beɪgəʊ), *sb.* (*a.*) [ad. Fox *wi·nepye·ko·ha*, lit. 'person of dirty water', an allusion to the muddy waters of the Fox River below Lake Winnebago, which became clogged with dead fish in the heat of the summer.] **1. a.** (A member of) a Siouan people of eastern Wisconsin. **b.** The language of this people. Also *attrib.* or as *adj.*

1766 J. CARVER *Jrnl.* 25 Sept. in J. Parker *Jrnls. J. Carver & Related Documents, 1766–70* (1976) I. 78 Arrivd at the great town of the Winebaygoes. *Ibid.* 79 The town of the Winebagoes is situate on the south east end of an island at the east end of the Winebago Lake. **1827** *Spirit of Seventy-Six* (Frankfort, Kentucky) 2 Aug. 2/1 An express reached here this moment from Galena..with information of hostilities having been commenced by the Winnebago Indians, on the settlers. **1835** C. F. HOFFMAN *Winter in West* I. 257 The Winnebago chief..[had] just left the establishment. **1839** H. R. SCHOOLCRAFT *Algic Researches* I. 13 The Winnebagoes are clearly of the Abanic stock. **1860** *Harper's Mag.* Sept. 568/2 As he could not speak Winnebago, the first thing to be done was to find an interpreter. **1881** *Encycl. Brit.* XII. 832/1 The Winnebagoes are a branch of the Dakota family. **1907** L. H. MORGAN *Anc. Society* III. iii. 440 In Winnebago and Achaotina she is 'my sister'. **1910** F. W. HODGE *Handbk. Amer. Indians* II. 958/1 The Winnebago have been known to the whites since 1634, when the Frenchman Nicollet found them in Wisconsin, on Green Bay. **1933** [see MANDAN *a.* and *sb.*]. **1966** A. C. HARDY *Divine Flame* iii. 65 Those tribes belonging to the great Sioux family such as the Omaha, Ponka, Kansas, Dakota, Iowa, Winnebago, etc. **1973** A. H. WHITEFORD *N. Amer. Indian Arts* 81 Winnebago women's mocassins have a flap over the toe. **1975** *Language* LI. 317 Ferguson.. suggests that Hockett's analysis of Winnebago is unusual.

2. Special Comb.: **Winnebago camper**, a motor vehicle with insulated panels used as living accommodation by campers (a proprietary term in the U.S.); also *ellipt.*

1966 *Mobile Home Jrnl.* Oct. (Advt., rear cover), Your most enjoyable travel companion is a Winnebago Pickup Camper Coach. **1970** *Official Gaz.* (U.S. Patent Office) 17 Nov. TM 132 Winnebago Industries, Inc., Forest City, Iowa. Filed Aug. 6, 1969. Winnebago... For Vehicles and Components..—Namely Motor Homes, Travel Trailers, House Trailers, Camper Coaches, [etc.]..First use April 1959. **1975** I. K. MARTIN *Regan & Manhattan File* 104 Regan..noted..a Winnibago camper parked to the rear... The back door of the Winnibago opened.

winnel, dial. form of WINDLE.

winner ('wɪnə(r)). [f. WIN *v.*[1] + -ER[1].] One who or that which wins, in various senses.

1. One who gains something, esp. by effort or merit; *spec.* one who gets (a living) by labour, an earner (*obs.* or *dial.* exc. in BREAD-WINNER); †one who makes profit, as by trading; †one who 'wins' (corn), a harvester, reaper (*fig.*).

1352 [see WASTER *sb.*[1] 1]. *c* **1375** *Sc. Leg. Saints* xxvii. (*Machor*) 860 Of goddis corne wynnare to be. **1393** LANGL. *P. Pl.* C. I. 222 Webbesters and walkers and wynners with handen. *c* **1456** *Pol. Poems* (Rolls) II. 235 Robberys now rewle ryȝtwysenesse, And wynnerys with her sothe sawe. **1483** *Cath. Angl.* 420/1 A Wynner, *lucrificus*. **1523–34** FITZHERB. *Husb.* §36 He that byeth grosse sale, and retayleth, muste nedes be a wynner. **1556** J. HEYWOOD *Spider & F.* lxxiii. 21 No fle therby winner, the worth of a straw. **1593** *Extr. Aberd. Reg.* (1848) II. 85 Knawin..to be wynneris of thair leving be sum honest moyen. **1630** R. N. tr. *Camden's Hist. Eliz.* IV. 173 Whereas Religion is the greatest winner of mens affections. **1836** HOR. SMITH *Tin Trump.* I. 257 The winner of a title generally deserves it. **1848** THACKERAY *Van. Fair* lxvii, The Major was disengaged too, and swore he would be the winner of her. **1876** SIR C. DILKE in *Life* (1917) I. xiii. 197 Holker..a great winner of verdicts from juries, was one of the dullest men. **1911** 'G. A. BIRMINGHAM' *Lighter Side Irish Life* i. 6 A woman, a careless winner of the hearts of men.

2. One who is victorious in a contest; a victor; *esp.* one who wins a game, a race, a prize, etc.; *spec.* a horse, dog, etc. that wins a race; in games of skill, the 'piece' that is nearest to a certain point, a winning shot, etc.; *colloq.* a thing that scores a success; a potentially successful project, enterprise, etc.

1456 SIR G. HAYE *Law Arms* (S.T.S.) 74 [If he] has tynt the bataill, tharfore he had the wrang, and the wynnar the rycht. **1546** J. HEYWOOD *Prov.* I. x. (1867) 24 Be they wynners or loosers, Folke saie alwaie, beggers should be no choosers. **1596** DALRYMPLE tr. *Leslie's Hist. Scot.* (S.T.S.) I. 156 The verie Romanis selfes, victorious winneris. **1596** SHAKS. *Tam. Shr.* v. ii. 187 'Twas I wonne the wager, though you hit the white, And being a winner, God giue you good night. **1598** —— *Hen. V*, III. vi. 120 When Lenitie and Crueltie play for a Kingdome, The gentler Gamester is the soonest winner. **1611** —— *Cymb.* III. v. 15 Sir, the Euent Is yet to name the winner. **1667** *Leathermore*: *Advice conc. Gaming* (1668) 10 It is not deny'd but most Gamesters have at one time or other a considerable run of winning, but..I could never hear of the Man that gave over a winner, (I mean to give over, as never to play again). **1710** *Act 9 Anne* c. 19 §2 It shall..be lawful..for any Person..to..recover the same [money],..with Costs..against such Winner. **1789** D. DAVIDSON *Seasons* 167 A leal shot ettled at the cock, Which shov'd the winner by. **1811** *Acc. Game Curling* 9 The stone nearest the tee..is called the winner. **1840** DICKENS *Old C. Shop* xxx, At length the play came to an end, and Mr. Isaac List rose the only winner. **1854** *Poultry Chron.* I. 371 Winners of the First Prizes. **1859** H. KINGSLEY *G. Hamlyn* xix, I'd ridden seven great winners before I was eighteen. **1874** J. D. HEATH *Croquet-Player* 83 It is..unfair to the winner, to tell him that he won only because you 'had a bad mallet'. **1876** *Coursing Calendar* 19 In a scrambling course, run partly out of sight, the early points of Moonshine doubtless landed her the winner. **1913** *Play Pictorial* No. 131 ¶p. iv/1 The Alhambra has also found a winner in its curiously named ['revue'] '8d. a mile'. **1934** *Punch* 14 Nov. 552/1 The growing function of the outlying theatres is to spot winners for the West-End. **1948** M. LASKI *Tory Heaven* v. 66 'I'd like to be a land-agent... I do really think I could have made a success of it.' 'I'm sure you would... It sounds like a winner to me.' **1958** *Times* 12 Sept. 13/1 The last crop of new ballets commissioned for the Edinburgh International Ballet company includes one winner, a near miss, and a very honourable mention. **1972** *Sunday Express* 9 Jan. 5/3 The warmth of wool plus good, classic styling, makes this coat a winner this winter. **1976** *Southern Even. Echo* (Southampton) 18 Nov. 4/3 Cyril Berry..must be on a winner with his latest book. **1985** *Woman's Own* 22 June 36/2 The actor believes that combining the strong with the sensitive is exactly what makes a man a winner—on screen and off.

3. ***winner-take(s)-all***, attrib. phr. used to denote contests or conflicts in which victory is outright or the successful competitor alone is rewarded; occas. (without hyphens) in non-attrib. use as an idiomatic sentence.

1969 *Listener* 10 Apr. 496/1 When you say war, I think that's what you mean: nations and empires clashing, and there will be one winner and one loser on clear-cut lines. I won, you lost. But here there's not supposed to be, the way I understand it, a winner-take-all-type thing. **1972** *National Observer* (U.S.) 27 May 5/1 Should McGovern win the June 6 California primary with its winner-take-all bag of 271 votes,..he then would be within easy range of a first-ballot nomination at the convention opening on July 10. **1972** *Guardian* 8 June 12/1 In California winner takes all. It will be almost impossible now to deny McGovern the nomination. **1973** *Times* 16 Nov. 1/1 The Government has accepted that there is no way out of a grim, winner-takes-all clash with the National Union of Mineworkers. **1976** 'H. CARMICHAEL' *False Evidence* iv. 63 There must've been a worthwhile rakeoff... The outcome was that winner took all. **1978** A. PRICE *'44 Vintage* xxiii. 264 A winner-takes-all lottery.

winning ('wɪnɪŋ), *vbl. sb.*[1] Forms: see WIN *v.*[1] [f. WIN *v.*[1] + -ING[1].] The action of WIN *v.*[1]; *concr.* something won.

1. Conquest, capture, taking (of a place); also, in early use, conquered territory (= CONQUEST *sb.* 4). *Obs.* or *arch.*

c **1320** *Sir Tristr.* 928 Rohand he left king Ouer al his wining þare. **1338** R. BRUNNE *Chron.* (1810) 296 Þritti reames men tolde, þat kyng Arthur wan. He parted his wynnyng tille his men largely. **1419** in *Documents Français* (1847) I. 227 Thei have wonne the forsaid toun by assaulte ..thorought the whiche wynninge my forsaid lord hath passage to Parys. *c* **1470** HENRY *Wallace* x. 577 Thow was gret caus off wynnyng off Scotland. **1577** HOLINSHED *Chron.* I. 34/2 Caius Iulius Cesar..determined to assay ye winning of Britain. **1622** PEACHAM *Compl. Gent.* xv. (1906) 184 Knighted at the winning of Edenburgh in Scotland. *a* **1660** *Contemp. Hist. Irel.* (Ir. Archæol. Soc.) I. 280 This noble warrior was soe eager for the wininge of that place. **1871** FREEMAN *Norm. Conq.* IV. xvii. 80 While the land which sent forth such goodly stores was in winning.

2. a. The action of gaining, getting, or obtaining; acquisition; †gain (in general, as opp. to *loss*); victory in a game or contest.

With various shades of meaning, in later use restricted as in the vb.

c **1320** *Sir Tristr.* 3006 In wining and in tin Trewe to ben ay. **1362** LANGL. *P. Pl.* A. v. 94 Of his leosinge I lauhwe.. Ac for his wynnynge I wepe. *c* **1374** CHAUCER *Troylus* I. 199 Swych labour as folk han yn wynnynge Of loue. *c* **1449** PECOCK *Repr.* III. xviii. 403 Bi biyng or bi wynnyng in waiouring or bi sum other fre maner of geting. **1508** DUNBAR

Flyting 19 It is nowthir wynning nor rewaird, Bot tinsale [etc.]. **1549** COVERDALE, etc. *Erasm. Par. James* i. 1–12 To counte losse of goodes, for the richeste wynnynge. **1610** SHAKS. *Temp.* I. ii. 451 Least too light winning Make the prize light. **1611** —— *Cymb.* II. iii. 8 Winning will put any man into courage. **1616** *Buccleuch MSS.* (Hist. MSS. Comm.) I. 183 Your Honour may guess that winning of time is their chiefest aim. **1630** J. TAYLOR (Water P.) *Gt. Eater Kent* Wks. I. 145/2 The vnexpected winning of the wager. **1667** [see WINNER 2]. **1813** SCOTT *Rokeby* III. xxx, Allen-a-Dale has no fleece for the spinning, Yet Allen-a-Dale has red gold for the winning. **1860** LÖWENTHAL *Morphy's Games Chess* 140 Ensuring the advance of the Queen's Pawn, which is almost equivalent to the winning of the game. **1885–94** BRIDGES *Eros & Psyche* Dec. ix, And in one winning all her woes redeem.

†**b.** Getting of money or wealth; gain, profit; money-making. *Obs.* as a specific sense.

a **1300** *Cursor M.* 25803 Man þou has ben to couetus Abote werlds wining fuus. *c* **1382** *Pol. Poems* (Rolls) I. 252 Mony for wynnyng wold bitraye Father and moder. *a* **1450** MYRC *Par. Pr.* (1868) 22/705 Vsureres that by cause of wynnyng lene her catall to her eine cristen. *c* **1480** HENRYSON *Want of Wyse Men* 22 (Bannatyne MS.) For warldly wonyng sic walkis, quhen wysar winkis. *a* **1533** LD. BERNERS *Gold. Bk. M. Aurel.* (1546) N vij, Of the vnlawful winnyng of the fathers, there folowethe the iuste loss to theyr children. **1536** BELLENDEN *Cron. Scot.* (1821) I. p. xxiv, To thair gret proffet and winning. *c* **1730** RAMSAY *Maltman* iii, He may crack of his winning, When he clears scores with me.

c. Getting by labour, earning. *Obs.* exc. *dial.*

c **1400** *Rule St. Benet* (verse) 2058 If ony woman can oght do þat ony wining falles vnto. **1545** in *Reg. Mag. Sig. Scot. 1546*, 757/2 Concerning the wynning of thair leving.

†**d.** Profit (in general), advantage. *Obs.*

c **1375** *Sc. Leg. Saints* xl. (*Ninian*) 1151 Quhat wynnyng had ȝe, þo ȝe had mycht to sla me? **1477** EARL RIVERS (Caxton) *Dictes* 6 b, Yf ye do so all your lyf, it shalbe to you a grete prouffitable wynnyng. *a* **1578** LINDESAY (Pitscottie) *Chron. Scot.* (S.T.S.) I. 37 Regairding our awin prevat wining mair nor the weillfair of the realme.

3. *concr.* That which is won; a thing or amount obtained or gained; gain, profit (as acquired); †in early use *occas.* spoil, booty; emolument, earnings. Now *rare* or *Obs.* exc. as in 4.

a **1300** *Cursor M.* 968 O þi winning giue me þe tend. *c* **1330** *Arth. & Merl.* 8393 Whar ȝe schul win wining, Ȝe nold it ȝeue for no þing! *c* **1386** CHAUCER *Prol.* 275 Hise resons he spak ful solempnely Sownynge alway thencrees of his wynnyng. *c* **1400** *26 Pol. Poems* xix. 77 Þy wrong wynnyng aȝen restore. **14..** *Sc. Acts Parlt.* (1814) I. 736/2 And þat of all his wynnying . . he sal nocht halde bot .ij.d. *c* **1450** *Merlin* xiv. 224 Ther was founde grete wynnynge; and the kynge made it to be . . presented to the sowdiours. **1488** *Burgh Rec. Edinb.* (1869) I. 55 And thai to dele thairvpoun vyning and tynsell. **1509** BARCLAY *Shyp of Folys* (1874) II. 83 Eche of them askyth Lucre and wynnynge. **1546** J. HEYWOOD *Prov.* (1867) 34, I might put my winnyng in mine eye. **1585** HIGINS *Junius' Nomencl.* 321/2 *Brauium*, . . the price or winning giuen to one that ouercommeth in plaies and games. **1860** PUSEY *Min. Proph.* 281 'Keep the winning, keep the sinning.' . . We cannot keep the gain, and escape the loss.

4. *pl.*: usually *concr.*, as pl. of 3 (mostly in collective sense), Things or sums gained, gains, profits; earnings (*obs.* or *dial.*); in mod. use chiefly applied to money won by gaming or betting; more rarely in abstract sense, as pl. of 2, Acts of gaining, gains as opp. to losses.

c **1380** WYCLIF *Sel. Wks.* I. 11 Defaute in al þis comiþ of ypocrisye of prelatis, þat shulden teche pleynly Goddis lawe and not þer erþly wynnynges. *c* **1449** PECOCK *Repr.* III. xvii. 391 Tithis going out fro her wynnyngis. **1557** TUSSER *100 Points Husb.* xiii, But chopping and chaungeing, may make such a breck, That gone is thy winninges, for sauing thy neck. **1616** DRAXE *Bibl. Scholast.* 78 Hee may put his winnings into his eye, and see neuer the worse. **1697** DRYDEN *Virg. Georg.* Ded. ¶2 b, One loss may be of more consequence to him, than all his former winnings. **1716** ADDISON *Freeholder* No. 40 ⁋3 A Buttering-Gamester, that stakes all his Winnings upon every Cast. **1725** J. GLANVILL *Poems* 63 When hapless France shall meet with no Repair From Losings here, by healing Winnings there. **1838** DICKENS *O. Twist* xxxix, Mr. Toby Crackit swept up his winnings [at cribbage], and crammed them into his waistcoat pocket. **1885** *Law Rep.* Weekly Notes 145/2 The defendant . . having won on those bets received the winnings from the persons with whom he had betted.

5. *spec.* Getting, gathering, taking (of produce, fish, coal, stone, etc.); also, in *Mining*, the process of excavation and other preparation for working a bed of coal or other mineral: see WIN *v.*^{1} 7 f, g.

1473 *Rental Bk. Cupar-Angus* (1879) I. 192 To mak ma tenandis for wenyng and laboryng of the ground. **1501** *Reg. Privy Seal Scot.* I. 100/1 To sustene ony skaith in the wynnyng of the saidis fischingis. **1506** *Acc. Ld. High Treas. Scot.* III. 87 To Andro Matheson, to the colheuch wynnyng in Faukland v li. **1553–4** *Burgh Rec. Edin.* (1871) II. 286 To Denne Morisoun for wynnyng of thre lintellis to the saids yeittis. **1630** *Burgh Rec. Glasgow* (1876) 374 For the wyning and leiding of certane stonis for mending of the commoun loche. *c* **1790** *Encycl. Brit.* (1797) V. 99/1 Where a level can be drove . . to drain a sufficient tract of coal, it is then the most eligible method of winning. **1825** E. MACKENZIE *View Northumbld.* (ed. 2) I. 87 The winning of a colliery is the draining of a field of coal, so as to render the several seams accessible. **1881** *Nature* 27 Jan. 308 Deep winning of coal in South Wales. **1891** *Times* 10 Oct., The winning of oats in the northern parts of England.

b. *concr.* (*Mining.*) A shaft or pit together with the associated apparatus for 'winning' the coal or other mineral; a portion of a coal-field or mine laid out for working.

1708 J. C. *Compl. Collier* (1845) 42 How much to allow for a Winning. **1768** *Ann. Reg., Chron.* 62 The vast quantity of water expected in this new winning. **1865** *Pall Mall Gaz.* 26 Sept. 7/2 The construction of new winnings, the colliery population, and the production of coal have considerably augmented.

6. Gaining of a person's affection or allegiance; gaining of an adherent or convert; also with *over*.

c **1375** *Sc. Leg. Saints* xxxiii. (*George*) 864 For of a martyre þe pynynge Of a thousand wes wynnynge. *c* **1380** WYCLIF *Wks.* (1880) 93 Þei loue more here owen worldly wynnynge . . þan wynnynge of soulis to blisse. *a* **1586** SIDNEY *Apol. Poetrie* (Arb.) 40 The winning of the mind from wickednesse to vertue. **1605** BACON *Adv. Learn.* I. iv. §2 The great labour that then was with the people . . for the winning and perswading of them. **1643** MILTON *Divorce* viii. Wks. 1851 IV. 47 The uncertain winning of an obdur'd heretick. **1899** HEDDLE *Marget at Manse* 91, I had forgotten all about Andrew and his proposed winning-over. **1918** *Nation* (N.Y.) 7 Feb. 134/1 All the sordid details that counted in the winning over of Italy.

†**7.** Deliverance, redemption: cf. WIN *v.*^{1} 8. *Obs.*

c **1400** *26 Pol. Poems* xxiv. 281 In helle is no wynnyng, Ne non aȝeynbyynge to pes.

8. The action of making one's way or getting somewhere. *Sc.* and *dial.*

1651 SIR A. JOHNSTON *Diary* (S.H.S.) II. 89 [It] might prevent . . his wining to my wyfe. **1818** SCOTT *Hrt. Midl.* xiii, Ye'll find it's easier wunnin in than wunnin out here.

9. *attrib.* Pertaining to or connected with winning, or at which something is won (sometimes practically coincident with WINNING *ppl. a.* 2, q.v.): **winning-chair**, the umpire's seat at the goal of a race-course (cf. *winning-post*); **winning-gallery** (*Real Tennis*), the last gallery on the hazard-side of a tennis-court; **winning headway** (*Coal-mining*), see quots., and cf. sense 5 and WIN *v.*^{1} 7 g; so ***winning mine***, ***pit***; **winning opening** (*Real Tennis*), see quots.; **winning-post**, a post set up at the goal of a race-course, the racer who first passes it being the winner; also *fig.*; **winning streak**: see STREAK *sb.* 6 b.

1835 W. DYOTT *Diary* Oct. (1907) II. 212 A platform was erected in front of the *winning chair [on Lichfield Race Course] to accommodate the ladies who were to deliver the standards [to a regiment]. **1856** 'STONEHENGE' *Brit. Sports* II. I. x. §4. 358/1 They will not leave their horses when called upon, in order to pass the winning-chair first. **1857** G. A. LAWRENCE *Guy Liv.* iv, His horse . . came down heavily into the ditch of the *winning field. **1878** *Winning-gallery [see GALLERY *sb.* 9]. **1891** [see HAZARD *sb.* 6]. *c* **1790** *Encycl. Brit.* (1797) V. 101/1 The first working or excavation made from the coal-pit, commonly called the winning mine or *winning headway. **1846** BROCKETT *N.C. Gloss.* (ed. 3), *Winning headways*, two parallel excavations... The principal exploring drifts of a colliery, for opening out the seams for the daily supply. **1878** J. MARSHALL *Ann. Tennis* 160 **Winning-openings*, the dedans, winning-gallery, and grille. *Ibid.* 163 (Laws §20) Either player wins a chase if he serve or return the ball so that it enter a winning opening. **1895** *Daily Tel.* 12 Nov. 6/7 A *winning pit of the Blackwell Colliery Company. **1759** A. MURPHY *Let.* 22 July in D. Garrick *Private Corr.* (1831) I. 101 You must judge whether they [*sc.* horses] are *marketable*, or likely to tire before they come to the *winning-post. **1790** T. WILKINSON *Mem.* II. 194 Miss Notable and Miss Prue from the archness and excellent acting of Mrs Abington, seemed to have the decision at the winning post for fame. **1820** COMBE *Syntax* xx. 164 In learned labours some proceed, But I prefer the racing steed: . . Others some pow'rful station boast; But let me gain the winning-post. **1824** SCOTT *St. Ronan's* x, The best horse ever started may slip a shoulder before he get to the winning-post. **1886** C. E. PASCOE *London of To-day* xviii. (ed. 3) 170 The starting-point at Putney Bridge, . . the winning-post at Mortlake. **1951** *Times* (Weekly Ed.) 30 May 3 Meals are landmarks, milestones which must be passed before the winnning-post of bed-time is finally and thankfully reached.

†'**winning**, *vbl. sb.*^{2} *Sc. Obs.* [f. WIN *v.*^{2} + -ING^1.] Dwelling, habitation. Also *attrib.*

c **1375** *Sc. Leg. Saints* xl. (*Ninian*) 1101 Ilkane a sere gat held away, Til þai come til þare wynny[n]g-place. *c* **1425** WYNTOUN *Cron.* xxvi. 665 His wynnyng þare he thocht to ma. *c* **1475** *Rauf Coilȝear* 227 Quhair is thy maist wynning? **1513** DOUGLAS *Æneis* v. iv. 103 Als swiftlie as the dow affrait doith fle Furth of hir hole, and rycht darn wynning wane. *c* **1575** *Balfour's Practicks* (1754) 541 His awin proper house, quhair he has his winning, rising, and lying day and nicht.

'**winning**, *vbl. sb.*^{3} *Sc.* and *dial.* [f. WIN *v.*^{3} + -ING^1.] The action of WIN *v.*^{3}

1844 H. STEPHENS *Bk. Farm* II. 242 Better it do that than become again damp after only a partial winning, when the meat loses much of its flavour.

'**winning**, *ppl. a.* [f. WIN *v.*^{1} + -ING^2.] That wins, in various senses.

†**1.** Gaining, or by which one gains, money or wealth; profitable, lucrative. *Obs.*

1435 MISYN *Fire of Love* I. xi. 24 Full hard treuly it is a wynnynge craft or office to haue & not to be couetus. **1530** PALSGR. 329/2 Wynnyng, gaynyng, *questueux*.

2. Gaining, or resulting in, victory or superiority in a contest or competition; victorious. In U.S. colloq. use also in superlative. ***winning hazard***: see HAZARD *sb.* 7 b. ***winning stroke***, a stroke that gains a point in a game, or one by which the game is won.

1592 SHAKS. *Rom. & Jul.* III. ii. 12 Learne me how to loose a winning match. **1609** HOLLAND *Amm. Marcell.* 290 Contemning that Emperour who everie where in civile warre went away on the winning hand. **1822** SCOTT *Nigel* Introd. Epist., I am not displeased to find the game a winning one. **1855** *Poultry Chron.* II. 486 Neither should I have given the first place to the winning Dorking cock. **1860** LÖWENTHAL *Morphy's Games Chess* 56 The winning move. **1884** *Marshall's Tennis Cuts* 114 In playing against a fine player, it is imperative to go for a winning-stroke whenever there is a fair opening. **1974** *State* (Columbia, S. Carolina) 5 Mar. 6-A/7 John Bates, coach of Maryland-Eastern Shore, at 26–1 the winningest college basketball team in the nation. **1979** *Tucson* (Arizona) *Citizen* 20 Sept. 5D/1 Slota defeated Sarah Cap, the winningest active greyhound with 113 career victories. **1985** *Dirt Bike* Mar. 23/2 (Advt.), That's the moment you know what the winningest racers and most satisfied riders know.

3. Persuasive (now *rare* or *obs.*); alluring, attractive, 'taking'. †Also *advb.*, winningly.

1596 *Edward III*, I. ii. 140 What needs a tongue to such a speaking eie, That more perswads then winning Oratorie? *c* **1620** FLETCHER *False One* III. ii, Eyes that are the winningst Orators. **1667** MILTON *P.L.* IV. 479 Less faire, Less winning soft, less amiable milde. **1700** T. BROWN *Amusem. Ser. & Com.* Wks. 1720 III. 54 The Winning Air, the Bewitching Glance, the Amorous Smirk. **1713** ADDISON *Cato* I. iv, While winning Mildness and attractive Smiles Dwell in her Looks. **1809** MALKIN *Gil Blas* VII. xii. ⁋6 You have very winning ways with you; you make me do just whatever you please. **1880** 'MARK TWAIN' *Tramp Abr.* xviii, There is a friendly something about the German character which is very winning.

Hence (in sense 3) '**winningly** *adv.*, '**winningness**.

1663 COWLEY *Cutter Colman St.* IV. i, I know thou canst speak *winningly. **1803** JANE AUSTEN *Susan* vi. (1879) 213 Her voice and manner winningly mild. **1934** G. B. SHAW *On Rocks* I. 208 *Sir Arthur* [*winningly*] And do you, Miss Brollikins, feel that you have got nothing? **1980** *Times Lit. Suppl.* 20 June 702/2 Clothes and hair styles [of petty criminals in the 1870s] repay scrutiny: no one ever dressed up or posed winningly for these pictures. **1727** BAILEY vol. II, *Insinuatingness* . . insinuating Nature, . . *Winningness. **1796** MME. D'ARBLAY *Camilla* I. ii, I think Camilla's [face] so much prettier; I mean in point of winningness. **1864** PUSEY *Daniel* viii. 541 Error has no intrinsic winningness for man.

†'**winninghead.** *Obs. rare.* In 4 **wynnynghede.** [f. WINNING *ppl. a.* + -HEAD.] Disposition to get gain; covetousness.

c **1315** SHOREHAM III. 286 Al hys þefte þat man teȝt Myd wyl of wynnynghede.

‖**winninish.** Also **winin(n)ish**, **-anishe**, **winnonish**, **-iche**, **wen-**, **wan(n)anishe**, **-oniche**, etc. Anglicized forms of the native name of the Labrador fresh-water salmon: see OUANANICHE.

1883 *Fisheries Exhib. Catal.* (ed. 4) 160 A Winnoniche. **1888** GOODE *Amer. Fishes* 445 In the Saguenay the Winninish has easy . . access to the sea.

Winnipeg ('wɪnɪpɛg). The name of the capital of Manitoba, Canada, used *attrib.* in ***Winnipeg couch***, a couch convertible into a double bed.

1954 S. M. RUSSELL *Living Earth* 233 He sat on the Winnipeg couch that stood at one end of the room. **1962** J. ONSLOW *Bowler-Hatted Cowboy* viii. 74 Beneath an old army blanket I drowsed to sleep on my Winnipeg couch. **1973** B. BROADFOOT *Ten Lost Years* xiii. 153 A couch, one of those Winnipeg couch things in the living room.

Hence '**Winnipegger**, a native or inhabitant of Winnipeg.

1882 G. M. GRANT *Picturesque Canada* I. 288 Winnipeggers . . never make comparisons with any city smaller than Chicago. **1936** MENCKEN *Amer. Lang.* (ed. 4) x. 549 Richmonder, Winnipegger, Montrealer, Lynner. **1971** J. GRAY *Red Lights* ii. 27 They watched Winnipeggers frantically planting trees all over the place.

winnle, Sc. and dial. form of WINDLE.

winnock ('wɪnək). *Sc.* Forms: 5 **wyndok**, 6 **vynd-**, **windok**, **vind-**, **wyndak**, **vindock**, **wink** (7 **windick**, 9 **windock**), 6– **winnock**. [Sc. development of *windoȝe*, WINDOW *sb.*; cf. *elbock* for **elboȝe*, ELBOW *sb.*, and WARLOCK. Cf. Gael. *uinneag*, Ir. *fuinneog*.] A window.

1492 *Acc. Ld. High Treas. Scot.* I. 200 Gevin . . for Estland burdis to durris and wyndokis . . v li. **1535** STEWART *Cron. Scot.* (Rolls) III. 477 To ane windok of the presoun scho ȝeid. **1582** in Campbell *Church of Kirkaldy* vii. (1904) 63 Yat William Crosby mak ye kirk and glaissen winkes clean ilk Setterday. **1596** DALRYMPLE tr. *Leslie's Hist. Seot.* (S.T.S.) II. 436 A gret cannoun Bullat . . cam in at the Kirk winnock. **1682** *Rec. Burgh Lanark* (1893) 210 That furthwith ther be ports provydit for four ports . . with windicks. *c* **1730** RAMSAY *To Æolus* 6 To fuff at winnocks and cry 'Wow!' **1816** SCOTT *Old Mort.* xxv, Mony a time I hae helped Jenny Dennison out o' the winnock. **1819** W. TENNANT *Papistry Storm'd* (1827) 132 The windocks scarce wi' beams did lauff, Whan bangit up Sir Tullidaff.

b. *attrib.*, as ***winnock-bunker*** [BUNKER 1], ***-nail***, ***-pane***, ***-sole*** (= WINDOW-SOLE); **winnock-bred**, **-brod** [BRED *sb.*, BROD *sb.*^{2}], a window-shutter.

1513 *Rentale Dunkeldense* (S.H.S. 1915) 281, 60 lie windok naile. **1546** *Acc. Ld. High Treas. Scot.* VIII. 453 For glew to the wyndak breddis. **1790** A. WILSON *2nd Ep. to Jas. Kennedy* Poet. Wks. (1846) 118 And Natures' winnock-brods are closin' Across the lift. **1790** BURNS *Tam o' Shanter* 119 A winnock-bunker in the east. **1896** CROCKETT *Grey Man* i. 10 Put the Bible for a keepsake in your winnock sole.

winnow ('wɪnəʊ), *sb.* Also 6 **-owe**. [f. next.]

1. A contrivance for winnowing grain, etc.; a winnowing-fan or the like.

1580 H. F. *Pelegrom. Syn. Sylva* 126 A Fan or a Winnowe. 1766 *Compl. Farmer* s.v. *Threshing*, The casting-shovel is much more expeditious than..the common winnow with sails. 1818 R. P. KNIGHT *Symb. Lang.* 132 Osiris has the winnow in one hand, and the hook of attraction in the other. 1890 *Sci. Amer.* 14 June 374/2 [Leaves of Palmyra palm] largely employed for making pans, bags, winnows [etc.].

2. An act of winnowing or a motion resembling it, as the swing of a pendent mass, the sweep of wings.

1802 COLERIDGE *Picture* 148 How solemnly the pendent ivy-mass Swings in its winnow. 1829 *Good's Study Med.* (ed. 3) III. 454 Some degree of humidity..which should be swept away by the winnow of a stirring breeze. *a* 1851 MOIR *Birth of Flowers* v, From every winnow of her wings.

winnow ('wɪnəʊ), *v.* Forms: α. 1 **windwian**, 2 **windwin**, 3 **-en**, *Orm.* **winndwenn**, 4 **wyn-**, **windewe**, **wyndwe**, 4–5 **wyndowe**, 4–7 **windowe**, 5 **wyndou**, **-oe**, 5–6 **wyndo**, (6 **wyendo**, **wyondo**, *Sc.* **vyndou**, **wando**), 5– (now *north. dial.*) **window** (9 **winder**). β. 4–5 **wynwe**, **wynnewe**, 4–6 **wynewe**, 5 **wynou**, **wenowe**, 5–6 **wynowe**, 6 **wynew**, **wynnow(e**, **winowe**, *Sc.* **wonnow**, 6–7 **winnowe**, (8 *dial.* **winner**), 6– **winnow**. [OE. *windwian*, f. *wind* WIND *sb.*[1]; cf. OE. *windwiȝceaf* chaff, *windwiȝsife* winnowing-sieve. Other verbal formations of the same meaning are Goth. *diswinþjan* to scatter like chaff, ON. *vinza* (:—**windisôjan*), and L. *ventilare* (f. *ventus* wind). See also WIND *v.*[3]]

1. *trans.* To expose (grain or other substances) to the wind or to a current of air so that the lighter particles (as chaff or other refuse matter) are separated or blown away; to clear of refuse material by this method.

α. *a* 900 *O.E. Martyrol.* 7 Mar. 36 He..corn þærsc & þæt windwode. *c* 1175 *Lamb. Hom.* 85 In þe deie of liureisun hwense god almihtin wule windwin þet er wes iþor[s]chen. *c* 1200 ORMIN 1530 þa winndwesst tu þin þrosshenn corn. *a* 1225 *Ancr. R.* 270 Ane wummon..þet windwede hweate. *c* 1400 MAUNDEV. xiii. (1919) I. 71 He..let wyndwe the askes in the wynd. *c* 1420 *Liber Cocorum* (1862) 7 Þen wyndo hit wele, nede þou mot. 1469 *Plumpton Corr.* (Camden) 21 Also that you gar the malt be windowd. 1549 *Rec. Elgin* (New Spald. Cl. 1903) I. 96 Quhatsumever personn was apprehendit wandoand corne in the hie gett. 1579 *Nottingham Rec.* IV. 190 No mann shall wyndo aney corne in the strettes. 1614 *Manchester Crt. Leet Rec.* (1885) II. 296 Inconvenience by ye often vsinge to Windowe..Corne in the Streets. 1729 P. WALKDEN *Diary* (1866) 45 Windowed my wheat the chaff out of it.

β. 1382 WYCLIF *Ruth* iii. 2 In this nyȝt he wynnewith the flore of his barli. *c* 1440 *Promp. Parv.* 530/1 Wynwyn' (*P.* wynowin), *ventilo*. *c* 1450 *Mirk's Festial* 185 Then made he to take vp þe bonys..and bren hom, and aftyr wynou ham yn þe wynde. 1523–34 FITZHERB. *Husb.* §35 In some countreys..they do fan theyr corne,..if it be well wynowed or fande, it wyll be solde the derer. 1573–80 TUSSER *Husb.* (1878) 125 More often ye turne, more pease ye out spurne, Yet winnow them in, er carrege begin. 1697 DRYDEN *Virg. Georg.* I. 400 And in the Sun your golden Grain display, And thrash it out, and winnow it by Day. 1825 *Gentl. Mag.* Mar. 216 It [*sc.* the coffee-berry] is then winnowed, and goes into the hands of the pickers. 1855 E. FORBES *Lit. Papers* ix. 231 The tea is afterwards winnowed and sifted, so as to free it from impurities. 1893 BRIDGES *Winnowers* v, A steady muffled din, By which we knew that threshed corn Was winnowing.

b. *fig.* To subject to a process likened to the winnowing of grain, in order to separate the various parts or elements, esp. the good from the bad; hence, to clear of worthless or inferior elements.

1382 WYCLIF *Jer.* li. 2 Y shal sende in to Babilon wyneweres [1388 wyndeweris] and thei shul wynewe [1388 wyndewe] it. 1548 UDALL *Erasm. Par. Luke* iii. 15–18 He shall..there winnowe euery creature, triyng them with the wynde of the crosse and of afflictions. 1597 SHAKS. *2 Hen. IV*, IV. i. 194. 1613 —— *Hen. VIII*, V. i. 111. 1646 J. WHITAKER *Uzziah* Ded. A 3 b, His [*sc.* Satan's] desire is to winnow you; if he can ruin you he knows he ruins the Kingdom. 1681 DRYDEN *Abs. & Achit.* I. 112 That Plot,.. Not weigh'd or winnow'd by the Multitude, But swallow'd in the Mass. 1699 BENTLEY *Phal.* 407, I cannot abuse my Reader's Patience in winnowing and sifting it, since the whole is nothing but Chaff. 1829 SOUTHEY *Sir T. More* (1831) I. 335, I wish it had been deemed advisable to have winnowed the Kalendar. 1844 H. H. WILSON *Brit. India* III. 456 After winnowing the list and excluding those who were considered not entitled to vote. 1875 MERIVALE *Gen. Hist. Rome* lxix. 563 The storm had no doubt the effect of winnowing the multitude of professing disciples.

c. *absol.* or *intr.*

c 1200 ORMIN 10483 Þat ure Laferrd Iesu Crist... Himm shollde brinngenn inn hiss hannd hiss winndell forr to winndwenn. 1388 WYCLIF *Ecclus.* v. 11 Wyndewe thee not in to ech wynd. 1573–80 TUSSER *Husb.* (1878) 56 Some vseth to winnow, some vseth to fan. 1621 J. TAYLOR (Water P.) *Superbiæ Flagellum* C 1 b, Plant, graft, hedg, ditch, thresh, winnow, buy & sel. 1647 FULLER *Good Th. in Worse Times* 92 He would Fan, as he doth winnow. 1825 *Yorks. Garland* etc. 16 Ah can milk, kern, fother, beeak, brew, sheear, winder. 1852 MRS. E. M. PITMAN *Mission Life in Greece* (1881) 145 To help them so to winnow that they cast not away the wheat with the chaff.

2. *trans.* (with that which is separated as obj.)

a. To separate or drive off (lighter or refuse particles) by the process described in 1; *fig.* to separate (the worthless part *from* the valuable); to get rid of, clear away, eliminate (something undesirable).

In the earliest quots. a literalism from L. *ventilare*.

c 825 *Vesp. Psalter* xliii. 6 [xliv. 5] In ðe fiond ure we windwiað. 1382 WYCLIF *Deut.* xxxiii. 17 In hem he shal wyndowe gentilys, vnto the teermes of the erthe. 1382 —— *Jer.* xlix. 36 Y shal wynewe [1388 wyndewe] them in to alle these windus. 1387 TREVISA *Higden* (Rolls) IV. 341 Þey.. wynewede þe askes awey with þe wynde. *c* 1390 *Form of Cury* in Warner *Antiq. Culin.* (1791) 4 Hule hem wele, and windewe out the hulkes. 1606 SHAKS. *Tr. & Cr.* I. iii. 28 Distinction with a lowd and powrefull fan, Puffing at all, winnowes the light away. 1642 MILTON *Apol. Smect.* xii. 53 Do but winnow their chaffe from their wheat, ye shall see their great heape shrink. 1781 COWPER *Hope* 417 Your office is to winnow false from true. 1869 LOWELL *Under the Willows* 229 And lets the kind breeze, with its delicate fan, Winnow the heat from out his dank grey hair. 1884 TENNYSON *Becket* I. i. 84 And all my doubts I fling from me like dust, Winnow and scatter all scruples to the wind. 1893 LIDDON, etc. *Pusey* I. xvi. 359 The appointment.. winnowed out the merely sentimental element from among adherents of the young Movement.

b. To separate (the valuable part *from* the worthless); (now esp. with *out*) to extract, select, or obtain (something desirable) by such separation.

1611 SHAKS. *Cymb.* v. v. 134 Giue answer to this Boy, and do it freely, Or..bitter torture shall Winnow the truth from falshood. 1647 MAY *Hist. Parlt.* I. vii. 73 These inventions were but sives, made of purpose to winnow the best men. 1685 BAXTER *Paraphr. N.T.* Matt. iii. 12 He will winnow and throughly separate the wheat from the Chaff, the Faithful from the Rebellious. *a* 1797 H. WALPOLE *Geo. II* (1847) II. vii. 244, I live too near the times..to be able..to winnow the truth from such a variety of interested.. relations. 1827 SCOTT *Chron. Canongate* Introd., In winnowing out the few grains of truth which are contained in this mass of empty fiction. 1843 CARLYLE *Past & Pr.* II. viii, To winnow out the man that is to govern them. 1897 *Allbutt's Syst. Med.* II. 905 Such persons are probably many, but there is no means of winnowing them out.

c. To waft, diffuse. *poet.*

1764 GOLDSM. *Trav.* 122 While sea-born gales their gelid wings expand To winnow fragrance round the smiling land. 1821 CLARE *Vill. Minstr.* II. 22 The woolly clouds..Keep winnowing down their drifting sleet and snows. 1871 B. TAYLOR *Faust* I. i. 23 With wings that winnow blessing From Heaven through Earth I see them pressing.

3. In various transf. uses (cf. L. *ventilare* and FAN *v.* 2–5): **a.** †To brandish or flourish (*obs.*); to beat (the air) with or as with wings; to flap (the wings), to wave (the fins); also *intr.* or with cognate obj., to follow a course with flapping wings, or the like.

1579 GOSSON *Sch. Abuse* Apol. (Arb.) 75 Players haue chosen such a Champion, as when I giue the Allarm, winnowes his weapon. 1667 MILTON *P.L.* v. 270 He..Sailes between worlds & worlds, with steddie wing Now on the polar windes, then with quick Fann Winnows the buxom Air. 1728–46 THOMSON *Spring* 745 Their self-taught wings Winnow the waving element. 1793 [see WINNOWING *ppl. a.*]. 1795 BURNS '*Now spring has clad the groves in green*' iv, The waken'd lav'rock..Winnowing blythe her dewy wings In morning's rosy eye. 1820 SHELLEY *Prometh. Unb.* II. i. 27 Her sea-green plumes Winnowing the crimson dawn. 1844, 1856 [see WINNOWING *vbl. sb.* 2]. 1852 MRS. C. MEREDITH *My Home in Tasmania* II. xviii. 252 Their [*sc.* owls'] ghostly shapes winnowing silently around in the twilight. 1865 [see WINNOWING *ppl. a.*]. 1873 GEIKIE *Geol. Sketches* iv. (1882) 78 In winnowing the air with his arms, he had struck against a waggon standing on the roadway. 1887 NEWTON in *Encycl. Brit.* XXII. 200/1 After..reaching a height at which it appears a mere speck, where it winnows a random zigzag course, it..shoots downwards.

b. Of the air, etc.: *trans.* To fan with a breeze. *intr.* To blow fitfully or in gusts.

1796 CAMPBELL *Caroline* II. ix, Where, winnowed by the gentle air, Her silken tresses darkly flow. 1820 [see WINNOWING *ppl. a.*]. 1827 CLARE *Sheph. Cal.* 7 Falling snows that winnow by. 1892 AMÉLIE RIVES *Barbara Dering* xxvii, Here upon this great crest a purer air came winnowing in.

winnow-cloth. Forms: see WINNOW *v.* and CLOTH. A winnowing-sheet.

α. 1404 *Durham Acc. Rolls* (Surtees) 398, 1 wyndowclath. 1547 *Reg. Mag. Sig. Scot.* 20/2 *note*, Ane windo clath contenand 12 ellis. 1599 in *Antiquary* XXXII. 243 One window cloth. 1894 *Northumbld. Gloss.*, *Winda-claith*, winnowing cloth; now called a barn-sheet.

β. 1552 HULOET, Wynew cloth, *ventilabrum*. 1588–9 *Extr. Burgh Rec. Glasgow* (1876) I. 129 Item, ane wonnow clayth, ane seif, ane sek, ane riddill, price xl s. 1608 TOPSELL *Serpents* 262 Vnder her head a hard Oken-logge, with the Winnow-cloth, and the one end of an old Hop-bagge, cast ouer in steed of a Couerlet. 1790 GROSE *Prov. Gloss.* (ed. 2), *Winner-cloth*, a large cloth on which corn is dighted or winnowed.

winnowed ('wɪnəʊd), *ppl. a.* [f. WINNOW *v.* + -ED[1].] In various senses of the verb.

The interpretation of quot. 1602 has been much disputed; the passage is perh. corrupt.

1602 SHAKS. *Ham.* v. ii. 201 The most fond and winnowed opinions. 1606 —— *Tr. & Cr.* III. ii. 174 Such a winnowed puritie in loue. 1611 FLORIO, *Ago*,..the chaffe comming from winnowed or bolted corne. 1697 DRYDEN *Virg. Georg.* III. 217 When..winnow'd Chaff, by western winds is blown. 1791 COWPER *Iliad* v. 229 Their steeds..eating winnowed grain. 1900 MORLEY *Cromwell* II. v. 183 Faith that the God of Battles was on their side nerved its chosen and winnowed ranks with stern confidence.

winnower ('wɪnəʊə(r)). [f. WINNOW *v.* + -ER[1].]

1. One who winnows; a person engaged in winnowing; also *fig.* (cf. next 1 b).

1382 [see WINNOW *v.* 1 b]. 1538 ELYOT, *Ventilator*, a vanner or wynnower of corne. 1548 UDALL *Erasm. Par. Luke* Pref. B ij b, As a wynnower pourgeth the chaffe from the corne. *c* 1611 CHAPMAN *Iliad* v. 497 As in sacred floores of barnes, vpon corne-winnowers flies The chaffe. 1765 *Museum Rust.* IV. 209 The seed carried into an heap near the winnowers is shook up a little by a caver. 1849 WHITTIER *Leg. St. Mark* xiv, Scattered..Like chaff before the winnower's fan. 1871 R. B. VAUGHAN *S. Thomas of Aquin* II. 646 He did not take for granted, like the Sophist... He was a winnower and a sifter. 1915 F. S. OLIVER *Ordeal by Battle* II. vii. 176 [War] is a great winnower of true men from shams.

2. An apparatus for winnowing; a winnowing-machine.

1605–6 in *Archdeaconry of Stow Wills 1603–6* lf. 110 (MS.) To my sonne Thomas Collinsonne my wyndyers wth the best of my tooles. 1862 J. WILSON *Farming* 164 The winnowers used in such cases do not differ in construction from those worked by hand. 1883 *Cassell's Fam. Mag.* Aug. 528/1 The beans [of coffee are] then put through a winnower. 1890 *Engineer* 12 Dec. 472/1 Threshing machines are popular here, because the grain does not have to run through a winnower.

winnowing ('wɪnəʊɪŋ), *vbl. sb.* [f. WINNOW *v.* + -ING[1].]

1. The process described s.v. WINNOW *v.* 1.

a 1225 *Ancr. R.* 270 Recabes sunen..ifunden þe wummon astunt of hire windwunge & iueollen aslepe. 1435 MISYN *Fire of Love* I. ix. 18 In þe wyndouynge þe caff is oute cast. 1538 ELYOT, *Ventilatio*, a fannynge or wynnowynge. 1586 *Shuttleworths' Acc.* (Chetham Soc.) 25 Wyndoinge of barlie. 1695 *Rector's Bk. Clayworth* (1910) 113 We look'd in to ye wheat..& upon winnowing in order to sale, found it in good condition. 1755 in *6th Rep. Dep. Kpr. Rec.* App. II. 128 [A machine] for the Dressing, Winnowing, and Cleansing of Flax. 1866 ROGERS *Agric. & Prices* I. xv. 261 The winnowing was done by women.

b. *fig.*: see WINNOW *v.* 1 b.

a 1400 *Minor Poems fr. Vernon MS.* xxiii. 437 Whon þe wynewyng schal be-ginne To parte euel from good. 1636 T. GOODWIN *Child of Light* 44 In these commotions & winnowings of spirit. 1679 in *Jrnl. Friends Hist. Soc.* (1919) XVI. 146 This being a time of Trying & winnowing doth onely blow away the chaffe. 1851 GALLENGA *Italy* v. 303 Instead of undergoing a thorough sifting and winnowing, the free corps fell every day into a more deplorable state of disorder. 1913 *Athenæum* 7 June 609/1 He has..subjected the correspondence..to a rigorous winnowing.

2. Of wings, etc.: see WINNOW *v.* 3. Chiefly *poet.*

1844 MRS. BROWNING *Rhyme of Duchess May* Concl. iv, Angel-wings, with their holy winnowings. 1856 KINGSLEY *Glaucus* (ed. 3) 120 Small cuttle-fish..put into a jar, will hover and dart in the water..by rapid winnowings of their glassy side-fins. 1897 F. THOMPSON *New Poems* 52 The wings Hear I not in prævenient winnowings Of coming songs, that lift my hair and stir it?

3. *attrib.* and *Comb.* (in sense 1), as ***winnowing operation***, ***place***; esp. in names of appliances for winnowing, as ***winnowing-basket***, ***-cloth***, ***-fan*** (see FAN *sb.*[1] 1), ***-machine***, ***-mill***, ***-sheet***, ***-shovel***.

1375 *Doc. Doune Manor, Wandsworth* (Westm. Chapter Munim.), 1 wyndwyngschete debilis. 1378 *Ibid.*, 1 Wynfynschete de Canabis. 1382 WYCLIF *Matt.* iii. 12 Whos wynwing cloth [is] in his hond. 1382 —— *Luke* iii. 17 Whos wynewyng tool in his hond. 1388 —— *Jer.* xv. 7 A wyndewynge instrument. 1548 UDALL *Erasm. Par. Luke* iii. 15–18 He shall make clene the floore of his winnowyng place. 1710 O. SANSOM *Acc. Life* 35 They took away my Winnowing-Fan, which was worth 8*s.* 1773 *Pennsylv. Gaz.* 3 Feb. Suppl. 2/3 A winnowing-mill. 1780 EDMONDSON *Her.* II. Gloss. s.v. *Basket*, A Winnowing-Basket. 1805 R. W. DICKSON *Pract. Agric.* I. 31 Winnowing-Machines. Machines of this sort are in pretty general use, where thrashing mills..are not erected. 1862 RAMSAY *Remin.* vi. (ed. 8) 243 The..man surceased his winnowing operations. 1879 B. TAYLOR *Germ. Lit.* viii. 253 The winnowing-mill of Time makes sad havoc with works considered immortal in their day. 1886 *S. W. Linc. Gloss.* s.v., A windering sheet.

'winnowing, *ppl. a.* [f. as prec. + -ING[2].] That winnows, in various senses of the verb.

1651 J. READING *Guide to Holy City* 347 Tentation only burneth out the drosse: it is as a winnowing winde. 1651 RUTHERFORD *Let. to Lady Kenmure* 28 Sept., We are fallen in winnowing & trying times. 1793 WOLCOT (P. Pindar) *Ode to Innoc.* Wks. 1812 III. 223 The winnowing Butterfly with painted wing. 1820 KEATS *Autumn* ii, Thy hair soft-lifted by the winnowing wind. 1865 SWINBURNE *Poems & Ball.*, *Faustine* 110 After change of soaring feather And winnowing fin.

Hence **'winnowingly** *adv.*

1834 M. SCOTT *Cruise Midge* (1859) 265 The wing of the slow-sailing owl flitted winnowingly across.

†**winnow-sheet.** *Obs.* [f. WINNOW *v.*] A winnowing-sheet.

c 1394 *P. Pl. Crede* 435 His wijf walked him wiþ..In a cutted cote..Wrapped in a wynwe schete to weren hire fro weders. 14.. *Voc.* in Wr.-Wülcker 618/38 *Ventilabrum*.., a wynue [*printed* wynne] shete. 1577 in H. Hall *Soc. Eliz. Age* (1886) App. I. 154, 16 sacks & two window sheets. 1688 HOLME *Armoury* III. iii. 74/1 To make Wind with a Winnow sheet. 1808 *Sporting Mag.* XXXI. 113 Covered with a winnow-sheet.

†**'winnowster.** Chiefly *Sc. Obs.* Also 4 **wynewestere**; *Sc.* 6 **vyndoustar**, **windostar**, 7 **windister**; 9 **winnister**. [f. WINNOW *v.* + -STER.] = WINNOWER (orig. applied to a woman).

c 1325 *Gloss. W. de Bibbesw.* in Wright *Voc.* 148 Par ventresse [*gloss* a wynewestere] en ventre Payn de furment entre. 1505 *Exchequer Rolls Scot.* XII. 673 Item to the vyndoustaris iiij bollis aitis. 1508 *Rentale Dunkeldense* (S.H.S. 1915) 251 For the windostaris, 2 b[olls]. 1618 in A. L. Ritchie *Churches St. Baldred* (1880) 170 That some women..being ye Ladies windisteris, did spred muick ye last Sabbothe at efternoone. 1825 JAMIESON, *Winnowster*, *winnister*, *sb.*, a machine for winnowing corn. *Aberd.*

winny ('wɪnɪ). *U.S. slang.* Var. WIENIE. Also *Comb.*, as *winny-wurst.* Cf. WEENY *sb.*[2]

1867 J. CHRISTISON *Crime & Criminals* 37 For a week longer he served at his usual business, which was that of peddling 'winnies', mostly among the saloons. **1914** B. TARKINGTON *Penrod* xix. 199 Winnies! *Here's* your hot winnies! Hot winny-*wurst!* **1929** T. WOLFE *Look Homeward, Angel* xx. 272 Fortune out of winnies. They're hot, they're hot.

winny, obs. or dial. var. WHINNY.

wino ('waɪnəʊ). *slang* (orig. *U.S.*). [f. WIN(E *sb.*[1] + -O[2].] An habitual drinker of cheap wine; an alcoholic or drunkard, esp. one who is destitute.

1915 *World* (N.Y.) *Mag.* 9 May 14/3 *Wineoe*, a wine bum; known on the Pacific Coast, especially in California. **1926** J. BLACK *You can't Win* xii. 153 The wine dumps, where wine bums or 'winos' hung out. **1946** [see JUICED *a.* 2]. **1957** J. KEROUAC *On Road* I. i. 9 Working.. without pause eight hours a night.. in greasy wino pants with a frayed fur-lined jacket and beat shoes that flap. **1958** *Times* 24 Nov. p. viii/5 In fact, Canadians have reserved the term 'wino' for the most reprehensible of their drinkers. **1961** *Guardian* 28 Feb. 8/7 A conglomeration of hop-heads, winos, overworked policemen. **1967** *Sunday Truth* (Austral.) 16 July 28/4 To save gas she washes in public toilets, and if she feels like a drink she has a swig from a wino's bottle at South Brisbane. **1973** 'J. MARKS' *Mick Jagger* (1974) 106 That sonuvabitch Dean Martin.. that lousy wino wop! **1979** *Evening Standard* 2 Mar. 19/4, I am in sympathy with the plea by Mrs A. L. Hughes for the survival of buskers, but feel her attack on 'winos' is both misdirected and lacking in human understanding. **1981** M. LEITCH *Silver's City* xii. 103 He saw the winos watching him out of bleary eyes as they huddled on their benches passing their brown bottles to and fro.

winraw, winrow: see WINDROW.

winsome ('wɪnsəm), *a.* Forms: 1, 5 **wynsum**, 2–3 **wunsum**, 2, 4 **winsum**, 3 **wonsom**, 4 **winsom**, **wonsum**; 7–9 *n. dial.* **wunsome**, 8- (in 8 only *Sc.*) **winsome**. [OE. *wynsum* = OS. *wunsam*, OHG. *wunnisam* (MHG. *wun(ne)sam*), f. *wyn(n* WIN *sb.*[2] + *-sum* -SOME. Sense 3 came into the literary language from northern dialects.]

I. OE. and ME. senses.

†**1.** Pleasant, delightful, agreeable. *Obs.*

Beowulf 612 Ðær wæs hæleþa hleahtor, hlyn swynsode, word wæron wynsume. *a* **900** *O.E. Martyrol.* 3 May, þær com upp of þære eorðan wynsumes stences rec. *a* **1000** *Phœnix* 13 Þæt is wynsum wong, wealdas grene. *c* **1175** *Lamb. Hom.* 35 Hit walð me þunchen þet softeste beð, and þet wunsemeste þet ic efre ibad. *c* **1205** LAY. 1187 He makede bi þon weofede a swiðe wunsum [*c* **1275** wonsom] fur. *a* **1225** *Juliana* 70 Hit colede anan ant warð hire as wunsum as euer eni wlech weter. *a* **1300** *Cursor M.* 5792 A wonsun [*sic*] thede, A land rinnand bath honi and milk.

†**2.** Kindly, gracious; merciful. *Obs. rare.*

c **900** tr. *Bæda's Hist.* v. xxii. (1890) 472 He wæs se swetesta lareow & se wynsumesta [L. *suavissimus*]. *c* **1205** LAY. 153 Feier wes þe wimmon & wunsum hire monnen. *a* **1300** *E.E. Psalter* ci[i]. 3 Þat winsom es to alle þine wickenesses.

II. Modern senses.

3. Pleasing or attractive in appearance, handsome, comely; of attractive nature or disposition, of winning character or manners.

1677 W. NICOLSON in *Trans. R. Soc. Lit.* (1870) Ser. II. IX. 322 *Wunsome*, neat, pleasant. **1724** W. HAMILTON *Braes of Yarrow* i, Busk ye, busk ye, my bony bony bride; Busk ye, busk ye, my winsome marrow. **1792** BURNS *My Wife's a winsome wee thing* i, She is a winsome wee thing, She is a handsome wee thing, She is a bonnie wee thing. **1818** SCOTT *Br. Lamm.* xiv, If the young folk liked ane anither, they wad make a winsome couple. **1833** H. COLERIDGE *Poems, Sonn.* viii, The rugged root that bare the winsome flower Is weak and wither'd. **1843** LYTTON *Last Bar.* IV. viii, I know thou art fair and winsome. **1873** DIXON *Two Queens* v. vi. I. 276 Henry broke into his winsome laugh. **1889** BUCHANAN *Heir of Linne* xix, She looked very winsome in her plain black dress.

4. Cheerful, joyous, gay. *dial.*

1787 GROSE *Prov. Gloss.*, *Wunsome*, smart, trimly dressed, lively, joyous. N. **1825** BROCKETT *N.C. Gloss.*, *Winsome, wunsome*, lively, cheerful, gay.

Hence '**winsomely** *adv.*, '**winsomeness** in senses 3 and 4 of the adj. (OE. *wynsumlíce*, *wynsumnes* did not survive.)

17.. *Jock o the Side* xxv. in Child *Ballads* VI. 480 O Jock, sae winsomely's ye ride, Wi baith your feet upo ae side! **1825** JAMIESON, *Winsomelie*, in a cheerful and engaging way. *Winsomeness*, cheerfulness and engaging sweetness. **1875** MRS. RANDOLPH *Wild Hyacinth* i, She could not have been called beautiful, but there was a winsomeness in Hyacinth Ettrick's face that rendered criticism a hard and ungracious task. **1883** MRS. BISHOP in *Leisure Hour* 83/1 Who came forward and most winsomely shook hands with us.

Winstonian (wɪn'stəʊnɪən), *a.* [f. the name of Sir *Winston* Leonard Spencer Churchill, British prime minister 1940–5 and 1951–5: see -IAN.] Of, pertaining to, or characteristic of Sir Winston Churchill. Cf. CHURCHILLIAN *a.*

1905 W. S. CHURCHILL *Let.* 9 May in R. S. Churchill *Winston S. Churchill* (1969) II. Compan. I. 391 It is vy kind of you to write me such a long letter. It will be carefully preserved among the Winstonian archives. **1945** S. SASSOON *Siegfried's Journey* viii. 79 The Winstonian exposition continued until Eddie reappeared with an apologetic intimation that Lord Fisher was growing restive. **1967** *Guardian* 16 May 8/6 Winstonian echoes to match the countless plaster busts in shop windows.

wint, obs. f. WIND *sb.*[1]; obs. 3 sing. of WIND *v.*[1]

wint, var. WENT.

winter ('wɪntə(r)), *sb.*[1] Forms: *Sing.* 1- **winter**; 3 *Orm.* **winnterr**, 3–7 **wynter**, (4 **weinter**, *Sc.* **vyntir**), 4–5 **wintur**, **wintre**, **wyntre**, **wyntir**, **-ur**, **-yr(e**, (4–6 **vynter**, *Sc.* **vintir**), 5 **wintir**, (**wintare**, **winttur**, **whynter**, **vyntyr**, 6 **vintter**). *Plural.* 1 **wintru** (*gen.* **wintra**), 2–5 **wintre**, 4–5 **wyntre**; *dat.* 1 **wintrum**, 2 **wintron**, 2–3 **-en**; 1–6 **winter**, (3 *Orm.* **winnterr**, 4 **vynter**, etc. as in sing.), 4–6 **wynter**; 1 **wintras**, 3–5 **wintres**, 4–5 **wyntres**, (4 **winteris**, **-es**, etc.), 4- **winters**; 4–5 **wyntren**. [OE. *winter* str. m. = OFris. *winter*, OS. *wintar* (MLG., MDu., LG., Du. *winter*), OHG. *wintar* (MHG., G. *winter*), ON. *vetr*, earlier *vettr*, *vittr* (Sw., Da. *vinter*, from LG.), Goth. *wintrus* :—**wentrus*, prob. f. nasalized form of the Indo-Eur. base *wed-*, *wod-*, *ud-* to be wet, found in WET *a.*, WATER *sb.*, OTTER.

Originally a *u*-stem, OE. *winter* had regularly gen. (rare) and dat. sing. in *-a*; but the ordinary gen. sing. in *-es*, dat. sing. in *-e*, and nom. pl. in *-as*, in *-u*, and without inflection, show general assimilation to other declensions.]

1. a. The fourth and coldest season of the year, coming between autumn and spring; reckoned astronomically from the winter solstice to the vernal equinox, i.e. in the northern hemisphere from the 22nd of December to the 20th of March; in popular use comprising the months of December, January, and February (or, according to some, November, December, and January); also often in contradistinction to *summer*, the colder half of the year (cf. MIDWINTER). In the southern hemisphere corresponding in time to the northern summer.

(*a*) In general use. (Also personified.)

c **888** ÆLFRED *Boeth.* xxi. §1 On sumera hit bið wearm, & on wintra ceald. *a* **1000**, *c* **1200**, *a* **1225** [see SUMMER *sb.*[1] 1 (*a*)]. *a* **1250** *Owl & Night.* 458 Ne recche ich nouht of wintres teone. **1377** LANGL. *P. Pl.* B. XVII. 226 As men may se in wyntre Ysekeles in eueses þorw hete of þe sonne, Melteth in a mynut while. **1382** WYCLIF *Isa.* xviii. 6 Alle the bestes of erthe vp on hym shal dwelle al wynter. *c* **1450** CAPGRAVE *Life St. Gilbert* (1910) 70 He wered no mo clothis in Wyntir þann in Somyr. *c* **1460** J. RUSSELL *Bk. Nurture* 766 Wyntur with his lokkys grey febille & old. *c* **1530** *Songs, Carols*, etc. (E.E.T.S.) 133 Wynter etythe, that somer getith. **1532–3** *Durham Househ. Bk.* (Surtees) 192 In agestamento unius equi in vynter,..16 d. **1551** RECORDE *Cast. Knowl.* (1556) 32 Haruest..continueth till the twelft day of December, and then doth the Son entre into Capricorn, & Winter beginneth. **1600** SHAKS. *A.Y.L.* v. iv. 142 You and you, are sure together, As the Winter to fowle Weather. **1647** COWLEY *Mistr.*, *Bathing in River* 28 When rig'orous Winter binds you up with Frost. **1719** [see SUMMER *sb.*[1] 1 (*a*)]. **1786** BURNS *Twa Dogs* 192 Thro' winter's cauld, or simmer's heat. **1820** SHELLEY *Sensit. Pl.* III. 86 Winter came: the wind was his whip: One choppy finger was on his lip. **1824** LOUDON *Encycl. Gardening* (ed. 2) 893 The season called winter by the natives of South America, lasting from May to November. **1840** DICKENS *Old C. Shop* lii, Store of fire-wood for the winter.

(*b*) In particularized use, esp. with qualification, or as denoting this season in a certain year.

Beowulf 1128 Hengest ða ȝyt wælfaȝne winter wunode mid Finn. **971** *Blickl. Hom.* 213 Wæs se winter eac þy ȝeare toþæs grim þæt maniȝ man his feorh.. ȝesealde. *c* **1205** LAY. 6034 Auere alche wintre inne Wales heo wuneden. **1375** BARBOUR *Bruce* IV. 338 In Rauchryne..[he] Lay till the vyntir neir wes gane. **1393** LANGL. *P. Pl.* C. XIII. 198 After an hard wynter. **1398** TREVISA *Barth. De P.R.* IV. iv. (Add. MS. 27944) If þe wintir tofore honde was as springinge tyme hote and moyst. **1590** SHAKS. *Com. Err.* III. ii. 100, I warrant, her ragges and the Tallow in them, will burne a Poland Winter. **1634** LAUD *Diary* Oct.–Dec., God bless us in the spring, after this green winter. **1740** C'TESS POMFRET in *C'tess Hartford's Corr.* (1805) II. 161 Mr. Walpole and Mr. Dashwood stay the winter. **1810** CRABBE *Borough* xxii. 232 A winter pass'd since Peter saw the town, And summer-lodgers were again come down.

(*c*) Phr. ***winter and summer***: see SUMMER *sb.*[1] 1 (*c*).

b. With reference to the chilling or injurious effect of winter, esp. on plants; *transf.* a period resembling winter, wintry or cold weather.

c **1000** *Sax. Leechd.* III. 274 Se wind [zephirus] towyrpð & ðawað ælcne winter. **1599** DALLAM in *Early Voy. Levant* (Hakl. Soc.) 84 This day we had bothe wynter and somer. **1607** SHAKS. *Timon* III. vi. 33 The Swallow followes not Summer more willing, then we your Lordship. *Tim.* Nor more willingly leaues Winter, such Summer Birds are men. **1697** DRYDEN *Æneis* IX. 913 When..bellowing Clouds.. with an armed Winter strew the Ground. **1757** [BURKE] *Europ. Settlem. Amer.* VII. xxii. II. 241 The second sort, which..bears the winter better, is a more tall and vigorous plant. **1801** *Farmer's Mag.* Nov. 467 They stood the Winter well.

c. In fig. and allusive use, esp. in reference to old age, or to a time or state of affliction or distress.

1590 GREENE *Never too Late* (1600) D 1, I am driuen in the winter of my yeares to abide the brunt of all stormes. **1594** SHAKS. *Rich. III*, I. i. 1 Now is the Winter of our Discontent, Made glorious Summer by this Son of Yorke. **1606** —— *Tr. & Cr.* IV. v. 24. **1668** R. STEELE *Husbandman's Calling* iii. (1672) 35 Prosperity..nourisheth so many weeds, that the winter of affliction hath much ado to master them. **1746** SHENSTONE *Song, Winter* 16 When will relenting Delia chase The winter of my soul? **1829** I. TAYLOR *Enthus.* x. 296 What has been done is not lost; the seed sown may spring up, even after a century of winter. **1849** FROUDE *Nem. Faith* vii. (ed. 2) 48 It is night and day..with all of us, if we want to keep in health. To be sure, now and then there will come a North Pole winter. **1869** TENNYSON *Passing of Arthur* 4 When the man was..In the white winter of his age.

2. Put for 'year': nearly always *pl.* with a numeral; often in expressions referring to a person's age.

In early use as a mere synonym of 'year'; later *poet.* or *rhet.*, chiefly in reference to advanced age or to a protracted period of hardship or misfortune (cf. 1 c, and SUMMER *sb.*[1] 2). See also THRINTER, TWINTER.

Beowulf 2209 Syððan Beowulfe bræde rice on hand ȝehwearf; he ȝeheold tela fiftiȝ wintru. *a* **900** *Saxon Geneal.* in *O.E. Texts* 179 Ða wæs agan his eldo xxiii wintra. *c* **1000** *Ags. Gosp.* John ii. 20 Þis tempel wæs ȝetimbrod on six & feowertiȝon wintron [*Hatton* wintren]. **1154** *O.E. Chron.* (Laud MS.) an. 1137, & ðet lastede þa xix wintre wile Stephne was king. *a* **1200** *Moral Ode* 4 in *Lamb. Hom.* 159 Þah ich bo a wintre ald to ȝung ich em on rede. *c* **1205** LAY. 9028 Tou and twenti wintre þis lond he iwalde. *Ibid.* 9695 Ah al oðer hit iwarð inne þan twam wintren. *c* **1275** *Passion of our Lord* 132 in *O.E. Misc.* 41 Vele wintre hit is ago þe prophete hit seyde. **1377** LANGL. *P. Pl.* B. XII. 3, I haue folwed þe in feithe þis fyue and fourty wyntre.

c **893** ÆLFRED *Oros.* I. xiv, Þa Læcedemonia besætan þa burȝ Mæs[ian]e x winter. *a* **1000** *Be monna wyrdum* 9 God ana wat hwæt him weaxendum winter bringað. *c* **1200** ORMIN 15594 Fowwerrtiȝ winnterr ȝedenn forþ & ȝet tær tekenn sexe. *c* **1250** *Gen. & Ex.* 919 Loth was fifti winter hold. **13..** *Northern Passion* 935 (Camb. Gg. 5. 31) Þis thre vynter. *c* **1386** CHAUCER *Monk's T.* 69 Fully twenty wynter yeer by yeere He hadde of Israel the gouernance. *c* **1400** *Rule St. Benet* (prose) lxx. 46 Til þai be o fiftene winter elde. **14..** *Pol. Rel. & L. Poems* (1903) 128/175 The elder broþer hade a Sonne to clerke, Well of fyftene wynter of age. **1509** BARCLAY *Shyp of Folys* (1874) I. 42 An hundreth wynter [*ed.* 1570 winters]. **1522** *World & Child* (facs.) A iij b, Now I am .xix. wynter olde.

c **1250** *Gen. & Ex.* 1211 Wintres forð-wexen on ysaac. **13..** *Cursor M.* 20832 (Edin.) Þis leuedi..liuid bot winteris .vij. and .ix. *c* **1380** WYCLIF *Sel. Wks.* III. 502 Holy Kirke hafs ben in erroure mony hundred wynters. *c* **1400** *St. Alexius* (Cotton) 261 A gayne xvij wyntersende. **1470–85** MALORY *Arthur* x. xxxiii. 467 Thus Anglydes endured yeres and wynters tyl Alysander was bygge and stronge. **1593** SHAKS. *Rich. II*, I. iii. 260 What is sixe Winters, they are quickely gone? **1612** *Two Noble K.* v. i. 114, I knew a man Of eightie winters. **1784** COWPER *Tiroc.* 210 Ere sixteen winters old. **1833** TENNYSON *Palace of Art* 139 A hundred winters snowed upon his breast.

c **1400** *St. Jer.* 15 *Tokens* 22 In þilk age he schal arise þat god was inne ded, Of litel more þan xxx[ti] wyntren.

sing. *c* **1412** HOCCLEVE *De Reg. Princ.* 5217 The ryot þat haþ ben with-in þis lande..many a wyntres space. *c* **1460** METHAM *Wks.* (1916) 84 Jon Metham..tranlatyd yt in-to Englysch the xxv[ti] wyntyr off hys age.

3. *attrib.* passing into *adj.* **a.** = Of, pertaining to, or characteristic of winter; adapted or appropriate to, used or occupied in, winter; existing, appearing, active, flourishing, or performed in winter.

(*a*) of natural phenomena, animals, plants, etc.

a **1000** *Phœnix* 18 Ne wearm weder ne winterscur. **1390** GOWER *Conf.* I. 35 The stormy wynter shoures. *c* **1400** *Laud Troy Bk.* 3576 Wyntir-wedur. **1576–7** *Wills & Inv. Durham* (Surtees) II. 318, v whyes, of iiij yeres olde, vj winter whies, 18*l.* **1585** HIGINS *Junius' Nomencl.* 55/2 *Alcedo, alcyon*,..a winter birde commonly called the kings fisher. **1596** SHAKS. *Tam. Shr.* IV. iii. 110 Thou Flea, thou Nit, thou winter cricket thou. **1600** *Knaresb. Wills* (Surtees) I. 223, I geve to Anne..one old winter stocke of bees. **1600** SHAKS. *A.Y.L.* II. vii. 174 Blow, blow, thou winter winde. **1637** RUTHERFORD *Let. to R. Stuart* 17 June, The winter-well will goe dry again in summer. **1639** J. CLARKE *Parœm.* 263 Winter thunder, is old mens wonder. **1653** WALTON *Angler* To Rdr. A 7, Winter-flies, all Anglers know,..are as useful as an Almanack out of date. **1717** POPE *Iliad* x. 507 His Coursers..white as Winter-Snow. **1717** PRIOR *Alma* II. 534 Cast your Eye By Night upon a Winter-Sky. **1751** YOUNG *Nt. Th.* VII. 34 Repelling Winter Blasts with Mud and Straw. **1773** G. WHITE *Selborne, To Pennant* 9 Nov., The.. stock-dove..seldom appearing till towards the end of November; is usually the latest winter-bird of passage. **1813** SCOTT *Rokeby* III. xxviii, The rose..shall bloom in winter snow, Ere we two meet again. **1850** *Beck's Florist* 115 A pleasing and interesting winter-tree is the Glastonbury Thorn. **1856** KANE *Arctic Expl.* I. xx. 244 The most solid winter-ice is open here and there. **1869** TOZER *Highl. Turkey* II. 136 A..bridge..across the bed of a winter torrent. **1869** TENNYSON *Passing of Arthur* 221 The winter moon, Brightening the skirts of a long cloud.

(*b*) of clothing, provisions, etc., accommodation (also WINTER-HOUSE, WINTER QUARTERS); of localities in their winter state and things serviceable in winter.

c **893** ÆLFRED *Oros.* IV. viii, Þæt he buton sorȝe mehte on þæm wintersetle ȝewunian. *a* **1000** *Phœnix* 250 Forst & snaw ..eorþan þeccað wintergewædum. *c* **1000** *Rectitudines* ix. (Liebermann 450), VIII pund cornes to mete, i sceap oððe III p.' to wintersufle. **1395** *Cartular. Abb. de Whiteby* (Surtees 1881) II. 568 De wynterfare..xxvis. De lentynfare..xi *li.* xs. iid. De halfare..xviiis. ?*c* **1400** LYDG. *Æsop's Fab.* iii. 98 The lawe dide hym compelle..his wynter flees to selle. *c* **1440** *Pallad. on Husb.* I. 331 The wintir wonyng. **1473** *Rental Bk. Cupar-Angus* (1879) I. 188 Pasture..reseruyt to the abbay, safe the wynter pastur. **1483** *Cath. Angl.* 420/1 A Wyntir haule, *hibernium, hibernaculum.* **1538** ELYOT *Dict.*, *Tablinum*, was a wynter parlour, wherein were painted tables and bokes of stories. **1568** KNOLLYS in *Cal. Scott. Pap.* (1900) II. 513 Unprovided of sufficient wynter garments. **1575** *Wills & Inv. N.C.* (Surtees 1835) I. 406 Another Close for Winter ground. **1593** SHAKS. *Lucr.* 1218 As winter meads when sun doth melt their snow. **1628** MAY *Virg. Georg.* I. 15 Some sit up late at winter-fires. **1628** F. DRAKE *World Encompassed* 64 Notwithstanding it was in the height of Summer..we could..haue beene contented to haue kept about vs still our Winter clothes. **1653** Walton *Angler* xii. 222 A winter bait for a Roch. **1675** Hannah Woolley *Gentlew. Comp.* 215 Provide your Winter-Butter and Cheese in the Summer. **1694** Motteux *Rabelais* iv. xxiv. 102 Have some winter Boots made of it, they'le never take in a drop of Water. **1713** C'tess Winchilsea *Misc. Poems* 36 Birds have dropt their Winter-plumes. **1727** Gay *Begg. Op.* iii. vi. 46 Black Velvet Scarfs.. are a handsome Winter-wear. **1729** Fenton in *Waller's Wks.* Observ. p. xxxiv, When the Sun retir'd.. to the six Winter-Signs of the Zodiac; short'ning the days. **1735** Somerville *Chase* iii. 97 So Ships in Winter-Seas.. defy the Storm. **1759** G. Clough *Let.* 30 Sept. in *Essex Inst. Hist. Coll.* (1861) III. 104/1 Cold weather.. will make us.. put on our Winter Clothing. **1760**, **1791** Winter-lodge [see hibernaculum 3, hibernacle]. **1818** Scott *Rob Roy* xxvi, Sic as folk tell ower at a winter-ingle. **1819** Keats *Eve of St. Mark* 77 The warm angled winter-screen. **1838** *Workwoman's Guide* in Walkley & Foster *Crinolines & Crimping Irons* (1978) xi. 165 Care should be taken to separate.. winter clothing from that worn in summer. **1842** W. F. Ainsworth *Trav. Asia Minor* II. 394 The winter road.. takes the longer portion of valley. **1842** Loudon *Suburban Hort.* 677 [Celery] is.. cultivated as a winter salad. **1844** H. Stephens *Bk. Farm* II. 484 To harrow it before cross-ploughing the winter-furrow. **1847** W. C. L. Martin *Ox* 35/2 After being kept on winter-fodder, they are turned out to graze in the spring. **1850** Tennyson *In Mem.* xxx, The winds.. We heard them sweep the winter land. **1855** *Orr's Circ. Sci., Inorg. Nat.* 38 A glacier.. is the outlet of.. vast reservoirs of snow, being a prolongation of the winter-world above. **1870** E. G. E. Ward *Jrnl.* 9 Nov. in D. P. Carew *Many Years, Many Girls* (1967) i. 33, I have been able to-day to send my children in England some winter clothes. **1874** Geo. Eliot *Let.* 16 June (1956) VI. 57 The cold winds.. have forced us to put on winter clothing. **1876** C. M. Yonge *Three Brides* I. iii. 35 Her hair and pretty Parisian winter dress arranged to perfection. **1892** *Daily News* 12 Dec. 1/2 (Advt.), Gentlemen's undervests. Winter weight, 32 in. to 48 in. chests. **1904** Bridges *Demeter* I. 282, I think he watch'd a summer-butterfly Creep out all crumpled from his winter-case. **1911** J. Ward *Roman Era Brit.* iv. 77 There was a 'winter-room' on the south side. **1934** G. B. Shaw *On Rocks* ii. 226 There is a generous fire in the grate; and the visitors wear winter clothes. **1940** L. I. Wilder *Long Winter* ix. 73 They dressed carefully in their woolen winter dresses. **1979** T. Barling *Olympic Sleeper* xi. 138 He was warm in his winterweight pin-striped suit. **1984** W. Beechey *Rich Mrs. Robinson* xii. 89 He needs some winter vests badly.

(*c*) of times and seasons. (See also winter-day, -tide, -time.)

a **1000** *Genesis* 370, & moste [ic] ane tid ute weorþan, wesan ane winterstunde. **1390** Gower *Conf.* I. 81 The blake wynter nyht. *c* **1400** *Brut* i. 194 He wolde nouȝt abide in Scotland in wynter seson. **1508** Dunbar *Tua Mariit Wemen* 77 The lang winter nicht. **1559** W. Cuningham *Cosmogr. Glasse* 34 The wynter tropike or circle of retorning from the South. **1577** Googe *Heresbach's Husb.* i. 11 Thinges doone .. in the Winter morninges. *Ibid.* 41 The Male [Hemp].. is made vp in bundels to be knockt and shaled in Winter euenynges. **1707** Freind *Peterborow's Cond. Sp.* 223 Marching in the stony Mountains, and in a Winter-season. **1825** Hook *Sayings* Ser. ii. I. *Man of many Friends* 156 The rosy May, though fashionably a winter month, led on the smiling summer of nature, and June.. was fast approaching. **1869** Lowell (*title of poem*), A Winter Evening Hymn to my Fire. *a* **1889** G. M. Hopkins in *Dublin Rev.* (1920) July–Sept. 46 They came from the south, Where winter-while is all forgot.

(*d*) of actions or conditions.

a **1310** in Wright *Lyric P.* xiii. 43 A-way is huere wynter wo. **1616** Surfl. & Markh. *Country Farm* v. xviii. 555 In October you shall giue it the fourth ardor or earing, which is called Winter-ridging. **1625** Bacon *Ess., Prophecies* (Arb.) 537 They ought.. to serue, but for Winter Talke, by the Fire side. **1677** Hubbard *Pres. St. New-Eng.* (1865) I. 165 Some of the stoutest of the Narhagansets that had escaped the Winter-brunt. *a* **1700** Evelyn *Diary* 14 Nov. 1666, I went my winter circle thro' my district. **1711** Swift *Cond. Allies* 52 Eight Thousand Men, for whose Winter Campaign the Queen was willing to give forty Thousand Pounds. **1725** Winter pruning [see summer *sb.*^{1} 4 a (*e*)]. **1726–46** Thomson *Winter* 573 Thus in some deep retirement would I pass The winter-glooms with friends of pliant soul. **1809** *Phil. Trans.* XCIX. 317 That very common.. disease of our climate, the winter cough. **1836–9** M. Hall in *Todd's Cycl. Anat.* II. 768/2 The winter-sleep and the summer-sleep of hibernating animals. **1842** Dickens *Amer. Notes* xv, [The emigrants] had had a long winter-passage out. **1934** Winter cruise [see *front-pager* s.v. front *sb.* (and *a.*) 14]. **1976** *Liverpool Echo* 6 Dec. 7/1 Aznar Line are having a record breaking season with their winter cruises out of Liverpool.

(*e*) with agent-nouns or other descriptive designations.

1654 G. Goddard in *T. Burton's Diary* (1828) I. Introd. p. lxxviii, Some part of the sea-forces were already struck off, and the winter-guard reduced. **1783** Crabbe *Village* i. 201 When he tends the sheep, His winter-charge. **1854** *Poultry Chron.* I. 363 The Cochins.. proved themselves the best possible 'winter-layers'.

b. The possessive *winter's* is similarly used, chiefly with *day*, *night*, *morning*, *evening*. ***winter's tale***: see *winter-tale* in 5.

835 *Charter* in *O.E. Texts* 449 ȝif hi wintres deȝ sie. **1390** Gower *Conf.* II. 327 Sche.. halt hir clos the wyntres day. *c* **1430** Lydg. *Min. Poems* (Percy Soc.) 212 The coold wynterys nyght. **1577** Harrison *England* i. xiii. 37 b/2 in *Holinshed*, Blewe claye.. (which hardlye drinketh vppe the winters water in long season). *a* **1593** Marlowe & Nashe *Dido* iii. iii, Who would not vndergoe all kind of toyle, To be well stor'd with such a winter's tale? **1593** Shaks. *3 Hen. VI*, v. v. 25 Let Æsop fable in a Winters Night. **1600** —— *A.Y.L.* ii. i. 7 The.. churlish chiding of the winters winde. **1605** —— *Macb.* iii. iv. 65 O, these flawes and starts.. would well become A womans story, at a Winters fire. **1654** Whitlock *Zootomia* 300 A pretty upshot of all ambitious Designes.. to be made at length a Winters Tale, and Chimney-corner Discourse. **1795** Cowper *Pairing Time Anticipated* 9 It chanced then on a winter's day, But warm, and bright, and calm as May. **1796** Grose *Dict. Vulgar T.* (ed. 3) s.v., He is like a winter's day, short and dirty.

c. Applied to autumn-sown crops that stand through the winter; also to fruits that ripen late, or keep well until or during winter; *spec.* in names of late-ripening apples, pears, etc. (See also 5 b.)

1398 Trevisa *Barth. De P.R.* xvii. cxv. (Add. MS. 27944), Barliche hatte Ordeum.. þis corn we clepith wynter bore. **1398** Winter seede [see summer *sb.*^{1} 4 c]. **1530** Palsgr. 289/2 Wynter frute, *fruit de yuer*. **1573–80** Tusser *Husb.* (1878) 40 Winter fruit gather when Mihel is past. **1577** Googe *Heresbach's Husb.* i. 28 Winter Barley.. is to be sowed in September. **1609** Dekker *Ravens Almanack* B 3 b, When winter plomes are ripe and ready to be gathered. **1676** Worlidge *Cyder* 170 Bings-pear, Winter-Poppering, Thorn-pear [etc.] are all very good Winter-pears. **1697** Dryden *Virg. Georg.* i. 300 When Astrea's Ballance, hung on high, Betwixt the Nights and Days divides the Sky, Then .. sow your Winter Grain. **1707** Mortimer *Husb.*, *Kalendar* Jan., Apples... Winter Queenings,.. Winter Pearmain... Pears. Winter Musk,.. Winter Norwich,.. Winter Burgamot, Winter Bon-Chrestien. **1762** Mills *Syst. Pract. Husb.* I. 466 The gray and other large winter peas. **1844** H. Stephens *Bk. Farm* II. 514 The state of the winter-wheat depends entirely on the sort of weather it had to encounter in winter and early spring. **1870** Yeats *Nat. Hist. Comm.* 63 In Egypt, wheat is a winter crop. **1939** *WPA Guide to Florida* (Federal Writers' Project) i. 7 The traveler.. may detour inland to discover the hidden winter-vegetable kingdom on the muck lands.

d. In figurative applications (cf. 1 c); †in quots. 1593, 1682 = old, aged.

1593 Shaks. *2 Hen. VI*, v. iii. 2 Salisbury,.. That Winter Lyon, who in rage forgets Aged contusions. **1651** N. Bacon *Disc. Govt. Eng.* ii. i. 6 The worst of his fate was, to live to his Winter age. **1682** Otway *Venice Preserved* iii. ii. 34 That mortify'd old wither'd Winter Rogue. **1709** Pope *Jan. & May* 104 The tasteless, dry embrace Of a stale virgin with a winter face. **1745** Young *Nt. Th.* ix. 410 The Crown of Manhood is a Winter-Joy; An Evergreen, that.. blossoms in the Rigour of our Fate.

4. *Comb.*: objective, as ***winter-boding***, ***-loving*** adjs.; indirect objective, as ***winter-like***, ***-proof***, ***-verging*** adjs.; instrumental, as ***winter-beaten***, ***-blasted***, ***-bound***, ***-chilled***, ***-heavy***, ***-left***, ***-locked***, ***-shaken***, ***-starved***, ***-swollen***, ***-thin***, ***-wasted***, ***-wearied***, ***-weary***, ***-weighed***, ***-withered***, ***-worn*** pa. pples. and adjs.; similative, as ***winter-blue***, ***-chill***, ***-cold***, ***-seeming***, ***-visaged***, ***-white*** adjs.; 'in or during winter', as ***winter-blooming***, ***-fattened***, ***-felled***, ***-flowering***, ***-hardy***, ***-made***, ***-pruned***, ***-sown***, ***-standing*** pples. and adjs.; ***winter-cut*** vb.; appositive, as ***winter-spring***.

1579 Spenser *Sheph. Cal.* Jan., Argt., He compareth his carefull case to the sadde season of the yeare,.. and to his owne *winterbeaten flocke. **1827** Clare *Sheph. Cal.* 23 Crab, hip and *winter-bitten sloe. **1597** Drayton *Heroic. Ep.*, *Rosamond* 40 The cold badge of *winter-blasted haires. **1632** Lithgow *Trav.* ii. 71 A roofe to my Winter-blasted lodging. *a* **1847** Eliza Cook *Song of Dying Old Man* vi, The spring-flower clinging round the *winter-blighted tree. **1855** *Poultry Chron.* III. 303 Cyclamen (especially the *winter-blooming kind) may be sheltered. **1936** R. Frost *Let.* 6 Feb. (1964) 270 And Sirius is a *winterbluegreen star. **1958** J. W. Day *Lady Houston* xv. 225 Never had.. the winter-blue woods of Kimbolton or the generous warmth of Brampton Park.. beckoned more seductively. **1892** W. Watson *Poems*, *Autumn* 36 And spectral seem thy *winter-boding trees. **1791** Burns *Lovely Davies* ii, As the wretch looks o'er Siberia's shore, When *winter-bound the wave is. **1904** Phillips Oppenheim *Betrayal* xxi. 179 A country silent and winterbound. **1605** Sylvester *Du Bartas* ii. iii. iv. *Captains* 482 My flesh (too-*Winter-chill) My spirit's small sparkles doth extinguish still. **1669** Worlidge *Syst. Agric.* vi. 72 In the Spring yielding a reviving Cordial to your *Winter-chilled spirit. **1944** E. Sitwell *Green Song* 7 Henry thought me *winter-cold When to keep his love I turned from him as the world Turns from the sun. **1784** G. White *Selborne*, *To Pennant* ix, A very large fall of timber, consisting of about one thousand oaks, has been cut... These trees.. were *winter-cut, viz. in February and March. **1840** Buel *Farmer's Comp.* 164 English beef and mutton.. is mostly *winter-fattened.. upon roots and straw. **1742** Ellis *Timber-Tree* II. 13 From whence they infer, that the worm can't breed so soon in a Summer-fell'd Tree, as in a *Winter-fell'd one. **1804** *Phil. Trans.* XCV. 89 This superiority in winter-felled wood. **1794** *Winter-flowering [see aconite 3]. **1872** *Routledge's Ev. Boy's Ann.* 101/2 Winter-flowering plants. **1960** *Farmer & Stockbreeder* 5 Jan. 43/1 We may.. be given a more *winter-hardy, leafier kale. **1975** *Daily Colonist* (Victoria, B.C.) 20 July 22/7 As it is not winter-hardy here, it is commonly grown as an annual. **1920** D. H. Lawrence *Women in Love* xxix. 435 This was an old world she was still journeying through, *winter-heavy and dreary. **1955** S. Spender *Coll. Poems 1928–53* ix. 173 Its vermilion seems A Red Admiral's wing, with veins Of lichen and rust, an underwing Of *winter-left leaves. **1611** Speed *Theat. Gt. Brit.* xli. 79 *Winter-like dispositions of weather. **1740** T. Smith *Jrnl.* (1849) 268, I believe no man ever knew so winter-like a spell so early in the year. **1926** S. Leslie *Cantab* xv. 183 He sobbed like a *winter-locked river hastening over the weir at the first warmth of spring. **1946** Dylan Thomas *Deaths & Entrances* 34 Two proud, blacked brothers cry, Winter-locked side by side. **1800** Hurdis *Fav. Village* 134 The *winter-loving moss. **1830** *Cumbld. Farm Rep.* 58 in *Libr. Usef. Knowl.*, *Husb.* III, The manure made in summer.. is always of better quality than *winter-made dung. **1830** Doyle in W. J. Fitz-Patrick *Life* (1880) II. 221, I.. hope I am now *winter-proof. **1842** Loudon *Suburban Hort.* 459 Canes *winter-pruned, or cut back. *a* **1631** Donne *Loves Alchymie* 12 A *winter-seeming summers night. **1605** Sylvester *Du Bartas* ii. iii. i. *Vocation* 483 Peasants *Winter-shaken. **1605** R. R. *Commend. Poem* in *Sylvester's Wks.*, Winter-shaken Leaues. **1707** Mortimer *Husb.* 316 *Winter sown Seed. **1960** *Farmer & Stockbreeder* 15 Mar. 141/3 Tri-Farmon 41 effectively controls the widest possible range of weeds in winter and spring-sown wheat. **1888** W. D. Hay *Blood* vii. 29 Although it was so late in the *winter-spring season, the weather was wild and wintry. **1967** *Oceanogr. & Marine Biol.* XVI. 409 The 'Atlanto-Scandian' winter-spring spawning stocks. **1598** Grenewey *Tacitus, Ann.* ii. vi. (1622) 40 The souldiers were brought backe to their *winter-standing camps. **1581** Sidney *Apol. Poetrie* (Arb.) 68 Figures and flowers, extreamelie *winter-starued. **1597** Drayton *Heroic. Ep.*, *Henry to Rosamond* 101 The hungry winter-starued earth. **1603** H. Crosse *Vertues Commw.* (1878) 92 A number of poore winterstarued people. **1849** Rock *Ch. Fathers* II. 465 Did the good man.. wade through the *winter-swollen brook? **1820** Keats *Fancy* 57 The snake all *winter-thin Cast on sunny bank its skin. **1824** Fenby *To a Redbreast* v, The *winter-verging autumn morn. **1898** Meredith *Odes Fr. Hist.* 87 The maimed, Torn, tortured, *winter-visaged. **1885** H. Tennyson in *Macm. Mag.* Mar. 345 As we fare.. forth.. From out our *winter-wasted Northern Isle. **1892** J. G. Whittier *At Sundown* 58 This stormy interlude Gives to our *winter-wearied hearts a reason For trustful gratitude. **1917** D. H. Lawrence *Look! we have come Through!* 160 We who are winter-weary in the winter of the world. **1866** J. G. Whittier *Snow-Bound* 46 And woodland paths that wound between Snow drooping pine-boughs *winter-weighed. **1915** E. Sitwell *Mother* 16 Her ice-cold breast was *winter-white. **1906** Hardy *Dynasts* ii. i. vi, *Winter-whitened bones. **1592** Daniel *Delia* xxx[viii], Her glas.. then presents her *winter-withered hew. **1872** Geo. Eliot *Middlem.* xxxvii, The common jealousy of a *winter-worn husband. *a* **1560** Phaer *Æneid* viii. (1562) Bb iij, Three *winter-wrested showres.

5. a. Special Combs.: **winter annual** (see quot. 1900); **winter bud** *Zool.*, a statoblast (formed at the approach of, or quiescent during, winter); **winter carnival** *Canad.*, 'an organized winter social activity featuring winter sports, beauty contests, ice-sculpture, etc.' (*Dict. Canadianisms*); **winter-clad** *a.*, clothed warmly for the winter; † **winter-close** *v.*, *trans.* to shut close against the cold of winter; **winter coat**, (*a*) the coat of an animal in winter, where this differs from that in summer; (*b*) a (woman's) coat suitable for winter weather; **winter count**, a pictorial record or chronicle of the events of a year, kept by a N. American Indian people; **winter country** *N.Z.*, land where livestock can be wintered; **winter eggs** = *winter ova*; **winter garden**, (*a*) a garden of plants that flourish in winter, as evergreens; (*b*) a greenhouse or conservatory in which plants are kept flourishing in winter; (*c*) a building used for concerts, plays, dances, etc., at a seaside resort; **winter-hained** *a.* [hain *v.*^{1}], of pasture, preserved from grazing during the winter; so **winter-haining** *vbl. sb.*; **winter-killed** *pa. pple.* and *a.* (*U.S.*), killed or blasted by the cold of winter: said esp. of grain or other crops; so **winter-killing**; also **winter-kill** *v. intr.*, to become winter-killed; *trans.*, to make winter-killed; also *absol.* and **winter-kill** *sb.*; **winter-long** *a.*, as (tediously) long as winter; *adv.*, through a whole winter; **winter-love**, cold or conventional love; **winter oil**, edible oil that remains clear at low temperatures owing to the removal of constituents that would have caused congelation or precipitation; **winter-old** *a.*, that has lasted since the beginning of winter; **Winter Olympic Games**, **Winter Olympics**, international competitive winter sports held under the auspices of the International Olympic Committee, usually every four years; **winter ova**, eggs produced by certain invertebrates at the approach of winter (cf. *summer ova* s.v. summer *sb.*^{1} 6); **winter packet** *Canad.* (*Obs.* exc. *Hist.*), a boat or land party carrying mail in winter-time between trading posts; the mail itself; **winter-piece** [piece *sb.* 17 b, d], a picture or description of a winter scene; **winter-pride**, the condition of being winter-proud; **winter-proud** *a.*, (of wheat or other crops) too luxuriant in winter; **winter-rig** *v.* (now *dial.*), *trans.* to plough (land) in ridges and lay it fallow for the winter (cf. winter-fallow); **winter road** *Canad.*, a road or a route used in winter when the ground is frozen or there is snow; **winter-rot** [rot *sb.*^{1} 2], a disease incident to sheep in the winter; † **winter-stall**, a hive in which bees are kept during the winter; † **winter story**, **tale**, an idle tale (also *winter's tale*: see 3 b); **Winter War** (also with small initials), the war between the U.S.S.R. and Finland in 1939–40; **winter woollies**: see woolly *sb.* 1.

1900 B. D. Jackson *Gloss. Bot. Terms* 290/2 **Winter-annual*, a plant which germinates in autumn, and living through the winter, fruits and dies. **1977** J. L. Harper *Population Biol. Plants* xviii. 547 A single population [of *Papaver dubium*] includes winter annuals and spring annuals. **1888** Rolleston & Jackson *Anim. Life* 709 The *Phylactolaemata* [among *Polyzoa*] also reproduce by statoblasts or *winter buds. **1884** *Outing* (U.S.) Feb. 400/2 The *winter carnival at Montreal, which was so successfully inaugurated last year, will open on February 4. **1973** *Globe & Mail* (Toronto) 13 Jan. 33/1 Most winter carnivals in Ontario rely less heavily on the snowmobile for their fun weekends. **1847** TENNYSON *Princess* II. 105 The man; Tattoo'd or woaded, *winter-clad in skins. *c* **1440** *Pallad. on Husb.* I. 507 *Winter close hit al To holde out colde. **1894** ARMATAGE *Horse* v. 73 A horse with his natural *winter coat. **1920** [see *bear fur* s.v. BEAR *sb.*[1] 9]. **1956** R. MACAULAY *Towers of Trebizond* viii. 78 The camel.. was very smooth, having just shed its winter coat. **1982** C. FREMLIN *Parasite Person* xix. 128 Helen felt the warmth of the sun.. through her thick winter coat. **1895** HOFFMAN *Beginnings of Writing* 35 These chronological records are designated '*winter counts', as each event covers that period of time between the end of one summer and the beginning of the next. **1898** MORRIS *Austral English* 513/1 **Winter country*, in New Zealand (South Island), land so far unaffected by snow that stock is wintered on it. **1912** A. WALL *Century N.Z.'s Praise* 80 Good winter-country, where sweet grasses grow. **1949** P. NEWTON *High Country Days* 197 Safe country which is saved for the winter is 'winter country'. **1872** H. C. BASTIAN *Begin. Life* II. 514 The so-called '*winter-eggs' of the beautiful.. Rotifer.. *Hydatina senta*. **1712** ADDISON *Spect.* No. 477 ¶1 A *Winter Garden, which would consist of such Trees only as never cast their Leaves. **1762** KAMES *Elem. Crit.* xxiv. (1774) 448 In a cold country, the capital object should be a winter-garden, open to the sun, sheltered from wind, dry under foot, and having the appearance of summer by variety of evergreens. **1783** T. BLAIKIE *Diary of Scotch Gardener* (1931) 179 The winter Garden adjoining to the Hott houses, was more Beautifull than Elegant. **1889** GUNTER *That Frenchman* xvi. 197 The great conservatory, or winter garden, as it is called in that country, and without which no grand Russian house is complete. **1896** *Ward & Lock's Illustr. Guide Bournemouth* etc. 22 Not far from the pier entrance is the Winter Garden and Pavilion. **1951** *Dict. Gardening* (R. Hort. Soc.) IV. 2282/2 The Winter Garden is usually of sufficient size to allow the central part of the interior being laid out in walks and large beds. **1977** *Lancs. Life* Nov. 81/1 The Palace incorporated a winter garden from which the stage could be seen without spectators needing to go through into the auditorium. **1886** C. SCOTT *Sheep-farming* 86 To have in reserve a *winter-hained old pasture, which the ewes and lambs can fall back on. **1667–8** *Act 19–20 Chas. II*, c. 8 §10 The time of the *Winter heyning (that is to say) from the Eleventh day of November to the Three and twentieth day of Aprill. **1743** R. MAXWELL *Sel. Trans. Agric. Scot.* 37 The Dung of these [sheep] in Summer, with Winter-haining, will keep the Ground in good Heart. **1845** *Farmers' Cabinet* 15 Feb. 202/2 It is not so hardy as some varieties: it is more subject to *winter-kill. **1846** E. EMMONS *Agric. N.Y.* I. 281 The grain very rarely winter-kills. **1849** *Ex. Doc. 31st U.S. Congress 1 Sess. House* No. 5. II. 653 The.. snow which lies upon the ground nearly six months in the year would be likely to 'winter-kill' it. **1918** S. S. VISHER *Geogr. S. Dakota* 56 Red clover is not a success.. largely because it winter-kills. **1945** *Ecol. Monogr.* XV. 343 (*heading*) Limnological conditions in ice-covered lakes, especially as related to winter-kill of fish. **1977** *Chicago Tribune* 2 Oct. XI. 1/4 High nitrogen fertilizer.. would only promote late growth that would winterkill. **1980** *Northeast Woods & Waters* Dec. 18/1 Last year's rate of winterkill was lower than usual because of the relatively mild weather conditions. **1817** S. BROWN *Western Gaz.* 49 That wheat.. never gets *winter-killed or smutty. **1868** *Rep. U.S. Comm. Agric.* (1869) 405 The White Mediterranean and Sandomirka wheats were badly winter-killed. **1845** *Farmers' Cabinet* 15 Jan. 195/1 This blight is not to be confounded with *winter-killing. **1868** *Rep. U.S. Comm. Agric.* (1869) 17 The early reports.. were generally favorable, and noted by the absence of winter-killing. *c* **1325** *Lai le Freine* 143 Al the *winter-long night. **1876** MORRIS *Æneids* IV. 193 How winter-long between them there the sweets of sloth they nursed. **1636** B. JONSON *Discov., Jactura vitæ*, What a deale of cold busines doth a man mis-spend the better part of life in! in scattering complements, tendring visits,.. making a little *winter-love in a darke corner. **1894** C. R. A. WRIGHT *Animal & Veg. Oils* xi. 257 Oils that have been thus treated are sometimes termed '*winter oils'. **1920**, **1939** Winter oil [see DEMARGARINATED *a.*]. **1970** T. J. WEISS *Food Oils* iii. 59 The solid portion of the oil which had set up in storage tanks in the winter at 40°–42° F.. was settled out and removed, leaving an oil which would remain clear when chilled. Cottonseed oils were thus divided into *summer* and *winter* oils. **1897** tr. *Nansen's Farthest North* II. v. 194 Ice which can hardly be *winter-old, or at any rate has been formed since last summer. [**1928** *Times* 17 Feb. 6/4 The usual clean crisp snow has given place to an earthy slush, and as a result the second celebration of a Winter Olympiad has come to an abrupt standstill.] **1932** *Times* 1 Feb. 7/4 A thaw which has set in threatens to destroy.. the third *winter Olympic Games. **1936** *Times* 27 Jan. 5/1 The Lake Placid bob-run.. provided some of the most exciting spectacles at the 1932 Winter Olympics. **1956** *Times* 6 Jan. 9/5 In 1948.. I won a bronze medal in the Winter Olympic Games. **1981** 'E. LATHEN' *Going for Gold* i. 11 It took the Winter Olympics to keep him in the continental United States in February. **1852** *Zoologist* X. 3406 He pointed out the difference between the ordinary ova and those called '*winter ova', which last he proposed to call ephippial ova. **1877** [see *summer ova* s.v. SUMMER *sb.*[1] 6]. **1888** ROLLESTON & JACKSON *Anim. Life* 634 The ova [of Rotifers] are of three kinds, small male ova, thin-shelled summer ova, and thick-shelled winter or, better, resting ova. **1831** E. SMITH *Let.* 25 Nov. in *Champlain Soc. Publ.* (1938) XXIV. 79 Our *Winter Packet being now preparing to Travell on to your Quarter, I will not let it go without acknowleging the receipt of your friendly epistile. **1971** J. MCDOUGALL *Parsons on Plains* xi. 92 We saw the flicker of a campfire. We found that it was the one winter packet from the east on its way to Edmonton. **1666** PEPYS *Diary* 17 July, To agree with.. (the Dutch paynter..) for a *winter piece of snow. **1697** ADDISON *Ess. Virgil's Georgics* ¶12 The Scythian Winter-piece appears so very cold and bleak to the Eye, that a Man can scarce look on it without shivering. **1797** HOLCROFT tr. *Stolberg's Trav.* (ed. 2) II. xlii. 70 The third [painting] is a winter piece. *a* **1722** LISLE *Husb.* (1757) 93 Sow old wheat at the first and earliest sowing, if you fear *winter-pride. **1601** HOLLAND *Pliny* XVII. ii. I. 501 When either corne is *winter-prowd, or other plants put forth and bud too earely, by reason of the mild and warme aire. **1799** J. ROBERTSON *Agric. Perth* 146 When the wheat is winter-proud, which commonly happens after a mild season.., that luxuriance.. ought to be checked by eating it down with sheep. **1846** J. BAXTER *Libr. Pract. Agric.* (ed. 4) II. 397 There is danger of the crop running to straw, or becoming what is called winter-proud. **1661** M. STEVENSON *Twelve Months* 39 At the end of this moneth [August] begin to *winter-rig all fruitful soyls. **1801** A. MACKENZIE *Voy. from Montreal* vi. 84 One of the natives who followed us, called it the *Winter Road River. **1808** H. GRAY *Lett. from Canada* (1809) 254 The country people who first form the winter roads on the snow, direct their *Carioles* by the nearest course where the snow is most level; and they go in as straight a line as possible, to the place where they are destined. **1916** *Yukon Territory* 194 In the summer of 1902 the government built a winter road between Dawson and Whitehorse, a distance of approximately 333 miles. **1971** *Country Life* 24 June 1572/1 We had been told to follow a path until it joined a 'winter road' which would in turn lead us to the marsh. **1973** *Kingston* (Ontario) *Whig-Standard* 26 Jan. 7/2 The winter road over the ice is about four lanes wide and is 'brushed' with evergreens at the sides as a guide during swirling snow storms. **1979** A. M. TIZZARD *On Sloping Ground* ix. 130 The bay would be frozen over and there was always a good winter road across Twillingate Island. **1577** GOOGE *Heresbach's Husb.* III. 140 Against the *winter rotte, or hunger rotte, you must prouide to feede them [*sc.* sheep] at home in Cratches. *c* **1275** *xi Pains of Hell* 40 in *O.E. Misc.* 148 þickure hi hongeþ.. þan don been in *wynterstal. **1587–8** *Wills & Inv. Durh.* (Surtees) II. 312, iij wynter stales of bees. **1824** [see STALL *sb.*[4]]. **1659** BP. WALTON *Consid. Considered* 239 A mere *winter-story without any ground or reason. **1556** OLDE *Antichrist* 7 According to olde wiues fables and *winter tales. **1637** C. DOW *Answ. to H. Burton* 120 b, Such winter tales as it were too great a mispence of time and words to refute them. **1942** F. OWEN in W. P. & Z. Coates *Soviet-Finnish Campaign* p. i, What about the Finns? In the *Winter War they gained a deserved fame for valour and military skill. **1957** *Times Lit. Suppl.* 11 Oct. 603/2 The so-called 'Winter War', resulting from the Soviet attack on Finland in November, 1939, and ending with the Finnish surrender of March, 1940. **1971** W. H. MCNEILL in A. Bullock *20th Century* 49/2 The Finns' success in holding the Russians at bay for the long weeks of the so-called 'winter war' (1939–40). **1973** J. FLEMING *You won't let me Finish* x. 82 The cook came here during the Winter War.

b. In names of animals and plants that are active or flourish in winter or in the winter half of the year (often rendering L. *hiemalis* as a specific name), or of late-ripening fruits (cf. 3 c): **winter-bloom**, (*a*) a late-flowering species of *Azalea*; (*b*) the American witch-hazel, *Hamamelis virginica*, which blossoms late in autumn and ripens its fruit the following year; **winter bunting**, the snow bunting (see BUNTING *sb.*[1] 1); **winter clover**, the partridge-berry, *Mitchella repens*; **winter-crack** (see quot. 1898); **winter daffodil**, a late-blooming yellow-flowered amaryllid, *Sternbergia lutea*, cultivated in gardens; **winter duck**, (*a*) the pin-tail duck (see PINTAIL 2); (*b*) in *U.S.*, the long-tailed duck, *Harelda glacialis*; **winter falcon**, the young of the red-shouldered buzzard, *Buteo lineatus*; **winter finch**, a N. American species of finch (see quot.); **winter flounder** (see quot.); **winter-flower**, (*a*) *gen.* a flower blooming in winter; (*b*) *spec.* the early-blooming Japan allspice, *Chimonanthus fragrans* [a rendering of the generic name]; †**winter gillyflower**, the wallflower (see quot. 1597); **winter gnat** = *winter midge*; **winter grape**, an American species of grape-vine, *Vitis cordifolia*; **winter-gull**, any species of gull which appears in winter in a particular locality, as the common gull, the black-headed gull, or the herring-gull; **winter hawk**, the red-shouldered buzzard (cf. *winter falcon*); **winter heath** (see quot.); **winter-mew** = *winter-gull*; **winter midge** (see quot.); **winter-moth**, any of various geometer moths which come forth in winter, esp. *Cheimatobia brumata*; **winter peach**, the fruit of a peach-tree cultivated in a greenhouse and fruiting during autumn or winter; **winter-pick** [? PICK *v.*[1] 5], a local name for the sloe when mellowed by frost, used for making a rustic wine; **winter queening**, a late-ripening variety of apple, which keeps well through the winter; **winter redbird** *local*, the cardinal grosbeak, *Cardinalis virginianus*, which winters in some parts of N. America (cf. *summer redbird* s.v. SUMMER *sb.*[1] 6 b); **winter rocket**, the common winter-cress, *Barbarea vulgaris* (see ROCKET *sb.*[2] 3); **winter rose**, (*a*) a rose blooming in winter; (*b*) ? the Christmas rose, *Helleborus niger*; **winter-shad**, the mud-shad, *Dorosoma copedianum*; **winter sleeper**, an animal that hibernates; **winter snipe**, the purple sandpiper or rock-snipe, *Tringa striata* or *maritima* (cf. *summer snipe* s.v. SUMMER *sb.*[1] 6 b); **winter squash**, a species of pumpkin, *Cucurbita maxima* (cf. *summer squash* s.v. SUMMER *sb.*[1] 6 b); **winter strawberry**, the strawberry-tree = ARBUTUS 1; **winter-sweet**, (*a*) = *winter sweet marjoram* (see MARJORAM); (*b*) a shrub, *Chimonanthus præcox*, of the family Calycanthaceæ, native to China and bearing pale yellow fragrant flowers in winter before the leaves appear; **winter teal**, the green-winged teal (see TEAL 2): cf. *summer teal* s.v. SUMMER *sb.*[1] 6 b; **winter-thorn**, a late-ripening variety of pear; **winter-weed**, any one of various small weeds which survive and flourish in winter; *esp.* the ivy-leaved and field speedwells, *Veronica hederæfolia* and *V. agrestis*. See also *winter* ACONITE, HELIOTROPE, HELLEBORE, HEMP, MARJORAM, RAPE (*sb.*[5]), SAVORY, WAGTAIL, WREN[1].

1760 J. LEE *Introd. Bot.* App. 332 *Winter Bloom. *Azalea*. **1884** MILLER *Plant-n.*, *Hamamelis virginica*, American Witch-Hazel,.. Winter-bloom. **1815** STEPHENS in Shaw's *Gen. Zool.* IX. 367 *Winter Bunting (*Emberiza hyemalis*). **1884** MILLER *Plant-n.*, *Mitchella repens*, Chequer-berry, Partridge-berry,.. *Winter Clover. **1877** E. PEACOCK *Gloss. Words Manley & Corringham, Lincs.* 276/2 **Wintercrack*, a small green plum, the fruit of which ripens very late. **1898** *N. & Q.* 13 Aug. 235/2 A fair-sized round, yellowish plum, only fully ripe in November, is known in Derbyshire as the 'winter-crack'. They are called 'cracks' because with the first frosts the fruit cracks on one side, being then fully ripe. **1914** D. H. LAWRENCE *Prussian Officer* 282 There were some.. winter-crack trees. **1884** MILLER *Plant-n.*, *Sternbergia lutea*, *Winter Daffodil. **1804** BEWICK *Brit. Birds* II. 360 Pintail Duck. Sea Pheasant, Cracker, or *Winter Duck. **1885**, **1917** Winter duck [see LADYBIRD 3]. **1785** PENNANT *Arctic Zool.* II. 209 *Winter Falcon... With a black bill; yellow cere:.. appears at approach of winter, and retires in the spring. **1783** LATHAM *Gen. Syn. Birds* III. 274 *Winter Finch... Found at New York, in the winter. **1809** EDMONDSTON *Zetland Isl.* I. 240 Ling.. are known by the name of *winter fish. **1814** S. L. MITCHILL *Fishes N.Y.* 387 New-York Flatfish.. is called the *winter flounder. **1873** T. GILL *Catal. Fishes E. Coast N. Amer.* 16 *Pseudopleuronectes americanus*... Common flounder; winter-flounder; mud dab. **1733** POPE *Let. to Richardson* 10 June, I hope to see you.. before this *Winter-flower is faded. I will defer her Interment till Tomorrow Night. **1597** GERARDE *Herbal* II. cxiii. 371 The people in Cheshire do call them *Winter Gilloflowers. **1615** W. LAWSON *Orch. & Gard.* vi. (1623) 12 Wall-flowers, commonly called Bee-flowers, or winter Gilly-flowers. **1899** D. SHARP in Harmer & Shipley *Cambr. Nat. Hist.* VI. vii. 473 The *winter gnats of the genus *Trichocera* are a fair sample of this sub-family. **1926** A. H. HAMM in J. J. Walker *Nat. Hist. Oxf. District* 257 Four species of 'Winter-gnats' are always common from autumn to spring. **1968** *Oxf. Bk. Insects* 122/1 There are ten British Winter Gnats, which belong to the family Trichoceridae and look like small crane-flies. They get their English name from their way of 'dancing' in large swarms on winter afternoons. **1771** G. WASHINGTON *Diary* 20 Nov. (1925) II. 43 Began to Plant Cuttings of the *Winter Grape. **1789** [see *frost-grape* s.v. FROST *sb.* 7 c]. **1814** PURSH *Flora Amer. Septentr.* I. 169 *Vitis cordifolia*.. commonly called Winter-grape or Chicken-grape. **1949** *Amer. Photogr.* Apr. 244/2 Winter grape is one of our commonest species from northern New York to Michigan. **1804** BEWICK *Brit. Birds* II. 221 *Winter Gull. Winter Mew, or Coddy Moddy. **1831** AUDUBON *Ornithol. Biog.* I. 364 The *Winter Hawk. *Falco hyemalis*, Gmel. **1882** *Garden* 14 Jan. 17/1 The *Winter Heath (*E*[*rica*] *carnea*) as a low-growing.. shrub is one of the best of all winter blooming plants. **1678** RAY *Willughby's Ornith.* 350 The *Winter-Mew, called in Cambridge-shire the Coddy-Moddy. **1854** J. HOGG *Microsc.* II. ii. 288 The appearance of gnats. The first that appear are called *winter midges (*Trichocera hyemalis*). **1819** SAMOUELLE *Entomol. Compend.* 359 *Smerinthus brumaria*. The *Winter Moth. **1869** E. NEWMAN *Brit. Moths* 106 The Winter Moth (*Chimatobia brumata*). **1787** J. WOODFORDE *Diary* 31 Oct. (1926) II. 354 Mr. Custances Garden brought us this Morning a Basket of *Winter Peaches. **1960** I. WALLACH *Absence of Cello* (1961) 199 Marian wanted a winter peach. **1862** W. S. COLEMAN *Woodlands* 118 '*Winterpick-wine' takes the place of port in the rustic 'cellar'. **1664** EVELYN *Kal. Hort.* Jan. (1669) 21 Apples.. Holland-pepin, John-apple, *Winter-Queening. **1714** J. LAWSON *Carolina* 108 Winter Queening is a durable Apple, and makes good Cider. **1889** *Science-Gossip* XXV. 146/1 Our lively cardinal grosbeak.. is known as the '*winter red bird', because.. more of a songster in December than in June. **1742** YOUNG *Nt. Th.* II. 240 The *winter Rose must blow, the Sun put on A brighter Beam in Leo. **1891** KIPLING *Life's Handicap* iv. 88 Clumps of winter-roses lay between the silver candlesticks. **1888** GOODE *Amer. Fishes* 409 In the Chesapeake region it is known as the 'Mud-Shad', '*Winter-Shad', or 'Stink Shad'. **1709** T. ROBINSON *Vind. Mosaick Syst.* 89 Those [creatures] that are *Winter-Sleepers, when the Summer warmth abates,.. draw to.. Winter-Quarters. **1911** J. A. THOMSON *Biol. Seasons* IV. 333 A survey of the Winter-sleepers seems to show that the life-saving reaction must have arisen by.. natural selection. **1775** *Boston Transcript* 26 Apr. III. 12/7, I have a fine prospect of a Crop of.. *winter Squashes this fall. **1809** KENDALL *Trav.* III. lxx. 109 The vine of a species of pompion called by the colonists winter squash. **1969** *Oxf. Bk. Food Plants* 122/2 Winter squashes are cut in the autumn and can be kept for 3 or 4 months or longer. *a* **1746** HOLDSWORTH *Remarks on Virgil* (1768) 29 The Arbutus cannot here mean the *Winter-Strawberry. **1840** PAXTON *Bot. Dict.*, *Winter sweet, *Origanum heracleoticum*. **1893** W. ROBINSON *Eng. Flower Garden* (ed. 3) 325/2 Winter Sweet is a lovely shrub which in our country requires a wall. It flowers in December and January; beautiful, and of delicious fragrance. **1934** LD. BERNERS *First Childhood* ii. 20 Just outside the windows there grew a shrub of the early-blossoming chimonanthus. (Winter-sweet it was called in the days before gardeners grew so refined.) **1955** [see CHIMONANTHUS]. **1980** *Gardener's Dozen* 12 My winter-sweet.. sometimes gets knocked about by the frost and snow. **1766** *Compl. Farmer* s.v. *Pear* 5 Y 4/2 The *winter-thorn.

'winter, *sb.*[2] [Origin uncertain.

Perhaps originating as a jocular antithesis to the *summer* or upper rail or cross-bar of the hand-printing press (SUMMER *sb.*[2] 3 e). Connexion with north. dial. *winter* = trivet is uncertain.]

In a hand-printing press, a block of wood about nine inches broad by nine deep, supporting the carriage and having a tenon at each end to fit into corresponding mortices in the cheeks.

1683 MOXON *Mech. Exerc., Printing* x. ¶4 The Length of the Winter besides the Tennants, is one Foot nine Inches. **1770** LUCKOMBE *Hist. Printing* 298. **1888** JACOBI *Printers' Voc.* 156.

'winter, *v.* [f. WINTER *sb.*^{1} after L. *hiemare* (in senses 1, 2), *hibernare* (in sense 1); cf. MHG., MLG., Du. *winteren* (G. *wintern*), ON. *vetra.*]

1. *intr.* To pass or spend the winter; to stay or reside (at a specified place) during the winter; (of animals) to find, or be provided with, food and shelter in the winter. Also (*Canad.*) with *out*.

1382 WYCLIF *Acts* xxvii. 12 If on ony maner thei myȝten come to Fenyce, for to wynterne in the hauene of Crete. **1526** TINDALE *Acts* xxvii. 12 The haven was nott commodius to wynter in. **1535** COVERDALE *Isa.* xviii. 6 The beastes of the earth wyntered there. **1668** DRYDEN *Even. Love* II. i, Birds that breed in one Countrie, and goe to winter in another. **1726** SWIFT *Gulliver* II. i, Discovering a Leak we unshipped our Goods and winter'd there. **1801** A. MACKENZIE *Voy. Montreal* Fur Trade p. xxvii, About a third of these [middlemen] went to winter, and had more than double the above wages. **1826** LAMB *Elia* Ser. II. *Pop. Fallacies* xv, What savage unsocial nights must our ancestors have spent, wintering in caves and unillumined fastnesses! **1828** DARVILL *Engl. Race Horse* Introd. p. ix, Mr. Crooke had a farm at Redland, in Gloucestershire, at which place his horses usually wintered. **1867** FREEMAN *Norm. Conq.* I. ii. 46 The heathen men wintered for the first time in the Isle of Sheppey. **1870** in C. Wilson *Campbell of Yukon* (1970) 165, I..had long consultations with most of the Freemen, wintering out in this quarter. **1968** E. RUSSENHOLT *Heart of Continent* viii. 132 When November [comes]..the population of Assiniboia is 'at home'—excepting only, those hundreds who elect to 'winter out' on the plains and along the waterways. **1970** R. SYMONS *Broken Snare* xvi. 112 He [*sc.* a steer] had found a bunch of wild horses... So he had wintered out quite happily with his kind hosts.

fig. **1835** DICKENS *Sk. Boz, Parish* iii, The Miss Willises.. seemed to have no separate existence, but to have made up their minds just to winter through life together.

2. a. *trans.* To keep or maintain during winter; *esp.* to provide (animals) with food and shelter in winter. (Also said of the food, or of the land.)

c **1440** *Promp. Parv.* 530/1 Wyntryn', or kepe a thynge al the wyntyr, *yemo.* **1550–1** *Test. Ebor.* (Surtees) VI. 306 To wynter theme [*sc.* two ox twinters] unto such tyme as thei be able to drawe. **1570–1** in Willis & Clark *Cambridge* (1886) III. 594 For vppyng ye Swannes and wynteryng them.. xxiij^{s}. **1580** *Knaresb. Wills* (Surtees) I. 139 To..my wief a cowe and asmoche haie as will wynter hir. **1607** TOPSELL *Four-f. Beasts* 605 They summered them [*sc.* sheep] in Apulia, they wintered them in Samnius. **1710** HILMAN *Tusser Rediv.* Oct. (1744) 135 If I keep more Sheep than I can Winter. **1824** LOUDON *Green-house Comp.* I. 15 The sickly condition of plants wintered in such of these houses as still exist. **1882** *Garden* 18 Mar. 187/3, I have given up wintering Cauliflower plants. **1883** *Standard* 3 Apr. 3/5 It should be the aim of the grass-land farmer to summer as many and winter as few animals as possible.

†**b.** *fig.* To maintain (an opinion) through a period of trial. (Cf. *to summer and winter* s.v. SUMMER *v.*^{1} 3 b.) *Obs. rare.*

1608 BP. HALL *Charac.* II. 108 The Vnconstant..what he will be next, as yet he knoweth not; but ere hee haue Wintred his opinion, it will be manifest. **1618** T. ADAMS *Serm. Heb. xiii. 8* Wks. (1629) 853 To winter an opinion is too tedious: hee hath beene many things; what hee will bee, you shall scarce know, till hee is nothing.

c. With *over.* = OVER-WINTER *v.* 4. Also *intr.*

1979 C. KILIAN *Icequake* iv. 42 How are we supposed to winter over on a goddam iceberg? **1982** 'E. LATHEN' *Green grow Dollars* i. 12 A tomato that could be planted, wintered over, then harvested.

†**3.** *intr.* To be or become wintry. *Obs. rare.*

1483 *Cath. Angl.* 420/1 To Wyntyr, *brumare, brumescere.*

†**4.** *pa. pple.* Detained by winter weather, winter-bound. *Obs. rare.*

1555 EDEN *Decades* (Arb.) 251 They sayled to the .49. degree and a halfe vnder the pole Antartyke; where beinge wyntered, they were inforced to remayne.

5. *trans.* To affect like winter, subject to wintry conditions; to make wintry; to chill, freeze. Chiefly *fig.* (cf. WINTER *sb.*^{1} 1 c).

1622 J. TAYLOR (Water P.) *Sir G. Nonsence* Wks. (1630) II. 3/2 Time that now summers him, wil one day winter him. **1628** FORD *Lover's Mel.* IV. iii, I am so..wintred with the tempests of affliction. **1797** ANNA SEWARD *Lett.* (1811) IV. 355 Experience has wintered the aspect of the future. **1857** MEREDITH *Farina* (1894) 304 They uttered noises that wintered the blood.

winterage ('wɪntərɪdʒ). *local.* Also **-idge.** [f. WINTER *v.* + -AGE.] The action of wintering cattle; food or pasture for cattle in winter.

1828 *Craven Gloss.*, *Winteridge*..the same as average. **1888** *Times* 8 Nov. 5/6 [In Galway] 'Winterage' is land hired to place cattle on in the winter months.

†**winteran.** *Obs.* In **winteran bark** [tr. mod.L. *cortex Winteranus*], erron. ***bark of Winteran*** = WINTER'S BARK.

1651 FRENCH *Distill.* ii. 58 Of the bark of Winteran half a pound. **1694** PECHEY *Compl. Herbal* 348 Winteranbark.

winterberry ('wɪntəˌbɛrɪ). Any of several N. American species of holly (*Ilex*, formerly *Prinos*) with berries, usually scarlet, which persist through the winter; esp. *Ilex verticillata* (also called Black Alder) and *I. lævigata* (Smooth Winterberry). Also, the fruit of any of these.

1759 MILLER *Gard. Dict.* (ed. 7), *Prinos.* Winterberry. **1770** J. R. FORSTER tr. *Kalm's Trav. N. Amer.* I. 67 *Prinos verticillatus*, the winterberry tree in swamps. **1832** J. BREE *St. Herbert's Isle* 147 Brambled paths, where winter-berries hang. **1889** *Science-Gossip* XXV. 171 A vigorous growth of winter-berry, laden with its crimson fruit.

winterbourne ('wɪntəbɔən). [OE. *winterburna*, f. WINTER *sb.*^{1} + *burna*, BOURN(E *sb.*^{1}, BURN *sb.*^{1} As a place-name *Winterbourne* is distributed over Wiltshire and Dorset together with s.w. Berks and s.w. Gloucestershire; there is also a *Winterburn* in North Yorkshire. The mod. use of the word as a common name has not been satisfactorily accounted for.] An intermittent stream, such as those found in chalk and limestone districts, which flows only in winter or at long intervals.

930 in Birch *Cartul. Sax.* II. 348 [Gloucestershire] In winterburnan..swa on oðærne winterburnan. *c* **950** *Lindisf. Gosp.* John xviii. 1 Ofer þæt burna *vel* uinterburna [L. *trans torrentem*].

[**1774** J. HUTCHINS *Hist. Dorset* I. Introd. p. lxxv, Winterborn N. rises at Winterborn Howton... This rivulet seldom runs farther than Clenston in the summer, and thus answers to its Saxon name Wintreburn.]

1851 KINGSLEY *Yeast* i, One of those noble springs known as winter-bournes in the chalk ranges. **1884** JUKES-BROWNE *Phys. Geol.* 86 The nailbournes [see EYLEBOURN] and winterbournes of the south of England are caused by a gradual rise in the line of saturation under the chalk-hills till the water reaches a level at which there is free egress into some valley or depression. **1895** SAINTSBURY *Ess. Engl. Lit.* Ser. II. 79 The flashing of the winterbournes as they spring from the turf where they have lain hid.

winter cherry.

1. Name for several plants of the nightshade tribe (N.O. *Solanaceæ*) with cherry-like fruit which is ripe in winter; also, the fruit itself.

a. The common English name of ALKEKENGI, a European herb bearing a round scarlet fruit inclosed in a red bladder-like envelope formed of the enlarged calyx; also of other species of *Physalis*, as the Cape Gooseberry, *P. edulis.*

1548 TURNER *Names of Herbes* (E.D.S.) 75 *Solanum vesicarium*..in englishe Alcakeng or wynter cheries. **1575** J. BANISTER *Chyrurg.* 96 b, *Alcakengi*, Winter cherie, a kynde of nightshade. **1640** PARKINSON *Theat. Bot.* 462 *Halicacabum sive Alkakengi.* Winter Cherries. **1721** MORTIMER *Husb.* II. 178 Winter Cherries are increased from the Roots by Sprouts or Runners. **1731** MILLER *Gard. Dict.* s.v. *Alkekengi*, The common medicinal Winter-Cherry. **1840** F. D. BENNETT *Whaling Voy.* II. 328 *Physalis edulis*—Cape Gooseberry or Winter Cherry.

b. Applied to species of *Solanum* with cherry-like fruit, as *S. Pseudo-capsicum*, also called Jerusalem Cherry.

1629 PARKINSON *Parad.* 431 *Amonum Plinij seu Pseudo-capsicum.* Tree Night shade or the Winter Cherry tree. **1731** MILLER *Gard. Dict.* s.v. *Solanum.* **1850** G. GLENNY *Handbk. Flower-Garden* 129 *Solanum pseudo-capsicum* is the Winter Cherry, a greenhouse bush, grown for its red cherry-like berries in winter.

2. Applied to species of *Cardiospermum* or Heartseed (N.O. *Sapindaceæ*), having fruit inclosed in an inflated calyx like that of *Physalis* (see 1); esp. *C. Halicacabum*, also called Balloon Vine.

1597 GERARDE *Herbal* II. lii. §2. 270 The blacke winter Cherrie hath weake and slender stalkes somewhat crested, and like vnto the tendrels of the Vine. **1866** [see *heart-pea*, HEART *sb.* 56 b].

winter corn. [Cf. Du. *winterkoren*, G. *winterkorn.*] Corn sown in winter, or in autumn and remaining in the ground through the winter.

c **1450** *Godstow Reg.* 351 On halfe acre of wyntur corne. **1523–34** FITZHERB. *Husb.* §8 If thou sowe it with winter-corne, as whete or ry. **1577** GOOGE *Heresbach's Husb.* I. 25 b, The Winter Corne when it is sowed before Winter, appeareth aboue the ground somtimes within a seuennight after. **1608** WILLET *Hexapla Exod.* 113 Our wheate and rie, which wee call winter corne. **1707** MORTIMER *Husb.* 60 These Lands are very subject to worms which destroys both the Corn and the Grass very much, especially the Winter-corn. **1764** *Museum Rust.* IV. 7 If it is to be winter corn, one ploughing more, which is the third only, makes it in fine order for the seed.

attrib. and *Comb.* *a* **1450** *Mankind* 54 in *Macro Plays* 3 A wyntur corn-threscher. **1611** in G. A. Carthew *Hund. Launditch* III. (1879) 26 In the tyme of wyntercorne harvest.

'winter-cress. [After Du. *winterkers.*] Any of the cruciferous herbs of the genus *Barbarea*, the leaves of which were formerly used as a winter salad; esp. *B. vulgaris* (Winter Rocket, Yellow R.).

1548 TURNER *Names of Herbes* (E.D.S.) 44 Irio..in englishe wynter cresse. **1578** LYTE *Dodoens* V. lxi. 626. **1597** GERARDE *Herbal* II. viii. 189 The seede of winter Cresse.. helpeth the strangurie. **1650** [W. HOWE] *Phytol. Brit.* 14 Barbarea, Pseudobunias,..Winter Cresses. **1785** MARTYN *Lett. Bot.* xxiii. (1794) 323 Winter Cress with lyrate leaves.. and spikes of yellow flowers, growing by ditch-sides. **1858** HOGG *Veg. Kingd.* 63.

winter day. [OE. *winterdæȝ* = MLG., MDu. *winterdach, -dagh* (Du. *winterdag*, G. *wintertag*), ON. *vetrardagr.*] A day in winter. (More commonly *winter's day*: see WINTER *sb.*^{1} 3 b.)

c **888** ÆLFRED *Boeth.* iv. §1 þu þe ðam winterdaȝum selest scorte tida. *c* **1375** *Sc. Leg. Saints* xxviii. (*Margaret*) 345 Eftyre sown þe blud fel Als clere of hyre as of a wel As dois watir one wyntir day. **1721** MORTIMER *Husb.* II. 116 To expose them to the Sun in such Winter-days as prove clear. **1726–46** THOMSON *Winter* 692 Behold, the joyous winter-days Frosty succeed. **1842** DICKENS *Amer. Notes* vi, The darkest winter-day that ever glimmered. *a* **1876** AIRD *Poet. Wks.* (1878) 145 On gurly winter days.

winterden, corrupt form of WITEREDEN.

wintered ('wɪntəd), *a.* Forms: (1 **ȝewintred**), 3 **wintred,** (*Orm.*) **winntredd,** 6–9 **wintred,** 6– **wintered.** [OE. *ȝewintred*, f. *ȝe-* Y- + *winter* WINTER *sb.*^{1} + *-ed*, -ED.]

†**1.** Having lived through or experienced many winters or years (cf. WINTER *sb.*^{1} 2); aged; veteran. In OE. also = 'of age', grown up. *Obs.*

The meaning in the last quot. is doubtful.

688–95 *Laws of Ine* xxxviii. (Liebermann), Healden þa mægas þone frumstol, Oð ðæt hit [*sc.* the child] ȝewintred sie. *c* **893** ÆLFRED *Oros.* VI. xxxi. §1 Hi hiene nieddon to leornunga, þeh he ȝewintred wære. *c* **1200** ORMIN 746 Sannt Johan wass streonedd ta þurrh faderr & þurrh moderr, þatt time þatt teȝȝ wærenn ba Winntrede menn & alde. **1594** KYD *Cornelia* IV. i, Backt With wintered souldiers vs'd to conquering [Garnier *vne armee, De fieres legions à vaincre accoustumee*]. **1599** NASHE *Lenten Stuffe* 66 The action is entred, the complaint of her [*sc.* a turbot's] wintered browes presented.

2. Exposed to the influence of winter; subjected to wintry conditions; chilled or blasted by winter.

c **1205** LAY. 101 þa scipen foren wide ȝeon þare wintrede sæ. **1556** J. HEYWOOD *Spider & F.* i. 4 In field so florishing That wintered withered stalks stand in couart. **1596** LODGE *Marg. Amer.* 21 First shall the sunne be seene without his flame, The wintred mountaines without frost or ice. **1804** ANNA SEWARD *Mem. Darwin* 293 The late and wintered period of Autumn. **1879** G. MACDONALD *Sir Gibbie* III. xv. 241 Something like a flash of cold moonlight on wintred water gleamed over..his poor focusless eyes. **1889** MRS. LYNN LINTON *Thro' Long Night* II. xx, He would welcome her as the wintered earth welcomes the fresh young spring.

†**3.** Adapted for or used in winter. *Obs. rare*$^{-1}$.

1600 SHAKS. *A.Y.L.* III. ii. 111 Wintred garments must be linde.

winterer ('wɪntərə(r)). [f. WINTER *v.* (or *sb.*^{1}) + -ER^{1}.] One who winters, in various senses.

1. a. One who spends the winter in a specified place; a winter visitor or resident; *spec.* a servant of the Hudson's Bay Company who was employed in the far interior of N. America. Also applied to birds (*spec.* the jerfalcon: see quot. 1831).

1801 A. MACKENZIE *Voy. Montreal* Fur Trade p. xxviii, Those are called North Men or Winterers. **1831** SWAINSON & RICHARDSON *Fauna Bor.-Amer.* II. 27 The Jerfalcon is a constant resident in the Hudson's Bay territories, where it is known by the name of the 'Speckled Partridge Hawk', or by that of the 'Winterer'. **1876** *Fortn. Rev.* Mar. 363 Davos, with its five hundred winterers. **1882** *Standard* 14 Apr. 6 Doubtless, the winterers in Smith's Sound..will have a curious tale to tell. **1923** *Times Lit. Suppl.* 15 Mar. 176/3 The whinchat hardly deserves to be ranked as a regular winterer, even in Cornwall.

b. *spec.* An animal, as a horse, ox, or sheep, 'kept to feed in a particular place during winter' (Jam.). *Sc.*

1795 G. ROBERTSON *Agric. Surv. Mid-Lothian* 41 In farms where no winterers are kept, the dunghill is placed behind the stables, out of view. **1801** *Farmer's Mag.* Aug. 251 Winterers, or straw-yard cattle, intended for next summer's grass. **1827** SCOTT *Two Drovers* ii, If you let me have six stots for winterers.

c. A hibernating animal.

1930 *Observer* 6 Apr. 24/2 Sudden warmth..may awake a winterer too precociously.

2. One who tends animals during winter.

1832 *Boston Her.* 8 May 3/5 Graziers and winterers of stock.

'winter-ˌfallow, *sb.* [Cf. MLG. *wintervalligen*, G. *winterfalgen.*] A lying fallow, or land that lies fallow, during the winter. So **'winter-ˌfallow** *v.*, *trans.* to lay (land) fallow during the winter; hence **'winter-ˌfallowing** *vbl. sb.*

1707 MORTIMER *Husb.* 45 The rougher it lies for a Winter fallow the better. *Ibid.* 47 In Staffordshire they often give their Lands a Winter fallowing, besides the three summer fallowings. *a* **1722** LISLE *Husb.* (1757) 54 Spring-corn, for which last three they winter-fallow only. **1763** *Museum Rust.* I. 33 Let the land be then Winter-fallowed. **1813** VANCOUVER *Agric. Devon* 166 The wheat-stubbles are.. winter-fallowed.

'winter-feed, *v. trans.* To feed or maintain (animals, etc.) during winter. Hence **'winter-ˌfeeding** *vbl. sb.*; also **'winter-feed** *sb.*, food supplied to animals during winter.

1605 SYLVESTER *Du Bartas* II. iii. IV. *Captains* 947 The wide-straddling Mower; That..Cuts-cross the swathes to winter-feed his Farm. *a* **1722** LISLE *Husb.* (1757) 276, I was saying that I had winter-feed..for more beasts than I had. **1762** MILLS *Syst. Pract. Husb.* I. 373 In Leicestershire, where they absurdly winter-feed their wheat by consent. **1765** *Museum Rust.* IV. 400 Deduct for the ewes winter-feed ..3 8 0. **1805** FORSYTH *Beauties Scot.* II. 221 Stall or winter-feeding of cattle or sheep. **1887** ROGERS *Agric. & Prices* V. 180 In 1595–6, peas and beans..were generally purchased for winter feed in the stable.

wintergreen (ˈwɪntəgriːn). [After Du. *wintergroen*, G. *wintergrün*.]

1. Name for various plants of low growth or creeping habit whose leaves remain green in winter. **a.** Any plant of the genus *Pyrola*, esp. *P. minor*, a woodland plant with roundish drooping white flowers. Also applied to plants of the allied genus *Chimaphila*, as *C.* (*P.*) *maculata* (Spotted W.), and *C.* (*P.*) *umbellata* (Pipsissewa or Prince's Pine).

Also in *pl.* as a collective name for the order *Pyrolaceæ* = the suborder *Pyroleæ* of *Ericaceæ*.

1548 TURNER *Names of Herbes* (E.D.S.) 48 *Limonium* named of the Herbaries Pyrola, is named in duch wintergrowen... It maye be called in englishe wyntergrene. **1640** PARKINSON *Theat. Bot.* 508 *Pyrola nostra vulgaris.* Our ordinary Winter greene... *Pyrola tenerior.* Slender Winter greene. **1771** J. R. FORSTER *Flora Amer. Septentr.* 20 Pyrola rotundifolia. Winter-green, round-leaved. Virginia. **1814** PURSH *Flora Amer. Septentr.* I. 300 *Chimaphila maculata*... *C. corymbosa*... Both species are handsome evergreens, and known by the name of Winter-green. **1861** S. THOMSON *Wild Fl.* III. (ed. 4) 222 The *Pyrolas*, or winter-greens. **1872** MACMILLAN *True Vine* vii. 285 The winter-green and the palmy shield-fern creep into the solitude of the pine-wood.

b. The N. American plant *Gaultheria procumbens* (Aromatic, Creeping, or Spring W.), bearing drooping white flowers and edible scarlet berries; also called Checkerberry, Partridge-berry, Tea-berry, etc.

oil of wintergreen, *wintergreen oil*, a heavy volatile oil obtained from the leaves of this plant, used medicinally as an aromatic stimulant, and for flavouring confectionery, etc.

1778 J. CARVER *Trav. N. Amer.* xix. 509 Winter Green.. is an ever-green.. found on dry heaths;.. in the winter it is full of red berries about the size of a sloe. *a* **1841** BRYANT *Strange Lady* 31 Where cornels arch their cool dark boughs o'er beds of winter green. **1845–50** MRS. LINCOLN *Lect. Bot.* 121 Among these oils are those of the orange,.. peppermint, and wintergreen. **1866** ODLING *Anim. Chem.* 87 Wood-spirit is a constituent residue of the essential oil of winter-green. **1909** *Chem. & Druggist* 20 Feb. 315/1 The methyl salicylate in the wintergreen oil.

c. chickweed wintergreen, either species of *Trientalis* (*T. europæa* or *americana*), woodland plants of high latitudes or altitudes.

1760 J. LEE *Introd. Bot.* App. 332 Winter Green, with Chickweed Flowers. **1789** AITON *Hortus Kew.* I. 493 Common Trientalis, or Chickweed Winter-green. **1840** BREMNER *Excurs. Denmark* etc. I. 370 The Wintergreen (Trientalis Europæa), the loveliest of all the flowers of the northern flora.

d. flowering wintergreen, the Fringed Milkwort of N. America, *Polygala paucifolia*.

1856 A. GRAY *Man. Bot. U.S.* (1860) 88.

2. Usually *pl.* (with hyphen, or as two words). An evergreen. Also *fig.* ? *Obs.*

1681 COTTON *Wond. Peak* 83 For Winter-Greens the Yew, Holly, and Box. **1707** MORTIMER *Husb.* 383 The best time for the removing of all Trees, except Winter Greens.. is either in October or February. **1729** SAVAGE *Wanderer* I. 196 Thick on this Top o'ergrown for Walks are seen Grey, leafless Wood, and winter Greens between! **1850** HAWTHORNE *Scarlet Let.* Introd. (1883) 33 This Inspector ..was.. one of the most wonderful specimens of winter-green that you would be likely to discover in a life-time's search.

3. (As two words or hyphened.) Greens for winter use.

1846 J. BAXTER *Libr. Pract. Agric.* (ed. 4) I. 149 Winter greens comprise those varieties of the Brassica tribe, which authors are in the habit of describing as Coleworts, Borecole, Savoys, Scotch Kale, Sprouts, &c. **1886** HARDY *Woodlanders* iv, Rabbits that had been eating the winter-greens in the gardens.

winter-ground, *v.*

Assumed by G. Steevens (ed. of Shakespeare, 1773, IX. 257) in *Cymb.* IV. ii. 229, where the 1st Folio has 'the Raddocke would.. bring thee all this, Yea, and furr'd Mosse besides. When Flowres are none To winter-ground thy Coarse —— *Gui.* Prythee haue done', and explained by him as meaning: 'To protect (a plant) from the inclemency of the winter-season, by straw, dung, &c. laid over it.' (Hence in Dicts. from Worcester, 1860, onwards.)

Winterhalter (ˈvɪntəhaltə(r)). The name of Franz Xavier *Winterhalter* (1806–73), German portrait painter of royalty, used *attrib.* to designate things characteristic of his pictures, esp. court settings and a style of women's formal dress.

1923 *Daily Mail* 11 Sept. 11/2 The 'period' dress, Winterhalter or Velasquez, is almost entirely restricted to dinner, or formal afternoon, wear. **1937** H. NICOLSON *Helen's Tower* vii. 146 How did she cope with the Winterhalter atmosphere of that decaying court? **1944** 'BRAHMS' & 'SIMON' *No Nightingales* xxvii. 155 An.. old lady tottering but aristocratic, at grips with a son-in-law too mean to buy a Winterhalter ball-gown for dining *en famille*. **1957** M. B. PICKEN *Fashion Dict.* 376/2 *Winterhalter*, name applied to costumes characterized by off-shoulder necklines, corseleted waistlines, crinoline skirts with flounces. **1970** R. T. WILCOX *Dict. Costume* 398/2 *Winter-halter*, another term for the crinoline period.

ˈwinter-ˌhouse. [OE. *winterhús*. Cf. G. *winterhaus*.] A house for winter occupation. (Cf. SUMMER-HOUSE 1.)

c **1000** ÆLFRIC *Saints' Lives* xxxvi. 98 Winterhus and sumorhus and wynsume buras. *c* **1440** *Promp. Parv.* 530/1 Wyntyr howse, or halle.. *hibernaculum*. **1539** *Bible* (Great) Ecclus. xxii. 17–18 A fayre playstred wall in a wynter house. **1611** *Bible* Jer. xxxvi. 22 The king sate in the winter house, .. & there was a fire on the hearth burning before him. **1688** BOYLE *Final Causes* iv. 173 Beavers.. lay these together so as to build themselves strong winter-houses. **1771** BURNEY *Pres. St. Mus. France & Italy* 256 He has a winter-house in Florence. **1865** LUBBOCK *Preh. Times* 392 These circles were at first supposed to be the remains of winter-houses.

So † **winter-housing.** *rare.*

c **1440** *Pallad. on Husb.* Tab. 18 Bildynge of wyntir housynge.

winteridge: see WINTERAGE.

winterim (ˈwɪntərɪm), *a.* and *sb. U.S.* [Blend of WINTER *sb.*[1] and INTERIM *adv.*, *sb.*, and *adj.*] (Of or pertaining to) a short winter term in some private schools in the U.S., part of which is spent by some pupils on projects away from the school.

1972 *Handbk. Private Schools* (ed. 53) 1079 A four-week 'Winterim' in which juniors and seniors may go off campus and a special program is run for freshmen and sophomores. **1976** *National Observer* (U.S.) 22 May 15/1 (Advt.), Winterim on-and-off campus work/study program—Thorough college preparation. **1979** *N.Y. Times Mag.* 30 Sept. 91/2 (Advt.), Interscholastic and recreational sports —On and off campus Winterim. **1980** L. BIRNBACH et al. *Official Preppy Handbk.* 52/2 Winterim session spent skiing.

wintering (ˈwɪntərɪŋ), *vbl. sb.* [f. WINTER *v.* or *sb.*[1] + -ING[1].]

I. The action of WINTER *v.* in various senses.

1. a. The keeping or tending of cattle, etc. during winter; provision of food and shelter for animals in winter.

1477 [see SUMMERING *vbl. sb.*[1] 1]. **1504** *Nottingham Rec.* III. 320 For wynttering of the commond bull' iij s. viij d. **1583** *Shuttleworths' Acc.* (Chetham Soc.) 15 The wynterynge and sommerynge of a styrke. **1617** *Ibid.* 253 Winteringe of a mare at Copthurst, xˢ. **1707** MORTIMER *Husb.* 171 Young, lean Cattel.. may by their growth pay for their Wintering. **1855** *Poultry Chron.* II. 415 The successful wintering of bees. **1886** C. SCOTT *Sheep-Farming* 123 The wintering of hill sheep.

† **b.** *transf.* or *gen.* Provision of food, clothing, or shelter for persons in winter. *Obs.*

1586 FERNE *Blaz. Gentrie* 158 If thou hast a shrewd wyfe, giue her as shrewde a wintring, and turne her off to hard meat. *c* **1590** *Trag. Rich. II.* (1870) 43 We haue all need of some kynd winteringe. We are besett.. with many stormes.

† **2.** Winter weather (of a certain kind). *nonce-use.*

1545 RAYNALDE *Byrth Mankynde* 89 When so euer the wynter is hote & moyst,.. when that such wintering chaunseth, the hote & moyste whether heateth and moysteth the womans body.

3. The action of passing the winter in a particular place; a stay or residence during winter.

a **1593** MARLOWE tr. *Lucan* I. 303 Our wintering Vnder the Alpes. **1621** in Foster *Engl. Factories Ind.* (1906) 240 The Red Sea intended for our shipps wintering. *a* **1674** MILTON *Hist. Moscovia* v. Wks. 1851 VIII. 505 Thir two years wintring in Lapland. **1740** RICHARDSON *Pamela* (1824) I. xxiii. 276 Whose heart is set upon the hope of her wintering with us in town. **1861** J. H. BENNET *Shores Mediterr.* I. vi. (1875) 155, I had not seen the good results from wintering abroad that I have since experienced. **1887** *Spectator* 8 Oct. 1340 In the Arctic seas, the art of wintering on the ice is so well understood.

II. Concrete senses.

4. = WINTERLING. (See WINTER *sb.*[1] 2, and cf. SUMMERING *vbl. sb.*[1] 3 c.) *Sc.*

Cf. ON. *vetrungr*.

1717 *Forfeited Estates Papers* (S.H.S. 1909) Introd. p. xxix, Winterings, 30 at 2s. 9½d. per Wintering. **1825** JAMIESON, *Winterin, Winterling.*

5. An animal that is wintered in a particular place.

1901 *Scotsman* 1 Apr. 9/2 To add to the anxieties of sheep-owners, the winterings are on the way from the low countries.

6. Land where livestock may be wintered.

1937 A. FRASER *Sheep Farming* iv. 46 The ewes can be helped if the hill is cleared as much and as early as possible .. by getting the ewe hoggs to their wintering at the earliest possible date. **1978** *Dumfries & Galloway Standard* 21 Oct. 21/3 (Advt.), Wintering wanted for 45 Blackface Ewe Lambs from November till 1st March 1979.

III. 7. *attrib.*, as (in sense 3) ***wintering-ground***, **†*-harbour*** (HARBOUR *sb.*[1] 2), ***-house***, ***-place***, ***-region***, ***-station***; (in sense 1) **†*wintering-meat*** (MEAT *sb.* 1).

c **1520** BARCLAY *Jugurth* xxxviii. 52 b, Worthy men of his army.. to be called togyder.. from their wyntring places. **1600** HOLLAND *Livy* V. ii. 180 The Romane captaines.. began to build wintring harbours. **1606–7** *Act 4 Jas. I* c. 11 §1 The Oxen and Kyne.. must be sold awaye for wante of winteringe Meate. **1611** in *Voy. L. Foxe & James* (Hakl. Soc.) II. 630 The certaine tyme of the Ship's comming owte of the wintring port, he remembreth not. **1629** LE GRYS tr. *Barclay's Argenis* 291 As in perpetuall wintering stations. **1780** COXE *Russ. Discov.* 254 This wintering place was observed to lie in 53° 29′ North latitude. **1805** Z. M. PIKE *Jrnl.* 15 Oct. in *Acct. Expeditions Sources Mississippi* (1810) I. 33 This day's march made me think seriously of our wintering ground. **1817** J. BRADBURY *Trav. Amer.* 51, I set out.. at sunrise, for the wintering house. **1841** CATLIN *N. Amer. Ind.* II. lii. 149 The wintering post of Colonel Kearney. *c* **1890** R. CAMPBELL in C. Wilson *Campbell of Yukon* (1970) xi. 104 Do away with a wintering ground which, from the starvation so frequently experienced there, our men hold in actual dread and abhorrence. **1977** *Monitor* (McAllen, Texas) 9 Jan. B 8/4 The request for Texas biologists to investigate the whitewing wintering grounds came from the International Whitewinged Dove Council.

ˈwintering, *ppl. a.* [f. WINTER *v.* + -ING[2].] That winters, in various senses.

1. Passing the winter in a particular place: *spec.* of cattle, etc. that are being tended in the winter.

1808 J. C. CURWEN *Feeding Stock* 55 Feeding the wintering Highland cattle with them [*sc.* turnips]. **1876** 'OUIDA' *Winter City* vii, The wintering-swallows had never been so fluttered. **1889** *Pall Mall Gaz.* 16 Feb. 5/2 Competent scientific men.. would be taken on board and left with the wintering party.

2. *poet.* used vaguely for 'wintry'.

1865 SWINBURNE *Atalanta* 268 As a windy and wintering moon Seen through blown cloud. **1876** —— *Erechtheus* 732 Thicker set with fence of thorn-edged spears Than sands are whirled about the wintering beach.

winterish (ˈwɪntərɪʃ), *a.* [f. WINTER *sb.*[1] + -ISH[1].] †**a.** Belonging to winter. **b.** Having a quality of winter: (somewhat) winterly or wintry.

1530 PALSGR. 329/2 Wynterysshe,.. *yvernal*. **1610** HOLLAND *Camden's Brit.* I. 220 In winter it may.. be called, a winterish region so wet.. it is. **1885** *Harper's Mag.* Jan. 199/1 Gray and winterish as it [*sc.* a barberry bush] had been on her approach, when she looked at it from the other side it seemed to be glowing with rubies.

ˈwinterishly, *adv.* [f. WINTERISH *a.* + -LY[2].] In a manner suggestive of winter.

1905 *Smart Set* Oct. 26/1 Though by good rights the day might have been winterishly cold it was of a balmy mildness.

winterize (ˈwɪntəraɪz), *v.* orig. and chiefly *U.S.* [f. WINTER *sb.*[1] + -IZE.] *trans.* To adapt or prepare (something) for operation or use in cold weather.

1938 *Amer. Speech* XIII. 160/1 A radio announcer... urged his listeners to have their cars winterized. **1949** A. HAYES *Girl on Flaminia* iv. 90 She sat on the hard canvas cushion of the jeep, and she must have felt exposed. The jeep had not been winterized. **1950** *Jane's Fighting Ships 1950–1* 454 *Arneb* has been refitted for Arctic Service... Other vessels are also to be 'winterized'. **1954** E. W. ECKEY *Veg. Fats & Oils* iii. 124 The temperature below which no portion of the oil should be chilled is a little above the cloud point of the oil to be winterized. **1964** S. BELLOW *Herzog* 96 This is a fine house you have... Summer only, isn't it? You could winterize it easily. **1973** B. WRIGHT *Four Seasons North* 42 Sam winterized the rifles, wiping away all the lubrication, which would freeze if left in the guns. **1980** L. AUCHINCLOSS *House of Prophet* vii. 101 We agreed to take over my parents' summer house in Seal Cove and winterize it.

Hence **ˈwinterized** *ppl. a.*, **ˈwinterizing** *vbl. sb.*; **winteriˈzation**.

1926 *Jrnl. Oil & Fat Industries* III. 421/1 Some of the cottonseed stearine made by the winterizing process and the hydrogenated oil are used in margarine. **1927** *Oil & Fat Industries* IV. 301/2 Depending upon the length of time winterized oil will stand clear, brilliant and limpid when exposed to the so-called Winter Oil Test, an oil is more or less suitable for.. salad oil and mayonnaise manufacturers. **1940** *PM* 29 Nov. 14/3 Instead of having an entire company of trainees, even one 'winterized tent' of trainees, all together,.. there will be throughout the 44th Division scads of veterans surrounding each new man. **1940** *Capital* (Topeka) 8 Dec. 2A (Advt.), Buy any car... Plus complete winterization. **1943** *Oil & Soap* July 131/2 The present slow and inefficient winterization process for cottonseed oil. **1955** SMALLEY & KLOHR in F. S. Mallette *Probl. & Control of Air Pollution* xvii. 199 (*caption*) Winterized sulfur recovery plant. **1957** *Encycl. Brit.* VI. 584/2 Winterization is a process by which a portion of the refined and bleached oil is solidified by chilling and filtered off. **1966** *Economist* 22 Jan. 341/3 Builders.. are showing considerable interest in 'winterisation'... Over a third now have some degree of lighting on site. **1970** *Toronto Daily Star* 24 Sept. 39/7 (Advt.), Winterized jackets have the accent on fashion with bright colours. **1971** C. BONINGTON *Annapurna South Face* 286 All the cameras functioned well, and although only the Nikons were winterized, there was no trouble from freezing up. **1978** *N.Y. Times* 30 Mar. B15/2 (Advt.), Two 5 rm winterized cottages. **1979** *Farmington* (New Mexico) *Daily Times* 27 May 6C/3 (Advt.), Experiments on winterizing and solar energy retrofits.

ˈwinterless, *a.* [f. as WINTERISH *a.* + -LESS.] Having no winter; free from or not experiencing winter.

1845 BAILEY *Festus* (ed. 2) 193 Such dew as gemmed the everduring blooms Of Eden winterless. **1869** RUSKIN *Q. of Air* §88 Glossy surfaces [of leaves], green with pure strength, and winterless delight. **1883** *Century Mag.* June 200/2 The sunny, delicious, winterless Californian sky.

ˈwinterling. [f. as prec. + -LING.] An ox, sheep, or other animal of a year old; a yearling.

1825 [see WINTERING *vbl. sb.* 4]. **1881** SIR G. W. COX *Compar. Mythol.* 156 A Chimaira is thus, strictly, a winterling, that is, a yearling.

winterly (ˈwɪntəlɪ), *a.* [OE. *winterlic* = OHG. *wintarlîh* (G. *winterlich*), ON. *vetrligr*, etc., f. WINTER *sb.*[1] + -LY[1]; but in modern use a new formation (cf. *summerly*).]

1. Of, belonging to, or occurring in winter. (Not always distinguishable from sense 2.)

c **1000** ÆLFRIC *Saints' Lives* xi. 144 On þam timan wæs swiþe hefigtime wynter.. and se winterlica wind wan mid þam forste.

1559 W. CUNINGHAM *Cosmogr. Glasse* 34 Into whiche [*sc.* tropic of winter] whan he [*sc.* the sun] doth enter, he maketh his wynterly retorne backwarde. **1622** WITHER *Faire-Virtue*, etc. O 7 b, Those tresses of Haire, which thy youth doe adorne, Will looke like the Meads in a Winterly morne. **1628** VENNER *Baths* Advt. 13 For them..that are subiect to..cold winterly diseases. **1665** MANLEY *Grotius' Low C. Wars* III. 307 The Winterly Waters, and frequent shoures. **1822** T. TAYLOR *Apuleius* 215 The winterly frosts of Capricorn. **1889** MRS. OLIPHANT *Poor Gentleman* I. xii. 222 Even the winterly birds in the trees..were silent to-day.

2. Having the character of, or characteristic of, winter; resembling winter or that of winter; cold and cheerless; wintry.

a **1661** FULLER *Worthies, Somerset* (1662) 17 The Earth [of Somerset] in winter is as winterly, deep and dirty, as any in England. **1675** tr. *Camden's Hist. Eliz.* (ed. 3) 500 The Air growing more winterly in the Month of Aprill. **1703** S. SEWALL *Diary* 16 Mar., All things look horribly winterly by reason of a great storm of Snow. **1816** KIRBY & SP. *Entomol.* xviii. (1818) II. 112 Though the summer has been so wet, and one may almost say winterly. **1858** MRS. OLIPHANT *Laird of Norlaw* II. 223 The winterly brown aspect of the trees. **1876** J. GRANT *Burgh Sch. Scot.* II. v. 191 The fields wear a winterly face.

b. *fig.*

1611 SHAKS. *Cymb.* III. iv. 13 If't be Summer Newes Smile too't before: if Winterly, thou need'st But keepe that count'nance stil. **1680** ALSOP *Mischief Impos.* vi. 40 Incendiaries who..will suffer none to be cool that are in them-selves of a more winterly temper. **1798** MARY WOLLSTONECR. *Posth. Wks.* IV. 76 Your note..produced a kind of winterly smile. **1864** W. J. LINTON *Claribel* I. iii, Let thy sweet spring smile Shine on me through this winterly contempt.

Hence **'winterliness**.

1891 W. SHARP in *Mem.* (1910) 174 With all the sunlit but yet sombre winterliness around.

'winter 'quarters. (Also with hyphen.) [See QUARTER *sb.* 15.]

1. a. The place of stay, or lodgings, occupied by troops, or by the members of an expedition, during the winter (between two campaigns or periods of activity or travel). Also, such a place occupied by any travelling company or by private individuals.

[**1641** EVELYN *Diary* 8 Sept., Seedam, where was at that time Coll. Goring's winter-quarters.] **1650** STAPYLTON *Strada's Low C. Wars* VIII. 8 The like..was done..by the Nervians, when they besieged the winter-quarters of Quintus Cicero. **1714** W. VICKERS *Let.* 21 Sept. in M. M. Verney *Verney Lett.* (1930) II. xxi. 16 Miss Pen comes to our winter quarters in the middle of next week. **1769** *Lond. Chron.* 9–11 Nov. 456/1 According to advices from the Russian Army..it will soon go into winter quarters in the centre of the kingdom. **1777** R. WATSON *Philip II* (1839) 423 His troops were no sooner distributed into winter-quarters, than Leicester returned with his army towards Zutphen. **1867** SMYTH *Sailor's Word-bk., Winter-quarters*, ..in Arctic parlance, the spot where ships are to remain housed during the winter months—from the 1st October to the 1st July or August. **1878** A. H. MARKHAM *Gt. Frozen Sea* xiii. 154 Altogether the neighbourhood of our winter quarters had the appearance of a young thriving settlement. **1897** A. BEARDSLEY *Let.* 29 July (1970) 353 At the end of this week I shall move to Paris, and then into winter quarters as soon as possible. **1939** *Florida* (Federal Writers' Project) III. 395 Bailey circus winter quarters.

†**b.** *transf.* The interval of time during which troops are in winter quarters. *Obs.*

1706 PHILLIPS s.v. *Quarters, Winter-Quarters*,..the Space of Time between two Campaigns. **1734** tr. *Rollin's Rom. Hist.* III. 402 Which he divides into campaigns and winter-quarters. **1797** *Encycl. Brit.* (ed. 3) XV. 751.

2. The place in which certain animals find shelter during the winter. (Rarely of plants.)

1697 DRYDEN *Virg. Georg.* IV. 357 Lazy Drones,..In Winter Quarters free, devour the Gain. **1709** T. ROBINSON *Vind. Mosaick Syst.* 89, I saw infinite Numbers of Frogs coming out of their Winter-Quarters, which was a vast heap of loose Stones. **1856** DELAMER *Fl. Gard.* (1861) 165 Remove dahlia-roots from their winter quarters. **1890** *Science-Gossip* XXVI. 34 A frost of several days' duration..sent most of these snails into winter-quarters.

Hence **winter-quarter** *v.*, *intr.* to go into or reside in winter quarters. *rare.*

1706 LUTTRELL *Brief Rel.* (1857) VI. 90, 25 000 of the allies are to winter quarter in Brabant.

winters ('wɪntəz), *adv. U.S.* [Pl. of WINTER *sb.*^{1}] During the winter.

1907 'MARK TWAIN' *Christian Sci.* II. 235 It can appoint its own furnace-stoker, winters. **1978** *Chicago* June 158/1 Winters, William is the tennis director at the Genesee Valley Tennis Club in Flint.

Winter's bark. [= mod.L. *cortex Winteranus* (see WINTERAN), named from its discoverer Captain William *Winter*, who accompanied Francis Drake to the Magellan Straits in 1578 (Clusius).] **a.** The pungent aromatic bark of *Drimys Winteri*, a magnoliaceous tree of the mountainous parts of western America from Mexico southwards; used as a stimulant tonic and antiscorbutic; also called **Winter's cinnamon**, from its flavour. **b.** Extended to other medicinal barks, as that of the W. Indian whitewood or wild cinnamon, *Canella alba* (*false Winter's bark*). **c.** Any of the trees themselves.

1622 R. HAWKINS *Voy. S. Sea* xxxvi. 88 A learned Country-man of ours, Doctor Turner, hath written of it, by the name of Winters barke. **1640** PARKINSON *Theat. Bot.* 1662 Captaine Winters Cinamon. **1679** TRAPHAM *Disc. Health Jamaica* 38 Our Winter Bark or West Indian Cinnamon Tree. **1712** tr. *Pomet's Hist. Drugs* IV. I. 74 White Cinamon, to which some give the Name..Winter's Bark, or Winter's Cinamon. **1776** *Med. Observ. & Inq.* V. 46 The Winter's Bark-tree, *Winterana Aromatica*. **1830** LINDLEY *Nat. Syst. Bot.* 121 The false Winter's Bark, a good tonic and stimulant, not much known.

'winter 'solstice. The time at which the sun reaches the winter tropic, i.e. in the northern hemisphere the tropic of Capricorn, in the southern the tropic of Cancer; the middle of the winter half of the year, midway between the autumnal and vernal equinoxes.

a **1633** AUSTIN *Medit.* (1635) 42 This night [*sc.* Christmas] was shortly after the Winter Solstice; when Night growes shorter, and Day longer. **1658** SIR T. BROWNE *Gard. Cyrus* iii. 48 Even the Autumnal buds, which await the return of the Sun, do after the winter solstice multiply their calicular leaves. **1729** FENTON in *Waller's Wks.* Observ. p. xvi, At the time of their breeding (which is about the winter-solstice,) the sea is calm. **1843** *Penny Cycl.* XXVII. 471/2 Winter begins at the winter solstice.

'wintersome, *a. rare*$^{-1}$. [f. WINTER *sb.*^{1} + -SOME^1.] = WINTRY *a.*

1864 TROLLOPE *Small Ho. Allington* II. xv. 148 The fourteenth of February in London was quite as black, and cold, and as wintersome as it was at Allington.

winter sport. a. A sport enjoyed in the winter; *spec.* an outdoor sport on snow or ice, such as skiing or skating. Usu. *pl.*

1828 *Ladies' Mag.* Mar. 141 (*heading*) Children at their winter sports. **1847** C. M. YONGE *Scenes & Characters* xiii. 163 Intent upon the various winter sports in which William and Lord Rotherwood allowed him to share [at an English country house]. **1879** H. CHADWICK (*title*) Handbook of winter sports. Embracing: skating (on ice and on rollers,) rink-ball, curling, ice-boating, and American football. **1906** *Dress* Dec. 18/1 Tobogganing, another favorite winter sport introduced from Canada, has many devotees. **1934** F. SCOTT FITZGERALD *Tender is Night* I. iii. 17 Vivid advertising cards of the railroad companies..winter sports at Chamonix. **1956** A. H. COMPTON *Atomic Quest* 213 Winter sports, especially skiing, were popular. **1975** *Oxf. Compan. Sports* 950/2 Skibobbing is a new winter sport, combining the virtues of the ski, the bobsleigh, and the velocipede in a downhill run.

b. *attrib.* (in *sing.* and *pl.*).

1908 E. & M. SYERS *Bk. Winter Sports* 323 Some notes on winter-sport resorts. **1922** *Cook's Continental Timetable* Jan. 377 (Advt.), Central position. Close to all Winter Sports places. **1950** E. HEMINGWAY *Across River* xxxiii. 207 It would be just like any winter-sports hotel. **1966** N. FREELING *King of Rainy Country* 38 She had gone..on a wintersport holiday. **1975** *Country Life* 30 Oct. 1192/2 A really beautiful collection of winter sports clothes.

Hence **winter-sport** *v. intr.*, to engage in winter sports; **winter-sporting** *vbl. sb.*

1948 M. LASKI *Tory Heaven* ix. 128 I'd like to go winter-sporting in January. **1955** T. H. PEAR *Eng. Social Differences* xi. 265 Few who 'winter-sport'..feel that their social rating is thereby raised. **1961** *Times* 13 May 11/2 The famous winter-sporting centres. **1974** *Guardian* 23 Mar. 14/2 If you've fished in Scotland, if you've winter sported in Switzerland, you can do it all in Sweden.

'winter-tide. Now somewhat *arch.* [OE. *wintertíd* (WINTER *sb.*^{1}, TIDE *sb.*): cf. OHG. *winterzît* (G. *winterzeit*), MLG., MDu. *wintertît* (Du. *wintertijd*), ON. *vetrartíð*, etc.; in modern use a new formation (cf. *summer-tide*).] = next.

c **900** tr. *Bæda's Hist.* II. xiii. (1890) 134 Swylc swa ðu æt swæsendum sitte mid ðinum ealdormannum ond ðeȝnum on wintertide, and sie fyr onælæd. *c* **1000** ÆLFRIC *Saints' Lives* iv. 35 Hit is wintertid nu, and ic wundrie pearle hwanon þes wyrtbræð þus wynsumlice steme. **1338** R. BRUNNE *Chron.* (1810) 240 In Wales it is fulle strong to werre in Winter tide. **1375** BARBOUR *Bruce* v. 1 Quhen vyntir tyde Vith his blastis ..Wes ourdriffin. *c* **1400** *Laud Troy Bk.* 634 The trees that ware In wynter-tyde naked & bare. **1590** GREENE *Neuer too late* Wks. (Grosart) VIII. 227 The daies growes short, then hasts the winter tide.

1830 TENNYSON *Ode to Memory* 19 Earliest shoots Of orient green,..Which in wintertide shall star The black earth with brilliance rare. **1904** A. GRIFFITHS *50 Yrs. Public Service* xii. 167, I shall never forget those church parades in the dull grey light of wintertide.

'winter-time. [Cf. ON. *vetrartími.*] The season of winter.

1393 LANGL. *P. Pl.* C. XIII. 189 With forste[s] With wyndes ne with wederes as in wynter-tyme. *c* **1400** *Brut* ccxxiv. 291 He wente aȝen into Scotland in þe wynter tyme. **1523–34** FITZHERB. *Husb.* §16 Yf the lande be falowed in wynter tyme, it is farre the worse. **1610** HOLLAND *Camden's Brit.* 631 All Winter time almost it is continually cloudy and misty weather. **1716** [? ARBUTHNOT] *Petit. Colliers* Swift's Misc. 1732 III. 73 Warming of Cellars and Dressing of Suppers in the Winter-time. **1835** DICKENS *Sk. Boz, Parish* v, If it's winter time, they just give you fire enough to make you think you'd like more. **1896** BADEN-POWELL *Matabele Campaign* xiii, A pair of skates..which..came in useful when he got up to Kandahar in the winter-time.

'winterward(s, *adv.* [f. WINTER *sb.*^{1}: see -WARD(S.] Towards winter.

1891 *Advance* (Chicago) 9 Apr., Winterward [see SUMMERWARD]. **1906** E. F. BENSON *Challoners* xii, Till to-day all had been grey and brown, all still pointed backwards, winter-wards.

wintery: see WINTRY.

wintle ('wɪnt(ə)l), *v. Sc.* Also 9 **wuntle.** [a. early Flem. *windtelen*, *wend(t)elen* 'voluere, volutare' (Kilian), f. *winden* WIND *v.*^{1}]

1. *intr.* To roll or swing from side to side.

1786 BURNS *To Auld Mare* vii, Tho' now ye dow but hoyte and hoble, An' wintle like a saumont-coble. **1790** —— *Verses to J. Rankine* 8 From him that wears the star and garter, To him that wintles in a halter. **1819** W. TENNANT *Papistry Storm'd* (1827) 173 And wi' his prickin' gude pyk-staff Made them rebound and wintle aff.

2. To tumble, capsize, be upset.

1867 J. K. HUNTER *Retrosp. Artist's Life* xxx. (1912) 315, I..wintled over beyond him in the bed. **1890** SERVICE *Thir Notandums* v. 28 At the whilk observe of mine, I thocht that his Lordship would have wuntled aff his cheyre.

Hence **'wintle** *sb.*, a rolling or staggering movement.

1785 BURNS *Halloween* xix, He by his shouther gae a keek, An' tumbl'd wi' a wintle. **1882** JAS. WALKER *Sc. Poems* 127 With rocking wintle near the shipping quay The Granton steamboat at our service lay.

†**wintrous,** *a. Obs. rare*$^{-1}$. [f. WINTER *sb.*^{1} + -OUS.] = next.

1629 Z. BOYD *Last Battell* 283 The more wintrous the Season of the life hath beene, look to the fairer Summer of pleasures for evermore.

wintry ('wɪntrɪ), *a.* Also 7 **winterie**, 9 **-y.** [OE. *wintriȝ*, = OHG. *wintirig*, etc., f. WINTER *sb.*^{1} + -Y^1; but in modern use a new formation.]

1. Of or pertaining to winter; occurring, existing, or found in winter; adapted or suitable for winter. Now *rare* or merged in 2, being replaced by 'winter' *attrib.* (WINTER *sb.*^{1} 3).

c **888** ÆLFRED *Boeth.* v. §2 Swa deð eac se ðe wintreȝum wederum wile blostman secan. *c* **893** —— *Oros.* I. i. 12 On þæm wintreȝum tidum.

1611 COTGR., *Hyvernal*, winterie, winterlie. *c* **1630** MILTON *Passion* 6 In Wintry solstice like the shortn'd light Soon swallow'd up in dark and long out-living night. **1697** DRYDEN *Virg. Georg.* I. 271 The wise Ant her wintry Store provides. **1697** —— *Æneis* VI. 298 The wintry Misleto. **1770** GOLDSM. *Des. Vill.* 133 To pick her wintry faggot from the thorn. **1795** COWPER *Needless Alarm* 20 Her berries red, With which the fieldfare, wint'ry guest, is fed. **1860** TYNDALL *Glac.* I. v. 40 Where the wintry edifices had fallen.

2. Having the quality of winter; of such a kind as occurs in winter; characteristic of winter.

1590 SPENSER *F.Q.* I. xi. 21 When wintry storme his wrathfull wreck does threat. **1713** ROWE *Jane Shore* II. 24 The Wintry Sky Descends in Storms. *c* **1781** BURNS *Winter* i, The wintry west extends his blast. **1825** SCOTT *Betrothed* ii, A barbed horse and his rider will fear to stem the wintry flood. **1830** LYELL *Princ. Geol.* I. 120 At this period, the climate of equinoctial lands might resemble that of the present temperate zone, or perhaps be far more wintery. **1856** KANE *Arctic Expl.* I. xxvii. 355 This mossing..is a frightfully wintry operation. **1876** C. F. HALL *Polar Exped.* 415 Great ice-crystals..gave the vessel a wintry appearance.

3. Exposed or subject to the effect or influence of winter; chilled or blasted by winter.

1697 DRYDEN *Æneis* IV. 205 When he leaves the frost Of wintry Xanthus. **1803** HEBER *Palestine* 56 The wintry top of giant Lebanon. **1817** SHELLEY *Rev. Islam* VI. xxviii, The wintry loneliness Of those dead leaves. **1853** DICKENS *Bleak Ho.* xii, Endless avenues and cross-avenues of wintry trees. **1918** *Blackw. Mag.* Oct. 464/2 You saw nothing but a field or two of bleached wintry grass.

4. *fig.* with various shades of meaning; *esp.* (*a*) Aged, infirm or withered from age; (of hair) white with age, 'snowy'; (*b*) devoid of fervour or affection, 'cold', 'chilling'; (*c*) destitute of warmth or brightness, dismal, dreary, cheerless.

1633 P. FLETCHER *Pisc. Ecl.* VII. i, Cold, wintry, wither'd Tithon. **1748** RICHARDSON *Clarissa* lvi. (1768) III. 281 Nodding at each other in opposite chimney-corners in a winter-evening, and over a wintry Love. **1822** SHELLEY *Scenes fr. Faust* ii. 15 Nothing of such an influence do I feel. My body is all wintry. **1846** MRS. A. MARSH *Fr. Darcy* xliii, A faint wintry kind of hope. **1847** TENNYSON *Princess* VI. 310 So she, and turn'd askance a wintry eye. **1876** BESANT & RICE *Golden Butterfly* vi, Her cold face shone..with the wintry light of a forced smile. **1895** *Pall Mall Gaz.* 5 Oct. 3/3 His latest work met with a somewhat wintry welcome. **1902** W. ADAMSON *Life Jos. Parker* xv. 192 The..wintry locks of wisdom.

5. Used *advb.* qualifying another adj. *poet.*

1892 W. WATSON *Poems* 9 Thine..Is wintry chill.

Hence **'wintrify** (-faɪ) *v.*, *trans.* to make wintry (*rare*); **'wintrily** *adv.*, in a wintry manner (*lit.* and *fig.*); **'wintriness**, wintry quality or condition (*lit.* and *fig.*).

1855 LYNCH *Lett. to Scattered* vi. 88 Wise divine Love.. re-imparting to a world which hate had *wintrified the summer warmth of life. *c* **1822** BEDDOES *Poems, Pygmalion* 159 Thou..dost shiver *Wintrily sad. **1867–8** J. THOMSON *In the Room* ii, Flies..now slept wintrily abashed. **1884** *Harper's Mag.* Sept. 613/1 She..began..to smile wintrily. **1824** in *Spirit Publ. Jrnls.* (1825) 512 With all this *winteryness, he is still a boy. **1853** KANE *Grinnell Exp.* xxxii. (1856) 277 To the east and west there is no such interception to our winteryness. **1916** *Spectator* 18 Mar. 383/1 On some morning when the harvest's done, And autumn its first wintriness reveals.

†**winx,** *v. Obs.* [Cf. dial. *whink* to bark, yelp, *whinnock* to whine, neigh, whinny.] *intr.* To bray as an ass.

14.. *Hortus Vocab.* (MS. Harl. 2257), *Mugio*, to lowe as a oxe. *Mugilo*, to wynx as a asse.

winy, winey ('waɪnɪ), *a.* Also 4, 6–7 **wyny,** 6 **wynie,** 6–7 **winie.** [f. WINE *sb.*[1] + -Y[1].]

1. Of, belonging to, or characteristic of wine; having the nature or properties (taste, colour, etc.) of wine; *occas.* producing wine; vinous.

1390 GOWER *Conf.* III. 371 The wyny grape. **1570** LEVINS *Manip.* 102/43 Wynie, *vinosus.* **1578** LYTE *Dodoens* VI. iv. 660 Ful of a redde wynie sappe or iuyce. *a* **1586** SIDNEY *Ps.* LXXV. iv, A troubled cupp..Where wine and wyny lees compounded stand. **1586** BRIGHT *Melanch.* 159 This waye melancholie carrying a winie and aromaticall spirit,..may procure an harty laughter. **1626** BACON *Sylva* §486 Take Cucumbers..and set them..amongst Muske-Melons, and see whether the Melons will not be more Winy, and better tasted. **1644** DIGBY *Nat. Bodies* xxxviii. §2. 328 It is said that sufficient tartar putt at the roote of a tree, will make the fruite haue a winy tast. **1660** tr. *Paracelsus' Archidoxis* I. VI. 92 There are Two Substances..in Wine; the one is Winey, in which the Spirit of the Wine is..; the other is Phlegmatick. **1710** T. FULLER *Pharmacopœia* (1719) 1 Middling Ale..that..is of Age just to leave its Malty Taste [and] grow Winey. **1725** POPE *Odyss.* XIX. 143 A winy vapour melting in a tear. **1817** L. HUNT *On Avon* Poems (1860) 257 The rich orchards in their sunniest robes Are pouting thick with all their winy globes. **1902** R. W. CHAMBERS *Cardigan* ix, I knew the risk.., but the hazard had a winy flavour withal. **1918** BART KENNEDY in *Chamb. Jrnl.* Sept. 593/1 His winey face took on a still deeper and more winey tinge.

2. a. Accompanied by the drinking of wine. *rare.*

a **1586** SIDNEY *Arcadia* II. xxvii. (1912) 322 There was no matter their eares had ever heard of that grew not to be a subject of their winie conference.

b. Affected by or due to (excessive) consumption of wine.

1594 NASHE *Terrors Nt.* To Rdr., If their winy wits must needs be working. **1840** LADY C. BURY *Hist. Flirt* xxi, A man who is perhaps a little winey. **1852** R. S. SURTEES *Sponge's Sp. Tour* xlvi, Ere he thought he had got rid of as much of his winy headache as fitful sleep would carry off. **1873** LELAND *Egypt. Sketch-Bk.* 61 When the old gentlemen were comfortably fed and amiably winey.

†**winyard.** *Obs.* Forms: 1–2 **winᵹeard,** 2 **winiærd,** 3 **winȝeard, -yard, -yherde, wynyarde,** 4 **wine-y(h)erd, wineierd, -yerd, wynȝard, -ȝord.** [OE. *winᵹeard* = OS. *wîngardo* (Du. *wijngaard*), OHG. *wîngart*, ON. *víngarðr*, Goth. *weinagards*: see WINE *sb.*[1] and YARD *sb.*[1]] = VINEYARD (*lit.* and *fig.*).

c **888** ÆLFRED *Boeth.* xxxii. §3 Ealle men witon þæt hit þær ne weaxð þe ma ðe ᵹimmas weaxað on winᵹeardum. **971** *Blickl. Hom.* 51 Ure hwæte, & ure winᵹeardas, & ealle ure eorþan wæstmas. **1154** *O.E. Chron.* (Laud MS.) an. 1137 He makede manie munekes & plantede winiærd. *a* **1225** *Ancr. R.* 294 þet beoð þe erest prokunges þet sturieð þe winȝeardes,..þet beoð ure soulen. *c* **1250** *Kent. Serm.* in *O.E. Misc.* 34 Se winyard be-tockneþ þe seruise of ure lorde. *a* **1310** in Wright *Lyric P.* xii. 41 Tho he the wynȝord whrohte. **1331** *MS. Chapter Acts Lincoln* lf. 23 b, Quamdam placeam clausam quæ vocatur le Wineierd. *a* **1400** *Minor Poems fr. Vernon MS.* 456/186 Mi deore wynȝard.

winze[1] (wɪnz). *Mining.* Also 8 **winds.** [The earliest recorded spelling suggests derivation from WIND *sb.*[2]] A shaft or an inclined passage sunk from one level to another, but not rising to the surface.

1757 BORLASE in *Phil. Trans.* L. 503 The stage-boards of the little winds or shafts 20 fathoms deep were perceived to move. **1778** PRYCE *Min. Cornub.* 164 The under-ground Shaft or Winds, is worked by hand, with a windlass only. **1839** *Penny Cycl.* XV. 244/2 The common windlass..is much used..in sinking winzes. **1871** *Daily News* 22 Sept., The footway winze leading from the 70 to the 80 has been completed. **1889** C. G. W. LOCK *Gold-Mining* 283 A winze or an incline, the winze being preferable, is made through the bed-rock to the gravel.

winze[2] (wɪnz). *Sc.* [a. early Flem. *wensch* 'imprecatio' (Kilian): see WISH *v.*] An imprecation, a curse.

1785 BURNS *Halloween* xxiii, He..loot a winze, an' drew a stroke. **1819** W. TENNANT *Papistry Storm'd* (1827) 186 Wi' bitter winze and ban.

winze[3]. *Cornwall.* Also **winz.** Altered f. WINCH *sb.*[1] Also *attrib.*

1839 DE LA BECHE *Rep. Geol. Cornwall*, etc. xv. 529 The miners were..taken up in a stirrup by two men, who wound the rope, probably over a winze. **1855** LEIFCHILD *Cornwall* 36 Upon this platform was fixed a winz for four men. **1875** J. H. COLLINS *Metal Mining* 7/4 The small kibbles used with the tackle are called 'winze-kibbles'.

wip, obs. pa. t. of WEEP *v.*; Sc. and dial. form of WHIP *v.*; obs. f. WIPE *v.*

†**wipard.** *Obs. nonce-wd.* [f. WIPE *v.* + -ARD.] An article for wiping.

1653 URQUHART *Rabelais* II. xv. 107 A good wiper, who in wiping continually, wipeth with his wipard [orig. *mouchet*].

wipe (waɪp), *sb.* Also 6–7 **wype.** [f. WIPE *v.*]

1. a. An act of wiping (in senses 1–3 of WIPE *v.*).

In first quot. in fig. phr.: see WIPE *v.* 10 a.

1642 FULLER *Holy & Prof. St.* v. vii. 388 That which hath sharpned the pens of many against him, is his giving so many cleanly wipes to the foul noses of the Pope and Italian Prelacy. **1849** CUPPLES *Green Hand* x, Here the worthy man took off his large spectacles, gave them a wipe, and put them on again. **1859** *Househ. Encycl.* II. 401/2 If the spit is carefully wiped after roasting,..it will require nothing more than a wipe before using. **1885** J. B. GOUGH *Platform Echoes* 69 He had been in the mine, and had evidently given himself a splash and a wipe. **1888** J. W. CLARKE *Mod. Plumbing Pract.* (1914) I. 168 Some men can take longer 'wipes' than others, but the wipes should always be done as quickly as possible.

b. With advs., in various *lit.* and *fig.* senses.

1822 [? EGAN] *Real Life Lond.* I. 322 A brush to give the gemman a wipe down. **1884** D. KEMP *Yacht & Boat Sailing* (ed. 4) 165 Do not wait until her bowsprit is over your quarter before you luff, but take a wipe out across her when she is fifty yards off or so. **1894** H. NISBET *Bush Girl's Rom.* 138 Those more particular gave them [*sc.* the tin platters] a rough wipe-out with a piece of paper. **1912** D. CRAWFORD *Thinking Black* xviii. 371 This vile fly means sleeping sickness, and sleeping sickness means a wipe-out.

c. *Cinemat.* and *Television.* An effect in which an existing picture seems to be wiped out by a new one as the boundary between them moves across the screen (the pictures themselves remaining stationary). orig. ***wipe-dissolve.***

1933 *Cinema Q.* II. I. 43, I..deplored the constant use of wipe-dissolves to cover the weak continuity. **1934** C. LAMBERT *Music Ho!* IV. 263 There is no real equivalent in music even of the 'wipe-dissolve' which leads the eye gently but quickly from one scene to another. **1936** A. BRUNEL *Film Production* 43 It may be argued that wipes are not easily achieved. **1960** *Guardian* 8 June 7/3 A special effects generator..enables 20,000 different shades of 'wipe' to be deployed... It makes a fascinating variety of shapes and devices upon the screen. **1979** *Broadcast* 1 Oct. 54/2 Within the SqueeZoomed sequence of archive TV shots..Tony Rayner inserted two wipes to blue..which allow live 'headline' shots from that day's programme to be chromakeyed in.

2. a. A slashing blow, a sweeping cut, a swipe; also *fig.* (in early use esp. in phraseological expressions, e.g. ***a wipe over the shins***; also, a 'blow of Fortune', a stroke of misfortune; ***a wipe in the eye***: a disappointment or rebuff; = *smack in the eye* s.v. SMACK *sb.*[2] 3 a; cf. WIPE *v.* 10 d).

1550 BALE *Image Both Ch.* II. 66 b, He [*sc.* the Beast] had a greuouse wype with the sworde (which is the lyuynge worde of the lorde) whan he lost his monks [etc.]. **1568** T. HOWELL *Newe Sonets* (1879) 117 When cruell fate them cleane cut of, at one most soden wipe. **1574** HELLOWES *Gueuara's Fam. Ep.* (1577) 235 The beginners of quarels do sometime catch a wipe. **1589** *Marprel. Epit.* B, He hath giuen the cause sicken a wipe in his bricke,..that the cause will be the warmer..for it. **1590** *Pasquil's Apol.* I. C ij, The second venue the Welch-man hath bestowed vpon vs, is a wipe ouer the shinnes of the Non Residents. **1635** BROME *Sparagus Garden* IV. x, So much for single Rapier: now for your secret wipe at Back-sword. **1644** BP. HALL *Serm., Eph. iv. 30* Rem. Wks. (1660) 107 The least wipe of the eye troubles us more then a hard stroak upon the back. **1785** GROSE *Dict. Vulgar T.* s.v., That story gave him a fine wipe. **1788** THICKNESSE *Sk. Life Gainsborough* 43 When a certain Duchess sent to know the reason why her picture was not sent home? he gave it a wipe in the face with his back-ground-brush. **1808** SIR J. MOORE in Jas. C. Moore *Narr. Campaign* (1809) 297 It will be very agreeable to give a wipe to such a corps. **1851** MAYHEW *Lond. Labour* I. 39/1 The cove used to fetch me a wipe over the knuckles with his stick. **1891** KIPLING *Light that Failed* vi. 100 There's the scar of the wipe he got when he was cut over. **1926** T. E. LAWRENCE *Let.* 6 Apr. (1938) 495 Your statement that the hospital passage would be a wipe in the eye for 19 readers out of 20 puts it out of court. **1949** D. M. DAVIN *Roads from Home* III. iii. 236 It was a wipe in the eye for John the way he was getting out.

†**b.** *transf.* A mark as of a blow or lash; a scar or brand. *poet. Obs.*

1593 SHAKS. *Lucr.* 537 The blemish..Worse then a slauish wipe or birth howrs blot.

†**c.** *colloq.* An act of drinking: cf. SWIPE *sb.*[2] 3.

1600 ROWLANDS *Lett. Humours Blood* Sat. vi. E 6 b, We gaue the Brewers Diet-drinke a wipe.

3. *fig.* A cutting remark; a sarcastic reproof or rebuff; a jeer, jibe.

In quot. 1596 in colourless sense, = 'remark'.

1596 DALRYMPLE tr. *Leslie's Hist. Scot.* (S.T.S.) I. 39 This as a wype be the way [orig. *ut hoc obiter dicam*]. *Ibid.* 263. **1606** *Proc. agst. Late Traitors* 286 For his labour [he] receives a wipe at the hands of Bellarmine. **1653** A. WILSON *James I*, 96 The Lord Treasurer gave him a wipe, for suffering his Coachman to ride bare before him in the streets. **1659** *Burton's Diary* (1828) IV. 333 It was an ill wipe to Mr. Grove who brought in the Declaration. **1705** VANBRUGH *Confederacy* V. ii, So, that's a wipe for me now, because I did not give her a New-Years-Gift last time. **1733** SWIFT *On Poetry* 95 To statesmen would you give a wipe, You print it in Italic type. **1822** GALT *Provost* xxxi, I did not much like this bantering of Mr. M'Queerie..I said, 'Come, come, neighbour, none of your wipes.' **1897** *Westm. Gaz.* 25 Oct. 2/2, The extraordinary 'wipe' (there is no other word for it) which the staid old *Quarterly* administers..to the Poet Laureate.

4. a. *slang.* A handkerchief. (Superseding the earlier WIPER 2.) Also in *comb.*

1708 *Memoirs of John Hall* 23 *Wipe*, a Handkerchief. **1789** G. PARKER *Life's Painter* (ed. 2) 136, I only napt a couple of birds eye wipes. **1800** *Sporting Mag.* XVI. 26 Three boys brought in for prigging of wipes. **1800** in *Spirit Publ. Jrnls.* IV. 254 The wipe-nabbers made a tolerable gleaning. **1838** DICKENS *O. Twist* viii, 'Is Fagin upstairs?' 'Yes, he's a sortin' the wipes.' **1859** SALA *Tw. round Clock* 125 The 'case of wipes', as an irreverent bystander called the *procès* of the pickpocket.

b. A disposable piece of soft absorbent cloth or tissue, sometimes impregnated with a cleansing agent, for wiping clean one's hands or anything small.

1971 *Textile Industries* Dec. 50/1 Towels, Covers, Pads, and Wipes. **1974** HAWKEY & BINGHAM *Wild Card* ix. 87 Half-empty boxes of medical wipes lying on the ultra-centrifuge. **1978** 'M. YORKE' *Point of Murder* ii. 19 Kate's hands had got oily..but she kept some tissue wipes in the car. **1980** *Chem. in Brit.* XVI. 449/4 For situations where protective gloves are inconvenient, Chicopee has brought out Dermawipe impregnated hand wipes.

5. = WIPER 5. Also *attrib.*

[**1873** MAXWELL *Electr. & Magn.* II. 375 A piece of mechanism (commonly called a Commutator, or *wippe*).] **1884** W. H. GREENWOOD *Steel & Iron* xvi. 308 The cam.. is a revolving wheel with twelve or fourteen projecting teeth or wipes. **1905** *Motor Year-bk.* 221 The wipe commutator is placed inside the bonnet projecting upwards.

wipe (waɪp), *v.* Pa. t. and pple. **wiped** (waɪpt). Forms: 1 **wipian,** 3–6 **wype,** (4 **whype,** 5 **whipe, wyp,** 6 **wip),** 2– **wipe.** *β.* 4–5 **wepe,** 5 **weype,** 7 **weipe, weepe.** *Pa. t.* 1 **wipode,** 3–4 **wipede, wypede,** 4–7 **wyped** (etc.), 3– **wiped.** *β.* 4 **wipped, wyppit,** 4–5 **wipte,** 5–6 **wypt,** 5–7 **wipt.** *γ.* 4 **weped,** 5 **weput.** *Pa. pple.* 2–4 **i-wipet,** 3–4 **i-wyped;** 5–7 **wyped** (5 **weyped**), 6– **wiped.** *β.* 4 **wipped, wypped,** 5–6 **wypt,** 6–7 **wipt(e, wip't.** [OE. *wípian* = OHG. *wîfan* (MHG. *wîfen*) to wind round, Goth. *weipan* to crown; further related to OHG. *waif* bandage, ON. *veipr* head-covering, Goth. *waips* wreath, and the forms enumerated s.v. WHIP: f. the base *wib-*, as in L. *vibrāre* to brandish, shake.]

1. a. *trans.* To rub (something) gently with a soft cloth or the like, or *on* something, so as to clear its surface of dust, dirt, moisture, etc.; to clean or dry in this way. Also with compl.

c **960** ÆTHELWOLD *Rule St. Benet* (Schröer 1885) xxxv. 59 Wæterclaðas..þe hy heora handa and fet mid wipedan. *c* **1000** ÆLFRIC *Hom.* I. 426 Ic ᵹeseo Godes engel standende ætforan ðe mid hand-claðe, and wipaþ ðine swatiᵹan limu. *c* **1200** *Vices & Virtues* 125 Wassce and wipe wol clane ða eiȝene. *c* **1205** LAY. 22289 Heo wipeden hors leoue mid linnene claðe. *a* **1300** *Cursor M.* 15300 And wit his tueil efterward þair fete he weped clene. *Ibid.* 17683 Quen he wipped had mi face. *c* **1300** *K. Horn* 622 (Laud MS.) Horn gan hys swerd gripe And on his arm hyt wipe. **1362** LANGL. *P. Pl.* A. v. 195 I-wipet with a wesp of Firsen. **1375** BARBOUR *Bruce* v. 647 Quhen the king saw thai war ded,.. he wyppit his brand. *c* **1400** MAUNDEV. xxvii. [xxiii.] (1919) 165 Whan þei han eten, þei wypen hire hondes vpon hire skirtes. **1486** *Bk. St. Albans* C viij, She bekyth when she sewith: that is to say she wypith hir beke. *c* **1500** *Young Children's Bk.* 105 in *Babees Bk.* 23 Wype thi mouthe when þou wyll drinke. **1508** STANBRIDGE *Vulgaria* (W. de W.) B iij, Wype thy nose. **1509** HAWES *Past. Pleas.* XXIX. (Percy Soc.) 136 Whan she lacketh cloutes, without any fayle She wyped her disshes wyth her dogges tayle. **1600** SHAKS. *A.Y.L.* II. vii. 122 We haue..sat at good mens feasts, and wip'd our eies Of drops, that sacred pity hath engendred. **1610** *Shuttleworths' Acc.* (Chetham Soc.) 191 To a boie that wyped bootes, iij[d]. **1781** COWPER *Expost.* 385 Though a bishop toil to cleanse the stain, He wipes and scours the silver cup in vain. **1806** J. CARR *Stranger in Ireland* 269 A large Newfoundland dog..walks round the table for the guests to wipe their fingers upon. **1831** SCOTT *Cast. Dang.* xiii, Wiping his lips, after having finished his draught. **1848** DICKENS *Dombey* liii, Stopping on the mat to wipe his shoes all round. **1859** H. KINGSLEY *G. Hamlyn* xxii, The Major had swum out and was standing on the rock wiping himself.

absol. **1614** EARL STIRLING *Domesday* II. xcix, Thus waters wash, winds wipe, and both conspire, That th' earth (so purg'd) may be prepar'd for fire.

†**b.** To rub, stroke. *Obs.*

1362 LANGL. *P. Pl.* A. v. 212 þenne he wakede of his wynk and wypede his eiȝen. *a* **1375** *Joseph Arim.* 30 Thenne he toke me by the hande frome the grounde and wyped my face with a rose and kyssed me. *c* **1450** *Mirk's Festial* 265 Then toke Iude þe lettyr þat Cryst send to þe kyng befor, and weput þe kyngys forhede þerwyth.

c. *absol.* = DRY *v.* 1 c. Also with *up*. Cf. WASH *v.* 1 i.

1943, 1962 [see WASH *v.* 1 i]. **1968** R. V. BESTE *Repeat the Instructions* ii. 19 He wiped while Huskion..scrubbed away in the sink. **1974** M. BIRMINGHAM *You can help Me* vii. 169, I was helping Mrs Hope wipe up in the kitchen. **1981** A. WILSON in T. Thompson *Edwardian Childhoods* iii. 78 One'd wipe and one'd wash—we didn't make hard work of it.

d. (*a*) To demagnetize (a ship) by passing a horizontal current-carrying cable up and down the hull. (*b*) To remove a recording from (magnetic tape).

1946 'L. LUARD' *Changing Horizons* 145 'No complaints, except she's steel.' 'And not wiped or degaussed,' the Skipper commented. **1947** CROWTHER & WHIDDINGTON *Science at War* 171 He arranged that ships should be 'wiped' with temporary horizontal coils. **1962** R. W. CLARK *Rise of Boffins* iv. 95 Demagnetizing the ships..by 'wiping' the sides..with a horizontal cable carrying a strong current. **1962** E. SALTER *Voice of Peacock* xx. 203 In the case of auditions, the tape was sometimes wiped so's it could be used again. **1965** D. FRANCIS *Odds Against* x. 137, I wiped the tape clean. **1980** *Listener* 8 May 594/2, I presume the BBC wiped, as they say, the original tape.

2. a. To remove or clear away (moisture, dust, etc.) from something by the action described in 1. Often with *away*, *off*, *up*.

Also formerly in extended sense, *e.g.* of a cleansing substance.

c **1000** *Sax. Leechd.* III. 4 Leᵹe on huniᵹ ðreo niht, nim þonne & wipa þæt huniᵹ of. *a* **1240** *Sawles Warde* in *O.E. Hom.* I. 261 þat haueð alle teares iwipet of hare ehnen. *a* **1300** *K. Horn* 1203 (Camb.) He wipede þat blake of his swere. *c* **1400** *Destr. Troy* 3380 Whipe vp þi teris. *c* **1450** *Mirk's Festial* 188 He had a cloth.., forto wepen away þe terys. **1535** COVERDALE *Isa.* xxv. 8 The Lorde God shal wipe awaye the teares from all faces. **1583** HOLLYBAND *Campo di Fior* 375 Hauing first wipt of the dust well. **1590** SPENSER *F.Q.* III. i. 38 The Goddesse..With her soft garment wipes away the gore. **1646** CRASHAW *Sospetto d'Herode* xlix, With her soft wing wipt from the browes of men Day's sweat. **1762** STERNE *Tr. Shandy* VI. ii, They should have wiped it up, said my uncle Toby, and said no more about it. **1838** DICKENS *O. Twist* xxxviii, Now he took courage to wipe off the perspiration which had been trickling over his nose. **1882** BESANT *All Sorts* xx, She groaned and wiped away a tear.

†**b.** (with *away*, *out*) To obliterate, efface, erase. *Obs.* as a specific sense.

1535 COVERDALE *Ps.* lxviii[i]. 28 Let them be wyped out of yᵉ boke of the liuynge. **1542** UDALL *Erasm. Apoph.* 232 b, Augustus had writen a tragedie entitleed Aiax, and yᵉ same tragedie..(because it myslyked hym) he wyped out with a spounge. **1587** GOLDING *De Mornay* xiii. 217 If ye meane fortune as she is peynted by the Poets,..it is as easie to wype her away as to paynt her. **1698** FRYER *Acc. E. India & P.* 112 They are allowed a Board plastered over, which with Cotton they wipe out, when full, as we do from Slates. **1826** LANDOR *Imag. Conv.*, *Emp. Alex. & Capo D'Istria* I. 447 Your Majesty has wiped away with the soft part of the pen, what the British Minister thought he had written so deeply.

†**c.** *transf.* and *gen.* To remove, clear *away* or *off* (something deleterious or offensive). *Obs.*

1398 TREVISA *Barth. De P.R.* XIII. i. (1495) Lij b/1 Water ..wypeth of fylthe and wasshyth awaye synnes. **1590** SPENSER *F.Q.* II. v. 30 Whiles creeping slomber made him to forget His former paine, and wypt away his toylsom sweat. **1600** SURFLET *Country Farm* II. xxxiv. 243 That turneps.. wipe away the spots of the face. **1633** P. FLETCHER *Purple Isl.* XI. xi, Till coldest aire..And heav'ns cleare forehead now wipes off her former lowres. **1641** MILTON *Animadv.* Wks. 1851 III. 246 Wipe your fat corpulencies out of our light. *a* **1660** *Contemp. Hist. Irel.* (Ir. Archæol. Soc.) III. 39 To weepe off this manchinge staine.

d. To erase (a magnetic recording, or data stored on a magnetic medium). Freq. with *off*, *out*.

1900 *Engin. Mag.* XIX. 758/1 When it is desired to wipe out a record, the electromagnet..is attached to a constant battery and run over the wire, thus magnetising it uniformly once more and preparing it to receive a new message. **1934** *Wireless World* 5 Jan. 8/3 When a record is no longer required, the programme recorded on the strip can be 'wiped out'. **1976** *Broadcast* 23 Aug. 10/3 He was staggered at the quantity of programmes in which James MacTaggart had been involved. Most of it has been wiped. **1981** *Times* 4 July 10/3 This is a three-hour reusable tape with an hour's quite sophisticated cabaret already recorded, which you can keep or wipe off. **1984** *Computerworld* 26 Mar. 14/2 If one formats an IBM Personal Computer XT and does not indicate which drive to format, the machine formats the hard disk and wipes out all data on it.

e. (Without *prep.*) To dismiss, reject, repudiate (esp. a person). *Austral.* and *N.Z. slang.*

1941 K. TENNANT *Battlers* 196 Giving her money..in the casual manner that wiped her from all consideration as a human being. **1946** *Coast to Coast 1945* 123 Listen pal—your girl wiped you, didn't she? **1948** *Landfall* June 111 Hands in pockets, shoulders hunched, he strode bitterly up the street from the pub. He'd wipe them, have nothing to do with the morons. **1954** T. A. G. HUNGERFORD *Sowers of Wind* 162 She dumped me, wiped me like a dirty nose. **1967** F. SARGESON *Hangover* xiv. 124 If it came to that one of his reasons for wiping university was a senior lecturer who had failed to avoid the same gross error. **1975** R. BEILBY *Brown Land Crying* 295 You can wipe that idea, if that's what you're thinking.

3. To apply or spread a soft or liquid substance over the surface of a body by rubbing it on with a cloth, pad, or the like (with the substance or the body as obj.); *spec.* in *Plumbing*, to apply solder by this method so as to unite and finish off a joint.

1799 G. SMITH *Laboratory* I. 98 With this liquid wipe over your gilding. **1837** WHITTOCK, etc. *Bk. Trades* (1842) 287 (*Gun-maker*) Nitrous acid, which contains gas, and is slightly wiped on in stripes. **1888** J. W. CLARKE *Mod. Plumbing Pract.* (1914) I. 100 If the cloths are of a good thickness the joints can be wiped much truer.

4. *fig.* (from 1.) To clear, cleanse (*from* or *of* something); in the biblical passage, to empty completely, lay waste.

c **1400** *Pety Job* 211 in *26 Pol. Poems* 127 Thus with wepyng haue I wypt My soule..from dedly synne. **1535** COVERDALE *2 Kings* xxi. 13, I..wyll wype out Ierusalem, euen as one wypeth a platter [**1560** (Geneva), I wil wipe Ierusalem, as a man wipeth a dish]. **1899** F. T. BULLEN *Way Navy* 94 The happy..faculty of wiping their minds clear of harassing thought.

†**5.** To deprive, rob, cheat, defraud, do out of some possession or advantage. Const. *beside* (BESIDE B. 4 c), *of*; rarely *for* (FOR *prep.* 23 d), *from*.

1549 COVERDALE, etc. *Erasm. Par. James* i. 1–12 He shall ..bee wyped besydes al his goodes. **1577–82** BRETON *Floorish upon Fancie* Wks. (Grosart) I. 30/1 My Ladies Maides will wipe the Page, Alwayes of such an heritage. **1594** [? GREENE] *Selimus* E 2, To wipe me cleane for euer being king. *Ibid.* F 2 b, Hath he not wip't me from the Turkish crowne? **1596** SPENSER *State Irel.* Wks. (Globe) 612/1 The English, which they thinke lye still in wayte to wipe them out of theyr landes. **1622** FLETCHER *Span. Cur.* IV. v, You fool us of our moneys.., in every Quiddit wipe us. **1678** *Donna Olimpia* 84 Seeing her self clearly wiped of that Interest. **1746** FRANCIS tr. *Hor.*, *Sat.* I. x. 56 The wily Harlot, and the Slave, who join To wipe the Miser of his darling Coin.

6. (from 2.) To clear away, remove: most commonly with adv. (*away*, *off*, *out*). **a.** To take away, put away (something figured as a stain or defilement); to remove the guilt, blame, or dishonour of; to clear a person, or oneself, of (a charge or imputation).

1387 TREVISA *Higden* (Rolls) VIII. 131 Whanne þe mescheef of his takynge was i-wyped of. *c* **1410** HOCCLEVE *Mother of God* 31 O blessid lady,..þat by prayere wypest cleene away The filthes of our synful wikkidnesse. **1526** *Pilgr. Perf.* (W. de W. 1531) 42 The good lyfe..wypeth awaye the synnes. **1591** SHAKS. *1 Hen. VI*, II. iv. 117 This blot that they obiect against your House, Shall be wiped [*Fol.* whipt] out in the next Parliament. **1606** G. W[OODCOCKE] *Hist. Justine* XXXVI. 114 To the entent to wipe that spot of cowardice wherewith hee had blemished his reputation. **1649** MILTON *Eikon.* xv. 140 To wipe off jealousies and scandals, the best way had bin by clear Actions. **1725** DE FOE *Voy. round World* (1840) 61 By his fidelity to wipe out all that was past. **1841** ELPHINSTONE *Hist. India* II. 149 One of those chiefs, indignant at the imputation, determined..to wipe it off at any risk. **1867** FREEMAN *Norm. Conq.* I. v. 431 There died Godwine,.. wiping out, by a valiant death, the errors of an earlier stage of his life.

†**b.** To take away completely, as by theft or fraud; to make off with. (Cf. 5.) *Obs.*

c **1290** *S. Eng. Leg.* 286/296 Al þat ich habbe i-wonne a-day.., I-wyped it is al clene a-wey ase it neuere nere. **1540** PALSGR. *Acolastus* IV. iii. S iv b, That he maye wype awaye all the money of this man. **1556** OLDE *Antichrist* 74 They deceatfully & fraudulently wyped their money from them. **1599** SIR J. HAYWARD *1st Pt. Hen. IV* 55 Hee wiped away from the people such heapes of money as [etc.]. **1648** GAGE *West Ind.* 151 The Priest..wipes away to his chamber all that which the poor..Indians had offered.

c. To destroy the trace of, obliterate, efface; to destroy the effect or value of, bring to nought.

1564 *Brief Exam.* *iij b, I must nedes wype a great many out of their brotherhood. **1597** SHAKS. *2 Hen. IV*, I. i. 211, I knew of this before. But..This present greefe had wip'd it from my minde. **1611** —— *Wint. T.* IV. ii. 11 As thou lou'st me (Camillo) wipe not out the rest of thy seruices, by leauing me now. **1704** C. LESLIE *Wolf Stript* 50 But all they have done before, is wip'd clean off! **1875** WHITNEY *Life Lang.* vii. 125 Every period of linguistic life..wipes out a part of the intermediates which connect a derived element with its original. **1898** 'H. S. MERRIMAN' *Roden's Corner* v. 47 The anxiety wiped away from his face as if by magic. **1901** *Scotsman* 1 Mar. 7/4 Last week the questions reached a total which had never before been known. This afternoon that record was wiped out, and another established.

d. To do away with, put an end to, abolish, annihilate. Now always with *out*.

1538 STARKEY *England* (1878) 194 The tyrannycal.. instytutyonys..left here among vs, whych al schold be wypt away by the receyuyng of thys wych we cal the veray cyuyle law. **1567** JEWEL *Def. Apol.* 468 If yee had not vtterly wypte al shame from your faces. **1579** SPENSER *Sheph. Cal.* Dec. 108 My haruest wast, my hope away dyd wipe. **1841** BROWNING *Pippa Passes* II. 212 And wipe with the first lunge My foe's whole life out, like a sponge. *a* **1842** ARNOLD in Stanley *Life* (1845) I. iv. 237 So completely wiping a man out of existence. **1903** *Athenæum* 17 Jan. 71/3 The competition of railways, which has wiped out the steamers of the Mississippi.

e. *spec.* To put all to death, destroy completely, exterminate (a body of persons); usually with *out*. Also (*slang*), to kill (a person); also with *out*.

1577 tr. *Bullinger's Decades* 105/2 The Chananites were wiped away because of their incest. **1861** *Jrnl. Discourses* (1862) IX. 112 Many of the officers went away saying, 'We will come by-and-by and wipe you out.' **1865** SWINBURNE *Poems & Ball.*, *Hymn to Proserpine* 14 O Gods dethroned and deceased, cast forth, wiped out in a day. **1889** KIPLING *Willie Winkie*, *Drums of Fore & Aft* 103 But for want of fresh troops, the Afghans would have been wiped off the earth. **1898** *Century Mag.* Apr. 925/2 A tragedy which wiped out an entire crew. **1968** J. PHILIPS *Hot Summer Killing* III. i. 129 Is he the one who was wiped earlier tonight in the Molyneaux Hotel? **1969** C. BURKE *God is Beautiful, Man* (1970) 47 They decided to find a way to get rid of him, to wipe him out. **1977** *Time* 12 Sept. 40/2 You could be wiped out if you moved a single inch. **1980** J. MCCLURE *Blood of Englishman* ii. 18 Someone tried to wipe Bradshaw... The shot caught him here in the collar-bone.

f. (with *off*, rarely †*out*) To cancel (an account or score); to discharge, pay off (a debt).

1667 DRYDEN & DK. NEWC. *Sir M. Mar-all* II. ii, All this is since the last reckoning was wip'd out. **1668** DRYDEN *Even. Love* III. i, For this time I wipe off your score, till you are caught tripping in some new amour. **1748** RICHARDSON *Clarissa* II. xxi. 133 Lovelace..like an absolved confessionaire, wipes off, as he goes along, one score, to begin another. **1831** JAMES *Philip Aug.* xliii, Many an old score of rebellion not yet wiped off between himself and the king. **1886** W. J. TUCKER *E. Europe* 187 A sum which has to go to wipe off a few of your most pressing mortgages.

†**g.** (with *off*) To get quit or clear of (an unpleasant task). *Obs. rare.*

1655 in *Verney Mem.* (1907) II. 13, I am glad..that you have wipt off that dirty & wett journey so fairely without prejudice to yoʳ health.

h. *to wipe* (an expression, esp. a smile) *off a person's* or *one's face*: (to cause him) to cease showing it. *slang.*

[**1567**: cf. sense 6 d above.] **1895** CONRAD *Almayer's Folly* xii. 256 A face from which all feelings and all expression are suddenly wiped off by the hand of unexpected death. [**1898**: cf. sense 6 c above.] **1935** *Time* 24 June 28/1 Wipe dat smile offen his face! **1936** D. CARNEGIE *How to win Friends & influence People* II. ii. 99 Bill, you are going to wipe the scowl off that sour puss of yours today. **1972** D. S. VISCOTT *Making of Psychiatrist* ii. 37 Terry O'Conner seemed to think it was funny but wiped the smile off her face every time her eye caught Larry's. **1977** *Observer* 14 Aug. 3/7 Only one sentence would have wiped the smile off Mason's face. **1978** G. GREENE *Human Factor* VI. i. 305 She realised she was smiling at the telephone—thank God, they hadn't yet invented a visual telephone, but all the same she wiped the smile off her face.

i. *pass.* or *intr. Surfing.* To be knocked from one's surfboard. With *out*. *slang.*

1962 T. MASTERS *Surfing made Easy* 66 *Wiped out*, getting knocked off of a surfboard, usually by a wave. **1965** [see LOCKED *ppl. a.* g]. **1966** *Weekly News* (N.Z.) 19 Jan. 6/3 When 'wiping-out' a surfer should try to hold his board. **1968** *Surfer Mag.* Jan. 48/2 Frye misjudged one of his turns high in the curl and wiped-out in the white water.

7. a. To strike, beat, or attack (with blows, or with mockery, sarcasm, rebuke, or the like). Now *dial.* or *slang.*

1523 LD. BERNERS *Froiss.* I. lxxxvi. h ij b/1 They wolde come to the walles, and wype them in derysion, sayeng [etc.]. *c* **1550** *Thersytes* (facs.) D j b, Thom tombler of tewxbury turninge at a tryce Wyll wype wylliam waterman if he be not wyse. **1589** R. HARVEY *Pl. Perc.* (1590) 22 You see my quarter staffe... A washing blow of this..can wipe a fellow ouer the thumbs. **1620** I. C. *Two Merry Milk-maids* IV. i, *Cal.* Something crost my Nose. *Ran.* A Dore, a Dore, the fields are full of them... There was another wip't me in the same place. *a* **1625** FLETCHER *Woman's Prize* I. i, *Tra.* You have wip'd him now. *Soph.* So will he never the wench, I hope. **1643** MILTON *Divorce* II. x. Wks. 1851 IV. 88 That such a hainous fault..should be onely wipt with an implicit and oblique touch. **1663** LAMONT *Diary* (Maitl. Club) 164 [He] found them out in bed togither, wher he abused his brother for such a lewd prancke, and did weipe hir with his rodde. **1846** *Bentley's Misc.* Oct. 366 If you don't shell out on the minute I'll wipe your throat with my bowy-knife. **1882** *Jamieson's Sc. Dict.*, *Wipe*, to strike, to whip. Clydes.

†**b.** (with *away*, *off*) To strike off, cut off at a blow. *Obs. rare.*

1596 SPENSER *F.Q.* V. xi. 27 Her Lions clawes he from her feete away did wipe. **1672** MARVELL *Reh. Transp.* I. 130 Nor that a Nonconformists head must be wip'd off as oft as your nose drivles.

8. *intr.* for *pass.* (*lit.* or *fig.*: see 2, 6).

a **1300** *Cursor M.* 8952 If þat ani vertu be Of halines wit-in þat tre, Wit sinful mens fett..On ganging it sal wipe a-wai. **1426** AUDELAY *Poems* 21 Al the worchyp of this word hit wyl wype sone away, Hit fallus and fadys forth. **1827** POLLOK *Course T.* VIII. 138 He had on his hands The blood of souls, that would not wipe away. *Mod. colloq.* The spots will easily wipe off.

9. *Cinemat.* and *Television.* To pass from or *from* one scene to another by means of a wipe; to employ a wipe.

1951 HALAS & PRIVETT *How to cartoon for Amateur Films* 118 We now wish to wipe from one scene to another. **1952** *Cinema* 7 Jan. 97/1 [The Director] can cut, fade, wipe or mix at will.

10. Phrases (with various nouns as obj.). **a.** *to wipe* a person's *nose*: †(*a*) see NOSE *sb.* 10, 10 b (cf. sense 5 above); occas., to treat with contempt or indignity; (*b*) in mod. use = d (*a*). †**b.** *to wipe the mouth of*: to exonerate, prove or assert the innocence of: cf. Prov. xxx. 20. **c.** *to wipe one's hands of* = *to wash one's hands of* (WASH *v.* 3 e). Similarly *to wipe one's lips of*. **d.** *to wipe* a person's *eye* (slang or colloq.): (*a*) Sporting, etc. (see quot. 1823); hence, to get the better of, 'score off'; (*b*) to 'give a black eye to'. **e.** *to wipe one's boots on*: to inflict the utmost indignity upon. *to wipe the floor with*: to 'bring to the ground' utterly, inflict a crushing defeat upon; also *to wipe up the floor* or *ground with*.

a. **1437**– [see NOSE *sb.* 10]. **1568** tr. *Gonsalvius' Inquis.* 10 The party must..seeke to wipe their noses by shaping them a shorte aunswere. **1577** HOLINSHED *Chron.* II. 323/2 Hee deuised a shifte howe to wype the Byshoppes nose of some of his Golde. **1598–1721** [see NOSE *sb.* 10 b]. **1599–1600** *Minutes Archdeaconry of Colchester* Jan. lf. 247 (MS.) Her husband..dyd saye that 'I will wype the noses of you all'. **1842** *Asiatic Jrnl.* XXXVII. I. 235 He once or twice, to borrow a not very delicate sporting phrase, 'wiped my nose' in a very off-hand manner. **1850** R. S. SURTEES *Sponge's Sp. Tour* lvii, 'I could have wiped your nose', exclaimed Mr. Sponge, covering the hare with a hedge stake placed to his shoulder like a gun.

b. **1687** *Good Advice* 8, I know she flatters herself..she is a Bulwark against Popery; and with that,..wipes her Mouth of all old scores. **1690** C. NESSE *O. & N. Test.* I. 95 This is alledged by the Romanists to wipe the mouth of the pope from being called the Antichrist.

c. **1785** TRUSLER *Mod. Times* III. 98, I was determined to wipe my hands of it. **1851** D. JERROLD *St. Giles* xvi, With a late and hesitating virtue, they wiped their lips of the murderer's malt, and consented to believe him very bad indeed. **1855** TROLLOPE *Warden* x, That he could..wipe his hands altogether of so sorrow-stirring a concern.

d. **1823** MOOR *Suffolk Words* s.v., In shooting, if one miss the bird, and a companion, firing after, kill it, the lucky, or more skilful gunner, is said to wipe the eye of his disappointed friend. **1860** W. W. READE *Liberty Hall* II. 207 If there is anything,..you shoot first, old boy, as it's your find: I'll stand by and wipe your eye. **1869** *Athenæum* 14 Aug. 214/1 The personal question between the Society and its agents, of what is due from the latter to the former when its eye is to be wiped in the fashion above told. **1874** R. H. BELCHER *Cramleigh Coll.* I. 89 Hullo! Cheeky! it's Sunday, or else I'd wipe your eye for you. **1899** *Spectator* 18 Mar. 385 Never so well-pleased as when he is wiping the eye of the professional burglar. **1928** D. L. SAYERS *Unpleasantness at Bellona Club* xiv. 168 'I'm glad somebody appreciates me. Anyhow,' he added viciously, 'I bet that's wiped old Pritchard's eye.' **1929** F. M. FORD *Let.* 11 Sept. (1965) 187 He had only got me away from Duckworth in order to wipe Gerald's eye. **1949** N. MITFORD *Love in Cold Climate* I. vi. 60 At teatime the village policeman reappeared.., having wiped the eye of all the grand detectives who had come from London in their shiny cars. He produced a perfect jumble-sale heap of objects which had been discarded by the burglars. **1956** 'A. GILBERT' *And Death came Too* xiv. 146

Eventually he agreed to take the case (his heel of Achilles being an inability to pass up a chance of wiping the official eye).

e. **1887** *Courier-Jrnl.* (Louisville, Kentucky) 4 Jan. 2/6 Two brothers wipe up the floor with a Missouri newspaper man. **1888** in Farmer & Henley *Slang* (1903) VII. 359 The Scroggin boy was as tough as a dog-wood knot. He'd wipe up the ground with him; he'd walk all over him. **1896** *Dialect Notes* I. 427 *Wipe the floor with*, to defeat. **1897** *Nat. Police Gaz.* 26 May 7/4 Green fairly wiped the floor with Roberts in the first two rounds. **1899** MACKAIL *Morris* II. 346 Though he often wiped his boots on a man, he never showed him the more stinging insolence of condescension. **1905** 'G. THORNE' *Lost Cause* ix, His only grief was that he was not allowed to 'wipe the floor with that there Hamlyn'. **1908** *Magnet* I. 1. 3/1 I've wiped up the ground with bigger fellows than you, for far less cheek than you've given me. **1918** 'G. A. BIRMINGHAM' *Island Myst.* xxiv. 231 He was so infernally certain that the Emperor would wipe the floor with us.

11. The vb.-stem in combination, as **wipe-clean** *attrib.* or as *adj.*, designating fabrics or furnishings that may be cleaned simply by wiping.

1962 *N.Y. Times Mag.* 9 Sept. 102 In new wipe-clean Boltaflex Vinyl Suede. **1965** *Economist* 13 Feb. 700/2 The [synthetic] shoes, although theoretically 'wipe-clean', tend to look grubby when unpolished. **1970** *Vogue* Jan. 25/1 Lovely cookers with plain glass tops—put the pan down.. and you are on the hob, yet this is a wipe-clean glass surface. **1977** *Austral. House & Garden* Jan. 114 (Advt.), Interiors are wipe clean, white melamine laminate, edged in white P.V.C. **1983** *Which?* Dec. (Publications Suppl.), Both binders are hardwearing and have wipe-clean covers.

Hence **wiped** (waɪpt) *ppl. a.* (see sense 3).

1884 KNIGHT *Dict. Mech.* Suppl., *Wiped Joint (Plumbing)*, one made by placing the parts in the required juxtaposition and covering the joint with a mass of solder.

wipe, obs. f. WEEP *v.*; var. WYPE, lapwing.

'wipeable, *a.* Also **wipable**. [f. WIPE *v.* + -ABLE.] Capable of being wiped.

1926 *Pocket Oxf. Dict.* s.v. *Wipe*, Wipable. **1979** *Personal Computer World* July 23/2 The single unit.. has a wipeable light brown plastic housing with a robust typewriter style keyboard and separate numerical key-pad. **1981** *Washington Post* 26 Aug. B5/2 For the latest in lunch carriers this fall, go with this wipeable tote decorated with elephants, sailboats or pigs. **1982** *Times* 20 Feb. 11/5 The tape.. will be wipeable, leaving a tape.. pristine for one's own recording.

wipe-out ('waɪpaʊt). [f. vbl. phr. *to wipe out*: see WIPE *v.* 6.] **1.** *Radio.* The condition in which a strong received signal renders impossible the reception of other signals (either wanted ones or interference).

1921 *Wireless World* IX. 13/1 With radiotelephony the case is worse, as the wipe out is continuous if it occurs at all. **1929** *Encycl. Brit.* IV. 218/2 Within a 'wipe-out' area uninterrupted service can be guaranteed, unless the interference is produced by listeners themselves. **1940** *Amateur Radio Handbk.* (ed. 2) x. 160/1 There are three types of interference that may be caused in neighbouring receivers working on broadcast waves, by an amateur telegraphy transmitter. First, the 'wipe-out' effect, where the signal from the transmitter 'blocks' the receiver due to either the excessive field strength of the transmitter, or the inselectivity of the receiver, or both.

2. *Surfing.* A fall from one's surfboard as a result of a collision with another surfer or a wave. Cf. WIPE *v.* 6 i. *slang.*

1962 *Austral. Women's Weekly* 24 Oct. Suppl. 3/4 *Wipeout*, a dramatic fall off a board when a rider is trying to catch a wave. **1963** [see SURFIE]. **1969** *Observer* 3 Aug. 33/1 The biggest danger always lies in a 'wipe-out', with a loose board which may hit the rider or other surfers. **1970** *People* (Austral.) 26 Aug. 20/1 One bad wipeout—at Sunset Beach, Hawaii—earned him broken ribs.

3. Destruction, annihilation; a killing; a crushing defeat; an overwhelming experience. *slang* (orig. *U.S.*).

1968 *Sun* (Baltimore) 7 July 5/2 Charlie is 1810. We had a wipeout... *Translation.* Girl: Charlie is old news. We broke up. **1971** J. HENDERSON *Copperhead* vi. 71 Less than thirty-six hours to incapacitate 85 percent of the population. The remaining 15 percent would take a little more than a week. Strategically it would be a wipe-out. **1972** *Jazz & Blues* Sept. 8/1 When I heard Art it was a wipeout. He just wiped me out man. **1977** *Daily Mirror* 12 Apr. 27/7 A record 140,000 [motor-cycling] fans have watched the embarrassing wipe-out by 410 points to 379. **1979** L. MEYER *False Front* iii. 24 This is something like the wipeout of a personal fortune. **1984** 'M. HEBDEN' *Pel & Pirates* xviii. 143 Think it was a gang wipe-out, Patron?

wiper ('waɪpə(r)). Also 6 (9 in sense 5) **wyper**. [f. WIPE *v.* + -ER[1].]

1. A person who wipes; *spec.* in various industries, a workman employed in wiping something clean or dry. Also with adv., as *away*, *out*.

1552 HULOET, Wyper a waye of fylth from a mans body. **1842** BROWNING *Pied Piper* xv, Let me and you be wipers Of scores out with all men. **1875** DORA GREENWELL *Liber Humanitatis* 141 A wiper away of the tears that none other but he and God behold. **1881** *Instr. Census Clerks* (1885) 89 Glass Manufacture.. Wiper-out. **1888** J. W. CLARKE *Mod. Plumbing Pract.* (1914) I. 99 So that when wiping the joint the solder will not burn the little finger of the wiper's hand. **1889** *Scribner's Mag.* Aug. 220/2 (Locomotive) For wipers and watchmen.

2. a. A cloth or other appliance used for wiping; in *slang* use, a handkerchief (later replaced by WIPE *sb.* 4).

1587 *Acc. Mary Q. Scots* (Camden) 59 For v ells canvas for butter clothes and wipers, iiij s. **1626** B. JONSON *Masque of Owls* 127 The wipers for their noses. **1685** *Phil. Trans.* XV. 1158 The fifth he calls the Wiper, supposing that by it they wipe off the honie from the flowers. *a* **1700** B. E. *Dict. Cant. Crew*, *Wiper*, a Handkerchief. **1841** CATLIN *N. Amer. Ind.* xli. II. 63, I rolled it up with my wiper. **1870** *Daily News* 23 Sept., The women in Holland clean their steps with an appliance combining the brush and wiper. **1890** *Sci. Amer.* 8 Nov. 297/1 Another movement [of a soldering machine] carries the can body across the wiper, which removes the superfluous solder.

b. = *wiping-rod*: see WIPING *vbl. sb.* 3.

1826 *Price List* in *Austin Papers* (1924) 1369 To wiper claw for rifle.. 50. **1827** J. KERR *Let.* 27 Feb. in *Ibid.* 1607 Thimble rod and socket end of wipers lost... 50. **1875** KNIGHT *Dict. Mech.*

c. = *windscreen wiper* s.v. WIND *sb.* 32. Also *attrib.*, as ***wiper blade, switch***.

1929 *Times* 2 Nov. 4/7 The driver has an all-enclosed cab, with.. a sloped adjustable screen, with a wiper, in front. **1942** W. FAULKNER *Go down, Moses* 337 It was the youngest face of them all,.. staring sombrely through the streaming windshield across which the twin wipers flicked and flicked. **1953** L. DURRELL *Balthazar* iv. 67 The wind-screen became gradually snowed-up and he switched on the wipers to keep it clear. **1959** *Times* 25 Sept. 8/2 Wiper blades dry the screen and then park automatically. **1970** *Motoring Which?* July 93/1 On the 1800s and 1800Ss the lights or wiper switches collapsed in about one in four cars. **1976** H. KEMELMAN *Wednesday the Rabbi got Wet* xiii. 80 It was coming down so fast that my wipers couldn't handle it.

3. One who or that which strikes or assails; in quots. applied to weapons. *slang.*

1611 BEAUM. & FL. *Philaster* v. iv, I could hulk your Grace, and hang you up cross-leg'd, Like a Hare at a Poulters, and do this with this wiper. **1890** CONAN DOYLE *Sign of Four* vii. 85, I have a wiper in this bag, an' I'll drop it on your 'ead if you don't hook it!.. Stand clear, for when I say 'three': down goes the wiper.

4. 'A severe blow; also, a sharp rejoinder or taunt' (Jam. 1882): = WIPE *sb.* 2, 3. *slang* or *colloq.*

1846 JAMES *Step-mother* lxv. III. 144, I say, Jack, that was a wiper you gave me between the eyes.

5. In machinery, a projecting piece fixed on a rotating or oscillating part, as an axle or wheel, and periodically communicating movement by a rubbing action to some other part; a cam, eccentric, or tappet; *esp.* one serving to lift a hammer, stamper, valve-rod, etc. which in the intervals falls by its own weight.

1796 *Abridgm. Specif. Patents, Weaving* (1861) 31 The treadles are worked by 'wipers' fastened on the main shaft. **1806** O. GREGORY *Treat. Mechanics* II. 11 A great forge, where the engineer.. formed the wipers into spirals, which communicated motion to the hammer almost without any jolt whatever. **1859** *Abridgm. Specif. Patents, Weaving* 969 Over these treadles is a shaft carrying four double wypers containing two segments each.

attrib. **1835** URE *Philos. Manuf.* 152 The upper roller is furnished with wiper-wings. **1839** —— *Dict. Arts* 367 The wooden wiper-rollers covered with flannel. **1844** H. STEPHENS *Bk. Farm* II. 314 The steam is admitted both above and below the piston, by moving the slide with the handle of the wiper-shaft.

6. A pivoted arm that automatically rotates through an arc to make electrical contact with any of a curved row of terminals in a telephone exchange; also, the rotary or sliding contact of a potentiometer.

1906 J. POOLE *Pract. Telephone Handbk.* (ed. 3) xxx. 483 Opposite the lower part of each 'bank' a short arm is fitted, on the ends of which are 2 springs, which, when the rod is rotated, sweep over and under the strips of contacts, and are, therefore, called 'wipers'... The circular ratchet teeth.. enable the vertical rod with the wipers to be raised. **1926** [see BANK *sb.*[2] 10 b]. **1969** [see *slide-wire* s.v. SLIDE- a]. **1975** C. D. TODD *Potentiometer Handbk.* vii. 166/2 Many different variations of the mechanical means which moves the wiper across the resistive element are possible. **1976** T. H. FLOWERS *Introd. Exchange Systems* iii. 82 In the L. M. Ericsson five-hundred-line switch, a stick carrying a set of wipers is rotated.. to point in one of twenty-five angular directions,.. then the stick is slid linearly outwards for the wipers to engage with one of twenty sets of fixed contacts.

7. *Comb.*: **wiper arm** = sense 6 above.

1933 K. B. MILLER *Telephone Theory & Practice* i. 2 The subscriber,.. by sending the proper number of impulses over one of his line wires, could cause the wiper arm of his switch to step *up* to the row containing the contact of the line desired and then.. to step *around* to engage the particular one. **1967** D. EADIE *Introd. Basic Computer* xv. 348 A full-fledged analog multiplier.. can be constructed if we take the pot just described and drive the wiper arm with a servomotor.

wiping ('waɪpɪŋ), *vbl. sb.* [f. WIPE *v.* + -ING[1].]

1. The action of the verb WIPE, q.v. (*lit.* or *fig.*) Also with advs.

1398 TREVISA *Barth. De P.R.* XVI. lxxx. (1495) L viij/1 Wyth wypynge & clensynge this vncleннes of leed may be taken away. *c* **1440** *Promp. Parv.* 530/1 Wypynge, of handys.., *tersura*. **1448–9** METHAM *Amoryus & Cl.* 1632 This lyoun.. in hys welteryng Made alle blody Cleopes kerchyff in hys wypyng. **1553** T. WILSON *Rhet.* 4 b, The Confutacion, is a dissoluyng or wipyng awaie, of all suche reasons as make against vs. **1815** J. SMITH *Panorama Sci. & Art* II. 207 When they require wiping, a warm piece of silk.. is the most suitable material to use. **1868** FREEMAN *Norm. Conq.* II. x. 499 This Gemót was meant to be a wiping out of old scores. **1890** JACOBI *Printing* 232 *Packing the rollers.*—This is sometimes necessary to avoid the 'wiping' of the roller on the extreme edges of the type, which causes an excess of ink.

2. *concr.* (*pl.*): see quot. 1888.

1888 JACOBI *Printers' Voc.* 156 *Wipings*, cotton refuse used for wiping up and cleansing machinery. **1905** *Daily News* 4 Mar. 6 There is sometimes spontaneous combustion.. in the ink and wipings at a printer's.

3. *attrib.* and *Comb.* Used for wiping, as ***wiping-handkerchief, -towel***; **wiping-bar** *Glass-making*: see quot.; **wiping-cloth** (*spec.* in *Plumbing*: see WIPE *v.* 3); **wiping head**, a head (HEAD *sb.*[1] 11 g) for removing any recording from a magnetic tape or wire; an erase head; **wiping-rod, -stick**, a rod fitted with a piece of cloth or tow for cleaning out the bore of a gun.

1839 URE *Dict. Arts* 590 (*Glass-making*) The *wiping bar.. wrapped in linen, to remove dust. **1591** PERCIVALL *Sp. Dict.*, *Almayzar*, a *wiping cloth of haire. **1888** J. W. CLARKE *Mod. Plumbing Pract.* (1914) I. 58 The wiping-cloth following the iron so as to pull or push the solder upwards as it runs downwards on being heated. **1647** TRAPP *Comm. James* v. 1 (1656) 913 Better weep here, where there are *wiping-handkerchiefs in the hand of Christ, then to have your eyes whipt out in hell. **1938** *Jrnl. Inst. Electr. Engineers* LXXXII. 266/2 The *wiping head carries a direct current adequate to saturate the tape completely, so that it leaves the head fully magnetized. **1950** [see *record button* s.v. RECORD *v.*[1] 12 a]. **1875** KNIGHT *Dict. Mech.* s.v. *Rod*, The.. *wiping-rod,.. used by gun-smiths. **1817** J. BRADBURY *Trav. Amer.* 167 They often take from them the furs they have collected, and beat them severely with their *wiping sticks. **1848** *Blackw. Mag.* July 18/1 Pete was in the act of forcing down the ball with his long hickory wiping-stick. **1582** STANYHURST *Æneis* I. (Arb.) 40 Thee wayting seruaunts.. doe carrye.. *wyping towels. **1911** KATE D. WIGGIN *Mother Carey* xiii, She.. gave the wiping towels to Julia.

'wiping, *ppl. a.* [f. as prec. + -ING[2].] That wipes, in various senses: see the verb.

1483 *Cath. Angl.* 420/1 Wypynge, *tergosus*. **1597** GERARDE *Herbal* I. lxxv. 114 A certaine wiping, cleansing, and attracting facultie. **1599** MARSTON *Sco. Villanie* III. xi, The quick change, with wiping mandritta. **1902** *Engineering Mag.* XIX. 758/1 A wiping-out electromagnet, which removes all traces of the record.

wipiti: see WAPITI.

wippe, obs. pa. t. of WEEP *v.*; obs. f. WHIP.

wipped, wipt(e, obs. pa. t. and pple. of WIPE *v.*

wips, obs. form of WISP.

wirble ('wɜːb(ə)l), *v.* Also **wirbel**. [ad. G. *wirbeln*.] *intr.* To turn round and round; to whirl; to eddy. So **'wirble** *sb.*, whirl.

1848 LYTTON *Harold* IV. ii, I was girt round with dead men's bones; and the bones moved round me, undulating, as the dry leaves that wirble round in the winds of the winter. *Ibid.* IX. vii, The gibe and the wirble of the dead men's bones. **1849** —— *K. Arthur* XII. cxv, And here and there, and wirbelling to and fro,.. pale thousands spread the plain. **1860** LD. LYTTON *Lucile* I. iv. §6. 9 The waters went wirbling above and around. **1932** J. JOYCE *Let.* 1 Aug. (1966) III. 251 But what about me in my present wirbel of worries.

wirch, -er, etc., obs. ff. WORK, WORKER, etc.

wirchep, -ip, obs. ff. WORSHIP.

wird: see WEIRD, WERED, WORD, WORTH.

wire (waɪə(r)), *sb.* Forms: 1–4 **wir**, 4–5, 7 *Sc.* **wyr**, 4–7 **wyre**, 5–7 **wyer**, (5 **were, whir**, 6 **wyere, wheire, wiar**; *Sc.* 6 **wyir**, 7 **vyr, weyer**), 6–7 **wier, wyar**, 5– **wire** (*Sc.* 8 **weyr**, 9 **weir**). [OE. *wír*, corresp. to MLG. *wîre* (LG. *wîr*), ON. **virr* in *víravirki* filigree work, related further to OHG. *wiara* (MHG. *wiere*) finest gold, ornament of this: referred to the base *wi-* of L. *viēre* to plait, weave, etc. (cf. WITHE *sb.*).]

I. Denoting the substance.

1. Metal wrought into the form of a slender rod or thread, formerly by hammering, now by the operation of wire-drawing. **a.** of precious metal, esp. gold, used chiefly in ornamentation.

From the 13th to the 16th century golden hair was freq. poetically likened to gold wire.

a **1000** *Riddles* xxvii. 14 Wrætlic weorc smiþa wire bifongen. *c* **1205** gold wir [see GOLD[1] 8 a]. **1377** LANGL. *P. Pl.* B. II. 11 Fetislich hir fyngres were fretted with golde wyre, And þere-on red rubyes. *c* **1400** *Ywaine & Gaw.* 2967 Many maidens thar he sese, Wirkand silk and gold wir. *c* **1420** ? LYDG. *Assembly of Gods* 373 Dame Venus.. Whoos long here shone as wyre of goold bryght. **1423** JAS. I *Kingis Q.* i, In Aquary, Cinthia the clere, Rynsid hir tressis like the goldin wyre. **1618** in *Archaeologia* XLI. 254 All his silver made up in wyer. **1717** LADY M. W. MONTAGU *Let. to Mrs. Thistlethwayte* 1 Apr., [The] cushions.. are generally brocade, or embroidery of gold wire upon satin. **1879** S. C. BARTLETT *Egypt to Pal.* iv. 73 Silver wire is thirty-three hundred years old, and gold wire six hundred years older.

b. of any metal, esp. iron, brass, or copper, drawn out into a rod or thread.

1348 *Acc. Exch. K.R.* 470/18 m. 6 (P.R.O.) In Wir empt[o] pro fistula conducti mundanda iiij. d. **1387–8** [see WIRE-DRAWER 1]. **1435** *Cov. Leet Bk.* 182 And yif the cardwire-drawer were ones or twies disseyued withe ontrewe wire he wolde be warre. **1482** *York Myst.* Introd. 40 [Pynners and Wyredrawers] makes pynnes or drawen wyre. **1497** *Naval Acc. Hen. VII* (1896) 100 Wire for prymers. **1508** *Acc. Ld. High Treas. Scot.* IV. 113 Item.. for wyir to the pottar of Strivelin to bind the gun muld v s. **1572** in Feuillerat *Revels Q. Eliz.* (1908) 159, ij lb of drawen wyer—iijs. iiij d. **1600** FAIRFAX *Tasso* II. xxvi, They.. bound her tender armes in twisted wire. **1677** MOXON *Mech. Exerc.* i. 14 Iron used for making of Wyer, which of all other sorts is the softest and toughest. **1815** J. SMITH *Panorama Sci. & Art* II. 786 The parts are then to be joined properly together, and kept in that state, by means of wire. **1839** URE *Dict. Arts* 955 A pin is a small bit of wire, commonly brass, with a point at one end, and a spherical head at the other. **1888** *Encycl. Brit.* XXIV. 615/1 The metals suitable for wire, possessing almost equal ductility, are platinum, silver, iron, copper, and gold.

c. with qualification denoting (*a*) the metal, as ***brass, copper, iron, magnesium, platinum wire***, (*b*) the form or colour, as ***black, small, white wire***, (*c*) its use, as ***binding, electric, fuse, joint, pinion wire***; also ***lapland wire*** (see quot. 1755).

14.. in Wr.-Wülcker 582/48 *Ferrifilum*, wyre of yre. **1435** *Cov. Leet Bk.* 183 Ne Cardwyre ne mystermannes wyre. **1463** *Act 3 Edw. IV*, c. 4. §4 Blanc file de ferre vulgarement nomme whitewyre. **1530** PALSGR. 288/2 Wyar of brasse, *fil darcal, fil de laton.* **1590** SPENSER *F.Q.* II. iv. 15 [He] Shakt his long lockes, colourd like copper-wire. **1669** STURMY *Mariner's Mag., Penalties & Forfeitures* 2 Iron Wyre, or whited Wyre, are forfeited if any such be Imported. **1755** *Dict. Arts & Sci.* s.v. *Wire, Wire of Lapland*..called..lapland-wire. It is made of the sinews of the reindeer..spun into a sort of thread..covered with tin. **1837** HEBERT *Engin. & Mech. Encycl.* II. 906 Rolled or 'black wire,' (as it is sometimes called, to distinguish it from the bright, or drawn-wire). **1843** HOLTZAPFFEL *Turning* I. 429 The drawn tube called joint-wire, ..used by the silversmiths, for hinges and joints. *Ibid.* 433 In hard-soldering, it is..necessary to bind the works together in their respective positions; this is done with soft iron binding-wire.

†**d.** as the material of a lash or scourge. *Obs.*

1606 SHAKS. *Ant. & Cl.* II. v. 65 Thou shalt be whipt with Wyer. **1622** MIDDLETON & ROWLEY *Changeling* I. ii, *Alib.* Peace, peace, or the wyer comes. **1648** GAGE *West Ind.* xiii. 70 Disciplines of wyar, rods of iron, haire-cloths.

e. used for fencing; esp. ***barbed*** (earlier ***barb***) ***wire***, later often simply *wire*: a fencing wire composed of two or more strands twisted together, with barbs or short spikes fastened a few inches apart in the strands; also, the fencing or defence so constructed; also *attrib.*

1876 *Field* 16 Dec. 714/2, I was in hopes that a country like the Bicester (where every farmer seems to enjoy the chase) would be free of such an enemy as wire. **1883** J. SCOTT *Farm Roads*, etc. 88 Barb wire fencing should consist of at least two barbs, used in connection with two wires twisted together. *Ibid.* 89 With cattle the great advantage of barbed wire is that it keeps them in; with sheep, it keeps their enemies out. **1900** KINNEAR *Modder River* xi. 93 The mere automatic discharging of their guns at the hustling crowd of human deer impaled upon Cronje's wicked barbed wire. **1915** *Daily News* 6 Jan. 4 Four German snipers were shot on our wire. **1917** H. GIBSON *Diplom. Diary* 168 Tremendous barbed wire entanglements form a broad barrier.

II. Denoting an individual object.

*** 2. a.** A piece, length, or line of wire used for various purposes (see quots.; some early uses are obsolete).

Beowulf 2413 Se [eorðseie] wæs innan full wrætta and wira. *c* **1374** CHAUCER *Troylus* III. 1636 For worldly Ioye halt not but by a wir; That preueth wel it brest alday so ofte; For-þi nede is to werke wiþ it softe. *c* **1385** —— *L.G.W.* 1205 *Dido*, Vp on a courser, stertelynge as the fyr, Men myghte turne hym with a litil wyr, Sit Enyas. *c* **1391** —— *Astrol.* II. §38. 46 In centre of the compas stike an euene pyn or a whir vp-riht. **1426–7** *Rec. St. Mary at Hill* 63 First payd for the sepulcre for diuers naylis & wyres & glu ix d. **1469** *Rolls of Parlt.* VI. 232 A Image of lede..broken in the myddes, and made fast with a Wyre. *a* **1548** HALL *Chron., Hen. VIII* 52, I haue distroyed Rycharde Hun... I put a wyre in his nose. **1572** in Feuillerat *Revels Q. Eliz.* (1908) 159 Greate wyers that went crosse the hall. **1581** W. BOROUGH *Disc. Var. Cumpas* ii. B ij, The Flye of the Cumpas of Variation, is so turned by vertue of the Magneticall wiers, that the North poinct thereof doeth shew the Pole of the Magnes. **1583** [see SUPPORTASSE]. **1585** HIGINS *Junius' Nomencl.* 7/2 *Graphium*, ..a writing wyer, or a steele where-with to write. **1616** A. RATHBORNE *Surveyor* 126 On the head or top of which shorter sight, must be placed a wyer or brasse pin. **1680** MOXON *Mech. Exerc.* x. 179 Through this Button should be fastned an Iron Wyer. **1695** J. EDWARDS *Author. O. & N. Test.* III. 244 Round Wires of Gold put into the Ears. **1753** MRS. DELANY *Let.* 17 Feb. in *Autobiogr.* (1861) III. 206 Mr. Maddox, who does surprising feats of activity on a wire. **1811** *Bk. Trades* III. (ed. 4) 67 The mould, which the paper-maker has in his hand, is composed of many wires set in a frame close together. **1827** FARADAY *Chem. Manip.* xvi. (1842) 425 The open limb is afterwards to be wiped clean.. with a wire and tow. **1840** LARDNER *Geom.* xv. 193 One of these cylindrical cards, which, as it revolves, carries away the wool spread upon the points of its wires. **1857** MILLER *Elem. Chem., Org.* (1862) iv. §1. 270 [The soap] is cut up with wires into bars. **1880** R. WARD *Sportsman's Handbk.* 62 [In setting up birds] the leg wires should be half as stout again as the body wire. **1897** *Times* 18 Sept. 8/2 The [wireless] messages being transmitted from a vertical wire carried up a pole.

b. *spec.* One of the fine platinum cross-wires fixed horizontally and vertically at the focus of a telescope: see COLLIMATOR 1.

1774 M. MACKENZIE *Marine Surv.* I. (1819) 52 If, while the vertical wire runs along the pole, the horizontal wire runs exactly along..the cross-piece [on the pole].., the quadrant and telescope are right. **1878** ABNEY *Photogr.* xxxvi. 294 Securing a sharp image of the sun together with that of the cross-wires or ruled gratings.

c. connecting a bell with the bell-pull or -push.

1837 DICKENS *Pickw.* xxxvi, 'There ain't a bell, is there, ma'am?'.. 'It's only a handle', said Mrs. Dowler; 'the wire's broken.' **1883** MISS BROUGHTON *Belinda* III. ix, The door-bell may ring itself off its wire.

d. *U.S.* A wire stretched across and above the track at the start and finish of a racecourse. Freq. in phrases: ***down to the wire***, up to, or all the way to, the finishing-line; freq. *transf.* and *fig.*; (***from***) ***wire to wire***, from start to finish of a race; also *transf.* and *attrib.*; ***under the wire***, at the finishing-line; *fig.*, (to fall) within the limits or scope of something.

1887 *Courier-Journal* (Louisville, Ky.) 5 May 1/1 Eva K., Little Munch..were first under the wire. **1901** 'H. MCHUGH' *Down the Line* 93 Swift often told himself that he could give Marshall P. Wilder six sure-fires and beat him down to the wire. **1920** C. SANDBURG *Smoke & Steel* 138 He flashed his heels to other ponies..and hardly ever came under the wire behind the other runners. **1929** M. C. WORK *Compl. Contract Bridge* v. 75 There are some hands which may just 'get under the wire' of the above definitions. **1950** *Keowee Courier* (Walhalla, S.C.) 31 Aug. 2/2 Baseball season is coming down to the wire, and the leading teams are about as close as two Scotchmen on bargain day. **1974** *State* (Columbia, S.C.) 15 Feb. 4-B/5 Nicklaus..led from wire to wire in the Hawaiian Open [Golf Tournament]. **1975** *New Yorker* 10 Nov. 137/2 Bertram Firestone's Honest Pleasure wound up his racing for the year with a wire-to-wire victory in the Laurel Futurity last weekend. **1982** 'E. LATHEN' *Green grow Dollars* xviii. 151 We're going to force Vandam's into court as fast as we can. I think we'll just make it under the wire. **1984** *Miami Herald* 6 Apr. 22A/1 Odds remain good that the Democrats' race will go down to the wire.

†**e.** ***the straight wire***: the honest truth; also used without article as a phrase emphasizing the truth of an assertion. *Austral. slang. Obs.*

1892 'J. MILLER' *Workingman's Paradise* 203 When it's all over you'll remember what I say and know it's the straight wire. **1909** A. WRIGHT *Rogue's Luck* 70 'Now, no kid, Harry,' said Ned anxiously. 'Straight wire, did you beat him?' **1936** M. FRANKLIN *All that Swagger* xlii. 394 'Will you?' said Humphrey... 'Straight wire, I will.'

f. ***to pull one's wire***: see PULL *v.* 20 i.

3. a. A line of wire used as a conductor of electric current.

live wire, a wire charged with electricity; *fig.* (*colloq.*) an energetic or vigorously active person: see LIVE *a.* 9.

1747 [see ELECTRIZE *v.*]. **1796** *Imison's Sch. Arts* (ed. 4) 91 When the shocks are to be given with this apparatus..two slender and pliable wires..are to be fastened [etc.]. **1807** CRABBE *Par. Reg.* II. 380 So two cold limbs, touch'd by Galvani's wire, Move with new life. **1817** BYRON *Mazeppa* vi. 11 Conveying, as the electric wire, We know not how, the absorbing fire. **1886** A. A. C. SWINTON *Elem. Princ. Electr. Lighting* 26 The conducting wires for electric lighting are almost invariably made of copper... They are usually covered with an insulating coat of india-rubber and tape. **1890** live electric wire [see LIVE *a.* 4].

fig. **1876** GEO. ELIOT *Deronda* xlviii, Political and social movements touched him only through the wire of his rental.

b. *spec.* The line of wire connecting the transmitting and receiving instruments of a telegraph or telephone. ***crossed wires***: see CROSS *v.* 5 c.

1846 *Punch* 5 Dec. 238/2 If this plan of Electric Telegraphs for the million should be carried out, the Post Office..might be turned into a central terminus for all the wires. **1854** telegraphic wires [see TELEGRAPHIC *a.* 1 b]. **1860** G. PRESCOTT *Electr. Telegr.* Pref. p. vi, The wires..are creeping over the Rocky Mountains, and erelong we shall have momentary advices from the Pacific States.

c. *transf.* The telegraphic system. ***by wire*** (formerly ***by the wires***): by means of a telegraphic message. Hence (*colloq.*) a telegraphic message, a telegram.

1859 LEVER *Dav. Dunn* xlix, He then telegraphed to his man of business, ..to ascertain..the latest accounts of Lord Lackington's health, and answer 'by wire'. **1860** TROLLOPE *Framley P.* xviii, You had better come up yourself; but say the word 'Yes', or 'No', by the wires. **1876** 'E. PINTO' *Ye outside Fools!* 76 Gusher, of the *Bellowgraphic*, may have a wire from his sub-editor. **1883** *Harper's Mag.* July 255/1 The forte of the *Enquirer* is its voluminous correspondence, both by wire and mail. **1889** CONAN DOYLE *Sign of Four* viii, We pulled up at the Great Peter Street post-office, and Holmes dispatched his wire.

d. The telephone system; an individual telephone connection. Freq. in phrases ***over the wire*** (or †***wires***), ***on the wire***.

Now somewhat old-fashioned.

1902 *Chambers's Jrnl.* Feb. 128/2 A Parisian dentist had discovered a process of 'seeing by wire', which..means that he can while speaking through the telephone *see* his correspondent at the other end of the line of communication. **1925** H. CRANE *Let.* 4 June (1965) 207, I did enjoy that talk with you over the wires to Cleveland! Your voice is so much better than ink and paper. **1925** F. SCOTT FITZGERALD *Great Gatsby* viii. 186, I tried [Gatsby's house] four times; finally an exasperated central told me the wire was being kept open for long distance from Detroit. **1929** 'E. QUEEN' *Roman Hat Mystery* xiv. 211 I'll get the newspaper boys on the wire and ask them to ballyhoo the opening. **1932** [see NUMBER *sb.* 4 f]. **1935** W. CATHER *Lucy Gayheart* I. vii. 51 Every day his concert agent..called him up as soon as his wire was open. **1947** S. BELLOW *Victim* xxiii. 280 He ought to have spoken to Nunez about the broken chain while he was on the wire. **1974** WODEHOUSE *Aunts aren't Gentlemen* iii. 24 And now for heaven's sake get off the wire, I'm busy.

e. A private warning or message. Chiefly in phr. ***to give the wire***. *slang.*

1925 FRASER & GIBBONS *Soldier & Sailor Words* 307 *Wire, to give the*, to give a secret warning. **1930** E. H. LAVINE *Third Degree* xvi. 210 The real thieves get 'a wire', and play poker. **1936** J. CURTIS *Gilt Kid* vi. 60 He'd been straight with her and had given her the wire right in the beginning. **1972** R. BUSBY *Reasonable Man* xviii. 161 He gave me the wire that there was a big one coming off.

****** Senses used mainly in pl. or collect. sing.

4. Metallic strings (of a musical instrument).

1387 TREVISA *Higden* (Rolls) I. 355 Irische men beþ connyng..in harpe and tymbre þat is i-armed wiþ wire and wiþ strenges of bras. **1599** PEELE *David & Bethsabe* B j, When his consecrated fingers strooke The golden wiers of his rauishing harpe. *Ibid.* E iij, His haire is lyke the wyer of Dauids Harpe. **1628** MILTON *Vac. Exerc.* 38 Apollo sings To th' touch of golden wires. *a* **1718** PRIOR *Power* 656 They breath the Flute, or strike the vocal Wire. **1780** COWPER *Progr. Err.* 126 When he has pray'd and preach'd the sabbath down, With wire and catgut he concludes the day. **1818** BYRON *Ch. Har.* IV. xxxviii, His country's creaking lyre, That whetstone of the teeth—monotony in wire! **1818** SHELLEY *Rosal. & Helen* 1164 From the twinkling wires among, My languid fingers drew and flung Circles of life-dissolving sound. **1875** *Encycl. Brit.* I. 112/2 In the violin and in the pianoforte, the lower notes are obtained from wires formed of denser material.

5. Metallic bars (of a cage).

1656 BEALE *Heref. Orchards* (1657) 8 A constant aviary of sweet singers, which are here retained without the charge or violence of the Italian Wiers. **1748** RICHARDSON *Clarissa* III. lxxv. 348 It [*sc.* a captive bird] beats and bruises itself against its wires. **1848** DICKENS *Dombey* vii, A new cage with gilded wires.

6. *Croquet.* The iron hoops or arches through which the balls are driven. Now *rare.*

1868 *Chambers's Encycl.* X. 483/2 The implements used in croquet are mallets, balls, posts (or sticks), and hoops (which are called indifferently hoops, wires, or arches). **1904** E. F. BENSON *Challoners* i, Martin..struck wildly in the hopes of an impossible cannon off the wire.

7. Knitting needles. *Sc.*

a **1774** FERGUSSON *Hallowfair* Poems (1845) 14, I wyt they are as pretty hose As come frae weyr or leem. **1797** *Encycl. Brit.* (ed. 3) XVII. 805/1 The method of knitting stockings by wires or needles. **1827** SCOTT *Chron. Canongate* v, Knitting her stocking systematically, as if she meant every twist of her thread, and inclination of the wires, to bear burden to the cadence of my voice. *a* **1878** in D. H. Edwards *Mod. Scott. Poets* (1880) I. 39 She's handy an' quick wi' her weirs an' her needles.

8. a. The metallic lines by which puppets are worked. Chiefly *fig.* in the phrase ***to pull*** (or ***move***) ***the wires*** (see WIRE-PULLER).

1607 BEAUM. & FL. *Woman Hater* III. i, Like dead motions moving upon wyers. *a* **1680** GLANVILL *Sadducismus* II. (1681) 35 [Miracles] were so easy to be done..by Wiers and Juggling. *a* **1704** T. BROWN *Walk Lond. & Westm.* Wks. 1720 III. 285 A Guide that..can do no more for them, than the Wire in the Finger of the Poppet-Player. **1813** *Deb. & Proc. Congr. U.S.* 5 Jan. (1853) 12th Congr. 2nd Sess. 562 When those who pulled the wires saw fit, they passed away. **1826** *Mass. Spy* 12 Apr. 2/6 Mr. McDuffie said..that he was perfectly aware..who was the skulking manager who moved the wires. **1834** S. ROGERS *Let. to Ld. Holland* 28 Oct. in *Pearson's 76th Catal.* (1894) 51 Lord Durham appears to be pulling at 3 wires at the same time—not that the 3 papers —the Times, Examiner and Spectator are his puppets, but they speak his opinions. **1862** *Fraser's Mag.* July 28 To charge him, in the technical language of his party, with 'pulling wires', and 'laying pipes' for the Presidency. **1888** BRYCE *Amer. Commw.* v. xciv. III. 321 A demagogue of greater talent..may practically pull the wires of a President whom he has put into the chair.

b. ***to be*** (***all***) ***on wires*** (fig.), to be in a state of nervous excitement or 'jumpiness'.

1869 *Chamb. Jrnl.* 2 Oct. 639/1 Here's another for T. P.; a man this time, all on wires.

III. Network or framework of wire.

9. a. Wirework; now usually, wire netting.

1547 in Feuillerat *Revels Edw. VI* (1914) 12 Twoo hattes ..the Turffes of wyer couerid with clothe of golde. **1617** MORYSON *Itin.* I. 111 Also there is a delicate cage of birds, wrought about with thick wyer. *a* **1700** EVELYN *Diary* 23 Apr. 1646, In the middle of this garden was a cupola made of wyre, supported by slender pillars of brick. **1716** HEARNE *Collect.* (O.H.S.) V. 260 It is pity the Windows of Fairford are not secured with Wire. **1833** LOUDON *Encycl. Archit.* §853 The dairy, the pantry, and the store room to have fly wire (wirecloth to exclude flies) inside of the windows. **1854** *Poultry Chron.* II. 303 Birds..in new and commodious pens, with galvanised wire fronts.

†**b.** A frame of wire (*a*) to support the hair; (*b*) to support the ruff, = SUPPORTER 3 b, SUPPORTASSE. *Obs.*

1583 STUBBES *Anat. Abus.* 67 Least it [*sc.* the hair] should fall down it is vnder propped with forks, wyers, and I can not tel what. **1595** GOSSON *Pleas. Quips* (Percy Soc.) 5 These flaming heads with staring haire, these wyers turnde like hornes of ram. **1603** in *10th Rep. Hist. MSS. Comm.* App. I. 31 For ane corldit wyr to ver on my haed, x s. *Ibid.*, For ane vyr to ver with ane French rouf v s.; item, for thri vyrs to uer vith Inglich roufs iii s. **1607, 1612** [see REBATO c]. **1619** FLETCHER *Knt. Malta* I. i, Unfledge 'em of their tyres, Their wires, ..pins, and Periwigs, And they appear like bald cootes, in the nest. **1690** D'URFEY *Collin's Walk Lond.* III. 115 Like buxom Lass, that trips Curanto With Wires, Comodes, and Topknots flaring. **1690** M. EVELYN *Fop-Dict., Palisade*, a Wire sustaining the Hair next to the Duchess, or first Knot. [**1893** GEORGIANA HILL *Hist. Engl. Dress* I. iii. 197 In addition to the starch, wires were used to stiffen the ruff. The wires were covered with silk or gold and silver thread, and came round the neck under the ruff.]

c. *Paper-making.* Woven brass wire-cloth.

a **1700** EVELYN *Diary* 24 Aug. 1678, On this [frame] they take up the papp, the superfluous water draining thro' the wyre... The mark we find on the sheets is formed in the wyre. **1881** *Spons' Encycl. Industr. Arts* IV. 1497 The 'wire' is an endless cloth made of very fine wire... The mesh varies from 60 to 70 and even more threads to the inch.

d. A snare for hares or rabbits.

1749 FIELDING *Tom Jones* VI. xii, He himself had passed through that Field, in order to lay Wires for Hares. **1815** *Sporting Mag.* XLV. 109 Hares are caught..in purse-nets or wires. **1819** *Ibid.* (N.S.) IV. 210 Fix here and there a large bush..and close to each bush two 'wires'.

IV. Transferred and miscellaneous uses.

10. Something resembling wire or a wire; e.g. a long thin plant-stem, as a strawberry runner;

†a branch-like appendage of a star-stone; a cylindrical piece of native silver.

1601, 1879 strawberry wire [see STRAWBERRY 9]. **1696** *Phil. Trans.* XIX. 294 Capillaries..creeping on..the Ground, with Wires after the manner of Strawberries. **1712** tr. *Pomet's Hist. Drugs* I. 36 Cinquefoil..produces its Leaves ..on a Stem, or Wire. *a* **1728** WOODWARD *Nat. Hist. Fossils* (1729) I. II. 81 Several [Asteriæ], with some of those Branches that are wont to arise from them, call'd, by some, Wires. **1793** J. LODGE *Introd. Topogr. Hist. Heref.* 37 That when the wires or vines [of hops] spring up, they may not be too far separated to run up the poles. **1805** R. W. DICKSON *Pract. Agric.* II. 603 It is only in such as possess a..good carbonic earthy matter, that they [*sc.* potatoes] are enabled to propagate their subterraneous wires or root-buds. **1859** W. S. COLEMAN *Woodlands* (1866) 128 There may they be seen knee-deep in the wires or clambering over the broken grey rocks. **1882** *Rep. Prec. Metals U.S.* 200 The quartz shows much free gold and silver. The latter is in the form of nuggets and wires. **1897** H. CLIFFORD *In Court & Kampong* 69 The bristling wires of whisker, the long cruel teeth [of a tiger].

11. *pl.* Applied to hairs, or rays, as resembling shining wires (cf. 1 a). *poet.* and *rhet.* Now *rare.*

1589 GREENE *Menaphon* (Arb.) 79 Apollo..Cut off his lockes, and left them on her head, And said; I plant these wires in Natures scorne. **1590** —— *Never too late* 49 (*bis*) The golden wyers that checkers in the day, Inferiour to the tresses of her haire. [*c* **1600** SHAKS. *Sonn.* cxxx, If haires be wiers, black wiers grow on her head.] **1876** HARDY *Ethelberta* xv, The sun was peeping out just previous to departure, and sent gold wires of light across the glades.

†**12.** ***city wire***: a 'city wife' who wears wires (sense 9 b) in her hair or ruff: used opprobriously.

1609 B. JONSON *Silent Wom.* Prol. 23 Some [cates] for lords, knights, squires, Some for your waiting wench, and citie-wires. **1632** MARMION *Holland's Leaguer* II. iii, All the City wires, And Summer birds in Towne, that once a yeare Come up to moulter.

13. *slang.* A pickpocket.

So called from the practice of extracting handkerchiefs from pockets with a piece of wire.

1851 MAYHEW *Lond. Labour* I. Introd. 25 'Wires', or those who pick ladies' pockets. **1862** *Cornh. Mag.* Nov. 644 The boy has now become a single-handed street wire. **1921** *Chamb. Jrnl.* June 410/1 When the 'wire' (that is, the man who actually picks the pocket) has helped himself he passes the 'swag' to his confederate.

14. Short for: **a.** Wire rope or cable.

1882 NARES *Seamanship* (ed. 6) 26 Steel wire is made of six strands, with a hemp heart in the centre. **1883** GRESLEY *Gloss. Coal-mining, Wire* (W.), a hauling rope.

b. A wire-haired fox terrier or dachshund.

1892 *Brit. Fancier* 19 Feb. 79/2 Mr. F. H. Field judged the Wires. **1938** *Times* 1 Jan. 1/6 (Advt.), Beautiful Corgis,.. Wires, Dachshunds, [etc.]. **1975** *Country Life* 6 Feb. (Advt. Suppl.) 27/1 Puppies for sale..Long Haired Wires.

V. *attrib.* and *Comb.* **15. a.** Simple attrib.: made of wire or wirework, as ***wire basket, blind, bolter, cable, cage, cloth, fence, fencing, gauze, grate, guard, lattice, mattress, mesh*** (also *attrib.*), ***net, netting, network, riddle, rigging, rope, shirt, sieve, spring, staple, trap, trolley, web, whip***; concerned with wire-drawing, as ***wire-gauge, -manufactory, manufacture, -manufacturer, -mill***; supported or running on wire, as ***wire railway, tramway.*** **b.** Parasynthetic and instrumental, as ***wire-caged, -framed, -guarded, -hung, -mended, -netted, -rimmed, -safed, -sewn*** adjs. **c.** Objective, with agent-nouns (applied to persons or to appliances) and vbl. sbs., as ***wire-clipper, -cutter, -cutting, -milker*** (see MILK *v.* 4 d), ***-monger, -nippers, -weaver***; also ***wire-like*** adj.

1845 E. ACTON *Mod. Cookery* vii. 196 A *wire basket..is convenient for frying parsley and other herbs. **1961** J. STROUD *Touch & Go* vii. 69 The people..carry the same wire baskets round the same Supermarket. **1964** D. FRANCIS *Nerve* ii. 16 There were a few letters..in the wire basket on the inner side of the door. **1977** C. MCCULLOUGH *Thorn Birds* ii. 31 A piece of boned fish..fried in the smoking well of liquid fat along with the chips, only in a separate wire basket. **1833** LOUDON *Encycl. Archit.* §560 With *wire blinds, the heat and great part of the light might be excluded. **1801** *Farmer's Mag.* Apr. 216 The flour mill.. had received a most valuable addition of a *wire boulter. **1860** *Ure's Dict. Arts* II. 113 The Atlantic telegraph cable.. is a single *wire cable. **1772** T. SIMPSON *Vermin-Killer* 5 Let the wire-maker make a *wire cage. **1858** GREENER *Gunnery* Advt. 14 [In the wire cartridge] the shot is packed within a wire cage. **1871** G. MACDONALD *Roadside Poems, A Manchester Poem* xiv. 17 The dark bird..which hangs *wire-caged. **1916** H. L. WILSON *Somewhere in Red Gap* iii. 109 That fresh bunch of campers..had a pair of *wire clippers in the whip socket. **1798** *Wire Cloth [see CLOTH *sb.* 9 b]. **1833** [see 9 a]. **1885** *Encycl. Brit.* XVIII. 224/2 This [mould] consists of a framework of fine wirecloth with a 'deckle' or movable frame of wood all round it. **1832** W. S. GILPIN *Landscape Gard.* vi. 209, I have lately seen..a *wire fence, which appears to me likely to reconcile the contending objects of beauty and expense. **1854** *Poultry Chron.* I. 540 Patent *Wire Fencing, strong enough to keep out Sheep, &c., and close enough for Dogs, Rabbits, Poultry, &c. **1971** S. HILL *Strange Meeting* i. 28 The sound of the man sleeping above him in the *wire-framed bunk. **1979** B. MALAMUD *Dubin's Lives* i. 6 She wore wire-framed blue-tinted glasses. **1833** HOLLAND *Manuf. Metal* II. xiv. 327 Stub's *wire gauges. **1888** *Lockwood's Dict. Terms Mech. Engin., Wire Gauge*, a notched plate having a series of gauged slots, numbered according to the sizes of wire and sheet metal manufactured. **1816** SIR H. DAVY in *Phil. Trans.* CVI. 23 A lighted lamp or candle screwed into a ring soldered to a cylinder of *wire gauze. **1877** RAYMOND *Statist. Mines & Mining* 430 The ore-bed, formed of wire-gauze tubes, which are set in a frame a short distance apart, thus allowing the ore to descend between them. **1819** REES *Cycl.*, **Wire-Grates*,..contrivances formed of fine wire-work, and used for keeping various kinds of large insects out of vineries,..and such places. **1841** LYTTON *Nt. & Morn.* v. xii, Just looking into the parlour..to convince herself that.. the *wire-guard was on the fire. **1907** H. WYNDHAM *Flare of Footlights* vi, *Wire-guarded gas brackets. **1856** H. H. DIXON *Post & Paddock* ii. 38 That springy *wire-hung action, which..distinguishes the stock of the great 'Rawcliffe Horse'. **1726** SWIFT *Gulliver* II. viii, He.. observed my Windows, and *wire Lettices that defended them. **1787** WITHERING *Brit. Plants* (1796) II. 857 Branches reddish, and *wire-like at the base. **1952** E. POUND *Personae* 180 The wire-like bands of colour involute mount from my fingers. **1825** J. NICHOLSON *Oper. Mech.* 349 The *wire manufactory..situated at L'Aigle,..is one of the most considerable in France. **1818** *Mathews's Bristol Directory* 67 *Wire manufacturer. **1875** KNIGHT *Dict. Mech.*, **Wire-mattress*, one having a web of wire-cloth or chain stretched in a frame for supporting a bed. **1891** *Scribner's Mag.* Sept. 318/1 A padlock with a *wire-mended chain. **1932** J. DOS PASSOS *1919* 271 There were knots of police in blue standing about..outside and inside the *wiremesh gates huskylooking young men in khaki. **1944** *Living off Land* v. 109 Tanks..are best dealt with by screening all openings with a protective wire mesh. **1974** T. HUGHES in *Listener* 4 Apr. 438/2 The sheep..in her wire-mesh compound. **1899** C. HYNE *Further Adv. Capt. Kettle* vi. 131 The *wire-milkers. **1825** J. NICHOLSON *Oper. Mech.* 346 Three of these machines..are, in general, employed in a *wire-mill. **1479** in H. Stewart *Co. Gold & Silver Wyre-drawers* (1891) 16 The petition of the Wyre-drawers, and Chape-makers that they may be made into one Company, and called *Wyre-mongers. **1871** *Man. Field Fortif.* §177 Gabions of galvanized iron *wire net. **1910** *Daily Chron.* 11 Mar. 6/4 Then why could not the coverts be *wire-netted from March to October? **1801** in *Deb. & Proc. Congr. U.S.* 21 Dec. (1851) 7th Congr. 2nd Sess. 1292 The books shall be.. set up in portable cases..with *wire-netting doors and locks. **1854** *Poultry Chron.* I. 468 Ordinary Wire Netting, from 2½d. per yard, 2 feet wide. **1843** *Penny Cycl.* XXVII. 478/2 *Wire net-work formerly employed for screens. **1914** B. M. BOWER *Flying U Ranch* 168 Want me to go back and get the *wire nippers? **1890** W. J. GORDON *Foundry* 12 We see a *wire railway to the left, or rather—for the wires are invisible—the trucks go floating through the air like rectangular balloons. **1844** H. STEPHENS *Bk. Farm* II. 281 A barley *wire-riddle answers for beans. **1883** *Man. Seamanship for Boys* 111 In turning a dead-eye, in *wire rigging, what seizings do you use? **1974** A. LURIE *War between Tates* (1977) ix. 185 Slouched down on the sofa..is a skinny adolescent boy with thick *wire-rimmed spectacles. **1841** *Penny Cycl.* XX. 156/2 Iron is the material usually employed for *wire ropes. **1859** R. HUNT *Guide Mus. Pract. Geol.* (ed. 2) 273 A flat Wire Rope Pulley. *c* **1824** L. HUNT *World of Bks., My Bks.* (1899) 20 With books all in Museum order, especially *wire-safed. **1888** JACOBI *Printers' Vocab.*, **Wire sewn*, books sewn with wire instead of thread. **1869** BROWNING *Ring & Bk.* IX. 1207 For the warm arms, were wont enfold thy flesh, Let *wire-shirt plough, and whip-cord discipline. **1665–76** J. REA *Flora* 126 The earth being first sifted through a *wyer seive. **1833** LOUDON *Encycl. Archit.* §665 *Wire Springs for stuffing are nothing more than spiral coils of wire. **1884** 'EDNA LYALL' *We Two* v, Tom ..says I am made on wire springs like a twelfth-cake butterfly. **1667** *Phil. Trans.* II. 440 A long *Wire-staple. **1626** BACON *Sylva* §171 Which Strings we call False, being bigger in one Place than in another; And therefore *Wire-strings are neuer False. *a* **1700** EVELYN *Diary* 20 Nov. 1679, The *viol d'amore* of 5 wyre-strings plaied on with a bow. **1887** *Sci. Amer.* 19 Feb. 121/1 The zither..having 24 wire strings. **1768** PENNANT *Brit. Zool.* I. 105 One that was seduced into a *wire-trap, by placing its brood in it. **1976** *Southern Even. Echo* (Southampton) 17 Nov. 13/3 She had separated the meat and cold goods into a bag to stop them contaminating sugar in the *wire trolley. **1818** *Mathews's Bristol Directory* 52 Coulsting John, *Wire-weaver and Worker. **1840** *Penny Cycl.* XVII. 209/1 The *wire-web moves forward with a motion so regulated, as..to determine the thickness of the paper. *a* **1627** H. SHIRLEY *Mart. Souldier* III. ii. (1638) E 3, *Wyer-whips shall drive you.

16. a. Special comb.: **wire act**, an acrobatic act performed on a tightrope; **wire bar**, a bar of copper cast into a suitable form for drawing into wire; **wire bed**, (*a*) a bed fitted with a wire spring base or mattress; (*b*) in papermaking, a moving bed of wire over which the pulp is passed, its fibres at this stage beginning to form a web; †**wire-bell**, a metal bar or rod used for producing a bell-like sound when struck; **wire birch** *Canad.*, a small birch, *Betula populifolia*, which has light-coloured bark and is found in eastern North America; **wire-bird**, a Ringed Plover, *Ægialitis sanctæ-helenæ*, found only on the wire-grass plains of St. Helena; **wire bridge**, (*a*) a suspension bridge supported by wires; (*b*) a kind of electric bridge furnished with a wire and a graduated scale; **wire brush**, (*a*) *Jazz* = BRUSH *sb.*^{2} 1 b; (*b*) a brush with stiff wire bristles used in cleaning, esp. for removing rust; hence **wire-brush** *v. trans.*, to clean with a wire brush; so **wire-brushed** *ppl. a.*, **-brushing** *vbl. sb.*; †**wire candle**, = *wired candle* (see WIRED *ppl. a.* 1, quot 1413); **wire-cartridge** (see quot. 1858); **wire-cut (brick)**, a machine-made brick cut by means of a steam power wire-cutter; **wire-cutter**, (*a*) nippers or pliers for cutting wire; also, a man employed to cut a wire or wires, e.g. in war operations; (*b*) an appliance for cutting bricks with wire in brick-making; so **wire-cutting** (also *attrib.*); †**wire-dancer**, one who dances or performs acrobatic feats on a wire rope; so **wire-dancing**; **wire edge**, the turned-over strip of metal produced on the edge of a cutting tool by faulty grinding or honing; also *fig.*; **wire-edged** *a.*, having a wire edge; also applied to a class of picotees having a line of deeper colour round the edge of the petals; **wire entanglement** *Mil.*, an abatis of (barbed) wire stretched over the ground in order to impede the advance of an enemy; **wire-feed, -feeding**, used attrib. in the names of machines with apparatus for maintaining a 'feed' or continuous supply of wire; **wire-finder**, an instrument for testing the insulation of electric wires; **wire-frame** *a.*, (*a*) applied to a picture (usu. computer-generated) in which every edge of an object is depicted, regardless of its visibility on the object itself, and nothing else; also *ellipt.*, (*b*) (of spectacles) having a frame made of wire; **wire-glass**, sheet glass in which wire netting is embedded; **wire ground** (see quot.); **wire grub** = WIREWORM; **wire-guided** *ppl. a.*, directed (in quot. 1922, carried out) by means of electric signals transmitted along a wire; *spec.* applied to a missile connected to a control point by a wire; **wire gun**, a wire-wound gun; **wire-hair**, short for 'wire-haired terrier'; **wire-haired** *a.*, having a rough coat of a hard and wiry texture, esp. designating a kind of fox-terrier as distinguished from the smooth-haired variety; **wire heel**, contracted quarters of the heel, a defect incident to the feet of horses and cattle; **wire house** *U.S.*, a brokerage firm having branch offices connected to its main office by private telephone and telegraph wires; **wire instrument**, †(*a*) a musical instrument with wire strings; (*b*) see quot. 1884; **wire iron**, rod iron for the manufacture of wire; **wire-mark** *Paper-making*, (*a*) *pl.*, the faint lines made by the impression of the wires of the mould in the substance of laid paper; (*b*) = WATER-MARK 5; **wire micrometer**, one with horizontal and vertical wires across the field; **wire money** *Numism.* (see quot.); **wire nail**, a nail circular in section, not tapering but pointed, and having a thin circular swaged head; **wire-nailing** (see quot.); **wire pliers**, pliers for shaping wire into curves and loops (see quot.); **wire puzzle**, a toy consisting of two or more wire patterns joined together in such a way as to puzzle one's ingenuity in disentangling them; **wire recorder**, an apparatus for magnetically recording sounds, etc., on wire and afterwards reproducing them; so **wire recording**, a recording so made, or the process of making one; **wire-rim** *a.* = *wire-frame* adj. (*b*) above; also *ellipt.*; **wire saw**, a kind of saw of which the cutting part is made of wire; **wire service** *U.S.*, a news agency that supplies syndicated news by wire to its subscribers; **wire silver**, native silver found in wire-shaped pieces; **wire-stitcher**, an automatic stapling machine which takes continuous wire and forms the staples as an integral part of the stapling operation; so **wire-stitching** (also *attrib.*); hence (as back-formations) **wire-stitch** *v. trans.*, **wire-stitched** *ppl. a.*; **wire story** *Journalism*, a story distributed by a wire service; **wire-strainer** *Austral.* and *N.Z.* = *wire-stretcher* below; **wire-stretcher** chiefly *N. Amer.*, a tool for making taut the wire of a fence or the like; **wire-tailed** *a.*, having wire-shafted tail-quills; **wire-twist**, a composition of iron and steel welded together and rolled into rods, used for gun-barrels; **wire-walker**, an acrobat who performs feats on a wire rope; so **wire-walking**; **wireway**, a channel or duct for enclosing lengths of wiring, esp. one made of sheet metal; ducting of this nature; **wire wheel**, a car wheel having wire spokes (used esp. on sports models); **wire wool**, matted thin wire, used esp. for scouring kitchen utensils; **wire-wound** *a.*, wound or encircled with wire.

1906 *Variety* 13 Jan. 7/2 The Roses..have a *wire act with some good tricks. **1912** C. MACKENZIE *Carnival* xi. 136 They did not object to interminable wire-acts, and put up with divination feats of the most exhausting dullness. **1976** *National Observer* (U.S.) 24 Jan. 18/5 You always knew a wire act would open the show. **1868** JOYNSON *Metals* 99 The copper, when at the proper state of refining, is cast into 'ingots', 'tiles', or '*wire bars'. **1882** W. WHITMAN *Daybks. & Notebks.* (1978) II. 296 *Wire-beds—829 no. 10th st. **1918** W. OWEN *Let.* 31 Oct. (1967) 591 Other officers repose on wire beds behind me. **1962** F. T. DAY *Introd. Paper* iv. 38 The wire bed is kept perfectly level while it oscillates to bring about the interlacing of fibres in the pulp. **1668** [STEDMAN] *Tintinnalogia* (1671) 3 Let him learn on some Instrument, or *Wyer-Bells, to know a Third, Fifth, and Eighth, which are the principal Concords. **1917** B. R. MORTON *Native Trees of Canada* 68 *Betula Populifolia*.. White birch, grey birch, *wire birch. **1956** [see *Indian pear* s.v. INDIAN *a.* 4b]. **1974** J. DOWELL *Look-Off Bear* p. viii, Beyond our grove of pines there were mixed growths of wire-birch, swamp willow, [etc.]. **1873** J. E. HARTING in *Ibis* July 260 The St.-Helena bird, popularly known in the island as the '*Wire-bird'. **1816** *Portfolio* (Philad.) June 521 The *wire bridge near Philadelphia..is supported by six wires each 3-8ths of an inch in diameter. **1842** *Penny Cycl.* XXIII. 334/1 Another wire bridge..was built in 1817, across the Tweed. **1891** *Cent. Dict.* s.v. *Wire*, *Wire bridge*, in *elect.*, a kind of Wheatstone bridge in which two adjacent resistances are formed by a wire. **1927** *Melody Maker* Apr. 389/1 In quiet passages, the *wire brush on a Chinese cymbal gives a very pleasing effect. *a* **1935** T. E. LAWRENCE *Mint* (1955) I. xxii. 76 Our job was to wire-brush and repaint a lot of salvaged sheeting... A good job, it looked. Six of us and six wire brushes. **1957** MANVELL & HUNTLEY *Film Music* iii. 98 Wire-brush percussion. **1974** A. ROSS *Bradford Business* 76 Even the short heavy bolts had been rubbed up with a wire brush. **1978** J. WAINWRIGHT *Thief of Time* 210, I should.. check the trays of seed potatoes... Wire-brush the seed-trays. **1955** *Archit. Rev.* CXVII. 68 Construction: reinforced concrete frame with mainly brick walls, but certain panels of *wire-brushed concrete. **1978** *Country Life* 28 Dec. 2212/1 The furniture in wire-brushed carved oak. **1978** E. GUNDREY *Simple Plumbing* 22 Rust removal involves *wire-brushing. **1980** *Yachts & Yachting* 29 Feb. 672/2 Lead is perhaps the easiest needing only one coat of undercoat and one of Metallic Primocon between wirebrushing (or rubbing down) and the new antifoul. **1419** *Churchwardens' Acc. St. Michael's Church, Oxford* (MS.), *Wyrecandel ante crucem ad Lux Fulgebit. **1839** W. WATT (*title*) Remarks on shooting, in verse, comprehending..the recent and admirable invention of the patent *wire cartridge. **1858** *Greener's Gunnery* Advt. 14 The advantages to be derived from the use of the Wire Cartridge, in the pursuit of..game... The shot is packed within a wire cage, which is constructed so as to allow them to escape from it gradually while the charge is in motion. **1892** *Labour Commission* Gloss., *Wire-cut Brick. **1910** *Encycl. Brit.* IV. 519/2 In all cases bricks thus made are known as 'wire-cuts'. **1875** KNIGHT *Dict. Mech.*, **Wire-cutter*, a nippers for cutting off wire. **1888** in W. P. Webb *Great Plains* (1931) 314 While a man was putting up his fence one day in a hollow a crowd of wire-cutters was cutting it behind him in another hollow. **1905** H. G. WELLS *Kipps* I. vi. §4 Pearce, the dog! had a wire-cutter in his pocket-knife. **1922** *Encycl. Brit.* XXXII. 919/1 Detachments of wire-cutters, and pioneers, about 50 strong. **1875** KNIGHT *Dict. Mech.*, **Wire-Cutting Plyers*. **1895** *Westm. Gaz.* 24 Jan. 5/2 The Tramway Strike at Brooklyn... The militia are now using search-lights to detect wire-cutting. **1728** BAKER *Biogr. Dram.* (1782) I. 88 Mr. Maddox, the celebrated *wire-dancer. **1768** TUCKER *Lt. Nat.* (1834) II. 362 The application of the pick-pocket, the wire-dancer, and the balance-master, to become expert in their several arts. **1785** *Daily Universal Reg.* 1 Jan. 4/1 Must he [*sc.* an editor]...have writers of tumbling—*wire dancing—and hurly burly description? **1801** STRUTT *Sports & Past.* III. v. §22. 175 Wire-dancing..consists rather of various feats of balancing..upon the wire. [**1698** *Phil. Trans.* XX. 418 The Edge being whet away to a Wire, as they term it.] **1807** H. H. BRACKENRIDGE *Mod. Chivalry* II. iv. 21 In the course of mixing with good company, the *wire edge of art would wear off, and an ease of demeanor be attained. **1846** HOLTZAPFFEL *Turning* II. 496 Lastly, the flat face of the [plane-] iron is laid quite flat on the oilstone, to remove the wire edge. **1847** BROWNSON *Two Brothers* Wks. VI. 246 Time had hardly worn off the wire-edge of his grief. **1861** CAMPIN *Pract. Hand-turning* ii. 41 The tool..should ..be so held that the grindstone is driven from the edge towards the handle..otherwise it will discover a great liability to become *wire-edged. **1898** *Gardener's Mag.* 3 Sept. 571/2 Time was when there was a distinct section of wire-edged yellow-ground picotees. **1876** VOYLE & STEVENSON *Milit. Dict.* (ed. 3) 470/2 *Wire Entanglement. **1879** HENSMAN *Afghan War* (1881) 215 Wire entanglements, made with telegraph wire and tent-pegs. **1875** KNIGHT *Dict. Mech.*, **Wire-feed Screw-machine*, a machine for making screws from a continuous length of wire. **1884** *Ibid.* Suppl. 950/1 A screw machine... It has an adjustable chuck and *wire-feeding apparatus. **1877** *Jrnl. Soc. Telegr. Engineers* VI. 522 A new *wire-finder. **1963** *AFIPS Conf. Proc.* XXIII. 348 A prototype graphical communications system capable of manipulating straight line, '*wire frame', figures in three-dimensional space is now in operation. **1977** E. LEONARD *Unknown Man No. 89* ii. 13 His tinted wire-frame glasses glistened. **1982** BALLARD & BROWN *Computer Vision* ix. 292 A set of vertices or edges can define many different solids. (It is possible, however, to determine algorithmically all possible polyhedral boundaries described by a three-dimensional wireframe.) **1982** J. E. SCOTT *Introd. Interactive Computer Graphics* viii. 135 A wire-frame drawing is less pleasing visually, but it is considerably faster for the computer to produce. **1983** *New Scientist* 24 Mar. 819/1 The more detail in a wire frame, the harder it is to understand. **1983** L. DEIGHTON *Berlin Game* viii. 83 Bret put his wire-frame glasses into their case. **1900** *Engineering Mag.* XIX. 761/1 Mr. Murphy proposes..to have a section of the roof made of *wire-glass. **1865** F. B. PALLISER *Hist. Lace* iii. 27 The honeycomb network or ground..is of various kinds; *wire ground, Brussels ground, [etc.]. **1882** CAULFEILD & SAWARD *Dict. Needlework*, *Wire ground*..is sometimes used in Brussels Lace; it is made of silk, with its net-patterned meshes partly raised and arched, and is worked separately from the design. *a* **1846** LOUDON (Worc.) *Wire grub. **1922** *Encycl. Brit.* XXXII. 1022/1 *Wire-guided high frequency telegraphy and telephony. **1958** C. C. ADAMS *Space Flight* 52 The latter two [rockets] ..are wire-guided. **1972** [see *TOW* s.v. T 6a]. **1982** *Sci. Amer.* May 103 (Advt.), The wire enables the Hughes TOW to have one of the highest velocities and longest ranges (2·3 miles) of any wire-guided missile in the world. **1982** *Daily Tel.* 10 May 4/3 Two wire-guided torpedoes of the Tigerfish type. **1895** *Daily News* 1 Feb. 3/1 The Majestic will probably be the first ship to be fitted with the new 12-inch *wire guns. **1884** *Live Stock Jrnl.* 5 Sept. 227/2 Heather, another *wire-hair, came second. **1801** *Sporting Mag.* XVIII. 85 The rough *wire-haired hound. **1818** *Ibid.* (N.S.) I. 157 Scotch terriers, rough, wire-haired, with long backs and short legs. **1881** V. SHAW *Bk. Dog* 299 Some excellent wire-haired Fox-terriers. **1819** REES *Cycl.*, *Wire-Heels. **1904** *N.Y. Evening Post* 18 June (Financial Sect.) 1/7 The so-called '*wire house'..is a product of the boom times. **1966** *Economist* 25 June 1436/1 It [*sc.* the New York Stock Exchange] has been firing salvos..about possibly setting up an auxiliary trading floor somewhere in New Jersey... Several larger nation-wide 'wire' houses have already said that they are considering some such plans to relocate. **1982** *Times* 27 July 15/4 United States banks..in the past have left financial futures very much to the brokers and major 'wire houses' such as Bache or Hutton. **1654** WOOD *Life* (O.H.S.) I. 190 John Trap of Trinity, [who played] on the citerne; and Georg Mason..on another *wyer instrument. **1884** KNIGHT *Dict. Mech.* Suppl., *Wire Instruments*..for manipulating wire in surgical practice. **1858** SIMMONDS *Dict. Trade*, **Wire-iron*, black rod iron made in South Staffordshire, and used for drawing out into wire. **1815** J. SMITH *Panorama Sci. & Art* II. 697 The kind of paper most proper..is..yellow wove, as the *wire-marks which are in the other sort, are an impediment to the point of the pencil. **1840** *Penny Cycl.* XVII. 209/2 Various wire-marks, or water-marks, as they are called. **1813** D. BREWSTER *New Philos. Instrum.* 5 The *wire micrometer. **1853** H. N. HUMPHREYS *Coin-coll. Man.* II. 492 A small issue of shillings, sixpences, and Maundy money, took place in 1797 and 1798... They are known among collectors as the *wire money, from the very slender numerals on the Maundy pieces. **1875** KNIGHT *Dict. Mech.*, *Wire-nail. *Ibid.*, **Wire-nailing Machine*, a machine for closing shoes with wire. **1888** *Lockwood's Dict. Terms Mech. Engin.*, **Wire Pliers*, pliers in which a pair of smooth jaws, circular in section and tapered lengthways, are substituted for the ordinary flat and roughened jaws. **1898** 'H. S. MERRIMAN' *Roden's Corner* vii. 69 It happened to be a *wire-puzzle winter, and Cornish had the best collection of rings on impossible wire mazes. **1942** *Frontier* Sept. 3/1 (*caption*) The *wire sound recorder developed by Armour Research Foundation differs from previous types in the type of recording head. **1957** *Encycl. Brit.* XI. 29/2 Three types of recording systems are in common use: (1) mechanical, as in the disk phonograph; (2) optical, as in the sound film; and (3) magnetic, as in the tape or wire recorder. **1978** 'D. KYLE' *Black Camelot* ix. 130 'I think we'd better record this as we go along.'.. The wire recorder had been produced and checked. **1933** *Amer. Speech* VIII. II. 77/1 Similar information should be given for film, strip, and *wire recordings. **1943** *Electronics* Oct. 236 (*caption*) A wire recording of the Army Hour is taken off the air by..engineers. **1966** *McGraw-Hill Encycl. Sci. & Technol.* XIV. 518/2 Except for minor details, the techniques and systems used for magnetic wire recording are similar to those for magnetic tape. **1982** *Sunday Tel.* (Colour Suppl.) 21 Nov. 8/2, I just read the words, they were recorded straight on to disc, then transferred on to wire recording tape and that was the end of it. **1977** *Sat. Rev.* 23 July 10/2 Slender, with a trim beard and *wire-rim glasses. **1982** J. VALIN *Day of Wrath* (1983) xvii. 131 He's got long hair, wears wire rims, muttonchops. **1688** HOLME *Armoury* 501 *Wyer Saw. **1901** *Nature* 28 Nov. 84/2 The helicoidal wire saw has been employed for quarrying marble in Belgium and in Italy for some years. **1950** *Mag. of Fantasy & S.F.* Fall 7, I monitored a couple of newscasts; the second one carried a story by another *wire service on the domes. **1962** E. LACY *Freeloaders* viii. 181, I didn't think the *Herald Tribune* used wire services for Europe. **1976** *National Observer* (U.S.) 6 Nov. 24/1 A morning newspaper in the East, using a wire service's totals, had Rockefeller ahead. **1985** *Times* 11 May 21/1 Reuters is keeping a close watch on its troubled American wire service rival, United Press International. **1882** *Rep. Prec. Metals U.S.* 177 Well-defined veins, carrying ruby silver, black sulphuret,..and *wire silver. **1902** *Census Bull.* (U.S.) No. 216. 65 A.. combination folding and wire-stitching machine, which by a continuous and automatic operation takes the sheets from the feeders, and folds, gathers, collates, covers and *wire-stitches copies of magazines and pamphlets. **1921** T. J. WISE *Bibliogr. Writings Joseph Conrad* (rev. ed.) I. 27 There are no signatures, the pamphlet being composed of a single halfsheet..issued *wire-stitched. **1887** *Courier-Journal* (Louisville, Ky.) 20 Feb. 3/2 Printing-Office... Card Cutter, *Wire Stitcher [etc.]. **1967** Wire stitcher [see SHORT RUN *sb.* 4]. **1881** *Even. News* 26 July 4 (Advt.), Over one hundred machines in motion [in a printing and paper-making exhibition]... *Wire stitching, paging, gumming, etc. **1957** *Encycl. Brit.* III. 859/2 The automatic assembling, wire-stitching and covering machine units complete the operation of pamphlet binding. **1943** *Wire story [see HOT-SHOT 1b]. **1979** J. CROSBY *Party of Year* (1980) iii. 25 The foreign desk was behind a glass screen... Feinberg was editing a wire story. **1882** ARMSTRONG & CAMPBELL *Austral. Sheep Husbandry* xviii. 204 Novel *Wire Strainer... This instrument..should be made of light iron... Three short spikes, or legs, should be fixed behind, so as to give the instrument a grip of the post as soon as the wire is tightened. **1959** A. UPFIELD *Bony & Black Virgin* xxiii. 215 The big man studied the method of joining the cut wires... 'Chain wire-strainer was used.' **1975** *N.Z. Jrnl. Agric.* Sept. 57/1 The installation of permanent wire strainers on each strand of a new fence..would overcome this difficulty. *a* **1877** KNIGHT *Dict. Mech.* III. 2797/2 **Wire-stretcher*, a tool for straining lightly telegraph or fence wires. **1954** W. FAULKNER *Fable* 187 Cowboy..exterminated from the earth by a tide of men with wire-stretchers and pockets full of staples. **1958** J. G. MACGREGOR *North-West of 16* ix. 132 Then it [*sc.* barbed wire] had to be tightened with our wire-stretchers (a simple block-and-tackle arrangement) until when you plucked it, it sang like a fiddle string. **1981** *Farmstead Mag.* Winter 43/4, I assemble my supplies for next year's battle: my fence staples, spare wire, my fencing pliers and wire stretcher. **1823** LATHAM *Gen. Hist. Birds* VII. 309 *Wire-tailed Swallow... Inhabits India. **1835** GREENER *Gun* ii. 14 Damascus being a variety or mixture, made from the composition named *wire-twist iron. *Ibid.*, The making of wire-twist barrels. **1762** GOLDSM. *Cit. W.* lxxxv, Stage-players, fire-eaters, singing women, dancing dogs, wild beasts, and *wire-walkers. **1895** *Pall Mall Gaz.* 1 Feb. 4/2 Miss Virginia Aragon is the most finished wire-walker that we can remember. **1898** *Pearson's Mag.* Sept. 332 *Wire-walking..must always retain a greater amount of fascination. **1920** *Variety* 31 Dec. 124 She learned acrobatics..wire walking and aerial work. **1932** A. L. ABBOTT *National Electr. Code Handbk.* viii. 97 (*caption*) A length of *wireway with hinged cover. *Ibid.* 99 Wireways may extend transversely through dry walls. **1953** H. A. CHINN *Television Broadcasting* xv. 606 In order to provide protection for audio, video, communications, control, and a-c cables..it is customary to instal such cables in conduit, raceways, pipe shafts,..and similar wireways. **1964** R. F. FICCHI *Electrical Interference* x. 192 A bare ground wire rubbing against a chassis or wireway can cause a considerable amount of noise in a system. **1909** *Westm. Gaz.* 9 Feb. 4/2 The Humber detachable *wire wheel..is said to be 50 per cent. stronger than wood. **1912** *Motor Manual* (ed. 14) (Advt., rear cover), Rudge-Whitworth detachable wire wheels lengthen the life of tyres 70%. **1926** *Daily Colonist* (Victoria, B.C.) 4 July 26/4 (Advt.), Sport Roadster $675 delivered. Racy streamlines, wire wheels, [etc.]. **1963** [see GAS *sb.*[1] 5d]. **1976** N. THORNBURG *Cutter & Bone* i. 8 A classic 1948 MG-TC with running board and wire wheels. **1958** J. CANNAN *And be Villain* iii. 71 A cupboard where detergents, a reserve of dishcloths and the rolls of *wire wool were kept. **1977** 'J. LE CARRÉ' *Hon. Schoolboy* xii. 264 His hair was like wire wool crimped into small trenches. **1894** *Westm. Gaz.* 22 Jan. 4/3 These *wire-wound guns have been approved of, and are supposed to be nearly 40 per cent. stronger than the present type of heavy ordnance. **1910** H. M. HOBART *Dict. Electr. Engin.* I. 32/1 Wire-wound Armature, the armature of an electric generator or motor which is wound with wire, in contradistinction to one of which the winding consists of bars. **1931** *Boys' Mag.* XLV. 125/2 The potentiometer should be a 'Colvern', wire wound. **1946** *Nature* 30 Nov. 799/2 The development of a vitreous enamel coating for fixed wire-wound resistors. **1975** D. G. FINK *Electronics Engineers' Handbk.* VII. 7 Rheostat (Power). These are variable wire-wound resistors used as speed controls.

b. In the names of various plants with slender wiry stems (see quots. and WIRE-GRASS).

1756 P. BROWNE *Jamaica* 126 The small Wire-rush. The larger Wire-rush. Both these little plants are very frequent in the swamps of Jamaica. **1797** J. BAILEY & CULLEY *Agric. Northumbld.* 127 *Nardus stricta.* Wirebent. **1827** in Bischoff *Van Diemen's Land* (1832) 167 We were several hours struggling through thick scrub and wireweed. *a* **1850** BROMFIELD *Flora Vect.* (1856) 434 *Polygonum aviculare*.. Wire-weed. **1866** *Treas. Bot.*, Wire-bent.

¶ From the 15th to the 17th century examples of *wire* occur app. with the sense 'iron', ? by confusion with the old form *ire*. (Cf. WIRY ¶.)

1406 *York Wills* (Surtees) I. 343 Lego Roberto Brid j wyrehatt cum j Carlele ax. **1455** in *Archæologia* XVI. 126 A Wyre hatt garnysshed yᵉ bordour Serkyll. **1567** *Aldeburgh Rec.* in *N. & Q.* 12th Ser. VII. 142/2 Makynge wheire gudgyons. **1582** N. LICHEFIELD tr. *Castanheda's Conq. E. Ind.* 42 A wether cock, made likewise of wier [orig. *di bronzo*]. **1630** *Maldon (Essex) Docts.* Bundle 217. No. 22 (MS.), iiii. Wyer candlesticks, 8*d.* **1682** in H. More *Contn. Remark. Stories* 63 That a Wier-Candlestick..might be turned into Brass.

wire (waɪə(r)), *v.* [f. WIRE *sb.*]

†**1. a.** To adorn with (gold) wire. *Obs. rare.*

13.. *K. Alis.* 208 (MS. Laud) Her ȝelewe her was faire atired, Mid riche strenges of golde wyred.

†**b.** To entwine. *Obs. rare.*

c **1645** HOWELL *Lett.* I. xiv. (1650) I. 23 As the Vine her lovely Elm doth wire.

†**c.** *intr.* To wind or twist about. *Obs. rare.*

1633 P. FLETCHER *Purple Isl.* IV. xxi, In small streams (through all the Island wiring).

2. *trans.* To furnish with a wire or wires. **a.** To fasten, join, or fit with wire or wires; *spec.* to secure (the cork of a bottle, the bottle itself) with wire.

1435 *Churchw. Acc. St. Michael's, Oxford* (MS.) i lib. of talow candell y-wyrede to the rode soler. **1551–2** in Feuillerat *Revels Edw. VI* (1914) 73 For vj mouldes for serpentes for the same hedpeces—ijˢ. and for wyeryng of xj of those serpentes at viijᵈ the pece—vijˢ. iiijᵈ. **1683** LORRAIN tr. *Muret's Rites Funeral* To Rdr. A4b, A Skeleton how neatly soever hung and wir'd together, is not an Object so entertaining as a Venus. *a* **1700** EVELYN *Diary* 24 Aug. 1678, They..then put it [*sc.* pulp] into a vessell of water, in which they dip a frame closely wyred with wyre as small as a haire. **1706** HEARNE *Collect.* (O.H.S.) I. 226 One of the Sceleton's in yᵉ Anatomy Schoole was wired by one Wells a Smith. **1796** M. EDGEWORTH *Parent's Assistant* (ed. 2) I. 74 Did not I order you..to carry these bottles to the cellar; and did not I charge you to wire the corks? **1828–32** WEBSTER, *Wire*,.. to apply wire to, as in bottling liquors. **1830** M. DONOVAN *Dom. Econ.* I. 295 The bottles should be wired down, and laid on their sides. **1837** MISS MITFORD *Country Stories* (1850) 124 He had written the label and wired the root. **1879** *St. George's Hosp. Rep.* IX. 377 Jaw retained in position by wiring the fragments together.

b. To furnish with a wire support; to stiffen with wire.

1834 PLANCHÉ *Brit. Costume* 274 The ruff was..starched and wired as usual. **1882** J. ASHTON *Soc. Life Reign Q. Anne* I. xiii. 151 In 1711 the coats used to be wired to make them stick out. **1891** *Daily News* 29 Apr. 7/1 Even ribbon loops are wired for hat and bonnet trimming.

c. To fence with wire: chiefly ***to wire in***, to enclose with a wire fence. Also, to cover *over* with wire.

1691 J. GIBSON in *Archæologia* XII. 184 The enclosure wired-in for white pheasants and partridges. **1774** J. WESLEY *Let.* 26 July (1931) VI. 104 You must..wire over the cupola. **1851** RUSKIN *Stones Venice* I. viii. §17. 93 They will look as if they were meant to keep the central shaft together by wiring or caging it in; like iron rods set round a supple cylinder. **1854** *Poultry Chron.* II. 60 A range of tables, the under part of which was wired in to form pens for the geese.

d. To strengthen or protect with (barbed) wire.

1881 MRS. P. O'DONOGHUE *Ladies on Horseback* 181 Wire the fences if necessary; but at the commencement of the hunting season, cut away, say twenty yards of the wiring. **1917** *Blackw. Mag.* May 737/2 Every night parties sallied forth, some to wire, others to repair the parapet.

e. To furnish with electric wires; to make electrical connections to; to connect electrically *to*; to provide *with* by means of connecting wires; *spec.* to fit with a concealed listening device. Also with *up*.

1891 E. I. Bax *Pop. Electr. Lighting* iv. 27 To admit of this the expense of wiring the room will have to be increased. **1892** A. Fahie *House Lighting by Electr.* 77 The..cost of wiring houses of different sizes. **1898** *Daily News* 27 Aug. 6/4 Nearly every street of importance had been wired. **1923** *Wireless World* 19 May 205/2 It is preferable to wire the valve panel before fixing it to the baseboard. **1960** *Practical Wireless* XXXVI. 393/1 The heater circuit is best wired first, leads being run close against the chassis. **1970** J. Earl *Tuners & Amplifiers* vi. 140 It is not usually difficult to wire the stereo loudspeaker pair and programme sources for the correct left and right channels. **1978** S. Brill *Teamsters* iv. 144 The prosecutor wired Henderson's phone so that there would be tapes of Faugno and Andretta threatening him. **1978** *Australian* 21 Aug. 9/2 One in every five homes with television are wired to a cable system. **1982** *Sci. Amer.* Sept. 68/2 The explosive charge is wired with electric blasting caps and detonated from a safe distance. **1983** J. Fuller *Convergence* xxx. 303 Just tell the truth... We have to wire you up.

f. To incorporate (a facility, etc.) *into* a device by electric wiring. Cf. wired-in *a.* 2.

1962 *Communications Assoc. Computing Machinery* V. 159/1 A scheme for wiring binary-to-decimal conversion into a machine at a small cost.

3. To catch or trap in a wire snare. Also *fig.*

1749 Fielding *Tom Jones* iii. x, He said that George had wired Hares. **1771** in Hone *Every-day Bk.* (1827) II. 207 *Court.* A sturdy beggar! We must find out some means of wiring that fellow! **1798** Southey *Engl. Ecl., Sailor's Mother* 110 But he was caught In wiring hares at last. **1836** Haliburton *Clockm.* Ser. i. xx, Why, if he aint snared, Sam; he is properly wired, I declare. **1851** Newland *Erne* v. 136, I recollect wiring a great lumping chubb once. I caught him asleep.

4. *pass.* and *intr.* (also with *in*) Of a horse's foot: To be contracted in the heel; to be affected with 'wire heel'; also *trans.*, to cause to be 'wired'.

1614, etc. [see wired *ppl. a.* 4]. **1753** J. Bartlet *Gentl. Farriery* (1754) 309 This turns them narrow above, wires their heels, and dries..the frog. **1831** Youatt *Horse* 293 Many persons reject a horse..if the quarters are wiring in.

5. *Croquet.* To place one's own or an opponent's ball so that a hoop intervenes between it and its object: with ball or player as obj. Chiefly *pass.*

1866 *Croquet: Implements & Laws* 10 A ball is Wired when it cannot effect the stroke desired on account of the leg of a hoop (wire) intervening. **1868** W. J. Whitmore *Croquet Tactics* 21 *To be wired* is to have your ball in such a position that you cannot hit some other ball, or get through your hoop, because of a wire intervening. **1874** J. D. Heath *Croquet-player* 54 It is useless to wire a ball from the player, if another ball, at which he would be more likely to shoot, is left unwired or 'open'. *Ibid.* 71 Red..has wired the player for all the balls. **1904** E. F. Benson *Challoners* i, Helen was standing close by her brother in the proud calm consciousness of having wired him with complete success.

6. To send (a message) 'over the wires', to telegraph; also *absol.* or *intr.*; *transf.* to send a telegraph message to; = telegraph *v.* 1. *colloq.*

1859 *Edin. Rev.* Apr. 378 Another party, who are striving to debase the language by introducing the verb 'to wire', instead of the word hitherto used, 'to telegraph'. **1863** Dicey *Federal St.* I. 247 No intelligence could be 'wired', according to the American phrase. **1876** 'E. Pinto' *Ye outside Fools!* 17, I am going to wire my broker fellow to buy a couple of thousand Bs and Cs. **1883** D. C. Murray *Hearts* xii, I want you to wire to Tom and demand the truth about the matter. **1883** *Leisure Hour* 282/2 The relief train came up, news of the difficulty having been wired on. **1891** 'Annie Thomas' *That Affair* x, He was wired for to go and look at a pony.

7. intr. *to wire in* (rarely *away*), to get to work with a will, to apply oneself energetically to something; *to wire into* (a meal, etc.), to set about it with avidity. *colloq.* or *slang.*

Origin uncertain; cf. quot. 1870 and *Slang Dict.*, 1874, where it is said that the orig. phr. is 'wire in and get your name up', an invitation to enter the ring for a contest.

1865 *Slang Dict.* (ed. 3), *Wire-in*, a London street phrase in general use at the present time. **1870** *Daily News* 16 Apr., We were politely told by Sandy to 'wire in'—digger's phraseology for an invitation to commence. **1888** *Fortn. Rev.* Jan. 93 In one fashion or another he 'keeps wiring away'. **1891** 'R. Boldrewood' *Sydney-side Saxon* vi, I asked for work at the first station I came to, and though I was strange to it, I wired in with a will. **1894** Astley *Fifty Yrs. Life* II. 252 After wiring into a leg of mutton and rice-pudding, [I] turned into a..welcome bed.

8. [Cf. wire *sb.* 13.] *intr.* To practise pick-pocketing; *trans.*, to pick the pocket of. *slang.*

1853 M. Carpenter *Juvenile Delinquents* i. 40 There are..at least ten times as many boys 'wiring' (picking pockets) as when I was young. *Ibid.* iv. 145 If he was bigger he could wire a man of his poke. **1891** 'F. W. Carew' *No. 747* xxxv. 414, I used to go wirin' in the main-thoroughfares.

wire, var. vire *sb.*[2] *Obs.*, virus.

wired (waɪəd), *ppl. a.* [f. wire *sb.* or *v.* + -ed.]

1. Supported, strengthened, or stiffened with wire; *spec.* of glass.

1413 *Churchw. Acc. St. Michael's, Oxford* (MS.) Pro xiiii libris de wyred candel iis. xi.d. **1480** in *Berks, Bucks & Oxon Archaeol. Jrnl.* (1913) Oct. 85 Paied yᵉ same John for wyred candell at Cristmas vᵈ. **1654** Webster *Appius & Virg.* v. ii, He that would tame a Lion, doth not use the goad or wierd whip, but a sweet voice. **1844** Noad *Electricity* (ed. 2) 88 The box contains a reel round which the wired string is wound. **1885** 'Mrs. Alexander' *Valerie's Fate* iv, A lovely bouquet came for me—not a nasty wired affair, but just a lot of loose flowers. **1908** Rosenhain *Glass Manuf.* 27 In wired plate glass..an entire layer of wire netting is interposed between two layers of glass. **1930** *Engineering* 12 Dec. 755/1 Plate glass, rolled figured glass, corrugated glass, and wired glass, all produced by rolling. **1979** P. Way *Sunrise* xi. 116 He had pushed through the wired-glass door.

2. Furnished with or consisting of a wire fence or netting for confinement or protection.

1748 Richardson *Clarissa* III. lxxv. 348 It [*sc.* a captive bird]..with meditating eyes, first surveys, and then attempts, its wired canopy. **1816** in J. Scott *Vis. Paris* xv. (ed. 5) 237 The lower shelves only are protected by doors and wired frames. **1820** Shelley *Witch Atl.* xvi, As bats at the wired window of a dairy, They beat their vans. **1880** Carnegie *Pract. Trap.* 43 Traps..placed round a wired pheasant inclosure ought to be effective. **1903** T. F. Dale *Fox-hunting in Shires* 21 A hunting crowd melts away..when the country is open. A wired district, however, will soon bring them together again. **1918** *Daily Mail* 12 Aug. 2/6 The troops..held up by deep gullies and wired woods. **1919** *Blackw. Mag.* June 831/1 The wired-over, sandy road.

3. Fastened or secured with wire. Also with *up*, and *fig.*

wired on, designating a kind of tyre which is secured to the wheel-rim by means of wire.

In first quot., Contained in a bottle having a wired cork.

1798 Lady Hunter in *Sir M. Hunter's Jrnl.* 19 Sept. (1894) 119 Had Majors Wemyss and Gordon to eat cold tongue and drink wired porter..at twelve. **1850** H. Melville *White Jacket* II. xlvi. 308 The Surgeon stalked over the side, the wired skeleton carried in his wake by his cot-boy. **1865** *Athenæum* 9 Dec. 803/1 Birch wine,..the native impetuosity of which had to be restrained by wired corks. **1897** Pemberton *Complete Cyclist* 82 The most suitable rim for any kind of wired-on tyre. **1946** *Coast to Coast 1945* 216 The gate was thoroughly wired up—three Queensland hitches of No. 8 wire. **1975** *Washington Post* 29 Sept. a-20/4 Let us..concede that point for a moment—although it shouldn't be conceded until it is properly wired up with all sorts of qualifications.

4. Of a horse's foot (see wire *v.* 4).

1614 Markham *Cheap Husb.* i. i. 3 Chuse him [i.e. a horse] that is..strong ioynted, and hollow houes, of which the long is best, if they be not wierd. **1696** *Lond. Gaz.* No. 3211/4 A Chesnut Mare Colt, two years old,..the hind feet and one before white, wired behind. **1864** E. Mayhew *Horse Managem.* 463 Where the heels have become 'wired in'.

5. *Croquet.* (See wire *v.* 5.)

1868 *Chamb. Encycl.* X. 485/2 A Wired Ball is one which cannot be croqued, by reason of the leg of the hoop intervening.

6. a. Employing wires or similar physical connections to convey electric signals, *spec.* for television or radio.

1924 *Telegraph & Telephone Jrnl.* XI. 6/1 Here are some extremely interesting particulars regarding 'Wired Radio' Broadcasting. **1930** E. E. Hunt *Audit Amer.* 20 In 1913 there were only 48 wired homes per 1,000 of the non-farm population. **1937** *Wireless World* 2 Dec. 565/2 (*heading*) Wired television. **1958** *Oxford Mail* 26 Aug. 3/6 In a discussion on wired television..Coun. W. G. White asked if the present or any future council was going to bar the television aerial from its housing estates. **1960** Gregory & Van Horn *Automatic Data-Processing Systems* ii. 61 Computers with externally stored programs..get their operating instructions from wired plugboards. **1960** *Electronics Weekly* 30 Nov. 2/4 A wired sound and television service may soon be provided..for Leicester. **1969** *Electr. Communications* XLIV. i. 14/1 The best compromise was sought between wired-logic control, which is very efficient but inflexible, and stored-program control. **1971** *New Scientist* 1 July 19/2 It is often argued that the provision of more radio and TV channels, particularly on the greatly expanded scale of the 'wired city', will lower standards. **1972** *Listener* 6 July 3/2 As America becomes increasingly a wired nation, with cables reaching out already into millions of homes, the channel limitations of over-the-air television are being superseded. **1976** Brzozowski & Yoeli *Digital Networks* ii. 30 Wired logic refers to the capability of tying together the outputs of gates to realize either the and..or the or..function without additional hardware.

b. Fitted with, or wearing, an electronic listening device; more fully ***wired for sound***. Also *fig. colloq.*

1957 J. D. MacDonald *Man of Affairs* ix. 141 The joint is wired, he says... The next step is cameras and infra red and tape recorders, I guess. **1967** *Boston Sunday Globe* 23 Apr. 18/3 Several agreed with the words of one who said he knew enough 'to stay away from Karafin... He's wired for sound 24 hours a day... He can keep stories out of the paper or get them in.' **1982** G. Lyall *Conduct of Major Maxim* xiv. 129 The very idea of being 'off the record' was nonsense, since the room was almost certainly wired.

c. With *up* in either of prec. senses.

1971 *New Scientist* 16 Sept. 614 (*heading*) The visual systems in their brain are wired up to match the visual world that is important to them. **1972** D. Bloodworth *Any Number can Play* xix. 197 That one-sided chat you had with the wired-up Goddess of Mercy. **1982** P. D. James *Skull beneath Skin* xxv. 210 She was glad that she wasn't wired up to a lie machine. **1984** *Listener* 26 July 20/1 Dr Glover came to the orchestra on the strength of being well wired-up with broadcasting contacts.

wired, obs. form of weird *sb.*

wired-in (stress variable), *a.* [f. wired *ppl. a.* + in *adv.*] **1.** Bounded by wire, in the form of netting or fencing. Cf. wire *v.* 2 c.

1855 *Poultry Chron.* III. 508 A moveable house and wired-in run which..is tenanted by a pair of Bantams. **1973** J. Thomson *Death Cap* ix. 128 She was feeding the chickens ..in the wired-in run. **1975** J. McClure *Snake* ix. 118 Wessels..hid behind the wired-in back of a parked truck.

2. Incorporated in or connected to a device or system by means of wiring. Also *fig.*

1957 C. E. Osgood et al. *Measurement of Meaning* i. 5 Certain stimulus patterns have a 'wired-in' connection with certain behaviour patterns (unconditional reflexes) and additional stimuli have acquired this capacity (conditional reflexes). **1962** *Commun. Assoc. Computing Machinery* V. 159/1 (*heading*) On a wired-in binary-to-decimal conversion scheme. **1975** P. Elbow *Oppositions in Chaucer* v. 120 His predilection for language and thought frees him..from a single, rigid, programmed, or wired-in response to a fox. **1975** *Language for Life* (Dept. Educ. & Sci.) xv. 234 This should be fitted with sound-proof projector booth, wired-in good quality speakers, and a large permanent screen. **1982** *Data Communications* Oct. 119/2 These terminals are dedicated to specific tasks through specific wired-in instructions and have no built-in intelligence. **1984** *Science* 22 June 1304/3 The wired-in semantics of these connections substitutes for the time-consuming interpretation process needed in systems that pass symbolic information.

wire-draw (ˈwaɪədrɔː), *v.* Now *rare.* [Back-formation from wire-drawer.]

1. *trans.* To draw out (metal) into wire: see wire-drawing *vbl. sb.* 1. *rare.*

1666 Boyle *Orig. Formes & Qual.* 96 Though out of a wedge of Gold one cannot immediately make a Ring, yet by ..Wyre-drawing that Wedge by degrees,..That thing may easily be effected. **1706** Phillips (ed. Kersey), To *Wire-draw*, to draw out Gold or Silver-Thread. **1755** Johnson, To *Wiredraw*. 1. To spin into wire. **1828–32** Webster.

2. *transf.* To draw out (a material thing) to an elongated form; to stretch, elongate.

1598 Florio, *Stringare*..to wyre-draw a thing. **1648** *Hunting of Fox* 23 To tug and wire-draw as Shoe-makers ordinarily do their leather between their hands and their teeth. **1656** Flecknoe *Diarium* 86 Such an art as his, Who wire-draw'd Simon to Simonides. *Ibid.* 92 But loath I am to stretch mine eares so far, As if they wire-drawn, or tenter'd were. **1656** F. Hawkins *Youths Behav.* (1661) 51 Perforations, through which Nature is wont to wyer draw spare humors into a fine spun excrescency [*sc.* hair]. *a* **1658** Cleveland *London Lady* 49 He wire-draws up his Jaws, and snuffs and grins. *a* **1701** Maundrell *Journ. Jerus.* (1721) 42 He never desisted from pulling his Beard, till he had wiredrawn it down to his Feet. **1849** D. J. Browne *Amer. Poultry Yd.* (1855) 163 The bird..has been actually wire-drawn. It has grown all the hours you have neglected it, without anything to grow from.

b. To cause (steam or water) to pass through a small aperture, thereby diminishing its pressure.

1744 Desaguliers *Course Exper. Philos.* II. 522 It must not be taken for a general Rule, that Wire-drawing the Water, as it is call'd, is always a Fault. **1787** M. Boulton *Let. to Jas. Watt* 1 Oct., Briggan always expanded the steam, great Poldice wiredraws it, as the valve opens very little indeed. **1802** *Specif. Trevethick's Patent* No. 2599. 2 This passage has a throttle valve..to wiredraw the steam.

3. *fig.* **a.** To draw or prolong to an inordinate length; to protract excessively, spin out.

1598 Florio, *Puntare*,..to wyre-draw any matter. **1611** Cotgr., *Tardiver*, to linger, foreslow, slacke, delay, wire-draw it. **1621** Burton *Anat. Mel.* ii. i. iv. i. 299 As an hungry Surgeon often doth prolong & wierdraw his cure so long as there is any hope of pay. **1641** J. Jackson *True Evang. T.* i. 40 His torments were so lengthened, and wire-drawne, to the end Christians might feele themselves dye. *a* **1693** *Urquhart's Rabelais* iii. xl. 332, I prorogate,..wyre-draw, and shift off the Time. **1782** Miss Burney *Cecilia* i. iii, They may contrive to fill up the middle and end of the evening by wire-drawing the comments afforded by the beginning. **1785** in Grose *Dict. Vulgar T.*

b. To draw out to an extreme tenuity; to reduce to a subtle fineness; to attenuate.

1660 Gauden *God's Gt. Demonstr.* 18 The superfluity of mans wit and eloquence glories to find out many inventions, definitions and distinctions, even in plain things; wire-drawing religion into fine threads. **1683** Cave *Ecclesiastici* 313 Having wiredrawn the Article concerning the Son of God into infinite Controversies and Disputes. **1796** Lamb *Let. to Coleridge* 13 June, Sonnets and all, they won't make a thousand lines as I propose completing 'em, and the substance must be wire-drawn. **1864** Lowell *Biglow P.* Introd., Poems 1890 II. 161 The school of Pope in verse ended by wire-drawing its phrase to such thinness that it could bear no weight of meaning whatever.

c. To strain, force, or wrest by subtle argument or the like.

1610 Carleton *Jurisd.* 288 Such as would proue this Iurisdiction from certaine texts of Scripture, as:..*oraui pro te Petre, &c.* And such like which are wire-drawen to countenance this Papall Iurisdiction. **1653** Gauden *Hierasp.* 530 He needes not wiredraw his conscience, till it fits every State passage. **1663** South *Serm.* (1717) V. 59 Nor am I for forcing, or wiredrawing the Sense of the Text. **1687** *Good Advice* 59 For while a man is out of Office, he is Test-free, but the hour he is chosen to any station..he must wyredraw his Conscience to hold it. **1700** Dryden *Fables* Pref. *A 2, Where I have been wrongfully accus'd, and my Sense wire-drawn into Blasphemy or Bawdry. **1765** Wesley *Let.* 14 May, Do not wrest, and wiredraw, and colour my words. **1812–29** Coleridge in *Lit. Rem.* (1838) III. 155 If our old divines..wire-drew their text, in the anxiety to evolve out of the words the fulness of the meaning. **1873** H. Rogers *Orig. Bible* iii. 115 Questions..which only tend to wiredraw the judgment.

absol. **1831** Emerson *Jrnl.* 25 Dec. (1909) II. 440 The rough and tumble old fellows, Bacons, Miltons, and Burkes don't wire-draw.

†d. To draw, bring, get, induce, extract, introduce, etc. by some subtle device. *Obs.*

1633 Marmion *Fine Comp.* iii. i, Although her husband be penurious,..Yet she can make him malleable, and worke him, And turne, and hammer him, and wire-draw him. **1650** Stapylton tr. *Strada's Low C. Wars* ii. 46 The Prince of Orange,..to wyer-draw the whole business out of the King, takes upon him to have been privy to the plot. *a* **1662** Heylin *Laud* (1668) 482 It was no hard matter for the Houses of Parliament to wire-draw him by degrees to such Condescensions. **1705** in Perry *Hist. Coll. Amer. Col. Ch.* (1870) I. 173 Among Mʳ. Commʸˢ 5 Arguments..is wire-drawn in a Sly ill look't insinuation. *a* **1734** North *Exam.* i. iii. §26. (1740) 138, I grant that Matter very fit to be taken

Notice of in the History of that Time; but then.. truly, as it was, and not only, as here is done, to wire-draw a Reflection from it. **1748** RICHARDSON *Clarissa* I. xliii. 303 If..I.. suspected, that she sought only to gain time, in order to wire-draw me into a consent.

†**e.** To draw or spin out *into* (also with colouring from c). *Obs.*

1648 HEYLIN *Relat. & Observ.* I. 135 In conclusion, after a tedious debate, the desires of the Citizens were referred to a Committee of the House to be wyer-drawne into an Ordinance. **1756** *Connoisseur* No. 118 ⁋8 [He] wire-drawed the books of Moses into a complete system of Natural Philosophy.

†**f.** *intr.* To be penurious or stingy; *trans.* to be overreaching or extortionate with. *Obs.*

1610 BEAUM. & FL. *Scornf. Lady* v. i, Thou hadst land and thousands, thou spendst, and flungst away, and yet it flows in double: I purchased, wrung, and wierdraw'd, for my wealth, lost, and was cozen'd. **1642** D. ROGERS *Naaman* 162 Seeing us wire-draw and castabout every way, rather then we will part with anything. *a* **1700** B. E. *Dict. Cant. Crew, Wire-draw*, to screw, over-reach, or deal hard with.

wire-drawer ('waɪə,drɔːə(r)). [f. WIRE *sb.* + DRAWER.]

1. One who draws metal into wire; one who practises or is skilled in wire-drawing.

1265 in C. W. Bardsley *Dict. Surnames*, Robert le Wyrdraere. **1320** in *Cal. Letter-bk. E. London* (1903) 136 [Emma, daughter of William] le Wirdrawiere. **1387-8** T. USK *Test. Love* III. vii. (Skeat) l. 103 The even draught of the wyr-drawer maketh the wyr to ben even and supple-werchinge. **1480** *Wardr. Acc. Edw. IV* (1830) 121 Rauff Vnderwood wyre-drawer for iij lb. and a quarteron of wyre of iren. **1589** [? LYLY] *Pappe w. Hatchet* 27 O, what a braue state of the Church it would be for all Ecclesiasticall causes to come before Weauers and Wierdrawers. **1656** T. VIOLET *Proposals* 52 Not to suffer either Refiner, Goldsmith or Wyer-drawer to melt the Coyn or Plate of the Nation, to make Gold or Silver Wyer. **1702** *Lond. Gaz.* No. 3810/8 The Master, Wardens, and Assistants of the Company of Gold and Silver Wire-Drawers. **1768** TUCKER *Lt. Nat.* (1834) I. 499 Like a wire-drawer, who takes a little bar of silver,.. and by driving it successively through smaller and smaller holes, brings it to a fineness fit for winding round a thread of silk. **1833** J. HOLLAND *Manuf. Metal* II. 346 It has all requisite qualities given to it in the workshop of the wire-drawer. **1881** *Instr. Census Clerks* 44 Wire Drawers' Plate Maker.

†**2.** In allusive phr. (***to go to the wire-drawer's***, etc.) or directly *fig.*, applied to one who spins out a matter to extreme length or draws it fine. *Obs.*

1566 Q. ELIZ. in Ellis *Orig. Lett.* Ser. I. II. 226 *note*, Are my wordes like lawiers bokes which nowe a dayes go to the wiar drawers to make subtall doings more plain? **1579** LYLY *Euphues* (Arb.) 106 Shee.. will either shut me out for a Wrangler, or cast mee off for a Wiredrawer. **1584** —— *Alex. & Camp.* v. iii, I meane to inioy the world, and to draw out my life at the wiredrawers, not to curtall it off at the Cuttelers. **1609** [BP. W. BARLOW] *Answ. Nameless Cath.* 309 For Tortus, according to his name, plaies the wire-drawer, and will needs stretch the resemblance, into an identity. **1623** WEBSTER *Duchess Malfi* I. ii, You play the wire-drawer with her commendations. **1805** W. TAYLOR in *Ann. Rev.* III. 649/1 The arts of amplification and illustration they cultivate in various manners; but they are still wire-drawers.

†**3.** One who plays on a stringed instrument. *jocular nonce-use.*

16.. MIDDLETON, etc. *Old Law* IV. i, *Clowne.* Is there no Musick in the house? *Drawer.* Yes sir, heere are sweet wire drawers.

4. *dial.* (See quot. and cf. WIRE-DRAW 3 f.)

1828 *Craven Gloss., Wire-drawer*, a covetous person, a penurious wretch.

5. *Comb.*, as ***wire-drawer-like*** adv. (cf. 2).

1611 COTGR. s.v. *Petit, Petit à petit*, faire and softly, now one and then one, wiredrawer-like.

'**wire-,drawing**, *vbl. sb.* [f. WIRE-DRAWER: see -ING[1].]

1. The action or operation of making wire by drawing a piece of ductile metal through a series of holes, successively decreasing in diameter, in a steel plate called a draw-plate. Also *attrib.*

1712 ARBUTHNOT *John Bull* III. viii. 33 Such Fellows are like your Wire-drawing Mills; if they get hold of a Man's Finger, they will pull in his whole Body at last. **1797** W. JOHNSTON tr. *Beckmann's Invent.* II. 232 The invention of the drawing-iron or proper wire-drawing. **1840** LARDNER *Geom.* xv. 177 The process of wire-drawing.. in which a cylindrical form.. is required to be imparted to the metal of which the wire is made. **1876** ROCK *Text. Fabr.* 22 The first use of a wire-drawing machine seems to have been about the year 1360, at Nuremberg.

2. *transf.* (See quots. and WIRE-DRAW *v.* 2 b.)

1660 D'ACRES *Water-Drawing* 35 The forceing & crowding of the water contrary to its own natural porousnesse, and as I may properly term it (as it were) a wyer-drawing of the water. **1875** R. F. MARTIN *Havrez' Winding Mach.* 90 Wire-drawing of the steam from passing through a contracted orifice. **1887** *Encycl. Brit.* XXII. 487/1 Wire-drawing of steam is.. a case of imperfectly-resisted expansion.

3. *fig.* (see WIRE-DRAW *v.* 3).

1640 DIGBY in *Lismore Papers* Ser. II. (1888) IV. 139, I am sorry to see thinges gotten by wyre drauing, which one may be sure before hand must be granted. **1648** C. WALKER *Hist. Independ.* I. 54 At length after much wyer-drawing of the businesse, one Warrant was shewn to Master Baynton. **1732** BERKELEY *Alciphr.* VII. §12 What Footsteps are there in the Holy Scripture to make us think, that the wiredrawing of abstract Ideas was a Task injoined either Jews or Christians? **1831** CARLYLE *Sart. Res.* III. x, We have often blamed him for a habit of wire-drawing and over-refining. **1877** CONDER *Basis Faith* ii. 68 To refine this discussion into the wire-drawing of verbal controversy.

So '**wire-,drawing** *ppl. a.* in fig. senses.

1741 RICHARDSON *Pamela* IV. vi. 37, I know the pretty wire-drawing ways of your Sex. **1756** BURKE *Vind. Nat. Soc.* Wks. 1906 I. 12 The history.. does not afford matter enough to fill ten pages, though it should be spun out by the wire-drawing amplification of a Guicciardini himself. **1831** CARLYLE *Sart. Res.* I. vi, An idle wire-drawing spirit.. is too clearly discernible.

wire-drawn ('waɪədrɔːn), *ppl. a.* [pa. pple. of WIRE-DRAW *v.*]

1. Drawn out to a great length or with subtle ingenuity; fine-spun; elaborately subtle, ingenious, or refined.

1603 FLORIO *Montaigne* I. xxvii. 96 A subject, common, bare-worne, and wyer-drawne [orig. *tracassé*] in a thousand bookes. **1610** B. JONSON *Alch.* III. ii, To.. shorten so your eares, against the hearing Of the next wire-drawne grace. **1642** D. ROGERS *Naaman* 138 The.. more subtill and wire-drawne selfe hath beene in deceiving the soule, the more the soule may abhorre her. **1662** HIBBERT *Syntagma Theol.* I. 196 There is no more certain signe of a bad cause than extended testimonies and wire-drawn arguments. **1715** FELTON *On the Classics* (1718) 137 What they call Improvement, is generally.. spinning out their Author's Sense, till 'tis wire-drawn, that is, weak and slender. **1732** BERKELEY *Alciphr.* v. §24 The.. wire-drawn distinctions.. of the Schoolmen. **1817** DIBDIN *Bibliogr. Decam.* I. 380 A very long note might grow out of this observation, but there is no necessity to be outrageously wire-drawn upon it. **1851** CARLYLE *Sterling* III. v, Courtly delicate manners, verging towards the wiredrawn and elaborate. **1873** HELPS *Anim. & Mast.* iv. 110 What a relief it is to come from the wiredrawn nonsense of Seneca, Thomas Aquinas, and Descartes, to the broad common sense of this thoughtful Scotchman [*sc.* Hume].

2. Of steam, water: see WIRE-DRAW *v.* 2 b.

1744 DESAGULIERS *Course Exper. Philos.* II. 522 Unless this wire-drawn water goes faster than at the Rate of four Feet in a Second, the Motion is not too swift. **1875** KNIGHT *Dict. Mech., Wire-drawn*.., the condition of steam when the pipes or ports leading to the cylinder have not sufficient carrying capacity. **1885** C. G. W. LOCK *Workshop Rec.* Ser. IV. 101/2 When the suction- or delivery-pipe is too small,.. the water is then called 'wire-drawn'.

3. Of a metal: Drawn into wire. *rare.*

1826 ADAMSON *Rail-Roads* 7 The under part will approach nearer to the condition of wire-drawn iron.

4. *nonce-uses.* Attenuated; 'weak'; 'thin'.

1856 DELAMER *Fl. Gard.* (1861) 12 A difficulty in town gardens is to keep things from being wire-drawn. **1876** HARDY *Ethelberta* xiii, 'I—am glad to see you!' Christopher stammered, with a wire-drawn, radically different smile from the one he had intended. **1897** CROCKETT *Lad's Love* iii, The keen, thin, wire-drawn voice of Peter Chrystie.

'**wire-grass.** [f. WIRE *sb.* + GRASS *sb.*] A name for various grasses or grass-like plants having wiry stems.

1. *U.S.* The British flat-stemmed meadow-grass *Poa compressa*, or the annual grass *Eleusine indica*, naturalized in North America.

1793 M. CUTLER in *Life*, etc. (1888) II. 294 Wire-grass, which is Poa compressa. **1856** OLMSTED *Slave States* 341 The wire-grass, which grew among the trees the previous year, is frequently set on fire.. in the spring. **1856** GRAY *Man. Bot.* (1860) 554 *Eleusine Indica.* Dog's-tail or Wire Grass. **1883** *Harper's Mag.* Oct. 710/2 The wire-grass had been roughly plaited into a little mat.

2. One of several other plants, as the West Indian *Paspalum filiforme*, the Australian *Tetrarrhena* (or *Ehrharta*) *juncea*, the North American *Sporobolus junceus* and species of *Aristida*.

1790 W. BLIGH *Narr. Mutiny on Board H.M.S. Bounty* 48 In the hollow of the land there grew some wire grass. **1824** BURCHELL *Trav.* II. 5 The Wire-grass of the island of St. Helena. **1864** GRISEBACH *Flora W. Ind. Isl.* 789 Wire-grass, *Paspalum filiforme*. **1883** E. M. CURR *Recoll. Squatting Victoria* viii. 81 The wire-grass, however, largely predominating over the kangaroo grass.

wireless ('waɪəlɪs), *a.* (*sb.*) [f. WIRE *sb.* + -LESS.]

A. *adj.* Without a wire or wires; spec. *Electr*, dispensing with the use of a conducting wire. ***wireless telegraphy***, a system of telegraphy (as that patented by Guglielmo Marconi in 1897) in which no conducting wire is used between the transmitting and receiving stations, the signals or messages being transmitted through space by means of electric waves; also, in British law, used to include wireless telephony; ***wireless telephony***: the transmission of speech and other uncoded signals by means of radio waves; = RADIO-TELEPHONY. Also ***wireless telegraph, telephone***. Now chiefly *hist.*, having been superseded by *radio*(-).

1894 *Westm. Gaz.* 22 Feb. 8/1 Not only may man be able some day to communicate by wireless telephone with the planets, but [etc.]. **1897** *Times* 18 Sept. 8/2 An electric bell was rung at the lighthouse by means of the wireless current. **1898** *Electrical Rev.* 20 May 688/2 The first installation of Marconi's wireless telegraph system in Ireland for business purposes was made.. last week. *Ibid.* 22 July 129/2 The wireless messages were sent from a steam tug, which followed the races. **1898** *Jrnl. Inst. Electr. Engineers* XXVII. 799 The general principles of electric space telegraphy—or wireless telegraphy, as it seems to wish to be called. **1903** C. H. SEWALL *Wireless Telegr.* I. 88 Wireless telephony. Telephoning without wires has not gained by the great developments in its sister-art. **1904** *Act 4 Edw. VII* c. 24 (*title*) An Act to provide for the regulation of Wireless Telegraphy. *Ibid.* §78 The expression 'wireless telegraphy' means any system of communication by telegraph.. without the aid of any wire connecting the points from and at which the messages or other communications are sent and received. **1906** S. R. BOTTONE tr. *Mazzotto's Wireless Telegr. & Teleph.* xi. 390 After the discovery of wireless telegraphy by means of electric waves, many attempts were made to apply the same principle to telephony. **1913** A. H. VERRILL *Harper's Wireless Bk.* xiii. 113 There is no reason to suppose that wireless telephony will not soon have the range of wireless telegraphy. **1922** JOYCE *Ulysses* 702 A private wireless telegraph which would transmit by dot and dash system the result of a national equine handicap. **1923** A. HUXLEY *On Margin* 49 If they are a little more up-to-date they adjust their wireless telephone to the right wave-length and listen-in to the fruity contralto at Marconi House, singing 'The Gleaner's Slumber Song'. **1936** G. B. SHAW *Simpleton Unexpected Isles* II. 51 (*stage-direction*) A writing table littered with papers and furnished with a wireless telephone. **1949** *Act 12 & 13 Geo. VI* c. 54. §685 The expression 'wireless telegraphy' means the emitting or receiving, over paths which are not provided by any material substance.. of electromagnetic energy of a frequency not exceeding three million megacycles a second, being energy which either—*a*) serves for the conveying of messages, sound or visual images.. or *b*) is used in connection with the determination of position, bearing or distance, or for the gaining of information as to the presence.. of any object. **1952** [see *sound radio* s.v. SOUND *sb.*[3] 8 b]. **1960** *Practical Wireless* XXXVI. 403/1 This station, which was built by Guglielmo Marconi, was the first to span the Atlantic with wireless telegraphy. **1981** *Daily Tel.* 12 Feb. 9/1 HMS Inskip, the Navy's wireless-telegraphy station, near Preston, Lancs.

B. *sb.* **1.** Wireless telegraphy or (esp.) telephony; sound broadcasting; = RADIO *sb.* 2 a, b; also, a particular radio station (= RADIO *sb.* 2 c).

Largely superseded by *radio* exc. in *hist.* contexts.

1903 *N.Y. Commercial Advertiser* 31 Jan. S 2/2 First in this great field of making the 'wireless' a handmaid of commerce is the de Forrest system, which has won the approval also of the United States government. **1904** *Times* 15 June 4/1 The country is full of wireless. **1915** GRAHAME-WHITE & HARPER *Aircraft in Gt. War* IV. xi. 150 The application of wireless to aeroplanes has, in the British Flying Corps, been studied very carefully. **1922** [see BROADCASTER 1]. **1924** [see SUPRANATIONAL *a.*]. **1927** C. CONNOLLY *Let.* 27 Jan. in *Romantic Friendship* (1975) 231 Chesterton is trying to be funny over the wireless. **1932** R. A. KNOX *Broadcast Minds* i. 13 We say 'the' wireless... For the wireless, in England, is a unique force; there is no question of two wirelesses differing, as two newspapers may differ in their outlook. **1939** *Daily Tel.* 18 Dec. 1/5 Moscow wireless claims advances in the Murmansk district. **1951** *Sport* 27 Apr.-3 May 2/1 Photos in the papers and interviews on the wireless. **1952** *Times Rev. of Year* 1 Jan. p. v/2 Sound radio (wireless declined farther towards archaism) has done much during the year. **1971** *Daily Tel.* 20 Jan. 10/3 [The Misses Waters] belong to the days when radio was 'the wireless'. **1978** E. BLISHEN *Sorry, Dad* II. i. 40 Wireless was still quite raw and improbable. The Dockrees next door had one... It was a crystal set. **1980** *Bookseller* 5 Jan. 23 The table shows the books recorded in December... Wireless and Television.. 42.

2. A radio-telegram.

1904 *Everybody's Mag.* Aug. 161/2 This is how it is taken down in those unerring short-hand notes of the recording angel and sent by special wireless to the typewriter for His Majesty of the Sulphur Trust. **1905** *Daily News* 28 Aug. 7 M. Witte admitted that my 'wireless' was correct. **1911** G. STRATTON-PORTER *Harvester* xvi. 351 Is Ajax [*sc.* a peacock] now sending a wireless to Ceylon asking for a mate? **1926** GALSWORTHY in *Scribner's Mag.* Aug. 192/1 Going home to have a look at Kit and send Fleur a wireless, he passed four musicians. **1940** N. MARSH *Surfeit of Lampreys* (1941) ii. 25 The steward gave her two [letters] and a wireless message. She opened the wireless first.

3. Short for *wireless set* (see sense 4 below); a radio.

1927 T. E. LAWRENCE *Let.* 4 Oct. (1938) 543 We have no wireless, and I don't look at papers. **1933** A. THIRKELL *High Rising* i. 16 He could.. repair the headmaster's wireless and drive his car. *a* **1944** K. DOUGLAS *Alamein to Zem Zem* (1946) 49 The wirelesses in the new tanks had to be checked. **1954** W. FAULKNER *Fable* 166 It's too bad every house he passes don't have a wireless, like ships do. **1971** *Daily Tel.* 13 May 7/1 As a child I used to stand alone in front of that big brown box that used to be called a 'wireless' and conduct symphony concerts. **1972** M. GILBERT *Petrella at Q* (1977) 37 P. C. Owers.. summoned assistance on his pocket wireless. **1973** [see *radio play* s.v. RADIO *sb.* 5 b].

4. *attrib.* and *Comb.*, in senses 1 and 3 above (in U.S., and increasingly in British use, replaced by the corresponding Combs. with *radio*), as ***wireless aerial, announcer, battery, broadcast, broadcasting, mast, operator, room, set, station, transmitter, valve***; ***wireless-equipped*** adj.; in the sense 'transmitted or broadcast by wireless', as ***wireless concert, news, play, programme, talk***; **wireless cabinet**, a cabinet incorporating a radio; **wireless licence**, an official permit needed for the possession of a radio; **wireless shack** = *radio shack* s.v. RADIO *sb.* 7; **wireless silence** = *radio silence* s.v. RADIO *sb.* 7; **wireless wave** = *radio wave* s.v. RADIO *sb.* 7.

1924 *Radio Times* 12 Dec. 527 (*caption*) Them's 'is wireless aerials. **1937** *Discovery* Feb. 37/1 The wireless aerial and its stays would become coated with an almost uniform layer of this frost. **1983** C. DEXTER *Riddle of Third Mile* i. 12 The voice.. of a pre-war wireless announcer... What they called an 'Oxford' accent. **1933** *Radio Times* 14 Apr. 83 (Advt.), Ever Ready wireless batteries. **1930** G. B. SHAW *Apple Cart* p. xi, Last October (1929) I was asked to address the enormous audience created by the new invention of Wireless Broadcast. **1980** J. LEES-MILNE *Harold Nicolson* I. xi. 205 On the 2nd May [1923]..he..heard a wireless broadcast over the air for the first time. **1923** *Radio Times* 28 Sept. 6 Wireless broadcasting service. **1930** KIPLING *Limits & Renewals* (1932) 208 [He] came back with a couple of cigarettes from the store behind the wireless cabinet. **1923** *Radio Times* 28 Sept. 18/1 Much has..been written on the subject of wireless concerts. **1920** *Conquest* May 328/1 Regular messages..from wireless-equipped vessels out in the Atlantic. **1920** *Radiograph* May 147 (Advt.), Applicants for wireless licence who specify them will not be required to furnish diagrams. **1928** *Melody Maker* Feb. 187 *(heading)* The over-taxed Frenchman! Wireless licences two-pence per annum. **1958** *Whitaker's Almanack 1959* 1098/1 If application is made at any other office which conducts wireless licence business, arrangements can be made for a licence to be issued at a Head Post Office. **1943** F. THOMPSON *Candleford Green* x. 167 Now..a wireless mast in every back garden. **1948** Wireless mast [see *rev-counter* s.v. REV *sb.* 2]. *c* **1919** H. C. WITWER *Smile a Minute* IV. iii. 158 Joe, I have just seen the wireless news [received on board ship]. **1926** in *Listener* (1974) 25 Apr. 519 Wireless news will be broadcasted by the B.B.C. **1942** E. WAUGH *Put out More Flags* ii. 139 She sat..listening to wireless news from Germany. **1978** P. G. WINSLOW *Coppergold* 127 Joss's death..had been on the wireless news. **1910** D. H. BERNARD *Signalling* 33 He..requested the wireless operator to ascertain the reason of the strange procedure. **1929** *Daily Express* 7 Nov. 1/1 Crew. Flight-Captain Rod Schinka..(first pilot)... Herr Niklas ..(wireless operator). **1978** F. MACLEAN *Take Nine Spies* iv. 138 Their mission had been joined by a second wireless-operator. **1929** *Radio Times* 8 Nov. 406/1 *Journey's End* was written for stage representation and is, therefore, not in the more restricted sense a 'wireless play'. **1948** D. WELCH *Jrnl.* 7 July (1952) 259 Last week there was a wireless programme on Marie Bashkirtseff. **1906** *Daily Chron.* 21 Aug. 4/3 The captain was absorbed in the 'wireless' room... As he himself said, he was 'so occupied with the wireless operations'. **1923** J. REITH *Diary* 19 Mar. (1975) ii. 131, I was standing talking to them with the wireless set at my back and I pushed the switch. *a* **1944** K. DOUGLAS *Alamein to Zem Zem* (1946) 25 About dusk the wireless sets in all tanks were switched on. **1978** *Dumfries Courier* 13 Oct. 10/4 In the 20 years up to 1950 the radio set—or wireless set as it was affectionately called—was the focal point of home entertainment. **1937** G. H. GRANT *Heels of Gale* vi. 59 The wireless shack..had been lifted on board by a crane on the day before sailing and bolted to the wooden planks. **1961** J. BISSET *Commodore* xxvii. 281 On this deck also was the Wireless Shack. **1915** LD. FISHER 12 Apr. in M. Gilbert *Winston S. Churchill* (1972) III. Compan. I. 793 It seems to me that the positions are all well chosen for all our different activities, and Jellicoe fully alive to wireless silence. *a* **1944** K. DOUGLAS *Alamein to Zem Zem* (1946) 49 Wireless silence was in force. **1909** *Chambers's Jrnl.* July 428/2 At Aldershot..there is a powerful wireless station. **1926** T. E. LAWRENCE *Seven Pillars* (1935) III. xxix. 170 My life was spent in moving back and forth..to the town, the port, the wireless station. **1978** D. A. STANWOOD *Memory of Eva Ryker* xxvi. 251 The Cape Race Wireless Station has a record of the message... It was transmitted from the *Titanic* five minutes before she struck ice. **1930** J. S. HUXLEY *Bird-Watching & Bird Behaviour* p. vii, Six wireless talks. **1923** *Radio Times* 28 Sept. 26/3 A small wireless transmitter will be installed at the 'Old Vic'. **1978** F. MACLEAN *Take Nine Spies* iv. 144 Bernhardt had established two wireless transmitters. **1923** *Radio Times* 28 Sept. 33 (Advt.), A new wireless valve. **1915** H. H. TURNER *Voyage in Space* vi. 250 Suppose you pretend that a second is itself like a year; divide it into..30 million parts; one of these tiny parts will be about the time that what we may call a 'wireless' wave of electricity takes to vibrate. **1936** *Discovery* Sept. 285/1 The reason why wireless waves travel round the earth's surface instead of disappearing into space has been explained by investigations of the properties of the upper atmosphere. **1960** *Practical Wireless* XXXVI. 403/1 Marconi announced that signals from Poldhu had bridged the Atlantic... That news..confounded the many learned critics who had said that wireless waves would never reach beyond the horizon.

Hence **'wireless** *v. intr.* to send a message by wireless; *trans.* to send (a message) or inform (a person) by wireless; **'wirelessly** *adv.*, by wireless.

1898 *Electrical Rev.* 17 June 834/2 The first news of the resolution..was conveyed wirelessly to St. Thomas's Hospital. **1899** *Westm. Gaz.* 6 Apr. 8/1 Touters may soon be able to wireless..from pole to pole. **1915** *Morning Post* 10 Apr. 9/5 A French man of war, which had left on Sunday, was wirelessed to come back. **1916** *Times* 14 Feb. 4/5 The watching British cruiser saw the manœuvre, but before it could wireless the news..the following order flashed out.

wireline ('waɪəlaɪn). Also wire line. [f. WIRE *sb.* + LINE *sb.*[2]] **1.** = *wire-mark (a)* s.v. WIRE *sb.* 16 a.

1858 *Sotheby's Principia Typogr.* III. 105 Owing to the leaves having been backed, the wire-lines could not be traced.

2. *Oil Industry.* **a.** A cable for lowering and raising tools and the like in a well shaft. Freq. *attrib.*

1916 A. B. THOMPSON *Oil-Field Devel. & Petroleum Mining* x. 468 At each pulley a short length of chain is inserted to accommodate the change of direction, and at each well a wire line can be led over the top derrick pulley and direct on to the pump. **1948** *Petroleum Handbk.* (Shell Internat. Petroleum Co.) (ed. 3) v. 92 Where a core head can drill more than 20 feet without getting dull, a retractable or 'wire line' inner-core barrel is used. After a core has been cut, the inner barrel containing the core can be brought to the surface with a wire line lowered inside the drill pipe. **1977** *Offshore Engineer* May 11/1 To prepare the well, the 'Christmas tree'..is..replaced with a temporary single-pipe ram preventer which allows wireline tools to be introduced.

b. An electric cable used to connect measuring devices in a well with indicating or recording instruments at the surface.

1972 L. M. HARRIS *Introd. Deepwater Floating Drilling Operations* ii. 6 Logging or other wireline operations. **1974** P. L. MOORE et al. *Drilling Practices Manual* xi. 279 The use of wireline logs for determining pore pressures is well documented. **1977** *Offshore Engineer* May 60/3 Various methods for monitoring grouting were used, including a radio-active isotope scheme.., and more conventional wireline temperature surveys.

3. A telegraph or telephone line of wire.

1934 in WEBSTER. **1947** *Trans. Amer. Inst. Electr. Engineers* LXVI. 492/3 The necessary frequency space for wide-band operation usually is not justified economically for wire line operation. **1983** *Mini-Micro Systems* July 240/2 The FCC is currently examining applications from wire-line and non-wire-line carriers for licenses to provide cellular mobile phone service in 30 large U.S. cities.

4. A fishing line of metal wire.

1974 *Encycl. Brit. Macropædia* VII. 374/1 Wire lines created from extruded Monel Metal or stainless steel assist in the sinking of a moving lure... But fish caught on metal or metal core lines are not eligible for International Game Fish Association records. **1984** *Miami Herald* 6 Apr. 9F/6 Boats are limited to four fishing lines... 'We allow use of the kite rig but do not permit use of wireline.'

wireman ('waɪəmən). [f. WIRE *sb.* + MAN *sb.*[1]] †**1.** One who makes or works in wire. *Obs.*

1547–8 in Feuillerat *Revels Edw. VI* (1914) 31 To Iohn west wyerman for ix[lb] of wyer. **1616** B. JONSON *Masques, Love restored*, Fortie other deuices I had, of Wyre-men. **1668** *Churchw. Acc. St. Margaret's, Westminster* (Nichols 1797) 70 To Christopher Davison, wyreman, for covering the vestry windows with wyre.

2. a. A workman who fixes and attends to the conducting wires of an electric service.

1881 *Instr. Census Clerks* (1885) 47 Telegraph Fitter, Wireman. **1902** F. C. RAPHAEL *'The Electrician Wireman's Pocket Bk.* Ed. Note, Such..Memoranda as would be useful to the Electric Light Wireman in his work.

b. A wire-tapper. *colloq.*

1973 *Telegraph* (Brisbane) 24 May 12/4 Watergate conspirator James McCord was one of the best 'wiremen' in the eavesdropping game. **1977** *Time* 21 Feb. 19 He had been one of the most sought-after 'wiremen', or electronic eavesdroppers, in the East, supplying bugging and recording devices to clients on both sides of the law.

3. A journalist working for a telegraphic news agency.

1973 D. MAY *Laughter in Djakarta* iv. 61 An American wire-man..who lived in Djakarta. **1977** 'J. LE CARRÉ' *Hon. Schoolboy* xv. 338 Keller was..a wireman..and Jerry knew him from other wars.

†**wiren**, *a. Obs.* In 6 *Sc.* wyrin. [f. WIRE *sb.* + -EN[4].] ***gold wiren***, of gold wire.

1513 DOUGLAS *Æneis* IV. iv. 19 Hir brycht tressis envolupit war and wound Intill a kuafe of fyne gold wyrin threid.

wirephoto ('waɪəfəʊtəʊ). orig. *U.S.* Also with hyphen and as two words. [f. WIRE *sb.* + PHOTO.] A facsimile process for transmitting pictures over telephone lines; also (*colloq.*), a photograph transmitted by this means.

1939 WEBSTER *Add.*, Wirephoto. **1940** *Chicago Daily Tribune* 11 May 1/3 All these pictures were sent..by radio and wirephoto. **1964** M. MCLUHAN *Understanding Media* II. xx. 203 The newspaper mesh of dots that is called 'wirephoto'. **1972** T. ARDIES *This Suitcase* xvii. 189 A picture of the teenaged Helmut Stern..came in last night via wirephoto. **1973** C. SAGAN *Cosmic Connection* (1974) xv. 109 The television pictures from *Mariner 9* were radioed from Mars to Earth in much the same way that a newsprint wire-photo is transmitted on Earth. **1981** 'D. SHANNON' *Murder Most Strange* vii. 147 The wire photo came in..and Higgins took it to show the Ortiz girl and she identified it.

So **wire-photograph**.

1962 *Listener* 12 July 57/1 Cartoonists in the United States rely for day-to-day material on newspaper morgues and wire-photographs. **1968** J. SANGSTER *Touchfeather* ix. 92 'Come and look at this.' The 'this' was a wire photograph... The transmission hadn't been up to much.

'wire-pull, *v.* [Back-formation from next.] *trans.* To actuate or promote by wire-pulling. Hence **'wire-pulled** *ppl. a.*

1883 *St. James's Gaz.* 28 Dec. 3/1 The whole company of wire-pulling and wire-pulled Radicals. **1888** *Engl. Hist. Rev.* Oct. 739 The King was but the crank by which Wildman wire-pulled the English royalists. **1896** SIR W. HARCOURT in *Westm. Gaz.* 8 May 7/1 They knew that the agitation was conducted, wire-pulled, and financed from the office of the Chartered Company in Capetown.

wire-puller ('waɪə,pʊlə(r)). [orig. U.S.; see WIRE *sb.* 8 a and PULL *v.* 7.] One who 'pulls the wires'; one who works secretly to further the interests of a person or party; *esp.* a politician or political agent who privately influences and directs others.

1833 in J. R. Commons et al. *Documentary Hist. Amer. Industr. Soc.* (1910) VIII. 340 Wire-pullers..for the furtherance of..party interest. **1848** *N.Y. Mirror* 5 June (Bartlett) Already that city [Philadelphia] is filled with wire-pullers,..and the whole brood of political make-shifts. **1859** GREEN *Oxf. Stud.* iv. (O.H.S.) 263 This youth breaks out..in a passionate loyalty to academical wire-pullers. **1898** G. W. E. RUSSELL *Coll. & Recoll.* iii. 35 The type of politician who is the despair of the official wire-puller.

So **'wire-,pulling** *vbl. sb.* and *ppl. a.*

1847 *Congressional Globe* 26 Jan. 262/3 Neither by demonstrations here, nor by figuring and wire-pulling at home, am I engaged to the support of this bill. **1876** 'E. PINTO' *Ye outside Fools!* 36 Let your clients try their best against the wire-pulling usurers. **1878** *N. Amer. Rev.* CXXVII. 9 Wretched, wire-pulling demagogues. **1887** *Sat. Rev.* 14 May 705/2 Literary wire-pulling and bargaining with publishers.

wirer ('waɪərə(r)). [f. WIRE *v.* or *sb.* + -ER[1].] One who wires (in various senses of the vb.); also (*slang*), one who picks pockets with a wire.

1857 DUCANGE ANGLICUS *Vulgar T.* 24 Wirer, pickpocket. **1864** TENNYSON *Aylmer's Field* 490 The nightly wirer of their innocent hare. **1881** *Instr. Census Clerks* (1885) 74 Straw Hat and Bonnet Making:..Presser, Liner, Wirer. **1901** *Daily Chron.* 10 Sept. 9/1 Mineral Water Trade.—Wanted..wirers, and bottlers. **1916** *Blackw. Mag.* Aug. 264/1 Then the wirers..began..to panic terribly, in code.

wirescape ('waɪəskeɪp). [f. WIRE *sb.* + SCAPE *sb.*[3], after *landscape*.] Scenery, or a scene, dominated by overhead wires and their supports.

1951 *Archit. Rev.* CX. 377 Wire, lots of wire, lining streets, crossing fields, acting as totems in villages and skeleton umbrellas on towns, by reducing the endless variety of the human and natural scene to the common denominator— wirescape—has made a dreadful uniformity out of the world it seeks to unite. **1959** *Times Lit. Suppl.* 9 Jan. 16/1 Each year the demands of the new industrial revolution gnaw away more insistently at the countryside... How many of us realize the Wirescape that impends? **1965** *New Statesman* 5 Nov. 713/1 The visual squalor, of which a notable feature is the appalling wirescape, of New York's periphery. **1969** E. SANDON *View into Village* x. 86 In the street is also to be seen that typically modern feature—an appalling wirescape. **1978** *Gold Coast Bulletin* (Austral.) 29 Sept. 7/1, I think we should be removing these unsightly wirescapes from the central precincts of the city.

wire-tap ('waɪətæp), *sb.* [Back-formation from next.] An act of tapping a telephone line, esp. as a form of surveillance; also, the device by which this is done.

1955 H. ROTH *Sleeper* xiv. 113 He had..refrained from any discussion of wire taps or followers. **1963** L. DEIGHTON *Horse under Water* xvii. 72 He has R.N. Signals Gibraltar doing a wire-tap job on me. **1976** *Billings* (Montana) *Gaz.* 11 July 7-A/1 Agents risked doing such things as roughing up antiwar radicals or placing illegal wiretaps. **1978** S. BRILL *Teamsters* iii. 103 The wiretaps were to end on March 6. **1982** H. KISSINGER *Years of Upheaval* iv. 103 The next morning it became apparent that Nixon had been talking about the wiretap records.

'wire-tapper. [f. WIRE *sb.* + TAPPER[1]. Cf. TAP *v.*[1] 2 c.] One who makes a (usually secret) connection to a telephone or telegraph circuit in order to intercept messages or eavesdrop.

1893 *Blue & Gray* Apr. 313/2 In that band of wire-tappers I had the honor to serve for four years. In 1863 I was appointed or employed as a telegraph operator in the field. **1894** *Columbus* (Ohio) *Disp.* 5 Jan., An attempt to tap the wires and 'work' the bookmakers..has been foiled... The wire tappers escaped. **1906** *N.Y. Tribune* 1 Feb. 8/2 On the day he bet his money, the wiretappers made it appear to Felix..that such sportsmen as James R. Keene and John W. Gates were betting thousands on Old Stone, through them, and advised him to 'get in on the good thing', too. **1910** 'O. HENRY' *Strictly Business* 36 Who wears the diamonds in this town? Why, Winnie, the Wiretapper's wife. **1929** *U.S. Rep.* CCLXXVII. 453 The wire tapper destroys this privacy... Does not wire tapping involve an 'unreasonable search' of the 'house' and of the 'person'? **1953** 'S. RANSOME' *Drag Dark* (1954) xv. 146 A call..couched in cryptic terms calculated to fool a wire tapper. **1969** *N.Y. Rev. Books* 2 Jan. 41/2 In the process, Macdonald proves himself more reprehensible than a wiretapper, for he uses intimacy, rather than electronics, to do his dirty work. **1977** 'J. D. WHITE' *Salzburg Affair* vi. 52 He could only drive on, find another telephone, in case the M.F.S. wire-tappers had traced the first call.

So **wire-tapping** *vbl. sb.*, the practice or activity of a wire-tapper; (as a back-formation) **'wire-tap** *v. trans.*, to tap the telephone line of; to monitor (a call) by means of a wire-tap.

1904 *Outing* Dec. 334/1 Despite the habitual exposure in American newspapers of the..'wire-tapping' swindle, the victim continues to be parted from his thousands with painful frequency. **1929** *U.S. Rep.* CCLXXVII. 474 The progress of science in furnishing the Government with means of espionage is not likely to stop with wire-tapping. **1952** W. R. BURNETT *Vanity Fair* vi. 56 Chad Bayliss did not want to discuss anything as important..over his apartment house phone... There had been a rash of wire-tapping. **1959** A. HARRINGTON *Life in 'Crystal Palace'* (1960) iv. 75 The private citizen is..being wire-tapped while he is looking for a job. **1973** *Times* 23 May 8/4 His telephone calls had not been wiretapped. **1973** *Black Panther* 21 July 2/3 The FBI, through their wire-tapping,..was practicing electronic surveillance. **1976** *National Observer* (U.S.) 27 Mar. 2/4 The U.S. Army may not wire tap American civilians in foreign countries unless it first gets a warrant from an American judge. **1978** R. NIXON *Memoirs* 388, I authorized Hoover to take the necessary steps—including wiretapping—to investigate the leaks. **1985** *Sunday Times* 20 Jan. 9/4 The U.S. customs officials say that his allegation of illegal wiretapping has been totally disproved.

wirework ('waɪəwɜːk).

1. The making of wire; work done in or with wire; fabrics or objects made of wire.

1587 in Feuillerat *Revels Q. Eliz.* (1908) 380 Edmond Burchall wierdrauer for wierworke. **1674** RAY *Coll. Words* 132 The manner of the Wire-work at Tintern in Monmouthshire. **1690** M. EVELYN *Fop-Dict.* 18 *Fil-grain'd*, dressing-Boxes, Baskets, or whatever else is made of Silver Wire-work. **1771** *Phil. Trans.* LXI. 322 Observe to clean the rails and wireworks, in the water-courses, of the weeds and grass. **1849** *Kelly's Builder's Price Bk.* 157 Brass trellis wire-work, for bookcases. **1854** *Poultry Chron.* I. 348 Wire work..to enclose poultry. **1908** *Act 8 Edw. VII* c. 28 Sched. 1 Erection of wireworks in hop gardens.

attrib. **1897** Mary Kingsley *W. Africa* xxviii. 611 Flower-stands..with wire-work legs.

2. *pl.* An establishment where wire is made or where wire goods are manufactured.

1598 *Acts Privy Counc.* (N.S.) XXVIII. 594 That the said Hanbery..should..deliver..at the said wyerwoorkes the number of 150 tonnes of..mallyable iron.

3. Wire-walking.

1906 *Variety* 3 Mar. 21/2 For sensationalism, the Meers in their wire work make the heart beat quicker. **1928** *Daily Express* 13 June 13/3, I learned acrobatics, wire work, dancing, and juggling.

wire-worker (ˈwaɪəˌwɜːkə(r)).

1. An artisan who works in wire.

1670 [Charter of Wire-workers of London]. **1792** *New Bath Directory* 24 Painter, Glazier, & Wire-worker. **1814** W. Johnston *Beckmann's Invent.* (ed. 2) IV. 309 Wire-workers, and other artists who use wire. **1846** McCulloch *Acc. Brit. Empire* (1854) I. 748 The paper manufacture creates a considerable demand for the labour of..wire-workers.

2. a. One who pulls the wires of a puppet-show. In quot. *fig.*

a **1843** Southey *Comm.-Pl. Bk.* (1851) IV. 260 Milton has *not* used machinery—for the supernatural powers are the characters of his poems, the agents themselves, not the wire-workers.

b. *U.S.* An earlier synonym of wire-puller.

1835 *Col. Crockett's Tour* (Phila.) 172 He is the wire-worker, the very mover and organ of all those high-handed and lawless measures. **1842** *Congressional Globe* App. 319/1 Should this be a party move,.. I tell the 'wire-workers' of that party that they are raising a storm of indignation. **1883** C. F. Wilder *Sister Ridnour's Sacrifice* 130 The politician grasps the hand of his wire-worker and tool.

3. = *wire-walker* s.v. wire *sb.* 16 a.

1970 M. Kelly *Spinifex* v. 91 She was one of the Flying Volantes, a bloody good wire worker.

So **ˈwire-ˌworking** *vbl. sb.* (*a*) the making of wire; (*b*) wire-pulling; also as *ppl. a*; hence also as back-formation) **wire-work** *v. trans.*, to influence by pulling wires.

1831 *American* (Harrodsburg, Ky.) 28 Jan. 3/2 One of the *wire-working* writers in the Union, seems disposed to consider it a little less than treason. **1835** Ure *Philos. Manuf.* 62 Rope-making and wire-working. **1843** J. Q. Adams *Diary* 23 Mar. (1876) XI. xxii. 343 James Monroe was recalled by President Washington through Thomas Pickering, wireworked by Alexander Hamilton. **1857** B. Hayes *Diary* 11 Sept. (1929) v. 167, I have kept aloof from the wire-working as well as from the more stormy scenes of politics. **1909** *Westm. Gaz.* 23 Feb. 2/2 Reducing to a minimum the ..wire-working that would follow, if details as to the schedules were permitted to leak out piecemeal.

wireworm (ˈwaɪəwɜːm).

1. The slender hard-skinned larva of any of the click-beetles (family *Elateridæ*), which is destructive to the roots of plants; also applied to similar larvæ, *esp.* the leather-jacket grub of the crane-fly.

1790 *Trans. Soc. Arts* VIII. 302 The person who shall discover to the Society an effectual method..of destroying the insect called the Wire-Worm. **1815** Kirby & Sp. *Entomol.* I. vi. 181 The wire-worm..destroying indiscriminately wheat, rye, oats, and grass. **1882** *Garden* 18 Mar. 189/3, I..found the crop quite eaten up with wireworm.

2. A myriapod, esp. one belonging to the genus *Iulus*; a millepede.

1875 Melliss *St. Helena* 202 *Julus pulchellus*, Leach.—The Wire Worm, well known as one of the most destructive insects in the Island to all root-crops.

ˈwire-wove, *ppl. a.* (occas. **-woven.**) [f. wire *sb.* + wove, pa. pple. of weave *v.*]

1. Denoting a very fine kind of paper used chiefly for letter-paper. (See wove.)

1799 *Spirit Publ. Jrnls.* III. 65 The splendours of gold leaf, wire-wove paper, and Morocco leather. **1808** [W. Gifford] *Heroic Epist. Winsor* Advt. to Rdr., I intend to print the Text upon a fine wire-woven hot-pressed paper. **1877** S. Redgrave *Descr. Catal. Water-Col. Paintings* 17 The papers..were chiefly of the description termed wire-wove.

2. Made of woven wire.

1888 *Builder* 3 Nov. 326/2 The roof of the Aquarium was being covered..with..'Patent Wire Wove Roofing'. **1897** *Allbutt's Syst. Med.* II. 169 A horse-hair mattress.. supported on a chain or wire-wove under-mattress.

wirey, obs. form of wiry *a.*

wirgine, -yne, obs. Sc. ff. virgin.

wirie, obs. form of worry.

wirily (ˈwaɪərɪlɪ), *adv.* [f. wiry *a.* + -ly².] In a wiry manner, like wire.

1846 Landor *Imag. Conv., Q. Eliz. & Dk. Anjou* Wks. II. 175/2 My grandfather, albeit spare, was wirily elastic. **1853** C. Brontë *Villette* xxii, A composite feeling..wound itself wirily round my heart.

wiriness (ˈwaɪərɪnɪs). [f. wiry *a.* + -ness.] The quality or condition of being wiry.

1801 *Med. Jrnl.* V. 210 Notwithstanding the rapidity of the circulation, and the apparent wiriness of the pulse. **1824-9** Good *Study Med.* (ed. 3) II. 46 Hardness and softness of the pulse, together with that vibratory thrill which has been called wiriness. **1831** *Examiner* 242/1 There is no marked change in her voice, except the absence of the wiriness and tremulousness which characterized it last year. *a* **1870** Stubbs *Lect. Eur. Hist.* I. xi. 135 There was..more wiriness than tenderness about his conscience. **1883** Miss M. Betham-Edwards *Disarmed* vi, You look wiriness itself.

wiring (ˈwaɪərɪŋ), *vbl. sb.* [f. wire *v.* + -ing¹.]

1. The action of the verb wire in various senses.

1809 Syd. Smith *Charac. Fox* Wks. 1859 I. 153/2 All the decretals of our ancestors respecting the wiring of hares. **1831** Youatt *Horse* 294 Lameness..does not always exist when the *wiring in* is slow or of long standing. **1872** *Punch* 29 June 269/2 Unless he telegraphs, which, when once you've started him at what he calls 'wiring', he generally does three or four times a day. **1874** J. D. Heath *Croquet-player* 71 Red, instead of playing thus,..completes the wiring, remaining near the hoop as before. **1890** *Pall Mall Gaz.* 29 Sept. 3/1 It discouraged scamped contract work in the [electric light] wiring of houses.

2. *concr.* Wires collectively; wirework; esp. the electric wires in an apparatus or building.

1809 Scott *Poacher* 79 Cordage for toils, and wiring for the snare. **1881** [see wire *v.* 2 d]. **1887** *Jrnl. Soc. Telegr.-Engineers* XVI. 182 This would be supplied from central stations (but without any outlay for insulated conductors beyond the 'wiring' of the actual domiciles to the extent rendered necessary by the number and position of the lamps required). **1897** S. Crane *Third Violet* xxv. 171 The cashier of the *Gamin* office looked under his respectable brass wiring and said [etc.]. **1915** *Sci. Amer.* 30 Jan. 95/2 A complicated 8-cylinder machine with its multiplication of wiring. **1923** *Wireless World* 5 May 135 (*caption*) The underside of the panel, showing the arrangement of the components and the wiring. **1958** C. Fremlin *Hours before Dawn* iii. 29 A rather cultured way of making me put a two-bar fire in her room. .. It's a matter of the wiring on the top floor. **1979** V. Capel *Burglar Alarm Systems* x. 107 This is about the worst place, as an intruder could soon silence the alarm by..cutting the bell wiring.

b. (See quot.)

1878 D. Kemp *Yacht & Boat Sailing* 380 *Wiring*, a stringer or ledge running fore and aft in a boat to support the thwarts.

3. *attrib.*, as ***wiring machine, system***; *Mil.* concerned with barbed-wire operations, as ***wiring party***; **wiring diagram,** a diagram of the wiring of an electrical installation or device, showing the electrical relationship of connections and components and usu. also their physical disposition; also *fig.*

1875 Knight *Dict. Mech.*, *Wiring-machine*,..a machine turning the edge of a tin-pan over a stiffening-wire. **1887** *Manch. Exhib. Catal.* 126 Complete Plants for the Manufacture of Aerated Waters,..Wiring Machine, [etc.]. **1902** W. C. Clinton *Electric Wiring* iii. 52 Wiring Systems. **1916** *Blackw. Mag.* May 705/2 Four nights previously Angus had been sent out in charge of a wiring-party. **1946** G. M. Chute *Electronics in Industry* viii. 63 Another kind of diagram..is called the connection or wiring diagram, because it shows the wire connections between the various parts. **1967** 'A. Cordell' *Bright Cantonese* xvii. 203 'There must be a switch assembly somewhere.'.. 'She gave me a wiring diagram.' **1969** *Times* 13 Feb. 10/3 He believes that until more is known about how the wiring diagram is modified, there can be little evidence in support of theories assuming that changes in nerve connexions are the basis of learning and memory. **1979** B. Scaddan *Mod. Electr. Installation* II. iv. 63 A circuit diagram shows how the system *functions*... A wiring diagram shows how the system is to be *wired*, and all components of the circuit should be shown in their correct places.

wirk(e, obs. forms of work.

wirken, dial. f. querken *v.*; obs. f. work *v.*

wirling (ˈwɜːlɪŋ). Now *Sc.* or *dial.* Forms: 4–6 **wyrling,** 5–6 **wirling,** (5 **wirlyng, wyrlyng(e, worling,** 6 **worlin,** 9 *Sc.* **wurlyon).** See also urling². [Origin unknown.] A term of abuse = 'wretch'; in mod. dial. use, a dwarfish or puny creature.

13.. *Metr. Hom.* (Vernon MS.) in Herrig's *Archiv* LVII. 270 Crist, his sone, God wolde not spare To beo fondet.. And sipen slen him as wyrling. *a* **1400-50** *Wars Alex.* 1706 A wirling, a wayryngle, a wawil-ȝeid shrewe. *Ibid.* 1733 A selly nounbre Of wrichis & wirlingis. **1436** *Libel Engl. Policy* in *Pol. Poems* (Rolls) II. 187 God forbede that a wylde Yrishe wyrlynge Shulde be chosene for to be there kynge. **1508** Dunbar *Flyting* 193 Forworthin wirling. *a* **1585** Montgomerie *Flyting* 446 Sauing, nixt, how the nunnes that worlin sould name. **1587** Harrison *Descr. Brit.* III. xiv. in *Holinshed*, The fridaie being commonlie called among the vulgar sort either king or worling, bicause it is either the fairest or foulest of the seauen [days]. [**1691-:** see urling².] **1819** [Rennie] *St. Patrick* II. xvi. 313 Haud abye! ye scruntet like wurlyon o' the pit.

wirlyk, wirm, wiroans, obs. forms of warlike, worm, werowance.

wirra (ˈwɪrə), *int. Irish.* Also **wurrah, whirra.** [Preceded by *oh*, = Ir. *a muire.*] An exclamation of sorrow or lament.

1829 G. Griffin *Collegians* I. vii. 153 O, wirra, Eily! this is the black day to your ould father. **1839** Carleton *Fardorougha* xii, Oh, wurrah, wurrah, this night! **1842** Lover *Handy Andy* xxii, And what was it at all? an upset, was it? oh, wirra! and wasn't it lucky he wasn't killed? **1908** Weyman *Wild Geese* xxiii. 366 'Oh, whirra, whirra, what'll I do?' the Irishman exclaimed, helplessly wringing his hands.

So **wirrasthru** (wɪrəsˈθruː) [Ir. *a muire is truaige*].

c **1874** D. Boucicault in M. R. Booth *Eng. Plays of 19th Cent.* (1969) II. 190 Ses he, 'You won't see home for six months.' Then I set up a wierasthru. *Ibid.* 214 Oh, weir asthru! What'll I do! **1892** T. E. Brown *Lett.* (1900) I. 158 He..rushed forth to catch the train,..with some wild wirrasthru of farewell.

wirra (ˈwɪrə), *sb. Austral.* [Aboriginal.] **1.** A species of acacia, *Acacia salicina*, burnt by Aborigines for its ash; = couba.

1906 J. H. Maiden *Wattles & Wattle-Barter* (ed. 3) 90 *A. salicina*, Lindl... Following are some additional aboriginal names..'Wirrha', Cooper's Creek, near Lake Eyre. **1941** I. L. Idriess *Great Boomerang* xiv. 102 Burned leaves of the wirra (a species of acacia, the leaves of which when burned yield a powder of potash).

2. A shallow wooden scoop used by Aborigines.

1935 H. H. Finlayson *Red Centre* vii. 74 A hunting party may decide suddenly to move on to another ground. Without more ado, the men reach for their spears and walk away, and their women follow, carrying no more than a yamstick, a *wirra*, and their youngest child. **1956** *Landfall* June 99 She carried two large pitchi, her four-foot-long mulga digging-stick, which she had freshly sharpened..by charring..; and her wirra, a shallow wood scoop.

wirrah (ˈwɪrə). *Austral.* [Aboriginal.] An Australian saltwater fish, *Acanthistius serratus* (family Serranidæ) that is greenish brown with blue spots.

1882 J. E. Tenison-Woods *Fish & Fisheries N.S.W.* 34 'Wirrah' or Plectropoma is a genus similar to that of Serranus, but armed with a row of spinous teeth on the lower jaw..besides the pair of canines above. **1933** *Bulletin* (Sydney) 11 Jan. 21 We had caught a number of more genteel fish, so we heaved the common wirrahs and leather-jackets overboard. **1978** J. M. Thomson *Field Guide Common Sea & Estuary Fishes Non-Tropical Austral.* 100 Except for the Wirrah most of the rock cods are regarded as good eating.

wirrangle, wirricow, wirrie: see wariangle, worricow, worry.

wirrock (ˈwɪrək). *Sc.* Also 6 **wyrok, virrok,** 9 **weerock.** [a. early Flem. *weerooghe* 'chalaza, chalazion' (Kilian), f. *weer* callosity (see warre) + *ooghe* eye *sb.*¹] A corn on the foot. Also *attrib.*

1500-20 Dunbar *Poems* xxviii. 18 A flyrok, That hes vpoun his feit a wyrok. *Ibid.* lx. 54 With his wawill-feitt and virrok taiss. **1801** Leyden *Compl. Scot.* Gloss. 380 *Virrok* [in Dunbar]..signifies a corn, or bony excrescence on the feet. It is in common use, and pronounced *wirrok.* **1839** W. McDowall *Poems* 154 (E.D.D.) Mary Hay, Wha had a weerock on each tae As big's a plum.

‖**wirrwarr** (ˈvɪrvar). [G. *wirrwarr.*] A welter.

1865 J. Grote *Moral Ideals* (1876) 392 The *wirrwarr* of the Newtonian or true view of the material universe. **1911** *Expositor* May 439 The strange and arid prejudice that history is only a wirr-warr of beings, happenings, relations.

wirs(s)at, -et, wirschep, wirsle, wirstill, wirst, wirsum: see worsted, worship, wrestle, wrist, worsum (*Obs.*, pus).

‖**Wirt** (vɪrt). In 9 **Wirth.** [Ger.] The landlord of a German inn.

1858 Geo. Eliot *Jrnl.* July in J. W. Cross *Life* (1885) II. viii. 48 The stout, red-faced *Wirth.* **1970** *Guardian* 28 Feb. 12/4 The Swabian *Weinstube* is a cosy place... The *Wirt* will make his round to bid every one of his guests a personal good evening.

wirt, obs. var. wherret.

1612 *North's Plutarch, Brutus* 994 Cassius..gaue him two good wirts on the eare.

wirt, wirtin, obs. forms of writ, written.

wirth, -y, obs. forms of worth, worthy.

‖**Wirtschaft** (ˈvɪrtʃaft). *rare.* In 9 **Wirth-.** [Ger.] **1.** Domestic economy, housekeeping.

1850 C. M. Yonge *Henrietta's Wish* ii. 21 The house.. was very soon pretty and cheerful, and the *wirthschaft*..well ordered and economical. **1889** —— *Reputed Changeling* I. viii. 138 The Doctor..[asked] whether the ladies abroad were given to housewifery. 'The German dames make a great ado about their *Wirthschaft*, as they call it..but as to the result! pah!'

2. [Ger., short for *gastwirtschaft*, f. *gast* guest *sb.*] = Wirtshaus.

1903 G. W. Hartley *Wild Sport* iii. 60 They had some beer at a snug little *wirtschaft*, and then they all fished. **1950** E. Hemingway *Across River* xxxviii. 269 What is there to eat in this *Wirtschaft*?

Hence **ˈWirtschaftswunder,** (*erron.*) **-schaftwunder** (-ˌvʊndər), the 'economic miracle' of West Germany, i.e. the substantial and lasting recovery in its economic state and standard of living following the war of 1939–45; also *transf.*

1959 *Times* 13 Mar. 16/3 Some of the pot-holes in the present age of prosperity, the *Wirtschaftswunder*, are laid bare in a manner that leaves little to the imagination. **1961** *Times* 10 Apr. 11/6 A *Wirtschaftswunder* incomparably greater than the Federal Republic's. **1965** *Punch* 22 Sept. 411/1 The peoples of both India and Pakistan are shockingly poor... There is no possibility here of miraculous recovery, the *Wirtschaftwunder.* **1980** 'D. Grant' *Emerald Decision* i. 14 My daughters..are products of the Socialist *wirtschaftwunder.* **1983** *London Mag.* July 62/1 The Germany of the mind's eye; not..the concrete cities of the Wirtschaftswunder.

‖**Wirtshaus** ('vɪrtshaʊs). In 9 Wirths-. Pl. **Wirtshäuser** (-hɔʏzər). [Ger.] In German-speaking countries: a hostelry, inn.

1829 C. Wilmot *Jrnl.* 6 Sept. (1935) 330 They..have a Wirthshaus and tables and chairs to eat and drink and be merry. **1967** *Sat. Rev.* 22 Apr. 37/2 They returned home with precious addresses of tiny bistros and *brasseries* and *osterias* and *Wirtshäuser.* **1982** G. Lyall *Conduct of Major Maxim* xx. 179, I have an unfinished beer at the *Wirtshaus.* Would you like to join me?

wirwe, obs. form of worry.

wiry ('waɪərɪ), *a.* Also 6-7 wy(e)rie, wiery, 8-9 wirey. [f. wire *sb.* + -y¹.]

1. Made or consisting of wire; in the form of wire.

1588 T. D[eloney] *Ballet Whips Spaniards* in *Roxb. Ballads* (1889) VI. 387 One sorte of whips they had for men, ..The strings whereof with wyerie knots like rowels they did frame. **1591** Spenser *Ruins of Time* 10 Her yeolow locks, like wyrie golde, About her shoulders careleslie downe trailing. **1598** Sylvester *Du Bartas* ii. ii. ii. *Babylon* 350 Jayes, that in their wyerie gail Can ask for victuals, and unvictual'd rail. *a* **1631** Donne *Eleg.* xix. 15 Off with that wyerie Coronet and shew The haiery Diademe which on you doth grow. **1720** Gay *Ep. to P. Methuen* 95 My song confines me to the wiry cage. **1816** Byron *Ch. Har.* iii. xv, The barr'd up bird will beat His breast and beak against his wiry dome. **1834** Landor *Exam. Shaks.* Wks. 1846 II. 272/1 To slit an ear or two, or inflict a wiry scourging. [See wire *sb.* 1 d.]

2. Resembling wire in form and consistence; tough and flexible: said esp. of hair (hence of a dog's coat), grass, stems of plants.

1595 Shaks. *John* iii. iv. 64 O what loue I note In the faire multitude of those her haires; Where but by chance a siluer drop hath falne, Euen to that drop ten thousand wiery friends Doe glew themselues in sociable griefe. **1807** Crabbe *Birth of Flattery* 308 The wiry moss, that whitens all the hill. **1812** —— *Tales* x. 120 Here on its wiry stem, in rigid bloom, Grows the salt lavender that lacks perfume. **1834** W. H. Ainsworth *Rookwood* i. i, A strange superannuated terrier, with a wiry back. **1844** *Jrnl. R. Agric. Soc.* V. i. 114 Clods of couch and wiry turf. **1880** Blackmore *Mary Anerley* xxv, While he was rubbing his wiry head with irritation.

b. *transf.* and *fig.*

1770 Armstrong *Misc.* I. 199 Your solid wirey nerves are asleep it would seem to the lute. **1809** W. Blake *Descr. Catal.* 63 The more distinct, sharp, and wirey the bounding line, the more perfect the work of art. **1815** J. Smith *Panorama Sci. & Art* II. 773 In the common method of etching,..those so tinted..always present a wiry hard effect. **1830** Lytton *Paul Clifford* iv, 'Knock him down'. There is something peculiarly harsh and stunning in those three, hard—wirey—sturdy—stubborn monosyllables.

c. *Med.* of the pulse: Small and tense.

1801 [implied in wiriness]. **1897** *Allbutt's Syst. Med.* III. 621 The pulse becomes small, sharp, wiry or thready.

3. Of sound: Produced by or as by the plucking or vibration of a wire; sometimes, of music, played on string instruments; of a voice, thin and metallic.

1819 [H. Busk] *Vestriad* iv. 767 Stridulous guitar with wiry twang. **1830** *Examiner* 388/1 He has..softened his voice, the tones of which were sharp and wiry. **1840** *Penny Cycl.* XVIII. 140/1 The tone of this piano-forte was thin and *wiry.* **1841** [see windy *a.* 1 b]. **1883** in *Royal Acad. Catal.* 222 With thy sweet fingers when thou gently sway'st The wiry concord.

4. Of a person or animal: Lean, tough, and sinewy. Hence *fig.* of personal attributes.

1808 Scott *Marm.* v. Introd. 11 Wiry terrier, rough and grim. **1848** Dickens *Dombey* xi, Mrs. Blimber..was a lady of great suavity, and a wiry figure. *a* **1870** Stubbs *Lect. Eur. Hist.* i. xi. 138 A wiry pertinacity was the distinctive feature of Charles's character. **1878** Black *Green Past.* xiii, The wiry little pony he rode.

5. *Comb.* (chiefly in sense 2), as ***wiry-coated, -haired, -leaved, -looking*** adjs.

1832 Carlyle *Remin.* (1881) I. 30 A slightish, wiry-looking old man. **1835** C. F. Hoffman *Winter in West* I. 155 A brindled, wiry-haired dog. **1854** R. S. Surtees *Handley Cr.* i, A wiry-looking bay mare. **1880** J. Buchanan *Indig. Grasses N.Z.* Pl. xxxi, *Danthonia Australis*,..Wiry-leaved Oat Grass.

¶ Used for: Made of iron: cf. wire *sb.* ¶ (at end).

1598 Sylvester *Du Bartas* ii. i. iv. *Handie-Crafts* 567 Wiery Cymbals [orig. *Des Cimbales le fer*].

wiry, wirykow: see worry, worricow.

†**wis**, *sb. Obs.* Also 4 wys. [Usually in inflected form *wisse, wysse*: absol. use of OE. *wis(s* adj. certain, in advb. phr. (see below). Cf. iwis C.] Phr. ***to wis(se)***, OE. *tó wissum* (for **tó (ʒe)wissum þinge*), ***mid wisse***, occas. ***in wis***: of a certainty, for certain. (Cf. wis *adv.*)

c **1000** Ælfric *Saints' Lives* xvii. 174 Ac wite ʒe to wissan þæt se wælhreowa deofol ne mæʒ mannum derian. *a* **1100** *Aldhelm Gloss.* i. 420 (Napier 13/1) *Præsertim, i. maxime, vel* to wissan. *Ibid.* 1051 (29/1) *Profecto, i. omnino,* to wissum. *a* **1200** *Moral Ode* 236 Nute hi hweþer hom deþ wurs mid [*v.r.* to] neure nane wisse. *c* **1200** Ormin 8460 Godess enngell comm himm to & seȝȝde himm þa to wisse Whillc ende off Issraæless land He shollde þanne sekenn. *c* **1200** *Trin. Coll. Hom.* 25 Ac sunderlepes he is here fader mid wisse. *c* **1250** *Gen. & Ex.* 1515 Oc god him sente reed in wis Ðat he bilef in gerasis. *c* **1380** *Sir Ferumb.* 120 Y knowe him wel to wisse. *Ibid.* 3763 Ther is non of ȝow þat wot to wys Wather he ys quyke or ded.

†**wis**, *v.*¹ *Obs.* Forms: 1 wissian, 2-3 wissien, (2 -ine), 3 wissi(n, wyssye, 3-5 wisse(n, 4 wiss, 4-5 wyssen, wis, 4-6 wys(se, 5 wyss. *β.* 5 wissh(e, wysshe, wysh, wish (wych), 5-6 wyshe, 6 *Sc.* wische. [OE. *wissian*, f. *wis* certain (cf. wis *sb.*) + *-ian*, -y²: a late formation on the model of the synonymous *wísian* wise *v.*¹]

1. *trans.* To make known, give information of, indicate; *esp.* to show, point out (the way).

c **1000** Ælfric *Gen.* xxxiii. 15 Ic bidde ðe þæt ðu nyme þe ladmenn of minum ʒeferum ðæt þe weʒas wission. *a* **1250** *Prov. Alfred* 29 in *O.E. Misc.* 104 He ou wolde wyssye wisliche þinges. *a* **1300** *Cursor M.* 25447 Lauerd..wiss me waies þare þare santes has þair seli sete. **1362** Langl. *P. Pl.* A. vi. 24 Const þou wissen vs þe wey wher þat he dwelleþ? *c* **1375** *Sc. Leg. Saints* xxxviii. (*Adrian*) 619, I sal wis ȝou þe rycht way. *a* **1400-50** *Wars Alex.* 689 Is oȝt þi werid to þe wissid [*v.r.* wist]? *Ibid.* 4997 And quat þou will of þaim to wete wis in þi saghe. *c* **1440** Capgrave *Life St. Kath.* v. 1929 þat she may vs wisse A stedefast lore for to amende oure mysse. **1460** *Paston Lett.* I. 518 If my feodaryes..may ought wisse therin, lete them se it.

β. *c* **1400** *Beryn* 3290 Met I nevir creature þat me coude wissh or say Reedynes of my ffadir, dede othir a-lyve. *c* **1460** *Towneley Myst.* xv. 156 He that this warld began, wysh vs the way! **1535** Lyndesay *Satyre* 1929 Wische me the richt way till Sanct-Androes.

b. Const. dependent interrog. clause.

c **1000** Ælfric *Saints' Lives* v. 253 Se cræft sceolde wissian ʒewisslice be steorrum hwæt ʒehwilcum menn ʒelumpe on his lifes endebyrdnysse. *c* **1175** *Lamb. Hom.* 37 He is iset bi-twihan god almihtin and þe for þe wissine hu þu scalt et god seolf habben þine sunne forȝeuene. *c* **1325** *Spec. Gy Warw.* 119 What it is i wole þe wisse. **1362** Langl. *P. Pl.* A. xii. 40 She wolde me wisse wher þe toun were. *c* **1412** Hoccleve *De Reg. Princ.* 1245 Wisseth me how to gete a golden salue. *c* **1450** *St. Cuthbert* (Surtees) 2633 þou may me wysse How lang þe kyngdome sall be hyss.

2. To show the way to (a person); to direct, guide; to lead, conduct (*lit.* or *fig.*). Also *absol.*

c **1000** Ælfric *Hom.* I. 324 Ælces mannes weorc cyðað hwilc gast hine wissað. *a* **1023** Wulfstan *Hom.* xix. (1883) 108 þa ðe him betæhte sindon for gode to wissianne. *c* **1175** *Lamb. Hom.* 89 Godes ȝife us wissað [Ælfric *Hom.* I. 312 ʒewissað] to his willen. *c* **1290** *S. Eng. Leg.* I. 390/41 God.. us leue..ore lif so wisse þat we..comen to heouene blisse. **1340** Hampole *Pr. Consc.* 9304 God..þat þam gun wysse Til mekenes. **1340-70** *Alisaunder* 806 Amon þe grete God.. Schall þee wisse fro wo. **13..** *Gaw. & Gr. Knt.* 739 þe knyȝt ..To Mary made his mone, þat ho..wysse hym to sum wone. *c* **1425** *Engl. Conq. Ireland* 95 He wissed the hors sydlynge ayeynes the watyr asquynt. *c* **1425** *Seven Sag.* (P.) 2366 Thy seven Clerkys, That wyssys the to wykkyd werkys. *c* **1430** *Pistill of Susan* 213 (Cott. MS.) Wylyly hyr wenches she wyssed a-way. *c* **1440** *York Myst.* i. 157 To all I sall wirke be ȝhe wysshyng. *c* **1530** *Songs, Carols,* etc. (E.E.T.S.) 51, & vertuosly me wysse to godward! *c* **1550** Wever *Lusty Juventus* (facs. Awdely) A ij b, I pray you wyshe me thether, For I am going to seeke them.

b. To manage, rule, govern, control.

c **1000** Ælfric in Morris *O.E. Hom.* I. 302 Rex we cwæþað cyning, þæt is ʒecweden wissiʒend, forþam þe he sceal wissiʒan mid wisdome his folce. *c* **1205** Lay. 5280 þe sculden witen þat lond & wissien þa leoden. *c* **1290** *Beket* 1059 in *S. Eng. Leg.* 136 Vnneþe he miȝte with is hondene þeos þre þingus do; blessi þat folk and bere þe croiz and is bridel wisse. *a* **1300** *Cursor M.* 5292 þe lauerd-hed of al his land To wiss and ledd. *a* **1470** Harding *Chron.* cxx. xxii. (1812) 232 He made duke Harold protectoure Of his cousyne, to gouerne and to wysse Edgar Athelyng.

3. with person as obj. (orig. dat.) and (freq.) inf. with *to*: To give directions or instructions to; to direct, order; to instruct, show how (*to do* something); also *gen.* to teach, instruct.

c **1000** Ælfric *Num.* xxiii. 8 He witeʒode þa, swa him wissode god. *c* **1200** *Trin. Coll. Hom.* 7 He..wisseþ us to leden ure lif on clennesse. *a* **1300** *Cursor M.* 17201 If þou wil werc als i þe wiss. *Ibid.* 20536 Thritti winter and sumdel mare, I lenged man to wiss in lare. *c* **1374** Chaucer *Troylus* i. 622 Thow koudest neuere yn loue þyn seluen wysse. **1399** Langl. *Rich. Redeles* Prol. 31 For to written him a writte to wissen him better. ? *a* **1400** *Morte Arth.* 9 And wysse me to werpe owte some worde. **1486** *Bk. St. Albans* e iv, And ye speke of the Bucke the fyrst yere he is A fawne sowkyng on his dam say, as I yow wis.

wis (wɪs), *v.*² *pseudo-arch.* Also 7 (3 *pers. sing.*) wisses, 9 wiss. Orig. in *I wis* = iwis *adv.* (q.v.) erron. taken as = 'I know'; hence occas. as a synonym of 'know' in other parts of the verb, being apprehended as the present of *wist*, pa. t. of wit *v.*¹

[The following show various stages of corruption of *iwis*:—

1508 Dunbar *Tua Mariit Wemen* 37 Ane wes ane wedow, I wist. *Ibid.* 414 Now am I a wedow, I wise. **1591** Shaks. *1 Hen. VI*, iv. i. 180 And if I wish he did. But let it rest. **1614** W. Browne *Sheph. Pipe* C 6, Better cannot be I wist, Descant on it he that list. **1615** Brathwait *Strappado* 115 Strange the Proiect was I wish Of this Metamorphosis. **1798** Coleridge *Anc. Mar.* iii. ii, It moved and moved, and took at last A certain shape, I wist. **1818** Byron *To Mr. Murray* v, Tours, Travels, Essays, too, I wist, And Sermons to thy mill bring grist. **1893** F. Thompson *Poems* 15 Wings, I wist, Whose amethyst Trepidations have forgone me.]

1606 *Lyly's Euphues* (1613) Y 1 b, You gall mee more with these tearmes then you wisse [*ed.* 1580 wist, 1597 wish]. **1642** Milton *Apol. Smect.* 13 Where my morning haunts are he wisses not. [Cf. **1642** [? J. Hall] *Modest Confut.* To Rdr. A iij b, Where his morning haunts are I wist not.] **1662** A. Cooper *Stratologia* ii. 47 Morgan more valorous than hee wis'd or wil'd. **1803** W. S. Rose *Amadis* 31 Full well I wiss To serve your princely will were perfect bliss. *c* **1830** Coleridge *Alice Du Clos* 77 And, bonny boy, you wis, Lord Julian is a hasty man. **1844** Mrs. Browning *Romaunt of Page* xxiii, In the dark chambère, if the bride was fair, Ye wis, I could not see.

†**wis**, *adv. Obs.* Also 3-4 wiss, 4-5 wys, 6 wusse. [Aphetic form of iwis, q.v. (cf. wis *sb.*).] Certainly, assuredly.

c **1200** Ormin 2866 Wiss to soþe. *Ibid.* 7410 þeȝȝ sindenn wiss hundess & swin þurrh þeȝȝre laþe sinness. *a* **1225** *Ancr. R.* 38 Alse wis ase iðen ilke flesche þet he nom of þe nes neuer sunne [etc.]. *a* **1300** *Cursor M.* 1863 þat mighti king, ful son and wiss, Did turn þair baret in-to blis. *c* **1330** *Amis & Amil.* 1292 The steward swore the pople among, As wis as he seyd no wrong, God help him at his nede! *c* **1386** Chaucer *Frankl. T.* 742 God helpe me so as wys This is to muche. **1390** Gower *Conf.* II. 276 Als so wiss mot I be schrive. *c* **1400** *Rom. Rose* 6433 God so wys be my socour [orig. *si m'aist Diex*]. **1598** B. Jonson *Ev. Man in Hum.* i. i, *Kno.* Why, I hope you will not a hawking now, will you? *Ste.* No wusse.

wis, obs. f. wise; obs. Sc. f. wish.

wisage, obs. Sc. f. visage.

wisall, obs. var. of wizle *dial.*

wisard, obs. f. wizard.

wisch(e, obs. Sc. pa. t. of wash *v.*; var. wis *v.*¹; obs. f. wish *sb.* and *v.*

wischcraft, wischeaf, wischeall, obs. Sc. ff. witchcraft, vouchsafe, vessel.

Wisconsin (wɪs'kɒnsɪn). *Geol.* The name of a state of the north central U.S.A., used *attrib.* and *absol.* to designate (the time of) the fourth and final Pleistocene glaciation of North America, corresponding to the Würm glaciation of the Alps.

[**1894** T. C. Chamberlin in J. Geikie *Gt. Ice Age* (ed. 3) xlii. 763 All this complex is grouped under a single term —the East-Wisconsin formation—because the grounds for a formal subdivision are not yet sufficiently clear.] **1895** *Amer. Naturalist* XXIX. 240 The second, third, and fourth glacial stages of the European Ice age..were probably also time equivalents, respectively, with the Kansan, Iowa, and Wisconsin stages in the United States and Canada. **1896,** etc. [see Illinoian *a.*]. **1967** E. B. Leopold in Martin & Wright *Pleistocene Extinctions* 235 Taylor considers that the Pliocene and Quaternary climates before the late Wisconsin were much less continental than now. **1981** J. E. Sanders *Princ. Physical Geol.* xiii. 332 The last ice mass to cover the Great Lakes basin arrived during the late Wisconsin Stage, starting 20,000 years ago.

Hence **Wi'sconsinan** *a.* (also *absol.*).

1968 [see Weichsel]. **1978** *Nature* 8 June 456/2 These volcanics are thought to have been formed under ice of Wisconsinan age. **1981** F. W. Shotton in Neale & Flenley *Quaternary in Brit.* xiii. 142 This is the way the Wisconsinan ice invading the U.S.A. from the Canadian Shield is interpreted.

wisdom ('wɪzdəm). Forms: 1- wisdom; 3 (*Orm.*) wissdom, (wistom), 3-5 wysdom, wisdam, 3-7 wisedom, wisdome, 4 wisdame, (wijsdam), 4-6 wysdome, (*Sc.* visdome), 4-7 wisedome, 5 wisedam, wysdam(e, wysedom, (wijsdom, wysedomme, wiesdom, vysdome, whysdom), 5-6 wysedome, (6 wisdoume, -dum(e, wisz-, wyszdome, 7 *Sc.* wosdome). [OE. *wísdóm* = OFris., OS. *wîsdôm*, MDu. *wijsdom*, OHG., MHG. *wîstuom* (G. *weistum* legal sentence, precedent), ON. *vísdómr* (Sw., Da. *visdom*): see wise *a.* and -dom.] The quality or character of being wise, or something in which this is exhibited.

1. a. Capacity of judging rightly in matters relating to life and conduct; soundness of judgement in the choice of means and ends; sometimes, less strictly, sound sense, esp. in practical affairs: opp. to *folly.*

Beowulf 1959 Offa wæs..wide geweorðod, wisdome heold eðel sinne. *c* **1000** *Inst. Polity* ii. in Thorpe *Laws* II. 306 Ðurh cyningces wisdom folc wyrð ʒesælig, ʒesundful, & siʒefæst. *c* **1175** *Lamb. Hom.* 123 þet wit and þene wisdom þe ure drihten us sende. *c* **1200** Ormin 8974 Hire sune wex & þraf i wissdom & inn elde. *a* **1225** *Ancr. R.* 6 He mai þe vttre riwle chaungen, efter wisdom. *a* **1225** *Leg. Kath.* 485 Ichulle fordon þe wisdom of þeos wise worldmen. *a* **1300** *Cursor M.* 8857 Godd ne had him sli wisdom Giuen, als he gaf salamon. **1340-70** *Alex. & Dind.* 102 ȝif god sente euery gome.. Wordliche wisdam & wittus iliche. *a* **1375** *Cato* 409 in *Minor Poems fr. Vernon MS.* 587 Forþure þi wille wiþ wisdam. *c* **1400** *26 Pol. Poems* x. 21 At þe tre of wysdom, foly þou souȝt. **1450-1530** *Myrr. our Ladye* ii. 183 The mooste wyse wysdome of god. **1513** More *Edw. V* in Hall *Chron., Edw. V* (1548) 2 b, Yf grace turne hym to wisedome. **1535** Coverdale *Prov.* ix. 10 The feare of the Lorde is the begynnynge of wysdome. **1563** *Homilies, Rogation Wk.* iii. Rrrrj, Thys wisdome can not be atteyned, but by the direction of the spirite of God, and therefore it is called spirituall wisdome. **1594** Shaks. *Rich. III*, iii. vii. 16 Your Discipline in Warre, Wisdome in Peace. **1597** Hooker *Eccl. Pol.* v. lvi. §5 That which moueth God to worke is goodnes, and that which ordereth his worke is wisedome. **1633** G. Herbert *Temple, Providence* xvi, Each creature hath a wisdome for his good. **1640** Wilkins *Disc. New Planet* ix. 204 Wee allow every Watch-maker so much wisdome as not to put any motion in his Instrument, which is superfluous. *a* **1708** Beveridge *Thes. Theol.* (1711) III. 28 By wisdom, I mean that attribute in God, whereby He orders and manages whatsoever He takes in hand, by the best means, in the best manner and to the best end. **1784** Cowper *Task* vi. 88 Knowledge and Wisdom, far from being one, Have ofttimes no connexion. **1875** Manning *Mission Holy Ghost*

xiv. 385 Illumination of the intellect, together with charity inflaming the heart, constitute the gift of wisdom.

b. personified (almost always as feminine).

c **888** ÆLFRED *Boeth.* iii. §1 Þa com þær gan in to me heofencund Wisdom. *c* **1000** *Ags. Gosp.* Matt. xi. 19 Wisdom ys ȝerihtwisud fram heora bearnum. **1362** LANGL. *P. Pl.* A. IV. 87 He haþ waget me a-mendes as wisdam him tauhte. **1535** COVERDALE *Prov.* viii. 1 Doth not wysdome crie? doth not vnderstondinge put forth hir voyce? **1597** HOOKER *Eccl. Pol.* V. viii. §1 To prescribe the order of doing ..is a peculiar prerogatiue which Wisedome hath, as Queene or soueraigne commandresse ouer other vertues. **1611** *Bible* Transl. Pref. ¶4 Loue the Scriptures, and wisedome will loue thee. **1742** GRAY *Adversity* 25 Wisdom in sable garb array'd Immers'd in rapt'rous thought profound. **1784** COWPER *Task* VI. 97 Knowledge is proud that he has learned so much, Wisdom is humble that he knows no more. **1802** WORDSW. '*I grieved for Buonaparté*' 9 Wisdom doth live with children round her knees. **1850** TENNYSON *In Mem.* CXIV. 22 For she [*sc.* Knowledge] is earthly of the mind, But Wisdom heavenly of the soul.

c. as one of the manifestations of the divine nature in Jesus Christ (cf. 1 Cor. i. 24, 30, etc.); hence used as a title of the second person of the Trinity (***the Wisdom of the Father***); also occas. applied to God or the Trinity.

c **888** ÆLFRED *Boeth.* xli. §4 Se wisdom mæȝ us eallunga onȝitan swylce swylce we sint..forðæm se wisdom is God. *a* **1175** *Cott. Hom.* 219 Þurh his wisdom (se sune) heo ȝe-worhte alle þing. *c* **1200** *Vices & Virtues* 25 Ðe sune of ðe fader akenned, al swa his wisedom. *a* **1225** *Ancr. R.* 26 Almihti God, Feder, & Sune, & soðfest Holi Gost, also ȝe þreo beoð o God, & o mihte, o wisdom, & o luue. *a* **1300** *Cursor M.* 9730. **1402** *Jacke Upland* in *Pol. Poems* (Rolls) II. 36 Christ, that is the wisedome of God the Father. **1587** GOLDING *De Mornay* v. (1592) 53 We call him also the wisedome of the Father, yea, and euen meerely and simply wisedome. **1833** NEWMAN *Arians* II. iii. (1876) 169 It would appear that our Lord is called the Word or Wisdom in two respects; first, to denote His essential presence in the Father ..: secondly, His mediatorship. **1855** LYNCH *Lett. to Scattered* ii. (1872) 32 Wisdom is alive: it is not a thing or quality. It is God. It is God and Man, for it is Christ.

d. Contextually, usually predicative with following inf.: = a wise thing to do; also with *a* and *pl.*, a piece of wisdom; a wise action or proceeding. (Opp. to FOLLY *sb.*^{1} 1 c.) *arch.*

1362 LANGL. *P. Pl.* A. VII. 201 Here nou..and holde hit for wisdam. *c* **1420** HOCCLEVE *Min. Poems* xxiv. 215 Is it wysdam as þat it seemeth yow, Were it on your fyngir continuelly? **1482** *Cely Papers* (Camden) 87 Hyt wylbe whysdom to be sewyr of mo. **1593** SHAKS. *3 Hen. VI*, IV. vii. 60 Till then, 'tis wisdome to conceale our meaning. *a* **1628** F. GREVIL *Sidney* (1652) 2 Had I grounded my ends upon active Wisedomes of the present. **1764** PRIESTLEY *Lect. Hist., Ess. Educ.* (1788) p. xv, It is certainly our wisdom to contrive that the studies of youth should tend to fit them for the business of manhood. **1831** SCOTT *Ct. Rob.* xviii, It is wisdom to choose a better protector. **1884** HELEN JACKSON *Ramona* i, If she had ever said anything about herself, which she never did—one of her many wisdoms.

e. (*a*) *pl.* as attribute of a number of persons; hence, with possessive, as a title of dignity or respect, esp. for the members of a deliberative assembly; also jocularly or ironically. Similarly, without possessive, as in ***the best wisdoms*** = the wisest men.

1432 *Rolls of Parlt.* IV. 403/2 To the right wyse and discrete Commens of this present Parlement... Please hit unto youre worthy and noble wisdoms and discretions [etc.]. **1447–8** *Shillingford's Lett.* (Camden) 108 As hit appereth of recorde the whiche they remytte to your wysedomys. **1536** CROMWELL in Merriman *Life & Lett.* (1902) II. 2 As by your wisedomes ye shall thinke may best serue for the kinges highnes purpose. **1587** D. FENNER *Def. Ministers* 60 It may please their wisedomes, who are to be Iudges, to consider. **1619** J. DENISON *Heav. Banquet* etc. 317, I will leaue that to their wisedomes who haue place of gouernment. **1631** MARKHAM *Country Contentm.* I. xix. (ed. 4) 103 Many of the best wisedomes of our Nation. **1794** WOLCOT (P. Pindar) *Ode to Tyrants* Wks. 1812 III. 253 Even Folly..freely on your Wisdoms cracks her jokes.

(*b*) Less commonly in *sing.* of a single person.

1447–8 *Shillingford's Lett.* (Camden) 42 Not likely by that mene to be ended lightly, as your wysedom knowyth well. **1598** HAKLUYT *Voy.* Ep. Ded. ¶3 The chiefe motiues which induced his princely wisedome hereunto. **1612** J. COTTA *Disc. Dang. Pract. Phys.* I. ix. 72 The parents..sent for a wisewoman, & her wisedome came vnto them. *a* **1652** A. WILSON in Peck *Desid. Curiosa* (1735) II. XII. 24 The Maior's Wisdom said, hee knew not my Lord's Hand. **1831** SCOTT *Ct. Rob.* viii, Can your wisdom possibly entertain a wish to converse with me?

f. Phr. ***in his*** (or ***its,*** etc.) ***wisdom***: now usually ironic.

1852 QUEEN VICTORIA in *Hansard* CXXIII. 20 To enable the Industry of the Country to meet successfully that unrestricted Competition to which Parliament, in its Wisdom, has decided that it should be subjected. **1863** N. HAWTHORNE *Our Old Home* 397 Possibly his Lordship thought, in his wisdom, that the good feeling which was sure to be expressed by a company of well-bred Englishmen, at his august and far-famed dinner table, might have an appreciable influence on the grand result. **1930** W. FAULKNER *As I lay Dying* 68 If you have no son, it's because the Lord has decreed otherwise in His wisdom. **1974** K. CLARK *Another Part of Wood* vi. 232 In the 1930's, when the country was at least ten times as rich as it is today, the Treasury 'in its wisdom' twice found it necessary to cut off our annual purchase grant altogether.

2. a. Knowledge (esp. of a high or abstruse kind); enlightenment, learning, erudition; in early use often = philosophy, science. †Also, practical knowledge or understanding, expertness in an art. Now only *Hist.*

c **950** *Lindisf. Gosp.* Luke xi. 52 *Tulistis clauem scientiae*, ȝie nomon cæȝo wisdomes. **1382** WYCLIF *1 Cor.* ii. 13 Not in tauȝt wordis of mannis wysdom, but in doctryne of the spirit. *c* **1386** CHAUCER *Prol.* 575 The wisdom of an heepe of lerned men Of maistres hadde he mo than thries ten. **1460–70** *Bk. Quinte Essence* 1 Þe wijsdom and þe science of þis book schulde..be..preserued. **1526** TINDALE *Acts* vii. 22 Moses was learned in all manner off wisdom of the Egipcians. **1557** in Lodge *Illustr. Brit. Hist.* (1791) I. 276 The Quene's Matie, knowing the wysdome and skyll of John Brende, Esquier, in the leading and ordering of footemen. **1662** J. CHANDLER *Van Helmont's Oriat.* 163 This..was Zoosophie or the wisdom of keeping living Creatures together. **1770** LANGHORNE *Plutarch* (1879) I. 130/1 What was then called wisdom, which consisted in a knowledge of the arts of government, and the practical part of political prudence. **1875** LIGHTFOOT *Comm. Coloss.* 99 'Wisdom' in Gnostic teaching was the exclusive possession of the few.

b. *pl.* Kinds of learning, branches of knowledge. *rare.*

c **888** ÆLFRED *Boeth.* vii. §3 Mine þeowas sindon wisdomas & cræftas & soðe welan. *a* **1300** *Cursor M.* 8482 Of all wisdoms [Solomon] had i-nogh. **1853** F. W. FABER *All for Jesus* (1854) 130 The Corinthians could not come near us in the variety of our wisdoms and our gifts.

c. In renderings of med.L. names of substances prepared or used by the alchemists, as ***lute of wisdom*** (see LUTE *sb.*^{2} 1), ***salt of wisdom*** = ALEMBROTH.

(Cf. PHILOSOPHER 4, 5 b, PHILOSOPHICAL 4.)

1460–70 [see LUTE *sb.*^{2} 1]. **1576** BAKER *Gesner's Jewell of Health* 37 The Lute of Wysedome, which resisteth the fire marveylously. **1800** tr. *Lagrange's Chem.* II. 23 Alembroth, Salt of the Art, Salt of Wisdom.

3. a. Wise discourse or teaching; with *a* and *pl.*, a wise saying or precept. Now *rare* or *arch.*

c **1175** *Lamb. Hom.* 125 Imong þan muchela wisdoma þe ure drihten lerde his apostles. *c* **1205** LAY. 25628 Ælc bi his witte wisdom sæiden. *c* **1250** *Gen. & Ex.* 462 On two tables of tiȝel and bras Wrot he ðat wistom. **1303** R. BRUNNE *Handl. Synne* 1179 Anoþer wysdom a clerk vs telleþ. *c* **1400** LYDG. *Chorle & Bird* 274 Min. Poems (Percy Soc.) 189 To here a wisdom thyn eres been half deef. **1493** [H. PARKER] *Dives & Pauper* (1496) IX. iv. 350/2, I shall teche the thre wysedomes whiche yf thou kepe them well they shall do the moche proufyte. **1531** ELYOT *Gov.* III. xxv, In his fables the foxe, the hare, and the wolfe, though they neuer spoke, do teache many good wysedomes. **1860** SALA *Badd. Peer.* I. vii. 127 Listen then, to the wisdom of Pollybank.

b. In the titles of two books of the Apocrypha, viz. ***The Wisdom of Solomon*** (often abbrev. ***Wisdom*** or ***The Book of Wisdom***), and ***The Wisdom of Jesus the son of Sirach*** (commonly called *Ecclesiasticus*). Cf. also *Wisdom literature*, etc. in 5.

1430–40 *Wycliffite Bible* Wisd. (*heading*) Heer gynneth the prolog in the booc of Wisdam. **1611** *Bible* (*title*) The Wisedome of Solomon. *Ibid.* (*title*) The Wisdome of Iesus the sonne of Sirach, or Ecclesiasticus. **1875** PLUMPTRE in *Expositor* I. 336 Those [words] which are found in Philo and in the Epistle, but not in Wisdom. **1912** E. C. SELWYN *Oracles N.T.* iii. 78 The fact that Wisdom also contains an anticipation of one of the three Temptations of Christ.

†**4.** Sanity, 'reason'. (Cf. WISE *a.* 4.) *Obs. rare.*

1603 SHAKS. *Meas. for M.* IV. iv. 5 Pray heauen his wisedome bee not tainted.

5. *Comb.* **a.** attrib., as ***wisdom-book***, ***-lecture***, etc.; ***Wisdom literature***, a collective term for the biblical books of Job, Proverbs, Ecclesiastes, Wisdom of Solomon, and Ecclesiasticus, and the Epistle of James; so ***Wisdom books***, ***poetry***, ***versification***. (See also WISDOM TOOTH.) **b.** instrumental, objective, etc., as ***wisdom-bred***, ***-giving***, ***-seasoned***, ***-seeming***, ***-working*** adjs.

c **1200** *Trin. Coll. Hom.* 187 Of þe strengðe þe ure drihten us to munegeð specð *wisdom boc and seið, *Fortitudo simplicis uia domini.* **1887** CHEYNE *Job & Solomon* 180 The Wisdom-books of the Old Testament proper. **1832** TENNYSON *Œnone* 121 Power..; *wisdom-bred And throned of wisdom. **1667** MILTON *P.L.* IX. 679 O Sacred, Wise, and *Wisdom-giving Plant, Mother of Science. *a* **1644** QUARLES *Sol. Recant.* ch. xii. 9 Because his true repentant soul was wise, He read this *wisdome-lecture. **1887** CHEYNE *Job & Solomon* 180 The book now before us —the largest and most comprehensive in the *Wisdom-literature. **1809–10** COLERIDGE *Friend* (1818) III. 112 The title of sophist,..a *wisdom-monger, in the same sense as we say, an iron-monger. **1895** R. G. MOULTON *Proverbs* 169 The metres of *Wisdom poetry. *a* **1644** QUARLES *Sol. Recant.* Sol. xi. 1 Thy *wisdome-seasoned brest. **1826** E. IRVING *Babylon* I. II. 74 A *wisdom-seeming ignorance. **1816** SHELLEY *Sunset* 36 To make hard hearts Dissolve away in *wisdom-working grief.

Hence **ˈwisdomful** *a.*, full of wisdom; †**ˈwisdomhood**, wisdom; **ˈwisdomless** *a.*, destitute of wisdom; †**ˈwisdomness**, (*a*) contained wisdom, wise signification or implication; (*b*) affected or spurious wisdom; **ˈwisdomship**, (with possessive) as a title of (ironical) respect (cf. 1 e).

1845 *Blackw. Mag.* Feb. 156/2 Its wondrous *wisdomful speech. **138.** WYCLIF *Sel. Wks.* III. 99 As Seynt Poul seyþ, In him beþ alle tresoures of kunnyng and of *wysdomhud. **1608** MACHIN *Dumb Knt.* IV. i, I am mad,..all wit-stung, *wisdomlesse. **1589** *Marprel. Epit.* (1843) 21 It is a hard matter..to conceiue all the *wisdomnes of this syllogisme. **1668** E. KEMP *Reas. Use Ch. Prayers in Publick* 14 So impertinent a piece of gravity, so unseasonable a piece of wisdomness. **1692** *Vindication* Pref. A 2, Their cool *Wisdomships can be as Hot as their Neighbours in their own Concerns.

wisdom tooth. [Usually pl.; orig. *teeth of wisdom*, rendering mod.L. *dentes sapientiæ*, = Arab. *aḍrāsu 'lḥikmi* (f. *ḍirs* tooth, *ḥikm* wisdom), after Gr. σωφρονιστῆρες (Hippocrates): so called as not appearing till the attainment of years of discretion.] The hindmost molar tooth on each side of both upper and lower jaws in man, usually 'cut' about the age of twenty. Often in phr. ***to cut one's wisdom teeth***, to attain to wisdom or discretion.

[**1668** CULPEPPER & COLE *Barthol. Anat.* Man. IV. xiii. 349 The two last are termed *Dentes Sapientiæ*, the Teeth of Wisedom. **1771** J. S. tr. *Le Dran's Observ. Surg.* (ed. 4) Dict. Cc 8 b, *Sophronesteres*, the..Teeth of Wisdom. **1809** MALKIN *Gil Blas* X. x. ¶32 The gamester, finding that I had cut my teeth of wisdom sooner than suited his purpose.]

1848 *Quain's Elem. Anat.* (ed. 5) II. 971 The last molar in each range, owing to its late appearance through the gums, is called the wisdom-tooth. **1863** MRS. GASKELL *Sylvia's L.* xxi, He's noane cut his wisdom-teeth yet. **1868** WHYTE-MELVILLE *White Rose* III. 205 It seems..they're all born with their wisdom-teeth cut and their whiskers growed. **1872** L. P. MEREDITH *Teeth* (1878) 49 The wisdom teeth occasionally erupt as late as the fortieth or fiftieth year.

wise (waɪz), *sb.*^{1} *arch.* Forms: 1– **wise**, 1, 3–4 (5–6 *Sc.*) **wis**, 1, 3–6 **wyse**, (3–4 **wisse**, 4 **wice**, *Sc.* **viss**, **vijs**, **vyijs**, **vyise**), 4–5 **wys**, (*Sc.* **wiss**, **vyse**, **vice**, 4–6 *Sc.* **wyis** (6 **-iss**), 5 **wyesse**, **whyse**, 5–6 *Sc.* **wyss(e**, **vise**, 6 **wize**, **weysse**). [OE. *wíse* wk. fem. (rarely *wís* str. fem.) manner, mode, condition, thing, affair, cause, reason, (occas.) song = OFris. *wîs*, OS. *wîsa* wk. and str. (MLG. *wîse*, *wîs*, MDu. *wîze*, *wijs*, Du. *wijze*), OHG. *wîsa*, and *wîs* manner, custom, tune (MHG. *wîse*, G. *weise*), ON. *vísa* wk. fem. stanza, **vís* manner in *öðruvís* otherwise (Sw. *visa*, Da. *vise* song; also Sw., Da. *vis* way, manner):—OTeut. **wīsōn-*, **wīsō*: f. *wit-* WIT *v.*^{1} (for the sense cf. the cognate Gr. εἶδος form, shape, kind, state of things, course of action).]

I. †**1. a.** Manner, mode, fashion, style; *spec.* habitual manner of action, habit, custom (cf. WAY *sb.* 22). *Obs.* (in later use *Sc.*): see also II.

971 *Blickl. Hom.* 55 Maniȝes mannes wise bið þæt he wile symle to his nehstan sprecan þa word þe he wenþ þæt him leofoste syn to ȝehyrenne. *c* **1205** LAY. 25426 An hundred þusende iwepnede þeines ohte on heore londes wise. *c* **1220** *Bestiary* 468 Ðe spinnere..werpeð ðus hire web, and weueð on hire wise. *a* **1250** *Owl & Night.* 1029 For heom ne may halter ne bridel Bringe from here wode wyse. **1297** R. GLOUC. (Rolls) 1213 Þat folc verst in is wise, To hor godes as hii wolde, dude hor sacrefice. **1393** LANGL. *P. Pl.* C. xx. 263 Þis is þe worste wise þat eny wight myghte Synegen aȝens þe *seynt espirit*. *c* **1400** MAUNDEV. (1919) xi. 49, & ȝit þei ben in moornynge in the wise þat þei maden here lamentacioun for him the firste tyme. *c* **1470** HENRY *Wallace* II. 25 Our all ye toune rewlyng on thair awne wis. **1572** *Satir. Poems Reform.* xxxiv. 3 Quho list to mark the Scottisch gyse..Sall weill persave thair craftie wyse.

†**b.** phr. ***to do, make one's wise***: to do what one can. ***in wise of***: after the fashion of; in respect of. ***in wise that***: in such a manner that, so that.

c **1290** *Beket* 1279 in *S. Eng. Leg.* 143 Þo he hadde al is tale itold and imaked is grete wise [*v.r.* al his wise], He sat adoun. *c* **1374** CHAUCER *Troylus* v. 64 This Troylus, yn wyse of curtasie,..rod and dide here compaynye. **1454** *Paston Lett.* I. 297 Ledam wulde a do hys wyse to a mad a complent to Pryothe in the scher-howse of yow. *c* **1470** HENRY *Wallace* VI. 565 All Wallace folk in wys off wer was gud. **1561** HOBY tr. *Castiglione's Courtyer* III. (1577) P v, Wyth the wayes whyche she ordeined, those Realmes are still ruled, in wise that albeit hir life wanteth, yet hir authoritie liueth.

†**2.** Song, melody. *Obs.*

a **1000** *Menologium* 70 Wrecan wordum forð, wise [*MS.* wisse] ȝesingan. *a* **1250** *Owl & Night.* 519 So sone so þu sittest a brode þu forleost al þine wise.

II. OE. *wíse* manner, fashion, like the cognate forms in other Germanic languages (see the respective sections below), was used in various kinds of advb. expressions meaning 'in such-and-such a manner, way, or respect', in which it was qualified by an adj. or a sb. with or without a governing preposition. Several of these expressions, with others formed on their pattern in later periods, have survived as simple words, e.g. *anywise*, *crosswise*, *leastwise*, *likewise*, *nowise*, *otherwise*, *slantwise*, in which *-wise* has the appearance of a suffix, and, in so far as it could or can still be freely combined with an adj. or a sb. (as in 1 b, 3 b), it has actually performed the function of a suffix. The free use of the various forms, i.e. apart from the established simple words, is now only archaic exc. in sense 3 b.

1. a. With demonstrative, interrogative, or indefinite adj. in an oblique case. (†rarely *pl.*)

In O.E. *óðre wísan* varies with *on óðre wísan* (see OTHERWISE), but most later expressions of this form, e.g. LIKEWISE, THISWISE, WHAT-WISE, resulted from ellipses of the prep. in expressions of the type in 2 a. THUSWISE is an analogical combination with an adv.

Cf. OFris. *hûdêne wîs*, OS. *hû wîs(e*, OHG. *andar wîs*, *einic wîs*, MHG. *neheine wîs*, *der selben wîs*, *manege(n wîs*.

971 *Blickl. Hom.* 177 Þe læs þe oðre wisan æniȝ man leoȝe. *c* **1205** LAY. 32018 Wulchere wise he mihte wið Aðelstane fihte. *a* **1300** *Cursor M.* 17473 All fals sal far þat ilk wise. *a* **1300** [see WHAT-WISE]. **13..** *Bonaventura's Medit.* 154 Þat he to hys treytur dyd þe same wyse. **13..–1530** this wise [see

THISWISE]. **1375** BARBOUR *Bruce* v. 78 His menȝe.. That vs dispytis mony vis. *c* **1375**, **1556** suche wise [see SUCHWISE]. *c* **1420** ? LYDG. *Assembly of Gods* 198 Syth that hit woll none other wyse be. *c* **1450** *Cursor M.* 9896 (Laud) This castelle ..is feyror many wyse [*Cott.* on mani wise] Then tong can telle. **1500-20** DUNBAR *Poems* xix. 1 How sowld I rewill me, or quhat wyiss. *Ibid.* lxxviii. 15 It will nocht walkin me no wise. **1513** DOUGLAS *Æneis* VI. x. 93 And as thai flokkit about Enee, als tyte Sic vise ontil thaim carpis Sibilla. **1513** quhat wyse [see WHAT-WISE]. **1524** in Strype *Eccl. Mem.* (1721) I. App. xiii. 30 The delaying..of this matier may do moche harme, and prejudice sundry wises. **1530** *Ibid.* III. App. x. 20, I haue prayed no other wysse then the trewth. **1538** STARKEY *England* (1878) 16 Thys law..must..be referryd, non other wyse then the conclusyonys of artys mathematical are euer referryd to theyr pryncypullys. **1560** *Abst. Protocols Town Clerks of Glasgow* (1896) II. 84 All reicht..quhilk he had or ony wyis mycht haif. **1649** C. WASE *Sophocles, Electra* 12 Whilst things stand this wise with me. **1693** EVELYN *De La Quint. Compl. Gard.* I. 36 The Houses, that can no wise afford above one Garden. **1799** UNDERWOOD *Dis. Childh.* (ed. 4) II. 242 A bougie..would be every wise as proper. **1856** MRS. BROWNING *Aur. Leigh* III. 810 No wise beautiful Was Marian Erle. **1883** L. OLIPHANT *Altiora Peto* xviii, He did it this wise.

b. With general adjs., often forming an equivalent of -LY[2], as † ***humble wise*** = humbly, ***despiteful-wise*** = despitefully: in later use hyphened or as one word.

Cf. MHG. *glîcher wîse* (G. *gleicherweise*), G. *glücklicherweise*, *irrtümlicherweise*, *törichterweise*, *zufälligerweise*, etc.; *normaler weise*, etc.

Beowulf 1865 Ic þa leode wat..fæste ȝeworhte, æȝhwæs untæle ealde wisan. *a* **1300** *Cursor M.* 21277 Þe queles er draun diuerse wise. *c* **1386** CHAUCER *Knt.'s T.* 480 The nyghtes longe Encressen double wise the peynes stronge. **1475** *Rolls of Parlt.* VI. 129/1 Service, the which the seid Galiard..had doon dyvers wise to your goode grace. *c* **1475** *Rauf Coilȝear* 929 Thus may thow, and thow will, wirk the best wise. **1592** CONSTABLE *Diana* I. i. 2 Humble wise To thee my sighes in verse I sacrifise. **1635** J. HAYWARD tr. *Biondi's Banish'd Virg.* 157 It was formed hooked-wise. **1866** *Church & State Rev.* 11 May 298/2 It is no dull good-boy book, to be taken teetotalwise. **1876** STEDMAN *Vict. Poets* vi. 220 'The Princess' and 'The Idylls of the King', are written Dorian-wise. **1903** KIPLING *Five Nations, S. Africa* vi, She..Treated them despiteful-wise.

2. a. (*a*) With prep. (orig. *on*, arch. since 16th cent.; OE. also *of*; from 14th cent. *in*) and demonstrative, interrogative, or indefinite adj., as *on náne wísan* in no way, NOWISE, *of þisse wísan* in this way, THISWISE. (Cf. 1 a.) Sometimes illogically written as one word or with hyphen.

Cf. OS. *an negana wîsa*, MLG. *in wat wîs(e*, OHG. *in thesa*, *alla*, *managa*, *zwei wîs*, *ze dero*, *andrero*, *welero wîs*, etc., G. *auf andere*, *solche*, *welche weise*, etc.

c **888** ÆLFRED *Boeth.* xvi. §2 On nane wisan. *c* **900** tr. *Bæda's Hist.* I. xxvii. (1890) 72 Ne meaht þu on oðre wisan biscop halȝian buton oðrum biscopum. *c* **950** *Lindisf. Gosp.* Luke xv. 10 *Ita*, on ða wisa. **971** *Blickl. Hom.* 31 Þas cyþnesse Drihten nam of þisse wisan. *c* **1050** *Voc.* in Wr.-Wülcker 341/26 *Aliter*, on æniȝe oðre wisan. *c* **1175** *Lamb. Hom.* 109 On monie wisen mon mei wurchen elmessan. *c* **1200** *Trin. Coll. Hom.* 203 Alle he laðeð ech a sume wise to endelese blisse. *c* **1200** ORMIN 2534 Herrsumm onn alle wise. *c* **1350** in what wise [see WHAT-WISE]. *c* **1400** *Destr. Troy* 8440 Andromaca..prayet the prinse..On nowise in thys world the walles to passe. *c* **1400** *Rom. Rose* 5940 Ben thanne siche marchauntz wise, No, but fooles in euery wise. *c* **1440** *Generydes* 102, I am come here, in lyke wyse as ye see. **1472**, **1563** in any wise [see ANYWISE]. **1526** TINDALE *Rom.* iii. 9 Are we better then they? No in no wyse. **1581** BURNE *Disput.* in *Cath. Tract.* (S.T.S.) 112 Thay..vil in nauyse suffer onie man to..preache aganis the same. **1639** ROUSE *Heav. Univ.* Advt. (1702) 2 One who was in no wise averse to that common Learning. **1732** LEDIARD *Sethos* II. IX. 269 Provided, however, it were in no-wise an obstacle. **1800** *Med. Jrnl.* IV. 318 The abdominal ring is in nowise concerned in the disease. **1844** DISRAELI *Coningsby* IV. vii, In this wise, affairs had gone on for a month. **1848**, **1865** in somewise [see SOMEWISE]. **1879** M. ARNOLD *Mixed Ess., Milton* 238 Whoever comes to the Essay on Milton..will feel that the essay in nowise helps hims. **1905** in what-wise [see WHAT-WISE].

(*b*) with *a* or a numeral, or *pl.*

a **1000** *Colloq. Ælfric* in Wright *Voc.* (1857) I. 7 On feala wisan ic beswice fuȝelas. *c* **1000** ÆLFRIC *Gram.* xxxviii. (Z.) 237 *Bifariam*, on twa wisan. *c* **1175** *Lamb. Hom.* 77 Þe fader is ine þe sune on þre wise. *c* **1200** *Trin. Coll. Hom.* 9 Teȝenes ure emcristene we sulle laden ure lif edmodeliche on two wise. *a* **1225** *Ancr. R.* 6 Alle ne muwe nout..holden on one wise ðe vtture riwle. *a* **1300** *Cursor M.* 29506 O thrijn wijs Mai cursing be tald on right wijs. **1340** *Ayenb.* 62 Þe dyeuel ..him chongeþ in uele wysen þet uolk uor to gyly. **13..** *E.E. Allit. P.* B. 1805 Þus vpon þrynne wyses I haf yow þro schewed, Þat vnclannes to cleues in corage dere. *c* **1375** *Sc. Leg. Saints* xii. (*Mathias*) 99, & In a vice to-gyddyr fede & in ane aray in bak & bede. **1430-40** LYDG. *Bochas* IX. ii. (1554) 197/1 Disceiuable in many sondry wyses. *c* **1449** PECOCK *Repr.* V. xii. 548 Bi manye wijsis. **1520** *Rolls of Parlt.* V. 437/1 In other divers manere of wyses.

b. With general adjs.: cf. 1 b. (occas. illogically as one word or with hyphen.)

Cf. *in likewise* (LIKEWISE 1), and OFris. *to lîkere wîs* (*and*).

971 *Blickl. Hom.* 189 Þa cwæþ Neron, On ða betstan wisan þu demest. *a* **1100** *Aldhelm Gloss.* I. 1252 (Napier 34) *Mirum in modum*, on wunderlicum ȝemete [*in another hand* wise]. *c* **1205** LAY. 27834 Wes þe kaisere of-slæȝen a seolcuðe wisen. *a* **1300** *Cursor M.* 10948 Als lagh was þan on ald wise. **13..** *E.E. Allit. P.* A. 1095 So sodanly on a wonder wyse, I was war of a prosessyoun. *c* **1385** CHAUCER *L.G.W.* 20 In euery skylful wyse. *c* **1400** *Cursor M.* 28028 (Cotton Galba) Ȝe oft sithes on wonderwise Biswikes þam. **1423** JAS. I *Kingis Q.* xcvii, That coude his office doon In connyng wise. **1456** SIR G. HAYE *Law Arms* (S.T.S.) 153 Thareto I ansuere in double wis. **1470-85** MALORY *Arthur* XI. vii. 580, I will.. that ye be wel bisene in the rychest wyse. **1480** *Cely Papers* (Camden) 29 In as lovynge whyse as harte cone thynke. **1500-20** DUNBAR *Poems* xxv. 3 We..To ȝow that ar in purgatory Commendis ws on our hairtly wyiss. **1526** *Pilgr. Perf.* (W. de W. 1531) 2, I shall praye for you in lyke wyse. **1597** MORLEY *Introd. Mus.* 87 You take a discord for the first part, & not in binding wise. **1600** W. WATSON *Decacordon* (1602) 360 Some in scoffing manner; others in malicious wise. **1610** HOLLAND *Camden's Brit.* I. 98 These letters in scattering wise, C A E R A T I C. **1684** BUNYAN *Pilgr.* II. Introd., By all means in all Loving-wise, them greet. **1782** TRUMBULL *McFingal* IV. (1795) 94 In mournful wise. **1865** SWINBURNE *Chastelard* I. i. (1894) 13 You praise her in too lover-like a wise. **1870** MORRIS *Earthly Par.* II. III. 46 A while in gentle wise they went.

3. a. With prep. (see 2) and sb. in (non-syntactical) combination with *wise*, e.g. OE. *on scipwísan* in the manner of a ship, like a ship.

Cf. OS. *an kuningwîsa(n* like a king, MHG. *in kriuzewîs*, MSw. *i korsvîs* crosswise.

c **890** WÆRFERTH tr. *Gregory's Dial.* (1900) 343 Tweȝen oflæthlafas on beaȝwisan abacene. *a* **950** *Guthlac* ii. (Prose) 107 Mid þam þe seo yld com þæt hit sprecan mihte æfter cnihtwisan. *c* **1000** ÆLFRIC *Saints' Lives* vi. 247 On munucwisan ȝescryd. *c* **1070** in Thorpe *Charters* (1865) 430 Mycel Englisc boc..on leoðwisan ȝeworht. **1377** LANGL. *P. Pl.* B. XIX. 138 Kulleden hym on-crosse-wyse. **1393** *Ibid.* C. VIII. 163 In a weythwynde wyse ywryþe al aboute. *c* **1400** *Destr. Troy* 175 Ayre vp the erthe on ardagh wise. *Ibid.* 4762 The grekes..At wyndous on yche syde-wise a wondurfull nombur. *c* **1407** LYDG. *Reson & Sens.* 5245 In karol wise I saugh hem goon. **1495** *Acta Dom. Conc.* (1839) 427/2 In Indenture wise. **1571** GOLDING *Calvin on Ps.* XXXV. 20 By the clifts of the earth wee may in metaphorwyse vnderstande miserable men..broken and maymed. **1589** in ballade wise [see *ballad-wise* s.v. BALLAD *sb.* 6]. **1596** *Edw. III*, v. 137 Heere twise as many pikes in quadrant wise. **1606** W. CRASHAW *Rom. Forgeries* To Rdr. D 4 b, The reuerend Master Iohn Ferus..did in Sermon-wise explane the bookes of Iob vnto the Citizens. **1622** MABBE tr. *Aleman's Guzman d'Alf.* II. 333 The points of the Hornes meeting.. in a kinde of circle-wise. **1800** COLERIDGE *Christabel* II. 573 Geraldine, in maiden wise,..turned her from Sir Leoline. **1916** H. E. G. ROPE *Relig. Ancilla* 54 We trod the pilgrim road in pilgrim wise.

b. without prep. (variously written).

(i) The meaning is 'in the manner of', 'in the..manner'. Cf. MLG. *crûcewîs*, Du. *kruiswijs*, MHG. *kriuzewîse*, G. *kreuzweise*, *pfandweise*, etc.

1398 [see CROSSWISE 1]. **1459** *Paston Lett.* I. 475 A goune ..with side slevis, sirples wise. **1474** [see CORNERWISE]. *c* **1530** *Crt. of Love* 1354 Within a temple shapen hauthorn wise. **1530** [see LOZENGEWISE]. **1545-1616** compass-wise [see COMPASS *sb.*[1] D]. **1577** GOOGE *Heresbach's Husb.* I. 37 To order it garden wyse, castyng it into beddes. **1591** SAVILE *Tacitus, Hist.* I. lv. 32 No man presumed to make any solemne oration assembly-wise [L. *in modum concionis*]. **1625** Antheme-wise [see ANTHEM *sb.* 4]. **1631** in Courridge *Ye Olde Streete of Pavement* (*c* 1890) 177/1 Let them tie upon a stick, posie wise, a little piece of sponge. **1657** SPARROW *Bk. Com. Prayer* (1661) 100 Then the Priest Collect-wise makes a Prayer. **1677** W. HUGHES *Man of Sin* III. iii. 61 Let us try once more to argue Cardinalwise. **1725** *Fam. Dict.* s.v. *Cutting*, They do at other Times cut sloaping, and Hind-foot-wise. **1743** SHENSTONE *Let. to Graves* 23 Dec., The sides [of an alcove] ornamented with sheeps-bones, jaws, sculls, &c. festoon-wise. **1851** H. MELVILLE *Moby Dick* II. xxviii. 192 Ahab..took Stubb's long spade..and striking it into the lower part of the half-suspended mass, placed its other end crutch-wise under one arm. **1854** H. D. THOREAU *Walden* 21 Waiting at evening on the hill-tops for the sky to fall, that I might catch something, though I never caught much, and that, manna-wise, would dissolve again in the sun. **1876** [O. H. B.] *White Cross* xlviii, 'Oh, only in a brotherly way.'.. 'Timothy or Titus-wise, you know.' **1885** *Cornhill Mag.* Mar. 283 Priests sitting with their legs tucked up tailor-wise, in the attitude of Buddha. **1919** R. FIRBANK *Valmouth* iv. 52 Flecked with wood shavings, Saint Joseph-wise, it [*sc.* a gown] brought with it suggestions of Eastern men. **1921** KASTNER & CHARLTON *Poetical Wks. of Sir Wm. Alexander* I. p. lvii, The style throughout, Seneca-wise, ought to be magnificent and grave. **1923** R. MACAULAY *Told by an Idiot* I. ii. 11 Her mass of chestnut hair parted Rosetti-wise in the middle. **1940** 'GUN BUSTER' *Return via Dunkirk* II. iv. 117 In a few minutes our vehicles were coiled serpent-wise round the château.

(ii) Used in the same way but with the sense: as regards, in respect of. *colloq.* (orig. *U.S.*).

1942 E. R. ALLEN in J. J. Mattiello *Protective & Decorative Coatings* II. viii. 252 It should be noted that there are two types of hydrogen atoms positionwise. **1948** *Sat. Rev.* 6 Mar. 16/3 Plotwise, it offers little more or little less of what-happens-next interest than may be found [etc.]. **1958** *Spectator* 10 Jan. 37/2 John Robert Russell, 13th Duke of Bedford..in twelve TV performances, was the greatest, successwise, among the aristocrats. **1958** *Times* 5 Sept. 11/5 An ill-disciplined, over-paid, frustrated youth, whose life chances have been vastly improved moneywise without commensurate social adjustment. **1961** *Far East Film News* (Tokyo) Apr. 5/1, 1961 so far has been UA [*sc.* United Artists] all the way prize-wise with this company taking an even dozen Oscars. **1976** J. I. M. STEWART *Memorial Service* xii. 184 These were a gentle race..desperately worried over the grim state of the market job-wise. **1981** *Gossip* (Holiday Special) 24/1 Acting-wise, I like Katharine Hepburn, Joanne Woodward, Judy Garland and, of course, Marilyn.

c. with prep. and sb. in the genitive.

Cf. OFris. *thiaveswîse* like a thief, MLG. (*in*) *dieves wîse*, *in pelegrimes wîse*, *gastes wîse* as a guest, OHG. *in eseles wîs* like an ass, MHG. *in kriuzes wîs* crosswise, *ze gesellen wîs* like comrades.

c **1250** *Gen. & Ex.* 2961 It was on fendes wise wroȝt. *a* **1300** *K. Horn* 360 On a squieres wise. **1362** LANGL. *P. Pl.* A. II. 148 On Palfreis wyse. *Ibid.* VI. 9 In A weþe-bondes wyse I-wriþen aboute [cf. quot. 1393 in 3]. *Ibid.* VII. 53 In pilgrimes wyse. **1423** JAS. I *Kingis Q.* cxvii, In thaire flouris wise. **1865** SWINBURNE *Chastelard* I. iii. (1894) 46 On peaceable men's wise.

†**d.** with formations in *-kin(s*, *manner*. *Obs.*

c **1200** *Vices & Virtues* 25 On alles kennes wisen. *a* **1300** *Cursor M.* 7984 On quatkin wise. *Ibid.* 9486 He ne mai be fre on nakins wis [*v.r.* nan-kin wise]. *c* **1350** *Will. Palerne* 4380 In no maner wice. *c* **1375** *Sc. Leg. Saints* ix. (*Bertholomeus*) 129 One foure-kine wise. *c* **1400** *Apol. Loll.* 91 On mani maner wis. *c* **1520** SKELTON *Garl. Laurel* 647 In lyke maner of wyse. **1523** LD. BERNERS *Froiss.* I. ccccviii. 287 b/1 In some maner awyse. **1535** *Goodly Primer* Ps. cxix, In no maner wyse. **1563** P. WHITEHORNE *Onosandro Platon.* 31 In no maner of wyse.

4. The synonymy of *-wise* and *-ways* in such advs. as *likeways*, *likewise*, *noways*, *nowise*, led to their interchange and consequently the illogical use of *-wise* for *-ways*: see -WAYS 3.

wise, *sb.*[2] *Obs.* exc. *dial.* Also **wyse**. [OE. *wíse*; cf. ON. *vísir*: ultimate relations doubtful.] The stalk or stem of a plant; *esp.* a trailing stem or runner, as of the strawberry.

a **1000** *Riddles* lxvi. 4 Æȝhwa mec reafað,..min heafod sciréþ, biteð mec on bær lic, briceð mine wisan. *c* **1000** *Sax. Leechd.* II. 36 Streawberȝean wise. *c* **1050** *Voc.* in Wr.-Wülcker 415/34 *Gesce*, eall hwite wysan. *c* **1425** *Pol. Rel. & L. Poems* (1903) 310 Tak an handful of Bugyl, an oþer of strawebery wyse. *c* **1440** *MS. Lincoln A.* i. 17 lf. 280 (Halliw.), Take the wyse of tormentile, and bray it. *c* **1440** *Promp. Parv.* 531/1 Wyse, of strawbery (*P.* or pesyn), *fragus*. *c* **1450** [see *strawberry wise*, STRAWBERRY 8].

wise (waɪz), *a.* (*sb.*[3], *adv.*) Forms: 1-5 (6 *Sc.*) **wis**, 3-5 (6 *Sc.*) **wys**, 4-7 **wyse**, 4- **wise**; also 3-5 **wiis**, 4 **wiys**, **wyys**, **wyese**, **-esse**, **weysse**, *Sc.* **viss**, **vyijs**, 4-5 **wijs**, **wyes**, **wiss**, 4-5 (6 *Sc.*) **wyss**, **wice**, 4-6 *Sc.* **vyise**, 4, 7 **wiese**, 5 **wijse**, **wies**, **weise**, **wiesse**, **wisse**, **wysse**, **vise**, **vice**, **viese**, *Sc.* **vyis**, 5 (6 *Sc.*) **wyis**, **wyce**, **vyse**, 6 *Sc.* **wisz**, **wyise**, **-ice**, **-iss**, **vyiss**, **vyce**. [OE. *wís* = OFris., OS., OHG. (MLG., MDu., MHG.) *wîs*, (Du. *wijs*, G. *weis* in phr. *einen weis machen*), ON. *víss* (Sw., Da. *vis*), Goth. *weis* (in compounds):—OTeut. **wīsaz*:—pre-Teut. **wīttos*, f. Indo-Eur. *weid-* (see WIT *v.*[1]) + ppl. suffix *-to-*.

OHG. *wîsi* (MHG. *wîse*, G. *weise*) is from a parallel formation with *j*-suffix.

The standard pronunciation with voiced *s* (z) is presumably derived from the oblique cases. The normal representative of OE. *wís* with (s), as in *ice* (OE. *ís*), survives in some northern dialects; the regular Sc. pronunciation is (weis).]

1. a. Having or exercising sound judgement or discernment; capable of judging truly concerning what is right or fitting, and disposed to act accordingly; having the ability to perceive and adopt the best means for accomplishing an end; characterized by good sense and prudence. Opp. to *foolish*. (See also WISE MAN 1.) Also in phr. ***wise old man***; spec. = WISE MAN 4.

In ME. often in collocation with WARE *a.*

Beowulf 1845 Mæȝenes strang and on mode frod, wis wordcwida. *c* **1000** *Rule of Chrodegang* liv, Preostas sceolon ȝemunan þæt hiȝ ne synt..wisran þonne Salomon. *a* **1122** *O.E. Chron.* (Laud MS.) an. 656 Theodorus, swiðe god man & wis. *c* **1205** LAY. 6303 Heo wes swiðe wis of wordliche dome. *a* **1225** *Ancr. R.* 90 Salomon þe wise. *a* **1250** *Owl & Night.* 192 He is wis and war of worde. **1297** R. GLOUC. (Rolls) 5388 King alfred was wisost king þat longe was biuore. **1375** BARBOUR *Bruce* IX. 327 The viss king, that ves vicht and bald. *c* **1386** CHAUCER *Prol.* 68 Though þat he were worthy he was wys. *Ibid.* 309 A Sergeant of the Lawe war and wys. *c* **1400** *Destr. Troy* 1463 A man witty & wise, wight, wildist in armes. **1434** MISYN *Mending Life* iv. 113 In meet & drynke be þow scars & wisse. *c* **1440** *Promp. Parv.* 526/1 Wyce, in werkynge and ware.., *discretus*, *providus*. **1500-20** DUNBAR *Poems* xxxix. 39 And quha can reive vthir menis rowmis..Is now ane active man and wyice. **1508** —— *Tua mariit wemen* 294 As wis woman ay I wrought & not as wod fule. **1526** *Pilgr. Perf.* (W. de W. 1531) 131 We sholde also be wele ware or wyse, as is y[e] serpent. **1526** TINDALE *Matt.* xxv. 2 Fyve of them were folysshe, and fyve were wyse. **1599** SHAKS. *Much Ado* II. iii. 167 *Claudio.* And she is exceeding wise. *Prince.* In euery thing, but in louing Benedicke. **1639** J. TAYLOR (Water P.) *Pt. Summers Trav.* 42 To tempt and draw the wisest men to folly. *a* **1732** GAY *Fables* II. v. 1 That man must daily wiser grow, Whose search is bent himself to know. **1798** SOUTHEY *Well of St. Keyne* 51 She had been wiser than me, For she took a bottle to Church. **1818** COLERIDGE *Friend* II. i. 23 The first duty of a wise advocate is to convince his opponents, that he understands their arguments and sympathizes with their just feelings. **1872** TENNYSON *In Childr. Hosp.* vi, 'If I,' said the wise little Annie, 'was you, I should cry to the dear Lord Jesus to help me.' **1875** MANNING *Mission Holy Ghost* xiv. 383 The wisest of all the sons of men before the Incarnation of the Son of God was Solomon, king of Israel. **1940** [see SHADOW *sb.* 1 d]. **1956** R. F. C. HULL tr. *Jung's Symbols of Transformation* in *Coll. Wks.* V. II. vii. 332 The archetype of the wise old man first appears in the father, being a personification of meaning and spirit in its procreative sense. **1961** G. ADLER *Living Symbol* xvii. 397 The more remote and more powerful figure of the 'wise old man' represents a further step..to a higher and more comprehensive wisdom. **1968** 'A. WHITNEY' *Every Man has his Price* viii. 61 Now he was a wise old man, greatly feared, much respected. **1975** D. DANIELL *Interpreter's House* iii. 60 There is a Wise Old Man..blind and of immense strength who..blesses John Burnet. **1977** M. GREEN *Children of Sun* i. 36 A whole movement focuses passionate values..on them [*sc.* young men]—as opposed to focusing them on the wise old man.

(*b*) of God.

c **1250** *Gen. & Ex.* 260 Ihesus, god and man so wis. *c* **1400** tr. *Secr. Secr., Gov. Lordsh.* 92 God ys wys and conynge. **1526** TINDALE *Jude* 25 To God oure saveour, whyche only ys wyse [**1611** to the onely wise God our Sauiour], be glory, maiestie, dominion, and power. **1606** SHAKS. *Ant. & Cl.* II. i. 6 We ignorant of our selues, Begge often our owne harmes, which the wise Powres Deny vs for our good. **1719** Watts *Ps.* lxiii. (L.M.) ii, Thou Great and Good, thou Just and Wise, Thou art my Father and my God!

(*c*) of animals.

a **1000** *Boeth. Metr.* xviii. 5 Sio wilde beo, þeah wis sie [etc.]. **1560** *Bible* (Genev.) Prov. xxx. 24 These be foure smal things.., yet thei are wise and ful of wisdome. **1697** Dryden *Virg. Georg.* i. 271 The wise Ant her wintry Store provides. **1863** Kingsley *Water-Bab.* ii, The wise dog took them over the moor.

(*d*) of superhuman beings and personifications.

c **1400** *Rom. Rose* 4621 Resoun Discrete and wijs and full pleasaunt. **1611** Shaks. *Cymb.* v. v. 367 He.. hath vpon him still that naturall stampe: It was wise Natures end.. To be his euidence now. **1647** H. More *Song of Soul* ii. *Infin. Worlds* cv, Wise preventing Destinie. **1796** H. Hunter tr. *St. Pierre's Study Nat.* (1799) I. 382 Wise Nature, in giving so much force to early habits, intended that our happiness should depend on those who are most concerned to promote it. **1833** Tennyson *Dream Fair Wom.* xxiv, No one can be more wise than destiny.

(*e*) const. *to* (with sb. or inf.), *unto*. *arch.*

a **1300** *Cursor M.* 8544 Was neuer nan wiser lagh to lede. *c* **1449** Pecock *Repr.* iv. i. 420 Hem that made hem silf seme wijse forto condempne mennis lawe. **1526** Tindale *Rom.* xvi. 19, I wolde have you wyse vnto that which is good. And to be innocent as concernynge evyll. —— *2 Tim.* iii. 15 Which is able to make the wyse vnto health. **1560** *Bible* (Genev.) Jer. iv. 22 Thei are wise to do euil, but to do wel thei haue no knowledge. **1583** Melbancke *Philotimus* K iv b, It makes my harte bleede to see thee so wise to wickednes. **1667** Milton *P.L.* ii. 193 Wise to frustrate all our plots and wiles. **1781** Cowper *Charity* 87 Wise to promote whatever end he means, God opens fruitful nature's various scenes.

(*f*) in proverbs and proverbial sayings. (See also 6 c.)

1303 R. Brunne *Handl. Synne* 9884 Wyys ys þat ware ys. **1526** Tindale *Luke* xvi. 8 The chyldren of this worlde, are in their kynde [1611 generation] wyser then the chyldren off light. **1539** Taverner *Erasm. Prov.* 18 He is in vayne wyse y^{t} is not wyse for hym selfe. [See *Prov.* ix. 12.] **1562** J. Heywood *Prov. & Epigr.* (1867) 132 Who wedth ere he be wise, shall die ere he thriue. **1596** Shaks. *Merch. V.* ii. ii. 83 It is a wise Father that knowes his owne childe. **1617** B. Rich *Irish Hubbub* 16 We were wont to say, it was a wise childe that did know the owne Father. **1717** Wodrow *Corr.* (1843) II. 319 The proverb of being wise behind the time. **1745** B. Franklin *Poor Richard* (1890) 157 Fools make feasts and wise men eat them. **1879** Dixon *Windsor* II. xix. 204 Men who are wise are wise in time. **1881** Saintsbury *Dryden* i. 10 Sir Gilbert Pickering.. was wiser in his generation.

b. Of action, speech, personal attributes, etc.: Proceeding from, indicating, or suggesting sound judgement or good sense; 'becoming a wise man' (J.); sage.

a **900** Cynewulf *Crist* 922 þam þe hafað wisne ʒeþoht. *a* **1225** *Ancr. R.* 198 So þet non wisure read ne mei bringen hire ut of hire riote. *Ibid.* 338 Of þe axunge mei uallen vuel bute ȝif þe axunge beo þe wisre. **1362** Langl. *P. Pl.* A. x. 71 Vche wiȝt in þis world þat haþ wys vnderstondinge. **1422** Yonge tr. *Secr. Secr.* 134 Anothyr yewyth a vyse consail. *c* **1480** Henryson *Fables* Prol. 17 (Makculloch MS.), A doctryne wiss anewch, and ful of fruyt. **1597** Shaks. *2 Hen. IV*, v. i. 84 It is certaine, that either wise bearing, or ignorant Carriage is caught, as men take diseases, one of another. **1600** —— *A.Y.L.* ii. vii. 156 Full of wise sawes, and moderne instances. **1667** Milton *P.L.* xi. 666 One.. eminent In wise deport, spake much of Right and Wrong. *a* **1672** Wilkins *Nat. Relig.* i. vi. (1675) 84 It must be a Wise Being that is the Cause of those Wise Effects. **1753–4** Richardson *Grandison* II. xxiii. 166 My father also thought fit (perhaps for wise reasons) to acquaint us, that he designed for us but small fortunes. **1821** Scott *Kenilw.* xvi, Teach your affection to see with a wiser eye. **1849** Macaulay *Hist. Eng.* vi. II. 89 By a wise dispensation of Providence. **1860** Tyndall *Glac.* i. xi. 71 He thought it wise not to attempt the ascent farther.

ironically. **1535** Joye *Apol. Tindale* (Arb.) 28 S. Paule (by this wyse reason) playd bo peep wythe hys pistle to the hebrews. **1822** Shelley *Scenes fr. Faust* ii. 227 'Twere a wise feat indeed to wander out Into the Brocken upon May-day night.

†**2. a.** Having practical understanding and ability; skilful, clever; skilled, expert (const. *of*). *Obs.*

a **900** Cynewulf *Elene* 592 Wordcræftes wis. *c* **1300** *Havelok* 282 Of alle þewes was she wis, þat gode weren. *c* **1320** *Sir Tristr.* 1270 In warld was non so wiis Of craft þat men knewe. ?*a* **1400** *Morte Arth.* 2745, I rede ȝe wyrke aftyre witte, as wyesse men of armes. *c* **1400** *Destr. Troy* 1530 Wise wrightis to wale, werkys to caste. **1508** Dunbar *Tua mariit wemen* 462 Ȝit am I wise in sic werk. *a* **1548** Hall *Chron., Hen. VII* 32 b, He secretly sent wise espialles.. to searche & prye oute of what progeny thys.. Rycharde was dissended.

b. *spec.* Skilled in magic or hidden arts. Now only *dial.*, as in ***wise wife***, wise man 3, wise woman 1.

a **1639** Spottiswood *Hist. Ch. Scot.* vi. (1655) 383 Agnes Samson (commonly called the wise wife of Keith) was.. a woman not of the base and ignorant sort of Witches. **1653** H. More *Antid. Ath.* iii. vi. §6 (1712) 102 While he wish'd to himself that some wise body would help him to his.. money again there appeared unto him a Spirit.

3. a. Having knowledge, well-informed; instructed, learned (*in*, earlier *of*, *upon*). *Obs.* exc. as in b. (See also wise man 2 a, wise woman 1.)

c **1000** *Sax. Leechd.* II. 146 Læcas lærdon, þa þe wisoste wæron, þæt nan man on þam monþe ne drenc ne drunce. *c* **1250** *Gen. & Ex.* 331 Sone ȝe it ðor of hauen eten,.. ȝe.. sulen.. ben so wise alle euene So ðo ðe wunen a-buuen in heuone. **13..** *Gaw. & Gr. Knt.* 1605 Wys vpon wod-craftez. *c* **1375** *Sc. Leg. Saints* xxxi. (*Eugenia*) 61 In al science at dewyce, þar mycht na woman wysare be. *c* **1400** *Rule St. Benet* (prose) lxiv. 42 Sho aȝht at be wise in goddis law. *c* **1505** (*title*) Here begynneth thystorye of y^{e} .vii. Wyse Maysters of rome. **1591** Shaks. *1 Hen. VI*, ii. iv. 18 But in these nice sharpe Quillets of the Law, Good faith I am no wiser then a Daw. **1651** Hobbes *Leviathan* ii. xxx. 179 Wiser and better learned in cases of Law,.. than them-selves. **1742** Gray *Eton* 100 Where ignorance is bliss, 'Tis folly to be wise.

b. (*a*) Informed or aware *of* something specified or implied. Now only in such phrases as ***none the wiser***, ***as wise as before*** = knowing no more than before (i.e., usually, nothing) about the matter.

c **1200** Ormin 2279 Forrþi wollde ȝho ben wis off þatt þurrh Godess enngell. *c* **1220** *Bestiary* 799 In water ȝe is wis of heuekes come. *c* **1375** *Sc. Leg. Saints* ii. (*Paulus*) 424 þat god wyss þame wald make Peteris banis quhilk war of þai, And quhilk war paulis banis alsa. **1377** Langl. *P. Pl.* B. x. 372 þis is a longe lessoun,.. and litel am I þe wyser. *c* **1470** Henry *Wallace* viii. 580 Thai maid him wys off all that suttell cace. **1599** Shaks. *Hen. V* iv. i. 206. **1616** *Withals' Dict.* 574 *Obscurum per obscurius*, I am as wise as I was before. **1635** D. Dickson *Hebr.* viii. 8. 156 The Church was made wyse of the imperfection of the Olde Covenant. **1712–13** Swift *Jrnl. to Stella* 2 Mar., I went into the city to see Pat Rolt, who lodges with a city cousin, a daughter of cousin Cleve (you are much the wiser). **1714** —— *Let. to Miss Vanomrigh* 8 June, The pretender, or duke of Cambridge, may both be landed, and I never the wiser. **1838** Dickens *O. Twist* xxxi, Messrs. Blathers and Duff came back again as wise as they went. **1889** *Century Mag.* July 343/1 Not one whit the wiser of the world than when he left home.

(*b*) *colloq.* (orig. *U.S.*). ***to be*** (or ***get***) ***wise to***, to be (or become) aware of; ***to put*** (one) ***wise*** (***to***), to inform one (of), enlighten one (concerning).

1896 Ade *Artie* ii. 14, I told him that when he wanted to get wise to what was in my hand all he had to do was to dig up his bit and come in. *Ibid.* xvii. 155 There was somethin' ailed me, but I was n't wise to it. **1901** H. McHugh *John Henry* 69 When I hear a pool-room comedian speaking lines about getting seasick on the B. & O., I'm wise to the fact that he dips in the Farmers' Almanac for his comedy stuff. **1913** A. Bennett *Regent* x. 296 'Tell me,.. she hasn't got herself arrested yet, has she?' 'No. And she won't!' 'Why not?' 'The police have been put wise.' **1918** Bindloss *Agatha's Fortune* xvii. 158, I suppose it was because the drummer put you wise that you went to Miss Strange? **1923** F. H. Kitchen *Divers. Dawson* 103 There would be the very devil to pay if Crutchley.. got wise to their existence. **1937** G. Heyer *They found Him Dead* ii. 41 Say, sister, get wise to this! You can't put nothin' across on me! **1950** G. Greene *Third Man* ii. 21, I met him my first term at school... He was a year older and knew the ropes. He put me wise to a lot of things. **1955** M. Gilbert *Sky High* xv. 210, I suppose Bill had just about got wise to you. **1977** F. Parrish *Fire in Barley* v. 49 Dan wondered if the arty woman was wise to him.

c. ***wise guy*** (colloq., orig. *U.S.*): an experienced or knowledgeable man; usu. ironic or derog., a know-all, a wiseacre; someone who makes sarcastic or annoying remarks; also (with reversal of meaning), someone easily duped; also *attrib.*

1896 Ade *Artie* xvi. 150 He was the wise guy and I was the soft mark. **1903** H. Hapgood *Autobiogr. of Thief* iv. 82 When these Rufus's up the State get a Yorker or a wise guy, they'll strip him down to his socks. **1910** W. M. Raine *Bucky O'Connor* ii. 28 You're wise guys, gents, both of yez. **1920** B. Tarkington in *On Plays, Playwrights & Playgoers* (1959) 42 However, they'd made the crowd aware of wise guy superiority. **1922** Wodehouse *Adventures of Sally* xiii. 219 Obviously one of the Wise Guys of whom her friend the sporting office-boy had spoken, he was frankly dissatisfied with the exhibition. **1929** W. T. Scanlon *God have Mercy on Us!* lvi. 331 We had positive orders not to pick up any form of documents and to leave them for the Intelligence Section—the 'Wise Guy Section', as we called it. **1932** [see con *v.*]. **1935** [see easy *a.* 13 b]. **1941** B. Schulberg *What makes Sammy Run?* (1943) i. 7 Listen, wise guy,.. if you found something wrong.. why didn't you come and tell me? **1959** C. Williams *Man in Motion* xi. 150 'What're you, a wise guy?' he snarled. **1972** *Village Voice* (N.Y.) 1 June 50/3 The cop.. told Rob he didn't think it was funny, portfolio or not, declared that he was a clear-cut wise guy and placed him under arrest. **1976** *National Observer* (U.S.) 7 Aug. 17/1 Kramer and Roberts seem unable to shake off the brittle, knowing, wise-guy tone of voice.

4. In one's right mind, sane. Now *Sc.* and *dial.*

So Du. *wijs*. Cf. wisdom 4.

Cf. *Beowulf* 3094 wis and ʒewittiʒ (= fully conscious).

c **1290** *S. Eng. Leg.* I. 412 Here men miȝhten iseo Hou he pleiȝez with þis ȝongue brid; he ne miȝhte nouȝt wys beo. *a* **1400**, **1481** [implied in unwise 3]. *a* **1598** D. Fergusson *Scot. Prov.* (S.T.S.) 8 Anes wood, never wise. **1604** Shaks. *Oth.* iv. i. 245 *Oth.* Fire, and brimestone. *Des.* My Lord. *Oth.* Are you wise?.. *Des.* My Lord? *Oth.* I am glad to see you mad. **1881** 'Sarah Tytler' *Three Frights* (1882) 9 They were each, according to a significant old Scotch phrase, 'wise (pronounced *wice*, and meaning rather rational than sagacious) and warld-like'.

5. †**a.** ***to make it wise*** (see make *v.*[1] 68 b): to deliberate, hesitate. *Obs.*

c **1386** Chaucer *Prol.* 785 Vs thoughte it was noght worth to make it wys And graunted hym wit outen moore auys.

b. ***to make wise*** (see make *v.*[1] 69): to behave as if one were 'wise' about a matter; to pretend, 'make *as if*...' *Obs.* exc. *dial.*

1447 Shillingford *Lett.* (Camden) 14 Hengston seide but litell therto, but made wyse as thogh hit were yes. **1561** Hoby tr. *Castiglione's Courtyer* ii. (1577) M vj, The two.. wente to bed darkelong, laughing and making wise to beleeue that hee wente about to mocke them. **1589** Puttenham *Engl. Poesie* iii. xxii. (Arb.) 265 He makes wise, as if he had not bene a man learned in some of the mathematickes. **1604** Hieron *Preachers Plea* Wks. 1614 I. 511 Hee.. made wise, as if he could haue tolde great tydings. **1834** Mrs. Bray *Warleigh* x, Whether she really felt desirous to take this opportunity of gaining repose, or whether, to use a Devonshire phrase, she only 'made wise' to do so.

6. *absol.* or as *sb.* †**a.** *sing.* usually with def. article or demonstrative: A or the wise man; *spec.* a sage. *Obs.*

c **897** Ælfred *Gregory's Past. C.* xxxiii. 220 Se dyseʒa.. all his inʒeðonc he ʒeypt, ac se wisa hit ieldcað. *a* **1250** *Owl & Night.* 176 Wel fyht þat wel flyhþ, seyþ þe wise. *c* **1374** Chaucer *Troylus* i. 79 þis forknowyng wyse. **1390** Gower *Conf.* I. 268 Upon the fol, upon the wise Siknesse and hele entrecomune. **1401** *26 Pol. Poems* iii. 12 Do euene lawe to fooll and wyse. *c* **1440** *Alphabet of Tales* 484 þe wise sayd vnto hym: 'þis way is bothe fayr & gude'.

b. *pl.* Wise men or persons: now always with *the*; †formerly also with demonstrative, possessive, etc.

c **1000** *Ags. Gosp.* Matt. xi. 25 þu þe behyddyst þas þing fram wisun & gleawun. *c* **1205** Lay. 16817 He bi-heold.. wulc of wiisen ærest spæken wolden. *a* **1300** *Cursor M.* 20794 Disput, he sais, es na mister, Bituix te wis in swilk a wer. **1340–70** *Alex. & Dind.* 973 Dindimus þe dere king, the docktour of wise. **1390** Gower *Conf.* I. 1 Som matiere, Essampled of these olde wyse. *Ibid.* 26 The wiseste of Caldee Ne cowthen wite what it mente. *c* **1400** *26 Pol. Poems* i. 167 Fle fro fooles, and folwe wise. **1535** Coverdale *Isa.* xxix. 14, I wil destroye the wisdome of their wise. **1670** Dryden *1st Pt. Conq. Granada* ii. (1672) 21 The bold are but the Instruments o' th' wise. **1784** Cowper *Task* iii. 562 The learn'd and wise Sarcastic would exclaim. **1833** Tennyson *Pal. Art* 195 O silent faces of the Great and Wise.

c. ***a word to the wise*** (***is enough***): = verbum sap. Also †***few words to the wise suffice***, etc.

1500–20 Dunbar *Poems* xv. 24 Few wordis may serve the wyis. **1562** Mountgomery in *Archaeologia* XLVII. 241 Feawe woordes to the wise doeth suffice. **1639** J. Clarke *Parœm.* 51 Few words to the wise suffice. *Verbum sapienti sat est.* A word to the wise. **1754** Richardson *Grandison* I. xix. 127 Nay, if she can withstand him—But a word to the wise, Mr. Reeves! Hem!

d. The comp. ***wiser*** as sb. (with pl. ***wisers***): One who is wiser; usually with possessive, (one's) superior in wisdom. Now *rare.*

(Cf. better A. 7, elder *sb.*[3] 2, greater C b.)

a **1300** *Cursor M.* 26180 Ga til a wijser to sceu þi wond. *c* **1385** Chaucer *L.G.W.* 2634 *Hypermnestra*, And werke aftyr thyn wisere euere mo. **1447** Bokenham *Seyntys* v. 292 And of þi wysers lern bettyr gouernaunce. *c* **1480** Henryson *Want of Wise Men* 22 For warldly wyn sik walkis, quhen wysar wynkis. **1818** Scott *Hrt. Midl.* i, Since it is well known these Delilahs seduce my wisers and my betters. **1838** Hare *Guesses* Ser. i. (1847) 161 All writers who feel an itching.. to be carping at their wisers and betters. **1843** Carlyle *Past & Pr.* iii. xiii, If thou really art my Senior, Seigneur, my Elder,.. if thou art in very deed my Wiser.

7. Used as *adv.* = wisely. In later use only in comparative. *rare.*

1375 Barbour *Bruce* xvii. 52 Thou vroucht has vis, That thou discouerit first till me. **1600** Shaks. *A.Y.L.* ii. iv. 58 Thou speak'st wiser then thou art ware of. **1797** Mrs. M. Robinson *Walsingham* IV. 153, I cannot act wiser than to take the little Welsh girl off the hands of her dragon.

8. *Comb.* **a.** advb. with adj. or pple., as ***wise-bold***, ***-hardy*** (opp. to foolhardy), ***-valiant***; ***wise-framed***, ***-judging***, ***-reflecting***, ***-said***. **b.** attrib. with sb., as ***wise-ass*** sb. and adj. (cf. smart-arse, -ass); ***wisebones*** sb. (humorous appellation for a wiseacre), ***wise-heart*** adj. (= wise-hearted). **c.** parasynthetic, as ***wise-assed***, ***-hearted***, ***-lipped***, ***-worded*** (ME. *wis iworded*).

1971 *Current Slang* V. iv. 21 **Wise ass*, n., a wise guy. **1972** J. Poyer *Chinese Agenda* iii. 17 Listen to what I have to say, then you can make all the wise-ass remarks you want. **1978** J. Irving *World according to Garp* iv. 66 Benny Potter from New York—a *born* wise-ass. *Ibid.* 67 It was unfortunate that wise-ass Benny Potter was the first to tell Garp the news. **1967** P. Tamony *Americanisms* (typescript) No. 18. 2 A fantastic display of brash male and female *wise-assed mediocrity. **1976** 'Trevanian' *Main* xii. 260 Some wiseassed note about the bad luck of getting a parking ticket the same night you get killed. **1600** Tourneur *Transf. Metam.* liv, With a *wise-bold heed. **1894** Alma-Tadema *Wings of Icarus* v. 26 There you go, old *wisebones! Here's a storm in a tea-cup! **1642** H. More *Song of Soul* iii. ii. xli, *Wise framed questions. **1575** Laneham *Let.* (1871) 44 Valiant, & *wizehardy. **1587** Holinshed *Chron.* III. 583/2 Of courage inuincible,.. wise-hardie alwaies. **1887** Morris *Odyssey* viii. 327 The cunning of *wise-heart Hephæstus' snare. **1535** Coverdale *Exod.* xxxv. 26 Soch wemen as were *wyse herted. **1867** Morris *Jason* ii. 862 Men there are Wise-hearted. **1644** Milton *Divorce* ii. xvii. (ed. 2) 66 Why men so disesteem this *wise judging Law of God. **1821** Scott *Kenilw.* vii, Many wise-judging men. **1818** Milman *Samor* i. 384 *Wise-lipp'd chief. **1848** Buckley *Iliad* vi. 110 By no means could she persuade just-minded, *wise-reflecting Bellerophon. **1597** *Pilgr. Parnass.* i. 113 Youre *wise-said says Keepe mee from devious.. wayes! *a* **1586** Sidney *Astr. & Stella* lxxv, He could young wise, *wise valliant frame His Syres revenge. *a* **1225** *Ancr. R.* 64 Sum is so wel ilered, oðer se *wis iworded [etc.].

wise (waiz), *v.*[1] *Obs.* exc. *Sc.* and *north. dial.* Forms: 1 **wisian**, 3 **wisie**, 4–6 (8–9 *Sc.* and *dial.*) **wyse**, (5 **vyse**, 6 *pa. pple.* **wizde**), 7 (9 *dial.*) **wize**, 3–7 (9 *dial.*) **wise**, 9 *Sc.* **weise**, **weize**. [OE. *wísian* to show the way = OFris. *wîsa*, OS. *wîsian*, MLG., MDu. *wîsen* (Du. *wijzen*), OHG. *wîsan* (MHG. *wîsen*, G. *weisen*, now conjugated as a str. vb.), ON. *vísa* (Sw. *visa*, Da. *vise*). Goth.

fulla-weisjan πείθειν: f. OTeut. **wîsaz* WISE *a.* (Cf. WIS *v.*[1])]

1. *trans.* To show the way to (a person); to guide, direct; †hence, to direct or manage the affairs of, govern, rule (*obs.*); also in mod. dial., to induce, entice *away*, *from*...; to instruct, inform.

Beowulf 320 Stræt wæs stanfah, stiȝ wisode gumum ætgædere. *c* **1000** ÆLFRIC *Gen.* xxxv. 5 Iacob ferde þa mid ealre his hiwrædene, swa him god wisode. *c* **1205** LAY. 1200 Wise mi & witere.. whuder ich mæi liðan. *a* **1250** *Owl & Night.* 973 þu.. seist þu uisest [*v.r.* wisest] mankunne þat hi biwepen hore sunne. *c* **1250** *Prayer to Our Lady* 2 in *O.E. Misc.* 192 þu wisie me nuþe for ich eom eirede. **1297** R. GLOUC. (Rolls) 10755 Sire steuene of segraue was imad þo hei iustise In sire hubertes stude de boru þut lond wel to wise. **13..** *Cursor M.* 17931 (Gött.) Quen i þe gan wis To þe ȝatis of paradis. *c* **1320** *Cast. Love* 297 Wiþ-oute whom he ne mai His kindom wiþ pees wysen. *a* **1400–50** *Wars Alex.* 2988 Alexander.. trottis him to þe trod-gate, as him þe torche wyssis [*Dubl.* vysys]. *c* **1400** *Song Roland* 303 'Now wise vs crist!' quod Roulond. *c* **1460** *Towneley Myst.* ix. 122 Mahowne he wyse the on thi way. **1575** TURBERV. *Faulconrie* 130 Alwayes wysing and making your hawke to leane in vpon you. **1594** CAREW *Tasso* II. xli, To be wizde what cause her thither drew. **1604** H. BROUGHTON *Advt. Corrupt. Relig.* E 3 b, Tremelius might haue wised M. Liuely. **1606** N. BAXTER *Sidney's Ourania* D 2, She [*sc.* the Moon] wizeth Surgeons when to ope a veine. **1610** H. BROUGHTON *Job* xxxv. 11 Who doth teach us more than the beasts of the earth: and wiseth us above the foules of the heaven. **1657** TRAPP *Comm. Ezra* viii. 16 Being themselves wise, and willing to wise others. *a* **1810** TANNAHILL *Song, Dear Highland Laddie* ii, The Laird's wys'd awa' by braw Highland laddie, O. **1821** GALT *Ann. Parish* xxxviii. 310 She ..took me by the hand, and wised me to go back. **1825** BROCKETT *N.C. Gloss., Wise*, to shew or direct. 'Wise him in.' 'Wise him out.'

2. To direct the course or movement of; to move in some direction or into some position; to convey, conduct; to turn (in various connexions: see quots.); also *fig.*

a **1300** *Cursor M.* 21272 A..wain men wit four quelis wises. *c* **1330** R. BRUNNE *Chron. Wace* (Rolls) 13698 His hors on hym [*sc.* Bokkus] his bridel wysed. *c* **1440** *Pallad. on Husb.* II. 78 The forgh is best, ille humour out to wise. **1606** N. BAXTER *Sidney's Ourania* C 3, Planets.. Knowne to each Figure-flinger.. That wize from thence many an vncouth-tale. **1816** SCOTT *Antiq.* vii, Now, weize yoursell a wee easel-ward—a wee mair yet to that ither stane. **1825** BROCKETT *N.C. Gloss.* s.v., Wise off that rope there. *a* **1827** in Scott *Jrnl.* 2 Aug., Stuff with moss, and clog with clay, And that will weize the water away. **1830** GALT *Lawrie T.* IV. x. (1849) 179 Mr. Bell quietly wised the conversation upon juvenile indiscretions. **1862** SMILES *Engineers* III. 113 Wise on the Hydrogen, Nichol! **1862** HISLOP *Prov. Scot.* 58 Every miller wad weise the water to his ain mill. **1867** J. K. HUNTER *Retrospect Artist's Life* xiv. (1912) 135 The little fish rushed to the shore before him, as he quietly wysed them shoreward.

b. To direct, aim, 'send', shoot (a missile) (*Sc.*); †*fig.* to utter.

a **1300** *Cursor M.* 24103 Quen i wend word to wise. **1721** RAMSAY *Ode to Ph——* ii, Fowk wysing a Jee The Byass Bouls on Tamson's Green. **1814** SCOTT *Wav.* lviii, Mony o' them wadna mind a bawbee the weising a ball through the Prince himsell.

c. *intr.* for *refl.* To direct one's course, make one's way, betake oneself, go.

c **1330** R. BRUNNE *Chron. Wace* (Rolls) 10956 Vnto þer contres he bad þem wyse. **1721** RAMSAY *Richy & Sandy* 69 But see the Sheep are wysing to the Cleugh.

3. *trans.* To show, point out (the way). †Also, to cause to be seen, show, reveal (*obs.*).

13.. *E.E. Allit. P.* A. 1135 A wounde ful wyde.. con wyse An-ende hys hert þurȝ hyde to-rente. *c* **1400** *Rule St. Benet* (verse) 138 Wysand vs þe way to heuen. *c* **1450** *Pol. Poems* (Rolls) II. 226 The printe of a palsy wisith the thy way. **1818** SCOTT *Rob Roy* xxiii, I'll hae somebody waiting to weise ye the gate to the place.

wise (waɪz), *v.*[2] [f. WISE *a.* 3 b (*b*).] **1.** *to wise up* (U.S. slang): to 'get wise'; to 'put wise'. Freq. const. *on* or *to*. Also *refl.*

1905 R. BEACH *Pardners* iv. 113, I cast the bad eye on the boys to wise 'em up. **1919** J. BUCHAN *Mr. Standfast* iii. 70 You've got to wise up about Gresson with the whole forces of the British State arrayed officially against you. **1922** P. G. WODEHOUSE *Girl on Boat* i. 25 You won't wise him up that I threw a spanner into the machinery? **1925** F. SCOTT FITZGERALD *Great Gatsby* vii. 124, I just got wised up to something funny the last few days. **1929** *Princeton Alumni Weekly* 24 May 982/2 To stick out one's neck is to commit an unpardonable error, to lay oneself open to criticism... A persistent offender should wise up on himself. **1955** W. GADDIS *Recognitions* I. iv. 158 Yeah, you got to wise up to yourself, see? **1960** C. MACINNES *Mr Love & Justice* 26 That's.. what I'm wising myself up on. **1971** *Wall St. Jrnl.* (Eastern ed.) 10 Mar. 1/4 Antique dealers are wising up to the growing demand for old radios. **1984** *Listener* 7 June 36/3 'Write a poem about it,' he suggests. 'Wise up, sir,' the new generation tells him.

2. *to wise off* (U.S. slang): to make wisecracks *at* someone.

1943 *Yank* 2 July 10 I'd love to have one of those acting noncoms wise off at me. **1981** 'P. MALLORY' *Killing Matter* xiii. 136 He's a real meanie. I wouldn't be wising off at him if I were you.

Hence **wised-up** *ppl. a.*

1926 J. BLACK *You can't Win* xx. 301, I could make a living without taking tough chances against wised-up city police. **1952** M. MCCARTHY *Groves of Academe* (1953) x. 205 His wised-up air was as irritating.. as Donna's exaggerations. **1973** R. PARKES *Guardians* ix. 172 It's nasty. Very nasty. But at least I'm wised up now.

Wise: see VAISYA.

wise, obs. f. VICE *sb.*[1] and [2], VISE *v.*[1]

-wise: see WISE *sb.*[1] II.

wiseacre ('waɪzˌeɪkə(r)). Forms: 6–7 **wise-aker, 7 wiseaker, wisacre, 7–8 wise acre, 7– wise-acre, wiseacre.** [ad. (with unexplained assimilation to *acre*) MDu. *wijsseggher* ('waɪsˌzɛgər) soothsayer, app. ad. OHG. *wîzago*, MHG. *wîzage* (= OE. *wítega* WITIE *sb.*), with assimilation to *wijs* WISE *a.* and *segghher* SAYER.]

1. One who thinks himself, or wishes to be thought, wise; a pretender to wisdom; a foolish person with an air or affectation of wisdom.

1595 *Enq. Tripe-wife* (1881) 146 Shall he run vp and downe the town,.. accompanied with some such wise-akers as himselfe. **1609** DEKKER *Gulls Horn-bk.* Proemium 5 Thou Lady of Clownes and Carters, Schoolemistres of fooles and wisacres. **1654** WHITLOCK *Zootomia* 47 Syrupe of Poppy, (that edged Tool in the hands of such Doctor Wise-akers). **1711** STEELE *Spect.* No. 138 ¶6 This Wiseacre was reckoned by the Parish, who did not understand him, a most excellent Preacher. **1810** SCOTT *Fam. Lett.* 31 Dec. (1894) I. vi. 202 This wise-acre thinks he should have a finger in every man's pie. **1852** THACKERAY *Esmond* I. xiii, I have heard politicians and coffee-house wise-acres talking over the newspaper. **1874** MICKLETHWAITE *Mod. Par. Churches* 115 The architect.. is lectured on his own art by wiseacres, whose whole stock of knowledge is got up from 'Parker's Glossary'.

†**b.** Used in pl. form of a single person; sometimes as a *quasi*-proper name. *Obs.*

? **1613** J. TAYLOR (Water P.) *Laugh & be fat* Wks. (1630) II. 71/1 A learned wiseakers. **1615** TOFTE *Varchi's Blazon Jealousie* 24 *note*, Wiseakers her Husband, neuer so much as once doubting or dreaming of any such matter. **1673** *S'too him Bayes* 9 When he has done (like a wise-acres) he makes nothing of it.

¶**c.** With allusion to *acres* as = 'lands'; in first quot. app. applied to a landed estate.

1608 *Yorksh. Trag.* I. iii, Is the rubbish sold, those wise-akers your lands? *a* **1734** NORTH *Exam.* II. v. §128 (1740) 394 If wise by their Acres, or, in a word Wiseacres, it was expected the Guineys should come out, for the Uses of Mobbing.

2. A wise or learned person, a sage. (Usually contemptuous.)

1753 in *Gentl. Mag.* XXIII. 417 (spuriously archaic) Pythagoras lerned muche—becomming a myghtye wyse-acre. **1814** *Sporting Mag.* XLIV. 271 The concourse of wiseacres.. was truly astonishing. **1842** THACKERAY *Fitz-Boodle's Conf.* Pref., It requires no great wiseacre to know that. **1902** *Sat. Rev.* 29 Nov. 677/2 The stoic paradox that the cobbler who has got wisdom is the universal wiseacre.

Hence (*nonce-wds.*) **'wiseˌacred** (-əd) *a.*, having the character of a wiseacre (in quot. with allusion to *acre*: cf. 1 c above), whence ***wiseacredness***; **'wiseˌacredom**, the realm of wiseacres, wiseacres collectively; **'wiseˌacreish** (-ərɪʃ) *a.*, like or characteristic of a wiseacre (whence ***wiseacreishness***); **'wiseˌacreism** (-ərɪz(ə)m), **'wiseˌacrery** (-ərɪ), something characteristic of a wiseacre; pretension to or affectation of wisdom, or a remark exhibiting this.

1603 DEKKER *Wonderful Year* B 3, Each *wise-acred Landlord. **1848** EARL NORTHBROOK in Mallet *Mem.* (1908) 39 The conceited phraseology and would-be *wiseacredness of its professors. **1885** A. DOBSON *Don Quix.* in *Sign of Lyre* 93 To make *Wiseacredom, both high and low, Rub purblind eyes. **1834** J. WILSON in *Blackw. Mag.* XXXVI. 415 He.. then perpends, in a *wiseacreish pause, to consider if they are all to be found. **1895** SAINTSBURY *Corrected Impr.* ii. 12 *Ex post facto* *wiseacre-ishness. **1861** T. L. PEACOCK *Gryll Grange* xxiii, Whist is more consentaneous to modern solemnity: there is more *wiseacre-ism about it. **1917** SAINTSBURY *Hist. Fr. Novel* I. 371 Interrupting his vizier and the other tale-tellers with *wiseacreries.

wisecrack ('waɪzkræk). *colloq.* (orig. *U.S.*). Also **wise crack, wise-crack.** [CRACK *sb.* 5.] A clever, pithy witticism or remark. Also as quasi-*adj.*

1924 G. ADE *Let.* 20 Dec. (1973) 101 When Geraghty came yesterday, both of us had thought of putting in another character, a young wise-crack small town loafer,.. who thinks he is very sly. **1925** *Sat. Even. Post* 14 Feb. 44 The Palace, Chicago, will howl at a wise crack, a nifty, that Duluth audiences won't even flag as it flies over their heads. **1950** G. B. SHAW *Buoyant Billions* 98 The satirical humor of Aristophanes, the wisecracks of Confucius, the precepts of the Buddha. **1959** I. & P. OPIE *Lore & Lang. Schoolch.* ix. 174 He might.. have seen sense in the wisecracks which.. scientifically minded boys indulge in..: 'What is the matter?' 'That which occupies space.' **1977** *Rep. Comm. Future of Broadcasting* (Cmnd. 6753) ii. 15 Lord Hill.. saw no reason why the BBC should have been expected to apologise for a wisecrack in a satire programme.. that if you can see the Prime Minister's lips moving you know he is lying. **1979** R. JAFFE *Class Reunion* (1980) I. viii. 109 Say only nice, polite, ladylike things, no nasty wisecracks.

So **'wisecrack** *v. intr.*, to make wisecracks; also *trans.*, with quoted words as obj.; **'wisecracking** *ppl. a.* and *vbl. sb.*; also **'wisecracker**, one given to making wisecracks.

1915 *Call* (San Francisco) 30 Apr. 17 Wisecrackin' city fellers ain't got nuthin' on you. **1923** *N.Y. Times* 9 Sept. VII. 2 *Wise-cracker*, a city fellow who makes wise remarks. **1924** P. MARKS *Plastic Age* 28 The lights flashed on and the crowd filed out, 'wise-cracking' about the picture. *Ibid.* 113 Carl the flippant, the voluble, the 'wise-cracker', lost his tongue. **1927** *New Republic* 12 Oct. 218/2 He has the knack of wise-cracking, and his dialogue is of that slick and well oiled kind that you may meet in good vaudeville. **1939** JOYCE *Finnegans Wake* 33 It has been blurtingly bruited by certain wisecrackers.. that he suffered from a vile disease. **1940** GRAVES & HODGE *Long Week-End* xx. 345 Everyday life could be made interesting on the screen without fictitious drama or wise-cracking comment. **1946** *Sat. Rev. Lit.* 2 Nov. 41/1 Both authors wisecrack their way through adverse circumstances. **1949** H. ROBBINS *Dream Merchants* (1950) 144 Jane saw him come into the office. 'If it ain't the vice-president himself!' she wisecracked. 'How's the picture business?' **1949** G. B. SHAW *Sixteen Self Sketches* xiv. 82 Without him I might have been a mere literary wise-cracker, like Carlyle and Ruskin. **1977** *Rolling Stone* 21 Apr. 58/1 Jim Rockford is a worldly wisecracker. **1979** *Fortune* 21 May 71/1 Fraser wisecracks that the Carter Administration's voluntary wage guidelines have 'self-destructed'. **1982** *Daily Tel.* 11 May 14 He has defended rioters.. with such vigour as to alarm his fellow lawyers, one of whom wisecracked to me: 'Who will rid us of this turbulent pest?' **1982** E. NORTH *Ancient Enemies* viii. 105 Liz reminds me.. of Tammy, who was tough and wise-cracking.

wisedam, -dom(e, obs. ff. WISDOM.

wisehead ('waɪzhɛd). [f. WISE *a.* + HEAD *sb.*[1]] One who has a wise head; always in ironical sense, One who fancies himself wise, a wiseacre.

[**1378** *Poll Tax Yorks* 158 in Bardsley *Surnames*, Johannes Wysehede.] **1756** *Monitor* No. 64. II. 123 The wise-heads.. have been a good deal troubled to invent proper subjects for this purpose. **1862** MISS BRADDON *Lady Audley* xxxvi, The wiseheads of the servants' hall. **1875** H. JAMES *Rod. Hudson* iii. 94 There were naturally a great many wiseheads who smiled at his precipitancy.

† **'wisehede.** *Obs. rare.* In 4–5 **wys-.** [f. WISE *a.* + *-hede*, -HEAD. Cf. OFris. *wîshêd*, Du. *wijsheid*, G. *weisheit.*] Wisdom.

1340 *Ayenb.* 68 Zuyche uolke þet wylleþ him benyme his lhordssip and his wyshede. **1481** CAXTON *Reynard* xxviii. (Arb.) 68 The ouerest wysehede.

wise-like ('waɪzlaɪk, *dial.* 'waɪs-, 'weis-), *a.* (*adv.*) *Sc.* and *dial.* [f. WISE *a.* + -LIKE 2.]

1. Reasonable, rational.

1816 SCOTT *Old Mort.* xiv, It wad hae been lang or my Leddy Margaret.. wad hae fund out sic a wise-like doctrine in the Bible! **1818** SUSAN FERRIER *Marriage* I. xii, It wad set her better to be carrying a wise-like wean in her arms, than trailing aboot wi' thae confoonded dougs an' paurits. **1893–4** *Northumbld. Gloss.* s.v., That's a wise-like dog o' yors.

2. Becoming, seemly, respectable, proper: esp. in appearance.

1820 *Blackw. Mag.* Nov. 148 Talking..o thrashing ripe rigs wi' the west wind.. may look very wiselike in rhyme. **1842** J. AITON *Dom. Econ.* (1857) 123 Make it something 'wiselike' and substantial, that it may remain as a monument of your own liberality and good sense. **1881** *Academy* 15 Oct. 289/3 Jane.. wice-like rather than pretty. **1894** *Blackw. Mag.* June 754/1 He was considered by.. many ladies of the parish to be a very personable man, comely.., and altogether a wyss-like man.

B. as *adv.* Fittingly, becomingly, respectably,

1822 *Blackw. Mag.* Sept. 315 They ought to hire a chaise, and gang in till Edinburgh wiselike. **1841** *Fraser's Mag.* Jan. 109/2 Dinna gang ramstam in, saying, 'Janet, here's meal; and Janet, here's butter';.. slip cannily and wiselike in.

wiseling ('waɪzlɪŋ). Now *rare.* [f. WISE *a.* + -LING[1] 2.] A pretender to wisdom; a wiseacre.

1633 J. DONE *Hist. Septuagint* 214 These wiselings, that shew themselues fooles in so speaking, and discoursing with-out Discourse. **1649** J. ELLISTONE tr. *Behmen's Epist.* (1886) 3 Those Luciferian wiselings that thought none could teach them anything. **1765** LAW *Behmen's Myst. Magnum* xxxix. 222 Let Master Sophister or Wiseling of Babel look us right in the Face. **1914** NELLEN & CRAIG tr. *Ozanam's Francisc. Poets Italy* v. 245 He praises the wisdom which shrinks from the wiselings.

wisell, var. WIZLE, stalk, etc.

† **'wisely,** *a. Obs. rare.* Forms: 1 **wislic,** 3 **wislich,** 4 *comp.* **wislier,** 5 **wysely,** 6 **wysley,** 7 **wisely.** [OE. *wíslic*: see WISE *a.* and -LY[1].] = WISE *a.* I.

c **900** tr. *Bæda's Hist.* II. xiii. (1890) 134 Me þynceð wislic, ȝif þu ȝeseo þa þing beteran,.. þæt we þam onfon. *a* **1023** WULFSTAN *Hom.* i. (1883) 4 Ðonne is eac wislic ræd, þæt manna ȝehwylc ȝeornlice smeaȝe. *a* **1300** *Cursor M.* 28116 Wit wislier þat i was amang Haue i striued oft-sithes wrang. **1436** *Libel Engl. Policy* in *Pol. Poems* (Rolls) II. 183 Yf men were wysely, the Frenshmen and Flemmynge Shulde bere no state in see by werrynge. **1556** *J. de Flores' Aurelio & Isab.* E 8, Vnto howre wysley wordes.

wisely ('waɪzlɪ), *adv.* Forms: see WISE *a.* and -LY[2]; also 5 **wisily, vi-, vysilie,** 5–6 **wys(e)-. wyislie,** 6 **wyslye, wislie.** [OE. *wíslíce* = OS. *wîslîco*, MLG., MDu. *wîslîk* (Du. *wijzelijk*), OHG. *wîslîcho* (MHG. *wîslîche*), ON. *vísliga* (in the sense of *vissuliga* certainly): f. WISE *a.* + -LY[2].] In a wise manner.

1. With wisdom, sound judgement, or sagacity. Also more widely, with good sense or discretion.

c **888** ÆLFRED *Boeth.* xviii. §1 Se þe wile wislice & ȝeornlice æfter þam hlisan spyrian. *c* **897** —— *Gregory's Past. C.* xviii. 131 Ðæt he meahte ðæt folc ðy wislicor & ðy rædlicor læran. *c* **1175** *Lamb. Hom.* 105 þet mon wisliche spene þa þing þe him god lene on þisse liue to brukene. *c* **1200** ORMIN 2199 ȝho toc wisliȝ to fraȝȝnenn himm whatt itt bitacnenn mihhte. *c* **1250** *Gen. & Ex.* 1091 Loth hem warnede, wislike and wel, Oc he ne troweden him neuere a del. *a* **1300** *Cursor M.* 18852 Clerli spak he þat he wald, And al his skil wiseli he tald. *c* **1374** CHAUCER *Troylus* I. 956 He hasteþ wel þat wysly kan a-byde. *c* **1400** *Lanfranc's Cirurg.* 70 Alle þese þingis I haue told, þat he þat rediþ hem mai þe visiloker [*v.r.* wyslocor] in semblable causis worchen. *a* **1450** *Le Morte Arth.* 1158 Thou ne woste not Ryght wiseliche What harme hathe falle. *c* **1489** CAXTON *Sonnes of Aymon* xxv. 539 See that ye revenge yourself wysly. **1551** ROBINSON tr. *More's Utopia* I. (1895) 113 Thys I suppose is the chiefe cause whie theyr common wealthes be wyselyere gouerned. *a* **1586** SIDNEY *Arcadia* III. (1922) 78 Young men, who thinke, then they speake wiseliest, when they cannot understand themselves. **1604** SHAKS. *Oth.* v. ii. 344 One that lou'd not wisely, but too well. **1610** —— *Temp.* II. i. 21 *Gon...* You haue spoken truer then you purpos'd. *Seb.* You haue taken it wiselier then I meant you should. **1667** MILTON *P.L.* x. 1023 Doubt not but God Hath wiselier arm'd his vengeful ire then so To be forestall'd. **1765** A. DICKSON *Treat. Agric.* (ed. 2) 63 This method of conveying the vegetable food from the earth to the air, and from the air to the earth, is wisely established, for making a just distribution of it upon all parts of the earth. **1829** SOUTHEY *Sir T. More* I. 280 Men judge wiseliest, when they judge most charitably. **1847** HELPS *Friends in C.* I. v. 85 From a genial, wisely-developed man, good things radiate. **1925** E. PHILLPOTTS *Voice from Dark* xvi. 199 He would have done wiselier to be home before it came.

b. With an air or assumption of wisdom; sagely, knowingly.

1585 T. WASHINGTON tr. *Nicholay's Voy.* IV. xiii. 126 b, [I asked him .. what religion he kept, wherupon wisely he gaue me to vnderstand that [etc.]. **1600** SHAKS. *A.Y.L.* II. vii. 22 He .. looking on it, with lacke-lustre eye, Sayes, very wisely, it is ten a clocke. **1888** 'J. S. WINTER' *Bootle's Childr.* iv, 'Ah! but there's very few Captain Ferrers about,' said Lassie wisely.

†**2.** Attentively, carefully, heedfully. *Obs.*

c **1000** *Inst. Polity* x. in Thorpe *Laws* II. 318 Beþencan heora dæda wislice & wærlice. *a* **1225** *Ancr. R.* 104 Þe heorte is wel iloked ȝif muð & eien & earen wisliche beoð ilokene. *a* **1225** *Leg. Kath.* 82 Ha heold hire aldrene hird wisliche & warliche. **1377** LANGL. *P. Pl.* B. XIII. 343, I wayted wisloker. ? *a* **1400** *Morte Arth.* 1613 That they be weisely wachede and in warde holdene. *c* **1400** MAUNDEV. (Roxb.) xxvi. 123 Qwhen þai ga to were, þai hafe þam riȝt warly and wysely. *c* **1475** *Rauf Coilȝear* 587, I raid on full richt, To watche wyselie the wayis. **1558** WARDE tr. *Alexis' Secr.* 111 Powre the said water fynely and wisely into some other vessel that is cleane. **1594** PLAT *Jewell-ho.* III. 28 If you holde the same [glass] wisely .. you shall see the wine ascende in the forme of a clowd.

†**3.** Skilfully, cleverly, ingeniously; cunningly.

a **1000** *Cædmon's Gen.* 456 Oð ðæt he Adam on eorðrice, godes handȝesceaft ȝearone funde, wislice ȝeworht, & his wif somed. *a* **1000** *Boeth. Metr.* xx. 15 Þu þe unstilla aȝna ȝesceafta to ðinum willan wislice astyrest. *c* **1250** *Gen. & Ex.* 3630 God it taȝte al ear moysen Wislike hu it wroȝt sulde ben. **1390** GOWER *Conf.* I. 255 With his wordes slyhe and queinte, The whiche he cowthe wysly peinte. *c* **1430** *Pilgr. Lyf Manhode* I. lxxiv. (1869) 44 She wolde it were so wysliche moolded and so subtylliche that bi seemynge it were litel. *a* **1586** SIDNEY *Arcadia* Ecl. ii. (1922) 231 The hives of wisely painfull Bees. **1601** SHAKS. *Twel. N.* I. v. 33 Here comes my Lady: make your excuse wisely, you were best.

wise man. (Formerly often as one word, or with hyphen; cf. the surname *Wiseman.*)

1. a. *gen.* A man who is wise; a man of good judgement or discernment; a discreet or prudent man. (Often opposed to *fool.*)

worldly wiseman: see WORLDLY.

c **888** ÆLFRED *Boeth.* xl. §3 Forðy ne scyle nan wis mon forhiȝan ne to swiðe ymb þæt gnornian, to hwæm his wise weorðe. *c* **1000** ÆLFRIC *Saints' Lives* xiii. 116 Ne sceal se wise mann beon butan godum weorcum. *a* **1225** *Ancr. R.* 214 Wel understond euerich wis mon þis. *c* **1300** *Havelok* 180 Wis man of red, wis man of dede. **1390** GOWER *Conf.* I. 46 It myhte make a wisman madd. *c* **1400** *Rule St. Benet* (prose) 15 Þe wyse man musters hym wid fa wordis & welle sitande. **1481** CAXTON *Godfrey* xxv. 57 There ben more fooles than wysemen. *a* **1548** HALL *Chron., Edw. IV* 207 This mariage semed very straunge to wise men. **1549** *Compl. Scot.* Prol. 16, I hope that vyise men vil reput my ignorance for ane mortifeit prudens. *a* **1619** FOTHERBY *Atheom.* I. xiv. §3. (1622) 150 Wisemen indeed haue euer reputed them, for no better then mad-men. **1702** H. DODWELL *Apol.* §13 in S. Parker *Cicero's De Finibus*, He took Cato for a perfect Stoick, and for a Wiseman, in the Sense of the Philosophers. **1770** BRIDGES *Burlesque Transl. Homer* II. 26 Old Nestor, .. Who always counted was a Wise-man. **1853** LYNCH *Self-Improvem.* i. 2 He is a wise man who has an instructed mind and a regulated choice. **1859** GEO. ELIOT *Adam Bede* xix, A fool 'ull hit on't sometimes when a wise man misses.

b. Ironically applied to a fool or simpleton, as in ***the wise men of Gotham*** (see GOTHAM 1).

[**1471** *Paston Lett.* III. 32 Yonge Wyseman othyrwy[s]e callyd Foole.] **1526**, *c* **1560** [see GOTHAM 1]. **1596** RALEIGH *Discov. Guiana* 5 Who like Wise men in the absence of their Captaine followed the Indians. **1711** *Countrey-Mans Lett. to Curate* 32 It were .. too Churlish to grudge these talkers the Character of the only Wisemen of G——.

2. *spec.* **a.** A man deeply versed in some subject of study, or in studies generally; a learned man, scholar, philosopher, sage. Now *rare* or *arch.*

the seven wise men = the seven sages: see SAGE *sb.*[2] 1.

a **1000** *Cædmon's Exod.* 377 Wise men wordum secgað, þæt from Noe niȝoða wære fæder Abrahames on folctale. **1338** R. BRUNNE *Chron.* (1810) 114 Wis man in þe lawe. **1379** *Glouc. Cath. MS.* *19* I. I. iv. lf 1 Iff þ[u] will wysman be in demyng of vryn. **1387** TREVISA *Higden* (Rolls) III. 63 Tales Millesus .. þe firste of þe seuene wise men. **1450–80** tr. *Secr. Secr.* iii. 6 His philesofris and grete wise-men of clergie. **1588** KYD *Househ. Philos.* Index, Thales one of the seauen wise men of Greece. **1655** STANLEY *Hist. Philos.* Pref. (1687) 2 Hermippus in his Treatise of the seven wise Men saith, they were in all seventeen, of which seven were variously named. **1656** BLOUNT *Glossogr.*, *Solon*, one of the seven wisemen of Greece. **1842** W. C. TAYLOR *Anc. Hist.* ix. §5 (ed. 3) 240 Periander, who is sometimes ranked among the Seven Wise Men of Greece. **1850** LD. KELVIN in S. P. Thompson *Life* (1910) I. v. 223 The steamer appeared about 4 P.M.—contrary to the expectation of the nautical wise men about the harbour.

b. A man who utters wise sayings or maxims; *esp.* as a title for any of the writers of the Jewish 'Wisdom Literature'.

a **1225** *Ancr. R.* 64 Þe wise mon [*sc.* Solomon] askeð in his boc hweðer [etc.]. **1375** BARBOUR *Bruce* I. 121 And wys men sayis he is happy, That be othir will him chasty. *c* **1400** *Rule St. Benet* (verse) 1080 Þus þe wisman sais þerbi. **1542** BOORDE *Dyetary* ix. (1870) 251 The wyse man sayth, that surfetes do kyll many men. **1587** T. NEWTON *Herbal for Bible* I. 274 So doth the Wiseman [*marg.* Eccle. i. 24] vse it, whereby he promiseth felicitie .. to him that .. embraceth Wisedom. **1611** *Bible* Transl. Pref. ¶3 There is no new thing vnder the Sunne, saith the wiseman. **1649** WILKINS *Beauty Provid.* 92 Like snow in Harvest (as the Wiseman speaks). **1659** *Gentl. Calling* v. §13 The wise-man hath assured us this, Prov. 11. 4. Riches profit not in the day of wrath. *c* **1705** POPE *Jan. & May* 153 Yet you pursue sage Solomon's advice, .. But, with the wiseman's leave, I must protest. *c* **1750** *New Whole Duty of Man* viii, The threatening of the Wise-man, who .. declares, that the eye that mocketh his father, .. the ravens of the valley shall pick it out.

c. One of a body of men chosen for their sagacity as advisers in matters of state; a councillor. *colloq.* in mod. use.

By 16th–18th century historians used in pl. to render WITAN.

c **1250** *Gen. & Ex.* 2649 Ðe king wið-stod & an wisman, He seide, 'ðe child doð als he can'. **1488** *Cely Papers* (Camden) 169 That eueryche of thes contreys doo send .. serten wyse-men w[t] full auctoryte .. for to coomen .. w[t] the Gauntnersse. **1502** ARNOLDE *Chron.* (1811) p. xx, This yere wer chosen be wise men of the cite, xxxv men, .. sworne to mayntene the Assisis. **1591** LAMBARDE *Archeion* (1635) 256 All the Acts are said to passe from the King, and his Wisemen both of the Clergie and Laitie. **1648** PRYNNE *Plea for Lords* 3 Lordes and Peeres; anciently stiled Aldermen, Heretockes, Senators, Wisemen, .. by our Historians. **1714** FORTESCUE-ALAND *Pref. Fortescue's Abs. & Lim. Mon.* 18 King Alfred .. with the Thought, i.e. Advice of his Wisemen, or Parliament. **1959** J. BALOGH in H. Thomas *Establishment* 98 In the negotiations on the finance of NATO rearmament in Lisbon the British representative 'wise man' accepted a contribution wholly out of line with the relative capacities to bear the burden. **1969** D. ACHESON *Present at Creation* xxxi. 277 Lester Pearson has continually urged the council to set up committees of 'wise men' to find a use for it [*sc.* Article 2 of the North Atlantic Treaty]. **1973** *Times* 5 May 4/4 The appointment of two independent 'wise men' by the United States and the European Community to prepare the ground for the forthcoming round of international trade talks, was suggested. **1983** *Times* 24 Feb. 6/8 A socialist leader .. has been nominated to the elite body of nine 'wise men' who form France's Constitutional Council. **1984** *Times* 29 Oct. 1/3 The Gaddafi affair .. is unlikely to go away as quickly as the TUC's 'four wise men' monitoring the dispute would wish.

3. A man versed or skilled in hidden arts, as magic, witchcraft, and the like; a magician, wizard; *spec.* applied in biblical versions and allusions to the three Oriental astrologers or Magi (see MAGUS 2) who came to worship the infant Jesus. In general sense now *dial.* or *vulgar* (cf. WISE WOMAN 1).

1382 WYCLIF *Matt.* ii. 1 When Jhesus was born in Bethlem .. loo! kyngis, or wijs men [1388 astronomyenes; Vulg. *Magi*], camen fro the eest. **1552** LATIMER *Serm. Lincs.* v. (1562) 100 b, Whan we be in trouble, or sicknes, or lose any thing: we runne hither and thither to wyssardes, or sorcerers, whome we call wyse men. **1561** S. WYTHERS tr. *Calvin's Treat. Relics* G iv b, Y[e] wysmen which came to worshipe our lord Iesus after his natiuitie. **1573** TWYNE *Æneid., Life Virgil* A 3, That he was at the first couenaunt seruant w[t] a traueilinge wyseman. **1595** PEELE *Old Wives T.* (facs.) C 1 b, I pray you tell where the wise man the Coniurer dwells? **1612** COTTA *Discov. Dang. Pract. Phys.* I. ix. 71 A sort of practitioners, whom our custome .. doth call wisemen and wisewomen, reputed a kind of good .. harmles witches or wisards, who by good words .. promise to allay .. diuels, practises of other witches, and the forces of many diseases. **1731** *Flying Post* 29 Apr. 2/1 George Raunsforth, .. a reputed Conjurer, or (as the Country People call him) a Wise Man. **1802** R. ANDERSON *Cumbld. Ball.* 39 The wise man lives nit far frae this, .. He telt Nan Dobson whee she'd wed. **1839** [see MAGUS 2].

4. (*old*) ***wise man***: an archetypal figure appearing in myths, folklore, etc., representing wisdom or meaning, esp., in the theory of C. G. Jung, one of the archetypes of the collective unconscious; cf. *wise old man* s.v. WISE *a.* (*sb.*[3], *adv.*) 1 a.

1692 W. SALMON tr. 'Hermes Trismegistus' in *Practical Physick* v. 203/1 But if thou shalt say, that Wisdom or the Wise Man does Rule or Command among all Mankind. **1940** S. DELL tr. *Jung's Integration of Personality* iii. 87 The magician is the archetype of the old wise man. *Ibid.* 88, I have been content to call it the archetype of the old wise man or of meaning. **1973** J. SINGER *Boundaries of Soul* x. 262 The archetype of the mana-personality, an Old Wise Man whose power is born of understanding the timeless life processes.

wisen, obs. form of WIZEN *v.*

wiseness ('waɪznɪs). *rare.* [f. WISE *a.* + -NESS. Cf. OE. *unwísnes.*] The quality of being wise; wisdom; occas. *ironical.*

c **1320** *Cast. Love* 292 To vchone sunderlyng He ȝaf a dole of .. his wysnesse. **1387–8** T. USK *Test. Love* II. vi. (Skeat) l. 119 For his goodnesse and wysnesse wolt thou nat do him worship? **1579** E. K. *Ded. to Spenser's Sheph. Cal.* §1 His morall wisenesse. **1602** SHAKS. *Ham.* v. i. 286 Yet haue I something in me dangerous, Which let thy wisenesse feare. **1634** MASSINGER *Very Woman* III. ii, Your wives wonderful wiseness. **1796** MME. D'ARBLAY *Camilla* VII. viii, Which is a wiseness that does honour to her education. **1820** COLERIDGE in *Blackw. Mag.* Sept. 629 This chilly, doubting, qualifying *wiseness.* **1907** *Sat. Rev.* 8 June 702/2 This report .. is full of touches that illustrate his wiseness.

¶ ***right wiseness***, erron. division of *right-wiseness*, RIGHTEOUSNESS.

1447 *Shillingford Lett.* (Camden) 134 Of your grete right wisnesse and speciall grace. **1493** *Festivall* (W. de W. 1515) 49 Come to this byleve by doynge of werkes of ryght wysenes. **15..** *New Notbroune Mayd* 172 in Hazl. *E.P.P.* III. 8 By ryght wysenes. **1638** *Dial. on Laws of Eng.* I. xv. 26 b, Truth in his word, & right wisenes in his deed.

wisenheimer ('waɪzənhaɪmə(r)). *U.S. slang.* Also **weisen-, wise-**. [f. WISE *a.* + *-enheimer*, as in German names such as *Oppenheimer.*] A wiseacre, a 'clever dick'. Also *attrib.* or as *adj.*

1904 R. L. MCCARDELL *Show Girl & her Friends* 51 He wants to know some good way to reduce his weight... You don't know any such a way? No? Why, I thought you was a wiseheimer. **1919** MENCKEN *Amer. Lang.* v. 151 Several years ago *-heimer* had a great vogue in slang, and was rapidly done to death. But *wiseheimer* remains in colloquial use as a facetious synonym for *smart-aleck*, and after awhile it may gradually acquire dignity. **1919** *National Police Gaz.* (U.S.) 4 Jan. 3/1 Cawkins .. like a true Wisenheimer, considered the gentle, goosey kind of a beautiful girl the most appetizing. **1922** S. LEWIS *Babbitt* xxiv. 287 The wisenheimers grab a look at a fellow's nails when they want to tell if he's a tinhorn or a real gent! **1937** *Amer. Speech* XII. 9/2 Some wiseheimer American newspaper man has picked this up and tagged it onto President Hoover. **1957** J. D. SALINGER *Franny & Zooey* (1964) 65 We were nervous .. at the statistics on child pedants and academic weisenheimers who grow up into faculty-recreation-room savants. **1959** *Washington Post* 26 Dec. A19/2 Then some wisenheimer from the agency decided we needed a trailer. **1975** *Times Lit. Suppl.* 21 Feb. 185/1 The wisenheimer who gets his ornate come-uppance. **1977** M. BABSON *Murder, Murder, Little Star* vii. 50, I shoulda listened to her. But .. I was too wisenheimer.

wisent ('wiːzənt). *Antiq.* [a. G. *wisent* (OHG. *wisunt*): see BISON.] The aurochs.

1866 J. E. LEE tr. *F. Keller's Lake Dwellings* 356 The urus .. as well as the bison (or wisent) .. are found to have been the most abundant animals in the forests of the stone age. **1889** I. TAYLOR *Orig. Aryans* iii. 152. **1893** LYDEKKER *Horns & Hoofs* 31 The true, or European, bison .. also known as the wisent or zubr.

wise woman. (For the general sense 'a woman who is wise' see WISE *a.* 1.)

1. A woman skilled in magic or hidden arts; a female magician, soothsayer, etc.; a witch, sorceress; *esp.* a harmless or beneficent one, who deals in charms against disease, misfortune, or malignant witchcraft. Now *dial.* or *arch.*

1382 WYCLIF *2 Sam.* xiv. 2 Joab .. sente to Thekuam, and took thens a wise womman. **1552** HULOET, Wise woman that telleth fortune. **1598** SHAKS. *Merry W.* IV. v. 27 Was't not the Wise-woman of Brainford? **1601** W. PERCY *Cuckqueanes & Cuckolds Errants* v. vi. (Roxb.) 74, I haue haunted a wise woman of our Parish in Maldon, hath taught mee the spell of eury each of them. **1612** [see WISEMAN 3]. **1653** H. MORE *Antid. Ath.* III. vii. §8 (1712) 107 The help and skill of the Witch or Wise-woman. **1828** HONE *Table Bk.* II. 777 An old woman .. who was .. accounted a wise woman, and a practiser of the 'art that none may name'. **1875** in Miss Jackson *Shropsh. Folk-lore* (1883) 146, I asked him if Mrs. P—— was a witch? He answered, she was a wise woman, and only used her knowledge to stop others doing wrong. **1885** A. H. BULLEN in *Dict. Nat. Biog.* I. 112/2 In his extremity he sought the assistance of a wisewoman, Alison Pearson, who treated him so successfully that he completely recovered. His enemies ascribed his cure to witchcraft.

2. A midwife (= F. *sage-femme*): cf. SAGE *a.* 2 b.

1821 SCOTT *Kenilw.* xxiv, 'O, what, you have got the wise woman, then?' said Varney.

wish (wɪʃ), *sb.*[1] [f. WISH *v.*, q.v. for forms.]

1. a. An instance of wishing; a feeling in the mind directed towards something which one believes would give satisfaction if attained, possessed, or realized. (With const. as in WISH *v.* 1 (*b*), (*c*), (*d*).)

Most commonly denoting a desire for something not attainable by one's own effort, felt in the mind but not impelling to action; a passive or inactive desire.

The ordinary word for this affection of the mind; less emphatic than *craving*, *longing*, or *yearning*, but including these as particular cases.

1390 GOWER *Conf.* III. 254 Bot if mi wisshes myhte availe, I wolde it were a groundles pet. *c* **1440** *Promp. Parv.* 535/1 Wusche, or wuschynge, *exoptacio.* *c* **1480** HENRYSON *Prais of Aige* 6 My wys Of al þis warld to mak me lord & kyng. **1530** PALSGR. 289/2 Wysshe desyre, *souhait.* **1591** SHAKS. *Two Gent.* I. iii. 62 As one relying on your Lordships will, And not depending on his friendly wish. **1597** —— *2 Hen. IV*, IV. v. 93 Thy wish was Father (Harry) to that thought. **1600** DEKKER *Old Fortunatus* D 2 b, This Hat .. clapt vpon my head, I (onely with a wish) am through the ayre, Transported in a moment ouer Seas. **1648** FANSHAWE *Il Pastor Fido* II. iv. 64 Fortune beyond my wish hath favoured me. **1694** ATTERBURY *Serm., Prov. xiv. 6* (1726) I. 191 He comes with strong Wishes that he may find it all a Mistake. **1750** GRAY *Elegy* 74 Their sober wishes never learn'd to stray. **1751** JOHNSON *Rambler* No. 178 ¶12 The whole world is put in motion by the wish for riches, and the dread of poverty. **1825** SCOTT *Betrothed* v, Form but a wish for her advantage, and it shall be fulfilled. **1850** TENNYSON *In Mem.* LV. 1 The wish, that of the living whole No life may fail beyond the grave. *Ibid.* xc. 24, I find not yet one lonely thought That cries against my wish for thee. **1850** G. C. LEWIS *Lett.* (1870) 223 He .. has no wish to be a Church dignitary. **1876** MOZLEY *Univ. Serm.* xi. 213 The power of prayer..is..the power of strong wishes.

Proverbs. **1665** WITHER *Lord's Prayer* 50 If (as the Proverb is) wishes were Thrushes, we might all eat Birds. **1670** RAY *Prov.* 157 If wishes would bide, beggers would ride. **1721** KELLY *Sc. Prov.* 178 If Wishes were Horses, Beggars would ride. **1880** MEREDITH *Tragic Com.* (1881) 89 He had a saying: Two wishes make a will.

†**b.** in generalized use: Desire. *Obs. rare.*

c **1430** *Hymns Virgin* (1867) 62 Pride..ȝeueþ but woo & wyssche to wage. *a* **1716** SOUTH *Serm., Matt. xxvi. 41* (1717) VI. 416 Prayer..was never designed to supply the room of Watchfulness, or to make Wish instead of Endeavour.

c. In phrases with prepositions. †*with* or *upon one's wish* or *wishes*, †*at wish*, according to one's wish, just as one wishes; in readiness for one as one wishes, at one's disposal (= *at will*, WILL *sb.*[1] 15 b, c). †*at high wish*, at the height of the fulfilment of one's wishes. *to* (*one's*) *wish* (rarely *wishes*), as one wishes; *esp.* to the full extent of one's desire, as much as one wishes. (Now *rare* or *Obs.*) *to a wish* (*Sc.*), †*till a wish*, just as one would wish, perfectly, exactly.

13.. *Cursor M.* 23412 All þat wit-standand þe es Thoru sal þou thril it wit þi wiss [*Gött.* Thoru sal þou thril wid þi suiftnes]. **1390** GOWER *Conf.* I. 330, I have ben ofte moeved so, That with my wisshes if I myhte,..I hadde storven in a day. *Ibid.* II. 39 He ne wol no travail take To ryde for his ladi sake, Bot liveth al upon his wisshes. *c* **1450** HOLLAND *Howlat* 847 All thus thir hathillis in hall heirly remanit, With all welthis at wiss. *c* **1489** CAXTON *Blanchardyn* ix. 37 Well syttyng on horsbacke, and tyl a wysshe wel shapen of alle membres. *a* **1542** WYATT *Poems*, '*Unstable Dream*' 13 Where it was at wysshe it could not remain. *a* **1568** ASCHAM *Scholem.* (Arb.) 40 Though a child haue all the giftes of nature at wishe. **1586** WHITNEY *Choice Emblems* 144 [He] to his wishe, of pilottes made his choise. **1601** SHAKS. *Jul. C.* III. ii. 271 He comes vpon a wish. **1607** —— *Timon* IV. iii. 245 The one is filling still, neuer compleat; The other, at high wish. **1667** MILTON *P.L.* IX. 423 When to his wish, Beyond his hope, Eve separate he spies. *a* **1674** CLARENDON *Hist. Reb.* VIII. §153 Though the relief of Banbury succeeded to wish, yet the King paid dear for it soon after. **1779** FORREST *Voy. N. Guinea* 56 The people, who assisted us so opportunely, were rewarded to their wish. **1787** [J. BEATTIE] *Scoticisms* 106 Every thing succeeds to a wish. **1823** BYRON *Juan* XV. lxviii, A dish Of which perhaps the cookery rather varies, So every one may dress it to his wish.

2. a. A desire expressed in words, or the expression of such; sometimes nearly = 'request': = DESIRE *sb.* 4. (Cf. WISH *v.* 3–5.)

1513 DOUGLAS *Æneis* VIII. ix. 31 The wyssis and avowis.. By women and the matronys doublit were. *a* **1533** LD. BERNERS *Huon* lxxxiv. 264 He sayd 'I wysshe them here on this table'. He had no sooner made his wysshe but they were set on the table. **1598** J. MELVILL *Autob. & Diary* (Wodrow Soc.) 443 My opinioun and wis was, ther sould be na generall meittings. **1714** POPE *Let. to Jervas* 27 Aug., I admire your whig principles of resistance exceedingly, in the spirit of the Barcelonians; I join in your wish for them. **1819** SHELLEY *Cenci* I. iii. 27 One supplication, one desire, one hope, That he would grant a wish for his two sons. **1908** R. BAGOT *A. Cuthbert* xxvi. 339 At Anthony's wish she wore the Cuthbert diamonds.

b. *spec.* An expression of desire for another's welfare: often as a farewell greeting. Usually, now always, in *pl.*

1593 SHAKS. *Rich. II*, I. iii. 94 Take from my mouth, the wish of happy yeares. **1601** —— *All's Well* I. i. 68 Maddam I desire your holie wishes. **1627** J. TAYLOR (Water P.) *Armado* Ep. Ded., With my best wishes for the perpetuity of your..felicity. **1753** POPE *Let.* Sept., Wks. 1741 II. 148 Pray tell him my best wishes for his health and long life. **1860** TYNDALL *Glac.* I. xxv. 177 We quitted Chamouni, bearing with us the good wishes of a portion of its inhabitants. **1833** D. C. MURRAY *Hearts* v, I know nothing about it, Tom,.. but you have my best wishes.

c. An imprecation, a malediction. *Obs.* or *dial.*

1592 SHAKS. *Rom. & Jul.* III. ii. 91 Blister'd be thy tongue For such a wish, he was not borne to shame. **1594** —— *Rich. III*, IV. i. 72 This was my Wish: Be thou (quoth I) accurst. **1820** *Marmaiden of Clyde* x. in *Edin. Mag.* VI. 423, I flang the renyie on his neck With a wiss that sould nae been. **1854** MISS BAKER *Northampt. Gloss.* s.v., 'He took a many wishes', was an expression used by a witness in the Sessions Court at Northampton.

3. *transf.* An object of desire; what one wishes or wishes for: = DESIRE *sb.* 5.

a **1300** *Cursor M.* 10406 Þai þat stad er in þair blis, Witvten want has alle þair wis. *c* **1400** MAUNDEV. xvii. [xiii.] (1919) 97 Þat faire lady schal ȝeuen him..the first wyssche þat he wil wyssche of erthely thinges. **1591** SHAKS. *Two Gent.* IV. ii. 93 *Sil.* What's your will? *Pro.* That I may compasse yours. *Sil.* You haue your wish. **1611** —— *Cymb.* III. v. 20 Your valiant Britaines haue their wishes in it. **1667** MILTON *P.L.* VIII. 451 Thy fit help, thy other self, Thy wish, exactly to thy hearts desire. **1713** ADDISON *Cato* IV. iii. 80 My joy! my best belov'd! my only wish! [**1761** FOOTE *Lyar* I. ii. (1786) 15 Surely, the wish of every decent woman is to be unnotic'd in public. **1849** MACAULAY *Hist. Eng.* v. I. 566 The wish of the government was that he should be executed in England.]

4. *Comb.*: **wish book** *N. Amer. slang*, a mail-order catalogue; **wish card** *rare*, in fortune-telling, a card which predicts the attainment of a desired end; **wish-dream** [cf. G. *Wunschtraum*], a dream or fantasy that reflects some hidden wish; also *attrib.*; **wish list**, a list of desired objects or occurrences; **wish-thinking** = *wishful thinking* s.v. WISHFUL *a.* 2 a; **wish-wife** [after ON. *óskmær* (see WISHMAY)], a light woman.

1933 *Amer. Speech* VIII. 32/1 *Wishbook, a mail-order catalogue. **1971** *Alberta Hist. Rev.* Summer 25/1 That was when we would look at our 'Wish Book', the mail order catalogue, until it was out of date, and then tear the pages out in the 'House of Parliament'. **1922** JOYCE *Ulysses* 761 I'll throw them the 1st thing in the morning till I see if the *wishcard comes out. **1934** R. CAMPBELL *Broken Record* i. 9 *Wish-dreams might account for this desire to 'headlong-hall' me into the next world. **1945** KOESTLER *Yogi & Commissar* I. iii. 31 She is not necessarily the wishdream-girl of suburban circulating libraries. **1953** *Encounter* Nov. 25/2 The wish-dream world of the Stockholm peace campaigner. **1966** *New Scientist* 28 July 222/1 Black gold in the back lot must be the standard rags-to-riches wishdream in the United States. **1972** *Times* 30 May 19/2 It had a presently confidential '*wish list' of programmes it would like to see abandoned. **1976** *National Observer* (U.S.) 10 July 9/3 Wholesale replacement of the nation's taxi fleet is hardly at the top of operators' wish lists. **1930** J. JASTROW *Piloting your Life* 170 It would take not a chapter but a volume to describe all the varieties of impediments of thought. If reduced to a schedule they might read like this:..*Wish Thinking*, believing what you hope or want to be true; [etc.]. **1945** R. KNOX *God & Atom* viii. 115 Most people who are capable of thinking, and are not deceived by wish-thinking, agree that the world is in ferment. **1958** J. LODWICK *Bid Soldiers Shoot* viii. 268 In matters of wish-thinking..the Victor of the Pacific, MacArthur, had met his match. **1886** CORBETT *Fall of Asgard* I. 227 Her wouldst thou profane as though she were some *wish-wife.

wish (wɪʃ), *sb.*[2] *local* (now Sussex). [OE. *wisc*, corresp. to OLG. *wisc* (in place-names), (M)LG. *wisch*(*e*, *wisk*(*e*, repr. OTeut. **wisko-*, f. *wais-*: *wis-*, whence OE. *wás* OOZE, G. *wiese* meadow.] A piece of meadow, now of marshy meadow; a piece of flat ground lying in the bend of a river and thus liable to be flooded.

898 in Birch *Cart. Sax.* II. 219 Concedo..terram..in loco qui dicitur Fearnleaȝ & an miclan wisce vi æceres mæde. *c* **1150** in Kemble *Cod. Dipl.* III. 175 To stucan wisc æt ðæne mearcbeorh. **1516–17** *Ledger Bk. Battle Abbey* in *Trans. Philol. Soc. 1895–8* 542 Menewyssh..Borderswyssh ..Hodisdaliswyssh. *a* **1600** in *Sussex Archæol. Collect.* (1851) IV. 306 A true & certeine note how yᵉ Drinker dooth faule to every-mans lande or yard wishe in the parishe of Kingston, nigh Lewis, at yᵉ time of trading of yᵉ wishe. **1651** *Ibid.* (1872) XXIV. 282 Lands settled vpon her by the name of Marshland, called Castle Wish als Colbrands lying within the parish of Westham. **1696–7** *Ibid.* (1849) II. 121 Yᵉ two acres croppe in yᵉ Northwish. **1850** *Ibid.* IV. 305 In both these parishes [*sc.* Lewes and Southease] were particular brooks [*i.e.* marshes] called Wishes, and in each also there was a small piece of brookland called the Drinker. **1857** *Ibid.* IX. 156 'The Wish' in East Bourn, close to the sea.

wish, *a.* (*dial.*): see WISHT.

wish (wɪʃ), *v.* Pa. t. and pa. pple. **wished** (wɪʃt). Forms: α. **1 wyscan, wiscan, 3–5 wussche, 4–5 wysche, (7** *Sc.*) **wische, 4–6 wisshe, 5–6 wys(s)he, (3 wusse, wisse, 4 wussche, whusshe, wiche, wesche, wesse, 5 wusche, wiesshe, wosshe, weesshe, 6 wys(c)h, wishe, whysshe, wyszhe), 6– wish.** β. *Sc.* (and *north.*) **4–6 wisse, wis, 4–9 wiss, 6 wys(s, whiss, 6–7 viss, 7 wosse, 9 wuss.** *Pa. t.* **1 wyscte, wiscte, 5 wyst, weste, 6 (9) wist; 3 wissede, etc., 4–6 wisshed, 5–6** *Sc.* **wissit, etc., 6– wished.** *Pa. pple.* **3 iwist, 6 wysht, 6–8 wisht; 4–6 wisshed, etc., 6– wished.** [OE. *wýscan* = OHG. *wunsken* (MHG., G. *wünschen*), ON. *æskja* (MSw. *yskia*, Sw. *önska*, Da. *önske*):—OTeut. **wunskjan*, f. **wunska-*, *-skô-* (represented by OE. *wúsc*, OHG. *wunsc*, MHG., G. *wunsch*, ON. *ósk*); cf. Skr. *vāñchā*:—**wānskā-*: f. base *wen-* to hold dear, love, desire, whence also WINE *sb.*[2], WIN *sb.*[2], WEEN *sb.* and *v.*, WONE.

Another form of the stem appears in (M)Du. *wensch*: see WINZE[2].]

1. a. *trans.* To have or feel a wish for; to desire.

The ordinary word for this; now always less emphatic than the synonyms *covet*, *crave*, *long* (*for*), *yearn* (*for*); in earlier use occas. in the sense of these. Sometimes softened by *could* or *should* (*would*): cf. CAN *v.*[1] 7, SHALL *v.* 19 c, WILL *v.*[1] 40 b; or strengthened before a dependent clause (*b*, *c*) by such phrases as *to God*, *to goodness*, *to heaven*.

(*a*) with simple obj. (in OE. usually in the genitive). Now *dial.*; superseded in standard English by *wish for* (see 2), or colloq. in certain contexts by *want* (WANT *v.* 5).

c **897** ÆLFRED *Gregory's Past. C.* i. 29 Ne cuæð he ðæt forðdyðe he æneȝum men ðæs wyscte oððe wilnode. **971** *Blickl. Hom.* 103 [Hie] his tocymes wyscton. *c* **1000** ÆLFRIC *Hom.* I. 594 Ic sceal his rode sigor swiðor wiscan ðonne ondrædan. *c* **1200** *Trin. Coll. Hom.* 165 Ðe sune wussheð þe fader deað, ar his dai cume. **13..** *E.E. Allit. P.* A. 14 Ofte haf I wayted wyschande þat wele. *c* **1470** HENRY *Wallace* IX. 1413 Sum wald haiff had Boyd at the suerdis lenth; Sum wyst [*ed.* **1570** wissit] Lundy. *c* **1489** CAXTON *Sonnes of Aymon* xxiii. 496 Now have I that I desired and wysshed soo longe. *a* **1510** DOUGLAS *K. Hart* II. 3 [He] wantis nocht in warld, that he wald wis. **1567** *Gude & Godlie B.* (S.T.S.) 9 Thy nychtbouris wyfe..Thow couet not to the, nor wis His hors, his oxe, [etc.] **1597** MORLEY *Introd. Mus.* 116 Causing you thinke the night long and wish the daylight. **1610** SHAKS. *Temp.* III. i. 54, I would not wish Any Companion in the world but you. **1651** HOBBES *Leviath.* II. xxvii. 159 Not as wishing liberty of private revenges. **1748** RICHARDSON *Clarissa* VI. lxxxiii. 305, I charge you,..as you wish my peace, not to say any-thing of a letter you have from me. **1816** SCOTT *Bl. Dwarf* i, 'Wussing your health, sirs,' said the shepherd. **1819** SHELLEY *Cenci* I. ii. 40 You know My zeal for all you wish, sweet Beatrice. **1854** DICKENS *Hard T.* II. i, Would you wish a little more hot water, ma'am? **1901** W. R. H. TROWBRIDGE *Lett. her Mother to Eliz.* xxix. 144 [The maid] flew into a rage, and wanted to know if I wished a month's notice.

(*b*) with obj. clause with *may* or (formerly) pres. subj., occas. indic.: expressing a desire that the event may happen or that the fact may prove to be so, and often implying some want of confidence or fear of the opposite (now commonly expressed by *hope*: see HOPE *v.* 3 b). Also expressing a request (see 5).

a **1000** *Deor* 25 Secg moniȝ..wyscte ȝeneahhe þæt þæs cynerices ofercumen wære. *c* **1000** ÆLFRIC *Gen.* xvii. 18 Ic wisce þæt Ismahel lybbe ætforan ðe. *a* **1586** SIDNEY *Arcadia* II. x. (1912) 208, I wish that it may not prove ominous foretoken of misfortune. **1591** SHAKS. *Two Gent.* IV. iii. 41, I wish all good befortune you. **1649** in *Spalding Club Misc.* (1852) V. 381, I heartellie wosse that anie that lowes religione..keepe themselwes free of anie accessione..to swche wnhape men. **1661** P. HENRY *Diaries & Lett.* (1882) 86, I wish I suffer no prejudice by it. **1691** SHADWELL *Scowrers* IV, I wish the house is not robb'd. **1715** ADDISON *Drummer* II. i, He say's he's a Conjurer, but he looks very suspicious; I wish he ben't a Jesuit. **1756** *Monitor* No. 35. I. 325 He is certainly bewitched: I wish the old hag upon the green has done him no mischief. **1808** JANE AUSTEN *Lett.* (1884) II. 6 She hears that Miss Bigg is to be married in a fortnight. I wish it may be so. **1823** SCOTT *Quentin D.* xxi, I wish we have not got King Stork, instead of King Log. **1860** EMILY EDEN *Semi-attached Couple* xii, Mrs. Tomkinson wished to goodness there might soon be..'a little staying company' in the house. **1872** GEO. ELIOT in J. W. Cross *Life* (1885) III. 157, I wish that you may happen to know her.

(*c*) with obj. clause with past subj. (or indic., e.g. *was* for *were*): expressing an unrealized or unrealizable desire (see also WILL *v.*[1] 46), or in mod. use sometimes a mild request (cf. 5). *to wish to God*: to wish intensely.

971 *Blickl. Hom.* 93 Hie..wyscaþ þæt hie næfre næron acennede from fæder ne from meder. *c* **1000** ÆLFRIC *Deut.* xxxii. 29 Ic wisce ðæt hi wiston & underȝeaton..hyra ende [Vulg. *utinam saperent*]. **1340** *Ayenb.* 56 Hi wesseþ þet hi hedden nykken of crane and wombe of cou. **1362** LANGL. *P. Pl.* A. v. 92 Þenne I wussche hit weore myn. *c* **1385** CHAUCER *L.G.W.* 755 *Thisbe*, Thys wall they woldyn threte And wysshe to god hyt were doun ybete. **1476** *Stonor Papers* (Camden) II. 11 Wherfore I wyst fulle hertly dyuerse tymez þat ȝe hadde ben here. *a* **1562** G. CAVENDISH *Poems* (1825) II. 40 Therfor my frayltie I may both curse and ban, Whissyng to God I had never known man. **1579** LYLY *Euphues* 31, I wish my wish were as effectually ended as it is heartely looked for. **1605** SHAKS. *Macb.* I. v. 26 That which rather thou do'st feare to doe, Then wishest should be vndone. **1624** USSHER *Lett.* (1686) 315, I could wish that Mr. Lisle would take some pains in translating the Saxon Annals into our English Tongue. **1681** in *10th Rep. Hist. MSS. Comm.* App. I. 133, I haiue gotten a tasch upon me that I wisch from my hart it was well of my handes to your satisfaction. **1711** I could wish [see CAN *v.*[1] 7]. **1817** BYRON *Let. to Moore* 25 Mar., Heigh ho! I wish I was drunk—but I have nothing but this damned barley-water before me. **1833** TENNYSON *May Queen, New Year's Eve* iv, I wish the snow would melt... I long to see a flower so. **1885** 'F. ANSTEY' *Tinted Venus* ii. 24, 'I wish to heaven I did,' cried the manager. **1890** [see GOODNESS 5]. **1932** 'N. SHUTE' *Lonely Road* vii. 178, I wish to God we'd gone back to the boat. **1941** L. A. G. STRONG *Bay* 7, I wish to God I knew how to begin. **1976** *Daily Mirror* 11 Mar. 7/2 Christopher..has been sent to Borstal... His mother said: 'I wish to God we had checked up on him.'

(*d*) with inf. as obj. (usually, now always, with *to*).

Occas. with admixture of the idea of intention or request for permission (cf. 5), as 'I wish to say a few words'.

c **1250** *Gen. & Ex.* 1060 He wisten him bergen fro ðe dead. **1390** GOWER *Conf.* I. 149 Sche wissheth forto ben unbore. *c* **1450** *Merlin* vii. 113 So that the moste hardy of hem.. sholde wiesshe to be at home in his owne contree. **1500–20** DUNBAR *Poems* liii. 33, I wissitt to be The grytast erle, or duik, in France. **1513** DOUGLAS *Æneis* XII. xiv. 17 Wys now to fle vp to the starnis on hycht. **1560** *Bible* (Geneva) Jonah iv. 8 Ionah fainted, and wished in his heart to dye. **1611** SHAKS. *Wint. T.* II. i. 123, I neuer wish'd to see you sorry, now I trust I shall. **1630** MILTON *On Shakespear* 16 Kings for such a Tomb would wish to die. **1776** *Trial of Nundocomar* 23/2 Any body that wishes to see him may. **1850** MISS MULOCK *Olive* xxv, I wish to talk to you. **1876** MOZLEY *Univ. Serm.* xi. 213 If men really wish to be good, they will become good. **1893** *Law Times* XCV. 305/2 If she wished to be sure of her income she should of all things avoid dabbling in the shares of new companies.

(*e*) with acc. and inf., or in pass. with inf. (usually, now always, with *to*).

Sometimes expressing a request: see 5 b.

1538 STARKEY *England* II. i. (1878) 176 Aftur a maner.. the wych I wold wysch to be put in vse wyth vs. *c* **1560** A. SCOTT *Poems* (S.T.S.) xv. 39 Away I went,..Wissing all luvaris leill to haif sic chance. ? **1567** [M. PARKER] *Whole Psalter* cx. vii, Pursued to death, and wysht to sinke. *a* **1586** SIDNEY *Astr. & Stella* x, I rather wish thee climbe the Muses hill. **1603** SHAKS. *Meas. for M.* IV. iii. 138 If you can pace your wisdome, In that good path that I would wish it go. **1657** J. SERGEANT *Schism Dispach't* 406, I love the Presbyterians so well as not to wish them renounce their reason. **1753–4** RICHARDSON *Grandison* I. xix. 130 [He said that] every man who saw me must wish me to be his. **1891** FARRAR *Darkn. & Dawn* xv, Nero..wished Junia Silana and Calvia Crispinilla to be of the party.

(*f*) with obj. and compl. (sb., adj., pple., advb. phrase): now chiefly in imprecations or the like.

14.. *How Plowman learned Paternoster* 152 in Hazl. *E.P.P.* I. 215 He wysshed them at the devyll therfore. **1477** *Stonor Papers* (Camden) II. 22, I thank you hertely þat hyt plesyd you to wyshe me with you. *c* **1520** SKELTON *Magnyf.* 2306, I se well there is no better rede, But sygh, and sorowe, and wysshe my selfe dede. **1532** TINDALE *Exp. Matt.* v–vii vii. (? 1550) 88 b, Who is so wel beloued..but that ther be ynow..that woulde, for hys good, wishe him to hel? *a* **1533** [see WISH *sb.*[1] 2]. **1579** LYLY *Euphues* (Arb.) 70, I wyshed my selfe heere. **1591** SHAKS. *Two Gent.* I. i. 14 Wish me partaker in thy happinesse, When thou do'st meet good hap. **1605** —— *Macb.* v. viii. 49 Had I as many Sonnes, as I haue haires, I would not wish them to a fairer death. **1621** [see FURTHER *adv.* 4 b]. **1711** STEELE *Spect.* No. 27 ⁋2 We every day wish ourselves disengaged from its allurements. **1724** RAMSAY *Vision* ix, Mailpayers wiss it to the devil. **1797** JANE AUSTEN *Sense & Sensib.* xxxvii, We all wish her extremely happy. **1819** CRABBE *T. of Hall* XVII. 364 Perch that were wish'd to salmon for her sake. **1823** LAMB *Let. to Southey* 21 Nov., I wished both magazine and review at the bottom of the sea. **1848** DICKENS *Dombey* xxii, Let us remember James by name, and wish him happy. **1902** 'VIOLET JACOB' *Sheep-Stealers* xi, She could only move uneasily on her seat, and wish him miles away.

(*g*) after *as* or *than*: often *ellipt.* (so also with rel.) for various constructions, esp. (*c*), (*d*), (*e*).

1523 LD. BERNERS *Froiss.* I. clxiv. 83/1 The aduentures of amours and of war, are more fortunate and maruelous, than any man canne thynke or wysshe. **1530** PALSGR. 783/1, I am as well nowe, I thanke God, as I coulde wysshe. **1560** *Bible* (Geneva) Ps. lxxiii. 7 They haue more then heart can wish. **1698** COLLIER *Immor. Stage* 227 He..goes off as like a Town Spark as you would wish. **1750** GRAY *Elegy* Ep. 8 He gain'd from Heav'n ('twas all he wish'd) a friend. **1866** GEO. ELIOT *Felix Holt* i, Nothing had come just as she had wished. **1868** LOUISA M. ALCOTT *Little Women* xiii, You should do just what your grandfather wishes.

(*h*) in passive: esp. in predicative phr. *to be wished* = desirable.

1531 ELYOT *Gov.* II. ix, It is to be wisshed, that they, whiche..haue any autoritie, maye be like to the lawes, whiche in correctynge be ladde only by equitie. **1597** MORLEY *Introd. Mus.* Ded., More to be wished and much more durable. **1602** SHAKS. *Ham.* III. i. 64 'Tis a consummation Deuoutly to be wish'd. **1697** DE FOE *Ess. Projects* 232 'Twere to be wish'd our Gentry were so much Lovers of Learning, that Birth might always be join'd with Capacity. **1788** CLARA REEVE *Exiles* II. 124 At length the day so long wished and expected came. **1876** *Jrnl. Soc. Arts* 2 June 708/1 The returns from the Cheltenham district were not so complete as might be wished. **1918** *Pall Mall Gaz.* 29 June 8/1 The first venture..was not, perhaps, as successful as could have been wished.

†**b.** *fig.* of a thing: To 'require': = DESIRE *v.* 3.

1600 ABBOT *Jonah* 599, I do not find that expositors speake so fully to the matter of this wind, as me seemeth this text doth wish.

2. *intr.* To have or feel a wish; in early use often, to long, yearn. **a.** with *after* (obs.), *for*: = 1 (*a*); also *indir. pass.* = 1 (*h*).

c **1200** *Trin. Coll. Hom.* 3 Men..wisten ȝerne after ure lauerd ihesu cristes tocume. *Ibid.* 135 þu hauest longe iwist after strene, and god haueð herd þine bede. **13..** *Cursor M.* 23548 (Edinb.) Ilk man sal haf til his, Al þat he wil eftir wis. **1481** CAXTON *Myrr.* 107 The deth wold they haue and weesshe after it incessantly. **1526** TINDALE *Acts* xxvii. 29 They cast iiij. ancres out of the sterne: and wysshed for the daye. **1579** LYLY *Euphues* (Arb.) 69 By so much the more you are welcome, by how much the more you were wished for. **1740** RICHARDSON *Pamela* II. 163, I can only wish for more worthiness. **1757** ELIZ. GRIFFITH *Lett. Henry & Frances* (1767) I. 84, I wished for you..in vain all night, the life-long night. **1834** DICKENS *Sk. Boz, Boarding-ho.* ii, Having nothing to do and nothing to wish for, she naturally imagined she must be very ill. **1867** SPEDDING *Publ. & Authors* 75 Buy the volumes as they come out, if you wish for them.

b. *absol.*

1546 J. HEYWOOD *Prov.* (1867) 50 Better to haue then wishe. **1570** *Satir. Poems Reform.* xii. 185 Than war I fane, bot all in vane, To wis and will nocht be. **1596** DALRYMPLE tr. *Leslie's Hist. Scot.* (S.T.S.) I. 228 Quha can wiss aboue thir thrie? **1601** SHAKS. *All's Well* I. iii. 218 If your selfe.. Did euer, in so true a flame of liking, Wish chastly, and loue dearely. **1850** MISS MULOCK *Olive* xxi, It had been one of her childish superstitions always 'to wish at the new moon'. **1904** W. W. JACOBS *Dialstone Lane* iii. 37, 'I could see it at any time I wished', she said sharply. 'Well, wish now', entreated Mr. Tredgold.

c. *trans.* with cognate obj.

c **1400** [see WISH *sb.*[1] 3]. **1588** SHAKS. *L.L.L.* II. i. 179 Thy own wish wish I thee, in euery place. **1849** MRS. GASKELL *Lizzie Leigh*, etc. (1913) 426 Wishing all manner of idle wishes. **1914** 'IAN HAY' *Knt. on Wheels* xi, If you wish a wish and then feel in my pocket, old lady, you may find something.

3. *trans.* To express a wish for; to say that one wishes...(with various const. as in 1); *spec.* to imprecate, invoke (an evil or curse).

c **1000** ÆLFRIC *Hom.* II. 308 Alexander ða wiscte: 'Eala ȝif ðu wære hund!' **1476** *Paston Lett.* Suppl. (1901) 149, I wysshed to hym that he and I hadde been at Norwyche. **1526** *Pilgr. Perf.* (W. de W. 1531) 7 Than he cryeth out and wyssheth that he neuer had had eyes to se. **1560** *Bible* (Geneva) Job xxxi. 30 Nether haue I suffred my mouth to sinne, by wishing a cursse vnto his soule. **1594** SHAKS. *Rich. III*, I. iii. 218 If Heauen haue any grieuous plague in store, Exceeding those that I can wish vpon thee. **1673** CAVE *Prim. Chr.* III. i. 221 He was consumed by such a disease as he had wished upon himself. **1715** ATTERBURY *Serm., Matt.* xxvii. 25 (1734) I. 134 The profane Folly..of wishing that Damnation to ourselves, which we otherways but too well deserve. **1724** RAMSAY *Vision* xxvii, He..wischt I happyness micht bruke. **1781** in *Jrnl. Friends Hist. Soc.* (1918) 72 She was senceable to the last..often wished she might be like her..D[ea]r Grandmother.

4. *spec.* (with *to* or simple object) To desire (something, usually good) for or on behalf of a person, etc.: esp. in formulæ of greeting or expressions of goodwill; hence as in 3, to express such a wish for, esp. as a formal greeting:

e.g. *to wish (one) good morning, good-bye* (= BID *v.*[1] 9), *a merry Christmas, a happy New Year, many happy returns of the day* (see RETURN *sb.* 2 b), etc.; also intr. in *to wish (one) well* (see WELL *adv.* 2 d), and intr. or trans. (usually with neg.) in *to wish (one) ill* (where *ill* may be taken as adv. or sb.). *to wish (one) joy of*: see JOY *sb.* 9 d.

c **900** *Laws Alfred* Introd. xlix. §3 Ða apostolas & þa eldran broðor hælo eow wyscað. *c* **1374** CHAUCER *Troylus* II. 406, I bidde wisshe yow no more sorwe. **1393** LANGL. *P. Pl.* C. xx. 328 þer ne is syk ne sory..þat he ne may..boþe wusshen and wylnen Alle manere of men mercy and for-ȝeuenesse. **1516** *State Papers Hen. VIII*, VI. 50 Not to thintent he schulde have hys parte off thys intolerable troble.., for I wolde not wysche itt to a dogge. **1535** COVERDALE *Ps.* cxxix. 8 We wish you good lucke in the name of the Lorde. —— *Job* xxxi. 30, I neuer suffred my mouth to do soch a sinne, as to wysh him euell. **1552** HULOET, Wyshe ille to any thinge, *fascino.* **1579** LYLY *Euphues* (Arb.) 97, I would neither wish thee a greater plague, nor him a deadlyer poyson. *a* **1586** SIDNEY *Apol. Poetrie* (Arb.) 72, I will not wish vnto you.. to be rimed to death. **1596** DALRYMPLE tr. *Leslie's Hist. Scot.* x. (S.T.S.) II. 359 To salute thame baith, wisse thame gude morne. **1610** SHAKS. *Temp.* v. i. 215 Let griefe and sorrow still embrace his heart, That doth not wish you ioy. **1623** HEMINGE & CONDELL *Shaks. Wks.* To Rdrs., And such Readers we wish him. *c* **1720** DE FOE *Mem. Cavalier* I. 39 They wished the Swedes Success. **1816** JANE AUSTEN *Emma* x, I wish Jane Fairfax very well; but she tires me to death. **1821** SCOTT *Kenilw.* vii, I have been prayed for, and wished well to, in your congregations. **1885** *Law Times* LXXIX. 345/2 [He] wished the officials good night, and left the room.

b. To desire, or express a desire for, the welfare or misfortune of (a person); only in *evil wished*, ILL-WISH *v.*, WELL-WISHED.

1577 HELLOWES *Gueuara's Chron.* 325 All three were so euil wished in the Common wealth, that the least euill which they would them..was but death. **1604** BODLEY in *Buccleuch MSS.* (Hist. MSS. Comm.) I. 48, I leave you both as well wished, as if you were to enjoy the best wishes bestowed this new year's day in England.

5. In expressions of desire for something to be done by another, thus conveying a request; hence, to request, entreat; formerly sometimes, to bid, command: **a.** a thing or action (with various const. as in 1): cf. DESIRE *v.* 5.

a **1533** LD. BERNERS *Huon* lxxxiii. 259 He came to Huon & wysshyd yᵉ fetters fro all there fete [orig. *soubhaita leurs fers hors de leurs iambes*]. **1553** T. WILSON *Rhet.* 38 To wishe of God to purge oure hartes from all filthines and vngodlie dealinge. **1596** DALRYMPLE tr. *Leslie's Hist. Scot.* IX. (S.T.S.) II. 236, I wisse rather..that in hope of barnes he take Margaret rather than Magdalen for his bedfallow. **1596** BACON *Max. Com. Law* ix. (1636) 36 The Statute of 27. H. 8. of uses, that wisheth that the *cestui que use* shall have the possession in quality and degree as hee had the use. **1671** MILTON *Samson* 1414 Brethren farewel, your company along I will not wish. *a* **1674** CLARENDON *Hist. Reb.* VIII. §272 To confer with lord Digby, who..should find the best way to make the earl of Antrim to communicate the affair to him, and to wish his assistance. **1842** DICKENS *Amer. Notes* xiv, Whatever we wished done was done with great civility and readiness. **1875** JOWETT *Plato* (ed. 2) I. 429, I wish that you would tell me about his death.

b. a person *to do* something: cf. DESIRE *v.* 6.

1583 STOCKER *Civ. Warres Lowe C.* IV. 55 [The] Captaine ..wished them quietly departe, without thei liked to be saluted with Cannon shotte. **1603** SHAKS. *Meas. for M.* v. i. 79 *Duk.* You were not bid to speake. *Luc.* No,..Nor wish'd to hold my peace. **1604** DEKKER & MIDDLETON *Honest Wh.* I. C 2 b, Hie to the Constable, And in all calme order wish him to attach them. **1716** SWIFT *Poems, Phyllis* 35 The Groom was wish'd to saddle Crop. **1854** DICKENS *Hard T.* II. i, Would you wish the gentleman to be shewn in, ma'am? **1859** RUSKIN *Two Paths* i. §35 There is another thing I wish you to notice specially in these statues.

†**c.** To invite, 'bid' (a person to a place). *Obs. rare.*

a **1533** LD. BERNERS *Huon* lxxxiii. 259 He..causyd them to syt downe at his owne table that he had wysshyd thether [orig. *eut fait venir*].

6. To recommend (a person) *to* another, or *to* a place, etc. *Obs.* or *dial.*

orig. prob. belonging to WIS *v.*[1] 2, to direct.

1596 SHAKS. *Tam. Shr.* I. i. 113 If I can by any meanes light on a fit man to teach her that wherein she delights, I will wish him to her father. **1610** B. JONSON *Alch.* I. iii, I was wish'd to your worship, by a gentleman,..That say's you know mens planets. **1633** ROWLEY *Match at Mid-n.* IV. i, He sayes he was wisht to [a] very wealthy Widdow, but of you he has heard much Histories, that he will marry you. **1751** ELIZA HEYWOOD *Betsy Thoughtless* I. xvi. 196 Now I have been wished to several fine women, but my fancy gives the preference to you. **1818** SCOTT *Hrt. Midl.* xxiii, She passed that interval of time in the lodging of a woman, an acquaintance of that person who had wished her to that place. **1846** BROCKETT *N.C. Gloss.* (ed. 3) s.v., Can you wish me to a customer?

7. To influence in a magical or occult way by wishing; to bewitch by a desire or imprecation. *dial.*

1848 MRS. GASKELL *Mary Barton* vii, We mun get him away from his mother. He cannot die while she's wishing him. **1865** TYLOR *Early Hist. Man.* vi. 134 When he hears that he has been 'wished,' he..takes to his bed at once.

8. To foist or impose (something or someone) *on* (*to*) someone; to endow with at another's wish.

1915 N. L. MCCLUNG *In Times like These* x. 164 Women have never chosen the liquor business... It has been wished on them. **1926** *Publishers' Weekly* 22 May 1725/1 Mr. Remington..has not been able to be with us... That is why we are able to wish that good job on him. **1934** E. WAUGH *Handful of Dust* i. 20 Who was the old girl you wished on me at that party last night? **1954** 'N. SHUTE' *Slide Rule* 1 An unwanted kitten that they had wished on to my children. **1962** *Listener* 5 July 14/2 The plan was to build a much larger school than was needed, at the same time 'wishing' additional housing on the village to justify it. **1971** *Guardian* 9 Jan. 13/2 We owed money everywhere... I wouldn't wish that on any of today's young housewives. **1983** M. BABSON *Fool for Murder* xviii. 166 It really was most unfair of Uncle Wilmer to wish it on Wanda-Lu... He wasn't the one who'd have to keep the place tidy.

¶ *I wish*, corrupt form of *iwis*: see WIS *v.*[2]

wish, var. WIS *v.*[1] *Obs.*

wisha ('wɪʃə), *int.* *Anglo-Ir. colloq.* [ad. Ir. *mhuise* indeed (the unlenited form *muise* gives anglicized *musha* MUSHA).] An exclamation indicating dismay, emphasis, or surprise.

1826 M. WILMOT *Let.* 29 Feb. (1935) 234 O 'wisha' 'wisha', shall I ever arrive at the ball I promised you! **1842** S. LOVER *Handy Andy* vi. 70 I'm afeard o' my life to go to bed!.. Wisha! but I'd give the world it was mornin'. **1898** J. D. BRAYSHAW *Slum Silhouettes* 49 Oh, wisha! didn't he break the leg of me wid his stick? **1914** JOYCE *Dubliners* 157 'Wisha! wisha,' says I. 'A pound of chops..coming into the Mansion House.' **1936** 'F. O'CONNOR' *Bones of Contention* 8 Wisha, for goodness' sake will you come down and leave the girl sleep? **1965** *N. Munster Antiquarian Jrnl.* IX. IV. 186 Wisha, I don't know what to say. **1978** 'M. M. KAYE' *Far Pavilions* lviii. 812 Wisha, but it's a gloomy devil you are an' all.

wishable ('wɪʃəb(ə)l), *a. rare.* [f. WISH *v.* + -ABLE.] That may be wished for; desirable.

1548 UDALL *Erasm. Par. Luke* iv. 20–24 The glad & wishable tidynges of saluacion. **1611** COTGR., *Souhaitable*,.. wishable, desirable. **1905** W. A. ELLIS *R. Wagner to M. Wesendonck* 165 Wisdom is so excellent and wishable.

wish-bone. Also wishbone. [f. WISH *sb.*[1] + BONE *sb.*] = MERRYTHOUGHT (q.v. for reason of the name).

1860 BARTLETT *Dict. Amer.* (ed. 3), Wish-Bone. **1884** ROE *Nat. Ser. Story* vi, If I bring you a canvas-back [duck], Amy, will you put the wish-bone over the door?

2. *Naut.* A boom composed of two halves that curve outward from the mast, on either side of the sail, and in again, the clew of the sail that lies between them being attached to the point where they meet aft. Freq. *attrib.*, designating a sail or a boat with such a boom.

1934 U. FOX *Sailing, Seamanship & Yacht Construction* I. 54 (*caption*) Wishbone gaff. **1935** *Yachting Monthly* Feb. 306/1 The working sail area of the 'wishbone' ketch rig shown totals 2,794 sq. ft. **1954** D. H. C. PHILLIPS-BIRT *Rigs & Rigging of Yachts* ii. 60 The wishbone ketch is the result of combining an unusual form of staysail ketch rig devised by Mr. F. Fenger..with the wishbone spar invented by Nathaniel Herreshoff. **1958** *Times* 27 Oct. 10/6 The fishermen..were already launching their dug-out canoes, some under the traditional wish-bone sprit-sail. **1981** B. WEBB *Schult's Sailing Dict.* 327/1 Sailboards have wishbone booms. **1984** *Times* 25 Aug. 11 The next stop was to pick a point to steer for, ease the rig (the mast, sail and wishbone) towards me until I was looking through the transparent panel in the sail.

3. A wishbone-shaped element in the independent suspension of a motor vehicle, the two arms of which are hinged to the chassis and their join hinged to the wheel; freq. *attrib.*

1934 *Automobile Engineer* XXIV. 289/3 The American types..do not use the longitudinal radius links, and thus the wheel position depends entirely on the 'wishbone' link bearings. **1959** *Times* 27 Apr. (Rubber Industry Suppl.) p. vi/1 Such bushes are now almost universally used for springs, torque arms, and in some forms of wishbone suspension. **1983** 'D. RUTHERFORD' *Stop at Nothing* ix. 165 It took me an hour and a half to put the Saab to rights. The front wishbone had been seriously distorted.

4. *U.S. Football.* Used *attrib.* and *absol.* to designate an offensive formation in which the full back lines up ahead of the half-backs in an alignment that resembles the shape of a wishbone.

1972 *N.Y. Times* 3 Nov. 48/2 Dartmouth's best hope lies in shutting off Yale's wishbone offense as engineered by Dick Jauron. **1974** *Spartanburg* (S. Carolina) *Herald-Jrnl.* 21 Apr. 134/3 The white team ran the wishbone that UCLA used last year. **1979** *Tucson* (Arizona) *Citizen* 20 Sept. 10D/3 The fullback in the Santa Rita Wishbone has averaged nearly 30 carries per game in the first two contests.

wishe, obs. pa. t. of WASH *v.*; obs. f. WISH.

wished (wɪʃt, *poet.* also 'wɪʃɪd), *ppl. a.* [f. WISH *v.* + -ED[1].]

1. That is the object of a wish; desired, longed-for. Now *rare* exc. as in b.

15.. *Fickle Estate of Our Vncertayn Lyfe* (MS. Rawl. poet. 112, lf. 10 b), What if a day or A moneth or a yeare Crowne thy delightes with a thowsand wisht contentinges? **1577** GRANGE *Golden Aphrod.* etc. P iv b, So friendly Venus is, so friendly Cupid was, That fancie brought hir soone, vnto my wisshed passe. **1583** MELBANCKE *Philotimus* C c ij, My wished frend, and welcomde guest. **1602** MARSTON *Antonio's Rev.* III. ii, We touch the shore Of wisht revenge. **1667** MILTON *P.L.* I. 208 While Night Invests the Sea, and wished Morn delayes. **1748** RICHARDSON *Clarissa* VII. lxii. 221 At length..every thing is in the wished train. **1811** W. R. SPENCER *Poems* 17 Oh! why so late thy wish'd return? **1812** CARY *Dante, Par.* XXIII. 4 The bird..With her sweet brood; impatient to descry Their wished looks. **1906** CHARL. MANSFIELD *Girl & Gods* xxvii, Psyche..held out her hand in token of a wished farewell.

b. with *for*: cf. WISH *v.* 2 a.

1586 T. B. *La Primaud. Fr. Acad.* I. 1 The wished-for newes of peace. **1725** RAMSAY *Gentle Sheph.* III. iv, When wished-for pleasures rise like morning light. **1812** BYRON *Ch. Har.* I. xlv, Yet is she free—the spoiler's wish'd-for prey! **1888** BURGON *Lives 12 Gd. Men* I. i. 32 [They] declared their inability to render America the wished for assistance.

2. Entertained as a wish: cf. WISH *v.* 2 c. *rare.*

1580 LYLY *Euphues* (Arb.) 467 Hauing thus made ech other priuie to our wished desires.

wishedly ('wɪʃɪdlɪ), *adv.* Now *rare* or *Obs.* [f. WISHED *ppl. a.* + -LY^2.] As is or was wished; according to desire.

1573 Twyne *Æneid.* x. E e 3, Like as wisshedly when winds in sommer season blowe. **1603** Knolles *Hist. Turks* (1621) 620 What could have happened unto him more wishedly? **1624** Capt. J. Smith *Virginia* v. 174 Sir George Somers..most wishedly and happily descried land. **1633** Heywood *Eng. Trav.* iv. G 4 b, Of all my friends to me Most wishedly, you are welcome.

wisher ('wɪʃə(r)). Now *rare.* [f. WISH *v.* + -ER^1.] One who wishes.

† ***wishers and woulders***: see WOULDER.

15.. *Parl. Byrdes* 91 in Hazl. *E.P.P.* III. 171 Wysshers want wyll. *a* **1586** Sidney *Arcadia* iii. (1922) 15 Many times he wished himself the back of an Asse,..(an unfortunate wisher, for if he had as well wished the head, it had bene graunted him). **1606** Shaks. *Ant. & Cl.* iv. xv. 37 Wishers were euer Fooles. **1670** Eachard *Cont. Clergy* To Rdr., I am ..only an honest and hearty wisher, that the best of our clergy might forever continue as they are. **1760** Sterne *Tr. Shandy* III. i, The safest way..to take off the force of the wish, is..to..wish the wisher something in return. **1846** Denham *Prov.* (Percy Soc.) 31 A March wisher is never a good fisher. **1905** Flor. Maybrick *My Fifteen Lost Yrs.* 133 If a prisoner has any complaint to make or wishes to seek advice, she asks to have her name put down to see the governor. She is then termed a 'wisher' and is 'seen' by him in his office in the presence of the chief matron.

b. qualified by *evil*, *ill*, *well* (see ILL-WISHER, WELL-WISHER).

1656 Earl Monm. tr. *Boccalini's Advts. fr. Parnass.* ii. lxxxviii. (1674) 241 To take an evil wishers life away. **1746** H. Walpole *Let. to Mann* 1 Aug., When the Peers were going to vote Lord Foley withdrew as too well a wisher.

wishful ('wɪʃfʊl), *a.* [f. WISH *sb.*^{1} + -FUL.]

†**1.** Such as is, or is to be, wished; desirable; desired, longed-for. (Cf. DESIROUS 5.) *Obs.*

1523 Cromwell in Merriman *Life & Lett.* (1902) I. 31 This so glorious, so profyttable and so wysshefull an enterpryse. **1565** Stapleton tr. *Bede's Hist. Ch. Eng.* 110 We haue receiued your excellencies wishefull letters. **1596** Spenser *F.Q.* vi. xi. 50 The ioyous light, Whereof she long had lackt the wishfull sight. *c* **1616** Chapman *Homer's Hymn Hermes* 185 Many a field Pleasant and wishful. *c* **1645** Howell *Lett.* I. vi. 4 Having so wishful an Opportunity.. I could not but send you this Friendly Salute.

2. a. Of the eye or look, tone, feeling, etc.: Full of desire; longing, yearning, wistful. (Cf. DESIROUS 2.)

1593 Shaks. *3 Hen. VI*, iii. i. 14 To greet mine owne Land with my wishfull sight. **1711** *Spectator* No. 250 ⁋6 You can't behold a covetous Spirit walk by a Goldsmith's Shop without casting a wishful Eye at the Heaps upon the Counter. **1739** C. Wesley *Hymn*, Hail the Day that sees Him rise, Ravish'd from our wishful Eyes. **1810** E. D. Clarke *Trav. Russia* (1839) 5/1 It has probably happened to others, as to myself, to cast an eye of wishful curiosity towards the eastern boundaries of Europe. **1827** C. Bridges *Exp. Ps. cxix.* verse 67. 173 The forlorn wandering child casting a wishful, penitent look towards his Father's house.

(*b*) In mod. use in weaker sense: expressing or indicative of a wish; chiefly in ***wishful thinking***, thinking, esp. belief or expectation, that is influenced by one's wishes to the extent that relevant (consciously) known facts are (subconsciously) ignored or distorted; also as *adj.*; so ***wishful thinker***.

1932 *Sat. Rev. Lit.* 2 July 817/4 At two vitally important points Glenn Frank's incisive analysis fades away in a vague realm of hope or even of wishful thinking. **1940** *Illustr. London News* CXCVI. 498/2 The possibility of any relief in that direction can only exist in the minds of wishful-thinkers. **1940** L. D. Weatherhead *This is Victory* ii. 58, I do not mean that that which is believed has no other support than man's wishful thinking. **1941** Auden *New Year Letter* i. 17 Twelve months ago in Brussels I heard the same wishful-thinking sigh. **1942** C. S. Lewis *Screwtape Lett.* ix. 50 It all depends on whether your man is..of the wishful-thinking type who can be assured that all is well. **1951** 'A. Garve' *Murder in Moscow* i. 20 He was a woolly wishful-thinker who happened to be inordinately vain as well. **1958** *Spectator* 6 June 724/1 He [*sc.* a prisoner] hoarded these glimpses of past happiness, rationing his wishful reminiscing to half an hour a day. **1958** *Listener* 25 Sept. 478/1 There are some embarrassingly wishful statements... 'The day when Joyce embarked in Dublin..they were burning his first book... He could see the smoke of the bonfire.'.. *Dubliners* was not burned: it was pulped. **1970** *Guardian* 10 Dec. 4/4 It is hard to reconcile this sort of picture with the one presented by the wishful-thinkers in Saigon. **1974** E. Ambler *Dr Frigo* ii. 117 I'm not a wishful-thinking idiot. **1980** *Sunday Times* (Colour Suppl.) 30 Mar. 55/2 An evocation of youth's transitoriness and innocent wishful-thinking.

b. Of a person: Possessed by a wish for something specified or implied; wishing, desirous. Now *rare* in literary prose.

1733 Whitehead *St. Dunces* Poems (1777) 18 Lo! o'er yon flood H——e casts his low'ring eyes, And wishful sees the rev'rend turrets rise. **1825** Waterton *Wand. S. Amer.* iii. ii. 236 Wishful to see how he worked, I allowed him to take possession. **1852** Dickens *Bleak Ho.* xlii, I was wishful to say a word to you, sir. **1867** Morris *Jason* i. 314, I am but Jason, who dwell here alone.. Wishful for happy days. **1875** Browning *Aristoph. Apol.* 1703 Wishful from my soul That truth should triumph. **1888** Bryce *Amer. Commw.* I. 165 A second chamber well qualified for the duty of revision, and wishful to discharge it.

'wish-fulfilment. [tr. G. *wunscherfüllung* (S. Freud *Die Traumdeutung* (1900) i. 64).] The imaginary fulfilment of acknowledged or unconscious wishes in dreams and fantasies; a dream or other event or object in which the fulfilment of a wish is given (usu. imaginary or symbolic) expression.

[**1901** H. Ellis in *Jrnl. Mental Sci.* XLVII. 370 The author [*sc.* Freud] points out that..we may with much more reason regard them [*sc.* dreams] as the protectors of sleep, willing us to repose with an imagined fulfilment of our wishes.] **1908** *Jrnl. Abnormal Psychol.* III. 237 This is a hyperbolic realization of his reveries, corresponding to the wish-fulfilment of the normal dream. **1916** A. A. Brill tr. *Freud's Wit & its Relation to Unconscious* vi. 250 Wider reading circles have contented themselves to reduce the contents [of *The Interpretation of Dreams*]..to a catchword, 'Wish fulfilment'—a term easily remembered and easily abused. **1928** C. H. Dodd *Authority of Bible* iii. 66 Behind the song lies..a longing for the down-fall of an implacable enemy, which finds in the picture of disaster a 'wish-fulfilment'. **1939** D. Cecil *Young Melbourne* iv. 106 Living wholly in a wish-fulfilment world of her own creation, she insisted it was the real one. **1953** A. Huxley *Let.* 31 Oct. (1969) 687 The jewelled palaces are partly, no doubt, wish fulfilments—the opposite of everyday experience. **1956** E. L. Mascall *Christian Theol. & Natural Science* vi. 217 More careful examination would enable us to sift out those beliefs which had a rational justification for those which were mere wish-fulfilments. **1958** E. A. Armstrong *Folklore of Birds* iii. 55 It is a man's wish-fulfilment story, as Cinderella is a woman's. **1958** *Punch* 25 June 852/2 She is gentle, charming, childlike, submissive, a young man's wish-fulfilment. **1978** M. Levey *Case of Walter Pater* xiv. 198 All Pater's dreams, nightmares as well as wish-fulfilments, find expression here.

So **'wish-fulfilling** *a.*

1922 R. S. Woodworth *Psychol.* xix. 501 They [*sc.* dreams] are 'wish-fulfilling'. **1945** D. L. Moore *Vulgar Heart* i. 14 The wish-fulfilling assumption that such honours will be deserved. **1976** *Listener* 8 Apr. 447/3 A serenity that accepts as self-evident truth what we reject as wish-fulfilling illusion.

wishfully ('wɪʃfʊlɪ), *adv.* [f. WISHFUL *a.* + -LY^2.]

1. In a wishful manner; with desire; longingly. Most commonly qualifying *look* or equivalent; sometimes app. associated with *wistfully*.

1598 Chapman *Iliad* iv. [viii.] 497 All did wishfullie expect the siluer-throned morne. **1722** De Foe *Col. Jack* ii, Well, young gentleman,..you look wishfully. **1773** Boswell *Tour Hebr.* (1785) 98, I was weary of this day, and began to think wishfully of being again in motion. **1791** Burns *Bonie Wee Thing* 5 Wishfully I look and languish In that bonie face o' thine. **1831** Southey in *Corr. w. C. Bowles* (1881) 272, I am looking daily and wishfully for your little book. **1878** Mrs. Stowe *Poganuc P.* i, Dolly still hung about wishfully.

†**2.** According to wish or desire. *Obs.*

1602 Middleton, etc. *Phœnix* iii. i. G 2 b, I doubt now We shall not gaine accesse vnto your loue or she to vs. *Fid.* Most wishfully here she comes.

So **'wishfulness**.

1801 Southey in Robberds *Mem. W. Taylor* (1843) I. 371, I expect with some wishfulness your remarks on the second volume. **1863** Trollope *Rachel Ray* I. 170 The longing loving wishfulness which used to make so many of her questions sweet to her mother's ears. **1892** *Sat. Rev.* 8 Oct. 422/1 A sweet wishfulness to please.

wish-hounds, *sb. pl.* Also **whished, whisht, wished.** [WISHT *a.* 2.] Local name for a ghostly pack of hounds popularly believed to hunt over Dartmoor (Devon) by night. So **'wish-hunt**, **'wish-hunter**.

1847 *Athenæum* 27 Mar. 334/2 The Abbot's Way..is the especial haunt of the Wish, or Wisked [*sic*] Hounds. **1865** R. Hunt *Pop. Rom. W. Eng.* Ser. i. Introd. p. xix, Wistman's Wood..is the very home of the *Wish hounds*, which hunt so fiercely over the Moor. **1863** Baring-Gould *Iceland* 202 On Dartmoor..the [Wild Huntsman's] chase continues: it is called the Wisht hunt. **1865** —— *Were-wolves* viii, On Heathfield, near Tavistock, the wild huntsman rides by full moon with his 'wush hounds'. **1897** —— *Guavas* xiv, 'Tis no Wish Hunter's gold.

wishill, obs. form of WISSEL.

wishing ('wɪʃɪŋ), *vbl. sb.* [f. WISH *v.* + -ING^1.]

a. The action of the verb WISH; desire; sometimes *spec.* †(*a*) evil desire, concupiscence; (*b*) imprecation.

c **1200** *Trin. Coll. Hom.* 179 Ne wrec þu þe mid wussinge ne mid warienge. *c* **1220** *Bestiary* 334 Golsipe and ȝiscing, ȝiuernesse and wissing. **1390** Gower *Conf.* I. 319 He set the herte in jeupartie With wihssinge and with fantasie. *c* **1500** *Melusine* 177 Our desyre and wysshyng is brought to effect. **1525** Ld. Berners *Froiss.* II. lxxviii. [lxxiv.] 90 b/1 Theyr horses serued them at theyr wysshyng. **1590** Stockwood *Rules Constr.* 3 Some aduerbe of wishing, as *vtinam.* **1599** Shaks. *Much Ado* iv. i. 329, I cannot be a man with wishing, therfore I will die a woman with grieuing. **1742** Young *Nt. Th.* iv. 71 Wishing, of all employments, is the worst. **1842** Newman *Par. Serm.* VI. xii. 154 Wishing will not serve instead of coming. **1869** Tozer *Highl. Turkey* II. 264 The power of obtaining anything by wishing.

b. An instance of this, a wish; formerly sometimes passing into the sense 'a request, petition': cf. WISH *sb.*^{1} 2, *v.* 5.

1377 Langl. *P. Pl.* B. ii. 90 In wedes and in wisshynges and with ydel thouȝtes. **1426** Lydg. *De Guil. Pilgr.* 6231 My desyr & my wysshynges Resten fully in thys thynges. **1548** Udall *Erasm. Par.* Pref. to Edw. VI, a ij, Our daily wysshinges and praiers. **1561** Hoby tr. *Castiglione's Courtyer* i. (1577) F v b, A wishing for that hee thought he had not. **1648** Fanshawe *Il Pastor Fido* ii. iv. 64 They.. Who not with wishings onely seek her favour. **1719** De Foe *Crusoe* i. (Globe) 191 Such were these earnest Wishings. **1877** Meredith *Gen. Ople* viii, Our young barbarians.. interest us in their wishings, their weepings, and..their kissings.

†**c.** ***wishing*(*s and wouldin*g(*s***: see WOULDING.

d. *attrib.* and *Comb.* in many designations of objects supposed to be capable of magically conferring the fulfilment of one's wishes, as ***wishing-bone*** (= wish-bone, WISH *sb.*^{1} 4), ***-cap***, ***-gate***, ***-hat***, ***-purse***, ***-rod***, ***-stone***, ***-tree***, ***-well***.

1860 Bartlett *Dict. Amer.* (ed. 3), *Wishing-Bone. **1600** Dekker *Old Fortunatus* E 4 b, Hauing this mint [*sc.* the purse] about me, I shall want no *wishing Cap. *a* **1674** Traherne *Chr. Ethics* (1675) 436 The fools wishing cap and the philosophers stone are but trifles. **1825** Scott *Jrnl.* 27 Dec., I have worn a wishing-cap, the power of which has been to divert present griefs. **1828** Wordsw. *Wishing-gate* 18 The rustic *Wishing-gate. **1600** Dekker *Old Fortunatus* H 1, Ile steale his *wishing Hat. **1855** Motley *Dutch Rep.* vi. i. III. 396 The *wishing purse in his hand. **1850** Lettsom *Fall Nibelungers* mclx. 197 The *wishing-rod of gold. **1859** G. W. Dasent *Pop. Tales from Norse* (ed. 2) p. xcii, Thus, we have *oska-steinn*, *wishing-stone, *i.e.* a stone which plays the part of a divining rod. **1908** *Daily Chron.* 20 Oct. 1/3 A wishing-stone. *a* **1586** Sidney *Arcadia* iii. (1922) 22 That she might have the first possession of the *wishing tree. **1792** J. Moore *Monast. Rem.* 2 The *wishing wells still remain. **1891** Atkinson *Moorland Par.* 235 One of these now unsuspected..wishing-wells or hâlikelds.

'wishing, *ppl. a.* [f. WISH *v.* + -ING^2.] That wishes, longing, desirous; expressing a wish.

† ***wishing and woulding*** (quot. 1620): cf. prec. c.

1530 Palsgr. 329/2 Wysshynge, *optatif.* **1579–80** North *Plutarch, Solon & Publicola* (1595) 121 In wishing manner, he would his end should be lamented to his praise. **1620** J. King *Serm. 24 Mar.* 3 It is not a wishing and woulding mercy, but a preuailing, speeding, releeuing mercy. **1662** Howell *New Engl. Gram.* 62 The Optatif or wishing Mood. **1703** Rowe *Ulysses* i. i, The wishing Warmth of Youth. **1725** Ramsay *Gentle Sheph.* iii. iv, Return'd to cheer his wishing tenant's sight. **1819** Shelley *Peter Bell 3rd* v. vi, Now Peter..Would..balk Some wishing guest of knife or fork.

Hence **'wishingly** *adv.*, desirously, longingly; in quot. 1571, optatively.

1571 Golding *Calvin on Ps.* lxxii. 2. 269 b, Some reade it wishingly; Othersome reteine the future tence, so as it should bee a prophesie. **1731** Bailey (ed. 5), *Desirously*, wishingly.

wishless ('wɪʃlɪs), *a. rare.* [f. WISH *sb.*^{1} + -LESS.] Having no wishes; void of or free from desire.

1820 Coleridge in *Blackw. Mag.* VII. 629 What a heartless, hopeless, almost wishless barrenness of spirit! *a* **1893** Chr. G. Rossetti *New Jerus.* Poet. Wks. (1904) 208/1 Where we shall be..Wishless in the sanctuary of Christ's embrace.

†**'wishly**, *a. Obs. rare.* [? f. next.] ? Steadfast.

1578 T. Procter *Gorg. Gallery Invent.* H ij, Vlisses wife shall mate the sore, whose wishly troth doth shine.

wishly ('wɪʃlɪ), *adv. Obs.* exc. *dial.* Also 6 **wysh(e)-, wishe-,** 7 **wishtly**. [? Alteration of WISTLY *adv.* influenced by *wish.*] Steadfastly, fixedly, intently; occas. longingly. (Almost always qualifying *look* or some equivalent: cf. *wistfully.*)

1530 Palsgr. fol. 183, I cast my syght vpon a thyng to beholde it wyshely. *Ibid.*, And sodaynly he caste his syght wyshely vpon me. **1533** More *Answ. Poysoned Bk.* v. ii. Wks. 1134/2 Causing hym to putte on his spectacles, and pore better and more wishely with his olde eyen vpon saynt Iohns ghospell. *c* **1611** Chapman *Iliad* xi. 522 Æacides, that wishly did intend..how deepe the skirmish drew Amongst the Greeks. **1622** J. Abernethy *Chr. Treat. Physick Soule* v. 73 Thou must bee wishly exstimulate in thy conscience. **1647** Trapp *Comm. Matt.* vi. 4. 186 He looketh wishtly, fixedly, steddily. **1660** S. Ford *Loyal Subj. Exult.* 21 Those thousands of loyall Subjects, who..had looked wishtly towards the royall Palace. **1680** R. L'Estrange *Erasm. Colloq.* xiii. 186 Looking wishly up into the Air [orig. *intentis in cœlum oculis*]. **1683** Cave *Ecclesiastici* App. 27 Woman, said he, tell me why dost thee so wishly behold me? *a* **1825** Forby *Voc. E. Anglia*, *Wishly*, earnestly; wishfully; with longing... 'The children eyed the plum-pudding wishly.' **1902** *Longman's Mag.* Nov. 40, I seed him yesterday a-cranen' over th' wall and eyen' on her wishly.

wishmay ('wɪʃmeɪ). [transl. ON. *óskmær*, f. *ósk* wish (see WISH *v.*) + *mær* maiden, MAY *sb.*^{1}] A Valkyrie.

1863 W. K. Kelly *Curios. Indo-Europ. Tradit.* 216 The Wishmays or Valkyries. **1889** R. B. Anderson tr. *Rydberg's Teut. Mythol.* 156 A giantess who had been adopted in Asgard as Odin's 'wish-may'.

Wishram ('wɪʃræm). Also 9 **Wish-ham.** [ad. Sahaptin *Wíšxam.*] **a.** (A member of) an American Indian people living in the southern part of the state of Washington. **b.** The language spoken by this people, a dialect of Upper Chinook.

[**1836** W. Irving *Astoria* I. 109 We would make special mention of the village of Wish-ram.] **1855** *Rep. Commissioner Indian Affairs 1857* 351 They are divided into three principal bands, namely: the Wish-hams, Click-a-hut, and Skien bands. **1907** *Amer. Anthropologist* IX. 533 The Indians formerly living on the northern shore of Columbia river..are known by their Yakima and Klikitat neighbours ..as *Wúcxam*, which, in its anglicized form of Wishram, or Wishham, is their common appellation today. *Ibid.* 535 The Wishram is prevailingly sonant in its use of stops. **1930** Spier & Sapir *Wishram Ethnography* 153 The Wishram were one of the earliest groups known to explorers of the Columbia River Basin... Only a few Wishram still remain.

1962 *Anthropol. & Human Behavior* (Anthropological Soc. Washington) 25 'Cussing out', a Wishram Chinook's English label for a class of aboriginal speech events. **1972** *Language* XLVIII. 378, I have drawn extensively upon my field research on the Wishram-Wasco dialect of Chinook.

wisht (wɪʃt), *a.* Chiefly *s.w. dial.* Also **whisht, whished, w(h)ish, whist, wist, weist, weest.** [Of obscure origin.]

1. Dreary, dismal; melancholy, wretched.

1829 T. Moore *Hist. Devon* I. 510 *Wish*, inapt, bad, unfit, as 'wish weather'. **1849** Kemble *Saxons in Eng.* I. 346 In Devonshire..a bad or unfortunate day is a *wisht* day. **1893** 'Q' *Delect. Duchy* 306 Ah, the poor body! his was a wisht case.

2. Uncanny, eerie, weird. (Cf. wish-hounds.)

c **1800** [implied in wishtness]. **1872** Mrs. Lynn Linton *Joshua Davidson* iii. 33 A wild whisht country that does not invite much night walking. **1891** Atkinson *Last of Giant-killers* 165 Their steps and hushed voices sounding very hollow and wisht all the time.

3. Sickly, wan.

1868 'Holme Lee' *B. Godfrey* lxvii, She is very whist and white. **1884** Fenn *Sweet Mace* III. xiii. 217 'I don't quite like the old woman to be burnt. How wist she looks!'

Hence **'wishtness**, melancholy; something uncanny or supernatural.

c **1800** Polwhele *Wishful Swain of Devon* in R. Hunt *Pop. Rom. W. Eng.* Ser. I. (1865) 150 He sought the dark-green lane,..Sighing..'Wishness! oh, wishness, walketh here'. **1839** *Mrs. Palmer's Devon. Dial.* Gloss., *Wishness*, melancholy. **1849** Kemble *Saxons in Eng.* I. 346 In Devonshire to this day all magical or supernatural dealings go under the common name of *Wishtness*.

wishtly, obs. form of wishly *adv.*

wishtonwish ('wɪʃtənwɪʃ). Also **wiston-**. [Imitative, from the cry of the animal.] Native name for the prairie-dog of N. America.

Used by Fenimore Cooper for *whip-poor-will*.

1806 Pike *Sources Mississ.* (1811) 207 Some prairie squirrels, or wish-ton-wishes. **1826** J. F. Cooper *Last of Mohicans* xxii, ''Tis a pleasing bird,..and has a soft and melancholy note.'..'He speaks of the wish-ton-wish', said the scout. **1829** J. Richardson *Fauna Bor.-Amer.* I. 154 The Wistonwish.

wish-wash ('wɪʃwɒʃ), *sb.* [Reduplicated formation from wash *sb.* (cf. sense 11 s.v.).]

1. A contemptuous name for weak, insipid, or unsubstantial drink (or liquid food). Also *attrib.* or *adj.* = wishy-washy 1.

1786 Mrs. A. M. Bennett *Juvenile Indiscr.* II. 36 The fish was ill-dressed, the soup mere wishwash. **1803** Mary Charlton *Wife & Mistress* IV. 50, I an't been used to her wish-washes, and her Cocoa. **18..** in Smyth *Sailor's Word-bk.* (1867) 736 His drink a wish-wash of six-water grog. **1896** Baring-Gould *Broom-Squire* xvi. 120 He must have ale, not wish-wash tea.

2. *fig.* Wishy-washy talk or writing.

1842 Howitt *Rur. & Dom. Life Germany* 479 You also find the trashiest wish-wash of Lady Blessington..just as much in vogue. **1885** Stopf. Brooke in Jacks *Life* (1917) II. 378, I talked sense, and was grimly resolved to give the exact opposite of ——'s wish-wash.

† **'wish-,washy**, *a. Obs.* [f. wish-wash *sb.* + -y¹.] = wishy-washy *a.*

a **1814** *Sixteen & Sixty* I. ii. in *New Brit. Theatre* II. 385 First he tuold I that losing a leg or a wing Were considered but wish-washy matters. **1816** Scott *Let.* in *Lockhart* (1837) IV. i. 27 There are two tales..the first is wish-washy enough. **1821** *Blackw. Mag.* IX. 60 None ever throve on the wish-washy draughts of the Muses.

wishy-washy ('wɪʃɪ,wɒʃɪ), *a.* (*int.*, *sb.*) [Reduplicated formation on washy *a.* (sense 2); cf. the earlier swish-swash (wishy-washy drink).]

1. Of drink (or liquid food): Weak and insipid; sloppy. Also *dial.* as *sb.* (see quot. 1824).

1791 *Massachusetts Spy* 12 May 2/1 He..looked at the broth—and d——d it for wishy washy stuff. **1824** Mactaggart *Gallovid. Encycl.* 481 *Wishie-washie*, small drink; ale with-out foam; whisky without bells. **1854** R. S. Surtees *Handley Cr.* xxvii, None of your flagon-of-ale and round-of-beef breakfasts nowadays—slip-slop, wishy-washy, milk-and-water, effeminate stuff. **1898** A. Balfour *To Arms* vii, Their wishy-washy, watery wine.

2. *fig.* **a.** Feeble or poor in constitution, condition, or aspect; weakly, sickly, 'washed-out'. Now *rare* or *Obs.*

1703 Steele *Tender Husb.* I. (1705) 12 Pray, Brother, observe his Make, none of your Lath-back'd wishy washy Breed. **1748** Smollett *Rod. Rand.* xxiv, A good seaman he is..; none of your guinea pigs,—nor your fresh-water, wishy-washy, fair-weather fowls. **1838** Lady Granville *Lett.* (1894) II. 261, I am quite well now, only rather wishy-washy. **1856** Hawthorne *Engl. Note-bks.* (1870) II. 163 A wishy-washy woman's face.

b. Feeble or poor in quality or character; trifling, unsubstantial, trashy, 'milk-and-watery'. †Also rarely as *int.* = pish! tush!

a **1693** Urquhart's *Rabelais* III. xxxvi. 298 *Pan.* Wishy, washy; Trolly, trolly [orig. *Tarabin, tarabas!*]. **1797** G. Colman *Heir at Law* II. ii, A lord without money be but a foolish, wishy washy kind of a thing a'ter all. **1801** T. Dibdin *Il Bondocani* III. ii, None of your wishy washy sparks that mince their steps. **1867** Trollope *Chron. Barset* I. vii. 55 A weak, wishy-washy man, who had hardly any mind of his own to speak of. **1865** Miss Braddon *Doctor's Wife* iii, Isabel painted wishy-washy looking flowers on Bristol-board from Nature. **1893** *Nation* (N.Y.) 9 Feb. 106/3 A silly, wishy-washy, inconclusive..style of writing.

Hence **'wishy-,washiness.**

1891 Lounsbury *Studies Chaucer* III. vii. 193 He had..every..personal inducement to go on diluting his original to the utmost limit of wishi-washiness.

wisie, obs. form of vizy *v. Sc.*

† **wisify** ('waɪzɪfaɪ), *v. Obs. nonce-wd.* [f. wise *a.* + -(i)fy.] *trans.* To make wise.

1694 Motteux *Rabelais* v. Author's Prol. A3b, The World therefore, wisifying it self [orig. *en sagissant*], shall no longer dread the..Blossoms of Beans every coming Spring.

Wisigoth, -ic, var. Visigoth, -ic.

wisioun, wisit, obs. ff. vision, visit.

wisk, obs. form of whisk.

wiskajon, var. whisky john.

wisker, obs. form of whisker.

wisket, whisket ('wɪskɪt, hw-). *dial.* Also 6 wysket(e, -cet, wiskyt, wiscat, 7–8 wiskett, 9 w(h)iskit, whiskett. [orig. and mainly north. dial.; ? derived (with -et¹) from the stem represented by the Scand. forms quoted s.v. whisk *sb.*¹] Local name for a basket, of various kinds and uses.

1542 in *Lanc. Wills* (Chetham Soc. 1857) 81, iiij stone and a half in ij grete wyscettis of wole; in another wisket xxx pond..; in another wisket xxᵗⁱ pound. **1570** Levins *Manip.* 87/23 A Wysket, *sportula.* **1674** Ray *N.C. Words* 53 A *Whisket*, a Basket, a skuttle, or shallow Ped. **1688** Holme *Armoury* II. 173/2 A Wisket, or Straw-basket, in which Provender is given Cows or Oxen. **1747** Hooson *Miner's Dict.* E2, Poor people..that go daily to the Mines, carry a small Wiskett and a Hammer along with them. **1828** *Craven Gloss.*, *Whisket*, a small clothes basket. **1838** R. Owen in *Life* (1894) I. iv. 139 A wisket of lovely grapes. **1897** 'O. Rhoscomyl' *White Rose Arno* 243 They'll tumble up from below like whelps from a wisket.

Comb. **1621** *Shuttleworths' Acc.* (Chetham Soc.) 248 To the wiskett maker,..iijᵈ.

Wiskinkie (wɪ'skɪŋkɪ). *U.S.* Also **Wiskinky, Wiskinski.** [Etym. unknown.] The official of the Tammany Society of New York charged with the office of door-keeper.

1800 *Commercial Advertiser* (N.Y.) 3 Jan. 2/3 Tammany Society, in the following order: 1st, The Wiskinkie, supporting the Cap of Liberty veiled in crape. **1843** *New Mirror* 15 Apr. 18/2 They were placed in charge of the Wiskinski of the wigwam. **1864** C. G. Halpine *Life & Adventures of Private Miles O'Reilly* 191 He had been a brave when the present Grand Sachems, Wiskinkies and Sagamores were no more than little papooses. **1905** W. L. Riordon *Plunkitt* 99 Dan Donegan, who used to be the Wiskinskie of the Tammany Society, and received contributions from grateful office holders. **1938** J. W. Norwood *Tammany Legend* xi. 145 The chief of a 'Tribe' was its Sachem; the master of ceremonies, the Sagamore; the Sergeant at Arms, the Wiskinskie. **1967** Connable & Silberfarb *Tigers of Tammany* i. 28 The Wiskinkie (sergeant-at-arms) swore an oath to preserve the Society from 'intruders and eavesdroppers'.

wisling, -yng: see wissel *v.*

† **'wisly**, *a. Obs.* Forms: 1 wislic, 3 (*Orm.*) wisslik. [OE. *wislic*, f. *wis(s* adj. (see wis *sb.*) + *-lic*, -ly¹.] Certain.

Phr. *wisslikess þingess* (gen. sing.), of a certainty, certainly.

c **1000** *Ags. Ps.* (Thorpe) lxxii[i]. 3 [4] Ne heora wites bið wislic trymnes [orig. *nec est firmamentum in plaga eorum*]. *c* **1200** Ormin 3186 Wisslikess þingess Godess hannd was wiþþ þatt child.

† **'wisly**, *adv. Obs.* Forms: 1 wis(s)lice, 2–4 wisliche, 4–5 wisly, wissely, (3 wysslych, *Orm.* wisslı3, -like, 4 wislike, -lich, -li, wissly, wysly, 5 wisselich, wysslie, wischli). [OE. *wislice*, f. *wis(s* adj. (see wis *sb.*) + *-lice*, -ly².] Certainly, surely; assuredly; verily.

c **1000** *Ags. Ps.* (Thorpe) lviii[i]. 13 Hi wisslice witon. *Ibid.* xcix. 2 [c. 3] Witað wislice, þæt [etc.]. *c* **1175** *Lamb. Hom.* 63 þe luste nulleð þesne red, wisliche he scal wurðen ded. *c* **1200** *Trin. Coll. Hom.* 189 þe holi man..on oðer stede wisluker þerof specð. *c* **1200** Ormin 928 He falleþþ wisslı3 forr þatt gillt i Godess wraþþe & wræche. **1340–70** *Alex. & Dind.* 844 Many wondurful wonus wisli we knowen. *c* **1386** Chaucer *Reeve's T.* 74 Men wenden wisly that he sholde dye. —— *Frankl. T.* 61 She to hym ful wisly gan to swere That neuere sholde ther be defaute in here. *c* **1400** *Destr. Troy* 3567 Vnto þat worthy he went wisly anon.

b. *esp.* with *as* (*alse, also*) or *so* in asseverations.

c **1200** *Trin. Coll. Hom.* 167 Vre lafdi Seinte Marie, alse wisliche alse hie þis dai was houen in to heuene, bere ure arende to ure louerd ihesu crist. **1303** R. Brunne *Handl. Synne* 9673 As wysly as he become a chylde. ? *a* **1366** Chaucer *Rom. Rose* 632 Now also wisly god me blesse. **14..** *Pol. Rel. & L. Poems* (1903) 79/104 For as wischli as euer y cum too blisse, My will is goode. *c* **1470** Henry *Wallace* IV. 63 Als wisly God me sawe.

wisment, Sc. var. visement *Obs.*, consideration.

c **1425** Wyntoun *Cron.* v. v. 988 He askyt thre dayis to wisment.

† **'wismuth.** *Obs.* Also [6 wisemute], 7 wismut, wismodt. = Bismuth.

[**1587** Harrison *England* III. xi. 238/2 in *Holinshed*, A mettall..the verie same which Encelius calleth *Plumbum cinereum*, the Germans wisemute, mithan, & counterfeie.] **1650** J. F[rench] *Chym. Dict.*, *Wismodt* is [*printed* in] Tin that is foule and immalleable, and cannot be wrought upon. **1651** French *Distill.* v. 168 Common copper makes a sea-green; Wismut common blew. **1783** *Phil. Trans.* LXXIII. 83 Wismuth forms a slight precipitate in the nitrous solution of arsenic.

wisnand, -nyt: see wizened.

'wisome. *dial.* Also 8 wissum, 9 wysan. [f. wise *sb.*², after risom.] = wizle.

1688 [see wizle]. *c* **1710** Celia Fiennes *Diary* (1888) 136 The greenes they [*sc.* the country people] Call Wissums and on these wissums the Deer Brouse in yᵉ winter. **1888** H. Wedgwood in *N. & Q.* 7th Ser. VI. 314 In North Staffordshire..the labouring man would speak of cranberry-wysans, bilberry-wysans. The runners of strawberries would be strawberry-wysans, and potato-halms were potato-wysans.

wisp (wɪsp), *sb.*¹ Forms: 4–5, 8–9 *dial.* wips, weps (5 wyps), 8–9 *dial.* whips; 4–5 (6, 8 *Sc.*) wysp, 4–6 wyspe, 4–7 wispe, (6 wysppe), 5–6 *Sc.* wosp, wasp, 6–9 whisp, 4– wisp. [Of uncertain origin; perh. an unrecorded OE. **wips*, **wisp*:—**wipisa-*, f. base *wip-* in the sense 'wind or bind round', for derivatives of which see whip *v.*

Cf. WFris. *wisp* wisp, twig, handful of straw. For the forms current in other Germ. langs. see whisk *sb.*¹]

1. A handful, bunch, or small bundle (of hay, straw, grass, etc.).

13.. in Horstm. *Altengl. Leg.* (1875) 91 þer inne oure ledi him wond and bond him wiþ aliste, And leide him on awisp of hei [*v.r.* a wips of heye]. *c* **1460** *Towneley Myst.* ii. 438 Yey, gif don, thyne hors, a wisp of hay. **1577** tr. *Bullinger's Decades* (1592) 579 These champions..bringing foorth a speare made of a wrapt vp wisp of hay. **1639** J. Clarke *Parœm.* 215 All's alike at th' latter day, a bag of gold and wispe of hay. **1779** G. Keate *Sketches fr. Nat.* (ed. 2) I. 42 But why do we stop?.. Only to give the horses a pail of water, replies the postillion... Nay, prithee boy, says my friend, add a whisp of hay to it. **1858** Carlyle *Fredk. Gt.* v. viii. (1873) II. 132 As if we were a starved coach-horse, to be quickened along by a wisp of hay put upon the coach-pole close ahead of us always! **1879** J. Beerbohm *Patagonia* iv. 53 Made soft for the young chicks by a few wisps of grass.

b. used to wipe something dry or clean; now chiefly to rub down a horse.

In quot. 1589 with allusion to hanging.

1362 Langl. *P. Pl.* A. v. 195 Alle þat herde þe horn heolden heore nose after, And weschte þat hit weore I-wipet with a wesp [*v.rr.* wips, wysp(e) of Firsen [C. vii. 402 Wips [*v.r.* weps] of breres]. *c* **1410** *Master of Game* (MS. Digby 182) xx, þenne kembe euery hounde after oþer and wype hem with a gret wyspe of strawe. **14..** in Wr.-Wülcker 595/35 *Mempirium* [= *anitergium*], a wyps. **1508** Dunbar *Flyting* 64 For wit and wisdome ane wisp fra the may rub. **1589** [? Lyly] *Pappe w. Hatchet* Lyly's Wks. III. 404 If he driuell so at the mouth and nose, weele haue him wipte [= wiped] with a hempen wispe. **1596** Nashe *Saffron Walden* Sj, A maulkin or wispe to wype her shooes with. **1600** Surflet *Country Farm* vii. xxii. 840 For lice..wash them [*sc.* dogs] and rub them with a wispe. **1611** Cotgr., *Torche-cul*, a wispe for the tayle. **1660** Bonde *Scut. Reg.* 214 There you shall burn like wisps, which have done scouring the better vessels. **1725** *Bradley's Fam. Dict.* s.v. *Embrocation*, Take the Soldiers Ointment,..and anoint the Part affected therewith, being first well rubbed with soft Whisps of Hay. **1864** E. Mayhew *Horse Managem.* 378 The curry-comb is abolished; but the generality of grooms also require to be cautioned concerning the use of the whisp and the brush. **1901** Fitzwyram *Horses & Stables* vi.

c. in various special uses, e.g. as an ale-house sign; hung outside a house as a sign of the plague; as a plug, strainer, or wad; (of herbs) as a perfume or deodorant.

1508 Dunbar *Tua Mariit Wemen* 335 3it tuk I neuir the wosp clene out of my wyde throte, Quhill I oucht wantit of my will. **1508** —— *Test. Andro Kennedy* 110, I will..na bellis for me ring,..Bot a bag pipe to play a spryng, Et unum ail wosp ante me. **1518** in W. H. Turner *Select. Rec. Oxford* (1880) 18 The inhabitants of thos howses that be..infectyd shall kepe in, pott owt wyspes and ber whyt roddys. **1596** Nashe *Saffron Walden* N3, His Muse, from the first peeping foorth, hath stood at Liuery at an Ale-house wispe. *a* **1598** D. Fergusson *Scot. Prov.* (S.T.S.) 34 Good wine needs not a wispe. **1626** Bacon *Sylva* §934 The same Man vsed to haue continually, a great Wispe of Herbes, that he smelled on. **1650** Stapylton *Strada's Low-C. Wars* ix. 41 [He] put forth..a wisp of straw, upon the end of a white Rod, as if he would, according to the custome of the Countrey, give notice..that the house was visited with the plague. **1658** tr. *Porta's Nat. Magic* v. ix. 176 Strain the vinegar through a wisp. **1688** Holme *Armoury* III. xviii. (Roxb.) 141/1 A wisp or wad, is either hay or straw to put in after the powder. **1855** Delamer *Kitch. Gard.* (1861) 25 If the potatoes are moist,..it will be well to leave a wisp of straw sticking out at the top [of the ridge]. **1901** Rhys *Celtic Folklore* I. iv. 299 He gave them herbs..and..sold them wisps to place under their pillows.

†**d.** in proverbial phr. **as wise as a wisp.** *Obs.*

1550 Bale *Engl. Votaries* II. 84 Than as wyse as ij wyspes, and as godly as ij goselynges, they examined her what her beleue was in the sacrament. **1655** H. More *Second Lash* 218 When we say that one is as wise as a wisp, does that imply the wisp is wise? **1682** —— *Annot. Glanvill's Lux O.* 35 They would have rose out of their sleep no more wise than a Wisp.

2. A twisted band, esp. of hay or straw; a ring or wreath of twisted material, used as a pad.

1398 Trevisa *Barth. De P.R.* III. xviii. (1495) Dvb/1 [The] gristylbone..in yᵉ eere..is wound & wrapped as a wyspe, leest the spyrite of heringe were..hurt by sodayn..smytynge. *c* **1440** *Promp. Parv.* 530/2 Wyspe, *torques*,.. *torquillus.* **1483** Caxton *Gold. Leg.* 239/2 [They] mocked hym..and bond behynd hym wyspes of strawe. **1607** Markham *Cavel.* iv. ix. 48 As you rid him with the tramels, so you shall ride him with these wispes [*sc.* thick 'thumb-ropes' of hay round his pasterns]. **1611** COTGR., *Torche*,.. the wreathed clowt, wispe, or wad of straw, layed by wenches betweene their heads, and the things which they carrie on them. **1725** POPE *Odyss.* x. 194 An ell in length the pliant wisp I weaved, And the huge body on my shoulders heaved. **1876** SMILES *Sc. Natur.* i. 10 His mother tied him firmly to the table leg with a thick wisp of thrums. **1908** *J. Gunn's Orkney Book* 394 'Wisps' (the local name for great rolls of heather 'simmons', or ropes, used in thatching houses).

†**b.** A twist or figure of straw for a scold to rail at. *Obs.*

a **1450** *Knt. de la Tour* xv. 21 He writhed a litell wipse of strawe, and sette it afore her, and saide, ladi, yef that ye will chide more, chide with that straw. **1566** DRANT *Horace, Sat.* VII. D 7 b, Women.. Whose tatling tongues, had won a wispe. **1593** SHAKS. *3 Hen. VI*, II. ii. 144. **1626** H. PARROT *Cures for the Itch* B 5 b, Theres nothing mads.. her [*sc.* a scold] more.. then but the very naming of a wispe. **1698** [R. FERGUSSON] *View Eccl.* 27 As a Wisp.. is a Theame copious enough to engage an Harangue for an hour long to a well studied Scold.

3. A bunch or twisted bundle of hay or straw, used for burning as a torch, etc.

1412–20 LYDG. *Chron. Troy* IV. 4984 þei faren as a wisp a-fire: Whanne it brenneþ bri3test in his blase, Sodeinly it wasteþ. **15..** *Wyf of Auchtirmuchty* 29 (Bannatyne MS.) Yeis lay ane soft wisp to the kill. **1572** MASCALL *Plant. & Graff.* (1592) 49 Ye shall.. with a wispe on a Poles ende, set fire on all. **1682** *Lond. Gaz.* No. 1688/4 Some rascally Boys.. who made some wisps of Straw, and burnt them in the dark night. **1806** [J. BLACK] *Falls of Clyde* 169 Fie light a wisp, and look below the bed! **1846** J. BAXTER *Libr. Pract. Agric.* (ed. 4) II. 268 It should be put into the oven, moderately heated with a few wisps of straw.

b. A marsh-fire, WILL-O'-THE-WISP; also the light supposed to be carried by the sprite. In more recent use *poet.*

[**1608**–: see WILL-O'-THE-WISP.] **1618** BP. HALL *Contempl., N.T.* I. *Sages and Star*, Philosophy without the star, is but the wispe of error. **1650** in H. Cary *Mem. Gt. Civ. War* (1832) II. 226 It is the saints' minimum quoddam naturale; a Nol with the wisp. **1821** CLARE *Vill. Minstrel* vii, 'Jack-a-lantern' with his wisp alight. **1822** BYRON *Vis. Judgem.* cv, Light as an elf, Or wisp that flits o'er a morass. **1847** TENNYSON *Princess* IV. 339 We did not know the real light, but chased The wisp that flickers where no foot can tread.

4. A bundle or parcel containing a definite quantity (of certain commodities: see quots.). *Sc.* and *north.* (Presumably so named from being orig. tied in a bundle with a wisp or wisps of straw or hay: cf. WIDDY 3, and the analogous SHEAF *sb.* 2 a, b, c.) **a.** of steel and glass.

1470 in *Fabric Rolls York Minster* (Surtees) 73 Pro j les wysp vitri rubii, 16 d. **1496** *Acc. Ld. High Treas. Scot.* I. 292 Item.. for vij wosp of steil to pykkis and mattokkis xiiij s. **1511–12** *Ibid.* IV. 273 Ane wisp of Lambart steile, price iiij s. **15..** *Aberdeen Reg.* (Jam.), Ane wosp of glas. **1612** *Sc. Bk. Rates in Halyburton's Ledger* (1867) 330 Wisp steill the wisp, x s. **1621** in *Reg. Privy Council Scot.* (1895) XII. 439 Thay fand that the.. caissis of the said glasse contenis fyfteene wispis and that in everie wisp thair is three tablis. **1657** [see *wisp-steel* in 6].

b. of other things, e.g. fish.

1521 *Aberdeen Reg.* XI. (Jam.), Four wospe of malt. **1557** *Rec. Inverness* (New Spalding Club) I. 8 This is the pricis [of fish]: for the gret wasp iij s., the small wasp xxx d. **1910** *Aberd. Jrnl. Notes & Q.* III. 150/2 *Weesp*, a quantity of fish; 'I hae naething bit a weesp o' eels' as the result of my fishing —Moray.

c. *transf.* A flock (of birds, esp. snipe).

1806 P. NEILL *Tour Orkney* etc. 59 The sportsman.. will not pass a marsh without starting several wisps of snipe. *c* **1810** A. MACKINTOSH *Driffield Angler* 294 Wisp, or whisp, of snipes. **1886** P. ROBINSON *Teetotum Trees* 159 A barrelful of shot emptied into a wisp of larks.

5. In various transferred and allusive senses.

a. A twist of paper. **b.** A heap or bundle (of clothes). **c.** (See quot.) **d.** A thin, narrow, filmy, or slight piece, fragment, or portion (*of* something); a mere shred or 'slip' *of*. **e.** A small broom; a whisk.

a. 1597 *Return fr. Parnass.* v. i. 1434 What, you saucye groome, are you bringinge mee such paper wisps? **1800** in *Spirit Publ. Jrnls.* IV. 264 And soar like a wisp to the tail of his kite. **1861** FLOR. NIGHTINGALE *Nursing* 24 If you have a fire-place, would you cram it up.. with a great wisp of brown paper? **1865** DICKENS *Mut. Fr.* I. xiii, The bare-armed Bob, leading the way with a flaming wisp of paper.

b. 1736 PEGGE *Kenticisms* (E.D.S.) s.v. *Wips*, 'The cloaths lie in a whips', i.e. tumbl'd in disorder. **1784** tr. *Beckford's Vathek* (1786) 106 At last, he was drawn forth, almost smothered, from the wisp of linen. **1810** T. WILLIAMSON *E. Ind. Vade Mecum* I. 245 [The clothes] are folded up into whisps, or bundles.

c. 1787 W. H. MARSHALL *Rur. Econ. Norfolk* (1795) II. 391 *Wisp*, a rowel, or seton.

d. 1836 DICKENS *Sk. Boz, Vauxhall-Gardens*, A rusty black neckerchief with a red border, tied in a narrow wisp round his neck. **1836** MRS. SOMERVILLE *Connex. Phys. Sci.* xxxvi. (ed. 3) 398 Some [nebulæ] cling to stars like wisps of cloud. **1848** THACKERAY *Our Street* 14 She had a large casque with a red horse-hair plume (I thought it had been a wisp of her brother's beard at first). **1883** *Century Mag.* Sept. 719/1 Tufted with ferns and brambles and wisps of delicate long grass. **1883** STEVENSON *Silverado Sq.* 22 That great mountain.. weaving vapours, wisp after wisp growing, trembling, fleeting, and fading in the blue. **1889** CONAN DOYLE *Micah Clarke* xii, As we approached this lonely gibbet, we saw that a dried-up wisp of a thing.. was dangling from the centre of it. **1893** STEVENSON *Catriona* xxviii, The sun had gone down, a little wisp of a new moon was following it. **1919** *Blackw. Mag.* Aug. 244/1 Dawson pointed to a thin wisp of smoke on the horizon.

e. 1875 KNIGHT *Dict. Mech.*, *Wisp*, a besom, a small broom. **1908** RIDER HAGGARD *Ghost Kings* xv. 209 A fly wisp made of the tip of an elephant's tail shrunk on to a handle of rhinoceros horn.

6. *Comb.*, as ***wisp-like*** adj.; **wisp bacillus** (see quot. 1916); **wisp-light**, a will-o'-the-wisp; †**wisp-steel**, steel sold in wisps.

1915 *Lancet* 18 Sept. 639/1 The non-sporing bacteria of fæcal origin—e.g., strepto-cocci, B. proteus, '*wisp' bacilli, &c. **1916** *Ibid.* 8 Jan. 75/1 The so-called 'wisp bacillus'.. is the B. ramosus or a member of its group. *a* **1847** ELIZA COOK *To the Spirit of Song* iv, When *wisp-lights dance on the moor and fen. **1883** SAVILLE-KENT in *Fisheries Bahamas* 36 A twisted *wisp-like bundle of long silicious spicules. **1612** *wisp steill [see sense 4 a]. **1617** *Rates of Marchandizes* L 2, Steele vocat. Long-steele, Wisp-steele [etc.]. **1657** *Acts Interregn.* (1911) II. 1220 Steel called Steel Wisp or Long.

wisp (wɪsp), *sb.*[2] *dial.* Also 6 **wyspe**, 8–9 **whisp**. [Of doubtful origin; perh. a use of prec.]

a. A disease in cattle, causing lameness or soreness near the hoof. (Cf. ANGLEBERRY, FOUL *sb.* 2.)

1577 GOOGE *Heresbach's Husb.* III. 132 This disease, as I take it, the countrey people call the Fowle, or the Wyspe. **1684** J. S. *Profit & Pleas. United* 24. **1696** AUBREY *Misc.* 109 To Cure a Bullock, that hath the Wisp, (that is) Lame between the Clees. **1847** HALLIWELL, *Whisp.. Wisp.*

b. = STY *sb.*[4] (Cf. earlier and dial. WEST *sb.*[2] and dial. *wish.*)

1789 A. C. BOWER *Diaries & Corr.* (1903) 57, I am blind in one Eye nearly from a Whisp on the Eye lid. **1888** *Berksh. Gloss.*, *Stye*, a 'wisp' on the eye.

wisp (wɪsp), *sb.*[3] [f. WISP *v.*] An act of wisping. *a wisp down*, a rub down with a wisp.

1844 H. STEPHENS *Bk. Farm* II. 180 They should give the horses a slight wisp down.

wisp (wɪsp), *v.* Also 7, 9 **whisp**. [f. WISP *sb.*[1]]

1. *trans.* To rub (an animal, esp. a horse) *down* or *over* with a wisp.

a **1598** D. FERGUSSON *Scot. Prov.* (S.T.S.) 6 A fair bryde is soon buskt, and a short horse soone wispt. **1834** *New Monthly Mag.* XLII. 436 Wisp her and curry her, feed her and train her!.. and what is she after all but a *mule*! **1844** H. STEPHENS *Bk. Farm* II. 217 The whole body should then be wisped down with straw. *Ibid.*, Of wisping and brushing, wisping is the more beneficial to the legs, where the hair is short. **1844** *Queen's Regul. & Ord. Army* 351 They are to remain saddled.., time being allowed for wisping them over. **1856** 'STONEHENGE' *Brit. Sports* II. I. xi. §1. 361/1 Beginning with the head, which should be first brushed over, then well whisped with a handful of hay.

†**2.** To put a twisted band of hay upon (the legs of a horse). Also with *up*. *Obs.*

1607 MARKHAM *Cavel.* IV. ix. 48 Hauing thus wispt al his foure legs,.. you shall then mount vpon him [etc.]. **1639** T. DE GREY *Compl. Horsem.* 32 Whisp him up round with small whisps.

3. To twist into or as a wisp; *dial.* to rumple.

1753 HOGARTH *Anal. Beauty* v. 28 The very same head of hair, wisp'd, and matted together, would make the most disagreeable figure. **1823** E. MOOR *Suffolk Words* 487 *Wisp* is used with us, in the farther sense of rudely handling any delicate thing—'Dont wisp it'. **1870** 'OUIDA' *Puck* vi, 'Ye'r wispin' tha ribbon, ma dear,' said Dick. **1880** *Daily Tel.* 2 Mar. 5/2 A cloth, degenerating into a rag, is wisped round his head.

4. *intr.* To pass *away*, as a wisp of vapour.

1883 MEREDITH *Poems Joy of Earth* 12 Whish! the phantom wisps away. **1898** G. W. STEEVENS *With Kitchener to Khartum* 278 Magically the rifles hushed, the stinging powder smoke wisped away.

5. *intr.* Of hair, etc.: to hang or twine in wisps. Hence **wisped** (wɪspt) *ppl. a.*

1913 W. DE LA MARE *Peacock Pie* 31 Topknot to love-curl The hair wisps down. **1922** A. S. M. HUTCHINSON *This Freedom* II. ix. 164 Her face flushed; her hat awry; her hair escaped and wisped about her eyes. **1976** 'A. YORK' *Dark Passage* iv. 56 Long, straight hair which wisped on her shoulders.

†**'wispen**, *a. Obs. rare.* [f. WISP *sb.*[1] + -EN[4].] Made of a wisp or wisps.

1593 G. HARVEY *Pierces Super.* 145 She hath already put-on her wispen garland ouer her powting Cros-cloth.

wisper, obs. form of WHISPER.

wispish ('wɪspɪʃ), *a.* [f. WISP *sb.*[1] + -ISH[1].] Of the nature of or resembling a wisp.

1896 SARA J. DUNCAN *His Honor & a Lady* xi, Involuntarily she put a wispish curl in its place. **1923** E. BRAMAH *Eyes of Max Carrados* iii. 113 With ungainly movements of her long, wispish arms. **1925** *Chamb. Jrnl.* Jan. 53/1 A small man.. with a wispish tawny beard.

wispy ('wɪspɪ), *a.* [f. WISP *sb.*[1] + -Y[1].] Consisting of or resembling a wisp or wisps.

In early quots. with allusion to *will-o'-the wisp.*

a **1717** PARNELL *Fairy Tale* xxvii, Will, who bears the wispy fire To trail the swains among the mire. **1830** AIRD *Demoniac* iii. 31 Miriam saw white wispy fires dance. **1830** —— *Captive of Fez* III. ii. 6 The skirring moon.. from her horn-tips tossed the wispy rack. **1839** J. WILSON in J. Hamilton *Mem.* vi. (1859) 208 These [cribs of the Cameleopards] are.. filled with a dry wispy-looking plant, neither hay nor clover. **1888** F. COWPER *Caedwallan* 141 A few locks of wispy hair hung down over the forehead. **1894** *Athenæum* 24 Nov. 719 Nebulous matter, which.. attaches itself to the.. stars and is of a wispy and streaky nature.

Hence **'wispily** *adv.*

1923 A. HUXLEY *Antic Hay* 30 His long grey hair floated wispily about his head. **1985** M. WESLEY *Harnessing Peacocks* ix. 76 His hair hung wispily round his collar.

wiss, var. WIS *v.*[1] and [2]; obs. f. WISE; obs. or Sc. f. WISH.

wissard, obs. f. WIZARD.

wissch(e, obs. ff. pa. t. of WASH.

wisse, obs. f. VICE *sb.*[1]; var. WIS *v.*[1] *Obs.*; obs. f. WISE *sb.*[1] and *a.*, WISH *v.*

wissel ('wɪs(ə)l), *sb.* Chiefly *Sc.* Forms: see next. [a. MLG. *wissele*, *wessele* (M)Du. *wissel*, corresp. to OFris. *wix(e)le*, OHG. *wehsal* (MHG. *wehsel*, G. *wechsel*), ON. *vixl*: see next.]

†**1.** = EXCHANGE *sb.* 10. *Obs.*

1482 *Cely Papers* (Camden) 104 The Kyng.. wylle hawe iij whystylles whon at Bregys another at Callez the thyrd at London. **1498** HALYBURTON *Ledger* (1867) 173 Sald tham [*sc.* xv lycht crounis] in the Wissil off Brugis for 3 li. 6s. 5.

2. Change for an amount of money; esp. in phr. ***to get the wissel of one's groat***, fig. to be 'paid out'.

1721 RAMSAY *Prosp. Plenty* 134 Nor can we wyt them, since they had our Vote; But now they'se get the Wistle of their Groat. **1722** W. HAMILTON *Wallace* 36 Wallace quickly brought the Culzeon back, And there gave him the Whissle of his Plack. **1786** BURNS *Ep. John Rankine* ix, I.. gat the whissle o' my groat, An' pay't the fee. **1808** JAMIESON s.v. *Quhissel*, 'Gie me my wissel'.

wissel ('wɪs(ə)l), *v. Sc.* and *north.* Forms: 4 **wesle**, **wisle**, 4–5 **vissill**, 5 **w(h)ystyll**, **wys(s)yll**, **whystel**, 5–6 **wyssil(l**, **wissle**, **wishill**, **quhissel**, 5–7 **wissil**, 7 **-ell**, **wyschell**, **wirsle**, 6–7, 9 **wissel**, 8 **w(h)istle**, 8–9 **whissle**, 9 **wissle**. [a. MLG. (MDu.) *wisselen*, *wesselen*, *weslen*, corresp. to OFris. *wixlia*, OS. *wehslôn*, OHG. *wehslôn* (MHG. *wehseln*, *wihseln*, G. *wechseln*), ON. *vixla*:—OTeut. **wixslōjan*, f. *wīk-* (cf. WEEK *sb.*, WIKE) + suffix *-sla-*.]

†**1.** *trans.* To exchange for something else. *Obs.*

1375 BARBOUR *Bruce* XII. 580 Mony men of gret valour With speris, macys, and with knyvis, And othir vapnys vissill [*v.r.* wysyllyt] thair lyvis. **1513** DOUGLAS *Æneis* IX. iv. 92 Heyr is.. A forcy spreit.. Quhilk reputtis fayr to wyssill, apon sik wys Wyth this honour thou thus pretendis to wyn, This mortale stait and life that we bene in. *a* **1583** MONTGOMERIE *Flyting* 578 Appardon mee, poets, to alter my style, And wissle my verse, for fyling the aire.

b. To exchange (words) *with* a person.

1571 A. STEWART *Let.* in *Bannatyne's Memorials* (Bann. Club) 152 Thow seames in the begyning to schaw thy vnwillingnes to wissil [*ed.* 1806 wishill] wordis in our querall. ? *a* **1603** MOYSIE *Mem.* (Bannatyne Club) 131 Some wordis wer wissellit at the first betuix the erle of Mar and lord Lyndsay. **1819** [ALEX. BALFOUR] *Campbell* I. xviii. 332 He.. sware a gryte aith, that he wad never wissle words wi' him till he changed his mind.

2. To change (money).

1483 *Acta Audit.* in *Acta Dom. Conc.* II. Introd. 130 The some of viij Henre nobles quhilk.. Issabell allegit.. was wissilit and changit be the said Johne and nocht laid wed. **1666** *Despauterii Gramm. Instit.* v. (1677) G vij b, *Cambio*, to wissel or change money. *c* **1700** KENNETT *MS. Lansd. 1033* lf. 432 b, *Wirsle*, to exchange, or, change, Northumb. in *Wirsle me this half-crown.* **1721** RAMSAY *Poems* Gloss., *Wistle*, to exchange (Money).

†**'wisseler.** *Obs.* Also 5 **whysteler**, **westelur**, **wislare**, 6 **wisler**, **quhysselar**, etc. [f. prec. + -ER[1], ad. or after MLG., MDu. *wisselere*, *wesselere*, *weslere*.] A money-changer; also, a retailer.

In the prose *Merlin* *c* 1450 (E.E.T.S.) 168 [A] regrater and a wyssher [so MS.], ? read *wyssler*.

1481 *Cely Papers* (Camden) 74 God.. pwt hyt in yowr mynd to have the c xxx li howt of the whystelers handys.. at Bregys. **1487** *Sc. Acts Jas. III.* (1814) II. 182/2 That his hienes deput.. ane vthir to be wislare & changeour. **1573** BARET *Alv.* H 654 An Huckster, a regrater: a seller by retaile: a wifler [*read* wisler], *propola*.

So †**'wisseling** *vbl. sb. Sc. Obs.* [= MDu. *wisselinghe*], exchange.

c **1375** *Sc. Leg. Saints* xxiv. (*Alexis*) 164 Al þe gold.. He gaf to pure, & his clething He gaf fore ware in weslyng. **1463** *Extr. Aberdeen Regr.* (1844) I. 405, v s. vi d. the quhilk he tuke fra him in wisling of a farthing of an Inglis nobill. **1540** *Sc. Acts Jas. V*, II. 373/2 Sindry personis havand quhite siluir will not change for gold bot takkis þairfor xij d or mair for wissilling of þe samine. **1629** *Reg. Privy Council Scot.* Ser. II. III. 20 That nane.. ressave anie of the saidis dollours in payment of debts nor in exchange or wissilling.

wissened, obs. Sc. f. WIZENED.

‖**Wissenschaft** ('vɪsənʃaft). [Ger.] (The systematic pursuit of) knowledge; learning, scholarship; science. Hence ‖**'Wissenschaftslehre** (-le:rə), a theory or philosophy of knowledge (used with reference to the work of J. G. Fichte, author of *Grundlage der gesammten Wissenschaftslehre* (1794)).

1834 F. D. MAURICE *Let.* 24 July in F. Maurice *Life* (1884) I. xi. 168 My friend adds, '.. They all seem to think *Wissenschaft*.. more important than soundness of creed.' **1846** J. D. MOREAU *Hist. & Crit. View Speculative Philos.* II. v. 72 Fichte's object was.. to erect a system.. of rigid scientific knowledge... Hence it was that, in place of 'Philosophy' he assumed the term 'Wissenschaftslehre', as most designative of his great purpose. **1896** W. CALDWELL *Schopenhauer's System* ix. 503 That most vicious aspect of

German philosophy, so prominent in the Hegelian dialectic and Fichte's *Wissenschaftslehre*, whereby it always seems to be telling us what a fact *must be* before we know what it *is*. **1961** D. G. JAMES *Matt. Arnold* iv. 93 By 'science' he does not, of course, mean 'science' as we now ordinarily understand it; he means *Wissenschaft*, that is, as he says elsewhere, 'knowledge systematically pursued and prized in and for itself'. **1976** B. WILLIAMS *Making of Manchester Jewry* iv. 108 The emergence of Theodores as..a major English representative of the German *Wissenschaft*. **1982** C. CLEMEAU *Ariadne Clue* (1983) xi. 120 These fragments are painstakingly collected, published..and roundly applauded as the choicest fruits of philological *Wissenschaft*.

Wissentide, obs. f. WHITSUNTIDE.

† **'wisser.** *Obs.* In 5 -are. [f. WIS *v.*[1] + -ER[1].] A leader, director, guide.

c **1440** *Promp. Parv.* 530/1 Wyssare, or ledare.

wissh(e, obs. pa. t. of WASH *v.*; var. WIS *v.*[1] *Obs.*; obs. f. WISH.

† **'wissing**, *vbl. sb. Obs.* [f. WIS *v.*[1] + -ING[1].] The action of WIS *v.*[1], in various senses.

1. Guidance, direction, instruction.

c **1000** ÆLFRIC *Pastoral Epist.* xx. in *Ags. Laws* (Thorpe) II. 370 Hi ealle þa lare þe we leornioð on bocum awriton and ȝesetton be Godes aȝenre wissunge. *c* **1200** *Trin. Coll. Hom.* 95 þe man þe..shewed preste his sinnes..nimeð þerof god wissinge. *Ibid.* 99 Bi shriftes wissenge. *c* **1200** ORMIN 11830 Uss birrþ sone þannkenn himm Hiss wissinng & hiss lare. **1377** LANGL. *P. Pl.* B. xi. 58 By wissynge of þis wenche I wrouȝte. *c* **1400** *Destr. Troy* 8151 This wot I full well, thurgh wisshyng of hom. **1493** [H. PARKER] *Dives & Pauper* I. xviii. B viij/2 To gouerne them selfe..by the lyght and wyssynge of tyme. **1670** NARBOROUGH *Jrnl.* in *Acc. Sev. Late Voy.* I. (1694) 79, I called them *The Islands of Direction*; they are good wishing to fall with the Mouth of the Streight.

b. Leading astray, enticement. (Cf. WISE *v.*[1] I.)

1357 *Lay Folks Catech.* (T.) 542 Idelnesse is..witter wissyng and wai till alkyns vices.

c. Conduction, conveyance. Also *concr.* a conduit.

a **1300** *Cursor M.* 11942 þe water wissing gan he ditt, þat water to þe lak broght. *c* **1400** *Destr. Troy* 1606 The water by wisshyng went vnder houses.

2. Command, ordinance; rule, government.

c **1000** ÆLFRIC in Assmann *Ags. Hom.* (1889) 39 þa munecas, þe..gode þeowiað under abbodes wissunge æfter þam regole. *c* **1175** *Lamb. Hom.* 73 Hit wes iloked bi godes wissunge ine halie chirche. *a* **1225** *Leg. Kath.* 190 As al þe world is iwald þurh his wissunge. *a* **1400–50** *Wars Alex.* 3256 þe wyssyng of þe wale god þat wist all before.

wissit, obs. Sc. pa. t. of VISIT *v.*

c **1425** WYNTOUN *Cron.* v. x. 1887 þis lady wowit gret pilgramage,..And wissit hir goddis, ane and ane.

Wissonday, obs. f. WHIT SUNDAY.

wist (wɪst), *sb. local.* [In Anglo-Latin *wista*, *wysta*; ? a use of OE. *wist* provision, sustenance, applied orig. to an area which provided sustenance for a community of a certain size.] A Sussex land measure of area, the extent of which has been variously computed (see quots. and J. Tout in *Engl. Hist. Rev.* XVIII. 705 ff.).

c **1180** *Chron. Monast. de Bello* (1846) 11 Octo itaque virgatæ unam hidam faciunt. Wista vero quatuor virgatis constat. *Ibid.* 17 Dividitur igitur leuga per wistas, quæ aliis in locis virgatæ vocantur. *Ibid.* 19 In Petlee est una wista in dominio... Ista enim quadraginta viii. acris constat. *c* **1300** in *Custumals Battle Abbey* (Camden) 26 Radulphus Bedellus tenet j wistam. Idem tenet j magnam wistam. *c* **1312** *Ibid.* 100 Virgata seu wysta est sextadecima pars unius feodi militis. Quatuor virgatæ seu wystæ faciunt unam hydam. *c* **1650** in *Sussex Archæol. Collect.* (1853) VI. 236, I doo allowe tithe free, to my Parishioners, for euery Wist of land that they till, one oxe pasture upon the lease. **1799** *Book of Surveys of D. of Dorset's lands in Sussex* (MS), under 'Lullington', Upon this Tenant Down the D. of Dorset has a right to stock for two Wists & a half of land sixty sheep for each Wist. **1853** *Sussex Archæol. Collect.* VI. 236 A 'wist' in Berwick, according to..the Rev. John Hawes, was ordinarily 16 acres; but he afterwards found that in some of the farms it was 18 acres. In Saxon times the wist was 4 virgates or 60 acres. **1892** VINOGRADOFF *Villainage in Eng.* 255.

† **wist**, *a. Obs. rare.* [app. back-formation from WISTLY *adv.*] Attentive, intent.

1615 CROOKE *Body of Man* 550 *Motus Tonicus*, wee in our Language cal it a Set or wist-looke.

wist, *v. pseudo-arch.* [Partly from *I wist*, corrupt form of *iwis* (see WIS *v.*[2]); partly erron. use of pa. t. *wist* of WIT *v.*[1]] To know; in quot. 1594 in *pa. pple.* = caused to know, informed.

[**1508**, **1614**, **1798**, **1893**: see WIS *v.*[2]] **1580** LYLY *Euphues* 98 b, You gall mee more with these tearmes, then you wist [*ed.* 1597 wish, 1606 wisse]. **1594** CAREW *Huarte's Exam. Wits* 255 Samuel now wisted [orig. *como ya estaua aduertido*], that a great stature was no sure token, caused him to be sent for. **1858** BUCKLE *Infl. Women Progr. Knowl.* Misc. Wks. 1885 I. 68 Though he [*sc.* Hamlet] wists not of this, he is moved.., and he, like Göthe, takes up a skull, and his speculative faculties begin to work.

wist, var. WISHT *a.*; pa. t. and pple. of WIT *v.*[1]; erron f. *wift*, var. of WITHE.

Wistar ('wɪstə(r), -ɑː(r)). *Med.* and *Biol.* The name of the *Wistar* Institute of Anatomy and Biology, Philadelphia (founded by I. J. Wistar (1827–1905), grandnephew of Caspar Wistar (see WISTARIA)), used *attrib.* to designate rats bred from a strain developed at the Institute for laboratory purposes.

1938 *Amer. Jrnl. Cancer* XXXIV. 353 The Wistar rats used in this series were from the Experimental Colony strain of the Wistar Institute. **1956** *Nature* 10 Mar. 453/2 One series of irradiated mice was injected with a suspension of bone-marrow cells of the Wistar rat. **1970** *Jrnl. Gen. Psychol.* LXXXII. 28 This kind of preference is the same as has been found by Wagner..and Rowntree with Long-Evans and Wistar albino rats.

wistaria (wɪ'stɛərɪə). Also wisteria; *erron.* **wysteria, westeria.** [mod.L., f. name of Caspar *Wistar* (or *Wister*) 1761–1818, American anatomist; named by T. Nuttall in 1818: see -IA[1].] **a.** Any plant of the genus *Wistaria* (N.O. *Leguminosæ*), native to N. America, Japan, and China, the species of which are hardy, climbing, deciduous shrubs bearing racemes of blue-lilac papilionaceous flowers, the best known being *W. sinensis* (or *chinensis*), formerly *Glycine chinensis*.

1842 LOUDON *Suburban Hort.* 376 Vines, roses, Wistarias, or other luxuriant climbers. **1843** *Penny Cycl.* XXVII. 486/1 *Wistaria frutescens*, Shrubby Wistaria... *W. Chinensis*, Chinese Wistaria. **1876** BLACK *Madcap Violet* vii. 59 The pale purple blossoms of the wysteria hanging in front of the sunlit walls. **1878** SUSAN PHILLIPS *On Seaboard* 173 The great Westeria's purple blooms.

attrib. **1888** J. C. HARRIS *Free Joe* 199 A wisteria vine running helter-skelter across the roof of the little cabin. **1895** A. DOBSON *At Convent Gate* i. in *Story of Rosina* 97 Wistaria blossoms trail and fall Above the length of barrier wall.

b. A light blue-purple shade, the colour of wistaria blossom.

1911 *Daily Colonist* (Victoria, B.C.) 5 Apr. 24/1 (Advt.), Important Silk Purchase..in colors of rose, Persian blue.., wisteria. **1927** *Observer* 3 Apr. 25/5 (Advt.), Sunrise, geranium, wisteria, russet. **1974** *Country Life* 25 Apr. 1025/2 Her best colours..are wistaria, ice blue..and lemon yellow.

wistful ('wɪstfʊl), *a.* [app. f. WISTLY *adv.* (where cf. quot. 1613–16) + -FUL, with reminiscence of *wishful*. In early use mainly poetical.]

† **1.** Closely attentive, intent. *Obs.*

1613–16 W. BROWNE *Brit. Past.* II. ii. 544 A Christall Riuer..chid The artlesse Songsters, that their Musicke still Should charme the sweet Dale, and the wistfull Hill. **1711** STEELE *Spect.* No. 113 ¶3 [She] bore the Whispers of all around the Court with such a pretty Uneasiness,..and then recovered her self from one Eye to another, 'till she was perfectly confused by meeting something so wistful in all she encountered.

2. Expectantly or yearningly eager, watchful, or intent; mournfully expectant or longing. (Chiefly in reference to the look.)

1714 GAY *Sheph. Week* v. 1 Why, Grubbinol, dost thou so wistful seem? There's Sorrow in thy Look, if right I deem. **1725** POPE *Odyss.* x. 484 My sad companions on the beach I found, Their wistful eyes in floods of sorrow drown'd. **1726** SWIFT *Gulliver* II. viii, I..lifting up one of my Sashes, cast many a wistful melancholy Look towards the Sea. **1799** CAMPBELL *Pleas. Hope* I. 88 His faithful dog..Points to his master's eyes (where'er they roam) His wistful face, and whines a welcome home. **1878** BLACK *Green Past.* xxi, For a moment she hesitated, eager, disappointed and wistful.

Comb. **1873** BLACK *Pr. Thule* iii, This fair-haired, wistful-eyed girl. **1889** CONAN DOYLE *Micah Clarke* xxiii, The wistful-eyed red Somerset kine.

advb. **1795** SOUTHEY *Joan of Arc* I. 258 His eyes gazed wistful round. **1848** LYTTON *Harold* I. i, The terror that seized the girl as she gazed long and wistful upon the knight.

wistfully ('wɪstfʊlɪ), *adv.* [f. prec. + -LY[2].]

† **1.** With close attention, intently; with an inquiring look. *Obs.*

1664 BUTLER *Hud.* II. III. 464 With that he fell again to pry Through Perspective more wistfully. **1713** ADDISON *Guardian* No. 139 ¶2 [The lion] after having regarded him [*sc.* Androcles] a little wistfully, fell to the ground, and crept towards his feet. **1759** STERNE *Tr. Shandy* II. xii, Brother Shandy, answered my uncle Toby, looking wistfully in his face,—you are much mistaken. **1833** HT. MARTINEAU *Manch. Strike* x. 115 Martha looked wistfully from one to the other, not understanding the grounds of the dispute.

2. With expectant or yearning eagerness; with mournful expectancy or longing.

1663 BUTLER *Hud.* I. III. 191 Eccho..His doleful wailings did resound, More wistfully by many times, Than in small Poets splay-foot Rhimes. **1758** GOLDSM. *Mem. Prot.* (1895) I. 256 Two of the Grenadiers passing by..and looking wistfully at the House; said one to the other, Comrade, let us halt, and take a little drop of Dram. **1760–72** H. BROOKE *Fool of Qual.* (1809) III. 90 Sore and shackled as I was, I got..on deck, and looked wistfully out at sea. **1823** BYRON *Island* III. vi, He..strode to where young Torquil stood,..Seized his hand wistfully, but did not press. **1858** FROUDE *Hist. Eng.* IV. xviii. 53 The Catholic league gazed wistfully from Flanders at their intended prey. **1883** RUSKIN *Fors Clav.* xc. 165 The girl wandered about wistfully a year or two longer, then died.

So **'wistfulness.**

1775 ASH. **1847** FLOR. NIGHTINGALE in Sir E. Cook *Life* (1913) I. I. v. 71 There is an uncertainty, a wistfulness in her eyes. **1887** HALL CAINE *Son of Hagar* I. ii, The lucent eyes were full of a dewy wistfulness.

wistiti ('wɪstɪtɪ). Also ouistiti(s. [ad. F. *ouistiti* (imitative); named by Buffon (*Hist. Nat.* 1767 XV. 96) from the cry of the animal.] A S. American monkey of the family *Hapalidæ*; a marmoset, esp. the Common Marmoset, *Hapale jacchus*.

1774 GOLDSM. *Nat. Hist.* IV. 237 Of the sagoins with feeble tails, there are six kinds... The third is the Wistiti; remarkable for the large tufts of hair upon its face, and its annulated tail. **1834** McMURTRIE *Cuvier's Anim. Kingd.* 49 *Simia jacchus*, Linnæus; the Common Ouistitis... This species is found in Paraguay, and nearly every part of South America. **1847–9** *Todd's Cycl. Anat.* IV. 212/1 This general resemblance to the human skull is still greater in the Ouistitis.

† **'wistless**, *a. poet. Obs.* [irreg. f. WISTLY *adv.* or WISTFUL + -LESS.] Inattentive, unobservant.

1747 [G. RIDLEY] *Psyche* xix. in *Museum* III. 86 So ore Avernus, or the Lucrine Lake, The wistless bird pursues his purpos'd Flight. **1795** SOUTHEY *Joan of Arc* I. 405, I held it, ..And, wistless what I did, half from the sheath Drew the well-temper'd blade. *Ibid.* IV. 61 Wistless that every eye dwelt on her form, With stately step she paced. **1814** CARY *Dante, Parad.* XI. 10 One, moiling, lay Tangled in net of sensual delight; And one to wistless indolence resigned.

† **'wistly**, *adv. Obs.* Forms: 6 wystly, wistle, wistlie, 6–9 wistly. [Origin doubtful; perh. a variant of WHISTLY, WHISHTLY *advs.* silently, hushedly.] With close attention; intently.

Occas. with implication of WISTFULLY 2.

a **1500** *Gest of Robyn Hode* ccccx, Robyn behelde our comly kynge Wystly in the face. **1583** MELBANCKE *Philotimus* O j, With that Castibula looking wistly vpon him, in furious rage flange hastilye from him. **1596** *Edw. III*, III. v. 109 Now lies it on an vpshot; therefore strike, And wistlie follow, whiles the games on foote. **1600** HOLLAND *Livy* IX. xxxii. 337 For a good while they stood on both sides, wistly looking, & waiting that the shout and charge should begin from the adverse part. **1613–16** W. BROWNE *Brit. Past.* II. v. 435 What time the new-cloath'd trees by gusts of winde Vnmou'd, stand wistly listning to those layes. **1641** H. L'ESTRANGE *God's Sabbath* 23 If you look wistly upon Calvines words, you shall find him not repugnant to what I have here delivered. **1675** N. LEE *Nero* III. i. 23 Do you know me, Sir? Look wistly on me. **1724** S. KNIGHT *Life J. Colet* 54 He look'd wistly upon me, to observe whether I spoke in jest, or earnest. **1730** T. BOSTON *View World* (1799) 281 In your..wrestling with temptations, have ye not sometimes looked wistly for death's relief?

wistonwish, var. WISHTONWISH.

wisy, obs. f. VIZY *v. Sc.*

wit (wɪt), *sb.* Forms: 1– wit, 3–6 wyt, 3 (*Orm.*), 4–8 witt, 4–6 wytt, wyte, 4–7 witte, wytte, (4 wiit, wijt, whit, 4, 6 wite, *Sc.* vit, vyt, 5 whytt, wette, 6 *Sc.* wott, 7 weet). [OE. *wit* neut., more commonly *ȝewit(t* I-WIT *sb.*, corresp. to OFris. *wit*, OS., (M)LG. *wit*, OHG. *wizzi* (MHG. *witz(e*, G. *witz*), ON. *vit* (Sw. *vet*, Da. *vid*), Goth. *un-witi* ἀφροσύνη, ἀγνοία: f. *wit-* (see WIT *v.*[1]).]

I. Denoting a faculty (or the person possessing it).

† **1.** The seat of consciousness or thought, the mind: sometimes connoting one of its functions, as memory or attention. *Obs.*

a **1000** *Boeth. Metr.* viii. 45 Ðeos ȝitsunc hafað gumena ȝehwelces mod amerred,..ac hit on witte weallende byrnð. *c* **1175** *Lamb. Hom.* 71 ȝif us eni ufel bitit þonke we gode in ure wit. *a* **1300** *Cursor M.* 324 First in his witte he all purueid His werc. *c* **1375** *Sc. Leg. Saints* xxvii. (*Machor*) 338 [He] in his hart wele held It, Ay retentywe he had a wyt. *a* **1400** *N.T.* (Paues) Eph. iv. 17 Mysblyfed men, þat walkeþ in vanyte of hure wyt. *c* **1449** PECOCK *Repr.* III. iv. 295 His ouer greet trust which in his witt he bisettid upon hem. **1513** DOUGLAS *Æneis* XII. i. 67 And sammyn prent thir sawis in thy wyt. **1548–9** *Bk. Com. Prayer, Ordering of Priests*, O holy ghoste into oure wittes, sende downe thyne heauenly lyght. **1575** LANEHAM *Let.* (1871) 35 A! stay a while! see a short wit: by my trooth I had almost forgot. **1612** BACON *Ess., Studies* (Arb.) 13 If a mans wit be wandring, let him study the Mathematiks. *a* **1660** *Contemp. Hist. Irel.* (Ir. Archæol. Soc.) I. 110 Our Catholicke General did now examen the secret retirements of his witte, to be enformed what best to doe in this extreamitie.

2. a. The faculty of thinking and reasoning in general; mental capacity, understanding, intellect, reason. *arch.* (now esp. in phr. ***the wit of man*** = human understanding).

For the corresponding pregnant uses see 5 and 6.

Beowulf 589 þæs þu in helle scealt werhðo dreoȝan, þeah þin wit duȝe. *c* **1230** *Hali Meid.* (1922) 21 Hwil þi wit atstond & chastieð þi wil..ne harmeð hit te nawiht. **1297** R. GLOUC. (Rolls) 9389 Is brayn & wit is so feble, þat þer nis of him no drede. *c* **1305** *St. Kenelm* 220 in *E.E.P.* (1862) 53 A dombe best wiþoute witte. *c* **1375** *Lay Folks Mass Bk.* (MS. B) 343 My lyue, my lymmes þou has me lent, My right witt þou has me sent. **1377** LANGL. *P. Pl.* B. xx. 266 Kynde witte me telleth, It is wikked to wage ȝow. *c* **1400** *Pety Job* 184 in *26 Pol. Poems* 127 To gouerne me thow yaue me wyt. *c* **1470** HENRY *Wallace* XI. 481 To mychty God,..sen I had wit off man, Befor my werk, to ȝeild me I began. **1526** TINDALE *1 Cor.* xiv. 20 Brethren be not children in witte. **1568** GRAFTON *Chron.* II. 193 He was verie pregnant and had an excellent wyt. **1590** SHAKS. *Mids. N.* IV. i. 211, I had a dreame, past the wit of man, to say, what dreame it was. **1665** GLANVILL *Scepsis Sci.* 99 A good will, help'd by a good wit, can find Truth any where. **1675** BAXTER *Cath. Theol.* II. VIII. 167 God were not God, if mans shallow wit could comprehend him. **1732** POPE *Epitaph Gay*, Of Manners gentle, of Affections mild; In Wit, a Man; Simplicity, a Child. **1842** R. S. WILBERFORCE *Rutilius & Lucius* 139 We profess not to discover the truth by our own wit. **1879** McCARTHY *Own Times* xx. II. 98 The wit of man could suggest nothing satisfactory. **1879** E. ARNOLD *Lt. Asia* VIII. 232 Shun drugs and drinks which work the wit abuse.

b. In plural, in reference to a number of persons.

a **1300** *Cursor M.* 23759 Crist[es] help sal be us ner, His helpes and vr wittes eke. **1463** *Bury Wills* (Camden) 27 To fynde remydyes and weyes as by there wittes may be fowunde moost sewr. **1526** TINDALE *Luke* xxiv. 45 Then openned he their wyttes, that they myght vnderstond the scriptures. **1591** SAVILE *Tacitus, Agricola* 242 That militare wittes are not refined to that sharpenesse and suttelty, that is practised in.. courtes of iustice. **1664** POWER *Exp. Philos.* Pref. b 2, Herein we can see what the illustrious wits of the Atomical and Corpuscularian Philosophers durst but imagine. **1700** T. BROWN tr. *Fresny's Amusem.* 7 Some Men can never be brought to write correctly in this Age, till they have formed their Wits upon the Ancients.

c. Often denoting indifferently the faculty or the person possessing it, and hence sometimes used definitely for the person in respect of this faculty. Almost always in plural, of a number of persons, and commonly with qualifying adj. *arch.*

For the corresponding pregnant uses see 9 and 10.

1536 *Act 27 Hen. VIII* c. 42 §1 In his Unyversities of Oxforde and Cambridge.. where yowth and good wyttes be educate. **1542** UDALL *Erasm. Apoph.* Pref. **v b, A sence not comen for euerie witte to picke out. *a* **1568** ASCHAM *Scholem.* Pref. (Arb.) 19 Many yong wittes be driuen to hate learninge, before they know what learninge is. **1610** HOLLAND *Camden's Brit.* I. 274 Gods-Hill, in which Iohn Worsley erected a schole for the training up of young wits. **1750** JOHNSON *Rambler* No. 24 ¶7 The great Praise of Socrates is, that he drew the Wits of Greece.. from the vain Pursuit of natural Philosophy to moral Inquiries. **1874** BLACKIE *Self-Cult.* 58 The rock, on which great wits are often wrecked for want of a little kindly culture of unselfishness.

d. Phr. ***at one's wit's end*** (occas. ***ends***): utterly perplexed; at a loss what to think or what to do. So ***to bring*** (***drive,*** or ***put***) ***to one's wit's end***: to perplex utterly.

Now commonly taken as 2 c, the word being written as gen. pl. (*wits'*) even in ref. to a single person.

1377 LANGL. *P. Pl.* B. xv. 363 Astrymyanes also aren at her wittes ende. *c* **1420** ? LYDG. *Assembly of Gods* 1665 When they were dreuyn to her wyttes ende. **1535** COVERDALE *Isa.* xx. 5 They shalbe also at their wittes ende, and ashamed one of another. **1550** *Respublica* I. iii. 240 & she att hir wittes endes what for to saie or doe. **1598** R. BERNARD tr. *Terence, Andria* II. iv, You bring him to his wits end. **1681** FLAVEL *Meth. Grace* iii. 54 What shall we do? is the doleful cry of men at their wits end. **1712** ADDISON *Spect.* No. 311 ¶1, I am at my Wits End for fear of any sudden Surprize. **1782** MISS BURNEY *Cecilia* IX. iv, Two ladies.. are quite, as one may say, at their wit's ends. **1826** GALT *Last of Lairds* xl. 360 The old Laird.. fairly finding himself driven to his wit's-end. **1853** KINGSLEY *Hypatia* xiii, Raphael, utterly at his wits' end.

†**e.** ***wit, whither wilt thou?***: phr. addressed to a person who is letting his tongue run away with him.

1600 SHAKS. *A.Y.L.* IV. i. 167 A man that had a wife with such a wit, he might say, wit whether wil't? [*Ibid.* I. ii. 60 How now Witte, whether wander you?] **1602** DEKKER *Satirom.* I. i, Th'art within a haire of it, my sweet Wit whether wilt thou? my delicate Poeticall Furie. **1617** *Greene's Groat's W. Wit* Pref. A 2, This olde Ballad made in Hell: *Ingenio perij, qui miser ipse meo*: Wit, whither wilt thou? woe is me. **1623** MIDDLETON *More Dissemblers* IV. i, *Cap.* Wit whether wilt thou? *Dond.* Marry to the next pocket I can come at. **1637** HEYWOOD *Royall King* I. i. C 2, *Cap.* Wit: is the word strange to you, wit? *Bon.* Whither wilt thou?

†**f.** ***wit and reason***: name of an old card-game.

1680 COTTON *Compl. Gamester* xvi. (ed. 2) 97 Wit and Reason.. is a Game something like one and thirty.

†**3. a.** Any one of certain particular faculties of perception, classified as *outer* (*outward*) or *bodily*, and *inner* (*inward*) or *ghostly*, and commonly reckoned as five of each kind (see b): = SENSE *sb.* 1, 7 (see also INWIT 2 b). Also ***common wit*** = COMMON SENSE 1. (In early use occas. loosely extended to include other bodily faculties, as speech and locomotion.) *Obs.* exc. as in b and c.

a **1225** *Ancr. R.* 64 þis is nu inouh of þisse witte [*sc.* sight]. *a* **1300** *Cursor M.* 23999 O wijttes all me wantid might, Gang, and steyuen, and tung, and sight. **1340** *Ayenb.* 251 þe wyttes of þe zaule. **1387** TREVISA *Higden* (Rolls) III. 467 Nesche is i-knowe by meny wittes, for it is knowe boþe by gropynge and by si3t. **1422** YONGE tr. *Secr. Secr.* 242 Al the wittis and meuynges of the body. *c* **1449** PECOCK *Repr.* V. vii. 519 Inward sensityue wittis and outward sensityue wittis. **1509** HAWES *Past. Pleas.* XXIV. ii. (Percy Soc.) 108 These are the .v. wyttes remeuing inwardly: Fyrst, commyn wytte, and than ymaginacyon, Fantasy, and estymacyon truely, And memory. **1541** COPLAND *Guydon's Quest. Cyrurg.* E j b, In whiche of the ventrycles is the wyt of smellynge founded? **1592** SHAKS. *Rom. & Jul.* II. iv. 77 Thou hast more of the Wild-Goose in one of thy wits, then I am sure I haue in my whole fiue.

b. ***five wits***: usually, the five (bodily) senses; often vaguely, the perceptions or mental faculties generally, = *wits* (in sense 3 c or 4 b). Also (jocularly) ***fifteen wits.*** *Obs.* or *rare arch.*

c **1200** *Vices & Virtues* 17 Ða fif wittes ðe god me betahte to lokin of mine wrecche lichame. *a* **1300** *Cursor M.* 17018 Hering, sight, smelling and fele, cheuing, er wittes five. *c* **1380** WYCLIF *Sel. Wks.* III. 117 þy fyve wyttys, þe uttyr and þe ynnyr. *c* **1460** *Wisdom* 163 in *Macro Plays* 41 þe v. wyttis of my sowll with-inne. *c* **1515** *Interl. Four Elem.* (Percy Soc.) 19, I comforte the wyttes fyve, The tastyng, smellyng, and herynge; I refresh the syght and felynge To all creaturs alyve. **1532** TINDALE *Expos. v–vii. Matt.* vii. 98 b, There is no breade in the sacrament, nor wine, though the five wittes saye all ye. **1570** FOXE *A. & M.* (ed. 2) 960 The v. wittes bodely and ghostlye. **1570** BUCHANAN *Admonitioun* Wks. (S.T.S.) 33 Quhen yai bendit all yair fyve wittis to stop ye regent. **1606** *Sir G. Goosecappe* V. i, Haue you no pittie in your villanous iests, but runne a man quite from his fifteene witts? **1610** A. COOKE *Pope Joan* 113 Though men.. had bene.. bewitched and distract of their fiue wits. **1830** TENNYSON *Owl* I. 6 Alone and warming his five wits, The white owl in the belfry sits. **1878** MORLEY *Diderot* I. iv. 86 Everybody now has learnt that morality depends not merely on the five wits, but on the mental constitution within, and on the social conditions without.

c. *pl.* Mental faculties, intellectual powers (of a single person or a number of persons: cf. 2 b); often practically equivalent to the sing. in sense 2.

to have one's wits about one: to have one's mental powers in full exercise, to be mentally alert. ***to live by one's wits***: to get one's living by clever or (now esp.) crafty devices, without any settled occupation.

13.. *E.E. Allit. P.* B. 515, I se wel þat hit is sothe, þat alle mannez wyttez To vn-thryfte arn alle þrawen. **1362** LANGL. *P. Pl.* A. I. 129 þou dotest daffe,.. Dulle are þi wittes. **1450–1530** *Myrr. our Ladye* I. vii. 21 To be full besy in all the wyttes and mightes of youre soulle. **1533** GAU *Richt Vay* 87 Quhen our hart and vittis are ful of sorow. **1576** FLEMING *Panopl. Epist.* 14 So soone as I gathered my wits together. **1612** B. JONSON *Alch.* III. iv, How doe they liue by their wits, there, that haue vented Sixe times your fortunes? **1622** MABBE tr. *Aleman's Guzman d'Alf.* II. 99, I had my wits about me; and a hand that was able to finde me worke. **1681** DRYDEN *Abs. & Achit.* I. 163 Great Wits are sure to Madness near alli'd. **1748** RICHARDSON *Clarissa* VII. 326 That my wits may not be sent a wooll-gathering. **1809** MALKIN *Gil Blas* V. i. ¶18 Have all your wits about you,.. you are nursing a viper in your bosom. **1820** L. HUNT *Indicator* No. 14. I. 111 That letter touched her kind wits. **1840** DICKENS *Old Cur. Shop* lxxiii, Living by his wits—which means by the abuse of every faculty that worthily employed raises man above the beasts. **1883** STEVENSON *Silverado Sq.* 146 This expression.. at last penetrated his obdurate wits.

†**d.** *sing.* and *pl.* Consciousness; sensation: cf. SENSE *sb.* 3, 6. *Obs. rare.*

c **1290** *St. Brendan* 12 in *S. Eng. Leg.* 220 Seint brendan.. cride on him al for-to is wit him cam. **13..** *Gaw. & Gr. Knt.* 1755 He keuered his wyttes, Swenges out of þe sweuenes. *c* **1385** CHAUCER *L.G.W.* 1815 *Lucrece*, Sche loste at onys bothe wit & breth, And in a swo she lay. *c* **1450** *St. Cuthbert* (Surtees) 6047 Withouten witt he was ligyng.

4. The understanding or mental faculties in respect of their condition; chiefly = 'right mind', 'reason', 'senses', sanity. †**a.** *sing.*: esp. in phrases ***in*** (*one's* ***right***) ***wit***, sane, of sound mind; chiefly ***out of*** (*by, from, of*) ***wit*** or ***one's wit***, insane, mad, out of one's mind; also ***out of wit*** advb., madly, furiously. *Obs.* (or *dial.*).

c **1000** ÆLFRIC *Saints' Lives* xv. 7 Wode he ȝehælde and on witte ȝebrohte. *c* **1205** LAY. 1661 Swa swiðe wa him was þat al his wit he for-læs. *c* **1290** *St. Dunstan* 600 in *S. Eng. Leg.* 19 Heo iwerth a-non out of hire witte, and feol a-doun ri3t þer. **1297** R. GLOUC. (Rolls) 10872 He made him as bi wit. *a* **1300** *Cursor M.* 27168 Man in wiit Or man mai falle was vte of itt. *c* **1350** *Will. Palerne* 1483 Nei3h wod of witte. *c* **1374** CHAUCER *Anel. & Arc.* 102 Arcyte.. swore he wold dey.. Or from his witte he wold twynne. **1425** *E.E. Wills* (1882) 66 Wiþ witte and good mende. **1470–85** MALORY *Arthur* I. xi. 50 They were wrothe out of wyt. *c* **1489** CAXTON *Blanchardyn* xlvi. 178 Arte thou now dronke, or folyshe, or from thy witte? **1561** T. NORTON *Calvin's Inst.* III. 207 As no man in his right wit wil graunt. *a* **1619** FOTHERBY *Atheom.* I. xiv. §3 (1622) 151 It is a thing so euident, that there is a God; that whosoeuer denieth it, is (surely) out of his wit. **1724** RAMSAY *Tea-t. Misc.* (1733) I. 86 The wife was wood, and out o' her wit.

b. *pl.* = SENSE *sb.* 10: esp. in phr. ***in*** or ***out of one's wits.***

1340 HAMPOLE *Pr. Consc.* 785 His wyttes fayles, and he ofte dotes. **1431** *E.E. Wills* (1882) 87 Beyng yn goode heale and yn my full wittes. *c* **1450** CAPGRAVE *Life St. Aug.* xxiii. 32 For a tyme it had a-wey hir wittis. **1526** TINDALE *1 Cor.* xiv. 23 Will they not saye that ye are out off youre wittes? **1568** GRAFTON *Chron.* II. 107 Such a one as lacketh his right wittes. **1601** SHAKS. *Twel. N.* IV. ii. 95, I am as well in my wits (foole) as thou art. **1604** DEKKER *Honest Wh.* I. xiii. (1635) I 4, How fell he from his wits? **1622** BACON *Hen. VII*, 226 Ioan.. was vnable.. to beare the Griefe of his Decease, and fell distracted of her Wittes. *a* **1661** FULLER *Worthies*, *York* III. (1662) 228 Seeing his wits is nearer and dearer to any man then his wealth. **1736** BUTLER *Anal.* Diss. i. 306 Nor is it possible for a Person in his wits, to alter his Conduct,.. from a Suspicion, that [etc.]. **1840** MACAULAY *Ess., Clive* (1880) 518 The governor.. was frightened out of his wits.

fig. **1598** SHAKS. *Merry W.* II. i. 143 Heere's a fellow frights English out of his wits. **1656** R. SHORT *Drinking Water* 62 Our small beer, or water skared out of its wits.

II. Denoting a quality (or the possessor of it).

* **5. a.** Good or great mental capacity; intellectual ability; genius, talent, cleverness; mental quickness or sharpness, acumen. *arch.*

The earliest quots. may belong to other senses, e.g. 6 or 11.

1297 R. GLOUC. (Rolls) 10812 þo.. he vnderstod of is wit, & of is wisdom, Him þo3te it was a gret lere to al is kinedom. *a* **1300** *Cursor M.* 8543 Salamon.. was a borli bachelere,.. O wijt o wisdom Was neuer nan wiser. *c* **1320** *Cast. Love* 1080 Of whom and hou comeþ hit, Such reson and such wit, þat þou.. darst nymen þe Forte dispute a-3eynes me? *c* **1400** MAUNDEV. (1839) vii. 78 Nyghe that Awtier is a place.. where the Holy Croys was founden, be the Wytt of Seynte Elyne. *c* **1450** *Mirk's Festial* 27 þay began to dyspute wyth hym; but.. þay haden no wytte ne no powste forto 3eynestonde hym. **1526** TINDALE *Rev.* xiii. 18 Let hym that hath wytt count the nombre off the beest. **1603** SHAKS. *Meas. for M.* II. i. 282 Are there not men in your Ward sufficient to serue it? *Elb.* Faith sir, few of any wit in such matters. **1630** *R. Johnson's Kingd. & Commw.* 13 The weake constitutions of the Southerne Nations are supplied by the extraordinarie gifts of the minde: terme them what you please, either wit, or subtiltie. **1709** POPE *Ess. Crit.* 17 Authors are partial to their wit, 'tis true, But are not Critics to their judgment too? **1837** DICKENS *Pickw.* xi, Where was the wit of the sharp-sighted men of sound mind? Where the dexterity of the lawyers? **1874** MAURICE *Friendsh. Bks.* vi. 163 The blessing of wit and foresight.

†**b.** Practical talent or cleverness; constructive or mechanical ability; ingenuity, skill. *Obs.* as a specific sense.

c **1325** *Spec. Gy Warw.* 212 God.. 3eueþ wit in alle craftes. *c* **1400** *Destr. Troy* 1632 A pales gert make.. Full worthely wroght & by wit caste. **1590** SPENSER *F.Q.* I. iv. 5 It was a goodly heape for to behould, And spake the praises of the workmans wit. **1648** J. BEAUMONT *Psyche* (1702) XI. xxv, Those Engins which so strangely spit Death's multiply'd and deadlyer made by Wit. **1691** RAY *Creation* I. (1692) 4 The best Telescopes that could possibly be invented or polished by the Wit and Hand of an Angel. **1726** LEONI *Alberti's Archit.* Pref. 4 The Enemy was oftener overcome.. by the Architect's Wit, without the Captain's Arms, than by the Captain's Arms without the Architect's Wit.

†**c.** Of animals: Intelligence, sagacity. *Obs.*

c **1400** *26 Pol. Poems* ii. 61 þere [*i.e.* the drones'] wit is wane To stroi3e the hony. **1577** GOOGE *Heresbach's Husb.* III. 145 The witte of this beast Nutianus reporteth, he once had experience of. **1607** TOPSELL *Four-f. Beasts* 658 The admirable witte of this beast appeareth in her swimming or passing ouer the Waters. **1610** GUILLIM *Heraldry* III. xii. 122 The Fox is full of wit.

6. a. Wisdom, good judgement, discretion, prudence: = SENSE *sb.* 11. *Obs.* exc. in phr. like ***to have the wit to***, which combines the notions of intelligence and good sense.

The phr. in quot. 1602 has become proverbial, though commonly taken in sense 8.

c **1200** ORMIN 3040 Godess Sune.. iss.. Godess word, & Godess witt. **1297** R. GLOUC. (Rolls) 9391 Vor wat he aþ Manliche bigonne he it aþ bileued Wommanliche as vor defaute of wit in his heued. *a* **1300** *Cursor M.* 285 þat he ordaind wit his witte He multiplis and gouerns itte. *Ibid.* 3079 Quen [ysmael] was of age and witte A wijf he spused of egipte. *Ibid.* 29204 þe gift o wijt of vnder-standing, O consail, strenght, o gode dreding, O conand-scipe, and o pite. *c* **1430** *Hymns Virgin* (1867) 5 Heil welle of witt and of merci! **1552** T. WILSON *Logic* (ed. 2) 22 As vertue is contrarie vnto vice, witte vnto folie, manhode vnto Cowardise. **1562** J. HEYWOOD *Prov. & Epigr.* (1867) 153 When ale is in, wyt is out. When ale is out, wyt is in. **1602** SHAKS. *Ham.* II. ii. 90 Since Breuitie is the Soule of Wit, And tediousnesse, the limbes and outward flourishes, I will be breefe. **1681** DRYDEN *Abs. & Achit.* I. 386 For Lavish Grants suppose a Monarch tame And more his Goodness than his Wit proclaim. **1701** SWIFT *Contests Athens & Rome* ii. Misc. (1711) 26 But, however, they had the Wit to recal him [*sc.* Aristides]. **1725** DE FOE *Voy. round World* (1840) 326 But they were taught more wit, to their cost, in two or three days. **1886** RUSKIN *Præterita* I. xi. 376 One piece of good fortune, of which I had the wit to take advantage. **1926** S. BALDWIN in *Morn. Post* 8 Oct. 15/3 Men.. who.. had formed his Majesty's Government.. and who had the wit to understand what the challenge meant.

†**b.** Contextually in predicative use: A piece of wisdom or prudence, a wise thing to do; also, something demanding or showing wisdom, a matter of practical wisdom. *Obs.*

1375 BARBOUR *Bruce* I. 344 To fenyhe foly quhile is wyt. *c* **1400** *Rule St. Benet* (verse) 1609 þarfor es wit, to lest & mast, Wine or aile softly to tast. **1421–2** HOCCLEVE *Min. Poems* xx. 115 Whane that a man is in prosperite, To drede a fall comynge it is a wit. **1562** in *Archaeologia* XLVII. 229 Gettinge ys a chaunce and keapinge a witte.

†**c.** A prudent measure or proceeding; an ingenious plan or device. *Obs.*

The uses exemplified by the quots. are prob. of various or mixed origin.

1340 *Ayenb.* 257 þe ilke eddre ous tekþ a wel grat wyt þet we ne hyere na3t þane charmere. *c* **1385** CHAUCER *L.G.W.* 1420 *Hypsip. & Medea*, To syndyn hym into sum fer cuntre Here as this Iason may distroyed be. This was his wit. *c* **1440** *Gesta Rom.* vi. 16, I shall shew þe a goode wit in þis cas; and if þou wolt do after my conseile, þou shalt not repente. **1607** DEKKER & WEBSTER *Northw. Hoe* V. i, Was't not a pritty wit of mine.. to haue had him rod into Puckridge, with a horne before him?

7. Quickness of intellect or liveliness of fancy, with capacity of apt expression; talent for saying brilliant or sparkling things, esp. in an amusing way. *arch.* (Cf. sense 8.)

Formerly sometimes opp. to *wisdom* or *judgement*; often distinguished from *humour* (see quots., and note s.v. HUMOUR *sb.* 7).

1579 LYLY *Euphues* (Arb.) 61 As the Bee is oftentimes hurt with hir owne Honny, so is witte not seldome plagued with his owne conceipt. **1597** SHAKS. *2 Hen. IV*, I. ii. 11 Men of all sorts take a pride to gird at mee:.. I am not onely witty in my selfe, but the cause that wit is in other men. **1650** DAVENANT *Gondibert* Pref. (1651) 27 Wit is not only the luck and labour, but also the dexterity of thought. **1665** BOYLE *Occas. Refl.* I. III. iii. 37 That nimble and acceptable Faculty of the Mind, whereby some Men have a readiness, and subtilty, in conceiving things, and a quickness, and neatness, in expressing them, all which the custom of speaking comprehends under the name of Wit. **1704** YALDEN *Sir W. Aston* 187 His flowing wit, with solid judgment join'd, Talents united rarely in a mind, Had all the graces and engaging art, That charm the ear and captivate the heart. **1765** CHESTERF. *Lett. to Godson* (1890) 180 If you have real wit it will flow spontaneously and you need not aim at it... Wit is so shining a quality, that everybody admires it, most people aim at it, all people fear it, and few love it unless in themselves. **1777** M. MORGANN *Ess. Dram. Char. Falstaff* 163 It being very possible, I suppose, to be a man of humour without wit; but I think not a man of wit without humour. **1782** COWPER *Gilpin* 169 Now Gilpin had a pleasant wit And lov'd a timely joke.

8. a. That quality of speech or writing which consists in the apt association of thought and expression, calculated to surprise and delight by its unexpectedness (for particular applications in 17th and 18th century criticism see esp. quots. 1650, 1677, 1685, 1690, 1704, 1709); later always with reference to the utterance of brilliant or sparkling things in an amusing way.

1542 UDALL *Erasm. Apoph.* Pref. **vij b, Neither dooe I esteme it a thyng worthie blame.. with laughter to refreshe the mynde.., so that the matier to laugh at bee pure witte and honeste [orig. *modo risus sit argutus ac liberalis*]. **1599** SHAKS. *Much Ado* I. i. 64 They neuer meet, but there's a skirmish of wit between them. **1606** CHAPMAN *Monsieur D'Olive* I. i, Crittickes, Essayists, Linguists, Poets, and other professors of that facultie of wit. **1633** G. HERBERT *Temple, Ch.-Porch* xxxix, Laugh not too much: the wittie man laughs least: For wit is newes onely to ignorance. **1650** DAVENANT *Gondibert* Pref. (1651) 26 Wit is the laborious, and the lucky resultances of thought having towards its excellence.. as well a happinesse, as care. **1664** FLECKNOE *Short Disc. Engl. Stage* G 6, Comparing him [Jonson] with Shakespear, you shall see the difference betwixt Nature and Art; and with Fletcher, the difference betwixt Wit and Judgement. **1677** DRYDEN *State Innoc., Apol. Her. Poetry* c 2 b, The definition of Wit.. is only this: That it is a propriety of Thoughts and Words; or in other terms, Thought and Words, elegantly adapted to the Subject. **1683** WOOD *Life* (O.H.S.) III. 16 Apr., Lord Chief Justice asked him 'if it were Oxford Wit', that also 'he should say that if *Magna Charta* would not do it *Longa Sparta* should do the busines'. **1685** DRYDEN *Sylvæ* Pref. A 6, I drew my definition of Poetical Wit from my particular consideration of him [Virgil]. **1690** LOCKE *Hum. Und.* II. xi. §2 Wit lying most in the assemblage of Ideas, and putting those together with quickness and variety. **1693** DENNIS *Misc.* Pref. a 2 b, A true description of Wit; which is a just mixture of Reason and Extravagance. **1697** DRYDEN *Æneis* Ded. (e) 3 b, *Les Petits Esprits*:.. who like nothing but the Husk and Rhind of Wit; preferr a Quibble, a Conceit, an Epigram, before solid Sense and Elegant Expression. **1704** POPE *Let. to Wycherley* 26 Dec., True Wit, I believe, may be defined a justness of thought, and a facility of expression. **1709** —— *Ess. Crit.* 297 True Wit is Nature to advantage dress'd, What oft was thought, but ne'er so well express'd. **1711** ADDISON *Spect.* No. 62 ¶2 Mr. Lock's Account of Wit, with this short Explanation, comprehends most of the Species of Wit, as Metaphors, Similitudes, Allegories, Ænigmas, Mottos, Parables, Fables, Dreams, Visions, dramatick Writings, Burlesque, and all the Methods of Allusion. **1744** CORBYN THOMAS *(title)* An Essay Towards Fixing the True Standards of Wit, Humour, Raillery, Satire, and Ridicule. **1858** O. W. HOLMES *Aut. Breakf.-t.* iii. 19 We get beautiful effects from wit,—all the prismatic colours,—but never the object as it is in fair daylight. *a* **1859** LEIGH HUNT in *Jrnl. Educ.* (1884) 1 Feb. 79 Wit consists in the arbitrary juxtaposition of dissimilar ideas for some lively purpose of assimilation or contrast, generally of both. **1900** HAMMERTON *J. M. Barrie & his Bks.* 78 There is more 'heart' in humour, and more 'head' in wit.

b. With qualification (see quots. and *sheer wit* s.v. SHEER *a.* 8 b).

1633 G. HERBERT *Temple, Ch.-Porch* xi, When thou dost tell anothers jest, therein Omit the oathes, which true wit cannot need. **1653** FLECKNOE *Misc., Disc. Lang.* 100 Jests, Clenches, Quibbles, Bulls, &c.,.. which although properly they be not Wit (excepting Jests onely, which is a kind of sportive and wanton wit). **1682** SHEFFIELD (Dk. Buckhm.) *Ess. Poetry* 12 True Wit is everlasting, like the Sun. **1693** DENNIS *Misc.* Pref. a 4 b, Scarron's Burlesque has nothing of a Gentleman in it, little of good Sense, and consequently little of true Wit. **1711** GAY *Pres. St. Wit* in Arb. *Garner* VI. 511 The *Spectator*, whom we regard as our Shelter from that flood of false wit and impertinence. **1717** ADDISON *Ovid's Met.* III. v. *note*, Wks. 1721 I. 243 As True wit is nothing else but a similitude in Ideas, so is False wit the similitude in Words. *Ibid.* 244 Ovid, who is the greatest admirer of this mixed wit of all the Ancients, as our Cowley is among the Moderns. **1765** CHESTERF. *Lett. to Godson* (1890) 182 There is a species of minor wit, which is much used,.. I mean Raillery. **1779** JOHNSON *L.P., Cowley* (1868) 20 These conceits Addison calls mixed wit; that is, wit which consists of thoughts true in one sense of the expression, and false in the other. **1792** D. STEWART *Elem. Philos. Hum. Mind* v. I. 305 *note*, I speak here of pure and unmixed wit, and not of wit, blended, as is most commonly, with some degree of humour.

†**c.** A witty saying or story; a *jeu d'esprit*: in the collocation *wits, fits, and fancies*. *Obs.*

1595 A. C[OPLEY] *(title)* Wits, Fittes and Fancies. Fronted and entermedled with Presidentes of Honour and Wisdome. **1626** W. VAUGHAN *Golden Fleece* I. 12 Except you season your *Auisoes* with some light passages with wits, fits, & fancies. **1632** BROME *Northern Lasse* I. ii. B 2 b, Hee.. breakes as many good iests as all the Wits, Fits, and Fancies about the Towne.

** **9.** (*transf.* from 5.) A person of great mental ability; a learned, clever, or intellectual person; a man of talent or intellect; a genius. *arch.* or *Hist.*

c **1470** *Gol. & Gaw.* 1137 Wourschipfull Wawane, the wit of our were. **1567** *Satir. Poems Reform.* vii. 185 Quhair is the wittis wont to reule Scotland? **1591** SYLVESTER *Du Bartas* I. v. 60 You divine wits of elder Dayes, from whom The deep Invention of rare Works hath com. *c* **1600** SHAKS. *Sonn.* lix. 13 The wits of former daies, To subiects worse haue giuen admiring praise. **1638** BRATHWAIT *Spir. Spicerie* 433 There goes an Author! One of the Wits! **1653** H. MORE *Antid. Ath.* III. xi. (1712) 124 Cartesius, that stupendious Mechanical Wit. **1698** FRYER *Acc. E. India & P.* 181 There are a sort of sublimated Wits that will own neither God nor Devil. **1779** JOHNSON *L.P., Milton* Wks. II. 131 Milton, the scholar and the wit. **1806** WOLCOT (P. Pindar) *Tristia* 20 The world.. Makes wits of fools, and sanctifies a sinner! **1842** LYTTON *Zanoni* I. vi, One evening, at Paris,.. there was a reunion of some of the most eminent wits of the time. **1867** 'OUIDA' *Cecil Castlemaine's Gage* 2 A circle of wits gathered 'within the steam of the coffee-pot' at Will's.

10. (*transf.* from 7.) A person of lively fancy, who has the faculty of saying smart or brilliant things, now always so as to amuse; a witty person.

1692 R. L'ESTRANGE *Fables* ccclxxi. 343 Intemperate Wits will spare neither Friend nor Foe. **1727** GAY *Fables* I. x, Wits are game-cocks to one another. **1824** W. IRVING *T. Trav.* I. 180 There is no character that succeeds so well among wits as that of a good listener. **1835** DICKENS *Sk. Boz, Lond. Recreations*, Uncle Bill.. is evidently the wit of the party. **1848** THACKERAY *Van. Fair* xviii, Go on joking, Ann. You're the wit of the family.

III. Senses, chiefly obsolete, corresponding to those of L. *scientia* and *sententia*.

11. †**a.** Knowledge; learning; *pl.* departments of knowledge, sciences. *Obs.*

1297 R. GLOUC. (Rolls) 4818 Þe bissopes him ansuerede.. Al wiþ grete reysons & wit of hor boc. **13..** *Cursor M.* 18940 (Arundel MS.) Þe holy goost ȝaf hem.. Of alle wittis to touche and tast. **1387-8** T. USK *Test. Love* II. ii. (Skeat) 43 Poore clerkes, for witte of schole, I sette in churches, and made suche persones to preche. **1565** *Creation of Eve* in *Non-Cycle Myst. Plays* (1909) 15 The tre is pleasante to gett wysedome & wytt.

†**b.** The fact of knowing, knowledge, awareness.

13.. *Guy Warw.* (A.) 799 No,.. bi mine wite, Y no herd þer-of neuer ȝete. *c* **1425** WYNTOUN *Cron.* v. x. 1936 God has reserwit til hym all þe wit of þat þat is to fal. **1483** in *Acts Parlt. Scot.* (1875) XII. 32/1 Be counsaile command wit or consent of his hienez. [**1648** HEXHAM, *Mijns wetens niet*, not with My weet, or knowledge.]

c. Knowledge communicated, 'intelligence', information, esp. in phr. *to get wit of*. *Sc.* and *north.*

1375 BARBOUR *Bruce* XIX. 443 The lord Dowglas.. Gat wit of thair enbuschement. *c* **1470** HENRY *Wallace* IV. 515 In the toun no wit of this had thai. *Ibid.* XI. 1032 Quhill witt tharoff is in till Ingland gane. **1504-5** *Acc. Ld. High Treas. Scot.* II. 474 The men that cersit and sought and gat wit of the silver disch that wes stollin. *a* **1578** LINDESAY (Pitscottie) *Chron. Scot.* (S.T.S.) I. 188 Bot on nowayis could they gett wott of him. **1633** M. P. *King & Poor Northern Man* 123 Belike the King of me has gotten some weet. *a* **1700** *Laidley Worm of Spindleston Heughs* xiv. in Child *Ballads* I. 312 The Child of Wynd got wit of it. **1825** BROCKETT *N.C. Gloss.* s.v., 'He got wit'—he obtained intelligence.

†**12.** Meaning, signification: = SENSE *sb.* 19–21.

a **1340** HAMPOLE *Psalter* ii. 5 And is þis þe wit. **1340** *Ayenb.* 96 Þe boȝes of þo traue ine one wytte byeþ alle þe ychosene þet euere were. **13..** *E.E. Allit. P.* B. 1630, I fayn wolde Wyt þe wytte of þe wryt. *c* **1380** WYCLIF *Sel. Wks.* II. 277 þe secounde witt is allegoryke.

†**13.** Way of thinking, opinion, judgement: = MIND *sb.*[1] 8, 9, SENSE *sb.* 18. *Obs.*

c **1374** CHAUCER *Troylus* IV. 1425 And verraylich hym semed þat he hadde The same wit. *c* **1380** *Sir Ferumb.* 1649 Þan were þay alle in wittes tweyne. *c* **1386** CHAUCER *Sqr.'s T.* 195 As many heddes, as manye wittes ther been. *c* **1386** —— *Frankl. T.* 147 It dooth no good to my wit, but anoyeth. *c* **1400** *Laud Troy Bk.* 8135 What is ȝoure wit? how thenke ȝow? **1555** PHAER *Æneid* II. (1558) C iv, The comons into sondry wittes diuided wer and stood. **1581** J. BELL *Haddon's Answ. Osor.* 282 The old Proverbe.. : so many heades, so many wittes.

IV. 14. Combinations. **a.** attrib., as ***wit-battle, -combat, -contest, -pride, -sally, -shaft, -sponge, -trap, -work***. **b.** objective, as ***wit-carrier, -gathering, -stealer; wit-writing; wit-assailing, -cherishing, -gracing, -infusing, -oppressing*** adjs. **c.** instrumental, as ***wit-abused, -beaten, -drawn, -fraught(ed, -pointed*** adjs. **d.** adverbial (= in, or with respect to, the wit or wits), as ***wit-foundered, -starved, -stung, -wondrous, -worn*** adjs. **e.** Special Combs.: **wit-crack**, the 'cracking' of a joke (cf. CRACK *v.* 5), a brisk witticism; so **wit-cracker**, one who makes witty or sarcastic remarks; **wit-craft**, †(*a*) the art of using one's 'wit' or intellect in reasoning, logic; (*b*) exercise of one's wits; **wit-jar**, an imaginary vessel humorously feigned to contain the wits or senses (in allusion to Ariosto's *Orlando Furioso* XXXIX. lvii); †**wit-lost** *a.*, having lost wit, senseless, foolish; **wit-monger**, a 'dealer' in wit, an utterer of witty sayings (*contemptuous*); †**wit-rack** *nonce-wd.*, a faculty of eliciting speech by wit (as a rack elicits a confession); †**wit-snapper** = *wit-cracker*; †**wit-stand**, in phr. *at a wit-stand* (cf. STAND *sb.*[1] 6), = at one's wit's end (see 2 d); †**wit-state**, state of being in one's wits, condition of sanity; †**wit-tooth** = WISDOM TOOTH; **wit-wanton** *a.*, making a wanton use of the 'wit' or understanding; also as *sb.*; †**wit-wanton** *v. intr.* (with *it*) (*obs.* exc. *arch.*), to exercise the understanding wantonly; also, to indulge in wanton wit; **wit-worm** (now *rare*), one who has developed into a wit (like a 'worm' or caterpillar emerging from the egg); †**wit-worship**, worship devised by human 'wit' or intellect without divine authority or sanction (cf. WILL-WORSHIP); †**wit-would**, †**wit-would-be**, a pretender to wit, a would-be wit; †**wit-wright**, a maker of wit, an author of witty sayings.

1603 J. DAVIES (Heref.) *Microcosmos* 40 The will *witt-abus'd. **1601** CHESTER *Love's Mart.* (1878) 106 The *wit-assailing Frenzie. **1693** DRYDEN *Juvenal* Ded. (1697) p. lxxii, The *Wit-battel of the two Buffoons. **1599** PORTER *Angry Wom. Abington* (Percy Soc.) 50 Sheele persecute the poore *wit beaten man. **1702** *Engl. Theophrastus* 7 *Wit-carriers, whose business is, to export the fine Things they hear. **1594** NASHE *Unfort. Trav.* D 4, That kinde *wit-cherishing climate. *a* **1661** FULLER *Worthies, Warwickshire* III. (1662) 126 Many were the *wit-combates betwixt him [*sc.* Shakspere] and Ben Johnson. **1892** CHILD *Ballads* VIII. 439/1 *Wit-contests in verse. **1662** GURNALL *Chr. in Arm.* III. xxx. §2. 256 Satan budges not for a thousand such Squibs and *Wit-cracks. **1599** SHAKS. *Much Ado* V. iv. 102 A Colledge of *witte-crackers cannot flout mee out of my humour, dost thou think I care for a Satyre or an Epigram? **1573** R. LEVER *(title)* The Arte of Reason, rightly termed, **Witcraft*. **1605** CAMDEN *Rem., Rebus* 146 He was no body that coulde not hammer out of his name an invention by this wit-craft. **1903** HARDY *Dynasts* I. I. iii, A witcraft marked by nothing more of weight Than ignorant irregularity! **1681** W. ROBERTSON *Phraseol. Gen.* 386 *Wit-drawn, wire-drawn curiosities. **1613** BOYS *Expos. Last Ps.* (1615) 7 The *wit-foundred drunkard. **1623** L. DIGGES in *Shaks. 1st Folio*, Thy *wit-fraught Booke. **1603** DEEBLE *Commend. Poems* in J. Davies (Heref.) *Microcosmos* Oo 2 b, His *witt-fraughted workes. **1893** MAX PEMBERTON *Iron Pirate* iii, I sat up in bed, uncertain in the effort of *wit-gathering if night had not given me a dream rather than an experience. **1591** SYLVESTER *Du Bartas* I. iv. 34 Your *Wit-gracing Skill. **1603** J. DAVIES (Heref.) *Microcosmos* 65 *Wit-infusing Mercury. **1748** RICHARDSON *Clarissa* VII. lxxxviii. 326 Dr. Hale.. was my good Astolfo (you read Ariosto, Jack) and has brought me back my *wit-jar. **1599** PORTER *Angry Wom. Abington* (Percy Soc.) 13 Ill report doth like a bailiffe stand, To pound the straying and the *wit-lost tongue. **1620** SHELTON *2nd Pt. Don Quix.* xxxi. 203 The Prater and *Wit-monger. **1691** WOOD *Ath. Oxon.* II. 620 [He] was.. cried up as the main witmonger surviving to the fanatical party. **1601** CHESTER *Love's Mart.* (1878) 102 *Wit-oppressing Drunkennesse. **1869** *Routledge's Ev. Boy's Ann.* 546 The butt of their *wit-pointed pencils. **1591** SYLVESTER *Du Bartas* I. ii. 1151 All the golden *Wit-pride of Humanity, Wherewith men burnish their erroneous vanity. **1642** FULLER *Holy & Prof. St.* IV. vi. 269 He had a pretty *wit-rack in himself,.. to draw speech out of the most sullen and silent guest. **1549** CHALONER *Erasm. on Folly* T iij, A certain passion muche lyke to madnesse or *witrauyng. **1907** RALEIGH *Shakespeare* 174 The *wit-sallies of Beatrice and Rosalind. **1881** SWINBURNE *Mary Stuart* I. iii. 64 Our keeper's *wit-shaft is too keen for ours To match with pointless iron. **1596** SHAKS. *Merch. V.* III. v. 54 What a *witte-snapper are you. **1632** BROME *Crt. Beggar* II. i. (1653) O 6 b, This humorous wity Lady is a *wit-sponge, that suckes up wit from some, and holds as her own. *a* **1670** HACKET *Abp. Williams* I. (1693) 188 They were at a *wit-stand. **1828-32** WEBSTER, **Wit-starved*, barren of wit; destitute of genius. *Examiner*. *c* **1450** *St. Cuthbert* (Surtees) 7237 Sho lost hir *witt state. **1886** CORBETT *Fall of Asgard* xxxv, Surely is ale a great *wit-stealer. **1608** MACHIN *Dumb Knt.* IV. i, Fie I am mad, Sham'd and disgrac't, all *wit-stung, wisdomlesse. **1601** HOLLAND *Pliny* XI. xxxvii. I. 338 The farthest cheek-teeth in a mans head, which be called *Genuini*, (*i.* the *Wit-teeth). **1750** FIELDING *Author's Farce* I. vi, Nor was it cram'd with a pack of *Wit-traps, like Congreve and Wycherly, where every one knows when the joke was coming. **1612** SYLVESTER *Lachr. Lachr.* 99 Epicures, *Wit-wantons, Atheists. **1655** FULLER *Ch. Hist.* x. iv. §4. 62 How dangerous it is for wit-wanton Men, to dance with their nice Distinctions, on such Mysticall Precipices. **1642** —— *Holy & Prof. St.* III. ii. 155 More dangerous it is to *wit-wanton it with the Majestie of God. **1795** SOUTHEY *Joan of Arc* IX. 268 Wretched Maid!.. England's inhuman Chiefs Shall.. black thy spotless fame, Wit-wanton it with lewd barbarity. **1922** JOYCE *Ulysses* 388 And Master Lynch bade him have a care to flout and witwanton. **1922** E. R. EDDISON *Worm* xv. 209, I will not suffer mine indignation so to witwanton with fair justice as persuade me to put the wite on Witchland. **1598** SYLVESTER *Du Bartas* II. ii. II. *Babylon* 584 *Wit-wondrous Salomon. **1632** B. JONSON *Magn. Lady* I. i, You're sure to have lesse-*wit-worke, gentle brother. **1611** —— *Catiline* II. i, What hast thou done With thy poore innocent selfe?.. Thus to come forth, so sodainly, a *wit-worme? **1647** C. HARVEY *Schola Cordis* (1778) 153 That which worldly wit-worms call nonsense. **1932** F. SCOTT FITZGERALD *Let.* 2 Aug. (1964) 498, I did not destinate to signify that you were a wiseacre ..but..that you were..a longhead,..are so many epigrammatists, wit-worms, [etc.]. **1617** *Greene's Groat's W. Wit* Pref. A 2, So many *Witworn Ideots. *a* **1629** HINDE *J. Bruen* xxx. (1641) 93 That such service unto Saints, is but *witt-worship, will-worship, and Idol-service. **1641** SANDERSON *Serm., Ad Clerum* (1681) II. 4 God will not approve of, nor accept any Wit-worship, or Will-worship, forged or devised by man. **1700** CONGREVE *Way of World* Ded., This Play had been Acted two or three Days, before some of these hasty Judges cou'd find the leisure to distinguish betwixt the Character of a **Wit-woud* and a *Truewit*. *a* **1763** SHENSTONE *Ess. Men & Manners* lxxxvi. Wks. 1765 II. 225 A wit-would cannot afford to discard a frivolous conceit. **1771** SHERIDAN in *Rival Beauties* 16 Then grinning Witwould—tho' no Teague—Who more successful in intrigue? **1681** H. MORE *Let.* 15 in Glanvill *Sadducismus*, Our professed *Wit-would-be's of this present Age. **1655** STRODE *Floating Isl.* Ded. A 2 b, If..*wit-wrights Poets be. **1666** DRYDEN *Ann. Mirab.* Pref., Ess. (1900) I. 14 Wit in the poet, or *Wit writing, (if you will give me leave to use a school-distinction). **1947** C. DAY LEWIS *Poetic Image* ii. 50 The conceits of the Metaphysicals are in a way wit-writing too.

†**wit**, *pron. Obs.* Also 1 wyt, 3 wet, (*Orm.*) witt. [OE. *wit* = OFris. **wit* (NFris, *wat, wæt*), OS. *wit*, ON. (MSw.) *vit*, Goth. *wit*: f. unstressed form of WE *pron.* with obscure dental element.] We two.

Beowulf 535 Wit þæt ȝecwædon cnihtwesende. *c* **1000** *Ags. Gosp.* Matt. xx. 22 Maȝe ȝyt drincan þone calic ðe ic to drincenne hæbbe? Þa cwædon hiȝ: Wyt maȝon. *c* **1175** *Lamb. Hom.* 33 3if.. wit beon anes lauerdes men. *c* **1200** ORMIN 201 Witt sinndenn off swillc elde nu þatt witt ne muȝhenn tæmenn. *c* **1205** LAY. 23653 Wit tweie. *Ibid.* 23663

Fehten wet scullen unc seoluen. *Ibid.* 26263 Fare wit [*c* 1275 we two] to uihte. *c* **1250** *Gen. & Ex.* 1775 Frend sule wit ben, And trewðe pliȝt nu unc bi-twen.

wit, *v.*[1] *arch.* exc. in legal use: see 10 c (b). Pres. t. **wot** (*Sc.* and *north. dial.* **wat**); pa. t. and pple. **wist**. Forms: see below. [A Com. Teut. preterite-present verb: OE. *witan*, 1st and 3rd sing. pres. ind. *wát*, 2nd pers. *wást*, pl. *witon*, pa. t. *wisse*, *wiste*, pa. pple. *ʒewiten*, OFris. *wita*, *wêt*, **wast*, **witon*, *witen* and *witath*, *wiste* (mod. Fris. dialects have various analogical forms, e.g. pa. pple. *wist*, *wust*), OS. *witan*, *wêt*, *wêst*, *witun*, *wissa* (MLG., MDu. *wêten*, *weet*, *weets*, *weten*, *wiste*, *gheweten*, LG., Du. *weten*), OHG. *wizzan*, *wizan*, *weiz*, *wiz(z)umês*, *wiz(z)un*, *wissa*, *wista*, *(gi)wizan* (MHG. *wizzen*, *weiz*, *wizzen*, *wisse*, *wiste*, *wesse*, *weste*, *wuste*, *gewizzen*, *gewist*, G. *wissen*, *weiss*, *weisst*, *wissen*, *wusste*, *gewusst*), ON. *vita*, *veit*, *veizt*, *vitum*, *vissa*, *vitaðr*, (Sw. *veta*, *vet*, *visste*, *vetat*, Da. *vide*, *ved*, *vidste*, *vidst*), Goth. *witan*, *wait*, *waist*, *witum*, *wissa*: f. OTeut. *wait-*, *wĭt-*:—Indo-Eur. *woid-*, *weid-*, *wid-* to see (? orig. to find), also found in OE. adj. *wis* (see WIS *sb.*), WISE *sb.*[1], WISE *a.*, WITE.

The OE. preterite-pres. *wát*, *wást*, *witon*, and their equivalents in the other Germanic langs. (= properly, I have seen, hence, I know), correspond to Skr. *véda*, *véttha*, *vidmá*, Gr. *οἶδα*, *οἶσθα*, *οἶδε*, *ἴδμεν* (*ἴσμεν*), OSl. *vědě*, *věsi*, etc., OPruss. 2nd sing. *waisei*, 1st pl. *waidimai*, and are based on Indo-Eur. *woid-*, *wid-*. OE. 2nd pers. sing. *wást* (see A. 2 b below) is an altered form of **wás* by analogy with *meaht* (2nd sing. pres. of MAY *v.*[1]). Similarly OE. *wiste* is an altered form of earlier *wisse* after regular weak forms in *-te*.

Indo-Eur. *woid-*, *weid-*, *wid-* is represented also by Skr. *veda* knowledge (see VEDA), *vitta-* known, *vittá-* found, Gr. *εἶδος* appearance, shape, *ἰδέα* form, *εἶδον* (:—**ἔϝιδον*) I saw, *ἀείδελος* invisible, *εἰδέναι* to know, *ἰδεῖν* to see, *ἄιστος* unseen, unknown, L. *vidēre* to see, OIr. *fiad* 'coram', *fiadu* witness, *adfiadat* they relate, *rofetar* I know, *fiss* knowledge, W. *gwydd* presence, *gwyddom* we know, OSl. *viděti* to see, *věděti* to know, Lith. *véidas* face, Arm. *gitem* I know, *egit* he found; and (with nasal infix) Skr. *vindáti* finds, Gr. *ἰνδάλλεσθαι* to appear, OIr. *finnaim* I find out.

The original conjugation, typically represented by *to wit* or *wete*, pres. *I* and *he wot*, *thou wost*, *we*, *ye*, and *they wite*, pa. t. *wist*, pa. pple. *witen*, presented many apparent anomalies, and various attempts at normalization were made by means of analogical formations and irregular extension of the use of certain forms, with the result that new infinitive and present-stem forms came into existence which it is necessary to treat separately: see WIS *v.*[1], WIST *v.*, WOT *v.*, and the archaistic WEET *v.*[1] (For forms combined with prefixed negative *ne* see NETE, NIST, NITEN, NOST, NOT *v.*[2], NUTE.)]

A. Inflexional Forms.

1. Infinitive. *α.*[1] 1 **witan** (**witenne**, **-an(n)e**, **-on(n)e**), 2–5 **witen**, 3–5 **wyten**, **wite**, 4–5 **wytene**, (**whyte**, **wiet**), 4–6 **wyt(e**, **wytte**, **witte**, *Sc.* **vit**, (1 **wiotan**, **wietan**, *Northumb.* **wuta**, 3 **witene**, *Orm.* **witenn**, 4 **witin**, **witten**, **wijt**, **wyete**, *Sc.* **vyt**, **-e**, 5 **wiete**, **whitte**), 4–7 **witt**, 5–6 **wytt**, 4– **wit**. *α.*[2] 4–6 **wet**, **wette**, (4 *Sc.* **vet**), 5 **wetten**. *β.* 4–5 **wetyn**, 4–6 **weit(e**, 4–7 **wete**, 5 **weten(e**, 5–7 **weete**, (8–9 *arch.*) **weet**, (6 *arch.* **weeten**). (See also WEET *v.*[1], WOT.)

α. [1] *c* **888** ÆLFRED *Boeth.* vii. § 1 Ʒif þu þonne heora þeawas witan wilt. *c* **897** —— *Gregory's Past. C.* Pref. 7 Ða ðe niedbeðearfosta sien eallum monnum to wiotonne. *Ibid.* xv. 92 Mare to wietenne ðonne eow ðearf sie. *c* **1100** *O.E. Chron.* an. 1050 (MS. D) Hit is earfoð to witane þara biscopa þe þærtocomon. *c* **1175** *Lamb. Hom.* 9 Ȝef..me hit mihte witen. *c* **1205** LAY. 26607 Heo wolden wite þat soðe of Walwain. *c* **1290** *St. Clement* 128 in *S. Eng. Leg.* 326 He wilnede muche to wyten of god. *a* **1300** *Cursor M.* 8301 Þou sal wijt on quatkin wise [etc.]. **1340** HAMPOLE *Pr. Consc.* 3763 Na man..may wytte Whether [etc.]. **1340** *Ayenb.* 1 Þet is to wytene. **13..** *Cursor M.* 12204 (Gött.) Hu sal he witt quat tav mai be? *Ibid.* 19779 (Edin.) Þat petir moȝte witte quat sco were. *Ibid.* 23635 If þai oht mai witin [*v.r.* witten] þar. **13..** *Gaw. & Gr. Knt.* 131 Vch wyȝ e may wel wit. **1362** LANGL. *P. Pl.* A. II. 27 Þat þou miht wyte..whuche þei ben. *c* **1375** *Sc. Leg. Saints* xix. (*Cristofore*) 401 Gyf þu vit wil myn cunctre. *c* **1380** *Sir Ferumb.* 1367 To whyte what hure wille were. ? *a* **1400** *Morte Arth.* 420 Late hyme wiet..I salle ..take leue. **1426** LYDG. *De Guil. Pilgr.* 4492 To wyten whether..Myn hamer hem touchyd. *c* **1450** *Merlin* 82 She wolde gladly witen what a-mendes the kynge wolde do. ? **1475** *Stonor Papers* (Camden) I. 156, I lett you whitte I am grette with the Kyng. *c* **1500** *Three Kings' Sons* 168 There be none..but wold be glad to wite me do wele. **1526** TINDALE *Matt.* xxiii. 8 One ys youre master, that is to wytt Christ. **1533** GAU *Richt Vay* (S.T.S.) 55 Desir notht to vit. **1577** FULKE *Confut. Purg.* 393 You must witte. **1580** wytte [see *β.* 1531]. **1628** DIGBY *Voy. Mediterr.* (Camden) 31 To witt. **1795** wit [see B. 3 c].

α.[2] **13..** *Cursor M.* 22556 (Edin.) Quen nan sal wet quar þam to nest. *c* **1375** *Sc. Leg. Saints* xviii. (*Egipciane*) 404 God has send me..þi lyfe, þe stat, al hal to vet. ? *a* **1400** *Morte Arth.* 948 To wette of the warlawe, whare that he lengez. *c* **1460** *Play Sacram.* 188 in *Non-Cycle Myst. Pl.* 63 Off yower welfare fayn wet wold we. **1520** SIR R. GRESHAM in Ellis *Orig. Lett.* Ser. III. I. 234 Yt may pleasse your Grace to wette I have [etc.].

β. *a* **1300** *Cursor M.* 1875 (Cott.) How sal we o þis waters weit [*Fairf.* wete] Quedir þai be fulli fallen yeit? **13..** *Northern Passion* (MS. I) 648 *a* Wele maye we alle wetyn and se þat it myghte neuyr so be. *c* **1400** *Anturs Arth.* 237 (Douce MS.) Yit wetene I wolde What wrathede god moste. *c* **1400** *Melayne* 120 He dose þe wele to weite. *c* **1425** *Noah's Ark* 131 in *Non-Cycle Myst. Pl.* 23 How Thou shalt weet all his will. *c* **1440** *Promp. Parv.* 531/1 Wytyn', or wetyn', or knowyn'. **1475** SIR J. PASTON in *P. Lett.* III. 130 It pleasyd yow to weete of myn heele. **1531** ELYOT *Gov.* I. ix, Lettinge you weete [*ed.* 1580 wytte] that we haue a sonne borne. **1596** weeten [see B. 10 c (*b*)]. **1600** weete [see B. 9 b]. **1610** in Picton *L'pool Munic. Rec.* (1883) I. 121 You shall..do the Maior..to wete thereof. **1748**, **1819** weet [see B. 10 c (*a*)].

2. Indicative Present. **a.** *1st and 3rd pers. sing.* *α.* 1–6 (8–9 *Sc.*) **wat**, 1, 4–6 **watt**, (1 **uat**, 1, 3 **wæt**, 3 **what**, **waht**, 4 *north.* **waite**, **wayte**, **quat**, **-e**, *Sc.* **vat**), 4–5 **watte**, 4–7 (8 *Sc.*) **wate**, 5–9 *Sc.* and *n. dial.* **wait** (6 **vait**). *β.* 3–9 **wot**, (3 **wod**, 4 **woth**), 4–5 **woot**, (**whot**, 5 **whotte**, **wout**), 4–6, 8 **wote**, 5–6 **woote**, **wotte**, 5–7 **wott**. Also in 1st pers. combined with prefixed pronoun (**ichot**, **chote**): see I *pron.* A. *β*[2] and CH *pron.*

α. *c* **950** *Lindisf. Gosp.* John viii. 55 Ic..conn *vel* wat [*c* **975** *Rushw. Gosp.* watt] hine. *c* **1200** *Vices & Virtues* 21 He hit wat ðe wat alle þing. *c* **1205** LAY. 7262 Wel ich hit wæt what Bruttis wæs. *Ibid.* 28088 Ich what..agan is al mi blisse. *a* **1300** *Cursor M.* 5060 Mi fader..fars well, i watte. **13..** *Ibid.* 12219 (Gött.) Fire i quat him mai noght brin. **13..** *Northern Passion* (Camb. Gg. 5. 31) 356, I hafe done I ne wate what. *Ibid.* 1654 Onone pilate a lettyr he wrate, So says saynt Iohne þat wele wayte. *c* **1425** WYNTOUN *Cron.* cxviii. 1987 (MS. W.) Quheþer it sa were..I wait nocht. **1583** *Leg. Bp. St. Androis* 172, I watt now what the propheit menis. **1615** BRATHWAIT *Strappado* (1878) 129 Wele I wate. **1724** RAMSAY *Tea-t. Misc.* (1733) I. 25 And that's an unco faut I wate. **1785** BURNS *Halloween* xii, I wat she made nae jaukin. **1825** BROCKETT *N.C. Gloss.*, *Wait*, wot.

β. *a* **1225** *Ancr. R.* 52 Þeo..wot betere þen ich wot. *a* **1250** *Owl & Night.* 1190 Ich..wod al þat to kumen is. *a* **1300** *Cursor M.* 8298 Wil i wote al þi yerning. **13..** *Ibid.* 2378 (Gött.) His catel wele i woth [*Trin.* I woot]. **13..** *Guy Warw.* (A.) 590 Ichot for soþe he wil me sle. *c* **1380** WYCLIF *Wks.* (1880) 77 No prelat whot where he schal be dampnyd. *c* **1385** CHAUCER *L.G.W.* 1359 *Dido*, Wel I woot hit is al in vayne. *c* **1400** *Destr. Troy* 11359, I wotte hit full wele. **1426** AUDELAY *Poems* 15 He whot never hou sone God wyl here his bone. **1526** TINDALE *Luke* xvi. 4, I woote what to do. **1600** HOLLAND *Livy* I. i, Neither wote I well, nor if I wist, dare I advouch. **1775** J. TAIT *Land of Liberty* I. xlv. 23 Here oft, I wote, dame Ignorance was seen. **1862** H. A. KENNEDY *Waifs & Strays* 137, I well wot.

b. *2nd pers. sing.* *α.* 1–4 **wast**, (1 **wæst**, **uast**, 3 *Orm.* **wasst**), 3–5 **wost**, 4–5 **woost**, **woste**. Also combined with foll. pron.: 1 **wastu**, 3 **wostu**, 4–5 **wostow(e**. *β.* See WOT *v.* *γ.* 4 *Sc.* **vittis**.

α. *a* **900** *Andreas* 1186 Wæst þe bæles cwealm hatne in helle? *c* **975** *Rushw. Gosp.* John iii. 8 Ne wastu hwona cymeð & hwider gað. *c* **1000** *Ags. Gosp.* John xiii. 7 Þu nast nu þæt ic do, ac þu wast syððan. *c* **1205** LAY. 15836 Nu þu hit wost. *a* **1250** *Owl & Night.* 716 Wostu to wan man was ibore? *a* **1300** *Cursor M.* 25477 Vnworthi am i, wel þou wast. *c* **1380** WYCLIF *Serm.* Sel. Wks. II. 79 Þou woost wel þat Fariseis.. ben sclaundrid. *c* **1400** *Rom. Rose* 6075, I bidde thee teche hem, wostowe howe. **1483** CAXTON *Gold. Leg.* 124/2 Thou woste not what thou sayest.

γ. *c* **1375** *Sc. Leg. Saints* iii. (*Andreas*) 508 Bot-gyf þu will hertly trow, þu vittis nocht þu speris now [*nunquam tu ad imaginem hujus veritatis attinges*].

c. *Plural.* *α.*[1] 1 **witon**, **weotan**, **uutu(n**, **-on**, **wut(t)on**, 2 **witan**, 2–5 **witen** (3 *Orm.* **-enn**, **wuten**), 3–5 **wyten** (3 **wuyten**, 4 **whiten**, 5 **wittin**); 3–5 **wite**, 4 **witte**, 5 **wyte**, **wytte**; 4 **weten**, **-in**, 5 **wet**, **weet**, **wete**. *α.*[2] 1 **wutaþ**, **witaþ**, **witteð**, **wutas**, 3 **wutez**, 3–4 **wuteþ**, 3–5 **witeþ** (4 **-yþ**, **wyteþ**, **wteþ**, **wites**, 5 **whiteþ**, **wittis**; 5 **weteþ**, **-iþ**, **-yþ**). *β.* See WOT *v.*

α.[1] *c* **900** tr. *Bæda's Hist.* II. v, We weotan þæt we þæs þearfe nabbað. *c* **950** *Lindisf. Gosp.* Matt. xx. 22 Ne uutuʒe huæt ʒe ʒiwas. *c* **1000** *Ags. Gosp.* John xvi. 30 Nu we witon þæt þu wast ealle ðing. **1154** *O.E. Chron.* (Laud) Introd. 3 We witan oþer eʒland. *c* **1175** *Lamb. Hom.* 19 Nusten heo nawiht swa muchel of him swa we witen. *c* **1200** ORMIN 7932 Þatt witenn menn inoȝhe. *c* **1200** *Trin. Coll. Hom.* 161 Hie wuten..wuderward hie sullen weie holden. *c* **1250** *Gen. & Ex.* 390 Adam and eue it wite ful ȝare. *c* **1275** *Passion our Lord* 261 in *O.E. Misc.* 44 Hwat ich to heom seyde, wel wyten heo. *c* **1290** *Beket* 1025 in *S. Eng. Leg.* 136 Ȝe wuyten wel. *c* **1380** WYCLIF *Wks.* (1880) 77 Siþ prelatis witte not where here preiere be acceptable. **1387–8** T. USK *Test. Love* I. viii. (Skeat) l. 80 Ye weten wel..that..I defouled never my conscience. *c* **1400** *26 Pol. Poems* iii. 101 Lordis wet neuere what comouns greues. *c* **1400** *Pride of Life* 483 in *Non-Cycle Myst. Pl.* 104 Ȝe wittin wel þat he is king. **1402** *Jack Upland* in *Pol. Poems* (Rolls) II. 17 These wretches weet never where to been. **1426** LYDG. *De Guil. Pilgr.* 5528 Ye wyte wel.

α.[2] *c* **950** *Lindisf. Gosp.* Mark ii. 10 Þætte..wutað [*Rushw.* witaþ] ʒie ðætte he mæht hæfeð sunu monnes. *Ibid.* x. 41 *Scitis*, wutasʒie [*c* **1000** *Ags. Gosp.* wite ʒe]. —— Luke xxi. 30 Witteð [*Rushw.* wutað] ʒie þætte neh is ðe summer. *c* **975** *Rushw. Gosp.* John iv. 22 We worðiʒað þætte we wutun. *a* **1225** *Ancr. R.* 252 To wel we hit wuteð. *c* **1290** *Beket* 1005 in *S. Eng. Leg.* 135 Wel we wutez. *a* **1300** *Leg. Rood* 18 As ȝe witeþ wel. *a* **1340** HAMPOLE *Psalter* iv. 4 Ȝe seke vanytes: and wites that it is vayne that ȝe luf. *c* **1380** WYCLIF *Wks.* (1880) 89 Men wityþ neuere what it meneþ. *a* **1400–40** *R. Glouc. Chron.* (Rolls) 122 Ȝe wyteþ [*v.rr.* weteþ, wetyth, whiteþ]. **1409** in *Exch. Rolls Scot.* IV. Pref. 209 Gif ony of the foresaide lordis wittis..ony maner of grefe..apperand til other.

3. *Subjunctive Present.* 1–5 **wite** (*pl.* **witen**), (1 **wiete**, *Northumb.* **witto**, **-e**, **-u**, 3 **wute**, 4 **wijt**, **witte**, **vit**), 4–5 **wyt**, 4–6 **wit**, **wyte**, **wete**, 5 **weete**.

c **897** ÆLFRED *Gregory's Past. C.* xxviii. 191 Sua sua hie selfe wieten..ðæt hi hit for Gode don. *c* **950** *Lindisf. Gosp.* Luke i. 18 *Unde hoc sciam*, huona ðis witto? *c* **1000** *Rule St. Benet* (1888) 16 He wite þæt he..iarcie hine to ʒescead aʒeldenne. *c* **1200** ORMIN 5710 Þatt tu ne wite nan. *a* **1225** *Ancr. R.* 250 God hit wute & he hit wot. **13..** in Sir W. Pole *Old Evid.* (? 1840) 1 Vit alle men þat þis skrite heris and ses. **1340** *Ayenb.* 5 Þis boc is ywrite uor englisse men, þet hi wyte hou hi ssolle ham-zelue ssriue. *c* **1380** WYCLIF *Wks.* (1880) 372 Wete lordis well þat [etc.]. *c* **1400** *Gamelyn* 644 It is good that we witen what men they be. *a* **1425** *Cursor M.* 14348 (Trin.), I wol þat alle witen. **1447** BOKENHAM *Seyntys* (Roxb.) 33, I wil ye wete Two precyous relykys I her have wyth me. **1470–85** MALORY *Arthur* VI. viii. 195, I wyl that thou wete and knowe that I am Launcelot du lake. **1545** ASCHAM *Toxoph.* II. (Arb.) 145 Awaye or a man wite. **1596** DALRYMPLE tr. *Leslie's Hist. Scot.* VIII. (S.T.S.) II. 104 To defend him selfe, that..tha steil him nocht doune or he wit.

4. *Past tense* (*indic.* and *subj.*). *α.* 1 **wisse**, 1–6 **wiste**, (1, 3 *Orm.* **wisste**), 3–6 **wyste**, 4–6 **wyst**, (4 **wijst**, *Sc.* **viste**, 4–6 *Sc.* **vist**, **vyst**, 5 **wyssste**), 4– **wist**. Also in 3rd pers. pl. combined with foll. pron. 4 **wistey**, **wystey**. *β.* 1 *pl.* **westan**, 4–6 **west** (4–5 **weste**), 6 *Sc.* **weist**. *γ.* 1 **wyste**, 3–5 **wuste**, (3 **wste**), 4–6 **wust**. *δ.* 4–5 **wost(e**. *ε.* 4 *Sc.* **wyttyt**.

α. *Beowulf* 181 Ne wiston hie drihten god. *Ibid.* 246 Ne ʒe leafnesword guðfremmendra ʒearwe ne wisson. *Ibid.* 2519 Ʒif ic wiste. *c* **950** *Lindisf. Gosp.* Matt. xxvii. 18 He wisse forðon þæt ðerh æfist saldon hine. *c* **1175** *Lamb. Hom.* 19 Heo wisten..þet he wes hali. *c* **1200** ORMIN 521 Illc an.. Wisste full wel. *c* **1275** *Passion our Lord* 160 in *O.E. Misc.* 42 He wyste þat þe Gywes hyne þouhte spille. *a* **1300** *Cursor M.* 15953 Þan wijst he cummen his maister word. *Ibid.* 16054 Sir pilate..Wist þam was leif to lei. *c* **1330** R. BRUNNE *Chron. Wace* (Rolls) 5068 Bettere wistey nought what for to do. *Ibid.* 8021 wystey. *a* **1352** MINOT *Poems* (ed. Hall) iii. 52 Men..þat wist both of wele and wo. **13..** *E.E. Allit. P.* B. 152 He ne wyst on worde what he warp schulde. **13..** *Gaw. & Gr. Knt.* 461 Neuer more þen þay wyste fram queþen he was wonnen. **1375** BARBOUR *Bruce* IV. 771 Quhethir scho.. Wenit, or vist it vitterly. *c* **1375** *Sc. Leg. Saints* xviii. (*Egipciane*) 1327 He..vyst it was scho. *c* **1400** *Destr. Troy* 13839 All wiston tho wise..He shuld duly be ded. *c* **1450** *Merlin* 25 When these..men wisten that Vortiger sholde be kynge. **1537** Q. MARGARET in *St. Papers Hen. VIII*, V. 120 And..thys Raulme vyst that Ze vold be dysplesyd. **1556** *Aurelio & Isab.* (1608) B v, She shewed..all that she wiste. **1576** R. PETERSON *G. della Casa's Galateo* 12 The Count.. neuer wyst of his fault. **1865** SWINBURNE *Chastelard* I. ii. 200 And that, God wot, I wist not.

β. *a* **1000** *Judith* 207 Westan beʒen þæt [etc.]. **1340** *Ayenb.* 72 Þet hi westen be hare wylle. **1539** *St. Papers Hen. VIII*, VIII. 172 He west not, whether [etc.]. *a* **1585** MONTGOMERIE *Cherrie & Slae* 178, I..weist not what it meind.

γ. *c* **1000** *Ags. Ps.* (Th.) cvi. 29 Swa he hira willan wyste fyrmest. *c* **1205** LAY. 525 He..wuste, þat þe king..forð sculde iwenden. *Ibid.* 1167 His sæ-monnen, þe..þa lawen wusten. *a* **1250** *Owl & Night.* 10 Eiþer seide of oþeres custe þat alere worste þat hi wuste. **1297** R. GLOUC. (Rolls) 2025 Þo he wste wat he was. **1362** LANGL. *P. Pl.* A. III. 52 Wust I þat,..þer nis nouþur Wyndou ne Auter, þat I ne schulde maken oþur mende. *c* **1400** *St. Alexius* (Vernon) 326 He wuste he scholde heþen wende. **1555** PHAER *Æneid.* II. (1558) D iij b, Nor what to do I wust.

δ. **1387** TREVISA *Higden* (Rolls) VII. 55 Me wost not where me myȝte mete hem. *a* **1450** *Knt. de la Tour* (1868) 6 Whanne her fader wost she was with childe. **1492** *Acta Dom. Conc.* (1839) 274/2 Robert..maid faith he wost nocht quhare It wes.

ε. **1375** BARBOUR *Bruce* XII. 156 He wyttyt [*v.r.* askit] at thaim of thair far.

b. *2nd pers. sing.* 1, 4, 6 **wistest** (1 **wistes**, *subj.* **wisse**, **wiste**), 4 **wystest**, (**vistes**), **wiste**, 4–5 **wyste**, **wist**, 6 **wyst**.

c **888** ÆLFRED *Boeth.* v. § 3 Ic wolde þæt þu me sædest hwæþer ðu wisse hwæt þu self wære. *c* **950** *Lindisf. Gosp.* John i. 48 Huona..mec wistes ðu? *c* **1000** *Ags. Gosp.* Matt. xxv. 26 Ðu wistest þæt ic rype þær ic ne sawe. **13..** *K. Horn* 240 (Harl.) Tech him alle þe listes þat þou euer wystest [*Laud MS.* vistes]. **1387–8** T. USK *Test. Love* I. viii. (Skeat) l. 31 In as fer as thou hem wistest false. **1423** JAS. I *Kingis Q.* xiv, Wist thou thy payne to cum..wele myght thou wepe. *c* **1430** *Chev. Assigne* 186 If þou here dome wyste. *c* **1500** *Melusine* 24 Yf thou wyst and knew the grette meruaylles. **1587** GOLDING *De Mornay* ii. (1592) 21 If thou wistest how to vse them.

5. *Imperative.* Stem as in 1; endings: *sing.* 1–6 **-e**; occas. combined with foll. pron. 4 **witow**; *pl.* 1 **-aþ**, 1–5 **-e** (in *wite ȝe*), 1, 4–5 **-eþ**, 4–5 **-eth**, 5 **-iþ**, **-yþ**; *north.* 1 **-as**, 4 **-s**, 5 **-is**, **-ys**; also sing. and (4–) pl. without ending.

a **900** CYNEWULF *Elene* 945 Wite ðu þe ʒearwor þæt ðu.. anforlete..lufan dryhtnes. *c* **900** tr. *Bæda's Hist.* IV. viii, Witað ʒe þæt hit swa nis. **971** *Blickl. Hom.* 183 Wit þu þonne þæt ic eom dry. *c* **1000** *Ags. Ps.* (Th.) iv. 4 [3] Wite ʒe [*scitote*] þæt God ʒemyclade his ðone ʒehalʒodan. *c* **1175** *Lamb. Hom.* 9 Wite ȝe hwet wes sinagoge on þam alde laȝe. *c* **1200** ORMIN 205 Witt tu þatt icc amm Gabriæl. *c* **1205** wite þu [see B. 5]. *a* **1300** *Cursor M.* 4727 Wijt [*Gött.* wit] yee wel. *Ibid.* 20275 Has na dred, bot wijts it wele. **13..** *Bonaventura's Medit.* 254 Weteþ þat he me hated ar ȝow. *c* **1325** *Spec. Gy Warw.* 312 Wete þu wel. *c* **1350** *Will. Palerne* 68 A gladere wommon..no miȝt go on erþe..witow for soþe. *c* **1400** MAUNDEV. vi. [v.] (1919) I. 23 And wyte ȝee wel þat [etc.]. *c* **1400** *Destr. Troy* 2775 Wetys hit all wele ..þat þe dayens you derit. **1441** in *Reg. Mag. Sig. Scot.* *1450*, 69/2 Wittis me to hafe gevin [etc.]. **1450–80** tr. *Secr. Secr.* Prol. 3 Witith welle that Aristotille made..many wondres. *c* **1489** CAXTON *Sonnes of Aymon* xvii. 396 Syr, wyte that charlemagne is come wyth his oost. **1508** DUNBAR *Gold. Targe* 177 Wit ye thay did thair baner hye display.

6. *Present Participle.* *α.* 1, 4 **witende**, (1 **wittende**, **weotende**), 4 *n. dial.* **witand**, **wetand** (*Sc.* **vittand**), 4–6 *Sc.* **wittand**; 4–6 **witing**, **wyt-**, etc., 5–6 **weting**, **-yng(e**, 6– **witting**.

c **900** tr. *Bæda's Hist.* I. xxvii. (ed. Schipper) 95/1 No witende [orig. *nesciens*]. *Ibid.* IV. iii. (1890) 270 Ne weotendum [orig. *nescientibus*]. *c* **950** *Lindisf. Gosp.* John, Introd. 2 *Scienti*, uitend. *a* **1340** HAMPOLE *Psalter* x. 4 Witand his priuytes. *c* **1375** *Sc. Leg. Saints* v. (*Johannes*) 86 Wittand na wa. **1412–20** LYDG. *Chron. Troy* I. 2714 Noon . . wetyng what sche ment. **1548** UDALL *Erasm. Par. N.T.* Pref. 8 Well wetyng that [etc.]. **1867** BAILEY *Universal Hymn* 8 Witting nought.

7. *Past Participle.* α. 1–5 **witen,** (2 **wy-**, 4 **-in**), 4–5 **witten,** 5 **wytene, wetyn, -un, -en(e,** *Sc.* 5 **witting,** 5–6 **-in, witne,** 6 *Sc.* **wyttin,** 8 (?) **wit.** β. 3, 5 **west,** 4 **weste,** 4–6 **wyst,** 5 **wyste, wiste,** 4– **wist.**

α. *c* **1000** *Ags. Gosp.* Luke xii. 2 Nis nan þing . . behydd þæt ne sy witen [*Hatton Gosp.* ȝewyten]. *a* **1300** *Cursor M.* 6996 In his time war þe fabus written, þat yeit er thoru þe bokes witten [*Gött.* witin, *Trin.* witen]. *a* **1400** *Morte Arth.* 869 Hade I wytene of this. *c* **1400** *Ywaine & Gaw.* 1810 Sho lete als sho him noght had sene, Ne wetyn that he thar had bene. *c* **1425** WYNTOUN *Cron.* cxxxviii. 435 Gif þai had witting, herd, or sene. *c* **1470** HARDING *Chron.* LXXVI. v, To be written . . euer to be knowen and weten. *c* **1475** *Rauf Coilȝear* 604 And I had wittin. *c* **1560** A. SCOTT *Poems* (S.T.S.) ii. 32, I wald þat it wer wittin. **1596** DALRYMPLE tr. *Leslie's Hist. Scot.* x. (S.T.S.) II. 444 Gif the peple had witne. **17..** *Jamie Douglas* ii. in Child *Ballads* IV. 98 An I had wit what I wit now.

β. *a* **1300** *Cursor M.* 18130 Als he had wist it noght. *c* **1300** *Harrow. Hell* 33 (Digby MS.) Suþþen haui þoled and west [*Harl. MS.* wyst] Boþe chele, hounger and þurst. *a* **1320** *K. Horn.* 1484 (Harl.) Knyhtes of þe beste þat he euer hede of weste. *c* **1449** PECOCK *Repr.* I. xiii. 67 Y haue wiste suche men. ? **1482** *Cely Papers* (Camden) 131 And y had west that ȝe would a taked so sor. **1526** wyst [see HAD-I-WIST]. **1792** [see B. 7]. **1844** wist [see B. 1 d].

B. Signification.

I. Simple senses.

1. *trans.* To have cognizance or knowledge of; to be aware of; to know (as a fact or an existing thing). **a.** with simple obj.: = KNOW *v.* 8, 11 f.

971 *Blickl. Hom.* 117 Frunan maran þinges þonne ænȝes mannes ȝemet wære her on eorðan, þæt hit witan mihte. *c* **1000** *Ags. Gosp.* John iv. 10 Ȝif þu wistest godes ȝyfe, & hwæt se is þe cwið to þe, syle me drincan. *c* **1175** *Lamb. Hom.* 35 Nis nan sunne þet he [*sc.* the priest] ne con; oðer he heo wat ðurh, þet he heo dude him seolf. *a* **1200** *Moral Ode* 112 in *O.E. Hom.* I. 167 Þe ðe lest wat biseið ofte mest, þe hit al wat is stille. *c* **1200** ORMIN 11259 Þiss wast tu wel to soþe. *c* **1250** *Hymn to God* 12 in *Trin. Coll. Hom.* App. 258 Þu þe wost al ure þoucht, louerd drauȝ us neor þe. **13..** *E.E. Allit. P.* C. 129 Þe welder of wyt, þat wot alle þynges. *c* **1380** *Sir Ferumb.* 638 A bettere kniȝt wot y non. *c* **1386** CHAUCER *Prol.* 389 For aught I woot, he was of Dertemouthe. *Ibid.* 595 Wel wiste he by the droghte, and by the reyn, The yeldynge of his seed, and of his greyn. *c* **1420** *Sir Amadace* (Camden) xxix, The trauthe fulle litulle thay wote. *c* **1460** *Play Sacram.* 679 The best Counsayle that I now wott. *c* **1500** *Lancelot* 225 None wist his nome. **1530** TINDALE *Lev.* v. 17 Though he wist it not, he hath yet offended. **1568** GRAFTON *Chron.* II. 105 If ye had wist the cause of our comming. **1590** SPENSER *F.Q.* I. i. 13 The perill of this place I better wot then you. **1642** H. MORE *Song of Soul* II. liii, You are Heavens Privy-Counsellour, I understond, Which I wist not before. **1753** RICHARDSON *Grandison* III. xxxi. 347 Wot ye not the indelicacy of an early present, which you are not obliged to make? **1821** SCOTT *Kenilw.* xxix, I wot that but too well.

b. with dependent statement (sometimes anticipated by a pronoun (*it, this*) as obj., which in the pass. const. becomes the subj.): = KNOW *v.* 11 a.

Beowulf 821 Grendel . . wiste þe geornor þæt his aldres wæs ende gegongen. **971** *Blickl. Hom.* 121 Hie wiston þæt heora eþel . . sceolde . . ȝeseted weorþan mid halȝum sawlum. *c* **1000** ÆLFRIC *Gen.* xv. 8 Hu mæȝ ic witan þæt ic hyt aȝan sceal? *c* **1000** *Ags. Gosp.* Matt. xxv. 24 Ic wat þæt ðu eart heard mann. *c* **1200** *Trin. Coll. Hom.* 147 He wiste siker þat hit wurðen solde. *a* **1250** *Owl & Night.* 61 Ich wot þat þu art vnMilde Wiþ heom þat ne Muwe from þe schilde. *c* **1250** *Gen. & Ex.* 3054 Nu ic wot we haue mis-don. *c* **1300** *Havelok* 1345, I wot, he wilen þe nouth werne. *c* **1330** R. BRUNNE *Chron. Wace* (Rolls) 5151 Hit haþ ofte be wyst & sen, þat wraþe bytwyxte kynde haþ ben. **1375** BARBOUR *Bruce* I. 509, I will blythly apon me ta The state, for I wate that I have rycht. *a* **1400** *Hymns Virg.* (1867) 87 Þou woost not to-day þat þou schalt lyue to-morowe. **1426** LYDG. *De Guil. Pilgr.* 8776, I wot my sylff yt ys nat so. **1456** SIR G. HAYE *Law Arms* (S.T.S.) 22 Efter Leoun, was chosin a woman pape nocht wittand that scho was a woman. *a* **1516** MORE *Rich. III* Wks. 37/1 Whose death kyng Edwarde . . when he wist it was done, pitiously bewailed. **1530** TINDALE *Gen.* xx. 6, I wot it well that thou dydest it in purenesse of thi herte. **1591** SHAKS. *1 Hen. VI*, II. v. 16 As witting I no other comfort haue. **1724** RAMSAY *Tea-t. Misc.* (1733) I. 8, I wat on him she did na gloom. **1816** SCOTT *Old Mort.* v, Well wot I thou hast not heard the call of a true preacher. **1899** *Century Mag.* Dec. 300/2 They . . witting little that the tide has long since turned.

c. with dependent question (also *ellipt.*): = KNOW *v.* 11 b.

See also WHAT *pron.* 8 b (quots. *a* 1000, *c* 1560, 1568, 1570, 1603) and WATNA-WHAT.

Beowulf 2519 Nolde ic sweord beran, . . ȝif ic wiste hu wið ðam aȝlæcean elles meahte ȝylpe wiðgripan. *c* **950** *Lindisf. Gosp.* John viii. 14 Ic uat huona ic cuom & huidder ic ȝeonge. *c* **1175** *Lamb. Hom.* 45 Wel ic wat hwer ic sceal milcien. *a* **1225** *Ancr. R.* 96 Ne schalt tu neuer more eft witen hu me stont. *a* **1250** *Owl & Night.* 1201 Ich wot ȝef treon schule blowe; Ich wat ȝef cornes schule growe. *a* **1300** *Cursor M.* 64 Wydur to wende ne wat he noght. **1340** *Ayenb.* 9 To yelde þet he heþ of oþre manne kueadliche, yef he wot to huam. **1362** LANGL. *P. Pl.* A. Prol. 12 Þat I was in A Wildernesse, wuste I neuer where. *c* **1380** WYCLIF *Sel. Wks.* III. 452 It is reservyd to God, to wete wiche [sin] is dedly and which is venyal. *c* **1450** *St. Cuthbert* (Surtees) 6646 At Rypoun hostelere he was, I ne wate how many ȝere. **1544** *St. Papers Hen. VIII*, X. 138 Forbicause . . that two of his servauntes wer sick, he wist not wherof [etc.]. **1818** SCOTT *Rob Roy* xxvi, Whether they speak Gaelic or no I wotna. **1842** MACAULAY *Battle of Lake Regillus* xix, And none wist where he lay.

d. with obj. and compl., or acc. and inf.: = KNOW *v.* 11 c.

Beowulf 1309 Syðþan he aldorþeȝn unlyfiȝendne, þone deorestan deadne wisse. *c* **888** ÆLFRED *Boeth.* xxvii. §1 Forðæm he hine wiste swiðe unȝesceadwisne. *a* **1000** *Colloq. Ælfric* in Wr.-Wülcker 90/2 We witan þe bilewitne wesan. *c* **1205** LAY. 15060 Anan swa heo me þer witen, awæi heo wulleð wenden. **1297** R. GLOUC. (Rolls) 1905 Maxencius þo he wste him come he adde of him gret doute. **13..** *K. Horn* 1372 (Harl.) Of ioie hue ne miste, O lyue ȝef hue þe wiste. *c* **1400** *Destr. Troy* 629, I wot me vnworthy þis wirdis to ffall. *c* **1462** *Paston Lett.* II. 87 In faith, my Lorde dyd quyte hym als curageously as ever I wist man do. **1552** LYNDESAY *Monarche* 2698, I haue wyttin gud wemen passe fra hame. *c* **1560** A. SCOTT *Poems* (S.T.S.) xxii. 10 It dois ȝow ay delyt To wit me in distress. **1571** CAMPION *Hist. Irel.* vi. (1633) 15 Hee never wist the matter to bee haynous. **1614** SYLVESTER *Bethulia's Rescue* VI. 276 Judith . . Whom now the Murdress of his Lord hee wist. **1844** MRS. BROWNING *Lay of Brown Rosary* I. iv, The grey border-stone that is wist To dilate and assume a wild shape in the mist.

e. *absol.*, or in parenthetic phrases (see also 11): = KNOW *v.* 11 e. (See also HAD-I-WIST.)

I wot (occas. *I wit*), dial. *awat* (*awyte*), is often equivalent virtually to *I wis* (see WIS *v.*[2]).

c **1000** *Ags. Ps.* (Th.) lxxxi[i]. 5 Ne onȝeatan hi, ne ȝeara wistan. *a* **1300** *Cursor M.* 13607 'Hu es it sua þat he seis nu?' 'We ne wat, bot ask him-seluen hu.' *a* **1300**, **1724** [see A. 2 α]. *c* **1300** *Havelok* 2708 Þou wost ful wel, yif þu wilt wite, þat aþelwold þe dide site On knes. *c* **1320** *Sir Tristr.* 867 Þou lext, ich vnder stand And wot! *c* **1386** CHAUCER *Sompn. T.* 182 Elye, wel ye witen In mount Oreb . . He fasted longe. *c* **1400** *Beryn* 509 What dogg is þat? . . wost þou ere? *c* **1450** HOLLAND *Howlat* 429, I wryt as I wait. *c* **1475** *Rauf Coilȝear* 262 Als far as I wait, the nicht is furth gane. **1590** SPENSER *F.Q.* I. viii. 44 Them to renew, I wote, breeds no delight. **1602** WARNER *Alb. Eng.* XI. lxiii. 275 But, well I wot, Loue is a Lordly Feast. **1748** THOMSON *Cast. Indol.* I. lxxiv, He led, I wot, the softest way to death. *a* **1774** I wyt [see WIRE *sb.* 7]. **1775** [see A. 2 β]. **1830** TENNYSON *Second Song Owl*, Thy tuwhits are lull'd, I wot.

†(*b*) in subjunctive in phr. ***God*** or ***Crist wite***. Cf. MHG. *wizze Crist*, etc.

c **1175** *Lamb. Hom.* 29 Eft, wite crist, heo is ful biter to betene. *a* **1225** *Ancr. R.* 250 God hit wute & he hit wot [etc.]. *c* **1300** *Havelok* 517 God it wite, he shal ben ded.

2. *intr.* with *of*: To be aware of (as existing, or as happening or having happened); to know of (KNOW *v.* 18 b). With negative, (*a*) to have no idea of, not to suspect; (*b*) to be unaware or unconscious of.

In later use chiefly in the phr. ***that I, you*** (etc.) ***wot of***.

c **1205** LAY. 17174 Ich what a wærc mid wundere bistonde. *a* **1225** *Ancr. R.* 88 Ȝare hit is þet ich wuste herof. *c* **1385** CHAUCER *L.G.W.* 7 Non . . may of it non othere weyis wytyn But as he hath herd seyd or founde it wrytyn. *c* **1400** *Apol. Loll.* 40 He þat presumiþ and weniþ to wete verily of a þing. *c* **1460** *Emare* 579 He . . wyste of no treson. **1470–85** MALORY *Arthur* I. x. 49, I wold I had wyst of hem, they shold not haue escaped so. **1596** DALRYMPLE tr. *Leslie's Hist. Scot.* x. (S.T.S.) II. 286 Our folk . . met with thame . . be chance the ane not witting of the vther. **1607** T. ROGERS *39 Art.* Pref. (1625) ¶¶1 We not weeting, nor . . dreaming of any such matter. **1801** WORDSW. *Prioress' T.* xxvi, Those bad Jews . . That of this murder wist. **1866** ALGER *Solit. Nat.* II. 58 Inspired by a splendid hope, . . he wist not of hunger or of sneers. **1876** WHITNEY *Sights & Insights* II. iii. 363 We wit well of many things that we would never prove.

†**b.** To have experience *of*: cf. KNOW *v.* 18 a.

13.. *Cursor M.* 20508 (Gött.), I sal fare þat i sal neuer witt of care. *c* **1400** *Sowdone Bab.* 3270 Gode lete hem never wete of woo! **1423** JAS. I *Kingis Q.* xliv, A . . prisoner . . That . . wote of noght bot wo. **1426** AUDELAY *Poems* 2 His soul never schal ponyschyd be, ne never wyt of wo.

†**3.** Passing into the sense: To become aware of, gain knowledge of, get or come to know; to find out, ascertain, discover; to be informed of, learn, 'hear' (*at* or *of* a person), esp. in answer to inquiry; hence sometimes virtually equivalent to 'inquire, ask'. Cf. KNOW *v.* 8, 18 b (obs. uses). *Obs.*

Often not distinguishable from the simple sense 'know' (1 or 2), esp. with *will* or *would* (= wish, would like), or with *ere, or* (= before).

a. *trans.* with simple obj., or in passive.

c **1000** [see A. 7 α]. *a* **1225** *Leg. Kath.* 562 Ȝef ha þe ȝet wule, þen ha wat hire woh, wiðstonden aȝein us. *a* **1300** *K. Horn* 288 (Camb.) To speke wiþ Rymenhild . . & witen hure wille. **1340–70** *Alex. & Dind.* 4 To oridrace . . alixandre wendus, þere wilde contre was wist & wondurful peple. *c* **1374** CHAUCER *Troylus* I. 615 Harmes myghte folwen . . If it were wyst. **1387** TREVISA *Higden* (Rolls) IV. 427 Nero . . wolde wite . . þe nombre of Iewes þat were at Ierusalem. *c* **1400** *Destr. Troy* 13486 Þai . . Made hym wise of þe werke, þat þai wiste hade. **1450** *Paston Lett.* I. 111 They . . sent in to me to weten if thei mytȝ speken with me. **1483** CAXTON *Gold. Leg.* 197 b/1 Anone as she wyste the comyng of the holy virgyne she wente to hir. **1535** LYNDESAY *Satyre* 291 Of my name wald ȝe wit the veritie, Forsuith, thay call me Sensualitie. *c* **1560** A. SCOTT *Poems* (S.T.S.) iii. 19 Lat non knaw ȝo[r] intentis; Be verry war or that thay wit ȝo[r] myndis.

b. with dependent statement or question or obj. and compl. (as in 1 b, c).

1132 *O.E. Chron.* (Laud MS.), Þa wiste þe king ðat he feorde mid suicdom. *c* **1175** *Lamb. Hom.* 41 Ȝif hwa wule witen hwa erest bi-won reste þam wrecche saule . . ic eow segge. *c* **1205** LAY. 271 Witen he wolde þurh þa wiþer-craftes wat þing hit were. **1297** R. GLOUC. (Rolls) 1185 Þe pikes smite hom þoru out ar hii wuste wat hit were. *a* **1300** *Cursor M.* 13082 Iohn bigan at þam to wijt Quer iesus crist . . yeitt Bigan wit werckes him to kiþe. *c* **1350** *Will. Palerne* 145 Whanne þis witty werwolf wiste him so schaped. *c* **1375** *Sc. Leg. Saints* xi. (*Simon & Judas*) 366, & bad þe duk þat þai suld vyte quhat he wes þat [þat] had done. **1377** LANGL. *P. Pl.* B. VI. 213 Now wolde I witen of þe what were þe best. *c* **1430** *Chev. Assigne* 35 Whenne he wysste her with chylde. **1471** CAXTON *Recuyell* (Sommer) 136 He began to caste his eyen vpon his peple . . for to wete how they were of nombre. **1530** TINDALE *Gen.* ix. 24 As soone as Noe was awaked . . and wyst what his yongest sonne had done. **1531** *Dial. on Laws Eng.* I. xvi. 38, I wolde wytte whether the partie shal be also dischargyd in the common lawe. **1535** COVERDALE *Exod.* ii. 4 His sister stode a farre of, to wete what wolde come of him. **1616** R. C. *Times' Whistle* v. 2094 Diligent enquirie made, they wist At length what was become of him. **1690** W. WALKER *Idiomat. Anglo-Lat.* 524 He stood to wit what would be done.

c. *absol.* or *intr.* with *of*.

1297 R. GLOUC. (Rolls) 689 Alle þre he broȝte þe doȝtren bi vore him to witen of hor þoȝte. *a* **1300** *Cursor M.* 20194 Quat es ti name . . ? Gladli þar-of wijt wald i. **1375** [see A. 4 ε]. *a* **1400–50** *Wars Alex.* 509 Þis egg, or þe kyng wyst, to þe erth fallis. *c* **1400** *26 Pol. Poems* i. 49 And ȝe wole wyte, thus mowe ȝe lere. *a* **1450** *How Merch. dyd Wyfe betray* 103 in Hazl. *E.P.P.* I. 201 Yf he wylle algatys wytt, Say in my chaumbyr y lye sore syke. *c* **1520** SKELTON *Magnyf.* 22 Where wonnys Welthe, and a man wolde wyt? *Ibid.* 1654, I speke the softlyer, because he sholde not wete. **1570** *Satir. Poems Reform.* x. 279 He come hame agane or euer thay wist. **1629** MAXWELL tr. *Herodian* (1635) 52 On a sudden (ere any wist) there rusht among the people the Emperors armed Horsemen. **1795** BURNS *'O Lassie'* 2 O Lassie, are ye sleepin yet, Or are ye waukin, I wad wit?

†**4.** *trans.* To have practical knowledge of; to be conversant with or versed in: = KNOW *v.* 9. *Obs.*

a **1000** *Cædmon's Gen.* 445 He . . wiste . . spræca fela. *a* **1250** *Owl & Night.* 195 He wot insiȝt in eche songe Wo singet wel, wo singet wronge. *a* **1300** *Cursor M.* 18938 For wel þai all langage wist. *c* **1330** R. BRUNNE *Chron. Wace* (Rolls) 7166 Tak & lef as þou sest skyle, . . Bettere þan y þou wost þe dede. **1340–70** *Alex. & Dind.* 516 Swiche maner lorus, þat þou miht . . þe beste lawe kenne. Whan þou hit wisliche wost, wilne hit in herte.

b. with *to* and inf.: To know how, be able: = KNOW *v.* 12.

1340–70 *Alex. & Dind.* 99 Sin we wetin hur wil to worchen . . We mowe be soþliche isaid hur seruauntus. *c* **1440** *Generydes* 53 He wyste not them to fynde. **1576** FOXE *A. & M.* (ed. 3) I. 14/2 He either wist not, or lyste not to shew his cunnyng therin. **1594** CAREW *Huarte's Exam. Wits* v. (1596) 58 No Philosopher as yet wist to giue to euery difference of wit determinatly that which was his. **1893** F. THOMPSON *Hound of Heaven* 24 Fear wist not to evade, as Love wist to pursue.

†**5.** In imperative = 'be assured', 'you may be certain', and later in monitory formulæ and polite phrases (e.g. *ye shall wit, please it you to wit*) = 'you must know', 'let me tell you', 'allow me to inform you'. *Obs.*

a **900–1000** [see A. 5]. *c* **1205** LAY. 15090 Wite þu . . þat dead is Vortimer. *c* **1275** *Passion our Lord* 356 in *O.E. Misc.* 47 Yf Mi kyneriche were ine worlde þisse, Mine men wolde wyþstonde, wite þu myd iwisse. *a* **1300** *Cursor M.* 10185 Was neuer nan for-soth wijt yee Men of sua mikel cherite. **1362** LANGL. *P. Pl.* A. II. 60 Hit witen and witnessen þat woneþ vppon eorþe, þat I, Fauuel [etc.]. *c* **1400** *Rom. Rose* 4782 Wite thou this, If thou fle it, it shal flee thee. *c* **1400** MAUNDEV. vi. [v.] (1919) I. 26 Wyteth wel þat the rewme of Arabye is a full gret contree. **1417** HEN. V in Ellis *Orig. Lett.* Ser. III. I. 61 We grete yow wel, and wol ye wite that thambassiatours . . have been here. **1425** *Paston Lett.* I. 21 Preyeng yow to wite that I have resceyved yowr goodly lettres. *c* **1450** *Merlin* 13 Wite well that god shall helpe yow. **1456** SIR G. HAYE *Law Arms* (S.T.S.) 15 Ȝe sall witt that the sevyn angelis signifyis the sevin partis of the tyme. *c* **1470** *Gol. & Gaw.* 98 Thow sall rew in thi ruse, wit thow but wene. **1476** *Stonor Papers* (Camden) II. 2 Ples it you to wete, this same day I depart to Cales wardes. **1539** CROMWELL in Merriman *Life & Lett.* (1902) II. 196 Please it your excellente Maiestie to witte that [etc.]. **1570** *Satir. Poems Reform.* x. 57 First thow sall wit, he was sone natural To James the Fyft. **1608** SHAKS. *Per.* IV. iv. 31 Please you wit: The Epitaph is for Marina writ.

†**6.** with *to* and inf.: To be certain or confident, feel sure, expect confidently. (Cf. KNOW *v.* 10.) *Obs.*

1297 R. GLOUC. (Rolls) 2057 He was glad, uor he wuste wel to winne al is wille. *c* **1386** CHAUCER *Prol.* 224 He was an esy man to yeue penaunce Ther as he wiste to haue a good pitaunce. *c* **1400** *26 Pol. Poems* vii. 41 Ȝif he wiste to heuene to go. *c* **1440** *Jacob's Well* 177 My conscyens telde me, þat ȝif I had wyst to haue lyued, I wolde noȝt have sorwyd for my synnes.

†**7.** To experience: = KNOW *v.* 5 c. *Obs. rare.*

a **1450** *Le Morte Arth.* 8 Oure eldris . . That mykell wiste of wo and wele. *a* **1510** DOUGLAS *K. Hart* I. 86 This cumlie court . . No wandreth wait, ay wenis welth endure. **1792** A. WILSON *Watty & Meg* 138 Meg . . Sic a change had never wist.

8. To recognize; to distinguish, discern, detect: = KNOW *v.* 1, 1 b, 4. *Obs.* or *rare arch.*

a **1300** *Cursor M.* 781 O wityng bath god and ill Ȝee suld be lauerds at ȝour will. **1340–70** *Alex. & Dind.* 1002 Men han wit for to wite þe wikke & þe gode. *a* **1352** MINOT *Poems* (ed. Hall) iv. 44 In þat morning fell a myst, And when oure Ingliss men it wist, It changed all þaire chere. **1555** PHAER *Æneid.* I. (1558) B ij, Whan he his mother wist, He folowed fast and cald (alas) what mean you, thus to list In fayned shapps . . to apeare? **1842** MRS. BROWNING *Grk. Chr. Poets* (1863) 98 If by chance an Attic voice be wist.

II. Phrases.

9. †**a. do to wit,** also without *to* (DO *v.* 22 c): to cause (a person) to know, make known to, inform. Also (rarely) ***give to wit*** (GIVE *v.* 29 c). Const. as in 1 and 2. *Obs.*

c **1205** LAY. 3163 Ich do þe wel to witene, . . þat mi drihliche lond atwa ich habbe ideled. *Ibid.* 27150 Arður hafde his hauwares . . and sone duden him to witen whuder he wolde wenden. c 1250 *Gen. & Ex.* 1302 He saȝt ðe stede Ðe god him witen in herte dede. c 1330 R. Brunne *Chron. Wace* (Rolls) 14782 Seint Bede doþ vs to wyten Whilk were gode, whilke were elles. 1377 Langl. *P. Pl.* B. viii. 13, I.. preyed hem.. If þei knewe any contre.. Where þat dowel dwelleth, doth me to wytene. c 1400 Maundev. (Roxb.) iii. 8, I do ȝow to wit þat Constantinople es riȝt a faire citee. 1470–85 Malory *Arthur* vii. xxvi. 253 Ye myght haue done me to wete of his comynge. 1524 in Hakluyt *Voy.* (1599) II. 77 Wee giue you to weet, that we haue receiued your letters. 1526 Tindale *1 Cor.* xv. 2, I do you to witt [1611 I declare vnto you] after what maner I preached vnto you. 1600 Holland *Livy* xxix. xxiv, He did them to weete and understand, that hee intended.. to conduct his armada to Lilybæum. a 1604 Hanmer *Chron. Irel.* (1633) 193 We doe you wit, that such a Law and Custome is in England. 1674 [see do *v.* 22 c].

b. let wit, rarely † *let to wit* (let *v.*[1] 12, 13): to let (a person) know (a thing): (*a*) to inform (one), or to make (something) known (= a); (*b*) to allow (one) to know, or (something) to be known, to disclose, reveal; † (*c*) occas. to show, exhibit. Const. as in a. *Obs.* exc. *dial.*

c 1205 [see let *v.*[1] 13]. 1297 R. Glouc. (Rolls) 9788 þe point of is suerd.. at canterbury þe monekes lateþ wite, Vor honour of þe holi man. c 1340 Hampole *Prose Treat.* 4 He lett me wyete.. þat he ne is fundene in þe lande of softly lyfande. c 1400 *Rom. Rose* 3145 Thou art wel worthy to haue maugree To late hym of the Roser wite. c 1440 *Generydes* 4153 If ye knowe wher that I may hym fynde, Now lete me wete, I prae yow. a 1533 Ld. Berners *Gold. Bk. M. Aurel.* (1546) C, I lette the to witte, that the Rodyan people are curteis. a 1547 Surrey in *Tottel's Misc.* (Arb.) 219, I let the wete thou shalt not play with me. 1592 Kyd *Sp. Trag.* iv. iv, Solyman saluteth thee, And lets thee wit by me his highnes will. 1600 Fairfax *Tasso* v. lxxxvi, From Egypt come they all, this lets thee weete [*rime* fleete]. 1794 [see let *v.*[1] 13]. 1825 Brockett *N.C. Gloss.* s.v., 'I'll ne'er let wit', I'll not inform, or I'll keep it secret. 1890 Hall Caine *Bondman* ii. i, [He] never let wit of his intention.

10. to wit. † **a.** *it is to wit* (also *to witting*): it is to be observed, noted, or ascertained; so *it were to wit*, it needs investigation, one ought to know. *Obs.*

c 1320 *Cast. Love* 783 Of þe middel heuȝ is to wite þe swetnesse and þe feirschipe. c 1330 R. Brunne *Chron. Wace* (Rolls) 431 Hit were to witen Whi þe bataille of Troye was smiten. c 1380 Wyclif *Serm.* Sel. Wks. I. 114 It were to wite þe moral sense of þese wordis. c 1380 —— *Wks.* (1880) 328 It were to wite.. wheþer priue confession made to prestis be nedeful. 1398 Trevisa *Barth. De P.R.* iii. ii. (Tollem. MS.), Firste it is to wetynge what þinge the soule is. *Ibid.* xvii. ii. (Add. MS. 27944), It is to wytynge [*ed.* 1495 wyte] þat a graffe.. chaungeþ þe.. qualite of þe stok in to his owne.. qualite. c 1449 Pecock *Repr.* ii. xiii. 223 For the more cleering of this present answere, it is to wite that a thing is holi in three maners. 1456 Sir G. Haye *Law Arms* (S.T.S.) 246 Bot quhethir his awin legis ar behaldyn to kepe his assuraunce, in that poynt it is to wit. 1511 *Guylforde's Pilgr.* (Camden) 47 It is to wyt that the Holy Londe.. in parte.. was called y[e] kyngdome of Jude. 1628 Coke *On Litt.* 16 And it is to wit, that this word (*inheritance*) is not only intended where a man hath Lands or Tenements by discent of inheritage. [Comm.] *Et est ascauoire.* This kinde of speech is vsed.. oftentimes by our Authour.. and euer teacheth vs some rule of Law, or generall or sure leading point.

† **b.** *that is to wit* (also *to witting*) = AF. *cestasavoir* literally 'that is to know': that is to say, that is, namely: = L. *scilicet*, *videlicet* (*viz.*); occas. = *id est* (*i.e.*). *Obs.* replaced by the simple *to wit*, c (*b*).

1340 *Ayenb.* 1 Tuaye lettres of þe abece, þet is to wytene A. and b. c 1375 *Sc. Leg. Saints* i. (*Petrus*) 403 Twa substance, þat is to wyt, Of devel and man, to-gyddir knete. a 1400 *Engl. Gilds* (1870) 349 Þese ben þe olde vsages of þe Cite of Wynchestre.. þat is to wetynge, þat [etc.]. 1440 in *3rd Rep. Hist. MSS. Comm.* 360/2 Ȝeldynge there of by the ȝere to the forseyde Johan, that ys to wetynge, the furste ȝere [6*s.* 8*d.*] and every ȝere after [13*s.* 4*d.*]. 1484 Caxton *Fables of Poge* v, The whiche parte was iumelle that is to wete double. 1496 *Bk. St. Albans, Fishing* h j, Your harnays. That is to wyte your rodde: your lynes. 1526 Tindale *Matt.* xxiii. 8 For one ys youre master, that is to wytt Christ. 1562 Turner *Herbal* ii. 75 Where of we haue hearde a grete wonder, that is to wete, that that same kynde dieth & lyueth agayn. 1579–80 North *Plutarch, Theseus* (1595) 8 Vpon conditions agreed betweene them: that is to wit, that the Athenians should furnish them with a shippe.

c. *to wit*: (*a*) 'To be sure', as one may know, truly, indeed. *Obs.* or *rare arch.*

c 1400 *Song of Roland* 850 Ther fell.. A straung wedur. A gret derk myst in the myd-day-tym,.. the erthe dynnyd doillfully to wet. c 1400 *Melayne* 222 Þay.. bade hym come owte with þam to fyghte, To witt with owtten wene. c 1400 *Destr. Troy* 14002 The worthiest to wete, þat in wer deghit. 1581 A. Hall *Iliad* ix. 166 No fault so great to wit, Which at the prayer of faultie folkes the Gods do not remit. 1748 Thomson *Cast. Indol.* i. xxv, He was, to weet, a little roguish Page. 1819 Keats *On Charles Armitage Brown* i, He is to weet a melancholy carle.

(*b*) That is, namely, *scilicet.*

In former law practice used to indicate (and placed after the name of) the venue of a trial.

1577 Wolton *Cast. Christians* B viij b, That common saying.., that the beginning of vertue is of Nature, to wyt of Perfect Nature. 1579 W. Wilkinson *Confut. Fam. Love* B j, The same testimonye that ye alledge, to weete, that they had Moses and the Prophets. 1596 Spenser *F.Q.* v. x. 1 Some Clarkes doe doubt.. Whether this heauenly thing, whereof I treat, To weeten Mercie, be of Iustice part. 1608 J. King *Serm. 24 Mar.* 12 He.. reigned long, to weete, fourty years. 1621 T. Granger *Eccles.* vi. 3. 137 An abortiue child, to wit, one that is borne before his time, and dyeth in his birth. 1657 Style *Reg. Pract.* 351 Incertain words in the Count or Declaration, may be made good.. by a plea in Bar. *Hill 22 Car. B. r.* To wit, by the Defendants taking notice of the meaning of them in his plea. 1711 Steele *Spect.* No. 43 ¶ 9 Accounting for what we frequently see, to wit, that dull Fellows prove very good Men of Business. 1756 C. Lucas *Ess. Waters* I. 39 In certain degrees of heat, to wit, in thirty three of Fahrenheit's thermometer, and upwards, water is always fluid. 1765 G. Wilson *Raymond's Entries* III. 168 Allen against Harris... Kent, (to wit). 1823 *Broadsheet* (Bodl. G. A. Oxon. b. 112, lf. 80), Oxfordshire to Wit. Sentences of the Prisoners, Who were tried at the Summer Assizes at Oxford. 1832 Bingham *Rep. Comm. Pleas* VIII. 235 At Martinmas 1830, to wit, on the 23d of November 1830. 1852 *Oxford Chron.* 3 July 1/5 advt., Oxfordshire Election. Proclamation for a Special County Court. Oxfordshire to wit. 1875 Maine *Hist. Instit.* iv. 114 Thrice nine ridges.., to wit, nine of bog, nine of smooth and nine of wood.

11. God wot (also † *God it wot*; † *Godwot, God ote*, goddot): God knows. **a.** Used to emphasize the truth of a statement. *arch.* So † *wot Christ.*

a 1225 *Ancr. R.* 54 God hit wot,.. more wunder ilomp. *Ibid.* 330 Wat Crist hit is god riht þet us scheome biuoren monne. c 1300 *Havelok* 2527 For he it made, god it woth! a 1300–1859 [see god *sb.* 10 a]. c 1400 *Anturs Arth.* 547 (Ireland MS.) 'Greselle', quod Gauan, 'gone is, God ote!' 1865 [see A. 4 *a*]. 1883 Miss Broughton *Belinda* III. 83 She has good reasons enough, God wot! 1893 T. E. Brown *Old John* etc. 177 A garden is a lovesome thing, God wot!

† **b.** With dependent interrogative or *absol.*, implying that the thing spoken of is utterly unknown.

1390 Gower *Conf.* I. 3 What schal befalle hierafterward God wot. c 1400 *Beryn* 1201, I am I-weddit! ȝe, God woot beste, in what maner & howe! c 1400 Maundev. (Roxb.) xii. 53, I wate noȝt; God wate. a 1500 *Peblis to the Play* 7 God wait þai wald þai do þat stound. 1570 *Satir. Poems Reform.* xiii. 134 God wait gif ȝe be Jaips to hald in stoir. 1646 [see god *sb.* 10 b].

† **12.** *to wit* (a person) *to say*: to inform or instruct him. *Obs.*

? A misuse due to confusion with *witere*, witter *v.* (cf. the reading of later text in quot. c 1205 s.v.).

a 1400–50 *Wars Alex.* 241 Þat semely qwene Ai of Egipt erd enquirid if he were,.. scho wetis if he wald wete hire to say. c 1400 *Destr. Troy* 11467 He shuld.. spir at hom specially of hor spede fer; If þai hade wille to þe werke, wete hom to say,.. glose hit not lengur. *Ibid.* 13580 He fraynet at þe freke.., Wat whe þat he was, wete hym to say.

† **wit**, *v.*[2] *Obs.* Also 5 **wyte**, 5–6 **wyt(t**, 6 **witt(e**; 5 *pa. t.* **wytte**; 6 *pa. pple.* **witte**. [app. inferred from witword testament, bequest. Cf. *bewit(t* (1436 and 1587), by-forms of bequeathe by contamination with this.] *trans.* To bequeath. Hence † **witting** *vbl. sb.*, bequest.

1393 *Test. Ebor.* (Surtees) I. 184, I wyte and I commend my saule to all myghty God & to our lady synte Mary. 1406 *E.E. Wills* (1882) 12, Y wyt to the person of my paryssh vj s. viij d. c 1420 *Lay Folks Mass Bk.* 86 He wytte his saul to his fadyr. c 1450 *Ibid.* 71 All.. þat.. in testment wytes any gode in mayntenyng of þis kirk. 1483 *Cath. Angl.* 421/1 To Wytt gude, *legare.* 1504 *Will* in *Ripon Ch. Acts* (Surtees) 295 The residue of my gude nott witte. 1547 *Test. Ebor.* (Surtees) VI. 257, I give and wit my soule unto Almighty God.

wit, *v.*[3] [f. wit *sb.*] **a.** *intr.* with *it*: To play the wit; to make witty remarks. **b.** *trans.* as a meaningless repetition of the word just used, by way of a vague threat. **c.** *trans.* To call (a person) a wit, attribute wit to. (All nonce-uses.)

1654 Gayton *Pleas. Notes* iii. v. 92 They beginne to be wanton, and to wit it one upon another. a 1662 Heylin *Laud* (1668) 260 Others.. impute the Republishing of this Declaration to the new Archbishop,.. after he took possession of his *Graceship*, as Burton doth pretend to wit it in his Pulpit Libell. 1679 Shadwell *True Widow* ii. 30 *Sel.* .. I think they are all out of their wits... *Prig.* Prithee Stanmore be my Second, I'll wit him with a Pox to him. 1778 Mme. D'Arblay *Diary* 26 Sept., *Dr. Johnson.* 'Why, did Dr. Jebb forbid her wine?' *F. B.* 'Yes, sir.' *Dr. Johnson.* 'Well, he was in the right; he knows how apt wits are to transgress that way...' In this sort of ridiculous manner he *wits* me eternally.

wit: see whit, white, wight, wite, with.

wital(l, witaldrie: see wittol, wittoldry.

witale, obs. Sc. form of victual.

witan ('wɪtən). *Hist.* [OE., pl. of *wita* wite *sb.*[1]] The members of the national council in Anglo-Saxon times; the council itself, the witenagemot. Also *transf.*

1807 S. Turner *Hist. Anglo-Saxons* x. iv. II. 226 The treaty.. is said to have been made by the king and his witan. 1839 Keightley *Hist. Eng.* I. 36 Edward, the Elder,.. was chosen by the Witan to succeed his father, Alfred. 1874 Green *Short Hist.* i. § 1. 4 Their homesteads clustered round a moot-hill.. Here, too, the 'witan', the Wise Men of the village, met to settle questions of peace and war. 1877 Tennyson *Harold* ii. ii, *William.* Good, good, and thou wilt help me to the crown. *Harold.* Ay.. if the Witan will consent to this.

witan, variant of whitten.

witand, -ly: see witting *ppl. a.*, wittingly.

‖ **witblits** ('vɪtblɪts). *S. Afr.* Also **witblitz** and as two words. [Afrikaans, irreg. f. Du. *wit* white + G. *blitz* lightning.] Home-brewed brandy, a strong and colourless raw spirit.

1934 *Sunday Times* (Johannesburg) 8 Apr., 'Wit blits' (white lightning) was the name given to peach brandy in the Johannesburg Magistrate's Court yesterday. 1948 *Cape Times* 21 July 16/3 In cases of snakebite people on the platteland have always run for the witblitz. 1955 L. G. Green *Karoo* ix. 105 Farmers are allowed to distill small quantities of witblits for their own use. *Ibid.*, *Witblits*, of course, is home-distilled dop brandy with a high alcoholic content. 1966 *Economist* 12 Mar. 1044/3 Coloured people are drinking less [in South Africa], particularly the favoured types of plonk known affectionately as *witblitz*.. and *skokiaan.*

witch (wɪtʃ), *sb.*[1] Now only *dial.* Forms: 1 **wicca, wycca**, 3–6 **wiche**, etc. (as next). [OE. *wicca* wk. masc. (see next).] A man who practises witchcraft or magic; a magician, sorcerer, wizard. See also white witch.

c 890 *Laws of Ælfred* xxx, Ða fæmnan, þe ȝewuniað onfon ȝealdorcræftiȝan, & scinlæcan, & wiccan. c 1100 *Gloss.* in Wr.-Wülcker 183/31 *Augur* uel *ariolus*, wicca. a 1225 *Juliana* 41 Ich hit am þat spec þurh simunes muð þe wicche. c 1250 *Gen. & Ex.* 3028 Ðe wicches hidden hem for-ðan, Biforen pharaun nolden he ben. c 1375 *Sc. Leg. Saints* xxi. (*Clement*) 532 Sayand he was ane enchantore, A wech and a trigetouyre. 1377 Langl. *P. Pl.* B. xviii. 46 'Crucifige', quod a cacchepolle 'I warante hym a wicche!' c 1400 *Three Kings Cologne* 84 Þe paynyms.. cleped þes iij kyngis *Magos*, þat is to seye wicchis. 1470–85 Malory *Arthur* i. viii. 45 Som of hem lough hym [*sc.* Merlin] to scorne,.. and mo other called hym a wytche. c 1533 More *Answ. Poys. Bk.* Wks. 1063/2 The turning of Aarons rod.. into suche a serpent as deuoured vp all ye serpentes of ye Egipciane witches. 1563 Winȝet *Vincent. Lirin.* xxx. Wks. (S.T.S.) II. 63/7 Simon the weche, quha wes strukin be the Apostolis cursing. 1627 R. Bernard *Guide Grand-Jury Men* 240 The examination of that grand Witch, Lewis Gaufredy, before noble Commissioners. 1668 Rolle *Abridgment* i. 44 Home dit que I. S. Is a Witch, and I will prove him so. 1712 Swift *Jrnl. to Stella* 17 June, Am I a Laplander? am I witch?.. can I make easterly winds? 1828 Carr *Craven Gloss.*, *Witch*, this word.. is frequently used for wizard, or fortune teller. 1913 in *Expositor* (1914) Jan. 20 [Near Criccieth] there lives a long-haired, haggard old man whom the people about speak of as a 'witch'.

b. *fig.*

1832 Carlyle *Misc.*, *Boswell's Johnson* (1857) III. 51 The Editor is clearly no witch at a riddle. 1840 Haliburton *Clockm.* Ser. iii. viii, And she keeps a-sayin'—Well, he's a witch! Well, how strange!

witch (wɪtʃ), *sb.*[2] Forms: 1–2 **wicce, wycce**, 2–6 **wicche**, 3 **wichche**, 3–4 **wychche**, 3–5 **wycche**, 3–6 **wiche**, 4–5 **wyche, wech**, 4–6 **wich, wytche, wych**, 4–7 **witche**, 5–6 **weche**, (4 **wecch**, *Sc.* **wesch-, wisch-**, 4, 6 **which(e**, 5 **whitche, wheche**, 6 **wytch**, *Sc.* **vytche, vyche, weyche**), 6– **witch**. [OE. *wicce* fem., corresponding to *wicca* witch *sb.*[1], both of which are app. derivatives of *wiccian* witch *v.*[1]]

1. a. A female magician, sorceress; in later use *esp.* a woman supposed to have dealings with the devil or evil spirits and to be able by their co-operation to perform supernatural acts. See also white witch.

c 1000 Ælfric *Saints' Lives* vii. 209 Animað.. þa reðan wiccan, Seo þe ðus awent þurh wiccecræft manna mod. a 1100 *Aldhelm Gloss.* i. 1926 (Napier 52/1) *P(h)itonissam*, .i. *diuinatricem*, helhrunan, wiccan. c 1290 *St. Kath.* 279 in *S. Eng. Leg.* 100 Faste ȝe schulle þe wychche binde,.. And smitez of hire heued a-non. 1303 R. Brunne *Handl. Synne* 499 Lo here a tale of a wycche, þat leued no better þan a bycche. c 1375 *Sc. Leg. Saints* l. (*Katerine*) 1088 [He] gert þis katrine till hyme feite, & sad hir: 'þu wikide wiche, Quhat wenis þu ws lang to preche?' c 1400 *Destr. Troy* 11182 The worthy, þat wicche hase wastid to dethe. 1440 Wyrcester in *Wars Eng. in Fr.* (Rolls) II. ii. 763 Alia mulier magica, vocata vulgariter Wyche of Eye,.. capta est.., et apud Smythfeld cremata. 1471 Caxton *Recuyell* (Sommer) 243 Iuno the false wycche and sorceresse. 1500–20 Dunbar *Poems* xxxv. 35 Jonet the weido on ane bussome rydand, Off wichiss with ane windir garesoun. 1591 Shaks. *1 Hen. VI*, v. iii. 34 See how the vgly Witch doth bend her browes, As if with Circe, she would change my shape. 1656 W. Coles *Art of Simpling* 67 Leaves of Elder.. which to disappoint the Charmes of Witches, they had affixed to their Doores and Windowes. 1711 Addison *Spect.* No. 117 ¶ 10 When an old Woman begins to doat, and grow chargeable to a Parish, she is generally turned into a Witch. 1790 Burns *Tam o' Shanter* 200 The witches follow, Wi' mony an eldritch skriech and hollo. 1868 Tennyson *Lucretius* 15 She.. Dreaming some rival, sought and found a witch Who brew'd the philtre. 1901 Rhys *Celtic Folklore* iv. 294, I have heard of one old witch changing herself into a pigeon.

b. With masculine prefix.

1601 *Strange Rep. Sixe Notorious Witches* B ij, Men-Witches. 1653 Gataker *Vind. Annot. Jer.* 108 No pure Astrologer, but a meer Magitian in plain English, an He-witch.

c. *a witch of Endor* (in allusion to 1 Sam. xxviii. 7): a fanciful term for (*a*) a bewitching person; (*b*) a medium.

1819 C'tess Spencer *Let.* 15 Nov. in *Sarah, Lady Lyttleton's Corr.* (1912) viii. 217 That witch of Endor, the Duchess of Devon, has been doing mischief of another kind. 1919 R. R. Marett in *Q. Rev.* Apr. 458 In the West End a *séance* with a Witch of Endor is doubtless to be obtained for a suitable fee.

d. Phrases. *the witch is in it*: it is bewitched. *as nervous as a witch*: a New England phrase, applied to a very restless person.

a 1654 Selden *Table-talk* (Arb.) 82 When a Country-wench cannot get her Butter to come, she says, The Witch is in her Churn. 1885 Howells *Silas Lapham* xvii. 325 She rose from her struggle with the problem, and said aloud to herself, 'Well, the witch is in it'. 1911 F. M. Crawford *Uncanny Tales, Man Overboard* (1917) 132 She's been as nervous as a witch all day. 1918 Eleanor H. Porter *Oh, Money! Money!* xvii, He's nervous as a witch. He can't keep still a minute.

† **2.** *transf.* The nightmare. *Obs.*

c **1440** *Promp. Parv.* 526/2 Wytche, clepyd nyghte mare.., *epialtes.* **1585** Higins *Junius' Nomencl.* 427/1 *Incubus, ephialtes*,..a kinde of disease called the night mare or witch. [Cf. **1847** Halliwell, *Riding of the Witch*, a popular phrase for the nightmare, still in use.]

3. *fig.* **a.** *gen.*

1659 W. Brough *Sacr. Princ.* 240 Save me from vain pleasures, the great witches of the world. **1708** *Brit. Apollo* I. Quarterly Paper No. 2. 8/1 The Four of Clubs [is] call'd *Wibling's Witch*..from one James Wibling, who in the Reign of..James the First, grew Rich by..Gaming, and was commonly observ'd to have the Card..in his Hand. **1820** Shelley *Gisborne* 132 The quaint witch Memory sees, In vacant chairs, your absent images.

b. (*a*) A young woman or girl of bewitching aspect or manners.

1740 Richardson *Pamela* (1824) I. xxiv. 37 Mrs. Jervis, said he, take the little witch from me. **1800** T. D. Whitaker *Whalley* I. 184 *note*, In..1634 was acted..a play entitled *The Witches of Lancaster*... The term has since been transferred to a gentler species of fascination, which my fair countrywomen still continue to exert in full force. **1834** Lytton *Pompeii* I. ii, For my part I find every woman a witch. **1845** Mrs. S. C. Hall *Whiteboy* ix. 69, I own I have abused Miss Ellen, and good right I had—a young witch, driving the world through heaven's windows. **1888** 'J. S Winter' *Bootles' Childr.* vii, She who had been the blithest little witch he had ever known.

(*b*) ***old witch***: a contemptuous appellation for a malevolent or repulsive-looking old woman.

c **1430** Lydg. *Min. Poems* (Percy Soc.) 168 A lusti galaunt that weddithe an olde wiche. *a* **1536** *Calisto & Melib.* 825 Thow old which thou bryngyst me in grete dole. **1831** Coleridge *Table-t.* 7 July, There are only three classes into which all the women past seventy that ever I knew were to be divided:—1. That dear old soul: 2. That old woman: 3. That old witch. **1884** F. M. Crawford *Roman Singer* i, Mariuccia is an old witch.

4. Applied to various animals and objects.

a. The stormy petrel. **b.** A West Indian name for *Crotophaga ani*, a black bird of the cuckoo family. **c.** A kind of snail. **d.** In a loom: = dobby 3. **e.** ***witch of Agnesi*** (*Math.*): a plane curve named after M. G. Agnesi (1718–99) of the university of Bologna.

a. 1784 Pennant *Arctic Zool.* (1792) II. 255 Stormy Petrel...hated by the sailors, who call them Witches, imagining they forbode a storm. **1885** Swainson *Prov. Names Birds* 211 Storm-Petrel...Witch, or Water-witch.

b. 1884 Coues *N. Amer. Birds* 472 Black Witch. Savanna Blackbird.

c. 1815 Burrow *Elem. Conchol.* 204 *Helix Scarabæus*, Witch or Cockchafer.

d. 1883 *Almondbury & Huddersfield Gloss.*, *Witch*, a machine which stands on the top of a loom, and was used previously to the jacquard machine for the purpose of figuring the cloth. **1909** *Century Dict.* Suppl., *Witch*,..a dobby or index-machine.

e. 1875 B. Williamson *Integral Calculus* vii. 173 Find the area between the witch of Agnesi $xy^2 = 4a^2(2a - x)$ and its asymptote. **1901** A. B. Basset *Elem. Cubic & Quartic Curves* 96 Then the locus of P is a cubic called the witch of Agnesi.

5. *attrib.* and *Comb.* **a.** General combs.: simple attrib., as ***witch-act*** (act *sb.* 5), ***gang***, ***-legion***, ***-lore***, ***-plot***, ***-pupil***, ***-trial***; with the meaning 'used in witchcraft or by witches in their enchantments', as ***witch-broth***, ***-charming***, ***-ointment***, ***-sabbath*** (Sabbath 3), ***-salve***, ***thing***; appositive, as ***witch-bird*** (bird *sb.* 4), ***-bride***, ***carline***, ***cummer***, ***-hag***, ***-hare***, ***-huntress***, ***-maid***, ***-maiden***, ***-people***, ***-wife***, ***-wolf***, ***-woman***; objective, etc., as ***witch-advocate***, ***-burner***, ***-master***, ***-pricker*** (pricker 1), ***-searcher***, ***-seeker***, ***-trier***; ***witch-burning***, ***-roasting***; also ***witch-like*** adj. and adv.; instrumental, as ***witch-held***, ***-ridden***, ***stricken***, adjs.; similative, as ***witch-wise*** adj. **b.** Special combs.: **witch-ball**, (*a*) (see quot. 1866); (*b*) a hollow ball of (usu. coloured or silvered) glass, formerly displayed in a house as a charm against witchcraft and now for decorative purposes; **witch-bell(s**, *Sc.*, a name for the harebell, *Campanula rotundifolia*; **witch bottle**, a stone or glass bottle, filled with urine, nails, hair, etc., which was either burned or heated for the purpose of repelling or breaking a witch's power over her victim; **witch-bowl**, a decorative circular glass bowl; **witch broom**, **butter** = *witches' broom*, *butter* (see c below); **witch cake**, a preparation used to test a supposed witch, or made by a witch for the purposes of incantation; **witch-chap** *dial.* = *plough-witch* (see plough *sb.*[1] 8); **witch dance**, a ritual dance performed by witches; **witch-fire** = corposant; **witch gowan** (see gowan 2); **witch-grass** *U.S.*, (*a*) *Panicum capillare*, a weed-grass found throughout the U.S., also called *old-witch grass*; (*b*) couch-grass, *Triticum* (*Agropyrum*) *repens*; **witch-hat**, a hat with a conical crown and flat brim, represented as worn by witches; **witch-hopple** *U.S.* = hobble-bush; **witch-hunter** = witch-finder; so *witch-hunting*; **witch-lock** = witch-knot 1; also *transf.*; **witch-loom** (see 4 d above); **witch-man**, (*a*) a wizard; (*b*) *dial.* = *witch-chap*; **witch-mania**, a mania or craze for witches and witchcraft; **witch-mark**, a mark on the body, supposed by witch-finders to denote that its possessor was a witch; **witch-meal** = lycopodium 2; **witch-meeting** = *witches' meeting* (see c below); **witch-pap** (see quots.); **witch-post**, in Yorkshire, a wooden post, usually of mountain ash, marked with a cross and built into a house as a protection against witches; **witch-riding**, the nightmare; **witch-smelling**, the smelling out of witches; also *fig.*, witch-hunting; **witch stitch** (see quot.); **witch-stone**, a flat stone with a natural perforation, used as a charm against witchcraft; †**witch-water**, contemptuous name for holy water; **witch-weed** *S. Afr.*, a parasitic plant, *Striga lutea*; **witchwork**, witchcraft.

1758 M. W. Montague *Let.* 14 Nov. (1967) III. 188, I.. am convinced of the necessity of the repeal of the *Witch-act (as it is commonly called). **1777** Brand *Pop. Antiq.* App. 319 The Witch-Act..was not repealed till the Year 1736. *a* **1680** Glanvill *Sadducismus* II. (1681) 9, I have..almost spoiled all Mr. Webster's..and the other *Witch-Advocate Books. **1815** Scott *Guy M.* xi, Witch-advocates, atheists, and misbelievers of all kinds. **1866** *Treas. Bot.*, **Witch-balls*, interwoven roller-masses of the stems of herbaceous plants, often met with in the steppes of Tartary. **1916** J. H. Yoxall *Collecting Old Glass* v. 38 Witch-balls seem to have been made at Bristol,..at Nailsea..and at Wrockwardine... These balls, it is said, were hung at each door and window, 'to keep the witches out'. **1927** *Daily Express* 22 June 9/4 There is a fashion just now to collect the deep blue or silver glass balls which our forefathers hung about the house to keep witches away. 'Witch balls' they were called. **1952** L. MacNeice *Autumn Leaves* 19 The witch-ball on the stairs. **1978** E. Ellenbogen tr. *Simenon's Maigret & Toy Village* ii. 34 Its houses..its tiny carefully-tended gardens, its clay animals and glass witchballs. **1808** Jamieson, **Witch-bell*, round-leaved Bell-flower, *Campanula rotundifolia*. **1826** Hogg *Love's Jubilee* 112 The witch-bell blue. **1698** *Prestwick Kirk Sess. Rec.* (MS.), Margaret Hood accused of calling Agnes Cuthbertson a '*witch-bird'. **1893** *Jrnl. Brit. Archaeol. Assoc.* XLIX. 267 Nails were formerly placed in an earthen vessel, and buried beneath the floor, near the hearth, to keep away the witches, and to afford protection from the 'evil eye'; hence such vessels were called 'witch-jugs' or '*witch-bottles'. **1908** E. Smith in A. C. Kelway *Memorials Old Essex* 252 An old witch-bottle..found 'below the floor and very near the fireplace'..contained some water, about fourteen horse-nails, and twenty thorns! **1966** G. E. Evans *Pattern under Plough* vi. 74 Under the hearthstone was the spot most frequently chosen to bury the witch-bottle. **1980** *Rescue News* Sept. 2/3 Both pots must have been buried on purpose, perhaps as charms but the bellarmine is thought to be rather too early to be a witch-bottle. **1955** *Times* 13 May 12/5 Along with salt-cellars, ash-trays, *witch-bowls, and the curious jam dishes. **1964** G. Sims *Terrible Door* xiv. 75 What looked like a fish-bowl was a 'witch bowl' with glass fishes suspended from floating glass bubbles in stagnant water. **1817** Scott *Harold* vi. vi, There of the *witch-brides lay each skeleton. **1849** H. Mayo *Pop. Superst.* 125 The witches..by *witch-broths..would induce in themselves and in their pupils a heavy stupor. **1892** *Review of Reviews* Feb. 170/1 (*heading*) A plea for the *witch-burners. **1894** *Advance* (Chicago) 26 Apr., Do we ever hear of Episcopalians as witch burners? **1909** *Strand Mag.* XXXVIII. 692/1 They had taken to *witch-burning. **1928** G. Ade *Let.* 10 July (1973) 135 Sooner or later we should elect a Catholic to the Presidency just to prove that we are living in the 20th century instead of the 18th and that witch-burning and religious persecutions are no longer the pastimes of a free and intelligent people. **1849** H. Mayo *Pop. Superst.* 126 The so-called *witch-butter found in the fields. **1693** I. Mather *Cases Consc.* 52 Many..Magical experiments have been used to try witches by. Of this sort is that of..making a *witch-cake with that urine. **1810** R. H. Cromek *Nithsdale & Galloway Song* 282 The baking of the 'Witch Cake', with its pernicious virtues, is a curious process. **1535** *Witche Carling [see carline[1] b]. **1827** Clare *Sheph. Cal.* 156 'Keep secrets, Sim', she said, 'I need them now, The *witch-chaps come'. ? **16..** in P. H. Waddell *Old Kirk Chron.* (1893) 70 Such treatment was condemned by the Session under the head of '*witch-charming'. **1818** Scott *Br. Lamm.* xxiv, Her ain *witch cummers would soon whirl her out of her shroud. **1921** M. Murray *Witch-Cult in Western Europe* v. 132 The round dance was..essentially a *witch dance. **1971** *Country Life* 9 Sept. 633/3 The round reel survives from the prehistoric witch-dance. **1893** Kipling *Seven Seas, Merchantmen* 55 The *witch-fire climbed our channels, And flared on vane and truck. **1693** C. Mather *Wond. Invis. World* 43 Some of the *Witch Gang have been fairly Executed. **1840** Buel *Farmer's Comp.* 232 The quack, switch, or *witch grass, a variety of the fiorin, is highly nutritious, roots and all. **1855** Lowell *Lett.* (1894) I. 269 That witch-grass which is the pest of all child-gardens. **1826** Hor. Smith *Tor Hill* (1838) I. 131 During the reign of the *witch-hag all the herbs around the cave were blighted. **1884** *Folk-Lore Jrnl.* II. 258 A dog cannot catch a *witch hare. **1898** R. Blakeborough *Wit, Char. N. Riding* 160 One of the houses was suspected of being *witch-held, and every thing about the place witch-stricken. **1840** C. F. Hoffman *Greyslaer* II. 44 Tangled thickets of moss wood and *wytch-hopple gave now the springy footing the tired hunter loves. **1943** R. Peattie *Great Smokies* 283 This is the hobblebush or witch hobble [*sic*], an abundant high-mountain shrub whose large rounding leaves reach their color peak in September. **1819** Shelley *Faust* ii. 209 *Witch-legions thicken around and around. **1723** Blackmore *Alfred* xii. 101 Rebellion's *Witch-like Charms the Senses bind. **1815** Scott *Guy M.* xxiii, She was..the same witch-like figure as when we first introduced her. **1880** L. Wallace *Ben-Hur* 412 Nor was it possible to have told which was mother, which daughter; both alike seemed witch-like old. **1682** H. More *Cont. Remark. Stories* 41 This Magical matting of the Daughter's hair into a *Witch-lock. **1914** 'Amélie Rives' *World's-End* xvii, Wild witch-locks of ravelled cloud. **1898** Posselt *Rec. Impr. Textile Mach.* i. 44 Box-motion for *Witch Looms. **1891** Atkinson *Moorland Parish* (ed. 2) 87 The copious *witch-lore of the district. **1855** Kingsley *Heroes, Argon.* iv, This is your doing, false *witch-maid! *Ibid.*, Medeia the *witch-maiden. **1851** T. Sternberg *Dial. & Folk-Lore Northampt.*, **Witch-men*, guisers who go about on Plough-Monday. **1882** in *Folk-Lore Jrnl.* (1883) I. 91 A farmer, having a horse taken ill, sent for a well-known witchman. **1855** Smedley *Occult Sci.* 169 Scotland was sunk into barbarism and ignorance... Never did the *witch-mania enter a nation better suited for its reception. **1677** J. Webster *Displ. Witchcraft* v. 82 Now if all these [*sc.* warts, etc.] were *Witch-marks, then few would go free. **1903** F. W. H. Myers *Hum. Pers.* I. 164 Patches of anæsthesia found upon hysterical subjects—the 'witch-marks' of our ancestors. **1910** Kipling *Rewards & Fairies* 96 'What's a *Witch-master?'.. 'A master of witches, of course.' **1931** V. Randolph in B. A. Botkin *Folk-Say* 86 My pappy follered gunsmithin' mostly, but he was a witch-master too. **1792** *Phil. Trans.* LXXXII. 66 *Semen lycopodii*, commonly called *witch-meal. **1693** C. Mather *Wond. Invis. World* 82 She confessed, that the Devil carry'd them on a pole, to a *Witch-meeting. **1853** Dickens *Bleak Ho.* xi, The iron gate, on which the poisoned air deposits its *witch-ointment slimy to the touch! **1871** Tylor *Prim. Cult.* II. xviii. 379 The mediæval witch-ointments which brought visionary beings into the presence of the patient. **1664** in Hale *Coll. Mod. Relat.* i. (1693) 58, I have, I confess, a *Witch-pap, which is Sucked by the Unclean Spirit. **1886** *Cheshire Gloss.*, *Witch-pap*, a mole which hangs or projects from the skin. **1895** Kipling *2nd Jungle Bk.* 163 Spirits, goblins, and *witch-people. **1693** C. Mather *Invis. World, Enchantments Encountered* 7 Which may perhaps prove no small part of the *Witch-Plot in the issue. *a* **1944** J. Ford *Some Reminiscences of Danby Parish* (1953) 96 It was the custom of the Priest to cut the Roman X on the upright oak post which went up to the low ceiling... They came to be called '*Witch Posts'. **1957** E. E. Evans *Irish Folk Ways* v. 64 In north Yorkshire the jamb post, called the witch post, is occasionally found to be covered with designs intended to protect the hearth from evil spirits. **1971** K. Thomas *Religion & Decline Magic* xvii. 543 Other preservatives included 'witch-posts' built into the structure of the house. **1899** Crockett *Black Douglas* vii. 50 Malise MacKim, a *witch pricker!.. Will he go..peering into ladies' eyes for sorceries? **1621** *witch-ridden [see incubus 2]. **1795** W. Hutton *Hist. Derby* 226 That weak and witch-ridden monarch, James the First. **1821** Lamb *Elia* Ser. i. *Witches & other night-fears*, I durst not..enter the chamber.. without my face turned..aversely from the bed where my witch-ridden pillow was. **1704** *Athenian Oracle* (ed. 2) I. 292 Q. Whether there's any such thing as a Hag, which the Common People fancy to be *Witch-riding, when they are in their Bed in the Night time? **1922** Joyce *Ulysses* 202 A Scotch philosophaster with a turn for *witchroasting. **1841** W. Spalding *Italy* III. 253 In the South, the *witchsabbaths are believed to be held around the Sacred Walnut-tree of Benevento. **1860** R. A. Vaughan *Mystics* II. 256 They fare like Lucius..to whom Fotis has given the wrong *witch-salve. **1646** Gaule *Cases Consc.* 5–6 This suspition, though it bee but late,..yet is it enough to send for the *Witch-searchers, or *witch-seekers. **1937** H. G. Wells *Star Begotten* vii. 130 Some sort of world-wide *witch-smelling for Martians everywhere... You could tell them because *instinctively* you dislike them. **1940** 'G. Orwell' *Inside Whale* 157 Frenzied witch-smellings after 'Bolshevism'. **1953** J. S. Huxley *Evolution in Action* vi. 141 The witch-smelling ordeals of Africa. **1882** Caulfeild & Saward *Dict. Needlework*, **Witch stitch*, the name given to Herringbone when used in Fancy Embroidery. **1855** G. Borrow *Jrnl.* 23 Aug. in *Exped. to Isle of Man* (1915) 8 What could those *witch-stones be? **1870** 'Ouida' *Puck* vi, The old soul have a bit of belief like in witch-stones, and allus sets one aside her spinnin' jenny. **1852** Mrs. Stowe *Uncle Tom's C.* xxxv, 'It's a *witch thing, mas'r!' 'A what?' 'Something that niggers gets from witches'. **1830** Pitcairn *Crim. Trials* (1833) III. ii. 603 *note*, This symbolical mode of taking the ..produce of land, &c., is frequently alluded to in *Witch-Trials. **1649** Whitelocke *Mem.* 13 Dec. (1853) III. 128 That the *witch-trier taking a pin, and thrusting it into the skin in many parts of their bodies, they were insensible of it. **1659** Baxter *Key Cath.* xxix. 186 The Priest exorcised him ..washing him with Holy water, *Witch water. **1904** *Times* 25 July 12/3 Complaints..were constantly being received.. of damage done..to the mealie..crop by..rooi-bloom or *witch weed. **1804** R. Anderson *Cumbld. Ball.* 79 The *witch weyfe begg'd in our backseyde. **1867** Morris *Jason* v. 139 As poisonous herbs..Are pounded by some witch-wife on the shore Of Pontus. **1781** C. Johnston *Hist. J. Juniper* II. 139 The Nabob..had as constitutional an aversion to cold iron, as *witch-wise Solomon. **1609** Healey *Discov. New World* iii. iv. 155 Here shall you haue your *Witch-wolues in aboundance. *a* **1765** '*Northumbld. betrayd by Dowglas*' xxvi. in Child *Ballads* (1889) III. 412/2 My mother, shee was a *witch woman. **1897** *Edin. Rev.* Oct. 394 Lapland witch-women. **1859** H. Kingsley *G. Hamlyn* xiii, I suppose you keep him [*sc.* a black tom-cat] for some of your *witchwork.

c. Combs. with *witch's*, *witches'*: **witch's bells**, the foxglove (cf. *witch-bell* in b above); **witches' besom**, **broom**, a bushy tuft developed on the branches of trees by a fungus (see quots.); **witches' bridle**, an iron collar and gag formerly used as an instrument of torture in Scottish witch-trials; **witches' butter**, a popular name for certain gelatinous algæ and fungi, esp. *Tremella Nostoc*; **witches' coral**, **witch's cradle** (see quots.); **witch's elm** = wych elm; **witch's horse**, **witches' horses** (see quots.); **witches' knot** = witch-knot 2; **witch's mark** = *witch-mark* (see b); **witches' meat** = *witches' butter*; **witches' meeting** = *witches' Sabbath*; **witches' night** (see quot.); **witches' prayer** (see quot. 1711); **witches' Sabbath** = Sabbath 3; **witches' thimble**, a local name for various plants with tubular flowers; **witch's tit**: in fanciful proverbial phr. (*as*) ***cold as a witch's tit***, extremely cold.

1884 R. Folkard *Plant Lore* 345 The witches are popularly supposed to have..decorated their fingers with its [*sc.* the foxglove's] largest bells, thence called '*Witches' Bells'. **1866** *Treas. Bot.*, **Witches' besoms*, this name is given to the tufted bunches of branches,..developed on the Silver Fir in consequence of the attack of *Peridermium elatinum*.

1887 W. PHILLIPS *Brit. Discomycetes* 401 *Exoascus deformans* . . Sadebeck says that this species produces the 'witches' besoms' on [species of] *Prunus*. **1829** PITCAIRN *Crim. Trials* (1833) I. II. 50 Iron collars, or '*Witches bridles', are still preserved in various parts of Scotland. **1881** ELEANOR A. ORMEROD *Man. Inj. Insects* 179 'Witch Knots' or '*Witches' Brooms' are caused by this Gall-mite. **1882** VINES tr. *Sachs' Bot.* 332 The formation of 'witches-brooms' in Firs by the growth of *Æcidium elatinum*. **1836** BERKELEY *Fungi* 218 *Exidia glandulosa*. (*Witches' Butter.) **1861** H. MACMILLAN *Footn. Page Nat.* 288 The wrinkled, quaking, gelatinous mass of the witches' butter. **1842** DICKENS *Amer. Notes* xiv, Where poisonous fungus . . sprouts like *witches' coral, from the crevices in the cabin wall and floor. **1880** *Antrim & Down Gloss.*, **Witch's cradle*, a Lias fossil, *Gryphea incurva*. **1821** SCOTT *Kenilw.* ix, I have sewn a sprig of *witch's elm in the neck of un's doublet. **1865** KINGSLEY *Herew.* xx, The silence was broken by a long wild cry from the forest. . . It was the howl of a wolf. 'Hark to the *witch's horse!' **1894** *Harper's Mag.* Feb. 456 [The walking stick insect] which the country people near Salem, Massachusetts . . call '*witches' horses'. **1825** JAMIESON, **Witches knots*, a sort of matted bunches, resembling the nests of birds, frequently seen on stunted thorns or birches. **1627** R. BERNARD *Guide Grand-Jury Men* 218 The Witch thus in league . . with the Deuill, is conuicted . . 1. By a *Witches marke. . . This is insensible, and being pricked will not bleede. **1867** *Chamb. Encycl.* IX. 531/2 *Tremella* . . Several species are found in Britain. In some places, they receive such popular names as *Witches' Meat and Witches' Butter. *a* **1676** HALE *Coll. Mod. Relat.* (1693) I. 29 This Love of hers had . . carried her at Nights to the *Witches Meetings in great Castles. **1767** HUTCHINSON *Hist. Mass.* (1795) II. 38. **1686–7** AUBREY *Rem. Gentilism* (1881) 133 'Tis Midsommer-night or Midsommer-eve (St. Jo. Baptist) is counted or called the *Witches night. **1663** BUTLER *Hud.* I. iii. 344 He that gets her by heart must say her The back-way, like a *Witches Prayer. **1711** ADDISON *Spect.* No. 61 ⁋5 To which I must . . add a little Epigram called the Witches Prayer, that fell into Verse when it was read either backward or forward, excepting only that it Cursed one way and Blessed the other. **1864** G. A. LAWRENCE *Maurice Dering* II. 218 My good wishes of late have been fearfully like witches' prayers. *a* **1676** HALE *Coll. Mod. Relat.* (1693) I. 29 The *Witches Sabbaths or Assemblies, which were held in the Night. **1853** DICKENS *Bleak Ho.* viii, Such . . as was never dreamed of in the wildest visions of a Witch's Sabbath. **1820** *Edin. Mag.* Apr. 344/1 The mother . . pulled some *witches thimbles, or foxglove. **1853** G. JOHNSTON *Bot. E. Borders* 40 *S[ilene] maritima*, . . Witches'-Thimbles. **1866** SOWERBY *Eng. Bot.* VI. 13 *Campanula rotundifolia*. . . Hare-bell. . . A common rustic name for them is 'witches' thimbles'. **1886** BRITTEN & HOLLAND *Plant-n.*, Witches' Thimble . . 4 *Centaurea Cyanus*. **1932** VAN WYCK MASON *Spider House* xviii. 210 It's cold as a *witch's tit outside. **1974** *Times* 17 Aug. 7/3 It was cold as a witch's tit, so I sat there and shivered. **1980** R. L. DUNCAN *Brimstone* viii. 200 Just listening to a weather report. . . Albuquerque's clear but cold as a witch's tit.

d. *attrib.* passing into *adj.* Magic, magical.

c **1400** *Apol. Loll.* 93 þei þat . . tenden to wiche falsnes [L. *magicis falsitatibus*] in hailes or tempestis. **1535** COVERDALE *Judges* ix. 37 One bonde of men commeth by the waye to ye witch Oke. **1801** SCOTT *Glenfinlas* lvi, And, bending o'er his harp, he flung His wildest witch-notes on the wind.

witch, wych (wɪtʃ), *sb.*[3] Forms: 1 **wice, wic, wyc,** 5–7 **wyche,** 6–8 **wich,** (6 **wi(t)che, wiech, wech(e, weach,** 7 **weech),** 6– **wych, witch.** [OE. *wice* and *wic*; app. f. Teut. *wik-* to bend (see WIKE, WEEK *sb.*, WEAK *a.*).] Applied generally or vaguely to various trees having pliant branches: *esp.* †**a.** the WYCH ELM, *Ulmus montana* (of which bows were made); **b.** (now *dial.*) the mountain ash, *Pyrus aucuparia*. Also *attrib.*; **witch alder**, a witch hazel with alder-like leaves, *Fothergilla alnifolia*, native to Virginia and North Carolina. (See also WITCH HAZEL.)

c **725** *Corpus Gloss.* (Hessels) C 106 *Cariscus*, cuicbeam, uuice. *a* **1000** *Ags. Voc.* in Wr.-Wülcker 200/20 *Cariscus*, . . wic, *uel* cwicbeam. *c* **1000** *Sax. Leechd.* II. 86 Ȝenim cwicbeam rinde . . wir, wice, ac, [etc.]. *c* **1440** *Promp. Parv.* 526/1 Wyche, tre, *ulmus*. **1534** *Star Chamber Cases* (Selden Soc.) II. 308 Mulso . . wrongfully fellid xxvij trees of asche and wyche. **1537** *St. Papers Hen. VIII*, II. 483 That 3 or 4000 wyche bowes . . be brought hyther. **1548** TURNER *Names Herbes* (1881) 81 Vlmus is called . . in englishe an Elme tree, or a Wich tree. **1556** WITHALS *Dict.* (1562) 23/2 A witche tree, *opulus*. **1579** SPENSER *Sheph. Cal.* June 20 Nor holybush, nor brere, nor winding witche. **1613** [STANDISH] *New Direct. Planting* 11 As of Elme, so of Wyche, being a wood as apt to grow speedily as any other wood. **1616** T. SCOT *Philomythie* II. B 4 b, The cursed Eldar and the fatall Yewe, With Witch, and Nightshade in their shadowes grew. **1845–50** MRS. LINCOLN *Lect. Bot.* App. 103 *Fothergilla alnifolia* (witch-alder). **1861** D. H. HAIGH *Conq. Brit.* 78 The mountain-ash, rown, or witch. **1868** ATKINSON *Cleveland Gloss.*, *Witch-wood*, the mountain ash or rowan-tree. **1869** *Lonsdale Gloss.*, *Witch-wand*, a twig of the mountain ash, once used to find minerals.

witch (wɪtʃ), *sb.*[4] *local.* Also **whitch.** [prob. a use of WITCH *sb.*[2], the name being given on account of the uncanny appearance of the fish; cf. uses of L. *sāga*, F. *sorcière*, It. *strega*.] The flatfish *Pleuronectes cynoglossus*, resembling the lemon sole; applied also to similar fishes.

1879 SATCHELL *Provis. Index Fish Names* 9 *Pleuronectes microcephalus* . . Lemon-Dab, Lemon-Sole, . . Witch. *Hippoglossoides limandoides*, . . Long-Fleuk, . . Witch. **1882** *Academy* 14 Oct. 280 Whitches.—These fish, well known in Grimsby and Manchester, . . The term is used . . to denote . . the craig-fluke (*Pleuronectes cynoglossus*, Lin.), a kind of dab, which is taken in considerable numbers in the North Sea . . These fish are sometimes called white soles. **1903** *Times* 21 Feb. 17/3 Plaice, witches, smelts, and herrings.

witch (wɪtʃ), *v.*[1] Forms: 1 **wiccian,** 4 **wicc(h)e,** (4 **witche,** *Sc.* **weche,** 4–5 **wiche, wyche,** 5 **wyc(c)hyn, wysshyn),** 5–6 **wytche,** 6– **witch.** [OE. *wiccian*, corresp. to MG., LG. *wikken*, *wicken*, of obscure origin. In the senses arising in ME. and later prob. aphetic from *bewitch*.]

†**1.** *intr.* To practise witchcraft; to use sorcery or enchantment. *Obs.*

c **1000** *Pœnit. Ecgbert* xviii. in Thorpe *Laws* (1840) II. 208 Ȝif hwa wicciȝe ymbe æniȝes mannes lufe. *a* **1300** *E.E. Psalter* lvii[i]. 5 A neddre def . . þat noght sal here þe steuen of wicchand. *c* **1350** *Will. Palerne* 2539 Were þei boþe here, þei schuld wicche wel ȝif þei a-wei went. **1623** T. SCOTT *Projector* 30 Hath not Iesabell painted, and whored, and plotted, and witched, and waded through blood?

2. *trans.* To affect (a person) with witchcraft or sorcery; to put a spell upon; = BEWITCH 1.

13.. *Evang. Nicod.* 216 in Herrig's *Archiv* LIII. 395 Wyched þi wyf has he. *c* **1350** *Will. Palerne* 4427 Þat neuer man vpon mold miȝt it [*sc.* the ring] him on haue, ne schuld he with wicchecraft be wicched neuer-more. *c* **1375** *Sc. Leg. Saints* iii. (*Andreas*) 64 Þane þat ȝong manis kyne in hy Sad, he was wechyt, sekyrly! *c* **1400** *Rowland & Otuel* 1151 Foully there thou wichede was. **1525** LD. BERNERS *Froiss.* II. ccxx. [ccxvi.] 282 b/1 They . . sayd, that the duchesse Ualentyne of Orlyaunce, doughter to the duke of Myllayn, hadde witched the kynge. **1596** in *Spalding Club Misc.* I. 87 His wyiff was witchit be his narrest nychtbour. **1605** *London Prodigal* I. ii. 63, I thinke I am sure crossed, or witcht with an owle. **1647** J. MARCH *Actions for Slaunder* 15 Thou art a Witch . . and diddest procure Mother Bale to witch the Cattell of J. S. **1883** *Folk-Lore Jrnl.* I. 354 A servant . . told me when her mother was confined a man in the village 'witched her', so that she could not move in bed. **1884** TENNYSON *Becket* III. ii, Our woodland Circe that hath witch'd the King. **1884** MARK TWAIN *Huck. Finn* xxxiv, He said the witches was pestering him . . and he didn't believe he was ever witched so long, before, in his life.

b. (with prep. or adv.) To bring, draw, put, or change by witchcraft.

1597 JAS. VI *Dæmonol.* II. i. 28 If Witches had such power of Witching of folkes to death (as they say they haue). **1608** CHAPMAN *Byron's Trag.* IV. i. O 2, O that in mine eyes Were all the Sorcerous poyson of my woes, That I might witch ye headlong from your height. **1693** I. MATHER *Cases Consc.* 26 See if you can Witch them into a Fit, . . and . . Witch them well again. **1855** MEREDITH *Shav. Shagpat* (1909) 223 He's witched there for an ill purpose. **1871** TYLOR *Prim. Cult.* I. iv. 103 Hindus settled in Chota-Nagpur . . believe that the Mundas . . can witch away the lives of man and beast. **1892** NORTHALL *Eng. Folk-Rhymes* 59 People say that the remarkable stones at Rollwright . . are a regiment of soldiers witched into stones.

3. *fig.* To influence as by witchcraft; to enchant, charm; = BEWITCH 2. Also with prep. or adv.

1590 SPENSER *F.Q.* II. vii. 10 Thy . . pleasing charmes, With which weake men thou witchest, to attend. **1592** GREENE *Groat's W. Wit* (1617) 10 [Loue] Witching chast eares with trothless tongs of men. **1596** SHAKS. *1 Hen. IV*, IV. i. 110 As if an Angell dropt downe from the Clouds, To . . witch the World with Noble Horsemanship. **1611** BEAUM. & FL. *King & No K.* 111, With her eyes She witches people. **1812** CARY *Dante, Purg.* XIV. 112 The ladies and the knights, the toils and ease, That witch'd us into love and courtesy. **1824** CAMPBELL *Theodric* 30 Her fingers witch'd the chords they passed along. **1876** GEO. ELIOT *Dan. Der.* I. iv, Her witching the world with her grace on horseback.

b. *intr.* To use enchanting wiles; to practise fascination.

1580 LYLY *Euphues* (Arb.) 407 Applied to those that witch with the eyes, not to those that wooe with their eyes. **1824** BYRON *Juan* XVI. xcv, Adeline was . . watching, witching, condescending.

witch (wɪtʃ), *v.*[2] *U.S.* [f. WITCH *sb.*[3]] *intr.* and *trans.* To dowse for water with a divining rod. Hence **'witcher**, a dowser.

1963 G. THOMSON *Crocus Country* xi. 74 The term to 'witch for water' is said to come from the fact that it was usually done with a witch-hazel wand. *Ibid.*, The witcher would walk up and down in the general area where a well was needed, with the ends of a forked hazel twig held firmly in his hands. **1970** J. BLACKBURN *Land of Promise* ii. 32 The witcher came to a place where the stem of the willow could no longer be held upright. **1978** *Country Life* 7 Dec. 1953/3 He got a well-digger to survey the site. . . The first driller and others consulted all 'witched' the situation.

witchaff, obs. Sc. f. VOUCHSAFE.

1596 J. MELVILL *Autob. & Diary* (Wodrow Soc.) 367 The doctrine quhilk God . . sall witchaff to grant.

witchcraft ('wɪtʃkrɑːft, -æ-). Forms: see WITCH *sb.*[2] [OE. *wiccecræft*, f. *wicca*, *wicce* WITCH *sb.*[1] and [2] + *cræft* CRAFT *sb.*]

1. The practices of a witch or witches; the exercise of supernatural power supposed to be possessed by persons in league with the devil or evil spirits.

c **1000** [see WITCH *sb.*[2] 1]. *a* **1100** *Aldhelm Gloss.* I. 4055 (Napier 107/2) *Necromantia*, .i. *demonum inuocatio*, ȝaldre, wiccecræfte. *a* **1250** *Owl & Night.* 1301 Þu yelpest of selliche wisdome; þu nustest hwenne hit þe come Bute hit of wicchecrafte were. *a* **1300** *Cursor M.* 28310, I . . folud wichecrafte and frete, And charmyng. *c* **1350** *Will. Palerne* 4044 His wif with wichecraft to a wolf him schaped. *c* **1375** *Sc. Leg. Saints* xxi. (*Clement*) 705 He . . wend [þat] he begabbit had bene Be wesch-crafte. *c* **1449** PECOCK *Repr.* V. xv. 563 Whiche sacramentis and her vsis summe of the lay peple holden to be pointis of wicche craft and blindingis. **1533** GAU *Richt Vay* (S.T.S.) 12 Thay sine aganis this [first] command quhilk wsis wich craft. **1651** HOBBES *Leviath.* I. ii. 7 As for Witches, I think not that their witchcraft is any reall power. **1671** SALMON *Syn. Med.* I. xxv. 51 The Sickness is more than natural, and Witchcraft is to be feared. **1711** ADDISON *Spect.* No. 117 ⁋2, I cannot forbear thinking that there is such an Intercourse and Commerce with Evil Spirits, as that which we express by the Name of Witchcraft. **1769** BLACKSTONE *Comm.* IV. iv. 60 To deny the possibility, nay, actual existence, of witchcraft and sorcery, is . . to contradict the revealed word of God. *a* **1862** BUCKLE *Misc. Wks.* (1872) I. 425 There are few superstitions which have been so universal as a belief in witchcraft.

b. *pl.* Acts or instances of this; magic arts; also †occas. with *a*, a kind of magic.

c **935** *Laws of Athelstan* I. vi, We cwædon be þam wiccecræftum & be liblacum [etc.]. *c* **1200** ORMIN 7077 Driȝmenn, weppmenn & wifmenn ec, þatt follȝhenn wicche crafftess. *a* **1225** *Ancr. R.* 268 Hit bringeð to nout alle þes deofles wieles, . . his wrenchfule wicchecreftes. **1398** TREVISA *Barth. De P.R.* XVIII. lx. (Bodl. MS.), Wicches also vse þe herte and þee lyuoure of þis beeste in many wicchecraftes. *c* **1400** *Apol. Loll.* 93 Wit þer wichecraftis and enchauntingis. *a* **1500** *Hist. K. Boccus & Sydracke* (? 1510) D iv b, Us thou hast now forsakyn And to a wychcrafte the takyn. **1569** in *10th Rep. Hist. MSS. Comm.* App. I. 43 Scho will confess no wytchcreftis nor gilt. **1617** MORYSON *Itin.* III. 45 All these witchcrafts ceased after the comming of Christ. **1670** R. T. *Opinion of Witchcraft Vind.* 43 Killing of Men or Beasts by Witchcrafts. **1767** T. HUTCHINSON *Hist. Mass.* II. i. 49 Commissioners . . were appointed for the trial of witchcrafts.

2. *fig.* Power or influence like that of a magician; bewitching or fascinating attraction or charm.

1599 SHAKS. *Hen. V*, V. ii. 301 You haue Witch-craft in your Lippes, Kate. **1613** —— *Hen. VIII*, III. ii. 18 He hath a Witchcraft Ouer the King in's Tongue. **1647** COWLEY *Mistr.*, *Vain Love* 1 What new-found Witchcraft was in thee, With thine own Cold to kindle Me? *a* **1674** CLARENDON *Hist. Reb.* x. §126 Whether the raising this spirit [of the Levellers] was a piece of Cromwell's ordinary witchcraft, in order to some of his designs, or whether [etc.]. **1747** RICHARDSON *Clarissa* I. viii. 47, I tell you, I see thro' your *witchcrafts*—that was her strange word. **1818** SHELLEY *Rosal. & Helen* 652 The subtle witchcraft of his tongue Unlocked the hearts of those who keep Gold. **1844** KINGLAKE *Eothen* iii, By some unfailing witchcraft she [*sc.* the sea] entices the breezes to follow her.

3. *attrib.* and *Comb.*

1654 WHITLOCK *Zootomia* 265 His Blindnesse and Infidelity betrayeth him to this Stupidity, and Witchcraft-adhæsion to the Creature. **1796** G. M. WOODWARD *Eccentric Excurs.* 135 Among the most approved witchcraft remedies, we find nailing horse-shoes at the thresholds of doors. **1797** *Encycl. Brit.* (ed. 3) XVIII. 877/1 The latest witchcraft frenzy was in New England, about 1692. **1897** MARY KINGSLEY *W. Africa* 452 Human sacrifice is very rare in Congo Français, the killing of people being nine times in ten a witchcraft palaver.

Hence †**witchcraftical** *a.* (*nonce-wd.*).

1676 *Doctrine of Devils* 84 Away with witchcraftical Doctors, away with the doctrine of Devils.

'witch-ˌdoctor. 1. a. One who professes to cure disease and to counteract witchcraft by magic arts.

1718 F. HUTCHINSON *Witchcraft* viii. 110 The said Dorothy Durent, having been with a Witch-Doctor, acknowledges . . that [etc.]. **1901** *Lancet* 19 Oct. 1085/2 He was considered to be a 'witch doctor' and . . farmers and females went to him to have the 'evil eye' removed.

b. A magician among African tribes, whose business it is to detect witches, and to counteract the effects of magic. (Cf. *medicine-man*.)

1836 R. M. MARTIN *Hist. S. Africa* I. iv. 168 So infatuated [are the Kaffirs] in a belief of the infallibility of the wizard or witch doctor. **1897** MARY KINGSLEY *W. Africa* 445 One witch doctor may have . . particular influence over one class of spirit and another over another class.

2. *Mil. slang.* A psychiatrist.

1966 *Listener* 29 Dec. 960/3, I did not again rub shoulders with . . the fraternity until I entered the army . . , where they were known . . as 'trick-cyclists', 'head-shrinkers', or 'witch-doctors'. **1979** D. ANTHONY *Long Hard Cure* vi. 58 That sounds like one of your witch doctors at the Retreat.

Hence **witch-doctoring** *vbl. sb.*, **-doctory** (also *fig.*); **'witch-ˌdoctress.**

1892 RIDER HAGGARD *Nada* vii, The most famous witch-doctress . . a woman whose scent was as keen as a dog's. **1924** KIPLING *Debits & Credits* (1926) 182 All the cars I met were 'protected' [with a label] as mine was—till I reached . . the limit of the witch-doctoring. **1927** G. B. SHAW in *Sunday Express* 7 Aug. 7/7 The dismal survivals of augury and witch-doctoring. **1944** J. S. HUXLEY *On Living in Revolution* iv. 45 As irreconcilable as is . . witch-doctoring with preventive medicine, or number-mysticism with higher mathematics. **1962** *Observer* 13 May 6/5 'Organisation and management' was for a long time regarded—as one Treasury man put it—as 'third-rate witchdoctory'. **1972** H. A. WILLIAMS *True Resurrection* ii. 22 And this was called scientific medicine as opposed to all forms of witch-doctory. **1977** P. JOHNSON *Enemies of Society* xv. 197 Those who practise psychiatric medicine are in the position of early-nineteenth-century doctors, trying to get round as yet unsolved difficulties by witch-doctoring.

†**'witchdom.** *Obs. rare.* [OE. *wiccedóm*: see WITCH *sb.*[1] and [2] and -DOM.] Witchcraft.

a **1050** in Assmann *Ags. Hom.* 143 Ne on wiȝlunge ne on wiccedome. *c* **1425** *Seven Sages* (MS. Cantab. Ff. ii. 38. lf. 146 b) So they lad hym wyth trecherye Wyth wychdome & wyth sorcerye.

witched (wɪtʃt, *poet.* 'wɪtʃɪd), *ppl. a.* [f. WITCH *v.*[1] + -ED[1].] Influenced by witchcraft; that is under a magic spell; also, possessed of magic power; full of witchery.

1591 *Troub. Raigne K. John* (1611) 66 False dreamer, perish with thy witched newes. *a* **1618** SYLVESTER *Simile* xviii. Wks. (Grosart) II. 254 Wee (wretched, witched

Elves). **1633** MARMION *Antiquary* II. (1641) E 2, That never such a witched passion [as love] should arise in any human brest again. **1886** JEROME *Idle Thoughts* 88 They hear the weird, witched music, and must follow.

Hence †'**witchedly** *adv.*, with witchcraft.

1650 A. B. *Mutatus Polemo* 34 We have not a people so witchedly besotted.

witch elm: see WYCH ELM.

witchen ('wɪtʃən). Now *dial.* Also 7 **whitchen**. [f. WITCH *sb.*[3] + -EN[4].]

1. In full ***witchen elm***; = WYCH ELM. Also *attrib.*

1594 PLAT *Jewell-ho.* II. 53 Another tree, that somewhat resembleth our Witchen Elmes. **1615** MARKHAM *Country Contentm.* I. viii. 108 The best bowe is either Spanish or English yewe, and the worst of Witchen or Elme. **1621** —— *Hungers Prevention* 39 A very good stiffe young growne Plant of Hazell, Elme, or Witchen. **1820** CLARE *Rural Life* (ed. 3) 53 And the witchen-branches nigh, O'er my snug box towering high. **1821** —— *Vill. Minstrel* II. 121 The rooks, where yonder witchens spread, Quawk clamorous to the spring's approach.

2. The mountain ash, *Pyrus aucuparia*. Cf. QUICKEN *sb.*[1] (*whicken*), WHITTEN.

1664 EVELYN *Sylvia* xiv. 31 The Quick-beam [Ornus] or (as others term it) the Whitchen [**1676** Witchen]. **1676** M. COOK *Forest-Trees* xxii. 75 The Quickbeam, Whitchen, or Wild-ash,..is pretty plentifull in some parts of the North. **1861** MISS PRATT *Flower. Pl.* II. 262 *Pyrus aucuparia* (Mountain Ash)..This tree has also the old names of Quicken-tree..and Witchen-tree.

'**witchering**. *nonce-wd.* [Formed on WITCHERY with -ING[1].] A deed of witchcraft.

1818 SCOTT *Hrt. Midl.* xl, Hast no done mischief enow already, wi' thy murders and thy witcherings?

witchert, var. WICHERT.

witchery ('wɪtʃərɪ). [f. WITCH *sb.*[2] or *v.*[1] + -ERY.]

1. The use or practice of witchcraft.

1546 BALE *Engl. Votaries* I. 35 b, Besydes the art Magyck, Sortilege..Geomancye, and witcherye, that was taught there also. **1584** R. SCOT *Discov. Witchcr.* III. x. 57 She sawe not anie one carrieng a faggot to the fier, but she would saie it was to make a fier to burne hir for witcherie. **1637** B. JONSON *Sad Shepherd* II. vi, *Cla.* What devil's pater noster mumbles she? *Alk.* Stay, you will heare more of her witcherie. **1727** DE FOE *Syst. Magic* I. i. (1840) 32 There is a manifest difference between magic, which is wisdom and supernatural knowledge, and the witchery and conjuring by which we now understand the word. **1810** SOUTHEY *Kehama* IV. iii, While young and old assembled round, Listened, as if by witchery bound. **1854** MILMAN *Lat. Christ.* II. 328 No one answering the citation to accuse the Empress of adultery or witchery.

attrib. **1627** R. BERNARD *Guide Grand-Jury Men* 19 The parents..sent for a wise woman, who played her witchery trickes. **1650** A. B. *Mutatus Polemo* 12 Like the blacke Prince of the ayre in his witchery Apparitions. **1906** *Daily Chron.* 28 Aug. 6/2 Prisoner burnt some candles over the fire,..and used some witchery words.

b. *pl.* Deeds of witchcraft.

1591 PERCIVALL *Sp. Dict., Hechizos*, witcheries, witchcraft. **1613** PURCHAS *Pilgrimage* VII. vii. 575 The Heathens in those parts are giuen to Auguries and Witcheries. **1634** MILTON *Comus* 523 Great Comus, Deep skill'd in all his mothers witcheries. **1781** COWPER *Expost.* 494 As dark as witch'ries of the night. **1819** SCOTT *Ivanhoe* xxxvii, Rebecca, daughter of Isaac of York—a woman infamous for sortileges and for witcheries. **1874** H. H. COLE *Catal. Ind. Art S. Kens. Mus.* App. 306 Spells, enchantments, and witcheries are supposed to be incessantly at work.

2. *fig.* Charming or fascinating power or influence.

1582 G. HARVEY *Marginalia* (1913) 191 Ye sweet bayte, & lure of curtesy: The cunningist and most intellectual witchery of all other. *a* **1677** BARROW *Serm. Ps. cxix. 60* Wks. 1686 III. 194 If we can disengage our selves from the witcheries of present allurement. **1798** WORDSW. *P. Bell* I. 265 He never felt The witchery of the soft blue sky! **1834** A. CUNNINGHAM *Burns' Wks.* I. Life 355 The witchery of his conversation, and the magic of his songs, were too powerful for the resolution of some. **1844** KINGLAKE *Eothen* v, A beautiful Greek woman..soothing him with the witchery of her guitar.

b. *jocular.* A body of bewitching women.

1777 T. TWINING in *Recreat. & Stud.* (1882) 54 Remember me to Mrs. B. and the whole witchery.

witchet ('wɪtʃɪt). *local.* [? repr. a variant *wichet of AF. *wiket* WICKET.] A wide 'head' or working-place in a coal mine; = WICKET 5 b.

1677 *Phil. Trans.* XII. 895 A Witchet or Cave was driven out in the middle of it upon a level for gaining of room to work. **1883** GRESLEY *Gloss. Coal-mining, Wichet* (N[orth] W[ales]), a working place in the shape of a wide heading or board, sometimes 60 or 70 feet in width.

witchetty ('wɪtʃɪtɪ). *Austral.* Also (*rare*) **wichetty, widgety**. [Native name.] In full ***witchetty grub***. A large white grub (the larva of certain moths and other insects) which infests the roots and stem of the ***witchetty bush*** (= MULGA 1 a), from which it is extracted for use as food by Aboriginals and as bait by fishermen.

1891 STIRLING in *Trans. Roy. Soc. South Australia* XIV. 158. **1894** R. LYDEKKER *Marsupialia* 191 The Marsupial Mole..was fed on the 'witchetty'. **1899** *Contemp. Rev.* Mar. 407 In the witchetty grub totem this sacred painting tallies with..a stone kist at Tillicoutry. **1935** H. H. FINLAYSON *Red Centre* iii. 30 The broad-leafed mulga or witchetty bush, the roots of which harbour a grub beloved by the blacks. **1944** F. CLUNE *Red Heart* 37 The sun gleamed on a motor-bike beneath a clump of witchetty bushes. **1954** B. MILES *Stars my Blanket* viii. 50 The widgetty grub tree at the roots of which the natives dig for the grubs which are like fat white slugs. **1960** *Times* 5 July 11/7 'Witchetty' bushes, a kind of wattle with bright yellow blossom. **1961** P. WHITE *Riders in Chariot* xi. 373 You look to me..like you was made out of old wichetty grubs. **1962** *Oxf. Univ. Gaz.* 19 Mar. 849/1 It is a pointed, oval, red-ochre-coloured, wooden bullroarer with designs of witchetty-grubs. **1968** M. PYKE *Food & Society* iv. 42 Witchetty grubs are famous as an article of diet eaten by aborigines. **1977** C. MCCULLOUGH *Thorn Birds* viii. 178 There were witchetty grubs, fat and white and loathsome.

'**witch-ˌfinder**. One formerly employed to search for and obtain evidence against witches.

1646 GAULE *Cases Consc.* 6 To save the trouble and Charges of the witch-finder, they will undertake to try the Witch of themselves. **1647** M. HOPKINS (*title*) The Discovery of Witches..now published by Matthew Hopkins, Witchfinder. For the Benefit of the whole Kingdome. **1797** *Encycl. Brit.* (ed. 3) XVIII. 876/1 Want of tears was, by the witch-finders,..considered as a very substantial proof of guilt. **1855** SMEDLEY *Occult Sciences* 169 Dr. Harsnett..exposed the pretensions of the celebrated exorcist and witch-finder, Darrel.

b. An African witch-doctor.

1892 RIDER HAGGARD *Nada* ii, I saw that the witch-finders and the medicine-men were feared in the land.

So '**witch-ˌfinding**.

1646 GAULE *Cases Consc.* 63 Oft times he marries them.. by the Book of Common Prayer (as a pretender to witch-finding lately told me).

witch hazel, wych hazel. [WITCH *sb.*[3]]

1. = WITCH *sb.*[3] a. Also, the hornbeam.

1541–2 *Act 33 Hen. VIII* c. 9 §3 That everie bowyer..for every bowe that he maketh of Ewe, make fower other bowes ..of Elme, wyche hasill, ashe, or other Wood. **1580** HOLLYBAND *Treas. Fr. Tong, Obier*,..a Wych hasell, as some thinke. **1588** HARRIOT *Brief Rep. Virginia* D 4 b, Maple, and also Wich-hazle, wherof the inhabitants vse to make their bowes. **1597** GERARDE *Herbal* III. cix. 1296 Called..Hornbeame, Hardbeame, Yoke Elme, and in some places Witch hasell. **1633** T. JOHNSON *Gerarde's Herbal* III. cxvi. 1481 *Vlmus folio latissimo scabro.* Witch Hasell, or the broadest leaued Elme... This hath little affinitie with *Carpinus*, which in Essex is called Witch Hasell. *c* **1767** G. WHITE *Selborne, To Pennant* ii, In the court of Norton farmhouse..stood within these twenty years a broad-leaved elm, or wych hazel. **1830** STRUTT *Sylva Brit.* 66 The Wych Elm, or Wych Hazel, as it is sometimes called. **1855** BAILEY *Mystic* 85 Wych-hazel, for divining treasures used.

attrib. **1886** A. WINCHELL *Geol. Talks* 137 Some men.. even resorted to the witch-hazel fork in quest of knowledge on which capital might venture investment.

2. A North American shrub, *Hamamelis virginica*; also, an extract of the leaves and bark of this shrub, used as an astringent remedy.

1760 J. LEE *Introd. Bot.* App. 332 Witch Hazel, *Hamamelis.* **1778** J. CARVER *Trav. N. Amer.* xix. 508 The Witch Hazle... It has been said, that it is possessed of the power of attracting gold or silver, and that twigs of it are made use of to discover where the veins of these metals lie hid. **1824** LONGF. *Autumn* 26 The purple finch..pecks by the witch-hazel. **1908** R. W. CHAMBERS *Firing Line* viii, 'Sentiment? Yes,' she said; 'but oh! it's the kind that offers witch-hazel and hot-water bottles to the best beloved!'

'**witch-hunt**, *sb.* Also **witch hunt, witchhunt**. [WITCH *sb.*[2]] 1. A search for witches, or for someone suspected or accused of witchcraft.

1885 R. HAGGARD *K. Solomon's Mines* x. 151 To-night ye will see. It is the great witch-hunt, and many will be smelt out as wizards and slain. **1927** J. BUCHAN *Witch Wood* xvi. 272 David had..seen a witch hunt..as a boy—and then there had been a furious and noisy crowd. **1960** D. HUDSON *Forgotten King* 17 Elizabethan inns and beards and witch hunts give place to the coffee house and the Restoration theatre. **1975** A. FRASER *Whistler's Lane* 9 Her mind had been..on the witch hunts of the early seventeenth century.

fig. **1915** 'I. HAY' *First Hundred Thousand* xiii. 178 Platoon commanders were bidden to hold a witch hunt, and smell out a chiropodist.

2. a. A single-minded and uncompromising campaign against a group of people with unacceptable views or behaviour, *spec.* communists; *esp.* one regarded as unfair or malicious persecution.

1938 'G. ORWELL' *Homage to Catalonia* xi. 241 Rank-and-file Communists everywhere are led away on a senseless witch-hunt after 'Trotskyists'. **1947** *Partisan Rev.* XIV. 344, I don't like Stalin's methods, but I shall never, never join in that witch-hunt. **1950** *Here & Now* (N.Z.) Dec. 8/1 Inside the Labour Party there was a witch-hunt of unbelievable viciousness against the Government's critics. **1958** *Times Lit. Suppl.* 21 Nov. 669/4 The story of a security officer in America in the days when McCarthy witch-hunts were frequent and when communists lurked..under every bed. **1972** *Guardian* 31 Aug. 6/7 Delegates to the annual Conference at the TUC at Brighton next week are urged.. not to indulge in a witch hunt..when discussing the 34 affiliated unions which have remained on the register of trade unions. **1976** *Survey* Spring 179 Literary zealots.. then took part in the anti-zionist and anti-revisionist witch-hunt. **1977** *Gay News* 24 Mar. 3/1 During the operation —labelled a 'witch-hunt' by the local gay community—28 men were arrested. **1977** *Times* 28 Apr. 2/1 Mr Orme, Minister for Social Security,..said he was not prepared to countenance a witch-hunt against claimants. **1979** A. PRICE *Tomorrow's Ghost* vii. 120 We must be absolutely fair... This isn't a witch-hunt. **1983** P. USTINOV *My Russia* i. 8 It is fashionable today to conduct a moderate witchhunt for that pro-Soviet bunch of Cambridge undergraduates..who spied for Russia.

b. A campaign *against* an individual.

1960 *Daily Tel.* 29 Jan. 1/2 The Opposition Front Bench do not intend to conduct a 'witch-hunt' against Mr Marples over his business connections. **1973** C. BONINGTON *Next Horizon* i. 20 The argument had developed into a witch-hunt against Barrie with, I suspect, very little justice. **1977** *Daily Mirror* 30 Mar. 31/1 After the Germans had strolled home 5-1, the controversial Neale accused non-playing captain Peter Simpson of leading a 'witch-hunt' against him.

'**witch-ˌhunter**. 1. = WITCH-FINDER a.

1867 HARLAND & WILKINSON *Lancs. Folk-Lore* I. 184 Dr. John Webster (who detected Robinson, the Lancashire witch-hunter).

2. One who takes part in or publicly advocates a witch-hunt (sense 2).

1935 *New Republic* 19 June 158 (*heading*) Witch-hunters at work. **1940** H. L. ICKES *Diary* 22 Feb. (1954) III. 139 Probably the witch-hunters are largely responsible for this. No one likes to be called a Communist and yet that is what every liberal has to submit to. **1960** *Encounter* Mar. 78/2 It is..necessary to that public to learn that its witch-hunters are corrupt. **1980** J. O'FAOLAIN *No Country for Young Men* xvi. 347 Obsessed as a pair of witch-hunters, minds zipping along their single track, they challenged him.

'**witch-ˌhunting**, *vbl. sb.* 1. The activity of seeking out witches and obtaining evidence against them.

1640 B. JONSON *Sad Shepherd* II. vii, in *Workes* II. 149 You speake, Alken, as if you knew the sport of Witch-hunting, Or starting of a Hag. **1885** RIDER HAGGARD *King Solomon's Mines* xv. 249 Ignosi..reaffirmed the promises.. that witch-hunting should cease. **1935** B. RUSSELL *Relig. & Sci.* iv. 99 In New England, a fierce outbreak of witch-hunting occurred at the end of the seventeenth century. **1950** AUDEN *Enchafèd Flood* (1951) ii. 51 The actual horrors of persecution, witch-hunting, and provincial superstition from which they were trying to deliver mankind. **1981** M. WARNER *Joan of Arc* v. 114 Double-think is..endemic to the business of witch-hunting, for..the witch-hunter is the alleged witch's most committed believer.

2. Participation in or advocacy of a witch-hunt (sense 2).

1932 J. F. CARTER *What we are about to Receive* xviii. 204 Once the election is over..we shall quietly lay aside our witch hunting. **1943** G. GREENE *Ministry of Fear* II. i. 125 You can't avoid witch-hunting in war-time. **1968** *Daily Tel.* 16 Nov. 16/3 We have been treated to a plethora of half-truths, innuendo, witch-hunting and ignorance. **1977** *Socialist Press* 2 Mar. 5/5 Despite this combination of administrative hysteria, right wing witch hunting and Stalinist betrayal, the fees issue is still alive at Essex.

Also as *ppl. a.* Hence (as a back-formation) '**witch-hunt** *v.*, (*a*) *trans.*, to subject to a witch-hunt (sense 2); (*b*) *intr.*, to take part in a witch-hunt.

1889 W. H. D. ADAMS *Witch, Warlock & Magician* II. v. 402 Our witch-hunting King offers an explanation of a peculiarity which..our readers have already noted. **1946** *Sun* (Baltimore) 19 July 20/1 The War Department hasn't gone off half-cocked to 'witch hunt, red bait or to bust' unions. **1948** 'J. TEY' *Franchise Affair* v. 49 Give those Midland morons a good excuse and they'll witch-hunt with the best. **1960** *Twentieth Century* Apr. 380 Assorted political personages (including a witch-hunting Senator). **1960** *News Chron.* 29 June 6/7 That uncouth, witch-hunting and paederastic gowk [*sc.* James I]. **1975** *Listener* 4 Dec. 754/2 David Niven..has severe words for it [*sc.* Hollywood]..for letting itself be..libelled and witch-hunted by..gossip columnists. **1980** *Jrnl. R. Soc. Arts* Mar. 180/1 There is.. a tendency to witch-hunt when any disaster happens. **1983** W. MCILVANNEY *Papers of Tony Veitch* x. 59 'When did you join the vigilantes, Jack?' 'Never. I'm not witch-hunting whoever did it.'

witching ('wɪtʃɪŋ), *vbl. sb.* [OE. *wiccung*, vbl. n. of *wiccian* WITCH *v.*[1]: see -ING[1].]

1. The use or practice of witchcraft.

c **1000** *Confess. Ecgberti* xxix. in Thorpe *Laws* (1840) II. 154 Ȝif hwylc wif wiccunga bega. *c* **1200** *Trin. Coll. Hom.* 213 Wicching & swikedom stale & leoð & lesiug & refloc, & alle þe luðere lastes þe man hafeð þurch deules lore. *c* **1290** *St. Lucy* 126 in *S. Eng. Leg.* 104 þou art strong wichche,.. Mine clerkes and mine enchauntours, bi-nime schullen þi wichchingue. **1382** WYCLIF *Acts* viii. 11 Moche tyme he hadde maad hem mad,..with his wicchingis [1388 witche craftis]. **1578** LYTE *Dodoens* I. lxxxi. 121 All the enchantments or witchings of Circe. **1584** R. SCOT *Discov. Witchcr.* I. iii. 8 Bodin himselfe confesseth, that not aboue two in a hundred of their witchings or wishings take effect. **1603** HARSNET *Pop. Impost.* 137 Geoffry Chaucer,..spying that all these brainlesse imaginations, of witchings, possessings, house-hanting, and the rest, were the forgeries ..of craftie priests. **1896** GRATIANA CHANTER *Witch of Withyford* viii. 86 Why be the folks always telling of witches and witching? **1914** J. MACKAY *Ch. in Highl.* IV. 152 Witching and charming were severely punished [in 17th c.].

2. *fig.* Enchantment, fascination.

1827–44 N. P. WILLIS *Contempl.* 26 Life had been like the witching of a dream. **1882** 'F. ANSTEY' *Vice Versa* iii, He felt far from hungry, and was conscious that his palate would require the adroitest witching.

witching ('wɪtʃɪŋ), *ppl. a.* [f. as prec. + -ING[2].]

1. That casts a spell; enchanting, bewitching.

In quot. 1387 *wycchen* is of uncertain origin.

1387 TREVISA *Higden* (Rolls) II. 187 In Affrica beeþ meyneys þat haueþ wycchen [*v.r.* wicching] tonges [*linguas fascinantes*]. ? *c* **1600** *Distr. Emperor* II. i. in Bullen *Old Pl.* (1884) III. 185 Nor her wytchinge eie..Can challendge any share in my disgrace. **1633** P. FLETCHER *Pisc. Ecl.* v. 5 Her witching eye the boy, and boat hath charm'd. **1747** W. DUNKIN in Francis tr. *Hor., Ep.* II. ii. 317 Witching Imps of Hell.

2. *transf.* Of or belonging to witchcraft; concerned with the practice of witchcraft or sorcery.

1584 R. Scot *Discov. Witchcr.* v. vii. 104 But they haue lesse reason that build vpon..the supernaturall frame of transubstantiation; as almost all our witching writers doo. *Ibid.* xii. vii. 228 They burst the snakes with witching words. **1713** Rowe *Jane Shore* iv. i, Those damnable Contrivers, Who shall with Potions, Charms, and witching Drugs, Practise against our Person and our Life.

b. *spec.* Of time: Belonging or appropriate to the deeds of witches and witchcraft, and hence to supposed supernatural occurrences.

In later use echoing Shaks.

1602 Shaks. *Ham.* iii. ii. 406 'Tis now the verie witching time of night, When Churchyards yawne, and Hell it selfe breaths out Contagion to this world. **1742** Blair *Grave* 55 Such Tales their Chear, at Wake or Gossiping, When it draws near to Witching Time of Night. **1835** Lytton *Rienzi* i. xii, It was now the witching hour consecrated to ghost and spirit. **1849** —— *K. Arthur* vi. lxvii, Just as the witching night begins to fall.

3. *fig.* 'Bewitching', fascinating.

?*a* **1600** in *Lyly's Wks.* (1902) III. 497 Witching Tobacco, I will fly to thee. **1607** Dekker *Whore of Babylon* G 2, On my modest cheekes, No witching smiles doe dwell. **1787** Burns *'A Prayer, in Prospect of Death'* 11 List'ning to their witching voice Has often led me wrong. **1812** Byron *Ch. Har.* i. lvii, Yet are Spain's maids..form'd for all the witching arts of love. **1890** *Spectator* 7 June 799/2 The spell of the witching land and its people grows on us.

b. *advb.* Bewitchingly.

1821 Clare *Vill. Minstrel* I. 144 She only answer'd with a look, But it was 'witching sweet.

Hence **'witchingly** *adv.*, bewitchingly.

1748 Thomson *Cast. Indol.* i. vi, The soft delights, that witchingly Instil a wanton sweetness through the breast. *a* **1868** Lowell *Nomades* viii, So witchingly her finger-tips To Wisdom..She kisses. **1878** *Tinsley's Mag.* XXIII. 518 She was about twenty-four, with a witchingly sweet face.

witchit, var. wichert.

witch knot.

1. a. A tangled knot of hair supposed to be made by witches: = elf-lock.

1598 Drayton *Heroic. Ep., El. Cobham* 112 O that I were a Witch..! I would..knit whole ropes of witchknots in her hayre. **17..** *Willie's Lady* xxxiv. in Child *Ballads* I. 87 Oh wha has loosed the nine witch knots That was amo that ladie's locks?

b. A knot tied for the purpose of making or averting a spell.

1884 A. Lang in M. Hunt *Grimm's Household Tales* I. p. xlvi, All over the world savages..tie 'witch-knots'. **1947** A. Runeberg tr. E. H. Meyer in *Witches & Demons in West-European Folk Belief* vii. 95 Witches..twist twigs into witchknots, and leave the fairy rings in the grass after their dances. **1957** E. E. Evans *Irish Folk Ways* xxi. 304 The cow-doctor uses sympathetic magic..by drawing apart over the animal's back the loose ends of a string tied in a complicated witch-knot or 'bat',..which comes undone when pulled.

2. A bushy tuft of twigs on a tree: = *witches' besom* (see witch *sb.*[2] 5 c).

1806 J. Grahame *Birds Scot.* 51 The simple boy.. Mistakes the witch-knots for the cushat's nest. **1880** F. P. Pascoe *Zool. Classif.* (ed. 2) 96 The 'witch-knot' found on the birch, and resembling a great mass of twigs like a bird's nest, is an abnormal growth..caused by *Phytopti*.

witchmonger ('wɪtʃ,mʌŋgə(r)). [f. witch *sb.*[2] + monger *sb.*[1]] One who has dealings with witches, or who believes in witchcraft.

1584 R. Scot (*title*) The discouerie of witchcraft, Wherein the lewde dealing of witches and witchmongers is notablie detected. **1677** J. Webster *Displ. Witchcraft* i. 17 To attribute these stupendious effects (as the Vulgar and Witchmongers use to do) unto the Devil. **1868** Lowell *Among my Bks., Witchcraft* (1870) 110 The witchmongers were put to strange shifts by way of accounting for it. **1903** *Sat. Rev.* 24 Jan. 110/2 Mr. Podmore..traces its pedigree through Rosicrucians, witchmongers,..and Swedenborg.

witchy ('wɪtʃɪ), *a.* [f. witch *sb.*[2] + -y[1].] Having the nature of or resembling a witch; characteristic or suggestive of a witch.

1666 *Third Advice to a Painter* 18 When he with Earthy Hounds, and Horn of Air, Pursues in Fountebleau the witchy Hare. **1903** *Contemp. Rev.* Sept. 331 Thiers..looked not a man, but a witchy old woman in man's clothes. **1968** S. Plath in *Atlantic Monthly* Sept. 54/2 Over the trees at the far side of the Common the..torch flare flattens and recovers under some witchy invisible push. **1975** M. Drabble *Realms of Gold* iii. 241 It [*sc.* a figurine] had a witchy, androgynous, yet friendly look. **1976** *Listener* 4 Nov. 590/2 The witchy black of the Grimm forests.

†**wite**, *sb.*[1] *Obs.* Forms: 1 **wita, wiota, weota, wuta,** 3 **weote, wite,** 4 **wete;** 8 *pl.* (*Hist.*) **wites.** [OE. *wita* wk. masc. (also *ȝewita* witness) = OFris. *wita*, OS. *gi-wito* (MLG. *wete*) witness, OHG. *wizo* (*giwizo* witness), Goth. *-wita* (in *fullawita*, *unwita*):—OTeut. **witon-*: see wit *v.*[1]]

1. A wise man, sage; a councillor; *spec.* one of the witan, q.v.

c **900** tr. *Bæda's Hist.* v. xix. (1890) 454 To freondscipe.. Bonefatius archidiacones, se wæs eac swylce wita & ȝeþeahtere þæs apostolican papan. *c* **950** *Lindisf. Gosp.* Luke vii. 30 *Legis periti*, æs wuto. *c* **1000** Ælfric *Saints' Lives* xiii. 131 Ne bið se na wita þe unwisliche leofað. *c* **1200** Ormin 8762 All bilammp þatt widdwe þa swa summ þe wite seȝȝde. *c* **1315** Shoreham i. 631 Wet hys mystyke ne mey non wete Be no þynge a-founde.

1701 *Cowel's Interpr., Wites, Witen*, the Title among our Saxon Ancestors for their chief Lords or Thanes, their wise and their noble Men. **1762** Hume *Hist. Eng., Jul. C. to Hen. VII*, I. App. i. 144 Besides the prelates and aldermen, there is also mention of the wites or wise men.

2. A witness.

c **900** tr. *Bæda's Hist.* Pref., Nalæs mid anes mannes ȝeþeahte ac mid ȝesæȝene unrim ȝeleaffulra witena. *c* **950** *Lindisf. Gosp.* Matt. xxvi. 60 Lycce witnesa *vel* wutu. *c* **1225** *Ancr. R.* 204 Beon waite [*v.r.* weote] & witnesse þerof.

wite, wyte (waɪt), *sb.*[2] *Obs.* exc. *Hist.* and *dial.* Forms: 1- **wite;** also 3, 5 **wijt,** 4-6 **witte,** 4, 6-7 **wyt,** 3-4, 6, 8 **wit** (4 **wyȝte, witt, wijtte,** 5 **wijte, wytte,** 5-6 **wyght,** 6 **wyit, wycht, wight, quhyt,** 7 **weit, wayt, waite,** 7-8 **white**), 4- **wyte.** [OE. *wíte* = OFris. *wîte*, OS. *wîti* (MLG. *wîte*, Du. *wijte*), OHG. *wîzi* (MHG. *wîze*), ON. *víti*: see wite *v.*[1]]

†**1. a.** Punishment; penalty; pain inflicted in punishment or torture, *esp.* the torments of hell. (Cf. OE. *helle-wíte*, etc.) *Obs.*

c **825** *Vesp. Psalter* xxxviii. 11 Awend from me witu ðin. *c* **888** Ælfred *Boeth.* xxxvii. §3 Ne þearf nænne wisne mon tweoȝan þæt ða yflan næbben eac ecu edlean hiora yfles; þæt bið ece wite. *a* **1000** *Cædmon's Gen.* 2542 þa ic sendan ȝefræȝn..sweartne liȝ werum to wite, weallende fyr. *a* **1175** *Cott. Hom.* 219 þa wile ȝearcode se almihti sceappende him and his iferen helle wite. *c* **1200** Ormin 3295 Swa þatt he ȝæn þe Kaserrking ne felle nohht i wite. *a* **1225** *Ancr. R.* 202 þe Vox of ȝiscunge haueð þeos hweolpes: Tricherie & Gile, þeofðe, Reflac, Wite, & Herrure strencðe. *a* **1300** *Cursor M.* 6714 þis beists lauerd þan sal bi quit Of alkin oncall, and oþer wijt. *Ibid.* 15802 He þat smitand es wit suerd, O suerd sal ha þe wite.

b. In Anglo-Saxon law, a fine imposed for certain offences or privileges; often as second element in compounds, as bloodwite, *ferdwite* (see ferd *sb.*[1] 4), *fyhtwite* (see fight *sb.* 7), lairwite. Now *Hist.*

c **890** *Laws Ælfred* ix, Sie þæt wite lx scill. *c* **1205** Lay. 5118 þat al comen to Lundene uppe wite of feowerti punden. **1387** Trevisa *Higden* (Rolls) II. 95 Fightynge wyte, amersement for fightynge. ?**1473** *Stonor Papers* (Camden) I. 130 That they schol noȝt pay no ale wytys to me.

1614 Selden *Titles Hon.* 262. **1628** Coke *On Litt.* 127. **1872** E. W. Robertson *Hist. Ess.* ii. vi. 64 The lesser wite or ordinary fine of the Hundred-Court. **1897** Maitland *Domesday Bk. & Beyond* 102 In any case their lord is to have their wites.

2. Blame, reproach; blameworthiness, fault. Now *Sc.* and *north. dial.*

Phr. *to have the wite, to put the wite in, to put* (a person) *in wite, to give* (one) *the wite* (*of*), *to lay the wite on.*

a **1225** *Ancr. R.* 4 Cleane schir in wit, wiðute wite of sunne. *c* **1250** *Gen. & Ex.* 2035 Ðe wite is hise, ðe right is hire. *a* **1300** *Cursor M.* 5667 He said til him þat bare þe wite, 'How dare þou sua þi broþer smite!' *c* **1386** Chaucer *Can. Yeom. Prol. & T.* 400 And but I do, lat me han the wite. —— *Wife's Prol.* 806 That I haue doon it is thy self to wyte. *c* **1400** *Melayne* 555 þe wyte is all in the. *c* **1403** Lydg. *Temple of Glas* 166 Some also þat putten ful grete wite On double louers. *c* **1440** *Generydes* 869 What cause haue ye to putte me in this witte? *c* **1449** Pecock *Repr.* iii. xvi. 386 Sithen hise successouris ben not ȝit founde in wijte or defaute. *Ibid.* 515 This gouernaunce deserueth not bi hir wijt to be kut away. *c* **1450** Holland *Howlat* 68, I se be my schadowe my schape has the wyte. **1470-85** Malory *Arthur* ii. x. 88 Kynge Pellinore bare the wytte of the deth of kynge Lott. **1528** More *Dyaloge Heresyes* iv. xii. (1529) 116 b, Our mother Eue layd the wyght of her synne to the serpent. **1550** *Reg. Privy Council Scot.* I. 104 The witte salbe imputt to him as accordis. *a* **1578** Lindesay (Pitscottie) *Chron. Scot.* (S.T.S.) II. 157 They gif ȝow the haill quhyt..that they ar persewit be the quene. **1583** *Leg. Bp. St. Androis* 1063 George Gipsones Iskie bae Had all the wyte he womit sae. **1596** Spenser *F.Q.* vi. iii. 16 Sith his own thought he knew most cleare from wite. **1600** Holland *Livy* viii. xxxiv. 306 The posteritie hereafter should lay the waite and blame..in the Tribunes. **1637-50** Row *Hist. Kirk* (Wodrow Soc.) 409 The Bishop,..crying to the people, That he had no wyt of the matter. **1674** Ray *N.C. Words* 53 You lean all the white off your self. **1722** Ramsay *Twa Cut-purses* 34 Ye canna lay the Wyte on me. **1787** Grose *Prov. Gloss.* s.v. *White*, You lean all the white off yourself. **1818** Scott *Hrt. Midl.* xxxii, This is a' your wyte, Miss Jeanie Deans. **1823** Galt *R. Gilhaize* xli, About seven months after he left the town twa misfortunate creatures gave him the wyte of their bairns. **1886** Stevenson *Kidnapped* xix, But now it's done, Alan; and who's to bear the wyte of it?

†**b.** The source or origin of blame; the person or thing that is to blame. *Sc. Obs.*

1513 Douglas *Æneid* i. Prol. 366 Quhilk in sum part is the caus and the wite, Quhy that of Virgillis vers the ornate bewtie Intill our toung may nocht obseruit be. **1560** Rolland *Seven Sages* (Bann. Club) 75, I am the wite now of hir deid doutles. *c* **1560** A. Scott *Poems* (1902) 94 ȝour twa fair ene is wycht of all my wo. **1725** Ramsay *Gentle Sheph.* iv. i, She abusing first, was a' the wyte Of what has happen'd.

†**3.** *transf.* Offence, trespass; wrong. *Obs.*

c **1175** *Lamb. Hom.* 15 Ne do he þe neure swa muchelne teone ne wite on þisse liue ne beo þu nefre ene wrað þer fore. *a* **1300** *Cursor M.* 4586 þou sal god office haue ful tite, And all forgiuen þe þi wijtte. *Ibid.* 10393 Iesu crist was tan, And don on rode for our wite. **13..** *Guy Warw.* (A.) 304 He wald anon mine heued of smite,..for that wite. **1390** Gower *Conf.* II. 89 Of tomoche or of tolyte Ther is algate founde a wyte. *c* **1412** Hoccleve *De Reg. Princ.* 2720 þat haþ I-do þe tres-pase, or the wyte.

4. *attrib.* and *Comb.*, as (sense 1 b) *wite-exacting*, *-free* adjs.

1897 Maitland *Domesday Bk. & Beyond* 87 A tract over which a lord has..a *wite-exacting power. **1205** *Rot. Chart.* (1837) 153/2 Wrecfri et *witefri et lestagefri. **1278** [see lovecop]. **1395** [see lastage *sb.* 7]. **1672** *Cowel's Interpr.*, *Wite*... Hence *Wite* or *Witfree*, one of the terms of Priviledge granted to our Portsmen.

wite, wyte (waɪt), *v.*[1] *Obs.* exc. *Sc.* and *north. dial.* Forms: 1 **witan,** 2-4 **witen,** 2-7 **wite,** 3-5 (6 *arch.*) **wyten,** 4-7, 8-9 *Sc.* **wyte** (3 **hwite?,** 4 **wytte,** *pa. t.* and *pa. pple.* **wijt, wit(t,** 4-6 **wit,** 4-7 **white,** 4-8 chiefly *Sc.* **wyt,** 5 **wytt, wiyte, wijte, wyet, wyth,** 6 **wiht,** *Sc.* **wyit, veit, vyit,** 7 *Sc. pa. t.* **wate**). [OE. *wítan*, pa. t. **wát*, *witon* (superseded by weak inflexions in ME.), also *ætwítan* (*-wát*, *-witon*, pa. pple. *-witen*, ME. pa. t. *atwiste*, pa. pple. *atwist*) atwite *v.*[1], *edwítan* (pa. pl. *-witon*, and wk. *-wítte*, Vesp. Ps.) edwite *v.*: = OS. *wîtan*, MLG., MD. *wîten* (Du. *wijten*), OHG. *wîzan* (MHG. *wîzen*, G. *verweissen* to reproach), Goth. *-weitan* in *fraweitan* to avenge; f. Teut. *wît-*: see wit *v.*[1] The sense-development is paralleled in L. *animadvertere* to observe, consider, censure, blame, punish.]

1. *trans.* To impute the guilt or lay the blame of (something) to or upon a person (his action, conduct, or character) or a thing, condition, or event (orig. dat., later also with *to*, *on*, *upon*).

Beowulf 2741 For ðam me witan ne ðearf waldend fira morðorbealo maga. *c* **893** Ælfred *Oros.* vi. iv, Romane witan Claudiuse þone hunger. *a* **1225** *Ancr. R.* 304 ȝif þu witest eni þing þine sunne bute þi suluen, þu ne schriuest þe nout. *a* **1250** *Owl & Night.* 1249 Schal he his mishap wite me? **13..** *K. Alis.* 1725 Thou konst no gode; Y wyt hit all thy yonge blode. *c* **1320** *Sir Tristr.* 369 Her sorwen and her care þai witt þat frely fode. *c* **1386** Chaucer *Monk's T.* 456 Allas Fortune..Thy false wheel my wo al may I wyte. —— *Miller's Prol.* 32 If that I mysspeke or seye Wyte it the Ale of Southwerk. *a* **1400** *Leg. Rood* (1871) 134 His wo I wyte hit sinne. *c* **1400** *Beryn* 2016, I may wit it þe, þat I have lost my siȝte. **14..** *Sir Beues* (M.) 1893 Thou sholdiste on me be awreke And not wite on hym the gilte. *c* **1430** *Hymns Virgin* (1867) 35 Y wiyte my silf myne owne woo! *c* **1436** *Pol. Poems* (Rolls) II. 148 White thi owne falsnes alle thi myschance. **1481** Caxton *Godfrey* xx. 51 This felonnye that this fewe dyde was wyted alle the hoost. *c* **1500** *Melusine* 308 It shal not be wytted me to haue a brother of myn a monke. **1571** Golding *Calvin on Ps.* xl. 9 After the miseries which he abydeth are wyted vppon his owne fault. **1587** —— *De Mornay* xii. (1592) 181 They..reteine the faultines of that first fault, and cannot wit it vpon any other than the first Man. **1826** Galt *Last of Lairds* xxx. 268 He wyted it a' on the liberty and equality speerit o' the times.

†**b.** To impute as guilt; also in neutral sense: To impute. *Obs.*

1382 Wyclif *Judges* iv. 9 In this while victory shal not be witid to thee [Vulg. *non reputabitur tibi*]. **1382** —— *Rom.* v. 13 Synne was not wijtid, [*gloss*] or rettid, whanne lawe was not. *c* **1460** *Towneley Myst.* x. 332 Wyte thou no wyrkyng of Werkys wast, She hase consauyd the holy gast. **1533** tr. *Erasm. Playne Expos. Com. Crede* 31 b, Vnto it is to be wihted or imputed what so euer thynge..hathe ben done.. vertuosly.

2. To impute the guilt or fault to, blame (a person).

a **1000** *Ælfred's Boeth.* Proem, þæt he..him ne wite ȝif he hit rihtlicor onȝite þonne he mihte. *c* **1200** *Trin. Coll. Hom.* 67 He [*sc.* Christ] setteð þe synfulle on his lifthalf, and witeð hem þat hie bi here lif daȝes ne wolden him quemen. *a* **1300** *Cursor M.* 17445 If ani man yow witte, We sal yow saue and mak yow quite. *c* **1320** *Sir Tristr.* 619 þe porter gan him wite And seyd:—'Cherl! go oway'. *c* **1386** Chaucer *Merch. T.* 933 And though þat I be Ialous, wyte me noght. *c* **1400** *26 Pol. Poems* xvii. 119 And þou be lost, whom wiltow wyte? *c* **1449** Pecock *Repr.* i. i. 5 The errouris..bi which holding thei vniustly..wijten and blamen the clergie. **1469** *Paston Lett.* II. 348 And they myght pulle downe the howse on our hedys, I wyet hem not. *c* **1500** *Melusine* 310 He..blamed & wytted hym self. **1530** Palsgr. 783/1 Why wyte you me, and I am nat to blame? **1590** Spenser *F.Q.* ii. xii. 16 Scoffing at him, that did her iustly wite. **1721** Ramsay *Prospect of Plenty* 133 Nor can we wyt them, since they had our Vote. **1721** Kelly *Sc. Prov.* 357 Wite your self if your Wife be with Bairn. **1818** Scott *Rob Roy* xxvi, It wasna my faut; he canna wyte me. **1826** Galt *Last of Lairds* xviii. 161 She had got an injury and wyted me.

absol. **1340** *Ayenb.* 69 Zuo hit is huanne god his..chasteþ, and maugre hy wyteþ. *c* **1430** *Chev. Assigne* 136 Moche mone was therfore but no man wyte moste.

†**b.** Const. obj. and inf. (see to *prep.* B. 8): To blame a person for doing so-and-so. *Obs.*

c **1449** Pecock *Repr.* ii. iv. 155 Wijting..vsers of ymagis to be gilti of vntrewe feith. **1500-20** Dunbar *Poems* lxxxiv. 20 Quha sould thame wyte To serue thair beistlie lust? *c* **1560** A. Scott *Poems* (S.T.S.) xi. 51 To lufe ȝour ladeis quho can wyt ȝow? *a* **1585** Montgomerie *Cherrie & Slae* 759 Quhat tyme he wytit Will To be maist cause of his mischeif.

c. Const. *of*, later *for*, *with*, that in respect of which blame is incurred.

c **1290** *Beket* 2087 in *S. Eng. Leg.* 166 Non oþur gulti nis of þat ȝe witez me. *a* **1300** *Cursor M.* 17772 He o mani plight was wijt [*Gött.* witt]. **13..** *E.E. Allit. P.* C. 501 Wyte not me for þe werk þat I hit wolde help. *c* **1374** Chaucer *Anel. & Arc.* 110 Ther nas no lacke with wiche he myght her wite. **1481** Caxton *Reynard* viii. (Arb.) 17 None shal wyte me therof. **1533** Gau *Richt Vay* (S.T.S.) 90 Lat vsz noth veit the deuil..of ony aduersite quhilk cumis to vsz. **1549** Coverdale, etc. *Erasm. Par. Rom.* ix. 19-26 Nothyng had Pharao to wyte God withal. *c* **1550** Rolland *Crt. Venus* Prol. 197 Thay say it is fals destenie And wyitis Fortoun of thair misgouernance. **17..** *Gil Morrice* xxv. in Child *Ballads* II. 273 Neir wyte a man for violence That neir wate ye wi nane. **1816** Scott *Bl. Dwarf* ix, A' the wrang he can wyte me wi.

3. To lay the fault or blame upon (a thing). †Also with const. as in 2 c.

a **1300** *Cursor M.* 27769 He wites werd [*MS.* wend] and waris his time. *c* **1520** Skelton *Magnyf.* 2304 Alasse, my wyckydnesse, that may I wyte! **1528** Tindale *Obed. Chr.*

Man Prol. 22 To wite Gods worde and the true preachers of all the mischeve which their lying doctrine is the very cause of. **1549** *Compl. Scot.* iv. 64 Allace i vyit ȝour tua fayr ene. **1596** Spenser *F.Q.* v. xi. 57 Albe he earst did wyte His wauering mind. *a* **1598** D. Fergusson *Scot. Prov.* (S.T.S.) 12 All thing wytes that well not faires. **1603** *Philotus* clxx, Wyte ignorance that I did not invent.

4. *to wite* was freq. used predicatively in senses 2 and 3 = to blame, blameworthy, in fault, culpable.

a **1300** *Floris & Bl.* (Camb. MS.) 723 Of al þis gilt ihc am to wite. **13..** *E.E. Allit. P.* B. 76 More to wyte is her wrange, þen any wylle gentyl. **1390** Gower *Conf.* I. 116 Ha fol, how thou art forto wyte. *a* **1425** *Cursor M.* 876 (Trin.) þat þou hast þus don þis mis þi seluen is to wite [*Cott.* þiself þou wite þi wa]. *c* **1480** Henryson *Test. Cress.* 134 O fals Cupide, is nane to wyte bot thow.

Hence **'witer, 'witing** *vbl. sb.*[1]

c **1449** Pecock *Repr.* ii. ii. 143 Alle such ouerhastie iugers and wijters God amende. *Ibid.* ii. iv. 155 Thilk doom and thilk wijting..is vntrewe. **1825** Jamieson, *Witer*, one who blames another Clydesd.

† **wite**, *v.*[2] *Obs.* Forms: 1 **witan**, 2-4 **wite** (3 **witte**, *imper.* **wit**), 3-4 **wyte** (4 **white**); *pres. 3rd sing.* 2-3 **wit**; 3 **wat, wot**; *pa. t.* 2-4 **wiste**, 3-4 **wuste** (4 **wist, wust, wste**); *pa. pple.* 3-4 **iwust**, 4 **iwist**. [OE. *witan*, usually in compound *bewitan* (pres. *-wát*, pa. t. *-wiste*) biwit *v.*; cf. OFris. *wita*, OHG. *wizzên* in *giwizzên*, *irwizzên* to be observant, watch, Goth. *witan* (pa. t. *witaida*): f. Teut. *wit-*: see wit *v.*[1] In ME. dialects where the inf. ending *-ie(n* is not preserved, this verb is indistinguishable from witie *v.*[2] Some ME. forms point to OE. *wítan*.]

1. *trans.* To keep, keep safe, guard, preserve, defend. Also *refl.*

c **1000** *Sax. Leechd.* III. 154 Þæt bið god swefen, wite þu þæt ȝeorne on þinre heortan. *c* **1175** *Lamb. Hom.* 79 [He] brohte him to an hors huse, and bitahte hine þe hors horde to witene. *Ibid.* 85 Meiden þet hire meiden-hat wit. *a* **1200** *Moral Ode* 84 in *O.E. Hom.* I. 165 He wit and waleð alle þing. *c* **1200** *Trin. Coll. Hom.* 29 Witte wel hwat þu hauest. *Ibid.* 31 Herdes..wittende here oref. *Ibid.* 137 To witen him of alle flesliche lustes. *c* **1205** Lay. 21302 Nu him is al swa þere gat þer he þene hul wat [*c* **1275** wot]. *c* **1230** *Hali Meid.* (1922) 16 ȝef ha wit hire wiðute bruche. *c* **1275** *Passion our Lord* 18 in *O.E. Misc.* 37 Yf we vs wyteþ from heued-sunne. *a* **1300** *X Commandm.* 34 in *E.E.P.* (1862) 16 Wit þe fram licheri. *a* **1300** *Floris & Bl.* (Camb. MS.) 756 His engin whan þu hit wite, þe betere wiþ oþere þu miȝt þe wite. *c* **1320** *Cast. Love* 168 Two lawen Adam scholde i-wis Witen and holden in paradis. **1362** Langl. *P. Pl.* A. x. 67 Bote þei witen hem from wantounesse, whil þat þei ben ȝonge. *a* **1400** *Pol. Rel. & L. Poems* 255 Ley þou þi fet to my pappe, And wite þe from þe colde. *c* **1430** Lydg. *Min. Poems* (Percy Soc.) 33 Voydyng slaundre, wyte the of gelousye. *c* **1440** *Pallad. on Husb.* i. 546 This wol from the wesel wite hem well.

Illustration of pa. t. and pa. pple.

c **1175** *Lamb. Hom.* 43 An meiden.. þet wel wiste hire licome in alle clenesse. *c* **1205** Lay. 1693 Brutus..hine wel wuste. *a* **1225** *Ancr. R.* 48 Wite wel þine heorte, uor soule lif is in hire, ȝif heo is wel iwust. **13..** *St. Alexius* (Trin. MS.) 102 Hy þoȝte on crist day and nyȝt And wiste [*Laud MS.* kepte] here fro senne. *a* **1325** *MS. Rawl. B.* 520 lf. 32 That eueriche contreie..ben so i wuste þat [etc.]. *c* **1350** *Will. Palerne* 172 Ȝhe wist it as wel or bet as ȝif it were hire owne.

2. Const. clause: To take care, see (*that*).

a **1000** *Sec. Laws Cnut* lxxv, Wite se oðer.. þæt he hit bete. *c* **1000** *Sax. Leechd.* III. 154 Wite þæt þin ȝeþanc ne losiȝe. *c* **1175** *Lamb. Hom.* 11 Wite ȝe þet ȝe ȝemen þenne halie sunnedei. *Ibid.* 53 Witeð eow þet ȝe ne beo noht þe foaȝe neddre.

3. To see, observe. Also *intr.* to look *on*.

c **1320** *Cast. Love* 1256 Hose w^t þe swerd smite, Two kuynden he miȝte sen and wite [*rime* smite]. *c* **1330** R. Brunne *Chron. Wace* (Rolls) 15860 þat non ne scholde hem se ne wite [*rime* lite]. **13..** *Gaw. & Gr. Knt.* 2050 Þe wyȝe wynnez hym to, & wytez on his lyre.

Hence †**witing** *vbl. sb.*[2], keeping, custody.

a **1225** *Ancr. R.* 418 Of swuche witunge is i-kumen muchel vuel.

† **wite**, *v.*[3] *Obs.* Forms: 1 **witan**, 2-5 **wite**, 4 **wit(t**, 4-5 **wyte**, 5 **witte**. *Pa. t.* 3 **wot**, 4-5 **wat**; 4 **wited**, 5 **wyted, wit**. *Pa. pple.* 3 *Orm.* **witenn**, 4 **wite**. [OE. *wítan* (rare), usually *ȝewítan* i-wite *v.*[2], q.v.] *intr.* To go, go *away*, depart; to perish, vanish *away*.

a **1000** *Boeth. Metr.* xxiv. 52 Nylle ic æfre hionan ut witan. *a* **1175** *Cott. Hom.* 239 Witeð into ece fer. *c* **1200** Ormin 8222 Affterr þatt Herode king wass witenn ut off life. *c* **1200** *Trin. Coll. Hom.* 109 Abacuc, þe wunede on þis weorlde and eft þerof wot. *Ibid.* 123 Hider he cumeð on wowe and heðen wit on wowe. *a* **1300** *Cursor M.* 8968 Hu all þis werld sal wite awai. *Ibid.* 10551 Quen þis angel a-wai was wite. *Ibid.* 11262 þir angels wited þam ewai. *a* **1340** Hampole *Psalter* Prol., All gladnes & delite of erth..wytes til noght. *c* **1375** *Sc. Leg. Saints* xxxii. (*Justin*) 229 As a reke away he wat. ? *a* **1400** *Morte Arth.* 708, I may noghte wit of this woo. *c* **1400** *St. Alexius* (Laud 622) 191 Þe kniȝttes waten on & on To her owen cuntre. *c* **1420** *Prose Life Alex.* 90 Bi þe son settynge þay wyted a-way in-to þe erthe agayne. *c* **1425** Wyntoun *Cron.* cxii. 1187 Quhen þis wes said he wit away. *c* **1425** *Thomas Erceld.* 327 Whene a tree rote es dede The leues fadis þane & wytis a-waye. *c* **1480** Henryson in *Poems Gray MS.* vi. 65 (S.T.S.) 56 Full oft Is sene thir emotis in ane hillok ay Rinnand oute befor þin ene; with litill weit þai wit away.

wite, obs. f. wight, wit *v.*[1]

witeȝe, var. witie.

witel, obs. f. whittle *sb.*[1]

† **'witeless**, *a. Sc.* (and *north.*) ? *Obs.* [f. wite *sb.*[2] + -less.] Blameless.

1560 Rolland *Seven Sages* (Bann. Club) 18 Scho was wyteless, howbeit storme thame opprest. *c* **1575** *Diurn. Occurr.* (Bann. Club) 240 Wyteles of the halding thairof. **1579** Spenser *Sheph. Cal.* Aug. 136 Ne can Willye wite the witelesse herdgroome. **1617** in A. I. Ritchie *Churches St. Baldred* (1880) 162 Alexander Daviesone did draw his quhinger also, and so suld not be altogidder wytless. **1721** Kelly *Sc. Prov.* 202 If all be well, I's be wyteless. **1737** Ramsay *Sc. Prov.* (1750) 102 They wyte you and you no wytless.

† **'witen**, *v. Obs. rare.* Also 4 **witten**. [f. wite *v.*[1] + -en[5].] *trans.* **a.** To impute. **b.** To blame.

c **1350** *Will. Palerne* 3462 But holli williams werkes þei wittened it alle. **1589** Peele *Egl. Grat.* Bj, Least worthily, I moughten witned bee.

witenagemot ('wɪtənəgɪˌməʊt, *popularly* wɪtə'nægɪmɒt). *Hist.* Also 3 **witene imot**; 6 **wytena gemote**, 7 **weidenagamoot**, 7-9 **wittena-gemot(e**, (9 **witana-**). [OE. *witena ȝemót* assembly of wise men: see witan, wite *sb.*[1], and gemot(e, moot *sb.*[1]] The assembly of the witan, the national council of Anglo-Saxon times; *transf.* of modern parliaments or other deliberative assemblies.

[*c* **900** tr. *Bæda's Hist.* iii. v, On ȝemote hiora witena.] *c* **1000** Ælfric *Gram.* viii. (Z.) 30 *Haec sinodus*, þis witena ȝemot. **1050** *O.E. Chron.* (MS. C), þa hæfde Eadwerd cing witena ȝemot on Lunden to midlencten. *c* **1205** Lay. 11545 þet hustinge wes god, hit wes witene-imot.

1591 Lambarde *Archeion* (1635) 252 The word Witena.. doth include the Nobilitie and Commons, because they be Counsellors of the Realme,..in respect whereof the assembling of them, was of some called Wytena Gemote. **1614** Selden *Titles Hon.* 226 Their Wittenagemots or Mikel Synods. **1656** Harrington *Oceana* 35 *marg.*, Weidenagamoots. **1660** Waterhouse *Arms & Arm.* 181 The Wittena-gemote and great Councel of our wisdom, in the preamble to the Statute of 43 Eliz. c. 12. acknowledgeth it to have been the policy of this Realm. **1769** Blackstone *Comm.* IV. xxxiii. 405 The wittena-gemote, or *commune concilium* of the antient Germans. **1785** Cowper *Let. to J. Hill* 22 Jan., Shall I derive no other advantage from the great Wittena-Gemot of the nation, than merely to read their debates? **1833** Southey *Lett.* (1856) IV. 348 Having occasion to write to Sir T. Acland while he is attending the Witena-gemot at Cambridge, I sent him a fact for the geologists. **1855** Browning *Old Pict. in Florence* xxxiii, A kind of sober Witana-gemot [*rime* bag 'em hot]. **1899** Sir M. Foster *Presid. Addr. Brit. Assoc.* 22 The first select Witena-gemote of the science of the world.

witenonfa, var. wedenonfa'. *Obs.*

witer: see after wite *v.*[1]; var. witter.

'witereden. *Hist.* Also *corruptly* **winter-, wynter-, wit(t)erden(e, wateredden**. [OE. *witerǽden* (used in *Bæda's Hist.* iii. viii. in the gen. sense of punishment), f. *wíte* wite *sb.*[2] + *rǽden* -red.] A fine (erron. explained by antiquaries as a royal imposition or aid).

688-95 *Laws Ine* §50 Nah he þær nane witerædenne. **855** (MS. 12th cent.) *Grant of Ethelwulf* in Birch *Cartul. Sax.* II. 84 Ut sit tuta..ab omnibus secularibus servitutibus, necnon regalibus tributis majoribus et minoribus, sive taxationibus quod nos dicimus Witereden [*v.rr.* Winterden, Witeredden].

1650 Elderfield *Civil Right of Tythes* 72 [transl. quot. 855] No secular service, nor tribute..nor Winterdene (or Witterdene, a kind of imposition). **1672** *Cowel's Interpr.*, *Witerden*..a kind of Taxation among the West-Saxons. **1710** Prideaux *Orig. Tithes* iv. 177 *note*, Written variously Witerden, Wynterden and Wateredden. It was a Tax or Royal ayd. **1862** Miall *Title Deeds Ch. Eng.* 19 *note*, [comment on prec.].

witesafe, obs. form of vouchsafe.

Witeson(e, etc., obs. forms of Whitsun.

wit-ess. *nonce-wd.* [f. wit *sb.* + -ness.] A female wit.

1781 Han. More in *Mem.* (1835) I. 206 All the pride of London,—every wit, and every wit-ess.

witeword, var. witword.

witful ('wɪtfʊl), *a.* [In ME. aphetic for **iwitful*, OE. **ȝewitfull*, inferred from *unȝewitfull* (f. *unȝewitt* madness, folly); in mod.E. a new formation on wit *sb.* and -ful.]

† **1.** Wise, sagacious. *Obs.*

c **1205** Lay. 911 Membricius..wes..wys & witful. *Ibid.* 9095 þurh his wit-fulne cræfte. **1340** *Ayenb.* 150 He makeþ man wytuol and wys. **1544** Betham tr. *Purlilia's Precepts War* i. cxxx. G iv b, A wytfull capitayne wyll sende some of hys souldyours that be subtyle & wyttye, to..tempt the mynde of his enemies. **1587** Golding *De Mornay* v. (1592) 58 That is the marke of the witfull action, (that is to say, of the euerlasting word or conceit whereby God made them). **1614** Chapman *Masque Inns of Court* C 2, Tis passing miraculous, that your dul and blind worship should so sodainly turne both sightfull, and witfull.

2. Full of wit (in modern senses).

1765 J. Brown *Chr. Jrnl., Summer Day* 174 The poems of lofty Milton, witful Cowley, elegant Pope. **1872** *Daily News* 31 July, M. Thiers' utterances snap with witful shrewdness. **1924** *Countries of World* I. 639/2 The women deck these stands with witful skill. **1935** W. de la Mare *Early One Morning* 321 A willing and witful child. **1980** *N.Y. Times* 26 Aug. c-8/5 Ravel's Sonata for Violin and Cello... For pinpoint gestural precision and witful repartee, this sophisticated instrumental dialogue is an unending source of fascination.

witgat ('vɪtxat). *S. Afr.* [Afrikaans, f. *wit* white + *gat* hole.] Any of several trees of the genus *Boscia*, which have pale bark and are found in dry areas of southern Africa, esp. the evergreen *B. albitrunca*. Also ***witgatboom*** [Afrikaans *boom* tree].

1824 W. J. Burchell *Trav. Int. S. Afr.* II. 18 Their trunks..appeared at a little distance as if they had been whitewashed. From this singular character, they have gained the name of *Wit-gat boom*. **1860** Harvey & Sonder *Flora Capensis* I. 362 A tall tree called *Witgat* by the colonists. **1932** C. Fuller *Louis Trigardt's Trek* 47 We were standing under a *witgatboom*. **1966** E. Palmer *Plains of Camdeboo* iv. 54 Close to this grew a witgat tree not fifteen feet tall but with a thick, seamed, milk-white trunk and a dense grey-green crown of tough little leaves. *Ibid.* xvii. 271 They..made coffee from the roots of the witgat. **1972** Palmer & Pitman *Trees S. Afr.* I. 620 Witgat wood is heavy and tough. **1973** Y. Burgess *Life to Live* 25 Coffee made from the roots of the witgat tree.

with (wɪθ), *sb.* Also 8 **wyth, width, wieth**, 8- **withe**. [? Corruption of width.] A partition between flues in a chimney stack: locally termed *mid-feather*.

1708 *Act 7 Anne* c. 17 §10 All Withs the Inside of such Chimnies shall be Four Inches and an Half in Breadth. **1717** V. Mandey *Mellificium Mensionis* (1727) 382 The Breasts and Wings, and Wieths [of the chimneys]. **1734** *Builder's Dict.* s.v. *Chimney*, If they [*sc.* the Chimney-Shafts] be wrought nine Inches thick,..then you must account your Thickness one Brick and half, in consideration of Wyths and Pargetting, and Trouble in Scaffolding. **1736** R. Neve *Builder's Dict.* (ed. 3) s.v. *Chimney*, In Consideration of the Widths, Pargeting, and Scaffolding. **1748** B. Langley *Lond. Prices* 327 The Widths of Chimneys. **1844** *Act 7 & 8 Vict.* c. 84 Sched. (F) The Breast of every Chimney, and the Front, Back, Withe, or Partition of every Flue, must be at the least Four Inches in Thickness of sound Bricks. **1905** *Pract. Brickwork* (ed. P. N. Hasluck) xii. 100 It will be necessary to tie in the withs on the stretching course.

with (wɪð; chiefly *north.* wɪθ), *prep.*, (*adv.*, *conj.*). Forms: 1-3 **wið**, 1-5 **wiþ**, 3-5 **wyþ, wit, wid** (9- *colloq.* and *dial.* wid), 4-5 **wyt**, 4-6 **wyth(t, withe**, (3 **wyd, wiz, wih'**, *Orm.* **wiþþ**, 3-5 **wiht**, 4 **witt, wiȝt(h, wyht, wyȝt, whiþ**, *Sc.* **vith**, 4-5 **whit**, 5 **wyt(t)he, whyt(h, whith, witȝ, weþ**, *Sc.* **wygh(e, wyghte, wycht**, 6 **wight, witht**, *Sc.* **vitht, quhit, wutht**, 7-9 *n. dial.* **wud**, 8-9 *Sc.* and *n. dial.* **wi'**, 9 *dial.* **wiv, way**), 2- **with**; *abbreviated* 4-7 w^t, 5-7 w^{th} (6 **wth**). [OE. *wið* = OFris. *with*, OS. *wið*, ON. *við* (Sw. *vid*, Da. *ved*): app. a shortening (peculiar to the Anglo-Frisian and Scandinavian areas) of the Com. Teut. **wider-* (see s.v. wither *a.* and *adv.* and wither-[1]), perh. taking place orig. in compounds (cf. with- and the parallelism of OE. *wiþcéosan* and *wiþercéosan* to reject, *wiþstandan* and *wiþerstandan* to withstand, etc.).

As an adv., *with* occurs as the second element in composition with other advs. denoting direction, motion, or extension: forwith (forouth, forrow), forthwith, inwith, outwith (utouth), downwith, upwith.]

A. *prep.* The prevailing senses of this prep. in the earliest periods are those of opposition ('against') and of motion or rest in proximity ('towards', 'alongside'), which are now current only in certain traditional collocations or specific applications. These notions readily pass into fig. uses denoting various kinds of relations, among which those implying reciprocity are at first prominent. The most remarkable development in the signification of *with* consists in its having taken over in the ME. period the chief senses belonging properly to OE. *mid* mid *prep.*[1] (cognate with Gr. μετά with). These senses are mainly those denoting association, combination or union, instrumentality or means, and attendant circumstance. These are all important senses of ON. *við*, to which fact their currency and ultimate predominance in the English word are partly due. The last important stage was the extension of *with* from the instrument to the agent, in which use it was current for different periods along with *of* and *through*, and later with *by*, which finally superseded the other three. The range of meanings in general has no doubt been enlarged by association with L. *cum*. The interaction of senses and sense-groups has been such that the position of a particular sense in the order of development is often difficult to determine.

In common with other preps. *with* can be postponed to the end of an interrogative or relative clause introduced by its regimen; but in ME. it was freq. placed immediately after the verb in relative clauses, *e.g.* þes rentis þat þe fend haþ dowed *wiþ* clerkis = these revenues with which the Devil has endowed clerics. In postposition it was for a long period extensively replaced by WITHAL (q.v. B).

I. Denoting opposition and derived notions (separation; motion towards).

†**1. a.** In a position opposite to; over against: = AGAINST 1. Chiefly in advb. phrases with repeated sb., as *face with face*, where *to* is now

c **893** ÆLFRED *Oros.* I. i. §31 Be norðan is se sæ, þe æȝþer is ȝe nearo ȝe hreoh, wið Italia þam lande. *c* **950** *Lindisf. Gosp.* Mark xii. 41 Sætt se hælend wið..ðæs dores. *c* **1175** *Lamb. Hom.* 61 Cristes wille bo us bitwon neb wið neb for him to son. *c* **1200** *Trin. Coll. Hom.* 105 His wise wordes þe he wið hem spec muð wið muðe. *c* **1205** LAY. 1874 Breoste wið breoste banes þer crakeden. *a* **1300** [see FACE *sb.* 2d].

b. In exchange, return, or payment for: = AGAINST 14, FOR 6. *Obs.* exc. *dial.*

The related senses 'in compensation for', 'in comparison with' are only OE.

c **893** ÆLFRED *Oros.* IV. xiii. §1 Hit Scipia nolde him aliefan wið nanum oþrum þinge butan hie him ealle hiera wæpeno aȝeafen. **993** *Battle of Maldon* 35 We willað wið þam golde grið fæstnian. *c* **1000** ÆLFRIC *Exod.* xxi. 24 Eaȝe wið eaȝan, toþ wiþ teð. **1442** in *Reg. Mag. Sig. Scot. 1444* 64/1 The landis of..Pettendrech, the quhilkis war changeit with the landis of Dunottir. *a* **1568** ASCHAM *Scholem.* I. (Arb.) 27 If the childe misse, either in forgetting a worde, or in chaunging a good with a worse. **1570** in *Shropsh. Par. Doc.* (1903) 63 Rec. at the chaunge of the cupp wth the challeis vii^{s}. ii^{d}. **1637** RUTHERFORD *Lett., to M. Mowat* 7 Sept. (1671) 165 We might barter or niffer our lazie ease with a profitable cross.

2. Of conflict, antagonism, dispute, injury, reproof, competition, rivalry, and the like: In opposition to, adversely to: = AGAINST 12a, 12b, 12d.

Still the normal prep. with such words as *battle*, *chide*, *compete*, *conflict*, *contend*, *dispute*, *fight*, *quarrel*, *strive*, *struggle*, *vie*, *war*, and phrases like *go to law*, *at odds*, but now associated with or merged in 8, 13b, or 20.

Beowulf 152 Grendel wan hwile wið Hroþgar. *a* **900** CYNEWULF *Elene* 836 Hie wið Godes bearne nið ahofun. **900-30** *O.E. Chron.* an. 853 (Parker MS.), Ealhere mid Cantwarum, & Huda mid Suþriȝium ȝefuhton on Tenet wiþ hæþnum heriȝe. *a* **1000** *Gnomic Verses* II. 187 Weriȝ scealc wiþ winde roweþ. *c* **1175** *Lamb. Hom.* 19 Þet he ne misdude wið oderne. *Ibid.* 129 Of þan icompe þe ure drihten hefde wið þene feond. *c* **1200** ORMIN 16981 3iff þa mihhtenn witenn itt þatt haffdenn niþ wiþþ Criste. **1338** R. BRUNNE *Chron.* (1810) 57 He praied him for his nauy to help him with summ. *c* **1440** *Alphabet of Tales* 124 Þis knight askid hym if he kend oght with hym selfe. **1590** [see CONFLICT *sb.* 1]. **1596** *Edw. III*, II. ii, Poore shipskin, how it braules with him that beateth it! **1611** SHAKS. *Wint. T.* I ii. 355 One, Who in Rebellion with himselfe, will haue All that are his, so too. **1668** WALTON *Angler* iv. (ed. 4) 66 He [*sc.* the trout] may justly contend with all fresh-water-Fish, as the Mullet may with all Sea-Fish. **1719** DE FOE *Crusoe* II. (Globe) 357 Let us go and have t'other Brush with them. **1736** *Gentl. Mag.* VI. 334/1 Let the Boys be set a running, as it were, with one another, in getting without Book. **1851** NEWMAN *Pres. Pos. Cath.* vi. §7 Invention cannot run with prejudice. Prejudice wins. **1909** *Dublin Rev.* Jan. 128 Amazons at handgrips with a long-suffering police.

†**3.** Of resistance, defence, protection, warning, caution: = AGAINST 13a, 13b. *Obs.*

Beowulf 540 Wit unc wið hronfixas werian þohton. **971** *Blickl. Hom.* 171 Þa woldan hie on ecnesse hæle & trume wið deofla niþum & helle witum. *c* **1000** *Sax. Leechd.* II. 130 Wiþ bryne ȝenim finules niþeweardes. *c* **1040** *Bidding Prayer* in *Lay Folks Mass Bk.* 62 Þæt hy us ȝehealdan & ȝescyldan wið ealra feonda costnunga. *c* **1175** *Lamb. Hom.* 53 Þe feder and þe sune and þe halie gast iscilde us..wið alle sunnen. *a* **1225** *Ancr. R.* 224 Hu 3e schulen witen ou wið þes deofles wieles. *c* **1320** *Cast. Love* 826 Þe seue berbicans abouten,..witeþ þis Castel so wel Wiþ arwe and wiþ qwarel. *c* **1375** *Sc. Leg. Saints* xi. (*Symon & Iudas*) 203 For þat þu suld mar vnwar be Vith þi fais.

†**4.** Of separation or deliverance: = FROM 6, 6b. *Obs.* (See also 19c.)

Beowulf 2423 Sundur ȝedælan lif wið lice. *a* **1000** *Cædmon's Gen.* 127 Þa ȝesundrode siȝora waldend..leoht wið þeostrum, sceade wið sciman. *a* **1250** *Owl & Night.* 610 Me is lof to cristes huse To clansi hit wiþ fule muse.

5. †**a.** Towards, in the direction of: = AGAINST 5. (Only OE.) *Obs.*

Beowulf 213 Streamas wundon sund wið sande. *Ibid.* 1880 Ac him on hreþre hyȝebendum fæst æfter deorum men dyrne langað beorn wið blode. **900-30** *O.E. Chron.* an. 894 (Parker MS.), Þa wende he hine west wið Exanceastres. *a* **1000** *Riddles* iv. 42 Þonne scearp cymeð sceo wiþ oþrum, ecg wið ecge. *c* **1000** ÆLFRIC *Saints' Lives* xxvi. 204 Sum weȝfarende man ferde wið þone feld.

b. Near or close to, against, alongside. Now only *Naut.* with words denoting proximity and consequently belonging more properly to 18.

Beowulf 326 Setton..rondas reȝnhearde wið þæs recedes weal. *Ibid.* 2566 Stiðmod ȝestod wið steapne rond winia bealdor. **900-30** *O.E. Chron.* an. 878 (Parker MS.), Æt Alre, & þæt is wiþ Æþelingga eiȝe. *c* **1000** *Ags. Gosp.* Luke viii. 5 Þa he þæt seow sum feoll wið þæne weȝ. *c* **1050** *Voc.* in Wr.-Wülcker 447/25 *Murotenus*, wið ðone weall. **13..** *Gaw. & Gr. Knt.* 113 Bischop Bawdewyn abof bi-ginez þe table, & Ywan, Vryn son, ette wit hymseluen. **14..** *Sailing Directions* (Hakl. Soc.) 12 Than go your cours with the horse shoo south southwest. *Ibid.* 13 Fro Seint Margret steyers and ye will go with Dengenes, your best way is south south west. **1579-80** NORTH *Plutarch, Theseus* (1595) 10 By force of weather driven with the coast of Sicile. **1591** RALEIGH *Last Fight Rev.* (Arb.) 24 A fourth ranne her selfe with the shore to saue her men. **1625** PURCHAS *Pilgrims* II. 1133 An houre after Sunne rising, we were with a very long and faire point. **1708-** [see IN *adv.* 9b]. **1748** *Anson's Voy.* II. vii. 212 One of our prizes was ordered to stand close in with it [*sc.* the land]. **1788** J. WHITE *Jrnl. Voy. N.S. Wales* (1790) 108 As we run in with the land,..we were surprised to see..some small patches of snow. **1849** O'BYRNE *Naval Biogr. Dict.* 661/2 At the cutting out, close in with the enemy's batteries of *La Guépe* privateer. **1860** DICKENS *Uncomm. Trav.* ii, A man..saw..some dark troubled object close in with the land.

c. Into the presence or immediate proximity of (and in derived fig. uses): following such verbs as *encounter*, *fall in*, *meet*, etc., q.v. (Now associated with 19.)

†**6.** Governing a demonstrative pronoun, forming conjunctive phrases: ***with than*** (*the*, *that*), ***with that***, ***with thi*** (*that*), ***wiþi***, ***wyþy***, rarely ***with this*** (*that*) [see THAN *dem. pron.*, THAT *conj.* 1c, THY *adv.*]: **a.** On condition that, provided that, if.

c **1000** ÆLFRIC *Saints' Lives* xii. 118 Nolde he syllan ealle his æhta þeah þe he weliȝ wære, wið þan þe he libban moste. *a* **1200** *Moral Ode* 152 in *O.E. Hom.* I. 169 Eure he walde her inne wawe and ine wene wunien Wið þet he mihte helle pine bi-flien. *c* **1205** LAY. 8253 Al þine wille he wule don, wið þon þe þu him 3eue grið. *a* **1300** *Siriz* 192, Ich wile 3eve the riche mede With that hit be so. *a* **1300** *St. Thomas* 184 in Horstm. *Altengl. Leg.* (1881) 22 Grete bewtes to him he bed..Withi he wold dwell with him still. *c* **1300** *Havelok* 532, I shal maken þe fre,..With-þan þu wilt þis childe take. **1375** BARBOUR *Bruce* I. 493 With-thi 3e giff me all the land, That 3e haiff now in-till 3our hand. *c* **1400** *Beryn* 3972 Tomorow I woll be redy his hest to fulfill, With this I have save condit. **1473** *Paston Lett.* III. 100, I wolde he had it for vij. yeer, with thys that my moodre be agreable to the same. **1497** in *Somerset Med. Wills* (1901) 353, I will that Isabell my doughter, shal haue all suche stuffe [etc.] whit that she marie by thaduyce of my executours. *c* **1500** *Lancelot* 960, I grant yow leif, withthy Your name to me that 3e wil specify. *c* **1500** *Crow & Pie* v. in Child *Ballads* II. 478 Haue ye thys, my dere swetyng, With that ye wylbe lemman myn.

†**b.** With the intention that, in order that, to the end that. *Obs.*

c **888** ÆLFRED *Boeth.* xxxiii. §2 He..forlæt mæniȝne weoruldlust wið þæm þe he þone welan beȝete & ȝehealde. *Ibid.* xl. §5 Me wære leofre þæt ic onette wið þæs þæt ic þe moste ȝelæstan þæt ic þe ær ȝehet. *a* **1225** *Juliana* 3 Þe liflade of a meiden þat is of latin iturnd to englische leode, wið þon þat teos hali leafdi in heouene luuie us þe mare.

II. Denoting personal relation, agreement, association, connexion, union, addition.

* Senses denoting primarily activity towards or influence upon a person or thing.

7. a. After words denoting speech or other verbal communication between persons (with the person as obj.); properly of mutual communication, but formerly sometimes merely = *to*, as in quot. 1480.

Beowulf 365 Hy benan synt þæt hie..wið þe moton wordum wrixlan. *a* **1000** *Riddles* xl. 12 Ne hafað hio fot ne folm,..ne muð hafaþ ne wiþ monnum spræc. *c* **1205** LAY. 14069 He wolde wið þan kinge holden runinge. *c* **1300** *Harrow. Hell* 123 Y shal speke þe wyht Ant do þe to holde gryht. *c* **1386** CHAUCER *Melib.* ¶755, I prey yow lat me speke with youre Aduersaries in priuee place. *c* **1420** *Prose Life Alex.* 14 He went..for to consaile wit a godd þat þay called Amon. **1470-1760** [see QUESTION *v.* 2]. *c* **1480** HENRYSON *Bludy Serk* 106 Scho said nay, With men þat wald hir wed. **1500-20** DUNBAR *Poems* xiii. 15 Sum with his fallow rownis. **1555-** [see CONFERENCE 4]. **1588** SHAKS. *L.L.L.* v. ii. 230 White handed Mistris, one sweet word with thee. **1670** in *12th Rep. Hist. MSS. Comm.* App. v. 16 Give me leave to be ingennuous with your Honour, that mannifacture grows worse daylie. *a* **1700** EVELYN *Diary* 9 Feb. 1665, I had much discourse with his Lordship. **1753-4** RICHARDSON *Grandison* III. viii. 109 But, unseasonably, as the event shewed, Father Marescotti, being talked with, was earnest to be allowed to visit her. **1884** CONWAY *Bound Together* I. 181 For many years Mrs. Blatchford had held little communication with her family.

b. Followed by refl. pron., in reference to soliloquy, consideration, determination, etc. *arch.*

1530 PALSGR. 514/2 Whan I determyne with my selfe to do a thyng. **1553** [see WEIGH *v.*[1] 12c]. **1564** HARDING *Answ. Jewel* 180 Saye this with thy selfe. **1580** LYLY *Euphues* (Arb.) 443 Bicause you are braue, disdaine not those that are base, thinke with your selues that russet coates haue their Christendome. *a* **1592** GREENE *Alphonsus* IV. iii, Remember with your selues. **1707** *Curios. Husb. & Gard.* 201, I imagin'd with my self..that..we might multiply..the very same curious Plants. **1741** WATTS *Improv. Mind* I. i. §1 (1786) 5 Think seriously with yourselves how many follies and sorrows you had escaped.

†**c.** After *communicate*, *impart* (information), orig. = 'share' (cf. 20). *Obs.* (now replaced by *to*).

1559, **1704** [see COMMUNICATE *v.* 2]. **1571** [see IMPART *v.* 2]. **1612** BRINSLEY *Lud. Lit.* 4 More readie..to impart your experiments with me. **1623** BINGHAM *Xenophon* 65 He..communicated his dream with him.

8. a. After words expressing transaction or dealing between persons (with the person as obj.).

Beowulf 155 Grendel..sibbe ne wolde wið manna hwone mæȝenes Deniȝa. *c* **893** ÆLFRED *Oros.* III. v, Æfter þæm þe Perse frið ȝenaman wið Romanum. *a* **1300** *Cursor M.* 5848 (Gött.) Wid þe eldest folk of israel, Wid pharao þai went to dele. ?*c* **1360** *Alexius* 123 (MS. Ashmol. 42) in Horstm. *Altengl. Leg.* (1881) 177 He..chaungid..his riche wede Wiþ a beggar. *a* **1400-50-** [see COVENANT *sb.* 1γ]. *c* **1450-** [see TREATY *sb.* 2, 3]. **1481** *Cely Papers* (Camden) 72 Ye schall receyve..a lytyll fardell of felles that ys alowyd for iij felles with the costomer. **1591** SHAKS. *Two Gent.* III. i. 3 What's your will with me? **1637** RUTHERFORD *Lett., to A. Colvill* 19 Feb. (1671) 194, I will neither borrow nor lend with it [*sc.* this world]. **1659** in *Engl. Hist. Rev.* (1920) Apr. 254, I will keepe my dayes with you as long as I am able. **1661** in *Extr. St. Papers rel. Friends* Ser. II. (1911) 139 Such of his Maiesties freindes as euer had occasion with me. **1780** *Mirror* No. 110 ¶1 To do justice to those with whom they have had dealings. **1838** THIRLWALL *Hist. Greece* xl. V. 115 To give audience to all who had business to transact with him. **1861** M. PATTISON *Ess.* (1889) I. 41 During Edward's wars our commerce with France was wholly broken off.

b. After words expressing conduct or feeling towards (a person, etc.).

In some cases now replaced by other prepositions, e.g. envious *of*. In expressions of hostile action or feeling, this coincides with 2.

c **888** ÆLFRED *Boeth.* vii. §3 Hwi murcnast ðu wið min? *c* **1000** ÆLFRIC *Gen.* xii. 18 Hwi dydest ðu swa wið me? *c* **1175** *Lamb. Hom.* 27 3if þu ert swiðe for-gult wið þine eorðliche lauerd. *a* **1200** *Moral Ode* 216 in *O.E. Hom.* I. 173 Ac helle king is are-les with þa þe he mei binden. *a* **1250** *Owl & Night.* 62 Ich wot þat þu art unmilde Wiþ hom þat ne mu3e from þe schilde. *c* **1300** *Havelok* 2705 Godrich, wat is þe þat þou fare þus with me? *c* **1400** *Brut.* I. 18 Corneil his eldest dou3ter..was so annoyed wiþ him and wiþ his peple. **1470-85** MALORY *Arthur* X. xxvii. 457 Thenne was kyng Arthur wroth with kynge Marke. **1526** TINDALE *Matt.* xviii. 29 Have pacience with me, and I will paye the all. **1577-** in love with [see LOVE *sb.*[1] 7d]. **1599** B. JONSON *Ev. Man out of Hum.* II. vi, I am come to haue you play the Alchymist with me. **1601** SHAKS. *Twel. N.* II. v. 162 Be opposite with a kinsman, surly with seruants. **1601** —— *Jul. C.* III. i. 255 O pardon me..That I am meeke and gentle with these Butchers. **1636** *Bk. Com. Prayer, Catechism*, To..be in charity with all men. **1677** EARL ESSEX in *Essex Papers* (Camden) II. 108 Ye soldier being very rough with ye Corporall, and refusing to pay. **1709** ADDISON *Tatler* No. 108 ¶3 Out of Humour with [see HUMOUR *sb.* 8a]. **1736-** vesed with [see VEX *v.* 4b]. **1889** J. K. JEROME *Three Men in Boat* 172, I..lost my temper with him.

9. a. Expressing a general relation to a person or thing, usually as affected in some way by the action, etc. spoken of: In the matter of, in regard to, towards, to, at, upon, about, concerning; in regard to the condition or fortune of.

Sometimes approaching the instrumental use, 37; or (with personal obj.) 8b.

c **897** ÆLFRED *Gregory's Past. C.* xxix. 200 Ðæm ðeowan is to cyðonne ðæt he wiete ðæt he nis freoh wið his hlaford. *c* **1205** LAY. 19057 Þe king hire wende to..& hæfde him to done wið leofuest wimmonne. *c* **1300** *Havelok* 901 Þan men haueden holpen him doun With þe birþene of his croun. *c* **1394** *P. Pl. Crede* 742 Y mi3t tymen þo troiflardes to toilen wiþ þe erþe. *c* **1400** *26 Pol. Poems* iv. 8 How it is wiþ hym, y kan not say. **14..** *Tundale's Vis.* 2366 (MS. A.) How þei schuld be with don as Godus wyll wold. **1502** *Plumpton Corr.* (Camden) 164 There was a servant of yours..was myschevously made away with. **1595** SHAKS. *John* V. vii. 111 Let vs pay the time but needfull woe, Since it hath beene before hand with our greefes. **1595-** [see BEFOREHAND 1c]. **1596-** [see BEHIND *adv.* 5b]. **1603** SHAKS. *Meas. for M.* I. i. 33 Heauen doth with vs, as we, with Torches doe. **1610** B. JONSON *Alch.* I. iii, You shall deale much with mineralls. **1624** CAPT. J. SMITH *Virginia* I. 16 We tooke more Cod then we knew what to doe with. **1660** SOUTH *Serm., Matt. xiii. 52* (1727) IV. 27 When the Rooters and Through-Reformers made clean Work with the Church. *a* **1715** BURNET *Own Time* (1724) I. 557 He told me, it was not decent to be merry with such a matter. **1715-** [see MATTER *sb.*[1] 25b]. **1753-4** RICHARDSON *Grandison* II. xv. 116 Things,..that we have no business with. **1755** *Connoisseur* No. 100 ¶5 All these indignities I very patiently put up with. **1799** G. S. CAREY *Balnea* (ed. 2) 159 The walks..have been taken a great deal of pains with. **1802** MARIA EDGEWORTH *Moral T., Prussian Vase* (1816) I. 211 What do you want with me? **1814** WORDSW. *Excurs.* VII. 194 The..Master's hand Was busier with his task. **1816** LADY GRANVILLE *Lett.* (1894) I. 101 His manner is brusque and short, and I got on but little with him. **1818** SCOTT *Hrt. Midl.* xxxviii, He knows how to manage with her. **1823** SCORESBY *Jrnl.* 391 This anxiety with myself. **1841** BROWNING *Pippa Passes* I. 228 God's in his heaven—All's right with the world! **1865** KINGSLEY *Herew.* viii, He surpassed Ptolemy with the astrolabe. **1873** H. E. ROSCOE in *Owens Coll. Ess. & Addr.* (1874) 56 Experiments on the properties of vanadium..made with much larger quantities than it fell to the lot of the Swedish chemist to work with. **1887** LEWIS CARROLL *Game of Logic* iv. 95 She is perhaps a little over-doing it, in the way of lessons, with her children. **1923** *Times Lit. Suppl.* 18 Jan. 34/3 Getting through with work as quickly as possible.

(*b*) **1809** MALKIN *Gil Blas* I. vi. ¶4 Get along with you, and go to bed. **1897** go along with you [see GO *v.* 73a].

b. After an adv. or phr. with ellipsis of or equivalent to a verb, usually imperative: e.g. *away with it* = 'take it away', *down with it* = 'put or throw it down', etc.

c **1377** in *Minor Poems Vernon MS.* 718/99, I ou Rede ..þat vch a Mon vp wiþ þe hede, And Mayntene him boþe hei3e and lowe. *c* **1388** in *Wyclif's Sel. Wks.* III. 472 His proude clerkis schal downe wiþ þer pride. **1477** SIR J. PASTON in *P. Lett.* III. 199 My charges be gretter than I maye a weye with. **1528** *Impeachm. Wolsey* in Furniv. *Ballads from MSS.* I. 360 Down with thy tayle, and of with thy goldyn shone. **1535-** [see DOWN *adv.* 25b]. **1598** SHAKS. *Merry W.* IV. ii. 239 Come, to the Forge with it. **1603** —— *Meas. for M.* V. i. 121 To prison with her. *Ibid.* 313 To th' racke with him. **1708** [see IN *adv.* 1c]. **1843** *Blackw. Mag.* LIV. 75 To the foul fiend with Rosley Castle!

†**c.** In case of, in the event of. *Obs. rare.*

1625 PURCHAS *Pilgrims* II. 1140 A good Hauen with all weathers. **1751** R. PALTOCK *P. Wilkins* (1884) II. 209, I don't know what we should do with fires; we see the dread of them sufficiently.

d. In phr. ***with reference, regard, respect to***: see REFERENCE *sb.* 3b, REGARD *sb.* 13, RESPECT *sb.* 7. So †***with*** (now ***in***) ***comparison to***.

1669 *Hist. Pope's Nephews* (1673) I. 38 When once he had put on the habit of a Priest, he could hardly..know himself with comparison to what he was before.

e. ***what's with*** ——? what about, what are the circumstances of?; how are things with, what's the matter with? *colloq.* (orig. *U.S.*).

1940 J. O'HARA *Pal Joey* 125 What's with the free food? Explain. **1962** E. LININGTON *Extra Kill* viii. 122 He says ..'What's with Whalen?' When he hears Whalen's out, he gets mad. **1969** 'V. PACKER' *Don't rely on Gemini* (1970) viii. 62 'What's with you and these long baths?' Archie asked. **1978** K. AMIS *Jake's Thing* xv. 158 What's with Jake is that he can't get it up any more, and what's with Brenda is she thinks it's her fault for having gotten middle-aged and fat.

10. In the opinion, view, or estimation of; 'in the sight of'.

a **1000** *Cædmon's Gen.* 507 Nu þu..hæfst þe wið drihten dyrne ȝeworhtne. *c* **1000** ÆLFRIC *Saints' Lives* xxvii. 171 Scyldiȝ wið god. *a* **1300** *Cursor M.* 9521 He had an anlepe son, þat wit his fader was sa wele þat [he] wist his wisdom ilk dele. *c* **1430** *Life St. Kath.* (1884) 92 He was so gret wyth þe Emperour. **1474** *Stonor Papers* (Camden) I. 149 Remembryng how grettely in consette ye stonde..with a gentylwoman. **1572** *Treat. of Treasons agst. Q. Eliz.* 61 b, To discredite those Noble persons with the people. **1598** HAKLUYT *Voy.* I. 56 To slay men, to inuade the dominions of other people, and to rifle their goods..are with them no offences at all. **1608–** go down with [see GO *v.* 80 g]. **1611** *Bible* 1 Pet. ii. 20 This is acceptable with God. **1634** SIR T. HERBERT *Trav.* Table Gg 3/2 Cycala-Bassa..is out of credit with the Grand Signior. *c* **1646** MILTON *New Forcers Consc.* 10 Men whose Life, Learning, Faith and pure intent Would have been held in high esteem with Paul. **1681** DRYDEN *Abs. & Achit.* I. 558 Every man with him was God or Devil. **1709** POPE *Ess. Crit.* 338 Most by Numbers judge a Poet's song; And smooth or rough, with them is right or wrong. **1823** BYRON *Juan* XIII. xxiv, Juan stood well both with Ins and Outs. **1841** BROWNING *Pippa Passes* ad. fin., All service is the same with God.

11. a. In the practice or experience of, in the life or conduct or, in (one's) case; sometimes *spec.* in the language or statement of, according to. (With pl. obj. = AMONG A. 6.)

a **1310** in Wright *Lyric P.* v. 25 He is coral y-cud with cayser ant knyht. *a* **1352** MINOT *Poems* (ed. Hall) iii. 69 þan with þam was none oþer gle. ? **1478** *Stonor Papers* (Camden) II. 35 Schepe was neuer so der with vs. **1526** TINDALE *Matt.* xix. 26 With men this is vnpossyble, but with God all thinges are possyble. **1605** SHAKS. *Macb.* v. i. 32 It is an accustom'd action with her, to seeme thus washing her hands. **1615** T. MAXFIELD in *Cath. Rec. Soc. Publ.* (1906) III. 51 Julie the 16, wth y^u^ 26. **1676** DRYDEN *Aurengz.* III. i, 'Tis not with me as with a private Man. **1678** CUDWORTH *Intell. Syst.* I. iv. §32. 516 This notion was so familiar with these Pagans. **1796–7** JANE AUSTEN *Pride & Prej.* xliii, 'And this is always the way with him', she added. **1841** FITZGERALD *Lett.* (1889) I. 77 These fits of exaltation are not very common with me. **1864** MRS. H. WOOD *Trevlyn Hold* xli, 'Were the ricks insured?' 'No. There's the smart with Chattaway.' **1881** RUSSELL *Haigs* xiv. 426 With the rough-riding men on both sides of the frontier to meet was to fight. **1909** BYWATER *Aristotle on Art Poetry* 172 *Πολιτική* is with him the practical wisdom of the statesman. **1910** BOLLAND *Eyre of Kent* (Selden Soc.) I. Introd. 95 These omissions would be impossible with a copyist who read over what he had copied.

b. After words expressing influence or the like: sometimes replaceable by *over* or *upon*.

1573–80 BARET *Alv.* P 696 With whom when she could nothing preuaile. **1631** WEEVER *Anc. Funeral Mon.* 512 His all-potencie with the King. **1712** P. METCALFE *Life S. Winefride* (1917) 16 He had great Power and Authority with them. **1814** JANE AUSTEN *Mansf. Park* xiii, She has no influence with..my sisters that could be of any use. **1865** RUSKIN *Sesame* i. §4 Most honest men..would..acknowledge its leading power with them as a motive.

** Senses relating to agreement (or disagreement) in some respect.

Senses 16 and 18 are closely allied to those under ***, involving the idea of proximity or accompaniment in space or time.

12. Following words expressing comparison, likeness, equality, or identity.

In some cases varying with or now replaced by *to*, e.g. after *compare*, *comparison*, *equal*, *resemblance*; after *same*, *as* is more usual; but *with* is still regular after some derived sbs., as *equality*, *sameness*, and also after *even* adj., *identical*, *identity*, *level* adj., *one* adj., *rank* vb., etc. See the various words.

c **888** ÆLFRED *Boeth.* xvi. §2 Hu micle mare is ðonne þæs monnes lichoma to metenne wið þæt mod þonne seo mus wið ðone mon. *c* **1200** ORMIN 3090 þatt wass inoh all an wiþþ þatt þatt Godess enngell seȝȝde. *Ibid.* 7931 þeȝȝre sang iss lic wiþþ wop. **1387** TREVISA *Higden* (Rolls) II. 259 Of þe same age wiþ þe kyngdom of Assiries. *c* **1450** *Merlin* xx. 317 Thei ben so fewe that thei may not compare with hem. **1513** MORE *Rich. III*, Wks. 47/1 Waye [= weigh] the good that they dooe, with the hurte that commeth of them. **1526** TINDALE *Phil.* ii. 6 Which beynge in the shape off god, and thought it not robbery to be equall with god. **1677–** [see IDENTICAL 2]. **1710** HEARNE *Collect.* 24 Feb. (O.H.S.) II. 348 A sniveling Gentleman of not half the sense with the late poor spirited Dick Cromwell. **1836** MACAULAY *Life & Lett.* (1883) I. 456 His style affects me in something the same way with that of Gibbon. **1879** WHITNEY *Sanskrit Gram.* 337 Some of the apparent roots..with sibilant final are akin with the desideratives. **1885** *Act 48 & 49 Vict.* c. 58 §1 This Act shall be read as one with the Telegraph Acts, 1863 to 1878.

13. a. Following words expressing agreement, conformity, sympathy, and the like.

c **893** ÆLFRED *Oros.* IV. viii, For þon hie on symbel wið Romanum sibbe heoldon. *a* **1000** *Guthlac* 382 þæt frið wið hy ȝefreoþad wære. **1123** *O.E. Chron.* (Laud MS.) an. 1120 Se arceb[iscop] Turstein..wearð þurh þone papan wið þone cyng acordad. *c* **1200** *Trin. Coll. Hom.* 105 Hie ben þenne sahtnede wið þe heuenliche fader. **1390** GOWER *Conf.* I. 6 At his commandement, With whom myn herte is of accord. **1398** TREVISA *Barth. De P.R.* XVI. xliv. (1495) L ij/2 Yren hath agrement with the stone Adamas. *c* **1430** *Hymns Virgin* (1867) 13 God wiþ man is maade at oone. **1535** JOYE *Apol. Tindale* (Arb.) 11 Henrichus Bullyngerus..consenteth with me in the significacion of this worde. **1605** B. JONSON *Volpone* III. iv, There was but one sole man..With whom I ere could sympathise. **1611** SHAKS. *Cymb.* III. iii. 31 Hap'ly this life is best..Well corresponding With your stiffe Age. **1642–** fall in with [see FALL *v.* 91 b–e]. **1662–** [see SYMPATHY 3 b]. **1761** MRS. F. SHERIDAN *Sidney Bidulph* II. 310 How ill does the vanity of pomp suit with a house of mourning! **1796** *Ann. Reg., Hist.* 115 Spain was..on friendly terms with France. **1821** SHELLEY *Hellas* 537 The tiger leagues not with the stag at bay Against the hunter. **1849** MACAULAY *Hist. Eng.* i. I. 107 He declared his determination to govern in harmony with the Commons. **1913** W. M. RAMSAY *Teaching of Paul* 158 His heart became..more..sympathetic with their trials.

b. By extension, after words expressing disagreement.

1646 SIR T. BROWNE *Pseud. Ep.* I. viii. 30 It containeth impossibilities and things inconsistent with truth. **1735–8** BOLINGBROKE *On Parties* 81 They [*sc.* the Tories] had only differ'd with the Whigs about the Degree of Oppression. **1791–1823** D'ISRAELI *Cur. Lit.* (1866) 208 Every edition varies with the preceding ones. **1868** GLADSTONE *Juv. Mundi* i. (1870) 16 Testimony..in no case discordant with that of the Iliad.

14. a. On the side or party of; in favour of; on behalf of; 'for': opp. to AGAINST 12. (See also 22 c.)

c **1200** ORMIN 4675 Swa forrwerrpesst tu þin Godd, & haldesst wiþþ þatt ahhte. *c* **1300** *Havelok* 2308 He swore, þat he sholde with him halde Boþe ageynes stille and bolde. **1382** WYCLIF *Matt.* xii. 30 He that is nat with me, is aȝeinus me. *c* **1420** LYDG. *Assembly of Gods* 1058 Vertu was full heuy, when he sy Frewyll Take part with Vyce. **1478** *Acta Audit.* (1839) 66/2 Ilk baroun and freehaldare þat..geve voce with þe said dome. *c* **1489** CAXTON *Sonnes of Aymon* ix. 238 Nevertheles he came, and helde syde wyth his broder. **1509** FISHER *Serm.* Wks. (1876) 277 What sentence he shal gyue wheder with me or ayenst me. **1534** *Star Chamber Cases* (Selden Soc.) II. 317 They were at issue and by a substancyall Jury..Founde with the seid mulsho. **1582** *N.T.* (Rhem.) Acts xiv. 4 Certaine of them..were with the Jewes, but certaine with the Apostles. **1600** HOLLAND *Livy* XXIX. vi. 713 The citie of Locri..had sided also with the Carthaginians. **1633** EARL MANCH. *Al Mondo* (1636) 171 When a man comes to be judged; his life..shal give the evidence with, or against him. **1653** CROMWELL *Sp.* 4 July in *Carlyle*, He hath appeared with them. **1697** DRYDEN *Æneis* XII. 827 Jove is with us. **1709** STRYPE *Ann. Ref.* I. xlix. 492 There being with the bill 60, against it 75. **1842** DICKENS *Amer. Notes* xv, The soldiers rather laughed at this blade than with him. **1845** BROWNING *Lost Leader* 14 Shakespeare was of us, Milton was for us, Burns, Shelley, were with us. **1886** *Manch. Exam.* 9 Jan. 5/3 M. Granet, Minister of Posts and Telegraphs, has usually voted with M. Clemenceau.

b. In reference to wind, tide, etc.: Favourable to, in a favourable direction for.

1647 SANDERSON *Serm.* (1674) II. 218 As a Boat that (having wind and tide with it) runneth glib and merrily down the stream. **1719** DE FOE *Crusoe* II. (Globe) 378 They had..the Flood-Tide with them.

15. a. In the same way as; as —— does or did, is or was, etc.; like. (Cf. 17.)

c **1340** *Medit.* in *Hampole's Wks.* (1895) I. 94 So þat þoru þi merci and grace we moun repente of oure..mys-dedis with seint Petir. **1362** LANGL. *P. Pl.* A. VIII. 71 He is Fals with þe Fend. *c* **1400** *Rule St. Benet* (prose) 11 Of mekenes spekis sain benet..& sais with hali scripture: 'Omnis qui se exaltat &c.' **1433** LYDG. *S. Edmund & Fremund* 1034–6 in Horstm. *Altengl. Leg.* (1881) 395 He..Hadde with Nestor manly auysynesse;..With Tideus he hadde eek hardynesse. **1589** NASHE *Returne Pasquill* Wks. (Grosart) I. 121 A crooked generation, that loues to swym side-long with the Crabbe. **1600** —— *Summer's Last Will* Prol. 73 Euery man cannot, with Archimedes, make a heauen of brasse. **1634** RAINBOW *Labour* (1635) 35 With stomackefull children we bawle for Rattles. **1711** ADDISON *Spect.* No. 227 ¶ 5, I must cry out with Dido..'Ah! cruel Heaven, that made no Cure for Love!' **1809** BYRON *Bards & Rev.* 102 Better to err with Pope, than shine with Pye. **1861** PALEY *Æschylus* (ed. 2) 7 *agst. Thebes* 759 *note*, Hermann gives ἀλκὰν with one of the most recent MSS. **1905** CHESTERTON *Heretics* 37 Whether we should love everybody with Tolstoy, or spare nobody with Nietzsche.

b. Followed by *the* and a superlative used *absol.*: As well or thoroughly as; (as) one of, 'among', 'of': forming adverbial (or †predicative) phrases denoting 'to the full or fullest extent', '(nearly) as —— as any or as possible', 'very ——', 'highly ——': e.g. ***with the best*** = among the best, as well as any, very well; ***with the first***, as one of the first, very early, chiefly, especially (see FIRST 6 c); ***with the least*** = at the lowest estimate; †***with the most inclined*** = highly inclined. *Obs.* or *arch.*

a **1300** *K. Horn* 1119 (Harl.) þou shen[c]h vs wiþ þe vurste. **13..** *Seuyn Sag.* (W.) 1656 The king..kep the leuedi with the best. **1445** in *Anglia* XXVIII. 281 Why is not he redde with the worthiest? **1470–85** MALORY *Arthur* x. lxviii. 531 Soo that nyghte they were lodged with the best. **1477** *Paston Lett.* III. 183, I wold have hym [*sc.* a horse] sumwhat large, not with the largest. *a* **1533** LD. BERNERS *Huon* clxii. 634 Thyne armure is good and thy sworde is with the best. **1553** GRIMALDE *Cicero's Offices* I. (1556) 41 b, If ther be anie somewhat with the moste enclined to pleasures. **1573–80** TUSSER *Husb.* (1878) 51 Who pescods delighteth to haue with the furst, If now he do sowe them, I thinke it not wurst. **1577** GOOGE tr. *Heresbach's Husb.* 45 Not to mowe your Grasse with the latest, but before the seede be ripe. *a* **1592** GREENE *Jas. IV*, I. ii, A young stripling..that can sleep with the soundest, eate with the hungriest. **1629** GAULE *Pract. Theories* 376 Of all the difficulties of Truth and Faith, the Article of Christs Resurrection is with the formost. **1671** H. M. tr. *Erasm. Colloq.* 494 There was no year, wherein he did not gain a thousand Duckats, to speak with the least. **1826** *Priestley's Rudim.* 55 The preposition *with* is..sometimes used in conversation, to express a degree ..something less than the greatest; as 'They are with the widest.' **1859** TENNYSON *Grandm.* 20 At your age, Annie, I could have wept with the best.

16. Expressing simultaneous occurrence and association (cf. 25), often also implying causal connexion (cf. 39). **a.** At the same time as; at the time or instant of; on the occurrence of (often with implication 'and because of'); at, on, upon.

(*a*) Followed by a sb. (often qualified).

Before *occasion*, *opportunity*, now replaced by *on* or (less usually) *at*.

13.. *Cursor M.* 10462 (Gött.) Vtayne wid þis word gan tene. **1456** SIR G. HAYE *Law Arms* (S.T.S.) 145 The payment cessis with the impossibilitee of the service. **1592** SHAKS. *Ven. & Ad.* 900. **1655** *Theophania* 89 With a resolution to hire a ship,..and with the first occasion to follow her into Sicily. **1697** DRYDEN *Virg. Georg.* IV. 273 Nor ends their Work, but with declining Day. **1719** PHILLIPS tr. *Thirty-four Conferences* 338 He hath promised to send you a Copy with the first Opportunity. **1748** THOMSON *Cast. Indol.* II. x, Sometimes with early morn, he mounted gay The hunter-steed. **1822** T. L. PEACOCK *Maid Marian* x, John..was determining to take possession with the first light of morning. **1870** LOWELL *Study Wind.* (1871) 157 Browning..draws nearer to the all-for-point fashion of the *concettisti*, with every poem he writes. **1926** *Times* 15 Mar., With his death, his younger brother..becomes heir to the barony.

(*b*) Followed by a demonstrative pron.: ***with that*** (†***than***), when (and, often, because) that occurred, thereupon; †at that instant, just then (*obs.*); saying or having just said that; ***with this***, hereupon. Cf. HEREWITH 2, THEREWITH 2 c, WHEREWITH 4 b.

c **1250** *Gen. & Ex.* 1409 Laban and his moder wið-ðan Faȝneden wel ðis sondere man. *a* **1300** *Cursor M.* 1203 Wit þis [*Trin.* Here aftir] was born an hali child, Seth þat meke was and mild. *Ibid.* 3368 And þof sco scamful was, i-wiss, Sco tint na contenance wit þis. **1375** BARBOUR *Bruce* xv. 168 Syne..[The] myddis of the toune he tais, With that neir cummand war his fais. *c* **1425** WYNTOUN *Cron.* I. v. 203 A child..said, he saw a dere. Wiþ þat þe takill wp he drew. **1470–85** MALORY *Arthur* XVI. xvi. 687 With that Bors lyfte vp his hand & wold haue smyten his broder. **1592** SHAKS. *Ven. & Ad.* 25. **1603** in *Cath. Rec. Soc. Publ.* (1906) II. 218 And with this I byd you most hartely fare-well. **1681** DRYDEN *Abs. & Achit.* I. 717 'Take then my tears' (with that he wiped his Eyes). **1779** *Mirror* No. 35 ¶ 11 'Who shall decide when doctors disagree?' And, with that, he made one of the finest bows in the world. **1847** TENNYSON *Princess* II. 290 'Our mother, is she well?' With that she kiss'd His forehead.

b. Followed by a sb. or pron., forming a phrase equivalent to a clause with *when*, in which the sb. or pron. is the subj. (or obj.), and the vb. is identical with that in the principal clause; e.g. *our hopes died with him*, i.e. when (and because) he died; *to rise with the lark*, i.e. when the lark rises (= early in the morning): see LARK *sb.*[1] 1 b.

†Formerly also with vbs. of durative meaning: = contemporaneously with.

1432–50 tr. *Higden* (Rolls) VIII. 497 But mony abusions comme from Boemia into Englonde with this qwene. **1592** SHAKS. *Ven. & Ad.* 1019 He being dead, with him is beautie slaine. **1614** RALEIGH *Hist. World* III. v. §8. 57 Where the Persians, so many of them as lost not their wits with their courage [etc.]. **1697** DRYDEN *Virg. Georg.* IV. 673 His Griefs with Day begun. **1742** MIDDLETON *Cicero* (ed. 3) II. vi. 31 Lentulus and Metellus, whose consulship expired with the year. **1791** BOSWELL *Johnson* 10 Apr. an. 1775, What was said by Johnson, or other eminent persons who lived with him. **1812** CRABBE *Tales* xi. 376 With virtue, prudence fled. **1891** FARRAR *Darkn. & Dawn* xliii, I hear rumours that another large vessel..foundered at sea. I expect that some of the accusers of Paulus perished with her.

c. In the course or duration of, in process of, 'in' (time, etc.); often with admixture of the instrumental sense: By, or in consequence of, the passage or lapse of (cf. 37, 39).

c **1440** *Alphabet of Tales* 329 With a few yeris þai war passand riche men. **1560** WHITEHORNE tr. *Macchiavelli's Arte of Warre* 87 All other thyng..maie with tyme be ouercome, this onely with tyme ouercometh thee. **1610** SHAKS. *Temp.* IV. i. 164 Come with a thought. **1611** FENTON *Usurie* II. xiii. 95 Mans labours and skill wil faile with yeeres. **1627** W. D. tr. *Andiguier's Lisander* 15 To render you more signal offices, which, with time, I hope to performe. **1784** in B. Ward *Dawn Cath. Revival* (1909) I. iv. 81 [Prejudices] will die away with time. **1855** TENNYSON *Will* ii, Bettering not with time. **1875** M. ARNOLD *God & Bible* p. xxviii, Christianity's admixture of popular legend and illusion was sure to be cleared away with time. **1884** W. C. SMITH *Kildrostan* 74 Unripe fruit..mellows with the months.

d. After words denoting change or variation: At the same rate as; at a rate, or in a manner, corresponding to that of; in proportion to, according to.

1697 DRYDEN *Virg. Georg.* III. 322 His stout Stomach with his Food will grow. **1701** SWIFT *Contests Nobles & Comm.* iii, Their Insolence and Power encreased with their Number. **1712** ARBUTHNOT *John Bull* I. v, His Spirits rose and fell with the Weather-glass. **1838** DE MORGAN *Ess. Probab.* 140 The probability of an error diminishes with its magnitude. **1839–47** *Todd's Cycl. Anat.* III. 516/2 The diameter of the capillaries of muscle varies..with the size of the blood-particles of the animal. **1857** BUCKLE *Civiliz.* I. ii. 58 The rate of wages fluctuates with the population. **1910** H. A. DALLAS *Mors Janua Vitæ?* 17 Her conviction as to the importance of the script naturally increased with the evidence for its veridical character.

17. Expressing agreement or accordance, esp. in opinion or statement. ***to be with***, to be of the same opinion as, to agree with. (See also 15.)

1456 SIR G. HAYE *Gov. Princis* (S.T.S.) 99 Thai speke quhilum with the and othir quhilis aganis the. **1565** ALLEN *Def. Purg.* xi. 104, I am not afrade to vse the word Satisfaction, with Cyprian, Origen, Ambrose, Augustin.

1611 TOURNEUR *Ath. Trag.* IV. iv. I4b, *Enter the Watch. Belfo.* The Watch? Met with my wish. **1625-** run with [see RUN *v.* 71 b]. **1648** HEXHAM, *Ick ben Met u*, I am With you, or, I am of your opinion. **1796** in B. Edwards *Maroon Negroes* 20, I am perfectly with you, that the pin ought not to receive another screw. **1883** STEVENSON *Treas. Isl.* xxix, Ah, it's a fine dance—I'm with you there. **1886** W. S. BLUNT *Diary* 22 Apr. in *Land War Irel.* (1912) ii. 79 Morris is with me about Ireland. **1916** J. R. MOZLEY *Div. Aspect Hist.* I. ix. 235 It was heart beating with heart.

18. In the same direction as; along the course of: opp. to AGAINST 9: esp. in such phrases as *with the grain, with the hair, with the stream, with the tide, with the wind.*

c **1489-** [see STREAM *sb.* 2 f]. **1577-** [see WIND *sb.*[1] 30]. **1597** BACON *Coulers Good & Euill* Ess. (Arb.) 154 If it be with the streame or with the hill. **1651** H. MORE *Enthus. Tri.* (1712) 37 With thankfulnesse and reverence he doth receive whatever Divine Providence brings upon him, be it sweet or sour, with the hair, or against it. **1678** MOXON *Mech. Exerc.* iv. 66 As well upon the Traverse.. as with the Grain of the wood. **1688** [see METAL *sb.* 7]. *c* **1710** CELIA FIENNES *Diary* (1888) 75 The Gardens runns down a great way, you descend with them by severall stepps. **1712** with the tide [see SWIM *v.* 1 c]. *a* **1774** GOLDSM. *Surv. Exp. Philos.* (1776) II. 386 A field of corn, viewed with the wind, is of a different shade from the same field viewed against the wind. **1786, 1816** [see STROKE *v.*[1] 1 d]. **1810** CRABBE *Borough* xviii. 183 The black footway winding with the wall. **1840** with the tide [see DROP *v.* 8]. **1867** SMYTH *Sailor's Word-bk., With the sun*, ropes coiled from the left hand towards the right; but where the sun passes the meridian north of the observer, it is of course the reverse. **1891** with the tide [see GO *v.* 87 f].

*** Senses expressing accompaniment or addition.

19. a. Following words expressing such meanings as are indicated above, as *accompany* (see note s.v.), *ally, alternate, associate, blend, combine, confront, connect, couple, entangle, incorporate, join, link, marry, mix, partake, share, unite, wed* (etc.) vbs. (and derived sbs., as *association, connexion*, etc.); *communion, company, contact, intercourse* (etc.) sbs.; *together* adv.: see the various words. See also ALONG *adv.* 3.

Beowulf 1088 þæt hie healfre ȝeweald wið Eotena bearn aȝan moston. *c* **888** ÆLFRED *Boeth.* xxxvi. §8 Se yfla willa næfð nænne ȝeferscipe wið þa ȝesælða. *a* **900** CYNEWULF *Elene* 307 Swa ȝe modblinde mengan ongunnon liȝe wið soðe. *a* **1240** *Ureisun* in *O.E. Hom.* I. 201 Hwoa so euer wule habben lot wið þe of þine blisse, he mot delen wið þe of þine pine on eorðe. **13..** *Cursor M.* 18019 (Gött.) Aisel haue i blend wid gall. *c* **1400** *Lanfranc's Cirurg.* 201 þei ben maad fast wiþ þe botme of þe stomac. **1557** *Dunfermline Reg.* (Bann. Club) 400 To pay.. Twelf caponis to giddir wutht hariage careage and due serwice. **1665** WALTON *Hooker* Introd., About forty years past.. I began a happy affinity with William Cranmer. **1671** MILTON *P.R.* IV. 412 Fierce rain with lightning mixt, water with fire In ruine reconcil'd. **1759** GOLDSM. *Bee* No. 4 ¶6, I was once determined to throw off all connexions with taste. **1785** REID *Intell. Powers* II. xiv. 214 A kind of feeling, or immediate perception of things present, and in contact with the percipient. **1836** THIRLWALL *Greece* xvi. (1838) II. 345 The Lacedæmonians, whose force, together with the Tegeans and forty thousand light troops, amounted to upwards of fifty thousand men. **1889** SWINBURNE *Study B. Jonson* 87 The collocation of such names.. as those of Æglamour and Earine with such others as Marche and Maudlin.

b. Following words expressing acquaintance or familiarity. (After *accustome(d, known*, now replaced by *to*.)

c **1220** *Bestiary* 113 His muð is ȝet wel unkuð wið pater noster and crede. *a* **1225** *Juliana* 14 Ne ich neuer þat ich wite nes wið him icnawen. **1338** R. BRUNNE *Chron.* (1810) 225 þan went þis Ottobone þorghout þe cuntre, & quaynted him with ilkone. *c* **1369** CHAUCER *Dethe of Blaunche* 532, I.. gan me aqueynt With hym. *c* **1386** —— *Prol.* 216 Famulier was he With frankeleyns ouer al in his contree. **1535** COVERDALE *Ecclus.* xxiii. 9 Let not thy mouth be accustomed with swearinge. **1611** *Bible* Isa. liii. 3 He is.. a man of sorrows, and acquainted with griefe. **1719** in *10th Rep. Hist. MSS. Comm.* App. I. 197 They could not.. undergoe the fatigue that the natives were accustomed with. **1880** L. STEPHEN *Pope* iii. 61 Pope was not disinclined to pride himself upon his familiarity with the great.

c. By extension, following words expressing separation: e.g. *to break with* = to break off connexion with (BREAK *v.* 34); *to part with* = to cease to be with or to have with one (PART *v.* 6 c). (After *take leave* now replaced by *of*.)

a **1300** *Cursor M.* 17022 Kynd na saul suffers ar to part wit man o-liue. *c* **1485** *Digby Myst.* (1883) III. 102 O ye good fathyr of grete degre, thus to departe with your ryches. **1486** *Bk. St. Albans* E iij b, In iij. degrees he hem berith or he with hem twyn. **1607** SHAKS. *Cor.* IV. vi. 48 It cannot be The Volces dare breake with vs. *a* **1629** HINDE *J. Bruen* lxvii. (1641) 224 My wife.. and my selfe, came to take leave with him. **1808** SOUTHEY *Lett.* (1856) II. 110 For more than a year, Scott has cut with the Edinburgh Review. **1885** *Manch. Exam.* 28 Mar. 5/5 The imminence of a rupture with Russia.

20. Expressing association or participation in some act, proceeding, or experience; *spec.* = acting on the same side as (another lawyer) in an action at law.

c **1290-** [see SIN *v.* 1 c]. *a* **1300-** [see PLAY *v.* 10]. *c* **1440** *Jacob's Well* 201 ȝif þou be partenere in dede of thefte,.. or of ony oþer wronges, þat is for to seyne, in folowynge wyth suche doers. **1526** TINDALE *Rom.* xii. 15 Be mery with them that are mery. wepe with them that wepe. **1533** [see ADULTERY 1]. **1596** SHAKS. *Merch. V.* I. iii. 36, I will buy with you, sell with you, talke with you, walke with you, and so following: but I will not eate with you, drinke with you, nor pray with you. **1711** STEELE *Spect.* No. 53 ¶7, I will.. for the future be merry with the Vulgar. **1816** SCOTT *Old Mort.* xxxviii, My lot is cast with Evandale, and with him I am resolved to bear it. **1837** DICKENS *Pickw.* xxxiv, 'I am for the plaintiff, my Lord,' said Mr. Serjeant Buzfuz. 'Who is with you, brother Buzfuz?' said the judge. **1848** —— *Dombey* xxxviii, Rob.. ran sniggering off to get change, and tossed it away with a pieman. **1883** *Manchester Exam.* 7 Nov. 5/2 A new weekly mail service with Australia.

21. a. (with such vbs. as *bring, take, come, go*) Followed by a sb. or (most commonly) pron. denoting the person (vessel, etc.) that leads, conveys, or carries a person or thing, thus having it in charge (cf. 23, of which this use is the converse).

Also *fig.* after *take*: see TAKE *v.* 59 b, c.

c **1290** *St. Matthew* 9 in *S. Eng. Leg.* 77 He bi-lefde þo is weork, and wiz ore louerd eode. *c* **1290** *Beket* 1213 *ibid.* 141 With him a-morewe he nam his oste. *a* **1300** *Cursor M.* 5297 To mi lauerd yee com wit me, I sal yow do a-quentid be. **1432-50** tr. *Higden* (Rolls) I. 133 [Nilus] makethe the londe plentuous thro slycche that hit drawethe with hit. *c* **1475** *Rauf Coilȝear* 6 Thay past vnto Paris.. With mony Prelatis and Princis. **1591** SHAKS. *Two Gent.* IV. i. 74 Come, goe with vs, we'll bring thee to our Crewes. *a* **1596** *Sir T. More* I. ii. 28 Ten poundes.. To carie in your pursse about with ye. **1697** DRYDEN *Virg. Georg.* III. 534 The Shepherd last appears, And with him all his Patrimony bears. **1776** *Trial of Nundocomar* 68/1 My uncle used frequently to go to Maha Rajah's: when I was little I used to go with him. **1812** JEFFERSON *Writ.* (1830) IV. 178 The truth is that we brought with us the rights of men. **1869** FREEMAN *Norm. Conq.* III. xi. 61 They took with them no force capable of controlling.. the country.

b. In the possession, keeping, care, or charge of (a person); in the hands of. (*lit.* and *fig.*)

a **1300** *Cursor M.* 4403 His mantel es bi-left wit me. **1340-70** *Alex. & Dind.* 32 Whan no wordliche wele is wiþ us founde. **1528** in Pocock *Rec. Ref.* (1870) I. 81 Leaving with the master of the Rolls such things as might.. instruct him. **1649** BP. HALL *Cases Consc.* III. ix. 341 That.. commissionary authority, which is by Christ entrusted with them. *c* **1710** W. HAMILTON *Descr. Lanark & Renfrew* (Maitl. Club 1831) 64 Douglass parish.. continued with the Earles of Douglass untill their fatall forfeiture. **1776** *Trial of Nundocomar* 68/1 You have for a long time had my money; it shall remain no longer with you. **1825** JEFFERSON *Autobiog.* Wks. 1859 I. 6 The committee.. left it in charge with their chairman to forward them by express. **1828** WHATELY *Rhet.* (1850) I. iii. §2 The 'burden of proof' lies with the accusers. **1896** CONAN DOYLE *Expl. Gerard* iii. 121 The deal lay with him. **1911** *Act 1 & 2 Geo. V* c. 46 §17 The ownership of an author's manuscript after his death.. shall be primâ facie proof of the copyright being with the owner of the manuscript.

c. In the nature or character of; as a quality or attribute of. Now chiefly after *way*: see WAY *sb.*[1] 22 d. (The converse of 31.)

14.. *Tundale's Vis.* 31 With hym was no charyte. **1553** *Douglas' Æneis* IX. Prol. *marg.*, Vertue.. has euer this rewill with hyr: do as thou wald be done to. **1650** TRAPP *Comm. Gen.* xxv. 30 This hunter hath no ho with him. **1678** DRYDEN *Kind Keeper* I. i, She has a notable Smack with her! **1711** R. MARTIN in E. H. Burton *Life Bp. Challoner* (1909) I. iii. 33 He had such an honest way with him. **1848** NEWMAN *Loss & Gain* II. xx. (1904) 254 What a way those fellows have with them!

22. a. In the company, society, or presence of.

face to face with: see FACE *sb.* 2 d. *with God*, in heaven: see GOD 5 c. *with oneself* (*dial.*): by oneself. *with us, them*, alive, still living.

a **1300** *K. Horn* 363 (Camb.) He schal wiþ me bileue Til hit beo nir eue. *a* **1300** *Cursor M.* 5706 þat fot moyses ful skete, And wit þe preist raguel he ete. **13..** *Gosp. Nicod.* (S.) 1579 Withe me þis ilk day be þou sall, With me in heuenryke. **1377** LANGL. *P. Pl.* B. v. 234 Ones I was herberwed.. with an hep of chapmen. *a* **1400-50** *Wars Alex.* 1613 þan Wer þair common whit hym kyngez. *c* **1450** *Mirk's Festial* 61 Then sate scho done all othyr wyth. **1526** TINDALE *John* xii. 8 The poore all wayes shall ye have with you, butt me shall ye nott all wayes have. **1553** *Dioc. Reg. Glasgow* (1875) I. 209 The said contrak.. subscrivit wyth Schir Jhone Alaine, notair publik. **1611** BIBLE *Acts* ix. 39 All the widowes stood by him weeping, and shewing the coats and garments which Dorcas made, while shee was with them. **1709** STEELE *Tatler* No. 26 ¶11 This Gentleman who has arrived with you is a fool of his own making. **1791** BOSWELL *Johnson* June 1763 (1904) I. 267, I begged I might be allowed to pass an evening with him there soon. *a* **1814** *Sailors' Ret.* I. i. in *New Brit. Theatre* II. 313 This whipper-snapper of mine.. sets off with himself, and no one knows where. **1820** KEATS *St. Agnes* xvi, Alone with her good angels, far apart From wicked men like thee. **1857** M. ARNOLD *Rugby Chapel* 25, I.. think Of bygone autumns with thee. **1891** FARRAR *Darkn. & Dawn* lviii, He found Nero sitting with Poppæa and Tigellinus. **1914** 'IAN HAY' *Knt. on Wheels* xvii, I don't go very often... Perhaps it is because I have no one to go with. **1961** E. WILLIAMS *George* xxiii. 391 That Mr Bellis, he's gone dead, not that he had that much life in him when he was with us, poor fellow. **1966** *Listener* 3 Feb. 166/2 The English church at Shiraz.. was built entirely thanks to the enthusiasm of the then incumbent, who was a very learned man (is indeed still with us).

b. *spec.* At the house of, or in the same house or meeting-place as; in the household, retinue, or service of, attending upon; on a visit to, being the guest of (hence *be with* sometimes = 'visit', 'call upon').

c **1250** *Gen. & Ex.* 466 Sella wuneð oc lamech wið. *c* **1275** LAY. 6784 He wonede at Ernleie wid þan gode cniþte. *c* **1386** CHAUCER *Prol.* 65 This ilke worthy knyght hadde been also Somtyme with the lord of Palatye Agayn another hethen in Turkye. *a* **1400** in Halliwell *Early Hist. Freemasonry* (1840) 20 He most love.. his mayster also, that he ys wyth. *c* **1440** *Alphabet of Tales* 171 When sho had ligen þus many day sho dyed, & no body with hur. *c* **1440** *Jacob's Well* 286 þei.. weryn harberwyd wyth a ryȝt good man. *c* **1465** *Stonor Papers* (Camden) I. 71 Squier for þe body with Kynge H. **1482** *Cely Papers* (Camden) 121, I thank yow of the grette cher that ye dydde me at my laste beyng wytthe yow. **1551** ROBINSON tr. *More's Utopia* II. viii. (1895) 253 For them, whomewyth they be in wayges, they fyghte hardelye. **1583** in *Cath. Rec. Soc. Publ.* V. 38 Somtyme Apprentice with oon M[r] Bannester of Preston. **1651** CROMWELL *Let.* 12 Apr. in *Carlyle*, If Dick Cromwell and his Wife be with you, my dear love to them. **1711-12** SWIFT *Jrnl. to Stella* 22 Jan., He was glad to find I was not with James Broad. **1715** C'TESS COWPER *Diary* (1864) 44 This Day Madame Selnave was with me to thank me for her Affair being ended. *a* **1752** in *Jrnl. Friends' Hist. Soc.* (1918) 21 Went.. to Yealand Scool.. to learn Wrighting and Arithmatick with Michael Jenkinson. **1803** T. JEFFERSON *Let.* Writ. 1854 IV. 470 He will be with you in Philadelphia in two or three weeks. **1878** HARDY *Ret. Native* v. vi, Have you heard that Eustacia is not with me now?

c. *fig.* in reference to an abstract thing: *to be with*, to accompany, 'attend'. Also in reference to God, combining the ideas of presence or companionship and favour, assistance, or the like (cf. 14).

Cf. *God be with you*, GOOD-BYE.

13.. *Gosp. Nicod.* (G.) 1020 Goddes bliscing be all his puple with. **1382** WYCLIF *Judges* vi. 12 The Lord with thee, moost stroong of men. *c* **1400** MAUNDEV. (Roxb.) iii. 10 Godd be with þe, for Godd es with vs. **1526** TINDALE *Eph.* vi. 24 Grace be with all them which love oure lorde Jesus Christ. **1634** SIR T. HERBERT *Trav.* 7 This calme and immoderate heate continued with vs seuen dayes. **1788** BURNS '*Of a' the Airts*' i, Day and night my fancy's flight Is ever wi' my Jean. **1825** BROCKETT *N.C. Gloss.* s.v. *Wud*, 'God be wud her'—God rest her soul. **1896** HOUSMAN *Shropsh. Lad* xxxvii, Luck, my lads, be with you still. **1897** KIPLING *Recess.* i, Lord God of Hosts, be with us yet.

d. The phrase *to be with*, used in menace, etc. = to be avenged on, chastise, be even with (cf. 12), perh. belongs here (cf. VISIT *v.* 3), but has affinities with other senses.

1590 SHAKS. *Mids. N.* III. ii. 403, I will be with thee straight. **1592** —— *Rom. & Jul.* II. iv. 78 Was I with you there for the Goose? **1596** —— *Tam. Shr.* IV. i. 170 What, do you grumble? Ile be with you straight. **1825** JAMIESON s.v. *With*, 'I'll be wi' him for that yet', Roxb.

e. *to be with* (a person), to follow his line of reasoning, to keep up with and understand his explanation, instructions, etc. *colloq.*

1900 F. P. DUNNE *Mr. Dooley's Philos.* 248 We keep our thoughts fixed upon th' inanity iv th' finite in comparison with th' onthinkable truth with th' ondivided an' onimaginable reality. Boys ar-re ye with me? **1933** *Punch* 8 Feb. 150/3 'Does it look to you as if the Boss keeps his skeletons in any ice-boxes around here?' 'Huh?' she said, not quite with me yet. **1955** N. FITZGERALD *House is Falling* xi. 190 'I'm with you so far,' said Hugh who for the first time was really giving his mind to the problem. **1977** T. HEALD *Just Desserts* viii. 188 'She will have to be taken in hand. Which.. has been the point of the exercise all along.' 'I'm not with you.'

f. *to be with it*, to be within a particular fashionable or exclusive group or set, to be up-to-date or *au fait* with the latest news, ideas, etc.; to be mentally alert. Also *to get with it*, to become informed or up-to-date, etc. *slang* (orig. *U.S.*). Cf. WITH-IT *a.*

1931 *Amer. Mercury* Nov. 353/2 *Not with it*, said of an outsider. 'He's not with it.' **1959** R. CONDON *Manchurian Cand.* (1960) vii. 108 They are with it, Raymond. Believe me, they are even away ahead of me. **1960** *Guardian* 9 Dec. 13 The new *Time and Tide*, to borrow the language of the teen-ager, is 'with it'. **1961** J. O'HARA in *Assembly* 159 Bud come to see you, especially when you had a chance of winning? Get *with* it, boy. **1971** *Daily Mail* 6 May 24/4 Horne made a strong attempt to get with it. Result: the stronger emphasis on fashionwear. **1976** *Jrnl. R. Soc. Arts* CXXV. 17/1 The need to be in fashion—in the swim—up to date—'with it'—might not have been the least of our driving forces for general progress. **1981** M. DOODY in Martin & Mullen *No Alternative* iv. 37 What is 'with it' for one or two generations can seem palpable folly a hundred years later. **1985** W. J. BURLEY *Wycliffe & Four Jacks* vii. 149 There's an old man, living in a home... He's quite with it—I mean he's mentally alert.

23. a. Having in one's hold, keeping, or charge; having within its compass, limits, area, etc.; leading, bringing, conveying, carrying, wearing, containing, etc.

with bag and baggage: see BAG *sb.* 20. (*found* or *taken*) *with the mainour* (*manner*): see MAINOUR 1.

c **1300** *Havelok* 52 þanne micthe chapmen fare þuruth englond wit here ware. *a* **1400** *Pist. Susan* 5 His Innes and his orchardus were with a dep dich. *c* **1400** *Ywaine & Gaw.* 759 A pot with riche wine. *c* **1400** *Destr. Troy* 5564 Palomydon.. presit into hauyn,.. With xxx[ti] shippes full shene, shot full of pepull. *c* **1430** *Chev. Assigne* 23 A pore womman.. Withe two chylderen her by-fore. **1488** *Acc. Ld. High Treas. Scot.* I. 80 A poik of canwes with demyis contenand aucht hundreth ane les. **1523** LD. BERNERS *Froiss.* I. ccxxvi. 123 b/1 The erle.. toke hym a flagon with wyne, wherof he had dronke. **1539** *Bible* (Great) 2 Sam. xviii. 27 He is a good man, and commeth with good tydinges. **1596** SHAKS. *Merch. V.* II. ii. (*stage direction*) Enter old Gobbo with a Basket. **1722** *Lond. Gaz.* No. 6054/2 A tall.. Man,.. with Ruffles and a light bag Wig. **1849** MACAULAY *Hist. Eng.* v. I. 609 He ordered Grey to lead the way with the cavalry. **1888** BARRIE *Auld Licht Idylls* iv. 105 The crowd.. was back in a moment with a handful of small change.

b. In phr. *with child, with young*, etc., said of a pregnant woman or animal (also in fig. phr. from these).

See CHILD *sb.* 17, EGG *sb.* 4, FOAL *sb.* 1 b, WHELP *sb.*[1] 1 b, YOUNG B. 2 c; also BIG *a.* 4, 5, GREAT *a.* 3, PREGNANT *a.*[2] 1, 2 b, 4, 5 (where the sense approaches 39); BEGET *v.* 2 c, CONCEIVE *v.* 3, GET *v.* 27 c, GO *v.* 7.

*c*1200 Ormin 2455 Þu best wiþþ childe off Haliȝ Gast. *a*1300 *Cursor M.* 10572 Anna wit child was of a mai. *c*1450 *St. Cuthbert* (Surtees) 391 Þe childe mett a cowe with' calfe. 1491 *Acta Audit.* (1839) 148/1, xxxij ȝowis with lamb. 1504 *Lincoln Wills* (1914) I. 21 If my wyfe be wyth a sonne. ?1556 *Wills & Inv. N.C.* (Surtees 1835) I. 152, ix whies calved and w^{t} calve. 1575 Turberv. *Faulconrie* 269 When hawkes fall to laying egges, and to be with egge in the mewe. 1585 *Knaresb. Wills* (Surtees) I. 149 The childe my wief is now conceyvid with. 1633 G. Herbert *Temple, Ch. Porch* vi, He that is drunken, may his mother kill Bigge with his sister. *a*1756 Eliza Haywood *New Present* (1771) 23 If they are with egg, their vents will be open. *c*1850 *Arab. Nts.* (Rtldg.) 388, I have also to inform you, that I am with child, and if Heaven so much favours me as to give me a son [etc.].

†**c.** In ownership of, as owner of, having in possession. *Sc. Obs.*

1406 in *Reg. Mag. Sig. Scot. 1427* 17/2 Quhyl we remane wyth the said landis. 1483 *Acta Audit.* in *Acta Dom. Conc.* II. Introd. 114 The said Thomas sall remain with the said land and tenement.

d. In phr. ***with costs, with damages*** (in a lawsuit): in early use said in ref. to the winning party = 'in possession of', 'having as awarded'; later, in ref. to the verdict = 'accompanied by an order to the losing party to pay' (cf. 32).

1466 *Stonor Papers* (Camden) I. 76 Richard.. prayeth þat he may be dismissed out of this Courte with his costes and damages. 1775 G. Wilson *Cases Comm. Pleas* III. 319 A verdict was given for the plaintiff, with one pound eleven shillings and sixpence damages. 1830 Barnewall & Cresswell *Rep. K.B.* IX. 528 They..recovered 25*l.* penalty, together with taxed costs. 1866 *Scott. Law Reporter* III. 81 The defender [was] assoilzied with expenses.

24. a. Accompanied by; having as an addition; having in one's company. Often connecting the two sbs. or prons.: = 'and in addition', 'and besides', or simply 'and'. Occas. in compound place-names: = cum. †***with the mare*** (*Sc. obs.*): = and more, and something over: see more B. 4 d.

*c*1200 Ormin 14792 Faraon wiþþ all hiss ferd comm affterr-warrd. *a*1300 *E.E. Psalter* ciii. 27 [civ. 25] Bestes smaller with þe mare. 1370–80 *Visions St. Paul* 247 in *O.E. Misc.* 230 Þer as was wepyng wiþ muche vnseeþe. *c*1380 Wyclif *Sel. Wks.* I. 205 Þe Sixte, wiþ Clementyns, done myche harm to Goddis lawe, and enfeblen bileve. 1432–50 tr. *Higden* (Rolls) I. 367 The water was so habundante that hit pereschede þe woman with here childe. 1494 *Acta Audit.* (1839) 205/2 Alexander.. tuk fra him out of his maling v^{xx} of ȝowis with the may. 1502 *Reg. Privy Seal Scot.* I. 112/2 Half a ȝere, with the mare, befor the date hereof. 1563 T. Wilson *Logic* 54 Beauuis with Alexander are comprehended vnder manne, as their kinde and speciall. *a*1706 Evelyn *Hist. Relig.* (1850) I. 410 The permitting female slaves to be corrupted by their masters, with the like. 1719 De Foe *Crusoe* I. (Globe) 296 We readily agreed to follow him, as did also twelve other Gentlemen, with their Servants. 1859 'Geo. Eliot' *Adam Bede* xviii, These grey pews, with the buff-washed walls, gave a very pleasing tone to this shabby interior. 1911 *Act 1 & 2 Geo. V* c. 6 §1 Imprisonment with or without hard labour.

in *attrib. phr.* 1898 *Westm. Gaz.* 17 May 8/1 To inaugurate some with-profit scheme.

b. Comprising in the whole number or total; including.

*c*1250 *Gen. & Ex.* 86 Til ihesus crist fro helle nam His quemed wid eue and adam. 1836 Dickens *Sk. Boz, Tuggs's at Ramsgate*, 'What's the terms?'..'Five guineas a week, ma'am, with attendance.' *Mod.* 'How many were there in the party?' 'I should say about twenty, with the children.'

c. Accompanied by (favourable wind, weather, etc.); having the advantage of.

1536 in *Sel. Pleas Crt. Admiralty* (1894) I. 58 Goyng from the porte of London at a full see with a full wynde. 1600 Fairfax *Tasso* xv. xlv, This evening (if you make good speed) To that hils foote with day-light might you passe. 1686 tr. *Chardin's Trav. Persia* 75 We put again to Sea with fair Weather.

d. ***with-profit(s)*** adj., of a life assurance policy: allowing the insured to receive a share of the profits of the insurance company, usu. in the form of a bonus. Also applied to holders of such policies, the associated payments, etc. Cf. *without-profit(s)* adj. s.v. without *prep.* 7 c.

1924 Tayler & Tyler *Life Assurance* ii. 19 Nearly all the offices transacting life assurance business issue two great classes of policy—(*a*) Those which share in the profits, known as 'with-profit' or 'participating' policies; and (*b*) Those which do not share in the profits, known as 'without-profit' or 'non-participating' policies. 1944 S. d'E. Colam *Life Assurance for Agents* 16 Premiums for with profit policies are larger than for without profit policies. 1950 *Economist* 18 Nov. 840/2 In trying to assess the relative merits of with-profit contracts, the only firm basis of comparison is the actual amount paid. 1961 *Observer* 10 Dec. 4/3 A modest writing-up of book values would add to the good times which with-profit-holders can expect in the future in the form of bumper bonuses. 1965 *Economist* 24 July p. xxii/2 These profits go to the with-profits policyholders, as well as the profits on the with-profits business itself. 1979 *Financial Times* 20 Jan. 7/6 If you are shopping around for a with-profits policy, take a look at how insurance brokers work out projections of maturity value. 1982 *Equity & Law Life Assurance Co. Ann. Rep. 1981* 16 The rate of terminal bonus depends on the year of entry as a with-profit benefit and is applied to the with-profit sum (or annuity) and attaching bonus.

25. Expressing association, conjunction, or connexion in thought, action, or condition.

one** (**day**, etc.) **with another: see one 17 b.

1387 Trevisa *Higden* (Rolls) II. 91 And so is Cornewayle acounted wiþ þe oþere schires. 1472 *Stonor Papers* (Camden) I. 124 For the certente what my cosen shall have with her, yf God provide for them that they shall go throwe in mariage. 1678 Prideaux *Lett.* (Camden) 64 Livy may be read with him [*sc.* Dionysius of Halicarnassus]. 1784 *Unfortunate Sensibility* II. 7 One week with another she earned about half-a-crown. ?1807–8 Wordsw. *Somnambulist* 162 And thou, in lovers' hearts forgiven, Shalt take thy place with Yarrow! 1820 Shelley *To a Skylark* xvi, With thy clear keen joyance Languor cannot be. 1834 Dickens *Sk. Boz, Boarding-ho.* i, He was to his wife what the o is in 90—he was of some importance with her—he was nothing without her. 1918 *Act 8 Geo. V* c. 4 §6 This Act.. may be cited with the Trustee Savings Banks Acts 1863 to 1904.

26. a. Expressing collocation in space.

1480 *Cely Papers* (Camden) 54 Aull iij sortes lyes togyddyr whon w^{t} anothyr. 1480 *Acta Dom. Conc.* (1839) 47/1 Þe castin of petis in a mosse merchand with þe landis of Dalruskane. 1662 J. Davies tr. *Olearius' Voy. Ambass.* 21 We thought it enough to put it [*sc.* a paper] in with that of the Suedish Ambassadors. 1664 J. Webb *Stone-Heng* (1725) 105 The most conspicuous [entrance]..into the Work it self lyeth North-East, whereby it fronteth rightly with the publick or high Road. 1815 Wellington in Gurw. *Desp.* (1838) XII. 484, I send with this dispatch three eagles, taken by the troops in this action. 1831 Scott *Cast. Dang.* i, The bonnet usually worn with this showy dress. 1849 Ruskin *Samuel Prout* (1870) 8 The angle formed by St. Mark's Church with the Doge's palace. 1914 F. Gribble *Francis Joseph* xxxi. 331 The aristocracy dare not ask the professors to dinner for fear lest..they should wear green ties with their dress clothes.

b. (*a*) Expressing mixture or combination of material substances.

*c*1400 *Lanfranc's Cirurg.* 199 Ȝeue him tiriaca maior wiþ a litil musco. *c*1430 *Two Cookery-bks.* 13 Take gode Mylke of Almaundys, an drawe it wyth Wyne. *c*1440 *Pallad. on Husb.* III. 829 Take peres right mature, And with hool salt hem trede. 1697 Dryden *Virg. Georg.* IV. 194 Potherbs..Which ..bruis'd with Vervain, were his frugal Fare. 1753 *Chambers' Cycl.* Suppl. s.v. *Lime* ¶3 They work up the chalk rubbish into a sort of stiff paste with water. 1841 *Penny Cycl.* XX. 354/2 When hydrate of salicyle is heated with potash, an acid is formed.

(*b*) *ellipt.* in slang use, in ref. to liquor = mixed with sugar, having sugar added; usually in phr. ***hot (warm)*** or ***cold with***.

1835 Dickens *Sk. Boz, Miss Evans & Eagle*, Two glasses of rum-and-water 'warm with—'. 1854 Surtees *Handley Cr.* xiv, Fatch me up a glass of cold sherry *with*. *Ibid.* xxiv, 'Take a glass of brandy,' said she... ''Ot with? or cold without?'

†**27.** In addition to, besides; with neg., except.

*c*1305 *St. Edward* 8 in *E.E.P.* (1862) 106 He nadd neȝ him noþing For to ȝyue þis pore man wiþ a goldene ring. *c*1425 Wyntoun *Cron.* v. x. 2252 Thre ȝhere and monethis twa, And ful ellewyn dayis withe þai. 1426 Lydg. *De Guil. Pilgr.* 8703 A myghty kyng,..And wyth al thys, a famous knyht. *c*1470 Henry *Wallace* IX. 43 With that thai war a gudly cumpany Off waillit men. 1530 Tindale *Exod.* xx. 23 Ye shall not make therfore with me goddes of syluer nor goddes of golde. 1579–80 North *Plutarch, Agis & Cleom.* (1595) 484 Very wise,..and with his wisdome..very valiant. 1599 Thynne *Animadv.* 11 All whiche make xxx persons with Chaucer.

28. After a sb., in a qualifying phrase indicating a characteristic or distinctive part or adjunct: Having, possessing; having in or upon it, containing, bearing (cf. 23).

In this and sense 31 the phr. is sometimes equivalent to a descriptive adj.: e.g. *with corners* = 'angular'; *with four wheels* = 'four-wheeled'.

*c*1300 *Havelok* 701 Shep wit wolle, neth wit horn,..and gate wit berd. 1377 Langl. *P. Pl.* B. II. 16 Hire robe..With ribanes of red golde. 1398 Trevisa *Barth. De P.R.* XVII. cxlv. (1495) T v/1 Harde stalkes wyth corners. *a*1400 *Minor Poems fr. Vernon MS.* 626 His Innes & his orchardus were with a dep dich. *c*1400 Maundev. xxvi. [xxii.] (1919) I. 159 A charett with .iiij. wheles. 1432–50 tr. *Higden* (Rolls) VIII. App. 497 Schoone with longe pykes. 1500–20 Dunbar *Poems* liv. 5 My ladye with the mekle lippis. 1599 Shaks. *Much Ado* II. i. 15 With a good legge,..and money enough .., such a man would winne any woman in the world. 1663 Gerbier *Counsel* 28 Stone with Sandy veines. 1711 Addison *Spect.* No. 86 ¶2 A Man with a sour rivell'd Face. 1842 *Penny Cycl.* XXII. 429/2 The consonants are conveniently classed into those with and those without voice. 1848 Thackeray *Lett.* 28 July (1887) 9 A paper-knife with a mother of pearl blade. 1892 *Speaker* 3 Sept. 289/2 The high road, with its shrieking steam-tram.

29. Indicating a quality or attribute of the action spoken of: forming phrases equivalent to adverbs, e.g. *with one accord* or *consent* = unanimously, *with care* = carefully, *with ease* = easily, *with impunity* = L. *impune*, *with severity* = severely, etc. (Sometimes closely approaching the instrumental use 37, esp. in such phrases as *with a curious eye*, *with all one's heart*, etc.) Similarly after an adj., in phr. expressing a particular kind or degree of the quality denoted by the adj.

*c*1200 Ormin 1395 Enngless haffdenn heoffness ærd forrlorenn all wiþþ rihhte. *c*1250 *Gen. & Ex.* 1598 Fro bersabe he ferde wið sped. *Ibid.* 1668 Aske it wið skil and ðu salt hauen. *a*1300 *Cursor M.* 4430 Now es ioseph in prisun strang Don..wijt wrang. 13.. *Northern Passion* (1913) I. 5/16 Þe Iewys..sayd he ferid all wyth foly. 13.. *K. Horn* 1353 (Harl.) He louede horn wiþ mihte & he him wiþ ryhte. *c*1350 *Will. Palerne* 163 Alle wiȝth on hol hert. *c*1400 *Rule St. Benet* (prose) 45 Whit mekenes sal sho muster to þabbes hir sekenes. 1528 *Star Chamber Cases* (Selden Soc.) II. 174 To get hys money with crafte and suttully. 1535 Coverdale *Deut.* vi. 5 Thou shalt loue the Lorde thy God with all thy hart, with all thy soule, & with all thy mighte. 1599 Shaks. *Much Ado* I. i. 300, I look'd vpon her with a souldiers eie. 1660 R. Coke *Power & Subj.* 45 This unlimited power of doing anything with impunity. 1671 Milton *P.R.* I. 319 Who first with curious eye Perus'd him. 1710 Steele *Tatler* No. 208 ¶8 He replied with a very angry Tone. 1760–72 H. Brooke *Fool of Qual.* (1809) III. 116 A little stage was erected..that the spectators might see with the better advantage. 1771 Goldsm. *Hist. Eng.* III. 351 He always travelled with hurry. 1780 Cowper *Progr. Err.* 562 They sidle to the goal with awkward pace. 1848 Dickens *Dombey* xxxviii, Polly, who, with a woman's tact, understood this at once. 1856 Mrs. Carlyle *Lett.* II. 269 To-day I walked with effort one little mile. 1875 Jevons *Money* (1878) 25 We use a great many words with a total disregard of logical precision.

30. a. Indicating a feeling, purpose, or other mental state accompanying the action spoken of: e.g. *with approval*, *awe*, *horror*, *indifference*, *pleasure*, *regret*, (*due*) *respect*, etc.; *with* (*a*, *the*, etc.) *determination*, *hope*, *intent*(*ion*, *view*, etc.: see also the sbs.

The phrase thus formed is often equivalent to an adv., as in 29, from which this use is not always distinguishable.

*c*1250 *Gen. & Ex.* 128 God..bliscede it wid milde mood. *c*1330 *Spec. Gy de Warw.* 93 To don penaunce Wid sorwe at þin herte rote. *c*1350 *Libeaus Desc.* (Kaluza) 1029 Sir Giffroun..Was bore hom on his scheld Wiþ care and rufull roun. 1382 Wyclif *Phil.* ii. 12 Worche ȝe with drede and tremblinge ȝoure heelthe. 1526 Tindale *Heb.* xii. 28 Grace, wherby we maye serve god..with reverence and godly feare. 1581 Rich *Farew.* D ij b, With this resolution he began to relate [etc.]. 1601 Holland *Pliny* II. cv. I. 47 Shee approched neere to the altars, with purpose to sacrifice. 1714 in *Jrnl. Friends' Hist. Soc.* (1918) 28 We left New England with peace of mind. 1748 *Anson's Voy.* II. xiv. 285 They still remember, with the utmost horror, the sacking of their cities. 1786 tr. *Beckford's Vathek* (1868) 51 Vathek applied his ear with the hope of catching the sound of some latent runnel. 1798 Southey *Pious Painter* I. i, Still on his Madonnas the curious may gaze With applause and with pleasure. 1820 Keats *Lamia* II. 100 If, as now it seems, your vision rests With any pleasure on me. 1849 Macaulay *Hist. Eng.* vii. II. 183 A land of exile, visited with reluctance and quitted with delight. 1885 *Law Rep. 29 Chanc. Div.* 482 It is wholly immaterial with what object the lie is told.

b. In expressions of devotion, affection, or gratitude accompanying what is said or written, esp. by way of greeting, as in a message or the conclusion of a letter.

1454 *Paston Lett.* I. 273 Right wurshipfull and myn especiall good maister, I recomaund me to you with all service and prayer to my power. 1521 in *Acts Parlt. Scot.* (1875) XII. 40/1 Ȝoure humile oratouris and servandis with all lauchfull service. 1679 in *Jrnl. Friends' Hist. Soc.* (1912) IX. 191 G. F[ox] ordered me to signifie thus to thee with his deare Love. 1685 Pett in *Engl. Hist. Rev.* (1920) Jan. 114 Two Dorsetshire regiments..were dismissed..with thanks for their good service. 1744 in *10th Rep. Hist. MSS. Comm.* App. I. 283 Laying the aff^{r} before my Ld Harrington with my best complim^{ts} desiring the fav^{r} of him just to sound the Count upon it. 1789 [see remembrance *sb.* 4 d]. 1793 [see love *sb.*[1] 1 e]. 1835 [see regard *sb.* 10 c]. 1898 G. B. Shaw *Mrs. Warren's Prof.* 11, Here: take George his hat and stick with my compliments.

31. a. Indicating an attribute, quality, or condition of the person or thing spoken of: Having, possessing, characterized by. (Often scarcely distinguishable from 28 or 29.)

*c*1450 Holland *Howlat* 18 The land lowne was and le, with lyking and luf. 1587 Holinshed *Hist. Scot.* 246/2 The Englishmen (with the number of 1500, vnder the conduct.. of Talbot). 1593 Shaks. *2 Hen. VI*, I. i. 105 What meanes this passionate discourse? This peroration with such circumstance. 1610 —— *Temp.* II. ii. 52 She had a tongue with a tang. 1671 Milton *Samson* 271 Bondage with ease. 1702 De Foe *Shortest Way w. Dissenters* 28 Why shou'd the Papist with his Seven Sacraments be worse than the Quaker with no Sacraments at all? 1712 Steele *Spect.* No. 438 ¶4 A very learned Man with an erect Solemn Air. 1776 *Trial of Nundocomar* 32/2 He was then in a cool sweat, with a low pulse. 1812 Crabbe *Tales* xi. 385 Retiring late, at early hour to rise, With shrunken features, and with bloodshot eyes. 1864 Tennyson *Aylmer's Field* 387. 1883 *Law Times* 22 Sept. 356/1 A colony with a constitution like that of the Cape Colony. 1893 *Atlanta* Jan. 269 Many another man with less heart and less imagination.

b. With special implications: (*a*) Still having; without loss of or detriment to; so as to keep or retain; consistently with.

*c*1440 *Alphabet of Tales* 25 He vnnethis gatt away with his life. 1568 Grafton *Chron.* II. 224 He could not long continue in the seruice of princes with the sauetie of his lyfe. 1600 in J. Morris *Troubles Cath. Foref.* (1872) Ser. I. iv. 195 Another gentleman..was beaten down from his horse and hardly escaped with life. 1615 in *Buccleuch MSS.* (Hist. MSS. Comm.) I. 163 The King's letter was, that he..could not with his greatness answer the proposition. 1654 in J. Morris *Troubles Cath. Foref.* (1872) Ser. I. vi. 307 He said she could not pass the next winter with life, if she took not this remedy. 1865 Ruskin *Sesame* i. §31 A nation..cannot with impunity,..cannot with existence..go on.. concentrating its soul on Pence.

(*b*) Though having; notwithstanding, in spite of. (Usually followed by *all* qualifying the sb.; cf. for *prep.* 23 a, b.)

13.. *Sir Beues* (A.) 1105 Ȝet wiþ þan Ichauede þe leuer to me lemman,..Þan al þe gold þat Crist haþ maked. 1557 North *Gueuara's Diall Pr.* (1582) 409 All these things notwithstanding they are dishonest are sometimes tollerable.., so y^{t} with these faults they would be diligent to dispatch men. 1561 Hoby tr. *Castiglione's Courtyer* II. (1577) K j b, He hath suche straunge conceites.., that with all ye painting he hath he can not paint them. 1693 Dryden *Juvenal Sat.* Ded. (1697) p. lxxxv, Ancient Words..which, with all their Rusticity, had somewhat of Venerable in them. 1779 *Mirror* No. 34 ¶9 Umphraville, with all his dignity, his abilities, and his knowledge, felt himself uneasy and ridiculous. 1784 Cowper *Task* II. 206 England, with all thy faults, I love thee still. 1881 Stevenson *Virg. Puerisque* Ded., But, with the best will, no man can be twenty-five for ever. 1908 R. Bagot *A. Cuthbert* vi. 50 With all her apparent roughness of disposition . . she was by no means a heartless woman.

32. a. Indicating an accompanying or attendant circumstance, or a result following from the action expressed by the verb.

c **1350** *Will. Palerne* 1851 þe werwolf . . went to him euene, Wiþ a rude roring. **1500–20** DUNBAR *Poems* viii. 2 Thou may complain with sighis lamentable The death of Bernard Stewart. **1563** FOXE *A. & M.* 621/2 To passe it ouer with sylence. **1621** LADY M. WROTH *Urania* 459, I looked vpon him, and with teares told him, his censure was harder, then the Prince his. **1677** MOXON *Mech. Exerc.* i. 10 Afterwards smooth it with a Blood red Heat. **1703** ROWE *Fair Penit.* I. i, She, with Looks averse, and Eyes that froze me, Sadly reply'd. **1793** SMEATON *Edystone L.* §265 Our men went out with a declaration that they would not return till they had found the moorings. **1806–7** J. BERESFORD *Miseries Hum. Life* (1826) vii. 13 The frosty silence . . with which it is received by the different auditors. **1809** MALKIN *Gil Blas* I. xvii. ¶11, I do not in the least doubt it, interrupted Fabricio with a horse-laugh. **1872** MORLEY *Voltaire* (1886) 1 With as far-spreading and invincible an effect. **1912** *Engl. Hist. Rev.* Oct. 672 The value of a papal dispensation is considered, with the conclusion that it is valid in some cases but not in all.

b. (after *find*, *take*, etc.) In the actual commission of (a crime or misdemeanour). *Obs.* or *arch.*

c **1430** *Syr Tryam.* 185 Y trowed in hur no false-hedd, Tylle y fonde them with the dede. **1510** *Reg. Privy Seal Scot.* I. 314/2 Taken in redehand with any crime. **1530–1611** [see MAINOUR 2]. **1572** R. H. tr. *Lauaterus' Ghostes* (1596) 40 Albeit they were . . almost taken tardy with the deede doing. **1586** T. B. *La Primaud. Fr. Acad.* I. 227 His sonne being taken with the fact, . . Zaleucus would never suffer the punishment to be . . lessened.

33. Indicating something granted, received, or assumed: often with conditional implication, as in ***with your leave*** (or ***permission***) = 'if you will allow me'.

13.. *Gaw. & Gr. Knt.* 971 Wyth leue laȝt of þe lorde he went hem aȝaynes. *c* **1400** *Apol. Loll.* 70 Weþ þe lefe or conferming of þe kirk, swilk mariage is rate. **1436** in *Rep. Hist. MSS. Comm., Var. Coll.* IV. 199 To oaste this land oute of allereputacion . . yf so falle, as with oure Lord mercy it never shal falle. **1539** *Bible* (Great) 2 Chron. xviii. 12 The wordes of the prophetes speake good to the kyng with one assent. —— *Ps.* xviii. 29 Wt the helpe of my God I shall leape ouer the wall. **1610** B. JONSON *Alch.* IV. i, Madame, with your pardon, I kisse your vesture. **1648–9** in *Engl. Hist. Rev.* (1917) Oct. 570 Hee . . had alsoe the Keyes of the Castle (but not with Thompson's good will). **1660** *Act 12 Chas. II* c. 19 Bee it Enacted by the Kings most Excellent Majesty by and with the advice and consent of the Lords and Commons . . That [etc.]. **1779** *Mirror* No. 33 ¶4 We were accordingly married with the universal approbation of my friends. **1794** J. H. MOORE *Pract. Navig.* (ed. 10) 87 With the course and distance find the difference of latitude and departure. **1838** DICKENS *Nich. Nick.* xv, Another gentleman comes and collars that glass of punch, without a 'with your leave', or 'by your leave'. **1856** FROUDE *Hist. Eng.* I. i. 77 So the law of England remained . . with the deliberate approval of both the great parties. **1879** E. WATERTON *Pietas Mariana Brit.* 226 With these general data, I now proceed to examine some of the details.

34. Followed by a sb. denoting some alteration or modification, or something imposed in the way of a demand or requirement: e.g. *change*, *condition*, *exception*, *loss*, *proviso*, *qualification*, etc. (Before *condition* now replaced by *on*.)

c **1450** *Merlin* xiv. 203 We be come to serue yow, with this condicion, that ye desire not to knowe oure names. **1489** in *Trevelyan Papers* (Camden) 93 With the same condicions and provisoes. **1626** W. SCLATER *Exp. 2 Thess.* (1629) 210 With exception of the crosse. **1629** HOBBES *Thucyd.* I. 59 The Athenians . . made peace, with condition to haue their Prisoners released. **1779** *Mirror* No. 7 ¶2 With these qualifications, Sir, I am held in considerable estimation by the wits of both sexes. **1849** MACAULAY *Hist. Eng.* ii. I. 165 Such a body . . is composed, with scarcely an exception, of sincere persons. **1861** M. PATTISON *Ess.* (1889) I. 44 With the exception of a dwelling-house . . , the remainder of the area was covered with warehouses.

35. a. Followed by a sb. denoting misfortune or evil, in imprecations and intensive phrases: also *with a* WANION, *with a witness* (see WITNESS *sb.* 14). Now chiefly in *with a vengeance* (in intensive sense: see VENGEANCE *sb.* 4).

a **1300** *K. Horn* 326 (Camb.) Went [= go] vt of my bur Wiþ muchel mesauentur. *c* **1386** CHAUCER *Manciple's Prol.* 11 Is that a Cook of London, with meschance? *a* **1529** SKELTON *E. Rummyng* 346 As thou, wyth shamfull deth! **1538–** [see MISCHIEF *sb.* 9a]. **16..** MIDDLETON, etc. *Old Law* III. ii, *Ly.* I will send it through you with a powder. *Sim.* Let come, with a Pox! **1663** DRYDEN *Wild Gallant* I. ii, I'll put you out of your Pater Nosters, with a sorrow to you.

b. Introducing a refrain (often meaningless) in a poem or ballad.

[**13..** *Coer de L.* 2522 They rowede hard, and sungge ther too, With heuelow and rumbeloo.] *c* **1400** *Pety Job* 96 in *26 Pol. Poems* 124 Nowe yeue me mercy, and say nat nay, Wyth *Parce michi, domine*. **15..** [see HEY-HO]. **1519** [see HEY *int.* 2]. *a* **1529** SKELTON *E. Rummyng* 289 Wyth Hey and wyth howe. **1633, 1672** [see FADING *sb.*]. **1665**, *a* **1800** [see FA-LA a]. **1780** *British Grenadiers*, With a tow, row, row, row, row.

36. In various preceding senses, followed by object and complement (phr. with prep., pple., adj., adv., or inf. with *to*).

c **1290** *Beket* 1169 in *S. Eng. Leg.* 140 With one haltre ope þe mere forth rod þis holi man. **1375** BARBOUR *Bruce* VIII. 48 Thai saw in battale cum arayit The vaward with baner displayit. *c* **1386** CHAUCER *Doctor's T.* 211 With fadres pitee stikynge thurgh his herte. **1443–50** in W. P. Baildon *Sel. Cases Chanc.* (1896) 134 His purse with xxv.s. of money therin. *c* **1482** *Paston Lett.* III. 295 Fayne she wold be redde of it with hyr onowr savyd. **1527** *Test. Ebor.* (Surtees) VI. 13 The lesse leede with the hole in the bothom. **1534** MORE *Comf. agst. Trib.* III. xix. (1553) R vij, The . . prieste . . that had . . vsed to say *Dominus* with the seconde sillable long. **1611** SHAKS. *Cymb.* II. i. 26 You crow Cock, with your combe on. **1630** PAGITT *Christianogr.* I. iii. (1636) 133 Standing . . with their armes fouldеd. **1745** POCOCKE *Descr. East* II. II. 231 There are six youths in each room, with a master over them. **1760–2** GOLDSM. *Cit. W.* lxxi, He sat with rapture in his eye. **1831** SCOTT *Cast. Dang.* xiv, The shield represented an owl with its wings spread. **1842** TENNYSON *Lady Clare* xv, She went by dale, and she went by down, With a single rose in her hair. **1842** BROWNING *Through the Metidja to Abd-el-Kadr* i, As I ride, as I ride, With a full heart for my guide. **1848** DICKENS *Dombey* v, An iron-grey autumnal day, with a shrewd east wind blowing. **1859** GEO. ELIOT *Adam Bede* xviii, They . . stood with their hats off. **1866** RUSKIN *Let.* 10 May, Joan has written another long letter to you with something about me in it. **1870** MORRIS *Earthly Par.* III. 455 Life seemed not so cursed With this to think of.

III. Denoting instrumentality, causation, or agency.

37. a. (*a*) Indicating the means or instrument (material or immaterial) of any kind of action: By means of, by the use of.

c **1200** ORMIN 5524 Þe bodiȝ forr to pinenn wiþþ swinnc. *c* **1220** *Bestiary* 9 He . . Draȝeð dust wið his stert. *Ibid.* 627 He ne hauen no lið Ðat he muȝen risen wið. *a* **1250** *Prov. Alfred* 90 in *O.E. Misc.* 108 For to werie þat lond wiþ hunger and wiþ herivnge. *c* **1250** *Gen. & Ex.* 44 Al was ðat firme ðrosing in niȝt, Til he wit hise word made liȝt. *a* **1300** *K. Horn* 459 (Camb.) Wiþ seluer & wiþ golde Hit wurþ him wel iȝolde. *Ibid.* 514 Þin armes he haþ & scheld To fiȝte wiþ vpon þe feld. *a* **1300** *Cursor M.* 14427 Þat he suld flexs take o þair kin, For to ranscun wit adam sin. **13..** *E.E. Allit. P.* B. 1438 He with keyes vncloses kystes ful mony. **1382** WYCLIF *Mark* xiv. 58, I schal vndo this temple maad with hondis. *c* **1386** CHAUCER *Prol.* 1 Whan that Aprille with hise shoures soote The droghte of March hath perced to the roote. *c* **1400** MAUNDEV. (1919) xxvii. 165 A lytille whippe in hire hondes for to chacen with hire hors. **1413** *E.E. Wills* (1882) 22 The residue of my gode, y bequethe tho Amys my wyf, an my son, to kepe hem boþ wyt. **1479** *Cely Papers* (Camden) 18, vc or vj c baras canvase for to packe woll wyt. **1491** CAXTON *Vitas Patr.* (W. de W. 1495) II. 247/2 Oonly as moche as suffysed to bye with his brede cotydyan. **1523** LD. BERNERS *Froiss.* I. ccxxvi. 123/1 He lost euer after ye syght with that eye. **1526** TINDALE *Matt.* xx. 22 Are ye able . . to be baptised with the baptism that y shalbe baptised with? —— *Mark* ix. 49 Every sacryfyse shalbe seasoned with saltt. **1591** SPENSER *Virg. Gnat* 432 All slaine with darts. **1634** SIR T. HERBERT *Trav.* 145 They build with vnburnt clay. **1671** MILTON *Samson* 1621 The people with a shout Rifted the Air. **1748** *Anson's Voy.* I. i. 9 The ships were disappointed of provisions for want of a cargo to truck with. **1766** GOLDSM. *Vicar W.* iii, We lightened the fatigues of the road with philosophical disputes. **1855** MACAULAY *Hist. Eng.* xi. III. 44 Some acts which in the citizen are punished with fine or imprisonment must in the soldier be punished with death. **1877** RUSKIN *St. Mark's Rest* i. §18 There is nothing like a little work with the fingers for teaching the eyes. **1890** *Law Times' Rep.* LXIII. 691/2 A publican runs a greater risk of being cheated with false money than other tradesmen.

†(*b*) Through the medium of (a person). *rare.*

c **1000** ÆLFRIC *Gen.* xxxviii. 20 Iudas sende an ticcen wið hys Odolamitiscean hyrde. *a* **1300** *Cursor M.* 1274 He wald send me word wit þe. *c* **1375** *Sc. Leg. Saints* xxviii. (*Margaret*) 135 Tyne nocht my sawle with fellone mene. **1590** SHAKS. *Com. Err.* V. i. 230 He did arrest me with an Officer.

b. Formerly used in many cases where *by* (BY *prep.*, 30, 32) is now the usual or only construction; e.g. with obj. a person, or an action (esp. when expressed by a gerund or vbl. sb. in *-ing*).

a **1300** *Cursor M.* 882 Sco has me fild wit hir sin. **13..** *Guy Warw.* (A.) 129 He wald do nimen him anon, & wiþ strengþe him nim wolde. **1375** BARBOUR *Bruce* I. 521 Wes nocht all Troy with tresoune tane . . ? *c* **1386** CHAUCER *Doctor's T.* 217 To dyen with a swerd or with a knyf. *c* **1450** tr. *De Imitatione* II. xii. 57 It shal not lye in þy power to be esid ner delyuered wiþ no remedy ner no solace. *c* **1450** CAPGRAVE *Life St. Aug.* 112 Þou wer led in-to þis place witȝ þe handis of many men. **1513** BRADSHAW *St. Werburge* I. 2461 And it to confyrme . . With charters and dedes. **1523** LD. BERNERS *Froiss.* I. ccciii. 183 b/1 The towne was taken with assaute, and robbed. **1539** *Bible* (Great) 1 Kings vi. 8 Men went vp with windyng steares into the myddle chambre. **1571** DIGGES *Pantom.* IV. vi. Xj, If by the second rule ye diuide 100 with 24, the quotient is $4\frac{1}{6}$. **1667** DRYDEN tr. *Life S. Francis Xavier* VI. 667 Many sick persons . . were cur'd with only seeing it. *a* **1715** BURNET *Own Time* (1724) I. 409 With all this the King was convinced. **1750** JOHNSON *Rambler* No. 43 ¶10 Distant countries are united with canals. **1837** DICKENS *Pickw.* iii, Will you oblige us with proceeding with what you were going to relate? **1859** GEO. ELIOT *Adam Bede* xvi, I don't believe there's anything you can't prevail on people to do with kindness.

c. Used where other prepositions are now usual, as *at* (a charge or cost), *in* (a receptacle or something figured as such), *of* (a material or constituent, after *make*), *on* or *upon* (food, etc.).

a **1300** *Cursor M.* 11109 Ion . . liued wit rotes and wit gress, Wit honi o þe wildernes. *c* **1450** *Godstow Reg.* 530 The forsaid Adam shold susteyn the said mese . . with his owne costis. **1564** HARDING *Answ. Jewel* 40 S. Augustine vttereth the same thinge almost with the same wordes. *a* **1586** SIDNEY *Astr. & Stella* Sonn. xcix, When farre spent night perswades each mortal eie . . To laye his then marke wanting shaftes of sight, Clos'd with their quivers in Sleeps armorie. **1588** SHAKS. *L.L.L.* I. i. 303 You shall fast a Weeke with Branne and water. **1598** GRENEWEY *Tacitus, Ann.* I. xv. (1622) 29 Germanicus . . furnished the rest with his owne charges. **1617** MORYSON *Itin.* III. 83 They dine with dried pork. **1633** J. CLARKE *Two-fold Praxis*, I lived . . with sevenpence a day. **1709** STRYPE *Ann. Ref.* I. xl. 410 That she would wrap up all such matters with oblivion. *a* **1774** GOLDSM. *Surv. Exp. Philos.* (1776) II. 239 Burning instruments of this kind are usually made with glass. **1785** CUMBERLAND *Nat. Son* I. i, When he shall see what frippery a woman is made up with. **1801** STRUTT *Sports & Past.* III. vi. 221 Diminutive imitations of muskets made with wood. **1840** PEREIRA *Elem. Mat. Med.* II. 1269 A sinapism made with flour.

†**d.** In reference to procreation, with obj. either the male or the female parent: = BY *prep.* 32c.

c **1450** *Merlin* 20 Thow wast with childe with hym. **1593** in *Maitl. Club Misc.* I. 56 The barne gottin be him with the said Margaret Steyne. **1603** SHAKS. *Meas. for M.* II. ii. 143 Shee speakes, and 'tis such sence That my Sence breeds with it. *a* **1709** J. LISTER *Autobiog.* (1842) 51, I had but two children with my wife.

e. After *begin* or *end* and words of like sense, in various shades of meaning: indicating (*a*) that which constitutes the beginning or end, i.e. the initial or final part, element, stage, proceeding, etc. (after a personal subj. and before a gerund now *by*, as in b above); (*b*) a person or thing acted upon or treated first or last (coinciding with 9); (*c*) (after *begin*, *originate*, etc.) the agent or source from which something takes its rise (allied to 11).

Phr. (with ellipsis of obj.) ***to begin with***: to take what is mentioned or indicated as one's starting-point.

1412–20 LYDG. *Chron. Troy* I. 2414 For my behest with deth I schal conclude. *c* **1550** BALE *K. Johan* (Camden) 47 Fyrst to begyne with, we shall interdyte the lond. **1570** FOXE *A. & M.* (ed. 2) I. 494/2 First begynnyng with that godly man . . the autor of the boke. *a* **1619** in S. Atkinson *Gold Mynes Scot.* (Bann. Club) 2 It is true that 'say well and doe well ends both with one letter'. **1677** in *Essex Papers* (Camden) II. 110 The Commoners . . take distaste that anything which relates to mony, should . . begin with the Lords. **1683** TRYON *Way to Health* 642 Drawing towards a Conclusion of this Treatise, I shall put a period thereto with some unvulgar Considerations of the Nature of Sounds and Melody. **1713** BERKELEY *Guardian* No. 69 ¶2 He has ended his Discourse with a Prayer. **1768** STERNE *Sent. Journ.* II. 51 (*Le Patisser*) He finish'd the scene with winning my esteem. **1833** HT. MARTINEAU *Brooke Farm* i. 6, I must begin my lecture with you. **1843** *Fraser's Mag.* XXVIII. 657 The evening generally closed with music. **1861** T. L. PEACOCK *Gryll Grange* xxix, I will be bound every one of this company could . . find a quotation in point.—Miss Gryll, to begin with. **1879** RUSKIN *St. Mark's Rest* iv. §56 We may close her national history with the seventeenth century. **1887** 'L. CARROLL' *Game of Logic* i. §2. 22 'Middle' begins with 'm'. **1918** in *Engl. Hist. Rev.* (1919) July 442 Newcastle's response . . did not stop with sending Warren for the defence of the Northern Colonies.

38. After words of furnishing, filling, covering, adorning, and the like. (Allied to II. ***, involving the notion of addition.)

After *full* now replaced by *of*.

c **1200** ORMIN 994 Bulltedd bræd . . smeredd wel wiþþ elesæw. *c* **1290** *S. Eng. Leg.* I. 384/256 For-to . . crouni him with golde. *a* **1300** *Cursor M.* 852 God . . fild þis werld al wit his grace. *Ibid.* 1046 Wit gress and leues his he clad. *a* **1310** in Wright *Lyric P.* xxxiv. 96 To presente hyre sone With myrre, gold, ant encenz. ? *a* **1366** CHAUCER *Rom. Rose* 1076 It [*sc.* a robe] ful well With Orfrays leyd was euerydeell. *c* **1394** *P. Pl. Crede* 116 Cloþ to coveren wiþ our bones. *c* **1425** *Engl. Conq. Irel.* 130 Encombret whyth syn. **1445** in *Anglia* XXVIII. 277 Histirlonde he plantith with vyne. **1506** in *Mem. Hen. VII* (Rolls) 285 The third chamber . . was hanged with a very rich arras. *c* **1511** *1st Engl. Bk. Amer.* (Arb.) Introd. 28/1 Ledder to kyuer theyr members with. **1526–** [see ENDOW *v.* 3b.]. **1590** SHAKS. *Mids. N.* II. i. 131 Her wombe then rich with my yong squire. **1590** SPENSER *F.Q.* III. iii. 4 That doest ennoble with immortall name The warlike Worthies. **1610** SHAKS. *Temp.* I. ii. 154 Infused with a fortitude from heauen. *Ibid.* 283 Then was this Island . . not honour'd with A humane shape. **1621** LADY M. WROTH *Urania* 229 As full of spite and ill nature as a Spider with poyson. **1633** J. CLARKE *Two-fold Praxis* 63 It is very expedient for us scholars to be instructed with good manners. *c* **1646** MILTON *New Forcers Consc.* 7 To force our Consciences . . And ride us with a classic Hierarchy. **1713–** [see LITTER *v.* 5, 6a]. **1734** SALE *Koran* Prelim. Disc. §1. 3 A stony and barren valley, surrounded on all sides with mountains. **1849** ROBERTSON *Serm.* Ser. I. vi. (1866) 99 Christianity . . permeates all evil with good. **1878** HARDY *Ret. Native* VI. i, Wreathing it [*sc.* a pole] with wild-flowers. **1884** W. C. SMITH *Kildrostan* 86 A . . breeze . . Tippling the waves with foam.

39. a. Indicating the cause or reason: In consequence of, as a result of, by the action of; because of, by reason of, on account of; from, through, by.

In some cases now replaced by *of* (e.g. after COME *v.* 11c); in others *of* and *with* are used with distinction of meaning (see e.g. DIE *v.*[1] 1b, 7c, WEARY *a.* 1c, 2).

13.. *Cursor M.* 1058 (Gött.) For-þi was he witt þat for lorn. **13..** *K. Alis.* 930 Mony a baner . . rotled with the wynde. ? *a* **1400** *Arthur* 466 And deyde wyþ strokis þat þey hente. **1476** *Paston Lett.* III. 161, I ame somewhatt crased, what with the see and what wythe thys dyet heer. **1591** SHAKS. *Two Gent.* I. i. 69 Hart sick with thought. **1593** —— *2 Hen. VI*, IV. vii. 111, I feele remorse in my selfe with his words. **1596** —— *Tam. Shr.* III. ii. 243 Went they not quickly, I should die with laughing. **1600** G. ABBOT *Exp. Jonah* 54 These did perish in their owne sinne, although they perished with his fault. **1601** SHAKS. *Twel. N.* III. iv. 366 This comes with seeking you. *a* **1604** HANMER *Chron. Irel.* (1633) 202 The Lord Iames Audley . . dyed with the fall of a horse. **1671** in *12th Rep. Hist. MSS. Comm.* App. v. 23 She was so ill with wearing a paire of perfumed bodyes that she was forced to goe to bed. **1682** WOOD *Life* (O.H.S.) III. 12 July, Sir Jonas Moore . . died with a fall from his horse. **1784** COWPER *Tiroc.* 833 Flush'd with drunk'ness. **1816** BYRON *Pris. Chillon* 1 My hair is grey, but not with years. **1837** HAWTHORNE *Twice-told T., Gt. Carbuncle*, The . . branches . . mossy with age. **1889** J. K. JEROME *Three Men in*

Boat 4 Zymosis I had evidently been suffering with from boyhood. *Mod. colloq.* Harry Wood is in the Cottage Hospital with his knee.

b. After a trans. vb. (usually in pass.), or a pa. pple. or ppl. adj., indicating the immediate cause or ground of the action or state spoken of: often approaching or coinciding with 37 or 40 b.

After certain pples., as *pleased*, *surprised*, etc., varying with or now replaced by *at*. After *trouble* vb. sometimes approaching 9.

c **1250** *Gen. & Ex.* 3690 Ðor wurð ȝhe ðanne wið lepre smiten. *a* **1300** *Cursor M.* 4076 Þai soght him ai to greue wit wrang. **1387** TREVISA *Higden* (Rolls) VIII. 149 Þe pepil was i-plesed wiþ his faire speche. *c* **1400** *Rom. Rose* 5628 Contente with his pouerte. *c* **1440** *Generydes* 2221 With tho wordes the kyng liked full ill. **14..** in *Guillim's Heraldry* IV. vii. (1632) 296 Worne wud Age. **1535** COVERDALE *Prov.* vi. 25 Lest thou be taken with hir fayre lokes. **1533** T. WILSON *Rhet.* 115 b, Because I haue halfe weried the reader.., I will harten him agayne wyth a merye tale. **1603-** [see SPENT 3 b]. **1652** WADSWORTH tr. *Sandoval's Civ. Wars Spain* 342 Hugging himself with that small victorie. **1655-1768** [see SURPRISE *v.* 5]. *a* **1745** SWIFT *Ess. Faculties Mind* Ded., Wks. 1841 II. 284/2 To suppose you would be very much obliged with anything that was new. **1792** JEFFERSON *Writ.* (1859) III. 494, I am rejoiced with the account he gives me. **1807** EARL MALMESBURY *Diaries & Corr.* III. 363, I am..not surprised with the opiniativeness of Lord Grenville. **1839** THIRLWALL *Greece* li. VI. 243 His men and horses were now nearly spent with toil. **1891** CONAN DOYLE *White Company* xx, A face which was distorted with rage.

c. After an intr. (rarely a trans.) vb. or an adj., combining the sense 'by reason of' with 28 ('having in or upon it') or 38 ('filled, covered, etc. with'). Also more vaguely, indicating a substance (esp. a liquid) which is the logical subject of the vb.: e.g. *it is pouring with rain* = rain is pouring; (*flowers*) *dripping with dew* = having dew dripping from them.

1388 WYCLIF *Exod.* iii. 8 A lond that flowith with milk and hony. **1390** GOWER *Conf.* I. 98 Hire chekes ben with teres wet. *c* **1400** *Ywaine & Gaw.* 1397 The castel and cete rang With mynstralsi and nobil sang. *c* **1450** HOLLAND *Howlat* 5 With alkyn herbes..The feldis flurist. **1508** DUNBAR *Gold. Targe* 28 Doun throu the ryce a ryuir ran wyth stremys. **1513** DOUGLAS *Æneis* VII. viii. 93 Hir figoure sa grisly gret aboundis, Wyth glowand ene birnand of flawmis blak. **1565** COOPER *Thesaurus, Manantia vlcera*, sores runnyng with matter. **1606** SHAKS. *Ant. & Cl.* I. iii. 45 Our Italy, Shines o're with ciuill Swords. **1622-** [see HEAVY *a.* 4]. **1667** MILTON *P.L.* IV. 605 Now glow'd the Firmament With living Saphirs. **1697** DRYDEN *Virg. Georg.* III. 235 Th' Alburnian Groves, with Holly green. *Ibid.* 559 The Garment, stiff with Ice, at Hearths is thaw'd. **1746** SMOLLETT *Reproof* 28 Hallowed be the mouth That teems with moral zeal and dauntless truth! **1798** COLERIDGE *Kubla Khan* 8 Gardens bright with sinuous rills. **1799** WORDSW. *Fountain* viii, My eyes are dim with childish tears. **1849** [see POUR *v.* 6 b]. **1899** T. S. MOORE *Vinedresser* 6 Banks more soft with moss than any bed.

d. Following words of blame or the like (after *charge* orig. fig. from 38); also after *credit* vb.: indicating the ground of the charge, etc.

After *accuse*, *suspect*, now replaced by *of*.

c **1440** *Alph. Tales* 318 Þis preste..tolde hur cowncell, & vpbrayed hur þerwith. **1559** *Mirr. Mag., Dk. Clarence* l. 7 To charge me with offence. **1579-80** NORTH *Plutarch, Demetrius* (1595) 946 Hee..was most detected with this vice of lechery. **1591** *Troub. Raigne K. John* i. 147 A Man, Whom he accuseth with adulterie. **1665** DRYDEN *Ind. Emperor* III. ii, None shall tax me with base Perjury. **1670** STUBBE *Reply H. More* (1671) 75 The World will condemn you with Blasphemy for that comparison. **1715** DE FOE *Fam. Instruct.* (1841) II. I. i. 10 The blot with which I reproach myself. **1814** MRS. J. WEST *Alicia de Lacy* IV. 298 There seems no just cause for accusing the King with the premature fate of this nobleman. **1877** FROUDE *Short Stud.* (1883) IV. I. iii. 27 To credit him with a desire to reform the Church.

40. After a passive verb or participle, indicating the principal agent: = BY *prep.* 33.

a. (a person or animal). *Obs.* exc. *dial.*

c **1300** *Havelok* 2489 He was wit þe prestes shriue. **13..** *Cursor M.* 15908 (Gött.) Sare he dred þat syden fell Wid þaim he suld be slaine. **13..** *Gaw. & Gr. Knt.* 1229 Your honour..is hendely praysed With lordez, wyth ladyes, with alle þat lyf bere. **1375** BARBOUR *Bruce* XVIII. 128 And be the armys led wes he With twa men. *c* **1400** MAUNDEV. (Roxb.) vi. 19 Þis same sowdan..was slayne with his awen seruands. **1456** SIR G. HAYE *Law Arms* (S.T.S.) 38 The first quhete that ever was sawin with man. *c* **1489** CAXTON *Sonnes of Aymon* i. 52 They all were eten wyth bores and of lions. **1535** STEWART *Cron. Scot.* (Rolls) II. 56 So awful rumour..Wes neuir hard with no man in this erd. **1579** LYLY *Euphues* (Arb.) 110 There was a Towne in Spayne vndermined with Connyes, in Thessalia with Mowles, with Frogges in Fraunce. **1611** SHAKS. *Wint. T.* v. ii. 68 He was torne to pieces with a Beare. **1632** LITHGOW *Trav.* III. 86 It was miserably sacked, and burned with Turkes. **1670** DRYDEN *Conq. Granada* III. i, As I were stung with some tarantula. **1707** MORTIMER *Husb.* 165 If the Ass, you design to breed on, be suckled with a Mare. *a* **1715** BURNET *Own Time* (1724) I. 250 He rode thro' London, accompanied with the most popular men of his Court. **1727** *Philip Quarll* (1816) 19 This island is inhabited..with monkies and myself. **1735** J. HUGHES tr. *Fontenelle's Dial.* I. viii. (ed. 3) 32, I went attended with a numerous train. *Mod. dial.* You never hear of horses being bit with snakes.

†**b.** (a thing, material or immaterial). *Obs.*

c **1375** *Sc. Leg. Saints* xii. (*Mathias*) 65 With wawis castine to þe land. **1387** TREVISA *Higden* (Rolls) III. 295 Awaked wiþ crienge of gandres. *c* **1450** *St. Cuthbert* (Surtees) 5866 In to eland war þai kest with' a flowyng flode. **1571** DIGGES *Pantom.* I. xxxi. Kj, Intercepted with the perpendicular lyne. **1634** SIR T. HERBERT *Trav.* 94 Hyrcania..is limited on the North with the Caspian Sea. **1729** LAW *Serious C.* xix. 354 Her other entrails were much hurt by being crush'd together with her stays. **1760** R. BROWN *Compl. Farmer* II. 2 Overflowed with rivers or land-floods.

B. *adv.*

†**1. a.** With it (me, them, etc.); in collocation, company, or association; together; occas., at the same time, simultaneously. *Obs.*

c **888** ÆLFRED *Boeth.* xvi. §3 Hit nis nauht ȝecynde..þæt æniȝ wiðerweard þing bion ȝemenged wið oðrum wiðerweardum, oððe æniȝe ȝeferrædenne wið habban. *c* **1000** *Sax. Leechd.* II. 54 Meng þonne hwitcwudu wiþ. *c* **1440** *Pallad. on Husb.* I. 711 Ley nettelys vndir with. *Ibid.* VI. 10 Al doubil seed, as benes,..And other puls, a xl dayes floure, And greteth with [orig. *simulque grandescunt*]. *c* **1450** tr. *De Imitatione* III. lxiv. 150 Defende and kepe þe soule of þy..seruant..and, þy grace goyng wiþ [orig. *comitante gratia*], dyrecte hym by þe wey of pes.

†**b.** ***with also***: nonce-substitute for WITHAL (= 'also'). *Obs. rare.*

1586 G. WHETSTONE *Engl. Mirr.* I. xv. 95 Frauncis the second..beeing both very young, and with also married to the Queene of Scots.

†**2.** ***with and with***: **a.** Immediately, forthwith (= BY AND BY 3); **b.** From time to time, again and again, every now and then. *Obs.*

c **1200** ORMIN 5628 Ice wile wiþþ & wiþþ þa seoffne seollþess shæwenn. *c* **1205** LAY. 20747 We sendeð wið and wið and ȝeornen Arðures grið. *Ibid.* 30177 Adwine..seide auere wið and wið: ich wulle makien un-frið. *c* **1440** *Pallad. on Husb.* XI. 175 Delue hit ofte, and..Ay with and with lycour on hit to trete.

†**3.** With that, or with which; therewith, wherewith: = WITHAL *adv.* 2. *Obs.*

a **1300** *Cursor M.* 936 God mad þam kyrtels þan of hide, And cled þar flexs wit for to hide. *a* **1425** *Ibid.* 8597 (Trin.) Her modris..had no cradles ne wiþ to by. **1566** in Picton *L'pool Munic. Rec.* (1883) I. 48 The said earl..had a couple of partridges, and to drink with of his lordships cost.

†**C.** *conj.* **a.** To the time that, until. (Only OE.) **b.** During or at the time that; while; when. (Cf. sense 16 of the prep.) *Obs. rare.*

c **950** *Lindisf. Gosp.* Matt. x. 11 Ðer wunas wið ȝe ðona ȝeonga. **1375** BARBOUR *Bruce* XVII. 455 It wes nocht eyth till ta The toune, with [*v.rr.* quhill; *ed.* 1570 while] sic defens wes maid. *c* **1450** *St. Cuthbert* (Surtees) 1685 With þir thinges were done.

D. *Comb.*, as **with-worker** (*nonce-wd.* after G. *mitwerker*), a fellow-worker, co-worker.

1884 R. F. BURTON *Camoens, Lyricks* I. 4, I have been aided by a host of 'with-workers'.

with: see WITHE.

with, obs. form of WHITE, WIGHT.

with-, representing OE. *wiþ-* (see WITH *prep.*) used as a prefix to verbs (and derived sbs.) with the meanings: (1) away, back, as in OE. *wiþbláwan* to blow away, *wiþfaran* to escape, *wiþgán* to disappear, *wiþtéon* to withdraw; so WITHDRAW, WITHHOLD; a few modern words come under this heading, which are formed by substituting *with-* for *re-*, as *withcall*; (2) away from one, as in several OE. verbs meaning 'reject', 'refuse', *wiþcéosan*, *wiþcweþan*, *wiþhoȝian*, *wiþlecgan*, *wiþsacan* WITHSAKE *v.*, *wiþweorþan*; (3) against, in opposition, as in OE. *wiþfeohtend* adversary, *wiþhabban* to resist, *wiþlicgan* to oppose, *wiþsprecan* to contradict, *wiþstandan* WITHSTAND *v.*; (4) together, in *withjoin*.

The following is a list of the less important verbal formations (transitive verbs except where otherwise marked); mostly obs. (see quots.).

†**withbere** [BEAR *v.*[1]], to carry away; see also b; †**withboȝt** *pa. pple.* [BUY *v.*] redeemed; †**withbrast** *pa. t.* [BURST *v.*] *intr.* burst asunder; †**withbreide** [OE. *wiþbreȝdan*, BRAID *v.*[1]], to withdraw; †**withbuwe** [BOW *v.*[1]], to avoid; **withcall**, to recall; †**withclepe**, to recall, revoke, repeal; †**withdrive**, to drive away, repel; †**withhuhe** [OE. *wiþhoȝian*], to despise; †**withjoin**, to join together, conjoin (*intr.* and *trans.*); †**withleft** *pa. pple.* left behind; †**withlosen** *pa. pple.* [LEESE], lost; †**withnay** [NAY *v.*; cf. RENAY], to deny, refuse; †**withnim** [= L. *reprehendere*; see NIM *v.*], to reprove, rebuke; †**withpass**, to escape the lips of; †**withquethe**, to deny, contradict, refuse; †**withscape**, to escape; †**withschadowid** *pa. pple.*, darkened; †**withschild** [SHIELD *v.*], in *God w.*, God forbid; †**withscore**, to cut away, detach; †**withshonte** [SHUNT *v.*], *intr.* to shrink back; †**withslip**, to escape; †**withsoȝt** *pa. t.* [SEEK *v.*], pursued, persecuted; †**withsperre** *v.* [SPAR *v.*[1]], to bar (the way); †**withstad, -sted** *pa. pple.* [STEAD *v.*], beset; †**withstarte** [START *v.* 6], *intr.* to escape; **withstay** [STAY *v.*[1] III], to hold back, oppose, withstand; †**withstew** [STEW *v.*[1]], to check; **withstrain**, †(*a*) to constrict; (*b*) to restrain; †**withtee** [TEE *v.*[1]], to withdraw; *refl.* and *intr.* to abstain; †**withtelle**, to gainsay; †**withturn**, to avert.

c **1500** *Melusine* 196 Other thing ye shal not haue ne *withbere fro me. **1340** *Ayenb.* 186 Alle we byeþ *wiþboȝt of one zelue pris. **1448-9** METHAM *Amoryus & Cl.* 1520 The dragon..*with brast in þe myddys. *c* **890** WÆRFERTH tr. *Gregory's Dial.* (1900) 203 Þara oðre se cniht *wiðbræd..& þa oðre brohte to ðam Godes men. *c* **1000** ÆLFRIC *Hom.* I. 88 Ðæt hi heora handa fram ðam blodes gyte ne wiðbrudon. *c* **1230** *Hali Meid.* (1922) 11 In wunne stude þu hauest her ofte helle; & bute þu wið-breide þe, bredes te þat oðer. *a* **1225** *Ancr. R.* 116 Uorte *wiðbuwen sunne. *c* **1230** *Hali Meid.* (1922) 52 Hwase þencheð on al þis,..& nule wiðbuhe þet þing þet hit al of awakeneð. **1901** J. PRIOR *Forest Folk* x. 105 Do yo *withcall them saving tears shed years and years agoo, Sister Morris? **1904** 'H. S. MERRIMAN' *Flotsam* xiv. 159 The troops were withcalled. **13..** *K. Alis.* 1301 Y *withclepe and withstonde Theo truage of Grece londe. **1340** *Ayenb.* 189 Uor alle time y-confermed ne neure in none time wyþcleped. *Ibid.* 215 Þer me ssel wyþ-clepie his herte to him. **1387** TREVISA *Higden* (Rolls) VI. 267 He..wiþ-cleped al þat was i-doo by his predecessour. *c* **1440** *Promp. Parv.* 530/2 Wythe clepyn', or reuokyn. **1617** HOLYOKE *Rider's Dict.*, To Withclepe, *revoco*. *c* **1000** *Ags. Ps.* (Th.) xciii[i]. 13 [14] Næfre *wiðdrifeð Drihten ure his aȝen folc. **1527** ANDREW *Brunswyke's Distyll. Waters* II. ii. A ij/2 The same [Sorell] water withdryueth impetigines. *a* **1000** *Cædmon's Gen.* 2864 Nalles nerȝendes hæse *wiðhoȝode. *c* **1230** *Hali Meid.* (1922) 53 Nule wiðhuhe þat þing þat hit al of awakeneð. *c* **1450** *Merlin* 282 Holde we vs to-geder cloos and make semblaunte as we wolde *with Ioyne. **1630** J. HAYWARD *Edw. VI*, 10 It had bin agreed..they should withjoyne forces. *c* **1375** *Cursor M.* 4403 (Fairf.) Hys mantel ys *wiþleft [*Cott.* bileft] wiþ me. *a* **1300** *Ibid.* 10855 (Cott.) Ne sal þe nawight be *wit-losen þe maidenhed þat þou hast chosen. *Ibid.* 14109 Þe better lott has mari chosen, þat hir mai nagat be withlosin. **13..** *E.E. Allit. P.* A. 915 As þou art gloryous with-outen galle, *With-nay þou neuer my ruful bone. *c* **1440** *Pallad. on Husb.* III. 1151 If thai withnay Her fruit. *c* **1450** *Brut* II. 480 Then she withneyed and withseyd all the poyntez þat were put. *a* **1315** SHOREHAM *Poems* vii. 308 By ryȝtte he myȝtte be *wyþ-nome Ryȝt ase a qued. **13..** *S.E. Leg.* (MS. Bodl. 779) in Herrig's *Archiv* LXXXII. 374/297 Ic am a-knowe þat ic whyl-er þe wit-nom amys. **1340** *Ayenb.* 17 Þe more þet me him wy[þ]nimþ and blameþ..þe more he him wreþeþ. *Ibid.* 66 Efter þan comeþ þe wyþnymynges,..huanne me atwyt ane man oþer his zennes. *c* **1340** *Nominale* (Skeat) 290 Woman thretith and withnemyth. *a* **1340** HAMPOLE *Psalter* xxxviii. 2 Þat nane reprouabil word *withpassid me. *c* **888** ÆLFRED *Boeth.* x. §1 Ne mæȝ ic na *wiðcweðan ne andsa-ciȝan þæt þe þu me ær sædest. *c* **1200** *Trin. Coll. Hom.* 137 He wið-quað and sede *Non sum ego christus*. *a* **1300** *Cursor M.* 20726 *Witschap scho vs, we sal ha blam. *a* **1400** *Sir Degrev.* (Linc. MS.) 1180 (Luick) Withscapid nane hym fra. **1398** TREVISA *Barth. De P.R.* VIII. xl. (Tollem. MS.), [Light] putteþ nouȝt it selfe deep into a body þat is *with-schadowid [orig. *umbrosi*]. *a* **1300** *Cursor M.* 2893 Godd *wit schild ȝe do þat sin. **13..** *Ibid.* 5011 (Gött.). **1340** *Ayenb.* 254 *Wyþscore [*MS. Bodl. 283* fol. 178 kit a weye] and wyþdraȝ þine willes and zete ane brydel to þine couaytises. *a* **1400** *Pistill of Susan* 231 (Cott. MS.) Sche *withe-shonte for no shame. *a* **1300** *Cursor M.* 12900 Moght it nangat þe *witslip þat he-self said o þi wirscip. *c* **1375** *Ibid.* 16196 (Fairf.) Herode..asked him..Quy þai him squa *wiþsoȝt [*Cott.* bisoght]. **1330** R. BRUNNE *Chron. Wace* (Rolls) 15660 Toward þe southe he wolde haue fled, But Edwyn his weye *wyþ-sperd. *Ibid.* 13503 Þat weye þey haue vs *wyþ-sted þat y scholde ȝow haue inne y-led. **14..** *Tundale's Vis.* 1628 (MS. A.) In grett povertte was he *wiþstadde. *c* **1460** *Pol. Rel. & L. Poems* (1903) 204, I knowe wele I may nat *with-starte, I have so doone, I ought to dreede. **1854** S. DOBELL *Balder* iii, Death, careful of my learning, hath *withstayed His final presence. **1885-94** R. BRIDGES *Eros & Psyche* May v, It fill'd the passage of the rising glade, And there withstay'd the sun in dazzling sheen. *Ibid.* July xix, There was no repentance coud atone For her dishonour, nor her fate withstay. *c* **1175** *Lamb. Hom.* 15 Heore uuel þe heo doð þu aȝest to hetiene and *wið-stewen. *c* **1400** *Lanfranc's Cirurg.* 65 Þat poudre *wiþstreyneþ [orig. *constringit*] þe blood. **1904** RYLE *Holy Script. & Crit.* 122 With difficulty is the multitude withstrained from doing sacrifice. *c* **897** ÆLFRED *Gregory's Past C.* xxxvi. 254 Balaham..wolde feran ðær hiene mon bæd, ac his estfulnesse *wiðteah se esol þe he onuppan sæt. *c* **1175** *Lamb. Hom.* 143 Þa þe heom wið-teoð of flesliche lustes. *c* **1200** *Trin. Coll. Hom.* 63 Þe lichames festing is wiðtiȝing of estmetes. *Ibid.* 79 Þat he us wissie to wið-tien of alle flesliche lustes. *c* **1275** LAY. 13242 Nas þar neuere man so bold þat þis wolde *wiþ-telle. **1563** *Mirr. Mag., Ld. Hastings* lxxxvii, God of Justyce had *withturnd that fate.

b. In the earlier version of the Wycliffite Bible it is used in nonce-formations modelled upon L. compounds of *con-*, *co-*: see quots.

withheeȝing [HIE *v.*[1], to hasten] is an erron. rendering of L. *cum festinatione* with haste. ***withhilden*** covered over [HILL *v.*[1]] represents a L. compound of *ob-*.

1382 WYCLIF *Isa.* lxii. 9 Thei..that *with bern [*comportant*] it, shul drinken in myn hoeli porches. —— *Ecclus.* xii. 19 Many thingus grucchendeli whistrende shal *with chaunge [*commutabit*] his chere. *Ibid.* i. 24 Kunnyng and vnderstonding of prudence wisdam shal *with departen [*compartietur*]. —— *Ps.* xxxi[i]. 4, I am turned in my myseise, whil *with ficchid [*configitur*] is the thorn. —— *Gen.* xxiv. 59 The *withfolweris [*comites*] of hyr. —— *Ps.* lxxvii[i]. 33 The ȝeeris of hem [failiden] in *withheeȝing. ——Pref. Ep. vii. 70 Micheas of Moraschym, the *witheire [*coheres*] of Crist. —— *Gen.* vii. 24 The watris of the flood ..*with hilden [*obtinuerunt*] the erthe. —— *Gen.* xxi. 6 Who so euer shal here shal *with lawe to me [*corridebit mihi*]. —— *Ecclus.* li. 15, I shal preisen thi name bysyly, and I shal *withpreisen [*collaudabo*] it in confessioun. —— *Gen.* xxii. 3 Abraham on the nyȝt *with rysynge [*consurgens*], diȝte his asse.

withal (wɪˈðɔːl), *adv.* and *prep. arch.* [Properly two words, orig. *with al(le* (see WITH *prep.* and ALL A. 9 e); in the earliest instances predominantly northern; ultimately superseding the older *mid alle* (see MID *prep.*[1] 7 a). The spelling *withall* continued till nearly 1800.]

A. *adv.* **1.** Along with the rest; in addition; besides; moreover; likewise; as well. Often in the collocations ***and withal*** (so-and-so), ***and*** (so-and-so) ***withal***. See also FORTHWITHAL.

c **1200** ORMIN 2572 Ne nan ne beoþ..þatt muȝhe.. tredenn dun þe deofless mahht, swa summ ȝho tradd wiþþ alle. *Ibid.* 2997 þatt Godess Gast iss soþfasst Godd & Allmahhtiȝ wiþþ alle. *Ibid.* 4203 He beoþ all unnbeshorenn þa swa þwerrt ut wel wiþþ alle. **1297** R. GLOUC. (Rolls) 7012 Seint edward held at windelsore a uair feste wiþ alle. *a* **1300** *Cursor M.* 3491 He þat was rugh was rede wit-al. **13..** *K. Horn* 424 (Harl.) Ich am ybore þral, þy fader fundlyng wiþ al. **13..** *Guy Warw.* (A.) 2984 Romiraunt com forþ snelle A Sarrazin a strong wiþ elle. **1393** LANGL. *P. Pl.* C. XI. 143 The constable of þat castel..Is a wys knyght with-alle. *c* **1470** HENRY *Wallace* IV. 549 A bow he bair..And arrous als, bath lang and scharpe with aw. **1528** MORE *Dyaloge* III. Wks. 224/1 Thereupon they burne up the booke and sometime the good manne withall. **1542** UDALL *Erasm. Apoph.* 35 Meryly spoken & nippyngly withall. **1611** *Bible* Acts xxv. 27 It seemeth to me vnreasonable, to send a prisoner, and not withall to signifie the crimes laid against him. **1643** SIR T. BROWNE *Relig. Med.* II. §2. 139 He that shall consider how many thousand severall words have beene..composed out of 24. Letters; withall how many hundred lines there are to be drawn in the fabrick of one man; shall [etc.]. **1671** MILTON *P.R.* IV. 128, I shall, thou say'st, expel A brutish monster: what if I withal Expel a Devil who first made him such? **1771** FRANKLIN *Autobiog.* Wks. 1840 I. 11 When he played and sung withal, it was extremely agreeable to hear. **1808** SCOTT *Marm.* I. xxviii, Nor lord nor knight was there more tall Or had a statelier step withal. **1837** SOUTHEY *Let. to Wynn* 24 May, Withal I have not often read a book that interested me so much. **1883** D. C. MURRAY *Hearts* viii, She ..was so sweet and kind, and withal seemed..so dependent on him. **1897** MARY KINGSLEY *W. Africa* 266 Of such peculiar suppleness that you could wind it round anything, ..and as strong withal as a hawser.

b. Contextually: 'At the same time'; in spite of all; notwithstanding, nevertheless.

1596 DANETT tr. *Comines* VIII. v. 326 Yet is it verie troublesome for horsemen, because it is full of ditches like to Flaunders,..but withall it is much pleasanter. **1654** BP. BRAMHALL *Just Vind.* vi. (1661) 124 St. Gregory..disliked the Law, but withall according to his duty published it. **1794** SOUTHEY *Let. to G. C. Bedford* 11 May, They have shown me that happiness is attainable; but, withall, taught me by repeated disappointments never to build on so sandy a foundation. **1802** WORDSW. *To the Small Celandine* 17 Modest, yet withal an Elf Bold, and lavish of thyself. **1859** LANG *Wand. India* 161 He confessed that his master was rather severe, but withal a very good man. **1880** *Academy* 23 Oct. 299/2 This..impressive, though withal faulty, work.

2. = THEREWITH 2, 3.

a **1300** *Cursor M.* 12318 Iesus..bar it ham als in a ball, And present þan his moder wit-all. **1389** in *Engl. Gilds* (1870) 101 Ye Den schal gedren ye forseyde halpenys, and bywyht-al breed. **1390** GOWER *Conf.* I. 83 Lok thou dele noght withal. *c* **1400** *Rule St. Benet* (prose) 29/33 Yef any es tan wid-al. **1535** COVERDALE *1 Macc.* iv. 44 He toke aduysement, what he might do withall. **1586** T. B. *La Primaud. Fr. Acad.* I. 301 A Philosopher..taking a lanterne and a candle lighted at midday..was demanded what he ment to do withall. **1605** A. WOTTON *Answ. to late Popish Articles* 78 We are not ashamed of our small nomber: though the Papists twight vs with all, in comparison of their huge multitudes. **1657** SANDERSON *Serm.* Pref. §4 The Papists,.. escaping in the mean while Scot-free, seldome or never meddled withall in any of their Sermons. **1833** MRS. BROWNING *Prometh. Bound* 92 Having spoiled the gods Of honours, crown withal thy mortal men Who live a whole day out.

to begin withal: see WITH *prep.* 37 e.

1531 TINDALE *Expos. 1 John* v. (1538) 83 And to begynne wythall, they sayde *Confiteor*. **1553** BRADFORD *Serm. Repentance* (1574) B vij b, I wyll (to begyn withal) shew you what repentance is. **1590** MARLOWE *2nd Pt. Tamburl.* v. i, Then have at him, to begin withal.

†**b.** ***I cannot do withal***: I cannot help it.

1470–1611 [see DO *v.* 54].

B. *prep.* Substituted for WITH *prep.* in postposition, esp. at the end of a relative clause or its equivalent or of a direct or indirect question, governing a relative (expressed or implied) or an interrogative; †occas. = WHEREWITHAL 2 b.

The relative may be either expressed (e.g. *that..withal* = with whom or which; *as* after *such*, etc.) or not expressed (freq. in the inf. construction, e.g. *a rod to be beaten withal* = a rod with which to be beaten).

The advs. *herewithal, therewithal, wherewithal*, were modelled upon the earlier *herewith, therewith, wherewith*.

a **1300** *Cursor M.* 6374 Bot tel yew of his suinc i sall, He drou þat fraward folk wit-all. *c* **1400** MAUNDEV. (Roxb.) xxvi. 122 þai giffe a grete soume of monee for to bye oute þaire penaunce withall. **1477** EARL RIVERS (Caxton) *Dictes* 7 Leste ye resemble hym that seketh a rod to be betyn with all. **1517** in Glasscock *Rec. St. Michæl's, Bp.'s Stortford* (1882) 35 A skeyn to kefer w^t alle the same booke. **1523** LD. BERNERS *Froiss.* I. cxlvi. 71 b/2 And we be so sore strayned that we haue nat to lyue withall. **1526** TINDALE *Matt.* xvi. 26 What shall a man geve to redeme hys soule agayne with all? **1531** *Test. Ebor.* (Surtees) VI. 25 Suche tithes as I was behind withall. **1555** R. POWNALL *Musculus' Temporiser* i. B vj b, Yonder commeth he that I haue dyuers tymes desyred to talke withall. **1600** SHAKS. *A. Y. L.* III. ii. 328 *Ros.* Ile tel you who Time ambles withall, who Time trots withal, ..and who he stands stil withall. *Orl.* I prethee, who doth he trot withal? *a* **1628** PRESTON *Breastpl. Faith* (1630) 30 Whatsoever you part withall, you shall have a hundred fold in this life. **1665** in *Extr. St. Papers rel. Friends* Ser. III. (1912) 236 P. J...tooke one Rebecah who he liues withall as his wife. **1703** MOXON *Mech. Exerc.* 238 Which sort of Bricks, is commonly used..to pave Yards or Stables withal. *a* **1774** GOLDSM. *Surv. Exp. Philos.* (1776) I. 365 Though we took the best telescope to observe him withal. **1821** SCOTT *Kenilw.* iv, But for hurting a man I have drunk my morning's draught withal, 'tis clean against my conscience. **1884** LOWELL *Democr.* (1887) 6 Such eyes and ears as Nature had been pleased to endow me withal.

†**b.** in other cases, esp. with indirect passive.

1556 in Lodge *Illustr. Brit. Hist.* (1791) I. 215 Notwithstanding ther layt brags and doings, wherin they have ben somwhat met wth all. *a* **1568** ASCHAM *Scholem.* I. (Arb.) 45 Will in children, wiselie wrought withall, maie easelie be won. **1642** TASMAN *Jrnl.* in *Acc. Sev. Late Voy.* I. (1694) 141 From that time they were better to be spoken withal. **1680** ALLEN *Peace & Unity* Pref. p. xv, If such were indulgently dealt withal and tolerated. *c* **1685** *Roxb. Ball.* (1891) VII. 477 Full six legs she travels withal. **1700** T. BROWN tr. *Fresny's Amusem.* 28 The Devil's Broker may be spoken withal every Sunday.

Witham (ˈwɪtəm). Also 6 **wyttam, wittam, wittome,** 7 **wittham.** The name of certain villages in Lincolnshire and Essex. ***Little*** (or ***small***) ***Witham*** was used proverbially (with pun on WIT *sb.*) for a place of which the inhabitants were remarkable for stupidity. Hence (app.), without qualification, used for: A witless person, a fool.

1538 BALE *Thre Lawes* B ij, Small wyttam be your spede. **1562** J. HEYWOOD *Prov. & Epigr.* (1867) 182 Whens come great breeches? from little wittam. **1589** NASHE *Anat. Absurditie* C 3 b, Who so snatcheth vp follies too greedilie.. may happes proue a wittome whiles he fisheth for finer witte. **1589** *Martins Months Minde* G 2 b, I appoynt..to each of them an Aduouson: To the former of small Wittam: and to the other of little Brainford. **1589** *Almond for Parrat* D 4, G. W. of Wig. house, in the land of little Wittam, chosen to the place and function of a pastor. *a* **1661** FULLER *Worthies, Lincs.* (1662) 153 Lincolneshire..Proverbs. He was born at Little Wittham... It is applyed to such people as are not overstock'd with acutenesse.

withamite (ˈwɪðəmaɪt). *Min.* [f. the name of its discoverer, H. *Witham*: see -ITE¹.] A red or reddish-yellow variety of epidote, found at Glencoe in Scotland.

1825 D. BREWSTER in *Edin. Jrnl. Sci.* II. 218.

†**ˈwithbind.** *Obs. rare.* Forms: 1 **weoþobend,** 4 **weþebond, withbinde.** [OE. ***wiþobend,** *weoþobend* (cf. OLG. *widebinde* 'ligustrum'), f. *wiþ-* in WITHE + *bend* BEND *sb.*¹ (Cf. BINDWITH, BENDWITH.)] A name for certain plants having pliant stems.

c **1000** *Sax. Leechd.* II. 312 Nim þas wyrte, safenan & mersc mealwan..& weoþobend. **1362** LANGL. *P. Pl.* A. VI. 9 He bar a bordun I-bounde wiþ a brod lyste, In A weþe-bondes [*v.r.* wodebyndes] wyse I-wriþen aboute. [**1551**: see WEEDBIND.] **1648–58** HEXHAM, *Mondt-hout*,..Privet, Prime-print, or White-withbinde.

†**with-child,** *v. Obs. nonce-wd.* [WITH *prep.* 23 b.] *trans.* To 'get with child', make pregnant.

1591 SYLVESTER *Du Bartas* I. ii. 390 The lusty Heav'n with Earth doth company: And with a fruitfull seed..With-childes..his own lawfull wife. **1598** *Ibid.* II. ii. IV. 355.

withdraught. *Obs.* exc. *arch.* Forms: see WITH *prep.* and DRAUGHT *sb.*; also 5 **wedraught,** 6 **wyddra(u)ght, -drought, weydraught, widdrawte,** 6–7 (8–9 *arch.*) **wydraught,** 7 **widraught.** [f. WITH- + DRAUGHT *sb.*, after *withdraw*.]

1. Withdrawal.

1340 *Ayenb.* 240 þe castel of þe wombe..ne may him hyealde aye þane gost þanne he is asterued be uestinges and be wyþdraȝþes. **1437** *Rolls of Parlt.* IV. 508/2 The..hurtes ..doone..to you..in withdraught of your due Custumes. **1442** *Ibid.* V. 64/2 Withoute fraude, embeselyng or withdraught therof in eny wise. *c* **1475** *Partenay* 5927 Thys knight saw hir come, with-draught wold not gette. **1623** T. ADAMS *Peace-offering* (1624) 42 May not a withdraught of all Gods fauours..be..foreseen?

b. *spec.* Withdrawal from an action in court (= RETRAXIT); a fine or fee imposed for this.

Cf. WITHDRAW *sb.*, quot. 1444.

[? **1402, 1455**: see *Essex Rev.* (1907) XVI. 128, 133.] **1600** *Maldon (Essex) Docts.* Bundle 162 lf. 3 (MS.) Withdraughts. Item, they are charged with xxxiiii s. by them receyved for lycenses of concord in accions personalls. **1635** *Maldon (Essex) Borough Deeds* Bundle 80 No. 2 (MS.) Allowance to the said seriants for collectinge of withdrafts behind.

†**2.** A place of retirement or retreat; a retreat; a private chamber, retiring-room; a closet or recess.

1480 CAXTON *Myrr.* III. xxi. 175 He that hath none other wythdraughte ne other dwellyng place. **1481** BOTONER *Tulle on Old Age* (Caxton) b vj, [He] fled by the withdraught into the toure of the same castelle. **1509** *Will Earl of Oxford* (Prerog. Crt. Cant.), ij peces of Rede Worstede vsed to be in the Wydraught of my Chamber. **1530** PALSGR. 288/2 Wydraught, *basse chambre*; *ortraict*; *retraict*.

3. A privy; a sewer: = DRAUGHT *sb.* 45, 46.

Survives locally in leases.

1493–4 *Leicester Borough Rec.* (1901) II. 344 For borde & tymbre for the wedraught. *a* **1513** FABYAN *Chron.* VI. cciv. (1811) 215 Whan the Kynge was at the withdraught to purge nature. *c* **1516** in Willis & Clark *Cambridge* (1886) II. 245 A Hows for the comyn wyddrowght of the said College. **1559** *Boke Presidentes* 26 The sayde mesuage..with thappurtenances with the pauementes, and wydraughtes of the same. **1671** in Birch *Hist. Charters* (1884) 247 That no man shall make or continue any widraughts, seat or seats, for houses of easement. **1702** J. K. *New Eng. Dict.*, A *Wy-draught*, a Water-course, or Water-passage. **1846** (25 Aug.) *Lease* (Surrey), Privies, sinks, sewers, wydraughts, drains and houses of office. **1896** *Lease*, Fences, pavements, gutters, pipes, drains, wydraughts.

withdraw, *sb. rare.* [f. WITHDRAW *v.*] Withdrawal, removal; *spec.* = WITHDRAUGHT 1 b.

1444 *Maldon (Essex) Docts.* liber 'A' lf. 32b (MS.) For a defaute, or a withdrawe of courte, a freman shall be amerced at iii d. **1693** C. MATHER *Wonders Invis. World* 64 One of these Witnesses was over-perswaded by some Persons, to be out of the way upon G. B.'s Tryal; but he came afterwards with Sorrow for his withdraw. **1720** S. SEWALL *Diary* 11 Nov. (1882) III. 276 Went not to M^m. Winthrop's. This is the 2^d Withdraw. **1727** C. MATHER (*title*) Christian Loyalty, Or, some Suitable Sentiments On the Withdraw of King George the First,..and the Access of King George the Second.

withdraw (wɪðˈdrɔː, wɪθ-), *v.* Pa. t. **withdrew** (wɪðˈdruː); pa. pple. **withdrawn** (wɪðˈdrɔːn). Forms: see WITH *prep.* and DRAW *v.*; also 4 **widdraw;** *pa. t.* 4 **wid-drogh, widrouh;** *pa. pple.* 5 **othedraw,** 6 **withdrawed.** [f. WITH- (1) + DRAW *v.* (Cf. L. *retrahĕre* to RETRACT, RETRAY, F. *retirer* to RETIRE.)]

I. *trans.* **1.** To take back or away (something that has been given, granted, allowed, possessed, enjoyed, or experienced).

a **1225** *Ancr. R.* 230 Ure Louerd..wiðdraweð his grace, & his cumfort. *c* **1315** SHOREHAM *Poems* VII. 490 Ich mey ȝyuen, and eke wyþ-draȝe, Al þat myn hys. **13..** *Guy Warw.* (A.) 332 þat he no may his loue haue, Grete strengþe him doþ wiþ-drawe. **1390** GOWER *Conf.* II. 91 Lich unto the greene tree, If that men toke his rote aweie, Riht so myn herte scholde deie, If that mi love be withdrawe. *a* **1400** *Prymer* (1891) 41 The sonne with drowȝ his liȝt. *c* **1400** *Pilgr. Sowle* (Caxton 1483) IV. xx. 65 Now the from me withdraweth bytter deth. **1535** COVERDALE *1 Chron.* xvii[i]. 13, I wyl not withdrawe my mercy from him. **1597** HOOKER *Eccl. Pol.* v. lv. §3 Impossible it is that God should withdrawe his presence from any thing. **1602** MARSTON *Ant. & Mel.* II. Wks. 1856 I. 23 My mistresse..withdrewe her gratious aspect even now. **1611** *Bible* Transl. Pref. ¶1 Those noursing fathers and mothers..that withdraw from them who hang vpon their breasts..liuelyhood and support. **1815** SHELLEY *Alastor* 16 Withdraw No portion of your wonted favour. **1833** TENNYSON *Two Voices* 145 When Life her light withdraws. **1854** R. S. SURTEES *Handley Cr.* xxxvi. (1901) I. 288 They..said they'd withdraw their subscriptions from the hounds. **1874** GREEN *Short Hist.* ii. §8. 105 The office of sheriff was withdrawn from the great nobles of the shire. **1898** 'H. S. MERRIMAN' *Roden's Corner* xiv, Then you are not disposed to withdraw your name from the concern?

†**b.** To subtract (arithmetically). *Obs.*

c **1391** CHAUCER *Astrol.* II. §45 Vnder that nombere [1400] I wrote a 1397; þan withdrowe I the laste nombere owte of þat, and þan fond I þe residue was 3 ȝere. *c* **1400** *Pilgr. Sowle* (Caxton) v. xiv. (1859) 81 Where that it nedeth oughte to adden, or withdrawen. *c* **1430** *Art of Nombryng* (E.E.T.S.) 6 The figures that thow hast withdraw, adde them ayene to the omyst figures.

†**c.** To cause to decline, decrease, or disappear.

c **1450** CAPGRAVE *St. Augustine* xxxv. 45 þat ȝe schuld.. not be lettyd with no cold whech schuld withdrawe ȝour deuocion. **1546** *Gassar's Prognost.* b viij, The heat of Summer shalbegynne to be wythdrawne by rayne. **1563** SHUTE *Archit.* B ij b, It hath ben withdrawen and hidden (as almost al other knowlages..hath bene) through ignoraunce.

2. To draw back, take away, remove (a thing) *from* its place or position.

c **1250** *Gen. & Ex.* 3803 Aaron..ðis fier blessede and wið-droȝ. *c* **1386** CHAUCER *Can. Yeom. Prol. & T.* 870 Withdraweth the fir, lest it to faste brenne. **1387–8** T. USK *Test. Love* II. v. (Skeat) l. 129 Whan the see ebbeth and withdraweth the gravel. *c* **1400** tr. *Secr. Secr., Gov. Lordsh.* 70 Reubard..withdrawys þe fleume fro þe mouth of þe stomake. *c* **1400** MAUNDEV. (Roxb.) vi. 21 Syrus..withdrew þe water and destruyd þe citee. **1422** YONGE tr. *Secr. Secr.* 241 Whan a man sittyth atte mette he sholde wythdrawe his honde afor that he be y-fillit. *c* **1489** CAXTON *Sonnes of Aymon* xiv. 352/12 Whan charlemagne sawe that reynawde had wyth-drawe his baner, he was glad of it. **1648** GAGE *West Ind.* 176, I withdrew my foot a little. **1671** MILTON *Samson* 192 In prosperous days They swarm, but in adverse withdraw their head. **1834** HOOK *Gilbert Gurney* iii, This speech..induced me suddenly to withdraw my head. **1842** LOUDON *Suburban Hort.* 463 So as to admit of withdrawing, and reintroducing the vines without injuring them. **1848** DICKENS *Dombey* lviii, Harriet was withdrawing her hand to open the book, when Alice detained it for a moment. **1854** RONALDS & RICHARDSON *Chem. Technol.* (ed. 2) I. 168 The most appropriate spot for withdrawing the gases from this furnace. **1898** 'H. S. MERRIMAN' *Roden's Corner* xxv, As he spoke he had withdrawn from his pocket a folded paper.

b. To take (one's eyes, etc.) off something.

1477 EARL RIVERS (Caxton) *Dictes* 5 He is happy that with-draweth his ere & his eye from alle vyle thinges. **1542** ELYOT, *Oculorum remissio*, a withdrawyng of the loke. **1836** DICKENS *Sk. Boz, Tuggs's at Ramsgate*, As her eye caught that of Mr. Cymon Tuggs, she withdrew it from his features in bashful confusion. **1838** —— *O. Twist* xxxviii, Till even she, who was not easily cowed, was fain to withdraw her eyes, and turn them towards the ground.

c. To remove (money) *from* capital, or *from* a bank or other place of deposit.

1776 ADAM SMITH *W.N.* II. iii. I. 403 That part is, from that moment, withdrawn from his capital. **1828** *Act 9 Geo. IV* c. 92 §38 After having withdrawn any Sum or Sums of Money from or out of any Savings Banks. **1861** *Act 24 Vict.* c. 14 §4 The Officers of the Postmaster General..shall not disclose the Name of any Depositor nor the Amount deposited or withdrawn.

d. To draw (a veil, curtain, etc.) back or aside; to draw back (a bolt). Now *rare.*

1797 MRS. RADCLIFFE *Italian* xi, The veil was at length withdrawn. **1833** L. RITCHIE *Wand. Loire* 170 The sound of opening doors, withdrawing bolts, and hoarse voices hallooing from tower to tower. **1841** DICKENS *Barn. Rudge* ix, Withdrawing the little window curtain, she gazed out. **1878** Browning *La Saisiaz* 106 Here's the veil withdrawn from landscape.

3. *fig.* †**a.** To retract, revoke, rescind. *Obs.*

c **1290** *Beket* 1829 in *S. Eng. Leg.* 159 3if þov wenest wel for-to do, with-drauȝ þine dede sone. *c* **1290** *St. Nicholas* 265 ibid. 248 With-drauȝ þi red, ich þe rede. *c* **1400** *Ywaine & Gaw.* 3459 The king withdrogh his jugement. *c* **1480** Henryson *Test. Cress.* 327 Withdraw thy sentence, and be gracious.

b. To remove *from* the scope of an inquiry, *from* a particular category, or the like.

1725 Broome *Notes Pope's Odyss.* vi. 331 Nausicaa..is withdrawn, and a whole nation introduced for a more general praise of Ulysses. **1839** Hallam *Lit. Eur.* ii. v. §97 One [poem] by Hercules Rollock..is..equal, a few names withdrawn, to any of the contemporaneous poetry of France. **1848** H. R. Forster *Stowe Catal.* 236 The next two lots were withdrawn. **1869** Tozer *Highl. Turkey* II. 259 The marvellous element..withdraws the narrative..from the course of ordinary occurrences. **1895** *Law Times Rep.* LXXIII. 637/2 It was not a case which should have been withdrawn from the jury.

c. To take back, retract (one's words, an expression). Often *absol.* in imper., in parliamentary procedure, to demand the withdrawal by a member of an expression or a statement.

1793 in *Ld. Auckland's Corr.* (1862) III. 37 Burke got up twice, but the House was so satisfied, that it would hear nothing, and nothing was heard but *Withdraw, withdraw.* **1837** Dickens *Pickw.* i, The Chairman was quite sure the hon. Pickwickian would withdraw the expression he had just made use of. **1880** *Hansard's Parl. Deb.* 20 Aug. 1756, I call upon the hon. Member to withdraw the word 'offensive'... (Cries of 'Withdraw!')

d. To refrain from proceeding with or prosecuting (a course of action, a proposal, etc.); to cease to support or present (a candidate, etc.).

1781 Blackstone *Rep.* II. 1028 The Court allowed the Plaintiff to withdraw his Demurrer. **1834** Dickens *Sk. Boz, Steam Excurs.*, Mr. Alexander Briggs moved as an amendment, that [etc.]..; but after some debate consented to withdraw his opposition. **1844** H. H. Wilson *Brit. India* I. 555 The latter proposition was withdrawn. **1880** *Hansard's Parl. Deb.* 20 Aug. 1739 Amendment, by leave, withdrawn. **1891** Farrar *Darkn. & Dawn* xxiii, Nero.. neither repeated nor withdrew his command. **1913** *Act 3 & 4 Geo. V*, c. 6 §1 If the candidate is withdrawn or deemed to be withdrawn.

4. †**a.** To keep back or hold (one's hand); also, to withhold (a blow). *Obs.*

a **1300** *K. Horn* 859 (Camb.) His dent he gan wiþ-draȝe, For hi were neȝ aslaȝe. **1390** Gower *Conf.* I. 369 Achilles tho withdrowh his hond. *c* **1400** tr. *Secr. Secr., Gov. Lordsh.* 52 Whanne kynges..withdrawes her hondys frome þe.. poscessiouns of her subgitz.

†**b.** To keep back, withhold (something due, customary, or necessary); hence *gen.* to withhold.

a **1300** *Cursor M.* 21906 Þai serue him all apon þair wise, And man wit-draus his seruise. *c* **1386** Chaucer *Wife's Prol.* 617, I koude noght withdrawe My chambre of Venus from a good felawe. *c* **1450** *Godstow Reg.* 231 They haue preuyd þat þey with-drowe no dewete þat was wonyd & vsyd. **1510** in Leadam *Sel. Cases Star Chamber* (Selden Soc.) II. 70 The seid priour..withdraweth suche dueties as they of Right owght to take. **1526** *Pilgr. Perf.* (W. de W. 1531) 6 b, Whan god withdraweth his rayne,..than shall there be neyther oxe ne cowe. **1580** [see withdrawer].

†**c.** To keep back, restrain (a person, his desires, etc.). *Obs.*

1340 *Ayenb.* 254 Þe guode man and þe wyse wyþdraȝeþ hare wyl and hare lostes..be temperance. **1390** Gower *Conf.* II. 393 Withdrawh thi lust and hold the stille. *c* **1450** *Mirk's Festial* 96 Forto wythdraw all men of such oþes and wordys Seynt Poule..forbedyth yche cristen man not to speke all maner ydull speche. **1450–1530** *Myrr. our Ladye* I. xix. 51 Yf yt happe..that any..be dystracte from saynge.. eny..verse..and may not say yt, but yf he withdrawe his voyce from syngynge. **1530** Palsgr. 781/2 Let him go whan he wyll, he shall nat be withdrawen for me.

5. To draw away, deflect, divert (a person, his mind, etc.) *from* an object, pursuit, line of conduct, etc.; †also, to draw, attract; to distract. Now *rare.*

†Occas. const. inf.: To divert from doing something.

1340 *Ayenb.* 58 Þet hi myȝten his..uram þe guode þet hi habeþ y-conceyued wyþdraȝe. *Ibid.*, Yef þou be þine tonge wyþdraȝst ane man oþer a child wel to done. *c* **1380** Wyclif *Sel. Wks.* II. 215 Þat man leve no worldly goodis þat wiþ-drawiþ his wille fro God. ? **1477** *Stonor Papers* (Camden) II. 34 Parauenture more chargeful besynes hathe othedraw yower mynde. **1489** Caxton *Faytes of A.* i. xxix. F iv, Withdrawe towardys the, the hertes of straungers by yeftes. **1542** Elyot, *Auocamentum*,..recreation, that withdraweth the mynde from heuynes or melancholy. **1563** Golding *Cæsar* iii. (1565) 76 Those sorte of rascals whom hope of spoile..had wythdrawen from husbandrye and daylye labor. *a* **1592** Greene *Jas. IV*, ii. ii, With how contrarious thoughts am I withdrawne! Why linger I twixt hope and doubtfull feare? **1606** Shaks. *Tr. & Cr.* v. iv. 23 Aduantagious care Withdrew me from the oddes of multitude. **1606** *Reg. Privy Council Scot.* (1885) VII. 181 To alienat and withdraw thaim from thair due obedience to his Majestie. **1651** Hobbes *Leviath.* i. viii. 33 Whatsoever is new, or great,..withdrawes a man..from the intended way of his discourse. **1667** Milton *P.L.* vii. 612 They thought Thee to diminish, and from thee withdraw The number of thy worshippers. **1841** Elphinstone *Hist. India* I. 593 It would have been happy if he had never been withdrawn from those pursuits. **1859** W. Collins *Q. of Hearts* i, The circumstances which have withdrawn us from the world for the rest of our days.

6. To remove (a person) *from* a position; to cause to retire or recede; †occas. to take aside; *spec.* to cause (a force, troops) to retire *from* a position; to draw off *from* an engagement.

a **1450** *Knt. de la Tour* (1868) 107 Mani that haue be withdrawe oute of abbeyes, for thaire londes. **1471** Caxton *Recuyell* (Sommer) 149 Saturne wythdrowe his peple on that oon syde. *a* **1548** Hall *Chron., Edw. IV* 206 His onely sauegarde and comforte, were to withdrawe hym and his compaignie into Fraunce. *a* **1592** Greene *Jas. IV*, iii. iii, A shining blade Withdrawes a coward theefe that would inuade. **1615** in *Buccleuch MSS.* (Hist. MSS. Comm.) I. 160, I presently did withdraw him..until I had discovered that which I desired. **1621** Elsing *Debates Ho. Lords* (Camden) 87 The prisoner withdrawen. **1805** C. James *Milit. Dict.* (ed. 2), To *withdraw*, to call back; to make to retire. **1821** Shelley *Adonais* xlii, Where'er that Power may move Which has withdrawn his being to its own. **1823** Scott *Quentin D.* ix, A sounder..had..withdrawn in pursuit of him all the dogs..and the greater part of the huntsmen. **1836** Thirlwall *Greece* xxi. III. 175 She would be compelled to with-draw her forces from Lesbos. **1848** Thackeray *Van. Fair* lx, Walter Scape was withdrawn from Eton, and put into a merchant's house. **1891** Farrar *Darkn. & Dawn* xx, She has withdrawn her spies.

b. *Law.* To remove (a juror) from the panel in order to put an end to the proceedings.

a **1676** Hale *De Jure Maris* i. vi. (1787) 36 The court and the king's attorney-generall..were so well satisfied with the defendant's title, that they moved the defendant to consent to withdraw a juror. **1789** *New Lond. Mag.* Sept. 458/2 And Mrs. Phillips agreed on her part that a Juror should be withdrawn. **1866** Foster & Finlason *Nisi Prius Cases* IV. 942 The plaintiff's counsel proposed to withdraw a juror, which was assented to. **1881** Odgers *Libel & Slander* 550 Actions of defamation are often compromised before the judge comes to sum up the evidence. A juror is often withdrawn, sometimes at the suggestion of the judge.

†**7.** = *withdraw from* in various senses. *Obs. rare.*

1340–70 *Alex. & Dind.* 895 Sin ȝe maugray ȝour miht mote hit wiþ-drawe. *c* **1400** *Beryn* 1257 Yff þow wolt drawe the to wit, & rebawdry withdrawe. *c* **1450** *Godstow Reg.* 304 He with-drow the forsaid court, by the mean of a frendly accorde.

II. *refl.* **8.** To remove oneself *from* a place or position; = 12. Now *rare* or *arch.*

a **1300** *Cursor M.* 19175 Þai badd þat þai þam suld wit-drau Quils þai samen spak a thrau. **13..** *Ibid.* 21654 (Edinb.) Adam quen he wroȝt hauid woȝ Vndir þis tre he him wiþ-droȝ. **1390** Gower *Conf.* I. 73 He him withdrowh So prively that sche ne wiste Wher he becom. *c* **1410** *Master of Game* xxvi. (1904) 83 Þei ought to wiþdrawe hym in þe softest maner..and þan go preuyli to þei be vndir þe wynde. *c* **1450** Capgrave *Life St. Aug.* 39/19 He wepte, and with-drow him. **1485** *Rolls of Parlt.* VI. 314/1 The said William had withdrawn him out of thys Lande. **1530** Palsgr. 783/1 He hath withdrawen him selfe in some corner. **1593** Shaks. *Rich. II*, v. iii. 28 Withdraw your selues, and leaue vs here alone. **1610** Holland *Camden's Brit.* i. 627 Vortigern had withdrawen himselfe into these parts. **1718** Atterbury *Serm., Acts i. 3* (1734) I. 177 It was requisite that he should not withdraw himself from their Sight, at once. **1839** Lane *Arab. Nts.* I. 103 The King disguised himself, and.. withdrew himself from the midst of his troops.

†**b.** Of combatants, troops, etc.: = 12 b. *Obs.*

1297 R. Glouc. (Rolls) 3253 Þe brutons hom wiþdrowe, & þe saxons hom reste. *c* **1300** *K. Horn* 886 (Laud MS.) Hys feren gonnen hem wyt drawe. **1387** Trevisa *Higden* (Rolls) III. 169 Cirus..feyned hym to flee and wiþdrowȝ hym.

†**c.** Of water: = 12 c. *Obs.*

c **1400** Maundev. (Roxb.) xxiv. 111 Þe see, þat before bette apon þe mount, withdrewe it. **1422** Yonge tr. *Secr. Secr.* 196 The See meveth and hym wyth-drawyth aftyr the mewynge..of the mone.

9. To remove oneself *from* a condition, sphere, society, etc.; = 13. Now *rare* or *arch.*

a **1300** *Cursor M.* 28136 Oft als haue i me wit-draun Til vncuth pryst, and fra myn aun. **1553** Eden *Treat. Newe Ind.* G j b, Voyces of deuyls..withdrawing them from the right waye. **1560** Daus tr. *Sleidane's Comm.* 102 b, It is also to be feared lest suche as would haue ioyned them selues vnto this league, wyll be affrayde nowe of this, and withdrawe them selues. **1612** Sir J. Digby *Let.* 10 Oct. in *10th Rep. Hist. MSS. Comm.* App. i. 609 Some of the beste of them have withdrawen themselves from their trade. **1638** Junius *Paint. Ancients* 24 Let our Imagination therefore among multitudes of people..withdraw it selfe to some secrecie. **1663** *Sc. Acts Chas. II* (1820) VII. 455/2 All..persons who shall..wilfully withdraw and absent themselffs from the ordinary meitings of divine worship. **1770** *Junius Lett.* xxxix, He cannot withdraw himself from the Complaints.. of his Subjects. **1798** Malthus *Popul.* (1878) 448 Every man may..have the redress of withdrawing himself from the club. **1812** Belsham *Mem. Lindsey* 348 Withdrawing himself from an office the duties of which he was so fully competent to discharge. **1865** Dickens *Lett.* (1880) II. 233, I am withdrawing myself from engagements of all kinds.

†**10.** To cease, refrain; = 14. *Obs.*

c **1290** *St. James* 159 in *S. Eng. Leg.* 38 Of is luþere þouȝt þat he þouȝte for drede he him with drovȝ. **1297** R. Glouc. (Rolls) 10221 Þe king of alimayne sende..To king Ion, þat he wiþdrowe him of is wou. **1303** R. Brunne *Handl. Synne* 10872 Of þat man hyt ys grete drede, þat wyþdraghþ hym fro gode dede. **1340** *Ayenb.* 52 Huanne hi wyþ-draȝeþ to do wel. **1422** Yonge tr. *Secr. Secr.* 243 He that is custumet to ette two tymes in the day, yf he wythdrawe hym sodaynly, anone he may grevaunce take.

†**11.** To contact. *Obs. rare.*

1471 Caxton *Recuyell* (Sommer) 497 His synewis shronke and withdrewe them.

III. *intr.* **12.** To go away, depart, or retire *from* a place or position, *from* some one's presence, to another room or a private place, etc.; †to draw back or turn aside.

c **1250** *Gen. & Ex.* 3983 If ðin asse ne were wið-draȝen, Her suldes ðu nu wurðen slaȝen. [*Vulg.* nisi asina declinasset de via..te occidissem, Num. xxii. 33.] **1398** Trevisa *Barth. De P.R.* viii. xxii. [xi.] (Tollem. MS.), Nouȝt with-drawinge towarde þe lyfte side, oþer towarde þe ryȝt side. **1471** Caxton *Recuyell* (Sommer) 170 He made his marouners to saylle and rowe with alle diligence for to withdrawe fro the porte. *Ibid.* 239 Whan she was a lytill withdrawen fro the temple. **1577** Holinshed *Chron.* II. 302/2 The people with their goodes and Cattell being fled and withdrawen into the Wooddes and Mountaynes. **1599** Shaks. *Much Ado* iii. iv. 100 Madam, withdraw, the Prince..and all the gallants of the towne are come to fetch you to Church. **1600** *1st Pt. Sir J. Oldcastle* v. x. 43, I will withdraw into some other roome. **1691** Wood *Ath. Oxon.* II. 711 Who was there, but withdrawn under a hedge with the Prince and Duke. **1697** Dryden *Virg. Past.* viii. 19 Scarce from our upper World the Shades withdrew. **1711** Addison *Spect.* No. 108 ¶6 Upon with-drawing into my Room after Dinner. **1712** *Ibid.* 536 ¶1 She delivered the remaining part of her Message, and with-drew. **1749** Fielding *Tom Jones* xviii. xiii, Sophia now took the first Opportunity of withdrawing with the Ladies. **1781** Cowper *Retirem.* 447 A man..Who comes when call'd, and at a word withdraws. **1810** Scott *Lady of L.* ii xxxvii, The Minstrel..from the shore withdrew. **1828** Lytton *Pelham* III. iii, I bowed slightly, and she withdrew to the countess. **1860** Tyndall *Glac.* i. xxvii. 209 The men ..withdrew from me, and approached the eastern boundary of the glacier. **1874** Green *Short Hist.* iii. §3. 127 By the treaty of Lambeth, Lewis promised to withdraw from England.

b. Of combatants, troops, etc.: To retire *from* the field of battle or any contest, or *from* an advanced position.

1297 R. Glouc. (Rolls) 3681 Prest aȝen him he was & slou of hom to grounde, so þat hii gonne wiþ drawe. *c* **1330** R. Brunne *Chron. Wace* (Rolls) 12746 Lenger to iuste myght þey nought stande, But þem defended al wyþdrawande. *a* **1400–50** *Wars Alex.* 2015, I..will at þou knaw þat for na drede I with-draw. **1471** Caxton *Recuyell* (Sommer) 401 Whan the two oostes were withdrawen. *a* **1533** Ld. Berners *Huon* lix. 203 Cause your men to withdraw fro the batayle. **1594** Shaks. *Rich. III*, v. iv. 8 Withdraw my Lord, Ile helpe you to a Horse. **1697** Dryden *Æneis* xi. 559, I beg your Greatness..beaten, to withdraw. **1709** Steele *Tatler* No. 83 ¶10 The Confederates are preparing to withdraw into Winter Quarters. **1880** Hensman *Afghan War* (1881) 449 The Amir's troops..only withdrew at daylight.

†**c.** Of water: To subside, ebb. *Obs.*

c **1250** *Gen. & Ex.* 596 In armenie ðat arche stod, Ðo was wið-draȝen ðat ilc flod. *Ibid.* 599 Dunes wexen, ðe flod wið-droȝ. *a* **1300** *K. Horn* 1399 (Camb.) Whanne þe se wiþ droȝe. *c* **1400** *Destr. Troy* 2008 The wodenes of waghes wightly with droghe. **1471** Caxton *Recuyell* (Sommer) 280 Whan the see was withdrawen & ferre ebbed. **1525** Ld. Berners *Froiss.* II. liii. [lii]. 76/2 They founde yᵉ ryuers withdrawen. **1618** Bolton *Florus* iii. x. (1636) 199 The Tide withdrawing upon course.

13. To draw away *from* a person; to remove oneself or retire *from* a society or community, *from* publicity, etc.; to retire from participation in or pusuit of something; †to resign.

c **1385** Chaucer *L.G.W.* 257 [331] Thow..makyst wise folk fro me withdrawe. **1540** *Bible* (Cranmer) Prov. xix. 7 Hys awne frendes withdrawe from him. **1667** Marvell *Corr.* Wks. (Grosart) II. 227 A large petition from the Earle of Clarindon, intimating that he was withdrawn. **1677** *Reg. Privy Council Scot.* Ser. iii. (1912) V. 120 Withdrawing from the publik ordinances in their owne paroch kirkes. **1697** Dryden *Æneis* xii. 757 [He] wisely from th' infectious World withdrew. **1715** Pope *Iliad* ii. 448 Now great Achilles from our aid withdraws. **1746** Hervey *Medit.* (1818) 108 Wisely they withdrew from that immense multiplicity of learning. **1798** Ferriar *Illustr. Sterne* iii. 63 An ideal world, into which we can withdraw at pleasure. **1849** A. Scratchley *Build. Societies* 100 Desirous of with-drawing from the society. **1853** Newman *Hist. Sk.* (1873) II. i. iv. 174 Classes and ranks withdraw from each other more and more. **1870** J. E. T. Rogers *Hist. Glean.* Ser. ii. 23 Wiklif withdrew from his political and social projects. **1892** Gladstone in *Daily News* 4 Nov. 5/4, I have..withdrawn from all attendance at public banquets. **1911** Marett *Anthropology* ix. 237 No one has a chance of withdrawing into his own soul.

†**b.** Of an immaterial thing, a condition, etc.: To depart, disappear.

1297 R. Glouc. (Rolls) 6583 [He] biheld toward þe water, & is grete herte wiþdrou. *Ibid.* 9189 Þe verste tuo ȝer god cas & hap inou..com to king steuene, ac suþþe it wiþ drou. **13..** *Cursor M.* 4698 (Gött.) Bot alkines welth bigan wid-drau. **1426** Audelay *Poems* 25 Dredles deuocioun hit is with draw. **1450–1530** *Myrr. our Ladye* ii. 151 Then grace withdrawyth and the fende enteryth.

†**14.** Const. *of* of inf. To cease or refrain from, or from doing, something. *Obs.*

1297 R. Glouc. (Rolls) 10893 Seint edmond..ofte him bisouȝte þat he wiþdrowe of is dede. **1340** *Ayenb.* 53 Ich wille þet þou loki and wyþdraȝe. *c* **1375** *Cato Major* 523 in *Minor Poems fr. Vernon MS.* 598 Þou most with-drawe of diuers metes, And vse no glotenie. **1450–80** tr. *Secr. Secr.* v. 8 Whan he withdrawith forto take the goodis and possessiones of his sugetis.

withdrawable (wɪð'drɔːəb(ə)l), *a.* [f. prec. + -able.] Capable of being withdrawn.

1850 Herschel *Ess.* (1857) 392 Its deposits being withdrawable only at a market value. **1876** Gladstone in *Contemp. Rev.* June 6 All other rights..are called rights only by way of accommodation, for they are withdrawable at will. **1903** in *Q. Rev.* (1905) Jan. 67 Half..had to be invested in stock and the other half was withdrawable.

withdrawal (wɪð'drɔːəl). [f. as prec. + -al[1]. (Superseding withdrawment, which took the place of the earlier withdraught and withdraw *sb.*)]

1. a. The act of taking back or away what has been held, occupied, or enjoyed.

1839 Lane *Arab. Nts.* I. 80 Thou deservest..the withdrawal of protection from thee. **1860** Tyndall *Glac.* i. xxv.

189 The cold, resulting from the withdrawal of the sunbeams.

b. The removal of money or securities from a bank or other place of deposit.

1861 *Regulations P.O. Savings Banks* §15 If any person shall fraudulently represent himself to be a Depositor, and by forwarding the proper notice of withdrawal,..shall obtain any sum of money. **1884** *Manch. Exam.* 28 May 5/3 The bank was in difficulties through large withdrawals.

2. The act of withdrawing a person or thing *from* a place or position, *esp.* the removal of troops by way of retreat.

1838 MEESON & WELBY *Cases Exch.* II. 36 It was no part of the agreement between the parties that the withdrawal of a juror should put an end to the suit at all events. **1844** H. H. WILSON *Brit. India* II. 480 He urged the withdrawal of the British officers, as their presence was no longer necessary. **1877** HUXLEY *Physiogr.* 37 The artificial withdrawal of water to feed the canal. **1892** HARDY *Well-beloved* I. v, Their application for admission led to the withdrawal of a bolt.

3. The retraction of a statement, proposal, etc.

1835 T. HOOK *G. Gurney* xiv, I thought perhaps the news ..might have induced you to retract; and that you might have considered it a perfect justification of your withdrawal. **1885** *Law Times* LXXVIII. 384/2 In consequence of his resignation, and notwithstanding his withdrawal of it.

4. a. The act of retiring or retreating *from* a place or position.

1824 MISS MITFORD *Village* Ser. I. 190 Perhaps, indeed, Joel's rapid improvement might be one cause of William's withdrawal. **1836** *Act 6 & 7 Will. IV*, c. 32 §1 The Withdrawal of such Member [from a society]. **1848** DICKENS *Dombey* xxxvi, It was a sight to see her lord..hold the door open for the withdrawal of the ladies. **1884** BRYCE in *Hansard's Parl. Deb.* 15 Mar. 1716 A vote which..would accelerate..the withdrawal of England from Egypt. **1891** *Law Times Rep.* LXV. 603/1 Desertion implies an active with-drawal from a cohabitation that exists.

b. *Psychol.* The state or process of psychic retreat from objective reality or social involvement; also *transf.*

1916 C. E. LONG tr. *Jung's Coll. Papers on Anal. Psychol.* vi. 203 Autistic withdrawal into one's own phantasies is what I formerly designated as the obvious overgrowth of the phantasies of the complex. **1937** K. HORNEY *Neurotic Personality of our Time* v. 98 The fourth means of protection [*sc.* against the basic anxiety] is withdrawal. **1957** P. LAFITTE *Person in Psychol.* xii. 181 Withdrawal and regression..are general classes of behaviour as compared to the social specificity of striving for advancement or mendacity. **1970** TOURAINE & PÉCAUT in I. L. Horowitz *Masses in Lat. Amer.* iii. 90 At the lowest level, we find *withdrawal*, characterized by a rejection of the industrial world. **1973** *Jrnl. Genetic Psychol.* June 315 One type of children's fantasy is 'withdrawal'.

5. Cessation of use or provision of a drug; *spec.* the interruption of doses of an addictive drug, with resulting craving and physical reactions.

The 1897 example is an isolated one.

1897 [see INJECTOR 2]. **1929** D. HAMMETT *Dain Curse* xxi. 237 Tears were one of the symptoms of morphine withdrawal. **1965** WILNER & KASSEBAUM *Narcotics* vi. 96 Withdrawal of morphine by substitution and subsequent withdrawal of methadon. **1972** *Nature* 22 Dec. 443/1 Dr R. Ericsson..suggested that the criteria for a successful antispermatogenic drug were..return of fertility on withdrawal, and normal libido. **1977** *Lancet* 29 Jan. 255/1 Any doctor prescribing or patient receiving this potent drug should consider carefully the effect of withdrawal which has not, to my knowledge, been researched.

6. = *coitus interruptus* s.v. COITUS.

1889 W. T. STEAD *Diary* 20 Jan. in J. W. R. Scott *Life & Death of Newspaper* (1952) xix. 244, I have from the birth of Willie practised simple syringing with water. Of late always withdrawal. **1923** M. C. STOPES *Contraception* iv. 48 Vaginal stimulation consummating the ejaculation after withdrawal, commonly called '*coitus interruptus*'. **1963** M. MCCARTHY *Group* iii. 66 What method of contraception had been used..? 'Withdrawal,' murmured the doctor. **1978** G. CUNNINGHAM *New Woman & Victorian Novel* 6 Such methods as the safe period, the sheath, the sponge..and withdrawal.

7. *attrib.* and *Comb.*, as (sense 5) ***withdrawal pain, period, syndrome***, etc.; **withdrawal slip**, a form which must be filled in when withdrawing money from a bank or other place of deposit; **withdrawal symptom**, an unpleasant physiological reaction resulting from the process of ceasing to take an addictive drug; usu. *pl.*; also *fig.*

1924 *Brit. Jrnl. Inebriety* XXI. 88 The *withdrawal symptoms* of addiction disease. **1929** LIGHT & TORRANCE in *Arch. Internal Med.* XLIV. 11 The general behavior and symptomatology of these addicts were uniform during the forty-eight hour withdrawal period. *Ibid.* 14 Addicts will admit that when they are unable to obtain drugs and when withdrawal symptoms..become severe, the assurance of an available supply at a considerable distance will cause them to travel..with remarkable speed and efficiency. **1961** *Lancet* 23 Sept. 677/1 A steroid withdrawal syndrome occurs in patients who have stopped corticosteroid therapy. **1962** *Ibid.* 6 Jan. 54/2 Lobeline sulphate closely resembles nicotine in many of its pharmacological actions. Using it as a substitute for tobacco during the withdrawal phase, Dorsey found the results 'encouraging'. **1962** 'K. ORVIS' *Damned & Destroyed* xvi. 113, I had seen that stare and twitching frequently enough now..to be able to tag it as an indication of the degree of withdrawal sickness. **1965** *New Statesman* 7 May 716/1 Often these women directly sabotaged the programme. One flushed her son's withdrawal medication down the lavatory. *Ibid.* 3 Dec. 866/2, I asked him how long it was since the withdrawal pains had stopped. **1966** C. E. ISRAEL *Hostages* 94 She wouldn't have had the dreg end of her withdrawal agonies yet. **1967** *Guardian* 7 Dec. 1/6 Methedrine has been used in heroin withdrawal treatment. **1970** G. F. NEWMAN *Sir, You Bastard* v. 140 Morgan was entering the withdrawal stage and would soon be requiring another intravenous dose. **1970** G. GREER *Female Eunuch* 276 Mrs J. S. used up two supplies of pills in all innocence, and then discovered that she had withdrawal symptoms. **1973** 'E. MCBAIN' *Let's hear It* xv. 226 On the withdrawal slip before him, he wrote the date, and the number of his account, and then he filled in the amount. **1976** *Times* 18 Oct. 3/7 Sir Harold Wilson..the former Prime Minister..says he has suffered no 'withdrawal symptoms' since resigning. **1979** F. OLBRICH *Sweet & Deadly* ix. 110 The bank manager..showed Ramesh the withdrawal slip for four thousand rupees.

withdrawer (wɪð'drɔːə(r)). [f. as prec. + -ER[1].] One who withdraws, in various senses of the vb.; *spec.* in *Sc. Church Hist.*, one who did not conform to the established church in the 17th century.

1475 *Bk. Noblesse* (Roxb.) 46 Sethe that none suche were never sene withdrawers or fleers frome batailes. **1580** OUTRED tr. *M. Cope's Expos. Prov.* 192 b, Joseph..was not a withdrawer of the corne, but a seller. **1606** in J. Forbes *Cert. Rec. Kirk* (Wodrow Soc.) 519 Contempners of his Majesties lawes, withdrawers and corrupters of his Majestie's subjects hearts from his obedience. *c* **1639** BAILLIE in Boyd *Zion's Flowers* (1855) Introd. 43 They are ..withdrawers of their hands. **1677** *Reg. Privy Council Scot.* Ser. III. (1912) V. 121 Constant withdrawers and keepers of conventicles. **1823** J. BROWN *Hist. Brit. Ch.* (new ed.) II. 312 Parliament..enacted [in 1663] That..all with-drawers from the conform incumbents of their own parish, be punished.

withdrawing (wɪð'drɔːɪŋ), *vbl. sb.* [f. WITHDRAW *v.* + -ING[1].] The action of the vb. WITHDRAW in various senses.

c **1315** SHOREHAM IV. 344 Þorȝ cheste and mysdoynge And wyþ-drawynge of god. *c* **1340** HAMPOLE *Prose Treat.* 11 All manere of withdraweynge of oþer men thynges wrangwysely agaynes þaire wyll. **1340** *Ayenb.* 205 Be wyþdraȝinges of mete and of drinke. *c* **1380** WYCLIF *Sel. Wks.* III. 348 Þei maken londis bareyne for wiþdrawyng of werkmen. *c* **1430** *Art Nombryng* (E.E.T.S.) 4 In withdrawyng .2. nombres ben necessary. **1471** CAXTON *Recuyell* (Sommer) 262 At the departyng hercules passeth lightly the withdrawyng & departyng of alle hem that were there. **1561** T. NORTON tr. *Calvin's Inst.* II. iii. 22 Euen they that are well minded, are subiecte to so many withdrawynges of minde, that they easily..fal awaye. *a* **1651** C. LOVE *Combat Flesh & Spirit* (1654) 6 A double withdrawing of Gods Spirit. **1689** in *Acts Parlt. Scot.* (1875) XII. 65/1 The fyneing husbands for the wifes withdrawing from the church is contrair to Law. **1748** *Anson's Voy.* II. xi. 250 The withdrawing of the guard from the harbour's mouth. **1817** COLERIDGE in *Athenæum* (1894) 8 Dec. 791/2 The quiet withdrawing from any further connection with him. **1862** TRENCH *Mirac.* v. (ed. 7) 177 A withdrawing of the meaner thing, to make receptive of the better.

b. *attrib.* (also WITHDRAWING-CHAMBER, -ROOM).

1570 LAMBARDE *Peramb. Kent* (1576) 378 A certaine withdrawing house, called Otforde. *a* **1693** *Urquhart's Rabelais* III. ii. 31 Withdrawing Corners and Refuges to Robbers. **1803** MARY CHARLTON *Wife & Mistress* IV. 263 Miss Winteram..soon made her withdrawing curtsy. **1821** SCOTT *Kenilw.* vi, They went to the withdrawing apartment. **1898** *Century Mag.* Jan. 456/1 This withdrawing-ground.. was within the garden inclosure.

with'drawing, *ppl. a.* [f. WITHDRAW *v.* + -ING[2].] That withdraws (usually in intr. senses); drawing back, retiring, receding.

1611 *Bible* Neh. ix. 29 They..withdrew the shoulder [*marg.* gaue a withdrawing shoulder]. *a* **1748** THOMSON *Hymn Solitude* 23 Amid the long withdrawing vale. *a* **1846** HAYDON *Autob.* (1853) I. 179 'That I can't tell you,' said he, with a cold, withdrawing air. **1847** H. MILLER *First Impr. Eng.* ii. 27 By some long withdrawing arm of the sea. **1889** RUSKIN *Præterita* III. iv. 152 Sands which the sunset gilded with its withdrawing glow.

Hence **with'drawingness**, retiring disposition.

1795 *Jemima* I. 207 To shake off all this shyness and withdrawingness from your friends.

†**with'drawing-,chamber.** *Obs.* [f. prec. vbl. sb.] = next.

1392-3 *Rolls Parlt.* III. 300/2 Triours des Petitions.. tendront lour place en la Chapelle de la Withdrawyng Chambre. **1444** *Test. Ebor.* (Surtees) II. 102 Item lego eidem j. burded-bedd in le withdrawynchambre. **1589** GREENE *Menaphon* (Arb.) 73 Samela..flung away to her withdrawing chamber in a dissembled rage. *a* **1670** HACKET *Abp. Williams* II. (1693) 119 The Bishop being in a withdrawing Chamber, read over the Order so often, that..he got it by heart *verbatim*.

fig. **1621** BP. MOUNTAGU *Diatribæ* 7 In the *Lararijs*, and withdrawing chambers of your *History of Tithes*.

with'drawing-,room. *arch.* or *Hist.* [f. as prec.] A room to withdraw to; = DRAWING-ROOM[1] 1.

1591 HORSEY *Trav.* (Hakl. Soc.) 204 He was..had into a with-drawinge roem, where many of the lords wear. **1611** L. BARRY *Ram Alley* v. i, Ile waite in the with-drawing roome, Vntill you call. **1661** EARL ORRERY *St. Lett.* (1742) 37 Whilst we were in the withdrawing room, making preparations to go into the house of lords. **1748** RICHARDSON *Clarissa* III. xxxvi. 185 The apartments she has to let are..a withdrawing-room, two or three handsome bed-chambers. **1846** MRS. A. MARSH *Fr. Darcy* xxxii, He sat by her in the large withdrawing room, where she was at work. **1885** PAYN *Talk of Town* I. 110 It was William Henry's habit to quietly withdraw and seek Margaret in the withdrawing-room.

withdrawment (wɪð'drɔːmənt). Now *rare.* [f. WITHDRAW *v.* + -MENT.] = WITHDRAWAL in various senses; formerly *spec.* the withdrawal of divine illumination.

1640 O. SEDGWICK *Christs Counsell* 79 All the wrath of God, and the withdrawments of his love. **1666** G. ALSOP *Char. Prov. Mary-Land* (1869) 64, I am certainly confident, that England would as soon feel her feebleness by withdrawment of so great an upholder. **1677** GILPIN *Dæmonol.* III. xxiii. 195 An apparent withdrawment from Obedience. *a* **1709** J. LISTER *Autobiog.* (1842) 52 He would sometimes say to me in the times of God's withdrawments, 'O! son, I am not able to bear under God's absence'. **1754** EDWARDS *Freed. Will* II. iii. 41 The Withdrawment or Absence of the Sun. **1817** CHALMERS in *Edin. Rev.* Mar. 4 A great withdrawment of wealth from its former channels of distribution. **1885** *Manch. Exam.* 16 Sept. 5/2 The immediate withdrawment from an..expensive colonial policy.

withdrawn (wɪð'drɔːn), *ppl. a.* [pa. pple. of WITHDRAW *v.*] In various senses of the vb.; sometimes in a purely static sense, secluded; also of mental state, detached. Also *spec.* in *Psychol.*, characterized by isolation and loss of contact with objective reality. Cf. WITHDRAWAL 4 b.

1615 CHAPMAN *Odyss.* VI. 477 Where abide My Mother, with her withdrawne housewiferies. *Ibid.* XXIII. 8 Wake, Leaue this withdrawne roome. *a* **1651** SIR J. SKEFFINGTON *Heroe of Lorenzo* (1652) 13 She shut her self up in..the most withdrawn chamber of the Palace. **1713** C'TESS WINCHILSEA *Misc. Poems* 94 The withdrawn, the absent Mind. **1723** POPE *Let. to Swift* 12 Jan., Your withdrawn and separate state. **1849** A. SCRATCHLEY *Build. Societies* 100 Withdrawn shares (not wholly subscribed for). **1858** THOREAU *Maine Woods* ii. (1918) 157 The stream was so withdrawn..that my companions..concluded to go farther up it. **1895** *Westm. Gaz.* 22 Feb. 7/1 The withdrawn lot [of horses] includes Stowmarket and Indian Queen. **1932** *Smith. Coll. Stud. Social Work* III. 145 Only four of the patients..were of the..type often thought to be common among the pre-schizophrenic... Perhaps children of the withdrawn, timid type are only rarely referred to a child guidance clinic. **1950** *Times* 12 May 7/7 The emotional re-education of the severely withdrawn type was at best a tricky business, for which frequent consultation between the school staff and the psychologist was advisable. **1971** H. KOHUT *Analysis of Self* ix. 243 He not only would tend to become generally withdrawn..and diffusely depressed, but..also manifested a striking change in his dream pattern.

with'drawnness. [f. prec. + -NESS.] Withdrawn or retired character.

1927 *Public Opinion* Feb. 102/1 He has the curiosity and interest of a young man and has none of the settled habits and introspection and withdrawnness of an old man. **1976** *Classical Q.* XXVI. 161 A more general characteristic of the Homeric style, the restrained objectivity and aristocratic withdrawnness.

withe, with (wɪθ, wɪð, waɪð), *sb.* Forms: 1, 3 **wiððe, wiþþe**, 4–9 **wyth**, 5–6 **wythe**, (4 **withthe, wyþþe**, 5–6 **wythth(e**, 5 **witthe, whythe**, 6 **wethe**, 7 **wieth**, *Anglo-Ir.* **whitt**; *dial.* 5 **wyffe**, 6 **wifte, wyft**, 7, 9 **wift**, 9 **wiff, weef, wef**), 6– **with, withe.** [OE. *wiþþe*, corresp. to OFris. *withthe, witte*, MDu. *wisse* (WFlem. *wisse*, Du. *wis, wisch*), MLG., LG. *wedde*, OHG. *with, widh, wit* (MHG. *wit*), OHG. *withî, widî*, (MHG. *wide*), also in OHG. *khunawithi* (cf. OE. *cynewiþþe*), ON. *við* (gen. *viðjar*), *viðja* (Sw. *vidja*, Da. *vidje*):—OTeut. **wiþjôn-*, **wiþi-*. Other Teut. variants are represented by MLG. *wîde*, OHG. *wîda* (MHG. *wîde*, G. *weide*) willow, Goth. *wida* in *kunawida* chain, ON. *víðir* willow, OE. *wíþiȝ* WITHY, q.v. (The variant forms with *f* are mainly Kentish.)

Outside Germanic cognate words of similar meaning from Indo-Eur. *weit-, wit-* are:—Zend *vaêti-* willow, Gk. ἰτέα willow (:—*ϝειτεϝᾱ), ἴτυς felloe, L. *vītis* vine, Lith. *výtis* wand, OPruss. *witwan* willow, OSlav. *větvĭ branch, OIr. féith* 'fibra' (:—**weiti*). According to a widely accepted view *weit-* is a derivative of *wi-*, which is represented also by L. *viēre* to plait, WIRE *sb.*, and perh. WOUGH, wall.]

1. a. A band, tie, or shackle consisting of a tough flexible twig or branch, or of several twisted together; such a twig or branch, as of willow or osier, used for binding or tying, and sometimes for plaiting.

c **1000** ÆLFRIC *Hom.* I. 594 Egeas..bebead ðam cwellerum ðæt hi hine mid wiððum handum and fotum on ðære rode ȝebundon. *c* **1100** in Wr.-Wülcker *Voc.* 105/9 *Circus, uel circulus*, wiðþe. *Funiculus, uel funis*, rap. *Ibid.* 183/16 *Loramentum, uel tormentum*, wiððe. *c* **1200** ORMIN 15813, 5 Þe Laferrd wrohhte an swepe þær all alls itt wære off wiþþess, To tacnenn þatt hemm ȝarrkedd wass stranng pine i defless wiþþess. *c* **1205** LAY. 25973 Þat weore twælf swine iteied to-somne Mid wiðen swiðe grete y-wriðen al togadere. *a* **1400** *Sir Perc.* 423 Brydille hase he righte nane;.. Bot a wythe hase he tane, And keuylles his stede. *c* **1440** *Promp. Parv.* 531/1 Wythe bonde..*boia.* **1520** *MS. Acc. St. John's Hosp., Canterb.*, Paed for wyft & Roddis for the [thacker] vd. **1523-34** FITZHERB. *Husb.* §15 The fote-teame shall be fastened..with a shakyll, or a withe to drawe by. **1553** EDEN *Treat. Newe Ind.* C ij, Vnbrideled hauinge neither withe nor coller aboute theyr neckes. **1555** —— *Decades* 271 Theyr shyppes..are tide togyther..with cordes and wyththes. **1570** FOXE *A. & M.* (ed. 2) 2165 They found..a casket locked with a padlocke, and so cutting the wifte [*printed* wiste] thereof, opened it. **1592** NASHE *P. Penilesse* 16 Two Calues..that were coupled together by the neckes with an Oken With. **1600** HAKLUYT *Voy.* III. 192 The manner of their hanging vp of their fish and flesh with withes to dry. **1611** *Bible* Judges xvi. 7 If they binde me with seuen greene withs [*Great Bible* withes], that were neuer dried, then shall I be weake. 1617 MORYSON *Itin.* III. 181 These Rogues.. girding their swords to them by a with. 162. *Toke* (Kent) *Estate Accts.* (MS.) For 300 of wifts. 1639 T. DE GREY *Compl. Horsem.* 271 They haue taken a withe and put it through the hole of the said stone. *a* 1660 *Contemp. Hist. Irel.* (Ir. Archæol. Soc.) I. 241 Tyinge rope and whitts to either end thereof. 1693 EVELYN *De la Quint. Compl. Gard.* II. 166 We tie up first with Osier withs, and afterwards.. we ..wrap up with long Litter..some Spanish Cardons. 1712 E. COOKE *Voy. S. Sea* 270 For making of these Bridges, they twist Withes together, like Ropes. 1805 R. W. DICKSON *Pract. Agric.* II. 674 Proper wyths for tying them together. 1844 H. STEPHENS *Bk. Farm* II. 281 In fir rims, the wooden withes of the bottom are passed through splits. 1863 KINGSLEY *Water-Bab.* v. 180 A round cage of green withes. 1876 VOYLE & STEVENSON *Milit. Dict.*, *Withes*, twisted rods for securing the web of a gabion. 1877 W. JONES *Finger-ring* 383 A.. massive gold mourning-ring formed of two knotted withes twisted together. 1881 *Leics. Gloss.*, *Wiff*, var. pron. of 'withe', 'willow-wiffs'. 1885 M. ROSS & STONEHEWER-COOPER *Highl. Cantabria* 335 Rounded stones..with grooves around them, where the withe would have been twisted, to form a handle for its manipulation. 1887 *Kentish Gloss.* s.v. *Wiff*, The large kind of fagot, which went by the name of kiln-bush, was bound with two wiffs.

b. *gen.* A pliant twig or bough.

1817 JAS. MILL *Brit. India* II. vi. I. 245 As he rises from sleep, a Brahmen must rub his teeth with a proper withe. 1833 M. SCOTT *Tom Cringle* xii, The fork of the tree, from which the withe depended. 1881 MRS. C. PRAED *Policy & P.* vii, A trailing withe of orange begonia.

†**c.** A willow wand or garland carried into the sovereign's or a nobleman's house at Easter; hence, the ceremony or festivity itself. *Obs.*

1465 *Mann. & Househ. Exp.* (Roxb.) 509 Item, on Ester day my master gaff to John Kooke to the wythe, xxd. 1467 *Ibid.* 393 Item, on Estyr day, my mastyr gaffe to the wyffe in the Kenges howse, vj. s. viij. d. 1537 *Privy Purse Exp. Princ. Mary* (1831) 24 Geuen to the Kinges Cookes to thayr wythe at East[r]..xl *s.* 1559 *MS. Acc. Bk. Butchers Co. London*, Payd for xii men for y[e] brynging in of y[e] Quynes wythe. 1598 STOW *Surv.* 72 In the weeke before Easter had yee great shewes made for the fetching in of a twisted Tree, or With, ..out of the woodes into the kinges house.

d. With allusion to the story of Samson in *Judges* xvi. 7 (see sense 1, quot. 1611).

1835 FABER *Lett.* (1869) 39 My soul arose..and cracked in scorn the chains of darkness, like the green withs of the strong man. 1866 MRS. GASKELL *Wives & Dau.* xiv, I know that if I choose to exert myself, I can break through the withes of green flax with which they try to bind me. 1876 BLACKIE *Songs Relig.* 29 Strong by thee, like feeble withes he snapt The bonds of custom.

†**2.** A halter, properly one made with withes. *Obs.*

c 1205 LAY. 22833 Doð wiððe an his sweore & draȝeð hine to ane more. 1303 R. BRUNNE *Handl. Synne* 11551 Aboute þy nekke hanggeþ a wyþþe, þat haþ þe departed fro Goddys gryþþe. 1340 *Ayenb.* 135 Þe þief..yproued and y-nome and mid mo þanne an hondred misdedes þet heþ nieȝ þe wyþþe ine þe nykke. 1583 GOLDING *Calvin on Deut.* xviii. 21–22. 681/2 Who walked about the streetes as it were with a with about his necke. 1612 BEAUM. & FL. *Coxcomb* III. i, A wyth take him. 1625 BACON *Ess., Custom & Educ.* (Arb.) 371 That he might be hanged in a With, and not in a Halter, because it had beene so vsed, with former Rebels. 1675 T. BROOKS *Gold. Key* Wks. 1867 V. 441 [He] was condemned to the fire with others, only he should have the favour of going to the stake without a wyth. 1694 S. JOHNSON *Notes Past. Let. Bp. Burnet* I. 1 If the Highest Censures will not do it, we must do as is done in like Cases, we must Take a Wyth.

3. a. A willow. Now *dial.*

c 1340 *Nominale* (Skeat) 671 Wyth, brome, and quincetre. 1569 *Surrey & Kent Sewers Comm.* (L.C.C. 1909) 31 To Cut vppe the Wythes by the Banck syde. 1572 *Ibid.* 130 To cut vp his wethes & share his bankes throw his groundes. 1696–1864 [see WATER-WITHE]. 1741 *Compl. Fam.-Piece* II. ii. 330 A Rod..made of Red Sallow, Withe or Hazle. 1777 ROBERTSON *Hist. Amer.* IV. I. 328 The root of the *curare*, a species of withe.

b. The creeping plant *Heliotropium fruticosum*, of Jamaica, the stems of which are used for making baskets.

1657 R. LIGON *Barbadoes* 87 Worse then all weeds, Withs, which are of a stronger grouth then the Canes. 1740 *New Hist. Jamaica* (ed. 2) 316. 1847 GOSSE *Birds Jamaica* 373 The gradual predominance of marsh plants, sagittaria,.. bulrush, and black-withe.

4. *technical.* (See quots.)

1688 HOLME *Armoury* III. 360/2 A Glovers With..is a square Iron, writhen (as it were) like a Wreath..: Upon this they do use to rub and fret their Leather Skins to make them soft and plump; which kind of work from the name of the Instrument, they term Withing. 1867 SMYTH *Sailor's Word-bk.* 736 *With*, an iron instrument fitted to the end of a boom or mast, with a ring to it, through which another boom or mast is rigged out and secured. Also, in mechanics, the elastic withe handles of cold chisels, set-tools, &c., which prevent a jar to the assistant's wrist. 1880 *Encycl. Brit.* XI. 437/2 A blacksmith's chisel held in a hazel withe, and used for hot iron. 1892 *Labour Commission* Gloss., *Withes*, iron hoops or bands used for binding bales of cotton or rags.

5. *attrib.* and *Comb.* as ***withe axe***, ***handle***, ***patch***; ***withe-woven*** adj.; **withe-rod**, a deciduous shrub, *Viburnum nudum*, native to North America and bearing clusters of small white flowers; also, a thin flexible twig from this or a similar shrub.

1776 G CARTWRIGHT *Jrnl.* 19 Oct. (1792) II. 215 The people came down from the lodge, and brought..a bundle of white-rods [*sic*]. 1819 KEATS *Let.* 5 Sept. (1958) II. 156 At the days end his thoughts will run upon a withe axe if he ever had handled one. 1839 T. T. STODDART *Songs & P.* 21 The withe-woven pannier. 1846 G. B. EMERSON *Rep. Trees & Shrubs growing in Forests Mass.* 364 The Naked Viburnum. Withe Rod... A slender, erect shrub. 1865 TYLOR *Early Hist. Man.* viii. 199 Axes made..by grinding the edge of a suitable pebble, and fixing it in a withe handle. 1866 *Treas. Bot.* 1235/2 Withe-rod, *Viburnum nudum.* 1902 CORNISH *Naturalist Thames* 85, I once turned out a dozen water-hens, a brown owl, a woodcock, and a water-rail, from one little withe patch. 1943 R. PEATTIE *Great Smokies* 265 We recognize the..withe rod..and wintergreen.

withe, *v.* Now *dial.* and *U.S.* Also 4 **wyþe**, 5 **weþe**, 8 **wythe**, 9 **with.** [f. prec.]

1. *trans.* To twist like a withe. Also *fig.*

1398 TREVISA *Barth. De P.R.* XVII. cxliv. (MS. Add. 27944) Þey breketh nouȝt but þey beeþ ymade strengere with wyþynge [*Bodl. MS.* weþing] and wyndynge as þreede is with twynynge. 1523 FITZHERB. *Husb.* §15 The horses.. must haue..holmes withed about theyr neckes. 1809 J. BARLOW *Columb.* IX. 621 Bacon..Withes Proteus Matter in his arms of might.

2. To bind with a withe or withes; *U.S.* to take (deer) with a noose made of withes.

c 1630 BP. HALL *Def. Cruelty* Wks. 1634 II. 424 Stay but a while, and yee shall see him with'd, and halter'd, and stak't, and baited to death. 1732 ELLIS *Pract. Farmer* 133 Others..will drive in one Stake, and wythe it about the Tree. 1836 HALIBURTON *Clockm.* Ser. I. xvi, If their fences ..ain't [good], they ought to stake 'em up, and with them well. 1839 HOFFMAN *Wild Scenes* I. xix, What, Linus, you are not a-going to withe the deer? 1841 J. F. COOPER *Deerslayer* vi, Isn't it enough that I'm withed like a saw-log, that ye must choke too?

3. *technical.* (See prec. 4, quot. 1688.)

withe, var. WITH *sb.*

withele, var. WEOTHELE *Obs.*

withen ('wɪðən, 'waɪðən). *Obs.* exc. *dial.* (w. *midl.*) Also 4 **wythone, withiene**, 5, 9 **wythen**, 6 **withyn**, 7–8 **within**, 9 **wythin, withing.** [prob. orig. adj., f. WITHE *sb.* or WITHY *sb.* + -EN[4], after *aspen*, *beechen*, etc. The west-midland place-name *Withington* is app. f. this word.] A withy or willow. Also *attrib.* or *adj.*

For other uses see Eng. Dial. Dict.

c 1230 *Ancr. R.* MS. C.C.C.C. lf. 22 b, He is as þe wiðin þe spruteð ut þe betere þet me hine croppeð ofte. [Cf. quot. *a* 1225 s.v. WITHY *sb.* 1.] *a* 1360 in *10th Rep. Hist. MSS. Comm.* App. v. 246 Gayneth me no garlond of greene Bot hit ben of wythones [*printed* wythoues] ywroght. 1382 WYCLIF *Job* xl. 17 Withiene trees [Vulg. *salices*] of the strem. *c* 1450 *Mirk's Festial* 174/13 He come by a wythen-tre, and made þerof a goode ȝerde. 1569 *Brasenose Coll. Muniments* (MS.), A diche quicksetted with thornes and Withyns. 1602 in *Lancs. Q. Sess. Rec.* (Chetham Soc.) I. 145 [John Sorocolde entered a close..and cut and took thence] withins. 1635 BRERETON *Trav.* (Chetham Soc.) I. 172, I observed most part of the ground..planted with withens. 1688 HOLME *Armoury* III. 295/2 The Hoop Twigs are Withen Twigs Cloven. 1788 *Trans. Soc. Arts* VI. 162 That I should attempt making of Paper from the Bark of Withins. 1788 *Ann. Reg., Projects* 96 The bark or peel of within twigs. 1886 *Cheshire Gloss.*, *Withen* or *Withy*, a willow.

†**wither**, *sb.*[1] *Obs.* [OE. *wiþre* (once), f. *wiþer* WITHER *a.*] Opposition, hostility; adversity. *on wiðere*, adversely.

Beowulf 2953 [He] wiðres ne truwode, þæt he sæmannum onsacan mihte. *c* 1205 LAY. 1418 Þe heo wolden mid wiðere þan kinge wið-stonden. *Ibid.* 2884 Þe wind him com on wiðere. *Ibid.* 4678 Þat ich wes i wide sæ wiðer com toȝenes.

wither ('wɪðə(r)), *sb.*[2] Also 8 **wether.** [f. WITHER *v.*[2]]

†**1.** A disease of cows. *Obs.*

1652 W. POOLE *Country Farrier* 48 A Cow that hath the Wither. *a* 1722 LISLE *Observ. Husb.* (1757) 294 The wether that comes forth either before or after calving. [Cf. 1750 ELLIS *Cy. Housewife* 359 That fatal Malady that some call Withering, that is to say, her Bearing comes out behind.]

2. *Tea-manuf.* The process of withering (see WITHER *v.*[2] 4 c).

1897 D. CROLE *Tea* vii. 114 Should..the weather not be propitious for a natural wither, none of this leaf would be ready for rolling. 1903 C. BALD *Indian Tea* xv. (1917) 225 Leaf is ready for rolling when it has become absolutely soft and flaccid, without being in any sense dried up [*marg.* Good wither].

wither, *sb.*[3], occas. sing. of WITHERS.

'**wither**, *a.* and *adv.* *Obs.* or *dial.* Also 1, 3 **wiþer, wiðer**, 3 *Orm.* **wiþerr**, 4–5 **wyþer**, 5 **wethire, whiþer, wythyr.** [OE. *wiþer* adv. or adj. (rare), related to *wiþer* prep. = OFris. *wither*, OS. *withar* (MLG. *wêder*, *wedder*, MDu., Du. *weder*, *weer*), OHG. *widar* (MHG. *wider*, G. *wider* prep. and *wieder* adv.), ON. *viðr*, Goth. *wiþra*; OE. has also *wiþ(e)re* prep. = ONFris. *withere* (MDu. *wêdere*), OHG. *widari* (MHG. *widere*): f. Indo-Eur. *wi-* denoting separation or division + comp. suffix *-tero-* (cf. Skr. *vitarám* further). See also WITHER-[1].]

A. *adj.* **1.** Hostile, adverse; fierce.

[*c* 1000 *Gloss.* in *Germania* (N.S.) XI. 394/366 *Infensus*, wiþer.] *c* 1200 ORMIN 11389 Ga, wiþerr gast, o bacch fra me. *c* 1205 LAY. 9287 Þer he isæh Wiðe[r] king þe wiðer wes an compe. 1387 TREVISA *Higden* (Rolls) I. 275 Sicambri were afterward i-cleped Franci, as it were feranci, þat is wither and sterne. *c* 1746 J. COLLIER (Tim Bobbin) *View Lanc. Dial.* Wks. (1862) 60 O lusty wither Tyke. [Cf. 1847 HALLIWELL, *Wither*..a strong fellow. *Yorksh.*.. *Withering*, (1) strong; lusty. *Chesh.*]

2. Contrary, opposite; wrong (side).

c 1205 LAY. 11972 Þa aras heom a wind a þere wiðer side. 13.. *E.E. Allit. P.* A. 230 On wyþer half water com doun þe schore. *a* 1400–50 *Wars Alex.* 3355 Þat he wirke noȝt on þe wethire halfe.

†**B.** *adv.* Hostilely; perversely; fiercely. *Obs.*

c 1200 *Trin. Coll. Hom.* 121 Men bien swo wiðerfulle, þat swo he ȝerenluker clepeð hem to him, swo hie wiðere turneð froward him. *c* 1250 *Gen. & Ex.* 3386 Amalech folc faȝt hard and wiðer.

Hence '**witherly** *a.*, contrary, perverse; *adv.*, fiercely, violently. *Obs.* or *dial.*

13.. *E.E. Allit. P.* B. 198 Neuer ȝet in no boke breued I herde þat euer he wrek so wyþerly on werk þat he made. *Ibid.* C. 74 Al he wrathed in his wyt & wyþerly he þoȝt. 1790 GROSE *Prov. Gloss.* (ed. 2), *Witherly*, wilful, contrary. 1847 HALLIWELL, *Witherly*, hastily; violently. *Devon.*

†**wither**, *v.*[1] *Obs.* [OE. *wiþerian* = MDu. *wedderen*, OHG. *widarôn* (MHG. *wider(e)n*): f. *wiþer* (see prec.).] *intr.* To be hostile; to offer resistance, fight, struggle.

c 1000 ÆLFRIC *Hom.* I. 552 For ði synd ða ᵹesibsuman Godes bearn, forðan ðe nan ðing on him ne wiðeraþ onᵹean God. *c* 1200 *Trin. Coll. Hom.* 63 Ȝif we wiðerið on dede and on speche toȝenes ure chirche. *c* 1220 *Bestiary* 475 Til ðat ðer fleȝes faren and fallen ðer-inne, wiðeren in ðat web, and wilen ut wenden. *a* 1225 *St. Marher.* 14 Wrestlin ha moten ant wiðerin wið ham seoluen. 13.. *E.E. Allit. P.* C. 48 Þenne is me lyȝtloker hit lyke..Þenne wyþer wyth & be wroth.

wither ('wɪðə(r)), *v.*[2] Forms: α. 4–6 **wydder, widder**, (5 **widre**, 6 **wyddre, weder**). β. 6 **wyther**, (6–7 **whither**, 7 **weather**), 6– **wither.** See also WITHERED. [app. var. of WEATHER *v.* ultimately differentiated for certain senses.]

1. *intr.* Of a plant: To become dry and shrivel up. Often in fig. context or in comparisons. Also with advs.

α. 13.. *E.E. Allit. P.* C. 468, & wyddered was þe wodbynde bi þat þe wyȝe wakned. *c* 1400 *26 Pol. Poems* v. 5 Riȝt as hay, þey mon widre. 1483 CAXTON *Gold. Leg.* 378 b/1 They shal neuer fade ne wydder ne lose theyr sauour. 1508 FISHER *7 Penit. Ps.* cii. Wks. (1876) 146 Saynt Iames compareth the vanyte of this lyfe to the vapoure and sayth it shall perysshe and weder awaye as a floure in the hey season. 1521 —— *Serm. agst. Luther* ibid. 323 Trees whan they be wydred and theyr leues shaken from them. 1526 TINDALE *Matt.* xxi. 19 The fygge tree wyddered awaye. *a* 1533 LD. BERNERS *Gold. Bk. M. Aurel.* (1546) Bb vij b, The grenenes of youthe shall waste and wydder in age.

β. 1588 SHAKS. *L.L.L.* II. i. 54 Such short liu'd wits do wither as they grow. 1593 —— *Rich. II*, v. i. 8 See, or rather doe not see, My faire Rose wither. 1634 MILTON *Comus* 744 Like a neglected rose It withers on the stalk with languish't head. 1668 J. OWEN *Indwelling-Sin* xiii. 214 He melts down the lusts of men, causeth them to wither at the root. 1763 MILLS *Syst. Pract. Husb.* IV. 32 Before their necks are withered off, the bulbs should be taken up. 1788 GIBBON *Decl. & F.* xliii. IV. 331 The harvest and the vintage withered on the ground. 1807 CRABBE *Par. Reg.* III. 948 Like flowers we wither, and like leaves we fall. 1816 BYRON *Ch. Har.* III. xxxii, The tree will wither long before it fall. 1842 TENNYSON *Locksley Hall* 190 Now for me the woods may wither, now for me the roof-tree fall. 1888 BRYCE *Amer. Commw.* cxiv. III. 643 After a year or two of bloom, a town wilts and withers.

2. Of other animate things: To become dried up or shrivelled; to lose vigour from lack of animal moisture; to pine or fade *away* with age, disease, decay, etc.

α. *c* 1400 *Destr. Troy* 5301 Þe fre kyng Teutra Wex weike of his wound & widrit to dethe. *c* 1460 *Towneley Myst.* iii. 63 Now I wax old,..As muk apon mold I widder away.

β. 1582 *N.T.* (Rhem.) Mark ix. 18 He fometh, and gnasheth with the teeth, and withereth. 1748 R. JAMES *Diss. Fevers* (1778) 157 When the eruptions begin to subside and wither. 1817 SHELLEY *Rev. Islam* VI. xlix, All lips which I have kissed must surely wither, But Death's. 1848 DICKENS *Dombey* xv, Do a kindness to the sweet dear that is withering away. 1849 MACAULAY *Hist. Eng.* v. I. 652 Those more unfortunate men who were withering under the tropical sun. 1898 J. HUTCHINSON in *Archives Surg.* IX. 309 Many of the nodules are distinctly withering.

3. *fig.* Of persons, or of inanimate and immaterial things: To lose vigour or freshness, to languish, decline, pine *away*, fade, fall into decay.

α. 1508 FISHER *7 Penit. Ps.* cii. Wks. (1876) 147 Vnderstandynge wyll and reason..be so vtterly wedred and dryed vp, that no maner of moysture of deuocyon is in them. 1523 [COVERDALE] *Old God & New* (1534) B, Y[u]..doest not widder & dry vp w[t] ydelnes. 1559 *Mirr. Mag., Edw. IV*, v, As vanity to nought all is wyddred away.

β. 1535 COVERDALE *Ecclus.* x. 17 He hath caused them to wyther awaye, he hath brought them to naught. 1625 SANDERSON *Serm., Ad Magistr.* iii. (1632) 248 Men that.. are now arrived at the haven of their businesse, to wither [*later edd.* weather] for their pasports. *a* 1647 HABINGTON *Surv. Worcestershire* (1895) I. 70 An honest gentellman witheringe in pouerty. *a* 1656 HALES *Gold. Rem.* (1673) 123 An hope of excellent things..which..for want of cherishing fades and withers away. 1688 *Addr. fr. Winchester* in *Lond. Gaz.* No. 2350/1 This Ancient City, which is now again weathering by their Absence, which began to Flourish.. from being blessed with their Presence. 1725 POPE *Odyss.* XIX. 246 With'ring at heart to see the weeping Fair. 1781 COWPER *Expost.* 324 States thrive or wither, as moons wax and wane. 1812 CRABBE *Tales* xvi. 268 A hue like this the western sky displays, That glows awhile, and withers as we gaze. 1830 GALT *Lawrie T.* III. ii. (1849) 87 My heart withered as I contemplated the scene. 1850 MAURICE *Mor. & Met. Philos.* (ed. 2) 155 When that sense [of national union] is weakened it withers. 1874 STUBBS *Const. Hist.* I. i. 8 Christianity..withered under Frank patronage. 1901 *Scotsman* 6 Nov. 9/4 It would be absurd to expect Consols ..to stand..at a high level, when all other securities are withering in price.

b. *spec.* in phr. ***to wither away***, used with reference to the belief held in Marxist philosophy that when the dictatorship of the proletariat has effected the necessary changes in society, the state will eventually cease to be necessary and will therefore disappear; also used allusively or generally. So ***withering away***.

1919 tr. *Lenin's State & Revol.* i. 21 Engels speaks here of the *destruction* of the capitalist State by the proletarian revolution, while the words about its withering away refer to the remains of a *proletarian* State *after* the Socialist revolution. *Ibid.* 22 Only the proletarian State or semi-State withers away after the revolution. **1935** E. Burns tr. *Engels' Anti-Dühring* III. ii. 315 The government of persons is replaced by the administration of things and the direction of the process of production. The state is not 'abolished', it withers away. **1937** *Times* 7 July 17/6 The Marxist theory of the 'withering away' of the State. **1948** M. Laski *Tory Heaven* v. 81 Reynolds is an M.I.5 nark... Eventually, they say, all that sort of thing will just wither away. **1971** *Guardian* 9 Sept. 13/1 Stormont was designed to wither away. It was invented in the hope that the two parts of Ireland would become united within the British Empire. **1980** D. Fernbach tr. *Buci-Glucksmann's Gramsci & State* xii. 285 The transition from an inevitable 'productivist' phase to an integral state thus takes place by way of hegemony and the distant tendential perspective of a withering away of the state. *Ibid.* 289 A state that withers away to the extent that its function withers away.

†**4. a.** *intr.* and *pass.* Of a crop: To be dried, to dry. *Obs.*

1523 Fitzherb. *Husb.* §25 Hey,..whan it is wel wyddred on the ouersyde and drye, than turne it. *Ibid.* §31 Pees and beanes.. wrythen togyder, and wyde benethe, that they maye the better wyddre. **1573–80** Tusser *Husb.* (1878) 131 Corne being had downe..should wither as needeth, for burning in mow.

†**b.** *trans.* To air: = weather *v.* 1 b. *Obs.*

1544 Phaer *Pestilence* (1553) L vij, Nor weare any of their apparell, excepte they be well sunned, or wythered in the clean ayre. *a* **1613** Overbury *A Wife*, etc. (1638) 180 He withers his clothes on a stage as a Sale-man inforc't to does his sutes in Birchin-lane.

c. *Tea-manuf.* To dry (tea leaf) before roasting. Also *absol.* Also *intr.* of the leaf.

1753 F. Pigou *Of Tea* in A. Dalrymple *Oriental Repertory* (1797) II. 288 [Bohea-tea] is gathered, then put in Sieves, or Baskets,..and those put in the air, till the leaves wither, or give. *Ibid.*, Youngshaw..says, that the leaves of Souchon.. are beat with flat sticks,..after they have been withered, by the Sun, or Air. **1870** E. Money *Tea* xxiv. (1878) 108 Why wither at all? I made Tea..of 1st, totally unwithered leaves; and, of leaves but little withered. **1892** J. M. Walsh *Tea* (Philad.) 104 Two leaves only being picked at a time and 'withered' in the open air.

†**d.** *intr.* = weather *v.* 2 b. *Obs. rare.*

Cf. G. *verwittern*.

1796 Kirwan *Elem. Min.* (ed. 2) I. 224 [Wacken] withers by exposure to the atmosphere, and then becomes more grey. [**1834** L. Ritchie *Wand. Seine* 97 The deserted pile withered away stone by stone beneath the breath of heaven.]

5. *trans.* To cause (a plant, flower, etc.) to dry up and shrivel. Also in fig. context.

1555 Eden *Decades* 292, I..sawe the braunches of frutefull trees wythyred by the coulde. **1596** *Edw. III*, II. i. 390 The Sunne, that withers heye, doth nourish grasse. **1668** J. Owen *Indwelling-Sin* xv. 253 He makes their lives.. unfruitful to others, in weakening their root, and withering their fruit through his poisoning temptations. **1765** Goldsm. *Double Transform* 76 That dire disease, whose ruthless power Withers the beauty's transient flower. **1831** James *Philip Aug.* xxiv, On whose rosy cheek the touch of care had withered not a flower. **1840** Dickens *Old C. Shop* xlvi, Where a factory planted among fields withered the space about it, like a burning mountain. **1885** Clodd *Myths & Dr.* I. iii. 41 The fierce heat that withered the approaching harvest.

6. To cause (the body or the physical powers) to become wasted or decayed; to cause to shrink, become wrinkled, or lose freshness.

1599 Nashe *Lenten Stuffe* 13 [They] haue not withred vp their handes in signing and subscribing to their requests. **1606** Shaks. *Ant. & Cl.* II. ii. 240 Age cannot wither her. **1621** Burton *Anat. Mel.* I. ii. III. x. 149 They..attenuate our bodies, dry them, wither them. **1667** Milton *P.L.* VI. 850 Every eye..shot forth pernicious fire Among th' accurst, that witherd all thir strength. **1740** Dyer *Ruins Rome* 477 Enfeebling vice Withers each nerve. **1827** Scott *Highl. Widow* v, May the tongue that tells me of his death.. be withered in thy mouth.

7. *fig.* To destroy the vitality or vigour of; to cause to decline, decay, or waste; now somewhat *rare* exc. in hyperbolical use, to blight or paralyse with a look of scorn or the like. Also with †*out*.

1590 Shaks. *Mids. N.* I. i. 7 Like to a Step-dame, or a Dowager, Long withering out a yong mans reuennew. **1608** *Yorksh. Trag.* iii. 11 Himselfe withered with debts. **1700** Dryden *Pal. & Arc.* III. 303 Wild Amazement flung From out thy Chariot, withers ev'n the Strong. **1725** Pope *Odyss.* VIII. 120 Like Mars terrific,..When clad in wrath he withers hosts of foes. **1816** J. Wilson *City of Plague* II. iii, Repent! before the red-eyed Wrath Wither you to ghosts. **1837** Dickens *Pickw.* iii, Dr. Slammer..said nothing, but contented himself by withering the company with a look. **1854** J. S. C. Abbott *Napoleon* (1855) I. xxx. 462 The historian..would have been withered by the frowns which would have darkened upon him from the saloons of Versailles [etc.]. **1887** A. Jessopp *Arcady* 172 The world is getting quite too much for us—withering us, in fact.

wither, var. witter *sb.*[2]

wither-[1], *prefix*, repr. OE. *wiþer-*, OFris. *wither-*, OS. *withar-*, OHG. *widar-* (MHG., G. *wider-*), = the adv. *wiþer* (see wither *a.*) used with sbs., adjs., and verbs (cf. with- 3), chiefly in the sense (1) against, in opposition or hostility, as in OE. *wiþercrist* antichrist, *wiþercwide* contradiction, resistance, *wiþersaca* withersake, *wiþerwinna* witherwin; less commonly in the senses (2) in return or compensation, counter-, as in OE. *wiþerléan* recompense, *wiþertihtle* countercharge; and (3) in the opposite direction, back.

†**1.** In sense (1), used (esp. by Layamon) in compounds denoting hostile acts or contests, as **wiþerblench, -ded** [deed *sb.*], **-gome** [game *sb.*], **-hap, -ueht** [fight *sb.*], **wiþerstrencþ** resistance; also in the derived sense 'adverse, evil', as **wiþercraft, -laȝe** [law *sb.*[1]], and (in personal designations) **wiþerlaȝe** [cf. OFris. *witherlaga* opponent] persecutor, **wiþerþeod** [thede] enemy people; occas. with verbs, as **wiþerhalde** [hold *v.*] to hold out against, oppose. (Often indistinguishable from wither *a.*) *Obs.*

c **1200** Ormin 6905 ȝiff he léte waxenn þær awihht off wiþerrstrenncþe Onnȝæn hiss aȝhenn oferrking. *Ibid.* 10227 To fihhtenn forr þe leode, To werenn hemm wiþþ wiþerrþeod. *c* **1205** Lay. 272 Witen he wolde þurh þa wiþer-craftes [*later text* wise craftes] wat þing hit were. *Ibid.* 405 þar aros wale & win & wiðer-heppes feola. *Ibid.* 9175 ȝif þe king wolde wið heom wiðer-heolden. *Ibid.* 10968 þe hæfde þurh his wiðer-laȝen muchel of þine cunne of-slaȝen. *Ibid.* 16318 Cuð hit is wide of ure wiðer-deden. *Ibid.* 24700 Summe heo wræstleden and wiðer-gome makeden. *Ibid.* 28669 þa weoren wide to-floȝen: ut of þan wiðer-uehte. *a* **1225** *St. Marher.* 5 þe awaride wiðerlahen leiden swa luðerliche on hire leofliche lich, þet hit brec oueral. *c* **1250** *Long Life* 12 in *O.E. Misc.* 156 Nis non so strong..þat mai ago deaþes wiþer-blench.

2. In sense (2), †**witherweȝe** *v. trans.*, to weigh again; **witherweight** *Sc.* (also *wodderweght*), a counterbalancing weight. Cf. withernam.

1340 *Ayenb.* 137 To..wiþnyme his dedes..and telle, and weȝe, and *wyþperweȝe. **1642** Row *Hist. Kirk* (Wodrow Soc.) p. xx, A *wodderweght to our bell to mak it ring the better. **1808** Jamieson, *Witherweight*,..(*witherwecht*), the weight thrown into one scale, to counterbalance the paper, or vessel, in the opposite scale, which contains the goods bought. **1820** Hogg *Wint. Even. T.* I. 270 She's nae wotherweight nouther.

3. In sense (3), †**witherhoked** *a.*, barbed [cf. MHG. *widerhâke* barb, G. *-haken*, EFris. *wërhake*]; †**witherwise** *adv. Sc.* [wise *sb.*[1] II], = withershins.

c **1330** *Arth. & Merl.* 5666 þis dragoun hadde a long taile þat was *wiþþerhoked. **1643** in Dalyell *Darker Superst. Scot.* x. (1834) 459 Shoe turnit hirselff thrie severall tymes round *witherwys, about the fyre.

wither-[2] (*rare*), = wither *v.*[2] used in comb. in sense 'withered', as *wither-boned*, *-faced* adjs.

1592 Nashe *Strange Newes* Wks. (Grosart) II. 227 The wither-fac'd weather-beaten Mariner. **1821** Milman *Fazio* 9 Like some dry wither-boned anatomy.

withered ('wɪðəd), *ppl. a.* Forms: 5–6 **wyddred** (*Sc.* 5 **wydderit**, 5–6 **widderit**), 6 **wydred, widdered, wydderad, wyddurde, (wedred,** *Sc.* **vidthrid), wyth(e)red, withred (wethered),** 6–7 **witherd,** 6– **wither'd, withered.** [f. wither *v.*[2] + -ed[1].]

1. Of a plant, fruit, etc.: Shrivelled or shrunken through lack of moisture, and so deprived of its natural colour, freshness, or bloom; hence, of fields, or stretches of country, and *gen.*: Dried up, arid.

c **1470** Henry *Wallace* VIII. 1037 Thar awld bulwerk I se off wydderyt ayk. *c* **1480** Henryson *Two Mice* 222 Thir widderit peis and nuttis,..Will brek my teith. —— *Fox, Wolf, & Husb.* xix, It will not win ȝow worth ane widderit neip. **1508** Fisher *7 Penit. Ps.* cii. Wks. (1876) 148 Wedred grasse or hey. **1549** *Compl. Scot.* vii. 70 The vidthrid barran feildis. *a* **1560** Becon *Jewel of Joy* Pref., Wks. 1564 II. 2 A pece of grosse smokye bacon or saulte withered byefe. **1585** T. Washington tr. *Nicholay's Voy.* III. xxi. 110 Manye desartes, sandye, wythered, vnfruitefull. **1609** Shaks. *Temp.* I. ii. 463 Wither'd roots. **1637** Rutherford *Lett., to M. Mowat* 7 Sept. (1671) 166 Our Lord..shall water with his dew the withered hill of mount Zion in Scotland. **1682** Dryden & Lee *Dk. Guise* I. i, To the bare Commons of the wither'd Field. **1710** *Lond. Gaz.* No. 4777/4 A tall thin Man, with withered Hair. **1781** Cowper *Conversat.* 51 Wither'd stumps disgrace the sylvan scene. **1813** Scott *Trierm.* I. v, The wither'd leaves, That drop when no winds blow. **1861** Mrs. Browning *Nature's Remorses* x, Withered immortelles, long ago cut. **1864** Tennyson *En. Ard.* 676 But narrow breadth..Of wither'd holt or tilth.

2. Of men and animals: Physically shrunken, shrivelled, wasted, or decayed; deprived of animal vitality or vigour.

a **1500–34** *Cov. Corpus Christi Pl.* i. 839 Sey ye, wyddurde wyvis, whydder are ye a-wey? **1509** Hawes *Past. Pleas.* XXIX. (Percy Soc.) 143 An olde wydred wiche. **1526** Tindale *John* v. 3 A greate multitude off sicke folke, off blynde, halt, and wyddered. **1588** Shaks. *L.L.L.* IV. iii. 242 A withered Hermite, fiue-score winters worne. **1641** Milton *Animadv.* xiii. Wks. 1851 III. 233 They may as well sue for Nunneries, that they may have some convenient stowage for their wither'd daughters. **1700** Rowe *Amb. Step-Mother* III. i, Marks which Years set on the wither'd Sage. **1868** J. H. Blunt *Ref. Ch. Eng.* I. 421 A poor withered skeleton of humanity.

b. Of the body, or parts of it: Shrivelled or shrunken, esp. by the wasting of disease or age. Formerly, and now *colloq.* or *dial.*, often applied to a paralysed limb.

1513 [see wearish *a.* 2]. **1526** Tindale *Mark* iii. 1 There was a man which had a widdred honde. **1697** Dryden *Æneis* v. 644 Take the last Gift my wither'd Arms can yield. **1795–6** Wordsw. *Borderers* II. 890 Twice did I spring to grasp his withered throat. **1805** Scott *Last Minstrel* Introd. 3 His wither'd cheek, and tresses gray. **1813** J. Thomson *Lect. Inflam.* 539 The part affected became at first insensible and cold, and, in the progress of the disorder, dry, hard, and withered. **1877** Dowden *Shaks. Primer* vi. 79 So..fierce a human energy as that of Richard concentrated within one withered and distorted body. **1920** H. G. Wells *Outl. Hist.* 552/2 The figure of the new monarch [William II of Germany]..with a withered left arm ingeniously minimized.

3. *fig.* in immaterial sense: Deprived of or having lost vigour, freshness, or 'bloom'; shrunken and decayed; †formerly sometimes, reduced to poverty.

1561 Hoby tr. *Castiglione's Courtyer* II. Yiij, In my withered reasoninges. **1596** Raleigh *Discov. Guiana* A 3 b, I am returned a begger, and withered. **1637** Rutherford *Let. to Parishioners* 13 July, The Lord will..make this withered Kirk, to bud again like a rose. **1782** J. Brown in R. Mackenzie *Life* (1918) 237 Our sacrament is on the 5th Sabbath of June. Pray for our withered corner. **1810** Scott *Lady of L.* IV. xiii, Lay on him the curse of the wither'd heart. **1819** Keats *Fall of Hyperion* I. 288 The pale Omega of a wither'd race. **1860** Smiles *Self Help* xi. 285 The *blasé* youth turns from his withered pleasures. **1865** Dickens *Mut. Fr.* II. xv, A grey dusty withered evening in London.

†**4. a.** Worn out, ragged. *Obs. rare.*

c **1480** Henryson *Test. Cress.* 165 His widderit weid fra him the wind out woir.

†**b.** = weathered 1. *Obs. rare.*

1796 Kirwan *Elem. Min.* (ed. 2) I. 348 Withered gneiss has sometimes the appearance of a grey slaty mortar.

c. *Tea-manuf.* (see wither *v.*[2] 4 c).

1897 D. Crole *Tea* vii. 117 Trolly loads of withered leaf.

5. *Comb.*, as ***withered-looking*** adj.

1849 Eastwick *Dry Leaves* 179 His beard..stunted, tawny, and withered-looking.

Hence **'witheredly** *adv.*, in a withered manner; **'witheredness**, the condition of being withered; rarely *concr.* a withered part.

1535 Coverdale *Isa.* iii. 24 And for their bewty wythrednesse and sonneburnynge. **1621** T. Williamson tr. *Goulart's Wise Vieillard* 24 Old age..the unweldinesse or witherednesse of the body. **1658** A. Fox *Würtz' Surg.* III. xxiii. 293 That witheredness caused by a fall..I have annointed twice a day. **1659** Torriano, Witheredly, *seccamente*. **1722** J. Willison *Five Sacr. Serm.* Wks. (1852) 313/2 There usually follows, on God's withdrawing, great witheredness and barrenness on the souls of his people. **1883** G. Macdonald *Princess & Curdie* iii, Every trace of the decrepitude and witheredness she showed..had vanished.

witherer ('wɪðərə(r)). *rare.* [f. wither *v.*[2] + -er[1].] One who or that which withers.

1828 Landor *Imag. Conv., Engl. & Flor. Vis.* III. 427 Gifford is the Harriet Wilson of our literary world; the witherer of young names. *a* **1851** Moir *Miner of Peru*, Blancher of the hair, And witherer of the strength.

†**'witherful**, *a. Obs.* [f. wither *sb.*[1] + -ful.]

a. Hostile; wicked, evil. **b.** Bold, valiant. Hence †**'witherfulness**, wickedness.

c **1200** *Trin. Coll. Hom.* 51 Hise wiðerfulle hine, þo ben deules on helle. *Ibid.* 63 *Dissoluere colligaciones impietatis* ..þat unbindeð þe bendes of wiðerfulnesse. *c* **1205** Lay. 21520 To þan scipen wenden wiðer-fulle cheorles. *Ibid.* 25264 Arður his writ nom an honden mid wiðer-fulle worden.

withering ('wɪðərɪŋ), *vbl. sb.* [f. wither *v.*[2] + -ing[1].]

1. The action of wither *v.*[2], q.v.

1523 Fitzherb. *Husb.* §23 The yonger and the grener that the grasse is, the softer and the sweter it wyll be whan it is hey, but it wyll haue the more wyddrynge. *a* **1614** Donne *Βιαθανατος* (1644) 131 These enormous witherings of our bodies are allowable. **1658** A. Fox *Würtz' Surg.* III. xxiii. 289 A Withering, is a Symptom which is incident to joints wounded. **1796** in J. Robertson *Agric. Perth* (1799) 517 What fell off from the whins, broom, firs, &c. in the course of their withering. **1848** S. Ball *Tea* viii. 157 The peculiar red appearance of this tea is produced..by tossing the leaves on trays..to promote the withering. **1853** Maurice *Proph. & Kings* vii. 115 The withering of a hand which was cured again. **1862** Helps *Organization in Daily Life* 5 The waste of time, and the withering-up of enjoyment. **1866** G. Stephens *Runic Mon.* I. 25 The remaining withering-away of the N in Scandinavia is in the infinitive. **1899** *Allbutt's Syst. Med.* VIII. 845 Spontaneous withering or retrogression of certain of the tumours. **1903** C. Bald *Indian Tea* xv. (1917) 218 Withering in the sun is fatal to fine quality.

b. *attrib.*

1707 Mortimer *Husb.* 267 After the Malt has lain on the withering Floors about twelve or fourteen days. **1853** Dickens *Bleak Ho.* xix, The learned gentleman who does the withering business, and who blights all opponents with his gloomy sarcasm. **1897** D. Crole *Tea* vii. 114 A withering-house 100 yards long..will..accommodate about 140 maunds of leaf.

2. *concr.* Withered branches or brushwood, used in making fences, etc.

1852 C. W. Hoskyns *Talpa* 46 A man-made barrier of stakes and 'witherings'. **1854** R. S. Surtees *Handley Cr.* xiv. (1901) I. 104 The rotten stakes and witherings of a low ill-made-up gap.

'withering, *ppl. a.* [f. WITHER *v.*[2] + -ING[2].] That withers, in various senses.

1. Fading, decaying. *lit.* and *fig.*

1599 ALEX. HUME *Hymns* VII. 226 Widdring weids. **1621** T. WILLIAMSON tr. *Goulart's Wise Vieillard* 2 This withering and transitory life. **1668** J. OWEN *Indwelling-Sin* xiv. 235 There may be a withering member in the body. **1680** OTWAY *Orphan* IV. viii, Desire shall languish like a withering flower. **1783** CRABBE *Village* I. 185 The bare arms broken from the withering tree. **1784** COWPER *Task* VI. 938 There he fights, And there obtains fresh triumphs o'er himself, And never with'ring wreaths. **1821** SHELLEY *Adonais* xxxii, On the withering flower The killing sun smiles brightly.

2. Causing to fade or decay (*lit.* and *fig.*); *esp.* causing decay of vigour or paralysis of effort; blasting, blighting; often applied to the 'paralysing' effect of scornful looks, criticism, and the like, and to destructive gun-fire.

1579 E. K. in *Spenser's Sheph. Cal.* Feb. *Arg.*, A dry and withering cold. **1599** DANIEL *Musophilus* 167 Whereas he came planted in the Spring,.. We, set in th' Autumne, in the withering And sullen season of a cold defect, Must [etc.]. **16..** ? BRETON *C'tess Penbrook's Pass.* xlviii. (Grosart) 6/1 Wethering Winter gives her chillinge cheare. **1747** COLLINS *Ode Passions* 42 With a with'ring Look. **1792** S. ROGERS *Pleas. Mem.* II. 110 A withering scowl she wore. **1810** SOUTHEY *Kehama* XI. iv, Oh! hide him from that Witch's withering sight! **1813** BYRON *Corsair* II. x, The withering sense of evil unreveal'd. **1849** AYTOUN *Lays Scott. Cav.* 114 Vainly sped the withering volley 'Mongst the foremost of our band. **1857** KINGSLEY *Two Y. Ago* xv, Elsley.. cast on him a look which he intended to have been withering. *a* **1859** MACAULAY *Hist. Eng.* xxiv. V. 135 A blighting and withering dominion. **1884** COLBORNE *With Hicks Pasha in Soudan* 174 Our withering fire knocked the poor fellows over and over.

Hence **'witheringly** *adv.* (*lit.* and *fig.*).

1815 BYRON *Hebr. Mel., Wild Gazelle* iv, We must wander witheringly, In other lands to die. **1819** WIFFEN *Aonian Hours* (1820) 64 The gathered flower droops witheringly away. **1835** M. SCOTT in *Blackw. Mag.* XXXVII. 452 My uncle.. looked so witheringly at him. **1905** R. BAGOT *Passport* xiii. 116 'Then, may I ask, what is the use of sending me on a fool's errand?' the professor retorted, witheringly.

witherite ('wɪðəraɪt). *Min.* [Named by Werner after W. *Withering*, who first described and analysed it in 1784: see -ITE[1] 2 b.] Native barium carbonate.

1794 *Phil. Trans.* LXXXIV. 418, I could not discover any regular crystallized shape, like the witherite.

'witherling[1]. *Obs.* exc. *arch.* [OE. *wiþerling*, f. *wiþer* WITHER *a.* and *adv.* + -LING[1].] An adversary.

c **1000** *Cant. Ps.* Exod. xv. 7 þu forbriccest wiþerlingas. *c* **1300** *K. Horn* 156 (Laud) þat heþene king Ihesu cristes wiþerling. **1922** W. STEVENS *Let.* 21 Dec. (1967) 232, I have omitted many things, exercising the most fastidious choice, so far as that was possible among my witherlings.

† **'witherling**[2]. *Obs.* [f. WITHER *v.*[2] + -LING[1].] A withered branch; a shrivelled or stunted person.

1528 MORE *Dyaloge* II. Wks. 186/1 All these braunches of heritikes.. seme thei neuer so freshe & grene, bee yet in dede but witherlinges y[t] wyther, & shal drye vp. *a* **1624** CHAPMAN *Crown of Homer's Wks.* 30 No forspoke Dwarfe, nor downeward witherling.

withernam ('wɪðənɑːm). *Law.* Now *Hist.* Also 4–6 **wyther-**, (4 **-ir-**), 5–6 **wether-**, **wider-**, 4–7 **-name**. [Law-French (in Britton *wythernam*), presumably a. ON. *viðrnám* recorded only in the sense 'resistance' (but cf. early Da. *vedernam* pledge), f. *viðr-* WITHER-[1] + *nám* NAAM. The etymological meaning is 'reprisal'.] In an action of replevin, the reprisal of other goods in lieu of those taken by a first distress and eloigned; also, the writ (called *capias in withernam*) commanding the sheriff to take the reprisal.

1292 BRITTON I. xxviii. §3 Si les bestes soint.. chacez hors del counté, ou si le baillif autre desturbaunce troeffe, tauntost face prendre des bestes del deforceour a la double value cum wythernam. **1534** *Returna breuium* 418 De returno in replegiare lou le pleintyfe auera vne withernam. **1542–3** *Act 34 & 35 Hen. VIII*, c. 26 §29 The Shirief shall have.. for the making of Replegias twelvepence, and withernam upon the same twelve pence. **1543** tr. *Act 13 Edw. I*, c. 2 [A] courte, hauynge power to holde pleas of wythernam. **1579** *Expos. Terms Law* 72 b, The party vpon y[e] returne of the sherife shall haue a writte of Withernam, directed to the Sherif, that he take as many of hys beastes.. tyll y[t] hee hath made deliuerance of y[e] first distres. **1599** *Life of Sir T. More* in Wordsw. *Eccl. Biog.* (1853) II. 102 Whether chattell taken [in] withername may be replevied. **1618** J. WILKINSON *Treat. Off. Coroners* II. 153 b, Then the plaintife may have a Withernam, which must be made in this maner. *a* **1625** SIR H. FINCH *Law* (1636) 354 In a repleuin in the Countie Court,.. if the goods be conueyed away, so as at the Tenants suite they cannot be restored,.. processe of withernam lyeth. **1656** tr. *Noy's Rep.* 50 A Withernam was awarded, and executed, and now comes the Plaintiff and prays to declare, and prays a deliverance of the Withernam. **1767** BLACKSTONE *Comm.* III. ix. 149 Goods taken in withernam cannot be replevied, till the original distress is forthcoming.

b. A process of distress (or arrest) for debt, formerly current in the Cinque Ports (and other towns).

1314–15 *Cal. Letter-bks. Lond.* E. (1903) 42 [The sum of 40*s.* which had been taken by way of] Withernam [from] Thomas de Grantham de Dyvelyn. **1352** *Borough Customs* (Selden Soc.) I. 122 Al sute du dit playntif, ci deit le bailif par assignement des jurés prendre une Wythirname sur qicomque vienge de la dite vile ou cité. **1461–83** *Ibid.* I. 125 Bayle and jurates may take a wythername agaynst all his tenauntes. **1529** *Ibid.* I. 125 Yf eny man have take toll or custum of eny freman of Cawnterbery, he that ys grevid may have a widername at Caunterbury therfore. **1574** *Acts Privy Council* (N.S.) VIII. 313 A letter to the Mayour of Dover.. touching complaintes made against him by Fleminges for the arrest made by widernams. **1576** *Ibid.* IX. 215 Whereas Andrew Muller.. of Hamboroughe was arrested at Dover by a writt of withernam.

c. Reprisals taken at sea by letters of marque.

1714 FORTESCUE-ALAND *Pref. Fortescue's Abs. & Lim. Mon.* 50 This Word Withernam also signifies Reprisals taken at Sea, by Letters of Mart-ships.

withers ('wɪðəz), *sb. pl.*, occas. *sing.* **wither**. Also 7 **weather-**. [app. a reduced form of *widersome* or *-sone* (see quots. 1541–2, 1547), f. *wider-* = WITHER-[1] + an obscure element; cf. G. *widerrist* withers, f. *wider-* WITHER-[1] + *rist* WRIST.] **a.** In a horse, The highest part of the back, lying between the shoulder-blades. Also, the corresponding part in some other animals, as the ox or the sheep. Often in fig. context, esp. after Shaks. (quot. 1602), with allusion to the 'wringing' of a horse's withers.

1541–2 *Act 33 Hen. VIII*, c. 5 §1 Every horse.. to be.. in heyght xiiij handfulles.. measured from the nether parte of the here of the houghe unto the upper part of the Wydersomes, That is to saye, the upper parte of the Shulders. **1547** SALESBURY *Dict. Engl. Welsh*, *Yskwydd gudun*, the wyder sone.

1580 LYLY *Euphues* (Arb.) 249 Wring not a horse on the withers, with a false saddle. **1594** BLUNDEVIL *Exerc.* IV. xix. (1597) 221 b, In his [*sc.* the Bull's] necke toward the Withers are 7 starres. **1596** NASHE *Saffron Walden* P 4, That wrung him on the withers worse than all the rest. **1602** SHAKS. *Ham.* III. ii. 252 Let the gall'd iade winch: our withers are vnrung. **1607** DEKKER & WEBSTER *Westw. Hoe* V. i. H 2 b, Never were three innocent Citizens.. so abhominably wrung vnder the withers. **1649** G. DANIEL *Trinarch., Hen. IV*, cccxlvii, Though the chaine of Tyrranye.. gall'd the withers of their will. **1729** SWIFT *Direct. Serv.* v, Contrive that the Saddle may pinch the Beast in his Withers. **1838** LYTTON *Alice* V. iii, 'Tell me now', said Caroline pressing on the wrung withers, [etc.]. **1839** DARWIN *Voy. Nat.* ii. 25 The Vampire bat is often the cause of much trouble, by biting the horses on their withers. **1867** S. BAKER *Nile Trib.* xviii. 475 The shoulders [of the sable antelope].. are extremely high at the withers. **1886** SYMONDS *Renaiss. It., Cath. React.* (1898) VII. xi. 179 There is not a city of Italy which Tassoni did not wring in the withers of its self-conceit.

sing. **1607** TOPSELL *Four-f. Beasts* 597 The wither of the beast, I meane the top of his shoulder next to his necke. **1695** *Lond. Gaz.* No. 3096/4 A black Gelding,.. the Hair clipt on his Wither. **1770** G. WHITE *Selborne, To Pennant* Mar., I measured it [*sc.* the moose-deer], as they do an horse, and found that, from the ground to the wither, it was just five feet four inches. **1850** 'H. HIEOVER' *Pract. Horsemanship* 118 The saddle, pressing on the off side of the wither, would pinch the horse. **1908** *Animal Managem.* 160 A wide wither is nearly as troublesome as a high one.

b. *transf.* The part of a saddle which comes over the withers.

1764 T. WALLIS *Farrier's Dict.* s.v. *Bows of a Saddle*, The withers is the arch that rises two or three fingers over the horse's withers.

c. *attrib.* and *Comb.*, as ***wither-gall***, ***pad***, ***-strap***; **witherband**, **-lock** (see quots.); **witherwrung** *a.*, injured in the withers.

1656 EARL MONM. tr. *Boccalini's Advts. fr. Parnass.* I. xxxi. 54 A three-wheel'd Charret.. drawn by lean weather-wrung-Jades. **1764** T. WALLIS *Farrier's Dict.* s.v. *Bands of a Saddle*, Besides these two great bands, the fore-bow has a small one called the wither-band, and a crescent to keep up the wither arch. *Ibid.*, *Witherband*,.. a band or piece of iron, laid underneath a saddle, about four fingers above the withers of the horse, to keep tight the two pieces of wood that form the bow. **1767** S. PATERSON *Another Trav.* II. v. 57 A.. broken-winded.. wither-wrung.. horse. **1794** W. FELTON *Carriages* (1801) II. Gloss., *Wither Strap*, a part of the harness, which goes round the withers of the horse to hold up the collar. **1825** JAMIESON, *Witherlock*, that lock of hair in the mane, of which one takes hold when mounting on horse-back. **1886** *Cornh. Mag.* Sept. 299 Many of them had open kidney-sores and wither-galls. **1963** E. H. EDWARDS *Saddlery* xv. 112 Numnahs and wither pads are used in conjunction with saddles. **1976** *Horse & Hound* 3 Dec. 52 (Advt.), The John Ayres New Zealand Rug... Featuring a sheepskin wither pad.

† **'withersake**. *Obs.* [OE. *wiþersaca* = OFris. *withirseka*, OS. *wiðarsako*, OHG. *widarsahho* (MHG. *widersache*, MHG., G. *widersacher*): f. *wiþer-* WITHER-[1] + *-saca*, agent-n. f. stem *sak-* of SAKE *sb.*] An adversary, enemy.

In OE., simply and in phr. ***Godes wiþersaca***, often = apostate.

c **960** ÆTHELWOLD *Rule St. Benet* (Schroër 1885) lxii. 112 Ne beo he na sacerd ȝeteald ac Godes wiðersaca. *c* **1000** *Ags. Gosp.* Matt. xxvi. 14 Iudas se wiþersaca. *c* **1205** LAY. 1808 Geomagog.. þat was þe heihste Godes wiðer-saka. *Ibid.* 12620 þat is goddes wiðer-sake.

withershins, widdershins ('wɪðə-, 'wɪdəʃɪnz), *adv. dial.* (chiefly *Sc.*). Forms: 6– **widder-**, 7– **wither-**, (6 **widdir-**, **weddir-**, **wod(d)er-**, 6, 9 **wooder-**); 6–9 **-sins**, 6– **-shins**, (6 **-syns**, **-shynes**, **-shynnis**, **-son(n)is**, 6, 9 **-sinnis**, **-sones**, 7 **-shines**, 9 **-schynnes**). [a. MLG. *weddersin(ne)s* (cf. *wedersins* 'contrario modo', Kilian), a. MHG. *widersinnes*, f. *wider-* WITHER-[1] + gen. of *sin* (esp. MG.) = *sind*, *sint* way, direction (see SITHE *sb.*[1]): cf. MHG. *widersinnen* to return. In sense 2 associated with *son*, SUN *sb.*[1]]

† **1.** In a direction opposite to the usual; the wrong way; ***to stand*** or ***start withershins***, (of the hair) to 'stand on end'. *Obs.*

1513 DOUGLAS *Æneis* II. xii. 26 Abaisit I wolx, and widdersyns start my hair. *Ibid.* Directioun of Buik 29 And on the bak half writis widdirsinnis Plentie of lesyngis. **1570** R. BANNATYNE *Mem.* (Bannatyne Cl.) 11 That will gar thair hartis trumbill, and thair hair stand widdirshynes. **1583** *Leg. Bp. St. Androis* 704 Ane porter.. to the bischop his blissing gave, Betuixt the schoulders a royall route, Turning him wodderschins about. *a* **1583** MONTGOMERIE *Flyting* 580 Hairis blavin widdersins abauk. *a* **1600** —— *Sonn.* xxxiii. 6 Sho.. straikit bakuard wodershins my hair. **1685** G. SINCLAIR *Satans Invis. World* 211 His hair standing Widdershins in his head. **1721** RAMSAY *I'll never leave* v, The Starns shall gang withershins e'er I deceive thee.

2. In a direction contrary to the apparent course of the sun (considered as unlucky or causing disaster).

1545 *Rec. Elgin* (New Spalding Club 1903) I. 84 Sayand the said Margarat Baffour vas ane huyr and ane wyche and that sche ȝeid widersonnis about mennis hous sark alane. *a* **1583** MONTGOMERIE *Flyting* 418 Thir venerabill virginis quhome ȝe wald call wiches.. nyne tymes, wirdersones, about the thorne raid. **1596** *Spalding Club Misc.* (1841) I. 96, I find it wilbe ane deir yeir; the bled of the corne growis withersones; and quhan it growis sonegatis about, it wilbe ane gude chaip yeir. **1597** *Ibid.* 190 He is indyttit.. to haue taine ane birne of the corne on his bak, and careit it thrie tymmis woodersonis abowe the kill. **1685** G. SINCLAIR *Satans Invis. World* 25 [In a witch-dance] the men turned nine times Widder-shines about, and the Women six times. **1725** RAMSAY *Gentle Sheph.* II. ii, Mausy.. Rins withershins about the Hemlock Low. **1825** SCOTT *Talism.* xxviii, While the challenger rode around the lists in the course of the sun .. the defender made the same circuit *widdersins*. **1840** *New Statist. Acc. Scot.* (1845) XV. 141 The fishermen, when about to proceed to the fishing, think they would have bad luck, if they were to row the boat 'withershins' about. **1903** KIPLING *Five Nations* 10 So, widdershins circling the bridebed of death, Each fleereth her neighbour.

withershin(s), widdershin(s), *a.* [f. the adv.] Moving in an anticlockwise direction, contrary to the apparent course of the sun (considered as unlucky or sinister); unlucky, ill-fated, relating to the occult.

1926 D. H. LAWRENCE *Plumed Serpent* vi. 112 She made up her mind, to be alone, and to cut herself off from all the mechanical widdershin contacts. *Ibid.*, He, too, was widdershins, unwinding the sensations of disintegration and anti-life. **1936** DYLAN THOMAS *Twenty-Five Poems* 16 Shall I still be love's house on the widdershin earth, Woe to the windy mansions at my shelter? **1973** G. M. BROWN *Magnus* vi. 112 There is a black joy abroad, a dance of the deadly sins, a withershin rout. **1976** *Early Music* Oct. 399/1 The sentiments and rituals of the court can be grotesquely guyed by the spirits (widdershins dances, sick-caricature mimes to accompany the Sorceress's prophecies and provoke those ho-ho outbursts, etc.).

† **'witherward**, *a. Obs.* Also 5 **witerward**. [OE. *wiþerweard* (cf. OHG. *widarwart*, *-wert*, Goth. *wiþrawairþs*), f. *wiþer-*, WITHER-[1] + *-weard*, -WARD.] Hostile, inimical.

c **888** ÆLFRED *Boeth.* xi. §1 þeah hit nu hefiȝ sie & wiðerweard. **971** *Blickl. Hom.* 223 Him þa hæðnan men wiþerwearde wæron. *c* **1000** *Ags. Gosp.* Matt. xii. 25 Ælc ceaster oððe hus, þe byð wiþerweard onȝen hyt sylf, hyt ne stent. *c* **1200** ORMIN 9667 Wiþerrwarrd onnȝæness Godd. *c* **1205** LAY. 6875 Wið al folc he wes wiðerward. *c* **1250** *Gen. & Ex.* 2935 Ðis king him his wel wiðer-ward Agen ðis folc. **13..** A. DAVY *Dreams* 20 No strook ne ȝaf he aȝeinward To þilk þat hym weren wiþerward.

b. *absol.* (Cf. OE. *wiþerweard* adversary.)

a **1400–50** *Wars Alex.* 4297 þou wirkis bot on þa witerward, & worthis þaim ouire.

Hence † **'witherwardness**, hostility, enmity.

c **897** ÆLFRED *Gregory's Past. C.* iii. 36 He wearð eft swæ unȝemetlice grædiȝ ðæs godan deaðes, butan ælcre scylde & ælcre wiðerweardnesse wið hine. *c* **1175** *Cott. Hom.* 233 Hatrede and widerwardnesse.

† **'witherwards**, *adv. Sc. Obs. rare.* [f. WITHER-[1] + -WARDS.] = WITHERSHINS.

1624 *Orkney Witch Trial* in *Abbotsford Club Misc.* I. 144 To.. gang thryse woderwardis about the kow, and straik hir in the left syd. **1643** in Dalyell *Superst. of Scot.* (1834) 459 [He] yeid about his hous twys or thrys witherwardis.

† **'witherwin**. *Obs.* Forms: 1–3 **wiþer-**, **wiðer-**, 3–4 **wither-**, **wyþer-**, (4 **weþer-**, **wiþir-**, **withere-**, **-yre-**, **wiþþer-**, **quiþer-**, **wider-**, **wyder-**, **widdir-**, **whydyre-**), 4–5 **wedir-**, **wethir-**, 5 **witer-**; 1–2 **-winna**, 2–4 **-wine**, 3–4 **-win**, 3–5 **-wynne**, 5 **-wyn**, (**-un**), 4–5 **-wyne**. [OE. *wiþerwinna* = OHG. *widarwinno* (MHG. *-winne*), f. *wiþer-* WITHER-[1] + agent-n. of *winnan* WIN *v.*[1]] An enemy, adversary; *spec.* the Adversary, the Devil.

c **897** ÆLFRED *Gregory's Past. C.* XIX. 146 Ðylæs he sie onȝieten ðæt he sie wiðerwinna.. ðæs þe he bið ȝesewen ðeow on his ðeȝnunge. *c* **1000** ÆLFRIC *Hom.* (Assmann) I. 120 Ure wiðerwinna is witodlice se deofol. *c* **1205** LAY. 27326 Haðene hundes, goddes wiðer-iwinnen [*c* **1275** wiþerwynnes]. *a* **1225** *Ancr. R.* 196 Vre wiðerwines beoð þreo: þe ueond, þe world, & ure owune vleshs. **1297** R. GLOUC. (Rolls) 6648 þo þis quene was of londe ydriue þoru hire wiþerwine. *a* **1300** *Cursor M.* 6284 His folk he has al sauued sund, þair wiþerwins er broght to grund. *c* **1375** *Sc. Leg. Saints* xvi. (*Magdalena*) 246 How þe ded he tholyt syne, To safe ws fra þe wethirwyne. ? *a* **1400** *Morte Arth.* 2215 Wrothely he.. Woundes these whydyrewyns, werrayede knyghttes. *c* **1400** *Melayne* 695 Nowe arte þou werre þan any

Sarazene, Goddis awenn wedirwyne. *c* **1450** LOVELICH *Grail* xlvii. 42 Thike day Convertyd was.. A thowsend & Fyfty Sarrazines that to fore tyme weren wethir-wynes.

withery ('wɪðərɪ), *a. rare.* [f. WITHER *v.* + -Y[1].] Inclined to wither; wilting.

1621 R. BANISTER *Treat. 113 Dis. Eye* Breviary (1622) (b 3 b), Eyes darke, withery, and cloudy, presage death. **1861** GREEN *Lett.* (1901) II. 82 All else are waxing pale and withery under the Tartarian heat.

withey, variant of WITHY.

†**withfall.** *Obs. rare.* [f. WITH *adv.* + FALL *sb.*, after late L. *symptoma*, Gr. σύμπτωμα SYMPTOM.] A chance, casualty, accident; a symptom.

1562 TURNER *Herbal* II. 46 b, The vnrype apples eaten with theyr sede bryng dedely withfalles. **1572** J. JONES *Bathes Ayde* III. 22 Accident is that, which the Greekes call *Symptoma*, and wee properly in English, to fall and with fall.

†'**withgang**, *sb.*[1] *Sc. Obs.* [a. ON. *viðgangr* increase.] Success; advantage, profit. So '**withgate**[1] *Sc.* [GATE *sb.*[2]]

1456 SIR G. HAYE *Law Arms* (S.T.S.) 171 Wikkit men has oft tymes in this warld welth, and withgang. *c* **1480** HENRYSON *Wolf & Wether* xxii, Thay haif withgang, welth, and cherising. **1510** in *Rec. Earldom Orkney* (S.H.S. 1914) 86 Victh al profetis and v[i]gang [?; *printed* vgang] sene Schir Dauit deit. **1825** JAMIESON s.v. *With-gate, To get the with-gate*, to gain the advantage.

†'**withgang**, *sb.*[2] *Sc. Obs.* [a. ON. *viðganga* access, admission.] Free course; unlimited permission, licence, toleration. Also †'**withgang** *v.*, *trans.* to give licence to, tolerate.

a **1500** *Ratis Raving* 420, I gaif my hart euer withgange of al plesans. *Ibid.* 3747 Gyf men thaim withgang wantonly, Than wyll thai cowet the maistry. **1808** JAMIESON, *With-gang*, toleration, permission to pass with impunity. *Skene.*

So †'**withgate**[2]. *Sc.* [GATE *sb.*[2]]

1599 *Sc. Acts Jas. VI* (1816) IV. 187/1 The withgait and libertie quhilk sindry avaricious.. persones hes tane to exact ..sik exorbitant..proffite. **1606** *Ibid.* 284/1 Ane terror to the ewill disposit to give withgait to thair Inclinatioun. *Ibid.* 616/2 The withgait and libertie grantit vnto Suche shamefull scafferie and extorsioun.

†**with'go**, *v. Obs.* [f. WITH- + GO *v.*; in sense 1 OE. *wiþgán*.]

1. *trans.* To go against, act in opposition to, oppose; in *pa. pple.* opposed (to).

743–5 in Thorpe *Charters* (1865) 29 Ond næfre ic ne mine lastweardas..ʒeðristlæcen þæt heo hit [*sc.* a grant] onwenden oððe þon wiðgæn. *a* **1300** *Cursor M.* 27986 It [*sc.* lechery] es sua greif and god withgan þat [etc.]. *c* **1350** *Leg. Rood* iii. 152 Þe sin of vs twa allane Was so grete and god withgane.

2. *intr.* To pass away; *pa. pple.* ?passed on their way.

a **1300** *Cursor M.* 5085 Mi wret es me now al witgan [*Gött.* ouer-gan]. **14..** in *Tundale's Vis.* (1843) 158, I fared me furthe yn that frythe; I mett three comely kyngis with gone.

3. *pass.* To be possessed *with*.

c **1375** *Cursor M.* 8915 (Fairf.) Ho is wode & wiþ þe deuel withgane.

4. *intr.* To go with something else.

1608 SYLVESTER *Mem. Mortalitie* II. xxxvii, Th' hand bindeth not except the heart with-go.

5. *trans.* To forgo.

a **1677** BARROW *2nd Serm. Ps. xc. 12* Wks. 1686 III. 174 Who for one..mess of Pottage..did withgo his birthright.

withheld (wɪð'hɛld), *ppl. a.* [pa. pple. of WITHHOLD *v.*] Kept or held back.

1753–4 RICHARDSON *Grandison* III. xxviii. 177 My withheld breath raised my complexion, and swelled my features. **1914** AMÉLIE RIVES *World's-End* xl, His face had a curious, withheld look as he stooped to kiss her.

withhold (wɪð'həʊld), *v.* Forms and etym.: see WITH- and HOLD *v.*; 3–7 occas. as two words, 6–8 freq. with hyphen; also 3 **wiðealden**, 4 **withald**, 5–6 **-alde**, 5–8 **withold**; *pa. t.* 3 **wiðeld**, 5 **without**, 6 *pseudo-arch.* **with hault**; *pa. pple.* 4–5 **witholde**, 5–8 **witholden** (*withholden* was still freq. in the 19th century).

1. *trans.* To keep *from* doing something; to keep in check or under restraint; to hold back, restrain.

Formerly also const. inf. = from doing a thing.

c **1200** *Vices & Virtues* 107 Alle unwilles ðe cumeð of ðe manne, ðies hes atempreð, & wiðhalt te misdon. *Ibid.* 143 Godd..wiðeld alle reines þrie hier & six moneþes. *c* **1290** *Beket* 1254 in *S. Eng. Leg.* 142 The teres fullen out of is eiʒene, he ne miʒte with-holden heom nouʒt. **13..** *E.E. Allit. P.* B. 740, I schal..wyth-halde my honde for hortyng on lede. **1379** *Glouc. Cath. MS. 19. No. I.* i. iv. lf. 11 b, It.. letteth & withholdeth the colre froo his kind decoccion. **1390** GOWER *Conf.* II. 240 Jason..Ne mihte noght withholde his lok, Bot so good hiede on hire he tok, That [etc.]. *Ibid.* 284 To be withholde ayein largesse. *c* **1400** tr. *Secr. Secr., Gov. Lordsh.* 113 Y withdrew me, & ouercome my self, for to withholde my couetyse. **1535** COVERDALE *Job* xvii. 4 Thou hast with holden their hertes from vnder-stondinge. *a* **1548** HALL *Chron., Hen. V* 70 Forasmuche as our saied father is witholden with diuerse sicknes, in such maner as he maie not intende in his owne persone. **1595** SHAKS. *John* v. vi. 37 With hold thine indignation, mighty heauen. **1601** —— *Jul. C.* III. ii. 108 What cause with-holds you then to mourne for him? **1696** TATE & BRADY *Ps.* xl. 9 Nor did [I] ..my Lips with-hold. **1719** DE FOE *Crusoe* I. (Globe) 237 So I withheld my Passion, though I was indeed enrag'd to the highest Degree. **1742** JOHNSON *Sydenham* Wks. 1787 IV. 493 He was with-held from the university by the commencement of the war. **1742** FIELDING *J. Andrews* II. v, Had not some awe of the company..withheld his rage. **1749** —— *Tom Jones* v. ii, From serenading his Patient every Hunting Morning with the Horn.., it was impossible to withhold him. **1780** JOHNSON *Let. to Mrs. Thrale* 8 May, Such is the call for your presence; what is there to withhold you? **1868** LYNCH *Rivulet* CXVII. i, While darkness yet withheld the dawn. **1873** J. G. HOLLAND *A. Bonnic.* ii, I longed to go nearer it, but the prohibition withheld me. **1912** *Engl. Hist. Rev.* Jan. 53 Walpole..withheld Great Britain from giving support..to..Frederick William.

absol. **1382** WYCLIF *2 Thess.* ii. 6 Now what withholdith, ʒe witen, that he be schewid in his tyme. **1560** *Bible* (Genev.) 2 Thess. ii. 7 He which now withholdeth, shal let til he be taken out of the waye.

b. *refl.* To restrain oneself.

c **1200** *Vices & Virtues* 135 Ðe mann þe him wiðhalt..of ates & of drenches. *a* **1225** *Ancr. R.* 348 Ich halsie ou..þet ʒe wiðholden ou from vlesliche lustes. **1303** R. BRUNNE *Handl. Synne* 12623 3ow to withholde Fro þe synnes þat byfore are tolde. *c* **1400** MAUNDEV. (Roxb.) xxii. 99 If it be swa þat any man..withhald him fra þis feste. *c* **1400** tr. *Secr. Secr., Gov. Lordsh.* 73 With-holde þe from latynge of blood. *Ibid.* 116 He þat with-oldys him to sterne his hondes. *a* **1619** FOTHERBY *Atheom.* II. viii. §2 (1622) 283 He prayeth to God, to withhold him; because hee could not withhold himselfe. **1897** WARUNG *Tales Old Régime* 246 Blake,..though tempted, yet withheld himself from yielding.

†**c.** *intr.* To refrain *from*; occas. const. inf., or *trans.* with gerund. *Obs.*

1650 H. MORE *Observ.* in *Enthus. Tri.*, etc. (1656) 103 You could not with-hold from telling us that you are but a young man. *c* **1650** BRADFORD *Plymouth Plant.* (1856) 104 They withheld and did no more hurte. **1711** ADDISON *Spect.* No. 123 ¶5 He could no longer withhold making himself known to him. **1807** [? W. H. IRELAND] *Mod. Ship of Fools* 118 *note*, No man should withhold from extending his hand to support the falling. *Ibid.* 275 *note*, The fools will carefully withhold from the mention of their own fooleries. **1817** JAS. MILL *Brit. India* v. iv. II. 453 He was incapable of giving, or capable of withholding to give..an opinion.

†**d.** *trans.* To keep away or off, ward off. *Obs.*

13.. *K. Alis.* 2302 Glitoun..pulte forth a stelene scheld, Ny-gusars dunt withhuld. **1560** *1st Bk. Discipl. Ch. Scot.* (1621) 66 Every Kirk must have..thack able to with-hold raine.

†**e.** To hinder, prevent. (With dir. obj., clause, or acc. and inf.) *Obs.*

c **1400** tr. *Secr. Secr., Gov. Lordsh.* 93 Vnderstandynge.. ys luge wirkand, and withhaldand þat þat vndoynge bycomes. **1486** *Bk. St. Albans* c vj b, It is anoyus sekenes..and with holdeth hir strengthe. **1674** N. FAIRFAX *Bulk & Selv.* 39 Nothing with-holds, but that from an infinite tale of finites there may at length arise an infinite. **1754** RICHARDSON *Grandison* II. iii. 22 Nothing with-holds my wishes to be released, but my desire of seeing the darling.. happy.

f. To keep away or separated *from*. *rare.*

1513 DOUGLAS *Æneis* IV. vi. 150 Quham of the realm of Itail I defraud, And fra the ground to him promist withhad. **1854** PATMORE *Angel in Ho., Betrothal* 140 Like a ship frostbound and far Withheld in ice from the ocean's roar.

†**g.** To defer, postpone. *Obs. rare.*

1725 POPE *Odyss.* XXII. 258 She..willing longer to survey The sire and son's great acts, with-held the day.

2. To keep back; to keep in one's possession (what belongs to, is due to, or is desired by another); to refrain from giving, granting, or allowing. †Formerly with dat. of person. (The current sense.)

c **1200** *Vices & Virtues* 139 Ða þinges ðe ne sculen ben iʒiuen, þa bieð to wiðealden mid michele skele. *c* **1250** *Gen. & Ex.* 914 Wid-held he ðor-of neuere on del, Oc al ðat euere fel him to, Sac-les he let hin welden it so. *a* **1300** *Cursor M.* 28427 Gains godd i haue bene vn-hende, þat i wit-halden ha my tende. **1362** LANGL. *P. Pl.* A. vi. 42 He with-halt non hyne his huire. *c* **1380** *Sir Ferumb.* 5620 3eld me þe relyqes vp agayn, þat þou with-halst of myne. ? **1449** *Paston Lett.* Suppl. (1901) 22 The Pryore and Convent of Norwyche have wythhalden certeyn rent for landes that they halden of me. **1470–85** MALORY *Arthur* x. xli. 480 A knyghte that hyght Goneryes that withhelde her alle her landes. **1493** *Plumpton Corr.* (Camden) 105 That ye without your duty belonging to the sayd Mr. Lee. *a* **1548** HALL *Chron., Edw. IV* 232 Your old rightes & possessions, which wer from you ..wrongfully with holden. **1590** SPENSER *F.Q.* II. xi. 9 Soone as Titan gan his head exault, And soone againe as he his light with hault. **1634** SIR T. HERBERT *Trav.* 186 Blessings..not with-held from Pagan people. **1728** POPE *Dunc.* III. 276 These Fate reserv'd to grace thy reign divine, Foreseen by me, but ah! withheld from mine. **1794** R. J. SULIVAN *View Nat.* I. 480 From such an inference, I must ..withhold my assent. **1848** DICKENS *Dombey* xlvi, Perch the messenger..could not withhold the tribute of his admiration from this zealous conduct. **1861** BROUGHAM *Brit. Const.* xiii. 178 [Parliament's] acknowledged power to give or to withhold supplies. **1874** S. WILBERFORCE *Ess.* I. 381 The other branches of the Church Catholic, with which ..communion was..withholden from us. **1883** TYLOR in *Encycl. Brit.* XV. 199/1 Such divine beings as can..give or withhold the rain. **1911** *Act 1 & 2 Geo. V.* c. 46 §4 That by reason of such refusal [to republish] the work is withheld from the public.

absol. **1781** COWPER *Hope* 331 He will give freely, or he will withhold. **1859** WHITTIER *My Psalm* 42 All as God wills, who wisely heeds To give or to withhold.

†**3.** To detain; to keep in bondage, in custody, or under control. Also *fig. Obs.*

c **1250** *Gen. & Ex.* 3019 He [*sc.* Pharaoh] wið-held hem, and, al-so he [*sc.* Moses] it bead, Al ðe erf of egipt wurð dead. *c* **1374** CHAUCER *Troylus* IV. 597 It is no shame vn-to ʒow,.. Hire to with-holden þat ye loueth most. **1390** GOWER *Conf.* I. 308 If thou art on of alle, That with this vice hast ben withholde. **1422** YONGE tr. *Secr. Secr.* 161 Verite in this dayes is wyth-holde, bonde, and prisoner. *c* **1520** SKELTON *Garl. Laurell*, etc., Wks. 1843 I. 427 The twayne last [*sc.* Right and Reason] Be withholde so fast With mony, as men sayne, They can not come agayne. **1590** SHAKS. *Mids. N.* II. i. 26 She (perforce) with holds the loued boy. **1611** TOURNEUR *Ath. Trag.* I. ii, Your favour had by his duty beene preuented, If we had not with-held him in the way. **1714** *Orig. Canto Spenser* xxxvi, The strugling Fly he firmly doth with-hold. [Cf. quot. 1854 in 1 f.]

†**4.** To keep in use or possession; rarely, to keep in place; to retain; *esp.* to retain in the memory; occas. to reserve *to oneself*. *Obs.*

c **1200** *Vices & Virtues* 27 Hit is al ʒedwoll, and of haðenesse ʒiet wiðhealden. *c* **1374** CHAUCER *Boeth.* IV. pr. vi. (1868) 139 He wolde for-leten peraventure to continue innocence, by þe whiche he ne may nat wiþholden fortune. *c* **1386** —— *Pars. T.* ¶967 [The Pater noster] is short,..for to withholden it the moore esily in herte. **1387–8** T. USK *Test. Love* II. viii. (Skeat) l. 121 Al-though it be a whyle swete, it may not be with-holde. **1398** TREVISA *Barth. De P.R.* v. ii. (Tollem. MS.), Þe heed is sumdel comynge narow and hyʒe, and þat to with holde þe bagge of þe brayne. *c* **1400** tr. *Secr. Secr., Gov. Lordsh.* 78 Study..to kepe and witholde kyndly hete. *c* **1430** *Pilgr. Lyf Manhode* I. xv. (1869) 10 He hath with holde to him alle vengeaunces. **1483** CAXTON *G. de la Tour* li. e ij, I wold ye couthe and wel withheld the example of a knyght that had thre wyues.

†**b.** To keep attached to one's person or engaged in one's service; to retain for one's pleasure or profit, keep on one's side. *Obs.*

c **1300** *Havelok* 2356 A thusand knihtes ful wel o bon With-held þe king, with him to lede. *c* **1380** *Antecrist* in Todd *Three Treat. Wyclif* (1851) 150 Crist wiþhelde no men of lawe ne pleders at þe barr for robes and fees. *c* **1400** MAUNDEV. (1919) xxvi. 157 All the mynstrelles þat comen before hym..ben withholden with him as of his houshold. *c* **1412** HOCCLEVE *De Reg. Princ.* 1250 With-holde hir on þi side. **1423** *Acts Privy Council* III. 90 He has bene withholde and of retenue for a yere wyt the..noble Kyng Henry. **1424** *Paston Lett.* I. 17 [He] never was servaunt to the..Duc ..ne wythhaldyn in hese service. *c* **1500** *Three Kings Sons* 22 My lorde withhelde him for his seruaunt.

†**5.** To keep, maintain, preserve. *Obs.*

c **1200** *Vices & Virtues* 71 Ðat tu hes kunne wel ʒecnawen & mid godes fultume wiðhealden. *c* **1374** CHAUCER *Boeth.* IV. pr. vi. (1868) 142 God..hastiþ to wiþhalden þe þinges þat he haþ maked in to hys semblaunce. *c* **1386** —— *Prol.* 511 To seken hym a chauntrie for soules, Or with a bretherhed to been withholde. **1390** GOWER *Conf.* I. 7 Knyhthode.. Wherof the wyde worldes fame Write in Cronique is yit withholde. *c* **1418** *Pol. Poems* (Rolls) II. 244 Hem nedethe nether spere ne shulde, Ne in no castel to be withholde.

†**6. a.** To hold. **b.** To hold up, sustain. *Obs. rare.*

1513 DOUGLAS *Æneis* VIII. xi. 44 In thair hand wythhaldand, euery knycht, Twa javilling speris. **1760–72** H. BROOKE *Fool of Qual.* (1809) II. 159 [He] cut the hair that with-held me in twain; so down I thought I fell.

†**7.** *intr.* To hold or adhere to. *Obs. rare.*

a **1450** *Knt. de la Tour* Prol. 4 Forto flee euelle and withholde the good. *Ibid.* 54 Alle these men that kepithe hem selff clene..haue free hert to witholde good ensaumples of lyff.

Hence **with'holdable** *a.*, liable to be or capable of being withheld.

1810 BENTHAM *Packing* (1821) 248 The habitual, but ever withholdable bribes, with which they are fed.

withholden (wɪð'həʊldən), *ppl. a. arch.* [pa. pple. of WITHHOLD *v.*] = WITHHELD *ppl. a.*

c **1430** *Pol. Rel. & L. Poems* 213/349 With-holden hire aʒen þe riʒt Of þi seruanntis vpon þee crye. **1802–12** BENTHAM *Ration. Judic. Evid.* (1827) V. 97 The fallaciously offered and really withholden remedy. **1884** TENNYSON *Cup* I. i. 48 The long-withholden tribute.

withholder (wɪð'həʊldə(r)). [f. WITHHOLD *v.* + -ER[1].] One who withholds.

1483 *Acta Audit.* in *Acta Dom. Conc.* II. Introd. 107 That scho haue hir accioun agane the withaldaris of thame. **1516** *Reg. Privy Seal Scot.* I. 418/1 To compell the withhaldaris and intromettouris thairwith to deliuer the samyn to thaim. **1548** *Act 2 & 3 Edw. VI*, c. 13 §13 Yt shall not be laufull.. to..sue suche witholder of tithes..before any other Judge then ecclesiasticall. *a* **1648** LD. HERBERT *Hen. VIII* (1683) 117 If either Prince haue an intention to recouer any other Rights, against other with-holders. *a* **1674** TRAHERNE *Chr. Ethics* (1675) 555 He hath more Withholders to keep him from Sin. **1866** J. G. MURPHY *Comm. Exod.* xxii. 28 Whether he [*sc.* God] be regarded as the withholder of prosperity or the restrainer of crime. **1917** OUTHWAITE *Land or Revol.* iii. 21 To compel the urban land withholders to use or part with the land.

withholding (wɪð'həʊldɪŋ), *vbl. sb.* [f. as prec. + -ING[1].] **1.** The action of the verb WITHHOLD: retention, restraint, keeping back, etc.

c **1386** CHAUCER *Melib.* ¶267 How I shal gouerne me in the chesynge and in the withholdynge of my conseillours. *c* **1400** tr. *Secr. Secr., Gov. Lordsh.* 116 Broodnesse of brest, and greetnesse of sholdres..by-tokyns..hardynesse, with witholdynge of wyt, and vndyrstondynge. *c* **1430** *Pilgr. Lyf Manhode* I. lii. (1869) 96 So is to me an hevy blok the bodi, and a gret withholdinge. **1440–1** *Privy Counc. Proc.* (P.R.O.), Thendentures of his withholdyng bitwix the Kyng and him. *c* **1450** *Godstow Reg.* 351 That they shulde receyue the tythys..with-out ony with-holdynge. **1454** *Rolls of Parlt.* V. 254/1 That a notable some of monneye bee to me delivered..for the withholding and contenting of such Souldeours. **1526** *Reg. Privy Seal Scot.* I. 518/2 Thair tressonable assegeing, taking and withhalding of the Kingis castell. *a* **1651** C. LOVE *Combat Flesh & Spirit* (1654) 41 The withholdings of the Spirit. **1705** STANHOPE *Paraphr.* II. 350 His very Withholdings and Delays are kindly meant. **1837** LOCKHART *Scott* IV. i. 18 The with-holding of the avowal. *a* **1861** CLOUGH *Poems, Uranus* 3 The..blank profound, Which..holds All knowledge, ever by withholding holds. **1884** *Law Times Rep.* (N.S.) LI. 242/2 If a party..obtains the sanction of the court by withholding information which is material..such withholding amounts to fraud.

2. Special Comb.: **withholding rate** *U.S.*, the rate for a withholding tax; **withholding table** *U.S.*, a table showing amounts of tax to be deducted from a dividend payment, salary, etc.; **withholding tax** orig. *U.S.*, a tax deducted at source, *spec.* one levied by some countries on interest or dividends paid to a person resident outside that country.

1972 *Time* 17 Apr. 43/3 Spending has been held back in part because of a colossal blooper by the House Ways and Means Committee in setting the new withholding rates. **1976** *Billings* (Montana) *Gaz.* 30 June 6-A/1 The House unanimously passed and sent to President Ford Tuesday a two-month extension of current lower income tax withholding rates. **1947** *Sun* (Baltimore) 15 May 2/8 The Finance Committee halved the House bill for the current year and made the new withholding tables effective as of July 1. **1940** *U.S. Federal Rep.* 2nd Ser. CXII. 1000/2 Intra-company payments designated as 'interest' would not be so regarded..for the purpose of the withholding tax. *Ibid.*, The principal amount..was due complainant on account of withholding taxes. **1950** *Tax Cases* XXXIII. 346 The Appellant received her arrears of interest as follows: In June, 1943...$18,000 *Less*: U.S. withholding tax at 30 per cent...5,400. **1960** I. WALLACH *Absence of Cello* (1961) 7 Will you tell me why the hell you never paid the withholding taxes for your employees? **1971** *Financial Mail* (Johannesburg) 26 Feb. 717/1 Interest accruing to non-residents of the Republic is subject to deduction of a withholding tax at the rate of 10 per cent, exemption from the tax having been granted in respect of accruals of interest amounting to R20 or less in any one year. **1979** *Daily Tel.* 27 Oct. 27/1 Many foreign countries have tax laws, which, in principle, require the foreign payer of the dividends or interest to deduct a withholding tax when making the payment to a non-resident. **1984** *Times* 5 Oct. 25/1 The German withholding tax was introduced in 1965 to prevent an overvaluation of the Deutschemark injurious to exports.

So **with'holding** *ppl. a.*, that withholds.

c **1430** *Pilgr. Lyf Manhode* IV. xiii. (1869) 183 Withholdinge, and ful of cley, and..glewy is þilke. **1883** *Fortn. Rev.* Aug. 305 The eternal duel between the desiring flesh and the withholding spirit.

with'holdment. *rare.* [f. WITHHOLD *v.* + -MENT.] = WITHHOLDING *vbl. sb.*

1640 O. SEDGWICK *Christ's Counsell* 183 An avocation or withholdment from errours. **1851** W. ANDERSON *Exposure of Popery* (1878) 73 There..is an important withholdment made in the communication.

withi, var. *with thi*: see WITH *prep.* 6.

within (wɪ'ðɪn), *adv.*, *prep.*, (*adj.*). Forms (2-5 written as one or as two words): α. 1 **wiþinnan, wiðinnan**, 2-4 **wiðinne(n**, 3-5 **wiþinne**, etc. (see WITH and INNE *adv.*); also 3 **wiþ ine(n**, *Orm.* **wiþþinnenn**, 3-4 **widine**, 4-5 **withine**. β. 3 **wiðin**, 4-5 **wiþin**, etc. (see WITH and IN *adv.*; *abbreviated* 4-6 **wtin**, 7 **wthin**), 4- **within**. [Late OE. *wiþinnan*, f. *wiþ* WITH *prep.* = *innan* INNE, the second element being assimilated to IN *adv.* in ME. OE. *wiþinnan*, *wiþæftan* behind, *wiþforan* before, *wiþȝeondan* beyond, *wiþhindan* behind, *wiþufan* above, and *wiþútan* WITHOUT, form a group of words peculiar to English, corresp. to and perh. partly modelled on the synonymous group *beæftan*, *bæftan* BAFT *adv.*, *beforan* BEFORE, *beȝeondan* BEYOND, *behindan* BEHIND, *beinnan*, *binnan* BIN *adv.*, **beufan*, *bufan* BOVE *adv.*, *beútan*, *bútan* BOUT *adv.*, of which nearly all have cognates in West Germanic. Cf. the blended forms BYTHINNE, BYTHOUT.]

A. *adv.* (In most senses opp. to WITHOUT *adv.*)

1. a. In the inner part or interior, or on the inner side (of a receptacle or other material thing); inside, internally.

c **1000** ÆLFRIC *Gen.* vi. 14 Ðu wyrcst wununga binnan ðam arce & clæmst wiðinnan & wiðutan mid tyrwan. *c* **1250** *Gen. & Ex.* 640 Ðe rede wid-innen toknet on Wreche ðat sal ȝet wurðen sent. *a* **1300** *Cursor M.* 523 His heued with in has eien tuin, þe lift has son and mon wit-in. **1398** TREVISA *Barth. De P.R.* IV. iv. (1495) e vij, By heete werkynge alwaye within and wythoute bodyes ben consumyd and waasted. *c* **1430** *Two Cookery-bks.* 48 Bake on an ovyn, & coloure with-ynne & wyth-oute. **1596** SHAKS. *Merch. V.* I. ii. 105 Set a deepe glasse of Reinish-wine on the contrary Casket, for if the diuell be within, and that temptation without, I know he will choose it. **1796** STEDMAN *Surinam* II. xviii. 51 Small annulated black spots, which are white within. **1797** COLERIDGE *Christabel* I. 127 The gate that was ironed within and without. **1815** STEPHENS in *Shaw's Gen. Zool.* IX. I. 42 At the bend of the wing, just within, is a horn-coloured spine. **1827** FARADAY *Chem. Manip.* ix. 248 The instrument may be removed, and the fluid within transferred to any convenient vessel. **1866** GEO. ELIOT *F. Holt* xxxiii, The tradesmen..locked their doors and barricaded their windows within.

b. In the interior of the body or some part of it.

c **1220** *Bestiary* 318 Wiðinnen he haueð brenning. **1387** TREVISA *Higden* I. 59 Betynge of veynes is bettre i-knowe in þe vttre parties of bodies þan ynward and in þe myddel wiþynne. **1450-1530** *Myrr. our Ladye* II. 246 How al hys glorious body muste be tormented..wythin and wythoute. **1596** SHAKS. *Merch. V.* I. i. 83 Why should a man whose bloud is warme within, Sit like his Grandsire, cut in Alablaster? *a* **1639** CAREW *Poems, My Mistress commanding me to return her Letters* 68 Though the skin Be clos'd without, the wound festers within. [**1843** MACAULAY *Horatius* lxii, But his limbs were borne up bravely By the brave heart within.] **1844** MRS. BROWNING *Lay of Brown Rosary* III. xvi, The maidens' lips trembled from smiles shut within.

c. In this writing or document; herein. *Obs.* exc. in technical use.

1387 TREVISA *Higden* II. 35 As hit is i-saide wiþ ynne. *c* **1450** *Godstow Reg.* 368 As is I-write with-yn. **1498-1844** [see D. a]. **1519** *Indenture betw. Pynson and Horman* in *Trans. Philol. Soc.* (1867) 365 The parties wythin namede. **1651** tr. *Kitchin's Jurisd.* (1653) 550 We A. B. and C. D. Coroners..do certifie the Justices within written..that we have searched the Rolles.

†**d.** (with verb of motion) So as to go in or be inside: = IN *prep.* 1. *Obs. rare.*

1297 R. GLOUC. (Rolls) 7951 Hii wiþinne turnde aȝen & hom allenome. *c* **1420** *Liber Cocorum* (1862) 19 Poure hit withinne.

2. a. In the limits of, or in the inner part of, a space or region, esp. a city or country; in the place or realm.

a **1122** *O.E. Chron.* (Laud) an. 1048 [Hi] ofsloȝon æȝðer ȝe wiðinnan ȝe wiðutan ma þanne .xx. manna. *c* **1205** LAY. 18300 Vtheres cnihtes..wereden þene tun wið innen. **1390** GOWER *Conf.* III. 382 If a kyng wol justifie His lond and hem that beth withynne. **1474** CAXTON *Chesse* II. iv. (1883) 52 Scylla that was Duc of the Romayns wyth oute had many fayr victoyres agaynst the Romayns wyth Inne. **1697** DRYDEN *Æneis* IX. 1034 But whom they fear'd without, they found within. **1849** GROTE *Greece* II. xliv. V. 359 Traitors within, as well as exiles without. **1914** *Engl. Hist. Rev.* Oct. 751 Support for the royal power against the barons within and the papacy without.

b. In (or into) the house or dwelling, indoors: = IN *adv.* 5; also, in the inner part of the house, in an inner chamber; *Theatr.* (esp. in stage-directions), behind the scenes.

c **1275** LAY. 642 He..þrettede þan castle and þat folk wid ine. *c* **1290** *Beket* 1175 in *S. Eng. Leg.* 140 Al with-Inne seten is men as þei he lowest were. *c* **1430** *Syr. Tryam.* 531 To mete as they were sett in halle, Syr Marrok was there ferre withynne y-wys. **1546** J. HEYWOOD *Prov.* (1867) 32 She was within, but he was yet abrode. **1590** SHAKS. *Mids. N.* IV. i. 143 *stage dir.*, *Shout within, they all start up.* **1595** —— *John* IV. i. 85 Go stand within: let me alone with him. **1613** PURCHAS *Pilgrimage* II. xiv. 159 The mother keepeth within, six weeks. **1771** WESLEY *Jrnl.* 26 May (1827) III. 419 The rain obliged me to preach within. **1815** JANE AUSTEN *Emma* xxxii, Not being within when he called the other day. **1833** L. RITCHIE *Wand. Loire* 131 'Within, there! ho!' shouted the traveller. **1837** DICKENS *Pickw.* xxxiv, Apartments furnished for a single gentleman. Inquire within. **1855** MACAULAY *Hist. Eng.* xxi. IV. 559 A messenger went with the summons to the house of the Duke of Leeds, and was there informed that the Swiss was not within.

c. *transf.* In the number or membership of a class or community. (Cf. B. 1 e.) *rare.*

1526 [see WITHOUT *adv.* 2 b].

3. *fig.* In the inward being; in the mind, soul, or heart (sometimes implying 'in one's true character as opposed to outward appearance'); inwardly.

c **1000** ÆLFRIC *Gen.* vi. 6 Ʒehrepod mid heortan sarnysse wiðinnan. *c* **1000** —— *Hom.* I. 604 We beoð fram Gode ȝesewene æȝðer ȝe wiðutan ȝe wiðinnan. *c* **1175** *Lamb. Hom.* 95 Ʒif þe halia gast ne hearð þes monnes heorte and his mod wið-innan. *c* **1200** ORMIN 5751 Ʒiff þiss hallȝhe griþþ iss wel wiþþinnenn i þin herrte. *a* **1225** *Ancr. R.* 4 Vorto riwlen þe heorte wiðinnen. **1340** *Ayenb.* 10 Þe zixte heste uorbyet þe dede wyþ-oute, ac þis uorbyet þe grantinge wyþinne. *c* **1386** CHAUCER *Wife's T.* 87 Be we neuer so vicious with-Inne We wol been holden wise. **1421** *26 Pol. Poems* xviii. 118 Be suche wiþ-ynne, as ȝe outward seme. *a* **1548** HALL *Chron., 22 Hen. VIII*, 187 b, His graces sight was so quike..that he saw him, ye and saw through him, both within, and without. **1617** FLETCHER *Valentinian* IV. iv, Think not the worse.., I shed not teares, Great griefes lament within. **1676** DRYDEN *Aurengz.* IV. i, I..Stood firm collected in my Strength within. **1690** NORRIS *Beatitudes* (1692) 159 Look within, for within is the Fountain of Good. **1850** TENNYSON *In Mem.* xxxiii, Thou, that countest reason ripe In holding by the law within.

4. Preceded by *from* (†*out of*), in various senses.

c **1489** CAXTON *Sonnes of Aymon* xv. 357 Ye shall not goo oute of wythin, wythout my leve. **1645** GATAKER *God's Eye on Israel* 52 Nor any helper..; as no power from within, so no ayd from without. **1667** MILTON *P.L.* IV. 64 Other Powers..Fell not, but stand unshak'n, from within Or from without. **1810** WORDSW. *Sonn.* '*O'erweening Statesmen*', From *within* proceeds a Nation's health. **1837** P. KEITH *Bot. Lex.* 273 When the impression from without, or the stimulus from within,..excites the organs. **1896** J. DAVIDSON *Fleet St. Eclogues* Ser. II. 38 Be your own star, for strength is from within.

†**5.** Below the number or amount mentioned; less. (Cf. B. 7.) *Obs.*

c **1375** *Sc. Leg. Saints* xxxvi. (*Baptista*) 997 Al barnis..Of twa ȝere elde & withine. *a* **1425** *Cursor M.* 11567 (Trin.) Of two ȝeer or wiþynne þus [*Cott.* Tua yeir or less]. **1450** *Paston Lett.* I. 155 To bye it at the some of C. mark or wythynne. **1509** *Reg. Privy Seal Scot.* I. 286/2 To the nowmer of xii personis or within.

†**6. a.** In possession or occupation. *Obs. rare.*

1573 in Hone *Man. & Manor. Rec.* (1906) 191 Aforesaid Agnes survived him, and kept herself within, and was, and still is, seised thereof for term of her life.

B. *prep.*

1. a. In the inner part or interior of, inside of, in (a space, region, receptacle, etc.). (*a*) as a mere synonym of IN *prep.* 1. *arch.*

The use with gen. in 'þæt wiðinnan ys calicys' (*Ags. Gosp.* Matt. xxiii. 26) is a literalism of translation (Vulg. *quod intus est calicis* = τὸ ἐντὸς τοῦ ποτηρίου).

c **1175** *Lamb. Hom.* 89 Þa weren þer igedered wiðinne þere buruh of ierusalem trowfeste men. *a* **1240** *Ureisun* 49 in *O.E. Hom.* I. 193 Wið-inne paradise. *c* **1250** *Gen. & Ex.* 348 Vn-welde woren..Here owen limes hem wið-in. *Ibid.* 555 Ðo wex a flod ðis werlde wid-hin. *a* **1300** *Cursor M.* 2678 þou and þi childer.. And þat wons þi house witin. **1388** in *Archæologia* LII. 213 Wtin the said westre. *c* **1400** *Anturs Arth.* 136 Sei me..whi þou walkest þes wayes, þe wodes with-in? *c* **1489** CAXTON *Blanchardyn* viii. *heading*, To passe ouer the ryuere wythin a bote. **1513** DOUGLAS *Æneis* VII. Prol. 116 Wythin my bed I waikynnit quhair I lay. **1596** SHAKS. *Tam. Shr.* I. i. 94 Schoolemasters will I keepe within my house. **1611** *Bible* Ps. ci. 2, I will walke within my house with a perfect heart. **1697** DRYDEN *Virg. Georg.* III. 810 The Viper dead, within her Hole is found. **1768** STERNE *Sent. Journ.*, *Moulines*, Her head leaning on one side within her hand. **1820** KEATS *Isabella* xxxviii, It shall comfort me within the tomb. **1867** MORRIS *Jason* I. 86 The bath within the pool of some green rill.

(*b*) with emphasis on the restriction or confinement by limits or boundaries: In the limits of, not outside or beyond. Opp. to WITHOUT *prep.* 1. (The current use.)

1131 *O.E. Chron.* (Laud), Ealle þa ðing þa wæron wiðinne mynstre & wiðuten. *c* **1200** ORMIN 1084 He..ȝede upp to þatt allterr þatt wass wiþþinnenn waȝheriflt. *c* **1300** *K. Horn* 256 (Laud), Wit hinne þe curt and wit oute. **1390** GOWER *Conf.* III. 307 Every thing which was honeste With-innen house and ek withoute. *c* **1400** MAUNDEV. (1919) i. 5 The water of the see is fressch & holdeth his swetness .xx. myle within the see. *c* **1450** *Godstow Reg.* 665 In weyes and pathes ..with-in burgh and with-out burgh. **1539** *Bible* (Great) 1 Kings vi. 23 Within the Oracle he made two Cherubims of Oliue tree. **1551** CROWLEY *Pleas. & Payne* 110 Tyll all the good and fruitfull grounde Were hedged in whythin your mownde. **1585** T. WASHINGTON tr. *Nicholay's Voy.* I. xiv. 15 Many small houses very auunciently builded within the grounde [= underground]. **1711** STEELE *Spect.* No. 91 ⁋1 Within the Liberties of the City of Westminster. **1794** *Act 34 Geo. III*, c. 93 §63 The Mines and Minerals lying and being within or under the said Lands. **1849** MACAULAY *Hist. Eng.* ix. II. 437 Privileged districts, within which the Papal government had no more power than within the Louvre or the Escurial.

b. (*a*) In (an inclosure or inclosing boundary); so as to be included, contained, surrounded, or confined by. Also in *fig.* context (cf. 9).

within board (Naut.), in the inside of a ship: see BOARD *sb.* 12. *within the lists*: see LIST *sb.*[3] 9.

1387-8 T. USK *Test. Love* I. iii. (Skeat) I. 54 These broughten me within-borde of this shippe of Traveyle. *a* **1400** *Pistill of Susan* 10 Wiþ Inne the sercle of sees Of Erberi and Alees. *a* **1400-50** *Wars Alex.* 211 With-in þe merris of Messedoyn. **1559** W. CUNINGHAM *Cosmogr. Glasse* 17 A Circle is a plaine and flat figure comprehended within one line, which is called a circumference. **1596** DALRYMPLE tr. *Leslie's Hist. Scot.* (S.T.S.) I. 9 Scotlande..is hail wtin the sey, excepte that parte quhair it lyes to Ingland. **1598** STOW *Surv.* 242 First to speake of that part within the gate. **1638** BAKER tr. *Balzac's Lett.* (vol. II.) 5 To gain beleefe, one must keepe himselfe within the bounds of likelihood. **1725** WATTS *Logic* I. vi. §5 To leave Obscurities in the Sentence, by confining it within too narrow Limits. **1779** *Mirror* No. 10 ⁋11 A man who has confined his turn for enjoyment within the bounds pointed out by nature. **1831** CARLYLE *Sart. Res.* I. iii, The proud Grandee..reposes within damask Curtains. **1849** MACAULAY *Hist. Eng.* ii. I. 221 Whether the Declaration of Indulgence lay within or without the limit was the question. *Ibid.* v. 614 Five hundred prisoners had been crowded into the parish church of Weston Zoyland;..five expired within the consecrated walls. **1871** R. H. HUTTON *Theol. Ess.* (1888) i. 7 Those within the circle of its influence.

(*b*) Appended to names of places lying within a certain boundary or area, as *Bishopsgate Within* (i.e. within the walls of London), *Hensington Within* (i.e. within the borough of Woodstock).

1598 STOW *Surv.* 85 Aldersgate ward within and without. *Ibid.* 248 Faringdon Warde, Infra, or within. **1657** HOWELL *Londinop.* 87 We will..take a Survey of Bridge Ward within, so called of London-Bridge. **1745** *Kent's Lond. Directory* 93 Ware Nathaniel, Grocer, Bishopsgate within. **1837** DICKENS *Pickw.* xlv, The united parishes of Saint Simon Without, and Saint Walker Within. **1899** *Kelly's Direct. Oxon* 323 2 Hensington Within is a civil parish, formed..from the portion of the old parish in Woodstock municipal borough.

†**c.** ***within land***: in the interior of the country, at a distance from the coast or other boundary: = INLAND C. *Obs.*

1614 PURCHAS *Pilgrimage* IX. iv. (ed. 2) 840 The Pories dwell an hundred miles within Land. **1617** MORYSON *Itin.* III. 141 Coventry..at this day is the fairest City within-land. **1793** SMEATON *Edystone L.* §206 Though there is plenty of the same kind of stone to be found in Strata within land; yet ..the lime-burners can procure..sufficient quantity from the shelving sea-shore. **1815** SCOTT *Guy M.* xxxiv, It was too far within land, and I might have been scented.

d. On the inner (esp. landward) side of; further in than. (Cf. WITHOUT B. 1 c.) ? *Obs.*

1743 BULKELEY & CUMMINS *Voy. S. Seas* 120 The Cutter, being on the Beam, and four Miles within us. **1766** GOLDSM. *Vicar W.* iv, Three other apartments, one for my wife and me, another for our two daughters, within our own. **1793** SMEATON *Edystone L.* §336 At 116 yards within high-water mark. *c* **1804** JANE AUSTEN *The Watsons* in *Mem.* (1871) 321 The tea-room was a small room within the card-room.

e. *transf.* In the membership of (a class, society, etc.); (in predicate) included in, forming a part of. (Cf. IN *prep.* 7.)

1697 JOS. WOODWARD *Relig. Soc.* vi. (1701) 124 It is objected..That this is a Society within a Society, and a Refining upon a Reformed Church. **1799** *Monthly Rev.* XXX. 471 Compositions which may be arranged within this class. **1885** *Law Times Rep.* (N.S.) LII. 319/2 Criminal informations are within the mischief intended to be guarded against.

2. To the interior of; into. Also with the boundary as obj., as in 1 b. (Cf. IN *prep.* 31.) *Obs.* or *arch.*

c **1205** LAY. 5812 Belin & Brennes buȝen heom fram þan fuhte wih innen are muchele dic. *c* **1250** *Gen. & Ex.* 3775 Alle he sunken ðe erðe wiðin. **13..** *Cursor M.* 2303 (Gött.) Feindes crepe þas ymagis wid-in. **1390** GOWER *Conf.* I. 80 This Hors..Was broght withinne the Cite. **1423** JAS. I. *Kingis Q.* lxxvii, I was anon In broght Within a chamber. *c* **1480** HENRYSON *Wolf & Wether* 51 Was nouther Uolf, Uildcat, nor ȝit Tod Durst cum within thay boundis all about. **1508** DUNBAR *Gold. Targe* 92 Full lustily thir ladyes ..Enterit within this park. **1582** N. LICHEFIELD tr. *Castanheda's Conq. E. Ind.* I. v. 13 b, Going upon the friday within a certein harbour. **1610** SHAKS. *Temp.* I. ii. 11, I would Haue suncke the Sea within the Earth. **1844** LINGARD *Anglo-Saxon Ch.* (1858) I. vii. 291 Admission within the fold.

†3. In or into the midst of, among, with; *spec.* in the house of; hence, in the hands or possession of.

a **1240** *Ureisun* 26 in *O.E. Hom.* I. 191 Biuoren ðine leoue sune wið-innen seraphine. *c* **1425** *Engl. Conq. Irel.* 52 Whan thay myght nat wyth streynth spede, thay bethoght ham that wyth falshed & wyth treyson they wold come wyth-yn ham. **1428** *Engl. Misc.* (Surtees) 2 To serche what osmundes he had with in hym at yat tyme. *c* **1450** CAPGRAVE *Life St. Gilbert* xx. 92 So wer þese chanones fer sette fro þe nunnes þat þei schuld not come with-inne þe nunnes..but only for ministracion of þe sacramentis. **1474** *Cov. Leet Bk.* 399 Yf he kepe any Bawdery withinne hym his fyne is at euery tyme vj s. viij d. **1482** in *Engl. Hist. Rev.* Jan. (1910) 122 He shalle bynde and repayre alle bookes needefulle wythine vs. **1490** *Will J. Baker* (Somerset Ho.), Elisabeth..dwelling within me. **1493** *Mirk's Festyuall* 151/2 Some..men y^t had copyes of this bokis within hem at home. **1570** FOXE *A. & M.* (ed. 2) 2124/2 A woman that dwelleth within vs. **1609** TOURNEUR *Funeral Poem Sir F. Vere,* When occasion did present His observation with some accident Within the enemie, that did invite The side he served in to attempt a fight.

4. Various *transf.* uses, chiefly with reflexive pronoun. **†a.** In the limits of (not beyond or outside) the body, community, or collection of. ***within themselves*** (***ourselves***, etc.): among themselves (etc.), independently of others. *Obs.*

a **1300** *Cursor M.* 1914 Wit-in þeir auen kind to brede. **1484** *Cov. Leet Bk.* 522 Hit shal-be determyned & orderyd by all the Mairys withyn them selff. **1496** *Rolls of Parlt.* VI. 516/2 They, within theymselfe, shall make Colleccion of such Somes of Money as shall be assessed..to be levyed. **1591** SHAKS. *1 Hen. VI,* IV. i. 140 If they perceyue dissention in our lookes, And that within our selues we disagree. **1654** EARL MONM. tr. *Bentivoglio's Wars Flanders* 189 They differed within themselves in their votes. **1737** [S. BERINGTON] *G. di Lucca's Mem.* (1738) 113 Living entirely within themselves, free from all Mixture and Commerce with other People.

b. ***within oneself*** (***itself***, etc.): (*a*) so as to be self-contained or independent, without external connexion (now *dial.*); † (*b*) in self-command or self-control, not 'beside oneself'; (*c*) in the limits of one's own belongings or resources, without external supply or aid (now *dial.*); (*d*) not beyond one's normal capacity of exertion; without strain, or waste of energy or effort.

(*a*) **1518** *Star Chamber Cases* (Selden Soc.) II. 136 He seid ..that my lord of Peturburgh was lord and Kyng wythin hym self vnder the Kyng. **1727–46** THOMSON *Summer* 772 A world within itself, Disdaining all assault. **1815** SCOTT *Guy M.* xxxvi, Some efforts..towards building houses *within themselves,* as they are emphatically termed.

(*b*) **1606** SHAKS. *Ant. & Cl.* II. v. 75 Good Madam, keepe your selfe within your selfe.

(*c*) **1738** EARL OXFORD in *Portland Papers* (Hist. MSS. Comm.) VI. 171 The several officers have all within themselves for their use, cook, butler, housekeeper, wash house, laundry, brew house. **1757** [BURKE] *Europ. Settlem. Amer.* VII. xxi. II. 239 They drive a great many cattle from North Carolina..into Virginia, to be slaughtered there; and they kill and salt some beef, and..pork, for the West Indies, within themselves. **1801** *Farmer's Mag.* Aug. 309 They, for the most part, live entirely upon the produce of the farm, and think they do well when they can, (in their own words) 'live within themselves'; that is to say,..without buying any thing. **1824** CARR *Craven Gloss.*, *Within-oursells,* in our possession, without purchase.

(*d*) **1737** BRACKEN *Farriery Impr.* (1757) II. 148 The Sweat will not..appear so plentiful, provided he [*sc.* the horse] is quite run within himself. **1860** WHYTE-MELVILLE *Mkt. Harb.* x. 76 [The horse] going well on his haunches, and quite within himself. **1878** *Month* Aug. 463 They are rowing quite within themselves, in very good time, and have the race in hand.

5. *fig.* In the (inner) being, soul, or mind of. ***within oneself***, spec. (after *say*, *think*, etc.) = in thought, mentally, without outward expression.

c **1000** *Ags. Ps.* (Spelman) cii[i]. 1 Ealle ða ðe wiðinnan me synd [Vulg. *intra me sunt*]. *a* **1240** *Lofsong* in *O.E. Hom.* I. 211 Þi passiun acwenche þe passiun of sunnen þet wunieð wið inne me. *a* **1300** *Cursor M.* 807 Þe find..said wit hin his sari thoght, Ic haue him don to suinc for noght. **1303** R. BRUNNE *Handl. Synne* 326 Þe holy goste ys þe withynne. **1340** *Ayenb.* 153 Huanne þise tuo ziden of þe herte byeþ acorded..þet is þe scele and þet wyl þanne is þe man ordine wyþ-inne him-zelue. **1340–70** *Alex. & Dind.* 338 To ouyr-comen enemis þat arn þe wiþ-inne. **1382** WYCLIF *Matt.* ix. 21 She saide with ynne hir self, ȝif I touche oonly the clothis of hym, I shal be saaf. **1500–20** DUNBAR *Poems* lxix. 22 Hald Hoip and Treuthe within the fast. **1526** TINDALE *Luke* xxiv. 32 Did not oure hertes burne wyth in vs, whyll he talked with vs? **1600** SHAKS. *A.Y.L.* I. i. 24 The spirit of my Father, which I thinke is within mee, begins to mutinie against this seruitude. *a* **1668** LASSELS *Voy. Italy* II. (1698) 118 Laughing within himself. **1748** RICHARDSON *Clarissa* (1768) VI. 217 They will be moved on the slightest occasions, whether those offer from within or without them. **1836** LYTTON *Duchess de La Vallière* III. iii, How sinks my heart within me! **1853** ROCK *Ch. Fathers* II. xii. (1903) IV. 179 The priest prayed—by name, but within himself—for the then pope [etc.]. **1860** HAWTHORNE *Marble Faun* vii. (1865) 55 It irks my brain and heart to think of her, all shut up within herself. **1896** HOUSMAN *Shropsh. Lad* xxx, And fire and ice within me fight Beneath the suffocating night.

6. a. In the limits of (a period of time); most usually, before the end of, after not more than; also, since the beginning of, not more than... ago; or *gen.* between the beginning and end of, in the course of, during. So †***within a word*** = as soon as a word was uttered, at a word.

c **1175** *E.E.* (*Vesp.*) *Hom.* 89 Wiðinnen feower wucan comen [hi] to him. *c* **1205** LAY. 4955 Wið innen a lut ȝeren Brennes hine bi-ðohte. *c* **1290** *Beket* 1500 in *S. Eng. Leg.* 149 Euerech Abbod of greie Monekes to þulke chapitle cam With-Inne þre ȝer. **1303** R. BRUNNE *Handl. Synne* 7047 Sone aftyrward, with-yn a lytyl. **1377** LANGL. *P. Pl.* B. x. 149 He hath wedded a wyf with-Inne þis syx monethes. *c* **1385** CHAUCER *L.G.W.* 103, I fel a-slepe with-Inne an our or two. *c* **1400** MAUNDEV. (Roxb.) xxv. 119 He schall hafe worde within a day and a nyght. **1535** COVERDALE *Acts* i. 5 Ye shalbe baptysed with ye holy goost, & that within this few dayes. **1548** PATTEN *Exped. Scot.* Pref. b v b, How many meanes and weys hath my lord Protectours grace, within his tyme of gouernaunce..attempted..to shonne these warres. **1605** BACON *Adv. Learn.* II. To King §15 Things..which may be done in succession of ages, though not within the houre-glasse of one mans life. **1651** tr. *Kitchin's Jurisd.* (1653) 79 If the Owner do not come within a year and a day. **1757** MRS. GRIFFITH *Lett. Henry & Frances* (1767) IV. 247, I am, within these three Days, recovering Spirits and Appetite. **1822** *Act 3 Geo. IV* c. 39 §1 Within Twenty one Days after the Execution of such Warrant of Attorney. **1869** 'MARK TWAIN' *New Pilgr. Progr.* xi. (1870) 85 The cry went abroad of 'Ten minutes to dress for breakfast!'.. I was dressed within the ten minutes. **1871** FREEMAN *Norm. Conq.* xix. IV. 361 One of which was standing within the present generation. **1918** *Act 8 Geo. V* c. 2 (*title*), The Hours within which Marriages may be lawfully solemnized.

†b. ***within night***: after nightfall. *Obs.*

c **1400** *Laud Troy Bk.* 7894 The day was gon, thei hadde no lyght, For it was wel with-Inne nyght. **1523** LD. BERNERS *Froiss.* (1812) I. cccxl. 533 About two houres within night they armed them. **1632** LITHGOW *Trav.* IV. 142 The last howre of Prayer, is alwayes two or three howres within night. **1685** W. HEDGES *Diary* (Hakl. Soc.) I. 206 We.. arrived..a little within night.

†c. (without reference to limits) At some time during: = IN *prep.* 19. *Obs.*

1471 *Acta Audit.* (1839) 16/1 Þe last court quhen..þe dome was gevin was within feryale tyme onne gude Wednisday in passioun woulk. **1551–2** in Feuillerat *Revels Edw. VI* (1914) 74 Boughte of him within y^e moneth of december. **1599** SHAKS. *Hen. V,* I. ii. 60 King Pharamond.. died within the yeere of our Redemption, Foure hundred twentie six. **1651** tr. *Kitchin's Jurisd.* (1653) 79 He to whom the property is, may take him within the year. [**1850** TENNYSON *In Mem.* xcii, Tho' it spake and bared to view A fact within the coming year.]

d. ***a story within a story*** and varr., a story, performance, etc., complete in itself but occurring within another. Cf. *play within a play* s.v. PLAY *sb.* 14 a.

1961 WEBSTER s.v. *Within,* A musical within a musical. **1971** J. GORES in 'E. Queen' *Magicians of Mystery* (1976) 162 A new kind of procedural detective story..it uses the dream 'story-within-a-story' which antedates even..The Vision of Pierce Plowman. **1976** C. BERMANT *Coming Home* II. ii. 125 A plump, bespectacled woman..grasped him in a tearful embrace. Was this a drama within a drama, a man who had thought he'd lost his wife and would rather that she had stayed lost? **1978** *Listener* 19 Jan. 86/3 Fitzgerald was featured creating one of his..short stories... This device allowed for a film within a film. **1984** B. PAUL *Renewable Virgin* ii. 38 There was some sort of a crime-within-a-crime just waiting to be discovered.

7. a. (*a*) Not beyond or above (a specified or implied amount or degree); at, in, or of less than or not more than; so as not to exceed or surpass; *esp.* (*b*) in expressions of a small difference or margin of error from a larger amount: = with a difference of not more than (so much) above or, usually, below.

1388 WYCLIF *1 Chron.* xxvii. 23 Dauid nolde noumbre hem with ynne twenti ȝeer [1382 fro twenty ȝeer and benethen]. *c* **1400** MAUNDEV. (Roxb.) xxx. 137 Faire damysellz within þe elde of xv. ȝere. *c* **1450** *Mirk's Festial* 290 Wether þei ben cosynnes wythinne degre of mariage or no. **1489** *Acta Audit.* (1839) 131/2 Þe sereffis quhilkis prisit his gudis haid prisit þaim gretly within þe avale of þaim. **1512** *Act 4 Hen. VIII* c. 20 *Preamble,* Beyng of kyn..unto the said John..within the second and third degree. **1727** SWIFT *Let. to very young Lady* Misc. II. 337, I think you ought to be well informed how much your Husband's Revenue amounts to, and be so good a Computer as to keep within it. **1783** LD. PERCY in *G. Rose's Diaries* (1860) I. 58 Being..determined to live within my income. **1851, 1887** [see MARK *sb.*[1] 12 c]. **1885** *Law Rep. 29 Chanc. Div.* 453 The actions were commenced within a few days of each other.

(*b*) **1556** J. HEYWOOD *Spider & F.* lxxvi. 28 Thousands.. are gone..Till all: within fortie, weare flowne quight awaie. **1601** HOLLAND *Pliny* XIII. xv. I. 395 The..diametre..was foure foot within three quarters of an inch. **1606** SHAKS. *Tr. & Cr.* I. ii. 126 He is very yong, and yet will he within three pound lift as much as his brother Hector. **1711** STEELE *Spect.* No. 91 ⁋1 She has a tall Daughter within a Fortnight of Fifteen. **1886** E. C. ROBINS *Temple Sol.* (1887) 15 The extreme length of Solomon's Temple..is made (in his restoration of it) to agree with that of the Temple of Pæstum within 2 inches. **1920** *Conquest* Apr. 168 The unit of electrical current..was obtained..to within one point in 20,000.

†b. ***within age*** = of less than full age, under age. *Obs.*

c **1400** *Pilgr. Sowle* (Caxton) IV. xxxviii. (1859) 64 They.. gouerne hym, ryght as he were to yonge within age. **1450–1530** *Myrr. our Ladye* III. 317 Chyldren..that dye wythin age vncrystened. **1525** LD. BERNERS *Froiss.* (1812) II. ci. [xcvii.] 295 When kynge Rycharde was crowned..he was within age, and a kynge ought nat to gouerne a royalme tyll he be xxi. yeres of age. **1596** BACON *Use Com. Law* iii. (1630) 35 Leauing their heire within age, a Male within 21. and a female within 14. yeares.

c. Not beyond or outside (a specified distance); at or to a distance of less, or not more, than; nearer or not farther away than.

Often in fig. phrases, as ***within an ace, a hair's breadth of.***

c **1440** *Generydes* 3044 As sone as Ermones..Sawe that he was withynne his wepons length, Anon he smote Att hym. **1537** LAYTON in *Lett. Suppr. Monast.* (Camden) 157 Other doctor Lee or I have familier acqwayntance within x. or xij. mylles of hit. **1634** SIR T. HERBERT *Trav.* 25 [We] came within foure degrees of the Æquinoctiall. **1700** T. BROWN tr. *Fresny's Amusem.* 23 The least false Step brings them within an Ace of Death. **1726, 1839** [see INCH *sb.*[1] 2]. **1755, 1767** [see HAIR'S-BREADTH, HAIRBREADTH]. **1794** *Act 34 Geo. III* c. 93 §64 Within the Distance of Ten Yards. **1812** JEFFERSON *Writ.* (1830) IV. 178 Almost within striking distance of each other. **1863** WHYTE-MELVILLE *Gladiators* xxxvii, The German would not permit Esca to approach within spear's-length of his post. **1865** A. TROLLOPE *Belton Estate* xiii, Keeping within a few yards of his sister's chair.

8. a. In expressions referring to the physical range of some action or perception: Not beyond, not farther than the extent of: as ***within call***, near enough to hear a call; ***within reach***, near enough to reach, or to be reached; ***within sight,*** or ***hearing***, near enough to see or hear, to be seen or heard; etc. Often const. *of* (the agent or percipient, or the object of the action or perception). Cf. IN *prep.* 9 d.

a **1533** LD. BERNERS *Huon* lv. 188 He slewe..all that came within his stroke. *a* **1533–** [see SIGHT *sb.*[1] 4 e]. **1580–** [see CANNON-SHOT 3]. **1581** PETTIE tr. *Guazzo's Civ. Conv.* I. (1586) 25 Shoote not at every bird, but onely at those that are within reach to be hit. **1591** SHAKS. *Two Gent.* V. iv. 127 Come not within the measure of my wrath. **1607–** [see EARSHOT]. **1623** MASSINGER *Dk. Milan* IV. iii, Be within call. **1687** PRIOR *Hind. & P. Transv.* 5 Stand off and come not within my Swords point. **1712** ADDISON *Spect.* No. 311 ⁋4 A Man..talking loud within her Hearing. **1766, 1862** [see HEARING *vbl. sb.* 1 b]. **1826** J. F. COOPER *Last of Mohicans* xv, There is also a powerful force within a few hours' march of us. **1856** MRS. CARLYLE *Lett.* II. 280, I will never be 'within wind' of Scotsbrig without going to see Jamie.

b. Inside the guard, defence, or point of; near enough to come to grips with; *Fencing*, on the inside of (one's sword, arm, etc.). Also *fig.* Now *rare* or *Obs.*

156. *Robin Hood, Play* (ed. W. Copland) H ij b, Well I wote the horeson lepte within me And fro me he toke my purse. **1589** P. IVE *Fortif.* 105 The Spanyards with their Targets entred within our Switzers, under their Pikes, and constrained them to forsake their Pikes. **1590** SHAKS. *Com. Err.* V. i. 34 Some get within him, take his sword away. *a* **1697** SOUTH *Serm., Rom. i. 32* II. 256 When by such Insinuations they have once got within him, and are able to drill him on from one Lewdness to another. **1707** SIR W. HOPE *New Method Fencing* 99 The Single Feint within and above the Sword, called in the Schools *Volte Coupé.* **1711** STEELE *Spect.* No. 109 ⁋3 He came within the Target of the Gentleman who rode against him. **1809** ROLAND *Fencing* 34 When, upon joining blades with your adversary, you find your sword in a line between his sword-arm and the left side of his body..it is termed being within the arm. **1876** R. F. BURTON *New Syst. Sword Exerc.* 52 When the point is passed well under and within the sword-arm.

9. *fig.* In the extent of (something abstract figured as a region, or as having extension); *esp.* in, or not beyond, the scope or sphere of action of (authority, power, knowledge, a law, etc.). Cf. IN *prep.* 8, 9 d.

1493 *Acta Dom. Conc.* (1839) 272/2 He wes within our souerane lordis warde. **1512** *Act 4 Hen. VIII* c. 2 §1 Suche as ben within holy orders only excepte. **1560** DAUS tr. *Sleidane's Comm.* 38 Wythin hys jurisdiction. **1599** SHAKS. *Hen. V,* I. ii. 289 But this lyes all within the wil of God. **1610** B. JONSON *Alch.* I. i, You will bring him in Within the statute? **1643** [see SPHERE *sb.* 6 b]. *a* **1648** LD. HERBERT *Hen. VIII* (1683) 357 That none should have the benefit of this recourse to the Ordinary, but those who were within holy Orders. *a* **1654** SELDEN *Table-t.* (Arb.) 88 Eat within your Stomack, act within your Commission. **1710** STEELE *Tatler* No. 201 ⁋1 As they live within Rules, and as they transgress them. **1769** BLACKSTONE *Comm.* IV. xxviii. 365 Within the benefit of clergy. **1820** *Broderip & Bingham's Rep.* I. 436 Whether the party was a trader within the bankrupt laws. **1823** SCOTT *Quentin D.* viii, Who..will assert that..their place of retirement is within my knowledge? **1862** SPENCER *First Princ.* I. ii. §14. 43 Even..Atheism comes within the definition. **1869** FREEMAN *Norm. Conq.* xiii. III. 288 Did they deem the enterprise within his power? **1891** *Law Times' Rep.* LXIII. 776/1 The contract and the label together constituted a written warranty within the meaning of the above section.

C. *adj.* That is within; †(of a letter or document) enclosed. *rare.*

1748 RICHARDSON *Clarissa* (1768) III. 258 This is a favour you'll see by the within Letter. *a* **1766** MRS. F. SHERIDAN *Sidney Bidulph* IV. 233 Give him the within letter. **1794** *Bloomfield's Rep.* 11 Agreeably to the command of the within Writ. **1806** GEN. WILKINSON in Coues *Exped. Z. M. Pike* (1895) II. 574 You will not fail, in addition to the within talk, to enhance our paternal regard for this nation.

D. *Comb.* **a.** of the adv.; in quots. in sense 1 c, as †***within-bounden, within-named*** adjs. **b.** of the prep.: **within-bound** *a.* (*nonce-wd.*), confined or experienced within bounds (in a school).

1498 *Cov. Leet Bk.* 593 The condicion of þis obligacion is such that whereas certayn trauers is dependyng betwixt þe withinbounden Maire & Cominalte on the on partie and þe priour & Couent..on þe oþer partie [etc.]. **1570** in G. F. Townsend *Leominster* (n.d.) 300 The wthin-named John Ingle. **1706** De Foe *True Relat.* Pref., Wks. (1889) 436 The house in which the within-named Mrs. Bargrave lived. **1708** *Rec. Stitchill* (S.H.S. 1905) 159 The within-designed George Hamilton. **1834** Chitty *Forms* 165 As well the within-named plaintiff as the within-named defendant. **1839** W. Howitt *Boy's Country-Bk.* xvi. 227 What are all their within-bound enjoyments..to their monthly rural walks? **1844** A. B. Corner *Forms of Writs*, etc. 43 To be indorsed 'By Rule of Court,' (if so). At the instance of the within-named Appellants (or Respondents).

within (wɪˈðɪn), *sb.* [f. the adv.] That which is within or inside (esp. *fig.*).

1912 J. Stephens *Crock of Gold* xiii. 166 It [*sc.* anger] is not the beneficent blindness which prevents one from seeing without, but it is that desperate darkness which cloaks the within, and hides the heart and the brain from each other's husbandly and wifely recognition. **1938** L. MacNeice *Mod. Poetry* 28 Wyndham Lewis maintains that it is the artist's or writer's business to depict the Without of people and not their Within. **1973** *Times* 26 Nov. 15/8 Having every intention of looking again and again before the exhibition finally departs for its permanent home in the 'Great Within', or wherever—I feel I must compliment the compilers of the excellent catalogue.

wiˈthin-ˌdoor, *adv. phr.* (*a.*) Now *rare.* [See door *sb.* 5.] = next.

speak within door: 'do not clamour so as to be heard beyond the house' (J.).

1579 Gosson *Sch. Abuse* (Arb.) 31 Him..that hath a Conduite within doore, and fetcheth water without. **1604** Shaks. *Oth.* iv. ii. 144 Speake within doore. **1625** Bacon *Ess., Greatn. Kingd.* (Arb.) 481 Sedentary, and Within-doore [*ed.* 1612 within-doores] Arts. **1649** C. Wase *Sophocles, Electra* 4 Methinks within door,..I seemd to heare One of the maidens keep a groaning. **1821** Lamb *Elia* Ser. i. *Old Benchers*, I suspect he had his within-door reasons for the preference. **1884** Tennyson *Becket* i. i. 35 They [*sc.* moths] burn themselves *within*-door. **1954** M. Sharp *Gipsy in Parlour* xxi. 200 All female within-door work had been properly done.

wiˈthin(-)ˌdoors, *adv. phr.* (*adj., sb.*) *arch.* In (or into) the house: = indoors.

1581 Mulcaster *Positions* viii. (1888) 53 One to be vsed within dores, and the other abroade. *a* **1690** in Somers *Tracts* (1748) I. 264 It seems..odd..that [he] should..make his final Appeal to the People, before he had tried the Force of one of his Reasons within-doors. **1789** S. Shaw *Tour W. Eng.* 459 Rain confined us within doors several hours. **1842** Dickens *Amer. Notes* iii, All within-doors is very plain and simple. **1858** Hawthorne *Fr. & It. Jrnls.* (1871) II. 266 An English coal-fire, if we could see its honest face within doors, would compensate for all the unamiableness of the outside atmosphere. **1884** Black *Jud. Shakespeare* vi, Judith's father would have no serving-men..come within-doors. **1895** Hardy *Jude the Obscure* i. ii, An animated conversation in progress within-doors.

b. (with hyphen) †*attrib.* or as *adj.* = indoor 1; also as *sb.* that which is, or those who are, indoors.

1612 [see prec., quot. 1625]. **1630** *R. Johnson's Kingd. & Commw.* 29 That there be more addicted to arts manly, than unto sedentary and within-doores occupations. **1858** Hawthorne *Fr. & It. Note-bks.* II. 286 All the within-doors of the village empties itself there.

† **wiˈthinforth**, *adv. Obs.* Also with hyphen, or as two words (variously divided), or as three. [f. within *adv.* + forth *adv.* Cf. *withoutforth.*]

Properly, everywhere within, internally throughout (see forth *adv.* 2 b); but in use a mere synonym of *within*: = within *adv.* 1, 2, 3.

c **1374** Chaucer *Boeth.* v. pr. v. (1868) 168 Þe passioun of þe body..moeueþ..þe formes þat resten wiþ in forþe. **1382** Wyclif *Ezek.* ii. 9 A boke..writen withinforth and without-forth. *c* **1425** *St. Mary of Oignies* ii. i. in *Anglia* VIII. 151/3 Wiþ how mykel dyuerste of vertues she was arayed..wiþ-inforþe. **1467** in *Engl. Gilds* (1870) 373 That no citezen sewe another in a foreyn courte vnto the tyme he take his accyon wtynforth. **1470–85** Malory *Arthur* xx. xxii. 836 They withinforth kepte theyr walles, & deffended them whan nede was. **1526** *Pilgr. Perf.* (W. de W. 1531) 78 b, Wene you..that it is with me withinforth, as it appereth outwardly? **1545** Raynalde *Byrth Mankynde* 135 It is so harde to cause a chylde to take any thyng within furth. **1548** Udall *Erasm. Par. Luke* xi. 43 Ye outwardely beare a shewe of holynesse, yet..withinfoorth swell in ambicion. **1601** Holland *Pliny* xxi. xiv. II. 95 The..lid..ought to..have libertie to play up and downe behind, that it may be let downe farre within-forth. **1610** —— *Camden's Brit.* 102 The Romanes..when they were about to found..cities..yoked on the right hand a Bull, and within forth a Cow.

wiˈthinside, *adv., prep.,* (*sb.*). Now *arch.* or *dial.* (Also with hyphen, or rarely as two words.) [f. within + side *sb.*[1], after *inside.*] **A.** *adv.*

1. On the inner side: = inside *adv.* 1, within *adv.* 1 (in part). Also const. *of.*

a **1595** Southwell *Hundred Medit.* (1873) 70 The windows..were wider..withinside than without. **1651** French *Distill.* i. 38 The salt..which adheres to the neck of the Retort withinside. **1731** Miller *Gard. Dict.* s.v. *Greenhouse*, Within-side of the Windows..you should have good strong Shutters. **1772** Graves *Spir. Quix.* iv. xii, A small oval picture,..fixed in a pannel, within-side of the door. **1800** T. Green *Diary Lover Lit.* (1810) 204 He employs..the illustration of a man withinside, and another withoutside, of a sphere, disputing on its convexity or concavity. *c* **1850** *Rudim. Navig.* (Weale) 154 *String*, one or two planks withinside, next under the gunwale, answering to the sheer-strakes withoutside.

2. In (or to) the inner part or interior (*of*): = inside *adv.* 2, within *adv.* 1 (in part), 1 b, 1 d. Also, indoors: = within *adv.* 2 b.

1598 Barret *Theor. Warres* v. i. 126 Cauallero, or a mount withinside distant from the curtine. **1712** Steele *Spect.* No. 533 ¶2 What passes..within-side of those Vehicles. *a* **1723** Sir C. Wren in Lucy Phillimore *Mem.* (1881) 347 A Basis of squar'd stone fifty foot high..so contrived within-side as to form a very intricate Labyrinth. *a* **1774** Goldsm. *Surv. Exp. Philos.* (1776) I. 389 The diver..sate upon a small seat within-side. **1774** —— *Nat. Hist.* (1862) I. vi. xi. 464 The porcupine's quill is within-side spongy. **1801** Maria Edgeworth *Irish Bulls* vii, The imprudence of firing at the door of a house without having previously examined whether any one was withinside. **1806** R. Cumberland *Mem.* (1807) II. 153 An edifice, that requires a day to examine it within side and without. *Ibid.* 397 A gaudy equipage will attract notice, though it shall carry a dull company withinside of it. **1807** Southey *Espriella's Lett.* xxxvii. (1808) II. 78 We meant..to have forsaken the roof and taken our seats within-side. **1889** Stevenson *Master of Ballantrae* x. 260 My gentleman sat withinside tailor-wise and busily stitching.

3. *fig.* Within the limits *of.*

1856 J. Grote in *Cambr. Ess.* 104 The classical range is restricted withinside of Greek and Latin literature.

B. *prep.* = inside *prep.*

1. On the inner side of: = within *prep.* 1 b, d.

1760–72 H. Brooke *Fool of Qual.* (1809) III. 99 The stake..they run up withinside the spinal bone. *a* **1766** Mrs. F. Sheridan *Nourjahad* (1767) 25 It was within-side the walls of the temple. **1851** Borrow *Lavengro* xcix. (1893) 398 Various evolutions withinside the pale. **1852** Thackeray *Esmond* i. ix, Holiday music from within-side a prison wall.

2. In the inner part of: = within *prep.* 1.

1686 Plot *Staffordsh.* 198 Why may not these imperfect Metalls..grow..withoutside the stalks of Gorse, as well as the perfect both without and withinside other plants? **1782** Eliz. Blower *Geo. Bateman* II. 200 Permit her to stay within-side the house. **1815** Jane Austen *Emma* I. x, Harriet..had never..been within side the Vicarage. **1849** De Quincey *Engl. Mail Coach* Wks. 1863 IV. 348 *note*, Graves within-side the cathedrals.

†**C.** *sb.* The inner side: = inside *sb.* 1. *Obs. rare.*

a **1814** *Bandit* ii. in *New Brit. Theatre* I. 409 She fastens the within-side.

So **wiˈthinsides** *adv. arch.* or *dial.*

1891 Stevenson *Island Nts.' Entert., Bottle Imp* (1893) 154 Withinsides something obscurely moved. *a* **1894** —— *Fables* xviii. *Touchstone*, His soul withinsides was as little as a pea. **1910** Kipling *Rewards & Fairies* 74 That thought shrivelled me withinsides.

wiˈthinward, -wards, *advs. nonce-wds.* [f. within + -ward, -wards.] Towards the interior.

1611 Florio, *Adintra*, from within, withinward [Torriano (1659) from within-ward]. **1865** J. Grote *Explor. Philos.* i. 8 The communication being only withinwards from without, and not..withoutwards from within.

with-it (ˈwɪðɪt), *a. slang.* [f. vbl. phr. *to be with it*: see with *prep.* 22 f.] Fashionable, up-to-date.

1962 *Listener* 29 Nov. 909/2 Curtain designs for the really with-it 'contemporary home'. **1963** [see far-out *a.* b]. **1970** J. G. Vermandel *Dine with Devil* ix. 52 The with-it Mr. Angel enjoyed a more subtle turn of mind. **1977** J. I. M. Stewart *Madonna of Astrolabe* v. 94 The silly woman just thought it a with-it thing to say to a celebrated dramatist.

Hence **ˈwith-it-ness**.

1963 *Punch* 22 May 752/1 The headlong rush of..social notabilities to win themselves the TW badge of with-it-ness. *a* **1974** R. Crossman *Diaries* (1976) II. 445 This has all paid off in terms of the audience ratings where the B.B.C. has been doing well in the last six months, winning the battle for the audience by its with-itness.

withlich, obs. form of wightly *adv.*

withnay: see with-.

withness (ˈwɪðnɪs). *rare.* [f. with *prep.* + -ness.] The fact of being with some one or something; collocation, association.

1904 W. James *Ess. Rad. Empiricism* (1912) ii. 47 This imperfect intimacy, this bare relation of *withness* between some parts of the sum total of experience and other parts. **1907** W. James *Pragmatism* iv. 156 The lowest grade of universe would be a world of mere *withness.* **1912** *Contemp. Rev.* Jan. 99 This Withness, Together-witness, association,..brings us into the interior of the plan of the creation. **1929** A. N. Whitehead *Process & Reality* ii. ii. 88 The account..traces back these secondary qualities to their root in physical prehensions expressed by the 'witness of the body'. **1946** *Sci. & Society* X. 244 Conversely union and withness, the *ta-tong* of Chinese thought, has been the aim of democracies. **1962** *Times* 11 Dec. 11/4 The 'withness' is all.

withnim: see with-.

without (wɪˈðaʊt), *adv., prep., conj.* Forms (2–5 written as one or as two words): *α.* **wiðˑ, wiþutan,** 2–4 **wiþ-, withuten,** 3–5 **wiþouten,** etc. (see with and outen *adv.*), 4–6, 7–9 *arch.* **withouten;** also 3 **-utene, -utin,** 4–5 **-owtten(e,** 5 **-oughten, -owghten, -outene, -yn(e,** etc.; *abbreviated* 5 **wtouton, wtowtyn.** *β.* 2–4 **wiþute,** 3–4 **witute,** 3–6 **withoute,** (3 **widh wute, wiþ houte,** 4 **wit out(t)e,** 5 **witheoute),** etc. (cf. oute *adv.*); *abbreviated* 4, 6 **wt oute,** 5 **wtowte, wtou3te.** *γ.* 3 **wiþ vt,** 4–5 **wiþout,** etc. (see with and out *adv.*), 4– **without;** *abbreviated* 5–6 **wtout,** 5 **wtou3t, wtwt,** 6, 8 **w̄out,** 7 **wthout.** [Late OE. *wiþútan*, f. *wiþ* with *prep.* + *útan* outen *adv.*: see within.] **A.** *adv.*

I. Outside, in various senses: opp. to within *adv.* Now only *literary* and somewhat *arch.*

For instances of the ellipsis of the object of the prep., in which *without* has the appearance of an adv., and may be so construed, see B. 4 and 14.

1. On the outside or outer surface (of a material thing); externally.

c **1000** Ælfric *Hom.* I. 86 His lichama bærn wiðutan mid langsumere hætan. *c* **1250** *Gen. & Ex.* 3828 On a wond Wið-uten ðo wrot he wið hond Ðe twelfte names of ðat kin. **1340** Hampole *Pr. Consc.* 8047 A vesselle dypped..In water..Has water bath with-in and with-out. **1398** Trevisa *Barth. De P.R.* xvii. vii. (1495) N vj/2 A Rede..is..smothe wythout & holow within. **1419** in *Proc. Privy Council* (1834) II. 247 They were endosid wiþoutyn to suche persones as us liste assigne. *a* **1425** *Cursor M.* 17347 (Trin.) Þei..shutte þe dores at þe last Wiþinne & wiþoute loken so. **14..** *Why I can't be a Nun* 180 in *E.E.P.* (1862) 143 Hyt schyned wythe-owte so fayre and clere. **1596** Shaks. *Tam. Shr.* iv. i. 52 Be the Iackes faire within, the Gils faire with-out? **1611** Coryat *Crudities* 85 The Dukes Palace seemeth to be faire, but I was not in it, onely I saw it without. **1621** T. Williamson tr. *Goulart's Wise Vieillard* 82 The Images called Silenes, which a farre off, and without appeared to bee grossely carued. **1626** Bacon *Sylva* § 505 It is an ordinary Curiosity, to Forme Trees and Shrubs..into Sundry Shapes; which is done by Moulding them within, and Cutting them without. **1797** [see within A. 1].

2. a. Outside (or out of) the place mentioned or implied; *esp.* outside the house or room; out of doors.

a **1100** in Assmann *Ags. Hom.* xvi. 126 Þæt ðær ʒelamp, þæt hiʒ ealle in on þa burh foron, þæt ðær nan þyng þæs folces wyðutan belyfen næs. *c* **1100** *O.E. Chron.* (MS.F.) an. 992 Man scolde fandian ʒif man mihte betræppan þane here ahwar wiþutan. *c* **1205** Lay. 12562 Bruttes weoren wið innen..& Melga wið vten. *a* **1300** *Cursor M.* 996 A firin wall þar es a-bute, Mai nan win in þat es wit-oute. *Ibid.* 15082 'Welcum be þou lauerd', said þai, 'Duell þou noght wit-vte.' *c* **1380** *Sir Ferumb.* 2240 Naymes þanne with-oute ʒede & hadde þe kyng wiþ-inne. *c* **1400** Maundev. (Roxb.) v. 17 Fra þis citee til a hill withoute bare Sampson..þe ʒates of þe citee. **1526** Tindale *Matt.* xii. 47 Behold thy moder and thy brethren stond without. **1535** Coverdale *2 Kings* x. 24 Whan they came in to offer sacrifyces.., Iehu appoynted him foure score men without. **1654** Sir A. Johnston (Ld. Wariston) *Diary* (S.H.S.) II. 300 They wer al sett in the feilds, but M. J. L. absolutely refused to preach without. **1684** Bunyan *Pilgr.* ii. (1900) 175 All this time poor Mercy did stand without, trembling and crying for fear that she was rejected. **1749** Fielding *Tom Jones* x. iii, There is a Footman without with the Horses. **1768** Goldsm. *Goodn. Man* v, *Jar*...I'll go hasten things without. **1849** Macaulay *Hist. Eng.* x. II. 562 Meanwhile the throng without was..becoming more numerous and more savage. **1890** Bridges *Spring* ii. viii, When winds without make moan, I love my own fireside. **1892** Zangwill *Childr. Ghetto* i. xv, Pinchas..betook himself unceremoniously without.

b. *transf.* Outside of a class, body, or community; not in the number or membership; in an alien or foreign community. **those** (**that are**) **without** = 'outsiders'. Now only in echoes of *1 Cor.* v. 12.

1297 R. Glouc. (Rolls) 3024 Þe king..let rere up chirchen & to al þat lond aboute, & bissopes dude in hor poer, þat er were al wiþoute. ? *a* **1300** in *O.E. Misc.* 146/34, xxxij. schiren syndan on engelonde. And Norþhumbre is wiþ-vtan And loðen and westmaralond and Cumberlond And Cornwale. **1525** Ld. Berners *Froiss.* (1812) II. lxxiv. [lxx.] 224 The pryse was gyuen of them without, to syr Johne Holande. **1526** Tindale *1 Cor.* v. 12 What have I to do to iudge them that are with out? Do ye not iudge them that are with in? **1535** Coverdale *Deut.* xxv. 5 Then shall not ye wife of the deed take a straunge man without, but hir kynsman shal..take her to wyfe. **1676** W. Allen *Addr. Nonconf.* 67 The breaking the Churches Peace..and the bad effects of it, both among themselves and in reference to them without. **1846** Mrs. A. Marsh *Fr. Darcy* xxxix, The secrets of my trade..are not to be lightly communicated to those who are without. **1864** Pusey *Daniel* (1876) 300 To win those without to live according to the law.

3. *fig.* and *gen.* Outside of the inward being, soul, or mind; with regard to external actions or circumstances; in relation to others or to something other than the self; sometimes, in outward appearance as opposed to inward reality; outwardly.

c **1000** Ælfric *Hom.* II. 404 Swa sind ʒe eac æteowode wiðutan rihtwise on manna ʒesihðum. *a* **1225** *Ancr. R.* 4 Þe oðer riwle is al wiðuten, & riwleð þe licome & licomliche deden. **1340** *Ayenb.* 25 Ypocrisye..is a ʒenne þet makeþ to ssewy þe guod wyþoute þet ne is naʒt wyþinne. *a* **1400** *Relig. Pieces fr. Thornton MS.* (1914) 54 How þay sall bere þam with-owtten and with-in; howe to God, how to man. *c* **1400** Maundev. (Roxb.) xxvi. 123 Ne þare schuld na man luffe a creature for þe bewtee withouten. **1502** *Ord. Crysten Men* (W. de W.) i. iii, Some thynges they make in operacyon wythout all onely, the whiche thynges are not in the soule materyally. **1560** *Bible* (Geneva) 2 Cor. vii. 5 We were troubled on euerie side, fightings without, & terrours within. **1607** Grimestone tr. *Goulart's Admir. Hist.* 392 Rage..may..haue inward beginnings, without any accidentall contagion without. **1653** Bogan *Medit. Mirth Chr. Life* 209 When (for ought a man can see) by his countenance without, a godly man may be sad, and melancholick, and perplexed. **1692** E. Walker tr. *Epictetus' Mor.* xxvi, An injury To something else without, 'tis none to thee. **1832** Ht. Martineau *Hill & Valley* v. 84 Then you will be at ease without and at peace within. **1855** G. Macdonald (*title*) Within and Without: a dramatic poem.

4. Preceded by *from*, in above senses.

a **1400–50** *Wars Alex.* 1032 'Ʒe Calodoyns',..he callis fra with-oute. **1645–** [see within *adv.* 4]. **1722** Wollaston

Relig. Nat. ix. 190 The hints I received from without. **1768** Goldsm. *Good-nat. Man* v, He who seeks only for applause from without, has all his happiness in another's keeping. **1848** Dickens *Dombey* xxxvi, Doors opened smartly from without. **1849** Macaulay *Hist. Eng.* v. I. 548 An independent state, jealous of all interference from without. **1898** Illingworth *Div. Imman.* vi. 137 The man loses his power of self-determination, . . and is . . determined from without.

B. *prep.*

I. Outside of, beyond (in various senses): opp. to WITHIN *prep.* Now only *literary* or *arch.*

1. a. Outside of, on or at the outside of, in the space external to (a space, region, place, receptacle, inclosing boundary, etc.).

without board (Naut.): see BOARD *sb.* 12. See also WITHOUT DOOR(s below.

c **893** Ælfred *Oros.* II. iv. §7 Wiðutan þæm dice is ȝeworht tweȝea elna heah weall. *a* **1122** *O.E. Chron.* (Laud MS.) an. 1079 Se cyng Willelm ȝefeaht toȝeanes his sunu Rotbearde wiðutan Normandiȝe. *c* **1205** [see BOARD *sb.* 12]. *c* **1250** *Gen. & Ex.* 1367 At a welle wið-uten ðe tun. *c* **1375** *Cursor M.* 8196 (Fairf.) Ilkan to sette þaire pauylion . . wiþ-out [*Cott.* vtewit] þe toun. *c* **1400** *Rule St. Benet* (prose) 31 Obied widvten þe kirke dore to þe vre be sungen. **1410** *E.E. Wills* (1882) 16 The Cherch of seynt Clementis wyth-owtyn Templebarr. *a* **1425** *Cursor M.* 10989 (Trin.) þe folke þat were þe chirche wiþoute Wondride what he was aboute. **1426** *Cov. Leet Bk.* 111 As well withoute house as within. **1496** *Naval Acc. Hen. VII* (1896) 176 To pyche the said shipp without borde. **1497** *Ibid.* 250 Abourde the Regent withoute Portesmouth haven. **1571** Jewel *Def. Apol.* 711 No Bishop maie geeue orders without his owne Diocese. *a* **1572** Knox *Hist. Ref.* Wks. 1846 I. 205 Thare fell a schour of rane, . . so vehement, that no man mycht abyd without a house. **1632** Lithgow *Trav.* III. 94 A little Chappell a mile without the Village. *a* **1676** Hale *Prim. Orig. Man.* I. i. (1677) 20 We cannot know . . whether there be any Worlds without the compass of this. **1717** Berkeley *Jrnl. Tour Italy* Wks. 1871 IV. 530 The church of S[t.] Agnes without the City. **1745** *Kent's Lond. Directory* 83 Snow Thomas & Comp. Bankers, without Temple-bar. **1827** Hallam *Const. Hist.* xviii. II. 727 The Irish language was universally spoken without the pale. **1869** Tyndall *Notes Lect. Light* §292 The rays of greatest heat . . lie entirely without the visible spectrum. **1885** *Act 48 Vict.* c. 15. Sched. II. 2 A parish . . situate partly within and partly without the boundary.

b. (with verb of motion) So as to be outside of, to the outside of, out of. *Obs.* or *arch.*

c **1000** *Ags. Gosp.* Matt. xxi. 39 Ða namon hiȝ & ofsloȝon hyne & awurpon wið-utan þone win-ȝeard. *c* **1290** *Beket* 2226 in *S. Eng. Leg.* 170 With-oute þe ȝates ne cam he nouȝt. **1387** Trevisa *Higden* III. 91 Nabugodonosor . . slowȝ alle the strong men, . . and þrewe hem wiþ outen þe walles vnburied. *a* **1450** *Knt. de la Tour* 45 She yede without her place crieng on God. **1464–5** in *Acts Parl. Scot.* (1874) XII. 30/2 Sendand woll . . fra quhatsumeuir port . . within þe Realme of Scotland wtw[t] þe samyn Realme. **1889** Stevenson *Master of Ballantrae* xii. 317 He led me without the camp.

c. On the outer side of; further out than; (in or to the space) beyond. (Cf. WITHIN B. 1 d.)

1623 Bingham *Xenophon* 18 All the middest of his battell . . was extended without the left Wing of Cyrus his Troopes. **1712** W. Rogers *Voy.* (1718) 5 When I came without the Spit-end, I saluted the Hastings. **1777** W. Dalrymple *Trav. Sp. & Port.* xliii, The rest of the court form in a second circle without the ambassadors. **1779** Forrest *Voy. N. Guinea* 122 Off the rock of Sipsapa, are three spots of breakers, . . one without another. **1867** Smyth *Sailor's Word-bk.* 736 *Without*, outside, as, studding-sail without studding-sail.

†**d.** At more than, beyond (a specified distance).

1724 *Lond. Gaz.* No. 6290/3 To begin to Work without 70 Yards Distance from the Shoar.

2. *transf.* and *fig.* Outside of, not in the limits of, external(ly) to.

1028–60 *Laws Northumb. Priests* §61 þæt nan man ne wifiȝe on neahsibban men þonne wiðutan þam IIII. cneowe. **1357** *Lay Folks' Catech.* (T.) 105 Withouten halikirke nis na saule hele. *c* **1375** *Cursor M.* 13166 (Fairf.) Nauþer I aske þe hous ne lande Ne nane oþer þing wiþ-oute resoun [*Cott.* wit vnresun]. *c* **1400** *Rule St. Benet* (prose) 17 Ilke sunday widuten lentin sal þe cantikils be said. *c* **1450** Capgrave *Life St. Gilbert* vii, Whan he was vexed with ony materis, eythir with-oute þe religion or with-Inne. **1558** Knox *First Blast* (Arb.) 45 It was forbidden vnto them to marie without their owne tribe. **1618** Wither *Motto, Nec Curo* Juvenilia (1633) 544 He that beares an honest heart about him, Needs never feare what changes be without him. **1694** Stanhope *Epictetus' Morals* i. 11 The Object that moves our Affection, is without us. **1705** —— *Paraphr.* II. 138 Some [reasons] are without the compass of my present design. **1877** Sparrow *Serm.* xiv. 190 One whose sources of happiness are without him.

†**b.** So as to exceed; beyond. *Obs.*

The phr. ***without measure*** (= F. *sans* or *outre mesure*), 'immoderate(ly)', 'excessive(ly)', belongs here or under 10 a.

c **1400** [see MEASURE *sb.* 12 b]. *c* **1520** Skelton *Magnyf.* 1895 Somtyme without Measure he trusted in golde; And now without Measure he shal haue hunger and colde. *c* **1610** *Women Saints* (1886) 63 Beating and bouncing her without all measure.

†**3. a.** Beyond the extent of, outside the range of (some action or perception); beyond the scope or sphere of action of. *Obs.*

For *without comparison*, etc. see 10 d.

a **1548** [see REACH *sb.*[1] 5 b]. **1551** Turner *Herbal* I. Prol. A ij b, He beynge without the danger of gonne shot. **1577** Googe *Heresbach's Husb.* III. 151 b, Though it be without my commission to meddle with them. **1605** Bacon *Adv. Learn.* II. xxii. §3 Two thynges are without our commaund: Poyntes of Nature, and pointes of Fortune. *a* **1676** Hale *Prim. Orig. Man.* I. iii. (1677) 91 Conjectures of things without our knowledge. **1770** Sir J. Reynolds *Disc.* iii. (1876) 332 Beauties in our art that seem . . to lie without the reach of precept. **1809** Kendall *Trav.* I. vii. 70 The happy consequences . . are without description. **1809** *Levity & Sorrow* II. 221 To witness the elements jarring from above, and without their reach.

†**b.** Beyond the capacity or comprehension of (= BEYOND B. 5 b); outside the province of. *Obs.*

1599 B. Jonson *Cynthia's Rev.* I. iv, Oh, now I apprehend you; your phrase was without me before. **1603** —— *Sejanus* II. i, The ages that succeede . . shall admire And reckon it an act, without your Sexe.

4. Used *absol.* by ellipsis of obj., in opposition to *within* (or *in*) prep., where it has the appearance of an adv.

a **1300** *Cursor M.* 5933 Bath in huses and wit-vte. *c* **1300** *K. Horn* 256 (Laud) Wit hinne þe curt and wit oute. **1480** in *Cov. Leet Bk.* 446 Placez within the shire of Couentre & withoute. **1587** A. Fleming *Contn. Holinshed* III. 1399/1 Aliances either in Italie or without. **1830** Carlyle *Misc. Ess.*, *Richter again* (1872) III. 11 Is not God's Universe within our head, whether there be a torn skull-cap or a king's diadem without?

II. Senses intermediate between I. and III.

†**5.** In addition to, or with the addition of; besides. *Obs.*

c **1205** Lay. 366 We habbeð seoue þusund of gode cnihten, wið outen wifmen. **1297** R. Glouc. (Rolls) 4107 An hondred þousend hors . . Wiþ oute votmen þat were so vale þat þer nas of non ende. **1338** R. Brunne *Chron.* (1810) 54 With-outen alle þis a hundreth knyghtes he toke. *c* **1386** Chaucer *Prol.* 461 Housbondes . . she hadde fyue Withouten oother compaignye in youthe. **1387** Trevisa *Higden* VI. 93 Wiþ oute þe ful service he wolde every day seie þe sawter. **1436** in *Rep. Hist. MSS. Comm.* Var. Collect. IV. 197 There ys redy . . iiij[c] shippes of forstage wythoute other smal shipes. **1535** Coverdale *Isa.* xlv. 14 God (with out whom there is none other God).

†**6.** Exclusive of, not including, except. *Obs.*

c **1000** *Sax. Leechd.* I. 378 Nim . . þa wyrtas wærma, alla wiðutan sauina. *c* **1250** *Gen. & Ex.* 557 A flod . . ouerflowȝed men & deres kin, Wið-vten noe and hise ðre sunen. *c* **1300** *Havelok* 425 Godard was . . þe moste swike, þat eure in erþe shaped was, With-uten on, þe wike Iudas. *c* **1320** in *Rel. Ant.* I. 119 He wes the fayrest mon, With-outen Absolon, That seththe wes ant tho.

III. Expressing absence, privation, or negation: With or involving the absence or want of; in a state of not having, or so as not to have; so, or such, that there is no . . . Opp. to WITH *prep.* II ***. (The ordinary current use.)

7. a. (*a*) (with obj. a thing, material or immaterial) With absence of; not with the presence or addition of; not having with it or with one; not accompanied by; not combined or associated with; not having in one's charge; not carrying or wearing.

c **1200** Ormin 997 Bræd all þeorrf wiþþutenn berrme. **12..** *Prov. Alfred* 119 Wyþvte wysdome is weole wel vnwurþ. *a* **1352** Minot *Poems* (ed. Hall) vii. 138 Bisschoppes . . þat songen all withouten stole. **1382** Wyclif *Luke* xxii. 35 Whanne I sente ȝou with oute sachel and scrip, and schoon. **1393** Langl. *P. Pl.* C. XXI. 10 Barfot on an asse back, bootles . . With-oute spores oþer spere. **1426** Audelay *Poems* 15 Wele withoutyn woo. **1546** J. Heywood *Prov.* II. v. (1867) 57 There is no fyre without some smoke. **1565** Golding *Ovid's Met.* III. (1593) 68 A spring withouten mud as silver cleere. **1600** Nashe *Summer's Last Will* 16, I . . vse to go without money, without garters, without girdle. **1744** Berkeley *Siris* §196 Phosphorus burns equally, with and without air. **1864** Bryce *Holy Rom. Emp.* xvi. (1875) 276 A barbarism which had inherited all the vices of civilization without any of its virtues.

†(*b*) Less, minus (a certain amount). *Obs.*

c **1450** *Godstow Reg.* 435 In brede xiiij. elnys with out ynche.

b. (with obj. a person) In the absence of; in a state of absence from; not with the companionship or attendance of.

c **1385** Chaucer *L.G.W.* 969 *Dido*, Forth they gon . . His fere & he with-outyn any gyde. *c* **1450** tr. *De Imitatione* II. viii. 48 What may þe worlde auaile þe wiþoute ihesu? **1491** *Cartul. S. Nicholai Aberdon.* (New Spald. Cl.) I. 256 Nay mess salbe songit Withoutin xij personis and ye prest. *a* **1548** Hall *Chron.*, *14 Hen. VII*, 49 He . . began secretly to commen without any witnesses or arbitrers nere hond with the bishop alone. **1656** Stanley *Hist. Philos.*, *Plato* 33 He counsel'd Dionysius to give over the Tyranny, and live with-out a Guard. **1685** Lady R. Russell *Lett.* (1853) I. 165 Doubtless he is at rest, though I find none without him. **1750** Johnson *Rambler* No. 6 ¶11 Those to whom he has formerly been known will very patiently support his absence when they have tried a little to live without him. **1877** Mrs. Argles *Phyllis* xxvii. (1890) 337 If you can live without me, . . I would rather ten thousand times be dead, than exist without you.

c. ***without-profit***(*s*) adj., of a life assurance policy: providing normal cover but not allowing the insured to receive a share of the profits of the insurance company. Also applied to the associated funds, business, etc. Cf. *with profit*(*s*) adj. s.v. WITH *prep.* 24 d.

1924, **1944** [see WITH *prep.* (*adv.*, *conj.*) 24 d]. **1960** *Times* 24 Oct. (Financial Rev.) p. xiii/4 For without-profits contracts are tending to come down. **1965** *Economist* 24 July p. xxii, When interest rates are high and there is significant inflation, profits on the without-profits businesses are high, since the premiums were originally fixed on the basis of lower money returns than are now being earned. **1982** *London Life Association Ann. Rep.*, Total without profit funds.

8. a. In a state of not possessing; not having (as a possession of any kind, a part, an advantage, etc.); in want of, destitute of, lacking.

1297 R. Glouc. (Rolls) 991 Wanne man wiþoute eir of him sulue to deþe were ibroȝt His moder kun was is eir. *c* **1300** *Havelok* 2860 þe erl of cestre, . . þat was yung knith wituten wif. *c* **1386** Chaucer *Prol.* 343 With oute bake mete was neuere his hous. **1459** *Paston Lett.* I. 476, j. hood of russet felwet withougt a typpet. **1526** Tindale *Acts* ix. 9 And he was iij. dayes wyth out sight. *Ibid.* xiv. 17 He lefte not hym silfe with outen witnes. **1548** Udall *Erasm. Par. Luke* i. 11–12 The grief and pensifnesse of beeng without issue. **1650** Bulwer *Anthropomet.* xxii. (1653) 426 The shin-bone exposed to all encounters without any defence at all. **1667** Dryden & Dk. Newc. *Sir M. Mar-all* III. (1668) 32, I hate him worse than foul weather without a Coach. **1754** in *Nairne Peerage Evid.* (1874) 48 Deceased . . w'out issue of his body. **1766** Goldsm. *Vicar W.* xxi, Without cross or coin to bless yourself with! **1871** Geo. Eliot *Middlem.* xxxv. II. 212, I do believe you are better without the money. **1883** *Law Times* 20 Oct. 407/2 Preventing . . a litigant without a case from wantonly harassing his opponent.

b. Not with (something that might be given, granted, or obtained); not getting or receiving, or having got or received.

c **1200** *Vices & Virtues* 11 Ðat we sculen bliðeliche ȝiuen . ., wið-uten erðliche mede, alle ðe niede habbeð. *a* **1225** *Ancr. R.* 230 Lo hu heo [*sc.* the devils] ne muhten nout wiðuten leaue swenchen fule swin. **1390** Gower *Conf.* III. 377 Y was left with outen helpe. *c* **1420** *Prose Life Alex.* 41 He commanded þat he schulde wende hame to his felawes wit-owtten any harme. *c* **1450** *Merlin* iv. 69 Thus departed the messagers with-outen other ansuere. **1548–1765** [see LICENCE *sb.* 1]. **1697** Dryden *Virg. Georg.* III. 735 The Victim Ox . . Sunk of himself, without the Gods Command: Preventing the slow Sacrificer's Hand. **1707** Watts *Hymn* 'How beauteous are their feet' iv, Prophets and kings desir'd it long, But dy'd without the sight. **1723** Dk. Wharton *True Briton* No. 3. I. 19 They are all Guilty of Felony, without Benefit of the Clergy. **1842** Tennyson *Ld. Burleigh* 10 He to lips, that fondly falter, Presses his without reproof. **1849** Macaulay *Hist. Eng.* v. I. 623 He would as soon die without their absolution as with it.

c. In the construction of certain verbs: see DO *v.* 41, GO *v.* 69. Also *colloq.* with ellipsis.

1458– [see GO *v.* 69]. **1713–** [see DO *v.* 41]. **1899** R. Whiteing *5 John St.* 75 His one principle of conduct is to do without.

9. a. With no use, employment, or action of (an instrument, means, etc.); not using, or not being acted upon by.

without book: see BOOK *sb.* 15: hence (with hyphen) attrib. or as adj., recited without book or from memory.

a **1122** *O.E. Chron.* (Laud MS.) an. 1086 He hæfde Yrlande mid his werscipe ȝewunnon & wiðutan ælcon wæpnon. *c* **1200** Ormin 11329 Wiþþutenn mete & drinnch heold Crist hiss fasste þære fowwerrtiȝ daȝhess. **1471** Ripley *Comp. Alch.* VI. iv. in Ashm. (1652) 162 So that hyt lyke wax wyll melt . . Wythouten blast. **1597** Shaks. *Rom. & Jul.* I. iv. 7 (Qo.) Weele haue . . no withoutbooke Prologue faintly spoke After the Prompter, for our entrance. *c* **1615** Bacon *Advice to Sir G. Villiers* Wks. 1879 I. 519/1 The excess of diet . . would be avoided; wise men will do it without a law. **1673** E. Browne *Trav.* 130 Two sorts of Virgin Mercury; the one running out and discovering it self without labour, the other requiring some way of extraction and separation. **1731–8** Swift *Pol. Conversat.* Introd. 21 To pass the Evening without Cards. **1797** Coleridge *Christabel* I. 177 The moon shines dim . . But they without its light can see The chamber carved so curiously. **1798** —— *Anc. Mar.* 169 Withouten wind, withouten tide, She steddies with upright keel. **1849** Macaulay *Hist. Eng.* i. I. 150 The new parliament, which, having been called without the royal writ, is more accurately described as a convention. **1857** [see GET *v.* 71 h]. **1865** Swinburne *Masque of Queen Bersabe* 92 [The rushes] Grew wet withouten foot of men.

b. With no action or agency of (a person); *esp.* with no co-operation of, or support from.

1340 Hampole *Pr. Consc.* Prol. 44 Alle thyng thurgh his myght made he, For with-outen hym myght nathing be. **1382** Wyclif *John* xv. 5 For with outen me ȝe mown no thing do. *c* **1450** *Merlin* ii. 36 A childe born withouten fader. **1476** *Stonor Papers* (Camden) II. 19, I . . saide . . That . . I coulde not answere that mateer without yow. **1535** Coverdale *2 Kings* xviii. 25 Thinkest thou that I came vp hither without ye Lorde to destroye these cities? **1592** in J. Morris *Troubles Cath. Forefathers* (1877) 28 Imprisoned for burying a Catholic without a minister. **1598** in *Harington's Nugæ Ant.* (1804) I. 176 To make peace withouten his allyes and friends. **1697** Dryden *Virg. Georg.* III. 70 Without thee nothing lofty can I sing. **1712** Swift *Jrnl. to Stella* 13 Dec., We shall have a peace very soon; the Dutch are almost entirely agreed, and if they stop we shall make it without them. **1875** [see GET *v.* 71 h]. *Mod.* Come and help me with this job; I can't do it without you.

10. (with obj. an abstract thing, as a quality, attribute, action, condition, etc.): **a.** (depending on or referring to a verb) With absence or lack of, or freedom from; so that there is no . . . ; often forming phrases equivalent to negative adverbs, e.g. *without end* = endlessly, *without fail* = unfailingly, *without fear* = fearlessly, *without success* = unsuccessfully, etc.

Frequent in ME. in intensive or expletive phrases, as ***without***(***en dread***, ***lease*** (sb.[2]), ***leasing***, ***let***, ***letting***, ***lie*** (sb.[1]), ***miss*** (sb.[1]), ***strife***, etc. See also the various sbs.

c **1175** *Lamb. Hom.* 143 Iwarpen ine eche pine, wiþuten alesinge, and wið-uten milce. *c* **1220** *Bestiary* 412 For to winnen fode, derflike wiðuten dred. *a* **1250** *Owl & Night.* 183 Wit-ute cheste and bute fiȝte. *c* **1275–** [see DELAY *sb.* 2 a]. **1297–** [see FAIL *sb.*[2] 1]. *a* **1300** *Cursor M.* 10407 þai þat stad er in þair blis, Wit-vten want . ., Wit-vten seke, wit-vten sare. **1340** Hampole *Pr. Consc.* 3429 Swa parfitely may nane lyf here, With-outen veniel syns sere. **1377** Langl. *P. Pl.* B. XIV. 237 He is neuere murie, Withoute mornynge amonge, and mischief to bote. **1390** Gower *Conf.* I. 281 Sche seith me nay withouten oth. *a* **1450** Myrc *Par. Pr.* 24 Say þy serues wyþowten hast. *c* **1450** *Merlin* 129 With-outen cause ye be not come hider. **1549** *Compl. Scot.* 5 Quhen he purchessis pace ande concord, vytht out diminutione of his rycht. *a* **1553** UDALL *Royster D.* IV. vii. (Arb.) 74, I will take the lawe on hir withouten grace. **1614** GORGES *Lucan* VI. 219 Then Pompey's men withouten stop, Do mount vpon the trenches top. **1633** EARL MANCH. *Al Mondo* (1636) 162 It is just..that they who live without repentance, should dye without comfort. **1721** RAMSAY *Lucky Spence* x, Nane gathers gear withoutten care. **1779** *Mirror* No. 57 ⁋6, I hope I may say it without vanity. **1812** BYRON *Ch. Har.* I. xxxi, Far as the eye discerns, withouten end. **1820** MADDOCK *Rep. V.-C. Crt.* V. 35 Stating..'that the estates were to be sold without reserve.' **1834** NEWMAN *Par. Serm.* (1837) I. 101 Men can without trouble be brought to confess that they sin. **1849** MACAULAY *Hist. Eng.* v. I. 540 Great doubt has been thrown on his integrity, but without sufficient reason. **1862** *Law Jrnl. Rep.* 31 Ch. 676 *Primâ facie*, a party writing a letter, and using the expression 'without prejudice', means that he is not to be prejudiced. **1881** MISS BRADDON *Asphodel* III. 265 He..then let her go with-out a word. **1896** KIPLING *Seven Seas, Last Rhyme True Thomas* 130, I do well To love my love withouten fear.

b. (depending on or referring to a sb.) Characterized by absence of, lacking or free from, not having: often forming phrases equivalent to negative adjs. e.g. ***without end*** = endless, ***without fear*** = fearless, ***without number*** (†*tale*) = innumerable, etc.

c **1175** *Lamb. Hom.* 95 He deð þa þe beoð bilehwite and wið-utan ufelnesse. *c* **1230** *Hali Meid.* 15 He is leoflukest þing & wiðuten eauer euch bruche. *a* **1250** *Owl & Night.* 863 For nys no mon wiþvten sunne. **1297** R. GLOUC. (Rolls) 8903 þi louerd ssal abbe an name..vair wiþoute blame. *a* **1300** *Cursor M.* 102 Mild and mek, witouten gall. *c* **1380** *Sir Ferumb.* 4112 Neuere ne was he with-oute strif, Bot ay wykkeliche lyuede ys lyf. **1390** GOWER *Conf.* I. 45 To grounde I was withoute breth. **14..** *Tundale's Vis.* 32 He was a man withoute pyte. **1509** FISHER *Funeral Serm. C'tess Richmond* Wks. (1876) 309 Be not sad..as men with-outen hope. **1626** BACON *Sylva* §499 It is obserued by some, that there is a vertuous Bezoar, and another without vertue. **1690** LOCKE *Hum. Und.* I. iv. §1 There was a time, when the Mind was without those Principles. **1719** DE FOE *Crusoe* II. (Globe) 422 All sorts of Tools and Iron-work, they had without Tale. **1758** HUME *Ess., Eloquence* 66 'Tis vehement reasoning, without any appearance of art. **1859** HAWTHORNE *Fr. & It. Jrnls.* (1871) II. 284 It resembled an unspeakably bad dough nut, without any sweetening. **1869** RUSKIN *Q. of Air* §77 They are white, without purity;.. massive, without strength; and slender, without grace.

c. With no possibility of; so, or such, as not to admit of; so, or such, that there can be no...

a **1300** *Cursor M.* 25821 For þair wanhopping þai fall wit-vten vp-couering. *c* **1470** HENRY *Wallace* I. 113 Our men was slayne with outyn redemptioune. *Ibid.* 226 With out reskew he stekyt him to dede. **1530** PALSGR. 329/2 Without remedy, *irremediable*. **1670** [see CLERGY 6]. **1751** JOHNSON *Rambler* No. 174 ⁋14 These wounds..are without cure. **1762** HUME *Hist. Eng., Jul. C. to Hen. VII*, I. App. I. 151 The great lords and abbots among the Anglo-Saxons.. could punish without appeal any thieves..they caught. **1766** [see REMEDY *sb.* 3].

d. In such phrases as ***without comparison, controversy, doubt,*** † ***nay***, etc. the meaning app. varies between 'beyond' (sense 2 or 3) and 'involving the absence of', 'not admitting of', 'so that there is or can be no...'.

a **1300–** [see DOUBT *sb.*[1] 4 d]. **1340–1578** [see COMPARISON *sb.* 2 b]. **1547–1777** [see CONTROVERSY *sb.* 1 c]. **1557** *N.T.* (Geneva) Heb. vii. 7 Without all nay, he which is lesse, receaueth blessyng of hym which is greater. **1605** BACON *Adv. Learn.* II. xix. §3 These things are without Contradiction, and could not otherwise be. **1621–1709** [see COMPARE *sb.*[1] 2].

†**e.** ***without day*** = SINE DIE. *Obs.*

1607 COWEL *Interpr.* s.v. *Day*, To be dismissed with out day, is to be finally discharged the court. **1713** *Mod. Cases* VI. 262 He doubted of the Effect of a Nolle Pros'..if it discharged the Indictment, or only put the Defendant without Day.

11. a. Followed by a gerund or vbl. sb. in *-ing*: equivalent to 'so as not to' or 'and not' with the corresponding vb., or 'not' with the pres. pple.; e.g. *to pass by without seeing* = 'to pass by so as not to see', 'to pass by and not see', 'to pass by, not seeing'.

c **1320** *Sir Tristr.* 2620 Tristrem is went oway Wiþ outen coming o3ain. **1377** LANGL. *P. Pl.* B. XI. 144 He..wilned me were graunted Grace, wyth-outen any bede-byddynge. *c* **1400** *Destr. Troy* 2992 Tite, withoutyn tariyng, atirit were all. **1515** *Reg. Privy Seal Scot.* I. 407/1 To pas and repas als oft as thai ples..without ony..aresting. *a* **1548** HALL *Chron., 14 Edw. IV*, 235 The Frenche kyng..callyng for water, washed and rose without any answere makyng. **1639** S. DU VERGER tr. *Camus' Admir. Events* To Rdr. a vij, Drones which do but humme about flowers, without gathering any honey from them. **1734** BERKELEY *Let.* Wks. 1871 IV. 217, I can hardly stir abroad without catching cold. **1779** *Mirror* No. 2 ⁋1 No child ever heard from its nurse the story of Jack the Giant Killer's cap of darkness, without envying the pleasures of invisibility. **1836** DICKENS *Sk. Boz, Shops & Tenants*, We never passed at night without seeing the eldest girl at work. **1849** MACAULAY *Hist. Eng.* ii. I. 169 He was a slave without being a dupe. **1877** RUSKIN *St. Mark's Rest* iv. §51 A solemn piece of old Venetian wall.. which you might pass under twenty times without seeing. **1885** *Law Times* LXXIX. 119/2 No person was..to blast coal without the charge having been inspected by the underlooker.

†**b.** Governing an infinitive with *to*. [After Fr., etc.]

c **1489** CAXTON *Sonnes of Aymon* xxii. 470 That we maye retourne agen hole and sounde..wythoute to be dyshonoured. **1556** *J. de Flores' Aurelio & Isab.* F 6, Without to see it whiche is written.

c. By ellipsis of the gerund: Not counting, leaving out of account. *colloq.*

1871 GEO. ELIOT *Middlem.* xxxv. II. 212 My father has enough to do to keep the rest, without me.

†**12.** ***without mo*** or ***more***: in various senses (see MO B. 3 c, MORE *a.* B. 4 c). Often used as a tag.

c **1290**, etc. [see MO, MORE, as above]. *c* **1350** *Will. Palerne* 2573 þe werwolf..went wi3tly a-wei wit-oute any more. *c* **1350** *Leg. Rood* iii. 148 By þat ilk way went we twa, þi moder and I with-outen ma. **14..** *Guy Warw.* (Camb. MS.) 719 Wythowytyn more forthe they rode. *c* **1470** HENRY *Wallace* I. 61 Till Noram kirk he come with outyn mar. **1500–20** DUNBAR *Poems* xxxiv. 89 The Deuill said then, withouttin mair, 'Renunce 3our God, and cum to me.'

13. In senses 7–11 often with conditional implication (mostly with negative, expressed or implied): If one have (or had) not, if there be (or were) not, unless one have or there be, in the absence of, in default of, 'supposing the negation or omission of' (J.).

a **1300** *Cursor M.* 126 Na werc may stand Wit-outen grundwall to be lastand. **1387** TREVISA *Higden* III. 161 Noþer man ne womman schulde be punsched wiþ oute gilt. *c* **1450** CAPGRAVE *Life St. Aug.* 99 þat swech þingis myte not be do wit3-outen vertuous lyuyng. **1526** TINDALE *Heb.* xi. 6 With out faith it is vnpossible to please him. **1661** GODOLPHIN *View Adm. Jurisd.* Introd. a b, The Mariner.. may not sail without one Cat or more in his Vessel. **1748** THOMSON *Cast. Indol.* I. i, Withouten that would come an heavyer bale. **1766** GOLDSM. *Vicar W.* xv, What is genius or courage without an heart? **1834** MARRYAT *Peter Simple* xxxvii, Without a sense of your fault, how can repentance and amendment be expected? **1857** BUCKLE *Civiliz.* I. x. 617 The people believed that without the nobles there was no safety; the nobles believed that without the crown there was no honour.

14. a. With ellipsis of the obj. (cf. 4). Now *colloq.* (except in contrast with *with*).

In negative contexts, as in quots. 1733, 1898, virtually = otherwise; this use is further extended in unstudied speech, e.g.: 'You can go, if you can find somebody to go with,—not without'.

c **1400** *Rule St. Benet* (prose) 16 þe nihend-ferþe salme wid þe antefen ouþ ir wid-vten. **1597** SHAKS. *Lover's Compl.* 98 Smal shew of man was yet vpon his chinne..Yet..nice affections wauering stood in doubt If best were as it was, or best without. **1654** DOROTHY OSBORNE *Lett.* (1888) 233 Here is a ring:..'tis indifferent whether there be any word in't or not; only 'tis as well without. **1672** WISEMAN *Wounds* I. viii. 70 We threw out our Tent, and by Sarcoticks cured this wound without. **1681** T. FLATMAN *Heraclitus Ridens* No. 27 (1713) I. 178 Come, it is a great while since we had a Pindarick; have you never a one in your Budget? *Earn.* I am seldom without. **1720** LADY B. GERMAINE in *C'tess Suffolk's Lett.* (1824) I. 73 Though you should take the four [thousand pounds], still I shall have enough without. **1733** TULL *Horse-Hoeing Husb.* vii. 26 All the former Roots being broken off at the Ends in taking up (for 'tis impossible to do it without). **1741** RICHARDSON *Pamela* III. 27 Pray don't! You'll have enough on your hands without. **1800** MRS. HERVEY *Mourtray Fam.* IV. 57 Well, promise nothing, Mr. Chowles; but do it without. **1834** NEWMAN *Lett.* (1891) II. 48 [He] was afraid to tell me, and left Oxford without. **1878** E. A. FREEMAN *Let.* in W. R. W. Stephens *Life & Lett.* (1895) II. 161, I don't get any worship here; but I am better without. **1898** W. W. JACOBS *Sea Urchins, Grey Parrot* (1906) 208 You must have given him some encouragement. .. A man wouldn't offer to lend a lady his opera-glasses without.

b. *slang.* in reference to liquor: Not mixed with sugar: cf. WITH *prep.* 26 b (*b*).

1835 DICKENS *Sk. Boz. River*, Glasses of brandy-and-water cold without. **1837** BARHAM *Ingol. Leg., Execution* 71 There is 'punch,' 'cold without,' 'hot with,' 'heavy wet.' **1854** [see WITH *prep.* 26 b (*b*)].

15. Qualified by a negative: ***not without*** = not lacking, with or having some (implying or suggesting a somewhat slight or not very great amount).

Cf. *not* with negative adj. or adv. (NOT *adv.* 10 c).

1596 DALRYMPLE tr. *Leslie's Hist. Scot.* (S.T.S.) I. 42 Sa sure a havin..that nocht w[t]out cause the historiographours named it, the Porte of saifgaird and saiftie. **1605** SHAKS. *Macb.* I. v. 20 Thou would'st be great; Art not without Ambition. **1766** GOLDSM. *Vicar W.* iv, Nor were we without guests. **1807** SOUTHEY *Espriella's Lett.* xxxvii. (1808) II. 71, I looked back upon Birmingham not without satisfaction at thinking I should never enter it again. **1855** MACAULAY *Hist. Eng.* xi. III. 113 Many..were not without hopes that mild and liberal counsels might prevail. **1879** MCCARTHY *Donna Q.* I. 61 She remembered not without a pang that [etc.].

C. *conj.* (or in *conj. phr.*)

1. The prep. governing a clause introduced by *that*, so that ***without that*** becomes a conjunctional phr.: †**a.** (*a*) Except that. (*b*) In addition to the fact that. *Obs. rare.*

c **1200** ORMIN 1022 þatt wa3herifft wass henngedd tær, forr þatt itt hidenn shollde All þatt tatt tær wiþþinnenn wass ..Wiþþutenn þatt te bisscopp sellf..þær shollde cumenn o þe 3er ann siþe, & all himm ane. **1489** *Acc. Ld. High Treas. Scot.* I. 145 Laide downe in redy siluer for rybbanis to the King,..withowte at the Master of the Wardrop hes boycht v dussane of rybbanis..summa iij[li].

b. (in sense B. 10) Without its being the case that: now expressed by the construction with gerund (B. 11), with or without poss., e.g. *without that you shall need* = 'without your needing'; *without that he led me* = 'without leading me'. Now *rare* or *Obs.*

c **1450** in W. T. Barbour *Hist. Contract* (1914) 201 Withoute þat ever eny accord..were made or had bitwene þe seid John Mercer and John Halsnoth. **1471** FORTESCUE *Wks.* (1869) 525 Sainte Edwarde reyned..peseably..with oute eny clayme made vppon him, by hyr, or by her husbande, and with outen that eny of ther heirs have claymed this londe. *c* **1489** CAXTON *Sonnes of Aymon* xxvi. 560 The speres flew in peces wythout that ony of theym felle to the grounde. **1594** R. CAREW *Huarte's Exam. Wits* xiii. (1596) 203 Himselfe will deliuer them into your hands, without that you shall need to conquer them. **1596** DANETT tr. *Comines* (1614) 86, The captaine at the castell gate.. offred me a cup of wine, without that he led mee into the castell as he was accustomed. *a* **1648** LD. HERBERT *Hen. VIII* (1683) 162 This seemed to be done, without that the King was fully informed thereof. *Ibid.* 230 Your Actions (without that I or any else speak of them) make you a lyar. **1853** C. BRONTË *Villette* xii, It was next to impossible that a casket could be thrown into her garden..without..that she should have caught intimation [etc.].

†**c.** (with conditional implication as in B. 13) If it be or were not the case that, unless: = 2. *Obs.*

c **1440** *Generydes* 475 Withoute that she myght have his loue ageyn, She were on don for euere in certayne. *c* **1450** CAPGRAVE *Life St. Aug.* ii. 4 This myth not be do with-outen þat þei had substauns of possession. **1523** Q. MARG. in M. A. E. Green *Lett. Royal Ladies* (1846) I. 266 (MS.) The lordes wilbe..ferd to leve the governours wayes, with-out that they may fynd some suyrtie to take ther partt.

†**d.** ***without that*** (or ***this***) ***that***: legal phr. introducing an exception, *spec.* in pleading [tr. law-L. *absque hoc quod*, law-Fr. *sans ceo que*], a form, obsolete since 1852, whereby a defendant asserted special matter of exception or justification against the plaintiff's claim while reserving his denial of the whole cause of action.

1518 *Star Chamber Cases* (Selden Soc.) II. 150 That all the said mesuages and lendes shuld be in the rule..of the Chamberleyne..Without that that the said mesuages and londes extend to the yerely value of cxl li. **1592** *B.N.C.* (Oxf.) *Docts.* B 2 37 (MS.) Without that, that H.P. was never properly enfeoffed. **1601** FULBECKE *1st Pt. Parall.* 72 b, The plaintife replyed, that..the defendant..assaulted him and beate him..and the defendant reioined that..by their common accorde they played together, without that that he beate him in other maner. **1651** tr. *Kitchin's Jurisd.* (1653) 422 Conspiracy, he is alive, with out that, that he is dead. *Ibid.* 423 Where one pleads out of his Fee, the other saith within, without that, that it was out in manner and forme. **1824** H. J. STEPHEN *Treat. Princ. Pleading* ii. 211 The defendants delivered their petition to the common council, complaining of an undue election; *without this that* the jurisdiction..belonged to the court of the mayor and aldermen.

2. Hence, by omission of *that*, simply as a conjunction: If..not, except, unless. Also, chiefly in U.S. dial. use: unless, without its being the case that.

Formerly common in literary use, most frequently with verb in subjunctive; later *colloq.* ('not in use, except in conversation' J. 1755) or *arch.*, and now chiefly *illiterate.* Often replaceable by the const. with gerund (B. 11), e.g. *without he be compelled* = 'without being compelled'; esp. with clause referring to an attendant circumstance or result rather than a condition, as in quot. 1467.

1393 LANGL. *P. Pl.* C. v. 176 Quath conscience to þe kynge with-oute þe comune help, Hit is ful hard..þer-to hit to brynge. **1467** MARG. PASTON in *P. Lett.* II. 308 If I wer ther withought I had the mor..wurchepfull persones abought me..it shuld be to me but a vylney. **1477** *Stonor Papers* (Camden) II. 28 She is displeside and I know nat whereffore, with owte hir olde sekenes be fallen on hir agayn. **1523** LD. BERNERS *Froiss.* (1812) I. xii. 12 All the moost parte of the realme were right joyouse, withoute it were a fewe parsones..fauourable to syr Hewe Spencer. **1534** MORE *Comf. agst. Trib.* I. xii. (1553) C iij b, Good workes to godwarde woorketh no man without god woorke with him. **1565** *Reg. Privy Council Scot.* I. 410 [He] will nocht deliver..the said hors without he be compellit. **1591** SHAKS. *Com. Err.* III. ii. 92 Such a one, as a man may not speake of, without he say sir reuerence. *a* **1643** J. SHUTE *Judgem. & Mercy* (1645) 129 He may barke, but he cannot bite without a man come within his reach. **1695** CONGREVE *Love for L.* IV. i, If he can't be cur'd without I suck the Poyson from his Wounds. **1754** SHEBBEARE *Matrimony* (1766) I. 143 Do not think of marrying this young Lady, without you are convinced you can love her. **1787** BEATTIE *Scoticisms* 101, I will not go without I am paid for it. Scottish and obsolete and vulgar English. **1802** MRS. E. PARSONS *Myst. Visit* III. 51, I shall never intrude without you invite me. *a* **1814** *Fam. Politics* II. i. in *New Brit. Theatre* II. 207 I'm but a working woman, and cannot live without I gets my due. **1834** T. ARNOLD *Let.* 14 Apr. in Stanley *Life* (1898) I. vii. 328 Not allowing God's seal, without it be countersigned by one of their own forging. **1859** TENNYSON *Elaine* 1411 Not without She wills it. **1860** O. W. HOLMES *Elsie V.* xv. (1891) 211, I know these people.., so as all the science in the world can't know them, without it takes time about it. **1867** J. R. LOWELL *Biglow Papers* 2nd Ser. p. lvii, I don't git much done 'thout I bogue right in along 'th my men. **1868** J. H. BLUNT *Ref. Ch. Eng.* I. 437 No canons were to become law without they were assented to..by the crown. **1887** *Daily News* 21 Nov. 2/7 Without a great change takes place the meeting is sure to commence to-morrow. **1903** 'T. COLLINS' *Such is Life* (1937) i. 51 A man shouldn't make a dog of his self without he's well paid for it. That's my religion. **1955** F. O'CONNOR *Wise Blood* iii. 52 Everything she looked at was that child... She couldn't lie with that man without she saw it. **1962** E. ALBEE *Who's Afraid of V. Woolf?* (1964) I. 51 Man can put up with only so much without he descends a rung or two on the old evolutionary ladder. **1984** A. CARTER *Nights at Circus* ii. 46 No two deaths without a third follows.

D. *sb.* That which is external; the outside. *rare.*

1899 C. F. D'ARCY *Ideal. & Theol.* Introd. 22 Necessity is determination from without, determination by the not-self. It belongs therefore to whatever has a 'without.' **1938** [see WITHIN *sb.*].

without, obs. pa. t. of WITHHOLD *v.*

† **wi'thout ˌdoor,** *adv. phr.* (*adj.*) *Obs.* = next.

c **1205** LAY. 2382 þat neuer ne ferde heo wið uten dore. **1570** LEVINS *Manip.* 229/8 Wythout dore, *extrà, foris.* **1621** in Foster *Engl. Factories Ind.* (1906) 280 A storme of..rayne ..that wett these bales which weare without doare in the street. **1649** C. WASE *Sophocles, Electra* 30 Enter in, and let her without door Her own distresses, and her friends deplore. **1739** JOHNSON *Boerhaave* in *Gentl. Mag.* IX. 174/1 His..Friend..found him sitting without Door.

b. *attrib.* or as *adj.* (with hyphen). = OUT-DOOR *a.*; in quot. *transf.* or *fig.* relating to the outer world, outward, external.

1611 SHAKS. *Wint. T.* II. i. 69 Prayse her but for this her without-dore-Forme.

wi'thout ,doors, *adv. phr.* (*adj.*) *Obs.* or *rare arch.* (Also with hyphen.) [See WITHOUT *prep.* I. and DOOR 5.]

1. Out of doors, outside the house, in the open air.

1617 MORYSON *Itin.* I. 63 Our meat we bought our selues, ..and we fetched our beere without doores. **1663** GERBIER *Counsel* 27 At the latter end of the year..no brick-work without doores ought to be laid. **1695** A. TELFAIR *New Confut. Sadd.* (1696) 4 The Family being all without-doors. **1711** ADDISON *Spect.* No. 83 ¶1 When the Weather hinders me from taking my Diversions without Doors. **1796** MORSE *Amer. Geog.* II. 621 Without doors they use a kind of wooden patten. **1840** DICKENS *Old Cur. Shop* xxviii, The preparations without doors had not been neglected.

2. *transf.* and *fig.* Outside the community (family, nation, etc.); †*spec.* outside Parliament (= OUT-OF-DOOR, -DOORS A. 2 a).

1697 C. DAVENANT *Ess. E. India Trade* Wks. 1771 I. 96 Some persons (without doors)..profess themselves open enemies to the traffic in general. **1709** SWIFT *Adv. Relig.* Misc. (1711) 224 Senates are like to have little Regard for any Proposals that come from without Doors. **1723** DK. WHARTON *True Briton* No. 5. I. 43 Those who are Without-Doors should do their Duty by supporting such Patriots. **1769** *Junius Lett.* xvii. (1812) I. 181 It will not be necessary ..to take the trouble of answering..the quotation from a speech without doors. **1792** BURKE *Sp.* 11 May (1816) IV. 51 The House was untainted..by those false principles which had been so amply circulated without doors. **1823** SCOTT *Quentin D.* xiv, He who beat all enemies without doors, found a fair foe who could belabour him within.

3. *attrib.* or as *adj.* = prec. b.

1654 FULLER *Comm. Ruth* 139 The Daughters of Sarah, whom the meeknesse of their Sex hath priviledged from following without doors affairs.

†**wi'thoutforth,** *adv. Obs.* (or *rare arch.*) Also with hyphen, or as two words, or as three. [f. WITHOUT *adv.* + FORTH *adv.*] Properly, Everywhere without or outside (see FORTH *adv.* 2 b); but in use a mere synonym of *without.* (Opp. to WITHINFORTH.) **a.** = WITHOUT *adv.* 1.

c **1380** WYCLIF *Sel. Wks.* II. 384 Woo worþe ȝou,.. ypocritis, þat clensen wiþout-forþ of þe cuppe and of þe dishe. *c* **1380** —— *Wks.* (1880) 46 þei weren apeied wiþ o cote or kirtil with-ynne forþe & with-oute forþ. *c* **1450** *Mirk's Festial* 72 When þay wern alle in, God closud þe dore aftyr hom wythout-forth. **1474** in *Litt. Cantuar.* (Rolls) III. 272 Yowre powche and key-band with the keverynge; on the which are..set ij. porses with owteforth. **1511** *Guylforde's Pylgr.* (Camden) 23 Withoute forthe byfore the entre into this Temple. **1601** HOLLAND *Pliny* xxxv. vi. II. 528 The peeces of this earth, if a man doe breake, shew the own naturall colour which is not mixt: without-forth they be spotted. **1894** F. S. ELLIS *Reynard the Fox* 247 Withoutforth of the ring..A stone..of colours three.

b. = WITHOUT *adv.* 2, 2 b.

1382 WYCLIF *Matt.* xii. 46 His modir and his bretheren stoden with outeforth [**1388** withouteforth]. **1388** —— *Acts* v. 34 Gamaliel..comaundide the men to be put without forth. **1467** in *Engl. Gilds* (1870) 373 That euery citezein.. w^t^outforth paye alle maner chargs as citezens do that dwelle w^t^ynforth. **1470–85** MALORY *Arthur* xx. xxii. 836 They.. kepte the syege wyth lytel warre withoutforth. **1530** TINDALE *Deut.* xxxii. 25 Without forth, the swerde shall robbe them off theire childern. **1600** HOLLAND *Livy* VII. xxi, All was quiet withoutforth. **1609** —— *Amm. Marcell.* 132 The space..between the wall and the heape of earth cast up withoutforth.

c. = WITHOUT *adv.* 3.

1357 *Lay Folks Catech.* (L.) 758 Thou schalt not do leccherye noþer in consent in hert ne spekynge ne in countenaunce withowte-forþ. *c* **1374** CHAUCER *Boeth.* v. pr. iv. (1868) 164 þe wit comprehendiþ fro wiþ outen furþe þe figure of þe body of þe man. *c* **1400** LOVE *Bonavent. Mirr.* (1907) 123 The schame that sche hadde of hir synne was so grete withynneforth that sche forȝat al schame and reproue withouteforth. **1491** CAXTON *Vitas Patr.* (W. de W. 1495) I. i. 4 b/2 Faynynge wythoute fourthe by theyr couuert maners and symple habyllemens to be Innocentes. **1530** PALSGR. Introd. 34 The verbes actyves betokyng some acte to passe from the doer without forth.

d. quasi-*sb.* (preceded by *of*): That which is without; external region or action.

1474 CAXTON *Chesse* III. iv. (1883) 114 Hyt befelle that a marchant of withoute forth herd the..fame of this man. **1491** —— *Vitas Patr.* (W. de W. 1495) II. 277 b/2 That the werkes of withoutforth be fyrst withinforth ruled after the Iugement of right & reason.

e. *attrib.* or as *adj.* Outside, external.

c **1500** in Arnolde *Chron.* (1811) 9 The wythoutforth landys and tenementis.

wi'thoutside, *adv.* and *prep.* Now *rare* or *Obs.* (Also with hyphen, or as two words.) [f. WITHOUT + SIDE *sb.*, after *outside.*] Opp. to WITHINSIDE or WITHIN. **A.** *adv.*

1. On the outer side or surface: = OUTSIDE *adv.* 1 (in part), WITHOUT *adv.* 1.

1578 LYTE *Dodoens* I. v. 11 The roote is..blacke withoutside. **1668** H. MORE *Div. Dial.* II. v. (1713) 97 Nor do we our selves grow by being liquored without side, but within. **1695** CONGREVE *Love for L.* IV. i, Why does that Lawyer wear black?—Does he carry his Conscience withoutside? **1727–38** CHAMBERS *Cycl.* s.v. *Mould,* The Moulds..are of wax, supported within-side by what they call a core, and covered without-side with a cap or case. **1794** C. SMITH *Wand. Warwick* 19 Barricading the cabin door withoutside. **1849** CHR. G. ROSSETTI *Testimony* 20 Poet. Wks. (1904) 119 We build our houses on the sand Comely withoutside and within. *c* **1850** [see WITHINSIDE A. 1].

2. In (or to) the place or space without: = OUTSIDE *adv.* 1 (in part), 2, WITHOUT *adv.* 2.

a **1700** EVELYN *Diary* 21 Sept. 1644, The Cathedrall,.. full of sepulchres without-side. **1706** E. WARD *Hud. Rediv.* (1707) II. VI. 4 Without side warm, within side merry. **1710** MRS. CENTLIVRE *Marplot* II. Wks. 1760 II. 147 When I came without-side, I saw nobody there. **1800** *Ann. Reg., Chron.* 414 Within this temple is an altar, and without-side, near the entrance, another. **1831** TRELAWNY *Adv. Younger Son* I. xx. 148 A wild shout from without-side.

3. **withoutside of,** *prep. phr.* = *outside of,* OUTSIDE *adv.* 3 a.

1638 in *Collect. Mass. Hist. Soc.* Ser. III. VI. 23 Placing the Indians..without side of our soldiers in a ring battalia. **1711** in *10th Rep. Hist. MSS. Comm.* App. v. 169 A very narrow bridge,..without-side of the gate. **1751** R. PALTOCK *P. Wilkins* (1884) II. xi. 108 Without-side of these mountains, it was scarce darker than at my arkoe. **1769** J. BUSH *Hibernia Curiosa* 163 Wearing their shirts withoutside of their cloaths. **1865** W. G. PALGRAVE *Arabia* I. 345 All the world withoutside of Nejed.

B. *prep.* = A. 3, OUTSIDE *prep.* 1, 2, WITHOUT *prep.* 1, 1 b.

1686 [see WITHINSIDE B. 2]. **1760** *Impostors Detected* I. iv. I. 31 The monk's sandals which he had left without side the door. *a* **1774** GOLDSM. *Surv. Exp. Philos.* (1776) II. 176 Succeeding each other, one without side the other, like circles in disturbed water. **1809** A. HENRY *Trav.* 133 A fire was made without side the cabin, in the open air. **1831** T. HOPE *Ess. Origin Man* I. 8 Modifications existing withoutside my person.

†**wi'thout-take,** *prep. Obs. rare.* [f. WITHOUT *adv.* after OUT-TAKE *pple., prep.*] Except.

1422 YONGE tr. *Secr. Secr.* 185 With al the Princes and men of value of the lande, wythout-take the Pepill of Vllystere.

wi'thoutwards, *adv. nonce-wd.* [f. WITHOUT + -WARDS.] Towards the exterior.

1865 [see WITHINWARDS].

withpraise, etc.: see WITH- b.

withsafe, -saif, obs. ff. VOUCHSAFE.

†**withsake,** *v. Obs.* Forms: 1 **wiþsacan,** 3 **-saken;** *pa. t.* 3 **-soc(k,** *pa. pple.* 4 **-saken.** [OE. *wiþsacan,* f. WITH- + *sacan* to contend, dispute, deny; cf. MHG. *widersachen.*] = WITHSAY *v.* 1, 2, 3.

971 *Blickl. Hom.* 53 Wiþsacaþ nu þam leasum welum. *c* **1000** *Ags. Gosp.* Matt. x. 33 Se þe me wiðsæcð beforan mannun, & ic wiþsace hyne beforan minum fæder. *c* **1205** LAY. 10898 þa wiðsaken wolde cristindom he dude his marken him on. *Ibid.* 13000 Imong þan eorlen he stod & fastliche hit wið-soc. *a* **1225** *Ancr. R.* 88 Ich hit ne mei nout wið-saken. *a* **1375** *Joseph Arim.* 178 His grete folk þat him wiþ-saken hedde.

†**withsave,** obs. f. VOUCHSAFE, used by Wyatt in the sense: To preserve.

a **1542** WYATT *'Syns love ys suche'* 20 Henceforthe my fredome to withsave [*rime* have]. —— *'Now must I lerne'* 22 Now must I seke som other ways My self for to withsave.

†**withsaw.** *Obs.* [f. WITH- + SAW *sb.*[2], after WITHSAY *v.*] = WITHSAYING.

a **1225** *Ancr. R.* 288 Hwon þe delit iðe luste is igon so oueruorð þet ter nis non wiðsigginge [*v.r.* wiðsahe]. *a* **1300** *Cursor M.* 5877 Now wald þai mak þam a witsau Fra þair warkes for to drau. *a* **1325** *MS. Rawl. B.* 520, lf. 28 Manie lordes of wastes..habbez i ben desturbed þoru with sawe of hoere neȝeburs [orig. *per contradiccionem vicinorum*].

†**with'say,** *sb. Obs.* [f. next.] = prec.

c **1315** SHOREHAM VII. 369 þer nere stryf ne contekynge, Ne no wyþ-sey.

†**with'say,** *v. Obs.* [OE. (rare Northumb.) *wiðsæcga*: see WITH- and SAY *v.*[1] Cf. OFris. *withsedza.*]

1. *trans.* To renounce. *rare.*

c **960** *Rituale Dunelm.* (Surtees) 34 *Terrena desideria respuentes,* eardlico lvsto wiðsæcgende. *c* **1386** CHAUCER *Sec. Nun's T.* 447 Euery cristen wight shal hen penaunce But if that he his cristendom withseye. *Ibid.* 457 We that knowen thilke name [of Christian] so For vertuous, we may it nat withseye.

2. a. To affirm the contrary of, contradict, deny (a fact or statement); also, to deny the existence of.

a **1225** *Ancr. R.* 86 ȝif a mon..deð so much mis þat hit beo so open sunne þat he hit ne mei nonesweis allelunge wiðsiggen. **1297** R. GLOUC. (Rolls) 2309 To londone he gan him bringe, & sede he was purost eyr to be icrouned to kinge. Nomon ne miȝte it wel wiþ segge. **1303** R. BRUNNE *Handl. Synne* 9800 Syker ys, þat yn rolle ys leyde, For þan may hyt neuer be wyþseyde. **1387** TREVISA *Higden* (Rolls) I. 19 Sawes þat wiþseiþ nouȝt oure byleue. **1443–50** in W. P. Baildon *Sel. Cases Chanc.* (1896) 136 He withseieth not the matier conteigned in the seid bille of complainte. **1493** *Cov. Leet Bk.* 57 To which the Recordour..seid that he withseith not þe ffraunchis of Couentre, nor the allowance þerof had at Bristoll. **1530** PALSGR. 783/2 Sythe I have sayd it, I wyll never withsay it. **1567** TURBERV. *Ovid's Ep.* 136 That Dian witnesde thou canst not withsaye.

b. To contradict, deny the statement of (a person).

1297 R. GLOUC. (Rolls) 10349 Wan þou seist, quaþ þe king, þat þat was mi þouȝt, So gret louerd as þou art, Ine wiþsegge þe nouȝt. **1387–8** T. USK *Test. Love* I. ii. (Skeat) I. 184 To withsaye thilke men that of thee speken otherwyse than the sothe. **1426** LYDG. *De Guil. Pilgr.* 5594, I ne may Suffre..But that I muste yow with-seyn. **1530** RASTELL *Bk. Purgat.* I. vii, As beyng and not beynge be two contraryauntys [etc.] the one alway doth denye and with saye the other.

c. *intr.* To make denial or contradiction; to speak in opposition *to*; also *trans.* to utter by way of contradiction.

a **1300** *Cursor M.* 17288 + 11 In witnes þai ros with him, ..For þe Iews suld not with-say þat gart to ded him bring. **1382** WYCLIF *Job* xvi. 9 The false seiere is rered vp aȝen my face, withseiende to me. —— *Judith* i. 11 To alle these Nabugodonosor..sente messageres; the whiche alle with o wil withseiden. **1390** GOWER *Conf.* I. 341 Whan Nestor hath his tale seid, Ayein him was no word withseid. *a* **1400** *Engl. Gilds* (1870) 355 þat euerych bakere habbe hys seal y knowe vpon hys loff, þat he ne mowe wiþ-segge ȝif he is of take oþer þan weel. *c* **1430** *Pilgr. Lyf Manhode* I. lxxiii. (1869) 48, I may not to that of no thing wel withseye. **1463** *Cases bef. King's Council* (Selden) 113 b, Forasmoch as they withsey not by dedez and actez of their factours.

3. *trans.* To speak or act against, oppose, resist; = GAINSAY *v.* 3; occas. to say (a thing) in opposition. Also, to disallow, forbid. Also *absol.*

c **1200** ORMIN 17826 Fele þede modiliȝ wiþþstodenn, & wiþþseȝȝdenn..heffness lihht. *c* **1200** *Trin. Coll. Hom.* 139 Bi þo daȝes luuede herodes..his broðer wif, and binam hire him, and Seint Iohan hit wið seide. *a* **1225** *Ancr. R.* 204 Hwonne þe schil & te heorte ne wiðsiggeð nout. *c* **1275** *Passion our Lord* 422 in *O.E. Misc.* 49 Eueruych mon þat makeþ hym king..He wyþ-seyþ cesare. *c* **1380** WYCLIF *Wks.* (1880) 160 þat no man dar wiþ-seie hem in here wrong. *c* **1386** CHAUCER *Prol.* 805 Who so wole my Iuggement withseye. **1390** GOWER *Conf.* I. 312 Ther mai noman his happ withsein. **1471** CAXTON *Recuyell* (Sommer) 88 That ther be not oon man that is so hardy to withsaye ony thynge contrarye to my will. **1483** —— *G. de la Tour* xxix. c vj, He was..patron of the parysshe and the parson durst not withsaye hym. *Ibid.* cxxxiii. mij b, I defende and withsaye to them the kyssyng. **1523** LD. BERNERS *Froiss.* I. cclxxxiv. 174/1, I may nat nor dare nat withsay yor noble pleasure. *a* **1529** SKELTON *Sp. Parrot* 395 Moloc, that mawmett, there darre no man withsay.

4. a. To refuse to do or perform. Also *absol.*

a **1225** *Ancr. R.* 238 þeo..wiðseggeð þe graunt þerof mid unwille heorte. *a* **1225** *Juliana* 26 ȝet tu maht ȝef þu wult burhen þe seoluen, ant ȝef þu mare wiðseist [etc.]. **1297** R. GLOUC. (Rolls) 7689 To hom þat wolde is wille do debonere he was & milde & to hom þat wiþsede strong tirant & wilde. *c* **1385** CHAUCER *L.G.W.* Prol. 367 Or hym was bodyn make thilke tweye Of sum persone & durste it not with-seye. **1485** CAXTON *Chas. Gt.* 49 Gladly he wold haue doo the bataylle yf he had not wythsayed it..whan he was requyred.

b. To decline to give, grant, or allow; to refuse. Also with dat. of person (sometimes without dir. obj.).

1297 R. GLOUC. (Rolls) 4920 + 6 þe byssop yt nolde grante ac outlych yt wyþ seyde. **13..** *K. Alis.* 2905 (Laud MS.) Homage nolde hym non wiþsaye. **1402** HOCCLEVE *Let. Cupid* 108 She..So lyberal ys, she wol no wyght with-sey. *c* **1430** LYDG. *Min. Poems* (Percy Soc.) 32 She..Halsethe and kissethe and wol hym not with-seyne. *c* **1450** *Merlin* xiv. 204, I will in no wise with-sey that ye requere. *c* **1475** *Partenay* 86 No man shall ther-of you werne ne withsay. **1531** *Dial. on Laws Eng.* I. vi. 10 b, I wyll nat withsay thy desyre. **1545** ASCHAM *Toxoph.* (Arb.) 165 Thanke your selfe, whiche woulde haue me rather faulte..than..withsay your request. **16..** *Eger & Grine* 590 in Furniv. & Hales *Percy Folio* I. 372 Soe he desired that sword soe bright That shee was loth to with-say that Knight. **1661–85** in *Househ. Ord.* (1790) 372 This is in noe wise to bee withsaid, for it is the King's honour.

Hence †**with'sayer,** a gainsayer, opponent.

c **1420** *Wycliffite Bible* Pref. Ep. iii. 63 The withseieris to withstonde [orig. *contradicentes revincere*]. *c* **1450** *Godstow Reg.* 267 All withseyers and attemptours to breke this writyng.

†**with'saying,** *vbl. sb. Obs.* [f. WITHSAY *v.* + -ING[1].] Contradiction, gainsaying, opposition.

a **1225** [see WITHSAW]. **1340** *Ayenb.* 233 þou sselt louye god..mid ale þine wylle wyþ-oute wyþziginge. **1387** TREVISA *Higden* (Rolls) I. 71 Fame of Paradys haþ i-dured wiþoute wiþseienge sexe þowsand ȝere and more. *c* **1450** *Godstow Reg.* 194 To distreyne aftir their owne wil, without ony withseiyng of them or ther successours. *c* **1475** *Partenay* 482, I shal do With all my hole hert, without withsaing, Al that which ye wyll be me commaunding.

†**with'set,** *v. Obs.* [OE. *wiþsettan*: see WITH- and SET *v.*[1]]

1. *trans.* To resist, oppose, withstand. Also occas. const. inf.: To prevent from doing something.

c **1000** *Lambeth Ps.* xvi[i]. 9 ðescyld me fram ansyne arleasra þa þe me ȝeswenctun *vel* wiðsettun. *c* **1000** in Assmann *Ags. Hom.* vii. 186 Ðonne sende he heom fultum ðurh sumne deman, ðe wiðsette heoræ feondum. *c* **1175** *Lamb. Hom.* 113 *Deus superbis resistit*..Drihten widset þan prudan. *a* **1330** *Roland & V.* 834 No hadde ben þe bacinet, þat þe strok wiþ sett. *c* **1330** R. BRUNNE *Chron. Wace* (Rolls) 2921 Hauen to aryue þey hym wyþsette. **1393** LANGL. *P. Pl.* C. I. 174 Myȝte we with eny wyt hus wil with-sette, We myȝte be lordes aloft. *a* **1430** *Pol. Rel. & L. Poems* (1903) 215/394 Holi writt, þat cleerli schewiþ þee goostli liȝt, How þou schuldist deedli synne with-sett. *c* **1430** *Syr Gener.* (Roxb.) 4518 Generides and his feres to lete, And here entre to withsett. *c* **1440** *Promp. Parv.* 530/2 Wythe settyn', *obsto,* *obsisto.* c 1450 *Cov. Myst.* (Shaks. Soc.) 212 If thou with-sett the deuyl in his deede.

2. To beset (a way, etc.) so as to prevent a person from passing. (In early use with dat. of person.)

a 1300 *Cursor M.* 23727 Ded has vs wit-sett vr strete, Nil we, wil we, we sal mete. 1338 R. BRUNNE *Chron.* (1810) 337 Als þei fro kirke cam, þer way he þam withsette. 1375 BARBOUR *Bruce* XIV. 107 Twa of thame.. With-set ane place in-till his way.. With twa thousand of men. c 1400 *Ywaine & Gaw.* 1921 Sir Ywayne sone with-set the yate, That the eril myght noght in tharate. 1426 LYDG. *De Guil. Pilgr.* 10527 Thys .iii. confederat, Causen..a perillous mortal stryff To pylgrymes.. Ther weyes, when they ha wyth-set.

3. To seize in compensation for a debt, etc.

1445 *Paston Lett.* I. 58 He hathe suffrid the corne to ben with sette for viijs. of rentte..wich yowre fadre paide nevere. 1477 *Ibid.* III. 211 Mastras Clere hath sen down hyr men, and with set alle the stuff and wrekke.

Hence †**with'setting** *vbl. sb.*

1340 *Ayenb.* 39 Þe ualse yulemde þet..zecheþ wyþsetti[n]gges and respit uor to bynime oþren hare oȝen. c 1440 *Promp. Parv.* 530/2 Wythe settynge, *obsistencia.*

†**with'sit**, *v. Obs.* [f. WITH- + SIT *v.*]

1. *trans.* To oppose, resist, withstand. Also, to prevent; to ward off.

c 1300 *Havelok* 1683 Hauelok ne durste..Nouth withsitten þat ubbe bad. c 1330 R. BRUNNE *Chron. Wace* (Rolls) 8138 Ȝyf ȝe ne conne nought do hym wyte What þe fallyng may wyþ-syt. c 1330 *Arth. & Merl.* 9055 King Rion wiþsat þat dent. 1387–8 T. USK *Test. Love* III. viii. (Skeat) l. 87 This rightfulnesse..helpeth the spirit to withsitte the leude lustes of flesshly lykinge. 1393 LANGL. *P. Pl.* C. XIX. 251 Ich with-sat nat hus heste. 1412–20 LYDG. *Chron. Troy* I. 3003 To with-sitte þe force of sorcerye. c 1425 *Seven Sag.* (P.) 518 None durste wyth-sytte hys heste, Nouthir the lest no the moste. c 1430 *Pilgr. Lyf Manhode* II. liii. (1869) 96 He shulde not mown with sitte thee ne ayens stonde thee.

2. *intr.* To fail. *rare.*

c 1330 *Arth. & Merl.* 8457 Hir eiȝen turned, hir voice wiþsat.

Hence †**with'sitting** *vbl. sb.*, opposition.

1387–8 T. USK *Test. Love* II. vii. (Skeat) l. 142 The fleshly body of a man, over whiche have oftentyme flyes,..mokel might in grevaunce..withouten any withsittinge.

withstand (wɪð'stænd), *v.* Pa. t. and pa. pple. **withstood**. (Also 5 *pa. t.* **wiþstonded**.) [OE. *wiþstandan*, = OFris. *withstonda*, ON. *viðstanda*: see WITH- and STAND *v.* Cf. OS. *wiðarstandan* (MLG. *wedderstân*), OHG. *widarstân*. For the separable form *stand with* see STAND *v.* 79 a.]

1. *trans.* To stand or maintain one's or its position against; to offer resistance to, resist, oppose: often with implication that the resistance is successful or effectual.

(*a*) a person, his will, desire, power, etc.

c 888 ÆLFRED *Boeth.* vi. §1 Swa doð nu ða þeostro þinre ȝedrefednesse wiðstandan minum leohtum larum. 971 *Blickl. Hom.* 161 Hi cyningum & yfelum ricum ealdormannum wiþstandan mihtan. c 1000 ÆLFRIC *Hom.* II. 434 Nis nan ðing þe his mihte wiðstande. *a* 1122 *O.E. Chron.* (Laud MS.) Introd. 3 Ȝif hwa eow wiðstent, we eow fultumiað. c 1200 ORMIN 16143 & tatt all forr to cwemenn Godd & defell to wiþþstanndenn. *a* 1225 *Ancr. R.* 264 Þet we muhten wiðstonden þes deofles ferde, þet is so strong uppon vs. 1377 LANGL. *P. Pl.* B. Prol. 156 Myȝte we wiþ any witte his wille withstonde. c 1386 CHAUCER *Monk's Prol.* 32, I dar hire [*sc.* my wife] nat withstonde For she is bigg in Armes. 1434 in Ellis *Orig. Lett.* Ser. II. I. 111 To with-stand your enemyes in tyme of nede. c 1450 *Brut* 432 She withstode the Duke of Burgoyne and alle his malice. 1530 PALSGR. 783/2 All the worlde can nat withstande the wyll of God. 1581 J. BELL *Haddon's Answ. Osor.* 212 Seeing that not their willes, but Gods predestination withstandeth them so, that they cannot be able to come. 1592 SHAKS. *2 Hen. VI*, IV. v. 4 They haue wonne the Bridge, Killing all those that withstand them. 1642 J. TAYLOR (Water P.) *Mad Fashions* 3 Thou Lord of Hosts,..Thy foes (Thine Anti-christian foes) withstand. 1708 PRIOR *Turtle & Sparrow* 106 Grim Pluto will not be withstood By Force or Craft. 1857 BUCKLE *Civiliz.* I. vi. 296 His might nothing was able to withstand. 1882 MISS BRADDON *Mt. Royal* v, You have not the will to withstand your aunt.

(*b*) a blow, force, attack, impulse; a destructive, oppressive, or hostile agency or influence.

a 1000 *Wanderer* 15 Ne mæȝ weriȝ mod wyrde wiðstondan. c 1000 *Sax. Leechd.* II. 236 Þisse adle eac wiþstandeþ tosnidenre hreaþemuse blod. *a* 1300 *Cursor M.* 19105 Yur sin witstand, þat yee mai rise Wit þat parti þat es rightwise. 13.. *Ibid.* 10523 (Gött.) Ioseph..þat styward was,..wele widstode þe hunger þat egipt ouer-ȝode. 1390 GOWER *Conf.* I. 68 He was noght of such myht The strengthe of love to with-stonde. 1430–40 LYDG. *Bochas* VIII. vii. (1558) 4 b, The stroke of fortune withstant no creatures. 1558 PHAER *Æneid.* v. N ij b, And sturdy strokes he did withstand. 1593 SHAKS. *Rich. II*, I. i. 173 Rage must be withstood. 1610 HOLLAND *Camden's Brit.* 509 It valiantly withstood the siege. 1667 MILTON *P.L.* VI. 253 Such destruction to withstand He hasted. 1741 BUTLER *Serm.* Wks. 1874 II. 264 The love of liberty..carries us to withstand tyranny. 1842 DICKENS *Amer. Notes* viii, Having withstood such strong attacks upon my fortitude. 1852 MALPAS *Builder's Pocket-bk.* 56 The pressure is..withstood by the abutments. 1860 TYNDALL *Glac.* I. xi. 76 Ground to mud by an agency which the hardest rocks cannot withstand. 1912 *Sphere* 28 Dec. 326/2 Armour to withstand the terrific hitting power of the latest naval gun.

(*c*) a material thing.

a 1400 *Octouian* 1120 He ne fond neuer boon ne lyre Hys ax withstent. 1581 A. HALL *Iliad* II. 22 Yet they our Machins haue withstoode. 1638 JUNIUS *Paint. Ancients* 209 An oxe doth withstand the yoke, and a horse doth withstand the bridle. 1697 DRYDEN *Æneis* VIII. 396 Nor thy resistless Arm the Bull withstood. 1721 PRIOR *Predestination* 332 A Casual Fabric built upon the sand Which can nor winds nor falling rains withstand. 1870 BRYANT *Iliad* I. IV. 130 Their limbs Are not of stone or iron to withstand The trenchant steel ye wield.

†**b.** To oppose in statement; to controvert, contradict, deny. *Obs.*

1513 THOMAS LD. HOWARD in Ellis *Orig. Lett.* Ser. III. I. 160 Trustyng that ye woll..withstonde all ill reports undeserved made of me. 1526 *Pilgr. Perf.* (W. de W. 1531) 66 b, To withstande and stoppe the tonges of them that.. sclaundreth them. 1581 J. BELL *Haddon's Answ. Osor.* 170 b, This withstandeth our disputation of Necessitie nothyng at all.

c. To resist the attraction, influence, or cogency of; occas. to abstain from (doing something).

1725 DE FOE *Voy. round World* (1840) 292 A curiosity that I could scarce withstand. 1781 COWPER *Charity* 31 The wretch that slighted or withstood The tender argument of kindred blood. 1798 FERRIAR *Illustr. Sterne* ii. 25 Religious disputes were subjects of ridicule too tempting to be withstood. 1852 DISRAELI *Bentinck* 18 He could scarcely have withstood contemplating what might perhaps have been his own position. 1877 FREEMAN *Norm. Conq.* (ed. 3) I. App. 753 It seems impossible to withstand this evidence.

†**2. a.** To refuse to allow (a person) the possession of (something). *Obs.*

a 1300 *Cursor M.* 24772 (Edin.) [William] sloh þe king þat Harald hiht þat born was of þe danis blod For qui þe land he him wit stod.

†**b.** Const. inf. or clause: To prevent. *Obs.*

a 1300 *Cursor M.* 6973 Þai fand strang folk..þat..wit-stode þam þe land to win. c 1400 *Rom. Rose* 3807 He myght not his tunge withstonde Worse to reporte than he fonde. 1542 UDALL *Erasm. Apoph.* 278 *marg.*, What..Caesar saied vnto Metellus withstandyng that he should not take any money out of the treasourie [*Metello obsistenti ne pecunias ab ærario tolleret*]. 1581 J. BELL *Haddon's Answ. Osor.* 177 b, Nothyng withstandeth truely, but that both may bee true.

†**c.** To keep off or away, withhold, withdraw.

1398 TREVISA *Barth. De P.R.* v. xxiv. (Bodl. MS.), He haþ bondes and obstacles to withstonde & lette þe poudre. c 1485 *Digby Myst.* III. 284 Lord, with-stond þis duresse! 1508 FISHER *7 Penit. Ps.* xxxviii. Wks. (1876) 82 He may noo more withdrawe from them the bemes of his grace..than the sonne may withstande his bemes out of wyndowes whan they be open.

d. To stand in the way of; to oppose or hinder the performance, operation, or progress of. *Obs.* or merged in 1.

c 1385 CHAUCER *L.G.W.* 1183 *Dido*, Hyre systir Anne as she that coude hire good Seyde as hire thoughte & sumdel it with stod. *a* 1425 tr. *Arderne's Treat. Fistula*, etc. 51 When þer growed..any superflue flesch.., I withstode it or mette it with poudre of creoferoboron. *a* 1548 HALL *Chron.*, *Edw. V*, 1 b, He spared no mannes deathe, whose life withstode his purpose. 1584 COGAN *Haven Health* cix. (1636) 110 Raysons..concoct raw humors, and withstand putrifaction. 1621 G. SANDYS *Ovid's Met.* v. (1626) 90 His sword withstood Their re-ascent. c 1680 *Roxb. Ball.* (1891) VII. 358 Then prethee Love make no delay, let's not our precious time withstand. 1697 DRYDEN *Æneis* II. 155 The Wintry Seas, and Southern Winds, Withstood their passage home. 1737 GLOVER *Leonidas* I. 228 Leonidas awake! Shall these withstand The public safety? Lo! thy country calls. 1742 FIELDING *J. Andrews* II. iv, I hope you will not withstand your own preferment. 1814 SCOTT *Ld. of Isles* III. iv, His frantic mood Was scarcely by the news withstood, That Moray shared his sister's flight. 1825 —— *Talism.* xvii, The entrance of Queen Berengaria..was withstood..by the chamberlains.

3. *intr.* To offer resistance or opposition.

c 950 *Lindisf. Gosp.* Luke xi. 53 Ongunnun ða ældu.. hefiȝlice wiðstonda. *a* 1122 *O.E. Chron.* (Laud MS.) an. 1070 Þa utlaȝa..woldon into þam mynstre, & þa munecas wið-stoden þæt hi na mihton in cumen. c 1175 *Lamb. Hom.* 131 Ne mihte þer [in hell] nan wiðstonden, ne prophete ne patriarche. c 1200 *Vices & Virtues* 39 Strengþe to wiðstanden aȝeanes dieules fondinges. c 1250 *Gen. & Ex.* 2649 Ðe king wið-stod. 13.. *K. Alis.* 2062 (Laud MS.), Þise shulden wiþstonde hard And sauen al þe forme ward. 1340 *Ayenb.* 22 Huanne þe man wyþstant to alle ham þet guod him wolde. 1375 BARBOUR *Bruce* I. 456 Quhar God helpys, quhat may withstand? ? *a* 1400 *Morte Arth.* 1747 Ȝife we in the stour withstondene the better. 1530 PALSGR. 781/2 Agaynst the wyll of God no man may withstande. 1618 BOLTON *Florus* (1636) 183 The City was encouraged to withstand upon the news of Lucullus his approach. 1667 MILTON *P.L.* II. 610 They..wish..to reach The..stream, ..But fate withstands. 1676 S. SEWALL *Diary* (1876) I. 31 He was here with Mr. Broughton earnestly urging [etc.]... Mr. Broughton with-stood. 1874 GREEN *Short Hist.* iii. §2. 122 Langton prepared to withstand and rescue his country from the tyranny of John.

†**4.** To come to a stand, halt, stop. *Obs.*

c 1250 *Gen. & Ex.* 3646 Ðre daȝes and niȝtes faren it gan And wið-stod in ðe deserd pharan. c 1330 R. BRUNNE *Chron. Wace* (Rolls) 12780 Þey come & passed to þe wodes side, & þere wyþstode for to abyde. c 1430 *Pistill of Susan* 285 (Cott. MS.) Alle were a-stonyed and with-stood.

with'stander. [f. WITHSTAND *v.* + -ER[1].] One who withstands; a resister, opponent.

a 1325 *MS. Rawl. B.* 520 lf. 25 b, þe schirreue..sal.. chastise þe withstonderes þoru þe prison. 1382 WYCLIF *Num.* xxii. 33 Ȝyuynge stede to the withstonder. 1550 BALE *Engl. Votaries* II. 49 To terryfye their withstanders. 1567 *Reg. Privy Council Scot.* I. 569 A withstandar of his Hienes authoritie. 1588 *Marprel. Epist.* (Arb.) 6 Proud prelates, intolerable withstanders of reformation. *a* 1618 RALEIGH *Judic. & Sel. Ess.* II. (1650) 1 War..may be defined the exercise of violence under Soveraigne Command, against withstanders force. 1745 DODSLEY *Rex et Pontifex* Misc. I. 155 Silence every bold withstander That shall dare to disobey. 1820 *Examiner* No. 645. 530/1 It has seen him withstand the withstanders of those despotisms. 1877 MORLEY *Crit. Misc.* Ser. II. 199 Obstinate withstanders of all novelty.

with'standing, *vbl. sb.* [f. WITHSTAND *v.* + -ING[1].] The action of the verb WITHSTAND; opposition, resistance.

13.. *K. Alis.* 2168 (Laud MS.), Stif wiþstondyng & wiȝth fleiȝeyng. 1303 R. BRUNNE *Handl. Synne* 12049 Þy wyþ-stondyng haþ hym rafte Of hys temptyng alle þe crafte. 1340 *Ayenb.* 29 Wy[þ]stondinge, þet is hardnesse of herte. 1493 [H. PARKER] *Dives & Pauper* III. xiii. (1496) 148/2 They shall haue sotylte of bodye without ony withstandynge, for ther shal no thynge withstande them. 1525 LD. BERNERS *Froiss.* II. vi. 6 b/1 The first went with ladders in to the dykes. They founde no withstandyng. 1650 TRAPP *Comm. Deut.* xii. 3 Notwithstanding the withstandings of the rude rabble. 1696 AUBREY *Misc.* ii. 28 To make several withstandings against the Shock of Fortune. 1842 NEWMAN *Corr.* (1917) 174 No one can tell how much there is in sympathy, over and above the influence one may have in withstanding.

So **with'standing** *ppl. a.*, that withstands.

1711 SHAFTESB. *Charac.* III. Misc. I. ii. 15 The tumid Bladder.., bursts the withstanding Casements.

†**with'standing**, *prep.* (*conj.*) *Obs.* (Only in Caxton.) [pr. pple. of WITHSTAND used as a prep. (conj.) in imitation of OF. *obstant* (*que*). Cf. NOTWITHSTANDING (= F. *non obstant*).] Having regard to, on account of; seeing *that*.

c 1489 CAXTON *Sonnes of Aymon* xxvi. 566 Why dyde ye calle my fader of treyson, wythstandyng that men know well that he is one of the trueste knyghtes of the worlde? 1490 —— *Eneydos* xvi. 65 Thynkyng in hymselfe to be in daunger of his persone..wythstandyng the inuectyue monycyons doon to hym. 1491 —— *Vitas Patr.* (W. de W. 1495) II. 186 b/2 The marchaunt..wolde not by it withstandynge this that he knewe not how moche it myght well be worth.

withstart to **withstrain**: see WITH-.

†**with'take**, *v. Obs.* [f. WITH- + TAKE *v.* Cf. ON. *viðtaka* resistance.]

1. *trans.* To 'take up', reprove, rebuke.

a 1340 HAMPOLE *Psalter* xlix. 9 Noght in þi sacrifice i sall wiþtake þe [Vulg. *arguam te*]. c 1340 —— *Prose Treat.* 8 Þay ere in trauayle..with takand ydill mene. c 1400 *Titus & Vesp.* (Roxb.) 1403 For he withtoke hem in her lawe þei wratthede hem sore with his sawe.

2. ? To rescue.

c 1400 *Destr. Troy* 11036 Phylmen þe freke, þat fuersly withtakon,..Lut to þe lady.

3. To keep back, retain, or withhold unlawfully.

14.. *Siege Jerus.* (E.E.T.S.) 48 His tribute..þat þey with-take wolde. *a* 1450 MYRC *Par. Pr.* (1902) 1185 Hast þow werkemen oght wyth-tan Of any þynge þat þey schulde han?

Hence †**with'taker**, a rebuker, reprover.

a 1340 HAMPOLE *Psalter* ix. 24 Þat thynge has man delite to doe in þe whilk þai hafe sum louere & nan with takere.

†**withward**, *prep. Obs.* [f. WITH *adv.* + -WARD, after *toward*.] ? Along with.

a 1225 *Leg. Kath.* 1983 Þis pinfule gin wes o swuch wise iginet, þæt te twa turnden eiðer wiðward oðer.

'**withweed.** *Obs.* or *dial.* [A blending of WITHWIND and BINDWEED.] = next.

1567 MAPLET *Gr. Forest* 34 Bindweede, of some With-weede. 1766 *Compl. Farmer* s.v. *Bindweed* P 2/1, I had a very good crop of wheat; but a with-weed came up to every plant. [Reproducing Lisle *Husb.* (1757) 393, which, however, has *withwind.*]

withwind ('wɪθwaɪnd). Now *dial.* Forms: 1 **wiþo-**, **wiþewinde**, 2 **wiþwinde**, 4 **weþewinde**, **withe-**, **wythe-**, **weythwynde**, 6 **with-**, **wythwynde**, 6–7 **withwinde**, 6– **withwind**. [OE. *wiþowinde*, *wiþe-*, later *wiþwinde*, f. *wiþo-*, *wiþe-* (related to WITHE) + *winde* WIND *sb.*[2]; corresp. to OS. *withewind* 'caprifolium', MLG., MDu. *wedewinde* 'caprifolium', 'periclymena', 'hedera', 'ligustrum'; for the first element cf. OE. *weoþobend* WITHBIND, for the second, OE. *widuwinde* ivy, convolvulus; see also WITHYWIND.] Bindweed, *Convolvulus arveniss* or *C. sepium*; also *C. Soldanella* (Sea Withwind: see SEA *sb.* 23 f). Applied also, like BINDWEED, to other climbing plants, e.g. dodder, smilax, traveller's joy.

c 1000 *Sax. Leechd.* II. 34 Wiþ eaȝece ȝenim wiþowindan twiȝu. *Ibid.* 122 Wiþewindan twiȝ foreweard. c 1050 *Voc.* in Wr.-Wülcker 428/36 *Inuoluco*, wiþewinde. c 1100 *Gloss.* ibid. 138/28 *Uiticella*, wiþwinde. 1377 LANGL. *P. Pl.* B. v. 525 In a withewyndes wise ywounden aboute. 1398 TREVISA *Barth. De P.R.* XVIII. xxix. (Bodl. MS.), A tree þat is bi-clipped w[t] yuye oþer wiþ weþewinde. 1533 ELYOT *Cast. Helthe* (1541) 11 b, Thynges good for the Lyuer: Worme-wode: Wyth wynde. 1548 TURNER *Names Herbes* (E.D.S.) 30 Conuoluulus..called of the herbaries Volubilis, in english wythwynde or byndeweede. 1552 HULOET, Withwinde herbe, *cassutha, cascuta, cissampelos, conuoluulus.* 1580 T. NEWTON *Approved Medicines* 20 b, *Smilax hortensis*, Gardein withwinde. *a* 1722 LISLE *Husb.* (1757) 382 Giving their lands a second tillage, perhaps to destroy the withwind. 1899 R. BRIDGES *Idle Flowers* xiv, Thro' the hedgerow peer Withwind and Snapdragon.

attrib. 1891 HARDY *Noble Dames* ii. 90 One of those sweet-pea or with-wind natures which require a twig of stouter fibre than its own to hang upon and bloom.

withy ('wɪðɪ), *sb.* Forms: 1 **wiðiȝ**, 3 **wiði**, 4 **wiþie**, **wiþge**, (**w(h)itheye**, **wytie**, **weþie**), 4, 6–7 (9 *Sc.*)

withie, 5–6 **wythy**, 5–7 **withye**, **wythie**, 6 **wythye**, 6–7 **withee** (5 **withi**, **wethei**, **-ie**, *pl.* **wetheis**, **wethiss**, 5–6 **wethy**, **whythy**, 6 **wethye**, *pl.* **wythiese**), 7, 9 **withey**, 6– **withy**. [OE. *wíþiȝ* (= L. *vītex*, *vītic-* Agnus Castus), for the connexions of which see WITHE. Cf. WIDDY.]

1. A willow of any species: sometimes *spec.* the osier willow, *Salix viminalis*.

961 in Birch *Cartul. Sax.* III. 289 On þone haran wiðiȝ. *a* **1225** *Ancr. R.* 86 He is ase þe wiði þet sprutteð ut þe betere þet me hine ofte croppeð. **1325** in Kennett *Parochial Antiq.* (1695) 395 Tres acræ apud le Whitheyes. *Ibid.* 400 A quo quidem prato dimidia roda jacet atte Witheyes juxta pratum Prioris. *c* **1325** *Gloss. W. de Bibbesw.* in Wright *Voc.* 163 Sauz [*glossed* wytie (wilwe)]. **1382** WYCLIF *Lev.* xxiii. 40 ȝe shulen take to ȝow..withies of the rennynge water. **1398** TREVISA *Barth. De P.R.* XIII. xi. (Bodl. MS.), In som partie of his brymme he haþ plente of wiþges and of segge as it is seide. **1523** FITZHERB. *Husb.* §24 The rakes..be moste comynly made of hasel and withe [*ed.* **1534** withee]. **1578** LYTE *Dodoens* III. lxii. 403 [Polypody] growing vppon olde wythiese. *c* **1640** J. SMYTH *Lives Berkeleys* (1883) I. 123 To be a bendinge withy, not a stubborne Oke. **1661** BOYLE *Style Script.* 180 Withees, whilst they are sound grow Unregarded Trees; but when they once are Rotten, Shine in the Night. **1791** W. GILPIN *Forest Scenery* I. 64 The withy, or *salix fragilis*, is the most inconsiderable of it's tribe. **1866** BLACKMORE *Cradock Nowell* l, The witheys were gloved with silver and gold. **1889** CONAN DOYLE *Micah Clarke* xxix, The moaning of the breeze among the withies.

b. With qualification, applied to various species of willow; also to other plants, as the laserwort, *Laserpitium Siler*: see quots.

hoop withy: see HOOP *sb.*^{1} 13 b. †**rose withy** = WILLOW-HERB 2.

14.. *Metr. Voc.* in Wr.-Wülcker 629/9 Wythy, *ciler.* **1523–34** FITZHERB. *Husb.* §130 Whyte wethy..wyll not grow in marsshe ground. **1585** HIGINS *Junius' Nomencl.* 153/1 *Siler*,..spert withie, ozier withie, or small withie. **1612** R. CH. *Olde Thrift newly revived* 49 The Withie, of which are said to be 4 kinds, that is, the white withy, blacke Withie, and red Withie, osier Withie. **1650** [W. HOWE] *Phytol. Brit.* 27 Chamænerion sive Epilobium..Rosebay willow-herb, Rose withy, or Willow-flower. **1733** W. ELLIS *Chiltern & Vale Farm.* 191 This Withy often arrives to a large Stature, especially the red Sort. **1860** WARTER *Sea-board* II. 35 The yellow withy which lived on the moisture in the hollow. **1866** *Treas. Bot.* 1235/2 Withy, *Laserpitium Siler*:..—, Hoop, *Rivina octandra*.

2. A flexible branch of a willow, esp. as used for tying or binding, as a halter (cf. WIDDY 2), etc.; any similar flexible branch or twig; a leash, hoop, or the like made of a withy.

a **1400** *Sir Perc.* 444 Therto his mere he bande With the withy. *c* **1425** WYNTOUN *Cron.* VII. ix. 2874 Withe rapis and wetheis about þar hals. *c* **1460** SIR R. ROS *La Belle Dame* 186 With grene wythies ybounden. **1564** BULLEIN *Dial. agst. Pest.* (1573) 6, I had better be hangad in a withie or in a cowtaile, then be a rowfooted Scot. **1587** FLEMING *Contn. Holinshed* III. 1348/2 Which tempest..rent up manie great trees,..or woond them like withies. **1658** *N. Riding Rec.* VI. 34 He is a rogue and deserves a withy. **1727** A. HAMILTON *New Acc. E. Indies* II. xlv, 149 A Rattan Withy to lift them by. **1787** W. HUTTON *Courts of Requests* 324 The ties of honour..are as easily broken through, as Sampson's withies. **1790** GROSE *Prov. Gloss.* (ed. 2), *Withy*, a round hoop of osier. **1805** SOUTHEY *Madoc* I. v, Canes and withies formed the walls and roof. **1818** SCOTT *Br. Lamm.* vii, In order to save himself from the withie. **1865** W. G. PALGRAVE *Arabia* II. 219 Palm-huts unroofed, despite of their strong lacings and withies. **1893** CONAN DOYLE *Refugees* xxxiv, They were lashed to low posts with willow withies.

b. *coll. sing.* Withies as a material.

1833 HT. MARTINEAU *Brooke Farm* viii. 95 The harness was made of withy. **1915** *Q. Rev.* July 4 Pots of withy or of stout netting..are used for crabs.

†**3.** = WIDDY 3. *Obs.*

1438 *Exch. Rolls Scot.* V. 58 Pro fabrica septem wethyis erri. **1456** *Ibid.* VI. 278. **1484** *Ibid.* IX. 239.

4. *attrib.* and *Comb.*, as ***withy band***, ***basket***, ***bed***, ***blossom***, ***bough***, ***cutting***, ***holt***, ***labyrinth***, ***leaf***, ***pollard***, ***pot***, ***prison***, ***rope***, ***shoot***, ***tree***, ***twig***, ***wood***, etc.; ***withy-bound*** adj.; †**withy-cole**, ? charcoal made of willow wood; †**withy-cragged** [CRAGGED *a.*^{2}], see quots., **withy-fly**, an artificial fly used in angling; †**withy-herb**, purple loosestrife: = WILLOW-HERB 1.

a **1688** STRADLING *Serm.* (1692) 176 Those Shackles..which could no more hold him, than the *withy bands could Sampson. **1820** SHELLEY *Hymn Merc.* lxix, He..bound Stiff withy bands the infant's wrists around. **1891** HARDY *Tess* xlix, She..packed up as many of her belongings as would go into a *withy basket. **956** in Birch *Cartul. Sax.* III. 96 On ðæt *wiðiȝ bed. **1420** *Chertsey Cartulary* 41 b (P.R.O.), Duas acras terre et dimidiam super le Whythybed. **1583** in Wadley *Notes Wills Bristol* (1886) 237 The withie Bedd or twigg bedd. **1844** J. T. HEWLETT *Parsons & W.* xxxix, And now, sir, do you push on to that corner of this withy-bed. **1898** J. A. GIBBS *Cotswold Village* 106 When November frosts begin to attract snipes to the withybeds. **1707** MORTIMER *Husb.* 203 As soon as the Willow or *Withy Blossoms appear. *c* **1440** *Pallad. on Husb.* III. 412 An arm gret *withi bough. **1862** W. BARNES *Hwomely Rhymes* II. 85 Grey-leav'd withy-boughs. **1898** A. AUSTIN *Lamia's Winter Quarters* 8 The *withy-bound flask of ruby wine. **1657** REEVE *God's Plea* 254 Fumigations of Storax,..Nemphar, Dragagant, *Withy-cole. **1607** MARKHAM *Cavel.* III. ii. 14 His necke straight..and..of one peece with his bodie, and not (as my countrey-men say) *withie craggd, which is loose and plyant. **1766** *Complete Farmer* s.v. *Stable* 7 B 1/1 The continual lifting up of the head to feed out of the rack..makes him, as they express it, withy-cragged. **1813** VANCOUVER *Agric. Devon* 137 Two rows of *withy or sallow cuttings. **1799** G. SMITH *Laboratory* II. 298 Alder-fly, *withy-fly, or bastard-caddis. **1578** LYTE *Dodoens* I. li. 75 Red *Lysimachus*, or *wythie herbe. **1856** MRS. TENNYSON in *Mem. Ld. Tennyson* (1897) I. 412 Went to our *withy holt. **1633** P. FLETCHER *Purple Isl.* I. lv, When a fisher-swain..hath spi'd A big-grown Pike..He sets a *withy Labyrinth beside. *c* **1460** J. RUSSELL *Bk. Nurture* 995 *Wethy leves, grene otes boyled in fere fulle soft. **1578** LYTE *Dodoens* I. li. 72 The leaues be..like willow, or wythie leaues. **1863** KINGSLEY *Water-Bab.* iii, The great *withy pollard which hangs over the backwater. *a* **1700** EVELYN *Diary* 9 Feb. 1665, *Withy-potts or nests for the wild fowle to lay their eggs in. **1633** P. FLETCHER *Purple Isl.* III. ii, Thirsil from *withy prison..Lets out his flock. **1815** SIMOND *Tour Gt. Brit.* II. 240 The *withy rope lasts good two years. *a* **1722** LISLE *Husb.* (1757) 375, I gathered *withy-shoots over which the cart-wheel had run. **1398** TREVISA *Barth. De P.R.* XVII. cxliv. (Bodl. MS.), þerfor it [is] nouȝt seker to slepe vnder þe *weþie tree. **1664** EVELYN *Sylva* xxix. 82, A..Withy-tree..which is increased to a most stupendious bulk. **1820** SHELLEY *Hymn Merc.* xiii, He..bound them in a lump with *withy twigs. **1523** FITZHERB. *Husb.* §24 Than maye he..tothe the rakes with drye *wethy wode.

'withy, *a. rare.* Also **-ey**. [f. WITHE *sb.* + -Y^{1}.] Resembling a withe or withy in flexibility.

1598 FLORIO, *Vencido*, tractable, yeeldinge,..plyable, withie. **1756** P. BROWNE *Jamaica* 244 A strong withey shrub. **1822** W. IRVING *Braceb. Hall* xxxvii. (1845) 229 The long withy ends of the branches.

withywind ('wɪðɪwaɪnd). Now *dial.* [Alteration of WITHWIND, after WITHY *sb.*] = WITHWIND.

1578 LYTE *Dodoens* III. lii. 391 Of smothe Bindweede, or Withiwinde. The great white Bindeweede or soft withiwinde. *Ibid.* liii. 393 Of blacke Withiwinde, or Bindeweede. **1591** PERCIVALL *Sp. Dict.*, *Campanilla yerva*, withie winde, *Smilax*. **1621** BURTON *Anat. Mel.* III. ii. III. 610 Whiter Galat then the white withy-wind. **1658** tr. *Porta's Nat. Magic* III. xix. 105 The seed of withy-winde being planted neer to Basil, [etc.]. **1825** JENNINGS *Obs. Dial. W. Eng.*, *Withy-wine*, the plant bindweed. **1829** J. L. KNAPP *Jrnl. Nat.* 114 The clematis, the 'withy-wind' of our peasantry. **1878** HARDY *Ret. Native* I. x, You could twist him to your will like withywind, if you only had the mind.

†**'witie**, *sb. Obs.* Forms: 1 **wit(e)ȝa**, **-iȝa**, (2 **witȝe**, **-eȝa**), 2–3 **witiȝe**, **-eȝe**, **witie**, (3 **witeie**, **witti(e**, **-y**). [OE. *wít(e)ȝa*, *-iȝa* = OHG. *wîz(z)ago*, altered (by association with *wîs* WISE *a.* and *sagen* SAY *v.*^{1}) to *wîssago* (MHG. *wîssage*, *-ag*), ON. *vitke*: f. *wīt-*: see WIT *v.*^{1}] A prophet. Also *adj.*, prophetic.

c **897** ÆLFRED *Gregory's Past. C.* xxxii. 213 Ne eow..ne ondrædað for nanes monnes wordum, ne for nanes witȝan gæste. *c* **950** *Lindisf. Gosp.* Mark i. 2 Suæ awritten is in esaia ðone witȝo. *c* **1175** *Lamb. Hom.* 43 Of þas pinan spekeð dauid þe halie witeȝe. *c* **1200** *Trin. Coll. Hom.* 83 Salemon and alle wise witeȝe. *Ibid.* 127 þis childes witiȝe gost. *c* **1205** LAY. 15877 To þan kinge was ibroht Joram þe witie [*c* **1275** witty]. *a* **1225** *Juliana* 39 þen muchele witti witeȝe ysaie.

†**'witie**, *v.*^{1} *Obs.* In 1 **wit(e)ȝian**, 2–3 **witeȝen**. [OE. *wít(e)ȝian* = OFris. *wítgia* (MLG. *wittigen*), OHG. *wîzagôn* (MHG. *wîssagen*, G. *weissagen*); f. *wíteȝa* WITIE *sb.*] To prophesy.

c **950** *Lindisf. Gosp.* Matt. xxvi. 68 Witȝa us, crist, hua is se ðe ðec of-sloȝ. *c* **1000** ÆLFRIC *Num.* xi. 27 Ða hi witeȝodon on wicstowe. *c* **1175** *Lamb. Hom.* 7 þis he witeȝede bi drihtene þurh þene halie gast. *c* **1200** *Trin. Coll. Hom.* 127 Hie witeȝede..of ure louerd ihesu cristes to cume.

†**'witie**, *v.*^{2} *Obs.* Forms: 3 **witeȝen**, **-iȝe**, **-ien**, **-ye**, **wete** (?), 3–4 **witi(e**, **wytie**, 4 **-ye**, **wetye**; *pa. t.* 4 **wited**. [OE. **witian*, as in *bewitian* BIWITIE.] *trans.* To keep, guard, protect: = WITE *v.*^{2}

c **1205** LAY. 2753 Heo biȝeten men þe heom cuðen witen [*c* **1275** witie]. *Ibid.* 23738 þat he..mid his riht honde witeȝe me wið sconde. *Ibid.* 32155 þe pape hatte Sergius, he weteð Peteres hus. *a* **1290** *St. Eustace* 92 in Horstm. *Altengl. Leg.* (1881) 213 Wendeþ..godes way, Wytieþ oure soule niȝt and day. *c* **1290** *St. Brendan* 299 in *S. Eng. Leg.* 227 þat euerech frere of þat him leuez witiez to is soper. **1297** R. GLOUC. (Rolls) 9875 Saladin..let witie þe sepulcre þat no cristine ne com þer. **1340** *Ayenb.* 122 þe baylifs þet gouerneþ and wytyeþ þe kingriche. *c* **1350** *Will. Palerne* 176 þis litel barn..couþe..kepe alle here bestes,..& wited hem so wisly. *a* **1400** *Engl. Gilds* (1870) 357 And þat seluer..be y-take to sexe godemen..for þe Commune assent, and treweleche wetye, and trewleche spende.

Hence †**'witier**, protector, guardian; †**'witiing** *vbl. sb.*, guarding.

1340–70 *Alex. & Dind.* 678 [Bacus] wis witiere of win þat alle won bryngus. **13..** *Pol. Rel. & L. Poems* (1903) 268 Of vr vife wittes a wel witiynge.

witie, obs. form of WITTY.

†**'witieng**. *Obs.* Forms: 1 **witeȝung**, **witȝiung**, **witȝeong**, 2 **witeȝung**, 3 **witieng**, *Orm.* **witeȝhunnge**. [OE. *wíteȝung* (= OHG. *wîzagunga*, MHG. *wîssagunge*), f. *wíteȝian* WITIE *v.*^{1} + *-ung*, -ING^{1}.] Prophecy. Also *attrib.*

c **950** *Lindisf. Gosp.* Matt. xiii. 14 Witȝiung essaies. *c* **1000** ÆLFRIC *Saints' Lives* xxiv. 115 Hit is awriten be me on witeȝung bocum [etc.]. *c* **1200** *Trin. Coll. Hom.* 127 þis childes witiȝe gost lihte þe moder gost of witienge. *c* **1200** ORMIN 15174 All þatt witeȝhunnge wass þurrh himm onn erþe cwiddedd. *Ibid.* 15188 All þatt witeȝhunngeboc þatt witess haffdenn cwiddedd.

witin, obs. pa. pple. of WIT *v.*^{1}

witing, **-liche**, obs. ff. WITTING, -LY.

witless ('wɪtlɪs), *a.* Now only *literary* and somewhat *arch.* [OE. *witléas*, also *ȝewitléas*: see WIT *sb.*, IWIT, and -LESS.]

1. Lacking wisdom or sense; not guided by reason; unreasonable, foolish, heedless.

[*a* **1000** *Boeth. Metr.* xix. 46 Wenað þonne swa ȝewitlease ðæt hi þa soðan ȝesælða hæbben.] *c* **1200** ORMIN 6197 ȝiff þin macche iss wis & god, & tu wittlæs & wicke. *c* **1290** *S. Eng. Leg.* 248/263 þov witlese wrechche. *c* **1400** *26 Pol. Poems* iii. 90 Witteles wordes in ydel spoken. *c* **1400** *Brut* ccxiii. 249 Longe berde hertles, peyntede Hode witles, Gay cote graceles, makeþ Englissheman þriftles. **1559** *Mirr. Mag.*, *Dk. Clarence* xiii, I was witlesse, wanton, fond, and yong. **1581** BURNE in *Cath. Tractates* (S.T.S.) 170 Ane..confused rabil of vitles Bishopis. **1587** TURBERV. *Trag. Tales* 73 b, O wilfull witlesse acte, Which no man well aduisde would do. *a* **1676** HALE *Prim. Orig. Man.* (1677) 356 To keep in and regulate the extravagant and witless Spirit of Man. **1724** RAMSAY *Tea-t. Misc.* (1733) II. 149 Why did I, young witless maid Believe the flatt'ring tale? **1794** GODWIN *Cal. Williams* 42 Intended (witless and miserable precaution!) for the safeguards of the poor. **1803** JANE PORTER *Thaddeus* xxxvi, This witless coxcomb. **1860** MOTLEY *Netherl.* v. (1868) I. 153 It was witless to believe that Parma contemplated any such measure. **1879** BUTCHER & LANG *Odyssey* 25 Telemachus, even hereafter thou shalt not be craven or witless. **1910** *Times* 13 July 12/3 Mr. Rolls..had..to drop suddenly to the ground..owing to some witless spectators running into his way.

2. Mentally deficient or deranged; out of one's wits, crazy, lunatic. †Also, stupefied, dazed.

c **1000** *Sax. Leechd.* III. 146 On þam fiftan monþe he [*sc.* the fœtus] biþ cwica and weaxeð and seo modur lið witleas. *c* **1290** *Beket* 1906 in *S. Eng. Leg.* 161 He eode op and doun ase witles. **1297** R. GLOUC. (Rolls) 4414 He verde as a witles mon, hit was deol to be him ney. *c* **1375** *Sc. Leg. Saints* xxix. (*Placidas*) 440 Sa lang witlas stil he stud, Til þat nere he dronyt in þat flud. **1377** LANGL. *P. Pl.* B. XIII. 1, I awaked þere-with, witles nerehande. *c* **1470** *Gol. & Gaw.* 573 Wraithly wroht, as their war witlese and wode. **1571** GOLDING *Calvin on Ps.* xxxiv. 1 The woord (witlesse)..will well agree, bycause Dauid feyned himself too bee out of his wittes. **16..** *Young Musgrave* xix. in Child *Ballads* II. 249/2 She'll gae witless wud. **1900** H. SUTCLIFFE *Shameless Wayne* iii. (1905) 26 It would never do to leave this witless body to the night-rain and the cold.

†**3.** Devoid of understanding; having no intellectual faculty; irrational. *Obs.*

1382 WYCLIF *Wisd.* xv. 18 Thei most wrecchid herien bestes; witles forsothe, comparisouned to these. *c* **1395** *Plowman's T.* II. 528 They..liven wors than witles beestes. **1577** T. KENDALL *Flowers Epigr.* 50 This Image..Tongles and witles. **1587** GOLDING *De Mornay* xiv. 236 Sillie Soules which go on still like witlesse Beastes.

4. a. Deficient in understanding; having undeveloped or imperfect intellectual power; unintelligent, undiscerning; stupid, dull-witted.

1562 A. BROOKE *Romeus & Jul.* 2470 Euen from the hory head vnto the witles childe She wan the hartes of all. **1612** WOODALL *Surg. Mate* (1639) 6, I hold none so witlesse which cannot make use thereof, when they once see but the instrument. **1625** PURCHAS *Pilgrims* II. VI. i. 777 The Inhabitants..are most base and witlesse people. **1822** PRAED *Lillian* I. 140 The witless Child grew up alone. **1855** M. ARNOLD *Balder Dead* I. 98 Of ignorant witless mind Thou barest me, and unforeseeing soul.

b. Not understanding (something specified or implied); inapprehensive.

1614 R. WILKINSON *Paire Serm.* 2 Witlesse to discerne what he is himselfe. **1637** RUTHERFORD *Lett.*, *To Jas. Lindsay* 7 Sept. (1671) 138 A witless and lazie observer of the Lord's way and working. **1855** BROWNING *An Epistle* 143 The man is witless of..The value in proportion of all things. **1856** R. A. VAUGHAN *Mystics* III. iv. (1860) I. 85 The blue aether..at which to look up with smiles of witless wonder.

5. Not knowing; unaware, unconscious *of*.

In quot. 1827, incapable *of*.

1584 *Reg. Privy Council Scot.* III. 691 Ignorant and wytles of thair rysche and insolent behaviour. **1597** BEARD *Theatre God's Judgem.* I. ii. (1612) 232 Guiltlesse and witlesse of the crime. **1827** HOOD *Mids. Fairies* lxxxi, His pretty pouting mouth, witless of speech. **1850** P. CROOK *War of Hats* 34 Witless of the storm his words excite. **1872** BLACKIE *Lays Highl.* 82 He lay all witless of his doom.

6. Devoid of wit (WIT *sb.* 8). *rare.*

1753 RICHARDSON *Grandison* II. xxvi. 200 Repartee and smartness; the current wit of that witless place. **1859** *Habits of Gd. Society* 93 He can no longer claim exemption from solemn dinners,..and witless tea-parties.

7. Alluding to a state of extreme fear. Esp. in *colloq.* phr. ***to be scared witless***.

1975 D. BAGLEY *Snow Tiger* 19 It's the last job he'll ever have and he's scared witless that he'll lose it. **1982** S. BRETT *Murder Unprompted* ii. 19 'How are you feeling?'..'Scared witless, darling.'

Hence **'witlessly** *adv.*, foolishly, stupidly; **'witlessness**, senselessness, folly, stupidity.

a **1100** in Napier *OE. Glosses* (1902) 213 *Socordia*, *torpor*, *dementia*, witleasnes. **1598** FLORIO To Rdr. 7 Had not H. S...so witlessly prouoked me. **1599** SANDYS *Europæ Spec.* (1632) 178 Divine blessing, which accompanieth good causes, where wickednesse or wilfull witlessenesse doth not barre against it. **1608** T. MORTON *Preamb. Encounter* 72 Rather..accounted lyingly witty, than witlesly rash. **1766** FORDYCE *Serm. Yng. Women* (1767) I. vii. 302 The admiration raised by 'a set of features..', is often by the witlessness of the possessor thrown down in an instant. **1855** ANNE MANNING *Old Chelsea Bun-ho.* xix. 317 Everybody conceived themselves safe, as witlessly as they had previously held themselves to be in Danger. **1860** PUSEY *Min. Proph.* 239 Wisdom was turned into witlessness. **1879** BUTCHER & LANG *Odyssey* 282 He kicked Odysseus on the hip in his witlessness. **1910** *Times Lit. Suppl.* 10 Mar. 82/3 An artist..choosing to portray..the havoc and witlessness of mankind.

witling ('wɪtlɪŋ). [f. WIT *sb.* + -LING^{1} 2.] A petty wit (see WIT *sb.* 9, 10); one who fancies himself a wit; a pretender to wit (see WIT *sb.* 5, 7); one who utters light or feeble witticisms.

1693 DRYDEN *Persius* Sat. I. Prol. 17 Let Gain, that gilded Bait, be hung on high, The hungry Witlings have it in their Eye. **1702** *Engl. Theophrastus* 6 There are many impertinent Witlings at Will's. **1712–14** POPE *Rape of Lock* v. 59 A Beau and Witling perish'd in the throng, One died in metaphor, and one in song. **1807** W. IRVING *Salmag.* No. 2 ¶5 Does any witling want to distress the company with a miserable pun? **1876** MEREDITH *Beauchamp's Career* xx, 'What's in hand?'.. Luckily some witling said, 'Fours-in-hand!' and so drily that it passed for humour.

attrib. **1817** J. SCOTT *Paris Revisit.* (ed. 4) 228 The miserable witling captiousness of an opposition. **1845** MIALL in *Nonconf.* V. 45 A witling poet.

‖**witloof** ('wɪtlo:f). [Du., lit. 'white leaf'.] = CHICORY 1, SUCCORY 1. Also *attrib.*

1885 *Bazaar* 2 Jan. 7/2 Chicory, or witloof, as some choose to call it, is a useful winter salad plant. **1925** W. WATSON *Gard. Assist.* I. 79 Witloof Chicory... Large Brussels (Witloof).. has large leaves with wide midribs and stalks.

†'**witly**, *adv. Obs.* Also 5 **wittle**. (Of doubtful authenticity; in some instances perh. a spelling of *wittely* WITTILY, in others of *wihtly* WIGHTLY.)

c **1350** *Will. Palerne* 259 þe child witly þanne wende wiþoute ani more. *c* **1380** WYCLIF *Sel. Wks.* II. 275 Siþ þis martirdoom of Crist was so swete bifore God, Poul clepiþ it witly siche an offryng bifore God into smelling of swetnesse. **1426** AUDELAY *Poems* (Percy Soc.) 30 Wysele and witly and wittle the leud thai wyl here.

†'**witne**, *v. Obs.* Also 4 **witt(e)ne**, (**wythene**). [a. ON. *vitna*, related to *vitni* witness, f. *wit-* WIT *v.*[1] (Cf. etym. note s.v. WITNESS *v.*)]

1. *trans.* To bear witness to; to attest, testify. Also *absol.* or *intr.* to bear witness.

a **1225** *Ancr. R.* 30 þet ich þurh hore bonen mote habben þe tweolf bowes þet bloweð of cherite, ase seinte Powel witneð. *Ibid.* 384 Seint Powel witneð þet alle uttre herdschipes.. al is ase nout aȝean luue. **1340** HAMPOLE *Pr. Consc.* 5355 Als þe buke wythenes. *a* **1400–50** *Wars Alex.* 2900 With slike a reryd þan it rynnes, þe romance it witnes, þat, qua so tuke it in þat tyme, tint ware for euire. *c* **1400** *Rule St. Benet* (verse) 753 For þe wisman witnes & sais [etc.].

2. To invoke, entreat.

c **1200** *Trin. Coll. Hom.* 171 Iob witnede ure drihten, þat of þis deað him redde, on þe carefuldai.

3. To impute, ascribe.

c **1350** *Will. Palerne* 3462 Holli williams werkes þei wittened it alle, nade his douȝthi dedes be þei hade be dede alle.

witne, obs. pa. pple. of WIT *v.*[1]

witness ('wɪtnɪs), *sb.* Forms: 1–7 **witnes**, 3–5 **wittnesse**, 3 *Orm.*, 6 **wittness**, 3–6 **wittenes**, **wytnesse**, 3–7 **witnesse**, 4–5 **witenes**, 4–6 **wittnes**, **wytnes(s**, (2 **witnys**, 3 **-nesce**, 4 **wijtnes**, **wittenesse**, 4–5 **whitnes**, 4, 6 **vytnes**, **wetness(e**, **witnese**, (7 *Sc.*) **vitnes**, 5 **wytt(e)nesse**, **-(e)nes**, **witnesh**, **wetenesse**, **whetnesse**, **vitness(e)**), 5– **witness**. [OE. *witnes*, more freq. *ȝewitnes*, f. (*ȝe*)*wit* WIT *sb.*, IWIT + *-nes* -NESS. Cf. OHG. *giwiznessi*, MDu. *wetenisse*. The passage in sense from abstract to concrete is paralleled in F. *témoin* (:—L. *testimonium*). The uninflected pl. was frequent in early use; for separate illustration see sense 4.]

I. †**1.** Knowledge, understanding, wisdom. *Obs.*

c **950** *Rituale Eccl. Dunelm.* (Surtees) 194 Fore wisdom *vel* witnes ðæs biscop.. *propter scientiam episcopi*. *c* **1250** *Gen. & Ex.* 507 He sal.. wenden iewes.. To ðe wittenesse of iesus crist. *c* **1380** WYCLIF *Sel. Wks.* II. 225 Whanne a symple man seiþ a treuþe, we trowen it not for he seiþ it,.. but Crist is man of greet witnesse. **1382** —— *Prov.* viii. 5 Vnderstondeth, ȝee litle childer, witnesse [1388 wisdom; Vulg. *astutiam*]. **1433** *Rolls of Parlt.* V. 435/1 The connyng and witnes that resten in his persone. **1482** *Monk of Evesham* (Arb.) 27 His owne seyng that he had tolde before to a few persons of wytnesse [orig. *perpaucis arbitris*].

2. a. Attestation of a fact, event, or statement; testimony, evidence; †evidence given in a court of justice. See also 10.

c **950** *Lindisf. Gosp.* Matt. xv. 19 *Falsa testimonia*, leasa witnesa. *c* **1175** *Lamb. Hom.* 13 Ne spec þu aȝein þine nexta nane false witnesse. *a* **1300** *Cursor M.* 16280 His aun muth nu has him dempt, o wijtnes es na nede. **1340** *Ayenb.* 10 þou ne sselt zigge none ualse wytnesse aye þine emcristen. **1483** *Acta Audit.* in *Acta Dom. Conc.* II. Introd. 108 The Lordis .. ordanis the witnes now takin to be closit. **1525** LD. BERNERS *Froiss.* (1812) II. clxi. 446 If nede be I shall proue it by the wytnesse of hymselfe. **1526** TINDALE *Acts* x. 43 To hym geveth all the prophetes witnes. —— *1 John* v. 9 Yf we receave the witnes of men, the witnes of god is gretter. **1596** SHAKS. *Merch. V.* I. iii. 100 An euill soule producing holy witnesse, Is like a villaine with a smiling cheeke. **1611** *Bible* Transl. Pref. ¶6 That language [*sc.* the Greek] was fittest to containe the Scriptures, both for the first Preachers.. to appeale vnto for witnesse [etc.]. **1660** *Trial Regic.* 157 It is not that I would invalidate his witness. **1739** BUTLER *Serm.* Wks. 1874 II. 221 They are to make their choice, and abide by it: but which soever their choice be, the gospel is equally a witness to them; and the purposes of Providence are answered by this witness of the gospel. **1867** DK. ARGYLL *Reign of Law* vii. 360 Nature is called as a witness, and then the witness she gives is condemned. **1870** LOWELL *Study Wind.* 11 There is the most trustworthy witness to the imitative propensity of this bird. **1881** JOWETT *Thucyd.* I. 7 Agamemnon.. if the witness of Homer be accepted, brought the greatest number of ships himself.

†**b.** The action or condition of being an observer of an event. *Obs.*

a **1225** *Ancr. R.* 68 Wiðute witnesse of weopmen oðer of wummon þæt ou muwe iheren, ne speke ȝe mid none monne ofte ne longe. *c* **1400** *Brut* ccxxxii. 319 He was bound by othe afor notaries in presence and witnes of tho kynges.

c. Applied to the inward testimony of the conscience; after *2 Cor.* i. 12.

a **1340** HAMPOLE *Psalter* v. 12 Witnes þaire awn consciens and accusand þaim. *c* **1375** *Sc. Leg. Saints* xviii. (*Egipciane*) 175 Hafand his consciens vytnes How he in þat tyme liffand vas. *c* **1450** tr. *De Imitatione* II. vi. 46 The joye of a gode man is þe witnes of a gode conscience. **1598** SHAKS. *Merry W.* IV. ii. 220 May we with.. the witnesse of a good conscience, pursue him with any further reuenge?

†**d.** In some versions of the Bible: = TESTIMONY *sb.* 4. *Obs.*

1530 TINDALE *Exod.* xxxviii. 21 This is the summe of the habitacyon of witnese. *Ibid.* 30 The tabernacle of witnesse. **1535** COVERDALE *2 Kings* xi. 12 He.. set a crowne vpon his heade, and toke the witnes, and made him kynge. *Ibid.* xxiii. 4 That they shulde walke after the Lorde, and to kepe his commaundementes, witnesses, and ordinaunces.

3. Testimony by signature, oath, etc. Chiefly in phr. ***in*** (rarely †***into***) ***witness of, hereof, whereof***, etc.

1338 R. BRUNNE *Chron.* (1725) 214 þe chartre was forth brouht with wittnes enseled streit [orig. *Le rays.. mette sun sel en testmoynaunce*]. **1362** LANGL. *P. Pl.* A. II. 75 In witnesse of whuche þing wrong was þe furste.. In þe Date of þe deuel þe Deede was aselet. **1388** in J. H. Ramsay *Bamff Charters* (1915) 22 In the wetness of the forsayd partysyng Willame, Jon, [etc.]. **1410** in *E.E. Wills* (1882) 17 In wytnesse of þis dede I haue set þerto me sel. *c* **1450** *Godstow Reg.* 38 Into witnesse of this he put to his seale. *Ibid.* 48 To the whyche wrytynge hys seel I-put to is wytnes. **1525** *Test. Ebor.* (Surtees) VI. 12 In wittenes whereof.. I.. haith setto my seale. **1550** *Rental Bk. Cupar-Angus* (1880) 76 In witnes of the quhilk to this present writ, subscriuit with our handis. **1658** *Sir R. Hutton's Yng. Clerks Guide* I. (ed. 8) 240 In witnesse whereof I have hereunto set my hand and seal. **1871** FREEMAN *Norm. Conq.* IV. xvii. 27 The land was received as a fresh grant, which needed the writ and seal of King William as its witness.

4. a. One who gives evidence in relation to matters of fact under inquiry; *spec.* one who gives or is legally qualified to give evidence upon oath or affirmation in a court of justice or judicial inquiry.

hostile witness, one who gives evidence adverse to the party by whom he is called. ***ultroneous witness***, see ULTRONEOUS b.

c **950** *Lindisf. Gosp.* Matt. xxvi. 60 *Falsi testes*, lease *vel* lycce witnesa. *a* **1300** *Cursor M.* 19419 Tua wittnes fals þai þam puruaid, To tell he had o godd missaid. *c* **1380** WYCLIF *Wks.* (1880) 74 þei wolen.. brynge many false witnesses & notaries in his absence, & in presence speke no word. *c* **1400** *Cato's Morals 1* in *Cursor M.* App. IV, If þou be made wittenesse, For to say þat soþ is, Saue þine honour Als mikil as þou mai fra blame. *a* **1577** SIR T. SMITH *Commw. Eng.* II. xv. (1584) 61 Witnesses be sworne, & heard before them [*sc.* the jury].. openly. **1622** J. TAYLOR (Water P.) *Sir Gregory Nonsence* Wks. 1630 II. 4/2 Truth must be found, and witnesses produced. **1628** COKE *On Litt.* 6 b, When a tryall is by witnesses, regularly the affirmative ought to be proued by two or three witnesses... But when the tryall is by verdict of 12. men, there the iudgement is not giuen vpon witnesses. **1651** HOBBES *Leviath.* II. xxvi. 146 A Judge.. ought to take notice of the Fact, from none but the Witnesses. **1718** LADY M. W. MONTAGU *Lett.* (1887) I. 240 False witnesses are much cheaper than in Christendom. **1814** MRS. J. WEST *Alicia de Lacy* IV. 251 Many witnesses attested that he had borne arms. **1827** RYAN & MOODY *Cases Nisi Prius* 31 *marg.*, In an action by executors, a paid legatee is a competent witness to increase the estate. **1848** MRS. GASKELL *Mary Barton* xxxiv, How did you like standing witness? Ar'n't them lawyers impudent things, staring at one so? **1867** WHARTON *Law-Lex.* (ed. 4), Hostile witness. **1883** D. C. MURRAY *Hearts* xii, It was certainly an odd chance which would throw them together in a police-court as barrister and witness. **1885** MISS BRADDON *Wyllard's Weird* i, 'You can show that to the Coroner,' he said; 'of course, you will be a witness.' 'About the only one necessary, I should think', said the doctor. 'I saw her fall.'

uninflected pl. *c* **1440** *Generydes* 1510 He bad hym goo.. To the Sowdon, and telle hym the processe, And he wold be on of his cheff witnesse. **1483** *Acta Audit.* in *Acta Dom. Conc.* II. Introd. 104 The Lordis.. ordanis him to have letters to summond his witnes, and the party to here thame suorn. **1533** CRANMER *Let.* Misc. Writ. (Parker Soc.) 253 (MS.) That he hathe diuerse witnes, whiche culde make manyfeste deposicions concernyng the mattir. **1535** in *Lett. Suppr. Monast.* (Camden) 33 Your owne confession in thes lettres, besides the wittnes which ar against you, wolbe sufficient to condemne yow. **1713** SWIFT *Cadenus & Vanessa* 68 The pleader, having spoke his best, Had witness ready to attest.

b. *transf.* and *fig.*

a **1340** HAMPOLE *Psalter* xxiv. 11 þai [*sc.* the prophets and evangelists] ere witnes of his hightynge. **1578** H. WOTTON *Courtlie Controv.* 213 If you doubt thereof histories and fables with one voyce are witnes of my saying. **1588** SHAKS. *Tit. A.* v. i. 103 Well, let my Deeds be witnesse of my worth. **1635** D. DICKSON *Hebr.* xii. 1. 284 The Examples of God's Saynctes in Scripture, should stand as Witnesses agaynst vs, if wee run not as becommeth. **1667** MILTON *P.L.* IX. 317 Why shouldst not thou.. thy trial chuse With me, best witness of thy Vertue tri'd? **1781** COWPER *Heroism* 81 Sweet nature.. stands a witness at truth's awful bar, To prove you, there, destroyers as ye are. **1853** MAURICE *Proph. & Kings* vi. 91 This prophet.. is a true witness for the Lord God of Israel.

5. a. One who is called on, selected, or appointed to be present at a transaction, so as to be able to testify to its having taken place: *spec.* one who is present at the execution of a document and subscribes it in attestation thereof; more definitely, ***attesting*** or ***subscribing witness***.

Often in formulæ corresponding to med.L. *teste me ipso*, *teste rege*, *his testibus*, etc., AF. *tesmoin*...

[*a* **995** in Thorpe *Charters* (1865) 288 Her cyþ on þysum ȝewrite hu Wynflæd ȝelædde hyre ȝewitnesse.] *a* **1122** *O.E. Chron.* (Laud MS.) an. 656 Ic bidde þe broðer Æðelred & mine swustre Cyneburh & Cynesuuith.. þet ȝe beon witnesse & þæt ȝeo hit write mid iure fingre. *Ibid.* 675 Ic Theodorus ærcebiscop of Cantwarbyriȝ am witnesse of þas ȝewrite. **1258** *Proclam. Hen. III* in *Trans. Philol. Soc.* (1868) 21 Witnesse vs seluen [AF. *Tesmoin Meimeismes*] æt Lunden' þane Eȝtetenþe day on þe Monþe of Octobr'. *c* **1290** *Beket* 836 in *S. Eng. Leg.* 130 Ich was with him er wel inov .. þare ne tok ich no witnesse of þat us was bitweone. *a* **1450** *Knt. de la Tour* xxxiv, Ye are suoren to God and to youre husbonde atte the chirche dore afore witnesse that ye shalle neuer breke it. *c* **1450** *Godstow Reg.* 51 These beyng witnesse, Robert of Wytham, Sire walter, [etc.]. **1463** *Irish Act 3 Edw. IV*, c. 32 We have done to be made these oure lettres patentes Oureself beying witnesse. **1494** *Acc. Ld. High Treas. Scot.* I. 239 Item, the foure witnes [of the execution] expensis in Edinburgh,.. xl s. **1525** *Test. Ebor.* (Surtees) VI. 13 Thies wittenesses, Thomas Beamont, [etc.]. **1606** SHAKS. *Tr. & Cr.* III. ii. 205 Go too, a bargaine made: seale it... Ile be the witnesse. **1611** —— *Wint. T.* IV. iv. 401 But come-on, Contract vs fore these Witnesses. **1625** B. JONSON *Staple of News* v. ii, I haue your Deed... Is't not A perfect Act? and absolute in Law? Seal'd and deliuer'd before witnesses? **1630** PRYNNE *Anti-Armin.* 139 Seuerall witnesses auerre it vnder their hands and seales. **1664** in *Extr. St. Papers rel. Friends* Ser. III. (1912) 228 This.. wee haue made bold to Certefie Witnesse our hands this First day of December. *c* **1696** in W. M. Morison *Dict. Decis.* (1807) 16183 The communers and witnesses present, who fortify and adminiculate the same. **1710** O. SANSOM *Acc. Life* 73 He.. threatned me before Witness, That if I did not pay him, I must expect to go to Prison. **1720** T. INNES *Crit. Ess.* (1879) 111 As it is clear by many ancient charters, and chiefly by the donors and witnesses in the chartularies of our monasteries. **1754** in *Nairne Peerage Evid.* (1874) 53 James Fullarton merchant in Edinburgh and the s[d] John Strathie who also subscribe as witnesses. **1754** in Vesey *Reports* (1793) I. 11 Whether Testator's declaration before three witnesses, that it is his will, is equivalent to signing it before them. **1837** DICKENS *Pickw.* xvii, We find his name in the parish register as a witness to the marriage of Maria Lobbs to her cousin. **1839** LANE *Arab. Nts.* I. i. 76 *note*, These words, 'I give myself to thee', uttered by a woman to a man, even without the presence of witnesses,.. render her his lawful wife if [etc.]. **1855** [see SUBSCRIBING *ppl. a.*]. **1858** LD. ST. LEONARDS *Handy-Bk. Prop. Law* xviii. 141 The statute requires the witnesses to attest and subscribe the will.

†**b.** A sponsor or godparent at baptism. *Obs.*

orig. in Puritan use.

1597 HOOKER *Eccl. Pol.* v. lxiv. § 5 In the phrase of some kinde of men they vse to be termed *witnesses*, as if they came but to see and testifie what is done. It sauoureth more of pietie to giue them their old accustomed name of fathers and mothers in God. **1614** B. JONSON *Barth. Fair* I. iii, He was Witnesse, for Win, here, (they will not be call'd Godfathers), and nam'd her *Winne-the-fight*. **1643** SIR T. HOPE *Diary* (Bannatyne Club) 188 This day I wes witness to ane barne of the Lord Balgonies, callit Agnes. **1653** H. MORE *Antid. Ath.* III. ix. §2 (1712) 115 Four days before this mischance he being witness to a Child, said, that that was the last he should be ever witness to. **1837** *Dial. in Devon Dial.* Gloss., To *Witness* or to *Stand Witness* to, to stand sponsor to a child in baptism.

6. a. One who is or was present and is able to testify from personal observation; one present as a spectator or auditor. (Cf. EAR-WITNESS, EYE-WITNESS.) Usually with *of*, occas. *to*.

a **1225** *Ancr. R.* 144 No þinc nis witnesse þer of god þet we þeonne deð bute God one. *a* **1300** *Cursor M.* 19004 Fra ded to lijf nu risen es he, And þar-of wittnes all ar wee. **1382** WYCLIF *Heb.* xii. 1 Forsothe and we hauynge so greet a cloud of witnessis [Gr. νέφος μαρτύρων, L. *nubem testium*] put to. *c* **1400** *Rule St. Benet* (prose) 39 [They shall] make þaire peticiun, and bi-fore whitnes offir þaire childir. *c* **1450** CAPGRAVE *Life St. Gilbert* xxxvi. 113 þe Pope sayde a.. sermon of þe holynesse and þe myracles of Seynt Gilbert, rehersing þe witnes þere present. **1474** CAXTON *Cheese* III. iv. (1883) 113 This lyar coude not brynge no wytnessis. **1495** *Act II Hen. VII*, c. 10 §2, ij witnesses or moo that woll witnesse and testefie the seid payment. *a* **1533** LD. BERNERS *Gold Bk. M. Aurel.* (1546) B v b, They were witnesse by syght, and not by heryng of other. *a* **1548** HALL *Chron.*, *Hen. V* 35 Because I was nether a witnes of the facte, nor present at the deede I ouerpasse that matter. **1548** UDALL, etc. *Erasm. Par. John* vi. 66–71 Speciall witnesses and bruters abrode, of al the thynges that he wroughte. **1560** DAUS tr. *Sleidane's Comm.* 360 b, No man might haue accesse to him, nor speake w[t] him without a witnesse. *c* **1590** MARLOWE *Faustus* 209, 2. *Scholar*. Why, didst thou not say thou knewst? *Wagner*. Haue you any witnesse on't? 1. *Scholar*. Yes sirra, I heard you. **1591** SHAKS. *1 Hen. VI*, II. iii. 9 Faine would mine eyes be witnesse with mine eares, To giue their censure. **1682** J. NORRIS *Hierocles* 37 But had they no witness? I omit God.. but had they not themselves, and the testimony of Conscience? **1694** ATTERBURY *Serm.*, *Isa.* lx. 22 (1726) I. 152 Those Miracles being perform'd in the Desart, without any Witnesses but what were of that Nation. **1702** POPE *Dryope* 54, I saw, unhappy! what I now relate, And stood the helpless witness of thy fate. **1751** JOHNSON *Rambler* No. 142 ¶13 He is magnificent without witnesses. **1794** PALEY *Evid.* II. ix. (1817) 235 It was the credit given to original witnesses appealing for the truth of their accounts to what themselves had seen and heard. **1797** JANE AUSTEN *Sense & Sensib.* xxxv, Before such witnesses he dared not say half what he really felt. **1824** W. IRVING *T. Trav.* II. II. viii. 12, I will endeavour to act as if she were witness of my actions. **1842** T. WRIGHT *Biogr. Brit.*, *Anglo-Sax. Per.* 467 Turgar.. in his youth had been a witness of the destruction of the abbey. **1854** J. S. C. ABBOTT *Napoleon* (1855) I. xxiii. 367, I have been twenty times witness to the singular effect which the sound of a bell had upon Napoleon. **1860** F. W. ROBINSON *Grandmother's Money* v, The inhabitants of Blackman's Gardens.. were witness to one of the.. scenes. **1862** STANLEY *Jewish Ch.* I. xviii. 391 'He judged Israel all his life:' even after the Monarchy had sprung up, he [*sc.* Samuel] was still a witness of an earlier and more primitive state.

fig. **1780** COWPER *Progr. Err.* 174 Then to the dance, and make the sober moon Witness of joys that shun the sight of noon.

b. In asseverative formulæ, in which a deity or a human being is invoked as one who is cognizant of a fact; as ***God is my witness, be my witness that...*** Most often in phr. ***to call*** or ***take to*** (†one's) ***witness***: to call upon or appeal to as one's surety; to swear by.

[*c* **1200** *Vices & Virtues* 73 ȝif he godd hafð to iwitnesse ðat he mid hlutter herte hit doð.] **1297** R. GLOUC. (Rolls) 6934 Ich clupie god to witnesse.. þat ȝif ich of eni gulti am þat ich mote þoru þis fure Brenne.. & perissy. *a* **1300** *Cursor M.* 17496 þat soth it es We tak drightin til vr wittnes. *c* **1386** CHAUCER *Pard. T.* 155 The hooly writ take I to my wytnesse That luxurie is in wyn and dronkenesse. **14..** HOCCLEVE *Min. Poems* xvi. 10 And so wolde I, god take I to witnesse! **1535** COVERDALE *2 Esdras* ii. 5, I call vpon the for a wytnesse ouer the mother of these children, which wolde not kepe my couenaunt. *a* **1548** HALL *Chron., Hen. VI* 99, I take firste God to my witnesse, and afterwarde all the worlde, that I haue been at all tymes.. true man. **1555** in Strype *Eccl. Mem.* (1721) III. App. xlv. 133 God is my Wytnes, that my Harte wyll not suffer me.. to declare suche vyle Reportes. **1581** A. HALL *Iliad* VII. 123 To which (if so it needefull is) I loue to witnesse call. **1598** SHAKS. *Merry W.* IV. ii. 139 Heauen be my witnesse you doe. *c* **1600** —— *Sonn.* cxxiv, To this I witnes call the foles of time, Which die for goodnes, who haue liu'd for crime. **1667** MILTON *P.L.* I. 635 For me, be witness all the Host of Heav'n, If counsels different, or danger shun'd By me, have lost our hopes. **1700** DRYDEN *Sigismonda & G.* 397 That I have lov'd, I own; that still I love, I call to Witness al the Pow'rs above. **1833** HT. MARTINEAU *Loom & Lugger* II. i. 3 He had so often emphatically taken his neighbours to witness that he was weaving. **1840** DICKENS *Old Cur. Shop* xxv, The tall boy.. called those about him to witness that he had only shouted in a whisper. **1851** KINGSLEY *Yeast* xiii, Though, God's my witness, there's no spite in me for my own sake.

†**c.** Referring to, usually introducing, the designation of an authority for a statement. (Cf. 7 b.)

a **1300** *Cursor M.* 14791 Quarof was born þe king daui, þat es þe tun of bethleem, þe bok is wittnes for to tem. *c* **1386** CHAUCER *Pars. T.* ¶274 They been deceyued that seyn that they ne be nat tempted in hir body, witnesse on [*v.r.* of] Seint Iame the Apostel. *c* **1440** *Sir Gowther* 117 The chylde throfe and.. The duk sent after other sex, As wetnesse the storie. *c* **1460** *Towneley Myst.* xiv. 428 Lord, this is sothe, securely, wytnes the profett Isay. **1486** in *Surtees Misc.* (1890) 54 Shewing the rose to be principall of all floures, as witnesh Barthilmew. **1567** *Gude & Godlie B.* (S.T.S.) 42 [Jesus Christ] Sinnaris onlie Saluatioun, As witnes is thy word in write.

7. *fig.* Something that furnishes evidence or proof of the thing or fact mentioned; an evidential mark or sign, a token.

c **1250** *Gen. & Ex.* 3843 To sen gode witnesse ðor-on, Ðat wond was in ðat arche don. *c* **1380** WYCLIF *Sel. Wks.* III. 428 For freris.. suspect in þis heresye, men schulden not comyne wiþ hom bifore þei schewid þo fayth by sufficyent wittenes. **1414** *26 Pol. Poems* xii. 94 Lete werk be witnes ȝe can ȝoure Crede. **1585** T. WASHINGTON tr. *Nicholay's Voy.* II. iii. 33 For better witnesse of the antiquitie thereof, the inhabitaunts.. doe.. call all these old ruines Paleopolys. **1594** W. HARBERT in *Shaks. Cent. Praise* (1879) 12 Whose death was witnesse of her spotlesse life. **1597** HOOKER *Eccl. Pol.* v. lxviii. §3 Our kneeling.. is the gesture of pietie.. What doth better beseeme our bodies.. then to bee sensible witnesses to minds vnfainedly humbled? **1599** SHAKS. *Much Ado* II. iii. 48 It is the witnesse still of excellencie, To put a strange face on his owne perfection. **1599** —— *Hen. V*, IV. iii. 97 Vpon the which [graves], I trust Shall witnesse liue in Brasse of this dayes worke. **1601** SIR W. CORNWALLIS *Ess.* II. xxvii. ¶2, They.. smelt of oyle, the witnesse of an vnmanlike effeminate nicenesse. **1656** EARL MONM. tr. *Boccalini's Advts. fr. Parnass.* II. xxii. (1674) 170 [He bade them] remove away that unfortunate Witness of their ingratitude from the eyes of the World. **1815** SCOTT *Guy M.* li, Now, wipe these witnesses from your eyes. **1859** HAWTHORNE *Marble Faun* xxvii, Italian asseverations.., however true they may chance to be, have no witness of their truth in the faces of those who utter them. **1871** FREEMAN *Norm. Conq.* IV. xvii. 82 Gifts yet more costly were now the witness of his personal presence.

b. Introducing a name, designation, phrase, or clause denoting a person or thing that furnishes evidence of the fact or exemplifies the statement. Also ***as witness***, and, in early use, †***witness on***. (After L. *teste...*, F. *témoin...*)

a **1300** *Cursor M.* 11788 Bot we ne wrick þe wisliker, þe wark of him sua mai we dred, Als wittnes on vr eldres dede. *c* **1386** CHAUCER *Sec. Nun's T.* 277 Witnesse [L. *testis est*] Tyburces and Cecilies shrifte. *c* **1386** —— *Wife's T.* 95 Pardee we wommen konne no thyng hele, Witnesse on Myda, wol ye heere the tale. *c* **1394** *P. Pl. Crede* 528 Wytnesse on Wycliff þat warned hem wiþ trewþe. *c* **1420** LYDG. *Assembly of Gods* 366 Ioyntly to her Mercurius tooke hys see As came to hys course—wytnesse the zodyak. **1598** F. MERES *Palladis Tamia* 281 b, The sweete wittie soule of Ouid liues in mellifluous.. Shakespeare, witnes his *Venus* and *Adonis*. **1616** CHAMPNEY *Voc. Bps.* 24 The wisest, and greatest clarkes haue erred, as witnesse the lapsǝ of Tertullian, Origen, and Lucifer. **1642** FULLER *Holy & Prof. St.* III. xv. 192 Nature oftentimes recompenceth deform'd bodies with excellent wits. Witnesse Æsop. **1667** MILTON *P.L.* I. 503 When Night Darkens the Streets, then wander forth the Sons of Belial... Witness the Streets of Sodom. **1671** —— *Samson* 906 *Dal.* In argument with men a woman ever Goes by the worse... *Sam.* For want of words no doubt, or lack of breath, Witness when I was worried with thy peals. **1781** COWPER *Retirem.* 713 And novels (witness ev'ry month's review) Belie their name, and offer nothing new. **1852** THACKERAY *Esmond* II. ii, The strange, barbarous French which she and many other fine ladies of that time —witness her Grace of Portsmouth—employed. **1868** T. H. KEY *Philol. Ess.* 249 What progress is visible there is chiefly due to the energy of German, not French, scholarship, as witness the valuable collection of Greek authors that has proceeded from the press of Didot.

c. *spec.* In textual criticism, a manuscript or an early version which is regarded as evidence of authority for the text. (Usually in *pl.*)

1853 SCRIVENER *Collation MSS. Holy Gospels* Introd. i. p. xiii, The very rough and unsatisfactory process of counting the number of witnesses produced in behalf of each [reading]. **1870** URWICK tr. *Bleek's Introd. N.T.* II. 305 By comparing the received text with Greek MSS. of the N.T. and other witnesses. **1926** FRIEDRICHSEN *Gothic Vers. Gospels* 194 Wherever the Codex [Argenteus] simulates the Vulgate text, the majority of Old Latin witnesses go with it.

d. Technical uses (see quots.; cf. F. *témoin*).

1802 C. JAMES *Milit. Dict., Witnesses.* In fortification. (See Temoins.) [*Temoins, Fr.* In civil and military architecture, are pieces of earth left standing as marks or witnesses in the fosses or places which the workmen are emptying, that they may know.. how many cubical fathoms of earth have been carried.] **1825** J. NICHOLSON *Oper. Mech.* 763 If any silver be produced it must be deducted from the assay. This is called the witness. **1880** ZAEHNSDORF *Bookbinding* Gloss., *Witness*, when a volume is cut so as to show that it has not been so cut down, but that some of the leaves have still rough edges. These uncut leaves are called 'Witness'.

8. a. One who testifies for Christ or the Christian faith, esp. by death; a martyr. *Obs.* exc. as literal rendering of Gr. μάρτυς MARTYR.

The reference in Rev. xi. 3 is much disputed; see, e.g., Vigouroux *Dict. de la Bible* s.v. *Témoins*.

1382 WYCLIF *Rev.* xi. 3 And I shal ȝiue to my two witnesses, and thei shulen prophecie a thousynd dayes two hundrid and sixty. **1548–9** *Bk. Com. Prayer, Collect Innoc. Day*, Whose prayse this day, the young innocentes thy witnesses hath confessed, and shewed foorth.. in dying. **1557** *N.T.* (Geneva) Acts xxii. 20 And when the bloud of thy wytnes [*marg.* or, Martyr] Steuen was shed, I also stode by. **1637** RUTHERFORD *Lett.* (1671) 128 One of the softest pillowes Christ hath, is laid under his witnesses head. [*a* **1700** EVELYN *Diary* 26 Apr. 1689, My Lord St. Asaph consider'd the killing of the two witnesses, to be the utter destruction of the Cevennes Protestants.., and the other the Waldenses and Pyrenean Christians.]

b. = *Jehovah's Witness* s.v. JEHOVAH 2. orig. *U.S.*

1931 *Watchtower* 15 Oct. 316/2 If any one does become fearful and ceases to be a witness, he ceases to be of the remnant and of God's anointed or Christ. **1935** *Time* 18 Nov. 59/1 By last week 28 Witnesses of Jehovah had popped up in the U.S. public schools. Cora Foster.. faced dismissal after confessing that she, too, was a Witness. **1974** *Watchtower* 15 Jan. 56/1 Suddenly, under religious animosity, the young man whipped out a knife and stabbed the Witness to death. **1980** R. HILL *Spy's Wife* ii. 8 Charity collectors went away happy, and.. even Mormons and Witnesses had got enough courtesy to bring them back.

II. Phrases. (See also above.)

9. a. ***in witness***: as a testimony or piece of evidence. Now *rare* or *Obs.* exc. as in 3.

c **950** *Lindisf. Gosp.* Matt. viii. 4 In cyðnisse *vel* witnesa. [*c* **1000** *Ags. Gosp.* Luke ix. 5 þonne ȝe of þære ceastre gað, asceacað eower fota dust ofer hiȝ on witnesse.] *a* **1325** *MS. Rawl. B.* 520, lf. 54 b, In witnesse of wche þinges we habbez don maken þues oure opene lettres. **1362** LANGL. *P. Pl.* A. VIII. 95 In two lynes hit lay.. And was I-writen riht þus In witnesse of treuþe. **1390** GOWER *Conf.* I. 34 In tokne and in witnesse That ilke ymage bar liknesse Of man and of non other beste. **1528** TINDALE *Declar. Sacram.* a ij b, They cast vp an heape of stones in wytnesse & called it Gylyad: yᵉheape of wytnesse. **1600** SHAKS. *A.Y.L.* III. ii. 1 Hang there my verse, in witnesse of my loue. **1657** EARL MONM. tr. *Paruta's Pol. Disc.* 113 Venice doth at this day enjoy many great priviledges, in witness of her great worth and singular merit.

†**b.** ***to stand in witness***: to act as a witness. *Sc. Obs.*

1516 *Reg. Privy Seal Scot.* I. 422/2 The king.. rehablis the said Johne and Johne to stand in preif and witnes.

10. ***to bear witness***: (said properly of a person, a book, etc.) to give oral or written testimony or evidence; hence *fig.* to furnish or constitute evidence or proof; to testify, witness *to* (occas. *of*). ***to bear*** (one) ***witness***: to corroborate one's statement or be a witness of one's action. (Cf. ON. *bera vitni*, OF. *porter temoin*.)

c **1200** ORMIN 12616, I barr to þe leode Wittness off himm, þatt he wass wiss Crist Godess Sune. *c* **1205** LAY. 13231 Ich habbe his munekes.. þat sculleð witnesse beren eowe alle biuoren. *a* **1300** *Cursor M.* 6820 Tak þou noght wit tunge leier, Ne fals wittnes for felun ber. *Ibid.* 12582 Als lucas vs sais þe gospelere, þat wittnes lel es wont at bere. **1303** R. BRUNNE *Handl. Synne* 2356 Certys þefte ryȝt wykked ys Whan þe dede bereþ wytnes [*Pus qe ceo tesmoine le mort*]. *c* **1325** *Spec. Gy Warw.* 412 þe godspel þerof bereþ witnesse. **1340** HAMPOLE *Pr. Consc.* 3612 þus may saules, als þe buke beres wytnes, By helpyd by way of rightwysnes. *c* **1385** CHAUCER *L.G.W.* Prol. 527 Hire white coroun beryth of it witnesse. **1393** LANGL. *P. Pl.* C. xx. 29 þre persones parcelmele departable from oþer, And alle þre bote o god; thus abraam bereþ wittnesse. **1426** *Anc. Deed* A. 10383 (P.R.O.) This endentur tripartitit beres wittenes that [etc.]. *c* **1450** CAPGRAVE *Life St. Gilbert* xxxvi. 113 þe archbischop of Reymes was þere present.. and bare witnesse of þe holy lyf of Seynt Gilbert. **1500–20** DUNBAR *Poems* lxvi. 34 The pepill so wickit ar of feiris, The frutless erde all witness beiris. **1526** TINDALE *John* viii. 18, I am won that beare wittnes off my sylfe, and my father that sent me beareth witnes off me. **1590** SHAKS. *Com. Err.* IV. iv. 80 In veritie you did, my bones beares witnesse, That since haue felt the vigor of his rage. *Ibid.* 93 God and the Rope-maker beare me witnesse, That I was sent for nothing but a rope. **1610** —— *Temp.* III. i. 68 O earth, beare witnes to this sound, And crowne what I professe with kinde euent If I speake true. **1671** MILTON *Samson* 239 In seeking just occasion to provoke The Philistine.. Thou never wast remiss, I bear thee witness. **1773** GOLDSM. *Stoops to Conquer* 111, I can bear witness to that. **1839** KEMBLE *Resid. in Georgia* (1863) 59 Her dress.. bore witness to a far more improved taste. **1841** THACKERAY *Gt. Hoggarty Diam.* x, To speak of heaven.. and to bring it to bear witness to the lie in his mouth. **1842** TENNYSON *St. Sim. Styl.* 127 And I, in truth (thou wilt bear witness here) Have all in all endured as much. **1876** MELLOR *Priesthood* ii. 59 The striking witness which he [*sc.* Judas] bore to the innocence of the Lord.

†**11.** ***to take witness by*** or ***of***: to take example by.

c **1400** *Anturs Arth.* 165 (Thornton MS.) Thus am I lyke to Lucefere, takis witnes by mee. *Ibid.* 273 Takes witnes by Fraunce. *c* **1480** HENRYSON *Cock & Fox* 200 Tak witnes of the Feyndis Infernall, Quhilk houndit doun wes fra that heuinlie hall To Hellis hole.

†**12.** ***to bring, teem*** (TEEM *v.*¹) ***to witness***: to bring under examination. *Obs.*

c **1200** *Moral Ode* 108 (Trin. Coll. MS.) Elch man sal þar biclepien himselfen and ec demen Hic [*read* his] oȝen werc and his þanc to witnesse he sal temen. *c* **1400** *Apol. Loll.* 12 In how many gret casis may it be, þat now regniþ in þe kirk synful marchondise; bryng to witnes; examyn þe sawis; discusse þe dedis.

†**13.** ***to take witness of***: to call or take to witness (see 6 b); to appeal to as an authority or source of information. *Obs.*

c **1375** *Cursor M.* 22583 (Fairf.), I take witnes of saint austine þat tellis how þis werlde sal fine. **1390** GOWER *Conf.* I. 66 For this witnesse I take of god, that my corage Hath ben mor siek than my visage. *a* **1500** in Halliwell *Nugæ Poeticæ* (1844) 38, I take wyttenesse of Davyd kyng and at Salomon the wyse, That a woman for a litulle thyng ofte change hir servyse. *a* **1586** SIDNEY *Arcadia* II. xxvii. (1912) 322, I take witnes of the gods (who never leave perjuries unpunished) that I often cried out against their impudency.

14. ***with a witness***: with clear evidence, without a doubt, 'with a vengeance', 'and no mistake'. *Obs.* or *rare arch.*

1575 G. HARVEY *Letter-bk.* (Camden) 98 French Camarick Ruffes, deepe with a witnesse, starched to the purpose. **1596** SHAKS. *Tam. Shr.* V. i. 121 Here's packing with a witnesse to deceiue vs all. **1609** J. DAVIES *Triumphs Death* Wks. (Grosart) I. 49/1 For now we sinne (yea with a witnesse sinne, Witnesse our conscience). *a* **1641** BP. MOUNTAGU *Acts & Mon.* vi. (1642) 82 He was sent; but with a witnesse, as the saying is, to destroy. **1670** T. BROOKS *Wks.* (1867) VI. 198 That man is cursed with a witness that is cursed by Christ himself! **1690** LOCKE *2nd Let. Toleration* Wks. 1727 II. 270 The French King requires all his Subjects to come to Mass: Those who do not, are punished with a witness. **1717** PRIOR *Alma* I. 444 Gall is bitter with a Witness. **1816** HAZLITT *Pol. Ess.* (1819) 103 Here's a levelling rogue for you! The world turned inside out, with a witness! **1829** SCOTT *Anne of G.* xxiii, To every other person about her she plays countess and baroness with a witness. **1849** CUPPLES *Green Hand* x. (1856) 90 At midnight, it blew great guns, with a witness.

III. 15. *attrib.* and *Comb.*, as ***witness-bearer***, ***-bearing*** sb. and adj. (see 10), ***-heap*** (cf. quot. 1528 in 9 a), ***-judge***; **witness action**, an action in which witnesses are summoned, as distinguished from one in which only matters of law are argued; **witness-box**, an enclosed space in which a witness is placed while giving evidence; **witness chair**, a seat for witnesses at a court of inquiry; **witness-room**, an apartment in which witnesses assemble and remain while not giving evidence; **witness-stand** *U.S.*, the place where a witness is stationed while giving evidence.

1892 *Daily News* 16 July 7/1 Mr. Justice Kekewich.. ordered the motion to be set down as a *witness action. *c* **1440** *Promp. Parv.* 531/1 *Wyttenesse berare, *testis, testificator, testificatrix.* *c* **1440** *Jacob's Well* 59 Alle fals wytnes-bererys. **1563** FOXE *A. & M.* 1250/1 These vi. heauenly martyrs & witnes bearers of truthe. **1553** M. WOOD tr. *Gardiner's De Vera Obed.* 35 b, I folow Tullies meaning, who in the weighti importaunce of *witnes bearing, attributeth authoritie vnto such as be witte & welthy men. **1577** tr. *Bullinger's Decades* (1592) 8 The whole consent and witnessebearing of the great congregation. **1616** CHAPMAN tr. *Musæus* C 1, The witnesse-bearing-light Of Loues, that would not beare a humane sight. **1848** A. THOMSON *Orig. of Secession Ch.* iii. 96 Their resolute and unflinching witness-bearing. **1889** *Spectator* 2 Feb. 166/1 A very real kind of witness-bearing to what we call the supernatural. **1806** J. CARR *Stranger Irel.* 469, I was surprised to find.. that they had no *witness-box. The witness is hoisted upon the table. **1859** GEO. ELIOT *A. Bede* xliii, Mr. Irwine was in the witness-box, telling of Hetty's unblemished character. **1897** *Westm. Gaz.* 16 Feb. 7/2 The ex-Premier.. advanced to the *witness chair. **1528** TINDALE *Declar. Sacram.* a iij, And of al that couenant thei made that heape wytnesse, callenge it yᵉ*wetnessheppe. **1726** POPE *Odyss.* XIX. 576 My own experience shall their doom decide; A *witness-judge precludes a long appeal. **1848** MRS. GASKELL *Mary Barton* xxxii, She took her place in the *witness-room, worn and dispirited, but not anxious. **1853** THOREAU *Let.* 10 Apr. (1958) 304 Expect no trivial truth from me, unless I am in the *witness-stand. **1896** HOWELLS *Impressions & Exp.* 71 A young man.. was called to the witness-stand in behalf of the prosecution.

Hence **'witnessdom** (see quot. and cf. 8 above).

1877 RUSKIN *Fors Clav.* lxxxii. VII. 330 Our act may have the.. Virtue of Witness-dom, or as we.. translate it Martyrdom.

witness ('wɪtnɪs), *v.* Forms: see prec.; also 4 **witnis**, 5 **wythnesse, wittenessh**, 6 **wittenish**. [f. prec. In some ME. texts forms of the type *wittnes* (= witnesses) may be inflected forms of WITNE.]

1. *trans.* To bear witness to (a fact or statement); to testify to, attest; to furnish oral or written evidence of. (*a*) with simple obj.

a **1300** *Cursor M.* 13893 He and his lare will lasten ai, þis will he self wittnes and sai. *Ibid.* 23820 þat wittnes us all hali gosspelles. **1338** R. BRUNNE *Chron.* (1810) 82 William of Malmesbirie witnesse it in his writte. **1377** LANGL. *P. Pl.* B. Prol. 191 þat witnisseth holiwrite who-so wil it rede. *c* **1400** *Rom. Rose* 6958 We purchace, thurgh oure flateryng,.. Lettres, to witnesse oure bounte. **1474** CAXTON *Chesse* IV. iii. [ii] (1883) 171 Sidrac wythnesseth the same. **1509** FISHER *Funeral Serm. C'tess Richmond* Wks. (1876) 308 She.. openly dyde wytnesse this same thynge at the houre of her dethe. **1590** SHAKS. *Com. Err.* V. i. 220 That Goldsmith there, were he not pack'd with her, Could witnesse it: for he was with me then. **1653** H. MORE *Antid. Ath.* III. iii. §2 (1712) 91 Remigius writes that he had it witnessed to him by the free confession of near two hundred men. **1729** T. INNES *Crit. Ess.* (1879) 117 Thus we see the antiquity of the settlement of the Scots in Britain witnessed by our own country writers. **1920** *Discovery* Mar. 90/1 The records.. contain.. references to their Royal founder, witnessing his continued interest in the progress of Science.

(*b*) with obj. clause.

13.. *Guy Warw.* (A.) 6609 Ichil þe make messanger.. Ichil þat þou wittnesse me þat þe loue ste[de]fast be. **1390** GOWER *Conf.* I. 263 Senec witnesseth openly How that Envie proprely Is of the Court the comun wenche. *c* **1475** *Partenay* 1529, I witnesse you.. That he was A trew catholike person. **1563** *Homilies* II. *Prayer* II. 126b, He wytnesseth in another place, the Martirs.. were wont.. to be remembred.. of the Priest at diuine seruice. **1596** SHAKS. *Merch. V.* V. i. 271 Lorenzo heere Shall witnesse I set forth as soone as you. **1633** FORD *Love's Sacr.* II. ii. E, Were not the party her selfe aliue to witnesse that [etc.]. **1859** S. WILBERFORCE *Sp. Missions* (1874) 186 To witness.. to the next generation, that England can never be clear from the guilt.

†(*c*) with complement (*for*... or inf.). *Obs.*

13.. *Cursor M.* 12909 (Gött.) And þar-of es right no farlik, Quen he-self þe wittnes for slik. **1545** BALE *Image Both Ch.* I. 41, I will earnestly witnesse hym.. before my heauenly father.. for one of myne, to haue the inheritaunce with mee. **1565** SHACKLOCK tr. *Hosius' Hatchet of Heresies* 12b, Christ, whome the Scriptures wytnesse to haue bene incarnat. **1607** J. CARPENTER *Plaine Mans Plough* 26 Noah was witnessed to be A man righteous and perfect. **1642** FULLER *Holy & Prof. St.* V. vii. 387 Those that knew him witnesse him to be of honest life.

(*d*) in imperative or subjunctive, as a form of appeal. Now *rare.*

c **1400** *Destr. Troy* 608 What-euer ye deme me to do,.. I hete you full highly with hert to fulfille,.. wittenes our goddes. *Ibid.* 1488 The fyfte.. Was Troylus.. That mykell worship wan, witnes ye of story. **1590** SHAKS. *Com. Err.* V. i. 186 Ay me, it is my husband: witnesse you, That he is borne about inuisible. **1591** —— *Two Gent.* II. vi. 25 And Siluia (witnesse heauen that made her faire) Shewes Iulia but a swarthy Ethiope. **1697** DRYDEN *Virg. Past.* VIII. 28, While I my Nisa's perjur'd Faith deplore; Witness ye Pow'rs, by whom she falsly swore! **1838** DICKENS *O. Twist* l, Witness you three—I'm not afraid of him.

b. *transf.* Of a document: To furnish formally attested evidence of. Usually with obj. clause.

1474 *Anc. Deed* C. 5555 (P.R.O.) This bylle shalle wytnesse that I Thomas Ormond oweth to Hew Mathew [3*l.* 6*s.* 8*d.*]. *a* **1475** *Rolls of Parlt.* VI. 155/2 Cokettes of all such Clothes.. witnessyng the nombre of theym. **1503** *Ibid.* 527/2 This Indenture.. Wytnesseth That whereas [etc.]. **1551** *Cal. Anc. Rec. Dublin* (1889) 425 This byll, mad the xvi. day of Aprill.. wittenishit that whereas [etc.]. **1658** *Sir R. Hutton's Yng. Clerks Guide* I. (ed. 8) 1 This Indenture.. witnesseth, That [etc.]. **1759** STERNE *Tr. Shandy* I. xv, And this indenture farther witnesseth, That [etc.].

c. *fig.* To furnish evidence or proof of; to be a sign or mark of, betoken. Also with obj. clause.

1377 LANGL. *P. Pl.* B. XVIII. 240 [þe] water witnessed þat he was god, for he went [= walked] on it. **1450–1530** *Myrr. our Ladye* II. 253 The tremblynge of the erthe.. the darkynge of the sonne wytnesse hym maker of all thynges. *a* **1586** SIDNEY *Arcadia* I. vi. (1912) 41 All other tokens witnessed them to be of the lowest calling. **1591** SHAKS. *Two Gent.* IV. iv. 74 Thy face, and thy behauiour, Which.. Witnesse good bringing vp. **1599** T. STORER *Life & D. Wolsey* G 3, The stones may witnesse shee was there. **1600** SIR W. CORNWALLIS *Ess.* I. ii. C 5, The Director whose high erected scituation witnesseth his prerogatiue. **1630** RANDOLPH *Aristippus* 12 You cannot ride to Ware or to Barkway, but your Hackneyes sides must witnesse your iourneyes. **1653** H. COGAN tr. *Pinto's Trav.* iv. 8 As the wounds we have upon us can but too well witness. **1760–72** H. BROOKE *Fool of Qual.* (1792) III. 87 This tear will witness for me, that I do not mean to insult you. **1781** COWPER *Hope* 415 His shoulders witnessing by many a shrug How much his feelings suffer'd. **1796** CHARLOTTE SMITH *Marchmont* I. 259 The gilding and carving.. witnessed the expence that had once been lavished on it. **1813** EUSTACE *Class. Tour* 1821) I. viii. 292 The banks of the river, for many a mile, witnessed the rout of the Carthaginians. **1843** MACAULAY *Horatius* lxv, And there it stands unto this day To witness if I lie.

†**d.** To give evidence of by one's behaviour; to make evident; to evince. *Obs.*

1581 A. HALL *Iliad* IX. 168 His kinred and the mother chiefe did many a teare let fall Their woe to witnesse. *a* **1586** SIDNEY *Ps.* XXXV. vii, Even gnashing teeth, to witness more their spight. *a* **1625** FLETCHER *Laws of Candy* III. i, To finde occasion wherein I might witnesse My duty and obedience. **1660** PEPYS *Diary* 15 Apr., Captain Dekings, an anabaptist, and one that had witnessed a great deal of discontent with the present proceedings. **1671** MILTON *P.R.* III. 107, I seek not mine, but his Who sent me, and thereby witness whence I am. *a* **1700** DRYDEN *Cymon & Iph.* 112 Long mute he stood, and leaning on his Staff, His Wonder witness'd with an Ideot laugh. **1728** POPE *Dunc.* I. 105 (v.r.) He roll'd his eyes that witness'd huge dismay.

e. To show forth evidence of or as to (an object of allegiance) by faithful speech or conduct; to be a witness for. Also with cognate obj. Now *rare* or *Obs.*

1526 TINDALE *1 Tim.* vi. 13 Iesus Christ whych vnder Poncius Pilate witnessed a good witnessynge [1582 Rheims and 1611 Confession]. **1534** —— *John* v. 32, I know that the witnesse which he witnesseth of me, is true. **1659** SOUTH *Serm., Matt.* x. 33 (1697) I. 117 To be a Martyr signifies only to witness the truth of Christ. **1663** in *Jrnl. Friends Hist. Soc.* XIX. 22 The glorious truth of God witnessed out by those contemned Christians which.. are called Quakers. **1680** C. NESSE *Ch. Hist.* (1681) 333 John Baptist, who had Witnessed him into the World. **1833** *Tracts for Times* I. No. 10. 4 That very confirmation is another ordinance, in which the Bishop witnesses Christ.

2. *intr.* To bear oral or written witness; to testify. Now usually with *to* or *against.*

a **1300** *Cursor M.* 11075 Forþi of him witnes [? witnessis] þus Vr lauerd,.. 'O wijf', he said, 'was neuer born nan A gretter barn þan sant iohan'. *c* **1380** WYCLIF *Wks.* (1880) 268 þat, as ierome & anselm witnessen,.. here abitis ben ful of lesyngis. *c* **1380** —— *Sel. Wks.* III. 436 At þe day of dom.. Crist and hise lawe shal witnesse aȝen ȝou. *a* **1400** *Pistill of Susan* 363 þe pistel witnesseþ wel Of þat profete. *c* **1400** MAUNDEV. ii. (1919) 7 As the storye of Noe witnesseth whan þat the culuer broughte the braunche of Olyue. *c* **1450** *Merlin* 56 And as the boke witnessith, Vter venquysshed the bataile. *c* **1450** *Godstow Reg.* 131 As his vncles.. gaf & grauntid.. to þe fore-seide minchons, as her charturs witnessin. **1486** *Bk. St. Albans, Her.* a j, Many other notable.. thyngys to the plesure of noble personys shall be shewyd as the werkys folowyng witteneses. **1550** CROWLEY *Epigr.* 1056 Idlenes hath ben cause of much wyckednes, As Ecclesiasticus doeth playnely wytnes. **1595** SHAKS. *John* IV. ii. 218 Oh, when the last accompt twixt heauen & earth Is to be made, then shall this hand and Seale Witnesse against vs to damnation. **1611** —— *Wint. T.* IV. i. 11, I witnesse to The times that brought them in. **1710** ADDISON *Tatler* No. 259 ¶6 The Prisoner brought several Persons of good Credit to witness to her Reputation. **1771** GOLDSM. *Hist. Eng.* IV. 5 He avowed his innocence, called heaven to witness to his veracity. **1870** ROGERS *Hist. Gleanings* Ser. II. 27 His simplicity.. and earnestness are similarly witnessed to.

b. *fig.* (cf. 1 c).

1592 GREENE *Groat's W. Wit* F 2, Lette their owne works serue to witnesse against their owne wickednesse. **1611** *Bible* Isa. iii. 9 The shew of their countenance doeth witnesse against them. **1836** NEWMAN *Par. Serm.* III. vi. 93 Works of obedience witness to God's just claims upon us. **1844** MRS. BROWNING *Lost Bower* xlvii, The golden-hearted daisies Witnessed there.. To the truth of things. **1856** AYTOUN *Bothwell* V. xiv, How many churches, wrapped in flames, Have witnessed to the spoilers' power! **1860** MOZLEY *Univ. Serm.* vii. (1877) 153 So subtle an hypothesis.. witnesses to a curious phenomenon.

†**c.** In pres. pple. absolute: *witnessing* (so-and-so); = WITNESS *sb.* 7 b. *Obs.*

c **1400** MAUNDEV. Prol. (1839) 2 [The Holy Land] is the Herte and the myddes of all the World; wytnessynge the Philosophere, that seythe thus; *Vertus rerum in medio consistit.* *c* **1440** *Gesta Rom.* i. 4 To goo vndir the ȝoke of penance.. is not hard, witnessing þe sauiour.., wher he seithe.. Lo! my ȝoke.. is swete. **1526** *Pilgr. Perf.* III. xii. 43 Our sayd lorde wytnessynge and sayeng. Who so euer for my loue forsaketh father or mother [etc.].

3. *trans.* **a.** To give formal or sworn evidence of (a fact, etc.); to depose in evidence. Now *rare.*

a **1325** *MS. Rawl. B.* 520 lf. 65 b, þe avisurs of þe siknesse sullen ben destreined to comen to þe curt to witnessen hoere siȝt. **1428** *Munim. de Melros* (Bann.) 519, I wes requeryt.. for to wytnes vndir wryt þe thyng at wes determynyt befor me in iugement. **1560** *Bible* (Geneva) Mark xv. 4 Answerest thou nothing? beholde how manie things thei witnes against thee. **1581** A. HALL *Iliad* IX. 172 The Aiax hie and Heraults eke can witnesse well his minde,.. they heard the talke. **1601** SHAKS. *All's Well* V. iii. 200 Me thought you saide You saw one heere in Court could witnesse it. **1622** MABBE tr. *Aleman's Guzman d'Alf.* I. 177 They did all of them witnesse one and the same thing; That I was the sonne of a principall Cavallero. *a* **1715** BURNET *Own Time* III. (1724) I. 586 If they would not witness treasonable matter against Baillie.

b. To attest formally by signature; to sign (a document) as a witness of its execution. Also *absol.*

a **1325** *MS. Rawl. B.* 520, lf. 54 b, Witnessinde vs sulf at Gaunt þe vifte dai of Octobre. **1362** LANGL. *P. Pl.* A. II. 131 To weende with hem to westmunster to Witnesse þe deede. **1439** *Rolls of Parlt.* V. 32/2 Licence of the said Chifteyne wittenessed undre his seall. *c* **1450** *Godstow Reg.* 27 Thys wytnessyth Alysaunder, of lyncolne bysshop, and many odyr. *Ibid.* 275 To this present writyng their commune seale.. they have put to, witnessyng theire Chapiter. **1668** SHADWELL *Sullen Lovers* III. 46 *Sir Pos.* Come Sir, do you Witness it. *2 Clerk.* Ay Sir. *he sets his hand.* **1718** LADY M. W. MONTAGU *Lett.* (1887) I. 240 A writing is drawn and witnessed. **1776** *Trial of Nundocomar* 102/1 Maha Rajah said it was necessary to witness it to make it pukka. **1853** MRS. GASKELL *Ruth* xviii, There! that's what I call a will; witnessed according to law, and all. **1871** LE FANU *Rose & Key* II. 38 Lady Vernon.. sends for her secretary, and seals, signs, and delivers it in his presence... And now he has duly 'witnessed' it. **1912** *Engl. Hist. Rev.* Jan. 50 John Chishull witnesses as chancellor pretty constantly in the roll of 53 Henry III.

c. To be formally present as a witness of (a transaction).

1362 LANGL. *P. Pl.* A. II. 60 Hit witen and witnessen þat woneþ vppon eorþe, þat I, Fauuel, Feffe Fals to þat Mayden Meede. **1849** SIR J. STEPHEN *Eccl. Biog.* (1850) I. 43 By his side.. sat Agnes the Empress-mother, brought there to witness and to ratify the judgment to be pronounced on her only child. **1859** H. KINGSLEY *G. Hamlyn* xiii, I would be much obliged to you if you could step round to the.. Bank with me. I want you to witness what passes.

4. (*transf.* from 3 c.) To be a witness, spectator, or auditor of (something of interest, importance, or special concern); to experience by personal (esp. ocular) observation; to be present as an observer at; to see with one's own eyes. In early use said mainly of the eyes or the ears. (In loose writing often used merely as a synonym of 'see'.)

1582 STANYHURST *Æneis* II. (Arb.) 43 Thee Troians.. Whose fatal misery my sight hath wytnesed heauye. **1607** DEKKER & WEBSTER *Northw. Hoe* III. i, Take but that corner and stand close, and thine eyes shall witnesse it. **1657** COKAINE *Obst. Lady* V. iv, I will make known how much you are her Servant, and what affection my ears have witnessed. **1606** G. W[OODCOCKE] *Hist. Ivstine* XXXIII. 110 Others enclustred about him to dispatch him of his life, more enuious against him now, through his Noblenesse which they witnessed. **1613** CHAPMAN *Rev. Bussy d'Ambois* IV. H 3, I neuer witness'd a more noble loue, Nor a more ruthfull sorrow. **1667** MILTON *P.L.* III. 700 To witness with thine eyes what some perhaps Contented with report heare onely in heav'n. **1710** SHAFTESB. *Charac.* (1711) I. III. i. ii. 175 There is nothing ever so trivial.. that he is not desirous shou'd be witness'd by the Party, whose Grace.. he sollicits. **1784** COWPER *Task* I. 144 And witness, dear companion of my walks,.. a joy that thou hast doubled long. **1787** *Generous Attachment* I. 26, I witnessed the uneasiness Mr. Melville endured. **1792** G. WAKEFIELD *Mem.* (1804) I. 294, I met with an opportunity.. of witnessing a most extraordinary ventriloquist. **1796** SOUTHEY *Lett. fr. Spain* xii. (1799) 164 Never did I witness a more melancholy scene of devastation. **1827** MACAULAY *Ess., Machiavelli* (1843) I. 68 They witnessed the arrangement of the pullies, and the manufacture of the thunders. **1836** *Hints on Etiquette* (ed. 2) 30 Do not pick your teeth much at table, as.. to witness it is not a pleasant thing. **1873** L. STEPHEN *Ess. Freethinking* 8 We are, however, passing through a great change, of which no living man can expect to witness the end. **1878** MORLEY *Diderot* I. iv. 79 As he could not witness the experiment, he began to meditate on the subject. **1912** *Times* 19 Oct. 5/1 Large crowds witnessed their departure, but no demonstration occurred.

const. clause. **1825** SCOTT *Talism.* xxiii, Thou art wise.. and generous... I have witnessed that thou art both.

absol. **1810** WORDSW. *Descr. Lakes* (1822) 121 The Lake of Uri.. is disturbed from the bottom, as I was told, and indeed as I witnessed, without any apparent commotion in the air.

b. *fig.* Of a place, time, etc.: To be associated with (a fact or event); to be the scene or setting of; to 'see'.

1785 ANNA SEWARD *Lett.* (1811) I. 78 That immortal fountain and valley, which had witnessed the beauty of Laura. **1810** SCOTT *Lady of L.* VI. i, What various scenes.. Are witness'd by that red and struggling beam! **1813** EUSTACE *Class. Tour* (1821) III. iii. 104 These fertile plains.. once witnessed the defeat and death of a Gothic monarch. **1825** SCOTT *Betrothed* iii, March and October have witnessed me ever as they came round, for thirty years, deal with the best barley in Shropshire. **1864** BRYCE *Holy Rom. Emp.* xv. (1866) 264 The thirteenth [century] witnessed the rapid spread of the scholastic philosophy. **1881** FROUDE *Short Stud.* (1883) IV. II. iii. 194 The scenes which those harbours had witnessed thousands of years ago.

witnessable ('wɪtnɪsəb(ə)l), *a. rare.* [f. WITNESS *v.* + -ABLE.] That may be witnessed.

1870 *Eng. Mech.* 25 Feb. 580/1 If this be not a witnessable fact, it is at any rate a self-evident one. **1891** *Athenæum* 30 May 710/2 In one.. a great improvement is witnessable.

witnessed ('wɪtnɪst), *ppl. a.* [f. WITNESS *v.* + -ED[1].]

a. Furnished with evidence or proof. **b.** Attested by a witness or witnesses.

c **1586** C'TESS PEMBROKE *Ps.* CXIX. C. iv, All my delight Thy witnest will shall be. **1746** FRANCIS tr. *Hor., Sat.* II. v. 110 The son-in-law shall.. give the sire His witness'd will.

witnesser ('wɪtnɪsə(r)). Now *rare.* [f. WITNESS *v.* + -ER[1].] One who witnesses; a witness.

c **1400** *Pilgr. Sowle* (Caxton 1483) III. v. 53 Ye lyers forswerers and witnessers of falshede. *c* **1449** PECOCK *Repr.* I. v. 26 Whanne a mater.. is witnessid.. bi a reuerend.. witnesser or denouncer or rememberer (as is God, an Apostil, or a Doctour). *c* **1450** CAPGRAVE *Life St. Gilbert* xxxiv. 110 þoo cleped þei þe witnesses, or witnesseres,.. mad hem to swere þat þei schuld say soth in þat mater. *a* **1483** *Liber Niger* in *Househ. Ord.* (1790) 55 They sitte with hym at the bourd of doome.. as recorders and witnessers to the trouthe. *c* **1520** *Dial. Creatures Moralised* xxii. G iv, A false witnesser. **1554** T. MARTIN *Traictise Marr. Priests* Z iij, He was nowe so well become a constaunte witnesser of the passion of Christe, that.. he gaue an example of an heauenly conuersation vnto all his subiectes. **1658** in *Extr. St. Papers rel. Friends* Ser. I. (1910) 42 Lyers, and false witnessers. **1665** J. SERGEANT *Sure Footing* 19 An Eminent and Knowing Witnesser to Posterity of the Sence and Faith of the Church. **1874** W. P. MACKAY *Grace & Truth* 36 The blessed Spirit, the witnesser of Christ.

†'**witnessfully**, *adv. Obs. rare.* [f. assumed adj. **witnessful* + -LY[2].] Evidently, plainly.

c **1374** CHAUCER *Boeth.* IV. pr. v. (1868) 131 In þis wise more clerely and more witnesfully [L. *testatius*, v.r. *apertius*] is þe office of wise men ytretid.

witnessing ('wɪtnɪsɪŋ), *vbl. sb.* [f. WITNESS *v.* + -ING[1].]

1. The action of bearing witness or giving testimony. †*in witnessing of*, as a witness to; †*to bear witnessing*, to bear witness.

a **1300** *Cursor M.* 18894 O þis gadring be-houes us þan, In witnesing to ches a man Vn-to þe seruis of vr tale. *Ibid.* 27832 O couaitise.. cums.. fals witnesing,.. and lesing. **1382** WYCLIF *2 Cor.* i. 12 The witnessinge of oure conscience. *c* **1385** CHAUCER *L.G.W.* Prol. 299 To this flour.. Hire white corowne beryth the witnessynge. **1426** LYDG.

in *Pol. Poems* (Rolls) II. 132 Gladly he chevith what so he begynne,.. The fyne therof berith witnessing. **1474** CAXTON *Chesse* III. viii. (1883) 150, I haue put on eche keye a bille & writynge In witnessinge of the thynges abouesayd. **1526** TINDALE *Rev.* i. 9 Iohn..was in the yle of Pathmos for the worde of god, and for the witnessynge of Iesu Christe. **1563** *Reg. Privy Council Scot.* I. 254 Diverse personis wer summond..to beir witnessing in the said mater. **1659** SOUTH *Serm.* (1697) I. 117 The witnessing of the truth was then so generally attended with this Event, that Martyrdom now signifies..to witness by death. **1857** DICKENS *Dorrit* II. xxviii, I have it on the witnessing of these two madmen.. that you want me.

†**b.** In biblical use: = WITNESS *sb.* 2 d.

a **1340** HAMPOLE *Psalter* cxviii[i]. 2 Blisful þai þat ransakis his witnessyngis. **1382** WYCLIF *Ps.* xcviii[i]. 7 Thei kepten his witnessingus, and the heste that he ȝaf to hem.

†**2.** That which is uttered or stated in support of a fact or statement; evidence given. *Obs.*

a **1300** *Cursor M.* 16277 Vp þai ras and gaf a cri..Quat mister es o wijtnessing Again him for to lede? *c* **1330** *Arth. & Merl.* 1269 Telle ous now, what is þi name,..þat we se sum witnesseing Of þi dede. **1476** *Acta Audit.* (1839) 52/1 Þe sadis partijs beand personaly present and þare allegations and witnessingis..herd. **1478** *Acta Dom. Conc.* (1839) 20/2 Johne..sall bring sic..document and witnessing or testimoniale of his sesing þat he has. **1561** DAUS tr. *Bullinger on Apoc.* (1573) 260 b, The Apostles in the gospell are called witnesses: and the Gospell, a testimony or witnessyng. **1587** GOLDING *De Mornay* Pref. p. viii, Vnto men we wil bring the witnessings of men, euen the things that euerie man readeth in his owne nature. **1616** W. HAIG in J. Russell *Haigs* vii. 158 His habitude of lying, his noted perjury, [etc.]: qualities for which any man's witnessing were to be repelled in judgment.

3. Attestation (of a document). Chiefly in phr. †*in* or *into* (*the*) *witnessing of* = F. *en témoignage de*.

1405 *Rolls of Parlt.* III. 605/2 In Witnessing of whilk thyng, to thys presentes we have sette our forsaide Seal. **1422** in *E.E. Wills* (1882) 51 Into wytnessyng of which thyng, to this my present testament I haue put to my seell. **1561** in *Exch. Rolls Scot.* XIX. 481 Robert Hammiltoun.. for the mare witnessing hes subscrivit this his obligatioun with his hand.

4. The fact of being present and observing something.

1855 in *Cambr. Ess.* 154 The witnessing of the scenes. **1872** P'CESS ALICE *Mem.* (1884) 288 The witnessing of your grief rent my heart so deeply.

So **'witnessing** *ppl. a.* (*spec.* in *witnessing part*: see quot. 1844).

1844 WILLIAMS *Real Prop.* 143 The *testatum*, or witnessing part, 'Now this Indenture witnesseth'. [See WITNESS *v.* 1 b.] **1855** C. DAVIDSON *Prec. Convey.* (ed. 2) I. 64 When the instrument contains more than one witnessing part. **1859** RUSKIN *Two Paths* i. §4 Corruption festered to its loathsomest in the midst of the witnessing presence of a disciplined civilisation.

†**'witnessman.** *north.* and *Sc. Obs.* Forms: see WITNESS *sb.* [a. ON. *vitnismaðr* (f. *vitnis*, gen. of *vitni* witness + *maðr* MAN *sb.*[1]), accommodated in form to WITNESS *sb.* and MAN *sb.*[1]]

a. A witness. **b.** The (tenurial) duty of providing a witness in court.

10.. in *Reg. St. Bees Priory* (Surtees) 527 Myd bode and wytnesmann on thyylk stow. **1278** *Ibid.* 374 Pro witnesman et summonitoribus inveniendis ad faciendum districciones. **1292** *Anc. Deed* L. 458 (P.R.O.) [cf. *Ibid.* 374] Quieti de secta facienda ad Curiam meum..et de Bode et de Wyttenesman..que seruicia quondam petii de predictis Abbati et Conuentu. *c* **1375** *Sc. Leg. Saints* xii. (*Mathias*) 323 Þe sal of me be wytnes-mene In þe towne of Iersualem. **1451** *Extr. Aberd. Reg.* (1844) I. 19 The quhilk assise ripely avisit, and the witnesmen examynit and herd in the cause. **1493** *Acta Dom. Conc.* (1839) 319/2 Þe lard of Amisfelde sall cause his officiare witht twa witnesmen..to pynd apoun þe commoune þat is debatabile.

Witney ('wɪtnɪ). Also 8–9 **Whitney** (8 **-eye**). A heavy loose woollen material with a nap, manufactured and made up into blankets at Witney, a town in Oxfordshire; also, formerly, a kind of cloth or coating made there. Also *attrib.* esp. in *Witney blanket* (for which the simple *Witney* is occas. used).

The name has been applied to similar materials made elsewhere, but in 1909 a decision of the Courts in an action brought under the Merchandise Marks Act upheld the restriction of the name to blankets produced by the Witney manufacturers.

1716 GAY *Trivia* I. 47 True Witney Broad-cloth with it's Shag unshorn, Unpierc'd is in the lasting Tempest worn. **1737** in Alice M. Earle *Costume of Colonial Times* (1894) 256 Fine Whitneye at 53s a yard, Coarse Whitneye at 28s a yard. **1760** FOOTE *Minor* II. 50 Whitney blankets for exportation. **1792** *New Bath Directory* 16 Whitney Blanket Warehouse. **1860** S. JUBB *Shoddy-trade* 45 Witneys have been made in a variety of plain colours, mixtures, and fancy styles. **1866** GRONOW *Recoll.* Ser. IV. 155 He..wrapped himself up in a large Witney blanket. **1880** BLACKMORE *Mary Anerley* xl, Give him one of our new whitneys to go behind his saddle. **1883** *Yorks. Textile Direct.* 3 Presidents, naps, witneys &c. **1885** *Mistletoe Bough* 25/2 A thick witney coat.

witogie (vɪ'tʊəxɪ). *S. Afr.* Also **witoogie, witteoogje.** [Afrikaans, f. Du. *wit* white + *oog* eye + *-ie* diminutive suffix.] Any of several birds of the genus *Zosterops* found in southern Africa, esp. *Z. pallidus* (formerly *Z. capensis*).

1867 E. L. LAYARD *Birds S. Afr.* 116 *Zosterops Capensis*.. Witteoogje, lit. white eye. **1936** E. L. GILL *First Guide S. Afr. Birds* 37 Witogie... The Cape White-eye sings all through the summer. **1949** *Cape Argus* 15 Oct. (Mag. Sect.) 2/7 Those pretty little birds known as white-eyes or witogies ..are well-known in most parts of the country as small green or yellowish birds with a characteristic circle of white feathers round each eye. **1957** *Cape Times* 11 Dec. 11/2 This burly bird has had a couple of twittering *witoogies* in close attendance. **1963** M. KAVANAGH *We Merry Peasants* x. 110 The tiny *witogies* have for their own use a fruit-laden pomegranate tree.

witoten, witout(en, obs. ff. WITHOUT.

witring, obs. form of WITTERING.

†**witryff,** *a. Obs.* [f. WIT *sb.* + *ryff*, RIFE *a.*] Abounding in cunning.

1598 *Spalding Club Misc.* (1841) I. 122 The crawis ar witryff beastis, and the Devill will cum in thair liknes.

witsafe, -saffe, -saufe, -save, -schaif, obs. ff. VOUCHSAFE.

witsau, var. WITHSAW *Obs.*

†**'witship**[1]. *Obs. rare.* In 1–2 **witscipe,** 3 *Orm.* **wittshipe.** [OE. (*ȝe*)*witscipe* = OFris. *witskipe*, OS. *giwitscepi* (MLG. *gewitschap*), OHG. *giwizscaf*: see IWIT and -SHIP.] Witness, testimony; knowledge.

c **900** tr. *Bæda's Hist.* I. xxvii. (1890) 72 Þa þe æt biscopes halȝunge in witscipe [*v.r.* ȝewitscype] stonde[n]. *c* **1175** *Lamb. Hom.* 25 Gif he hit deð in his witscipe. *c* **1200** ORMIN 5709 Þatt all þin herrte beo þwerrt ut att tin wittshipe clene.

'witship[2]. [f. WIT *sb.* + -SHIP.] With possessive pron. used as a fanciful title for a witty person.

1636 DAVENANT *Wits* IV. i. H 2, A little to Increase your witships allowance of aire.

witson(e, -dai, -tyd, obs. ff. WHITSUN, etc.

wittail(e, -aill, -ale, etc., obs. ff. VICTUAL.

wittam: see WITHAM.

‖**witteboom** ('vɪtəbʊəm). *S. Afr.* [Cape Du. (*witte* WHITE *a.*, *boom* BEAM *sb.*[1])] = SILVER-TREE 1.

1799 A. BARNARD *Let.* 4 Apr. in *Lett. Lady Anne Barnard to Henry Dundas* (1973) 185 Her Ladyship..is soon to present the Regiment with their colors [*sic*], in which the Whittebomb [*sic*]..is Happily blended and united with the Royal oak. **1818** LATROBE *Jrnl. S. Afr.* 35 The foot..of.. Table-Mountain is well clothed with witteboom (protea argentea). **1926** C. G. BOTHA *Our S. Afr.* (1938) 85 *Witteboomen*..is the name of the well known silver trees found in the Cape Peninsula. **1972** PALMER & PITMAN *Trees S. Afr.* I. 493 Witteboom..is believed to grow naturally only in the Cape Peninsula.

witted ('wɪtɪd), *a.* Forms: see WIT *sb.*; also 4 **ywittede, wyttet,** 7 *erron.* **wittied, witti'd.** [f. WIT *sb.* + -ED[2].]

1. Having wit or wits (of a specified quality or amount): with qualifying adv., as WELL-WITTED, etc. (*obs.*), or in parasynthetic comb. with an adj., as *dull-, fine-, half-, gross-, light-, quick-, sharp-, slow-witted,* etc.; also in nonce-formations after *half-witted*, as *two-third-witted, whole-witted.*

†Also (in form *witti'd*, influenced by WITTY *a.*) in comb. *wealth-witti'd* (? whose wits consist in wealth).

1377 LANGL. *P. Pl.* B. x. 397 Wyse witted men and wel ylettred clerkes. **1387** TREVISA *Higden* (Rolls) III. 409 Þe scharpest witted men. **1393** LANGL. *P. Pl.* C. XII. 235 Ryght wel ywittede men and wel lettred clerkes. **1470–85** MALORY *Arthur* VII. xxvi. 253 He was merueillously wytted. **1528** MORE *Dyaloge* III. Wks. 213/2 Diuers yonge scolars.. properly witted, feately lerned. **1532** —— *Confut. Barnes* VIII. ibid. 749/2 Had he no learning at all, and wer witted but right meanely. **1610** HEALEY *St. Aug. Citie of God* v. xxvi. *Vives* 233 Claudian..was..elegantly wittied [**1620** witted]. **1624** A. HOLLAND in J. Davies (Heref.) *Scourge Paper-Persecutors* 3 Wealth witti'd Loobies. **1642** J. EATON *Honey-c. Free Justif.* 44 Conceiving it after a carnall humane-witted fashion. **1835** C. F. HOFFMAN *Winter in West* II. 25 A forward, two-third witted fellow. **1904** A. C. BRADLEY *Shakesp. Trag.* 313 A quick-witted though not whole-witted lad.

†**2.** Possessed of understanding or intelligence.

1528 MORE *Dyaloge* II. Wks. 201/1 Yet might a few witted men deuise and feine a thing of such a fashion that it would be beleued. **1606** MARSTON *Fawne* V. I iv, Renowmed, witted, Dulcimel.

†**wittee.** *Obs. nonce-wd.* [irreg. f. WITTOL: see -EE.] A wife whose adultery was forced upon her by her husband.

1654 GAYTON *Pleas. Notes* IV. vi. & vii. 202 Such arts those gamesters have, Their Wittals to their wittees to enslave. *Margin*, The Wittall prostitutes his wife to be Wittee.

wittely, obs. form of WITTILY.

witten, obs. inf. and pa. pple. of WIT *v.*[1]; var. WITEN *v. Obs.*; Sc. f. WITTING *vbl. sb.*[1]

wittenes, -nesse, obs. ff. WITNESS.

witter ('wɪtə(r)), *sb.*[1] *Sc.* and *north.* Also 6 **wittir,** 9 **waiter, wutter, wyttyr.** [prob. of Scand. origin: cf. Norw. *vitr*, *vitring* warning, sign (f. *vitra* to warn = ON. *vitra* to reveal), and WITTER *a.*[1] and *v.*]

1. Something that serves as a mark, sign, or token.

1513 DOUGLAS *Æneis* V. iii. 52 A mark or wittir of ane greyn aik tre. *a* **1578** LINDESAY (Pitscottie) *Chron. Scot.* (S.T.S.) I. 272 Ane wyspe wpoun ewerie speir heid to be ane signe and witter to thame. **1644** D. HUME *Hist. Douglas & Angus* 98 He snatched away his spear with his guidon or witter. **1798** J. NAISMITH *Agric. Clydesdale* 105 To leave 20 or 25 select trees, called reserves or witters,..at each cutting. **1808** JAMIESON, *Waiter*, a token, a sign. **1894** *Northumbld. Gloss.*, *Wutter*, the rod which is put in the tithe stooks of corn.

2. *Curling.* The tee (TEE *sb.*[3]) towards which the stones are aimed.

1789 D. DAVIDSON *Seasons* 166 Next Robin o' Mains, a leader good, Close to the witter drew. **1811** *Acc. Game Curling* 4 A..witter..is a small hole made in the ice, round which two circles of different diameters are drawn, that the relative distances of the stones from the tee may be calculated at sight.

3. *attrib.*: †**witter hole,** a hole serving as a mark in a *witter stone*; **witter length** *Curling*, as far as the tee; so **witter shot,** a shot that sends the stone exactly to the tee; †**witter stone,** a boundary stone, a 'march stone'.

1615 *Extr. Aberd. Reg.* (1848) II. 323 Ane great merche stane, havand four *witter hollis. **1824** MACTAGGART *Gallovid. Encycl.* 65 Old wary curlers..won't waste stones on the guards. They sail them past the sentinels, nigh *wutter length. **1823** JAS. KENNEDY *Poems* 29 Their outer, and their inner wicks, And *witter shot. **1824** MACTAGGART *Gallovid. Encycl.* 184 *Draw a Wutter Shot*, a curling phrase, signifying to give the stone so much strength, that it may slide the length of the mark, and no farther. **1615** *Extr. Aberd. Reg.* (1848) II. 322 Ane great *witter stane in the muir, merkit with four hollis. **1679** SIR J. LAUDER *Decis.* (1759) I. 66 The Lords..Find..that the stone called the witterstone is not a stone for the regulating thereof [*sc.* the 'regorging' of water].

witter ('wɪtə(r)), *sb.*[2] *Sc.* and *north.* Also 8 **wetter,** 9 **wither, w(h)utter,** etc. (see *E.D.D.*). [Of obscure origin; cf., however, ME. *wither-hoked* (WITHER-[1] 3) and dial. *witter-huked* (Lonsdale Gloss. 1869).] *pl.* The barbs of an arrow, fishing-spear, fish-hook, or the like. (*rare* in *sing.*) Hence **'wittered** *a.*, barbed.

1775 H. FOORD in *Trans. Soc. Arts* (1784) II. 197 The other [whale] was lost,..by the Wetters, or Feathers of the Harpoon, giving way and bending. *Ibid.* 198 With one Wetter towards the Fish's head, the other towards her tail. **1792** *Archaeol. Scot.* I. 392 In process of time, the lozenge form fell into disuse, and the arrow head was formed with two witters. **1815** SCOTT *Guy M.* xxvi, He deserved his paiks for't—to put out the light when the fish was on ane's witters! **1820** SCORESBY *Acc. Arctic Regions* II. 223 The harpoon.. consists of three conjoined parts, called the 'socket', 'shank', and 'mouth'; the latter of which includes the barbs or 'withers'. *a* **1824** in Mactaggart *Gallovid. Encycl.* 6 They'd soon be darting in him Mony a wittered poisonous stang. **1894** *Northumbld. Gloss.*, *Wuttered*, barbed.

†**'witter,** *a.*[1] *Obs.* Also 3–4 **witer,** 4 **wyter,** 4–5 **wittur.** [Late OE. or early ME., a. ON. *vitr* wise, f. OTeut. *wit-*: see WIT *v.*[1]] Knowing, cunning, wise. Also, cognizant, aware (cf. WISE *a.* 3 b).

c **1100** *O.E. Chron.* (MS.D) an. 1067 Se kyng..wislice hine beþohte swa he full witter wæs. *c* **1205** LAY. 9600 Heo wes witer, heo wes wis. *c* **1250** *Gen. & Ex.* 168 So made god wid witter miȝt, Al erue,..and wilde der. *Ibid.* 1308 Ðo wurð ðe child witter and war Ðat ðor sal offrende ben don. *Ibid.* 2330 Ne wiste ȝe noȝt Ðat ic am o wol witter ðoȝt? *a* **1300** *Cursor M.* 698 Ne þe nedder was noght bittur þan, Þowf he was euer wittur. *c* **1320** *Cast. Love* 75 Ac whose is witer and wys of wit. *a* **1400–50** *Wars Alex.* 629 Sone wex he witter & wyse.

Hence †**'witterhed** [-HEAD], †**'witterness,** wisdom, prudence, knowledge.

c **1250** *Gen. & Ex.* 3667 Ches ðe nu her seuenti Wise men to stonden ðe bi, And ic sal hem geuen witter-hed. *a* **1300** *Cursor M.* 9728 Fader,..þi sun i es O þi strenght and þi witernes. *Ibid.* 23510 Godd, þat all wate þat es..Vte of his witernes be þai neuer.

†**'witter,** *a.*[2] *Obs.* Also 3 *Orm.* **witerr.** [Back-formation from WITTERLY, or prec. adj. with meaning transferred from the same: cf. MSw. *vitterliker*, (1) = ON. *vitrligr* wise, (2) manifest (so also early Da. *vitterlig*).] Clear, evident, certain.

c **1200** ORMIN 3363 Her icc wile shæwenn ȝuw summ þing to witerr takenn. *c* **1250** *Gen. & Ex.* 2903 Min milche witter name eley He knewen wel. **1357** *Lay Folks Catech.* (T.) 542 Idelnesse is..witter wissyng and wai till alkyns vices.

†**'witter,** *v.*[1] *Obs.* (cf. next). Forms: 3–4 **witere,** 4–5 **wyter(e, wytter,** 5 **wyttyr(e, witter.** [f. WITTER *a.*[1] or [2]: cf. ON. *vitra* to reveal.] *trans.* To inform, instruct; in some early quots. perh. to make clear (to a person what to do).

c **1205** LAY. 1200 Heȝe Diana..wise me & witere [*c* 1275 witte me]..whuder ich mæi liðan. *a* **1225** *Juliana* 33 (Bodl.) Wite me & were & witere & wisse þurh þi wisdom to wite me wið sunne. **13..** *E.E. Allit. P.* B. 1552 To wayte þe wryt þat hit wolde & wyter hym to say. *Ibid.* 1587 When ho was wytered bi wyȝes what was þe cause. *a* **1375** *Joseph Arim.*

466 Ho has witered hire of þis? ?*a* **1400** *Morte Arth.* 1239, I witter þe þe emperour es entirde in-to Fraunce. *c* **1425** WYNTOUN *Cron.* VI. 2284 (Wemyss) þai thocht.. for to cum in prevate One him or he suld witterit [*Cott. MS.* wyttride] be.

witter ('wɪtə(r)), *v.*² *colloq.* (orig. *Sc.* and *dial.*) Also **whitter**. [Perh. a variant of WHITTER *v.*: cf. WHITTER *sb.*¹]

To chatter or mutter; to grumble; to speak with annoying lengthiness on trivial matters. Occas. *trans.* Freq. const. *on.*

1808 A. SCOTT *Poems* 82 The winking swankies whitter, An' fondly ee some female band. **1854** A. E. BAKER *Northamptonshire Gloss.*, *Whitter*, to murmur, to grumble, to complain... 'Don't *whitter* so.' **1886** R. E. G. COLE *Gloss. Words S.W. Lincs.* 168, I witter my-sen at times, and my husband tells me I'm a regular wittering old woman. **1925** E. C. SMITH *Mang Howes* 21 A clecken o guidweives at a gairdeen-yett whuttert ti other whan they eyed iz. **1959** [see *suicide blonde* s.v. SUICIDE *sb.*² d]. **1966** 'O. MILLS' *Enemies of Bride* ii. 16 You might.. try making the tea, instead of wittering on about Cordon Bleu methods. **1973** *Where* Jan. 13/2 Don't whitter away at every item [on the agenda], giving up at the first unsatisfactory explanation. Make your choice of issue, then take your time. **1981** R. D. EDWARDS *Corridors of Death* i. 4 The questions which those who had spotted him as the man-in-the-know were wittering at him. *Ibid.* xxxvi. 164 It wasn't like Robert to witter on like this. **1982** *Observer* 3 Oct. 9/2 If I wasn't going to hear the Tories wittering on in Brighton this week, I'd be in Frankfurt listening to publishers wittering on at the annual Book Fair.

Hence '**wittering** *ppl. a.*

1886 [see WITTER *v.*²]. **1983** *Listener* 20 Jan. 5/2 A really wittering, patronising speech programme is a worse insult to the intelligence than the most fatuous disc jockey.

'**wittering**, *vbl. sb. Sc.* and *north.* Also 4 **wit(e)ring, -iring**, *Sc.* **vittering, -yng.** [f. WITTER *v.* + -ING¹.] Information, cognizance; *mod. dial.* a sign, token (cf. WITTER *sb.*¹ 1), a hint.

a **1300** *Cursor M.* 21583 þat godd suld send hir witering [*Gött.* witring] sun, Quat he o þat cros wald ha don. **1375** BARBOUR *Bruce* v. 342 Iames of Douglas of thare cummyng .. had vittering. *c* **1425** WYNTOUN *Cron.* I. 411 Noe first send furþ þe rawin Till get wittering and knawlege Gif þat þe flud begouth to suage. **1513** DOUGLAS *Æneis* IV. iv. 79 And of thair cupling wittering schew the air. **17..** *Broomfield Hill* viii. in Child *Ballads* I. 394 That was to be wittering true That maiden she had gane. **1781** J. HUTTON *Tour to Caves* (E.D.S.), *Wittering*, an hint. **1828** *Craven Gloss.*, *Wittering*, a hint, a secret report. **1876** *Mid-Yorks. Gloss.* s.v., I got a wittering o' 't from him.

†'**witterly**, *adv. Obs.* Forms: 3-5 **wit(t)er-, wytter-**, (3 **witerr-**, 4 **wyter-, wit(t)ir-, wyttir-, witur-, weter-**, *Sc.* **vittir-**, 5 **wyt(t)ur- -yr-, wetir-, -ur-, witre-**, (**whiter-, wihtur-**); 3-4 **-like, -liche**, 3-5 **-li**, etc. (-LY²). [Of Scand. origin (cf. MSw. *vitterliga*, early Da. *vitter-, vider- lige*, corresp. to the respective adjs. MSw. *vitterliker*, chiefly neut. *-likit*, early Da. *vitter-, viderlig* clear, manifest): cf. WITTER *a.*² and *v.*] Clearly, plainly, evidently; certainly, for certain; without doubt, undoubtedly, truly.

Used esp. as a conventional addition in ME. verse, freq. with the verb *wit* (to know).

c **1200** ORMIN 785 & tatt wass witerrlike soþ þatt Godess enngell seȝȝde. *Ibid.* 1131 & witt tu wel þatt Latin boc Full witerrlike uss kiþeþþ, Whillc lac wass offredd forr þe preost. *Ibid.* 3446 [The Magi] wisstenn witerrliȝ þærþurrh þatt swillc new king wass awwnedd. *c* **1205** LAY. 17563 þu miht ileue me inoh, for þis is witerliche soð. *a* **1225** *Ancr. R.* 358 Lokeð nu hu witterliche ure Louerd sulf hit witneð. *c* **1250** *Gen. & Ex.* 791 Egipte clerkes.. hem lerede, witterlike, Astronomiȝe and arsmetike. *a* **1300** *Cursor M.* 2003 þe elleuend winter was, witerli, þer after. *Ibid.* 16259 Sai me son quer þat þou be godd sun or nan, þat i mai wijt it witerli. *c* **1350** *Leg. Rood* iii. 134 And pray him me to certify Of þe oile of mercy weterly. **13..** *Gaw. & Gr. Knt.* 1706 Wreȝande hym ful weterly with a wroth noyse. **1375** BARBOUR *Bruce* x. 350 Thai that I wat vittirly Eftir my wit rehers sall I. **1393** LANGL. *P. Pl.* C. I. 11 Al þe welþe of þis worlde & þe woo boþe, Wynkyng as it were wyterly ich saw hyt. *c* **1400** MAUNDEV. (Roxb.) x. 39 Helen wist noȝt witerly whilk was þe crosse þat Criste was done apon. *c* **1400** *Destr. Troy* 9180 Thies wordes, in his wo, witturly he said, Soberly to hym-selfe. *c* **1450** *St. Cuthbert* (Surtees) 5463 þat ilk place Whare þe fische lay dry, þat was cuthberts witterly. *a* **1500** *Ratis Raving* 3453 Suppos thai wyst It wytterly, Quhai suld that gold aw werraly.

Wittesontyde, obs. f. WHITSUNTIDE.

Wittgensteinian (ˌvɪtgənˈstaɪnɪən), *a.* and *sb.* [f. the name of the Austrian-born philosopher Ludwig *Wittgenstein* (1889-1951) + -IAN.]

A. *adj.* Of, pertaining to, or characteristic of Wittgenstein, or his theories or methods. **B.** *sb.* An adherent of Wittgenstein's ideas.

1946 *Mind* LV. 25 Unfortunately, for the outsider there exists no official and adequate statement of the Wittgensteinian technique. *Ibid.*, 'W——ns' will be used for 'Wittgensteinians'. **1954** [see RUSSELLIAN *a.* and *sb.*]. **1966** D. JENKINS *Educated Soc.* iii. 140 The Wittgensteinian line of concluding that when one cannot profitably speak one must perforce be silent. **1969** T. F. TORRANCE *Theol. Sci.* i. 19 To use Wittgensteinian language, are these 'images' 'pictures' or 'tools'? **1973** *Listener* 4 Jan. 21/2 A hard-line defence, by a leading Wittgensteinian, of the Pope's pronouncement on contraception. **1980** *Times Lit. Suppl.* 20 June 714/2 Professor Wright.. picks up some Wittgensteinian themes and explores how they might be developed. *Ibid.* 714/4 The question of whether.. a Wittgensteinian can defend the distinction between necessary and contingent propositions.

wittham: see WITHAM.

witti, obs. f. WITTY *a.*

witticaster (wɪtɪˈkæstə(r)). *nonce-wd.* [f. WIT *sb.* or WITTY *a.*, after CRITICASTER.] A petty or inferior wit, a witling.

First in Latham's Dict., 1872, where the following is quoted as from Milton on the authority of 'Ord MS.':—The mention of a nobleman seems quite sufficient to arouse the spleen of our witticaster.

Hence in later Dicts.

wittichenite ('wɪtɪkənaɪt). *Min.* [ad. G. *wittichenit* (Kenngott, 1853), f. *Wittichen* in Baden, where found: see -ITE¹.] Native sulphide of bismuth and copper.

1868 DANA *Min.* (ed. 5) 98.

witticism ('wɪtɪsɪz(ə)m). Also 7 **wittycism**. [Coined by Dryden, f. WITTY *a.*, after *criticism.*] A piece of wit; a witty saying or remark; a smart joke. In earlier use often *contemptuous* ('a mean attempt at wit' J.), or applied esp. to a joke made at another's expense, a jeer, a witty sarcasm.

1677 DRYDEN *State Innoc.*, *Apol. Her. Poetry* c 1 b, A mighty Wittycism, (if you will pardon a new word!) but there is some difference between a Laugher and a Critique. **1683** —— *Vind. Dk. Guise* 18 For the sake of a silly Witticism. **1683** E. HOOKER *Pref. Pordage's Mystic Div.* 15 What shal wee.. think of Cramp-words, or Criticisms, Jocs, or Witticisms, Railleries and Drolleries..? **1778** MISS BURNEY *Evelina* xlix. (1779) II. 161 I had many witticisms to endure from the Branghtons. **1802** MARIA EDGEWORTH *Moral T.*, *Good Fr. Governess* (1848) I. 286 Assailed.. by a variety of.. maternal witticisms upon his uncouth appearance. **1842** H. ROGERS *Ess.* I. i. 22 The profane heartless witticisms of those with whom nothing is sacred. **1874** BURNAND *My Time* xx, At this witticism, there was a burst of laughter.

So **witticize** ('wɪtɪsaɪz) *v. intr.*, to utter witticisms.

1773 WESLEY *Wks.* (1872) X. 423 It lies therefore upon Mr. Hill to answer Mr. Sellon before he witticizes upon me. **1833** *New Monthly Mag.* XXXVIII. 489 The sketching and witticising talent which characterizes so many of our modern travellers. **1881** *Dollar Instit. Mag.* Dec. 1 While we warble or witticise.

witti(e)d: see WITTED.

'**wittified**, *ppl. a. nonce-wd.* [f. WITTY *a.* + *-fied* (see -FY).] Possessed of wit.

a **1734** NORTH *Lives* (1826) I. 61 Those wittified ladies who were willing to come into the order [of wits].

†'**wittiful**, *a. Obs. nonce-wd.* [irreg. f. WITTY *a.* + -FUL.] Full of 'wit', wise, sensible.

1590 LODGE *Euphues' Golden Legacie* (1592) I 2 b, Oh, Rosader, then be thou wittifull [*rime* pitifull].

Wittig ('vɪtɪç, -ɪg). *Chem.* The name of Georg Friedrich Karl *Wittig* (b. 1897), German chemist, used *attrib.* to designate various synthetic techniques introduced by him, as **Wittig reaction**, a method for the preparation of substituted alkenes utilizing the action of an alkyl phosphorus ylide on a carbonyl compound (aldehyde or ketone); **Wittig rearrangement**, the conversion of benzyl or allyl ethers in the presence of a strong base to the corresponding secondary or tertiary alcohol.

1951 *Jrnl Amer. Chem. Soc.* LXXIII. 1437 The Wittig rearrangement of benzyl ethers by lithium phenyl. **1956** *Chem. Abstr.* L. 6443 The previous attempt to prep. a model vitamin D triene by the Wittig reaction.. has been continued. **1974** GILL & WILLIS *Pericyclic Reactions* vi. 195 This elegant experiment proved that the migration involves a *supra-supra* interaction in Wittig rearrangements. **1979** *Sci. Amer.* Dec. 74/1 Vitamin A is synthesized industrially using the Wittig reaction. **1980** *Chem. in Brit.* XVI. 466/3 Vitamin A acetate is produced industrially *via* the Wittig synthesis.

†'**wittihede**. *Obs. rare*⁻¹. [f. WITTY *a.* + *-hede*, -HEAD.] Wisdom, understanding.

c **1315** SHOREHAM *Poems* VII. 95 þe mytte hys fader.. Wysdom þe sone, for wytti-hede þat he forþ toke.

wittily ('wɪtɪlɪ), *adv.* Forms: see WITTY *a.*; also 4-6 **wittely** (4 **-li**, *Sc.* **vittely**), 5 **wyttely**. [f. WITTY *a.* + -LY².] In a witty manner.

†**1.** Intelligently, cleverly, ingeniously. *Obs.*

Not always easily distinguishable from 2.

c **1350** *Will. Palerne* 2602 þat wittily tauȝt hem þe weies whider þei wende scholde. **1362** LANGL. *P. Pl.* A. x. 4 Of Erþe and Eir hit is mad I-medelet to-gedere, Wiþ wynt and wiþ watur ful wittiliche I-Meint. *c* **1440** *Promp. Parv.* 531/1 Wyttyly, *ingeniose.* **1542** UDALL *Erasm. Apoph.* Pref. **vj, With fables and tales preatyly and wittyly feigned. **1578** LYTE *Dodoens* Epist. to Queen *ij b, By their diligent inquisition they wittily found out the vse of many [plants]. **1621** T. WILLIAMSON tr. *Goulart's Wise Vieillard* 184 Those women, who.. so cunningly and wittily twisted on your fine skaines and clues. **1675** J. SHEFFIELD (Dk. Buckhm.) *Ess. Satyre* 133 But is there any other Beast alive, Can his own Harm so wittily contrive? **1682** SIR T. BROWNE *Chr. Mor.* II. xii. (1716) 69 Of good natural parts,.. which did but arm their bad inclinations, and make them wittily wicked.

†**2.** Wisely, discreetly, sensibly. *Obs.*

c **1350** *Will. Palerne* 4142 Sende wittili to þi wif & warne hire fore. **1375** BARBOUR *Bruce* v. 264 Gude begynnyng.. And it be followit vittely, May [etc.]. *Ibid.* XIII. 571 Thai war gouernit full wittely. **1465** *Paston Lett.* Suppl. 91 Ye may verely understand that it is not guided wittely nor discretly. **1470-85** MALORY *Arthur* X. xxxvi. 472 Alysander fought wyldly and not wyttely. **1551** ROBINSON tr. *More's Utopia* I. (1895) 65 Whose lande is.. well and wyttelye gouerned. **1660** SHARROCK *Vegetables* 107 Lord Bacon wittily advises to sprinkle a little forrage seed on the strawberry bed. *a* **1700** EVELYN *Diary* 27 Feb. 1676, Dr. Pritchard.. preached.. very allegorically according to his manner, yet very gravely and wittily. **1702** C. MATHER *Magn. Chr.* III. II. xxiii. 136 How Learnedly he now conveyed all the Liberal Arts unto those that sat at his Feet; how Wittily he moderated their Disputations. **1825** SCOTT *Betrothed* vii, Thou hast studied some small revenge on me.. and.. I think thou hast taken it wittily enough.

3. In a manner characterized by wit (see WIT *sb.* 7, 8, WITTY *a.* 7, 8); in a cleverly amusing way; with smart jocosity.

1553 T. WILSON *Rhet.* II. 58 To beginne with some pleasaunt tale or take an occasion to iest wittely. **1581** PETTIE tr. *Guazzo's Civ. Conv.* II. (1586) 75 b, Hee.. can give quip for quip so wittilie that those which begin the skirmish with him boldlie, are faine to retire shamefullie. *a* **1586** SIDNEY *Arcadia* II. xviii. § 5 In conversation wittily pleasant, and pleasantly gamesome. **1691** SIR T. P. BLOUNT *Ess.* i. 19 Therefore one wittily calls these Indulgences Emulgences. **1759** GOLDSM. *Pres. St. Pol. Learn.* ix. Wks. (Globe) 440/1 When an unexpected similitude in two objects strikes the imagination—in other words, when a thing is wittily expressed. **1869** *Adam Smith's W.N.* II. ii. I. 326 *note*, Free trade in banking, it has been wisely and wittily said, is free trade in swindling. **1878** A. H. MARKHAM *Gt. Frozen Sea* ii. 25 As one of our men wittily remarked on seeing his first iceberg, it reminded him strongly of the isle of Wight (white). **1885** 'MRS. ALEXANDER' *At Bay* i, A good deal more talk, partly business, partly wittily told scandal.

†**4.** Knowingly, wittingly. *Obs. rare.*

1653 WHITFIELD *Treat. Sinf. Men* iii. 5 That which he willingly and wittily suffers to be done. **1654** FULLER *Two Serm.* 36 Not willingly, wittily, or wilfully.

¶**5.** irreg. as adj. = WITTY *a.* 4.

c **1400** *Rule St. Benet* (verse) 1079 þat we vs avise,.. To say our wil in wordes foune, And þat our wordes be wittely.

wittin: see WIT *v.*¹, WITTING *vbl. sb.*¹

wittiness ('wɪtɪnɪs). [f. WITTY + -NESS.] The quality or character of being witty; †intelligence, sagacity; †cleverness, ingenuity; †wisdom, good sense, etc. (see WITTY *a.* 2-8).

1533 J. HEYWOOD *Dial. Wit & Folly* (Percy Soc.) 1 Ye show some wytty wyttines. **1542** RECORDE *Gr. Artes* Pref. a iv, Wittynesse of beastes and byrdes. **1544** BETHAM tr. *Purlilia's Precepts War* I. clxxxviii. I iv, In which case the wittynesse of yᵉ capitayn & knowledge, is moch requyred. **1608** TOPSELL *Serpents* 264 Theyr [*sc.* spiders'] wittinesse, pollicie, quicknes and sharpnes of sence. **1656** TRAPP *Comm. Rom.* viii. 6. 635 *To be carnally*] The quintessence of the fleshes wittiness, or rather wickedness. **1685** BAXTER *Paraphr. N.T.* Mark vii. 28 Not for the Wittiness of her saying, but for her Faith and Importunity. *Mod.* The wittiness of his remarks was refreshing after the dullness of the previous speeches.

witting ('wɪtɪŋ), *vbl. sb.*¹ *Obs.* exc. *dial.* α. 4 **witand, wyttande**, 5 **wetand**; Sc. 5 **wyttyn**, 5-6 (9 *n. dial.*) **wittin**, 6, 9 **witten** (9 **wittance**, ? = *wittens*). β. *Ayenb.* **wytende, -inde.** γ. **witting**, etc. [Of mixed origin; in the forms *witand, wyttande, wetand*, a. ON. *vitand* consciousness, knowledge (f. *vita* WIT *v.*¹) in phr. *at minni, várri*, etc. *vitand* to my, our, etc. knowledge; this type is app. in part continued in the *Sc.* and *n. dial wyttyn*, etc.; in *Ayenbite* (see quots. 1340) in pres. ppl. form *wytende, -inde*; otherwise f. WIT *v.*¹ + -ING¹.]

1. The fact of knowing or being aware of something; knowledge, cognizance.

Most commonly with prep. and possessive (or *of*), as *at, by, of, to one's witting* (partly after OF. *a son escient*), to or with one's knowledge, as one knows; as far as one knows; knowingly, wittingly; ***without one's witting***, without one's knowledge, so that one does not know; also ***but witting***, without its being known; ***with witting***, wittingly.

α. *a* **1300** *Cursor M.* 29262 [He] mai noght þis cursing scape, þat comuns wit him þat þe pape Cursd has at his witand. *c* **1375** *Sc. Leg. Saints* xx. (*Blasius*) 114 þane rase þe chyld & a-va cane ga As he had wittine of na way. *a* **1400** *Pistill of Susan* 250, I wrapþed þe neuere, at my witand. *c* **1440** *York Myst.* xlv. 72 A! bredir, be my wetand and i-wisse so wer we. **1466** in *Reg. Mag. Sig. Scot.* *1471* 214/2 To gif us lele and trew counsale eftir thare wittin. **1474** *Acta Audit.* (1839) 32/1 Be wittin of vmquhile William of Striuelin. **1808** JAMIESON s.v., *Without my wittins*, without my knowledge. **1824** CARR *Craven Gloss.* 124 Bout my wittin, without my knowledge. **1828** MOIR *Mansie Wauch* vii. 57 Neither word nor wittens of a family, to perpetuate our name to future generations.

β. **1340** *Ayenb.* 8 Huo þet onworþeþ his uader and his moder be his wytinde.. zeneȝeth dyadliche. *Ibid.* 37 Wyþ-oute hare wytende and wyþ-oute hare wylle.

γ. **1338** R. BRUNNE *Chron.* (1810) 216 Withouten his conseile, or þe kynges wittyng. **13..** *Cursor M.* 23510 (Gött.) Forgiuen er þai [*sc.* man's sins] and neuer þe less.. Vte of his [*sc.* God's] witting [*Cott.* witernes, *Fairf.* witring] be þai neuer. *c* **1374** CHAUCER *Troylus* II. 236 Ye be the womman in þis world lyuynge With-oute paramours to my wytynge That I best loue. *Ibid.* IV. 991 That god shuld han no parfit cler witynge More þan we men, þat han doutous wenynge. *c* **1386** CHAUCER *Knt.'s T.* 753 With oute wityng of any oother wight. **1387-8** T. USK *Test. Love* III. iv. (Skeat) I. 63 [God's] weting and his before-weting is al oon. *c* **1400** *Apol. Loll.* 66 þei..þat are chargid to sey þe soþe to þer witing. *c* **1425** WYNTOUN *Cron.* V. iv. 676 þe Grekys..þe bodeis cast In til a cistern dep, qwhar þai Lay hid but wyttynge. **1445** tr. *Claudian* in *Anglia* XXVIII. 267 Iustice moevith to preferre right..& wronge nevir yive with wetyng. *a* **1450** MYRC 397 That heo avow no maner þynge But hyt be at hys wytynge. *c* **1450** *Merlin* 12 Gode lete me haue delyueraunce yef euer man, my witynge, hadde to do with me. *Ibid.* 18 The Iuges examyned the gode hermyte yef it were so, and he seide, 'Ye', as by his wetynge. **1502** *Ord. Crysten Men* (W. de W. 1506) I. vii. G vii b, Who so trespasseth vnto his wyttynge ony of the .x. commaundementes, is in deedly synne. *a* **1533** LD. BERNERS *Gold. Bk. M. Aurel.* (1546) Q iii b, He went fro Rome to Salon..without the witting of any person. **1560** *Acts Privy Counc. Irel.* (Hist. MSS. Comm.) 99 Without thassentes or witting of the saide freholders. **1574** *Reg. Privy Council Scot.* Ser. I. II. 400 [If they be] sufferit to remane thairintill ..be our witting. **1587** *Sc. Acts Jas. VI* (1814) III. 464/1 The cuntrie wherin the saidis guidis salbe ressett or remane for the space of tuelff houris of his witting. **1621** HAKEWILL *David's Vow* ii. 46 As..we have action implied in the Verb: so have wee witting, and willing,..implied in the Adverb. **1846** BROCKETT *N.C. Gloss.* (ed. 3), *Witting*, knowledge, judgment, wit.

2. Knowledge obtained or (esp.) communicated; information, intelligence, tidings, news; notice, warning. (Cf. WIT *v.*[1] 3.) Chiefly in *to get* or *have witting*.

1375 BARBOUR *Bruce* IV. 359 We sall cum thair sa preuely, That thai sall haff na persavyng, Na ȝeit witting of our cummyng. *Ibid.* v. 540 Quhen men schupe hym to betraiss, He gat vitting tharof alwayis. **1417** in Rymer *Foedera* (1710) IX. 427 Kepe this Matere..secre..that never Creature have Wittyng thereof. *c* **1450** *Merlin* 14 When thow shalte be brought oute ageyn to Iugement lete me haue wetynge. *Ibid.* 45 He merveyled..how merlin myght have witinge ther-of. **1497** *Merton Coll. Rec.* No. 1031, The same John Wreyght shall gyve wetyng and warnyng vnto the fermour then beyng. *a* **1513** FABYAN *Chron.* VI. clx. (1811) 150 The sonnis sent wittynge to the pope..requyrynge hym of ayde and counceyll. *a* **1529** SKELTON *Bouge of Court* 278 And I knowe ony erthly thynge That is agayne you, ye shall haue wetynge. *a* **1625** PURCHAS *Pilgrims* II. 1066 To giue him witting thereof. **1818** SCOTT *Rob Roy* xxii, What will come o' ye gin the bailies suld come to get witting? **1893** W. R. MACKINTOSH *Around Orkney Peat Fires* ii. (1905) 34 His scouts..gave him 'wittance' of the..scheme.

¶ Used for the infin. in phr. 'to wit'.

1398, *a* **1400**, **1440** [see WIT *v.*[1] B. 10 a, b].

witting, *vbl. sb.*[2], bequest: see WIT *v.*[2]

1483 *Cath. Angl.* 421/1 Wyttinge, *legacio*.

'witting, *ppl. a.* Forms: see WIT *v.*[1] A. 6. [f. WIT *v.*[1] + -ING[2].]

a. Chiefly in conjunction with *wilfully* or *willing* (see WILLING *ppl. a.* 2 f), advb. = WITTINGLY 1.

1377 LANGL. *P. Pl.* B. XIX. 368 Lyeres..þat were forsworen ofte, Wytynge [*v.r.* wytyngli] and willefully with þe false helden. *c* **1450** *Mirk's Festial* 138 þylke þat don aȝeyne þe constytucyons of holy chyrche wytyng, he ys acurset tyll he come to amendement. **1531** TINDALE *Expos. 1 John* ii. (1538) F viij b, He..whyche wyttynge and wyllynge shutteth hys eyes at the true lyght. **1538** STARKEY *England* (1878) 66 No man wyttyng and wyllyng wyl hurt hymselfe. **1582** T. WATSON *Centurie of Loue* lx, How he witting and wilfully followeth his owne hurt. **1600** HOLLAND *Livy* VI. xl. 245 We..have practised nothing, witting and willing,..prejudiciall to the Communaltie.

b. Chiefly *predicatively*: Aware, cognizant.

1500-20 DUNBAR *Poems* ix. 138 Both witting and vnwitting me. *a* **1586** SIDNEY *Two Pastorels* ii. 29 Seely shepheards are not witting What in art of Loue is fitting. *a* **1629** HINDE *J. Bruen* v. (1641) 19 Using men both witting and unwitting. **1894** F. S. ELLIS *Reynard Fox* 221 Hither.. I..came, To make you witting of the same. **1906** *Macm. Mag.* Oct. 885 Scarcely witting, he ran forward.

c. Conscious as an agent; that is consciously what the sb. denotes.

1678 LITTLETON *Dict., Eng.-Lat.*, A witwal or wittal, a witting cuckold. **1872** J. G. MURPHY *Comm. on Lev.* iv. 2 Witting and wilful transgressors. **1912** *Oxf. & Camb. Rev.* Nov. 48 [Synge] was a witting artist of marvellous skill.

d. *transf.* of the action: Done consciously (and so with responsibility), 'conscious', deliberate: often in conjunction with *willing*.

1553 BRADFORD *Serm. Repentance* (1574) H iij b, This willing and witting offending & synning. **1581** HANMER *Jesuites Banner* 4 b, Wee are all by nature the children of wrath, yet will you not confesse, that the corruption of nature is voluntary and witting. **1613** HOBY *Counter-snarle* 55 These his witting falsifications. **1629** H. BURTON *Truth's Tri.* 316 So..fore-knowledge of God, is his witting and willing act or decree. **1879** MAUDSLEY *Pathol. Mind* vi. 288 The notion of witting and wilful vice.

witting, obs. Sc. pa. pple. of WIT *v.*[1]

wittingite ('wɪtɪŋaɪt). *Min.* [ad. G. *wittingit* (Nordenskiöld, 1849), f. *Wittingi* in Finland, where found: see -ITE[1].] A variety of NEOTOCITE.

1868 DANA *Min.* 491. **1882** [see NEOTOCITE].

wittingly ('wɪtɪŋlɪ), *adv.* Forms: see WIT *v.*[1] A. 6 and WEETINGLY; also 4 **wytindeliche**. [f. WITTING *ppl. a.* + -LY[2].]

1. With knowledge or awareness of what one is doing; knowingly, consciously; often implying 'designedly, deliberately, intentionally'. (In earlier use freq. conjoined with *wilfully* or *willingly*.)

a **1340** HAMPOLE *Psalter* xciv. 11 þai erre in hert.. witandly & wilfully. **1340** *Ayenb.* 8 þet we ne wreþþi uader ne moder wytindeliche. *a* **1390** WYCLIF *Rom.* Prol., Greuousli to han trespassid, and witendely. *c* **1425** AUDELAY *XI Pains Hell* 114 in *O.E. Misc.* 214 þai foreswere ham wettanly. **1500-20** DUNBAR *Poems* xc. 21 Thow art nocht abill remissioun for to get, Wittandlie and thow suld ane syn forȝet. **1535** JOYE *Apol. Tindale* (Arb.) 23 Not willingly and wetingly to slip ouer siche fautes. **1583** STUBBES *Anat. Abus.* II. (1882) 14 If it were proued that he killed him wittingly, willingly and prepensedly. **1602** SHAKS. *Ham.* v. i. 13 She drown'd her selfe wittingly. **1603** KNOLLES *Hist. Turks* (1621) 524 After him..succeeded many valiant men.. whom for breuitee I wittingly passe ouer. **1670** *Act 22 Chas. II* c. 1 §4 Every person who shall wittingly and willingly suffer any such Conventicle..in his..House. **1713** DERHAM *Phys.-Theol.* v. ix. 347, I have endeavoured to say as little wittingly as I could. **1809** W. IRVING *Knickerb.* III. ix. (1861) 109, I would not wittingly dishonour my work by a single false-hood, misrepresentation, or prejudice. **1851** *Gloss. Cumberld.*, *Wittenly*, wottenly; designedly. **1872** PROCTOR *Ess. Astron.* ii. 26, I would by no means desire to imply that Sir John Herschel..wittingly overlooked known facts. **1872** FREEMAN *Engl. Const.* ii. 105 Wittingly or unwittingly, much of our best modern legislation has..been a case of advancing by the process of going back.

†**2.** With knowledge; skilfully; wisely. *Obs. rare.*

1375 BARBOUR *Bruce* XI. 594 Emang thame that fechtand weir, That thame defendit so vittandly. **1657** *Narr. late Parlt.* 28 As was learnedly & wittingly intimated by the Speaker.

wittite ('vɪtaɪt). *Min.* [ad. Sw. *wittit* (K. Johansson 1924, in *Ark. f. Kemi, Mineral. och Geol.* IX. IX. 2), f. the name of Th. *Witt*, Swedish mining engineer: see -ITE[1].] A mineral containing lead, bismuth, selenium, and sulphur and occurring as grey monoclinic crystals.

1924 *Mineral. Abstr.* II. 340 Wittite resembles molybdenite in appearance. **1980** [see WEIBULLITE].

wittol ('wɪtəl), *sb. Obs.* or *arch.* Forms: 5-6 **wetewold**, 6-7 **wittold**, **wittall**, **wit-wal**, 6-8 **wittal**, (6 **wittole**, **-oll**, **-ale**, **-ald**, **witall**, 7 **whittoll**), 7-8 **wital**, 6- **wittol**. [Late ME. *wetewold*, app. formed after *cokewold*, CUCKOLD, with substitution of *wete*, WIT *v.*[1] for the first part of the word.]

1. A man who is aware of and complaisant about the infidelity of his wife; a contented cuckold.

14.. ? LYDG. *Assembly of Gods* 710 Wetewoldes that suffre syn in her syghtes. *c* **1520** SKELTON *Garl. Laurel* 187 Some carefull cokwoldes..; Some famous wetewoldis, and they be moche wurs. **1597** BP. HALL *Sat.* I. vii, Fond wit-wal that wouldst lode thy wit-lesse head With timely hornes. **1598** SHAKS. *Merry W.* II. ii. 313 But Cuckold, Wittoll, Cuckold? the Diuell himselfe hath not such a name. **1614** W. BROWNE *Inner Temple Masque* ii, Come yee whose hornes the cuckold weares, The whittoll too, with asses eares. **1736** VAUGHAN *Voy.* (1760) I. 136 [He] being a good-humour'd easy Man, and a Wittol to boot, at their Tears and Entreaties, forgave 'em both. **1818** BYRON *Juan* I. xcix, A real husband [*MS.* wittol] always is suspicious. **1821** SCOTT *Kenilw.* xxxvi, She would not quit the estate and title of the wittol who had wedded her.

b. *transf.* (? with pun on *wit-all*.) One who has little sense; a half-witted person; a fool; occas. a witling.

1588 J. ASKE *Eliz. Triumphans* To Rdr. A 3, They..are.. accounted of as wittals, for spending their studies about such common deuises. **1599** T. M[OUFET] *Silkwormes* 34 To see great wittols little things despise. **1639** J. CLARKE *Parœm.* 151 He that's wicked is a witall [*stultus*]. **1721** AMHERST *Terræ-Filius* xxxix. (1726) II. 211 Heaven was crouded with religious punsters and witals. **1822** SCOTT *Pirate* xxxvi, He told them they should see what message he was about to send to the wittols [*sc.* the Mayor and Aldermen] of Kirkwall. **1866** KINGSLEY *Herew.* xxxiv, Gospatric! the wittol! the wood-cock!

2. *attrib.* That is a wittol, pertaining to or characteristic of a wittol; *transf.* half-witted, senseless.

1604 MARSTON *Malcontent* IV. iii. F 2 b, And do I liue to be the skoffe of men, To be their wittall cuckold..? **1703** ROWE *Fair Penit.* III. i, If thou wou'dst live, Without the Name of credulous, wittal Husband, Avoid thy Bride. **1780** BURKE *Sp. Ho. Comm.* 11 Feb. 76 What sums the nursing of that ill-thriven..and ill-favoured brat [*sc.* Nova Scotia], has cost to this wittol nation! **1796** —— *Regic. Peace* iii. (1892) 193 There are cases in which we may pretend to sleep: but the wittol rule has some sense in it, *Non omnibus dormio*. **1810** WIRT in J. P. Kennedy *Mem.* (1860) I. xviii. 258 As one of Congreve's wittol squires said.., it is a pleasure I would as soon be without. **1869** LOWELL *Winter-evening Hymn to Fire* iv, And thy down-trod instincts savage To stealthy insurrection creep, While thy wittol masters sleep.

Hence †**wittol** *v. trans.*, to make a wittol of.

1624 DAVENPORT *City Night-cap* I. i, He would wittal me, With a consent to my own Horns.

wittolly ('wɪtəlɪ), *a.* Also 7 **wittally**, **wittoldly**, 9 **wittoly**. [f. WITTOL *sb.* + -Y[1] or -LY[1].] Having the character, or characteristic, of a wittol.

1598 SHAKS. *Merry W.* II. ii. 284 They say the iealous wittolly-knaue hath masses of money. **1605** CHAPMAN *All Fooles* II. i. E 1, No, let me still be..thought A ielouse Asse, and not a wittally Knaue. **1614** PURCHAS *Pilgrimage* III. x. (ed. 2) 293 Her husband was hanged for his wittoldly permission. *a* **1652** BROME *City Wit* IV. i, You are a Wittally Cuckold I know. **1845** FORD *Handbk. Spain* I. 83 Most of this finger-talk, wittoly wit, as well as the figs [*sc.* 'a fig for you', digitally represented], is confined to the lower classes.

†**'wittolry**. *Obs.* Also 7 **witald-**, **wittoldrie**. [f. WITTOL *sb.* + -RY.] Complaisant cuckoldry; hence, extreme folly.

1592 WARNER *Alb. Eng.* VII. xxxvii. 168 Iust Guerdons for Ambition..For dastard Dotards, Wittolrie, and Harlots nice. **1611** COTGR. s.v. *Folie, En amour est folie et sens*, in loue there is both wit and witaldrie. **1624** HEYWOOD *Gunaik.* v. 257 Cabbas, a Roman (worthie for ever to be branded with base Wittoldrie).

wittome: see WITHAM.

witts (wɪts), *sb. pl. Mining.* Also **whits**. [Short for *tinwitts*: see TIN *sb.* 5.] Tin ore after the first dressing: see quot. 1853.

1853 URE *Dict. Arts* (ed. 4) II. 858 Tin witts... The clean 'witts' contain native oxide of tin; black tin or resin tin, and wolfram with iron and arsenical pyrites, generally containing some copper. **1855** [LEIFCHILD] *Cornwall* 208 This mixture of metallic matter, named Witts.

wittual, **wittule**, obs. ff. VICTUAL.

witty ('wɪtɪ), *a.* Forms: 1 **wit(t)iȝ**, 3 **witi(ȝ, -eȝ**, 3-5 **wytti**, 3-6 **witti**, 4-6 **wytty**, **wittye**, 4-7 **wittie**, (4 **witthi**, *Sc.* **vitty**, 5 **witte**, 6 **wyttie**, **-ye**, *Sc.* (*sup.*) **vittiast**), 3- **witty**. [OE. *wit(t)iȝ* (also *ȝewittiȝ*) = MLG. *wetig*, OHG. *wiz(z)ig* (MHG. *wizzic*), ON. *vitugr*: f. WIT *sb.* + -Y[1].]

†**1.** Having wisdom. **a.** Said of God or Christ: cf. WISE *a.* 1 (*b*). *Obs.*

Beowulf 685 Witiȝ god..haliȝ dryhten. *a* **1000** *Cædmon's Exod.* 25 Hu þas woruld worhte witiȝ drihten. **1340** HAMPOLE *Pr. Consc.* 6280 Swa witty and myghty es he þat nathyng til hym impossibel may be. **1380** *Lay Folks' Catech.* (L.) 531 This god is most myȝty þyng þat may be. The most wytty and most ryȝtful. *c* **1400** LOVE *Bonavent. Mirr.* i. (1908) 18 The persone of the sone [is] al wyse and witty. *c* **1480** HENRYSON *Swallow* vi, God in all his werkis wittie is.

†**b.** Of human beings: Having good judgement or discernment; wise, sagacious, discreet, prudent, sensible. *Obs.*

In quot. *a* 1562 *advb.* = wisely.

[**1027-34** *Laws Cnut* lxxvi, Hit wæs ær þyson, þæt þæt cild þe læȝ on cradele,..þa ȝitseras letan efen scyldiȝ & hit ȝewittiȝ wære.] **1340** HAMPOLE *Pr. Consc.* 588, I hald a man, noght witty þat here es over-prowde and ioly. *c* **1380** WYCLIF *Wks.* (1880) 10 In þat þei seyn þat an heþene philosofre..is wittiere and trewere þan almyȝti god. *c* **1400** *Destr. Troy* 3807 Wise in his wordys, witte of counsaille. *c* **1449** PECOCK *Repr.* I. v. 25 Ech witti man muste graunte that the first principal conclusioun bifore sett is trewe. **1531** ELYOT *Gov.* I. ii, Ioynynge to hym counsailours Nestor and the witty Ulisses. *a* **1562** G. CAVENDISH *Wolsey* (1893) 46 A ..warnyng to use thy self more wittier hereafter. *a* **1592** GREENE *Jas. IV*, 2022 To haue two meanes beseemes a wittie man. **1611** *Bible* Ecclus. xxi. 12 He that is not wise [*marg.* or, wittie], will not be taught.

2. a. (*a*) Having (good) intellectual ability; intelligent, clever, ingenious; skilful, expert, capable. *Obs.* exc. *dial.*

[*a* **1000** *Gifts of Men* 74 Sum bið ȝewittiȝ æt winþeȝe, beorhyrde god.] *a* **1100** *Aldhelm Gloss.* 39 in Napier *O.E. Glosses* 2/2 *Per gymnosophistas*, þurh wittiȝe pleȝmen *uel* gleawe gliȝmen. *c* **1205** LAY. 21134 He wes ihaten Wygar, þe witeȝe wurhte [*c* **1275** þe wittye wrohte]. **1362** LANGL. *P. Pl.* A. XI. 5 Wel artou witti,..wisdom to telle To Fayturs or to Fooles. *a* **1425** tr. *Arderne's Treat. Fistula*, etc. 28 A gode lech and a witty. *c* **1440** *Gesta Rom.* xiv. 45 A wise man, and witty in armys & in alle his werkys. **1553** EDEN *Treat. Newe Ind.* (Arb.) 24 In workemanship and artes they are marueylous wyttie. **1560** *Bible* (Geneva) Wisd. viii. 19, I was a wittie childe [*R.V.* a child of parts]. *a* **1586** SIDNEY *Arcadia* II. xxiii. §8 He (no more wittie to frame, then blinde to judge hopes). **1612** BACON *Ess.*, *Of Judicature* (Arb.) 451 Iudges ought to be more Learned, then Wittie. **1617** MORYSON *Itin.* III. 76 Witty Copernicus. *a* **1656** HALES *Golden Rem.* (1673) 196 God who is..πολύτροπος εἰς σωτηριὰν ἀνθρώπων..as Clemens speaks..is witty in inventing of means to bring us to him. **1709** PRIOR *Henry & Emma* 82 In gentle Verse, the Witty told their Flame. **1725** WATTS *Logic* I. ii. §4 When we say the Boy is strong or witty, these are proper or inherent Modes. **1784** COWPER *Task* I. 728 Now..show this queen of cities [*sc.* London], that so fair May yet be foul; so witty, yet not wise. **1886** *Cheshire Gloss.*

(*b*) Of animals: = WISE *a.* 1 (*c*): cf. WIT *sb.* 5 c.

1398 TREVISA *Barth. De P.R.* XVIII. xxiv. (Bodl. MS.), Noþing is more witty and besie þanne hounde. **1600** J. PORY tr. *Leo's Africa* IX. 336 This wittie beast [*sc.* the elephant] keepeth in the woods. **1606** B. JONSON *Hymen.*, *Barriers* 163 At her feet doe witty serpents moue. **1626** BACON *Sylva* §978 The Ape also is a Witty Beast, and hath a Dry Braine.

†**b.** In unfavourable sense: Crafty, cunning, wily, artful; skilful in contriving evil; also, foolishly ingenious in devising something to one's own hurt. *Obs.*

a **1425** tr. *Arderne's Treat. Fistula*, etc. 30 þat any oþer witty man perceyuyng his werk mow vsurpe it to hymself. **1580** VAUTROULLIER *Luther on Ep. Gal.* 282 They are maruelous witty and wily in finding fault with other mens doings. **1599** SHAKS. *Much Ado* IV. ii. 27 A maruellous witty fellow I assure you, but I will goe about with him. **1608** BP. HALL *Char.*, *Vnconstant* 111 He is..wittie to wrong himselfe. **1638** SIR T. HERBERT *Trav.* (ed. 2) 19 As simple as they seeme, they are witty enough in craft, revenge, and villany. *a* **1656** HALES *Golden Rem.* (1673) 123 They are unexpectedly, and..wonderfully prompt and witty to villany and wickedness. *a* **1683** OLDHAM *Passion of Byblis* Wks. (1686) 125 How came I witty to my ruin thus? *a* **1699** J. BEAUMONT *Psyche* XXI. iv, Witty too in Self delusion. **1706** MRS. CENTLIVRE *Love at a Venture* Epil., You Men are grown so witty in Deceit.

†**3. a.** Endowed with reason, rational. **b.** In full possession of one's wits, of sound mind. *rare.*

c **1000** ÆLFRIC *Saints Lives* vii. 428 Wearð..his suna wittiȝ. *c* **1300** *Kenelm* 219 in *E.E.P.* (1862) 53 Whan no man nolde þat witti was of him habbe munde A dombe best wiþoute witte hadde aȝe cunde. *c* **1350** *Will. Palerne* 158 þus was þis witty best werwolf ferst maked. **1672** WISEMAN *Wounds* I. x. 130 The Child returned to her friends perfectly in health, is a witty Girle, but it's doubted she will be but a dwarf.

†**4.** Having knowledge, knowing, learned. *Obs.*

a **1225** *Leg. Kath.* 532 Ha somet seiden, þt wittiest ha weren of alle þe meistres. **1340–70** *Alex. & Dind.* 1121 Wise & wittie of lorus. **1388** WYCLIF *Deut.* i. 13 Witti [Vulg. *gnaros*] in mennus thingis. **1393** LANGL. *P. Pl.* C. XVII. 219 The wyttiour that eny wight is..The biterour he shal abygge, bote yf he wel worche. **1456** SIR G. HAYE *Law Arms* (S.T.S.) 79 Men that war symple and nocht witty of perpetuale thingis.

†**5.** (*transf.* from 2.) Showing or demanding intellectual ability; (later, esp. of discourse) clever, ingenious, or subtle in conception or expression. Also *ironically*. *Obs.*

13.. *Cursor M.* 4677 (Gött.) Ioseph..comandid..Depe celers for to delue, And thoru his aun witti rede Fild þaim wid wines, quite and rede. **1463** *Stonor Papers* (Camden) I. 62 It [*sc.* the matter] must have wytty gydyng. **1551** RECORDE *Pathw. Knowl.* Pref., Neuer was arte so wonderfull witty..as is good Geometry. **1551** R. ROBINSON tr. *More's Utopia* Ep. Transl. (1895) 18 The wittie inuencion, and fine ..disposition of the matter. *a* **1562** G. CAVENDISH *Wolsey* (1893) 5 A mete & apte person to be preferred to wytty affayers. **1581** PETTIE tr. *Guazzo's Civ. Conv.* I. (1586) 20 The wittie answeres which hee made touching this purpose. **1611** *Bible* Prov. viii. 12, I wisedome dwell with prudence, and find out knowledge of witty inuentions. **1633** G. HERBERT *Temple, Forerunners* ii, If I please him, I write fine and wittie. **1653** H. MORE *Antid. Ath.* I. viii. §2 (1712) 22 That's the witty Fallacy his unwariness has intangled him in. **1700** LOCKE *Hum. Und.* IV. xvii. §4 (ed. 4) 409 The Fallacies that are often concealed in florid, witty or involved Discourses.

†**b.** Skilfully devised for an evil purpose; cunning, crafty; (of torment, etc.) ingeniously contrived, 'exquisite'. *Obs.*

1602 *2nd Pt. Return fr. Parnass.* I. i. 111 Stale sinnes are stale: now doth the world begin To take sole pleasure in a witty sinne. **1619** FLETCHER *Knt. Malta* v. i, Expect a witty, and a fell revenge! **1623** MASSINGER *Dk. Milan* v. ii, Let me pronounce vpon this wretch all torture That witty cruelty can inuent. **1649** JER. TAYLOR *Gt. Exemp.* I. Disc. iv. 128 Some..in witty torments excelled the cruelty of many of their persecutors. *c* **1670** HOBBES *Behemoth* (1679) 254 He call'd a Parliament, and gave it the Supreme Power, to the end that they should give it to him again; was not this witty? **1681–6** J. SCOTT *Chr. Life* (1747) III. 612 The most witty and exquisite Torments.

†**6.** (*transf.* from 1 b.) Showing, or springing from, good judgement or discernment; wise, discreet, sensible. *Obs.*

c **1380** WYCLIF *Wks.* (1880) 220 þei louen more..þe most witti reulis of ihū crist þan þe vnwitti constitucions of synful ..men. *a* **1475** G. ASHBY *Active Policy* 741 Your manly & wytti diligence. **1553** M. WOOD tr. *Gardiner's De Vera Obed., Bonner's Pref.* 3 b, What a witti part it is, for a man to suspend his iudgement, and not to be rashe in geuing of sentence. *c* **1560** INGELEND *Disob. Child* Peror. G iv, Here ye maye learne a wyttie lesson. *a* **1593** MARLOWE *Ovid's Elegies* I. viii, Trust me, to giue, it is a witty thing. **1656** R. FLETCHER tr. *Martial* IX. Epigr. vi, Thou very fain wouldst Priscus wed, I wonder not, 'tis witty so to doe. **1710** *Brit. Apollo* III. No. 79. 3/1 The Bold assert 'tis Witty to be Brave,..The Timerous Wittily decline all Strife.

7. Possessing wit (see WIT *sb.* 7); capable of or given to saying (or writing) brilliant or sparkling things, esp. in an amusing way; smartly jocose or facetious.

1590 SHAKS. *Com. Err.* III. i. 110, I know a wench of excellent discourse, Prettie and wittie. **1653** WALTON *Angler* ii. 45 *Viat.* Is not mine Hoste a witty man? *Pisc.* Sir, To speak truly, he is not to me; for most of his conceits were either Scripture-jests, or lascivious jests; for which I count no man witty. **1684** W. WINSTANLEY *England's Worthies* 345 Plautus,..by his conversing with jocular Wits,..became so famously witty, or wittily famous, as..he attained to an extraordinary height in the Comique strain. **1731–8** SWIFT *Pol. Conversat.* Introd. 14 Whatever Person would aspire to be completely witty, smart, humourous, and polite. **1849** FROUDE *Nem. Faith* (ed. 2) 103 We are witty if it be so, not for applause but for affection. **1878** BROWNING *La Saisiaz* 596 Learned for the nonce as Gibbon, witty as wit's self Voltaire.

†**b.** Sharply critical, censorious, sarcastic. *Obs.* or merged in prec. sense.

1601 SHAKS. *All's Well* II. iv. 32 Go too, thou art a wittie foole. **1632** G. HERBERT *Priest to Temple* xxvi. (1652) 106 Being partiall to themselves and witty to others. **1712** ADDISON *Spect.* No. 530 ¶2 Will Honeycomb, who was so unmercifully witty upon the Women. **1748** RICHARDSON *Clarissa* (1768) II. 75 My Mother..says, I am too witty; Anglicè, too pert.

8. Of speech or writing: Characterized by or full of wit (see WIT *sb.* 8); cleverly amusing, 'sparkling', smartly facetious or jocular; †sarcastic.

1588 SHAKS. *L.L.L.* v. i. 4 Your reasons..haue beene.. witty without affection, audacious without impudency. **1601** —— *Twel. N.* III. ii. 46 Be curst and briefe: it is no matter how wittie, so it bee eloquent, and full of inuention. **1639** N. N. tr. *Du Bosq's Compl. Woman* I. 30 The Melancholy [humour]..is..too grosse for witty conceits and apt replies. **1700** T. BROWN tr. *Fresny's Amusem.* 152 Your Gentlemen that speak sharp and witty Things. **1702** STEELE *Funeral* II. 27 This is not one of your Tringham Trangham Witty things, that your Poor Poets write. **1733** SWIFT *Apol. Lady Carteret* 146 The powder'd courtier's witty sneer. **1744** CORBYN THOMAS *Ess. Wit, Humour*, etc. 37 Satire is a witty and severe Attack of mischievous Habits or Vices. **1829** LYTTON *Devereux* I. i, He told the wittiest stories in the world without omitting anything in them but the point. **1880** 'OUIDA' *Moths* i, 'Of course! One always marries girls; how stupid you are', said Lady Dolly... The counsellor smiled grimly, 'And then you will be a grandmother', he said... 'I suppose you think that witty', said Lady Dolly.

9. *Comb.* (parasynthetic and adverbial), as ***witty-brained***, ***-conceited***, ***-feigned***, ***-pated***, ***-pretty*** adjs. (all in sense 2, and obs. or arch.).

1591 SYLVESTER *Du Bartas* I. vi. 746 Japhetus' witty-fained Son. **1599** NASHE *Lenten Stuffe* 50 Some politique delegatory Scipio, or witty pated Petito. **1600** BRETON *Strange Fortunes* 14 No lesse witty conceited of her dreame, then noting the cariage of her humor. **1606** SYLVESTER *Du Bartas* II. iv. II. *Magnificence* 684 Queint witty-pretty Toyes. **1818** SCOTT *Hrt. Midl.* xii, The smart witty-pated lawyers. **1820** —— *Monast.* xv, A witty-brained..and accomplished courtier.

wituper, Sc. var. VITUPER *sb. Obs.*

witute(n, obs. forms of WITHOUT.

witwall ('wɪtwɒl). Now *dial.* Forms: 6–7 **witwol**, 6–8 **witwal**, 8–9 **whitwall**, 6– **witwall**. [a. early mod.G. †*wittewal(e*, also †*weidewal* (Gesner), now *widewal*, *wiedewal*; = MLG. *weddewale*, early Flem. *widewael* (Kilian). Cf. WOODWALL.]

†**1.** The Golden Oriole, *Oriolus galbula*. *Obs.*

1544 TURNER *Avium Præcip.* I. 7, Χλωρίον, uireo,..Anglicè a uuituuol, Germanicè eyn witwol, oder eyn weidwail. **1601**, **1658**, **1676** [see LORIOT]. **1671** H. M. tr. *Erasm. Colloq.* 514 But one can hardly guess for what reason the..Raven and the Witwal [L. *chlorio*]..hate one the other. **1678** RAY *Willughby's Ornith.* 198 The Witwall, as it is by some called, *Galbula seu Picus nidum suspendens.*

2. The Green Woodpecker (*Gecinus viridis*) or the Greater Spotted Woodpecker (*Dendrocopus major*).

1668 CHARLETON *Onomast.* 86 *Picus viridis*..the Hickwall, Witwall, or Green-Wood-pecker. **1678** RAY *Willughby's Ornith.* 137 The greater spotted Woodpecker or Witwall. **1844** HOOD *Haunted House* I. 62 The ringing of the Whitwall's shrilly laughter.

†'**witword.** *Obs.* Chiefly *north.* Also 4 **wite-**, 4–6 **wyt-**, 5 **wytte-**, 6 **witt-**; 4–5 **-worde**; 6 **wytward.** [OE. *witword* contract, agreement, f. *wit-* WIT *v.*¹ + WORD *sb.*; later associated with WIT *v.*²] A will or testament; also, a covenant (in the scriptural sense): = TESTAMENT *sb.* 1, 4.

?**997** *Laws Æthelred* III. §3 Landcop & hlafordes ȝifu..& lahcop & witword & ȝewitnes, þæt þæt stande, þæt hit nan man ne awende. *c* **1080** *Charter Will. I* in Thorpe *Charters* (1865) 439 Ofer þæm landum ðe Ealdred ærcebiscop hæfð siðþan beȝitan..on witword oððe on caupland. *a* **1300** *E.E. Psalter* xxiv. [xxv.] 10 To sekand his witeword. **1338** R. BRUNNE *Chron.* (1810) 153 Fulfille I salle in dede þe kynges witworde. **1393** *Test. Ebor.* (Surtees) I. 186 In kase be that this wytword will noght perfurnysche, I will it be abrydged. **1411** *26 Pol. Poems* x. 101 Man, how darst þou..My wit word wiþ þy mouþ teche, And in þy werkis þou seyst hit nay? **1471** *Test. Ebor.* (Surtees) III. 180, I will that bothe my l^s wyll and my wytword be fulfyld of the hoole that is my propyr guddys at this tyme. **1555** *Churchw. Acc., Wigtoft, Linc.* (Nichols 1797) 199 Rec. for ye Wytword of Willm Brygthe 1^s.

†'**wity**, *a. Obs. rare.* [f. WITE *sb.*² + -Y¹.] Blameworthy.

1530 PALSGR. 329/2 Wytye in faulte for a thyng, *faulteux.*

†**witzchoura.** *Obs.* [a. F. *vitchoura*, a. Polish *wilczura* wolf-skin coat, f. *wilk* WOLF *sb.*] A style of lady's mantle (see quots.) fashionable *c* 1820–35. Also *attrib.*

1823 *La Belle Assemblée* Dec. 269/1 Witzchoura pelisse of *gros de Naples*,..trimmed with a very broad border of swansdown. **1833** *Ladies Pocket Mag.* I. 38 The *witchoura* is a very ample mantle, made with a very deep collar, and cape, and long, loose sleeves. **1835** *Court Mag.* VI. p. v/1 [The mantle] is of the Witzchoura form, drawn close at the back, with large Turkish sleeves, and a deep falling collar. [**1898** LADY M. LOYD tr. *Ozanne's Fashion in Paris* iii. 54 *Witzchouras* had not yet [*c* 1806] come into vogue.]

wiue, obs. form of WIFE *sb.*, WIVE *v.*

wiure *Her.*, var. *vivre* (F. *vivre*:—L. *vīpera* VIPER), a barrulet or cotise dancetté.

1688 HOLME *Armoury* I. ix. 90/2 He beareth Argent, a Wiure, Nebule, counter Nebule, Sable. A Wiure is much less than either Barrulett or Cotize. *Ibid.* I. x. 102/1 A Wiure nebulee between 2 Cotizes. *c* **1828** BERRY *Encycl. Her.* I. Gloss., Wiure, Wyer, Viure, Viurée, and Viurie.

wiv (wɪv). Representation of a vulg. pronunc. (esp. Cockney) of WITH *prep.* (*adv.*, *conj.*).

1898 J. D. BRAYSHAW *Slum Silhouettes* 1 Tall an' thin, yer say? Wot, wiv long white 'ands, an' black 'air—Yus! **1933** D. L. SAYERS *Murder must Advertise* xix. 332 You'll 'ave 'im steppin' aht ter meet me wiv' a crimson carpet and a bokay. **1981** 'J. GASH' *Vatican Rip* iv. 44 Want me to come wiv yer, Lovejoy?

wive (waɪv), *v.* Forms: 1 **wifian**, (3 **wifue**), 3–6 **wyue (-ve)**, 3–7 **wiue**, 7– **wive.** [OE. *wífian* (= MLG., MDu. *wîven*), f. *wíf* WIFE *sb.*]

1. *intr.* (†rarely *refl.*) To take a wife, get married, marry. Const. †*on* (*o*), *with*. Also occas. with *it*.

c **888** ÆLFRED *Boeth.* xi. §1 Maniȝe habbað ȝenoȝ ȝesælilice ȝewifod. *c* **1000** *Ælfric's Canons* vii. in Thorpe *Laws* (1840) II. 346 He ne moste on wydewum wifiȝan. *a* **1225** *Ancr. R.* 308 Judas..wiuede o Thamar. *a* **1225** *Juliana* 12 ȝef þat he..ne schal wiuen on me, wiue þer his wil is. *c* **1250** *Gen. & Ex.* 1588 Quad rebecca to hire were, Esau wifuede us to dere. **1297** R. GLOUC. (Rolls) 6459 þo adde hii boþe iwiued wel. *c* **1320** *Sir Tristr.* 2896 To wiue on our kinde. **1340** *Ayenb.* 225 Zaynte paul..zayþ to wodewon, 'huo þet guod is, he him hyealde ine þet stat; and yef hit him naȝt ne lykeþ, he him wyui'. *c* **1386** CHAUCER *Clerk's T.* 117 Ther as myn herte is set ther wol I wyue. *c* **1460** *Wisdom* 666 in *Macro Plays* 57 *Wndyrstondynge.* We haue þat nedyt vs, so thryve I; *Wyll.* And yff þat I care, neuer wyve I. **1546** J. HEYWOOD *Prov.* I. xi. 28 It is harde to wiue and thryue bothe in a yere. **1596** SHAKS. *Tam. Shr.* I. ii. 56, I haue thrust my selfe into this maze, Happily to wiue and thriue, as best I may. *Ibid.* 75, I come to wiue it wealthily in Padua. **1606** MARSTON *Parasit.* v. H 4, Goe thy waies & wiue with whome thou wilt for my part. **1774** JOHNSON *To Mrs. Thrale* 17 All who wisely wish to wive. **1817** BYRON *Beppo* xcii, With any other women did you wive? **1876** HARDY *Ethelberta* xxvii, Encouraging Neigh in his resolve to wive.

2. To be a wife, act as a wife. Also with *it*. *rare.*

1583 MELBANCKE *Philotimus* E j b, Were it not very absurd ..for maides being scarse borne, to begin to bride it, and say in so doing they woulde learne to wiue it? **1639** [see WIVING *ppl. a.*]. **1891** C. E. NORTON *Dante's Hell* i. 100 Many are the animals with which she [*sc.* a she-wolf] wives [orig. *a cui sammoglia*].

3. *trans.* To take to wife, make one's wife, marry, wed (a woman); *pa. pple.* made or become a wife, married (*to* a man).

1592 WARNER *Alb. Eng.* VII. xxxv. 152 He wyu'd a Lady passing faire. **1596** SHAKS. *Merch. V.* I. ii. 145, I had rather hee should shriue me then wiue me. **1676** HOBBES *Odyssey* II. 203 Many other ladies we could wive. **1848–9** LYTTON *K. Arthur* II. lxv, 'Wived to my son, the witch will soon be steady!' 'Wived to your son?—she is a wife already!' **1862** MEREDITH *Modern Love* xxxv, It is no vulgar nature I have wived. **1898** E. P. EVANS *Evol. Ethics* i. 52 The Magians continued to wive their sisters in conformity to ancient usage.

4. To furnish with a wife, obtain a wife for; to marry *to* a wife: chiefly in *pa. pple.* married (of a man). *Obs.* or *arch.*

1513 MORE *Rich. III* (1883) 61 Smal pleasure taketh a man of al that euer he hath beside, yf he bee wiued against his appetite. **1583** MELBANCKE *Philotimus* X iij b, They are euill horsed, and worse wiued, that ride on coltes & marrie younge giglittes. **1597** SHAKS. *2 Hen. IV*, I. ii. 61, I bought him in Paules, and hee'l buy mee a horse in Smithfield. If I could get mee a wife in the Stewes, I were Mann'd, Hors'd, and Wiu'd. **1604** —— *Oth.* II. i. 60 *Mon.* .. Is your Generall wiu'd? *Cassio.* Most fortunately: he hath atchieu'd a Maid That paragons description. **1608** —— *Per.* v. ii. 10 He is promisde to be wiued To faire Marina. **1670** MILTON *Hist. Eng.* III. Wks. 1851 V. 113 She..won so much upon his fancy, though already wiv'd, as to demand her in mariage. **1816** CRABBE *Flirtation* 372 His craft contrived To get the Priest with expedition wived. **1820** SCOTT *Monast.* xxxvii, I promise you..that young Bennygask shall be richly wived. **1851** W. B. MACCABE *Bertha* III. xiv. 376, I [Henry] can do more strange things than unwive myself, and wive you.

†**b.** with *it*: To obtain a wife *for*. *Obs. rare.*

1608 J. DAY *Humour out of Breath* I. i. B 3, *Oct.*.. Ile one day get A husband for thee... *Flo.*.. Wiue it for them [*sc.* my brothers], you shall not husband me.

5. To become the wife of, marry (a man; also *transf.* of an animal). *Obs.* or *arch.*

1621 G. SANDYS *Ovid's Met.* IX. (1626) 175 So haue I seene two Buls together close; The fairest Cow in all the pasture chose To wiue the Victor. **1812** CRABBE *Tales* xii. 283 Served by that Villain—by this Fury wived—What fate is mine!

6. *fig.* To 'wed', unite, couple. *rare.*

1886 LOWELL *Latest Lit. Ess.*, *Gray* (1891) 2 The thoughts, wived with words above their own level.

Hence **wived** (waɪvd), *ppl. a.*

1633 *Costlie Whore* IV. end, He shalbe intombed with a wived maid. **1876** *Encycl. Brit.* V. 293/2 Gregory VII.. determined..that no wived priest should celebrate or even assist at the Mass.

wivehood, -less, -ly: see WIFEHOOD, etc.

wivel(l, obs. forms of WEEVIL.

†'**wiven**, *a. Obs.* Forms: 4 **wyfyne**, 4–5 **wyuen(e.** [f. *wiv-*, WIFE *sb.* + -EN¹. (In some instances perh. wk. gen. pl. of *wife*.)] **a.** Womanly, feminine. **b.** Wifely.

1362 LANGL. *P. Pl.* A. v. 29 To..fette hom Felice From wyuene [*v.r.* wyuen] pyne. *c* **1375** *Sc. Leg. Saints* xxvi. (*Nicholas*) 178 His body waikly he fed, & wyfyne company ay fled. *c* **1400** *Trevisa's Higden* (Rolls) VI. 213 þanne þe queene byȝede here housbonde wiþ benygne [*v.rr.* wyvene, wyven] flaterynge [L. *uxoriis deliramentis*].

wiver¹ ('waɪvə(r)). *north. dial.* Also 6 **wywer.** [Identical with *waver*, *wafer*, *wefer*, †*waiver*, †*wayver*, †*weaver*, in WAVER *sb.*¹, SIDE-WAVER, and Northumb. dial. *inwaver*, *inwiver* (in sense a).] A long beam of wood. **a.** in the roof of a house; in †***wiver-tree***, SIDE-WAVER, ***top wiver***. **b.** in a boat (see quot. 1894).

c **1325** *Gloss. W. de Bibbesw.* in Wright *Voc.* 170 Amont heceler mettez la poutre [*glossed* the wiver-tre]. **1532** in *Priory of Finchale* (Surtees) 445/2 [Timber at Durham sawn into] wywers, rybbs, wynd balks. **1641** [see SIDE-WAVER 1]. **1641** BEST *Farm. Bks.* (Surtees) 148 They will sowe downe theire thatch in fower places, viz.; first close to the very wall plates, then two foote belowe the side wivers, then two foote above the side wivers, and lastly aboute a yarde or more belowe the rigge-tree. **1894** *Northumbld. Gloss., Wivere*, a long beam. The top wivere is the wind-balk or collar beam in a housetop. The side wivere is the long beam on which frame-houses formerly rested. (Obs.) [Misprinted *winere.*] *Ibid., Wiver*, one of the timbers or wales of a boat on which the seats rest.

wiver² (ˈwaɪvə(r)). *rare.* [f. WIVE *v.* + -ER¹.] One who takes a wife.

1888 DOUGHTY *Trav. Arabia Deserta* II. 214 The young negro found the old wiver in the palms.

wiver(e, wivern(e: see WYVER, WYVERN.

wivers, obs. f. VIVERS.

wives, pl. (and obs. gen. sing.) of WIFE *sb.*

wiving (ˈwaɪvɪŋ), *vbl. sb.* [f. WIVE *v.* + -ING¹.] The action of the verb WIVE; taking a wife, marrying, marriage.

1297 R. GLOUC. (Rolls) 5955 He biþoȝte him..ȝif þer miȝte be eny red þoru wiuinge..vor is wif was ded. **1377** LANGL. *P. Pl.* B. IX. 181 Whiles þow art ȝonge..Wreke þe with wyuynge ȝif þow wilt ben excused. **1398** TREVISA *Barth. De P.R.* II. ii. (1495) b ij b/1 Angels..for they ben spyrytuall & bodylesse, they nede nother weddynge ne wyuynge. **1542** UDALL *Erasm. Apoph.* 78 He allowed theim that wer towarde wiuyng, & yet wiued not. **1567** TURBERV. *Epit.*, etc. 73 b, Let wyuing go, lyue single aye. **1591** H. SMITH *Prepar. Marr.* 27 In wiuing and striuing, a man should take counsell of all the world. **1596** SHAKS. *Merch. V.* II. ix. 83 The ancient saying..Hanging and wiuing goes by destinie. **1628** WITHER *Brit. Rememb.* v. 1832 The wivings of the wise King Solomon. **1756** *Monitor* No. 35. I. 324 The consequence of so much wiving, was a numerous progeny. **1872** JEAFFRESON *Brides & Bridals* II. 54 In a priest the act of wiving was under no lawful circumstances positively sinful. **1910** A. HILLIERS *Master-Girl* vi. 152 Since the world and wiving began was there ever such a woman?

attrib. c**1610** MIDDLETON, etc. *Widow* v. i. (1652) 59 [He] Sayes I'm ordain'd for him;..And that this wiving fate speaks in me to him.

So ˈ**wiving** *ppl. a.*

1639 GLAPTHORNE *Wallenstein* III. iii, The wiving Vine that 'bout the friendly Elme, Twines her soft limbes.

wivish, obs. var. WIFISH.

wiwes, obs. pl. of WIFE *sb.*

wiwi¹ (ˈwiwi). [Maori, = 'rushes' (T. Kendall *Gram. & Vocab. N.Z.* (1820) 228).] A New Zealand rush used to make an outer covering for the roof and walls of a house.

1840 J. S. POLACK *Manners & Customs New Zealanders* II. 285 *Wi-wi*, kind of wiry grass that is pulled up in tufts, it also is the produce of the marsh. **1842** W. R. WADE *Journ. N. Isl. N.Z.* iii. 61 The roof [of the house] is usually completed with a thick covering of wiwi (a small rush). **1875** *Treas. Bot.* Suppl. **1970** MOORE & EDGAR *Flora N.Z.* II. 59 The Maori name for rushes and rush-like plants is *Wiwi.*

wi-wi² (ˈwiːwiː). *Austral. & N.Z. slang.* Also **wewi, wee-wee, oui-oui.** [ad. F. *oui, oui* yes, yes, taken as typical of the French language.] A Frenchman; also as *pl.* the French.

1841 E. J. WAKEFIELD in *N.Z. Jrnl.* II. XLV. 243/1 Should the *Wiwis*, or French, kill any of our Chiefs. **1845** E. J. WAKEFIELD *Adv. N.Z.* I. iv. 94 If I had sold the land to the White missionaries, might they not have sold it again to the *Wiwi* (Frenchmen) or Americans? **1852** MUNDY *Antipodes* (1857) 180 Young chiefs..who will,..like the 'Wi-wis' of Young France, indulge occasionally in what that volatile people style '*revolutions intestines!*' **1859** A. S. THOMSON *Story N.Z.* I. II. i. 236 The Wewis, as the French are now called. **1872** EARL PEMBROKE & G. H. KINGSLEY *S. Sea Bubbles* i, Would that the imperious 'Oui-oui' had never placed foot upon your sacred shores!

wiylde, wiys, obs. forms of WILD, WISE.

Wiyot (ˈwiːjɒt). [Wiyot *wíyat* (people of) the Eel River delta.] An American Indian people formerly living on the coast of northern California; the Macro-Algonquian language of this people. Also *attrib.* or as *adj.*

1851 G. GIBBS *Jrnl.* 9 Sept. in H. R. Schoolcraft *Information respecting Indian Tribes* (1853) III. iv(3). 127 The name given to this people by their neighbors is Weeyot. **1911** A. L. KROEBER *Lang. Coast Calif.* 384 The Wiyot occupied the Coast from the Bear River mountains north as far as to Little river. *Ibid.*, Wiyot is spoken indistinctly and lacks..phonetic clarity. **1918** *Univ. Calif. Publ. in Amer. Archaeol. & Ethnol.* XIV. III. 232 Cedar though present on Wiyot territory, is not abundant enough for the purposes for which a soft wood is needed. **1925** *Ibid.* XXII. I. 5 There are also some Wiyot living among the Athapascans at Blue Lake. *Ibid.* 6 The individual differences of Wiyot speech will be discussed. **1946** L. BLOOMFIELD in C. Osgood *Linguistic Structures Native Amer.* 201 Two languages of California, Wiyot and Yurok, have been suspected of kinship with Algonquian. **1961** H. DRIVER *Indians N. Amer.* xiv. 251 From the Wiyot to the Bella Coola, such usufruct was patricentered. **1964** R. H. ROBINS *Gen. Linguistics* 308 Isolated languages in the western states, Blackfoot..and Wiyot and Yurok (California). **1974** *Encycl. Brit. Micropædia* X. 720/1 Wiyot settlements were located on streams of bays, rather than on the ocean itself. **1977** *Language* LIII. 501/1 Pentland expands on Karl Teeter's suggestion..that the rule affricating dental stops which is operative in diminutives in Wiyot..as well as in Algonquian, should be ascribed to Proto-Algic.

wiz, var. WHIZZ, WHIZ *sb.*²

wizard (ˈwɪzəd), *sb.* and *a.* Forms: 5 **wys(e)ard, -sar,** 6 **-sarde, -zard, wyssarde, wissard,** *Sc.* **weser,** 6–7 **wisard,** (7 **wiseard, wizer**), 7–8 **wizzard,** (**vizard**), 6– **wizard.** [late ME. *wysar(d*, f. *wys, wis, wiss,* WISE *a.* + -ARD. The pronunciation with voiced *s* (z) follows *wisdom* and *wise.*]

A. *sb.*

†**1.** A philosopher, sage: = WISE MAN 2. Often *contemptuous. Obs.*

The second quot. may belong to sense 2.

c**1440** *Promp. Parv.* 530/1 Wysard (*K.* wysar), *sagaculus.* ?a**1500** *Chester Pl., Coming of Antichrist* 371 *Antechristus.* Out on the [*sc.* Enoch], wyseard [*v.rr.* rasarde, roysarde], with thy wyles! For falcsely my people thou begyles. **1547** BAULDWIN *Mor. Philos.* I. i. (1550) A ij, The Grecians..haue therin taken great paynes, naming it first Sophia, and suche as therin were skilled Sophistes or wysardes. **1594** [GREENE] *Selimus* 214 Perhaps you thinke that now forsooth you sit With some graue wisard in a pratling shade. **1596** SPENSER *F.Q.* IV. xii. 2 Therefore the antique wisards well inuented, That Venus of the fomy sea was bred. **1601** B. JONSON *Poetaster* IV. v. (1905) 82 *Albi.* I haue read in a booke, that to play the foole wisely, is high wisdome. *Gall.* How now, Vulcan! Will you be the first wizard? **1676** *Doctrine of Devils* 56 The Politicians, the Philosophers, the Wizers of the World. **1697** DRYDEN *Virg. Georg.* IV. 557 First the wily Wizard [*sc.* Proteus] must be caught, For unconstrain'd he nothing tells for naught. **1841** W. SPALDING *Italy* II. 99 Two young philosophers and wizards, called Phidias and Praxiteles.

2. a. A man who is skilled in occult arts; in later use, a man who practises witchcraft (the masculine correlative of WITCH *sb.*²): = WISE MAN 3.

†Occas. applied to a woman.

c**1550** CHEKE *Matt.* ii. 1 When Jesus was boorn in beethleem.., lo then yᵉ wisards cam from th'est parties to Jerusalem. **1552** [see WISE MAN 3]. c**1574** G. HARVEY *Marginalia* (1913) 163 Owr vulgar Astrologers, especially such, as ar commonly termed Cunning men or Artsmen. Sum call them wissards. **1596** in *Spalding Club Misc.* I. 84 Sche is convick..as a common weser and socerer, and ordint to be brunt. **1606** HOLLAND *Sueton.* 237 Yet to none was he more spitefully bent than to wiseards and Astrologers. **1621** [see WHITE WITCH]. **1629** MILTON *Nativity* 23 The Star-led Wisards haste with odours sweet. **1674** HOBBES *Odyssey* 73, I was forc't to come T' inquire of th' Wizard, old Tiresias, What the Fates say about my going home. **1713** SWIFT *Author upon Himself* 7 Clowns on Scholars as on Wizards look, And take a Folio for a conj'ring Book. **1751** *Tryal T. Collet* (ed. 3) 3 A large Mob..at Tring..declaring Revenge against Osborne and his Wife, as a Witch and a Vizard. **1825** HONE *Every-day Bk.* I. 942 In July, 1825, a man was 'swam for a wizard', at Wickham-Skeith, in Suffolk. **1851–61** MAYHEW *Lond. Labour* III. 107, I call myself a wizard as well; but that's only the polite term for conjurer; in fact, I should think that wizard meant an astrologer, and more of a fortune-teller. **1872** HARDWICK *Trad. Lanc.* 133 A wizard who had wrought sad havoc amongst his neighbour's cattle. **1897** F. THOMPSON *New Poems* 113 To dower her, past an eastern wizard's dreams.

b. *transf.* and *fig.*: *esp.* a man who 'does wonders' in his profession: in recent use often trivially applied to an expert. Also freq. as ***financial wizard***, a person skilled in making money, or in organizing financial affairs.

the Wizard of the North, Sir Walter Scott.

1620 SHELTON *2nd Pt. Don Quix.* xxxi. 201, I haue heard my Master say, who is the very Wizard of Histories,..when he came [etc.]. **1817** SHELLEY *Rev. Islam* VI. xxiii, The choicest winds of Heaven, which are enchanted To music, by the wand of Solitude, That wizard wild. **1858** HAWTHORNE *Fr. & It. Note-bks.* (1871) II. 35 Gerard Dow, and other old Dutch wizards, who painted..such earthern pots that they will surely hold water. **1869** R. WALTON *Random Recoll. Midl. Circuit* 134 Fortunately the 'Wizard of the North' came upon the spot [*sc.* Kenilworth], and 'Henceforth' (as a modern historian has it) 'the ruined place was to be sanctified [etc.]'. **1871** L. STEPHEN *Hours in Libr.*, *Scott* (1874) 218 Some reason for suspecting that the great 'Wizard' has lost some of his magic power. **1893** *Ladies' Home Jrnl.* May 27/2 Sir Walter Scott was called 'The Wizard of the North'. **1903** *Westm. Gaz.* 31 Aug. 7/2 The wizard of yacht-building. **1952** G. SARTON *Hist. Sci.* I. xix. 471 The eunuch, Hermeias, who began his career as a money-changer, was a kind of financial wizard and became very wealthy and powerful. **1967** G. F. FIENNES *I tried to run a Railway* v. 58, I had energy..to be the financial wizard on the parochial church council. **1975** *Times* 24 May 4/7 Judge Kennet..noted that Mr Tzour had been noted as a financial wizard.

c. A witch-doctor or medicine-man.

1845 DARWIN *Voy. Nat.* x. (1879) 214 Each family or tribe has a wizard or conjuring doctor. **1889** RIDER HAGGARD *Allan's Wife* 28 This man..had for some years occupied the position of Wizard-in-chief to the tribe.

†**d.** A professional conjuror. *U.S. Obs.*

1859 L. WRAXALL tr. *J. E. Robert-Houdin's Mem.* II. iv. 108 On my arrival in England, a conjuror of the name of Anderson, who assumed the title of *Great Wizard of The North*, had been performing for a long period at the little Strand Theatre. **1895** *N.Y. Dramatic News* 14 Dec. 6/1 The wonderful record established at the California theatre by Hermann the Great..has finally been broken..[by] the wonderful wizard [himself].

3. *attrib.* and *Comb.*, as ***wizard-craft, -finder, -man, -swarm; wizard-woven*** adj.

1819 SHELLEY *Faust* ii. 210 Wizard-swarms cover the heath all over. **1819** KEATS *Otho* III. ii, If he flames longer in this wise I shall believe in wizard-woven loves. **1876** H. BROOKS *Natal* 334 The wizard-finder is not unfrequently turned to account by the stronger men of a tribe. **1891** KIPLING *Life's Handicap* 277 He went to Juseen Dazé, the wizard-man who keeps the Talking Monkey's Head. **1897** *Folk-Lore* Mar. 53 Wizardcraft has the same ultimate origin as..the fairy belief.

B. *adj.* **1.** Having the powers or properties of a wizard; that practises wizardry; hence *gen.* having magical or witching power or influence.

1579 HAKE *Newes out of Powles* (1872) F iiij b, O wylie wincking wyzard Woolues. **1649** HAMMOND *Serm.* vi. Wks. 1684 IV. 506 That wizard flesh within us, that hath thus bewitch'd us to its false pleasures. **1679** DRYDEN & LEE *Œdipus* IV. i. 55 Thou blind old wizard Prophet. **1746** W. COLLINS *Ode to Liberty* Antistr. 2 Beyond the Measure vast of Thought, The Works, the Wizzard Time has wrought! **1747** —— *Ode to Manners* 11 Some Pow'r..At which the Wizzard Passions fly. **1794** MRS. RADCLIFFE *Myst. Udolpho* xlix, Or in some shadowy glen's romantic bower, Where wizard forms their mystic charms prepare. **1820** SHELLEY *Witch Atl.* xxvi, All day the wizard lady sate aloof, Spelling out scrolls of dread antiquity. **1835** LYTTON *Rienzi* III. ii, These wild and wizard extremes of life. **1897** *Daily News* 14 June 5/3 The artificial production of diamonds by the wizard chemist of to-day.

2. a. Of, pertaining to, or associated with wizards or wizardry; hence *gen.* magic, enchanted, bewitched.

1638 MILTON *Lycidas* 55 Nor on the shaggy top of Mona high, Nor yet where Deva spreads her wizard stream. c**1796** ROSCOE in Currie *Burns's Wks.* (1800) I. 343 And let Despair, with wizard light, Disclose the yawning gulf below. **1808** SCOTT *Marmion* III. xx, Lord Gifford..tarried not his garb to change, But, in his wizard habit strange, Came forth. **1813** —— *Trierm.* III. xxv, The wizard song at distance died, As if in ether borne astray. **1817** MOORE *Lalla Rookh, Fire-worshippers* II. 221 Those tow'rs sublime,..Were sever'd from the haunts of men By a wide, deep, and wizard glen. c**1820** S. ROGERS *Italy, Interview* 194 Tasso, Guarini, waved their wizard-wands, Peopling the groves from Arcady. **1850** TENNYSON *In Mem.* cxxii, The wizard lightnings deeply glow. **1918** N. MUNRO *Jaunty Jock* ii. 20 It was like as they were in some wizard fortress cut from rock.

b. *slang.* Excellent, marvellous, very good.

1922 S. LEWIS *Babbitt* xvii. 216 The Rev. Dr. John Jennison Drew..is a wizard soul-winner. **1932** E. WAUGH *Black Mischief* vii. 277 They..righted themselves and stopped dead within a few feet of danger. 'Wizard show that,' remarked the pilot. **1943** J. B. PRIESTLEY *Daylight on Saturday* i. 1 The roofs are nicely camouflaged, and the stiff coloured netting..is a wizard show. **1954** [see SUPER *a.* 3]. **1958** 'R. CROMPTON' *William's Television Show* vii. 189 Gosh, that party of Ginger's last Christmas was *wizard.* a**1966** 'M. NA GOPALEEN' *Best of Myles* (1968) 25 How awfully wizard being at the theatre with you! **1974** *Times* 17 Aug. 7/3 'How wizard!' they said... 'How absolutely super!'

3. *Comb.*: **wizard-like** *a.* = WIZARDLY *a.*

1859 GEO. ELIOT *Adam Bede* v, I know you are fond of queer, wizard-like stories.

Hence (*nonce-wds.*) ˈ**wizardess**, a female wizard, witch; ˈ**wizardism**, wizardry; †ˈ**wizardizing** *ppl. a.*, practising wizardry or witchcraft; ˈ**wizardship**, wizardry.

1789 H. WALPOLE *Let. Hannah More* 9 Aug., I wish my Macbethian *wizardess would tell me 'that Cowslip Dale should come to Strawberry Hill'. **1866** *Cornh. Mag.* Mar. 353 It was vaguely left to force the belief, that on this occasion our basket either carried a distinguished wizardess, or..a wondrous medium. **1682** W. RICHARDS *Wallogr.* 96 The study of *Wizzardism hath also been famous amongst them. **1726** DE FOE *Hist. Devil* II. ix, Whether Wizardism made them ugly, that were not so before. **1603** HARSNET *Pop. Impost.* xxi. 135 *Wisardizing Augurs, imposturizing South-sayers. **1882** MABEL COLLINS *Cobwebs* II. 252 Vansittart had learned the secrets of *wizardship during his travels.

wizard (ˈwɪzəd), *v. rare.* [f. prec. sb.]

†**1.** *trans.* To call 'wizard'. *Obs. nonce-use.*

1603 SIR C. HEYDON *Jud. Astrol.* iii. 111 If M. Chamber had considered that Aristotle and the Grecians had their chiefe knowledge from these nations that were Astrologers, he could neuer (for shame) haue wisarded them. *Ibid.* vi. 179.

2. To practise wizardry upon, to bewitch; to drive *away* as by magic.

1898 A. AUSTIN *Lamia's Winter-quarters* 61 The last lingering trails of mist were gradually wizarded away. **1900** *Folk-Lore* (1901) June 177 If yah be a wizard, wizard me.

So ˈ**wizarding** *vbl. sb.*, the practice of wizardry, witchcraft, or magic art.

1668 WILKINS *Real Char.* 337 Those..cheating Arts of Manteia or Wizarding, with which the world always hath been..abused. **1924** *Blackw. Mag.* Nov. 650/1 When the people think that the wizard half of him is not sufficiently potent in spells, they get Tzour to do the wizarding on their own account.

wizardly (ˈwɪzədlɪ), *a.* Now *rare.* [f. WIZARD *sb.* + -LY¹.] Of, pertaining to, characteristic of, or resembling a wizard or wizardry.

1588 J. HARVEY *Disc. Probl.* 23 O wyzardly dreame of dreames! **1596** NASHE *Saffron Walden* N 2 b, No wizardly astronomer of them all ever dreamed of any such calculations. **1613** PURCHAS *Pilgrimage* VIII. iv. 629 By wisardly and deuillish practises to vp-hold his owne greatnesse. a**1648** LD. HERBERT *Hen. VIII* (1683) 404 Divers feigned Miracles, accompanied with some Wisardly Unsooth sayings. **1652** GAULE *Magastrom.* 24, I count the Jewish wizzardly fable not here worth the relating. **1893** *Scribner's Mag.* May 597/2 A power which seemed sometimes to have a touch of the weird and wizardly in it. **1913** JAMES HOOPER *Souvenir of George Borrow Celebr.* 14 Sergeant Bagge's encounter with the wizardly creature.

wizardry (ˈwɪzədrɪ). [f. WIZARD *sb.* + -RY.]

1. a. The art or practice of a wizard or wizards; wizardly or magic skill; witchery, witchcraft.

1583 GOLDING *Calvin on Deut.* cix. 671/1 If these [inchanters or witches] be forbidden; we must vnderstand..

yt all other kinds of Wisardrie are deadly crimes. **1665** PATRICK *Pilgrim* vii. 23, I never used any other Wizzard[r]y to make my Land better than my neighbours, but what you will find to lye in these Spades, Ploughs, and Oxen. **1796** W. TAYLOR in *Monthly Rev.* XX. 535 The Arabic wizardry of the Italian, the elfen mythology of the German poet, seemed to offer rival resources for a supernatural machinery. **1855** BROWNING *Men & Women* I. *An Epistle* 249 The learned leech Perished in a tumult many years ago, Accused..of wizardry. **1861** S. THOMSON *Wild Fl.* III. (ed. 4) 239 All the witcheries and wizardries that found home in the imaginations of the people. **1877** SYMONDS *Renaiss. It.* vi. 343 As a physiognomist and diviner, he acquired a reputation bordering on wizardry.

b. *transf.* Magic lore.

1876 E. DOWDEN *Poems* 196 There I will sit, and score rare wisardry In characters vermilion, azure, gold.

2. *fig.* 'Magical' or 'bewitching' art, power, or influence; 'magic'. Also more *loosely*, skill, expertise, or the result of this.

1884 J. PARKER *Apost. Life* II. 265 Time..works its wondrous wizardry upon the mind. **1887** *Academy* 20 Aug. 113/3 So fascinating a writer is Mr. Matthew Arnold, so all conquering is his own wizardry. **1901** 'L. MALET' *Calmady* v. ii. You have employed a certain wizardry in the furnishing of that room. **1951** *Sport* 27 Jan.–2 Feb. 3/3 Rounding off the wing wizardry of Finney and Morrison are inside men Horton, Wayman and Bobby Beattie. **1974** W. J. BURLEY *Death in Stanley Street* viii. 142 Bits of electrical wizardry which must have come from a record player or a television set. **1979** *Arizona Daily Star* 5 Aug. (Comic Suppl.), Peter Parker uses his scientific wizardry.

wize, obs. f. or var. WISE.

wizen ('wɪz(ə)n), *a.* Also **wizzen**. [Clipped f. WIZENED, the resultant form suggesting a ppl. adj. in *-en*.] = WIZENED 2.

1786 MME. D'ARBLAY *Diary* 16 Aug., A thin, little, wizen old gentleman..came up. **1837** *Lett. fr. Madras* (1843) 49 The ladies are all young and wizen, and the gentlemen are all old and wizen. **1867** TROLLOPE *Chron. Barset* xxxvii, Her little wizen face was as sharp as ever. **1880** F. G. LEE *Ch. under Q. Eliz.* II. 336 Her now drawn and wizen features. *Comb.* **1819** M. EDGEWORTH *Let.* 17 Apr. (1971) 201 An old thin stupid wizzen looking Mr. Evelyn received us. **1837** BARHAM *Ingol. Leg., Spectre Tappington* ad fin., A dingy wizzen-faced portrait. **1888** FERGUS HUME *Mme. Midas* I. ii, A small, wizen-looking little man.

wizen ('wɪz(ə)n), *v.* Also 5 **wisen**, 6 **wisne**, 8–9 **wizzen**. [OE. *wisnian*, *weosnian* (also *áwisnian*, *forwisnian*) = OHG. *wesanên*, *-(e)nên*, also *ar-*, *ir-*, *firwesenên*, ON. *visna* (Sw. *vissna*, Da. *visne*); cf. ON. *visinn* (Sw., Da. *vissen*) withered, palsied: f. Teut. *wis-*, whence also MHG. *wesel* weak, perished; cf. Lith. *výsti* to wither, L. *viēscere* to wither, W. *gwyw* (:—**wiswo-*) withered, OIr. *feugud* 'marcor'.]

1. *intr.* Of plants: To dry up, shrivel, wither. Also *transf.* of persons, their features, etc. See also WIZENED.

c **890** WÆRFERTH *Gregory's Dial.* 134 Heo byð ȝeswenced, þæt heo weornað [*MS. O.* weosnað] & brosnaþ in hire sylfre. *c* **950** *Lindisf. Gosp.* John xv. 6 ðif huælc in mec ne wunas ȝesended bið buta suælce tuigga & dryȝeð *vel* wisneð. **971** *Blickl. Hom.* 115 þa he [*sc.* the world] þus fæȝer wæs..þa wisnode he on Cristes haliȝra heortum. *c* **1050** *Voc.* in Wr.-Wülcker 343 *Arida*, weosniendre.

a **1450** *MS. Cantab. Ff.* v. *48* lf. 90 þe tre weloid & wisened sone, & wex olde and dry.

1787 GROSE *Prov. Gloss.*, *Wizzen*, to wither. N. **1818** TODD, To *Wizen*, to wither; to become dry:..Common in several parts of the north of England. **1864** J. GILBERT & G. C. CHURCHILL *Dolomite Mountains* 493 After wizening with cold for an hour, we ran down to the hut for breakfast. **1883** D. C. MURRAY *Hearts* xxvi, His plump features wizened, and his rosy cheeks grew white.

2. *trans.* To cause to wither or shrivel. *Sc.*

1513 DOUGLAS *Æneis* VI. xii. 42 Tharfor thai suffir panis and turment,..Sum stentit bene in wisnand windis wak. *a* **1895** R. McL. CALDER *Berwicksh. Bard* (1897) 223 Self has gained the upper han', An' wizened up their hearts.

wizen, Sc. and north. f. WEASAND.

wizened ('wɪz(ə)nd), *a.* Forms: 6 **wysnit**, **-yt**, 8 **wissen'd**, 8–9 **wizen'd**, 9 **wiz(z)ened**, **wizzen'd**, **wizend**, **wizzent**, **wuzzent**. [orig. Sc. and north.: f. WIZEN *v.* + -ED[1].]

1. Of plants, foliage, wood, etc.: Dried up, withered, shrivelled.

1513 DOUGLAS *Æneis* VII. Prol. 124 In heych wysnit treis, The soir gled quhislis loud. **1721** RAMSAY *Prosp. Plenty* 93 The antient Nations..Maun study closs..Aff a' the wissen'd Leaves of Spite to shake. **1721** —— *Ode to Mr. F——* 7 The Nags and Nowt hate wissen'd Strae. **1826** G. BEATTIE *John O' Arnha* (ed. 5) 58 Their wizzent timbers stour'd like sneishin! **1853** HAWTHORNE *Tanglewood T.*, *Pomegranate Seeds* 196 He set down the golden salver, with the wizened pomegranate upon it. **1880** HOWELLS *Undiscov. Country* ix, The farmer had ceased to coax his wizened crops from the sterile soil. **1882** *Garden* 18 Mar. 183/3 There is some excuse for eating wizened Muscats.

2. Of persons or animals, their features, etc: Shrunken and dried up, thin and shrivelled. †Also of the throat, parched.

1513 DOUGLAS *Æneis* IX. ii. 70 [The wild wolf's] wysnyt throt, havand of blude sic thrist, Gendris of lang fast sic ane appetyte. **1728** RAMSAY *Last Sp. Miser* iv, The wissen'd beardless wights Wha herd the wives of eastern knights. **1785** BURNS *1st Epist. Davie* xi, I'll light now, and dight now, His [*sc.* Pegasus's] sweaty, wizen'd hide. **1818** SCOTT *Heart Midl.* xviii, Wadna I set my ten talents in your wuzzent face for that very word? **1866** G. MACDONALD *Ann. Q. Neighb.* xxx. (1878) 518 A little wizened creature, with more wrinkles than hairs. **1871** L. STEPHEN *Playgr. Eur.* (1894) x. 253 His..wizened face had a strong resemblance to the features of good-humoured goblins. **1903** MEREDITH *Lett.* (1912) II. 559 Your visit will give you a wizened old hen instead of the plump pullet you look for.

Comb. **1890** W. A. WALLACE *Only a Sister?* xxxi, I'll have a reckoning with the wizened-faced old rogue.

b. *transf.*

1862 MRS. BROWNING *Song Ragged Schools* 28 In God's liberal blue air Peter's dome itself looks wizened. **1895** MEREDITH *Amazing Marr.* I. xix. 209 Below the top bars of a wizened grate was a chilly fire. **1905** SIR F. TREVES *Other Side Lant.* (1906) II. xix. 123 A wizened old city hidden among the hills.

Hence **'wizenedness**.

1887 KIPLING *Plain Tales, Bisara of Pooree* (1924) 263 It was his wizenedness and worthlessness that made him fall..in love with Miss Hollis.

wize roy, wizir, obs. ff. VICEROY, VIZIER.

wizle ('waɪz(ə)l). *dial* (n.w. *midl.*) Forms: 7 **wisall**, **-ell**, 8–9 **wyzle**, 9 **w(e)isle**, **wysle**, **wisle**, **wizle**. [Obscurely f. WISE *sb.*[2] Cf. WISOME, *wizer* (Eng. Dial. Dict.).] The (green) top of a plant having an edible root.

Hence †**wisalled** *a. Her.*, having the wizles of a specified tincture.

1688 HOLME *Armoury* II. iii. 55/1 The tops of Carrats and Parsnips are by Gardiners termed Wisalls, and some Wisomes, so then according to the terms of Art, the Carrat is Or, Wisalled Vert. *Ibid.* ix. 181/2 Grass, Roots, Wisells, Grains. *c* **1746** J. COLLIER (Tim Bobbin) *View Lanc. Dial.* Gloss. Wks. (1775) K 1/2 *Wyzles*, stalks of potatoes, turnips, etc. **1886** *Cheshire Gloss.*, *Wyzles*, the stems of potatoes.

wizzard, obs. f. WIZARD.

wizzel(l, var. WEEZLE *Obs.*

wizzen: see WEASAND, WIZEN.

†**wlaffe**, *v. Obs.* [OE. *wlaffian*, of imitative origin. Cf. ME. *blaffere*, *blaffoorde* 'traulus' (Promp. Parv. 37).] *intr.* To stammer; to speak indistinctly. Hence †**'wlaffer**, †**'wlaffing** *vbl. sb.* and *ppl. a.* Also †**'wlaffering** *vbl. sb.* (? erron.).

1025–50 *Rule Chrodegang* lx. (1916) 74 Of þam deafiað þa earan & wleaffað seo tunge. *a* **1300** in Horstmann *Altengl. Leg.* (1875) 119 An old mon he fond, Bleryid & wlaffing. *c* **1325** *Gloss. W. de Bibbesw.* in Wright *Voc.* 173 A checun mot l'un balbeye, *gloss* wlaffes. **1340** *Ayenb.* 262 And þeruore ich ne ssolde by bote a wlaffere ne zigge þing to þe uolle. *c* **1340** *Nominale* (Skeat) 84 Man drauelith and wlaffyth. **1387** TREVISA *Higden* (Rolls) II. 159 By comyxtioun..wiþ Danes and..Normans, in meny þe contray longage is apayred, and som vseþ straunge wlafferynge [*Caxton* wlaffyng].

†**wlak, wlach**, *a. Obs.* Forms: 1 **wlacu**, **-o**, **wlæc**, 3 **wlec(c)h**, **wleach**, 3–4 **wlach**, 4 **wlak**, 5 **wlake**. [OE. *wlæc*, *wlacu* (an orig. *u*-stem) = MLG. *wlak* lukewarm (whence *wlacheit* 'tepor'); cf. OS. *wlakon*, MLG. *wla(c)ken* to be tepid; the ulterior relations are doubtful. For the phonology of the final consonant cf. FRECK *a.* (ME. *frek*, *frech*).] Lukewarm, tepid; also *fig.* Also advb. in ***wlach hot*** (cf. MLG. *wlakwarm*).

c **897** ÆLFRED *Gregory's Past. C.* xxxvii. 269 Ða ful oft beoð mid wlacum watre ȝelacnode. *Ibid.* lviii. 447 Se ðonne bið wearm, nalles wlaco, ðe god ȝeornlice onginð, & eac ȝeendað. *c* **1200** *Trin. Coll. Hom.* 151 Ðe wop þe man wepeð for his emcristenes wowe cumeð of þe wlache heorte. *a* **1225** *Ancr. R.* 400 Forði þet tu ert ase wlech bitweonen two, nouðer cold ne hot. *c* **1290** *S. Eng. Leg.* 319/695 ȝif þov nimst riȝt puyr hot watur and dost cold þar-to, þov miȝt it makien euene wlach [*MS. Harl.* wlak]. **1432–50** tr. *Higden* (Rolls) VII. 522 In comparisoun to that [hote brennyng] lyȝe, oure fier is but as it were wlache hoot. *c* **1450** *Bk. Hawking* in *Rel. Ant.* I. 304 Kepe it with wlake wyn unto the tyme.

wlanc(k, wlank(e, var. WLONK *Obs.*

†**wlappe**, *v. Obs.* [app. blending of *lappe*, LAP *v.*[2] with WRAP *v.*] *trans.* To wrap. Also *fig.*

c **1380** WYCLIF *Wks.* (1880) 97 Comunly þei ben..wlappid in pride. *Ibid.* 123 Siche on is a dede careyne gon out or his sepulcre wlappid with cloþis of mornynge. **1382** —— *Matt.* xxvii. 59. **1388** —— *2 Tim.* ii. 4 No man holdinge knyȝthod to God, wlappith [1382 inwlappith] hym silf with worldli nedis. *c* **1449** PECOCK *Repr.* III. v. 306 [Comm. 2 Tim. ii. 4: see prec. quot.] Forwhi grete lordis han lasse nede forto wlappe hem silf in worldli nedis. [**1829** J. HUNTER *Hallamshire Gloss.* s.v., In wlapping there is more of folding over, placing one layer over another, than in wrapping. We wrap up any thing in a silk handkerchief: the laundress wlaps up the shirt which she has ironed.]

†**wlat**, *sb. Obs.* [OE. *wlætta*, related to WLATE *v.* Cf. MLG. *wlate*.] Nausea, loathing, disgust.

c **960** ÆTHELWOLD *Rule St. Benet* (Schröer 1885) 68 þelæs he..hwylcne wleattan and soȝeðan on his heortan ne astyriȝe. *c* **1000** *Sax. Leechd.* I. 358 Wiþ spiwðan & wlættan ..ȝenim bares ȝelynde. *a* **1250** *Owl & Night.* 1506 If þu biþenchest hwo hire ofligge þu myht myd wlate þe este bugge.

†**wlat**, *a.* Also 3 **wlath**. [f. prec. or next.] Nauseous, loathsome. Hence †**'wlatness**, nausea.

c **1250** *Gen. & Ex.* 3300 A welle he funde at marath, Ðe water was biter and al wlath. **1398** TREVISA *Barth. De P.R.* XVII. lxx. (Tollem. MS.), I use þerof comforteþ..þe stomak, and abateþ wlatnesse [*Addit. MS.* wlatenesse; orig. *nauseam*].

†**wlate**, *v. Obs.* Also 4 **wlath**, 5 **wlatte**. [OE. *wlatian* = MLG. *wlaten*.]

1. *intr.* and *impers.* with *dat.* To feel disgust or loathing.

c **1000** ÆLFRIC *Num.* xxi. 5 Us wlataþ nu for ðisum eohtostan mete. *c* **1000** *Sax. Leechd.* II. 220 þonne hie mete þicgeað & drincað, þonne wlatað hie. *a* **1225** *Ancr. R.* 86 ȝif heo hit [*sc.* the filth of flattery] stunken, ham wolde wlatien þer aȝean. *Ibid.* 400 Forði þet tu ert ase wlech..þu makest me uorto wlatien. *a* **1250** *Owl & Night.* 354 Ouerfulle makeþ wlatie. **1303** R. BRUNNE *Handl. Synne* 3538 Swyche men god almyȝty hatys And with here foule synne hym wlatys. *Ibid.* 9932 ȝyf þou hym louest, with synne þou wlates. **13..** *E.E. Allit. P.* B. 305 With her vn-worþelych werk me wlatez with-inne. *c* **1450** *Mirk's Festial* 47 His hert wold wlaton and be aschamed of hymselfe, to þenk þat he wer conceyuet of so fowle þyng.

2. *trans.* To loathe, abhor.

a **1340** HAMPOLE *Psalter* v. 7 Man of blodes & swikel wlath sall lord. **1382** WYCLIF *Eccl.* ii. 18, I wlatede alle my bisynesse, that..most studiousli I trauailede. *c* **1395** *Plowman's T.* III. 1098 To worship god men wolde wlate. **1493** [H. PARKER] *Dives & Pauper* (Pynson) VI. xvii. t viii, The glose..seyth that it is amaner of spech to do wlate auoutre and shewynge that auoutrye is ful greuous.

3. To disgust.

c **1375** *Sc. Leg. Saints* xxxiv, (*Pelagia*) 187 Now me wlatis sa myn syne þat I for-sak it. *a* **1400–50** *Wars Alex.* 5634 It wald haue wlated any wee þat welth to be-hald.

†**'wlatful**, *a. Obs.* [f. WLAT *sb.* + -FUL.]

1. Nauseous, loathsome.

c **1230** *Hali Meid.* (1922) 35 (MS. Titus) Hit is wlateful þing for to þenke þron; & for to speke þer-of, ȝet wlatefulre. *a* **1300** *E.E. Psalter* xiii. 2 Forbroken and wlatful made þai are In þair thoghts. **1340** *Ayenb.* 241 þe wordle him hild uor uyl and uor wlatuol. *c* **1450** *Mirk's Festial* 47 þe sede þat he ys conceyuet of, þat ys so fowle yn hym-selfe and so wlatfull.

2. That has a loathing (*of* something). *rare.*

1387 TREVISA *Higden* (Rolls) II. 167 Ful vnpacient of pees ..and wlatful of sleuþe [L. *otium nauseat*].

†**'wlating**, *vbl. sb. Obs.* Forms: 1–3 **wlatung** (1 **uulatunc**), 3–5 **wlating(e**, **-yng(e**, (4 **-iynge**, **-iinge**, **wlath-**, **wlatt-**). [OE. *wlatung*, f. *wlatian* WLATE *v.*] Loathing, nausea; abhorrence, detestation; *occas.* an abomination.

c **725** *Corpus Gloss.* (Hessels) N 5 *Nausatio*, uulatunc. *c* **1000** *Sax. Leechd.* I. 80 ðenime weȝbrædan..& þyȝe hy; ðonne mid micelre wlatunge ȝewiteþ þæt sar on weȝ. *a* **1225** *Ancr. R.* 80 Habbeð wlatunge of þe muðe þet speoweð ut atter. *a* **1300** *E.E. Psalter* lxxxvii. 9 þai set me wlatinge to þam to be. *c* **1315** SHOREHAM I. 697 Hydous hyȝt were to þe syȝte, And to þe tast wlatynge And pyne. *a* **1340** HAMPOLE *Psalter* Cant. 516 In þaire wlathyngis þai mouyd [him] till wreth. **1340** *Ayenb.* 192 God heþ grat wlatiynge of zuych sacrefice. *c* **1400** *Lanfranc's Cirurg.* 98 þat may be knowe by ..wlattynge, whenne þat a man ys fastynge. *a* **1450** MYRC 894 [782] Koghe þow not..Lest heo suppose þow make þat fare, For wlatynge þat þou herest þare [in confession].

So †**'wlatingness**, abhorrence.

1382 WYCLIF *Dan.* ix. 11 Cursse droppide on vs, and wlatyngnesse [1388 wlatyng; Vulg. *detestatio*].

†**'wlatsome**, *a. Obs.* Forms: 4 **wlatsum**, **-som**, **wlatesome**, *Sc.* **vlatsum**, 4–5 **wlathsum**. [f. WLAT *sb.* + -SOME.] Loathsome, detestable.

a **1300** *Cursor M.* 23229 Fell dragons and tades bath þat ar apon to lok ful lath, Ful wlatsum on to here or se. **13..** *E.E. Allit. P.* B. 541 Lo! suche a wrakful wo for wlatsum dedez. *c* **1375** *Sc. Leg. Saints* x. (*Mathou*) 484 His wlatsum Infirmyte [*sc.* leprosy]. *Ibid.* xviii. (*Egipciane*) 418, I sal sa quhow myn saule vithine Is fylyt vith a vlatsum syne. *c* **1386** CHAUCER *Monk's T.* 634 Ful wlatsom was the stynk of his careyne. *c* **1386** —— *Nun's Priest's T.* 233 Mordre is so wlatsom and abhomynable To god. *c* **1430** *Pol. Rel. & L. Poems* (1903) 203 Man is but wlatsum erþe and clay. *c* **1492**, **1563** [see the erron. form WALTSOM(E)].

Hence †**'wlatsomeness**, loathing, disgust.

c **1375** *Sc. Leg. Saints* xxxi. (*Eugenia*) 351 þe abbot..Gat on his fete & stert hir fra,..Hafand at hyr gret wlatsumnes. *c* **1380** WYCLIF *Sel. Wks.* II. 195 Here sour dowȝ is savery þing þat fordoiþ wlatsunnesse [*sic*]. **1398** [see WALTSOM(E)].

wlaunke, -ness: see WLONK, -NESS.

wleach, wlec(c)h, var. WLAK *a. Obs.*

†**wlench**, *v. Obs.* [OE. *ȝewlencan*, f. *ȝe-* Y- + **wlaŋkjan* (f. *wlanc* WLONK; cf. OS. *giwlenkid*). Cf. FORWLENCH.] *trans.* To make proud; *refl.* to pride oneself.

c **1200** *Trin. Coll. Hom.* 189 And on þis fihte is ech man strong, þe awelt is lichame,..and wlencð his soule. *a* **1225** *Leg. Kath.* 1010 Leaf þi lease wit þæt tu wlenchest te in.

wlessche, obs. form of FLESH.

c **1315** SHOREHAM I. 1583 Ine wlessche ioyneþ man and wyf, Children to multeplye.

wlf, obs. f. WOLF.

wlga(i)r, obs. ff. VULGAR *a.*

†**wlisp**, *a. Obs. rare.* Also 4 **wlysp**. [OE. *wlisp*, *wlips* 'balbus', 'blæsus', related to **wlispian* to LISP.] Lisping.

c **1370** in *Pol. Poems* (Rolls) I. 185 Seduus, i. homo qui non potest bene dicere s., qui Anglice dicitur wlysp.

wlisp(e, obs. ff. LISP *v.*

†**'wlite**, *sb. Obs.* [OE. *wlite* m., beauty, splendour, appearance, form, corresp. to OFris. *wlite*, OS. *wliti* sheen, form, ON. *litr* colour,

countenance (see LIT *sb.*), Goth. *wlits* πρόσωπον, ὄψις, μορφή; also in the compound OE. *andwlite*, *onwlite*, beside *andwlita* (see ANLETH).]

1. Beauty; splendour.

c **825** *Vesp. Ps.* xxv[i]. 8 Ic lufade wlite huses ðines. **971** *Blickl. Hom.* 115 He [*sc.* the world] teah men to him þurh his wlite & þurh his fægernesse. *c* **1200** *Trin. Coll. Hom.* 19 þe fader is on þe sune on þrie wise, þat on is on westme,.. þat oðer is on wlite.. swo fair is ure louerd.. and þe þridde is on þewe. *c* **1205** LAY. 2934 Heo wes þa ȝungeste suster, a wliten alre vairest. *Ibid.* 22844 Keruеð of hire neose & heore wlite ga to lose. *a* **1250** *Owl & Night.* 439 þe lilie mid hire faire wlite Wolcumeþ me. *c* **1275** *Serving Christ* 68 in *O.E. Misc.* 92 þer wereþ vre wlite in wurmene won. *a* **1300** *E.E. Psalter* xliv. 5 þi wlite and fairehed ilike.

2. Face, countenance.

c **950** *Lindisf. Gosp.* Matt. xxii. 16 Wlit *vel* onsion monna [Vulg. *personam hominum*]. *a* **1225** [see WASTUM 2]. *c* **1250** *Gen. & Ex.* 2288 Sone he ȝede ut and stille he gret, Ðat al his wlite wurð teres wet.

Hence †**'wliti** *a.* [OE. *wlitiȝ*], beautiful.

c **1000** ÆLFRIC *Gen.* vi. 2 Ða ȝesawon Godes bearn.. manna dohtra, ðæt hi wæron wlitiȝe. *a* **1225** *Leg. Kath.* 313 He awundrede him of hire wliti westum.

†**wlite**, *v. Obs.* [? Imitative; cf. OE. *writian* and WRITELING.] *intr.* To pipe, chirp, warble.

c **1200** *Trin. Coll. Hom.* 215 ȝif he wliteð mid stefne for to liken wimmannen. *a* **1310** in Wright *Lyric P.* xiii. 43 This foules singeth ferly fele, Ant wlyteth on huere wynter [? *read* wynne] wele.

†**wlo.** *Obs.* [OE. *wlóh* = OS. *wlôh*, MLG., MDu. *vlo*, ON. *ló* (Norw., Sw. *lo*, Da. *lu*) nap of cloth.] A hem or fringe; a nap on cloth.

c **950** *Lindisf. Gosp.* Matt. ix. 20 *Fimbriam uestimenti eius*, fas *uel* wloh wedes his. *c* **1394** *P. Pl. Crede* 736 Somme of hem walkeþ Wiþ.. cloþes ful feble, Wel neiȝ for-werd & þe wlon offe.

†**wlonk**, *a.* (*sb.*) *Obs.* Forms: 1–4 **wlanc**, 1–3 **wlonc**, 2 **wlong**, 3–6 **wlonk**, 4 **wlanck**, **vlanck**, **wlanke**, **wlaunk**, **wlonke**, 4–5 **wlank**. [OE. *wlanc*, *wlonc* = OS. *wlank*: cf. WLENCH *v.*]

1. Proud, haughty.

Beowulf 341 Ellenrof.. wlanc Wedera leod.. heard under helme. *c* **1175** *Lamb. Hom.* 35 He wes prud & wlonc. *a* **1225** *Leg. Kath.* 844 Nawt wið wit ah wið wind of ane wlonke wordes. *a* **1300** *Cursor M.* 6397 þir Iuus þat o will war wlanck, þai cund him ai ful litell thanck.

2. Rich, splendid, fine, magnificent: in later use esp. as a conventional epithet in alliterative verse.

Beowulf 2833 Maðmæhta wlonc. *a* **1000** *Phœnix* 100 Fuȝel feþrum wlonc. *c* **1230** *Hali Meid.* (1922) 43 & tine wide wahes wlonke & welefulle. *a* **1250** *Owl & Night.* 489 Sumeres tide is alto wlonc. *c* **1325** *Song of Merci* 3 in *E.E.P.* (1862) 118 Wlanke deor on grounde gan glide. *c* **1350** *Will. Palerne* 1634 A while wol i stinte of þis wlonke murþe. **13..** *E.E. Allit. P.* A. 122 Wod & water & wlonk playnez. *Ibid.* 903, I schulde not tempte þy wyt so wlonc. *a* **1400–50** *Wars Alex.* 5089 A worthi wedow & a wlonk. *c* **1400** *Anturs Arth.* 347 Wlonkest in wede. *c* **1450** HOLLAND *Howlat* 553 Archebald the honorable.. Weddit that wlonk wicht. **15..** *Tayis Bank* 118 (Bann. MS.) Joy wes within and joy without, Vnder that wlonkest waw.

b. Rich in moisture or sap; rank; lush.

1398 TREVISA *Barth. De P.R.* XI. xi. (Tollem. MS.), Snow.. norischeþ and fedeþ good herbes and makeþ hem wlonke [orig. *impinguit*; *ed.* 1495 cranke; *ed.* 1535 ranke]. *c* **1440** *Pallad. on Husb.* III. 449 The potters cley, the wlonk *uliginosa*], or sondy lene,.. nys nought.

B. as *sb.* A fair or beautiful one.

? *a* **1400** *Morte Arth.* 3338, I went to that wlonke, and wynly hire gretis. *a* **1508** DUNBAR *Tua Mariit Wemen* 36 Of thir fair wlonkes,.. Ane wes ane wedow. *Ibid.* 150 The wedo to the tothir wlonk warpit ther wordis.

†**'wlonkful**, *a. Obs. rare.* [f. OE. *wlonc* pride + -FUL.] = WLONK.

c **1400** *Sege Jerus.* 394 In partyis four Of þis wlonfulle [*v.r.* wankille] worde.

So †**'wlonkhede, -ness**, pride.

c **1175** *Lamb. Hom.* 9 Al swa his festen þe swiðe ouerkimet þes flesces wlongnesse. *a* **1250** *Owl & Night.* 1400 (Jesus MS.) þar fleys drahþ nv men to drunkenesse & to wlonkhede & to golnesse. *c* **1325** *Poem Times Edw. II.* in *Pol. Songs* (Camden) 330 Wlaunknesse of wele hem hath al ablent.

†**wlouȝ, wlouh**, *a. Obs. rare.* [? OE. *ȝewlóh* adorned.] ? Opulent.

13.. *Minor Poems fr. Vernon MS.* xxxvii. 155 ȝif.. þou art riche mon and wlouȝ And of richesse hast inouh. *Ibid.* 464 Hou þou schalt.. riche mon bicome and wlouh.

wlt, wluine, wman: see VULT, WOLFEN *sb.*, WOMAN.

wm-, wn-: see UM-, UN-.

wnden, obs. pa. pple. of WIND *v.*[1]

wne, obs. Sc. form of OVEN.

1596 in *Spalding Cl. Misc.* I. 88 Rossin as in ane wne.

wne, obs. form of WONE.

wnse, obs. Sc. form of OUNCE *sb.*[1]

1563 *Aberd. Reg.* (Jam.), In weycht of ten wnsiss.

wnt, obs. Sc. form of WONT.

wnys, obs. form of ONCE.

1482 *Cely Papers* (Camden) 123 Wnys or twyse.

wo (wəʊ), *int.* [Variant of WHO *int.*]

1. In *wo ho, wo ha, wo ho ho, wo ha ho*: a falconer's call to a hawk; also allusively.

1588 *Marprel. Epistle* (Arb.) 33 Wohohow, brother London, do you remember Thomas Allen? **1596** SHAKS. *Merch. V.* v. i. 39 *Clo.* Sola, sola: wo ha ho, sola, sola. **1599** T. CUTWODE *Caltha Poet.* (Roxb.) cxxxvi, Come bird com.. come to me, With so ho ho, and wo ho ho cries she. **1606** CHAPMAN *Gentl. Usher* v. i, Ile rush vpon them With a most hideous cry, the Duke, the Duke, Ha, ha, ha, wo ho, come againe, I say. **1829** SCOTT *Anne of G.* xvii, A woodcock sprung from some bushes, and the young lady threw off her merlin in pursuit. 'Sa ho—sa ho—wo ha!' hollowed the falconer.

2. A call to a horse to stop (cf. WHO *int.*, WHOA, WOA, and WAY *int.*). Also used in conjunction with other interjections, as ***wo-back, wo-ho, hait-wo***.

Also dial. in various combinations with special applications; cf. quot. 1894.

1787 'G. GAMBADO' *Acad. Horsem.* (1809) 24 That he is docile, and will stop short with a 'Wohey'. *a* **1800** PEGGE *Anecd.* (1814) 11 When our waggoners and carmen make use of the terms *ge* and *wo* to their horses. **1801** G. COLMAN *Poor Gentl.* I. i. 1 *Farmer Harrowby, without.* Wo, ho! gently wi 'em! so there! **1823** E. MOOR *Suffolk Words*, *Wooh* or *Woo-e*, an imperative to stop cart horses. *a* **1825** Hait-wo [see HAIT *int.*]. **1834** WHATELY in *Life & Corr.* (1866) I. 247 It is stopping the Horse by a woo-ee instead of a sharp pull of the curb. **1837** DICKENS *Pickw.* v, 'Wo-o!' cried Mr. Pickwick, as the tall quadruped evinced a decided inclination to back into the coffee-room window. **1838** —— *Nickleby* vi, 'Wo ho!' cried the guard,.. running to the leaders' heads. **1840** THACKERAY *Barber Cox* Mar., I pulled very hard, and cried out, Wo! but he wouldn't: and on I went galloping for the dear life. **1871** [see GEE *int.*[1]]. **1879** JEFFERIES *Wild Life in S. Co.* 142 The carter's lads shouting 'Woaght!' to the horses as they steer through the gateway. **1894** *Northumbld. Gloss.*, *Wo, Wo-hay*, a cartman's order to his horse to stop or stand still. *Wo-hi* and *Wo-hick*, turn to left or near side. *Wo-hup* or *Wo-gee*, turn to right or off side.

Hence **wo** *v. intr.*, to call 'wo' to a horse; also in *vbl. sb.* (also ***wohohing***).

1883 *Good Words* 10 The wo-wo-ing of the ploughboy. **1885** RIDER HAGGARD *Witch's Head* xxxiii, Presently from the stables there arose a sound of kicking, plunging, and wohohing impossible to describe. **1889** T. E. BROWN *Manx Witch* 3 'You're very late on the road,' he says—and waein and woin.

wo, obs. form of HOW.

1476 *Stonor Papers* (Camden) II. 5, I cannat tell wo sone.

wo, obs. or arch. form of WOE.

woa (wəʊ), *int.* Also **woah**. [Variant of WHOA.] = WO *int.* 2. Hence **woa** *v.*, to stop (*trans.* and *intr.*) with the call of 'woa'.

1840 DICKENS *Old Cur. Shop* xxxviii, Woa-a-a then, will you? **1856** *Putnam's Monthly Mag.* Nov. 530/1 With a loud 'woah!' the man stopped the beast [*sc.* ass]. **1870** S. LANIER *Nine from eight* 31, I woa'd my mules mighty easy. **1871** M. LEGRAND *Cambr. Freshm.* 252 Woa, Princey, woa! But Prince wouldn't 'woa.' **1892** CHEVALIER *Wot Cher!* iv, 'Woa! steady! Neddy Woa!'

woad (wəʊd), *sb.*[1] Forms: α. 1–2, 5–7, 9 *dial.* **wad**, 2 **waad**, 5 *Sc.* **waid**, **wayde**, 5–7 **wadde**, 6 *Sc.* **vad**, 6–8 **wade**, 7 *Sc.* **wadd**. β. 3–4 **wod**, 4–5 **wode**, 5–6 **wood(e)**, 6 **wo(a)dde**, 6–8 **woade** (7 **waude**), 6–**woad**. γ. 5–6, 8 **ode**, 6–7 **oade**, 7 **oad**. [OE. *wád* = OFris. *wêd*, MLG., MDu. *wêt*, *wêde* (Du. *weede*), OHG., MHG. *weit*, *weid* (G. *waid*):—**waido-* (whence OF. *waide*, *gaide*, It. *guado*), by-form of **waizdo-* (whence med.L. *waizda*, *guaisdium*, etc., AF. *waisde*, OF. *guesde*, F. *guède*, formerly also *voide*, *vouède*, *voueide*), related to Goth. **wizdila* (recorded in L. forms *ouisdelem*, etc.).

Ulterior connexion with OE. *weard*, *werd* 'sandix', and (outside Germanic) with L. *vitrum*, Gr. ἰσάτις is doubtful. The hypothesis of a primitive loan may account for the remarkable phonological variations in pre-Germanic.]

1. A blue dye-stuff prepared from the leaves of *Isatis tinctoria* (see 2) powdered and fermented: now generally superseded by indigo, in the preparation of which it is still sometimes used.

c **1000** ÆLFRIC *Gram.* ix. (Z.) 72 *Hic sandyx*, þis wad. *a* **1100** *Aldhelm Gloss.* I. 1058 (Napier 29/2) *Ex.. iacintho*, of wade. *a* **1200** *Voc.* in Wr.-Wülcker 544/46 *Sandix*, wod. *a* **1250** *Owl & Night.* 76 þin eȝene boþ colblake & brode Riȝt swo ho weren ipeint mid wode. *c* **1374** CHAUCER *Former Age* 17 No Madyr welde or wod no litestere Ne knewh. **14..** *De Artic. Inquir.* in *Sc. Acts* (1844) I. 682/2 Item de tynctoribus Burgensibus ponentibus manus suas in le wadde. **1436** *Libel Engl. Policy* in *Pol. Poems* (Rolls) II. 180 The madre and woode that dyers take on hande. **1488–9** *Act 4 Hen. VII* c. 10 Wood called Tolowse Wode. **1494** in *Somerset Med. Wills* (1901) 322, ij mesers of Ode. **1495** HALYBURTON *Ledger* (1867) 45, 3 ton of waid. **1545** *Rates of Custome Ho.* d j, Woad of goscoyne the pipe .iii. pound vi.s. viii. d. Woad of the Ile of Surrey the ballet x. s. Woad of the Ile of Assorns [= Azores] the ballet x. s. *a* **1548** HALL *Chron., Hen. VIII*, 200 The Merchaunt straungers.. daily brought Oade, Oyle, Sylke,.. and other Merchaundyse into this Realme. **1563** GOLDING *Cæsar* (1565) 117 Al the Britons doe dye themselves wyth woade, which setteth a blewish color uppon them. **1601** B. JONSON *Poetaster* II. i. 59 He that respects to get, must relish all commodities alike; and admit no difference betwixt oade and frankincense. *a* **1618** *Rates of Marchandizes* F 4 b, Iland or green Woad.. Tholoze Woade. **1634** SIR T. HERBERT *Trav.* 224 Azores.. They affoord much Oade, which has made them most famous and best inriched them. **1715** GARTH *Claremont* 91 When Dress was monstrous, and Fig-leaves the Mode, And Quality put on no Paint but Woade. **1800** MARIA EDGEWORTH *The Will* iii, A gentleman who had set up an apparatus for manufacturing woad. **1867** MORRIS *Jason* VI. 327 Deep dyeing-earths, and woad and cinnabar. **1882** J. SMITH *Dict. Pop. Names Plants* 441 Woad.. is manufactured now only at Parsons Drove near Wisbech. **1894** VICKERMAN *Woollen Spinning* 102 The woad cut into small pieces is cast into the vat, which is then filled with water.

fig. **1667** WATERHOUSE *Fire Lond.* 42 This.. gives the judgement a tincture, nay, a deep woad of intense displeasure.

†*pl.* **1598** STOW *Survey* x. 64 The Marchants of Normandie made fine for licence to harbor their woads, till it was otherwise prouided. **1599** NASHE *Lenten Stuffe* 27 They returne wine and Woades, for which is alwaies paide ready Golde. **1622** BACON *Hen. VII*, 75 The King.. ordained; That wines and woads from.. Gascoigne and Languedocke, should not be brought but in English bottomes.

2. The plant *Isatis tinctoria*, formerly extensively cultivated for the blue colouring matter furnished by it (see 1). Sometimes called ***dyer's*** or ***garden woad***, and DYER'S WEED. Also applied to other species of the genus *Isatis*.

c **1000** *Sax. Leechd.* II. 94 Ȝenim wades croppan. **1538** ELYOT, *Glastum*, an herbe lyke to plantayne,.. some men englyshe it woadde. **1538** TURNER *Libellus*, *Isatis sive glastum*,.. *uulgus herbam appellat* wad. **1548** —— *Names Herbes* (E.D.S.) 40 Glastum is called.. in english wad, & not Ode as some corrupters of the englishe tonge do nike-name it. **1562** —— *Herbal* II. 11 The diers occupy the garden wadde.. in dyenge of wull and clothe. **1585** *Procl. agst. sowing of woad* 14 Oct., That no maner of person or persons.. shal.. breake vp.. any maner of grounde.. for the.. purpose to sowe or plant woade in. **1601** HOLLAND *Pliny* XXII. i. II. 114 An hearbe.. Glastum, (*i.* Woad) with the juice whereof the women of Brittaine.. annoint and die their bodies all over. *Ibid.* XXXIII. xiii. 484 These Azurs, receive first a dye, and are boiled with a certaine hearbe.. called Oad, the colour and juice whereof Azur is apt to drinke in and receive. **1633** *Costlie Whore* I. ii. in Bullen *O. Pl.* IV, To.. make our land beare woad instead of wheate. **1739** TROWELL *Treat. Husb.* etc. 33 Of Woad or Wade, the best Land for it. **1778** *Eng. Gazetteer* (ed. 2) s.v. *Bedfordshire*, Woad, a plant used by dyers, is also cultivated here. **1856** *Farmer's Mag.* Jan. 77 A long and explicit covenant [in a lease] against growing pernicious weeds, such as flax, hemp, woad.

b. wild woad, the plant *Reseda Lutcola*: = WELD *sb.*[1] 1. **bastard woad** = WELD *sb.*[1] 1 b.

1578 LYTE *Dodoens* I. xlvi. 66 There be two sortes of Woad: the one is of the garden... The other is wilde Woad. **1597** GERARDE *Herbal* II. cxxviii. 396 Of Sesamoides, or bastard Weld or Woade. **1611** COTGR., *Guesde sauvage*, wild woad, which growes of it selfe in grounds wherein th' other hath beene sowne; and differs not much from it but in staulke. **1796** WITHERING *Brit. Plants* (ed. 3) II. 445 Reseda Luteola.. Wild Woad. Dyers-weed. **1821** CLARE *Vill. Minstr.*, *Cowper Green* iv, Thy wild-woad on each road we see.

3. *attrib.* and *Comb.*, as ***woad-blue, -colour, -farm***, †***-fat*** (= vat) ***-gore*** (GORE *sb.*[1] 1), ***-house***, †***-lead, -man, -mark, -plant, -planter, -rose, -vat; woad-leaved, -painted*** adjs. †**woad-nut**, ? corruptly **-net**, ? a ball of woad.

a **1667** SIR W. PETTY in Sprat *Hist. Royal Soc.* 289 Nor is Allum used in many Colours, viz. In no *Woad or Indico Blews. **1658** ROWLAND tr. *Moufet's Theat. Ins.* 968 The outmost border of the innermost wings is sky or *woad-colour. *a* **1667** in Sprat *Hist. Royal Soc.* 301 An intense Woad-Colour is.. of a Damson-colour. **1892** *Daily News* 23 July 5/4 There are now only four *woad farms and factories in the entire kingdom. **1479** *Will of Swayne* (MS.), *Odefatis. **1496** *Bk. St. Albans, Fishing* h ij, Lete woode your heer in an woodefatte a lyght plunket colour. **1569** *Bury Wills* (Camden) 155 My woadfat coverynge. **1778** D. LOCH *Tour Scot.* 43 Adam Dickson, dyer and clothier,.. works two wood fats. **1856** *Morton's Cycl. Agric.* II. 1162 The hands.. weed the *woad-fields three times. **1419** *Liber Albus* (Rolls) I. 335 Qe nulle ne gette estreyin, poudre, fyms, *wodegor, nautre vilenye. **1705** tr. *Art of Dying* (1913) 350 Sheep should be put into the *Woad grounds to eat up the Grass and Weeds. **1829** [H. BEST] *Lit. Mem.* 456 We rode over the farm to the *woad-houses. **1485–6** *Durham Acc. Rolls* (Surtees) 157, ij s. pro operacione lxxix petr. plumbi operati in j *Wadlede. **1822** *Hortus Anglicus* II. 417 *Woad-leaved Centaury. **14..** in *York Myst.* Introd. p. xxvi, *Wadmen. **1799** A. YOUNG *Agric. Lincoln* 155 It [*sc.* the woad] becomes what the woadmen term *foxy*. **1800** J. HAIGH *Dyer's Assist.* 32 Woadman,.. the name given to the Journeyman Dyer, whose principal business is to conduct the woad. **1613** J. MAY *Decl. Estate Cloth* 30 Some colours haue a slight ground of woad, but farre too weake for the depth of that colour it beares, yet can set vp the *woade marke, or *woade rose, which is vpon the piece at a farre richer depth than the peice is woaded throughout. **1545** *Rates of Custome Ho.* c viij b, *Wodnuttes the C. li vi. s. viii. d. *Ibid.* d ij, Wodenuttes. **1583** *Ibid.* F vij, Wood-nets the c. **1642** *Rates of Merchandizes* 79 Wood-nets the hundred containing five score, 00 10 00. **1891** FARRAR *Darkn. & Dawn* xliv, But how could those *woad-painted fighters withstand the skill.. of our legionaries? **1799** A. YOUNG *Agric. Lincoln* 155 The colour resulting from the *woad plant. *Ibid.* 197 The *woad-planter gives 4 or £5. per acre per annum. **1800** J. HAIGH *Dyer's Assist.* 36 A *woad vat may be set without the addition of indigo. **1865–72** WATTS *Dict. Chem.* III. 252 Woad-vat (Pastel vat).

†**woad**, *sb.*[2] *local. Obs.* Also 7 **oade**. [Error for *woar*, *oare*, ORE[5], by confusion with prec.] ***woad of the sea***: seaweed.

1603 G. OWEN *Pembrokeshire* (1892) 55 Havinge lyme, sand, woade of the sea and divers other principall helpes to better the soile, where neede is. *Ibid.* 59 Oade of the sea. *Ibid.* 75 The sea ore, or woad as some call yt, which is verye weedes growinge vnder water in the sea.

woad (wəʊd), *v.* Also 7 wad, oad; 5 *pa. pple.* y-wooded. [f. WOAD *sb.*[1]]

1. *trans.* To dye, colour, or stain with woad, sometimes (in dyeing) as a ground for another colour. Often *fig.* or in fig. context (cf. *double-dyed*).

1464 *Rolls of Parlt.* V. 562/1 Cork may be used in dying uppon Wolle y wooded. **1549–50** *Act 3 & 4 Edw. VI*, c. 2 §1 Nor that any person shall..dye any Wooll to be converted into Cloth called Russettes [etc.], unlesse the same Wooll be perfectlie woaded boyled and maddered. **1603** HARSNET *Pop. Impost.* 132 His wit beeing deepe woaded with that melancholick blacke dye. **1613** [see *woad-mark*, WOAD *sb.*[1] 3]. *c* **1613** *Overbury's Wife*, etc. *Elegies* Wks. (1856) 6 Some murdering hand, oaded in guiltlesse blood. **1651** CLEVELAND *Poems, Upon Sir T. Martin* 31 Tom never oaded Squire, scarce Yeoman high, Is Tom twice dipt Knight of a double dy? **1655** GURNALL *Chr. in Arm.* II. 99 The hypocrite is not thus woaded with impudency, to sinne at noonday. **1660** FULLER *Mixt Contempl.* I. xlix. 76 It was never wet wadded, which giveth the fixation to a colour, and setteth it in the cloth. **1678** *Pol. Ballads* (1860) I. 206 Foul Error's motly vesture first Was oaded in a Northern blue. **1820** SOUTHEY *Wesley* I. ix. 306 The Picts were apparently an unconverted tribe of indigenous savages, still tattooed and woaded. **1847** TENNYSON *Princess* II. 105 Tattoo'd or woaded, winter-clad in skins. **1894** VICKERMAN *Woollen Spinning* 98 A piece is sent to the dyer with strict injunctions that it must be 'woaded,' that it must have a ground of indigo put upon it for making the colour of the cloth or wool more durable.

b. To treat with woad, in dyeing.

[**1579–1862**: see WOADED.] **1705** *Whole Art of Dying* (1913) 244 'Tis above all of great importance to take care to have a perfect Black, whether it be Madder'd or Woaded only. **1727–38** CHAMBERS *Cycl.* s.v. *Dyeing*, Bright green is first dyed blue,..and lastly woaded.

†**c.** *transf.* (*fig.*) To ingrain like a dye or stain.

1647 TRAPP *Comm. Matt.* xxi. 37. 511 Sin had woaded shamelesnes in their fore-heads. —— *Jude* i. 2 Sin having oaded an impudency in their faces. **1647** C. HARVEY *Schola Cordis* Ode xvii. (1674) 67 The stains of sin I see Are oaded all, or di'd in grain.

2. To plant (land) with woad. *rare.*

1799 A. YOUNG *Agric. Lincoln* 154 He has now between two and three hundred acres of arable, on land he does not woad, in a course of crops.

†**'woad-,ashes**, *sb. pl. Obs.* [f. WOAD *sb.*[1] + pl. of ASH *sb.*[2]: corresp. to MLG. *wed(e)asche*, MDu. *weedassche* (*weed-*, *weydasschen* 'cineres clavellati..cineres smigmatici', Kilian), MHG. *weidaschen* 'sandix', 'clavellati cineres' (G. *waidasche*), whence F. *védasse*, †*wedasse*. Sense b is properly *wood-ash*, but the formal similarity of *woad* and *wood*, and the double use of the MDu. form, produced confusion.] **a.** The ashes of burnt wine-lees, used by dyers: = med.L. *cineres clavati* or *clavellati*, OF. *cendres clavelés*, F. *cendres gravelées*. **b.** The ashes of burnt wood used to make a lye.

a **1387** *Sinon. Barth.* 16 *Cineres clavellate*, an. woode ashes. **1545** *Rates of Custome Ho.* a ij, Asshes called woad asshes the laste xx, s. **1562–3** *Act 5 Eliz.* c. 4 §23 The art or occupation of a..burner of Ore and woade ashes. **1583** *Rates of Custome Ho.* A iij b, Ashes called wood or sope Ashes. **1663** BOYLE *Usef. Exp. Nat. Philos.* II. 363 This way was only to mingle exquisitly a quantity of Sal-Armoniack, with about thrice its weight of strong Wood-ashes. **1705** tr. *Art of Dying* (1913) 113 A Perfect Description, of Pot and Woad-Ashes. *a* **1756** MRS. HAYWOOD *New Present* (1771) 267 Some persons at a great wash put ode, or pearl ashes tied in a cloth, and let it lie in the water. **1780** *Act 20 Geo. III*, c. 25 Preamble, Whereas Pot and Pearl Ashes, Wood and Weed Ashes, are essentially necessary in the whitening of Linen Cloth and Thread.

¶Forms representing the G. and LG. words are illustrated in the following:—

1705 tr. *Art of Dying* (1913) *title-p.*, A Discourse of Pot and Weyd Ashes, as well as several other Foreign Ingredients used in Dying. *Ibid.* 136 Wayd-Ashes are prepared in the same manner [as pot-ashes], from the Ashes of burnt Wayd, that is Willow. **1708** SEWEL *Dutch-Eng. Dict.*, *Weedasch*, Weed-ashes. **1780** [see above].

woaded ('wəʊdɪd), *ppl. a.* [f. WOAD *sb.*[1] or *v.* + -ED.] **a.** Of a colour or dye: Having a basis of, or treated with, woad. **b.** Of cloth, etc.: Dyed with woad or woaded dye.

1579–80 NORTH *Plutarch* (1595) 85 As a deepe woded die, which went to the bottome, and pearced into the tender wolle. **1580–1** *Act 23 Eliz.* c. 9 §2 A..perfitte couler of woaded and mathered Blacke. **1613** J. MAY *Decl. Estate Cloth* 30 The diers of London doe best obserue a true course in setting a woaded seale vpon woaded colours. **1615** S. WARD *Coal fr. Altar* 24 The set vp blewes haue made strangers loath the rich oaded blewes. **1653** BLITHE *Engl. Improver Impr.* xxxv. (ed. 3) 227 Woad..layes the foundation for the solidity of very many colours more: A Woaded colour is free from stayning. **1862** C. O'NEILL *Dict. Calico Printing* etc. 212 The term *woaded colours*, still in common use for colours which are supposed to be dyed upon a basis of woad blue. **1869** A. MACDONALD *Love, Law & Theol.* iv. 66 The glossy woaded blacks of the unique Webster, which usually adorn the backs of youthful Sneakers. **1894** *Times* 14 May 4/3 Some good parcels of woaded wool serges.

So **'woading** *vbl. sb.*

1613 J. MAY *Decl. Estate Cloth* 30 The ground of good colours is substantiall woading, without which diuers colours cannot be perfectly made, as blackes, russets,..and such like. **1894** VICKERMAN *Woollen Spinning* 111 The 'woading' of blacks in too many instances has become so much of a formality..that the old tests are no longer of any service.

woader ('wəʊdə(r)). *rare.* Also 5 **woder**. [f. as prec. + -ER[1].] **a.** A dyer with woad. **b.** A cultivator of woad.

1415 *Rolls of Parlt.* IV. 75/1 Deux Drapers, un Woder, & un Tinctour. **1424** *Will of John Rouwe* (Somerset Ho.) Tinctor siue Woder. **1616** *Rich Cabinet* 55 b, To goe afield with victuals to his woaders or weeders. **1830** *Withering's Brit. Plants* (ed. 7) III. 752 *note*, The gangs of people called Woaders, who make the culture of this herb their peculiar employment. **1881** *Instr. Census Clerks* (1885) 67 Silk Bleacher, Woader.

woad-waxen: see WOODWAXEN.

woag(e, obs. Sc. ff. VOYAGE.

woak, dial. f. OAK.

woald, var. WELD *sb.*[1]; obs. f. WOLD.

woan(e, var. WONE.

woant, obs. f. WANT *sb.*[1]

woar, variant of ORE[5], seaweed.

1586 J. HOOKER *Hist. Irel.* in *Holinshed* II. 43/1 The woars of the seas.

woar, obs. form of WOOER.

woat, obs. form of OAT *sb.*

1673 G. FOX in *Jrnl. Friends' Hist. Soc.* (1914) July 98 Pease & barly & woats 2 shilens a bueshell.

wob, wobat: see WEB *sb.*, WOUBIT.

wobbegong ('wɒbɪgɒŋ). Also **wobbygong, wobegong**. [Aboriginal name.] A brown carpet shark with buff markings, *Orectolobus maculatus*, found off the coast of Australia.

1852 G. C. MUNDY *Our Antipodes* I. xii. 392 The most hideous to behold of the shark tribe is the wobegong, or woe-begone, as the fishermen call it... His broad back is spotted over with leopard-like marks. **1882** J. E. TENISON-WOODS *Fish & Fisheries N.S.W.* iv. 94 The wobbegong..is chiefly nocturnal. **1917** *Chambers's Jrnl.* Sept. 588/1 There is also the well-known wobbygong, a creature of extraordinary and beautiful colouring. **1937** Z. GREY *Amer. Angler in Austral.* vi. 53 The most remarkable feature of the wobbegong is his teeth. **1956** S. HOPE *Diggers' Paradise* xx. 183 The worst types are the white pointer,..hammerhead and carpet shark, also called the wobbegong. **1981** B. STONEHOUSE *Sharks* iv. 46 Woggegongs..add to their camouflage by growing fronds that look like seaweed on their faces.

wobble ('wɒb(ə)l), *sb.* Also † **wabble**. [f. next.] **1. a.** The action or an act of wobbling; an unsteady rocking motion or movement; also *fig.*

1699 *Phil. Trans.* XXI. 286 That direction being nothing but a certain wabble in the Earth's Motion. **1842** FRANCIS *Dict. Arts* etc., *Wabble*, a hobbling unequal motion. **1867** F. FRANCIS *Bk. Angling* iv. 89 The long, slow wobble of a badly spinning bait. **1870** STEINMETZ *Gaming Table* II. v. 154 The mouth[s] of the pockets..are easier of access; and the chance of a wobble all but avoided. **1896** WELLS *Wheels of Chance* v, The bicycle..began an absolutely unprecedented wabble. **1911** *Sat. Rev.* 19 Aug. 223/1 That is a quite characteristic wobble on the part of Sir Wilfrid Laurier.

b. *pl.* (*Austral.*) A disease in cattle caused by eating the leaves of the palm-tree.

1895 *Queenslander* 7 Dec. 1090 Rickets or Wobbles in Cattle.

2. *Biochem.* The variable pairing that is possible between a base in a transfer RNA anticodon and the corresponding base in a messenger RNA codon. Freq. *attrib.*

1966 F. H. C. CRICK in *Jrnl. Molecular Biol.* XIX. 548 (*heading*) Codon–anticodon pairing: the wobble hypothesis. *Ibid.* 551, I now postulate that in the base-pairing of the third base of the codon there is a certain amount of play, or wobble, such that more than one position of pairing is possible. **1974** *Nature* 22 Feb. 517/2 tRNA$_f^{met}$ of *E. coli*, yeast and mouse ascites tumour cells has the ability to recognise both the codons A_pU_pG and G_pU_pG and to thus exhibit code degeneracy or 'wobble' at the third base (3' end) of the anticodon. **1982** K. H. MUENCH in T. M. Devlin *Textbk. Biochem.* xix. 921 According to the wobble rules 31 different tRNAs would suffice to read the 64 codons.

wobble ('wɒb(ə)l), *v.* Also † **wabble**, *Sc.* 8–9 **wauble**. [Corresponds to Upper, Middle, and Low G. *wab(b)eln*: cf. MHG. *wabelen* to move restlessly, and ON. *vafla* (synonymous with *vafra* WAVER *v.*): f. Teut. *wab-* (see WAVE *v.*). A parallel Teut. *wap-* appears in LG. *wappeln*, ON. *vappa* to waddle, OE. *wapolian* to bubble. (Cf. SWABBLE *v.*)]

1. a. *intr.* Of a person or animal: To move from side to side unsteadily or with uncertain direction.

1657 [see WOBBLING *ppl. a.*]. **1694** tr. *Marten's Voy. Spitzbergen* in *Acc. Sev. Late Voy.* (1711) II. 91 This Bird is a Diver..They go wabbling from side to side. *Ibid.* 101 When they go to fly up they wabble a great way before they can raise themselves upon the Wind. **1705** *Lond. Gaz.* No. 4178/4 Advt., Wabbles in his walking. **1749** MRS. DELANY *Autobiogr.* (1861) II. 515 James came wabbling on with the broken equipage, his Fribbleship much ruffled. **1786** BURNS *Auld Farmer's Salut. Mare* vii, Ye..ran them 'till they a' did wauble, Far, far, behin'. **1789** D. DAVIDSON *Seasons* 156 The snipe..Starts frae the slimy drain; and, to the spring.. now waubles fast. **1833** CARLYLE *Cagliostro* Ess. 1872 V. 73 'The two pinions on which History soars'—or flutters and wabbles. **1856** WHYTE-MELVILLE *Kate Cov.* vi. 69 Such a figure *I* never saw on a horse!..bumping when she trots, and wobbling, when she canters. **1896** WELLS *Wheels of Chance* viii, He resumed the treadles,..jolted over a stone, wabbled, recovered, and began riding faster.

b. Of a piece of mechanism, a top, a missile, etc.

1677 MOXON *Mech. Exerc.* iii. 45 The wheel..would not move perpendicularly, but wabble towards the Fore or Backsides of the Jack frame. **1680** *Ibid.* xii. 215 If in going about of your Work you find it Wabble, that is, that one side of the Flat incline either to the Right or Left Hand. **1706** PHILLIPS (ed. Kersey), To *Wabble*, to wriggle about as an Arrow sometimes does in the Air. **1806–7** J. BERESFORD *Miseries Hum. Life* IV. xv, [A] hat..which..wabbles over your eyes and ears. **1828–32** WEBSTER s.v., A top wabbles, when it is in motion, and deviates from a perpendicular direction; a spindle wabbles, when it moves one way and the other. **1884** E. P. ROE in *Harper's Mag.* June 88/1 Well now, watch the floats. If you see one bob under and wobble, a shad has struck the net near it. **1884** *Sat. Rev.* 6 Sept. 320/2 A projectile from a smoothbore is apt to 'wobble' and go wide.

c. To bubble; to boil. Now *dial.*

1725 *New Canting Dict.*, *Wobble*, to boil. The Pot wobbles, i.e. The Pot boils. **1825** T. HOOK *Sayings* Ser. II. *Passion & Princ.* xv. III. 397 Sir Frederick smoked his chilum..and whiffed and 'wobbled', and wore away the evening. **1854** MISS BAKER *Northampt. Gloss.*, *Wabble*, to boil fast.

d. To shake or quiver like a jelly or fleshy body.

1748 [see WOBBLING *ppl. a.*]. **1854** R. S. SURTEES *Handley Cr.* xxxvi, Away Jorrocks went, wobbling like a great shape of red Noyeau jelly. **1875** HOWELLS *Foregone Conclus.* xvii, Her chin wobbled pathetically. **1881** *Harper's Mag.* Apr. 643 He wabbled with laughter at the delicious absurdity of the reminiscence.

e. To move unsteadily from side to side or backwards and forwards (without progression). Also *fig.*

1858 H. MAYHEW *Upper Rhine* iv. 214 From the mouth of the..figure a long tongue..was made to wabble. **1865** BARING-GOULD *Werewolves* xv. 264 You see it well in old women: how the last teeth wobble. **1878** TYNDALL *Fragm. Sci.* (1879) II. xiii. 307 The field of the microscope is crowded with organisms, some wabbling slowly. **1895** S. CRANE *Red Badge* xiii, His knees wobbled. **1903** G. H. LORIMER *Lett. Self-made Merch.* xix. 288 He..shouted 'Hello!' in what he tried to make a big, brave voice, but it wobbled a little all the same.

2. *fig.* To hesitate or waver between different opinions or courses of action; to be inclined to favour first one side and then the other.

1884 *Bath Herald* 20 Sept. 3/1 The *Standard*..has.. wobbled back to its old ways. **1885** DILKE in *Life* (1917) II. 111 The other members of the Cabinet either wobbled backwards and forwards, or did not care. **1906** G. W. E. RUSSELL *Social Silhouettes* 161 If you wobble or rat or play the Candid Friend, you are only too likely to find yourself cast at the next election.

3. *trans.* To cause to move unsteadily from side to side.

1831 T. ALLEN *Hist. Co. York* III. 41 The convex surface, with its glass pieces, is then turned and wabbled in the concave basin by steam power. **1881** P. M. DUNCAN in *Academy* 23 Apr. 468/3 One of the rigidly armoured Silurian fishes which learned to snap at its prey and got more food by the attempt to wobble its cranium.

4. *U.S.* To crumple *up*.

1869 MRS. WHITNEY *We Girls* vi. (1874) 119 The dish-towels dirty, and the dish-cloth all wabbled up in the sink. **1884** E. P. ROE in *Harper's Mag.* June 88/1 To keep the net straight, and not all tangled and wobbled up.

5. *Comb.*: **wobble-heat**, a form of heat-energy caused by vibration; **wobble plate** = *swash-plate* s.v. SWASH *sb.*[1] 9; freq. *attrib.*; **wobble-saw**, a circular saw mounted askew on its spindle so as to cut a groove wider than its own thickness.

1899 LOCKYER in *Nature* 20 Apr. 585/2 To get concrete images of these effects we spoke of path-heat, spin-heat, and *wobble-heat. **1929** V. W. PAGÉ *Mod. Aviation Engines* II. xlvi. 1897 A peculiar '*wobble' plate mechanism replaces the usual crankshaft arrangement. *Ibid.* (*caption*) Wobble plate. *Ibid.* (*caption*) A typical example of a 'wobble' plate or barrel type engine. **1943** Wobble-platemeter [see NUTATE *v.*]. **1875** KNIGHT *Dict. Mech.* 2717 **Wabble-saw*. **1917** H. W. DURHAM *Saws* 53 'Drunken' or 'Wobble' saws.

wobbler ('wɒblə(r)). Also 8 **wabler**, 9 **wabbler**. [f. WOBBLE *v.* + -ER[1].] **1.** One who or that which wobbles; a person or animal that walks unsteadily; one who wavers or vacillates in opinion; also *spec.* (see quots. 1785, 1823, 1875).

1785 GROSE *Dict. Vulgar T.*, *Wabler*, foot wabler, a contemptuous term for a foot soldier, frequently used by those of the cavalry. **1823** 'JON BEE' *Dict. Turf*, *Wabbler*, a boiled leg of mutton, alluding to the noise made in dressing it. **1875** KNIGHT *Dict. Mech.* 2717 *Wabbler*, an elliptical cutter-head placed at such obliquity on the shaft as to revolve in a circular path. Sometimes called a *drunken cutter*. **1887** *Pall Mall Gaz.* 20 Aug. 1/1 Such a Government of Wobblers. **1897** BARRÈRE & LELAND *Dict. Slang*, *Wobbler*,.. a horse that swerves from side to side when trotting.

2. *Mech.* **a.** A projection on a roll in a rolling-mill, by means of which it may be turned.

1904 J. W. HALL in F. W. Harbord *Metallurgy of Steel* xvi. 294 At the outer end of each neck forming part of the casting is a 'wobbler', provided with either three or four prongs or corners, by means of which the roll is driven. **1919** *Jrnl. Inst. Metals* XXII. 383 Rolls.—These are usually of chilled cast iron or hardened steel. For wobbler ends, the four-horn design is the most general in use... A rule is suggested regarding length of spindles and clearance between wobbler and box. **1930** *Engineering* 25 Apr. 539/1 A driving bar socket for the wobbler drive is bolted to the face-plate. **1978**

W. L. ROBERTS *Cold Rolling of Steel* iii. 64 Wobblers are shown in Figure 3-3, and flat roll ends in Figure 3-4.

b. = *wobble plate* s.v. WOBBLE *v.* 5.

1950 W. E. WILSON *Positive-Displacement Pumps & Fluid Motors* iii. 42 Oil pressure forces the pistons against the nonrotating wobbler. The resultant force is transmitted through ball and roller bearings to the wobbler plate on the shaft and imparts a rotating action to it.

3. *Angling.* A lure that wobbles and does not spin.

1928 E. F. SPENCE *Pike Fisher* v. 55 The 'shining streak of silver' does not resemble any inhabitant of river or lake, but the 'wobbler' does look something like an injured fish. **1945** [see LEERVIS]. **1960** M. SHARCOTT *Place of Many Winds* vii. 120 'I bought a dozen new wobblers,' he says as he lifts the lid to reveal the shiny brass cohoe-spoons. **1977** *Best of Austral. Angler* 49/1 The wobbler and spoon type lure, however, whilst also being highly attractive to trout, are more suited to the physical requirements.

wobbling (ˈwɒblɪŋ), *vbl. sb.* [f. WOBBLE *v.* + -ING[1].] The action of the vb. WOBBLE.

1836 HALIBURTON *Clockm.* Ser. I. xxvii, No wabblin' of his hind parts, but steady as a pump bolt. *a* **1848** *N. Y. Com. Adv.* (Bartlett) Leverrier's calculations gave the mass of the unknown planet, by which the 'wabblings' of Herschell were to be set right, at so much. **1861** MISS E. A. BEAUFORT *Egypt. Sepulchres* II. xvi. 26 He nearly fell off his mule with the excess of the wabbling. **1876** VOYLE & STEVENSON *Milit. Dict.* (ed. 3), *Wobbling*, the unsteady motion of an elongated projectile through the air. **1907** *Athenæum* 27 Apr. 513/2 Here . . is a slight wobbling in the artist's intention.

wobbling (ˈwɒblɪŋ), *ppl. a.* [f. WOBBLE *v.* + -ING[2].] That wobbles, in senses of the vb.

1657 LIGON *Barbadoes* 62 Cockroches, a creature . . of a pure hair-colour, which would set him off the better, if he had not an ugly wabling gate. **1748** RICHARDSON *Clarissa* VI. 99 [An old man] Shaking his loose-flesh'd wabbling chaps. **1774** GOLDSM. *Nat. Hist.* IV. 140 Its [*sc.* the bat's] evening flight and its unsteady wabbling motion amuse the imagination. **1821** CLARE *Vill. Minstr., Rustic Fishing* 46 Still wobbling curves keep wavering like a bite. **1883** GROVE *Dict. Mus.* III. 509/2 His whole singing was a bad wobbling trill. **1884** J. H. WALSH *Mod. Sportsman's Gun* II. 7 When discharged from a smooth bore, . . an oscillating or 'wobbling' flight is produced. **1898** *Catholic News* 21 May 8/4 It cannot be said that the constituency is a wobbling one.

wobbly (ˈwɒblɪ), *a.* Also **wabbly**. [f. WOBBLE *v.* + -Y[1].] Inclined to wobble.

1851–61 MAYHEW *Lond. Labour* III. 149/1 The knees, which at first is weak and wabbly, gets strong. **1871** *Daily News* 11 Apr. 6 A brigade can fight as well if its line be slightly 'wobbly' as if it were dressed to death. **1873** MISS BROUGHTON *Nancy* I. 279 'Nancy!' cries Bobby, . . speaking in a wobbly, quivering voice. **1878** *Athenæum* 13 July 42/1 His English . . is decidedly 'wobbly'.

Hence **ˈwobbliness**, the state of being wobbly.

1880 MISS BROUGHTON *Second Thoughts* I. ii, General Tarlton is observing with chill misgiving a certain threatening wobbliness in the gait of his [top]. **1881** J. MORLEY *Recoll.* (1917) I. 174 A 'wobbliness' which nobody is more conscious of or more disgusted by, than I am.

ˈwobbly, *sb.*[1] orig. *U.S.* [Origin uncertain.] A member of the Industrial Workers of the World (see INDUSTRIAL *a.* e).

[**1913** *Miners Mag.* 24 Apr. 5 Joe Elton, Sabotist, Syndicalist and fearless I.W.W. with a red, flowing tie, with fire in his eye and fight in his backbone, the I Wobbily-Wobbily organizer . . is traveling the country delivering his message. **1914** *Rep. Calif. District Courts of Appeal* (1915) 402 He telegraphed. . . Send all speakers and wobbles [*sic*] possible. . . It appeared at the trial that the term 'wobbles' meant members of the I.W.W.] **1914** *Voice of People* (Portland, Oregon) 1 Oct. 2/4 The workers are . . asking why the wobblies are not holding meetings. **1921** *Outing* (U.S.) Nov. 94/3, I saw an angel and the devil standing side by side. The devil wore a 'Wobbly' (I.W.W.) button. **1923** *Nation* 5 Sept. 242/2 In Vancouver, in 1911, we had a number of Chinese members and one restaurant keeper would trust any member for meals. He could not pronounce the letter *w*, but called it *wobble*, and would ask: 'You *I. Wobble Wobble?*' and when the card was shown, credit was unlimited. Thereafter the laughing term among us was *I. Wobbly Wobbly*. **1932** E. WILSON *Devil take Hindmost* xxi. 218 The Wobbly leaders . . called the men out of the tunnels. **1948** V. PALMER *Golconda* xxx. 251 And sometimes he [*sc.* the Labour Party candidate] was bothered by young fellows, usually advocates of One Big Union, who tried to lure him into deep water. . . He came to recognize them in the end and to stop them with light thrusts before they had lured him too far. 'What're you fellows? Wobblies, aren't you? I.W.W.—I Won't Work, but listen to me talk, eh?' **1957** [see *I.W.W.* s.v. I III]. **1967** A. L. LLOYD *Folk Song in Eng.* v. 387 'The celebrated working man', a song of American origin . . was brought to Durham by a Wobbly collier from Kentucky. **1980** *Times* 21 June 6/1 A poor white American, probably a Wobbly—a member of the Industrial Workers of the World, a group of radical labour unions largely made up of itinerant workers.

ˈwobbly, *sb.*[2] *colloq.* [f. the adj.] ***to throw a wobbly***: to lose one's self-control in a fit of nerves, panic, temperament, annoyance, or the like; also, to act in an unexpected way, causing surprise or consternation.

1977 *Telegraph* (Brisbane) 13 Apr. 13/2 The world has used him, exploited his talent and brains and then discarded him . . . is it any wonder that he throws a wobbly? **1978** D. NORDEN in Muir & Norden *Take my Word for It* 59 Not only did she throw a wobbly at the slightest murmur of tango rhythms, even the sight of a piano-accordion brought her out in hives. **1981** *Radio Times* 22–28 Aug. 6/4 The debriefing . . seemed to take an inordinately long time. . . 'By lunch,' he [*sc.* Simeon Harris] says, 'I was getting a bit fed up, so I threw a wobbly.' **1982** *Guardian* 30 Oct. If the men heard my name called on the public address system all kinds of stories would go round. They'd say 'Someone's thrown a wobbly again.' **1987** *Daily Tel.* 28 Jan. 13/4 When Susannah was 15 Leslie threw the biggest wobbly of all. She uprooted the family from Kent . . and went to farthest Pembrokeshire.

wobbulator (ˈwɒbjʊleɪtə(r)). *Electronics.* Also **wobulator**. [f. WOBB(LE *sb.* or *v.* + MOD)ULATOR.] A device for producing a signal whose frequency varies rapidly and repeatedly between two limits.

1945 COOKE & MARKUS *Electronics Dict.* 428/1 Wobbulator. **1958** *Electronic Engin.* XXX. 541 A wobulator for amplitude testing often gives errors because of unwanted signal amplitude variations. **1977** S. W. AMOS *Radio, T.V. & Audio Technical Reference Bk.* xxxii. 9 Alignment should not be attempted on any u.h.f. tuner without the use of a u.h.f. wobbulator.

So **ˈwobbulated** *ppl. a.*, varied or produced by means of a wobbulator; **wobbuˈlation**, repeated variation of a frequency by a wobbulator.

1944 *Electronic Engin.* XVI. 327/3 A powerful high-frequency sound with a wobbulated effect might give the birds a disagreeable sensation. **1957** *Practical Wireless* XXXIII. 569/1 Apply a 10·7 Mc/s signal, wobbulated 300 kc/s, to a test point. **1965** *New Scientist* 15 Apr. 156/1 'Wobbulation' or the sweeping of the modulation frequency through 15 per cent either way of its mean value. **1982** *IEEE Jrnl. Solid-State Circuits* XVII. 671/1 The initial and final frequencies, the wobbulation rate, the ramp amplitude and frequency, and the wobbulation mode are all controlled from the input data.

woc, var. WOKE *a. Obs.*

woce, obs. Sc. f. VOICE.

woch(e: see VOUCH, WHICH, WOW (wall).

woch(e)safe, obs. ff. VOUCHSAFE.

wod, obs. f. WOOD *sb.* and *a.*; obs. pa. t. of WADE *v.*

wod, obs. Sc. form of VOID *v.*

1477 *Lydgate's Dietary* 54 in *Makculloch MS.* (S.T.S.) 31 Wod al dronkynness, learis & lechoris.

wod, obs. form of HOOD.

1559 *Inv.* (Warw.) in *N. & Q.* 12th Ser. II. 502/1 A crest cap and a wod to weyr upon his sholder iiij s.

wodake, obs. f. WOODHACK (woodpecker).

wodbill, -bin, -binde, -cok(ke, etc., obs. ff. WOODBILL, WOODBINE, WOODCOCK.

wodd(e, wodden, obs. ff. WOOD, WOODEN.

wodder, -ir, obs. ff. WEATHER.

wodderweght, obs. f. WITHERWEIGHT *Sc.*

woddie, obs. var. WIDDY, WOODY.

woddish, -y, obs. ff. WOODISH, -Y.

woddram, wodrome, early forms of WIDDENDREAM.

1644 in S. Hibbert *Shetl. Isl.* (1822) 594 The said sickness was taken off the said Marion and casten upon a young cow of the said John's, which took wodrome. *Ibid.*, An uther cow . . also died mad and in woddram.

wode, obs. Sc. f. VOID; obs. pa. t. of WADE *v.*; obs. f. WOAD, WOOD.

wodehouse: see WOODWOSE.

Wodehousian (wʊdˈhaʊsɪən), *sb.* and *a.* [f. the name of Sir Pelham Greville *Wodehouse* (1881–1975), British author + -IAN.]

A. *sb.* **a.** A typical character in one of the comic novels of P. G. Wodehouse. **b.** An admirer or an habitual reader of Wodehouse's novels. **B.** *adj.* Pertaining to or characteristic of Wodehouse or of his works.

1931 *Times Lit. Suppl.* 21 May 409/4 Berry Conway and Lord Biskerton, the lads who are after Big Money, are true Wodehousians, stamped with the authentic stamp. **1938** *Ibid.* 12 Feb. 107/3 One may wince at Wodehousian baronets taking lodgers. **1943** *Scrutiny* XI. 288 About every seven pages some Wodehousian character receives a severe and almost mortal shock. **1958** *Times Lit. Suppl.* 14 Feb. 85/4 An up-to-date version of gaily irresponsible Wodehousian farce. **1973** M. MUGGERIDGE *Infernal Grove* iv. 229 The broadcasts, in point of fact, are neither anti- nor pro-German, but just Wodehousian. **1979** *Daily Tel.* 2 Aug. 11/3 With some minor reservations. ., this addition to Wodehousian lore can safely be admitted. **1980** *Times* 2 Feb. 7/2 The experienced Wodehousian's heart leaps.

wodeland, -liche, -ness(e: see WOODLAND, WOODLY, WOODNESS.

Wodenism (ˈwəʊdənɪz(ə)m). *rare.* [f. *Woden* (see ODINISM) + -ISM.] Odinism.

1891 ATKINSON *Moorland Par.* 236 Wodenism was so completely vanquished that even the coming of the Danes failed to revive it.

Wodensday, obs. f. WEDNESDAY.

woder, obs. f. OTHER, WEATHER.

woderofe, -rove, -rowe, obs. ff. WOODRUFF.

wodershins, obs. f. WITHERSHINS.

wodeship, -sour, etc., **-wale, -ward**: see WOODSHIP, etc.

wodewe, obs. f. WIDOW.

wodewose: see WOODWOSE.

wodge (wɒdʒ). *colloq.* (orig. *dial.*). Also **wadge**. [Perh. phonæsthetic alteration of *wedge*: cf. WEDGE *sb.* 4 and *Eng. Dial. Dict.*] A bulky mass; a chunk or lump; a wad (of paper).

1860 *All Year Round* 28 July 368/2 The unhappy children [Blue-coat boys] . . are compelled . . to turn their skirts up and gird them in a great hot wadge about their loins. **1862** C. A. COLLINS *Cruise upon Wheels* xxiv. (1863) 413 That monstrous wadge of a dressing-gown. **1913** E. POUND *Let.* 7 Nov. (1971) 25, I don't want a great wadge of prose, but about double what we have at present. **1922** *Chambers's Jrnl.* Dec. 797/1 A 'wodge' in his left breast-pocket. **1949** D. SMITH *I capture Castle* II. viii. 112 You must take only one kind of food on the fork at a time; never a nice comfortable wodge of meat and vegetables together. **1958** HAYWARD & HARARI tr. *Pasternak's Dr. Zhivago* I. vii. 195 He held out a wadge of papers across the hand-rail. **1963** A. SMITH *Throw out Two Hands* iii. 39 We strode out into the rain with a wodge of well-stamped supplications. **1977** *Private Eye* 4 Mar. 7/3 True, there's a wadge of self-opinionated dolts who drive around in head scarves and Range Rovers. **1981** *Brit. Med. Jrnl.* 21 Mar. 968/1 A posterior pack is made from a wadge of gauze as large as the end of the patient's thumb, which is rammed tightly into the posterior choana. **1984** *Listener* 6 Dec. 35/1 These tomes are usually given a lively, busy design, with screaming wodges of colour. *Ibid.* 20–27 Dec. 7/2 Cross-headings, the lay reader should know, are those devices used to break a grey wodge of type and encourage you to keep reading.

wodginite (ˈwɒdʒɪnaɪt). *Min.* [f. *Wodgina*, name of a locality in Western Australia + -ITE[1].]

A rare oxide of tantalum, niobium, and manganese (usu. also containing tin and iron) which occurs as brown or black monoclinic crystals or grains.

1963 E. H. NICKEL et al. in *Canad. Mineralogist* VII. 390 The name wodginite is proposed for a mineral found at two widely separated localities—Wodgina, Australia and Bernic Lake, Manitoba. **1978** *Mineral. Rec.* IX. 18/2 (*caption*) Unusual twin crystal of wodginite/cassiterite. The size is about 6 × 4·5 × 3·5 cm.

wodgy (ˈwɒdʒɪ), *a.* [f. WODGE *sb.* + -Y[1].]

Solid, bulky. Also *fig.*

1907 PHYLLIS DARE *From School to Stage* v. 84 Not a London thin-bread-and-butter tea, but a great, wodgy, six-sliced repast. **1928** *Daily Express* 8 June 5/5 Wedding cakes . . are fattening and indigestible; they are 'wodgy' to the palate. **1978** *Daily Tel.* 30 Aug. 13 (*caption*) Swirl a piece of totally straight hair high, pin a little wodgy bun of bright crepe paper on over the kerby grips: that's Patrick Ales [*sic*] way. **1979** *Hi-Fi News* Dec. 169/2, I only wish I could be as totally enthusiastic about the recording. At average levels it is fine but sudden fortes come with a wodgy quality that is not at all pleasing; there are too many individual resonances for the ear to cope.

wodhacke, obs. f. WOODHACK.

wodhed, var. WOODHEAD.

Wodinsdai, obs. f. WEDNESDAY.

wodky, variant of VODKA.

wodland, -liche, -ly: see WOODLAND, WOODLY.

wodmell, obs. form of WADMAL.

1522 *Test. Ebor.* (Surtees) V. 154 A wodmell slope and a pare of breche of the same.

wodnes(s, var. WOODNESS.

wodou, obs. var. WOODOO.

wodowes, var. WOODWOSE.

wodowhod, obs. f. WIDOWHOOD.

wodrofe, -roffe, -rove: see WOODRUFF.

wodrome: see WODDRAM.

wodschipe, var. WOODSHIP, madness.

wodset(t, obs. ff. WADSET.

wodsore, -sour: see WOODSOUR.

wodur, obs. f. OTHER.

wodwale, -ward, -wose: see WOODWALE, WOODWARD, WOODWOSE.

woe (wəʊ), *int.*, *adv.*, *sb.*, *a.* Forms: α. 1–6, 8–9 *Sc.* and *north.* wa, 3–5, 9 *north.* waa, (*Sc.* or *north.* 4, 6, 9 way, 5 ua, 7 weay, 7–9 wea, 8 weea), 5– *Sc.* wae; (with *is*) *Sc.* 4, 6 wais, 6 waiss, wayis, 7 waies, wayes, 8 waes; (with *is the*) *Sc.* and *north.* 7 wee'st, 8 wae'st, wa-ist, wazist, 9 wa(a)st, waest; 5 *Sc. sup. of adj.* wast, wayest; 1 *Northumb.*, 3 *Lay.* wæ. β. 2– wo, (3 woa, wao, wuo, 4 who, 5 whoo, wooe, 6 *Sc.* voo, woi), 4–6 woo, 4– woe. γ. 3 *Orm.* waȝȝ, 2–3 wei, 3–4 wai, way, 4 weye, we. [Com. Indo-European interjection, used as a natural exclamation of lament; its forms fall into types distinguished by variety of vocalism, and reduplicated forms are characteristic of several of the Germanic langs.; most of these langs. have developed a substantival use of the simple forms (through such constructions as that in A. 6), and English and German have developed an adj. use.

OE. *wá*, also *wǽ*, corresp. to OS., MLG. *wê*, (M)Du. *wee*, OHG., MHG. *wê* (G. *weh*, also *wehe*), ON. *vei*, *vǽ* (Sw., Da. *ve*), Goth. *wai* οὐαί, and further to L. *væ*, Lett. *vai*, OIr. *fē*, W. *gwae*. (Arm. *vay* and late Gr. ὀά, οὐά, οὐαί are new formations.) Teut. **wai* is the source of the exclamations F. *ouais*, It. *guai*, Sp. *guay*.

The γ-forms are from ON. *vei* (cf. WELLAWAY). The spelling *wo* has been long prevalent in exclamatory use, and is still affected in poetry.

The forms properly substantival (as distinct from the above forms, which belong primarily to the int. and adv.) are:—OE. *wéa*, also the reduplicated *wáwa* WOWE, MLG. *wêwe*, OHG. *wêwo* m., *wêwa* f. (MHG. *wê*, gen. *wêwes* str. n., *wêwe*, *wéhe* wk. m., str. and wk. f.); otherwise the orig. interjectional forms are used as sbs.

OE. *wéa* entered into compounds in the sense of 'grievous, evil, bad'; one of these, *wéamód* peevish, survived into ME., see WEMOD; so Gothic *wai* in *waidēdja* ληστής (f. **waidēþs* = OE. *wéadǽd* crime), OHG. *wê* in *wêwurt* evil fate, misfortune; cf. Lett. *vājš* weak, ill.

Partially disguised compounds are WELLAWAY, WELLAWO, and WAIL *v*.]

A. *int.* and *adv.*

I. 1. a. As an exclamation of grief or lamentation: = Alas! Often in combination with another int., as *ah*, *lo* (see WALE *int.*, WELLAWO); cf. WAESUCKS. *arch.*

*c*725 *Corpus Gloss.* Int. 327 *Ua*, euwa [= eow + wa]. *c*1250 *Death* 167 in *O.E. Misc.* 178 Wai hwi noldestu er of þisse beon icnowe? 1297 R. GLOUC. (Rolls) 6446 Awey [*v.r.* awai] seli ȝonge þinges, frendles were hii þere. *c*1320 *Cast. Love* 188 A-wei, to sone he hit for-les. *c*1330 R. BRUNNE *Chron. Wace* (Rolls) 15879 Cried he neyþer wo ne way, But ded he was, & þer he lay.

*c*1400 *26 Pol. Poems* xxiv. 366 Allas, oure synnes..say, 'wo, wo, wo!' *c*1470 HENRY *Wallace* IV. 760 At hir he speryt giff scho forthocht it sar. 'Wa, ya', scho said. 1676 DRYDEN *Aurengz.* v. 76 Ah wo, wo, wo! the worst of woes I find! 1729 G. ADAMS tr. *Sophocles, Antig.* v. iv, Wo! and wo! Again, thou hast ruined an unhappy Man. 1854 PATMORE *Angel in Ho., Betrothal* 126 And if, ah woe, she loves alone.

†**b.** with following clause or phrase expressing the object of the lament. *Obs.*

*c*1175 *Lamb. Hom.* 21 O, seið þus þe boc, wei þet he eure hit wule iþenche in his þonke. *a*1250 *Owl & Night.* 120 Wai [*v.r.* way] þat hit nis þarof bireued. *c*1275 LAY. 8013 Wei þat ich nadde bi war. *a*1400 in *Minot's Poems* (ed. Hall) App. ii. 23 We for his Ending!

II. Construed with a dative (or, later, its equivalent), with or without a verb of being or happening, in sentences expressing the incidence of distress, affliction, or grief.

2. In prophetic or denunciatory utterances of the type of OE. *wá biþ þǽm mannum* = affliction or grief shall be the lot of the men; *woe be to us* = may affliction or distress light upon us; *woe is him* = cursed is he. *Obs.* or *arch.*

Beowulf 183 Wa bið þæm ðe sceal þurh sliðne nið sawle bescufan in fyres fæþm. 971 *Blickl. Hom.* 61 Wa biþ þonne þæm mannum þe ne onȝytaþ þisse worlde yrmþa. *a*1023 WULFSTAN *Hom.* xxx. (1883) 146 Wa byð ðam þe þær bið ȝeteohhod to. *c*1300 *Harrow. Hell* (Harl. MS.) 102 Wo ys him þat þe knowe ne shal! 13.. *Northern Passion* 249 (Camb. Gg.) Who be þat man At þat treson fyrst began. 1390 GOWER *Conf.* I. 98 Sche seide: 'Ha treson, wo thee be'. *a*1400–50 *Wars Alex.* 4564 Wailaway to wriches & wa is ȝow in erthe. *c*1400 MAUNDEV. (Roxb.) xiii. 55 Wa be to þe, Bethsaida! *c*1450 *Mirk's Festial* 4 Then woo schall be to hom þat schall here þys rebuke yn þat day. 1475 *Bk. Noblesse* (Roxb.) 41 Heh allas!..and woo be the tyme they saide, that ever we shulde put..trust to the Frenshe partie. 1533 FRITH *Mirr.* ii. A vij, Woe be to them that couple and knytte houses to gether. 1542 BOORDE *Dyetary* xvi. (1870) 273 Bacon is good for carters and plow-men,..but & yf they haue the stone,..they shall synge, 'wo be the pye!' *c*1560 A. SCOTT *Poems* (S.T.S.) xxxiv. 151 Waiss ȝow. 1567 *Gude & Godlie B.* (S.T.S.) 187 Way is the Hirdis of Israell. 1583 STUBBES *Anat. Abus.* II. (1882) 59 Woe were vs, if wee were at the rule and gouernement of creatures. 1636 EARL MANCH. *Al Mondo* (ed. 3) 162 Woe is him whose bed is made in hell. 1680 in *Proc. Soc. Antiq. Scot.* XLV. 246 Woes us that we can nether shew nor receive kindness without danger. 1748 RICHARDSON *Clarissa* (1768) V. 25 Wo be to the Villain, if he recollect not this! *c*1860 FABER *Child's Death* vi, Thou are welcome, thrice welcome:—yet woe is the day! 1880 BLACKMORE *Mary Anerley* xi, But woe is him, if a nasty foe ..smite him to the quick.

3. a. In merely declaratory statements of the type of OE. *him bið* or *is wá* = he will be or is distressed, afflicted, grieved, or sorrowful; ME. *him is (full) wo* = he is (much) distressed or grieved. *Obs.* exc. as in b.

*c*893 ÆLFRED *Oros.* III. vii, þæm folce wæs æȝþres waa, ȝe þæt hie þæt mæste yfel forberan sceoldon, ȝe eac þæt hie his sciran ne dorstan. *a*1000 *Sal. & Sat.* 104 Huru him bið æt heartan wa, ðonne he hangiende helle wisceð ðæs engestan eðelrices. *c*1200 *Trin. Coll. Hom.* 149 *Tedet anima mea uite mee.* Wuo is mi soule þat ich bide here swo longe. *c*1200 ORMIN 11904 Himm wass waȝȝ & ange Off þatt he nohht ne wisste off Crist. *c*1205 LAY. 1660 Swa swiðe wa him was þat al his wit he for-læs. *a*1225 *Ancr. R.* 96 Me is wo þet tu hit wost. *a*1250 *Owl & Night.* 882 þat beoþ her, wo is hom þes. *a*1300 *Cursor M.* 3749 Me es sua waa, almast i weede. *c*1380 *Sir Ferumb.* 209 Him was ful wo þan on is þoȝt, & ofte sekede amonge. ? *a*1400 *Morte Arth.* 2684 Be alle the welthe of the werlde, so woo was theme neuer! *c*1450 *St. Cuthbert* (Surtees) 816 Cuthbert sawe, him was full wa.

b. very freq. in ***woe is me*** (occas. †*to, unto me*): I am distressed, afflicted, unfortunate, grieved. Now only *arch.* and *dial.*

*c*1205 LAY. 28345 Wa is me þat ich was mon iboren. *a*1240 *Ureisun* in *O.E. Hom.* I. 185 Wa is me þet ic am swa fremede wiþ þe! *c*1375 *Sc. Leg. Saints* xxxiii. (*George*) 146 Wais me, douchtir, for þe. *a*1400–50 *Wars Alex.* 3075 'Wa is me!' quod he,..'wa is me vnhappy!' *c*1400 *Anturs Arth.* 196 (Douce MS.) 'Wo is me for þi wo!' quod Waynour. *c*1480 HENRYSON *Swallow & Other Birds* 265 Now ar þaj deid, and wo is me þairfore! 1513 DOUGLAS *Æneis* XI. i. 133 Bot netheles, quhat harm, ful wayis me! 1526 TINDALE *1 Cor.* ix. 16 Wo is it vnto me [WYCLIF wo to me, COVERDALE wo vnto me, 1611 Woe is vnto me] yf I preache not the gospell. 1579 SPENSER *Sheph. Cal.* Sept. 25 My sheepe bene wasted, (wae is me therefore). 1683 G. M[ERITON] *Yorks. Dial.* 6 Waies is me Husband, our awd Breads all gane. 1729 G. ADAMS tr. *Sophocles, Antig.* II. v, Wo is me a Wretch! 1785 BURNS *Death & Dr. Hornbook* xxiii, Waes me for Johnie Ged's Hole now..if that thae news be true! 1842 TENNYSON *Morte d' Arth.* 120 To whom replied King Arthur, much in wrath: 'Ah, miserable and unkind, untrue, ..Woe is me!' 1892 FURNIVALL *Hoccleve's Minor Poems* p. xliv, Lastly (woe is me!) I printed it in 1878 from [etc.].

4. a. ***woe worth*** (in 16th and 17th cent. sometimes hyphened): may evil befall or light upon; a curse upon; cursed be or shall be: often in phr. ***woe worth the day*** (***the while, the time***). *arch.*

*c*1205 LAY. 1562 Wa wrðe auer þene smið. *c*1230 *Hali Meid.* (1922) 37 Wa wurðe þat chaffere. *c*1275 LAY. 8011 Wo worþe onread [*earlier text* Wale wale vnræd]. 1340 HAMPOLE *Pr. Consc.* 7396 Cursed kaytif and wa worth þe. *c*1350 *Will. Palerne* 4118 And ȝif i wrong seie any word, wo worþ me euer. *a*1400 *Sir Perc.* 139 'Wo worthe wykkyde armour!' Percyvelle may say. *a*1470 HENRY *Wallace* IV. 744 Allace That I was maide, wa worthe the coursit cas! *a*1500 *Chaucer's Dreme* 1715 Alas my birth, wo worth my life. 1549 LATIMER *Ploughers* (Arb.) 34 Wo worth the, O Deuyll, wo worth the,..that thou haste made Englande to worshyppe false Goddes. 1563 *Homilies* II. *Passion* II. 199 May we not iustly crye wo worth the tyme that euer we synned? 1593 NASHE *Christ's T.* 66 Fall England, farewell peace, woe-worth our Weale and tranquillitie. 1683 G. M[ERITON] *Yorks. Dial.* 16 Weayworth this Trash. 1684 BUNYAN *Pilgr.* II. 7 Then they all wept again, and cryed out: Oh, Wo worth the day. 1714 GAY *Sheph. Week* I. 17 Woe worth the Tongue! may Blisters sore it gall, That names Buxoma, Blouzelind withal. 1785 BURNS *Sc. Drink* xv, Wae worth that brandy, burnin trash! 1810 SCOTT *Lady of L.* I. ix, Woe worth the chase, woe worth the day, That costs thy life, my gallant grey! 1870 LOWELL *Study Wind.* 244 Woe worth the hour that I beheld thee born.

†**b.** As an independent exclamation: = sense 1.

1553 T. WILSON *Rhet.* I. 43 Wo worthe, thei are dedde. 1598 MARSTON *Sco. Villanie* I. 23 Woe worth when trees drop in their proper kinde!

¶ **c.** ***woe worth me!*** used occas. loosely = *woe is me.*

1887 SWINBURNE *Locrine* v. ii, *Estrild.* Woe worth me! *Sabrina.* Nay, woe worth Her wickedness. 1891 CONAN DOYLE *White Company* ix, Wo worth me when Agatha the tire-woman sets eyes upon it!

d. Similarly, ***woe betide you*** (etc.). In mod. use *colloq.* with weakened sense: You (etc.) will get into trouble (if...). Also without obj.

1362 LANGL. *P. Pl.* A. II. 86 And ar þis weddyng beo wrouȝt wo þe beo-tyde! *Ibid.* III. 116 Er Ich wedde such a wyf wo me bi-tyde! 1588 SHAKS. *Tit. A.* IV. ii. 56 Now helpe, or woe betide thee euermore. 1808 [see BETIDE *v.* 1 c]. 1819 KEATS *La belle Dame sans Merci* ix, And there I dream'd, ah! woe betide, The latest dream I ever dream'd. 1819 SCOTT *Ivanhoe* xxvi[i], Go to the sick man's chamber..; and woe betide you if you again quit it without my permission! 1840 DICKENS *Old Cur. Shop* vi, If you're not sharp enough I'll creak the door, and wo betide you if I have to creak it much. 1868 [see BETIDE *v.* 1 c].

5. Without verb. **a.** const. dative (or its equivalent) = *woe be, woe worth, woe betide. arch.*

*c*897 ÆLFRED *Gregory's Past. C.* xliv. 328 Hit is ȝecweden: Wa eow þe gadriað hus to huse. *Ibid.* xlix. 378 Wa me ðæs ic swuȝode! 971 *Blickl. Hom.* 25 Wa eow þe nu hlihaþ. *c*1000 *Ags. Gosp.* Matt. xviii. 7 Wa þysum middan-ȝearde þurh swicdomas. *c*1200 *Vices & Virtues* 19 Wa hem ð att hie æure iscapene waren. 1382 WYCLIF *Rev.* viii. 13, I..herde the voys of an egle..seiynge..Wo! wo! wo! to the dwellinge men in erthe. 1390 GOWER *Conf.* II. 355 Wo the while, he was a thief! *c*1400 LOVE *Bonavent. Mirr.* (1908) 139 Woo to vs ȝif we wole folewe hym that wolde sette his fete in the hille of lordschippe. *c*1460 *Play Sacram.* 853 Woo the whyle that bargayn I dyd euer make. 1535 COVERDALE *1 Cor.* ix. 16 And wo vnto me [1611 woe is vnto me], yff I preach not the Gospell. 1589 GREENE *Menaphon* (Arb.) 55 Then woe mine eyes vnlesse they beautie see. 1610 SHAKS. *Temp.* I. ii. 15 O woe, the day. 1697 DRYDEN *Virg. Georg.* III. 389 Wo to him, that in the desart Land Of Lybia travels. 1721 RAMSAY *Prospect of Plenty* 25 Wae to that hand that dares..Defile the stream. 1794 BURNS *Song, Lovely Lass Inverness* 13 Now wae to thee, thou cruel lord, A bluidy man I trow thou be. 1829 DIGBY *Broad Stone Hon., Godefridus* 205 But woe the while! our fathers' minds are dead. 1842 LYTTON *Zanoni* I. ii, Woe to thine ears hadst thou heard the barbiton that night!

b. const. preps. *on*, *for*.

1823 SCOTT *Quentin D.* xxx, Some articles we will minute down with which he shall comply, or wo on his head! 1851 CARLYLE *Sterling* I. xiv, It has ended thus. Wo on it! 1852 MRS. STOWE *Uncle Tom's C.* xxvi, Oh, woe for them..when they shall wake!

†**6.** ***to do*** or ***work*** (a person) ***woe***: to inflict distress or trouble upon; to afflict; to do harm to. Also without regimen. *Obs.*

Orig. *woe* is adv. in this phr., but later apprehended as sb. (B. 1). (Cf. other langs., e.g. G. *weh(e tun.*)

*c*1000 *Ags. Ps.* (Th.) cxviii. 138 þa me grame wæron worda þinra, and me wa dydan. *a*1200 *Moral Ode* 289 in *O.E. Hom.* I. 177 Ac ȝet ne deð heom nout so wo in þo loþe biende bute þat hi witeð þat heore pine ne scal neure habben ende. *a*1225 *Ancr. R.* 364 Is hit nu wisdom mon to don so wo him suluen? *c*1230 *Hali Meid.* (1922) 49 Hu moni earmðen anan awakeneð þer-wið, þat wurcheð þe wa inoh. *c*1250 *Gen. & Ex.* 880 Abram hem folwede and wroȝte woa. *Ibid.* 2100 Ðeden ut-comen .vii. neet,..And .vii. lene after ðo, Ðe deden ðe .vii. fette wo. *a*1300 *Cursor M.* 5531 Bot ai þe mare þai did [þ]am wa þis folk multiplid ai maa. *c*1375 *Sc. Leg. Saints* xxx. (*Theodera*) 624 þe feynd, oure fa, Cesit nocht to wirk hyr way. *c*1400 *26 Pol. Poems* x. 65, I do þe wele, why dost me woo? *c*1425 WYNTOUN *Cron.* I. xvi. 1571 Iubiter sulde noucht..wyrk hym mar wa na dispyte. *a*1500 *Bernard. de cura rei fam.* III. 55 He kest the stone in þe watter, & bad it waa worghe. 1509 HAWES *Past. Pleas.* XVIII. (Percy Soc.) 86 It doth right well appere..that love hath done you wo. 1553 *Respublica* 1648 Theis ladies..prepare to weorke vs woo and doo vs all mischiefe.

B. *sb.* (See also A. 6.)

1. a. A condition of misery, affliction, or distress; misfortune, trouble; grievous or sorrowful state. *poet.* or *rhet.* Freq. in phr. ***tale of woe***, a narrative of (one's) misfortunes. Now usu. *joc.*

*c*1200 ORMIN 897 Baþe hemm fell to þolenn wa þurrh ifell wifess irre. *Ibid.* 4766 Tenn menn..Forrlæs þe gode Job þatt daȝȝ,..& ȝet bilammþ himm oþerr wa. *c*1250 *Gen. & Ex.* 237 Issa was hire firste name..Siðen ȝhe brocte us to woa, Adam gaf hire name eua. 1297 R. GLOUC. (Rolls) 7770 þe king & oþer riche men..wolde euere abbe ynou wanne þe pouere adde wo. *a*1300 *Cursor M.* 2196 Nembrot..þat in his time wroght mikel waa. 13.. *Ibid.* 22472 (Edin.) Quar-to sold we be born to-day, Quen al þing sal com to way? *c*1375 *Sc. Leg. Saints* vi. (*Thomas*) 250 He vald firste quyke þam fla, & bryne þame syne in doile & va. *c*1400 *Rom. Rose* 4951 Youthe hem putte in Iupardye, In perell and in mych woo. *c*1480 HENRYSON *Prais of Aige* 12 Wrechitnes has wroht all welthis wele to wo. 1523 LD. BERNERS *Froiss.* I. ccccxxxiv. 308 b/2 The capitayne..had dayly great payne and wo to defende their towne. 1592 SHAKS. *Rom. & Jul.* v. iii. 309 For neuer was a Storie of more Wo, Then this of Iuliet, and her Romeo. 1655 MILTON *Sonn. Massacre Piedmont* 14 From these may grow A hunder'd-fold, who.. Early may fly the Babylonian wo. 1667 —— *P.L.* I. 3 The Fruit Of that Forbidden Tree, whose mortal tast Brought Death into the World, and all our woe. 1770 GOLDSM. *Des. Vill.* 160 Pleased with his guests, the good man learned to glow, And quite forgot their vices in their woe. 1790 COLERIDGE *Genevieve* 8 Within your soul a voice there lives! It bids you hear the tale of Woe. 1813 BYRON *Giaour* 983 My days, though few, have pass'd below In much of joy, but more of woe. 1814 —— *Lara* I. ii, Lord of himself,—that heritage of woe. 1821 SCOTT *Kenilw.* xxii, A screech-owl denouncing some deed of terror and of wo. 1837 CARLYLE *Fr. Rev.* III. II. viii, This scene of wo. 1848 MRS. GASKELL *Mary Barton* iii, Her giddiness, her lightness of conduct, had wrought this woe. 1882 E. FIELD *Compl. Tribune Primer* 111 (*heading*) A tale of woe. 1951 *Sport* 16–22 Mar. 4/2 Listen to the tale of woe from Swindon Town, who.. suffered their 16th away league defeat... Swindon..lost goalkeeper Norman Uprichard at a goalless stage of the game. 1967 BAKER & JONES *Coffee, Tea or Me?* xvi. 199 Kelman savored a crisp piece of sausage pizza as he thought about our tale of woe. 1973 *Times* 11 June 18/8 Yet it is not all a tale of woe. An entirely new management structure has been brought into force, and Liverpool was the first port in the world to link a computer service to its cargo handling.

personified. *c*1400 *Rom. Rose* 4995 With hir labour and travaile Logged ben with sorwe and woo.

b. in conjunction with *weal*.

*c*1250 *Gen. & Ex.* 216 A fruit, ðe kenned wel and wo. 13.. *K. Alis.* 3449 There his folk come wel or weye, Him tofore nys bote deth. *a*1340 HAMPOLE *Psalter* i. 2 Day & nyght, þ[t] is assiduelly, in wele & wa. *c*1375 *Sc. Leg. Saints* xxxiii. (*George*) 235 Fore wele na way Of þis place sal I nocht ga. *c*1385 CHAUCER *L.G.W.* 687 *Cleopatra*, ȝe nere out of myn hertis remembraunce For wel or wo for carole or for daunce. *c*1400 *26 Pol. Poems* v. 66 God haþ lent ȝow discrecioun Boþe of wele and of woo. 1567 *Gude & Godlie B.* (S.T.S.) 182 Greit cause thay haif for till repent, Zot will thay nocht do so, Nouther for weill nor wo. 1812 J. WILSON *Isle of Palms* I. 351 Whate'er betide of weal or woe. 1860 MOTLEY *Netherl.* vi. I. 299 Two important commonwealths, upon whose action..the weal and wo of Christendom was hanging.

c. In particularized use; chiefly *pl.*, Misfortunes, troubles, griefs.

1382 WYCLIF *Rev.* ix. 12 Oo woo passid, and lo! ȝit comen two wos. 1567 *Satir. Poems Reform.* iii. 153 All the wois that Ouid in Ibin Into his pretty lytill buik did wryte. *a*1568 MONTGOMERIE *Misc. Poems* iii. 9 That curst inconstant cative till accuse, Quhais variance of all my wois I wyt. 1599 DRAYTON *Heroic. Ep., Q. Isab. to Mortimer* 16 One woe makes another woe seeme lesse. 1642 J. TAYLOR (Water P.) *Mad Fashions* A 2 b, Those Rebells that doe breed her [*sc.* Ireland's] woes. 1697 DRYDEN *Æneis* XII. 892 Latinus tears his Garments as he goes, Both for his publick, and his private Woes. 1714 YOUNG *Force Relig.* I. 258 Now she revolves within her anxious mind, What woe still lingers in reserve behind. *a*1720 SEWEL *Hist. Quakers* (1795) I. 61 The Lord sent me to you, to warn you of the woes that are coming upon you. 1832 W. IRVING *Alhambra* I. xii. 152 Who has not been touched with the woes of his lovely and gentle queen, subjected by him to a trial of life and death, on a false charge of infidelity? 1920 *Discovery* May 146 The most fundamental cause of all our present economic woes.

†**d.** *transf.* A cause of misfortune. *Obs. rare.*

*c*1400 *Beryn* 1176 My wele, my woo, my paradise, my lyvis sustenaunce!

†**2. a.** Physical pain or distress; disease or infirmity. *Obs.* or merged in sense 1.

a **1225** *Ancr. R.* 220 He lette ham þolien wo inouh—hunger & þurst, & muchel swinc. **1297** R. Glouc. (Rolls) 1918 He was.. pur mesel þo, & he bicom in is baptizinge hol of al is wo. **13..** *Northern Passion* 49 (Camb. Gg.) þai.. dyd hym tyll pyne and waa And euer þai thoght hym for to slaa. **1340–70** *Alex. & Dind.* 1033 A litil wetinge of watur his wo wol amende. *a* **1400–50** *Wars Alex.* 539, I am all in aunter sa akis me þe wame, Of werke well ne I wede & slike wa tholis. *c* **1425** *Hampole's Psalter* Metr. Pref. 36 Thys holy man.. keuord mony of hur wo, the doumbe, the defe, and other seke. [**1783** Crabbe *Village* I. 227 Thus groan the old, till, by disease oppress'd, They taste a final woe, and then they rest.]

b. With reference to the pains of hell.

c **1200** Ormin Ded. 209 To takenn ut off helle wa þa gode sawless alle. *Ibid.* 1400 Forr whatt teȝȝ fellenn sone dun off heoffne unntill helle Till eche wa. *c* **1290** *St. James* 77 in *S. Eng. Leg.* 36 þou sendest us þare we gret wo ifielde In gret torment and brenningue. *c* **1315** Shoreham vii. 534 þus þe deuel ydampned hys, And wyþ hym.. Deuelen wel mo;.. Moche hys þe pyne þat hem eyleþ, And eke þe who. *c* **1400** *26 Pol. Poems* i. 108 The more he dwelleth theryn long, To his soule he encreseth woo. **1781** *Transl. & Paraphr.* xli. 8 Who looks to him with lively faith is sav'd from endless woes.

†**3.** Sorrow, grief, anguish (as a state of mind or feeling). *Obs.* or merged in sense 1.

a **1300** *K. Horn* 263 Heo louede so horn child þat.. In heorte heo hadde wo. *c* **1350** *Will. Palerne* 1483 Neiȝh wod of witte for woo of þat sawe. **13..** *Gaw. & Gr. Knt.* 1717 With alle þe wo on lyue, To þe wod he [*sc.* the fox] went away. *c* **1400** *Destr. Troy* 1360 Mony wyues, for woo, of þere wit past. *c* **1410** Hoccleve *Mother of God* 57 Tendrely remembre on the wo & peyne, þat thow souffridist in his passioun. *c* **1530** *Crt. Love* 256 'For-soth, quod she, 'they wailen of their wo.' *c* **1560** A. Scott *Poems* (S.T.S.) xxv. 21 My hairt, tak nowdir pane nor wa, For Meg, for Meriory, or ȝit Mawis. **1620** J. Taylor (Water P.) *Jack a Lent* C 2, The poore Curres.. stinke for woe for feare that another Lent is come sodainely vpon them. [**1709** Prior *Henry & Emma* 118 His down-cast Eye reveals his inward Woes. **1719** Young *Busiris* i. i, While the big Woe lies throbbing at my Heart.]

†**4.** Lamentation, mourning. Chiefly in phr. *to make woe*. *Obs.*

c **1300** *Havelok* 465 Godard herde here wa, Ther-offe yaf he nouth a stra. **13..** *K. Alis.* 2360 (Laud MS.), Michel woo & grete wailynges Was made. *c* **1385** Chaucer *L.G.W.* 1839 *Lucrece*, The woo to telle hyt were impossible, That she and al hir frendes make attones. *c* **1412** Hoccleve *De Reg. Princ.* 1057 For shame! why makest þou al this wo? **1508** Dunbar *Tua Mariit Wemen* 437, I haif a water spunge for wa, within my wyde clokis, Than wring I it full wylely, & wetis my chekis.

5. An utterance of the word 'woe' in denunciation; an anathema, curse.

c **1400** *Apol. Loll.* p. xi, Her enden the eighte woois that God wishid to freris. Amen. **1546** Bale *Engl. Votaries* i. 75 He went fearcelye vpon them with wo vpon wo. **1637** Rutherford *Let. to Ld. Craighall* 10 Aug., There is a *woe, woe to him by whom offences come*: This woe came out of Christ's mouth. **1638** *Penit. Conf.* vii. (1657) 146 A necessity is laid upon us with a woe, and an Anathema, if we come not to confession. **1818** Scott *Hrt. Midl.* xxii, She bore a male-child, under circumstances which added treble bitterness to the wo denounced against our original mother. **1821** Mrs. Wheeler *App. Cumbld. Dial.* 9 Here it was (a way light on the pleace!) At first I got a gliff o' Betty's feace. **1867** Lady Herbert *Cradle L.* viii. 228 The woe.. pronounced by the Saviour—that woe so literally fulfilled.

6. *attrib.* and *Comb.*: simple attrib., as ***woe-hurricane***, ***-mark***, ***-trumpet*** (Rev. viii, ix); also adj. = woeful (cf. C), as †***woe-day***, †***-thing***, †***-word***; objective, as ***woe-begetting***, ***-boding***, ***-denouncing***, ***-foreboding***, ***-revolving*** adjs.; instrumental, as ***woe-adumbred***, ***-beseen***, ***-bested***, ***-cross-wounded*** (see cross- B), ***-dejected***, ***-delighted***, ***-embroidered***, ***-exhausted***, ***-fraught***, ***-illumed***, ***-infirmed***, ***-stricken***, ***-struck***, ***-surcharged***, ***-tied***, ***-wearied***, ***-weary***, ***-whelmed***, ***-worn*** adjs.; ***woe-enwrap***, ***-wrinkle*** vbs.; in other advb. relations, as ***woe-betrothed***, ***-destined***, ***-sprung***, ***-wedded*** adjs.; †***woe-heart*** [cf. C. 1 b, d], an affliction; also wosith.

1609 J. Davies *Holy Roode* I 1, Thy *Woe-adumbred Front. **1760–72** H. Brooke *Fool of Qual.* (1809) IV. 3 The natural progeny of that *wo-begetting parent. **1390** Gower *Conf.* III. 370 Al my face.. So riveled and so *wo besein. *c* **1470** Harding *Chron.* xliii. ii, Full *wo bystad.. with sorowe and with care. *c* **1510** More *Picus* Wks. 29 If thou be neuer so wo bestad. *c* **1530** *Crt. Love* 845 Ye made me wo-bestad. **1777** Potter *Æschylus, Supplicants* 75 My bursting heart.. *woe-betroth'd, fears e'en its friends. **1838** Eliza Cook *World* iv, The raven.. with its *woe-boding tone. **1609** J. Davies *Holy Roode* F 2, Comfort.. Her *woe-crosse-wounded Heart. *c* **1205** Lay. 8750 Nu is icumen þin *wa-dæi. *c* **1346** *Pol. Poems* (Rolls) I. 48 Ipsis sit Waleway, meschef tristissima woday. *a* **1796** Burns *Bannocks o' Barley*, Wha in his wae-days Were loyal to Charlie? **1786** —— *To Ruin* 4 Thy cruel, *woe-delighted train. **1809** Campbell *Gert. Wyoming* iii. xvi, [He] smote his breast with *woe-denouncing hand. **1796** Eliza Hamilton *Lett. Hindoo Rajah* (1811) I. 86 The.. years, which might change the abode of the souls of these tyrant whites into the frames of *woe-destined negroes. **1729** Savage *Wanderer* ii. 203 She muses o'er her *woe-embroider'd Vest. **1593** Nashe *Christ's T.* 26 Adams fall neuer so *woe-enwrapped the earth, as the relation of them shall. **1797** Mrs. M. Robinson *Walsingham* III. 56 The *woe-exhausted poet. **1854** J. S. C. Abbott *Napoleon* (1855) I. ii. 56 The beleaguered and woe-exhausted city. **1813** Scott *Rokeby* i. xxviii, Three banners.. The *woe-foreboding peasant sees. **1797** T. Park *Sonn.* 103 *Woe-fraught breast of kesar or of queen. **1818** Holder *Poems* 69 From whose woe-fraught bosom break Those dismal cries? **1639** Rutherford *Let. to Vsctess. Kenmure* 1 Oct., I hope that Christ, when he married you, married you and all the crosses and *wo hearts that follow you. **1818** Keats *Endym.* iv. 527 *Woe-hurricanes beat ever at the gate. **1820** Shelley *Prometh. Unb.* i. i. 637, I.. see more clear Thy works within my *woe-illumed mind. **1593** Nashe *Christ's T.* Ep. Ded., My *woe-infirmed Witte, conspired against me. **1848** Mrs. Gaskell *Mary Barton* ix, The distress.. which was crushing their lives out of them, and stamping *woe-marks over the land. **1824** Symmons tr. *Æschylus, Agamemnon* 65 Many a *woe-revolving year [πολύθρηνον αἰῶν']. **1776** Mickle tr. *Camoens' Lusiad* 276 Their *woe-sprung tears shall sue. **1850** Thackeray *Pendennis* lvii, Arthur could not see how pallid and *woe-stricken her face was. **1770** Hodson *Ded. Temple of Solomon* 5 The Fury of the *Woe-struck King. **1828** Carlyle *Misc., Werner* (1840) I. 169 A certain woestruck martyr zeal. **1615** Brathwait *Strappado* 97 A *Woe-surcharged heart. **1675** Cotton *Burlesque upon B.* 6 What! must I undergoe this *wo-thing, And suffer thus for doing nothing? **1619** Drayton *Bar. Wars* vi. xcv, Her *woe-ty'd Tongue. **1680** C. Nesse *Church-Hist.* 493 While the Church lay under the *Wo-Trumpets. **1826** E. Irving *Babylon* iii. I. 196 We expect the seventh trumpet, the last of the three woe trumpets. **1615** Chapman *Odyss.* xix. 700 When all poore men.. Would.. get their *wo-watcht pow'rs relieu'd. **1594** Shaks. *Rich. III*, iv. iv. 18 My *woe-wearied tongue. *c* **1350** *Will. Palerne* 793 He slod sliȝli a-doun a-slepe ful harde, as a *wo wery weiȝh for-waked to-fore. **1393** Langl. *P. Pl.* C. xxi. 1 Wo-werie and wet-schod wente ich forth after. **1613** J. Davies *Muses Teares* C 3, When thou.. Cam'st to espouse his Halfe; *wo-wedded now! **1777** Potter *Æschylus, Agamemnon* 255 On its woe-wedded [αἰνόλεκτρον] Paris' hated head. **1875** Browning *Aristoph. Apol., Herakles* 851 This.. I pondered, though *woe-whelmed. *a* **1225** *Ancr. R.* 306 Heren þat harde word, þat *waword. **1601** *Mary Magd. Lament.* ii. 132 Poore *wo-worn woman. **1799** *Cupid & Psyche* 46 These wan and woe-worn cheeks of mine. **1857** Mrs. Gaskell *C. Brontë* II. xiii. 324 She saw her husband's woe-worn face. **1871** Swinburne *Songs bef. Sunrise, Halt bef. Rome* 86 The woe-worn people. **1593** Nashe *Christ's T.* 29 Let me.. waxe olde and *woe-wrinckle my cheekes.

C. *adj.* (orig. and chiefly predicative).

This use has developed by a process common to the history of impersonal expressions in which an original dative has been converted into a nominative; *me is wo* became *I am wo*, as *me longeth* became *I long*.

1. a. Grieved, wretched, miserable, sorrowful. *Obs.* exc. *Sc.* and *north. dial.*

The first instance, like many more in early ME., is doubtful, because it is impossible to determine whether *sancte paul* is dative (See A. 3) or nominative.

c **1175** *Lamb. Hom.* 45 þa wes sancte paul swiðe wa and abeh him.. to his lauerdes fet. *c* **1200** *Trin. Coll. Hom.* 173 Ðanne stondeð þo wreches alse þo þe wo beð. *a* **1300** *Cursor M.* 14546 His disciplis þan war ful waa, þat þair maister was hated sua. **1340** Hampole *Pr. Consc.* 1452 Now er men wele, now er men wa. *c* **1375** *Sc. Leg. Saints* iii. (*Andreas*) 799 þan was egeas wondir wa, þat saw hym-self confundit sa. **1399** *Pol. Poems* (Rolls) I. 364 The swan is ded; his make is woo. *c* **1470** Henry *Wallace* i. 401 Willȝham was wa he had na wappynis thar. **1470–85** Malory *Arthur* viii. xxxix. 334 Ful wo was la Beale Isoud. **1515** *Let.* in *Douglas' Poet. Wks.* (1874) I. Biogr. Introd. p. xxiii, I am ryght sory and voo therfor. **1523–34** Fitzherb. *Husb.* §15 It is an olde saying, 'The oxe is neuer wo, tyll he to the harowe goo'. **1535** Coverdale *Jer.* xxii. 10 Mourne not ouer the deed, and be not wo for them. **1567** *Satir. Poems Reform.* iii. 10 My freind, quhat makis the sa way? **1632** Holland *Cyrupædia* 130 Cyrus understanding that Gadatas was long since full woe and even out of the world for feare. **1637** Rutherford *Lett., to T. Corbet* (1671) 173 If it be not so, I will be woe to be a witness against them. *a* **1648** Ld. Herbert *Hen. VIII* (1683) 515 He was woe that ever she came into England. **1700** Dryden *Wife of Bath's T.* 108 Woe was the Knight at this severe Command! **1721** Kelly *Sc. Prov.* 211, I am wae for your Skathe. **1816** Scott *Bl. Dwarf* vii, I'm wae ye suld hae cause to say sae. **1835** Mrs. Carlyle *Lett.* (1883) I. 44 Poor Queen!.. I was wae to look at her, wae to think of her. **1887** Hall Caine *Deemster* xxxv, She had grown 'wae' as folk said.

in comp. and sup. forms.

1375 Barbour *Bruce* xvi. 245 Micht no man se ane vrather [*MS. E.* waer] man. *a* **1400–50** *Wars Alex.* 2004 And he þe waest [*v.r.* woest] of þe werd. **14..** *Chaucer's Compl. Pite* 3 (Phillipps MS.) In this worlde was no wight woer. *c* **1450** Holland *Howlat* 963, I couth nocht won in to welth wretch wast [*v.r.* wayest]. *c* **1475** *Partenay* 2855 More neuer ne [? he] was woer at no stounde Then off that he hade wrethed so Raymounde.

b. Said of the heart or soul, and in phr. *woe in heart*, etc.; esp. in north. dial. phr. ***wae's t'heart*** (***wast-heart***, ***waestart***, etc.) = woe is me! alas!

The earliest quots. are doubtful: cf. 1 above.

c **1205** Lay. 2260 Corineus wes un-eðe & wa on his mode. *a* **1300** *K. Horn* 275 þe stuard was in herte wo, For he nuste what to do. *c* **1375** *Cursor M.* 12440 (Fairf.) For-soþ myne hert is wa. *c* **1400** *Gamelyn* 335 Gamelyn in his hert was ful woo. *c* **1420** *Chron. Vilod.* 3446 He nas neuer ere so sore aferde Ny neuer in hert half so wo. **1591** Drayton *Harmony Ch.* (Roxb.) 26 Oh holy blessed Sion hill! my heart is woe for thee. **1600** W. Watson *Decacordon* (1602) 266 How woe my hart was. **1695** [see wee't heart]. **1703** Thoresby *Let. to Ray* Gloss. (E.D.S.), *Wae'st heart*, a condolence to the same purport with *wae's me*, woe is the heart, &c. **1728** Ramsay *Anacreontic on Love* 11 With his complaint my soul grew wae. **1773** Fergusson *Ode Gowdspink* 21 'Mang men, wae's-heart! we aften find The brawest drest want peace o' mind. **1786** Burns *Twa Dogs* 94 An' mony a time my heart's been wae. **1829** J. Hunter *Hallamsh. Gloss., Wast-heart-a-day*, an expression of grief or of commiseration. **1854** *N. & Q.* 1st Ser. IX. 349/2 *Waestart*, a common expression of sorrow or condolence among the lower classes.. around Leeds. **1894** R. Bridges *A Robin* iv, She was not there, and my heart is woe.

†**c.** In exclamations similar to those in A. 2, 3.

a **1300** *Cursor M.* 22105 Corozaim, ai be ye waa! And sua be ye beth[s]aida! *c* **1340** Hampole *Wks.* (Horstman) I. 165 Wo is he þat wotnot [etc.]. *c* **1375** *Sc. Leg. Saints* vii. (*Jacobus Minor*) 332 Iervsalem, euir va þu be! *c* **1435** *Torr. Portugale* 1691 This Giaunt hym toke, wo he be! **1520** *Calisto & Melib.* C ij b, A baudy wych Callyd celystyne that wo myght she be.

d. In attrib. relation (cf. *woe-day*, etc. in B. 6). *Obs.* or *dial.*

a **1670** Spalding *Troub. Chas. I* (Bannatyne Club) I. 125 Some.. left their lodgeings desolate,.. with wae and sorry hearts. **1728** Theobald *Double Falsehood* iv. i, If he have a Mother,.. she's a Woe-woman for him at this Hour. **1778** H. Brooke *Female Officer* ii. iii, I am a woe woman this heavy day. **1913** N. Munro in *Blackw. Mag.* Dec. 784/2 The wae wee chirrup of the yellow-yite.

†**2.** Of an event, situation, etc.: Woeful, miserable, 'sorry'. *Obs.*

1588 *Marprel. Epist.* (Arb.) 38 Then alas, he was in a woe case. **1612** Day *Festivals* vi. (1615) 155 Were it not for Bread, it would be woe with Mankind. **1638** Heywood *Wise Woman* iii. i, I hope so, or else I were in a woe case. **1642** J. Eaton *Honey-c. Free Justif.* 69 If he did, it would soone bee woe with us all. **1795** Southey *Joan of Arc* vi. 256 Oh! woe it is to think So many men shall never see the sun Go down!

woe-begone ('wəʊbɪgɒn, -ɔː-), *a.* (*sb.*) [The construction out of which this word arose is illustrated by the quots. immediately following, in which an objective pron. is governed by a compound tense of bego (q.v. sense 8) with woe *sb.* as subject (*me is wo bigon* = woe has beset me):—

c **1330** *Amis & Amil.* 2150 Me nas neuer so woe bigon, Yif thou it wost vnderstond! For.. almost ichaue him slon. *c* **1386** Chaucer *Frankl. T.* 588 Noght wolde I telle how me is wo bigon But certes outher moste I dye or pleyne.

Subsequently a change of construction took place, parallel to the passing of *me is woe* into *I am woe* (see woe *a.*), *woe* and *begone* becoming consequently so indivisibly associated as to form a compound.

In the following quot. there seems to be a blend of the old and new constructions:

1593 T. Watson *Tears of Fancie* xxxviii, My hart doth whisper I am woe begone me.]

1. 'Beset with woe'; oppressed with misfortune, distress, sorrow, or grief. *Obs.* or *arch.*

13.. *Guy Warw.* (A.) 312 He went and trent his bed opon, So man þat is wo bigon. ? *a* **1366** Chaucer *Rom. Rose* 336 In worlde nys wyght so harde of herte.. That nolde haue had of her pyte So wo begone a thyng was she. **1390** Gower *Conf.* II. 272 Hellen.., Which of the See was wo bego, For pure drede hire herte hath lore. **13..** *Northern Passion* (1913) I. 140 Tyll anoynt with all his seke body þat waylid was and wa began. *c* **1430** *Pol. Rel. & L. Poems* (1903) 207 þou myȝtist haue holpe ȝong & oolde þat ben disesid and woo-bigoon. *c* **1460** *Towneley Myst.* xxiii. 257 Beestys, byrdys, alle haue thay rest, when thay ar wo begon. *c* **1480** Henryson *Sheep & Dog* 1291 So is mony one Now in this warld richt wonder wo be gone. **1513** Douglas *Æneis* x. xiii. 79 Sa wobegone becam this lusty man That salt teris fast our his chekis ran. **1597** Shaks. *2 Hen. IV*, i. i. 71 Euen such a man, so faint, so spiritlesse, So dull, so dead in looke, so woe-be-gone. **1603** J. Davies *Microcosmos* 192 To succour one another woe-begon. **1615** Brathwait *Strappado* (1878) 93 All wea-begane, thus liu'd the Shepheard long. **1805–6** Cary *Dante, Inf.* xviii. 83 That lofty shade, who.. seems too woe-begone to drop a tear. [**1852** Thackeray *Esmond* iii. ix, Poor Frank Castlewood, who Esmond thought might be wobegone on account of parting with his divine Clotilda.]

2. Of persons in respect of their looks, appearance, or manner: Exhibiting or betraying a state of distress, misery, anguish, or grief. Also *transf.* of inanimate objects.

The rise of this sense in the modern period was due to an archaistic revival of the word, perhaps with special reference to such contexts as that of quot. 1597 in sense 1.

1802 Mrs. E. Parsons *Myst. Visit* IV. 135 You have left all your woe-begone looks behind. **1809** W. Irving *Knickerb.* ii. v. (1849) 112 The wo-begone heroes.. eyed each other with rueful countenances. **1825** Waterton *Wand. S. Amer.* iv. 275 St. John's is the capital of Antigua... At present it appears sad and woe-begone. **1837** Lockhart *Scott* I. ii. 89 A poor mendicant approached, old and woebegone. **1862** Sala *Accepted Addr.* 153 It was the most woebegone excavation.. you ever saw. **1883** D. C. Murray *Hearts* viii, Remembering how sad and woe-begone the little man seemed at leaving England. **1891** 'J. S. Winter' *Mrs. Bob* xviii, 'And I dare say I should', she ended, laughing at this woe-begone picture of herself.

Comb. **1844** Kinglake *Eothen* ii, Some woe-begone looking fellows were.. laden with our baggage. **1858** R. S. Surtees *Ask Mamma* lxvi, A wretched, dilapidated woe-begone-looking place.

b. as *sb.* A woe-begone creature.

1879 E. Arnold *Lt. Asia* v. 117 Whom sadly eying spake our Lord to one, Chief of the woe-begones. **1893** Kinney in *The King's Business* (New Haven, Ct.) 138 The streaming tears of those woe-begones.

Hence **'woe-be,goneness**, **'woe-be,gonish** *a.*

1826 B. Hall in Lockhart *Scott* (1837) VI. 316 His countenance.. a little woe-begonish. *c* **1863** J. Brown *John Leech* etc., *Thackeray's Death* (1882) 187 A strange visage, staring at him with an expression of comical woebegoneness. **1885** H. O. Forbes *Nat. Wand. E. Archip.* 159 The intermittent 'All'-il-allahs'—whose very woe-begoneness made me smile.

woed, obs. form of wood *a.*

woeful ('wəʊfʊl), *a.* Also woful. [f. woe *sb.* + -ful. (Revived or newly formed *c* 1750.)]

1. Of persons, their attributes, actions, etc.: Full of woe; afflicted with sorrow, distress, or misfortune; sorrowful, mournful.

a **1300** *Cursor M.* 11564 Ful waful made he mani wijf! *c* **1384** Chaucer *H. Fame* i. 214 Wepynge with ful woful chere. **1390** GOWER *Conf.* III. 260 Wher thei myhten se The wofulleste upon this Molde. ? *a* **1400** *Morte Arth.* 950 A wery wafulle wedowe, wryngande hire handez. **1470–85** MALORY *Arthur* IV. vi. 126 Herynge aboute hym many complayntes of woful knyghtes. **1549** *Compl. Scot.* vii. 68 It aperit be hyr voful contenens, that sche vas in grite dout ande dreddour. *a* **1557** GRIMALDE in *Tottel's Misc.* (Arb.) 112 For Wilford felt the wayters wayfull wo. **1603** KNOLLES *Hist. Turks* Introd. (1621) A4, The infinite number of wofull Christians (whose grieuous groanings vnder the heauie yoke of infidelitie no tongue is able to expresse). **1655** FULLER *Ch. Hist.* I. v. §14 They dispatch Petition after Petition, Embassie on Embassie, representing their wofull estate. **1802** LEYDEN *Lord Soulis* xl, When Soulis thought on his merriemen now, A woeful wight was he. **1825** MACAULAY *Ess., Milton* ¶45 The haggard and woful stare of the eye. **1885** E. ARNOLD *Secret of Death* 10 Be sure that woeful father wept.

2. Of times, places, occurrences, etc.: Fraught with woe, affliction, or misery; miserable.

a **1300** *Cursor M.* 2882, I rede yow take Ensaumple bi þis waful wrake. *c* **1400** *Melayne* 260 Oure knyghtis one þ[e] gronde lyse With wondes wyde one wafull wyse. *c* **1480** HENRYSON *Want of Wyse Men* 7 This is a wofull werde. **1592** SHAKS. *Rom. & Jul.* IV. v. 49 O wo, O wofull, wofull, wofull day. **1610** HOLLAND *Camden's Brit.* I. 240 That wofull war betweene the houses of Lancaster and Yorke. **1630** *R. Johnson's Kingd. & Commw.* 554 In this wofull Towne dwell not above two or three hundred Inhabitants. **1642–3** *Petit. Gen. Assembly* 4 Jan. 1 In this wofull case, and lamentable condition of your Majesties Dominions. **1777** DALRYMPLE *Trav. Sp. & Port.* lvi, Many old palaces going to ruins, the woeful memorials of antient splendour. **1803** SCOTT *Gray Brother* xx, A woful place was that, I ween, As sorrow could desire. **1853** HAWTHORNE *Tanglewood T., Minotaur* 28 The wofulest anniversary in the whole year.

3. In weakened or trivial senses: Such as to excite commiseration or dissatisfaction; 'grievous', 'sad', unpleasant; very bad, poor, or mean; 'pitiful', 'deplorable', 'wretched'.

1619 J. TAYLOR (Water P.) *Kicksey Winsey* B5, These mens honesties are like their states, At piteous, wofull, and at low priz'd rates. **1647** in *Verney Mem.* (1907) I. 496 Mun, poore childe, is a woefull schollar. **1650** B. *Discolliminium* 2 It is a wofull while a coming. **1691** MRS. D'ANVERS *Academia* 53 She's in a woful taking, When once she comes to miss her Bacon. **1709** POPE *Ess. Crit.* 418 What woful stuff this madrigal would be. **1723** CHAMBERS tr. *Le Clerc's Archit.* I. 117 Two Imposts over each other wou'd have a woful Effect. **1798** S. & HT. LEE *Cant. T., Young Lady's T.* II. 546 [She] had many good qualities, but was a woeful manager of children. **1853** DICKENS *Bleak Ho.* lxiii, He.. has a woful consciousness upon him of being a scapegrace. **1863** W. C. BALDWIN *Afr. Hunting* ii. 44, I had to return to camp.. in a woful plight, minus my hat, and my shirt torn to ribbons. **1905** *Times Lit. Suppl.* 2 June 176/3 Wild dogs have.. made woful havoc of the sambar and spotted deer. **1920** *Ibid.* 2 Sept. 558/1 The woful results of uncritical thinking.

4. In comb. with another adj., as ***woeful-wan***; also advb. = WOEFULLY.

1750 GRAY *Elegy* 107 Now drooping, woeful-wan, like one forlorn. **1794** *Girlhood of M. J. Holroyd* (1896) 259 His others are woful bad. **1820** S. ROGERS *Hum. Life* 282 One woeful-wan, one merrier yet as mad.

woefully ('wəʊfʊlɪ), *adv.* Also **wofully**. [f. WOEFUL + -LY[2].]

1. In a woeful manner or condition; miserably, grievously; mournfully, sadly. *arch.*

1390 GOWER *Conf.* I. 198, I am A womman wofully bestad. *Ibid.* 267 Whan thei herde Hou wofully this cause ferde. *c* **1480** HENRYSON *Trial of Fox* 275 The ȝow.. Put out hir playnt on this wyis wofullie. **1526** *Pilgr. Perf.* (W. de W. 1531) 302 b, As thou were so wofully arayed. **1590** SPENSER *F.Q.* I. v. 33 Where many soules sit wailing woefully. **16..** MIDDLETON, etc. *Old Law* v. i, These that do lead this day of jollity Doe march with Musick.. Those that doe follow sad, and wofully. *a* **1656** BP. HALL *Specialities Life* Rem. Wks. (1660) 35 That wofully distracted Church. **1751** SMOLLETT *Per. Pickle* cxiii. [cv], I know.. what makes you laugh so woefully. **1865** TROLLOPE *Belton Estate* xiii, 'I suppose she thinks so of me,' said Belton wofully. **1876** SWINBURNE *Erechtheus* 570 Wofully wed in a snow strewn bed.

2. So as to excite commiseration or dissatisfaction; grievously, deplorably, 'sadly'.

Occas. as a mere intensive: cf. *awfully*, *terribly*.

1648 JENKYN *Blind Guide* iii. 58 You say but very little.. but in that little you wofully trifle. **1766** GOLDSM. *Vicar W.* xxiv, Thou hast once wofully, irreparably deceived me. **1831** JAMES *Philip Aug.* xix, Of defensive armour the supply was wofully small. **1843** *Peter Parley's Ann.* IV. 266 Mrs. Clinker, who was wofully, as she termed it, fond of pigs. **1885** *Truth* 11 June 928/1 The other exhibits are.. wofully bad, and deplorably uninteresting.

woefulness ('wəʊfʊlnɪs). *arch.* [f. WOEFUL + -NESS.] Woeful condition; sad misery.

1513 BRADSHAW *St. Werburge* I. 3171 O dredefull dethe.. Takynge our heed from vs.. Hath brought vs to threaldome, wofulnes and peyne. *a* **1586** SIDNEY *Arcadia* III. (1922) 61 The harte stuffed up with wofulnes. **1686** G. STUART *Jocoser. Disc.* 2 Their waedeum [*marg.* Wofulness] seem'd vanish't. **1867** MORRIS *Jason* XVII. 1118 He.. muttered low for fear and woefulness.

woele, obs. form of WHEEL.

†'**woeless**, *a. Obs. rare.* In 6 **woles**. [f. WOE *sb.* + -LESS.] Free from woe.

c **1560** A. SCOTT *Poems* (S.T.S.) iii. 28 Petously complene ȝo[r] woles pane.

woemen, obs. pl. of WOMAN.

†'**woeness.** *Obs. rare.* In 6 *Sc.* **wanes**. [f. WOE *sb.* + -NESS.] Grief, sorrow.

1535 STEWART *Cron. Scot.* (Rolls) I. 80 The wemen.. tuke sic melancoly, That sum for wanes lap into the se.

woer, woerd, woes: see WOOER, WORD, OOZE.

woesome ('wəʊsəm), *a.* Also *Sc.* **waesome**. [f. WOE *sb.* + -SOME.] Woeful.

1818 SCOTT *Hrt. Midl.* xliv, She kend her lot would be a waesome ane. **1867** G. MACDONALD *Songs Summer Nts.* I. iii, 'Tis not a flowing wind, I see—An ebbing woesome thing. **1897** *Outing* (U.S.) XXIX. 356/1 The copper blade passed through Lakanoo's breast-bone, cutting a woesome gash.

wof, obs. pa. t. and pa. pple. of WEAVE *v.*

woff, var. WAFF *v.*[3]

1570 LEVINS *Manip.* 156/40 To woff like a dog, *latritare*.

woffle, var. WAFFLE *v.*, *sb.*[2]

woft, Sc. var. WEFT *sb.*[1]

wog[1] (wɒg). *slang.* [Origin uncertain: often said to be an acronym, but none of the many suggested etymologies is satisfactorily supported by the evidence.] **1.** A vulgarly offensive name for a foreigner, esp. one of Arab extraction.

1929 F. BOWEN *Sea Slang* 153 *Wogs*, lower class Babu shipping clerks on the Indian coast. **1932** R. J. P. HEWISON *Essay on Oxford* 5 And here the *Ethiop* ranks, the wogs, we spy. **1937** F. STARK *Baghdad Sketches* 90 When I return, Nasir fixed me with real malignity in his little placid eyes. 'I knew she wanted me to go,' he said. 'I could see what she was thinking. They call us wogs.' **1942** C. HOLLINGWORTH *German Just behind Me* xiii. 258 King Zog Was always considered a bit of a Wog, Until Mussolini quite recently Behaved so indecently. **1944** [see COME *v.* 39e]. **1955** E. WAUGH *Officers & Gentlemen* II. 323 He turned up in western Abyssinia leading a group of wogs. **1958** *Times Lit. Suppl.* 11 Apr. p. vi/3 We have travelled some distance from the days when Wogs began at Calais. **1965** [see COMMIE]. **1982** J. SAVARIN *Water Hole* I. iv. 42 He hated Arabs... They were all wogs to him.

2. The Arabic language.

1977 P. RAYMOND *Matter of Assassination* vi. 63, I can't speak Wog and don't seems to be getting anywhere. **1982** 'W. HAGGARD' *Mischief-Makers* xiv. 157 'I've picked up a few words of wog, sir.'.. The driver spoke terrible barrack-room Arabic.

3. a. *attrib.* passing into *adj.*

a **1963** J. LUSBY in B. James *Austral. Short Stories* (1963) 236 Wog chappie scuttling around seeking safe side of the beast. **1970** G. F. NEWMAN *Sir, You Bastard* viii. 234 We were hawking, and getting treated like bleeding wog brush salesmen. **1973** *Daily Tel.* 31 May 3/2 Judge Sheldon heard that trouble started.. when white girlfriends of coloured soldiers.. were taunted by members of the Royal Scots as 'wog lovers'. **1977** *Drive* Sept.–Oct. 112/2 Any foreign car, even a Ferrari or a Mercedes, is a *wog motor*, unless it's a *Yank*.

b. *Comb.* **wogland** *derog.*, a foreign country.

1961 [see NIG, NIG *sb.*[3]]. **1967** 'J. MUNRO' *Money that Money can't Buy* ii. 24, I don't live in Wogland [*sc.* Spain] because I like it.

Hence also '**wogger**; '**woggy** *a.*

1922 JOYCE *Ulysses* 740 She called him wogger. *Ibid.* 741 She may have noticed her wogger people were always going away. **1973** M. CATTO *Sam Casanova* iv. 75, I met some kid in a night-club here, does some sort of Woggy belly-dance. **1979** REESE & FLINT *Trick 13* 100 That woggy fellow.. was cleaning up.

wog[2] (wɒg). *Austral. slang.* [Origin uncertain.] A germ or parasite; an insect; an illness or disease. Cf. BUG *sb.*[2] 3d.

1934 *Bulletin* (Sydney) 31 Oct. 20/4 Buckley's fluke.. is a wog that enters the nostrils of these snakes during hibernation. **1941** C. BARRETT *Coast of Adventure* iii. 51 Jolly little people.. popping into old jam tins a miscellany of wogs—from bull-ants to scorpions and centipedes. **1953** A. UPFIELD *Murder must Wait* xxi. 191 The wogs flying about the light. **1964** R. BRADDON *Year Angry Rabbit* i. 9 But find the wog, find the super-myxomatosis, the whatever-it-may-be that kills today's rabbits. **1976** D. FRANCIS *In Frame* viii. 126 A beastly stomach wog, so he couldn't come.

wog, obs. Sc. f. VOGUE *sb.*

c **1700** M'ALPIE *Cert. Cur. Poems* (1828) 6 For we declair it wnto yow, The man hes gott the wog.

Wogdon ('wɒgdən). Also erron. **Wogden**. The name of Robert *Wogdon* (fl. 1776–1800), a noted gunsmith, used *absol.* to designate a duelling pistol made by him.

c **1810** W. HICKEY *Mem.* (1923) III. 150 By God, Bill, you shall shoot the dirty little rascal through the head. I have a delicate pair of Wogdens that will do his business effectually. **1969** G. LYALL *Venus with Pistol* xxv. 161 Give it a little time for the word to go round that Bert Kemp had matched a pair of fancy Wogdons. **1981** 'J. STURROCK' *Suicide Most Foul* vi. 127 Had I been armed with only one of my Wogdons the end would have been different, but a gentleman does not take pistols to a ball.

woggle ('wɒg(ə)l), *v.* Variant of WAGGLE *v.*

1648 HEXHAM, *Loteren*, to Wagge, or to Woggle. **1918** *Blackw. Mag.* June 767/1, I woggle my machine [*sc.* an aeroplane] from side to side. **1921** S. GRAHAM *Europe—Whither bound?* 131 The miserable green waggons of open horse-trams woggled along the main ways.

woggle ('wɒg(ə)l), *sb.* [Origin unknown: cf. TOGGLE *sb.*] A loop or ring of leather, cord, etc., through which the ends of a Scout's neckerchief are threaded.

1930 *Daily News* 10 May 4/4 Woggles have now become an established part of Scout uniform, and I have seen some very good examples made by Scouts. **1977** *Grimsby Even. Tel.* 27 May 2/7 The woggle—the ring holding the neckerchief in place on the Scout uniform. **1983** J. DEFT *Beaver Leader's Handbk.* 32 You must decide yourself whether each new Beaver should be asked to pay for his scarf and woggle, or whether these should be provided by the Colony.

woȝte, obs. var. VAULT *sb.*[1]

wogue, obs. Sc. f. VOGUE.

Wogul, var. of VOGUL.

woh, var. WOUGH, WOW *sb.*[1] *Obs.*

wohe, obs. f. WOO.

wo hey, etc.: see WO.

Wöhler ('vɜːlə(r)). *Mech.* [The name of August *Wöhler* (1819–1914), German railway engineer.] ***Wöhler test***: a fatigue test in which a horizontal bar is rotated axially while supported at one end and loaded at the other.

[**1888** *Rep. Brit. Assoc. Adv. Sci. 1887* 434 (*caption*) Limits of stress from Wöhler's endurance tests.] **1911** *Jrnl. Iron & Steel Inst.* LXXXIV. 655 The testing machines include.. a rotary fatigue (Wöhler test) machine. **1948** P. F. FOSTER *Mech. Testing of Metals & Alloys* x. 203 One objection urged against the Wöhler test is that it is merely a skin test, since the major part of the section is but comparatively lightly stressed. **1980** *Proc. European Offshore Steels Res. Seminar 1978* (Welding Inst.) p. III/P7-2 The test programme included Wöhler tests (fatigue tests) with an alternating load.

woice, obs. f. VOICE.

woid(e, obs. Sc. ff. VOID, WOOD *a.*

woidie, var. VOISDIE.

woifen, obs. Sc. pa. pple. of WEAVE *v.*

wois, woise, obs. ff. WHOSE.

woitting, obs. Sc. f. VOTING.

woiwode, var. VOIVODE.

wok (wɒk). Also **wock**. [a. Chinese (Cantonese).] A bowl-shaped pan used in Chinese cookery.

1952 D. Y. H. FENG *Joy of Chinese Cooking* i. 37 A well-stocked Chinese kitchen usually has.. several convex-bottomed circular pans hammered out of thin iron or copper called *wock*. **1962** E.-M. WONG *Chinese Cookery* i. 4 For versatility and easy handling the wock is indispensable. **1969** *Britannica Bk. of Year* (U.S.) 801/1 *Wok*, a bowl-shaped cooking utensil used especially in the preparation of Chinese food. **1972** *Maclean's Mag.* Mar. 46/3 The Chinese wok technique is my mainstay of cooking, although I do it in a plain frypan. **1973** J. GORES *Final Notice* (1974) x. 61 The pixie-like waitress came in with a boardful of fresh vegetables for the *wok*. **1977** *Sunday Times* (Colour Suppl.) 4 Dec. 20/2 Wok cooking is about to sweep the Western world. **1983** *Listener* 30 June 17/1 By 1972 I needed a small pantechnicon to convey all my books on macrobiotic cookery, my plants, wall-hangings and floor cushions, my astrological tables, women's-lib posters and my wok.

†**woke**, *a. Obs.* Forms: *α.* 1–3 **wac** (1 **waac**, *infl.* **wake**), 4 *north.* **wak**, 4–5 **wake**; *β.* 2–3 **woc**, (3 **wooc**, *infl.* **woke**), 3–5 **wok**, 5 **woke**; 1 *comp.* **waccra**, *superl.* 1 **waccust**, 4 **wakkest**. [Com. Teut. (wanting in Goth. and Fris.): OE. *wác*, corresp. to OS., MLG. *wêk*, MDu. *weec* (Du. *week*), OHG. *weih* (MHG., G. *weich*) yielding, soft, ON. *veikr*, *vøyk-r* (Sw. *vek*, Da. *veg* soft, Norw. *veik*) weak:—OTeut. **waikwo-*, f. **waikw-*: **wikw-* to yield, give way: see WIKE *v.* Cf. WEAK *a.*, a. ON. *veikr*.

The word died out in the 15th c., being superseded by WEAK; if it had survived, its form in mod.Eng. would have been **wook* (wuk), the vowel being modified in quality by the initial (w) and shortened by the final (k).]

= WEAK *a.* in various senses. **a.** Pliant, flexible (only OE.). **b.** Lacking in strength, vigour, endurance, or courage; inferior physically or morally. **c.** Lowly in status or degree; insignificant.

c **897** ÆLFRED *Gregory's Past. C.* xlii. 306 Sua sua wac hreod & idel, ðe ælc hwiða windes mæᵹ awecggan. *a* **1000** *Wanderer* 67 Ne sceal no to hatheort ne to hrædwyrde ne to wac wiᵹa ne to wanhydiᵹ. *c* **1000** ÆLFRIC *Hom.* I. 2 Ic Ælfric munuc and mæssepreost, swa þeah waccre þonne swilcum hadum ᵹebyriᵹe. *c* **1050** *Suppl. Ælfric's Gloss.* in Wr.-Wülcker 191/19 *Lentus*, waac. **1050–73** *Charter* in Thorpe *Charters* (1865) 430, ii forealdode rædingbec swiðe wake, and .i. wac mæssereaf. *c* **1200** ORMIN 18328 Icc amm i me sellfenn wac & full off unntrummnesse. *c* **1205** LAY. 23593 Ah fehten ich wulle.. wið Arðure kinge, whaðer unkere swa beoð þere wakere sone he bið þe laðere. *a* **1225** *Ancr. R.* 12 Do wel & dem ðe suluen euer woc. *Ibid.* 52 Ofte a ful hawur smið smeoðið a ful woc knif. *c* **1230** *Hali Meid.* (1922) 9 Drehen se moni wa, for swa wac huire as te world forȝelt eauer at ten ende. *c* **1250** *Gen. & Ex.* 1197 ȝhe wurd wið child, on elde wac. *a* **1275** *Prov. Alfred* 581 in *O.E. Misc.* 135 Min hew falewidþ, and min wlite is wan, and min herte woc. **13..** *Gaw. & Gr. Knt.* 354, I am þe wakkest, I wot, and of wyt feblest. *c* **1375** *Sc. Leg. Saints* xvi. (*Magdalene*) 389 For þu art wak & gret with barne. *c* **1425** *Engl. Conq. Ireland* 146 The englysshe weren both argh & woke to assayllen and to fyght, þe Iresshe stronge & bold to wythstonde. *c* **1450** *Mirk's Festial* 196 Then callyd þe norys to þe modyr, and bade hur.. helpe hur forto folde þe chyldys cloþis; for scho was to woke, and myght not welde hom. **1457** HARDING *Chron.* i. in *Engl. Hist. Rev.* (1912) Oct. 743 With incurable mayme that maketh me wake.

d. *woke fish* [cf. G. *weichfisch*], dried cod, stockfish.

1386 in R. R. Sharpe *Cal. Letter-bk. H Lond.* (1907) 299 Stokfisshe [called] halfwoxefisshe [*sic*].

†**woke,** *v. Obs.* Forms: 1 **wacian**, 3 **wakien**, 3–4 **woke, wokie.** [OE. *wácian*, f. *wác* WOKE *a.*]

1. *intr.* To grow or become weak, to weaken; to become less severe, be mitigated.

993 *Battle of Maldon* 10 þe þam man mihte oncnawan þæt se cniht nolde wacian æt þam wiȝe. **1003** *O.E. Chron.* (Laud MS.), Ðonne se heretoȝa wacað, þonne bið eall se here swiðe ȝehindred. *c* **1205** Lay. 2938 þa ældede þe king & wakede an aðelan. *Ibid.* 13466 þa heo weore swa drunken þæt wakeden heore sconken. *Ibid.* 19798 His heorte gon to wakien [*c* **1275** wokie]. *c* **1275** *Signs of Death* 2 in *O.E. Misc.* 101 [H]wenne þin heou blokeþ And þi strengþe wokeþ. *c* **1374** [see WEAK *v.* 2].

2. *trans.* **a.** To dilute, water. **b.** To soften (in quot. *fig.*). **c.** To soak in water: = WEAK *v.* 1 b.

1377 Langl. *P. Pl.* B. xv. 332 As who so filled a tonne of a fresshe ryuer, And went forth with þat water to woke with themese. **1393** *Ibid.* C. xv. 25 Ac grace groweþ nat til goode wil gynne reyne, And wokie þorwe good werkes wikkede hertes. *Ibid.* xvii. 332 [He] with warme water of hus eyen wokeþ hit til hit white.

Hence †**woked** *ppl. a.*, steeped.

1408–9 in R. R. Sharpe *Cal. Letter-bk. I Lond.* (1909) 71 [A proclamation forbidding the sale by retail of watered fish] pessoun eawee [called in English] Wokedfyssh.

woke, obs. pa. t. of ACHE *v.*; pa. t. and pple. of WAKE *v.*; obs. form of OAK, WEEK.

†'**wokely,** *adv. Obs.* [OE. *wáclíce*, f. *wác* WOKE *a.*: see -LY^2.] Weakly, feebly, poorly.

a **1000** *Boeth. Metr.* v. 34 Ne eft to waclice ȝeortreowe æniȝes godes. *c* **1000** Ælfric *Hom.* I. 528 Ðehwam sceamað, ȝif he ȝelaðod bið to woruldlicum ȝyftum, ðæt he waclice ȝescryd cume. *a* **1225** *Ancr. R.* 294 3if þu .. werest te erest wocliche [*MS. C.* wachlichliche] & ȝiuest þe ueonde inȝong. *c* **1230** *Hali Meid.* (1922) 10 Þe poure, þe beoð wacliche iȝeuen and biset on vuele.

'**woken,** *ppl. a. rare.* [pa. pple. of WAKE *v.*] Awakened.

1649 C. Wase *Sophocles, Electra* 2 Birds with chirping Mattins call from bed The woken Suns already rising head. **1924** *Serena Blandish* vii. 120 Her newly woken spirit.

†'**wokeness.** *Obs.* [OE. *wácnes*, f. *wác* WOKE *a.*: see -NESS.]

1. Weakness, debility; (in OE. also) lowliness, inferiority.

c **1000** Ælfric *Hom.* I. 68 Hi bædon ðæt ða ȝymstanas awendon to heora wacnysse. *a* **1100** *Aldhelm Gloss.* I. 1384 (Napier 37) *Uilitas, abiectio*, wacnys. *c* **1200** *Vices & Virtues* 83 Þu hafdest me imaked glad and bliðe; ac ich hes haue forloren for mine wocnesse. *a* **1225** *Ancr. R.* 232 Þet we iknowen ure owune feblesce & ure owune muchele unstrencðe, & ure owune wocnesse. *a* **1240** *Wohunge* in *O.E. Hom.* I. 273 And te strengðe of þe helpe mi muchele wacnesse. **1547** *Test. Ebor.* (Surtees) VI. 258 The debilitie and wakenes of my bodie.

2. Moisture. (Cf. *wakness* s.v. WAK.)

1340 *Ayenb.* 95 Guod molde, wocnesse norissynde, and renable hete.

†**wokethistle.** *Obs.* [app. f. WOKE *v.* (2 c) + THISTLE *sb.*] The teasel (the upper leaves of which form a cup, which is usually full of water).

a **1387** *Sinon. Barthol.* (Anecd. Oxon.) 27 *Labrum veneris*, an. wokethistel.

†**wol(e, woll,** *adv. Obs.* Orig. unstressed form of WELL *adv.*

c **1250** *Gen. & Ex.* 1995 Putifar was wol riche man. **13..** *Coer de L.* 1280 A wol bold baroun. **1399** Langl. *Rich. Redeles* I. 67 Woll wo beth þe wones. *a* **1450** *Songs & Carols* (Warton Club) 75 My cause xal be wol i-doo. *c* **1460** *Play Sacram.* 178 Datis wole dulcett for to dresse.

wol(e: see WHILE, WILL, WOOL.

wolant, wolbede, etc., **wolcome,** obs. ff. VOLANT *a.*, WOUBIT, WELCOME.

wolchonskoite, wolk-, obs. varr. VOLKONSKOITE.

wold (wəʊld). Forms: α. 1, 3, 4–6 *Sc.* **wald**, 5 **walde**, 7– *dial.* **waud**, 8 *dial.* **wadd**, 9 *Sc.* **wauld.** β. 3– **wold**, 4–6 **wolde**, 5–8 **would**, 7 **wowld**, *pl.* **woles**, 8 **woald.** γ. 6–7 **old**, 7 **ould.** See also WEALD. [Com. Teut. (not extant in Gothic): OE. (Anglian) *wald* (WS. *weald*: see WEALD) str. masc. forest, wooded country = OFris. *wald* forest, MDu. *wout, woud-* (Du. *woud*), OS. *wald* forest, ? wilderness (MLG., LG. *wold*), OHG. *wald* forest, wilderness (MHG. *walt, wald-* forest, wood, timber, G. *wald* forest), ON. *völlr* untilled field, plain (Sw. *vall* pasture, Norw. *voll* grassy plain):—OTeut. **walþuz*, of which the ulterior relations are doubtful. (From Teut. is derived OF. *gua(l)d* woodland, scrub, untilled land, whence *gaudine* bower, grove.)

After the early 16th cent., the word ceased to be in general use and became restricted to localities in which it entered into the proper designation of characteristic tracts of country, probably at one time thickly wooded; thence arose the general literary (esp. poetical) use defined in sense 3.]

†**1.** Forest, forest land; wooded upland. *Obs.*

786 in Birch *Cartul. Sax.* (1885) I. 344 In limen wero wealdo, & in burh waro uualdo. *a* **1000** *Judith* 206 þæs se hlanca ȝefeah wulf in walde. *a* **1225** *St. Marher.* 10 Wilde deor þet on þeos wilde waldes wunieð. *c* **1300** in Stow *Surv. Lond.* (ed. Strype 1755) II. 280/2 *marg.*, Fabri de Waldis. ? **13..** in Somner *Roman Ports & Forts Kent* (1693) 110 Septem Dennas in sylva quæ vocatur Wald. *Ibid.* 113 Homines quoque de Walda debent unam domum æstivalem quod Anglicè dicitur Sumerhus, aut xx solidos dare. *a* **1400–50** *Wars Alex.* 3799 Þai droȝe furth be dissert & drinkles þai spill, Was nouthire waldis in þar walke ne water to fynde.

†**2.** A hill, down. *Obs.*

c **1205** Lay. 21530 Childric com sone ouer wald liðen [*later text* ouer dounes wende]. *Ibid.* 25758 Na whit heo ne funden quikes uppen wolden [*later text* vp þan hulle]. *c* **1250** *Gen. & Ex.* 938 Ðre der he toc, ilc ðre ȝer hold, And sacrede god on an wold. *c* **1275** *Passion our Lord* 27 in *O.E. Misc.* 38 Þe holy gost hyne ledde vp into þe wolde For to beon yuonded of sathanas. **1483** *Cath. Angl.* 406/2 Y^e Walde, *alpina*. *a* **1500** *Cov. Corpus Chr. Plays* 15/436 Hereby apon a wolde Scheppardis wachyng there fold. **1513** Douglas *Æneis* x. xiii. 111 The travellour ȝond vnder the wald Lurkand wythdrawis to sum sovir hald. [**1590** Camden *Britannia* 279 *Cotswold*.. Montes enim & colles *Woulds* olim dixerunt Angli, vnde Glossarium antiquum Alpes Italiæ *The Woulds of Italie* interpretatur.]

3. A piece of open country; a plain; in early use (with *the*) sometimes = 'the plain', the ground, the earth; in later use chiefly, an elevated tract of open country or moorland; also *collect. pl.* or *sing.* rolling uplands. (Frequent since *c* 1600 in vague poetical use.)

c **1205** Lay. 10001 Stod þe wundliche wude amidden ane wælde [*later text* wolde]. *Ibid.* 16461 Hengest bah a þene wald [*later text* Hii wende in to þan felde]. *Ibid.* 20842 Þenne he bið baldest ufenan þan walde. *c* **1220** *Bestiary* 606 Elpes .. to-gaddre gon o wolde, So sep ðat cumen ut of folde. *Ibid.* 757 Ilk der ðe him hereð to him cumeð, And foleȝeð him up one ðe wold. **1375** Barbour *Bruce* xviii. 555 Thair fayis, vith thair mycht, noyand, Quhill to the wald cummyn war thai. Syne northwarde tuk thai hame thar way, And distroyit, in thair repair, The vale haly of Beauvare. **1425** in *Rep. MSS. Ld. Middleton* (1911) 107 No man with comyn herd ne with sched herd com on the wold after gresse be mowen to it be maked and led away. *c* **1425** *Cast. Persev.* 826 in *Macro Plays* 102 Whyl he walkyth in worldly wolde, I, Bakbyter, am with hym holde. **1471** *Hist. Arrivall Edw. IV* (Camden 1838) 26 Aboute that place was a great and a fayre large playne, called a would. **1513** Douglas *Æneis* ix. xi. 13 Rane .. dois smyte apon the wald [orig. *humum*]. **1538** Starkey *England* (1878) 73 The wast groundys (as hethys, forestys, parkys and oldys). **1587** Harrison *England* II. xix. 206 in *Holinshed*, This may suffice for the vse of the word Wald, which now differeth much from Wold. For as that signifieth a woodie soile, so this betokeneth a soile without wood, or plaine champaine countrie, without anie store of trees. **1605** Shaks. *Lear* III. iv. 125 Swithold footed thrice the old. **1636** W. Denny in *Ann. Dubrensia* (1877) 16 Faire fleec'd Sheepe, which beautifie the Woulds. **1740** Somerville *Hobbinol.* I. 237 On the bleak Woald the new-born Infant lay, Expos'd to Winter Snows. **1810** Scott *Lady of L.* IV. xiii, Or who may dare on wold to wear The fairies' fatal green? **1812** Byron *Ch. Har.* II. lxix, Till he .. from his further bank Ætolia's wolds espied. **1832** Tennyson *To J. S.* i, The wind, that beats the mountain, blows More softly round the open wold. *a* **1845** Barham *Ingol. Leg.* Ser. III. *Blasphemer's Warn.* 5 With broad lands, pasture, arable, woodland, and wold. **1865** Kingsley *Herew.* Prel., Between the forests were open wolds. **1905** A. C. Benson *Thread of Gold* iii, Beyond all ran the long pure line of the rising wold.

b. *fig.*

1633 G. Herbert *Temple, Pilgrimage* iii, That led me to the wilde of passion, which Some call the wold. *a* **1640** Jackson *Creed* x. Notes to xxxi. 3141 Though I have cut up in the Wolds of Gentilism, and layd together a Turf or two. **1877** L. Morris *Epic of Hades* II. 117 The thick-leaved coverts deep And wind-worn wolds of life.

c. in alliterative conjunction with *wood* (occas. with *waste, wild*).

1813 Scott *Trierm.* I. xi, On vent'rous quest to ride, .. by wood and wold. **1821** —— *Pirate* xxvi, On they went, through wild and over wold. **1847** Longf. *Ev.* II. iv, The notes of the robin .. Sounded sweet upon wold and in wood. **1896** J. Davidson *Fleet St. Eclogues* Ser. II. 70 And waste and wold Took heart and shone.

4. Used in the specific designations of certain hilly tracts in England, viz. the hill country of North Yorkshire and Humberside (***Yorkshire Wolds***, †***York(e)swold***, †***York-wolds***), the Cotswold district, the hilly districts of Leicestershire and Lincolnshire.

1472–5 *Rolls of Parlt.* VI. 157/2 Fell called Shorlyng and Morlyng, growyng in Yorkeswold. **1548** *N. Country Wills* (Surtees 1908) 202 My manor in Willoughby upon the woldes. **1596** Lambarde *Peramb. Kent* (ed. 2) 408 Those large champaignes of Yorkswold, and Cotswolde. **1610** Holland *Camden's Brit.* I. 523 Part of it [*sc.* Leicestershire] is called the Wold, as being hilly without wood. **1622** Drayton *Poly-olb.* xxvi. Argt., Tow'rds Lester then her course she holds, And sailing o'er the pleasant Oulds, She fetcheth Soare down from her springs. **1622** W. Burton *Leicestersh.* 296 Waltham on the Wouldes. **1641** Best *Farm. Bks.* (Surtees) 28 Most of the grasse that groweth on the landes, and especially on the leyes of the wolds, is a small, sparrie, and dry grasse. **1669** *Phil. Trans.* IV. 1012 In some wooddy parts of the Woles in Lincoln-shire. **1697** Meriton *Praise York-sh. Ale* (ed. 3) 80 (East-Riding Yorks.) For *Wolds* or *Woulds* [they say] *Wauds*. **1725** *MSS. Dk. Portland* (Hist. MSS. Comm.) VI. 95 The Yorkshire Wolds, called here the Wadds. **1778** *Eng. Gazetteer* (ed. 2) s.v. *Yorkshire*, A large tract called the York-Woulds. **1891** Scrivener *Fields & Cities* 20 The north of Lincolnshire is .. high and dry. It is called the 'Wold'; but that does not mean big stones and heather. The Wold is not a moor; it is a succession of good turnip fields.

5. *attrib.* and *Comb.*, as ***wold-dweller, -fire, -hill, -land***; ***wold-like*** adj.; **wold-mouse**, a vole; **woldsman**, a dweller in the wolds.

1907 M. C. F. Morris *Nunburnholme* 12 The early *Wold-dwellers. **1813** Hogg *Queen's Wake* II. (1814) 147 Like *wold-fire, at midnight, that glares on the waste. **1850** 'Sylvanus' *Bye-lanes & Downs* Introd. p. ix, A view of pastures, turnip and corn-fields, and *wold-hills, terminating in a distant glimpse of the ocean. **1799** *View Agric. Lincoln.* 12 The *wold land about Louth. **1848** Lytton *Harold* I. iii, Lands .. wild and *wold-like. **1892** *Daily News* 18 Nov. 5/1 Voles, or '*wold-mice'. **1765** *Museum Rust.* IV. xxx. 138, I am told by the experienced *woldsmen, that there is as great difference as possible in the neatness of the making up the sheaves. **1895** *Naturalist* 322 The Louth woldsmen were in the habit of attending Lincoln [market].

Hence '**wolder** in ***Yorkshire wolder***, an inhabitant of the Yorkshire wolds.

1765 *Museum Rust.* IV. xxx. 139 The experience of our Yorkshire wolders.

wold, var. *quold*, pa. pple. of QUELL, to kill.

c **1250** *Gen. & Ex.* 255 Til he was on ðe rode wold, And biried in ðe rocke cold. *Ibid.* 420 Abel an hundred ȝer was hold, Ðan he was of is broðer wold. *Ibid.* 526 Ðor is writen quat aȝte a wold, Ðat ðis werld was water wold.

wold(e, obs. ff. OLD, WELD *sb.*^{2}, WIELD, WOOLD.

†**wolden-eiȝed,** *a. Obs. rare*$^{-1}$. [App. an alteration of *wald-eiȝed* WALL-EYED *a.*, due to the influence of ME. **walden*, OE. *ȝewealden* small. Cf. WALDENEIE.] ? = WALL-EYED *a.*

13.. *K. Alis.* 5274 (Laud MS.) Alle wolden-eiȝed hij [*sc.* the Albanians] beeþ By niȝth als a Catt hij seeþ.

wole, obs. f. WHOLE, WILL, WOLD, WOOL, WOOLD.

wolen, obs. form of WOOLLEN.

wolf (wʊlf), *sb.* Pl. **wolves** (wʊlvz). Forms: *Sing.* 1–6 **wulf**, 3–4 **wlf** (dat. **-ue**), 4–6 **wulfe**, 4–7 **woulf(e**, 4–8 **wolfe**, (1 **uulf**, 4 *Sc.* **volf**, 5 **wlfe, wulff**, *Sc.* **wouff**, 5–6 **wolff(e**, 5–8 **woolf(e**, 6 **wolphe**, *Sc.* **vuolfe, volue**, 6, 8 *Sc.* **wowf**, 7 **wolph**, in Comb. **wolve**, 8 *Sc.* **wouf**, 9 *Sc.* **woof**), 3– **wolf.** *Gen.* 1 **wulfes**, 3 **wulues**, etc., 4–6 **wolfes**, 5 **wolfys**, 6 **woulfes, woluis**, 6–7 **woolfes, -ues**, 7 **wolues**, 8 **wolve's**, 7– **wolf's.** *Pl.* 1 **wulfas**, 3–4 **wulues**, 3–7 **wolues**, 4–6 **woulfes**, 4–7 **wolfes**, (4 **woluys, -ez, wolwes**, *Sc.* **w(o)lfis**, 5 **woluess, vulves**, 6 **woulves, wolffes, wolfys, wulphes**, *Sc.* **woulfis, voulfis, wolffis, volf(f)is, voffis, voluis, vowis, wowes**), 7 **wolfs**, 7–8 **woolfs**, 4– **wolves.** [Com. Teut. and Indo-European: OE. *wulf* = OFris. *wolf*, OS., MLG. *wulf*, MDu. *wolf, wulf* (Du. *wolf*), OHG., MHG., G. *wolf*, ON. *ulfr* (Sw. *ulf*, Da. *ulv*), Goth. *wulfs*:—OTeut. **wulfaz*. Feminine formations in Germanic are OE. *wylf*, OHG. *wulpa* (MHG. *wülpe*), ON. *ylgr*.

Indo-Eur. **wl̥q^{w}o-* is represented outside Germanic by Skr. *vṛ́kas*, Zend *vəhrkō*, Gr. λύκος, Alb. *ul'k*, Arm. *gail*, L. (dial.) *lupus*, OSl. *vlŭkŭ*, OPruss. *wilkis*, Lith. *vilkas*, Lett. *vìlks*, and the corresp. fem. **wl̥q^{w}ī-* by Skr. *vṛkī́*, Lith. *vìlkė*, Russ. *volči-ca*.

Various details of these relationships have been much disputed, and the proposed ultimate connexion with Gr. ἕλκειν to draw, OSl. *vlěką*, Lith. *velkù* to tear, or L. *vellĕre* to pluck (see WOOL *sb.*) is problematical.]

1. a. A somewhat large canine animal (*Canis lupus*) found in Europe, Asia, and N. America, hunting in packs, and noted for its fierceness and rapacity. Also applied, with or without defining word, to various other species of *Canis* resembling or allied to this: see also PRAIRIE-*wolf*, TIMBER-*wolf*.

c **725** *Corpus Gloss.* (Hessels) L 332 *Lupus*, wulf. *c* **1000** *Be manna wyrdum* 12 (Gr.), Sceal hine wulf etan, har hæðstapa. *c* **1205** Lay. 21305 Þenne comed þe wlf wilde. **1297** R. Glouc. (Rolls) 5774 King edgar .. het þat he him sende ech ȝer .. þre þousend of wolues in name of truage. **1340** Hampole *Pr. Consc.* 1228 Lyons, libardes and wolwes kene. **1362** Langl. *P. Pl.* A. x. 207 Wandren as wolues, and wasten ȝif þei mouwen. ? *a* **1400** *Morte Arth.* 3446 The wolfes in the wode, and the whilde bestes. **1483** Caxton *Gold. Leg.* 16/2, I sought the, to thende that of the vulues ne of the euyll bestes thou were not eten ne all to torne. **1500–20** Dunbar *Poems* xxxii. 57 Throw hiddowis ȝowling of the wowf [*rime* growf]. **1516** *Kal. New Leg. Eng.* (Pynson) 5 b, Two wood wulphes. **1533** Gau *Richt Vay* (S.T.S.) 66 Etine with vowis lions and oder bestis. **1549** *Compl. Scot.* viii. 73 The beiris, lyons, voluis, foxis, and dogis. **1552** Huloet, Wolfes denne, *lupanarium*. **1593** Shaks. *3 Hen. VI*, I. i. 242 The trembling Lambe, inuironned with Wolues. **1607** Topsell *Four-f. Beasts* 753 The laps or fillets of a Wolues Liuer. **1624** Capt. Smith *Virginia* II. 27 The Woolues [are] not much bigger then our English Foxes. *c* **1643** Ld. Herbert *Autobiog.* (1824) 90 The Wolves, .. of which are found two sorts; the Mastiff Wolf thick and short ..; the Greyhound Wolf long and swift. *c* **1645** Howell *Lett.* I. III. 120 Two huge Woolfs. *a* **1718** Prior *Power* 306 The Wolve's Portion, or the Vulture's Prey. **1726–46** Thomson *Winter* 395 Assembling wolves in raging troops descend. **1730** Ramsay *Fables, Condemned Ass* 7 The wowf and tod. **1814** LEWIS & CLARK *Trav. Missouri* (1815) I. 206 We caught in a trap a large gray wolf. **1855** LONGF. *Hiaw.* xv. 48 The wolves howled from the prairies. **1858** BAIRD *Cycl. Nat. Sci.* 99 The American wolf, *Canis* (*lupus*) *occidentalis*. **1880** HUXLEY in *Proc. Zool. Soc.* 278 The Indian Wolf, *Lupus pallipes*,.. approaches the Jackals. **1888** F. COWPER *Caedwalla* 55, I have a wolf's snout hung about my neck, and no witch can hurt me. **1890** MIVART *Dogs, Jackals*, etc. 6 The size and proportions of the Wolf roughly resemble those of a large mastiff. **1891** FLOWER & LYDEKKER *Study of Mammals* 548 The true Wolves are (excluding some varieties of the domestic Dog) the largest members of the genus, and have a wide geographical range. **1902** *Nature* 30 Oct. 661/1 The South American maned wolf.. carrying its head very low.

b. In comparisons, with allusion to the fierceness or rapacity of the beast; often in contrast with the meekness of the sheep or lamb.

c **950** *Lindisf. Gosp.* Matt. x. 16 Heonu ic sendo iuih suæ scip in middum *vel* inmong uulfa. *c* **1205** LAY. 1545 Corineus heom rasde to swa þe rimie wulf. *a* **1225** *Leg. Kath.* 31 [He] Bigon anan ase wed wulf to weorrin hali chirche. **1297** R. GLOUC. (Rolls) 5680 No licchere is broþer him nas þane wolf is a lomb. *c* **1330** *Arth. & Merl.* 4047 Al so wolf þe schip gan driue, Arthour smot hem after swiþe. *c* **1400** *Destr. Troy* 10207 He fore with his fos in his felle angur, As a wolfe in his wodenes with wethurs in fold. **1562** WINȜET *Cert. Tractatis* i. Wks. (S.T.S.) I. 14 The reularis in the middis of it ar lyke woulfis rauisching thair pray. **1605** SHAKS. *Lear* III. iv. 96 Hog in sloth, Foxe in stealth, Wolfe in greedinesse. **1795** SOUTHEY *Joan of Arc* I. 176 Unhappy France! Fiercer than evening wolves thy bitter foes Rush o'er the land. **1815** BYRON *Destr. Sennacherib* 1 The Assyrian came down like the wolf on the fold. **1860** *All Year Round* No. 63. 307 I'm as hungry as a wolf; run, or I shall eat thee!

c. The skin or fur of the animal. (Chiefly *attrib.*: see sense 11 a below.)

1805 LEWIS & CLARK *Orig. Jrnls. Lewis & Clark Expedition* (1904) II. 377, I have also observed some robes among them of beaver, moonox, and small wolves. **1876** *Smithsonian Misc. Coll.* XIII. VI. 69 Furs... Wolf, (*Canis lupus*)—linings, rugs, and robes. **1940** *Chambers's Techn. Dict.* 911/1 *Wolf*, the dressed skin of one of the varieties of wolf. **1974**, etc. [see *wolf hat*, etc., sense 10 a below].

2. a. A figure or representation of a wolf.

1562 LEGH *Armory* 97 b, The fielde is Azure, a wolfe Saliaunte, Argent. **1610** GUILLIM *Heraldry* III. xv. 145 Hee beareth Gules, two Wolues passant, Argent. **1727** COLDEN *Hist. Five Ind. Nations* Introd. (1747) 1 Three Tribes or Families, who distinguish themselves by three different Arms or Ensigns, the Tortoise, the Bear, and the Wolf. **1870** C. C. BLACK tr. *Demmin's Weapons of War* 548 Another very usual [armourers'] mark is a wolf. **1885** E. CASTLE *Sch. Fence* Plate I, Grooved single-edged blade, with 'wolf' or 'fox' mark.

b. *Astron.* The constellation *Lupus* (LUPUS 2).

1551 RECORDE *Cast. Knowl.* IV. (1556) 270 This Centaure with his righte hande dooth holde a Wolfe, whiche is a seuerall constellation made of 19 starres. **1868** LOCKYER *Guillemin's Heavens* (ed. 3) 334 One detached branch of the Milky Way traverses the Wolf, and is lost in the Scorpion.

3. Applied to other animals in some way resembling wolves. **a.** (*a*) In S. Africa, a hyena: see also AARD-WOLF, STRAND-*wolf*, TIGER-*wolf*. (*b*) A Tasmanian marsupial, *Thylacinus cynocephalus*: see also ZEBRA-*wolf*. Freq. as ***Tasmanian wolf***; = THYLACINE.

[**1596** T. JOHNSON *Cornucopiæ* B 4, A certaine Wolfe called Hyena.] **1812** ANNE PLUMPTRE *Lichtenstein's S. Africa* II. 15 The spotted hyena, *hyæna crocuta*, is here called simply the wolf. **1891** *Guide Zool. Gard., Melbourne* (Morris) In this cage are two marsupial wolves, *Thylacinus cynocephalus*, or Tasmanian tigers as they are commonly called. **1908** RIDER HAGGARD *Ghost Kings* iv. 53 She saw the hyenas, two of them, wolves as they are called in South Africa. **1941** E. TROUGHTON *Furred Animals Austral.* 50 (*heading*) Tasmanian wolf or tiger. **1966** G. DURRELL *Two in Bush* vi. 178 The predators are represented by such things as the Tasmanian Wolf—not a true wolf, of course, but a marsupial, looking remarkably like its counterpart.

b. A name for various voracious fishes (after Gr. λύκος, L. *lupus*): see also SEA-WOLF 2, RIVER-*wolf*.

1555 EDEN *Decades* (Arb.) 251 Woolues of the sea which sum thynke to bee those fysshes that wee caule pikes. **1569** BLAGUE *Sch. Conceytes* 153 The Cockatrice on a time went to the sea side in the clothing of a Monke, and called to him the Wolf.. The Wolf fishe.. knowing what he was, sayde [etc.]. **1634** [? BRATHWAIT] *Strange Metam.* C 3, The Pike.. is called the Wolfe of the water. **1653** WALTON *Angler* vii. 144 Pikes.. called the Tyrant of the Rivers, or the Freshwater-wolf, by reason of his bold, greedy, devouring disposition. **1808** NEILL in *Mem. Wernerian N.H. Soc.* (1811) I. 539 *Trigla Gurnardus*. Grey Gurnard.. known.. as Captain, Hardhead, Goukmey, and Woof. **1896** *Westm. Gaz.* 16 Sept. 3/3 This defence of the 'wolf of the stream' will, we are afraid, be regarded in many quarters as nothing short of rank heresy.

†**c.** = *wolf-spider*: see 11 e. *Obs.*

1608 TOPSELL *Serpents* 247 Spyders.. which by reason of their rauenous gut.. haue purchased to themselues the names of wolfes, and hunting Spyders.

d. A name for various destructive insect larvæ, esp. that of the wolf-moth, which infests granaries.

1682 LISTER *Godartius Of Insects* 65 Live Wormes, which our Dutch Boors call Woolves. **1694** A. VAN LEUWENHOEK in *Phil. Trans.* XVIII. 194 The Wolf is a small white Worm armed with two red Sheers or Teeth.. wherewith it bores and feeds on the Grains of Corn. **1743** H. BAKER *Microscope* 223. **1815** KIRBY & SP. *Entomol.* ii. (1818) I. 32 Leeuwenhoek's wolf (*Tinea granella*).

4. = *wolf tree*, sense 11 e below.

1949 *Q. Jrnl. Forestry* XLIII. 127 Most props containing large knots have been prepared from quick-grown heavily branched trees such as wolves. **1966** *Times* 21 Apr. 16/7 Douglas fir plantations nearly always have some undesirable wolves which have to be cut out.

5. a. A person or being having the character of a wolf; one of a cruel, ferocious, or rapacious disposition. In early use applied esp. to the Devil or his agents (***wolf of hell***); later most freq., in allusion to certain biblical passages (e.g. Matt. vii. 15, Acts xx. 29), to enemies or persecutors attacking the 'flocks' of the faithful.

a **900** *O.E. Martyrol.* 24 Jan. 30 þu eart deofles wulf. *a* **900** *Cynewulf's Crist* 256 Hafað se awyrȝda wulf tostenced, deor dædscua, dryhten, þin eowde. *c* **1380** WYCLIF *Wks.* (1880) 149 Woluys of helle stranglen hem. *c* **1386** CHAUCER *Pars. T.* ¶694 As seith seint Augustyn, they been the deueles wolues that stranglen the sheepe of Ihesu crist. *c* **1450** *Godstow Reg.* 18 (Kalendar, June) Cyryce and Iulytte, kepe us fro þe wulfe. **1497** BP. ALCOCK *Mons Perfect.* A iij, It putteth from us the wulf the deuyll deuourer of mannes soule. **1577** KENDALL *Flowers Epigr.* 43 The feend the woulfe of hell.

c **1205** LAY. 21315 Ich am wulf & he is gat. *a* **1225** *Ancr. R.* 120 Mon wroð is wulf, oðer leun, oðer unicorne. **13..** *Cursor M.* 20935 (Edin.), Paul.. Eftirward bicom prechure, Schepe of wlue, meke of felle. *c* **1386** CHAUCER *Prol.* 513 [A priest] kepeth wel his folde So that the wolf ne made it nat myscarie. *c* **1450** *Cov. Myst.* vii. 102 From þe wulf to saue al shepe of his flok. *a* **1529** SKELTON *Col. Cloute* 153 The wolf from the dore To werryn and to kepe From theyr goostly shepe. **1577** [see 9 j]. *a* **1586** SIDNEY *Arcadia* IV. (1922) 134 Since such a slye wolfe was entred among them, that could make justice the cloake of tirannye. **1637** MILTON *Lycidas* 128 Besides what the grim Woolf with privy paw Daily devours apace. **1722** CROXALL *Fables Æsop* xlii. 79 If Wolves sometimes creep into the Church in Sheep's Cloathing. **1781** COWPER *Charity* 287 Let just restraint.. Chain up the wolves and tigers of mankind. **1847** TENNYSON *Princess* II. 173 Why who are these? a wolf within the fold! A pack of wolves! **1860** EMERSON *Cond. Life, Fate* Wks. (Bohn) II. 321 What good, honest, generous men at home, will be wolves and foxes on change!

†**b.** Applied to a person, etc. that should be hunted down like a wolf. (Cf. WOLF'S-HEAD.) *Obs.*

[**1375** BARBOUR *Bruce* VI. 470 To hunt hym out of the land, With hund and horn, rycht as he were A volf.] ? **1554** W. TURNER (*title*) The Huntyng of the Romyshe Vuolfe. **1593** SHAKS. *3 Hen VI*, II. iv. 13 Nay Warwicke, single out some other Chace, For I my selfe will hunt this Wolfe to death. **1606** DEKKER *Seven Deadly Sins* 9 Hunt these English Wolues to death. *a* **1638** BROWNLOW *Rep.* II. (1652) 113 He is called the Oppresser of the Poore, and *Fleta* calls him Woolfe which ought to be hunted from place to place.

c. *slang.* (*a*) A sexually aggressive male; a would-be seducer of women; (*b*) orig. *U.S.*, a male homosexual seducer or one who adopts an active role with a partner.

Occas. applied to a woman: see quot. 1968 s.v. WOLFESS 2.

(*a*) **1847** THACKERAY *Van. F.* (1848) xxxvii. 335 'Rawdon,' said Becky,..'I must have a sheep-dog... I mean a *moral* shepherd's dog.. to keep the wolves off me.' **1862** MRS. H. WOOD *Mrs. Haliburton's Troubles* II. ii. 23, I vowed I'd tell Mark what I had seen and heard, and what sort of a wolf she allowed to make her presents of fine clothes. **1945** S. LEWIS *Cass Timberlane* xix. 113 She was innocent, but this Roskinen was a wolf. **1968** [see KARATE *v.*]. **1973** 'E. PETERS' *City of Gold & Shadows* ii. 25 He did not look like a wolf, but he did look like a young man with an eye for a girl.

(*b*) **1917** *New Republic* 13 Jan. 293/2 The sodomist, the degenerate, the homosexual wolf. **1931**, etc. [see JOCKER]. **1950** PATTERSON & CONRAD *Scottsboro Boy* II. ii. 91, I learned men were having men. Old guys, they called them wolves, they saw me looking at this stuff and thought I might be a gal-boy. **1978** K. J. DOVER *Greek Homosexuality* II. 87 In prisons the 'wolf' is the active homosexual, and does not reverse roles with his partners.

6. a. As a type of a destructive or 'devouring' agency, esp. hunger or famine; often in such phrases as ***to keep the wolf from the door*** (now always = to ward off hunger or starvation).

c **1470** HARDING *Chron.* XCVIII. xii. (1812) 181 Endowe hym now, with noble sapience By whiche he maye the wolf werre [*v.r.* bete] frome the gate. **1555** *Instit. Gentl.* G ij, This manne can litle skyl.. to saue himself harmlesse from the perilous accidentes of this world, keping y[e] wulf from the doore (as they cal it). *c* **1645** HOWELL *Lett.* VI. lx. (1650) I. 254 That Hee or Shee should have wherewith to support both,.. at least to keep the Woolf from the door, otherwise 'twere a meer madnes to marry. **1679** J. GOODMAN *Penit. Pard.* I. ii. (1713) 31 That hungry Wolf, want and necessity, which now stands at his door. **1726** LEONI *Alberti's Archit.* I. 75/1 Poets call the Earth.. the Woolf of the Gods, because it devours and consumes every thing. **1755** *Mem. Capt. P. Drake* II. v. 176 Business began to flag, and the most I could do was to keep the Wolf from the Door. **1858** [see 9 a]. **1891** HERMAN *His Angel* 73 It makes a lot of difference to.. one's happiness if the wolf is not scratching at the door.

b. Applied to a ravenous appetite or craving for food.

1576 BAKER *Gesner's Jewell of Health* 66 b, The water cureth that sore feeding, which most men name the Wolfe. *c* **1600** *G. Peele's Merrie Jests* 18 Hauing as villanous a Wolfe in his belly as George. **1693** *Humours Town* 38 There is a monstrous Disease.. in Nature, which they.. call the Wolf, which makes the distemper'd eat beyond Reason. **1823** SCOTT *Quentin D.* x, I know thine appetite is a wolf... Canst thou yet hold out an hour without food? **1848** MRS. GASKELL *Mary Barton* vi, There was no breakfast to lounge over; their lounge was taken in bed, to try.. to deaden the gnawing wolf within.

7. a. A name for certain malignant or erosive diseases in men and animals (see quots.); *esp.* = LUPUS 4. *Obs.* or *dial.*

1559 MORWYNG *Evonymus* 86 Aqua vitae is commodious and profitable.. against the disease called the Wulfe. **1572** J. JONES *Bathes Buckstone* 16 b, Frettinge vlceres, wolues in the brest, and many daungerous pustles. **1576** TURBERV. *Venerie* (1908) 230 The disease called the Wolfe, which is a kernell or round bunch of flesh, which groweth.. vntill it kill the dogge. **1577** GOOGE *Heresbach's Husb.* III. 131 A disease [in cattle] which they call the Woolfe, others the Tayle [TAIL *sb.*[1] 10]. **1589** *Nottingham Rec.* IV. 225 A poore woman that had a woolfe in her legge. **1684** J. S. *Profit & Pleas. United* 207 (*Horse*), Wolf, or over-growing of the Flesh. *Ibid.* 208 The Shee-Wolf, or Boyls and Knobs on the Foot [of a horse]. **1709** *Brit. Apollo* II. No. 2. 2/2 What is call'd by.. Surgeons a Wolf, is a sort of Cancerous Ulcer, more properly so called when in the Legs. **1741** [see TAIL *sb.*[1] 10]. **1796** PEGGE *Anonym.* (1809) 108 The common people usually call a cancer in the breast a Wolf. **1801** *Sporting Mag.* XVII. 153 All sorts of cancers, wens, and wolves.

†**b.** = *wolf's-tooth*: see 11 f. *Obs.*

1607 MARKHAM *Cavel.* VII. xxxvii. 54 The woolfes.. are two sharp teeth more then nature allowes, growing out of the vpper iawes, nexte to the great teeth.

8. A name for apparatus of various kinds.

†**a.** An ancient military engine with sharp teeth, employed for grasping battering-rams used by besiegers. *Obs.*

1489 CAXTON *Faytes of A.* II. xxxvi. K vj, Men make another engyn whiche is called wolffe that hath an yron bowed with grete and sharp teeth whiche engyn is in suche manere sette to the walle that hyt cometh and gropith the maste of the mowton, and holdeth it so fast that hit can not be drawe nother forward nor bakward. **1632** HAYWARD tr. *Biondi's Eromena* 150 Nor had they as much as iron Wolves [orig. *lupi*] and Crows to graspe the Ram withall.

b. A kind of fishing-net: also *wolf-net* (see 11 e).

1725 *Bradley's Family Dict.*, *Wolf*, the name of a Net that is a great destroyer of Fish, as well in Rivers as in Ponds. **1847** HALLIWELL. **1867** SMYTH *Sailor's Word-bk.*, *Wolf*, a kind of fishing-net.

c. *Textile Manuf.* A willow or willy (WILLY *sb.*[1] 3). (Cf. G. *wolf*, Sw. *vulf*.)

1875 KNIGHT *Dict. Mech.*, *Wolf*, a beating or opening machine, for tearing apart the tussocks of cotton as delivered in the bale.

9. *Mus.* **a.** 'The harsh howling sound of certain chords on keyed instruments, particularly the organ, when tuned by any form of unequal temperament' (Grove's Dict. Mus.); a chord or interval characterized by such a sound.

After G. *wolf* (Arnolt Schlick, *Spiegel der Orgelmacher*, 1511).

1788 in *Abridgm. Specif. Patents, Music* (1871) 22 By this means the temperature of all thirds and 'fifths' can be highly improved, and what is called the 'wolfe' is entirely done away. **1889** HIPKINS in *Grove's Dict. Mus.* IV. 188 The G♯ to the E♭, he [*sc.* Schlick] calls the 'wolf', and says it is not used as a dominant chord to cadence C♯. *Ibid.* 485 In the mean-tone system.. there is one fifth out of tune to this extent [nearly half a semitone]... There are also four false thirds, which are sharp to about the same extent... All chords into which any of these five intervals enter are intolerable, and are 'wolves'.

b. In instruments of the viol class, a harsh sound due to faulty vibration in certain notes.

1876 STAINER & BARRETT *Dict. Mus. Terms.* **1884** HAWEIS *Mus. Life* 225 A slight mistake in position [of the sound-bar], a looseness, an inequality or roughness of finish, will produce that hollow teeth-on-edge growl called the 'wolf'. **1901** *Blackw. Mag.* July 15/2 There's a hantle o' wolfs on my father's strings.

10. Phrases. **a.** ***to cry 'wolf'***: to raise a false alarm (in allusion to the fable of the shepherd boy who deluded people with false cries of 'Wolf!'). **b.** ***to keep the wolf from the door***: see 6. **c.** ***to have*** or ***hold a wolf by the ears*** [= Gr. τῶν ὠτῶν ἔχειν τὸν λύκον, L. *lupum auribus tenēre*]: to be in a precarious situation or predicament (see quots.). †**d.** ***a hair of the same wolf***: cf. DOG *sb.*[1] 17 e. †**e.** ***to howl among wolves*** [= F. *hurler avec les loups*]: to adapt oneself to one's company, though one disapproves of it. **f.** ***a wolf in a lamb's skin, in sheep's clothing***, etc.: a person who conceals malicious intentions under an appearance of gentleness or friendliness (in allusion to Matt. vii. 15). †**g.** ***to be in the wolf's mouth*** [cf. F. *à la gueule du loup*]: to be in deadly peril. **h.** ***to see*** or ***have seen a wolf*** [= Gr. λύκον ἰδεῖν, etc.]: to be tongue-tied (from the old belief that a man on seeing a wolf lost his voice). **i.** ***to wake a sleeping wolf***: to invite trouble or disturbance (cf. DOG *sb.*[1] 17 k). **j.** In various proverbial expressions. **k.** ***to throw to the wolves***: to sacrifice (a subordinate, friend, ally, etc.) to one's enemies in order to save oneself. **l.** ***lone wolf***: see LONE *a.* 3 c.

a. [**1692** R. L'ESTRANGE *Fables* ccclx. 332 The Boy.. would be Crying *a Wolf, a Wolf*, when there was none, and then could not be Believed when there was.] **1858** MRS. CRAIK *Woman's Th.* xii. 316 She begins to suspect she is 'not so young as she used to be'; that after crying 'Wolf' ever since the respectable maturity of seventeen—.. the grim wolf, old age, is actually showing his teeth in the distance. **1886** BARING-GOULD *Court Royal* xxxviii, This is Beavis' cry of wolf, is it?

c. **1560** DAUS tr. *Sleidane's Comm.* 425 The Bishop of Rome,.. as the prouerbe is, helde the woulfe by both eares, ..he coueted to gratifie the kyng, and also feared themperours displeasure. **1631** QUARLES *Samson* xi. 63, I have a Wolfe by th' eares; I dare be bold, Neither with safety, to let goe, nor hold: What shall I doe? **1884** *Times* 29 Oct. 9/3 These expressions come from a man who has a wolf by the ears, whose task is well-nigh desperate.

d. **1614** B. JONSON *Bart. Fair* I. iii, 'Twas a hot night with some of vs, last night, Iohn: shal we pluck a hayre o' the same wolfe, to-day?

e. **1578** TIMME *Calvin on Gen.* vi. 181 This diuelishe prouerbe..we must howle among the Wolues. **1649** BP. HALL *Cases Consc.* (1650) 187 What do you howling amongst Wolves, if you be not one?

f. [*c* **1400** *Rom. Rose* 6260 Who-so toke a wethers skin, And wrapped a gredy wolf therin.] *c* **1460** *Wisdom* 490 in *Macro Plays* 51 Ther ys a wolffe in a lombys skyn. **1533** MORE *Debell. Salem* xvi. 87 He wyl play the woulfe in a lambes skynne. **1591** SHAKS. *1 Hen. VI*, I. iii. 55 Thou Wolfe in Sheepes array. **1718** BREVAL *Play is the Plot* I. i. 9 Mercy o' me! what have we here then? a Wolf in Sheep's cloathing? **1722** [see 5]. **1857** TROLLOPE *Three Clerks* xiv, Why had this tender lamb been allowed to wander out of the fold, while a wolf in sheep's clothing was invited into the pasture-ground?

g. **1338** R. BRUNNE *Chron.* (1810) 42 þan was Eilred in þe wolfes mouth.

h. [**1480** CAXTON *Mirrour* II. xv. 100 Yf a wulf and a man see that one other fro ferre, he that is first seen becometh anon aferd. **1562** LEGH *Armory* 98.] **1575** A. FLEMING *Virg. Bucol.* IX. 29 Mœris holdes his tounge, The wolfe hath spide out Mœris fyrst. **1697** DRYDEN *Virg. Past.* IX. 75 My Voice grows hoarse; I feel the Notes decay; As if the Wolves had seen me first to Day. **1767** FAWKES tr. *Idyll. Theocritus* xiv. 30 'What are you mute?' I said—a waggish guest, 'Perhaps she's seen a Wolf,' rejoin'd in jest. **1823** SCOTT *Quentin D.* xviii, Our young companion has seen a wolf,..and he has lost his tongue in consequence.

i. **1597** SHAKS. *2 Hen. IV*, I. ii. 174 Since al is wel, keep it so: wake not a sleeping Wolfe.

j. *c* **1412** HOCCLEVE *De Reg. Princ.* 3064 A fflye folweþ the honye; þe wolf, careyn. **1553** T. WILSON *Rhet.* (1580) 202 We saie whishte, the Woulfe is at hande, when the same man cometh in the meane season, of whom we spake before. [After L. *lupus in fabula*.] **1577** WOLTON *Cast. Christians* B iiij b, Lyons..doo not one encounter another, the Serpent stingeth no Serpent: but Man is a Woolfe to Man. **1643** J. TAYLOR (Water P.) *Let. sent to London* 6 It is a hard world when one Wolfe eates another. **1721** KELLY *Scot. Prov.* Y 67 You have given the Wolf the Wedder to keep. **1784** COWPER *Task* IV. 103, I mourn the pride And av'rice that make man a wolf to man. **1872** BROWNING *Fifine* ix, If hunger, proverbs say, allures the wolf from wood.

k. **1927** F. HARRIS *My Life & Loves* III. x. 146 But if Gladstone had had his letter back, I think the G.O.M. would have thrown Dilke to the wolves. **1958** *Listener* 6 Nov. 743/2 This able and agreeable doctor [*sc.* Lord Addison] was thrown to the wolves by a Prime Minister who had good reason to know that his own position was desperate. **1980** P. KINSLEY *Vatchman Switch* xli. 236 If anyone..showed disloyalty he would throw him to the wolves.

11. *attrib.* and *Comb.* **a.** Simple attrib., as ***wolf bark, bite, chase, den, eye, fur, growl, hair, hunt, kind, pack, pelt, pest, snow, tail, track, -trap***; appositive, as ***wolf ancestry, bitch, burd*** (= offspring), ***cub, dam, nurse, whelp***; in connexion with belief in lycanthropy or the association of human beings with wolves, as ***wolf boy, brethren, charm, child, clan, dance, devil, life, man, mask, people, race, totem, type, woman***; also with reference to the skin or fur of the animal, as ***wolf-belt, coat, collar, hat, jacket, -shirt***; **b.** Objective, as ***wolf-breeding, -catcher, -hunter, -hunting, -rider, -scaring, -slaying, -spearing*** sbs. and adjs. **c.** Agential or instrumental, as ***wolf-begotten, -haunted, -moved*** adjs. **d.** Similative and parasynthetic, as ***wolf-coloured, -eyed, -grey, -headed, -shaped*** adjs.; also ***wolf-like*** adj. and adv.

1860 O. W. HOLMES *Elsie V.* iii, The great cur showed his teeth,—and the devilish instincts of his old *wolf-ancestry looked out of his eyes. **1845** R. W. HAMILTON *Pop. Educ.* ix. 251 Was that the *wolf-bark of the Corsican dynasty? **1866** J. B. ROSE tr. *Ovid's Met.* 73 The *wolf-begotten Nape. **1883** STALLYBRASS *Grimm's Teut. Mythol.* III. 1094 Our oldest native notions make the assumption of wolf-shape depend on arraying oneself in a *wolf-belt or wolf-shirt. *c* **1410** *Master of Game* (MS. Digby 182) vi, When þe *wolfe bycche hath hir whelpes. **1820** SCOTT *Abbot* xix, He who speaks irreverently of the Holy Father..is the cub of a heretic wolf-bitch. **1873** FAYRER *Clin. Observ. India* 261 *Wolf Bite of the Forearm. **1857** DALTON (*title*) The *Wolf-Boy of China. **1889** W. B. YEATS *Wanderings of Oisin* 77 *Wolf-breeding mountains. **1892** RIDER HAGGARD *Nada* xiv, As yet the *Wolf-Brethren and their pack killed no men. **1827** SCOTT *Highl. Widow* v, There shall never be..dirge played, for thee or thy bloody *wolf-burd. **1611** COTGR., *Louvetier*, a *Wolfe-catcher. **1644** *Early Recs. Portsmouth, R.I.* (1901) 33 That the wolfe Catcher shall be payed out of the tresuery. **1921** *Chamb. Jrnl.* July 473/1 The *wolf-charms he used. **1824** in *Coll. Missouri Hist. Soc.* (1928) VI. 75 Had a *wolfe chase. **1835** C. F. HOFFMAN *Winter in West* I. 244 That most exciting of sports, a wolf-chase on horse-back. **1859** LANG *Wand. India* 268 In this district..'a *wolf child,' as the natives of India express it, was found some years ago. **1890** FRAZER *Golden Bough* iv. II. 351 The Indians of this part of America are divided into totem clans, of which the *Wolf clan is one of the principal. **1977** P. WAY *Super-Celeste* II. 117 She put on her Siberian *wolf coat. **1974** *Selfridge Christmas Catal.* 14 Leather coat with *wolf collar and hamster lining. **1779** FORREST *Voy. N. Guinea* 135 The largest bird of Paradise..The breast..is black, or *wolf-coloured. **1926** Wolf-coloured [see KEESHOND]. **1582** STANYHURST *Æneis* II. (Arb.) 55 Lyke rauening *woolfdams vpsoackt and gaunted in hunger. **1908** *Sunset Mag.* Apr. 566/1 A *wolf-dance [by] painted naked savages. *c* **1440** *Alphabet of Tales* 307 þai fand in þe wud a *wulfe den & þer was wulfe-whelpis þerin, bod þer dam was away. **1895** KIPLING *2nd Jungle Bk.* 70 We will teach them to shelter *Wolf-devils! **1922** JOYCE *Ulysses* 434 Her *wolfeyes shining. **1866** LYTTON *Lost Tales Miletus, Fate Catchas* 86 A *wolf-eyed rover. **1883** 'OUIDA' *Wanda* I. 15 The little fierce half-naked boy who in frost was wrapped in *wolf-fur. **1863** BARING-GOULD *Iceland* 118 Coarse *wolf grey hair. **1895** KIPLING *2nd Jungle Bk.* 223 A deep *wolf-growl that silenced the curs. **1865** BARING-GOULD *Werewolves* v. 59 When the *wolf-hair began to break out and his bodily shape to change. **1974** *Country Life* 3 Oct. 980/2 Natural wolf three-quarter length jacket worn with a *wolf hat. **1865** KINGSLEY *Herew.* Prel., The dark *wolf-haunted woods. **1898** *Saga-Bk. Viking Club* Jan. 35 Two *wolf-headed serpents. **1835** C. F. HOFFMAN *Winter in West* II. 12, I was on a *wolf-hunt by moonlight. **1841** *Ir. Penny Jrnl.* 8 May 355 He took the spear from the *wolf-hunter's hand. **1690** TEMPLE *Misc.* II. iv. 44 In his *Wolf-Huntings..when he used to be abroad in the Mountains three or four Days together. **1731–2** *Norwich Mercury* 19–26 Feb. 1/1 The King went a Wolf-hunting. **1841** *Ir. Penny Jrnl.* 8 May 353 No particular breed of dogs was ever kept for wolf-hunting in this country. **1976** *Jrnl.* (Newcastle) 26 Nov. (Advt.), Mink coat..also modern *wolf jacket with matching fox hat, both coats new. **1892** RIDER HAGGARD *Nada* xiv, Galazi asked him if he would..rule with him over the *wolf-kind. *Ibid.*, The desire of this *wolf-life. **1580** HOLLYBAND *Treas. Fr. Tong*, *Manger Louvichement*, to eate *Wolfe like. **1593** Q. ELIZ. *Boeth.* IV. pr. iii. 51 The violent robber of others goodes..swellith in coueting, & [thou] mayst call him woolf lyke, feerce & contentious. **1612** J. DAVIES *Muses Sacrif.* (Grosart) 82/2 Our Wolfe-like Appetites. **1725** POPE *Odyss.* x. 513 Will you..wolf-like howl away the midnight hour? **1844** KINGLAKE *Eothen* i, Big wolf-like dogs. **1610** HOLLAND *Camden's Brit.* II. (*Ireland*) 83 Some..doe affirme, that certaine men in this tract are yeerly turned into Wolves [*marg.* *Wolf-men]. **1892** RIDER HAGGARD *Nada* xiv, I have become a wolf-man. For with the wolves I hunt and raven. **1913** FRAZER *Golden Bough* xi. (ed. 3) II. 271 Indians dressed in wolf-skins and wearing *wolf-masks. **1868** MORRIS *Earthly Par.* I. II. 489 *Wolf-moved battered shields, O'er poor dead corpses. **1887** BOWEN *Virg. Æneid* I. 275 The yellow skin of his [*sc.* Romulus's] *wolf-nurse. **1923** D. H. LAWRENCE *Birds, Beasts & Flowers* 200 On to the fur of the *wolf-pelt that strews the plain. **1892** RIDER HAGGARD *Nada* xvi, That *wolf-people of yours. **1872** *Gentl. Mag.* Dec. 680 We hear no more of the *wolf-pest till the days of Queen Mary. **1911** A. LANG in *Encycl. Brit.* XIX. 137/1 The..totem of the *wolf-race of men. **1848** LYTTON *Harold* v. i, Belsta, and Heidr, and Hulla..the *wolf-riders. **1804** CAMPBELL *Soldier's Dream* 6 The *wolf-scaring faggot that guarded the slain. **1891** *Hardwick's Sci. Gossip* 1 Oct. 233/1 The *wolf-shaped Mänagarm. **1883** *wolf-shirt [see *wolf-belt*]. **1649** C. WASE *Sophocles, Electra* 1 [Apollo] the *wolf-slaying god. *c* **1878** G. M. HOPKINS *Poems* (1967) 73 There did storms not mingle?..*wolfsnow, worlds of it, wind there? **1855** MACAULAY *Hist. Eng.* xii. III. 136 *note*, In a poem published as late as 1719, and entitled Macdermot,..wolfhunting and *wolfspearing are represented as common sports in Munster. *a* **1674** MILTON *Hist. Moscovia* i. Wks. 1851 VIII. 431 The Russe of better sort goes..on his Sled ..drawn with a horse well deckt; with many Fox or *Wolve-tails about his neck. **1911** J. A. MACCULLOCH *Relig. Anc. Celts* xiv. 218 An early *wolf-totem. **1780** EDMONDSON *Her.* II. Gloss., **Wolf-Trap* is a German bearing. This trap is made of a stick, bent like the head of a pick-ax, and having in the centre a ring, whereto the collar is fixed. **1883** STEVENSON *Treas. Isl.* xxx, If we both get alive out of this wolf-trap, I'll do my best to save you. *c* **1440** *wolf-whelp [see *wolf-den*]. **1823** SCOTT *Quentin D.* xvi, He was the imprisoned wolf-whelp, which at the first opportunity broke his chain. **1863** W. K. KELLY *Curios. Indo-Europ. Tradit.* 252 Mention is made of a *wolfwoman in the Mabinogion.

e. Special Combs.: **wolf-berry**, a N. American shrub, *Symphoricarpus occidentalis*, allied to the snowberry; **wolf call** *colloq.* (orig. *U.S.*) = WOLF-WHISTLE; † **wolf-claw** = *wolf's-claw* (see f); **wolf-cry** [f. vbl. phr. *to cry 'wolf'*: see 10 a] = *false alarm* s.v. FALSE *a.* 14 c; **wolf cub**, (*a*) a young wolf; (*b*) = CUB *sb.*[1] 2 c; also *fig.*; **wolf-drum**, a drum with head made of wolfskin; † **wolf-fly**, a kind of large fly which preys upon other insects; **wolf-greyhound**, a greyhound used in hunting wolves; † **Wolfland**, a former nickname for Ireland; **wolf-madness**, a form of mania in which a man imagines himself to be a wolf (= LYCANTHROPY 1); **wolf-moth** (see quot., and cf. 3 d); **wolf-net** = 8 b; **wolf-note** = 9 b; **wolf pack**, a number of wolves naturally associating as a group, esp. for hunting; also *fig.*, esp. denoting an attacking group of German submarines in the war of 1939–45; **wolf pen** *U.S.*, a strong box made of logs used for trapping wolves; **wolf-platform** *Archæol.*, a hill-side embankment in the form of a platform, suggested to have been used as a means of defence against the wolves of the lowlands; † **wolf-sheep**, a tribute of a sheep paid by a tenant for protection against wolves; **wolf-spear**, a wolf-hunter's spear; **wolf-spider**, a spider of the family *Lycosidæ*, which hunts after and springs upon its prey; **wolf-stone** (cf. DOG-STONE); † **wolf-thistle** = *wolf's-thistle* (see f); **wolf-tick**, a tick of the genus *Ixodes* infesting wolves and dogs; **wolf-tooth** = *wolf's-tooth* (see f); **wolf tree**, a tree that is occupying more space than has been allowed for it, so restricting the growth of its neighbours (cf. sense 4 above;) **wolf-willow** *Canada*, any of several shrubs, esp. *Elæagnus commutata*, which has silver-grey foliage. See also WOLF-DOG etc.

1834 G. DON *Gen. Syst. Gard.* III. 451 *Wolf-berry. **1948** *Time* 27 Sept. 12/1 Grins, whistles, *wolf-calls..followed her in this exclusively male territory. **1958** *Spectator* 6 June 726/3 The streets are lined by groups of lounging youths watching the girls go by (but no whistles or wolf-calls). **1597** GERARDE *Herbal* III. clvii. 1374 *Woolfe claw Mosse. **1915** W. J. LOCKE *Jaffery* xxii. 315, I have a habit of losing things and setting the household in frantic search,..only to discover that I have had the wretched object in my pocket all the time. So accustomed is Barbara to this *wolf-cry that if I came up to her without my head and informed her that I had lost it, she would be profoundly sceptical. **1980** *Listener* 9 Oct. 462/3 The news that the Met season might have to be cancelled..is an annual threat, a wolf-cry. **1817** SCOTT *Harold* I. viii, A she-wolf, and her *wolf-cubs twain. **1860** G. H. K. *Vac. Tour.* 130 Five or six active wolf-cubs. **1916** R. BADEN-POWELL in *Wolf Cub* Dec. 2/1 Hullo, Wolf Cubs! What swells you are to have a newspaper all to yourselves! **1963** H. WILSON in *Times* 8 May 6/3 If we had to face a really dedicated and trained spy, not an overgrown wolf cub who had gone wrong, then the system would have been wide open in respect of security. **1981** E. LONGFORD *Queen Mother* ii. 35 (*caption*) Wellington: the Duchess of York inspects a pack of wolf cubs. **1598** SYLVESTER *Du Bartas* II. I. III. *Furies* 107 At the sound of *Wolf-Drum's rattling thunder Th'affrighted Sheep-skin-Drum doth rent in sunder. **1658** ROWLAND tr. *Moufet's Theat. Insectes* 934 The first..called in Latine, *Lupus*, in English, the *Wolf fly... feeds especially upon flies, if he cannot come by these he preys upon other Insects. **1753** *Chambers' Cycl. Suppl.* s.v. *Lupus*. **1829** *Glover's Hist. Derby* I. 177 *Asilus*, Wolf Fly. **1825** SCOTT *Talism.* vi, Three alans, as they were then called (*wolf-greyhounds, that is) of the largest size. **1692** *Advice to Painter* 20 A chilling Damp, And *Wolfe-land Howl, run thro' the rising Camp. **1855** MACAULAY *Hist. Eng.* xii. III. 136 *note*, In William's reign Ireland was sometimes called by the nick-name of Wolf land. **1662** BAYFIELD *Treat de Morb.* 49 *Lupina insania*, *Wolf-madness. **1854** *Jrnl. Mental Sci.* 52 Lycanthropy or Wolfmadness. **1863** WOOD *Illustr. Nat. Hist.* III. 544 Another species.., popularly called the *Wolf-moth (*Tinea granella*),..haunts granaries and malthouses, and does great damage by feeding on the grains and fastening them together with its silken web. **1819** REES *Cycl.*, **Wolf-Net*,..a kind of net used in fishing, which takes great numbers, and has its name from the destruction it causes. **1915** *Proc. Camb. Philos. Soc.* XVIII. 85 On all stringed instruments of the violin type a certain pitch can be found which it is difficult..to produce by bowing. This note is called the '*wolf-note'. **1895** SIR H. MAXWELL *Duke of Britain* viii. 105 Supposing the *wolf-pack over-whelmed you. **1941** *Hutchinson's Pict. Hist. War* 9 July–30 Sept. 270/1 The U-boat is now being used as a unit in a flotilla... We had a hint of it a year ago when the Berlin bulletins talked about 'wolf pack' attacks on convoys. **1951** W. STEVENS *Let.* 2 Oct. (1967) 731 There is probably a sort of wolf-pack that follows him [*sc.* Hermann Hesse] round. His idea of throwing out a poem or two to slow them up and invite them to devour each other sounds almost like folklore. **1977** *Time* 26 Sept. 9/2 What Andreas Baader and Ulrike Meinhof spawned as a small wolf pack of urban guerrillas has now become a scattered army of vicious malcontents, bent on destroying the society around them. **1980** 'D. GRANT' *Emerald Decision* vi. 129 They were headed for the perilous North Channel..if they survived the wolfpacks. **1647** in *Watertown* (Mass.) *Rec.* (1894) I. I. 12 The Towne gaue: to John Witherll: there Right in the palisado that inclosed the *woulfe pen. **1876** J. S. INGRAM *Centennial Expedition* 106 The places of interest are..the Aviary, the Fox Pens, the Wolf-Pens. **1906** *Cornh. Mag.* May 615 At [the] base [of the hill] the great *wolf platforms would be set in a position where a conflict might be carried on without stampeding the herds in the camp above. **1528** in *Archaeologia* LIII. 381 He hath yerely..one shepe of the best instede of a tolle called the *wolfe shepe, for the which ..he ys bownde to hunt the wolfe. **1823** MRS. HEMANS *Siege of Valencia* vi. *Cid's Battle Song*, That her sons..may.. sharpen the point of the red *wolf-spear. **1608** TOPSELL *Serpents* 270 One kind of Autumnall Lupi, or *Wolfe-Spyder. **1753** *Chambers' Cycl. Suppl.* s.v. *Lupus*. **1863** WOOD *Illustr. Nat. Hist.* III. 656 The Lycosidæ, or Wolf-spiders,..take their prey in fair chase instead of catching it in nets. *Ibid.* 657 About sixteen or seventeen British species of Wolf-spider are already known. **1640** in Entick *London* (1766) II. 181 For a dog-stone, 2.6. For a *wolf-stone, 2.0. **1525** *Grete Herbal* cxxii. (1529) H ij, De cameleonta. *Wolfe thystle. **1579** LANGHAM *Gard. Health* (1633) 683 Wolfthistle. **1861** HULME tr. *Moquin-Tandon* II. VI. iv. 302 The Ticks, or Ixodes... In France the two principal species are—1, the *Wolf Tick; 2, Reticulated Tick. **1753** *Chambers' Cycl. Suppl.*, *Wolf-Tooth. **1928** R. S. TROUP *Silvicultural Systems* xix. 187 The stands..were kept fairly dense in order to promote clean stems, congested thickets being thinned and *wolf-trees removed. **1966** D. WATERS *Forestry* xviii. 94 Wolf trees are large mis-shapen trees which do not provide good timber. **1889** J. G. DONKIN *Trooper & Redskin* 86 The luscious perfume of *wolf-willow and wild rose..come scampering on the western breeze. **1948** A. L. RAND *Mammals Eastern Rockies* 90 Wolf-willow clumps, gopher holes, odd stones, aspen bluffs. **1974** M. LAURENCE *Diviners* 357 There were these thin prairie maples and the wolf willow.

f. Combinations with genitive, as ***wolf's-hide*** (attrib.): **wolf's-claw**, a name for club-moss (= LYCOPODIUM 1); **wolf's-foot**, † (*a*) ? the sea-wolf, *Anarrichas lupus*; (*b*) = *wolf's-claw*; † **wolf's-thistle**, a species of carline thistle, *Carlina acaulis*; **wolf's-tooth**, *Farriery* [cf. MHG. *wolfzan*, G. *wolfszahn*] (see quots.); † **wolf's-wort** = WOLF-WORT a. See also WOLF'S-BANE, etc.

1578 LYTE *Dodoens* III. lxxi. 412 The fifth kinde of Mosse, called *Wolfes clawe. **1753** *Chambers' Cycl. Suppl.* s.v. *Lycopodium*, The common wolf's claw moss. **1861** S. THOMSON *Wild Fl.* III. (ed. 4) 289 The..common club-moss, or wolf's-claw, or 'stag's-horn.' **1443** in *Bekynton's Corr.* (Rolls) II. 238 Chattok dedit piscem vocatum Pedulupum aut *Wolfes-foote al. Luperius. **1597** GERARDE *Herbal* III. clvii. 1374 Called..in English Woolfes foote, or Woolfes clawe, and likewise Club Mosse. **1859** H. KINGSLEY *G. Hamlyn* vi, Crowd close, little snipes, among the cup-moss and wolf's foot. **1866** LYTTON *Lost Tales Miletus* 125 A *wolf's-hide mantle for his robe of state. *a* **1400–50** *Stockh. Med. MS.* 179 *Wolfys thystyl: *camalion*. **1597** GERARDE *Herbal* Suppl., Wooluisthistle is *Chamæleon*. **1565–6** BLUNDEVIL *Horsemanship* IV. xlvi. (1580) 19 b, A horse..hauing two extraordinarie teeth called the *Woolfes teeth, which be two little teeth growing in the vpper iawes, next vnto the great grinding teeth. **1737** BRACKEN *Farriery Impr.* (1756) I. 323 A Horse is said to have Wolves-Teeth, when his Teeth grow either Outwards or Inwards so that their Points prick and wound either the Tongue, or Gum when he eats. **1864** E. MAYHEW *Illustr. Horse Management* 146 At one year old,..frequently at birth, little nodules of bone, without fangs, merely attached to the gums, appear in front of each row of grinders. These are vulgarly denominated 'Wolves' Teeth'. **1575** BANISTER *Chyrurg.* 95 *Aconitum* *woulfes wort.

Hence **'wolfdom**, the realm or domain of wolves, wolves collectively; **'wolfhood**, the state or condition of being a wolf; **'wolfkin**, a young wolf; **'wolfless** *a.*, free from wolves; **'wolflessness** *nonce-wd.* [cf. 6 a], the state of 'not having the wolf at the door', i.e. being free of poverty.

1851 *Sun* 21 Jan. 3/2 Before the House of Hanover or Stuart,..Alfred or Boadicea, *Wolfdom was, and is and is to be. **1889** J. JACOBS *Fables of Æsop* I. 209 To him cunning was foxiness,..cruelty, *wolfhood. **1706** MRS. CENTLIVRE *Basset-Table* v. 59 Oh! thou *Wolfkin instead of Lambkin. **1864** TENNYSON *Boadicea* 15 Make the carcase a skeleton;..wolf and wolfkin, from the wilderness, wallow in it. **1893** L. STEPHEN in *Contemp. Rev.* Aug. 160 The sheep of a *wolfless region. **1928** D. H. LAWRENCE *Rawdon's Roof* 26 The perfect *wolflessness of Rawdon's door, the perfect windlessness of Rawdon's roof.

wolf (wʊlf), *v.* [f. WOLF *sb.*]

1. *trans.* To eat like a wolf; to devour ravenously.

1862 SALA *Seven Sons* III. xi. 272 [She] used to..wolf her food with her fingers. **1880** SPURGEON *Ploughm. Pict.* 105 Hungry dogs will wolf down any quantity of meat. **1903** *Speaker* 24 Jan. 419/1 The men..wolfing up meals of oyster stew in an atmosphere of perpetual dyspepsia.

2. *intr.* with *it*: To behave like a wolf; = WOLVE *v.* 1. Also without *const.*: cf. WOLF *sb.* 5 c. Occas. *trans.*

1865 W. G. PALGRAVE *Arabia* I. 126 While 'Obeyd was wolfing it in Kaseem. **1929** *World's Work* Nov. 40 The college boy (in 1929) knows a smoothie who wolfed on a friend and creamed his lady. **1934** G. & S. LORIMER *Stag Line* vii. 232 No matter how I feel, I wouldn't wolf a brother's girl. **1940** J. O'HARA *Pal Joey* 186, I give with the vocals and wolf around in a nite club.

3. *trans.* To delude with false alarms: cf. prec. 9 a.

1910 *Contemp. Rev.* Jan. 55 Those whose interest it was to wolf the credulous public out of their pence. **1917** 'CONTACT' *Airman's Outings* 4 The dwellers in the blinking hole, having been wolfed several times, are sceptical.

4. *trans. U.S. Blacks.* (See quots. and cf. WOOFING *vbl. sb.*) Occas. *intr.* with *at*.

1966 *Urban Education* II. ii. 108 *Wolf*, to make fun of someone. **1969** *Sports Illustr.* 3 Nov. 36/2, I turned round and started wolfing at the guy, and he just strolled off. **1971** E. E. LANDY *Underground Dict.* 199 *Wolf v.*, criticize; chop down. **1974** H. L. FOSTER *Ribbin', Jivin', & Playin' Dozens* iv. 172 *Wolf, wolf'n, woof, woofin, wolf ticket*, can mean anything from making fun of someone to challenging someone to a fight, a powerful person. **1978** *Detroit Free Press* 2 Apr. (Detroit Suppl.) 8/3 'C'mon, man,' they tell Balls, backing down, 'we was just wolfin' ya. We gotta be careful who we sell to.'

wolfbane: see WOLF'S-BANE.

'wolf-dog. [Cf. G. *wolfshund.*]

1. Any of several large varieties of dog formerly kept for hunting wolves, *esp.* the Irish greyhound or wolf-hound.

1652 *Order Ir. Privy Council* 27 Apr., Such great dogges as are commonly called Wolfe dogges,..which are useful for destroying of wolves. *a* **1700** EVELYN *Diary* 16 June 1670, The bulls did exceeding well, but the Irish wolfe-dog exceeded, which was a tall greyhound. **1796** MORSE *Amer. Geog.* II. 180 Wolf-dogs (once so useful and celebrated) were perhaps peculiar to Ireland, but that species is now nearly extinct. **1840** C. H. SMITH *Dogs* II. 139 The Great Wolf-dog is not common in central Europe; and appears at present almost confined to Spain. **1845** YOUATT *Dog* 66 The Italian or Pomeranian wolf-dog. **1884** TENNYSON *Becket* III. ii, When that horn sounds, a score of wolf-dogs are let loose.

2. A cross of a domestic dog and a wolf.

1736 AINSWORTH, *Lycisca*, a dog ingendered of a wolf and a bitch, or a shepherd's dog, a wolf dog. **1755** JOHNSON. **1896** M. MCNAUGHTON *Overland to Cariboo* 47 A large number of wolf-dogs were prowling about. **1910** *Encycl. Brit.* VIII. 377/1 The black wolfdog of Florida resembles the black wolf of the same region. **1924** R. ARUNDEL *Police Dogs* 6 The German Sheep Dog (known in this country as the Alsatian Wolf Dog). **1953** B. J. BANFILL *Labrador Nurse* 19 The mossy grass knolls were dotted with tethered wolf dogs.

wolfdom: see after WOLF *sb.*

wolfe, obs. ff. WOLF, WOOF.

wolfeite ('wʊlfaɪt). *Min.* [f. the name of Caleb W. *Wolfe* (1908–80), U.S. crystallographer + -ITE[1].] A basic phosphate of ferrous iron and bivalent manganese, $(Fe^{2+},Mn^{2+})_2(PO_4)(OH)$, that occurs as transparent or translucent monoclinic crystals and forms a series with triploidite.

1949 C. FRONDEL in *Amer. Mineralogist* XXXIV. 694 The name wolfeite is proposed for the mineral and is particularly appropriate in view of Professor Wolfe's studies of iron and manganese phosphates from Palermo and other localities. **1951** C. PALACHE et al. *Dana's Syst. Min.* (ed. 7) II. 853 The names triploidite and wolfeite are applied to those parts of the series with Mn > Fe and Fe > Mn, respectively. **1979** *Mineral. Mag.* XLIII. 507/1 Unlike wolfeite from the Palermo pegmatite, the wolfeite at Thackaringa [Australia] does not appear to be an alteration phase of a pre-existing phosphate and is a late stage phase in the core of the pegmatite.

†**'wolfen**, *sb. Obs. rare.* Forms: 1 **wylfen**, 3 **wuluene, wluine**, 6 *Sc.* **wolfyne**. [OE. *wylfen*, of which the normal representative would be **wilven*; f. *wulf* WOLF *sb.* + -EN[2]. Cf. MHG. *wülvinne* (G. *wölfin*), MDu. *wolvinne* (Du. *wolvin*), Da. *ulvinde*, etc.] A she-wolf.

c **1000** *Sax. Leechd.* I. 362 Ʒif he drinceð wylfene meolc. *a* **1225** *Ancr. R.* 120 Wummone wroð is wuluene, & mon wroð is wulf. *Ibid.*, þeo þet is iwend te wuluene, i Godes eien, & is ase wuluene stefne in his swete earen. *c* **1300** *Havelok* 573 Leoun or wlf, wluine or bere. **15..** *Henryson's Trial of Fox* 107 (Bannatyne MS.), The..wildcat, & the wild wolfyne.

'wolfen, *a. rare*[−1]. [f. WOLF *sb.* + -EN[4].] Pertaining to a wolf, wolfish.

1810 W. TAYLOR in *Monthly Mag.* XXIX. 320 To wreathe anew the bonds of love, Which strife with wolfen tooth No more shall gnaw in twain.

wolfer ('wʊlfə(r)). [f. WOLF *sb.* and *v.* + -ER[1]. Cf. WOLVER.]

1. A wolf-hunter.

1872 *Rep. Indian Affairs 1871* 410 A regular stampede took place out of that section of the country of 'Wolfers' and whiskey traders. **1877** HALLOCK *Sportsman's Gaz.* 13 The 'wolfers' proceed to gather up animals slain, carry them to camp [etc.]. **1888** *Century Mag.* Feb. 501/2 Trappers and wolfers, whose business is to poison wolves. **1930** C. M. MACINNES *In Shadow of Rockies* 66 Even more disreputable than the whisky traders were the wolfers. **1973** R. WIEBE *Temptations of Big Bear* II. iii. 101 Settlers ripping up land and knocking down trees and wolfers dashing about scattering poison and killing wolves and buffalo. **1976** *Times* 8 July 16/4 The ghoulish wolfers poisoned the plains with strychnine.

2. One who 'wolfs' food or drink. *rare*

1897 A. R. MARSHALL *Pomes* 118 (Farmer), The worn-out whiskey wolfer calmly slumbered through it all.

'wolfess. *rare.* Also 5 **woluesse, -as.** [f. WOLF *sb.* + -ESS[1].] **1.** A she-wolf.

1387 TREVISA *Higden* (Rolls) III. 43 A wolfesse [*v.rr.* wolvesse, woluas] þat hadde i-lost hir whelpes. **1550** W. LYNNE *Carion's Cron.* 25 b, By chaunce came a wolfesse out of the nexte mountaynes. **1820** W. TOOKE tr. *Lucian* I. 560 *note*, The wolf lives instinctively solitary..so that even his connection with the wolfess is but of short duration.

2. A woman who is sexually aggressive; a woman who seeks to seduce men.

1945 *Bulletin* (Philadelphia) 27 Nov. 42/1 A nice girl hasn't got a chance with a wolfess around. **1968** *Word Study* Dec. 4/2 *Wolf* suggests the sexually aggressive female as well as the sexually agressive male, though it is often expanded to *wolfess* when applied to a woman.

Wolffian ('wʊlfiən), *a. Anat.* and *Zool.* [f. the name of the German embryologist K. F. *Wolff* (1733–94) + -IAN.] In ***Wolffian body***, the mesonephron or primitive kidney; either of the two renal organs of the embryo of vertebrates; so ***Wolffian duct***. Also ***Wolffian ridge***, each of two longitudinal ridges on either side of the embryo on which the limb buds arise.

1844 HOBLYN *Dict. Med.*, *Wolffian Bodies*, false kidneys. .. The substance by which the kidneys are preceded in the embryo, and which was first remarked by Wolff. **1859** *Todd's Cycl. Anat.* V. 594/1 The parovarium is formed out of the Wolffian body. **1874** FOSTER & BALFOUR *Elements Embryol.* I. vi. 143 The somatopleure..is raised up..into a low rounded ridge which runs along nearly the whole length of the embryo from the neck to the tail... This ridge..is known as the Wolffian ridge. **1879** tr. *Haeckel's Evol. Man.* II. 414 The earlier, primitive kidney duct is distinguished as the 'Wolffian duct.' **1931** A. ROBINSON *Cunningham's Text-bk. Anat.* (ed. 6) 76 By the end of the first month..the Wolffian ridges have appeared. **1976** N. J. BERRILL *Development* xiv. 309 In amniotes the combined epidermal-mesenchymal thickening extends as a horizontal ridge along each side of the body (the Wolffian ridges). The intermediate part of the ridge later disappears, leaving anterior and posterior regions as the definitive limb areas.

'wolf-fish. [After L. *lupus* (see WOLF *sb.* 3 b). Cf. G. *wolfsfisch.*] A large and voracious sea-fish, *Anarrhichas lupus*, having numerous sharp teeth and edible flesh; also called *sea-wolf*. Also applied to other fishes of the same genus.

1569 BLAGUE *Sch. Conceytes* 153 Of the Cockatrice and Seawolf... The Wolf fishe marking him well..sayde [etc.]. **1605** R. F. *Dedekind's Sch. Slovenrie* (1904) 77 As for the Wolfe-fish, gluttons hold the taile to be the best. **1774** *Phil. Trans.* LXIV. 315 The mouth of the wolf-fish is almost paved with teeth. **1855** KINGSLEY *Glaucus* 64 In Torbay.. where no wolf-fish (*Anarrhicus lupus*) or other shell-crushing pairs of jaws wander.

wolfhood: see after WOLF *sb.*

'wolf-hound. = WOLF-DOG.

1823 SCOTT *Quentin D.* xxii, We have brought down the game at last, quoth my lady's brach to the wolf-hound. **1871** M. COLLINS *Marq. & Merch.* I. i. 27 An enormous Pyrenean wolf-hound. **1899** *Dogs, their Managem. & Treatm.* 20 The Irish wolfhound, as he is known to-day, will weigh as much as one hundred and fifty pounds. **1923** *Westm. Gaz.* 22 Mar., It was discovered when the Show opened that a valuable Alsatian wolf-hound had disappeared.

Wolfian ('vɒlfiən, 'wʊlfiən), *a.*[1] and *sb.*[1] Also **Wolffian.** [f. the name of the German philosopher Christian *Wolf* or *Wolff* (1679–1754) + -IAN.] **a.** *adj.* Pertaining to the philosophical system of Wolf, which was an eclectic adaptation of Leibnitzianism and scholasticism. **b.** *sb.* An adherent of this system. Hence **'Wolfianism**, the philosophical system of Wolf; **'Wolfianize** *v.*, *trans.* to render Wolfian.

1791 ENFIELD *Brucker's Hist. Philos.* II. 572 Almost every German university was inflamed with disputes on the subject of liberty and necessity; and the names of Wolfians and Anti-Wolfians were every where heard. **1843** *Eclectic Rev.* Feb. 163 The influence of the Wolfian philosophy. *Ibid.* 164 It is undoubtedly to Wolfianism that we are to trace, in great measure, that coldness and lifelessness which characterizes the sermons of the latter part of the preceding century. *Ibid.* 165 The already Wolfianized mind of the rising ministry. **1874** G. S. MORRIS tr. *Ueberweg's Hist. Philos.* II. 116 Lange..sought.. to demonstrate the Spinozistic and atheistic character of the Wolffian doctrine.

So **'Wolfio-Leib'nitzian** *a.*, characterized by a combination of Wolfian and Leibnitzian views.

1877 E. CAIRD *Philos. Kant* I. 150 The artificial harmonies of the Wolffio-Leibnitzian philosophy.

Wolfian ('vɒlfiən, 'wʊlfiən), *a.*[2] and *sb.*[2] [f. the name of the German philologist F. A. Wolf (1759–1824) + -IAN.] **a.** *adj.* Of or pertaining to F. A. Wolf or his theory regarding the Homeric poems (developed in his *Prolegomena ad Homerum*, 1795). **b.** *sb.* One who accepts this theory.

1824 DE QUINCEY in *London Mag.* Jan. 5/1 Was the Iliad the work of one mind, or (on the Wolfian hypothesis) of many? **1875** W. D. GEDDES in *Contemp. Rev.* July 234 The Wolfian theory..that the Homeric poems were a congeries of originally independent lays..moulded into a unity in the time of Pisistratus. *Ibid.* 235 Next to him [*sc.* G. Hermann] in importance among the later Wolfians..stands Lachmann.

wolfin, obs. Sc. form of WOVEN.

wolfing ('wʊlfɪŋ), *vbl. sb.* [f. WOLF *sb.* + -ING[1].] Hunting for wolves. Also *attrib.*

1875 F. T. BUCKLAND *Log-Bk.* 128 When the wolfing season has commenced on the prairies, the hunter impregnates the carcase of a buffalo..with strychnine and places it in a likely position. **1877** HALLOCK *Sportsman's Gaz.* 13 The stock in trade of a party engaged in 'wolfing' consists in flour, bacon and strychnine.

wolfish ('wʊlfɪʃ), *a.* Also 8 **woolf-**. [f. WOLF *sb.* + -ISH[1]. Cf. MHG. *wolfisch*, and WOLVISH.]

1. a. Of or pertaining to a wolf or wolves.

1570 LEVINS *Manip.* 146/8 Wolfish, *lupinus*. **1687** DRYDEN *Hind. & P.* I. 160 The wolfish race, Appear with belly Gaunt, and famish'd face. **1690** C. NESSE *O. & N. Test.* I. 213 Ye may beat a wolf..yet all this will not drive away his wolfish nature. **1868** *Cornh. Mag.* July 70 The bristles that ornamented him in his wolfish state. **1890** *Temple Bar* Nov. 355 So vigorously had the wolfish tribe been hunted down that only one couple survived.

b. Abounding in wolves. *nonce-use.*

1747 COLLINS *Ode Liberty* 72 Where Orcas howls, his wolfish mountains rounding.

2. a. Characteristic of, befitting, or resembling that of, a wolf.

1674 *Govt. Tongue* viii. 146 All the wolfish designs walk under this sheeps clothing. **1750** LARDNER *Wks.* (1838) III. 79 His..unsociable and wolfish disposition. **1842** DICKENS *Amer. Notes* vi, Grope your way with me into this wolfish den. **1848** LYTTON *Harold* VII. v, The eyes of the three men, with a fierce and wolfish glare.

b. In sense 8 b of WOLF *sb. rare.*

1889 *Grove's Dict. Mus.* IV. 89/1 Bad Tenors [*sc.* tenor violins] are worse than bad violins; they are unequal and 'wolfish'.

3. a. Resembling a wolf, wolf-like.

1775 ADAIR *Amer. Indians* 259 To keep the [Indian] wolf from our own doors, by engaging him with his wolfish neighbours. **1854** J. S. C. ABBOTT *Napoleon* (1855) II. xiv. 242 Swarms of Cossacks, on fleet and wolfish horses.

b. Ravenously hungry. *U.S. colloq.*

[**1842** *Fraser's Mag.* Dec. 652/2 My appetite was growing decidedly wolfish.] **1848** BARTLETT *Dict. Amer.*, *Wolfish*, savage, savagely hungry. **1894** FENN *In Alpine Valley* II. 133 I'm wolfish.

4. *Comb.*, as ***wolfish-faced, -looking, -visaged*** adjs.

c **1779** CRABBE *Midnight* 295 Avarice..A Woolfish-Visag'd Fiend. **1820** SCOTT *Ivanhoe* I. i. 14 A rugged wolfish-looking dog..half mastiff, half greyhound. **1851** MAYNE REID *Scalp Hunters* xxvii, [The animal] is wolfish-looking. **1894** MRS. CROKER *Village Tales* (1896) 162 The wolfish-faced crowd had melted away.

Hence **'wolfishly** *adv.*; **'wolfishness.**

1676 MARVELL *Mr. Smirke* 66 The Wolfishness of those which..ought to have been the Christian Pastors, but went on scattering their Flocks, if not devouring. **1831** J. WILSON in *Blackw. Mag.* XXIX. 703 The Red Rover yowls wolfishly to the moon. **1842** BORROW *Bible in Spain* xl, Wolfishly eager for booty. **1890** J. PULSFORD *Loyalty to Christ* I. 205 Compare..the consummate wolfishness of Christian Europe with the simpler wolfishness of heathen nations.

wolfkin, wolfless: see after WOLF *sb.*

wolfling ('wʊlflɪŋ). [f. WOLF *sb.* + -LING[1].] A young or little wolf. Also *fig.*

13.. *K. Alis.* 6256 (Laud MS.), Wulflynges he bischette also, Merueillous men ben þoo. **1570** FOXE *Serm. Christ Crucif.* 8 If a mighty hunter.. happenyng vppon the Wolfes denne, findeth there the young Wolfelynges. 1746 W. Horsley *Fool* (1748) I. 94 Wolflings the Lambs embrace. 1759 J. Downes in Tyerman *John Wesley* (1870) II. 342 Two bold, though beardless divines, so young, that they might rather be called wolflings than wolves. 1837 Carlyle *Fr. Rev.* III. v. iii, Young children were thrown in [the river], their mothers vainly pleading: 'Wolflings,' answered the Company of Marat, 'who would grow to be wolves.' 1895 Kipling *2nd Jungle Bk.* 204 Thou art a man, Little Brother, wolfling of my watching.

wolfram ('wʊlfrəm, 'vɒlfrəm). [a. G. *wolfram* (*wolform* in Mathesius, 1562, *wolffram* in Ercker, 1580, *volfram* in Wallerius, *Mineralogia*, 1747), of uncertain formation: generally assumed to be an old miners' term f. *wolf* wolf + *rahm* cream (cf. *rahmerz* foamy wad), and to be the source of mod.L. *lupi spuma* (Agricola *De Nat. Foss.*, 1546), which corresponds, however, to G. *wolfsschaum*; but perh. f. MHG. *râm* dirty mark, soot.

The variants of the G. word, e.g. *wolffram(m*, *wolf(f)ert*, *wolfart*, *wolfrath*, suggest association with proper names. Since Agricola describes the *lupi spuma* as a light 'stone', it is improbable that it was the mineral wolfram.]

1. *Min.* A native tungstate of iron and manganese.

1757 tr. *Henckel's Pyritologia* ix. 132 Though this tin ore be not easily separable from wolfram, a kind of mock-tin, or an irony tin mineral. 1787 Groschke tr. *Klaproth's Observ. Fossils Cornw.* 32 Wolfram of a foliated texture united to quartz and clay, is brought from Poldice. 1849 D. Campbell *Inorg. Chem.* 292 Oxide of tungsten... Preparation.—The mineral wolfram is reduced to the finest powder [etc.]. 1916 *Lancet* 8 Jan. 76/1 These electrodes are made..from a mixture of.. ores.., the chief one being a tungstate of iron and manganese, known as wolfram.

2. The metal tungsten, obtained from this mineral.

1845 W. Gregory *Outl. Inorg. Chem.* 197 Tungsten... Syn. Wolfram—Occurs in nature, chiefly in the mineral wolfram. 1907 *Proc. Soc. Antiquaries* 2 May 456 Wolfram, or tungsten, a metal which is used as an alloy for hardening steel.

3. *attrib.*, as ***wolfram mine***, ***ore***; **wolfram lamp**, **-steel** = TUNGSTEN *lamp*, *-steel*; **wolfram-ochre** = TUNGSTIC ochre, TUNGSTITE.

1862 wolfram-steel [see TUNGSTEN 3]. 1868 Watts *Dict. Chem.* V. 903 Trioxide of Tungsten..occurs native as tungstic ochre, wolfram-ochre, or wolframine. 1907 *Westm. Gaz.* 24 July 10/1 Dr. Auer..claims that the light obtained from the wolfram lamp is three or four times as brilliant as that given by the ordinary carbon lamp with the same consumption of electricity. 1914 *Brit. Mus. Return* 227 A large specimen of hübnerite from Huara wolfram mine. 1916 *Chamb. Jrnl.* 9 Sept. 655/2 Quantities of wolfram ore are also produced in Australia.

Hence **'wolframate**, = TUNGSTATE; **'wolframed** *a.*, having wolfram added; **wol'framic** *a.*, = TUNGSTIC; **'wolframine**, tungstic ochre, tungstite; **'wolframite**, = WOLFRAM 1.

1864 *Q. Jrnl. Sci.* I. 693 M. Le Guen has solicited attention to what he calls **wolframed pig-iron*. 1860 Mayne *Expos. Lex.* s.v. *Wolframiate*, *Wolframic acid. 1854 Dana *Min.* 143 *Wolframine. 1868 *Ibid.* 601 *Wolframite. 1914 *Brit. Mus. Return* 228 Wolframite and smoky quartz, from Burma.

Wolf-Rayet ('vɒlfrɛjɛ, wʊlf-). *Astr.* The names of C. J. E. *Wolf* (1827–1918) and G. A. P. *Rayet* (1839–1906), French astronomers, used *attrib.* to denote any of a class of hot white-to-blue stars (first described by them in 1867) which are characterized by bright, broad spectral lines due to hydrogen, helium, carbon, or nitrogen and are believed to be short-lived and unstable.

1890 A. M. Clerke *Syst. of Stars* v. 71 Accurate measurements of the three original Wolf-Rayet stars..were made. 1930 R. H. Baker *Astron.* ix. 356 The Wolf-Rayet stars are distinguished from the other Class O stars by the great width of the bright lines in their spectra. 1978 Pasachoff & Kutner *University Astron.* ii. 40 Astronomers think that the emission in Wolf-Rayet stars comes from shells of material that the star has ejected into the space surrounding it.

wolf's-bane ('wʊlfsbeɪn), †**wolfbane.** [f. *wolf's*, gen. of WOLF *sb.* + BANE *sb.*[1], rendering mod.L. *lycoctonum*, a. Gr. λυκοκτόνον lit. 'wolf-slayer'.] A plant of the genus *Aconitum*, esp. *A. lycoctonum*, with dull yellow flowers, occurring in mountainous regions in Europe. Also applied to *Arnica montana* (***winter wolf's-bane***), and to the winter aconite, *Eranthis hyemalis*.

1548 Turner *Names Herbes* (E.D.S.) 9 The other kynde [of Aconitum] is called Lycoctonum, & in englishe it maye be called wolfes bayne. But this kynde is deuided into two other kyndes, of whiche..the one may be called in englishe monkes coule or blewe wolfsbaine. The other kinde..may be called in Englishe yelowe wolfesbayn. 1578, 1597 [see MONK'S-HOOD 1]. 1629 Parkinson *Parad.* xxvi. 216 Most Herbarists call it *Aconitum hyemale*, and we in English thereafter, Winters Wolfesbane. 1656 W. Coles *Art of Simpling* 66 The Oyntment that Witches use is reported to be made..of the Juices of Smallage, Woolfsbaine and Cinquefoyle. 1760 J. Lee *Introd. Bot.* App. 332. 1785 Martyn *Lett. Bot.* xxi. (1794) 298 Wholesome Wolfsbane [*Aconitum Anthora*]..has five capsules,..and the flowers are sulphur-coloured. 1820 Keats *Melancholy* i, Go not to Lethe, neither twist Wolf's-bane, tight-rooted, for its poisonous wine. 1846–50 A. Wood *Class-bk. Bot.* 146 *Aconitum uncinatum.* American Wolf's-Bane. 1856–60 A. Gray *Man. Bot. N.U.S.* 13 *Aconitum reclinatum.* Trailing Wolfsbane. 1866 *Treas. Bot.* 1235/2.

†**wolf's-fist.** *Obs.* In 3 **wuluesfist**, 6 **woolfes fistes**, 7 **wolues fyste**; also 6 **wolfyst**, 7 **woolfist.** [f. gen. of WOLF *sb.* + FIST *sb.*[2], of which LYCOPERDON (Tournefort) is a translation.] The puffball, *Lycoperdon Bovista.* Also used as a term of abuse.

*c*1265 *Voc. Plants* in Wr.-Wülcker 556/45 *Fungus*, wulues-fist. 1530 Palsgr. 289/2 Wolfyst, *uesse de loup.* 1597 Gerarde *Herbal* III. clxii. 1386 Puffes Fistes, are commonly called in Latine *Lupi crepitus*, or Woolfes Fistes. 1606 *Wily Beguiled* Prol., Out you soust gurnet, you Woolfist. 1611 Cotgr., *Vesse de loup*..Wolues fyste.

'wolf's-head, wolf-head. Forms: see WOLF *sb.* and HEAD *sb.*[1]

1. The head of a wolf; a figure of this, e.g. as a heraldic bearing.

*c*1000 *Sax. Leechd.* I. 360 To slæpe, wulfes heafod leȝe under þone pyle. ?*a*1400 *Morte Arth.* 1093 Alle falterde þe flesche in his foule lyppys, Ilke wrethe as a wolfe-hevede, it wraythe owtt at ones! 1586 Ferne *Blaz. Gentrie* 230 Hugh the firste Earle of Chester, was surnamed de Loupe, because he bare a Wolfes head in his shield. 1610 Guillim *Heraldry* III. xv. 145 Hee beareth Azure, two Barres, Argent, on a Canton Sable, a Wolues head Errased of the second. 1875 F. T. Buckland *Log-Bk.* 5 A young man holding a wolf's head high up in the air. 1891 *Daily Tel.* 16 Apr. 7/2 Minnesota spent last year twenty-five thousand dollars in bounties on wolf-heads brought in.

2. *Old English Law.* A cry for the pursuit of an outlaw as one to be hunted down like a wolf; *transf.* (orig. in phr. ***to cry wolf's head***) an outlaw.

17th century law books have various corrupt forms, as ***wolferfod***, ***woolfeshered***, ***woolferthfod***, ***wolfetchsod***.

[*c*1000 *Laws Edw. Conf.* vi, Lupinum enim gerit caput a die utlagationis sue, quod ab Anglis uulfesheued nominatur.] ?*c*1300 *Mirr. Justices* IV. iv. (Selden Soc.) 125 E point ne vient, qe des adunc le tiegne lem pur lou e est criable Wolvesheved, pur ceo qe lou est beste haie de tote gent. *c*1400 *Gamelyn* 700 (Harl. MS.) Whan Gamelyn her lorde wolues-heed was cryed & made. 1430–40 Lydg. *Bochas* VII. 1261 Out of ther court banyshed was prudence, ..Cried woluis hed was vertuous sobirnesse. *c*1460 *Towneley Myst.* xxi. 139 Now wols-hede and out-horne on the be tane! 1865 Kingsley *Herew.* i, By that time I shall be a wolf's head, and out of the law. 1914 *Blackw. Mag.* Jan. 95/2 Vengeance on these cruel wolfheads.

'wolfskin. The skin or pelt of a wolf; a garment, etc. made of this. Also *attrib.*

*c*1410 *Master of Game* (MS. Digby 182) vi, þe wolfe skynn is hote forto make koffes or pylches. *a*1612 Harington *Sch. Salerne* II. (1624) 37 Garments..of Martyn or Wolfe-skinnes. 1734 *Free Briton* No. 255. 2/2 Multitudes believe..that a Sheep-skin Drum bursts asunder at the beat of a Wolf-skin Drum. 1805 Scott *Last Minstr.* III. xvi, His bugle-horn..in a wolf-skin baldric tied. 1859 Tennyson *Elaine* 809 His battle-writhen arms and mighty hands Lay naked on the wolfskin. 1918 *Blackw. Mag.* June 743/1 When our own ancestors were.. barbarians in wolfskins.

'wolf's-milk. [Cf. LG. *wulfsmelk*, MHG. *wolfmilch*, (G. *wolfs-*), Da. *ulvemelk*, etc.]

1. a. A spurge, esp. the sun-spurge, *Euphorbia Helioscopia*; so called from the acrid milky juice.

1575 Banister *Chyrurg.* 101 *Esula*, Woulfes milke. 1599 A. M. tr. *Gabelhouer's Bk. Physicke* 364/1 For the Felone of the Finger. Take the herbe called Woluesmilcke, tye the same with the Flowers on the Felon [etc.]. 1861 Miss Pratt *Flower. Pl.* V. 5 *Euphorbia helioscopia* (Sun Spurge).. Country people call it..Wolf's-milk. 1897 R. N. Bain tr. *Jókai's Pretty Michal* xxv. 201 The witch took freshly plucked wolf's-milk flowers.

b. The fungus *Lycogala.*

1861 H. Macmillan *Footn. Page Nat.* 288 The beautiful round vermilion balls of the Lycogala, or Wolf's milk.

2. The milk of a wolf.

1847 Tennyson *Princess* VII. 115 Half the wolf's-milk curdled in their veins. 1892 Rider Haggard *Nada* xvii, They have drunk wolf's milk.

'wolf-whistle. *colloq.* Also **wolf whistle.** [f. WOLF *sb.* 5c + WHISTLE *sb.* 3.] A distinctive whistle from a man expressing sexual admiration for a woman; also *transf.*

1952 *Time* 21 Jan. 29/3 No one took exception to U.S.N. wolf-whistles at the señoritas. 1953 N. Balchin *Sundry Creditors* 46 Some vulgar female person let out a low wolf-whistle as she passed him. 1958 *Daily Express* 13 Mar. 8/5 She heard one kid give a wolf whistle, and his chum exclaim: 'Coo, what a smashing car!' 1960 A. Kimmins *Lugs O'Leary* i. 11 They passed the pretty probationer. Lugs gave her a low wolf whistle. 1971 *New Scientist* 29 Apr. 246/1 A young housewife..recently asked for a reduction in the rates of her residence because of nuisance from wolf-whistles. 1980 'T. Hinde' *Daymare* vi. 61 Bob Smiles whistles at him..a hideous wolf-whistle.

Hence as *v.*, to utter a wolf-whistle (at); **'wolf-whistling** *vbl. sb.* and *ppl. a.*

1955 *Sun* (Baltimore) 2 Sept. 1/5 The Governor of Mississippi today called for a complete investigation of the kidnap-killing of a Negro youth who allegedly wolf-whistled at a white woman. 1958 L. Little *Dear Boys* 222 They had their heads and shoulders hanging dangerously out of the windows [of a coach], wolf-whistling the odd bints on the pavements. 1958 *Times* 2 Sept. 11/7 Surrounded as I am by thousands of barking dogs, wailing cats, and wolf-whistling budgerigars. 1961 Wodehouse *Ice in Bedroom* 41 Dolly Molloy unquestionably took the eye... Wolf-whisting is of course prohibited in the lobby of Barribault's Hotel so none of those present attempted this form of homage. 1976 J. Grenfell *Joyce Grenfell requests the Pleasure* i. 17 An American sailor wolf-whistled at her. 1981 G. Petrie *Tondeau of Chartres* i. 19 Julie and Elaine took their bows to a cacophony of wolf-whistling.

wolfwort ('wʊlfwɜːt). ? *Obs.* [f. WOLF *sb.* + WORT.] **a.** A plant of the genus *Aconitum*: = WOLF'S-BANE. **b.** A plant of the genus *Periploca*, the juice of which was used for poisoning wolves.

1611 Cotgr. s.v. *Loup*, *Herbe au loup*, Wolues-bane, wolfe-wort (a kind of Aconitum). 1658 [see LEOPARD'S BANE]. 1773 J. Hill *Vegetable Syst.* IX. 43 Wolfwort. Periploca.

wolfy ('wʊlfɪ), *a.* *U.S.* [f. WOLF *sb.* + -Y[1].] Wolf-like; characterized by, or suggestive of the presence of, wolves; ferocious, uncivilized.

1828 *Western Souvenir 1829* 314 'Couldn't you take a pack or two of wolves along?' said Pete, sneeringly. 'We can spare you a small gang. It's mighty wolfy about here.' 1831 J. K. Paulding *Lion of West* (1954) II. 54 Well, I hadn't had a fight for as much as ten days—felt as though I must kiver myself up in a salt bin to keep—'so wolfy' about the head and shoulders. 1838 B. Drake *Tales & Sk., from Queen City* 36, I say, Mr. Jack-of-knaves, it looks rather wolfy in these parts. 1927 C. M. Russell *Trails plowed Under* 114 This talk makes the whole bunch wolfy.

wolfyst: see WOLF'S-FIST.

wolhe, nolhe: see WILL *v.*[1] 50b.

wolken(e, -in, obs. ff. WELKIN.

woll: see WELL, WHILE, WILL, WOOL, WOOLD.

Wollaston ('wʊləstən). *Physics.* [The name of W. H. *Wollaston* (1766–1828), English physicist.] ***Wollaston('s) prism***: a prism made by cementing together two prisms of calcite or quartz with their optic axes perpendicular to each other and to the incident light, which is thereby separated into two diverging beams of polarized light.

1890 T. Preston *Theory of Light* xi. 258 Wollaston's Prism.—This prism differs from that of Rochon only in that the optic axis of the first prism ABD is parallel to the face AB, so that it is merely Rochon's prism turned through a right angle. 1970 *Nature* 18 July 264/2 The Wollaston prism, which splits the incident starlight into two beams, polarized in mutually perpendicular planes, was placed in an adjustable mounting above the spectrograph slit.

wollastonite ('wʊləstənaɪt). *Min.* [Named by Lehman (1818) after the chemist and physicist W. H. *Wollaston* (1766–1828): see -ITE[1].] Native metasilicate of calcium; tabular spar.

Applied also by T. Thomson to PECTOLITE.

1823 W. Phillips *Introd. Min.* (ed. 3) 211 Wollastonite... This substance occurs in the lava of Capo di Bove, near Rome, in small masses. 1836 T. Thomson *Outl. Min.* etc. I. 131 This was the reason which led me to give the appellation *Wollastonite* to the present species, which occurs..near Kilsyth... It is related to *table spar.* 1888 Rutley *Rock-Forming Min.* 183 Wollastonite..occurs as a rock-forming mineral chiefly in..rod-like or platy crystals.

wolle: see WALL *sb.*[1], WILL *v.*[1], WOOL.

wolle bode, obs. var. WOUBIT.

†**wolleyn,** suggested by Lyte [after WOOLLEN, q.v. ¶] as an alternative for MULLEIN.

1578 Lyte *Dodoens* I. lxxxi. 118 Mulleyn (or rather Wolleyn). *Ibid.* 119 Mulleyne, or rather Wulleyn.

wollop, var. WALLOP.

wollow, obs. form of WALLOW *v.*[1]

1622–5 *Essex Archdeaconries Depos. Bk.* lf. 129 (MS.) She was drunck and lay wollowing in the durt.

wolly ('wɒlɪ). *slang.* Also **wally.** [Origin unknown: cf. WALLY *sb.*[2]] A uniformed policeman, esp. a constable. Cf. WOOLLY *sb.* 3.

1970 G. F. Newman *Sir, you Bastard* 8 The wollies were out in their cars, patrolling for drunks and discontents. 1977 'D. Cory' *Bennett* ii. 69 The doorman..mentioned it to one of our wollies on the beat. 1983 J. B. Hilton *Asking Price* v. 33 These traffic Wollies make sure it all goes down, once they've licked their pencils.

wollyn, obs. form of WOOLLEN.

Wolof ('wəʊlɒf), *sb.* and *a.* Also **Jolof** ('jəʊlɒf), **Woloff**, etc. [Native name.] **A.** *sb.* **a.** (A member of) an African people of Senegal and the Gambia. **b.** The language of this people, belonging to the Niger-Congo family.

1745 F. Moore in *New Gen. Coll. Voy.* II. 227/2 The Natives, who were Jolloifs, had taken his chief Mate and Surgeon Prisoners. 1823 Mrs. H. Kilham (*title*) African lessons. Wolof and English. 1848 *Rep. Brit. Assoc. Adv. Sci.* 162 Here the Woloff has not only no particular affinities, but fewer miscellaneous ones than any other language. 1883, etc. [see PEULH *sb.* and *a.*]. 1908 T. G. Tucker *Introd. Nat. Hist. Lang.* 147 This process is common in Wolof. 1930 C. G. Seligman *Races of Afr.* iii. 58 The lower and middle portions of the Senegal River form the ethnic divide between Hamites and Negroes. Immediately south of the river the latter are represented by the Wolof (or Jolof). 1961 *Guardian* 25 Nov. 7 Senegal combines at least six different tribes... The largest is the Wolof numbering about 800,000. 1972 J. L. Dillard *Black Eng.* iii. 74 The widespread use of

Wolof, which seems to have a special *lingua franca* status among West African languages, in the thirteen colonies. **1976** *Times* 20 Nov. 11/4 The third largest group are the Wollofs, whose women . . are . . among the most beautiful in Africa.

B. *adj.* **a.** *gen.*

1828 MRS. H. KILHAM *Specimens African Languages Sierra Leone* p. vii, In the Jolof Language there are two sounds of the guttural kind. **1865** R. F. BURTON *Wit & Wisdom in W. Afr.* i. 2 (*heading*) Proverbs in the Wolof tongue. **1879** J. A. FARRER *Primitive Manners & Customs* iii. 92 The Wolof proverb, that 'lies, though many, will be caught by Truth as soon as she rises up'. **1918** *Harvard Afr. Studies* II. 98 De Rochebrune distinguishes the gluteal accumulation of fat commonly found in Wolof women and girls from true steatopygia. **1961** F. G. CASSIDY *Jamaica Talk* vii. 146 The word *juke*, as in the American *juke box* . . has been traced by Turner to Wolof *jug*, to misconduct oneself. **1977** J. WYLLIE *To catch a Viper* (1979) vii. 45 The original African ethnic groupings such as those represented by the Yoruba, the old nations of Ashanti, Dahomey and Goshi and the Mossi, Mende, Mandinka and Wolof peoples.

b. Special collocation: **jollof rice** (see quot. 1982).

1959 [see FUFU]. **1966** C. ACHEBE *Man of People* ii. 25 Whenever you allowed him a say in this matter he invariably came up with Jollof rice—his favourite dish. **1982** G. M. DALGISH *Dict. Africanisms* 76/1 *Jollof rice*, a West African dish, a stew of fish, chicken or beef, tomatoes, onions, rice, and chili peppers; said to be ultimately of Sierra Leone origin.

wolp, obs. form of WUP *v. Sc.*

wolron, var. WILRONE *Obs.*

wölsendorfite ('vɜːlzəndɔːfaɪt). *Min.* [a. F. *wölsendorfite* (J. Protas 1957, in *Compt. Rend.* CCXLIV. 2942), f. *Wölsendorf*, name of a locality in Bavaria: see -ITE[1].] A hydrated oxide of lead, calcium, and uranium, $(Pb,Ca)U_2O_7 . 2H_2O$, found as orange or red orthorhombic crystals.

1957 *Chem. Abstr.* LI. 13659 (*heading*) Wölsendorfite, a new uranium mineral. **1975** *Mineral Abstr.* XXVI. 321/1 Red and orange aggregates of wölsendorfite are described from the oxidation zone of a U-Mo ore deposit [in the U.S.S.R.].

wolsome, var. WILSOME *a.*[1]

wolsted, obs. form of WORSTED.

Wolstonian (wʊl'stəʊnɪən), *a. Geol.* [f. *Wolston*, name of the village in Warwickshire where the type site is situated: see -IAN.] Epithet of the penultimate Pleistocene glaciation in Britain (identified with the Saale of continental Europe), and of a stratigraphic stage of the Pleistocene lying above the Hoxnian and below the Ipswichian; of or belonging to this stage or glacial. Also *absol.*

1969 *Proc. Geol. Soc.* Aug. 152 It is recommended that for the Pleistocene and Holocene of the British Isles the following ages/stages be adopted as a regional scale. . . Pleistocene: Devensian, Ipswichian, Wolstonian [etc.]. **1975** *Nature* 9 Oct. 478/2 The Sugworth deposit lies topographically well above the Hanborough Terrace which has been ascribed both to the Hoxnian Interglacial and, more recently, to an early part of the Wolstonian. **1981** F. W. SHOTTON in Neale & Flenley *Quaternary in Brit.* xiii. 143 This makes the gravels post-Hoxnian or at least late-Hoxnian, and the overlying Wetton Till even later. So if the latter is pre-Devensian, it can only be Wolstonian.

wolt, obs. pa. t. of WIELD.

wolt(e, obs. var. VAULT *sb.*[1]; see WILL *v.*[1] A. 3.

woltou, -towe = *wilt thou*: see WILL *v.*[1] A. 6 a.

wolum, obs. Sc. f. VOLUME.

wolunte, var. VOLUNTY *Obs.*

wolve (wʊlv), *v.* [f. inflexional stem of WOLF *sb.*] **1.** *intr.* (also with *it*). To behave like a wolf, play the wolf.

1702 C. MATHER *Magn. Chr.* III. III. 187/2 If any Seducers were let loose to wolve it among the good people of Roxbury. *a* **1909** E. THOMPSON SETON *Billy* i. (C.D. Suppl.) A Wolf was 'wolving' on the east side of Sentinel Mountain.

2. Of an organ: To give forth a hollow wailing sound like the howl of a wolf, from deficient wind-supply.

1864 LE FANU *Uncle Silas* I. xxv. 325 What an awful storm! . . Don't you like the sound? What they used to call 'wolving' in the old organ at Dorminster! **1919** M. R. JAMES *Thin Ghost* 130 The organ wolved—you know what I mean: the wind died.

†'**wolveling.** *Obs. rare*[−1]. [f. *wolv-*, inflexional stem of WOLF *sb.* + -LING[1].] = WOLFLING.

1798 W. ROSCOE tr. *Tansillo's Nurse* I. (1800) 23 Whilst ten young wolvelings shelter find.

wolver ('wʊlvə(r)). *rare.* Also 6–7 wooluer. [f. WOLVE *v.* or inflexional stem of WOLF *sb.* + -ER[1].]

1. One who behaves like a wolf; a ravenous or savage creature.

1593 G. HARVEY *Pierce's Super.* 147 Three meales of a Lazarello, make the fourth a Woolner [*sic*]. **1604** T. M. *Black Bk.* Epistle to Rdr., Scylla and Charibdis, those two Cormorants and Woolners [*sic*] of the Sea. **1883** *Cornh. Mag.* Feb. 184 Jelly-fish, fierce little 'wolvers' throwing out their . . stings.

2. One who searches or hunts for wolves.

a **1909** E. THOMPSON SETON *Billy* i. (C.D. Suppl.) As the wolver rode down an adjoining cañon, he saw a Wolf come out of a hole. **1921** *Chambers's Jrnl.* July 473/1 The wolver, exploring unsurveyed territory.

wolverene, -ine (wʊlvə'riːn). Forms: 6–9 wolvering, 8– wolverene, -ine (6 wool-, ulvering(e, 7 woolverin(e, *Sc.* voluering). [app. f. *wolv-*, inflexional stem of WOLF *sb.*, but the formation is obscure.]

1. The glutton (*Gulo luscus*), now esp. the North American variety: see GLUTTON A. 4.

1574 in Feuillerat *Revels Q. Eliz.* (1908) 236 Furres of woolveringes for pedlers capps. **1591** G. FLETCHER *Russe Commw.* (Hakl. Soc.) 14 Their beasts . . are the losh, . . the beare, the wolvering or wood dogge. **1619** MIDDLETON *Love & Antiq.* D 1, Beasts bearing Furr, . . Racoone, Moashye, Wolverine. **1747** G. EDWARDS *Nat. Hist. Birds* II. 103 The Quick-Hatch, or Wolverene. **1812** J. SMYTH *Pract. Customs* (1821) 225 Wolvering is a large animal, almost equal in size to the wolf. **1820** HARMON *Jrnl. Voy. N. Amer.* 426 The carcajou or wolverine, in shape and the colour of the hair, greatly resembles the skunk. **1855** LONGF. *Hiaw.* xvi. 40 How the Wolverine, uprising, Made him ready for the encounter. **1896** KIPLING *Seven Seas, Song of Dead* 8 Where the wolverine tumbles their packs from the camp.

2. The fur of the wolverene.

1596 *Lanc. Wills* (Chetham Soc. 1861) 2 A cassocke of grogran edged wth ulveringe. **1612** *Sc. Bk. Rates* in *Halyburton's Ledger* (1867) 307 Furres called . . Volueringis the peice, vi li. **1833** *Act 3 & 4 Will. IV*, c. 56 Wolverings, undressed. **1890** *Daily News* 28 Jan. 7/1 It is already prophesied that wolverine is to be the favourite fur next winter. **1895** KIPLING *2nd Jungle Bk.* 158 The long wolverine-fur fringe of her ermine hood.

3. A nickname for an inhabitant of Michigan. So ***Wolverine State***, Michigan.

1835 C. F. HOFFMAN *Winter in Far West* I. 207 The genuine wolverine, or, naturalized Michiganian. **1847** *Congressional Globe* 5 Feb. 332/2 A great Government bank — . . a full-grown . . Wolverine wild-cat. **1875** *Chamb. Jrnl.* 13 Mar. 171/2 Michigan is Lake State or Wolverine State.

Wolves (wʊlvz). [pl. of WOLF *sb.*] Colloq. name for Wolverhampton Wanderers Football Club.

1908 O. SEAMAN *Salvage* 140, I hardly care at all Whether the Wolves break up the Throstles' wings. **1923** *Racing Record* 10 Feb. 3/2 Bradford City I take to defeat the Wolves. **1960** [see SLATE *sb.*[1] 2 b]. **1978** P. BAILEY *Leisure & Class in Victorian Eng.* vi. 139 A Church of England school team in Wolverhampton, later the Wolves.

wolvin, obs. Sc. form of WOVEN.

'**wolvish,** *a.* Also 5–6 wolw-, 6 woulu-, wollw-, *Sc.* volw-, 6–7 wo(o)lu-, 7–9 woolv-. [f. *wolv-*, inflexional stem of WOLF *sb.* + -ISH[1].]

1. = WOLFISH 2, 3.

c **1430** LYDG. *Min. Poems* (Percy Soc.) 174 Among wolvys be wolvysshe of corage. **15..** *Six Ballads with Burdens* (Percy Soc.) 5 This wollwysshe shepe. **1540–7** COVERDALE *Fruitful Less.* i. (1593) M 1, Iudas . . hauing woluish conditions vnder sheepes cloathing. *a* **1586** SIDNEY *Arcadia* v. (1922) 191 This woolvish sheepheard. **1604** *Supplic. Mass-priests, Ans.* K 2, The wooluish cruelty of popish Inquisitors. **1605** SHAKS. *Lear* I. iv. 330 With her nailes Shee'l flea thy Woluish visage. **1632** MASSINGER & FIELD *Fatal Dowry* II. i. D 3 b, Out you wooluish mungrells! **1692** R. L'ESTRANGE *Fables* I. clvi. 141 These Wolvish Back-Friends. **1817** COLERIDGE *Biog. Lit.* I. x. 181 If superstition and despotism have been suffered to let in their woolvish sheep. **1911** D. H. LAWRENCE *White Peacock* I. vi. 97 There was a report of two grey wolvish dogs. *a* **1945** E. R. EDDISON *Mezentian Gate* (1958) i. 16 'Nay, read it if you please: I had it but five minutes since.' And with a wolvish look he tossed the letter upon the table. **1978** J. UPDIKE *Coup* (1979) vii. 267 She tugged at his hand with that fretful, proprietorial impatience of her wolvish race.

2. = WOLFISH 1. Also *Comb.*, as ***wolvish-looking*** adj.

1565 *Satir. Poems Reform.* i. 133, I sawe the ffrendlie man wounde in a volwyshe weede. **1577** T. KENDALL *Flowers Epigr.* 87 The founder of the same [*sc.* Rome] with Wouluishe milke was fedde. **1793** BLAKE *Songs Exper., Little Girl Found* 51 Nor fear the wolvish howl Nor the lions' growl. **1954** J. R. R. TOLKIEN *Fellowship of Ring* iv. 101 Two wolvish-looking dogs sniffed at him suspiciously, and snarled.

Hence †'**wolvishly** *adv.*; '**wolvishness**; †'**wolvy** *a. Obs. rare*[−0].

1538 BALE *Three Lawes* 1211 Thy woluysshnesse by thre crownes wyll I hyde making the a pope. **1611** COTGR., *Louvier*, Woluie, Wolfe-like. **1628** WITHER *Brit. Rememb.* IV. 663 Some, wolvishly, did prey upon the quick. *a* **1945** E. R. EDDISON *Mezentian Gate* (1958) xxxvii. 191 God shield us from women on our councils of war. . . Besides, I mistrust Parry wolvishness. And bitch-wolf was ever more fell than dog-wolf.

wolward, obs. f. WOOLWARD.

wolwat, obs. f. VELVET.

wolx, obs. pa. t. of WAX *v.*

wom, obs. form of WHOM.

woman ('wʊmən), *sb.* Pl. **women** ('wɪmɪn). Forms (case-inflexions in OE. and early ME. as in MAN *sb.*[1]): *Sing.* α. 1–5 **wifman,** 2–3 **-mon,** 2–4 **wimman,** (3 **wim(m)on, wyman),** 3–4 **wymman,** 3–5 **wymmon** (4 **wyfman).** β. 3 **wummon,** 3–5 **wumman.** δ. 3–5 **womman, wommon,** 4–6 **voman,** 5 **vomman, woman(n)e,** 5–6 **wommane,** 7 **whoman,** (also 9 *dial.*) **wooman,** 3– **woman.** γ. 5 **oman,** 6 **owman** (?), 7 *Anglo-Welsh* **o'man,** 7–9 **uman,** 9 **'ooman, umman.** *Pl.* α. 1–4 **wifmen,** 1–4, 8 **wimmen,** 3–5 **wymmen,** (4 **wyfmen, wimen, wemmen,** 4–5 **wymen,** 5 **vymmen,** 7 *Anglo-Welsh* **ymen).** β. 3–4 **wummen.** γ. 3–5 **wommen,** 5 **womene, vommen, woymen,** 6–7 **woemen,** 4– **women.** δ. 4 *Sc.* **vemene,** 4–7 **wemen,** 5 **wemyn, whemen, weymen,** 5–7 **weomen,** 6 **vemen,** 6–7 **weemen,** 7 **weamen.** [OE. *wífmon(n, -man(n* masc., later fem., pl. *wífmen(n*, f. *wíf* woman, WIFE *sb.* + *mon(n, man(n* human being, MAN *sb.*[1] A formation peculiar to English, and not extant in the earliest period of OE., the ancient word being WIFE.

The regular ME. descendants of OE. *wífman, -men*, viz. *wimman, wimmen* (cf. OE. *léofman*, ME. *lemman*, LEMAN) continued in use until the 15th century. By *c* 1200 the rounding of *wi-* to *wu-* is clearly established, and is at that time characteristic of western ME. texts. The form *womman* appears in the late 13th century (first in western texts), and the corresponding pl. *wommen* in the late 14th. The simplification of *mm* in *womman, -en* and *wimman, -en*, and the consequent conversion of the first syllable into an open syllable gave rise to forms with *ō* and *ē*, which, continuing to the early modern period, provided the occasion for punning analyses of *wōman* and *wēmen* (see 1 k below). From *c* 1400 *woman* and *women* became regular spellings for sing. and pl., and have been retained as a properly corresponding pair to *man* and *men*; but in the standard speech the pronunciation (wu-) was ultimately appropriated to the sing. and (wi-) to the pl., probably through the associative influence of pairs like *foot* and *feet*.

From at least the 16th century, the only variety in the pronunciation of the pl. has been in respect of the quantity of the first vowel, which was either short or long in the 16th and 17th centuries; but in the same period no less than five pronunciations of the sing. are recognized by orthoepists, viz. ('wʊmən), ('wuːmən), ('wʌmən), and ('ɒmən), ('ʌmən), of which all but the first have now sunk to vulgar or dialectal status.

Examples of the δ-forms of the sing., without initial *w*, follow here; for illustration of the more normal forms see sense 1.

? **1455** *Paston Lett.* I. 343 Youre pore bede oman and cosyn, Alice Crane. **1558** CHARNOCK *Bk. Astron.* Title of Chapter (MS.) Is the theffe man or owman or bothe? **1623** SHAKS. *Merry W.* IV. i. 52 *Eua.* Leaue your prables (o'man) . . . *Eua.* O'man, forbeare. **1632** NABBES *Cov. Gard.* v. ii, Your Ladiships uman. **1749** FIELDING *Tom Jones* XV. x, When her Laship was so veri kind as to offar to mak mee hur one Uman. **1808** JAMIESON, *Uman*, the pron. of *woman*. **1837** DICKENS *Pickw.* xiii, Putting on his spectacles to look at a married 'ooman! **1838** JAS. GRANT *Sk. Lond.* 69 Bad luck to the 'ooman! **1898** G. W. E. RUSSELL *Coll. & Recoll.* 14 Like other high-bred people of his time, he [*sc.* Lord John Russell] . . called a woman an ''ooman'.]

I. 1. a. An adult female human being. (The context may or may not have special reference to sex or to adult age: cf. MAN *sb.*[1] 4 a, c, d.)

† ***man or*** (or ***and***) ***woman*** used appositionally = male or (and) female.

sing. α *c* **893** ÆLFRED *Oros.* III. vi. §2 Minutia hatte an wifmon, þe on heora wisan sceolde nunne beon. *c* **1000** ÆLFRIC *Gen.* ii. 22 God . . ȝeworhte ðæt rib, ðe he ȝenam of Adame, to anum wifmen. —— *Judges* iv. 22 Ða clipode seo wimman cuðlice him to. *c* **1175** *Lamb. Hom.* 15 ȝif þa laȝe weren nu, nalde na mon mis-don wið oðre, ne wepmon ne wifmon ne meiden. *c* **1200** *Trin. Coll. Hom.* 133 þe lif holi wimman sarra. *a* **1250** *Owl & Night.* 1357 If wymmon þencheþ luuye derne. *c* **1290** *S. Eng. Leg.* 486/53 Com ageyn & bring this swyn a-now To this pore wifman. *c* **1300** *Havelok* 1156 þe fayrest wymman under mone. **13..** *K. Horn* 552 (Harl. MS.) Er ne he eny wyf take Oþer wyþ wymmon forewart make. **1340** *Ayenb.* 31 He . . zayþ to þe manne and to þe wyfmanne [etc.].

β. *a* **1225** *Ancr. R.* 12 Hwarse wummon liueð oðer mon bi him one. *Ibid.* 58 þis is a swuðe dredlich word to wummen þet scheaweð hire to wepmones eien. *a* **1240** *Ureisun* in *O.E. Hom.* I. 191 Nis no wummon iboren þet ðe beo iliche. **13..** *Coer de L.* 3863 Man, wumman, every Sarasyn. **1499** *Promp. Parv.* 534/2 (ed. Pynson), Wumman.

γ. *c* **1275** LAY. 2237 Womman [*c* 1205 wifmon] þou hart hende. **1297** R. GLOUC. (Rolls) 211 Al vor a woman þat heleine was icluped þis bataile verst bigan. *a* **1300** *Cursor M.* 9000 Foluand a wicked womman will. *Ibid.* 20285 Quils scho spac þus, þat suet woman, . . saint iohan . . com. **1362** LANGL. *P. Pl.* A. VIII. 74 þei weddeþ no wommon þat þei with deleþ. **14..** in *Rel. Ant.* I. 275 To onpreyse womene yt were a shame, For a womane was thy dame. **1476** *Stonor Papers* (Camden) II. 7 And yff ye wold be a good etter off your mete allwaye, that ye myght waxe and grow ffast to be a woman. **1546** in J. Bulloch *Pynours* (1887) 63 Euery pynour baytht man and voman. **1588** SHAKS. *L.L.L.* IV. i. 125 One . . that was a woman when Queene Guinouer of Brittaine was a little wench. **1591** —— *Two Gent.* IV. iv. 165 Our youth got me to play the womans part, And I was trim'd in Madam Iulias gowne. **1667** DRYDEN & DK. NEWC. *Sir M. Mar-all* III. (1668) 26 A Woman's in a sad condition, that has nothing to trust to, but a Perriwig above, and a well-trim'd shoe below. **1697** CONGREVE *Mourn. Bride* III. ad. fin., Heav'n has no Rage, like Love to Hatred turn'd, Nor Hell a Fury, like a Woman scorn'd. **1735** POPE *Ep. Lady* 216 Men, some to Bus'ness, some to Pleasure take; But every Woman is at heart a Rake. **1780** J. BROWN *Toleration* (1803) 81 No ecclesiastical power can reside in a heathen, a woman, or a child. **1804** WORDSW. '*She was a Phantom*' 27 A perfect Woman, nobly planned, To warn, to comfort, and command. **1818** BYRON *Juan* I. lxi, Her stature tall—I hate a dumpy woman. **1835** HOOK *G. Gurney* vii. in *New Mo. Mag.* XLIV. 18 A girl of seventeen is a woman, when a man of seventeen is a boy. **1867** *Act 30 & 31 Vict.* c. 130 §3 In this Act..'Woman' shall mean a Female of the Age of Eighteen Years or upwards. **1887** *Act 50 & 51 Vict.* c. 58 §75 In this Act..'Woman' means a female of the age of sixteen years or upwards. **1889** 'J. S. WINTER' *Mrs. Bob* v, A girl she was not, but a woman of at least nine and twenty.

pl. α. *c*900 tr. *Bæda's Hist.* III. v. (1890) 162 Ծe wæpnedmen ȝe wimmen. *c*1000 *Christ's Descent* 48 Wifmonna þreat, fela fæmnena. **1154** *O.E. Chron.* (Laud MS.) an. 1137 þa namen hi..carl-men and wimmen & diden heom in prisun. *c*1200 *Trin. Coll. Hom.* 215 Ʒif þe hodede wliteð mid stefne for to liken wimmannen. *c*1290 *John* 196 in *S. Eng. Leg.* 408 Twelf þousend Men..With-oute children and wimmen. **1297** R. GLOUC. (Rolls) 2753 Ofte in wimmen [*v.rr.* wimmane, wommannes, wommanys, wommens] fourme hii comeþ to men al so. *a*1300 *Cursor M.* 7044, Zamazims..þe wimmen land wit-outen man. *a*1300 *K. Horn* 67 Of alle wymmane [*v.r.* wimmenne] Wurst was godhild þanne. **13..** *Cursor M.* 24644 (Edin.) Wit oþir wimen þat him soht. **1340** *Ayenb.* 10 To habbe uelaȝrede ulesllich mid wyfmen. *c*1375 *Cursor M.* 8583 *heading*, How ij. wemmen ware iugged for a childe þe tane slogh in hir bedde. **1470–85** MALORY *Arthur* II. vii. 83 For her sake I shal owe al wymmen the better loue. *c*1500 *God speed the plough* 87 Wymen commeth weping on the same Maner. *c*1620 *Welsh Embass.* IV. 1509 (Malone Soc.) Our valliant Comragues..so fright the ymen that [etc.]. **1790** MRS. WHEELER *Westmld. Dial.* 60 What is cum amang Wimmen an Lasses E this Parish?

β. *c*1205 LAY. 11718 Æc heo nomen wummen wunder ane monie. *a*1240 *Ureisun* in *O.E. Hom.* I. 191 þu ert briht and blisful ouer alle wummen. **13..** *Cursor M.* 23451 (Gött.) Man [has] gret liking..On wummen fair for to bihald.

γ. **1340–70** *Alex. & Dind.* 1016 Ʒoure fingrus of fin gold ȝe fullen wiþ ryngus, As is wommenus wone for wordliche glose. *c*1386 CHAUCER *Melib.* ¶91 Of alle wommen good womman foond I neuere. **1390** GOWER *Conf.* I. 58 Of body bothe and of visage Lik unto wommen of yong age. *c*1400 MAUNDEV. (1839) xiii. 143 Amazoyne, that is the Lond of Femynye, where that no man is, but only alle Wommen. *c*1430 LYDG. *Min. Poems* (Percy Soc.) 46 Here gynneth a dyté of women-his hornys. *c*1449 PECOCK *Repr.* I. xx. 119 Bi wering of wommennys couercheefis. *c*1450 *Mirk's Festial* 22 All good men and woymen. *c*1450 *Cursor M.* 10528 (Laud) Ouyr alle women to bere croun. **1553** *Respublica* 1454 Men shoulde kysse woomen. **1573** L. LLOYD *Pilgr. Princes* (1586) 55b, The fiftie virgins..certaine..baites being set of purpose by the gentlemen of Messena for their virginities, and now readie..being then maides, to bee made women that night. **1596** DALRYMPLE tr. *Leslie's Hist. Scot.* v. (S.T.S.) I. 290 Woemen quha had vowet chastitie. **1611** CORYAT *Crudities* 247 (*Venice*), I saw women acte, a thing that I neuer saw before. **1753–4** RICHARDSON *Grandison* II. viii. 51 Girls are said to be sooner women than boys are men. **1818** SHELLEY *Julian* 592 Like one of Shakespeare's women. **1874** HARDY *Far fr. Mad. Crowd* xxv, They were already loading hay, the women raking it into cocks, and windrows. **1904** MAX PEMBERTON *Red Morn* viii, The women first, and one by one... If any man goes out of his turn, I will shoot him like a dog.

δ. **1375** BARBOUR *Bruce* III. 734 Men mycht her wemen hely cry. *c*1375 *Sc. Leg. Saints* x. (*Mathou*) 347 Mariage.. To cople men & vemene. *c*1400 *Destr. Troy* 8056 Hit is a propertie apreuit..To all wemen in the world..To be vnstable. *Ibid.* 10904 The wemyn..welt hom to ground with swappis of hor swordes. **1456** *Cov. Leet Bk.* 288 Most excellent princes of weymen mortall. **1503–4** *Rec. St. Mary at Hill* (1904) 252 For the makkyng of the nev wemens pevys. **1512** WRIOTHESLEY *Chron.* (Camden) I. 8 Servantes, prentises, weomen, and all other to pay 4d. a peece. **1553** *Respublica* 1462 Thei bee weemen and perchaunce maye bee faced owte. **1617** MORYSON *Itin.* I. 168 The French Liberty of the Weomen makes the Italians judge them without shame. **1641** (*title*) The Petition of the Weamen of Middlesex. *a*1699 LADY A. HALKETT *Autobiog.* (Camden) 22, I dresed him in the women's habitt that was prepared, wch fitted his Highnesse very well.

b. *Generically* without article: The female human being; the female part of the human race, the female sex. Hence gen. ***woman's*** = womanly, female, feminine.

*c*950 *Lindisf. Gosp.* Matt. xix. 4 *Masculum et feminam fecit eos*, woepen-monn & wifmonn ȝeworhte hia. *c*1000 ÆLFRIC *Deut.* xxii. 5 Ne scryde nan wif hi mid wæpmannes reafe, ne wæpman mid wifmannes reafe. *a*1250 *Prov. Alfred* 281 in *O.E. Misc.* 118 Wymmon is word-woþ and haueþ tunge to swift. *c*1290 *S. Eng. Leg.* 29 þe beste bern..þat euere of womman was i-bore. *c*1386 CHAUCER *Melib.* ¶142 What is better than wisedoom? womman. And what is bettre than a good womman? no thyng. **1526** *Pilgr. Perf.* (W. de W. 1531) 271b, For in man as man is no assurance, & moche lesse in woman. **1697** DRYDEN *Æneis* IV. 820 Woman's a various and a changeful Thing! **1753–4** RICHARDSON *Grandison* III. xvii. 133 Woman is the glory of all created existence:—But you, madam, are *more* than woman! **1766** GOLDSM. *Vicar W.* xxiv. *Song*, When lovely woman stoops to folly. **1808** SCOTT *Marmion* VI. xxx. 1 O Woman! in our hours of ease, Uncertain, coy, and hard to please. **1823** —— *Quentin D.* xiv, Get thee gone with thy woman's ware! **1849** FROUDE *Nem. Faith* 224 All that woman's care or woman's affection could do to soften off her end was done. **1853** DICKENS *Bleak Ho.* xiv, 'But Wooman, lovely Wooman,' said Mr. Turveydrop,..'what a sex you are!' **1855** KINGSLEY in *Life* (1877) I. 453 Woman's heart is alike in all ranks. **1894** 'MAX O'RELL' *John Bull & Co.* 284 Of all the domestic animals invented for the service of man in South Africa, the most useful is woman.

c. *pl.* in pregnant use with reference to (irregular) intercourse with women.

*c*1200 *Vices & Virtues* 127 He..seið þat for ates ne for drinches ne for wifmanne..ne scal man naure ben forloren. **1420–22**, *a*1532, 1621, 1727, 1819 [see WINE *sb.*1 1 f (*b*)]. **1535** COVERDALE *1 Sam.* xxi. 4 Yf the yonge men haue onely refrained them selues from wemen. **1577** FRAMPTON *Joyful News* 15 Aboue all thynges let hym keepe hym self from Women.

d. As a mode of address. (Cf. MAN *sb.*1 4 e.) Now (except *dial.* and in renderings of foreign modes of speech) used chiefly derogatorily or jocularly.

*c*1230 *Hali Meid.* (1922) 42 Wummon, ȝef þu hauest were after þi wil. *a*1240 *Ureisun* in *O.E. Hom.* I. 189 Helpe me.. marie, moder and maiden, deorwurþ wimmon. *c*1250 *Kent. Serm.* in *O.E. Misc.* 29 Ure louerd..sede to hire, Wat be-longeth hit to me oþer to þe, wyman? *a*1300 *Cursor M.* 16651 Wimmen, wimmen, dos a-wai! wepe yee noght for me. **1377** LANGL. *P. Pl.* B. III. 105 Vnwittily, womman! wrouȝt hastow oft. **1382** WYCLIF *Matt.* xv. 28 O thou womman, thi feith is grete. *c*1440 *York Myst.* ix. 93 O! woman, arte þou woode? **1607** SHAKS. *Cor.* IV. i. 12 *Virg.* Oh heauens! O heauens! *Corio.* Nay, I prythee woman. **1667** MILTON *P.L.* IX. 343 O Woman, best are all things as the will Of God ordaind them. **1726** R. WEST *Hecuba* IV. 24 Oh Woman! thy Calamities are great. **1842** LOVER *Handy Andy* ix, Arrah, woman, don't be talkin' your balderdash to me. **1860** SALA *Badd. Peer.* I. iii. 63 'Will you hold your tongue, woman?' her husband..cried out..'Woman! hold my tongue! This language to me!' **1901** S. MACNAUGHTAN *Fortune of Christina M'Nab* i, 'Woman, you are just perfect', responded Colin, 'but you have not got the English tone.'

e. With allusion to qualities conventionally attributed to the female sex, as mutability, capriciousness, proneness to tears; also to their traditional consignment to a position of inferiority or subjection (phr. ***to make a woman of***, to bring into submission).

*c*1400 *Beryn* 872 She had done a vommans dede. *c*1400 *Anturs Arth.* 107 Hit waried, hit wayment as a womane. *c*1515 *Interl. Four Elem.* (Percy Soc.) 23 Then know I a lyghter mete than that... It is evyn a womans tounge, For that is ever sterynge! *a*1548 HALL *Chron.*, *Hen. VIII* 185b, This peace was called the womennes peace, for because that notwithstandyng this conclusion, yet neither the Emperoure trusted the Frenche kyng, nor he neither trusted nor loued hym. **1591** SHAKS. *Two Gent.* I. ii. 23 *Iul.* Your reason? *Lu.* I haue no other but a womans reason: I thinke him so, because I thinke him so. **1593** *Passionate Morrice* (1876) 79 At last, with a resolution, she played the woman, falling into so kinde a vaine of scoulding, as she had charged him with a thousand discourtesies. **1595** SHAKS. *John* V. vi. 22. **1596** —— *Tam. Shr.* IV. v. 36. **1596** —— *1 Hen. IV*, II. iii. 112. **1602** —— *Ham.* I. ii. 146 Frailty, thy name is woman. **1605** *1st Pt. Jeronimo* I. ii. 62 Be woman in all partes, saue in thy eies. **1612** FIELD (*title*) A Woman is a Weather-cocke. **1677** W. HUGHES *Man of Sin* II. viii. 125 O what great Bargains are these! and cheap enough in any Womans Conscience! **1742** *Col. Rec. Pennsylv.* IV. 579 We conquer'd You, we made Women of you. **1836** W. IRVING *Astoria* xxi. II. 40, I have seen your husband carrying wood into his lodge to make the fire. Where was his squaw, that he should be obliged to make a woman of himself? **1850** SMEDLEY *F. Fairlegh* xxvii, Don't make such a fuss; you're as bad as a woman. **1851** KINGSLEY *Three Fishers* 5 For men must work, and women must weep.

f. (Now always with *the*.) The essential qualities of a woman; womanly characteristics; that which makes a woman what she is; womanliness; *occas.* the feminine side or aspect; †predicatively = feminine, womanish.

1611 BEAUM. & FL. *King & No K.* IV. iv, But that my eyes Have more of woman in 'em than my heart, I would not weep. **1637** N. WHITING *Albino & Bellama* 18 Not in a fit of woman cry and whine. **1661** EVELYN *Tyrannus* 25 It is not possible to say which is the more Woman of the two Coated Sardanapalus's. **1676** DRYDEN *Aurengz.* v. 80 All the Woman work'd within your mind. **1771** MACKENZIE *Man Feel.* xxi. (1803) 28 Take away that girl,..she has woman about her, already. **1821** SCOTT *Kenilw.* xiv, It might be.. said, that the Earl of Sussex had been most serviceable to the Queen, while Leicester was most dear to the woman. **1834** SIR H. TAYLOR *Artevelde* I. II. iii, Teach her to subdue The woman in her nature. **1844** *Fraser's Mag.* XXX. 532/2 Liddy was really taking the woman upon her in earnest. **1885** 'MRS. ALEXANDER' *At Bay* vii, She knew that all the woman in her somewhat masculine nature had gone out, in maternal affection to her husband's nephew. **1894** 'G. EGERTON' *Keynotes* 188 To get at the woman under that infernal corset.

†**g.** ***one's own woman***: mistress of oneself, independent. (After MAN *sb.*1 41.) *Obs.*

1605 MARSTON *Dutch Courtezan* III. i, I assure you ile nere marry... Marry God forfend..ile liue my owne woman.

h. In contrast, explicit or implicit, with 'lady' (see LADY *sb.* 4).

1788 WESLEY *Wks.* (1872) VII. 34 Hunting, shooting, fishing, wherein not many women (I should say ladies) are concerned. **1837** DICKENS *Pickw.* xxxii, 'You are such an unreasonable woman,' remonstrated Mr. Benjamin Allen. 'I beg your parding, young man,' said Mrs. Raddle,..'but who do you call a woman?' **1847** *Athenæum* 30 Oct. 1128/1 Defendant pleaded..that the person described as a woman was in fact a lady. **1855** MRS. GASKELL *North & South* xxxix, So that was the lady you spoke of as a woman?.. You might have told me who she was.

i. With qualification denoting status, occupation, or character, *woman* enters into many compounds or collocations more or less permanent, corresponding to those of *man* (MAN *sb.*1 4 p) but much less numerous: see the various qualifying words and BONDWOMAN, CHARWOMAN, COUNTRYWOMAN, GENTLEWOMAN, HORSEWOMAN, MAN-WOMAN, NEEDLEWOMAN, OLD WOMAN, TIRE-WOMAN, TOWNSWOMAN, WISE WOMAN, YOUNG WOMAN, etc.

†*woman bond*, nonce-inversion of BONDWOMAN. ***first woman*** = PRIMA DONNA. ***little woman***: a female child, girl (cf. *little man*, MAN *sb.*1 4 f); also, an affectionate or playful form of address to a girl or young woman, esp. one in whom womanly qualities are conspicuous. ***new woman***: a woman of 'advanced' views, advocating the independence of her sex and defying convention; hence ***new-womandom***, ***new-womanish*** adj.

1675 HOBBES *Odyssey* IV. 12 The second wedding was his son's, Whom on a woman bond he had begot. **1827** EARL MOUNT-EDGCUMBE *Mus. Remin.* (ed. 2) 47 At one of the smaller theatres, however, the part of first woman in an intermezzo..was filled by a very promising singer,..who became in time one of the best first men. **1868** LOUISA M. ALCOTT (*title*) Little Women; or Meg, Jo, Beth, and Amy. **1880** [see PRIMA DONNA]. **1893** G. GISSING *Odd Women* I. viii. 235 A strong character, of course. More decidedly one of the new women than you yourself—isn't she? **1894** SARAH GRAND in *N. Amer. Rev.* March 271 Both the cow-woman and the scum-woman are well within the range of the comprehension of the Bawling Brotherhood, but the new woman is a little above him. **1894** 'OUIDA' *Ibid.* May 616 The elegant epithet of Cow-woman implies the contempt with which maternity is viewed by the New Woman. **1894** *Granta* 8 Dec. 122 The Alexandra (Dublin) ladies..are models of new womandom. **1896** *Harper's Mag.* XCIII. 32/1 She is not at all of an unsentimental nature—only fractious—new-womanish, perhaps. **1897** 'OUIDA' *Massarenes* iv, They were pretty babies, dear little men and women.

j. In phraseological collocations corresp. to those s.v. MAN *sb.*1 18, as ***woman of all work***, ***business***, ***colour***, ***fashion***, ***honour***, ***letters***, ***livelihood***, ***pleasure***, ***the people***, ***property***, ***sense***, ***the town***, ***the world***: see also these sbs. ***woman about town***: see TOWN *sb.* 8 b; ***woman in the street***: see STREET *sb.* 3 h; ***woman-to-woman***: cf. MAN *sb.*1 4 h.

1484 *Test. Ebor.* (Surtees) III. 257 Or ellis to marye hym till a woman of liveloд to his degre. **1697** DE FOE *Ess. Projects* 303 A Woman of Sense and Breeding. **1705** VANBRUGH *Country-ho.* II, You must behave yourself like a woman of honour, and keep your word. **1742** FIELDING *J. Andrews* I. vii, She resolved to preserve all the dignity of the woman of fashion to her servant. **1818** 'T. BROWN' *Brighton; or The Steyne* I. 20 She passes for a woman of letters. **1837** DICKENS *Pickw.* xxxii, The young woman of all work. **1838** —— *O. Twist* xlviii, 'Coming,'..'Ah, and so's the young 'ooman of property that's going to take a fancy to me.' **1847** L. HUNT *Men, Women & B.* (1876) 316 Our little woman of letters [*sc.* Lady Mary W. Montagu] read all the books she could lay her hands on. **1849** LYELL *2nd Visit U.S.* II. 11 The..pleasant expression of countenance of a young woman of colour. [**1859** LYTTON *What will he do with It?* III. VI. ix. 302 Talking thus, Arabella forgot the relationship of pupil and teacher; it was a woman to woman—girl to girl—friend to friend.] **1907** G. B. SHAW *Major Barbara* III. 274, I thought she was a woman of the people, and that a marriage with a professor of Greek would be far beyond the wildest social ambitions of her rank. **1929** J. B. PRIESTLEY *Good Companions* III. v. 586 'I should think you have news,' said Susie, smiling and being tremendously woman-to-woman. **1933** KIPLING *Souvenirs of France* ii. 44 A woman of the people led her away. **1935** E. BOWEN *House in Paris* II. iii. 114 Her round slate-blue eyes rolled in a woman-to-woman way. **1962** 'L. GREX' *Terror wears Smile* iv. 58 'There's not going to be any nonsense. You know what I mean.' Those words had been uttered in a quiet woman-to-woman chat some weeks before. **1982** H. INNES *Black Tide* v. iii. 272 If I told her, woman-to-woman, the sort of person Karen was... Perhaps she'd understand then.

†**k.** In the 16th and 17th centuries freq. with play on a pseudo-etymological association with *woe*; also, less freq., between *weemen* (= women) and *we men*. *Obs.*

?*a*1500 *Chester Plays, Creat.* 259 Woman,..soothe said I in prophesie when thou wast taken of my body, mans woe thou woldest be witlie, therfore thou wast so named. **1534** MORE *Comf. agst. Trib.* To Rdr., Man himselfe borne of a woman, is in deede a wo man, that is, ful of wo and miserie. **1546** J. HEYWOOD *Prov.* II. vii, A woman! As who saith, woe to the man! **1589** PUTTENHAM *Engl. Poesie* II. xviii. (Arb.) 147 Not money: nor many, Nor any: but any, Not weemen, but weemen beare the bell. **1601** in Bullen *More Lyrics* (1888) 143 Women, what are they?.. We men, what are we? **1616** R. C. *Times' Whistle* v. 1962 Woemen when they will Can weep. **1653** FLECKNOE *Misc.* 70 *Shep.* Woe has end, when 'tis alone: But in woman never none. *Nim.* Say of Woman worst ye can, What prolongs their woe, but man?

l. Proverbs.

*c*1425 *Cast. Persev.* 2650 in *Macro Plays* 156 þer wymmen arn, are many wordys. *c*1440 *Alphabet of Tales* 396 Socrates ..sayd þat womman, ay þe mor sho was bett, þe wars was sho. **1520** *Calisto & Melib.* A iij b, Yt is an old sayeng That women be the dyuells nets and hed of syn. **1541** *Schole-h. Women* 690 in Hazl. *E.P.P.* IV. 131 Women and dogges cause much strife. **1545** TAVERNER *Erasm. Prov.* 31b, Fyre, See, Woman, thre euyls. **1589** PUTTENHAM *Engl. Poesie* III. xix. (Arb.) 239 It..may be likened to the maner of women, who as the common saying is, will say nay and take it. *Ibid.* xxiv. 297 A woman will weepe for pitie to see a gosling goe barefoote. **1594** *Mirr. Policy* (1599) X ij, Is it not an old Prouerbe. That Women and Shippes are neuer so perfect but still there is somewhat to bee amended. **1599** SANDYS *Europæ Spec.* (1629) 194 Seeing as the Proverbe is, a dead woman will haue foure to cary her forth. **1639** J. CLARKE *Parœm.* 117 A woman, asse, and walnut-tree, the more you beat the better be. **1659** N. R. *Proverbs* 110 Three Women make a Market. *Ibid.* 120 Women laugh when they can, weep when they will. **1670** RAY *Prov.* 50 A womans work is never at an end. *Ibid.* 54 England is the Paradise of women. *c*1825 MRS. CAMERON *The Cradle* 12 You know they say 'A woman's business is never done.'

m. ***hell hath no fury like a woman scorned*** and var. (see SCORN *v.* 3 a, quot. 1697). Hence ***woman scorned***, used allusively; also as *attrib. phr.*

1868 J. G. SAXE *Poems* 291 In classic authors we are often warned, There's naught so savage as a 'woman scorned'. [**1886** M. H. E. BATES *Chamber over Gate* xxvi. 363 You know 'Hell hath no fury', etc. If your wife should ever wake up to the true state of the case..I'm afraid she'd be an ugly customer.] **1927** W. JOHNSTON *Affair in Duplex 9B* 60 The old idea of 'the woman scorned' on which Chilton had been relying this time failed utterly. **1932** W. McFee *Harbourmaster* xxi. 333 They say hell hath no fury like a woman scorned. **1940** G. H. Coxe *Glass Triangle* x. 126 If you really want to know who could have wanted to kill him, you might as well start with me... You've heard that one about hell having no fury like a woman scorned? Well, that was me. **1942** N. Marsh *Death & Dancing Footman* iii. 49 He broke out into..merriment calculated..to arouse in Chloris the pangs proper to a woman scorned. **1967** —— *Death at Dolphin* viii. 222 She really does bear out the Woman Scorned crack. She is..not all that charitably disposed at any time. **1971** 'J. Ripley' *Davis doesn't live here any More* 124 The discarded mistress—the 'woman scorned'—motive. **1973** I. Murdoch *Black Prince* 330 'Hell hath no fury like a woman scorned.' In a way I might have been flattered.

2. A female servant, *esp.* a lady's maid or personal attendant. Often *pl.* (†also = womenfolk).

a **766** *Pœnit. Abp. Egbert* iv. in Thorpe *Laws* (1840) II. 182 Ʒif hwylc wif..hire wifman swingð. *c* **1000** Ælfric *Gen.* xx. 18 God ʒewitnode ealle hys wimmen. **1340** *Ayenb.* 67 Þis zenne is ine uele maneres ase ine sergons aye hire lhordinges, ine wyfmen aye hare leuedis. *c* **1450** *Merlin* v. 90, I..require that as soone as it is born that ye take it to oon of youre moste secrete woman. **1565** *Cal. Scott. Papers* (1900) II. 142 To play a partie at a playe theie call the biles, my mestres Beton and I agaynste the Quene and my lord Darlye—the women to have the gayne of the wynninges. **1613** Shaks. *Hen. VIII*, i. iv. 93 Sir Thomas Bullens Daughter,..One of her Highnesse women. **1663** Dryden *Rival Ladies* i. ii, A Note put privately into my hand By Angellina's Woman. **1749** Fielding *Tom Jones* vii. viii, In Town I visit none but the Women of Women of Quality. **1809** Malkin *Gil Blas* x. ix. (Rtldg.) 360 Another coach and four, with Seraphina's women. **1893** 'Leslie Keith' *Lisbeth* iii, I wonder ye dare put such an affront on me before the women! **1898** Hichens *Londoners* x, From Mrs. Crouch, ma'am, her Grace's woman.

3. † **a.** A lady-love, mistress. *Obs.* **b.** A kept mistress, paramour.

13.. *K. Alis.* 7567 They toke and slowe Hirkan And yolde Kindeleke his woman. **1561** Hoby tr. *Castiglione's Courtyer* iii. (1577) Q vj, A feruent Dialogue full of the affection of a louer with his womanne. **1639** J. S. *Clidamas* 25 Agree to bee my woman, and I will consent to bee thy man. **1666** Pepys *Diary* 13 Oct., The Duke of York..leaves off care of business, what with his woman, my Lady Denham, and his hunting three times a week. **1719** De Foe *Crusoe* ii. (Globe) 384 If any of you take any of these Women, as a Woman or Wife,..he shall take but one. **1924** Galsworthy *White Monkey* iii. vii, They tell me Elderson keeps two women.

4. a. A wife. Now only *dial.* and *U.S.*

Cf. old woman 1 b and the corresp. use of *man* (man *sb.*[1] 8).

c **1450** *St. Cuthbert* (Surtees) 7041 A night be his woman [*cum uxore*] he lay. **1598** Shaks. *Merry W.* ii. ii. 305 See the hell of hauing a false woman: my bed shall be abus'd. *a* **1625** Fletcher *Nice Valour* ii. i, A man can in his lifetime make but one woman, But he can make his fifty Queanes a month. **1693** Dryden *Juvenal* vi. 295 Prepare thy Neck and put it in the Yoke: But for no mercy from thy Woman look. **1765** in *Buccleuch MSS.* (Hist. MSS. Comm.) I. 416 My poor little woman has been in the drooping mood for two or three days. **1841** Thackeray *Gt. Hoggarty Diam.* x, Gates and his woman thought that they should come for'ard..to help the kindest master and missus ever was. **1866** Carlyle *Remin.* (1881) II. 193, I persisted in them to the last, as did my woman. **1897** Kipling *Capt. Cour.* vii. 147 He married my woman's aunt.

† **b.** The female mate of an animal. *Obs. rare.*

1577 Googe *Heresbach's Husb.* iii. 144 b, The hee Goate, ..by a certayne instinct of nature,..goeth alwayes before his woman.

5. The reverse of a coin; in reference to the figure of Britannia (q.v.) upon it. (Cf. man *sb.*[1] 17.)

1785 Grose *Dict. Vulgar T.* s.v. *Harp*, Harp..is also the Irish expression for woman, or tail, used in tossing up in Ireland. **1835** Marryat *Olla Podr., Ill-Will* iii, *Thos.* Here goes—heads or tails? *John.* Woman for ever. **1888** 'R. Boldrewood' *Robbery under Arms* xi, I pulled out a shilling. 'If it's head we go, Jim; if it's woman, we stay here.'

II. *attrib.* and *Comb.*

6. a. Simple attrib. = 'of or characteristic of a woman or women, feminine, womanly': ***woman-city, -eye, -flesh, -godhead, -haunt, -luck***, etc.

1542 Udall *Erasm. Apoph.* 29 The woman sexe is no lesse apte to learne al maner thynges then menne are. **1621** Lady M. Wroth *Urania* 104 Woman modestie kept her silent. **1622** Fletcher *Prophetess* iii. iii, You'll find it but a woman-fit to try ye. **1631** Heywood *1st Pt. Fair Maid of West* iii. i. 31 In this woman shape Ile cudgell thee. **1726** Pope *Odyss.* xix. 82 Into the woman-state asquint to pry. **1810** Scott *Lady of L.* v. xxvi, The only man, in whom a foe My woman-mercy would not know. **1845** Clough *Poems*, 'Ὁ Θεὸς μετὰ σοῦ' 7, I shall see thy soft brown eyes dilate to wakening woman thought. **1846** Mrs. Carlyle in *Jane Welsh Carlyle* (1924) 278 What a contrast I often think betwixt that woman and Geraldine! the opposite poles of woman-nature! **1880** G. Meredith *Trag. Comedians* II. v. 83 Exactly what his appreciation, in womanflesh, would lead him to fix on. **1883** Browning *Joch. Hakkadosh* 310 The woman-nature—the soft sway Of undefinable omnipotence O'er our strong male-stuff. **1895** *Outing* (U.S.) XXVI. 346/2 The next moment he had taken the fair woman face between his hands. **1895** *Cath. Mag.* Dec. 453 Her shrewd woman-wit. **1897** 'H. S. Merriman' *In Kedar's Tents* xxvi. *heading*, Womancraft. **1915** D. H. Lawrence *Rainbow* iii. 81 He must get out of this oppressive, shut-down, woman-haunt. **1922** Joyce *Ulysses* 468 Under it lies the womancity. *Ibid.* 155 Mrs Breen's womaneyes said melancholily. **1923** D. H. Lawrence *Ladybird* 53 She could not finally believe in her own woman-godhead. **1946** Dylan Thomas *Deaths & Entrances* 40 The next-door sea dispelled Frogs and satans and woman-luck. **1971** V. Canning *Firecrest* vi. 83 He put his arm round her shoulder..and felt through silk the warmth and firmness of woman flesh.

b. appos. (*a*) = 'female', esp. with designations of occupation or profession: ***woman doctor, driver, -help, journalist, officer, p.c., police officer, -savage, teacher***, etc.

a **1300** *Cursor M.* 29420 If þou wit þi woman frend Find clerk be doand dede vn-hende. **1382** Wyclif *1 Kings* xvii. 9 A womman widowe. *c* **1400** *Three Kings Cologne* (1886) 33 A womman-paynym þat was his moder. **14..** *Lat.-Eng. Voc.* in Wr.-Wülcker 600/47 *Sacerdotissa patrina*, a wommangossyb. **1530** Palsgr. 289/2 Woman coke, *cuisiniere.* **1617** Moryson *Itin.* i. 258 The famous woman poet Sapho. **1632** Brome *Court Beggar* v. ii. (1653) S 3 b, What Woman Monster's this? **1659** D. Pell *Improv. Sea* Ep. Ded. d j, Wee are so wise now, that wee have our woman Politicians. **1675** T. Brooks *Gold. Key* Wks. 1867 V. 442 A woman-martyr who..offered herself to martyrdom. **1680** Shadwell (*title*) The Woman-Captain. **1693** Dryden *Juvenal* vi. Note 31 A Woman-Grammarian, who corrects her Husband for speaking false Latin. **1697** —— *Æneis* xi. 996 [1016] A Woman Warrior was too strong for thee. **1706** Prior *Ode to Queen* xxvi, The Woman Chief is Master of the War. **1717** Pope *Iliad* ix. 756 One Woman-Slave was ravish'd from thy Arms. **1805** Forsyth *Beauties Scot.* II. 54 A woman-shearer, through the harvest, is reckoned equal to the rent of a cottage and yard. **1847** Tennyson *Princess* iv. 540 The Princess with her monstrous woman-guard. **1853** Dickens *Child's Hist. Eng.* xxix, in *Househ. Words* 12 Mar. 48/2 Edward was now sinking in a rapid decline... They handed him over to a woman-doctor who pretended to be able to cure it. **1859** Geo. Eliot *Adam Bede* l, Lisbeth's obstinate refusal to have any woman-helper in the house. **1877** Black *Green Past.* i, With scarcely a woman-friend in the world. **1899** W. James *Talks to Teachers on Psychol.* ii. i. 227 What our girl-students and woman-teachers most need..is..the toning-down of their moral tensions. **1902** A. Bennett in *Academy* 21 June 635/1 The average woman-journalist is the most loyal, earnest and teachable person under the sun. **1911** D. H. Lawrence *White Peacock* i. ix. 158 At any rate the extra woman-help came. **1921** R. Macaulay *Dangerous Ages* iii. 65 Pamela bright and cool and firm, like a woman doctor. **1930** D. H. Lawrence *A Propos of Lady Chatterley's Lover* 25 We read of the woman-savage who wore three overcoats on top of one another to excite her man. **1968** R. L. Fish *Bridge that went Nowhere* iv. 44, I might have known it would be a woman driver! **1972** L. Lamb *Picture Frame* xviii. 154 A woman p.c. was clearing an outside drain. **1973** 'B. Mather' *Snowline* x. 121 I'll send a couple of woman officers along. **1976** R. Lewis *Witness my Death* i. 36 You've shown all the worst traits that can be expected in a woman doctor. **1976** *Southern Even. Echo* (Southampton) 11 Nov. 32/5 A chase through rush-hour crowds ended with a suspected shoplifter escaping into the darkness..as he was pursued by a woman police officer. **1982** D. Mackenzie *Raven's Revenge* xi. 104 A small car stopped... The woman driver was already crossing the pavement, house-keys in hand. **1982** A. Brookner *Providence* ix. 108, I wonder why they didn't send a woman teacher.

†(*b*) = 'having the character of a woman, feminine, womanly; effeminate'. *Obs.*

a **1586** Sidney *Arcadia* iii. xxv. (1912) 497 Rather then onely shew her selfe a woman-lover in fruitles lamentations. **1635–56** Cowley *Davideis* i. 319, I have been a pious fool, a Woman-King.

(*c*) With names of animals, forming designations of creatures having the qualities or properties of a woman and of the particular animal.

a **1625** Fletcher *Womans Prize* iv. iv, I..know her To be a Woman-wolfe by transmigration. **1673** *Lady's Calling* i. iii. §23 Nothing can be more unnatural, more odious, then a woman-tiger. **1889** Rider Haggard *Allan's Wife* xi, The brutes, acting under the direction of that woman-monkey. **1893** Rodway *Hand-bk. Brit. Guiana* 67 How such an unwieldy creature [as the manatee]..could ever have been figured as a woman-fish can hardly be understood by anyone who has seen it.

c. objective, as ***woman-follower, -killer, †-queller, -scorner, -slayer, -spiter, -worship, -worshipper, -wronger***; also ***woman-bearing, -churching, -degrading, -despising, -flogging, -murdering, †-quelling, -worshipping***, adjs.; ***woman-hating*** adj. and sb.; similative and parasynthetic, as ***woman breasted, -faced, -fair, -headed, -hearted, -proud, -vested*** adjs.; instrumental, as ***woman-bred, -built, -conquered, -daunted, -governed, -made, -ridden, -tended*** adjs.

1928 W. B. Yeats tr. *Sophocles' King Oedipus* 42 Oedipus overcame the *woman-breasted Fate. **1946** Dylan Thomas *Deaths & Entrances* 30 The woman breasted and the heaven headed Bird. **1848** Thackeray *Van. Fair* xxxviii, The boy grew up delicate, sensitive, imperious, *woman-bred. **1847** Tennyson *Princess* iv. 466 A new-world Babel, *woman-built. *a* **1693** *Urquhart's Rabelais* iii. xli. 336 An uprising or *Woman Churching Treatment. **1847** Tennyson *Princess* iii. 333 *Woman-conquer'd [stood] there The bearded Victor of ten-thousand hymns. **1598** Rowlands *Betraying Christ*, etc. D iv, *Woman-daunted Peter. **1895** G. Allen *Woman who did* (1906) 84 Their own vile *woman-degrading and prostituting morality. **1610** Healey *St. Aug. Citie of God* 686 Ausonius makes her [*sc.* the Sphinx] ..*woman-faced. **1866** Lytton *Lost Tales Miletus* 96 Beside him sate An image *woman-fair. **1794** Southey *Coleridge's Fall of Robespierre* iii. 181 The *woman-govern'd Roland. **1939** W. Fortescue *There's Rosemary* xii. 87, I even got personal praise from a *woman-hating Don who acted as dramatic critic for the 'Varsity magazine. **1973** E. Taylor *Serpent under It* xi. 172 He was really an old dear—all that woman-hating stuff was just a pose. **1902** *19th Cent.* Dec. 989 The *woman-headed serpent. **1813** H. G. Knight *Alashtar* iii. xiii, Well may the mild, the *woman-hearted fail. **1848** Thackeray *Van. Fair* xxix, Having a firm conviction in his own mind that he was a *woman-killer and destined to conquer. **1597** Shaks. *2 Hen. IV*, ii. i. 58 Thou art..a Man-queller, and a *woman-queller. **1611** J. Davies *Sco. Folly* (Grosart) 10/1 Bossus the woman-queller. **1852** Thackeray *Esmond* ii. iv, A weak priest-ridden, *woman-ridden man. **1935** Auden & Isherwood *Dog beneath Skin* i. v. 57 But perhaps you're a *woman-scorner. **1591** Harington *Orl. Fur.* xxix. xxxii, He had proud'd him selfe a *woman-slayre. **1847** Mrs. Gore *Castles in Air* v, A perpetual sense of aggression had converted me, not into a woman-hater, but a *woman-spiter. **1857** Ld. Dufferin *Lett. High Lat.* vi. 36 The elegance and comfort of a *woman-tended home. **1847** Tennyson *Princess* iv. 163 *Woman-vested as I was. **1848** Kingsley *Saint's Trag.* Introd. p. xviii, The *woman-worship of chivalry. **1856** Reade *Never too Late* ix, Next Lady-day, as the *woman-worshipper calls it. **1921** D. H. Lawrence *Sea & Sardinia* iii. 114 *Woman-worshipping Don Juans. **1596** Spenser *F.Q.* vi. vii. 7 Foule *womanwronger.

7. Special comb.: † **woman-actor**, (*a*) an actress; (*b*) an actor who takes women's parts; **woman-boat** = *women's boat* (10); **woman-body** *dial.*, a person of the female sex, woman; **woman-born** *a.*, born of woman; **woman-dangler**, one who dangles after women; † **woman-errant**, one who goes after women; **woman-grown** *a.*, that has become a woman; **woman-hour**, an hour's work done by a woman; † **woman-house** *Sc.*, a laundry: see also *women-house* (9 c); † **woman-keeper**, a female nurse; † **woman-louper** *Sc.*, a whoremonger; **woman-mad** *a.*, mad after women; **woman-man**, an effeminate man, or one who in some way resembles a woman; **woman-market**, a place for the sale (*lit.* or *fig.*) of women; **woman-movement**, the movement for the emancipation of women, or the recognition and extension of women's rights; **woman-palaver** *African*, illicit commerce with a woman or women; **woman-physician**, (*a*) a woman's doctor; (*b*) a woman-doctor; **woman-post**, a female messenger or courier; **woman-power**, (*a*) the exercise of authority by women; (*b*) the number of women available for work; the power of women in work; **woman question**, a controversy over the rights of women, esp. that in the nineteenth century; **woman-raving** *a.* = *woman-mad*; † **woman-reputation**, reputation with women; † **woman-shoemaker**, a maker of women's shoes; **woman-slaughter**, the killing of a woman by a human being; **woman-suffrage**, the right of women to vote in public affairs; hence **woman-suffragist**, an advocate of woman-suffrage; † **woman-surgeon**, one who beautifies women by the aid of paints, washes, etc.; † **woman-tired** *a.* [tire *v.*[2] 2], hen-pecked; **woman trouble** *colloq.*, (*a*) *U.S.*, gynæcological problems (cf. trouble *sb.* 4); (*b*) difficulties caused to a man by a relationship with a woman or women; †(*on*) **woman-ways, -wise** *advs.*, after the manner of a woman or women; **woman-year**, a year of a woman's life; esp. used as a cumulative measure in medical tests carried out on a number of different women.

1739 Cibber *Apol.* (1756) II. 146 (Dial. old Plays) Alexander Goffe, the *woman-actor at Blackfriers..used to be the jackall. **1895** Kipling *2nd Jungle Bk.* 146 Big skin '*woman-boats', when the dogs and the babies lay among the feet of the rowers. **1818** Scott *Hrt. Midl.* x, It was an awkward thing for a *woman-body to be standing among bundles o' barkened leather her lane, selling saddles and bridles. **1887** Hall Caine *Deemster* xii, The young woman-body is dead in child-bed. **1781** Cowper *Charity* 181 Canst thou..Buy what is *woman-born, and feel no shame? **1842** J. Wilson *Chr. North* (1857) I. 217 Nor in those days needed he [*sc.* Burns] help from woman-born. **1850** *Fraser's Mag.* Nov. 508/2 That when his back is turned the Senecas may not call him a thief as well as a *woman-dangler. **1628** Shirley *Witty Fair One* ii. ii, What make you here, my *woman errant? **1785** Burns *Cotter's Sat. Nt.* iv, Their Jenny, *woman-grown, In youthfu' bloom. **1864** Tennyson *Aylmer's F.* 108 The maiden woman-grown. **1961** *Guardian* 23 Mar. 24/6, I shudder to think how many man-hours and *woman-hours are spent..typing, 'Dear So-and-So'. **1979** M. McCarthy *Cannibals & Missionaries* i. 4 I'm doing a serious study of the woman-hours expended in this family. **1616** *Reg. Mag. Sig. Scot.* 555/2 Cameram lie *woman-hous. **1754** *State of Process, Mrs. Forbes v. D. Scot* (Jam.) Water lying on the floors of the woman-house and kitchen. **1552** Wriothesley *Chron.* (Camden) II. 80 Betwene euery xx children [of Christ's Hospital] [there was] one *woman keeper. **1630** ? Dekker *Blacke Rod* (1925) 217 No Women-keepers to rob you of your Goods, or to hasten you to your End. *a* **1568** in *Bannatyne MS.* (Hunter. Club.) 419 A *woman lowpar, landless. **1848** Buckley *Iliad* 249 Accursed Paris, *woman-mad, seducer. **1605** Sylvester *Du Bartas* ii. iii. i. *Vocation* 344 May one hope..In *Woman-Men a manly Constancie? **1621** J. Taylor (Water P.) *Superbiæ Flagellum* C 6, The Woman-man, Man-woman, chuse you whether, The Female-male, Male-female, both, yet neither. **1889** Tennyson *On one who affected an effeminate manner* 4 But friend, man-woman is not woman-man. **1760–72** H. Brooke *Fool of Qual.* (1809) III. 103 Another lady then demanded, if we had not a *woman-market. **1864** Tennyson *Aylmer's F.* 348 He never yet had set his daughter forth Here in the woman-markets of the west. **1883** *Harper's Mag.* Aug. 468/2 Whether the great progress of the '*woman movement'..is due to the agitation of 'woman's rights', or proceeds in spite of it. **1898** *Daily News* 14 Dec. 5/1 It is in educational affairs that the Woman

Movement appears to be making the most progress. **1897** HINDE *Congo Arabs* 32 What every African traveller knows as '*woman-palaver'. **1533** *MSS. Dk. Rutland* (Hist. MSS. Comm.) IV. 274 To a *woman phisician..iijs. iiij*d*. **1591** H. SMITH *Prepar. Marr.* 76 To helpe him in his sicknesse, like a woman Phisition. **1625** HART *Anat. Ur.* II. vi. 85 Much lesse then the ignorant Empiricke, the peticoate or woman-physitian. **1595** SHAKS. *John* I. i. 218 But who comes in such haste in riding robes? What *woman post is this? **1626** *Raleigh's Ghost* in *Harl. Misc.* (Malh.) III. 547 How he [*sc.* Gondomar]..answered the expectation..of..the king..shall be declared upon the next return of the woman-post, which passeth betwixt the English and the Spanish Jesuits. **1847** TENNYSON *Princess* IV. 357 A woman-post in flying raiment. **1927** *Amer. Jrnl. Philol.* XLVIII. 201 In the kingdoms established by the Successors in Egypt and in Syria women appear as co-rulers with their husbands and as regents during the minority of a son or the exile of a husband. This *woman-power is sometimes regarded as a Macedonian tradition. **1938** *Lancet* 5 Nov. 1071/2 If the aim is to use the woman-power of the countryside to the best advantage it will often be best for the women themselves to organise their work collectively. **1941** *New Yorker* 29 Mar. 46/3 The long-threatened drive to bring womanpower into the war effort. **1968** *Ramparts* May 8 If you had a cover on Black Power like your cover on Woman Power, it would be a picture of a sharecropper with a harmonica in one hand and a piece of watermelon in the other. **1973** *Black World* June 32 Woman power Is Black power Is Human power Is Always feeling. **1976** H. WILSON *Governance of Britain* 7 Ernest Bevin..was in charge of the industrial and military mobilization of Britain's manpower and woman-power. **1977** *Spare Rib* July 23 We're desperately short of woman-power on all areas of the magazine. **1984** *Sunday Times* (Colour Suppl.) 28 Oct. 80/2 The more progressive industries are beginning to realise that they can't afford to waste Britain's womanpower. **1857** GEO. ELIOT *Let.* 21 Sept. (1954) II. 383 Quite delivered from any necessity of giving a judgment on the *Woman Question or of reading newspapers about the Indian Mutinies. **1884** T. STANTON (*title*) The woman question in Europe. **1930** J. COLLIER *His Monkey Wife* ix. 119 A belated essayist on the Woman Question. **1981** R. TREMAIN *Cupboard* ii. 31 The attitude of men to the Woman Question. **1848** BUCKLEY *Iliad* 50 Cursed Paris, thou *woman-raving seducer. *a* **1641** BP. MOUNTAGU *Acts & Mon.* vii. (1642) 395 To which popular credit and *woman-reputation they attained..by their saint-seeming sanctity. **1704** *Lond. Gaz.* No. 4003/4 Robert Fleetwood, a *Woman Shoemaker. **1639** J. TAYLOR (Water P.) *Crabtree Lect.* 82 Least there should be man-slaughter, or *woman-slaughter committed. **1720** T. GORDON *Humourist* I. 169 But only be deem'd Woman-slaughter. **1844** J. T. HEWLETT *Parsons & W.* ix, They had never heard of a verdict of woman-slaughter in their lives. **1867** *Times* 11 Apr. 12/1 *Woman Suffrage. [Text of two petitions.] **1888** *Pall Mall Gaz.* 26 Jan. 10/1 The sunflower badge..has been adopted by the Iowa *woman suffragists. **1628** FORD *Lover's Mel.* I. ii, *Pel.* My nurse was a *woman-surgeon... *Rhe.* A she-surgeon, which is in effect a meere matter of colours. **1959** N. MAILER *Advts. for Myself* (1961) 95 She comes to see him about something or other, *woman trouble maybe, and he seduces her in his medical chambers. **1967** J. IRWIN *Murderous Welcome* vi. 51 She repudiated strongly any suggestion of discord between husband and wife and poured scorn on the mere idea of woman-trouble. **1977** L. MEYNELL *Hooky gets Wooden Spoon* xi. 127 'What's happening to Len Carron these days?'..'Woman trouble.' **1611** SHAKS. *Wint. T.* II. iii. 74 Thou dotard, thou art *woman-tyr'd: vnroosted By thy dame Partlet heere. *a* **1568** *Bannatyne MS.* (Hunter. Club) 174 With welwet bordour abowt his threidbair coit, On *woman-wayis weill toyit abowt his west. **1865** SWINBURNE *Atalanta* 2308 This man Died *woman-wise. **1959** *Science* 10 July 81/2 Sixteen certain and one probable pregnancy occurred in women taking the medication; this represented a rate of 2·7 pregnancies per 100 *woman-years.

8. Comb. with *woman's*, as ***woman's †poet, tailor***; **woman's boat** = *women's boat* (see 10); **woman's magazine**, a magazine designed primarily for women; also (*colloq.*) ***woman's mag***; freq. *attrib.*, esp. alluding to superficiality or stereotypical attitudes regarded as associated with such productions; **woman's man**, a lady's man, a gallant; **† woman's-meadwort** = MEADWORT 2; **woman's movement** = *woman-movement*, sense 7 above; **woman's page**, a page of a newspaper devoted to topics intended to be of special interest to women; **woman's woman**, a woman whose qualities are appreciated by other women, a woman who is popular with other women (cf. *man's man* s.v. MAN *sb.*[1] 21); **woman's work**, work traditionally undertaken by women.

1769 FALCONER *Dict. Marine* (1776) s.v. *Canoe, Umiak*, the *woman's-boat. **1912** *Magazine Maker* Sept. 7 (*title*) Making a *woman's magazine. **1944** U. ORANGE *Company in Evening* ii. 34 The woman's magazine short story market may be a footling one. **1958** *Observer* 23 Feb. 14/2 The play..fools about at woman's-mag-whimsy level of moral convention. *Ibid.* 25 May 16/7 A Miss Lonelyhearts on a foundering woman's mag. **1958** *Spectator* 13 June 768/2 Ophelia's infatuated woman's magazine royalism rings with a specially hollow tinkle in Glen Byam Shaw's production of *Hamlet*. **1959** J. BRAINE *Vodi* xxi. 231 Honestly, that woman's magazine stuff, just the sort of advice these damned aunties give. **1974** *Times Lit. Suppl.* 3 May 483/2 Without these pages of imaginative grace, the novel would be dangerously close to the woman's magazine level of romantic fiction with which it persistently flirts. **1599** BRETON *Wil of Wit* (Grosart) 57/1, I thinke it better to bee thought a good *womans man than an ill mans woman. **1693** CONGREVE *Old Bach.* IV. xiii, Railing is the best qualification in a woman's man. **1711** STEELE *Spect.* No. 156 ¶1 The Woman's Man is a Person in his Air and Behaviour quite different from the rest of our Species. **1729** T. COOKE *Tales*, etc. 93 And him the Women call'd a Woman's Man. **1818** FESSENDEN *Ladies' Monitor* 31 Nor will I sanction any plan T'annihilate your pretty woman's man. *a* **1400-50** *Stockholm Med. MS.* lf. 209 Freynch cresse or *wymmannys medewourth. [**1881** E. C. STANTON et al. *Hist. Woman Suffrage* I. xiv. 577 The 'Woman's Rights' Movement is a practical one.] **1894** J. E. SCHMAHL in *Englishwoman's Rev.* 16 Apr. 90 For many years Maria Deraismes was looked upon as the sole and undisputed head of the *woman's movement in France. **1906** C. P. GILMAN *Women & Economics* (ed. 5) iii. 49 So utterly has the status of woman been accepted as a sexual one that it has remained for the woman's movement of the nineteenth century to devote much contention to the claim that women are persons! **1933** E. WAUGH *Scoop* I. i. 15 Those carefree days when he had edited the *Woman's Page. **1952** M. STEEN *Phoenix Rising* iv. 87 An editor or a publisher or a woman's page-writer. **1971** Woman's page [see SEXISM]. **1620** B. JONSON *Masque, News fr. New World* (1641) 42 *Chro.* Is he a Mans Poet, or a *Womans Poet I pray you? *2 He.* Is there any such difference? *Fac.* Many, as betwixt your mans Taylor, and your womans Taylor. **1597** SHAKS. *2 Hen. IV*, III. ii. 161 What Trade are thou Feeble? *Feeble.* A *Womans Taylor sir. **1886** KIPLING *Plain Tales* (1888) 47 Mrs. Hauksbee was honest..and, but for her love of mischief, would have been a *woman's woman. **1923** G. ATHERTON *Black Oxen* xl. 246 She had never been a 'woman's woman', and it was patent that, as ever, she was far more animated in the company of men. **1976** 'M. NELSON' *Crusoe Test* i. 12 Elegant was the word for Carla Bayer... She was not a woman's woman. [**1670** *Woman's work: see sense 1 l.] **1890** A. J. ARMSTRONG *Ingleside Musings* 139 Thae bairns are just a woman's wark To keep them clean an' tidy. **1971** K. MILLETT *Sexual Politics* (1972) I. ii. 39 The 'woman's work' in which some two thirds of female population..are engaged is work that is not paid for.

9. Comb. with *women*: **a.** appos., serving as plurals of combs. with *woman* (see 6 b, 7): ***women doctors, drivers, friends, journalists, ministers, priests, professors, students***, etc.

13.. *Cursor M.* 2672 (Gött.) þat ilke lym quar-with þat þai er kend fra wimmen kith. **1382** WYCLIF *2 Sam.* xix. 35, I may here..the vois of men syngers and of wymmen syngers. **1494** in *Househ. Ord.* (1790) 125 The woemen officers for to receave it in the chamber. **1577** tr. *Bullinger's Decades* (1592) 1044 There is in the Church an order of women ministers called women-deacons. **1588** KYD *Househ. Phil.* Wks. (1901) 273 Homer, who..brought Penelope and Circes in the number of women weauers. **1600** J. PORY tr. *Leo's Africa* III. 148 The third kinde of diuiners are women-witches. *c* **1610** *Women Saints* (1886) 30 The moste famous women saints. **1614** PURCHAS *Pilgrimage* V. xvii. (ed. 2) 542 Ten women-slaues. **1622** PEACHAM *Compl. Gentl.* i. 11 Women Doctors (of whom for the most part there is more danger, then of the worst disease it selfe). **1625** HART *Anat. Ur.* I. i. 8 By the aduice of her women-gossips. **1632** BROME *Court Beggar* V. ii. (1653) S 2 b, Women-Actors now grow in request. **1661** WALTON *Angler* xviii. (ed. 3) 233 A Sticklebag..is good..only to make sport for boyes and women-Anglers. **1771** T. HULL *Sir W. Harrington* (1797) III. 226 A parcel of women-relations. **1859** GEO. ELIOT *Adam Bede* xlii, These poor silly women-things. **1878** *Harper's Mag.* Mar. 602/2 The established physicians shook their heads. They never believed in 'women doctors'. **1893** *Dict. Nat. Biogr.* XXXIV. 200 A procession, chiefly of women-workers. **1896** C. L. DODGSON (*title*) Resident women-students. **1898** *Daily News* 2 Dec. 5/1 The Guild of Women-Binders. **1930** A. BENNETT *Imperial Palace* xi. 63 A strong sex-bias which had persuaded him that women-drivers were capable of any enormity. **1935** D. L. SAYERS *Gaudy Night* vii. 147 There are much better ways of enjoying Oxford than fooling round..with the women students. **1941** J. D. CARR *Case of Constant Suicides* xi. 142 What kind of a professor are you, anyway? Running around with women professors from other colleges. **1956** A. S. C. Ross in M. Black *Importance of Lang.* (1962) 97 The custom is now obsolescent, save perhaps between close women-friends. **1967** L. MEYNELL *Mauve Front Door* xi. 138, I switched off the engine and climbed out of the cab; bloody women drivers, I thought. **1971** *Guardian* 15 Apr. 11/1 The diocese of Hong Kong, the only diocese out of 300 to have stated openly its support for the ordination of women priests. *Ibid.* 11/2 In the Congregationalist church..it can no longer be considered particularly unusual to have women ministers. **1975** *Ibid.* 21 Jan. 6/2 Creches should be provided at places where women journalists work. **1981** 'J. Ross' *Dark Blue & Dangerous* iv. 22 Did he have friends? Women friends? **1981** 'A. CROSS' *Death in Faculty* ix. 106 Most women students..don't really believe women professors actually exist.

b. objective, etc. synonymous with the corresp. combs. with *woman* (see 6 c, 7).

1748 RICHARDSON *Clarissa* (1768) IV. 159 As Daughters will (when women-grown especially). **1753-4** —— *Grandison* IV. xiii. 81 These women-frightening heroes. **1856** 'C. BEDE' *Tales of Coll. Life, Long-Vac. Vigil* x, The *Morning Post*..devoted..half a column to these women-absorbing topics. **1896** *Daily News* 26 Dec. 2/2 A nation of women-supported men.

c. Special comb.: **women-house** *Sc.*, a building set apart for women only; **women liberators**, women's liberationists (see sense 10 below); **† women-matters** *pl.*, matters relating to women; **women-men** *pl.* (see *woman-man*, 7); **womenpower**, = *woman-power*, sense 7 above; **† women-sleepers** *pl.*, female nurses (cf. *woman-keeper* in sense 7); **† women-strikers** *pl.* [STRIKER *sb.* 2 d], prostitutes; **women-suffrage** = *woman-suffrage* (see 7); **women-wise** *adv.*, in the fashion or way of women; **women-years**, *pl.* of ***woman-year***, sense 7 above.

1792 *Statist. Acc. Scot.* II. 149 At these [bleach-] fields,..there are a number of women not having families, nor residing in families, but in *women-houses, so called, erected on purpose. *c* **1865** J. SHAW in R. Wallace *Country Schoolm.* (1899) 154 Large central buildings of the public works called 'women-houses'. **1969** *Time* 21 Nov. 53 *Women Liberators at Atlantic City. **1632** B. JONSON *Magn. Lady* IV. ii, Keep these *women-matters..in our own verge. **1864** MEREDITH *Emilia* xxxvi, Are there men-women and *women men?..have we changed parts to-night? **1968** *Ramparts* Feb. 28 Her concept of *women power, then, is assimilation to achieve a grey-flannel equality for the purpose of bettering women's estate in society by having them beat the hell out of..the men at the Establishment game. **1978** *Daily Tel.* 3 May 17/2 Consultants to advise businesses on..how to improve their use of manpower (or womenpower for that matter). **1630** ? DEKKER *London looke back* (1925) 190 When the Bell hath ceast tolling for thee, and thy *Women-sleepers leaue gaping for thy Linnen. **1665** NEEDHAM *Med. Medicinæ* 73 [Zacutus] hardly grants any possibility of *Women-strikers escaping [pox]. **1867** *Times* 4 Mar. 6/4 Mr. Mill upon *Women Suffrage. **1930** *Women-wise [see *man-wise* s.v. MAN *sb.* 20 a]. **1977** *Lancet* 29 Oct. 922/1 The latest report is based on 206 689 *women-years of observation.

10. Comb. with *women's*: **women's-boat**, a boat to be used by women only = UMIAK; **women's college**, a university college that admits only women as students; **women's courses**, **† evil** = CATAMENIA; **women's group**, a group formed for the discussion or futherance of the interests of women; **Women's Institute**, an organization of women in rural areas who meet regularly and engage in various social and cultural activities; **† women's-kins**, of the female sex; **women's liberation**, the liberation of women from subservient social status and all forms of sexism; also (usu. with cap. initial) a militant movement with these aims; also abbrev. as **women's lib** (cf. LIB); hence **women's libber** [LIBBER], **liberationist**; **women's magazine** = *woman's magazine*, sense 8 above; similarly ***women's mag***; **women's men**, pl. of *woman's man* (see 8); **women's movement**, (*a*) = *woman-movement* s.v. WOMAN *sb.* 7; (*b*) the women's liberation movement (see above); **women's page** = *woman's page*, sense 8 above; **women's room** *U.S.* = *ladies* s.v. LADY *sb.* 4 f; **Women's Rural Institute**: see RURAL *a.* 6; **women's studies** orig. *U.S.*, academic studies concerning women, their role in society, etc.; **women's suffrage** = *woman-suffrage* (see 7); **women's wear**, clothing for women; **women's work** = *woman's work*, sense 8 above.

1823 SCORESBY *Jrnl.* p. xxx, They had made a three years excursion along the eastern coast in a *women's-boat. **1867** GEO. ELIOT *Let.* 22 Nov. (1956) IV. 401 There is a scheme on foot for a *women's college, or rather university..to be in connection with the Cambridge university. **1920** A. N. WHITEHEAD *Concept Nature* i. 7 Suppose that the expositor is in London, say in Regent's Park and in Bedford College, the great women's college which is situated in that park. **1948** M. LASKI *Tory Heaven* vii. 92 The women's colleges at Oxford..became reserved for B's. **1984** 'A. CROSS' *Sweet Death* xi. 129 Can you offer me one reason for women's colleges these days? **1615** CROOKE *Body of Man* 62 Where wee apply cupping glasses to bring down *womens courses. **1379** *MS. Glouc. Cathedr.* 19, I. iv. 2 b, Menstrua. In Englyssh *wymmens yvell. **1968** *Ramparts* May 8 Your attitude was condescending throughout, and your analysis of radical *women's groups..amounted to a movement fashion report. **1977** *Evening Post* (Nottingham) 27 Jan. 4/4 He is a solicitor..and while in Paris he was invited to talk to an American women's group. **1906** *Rep. Women's Institutes Province of Ontario* 69 After placing before them the aims and objects of the *Women's Institute..the warden kindly assured us that he was..in sympathy with our work. **1909** *Jrnl. Home Econ.* I. 161 The usual practice has been to hold the Women's Institute on the same day..as the institute for men. **1912** *Rep. Farm & Agricultural Schools & Colleges in France, Germany, & Belgium* (Board of Educ.) 20 The success which has followed the formation of Women's Institutes in Poland, the United States, and Canada incited some social and agricultural reformers in Belgium to organise similar means of education. *Ibid.* 20 The Women's Institute is an association of farmers' wives, daughters, and sisters who meet periodically..to hear lectures, read papers, and study books on professional subjects. **1921** *Daily Colonist* (Victoria, B.C.) 20 Mar. 32/2 The first general meeting of the Victoria Women's Institute..was held Friday afternoon. **1924** [see SCOUT *sb.*[4] 2 c (*a*)]. **1935** *N. & Q.* 2 Feb. 87/2 The Women's Institute of the old village of Cambo. **1982** *Daily Tel.* 25 Nov. 14/6 With reference to the letter from a Women's Institute member in Yorkshire regarding the splitting up of the Yorkshire federation [etc.]. **1534** *Will of Sir W. Butler* (Somerset Ho.), Euerye of my seruauntes as well menskynes as *womenskynnes. **1969** *Time* 21 Nov. 15 'My twelve-year-old son has been hearing a lot about *Women's Lib lately,' says Ruth. **1971** *Times* 17 July 5/8 Ecology..one Texas paper said recently, has replaced women's lib as the people's favourite cause. **1976** P. & W. PROCTOR *Women in Pulpit* i. 10 The earring criticism soon subsided as they got used to her and saw that she wasn't interested in staging women's lib demonstrations. **1971** *Women's libber [see LIBBER]. **1973** *Lancet* 24 Feb. 419/1 We have heard a lot lately from unhappy ones of one kind and another—the women's libbers, the occasional bleat from the male side, [etc.]. **1978** J. GALWAY *Autobiogr.* ii. 16 It sounds now like a good case for the women's libbers but my mother was essentially a happy woman. **1985** *Observer* (Colour Suppl.) 14 Apr. 23/2 What the women's libbers don't realise is that what they denigrate as domestic drudgery is exactly the right sort of thing to be doing when you are mucking around with the under-twos. **1966** *New Left Rev.* Nov./Dec. 12 Fourier was the most ardent and voluminous advocate of *women's liberation and of sexual freedom among the early socialists. **1967** *New Left Notes* 10 July 4/1 The SDS National Convention adopts the following statement and program as written by the Women's Liberation Workshop. **1974** L. DEIGHTON *Spy Story* v. 55 Women's Liberation..planned to march to Westminster. **1978** S. SHELDON *Bloodline* iv. 64 There were rumors that Hélène Roffe was an advocate of the women's liberation movement. **1969** *Leviathan* (Berkeley,

Calif.) June 43/1 The radical *women's liberationists believe that the true extent of women's oppression can be revealed and fought only if the women's liberation movement is dominated by working class women. **1979** R. RENDELL *Means of Evil* 147 Sheila singing lustily, Sylvia, the Women's Liberationist, with less assurance as if she doubted the ethics of lending her support to so..sexist a ceremony. **1959** *Observer* 18 Jan. 19/2 The daydream world of *women's mags. **1942** D. POWELL *Time to be Born* ii. 42 All Vicky could do was to read the *women's magazines and discover how other heroines had solved this problem. **1960** K. AMIS *New Maps of Hell* iii. 81 Art is mentioned..with a frequency not even paralleled in women's-magazine stories. **1981** J. B. HILTON *Playground of Death* vi. 72 There were shopping notes, memos..a pile of women's magazines. **1712** ADDISON *Spect.* No. 536 ¶2 That part of Mankind who are known by the Name of the *Womens-Men or Beaus. **1781** R. KING *Mod. Lond. Spy* 59 We now drank our tea, which, to what are called women's men, is at that time of the evening generally very agreeable. **1902** H. BLACKBURN *Women's Suffrage* vi. 107 The Married Women's Property Bill occupied the main attention of those engaged in the *women's movement. **1944** G. MYRDAL *American Dilemma* App. 5 The women's movement got much of its public support by reason of its affiliation with the Abolitionist movement. **1968** *Ramparts* Feb. 31 The most active of the new radical women's movements is in Berkeley—which should surprise no one. **1985** *Observer* (Colour Suppl.) 14 Apr. 18/3 She champions women who simply want to stay at home with their babies without a lot of pressure from the women's movement. **1929** E. LINKLATER *Poet's Pub* xiii. 154 She had had two or three articles accepted for the *women's page of the *Daily Day*. **1980** M. BABSON *Dangerous to Know* i. 8 There weren't all that many openings for Women's Page Editors around the Street these days. **1961** WEBSTER, *Women's room. **1977** M. FRENCH (*title*) The women's room. **1981** 'A. CROSS' *Death in Tenured Position* i. 5 The women's room on the ground floor. **1972** *Newsweek* 10 Dec. 124/3 In the classroom, many women think less of competing with men than of learning about themselves. '*Women's studies' was nearly unknown before 1970; now 78 institutions have complete women's studies programs. **1976** *Spare Rib* Nov. 14/2 Last year there was one women's studies course here. This year four are planned. **1868** *Times* 11 May 10/4 A branch of the National Society for *Women's Suffrage. **1919** MENCKEN *Amer. Lang.* iv. 121 *Women's wear, in English shops, is always ladies' wear. **1980** *Times* 22 Jan. 9/6 Austin Reed is planning to open a womenswear area in the Regent Street branch. **1974** R. ADAMS *Shardik* xxv. 209, I can't help wondering why he trims lamps at noon. Or why he trims lamps at all, if it comes to that, seeing it's *women's work and he has that girl to help him. **1977** *Undercurrents* June–July 41/3 Spinning, weaving, knitting, crocheting, sewing are women's work and are called crafts.

woman ('wʊmən), *v.* [f. prec.]

†**1.** Early nonce-uses. **a.** *intr.* To become woman-like; with *it*, to behave as a woman, be womanly. **b.** *trans.* To make like a woman in weakness or subservience. **c.** *pa. pple.* Accompanied by a woman. **d.** To make 'a woman' of, deprive of virginity.

1595 T. EDWARDS *Cephalus* (1878) 55 Her courage was euen then a womanning. **1601** SHAKS. *All's Well* III. ii. 53, I haue felt so many quirkes of ioy and greefe, That the first face of neither on the start Can woman me vntoo't. **1604** —— *Oth.* III. iv. 195, I..thinke it no addition nor my wish To haue him see me woman'd. **1611** HEYWOOD *Golden Age* III. i. G1b, I woman'd first Calisto, and made thee A grandfather. **1613** DANIEL *Hymen's Tri.* III. ii, This day I should Haue seene my daughter Siluia how she would Haue womand it.

2. *trans.* To furnish or provide with women; to equip with a staff of women. (After MAN *v.*)

1706 MRS. CENTLIVRE *Basset-Table* Epil., The Ship's well mann'd, and not ill Woman'd neither. **1830** WHEATON *Jrnl.* 271 The tops of the houses were manned and womaned for many a square. **1865** BURRITT *Walk to Land's End* 108 A sea-boat womanned by a set of Grace Darlings. **1894** *Daily Tel.* 7 Aug. 5/2 Our hospitals,..not manned, but womanned, with intelligent nurses.

3. To address as 'woman': see prec. 1 d.

So *to dear woman*, to address as 'dear woman'.

1740 RICHARDSON *Pamela* II. 269 She call'd her another time Fat-face and woman'd her most violently. **1822** *Blackw. Mag.* XI. 399 Whom call you woman? Dare to woman me! **1883** D. COOK *Paul Foster's Dau.* iii, Don't come dear womaning of me.

'woman-child. *arch.* Pl. **'women-,children.** [WOMAN *sb.* 6 b.] A female child.

1558 T. WATSON 7 *Sacram.* iii. 15 If it be a woman childe, than let the christener say thus, [etc.]. **1560** BECON *New Catech.* VI. Wks. 1564 I. 537 It is expedient, yt..scholes for women children be erected. **1625** K. LONG tr. *Barclay's Argenis* IV. viii. 265 The women, by stealth, put a woman-child into the Princes cradle. **1765** BLACKSTONE *Comm.* I. xvii. 449 The father might..assign a guardian to any woman-child under the age of sixteen. **1825** J. NEAL *Bro. Jonathan* I. 183 Such a temper—in one so young—..a child—a woman-child. **1866** LYTTON *Lost Tales Miletus* 108 An aged king, to whom the fates had spared But one fair woman-child.

womandom ('wʊməndəm). [f. WOMAN *sb.* + -DOM.] The realm of women; womankind.

1838 *New Monthly Mag.* LIII. 452 The whole womandom of the rooms is up in arms. **1891** *Pictorial World* 31 Oct. 19/1, I had a special brief for Fashion in the High Court of Womandom.

womanfully ('wʊmənfʊlɪ), *adv.* [f. WOMAN *sb.* after *manfully*.] With womanly courage or perseverance; like a woman of spirit.

1821 M. EDGEWORTH *Let.* 29 Jan. (1971) 236, I will trample..upon all the prickles of the impossibilities and flatten them womanfully. **1822** *Blackw. Mag.* XII. 660 Do all manfully and womanfully, good ladies and gentlemen, without let or gainsay. **1824** SOUTHEY *Let. to John May* 29 Aug. in *Life* (1849) I. 140 This she resisted most womanfully. **1870** TYNDALL *Imag. Sci.* 25 You will manfully and womanfully prolong your investigations.

'woman-,hater. Also (in pl.) women-. One who hates women; a misogynist.

1607 [FLETCHER] (*title*) The Woman Hater. **1629** MASSINGER *Picture* II. ii, Surely, madam, I am no woman-hater. **1698** COLLIER *Immor. Stage* iv. 171 This Coarseness [toward women] does not alwaies come from Clowns, and Women-haters. **1728** SWIFT *Jrnl. Mod. Lady* 8 Against the sex to write a satire, And brand me for a woman-hater. **1847** [see *woman-spiter* s.v. WOMAN *sb.* 6 c]. **1877** 'RITA' *Vivienne* I. i, I should scarcely think that the sudden introduction of a young and beautiful woman..into your domestic life was quite welcome to such a woman-hater as yourself. **1951** M. MCLUHAN *Mech. Bride* (1967) 99/1 The glamour business ..is crammed with both women-haters and men-haters of dubious sex polarity. **1982** J. FOX *White Mischief* xxi. 247 Colvile was a great woman hater.

†**'womanhead.** *Obs.* or *rare arch.* Forms and etym.: see WOMAN *sb.* and -HEAD. = next.

c **1374** CHAUCER *Anel. & Arc.* 299 (Fairf. MS.) And shal I prey, and weyve womanhede? *c* **1386** —— *Knt.'s T.* 890 The queene anon for verray wommanhede Gan for to wepe. *c* **1386** —— *Man of Law's T.* 753 Thow glorie of wommanhede, thow faire may. *c* **1448** HOCCLEVE *Min. Poems* (1892) 50 To recommande me..To hir benigne & humble wommanhede. *c* **1470** HENRY *Wallace* v. 691 Fra Inglismen to saiff my womanheid. **1496–7** *Plumpton Corr.* (Camden) 126 She is amyable and good, with great wysdome and womanhead. **1508** DUNBAR *Gold. Targe* 160 Suete Womanhede I saw cum in presence. **1570** DRANT *Serm.* D viij b, The Church of Christ is a woman, and hath womanhead towardes her beloued. **1597** in *J. Melvill's Autob. & Diary* (Wodrow Soc.) 432 Deir damiselles! leave af your dreirie mean, And grow in godlines to womanhead. **1627** DRAYTON *Moon-calf* Agincourt etc. 165 When I sawe her rampant to transcend All womenhead [*sic*]. *a* **1631** DONNE *Relique* 3 Graves have learn'd that woman-head To be to more then one a Bed. **1894** J. DAVIDSON *Ballads & Songs* 3 Now you surely know The wrongs of womanhead At last are fairly dead.

womanhood ('wʊmənhʊd). Forms and etym.: see WOMAN *sb.* and -HOOD.

1. The state or condition of being a woman.

c **1374** CHAUCER *Troylus* I. 283 Alle here lymes so wel answerynge Weren to womanhode. **1568** GRAFTON *Chron.* II. 545 She..,contrarie to Gods lawe, and the honest estate of womanhood, was clothed in mans apparell. **1598** SHAKS. *Merry W.* IV. ii. 220 May we with the warrant of womanhood..pursue him with any further reuenge? **1823** BYRON *Juan* IX. lxxi, Her womanhood In its meridian. **1859** TENNYSON *Marr. Geraint* 176 She..with all grace Of womanhood and queenhood, answer'd him. **1860** HAWTHORNE *Marble Faun* v, Her first conception of the stern Jewess had..been that of perfect womanhood.

b. (*a*) The state of being a grown woman; the period of life succeeding to girlhood.

1608 WILLET *Hexapla Exod.* 470 *Si appareant in ea signa pubertatis*, if the signes of her womanhood appeared. **1712** STEELE *Spect.* No. 534 ¶1 This has been my State, till I came toward Years of Womanhood. **1784** COWPER *Task* IV. 227 Misses..assume the dress Of womanhood. **1848** DICKENS *Dombey* xlvii, The change from childhood to womanhood. **1893** CROCKETT *Stickit Minister* 40 Janet grew to womanhood without a sweetheart.

(*b*) *attrib.* in ***womanhood suffrage***, formerly freq. used (after MANHOOD 7) for *woman-suffrage* (WOMAN *sb.* 7).

1892 *Daily News* 28 Apr. 3/2 A future system of manhood and womanhood suffrage.

2. The disposition, character, or qualities natural to a woman or womankind; womanliness.

c **1385** CHAUCER *L.G.W.* 1041 *Dido*, If that god..Wolde han a loue for beaute & goodnesse And womanhod [*v.r.* womanhede] & trouthe. **1552** HULOET, Womanhode, *muliebritas.* **1590** GREENE *Never too late* I. (1600) E2, Courage is knowne in extremities, womanhood in distresse. **1596** SHAKS. *1 Hen. IV*, III. iii. 125 There's neyther Faith, Truth, nor Woman-hood in me else. **1621** BRATHWAIT *Nat. Embassie* 160 To transgresse the bounds of womanhood. **1755** JOHNSON, *Womanhood, Womanhead*, the character and collective qualities of a woman. Obsolete. **1840** DICKENS *Old Cur. Shop* xxxiii, Miss Brass's maiden modesty and gentle womanhood. **1886** RUSKIN *Præterita* I. viii. 255 My mother..had sympathy with every passion of true womanhood.

3. Women collectively, womankind.

1523 SKELTON *Garl. Laurel* 992 Maydenly demure, Of womanhode the lure. **1718** *Freethinker* No. 39 They contribute to make this kind of Womanhood more universal, than it would otherwise be. **1858** MISS MULOCK *Woman's Th.* 71 The infinite wrongs, errors, and sufferings of this mass of womanhood. **1889** SKRINE *Mem. Thring* 203 Uppingham womanhood must next be taught to cook.

womanish ('wʊmənɪʃ), *a.* [-ISH[1] 2.]

1. Of or belonging to a woman or women; a woman's; used or done by women. Now *rare*.

1390 GOWER *Conf.* I. 58 With so swete a stevene Lik to the melodie of hevene In wommanysshe vois thei singe. **1555** LADY VANE in Foxe *A. & M.* (1563) 1445/1, I..doe prepare ..my womanishe backe to their burthens of reproufe. **1610** A. COOKE *Pope Joan* 100 They might haue pretended that they would not be subiect to a womanish and an whorish gouernment. **1624** HEYWOOD *Gunaik.* III. 130 Spinning, weaving, and the like womanish chares. *a* **1661** HOLYDAY *Juvenal* II. Notes (1673) 25 That this was a Womanish wear may be seen by the same Authors 97. Ep. of his I. L. **1678** CUDWORTH *Intell. Syst.* I. iv. 342 *Peplum* is properly a womanish Pall or Veil. **1896** F. HARRISON in *19th Cent.* Mar. 501 A separate degree-conferring and exclusively womanish university.

2. Characteristic of or proper to a woman or women; womanly, feminine.

c **1374** CHAUCER *Troylus* IV. 694 Tho wordes and þo wommannyssh [*v.r.* womanliche] þynges. **1390** GOWER *Conf.* I. 72 Wherof in wommanysshe drede Sche wok and nyste what to rede. *Ibid.* III. 304 Sche wolde hire goode name kepe For feere of wommanysshe schame. **1513** MORE *Rich. III* Wks. 46/1 The mothers drede and womannishe feare. *a* **1568** ASCHAM *Scholem.* I. (Arb.) 39 A voice, not softe, weake, piping, womannishe, but audible, stronge, and manlike. **1606** G. WOODCOCK *Lives Emperors* in *Hist. Ivstine* Kk4, Her priuat matters she had beene able to gouerne easily by her owne womannish wisedome. **1611** BEAUM. & FL. *Maid's Trag.* I, She has a brother..Like her, a face as womanish as hers. **1706** KENNETT *Hist. Eng.* III. 784 He had a particular Averseness to Dancing, and all Womanish Exercises. **1712** ADDISON *Spect.* No. 363 ¶9 Eve's Complaint..is wonderfully beautiful: The sentiments.. have something in them particularly soft and womanish. **1740** RICHARDSON *Pamela* I. 203 Nothing, said she, but Womanish Curiosity. **1844** KINGLAKE *Eothen* xvii, To love her [*sc.* the camel] for the sake of her gentle and womanish ways. **1866** MRS. H. WOOD *St. Martin's Eve* xix, The pale features, regular to a fault, were of almost womanish beauty.

b. In derogatory use.

1390 GOWER *Conf.* II. 229 As he which hath himself restreigned..Out of the manere of a man, And tok his wommannysshe chiere. **1532** MORE *Confut. Barnes* VIII. Wks. 760/2 Her questions..wer like to be but friuolous & womannish. **1534** —— *Comf. agst. Trib.* II. vi. (1553) Gj, Weping for our sinnes..they reckyn shame almost and womanyshe peuishnes. **1592** A. DAY *Engl. Secretorie* II. (1625) 46 Womanish encountrings, vnseemely lyings and childish threatenings. **1685** DRYDEN *Thren. August.* viii, So weak, so womanish a woe. **1771** GOLDSM. *Hist. Eng.* II. 207 She betrayed neither weakness, nor womanish submission. **1813** E. S. BARRETT *Heroine* x. (1909) 57, I do not like..his pencilled eyebrows and curled locks, they look so womanish. **1889** *Sat. Rev.* 6 Apr. 402/2 He must have been under the influence of fears which it would be an excess of flattery to call womanish.

3. Resembling a woman, womanlike: in later use chiefly derogatory; also of a girl, Like a grown woman in her ways.

1390 GOWER *Conf.* I. 93 He syh wher sat a creature, A lothly wommannysch figure. *c* **1470** HARDING *Chron.* LX. ii, Elyne..was..More Angelyke then womannyshe of hewe. **1604** T. WRIGHT *Passions* v. §2. 167 If musicke can make warriers womanish. **1788** WESLEY *Jrnl.* 10 June, This girl.. being then between fourteen and fifteen years old. But she was then quite a womanish girl. **1891** FARRAR *Darkn. & Dawn* lxv, Lascivious Otho, gluttonous Vitellius, savage Domitian, womanish Elagabalus.

†**4.** Having a great inclination or liking for women. *Obs. rare.*

1529 MORE *Dyaloge* I. xii. 18/1 A freer wylbe womanysh loke the holy horeson neuer so sayntly. **1579–80** [implied in WOMANISHNESS].

5. *Comb.*

1382 WYCLIF *1 Kings* XV. 12 He took awey the wommannysh maad men [*effeminatos*] of the loond. *a* **1623** FLETCHER *Love's Cure* III. ii, One so full of childish fear, And womanish-hearted.

Hence †**'womanish** *v. trans.*, to render womanish, to womanize.

1561 T. HOBY tr. *Castiglione's Courtyer* I. Iij, Men..who ought not with suche delicacies [as music] to womannishe their mindes. *a* **1586** SIDNEY *Arcadia* I. xii. §5 This effeminate love of a woman, doth so womanish [*so ed.* **1590**; *edd.* 1593–1674 womanize] a man, that (if he yeeld to it) it will..make him..a launder, a distaff-spinner.

womanishly ('wʊmənɪʃlɪ), *adv.* [f. WOMANISH *a.* + -LY[2].] In a womanish manner or style.

1573 BARET *Alv.* W 319 Womannishly, faintly, fearfully, *muliebriter.* **1579** TWYNE *Phis. agst. Fortune* II. lxvi. 242 When as she womanishly lamented that he should die an innocent. **1665** BRATHWAIT *Comm. Two Tales* (1901) 13 To have his hair curled, and so womanishly disheveled. **1731** G. JEFFREYS *Merope* I. i. 2 Are we sunk so womanishly low, That we can only mourn, and rail, and pray? *a* **1845** T. O. DAVIS *Life Curran* (1846) 69 They had..the same impassionate, womanishly sensitive hearts. **1860** SIR T. MARTIN *Horace* I. xxxvii. 65 A woman, yet not womanishly weak.

So **womanishness** ('wʊmənɪʃnɪs), the quality or state of being womanish.

1545 ASCHAM *Toxoph.* I. (Arb.) 41 The minstrelsie of lutes ..is farre more fitte for the womannishnesse of it to dwell in the courte among ladies. **1579–80** NORTH *Plutarch, Theseus & Romulus* (1595) 43 That his womanishenes was rather to satisfie lust, then of any great loue. **1607** MARKHAM *Cavel.* I. 25 Such as out of their flemye womanishnesse seeke for such secrets. **1664** H. MORE *Exp. 7 Epist.* Pref. cvj b, The more-then-ordinary Womanishness of the Church of Rome in that Intervall. **1858** *Househ. Words* XVIII. 414/1 There was no nonsense about Katie; no silly affectation of boyishness, no still sillier affectation of premature womanishness. **1860** *Sat. Rev.* 7 Jan. 12/2 The clergyman's acquired womanishness. **1883** J. HAWTHORNE *Dust* I. 207 A certain softness or womanishness in his nature, which his masculine taste condemned.

womanism ('wʊmənɪz(ə)m). [f. WOMAN *sb.* + -ISM.] Advocacy of or enthusiasm for the rights, achievements, etc. of women.

1863 LD. W. P. LENNOX *Biogr. Remin.* I. 286 It became quite the rage to quote the ambiguous passages of her worst productions..as reflecting the strong-minded womanism of the nineteenth century. **1880** BLACKMORE *Mary Anerley* xxvii. II. 165 That the mother of his daughter..should now turn round and take her part, from downright womanism, in the teeth of all reason.

†**'womanist.** *Obs. rare.* [f. WOMAN *sb.*: see -IST.] A womanizer.

1608 DAY *Law-Tricks* v. I2b, Hee's a sweet womanist.

womanity (wʊ'mænɪtɪ). *humorous.* [f. WOMAN *sb.* + -ITY, after *humanity.*] The normal disposition or character of womankind.

1843 MRS. BROWNING *Lett. R. H. Horne* (1877) I. xviii. 81, I will be secret beyond womanity, if you are frank beyond discretion. **1868** HELPS *Realmah* I. vi. 115 Mrs. Milverton and Lady Ellesmere are very like ordinary women. Womanity is strong in them. **1892** M. C. SALAMAN *Woman* 6 Each fresh experience of love..increases one's knowledge of 'Womanity'—if I may be allowed the term. **1896** *Daily Tel.* 4 Mar. 7/3 What will it profit a woman to gain an Oxford degree and lose her womanity?

womanize ('wʊmənaɪz), *v.* [f. WOMAN *sb.* + -IZE.]

1. *trans.* To make a woman of (a man); *gen.* to render effeminate, to emasculate.

1593 [see WOMANISH *v.*, quot. *a* 1586]. **1643** TORSHELL *Case Consc.* 9 Wee may not now suffer the thoughts of safety elsewhere to womanize our spirits. **1647** STAPYLTON *Juvenal* 19 *margin*, The Roman Sardinapali, men womanized. **1755** JOHNSON, *Womanise*, to emasculate; to effeminate; to soften. Proper, but not used. **1782** V. KNOX *Ess.* No. 156 ¶5 To vitiate their morals, to womanize their spirits. **1853** LYTTON in *Lett. Robt. 1st Earl Lytton* (1906) I. 40 Don't let Italy womanise you. **1881** MEREDITH *Tragic Com.* I. vii. 146 Men who have the woman in them without being womanized.

†**2.** *intr.* To become womanlike; to behave like a woman. *Obs.*

1604 EARL STIRLING *Crœsus* III. ii. F 3, From the height of Honour to digresse, To womanize with courtly vaine delights. **1613** WITHER *Abuses* II. Juvenilia (1633) 232 Such as can So much degenerate themselves from Man, In tyre and gesture both to womanize. **1736** BAILEY (fol.).

3. To consort illicitly with women. *colloq.*

1893 FARMER & HENLEY *Slang, Goose*..to go wenching: to womanize. **1914** C. MACKENZIE *Sinister St.* III. xii, The Bad Men went up to London and womanized.

Hence '**womanized** *ppl. a.*, in senses of the verb; also, rendered womanly; '**womanizing** *vbl. sb.* and *ppl. a.*; **womani'zation**; '**womanizer**, one who goes after or consorts illicitly with women.

1624 GEE *Foot out of Snare* 62 Fit..to act a womanized Chaerea in Terence his Eunuchus. **1633** DRUMM. OF HAWTH. *Entert. K. Chas.* iv. 31 Gorgeous rayments, womanising toyes. **1634** T. JOHNSON *Parey's Chirurg.* I. xi. (1678) 17 These are some womanizing or womanish men. **1775** ASH, *Womanizing*, the act of softening down to the qualities of a woman. **1839** MRS. KIRKLAND *New Home* xviii. 121 The womanized tone of the proud and happy mother. **1878** M. C. JACKSON *Chaperon's Cares* iii, She is a womanized likeness of poor Edward. **1914** A. HARRISON *Kaiser's War* v. 141 The growing softness of life beyond the Fatherland—the world's general womanization, as they [*sc.* Germans] called it. **1924** GALSWORTHY *White Monkey* II. ix, Somehow..I feel he's a womaniser.

† '**womankin.** *Obs.* In 3 (*Orm.*) wifmann-, wimmannkinn. [f. WOMAN *sb.* + KIN *sb.*[1]: cf. MANKIN[1].] = next, 1.

c **1200** ORMIN 2334 Wel ȝho sahh..þatt ȝho wass æðiȝ wimmann an all wimmannkinn bitwenenn. *Ibid.* 3058 Till weppmann & till wifmannkinn.

womankind ('wʊmənkaɪnd). [f. WOMAN *sb.* + KIND *sb.* Cf. WOMENKIND.]

1. The female part of the human race; the female sex; women in general.

c **1375** *Cursor M.* 9024 (Fairf.) For alle we come of womman kinde. **1387** TREVISA *Higden* (Rolls) II. 317 Pharao ..heelde womman kynde ful feble to be rebel. *a* **1400** *Prymer* (1891) 21 Byseche for the deuowte wommankynde [*Prymer* (1895) 6 wommans kyndel]. *c* **1450** *Bk. Curtasye* 259 in *Babees Bk.*, Speke neuer vnhonestly of woman kynde. **1500–20** DUNBAR *Poems* lxxxiv. 4 The foul delyte Off woman-kynd that dreidis for na schame. **1535** COVERDALE *Lev.* xviii. 22 Thou shalt not lye with mankynde as with womankynde. **1590** SPENSER *F.Q.* III. v. 52 In gentle Ladies brest, and bounteous race Of woman kind. *a* **1670** HACKET *Abp. Williams* II. (1692) 35 This man would suffer no woman-kind to do any service within his gates. **1760–72** H. BROOKE *Fool of Qual.* (1809) III. 9 In womankind, I can love nothing but you. **1782** COWPER *Gilpin* v, I do admire Of womankind but one. **1822** BYRON *Juan* VI. xxvii, My wish is ..That womankind had but one rosy mouth, To kiss them all at once from North to South. **1847** TENNYSON *Princess* VI. 290 The soft and milky rabble of womankind.

†**b.** appositively or predicatively: Female. *Obs.*

c **1570** R. COXE *Injunctions*, Their chyldren and seruauntes both mankinde and womankinde. **1577** BP. AYLMER *Articles to be enquired of* A 4 b, Any of his parish..either mankind or womankinde. **1614** R. TAILOR *Hog hath lost Pearl* II. D 2 b, Did I but only know her to be woman kind, I think it were sufficient.

2. The women of a family, household, company, country, etc.; female relatives and friends (sometimes also servants); (one's) women-folk.

1573 L. LLOYD *Pilgr. Princes* (1586) 8 Agreeing that the womankinde should passe away that night. **1825** SOUTHEY *Lett.* (1856) III. 518 My womankind join in kind regards. **1850** THACKERAY *Pendennis* lvi, Pen, chafing under the persecution which his womankind had inflicted upon him. **1862** KINGSTON *Three Midshipmen* viii, All the womankind in and out of the house, for a long way round.

†**3.** A female human being; a woman. *Obs.*

a **1685** *Warn. Married Women* xxviii. in Child *Ballads* (1892) IV. 363/2 Since that time the woman-kind Was never seen no more. **1711** *Acts & Laws Massachusetts* (1724) 270 Whosoever shall be convicted of Assaulting..any Woman or Woman-kind. **1816** SCOTT *Antiq.* ix, 'Where's the younger womankind?'.. 'Indeed, brother,.. Maria..set away to the Halket Craig-head—I wonder ye didna see her.' **1823** BYRON in Trelawny *Shelley* (1887) 213 If we had a womankind on board, she would set us all at loggerheads.

†**4.** Womanhood. (Cf. MANKIND A. 2.) *Obs. rare.*

1549 COVERDALE, etc. *Erasm. Par. 1 Peter* iii. 7 Let your wisdome succour the frailtie of their womankynde.

womanless ('wʊmənlɪs), *a.* [f. WOMAN *sb.* + -LESS.] Without a woman or women; having or containing no women.

1846 in WORCESTER. **1859** *Athenæum* 10 Dec. 771/2 It is a strange arena, the womanless world of cassocks. **1872** M. COLLINS *P'cess Clarice* I. xvi. 254 Arthur Swingate found himself womanless. **1912** *Engl. Rev.* June 494 A womanless play called *The New Sin.*

womanlike ('wʊmənlaɪk), *a.* and *adv.* [f. WOMAN *sb.* + -LIKE.] **A.** *adj.* Like, resembling, or characteristic of a woman or women; in derogatory use, womanish, effeminate.

c **1440** *Promp. Parv.* 154/2 Femynyne, or woman lyke, *muliebris.* **1550** CROWLEY *Way to Wealth* 315 Fingered ladies, whose womanlike behauiour..ought to be a lighte to al women. **1561** T. NORTON tr. *Calvin's Inst.* IV. xix. 156 b, Clerkes were commaunded..to sheare their head..that they should not beare any shewe of womanlyke trimming. **1597** DRAYTON *Heroical Ep., Isab. to Mortimer* Notes 20 b, His behauiour and attire euer so womanlike, to please the eye of his lasciuious Prince. **1624** CAPT. J. SMITH *Virginia* 31 Scorning to be seene in any woman-like exercise. **1647** HEXHAM I, Womanlike, delicate and tender. **1825** SCOTT *Talism.* xiv, Ashamed at being surprised in a womanlike expression of sorrow, Sir Kenneth dashed his tears indignantly aside. **1878** *Contemp. Rev.* Feb. 521 Trees were credited with woman-like inhabitants capable of doing good and ill. **1880** L. WALLACE *Ben-Hur* 516 The tearful woman-like face of the Christ.

B. *adv.* In a manner characteristic of women; after the fashion of women; like a woman.

c **1440** *Alphabet of Tales* 365 Sho was not ferd for swerd nor wownd, nor wepid wommanlyke. **1556** PHAER *Æneid.* IV. (1558) I iv b, This pranking Paris fyne..With grekishe wymple pynkyd, womanlyke. **1635** *Life Long Meg of Westm.* (1872) 43 She..dressed him full womanlike. **1743** FRANCIS tr. *Hor., Odes* I. xxxvii. 28 But she a nobler fate explored, Nor woman-like beheld the deathful sword. **1857** W. COLLINS *Dead Secret* v. iv. (1861) 221 'Of course', cried Rosamond, looking, womanlike, straight on to the purpose she had in view. **1898** 'H. S. MERRIMAN' *Roden's Corner* xxix. 303 He would not, it appeared, sit down without her permission. And, womanlike, she gave it.

womanliness ('wʊmənlɪnɪs). [f. WOMANLY *a.* + -NESS.] The quality of being womanly; womanly character; †effeminateness.

1538 ELYOT *Dict., Mollicies, et mollicia*,..womanlynesse. **1549** COVERDALE, etc. *Erasm. Par. 1 Pet.* iii. 1–6 The entier vpryghtnes, godlynes, womanlynes,.. and sufferaunce of the wyfe. **1596** DALRYMPLE tr. *Leslie's Hist. Scot.* IV. (S.T.S.) I. 214 Throuch the negligence of King Constantine, and his womanlines. **1647** HEXHAM I, Womanlienesse, *vrouwachtigheydt.* **1864** *Reader* 30 Apr. 564/2 The *Portia* of Mrs. Vezin is endued with the grace and womanliness that characterize all her performances. **1876** J. PARKER *Paracl.* I. xvi. 259 The womanliness of the Divine nature, its infinite grace and pathos. **1881** G. MEREDITH *Trag. Com.* I. vii. 146 The choicest women are those who yield not a feather of their womanliness for some amount of manlike strength.

† '**womanlish,** *a. Obs. rare.* [Blending of WOMANISH and WOMANLY *a.*] Womanlike, effeminate. '**womanlishly** *adv.*, '**womanlishness.**

1579 TWYNE *Phis. agst. Fortune* II. xii. 181 Womanlyshly glorying [she] shewed her her most precious and fayre Iewelles. **1647** HEXHAM I, Womanlish or effeminate, *vrouwachtigh.* Womanlishly, *vrouwachtighlick.* **1648** *Ibid.* II, *Wijflickheydt*, Womanlishnesse, or Effeminatenesse.

womanly ('wʊmənlɪ), *a.* [f. WOMAN *sb.* + -LY[1].]

1. a. Possessing the attributes proper to a woman; having the qualities (as of gentleness, devotion, fearfulness, etc.) held to be characteristic of women; also said of these qualities or of actions which exhibit them. Freq. in phr. ***womanly woman.***

c **1374** CHAUCER *Troylus* III. 106 .O. wommanlyche wyf. *Ibid.* IV. 694 (Camb. MS.) Þo wordis & þo wommanliche þyngis Sche herde riȝt nouȝt þow sche þere were. *c* **1385** —— *L.G.W.* 175 So wommanly so benygne & so meke. *c* **1386** —— *Knt.'s T.* 2225 Youre wommanly pitee. **1387–8** T. USK *Test. Love* II. xii. (Skeat) l. 114 So precious perle, as a womanly woman in her kynde. **1421** HOCCLEVE *Jereslaus's Wife* 466 A lady the womanlyeste Of cheere. *c* **1485** *Digby Myst.* III. 525 Your person, ittis so womanly. *a* **1548** HALL *Chron., Hen. VI* 115 b, Where was her womanly pitie? **1579** LYLY *Euphues* (Arb.) 69 She coulde scarcely conteine hir selfe from embracing him, had not womanly shamefastnes..stayed hir wisedome. **1614** B. JONSON *Barth. Fair* I. iii, Be womanly, Win; make an outcry to your mother, Win! **1676** DRYDEN *Aurengz.* IV. 54 Rage choaks my words: 'tis Womanly to weep. **1712** STEELE *Spect.* No. 272 ¶1 One who was growing up to the same womanly Virtues which shine to Perfection in her. **1805** SOUTHEY *Madoc* I. xvii. 132 Womanly sobs were heard, and manly cheeks Were wet with silent tears. **1852** MISS MITFORD in L'Estrange *Life* (1870) III. 235 Lady Goldsmid (that impersonation of all that is womanly and motherly). **1872** (*title*) Woman's rights and the wife at home. By a womanly woman. **1874** GREEN *Short Hist.* vii. §3. 368 Whatever womanly tenderness she [*sc.* Elizabeth] had, wrapt itself around Leicester. **1891** G. B. SHAW *Quintessence of Ibsenism* iii. 34 In real life a self-sacrificing woman, or, as Mr. Stead would put it, a womanly woman, is not only taken advantage of, but disliked as well for her pains. **1926** WODEHOUSE *Heart of Goof* iii. 96 The least you can do, as a good womanly woman, is to have a capable lawyer watching your interests. **1958** M. KENNEDY *Outlaws on Parnassus* xii. 196 Telemachus..upbraids his mother for not behaving like a womanly woman. **1978** J. PORTER *Dead Easy for Dover* vii. 78 The Brigadier..only exists to make Madame more credible as a womanly woman.

b. In derogatory use, with reference to the bad qualities attributed to women; †(of men) effeminate, womanish.

a **1225** *Ancr. R.* 274 Þet nis nout iwar ne waker ne nis nout monlich, auh is wummonlich. **1382** WYCLIF *1 Kings* xiv. 24 Men maad wommanlich weren in the loond. *a* **1400** *New Test.* (Paues) 1 Pet. iii. 7 Departynge to hem worschupe, as to a wommanlyche vessel þat is more febel þan ȝe beþ. **1519** HORMAN *Vulg.* 228 b, Nyce aray, and new fangled garmentis, welthy fare and ydelnes: make men to be womanly. **1538** ELYOT *Dict.* s.v. *Mollis, Mollis homo*, a man efffemynate, or womanlye. *a* **1548** HALL *Chron., Hen. V* 57 b, For very womanly malice, she set in the highest authoritie aboute the kyng her husband. **1558** KNOX *First Blast* (Arb.) 21 Lest that again she slide and fall by womanlie facilitie. **1615** G. SANDYS *Trav.* 23 Burning with a womanly spleen. **1716** LADY M. W. MONTAGU *Lett., to Lady X——* 1 Oct. (1887) I. 128 The womanly spirit of contradiction. **1830** JAMES *De L'Orme* xvii, Senor, are you a man? I would not, for very shame, have any one see you look so womanly. **1862** MISS BRADDON *Lady Audley* xix, Has she baffled me by some piece of womanly jugglery?

2. Having the character of, befitting or characteristic of, a woman as contrasted with a girl.

1709 STEELE *Tatler* No. 15 ¶2 The Girl was very proud of the Womanly Employment of a Nurse. **1732** ARBUTHNOT *Aliments, Rules of Diet* (1736) 408 Young Persons under a womanly Age. **1753–4** RICHARDSON *Grandison* II. xxxvi. 279 The girl begins to be womanly. **1848** DICKENS *Dombey* iii, A short, brown, womanly girl of fourteen. **1853** —— *Bleak Ho.* xv, A very little girl..wearing a womanly sort of bonnet much too large for her.

3. Belonging or proper to the female sex.

1863 GEO. ELIOT *Romola* xliv, Her early training had kept her aloof from such womanly labours. *a* **1873** LYTTON *Pausanias* (1876) 90 Cleonice..had enjoyed those advantages of womanly education wholly unknown at that time to the freeborn ladies of Greece. **1875** JOWETT *Plato* (ed. 2) III. 146 Many types of manly and womanly beauty.

'**womanly,** *adv. Obs.* or *arch.* [f. as prec.: see -LY[2].] In a womanly manner; like a woman.

1297 R. GLOUC. (Rolls) 9391 Wat he aþ Manliche bigonne, he it aþ bileued Wommanliche, as vor defaute of wit in his heued. *c* **1400** *Destr. Troy* 3994 Cassandra..was a Clene Maydon,..Womonly wroght. **1476** *Stonor Papers* (Camden) II. 7 Where as ye, ffull womanly and lyke a loffer, remembre me with manyffolde recommendacion in dyuersse maners. **1508** DUNBAR *Tua Mariit Wemen* 496 To euery man in speciall speke I sum wordis, So wisly, and so womanly, quhill warmys ther hertis. **1575** GASCOIGNE *Flowers, Lullabie of Lover* 4 And lullaby can I sing to, As womanly as can the best. **1612** T. TAYLOR *Comm. Titus* iii. 2 (1619) 578 For how womanly haue many behaued themselues. **1723** *Briton* No. 7 (1724) 28 You..then very Womanly expect a Consideration, for the Trouble we put you to in Swearing. **1844** MRS. BROWNING *Rom. Page* xxvii, Oh, womanly, she prayed in tent, When none beside did wake!

womanness ('wʊmənnɪs). *rare.* [f. WOMAN *sb.* + -NESS.] Womanliness; the quality of being a woman.

1845 MRS. CARLYLE in *Jane Welsh Carlyle* (1924) 230 The only chance of my getting any right good of him was to make him forget my womanness. **1881** *Blackw. Mag.* Oct. 433 Above..all stood her feminineness, her thorough womanness. **1926** D. H. LAWRENCE *Plumed Serpent* ii. 29 They hated her mechanically for the very fact that she was a woman. They hated her womanness. **1971** *Guardian* 2 Dec. 11/4 There may be something about 'woman-ness' which has to be defined in its own terms, not by reference to maleness.

'**woman-,servant.** Pl. women-servants. A female servant.

1529 *Sel. Cases Star Chamber* (Selden Soc.) II. 43 Other wymen and wymen seruands. **1539** *Bible* (Great) Gen. xx. 14 Men seruauntes & wemenseruauntes [**1560** *Geneva* women seruantes]. **1589** RIDER *Bibl. Schol.* 1670 A woman seruant. **1779–81** JOHNSON *L.P., Pope* Wks. 1787 IV. 15 She bribed a woman-servant to procure her a sword. **1838** DICKENS *O. Twist* xxxiv, At this, the two women-servants lifted up their hands and eyes. **1855** MRS. CARLYLE *Lett.* II. 263 A dirty woman-servant opened the door.

'**womanship.** *nonce-wd.* [f. WOMAN *sb.* + -SHIP.] ***her womanship***: jocular title for a woman.

1609 HEALEY *Discov. New World* II. ii. 99, I..told her Womanship that for my part I had [etc.].

'**womanshire.** *nonce-wd.* [f. WOMAN *sb.* + SHIRE *sb.*] The domain or sphere of women.

1606 *Wily Beguiled* 73 Thou hast got the merriest woer in all Womanshire.

woman's rights, women's rights. The rights claimed for women of equal privileges and opportunities with men. Also *attrib.*

1632 (*title*) The lawes resolutions of womens rights, or the lawes provision for woemen. [**1799** the rights of woman: see RIGHT *sb.* 10.] **1840** THACKERAY *Shabby-genteel Story* iv, One may sympathise with the advocates of woman's rights who point out this monstrous wrong. **1842** E. PEASE *Let.* 29 Mar. [MS. in Library of Society of Friends, London], I believe that the Chartists generally hold the doctrine of the equality of woman's rights. **1850** (*title*) Women's Rights Convention. **1859** A. J. MUNBY *Diary* 28 Jan. (1972) 18 Those who prate of women's rights, if they knew their own meaning, would honour such mighty daughters of the plough. **1864** 'ANNIE THOMAS' *D. Donne* III. 33 Even though Stephanie Fordyce was no woman's rights girl. 1876 H. JAMES *Roderick Hudson* xi. 378 Five unmarried sisters, one of whom gave lyceum-lectures on woman's rights. 1883 F. M. CRAWFORD *Dr. Claudius* v, We have seen something of the 'woman's rights' question in America. 1897 E. BELLAMY *Equality* xx. 119 There was a great stir about women's rights, but the programme then announced was by no means revolutionary. 1902 G. B. SHAW *Let.* 20 June (1972) II. 276 The Woman's Rights young lady. 1963 B. FRIEDAN *Feminine Mystique* i. 28 The fact is that no one today is muttering angrily about 'women's rights', even though more and more women have gone to college. 1977 *Socialist Press* 2 Mar. 4/1 The latest in a series of non-political jamborees organised around the question of women's rights took place at Alexandra Palace last Saturday. 1982 *N.Y. Times Mag.* 1 Aug. 6 Campaigning by the women's-rights movement to purge the English language of sexism.

Hence **woman's (women's) righter**, a believer in or supporter of woman's rights.

1858 J. J. BOYER *Let.* 9 July in *Lawrence* (Kansas) *Republican* 15 July 1/4 Capt. Holmes and lady joined us. She is a regular woman's righter, wears the Bloomer, and was quite indignant when informed that she was not allowed to stand on guard. 1885 *Pall Mall Gaz.* 23 Feb. 3/2 Women's righters in Germany. 1894 LE GALLIENNE *Retrosp. Rev.* (1896) II. 179 May she be saved from being a.. woman's-righter!

womanthrope ('wʊmənθrəʊp). [Joc. formation f. WOMAN *sb.* + *-thrope* as in MISANTHROPE.] A hater of women.

1891 O. WILDE *Intentions* 126 They would become confirmed misanthropes, or if I may borrow a phrase from one of the pretty Newnham graduates, confirmed womanthropes for the rest of their lives. 1902 'COLDSTREAMER' *Ballads of Boer War* iv. 35 I'm quite willing for to be Wot scholars calls a 'womanthrope'.

womar, var. WOOMERA.

womb (wu:m), *sb.* Forms: α. 1–2, 4 **wamb**, 4–5 **wambe**; see also WAME. β. 1– **womb**; 1 **uommb**, 3–7 **wombe**, 5 *north.* **vombe**, 6 *Sc.* **voyme**, **voymbe**. [Com. Teut.: OE. *wamb*, *womb* str. fem. = (M)LG., MDu. *wamme* (Du. *wam*), OHG. *wamba*, *wampa* (MHG. *wamme*, *wampe*, G. *wamme*, dial. *wampe*), ON. *vǫmb* (MSw. *vamb*), Goth. *wamba* κοιλία, γαστήρ: ulterior relations obscure.

For a Romance deriv. of the Teut. word see GAMBESON.]

†**1.** = BELLY. **a.** The abdomen. *Obs.*

c825 *Vesp. Ps.* xliii[i]. 25 *Adhesit in terra venter noster*, ætfalh in eorðan womb ur. a1000 *Riddles* xxxvii. 3 Ic wiht ȝeseah on weȝe feran, seo.. hæfde feowere fet under wombe. c1205 LAY. 19800 His neb bigon to blakien, his wombe gon to swellen. 1297 R. GLOUC. (Rolls) 10794 Wan richard þe marschal.. toward is fon in þe feld haþ is wombe iwent, Ssold he turne hom is rugh? c1305 *Judas Isc.* 141 in *E.E.P.* (1862) 111 His wombe to-berste amidde atuo. c1340 *Nominale* (Skeat) 66 Inwyth the wombe of man.. Is herte lyuer and longes. 13.. *Gaw. & Gr. Knt.* 144 His wombe & his wast were worthily smale. 1390 GOWER *Conf.* I. 24 Tharmes, The wombe and al doun to the kne, Of bras thei were. *Ibid.* III. 215 What man that.. wery is to swinke, Upon his wombe and lith to drinke, Forsak. a1425 *Voc.* in Wr.-Wülcker 635/33 *Hic uenter*, wambe. c1430 *Two Cookery-bks.* 39 Take þe Wombe of A luce, & seþe here wyl. c1440 *Pallad. on Husb.* I. 53 Her wombis [L. *venter, aut viscera*], sidis, reynys, swelle or ake. 1486 *Bk. St. Albans* e iij b, All thyng with in the wombe saue onli the gall. 1509 BARCLAY *Shyp of Folys* (1874) I. 12 If he haue a great wombe, and his Cofers ful. 1526 R. WHYTFORD *Martiloge* 100 They were racked,.. than were theyr wombes or belyes flayne the skynne of. 1597 SHAKS. *2 Hen. IV*, IV. iii. 25 And I had but a belly of any indifferencie, I were simply the most actiue fellow in Europe: my wombe, my wombe, my wombe vndoes mee. 1632 LITHGOW *Trav.* x. 462 The Tormentor.. drew violently with his hands, making my Wombe support the force of his feete. 1684 J. S. *Profit & Pleas. United* 35 As for your Mare; let her have a compleat Body, Indifferent Long with a large Womb.

†**b.** The stomach (as the receptacle of food).

c950 *Lindisf. Gosp.* Matt. xv. 17 Ne oncnauas ȝie forðon eȝhuelc þæt in muð inngaas in womb gaas? a1100 *Gloss.* in Wr.-Wülcker 159/27 *Aluus*, rif *uel* seo inre wamb. c1160 *Hatton Gosp.* Luke xv. 16 Ða ȝewilnede he his wambe fellen of þam beancoddan þe þa swin æten. a1200 *Moral Ode* 145 in *O.E. Hom.* I. 169 Ful wombe mei lihtliche speken of hunger & of festen. c1200 *Vices & Virtues* 137 Of here wombe hie makieð here godd. c1200 *Trin. Coll. Hom.* 37 Þe fule man þe foleȝeð his wombes wil. 13.. *Cursor M.* 536 (Gött.) Manes wambe all licur drinkis. 1340 *Ayenb.* 53 Þanne ssolle we betuene þe porse and þe wombe of þe glotoune habbe a uayr strif. 1362 LANGL. *P. Pl.* A. VII. 162 Hongur.. wrong him so be þe wombe, þat boþe his eȝen watreden. 13.. *E.E. Allit. P.* B. 462 He.. Fallez on þe foule flesch & fyllez his wombe. c1386 CHAUCER *Monk's T.* 447 Thanne sholde nat hunger in my wombe crepe. c1430 LYDG. *Min. Poems* (Percy Soc.) 170 Withe ful wombe they preche of abstynence. c1430 *Two Cookery-bks.* 39 Do in þe grete wombe of þe Schepe, þat is, the mawe. 1515 BARCLAY *Egloges* iv. (1570) C iij b/2 When ye be mery and stuffed is your wombe.. Then laude ye songes. 1601 HOLLAND *Pliny* XXVI. viii. II. 248 The wombe.. oftentimes in a day calleth unto us for victuals. 1603 J. DAVIES (Heref.) *Microcosmos* Wks. (Grosart) I. 58/2 If nought from without come in the wombe The Body needes must die. 1756 *Poor Robin* June B 1 b, Who makes a swill tub of his womb, Is but a speaking, prattling tomb.

†**c.** The bowels. *Obs.*

c1000 *Sax. Leechd.* II. 186 Se ȝeþiȝeda mete hefeȝaþ þone maȝan & he þone sammeltan þurh ða wambe utsent. c1400 MAUNDEV. (1919) xviii. 101 Men putten it in medicynes.. to make the Wombe lax. c1400 tr. *Secr. Secr., Gov. Lordsh.* 70 A potage nesshe and laxatyue to þe wombe. c1400 *Lanfranc's Cirurg.* 51 If þat he be feble.. voide þe fecis of his wombe bi clisterie. c1430 *Pilgr. Lyf Manhode* II. xxxiv. (1869) 88 Þou berest him to priuee chambres.. to voide his wombe. 1544 PHAER *Regim. Lyfe* (1560) M ij, It is holsome for you, every day once to procure the duety of the wombe.

†**d.** The belly-piece of a hide or skin. *Obs.*

1434 *Will of Ruddok* (Somerset Ho.) Calabir wombis. 1483 in *Antiq. Rep.* (1807) I. 32 A greete bordure and purfile of ermyne wombes. 1531 *Dunmow Churchw. MS.* lf. 11 b, Item, for a payer of wombs tande.., vi *d* ob. 1551–2 *Act 5 & 6 Edw. VI* c. 15 §3 Everie Girdler.. maye.. sell.. Neckes, Wombes and Shreddes of tanned Leather. 1592 GREENE *Upst. Courtier* Wks. (Grosart) XI. 269 Whereas you should only put the backs of skinnes into facing, you taw the wombs. 1612 *Sc. Bk. Rates* in *Halyburton's Ledger* (1867) 305 Beaver bellies or wombes the peice, viii s.

¶ (*a*) In translations of the Vulgate rendering *venter* in the sense of 'heart, soul'.

c825 *Vesp. Hymns* vi. 31 *Expavit venter meus*, forhtade womb min. 1382 WYCLIF *Ecclus.* li. 29 My wombe [*later version* soule] is disturbid in sechyng it.

(*b*) tr. L. *ventriculus* = VENTRICLE 1.

1398 TREVISA *Barth. De P.R.* v. xxxvi. (1495) i vij b/2 The herte hath two holownesses.. And thise two holownesses ben callyd the wombes of the herte [L. *ventriculi cordis*]. *Ibid.* i viij/1 In the wombe of the hert is a pyece shappe as an eere wythout.

2. The uterus.

c825 *Vesp. Ps.* cxxvi[i]. 3 *Fructus ventris*, westem wombe. c950 *Lindisf. Gosp.* Luke xxiii. 29 Eadȝo biðon ða unberendo & ða wombo ðaðe ne acendon. c1200 *Vices & Virtues* 87 Hv mai ðat moder forȝeten ðat child ðe hie bar in hire wombe? c1205 LAY. 199 Heuede Lauine þa quene kine-bearn on wombe. a1300 *Cursor M.* 3460 Childir tuin þat lai þer moder wamb wit-in. c1400 *Beryn* 859 A child gan stere in hir vombe. c1440 *Alphabet of Tales* 63 What wommans wambe myght bere so grete a light? a1548 HALL *Chron., Hen. VI* 134 They were his bretherne of one wombe descended. 1626 BACON *Sylva* §94 Birds, that are shaped without the Females Wombe, haue in the Egge.. Matter of Nourishment. 1718 PRIOR *Solomon* III. 115 Naked from the Womb We yesterday came forth. 1820 SHELLEY *Cloud* 83 Like a child from the womb. 1842 TENNYSON *Day-dream* 28 Like hints and echoes of the world To spirits folded in the womb.

b. Phr. ***womb-to-tomb***, esp. used *attrib.* to denote procedures, etc., which span a lifetime. Cf. *cradle-to-grave* s.v. CRADLE *sb.* 2.

1964 A. WYKES *Gambling* i. 8 During our womb-to-tomb progress we never stop gambling, for we cannot know the outcome of each of the many decisions we have to make every day. 1967 MCLUHAN & FIORE *Medium is Massage* 12 Electrical information devices for universal, tyrannical womb-to-tomb surveillance are causing a very serious dilemma between our claim to privacy and the community's need to know. 1968 G. JACKSON *Let.* 29 June in *Soledad Brother* (1971) 163 From the womb to the tomb this plays in our minds. We are not worth more than the amount of capital we can raise. 1979 *Bookseller* 23 June 2830/3 *Kane and Abel*.. is a womb-to-tomb tale.

3. *transf.* A hollow space or cavity, or something conceived as such (*e.g.* the depth of night); †also, a belly-shaped object or part.

969 in Birch *Cart. Sax.* III. 532 Þæt swa on east crofte þæt swa ondlong þære heȝe ræwe þæt on ondoncilles wombe. a1000 *Riddles* iv. 48 [Clouds] feallan lætað sweart sumsendu seaw of bosme, wætan of wombe. *Ibid.* xxxviii. 1 Ic þa wihte ȝeseah; womb wæs on hindan þriþum aþrinten. 1382 WYCLIF *Isa.* xix. 7 Nakened shal be the flod wombe [*alveus rivi*]. c1391 CHAUCER *Astrol.* I. §3 The moder of thin Astrelabie is þe thikkeste plate, perced with a large hole, þat resseyuyth in hir wombe the thynne plates. 1471 CAXTON *Recuyell* (Sommer) 56, I had moche leuer that the erthe wold opene and swalwe me in to his wombe. 1588 SHAKS. *Tit. A.* II. iii. 239, I may be pluckt into the swallowing wombe, Of this deepe pit, poore Bassianus graue. 1592 —— *Rom. & Jul.* v. i. 65 As violently, as hastie powder fier'd Doth hurry from the fatall Canons wombe. 1602 MARSTON *Antonio's Rev.* III. v, Yee sootie coursers of the night, Hurrie your chariot into hels black wombe. 1615 CHAPMAN *Odyss* x. 471 The fourth brought water, and made fuel shine In ruddy fires beneath a womb of brass. 1616 T. SCOT *Philomythie* I 3 b, And both these rudely enter The strong ships wombe. 1661 CHILDREY *Brit. Baconica* 141 When the wind is gathered into that hole, and tossed to and fro in the womb of it, there is to be heard as it were a musicall sound. 1697 DRYDEN *Æneis* XII. 1278 What Earth will open her devouring Womb, To rest a weary Goddess in the Tomb? 1715 tr. *Pancirollus' Mem. Things* II. x. 334 There was seen at Mecklin fifteen Pair of Dice.. in the Womb of a Cherry-Stone. 1722 SWIFT *Stella's Birthday* 68 As you raise it [*sc.* the bottle] from its Tomb, It drags behind a spacious Womb. 1797 J. CURR *Coal Viewer* 45 Inclosing it [*sc.* the boiler] with a circular wall 10 inches thick, as high as the womb of the boiler. 1827 KEBLE *Chr. Y., Palm Sunday* iii, Stones in earth's dark womb that rest. 1857 B. TAYLOR *Northern Trav.* xxx. (1858) 315 You can.. watch, through the vortex of whirling spray in its tortured womb, the starry coruscations which radiate from the bottom of the fall. 1863 —— *Poems, Poet's Jrnl., 2nd Eve in Winter*, Wait in the womb of the snow. 1887 IAN HAMILTON *Ballad of Hadji* 14 Then through the womb Of night I galloped.

4. *fig.* (from 2) A place or medium of conception and development; a place or point of origin and growth; sometimes *spec.*, as †the matrix of metals, etc.

1593 SHAKS. *Rich. II*, II. i. 51 This England, This Nurse, this teeming wombe of Royall Kings. *Ibid.* ii. 10 Some vnborne sorrow, ripe in fortunes wombe. 1604 —— *Oth.* I. iii. 377 There are many Euents in the Wombe of Time, which wilbe deliuered. 1622 J. TAYLOR (Water P.) *Shilling* C 6 b, Siluer.. from the wombe of vaust America. 1631 WIDDOWES *Nat. Philos.* 15 Elements are simple essences.. and are the wombs of mixed things. 1665 J. SPENCER *Vulg. Proph.* 8 There is not a more fruitful womb of seditions and confusions in States than the Opinion of such predictions is. 1667 MILTON *P.L.* I. 673 Undoubted sign That in his womb was hid metallic Ore, The work of Sulphur. a1708 BEVERIDGE *Thes. Theol.* (1711) III. 29 The empty Womb of Nothing delivered itself of that Lump and confused Chaos, which.. God.. digested into that.. Order we now see it in. 1757 [BURKE] *Europ. Settlem. Amer.* VII. xxix. II. 282 The cold womb of the earth is incapable of any better production than some miserable shrubs. 1776 J. LEE *Introd. Bot.* Explan. Terms 396 *Pericarpium*, the Womb of the Plant big with Seeds, which it emits when mature. 1810 COLERIDGE *Friend* No. 22 ¶8 The various unforeseen Events that are ripening in the womb of the Future. 1866 VENESS *El Dorado* ix. 95 The fulfilment of her destiny is in the womb of time.

5. *attrib.* and *Comb.*, as ***womb-element***, ***-fruit***, ***-land***, ***-life***, ***part***, ***passage***, ***-pipe***, ***side***; ***womb-enclosed***, ***-fibrilled***, ***-like***, ***-lodged*** adjs.; ***womb-ward*** adv.; †**womb ache**, belly-ache, stomach-ache; †**womb brother**, a uterine brother; †**womb-cake** = PLACENTA 1; †**wombȝate** [GATE *sb.*[1]], = VULVA 1; **womb-grain** [tr. G. *mutterkorn*], ergot of rye (Dunglison *Med. Lex.* 1848); †**womb-infant**, an unborn child; †**womb-joy**, gratification of the appetite, luxurious fare, belly-cheer; †**womb-liver** = *womb-cake*; †**womb-pancake** = *womb-cake*; †**womb-rope**, a belly-band of rope; **womb-stone**, a calcified fibroid tumour of the womb (Billings *Med. Dict.* 1890); **womb-syringe**, a uterine syringe; †**womb syrup** (see quot.); †**womb-tack** [cf. TACK *sb.*[1], *v.*[1]] = WOMB-TIE; †**womb-trumpet** [cf. G. *muttertrompete*], a Fallopian tube, oviduct.

1398 TREVISA *Barth. De P.R.* XVI. xlviii. (1495) f iij b/1 Gete.. swagyth *wombe ache. 1647 TRAPP *Comm. 2 Thess.* ii. 1 Brethren, *womb brethren, as near in nature as is possible. a1661 FULLER *Worthies, Hartfordshire* (1662) II. 19 Son to Queen Katherine by Owen Theodor, her second husband, womb-brother to King Henry the Sixth. 1668 CULPEPPER & COLE *Barthol. Anat.* Introd., The Navil-vein, receiving blood out of the *Womb-cake. 1743 R. POOLE *Journ. France* etc. (1744) I. 132 The Placenta or Womb Cake. 1923 D. H. LAWRENCE *Birds, Beasts & Flowers* 94 Who lies with the waters of his silent passion, *womb-element?—Fish in the waters. a1593 MARLOWE *Ovid's Elegies* II. xiv. 8 Thy *wombe-inclosed off-spring. 1923 *Womb-fibrilled [see INTURNED *ppl. a.*]. 1922 *Wombfruit [see QUICKENING *vbl. sb.*]. 1379 *Gloucester Cath. MS.* 19 Press No. 1 *Tentigo* ys ycalled paries vulue Anglice the *Wombeȝates wall. Or elles lingula vulue Anglice the Wombeȝates tunge. 1611 COTGR., *Vraque*, the pipe or passage whereby a *wombe-infants vrine is carried from it. c1380 WYCLIF *Wks.* (1880) 68 Prelatis.. sillen.. trewe prechynge for.. worldli lordschipe, & *wombe ioie and idelnesse. 1388 *Songs & Poems on Costume* (Percy Soc.) 45 Unthrifte and wombe-joye, *steriles et luxuriosi.* 1398 TREVISA *Barth. De P.R.* VI. vi. (Tollem. MS.) [Children] biþinkeþ only in wombe ioye, and knoweþ not þe mesure of here owen wombe. 1930 A. HUXLEY *Vulgarity in Literature* iv. 16 Those yearning popular songs which are the national anthems of *Wombland. 1876 G. M. HOPKINS *Wr. Deutschland* vii, in *Poems* (1967) 53 Warm-laid grave of a *womb-life grey. a1930 D. H. LAWRENCE *Last Poems* (1932) 308 The shell-like, *womb-like, convoluted shadow. 1981 J. WAINWRIGHT *All on a Summer's Day* 24 An Interview Room.. is womb-like in its complete isolation. 1668 CULPEPPER & COLE *Barthol. Anat.* I. xxxvi. 80 That same round mass is called Placenta Uteri, the Womb-pancake..; also the *Womb-liver. 1684 tr. *Bonet's Merc. Compit.* II. 2 On the seventh day she.. voided the placenta (or womb liver). 1611 COTGR. s.v. *Agneliere*, A *wombe-lodged infant. 1668 *Womb-pancake [see *womb-liver*]. 1598 FLORIO, *Vulva*,.. the *wombe part or *womb passage. 1860 MAYNE *Expos. Lex.*, *Womb-Passage*,.. common term for the *Vagina.* 1611 COTGR., *Vulve*, the *wombe-pipe, or priuie passage. c1325 *Gloss. W. de Bibbesw.* in Wright *Voc.* 168 Ke porte à dos une dossere [*gloss* rige-leyther], E au ventre une venter [*gloss* a *wombe-rop]. c1340 *Nominale* (Skeat) 882 *Sele coler et ventrere*, Sadul hamborwe and womberope. c1391 CHAUCER *Astrol.* II. §29 The lyne Meridional on the *wombe-side. c1450 *Two Cookery-bks.* 101 Ley the pike in A charger, the wombe side vpward. 1694 SALMON *Bate's Dispens.* (1713) 5/1 This Water is to be injected into.. the Womb with a *Womb-Syringe. *Ibid.* 609/1 *Syrupus Uterinus*, i.e. *Carannæ*, The *Womb Syrup, or Syrup of Gum Caranna. 1729 P. WALKDEN *Diary* (1866) 56 Henry Charnley viewed the horse, with packsaddle and *woontak, at £2 10s. 1703 *Etmullerus Abridged* 596 The Egg thus influenc'd, falls off into one of the *Womb-Trumpets. 1923 D. H. LAWRENCE *Birds, Beasts & Flowers* 19 There was a flower that flowered inward, *womb-ward.

womb (wu:m), *v.* [f. WOMB *sb.*]

1. *trans.* To enclose as in a womb.

1557 *Tottel's Misc.* (Arb.) 239 The hidden harme.. Wombed within our walles and realme about, As Grekes in Troy were in the Grekish beast. 1611 SHAKS. *Wint. T.* IV. iv. 501 Not.. for all the Sun sees, or The close earth wombes,.. will I breake my oath. 1855 SINGLETON *Virgil* I. 113 In this from out another tree A bud they womb. 1871 G. MACDONALD *Somnium Myst.* v. 30 A world that lay Wombed in its sun.

†**2.** To cause to swell *out*: = BELLY *v.* 1. *nonce-use.*

1628 FELTHAM *Resolves* I. [II.] lxi. 57 Once lanched forth, hee may.. find the blast, to wombe out his sailes more fully.

3. *pa. pple.* Impregnated *with*. *nonce-use.*

1786 J. COURTENAY *Poet. Rev. Char. Johnson* 16 As womb'd with fire the cloud electrick flies.

wombat ('wɒmbæt). Also **womat**, **wombach**, **wo(o)mback**. [Native Australian name.] Any of the burrowing marsupials of the genus *Phascolomys*, native to South Australia and Tasmania, characterized by a thick heavy body, short legs, and a general resemblance to a small bear.

1798 FLINDERS in *Voy. Terra Australis* (1814) Introd. p. cxxviii, Point Womat, a rocky projection of Cape-Barren Island, where a number of the new animals, called *womat*, were seen. [*Ibid.* p. cxxxv, Called by the natives, *womat*, *wombat*, or *womback*, according to the different dialects, or perhaps to the different rendering of the wood rangers who brought the information.] **1827** in Bischoff *Van Diemen's Land* (1832) 175 The dogs had caught them three kangaroos, and two badgers or woombacks. **1852** J. West *Hist. Tasmania* I. 324 The Wombat, commonly called in the colony Badger. **1896** Gosse *Critical Kit-Kats* 267 Pater has often reminded me of some such armadillo or wombat.

attrib. and *Comb.* **1847** G. F. Angas *Savage Life* I. 66 Wombat burrows. **1859** C. G. Rossetti *Goblin Market* xvii, Cat-like and rat-like, Ratel- and wombat-like. **1870** Gordon *Bush Ballads, From the Wreck* 24 Look out for the holes On the wombat hills.

† ˈ**wombclout.** *Obs.* Forms: 4 **wombecloute,** 5 **wamclowte, womclotte.** [f. womb *sb.* + clout *sb.*¹] The omentum; tripe. (Cf. *paunch-clout*, paunch *sb.*¹ 3.)

1377 Langl. *P. Pl.* B. xiii. 63 He eet many sondry metes mortrewes and puddynges, Wombe-cloutes and wylde braune. *c* **1440** *Promp. Parv.* 503/1 Trype (or pawncheclowt,..or wamclowte..), *scrutum*. *c* **1475** *Pict. Voc.* in Wr.-Wülcker 789/19 *Hoc omentum*, a womclotte.

wombed (wuːmd), *a.* [f. womb *sb.* + -ed².] Having a womb or belly (of a specified kind); also (quot. *c* 1430), great-bellied.

1297 R. Glouc. (Rolls) 7731 Suiþe þikke mon he was & of grete strengþe, Gret wombede & ballede. *c* **1430** *Pilgr. Lyf Manhode* ii. cvi. (1869) 115 Swollen and wombed thanne j bicome. **1602** Marston *Ant. & Mel.* iii. Wks. 1856 I. 32 This hollow wombed masse shall inly grone. **1791** Cowper *Odyss.* viii. 533 O'er the fire A tripod ample-womb'd.

† ˈ**wombful,** *sb. Obs.* [f. womb *sb.* + -ful.] As much as will fill the womb or the stomach.

1387 Trevisa *Higden* (Rolls) III. 437 Sche leved þere thrittene dayes in flescheliche likyng, and hadde her wombeful, and went hir wey [L. *impleto utero abscessit*]. **1637** Rutherford *Lett., to Parishioners* 13 July (1664) 7 The earth worme, who can never get his wombfull of clay. **1637** —— *Let. to A. Gordon* 234, I would break the door and be in upon him, to get a wombfull of love; for I am an hungered ..soul.

† ˈ**wombful,** *a. Obs. rare.* [f. womb *sb.* + full *a.*] Having a full stomach.

1450–80 tr. *Secr. Secr.* xlix. 30 He that lythe with women wombe fulle [*cf. ante* with fulle wombe].

wombill, womble, obs. ff. wimble.

Womble (ˈwɒmb(ə)l). [Shortening of *Wombledon*, fanciful alteration of Wimbledon.] An imaginary animal depicted as inhabiting Wimbledon Common (see quot. 1968). Also, a soft toy representing this creature. Also *transf.*

1968 E. Beresford *Wombles* (1974) (*dust-jacket*), The Wombles are a bit like teddy bears to look at but they have real claws and live underneath Wimbledon Common and devote their lives to 'tidying up' all the things those untidy Human Beings leave behind. **1975** *Sunday Express* 15 June 6/3 In addition to the Wombles pop group and the TV series, there are Womble jigsaws, Womble dolls, Womble T-shirts, Womble pillow cases... Now..there are Womble-approved crisps. **1977** *Lancashire Life* Dec. 77/2 Now she had locked herself in the ladies' with five rubber frogs and a selection of plastic Wombles and was refusing to come out. **1978** *Times* 26 Aug. 3 (*caption*) Members of the Outset youth service group felling and clearing dead trees on Wimbledon Common. These 'Wombles' have also assisted in pond clearing. **1982** *Buses* Sept. 393/2 The customers being predominantly senior citizens or 'wombles' in the London Transport vernacular.

womble, wombly, var. ff. wamble, wambly *a.*

† ˈ**wombling, -long,** *adv. Obs. rare.* [f. womb *sb.* + -ling, -long.] With the belly on the ground or along a surface.

13.. *K. Alis.* 5658 (Laud MS.) Þe Addres..to-cleueþ wombelyng. *c* **1460** J. Russell *Bk. Nurture* 451 Lay your cony wombelonge vche side to þe chyne.

† ˈ**womb-tie, -tow.** *Obs.* In 5 **wom(e)tye, wombtye,** 6 **womtoe.** [f. womb *sb.* + tie *sb.*, tow *sb.*² Cf. wame-tow, wanty.] A girth or belly-band.

1481–3 *Acc. Exch. K.R.* 496. No. 26 (P.R.O.) Bely girthez Wometyes. **1485** in *Compotus Rolls Obedientiaries St. Swithun's, Winch.* (1892) 383 Et in corda empta ad faciendum lez Wombtyes iiijd. **1587** *Wills & Inv. Durham* (Surtees) II. 150, ij load saddles, a womtoe and a halter.

womby (ˈwuːmɪ), *a.* [f. womb *sb.* + -y¹.] Having a womb-like cavity; hollow. Also *fig.*

1599 Shaks. *Hen. V*, ii. iv. 124 Caues and Wombie Vaultages of France. **1858** Singleton *Virgil* II. 536 To hide thee in the womby earth [orig. *cava..terra*]. **1934** Dylan Thomas *Let.* 2 May (1966) 117 I've a good mind to ferret an Old Boys' Society, & read them the waxiest and wombiest efforts that I've got. **1951** W. Sansom *Face of Innocence* xi. 150 The sense of round shapes about—the rounder mouldings of stone, the curves of boats..roundness, if you like, that is womby. **1977** *Time* 5 Sept. 44/1 It [*sc.* a van] is self-contained and self-containing, and its womby little room is packed with the motherly comforts of home.

wome, obs. form of whom.

womell, obs. form of wimble.

womenfolk (ˈwɪmɪnfəʊk). Also *dial.* and *U.S.* **-folks.** [f. *women*, pl. of woman *sb.* + folk.] **a.** Women collectively, womankind. Now *dial.* **b.** The women of a household, a party, or the like: *dial.* the female servants.

1833 T. Hook *Parson's Dau.* i. vii, You have been snubbed—the women-folk, as I call them, have driven you away. **1849** E. E. Napier *Excurs. S. Afr.* II. 389 Making your appearance in such a fashion, and that too, when you know there are women-folk in the house. **1851** J. J. Hooper *Widow Rugby Husband* 50 Such wimmen folks. **1877** Black *Green Past.* i, There was a stir among our women-folk. **1879** Burroughs *Locusts & Wild Honey* 131 We could gain no information from the 'women-folks'..nor from the men who had just come in. **1896** Rideal (*title*) Charles Dickens's Heroines and Women-Folk. **1911** *Times* 2 Aug. 3/2 Foreign residents have sent their women-folk by train to Mexico City.

ˈ**womenish,** *a.* [f. *women*, pl. of woman *sb.* + -ish¹.] Of, pertaining to, or characteristic of, women. Also in phr. ***wine and womenish***: cf. wine *sb.*¹ f (*b*).

1892 S. Hale *Let.* 28 Apr. (1919) 273 The day was so hot that it smelled perspiration of emigrant women-ish. **1920** D. H. Lawrence *Let.* 4 Jan. (1962) I. 606 At midnight the Monty crowd ordered champagne and tried to look wine and womenish.

† ˈ**womenkin.** *Obs.* [f. *women*, pl. of woman *sb.* + kin *sb.*¹] = next, 1.

1387 wommen kyn [see men-kind].

womenkind (ˈwɪmɪnkaɪnd). [f. as prec. + kind *sb.* Cf. men-kind.] **1.** = womankind 1.

1387 Trevisa *Higden* (Rolls) VI. 335 Þis pope is nouȝt i-rekened in þe book of poopes for he was of wommen kynde. **1577** Grange *Golden Aphrod.* F ij, I can not for thy sake but say and thinke well of all womenkinde. **1611** Beaum. & Fl. *Philaster* iii. i, 'Tis the truth that all womenkind is false. **1652** H. L'Estrange *Amer. no Jewes* 26 A curse entailed upon Eve, and all women kind ever since. **1694** Salmon *Bate's Dispens.* (1699) 599/2 It..cures the Green-sickness in Virgins, and most Diseases of the Womb in Women-kind. **1880** Blackmore *Mary Anerley* xxxvi. II. 300 The women-kind always do think that. **1883** *Harper's Mag.* Mar. 539/1 The..foot-warmers..used by all womenkind in Dutch churches. **1889** Mrs. E. Kennard *Landing a Prize* i. (1891) 1 This behaviour disgusted Mr. Bousfield with womenkind.

† **b.** = womankind 1 b. *Obs.*

1571 Grindal *Injunct., Laity* §10 Their children and seruaunts both menkinde and womenkinde. **1588** in Wadley *Notes Wills Bristol* (1886) 255 [Every servant] bothe men kinde and women kinde. **1596** Dalrymple tr. *Leslie's Hist. Scot.* ii. (S.T.S.) I. 133 Gif the king left successione behind him vndir xiiii ȝeiris in menkynd, and xii ȝeiris in womenkynd.

2. = womankind 3.

1648 Josselin *Diary* (Camden 1908) 59 Some of the women-kinde of the parrish. **1674** [see men-kind]. **1852** Miss Mulock *Agatha's Husb.* xiii. (1875) 159 The old gentleman evidently took a secret pride in his womenkind. **1905** W. B. Boulton *Gainsborough* 328 The patronage of gentlemen and their womenkind alone enabled him to live.

womens (ˈwɪmɪnz). *U.S. dial.* Non-standard pl. of woman *sb.*

1928 [see spade *sb.*² 3 a]. **1945** L. Saxon et al. *Gumbo Ya-Ya* i. 8 'It's damn funny' Fisher sniffed, 'how womens is.' **1967** *Boston Sunday Herald* 26 Apr. (Comic Section), Sometime I think wimmens is the strongest gender. **1970** R. D. Abrahams *Positively Black* iv. 84, I got so many womens I cannot call they name.

woment, var. wayment *v.*

womerah, womerar, varr. woomera.

womet, -it, obs. Sc. ff. vomit.

wommal, var. warnel *dial.*

wommil, -ill, obs. ff. wimble.

wommle, var. wamble.

womoonless (wʊˈmuːnlɪs), *a. nonce-word.* [See def.] Joc. combination of womanless *a.* and moonless *a.*

1922 Joyce *Ulysses* 278 Croak of vast manless moonless womoonless marsh.

wompam, wompom, obs. ff. wampum.

womple, wompyll, obs. Sc. ff. wimple.

womward(e, obs. forms of homeward *adv.*

1507 in Leadam *Sel. Cases Star Chamber* (Selden Soc.) I. 249 They..returnyd womward.

womyl, -ylle, obs. forms of wimble.

won, wone (wʌn, wəʊn), *v. Obs.* exc. *Sc.* and *north.*, and *arch.* Forms: 1 **wunian,** (1–2 **uni-**), 2–3 **wnien, wunen,** 3 **wunie(n, wunye(n, wune,** *Ormin* **wunenn,** 3–4 **wne;** 2–4 **wonien,** 3 **wonin,** 4 **wonen, woniȝe(n, wonȝe, wonie, -y,** 4–5 **-ye;** 4–8 **wonne,** 4–9 **won(n, wone,** 5 **wonon, -yn,** (5–7 **woon,** 7 **woone);** *Sc.* and *north.* 4 **vone, vonne,** 5–9 **wun,** 9 **woan(e, woon, wonne, wunn.** *Pa. t.* 1 **wunode,** 2 **wnede,** 3 **wunede;** 4 **wonid, wonyed, wonde,** *Sc.* **wonnyt,** 4–8 **wond,** 5 **wonyd, vonnyt,** 6 **woond,** (*pseudo-arch.* **wonne),** *Sc.* **wonnit,** 4– **wonned, wonn'd, woned, won'd.** *Pa. pple.*: see wont *pa. pple.*; also 5 **wunte.** See also win *v.*² [OE. *wunian*, corresp. to OFris. *wunia*, *wonia* to dwell, OS. *wunôn*, *wonôn*, (M)LG., (M)Du. *wonen*, OHG. *wonên* (MHG. *wonen*, G. *wohnen*) to be accustomed, remain, dwell, ON. *una* to rejoice, Goth. **wunan* in *unwunands* troubled:—**wunōjan*, *-æ̅jan*, f. Teut. *wun-*, for further relations of which see wean *v.*, win *sb.*², etc.]

I. 1. *intr.* To stay habitually, dwell, live (in a place or with some one).

Beowulf 1128 Hengest..wunode mid Finn. *c* **725** *Corpus Gloss.* 1140 *Inmoratur*, wunat. **971** *Blickl. Hom.* 57 Seo fæȝernes þære saule þe on ecnesse wunaþ on heofena rices ȝefean. *Ibid.* 105 Ac þær wunian mot [he]..mid engla sibbe on ecean wuldre. *c* **1000** *Ags. Gosp.* John i. 39 Hiȝ comon & ȝesawon hwar he wunode, & mid him wunodon on ðam dæȝe. *a* **1175** *Cott. Hom.* 231 His under-þeoden..on his cyne rice wuneden. *c* **1175** *Lamb. Hom.* 51 Þer wunieð fower cunnes wurmes inne þet fordoð nuðe al þeos midelerd. *c* **1205** Lay. 17681 Þene bezste læche þe wunede an æi londe. *c* **1220** *Bestiary* 517 Ðis fis [*sc.* whale] wuneð wið ðe se grund. *c* **1250** *Gen. & Ex.* 2742 Raguel Ietro ðat riche man, Was wuniende in madian. *a* **1300** *Cursor M.* 2678 Þou and þi childer it sal bigin And þat wons þi house wit in. **1338** R. Brunne *Chron.* (1810) 17 He com his eam to socour fro fer þer he gan wonne. **1377** Langl. *P. Pl.* B. ii. 232 He..is welcome whan he wil and woneth wyth hem oft. *c* **1440** *Alphabet of Tales* 54, I hafe wunte with þis knyght þis xiiij yere. **1513** Douglas *Æneis* xi. xi. 82 In maner of hyrdis in pasturage, On wild montanis he wonnit all his age. **1557** Phaer *Æneid.* vii. (1558) S iv, What people dwells hereby, what townes they keepe, and where they wonne. **1610** Holland *Camden's Brit.* i. 88 Wheresoever the Romane winneth..there he woneth, and inhabiteth. **1614** Gorges *Lucan* vi. 240 Dis that wooneth still below. **1621** Brathwait *Nat. Emb.*, etc. N 2, Simple and meane's the cottage where I won. **1667** Milton *P.L.* vii. 457 Out of the ground up rose As from his Laire the wilde Beast where he wonns In Forrest wilde. **1728** Ramsay *Monk & Miller's Wife* 5 An honest Miller wond in Fife. *c* **1746** J. Collier (Tim Bobbin) *View Lanc. Dial.* Wks. (1862) 46 There's o Gentlemon ot wooans abeawt three Mile off. **1810** Scott *Lady of L.* iv. xiii, Up spoke the moody Elfin king, Who won'd within the hill. **1827** Hood *Mids. Fairies* lii, Neither in forest haunts love I to won. **1848** H. Miller *First Impr. Eng.* v. (1857) 85 There wons a barber in Dudley..of whom I purchased several fine trilobites. **1867** Jean Ingelow *Gladys* 563 The wizard that wonned..underground.

b. *transf.* and *fig.*

Beowulf 2242 Beorh ealȝearo wunode on wonge. **971** *Blickl. Hom.* 111 We sceolan..þone rihtan ȝeleafan fæste staðelian on urum heortum þæt he ðær wunian mæȝe. *c* **1000** *Phœnix* 82 Þær se halȝa stenc wunaþ ȝeond wynlond. *c* **1175** *Lamb. Hom.* 7 3if we þis doð þenne wunet god almihti in us. *c* **1250** *Prov. Alfred* 391 in *O.E. Misc.* 126 Þeyh o mon wolde al þe worlde And al þe wunne þe þar-inne wunyeþ. *a* **1300** *Cursor M.* 9666 For pes mai nourquar abide Þar hate wons, or werr, or pride. *c* **1400** *Rule St. Benet* (prose) 2 He dos all to noht þe sinne þat wnis in his þoht. *a* **1529** Skelton *Col. Cloute* 141 They haue..ryght sklender connyng Within theyr heedes wonnyng. **1590** Spenser *F.Q.* iii. i. 3 Wastefull wayes, Where daungers dwelt, and perils most did wonne. *a* **1592** Greene *Jas. IV*, i. iii, Thy sight hath cleerd my thoughts Of many banefull troubles that there woond. **1622** Drayton *Poly-olb.* xix. 17 For in that happy soil, doth pleasure ever wonne. *a* **1641** Bp. Mountagu *Acts & Mon.* i. (1642) 56 And if it be blasphemy or Heresie, let them looke unto it, where it wonneth so familiarly with so many men. **1828** Hood '*Oh! well may poets make a fuss*' 81 Where are ye, London meads..And gardens redolent of flow'rs Wherein the Zephyr wons? *a* **1839** Lady Flora Hastings *Poems, Lay of Bell* 222 Ever within those sashless walls Sorrow woneth. **1852** Bailey *Festus* (ed. 5) 504 That Wisdom yet might wonn with them again.

† **2.** To continue to be, remain (in a certain state, condition, or way of life); to have existence, live.

Beowulf 1735 Wunað he on wiste, no hine wiht dweleð adl ne yldo. **971** *Blickl. Hom.* 155, & heo wæs fæmne ær hire beorþre & heo wunaþ fæmne æfter hire beorþre. *c* **1000** Ælfric *Saints' Lives* iii. 595 Se læce..cwæð þæt he ȝelyfan wolde..ȝif he wunode of[er] mid-dæȝ. *c* **1175** *Lamb. Hom.* 63 3ife us..þet he..mid his halie gast us lihte and in cherite to wnien inne. *c* **1200** *Trin. Coll. Hom.* 3 Men þe waren wunende on elche of þese þrie times. *Ibid.* 179 *Viuimus in labore*,..on swunche we here wunien. **1340** *Ayenb.* 54 Þo þet libbeþ be þe goste byeþ þo þet ine þe loue of god wonyeþ. *a* **1375** *Lay Folks Mass Bk.* App. iv. 205 3if þou wol wone in weole, Prey for þe prest. *c* **1450** Holland *Howlat* 963, I couth nocht won in to welth wretch wast, I was so wantoun of will. **1590** Spenser *F.Q.* i. vi. 39 How might that bee, And he the stoutest knight, that euer wonne? **1595** —— *Col. Clout* 307 Like as in this same world where we do wone. **1633** P. Fletcher *Purple Isl.* vii. xxvii, Fancie, a lad that all in feathers wons.

† **3.** To remain (in a place); to stay. *Obs.*

c **1000** Ælfric *Saints' Lives* ix. 146 Seo eadiȝa lucia on þære ylcan stowe wunode þe heo ofslaȝen wæs oðþæt sacerdas coman. *c* **1430** *How Good Wife taught Dau.* 83 in *Babees Bk.* (1868) 40 Wone at hom, douȝtir.

† **4.** *trans.* To dwell in, inhabit. *Obs.*

Beowulf 1260 Grendles modor..se þe wætereȝesan wunian scolde, cealde streamas. *a* **1000** *Phœnix* 172 Ðær he heanne beam on holtwuda wunað. **1565** Golding *Ovid's Met.* ii. (1593) 39 The fire he ay doth shon, And chooseth him the contrary continually to won. *a* **1586** Sidney *Arcadia* iii. (1922) 75 When all this Earth..Was onely won'd with such as beastes begot. **1600** Fairfax *Tasso* xii. xxv, The toure wherein she lay enclos'd, Was with her damsels onely wond and mee.

II. † **5.** *intr.* To be accustomed or used *to do* something. *Obs.* ***to be wont***: see wont *pa. pple.*

The regular form in this sense in OE. was *ȝewunian*.

c **1000** Ælfric *Gram.* xli. (Z.) 247 *Soleo* ic ȝewuniȝe [*v.rr.* iwunie, wuniȝe], *solens* wuniȝende. *c* **1440** *Promp. Parv.* 532/1 Wonon', or vse custummably, *usito*. **1579** Spenser *Sheph. Cal.* Feb. 119 And thereto aye wonned to repayre The shepheards daughters. **1590** —— *F.Q.* iii. ix. 21 Her well plighted frock, which she did won To tucke about her short, when she did ryde. **1642** H. More *Song of Soul* I. I. xxxii, These parts that won To drag in dirty earth.

†**6.** *trans.* To accustom (a person *to* something); *refl.* to accustom oneself, become or be accustomed.

c **1200** Ormin 19541 He wass sennd to fullhtnenn, To wunenn swa þe follc þærto, forr þatt teȝȝ sholldenn ȝernenn Affterr þe Laferrd Jesu Crist. *a* **1300** *Cursor M.* 12088 If þou ..wald luue þi sun, Til oþer thues þou suld him won. *c* **1440** *Promp. Parv.* 532/1 Wonon', or make to be custummyd or vsyd.., *assuefacio.* **1483** *Cath. Angl.* 423/1 To Wonne, *assuefacere.*

c **1200** *Trin. Coll. Hom.* 85 Seint nicholas þe on his chilhode wunede him to fasten. *a* **1225** *Ancr. R.* 412 Wunieð ou to lutel drunch. *a* **1250** *Prov. Alfred* 367 in *O.E. Misc.* 124 From lesynge þu þe wune. **1340** *Ayenb.* 7 Þe ilke þet mest him woneþ to zuerie mest zeneȝeþ. **1387** Trevisa *Higden* (Rolls) II. 167 Þey woneþ hem to glotonye. *c* **1400** *Rule St. Benet* (prose) 10 Ye sal wne yu til strate gate. *c* **1449** Pecock *Repr.* v. xiv. 559 For to sette thee and wone thee to not loue money.

won (wʌn), *ppl. a.* Also 6 **wonne**. Pa. pple. of win *v.*[1], in various senses of the vb.

1500–20 Ill-won [see ill- 7]. **1553** Becon *Reliques of Rome* (1563) 155b, An holy nation, a wonne people. **1598** Bernard tr. *Terence, Phormio* I. v, Whatsoeuer may happen vnlooked for, account that as wonne good. **1827** Scott *Surg. Dau.* v, A won battle. **1860** Löwenthal *Morphy's Games Chess* 56 A won game. **1883** *Mem. Sam. Miller* iv. 108 Rendering at last to God His own won heritage.

won (wɒn, wɔːn), *sb.* [ad. Korean *wån* in same sense.] The basic monetary unit of (North and South) Korea.

1950 *Times* 16 Nov. 7/7 Between June 25 and October 1 expenditure totalled 28,000m. *won*,..while revenue amounted to about 1,000m. *won.* **1952** R. Cutforth *Korean Reporter* x. 85, I gave him 20,000 won, patted him on the back and said goodbye. **1981** 'A. Hall' *Pekin Target* vii. 62, I declared 100,000 *won* and asked where I could change pounds sterling. **1984** *Times* 25 Jan. 6/8 Twelve South Korean herb medicine dealers were arrested for selling 1bn won (£850,000) worth of false cures.

won, obs. form of one, wan *a.*, when; pa. t. and pple. of win *v.*[1] and [3]; obs. pa. pple. of wind *v.*[1]; var. wone.

wonable *a.*, Sc. var. of winnable (see win *v.*[1] Forms *Inf.* β).

c **1610** Sir J. Melvil *Mem.* (1683) 125 So many of the King's Servants, as were thought to be most wonable.

wonce, obs. form of once.

1599 Harington in *Nugæ Ant.* (1804) I. 272 The rebell wonce in Rorie O More shewed himselfe.

†**wond,** *sb.*[1] *Obs. rare.* [a. ON. *vándr* bad, wicked (Sw., Da. *ond*, Norw. *vond*, mod.Icel. *vondr*).] The evil one, the devil. (So Da. *den onde.*)

c **1250** *Death* 112 in *O.E. Misc.* 174 Nu þu schalt in þe putte wunie wid þe wonde.

†**wond,** *sb.*[2] *Obs. rare.* In 4 **wa(a)nd.** [f. wonde *v.*] Hesitation.

a **1300** *Cursor M.* 8465 Man it clepes ecclesiastes, Þat spekes mast wit-vten waand, Hu fals þis werld es for to faand. *Ibid.* 11517 Þat þai faand, wit-vten wand Þai tok.

wond, south. ME. var. fond *v. Obs.*

1297 R. Glouc. (Rolls) 9600 King henri wondede muche to abbe men in offis..þat of conseil were..wis.

wond, south. ME. var. *fond*, pa. t. of find *v.*

1297 R. Glouc. (Rolls) 561 He astore wel is lond Wiþ homber kinges god þat me of his wond. *Ibid.* 3726 He..wan it [*sc.* Ireland] al clene to him & al þat he vonde [*v.r.* wond].

wond(e: see wand, wind, wone, wont, wound.

†**wonde,** *v.* Forms: 1–2 **wandian**, 4–5 **wand(e, wond(e,** (4 **waand, want,** 5 **whonde, wound(e, woonde;** *Sc.* 5 **waynd(e,** 5–6 **waind).** [OE. *wandian* to shrink, hesitate, refrain, spare, corresp. to ON. *vanda* to make elaborately, make difficulties, find fault (cf. *vandr* difficult, etc., *vandi* difficulty, etc.): app. f. *wand-, wend-* to turn (see wand *sb.*, wend *v.*, wind *v.*[1]; and cf. wandis *v.*).]

1. *intr.* To shrink or flinch for fear; to hesitate (esp. const. inf.); to refrain.

c **897** Ælfred *Gregory's Past. C.* xx. 149 Oft mon bið suiðe wandiȝende æt ælcum weorce & suiðe lætræde. **971** *Blickl. Hom.* 43 [Sins] swiþe unsyferlice þæt se man wandaþ þæt he hi æfre asecgge. *c* **1000** Ælfric *Gram.* xxvii. (Z.) 162 *Uereor* ic anðraciȝe oððe ic wandiȝe. *a* **1122** *O.E. Chron.* (Laud MS.) an. 1052 Ac he ne wandode na him metes to tylienne. *a* **1300** *Cursor M.* 4334 How sco broght him to þe fand, Forth to tell wil i noght waand. *Ibid.* 5293 For-þi, leue fader, want þou noght, Al þi will it sal be wroght. **1303** R. Brunne *Handl. Synne* 1693 Also shal þe womman wonde To take [in marriage] here godmodrys husbonde. *c* **1330** *King of Tars* 898 The soudan tok the prest bi the honde, And bad him go and nothing wonde. *c* **1350** *Will. Palerne* 4071 For drede of duresse nor of deth in erþe, nel i wonde in no wise what i þouȝt to seie. *c* **1385** Chaucer *L.G.W.* 1187 *Dido*, Loue wil loue, for no thing wele it wande. *c* **1400** *Destr. Troy* 590, I wole..Do my deuer yf I dar, & for no dethe wonde. *Ibid.* 3380 Wond of þi weping, whipe vp þi teris. *c* **1425** Wyntoun *Cron.* v. 3961 (MS. W.) Scho wayndit nocht þare feit to wesche. *c* **1470** Henry *Wallace* I. 198 Quhar he fand ane.. To cutt his throit, or steik hym sodanlye. He wayndyt nocht. *c* **1500** *Melusine* 219 But the duc Anthony wanded. *a* **1510** Douglas *K. Hart* I. 91 Richt as the rose vpspringis fro the rute,..Nor waindis nocht the levis to outschute.

2. *trans.* To refrain from; to shrink from, avoid, shun; to refuse.

13.. *Cursor M.* 8361 (Gött.) He..bad hir say, ne wond it noght, Quat war best as hir thoght. *c* **1315** Shoreham *Poems* I. 2031 Ne hy ne wondeþ messeday, Ne none holy tyde. **1390** Gower *Conf.* III. 268 This worthi kniht with swerd on honde His weie made, and thei him wonde. *c* **1430** *Syr Tryam.* 1526 My ryght name schalle y not wande. *c* **1450** *Erle Tolous* 1155 Soche wordes y rede thou wonde. ? *a* **1500** *Chester Plays* (E.E.T.S.) xxiii. 29 His wickednes he would not wonde [*v.r.* wound], Till he was taken and putt in Band.

Hence †**wonding** *vbl. sb.*, flinching, hesitation.

c **1440** *York Myst.* xxviii. 77 Nowe will we lere, Full warely to were ȝou fro alle wandynge.

wonde, irreg. pa. t. of win *v.*[1]

1571 Fortescue *Forest of Hist.* 65 Who so wonde [*ed.* 1576 wan] then the price.

wonder ('wʌndə(r)), *sb.* Forms: 1 **wundor**, 2–5 **wunder,** (3 **wnder,** *Orm.* **wunnderr,** 4 **wondere, wonþer),** 4–5 **wondre, wondur, wondire, -yr(e, wundyr,** 4–6 **wundir, woundir, -er,** *Sc.* **vounder, vondir,** 4–6, 8 *Sc.* **wondir,** (5 **wundur, wonther, wonþur,** 6 *Sc.* **winder, -ir),** 6–7 **woonder,** 8–9 *Sc.* **wonner,** 3– **wonder.** [OE. *wundor* neut. = OFris. *wunder*, OS. *wundar*, (M)Du. *wonder*, OHG. *wuntar* (MHG., G. *wunder*), ON. *undr* (Sw., Da. *under*): of unknown origin.]

I. Something that causes astonishment.

1. a. A marvellous object; a marvel, prodigy. ***the seven wonders of the world*** (= L. *septem mira, miracula*, or *spectacula*), the seven monuments regarded as the most remarkable structures of ancient times; so ***eighth wonder of the world*** (used hyperbolically of any impressive object, etc.); ***nine days' wonder***, and allusive uses: see nine *a.* 3a and 4b.

Beowulf 840 Ferdon folctoȝan..ȝeond widweȝas wundor sceawian, laþes lastas. *c* **700** Cædmon *Hymn* 3 Sue he uundra ȝihuaes..or astelidæ. *a* **1000** *Sal. & Sat.* 281 Ac hwæt is ðæt wundor ðe ȝeond ðas worold færeð, styrnenga gæð? *c* **1205** Lay. 21738 Þa..gunnen to fleonnen..into þan watere, þer wunderes beoð inoȝe. **1297** R. Glouc. (Rolls) 151 Mirabilia Anglie. Þre wondres beþ in engelond,..Þat water of baþe is þat on, þat euere is iliche hot. *Ibid.* 155 Vpe þe plein of salesbury þat oþer wonder is Þat ston heng is icluped. **1387** Trevisa *Higden* (Rolls) I. 43 For þey schulde ..write and certifie þe senatoures where and what wondres were i-founde. **1591** Shaks. *Two Gent.* I. i. 6, I rather would entreat thy company, To see the wonders of the world abroad. **1592** —— *Rom. & Jul.* III. iii. 36 Carrion Flies.. may seaze On the white wonder of deare Iuliets hand. **1616** R. Cocks *Diary* (Hakl. Soc.) I. 194, I doo esteem it [*sc.* the idol] to be bigger then that at Roads, which was taken for 1 of the 7 wonders of the world. **1681** [see Peak *sb.*[1] 3]. **1712–14** Pope *Rape Lock.* I. 142 The fair..Repairs her smiles,..And calls forth all the wonders of her face. **1774** Goldsm. *Nat. Hist.* (1776) I. 267 All the wonders of the Mediterranean sea are described in much higher colours than they merit. **1831** M. Edgeworth *Let.* 20 Jan. (1971) 473 A..spoiled child of 30 whose mother and father having not been able to conceal from him that they think him the 8th wonder of the world have at last brought him to acquiesce in their opinion. **1878** Browning *La Saisiaz* 71 We must have our journey marge Ample for the wayside wonders. **1930** *Amer. Speech* VI. *Eighth wonder of the world.* .. Ford runabout. **1977** H. Fast *Immigrants* IV. 267, I rode the first cable car on California Street... The Eighth Wonder of the World.

b. Marvellous character or quality; wonderfulness; marvels collectively. (Cf. marvel *sb.*[1] 2c.)

c **1220** *Bestiary* 266 Ȝet is wunder of ðis wirm [*sc.* the ant] More ðanne man weneð. **1605** Shaks. *Macb.* I. v. 6 Whiles I stood rapt in the wonder of it, came Missiues from the King. **1610** —— *Temp.* v. i. 181 *Mir.* O wonder! How many goodly creatures are there heere? **1613** —— *Hen. VIII*, v. v. 41 As when The Bird of Wonder dyes, the Mayden Phoenix, Her Ashes new create another Heyre. **1667** Milton *P.L.* VII. 70 Great things, and full of wonder in our eares. **1738** Gray *Tasso* 35 Great things and full of wonder in your ears I shall unfold. **1801** 'Monk' Lewis (*title*) Tales of Wonder. **1842** Tennyson *Locksley Hall* 16 When I dipt into the future..Saw the Vision of the world, and all the wonder that would be. **1872** Black *Adv. Phaeton* ix. 129 We went out into the bright wonder of the moonlight.

c. (*transf.* from 7.) The object of astonishment (usually implying profound admiration) for a particular country, people, age, or the like.

world's wonder: the Marvel of Peru. ***wonder of the world***, the ginseng, *Panax Shinseng* (Treas. Bot. 1866).

1591 Shaks. *1 Hen. VI*, IV. vii. 48 Hack their bones assunder, Whose life was Englands glory, Gallia's wonder. **1597** Hooker *Eccl. Pol.* v. xi. §1 The bewtie whereof..was such, that euen this was..the wonder of the whole world. **1607** *Ld. Coke's Sp. & Charge* F, This Sea-Inuyrond-Iland, the beauty, and wonder of the world. **1639** Mayne *City Match* I. iv, She's the wonder of the Court, And talke oth' Towne. **1671** Milton *P.R.* III. 280 Babylon the wonder of all tongues. **1706** Phillips (ed. Kersey), *Marvel of Peru*, a kind of Night-shade..with Flowers of such Variety that it is also call'd *The World's Wonder.* **1733** Pope *Ep. Cobham* 180 Wharton, the scorn and wonder of our days. **1831** E. Burton *Eccles. Hist.* vii. 205 In Ephesus this feeling found an additional vent in the pride of having their temple considered the wonder of the world.

d. A marvellous specimen or example (*of* something); in *Sc.* used contemptuously. ***boneless wonder***, a gymnast; *fig.*, someone or something lacking 'backbone'; ***chinless wonder***: see chinless *a.* b.

1721 Bradley *Philos. Acc. Wks. Nat.* 182 In this Wonder of a Garden there is neither Grass-work nor Gravel. **1786** Burns *Twa Dogs* 65 Our Whipper-in, wee blastit wonner, Poor worthless elf. **1855** Kingsley *Westw. Ho!* xxiii, But surely she was a very wonder of beauty! **1898** *Atlantic Monthly* LXXXII. 499/2 It was a wonder of beauty,..the fairest piece of earth my eye ever rested upon. **1931** W. S. Churchill in *Hansard Commons* 28 Jan. 1022, I remember, when I was a child, being taken to the celebrated Barnum's Circus... The exhibit on the programme which I most desired to see was the one described as 'The Boneless Wonder'. My parents judged that that spectacle would be too revolting and demoralising for my youthful eyes, and I have waited 50 years to see the boneless wonder sitting on the Treasury Bench. **1946** Boy wonder [see Chattertonian *a.* and *sb.*]. **1951** 'J. Tey' *Daughter of Time* xiv. 186 The spectacle of Dr. Gairdner trying to make his facts fit his theory was the most entertaining thing in gymnastics that Grant had witnessed... As a contortionist Dr. Gairdner was the original boneless wonder. **1963** *Guardian* 15 Feb. 20/6 One of those boneless wonders that go by the name of 'Observer' editorials. **1967** M. Shulman *Kill 3* IV. ii. 168 Reconciling more contradictory positions than could be broken up by a boneless wonder on a trapeze.

e. *U.S.* A kind of cake; = cruller.

1848 Drake *Pioneer Life in Kentucky* (1870) 97 Other dainties awaited us as the result of killing hogs. They were 'dough-nuts' and 'wonders'. **1859** Mrs. Stowe *Minister's Wooing* iv. 34 A plate of crullers or wonders, as a sort of sweet fried cake was commonly called.

2. a. A deed performed or an event brought about by miraculous or supernatural power; a miracle. ***to do*** or ***work wonders***, to perform miracles. *arch.*

c **950** *Lindisf. Gosp.* John ii. 11 Ðis uorhte frumma ðara uundra se hælend in ðær byriȝ. **971** *Blickl. Hom.* 15 Eal þæt folc þe þis wundor ȝeseah, his noman myccledon. *c* **1200** Ormin 9499 Crist..wrohhte wunndre miccle ma þann icc ȝuw maȝȝ nu tellenn. *c* **1275** *Passion our Lord* 60 in *O.E. Misc.* 39 Hi seyden..Alle his wndres þat he doþ is þurch þene vend. **1387** Trevisa *Higden* (Rolls) III. 125 By wycchecraft he schal wirche wondres. *c* **1400** Maundev. (Roxb.) xi. 43 With þat ilke ȝerde Moyses..didd many wonders. *c* **1450** Holland *Howlat* 785 He couth werk wounderis quhat way that he wald. **1526** *Pilgr. Perf.* (W. de W. 1531) 3 For they se hym in his great myracles & wonders. **1562** Winȝet *Cert. Tractatis* ii. Wks. (S.T.S.) I. 17 He send His Apostolis and seuinty-twa Discipulis..geuand thaim also power to wyrk wounderis. **1591** Shaks. *1 Hen. VI*, v. iv. 48 You iudge it straight a thing impossible To compasse Wonders, but by helpe of diuels. **1662** Stillingfl. *Orig. Sacræ* II. iii. §6 That doctrine which was confirmed by undoubted miracles, hath assured us of the coming of lying wonders. **1781** Cowper *Expost.* 155 They saw distemper heal'd, and life restor'd,..Confess'd the wonder. **1846** Trench *Mirac.* 6 The healing of the paralytic..was a wonder, for 'they were all amazed'.

†**b.** An extraordinary natural occurrence, esp. when regarded as supernatural or taken as an omen or portent. Chiefly *pl. Obs.*

1297 R. Glouc. (Rolls) 8612 Wanne me sede him of suche wondres þat god on erþe sende Þat it was vor is luþernesse to trufle he it wende. **1340** Hampole *Pr. Consc.* 4004 For wonders þat shuld falle, als I trow, Agayn þe worldes hende er sene now. *c* **1400** *Destr. Troy* 11827 When he wist of thies wondres, thies wordes he said: 'Yonder towne wilbe takon in a tyme short.' **1513** Douglas *Æneis* VIII. viii. 36 We haue bot sobir pissance, and no wonder, To help in battale. **1560** Daus tr. *Sleidane's Comm.* 422 He rekened vp the wonders that went before his death. **1596** Dalrymple tr. *Leslie's Hist. Scot.* (S.T.S.) I. 13 Mony sygnes be God war schawne and wonndiris. **1655** Stanley *Hist. Philos.* II. iii. (1687) 66/1 Of the Wonder [*sc.* a meteor] Aristotle gives a very slight account. **1681** Dryden *Abs. & Achit.* I. 320 My Father Governs with unquestion'd Right;..And Heav'n by Wonders has espous'd his Cause.

3. A marvellous act or achievement. ***to work, do,*** or ***perform wonders***: to do marvellous acts or bring about marvellous results; hence *gen.* to do surprising things.

c **1220** *Bestiary* 398 Listneð nu a wunder, Ðat tis der [*sc.* the fox] doð for hunger. **1390** Gower *Conf.* I. 5 This bok schal afterward ben ended Of love, which doth many a wonder. *Ibid.* 136 With strengthe he [*sc.* Nebuchadnezzar] putte kinges under, And wroghte of Pride many a wonder. **1471** Caxton *Recuyell* (Sommer) 378 In this bataill hercules dide wondres & meruailles. **1591** Shaks. *1 Hen. VI*, I. i. 122 Where valiant Talbot..Enacted wonders with his Sword and Lance. **1660** F. Brooke tr. *Le Blanc's Trav.* 295 Don Sebastian did wonders in his own person, but overpowred with number, he [etc.]. **1727** E. Laurence *Duty of Steward* 207 Lay on Twenty Loads of Chalk alone upon an Acre, and it will perform wonders. **1731** in *10th Rep. Hist. MSS. Comm.* App. I. 270 The Millypedes or Wood-lice have a sulphureous spirit in them w[ch] I have known do wonders on weak constitutions. **1784** Cowper *Tiroc.* 23 For her the fancy, roving unconfin'd,..Works magic wonders. **1784** —— *Task* IV. 87 Katterfelto, with his hair on end At his own wonders. **1827** Disraeli *Viv. Grey* v. vi, Inspired by your Ladyship's approbation, my steward has really done wonders. **1834** L. Ritchie *Wand. Seine* 192 Habit effects wonders.

4. a. *gen.* An astonishing occurrence, event, or fact; a surprising incident; a wonderful thing.

to hear, read, speak, talk wonders, to hear, etc., surprising accounts.

1297 R. Glouc. (Rolls) 319 A temple hii vovnde vair inou & a maumet amidde Þat ofte tolde wonder gret & ȝwat men bitidde. **1390** Gower *Conf.* II. 67 Who that wolde ensample take..Of many a wondre hiere he mihte. **1398** Trevisa *Barth. De P.R.* XVI. xlviii. (1495) L iij b/1 Gete..is kyndled in water and quenchid in oyle: and that is wonder. *a* **1425** *Cursor M.* 11 (Trin.) Man ȝernen..romaunce rede..Of kyng Arthour..Of wondris þat his knyȝtes felle. **1553** T. Wilson *Rhet.* 47b, I ought..not turne my tale to talke of Robbyn Hoode,..or to speake wounders of the man in the Mone. **1598** Shaks. *Merry W.* v. i. 13 Bee you in the Parke about midnight, at Hernes-Oake, and you shall see wonders.

1604 E. G[RIMSTONE] tr. *D'Acosta's Hist. Indies* III. xvi. 171 Some of these Lakes be very hote, which is another wonder. 1611 BEAUM. & FL. *Philaster* II. i, The love of boyes unto their Lords is strange, I have read wonders of it. 1686 tr. *Chardin's Trav. Persia* 136 They talk Wonders of her Beauty. 1784 COWPER *Task* IV. 563 The chilling tale Of midnight murder was a wonder..told to frighten babes. 1823 SCOTT *Quentin D.* xix, Why should you make a wonder of my wearing the badge of my company? 1890 HARTLAND *Science of Fairy Tales* i. (1891) 1 The weary hunters beguile the long silence of a desert night with the mirth and wonders of a tale.

†**b.** app. = MIRACLE *sb.* 4. *Obs.*

1435 MISYN *Fire of Love* 5 Nozt standyng in ydilnes, nor to plays no wondyrs rynnynge.

†**5. a.** Evil or shameful action; evil; *pl.* evil or horrible deeds. *Obs.*

1154 *O.E. Chron.* (Laud MS.) an. 1137, I ne can ne i ne mai tellen alle þe wunder ne alle þe pines ðæt hi diden wrecce men on þis land. *c*1200 *Vices & Virtues* 15 Ic ne mai rimen ..alle ðo sennes,..ne alle ðo wundren ðe ich, wrecche senfulle, habbe idon. *a*1225 *Ancr. R.* 72 Moni mon weneð to don wel þat he deð alto cweade [*MS. C.* wunder]. *c*1250 *Gen. & Ex.* 69 Pride made angel deuel dwale, Ðat made.. euerilc wunder, and euerilc wo. *Ibid.* 3588. *a*1300 *K. Horn* 1440 (Cott.) Fykenild me haþ gon vnder Ant do rymenild sum wonder.

†**b.** Destruction, disaster. *Obs.*

*c*1205 LAY. 7855 Þa scipen wenden to wundre oðer half hundred. *Ibid.* 12590 Heo slozen þer muchel wunder, twa & fifti hundred. 13.. *Gaw. & Gr. Knt.* 16 Bretayn..Where werre, & wrake, & wonder Bi syþez has wont þer-inne.

†**c.** Great distress or grief. *Obs.*

1303 R. BRUNNE *Handl. Synne* 5262 Yn þe put..He sagh so moche sorowe and wundyr, Of fendes fele þat þere wore. ?*c*1430 *Syr Tryam.* 190 (Percy Fo.), Of this..I haue great wonder; for sorrow my hart will breake assunder. *a*1600 *Northumberland Betrayed by Douglas* ii. in Child *Ball.* III. 411 As woe and wonder be them amonge!

6. Phraseological uses. †**a.** ***to wonder***: dreadfully, horribly, terribly. (Cf. sense 5.) *Obs.*

*c*1000 ÆLFRIC *Saints' Lives* xxiii. 654 Ealle men hine fram stowe to stowe brudon and to wundre tawedon. *c*1230 *Hali Meid.* (1922) 23 Leccherie seið 'schome þe menske of þi meidenhad,' & tukeð hire to wundre [*v.r.* al to wundre]. *a*1300 *Cursor M.* 22606 Heuen he sal se part in sundre, And he sal here it cri to wonder.

b. ***to a wonder***, in early use also †***to wonder*** [after F. *à merveille*], marvellously, wonderfully, marvellously well. *Obs.* or *arch.*

1661 GLANVILL *Van. Dogm.* 175 The unparallel'd Des-Cartes hath unridled their dark Physiology, and to wonder solv'd their Motions. 1698 CROWNE *Caligula* IV, Y'are to a wonder fair. *a*1700 EVELYN *Diary* 27 Jan. 1658, Sentences in Latin and Greeke, which on occasion he would produce even to wonder. 1751 *Female Foundling* II. 11 He is better to a Wonder. 1792 COWPER *Let. to Carwardine* 11 June, His motives were not, nor could be, of the amorous kind, for she was ugly to a wonder. 1828 LYTTON *Pelham* xxxi, I have flattered him to a wonder! 1843 THACKERAY *Mr. & Mrs. Berry* ii, He ties his white neckcloth to a wonder.

†**c.** ***to think wonder*** [THINK *v.*[1]] (const. dative of person): to seem a matter of astonishment (to); hence, of the person, to be astonished, to marvel, wonder. So, rarely, ***to think it wonder***, [THINK *v.*[2]] to be amazed at it. *Obs.*

971 *Blickl. Hom.* 33 Þonne ne þincþ us þæt nan wundor. *c*1000 ÆLFRIC *Hom.* II. 484 Wundor me ðincð eower ðingræden. *c*1200 ORMIN 218 All þe follc..þuhhte mikell wunnderr forrwhi þe preost swa lannge wass..att Godess allterr. *a*1225 *Ancr. R.* 8 Ʒif him þuncheð wunder & selkuð of swuch onswere. 1340 HAMPOLE *Pr. Consc.* 1786 Of þe dede here men may thynk wonder, For alle thyng it brestes in sonder. 1362 LANGL. *P. Pl.* A. III. 176 Whi þou wraþþest þe now wonder me þinkeþ. *a*1586 MONTGOMERIE *Misc. Poems* xl. 54 Quhat Natur works, we may not think it wonder.

d. ***it*** (or †***that***) ***is*** (***was, were,*** etc.) ***no wonder***: it is (etc.) not surprising; usually with dependent *that-* or *if-*clause. Similarly, ***it is*** †***great, little, small wonder***, it is very, not very surprising; ***it is*** (***a***) ***wonder, wonder it is***, it is wonderful.

† ***a wonder is to speak***, it is surprising to tell.. † ***make it no wonder***, do not be surprised at it.

*a*900 CYNEWULF *Crist* 1016 Forþon nis ænig wundor hu him woruldmonna seo unclæne gecynd cearum sorgende hearde ondrede. *c*1175 *Lamb. Hom.* 23 Hit nis nan wunder þah mon suneʒie oðer hwile unwaldes, ah hit is muchele mare wunder ʒif he nule nefre swiken. *c*1200 ORMIN 9327 & tatt nass wunnderr þwerrt ut nan þatt he wass wis o lare. 1297 R. GLOUC. (Rolls) 378, & lute wonder it was þat strange men in is owe lond dude a such trespas. 13.. *Cursor M.* 746 (Gött.) Wonþer was hu he þider wan. *c*1320 *Sir Tristr.* 2215 Sore him greued his vene, As it no wonder nes. 1362 LANGL. *P. Pl.* A. V. 102 Ʒif schrift schulde hit þenne swopen out, a gret wonder hit were. 1390 GOWER *Conf.* III. 382 Though god his grace caste aweie No wondir is. *a*1400–50 *Wars Alex.* 811 Þare slike wirschip he wan ware wonder to tell. *c*1400 *Brut* I. 1 Þere þey lyved in ioy and merthe y-now, that it was wonder to wete. *c*1520 SKELTON *Magnyf.* 85 And it is wonder that your wylde Insolence Can be content with Measure presence. *c*1540 tr. *Pol. Verg. Engl. Hist.* (Camden No. 29) 50 He went.. to the duke of Bedforde, whose arrivall, a wonder is to speake, how much it encouraged his owne frendes. *c*1560 A. SCOTT *Poems* (S.T.S.) ii. 167 For he affeird, it wes na winder, His cursour suld him cast. 1579 W. FULKE *Heskins' Parl.* 168 It was a woonder, howe the corporall nature passed through the impenetrable body. 1596 SHAKS. *Tam. Shr.* III. ii. 193, I must away to day before night come, Make it no wonder. 1600 E. BLOUNT tr. *Conestaggio* 268 It was therefore no woonder, if without the kings consent..he attempted many things. 1651 HOBBES *Leviath.* III. xxxv. 219 It were a wonder there is no greater notice taken of it. 1673 *Vinegar & Mustard* (1873) 19 That's a wonder you have none of your trollops with you. 1706 E. WARD *Wooden World Diss.* (1708) 100 If he has a Reversion clear of Incumbrances, it's a Wonder. 1741 WARBURTON *Div. Legat.* VI. vi. II. 639 It is no Wonder his Arguments should look asquint. 1749 FIELDING *Tom Jones* III. iv, 'No Man is wise at all Hours'; it is therefore no Wonder that a Boy is not so. 1860 THACKERAY *Lovel* ii, You consume more tea than all my family,..and as much sugar and butter—well, it's no wonder you are bilious!

e. Without verb, esp. in ***no wonder that, if,*** or ***though***; similarly, ***small wonder that*** (etc.), ***what wonder if..?*** Also interjectionally in (***and***) ***no wonder!, and what wonder!***

Cf. L. *nimirum*, Gr. *οὐ θαῦμα, θαῦμα οὐδέν.*

1390 GOWER *Conf.* I. 100 No wonder thogh he siketh ofte. *a*1400 *Pistill of Susan* 201 And heo wepte for wo, no wonder, I wene. *c*1400 T. CHESTRE *Launfal* 204 No wonther dough me smerte. *c*1440 *Promp. Parv.* 360/1 Nowundyr, (*P.* nowonder), *nimirum.* 1513 DOUGLAS *Æneis* III. viii. 103 Na wondir, this is the selcouth Caribdis. 1611 SHAKS. *Cymb.* III. vi. 11 Will poore Folkes lye..? Yes; no wonder, When Rich ones scarse tell true. 1667 MILTON *P.L.* III. 606 What wonder then if fields and regions here Breathe forth Elixir pure. 1795–6 WORDSW. *Borderers* II. 812 *Her.* I was alarmed. *Mar.* No wonder; this is a place That well may put some fears into *your* heart. 1853 DICKENS *Bleak Ho.* iv, Pa's miserable, and no wonder! 1862 H. KINGSLEY *Ravenshoe* xviii, She has given her honest little heart away—and what wonder! 1891 FARRAR *Darkn. & Dawn* xxxix, No wonder Nero loves her better than that pale sad lady who sits among the six Vestals. 1913 H. L. JACKSON *Eschatol. Jesus* 6 If 'the great authorities differ' small wonder that weaker minds are in doubt.

f. ***the wonder is..***, what is surprising is...

1605 SHAKS. *Lear* V. iii. 316 *Edg.* He is gon indeed. *Kent.* The wonder is, he hath endur'd so long. 1842 DICKENS *Amer. Notes* xi, The wonder is, not that there should be so many fatal accidents, but that any journey should be safely made. 1856 MISS YONGE *Daisy Chain* I. iv, The only wonder was, that it had not happened sooner.

g. ***for a wonder***: as an instance of a surprising fact; strange to say.

1782 BOSWELL *Jrnl.* 16 July in *Boswell, Laird of Auchinleck* (1977) 456 While she was out, my father and Lady Auchinleck called, for a wonder. 1811 PRINCESS CHARLOTTE *Let.* 13 Nov. (1949) 12 Soon for a wonder I plucked up courage & went in. 1856 READE *Never too Late* xxxvi, For a wonder he was not sea-sick. 1881 SAINTSBURY *Dryden* vii. 145 For a wonder Dryden resists..his unhappy tendency to exaggerate the coarseness of his subjects.

h. ***in the name of wonder***: used with an interrogative word to give emphasis to a question; also *colloq.* or *dial.* shortened to ***the wonder***.

1626 MASSINGER *Roman Actor* IV. ii, In the name of wonder, What's Cæsar's purpose? 1716 ADDISON *Freeholder* No. 9 ¶12 What in the name of wonder do you mean? 1862 MRS. H. WOOD *Mrs. Hallib.* xxxv, How the wonder do you manage it? 1889 R. BRIDGES *Feast of Bacchus* III. 814 Who in the name of wonder are these queer foreigners?

i. ***wonders will never cease***: that is indeed surprising; now freq. *ironic.*

1828 T. CREEVEY *Let.* 11 Feb. in *Creevey's Life & Times* (1934) xii. 258 Off he went with, 'Well, Creevey, wonders will never cease!' I met Lord Bathurst at the Duke of Buccleuch's [etc.]. 1837 DICKENS *Pickwick Papers* xlv. 489 Vonders vill never cease... I'm wery much mistaken if that 'ere Jingle worn't a doin' somethin' in the vater-cart vay! 1902 CONRAD *Typhoon* xxiv. 191 'Solomon says wonders will never cease,' cried Mrs. Rout joyously. 1962 M. SUMMERTON *Nightingale at Noon* (1963) viii. 105, I offered: I'll help you...' She..gave me a cheeky grin. 'Hear that! Wonders will never cease!' 1974 A. PRICE *Other Paths to Glory* I. vii. 88 Wonders will never cease... Early Tudor —practically untouched.

II. 7. a. The emotion excited by the perception of something novel and unexpected, or inexplicable; astonishment mingled with perplexity or bewildered curiosity. Also, the state of mind in which this emotion exists; †an instance of this, a fit of wonderment.

*c*1290 *St. Dunstan* 8 in *S. Eng. Leg.* 19 Þat folk stod al in gret wonder. 1382 WYCLIF *Luke* v. 26 And greet wondir took alle men, and thei magnyfieden God. *c*1450 *Mirk's Festial* 18 When Thomas had soo ydo, anon he criet for wondyr and for fere. 1561 HOBY tr. *Castiglione's Courtyer* II. (1577) K vij b, Then he turning about, and beholding him.. with a wonder [orig. *con marauiglia*] stayed a while wythout any word. 1599 SHAKS. *Hen. V*, II. iv. 135 You'le find a diff'rence, As we his Subiects haue in wonder found. 1611 *Bible* Acts iii. 10 They were filled with wonder and amazement at that which had happened vnto him. 1659 *Vulg. Err. Cens.* 31 Galen was husht into a wonder by some anatomicall observations. 1667 MILTON *P.L.* III. 542 Satan ..Looks down with wonder at the sudden view Of all this World at once. *a*1700 EVELYN *Diary* 23 Nov. 1690, Lord Godolphin, now resuming the commission of the Treasury to the wonder of all his friends. 1738 GRAY *Tasso* 25 Fix'd in wonder stood the warlike pair. 1770 GOLDSM. *Des. Vill.* 215 And still they gazed, and still the wonder grew, That one small head could carry all he knew. 1814 CARY *Dante, Parad.* XXXI. 31 The grim brood..Stood in mute wonder 'mid the works of Rome. 1848 THACKERAY *Van. Fair* lxv, Max and Fritz were at the door listening with wonder to Mrs. Becky's sobs and cries. 1870 LOWELL *Among my Books* Ser. I. 143 The faculty of wonder is not defunct, but is only getting more and more emancipated from the unnatural service of terror.

†**b.** ***to have wonder***, to be greatly surprised; to marvel: = WONDER *v.* 1, 2. *Obs.*

*a*1300 *Cursor M.* 17288 + 171 It was our lordez ordinans, for-þi no wonder has. 1375 BARBOUR *Bruce* III. 485 And quhen he hard sa blaw & cry, He had wondir quhat it mycht be. *c*1375 *Sc. Leg. Saints* x. (*Mathou*) 121 All þat harde hyme, ʒald or ʒynge, Had wondyre þat sik grace suld be In ony manne. 1470–85 MALORY *Arthur* I. xiv. 55 Thenne syre Arthur dyd so merueillously in armes that all men had wondyr. 1500–20 DUNBAR *Poems* lxxxi. 37 Thay saw that I nocht glaidder wax of cheir, And thairof had thai winder.

†**c.** Profound admiration. *Obs.*

*a*1586 SIDNEY *Apol. Poetry* (Arb.) 19 To so vnbeleeued a poynt hee proceeded, as that no earthly thing bred such wonder to a Prince, as to be a good horseman. 1588 SHAKS. *L.L.L.* IV. ii. 117 All ignorant that soule, that sees thee without wonder. 1605 —— *Macb.* I. iii. 92 His Wonders and his Prayses doe contend, Which should be thine, or his. 1607 BP. HALL *Holy Observ.* I. xx. (1609) 32 No man hath beene so exquisite, but some haue detracted from him, euen in those quallities which haue seemed most worthy of wonder to others.

8. [f. WONDER *v.* 2.] A state of wondering (*whether*, etc.). *rare.*

1853 MRS. GASKELL *Ruth* xix, Many profound secrets.. most of which related to their wonders if Jemima and Mr. Farquhar would ever be married. 1889 'J. S. WINTER' *Mrs. Bob* iv. (1891) 45 Haunted by..a wonder whether he would find his way to St. Eve's.

III. *attrib.* and *Comb.*

9. Simple attrib. (sometimes passing into adj.). **a.** = 'that is a wonder, marvel, or prodigy', as ***wonder-avenue, -beauty, boy, -child*** (after G. *wunderkind*), ***drug, -flower, -gleam, goal, -horse, -look, -night, -sight*** (after G. *wundergesicht*), ***-treasure, -woman.***

1838 LONGF. in *Life* (1891) I. 293 The great wonder-flowers bloom but once in a lifetime; as marriage and death. 1845 J. C. MANGAN *German Anthol.* I. 185 But, lo! a wonder-sight!—Ere long Rose, blooming,.. The fairest lily ever seen. 1866 HOWELLS *Venetian Life* viii. 120 That wonder-avenue of palaces [the Grand Canal]. 1890 'R. BOLDREWOOD' *Miner's Right* xli, You..discover so many wonder-treasures..that you will never consent to return. 1890 —— *Col. Reformer* xviii, A Pharos, a wonder-sign, an exemplar throughout all the civilised world. 1896 *Catholic Mag.* May 258 Hermann Cohen, by reason of his marvellous piano-playing, was looked upon as a 'wonder-child'. 1921 D. H. LAWRENCE *Sea & Sardinia* v. 210 Real fresh wonder-beauty all around. 1922 —— *Aaron's Rod* xviii. 269 The glimmer of the open flower, the wonder-look, still lasted. 1927 E. O'NEILL *Marco Millions* III. i. 167 Worth while your waiting, eh?.. Yes, my wonder boy! 1927 A. CONAN DOYLE *Case-Bk. Sherlock Holmes* 15 A wonder-woman in every way. 1929 R. BRIDGES *Test. Beauty* IV. 188 The shifting hues that sanctify the silent dawn with wonder-gleams. 1938 *Encycl. Brit. Bk. of Year* 38/2 The one signed work in the series..was the wonder-child of the project. 1939 *Time* 14 Aug. 50/2 Sulfanilamide, the 'wonder drug', introduced into the U.S. in 1936, is credited with remarkable cures. 1939 Wonder horse [see SECOND-GUESSER]. 1939 JOYCE *Finnegans Wake* 395 You know her, our angel being, one of romance's fadeless wonderwomen. 1948 Wonder drug [see SUBTILIN]. 1958 P. SCOTT *Mark of Warrior* I. 82 Old Ramsay's something of a wonder boy. He'll be top cadet of the course. 1975 *Daily Tel.* 18 June 2/8 Experts..began work on the vaccines following the failure of the post-war 'wonder drugs' such as sulphonamides and penicillin to wipe out these two diseases. 1976 *West Lancs. Evening Gaz.* 15 Dec. I. 4/7 He scored a superb hat trick with a wonder goal to round it off. 1976 *Liverpool Echo* 23 Nov. 7/1 Southport's golden sands, world famous as the training track of wonderhorse Red Rum. 1980 'R. B. DOMINIC' *Attending Physician* xiv. 117 Senator Gerald Ewell was a Democrat... 'What's Wonder Boy done this time?' demanded Tony. 1980 I. HUNTER *Malcolm Muggeridge* iv. 59 Various bizarre proposals to sort out and rearrange our genes so that everyone will become superman and wonderwoman. 1985 *Times* 2 Jan. 15/2 The word from the market is that a replacement 'wonder drug' is now in clinical trials.

b. = 'of wonder or wonders', as ***wonder-book, -city, -life, -literature, song, -story, -tale, -world*** (cf. G. *wunderwelt*).

1851 HAWTHORNE (*title*) A Wonder-Book for Girls and Boys, (including 'Tanglewood Tales'). 1851 H. MELVILLE *Whale* i. 7 The great flood-gates of the wonder-world swung open. 1854 *Zoologist* XII. 4487 A kind of wonder-story in zoology. 1865 TYLOR *Early Hist. Man.* vi. 144 The native wonder-tales must only be told in the winter. 1881 —— *Anthropol.* 380 It is known to be only a version of the.. wonder-tale told by Herodotus. 1895 KIPLING *Seven Seas* (1896) 84 The everlasting Wonder Song of Youth! 1896 *Tablet* 15 Feb. 257 That Asiatic wonder-world, the Indian Empire. 1896 J. DAVIDSON *Fleet St. Ecl.* Ser. II. 78 To wonder-worlds of old romance Our aching thoughts for solace run. 1905 ROOSEVELT *Outdoor Pastimes* xi. 339 To read and enjoy the wonder-book of nature. 1907 *Westm. Gaz.* 14 Sept. 6/2 All our wonder-literature. *Ibid.* 20 Sept. 2/1 Everything in that wonder-city [*sc.* Fez] was so like a half-remembered dream. 1929 R. BRIDGES *Test. Beauty* III. 105 With what other numberless wonder-lives of the Saints they wrote.

c. = 'miraculous, magic, magical', as ***wonder-offspring, -staff*** (cf. G. *wunderstab* magic wand), ***-stroke.***

1846 TRENCH *Mirac.* Introd. iv. §3. 46 By a mighty wonder-stroke of grace the polarity in the man is shifted. *Ibid.* xxix. 421 *note*, Sometimes [in early Christian art] he [*sc.* Jesus] is touching with his wonder-staff the head of Lazarus. 1907 *N. & Q.* 10th Ser. VIII. 208/2 The belief in such wonder-offspring was once as common in Europe.

10. a. Objective and obj. genitive, as ***wonder-bearing, -exciting, -hiding, -loving, -promising, -raising, -seeking, -stirring, -writing*** adjs.; †***wonders-doing*** adj.; ***wonder-hider, -seeker; wonder-worth, -worthy*** adjs; instrumental, as ***wonder-dumb, -fed, -ridden, -smit, -stricken, -struck,*** †***-strucken, -wide, -wounded*** adjs.; ***wonder-beaming, -striking, -teeming, -waiting*** adjs.; †***wonder-rap*** [RAP *v.*[3]], ***-strike*** vbs.

1799 CAMPBELL *Pleas. Hope* I. 130 Wilt thou, with him [*sc.* Newton],..watch the shrine with *wonder-beaming eye?

1552 HULOET, *Wonders doynge, *mirificus*. **1898** HARDY *Wessex Poems* 167 Shy birds stood Watching us, *wonder-dumb. **1855** MILMAN *Lat. Christ.* XIV. ii. (1864) IX. 77 This *wonder-fed and wonder-seeking worship. **1831** CARLYLE *Sart. Res.* III. viii, The deceptions, and *wonder-hiding stupefactions, which Space practises on us. **1851** *Zoologist* IX. 3167 The *wonder-loving and credulous Northmen. **1817** COLERIDGE *Biog. Lit.* viii. (Bohn) 64 The *wonder-promising Matter, that was to perform all these marvels. **1813** —— *Remorse* Epil. 28 Saintly hermits' *wonder-raising acts. **1612** J. DAVIES *Muses Sacrif.* Wks. (Grosart) II. 27/2 O sight of force to *wonder-rap all Eyes! **1791** COWPER *Odyssey* VI. 199 *Wonder-rapt I gaze. **1916** D. H. LAWRENCE *Amores* 76, I see each shadow start with recognition, and I Am *wonder-ridden. **1599** T. M[OUFET] *Silkwormes* 53 Then list a while, you *wonder-seekers great. **1856** FROUDE *Hist. Eng.* I. iv. 296 The phenomena known to modern wonder-seekers as those of somnambulism or clairvoyance. **1855** *Wonder-seeking [see *wonder-fed*]. **1615** SYLVESTER *Job Triumph.* III. 99 Therefore, before Him, am I *wonder-smit. **1799** *Cupid & Psyche* 33 He'll tell the *wonder-stirring tales. **1818** SHELLEY *Laon & Cythna* V. xliii. 114 The morning's golden mist, Which now the *wonder-stricken breezes kist With their cold lips, fled. **1855** SINGLETON *Virgil* I. 51 At whose lay wonder-stricken were the pards. **1856** HAWTHORNE *Engl. Note-bks.* (1870) II. 65 The..mysterious plan which perplexes and *wonder-strikes me in most cathedrals. **1644** VICARS *God in Mount* 4 The memorable and *wonder-striking Parliamentarie-mercies. **1598** SYLVESTER *Du Bartas* II. ii. I. *Noah* 597 Ashamed, *wonder-strook. **1638–56** COWLEY *Davideis* IV. 855 If wonder-strook I at your words appear, My wonder yet is Innocent of Fear. **1796** MME. D'ARBLAY *Camilla* II. xiii, [She] seemed wonder-struck, without knowing why. **1817** MALTHUS *Popul.* II. 210 Great and astonishing as this difference is, we ought not to be so wonder-struck at it. **1628** MURE *Doomesday* 562 *Wonder-strucken wights. **1798** SOUTHEY *Blenheim* v, With *wonder-waiting eyes. **1922** JOYCE *Ulysses* 530 Milly Bloom..calls, her young eyes *wonderwide. **1864** BROWNING *Dram. Pers.*, *Abt Vogler* 44 Had I painted the whole, Why, there it had stood, to see, nor the process so *wonder-worth. **1622** MIDDLETON *Honour & Virtue* Wks. (Bullen) VII. 361 Which is not the least *wonder-worthy note. **1905** G. BLOUNT *Rustic Renaiss.* i. 10 [This] is in itself a wonder-worthy paradox. **1602** SHAKS. *Ham.* V. i. 280 Like *wonder-wounded hearers. **1603** in J. Davies *Microcosmos* Wks. (Grosart) I. 103/1 His *wonder-writing Hand.

b. advb., = 'wonderfully'. (After G. *wundergross*, *wunderschön*, etc.; cf. WONDER *adv.*) ***wonder-fine***.

1872 J. PAYNE *Songs Life & Death* 214 Oh, wonder-lovely maidens were the seven! **1903** *Westm. Gaz.* 14 Feb. 2/1 Oh, how wonder-beautiful! **1904** *Ibid.* 12 Feb. 2/3 Delicate wonder-white crystals. **1929** R. BRIDGES *Test. Beauty* I. 29 Not to these look we with grateful pleasur or satisfaction of soul, wonder-fine tho' they be.

11. Special comb.: **wonder-bag**, a Negro amulet, = OBEAH I; **wonder-horn**, (*a*) a cornucopia of marvels; (*b*) a magical horn; **wonder-man**, a wonder-worker; also in weakened sense, a man whose achievements are admired; † **wonder-master**, a magician; † **wonder-maze** *v. intr.* and *trans.*, to be amazed, or to amaze, with wonder; **wonder rabbi**, in the Chasidic movement, a TSADDIK; **Wonder State** *U.S.*, a nickname for the state of Arkansas.

1793 WOLCOT (P. Pindar) *Ep. the Pope* Wks. 1812 III. 209 Quako..full of negro faith in conjuration, Loaded his jackass deep with *wonder-bags Of Monkeys' teeth, glass, horsehair, and red rags. **1864** LOWELL *Fireside Trav.* 178 Their world was a huge *wonder-horn. **1906** *Edin. Rev.* Jan. 231 Was it that the wonder-horn was still echoing from the far-off, summoning the man..to the soul-roads? **1883** STALLYBRASS tr. *Grimm's Teut. Mythol.* III. 1232 He was the greatest magician or *wonder-man of them all. **1901** *Daily News* 9 Feb. 6/1 Cornelius Drebbel, 'the wonder-man of Alkmaar'. **1933** *Amer. Speech* VIII. III. 39/2 *Wonderman*. Foreign fighters are often thus described [by sports writers]. **1935** WODEHOUSE *Luck of Bodkins* xv. 173 They get the idea that they are sort of wonder-men who can just look around and find talent where nobody else would suspect it. **1961** *Catholic Herald* 23 June 3/1 (*heading*) De Gaulle, hero and wonderman. **1962** A. SAMPSON *Anat. of Britain* xxvii. 450 In Whitehall he had the reputation of a wonderman, and had even been tipped by some as an eventual head of the Treasury. **1603** HARSNET *Pop. Impost.* 57 This foule *wonder-maister is too full of wonders euer to be good. **1603** in J. Davies *Microcosmos* Wks. (Grosart) I. 7/2 Men did *wonder-maze, Which wonderment, this later worke of thine (Not by detracting from it) doth deface. *a* **1618** J. DAVIES *Wit's Pilgr.* ibid. II. 51/1 Hee taught..Rights Ruines to repaire..with Words, that wonder-mazed men. **1907** I. ZANGWILL *Ghetto Comedies* 409 We *Chassidim* have no fear. Our *wonder-rabbi has power over all the spheres. **1970** C. KERSH *Aggravations of Minnie Ashe* i. 11 [Her] father had been a wonder rabbi in some obscure Jewish village in Galicia—a worker of miracles. **1923** *Gen. Acts Arkansas* 804 Be It Resolved by the Senate of the State of Arkansas... That hereafter Arkansas shall be known and styled 'The *Wonder State'.

† **'wonder**, *a. Obs.* Forms: see prec. [repr. OE. *wundor* WONDER *sb.* in compounds, as *wundorcræft* marvellous skill or power, *wundordǽd* miracle, *wundortácen* wondrous sign, miracle, prodigy (so OS. *wundarquâla* extreme torment, OHG. *wuntarsiht* 'spectaculum', MHG., G. *wundertat* miracle, ON. *undrsjón* spectacle, etc.; see also WONDER THING); cf. the similar origin of MAIN *a.*, and see WONDERS *a.*] Wonderful, wondrous, marvellous. ***on*** or ***in*** (***a***) ***wonder wise***, wonderfully (cf. MLG. *wunderwîs*(*e* adv.). See also WONDER THING, WONDER-WORK.

a **1175** *Cott. Hom.* 235 He cweð a wunder word to þar sawle bi þa witie ysaiam. *c* **1205** LAY. 1147 Heo dude wnder craftes. **1297** R. GLOUC. (Rolls) 6919 þat folc com þikke amorwe to se þis wonder dede. *Ibid.* 8593 þe sixte ȝer þer com also a wel wonder cas. *c* **1350** *Will. Palerne* 1873 So wonder a wilde best þat weldes no mynde. **13..** *E.E. Allit. P.* A. 1095 So sodanly on a wonder wyse, I was war of a prosessyoun. *c* **1374** CHAUCER *Troylus* I. 419 Allas what is þis wonder maladye. *c* **1382** *Pol. Poems* (Rolls) I. 250 This warnynges beoth wonder and feole. **1393** LANGL. *P. Pl.* C. II. 126 In wonderwyse holy wryt tellith how þei fullen. *a* **1400** *Hymns Virg.* (1895) 46 Wiyn of watir he makiþ blyue, And dooþ manye a wondir dede. *c* **1425** *Engl. Conq. Irel.* 130 About that tyme, befel a wonder aduentur yn a wodde of Myth. *c* **1425** *Seven Sag.* (P.) 2643 Thou schalt telle me of that cas; Hyt hys the wounderest that ever I herde. **1470–85** MALORY *Arthur* XVII. i. 689 He passed by a Castel where was a wonder turnement. *a* **1529** SKELTON *E. Rummyng* 73 With clothes vpon her hed..Wrythen in wonder wyse, After the Sarasyns gyse. **1535** COVERDALE *2 Chron.* xxxii. 24 And he prayed vnto the Lorde, which made him promes, and gaue him a wonder-token. *c* **1590** GREENE *Fr. Bacon* iv. 58 And, wonder Vandermast, welcome to me.

wonder ('wʌndə(r)), *v.* Forms: 1 **wundrian**, 3–4 **wondri**, 4–5 **woundre**, 4–6 **wondre**, **wondir**, (3 **wundren**, **wundre**, **wndre**, **wundrie**, **wondry**, *Orm.* **wunndrenn**, 4 **wondur**, 5 **wondyr**, **wundur**, **wunderon**, **wonderyn**), 5–6 **wunder**, **wounder**, **-ir**, 6–7 **woonder**, 4– **wonder**. [OE. *wundrian* = OS. *wundrôn*, (M)Du. *wonderen*, OHG. *wuntarôn* (MHG., G. *wundern*), ON. *undra* (Sw. *undra*, Da. *undre*): f. WONDER *sb.*]

1. *intr.* To feel or be affected with wonder; to be struck with surprise or astonishment, to marvel. Also *occas.* to express wonder in speech. **a.** in OE. const. genitive of the object of wonder, also with preps., now nearly always *at*, occas. *over*, formerly also *on*, *upon*, *of*.

c **888** ÆLFRED *Boeth.* xxxiv. §10, Hwa mæᵹ þæt he ne wundrie swelcra ᵹesceafta ures scyppendes? **971** *Blickl. Hom.* 33 Nis þæt to wundriᵹenne..þæt he acweald beon wolde. *Ibid.* 153 He ᵹehyrde heora þrowunga & he þa wundrode æfter þære ᵹesihþe. *a* **1000** *Phœnix* 331 Ðonne wundriað weras ofer eorþan wlite & wæstma. *c* **1000** *Ags. Gosp.* Mark vi. 2 Maneᵹe ᵹehyrdon & wundrodon on his lare. *c* **1200** ORMIN 7633 Josæp..& Marȝe..wundredenn baþe off all þatt hemm wass cwiddedd tære off Criste. *a* **1250** *Owl & Night* 228 þu fliȝst a niȝt and noȝt a-dai, þar-of ich wndri. *c* **1250** *Gen. & Ex.* 3716 Ȝetenisse men ben in ebron, Quilc men mai ȝet wundren on. **1297** R. GLOUC. (Rolls) 5353 In lepes & in coufles so moche viss hii ssolleþ hom bringe, þat ech mon ssal wondry of so gret cacchinge. *a* **1300** *Cursor M.* 18774 Godmen o galilee, apon quat thing sa wonder yee? *c* **1386** CHAUCER *Sqr.'s T.* 217 Somme of hem wondred on the Mirour..Hou men myghte in it swiche thynges se. *c* **1430** *Syr Gener.* (Roxb.) 7599 Mirabel wondred of hir woo, Whi hir ladie ferd soo. **1483** CAXTON *Gold. Leg.* 125 b/1 All the peple drewe to hym and wondred on hym. **1529** MORE *Dyaloge* x. 16 b/2 We nothyng wonder at the ebbyng and flowyng of the see. **1590** SHAKS. *Mids. N.* IV. i. 136, I wonder of this being heere together. *a* **1600** MONTGOMERIE *Misc. Poems* xxiv. 16 O, wareit be my weird, For wondring on a deitie divyne. **1667** MILTON *P.L.* IX. 856 Hast thou not wonderd, Adam, at my stay? **1753** RICHARDSON *Grandison* (1754) IV. 191, I wonder at you. **1780** COWPER *Progr. Err.* 191 Rufillus..Wonders at Clodio's follies, in a tone As tragical, as others at his own. **1818** J. W. CROKER *Jrnl.* 7 Dec. in *C. Papers* (1884) I. iv. 123, I cannot but wonder at her living here and bearding the Prince in a way so indelicate. **1844** EMERSON *Lect. New Eng. Ref.* Wks. (Bohn) I. 273 The unwise..wonders at what is unusual, the wise man wonders at the usual. **1919** B. CAPES *Skel. Key* xvii. 213 His benevolent truthfulness was a thing to wonder over.

b. with clause expressing the motive or object of wonder.

c **1000** *Ags. Gosp.* Luke i. 21 þæt folc wæs zachariam ᵹeanbidiende, & wundrodon þæt he on þam temple læt wæs. *c* **1386**, *c* **1430** [see a]. **1553** *Respublica* 602 Nowe I doe lesse woonder that lost men, life to save, Ferre from lande dooe Laboure againste the roring wave. **1596** DALRYMPLE tr. *Leslie's Hist. Scot.* (S.T.S.) I. 36 This causes men meruellouslie to wondir, that vndir that earth ar fund gret stokis..of wondirful akes and vthir tries. **1599** SHAKS. *Much Ado* I. i. 117, I wonder that you will still be talking, signior Benedicke, no body markes you. **1671** MILTON *Samson* 215, I oft have heard men wonder Why thou shouldst wed Philistian women rather Then of thine own Tribe fairer. **1676** in *12th Rep. Hist. MSS. Comm.* App. v. 33, I wonder my father would not ease himselfe from his Haddon inquietudes by staying at Belvoire. **1708** SWIFT *Bickerstaff Detected* 5 A Third Rogue tips me by the Elbow, and wonders how I have the Conscience to sneak abroad. **1846** GREENER *Sci. Gunnery* 133 We wonder the parties did not take a patent for the discovery. **1885** 'MRS. ALEXANDER' *At Bay* vii, I wonder he is not more confidential with you.

c. const. *to* with inf. (usually = *at* with gerund).

1604 E. G[RIMSTONE] tr. *D'Acosta's Hist. Indies* III. xix. 183 When wee goe..to the Indies, wee woonder to see the land so pleasant, greene and fresh. **1711** ADDISON *Spect.* No. 34 ¶4 He wondered to hear a Man of his Sense talk after that Manner. **1798** FERRIAR *Illustr. Sterne*, etc. 222 We cannot wonder to find a joint occasionally added to this part. **1840** THACKERAY *Pictorial Rhapsody* Concl., Wks. 1900 XIII. 354 The drawing is executed in a manner so loose and slovenly that one wonders to behold it.

d. in indirect passive (now only in ***to be wondered at*** as adj. or pred. phr.).

1532 MORE *Confut. Barnes* VIII. Wks. 741/2 He had so monstrouslye dressed himself because he would be wondred on. **1549** COVERDALE, etc. *Erasm. Par. Rom.* xii. 16–19 That to hymself..he seme a stoute felow and one to be wondered at. **1588** SHAKS. *L.L.L.* V. ii. 266 Are these the breed of wits so wondered at? *a* **1701** MAUNDRELL *Journ. Jerus.* (1732) 28 Nor is this ignorance to be much wondred at. **1825** SCOTT *Talism.* xi, It cannot be wondered at if he took such opportunities as offered.

e. Without construction. Now *rare*.

c **1205** LAY. 473 Ȝif heo wlleð frescipe bi-winnen ne wndre þou nawiht þer fore. **1297** R. GLOUC. (Rolls) 11409 A sterre ..þat comete icluped is Aros..þat ech man miȝte wondri þat þe sterre isei. *c* **1380** WYCLIF *Serm.* Sel. Wks. II. 306 Herfore þei alle abaishiden and woundriden. **1390** GOWER *Conf.* I. 185 Wherof thei merveile everychon, Bot Elda wondreth most of alle. **1533** FRITH *Answ. More* (1548) D vj b, They..vnderstoode not the Spirituall wordes of our Sauioure Christe, and therfore wondered and murmured. **1567** *Gude & Godlie B.* (S.T.S.) 100 Quhen men sall se this haistie suddand change, Than sall thay wunder. **1611** SHAKS. *Cymb.* I. vi. 81, Whil'st I am bound to wonder, I am bound To pitty too.

f. *pass.* (obs.) and *refl.* (obs. or dial.) in the same sense. Also †*impers.* (*me wondreth* = I wonder).

a **1225** *Ancr. R.* 376 Ne wundrie heo hire nowiht, ȝif heo nis nout Marie. *a* **1300** *Floriz & Bl.* 354 Muche he wule þonki þe And of þe suþe iwundred beo. *a* **1330** *Roland & V.* 161 Me wondreþ..þat þou comest nouȝt to do batayl. *c* **1330** R. BRUNNE *Chron. Wace* (Rolls) 4295 Vs wondreþ at ȝowre nurture of pris, þat swylke vilenie in þe now lys. *c* **1400** *Destr. Troy* 9821 þof þow wylne to þe wer, wonders vs noght. *a* **1400–50** *Wars Alex.* 2856 þai ware so woundird of þat werke. *c* **1430** *Pilgr. Lyf Manhode* I. iv. (1869) 3 Yit more j wundrede me of a thing that j seygh. **1533** TINDALE *Supper of Lord* B vj b, I wonder me, that hys scholemaister here fayled him so conynge as he maketh hym selfe therin.

g. ***I shouldn't wonder*** (*colloq.*): I should not be surprised (*if*, etc.).

1836 DICKENS *Sk. Boz*, *Gt. Winglebury Duel*, 'Do you think you could manage to leave a letter there?' interrogated Trott. 'Shouldn't wonder,' responded boots. **1875** JOWETT *Plato* (ed. 2) I. 19, I should not wonder if he who said this did not understand what he was saying. **1913** EDITH WHARTON *Custom of County* I. iii. 35 Saying..'I wouldn't wonder' when she thought any one was trying to astonish her.

2. Usually with clause: To ask oneself in wonderment; to feel some doubt or curiosity (*how*, *whether*, *why*, etc.); to be desirous to know or learn.

I wonder is often placed after a question which expresses the object of curiosity or doubt; e.g. 'How can that be, I wonder?' = I wonder how that can be. Also ***I wonder!***, colloq. exclamation expressing doubt, incredulity, or reserve of judgement.

1297 R. GLOUC. (Rolls) 160 þe stones stondeþ þere so grete..& oþere liggeþ heie aboue..þat eche man wondry may hou hii were ferst arered. **1377** LANGL. *P. Pl.* B. XIX. 199, I wondred what þat was. **1390** GOWER *Conf.* I. 210 Thei wondren what sche wolde mene, And riden after softe pas. *a* **1425** tr. *Arderne's Treat. Fistula* etc. 6 Ȝif the pacient considere or wondre or aske why that he putte hym so long a tyme of curyng. **1590** SHAKS. *Mids. N.* III. ii. 1, I wonder if Titania be awak't. **1611** —— *Wint. T.* III. iii. 71 What haue we heere? Mercy on's, a Barne?.. A boy, or a Childe I wonder? **1651** HOBBES *Leviath.* II. xxvi. 139 A man may wonder from whence proceed such opinions. **1681** EVELYN *Let. to Pepys* 6 Dec., P.'s Diary 1879 VI. 138, I know it has been wondered upon what pretence I should have sought to sit at the Navy Board. **1716** ADDISON *Freeholder* No. 43 ¶1 One would wonder how any Person endow'd with.. ordinary..Prudence..should [etc.]. **1782** COWPER *John Gilpin* 96 His horse..What thing upon his back had got Did wonder more and more. **1784** —— *Task* I. 469 The heart.. finds no music in the song,..and wonders why. **1847** TENNYSON in Ld. Tennyson *Mem.* (1897) I. 244, I wonder whether you can read this scrawl. **1853** DICKENS *Bleak Ho.* iv, I still remained before the fire, wondering and wondering about Bleak House. **1858** *Punch* XXXIV. 2 Well, I'm sure! What next, I wonder! **1864** MRS. H. WOOD *Ld. Oakburn's Dau.* xvii, 'But what is it all to me?' wondered the captain. **1885–94** R. BRIDGES *Eros & Psyche* Feb. v, Wondering of her wiles, and what the charge Shut in the dark obsidian pyx might be. **1898** J. K. JEROME *2nd Thoughts of Idle Fellow* 5 She wonders would they change it, if she went back. **1922** STORER CLOUSTON *Lunatic at large again* I. vi. 70 'Oh, it was entirely his own idea.' Mr. Mason threw him a curious look. 'I wonder!' said he.

† **3.** *trans.* To regard with wonder; to marvel at: often implying profound admiration (cf. WONDER *sb.* 7 c). *Obs.*

1535 COVERDALE *Ecclus.* ix. 8 Many a man wonderinge the bewtye of a straunge woman, haue bene cast out. **1567** PAINTER *Pal. Pleas.* II. 156 b, That which was more to be wondred in hym. **1593** R. BARNES *Parthenophil* xxvi. in *Arber's Garner* V. 354 If She be silent, every man in place With silence, wonders her! **1631** HEYWOOD *2nd Pt. Fair Maid West* I. C 2, *Goodl.* You wonder me. *Mull.* No, thou art dull, or fearfull, fare thee well. **1821** LAMB *Elia* Ser. I. *My first Play*, I knew nothing, understood nothing, discriminated nothing. I felt all, loved all, wondered all.

b. impers. pass. ***it is to be wondered*** = it is to be wondered at (1 d). Now *rare* or *Obs.*

1654 EARL MONM. tr. *Bentivoglio's Wars Flanders* 2 You shall see them so favour'd..as it is not to be wondred if they have made so long opposition. **1771** GOLDSM. *Hist. Eng.* I. 350 It is not then to be wondered, that there were many complaints. **1827** *Westm. Rev.* Apr. 284 If it is wondered that they abused what was in their power. **1886** SYMONDS *Renaiss. It., Cath. Reaction* II. 434 It is not to be wondered that..a mournful discouragement should have descended on the age.

† **4.** To affect or strike with wonder; to cause to marvel, amaze, astound. (See also 1 f.) *Obs.*

1558 G. CAVENDISH *Poems* (1825) II. 123 But how they durst presume it wonders me therefore. **1627** W. SCLATER *Expos. 2 Thess.* (1629) 187 It wonders me to hear the desperate inference. **1638** —— *Serm. Experimentall* 28 Of all passages in the story of Job, that one thing wonders me. **1788** MME. D'ARBLAY *Diary* 25 Oct., She alarms me sometimes for herself, at other times she has a sedateness that wonders me still more.

5. *intr.* To perform wonders. *nonce-use.*

1784 COWPER *Task* IV. 87 Katterfelto, with his hair on end At his own wonders, wond'ring for his bread.

'wonder, *adv. Obs.* or *arch.* (in later use *Sc.*). Forms: see WONDER *sb.* [Partly OE. *wundor* WONDER *sb.* in compounds, as *wundorágræfen* wonderfully carved (so in OFris. *wundergrât* wonderfully great, OHG. *wunterwas* very sharp, MHG. *wunderschœne* very beautiful); partly OE. *wundrum*, advb. dative pl. of *wundor* (cf. MHG. *wundernalt* very old, etc., and the similar use of gen. pl. of ON. *undr* in *undradigr*, *-hár* wondrously big, high, etc.).] Wondrously, marvellously, surprisingly; exceedingly, very.

c **1200** ORMIN 7284 Wunnderr mikell shame wass till Issraæle þede. *c* **1205** LAY. 1154 þa wnder creftie men. *Ibid.* 1744 þat feht wes wnder strong. **13..** *Cursor M.* 4448 (Gött.) þe king wid þaim was wonder wrath. *c* **1369** CHAUCER *Dethe Blaunche* 452 (Fairf.) Than founde I sitte even vpryght A wonder wel farynge knyght. *c* **1420** *Prose Life Alex.* 46 This prynce was a wyghte man..& wonder trewe till Alexander. *c* **1420** *Liber Cocorum* 23 Wasshe hom and hew hom wondur smalle. **1536** CRANMER *Let.* in *Misc. Writ.* (Parker Soc.) 322 Wherein I would wonder fain break my mind unto you. *a* **1550** *Freiris Berwik* 167 in *Dunbar's Poems* (S.T.S.) 290 With that scho smylit woundir lustely. **1596** DALRYMPLE tr. *Leslie's Hist. Scot.* II. (S.T.S.) I. 169 Hadrian heiring this, was woundir discontent. **1725** RAMSAY *Gentle Sheph.* II. iv, Now I believe ye like me wonder weel.

†**'wonderclout.** *Obs. rare.* [f. WONDER *sb.* + CLOUT *sb.*[1]] ? Something showy but worthless.

1570 LEVINS *Manip.* 228/46 A Wonderclout, blabbe, *garrulus, linguax.* **1593** HARVEY *Pierce's Super.* Z 1 b, O wretched Atheisme, Hell but a scarecrow, and Heauen but a woonderclout in their doctrine. *Ibid.* Ff 4, Her meritorious worke, a Wonderclowte.

wondered ('wʌndəd), *ppl. a.* [f. WONDER *sb.* or *v.* + -ED.]

†**1.** Wonderful, marvellous. *Obs.*

c **1586** C'TESS PEMBROKE *Ps.* XCVI. ii, Of his actes the wondred story Paint unto each people forth. *Ibid.* CVI. ix, God..Preserv'd them soe by miracles of might,..And wondred works. **1612** DRAYTON *Poly-olb.* viii. 448 Into what sundry gyres her wondered self she throws.

2. ***wondered-at***: see WONDER *v.* 1 a, d.

c **1611** CHAPMAN *Iliad* XXIV. 420 A great time Achilles gaz'd vpon His wonderd-at approch. **1615** —— *Odyss.* XI. 242 My Father..vsde no sumptuous beds, Wonderd at furnitures. **1637** RUTHERFORD *Lett.* 8 Aug. (1881) 96 My.. never-enough-wondered-at Lord Jesus.

¶ In the following, *wondred* is virtually in parasynthetic comb. ('performing such rare wonders').

1610 SHAKS. *Temp.* IV. i. 123 So rare a wondred Father.

†**'wonderel.** *Obs. rare.* In 5 **wunderelle, wundrel.** [Of Scand. origin (cf. MDa. *underls*): see WONDER *v.* and -ELS (cf. -LE 1 b).] A wonder, marvel.

c **1440** *Promp. Parv.* 534/2 Wunderelle (*K.* wundrel..), *prodigium.*

wonderer[1] ('wʌndərə(r)). [f. WONDER *v.* + -ER[1].] One who wonders *at* something.

1573 BARET *Alv.* W 323 A Wonderer: a marueler, *mirator.* [**1589** PUTTENHAM *Engl. Poesie* III. xix. (Arb.) 233 *Paradoxon*, or the Wondrer.] **1602** CHETTLE *Hoffman* III. (1631) F 4 b, That giddy wonderers may amazed stand. **1648** GAGE *West Ind.* 1 To advance that crackt-brain head in the conceits of his European wonderers. **1734** J. RICHARDSON *Milton's Par. Lost* p. xciii, Had the Bishop known This Story..he would not have been One of the Wonderers at Milton's Escape. **1797** JANE AUSTEN *Sense & Sensib.* xiv, She was a great wonderer, as every one must be who takes a very lively interest in all the comings and goings of all their acquaintance. **1852** R. B. MANSFIELD *Log Water-Lily* 19 At our start, crowds of wonderers hung over the bridge. **1865** DE MORGAN in *Athenæum* 25 Nov. 730/1 His backers and his quizzers, his admirers and his wonderers.

†**'wonderer**[2]. *Obs. rare.* [f. WONDER *sb.* + -ER[1].] A wonder-worker.

1647 TRAPP *Comm. Rev.* xiii. 4 The Pope can doe whatsoever Christ can doe; yea and more too, it should seem by these wise wonderers.

wonderful ('wʌndəfʊl), *a.*, (*sb.*), and *adv.* [late OE. *wunderfull*, f. WONDER *sb.* + -FUL; cf. MLG. *wonderfull*, MSw. *under(s)fulder*.] **A.** *adj.*

1. Full of wonder; such as to excite wonder or astonishment; marvellous; sometimes used trivially = surprisingly large, fine, excellent, etc.

a **1100** *Aldhelm Gloss.* I. 2757 (Napier 74/2) *Stupendo*, .i. *mirando*, mid wunderfulre, *spectaculo*, wæfersyne. *c* **1200** *Trin. Coll. Hom.* 177 Wunderliche ben þe sæ ut sondes, and wunderful is ure louerd on þeunesse. *c* **1275** LAY. 280 Hii funde..þat ȝe mid one sone was wonderfol to telle. **1297** R. GLOUC. (Rolls) 8575 God sende uor is luþernesse moni deoluol cas In þis lond & wonderuol. **1340** HAMPOLE *Pr. Consc.* 6404 Of þe day of dome..And of þe wondirful takens many, þat salle falle byfor þat day. *c* **1400** *Destr. Troy* 1355 There were wemen to wale, A wondurfull nowmbur. *a* **1425** *Cursor M.* 9314 (Trin.) Men shul him calle nomes sere Wondirful & counsellere. *c* **1450** *Mirk's Festial* 20 þer God worcheth mony wondyrfull myracles for hym. **1508** DUNBAR *Tua Mariit Wemen* 451 Wise women has.. wonderfull gydingis,..to beiaip ther ielyus husbandis. **1555** EDEN *Decades* (Arb.) 49 The wonderfull and sumptuous woorke of the sepulcher whiche Artemisia made. **1596** J. SMYTHE in *Lett. Lit. Men* (Camden) 91 Whereof ensued unto me..a wonderfull payne in my stomacke. **1611** *Bible* Prov. xxx. 18 There be three things which are too wonderfull for me; yea foure, which I know not. **1632** LITHGOW *Trav.* IV. 134 They made a wonderfull massacre of poore afflicted Christians. **1779** MRS. DELANY *Let. to Mrs. Port* 17 Apr., Give him the juice of clivers or goose grass, which is wonderfull, pounded with a little cold water. **1827** CARLYLE *Misc., Richter* (1872) I. 11 The unhappy man persuades himself that he has..become a new creature, of the wonderfulest symmetry. **1834** DICKENS *Sk. Boz, Boarding-ho.* ii, Mr. Tomkins..had a wonderful eye for the picturesque. **1840** FABER *Hymn*, My God, how wonderful Thou art! **1880** BLACKMORE *Mary Anerley* xxxvi. II. 303 Every Sunday morning, he trimmed his whiskers, and put on a wonderful waistcoat. **1884** RUSKIN *Pleas. Eng.* iii. §78 Robert Guiscard, the most wonderful soldier of that or any other time.

b. ***the wonderful***: that which is wonderful. †Also *sb. pl.* wonderful things.

1727 DE FOE *Syst. Magic* I. iii. (1840) 75 This temper of the people..drove the magicians..to a confederacy with the Devil for a supply of wonderfuls to delude the people. **1749** FIELDING *Tom Jones* VIII. i, Every Writer may be permitted to deal as much in the Wonderful as he pleases. **1815** W. H. IRELAND *Scribbleomania* 20 One unvarying predilection for the wonderful runs through the whole series of his poems.

†**2.** Filled with wonder or admiration. *Obs. rare.*

c **1380** WYCLIF *Wks.* (1880) 308 Makinge persones wondirful bi cause of here wynnyng. **1552** HULOET, Wonderfull,..*admirabundus.* **1583** HARSNET *Serm. Ezek.* in *R. Stuart's Serm.* etc. (1658) 132 The H[oly] Fathers are wonderfull in the contemplation of mans excellency at the first.

B. *adv.* = WONDERFULLY 1. Now *dial.*

c **1400** *Rowland & O.* 50 Now come þam..wondirfull hasty tythande. **14..** *Sir Beues* (M.) 3866 A wonderffull gret route. **1531** ELYOT *Gov.* I. xi. (1883) I. 79 Cosmographie is to all noble men, nat only pleasant, but..wonderfull necessary. **1625** BACON *Ess., Boldness* (Arb.) 518 Wonderfull like is the Case of Boldnesse, in Ciuill Businesse. **1722** HEARNE *Collect.* (O.H.S.) VII. 381 Being full of wooden Cutts, w[ch] makes the Book wonderfull curious. **1786** BURNS *Twa Dogs* 84 They're maistly wonderfu' contented. **1885** 'MRS. ALEXANDER' *At Bay* ix, She was wonderful fond of Elsie.

wonderfully ('wʌndəfʊlɪ), *adv.* [f. prec. + -LY[2].] In a wonderful manner.

1. So as to excite wonder; †miraculously; to a wonderful degree or extent; marvellously, astonishingly, surprisingly: often passing into a mere intensive = amazingly well or much; extraordinarily, exceedingly.

a **1300** *E.E. Psalter* xliv. [xlv]. 6 þy pouste shal laden þe wonderfulliche. **13..** *Cursor M.* 11424 (Gött.) þe stern went forwid þat þaim ledd, And wonþerfulli [*Cott.* ferlilic, *Fairf.*, *Trin.* wondirly] þan war þai fedd. *a* **1340** HAMPOLE *Psalter* xcvii. 1 God..þat wondirfully made man and wondirfullyere boght him. *a* **1400** *Prymer* (1891) 35 He was boren wonderfulliche of a mayde. *a* **1425** tr. *Arderne's Treat. Fistula* etc. 69 Ane emplastre of þe white of ane rawe ey and oile..is seid wonderfully for to be mitigatiue. *a* **1513** FABYAN *Chron.* VI. cc. (1533) 123 b/2 He arrered excedynge imposycyons of the people, and greued them wonderfully. **1596** DALRYMPLE tr. *Leslie's Hist. Scot.* IV. (S.T.S.) I. 237 Eugenie had ane onlie dauchtir,..quha wounderfullie was ..mouet with effectione of a religious lyfe. **1610** HOLLAND *Camden's Brit.* I. 813 A chappell wonderfully built out of a rocke hewen hollow. **1617** MORYSON *Itin.* III. 23 The conversation of the English abroad, is wonderfullie pleasing unto strangers. **1642** *Caldwell Papers* (Maitl. Club) I. 94, I pray God send her safe hither; wee wonderfully want her. **1719** DE FOE *Crusoe* II. (Globe) 336, I wonderfully lik'd the Man. **1765** *Museum Rust.* IV. 258 The seed being exceeding small, and to be sown wonderfully thin. **1789** MRS. PIOZZI *Journ. France* I. 149 Their wonderfully-situated metropolis [*sc.* Venice]. **1839** THACKERAY *Fatal Boots* Jan., It got through the measles wonderfully. **1885** 'MRS. ALEXANDER' *Valerie's Fate* iv, It was a capital play, too, and so wonderfully acted.

†**2.** With wonder or admiration. *Obs. rare.*

c **1450** *Merlin* xiii. 200 Ther dide Gawein soche merveiles in armes that wondirfully was he be-holden of hem of logres. **1570** J. DEE *Math. Pref.* *j, How Immateriall..Number is, who doth not perceaue? yea, who doth not wonderfully wonder at it? **1821** CLARE *Vill. Minstrel* I. 35 The crowd that wonderfully stares, To hear him talk of things in foreign land.

'wonderfulness. [f. as prec. + -NESS.] The quality or condition of being wonderful.

†**1.** The state of being filled with wonder. *Obs. rare.*

1387–8 T. USK *Test. Love* I. ii. (Skeat) l. 14 Angels ben adradde, not by ferdnes of drede,..[but] as [by] affeccion of wonderfulnesse and by service of obedience.

2. Wonderful character, marvellousness.

1574 tr. *Marlorat's Apoc.* 3 He called the Wyze men by a strange starre,..the Gentiles by the wonderfulnesse of Miracles. **1579** TWYNE *Phisicke agst. Fortune* I. xxx. 41 What by the wonderfulnesse and number of the woorkes, there was nothyng in all the whole world to be wondred at, but Rome. **1652** FRENCH *Yorksh. Spaw* iii. 32 The wonderfulnes of the waters that I shall mention, consists.. in the strangeness of their colours, tasts, [etc.]. **1674** ALLEN *Danger Enthus.* 100 The wonderfulness of his Birth of a Virgin. **1714** DERHAM *Astro-Theol.* IV. ii. (1769) 101 The wonderfulness of the things of the heavens or the earth. **1870** MAX MÜLLER *Sci. Relig.* (1873) 27 The Buddhist.. miracles, which in wonderfulness certainly surpass the miracles of any other religion. **1892** HENLEY *Song of Sword, Lond. Voluntaries* I. 39 Dispossessed of wonderfulness, they stand Beggared and common. **1908** *Athenæum* 22 Aug. 205/1 A knowledge of the wonderfulness of life.

wondering ('wʌndərɪŋ), *vbl. sb.* [f. WONDER *v.* + -ING[1].]

1. The action of the verb WONDER.

a **900** CYNEWULF *Crist* 89 Hwæt is þeos wundrung þe ȝe wafiað? *c* **1000** ÆLFRIC *Saints' Lives* xxiii. 627 þa þa he on þære micclan his modes wundrunge þær ȝestod. *a* **1300** *Cursor M.* 11453 þan þai gedir þam to-gedir, And spak hir-of wit gret wondring. **1382** WYCLIF *Acts* iii. 10 And thei weren fulfillid with wondryng, and exstasie. *c* **1386** CHAUCER *Sqr.'s T.* 300 Swich wondryng was ther on this hors of bras. *c* **1450** tr. *De Imitatione* III. lix. 139 He desiriþ..to do suche þinges wherof preisinge & wondring miȝt arise. **1471** CAXTON *Recuyell* (Sommer) 44 Whan he had herd their reasons & had seen their wondringes. *a* **1500** in Kingsford *Chron. Lond.* (1905) 221 Perkyn was conueyd ayen thorwth Candylwyke strete..with many a curse and wonderyng Inowth. **1600** SHAKS. *A.Y.L.* III. ii. 181 But didst thou heare without wondering, how thy name should be hang'd and carued vpon these trees? **1645** MILTON *Tetrach.* Wks. 1851 IV. 145 It may save the wondring why in this age many are so opposite both to human and to Christian liberty. **1848** DICKENS *Dombey* xxiii, Into her mind..there had stolen solemn wonderings and hopes. **1858** J. MARTINEAU *Stud. Christ.* 291 The infinite wonderings of the religious life.

†**2.** An object of wonder; a wonder, marvel, prodigy. *Obs. rare.*

a **1100** *Aldhelm Gloss.* I. 4370 (Napier 114/2) *Spectaculi*, wundrunge, wæfersyne. **1513** DOUGLAS *Æneis* VI. iv. 92 Witles Discord, that woundring maist crewell.

3. *attrib.*, as ***wondering food, stock*** (STOCK *sb.*[1] 59).

c **1550** G. WALKER *Dice-Play* (Percy Soc. 1850) 36 The poor boy..continued..a wondering-stock to all the house. **1570** FOXE *A. & M.* 72/2 Thus were the bodies of the Martyrs made a wondering stocke. **1571** GOLDING *Calvin on Ps.* lxxi. 7 He had..bin..counted as a wonderingstocke by reason of his miserable affliction. **1819** KEATS *Otho* I. ii. 111 Let me no longer be the wondering food Of all these eyes.

'wondering, *ppl. a.* [f. WONDER *v.* + -ING[2].] That wonders.

1592 TIMME *Ten Engl. Lepers* A 2, The woondring Queene of Sheba..presented the most wise Salomon with the golde of Ophyr. **1667** MILTON *P.L.* VIII. 257 Strait toward Heav'n my wondring Eyes I turnd. **1715** POPE *Iliad* I. 524 Then..the Monster Titan came,..Thro' wondring Skies enormous stalk'd along. **1810** SCOTT *Lady of L.* I. iii, The falcon, from her cairn on high, Cast on the rout a wondering eye. **1840** DICKENS *Old Cur. Shop* xiii, 'Where in the devil's name are they gone?' said the wondering Dick. **1846** MRS. A. MARSH *Fr. Darcy* xxxvi, The two priests could only look on him with a sort of wondering astonishment. **1872** MORLEY *Voltaire* 8 The..sinister method of assault upon religion which we of a later day watch with wondering eyes.

Comb. **1895** MRS. K. T. HINKSON *Miracle Plays* Proem, Thy little one and wondering-eyed.

wonderingly ('wʌndərɪŋlɪ), *adv.* [f. prec. + -LY[2].] In a wondering manner; in or with wonder.

1556 J. HEYWOOD *Spider & F.* lxii. 33 Two flies togither wondringlie..In talke betwene them selues, as folowith did saie. **1602** WARNER *Alb. Eng.* XI. lxii. (1612) 272 They, seeing vncouth Men, and Shippes, weare wondringly agaste. *a* **1736** in Spurgeon *Treas. Dav.* Ps. cxxvi. 1 They were looking on each other wonderingly, like sleepers on an empty dream. **1847** C. BRONTË *Jane Eyre* xv, I meditated wonderingly on this incident. **1881** STEVENSON *Virg. Puerisque, Some Portraits by Raeburn*, The little child who looks wonderingly on his grandfather's watch.

wonderland ('wʌndəlænd). (Also occas. with hyphen.) [f. WONDER *sb.* + LAND *sb.*[1] Cf. G. *wunderland*.] **a.** An imaginary realm of wonder and faery. **b.** A country, realm, or domain which is full of wonders or marvels.

1790 WOLCOT (P. Pindar) *Compl. Ep. James Bruce* 332 Wks. 1812 II. 368 Where other trav'lers, fraught with terror, roam, Lo! Bruce in Wonder-land is quite at home. **1866** 'LEWIS CARROLL' (*title*) Alice's Adventures in Wonderland. **1894** *Outing* (U.S.) Apr. 66/1 Every mile of my journey opened to me anew..the surprises of this wonder-land. **1902** *Westm. Gaz.* 24 May 9/1 That wonderland of the world, Egypt. **1903** AGNES M. CLERKE *Probl. Astrophysics* 6 The wonderland of molecular physics.

'wonderlandish, *a.* [f. WONDERLAND + -ISH[1].] Seemingly enchanted.

1929 J. B. PRIESTLEY *Good Companions* III. v. 590 He was beginning to feel wonderlandish again, what with Mr. Memsworth and the champagne.

'wonderless, *a. rare.* [f. WONDER *sb.* + -LESS.] Destitute of wonder.

1601 DEACON & WALKER *Answ. Darel* 47 A very world of wonderles wonders.

'wonderling. *rare nonce-wd.* [f. WONDER *sb.* + -LING.] A wonderful being.

1658 GURNALL *Chr. in Arm.* II. 190 This made Job such a wonderling to his wife. **1913** A. O'CONNOR *Poems* 8 Sweet wonderlings Of passing fancy, slight, too slight for birth, Yet dazzlingly alive with sudden mirth.

†**'wonderly,** *a. Obs.* Forms: see WONDER *sb.*; also 6 *Sc.* **wnderlie, vnderlie.** [OE. *wundorlic* = OS. *wundarlic* (MDu., MLG. *wunderlik*, Du. *wonderlijk*), OHG. *wuntarlih* (MHG., G. *wunderlich*), ON. *undrligr* (Sw., Da. *underlig*): f. WONDER *sb.* + -LY[1].] Wonderful.

c **893** ÆLFRED *Oros.* II. iv. §8 Nu seo burȝ swelc is þe ær wæs ealra weorca..wunderlecast & mærast. **971** *Blickl. Hom.* 181 þa færinga coman þær hundas forþ on wundorlicre mycelnesse. **1154** *O.E. Chron.* (Laud MS.) an. 1137 He maket..wunderlice & manifældlice miracles. *c* **1200** ORMIN

15645 þatt Godess Sune off heffne stah þurrh wunnderrliȝ mecnesse. **1387** TREVISA *Higden* (Rolls) I. 427 There is a roche wel wonderly. *c* **1475** *Partenay* 1241 The fyfte child.. had on ey and no mo,..wonderly to se. **1481** CAXTON *Reynard* xxvii. (Arb.) 61 Dame said the foxe, thauenture of the world is wonderly, it goth otherwhyle by wenyng. **1533** GAU *Richt Vay* (S.T.S.) 29 The vnderlie secret thyngis of God. *Ibid.* 40 His nayme sal be callit wnderlie consalour.

† ˈ**wonderly**, *adv. Obs.* Forms: see WONDER *sb.*; also 5 **wondarly**. [OE. *wunderlíce* = OS. *wundarlîco* (MLG., MDu. *wunderlîke*), OHG. *wuntarlîhho* (MHG. *wunderlîche*) f. WONDER *sb.* + -LY[2].] = WONDERFULLY 1. **a.** In a wonderful manner; marvellously.

c **897** ÆLFRED *Gregory's Past. C.* liv. 423 Swa wundorlice hit todælð..se godcunda wisdom be hira æȝðeres ȝeearnungum. *c* **1000** *Sax. Leechd.* I. 194 Wundurlice heo hæleþ. *c* **1205** LAY. 28627 Twa wimmen..wunderliche idihte. **1297** R. GLOUC. (Rolls) 10043 þat water suþþe heye aros..& mo þan ten þousend men wonderliche adrencte. *c* **1350** *Will. Palerne* 2535 Wonderli a werwolf ȝesterday hem saued. **1387** TREVISA *Higden* (Rolls) II. 207 Som tyme burþes beeþ i-bore wonderliche and wonderliche i-schape. *c* **1400** *26 Pol. Poems* xxiv. 374 Wiþ þy blod principal, Wonderly þou haste vs boȝt. *c* **1500** *Melusine* i. 5 Wherfore he punysshed them so secretly & so wounderly. *a* **1529** SKELTON *Bouge of Court* 283 Anone ther mette with him,..A man, but wonderly besene was he. *a* **1562** G. CAVENDISH *Wolsey* (1893) 32 The court.. was wonderly furnysshed with noble men and gentilmen.

b. To a wonderful extent or degree.

c **1000** ÆLFRIC *Saints' Lives* xxiii. 616 þær wearð þa ȝegade-rod wundorlice micel folc. *c* **1205** LAY. 7320 He wes wunderliche wrah [= wraþ]. *c* **1275** *Ibid.* 2677 He..one neuwe borh makede..wonderliche [*c* 1205 mærliche] fair. **1340** *Ayenb.* 267 þe profetes..and þe patriarkes wonderlyche glediynde ine blisse. *c* **1386** CHAUCER *Prol.* 84 Wonderly delyuere and of greet strengthe. *c* **1412** HOCCLEVE *De Reg. Princ.* 520 His garnamentes..hym becam wonderly wel. ? **1482** J. WATTON *Speculum Christiani* 46 b, Thair sence [= incense] was wonderly wrought With riche spices. **1556** J. HEYWOOD *Spider & F.* lxxxvii. 198 His hart wunderlie faynted.

wonderment (ˈwʌndəmənt). Chiefly *literary*. [f. WONDER *v.* + -MENT.]

1. The or a state of wonder; = WONDER *sb.* 7.

1535 in *Lett. Suppr. Monast.* (Camden) 78 After most shamefull rumors raysed uppe to theyre dyffamacion, with slaunderouse wonderment of the towne. **1569** GOLDING tr. *Heminge's Postill* 30 Wee must with holy wonderment embrace the heauenly Oracles. **1571** —— *Calvin on Ps.* viii. Contents, Dauid bethinking himself of Gods fatherly bountifulnesse towards mankinde..is rauished into a wonderment of it. **1590** SPENSER *F.Q.* I. xii. 9 Whom all admired, as from heauen sent, And gazd vpon with gaping wonderment. **1688** BUNYAN *Sol. Temple* xxii. 52 That which added to their adornment, was the wonderment of a Queen. **1787** MME. D'ARBLAY *Diary* 19 Feb., The wonderment with which they heard a proposal so new was diverting. **1799** COLERIDGE '*Nor cold, nor stern, my soul!*' 8 They gape for wonderment. **1815** WORDSW. *Prose Wks.* (1876) II. 119 Much of what his biographer deemed genuine admiration must in fact have been blind wonderment. **1879** LEWES *Study Psychol.* viii. 155 The mind passes from wonderment at the miraculous to the discernment of order.

b. An expression of wonder: chiefly in *to make a wonderment*, to express wonder.

1553 M. WOOD tr. *Gardiner's True Obed.* 54 b, Her parentes..would make suche a lyke wonderment, as these men seme to vse against me. *a* **1565** R. TURNER in Marbeck *Bk. Notes* (1581) 243 A great outcrie & wonderment was made against the Deacons & Priests of Constantinople. **1630** tr. *Camden's Hist. Eliz.* II. 2 (an. 1570) Much talke there was ..of the murther of the Regent, many making a wonderment at vaine things, as his mothers dreame. **1681** R. L'ESTRANGE *Tully's Offices* 110 What a wonderment is made of it. **1748** RICHARDSON *Clarissa* (1768) III. 71 Why, Jack, thou needest not make such a wonderment, as the girls say. **1838** *Bentley's Misc.* III. 331 After the usual wonderments, and mutual applauses of our marvellous good looks. **1840** MRS. TROLLOPE *Widow Married* xxiv, What wonderments you do make about nothing.

2. An object of or a matter for wonder; a wonderful thing; = WONDER *sb.* 1–4.

1542 UDALL *Erasm. Apoph.* 70 b, The games called Dionysiaca,..he called the greate woondrementes & gazynges of fooles. **1563** FOXE *A. & M.* 50/2 This obstinate and stoburn rebellion of tharchbishop stirred vp much anger.., that almost he was alone a wonderment to al the realme. **1568** GRAFTON *Chron.* II. 213 *marg.*, Sir Hugh Spencer the yonger lead about for wonderment, lyke a beast. **1584** CONSTABLE *Diana* VII. i, A flouring fielde, the world's sole wonderment. **1591** SPENSER *Ruins of Rome* 28 Seuen Romane Hils, the worlds 7. wonderments. **1618** ROWLANDS *Sacred Mem.* 8 Therefore in Heathens Images he spake, Wrought wonderments, and wrought them so from grace. **1628** PRYNNE *Love-lockes* 33 They turne themselues into.. so many Monsters, and wonderments of the World. **1643** TRAPP *Comm. Gen.* xxxv. 1 Deliverances, commonly, are but nine days wonderment, at utmost. **1757** FOOTE *Author* Prol., 'Tis Wonderment, them Boobies ben't asham'd. **1841** J. F. COOPER *Deerslayer* xv, It's a wonderment to me..how you got us off. **1859** REEVE *Brittany* 87 A shop with all sorts of household wonderments exposed for sale. **1915** H. JAMES *Sense of the Past* (1917) 150 To determine wonderments that should be beyond answering.

b. A wonderful example or instance (*of* something): = WONDER *sb.* 1 d.

1606 G. W[OODCOCKE] *Hist. Ivstine* v. 25 But vpon Alcibiades they threw down a wonderment of welcoms. **1607** BEAUM. & FL. *Woman Hater* IV. i, How many..have dedicated grave Works to Ladies, toothless, [etc.], and have call'd them..the patterns of perfection, and the wonderment of Women. **1917** *Blackw. Mag.* Aug. 253 The untended orchards are arrayed in a wonderment of blossom.

3. Wonderful quality: = WONDER *sb.* 1 b.

1596 SPENSER *F.Q.* IV. v. 20 That strange Dame, whose beauties wonderment She lesse esteem'd, then th' others vertuous gouernment. **1633** P. FLETCHER *Purple Isl.* III. xxxii, How should I..limme forth her vertues wonderment? **1647** N. BACON *Disc. Govt. Eng.* I. lxxi. 313 That King will be looked upon as a King of wonderment. **1801** SURR *Splendid Misery* III. 251 As a climax of wonderment, the Jacobin Winterton has succeeded with Lady Amelia. **1871** SMILES *Charac.* ii. (1876) 33 The child..opens his eyes upon things all of which are full of novelty and wonderment.

ˈ**wonder-ˌmonger.** [f. WONDER *sb.* + MONGER *sb.* 2.] One who deals in wonders; a wonder-worker, or relater of wonders.

1612 BP. HALL *Contempl., O.T.* IV. iv, How are the great wonder-mongers of Ægypt abashed. **1651** WITTIE tr. *Primrose's Pop. Err.* 436 Those Wondermongers cannot take away the Kings evill. **1745** ELIZA HAYWOOD *Female Spect.* No. 18 (1748) III. 281 Invention! cried our wonder-monger, do I not tell you, sir,..that I saw it with my own eyes! **1751** LAVINGTON *Enthus. Meth. & Papists* III. (1754) Pref., The God Proteus..famous for being a juggling Wonder-monger ..and turning himself into all Shapes. **1851** NEWMAN *Pres. Pos. Cath.* 231 Future story-tellers and wonder-mongers. **1863** DE MORGAN *Pref.* in *From Matter to Spirit* p. xii, That some tricky wonder-monger had stuck the bill of a duck upon the neck of a quadruped. **1867** SWINBURNE *Blake* (1868) 94 No wonder-monger of the low sort need here have hoped for a pupil.

Hence ˈ**wonder-ˌmongering**.

1886 GURNEY, etc. *Phantasms of Living* I. 128 Another instinct which tends directly to discourage wonder-mongering. **1911** W. DE MORGAN *Likely Story* iv. 112 That ..class of persons which, when its attention turns towards wonder-mongering,..loses its head promptly.

† ˈ**wonderness.** *Obs. rare.* In 3 **wundernesse.** [f. WONDER *sb.* + -NESS.] A wonder.

c **1275** *Wom. Samaria* 40 in *O.E. Misc.* 85 Bi-twene þis twam volke me þuncheþ a wundernesse.

† ˈ**wondernize**, *v. nonce-wd.* [irreg. f. WONDER + -IZE.] *trans.* To make a wonder or marvel of.

1599 PORTER *Angry Wom. Abingt.* F 1, Some iudgements ..wondernize the birth of common wit.

† ˈ**wonders,** *a.* and *adv. Obs.* Also 6 *Sc.* **wounderis**. [gen. of WONDER *sb.*; a Scand. idiom: cf. MSw. *unders*, gen. of *under* WONDER *sb.* in *unders miraculum, teken, thing* marvel, miracle, prodigy. Cf. *lives* alive (LIFE *sb.* 15). See also WONDROUS.]

A. *adj.* = WONDROUS *a.*

a **1300** *Cursor M.* 1529 þaa þat þa wonders [*Gött.* wonþer] werkes wroght..Tua pilers þa mad. *a* **1500** *Sir Beues* 1469 (Chetham MS.) A wonders thinge [13.. *MS. A.* wonder-þing] ye may here. **1509** HAWES *Past. Pleas.* xxxvi. (1555) z ij b, It was a wonders case. *c* **1511** *1st Engl. Bk. Amer.* (Arb.) Introd. 29/1 Many dyuers maner and wonders bestes. *c* **1520** SKELTON *Magnyf.* 89 A, ye be wonders men! *c* **1530** LD. BERNERS *Arth. Lyt. Bryt.* xxxv. (1814) 111 Whan the duke sawe these thre knyghtes do suche wonders meruayles in armes..he was..dyspleased. **1602** W. BASSE *Three Past. Elegies* i. (1893) 44 An Iuory boxe of wonders cost.

B. *adv.* = WONDROUS *adv.*

1387–8 T. USK *Test. Love* II. iii. (Skeat) l. 45 Ye..let light of that thing whiche firste ye maked to you wonders dere. *c* **1395** *Plowman's Tale* 699 in *Pol. Poems* (Rolls) I. 324 These folkes be wonders stout. *c* **1520** *Everyman* 7 This matter is wonders precyous. **1551** ROBINSON tr. *More's Utopia* II. (1895) 220 Hym they receyue and interteyne wonders gentyllye. **1567** *Gude & Godlie B.* (S.T.S.) 207 In danger of deith,..Do weill is harnessit, and wounderis bauld. ? *a* **1600** *Dialogue in Verse* in *Marlowe's Wks.* 1850 III. 304 But a' dances wonders well.

Hence † ˈ**wondersly** *adv.* wondrously.

1489 SKELTON *Dethe Erle Northumb.* 193 Operlese Prince ..! Which to thy resemblaunce wondersly hast wrought All mankynd. **1556** J. HEYWOOD *Spider & F.* xiv. 5 Be ye sure it doth wondersly well.

ˈ**wondersome**, *a. rare.* [f. WONDER *sb.* + -SOME.] Wonderful.

1774 DIBDIN *Waterman* I. i, I have often-times thought to myself, that it was a wondersome kind of thing, how it came to pass, that you two agree so badly.

wonderstone (ˈwʌndəstəʊn). [f. WONDER *sb.* + STONE *sb.*] **1.** (See quots.)

1824 *Trans. Geol. Soc.* I. 295 In the neighbourhood of Wells, and at Bleydon near the Bristol Channel, it [*sc.* the conglomerate] forms a beautiful breccia, called wonder-stone, consisting of yellow transparent crystals of carbonate of lime, disseminated equably through a dark-red earthy dolomite. **1887** H. B. WOODWARD *Geol. England & Wales* (ed. 2) II. 232 The road to Wookey Hole..and that leading to Dulcot..show in places in the Red Marl a bed termed the 'Wonder Stone'.

2. A soft bluish-grey rock of volcanic origin in South Africa that takes a high polish.

1936 *Mineral Resources Union S. Afr.* (Geol. Survey, Union S. Afr.) (ed. 2) 299 Wonderstone appears to be one of the most indestructible of building stones. **1952** *Archit. Rev.* CXI. 329/1 Some of the work in 1936 by Henry Moore in African wonderstone and by Barbara Hepworth was very derivative, in the best sense, of the shapes assumed by..the stone and pebble plants of the African Karoo. **1952** L. MACNEICE *Ten Burnt Offerings* 84 He was..Firm as a Rameses in African wonderstone. **1975** *Stand. Encycl. S. Afr.* XI. 490/1 Large quantities of high quality wonderstone are available in the Dominion Reef System, 10 km north of Ottosdal in the Western Transvaal.

† **wonder thing.** *Obs.* (Also as one word.) [f. WONDER *sb.* or *a.* Cf. G. *wunderding*, MSw. *unders thing* (see WONDERS *a.*).] A wonderful thing, wonder, marvel.

c **1290** *St. Brendan* 677 in *S. Eng. Leg.* 238 A wonder þing it was to seo..A so gret best a-boute wiende. **13..** *Sir Beues* (A.) 1527 A wonder-þing now ȝe may here. *a* **1340** HAMPOLE *Psalter* cxviii[i]. 18, I sall bihalde wondirthyngis [Vulg. *mirabilia*] of þi laghe. *c* **1435** *Torr. Portugale* 53 He sware.. Ther wase told hym a wondyr-thyng In hys chambyr to nyght. **1500–20** DUNBAR *Poems* xxxii. 2 This hindir nycht.. To me wes tawld ane windir thing. **1546** J. HEYWOOD *Prov.* (1867) 27 A wonder thing what thingis these olde thinges tell.

ˈ**wonder-ˌwork.** [OE. *wundorweorc* = WFris. *wonderwirk*, MHG. *wunderwerc* (G. *-werk*), MDa. *underværk*, etc., f. WONDER *sb.* + WORK *sb.* In ME. treated as two words (cf. WONDER *a.*); in the modern period, a new formation.]

1. A marvellous or miraculous act; = MIRACLE 1. Also *gen.* a wonderful achievement.

971 *Blickl. Hom.* 161 Hie..wundorweorcum swiþe wuldorlice ascinon. *a* **1000** *Andreas* 705 Swylce he [*sc.* Christ] oðerra unrim cyðde wundorworca on wera ȝesyhðe. **13..** *Evang. Nicod.* 39 in Herrig's *Archiv* LIII. 392 þan wirkes he wonder werkes new. **13..** *Cursor M.* 1529 (Gött.) þai þat þir wonþer werkes wroght. *c* **1375** *Sc. Leg. Saints* xxvii. (*Machar*) 30 In þis land we ken hym nocht, Quhare he wondir werkis wrocht. **1570** DEE *Math. Pref.* A j, By sundry meanes, this Wonderworke is wrought.

1846 TRENCH *Mirac.* 60 While the Christians,..on account of a few insignificant wonder-works, proclaim their Jesus for a god. **1889** JAS. GIBBONS *Our Chr. Heritage* 242 Saint John referring to the wonder-works of Christ.

2. A wonderful work or structure.

c **1275** LAY. 17376 þo gonnen hii wende..to þan hulle.. war stod þat wonder worc. **1387** TREVISA *Higden* (Rolls) VI. 275 He bygan to bulde Seynt Albons his grete chirche from the foundement of a wonder werk of brend tyle.

1816 BYRON *Ch. Har.* III. x, Fit speculation; such as..He found in wonder-works of God and Nature's hand. **1887** WALLIES *Throne of Fisherman* 150 Forums which should surpass Trajan's wonderwork. **1895** *Outing* (U.S.) XXVII. 238/1 These wonder works of the sea are broken..into the most fantastic forms. **1904** *Westm. Gaz.* 22 Oct. 2/3 The hotel is, like everything else here, a wonder-work.

3. Marvellous work or workmanship.

a **1513** FABYAN *Chron.* V. cxxxiii. (1811) 116 A beer of wonder warke, standith..ouer y[t] graue.

1863 *Pilgrimage over Prairies* II. 265 Impassive spirits.. whom the daily wonderwork of nature, her glorious displays of the solemn, the lovely and the wild, seem never..to affect. **1883** in Spurgeon *Treas. Dav.* Ps. cxxxvi. 4 God was alone in the wonderwork of Creation.

ˈ**wonder-ˌworker.** [f. WONDER *sb.* + WORKER.] One who performs wonders or marvellous things; *esp.* a worker of miracles; a thaumaturge.

1599 SANDYS *Europæ Spec.* (1632) 169 Some of their better Prælates have removed..an image of our Lady, upon the broaching of a report that it discovered it selfe for a Wonder-worker. **1641** S. FAWCET *Seasonable Serm.* 17 The praying generation are the wonder-workers of the world. **1668** H. MORE *Div. Dial.* III. xix. 427 That he may be accounted a stupendious Wonder-worker, a Creatour of his Creatour. **1718** ATTERBURY *Serm., Acts xxvi. 26* (1734) I. 18 In China and Japan these Wonder-workers may pretend to have done as many Miracles as they please. **1856** MISS YONGE *Daisy Chain* II. xviii. (1879) 546 A wonderworker in cloth. **1878** BOSW. SMITH *Carthage* 375 Hannibal..taking his place..among the great wall-builders and wonder-workers of Eastern history and legend. **1895** FR. MARIANUS *St. Anthony of Padua* 145 The saintly Friar, the Wonder-worker filled with love and sympathy.

So ˈ**wonder-ˌworking** *ppl. a.* and *vbl. sb.*

1594 *Selimus* 284 Your wisedomes ouerflowing wit, Digs deepe with learnings wonder-working spade. **1644** VICARS *God in Mount* 199 To the high honour of our great and wonder-working God. **1679** *Hist. Jetzer* 18 They fall down before this wonder-working Image. **1710** BROOME *Paraphr. Habakkuk iii.* iii, Waving his Wonder-working Wand. **1776** BURNEY *Hist. Mus.* I. 194 The music of Orpheus, Amphion, and such wonder-working bards. **1809** W. IRVING *Knickerb.* I. ii. (1861) 10 The wonder-working sword of Harlequin. **1847** KEBLE *Serm.* x. 270 In the mysterious and wonder-working Prayer of Consecration. **1895** *Catholic Mag.* Aug. 228 There came..the wonder-working body of St. Cuthbert. **1900** F. T. ELWORTHY *Horns of Honour* iii. 180 There is some confusion about the several stories told of its [*sc.* the hand of glory's] wonder-working.

wonderwyse: see WONDER *a.*

† ˈ**wondlich,** *a. Obs. rare.* In 3 **wandlich.** [app. a. ON. *vándsligr* bad, wicked, evil, f. *vándr*: see WOND *sb.*[1] and -LY[1].] app. Bad, evil.

c **1205** LAY. 6358 He hauede bi þare wimman enne swiðe wandliche sune [*later text* ohte man].

wondrous (ˈwʌndrəs), *a.* and *adv. literary.* Also 6–9 **wonderous**, 6 **wond(e)rouse, wo(u)nderus, woundrous**, 6–7 **woonderous**, 7–9 **wond'rous.** [Alteration of WONDERS *a.* by substitution of suffix -OUS, after *marvellous*.] Wonderful.

a **1500** *Chaucer's Dreme* 1898 The sede wex grene, And on the dry herse gan spring Which me thought a wondrous thing. **1509** HAWES *Past. Pleas.* iv. (1555) C iiij, The wonderous serpente Of the seuen metals, made by enchauntment. **1535** COVERDALE *Ps.* cxix. 18, & so shal I spie out wonderous thinges in thy lawe. **1590** SPENSER *F.Q.* II. viii. 5 A faire young man, Of wondrous beautie. *a* **1656** HALES *Gold. Rem.* (1673) 7 The Grecians, till barbarism began to steal in upon them, were men of wonderous subtlety of wit. **1667** MILTON *P.L.* VII. 483 Some of Serpent kinde Wondrous in length and corpulence. **1709** WATTS *Hymn*, When I survey the wondrous cross On which the Prince of glory dy'd. **1781** COWPER *Hope* 155 Hope..has the wondrous virtue to educe From emptiness itself a real use.

1844 Kinglake *Eothen* viii, For hours, and hours, this wondrous white woman poured forth her speech. **1864** Bryce *Holy Rom. Emp.* xix. (1875) 357 The German mind, just beginning to put forth the blossoms of its wondrous literature.

B. *adv.* = next. *arch.*

a **1557** Mrs. M. Basset tr. *More's Treat. Passion* M.'s Wks. 1391/2 An vrgent and woonderous necessarye cause. **1632** Lithgow *Trav.* v. 229 We found this auncient Well so wondrous deepe, that scarcely all our ropes could sinke our bucket in the water. **1678** Hobbes *Decam.* vii. 77 As he made some Bodies wondrous great, so he made others wondrous little. **1740** Richardson *Pamela* (1824) I. xxiii. 35 They tell me she is grown wondrous pretty. **1781** Cowper *Anti-Thelyphth.* 38 Some she would teach (for she was wondrous wise). **1843** James *Forest Days* vi, This horse eats so wondrous slow. **1856** Mrs. Browning *Aur. Leigh* II. 428 Lady, thou art wondrous fair.

wondrously ('wʌndrəslɪ), *adv. literary.* [f. prec. + -ly².] In a wondrous manner; to a wonderful degree; wonderfully, marvellously.

1500–20 Dunbar *Poems* lxxxi. 12 Thane thocht I thus, this is ane felloun phary, Or ellis my witt rycht woundrouslie dois varie. **1535** Coverdale *Wisd.* xvii. 3 They were..put to horrible feare & wonderously vexed. *c* **1586** C'tess Pembroke *Ps.* lxxiv. xiv, Thou wondrously didst cause.. From thirsty flynt a fountayne flow. **1607** Shaks. *Timon* III. iv. 71 My Lord leanes wondrously to discontent. **1667** Milton *P.L.* III. 587 So wondrously was set his Station bright. **1807** W. Irving *Salmag.* No. 17 (1824) 319 So wonderously adroit in pedestrian exercises. **1905** Treves *Other Side Lantern* II. ix. (1906) 83 The walls of the main building are wondrously carved.

So '**wondrousness**.

1851 Nichol *Archit. Heav.* 240 Because of the very wondrousness of this universe.

† '**wondsome**, *a. Obs. rare.* [Of Scand. origin (cf. MSw. *vandsamr* difficult, troublesome; Norw. *vandsam* difficult to please): see wonde *v.* and -some.] Beset with difficulty; in quot. quasi-sb. (see for *prep.* 10). So † '**wondsomely** (**wandsomdly**) *a.* [cf. MSw. *vandsamliker*].

? *a* **1400** *Morte Arth.* 3836 And for wondsome and wille alle his wit failede. *Ibid.* 4012 The waye vnto Wynchestre thay wente..Wery and wandsomdly.

† **wone**, *sb.*¹ *Obs.* Forms: 3–4 **wune**, 3–6 **wone**, 4–7 **won**, 4–8 **wonne**, (5 **wne**, **woone**, 6 **wun**). [ME. *wune*, *wōne*, aphetic f. i-wune, i-wone, OE. *ȝewuna* = OS. *giwono* (MDu. *ghewone*, MDu., (M)LG. *wone*), OHG. *giwona* (MHG. *gewon(e)*, related to MHG. *gewan*, ON. *vane*, which represent another grade: f. Teut. *ga-* y- + *wun-*, won, wone *v.*]

I. [See won *v.* II.] Habit, custom.

1. Habitual action or conduct (of a person); (one's) habits or practices collectively.

a **1225** *Ancr. R.* 266 [Heo] dude hit eft & eft, & feol so into ful wune þet heo lei & rotede þerinne. *c* **1275** Lay. 14017 Þe Peutes dude hire wone [*c* 1205 iwune]. **13..** *Guy W.* (A.) 230 Artow..Suward sone, þat of al godenes haþ þe wone? *c* **1320** *Cast. Love* 278 Þis kyng hedde a sone, Of such wit and of such wone..As was his fader. *c* **1386** Chaucer *Prol.* 335 To lyuen in delit was euere his wone, For he was Epicurus owene sone. *c* **1400** *Rule St. Benet* (prose) 6 Chasti þaim fra iuil wne, als þe fadir dos his sune. *c* **1425** *Engl. Conq. Irel.* 66 Mych horynesse or oryble synnes that..weren amendet, & yn better wonne I-broȝth. *c* **1440** *York Myst.* xxix. 252 His wonne was to wirke mekill woo. **1450–80** tr. *Secr. Secr.* xl. 26 He vsith not his custome [of eating twice a day] for þe stomak is out of his wone.

b. In particularized use; *pl.* habits.

c **1200** *Trin. Coll. Hom.* 85 Seint nicholas þe on his childhode wunede him to fasten, and þat wune heold to his liues ende. *a* **1250** *Owl & Night.* 272 Hit is min hiȝte, hit is mi wune, þat ich me draȝe to mine cunde. **13..** *K. Alis.* 2715 (Laud MS.), He was þe Emperoures sone, Wel to juste was his wone. **1362** Langl. *P. Pl.* A. viii. 29 Treuþe..Bad hem..wikkede wones wihtly to amende. *c* **1450** *Mirk's Festial* 79 He was wont before to stele, and cowþe not leue his old wone. *a* **1500** *Assemb. Ladies* 5 In a gardyn, about twayn after noon, Ther were ladyes walking, as was her wone.

2. Established usage or custom (of a people, country, etc.).

c **1200** *Trin. Coll. Hom.* 105 Seint iacob..nam ȝeme of þe wune þe weren þo, and ȝet bien mid mannen. *c* **1220** *Bestiary* 368 Ðis wune he [*sc.* harts] hauen hem bi-twen, Ðoȝ he an hundred to-giddre ben. *c* **1250** *Gen. & Ex.* 1681 Quat laban, 'long wune is her driuen, Firmest on elde, first ben giuen'. *Ibid.* 3137 Ðanne he lereden hem newe wunen. *c* **1290** *St. Edward* 12 in *S. Eng. Leg.* 47 Seint Edward..is sone Aftur him was king j-mad, ase lawe was and wone. *a* **1300** *Cursor M.* 10915 Þe lauerd es nu bicummen threll, þe doghter moder again al won. *c* **1385** Chaucer *L.G.W.* 714 *Thisbe*, There was but a ston wal hem be-tweene, As ofte in grete tounnys is the wone. *c* **1425** *Engl. Conq. Irel.* 34 Thay ne hadden no wone of warytres; & þerfor þey..drent ham. *c* **1450** *Mirour Saluacioun* (1888) 163 Dede mens bodyes to byrye with mirre was the olde wonne.

3. Phr. ***in wone***: as a matter of custom, customarily. ***to have in wone***: to be accustomed *to do* something; to practise habitually; so ***to be in wone, to have wone. to be of common wone***: to be common custom. ***by*** or ***with wone***: as a matter of custom; used as a tag (also ***in good wone***).

1297 R. Glouc. (Rolls) 4718 Hii dude hom vorþere in þis lond þan hii were in wone. *a* **1300** *Cursor M.* 21237 Marc was gospellere wit won. *c* **1330** *Assump. Virg.* (B. M. MS.) 20 He callide to hym seynt Iohan..And seide, 'womman, lo, here þi sone, And, man, take hure to moder in good wone'. **1390** Gower *Conf.* I. 284 Of comun wone In chambre thei togedre wone. *Ibid.* II. 143 At hom if that a man wol wone, This Fievere [*sc.* jealousy] is thanne of comun wone Most grevous in a mannes yhe. *c* **1400** *Titus & Vesp.* (Roxb.) 5058 Aftur hym regnede Titus his sone, The Emperour most curteys by wone. *c* **1425** Wyntoun *Cron.* VIII. 3292 (Cott.) He..had in won, By his wiff, oftsyis to ly Oþir syndry women by. **14..** *Guy Warw.* (C.) 230 'Bee ye', she seide, 'Sywardes sone, That all goodnesse hath in wone?' *c* **1436** *Libel Engl. Pol.* in *Pol. Poems* (Rolls) II. 196 In somere tide wolde he have in wone, And in custome, to be fulle redy sone, Wyth multitude of men. *c* **1460** *Towneley Myst.* ii. 116 All the good thou has in wone Of godis grace is bot a lone. **1562** Turner *Herbal* II. 31 They that vse to eat of it loke much more freshly then they had won to do.

II. [See won *v.* I.] The action of staying or remaining; place of dwelling.

4. Phr. ***withouten wone***, without delay. Cf. *withouten hone* (hone *sb.*²).

c **1440** *Bone Flor.* 215 And yf thou sende hur not soone, Hastelye, wythowten wone, Then ryseth ther a stryfe. *c* **1596** *King & Backer* in Hazl. *E.P.P.* I. 5 Gramercy, felow, seyde owr kyng, withowtyn eney wone.

5. A dwelling-place, abode; *spec.* this world: = wone *sb.*² 1, 3 b.

c **1205** Lay. 13492 Ne mæi i noht for muchele scome habben here þesne wone. *c* **1250** *Gen. & Ex.* 513 Or enoch wente fro werldes wune Matusale was boren is sune. *a* **1300** *XV Signa* 164 in *E.E.P.* (1862) 12 Wel aȝtist þe faire to lede Wile þou art in þis wreche wone [*rime* mone]. **1340–70** *Alisaunder* 598 Of any wightes in wonne wysest i-holde. *a* **1450** *Le Morte Arth.* 3377 Sythe bretayne owte of troy was sought And made in bretayne hys owne wonne. **1563** Sackville *Induct. Mirr. Mag.* xxiii, Howe she telde Both what she was, and where her wun she helde. **1590** Spenser *F.Q.* III. iii. 7 There the wise Merlin whylome wont (they say) To make his wonne. **1608** Topsell *Serpents* 269 She.. from the Center draweth a thred like wooll to lye vpon While double worke on euery part doth fortifie her wone. **1642** H. More *Song of Soul* I. II. xxii, That free light hath given a free wonne [*rimes* sun, shone, begun] To this dependent ray. *Ibid.* xxiii, Flocks of souls..that have their won Where they list most to graze. **1685** —— *Paralip. Prophet.* Pref. p. xxvi, The Wilderness the Won of Spirits and Ghosts. **1748** Thomson *Cast. Indol.* II. viii, With all the gods that love the rural wonne [*rimes* run, son, undone].

† **wone**, *sb.*² *Obs.* Chiefly *poet.* Forms: 3 **woan**, 3–4 **won**, 4–5 **woon**, **wone**. [Midland and Southern variant (with ɔː) of wane *sb.*², which is probably a. ON. *ván* hope, expectation, and therefore identical with wone *sb.*³ The germ of the sense of 'dwelling-place' is to be seen in ON. examples such as *þá er allar vánir vóru rannsakaðar* when all the 'expected places' (places where it might be expected to be) were searched; cf. Norw. *von* place where one expects to find something, fishing-place, hunting-ground. Association with won *v.* assisted the establishing and further development of the sense in ME.; cf. also wone *sb.*¹ II. The allocation of meaning in particular instances is often doubtful.]

1. A place of habitation or abode, dwelling-place.

c **1275** *Serving Christ* 68 in *O.E. Misc.* 92 Me graueþ þis gode, in greote and in ston, þer wereþ vre wlite in wurmene won. *a* **1310** in Wright *Lyric P.* xiv. 46 So wyde in world ys huere won, In uch a toune untrewe is on. *c* **1320** *Sir Tristr.* 2456 No hadde þai no won to wille Bot þe wode so grene. **14..** *Songs, Carols*, etc. (E.E.T.S.) 85/116 Pray we þat byrde so bright as bon..þat owr dwellyng may be in her wone, With hym that for owr sake was slone.

2. *sing.* and *pl.* A dwelling-house, dwelling, habitation: freq. applied to a palace.

a **1225** *Ancr. R.* 418 Wiðinnen ower woanes ne lete ȝe nenne mon slepen. *c* **1350** *Athelston* 755 Boþe in-same þey rod To Westemynstyr wone. **13..** *E.E. Allit. P.* B. 140 Hov wan þou into þis won in wedez so fowle? **13..** *Gaw. & Gr. Knt.* 2400 Ȝe schal in þis nwe ȝer aȝayn to my wonez. *c* **1394** *P. Pl. Crede* 172 A woon wonderlie well y-beld, Wiþ arches on eueriche half. *c* **1400** *Laud Troy Bk.* 18361 Thei caste al doun thes worthi wones, Led & tyle, sclat & stones. *c* **1430** *Pol. Rel. & L. Poems* (1903) 207 And al þe welþe withinne þi woon To susteine þee and þin householde. **1501** Douglas *Pal. Hon.* I. xxxiv, Reparrellit was that godlike plesand wone. **15..** *Flodden F.* lxxvii. in Furniv. *Percy Folio* I. 332 He tooke me from my father deere & keeped me within his woone. **1570** Levins *Manip.* 168/11 A Wone, *habitatio*.

b. *pl.* Rooms, chambers, apartments.

c **1325** *Orfeo* 351 Amyd the launde a castel he sye..Within were wyde wonys. **13..** *E.E. Allit. P.* A. 917 Haf ȝe no wonez in castel walle? *c* **1440** *Pallad. on Husb.* I. 331 The wynter wones on the sonny side. **14..** *Tundale's Vis.* 1623 Large and rownde were tho wones, Þe flore was paved with precioușe stones.

c. *sing.* and *pl.* (with sing. concord). A city.

? *a* **1400** *Morte Arth.* 2472 Thay had wonne that wone be theire awene strenghe! *c* **1400** *Destr. Troy* 9857 Yonder won [*sc.* Troy] for to wyn. *c* **1440** Capgrave *Life St. Kath.* I. 141 For the grete welthe þat was in þat wonys [*sc.* the city of Alexandria].

d. ***in*** or ***within one's wones***: in one's possession.

1390 Gower *Conf.* II. 76 He that stant to day alofte And al the world hath in hise wones. *Ibid.* 134 Thogh a man at ones Of al the world withinne his wones The tresor myhte have everydel.

3. *sing.* and *pl.* An inhabited place; a country, realm, territory, domain; *gen.* a place. Phr. ***within wones, in wone*** (freq. as a tag) = everywhere, anywhere.

c **1330** R. Brunne *Chron. Wace* (Rolls) 8951 Passent calanged his fader wones, Þe kyng for robberye of þe stones. **1338** —— *Chron.* (1810) 75 [He] fulle bare mas many wone, Of gode men er non left. *c* **1386** Chaucer *Sir Thopas* 90 He so longe hadde riden and goon That he foond in a pryue woon The contree of Fairye So wilde. **1390** Gower *Conf.* III. 295 Ther was ynowh withinne wones Of wepinge and of sorghe tho. **1393** Langl. *P. Pl.* C. I. 18 Deþ, as ich lyuede, Wonede in þo wones, and wyckede spiritus. **1399** —— *R. Redeles* II. 180 Wher so þey fferde be ffryth or be wones. *a* **1400** *Leg. Rood* viii. 347 Fadres and Modres þat walken in won. *c* **1400** *26 Pol. Poems* xxiii. 8 Prestes are lanterne hem to wysse þe wise weyes to heuene wones. **1412** *Ibid.* xi. 94 Hem thar not drede, where þey go, Here wele and worschip, in euery won. *c* **1440** Capgrave *Life St. Kath.* I. 26 A noble man,..Gracious in feld, peisible in wones. *c* **1450** Lovelich *Grail* liii. 126 Twelve the wysest Of Al that won. **14..** *How Good Wife taught Dau.* 44 in *Q. Eliz. Acad.* 45 Ne fayre wordes brake neuer bone, Ne neuer schall in no wone.

b. Applied to this world (esp. in ***worthly*** or ***worldly wone***); also to heaven (cf. also quots. 14.. in 1 and *c* 1400 in 3). Phr. ***worthly*** or ***worthy in wone***, distinguished in the world or in this life.

a **1310** in Wright *Lyric P.* xvi. 51 In al this wurhliche won, ..Never ȝete y nuste non lussomore in londe. *a* **1375** *Lay Folks Mass Bk.* App. IV. 637 From his blisse we schal be flemed Out of þat worþli won. *a* **1400** *Pistill of Susan* 54 Þo þouȝte þe wrecches to bewile þat worly [*v.rr.* worþi, wrthi] in wone. *Ibid.* 134 With wordus þei worshipe þat worliche in wone. *c* **1400** *Melayne* 168 Þose worthely men in wone. *c* **1400** *Anturs Arth.* xiii, Welcum, Waynor, i-wys wurlok in wone. **14..** T. Chestre *Launfal* 933 To wonye yn worldly wone. *c* **1460** *Towneley Myst.* i. 184 To walk here in this worthely wone.

† **wone**, *sb.*³ *Obs. poet.* Forms: 3–5 **won**, 3–7 **wone**, 4 **whon**, 4–5 **woon**, **wonne**, 5 **von**, **woone**; 5 **oon**, **one**; *Sc.* and *north.* 3–4 **wan**, 3–6 **wane**, 4–6 **wayn(e**, (4 **vayn**, 6 **vaine**). [ME. *wǭn*, app. a. ON. *ván* (see wone *sb.*²), but the earliest form with prefixed *i-* (y-), viz. i-won (q.v.), is remarkable in a word of Scand. origin.]

I. 1. Hope or expectation of a favourable issue; choice of alternative; hence, resource, expedient, course. Often in phr. ***to have, know, see***, etc. ***no other*** (or ***better***) ***wone***.

c **1290** *S. Eng. Leg.* I. 7/226 Þo he nuste non oþur won [*v.rr.* whon, iwon]. **1297** R. Glouc. (Rolls) 442 Þis gode folc of troye..flowe in to hor castles, vor hii nadde oþer won. *Ibid.* 1915 He him vnderstod of þe beste won. *Ibid.* 6540 He þoȝte of luþer won, Vor to sle þis godwine. *Ibid.* 10749 He of scapede to churche, as him þoȝte best won. *a* **1300** *Cursor M.* 5679 Moyses sagh na better wan Bot fled he in-to madian. *c* **1400** *St. Alexius* (Vernon) 247 Whon he sauȝ non oþur won, He bi-þouȝte him sone Anon, Wher him was best to be. *c* **1410** *Sir Cleges* 313 Sir Cleges sey non other von; Thereto he grauntyd sone anon. *c* **1425** Wyntoun *Cron.* III. vi. 874 Sen oþir succoure haf ȝhe nane, Na ȝhe can se na bettyr wayne. *c* **1435** *Torr. Portugale* 1295 The theff couth no better wonne, In to the see rennyth he sone. *c* **1450** *St. Cuthbert* (Surtees) 7779 He wist noȝt whilk was better wane, To dye in fire, or els be slane. **1535** Stewart *Cron. Scot.* (Rolls) I. 191 Flie mycht tha nocht, thair wes na vther wane. **1583** *Leg. Bp. St. Androis* 85 Than, when he had na vther vaine, He maid him for the kirk againe.

b. phr. (*north.*) ***will of wane*** [will *a.*] (less freq. ***wone***), occas. ***wilsome of wane***: at a loss, in bewilderment, without resource.

13.. *Cursor M.* 3051 (Gött.) Nou gas þat wreche wille of wane Wandrand in wildernes alane. **1375** Barbour *Bruce* VII. 2 The kyng toward the vod is gane, Wery for-swat and vill of vayn. *c* **1400** *Destr. Troy* 12823 All will of his wone his werdis to laite. *c* **1420** *Sir Amadace* (Camden) xxxiv, Nowe may wise men sitte atte home, Quen folus may walke full wille of wone. *c* **1450** Holland *Howlat* 43 Wa is me, wretche in this warld, wilsome of wane! **1535** Stewart *Cron. Scot.* (Rolls) II. 496 Preist or clerk that tyme tha sparit nane; Full mony one tha maid rycht will of wane.

2. Opinion, belief. (Cf. ween *sb.* 1.)

c **1300** *Havelok* 1711 More he louede hauelok one, Þan al denemark, bi mine wone! *Ibid.* 1972. **1370–80** *Visions of St. Paul* 207 in *O.E. Misc.* 229 Hose leeueþ not in wone þat Iesu crist, Godus sone, Tok Flesch and blod. *c* **1375** *Sc. Leg. Saints* xix. (*Cristofore*) 89 Trowand in wane, forowt wene, Þat þu þe maste master had bene.

II. Resources; abundance.

3. Phr. ***(full) good wone, (full) great wone***: a good number, a great quantity; used either in apposition (often following the sb. qualified), or with dependent *of*. Also advb., more or less vaguely, but chiefly with reference to the exercise of great force or speed. So *evil wone*, scarcity, dearth.

1297 R. Glouc. (Rolls) 17 Engelonde is vol inoȝ of frut & ek of tren..Of stel of yre & of bras, of god corn gret won. *Ibid.* 5359 His vissares.. so gret won of fisse him broȝte, þat wonder it was. *a* **1300** *Cursor M.* 7921 O scep he had ful mikel wan. *c* **1300** *Havelok* 1907 He leyden on heuedes, ful god won. *c* **1330** *King of Tars* 635 Whon thei weore bete ful good won. *c* **1350** *Leg. Rood* iii. 447 We sall gett water grete wane Here out of þis hard stane. **1377** Langl. *P. Pl.* B. xx. 170 Lyf..gaf hym golde, good woon, þat gladded his herte. *a* **1400** *Relig. Pieces fr. Thornton MS.* (1914) 102 Þou gafe thaym welthe mare wone þan þay euer hadde. **14..** T. Chestre *Launfal* 360 He..keste her well good won. **14..** *Sir Beues* (M.) 1344 Bred ne corne he ete none, But water had he good one. **14..** *Guy Warw.* (Cambr. MS.) 10329 Of harnes þou haste here gode oon. *c* **1470** Henry *Wallace* VIII. 948 Thir wermen tuk off venysoune gud wayn. ? *a* **1500** *Chester Pl., Balaam* 125 Yea, looke, thou het hym gold great wone [*v.r.* one], And riches for to lyve upon. *c* **1530** in *N. & Q.* 3rd Ser. XI. 7/2 Fruytes and corne shal fayle, gret woone. **1570** Levins *Manip.* 168/24 Good wone, *abundantia*. Euil wone, *inopia*.

4. Abundance, plenty. *in wone*: in abundance, plentifully.

a **1300** *Cursor M.* 2876 Thoru brennyng of þe brinstane, Quare-of þar es sa mikel wan. **13..** *Ibid.* 641 (Gött.) Þis is a stede of welthful wone, Of ioye ne blis ne wantis nane. *Ibid.* 4353 Worldes welth to welde in wone. **1340-70** *Alex. & Dind.* 499 Þere won walleþ of watur in þe welle-springus. *c* **1470** *Gol. & Gaw.* 37 All thair vittalis war gone, That thay weildit in wone.

5. Fortune, wealth, riches, possessions.

a **1300** *Florice & Bl.* (C.) 386 Þe ne faileþ non Gold ne seluer ne riche won. *c* **1300** *Prov. Hending* xxvi, 3ef þou haue þin oune won. *a* **1310** in Wright *Lyric P.* iv. 24 This worldes won. **13..** *K. Alis.* 5658 Hy ben y-clothed in alle wones. **13..** *Gaw. & Gr. Knt.* 1269 Were I worth al þe wone of wymmen alyue. *c* **1440** CAPGRAVE *Life St. Kath.* II. 1370 That ye shuld parte al this welthe and wone. *a* **1500** *Flower & Leaf* 201 The large wones Of Prester John, ne al his tresory Might not unneth have bought the tenth party.

†**wone**, *a. Obs.* Forms: α. 1–2 **ʒewuna**, 4 **ywon(e**, 5 **iwone**; β. 3 **wune**, 4–5 **won**, **wonne**, **wone**. [OE. *ʒewuna* = OS. *giwono* (MDu. *ghewône*, Du. *giwoon*), OHG. *giwon*: f. *ʒe-*, Y- + *wun-*, WON *v.*]

1. Accustomed, used, wont (*to do* something).

α. *c* **950** *Lindisf. Gosp.* Mark x. 1 *Sicut consueverat*, suæ þætte he ʒewuna wæs. *a* **1122** *O.E. Chron.* (Laud. MS.) an. 1006 Dydon eall swa hi ær ʒewuna wæron. *c* **1330** *Arth. & Merl.* 176 Why he nold with hem come, So he tofore was ywone. **13..** *Guy Warw.* (A.) 188 Þerl a gret fest held At Warwike in þat cite, Þat þan was y-won to be. *c* **1400** *Sowdone Bab.* 358 For ever he was thereto I-wone, To do Cristen men grete pyne.

β. *c* **1250** *Gen. & Ex.* 3569 And Iosu cam him a-gen, Als he was ilc dai wune to don. *a* **1300** *Cursor M.* 1384 Þe pine to bere a frut es won. *Ibid.* 2861 Þar þaa fiue cites war won to be Es noght now bot a stinkand see. *c* **1300** *Havelok* 2151 He..was here king, þat was hem wone Wel to yeme. **1375** BARBOUR *Bruce* IV. 246 [Satan] as he all tyme wes wone, In-to dissat maid his ansuer. *c* **1425** WYNTOUN *Cron.* VIII. xxxii. 5516 Folk, þat was noucht wone To se sic awant..Abayssit of þat sicht þai war. *c* **1450** CAPGRAVE *Life St. Aug.* 23 Þe heruest dayes wer ny whan skole is wone to cese. *a* **1500** *Hist. K. Boccus & Sydracke* (? 1510) U iij b, And hayle that to fal is wone The eyght daye of the mone.

2. Customary, usual. *rare.*

This is a doubtful sense assumed from such phrases as *as it is wone*, where *wone* is orig. and prob. always WONE *sb.*[1] (cf. quot. *c* 1290 in sense 2).

c **1205** LAY. 11184 He dude alse hit is wune, he streonede hire on enne sone. **1338** R. BRUNNE *Chron.* (1810) 83 Roberd Courthose his sonne he gaf all Normundie, To hold, as it was wonne, als heyre of ancestrie.

wone, *v.*[1]: see WON *v.*

†**wone**, *v.*[2] *Obs.* Forms: 1 **wanian**, 3 **wanenn** (*Ormin*), **wony**, **-ie**, **wone**, 3–4 **wane**. [OE. *wánian* = OFris. *wênia*, MLG. *wênen*, OHG. *weinôn* (MHG., G. *weinen*), ON. *veina* :—OTeut. **wainōjan*, f. *wai-* WOE.]

1. *trans.* To bewail, bemoan.

Beowulf 787 þara þe..ʒehyrdon..sar waniʒean hellehæfton. *a* **900** CYNEWULF *Juliana* 538 Siðfæt seofian, sar cwanian, wyrd wanian. *c* **1205** LAY. 25847 Þa fond he þer ane quene..wanede hire siðes þæt heo wæs on liues.

2. *intr.* To lament, moan. Also *transf.*

a **900** CYNEWULF *Crist* 992 Beornas gretað, wepað wanende wergum stefnum. *c* **1200** ORMIN 5653 Þe þridde seollþe doþ þe mann wepenn wiþþ skill & wanenn..forr hiss aʒhenn sinne. *a* **1225** *Owl & Night.* 975 Solde euch mon wonie and grede, Riʒt suich hi weren unlede. *c* **1275** LAY. 25827 Þo ihorde he..weape and wony [*c* 1205 weinen] reuliche beares. *c* **1275** *XI Pains of Hell* 187 in *O.E. Misc.* 152 Heo woneþ and groneþ day and nyht. *c* **1375** *Cursor M.* 12196 (Fairf.), I likkin ham to a brasin belle þat..wanis forþ wiþ-out resoun.

wone: see WANE.

woned: see WONT *pa. pple.*

wonene, var. WHENNE *Obs.*, whence.

woner: see WONNER.

†**'wonesome**, *a. Obs.* In 3 **wunsum**. [f. WON *v.* or WONE *sb.*[1] + -SOME.] Customary, usual.

c **1200** *Trin. Coll. Hom.* 181 Ac wowe beð wunsum þeih hit ne bie naht lefsum. *Ibid.* 203.

wong. *Obs.* exc. in place-names. Also **wang**. [OE. *wang, wong* = OS. *wang*, OHG. *wang*, only in *holzwangâ* 'campi nemorei' and in place-names, (G. dial. *wang* mountain slope), ON. *vangr* (Sw. dial. *vång*, Da. *vang*), Goth. *waggs* παράδεισος. (See WANG[1].)] A plain, field; a piece of meadow land; *spec.* a portion of unenclosed land under the open-field system: now surviving locally in the proper designations of certain fields or common lands.

Beowulf 2242 Beorh ealʒearo wunode on wonge wæteryðum neah. **971** *Blickl. Hom.* 105 Seoþþan heofonas tohlidon, & seo hea miht on þysne wang astaȝ. *a* **1000** *Phœnix* 13 Þæt is wynsum wong. *c* **1300** *Havelok* 1444 Borwes, tunes, wodes and wonges. ? **13..** in Spelman *Gloss. Arch.* (1664), Tres acræ terræ jacentes in lez wongs. **1371** in *Cal. Close Rolls* 351 [A third part of a furlong called the] Londmedewong..[a third part of a furlong called] Londwong. *c* **1440** *Promp. Parv.* 532/1 Wonge of londe, *territorium.* **1525** in *Lincoln Wills* (Linc. Rec. Soc. V) I. 157, ij acres landes lying in burgh callyd schothorne wang. **1528** *Ibid.* II. 97 A certeyn lande callyd Bawdwynwang. *a* **1825** FORBY *Voc. E. Anglia, Wong*, an agricultural division or district of some uninclosed parishes... In the parish of Horningtoft, in Norfolk, for instance, there is the How-wong, q.d. the wong by the hill. **1856** *N. & Q.* 2nd Ser. II. 79 At Tickhill [Yorks] are lands, all or mostly meadow, called the North Wongs, South Wongs, Saffron Wongs, and Church Wongs. **1877** *N.W. Linc. Gloss.* s.v., At Horncastle there is a piece of common land near the town called The Wong.

wong, obs. form of WANG[1], cheek.

wongai ('wɒŋgaɪ). *Austral.* [Aboriginal name.] A name used in the islands off the north coast of Australia for the jujube, *Zizyphus jujuba*. Also ***wongai tree.***

1947 I. L. IDRIESS *Isles of Despair* xxii. 146 All the yams and berries and wongais will soon ripen. **1959** K. TENNANT *All Proud Tribesmen* vii. 84 Wongai trees..have big dark berries like dates. **1968** *Courier-Mail* (Brisbane) 10 July 2/8 Thursday Island..has an informal charm and friendliness which easily tempts one to bite into the sticky fruit of the wongai tree. If you eat this fruit, legend says, you are bound to return.

‖**wonga-wonga** ('wɒŋgə'wɒŋgə). *Austral.* Also **wanga-wanga**. [Native name.]

1. An Australian pigeon, *Leucosarcia melanoleuca*. Also ***wonga(-wonga) pigeon.***

1821 L. MACQUARIE *Jrnl. of Tours* (1956) 223 Major Morisett has most kindly sent his young friend Lachlan the following very handsome presents of pets; vizt. four black swans..and one wanga-wanga pigeon. **1827** P. CUNNINGHAM *Two Yrs. N.S.W.* I. xvii. 321 A large pigeon named the *wanga-wanga*, of the size and appearance of the ringdove. **1846** J. L. STOKES *Discov. Australia* I. x. 314 At Captain King's table I tasted the wonga-wonga pigeon. **1887** W. S. S. TYRWHITT *New Chum in Queensland Bush* viii. 149 An occasional plain or scrub turkey, and wonga or squatter pigeons.

2. In full ***wonga(-wonga) vine.*** An evergreen climber, *Pandorea pandorana*, of the family Bignoniaceæ, native to Australia and bearing panicles of pale yellow or pink flowers.

1895 J. H. MAIDEN *Flowering Plants & Ferns N.S.W.* 33 The Wonga Wonga Vine... A tall, woody, glabrous climber with more or less twining branches. **1936** F. CLUNE *Roaming round Darling* xvii. 162 Another shrub was the wonga-wonga vine. It has white flowers, and the blacks used to hollow the stems and make whistles from them. **1946** K. TENNANT *Lost Haven* (1947) xvii. 278 The bells of the Wonga vine, milky with plum velvet in their throats.

wongen, variant of WANIGAN.

wonger(e, var. ff. WANGER *Obs.*

wongge tooth, obs. var. WANG-TOOTH.

wongi ('wɒŋgɪ). *Austral. local.* [Aboriginal.] A talk or chat; a speech.

1929 K. S. PRICHARD *Coonardoo* xxv. 243 He..had seen smoke..and come in for a bit of sugar and a wongie. **1939** X. HERBERT *Capricornia* xxiv. 354 'Give's a drink Joe —— I've rasped me old throat raw.'..'By cripes, Andy, that was a great wongi.' **1969** L. HADOW *Full Cycle* 178 If he asks you to have one..well, he's out for a wongi.

woning, *vbl. sb.*[1]: see WONNING.

†'**woning**, *vbl. sb.*[2] *Obs.* Forms: 1 **wanung**, 2–3 **waning**, 3–5 **woning(e**, **-yng(e**, 5 **wowenyng**. [OE. *wánung*, f. *wánian* WONE *v.*[2] + -ING[1].] Moaning, lamentation.

c **950** *Lindisf. Gosp.* Mark v. 38 Ðesaeh þæt wanung. *c* **1000** ÆLFRIC *Saints' Lives* xxiii. 104 La..hwæt mæȝ beon ȝeomrung and wanung ȝyf þæt næs se fulla æȝðres? *c* **1175** *Lamb. Hom.* 33 In helle..þer is waning and graming and toþen grisbating. *c* **1200** *Trin. Coll. Hom.* 177 Ðanne hauen wanspedie men on heorte wowe and on muðe woninge. *a* **1250** *Owl & Night.* 311 Þu..tellest þat ich ne can nouht singe Ac al my reorde is wonyng. *c* **1400** *Laud Troy Bk.* 15454 Achilles ligges..Ded In Troye In gret wowenyng. *c* **1425** *Engl. Conq. Irel.* 144 In al places was weylynge & wonynge, yollynge & crynge.

wonk[1] (wɒŋk). Also **wunk**. [Said to repr. pronunc. of Chin. *huáng gǒu* yellow dog.] In China, a dog. Also ***wonk dog.***

1900 H. A. GILES *Gloss. Subjects Far East* (ed. 3) 318 *Wunk*,..yellow dog. A term commonly applied by foreigners to the ordinary Chinese dog. From the Ningpo pronunciation *wou*[n] *kyi*, of the above two characters. **1909** J. O. P. BLAND *Houseboat Days in China* vii. 78 Particularly around the great cities you find him of the modern type, sporting a muzzle-loader..and a half-trained wonk. **1939** 'A. BRIDGE' *Four-Part Setting* i. 4 Away in the Chinese village a wonk dog bayed at the moon. *Ibid.* 5 There are all these Chinks and wonks about—you oughtn't to go alone. **1967** 'A. CORDELL' *Bright Cantonese* vi. 67 Starving wonk dogs, the scavengers of China.

wonk[2] (wɒŋk). *slang.* [In sense 1 related to WONKY *a.* The other senses may represent different words.] †**1.** In phr. ***all of a wonk***, nervous, upset. *Obs. rare.*

1918 [see DOODAH 1].

2. *Naut.* (See quots.)

1929 F. C. BOWEN *Sea Slang* 153 *Wonk*, a useless hand, or a young naval cadet who has not yet learnt the elements of his job. **1962** W. GRANVILLE *Dict. Sailors' Slang* 134/1 *Wonk*, midshipman.

3. *Austral.* **a.** A white person.

1938 X. HERBERT *Capricornia* 252 He went to the Dagoes and Roughs of second-class and won their friendship by..telling them how he had been cast out by the Wonks of the saloon. **1959** BAKER *Drum* 157 *Wonk*, a white man or white woman. Aborigines (esp. half-castes) use this pejorative much as whites use the word *boong* to denote an aboriginal.

b. An effeminate or homosexual man.

1945 BAKER *Austral. Lang.* vi. 123 An effeminate male is a ..gussie, spurge and wonk. **1970** P. WHITE *Vivisector* 213 I'd have to have a chauffeur to drive me about—with a good body—just for show, though. I wouldn't mind if the chauffeur was a wonk.

4. *U.S.* A disparaging term for a studious or hard-working person.

1962 *Sports Illustrated* 17 Dec. 21 A wonk, sometimes called a 'turkey' or a 'lunch', roughly corresponds to the 'meatball' of a decade ago. **1970** E. SEGAL *Love Story* 32 Who could Jenny be talking to that was worth appropriating moments set aside for a date with me? Some musical wonk? **1980** *N.Y. Times Mag.* 20 July 8 At Harvard the excessively studious student is derided as a 'wonk', which Amy Berman, Harvard '79, fancifully suggests may be 'know' spelled backward. (In British slang, 'wonky' means 'unsteady'.)

wonky ('wɒŋkɪ), *a. slang.* [Obscure: the G. element *wankel-* has similar force.] Of a person: shaky, groggy; unstable. Of a thing: faulty, unsound; unreliable.

1919 LD. NORTHCLIFFE *Let.* in *Hist. The Times* (1952) IV. I. xi. 507 Am weak, and wonky, as the telephone girls say, after a bad morning with the subscribers. **1923** H. C. BAILEY *Mr Fortune's Practice* iii. 81 'Who runs the "Daily Watchman?"..It's the wonkiest print on the market.'..'You said "on the market"... Corrupt?' 'Well, naturally.' **1925** E. WALLACE *Strange Countess* ix. 83 Financial adviser to some heads of departments, whose accounts went a little wonky. **1929** P. GIBBS *Hidden City* xvi. 79 It had made his heart jump in a wonky sort of way. **1932** KIPLING *Limits & Renewals* 127 Haman's headlight's wonky. Something *must* have happened. **1957** *Listener* 11 July 67 Despite the perfection of isolated lines and phrases..most of the poems seem slightly out of shape, wonky, as if the kiln had not been hot enough. **1958** *Observer* 23 Feb. 15/5 Would they really have sent her on a dangerous mission with an ankle still wonky from an old parachute fall? **1981** *Times Lit. Suppl.* 5 June 633/3 The vast majority of murderers are *ipso facto* acutely wonky, and most frequently wonky in dispiriting and unimaginative ways. **1983** D. BOGGIS *Woman they sent to Fight* ii. 17 The window fitted badly, and her chair was..wonky with one short leg. **1984** A. CARTER *Nights at Circus* II. vii. 156 'How's the wonky arm?' she enquired. He showed his sling.

Hence '**wonkiness**.

1982 *Times* 29 Apr. 10/8 Do not be disconcerted by its [*sc.* a book's] wonkiness of style.

wonly, obs. f. ONLY.

wonn(e, obs. ff. ONE, WAN *a.*, WHEN.

'**wonner**, '**woner**. *arch.* Also 4 **wonere**, **wonyer**. [f. WON *v.* + -ER[1]. Cf. G. *bewohner*, *einwohner*.] A dweller, an inhabitant.

a **1340** HAMPOLE *Psalter, Song of Moses* 506 All þe woners of chanaan wex starke. **1382** WYCLIF *Ps.* cxviii[i]. 19 A comeling wonere I am in the erthe. **1387** TREVISA *Higden* (Rolls) VII. 33 Þat is nouȝt plesynge to God, þat graunted þe place to þe olde wonyer. *a* **1513** FABYAN *Chron.* VI. cxcvi. (1811) 201 Wonner [citing Trevisa]. **1885** JEAN INGELOW *Sleep of Sigismund* xxvii, The shy wood-wonners.., bright-eyed furry things.

'**wonning**, '**woning**, *vbl. sb.*[1] *Obs., dial.*, or *arch.* Forms: 1 **wunung**, 2–3 **-ing**, **-ieng**, (3 **-(i)unge**, **-iȝinge**, **wun(n)ing**, **woniinge**, 4 **-yȝing**, **-enge**, **-(e)yinge**, **-iing**, *Sc.* **wonnyne**), 4–5 **wonyng(e**, **-inge**, **-iynge**, 4–6 **wonnyng(e**, (5 **wunnyng(e**, **vonyng**, 6 *arch.* **woonning**, 9 *dial.* **wunning**, **wunnen**), 4– **wonning**, **woning**. [OE. *wunung*, f. *wunian*: see WON, WONE *v.* and -ING[1].]

I. 1. The action or state of dwelling or abiding. ***to make one's woning***, to take up one's abode, to dwell.

c **960** ÆTHELWOLD *Rule St. Benet* (1885) 109 Ȝif he eft on æniȝne timan hine sylfne to mynstres wununge ȝefæstnian wile. **971** *Blickl. Hom.* 13 We þæs ȝelefað..þæt swa hwylc man swa mildheortnesse nafað, ne biþ þær Cristes..wunung on þære heortan. *c* **1200** *Trin. Coll. Hom.* 127 Þerefore he makede his wunienge in þe wilderne. *a* **1225** *Ancr. R.* 190 Mi cume & mi wuniunge, þauh hit þunche attri, hit is þauh healuwinde. **1297** R. GLOUC. (Rolls) 2604 In is stepmoder herte is woniinge he [*sc.* the Devil] nom. *a* **1300** *Cursor M.* 914 In womman sal mi wonning be. *Ibid.* 6157 Þair wonning þar..Four hundreth yere to þan had bene. *a* **1340** HAMPOLE *Psalter* lxxvii. 66 His wonnynge is amange men that has clene thoghtis. *c* **1375** *Sc. Leg. Saints* xxxvi. (*Baptista*) 761 Sum cristine þare wonnyne mais, þat þar propire kirkis hase. **1407** SCOGAN *Mor. Balade* 86 Let hem [*sc.* vices] have no wonning In your soules. *c* **1440** *York Myst.* iv. 3 The place That I haue graunte you..To haue your wonnyng in. *c* **1440** *Promp. Parv.* 532/1 Wonynge, or dwellynge, *mansio.*

2. A place of habitation, dwelling-place.

c **1000** ÆLFRIC *Saints' Lives* xxx. 315 Wæs seo wunung þær swyþe wynsum on to wicenne. *c* **1000** *Ags. Hom.* (Assmann) iii. 454 Se hælend sæde þæt on his fæder huse syndon maneȝa wununga. *c* **1200** *Trin. Coll. Hom.* 69 Þole me louerd alitelwan þat ich bimurne mi sor, er ich wite to þe þestere wunienge. **1297** R. GLOUC. (Rolls) 5572–3 To certein woniinge he hom broȝte boþe lowe & hey. So þat hor woniinge were al bi weste weye. **1340** *Ayenb.* 149 Þe erþe is woniynge of bestes and of men. **1398** TREVISA *Barth. De P.R.* VIII. iv. (Tollem. MS.), Þe..hyȝest heuen,..cuntrey and wonynge of blisful men. *c* **1400** *Lay Folks Mass Bk.* App. III. 123 His soule þat is þe wonyinge of crist. *c* **1430** *Hymns Virgin* (1867) 28 Ihesu! me brynge to þi woniynge. *c* **1470** HENRY *Wallace* IX. 442 In Gyan land full haistely couth ryd, Raissyt feill fyr, and waistyt wonnyngis wid. **1592** GREENE *Groat's W. Wit* (1617) 3 When I came first to this Cittie, my whole wardrope was onely a sute of white sheepe skins,..my woonning, the wide world. **1602** W. BASSE *Three Past. Elegies* ii. (1893) 66 My wonning is in yonder stall.

3. A dwelling-house or dwelling-room, dwelling, habitation.

c **1000** ÆLFRIC *Gen.* vi. 14 Wyrc ðe nu anne arc..& ðu wyrcst wununga binnan ðam arce. *a* **1225** *Ancr. R.* 74 *Habitatio eorum non habet januam*..Hore wunnunge naueð no ȝet. **1297** R. GLOUC. (Rolls) 594 He made hire vnder erþe a woniinge..& huld hire þere..priueliche. **13..** *E.E. Allit. P.* B. 921 Nov walle þe a wonnyng þat þe warisch myȝt. **1375** BARBOUR *Bruce* v. 177 The lady hir leif has tane, And went hyr hame to hir wonnyng. *c* **1450** CAPGRAVE *Life St. Gilbert* xlii. 28 Whan he say veryly þat he was hool he took leue and walkith on-to his wonyng. *a* **1529** SKELTON *E. Rummyng* 94 Her name Is Elynour Rummynge, At home in her wonnynge. **1824–8** *Craven Gloss.*, *Wunnen, Wunning*, a dwelling. In some parts of Craven this word is nearly extinct. When a cottage is divided into two parts, or habitations, it is called a house with two wunnings. **1901** G. MEREDITH *Reading of Life*, etc. 115 Clouds of them [*sc.* flies], under some herdsman's wonning, where there are the milk-pails.

II. 4. Custom, usage, habit. *rare.*

c **1440** *Promp. Parv.* 534/2 Wunnynge, or vsynge of custome, *frequentacio.* **1624** in *Cosin's Corr.* (Surtees) I. 23 He knoweth my woning, lett me se what he can say.

III. 5. *attrib.*: **won(n)ing-place, -stede** (STEAD *sb.*), **-wane** (WANE *sb.*^{2}; cf. *winning-wane*, WINNING *vbl. sb.*^{2}), a dwelling-place.

1303 R. BRUNNE *Handl. Synne* 1404 Here *wonynge placys yn joye were dyghte. **13..** *Cursor M.* 2076 (Gött.) Bi me au þu [*sc.* Cain] noght to duell, þi woning place es made in hell. *c* **1400** *Laud Troy Bk.* 18358 In helle mot be her wonyng-plas! *a* **1400–50** *Bk. Curtasye* 847 in *Babees Bk.* 327 Of alle oure synnes cryst be oure leche, And bryng vs to his vonyng place! *a* **1547** SURREY *Æneis* II. 842 For if the Gods my life wold haue proroged, They had reserued for me this wonning place. *a* **1300** *Cursor M.* 5375, I giue him *woningsted to wale For euermare. **1338** R. BRUNNE *Chron.* (1810) 76 So grete vengeance he nam..Fro ȝork vnto Durhem no wonyng stede was. *a* **1400–50** *Wars Alex.* 3734 Oure werkis & of oure wonynge-stede, if ȝe wald knawe, I sal declare ȝow þe cas. *a* **1500** *Hist. K. Boccus & Sydracke* (?1510) H iij, Where hath ye sowle..In mannys body his wonnyng-stede. *c* **1400** *Anturs Arth.* 316 (Th. MS.), For me buse wende one my waye,..Vn-to my *wonnynge wane. *c* **1500** *Gest Robyn Hode* cxlviii. in Child *Ballads* III. 63/2 Where is thy wonynge wane?

wonryde, var. WANDRETH *Obs.*

wons, obs. f. ONCE.

wonsom, obs. f. WINSOME *a.*

wonsped, var. WANSPEED *Obs.*

wonst: see ONCE *adv.* A. δ.

wont (wəʊnt; also (*now chiefly U.S.*) wʌnt), *sb. arch.* Also 6 **woont(e, wonte,** *Sc.* **wount.** [Early history and origin doubtful; perh. arose from a conflation of two synonymous constructions, *it is my wone* (WONE *sb.*) *to..*, and *I am wont* (WONT *pa. pple.*) *to..*, whence *it is my wont to..* (In view of the textual variants in the quot. from 'Cursor Mundi', this must be considered a dubious instance.) Johnson marks this word as 'out of use'.] Habitual or customary usage, custom, habit. ***use and wont***: see USE *sb.* 9 b; ***of* (†*in*) *wont***, customary, usual.

13.. *Cursor M.* 13693 (Gött.) For þiþer ȝode he ai vmstunt, þar to prai ofte was his wont [*other texts* was he wont].

1530 PALSGR. 290/1 Wont or custome to an yvell thyng, *amorse.* **1543** *Rental Bk. Cupar-Angus* (1880) II. 24 Payand zeirly..the sowm of xx^{ty} bollis..with all..vther dew seruice, vse and wont. *a* **1548** HALL *Chron., Hen. VIII* 196 b, After our old wont, we came together vpon our othe in the churche of S. Maturyne. **1548** GESTE *Agst. Priv. Masse* L iv, It was fyrst in wont that al the togethers assembled persones in ye church did communicat eche day. **1550** LATIMER *Serm. preached at Stamford* B ij, They [*sc.* the Pharisees] wolde be ordred by olde wont, customes, forfathers. **1593** SHAKS. *2 Hen. VI*, III. i. 2 'Tis not his wont to be the hindmost man. **1602** —— *Ham.* I. iv. 6 Then it drawes neere the season, Wherein the Spirit held his wont to walke. **1607** BEAUM. & FL. *Woman Hater* III. iv, She shall come in a white wastcoat, And—..And perhaps torn stockings, she hath left her old wont else. **1667–8** PEPYS *Diary* 10 Mar., As merry as that fellow Joyce could make us with his mad talking, after the old wont. **1818** SHELLEY *Julian & Maddalo* 13 A narrow space of level sand..Where 'twas our wont to ride. **1822** SCOTT *Nigel* xi, Her lodger..gave her, contrary to his wont, a signal to leave the room. **1848** LOWELL *Fable for Critics* liii, His wont Is to say very sharp things and do very blunt. **1850** NEWMAN *Serm. Var. Occas.* xii. (1881) 199 His commemoration is of daily wont in this neighbourhood. *a* **1866** WHEWELL in *Life* (1881) 563 Can I forget that this for thee too is Christmas, Christmas not as of wont—Christmas not of the earth? **1879** FARRAR *St. Paul* I. 385 They were..liable beyond the common wont of mobs to sudden gusts of feeling and impulse. **1903** *Times* 14 July 11/2 Bosnian use and wont and Oriental ideas were taken into full consideration. **1906** *Athenæum* 24 Nov. 665/2 The story is extravagant beyond the author's wont.

transf. **1581** A. HALL *Iliad* VI. 118 My heart to alter from his wont it also doth disdaine. **1594** HOOKER *Eccl. Pol.* I. iii. §5 When things naturall in that regard forget their ordinary naturall woont. **1637** C. DOW *Answ. to H. Burton* 128 Envy her selfe..would have lost her wont. *a* **1854** H. REED *Lect. Brit. Poets* ix. (1857) 312 It is the wont of hollow things to echo.

b. in particularized use.

1542 UDALL *Erasm. Apoph.* 135 b, Diogenes of a customable woonte auouched to bee a thynge muche more daungerous to falle in the handes of flaterers..then to lighte emong crowes. **1556** M. PARKER *Psalter* lxxviii. 226 To theyr old wontes they dyd retyre, as sturdy bow in bent. **1612** T. TAYLOR *Comm. Titus* iii. 3. 597 He is a foole still, he leaueth not his old wonts. **1674** N. FAIRFAX *Bulk & Selv.* 1 Whoever ..betakes himself to the scanning of bodies,..either as to their kinds of being or wonts of working. **1854** S. DOBELL *Balder* xxiii. 103 She [*sc.* Morn] won of God That ever when she walketh in the world It shall be Eden: and around her come The happy wonts of early Paradise.

wont (wəʊnt; also (*now chiefly U.S.*) wʌnt), *v. arch.* Forms: 5 **wunte, -on, wontyn,** 6 **wonte, wount,** *Sc. pa. t.* **vont,** 6–7 **woont,** 6– **wont;** *pa. t.* 6– **wonted, wont.** [f. WONT *pa. pple.* or back-formation f. WONTED.]

1. *trans.* To make (a person, etc.) accustomed or used *to* (occas. *with*); = ACCUSTOM 3, USE *v.* 19.

c **1440** *Alphabet of Tales* 228 Þat he mott wunte þaim & make þaim perfite in wirkyng of wull. *c* **1440** *Promp. Parv.* 534/2 Wunton, or gretely to ȝeue an other vse and custome (*P.* wontyn or greatly to vse and custom), *assuefacio, usito.* **1535** *Goodly Primer* Ps. xxv, Wont me to thy paths. **1544** BETHAM tr. *Purlilia's Precepts War* II. xxxii. K v, It shal not be vnprofitable to acquaynten and wount your horses..to suffer the sytter whyche is a gunner. **1600** SURFLET *Countrie Farme* VII. xlvii. 882 And so offring her such meat as is most easie, you shall woont her to eate of the said hart. **1606** PEACHAM *Art of Drawing* 12 Before you..have woonted and made your hand ready in proportions of all sorts. **1656** J. OWEN *Mortif. Sin* (1668) 108 Wont thy Heart to thoughts hereof. *c* **1682** in *Verney Mem.* (1907) II. 312 When I have visited her and a little wonted her to the place, I'll come home. **1916** *Contemp. Rev.* June 689 The various defence and relief committees..have wonted people to the notion of organising the community.

b. *refl.* (rarely *intr.* for *refl.*)

1603 HOLLAND *Plutarch's Mor.* 1213 He..woonteth himselfe to keepe farre from any unjust and unlawfull taking of money. **1614** T. ADAMS *Sinners Passing Bell* Wks. (1629) 268 So these, that in youth haue wonted themselues to the load of lesse sinnes. **1652** H. L'ESTRANGE *Amer. no Jewes* 18 To wont and accustome to the waters, they practising very much swimming. **1699** R. L'ESTRANGE *Erasm. Colloq.* (1725) 83 It is the best Course we can take to wont ourselves to that which is good. **1856** EMERSON *Engl. Traits* xvi. 275 We walked round the stones..to wont ourselves with their strange aspect.

†**2.** *trans.* To use habitually. *Obs. rare.*

1530 PALSGR. 784/1 It is no wysdome to wont a thyng that is nat honest.

3. *intr.* To be wont or accustomed; to be in the habit of (doing that which is expressed by the inf.). Chiefly in pa. t. = used (USE *v.* 21).

a **1547** SURREY *Poem in Add. MS. 17492* in *Anglia* XXIX. 337 Helpe to be walle the woffulle casse..off me that wontede to rejoyes the ffortwne offe my pleassante chyes. *a* **1578** LINDESAY (Pitscottie) *Chron. Scot.* (S.T.S.) I. 29 Flatteraris..spurit him to grettar tyrannie and oppressioun nor ony man vont to do befoir. **1591** SHAKS. *1 Hen. VI*, I. ii. 14 Talbot is taken, whom we wont to feare. **1592** NASHE *P. Penilesse* (ed. 2) 31 b, He determined..to poyson the streame, where this iolly Forester wonted to drink. **1632** LITHGOW *Trav.* Ded. A 4, And how often wont your euer blessed Father, graciously to peruse Lines of mine. **1671** MILTON *Samson* 1487 Sons wont to nurse thir Parents in old age, Thou in old age car'st how to nurse thy Son. *a* **1700** SEDLEY *Poet. Pieces* Wks. 1722 II. 10 To bouze old Wine, mad Pindar wonted. *a* **1703** BURKITT *On N.T.* Luke ii. 45 Had he not wonted to converse formerly with them, he had not now been sought amongst them. **1771** BEATTIE *Minstr.* I. xxxv, Where Fays of yore their revels wont to keep. **1837** WORDSW. *Cuckoo at Laverna* 60 With beast and bird..He wont to hold companionship so free. *a* **1851** MOIR *Sonn., Scottish Sabbath* v, With those he loved..He wont on Sabbath morn to cross the plain!

transf. **1599** THYNNE *Animadv.* Ded. (1875) 2 Not degeneratinge from youre former curtesye wontinge to accompanye all youre actions. **1640** R. BAILLIE *Canterb. Self-convict.* Pref. 13 England wont not..to bee so scant of faithfull witnesses. **1726** POPE *Odyss.* XIX. 11 His arms deform the roof they wont adorn. **1833** CHALMERS *Const. Man* (1835) II. vii. 46 In as far as this wont to consist of potatoes or grain. **1884** W. C. SMITH *Kildrostan* 43 He never can Bring back the glory that wont to be. **1885–94** R. BRIDGES *Eros & Psyche* Sept. 12 The merry pipe, That wont to cheer the harvesting, is mute.

b. *absol.* (without inf.)

1585 LAMBARDE in *Camden's Lett.* (1691) 28 Sorrowing that I may not now, as I wonted, dwell in the meditation of the same things. **1590** SPENSER *F.Q.* II. xi. 26 The villein turn'd his face, (As wonts the Tartar..When as the Russian him in fight does chace). **1590** SHAKS. *Com. Err.* IV. iv. 40, I beare it on my shoulders, as a begger woont her brat. **1593** NASHE *Christ's T.* 28 The Earth left to be so fruitfull as it wont. **1594** R. C[AREW] *Godfrey of Bvlloigne* (1881) 109 And with a semblant braue and nobellest, (As lightning wonts) he in his armour shines. **1598** SYLVESTER *Du Bartas* II. i. I. *Eden* 461 Ile not exact hard fines (as men shall woont). **1836** RUSKIN *Marcolini* II. iii. Wks. 1903 II. 494 Peace, he is here —Lo you, he comes not forward as he wont.

†**4.** To dwell habitually, have its habitat. *Obs.*

1692 R. L'ESTRANGE *Fables* I. clxvii. 140 The Kingfisher is a Solitary Bird, that Wonts commonly by the Water-side.

wont (wəʊnt; also (*now chiefly U.S.*) wʌnt), *pa. pple.* and *ppl. a.* Forms: α. 1 **ȝewunod, -ad, -ed,** 2–3 **iwuned,** 2–5 **iwoned,** 3–4 **ywoned,** 4–5 **ywond(e** (5 **i-, ywonyd**); 3 **wuned,** 4 **wonde,** 4–5 **woned, -yd,** 5 **woond,** 7 **won'd, wond, wouned.** β. 3 **iwunet, iwonet,** 4–5 **iwont** (4 **iwonte, ywont,** 5 **ywonet**); 4–6 **wunt, wount, wonte,** (4 **wonnt, wonþ,** *Sc.* **vont,** 4–5 **wnt,** 5 **won(n)et, w(o)unte,** 6 **wante**), 5–7 **woont(e,** 4– **wont.** [OE. *ȝewunod*, pa. pple. of *ȝewunian* WON *v.*]

A. *pa. pple.* †**1.** Accustomed, used *to*, familiar *with* (a thing, practice, or condition). *Obs.*

c **888** ÆLFRED *Boeth.* i, His mod..to þam woruldsælþum ȝewunod wæs. *c* **1000** ÆLFRIC *Hom.* II. 278 Næs þæt Israhela folc ȝewunod to hreawum flæsce. *c* **1200** *Trin. Coll. Hom.* 181 Ac hwanne hit [*sc.* the child] beð þarto wuned, hit wepeð þe lasse. *a* **1300** *Cursor M.* 28462 Til tauerne huse my-seluen was wont. *c* **1374** CHAUCER *Boeth.* IV. pr. iv. (1868) 128 Þei han hire eyen so wont to derkenesse of erþely þinges. *c* **1386** —— *Clerk's T.* 283 She neuere was to swiche gestes woned. *a* **1400** *Theophilus* xxi. in *Engl. Studien* XXXII. 8 For I was wont to noble fare Among prynces of londes. *c* **1450** HOLLAND *Howlat* 164 Cardinalis..With red hattis on hed, in haile takynning Off that deir dignite, with worschipe ay wont. *c* **1520** BARCLAY *Jugurth* lvii. 83 From his youth he was euer wont with hardnesse, hunger, thyrst, and labour.

2. (*a*) Conjugated with the verb 'to be', and const. inf. (with or less freq. without *to*): Accustomed, used; in the habit of (doing something).

α. *c* **1175** *Lamb. Hom.* 143 Vre drihten wile cumen..and wile for-berne alle his fon and heom þet beoð iwunede uuel to done. *c* **1200** ORMIN 12695 Ær wass he wunedd offte To cumenn till þe flumm till himm. **1297** R. GLOUC. (Rolls) 1431 Gwider vr king of þis lond is truage athuld sone Of rome þat is eldore were iwoned [*v.rr.* ywond, ywonte, wonnte, wonte] to done. **13..** *Sir Beues* (A.) 3776 Whan wer we woned be by-hinde? **1340** *Ayenb.* 106 Al þet me wes ywoned byuore to louie. *c* **1384** CHAUCER *H. Fame* III. 486 His clarioun..With which he wonde is to hiraude Hem that me list preised be. **1393** LANGL. *P. Pl.* C. VII. 143 Among wyues and wodewes ich am ywoned [*v.rr.* wonet to, wont to] sitte Yparroked in puwes. *c* **1450** *Godstow Reg.* 106 Iohn Waleys and Alice his wyf..quyteclaymed..ij. d. of yerely rente, the which they were I-wonyd to haue. **1483** CAXTON *Gold. Leg.* 111/1 Lyke as he was woond to telle and reherce. **1489** —— *Faytes of A.* III. xiii. 196 Of suche thynges men are woned to vse.

β. *a* **1240** *Sawles Warde* in *O.E. Hom.* I. 257 Ant al þat hird þat ha wes i wunet to dreaien efter hire. *c* **1290** *Beket* 247 in *S. Eng. Leg.* 113 With more nobleie he rod i-nouȝ þane he was i-wonet to do. *a* **1300** *Cursor M.* 3922 A godd..þe quilk þat he was wonnt anure. *Ibid.* 4452 To comforth þam wel was he wont. *Ibid.* 28223 My breth it wald be til vnhoue þat many man was wonto droue. **13..** *Bonaventura's Medit.* 975 Sone, y was wunt þe swetly to wrappe. **1375** BARBOUR *Bruce* I. 220 That folk, that euir wes fre, And in fredome wount for to be. *c* **1440** *Alphabet of Tales* 292 He forgatt hur,..nor did hur nott wurshup as he was wunte to doo. *a* **1450** MYRC *Par. Pr.* 1353 Art þow I-wont at lychwake Any pleyes for to make? *c* **1470** *Stonor Papers* (Camden) I. 110 Servantes be not so delygent as þei were wonto bee. *c* **1520** SKELTON *Magnyf.* 1890 He was wonte to boste, brage, and to brace. **1590** SPENSER *F.Q.* I. i. 16 Ay wont in desert darknesse to remaine. **1664** BUTLER *Hud.* II. III. 599 Your Ancient Conjurers were wont To make her from her Sphere dismount. **1741–2** GRAY *Agrip.* 108 Legions, wont to stem With stubborn nerves the tide. **1810** SCOTT *Lady of L.* VI. xxiv, The lark was wont my matins ring. **1814** JANE AUSTEN *Mansf. Park* xli, He might have more good qualities than she had been wont to suppose. **1850** TENNYSON *In Mem.* viii, Every pleasant spot In which we two were wont to meet. **1869** TOZER *Highl. Turkey* II. 350 The poet is wont to ignore the rivers when it suits his convenience to do so.

(*b*) predicated of things.

a **1200** *Moral Ode* 57 Vre swinc and ure tilþe is ofte iwoned [*v.rr.* iwuned, wuned] to swinden. **1303** R. BRUNNE *Handl. Synne* 914 And so, grete tempest secede al, þat on þeyr frutys was wnt to fal. **1387** TREVISA *Higden* (Rolls) I. 85 Parthia..was i-woned to conteyne al þe lond of foure contrees, of Assyria, of Media, of Persida, and of Carmania. *c* **1400** MAUNDEV. i. (1919) I. 5 Constantynoble þat was wont to be clept Bezanzon. **1444** *Rolls of Parlt.* V. 114/1 Al manere of Wynes..were woned and used to pass through a vessell. **1566** *S'hampton Crt. Leet Rec.* (1905) I. i. 44 Where the Backe was wante to stonde. **1647** in *Verney Mem.* (1907) I. 359 The longer your letters were the more they were woont to please mee. **1667** MILTON *P.L.* v. 123 Those looks That wont to be more chearful and serene. **1794** PALEY *Evid.* III. viii. (1817) 373 The prejudices which are wont to arise in our minds. **1875** WHITNEY *Life Lang.* vii. 127 Such a distinction is wont to be termed 'inorganic'.

b. Conjugated with the verb 'to have': in ***had wont***, had been accustomed. Now *rare.*

1594 O. B. *Quest. Profit. Concern.* 15 b, One of his good dames..who had wont to bestow the best roome..in her house on him. **1606** G. W[OODCOCKE] *Hist. Ivstine* XLIV. 137 A narrow path, where cattel had wont to go through. **1655** tr. *Sorel's Com. Hist. Francion* I. 16 My Couch had wont to be upon curious Satin Quilts. **1682** BUNYAN *Holy War* 239 The love-feasts that had wont to be between their Prince and them. **1870** J. BRUCE *Life of Gideon* vii. 120 He who had wont to come to the patriarchs..had actually come to him.

c. without inf.

c **1000** ÆLFRIC *Hom.* II. 138 Þes..halȝa wer wæs ȝewunod þæt he wolde gan on niht to sæ. *a* **1300** *Cursor M.* 3520 Esau went for till hunt, A day, sum he was oft wunt. *c* **1375** *Sc. Leg. Saints* x. (*Mathou*) 68 Þai cuth..Ger serpentis strik men ful sare, As befor-tyme wechis vont ware. *c* **1380** WYCLIF *Wks.* (1880) 321 Ȝif lif of þise newe ordris be more medeful þen mannes lif was woned. *c* **1470** HENRY *Wallace* XI. 349 Inglismen thocht he tuk mar boundandly Than he was wount at ony tym befor. **1535** COVERDALE *Ps.* cxviii[i]. 149 Quycken me acordinge as thou art wont. **1656** EARL MONM. tr. *Boccalini's Advts. fr. Parnass.* II. xv. (1674) 164 He found her not to have that Grace and Majesty which she had wont. **1719** YOUNG *Revenge* v. i, He fought as he was wont, and four he slew. **1812** CARY *Dante, Parad.* XVII. 52 The common cry, Will, as 'tis ever wont, affix the blame Unto the party injur'd. **1848** DICKENS *Dombey* xli, All is going on as it was wont.

†**B.** *ppl. a.* = WONTED B. *Obs.*

1382 WYCLIF *Jer.* xlviii. 33 The tredere of the grape the wont myrie song shal not synge. **14..** HOCCLEVE *Min. Poems* 70/107 Lady! Of thy wont bontee, keepe alway the cours! *c* **1450** tr. *De Imitatione* III. vii. 73 Þou..turnest anoon ayen to þe wont iapes of þyne herte. **1535** JOYE *Apol. Tindale* (Arb.) 17 Aftir his wont disdaynful maner. **1596** SPENSER *F.Q.* v. iii. 1 So comes it now to Florimell by tourne,..To tast of ioy, and to wont pleasures to retourne.

b. *ought and wont* (*Sc.*): due and customary. (Cf. *used and wont* s.v. USED *ppl. a.* 2 b.)

c 1450 Godstow Reg. 258 Yeldyng therof yerely to the chief lordis dewe and woned rentis. 1477 in Exch. Rolls Scot. IX. 102 All uthir dew service aucht and wount. 1535 Reg. Privy Seal Scot. II. 261/2 With uther service and dewiteis aucht and wonit alanerlie.

wont: see WANT, WEEN *v.*

won't (wəʊnt), colloq. contraction of *woll not* = *will not* (see WILL *v.*[1] A. 6 b). Also (cf. DON'T, SHAN'T) as *sb.* = refusal.

1902 Monthly Rev. Aug. 168 Already he was beginning to know the just value of a woman's won't, so he gave up the contest. 1911 B. HOLLAND Life Dk. Devonshire I. xiii. 293 Hartington's 'won't' was stronger than his 'will'.

b. In hyphened comb. with infins., forming sbs. (occas. adjs.), e.g. ***won't-learn***, one who refuses to learn; ***won't-work***; ***won't-wait***, that won't wait.

1857 R. M. BALLANTYNE Coral Islands xxiv, People .. who are sich born drivellin' won't-believers that they think [etc.]. 1868 FURNIVALL Babees Book 200 John Russell lets off his won't-learns very easily. 1904 Westm. Gaz. 20 Feb. 7/1 The 'unemployables' and the 'won't works' are the recipients of most of the relief. 1909 Daily Chron. 8 Apr. 1/7 Won't-wait agitators.

wonted ('wəʊntɪd; also (*now chiefly U.S.*) 'wʌntɪd), *pa. pple.* and *ppl. a.* [Either f. WONT *sb.* + -ED, or an extension of WONT *pa. pple.*, apprehended later as pa. pple. of WONT *v.*]

A. *pa. pple.* †**1.** = WONT *pa. pple.* 2. *Obs.*

a 1413 Chaucer's Troylus v. 277 (Campsall MS.) And whiten gan the Orisonte shene Al Estward as it wonted is to done [v.rr. Al Esturwarde as it wonte is to done; Al est-ward as it was wone to done]. c 1450 LOVELICH Merlin 6779 Lo, Sire, Merlyne Js comen to ȝow here, That ȝe Weren Wonted to loven so Wel. 1557 PHAER Æneid. v. (1558) N ij b, Syr Erix wonted was to giue combat. 1566 Acts Privy Counc. Irel. (Hist. MSS. Comm.) 152 Omagher to contribute to Occarrall, as hath been wonted, the thirde parte of the said bonnaght. 1583 STOCKER Civ. Warres Lowe C. I. 15 A great Image .. which was wonted to be set vp. 1606 G. W[OODCOCKE] Hist. Ivstine XXXII. 109 Being enticed with the sweeteness of the prey as men wonted to liue together vpon the spoile. 1612 R. SHELDON Serm. preached at S. Martins in the Fields 15 O theefe, wonted with violence to violate men.

2. = WONT *pa. pple.* 1. Now *U.S.*

1610 C. HAMPTON Serm. 2 He prouided .. a tent, whereunto it had beene wonted. 1614 SYLVESTER Parl. Vertues Royall 1305 The Angell, wonted to Heav'n's Blissefull Hall, Made little stay in this unholesome Stall. 1637 EARL MONM. tr. Malvezzi's Romulus & Tarquin 295 The Romanes were .. accustomed to war, wonted to victory. 1692 R. L'ESTRANGE Fables I. clxv. 138 She was wonted to the Place, she said, and would not Remove. 1847 EMERSON Repr. Men, Shakespeare Wks. (Bohn) I. 364 Dramatic materials to which the people were already wonted. 1851 HAWTHORNE Ho. Sev. Gables v. (1904) 98 Hepzibah had fully satisfied herself of the impossibility of ever becoming wonted to this .. obstreperous little bell. 1878 Scribner's Monthly XVI. 56/2 Afterward we grew wonted to their beauty. 1893 Harper's Mag. LXXXVI. 855/1 He became wonted to his new station.

b. *absol.* Made familiar with one's environment. Now *U.S.*

1610 MARKHAM Masterp. I. lxxvi. 159 Others vse to leade the horse to a .. sheepe-pen, where great store of sheepe are wonted. 1641 [see WONTING c]. 1870 LOWELL Study Wind. I. 14, I had crows... They grew so wonted as .. to tolerate my near approach. 1874 —— Lett. II. 138, I long to get back, and yet am just beginning to get wonted (as they say of babies and new cows) over here.

B. *ppl. a.* Accustomed, customary, usual. Now *arch.* or *U.S.*

1408 in Hakl. Voy. (1599) I. 177 According to their woonted maner. 1553 ASCHAM Rept. Germany A iij, Letters .. full of your wonted good will towardes me. 1574 in Hist. Fam. Fortescue (1869) II. 234 Savage did send into the grounds, with the hounds, but the wonted boy, with 2 keepers. 1576 in W. H. Turner Select. Rec. Oxford (1880) 384 The wonted streame .. ys .. taken awaye. 1624 CAPT. J. SMITH Virginia v. 199 It being growne past the wonted season of the comming in of ships. 1671 MILTON P.R. IV. 449 Out of the wood he starts in wonted shape. 1710 BERKELEY Princ. Hum. Knowl. §3 Wks. 1871 I. 138 The wonted indulgent methods of Providence. 1750 GRAY Elegy 92 E'en in our Ashes live their wonted Fires. 1823 SCOTT Quentin D. xxvi, The King .., in a threadbare cloak, with his wonted old high-crowned hat stuck full of images. 1848 LOWELL Fable for Critics lii, Archæologians .. Have tried to make out, with a zeal more than wonted, 'T was a kind of wild swine that our ancestors hunted. 1850 TENNYSON In Mem. ci. 22 As year by year the labourer tills His wonted glebe. 1860 MAURY Phys. Geog. xii. §539. 299 Which obstructions may prevent the winds from taking up .. their wonted supplies of moisture.

absol. 1837 CARLYLE Fr. Rev. III. v. i, The Wonted tumbles down; by imitation, by invention, the Unwonted hastily builds itself up.

'wontedly, *adv.* [f. prec. + -LY[2].] Customarily, habitually, usually.

1567 PAINTER Pal. Pleas. (1575) II. 182 [Her] hands wontedly were so cold both in Wynter and Sommer as the Mountayne ice. 1611 SPEED Hist. Gt. Brit. IX. ii. §25. 425 Wontedly the Land was defended by dint of Swords. 1625 JACKSON Creed v. l. 449 Oftimes more then wontedly pampering their wonted greene desires, vnder the shelter of a sable suite. 1653 R. SANDERS Physiogn. 189 If the sight appear not as formerly or wontedly it did. 1913 W. OWEN Let. 4 Jan. (1967) 175 The Vicar's presence (taciturn instead of wontedly gay) .. sat heavy on my soul the night. 1980 N.Y. Times 12 Dec. C-30/3 On Sunday at 7.30 P.M., South Street's 19th-century surroundings will be wontedly hushed, except at Bowne. 1981 Guardian 4 Oct. 21 Dexter was wontedly tough on some of the actors.

'wontedness. *rare.* [f. as prec. + -NESS.] Accustomedness, habituation.

1648 Eikon Bas. xvii. 92, I might suspect my Judgement to be biassed .. with some Prejudice and wontedness of Opinion. 1656 Artif. Handsom. 173 Wontednesse makes even Blackamores seem handsome to one another. 1868 A. D. T. WHITNEY Patience Strong's Outings iii, We shaded off our wontedness from one [carpet] into the other.

wonter, var. WANTER[2], mole-catcher.

1657 in Giles Bampton (1847) Suppl. 3 Within these two meadows are several Hams of meadow, viz. the Bull Ham, .. the Worden Ham, the Wonter's Ham [etc.].

wonti(e, obs. forms of WANT *v.*

'wonting, *vbl. sb.* [f. WONT *v.* + -ING[1].] The action of the verb WONT. **a.** The accustoming (of a person *to* something).

1692 R. L'ESTRANGE Fables Pref. A 2, The Wonting of us to the Use and Liking of these Levities, Leads .. us to a Misunderstanding of Things.

b. Custom, wont.

1667 COTTON Scarron. IV. 78 Æneas and the Queen have made .. A match to go, after her wonting, Into the Woods a Squirrel hunting.

c. *attrib.*: †**wonting penny**, wages paid to a cattle-herd for keeping beasts in a place until they are accustomed to it (cf. WONTED *pa. pple.* 2 b).

1641 BEST Farm. Bks. (Surtees) 120 The nowt heard hath for everie beast one pennie, which is called a wontinge pennie; hee .. keepeth them .. till they bee wonted and hanted togeather.

'wontless, *a. poet. Obs.* or *arch.* [f. WONT *sb.* + -LESS.] Unaccustomed, unwonted, unusual.

1587 T. HUGHES Misfort. Arthur I. ii, That both my hart and marrow quite be burnt, And synewes dried with force of woontlesse flames. 1596 SPENSER Hymn Hon. Beauty 2 What wontlesse fury dost thou now inspire Into my feeble breast? 1628 MURE Fancies Farewell i. 12 Mounted on wings of immortalitie, I feele my brest warmde with a wountless fire. 1795 SOUTHEY Joan of Arc VI. 349 He, .. all astonish'd at their force And wontless valour, rages round the field. 1855 SINGLETON Virgil VI. 21 Daedalus .. Along a wontless region floated off To th' icy Bears.

†**'wontlike**, *a. Obs. rare.* In 7 **woont-**. [f. WONT *sb.* or *ppl. a.* + -LIKE.] Wonted, accustomed.

1601 R. JOHNSON Kingd. & Commw. 64 He stirred not, neither with woontlike disdaine once offered to reuenge so great an indignitie.

†**'wontly**, *adv. Obs. rare.* [f. WONT *ppl. a.* + -LY[2].] According to custom, usually.

1654 VILVAIN Enchir. Epigr. v. li, Hot Fume .. Which Wind And Earthquake wontly breeds. Ibid. 191 b.

won ton (wɒn tɒn). Also **wan tan, wun tun**, and as one word. [Chinese (Cantonese), Pinyin *húntun*.] A small round roll or pocket of dough containing a savoury filling, eaten alone (after being deep-fried) or boiled in soup (***won ton soup***).

1948 R. W. DANA Where to eat in New York 66 The theater and night-club performers drop in late for chicken egg foo yong, a won ton soup, squab, or Chinese steak. 1952 W. Y. HONG Chinese Cook Bk. 37 Pick up about ½ teaspoon of meat (or fish) mixture and place on one corner of the won-ton skin. Roll almost to the opposite corner... The usual serving is 12 to 15 won-tons per person. Ibid. 38 Chicken Won-Ton Soup... 8 cups super soup stock... 2 cups chicken meat... 90 pieces of won-ton. 1956 'E. MCBAIN' Cop Hater (1958) xx. 172 The wonton soup was crisp with Chinese vegetables... The wontons were brown and crisp. 1972 K. LO Chinese Food I. 54 Well made wuntuns floating in clear soups resemble clouds. 1976 Times 20 Aug. 12/8 Two spring rolls for 25p, skins for Wan Tan dumpling at 60p a lb. 1976 Time 27 Sept. 63/2 The Chinese deep-fry everything from shrimp toast and wontons to beef and chicken.

†**'wontsomeness.** *Obs. rare.* [f. WONT *sb.* + *-someness* (see -SOME[1]).] Custom, habit.

c 1425 WYNTOUN Cron. lxx. 2124 Alkyne tame best .. ran .. To woddis and to wildernes, Leiffand thare avne wontsumnes [MS. Cott. awlde hamlynes].

wonus, obs. form of ONCE.

woo (wu:), *v.*[1] Now *literary*. Forms: 1 **woȝian**, 3 **wohe**, 3–4 **woȝe(n, wowen**, 3–6 **wowe**, (4 **wouwe**, 5 **wowyn, wogh**), 5–7 **wow, wooe**, 6–7 **wo**, 6–8 **woe**, 6– **woo**. [Late OE. *wóȝian* (also *áwóȝian* in trans. sense), of obscure origin.]

I. *intr.* (or *absol.*) **1.** To solicit or sue a woman in love; to court, make love.

a 1050 Liber Scintill. xiii. (1889) 68 Bearn worulde þissere woȝiað & hi beoð ȝesealde to gyftum. Ibid., Ne hi ne woȝiað ne hi ne lædað wif. Ibid. 70 Naht framað flæsc habban mæden ȝif on ȝeþance æniȝ woȝað. a 1225 Ancr. R. 388 Ase a mon þet woweð [MS. Titus wohes]—ase a king þet luuede one lefdi of feorrene londe. a 1300 K. Horn 793 (Camb.) Whan þu farst to woȝe, Tak him þine gloue. 1338 R. BRUNNE Chron. (1810) 40 Unto þe duke of Normundie he went for to wouwe. 1390 GOWER Conf. II. 7 Wher a womman is al one, It makth a man .. The more hardi forto wowe. 1500–20 DUNBAR Poems xiii. 44 Religious men of diuerss placis Cumis thair to wow and se fair facis. 1600 SHAKS. A.Y.L. v. ii. 3 Is't possible, that .. but seeing, you should loue her? And louing woo? and wooing, she should graunt? 1670 RAY Prov. 30 To wo is a pleasure in a young man, a fault in an old. 1792 BURNS Duncan Gray i, Duncan Gray came here to woo. 1822 CAMPBELL Maid's Remonstr. i, Never wedding, ever wooing, Still a love-lorn heart pursuing, .. Wed, or cease to woo. 1859 TENNYSON Marr. Geraint 442 A creature wholly given to brawls and wine, Drunk even when he woo'd.

b. Of animals.

a 1310 in Wright Lyric P. 44 Wowes this wilde drakes. Ibid., Wormes woweth under cloude. 1398 TREVISA Barth. De P.R. XII. i. (1495) A ij/1 Males [of birds] drawe to company of females .. and wowe wyth beckes & voyce.

c. in fig. context.

a 1225 Ancr. R. 400 Lo! þus ure Louerd woweð: nis heo to herd i-heorted þet a swuch woware ne mei turnen hire luue to him. 1390 GOWER Conf. II. 78 In loves court .. The povere vertu schal noght spiede, Wher that the riche vice woweth. c 1400 26 Pol. Poems xx. 120 He [sc. Christ] is worþy be loued, þat so dede wowe.

2. To make solicitation or entreaty; to sue *for*; to 'invite', 'call'. Also const. clause.

1615 BRATHWAIT Strappado (1878) 143 Th' Maide .. Wooing with teares .. That Ioue would giue this Monster th' ouer-throw. 1634 BP. HALL Contempl., N.T. IV. xv, Even after an ill harvest we must sow, and after denials we must woo for God. 1647 TRAPP Comm. 2 Cor. iv. 5 (1656) 711 We are Christs Paranymphs, or spokesmen, and must woo for him. 1877 MRS. FORRESTER Mignon I. 222 So poor George wooes and prays and pleads in vain. 1896 A. E. HOUSMAN Shropsh. Lad iv, Towns and countries woo together.

II. *trans.* **3.** To sue to or solicit (a woman) in love, esp. with a view to marriage; to pay court to, court.

[c 1000 ÆLFRIC Saints' Lives vii. 14 þa ða heo ȝewende of scole, ða awoȝode hi sum cniht. a 1020 in Thorpe Charters (1865) 312 þa foreward ðe Godwine worhte wið Byrhtric þa he his dohter awoȝode.]

c 1290 St. Matthew 84 in S. Eng. Leg. 80 A king .. wolde ire habbe to his spouse and wowede hire wel faste. a 1300 K. Horn 546 (Camb.) Ischal .. mi kniȝthod proue, Ar ihc þe ginne to woȝe. a 1300 Cursor M. 27998 If þou man nedd þe euer þar-till At force womman .. Or woud hir wit wordes slight. c 1385 CHAUCER L.G.W. 1247 Dido, He .. wowede hyre to han hire as his wyf. c 1440 Generydes 4442 Ther is a knyght hir wowith euery owre, Not for to wedde butt for his paramour. 1530 PALSGR. 783/2 Thou arte but a foole to wo her, she is nat for the. 1580 LYLY Euphues (Arb.) 307 Wooe hir, win hir, and weare hir. 1589 WARNER Alb. Eng. VI. xxix. (1612) 146 Thus wowde he her, thus wonne he her, thus wowde and wonne hee sped. 1590 SPENSER F.Q. III. vii. 59 Long thus I woo'd her with dew obseruance, In hope vnto my pleasure to haue won. 1714 T. LUCAS Mem. Gamesters (ed. 2) 41 He presum'd to woe a great Lady, who was a Widow. 1842 TENNYSON Dora 37 He woo'd and wed A labourer's daughter. 1861 GEO. ELIOT Silas M. iii, For four years he had thought of Nancy Lammeter, and wooed her with tacit patient worship.

b. Of animals.

1398 TREVISA Barth. De P.R. XVIII. i. (1495) X vj b/2 The males woweth & plesyth the females. 1684 J. S. Profit & Pleas. United 35 If she [sc. the Mare] refuse him .. you may put a small Stone Nag to wooe her. 1855 Poultry Chron. II. 412 [We] heard their loud gobbling on a sunny spring morning when wooing their mates.

†**c.** Said of the female: To solicit the love of.

c 1425 WYNTOUN Cron. II. v. 344 Scho .. Said Iosephe walde haf lyin hyr by, Qwhar to scho wowit hym besely. 1470–85 MALORY Arthur XIX. viii. 784 [She] wowed hym to haue layne by hym.

d. in fig. context.

a 1225 Ancr. R. 390 Iesu Crist .. þet al o þisse wise wowude ure soule. a 1240 Ureisun in O.E. Hom. I. 187 A swete ihesu .. hwine con ich þe woȝe [later text wowen þe] wiþ swete luue. c 1430 Hymns Virgin (1867) 69 In ȝougþe whanne y was wilde & stronge, þe fals world fair dide me wowe. 1601 SHAKS. All's Well II. i. 15 See that you come Not to wooe honour, but to wed it. 1672 DRYDEN 2nd Pt. Conq. Granada III. 113 In gaining him, I gain that Fortune too Which he has Wedded, and which I but Wooe. 1784 COWPER Task III. 126 They are lost In chase of fancied happiness, still woo'd And never won. 1844 KINGLAKE Eothen iii, Venice .. in old times would send forth the Chief of the State to woo and wed the reluctant sea.

4. To move or invite by alluring means; to entreat or solicit alluringly. (Said properly of persons, fig. of things.) **a.** const. obj. and inf.

c 1400 Song Roland 546 His bugle to blow, they hym wowid. 1593 NASHE Christ's T. 4 He .. wooed them (with many fayre promises) to repent. 1604 SHAKS. Oth. III. iii. 293 My wayward Husband hath a hundred times Woo'd me to steale it. 1621 ELSING Debates Ho. Lords (Camden) 81 He was wood to consent to the patent of Inns. 1629 MILTON Nativity 38 Only with speeches fair She [sc. Nature] woo's the gentle Air To hide her guilty front with innocent Snow. 1728–46 THOMSON Spring 1036 Then forth he walks, .. and wooes the bird of eve To mingle woes with his. 1791 COWPER Iliad I. 217 Begone!—I woo thee not to stay. 1820 W. IRVING Sketch Bk. II. 175 A mild air .. wooing every bud and flower to burst forth into .. beauty. 1864 TENNYSON Aylmer's F. 487 Him they lured Into their net .., wooing him to woo.

b. const. obj. and advb. phr. (or simple adv.).

1387 TREVISA Higden (Rolls) VI. 91 þey heo were .. bysylych ywowed to cosses and clippynge ..; ȝit sche lefte clene mayde. 1601 B. JONSON Poetaster II. ii, This gentlewoman is wooing Hermogenes for a song. 1612 Two Noble Kinsmen II. ii. 109 All those pleasures That wooe the wils of men to vanity. 1639 FULLER Holy War v. xxv. 272 With the oratorie of so pious a project to woo money out of peoples purses. 1682 BURTON Admirable Curiosities (1684) 23 To little purpose he woed the King and Queen for Reparation. 1703 ROWE Ulysses I. i, Well might you hope to woe me to your Wishes. 1781 COWPER Expost. 627 Those truths .. Invite thee, woo thee, to the bliss they share. 1820 BYRON Mar. Fal. IV. i. 17, I .. will woo my pillow For thoughts more tranquil. 1830 TENNYSON Owl II. ii, Thee to woo to thy tuwhit. 1875 MCLAREN Serm. Ser. II. vii. 121 In spite of every silvery voice that woos him aside. 1882 T. G. BOWLES Flotsam & Jetsam 8 A splendid summer day, wooing the very coat off your back.

5. To sue for or solicit the possession or achievement of; hence *fig.* to 'court', 'invite', 'tempt'.

c**1440** *Promp. Parv.* 533/1 Wowyn', *proco, procito.* **1570** Levins *Manip.* 180/1 To wowe, *procare, ambire.* a**1585** Montgomerie *Cherrie & Slae* 140 'Mak choice then of those then, Or of a thousand things';.. With that I wowd his wings. **1600** Shaks. *A.Y.L.* ii. vii. 10 What a life is this That your poore friends must woe your companie. **1613** —— *Hen. VIII*, v. i. 140 You take a Precepit for no leape of danger, And woe your owne destruction. **1625** Bacon *Ess., Honour & Reputation* (Arb.) 67/2 Some in their Actions, doe Wooe and affect Honour, and Reputation. **1639** Fuller *Holy War* i. iv. 5 Some.. rather wooed then waited for their own deaths. **1678** Butler *Hud.* iii. i. 90 Their Bones were drubb'd so sore They durst not wooe one Combat more. **1781** Cowper *Expost.* 413 All fasting else.. Is wooing mercy by renew'd offence. **1781** —— *Hope* 420 They that woo preferment. **1792** S. Rogers *Pleas. Mem.* i. 14 Whose hollow turret wooes the whistling breeze. **1820** Byron *Juan* iv. xliii, Pale, statue-like, and stern, she woo'd the blow. **1882** W. Ballantine *Exper.* xxiii. 224 A theatre which for years before had wooed in vain the patronage of the public. **1883** R. Bridges *Prometheus* 935 She fled Into the sea, preferring there to woo The choking waters.

Hence **wooable** ('wu:əb(ə)l) *a.*, suitable to be wooed.

1903 Zangwill *Grey Wig, Merely Mary Ann* 262 She was well-nigh of wooable age.

woo (wu:), *v.*^{2} [Origin unknown.] = mah jong *v.*

1922 H. Sterling *Standard Rules & Instr. Chinese Game Mah Chang* (ed. 4) 6 Experienced players invariably prefer to 'Woo' quickly with a small score rather than fail to 'Woo' at all. *Ibid.* 12 The Woo hand adds 2 points if he Woo with only one possible piece.. or if he hold one of his last pair and Woo with the other. **1943** K. S. Whitehead *Mah Jong Chinese Way* §59 A player whose hand contains a false set has a 'foul hand', and cannot woo. **1973** J. Scarne *Scarne's Encycl. Games* xxiii. 451 When he completes his hand, four sets and a pair, a player may *woo* or *mah-jongg* by showing his whole hand. He wins the deal, ending play.

woo (wu:), *sb.* [f. woo *v.*^{1}] (A spell of) caressing or love-making; esp. in phr. *to pitch a woo*: see pitch *v.*^{1} 17 d.

1937, etc. [see pitch *v.*^{1} 17 d]. **1938** N. Marsh *Artists in Crime* ix. 120 Hello, you two, what are you up to? Having a woo or something? **1959** —— *Singing in Shrouds* vi. 111 A pair of tango dancers.. strutted and stalked.. and frowned ineffably at each other. 'What an angry woo,' Tim said. **1968** *Guardian* 27 Nov. 9/6 Couples making woo in motor-cars should be careful not to rock them too much.

woo, var. whoo *int.*

woo, dial. f. wo *int.*

woo, woo', dial. ff. wool.

wooc, wooch, var. woke *a. Obs.*, woosh.

wood (wʊd), *sb.*^{1} Forms: 1 widu, wiodu, wudu, 2-3 wude, 3-6 (7 *Sc.*) wode, 4-6 wodd, woode, (7 *Sc.*) wod, wodde, (3 wd(d)e, 4 uud, *Sc.* vod, woud, voud, 5 woyd, whode, vode, voode, 6 wooddе, wud), 5-6 *Sc.* wid(d, 5- wood, (9 *Sc.* wudd). [OE. *widu, wiodu*, later *wudu* str. m. = OHG. *witu, wito* (MHG. *wite, wit*), ON. *viðr* (Sw., Da. *ved*):—OTeut. **widuz* (cf. OIr. *fid* tree, wood, Gael. *fiodh* timber, wood, wilderness, W. *gwŷdd* trees:—**widu-*).]

I. †1. a. A tree. *Obs.*

Beowulf 1364 Wudu wyrtum fæst. c**725** *Corpus Gloss.* P 420 *Pinus*, furhwudu. a**1000** *Phœnix* 37 Wintres & sumeres wudu bið gelice bledum gehongen. c**1220** *Bestiary* 245 Ilkines sed Boðen of wude and of wed. *Ibid.* 326 He werpeð er hise hornes In wude er in ðornes. [**1526** Tindale *Rev.* xxii. 2 Off ether syde off the ryver was there wode [Gr. ξύλον] off lyfe: which bare xij manner off frutes;.. and the leves off the wodde served to heale the people with all.]

†b. *transf.* applied to objects made from trees or their branches, e.g. a ship (in OE. freq.), a spear, the Cross. (Cf. tree *sb.* 3-6.) *Obs.*

In mod.arch. use associated with sense 7.

a**1000** *Dream of Rood* 27 Ongan sprecan wudu selesta. a**1400-50** *Wars Alex.* 798 So sare was þe semble þire seggis be-twene, þat al to-wraiste þai þar wode & werpis in-sondire. **1866** Neale *Sequences & Hymns* 46 His precious Body.. broken on The Wood.

2. a. A collection of trees growing more or less thickly together (esp. naturally, as distinguished from a *plantation*), of considerable extent, usually larger than a *grove* or *copse* (but including these), and smaller than a *forest*; a piece of ground covered with trees, with or without undergrowth.

† *honey of the wood*: = *wood-honey* (sense 10).

c**825** *Vesp. Psalter* ciii. 20 *Omnes bestiae silvarum*, alle wilddeor wuda. **858** *Grant* in Birch *Cartul. Sax.* II. 101 Butan ðem wioda ðe to ðem sealtern limpð. c**1000** Ælfric *Saints' Lives* xxx. 31 He.. ræsde into þam wudu þær he þiccost wæs. a**1122** *O.E. Chron.* (Laud MS.) an. 1112 Ðis wæs swiðe god ʒear & swiðe wistfull on wudan & on feldan. a**1200** *Moral Ode* 344 in *O.E. Hom.* I. 181 Hi muwen lihtliche gon... Ðurh ane godliese wude in-to ane bare felde. c**1290** *Kenelm* 150 in *S. Eng. Leg.* 349 He[o] wende to þe wode of clent. **1297** R. Glouc. (Rolls) 3887 In þe oþer half beþ grete wodes, lese & mede al so. a**1300** *Cursor M.* 8785 Mani wodds ha þai thoru gan, Bot suilk a tre ne fand þai nan. c**1380** Wyclif *Sermon* Sel. Wks. II. 4 Hony of þe woode. c**1385** Chaucer *L.G.W.* 806 *Thisbe*, There comyth a wilde lyones Out of the wode. c**1400** *Destr. Troy* 1350 Ouer hilles & hethes into holte woddes. **14..** *Stat. King's Forests* (Douce MS. 335 fol. 73) As touching the kinges veert that is to say the kinges wodes. **1426** Lydg. *De Guil. Pilgr.* 11606 Gladly ffolkys I conveye.. To ward the voode, to gadre fflours. c**1480** Henryson *Robene & Makyne* 11 Nathing of lufe I knaw, Bot keipis my scheip vndir ʒone wid. **1535** Coverdale *Ps.* lxxix. 13 The wilde bore out of the wod hath wrutt it vp. **1598** Manwood *Lawes Forest* viii. 41 Where the trees do grow scattering here and there one, so that those trees do not one of them touch an other, such places are called woods, but they are not properly to be called couerts. c**1614** Mure *Dido & Æneas* ii. 216 Then are those lovers two A hunting in the woddes resolv'd to goe. **1617** Moryson *Itin.* i. 203 Hils.. adorned with some pleasant woods (which in higher Germany are of firre). **1754** Gray *Poesy* 66 Woods, that wave o'er Delphi's steep. **1847** Tennyson *Princess* iv. 180, I.. push'd alone on foot.. Across the woods. **1860** Tyndall *Glac.* i. xxv. 177 We proceeded slowly upwards, through woods of pine. **1880** Stevenson *Across the Plains* ii. (1892) 81 All woods lure a rambler onwards.

b. *Woods and Forests*, more fully *Woods, Forests, and Land Revenues*, a department of the Civil Service (see quot. 1810; merged with the Forestry Commission in 1923).

1803 *Lond. Gaz.* No. 15547. 34/1 Surveyor-General of His Majesty's Woods, Oaks, Forests, and Chaces. **1810** *Act 50 Geo. III* c. 65 §1 Such Commissioners so to be appointed, shall be and be called 'The Commissioners of His Majesty's Woods, Forests, and Land Revenues'. **1812** *1st Rep. Comm. Woods, Forests*, etc. 18 Department of Woods and Forests. **1850** Carlyle *Latter-d. Pamph.* vii. (1858) 247 But as to Statues, I really think the Woods-and-Forests ought to interfere. **1853** Dickens *Bleak Ho.* xii, You can't offer him the Presidency of the Council,.. You can't put him in the Woods and Forests.

3. Without article, in general or collective sense: Wooded country, woodland; trees collectively (growing together). Now *rare* exc. as in brushwood 2, copsewood 2, underwood.

c**897** Ælfred *Gregory's Past. C.* xxi. 167 To wuda we gað mid urum freondum. a**1100** *Gerefa* in *Anglia* IX. 259 Ðe on dune, ʒe on wuda, ʒe on wætere. c**1200** Ormin 14568 Wude, & feld, & dale, & dun, all wass i waterr sunnkenn. c**1300** *K. Horn* 661 (Laud) þe king rod on huntingge, To wode he gan wende. c**1450** *Godstow Reg.* 33 In toftis in croftis, in wode and in mede. **1557** *Lanc. Wills* (1884) 58 Towe hundreth Acres of Pasture xx^{ta} acres of wooddе. **1615** G. Sandys *Trav.* 89 High land..: full of tall wood. **1686** tr. *Chardin's Trav. Persia* 199 Luarzab.. shut up the Passages by felling an infinite number of Wood. **1737** *Daily Gazetteer* 21 Feb. 2/2 Advt., To be Sold. A very large Quantity of all Sorts of Wood, with or without the Estate on which it stands. **1767** A. Young *Farmer's Lett. to People* 149 The real interest of the country requires that none but the worst lands be covered with wood. **1810** Scott *Lady of L.* iii. vi, Whole nights he spent by moon-light pale, To wood and stream his hap to wail.

4. *transf.* and *fig.* A collection or crowd of spears or the like (suggesting the trees of a wood); *gen.* a collection, crowd, 'lot', 'forest'. (After L. *silva.*) Now *rare* or *Obs.*

1584 Hudson *Du Bartas' Judith* v. 500 Though my buckler bore a wood of darts. **1610** B. Jonson *Alch.* iii. ii, The whole family, or wood of you. [**1664** H. More *Myst. Iniq.* 331, I might.. observe what is answerable in the Church of Rome to the *Vinalia, Robigalia, Terminalia, Parentalia, Proserpinalia*, and other Feasts of the Gentiles; but this wood is so wide, that I may easilier lose my self in it then get through it.] **1670** G. H. tr. *Hist. Cardinals* iii. iii. 328 Cardinal Savelli.. having discover'd his natural infirmities.., the whole Wood of his other good qualities were not sufficient to ballance them. **1670** Dryden *1st Pt. Conq. Granada* ii. (1672) 14 A wood of Launces. a**1674** Milton *Hist. Moscovia* Pref., Wks. 1851 VIII. 469 In such a wood of words. **1704** Norris *Ideal World* ii. ii. 79 What a wood of difficulties and objections this side of the question is incompassed with. **1798** Sotheby tr. *Wieland's Oberon* (1826) I. 2 A wood of threat'ning lances.

5. Phrases and Proverbs. †a. *in a wood*: in a difficulty, trouble, or perplexity; at a loss. So b. *out of the wood* (U.S. *woods*). (Cf. quot. 1664 in sense 4.) c. *to go to the woods*: to lose social status, be banished from society. d. *man of the woods*: = orang-outang. e. *a bird in the hand is better than two in the wood* (and similar phrases; now usually with substitution of *bush*, bush *sb.*^{1} 1 c): a smaller actual advantage is preferable to the mere chance of a larger one. †f. *to have an eye to the wood*: to be on the look-out for some advantage. g. *not to see the wood* (†*see wood*) *for the trees* (†*for trees*): to lose the view of the whole in the multitude of details. †h. *more ways to the wood than one*: different methods of attaining the same result (and similar phrases). i. *to have the wood on* (a person) and varr.: to have the upper hand, to have a hold on. *Austral.* and *N.Z. colloq.* Cf. *to have the goods on* s.v. good *a.* C. 8.

a. **1658-9** *Burton's Diary* (1828) III. 415, I am afraid we are in a wood. No wonder the nation is puzzled, when the wisdom of the nation is puzzled in this place. **1700** T. Brown tr. *Fresny's Amusem.* 115, I am in a Wood, there are so many of them [*sc.* coffee-houses] I know not which to enter. **1786** Mme. D'Arblay *Diary* 28 Nov., I assured him I was quite in a wood, and begged him to be more explicit.

b. **1792** Mme. D'Arblay *Let.* 20 Dec., Mr. Windham says we are not yet out of the wood, though we see the path through it. **1801** [see halloo *v.* 2 b]. a**1849** Poe *X-ing a Paragrab*, Dxn't crxw.. befxre yxu're xut xf the wxxds. **1887** *Times* (weekly ed.) 21 Oct. 8/3 It remains to be seen yet whether the Germans are not shouting before they are out of the wood. **1889** 'Edna Lyall' *Derrick Vaughan* i. 12 In a few months,.. I noticed a fresh sign that he was out of the wood. **1890** *Boston* (Mass.) *Jrnl.* 21 Nov. 2/2 The people of North Dakota seem not to be out of the woods in the matter of prohibition. **1902** Wister *Virginian* xxix, When a patient reaches this stage [of convalescence], he is out of the woods.

c. **1891** *Pall Mall Gaz.* 16 June 2/1 Two other gamblers whose social position was at least equal to Sir William's have gone.. 'to the woods'.

d. **1755** *Hist. Descr. Tower Lond.* 25 You are.. shewn in this Yard a Man of the Wood. **1774, 1836** [see orang-outang]. **1852** Ross tr. *Humboldt's Trav.* II. xx. 270 The hairy man of the woods.

e. c**1530** [see bird *sb.* 6]. **1546** J. Heywood *Prov.* i. xi. (1867) 30 Better one byrde in hande than ten in the wood. **1621** T. Granger *Eccles.* xi. 5. 297 A bird in the hand is far better then two in the wood.

f. **1578** H. Wotton *Courtlie Controv.* 292 The Damoysell making a signe to hir supplyante [*printed* supply oute] (who had alwayes an eie to the wood).

g. **1546** J. Heywood *Prov.* ii. iv. (1867) 51 Plentie is no deintie, ye see not your owne ease. I see, ye can not see the wood for trees. **1583** Melbancke *Philotimus* Sij b, Thou canst not or wilt not see wood for trees. **1640** Howell *Dodona's Gr.* 217 He could not have beene able as hee went along to have seene the Wood for Trees. **1751** *Affect. Narr. H.M.S. Wager* 92 This was like, not seeing the Wood for Trees. **1888** Pater *Ess. fr. Guardian* (1896) 95 Garrick.. bears no very distinct figure. One hardly sees the wood for the trees.

h. **1546** J. Heywood *Prov.* ii. ix. (1867) 75 Ye tooke The wrong way to wood. *Ibid.* 77 There be mo waies to the wood than one. **1569** Blague *Sch. Conceytes* 64 Couetous men, which studie all the wayes to the wood to saue their money. **1597** T. Morley *Introd. Mus.* 74 There bee (as the Prouerbe sayeth) more wayes to the Wood then one.

i. c**1926** 'Mixer' *Transport Workers' Song Bk.* 7, I hold the 'wood' on those who work. **1944** J. H. Fullarton *Troop Target* vi. xxii. 168 Then we've taken another hiding. And I thought we had the wood on Jerry today. **1954** T. A. G. Hungerford *Sowers of Wind* xxi. 264 Can't you realize I've got the wood on you? You've got two minutes. **1965** L. Haylen *Big Red* i. 55 It was another of her occasions of fear: she liked having the wood on you. **1974** D. Stuart *Prince of My Country* ix. 66 Father stands up. 'Look, Marney... Get down and be civil or shut up and get to hell out of it'! Mr Marney dismounts... Mr Molloy pours tea and makes room on the bench. It looks as if Father has the wood on this sour old man right from the start.

II. 6. a. The substance of which the roots, trunks, and branches of trees or shrubs consist; trunks or other parts of trees collectively (whether growing or cut down ready for use).

Also with qualification, as brushwood 1, talwood; *small wood, young wood.*

c**897** Ælfred *Gregory's Past. C.* xxi. 167 Se se ðe unwærlice ðone wuda hiewð, & sua his freond ofsliehð. a**1000** *Gnomic Verses* ii. 110 Wuda and wætres nyttað. c**1205** Lay. 8700 Heo bi-gunnen þene wude feollen. c**1400** tr. *Secr. Secr., Gov. Lordsh.* 97 Hewynge of wode. c**1440** Lydg. *Hors, Shepe & G.* 121 The hors is nedeful wode & stuff to carie. **14..** *Stat. King's Forests* (Douce MS. 335 fol. 73) If ther be ony man that.. caryeth a way ony smal wode. ?**1479** *Engl. Gilds* (1870) 425 That no wodde there be solde vntil the price be sett vpon it by the saide maire. **1482** *Stonor Papers* (Camden) II. 141 That non young vode be stryyd. **1547** Boorde *Introd. Knowl.* (1870) 121 In dyuers places in England there is wood the which doth turne into stone. **1573-80** Tusser *Husb.* (1878) 40 Fruit gathred too timely wil taste of the wood. **1611** Cotgr., *Bois de brin*, round, or vncleft-small-wood. **1642** Fuller *Holy & Prof. St.* v. xiv. 414 The wood will pay for the ground. **1756** C. Lucas *Ess. Waters* III. 64 This stone I took to be wood petrified. **1828** L. Kennedy & Grainger *Tenancy of Land* 151 Timber elm grows more commonly than any other kind of wood excepting beech. **1855** T. F. Hardwich *Phot. Chem.* (ed. 2) 289 Acetic Acid is.. produced.. by heating wood in close vessels.

b. as prepared for and used in arts and crafts.

In predicative use sometimes = wooden. (OE. regularly used *tréow* tree (*sb.* B. 2) in this sense.)

a**1300** *Cursor M.* 22543 Wodd and wall al dun sal drau. **1551-2** in Feuillerat *Revels Edw. VI* (1914) 80 Y^e scabbarde of wood turned. **1577** Googe tr. *Heresbach's Husb.* 46 Sythes we vse to sharpe with Whetstones or instruments of Wood. **1591** Shaks. *1 Hen. VI*, v. iii. 90 He talkes of wood: It is some Carpenter. **1622** J. Taylor (Water P.) *Merry Wherry-Ferry Voy.* Wks. (1630) ii. 15 Edwin.. pluck'd the Minster down that then was wood, And made it stone. **166.** Petty in Sprat *Hist. Roy. Soc.* (1667) 285 Colouring of Wood and Leather by Lime, Salt, and Liquors. **1687** A. Lovell tr. *Thevenot's Trav.* i. 22 The model of the Mosque in wood. a**1700** Evelyn *Diary* 4 Sept. 1677, The gates are wood.. plated over with iron. **1711** Addison *Spect.* No. 37 ¶1 Other Counterfeit Books upon the upper Shelves.. were carved in Wood. **1776** Gibbon *Decl. & F.* ii. (1782) I. 56 No wood, except cedar, very curiously carved, was employed in any part of the building. **1781** Crabbe *Library* 502 Bibles bound in wood. **1816** W. Y. Ottley *Hist. Engraving* I. i. 5 The Origin of Engraving in Wood. **1852** R. A. Willmott *Pleas. Lit.* (ed. 2) vii. 40 All the classic authors—in wood, with bright backs.

c. as used for fuel; firewood.

†Occas. *coll. sing.* faggots; locally, small coal (quot. 1805).

c**888** Ælfred *Boeth.* xxxix. §4 Ær he hi bewæʒ mid wuda utan & forbærnde þa mid fyre. a**1225** *Ancr. R.* 402 Gedereð wude þerto, mid þe poure wummon of Sarepte. **1340** Hampole *Pr. Consc.* 3189 Als wodde brinnes, þat es sadde and hevy. c**1425** *Voc.* in Wr.-Wülcker 657/15 *Hoc focale*, wode to the fyre. **1480** *Howard Househ. Bks.* (Roxb.) 18 Thei have received opon making of the iij. M. wode xiiij.s. viij.d. **1497** *Naval Acc. Hen. VII* (1896) 224, cc wode xij^d & iiij candell v^d. **1560** *Bible* (Geneva) Ezek. xxiv. 10 Heape on muche wood: kindle the fyre. a**1568** in *Bannatyne MS.* (Hunter. Club) 35 As fyre the wid we se Dois burne. **1639** J. Taylor (Water P.) *Part Summer's Trav.* 44 The miserable Stipend or Hireling wages will hardly buy wood to make a fire for him. **1805** Forsyth *Beauties Scot.* III. 511 The small coal used to heat the salt-pans is universally called wood by the salters on the eastern coast of Scotland. **1808**

Scott *Marm.* vi. Introd. 1 Heap on more wood!—the wind is chill.

d. *Hort.* The substance forming the head of a tree or shrub; branch-wood; also, branches collectively; in a fruit tree, primarily leaf-bearing, as distinguished from fruit-bearing, branches. (Cf. *wood-bud*, *-branch* in 10.)

1523–34 Fitzherb. *Husb.* §130 [Withies] be trees that wyll soone be nourysshed, and they wyll beare moche woodde. 1572 Mascall *Plant. & Graff.* 46 If there be in your trees certain branches of superfluous wood that ye will cut of. 1658 Evelyn *Fr. Gard.* (1675) 32 Every Bud which hath but a single leaf produces only wood. 1721 Mortimer *Husb.* II. 302 A Peach, the more it runs to Wood, .. the better it will bear. 1842 Loudon *Suburban Hort.* 705 Gardeners, when pruning for wood, cut farther back than when pruning for fruit. 1858 Glenny *Gard. Every-day Bk.* 211/1 When a Heath has done blooming, and before it makes its new wood, is the time for pruning it into shape.

e. As the material of an idol or image. (Biblical.)

1535 Coverdale *Ezek.* xx. 32 Wod & stone wil we worshipe. 1567 *Gude & Godlie B.* (S.T.S.) 236 Bewar, I am ane Ielous God, I am na Image, stock nor wod. 1682 *Letany for S. Omers* ii. ix, All Adorers of the Mass, Who bow to Wood, and Stone, and Brass. 1819 Heber *Hymn*, '*From Greenland's icy Mountains*', The Heathen, in his blindness, Bows down to wood and stone!

f. *spec.* (*Hort.* and *Bot.*) The hard compact fibrous substance lying between the bark outside and the pith within.

1600 Surflet *Country Farm* iii. xiv. 449 It is vsuall to graft betwixt the wood and the barke, when trees begin to put vp their sap. 1673–4 Grew *Anat. Pl.* (1682) 113 The next general Part of a Branch, is the Wood; which lyeth betwixt the Barque and the Pith. 1875 Laslett *Timber* 20 A drying up or wasting away of the wood immediately surrounding the pith. 1877 A. W. Bennett *Thomè's Bot.* 333 In the anatomical structure of the wood Gymnosperms resemble Dicotyledons in all essential particulars.

g. A particular kind of wood; freq. *pl.* kinds of wood. In *Pharmacy* formerly applied to particular kinds used medicinally: see quots.

Phr. † ***to tell what wood the ship is made of***, to be seasick.

1580 Lyly *Euphues* (Arb.) 248 Philautus not accustomed to these narrow Seas, was more redy to tell what wood the ship was made of, then to aunswer to Euphues discourse. 1581 A. Hall *Iliad* iv. 73 A wood full fit to forge the trolling wheeles Of chariots. 1602 W. S. *Thomas Ld. Cromwell* ii. ii, To my victtualles went the Sailers, and thinking me to bee a man of better experience then any in the shippe, asked mee what Woode the shippe was made of. [1608 Armin *Nest Ninn.* C 1 b, Iemy stood fearefull of euery calme billow, where it was no boote to bid him tell what the ship was made of, for he did it deuoutly.] 1661 Culpepper & Cole *Pharm. Lond.* 7/3 Cypress. This Wood laid amongst cloaths, secures them from Moths. 1687 Blome *Pres. St. Amer.* 14 Woods for the use of Dyers... Sweet smelling and curious Woods. 1712 tr. *Pomet's Hist. Drugs* I. 63 The Nephritic Wood is thick, without Knots. *a* 1774 Goldsm. *Surv. Exp. Philos.* (1776) I. 292 To ascertain how much friction some woods have more than other woods. 1829 Loudon *Encycl. Plants* 604 Many of the red Indian woods tra[n]sude a blood red juice. 1875 Laslett *Timber* 27 The hard and strong woods used for architectural purposes.

1772 Macbride *Th. & Pract. Physic* 635 A pint of decoction of the sudorific woods. 1799 Underwood *Dis. Childhood* (ed. 4) II. 15 A decoction of the woods. 1848 Dunglison *Med. Lex.*, *Woods, Sudorific*... This term is applied, collectively, to the guaiacum, sassafras, china, and sarsaparilla; which are often used together to form the sudorific decoction. 1890 Billings *Med. Dict.*, *Woods, the*, those formerly in repute as antisyphilitics.

h. *transf.* A hard substance found in the head of an elephant.

1829 C. Rose *Four Yrs. S. Africa* 236, I sat on one [elephant] while they searched for the wood in his head. It lies about an inch beneath the skin imbedded in fat, just above the eye, and has the appearance of a thorn, or a small piece of twig broken off.

i. In echoes of the L. proverb which appears in Erasmus's *Adagia* ii. v. xlvii in the form *Ne e quovis ligno Mercurius fiat* (see quot. *c* 1594, and cf. A. Otto *Sprichwörter der Römer* 220); hence, the 'material' or 'stuff' of which a person is 'made'.

Cf. similar uses of Gr. ὕλη, F. *bois*.

[1588 Shaks. *L.L.L.* iv. iii. 249 Is Ebonie like her? O word divine? A wife of such wood were felicitie.] *c* 1594 Bacon *Promus of Formularies & Elegancies* (1898) 19 A mercury cannot be made of every wood (bvt priapus may). 1594 —— *Let. to Ld. Puckering* in Spedding *Lett. & Life* (1861) I. 293, I hope you will think I am no unlikely piece of wood to shape you a true servant of. 1626 T. H[awkins] tr. *Caussin's Holy Crt.* 5 Vertue is a merueylous worke-woman, who can make Mercury of any wood. 1826 Disraeli *Viv. Grey* iv. i, I know better than most men of what wood a minister is made. 1831 Scott *Cast. Dang.* v, The wood of which a knight is made, and that is a squire.

7. Something made of wood: *spec.* **a.** The wooden part of something, as the shaft of a spear. **b.** A block of wood used for engraving or printing, as distinguished from a metal plate or type. **c.** The cask or barrel as a receptacle for liquor, as distinguished from the bottle. **d.** *slang.* The pulpit. **e.** The wooden wind-instruments in an orchestra collectively (also called *the woodwind*: see 10 below). **f.** Each of the bowls in the game of bowls. **g.** A golf club with a wooden head; a shot made with such a club (more commonly ***wood shot***). **h.** The wooden frame or handle of a racquet, with reference to a shot in which these parts are accidentally used instead of the strings.

a. 1683 Moxon *Mech. Exerc.*, *Printing* xv. ¶9 A long piece of .. Wyer .. fastned into the Wood of the under half of the Mold. 1697 Dryden *Æneis* xi. 1191 The Wood [of the javelin] she draws, the steely Point remains.

b. 1839 J. Jackson *Wood Engraving* viii. 720 Wood engraving is necessarily confined, by the size of the wood, to the execution of subjects of .. small dimensions. 1856 in Ruskin *Rossetti* (1899) 137 An engraving on wood of my picture .. there is an objection to sending 'the wood' travelling.

c. 1822 *Sunday Times* 20 Oct. 1/2 (Advt.), The long established system of serving wine from the wood, in full measures. 1826 J. Wilson *Noctes Ambr.* Wks. 1855 I. 174 When the speerit's been years in the wudd. 1882 J. Ashton *Social Life Reign Q. Anne* I. 199 Ordinary clarets from the wood.

d. 1854 Thackeray *Newcomes* xi, They say he's a pleasant fellow out of the wood. 1886 *Sat. Rev.* 10 July 45/2 Mr. Beecher's activity has not been altogether confined to what irreverent people call 'the wood'. 1897 Rye *Norfolk Songs* 129 You are very good in flannel, Sir. I'll come on Sunday, and see if you are as good in wood.

e. 1879 E. Prout *Instrum.* 77 The brass instruments, used .. in combination with strings or wood. 1901 W. J. Henderson *Orchestra* 81 The 'wood' .. in the modern orchestra consists of flutes, oboes, clarinets and bassoons.

f. 1884 Doherty *N. Barlow* viii. 49 Here ancient fogies .. tried To better aim their wandering 'woods' to guide. 1912 J. A. Manson *Compl. Bowler* 194 The skip may .. summon a player from the mat to look at the lie of the 'woods' before delivering his bowl.

g. 1915 A. W. Tillinghast *Cobble Valley Golf Yarns* 75 Hodge couldn't quite get there with two from his wood. 1927 Jones & Keeler *Down Fairway* xv. 203 For the drive with the wood, and for all normal wood shots, I play the ball opposite the arch of the left foot. 1928 *Evening News* 5 May 8/3, I do not think another professional golfer in America is hitting such terrific tee shots and full woods off the fairway as Gene. 1952 W. J. Cox *Play Better Golf* xi. 54 The normal flight of the ball from a No. 4 wood is high. 1971 'D. Halliday' *Dolly & Doctor Bird* viii. 104 Lady Edgecombe .. hit her first ball .. a good third of the distance, nicely placed for a wood shot fairly close to the green. 1977 *Times* 17 June 28/1 (Advt.), Uxbridge Golf Centre... 4 woods, Nos 1, 3, 4, 5 and Irons 3–9.

h. 1955 *Times* 30 June 4/1 Could Nielsen save the set? He did after a lucky one off the wood had been a help. 1961 [see *double-fault* vb. s.v. double *a.* C. 3]. 1974 Mills & Butler *Tackle Badminton* ii. 27 A fault can occur even when the shuttle is struck by the wood.

8. Phrases. †**a.** ***against the wood***: 'against the grain' (grain *sb.*[1] 16 b). †**b.** ***a piece of wood***: a contemptuous appellation for a stupid person; a blockhead. **c.** ***wood and wood***: see quots. **d.** ***to take in wood*** (local U.S. colloq.): see quot. **e.** In names of certain trees: ***wood of Jerusalem***, a variety of pear; ***wood of life*** = lignum vitæ 1. **f.** ***dead wood***: see as main entry. **g.** ***to touch wood***: see touch *v.* 29.

a. *a* 1568 Ascham *Scholem.* (Arb.) 35 Such a witte .. well handled by the mother, .. and wrought as it should, not ouer-thwartlie, and against the wood, by the scholemaster.

b. 1691 *New Disc. Old Intreague* xxv, Next him Sir Ralph, .. a very piece of Wood.

c. *a* 1625 Manwayring *Seaman's Dict.*, *Wood and Wood*, that is when two timbers are let into each other so close that the wood of the one doth join close to the other. 1688 Holme *Armoury* iii. 337/2 A straight Board, with a Staffe in the side, to draw over Corn in measureing, .. Which measureing is termed Wood and Wood. 1805 *Shipwright's Vade-m.* 142 *Wood and Wood.* This term implies that when a treenail, &c. is driven through, its point is directly even with the inside surface, whether plank or timber.

d. 1839 Marryat *Diary Amer.* Ser. i. II. 230 In the West, where steam-navigation is so abundant, when they ask you to drink they say, 'Stranger, will you take in wood?'

e. 1597 Gerarde *Herbal* iii. cxviii. 1309 Italian Lignum vitæ, or woode of Life, groweth to a faire and beautiful tree. 1600 Surflet *Country Farm* iii. xlix. 537 Peares, such as .. the wood of Hierusalem. 1688 Holme *Armoury* ii. 79/1 The Lignum Vite, or wood of Life, hath a smooth leaf. 1760 J. Lee *Introd. Bot.* App. 332.

III. *attrib.* and *Comb.*

9. General: **a.** *attrib.* or as *adj.* Made or consisting of wood, wooden.

1538 *Test. Ebor.* (Surtees) VI. 76 All wodde implementes. 1545 *Rates of Custome Ho.* d j, Wod crosses for bedes. 1578 *Knaresb. Wills* (Surtees) I. 133 Fower woodd bottels, one lether botle. *a* 1674 Milton *Hist. Moscovia* i. Wks. 1851 VIII. 471 The .. Sap of thir Wood-fewel burning on the fire. 1770 Luckombe *Hist. Printing* 316 This Wood Handle with long working often grows loose. 1846 Mrs. Gore *Engl. Char.* (1852) 3 Smooth as glass,—level as wood pavement. 1849 D. Campbell *Inorg. Chem.* 16 A wood match red immediately rekindles when dipped into a jar of [oxygen]. 1863 A. Young *Naut. Dict.* (ed. 2) 448 Wood-sheathing is used most generally for covering a vessel's bottom that has been partially wormed. 1879 E. Prout *Instrum.* 57 The 'wood instruments' in ordinary use in the orchestra. 1897 Mary Kingsley *W. Africa* 378 To store enough wood to go twenty miles you had to have wood billets everywhere; all over the deck, .. &c. 1901 *J. Black's Carp. & Build.*, *Home Handicr.* 61 Tarsia .. was a species of wood inlay or mosaic. 1912 T. D. Atkinson *Cathedrals* 180 The nave was covered with a wood ceiling.

b. attrib. (*a*) in sense 2 or 3, as ***wood country***, †***-dike***, †***-eaves***, ***-edge***, ***-end*** (end *sb.* 2), ***-ground***, ***-music***, ***-path***, ***-pathway***, ***-ride***, ***-riding***, †***-rim***, ***scenery***, ***-shadow***, ***-song***, ***-stream***, ***-top***, ***-walk***, ***-way***, ***-wonder***, ***-world***; dwelling in or haunting a wood or woods, sylvan, as ***wood-bird***, †***-burgess*** (*fig.*), ***-child***, ***chorister*** (*fig.*), ***-demon***, ***-folk***, ***fowl***, ***-god***, ***-goddess***, ***-knight***, ***-rhapsodist***, ***-tike***; growing in woods, as ***wood-moss***, ***root***, ***-weed***; ***-woman***; (*b*) in sense 6, as ***wood-bote*** (boot *sb.*[1] 5 b), ***-cell*** (cell *sb.*[1] 12), ***charcoal***, ***-fibre***, ***fire***, ***reek***, ***rick***, ***shide***, ***smoke***, ***stack***; in sense 6 d, as ***wood-shoot***; used for storing or conveying wood, as ***wood barge***, ***boat***, ***box***, ***cart***, ***cellar***, ***hoy***, ***loft***, ***sled***. **c.** objective, etc., (*a*) in sense 2 or 3, as ***wood-keeper***, ***-owner***; (*b*) in sense 6, as ***wood-bearer***, ***-broker***, ***-carrier***, ***-carter***, ***-chapman***, ***-chopper***, ***-cleaver***, ***-eater***, ***-feller***, ***-grower***, ***sculptor***, ***-seller***, ***-turner***, ***-worshipper***; ***wood-carting***, ***-chopping*** (cf. *wood-chop*, sense 10 a below), ***-eating***, ***-hewing***, ***sculpture***, ***-turning*** sbs. and adjs.; ***wood-like*** adj. **d.** locative, as (*a*) in sense 2, ***wood-creeper***, ***-dweller***, ***-retreat***, ***-rover***, ***-well***; ***wood-born***, ***-bred***, ***-embosomed*** adjs. (*b*) in sense 7 c, as ***wood port***. **e.** instrumental and parasynthetic, (*a*) in sense 2 or 3, as ***wood-crowned***, ***-encumbered***, ***-fringed***, ***-girt***, ***-grown***, ***-lost***, ***-skirted*** adjs.; (*b*) in sense 6, as ***wood-built***, ***-cased***, ***-faced***, ***-feeding***, ***-fired***, ***-hooped***, ***-keyed***, ***-panelled***, ***-paved***, ***-roofed***, ***-sheathed***, ***-tongued***, ***-walled*** adjs.; ***wood-pave*** vb.

1538 Elyot *Dict.*, *Ratariæ naues*, lyghters, or *woode barges. 1568 in Marsden *Sel. Pleas Court Admir.* (Selden) II. 139 A woodbarge alias the Woolfe of Dorney. *c* 1440 *Promp. Parv.* 531/2 *Wodeberare, or caryare of fowayl. 1536–7 *Privy Purse Exp. P'cess Mary* (1831) 10 My ladys grace wodberer. 1684 E. Chamberlayne *Pres. St. Eng.* i. (ed. 15) 159 Wood-bearer, one. 1590 Shaks. *Mids. N.* iv. i. 145 Begin these *wood birds but to couple now? 1709 T. Robinson *Vind. Mosaick Syst.* 97 The Wood-Birds feed upon the Fruits of Trees. 1839 Emerson *Poems*, *Problem* 25 Yon woodbird's nest Of leaves, and feathers. 1458 in *10th Rep.*, *Hist. MSS. Comm.* App. v. 299 Maistres of *wodbotes. 1691 *Andros Tracts* I. 142 Shallops and Wood-boats. 1883 'Mark Twain' *Life on Mississippi* xvi. 166 Those boats never halt a moment .. except .. to hitch thirty-cord wood-boats alongside. 1590 Spenser *F.Q.* i. vi. 16 The *wood-borne people .. worship her as Goddesse of the wood. 1746 Francis tr. *Hor.*, *Art P.* 347 The Wood-born Satyr. 1882 J. F. S. Gordon *Hist. Moray* III. 87 A forest, in which the burgesses had the privilege of *wood-bote granted to them. 1850 S. Judd *R. Edney* ix. 135 The Old Man romanced with the fire, making it seem how he could graduate it exactly to the necessities of the room, and the state of the *wood-box. 1893 *Outing* (U.S.) XXII. 135/1, I looked for a place to rest, but there was nothing but a large wood-box, with an old hemp sack to lie on. *c* 1586 C'tess Pembroke *Ps.* lxxx. iv, The *woodbred swine. 1597 in Feuillerat *Revels Q. Eliz.* (1908) 417 Thomas Jhones *woodbroker. 1861 Thackeray *Four Georges* i, A very humble *wood-built place. *c* 1586 C'tess Pembroke *Ps.* civ. ix, *Wood-burgesses .. Lions I meane. 1541 *Old Ways* (1892) 71 He see a *wod-carier come. 1921 *Daily Colonist* (Victoria, B.C.) 8 Oct. 9/1 (Advt.), Before you put on your slippers fill up one of our strong, attractive, useful, tidy Wood Carriers. It holds about six pieces of stove wood. *c* 1330 *Durham Acc. Rolls* (Surtees) 518 In 6. Coleris pro equis del *Wodecartes. 1377–8 *Ibid.* 586. 1898 *Atlantic Monthly* Apr. 462/1 The *wood-carter answering them in a neighbourly spirit. 1890 'R. Boldrewood' *Miner's Right* (1899) 58 Amos Burton .. at present does *wood carting. 1892 W. B. Yeats *Countess Kathleen* 71 Between the pepper-pot And *wood-cased hour glass. 1907 *Install. News* Dec. 21/1 The board .. is a D.P. Fuse and S.P. Switch wood-cased type. 1861 Bentley *Man. Bot.* 13 In the *wood-cells of some trees we find their walls present .. large circular dots or discs which encircle them. 1875 Bennett & Dyer *Sachs' Bot.* 98 To the Vascular forms belong the ducts and the vascular wood-cells or Tracheïdes. 1833 Loudon *Encycl. Cottage Archit.* §712 The coal and *wood cellar. *a* 1722 Lisle *Husb.* (1757) 368 The *wood-chapmen did not care to have their wood faggotted so early. 1857 Miller *Elem. Chem.*, *Org.* (1862) xiv. §2. 892 The specific heat of *wood charcoal. 1925 Blunden *Eng. Poems* 86 The *wood-child with man's torture racked Dares seek him out, if he'll retract. 1779 *Mass. Hist. Soc. Coll.* (1814) II. 458 The Century discov[er]ed a man creeping towards the *wood choppers. 1841 Emerson *Lect.*, *Man the Reformer* Wks. (Bohn) II. 239 My wood-chopper, my ploughman, .. have some sort of self-sufficiency. 1845 Thoreau *Jrnl.* 14 July in *Writings* (1906) VII. 367 He was going to do his *woodchopping. 1897 Henty *On the Irrawaddy* 163 The sound of wood-chopping. 1933 *Bulletin* (Sydney) 23 Aug. 35/3 Woodchopping .. is a fine, healthy and manly sport. 1642 H. More *Song of Soul* i. ii. lx, There the *wood-queristers sat on a row. 1589 R. Harvey *Pl. Perc.* (1590) 1 The medling Ape, that like a tall *wood cleauer, assaying to rend a .. billet in two peeces, did wedge in his pettitoes. 1657 Trapp *Comm. Ps.* cxli. 7. 918 As wood-cleavers make the shivers flye hither and thither. 1523–34 Fitzherb. *Husb.* §124 Gette thy quyckesettes in the *woode-countreye. 1570 Foxe *A. & M.* (ed. 2) 188/1 A certayne wood countrey in Somersetshire, called Etheling. *c* 1580 *Bugbears* iii. iii. 50 Som are called *folletti*, *foraboscki*, *forasiepi*, that ys *wood-crepers, hedg crepers, & the whyte & red fearye. 1727–46 Thomson *Summer* 559 The *wood-crowned hill. 1820 W. Irving *Sk. Bk.*, *Spectre Bridegroom* (1821) I. 297 Some talked of mountain sprites, of *wood-demons. 1591 *Exch. Rolls Scot.* XXII. 135 For uphalding of the *woddikis of Falkland. 1870 Morris *Earthly Par.* III. iv. 404 The abode of some stout *wood-dweller. 1693 S. Dale *Pharmacol.* 539 Teredo .. The *Wood-Eater. 1844 *Zoologist* II. 410 It is hard to attribute carnivorous propensities to so harmless a wood-eater as Hylobius. 1854 A. Adams, etc. *Man. Nat. Hist.* 202 *Wood-eating Snout-Beetles. *c* 1325 *wode-hevese [see eaves 1 b]. ? *a* 1400 *Morte Arth.* 3376 Cho wente to the welle by þe wode euis. *a* 1375 *Joseph Arim.* 475 He seiȝ vnder a *wode-egge .. Fyue hondred men of Armes. 1888 Stevenson *Black Arrow* 8 There was a stout fellow yonder in the wood-edge. 1805 Scott *Last Minstr.* iv. ix, High over Borthwick's mountain-flood His *wood-embosom'd mansion stood. 1817 Lady Morgan *France* (1818) II. 300 The Château .. so lonely, so wood-embosomed. 1808 Scott *Marm.* iii. ix, Kentucky's *wood-encumber'd brake. 1583

Reg. Privy Council Scot. Ser. I. III. 592 Hir duelling houss in the *Wodend callit Daveschaw. *c* **1640** J. Smyth *Lives Berkeleys* (1883) I. 331 Lands in Wixstowe at the woodend of Hill. **1919** J. Masefield *Reynard* 69 The wood-end rang with the clear voice crying. **1840** *Civil Eng. & Arch. Jrnl.* III. 402/1 The improved metallic wheel with *wood-faced tyre. **1946** *Nature* 9 Nov. 644/2 Protozoa and bacteria are essential for digestion in the *wood-feeding termites. **1974** W. Trager in K. Elliott et al. *Trypanosomiasis & Leishmaniasis* 247 Hypermastigote flagellates of the wood-feeding roach *Cryptocercus*.. have a whole variety of sexual phenomena. **14..** *Nom.* in Wr.-Wülcker 697/17 *Hic frondator*, a *wodfeller. **1569** Blague *Sch. Conceytes* 54 As a Woodfeller was cuttyng wood neere a riuer side, he lost his axe. **1786** tr. *Beckford's Vathek* (1868) 90 The wood-fellers who directed their route. **1875** Bennett & Dyer *Sachs' Bot.* 100 Whether *wood-fibres occur in Cryptogams is at least doubtful. **1493** *Festivall* (W. de W.) 131 b, A *wode fyre, for peple to syt & wake therby. **1794** Mrs. Radcliffe *Myst. Udolpho* xlii[i], The dying embers of a wood fire still glimmered on the hearth. **1823** J. Badcock *Dom. Amusem.* 185 Bugs never infest houses.. in which wood-fires only are used. **1956** *Railway Mag.* Mar. 163/1 The *wood-fired locomotives were never very efficient. **1978** M. Duffy *Housespy* vi. 157 I've built a wood-fired kiln. **1867** Morris *Jason* I. 262 All about The *wood-folk gathered. **1398** Trevisa *Barth. De P.R.* xii. i. (Bodl. MS.), *Wood foules.. dwelleþ in woodes and in þikke coppes of treen. **1787** Burns *'Admiring Nature in her wildest grace'* 13 The lawns *wood-fring'd in Nature's native taste. **1828** G. W. Bridges *Ann. Jamaica* II. xv. 227 Surprised to find their *wood-girt town surrounded by an armed force. **1590** Spenser *F.Q.* I. vi. 9 The wyld *woodgods. **1610** Fletcher *Faithf. Sheph.* I. i, No Goblin, Wood-god, Fairy, Elfe, or Fiend. **1820** Keats *Lamia* I. 34 Full of painful jealousies Of the Wood-Gods, and even the very trees. *c* **1843** Carlyle *Hist. Sketches* (1898) 270 The *wood-goddess with her nymphs. **1581** *Cov. Leet Bk.* 824 & so followe the broke into another *woodground. **1611** Cotgr., *Laie*, Wood-ground, by measure, or quantitie of *Arpens*. **1835** Ure *Philos. Manuf.* 258 [He] has to pay.. more for his timber, to protect the *wood-grower. **1922** W. B. Yeats *Trembling of Veil* 135 Little *wood-grown islands. **1956** R. Macaulay *Towers of Trebizond* xiii. 142 The white-walled, red-roofed town and the wood-grown height beyond it. **1851** Mayne Reid *Scalp-Hunters* vi. 48 The water-drawing, *wood-hewing pueblos. **1891** Hardy *Tess* xxvii, The *wood-hooped pails.. hung.. ready.. for the evening milking. **1537** *Wood hoy [see wend *v.* 6 c]. **1483** *Cath. Angl.* 423/1 A *Wodde keper, *lucarius*. **1519** *Pres. Juries* in *Surtees Misc.* (1890) 32 That noo wode kyeper take no swyn into the woddys for akecornes. **1868** 'Holme Lee' *B. Godfrey* xvii. 95 He is woodkeeper to Squire Gisborne. **1874** Thearle *Naval Archit.* 27 The pieces of which it is composed are connected by *wood-keyed hook scarphs. **1845** Browning *Flight of Duchess* xvii. 78 Like Orson the *wood-knight. **1548** Thomas *Ital. Dict.* (1550), *Seluaggio*, wilde, or *wooddelike. **1713** *Phil. Trans.* XXVIII. 224 A sort of sullen greenish Wood-like rust. **1785** Cowper *Let. to Newton* 19 Mar., We.. have.. more than two waggon loads of them in our *wood-loft. **1916** Blunden *Pastorals* 15 Voices of *wood-lost winds. **1796** T. Townshend *Poems* 104 For many a long and languid day Upon the *wood-moss laid. *a* **1586** Sidney *Arcadia* III. (1922) II. 74 The Nightingale *woodmusiques King. **1757** *Refl. Importation Bar-Iron* 17 The *Wood-Owner.. divides his Wood into a Number of Cuts. **1832** *Gentl. Mag.* CII. I. 578/2 The *wood panneled ceiling. **1827–35** N. P. Willis *Idleness* 60 *Woodpath or stream, or slope by hill or vale. **1856** Vaughan *Mystics* (1860) I. 139 These *wood-pathways.. led up a steep hill. **1842** *Civil Eng. & Arch. Jrnl.* V. 281/1 To *wood-pave all the turnpike roads. **1887** *Pall Mall Gaz.* 14 Nov. 2/1 The *wood-paved part of the Space. **1972** *House & Garden* Feb. 109/4 Each shipment of *wood ports will have a continuity of quality... Ruby, tawny and white ports are all matured in wood. *Beowulf* 3144 *Wudu-rec astah. [**1895** W. Morris *Beowulf* 109 The wood-reek went up.] **1898** *Pall Mall Mag.* May 87 That the blue wood-reek might chase away the flies. **1909** T. S. Eliot in *Harvard Advocate* 26 Jan. 135 As if one should meet A pensive lamia in some *wood-retreat. **1885** W. B. Yeats in *Dublin Univ. Rev.* May 82/1 The birds that nestle in the leaves are sad, Poor sad *wood-rhapsodists. **1869** Blackmore *Lorna D.* x, The bark from the *wood-ricks [being] washed down the gutters. **1827** Clare *Sheph. Cal.* 9 Beside the *woodride's lonely gate. **1928** Blunden *Retreat* 36 And wood-rides never reach the glittering gate. **1972** R. Adams *Watership Down* vii. 24 The head moved slowly, taking in the dusky lengths of the wood-ride in both directions. **1934** Blunden *Mind's Eye* 154 An abundant round of skilful practical doings, from the wagon-shed to the *wood-riding. **1943** *N. & Q.* 9 Oct. 234 *Wood-riding*, green way across a wood. Northants. **969** *Lease* in Birch *Cartul. Sax.* III. 528 Of swepelan streame west be *wudu riman. *c* **1205** Lay. 739, I þon wode rime. **1837** *Civil Eng. & Arch. Jrnl.* I. 24/1 The *wood-roofed house. *c* **1205** Lay. 467 Leouere heom his to libben bi þan *wode-roten. **1825** Hazlitt *Spirit of Age* i. Wks. 1902 IV. 198 Wreaths of snow under which the wild *wood-rovers bury themselves.. in winter. **1817** Lady Morgan *France* (1818) II. 309 Our celebrated landscape-painter, Robert,.. assisted me in laying out the grounds, and disposing of my *wood scenery. **1968** *Canad. Antiques Collector* Aug. 13/3 Quevillon, one of the leading *wood-sculptors of the early 19th century, worked at Longueil from 1818 to 1821. **1977** *Belfast Tel.* 27 Jan. 10/7 It's a new oak prie-dieu.. and it has taken wood sculptor Billy Graham and joiner Tommy Simons 120 man-hours to turn it out. **1974** *Saturday* (Charleston, S. Carolina) 20 Apr. 5-A/2 (Advt.), Children up to 15 are encouraged to come and participate free in learning to paint, make jewelery, *wood sculpture and other crafts with all materials free. **1479** in *Engl. Gilds* (1870) 425 Prouydid.. that the *woddesillers leve not the bak.. bare of wodde. **1554** in Wadley *Notes Wills Bristol* (1886) 189 Wodseller and Citesin of the Citie of Bristowe. **1755** Johnson, *Woodmonger*, a woodseller. **1828** Mrs. Hemans *Peasant Girl Rhone* 16 Sad and slow, Through the *wood-shadows, moved the knightly train. **1922** Joyce *Ulysses* 11 Woodshadows floated silently by through the morning peace. **1691** T. H[ale] *Acc. New Invent.* 9 *Wood-sheathed Ships. *c* **1440** *Promp. Parv.* 531/2 *Wodeschyde.., *teda*. **1577** in J. R. Boyle *Hedon* (1875) 65 For nailes and wodshiddes and two skottells vjd. **1842** J. Aiton *Dom. Econ.* (1857) 299 Take the *wood-shoots close by their roots, so that the bark may grow over the wound. **1822** Home *Fatal Discov.* III, On the *wood-skirted lawn. **1858** O. W. Holmes *Aut. Breakf.-t.* ix. (1891) 211 The creaking of the *wood-sleds, bringing their loads of oak and walnut. **1747** H. Glasse *Art of Cookery* ii. 42 Hang it up in a Chimney where *Wood-Smoke is. **1847** Mrs. Gore *Castles in Air* vii. (1857) 48 Smelling of fresh straw in summer, and wood-smoke in winter. **1601** *Death of Robt. Earl of Huntington* D 2, Fall to your *wod-songs therefore, yeomen bold. **1834** Mrs. Hemans *Poems, Happy Hour* 7 The sweet wood-song's penetrating flow. **1930** T. S. Eliot *Marina*, Those who suffer the ectasy of the animals, meaning Death Are become unsubstantial, reduced by a wind, A breath of pine, and the woodsong fog By this grace dissolved in place. **1538** Elyot *Dict.*, *Lignile*, fuell, or a *wodde stacke. **1707** Mortimer *Husb.* 379 The size of Faggots and Wood Stacks.. differs in most Countries. **1913** 'Q' *Hetty Wesley* II. v, The wood stack hid her from the Parsonage windows. *c* **1820** Mrs. Hemans *Tale 14th C.* 322 The *wood-stream's plaintive harmony. *a* **1583** Montgomerie *Flyting* 737 *Woodtyk, hoodpyk, ay like to liue in lacke! **1938** Dylan Thomas *Map of Love* (1939) 13 But I, Ann's bard on a raised hearth, call all The seas to service that her *wood-tongued virtue Babble like a bellbuoy over the hymning heads. **1794** Mrs. Radcliffe *Myst. Udolpho* xxxi[i], The passing gleam fell on the *wood-tops below. **1839** in *Inquiry, Yorksh. Deaf & Dumb* (1870) 22 William.. Sedgwick, *wood-turner. **1901** *Scotsman* 5 Apr. 7/2 *Wood-turning tools. **1791** Charlotte Smith *Celestina* (ed. 2) I. 228 Birds, who found food and shelter amid the shrubberies and *wood-walks. **1595** Markham *Trag. Sir R. Grinuile* (Arb.) 46 The *wood-walled Cittizens at sea. *c* **1325** in Kennett *Par. Antiq.* (1818) I. 566 Duæ acræ ..juxta le *wode wey. **1906** S. W. Mitchell *Pearl* 19 The beauty of those wood-ways green. **1850** *Household Words* I. 29/1 *Wood-weeds, river-weeds, and other weeds. **1920** E. Sitwell *Wooden Pegasus* 106 Dark *wood-wells. **1903** W. B. Yeats *In Seven Woods* 21 And the *wood-woman whose lover was changed to a blue-eyed hawk. **1925** Blunden *Eng. Poems* 92 Oh could it but be held by these *wood-wonders. *a* **1887** Jefferies *Field & Hedgerow* (1889) 331 The humble-bee the wide *wood-world may roam. **1579** Fulke *Conf. Sanders* 587 To proue them *woode worshippers and idolaters.

f. In ME. poetry, in combs. ***wood bough***, ***lay*** (lea *sb.*[1]) = ? glade or grove, ***lind*** (= tree), ***rise*** (rice *sb.*, small branch), esp. in phr. ***under wood bough***, etc. = in the woods, in the leafy shade: sometimes with allusion to secret love-making.

Cf. J. Hall's ed. of *King Horn* 1227 note.

a **1225** *Ancr. R.* 96 Euer is þe eie to þe wude leie [*v.r.* wodeleȝe], þerinne is þet ich luuie. *a* **1290** *S. Eustace* 20 in Horstm. *Altengl. Leg.* (1881) 212 Þe hert wes muchel.. þer he wes ounder wode linde. *Ibid.* 32 Þere he wes ounder wode leye. *Ibid.* 76 [He] wes ounder wode-bowe. **13..** *K. Horn* 1160 (Harl.) ȝef þou horn euer seȝe vnder wode leȝe. *c* **1320** *Sir Tristr.* 2485 Vnder wode bouȝ þai knewen day and niȝt. *c* **1330** R. Brunne *Chron. Wace* (Rolls) 4734 Wylde walkande by wode lyndes. **1387–8** T. Usk *Test. Love* III. vii. (Skeat) l. 53 Beware of thy lyfe, that thou no wodelay use, as in asking of thinges that strecchen in-to shame! *c* **1400** *Gamelyn* 633 Adam loked tho vndir wode bough. *Ibid.* 676 As men that ben.. hard be-stad vnder wode lynde. *c* **1470** *Gol. & Gaw.* 1344 Rachis can ryn vndir the wod rise.

g. attrib. uses and comb. of pl. (sense 2). *U.S.*

1849 F. Douglas *Life* 59, I stopped my oxen to open the woods gate. **1868** *Rep. U.S. Comm. Agric.* (1869) 391 Any land.. may be improved by the addition of vegetable matter, such as woods litter. **1880** S. Lanier *Hymns of Marshes, Sunrise* 47 The woods-smell. **1902** S. E. White *Blazed Trail* v, Bands of woods-creatures. **1904** —— *Forest* xiv, He was ..comparatively inexperienced in woods-walking. *Ibid.*, A good woods-walker progresses without apparent hurry. **1908** —— *Riverman* vii, Still lingering at the woods camps, ..five hundred woods-weary men.

h. similative, as ***wood-green***, ***-wild*** adjs.

1807 J. Barlow *Columbiad* v. 169 The sandy stream-bank and the woodgreen plain Raise into sight the new made seats of man. **1925** E. Sitwell et al. *Poor Young People* 10 His wood-green laughter. **1953** —— *Gardeners & Astronomers* 37 And is blown by the bright air Upon your wood-wild April-soft long hair.

10. a. Special Combs.: **wood-acid** = *wood-vinegar*; **wood-agate**, agatized wood (*Cent. Dict.*); **wood-alcohol** = wood-spirit 2; **wood-and-water joey** *Austral. slang*, an odd job man; **wood-axe**, an axe for hewing wood or felling trees; **wood-block**, (*a*) a block of wood, *esp.* one on which a design is cut for printing from (cf. *wood-engraving*, woodcut); (*b*) *Mus.*, a hollow wooden block used as a percussion instrument; cf. *Chinese block* s.v. Chinese *a.* 2 and *temple block* s.v. temple *sb.*[1] 6 c; **wood-block** *v.*, to pave with wood-blocks; † **wood-bone** [boon *sb.*[1] 6], ? a boon-day for wood-cutting; **wood-borer**, something that bores wood; *esp.* any one of certain insects and other invertebrates which make perforations in wood; so **wood-boring** *a.*; **wood-bound** *a.*, (*a*) bound or fastened with wood; (*b*) of land, encumbered with woody hedges or trees; (*c*) enclosed by woodland; (*d*) see quot. 1892; **wood-branch**, a branch of a fruit tree kept primarily for growth of wood (6 d); **wood brick**, a block of wood cut to the size and shape of a brick, inserted in the interior walls of a building as a hold for joinery (Gwilt); **wood-bud**, a bud forming the rudiment of a wood-branch; **wood-burner**, (*a*) a locomotive that is fuelled with wood; (*b*) a wood-burning stove or fire; **wood-burning** *a.*, using wood as fuel; † **wood-bush**[1] [buss *sb.*[1]], a vessel for conveying wood, a wood-barge; **wood-bush**[2] [bush *sb.*[1] 9], name of a wooded region in S. Africa; **wood-butcher** *U.S. slang*, an inexperienced carpenter; **wood-carpet**, (*a*) a floor-carpet made of thin pieces of wood arranged in patterns (Knight *Dict. Mech.* 1875); (*b*) the geometer moth *Melanippe rivata* (E. Newman, 1869); † **wood-carriage**, a tenurial obligation to carry wood; **wood-carving**, the ornamental carving of wooden utensils, furniture, etc.; *concr.* a piece of such carving; hence **wood-carved** *a.*, **-carver**; † **wood-cast** [cast *sb.* 13], a pile or stack of wood; **woodchip**, a chip of wood; also (in full ***woodchip paper***), wallpaper with woodchips, etc., embedded in it to give an uneven appearance; ***woodchip board*** = *chipboard* s.v. chip *sb.*[1] 9; **wood-chop** *Austral.* and *N.Z.*, a wood-chopping contest; **wood-colour**, the colour of wood; a pigment of such a colour; **wood-copper**, a wood-brown fibrous variety of olivenite; † **wood-corder** *U.S.*, a town official responsible for stacking cut wood for sale into standard 'cords' piles; **wood-corn**, 'some quantity of Oats or other Grain, paid by Customary Tenants to the Lord, for liberty to pick up dead or broken Wood' (*Cowel's Interpr.* 1701); **wood-draughtsman**, one who draws for wood-engraving; so **wood-drawing**; **wood-dried** *a.*, dried by the heat of burning wood; **wood-drink**, a decoction of some medicinal wood (cf. 6 g); **wood-engraver**, (*a*) one who engraves on wood, an artist who does wood-engraving; (*b*) a name for various species of N. American wood-boring beetles, esp. *Xyleborus cælatus*; **wood-engraving**, the process or art of engraving on wood or of making wood-cuts; *concr.* a design so cut upon a wood-block or obtained by impression from it, a woodcut; **woodfall**, a felling of trees for their wood, a cutting of timber; **wood-farm**, (*a*) a farm on which trees are grown for timber; † (*b*) an office in the Port of London, which dealt with the delivery of wood and other goods discharged; **wood-farmer** (see quot.); **wood-flat** *U.S.*, a raft or flat-bottomed boat used for transporting wood by water; **wood-flour**, (*a*) a substance obtained by grinding wood containing starchy matter, proposed as a substitute for flour; (*b*) a very fine sawdust obtained from pine-wood, used as an absorbent surgical dressing; † **wood-fold**, a wood-yard; **wood-forester** *Sc.*, one who has charge of woods; **wood-free** *a.* (*a*) [cf. free *a.* 27 b], entitled to take wood gratis; (*b*) *Paper-making*, made free from mechanical wood, though not necessarily from chemical wood; also as *sb.*, a wood-free paper; **wood-fretter** (cf. *wood-borer*); **wood-fungus**, a fungus that infests wood; † **wood-garth** = wood-yard; **wood-gas**, gas for illumination obtained from wood; † **wood-geld** [geld *sb.*], money paid for the privilege of cutting or gathering wood in a forest; also (according to 17th c. legal writers), the privilege of immunity from such payment; **wood-gum** = xylan; † **wood-hag** [hag *sb.*[3]], the right to cut wood; † **wood-hagger**, a wood-cutter, wood-hewer; **wood-hanging**, 'thin veneer on a paper backing, to be used as wall-paper' (Knight *Dict. Mech.* 1875); **wood-heap** *Austral.* = *wood-pile*; **wood-hewer**, (*a*) one who hews wood, a wood-cutter; (*b*) a bird of the family *Dendrocolaptidæ*, a South American tree-creeper; † **wood-hire**, payment or outrent for wood; **wood-hole**, a hole or recess in which wood is stored for fuel (cf. *coal-hole*); † **wood-honey** [OE. *wuduhuniᵹ* = L. *mel silvestre*, Gr. *μέλι ἄγριον*], wild honey; **wood-hook**, a hook for cutting off pieces of wood from trees; **wood-horse** *U.S.*, (*a*) a sawing-horse; (*b*) the walking-stick insect (*Cent. Dict.*); **wood-hung** *a.*, bordered with hanging woods; † **wood-iron**, ? iron smelted by means of wood; † **wood-leave** (Sc. *-leif*, *-lief*, *-leive*), leave or permission to cut or procure wood; *transf.* a duty charged for this; **wood-lock** *Naut.*, a piece of hard wood sheathed with copper, fitted closely beneath the pintle of a rudder to prevent the latter from rising; hence **wood-locked** *a.*, secured by a wood-lock; † **wood-lode**, the carriage or conveyance of wood; the right or privilege of carrying wood; **wood-lot** orig. *U.S.* [lot *sb.* 6 a], a plot of land containing or consisting of woodland; **wood-maid**, **-maiden**, a mythical female being dwelling in or haunting woods; † **wood-maker** = woodman 2; **wood-master**, now *Hist.* the master or overseer of a wood; **wood-meal**, (*a*) a kind of flour, resembling sawdust in appearance, prepared from the root of the manioc or cassava-plant; (*b*) the powdered wood produced by the wood-worm; **wood-money** (see quot.); **wood-mote**, now *Hist.*, a court for determining cases in forest law, later called *court of attachments* (ATTACHMENT 3); **wood-mould**, mould consisting of decayed wood; **wood naphtha** = WOOD-SPIRIT 2; **wood-note**, a natural untrained musical note or song like that of a wild bird in a wood (in later quots. echoing Milton); **wood offering**, an offering of wood to be burnt in sacrifice; **wood-opal** [G. *holzopal*], opal formed by petrifaction of wood, opalized or silicified wood; **wood-paper**, paper made from wood-pulp; **wood-peat**, peat formed from decayed wood (*Cent. Dict.*); † **wood-penny**, (*a*) ? = *wood-silver*; cf. *woodland penny*; (*b*) Paul's betony, *Veronica officinalis*; **wood-piercer**, **-piercing** *a.* = *wood-borer*, *-boring*; **wood-pile**, (*a*) a pile or stack of wood, esp. for fuel; (*b*) phr. ***a nigger in the woodpile***: see NIGGER *sb.* 1 d; also in allusive and euphemistic varr.; (*c*) *Mus. slang*, a xylophone; **wood-plant**, (*a*) a plant with woody stem and branches; (*b*) a plant that grows in woods, a woodland plant; † **wood-plea court**, ? = *wood-mote*; † **wood-pleck** [PLECK], ? an enclosure in which wood is stored; **wood post**, a station where wood is procured; **wood powder**, (*a*) powder made by disintegration of wood, as sawdust; (*b*) a kind of gunpowder made from light porous wood; **wood-print**, a print from an engraved wood-block, a woodcut; **wood-pulp**, a pulp made by mechanical or chemical disintegration of wood-fibre, and used for making paper; also *attrib.*; **wood-ranger** orig. and chiefly *U.S.*, one who ranges woods; a scout or sharpshooter in American armies (cf. RANGER *sb.* 3); **wood ray** *Bot.* (see quot. 1933); † **wood-rent**, ? = *wood-silver*; **wood-road**, a track or rough road through woods; **wood-rock**, a compact variety of asbestos resembling dry wood, also called *mountain wood* (Cent. Dict.); **wood rot**, a fungal disease that causes wood to rot; so **wood-rotting** *a.*; **wood-saw**, a saw for cutting wood, as a buck-saw (Knight 1875); **wood-sawyer**, (*a*) a man employed in sawing wood; (*b*) the larva of a wood-boring beetle or other insect, which cuts off twigs, etc. (*Cent. Dict.*); † **wood-scathe** [SCATHE *sb.* 1], a fiend or monster of the wood; **wood-screw**, a metallic screw specially adapted for fastening together parts of woodwork or wood and metal; **wood-service**, service as a wood-ranger; † **wood-silver**, ? a payment made in lieu of a supply of wood; cf. *woodland silver*; **woodskin**, a light canoe made of bark, used by native tribes in Guyana; in full ***woodskin canoe***; **wood-soot**, the soot of burnt wood, formerly recognized in the British Pharmacopœia as *fuligo ligni*, and used in dyeing; † **wood-speech** [SPEECH *sb.*[1] 10 b], a kind of wood-mote; **wood-still**, a still for distilling tar or turpentine from pine-wood (Knight *Dict. Mech.* 1875); **wood-stone**, petrified wood, *esp.* a form of quartz consisting of silicified wood; **wood-stove**, a stove adapted for burning wood (Knight 1875); **wood-sugar** = XYLOSE (*Cent. Dict. Suppl.*); † **wood-tale**, a quantity of wood supplied as a due; **wood-tar**, a bituminous liquid obtained in the destructive distillation of pines and other trees; **wood-tin** [G. *holzzinn*], a variety of cassiterite or tin-stone of brownish colour and fibrous structure, resembling dry wood; **wood-vessel**, (*a*) a vessel carrying a cargo of wood; (*b*) *Bot.* a sap-conducting vessel in the woody tissue of a plant; **wood-vinegar**, vinegar or crude acetic acid obtained by distillation of wood, also called *pyroligneous acid*; † **wood-waste** (meaning unknown); **wood-wharf**, a wharf at which cargoes of wood are landed or shipped; so ***wood-wharfing***; † **wood-whistle**, ? the bishop's weed, *Ammimajus*; **woodwind**, the wooden wind-instruments in an orchestra collectively (cf. 7 e above, and WIND *sb.*[1] 12 b; now often made of some other material); also, an individual instrument of this kind ; **wood-wing** *Theatr.*, a wing which is shaped and decorated so as to represent a tree or trees; **wood-wool**, † (*a*) cotton; (*b*) fine shavings of wood, usually pine-wood, used as a surgical dressing and for various other purposes; **woodwright**, a worker in wood, as a carpenter.

1858 SIMMONDS *Dict. Trade*, **Wood-acid*, an inferior pyroligneous acid, distilled from oak, beech, ash, &c. **1861** *Wood alcohol [see PYROLIGNEOUS]. **1887** *All Year Round* 30 July 67/2 A '*wood-and-water Joey' is a hanger about hotels, and a doer of odd jobs. **1930** V. PALMER *Passage* I. v. 42, I wanted you to be something different from a wood-and-water joey, earning a few pounds here and there. **1966** *Woman's Day* (Sydney) 31 Oct., He is a 'wood and water joey'—the lad who does the odd jobs around the homestead. *c* **1356** *Durham Acc. Rolls* 557 In factura unius *Wodeax. **1535** STEWART *Cron. Scot.* II. 454 With ane wod-ax thair tha straik of his heid. **1625** *Reg. Mag. Sig. Scot.* 300/2 Lie schaft of the wode aix. **1900** R. W. CHAMBERS *Cardigan* xxix, I.. unslung my wood-axe. He drew his hatchet. **1837** HEBERT *Engin. & Mech. Encycl.* II. 825 Two specimens of *wood-blocks, cut by Mr. Wightman. **1877** H. LAW & D. K. CLARK *Constr. Roads* 17 Following the experience of stone-set paving, the wood blocks of narrower dimensions answered better. **1883** *Builder* 24 Nov. 704/2 The prejudice against the use of good elm for purposes such as wood-block floors. **1930** *Étude* Sept. 620 (*caption*) The drummer in a modern theater orchestra uses the assortment of instruments here shown. There are.. Trap Console, Italian Tam Tam, and Wood Block. **1969** *Listener* 23 Jan. 121/2 The viola players also plays a woodblock, and the viola and cello bow a suspended cymbal. **1972** *Jazz & Blues* Oct. 28/2 The drummer accompanies on the drums, with woodblocks used to give tonal contrast. **1908** *Westm. Gaz.* 13 Aug. 4/2 The road leading from Shepherd's Bush to Uxbridge,.. the major part of which was *wood-blocked by the United Tramways Company. **1524** *Compotus of monastic property in Cottingham, Northants* (MS.), Vnu' *Wodbone in autumpno, vnam Gallinam ad Natale D'ni, et decem oua ad Pascha. **1850** A. WHITE *List Crustacea B. Mus.* 56 *Chelura terebrans.* Sea *Wood-Borer. **1815** KIRBY & SP. *Entomol.* viii. (1818) I. 240 The little *wood-boring beetles ..(*Anobium pertinax* and *striatum*) also attack books. **1875** KNIGHT *Dict. Mech.* 2275/1 *Spiral Bit*, a wood boring tool.. made of a twisted bar of metal. **1570** *Richmond Wills* (Surtees) 229 Two paire of *wood boune wheills. **1710** HILMAN *Tusser Rediv.* Mar. (1744) 35 Where it fronts the Sea, pois'nous Marshes, Wood-bound, over-shelter'd by Woods, and the like. **1796** MARSHALL *Planting* I. 56 High Hedges, and low Pollards, are the bane of corn fields.. in Norfolk, lands thus encumbered are.. said to be wood-bound. **1876** HARDY *Hand of Ethelberta* xv, Ethelberta and Christopher stood within the wood-bound circle alone. **1892** *Labour Commission* Gloss., *Wood-bound Trade*, in the coopering industry making packing casks in which to put bottles for export from breweries. **1706** LONDON & WISE *Retir'd Gard'ner* I. II. iii. 111 The *Wood-Branches are those that form the Shape of the Tree. **1842** *Wood Bricks [see NOG *sb.*[1]]. **1763** MILLS *Syst. Pract. Husb.* IV. 249 Care should.. be taken to cut them a little sloping behind a *wood bud, which may be easily distinguished from the blossom buds. **1840** *Penny Cycl.* XVII. 346/1 The flower-buds are plump and roundish; the wood-buds are more oblong and pointed. **1901** *World's Work* (N.Y.) Dec. 1518/2, I began when there was nothing but *wood-burners, big flaming smokestacks, and all that. **1965** G. MCINNES *Road to Gundagai* v. 81 A gas stove and an old fashioned woodburner. **1980** *Sunday Times* (Colour Suppl.) 30 Mar. 69/3 Finland's last wood-burner steams through an Arctic Circle blizzard. **1951** W. FAULKNER *Requiem for Nun* III. 225 The light-wheeled bulb-stacked *wood-burning engines shrieking among the swamps. *Ibid.* 251 The intractable and obsolescent of the town who still insisted on wood-burning ranges. **1960** *Times* 20 Oct. 15/2 A wood-burning river steamer. **1980** A. E. FISHER *Midnight Men* xv. 187 Sarah's studio.. was warm.. with a big wood-burning stove. **1587** *K.R. Mem. Roll 392* Mich. v. 3 Navis Angl' voc' *woodbushe. **1896** *Westm. Gaz.* 14 Sept. 2/3 Majajie, the mystical Queen of the *Wood-bush tribes. **1903** J. BUCHAN *Afr. Colony* 114 A delight in the Wood Bush is apt to spoil a man for other scenery. **1883** *Sporting Life* 27 May 4/3 What has he done to the New York *Clipper*'s *wood butcher that he should be thus caricatured? **1890** in Barrère & Leland *Dict. Slang* s.v., Counting carpenters and wood-butchers together, it is estimated that about 20,000 men make their living in London as carpenters and joiners. **1557** *Acts Privy Counc. Irel.* (Hist. MSS. Comm.) 39 The freholders.. hathe been accustomed.. to pay.. certain *woodd cariages and other duties. **1885** HALLIWELL *Life Shaks.* (ed. 5) 521 The elegant *wood-carved roof. **1859** W. S. COLEMAN *Woodlands* (1862) 62 The wood [of the alder].. is a favourite material for many purposes of the turner and the *wood-carver. **1847** LD. LINDSAY *Chr. Art* I. p. ccix, Artists in *wood-carving. **1862** *Catal. Internat. Exhib., Brit.* II. No. 5723, Book-case, wood-carvings, stone-sculpture. **1483** *Cath. Angl.* 423/1 A *Wodde caste, *strues.* **1612** *N. Riding Rec.* (1884) I. 259 Chr. Wright.. [presented] for building his wood-cast and laying his tymber in the Kinges street whereby the people.. cannot conveniently passe. **1958** *Times Rev. Industry* Dec. 61/3 Information service, covering all aspects of the production of *wood-chip board. **1973** *Nation Rev.* (Melbourne) 31 Aug. (Suppl.) 1/1 The impending threat to Australia's native forests from intensive forestry, and particularly from woodchip projects. **1976** *Dumfries & Galloway Standard* 25 Dec. 4 (Advt.), Top quality woodchip reduced from 49p to only 39p roll. **1976** *Milton Keynes Express* 18 June 14/1 (Advt.), Woodchip paper—ideal for overpainting. Sale price 37p. **1977** *Abingdon Herald* 2 June 9/2 (Advt.), Fine quality woodchip (ideal for overpainting) only 39p per roll. **1918** *Bulletin* (Sydney) 16 May 48/2 Bill Lucas will chop against a local champion... After the *wood-chop five rounds between. **1934** T. WOOD *Cobbers* xvi. 191, I saw a good wood-chop and some tumultuous steer-riding. **1964** *Courier-Mail* (Brisbane) 27 July 8/5 It will be dearer at this year's Show if you want to just drop in to see one or two woodchops. **1622** PEACHAM *Compl. Gent.* xii. 116 Your *Wood colours are compounded either of Vmber and White, Char-coale and White [etc.]. **1884** BOWER & SCOTT *De Bary's Phaner.* 507 The sap-wood.. has a light whitish or yellowish wood-colour. **1823** W. PHILLIPS *Introd. Min.* (ed. 3) 320 Hæmatitic Arseniate. *Wood Copper. **1681** *Rep. Record Commissioners City of Boston* (1881) VII. 143 Chosen.. Over-seers of *Wood Corders. **1781** *First Records Baltimore Town* (1905) 43 The Commissers had it [*sc.* an oath] administred to him and afterwards appointed him Wood-corder. **1850** *Knickerbocker* XXXVI. 105 When he has a long wand, he is a wood-corder. **1235–53** *Rentalia Glaston.* (Somerset Rec. Soc.) 76 Facit easdem consuetudines sicut Robertus de Stodlegh' preter *Wdecorn unum ferdellum. **1894** HERKOMER in *Daily News* 28 Apr. 6/7 Nearly all the *wood-draughtsmen of my time have become painters of eminence. *Ibid.*, He watches over the welfare of the artists now as much as he did in my *wood-drawings days. **1577** HARRISON *England* III. i. 96/1 The *woode dryed mault.. doth.. annoye the heade of him that is not vsed thereto because of the smoke. **1591** R. HITCHCOCK in Arb. *Garner* II. 216 Wood-dried malt will make unsavoury drink. **1611** FLORIO, *Pigliare il legno*, to take the *wood or dyet drinke for the pox. **1696** FLOYER *Humours* 190 Drinking Wine, and two parts of Water, or Wood-Drinks. **1816** OTTLEY *Hist. Engraving* I. 97 It appears that the old German *wood engravers manufactured prodigious quantities of these religious cuts. *Ibid.* 31 The professors of *wood engraving. *Ibid.* 32 Another large wood engraving, representing the Madonna. **1588** WALSINGHAM in *Collect.* (O.H.S.) I. 230 Yearely *woodfals in Middlesex. **1619** T. CLAY *Chorol. Disc.* 25 To see that the Woodfalls be made at seasonable times. **1767** A. YOUNG *Farmer's Lett. to People* (1771) I. iii. 153 *note*, *Wood-farms.. not being very common. **1812** J. SMYTH *Pract. Customs* (1821) 388 The business of the Woodfarm or River Office in the Port of London. **1831** LOUDON *Encycl. Agric.* (ed. 2) 1123 *Wood-farmers, such as rent woodlands, to be periodically cut for fuel [etc.]. **1785** in *Maryland Hist. Mag.* (1925) XX. 42 He hath gone up and down frequently in battans, scows and *wood-flats. **1838** *Jrnl. & Register* (Columbus, Ohio) 27 Apr. 2/5 There were no boats at hand except a few large and unmanageable wood flats which were carried to the relief of the sufferers.. by the few persons on the shore. **1883** 'MARK TWAIN' *Life on Mississippi* 237 The Pennsylvania was creeping along,.. towing a wood-flat which was fast being emptied. **1845** DODD *Brit. Manuf.* Ser. v. 18 The wood is next dried.., and is afterwards ground repeatedly, till it assumes the form of a rough flour. The *wood-flour is then formed into small flat cakes by the addition of water. **1885** *Buck's Handbk. Med. Sci.* I. 265/2 Wood-wool and wood-flour, the latter the finest, are made from pine wood. **1570** LEVINS *Manip.* 219/20 A *Wodfould, *lignarium.* **1865** Q. VICTORIA *More Leaves* (1884) 32 The Duke's head *wood-forester. **1899** CROCKETT *Kit Kennedy* 175 Kit's uncle Rob, the wood forester. **1554** *Charters rel. Glasgow* (1906) II. 513 Archinbalde salbe *wod fre and querell fre to the bigging.. of the saidis mylne and hir dame. **1904** *Jrnl. Soc. Chem. Industry* 15 Jan. 34/2 (*heading*) Manufacture of wood-free cardboard for printing. **1966** *Economist* 24 Sept. 1269/1 The mill will make.. good quality 'wood-frees'. **1979** *Morning News* (Karachi) 24 May 5/2 This variation is applied for woodfree and mechanical pulp. **1611** COTGR., *Tavelliere*, the little worme called a *Wood-fretter. **1876** PREECE *Telegraphy* 161 Dry-rot.. is due to a species of *wood-fungus—the *Merulius lachrymans*—which destroys the tensile and cohesive power of the wood, and gradually reduces it to.. a fine powder. **1343** *Durham Acc. Rolls* (Surtees) 39 Lapides pro paviamento del *Wodegarthe. **1570** LEVINS *Manip.* 34/5 Y^e Wodgarth, *lig*[*n*]*arium.* *c* **1865** LETHEBY in *Circ. Sci.* I. 125/2 The.. city of Heilbronn has recently been lighted up with *wood-gas. **1220** in Spelman *Gloss. Archæol.* (1664) 260 Et sint quieti.. de omnibus geldis, & danegeldis, & *vodegeldis. **1334** in *N. Riding Record Soc.* N.S. III. 108 Quod ipse et homines sui sint quieti de omnibus geldis.. Et de wodegeldis. **1594** CROMPTON *Jurisd.* 197 Woodgeld, is properly to be discharged of gathering within the forest, for the behoofe of the foresters, and other ministers there. **1628** COKE *On Litt.* 233 Pudzeld [*i.e.* þudȝeld] or Woodgeld is to be free from payment of money for taking of Wood in any Forest. **1894** MUIR & MORLEY *Watts' Dict. Chem.* IV. 868/1 Tree gum. *Wood gum. **1569** in *Reg. Mag. Sig. Scot. 1580*, 810 Cum.. lapicidiis, silvis, nemoribus cum lie *wode hage. **1569** *Charters Crosraguel Abbey* (1886) I. 195 Cum earundem silvis et nemoribus cum lie Wodhag. **1295** *Acc. Exch. K.R.* 5/8 m. 2 (P.R.O.) In stipendiis Walteri Le *Wodhagger pro meremio prosternendo in bosco de Stagholme. **1624** CAPT. J. SMITH *Virginia* III. vii. 69 Let no man thinke that.. these gentlemen spent their times as common wood-haggers at felling of trees. **1868** *Rep. U.S. Comm. Agric.* (1869) 15 The American *wood-hanging.. has been applied for the finish of the suite of rooms. **1943** K. TENNANT *Ride on Stranger* (1968) iii. 21 Get back to the *wood-heap. **1966** 'J. HACKSTON' *Father clears Out* 77 Father was out at the woodheap chopping Mother's wood for her. *c* **1000** ÆLFRIC *Deut.* xxix. 11 Butan *wudu-heawerum & ðam ðe wæter berað. **1300** *Rolls of Parlt.* I. 255/1 Roberto le Wodehyewere. **1483** *Cath. Angl.* 423/1 A Wodde hewer, *lignarius.* **1867** SCLATER & SALVIN *Exotic Ornith.* (1869) 71 *Xiphocolaptes major.* (Rusty Wood-hewer). **1361** in Blount *Fragm. Antiq.* (1815) 368 Pro *wodehyre ob'. **1438–9** *Durham Acc. Rolls* (Surtees) 74 Pro Wodhire apud Aldyngrige, Brome, et Rylley, hoc anno, iiij *d.* **1511–12** *Ibid.* (MS.), Pro Wodhire in Aldyngryge et Rylley, iij d. ob. **1668** ETHEREDGE *She Wou'd if she Cou'd* I. i, Creep into the *Wood-hole here. **1703** J. PHILIPS *Splendid Shilling* 44 Confounded, to the dark recess I fly Of wood-hole. *c* **950** *Lindisf. Gosp.* Mark i. 6 *Mel siluestrae*, *wudu huniȝ. **1398** TREVISA *Barth. De P.R.* XVII. lxiii. (1495) P vj/2 Been haunte the floures [of beech] and gadre wode hony in holowe trees. *c* **1450** *Mirk's Festial* 184/30 Saynt Ion ete leues, brod and rownd and whyt,.. and when þay byn frotude.. thay byn swete as hony.. and byn callyd wod-hony. *c* **1440** *Promp. Parv.* 531/2 *Wodehoke, or wedehoke, *sarculus.* **1598** BARRET *Theor. Warres* v. iii. 134, 1500 wood hookes, and tooles to make faggots. **1849** F. DOUGLAS *Life* 116 Mr. Johnson kindly let me have his *wood horse and saw. **1745** WARTON *Pleas. Melanch.* 315 *Wood-hung Menai, stream of druids old. **1536–7** *Durham Acc. Rolls* (Surtees) 694 Et in 4^{xx} petr. ferri de stauro dni Prioris pro le *Wodyron ad 4*d.*, 26*s.* 8*d.* **1503** *Acc. Ld. High Treas. Scot.* II. 283 Payit be the said Robert for *wod leif in France, xviij frankis. **1610** in *Rec. Convent. Burghs Scot.* (1870) II. 300 Dewteis for grundlieve and woodlieve. **1805** *Shipwright's Vade-m.* 142 **Wood-lock*, a piece of elm or oak,.. in the throating or score of the pintle, near the load-water line. **1867** SMYTH *Sailor's Word-bk.* 529 The pintles are hooks which enter the braces, and the rudder is then *wood-locked. **1263** *Cal. Inquis. p. M. Hen. III* (1904) 563, 15 s. 4 d. *wodelode. **1377** in *Somerset & Dorset N. & Q.* (1911) Dec. 342 Johannes Purdy tenet unam virgatam.. reddet per annum vij s- vj d. pro Wodelode iiij d. **1658** *Suffolk* (Mass.) *Deeds* (1885) III. No. 174, I heeretofore purchased.. all the rights to any *wood Lott. **1706** *Town Records* (Manchester, Mass.) (1889) I. 115 It is Voted and agreed to lay out 50 or 60 Acors of land at the west end of our common for a wood lot. **1742** in W. M. Sargent *Maine Wills* (1887) 473 A third part of a Wood Lott for Cutting of ye wood or for feeding. **1866** LOWELL *Among my Bks., Lessing* (1870) 304 He would soon be driven to the cutting of green stuff from his own wood-lot, more rich in smoke than fire. **1975** *N.Z. Jrnl. Agric.* Sept. 25/2 Burning requires fuel, but..piles of branches from the woodlots..are soon used up. **1976** *Shooting Times & Country Mag.* 18–24 Nov. 28/2 Not that Jim wouldn't shoot a woodcock that got up in front of him, or a pheasant from the plough between a couple of woodlots. **1616** *MS. Acc. St. John's Hosp., Canterb.*, For bread and drink to the teners and *wood makers. **15..** in Blount *Anc. Tenures* (1679) 168 The *Woodmaster and Kepers of Needwoode shale every yere mete at..Birkeley Lodgge..and Seynt Laurence dey; at which dey and place a Woodmoote shal be kept. **1826** Hor. Smith *Tor Hill* I. 292 A Woodmote having been held on the same day,..the wood-master and his men came to swell the procession. **1760–72** J. Adams tr. *Juan & Ulloa's Voy.* (ed. 3) II. 324 The common food of the inhabitants.. throughout Brazil, is the farina de Pau or *wood-meal, which is universally eaten instead of bread. **1852** J. J. Seidel *Organ* 121 Pipes..so completely eaten by the wood-worm, that the wind blows out the dust or wood-meal through all the holes. **1892** *Labour Comm.* Gloss. s.v. *Money*, Some yards in the barge-building industry allow the men to take home..small pieces of wood: others allow 2*d.* per day in lieu of wood; this is termed *wood money. **15.., 1826** *Woodmote [see *wood-master*]. *a* **1610** Manwood *Lawes Forest* xxii. §1 (1615) 207 The said Court of attachments then called the Wood-mote Court. **1768** Blackstone *Comm.* III. vi. 71 The court of attachments, wood-mote, or forty days court, is to be held before the verderors of the forest once in every forty days. **1900** J. Nisbet *Our Forests & Woodlands* i. 29 In the Charter of 1217 provision was made for a Court of Attachment or 'Woodmote' being held every forty days... Like the Woodmote, the Swainmote was originally held at irregular times. **1978** *Lancashire Life* Apr. 27/2 One named Ughtred Hodgkinson attended a woodmote at Whitewell in Bowland in 1570. **1868** *Rep. U.S. Comm. Agric.* (1869) 424 A small portion of the field was manured with a compost of night-soil and *wood-mold. **1842** *wood-naphtha [see wood-spirit 2]. **1632** Milton *L'Allegro* 134 If..sweetest Shakespear fancies childe, Warble his native *Wood-notes wilde. **1789** Burns *Let. to M'Auley* 4 June, Mrs. Burns.. has a glorious 'wood-note wild' at either old song or psalmody. **1887** S. Colvin *Keats* v. 105 Wild wood-notes of Celtic imagination. **1611** *Bible* Neh. x. 34 We cast the lots among the priests, the Leuites, and the people, for the *wood offering..to burne vpon the altar. **1816** R. Jameson *Syst. Min.* I. 246 *Wood-Opal. **1800** Koops *Hist. Acc. Inv. Paper* 88 The substance of the *Wood Paper on which these lines are printed. **1261** *Cal. Inquis. p. M. Hen. III* (1904) 502, 2d, *Wudepanies. **1570** Levins *Manip.* 102/29 Wodpenie, *betonica Pauli.* **1713** Petiver *Aquat. Anim. Amboinæ* Tab. 19/8 *Pholas Lignorum*..*Wood Peircer. **1802** Bingley *Anim. Biog.* (1813) III. 279 The *Wood-Piercing Bee. **1552** Huloet, *Woode pyle, *strues.* **1696** Aubrey *Misc.* vi. 68 The Cook Maid, going to the Wood-pile to fetch Wood to dress Supper. **1699** Dampier *Voy.* II. i. 107 They built a Town and fenced it round about with a kind of Wood-pile, or Wall of great Timber Trees. **1883** 'Mark Twain' *Life on Mississippi* xxi. 222 The seldomest spectacle on the Mississippi to-day is a wood-pile. **1936** *Metronome* Feb. 61/2 *Wood pile*, xylophone. **1936** W. Stevens *Let.* 13 May (1967) 311, I agree that there is something wrong in the woodpile. **1951** *Time* 22 Oct. 69 Red Norvo kept salting his half-hour stands with such tunes as..he used to rap out on his 'woodpile' (xylophone) with Paul Whiteman's band 20 years ago. **1977** 'J. D. White' *Salzburg Affair* xvi. 139 He was the odd man out, the African in the woodpile. **1773** *Holme on Spaldingmoor Incl. Act* 18 Banks, *Wood-Plants, Quicksets, or Fences. **1908** [Eliz. Fowler] *Betw. Trent & Ancholme* 19 Wood-plants flourish about this border. **1672** *Cowel's Interpr.*, **Woodplea-Court*, is a Court held twice in the year in the Forest of Clun in Con. Salop,..and perhaps was anciently the same with Woodmote-Court. **1521** *Cov. Leet Bk.* 668 That no inhabitant..make eny gardeyn or *wodpleck with-in xl[ti] fote [of the town wall]. **1904** *Brit. Med. Jrnl.* 17 Sept. 662 Leisha *wood post is on the bank of the river surrounded by forests. **1870** in *Boorde's Introd. Knowl.* 99 *Wood-powder, Boorde's remedy for Excoriation. **1881** Greener *Gun* 322 In combustion wood powder is far more rapid than black. **1816** W. Y. Ottley *Hist. Engraving* I. 91 The very early *wood-prints of Germany. **1908** *Dublin Rev.* July 216 The book is adorned with charming wood-prints. **1866** *Patents, Abridgm. Specif. Manuf. Paper* II. (1876) 427 Improvements in preparing ..*wood pulp for the manufacture of paper. **1734** in *Acct. Progress Colony Georgia* (1741) App. v. 51 [The French] have Five hundred Men in Pay, constantly employed as *Wood-Rangers, to keep their neighbouring *Indians* in Subjection. **1757** [Burke] *Europ. Settlem. Amer.* VII. xxvii. II. 270 A company of wood rangers..to scour the country near our settlements. **1896** *Harper's Mag.* XCII. 712/1 The white wood-rangers were as ruthless as their red foes. **1915** W. B. Yeats *Reveries* (1916) 137, I could not sleep..from my fear of the wood-ranger. **1933** *Trop. Woods* XXXVI. 3 **Wood ray* or *xylem ray*, the part of a ray internal to the cambium. **1975** *Sci. Amer.* July 102/2 Among the components of the cambium are what are called ray initials; the continuation of a ray initial down into the sapwood of a stem, a branch or a trunk is known as a wood ray. **1774** T. West *Antiq. Furness* 109 These [iron forges] were destroyed ..at the request of the customary tenants, who charged themselves with paying the rent of 20. l. by a rate which is now called *Woodrent or Bloomsmithy rent. **1821** J. F. Cooper *Spy* (1831) vii. 81 The English captain took the advice of this mysterious being and finding a *wood-road.. turned down its direction. **1891** *Century Mag.* Apr. 921, I moved camp, following the wood-road to the summit. **1954** C. Bruce *Channel Shore* 89 In early winters he and James had cut firewood there and hauled it out over the wood road he had swamped, and up the main road, home. **1926** *Rev. Appl. Mycol.* V. 521 The winter draws attention to the misleading impression created by the use of the term 'branch canker' for two totally distinct types of injury: one caused by the attacks of such organisms as *Macro-phoma theicola*, and the other resulting from a *wood rot. **1931** E. E. Hubert *Outline of Forest Path.* xi. 449 The classification of wood rots is largely based upon the colour changes produced in wood by fungi. The discolorations produced by wood-rot and sap-stain fungi..are responsible for a large part of the loss due to degrade in lumber. **1973** C. Bonington *Next Horizon* viii. 128 The garden bounded by a high hedge with an old wooden seat, softened with age and wood-rot. **1918** *Wood-rotting [see *sap-rot* s.v. sap *sb.*[1] 7 a]. **1971** P. H. B. Talbot *Princ. Fungal Taxonomy* i. 17 One can only conjecture how different the course of history might have been if the British fleet had not been laid low at times by the action of wood-rotting fungi. **1816** *Austin Papers* (1924) I. 264, 1 *Wood Saw. **1884** 'Mark Twain' *Huck. Finn* vi. 39, I found an old rusty wood-saw without any handle. **1815** *North Amer. Rev.* II. 143 Deaths by Violence. .. In New York Mr. John Wood, killed in the street by Patrick Hart, a *wood-sawyer, with a stick of wood. **1844** Emerson *New Eng. Reform.* Wks. (Bohn) I. 260 The labour of the porter and wood-sawyer. **1891** M. E. Wilkins *New Eng. Nun* 43 Matilda's antecedents had come of wood-sawyers and garden-laborers. *c* **1275** Lay. 25859 Wola þat þe *wode-scaþe haueþ þe þus for-fare. **1733** Tull *Horse-hoeing Husb.* xxiv. 402 What is meant by *Wood Screws, are taper Screws made with Iron, having very deep Threads, whereby they hold fast when screw'd into Wood. **1868** *Rep. to Govt. U.S. Munitions War* 222 These plates..are attached to the ship's side by a plentiful supply of wood-screws, screwed into the timber backing. **1757** R. Rogers *Jrnls.* (1769) 52 Volunteers in the regular troops, to be trained to the ranging, or *wood-service. *c* **1245** in Lysons *Environs Lond.* (1796) IV. 131 [In this survey two payments are mentioned called] *wodeselver [and] averselver [a composition for labour]. **1355–6** *Abingdon Obedientiars Acc.* (Camden) 5 De redditu de wodeseluer x li. iij s. **1510–11** in Eyton *Antiq. Shropsh.* (1856) III. 325. **1825** Waterton *Wand. S. Amer.* i. (1903) 32 There is neither curial nor canoe, nor purple-heart tree in the neighbourhood to make a *wood-skin to carry you over. **1904** W. H. Hudson *Green Mansions* xxi. 289 Some compassionate voyager would let me share his *wood-skin. **1934** E. Waugh *Handful of Dust* v. 287 The canoes were made of woodskin... They worked patiently but clumsily; one woodskin was split in getting it off the trunk. **1958** J. Carew *Wild Coast* iii. 44 He had to fetch his woodskins from Honey Reef. **1966** P. Sherlock *West Indian Folk-Tales* 37 Each morning the men of the tribe went out in their woodskin canoes. **166.** Sir W. Petty in Sprat *Hist. Roy. Soc.* (1667) 296 In Cloth Dying *wood-soot is of good use. **1728** Chambers *Cycl.* s.v. *Dy(e)ing*, Wood-soot, containing not only a colour, but a salt, needs nothing to..make it strike on the stuff. **1770** *Cook's Voy. round World* III. viii. (1773) 632 Of the colour of wood soot, or what is commonly called a chocolate colour. **1222–3** in Dugdale *Monast. Angl.* (1825) V. 268/1 In curiis nostris.. shiris, halemotis, et *wodespeches. **1796** Kirwan *Elem. Min.* (ed. 2) I. 315 *Woodstone..is commonly..the substance of petrified wood. **1839** Ure *Dict. Arts* 647 Hornstone occurs under three modifications; splintery hornstone, conchoidal hornstone, and woodstone. **1235–52** *Rentalia Glaston.* (Som. Rec. Soc.) 83 Et debet habere *wdetale contra Natale, scil. unum truncum [etc.]. **1857** Miller *Elem. Chem., Org.* iv. §6. 198 *Eupione*, which Reichenbach obtained during the rectification of the products from *wood-tar. **1787** Groschke tr. *Klaproth's Observ. Fossils Cornw.* 13 The most remarkable species of stream-tin is a tin-ore like haematites, or what is called *Wood-tin. **1855** Leifchild *Cornwall* 201 The famous wood-tin, so called from the woody appearance of some of the pebbles, was formerly found in the Loth stream works in abundance. **1796** Nelson 26 July in Nicolas *Disp.* (1845) II. 220 Not a *Wood-Vessel bound to Piombino would go out of the Port. **1883** McNab *Bot., Morphol. & Physiol.* ii. 42 The xylem..consists..of three sets of cells, viz. the wood vessels, the wood prosenchyma, and the wood parenchyma. **1837** Hebert *Engin. & Mech. Encycl.* II. 849 There are four principal kinds: namely, wine vinegar, malt vinegar, sugar vinegar, and *wood vinegar. **1235–52** *Rentalia Glaston.* (Som. Rec. Soc.) 135 Et debet cariare bladum cum careta sua per j diem et debet auxiliari ad *wddewaste. **1279** *Liber Cust.* (Rolls) 150 Qil serra lie au pilier qi estet en Tamise a *Wodehwarfe. **1594** Norden *Spec. Brit., Essex* (Camden) 10 Places wher they take in wood,..w[ch] places are called vpon the Thames, westward, haws or woodwharfes. *a* **1700** Evelyn *Diary* 5 Sept. 1666, The coale and wood wharfes. **1902** Cornish *Naturalist Thames* 212 A tug was taking a couple of deal-loaded barges to a woodwharf. **1840** *Evid. Hull Docks Comm.* 136, I propose what in the neighbourhood of Hull is called *wood-wharfing. *a* **1400** *Alphita* (Anecd. Oxon.) 8 *Ameos agreste*, similis fraxinarie, anglice, *wodewhisgle [*v.r.* wodewhistle]. **1876** *Wood wind [see wind *sb.*[1] 12 b]. **1901** W. J. Henderson *Orchestra* 19 Next in importance to the strings is the wood-wind, which is divided into three families—flutes, oboes, and clarinets. **1922** Joyce *Ulysses* 280 Double-basses, helpless, gashes in their sides. Woodwinds mooing cows. **1926** Whiteman & McBride *Jazz* ix. 195 Musicians recognize four general classes of instruments in speaking of the orchestra—strings, wood winds, brasses, and the battery of traps. **1967** T. Stoppard *Rosencrantz & Guildenstern are Dead* III. 83 One of the sailors has pursed his lips against a woodwind. **1978** *Early Music* July 333/2 Vivaldi had to rely on Austrian and German makers for the newer woodwinds. **1933** P. Godfrey *Back-Stage* i. 19 *Wood-wings are lugged into position. **1974** D. Smith *Look back with Love* xvi. 164 One of these quick-changes occurred during my first scene, and to cover it, I had..a short soliloquy, halfway through which a glance into the wood-wings showed me that our leading man was still three-quarters Lesurques when he should have been seven-eighths Dubosc. **1559** Morwyng *Evonymus* 323 With a little *wode woul dipte therein rub the teethe. **1885** [see *wood-flour*]. **1887** *Advance* (Chicago) 7 July 431 In workshops, the wood-wool is even replacing cotton waste for cleaning machinery. **1867** Morris *Jason* III. 75 All who chanced to know The *woodwright's craft. **1883** J. Parker *Tyne Chylde* 6 At a wood-wright's door, where I stood on a large block of old oak.

b. In names of animals, chiefly birds and insects: (i) that live in woods, as ***wood bee***, ***fly***, ***gnat***, ***hornet***, ***moth***; esp. in designations of particular species or groups, as ***wood Argus*** (Argus 3), ***dormouse***, ***fly***, ***lady*** (lady *sb.* 9), ***mite***, ***rattlesnake***, ***red-bird***, ***sandpiper***, ***swift*** (swift *sb.*[2] 4), ***tattler***, ***tiger*** (tiger *sb.* 11), ***wagtail*** (see quots.); *wood* mouse, pewee, pie (*sb.*[1] 3 b), swallow (*sb.*[1] 2 b); (ii) that live, bore, or burrow in wood; e.g. in local names of species of woodpecker, as ***wood-jobber***, ***-knacker***, ***-tapper***, and in *wood-borer*, *-fretter*, *-piercer*, *-sawyer* in 10; **wood-ant**, (*a*) a large ant, *Formica rufa*, living in woods; (*b*) a termite or white ant, which burrows in wood; **wood baboon** = drill *sb.*[3]; **wood-beetle**, a wood-boring beetle; **wood bison**, **wood buffalo**, a variety of American bison (*Bison bison athabascæ*) found in the wooded parts of the west of Canada; **wood-bug**, an insect of the genus *Pentatoma*; **wood-cat**, †(*a*) a fanciful name for the hare; (*b*) a wild cat living in woods, *spec.* the S. American species *Felis geoffroyi*; **wood-cracker** *dial.*, the nuthatch, *Sitta cæsia*; **wood-cricket**, a species of cricket found in woods, as *Nemobius sylvestris*; **wood-culver** = wood-pigeon; **wood-deer** = *wood-goat*; **wood-digger**, a West Indian insect (see quot.); **wood-drake**, the male of the *wood-duck*; **wood-duck**, a species of duck inhabiting woods, *esp.* the N. American summer duck, *Æx sponsa*, and the Australian *Bernicla jubata*; **wood-frog**, a species of frog found in woods, as the N. American *Rana sylvatica*; **wood-goat**, a S. African species of antelope, *Antilope sylvatica*; **wood-grouse**, (*a*) the capercailye *Tetrao urogallus* (see grouse *sb.*[1] 1); (*b*) the spotted Canada grouse, *Canace* (*Dendragapus*) *canadensis*, or allied species; **wood grub**, the larva of any of several wood-boring insects; †**wood hog** *U.S.*, a variety of pig which feeds in woods; **wood hoopoe**, any of several birds of the genus *Phœniculus* (or the family Phœniculidæ), native to Africa and distinguished by blue and green plumage and a long tail; **wood-ibis**, a stork of the subfamily *Tantalinæ*, esp. *Tantalus loculator*, which inhabits wooded swamps in southern U.S.; a wood-stork; **wood-kingfisher**, a name for birds allied to the kingfisher, living in woods: = *king-hunter* (king *sb.* 13 b); **wood-leopard** (*moth*), a species of spotted moth (*Zeuzera pyrina*), the larva of which bores into the wood of trees; = *leopard-moth* s.v. leopard 6 b; **wood-owl**, any species of owl living in woods, as the tawny or brown owl, *Syrnium aluco*; **wood-partridge** = *wood-grouse*; **wood-pelican** = *wood-ibis*; **wood-pheasant**, (*a*) = *wood-grouse* (a); (*b*) in Zanzibar (see quot. 1892); **wood(s)-pussy** *N. Amer. colloq.*, a skunk; **wood-quail**, any bird of the genus *Rollulus*, of the Malay archipelago; **wood-rabbit**, the common rabbit of U.S., *Lepus sylvaticus*, also called *cotton-tail*; also, any rabbit living in a wood; **wood-rat**, any rat of the American genus *Neotoma*; **wood-robin**, a local name of the American *wood-thrush*; **wood-shrike**, (*a*) = woodchat; (*b*) an African shrike of the genus *Prionops*; **wood-shrimp**, a crustacean of the family *Cheluridæ*, as *Chelura terebrans*, which bores in submerged wood; **wood-slave**, a West Indian lizard of the species *Mabouya*; **wood-snail**, any species of snail inhabiting woods, esp. *Helix nemoralis*; **wood-snake**, a snake that lives in woods, as those of the family *Dryophidæ*; **wood-snipe**, **-snite**, names for the woodcock (British or American); **wood-star**, a name for several species of humming-birds, as those of the genus *Calothorax* and the Bahama sheartail, *Doricha evelynæ*; **wood-stork** = *wood-ibis*; **wood-swine**, a swine living in woods; *spec.* the bosch-vark, a ferocious wild swine of S. and E. Africa; **wood-tantalus** = *wood-ibis*; **wood-thrush**, (*a*) a species of thrush of the eastern U.S., *Turdus* (*Hylocichla*) *mustelinus*, noted for its beautiful coloration and sweet song; (*b*) a local name of the missel-thrush, *T. viscivorus*; **wood-tick** [tick *sb.*[1]], a tick of the family *Ixodidæ*, found upon plants; **wood-warbler**, (*a*) the wood-wren, *Phylloscopus sibilatrix*; (*b*) a general name for the American warblers (warbler 2 b), esp. those of the genus *Dendrœca*; **wood-wasp**, (*a*) a wasp that lives in woods, as *Vespa sylvestris*; (*b*) a wasp that burrows in rotten wood, as some species of *Crabronidæ*, or a wasp-like insect whose larvæ bore in wood, as the horntails; **wood-worm**, an insect larva or other invertebrate, as the ship-worm (see Teredo), which bores in wood (also *fig.*); **wood-wren**, a species of warbler, *Phylloscopus sibilatrix*, or its congener the willow-wren, *P. trochilus*. See also woodcock, etc.

1709 T. Robinson *Vind. Mosaick Syst.* 90 The *Wood-Ant feeds upon Leaves. **1781** *Phil. Trans.* LXXI. 140 In the West Indies, [they are called] Wood Lice, Wood Ants, or White Ants. **1889** *Science-Gossip* XXV. 33 Length of the wood-ant (*F. rufa*) three-eighths of an inch. **1781** Pennant *Hist. Quadrup.* I. 176 *Wood Baboon... Inhabits Guinea. **1398** Trevisa *Barth. De P.R.* xviii. xii. (Bodl. MS.), Some beþ feelde been and some beþ *wood been. **1609** C. Butler *Fem. Mon.* H 5 b, The wood-pecker..doth more harme to wood-bees then garden-bees. **1836** *Southern Lit. Messenger* II. 96 The wood-bee revels on their sweets. **1953** A. Clarke *Coll. Plays* (1963) 344 The wood-bees court tangles of dew. **1795** Winterbotham *View U.S.* IV. 413 *Wood-beetle, Leptura. **1825** R. T. Gore *Blumenbach's Nat. Hist.* 190 Leptura.. I. Aquatica... The Wood-beetle... On aquatic plants of all kinds. **1843** Johnston in *Proc. Berw. Nat. Club* II. No. xi. 78 As thoroughly drilled as.. a piece of wood that has been eaten with the maggot of the wood-beetles. **1895** C. W. Whitney in *Harper's Mag.* Dec. 10/2 To hunt *wood-bison,.. now become the rarest game in the world. **1892** W. Pike *Barren Ground N. Canada* 143 These animals go by the name of *wood buffalo. **1897** E. Coves *New Light on Early Hist. Greater Northwest* II. xviii. 622 They are the wood buffalo, more shy and wild than those on the plains. **1961** W. P. Keller *Canada's Wild Glory* v. 274 One small pocket of pure wood buffalo persist in a remote corner of the area, and plans are afoot to establish new sanctuaries for these. **1972** Wood buffalo [see *plain(s) buffalo* s.v. PLAIN *sb.*[1] 10]. **1836** Redding *Hist. Mod. Wines* iii. (ed. 2) 47 A nauseous odour.. from a vast number of *wood bugs which had been.. crushed in the [wine] press. *c* **1280** *Names of Hare* in *Rel. Ant.* I. 133 The frendlese, the *wodecat. **1791** J. Long *Voyages* 41 The country every where abounds with wild animals, particularly.. otters, martins, minx, wood cats, racoons, [etc.]. **1892** W. H. Hudson *Nat. La Plata* 15 It is called wood-cat, and.. is an intruder from wooded districts north of the pampas. **1898** Stanley J. Weyman *Shrewsbury* xxvi, Speak, you viper, and don't stand there glowering like a wood-cat! **1677** Plot *Oxfordsh.* 175 A little Bird, somtimes seen, but oftner heard in the Park at Woodstock, from the noise that it makes, commonly called the *Wood-cracker. **1774** Goldsmith *Nat. Hist.* VII. 350 The *wood-cricket is the most timorous animal in nature. *a* **1100** *Gloss.* in Wr.-Wülcker 131/32 *Palumbus*, *wudeculfre. **1533** Elyot *Cast. Helthe* (1541) 15 Meates and drynkes makynge good juyce... Wodde culvers. **1662** J. Chandler *Van Helmont's Oriat.* 201 Mice, Dormice, and Swine do sooner perish with hunger, than they do eat of a Ring-Dove or Wood-Culver. **1812** Plumtre *Lichtenstein's S. Africa* I. 194 Large animals, such as buffalos, *wood-deer (*antilope sylvatica*). **1838** W. P. Hunter tr. *Azara's Nat. Hist. Paraguay* I. 145 Laborde says that his first species is called red deer and wood deer (*Cierba roxa y cierba de Bosques*) in Cayenne, being always met with in woods. **1756** P. Browne *Jamaica* 433 The *Wood-Digger. This insect.. digs frequently into soft places of timber, where it keeps a throbbing noise, not unlike our death-watches in Europe. **1801** Shaw *Gen. Zool.* II. 166 *Wood Dormouse. *Myoxus Dryas*... It is said to be a native of Russia, Georgia, &c. inhabiting woods, &c. **1777** *Wood duck [see NARRAGANSETT 2]. **1814** A. Wilson *Amer. Ornith.* VIII. 97 Summer Duck, or Wood Duck. *Anas sponsa.* **1847** Leichhardt *Jrnl.* v. 147 The wood-duck (Bernicla jubata) abounded on the larger water-holes. **1911** C. E. W. Bean *'Dreadnought' of Darling* vi. 57 Wood duck.. are really not duck at all, but Queensland goose. **1980** *Outdoor Life* (U.S.) (Northeast ed.) Oct. 80/1 Grain-fed mallards or pintails are superb table fare, as are wood ducks fattened on acorns. **1827** Clare *Sheph. Cal.* 54 Green *wood-fly, and blossom-haunting bee. **1854** A. Adams, etc. *Man. Nat. Hist.* 258 Wood-Flies (Platypezidæ). **1698** M. Lister *Journ. Paris* 73 Very large *Wood-Frog, with the extremity of the Toes webbed. **1895** Swettenham *Malay Sketches* 288 The fitful and plaintive croak of a wood-frog. **1882** *Cassell's Nat. Hist.* VI. 77 The *Wood Gnat (*Culex nemorosus*) frequents woods and does not come into houses. **1785** G. Forster tr. *Sparrman's Voy. Cape Gd. Hope* vii. I. 276 This *wood-goat, or, as it is called, *bosch-bok*. **1776** Pennant *Brit. Zool.* (ed. 4) I. 223 *Wood Grous... It inhabits wooded and mountanous countries. **1838** T. Need *Six Years in Bush* iv. 30 And the woods with partridges, wood-grouse, black squirrels and occasionally a turkey. *a* **1861** T. Winthrop *John Brent* (1862) xxii. 245 The brace of wood grouse he had shot that morning. **1917** T. G. Pearson *Birds Amer.* II. 14 Hudsonian Spruce Partridge. *Canachites canadensis canadensis*... Wood Grouse; Wood Partridge. **1956** *Numbers* (Wellington, N.Z.) May 8 The rotten wood.. split lengthwise and fell apart, baring the wet sawdust tunnels of *woodgrubs. **1964** R. Braddon *Year Angry Rabbit* (1967) xx. 158 Her husband fed their child with a wriggling wood grub. **1805** R. Parkinson *Tour in Amer.* 290 The real American hog is what is termed a *wood-hog: they are long in the leg, narrow on the back, [etc.]. **1840** *Cultivator* VII. 81 The next fall, *mast* was plenty, and 'wood hogs' were fat. **1908** Haagner & Ivy *Sk. S. Afr. Bird-Life* 26 The *Wood Hoopoes.. are represented in South Africa by two well-marked species. **1953** R. Campbell *Mamba's Precipice* xi. 115 A whole flock of wood-hoopoes with scarlet beaks and silk-shot, glossy, green and purple feathers were raising the most amazing din in the tree. **1964** A. L. Thomson *New Dict. Birds* 894/2 The wood-hoopoes.. are very unlike the true hoopoes in general appearance. **1658** Rowland tr. *Moufet's Theat. Ins.* 928 The *wood or wilde Hornet (saith Pliny) live in hollow trees all the winter. **1785** Latham *Gen. Syn. Birds* V. 104 *Wood Ibis... found in Carolina, and in various parts of South America. **1875–84** *Layard's Birds S. Afr.* 735 *Pseudo-tantalus ibis.* African Wood-Ibis. **1819** *Wood leopard-moth [see LEOPARD 6 b]. **1856** *Knight's Eng. Cycl., Nat. Hist.* IV. 1276 *Zeuzera Æsculi*, the Wood-Leopard, is a rare species, of a white colour, with numerous steel-blue spots. **1854** A. Adams, etc. *Man. Nat. Hist.* 277 *Wood-Mites (Orbitidæ). *a* **1678** Marvell *Appleton Ho.* 542 The hewel.. Doth from the bark the *wood-moths glean. **1916** A. Huxley *Burning Wheel* 24 Mottled and grey and brown they pass, The wood-moths, wheeling, fluttering. **1601** Holland *Pliny* xxx. viii. II. 384 If the seat be galled, it is thought that the ashes of the *wood-Mouse tempered with honey, cureth the same. **1834** Mary Howitt in *Tait's Mag.* I. 445/2, I saw a little Wood-mouse.. Sit under a mushroom tall. **1809** Shaw *Gen. Zool.* VII. 253 *Wood Owl... As the bird seems to be the only British species.. more particularly found in woody than in other situations, the title of Wood Owl seems best adapted to its nature. **1772** *Phil. Trans.* LXII. 389 *Woodpartridge. **1830** Galt *Lawrie T.* VIII. v. (1849) 370, I heard the wood-partridge drumming on a neighbouring tree. **1754** Catesby *Carolina* I. pl. 81 *Pelicanus Sylvaticus.* The *Wood Pelican. **1810** A. Wilson *Amer. Ornith.* II. 81 *Wood Pewee Fly-catcher. *Muscicapa rapax.* **1705** tr. *Sir J. Ware's Antiq. Irel.* vii. 20 The Cock of the Wood, which Giraldus Cambrensis calls the *Wood Pheasant. **1892** *Pall Mall Gaz.* 12 Nov. 3/1 What is called the 'wood-pheasant' is a big long-tailed bush cuckoo. **1899** F. D. Bergen *Anim & Plant Lore* 61 *Wood pussy, skunk. **1950** *Chicago Daily News* 16 Feb. 5/1 Miss Bennett paid $35 for the deodorized house-broken wood pussy. **1972** *Islander* (Victoria, B.C.) 18 June 9/2 You would never have known that said woods pussy had met its doom and left so many 'scents' behind in its will. **1891** *Cent. Dict.* s.v. *Rollulus*, The red-crested *wood-quail is *R. cristatus* or *roulroul*. *Ibid.*, *Wood-rabbit. **1902** Cornish *Naturalist Thames* 73 These wood-rabbits differ in their way of life from those in the open warren outside. **1766** J. Bartram *Jrnl.* 10 Jan. 30 We found a great nest of a *wood-rat, built of long pieces of dry sticks. **1879** W. L. Lindsay *Mind in Lower Animals* II. xi. 151 The Californian wood-rat. **1802** Shaw *Gen. Zool.* III. 335 *Wood Rattle-Snake. *Crotalus Dryinas.* **1805** Mitchell & Miller *Med. Repos.* 122 Fire-bird or *wood red-bird with blue wings. **1808** A. Wilson *Amer. Ornith.* I. 29 Wood Thrush. *Turdus melodus*... It is called by some the *Wood Robin. **1882** *Garden* 11 Nov. 425/1 The chief bird friend and companion of the wanderer in the New Zealand bush is the wood robin. **1784** Pennant *Arctic Zool.* II. 482 *Wood.. Sandpiper... *Tringa Glareola.* .. Inhabits the moist woods of Sweden. **1824** [see SANDPIPER 1]. **1875–84** *Layard's Birds S. Afr.* 401 *Bradyornis mariquensis.* Mariqua *Wood-Shrike. **1725** Sloane *Jamaica* II. 185, I saw one of these Spiders eat a small lizard call'd a *Wood-slave. **1864** *N. Brit. Rev.* Dec. 404 The baleful race of woodslave and slippery-back, those hideous brown and yellow lizards of the West Indies. **1831** Audubon *Ornith. Biog.* I. 19 They now and then descend.. to pick up a *wood-snail or a beetle. **1865** Gosse *Land & Sea* (1874) 118 The pretty banded wood-snail (*Helix nemoralis*). **1585** Higins *Junius' Nomencl.* 75/2 *Coluber*,.. a landsnake or *woodsnake. **1887** *St. James's Gaz.* 14 Mar. 6/1 It would seem that in times past the '*woodsnipe' was considered a stupid bird. *c* **1050** *Voc.* in Wr.-Wülcker 363/27 *Cardiolus*, *wudusnite. **1655** Moufet & Bennet *Health's Improv.* xi. 96 There is a kind of Wood-Snite in Devonshire, greater than the common Snite. **1859–62** Sir J. Richardson, etc. *Mus. Nat. Hist.* (1868) I. 311 The Short-tailed *Woodstar (*Calothorax macrurus*).. is one of the most diminutive even in the family of dwarfs, measuring rather less than two inches and a half in length. **1884** Coues *N. Amer. Birds* (ed. 2) 653 American *Wood Stork. **1854** A. Adams, etc. *Man. Nat. Hist.* 37 *Wood-Swallows (*Artamidæ*). **1869** E. Newman *Brit. Moths* 19 The *Wood Swift (*Hepialus sylvinus*). *c* **1480** Henryson *Trial of Fox* 894 The Uild *wod Swyne. **1785** G. Forster tr. *Sparrman's Voy. Cape Gd. Hope* x. II. 23, I saw.. a herd of *bosch-varkens*, or, as they are likewise called, *wilde-varkens*, (wood-swine, or wild-swine). **1834** [see *bosch-vark* s.v. BOSCH[1]]. **1824** Stephens in Shaw's *Gen. Zool.* XII. 3 *Wood Tantalus. (*Tantalus loculator.*) **1852** Macgillivray *Brit. Birds* IV. 346 *Totanus Glareola.* *Wood Tatler. **1791** W. Bartram *Trav. N. & S. Carolina* (1792) 179 The shrill tuneful songs of the *wood-thrush! **1817** Stephens in Shaw's *Gen. Zool.* X. 179 Wood Thrush. (*Turdus melodes.*) **1841** W. C. Bryant *Earth's Children* 11 Wks. 44 Dark maples where the wood-thrush sings. **1668** Charleton *Onomast.* 49 *Ricinus*.. the *Wood Teek, or, Dogs Teek. **1819** D. B. Warden *Acc. United States* II. 180 The wood tick.. resembles a bug, and lives upon trees and rushes. **1869** E. Newman *Brit. Moths* 32 The *Wood Tiger ..(*Chelonia Plantaginis*). **1868** J. Burroughs *Wake-robin* v. (1884) 207 The well-known golden-crowned thrush (*Sciurus aurocapillus*) or *wood-wagtail. *Ibid.* viii. 296 [see WAGTAIL 2 a]. **1817** Stephens in Shaw's *Gen. Zool.* X. 748 *Wood Warbler. (*Sylvia Sylvicola.*) **1868** *Rep. U.S. Comm. Agric.* (1869) 310 The *wood-wasps.. are often seen resting on leaves in the sunshine. **1871** Staveley *Brit. Insects* 203 The second division of the predaceous stinging Hymenoptera, known as *Fossores* or diggers, consists of the Sand-wasps and Wood-wasps. **1895** Rider Haggard *Heart of World* x. (1899) 135 Tiny grey flies, wood-wasps, and ants ..tormented us with their bites and stings. **1540** *Septem Ling. Dict.* D vj, Teredo.. a *woodworme. **1607** B. Barnes *Divils Charter* (ed. McKerrow) 1376 Now skelder yee scounderels,.. you wood-wormes. **1725** Swift *Wood an Insect* 17 An Insect we call a Wood-Worm, That lies in old Wood like a Hare in her Form. **1855** Browning *Mesmerism* 7 At night, when.. the wood-worm picks, And the death-watch ticks. **1792** T. Lamb in *Trans. Linnean Soc.* (1794) II. 245 A New Species of Warbler, called the *Wood Wren... It.. comes with the rest of the summer warblers. **1839** Macgillivray *Brit. Birds* II. 371 *Phyllopneuste Trochilus.* The Willow Woodwren.

c. In names of plants or their products (usually designating particular species) growing in woods, as ***wood calamint***, ***fern***, ***germander***, ***horsetail***, ***hyacinth***, ***liverwort***, ***pea***, ***pimpernel***, ***rasp***, ***reed***, ***rose***, ***sedge***, ***violet***, etc. (see quots. and CALAMINT, etc.); **wood-almond**, a West Indian shrub, *Hippocratea comosa*, producing edible seeds like almonds; **wood-anemone**, the common wild anemone, *A. nemorosa*, abundant in woods, and blossoming in early spring; also applied to other species; **wood-apple**, (*a*) a wild apple, crab-apple; (*b*) the fruit of *Feronia elephantum*, an East Indian gum-yielding tree allied to the orange, or the tree itself; also called *elephant-apple*; **wood betony**, (*a*) the common betony, *Stachys Betonica*; (*b*) *N. Amer.*, a kind of lousewort, *Pedicularis canadensis*; **wood crab** = *wood-apple* (a); **wood cranesbill**, *Geranium sylvaticum*, a wild species with light purple flowers; **wood-grass**, any species of grass growing in woods; **wood-lily**, †(*a*) ? the meadow-saffron, *Colchicum autumnale*; (*b*) the lily-of-the-valley, *Convallaria majalis*; (*c*) the common winter-green, *Pyrola minor*; (*d*) any plant of the N. American genus *Trillium*, grown in the U.K. as a spring-flowering perennial; †**wood-march** [OE. *wudumerce*: see MARCH *sb.*[1]], the common or wood sanicle, *Sanicula europæa*; †**wood-mint**, pennyroyal, *Mentha Pulegium*; †**wood-nep** [NEP *sb.*[1] or [2]], see quots.; **wood nut (tree)**, the hazel, *Corylus avellana*; **wood sanicle**: see SANICLE 1; **wood-spurge**, a species of spurge, *Euphorbia amygdaloides*, with greenish-yellow flowers; **wood strawberry**, the common wild strawberry, *Fragaria vesca*; **wood-vetch**, any species of vetch growing in woods, esp. *Vicia sylvatica*, with pink or white flowers streaked with purple; **wood-vine**, (*a*) the bryony, *Bryonia dioica*; (*b*) *yellow wood-vine*, a species of mulberry, *Morus Calcar-galli*. See also main words.

1657 W. Coles *Adam in Eden* ccxci, The *Wood Anemone or Wind-flower. **1816–20** T. Green *Univ. Herbal* I. 100 *Anemone Ranunculoides*; Yellow Wood Anemone. *c* **1000** *Sax. Leechd.* II. 190 Ȝesodene *wudu æpla. **1430** in *Engl. Hist. Rev.* (1899) July 514 Ooke, esshe, holyn, wodapiltre and crabtre. **1858** Simmonds *Dict. Trade*, *Vellanga, Yelanga*, vernacular Indian names for the wood-apple, *Feronia Elephantum*. **1859** Miss Pratt *Brit. Grasses* 121 *Hordeum sylvaticum* (Lyme-grass, or *Wood Barley). **1657** S. Purchas *Pol. Flying-Ins.* I. xv. 92 Bees gather not of flowers which have deep sockets, as.. *Wood-bettony. **1747** Wesley *Prim. Physick* (1762) 117 Apply Wood Betony bruised. **1886** *Harper's Mag.* Dec. 99/1 The wood-betony, it is called—to select its worthier title—a common early flower of our woods. **1976** *Hortus Third* (L. H. Bailey Hortorium) 832/1 Wood betony. Pubescent per., to 1½ ft... Spring. Que. to Fla., W. To Tex. and n. Mex. **1712** J. James tr. *Le Blond's Gardening* 152 The Box proper for planting Palisades, is the *Wood-Box. **14..** *Nom.* in Wr.-Wülcker 715/38 *Hec arbitus*, *wodcrabtre. **1483** *Cath. Angl.* 423/1 A Wodde crab, *acroma*. **1525** *Grete Herbal* cclxxxiii. (1529) Q ij, Wood crabbes, or wyldynges. **1796** Withering *Brit. Plants* (ed. 3) III. 602 *Geranium batrachoides alterum*... *Wood Cranesbill. **1863** Baring-Gould *Iceland* 214 A hill purpled with wood cranesbill. **1884** Miller *Plant-n.*, *Aspidium nevadense*, Nevada *Wood-fern. *Ibid.*, *Polypodium vulgare*, Adder's Fern, Common Polypody,.. Wood Fern. **1844** Whittier *Pumpkin* 26 When *wood-grapes were purpling. **1597** Gerarde *Herbal* I. vi. 7 *Wood grasse hath many thicke and threadie rootes. *Ibid.* 8 *Gramen sylvaticum* ..is called in our toong Wood grasse or Shadow grasse. **1882** *Proc. Berw. Nat. Club* IX. No. iii. 475 *Listera ovata* was plentiful, as well as *Calamintha Clinopodium*, and several wood-grasses. **1597** Gerarde *Herbal* II. ccccxlii. 957 *Wood Horse taile. **1871** Ruskin *Fors Clav.* vi. 7 The *wood-hyacinth is the best English representative of the tribe of flowers which the Greeks called 'Asphodel'. *a* **1400** *Stockholm Med. MS.* ii. 517 in *Anglia* XVIII. 320 *Wode-lilie with.. Blo purpre flowres, no lefe on stele. **1579** Langham *Gard. Health* 679 Wood-lillie, or Lillie conuaile. **1882** *Garden* 20 May 352/1 The Virginian Cowslip.. attains true development in semi-shady spots.. and so does the large white Wood Lily. **1884** Miller *Plant-n.*, *Pyrola minor*, Common Winter-green, Wood Lily. *Ibid.*, *Trillium*, American Wood-lily. *c* **1000** *Sax. Leechd.* II. 22 Ȝenim ..*wudumerce. *c* **1265** *Voc. Plants* in Wr.-Wülcker 554/8 *Saniculum, i. sanicle, i.* wudemerch. *a* **1387** *Sinon. Barthol.* (Anecd. Oxon.) 38 *Sanicula*, i. wode-merche. **1597** Gerarde *Herbal* Suppl., Wood March is Sanickle. *c* **1265** *Voc. Plants* in Wr.-Wülcker 557/20 *Origanum, i. puliol real, i.* *wde-minte. **1525** *Grete Herbal* xlviii. (1529) C v b, Ameos, *woodnep, or penywort. **1599** Gerarde *Catal. in horto* 19 *Sison.* Wood Nep. **1597** —— *Herbal* II. lviii. 279 The later Herbarists haue named this plant *Dulcamara*, *Amarodulcis*, and *Amaradulcis*.. we call it Bitter sweete, and *Woodnightshade. **1578** *Wood Nut tree [see HAZEL[1] 1]. **1634** T. Johnson *Merc. Bot.* 24 *Astragalus sylvaticus.* *Wood-pease, or Heath-pease. **1820** Hogg *Tales, Bridal of Polmood* (1836) II. 82 Gathering *wood-rasps for a delicate preserve. **1816–20** T. Green *Univ. Herbal* I. 129 *Arundo Calamagrostis.* *Wood Reed-grass. *c* **1000** *Sax. Leechd.* II. 90 Ȝenim *wudu rosan. **1614** Markham *Cheap Husb.* Table Hard Words, Woodrose or wilde-Eglantine. **1705** tr. *Cowley's Plants* Wks. 1711 III. 363 Nought by Experience than the Wood-Rose found, Better to cure a mad Dog's poisonous Wound. **1597** Gerarde *Herbal* I. xvi. 20 *Wood Rushie grasse. **1793** J. Sowerby *Eng. Bot.* II. 98 (*table*) Sanicula europæa **Wood Sanicle*... Common enough in woods, growing among dead leaves of trees. **1857** A. Pratt *Flowering Plants & Ferns* III. 12 *S[anicula] Europæa* (Wood Sanicle). **1961** R. W. Butcher *New Illustr. Brit. Flora* I. 816 The Wood Sanicle is a perennial plant with erect, ribbed stems. **1816–20** T. Green *Univ. Herbal* I. 256 *Carex Sylvatica*; *Wood Sedge. **1597** Gerarde *Herbal* II. cxxxii. 403 Sweete *wood Spurge... Vnsauorie wood Spurge. **1707** *Curios. Husb. & Gard.* 154 Spurges of Different Kinds.. the Wood-Spurge, the Cipress-Spurge, and the Mirtle-Spurge. *a* **1869** Rossetti *Songs, Woodspurge* 12 Among those few.. The woodspurge flowered, three cups in one. **1731** Miller *Gard. Dict.*, *Fragaria vulgaris.* Common or *Wood-Strawberry. **1766** *Complete Farmer* s.v. *Pulse* 6 G 1/2 Dr. Lister.. recommends for the improvement of sandy, light ground,.. all plants of the.. pea kind, and particularly.. the *wood vetch. **1813** Scott *Rokeby* IV. ii, Where profuse the wood-vetch clings Round ash and elm,.. Its pale and azure-pencill'd flower Should canopy Titania's bower. **1861** Miss Pratt *Flower. Pl.* II. 312 This Bryony is commonly called also Wild Vine, or *Wood-vine. **1866** *Treas. Bot.* s.v., Woodvine, Yellow, *Morus calcar galli*.

d. *pl.* used *attrib.* in senses 2 or 3, as **woods boss** *N. Amer. Lumbering*, a foreman in charge of lumberjacks; **woods colt** *U.S. colloq.*, a horse of unknown paternity; also, a foundling; an illegitimate child.

1928 C. Perry *Two Reds of Travoy* 44 'He's a scrapper from way back. Sort of a bully in the village, I guess.' 'Derosier's woods boss,' breathed Gwen. **1946** K. Tennant *Lost Haven* (1947) xiv. 231 Alec strolled ashore to talk with the 'woods boss'. **1970** *Islander* (Victoria B.C.) 17 May 6/3 Pete Haramboure became manager and his son, John, woods boss. **1895** *Dial. Notes* I. 395 *Woods colt*, foundling, Winchester, Ky. **1903** *Ibid.* II. 337 *Woods colt*, a horse of unknown paternity. Also applied to a person of illegitimate birth. **1913** [see OUTSIDER 1 c]. **1959** W. Faulkner *Mansion* i. 4 Will Varner was going to have to marry her off.. quick, if he didn't want a woods colt in his back yard next grass.

wood, *a.* (*sb.*², *adv.*) *Obs.* exc. *dial.* or *rare arch.* Forms: 1–6 (9 *Sc.*) wod, 3–7 (9 *arch.*) wode, (4 *Sc.* vode), 4–5 woed, 4–6 woode, woud(e, wodde, (5 ode, oothe, *Sc.* woide, void, 5–7 *Sc.* woid), 6 wodd, (oode, wyd, *Sc.* vod, wuid), 6–7 woodde, (6, 9 *Sc.* wid, 7 would, 8– *Sc.* and *dial.* wud), 4– wood. [OE. *wód* = OHG. *wuot* (in *ferwuot* raging, frantic), ON. *óðr*, Goth. *wôd-*, **wōþs* possessed (cf. OHG., MHG. *wuot*, G. *wut* rage); f. Teut. *wōð-* (to which belong also OE. *wóþ* song, sound, ON. *óðr* poetry, and WODEN) :—Indo-Eur. *wāt-*, represented by L. *vātēs* seer, poet, OIr. *fáith* poet, W. *gwawd* song of praise, the fundamental meaning being 'to be excited or inspired'. From the mutated stem are OE. *wéde* mad, *wédan* WEDE *v.*, *wéden* in WEDENONFA', WIDDENDREAM. The form *oothe* is from Scand. Compounds are BRAIN-WOOD, RED-WOOD *a.*]

1. Out of one's mind, insane, lunatic: = MAD *a.* 1.

c **725** *Corpus Gloss.* (Hessels) E 249 *Epilenticus*, woda. *c* **1000** *Ags. Gosp.* John x. 21 Ne synt na þis wodes mannes word. *c* **1200** ORMIN 15506 He draf ut off wode menn Defless. **1303** R. BRUNNE *Handl. Synne* 11026 A wode man touched on hys bere,..And a-none he hadde botenyng. *c* **1350** *Will. Palerne* 554 ȝif i told him treuli my tene..He wold wene i were wod. *c* **1430** *Hymns Virgin* (1867) 46 Woode men, he ȝeueþ hem þer mynde, And makiþ mesels hool. *c* **1440** *York Myst.* xi. 334 His folke sall no ferre Yf he go welland woode. *c* **1440** *Promp. Parv.* 372/2 Oothe, or woode, *amens.* **1540** HYRDE tr. *Vives' Instr. Chr. Wom.* (1592) G, They bee bitten of the wood dog the devil, & be fallen wood themselves. **1572** *Satir. Poems Reform.* xxxviii. 101 Anis wod and ay the war. **1590** SPENSER *F.Q.* I. iv. 34 Through vnaduized rashnesse woxen wood. **1609** SKENE *Reg. Maj.* 82 b, Gif any man is Lunatick, wodde, or furious, with space of manifest wit and judgement betwix ilk time. **1627** J. TAYLOR (Water P.) *Armado* D 1 b, In the North parts of England,..when they thinke that a man is distracted or frenzy, they will say the man is Wood. **1724** RAMSAY *Tea-t. Misc.* (1733) I. 86 The wife was wood, and out o' her wit. *c* **1730** —— *Betty & Kate* iv, That's like to put us wood. **1816** SCOTT *Old Mort.* xxxvii, Some folk say, that pride and anger hae driven him clean wud. **1828** *Craven Gloss.*, *Wood*, mad, rhyming with *food*. This word is rarely used. **1843** LYTTON *Last Bar.* I. ix, Am I dement? Stark wode?

b. Of a dog or other beast: Rabid: = MAD *a.* 6.

c **1000** *Sax. Leechd.* I. 4 Wið woden hundes slite. **1398** TREVISA *Barth. De P.R.* XII. iv. (Tollem. MS.), [Honey] heleþ þe bitynge of a wood hounde. **1481** CAXTON *Reynard* xviii. (Arb.) 44 Ye sawe neuer wood dogges do more harme. **1549** *Compl. Scot.* vi. 57 Quhen it [*sc.* the dog-star] ringis in our hemispere, than dogis ar in dangeir to ryn vod. **1551** TURNER *Herbal* I. B v, Garlyke..is good agaynst the bitinges of madd or weod beastes. **1608** *Melrose Regality Rec.* (S.H.S. 1914) 60 Scho [*sc.* a mare] ran woid and drouneit hirself in Tueid. **1610** FLETCHER *Faithf. Sheph.* II, Bitten by a wood-Dogs venom'd tooth. **1733** *Culross Town Rec.* (MS.), There has been some wood dogs going through the town. **1856** G. HENDERSON *Pop. Rhymes* 58 The bull ran wud. *a* **1869** SPENCE *Braes of Carse* (1898) 181 The dog ran wud that barkit at her.

c. In phr. of comparison, often expressing fury or violence (cf. 3): e.g. *as* (*if*) *he* (etc.) *were wood*; *as* or *like wood* (cf. MAD *a.* 1 c).

c **1220** *Bestiary* 338 We brennen in mod, And wurðen so we weren wod. *c* **1300** *Havelok* 508 Starinde als he were wod. **1340** *Ayenb.* 140 Hi yerneþ hi lheapeþ ase wode. *c* **1420** *Chron. Vilod.* 3859 He cryedde & rorede as þaw he were wode. *a* **1450** *Knt. de la Tour* xxviii, They..beganne to crye lyke wode folke. *c* **1460** *Play Sacram.* 403 in *Non-Cycle Myst. Plays* (1909) 70 Yt bledyth as yt were woode, I wys. *a* **1510** DOUGLAS *K. Hart* I. 224 Thai preik, thai prance, as princis that war woude. **1568** T. HOWELL *Newe Sonets* (1879) 121 From me he fled as woode. **1591** SHAKS. *Two Gent.* II. iii. 30 Like a would-woman. **1647** H. MORE *Song of Soul* I. II. xciii, Thou..rav'st as thou wert wood. **1721** RAMSAY *To Earl Dalhousie* 13 Some like to..gar the Courser rin like wood.

d. With qualification, as *half*, *near* (*nigh*), *worse than*, etc., the combined phrase becoming virtually equivalent to one of the derived senses below.

1297 R. GLOUC. (Rolls) 3840 He was ney uor wraþþe wod. *c* **1350** *Will. Palerne* 36 He gan to berke on þat barn..þat it wax neiȝ of his witt wod for fere. **14..** *Childh. Jesus* 133 in Horstm. *Altengl. Leg.* (1878) 113 Frawdys was wroþ & nydel ode [*v.r.* nerehande wode]. *c* **1440** *Gesta Rom.* xxvi. 99 þe knight was halfe woode for wo. *c* **1470** HENRY *Wallace* VI. 418 In propyr ire he wox ner wode for teyne.

2. Going beyond all reasonable bounds; utterly senseless; extremely rash or reckless, wild; vehemently excited: = MAD *a.* 2, 4, 7.

c **900** ÆLFRED *Solil. August.* (1922) 25 Hwa is swa wod þæt he dyrre cweðan þæt God ne sy æce? *c* **1205** LAY. 1714 Swa wod he was to fehte. *a* **1225** *Ancr. R.* 120 þet tu schalt demen þi suluen wod, þo þu þer touward þouhtest. **1340** HAMPOLE *Pr. Consc.* 99 þat man may be halden wode, þat cheses þe ille and leves þe gude. ?*a* **1366** CHAUCER *Rom. Rose* 203 Coueitise is euere wode, To gripen other folkis gode. **1390** GOWER *Conf.* I. 164 Aweie he fledde..As he that was for love wod. *c* **1400** *Pride of Life* 499 in *Non-Cycle Myst. Plays* 104 Be he so hardy or so wode In his londe to aryue, He wol se his herte blode. *c* **1430** LYDG. *Min. Poems* (Percy Soc.) 76 A woode wisdom, and a wise woodenesse. **1435** MISYN *Fire of Love* II. viii. 89 Wode luste, made lufe. **1509** BARCLAY *Shyp of Folys* (1874) I. 116 Whiche of theyr myndes ar so blynde and wode And so reted in theyr errour and foly. **1579** SPENSER *Sheph. Cal.* Mar. 55 Thelf was so wanton and so wood. **1584** *Mirr. Mag.* 26 b, Incontinent desire maketh him wood of their societie. **1617** COLLINS *Def. Bp. Ely* II. x. 413 Vnles you wil be so wood now, as to adde brutish Ubiquitisme, to your barbarous Cyclopisme. *a* **1708** T. WARD *Eng. Ref.* 14 What sees he in her, he's so wood for? **1818** SCOTT *Rob Roy* xiv, The folk in Lunnun are a' clean wud about this bit job. **1895** CROCKETT *Men of Moss-Hags* liv. 382 The lassie's gane wud! There's nae reason in her.

¶ **b.** Used inaccurately to render L. *furialis.*

1387 TREVISA *Higden* (Rolls) I. 197 In þat lond is a lake wonderful and wood [L. *furialis*], for who þat drynkeþ þerof he schal brenne in woodnesse of leccherie.

3. a. Extremely fierce or violent, ferocious; irascible, passionate.

a **1225** *Ancr. R.* 66 Monie cumeð..ischrud mid lombes fleose, & beoð wode wulues. **1340** HAMPOLE *Pr. Consc.* 2224 Als wode lyons þai sal þan fare. **1435** MISYN *Fire of Love* II. viii. 89 A scheep cled in foxis skyn, & a dowe wodar þen any wode best. *c* **1480** HENRYSON *Cock & Fox* 195 A nyce proud man, void and vaneglorious. **1538** STARKEY *England* (1878) 12 Ther ys no best..so wyld, oode, or cruel, but to man by wysdom he ys subduyd. **1556** LAUDER *Tractate of Kyngis* 286 ȝe sulde nocht chuse vnto that cure Ane Vinolent nor wod Pasture. **1590** BARROUGH *Meth. Phisick* I. xxvii. (1596) 44 They that haue this disease [*sc.* mania] be wood & vnruly like wilde beasts. **1747** UPTON *New Canto Spenser's F.Q.* xxvi, Guileful Dissimulation, and pale Fear, And Discord wood.

b. Violently angry or irritated; enraged, furious.

c **1205** LAY. 2189 Humber wes swa swiðe wod for al þat lond on him stod. **1297** R. GLOUC. (Rolls) 5979 Suan..þo he hurde of þis cas Made him wroþ & wod ynou. *c* **1380** WYCLIF *Wks.* (1880) 25 þei..ben wode ȝif men speken treuly aȝenst here cursed synnes. **1422** YONGE tr. *Secr. Secr.* 229 Tho that haue a brandynge colure like the lye of fyre, lightly wexen woode. **1481** CAXTON *Godfrey* lxvii. 112 The grete stedes.. becam alle araged and wood for thurst. *a* **1540** BARNES *Wks.* (1573) 282 Yᵉ more it is preached the more they grudge, and the woodder bee they. *a* **1578** LINDESAY (Pitscottie) *Chron. Scot.* (S.T.S.) I. 146 To quhome scho turnit about witht ane wode and furieous contienance. **1590** SHAKS. *Mids. N.* II. i. 192 Heere am I, and wood within this wood, Because I cannot meet my Hermia. **1654** GAYTON *Pleas. Notes* IV. xix. 267 Be not thou wood too, nor a jot inraged. **1682** SHADWELL *Lanc. Witches* I, Pray now do not say ought to my Lady, by th' Mass who'l be e'en stark wood an who hears on't. **1786** BURNS *Sc. Drink* xiii, When neebors anger at a plea, An' just as wud as wud can be. **1816** SCOTT *Old Mort.* xlii, Now he's anes wud and aye waur, and roars for revenge. **1858** KINGSLEY *Red King* 23 King William sterte up wroth and wood.

c. *transf.* of rage, pain, etc. (Cf. MAD *a.* 5.)

1297 R. GLOUC. (Rolls) 4415 In is wod rage he wende Vor to awreke is vncle deþ. *c* **1374** CHAUCER *Boeth.* III. met. ii. (1868) 68 þe woode wraþþes of hem. **1390** GOWER *Conf.* I. 287 In this wilde wode peine. *a* **1400–50** *Wars Alex.* 1168 þar is na wa in þe werd to þe wode hunger. *c* **1500** *Lancelot* 2695 Thar was the batell furyous and woud. **1607** J. CARPENTER *Plaine Mans Plough* 193 To execute..against them (in his wood furie) whatsoever he listeth.

d. *fig.* of inanimate things, as the sea, wind, fire: Violently agitated; 'furious', 'raging'. (Cf. MAD *a.* 7 b.)

c **1100** *O.E. Chron.* an. 1075 (MS. D) Seo wode sæ & se stranga wind hi on þæt land awearp. *c* **1320** *Sir Tristr.* 371 þe wawes were so wode Wiþ winde. *c* **1386** CHAUCER *Miller's T.* 331 A reyn..so wilde and wood That half so greet was neuere Noees flood. *c* **1400** *St. Alexius* (Laud 622) 593 Wynde aroos wiþ wood rage. **1477** NORTON *Ord. Alch.* vi. in Ashm. (1652) 98 Flames brenning fierce and woode. **1490** CAXTON *Eneydos* x. 39 Temppestes horrible of the woode see. *a* **1510** DOUGLAS *K. Hart* I. 75 About the wall thair ran ane water void, Blak, stinkand, sowr, and salt as is the sey. **1593** Q. ELIZ. *Boeth.* I. met. iv. 7 Wood Vesevus..that burstz out his smoky fires.

† **B.** quasi-*sb.* (*a*) madness; (*b*) in phr. *for wood* (see FOR- *pref.*¹ 10), 'like mad', madly, furiously.

c **1275** *xi Pains of Hell* 48 in *O.E. Misc.* 148 Snaken and neddren stingeþ for wod. **1297** R. GLOUC. (Rolls) 6201 þeruore hii flowe vor wod. ?*a* **1366** CHAUCER *Rom. Rose* 276 She..hath such wo, whan folk doth good, That nygh she meltith for pure wood. *c* **1384** —— *H. Fame* III. 657 Lat vs ..seme..That wommen louen vs for wode. **1390** GOWER *Conf.* I. 286 Betwen the wawe of wod and wroth Into his dowhtres chambre he goth. *c* **1430** *Syr Gener.* (Roxb.) 5777 Out of witt he was for wode.

† **C.** *adv.* Madly, frantically, furiously (chiefly in *wood wroth*). *Obs.*

1297 R. GLOUC. (Rolls) 6109 þe king knout wiþ hom was þo so wod wroþ. *c* **1380** WYCLIF *Wks.* (1880) 5 ȝif þei..haten and ben woode wroþ with men þat trewly dispisen synne. *c* **1425** *Engl. Conq. Irel.* xxxviii. 94 The knyght..bytwene twe perylle: on on halue, þe wode-yernynge watyr so grysly; on other halue, hys fomen. *c* **1430** *Syr Gener.* (Roxb.) 4913 The king of kinges quooke woode That any shuld be hold.. bettre than him self were. *a* **1513** FABYAN *Chron.* VII. (1811) 515 The more the Kynge spake for the Englysshe men, the more woder were they dysposyd agayne them. **1513** DOUGLAS *Æneis* XII. vii. 9 Wod wroth he worthis, for dysdene and dyspyte That he ne mycht his feris succur. **1535** COVERDALE *Hosea* vii. 5 They begynne to be woode droncken thorow wyne. **1569** BLAGUE *Sch. Conceytes* 94 The pacient hearing this..was wood angrie, and commaunded all yᵉ Phisitians to be put out of doores. **1601** DENT *Pathw. Heaven* (1831) 142 They are so extraordinarily enamoured ..and are so wood-mad of it, that they will have it.

D. *Comb.*: † **wood-like** *a.* = WOODLY *a.*; † **woodsek** [SICK *a.*], mad. See also WOODMAN².

1578 T. PROCTOR *Gorg. Gallery* O iv b, Wherwith distrest with *woodlike rage, the[se] words he out abrade. *c* **890** WÆRFERTH tr. *Gregory's Dial.* (1900) 135 þa wæs ȝelæded se *wodseoca [*v.r.* wedendseoca] man to..Benedicte. **14..** in Wr.-Wülcker 595/25 *Meger*, wode sek.

Wood (wʊd), *sb.*³ The name of B. *Wood* (see quot. 1860¹) used in the possessive to designate an easily melted alloy consisting of bismuth, lead, tin, and cadmium in decreasing proportions and used esp. for soldering.

Patented by Wood in *U.S. Patent 27,590* (1860).

1860 *Amer. Jrnl. Sci.* LXXX. 271 [New 'fusible metal'. —Dr. B. Wood of Nashville, Tenn., has secured a patent (Weekly Scientific Artizan, Cincinnati, May 5th, 1860,) for an alloy composed of cadmium, tin, lead and bismuth, which fuses at a temperature between 150° and 160° F.] *Ibid.* 272 We have had time only to repeat a few of Dr. Wood's interesting experiments... The alloy made by fusing together two parts of cadmium, two parts tin, four parts lead and eight parts bismuth melts at a temperature varying not far from 70° C. (158° F.) It may appropriately be called 'Wood's fusible metal'.—Eds. **1876** *Jrnl. Chem. Soc.* XXX. 592 The author then describes the method adopted by himself to measure the volumes of the four following fusible alloys at temperatures between 0° and 120°:——...III. Wood's alloy, the composition of which is represented by the formula $Bi_4Pb\,Cd_2\,Sn_2$. **1947** J. C. RICH *Materials & Methods of Sculpture* vi. 192 Wood's metal is rarely employed sculpturally although the material could be used as a casting medium because of its low melting point. **1974** *Nature* 11 Oct. 506/2 One eye was centred on a projection perimeter..and the visuotectal representation for that eye on the right tectum mapped with a Woodsmetal microelectrode.

Wood (wʊd), *sb.*⁴ *Med.* The name of Robert W. *Wood* (1868–1955), U.S. physicist, used in the possessive to designate (*a*) a special glass that is opaque to visible light but transmits ultraviolet, and (*b*) ultraviolet light obtained by using this glass as a filter to remove visible components.

1925 *Index Medicus* X. 988/1 Experimental tumours studied by Wood's light. **1927** *Brit. Jrnl. Actinotherapy* Jan. 24/2 The healthy scalp under Wood's light gives only a feeble fluorescence of a dark violet colour. **1927** *Brit. Jrnl. Dermatol. & Syphilis* XXXIX. 352 Wood's glass costs about 1*s.* 6*d.* per square inch, but only a small piece is required. **1951** WHITBY & HYNES *Med. Bacteriol.* (ed. 5) xiv. 261 The microscope is illuminated by a mercury-vapour lamp with a Wood's glass filter which transmits ultraviolet but not visible light. **1958** *New Biol.* XXVII. 56 In 1925 two French workers discovered that *Microsporum*-infected hairs showed a very characteristic greenish fluorescence in ultra-violet light which had been filtered through glass containing nickel oxide, the so-called Wood's Light. **1961** R. D. BAKER *Essent. Path.* ix. 223 (*caption*) A Negro child developed papular white scaly oval lesions... The involved regions fluoresced with Wood's light. **1983** *Oxf. Textbk. Med.* I. v. 371/1 When large numbers of children are involved, screening of scalp infections with a filtered ultra-violet (Wood's light) lamp is useful.

† **wood**, *v.*¹ *Obs.* Also 4–5 wode. [f. prec.] *intr.* To go mad; to rave, rage (also *fig.*).

c **1374** CHAUCER *Boeth.* IV. met. iii. (1868) 123 þouȝ þei ne anoye nat þe body, ȝitte vices wooden to distroien men by wounde of þouȝt. *c* **1386** —— *Sec. Nun's T.* 467 He stareth and he woodeth in his Aduertence. **1390** GOWER *Conf.* I. 282 Whan I ne may my ladi se, The more I am redy to wraththe, ..I wode as doth the wylde Se. *c* **1430** *Pilgr. Lyf Manhode* I. cxvi. (1869) 61 Deth is a beste so wylde that who so seeth it he woodeth. *c* **1440** *Ipomydon* 1144 The kynge..began to wode, That his knyghtes bore downe were.

wood (wʊd), *v.*² [f. WOOD *sb.*¹ (Cf. OE. *wudian* to fell wood.)]

I. † **1.** *trans.* To surround with or inclose in a wood or trees; *refl.* and *intr.* to hide or take refuge in a wood. *Obs.*

1538 in *Letters Suppr. Monast.* (Camden) 195 The howse.. ys metely wodeyd in hege rowys. *a* **1589** R. LANE in *Hakluyt's Voy.* 741 The Sauages..betooke themselues to flight: we..followed for a smal time after them, who had wooded themselues we know not where. **1645** *City Alarum* 13 We should not tread those Mazes of fortune, wherein we have often wooded.

2. *trans.* To cover (land) with wood, as trees; to plant with trees, convert into woodland.

In this sense a back-formation from WOODED *ppl. a.*, q.v. for earlier quots.; cf. also WOODING 2.

1807 SOUTHEY *Espriella's Lett.* xxxiv. (1808) II. 36, I was delighted with the fine pear-trees which wooded the country. **1828** STEUART *Planter's Guide* (ed. 2) 10 Transplanting could do this;..an entire Park could be thus wooded at once. **1896** HOWELLS *Impressions & Exp.* 6 The primeval forests densely wooding the vast levels.

II. 3. a. *trans.* To supply with wood for fuel; to load (a vessel) with wood.

1628 in Foster *Engl. Factories India* (1909) III. 260 Wee wooddied and ballasted our shipps. **1712** E. COOKE *Voy. S. Sea* 117 This Island where we careen'd, wooded, water'd, and fitted our Ships. **1748** *Anson's Voy.* I. v. 42 Our next employment was wooding and watering our squadron. **1804** NELSON 22 Mar. in Nicolas *Disp.* (1845) V. 471 Seahorse being in want of wood, to be ordered..to the Island of Asinara, to cut wood, for which purpose she may remain forty-eight hours. In much less time the Victory could be wooded. **1902** LENNOX *James Chalmers* x. 72 The people helped in wooding the vessel.

b. *intr.* To procure or take in a supply of wood for fuel. Also (in mod. use) with *up*.

1630 CAPT. J. SMITH *Trav. & Adv.* II. 57 In this little Ile of Mevis,..I have remained..to wod and water and refresh my men. **1726** SHELVOCKE *Voy. round World* 76 In this river I imagined we might wood and water. **1856** OLMSTED *Slave States* 369 Soon after leaving, we passed the Zephyr, wooding-up: an hour later, our own boat was run to the bank,..and we also commenced wooding. **1891** C. ROBERTS *Adrift Amer.* 220 We went on down the river,..stopping.. occasionally to 'wood up', as taking in fuel was termed. **1921** W. P. LIVINGSTONE *Laws of Livingstonia* 56 The vessel was wooding..with rosemary and ebony logs.

4. Bowls. *to be wooded*: see quot.

1897 *Encycl. Sport* I. 130/2 The jack is said to be 'wooded' when surrounded by bowls.

5. *trans.* To furnish with a wooden support; to prop with wood.

1918 *Glasgow Her.* 14 June 6 Simpson wooded the place [in a coal-mine] temporarily, in order.. to prevent a further fall.

wood, obs. form of WOAD.

†**woodage.** *Obs. rare.* [f. WOOD *sb.*[1] + -AGE.]

1611 COTGR., *Lignade*, wooddage; prouision of wood.

'wood-ash. *Pl.* **-ashes.** [WOOD *sb.*[1], ASH *sb.*[2]] The ash or ashes of burnt wood.

1748 *Anson's Voy.* II. ii. 135 This oil served.., when mixed with wood-ashes, to supply the use of tallow. **1836** C. WORDSWORTH *Athens* v. (1855) 26 Kneading some cakes to be placed among the wood-ashes of the fire, and baked. **1884** *Littell's Living Age* 659 Natives who had rubbed themselves with wood-ash until their complexions were 'the color of slate-pencil'.

¶ See WOAD-ASHES.

wood-bill ('wʊdbɪl). [OE. *wudubil(l*: see WOOD *sb.*[1] and BILL *sb.*[1]] An implement used for cutting wood, pruning, etc.: = BILL *sb.*[1] 4.

*c***725** *Corpus Gloss.* (Hessels) F 48 *Falcastrum*, wudubil. *c***890** WÆRFERTH tr. *Gregory's Dial.* (1900) 113 Sume dæȝe sealde he him irenȝeloman, þæt is haten wudubill. **1356** in Riley *Mem. Lond.* (1868) 284, 3 twybilles, 3 wodbilles. **1485** in *Ripon Ch. Acts* (Surtees) 373, j wodbill. **1660** BLOUNT *Boscobel* I. (1680) 44 His Name was agreed to be Wil-Jones, and His arms a wood-Bill. **1788** COWPER *Let.* 28 July, The axe and the woodbill.. have.. been constantly employed.

woodbine ('wʊdbaɪn), **woodbind** (-baɪnd). Forms: see WOOD *sb.*[1]: α. 1 **-bind, -bend,** 1–6 **-binde,** 4–7 **-bynde,** 5 **-bende,** 5–6 **-bynd,** 6– **woodbind;** β. 6 **-byne, -bin,** (9 *dial.* **wid(d)bin**), 6– **woodbine.** (Also with hyphen, formerly occas. as two words.) [OE. *wudubind, -binde*, also *-bend*, f. *wudu* WOOD *sb.*[1] + root of BIND *v.* (*bend-, band-*); cf. Da. *vedbende* ivy, and, for the second element, WITHBIND. For the loss of final *d* cf. *line* for *lind, rine* for *rind*.

Similar formations are OE. *widuwinde* 'volvola', 'edera', 'viburna', 'convolvulus', *widubindle* 'involuco', ON. *viðvindill* ivy, Norw. *vi(d)vendel, vivendel, vibendel* 'caprifolium'.]

1. A name for various plants of a climbing habit; in early use (later only dial.), convolvulus and ivy; now chiefly (*U.S.*) the Virginia Creeper *Ampelopsis quinquefolia*, and the West Indian *Ipomœa tuberosa* (Spanish Woodbine).

α. *c***875** *Erfurt Gloss.* 1059 *Volvola*, uuidubindae. *Ibid.* 1082 *Viburnum*, uuidubindae. *c***950** *Lindisf. Gosp.* Mark i. 6 Wudu huniȝ þæt wæxes on wudu binde [*Rushw.* wudebendum]. *c***1000** *Sax. Leechd.* I. 302 Ðenim þysse wyrte wyrttruman þe man capparis & oþrum naman wudubend hateð. *Ibid.* II. 34 Wyrc eaȝsealfe wudubindes leaf. *c***1050** *Voc.* in Wr.-Wülcker 418/25 *Hedera nigra*, wudubind, eorþifiȝ. *c***1425** tr. *Arderne's Treat. Fistula*, etc. 30 Recipe—þe Iuyse of smalache or merch, wormode,.. petite consoude, wodbynd. **1525** *Grete Herbal* ccccxvii. (1529) Aa iv b, *De Volubilis.* Woodbynde. **1562** PILKINGTON *Expos. Abdyas* Pref. A a iij, The woodbinde.. climbes vp & spreades it selfe ouer all the branches, vnto it haue ouergrowen and kylled the hole tree. **1562** BULLEIN *Bulwark, Bk. Simples* (1579) 21 b, This is called *Helxine, Smilax*, or *Campenella*, or the Bell Wodbinde. **1570** BUCHANAN *Chamæleon* Wks. (S.T.S.) 44 As ye wod bind clymeth on ye oik and syne with tyme distroyis ye tre. **1597** GERARDE *Herbal* Table Eng. Names, Blew Woodbind, or ladies bower. **1624** CAPT. J. SMITH *Virginia* v. 170 A kinde of Wood-bind.. which runnes vpon trees, twining it selfe like a Vine: the fruit.. eaten worketh.. in the nature of a purge. **1625** GORDON *Pharmaco-pinax* 11 *Baccæ Hederæ.* Berries of Wood-bind. **1760** J. LEE *Introd. Bot.* App. 332 Woodbind, Spanish, *Ipomoea.*

β. **1573** TUSSER *Husb.* (1878) 97 Necessarie herbes to growe in the garden for Physick... 23 Stitchwort. 24 Valerian. 25 Woodbine. **1846–50** A. WOOD *Class-bk. Bot.* 212 *Ampelopsis quinquefolia*.. has long been cultivated as a covering for walls, and is best known by the name of Woodbine.

2. *esp.* The common honeysuckle, *Lonicera Periclymenum*, a climbing shrub with pale yellow fragrant flowers; also extended to other species, as the N. American *L. grata.*

*a c***1265** *Voc. Plants* in Wr.-Wülcker 556/39 *Mater silua, i. cheuefoil, i.* wudebi[n]de. *c***1374** CHAUCER *Troylus* III. 1231 As abowte a tre.. wryþe the soote wode bynde. *a* **1387** *Sinon. Barth.* (Anecd. Oxon.) 14 *Caprifolium*, wodebinde. **1562** TURNER *Herbal* II. 82 Wodbynde or Honysuckle.. windeth it self about busshes. **1624–5** SHIRLEY *Sch. Complement* II. (1631) 18 The Honey Wood-bind, Circling a withered Bryer. **1776** R. GRAVES *Euphrosyne* I. 159 See! how that woodbind round the door And lattice blooms! **1785** MARTYN *Lett. Bot.* xvi. (1794) 204 The Woodbind has.. slender trailing branches, twining round the boughs of trees.

β. **1548** ELYOT, *Periclymenon*, an herbe called woodbyne, whiche beareth the honysuckle. **1590** SHAKS. *Mids. N.* II. i. 251, I know a banke where the wilde time blowes,.. Quite ouer-canoped with luscious woodbine. **1637** MILTON *Lycidas* 146 The Musk-rose, and the well attir'd Woodbine. **1718** LADY M. W. MONTAGU *Let. to Abbé Conti* 19 May, The walls are in the nature of lattices; and, on the outside of them, vines and woodbines planted. **1847–60** DARLINGTON *Amer. Weeds* 160 Agreeable Lonicera. Wild Honeysuckle. American Woodbine. **1856** MISS MULOCK *John Halifax* ix, There was a yellow jasmine over the porch at one front door, and a woodbine at the other.

3. a. (Normally **Woodbine.**) A proprietary name for a brand of cheap cigarettes; a cigarette of this brand.

[**1886** *Trade Marks Jrnl.* 6 Jan. 8 *Wild Woodbine Cigarettes.* W. D. & H. O. Wills, Bristol & London.] **1907** *Ibid.* 11 Sept. 1602 *Woodbine*... Tobacco whether manufactured or unmanufactured. The Imperial Tobacco Company.., Bedminster, Bristol. **1910** *Sessions Paper of Central Criminal Court* 16 Nov. 18 Prisoner asked for a packet of Woodbine cigarettes (1 d). **1914** *Autocar* 21 Nov. 736/1 'Woodbine! This is a bit of luck,' he exclaimed, taking a cigarette. **1924** H. DE SÉLINCOURT *Cricket Match* ii. 21 He picked a woodbine out of its paper on the mantelpiece. **1939** JOYCE *Finnegans Wake* 587 First a couple of Mountjoys and nutty woodbines.. in the snug at the Cambridge Arms. **1970** B. CARTLAND *We danced All Night* vii. 198 It was only during the war [of 1914–18] that Tommies had got used to the cheaper type, especially Woodbines. **1979** 'P. O'CONNOR' *Into Strong City* x. 29 A Woodbine cigarette found in my pocket. **1983** J. CROALL *Neill* viii. 148 As long as.. he had enough for a packet of Woodbines, he was fine.

b. An Englishman, esp. a soldier, considered as a habitual smoker of Woodbine cigarettes. *Austral. slang.*

1919 W. H. DOWNING *Digger Dial.* 54 *Woodbine*, an English soldier, so called from the name of a cheap brand of cigarette favored by Englishmen. **1937** E. HILL *Water into Gold* 192 Bagtown became 'Woodbine Ave'.. so-called for the number of English settlers in residence. [**1978** R. BEILBY *Gunner* 43 'Inglesi,' he grinned. 'Pommies. Chooms. 'Bines. That's what we call them.']

4. *attrib.* and *Comb.*

1588 SPENSER *Virgils Gnat* 82 Others.. brouze the woodbine twigges. **1599** SHAKS. *Much Ado* III. i. 30 Beatrice.. Is couched in the wood-bine couerture. **1599** CUTWODE *Caltha Poet.* lxxxiv. C 6 b, She commeth to the woodbind tree. *Ibid.* cxvi. E 8, She goes vnto the Woodbine Tree. **1704** POPE *Spring* 97 Haste to yonder woodbine bow'rs. **1713** *Guardian* No. 125 To taste the odours of the wood-bine grove. **1727–46** THOMSON *Summer* 461 In the gelid caverns, woodbine-wrought. **1845** J. E. CARPENTER *Poems & Lyrics* 93 The cottage.. With porch—all woodbine-clad. **1855** TENNYSON *Maud* I. XXII. i, The woodbine spices are wafted abroad. **1895** R. W. CHAMBERS *King in Yellow, Street of Our Lady of Fields* ii. (1909) 232 A white house and woodbine-covered piazza. **1908** [ELIZ. FOWLER] *Betw. Trent & Ancholme* 141 Across a woodbine hedge.

Hence **'woodbined** (-baɪnd) *a.*, overgrown or adorned with woodbine.

1795 SOUTHEY *Joan of Arc* v. 104 The woodbined wall. **1895** 'COTSWOLD ISYS' *Lyra Piscat.* 109 Those woodbined oriels.

'wood-brown. Also 3 **wudebrune,** 4 **wodebron,** 4–5 **-broun,** 6 (? *erron.*) **woodbroney.** [f. WOOD *sb.*[1] 6 + BROWN.]

†**1.** The herb bugle, *Ajuga reptans*, in reference to the brownish tint of the leaves. *Obs.*

*c***1265** *Voc. Plants* in Wr.-Wülcker 554/7 *Buglosa, i. bugle, i.* wudebrune. *a* **1387** *Sinon. Barthol.* (Anecd. Oxon.) 13 *Bugla*, bugle, i. uodebroun.

¶ Glossing L. *fraxinus* ash-tree.

a **1400** *Stockh. Med. MS.* 188 Hertwourt or wodebroun, *f[r]axinus.* **1597** GERARDE *Herbal* Suppl., Woodbroney is *Fraxinus.*

2. [partly after G. *holzbraun.*] The brown colour characteristic of wood (see quot. 1805). Also as *adj.*

1805 T. WEAVER *Werner's Ext. Charact. Fossils* 63 Wood-brown is a very pale colour, being a mixture of yellowish-brown and much ashes-grey. **1839** MACGILLIVRAY *Brit. Birds* II. 367 The wings and tail wood-brown. **1866** MRS. WHITNEY *Leslie Goldthwaite* ii, The loveliest balmoral I ever saw in my life!.. Why, you'll look like a hamadryad, all in these wood-browns!

Woodbury ('wʊdbərɪ). The name of Walter Bentley *Woodbury* (1834–1885), inventor of many contrivances connected with photography, used attrib. in designations of processes invented by him, as ***Woodbury-gravure, -process***; esp. **Woodburytype** ('wʊdbərɪ,taɪp) [see -TYPE], a process in which a design on a film of gelatine, obtained from a photographic negative, is transferred by heavy pressure to a metal plate from which it may be printed; a print thus produced; also *attrib.*

1869 *Photogr. Jrnl.* 16 Jan. 218/2 The Woodbury Type Company. **1872** WOODBURY *Patent Specif.* 4 Dec., in *Ure's Dict. Arts* (ed. 7) III. 565 The ordinary Woodbury printing-press. **1875** tr. *Vogel's Chem. Light* xv. 245 Woodbury printing. **1878** ABNEY *Treat. Photogr.* 174 The Woodbury-type process. **1881** *Athenæum* 22 Jan. 134/1 This book.. is illustrated by Woodburytype reproductions of contemporary views of the Tower of London. **1881** *Nation* (N.Y.) XXXII. 219 A two-page Woodburytype of a Caxton eaten.. by book-worms. **1892** *Hazell's Annual* 559 It is an improvement upon the well known Woodbury process, and has been given the name of Woodbury-gravure.

wood-carne, -cerne, obs. ff. WOOD-KERN.

woodchat ('wʊdtʃæt). [First found in a posthumous work of Ray's (see first quot.), where it appears to be for **wood-cat*, a literal rendering of G. *waldkatze* (Naumann) or *waldkater* (Brehm): thus not connected with CHAT *sb.*[2]] A species of shrike, *Lanius rutilus* (*rufus*, or *auriculatus*), a rare summer visitor to England; also called **woodchat-shrike.**

a **1705** RAY *Synops. Meth. Av.* (1713) 19 The lesser Ash-coloured Butcher-bird with a white Spot on each Shoulder: The Wood-chat. **1774** GOLDSM. *Nat. Hist.* V. 136 The wood-chat resembles the [red backed butcher-bird] except in the colour of the back, which is brown and not red as in the other. **1781** LATHAM *Syn. Birds* I. I. 169 Wood chat shrike. *La Pie-griesche rousse.* **1862** WOOD *Illustr. Nat. Hist.* II. 376 The Woodchat Shrike has occasionally but very rarely been found in England. **1894** NEWTON *Dict. Birds* 845 The Woodchat,.. with a bright bay crown and nape, and the rest of its plumage black, grey and white.

woodchuck ('wʊdtʃʌk). [Alteration, by association with WOOD *sb.*[1], of American Indian name: cf. Cree *wuchak* (Watkins), *otchock* (J. Richardson), WEJACK.] **a.** A common N. American species of marmot, *Marmota monax*, of a large stout form, which burrows in the ground, and hibernates in winter.

1674 *Cal. State Papers, Amer. & W. Indies* (1889) VII. 581 The natural inhabitants of the woods, hills, and swamps, are.. rabbits, hares, and woodchucks. **1689** in *Hist. Coll. Essex Inst.* (Mass.) IV. 236/1 A parcell of meadow commonly called Woodchuck meadow. **1778** J. CARVER *Trav. N. Amer.* xviii. 454 The Woodchuck is a ground animal of the fur kind, about the size of a martin. **1819** WARDEN *Acc. U.S.* I. 225 Marmot of Maryland, *Arctomys monax*,.. known by the names of woodchuck and ground hog. **1855** LONGF. *Hiaw.* vi. 125 O'er these logs we cannot clamber; Not a woodchuck could get through them. *a* **1864** HAWTHORNE *Septimius* (1883) 230 Caverns which they had dug out for their shelter, like swallows and woodchucks.

b. ***woodchuck hole.***

1853 H. D. THOREAU *Jrnl.* 29 Mar. (1949) V. 62 Looking at the mouth of a woodchuck-hole.. [I see] that those places are sprinkled with.. salt-shaped masses of frost. **1974** P. GZOWSKI *Bk. about this Country* 43/2 The hay wagon had dropped into a woodchuck hole.

'wood-coal.

1. Charcoal obtained from wood; with *pl.*, a piece of this: = COAL *sb.* 4. *arch.* or *Hist.*

1653 [see COAL *sb.* 4]. **1727** [DORRINGTON] *Philip Quarll* (1816) 14 In both.. places appeared to have been fire made.. by wood coals. **1855** BROWNING *Fra Lippo* 38 It's not your chance to have a bit of chalk, A wood-coal or the like?

2. = LIGNITE.

1799 KIRWIN *Geol. Ess.* 348 Coal.. is often.. found under basalt:—Wood coal is sometimes found under both. **1830** HERSCHEL *Study Nat. Phil.* I. iii. (1851) 45 Thin seams.. of fossil-wood and wood-coal.

Hence †**'wood-,coaler, -,collier,** a maker of or dealer in 'wood-coal' (sense 1): = COLLIER 1, 2.

1600 *West Riding Sessions Rolls* (Yorks. Rec. Ser. III.) 216 Robertus Scoorer nuper de Emley.. woodcollier. **1659** in Marshall *Edwinstow Reg.* (1891) 32 Elizabeth Childe wood coallers wife. **1708** *Lond. Gaz.* No. 4447/4 Richard Badily, a Wood-Collier.

woodcock ('wʊdkɒk), *sb.* Forms: see WOOD *sb.*[1] and COCK *sb.*[1]; also 2–3 **wide cok,** 4–5 **wodekoc,** 5 **-kok, wodkoke,** 6 **wodkoce,** *Sc.* **widcoik.** [Late OE. *wudu-, wudecoc(c*, f. WOOD *sb.*[1] and COCK *sb.*[1] Appears in OF. as *huitecox, witecos, videcos*, etc., and in Norman dial. as *videcoq.*]

1. a. A migratory bird, *Scolopax rusticula*, allied to the snipe, common in Europe and the British Islands, having a long bill, large eyes, and variegated plumage, and much esteemed as food. Also, the allied *Philohela minor* of N. America, similar in appearance and habits but smaller.

Properly denoting the male bird, but commonly applied to both sexes; cf. WOOD-HEN 1. In sportsman's use with collective pl. *woodcock*; cf. *grouse, snipe, teal*, etc.

*c***1050** *Voc.* in Wr.-Wülcker 258/5 *Acega*, wuducoc. *a* **1100** *Gloss.* ibid. 132/20 *Aceta*, snite, *uel* wudecocc. **1273** *Liber Cust.* (Rolls) 82, ii wodecokes pro iii obolis. **1321** *Ibid.* 304 Le bon widecoke pur i denier. *c* **1325** *Gloss. W. de Bibbesw.* in Wright *Voc.* 164 Un arscye [*gloss* a wode-koc]. *Ibid.* 174 Assez [*gloss* wodekok]. **1347** *Durham Acc. Rolls* (Surtees) 41, ix pluuers, ij Wodekokes. *c* **1420** *Liber Cocorum* (1862) 35 Þo crane schalle.. be.. Draȝun at þo syde as wodcockis. **1486** *Bk. St. Albans, Hawking* d i, The wodecok is comborous to sle: bot if ther be crafte. **1533** ELYOT *Cast. Helthe* (1539) 30 Woodcockes, are of a good temperaunce, and metely lyghte in dygestion. **1538** *Burgh Rec. Edinb.* (1871) II. 92 A mure fowle viij d, a widcoik viij d. **1658** in *10th Rep. Hist. MSS. Comm.* App. I. 58 Send to the fouller and sie if he can get moor fowles or plivers or partridges or woodcokis. **1700** T. BROWN tr. *Fresny's Amusem.* 28 Mayors and Woodcocks come in about Michaelmas. **1768** PENNANT *Brit. Zool.* II. 348 Woodcocks generally arrive here in flocks. **1819** BYRON *Juan* II. lxvii, He cannot live, like woodcocks, upon suction. **1872** COUES *N. Amer. Birds* 249 In woodcock and true snipe.. the eye.. is placed far back and high up. **1902** BUCHAN *Watcher by Threshold* 152 The woodcock are notoriously late.

b. Applied to other birds.

(*a*) Local name for the pileated woodpecker of N. America, also called *log-cock*. (*b*) ***little woodcock***: = woodcock-snipe (see 4). (*c*) ***sea woodcock***: see SEA *sb.* 23 c.

a **1813** A. WILSON *Foresters* Poet. Wks. (1846) 228 Crested wood-cocks hammer from on high. **1885** SWAINSON *Prov. Names Birds* 191 Great Snipe (*Gallinago major*).. Little woodcock, Woodcock snipe (Ireland). **1888** G. TRUMBULL *Bird Names* 151.

2. In allusive use (from the ease with which the woodcock is taken in a snare or net), in reference to capture by some trickery, or as a type of gullibility or folly; hence applied to a person: a fool, simpleton, dupe. *Obs.* or *arch.*

c **1430** LYDG. in *Pol. Rel. & L. Poems* (1903) 48 With wodcokkes, lerne for to dare. *a* **1500–34** *Cov. Corp. Christi Pl.* ii. 432 For, dame, woll I neuer vast my wyttis, To wayte or pry where the wodkoce syttis. **1533** MORE *Debell. Salem* Wks. 958/2 As though he trusted that all the worlde wer woodcockes saue himselfe. **1579** GOSSON *Sch. Abuse* Apol. (Arb.) 72 Cupide sets vpp a Springe for Woodcockes, which are entangled ere they descrie the line. **1601** SHAKS. *Twel. N.*

(Arb.) 72 Cupide sets vpp a Springe for Woodcockes, which are entangled ere they descrie the line. **1601** SHAKS. *Twel. N.* II. v. 92 Now is the Woodcocke neere the gin. **1645** MILTON *Colast.* Wks. 1851 IV. 376 This most incogitant woodcock. **1654** T. WASHBOURNE *Div. Poems* 1 Or like the Wood-cock hide their heads, and then, 'Cause they see none, think none sees them agen. **1679** *Hist. Jetzer* 25 What have the wise Woodcocks of the Council to do with our Affairs? **1708** *Brit. Apollo* No. 3. 2/2 That he shou'd not, In his own Trade appear a Woodcock. **1828** SCOTT *F.M. Perth* xxxii, Poor woodcock, thou art snared! **1877** TENNYSON *Harold* II. ii, We hold our Saxon woodcock in the springe, But he begins to flutter.

3. Various transferred uses. **a.** = *woodcock-shell* (see 4); more fully ***thorny woodcock***. **b.** A variety of apple. **c.** = *woodcock soil* (see 4). **d.** ***Scotch woodcock***: fancy name for a savoury dish: see quot.

a. 1815 S. BROOKES *Introd. Conchol.* 157 Woodcock, *Murex Haustellum.* **1815** BURROW *Elem. Conchol.* 202 *Murex Tribulus*, Thorny Woodcock or Venus Comb.

b. 1700 NOURSE *Disc. Benefits Husb.* x. 148 The Woodcock is a fair large Apple, and produces an excellent Cyder. **1803** *Trans. Soc. Arts* XXI. 262 The old pauson, woodcock, and red musk, are generally large apples.

c. 1764 *Museum Rust.* III. xlvii. 197 Our soils are, in general, either a loam, brick earth, or woodcock, and under them clay.

d. 1861 MRS. BEETON *Bk. Househ. Managem.* xxxiii. 822 (*heading*) Scotch woodcock. **1879** *Birmingham Weekly Post* 24 May 1/4 'Scotch Woodcock'..consists of hard boiled eggs chopped up, mixed with..anchovy sauce, and then laid on slices of hot buttered toast.

4. *attrib.* and *Comb.*, as ***woodcock-pie***, ***-shooting***; **woodcock clay** = *woodcock soil*; **woodcock-eye**, = SNAP-HOOK 2; **woodcock-fish** = SNIPE-FISH 1; **woodcock-fly**, a fly used by anglers (see quot.); **woodcock gun**, a gun used for shooting woodcocks; **woodcock owl**, a local name for the short-eared owl; **woodcock('s) pilot**, a local name for the golden-crested wren (see quot. 1893); **woodcock-shell**, one of several species of *Murex* having a long spout resembling a woodcock's bill; **woodcock-snipe**, the great snipe, *Scolopax major*; **woodcock soil**, a loose soil consisting of a mixture of clay and gravel; **woodcock wing**, (*a*) the wing of a woodcock; (*b*) = *woodcock fly*.

1780 YOUNG *Tour Irel.* II. 8 A hill..which is wet *woodcock clay. **1794** W. FELTON *Carriages* (1801) II. 155 Having the trace-rings..made with a screw, whereby they may be changed, and *woodcock eyes substituted in their place. **1880–4** DAY *Fishes Gt. Brit. & Irel.* I. 250 *Centriscus scolopax*.. The trumpet, bellows-fish, *woodcock or snipe-fish. **1787** BEST *Angling* (ed. 2) 24 Oakfly, Ash-fly, or *Woodcock-fly, found on the body of an Oak or Ash..is a brownish fly and is taken from the beginning of May till the end of August. **1858** GREENER *Gunnery* 205 If making *woodcock guns, less elevation is required, the distance of shooting being shorter. **1840** MACGILLIVRAY *Brit. Birds* III. 461 *Asio brachyotos.* The Streaked Tufted-Owl... *Woodcock Owl. Mouse-hawk. **1598** *Mucedorus* v. ii. 86 Now wee maie goe to breakefast with a *woodcoke pie. **1906** *Westm. Gaz.* 24 Dec. 11/1 Woodcock-pie is..a famous Christmas dish at the Palace. **1871** *East Anglian* IV. 112 '*Woodcock Pilot'. **1893** NEWTON *Dict. Birds* 368 The bird [*sc.* Golden-crested Wren] in autumn visits the east coast in enormous flocks,..they are well known to the fishermen as 'Woodcock's Pilots,' from their generally preceding by a few days the advent of those regular immigrants. **1907** *Athenæum* 11 May 570/2 The most interesting of these local terms is that of 'woodcock pilot', by which the goldcrest is known to all the wild fowlers. **1850** R. G. CUMMING *Hunter's Life S. Afr.* (1902) 98/1 Taking my breakfast..with as much indifference as if I were going *woodcock-shooting. **1885** *Woodcock snipe [see 1 b]. **1764** YOUNG in *Museum Rust.* III. lxiii. 284 Loose, *woodcock, brick-earth soils. **1775** N. KENT *Hints to Gentl.* 14 Woodcock-soil generally consists of yellow, or white clay, with a mixture of gravel; is seldom fruitful. **1535** LYNDESAY *Satyre* 3528 Except God make me lichter nor ane fedder, Or send me doun gude *Widcok wingis to flie. **1888** *Pall Mall Gaz.* 7 Apr. 6/1 A bull trout..succumbs to the woodcock wing.

Hence (*nonce-wds.*) **'woodcock** *v.*, *intr.* to act like a woodcock (see quot., and cf. quot. 1654 in 2 above); **'woodcockize** *v.*, *trans.* to make a 'woodcock' of, to befool.

1817 MARIA EDGEWORTH *Ormond* vi, Like all cunning people, he **woodcocks*—hides his head, and forgets his body can be seen. **1611** COTGR., *Beccassé*, gulled, abused, *woodcockised, make a woodcocke.

woodcraft ('wʊdkrɑːft, -æ-). (Also *U.S.* **woodscraft**: see WOOD *sb.*[1] 9 g.) [f. WOOD *sb.*[1] + CRAFT *sb.*]

1. Skill in, or skilled practice of, matters pertaining to woods or forests, esp. (in early use) to the chase; now (chiefly *N. Amer.*, *Austral.*, etc.) applied esp. to such knowledge of forest conditions as enables one to maintain oneself or make one's way.

13.. *Gaw. & Gr. Knt.* 1605 A wyȝe þat was wys vpon wod craftez To vnlace þis bor lufly bigynnez. *c* **1386** CHAUCER *Prol.* 110 Of woodecraft wel koude he al the vsage..A Forster was he.

1823 SCOTT *Quentin D.* ix, Thou hast begun thy woodcraft well. **1835** W. IRVING *Tour Prairies* xxxiv, One or two other leaders of the camp, versed in woodcraft, examined with learned eye the trees. **1870** BRET HARTE *Idyl of Red Gulch* Wks. (1872) 58 When he had built a fire against a tree, and had shown them other mysteries of wood-craft. **1890** 'R. BOLDREWOOD' *Col. Reformer* xi, The..steering straight in a country without a landmark, was likely to bear hard upon his woodcraft. **1902** S. E. WHITE *Blazed Trail* xviii, He was full of delight over everything that savored of the woods or woodcraft.

2. Skill in woodwork, or in constructing something of wood.

1833 MRS. BROWNING *Prometh. Bound* 525 They..Nor knew to build a house..With wicketed sides, nor any wood-craft knew. **1891** E. PEACOCK *N. Brendon* I. viii. 127 The chief carpenter [has] some good books on woodcraft.

Wood Cree. Also **Woods Cree.** [f. WOOD *sb.*[1] + CREE *sb.* and *a.*: a shortening of earlier *Strong* (also *Thick*) *Woods Cree*, tr. a Wood Cree name.] **1. a.** One of the major divisions of the Cree Indians, inhabiting woodland areas of Saskatchewan and Manitoba in Canada. **b.** A member of this people. Cf. PLAINS CREE.

1885 *Boston Jrnl.* 23 June 1/8 The Wood Crees have gone back to get a cache of provisions. **1910** F. W. HODGE *Handbk. Amer. Indians* II. 414/1 *Sakawithiniwuk* ('people of the woods'). The Wood Cree, one of the several divisions of the Cree. **1947** *Beaver* June 15/1 The Wood Crees, who were in the minority, were, in general, less troublesome. **1972** [see PLAINS CREE].

2. The language spoken by the Wood Cree.

1958 R. A. LOGAN *Cree Lang.* 4 One dialect (Moose Cree) uses the sound of L where another dialect (Northern or Woods Cree) uses the sound of TH... Only Northern Cree uses TH. **1978** D. H. PENTLAND in Cook & Kaye *Ling. Stud. Native Canada* 190 Woods Cree is now spoken by about five per cent of the total number of Cree Speakers.

woodcut ('wʊdkʌt). [f. WOOD *sb.*[1] + CUT *sb.*[2] 22.] A design cut in relief on a block of wood, for printing from; a print or impression obtained from this; a wood-engraving. (Formerly more freq. called *wooden cut*: see WOODEN *a.* 4.)

1662 EVELYN *Chalcogr.* 84 All those excellent Wood Cuts of Hans Schirstyn and Adam Altorf. **1816** OTTLEY *Hist. Engraving* I. 102 The wood-cuts, which constitute what are termed the old block-books. **1835** DICKENS *Let. to Miss Hogarth*, A new publication..each number to contain four woodcuts. **1857** H. SPENCER in *Westm. Rev.* Apr. 460 The woodcuts of the *Illustrated London News*.

attrib. **1865** WAY *Promp. Parv.* p. xlv, The well-known wood-cut device used by Wynkyn de Worde. **1887** R. R. BOWKER in *Harper's Mag.* July 182/1 Charles Knight's popular illustrated books..again revived wood-cut work.

wood-cutter ('wʊd,kʌtə(r)).

1. One who cuts wood; one who cuts down or fells trees, or cuts off their branches, for the wood; a wood-hewer.

1774 *Pennsylv. Gaz.* 14 Dec. Suppl. 2/3 Cross-cut, pit, hand, woodcutters, tennon, and a variety of other saws. **1775** LYNCH in Sparks *Corr. Amer. Rev.* (1853) I. 84 Will it be right to keep your heroes for wood-cutters? **1837–42** HAWTHORNE *Twice-told T.* (1851) II. ix. 129 The axe of the woodcutter echoes..in the forest. **1844** DICKENS *Mart. Chuz.* xxiii, The huts of the wood-cutters, where the vessel stopped for fuel.

2. A maker of woodcuts, a wood-engraver.

1821 T. G. WAINEWRIGHT *Ess. & Crit.* (1880) 194 Our historical wood-cutters have thought it much to follow..those lines ready-pencilled by the inventor on the blocks. **1924** *Times Lit. Suppl.* 12 June 365/2 Mr. Maudslay interpreting the stone carvings, and the woodcutters interpreting Mr. Maudslay.

'wood-,cutting, *sb.*

1. Wood-engraving. Also *attrib.*

1722 *Hearne's Collect.* (O.H.S.) VII. 381 Wood-cutting being not so much used since ingraving came up. **1871** ALABASTER *Wheel of Law* liv, The arts of printing and woodcutting have, in China and Japan, made books very cheap. **1890** *Athenæum* 1 Mar. 281/2 Many inequalities..observed in the output of woodcutting *botteghe*.

2. The action or employment of cutting down trees for wood, or of cutting wood with saws or other appliances. Also *attrib.*

1872 J. RICHARDS *Wood-working Machines* 32 Wood-cutting Machines. **1893** RODWAY *Hand-bk. Brit. Guiana* 49 Wood-cutting grants are obtainable. **1899** —— *Guiana Wilds* 19 Now and again he did a little wood-cutting.

wooddie, -y, -ish, obs. ff. WOODY, WOODISH.

'wood-dove. [Cf. Du. *houtduif*, G. *holztaube*.] = WOOD-PIGEON. Also applied to certain S. African birds allied to this (see quot. 1875–84).

c **1386** CHAUCER *Sir Thopas* 59 The wodedowue vpon a spray She sang ful loude and cleere. *c* **1440** *Promp. Parv.* 531/2 Wode Dowe, or stokk dowe, *palumba*. *c* **1530** *Songs, Carols*, etc. (E.E.T.S.) 114 Whan..curlews cary clothes, ..& woddowes were wodknyffis, theves to kyll,..Than put in a woman your trust & confidence. **1729** SAVAGE *Wanderer* v. 92 While the soft-murm'ring am'rous Wood-Dove cooes. **1837** MACGILLIVRAY *Hist. Brit. Birds* I. 287 *Columbas Œnas*. .. Stock Dove. Wood Dove. *c* **1843** CARLYLE *Hist. Sk. Jas. I & Chas. I* (1898) 74 Melodious as the voice of wood-doves. **1875–84** *Layard's Birds S. Afr.* 564 *Haplopelia larvata*. Rufous-breasted Wood-Dove. *Ibid.* 570 *Chalcopelia afra*. Emerald-spotted Wood Dove. *Ibid.* 571 *Tympanistria tympanistria*. White-breasted Wood Dove.

woode, obs. form of WOAD, WOOD.

wooded ('wʊdɪd), *ppl. a.* [f. WOOD *sb.*[1] or *v.*[2] + -ED.] Furnished with wood or woods; covered with growing trees; abounding in woods or forests. (*a*) predicative, in ppl. construction; in later use giving rise to sense 2 of WOOD *v.*[2], of which it may be taken as the pa. pple. Usually with adv.

1605 CAMDEN *Rem.* 1 Isle of Britaine..aboundant in pasture,..plentifully wooded. **1625** MASSINGER *New Way* IV. i, It is well wooded, and well watered,—the acres Fertile and rich. *a* **1700** EVELYN *Diary* Introd., His estate was..well wooded and full of timber. **1796** MORSE *Amer. Geog.* I. 141 The land is flat, marshy and wooded with pines, birch, larch and willows. **1855** MACAULAY *Hist. Eng.* xii. III. 137 The neighbourhood of Kenmare was then richly wooded.

fig. *a* **1616** BEAUM. & FL. *Bonduca* I. ii, The hills are wooded with their partizans. And all the valleys overgrown with darts, As moors are with rank rushes.

(*b*) in attrib. construction, preceding the sb.

1782 PENNANT *Journ. Chester to Lond.* 292 Some pretty pieces of water, winding along a fine wooded dell. **1821** SCOTT *Kenilw.* iii, In a wooded park..was situated the ancient mansion. **1920** *Blackw. Mag.* Jan. 107/2 The..Ganges Canal..runs straight as a die between its wooded banks.

wooden ('wʊd(ə)n), *a.* Also 6–7 **wodden**, **woodden**, 6–8 **woden**. [f. WOOD *sb.*[1] + -EN[4].]

I. 1. a. Made or consisting of wood.

1538 ELYOT *Dict.*, *Durateus*, wodden. **1577** GOOGE *Heresbach's Husb.* I. 37 Raking them with woodden Rakes. **1577** tr. *Bullinger's Decades* II. ii. (1592) 121 To fall downe prostrate before a wooden Idoll. **1611** CORYAT *Crudities* 34 The images of many of the French Kings, set in certain wodden [*ed.* **1776** woden] cupbords. **1683** MOXON *Mech. Exerc.*, *Printing* xxiv. ¶ 1 If the Joyner performed his Work well in making the Wooden-work. **1683** J. REID *Scots Gard'ner* (1907) 40 Beat every two or three rows of turf, while moist, with the wooden-beater. **1726** SWIFT *Gulliver* II. vii, A kind of wooden Machine. **1831** SCOTT *Ct. Rob.* xv, A massive wooden stool. **1860** TYNDALL *Glac.* I. xxvii. 197, I reached a wooden hut. **1898** A. AUSTIN *Lamia's Winter Quarters* 69 The slowly-rolling wheels of a wooden wain..with wooden wheels, wooden pole, and wooden yoke.

b. *transf.* in various occas. senses: Made or produced by means of wood; dull or dead, as the sound of wood when struck; relating to or occupied with wood; full of objects made of wood; hard and stiff like wood.

1606 SHAKS. *Tr. & Cr.* I. iii. 155 Like a strutting Player..To heare the woodden Dialogue and sound 'Twixt his stretcht footing, and the Scaffolage. **1610** —— *Temp.* III. i. 62, I..would no more endure This wodden slauerie [*sc.* piling logs]. **1663** BUTLER *Hud.* I. ii. 699 Secure from Wooden Blow. **1677** MOXON *Mech. Exerc.* iii. 57 Put the whole lump into a wooden Fire. **1703** T. N. *City & C. Purchaser* 261 Trees..useful for the Carpenter, Joyner, or other wooden Tradesman to work upon. **1897** HOWELLS *Landlord at Lion's Head* 442 In the woodenest outskirts of North Cambridge. **1897** *Allbutt's Syst. Med.* IV. 762 A feeling as if the throat were 'wooden'. **1899** J. HUTCHINSON in *Archives Surg.* X. No. 38 Descr. Plate xvii, The fingers have..become slender, pale and wooden.

2. *fig.* Having some quality likened to the hard dry consistence of wood, or to its inferior value as compared with precious metal or the like.

a. Lacking grace, liveliness, interest, or the like; expressionless, spiritless; dull and inert; stiff and lifeless.

a **1566** R. EDWARDS *Damon & Pithias* (1571) B 3 b, He wyll neuer blush, he hath a wooden face. **1625** BACON *Ess.*, *Boldness* (Arb.) 519 When a Bold Fellow is out of Countenance;..that puts his Face into a most Shruncken, and woodden Posture. **1813** R. H. in *Examiner* 17 May 315/2 The drawing and character are..in some parts feeble and wooden. **1863** KINGLAKE *Crimea* I. xiv. 215 The seeming poverty of his intellect, his blank wooden looks. **1887** SAINTSBURY *Hist. Elizab. Lit.* iv. (1890) 130 This earlier and woodener matter [of poetry]. **1899** *Athenæum* 29 Apr. 526/1 A dryasdust antiquary of the most wooden type.

b. Of persons or their attributes: Mentally dull; insensitive, inapprehensive; unintelligent, blockish.

a **1586** SIDNEY *Astr. & Stella* Sonn. vii, Who have so leaden eyes, as not to see sweete Beauties showe: Or seeing, have so wooden wits as not that worth to knowe. **1591** SHAKS. *1 Hen. VI*, v. iii. 89 Ile win this Lady Margaret. For whom? Why for my King: Tush, that's a woodden thing. **1659** S. LEE *Temple of Solomon* 194 Their lying wonders..so often recited in their wooden Legends. *a* **1697** AUBREY *Lett. Eminent Persons* (1813) II. 453 *note*, The Rumpe of a House, 'twas the wooden invention of Generall Browne (a woodmonger). **1698** *Christ Exalted* 40 To talk of a Law that admits of Sin, is to make the Maker of such a wooden Law to be little better than a wooden God. **1805** MOORE *To Lady Heathcote* 51 Those fops..With heads as wooden as thy ware, And, Heaven knows! not half so polish'd. **1830** GALT *Lawrie T.* IV. ii. (1849) 150 The sight of that wooden old man, as I had often spoken of him..weeping like a woman ..suprised me. **1833** CARLYLE *Ess.*, *Diderot* (1872) V. 7 Withal, however, he is wooden; thoroughly mechanical. **1859** GEO. ELIOT *Adam Bede* v, He's got a bad ear for music. .. When people have wooden heads..it can't be helped. **1871** EARLE *Philol. Engl. Tongue* iv. 178 The wooden notion that it is an inherent quality in a word to be of this or that part of speech.

†**c.** Of inferior character, poor, worthless.

1592 LYLY *Gallanthea* II. iii, I shall haue but wodden lucke. *c* **1630** RISDON *Surv. Devon* §104 (1810) 100 In old time were golden prelates, and wooden chalices, but in this time, wooden prelates and golden chalices. [Cf. CHALICE 2 γ, quot. 1528.] **1719** DE FOE *Crusoe* I. (Globe) 119 Making a wooden Spade..; but this did my Work in but a wooden manner.

†**3. a.** Belonging to the woods, sylvan. *Obs. rare.*

1606 CHAPMAN *Gentl. Usher* I. B 2 b, Syluanas..this wodden god.

b. *U.S.* = WOODED *ppl. a.* ? *Obs.*

1816 U. BROWN *Jrnl.* 15 Aug. in *Maryland Hist. Mag.* (1910) X. 358 To Smith field a Wooden Town in a Wooden Country & a wooden bred set of Tavern-keepers. **1843**

Carlton *New Purchase* 115 Religious meetings in the wooden world. **1843** Carlton *New Purchase* 50 Our wooden country's mighty rough . . for some folks. **1891** M. E. Ryan *Pagan of Alleghanies* i. 12 And then there are others more seldom seen, the women from the 'wooden' country of the interior.

II. Special Collocations. †**4. wooden cut**: = woodcut. So ***wooden picture, print****. Obs.*

1683 Moxon *Mech. Exerc., Printing* 1 Cutting their Letters upon Blocks in whole Pages or Forms, as among us our Wooden Pictures are Cut. **1691** Wood *Ath. Oxon.* I. 31 Printed from a Wooden Cut the Picture of a Bear baited by six Dogs. **1706** Hearne *Collect.* 25 Feb. (O.H.S.) I. 194 Raphael, a Wooden Print. **1770** Luckombe *Hist. Printing* 92 Elegant initial letters, and fine wooden cuts. **1837** Hallam *Lit. Eur.* I. i. ix. §18. 470 Otto Bremfels of Strasburg . . published a . . work in three volumes folio, with 238 wooden cuts of plants. [**1848** Lowell *Fab. Critics* 1596 *note*, Cuts rightly called wooden, as all must admit.]

5. wooden horse. **a.** [cf. L. *equus ligneus*.] A designation for a ship. *Obs.* or *arch.*

1599 Nashe *Lenten Stuffe* 29 They are glad on their wodden horses to post after [the herring]. **1639** Fuller *Holy War* v. xxi. (1647) 264 The Low-countreys, the best stable of woodden horses, and most potent in Shipping. **1824** Scott *Redgauntlet* ch. xv, [He] saw nothing in this worse than an ordinary fit of sea-sickness... He assured his passenger . . that he hoped to drink a can . . with him . . for all that he felt a little out of the way for riding the wooden

b. An instrument of punishment, chiefly military, formerly in use (= horse *sb.* 6 b): see quot. 1688. *Hist.*

1629 *Lex Scripta Isle of Man* (1819) 103 The Offender [for theft] . . under the Value [of 6½d.] to be whipped, or sett upon a Wooden Horse ordained for such Offenders. **1648** in Rushw. *Hist. Coll.* iv. II. 1369 Henry Matthews and Robert Rowe were . . tried by Court Marshal and sentenced to ride the Wooden-Horse at the Royal Exchange. **1678** Butler *Hud.* iii. iii. 212 Worse Than mannaging a Wooden Horse. **1688** Holme *Armoury* iii. xix. (Roxb.) 220/1 Moderne punishments used among the Souldiery... Ridding the wooden horse; setting him on an horse made of wood with a sharp rigged back, his hands tyed behind him, and Musketts or weights hung at his feet. *c* **1700** J. Lewis *Mem. Pr. William Henry* (1789) 11 The Duke bid his boys . . put the taylor on the wooden horse, which stood in the presence-room for the punishment of offenders, as is usual in martial law. **1760** *Cautions & Advices to Officers of Army* 44 Punishments . . inflicted by Officers without the Sentence of a Court-Martial, . . Picketting—tying neck and heels, and riding the wooden horse. **1899** Baldock *Cromwell* 360 Two soldiers of Dean's regiment rode the 'wooden horse' for an hour.

†**c.** A name for the scaffold or gallows; also for an instrument of torture: = horse *sb.* 25. *Obs.*

1642 [see horse *sb.* 25]. **1731** Chandler tr. *Limborch's Hist. Inquis.* II. 222 A Wooden Bench, which they call the Wooden Horse [described at length].

d. The wooden figure of a horse (*ἵππος δουράτεος*, Odyssey viii. 492, 512) in which the Greek invaders were concealed at the siege of Troy. Hence †**wooden-horse** *v.* (*nonce-wd.*), *trans.* to capture by means of this.

1622 J. Taylor (Water P.) *Sir Gregory Nonsence* Wks. (1630) ii. 3/2 Vntill the Woodden Horse of trusty Synon, Foald a whole litter of mad Colts in Harnesse. **1666** *Third Advice to Painter* 32 Hark to Cassandraes Song, e're Fate destroy, By their own Navyes; Wooden-horse thy Troy. **1835** Thirlwall *Greece* I. vi. 226 Epeus was celebrated as the builder of the wooden horse in which the heroes were concealed.

e. A wooden structure in a gymnasium, for vaulting exercise: = horse *sb.* 6 c.

1854 G. Roland *Gymnastics* 27 The wooden horse . . interesting from the number of exercises practised upon it.

6. wooden shoe: a shoe made of wood, as the French sabot; in the 18th c. popularly taken as typical of the miserable condition of the French peasantry.

1607 [see sabot 1]. **1701** De Foe *Trueborn Eng.* i. 268 Two hundred Thousand Pair of Wooden Shooes, Who God be thanked, had nothing left to lose. **1715** Addison *Drummer* Prol. 8 Round-heads and Wooden-shoes are standing Jokes. **1766** Goldsm. *Vicar W.* xix, What! give up liberty, property, and, as the Gazetteer says, lie down to be saddled with wooden shoes! **1807–8** Syd. Smith *Plymley's Lett.* iii. (1852) 29 He calls all hands on deck; talks to them of king, country, glory, sweethearts, gin, French prison, wooden shoes, Old England, and hearts of oak. **1818** Scott *Rob Roy* ix, King William . . our immortal deliverer from papists and pretenders, and wooden shoes and warming pans. **1859** W. S. Coleman *Woodlands* (1862) 62 In France great numbers of the peculiar wooden shoes, called '*sabots*', are made of Alder.

7. wooden spoon: a spoon made of wood; *spec.* one presented by custom at Cambridge to the last of the Junior Optimes, i.e. the lowest of those taking honours in the Mathematical Tripos; hence, this position in the examination, or the person who takes it. Also in extended use, referring to the lowest of a list or set in other connexions. Hence **wooden-spooner**, **-spoonist**, a competitor who is awarded the 'wooden spoon'; a loser.

'At Yale, formerly, the student who took the last appointment in the Junior Exhibition; later, the most popular student in a class' (*Cent. Dict.*).

1803 *Gradus ad Cantab.* 137 Wooden Spoon, for wooden heads: . . the lowest of the Junior Optimes. **1820** Byron *Juan* iii. cx, Sure my invention must be down at zero, And I grown one of many 'wooden spoons' Of verse (the name with which we Cantabs please To dub the last of honours in degrees). **1858** Earl Malmesbury *Mem.* (1884) II. 127 The 'wooden spoon' which is given to the Minister in the House of Commons who has been in the fewest divisions. **1883** in *Standard* 20 June 2/7 There was no opposition to the presentation of the time-honoured 'Wooden Spoon'. **1900** *Westm. Gaz.* 19 Mar. 8/2 The international matches . . have now all been played, . . Ireland, who won the championship last year . . have only 1 point, and take the 'wooden spoon'. **1927** *Daily Express* 23 Mar. 13/3 Champions and wooden spoonists of the Isthmian League last season were opposed on the Civil Service ground at Chiswick. **1954** J. Fingleton *Ashes crown Year* 275 Somerset were wooden-spooners last summer and will be so again. **1973** *Nation Rev.* (Melbourne) 31 Aug. 1442/3 4BH slips to fourth place in the five station market, with perennial wooden spooners, 4BK, only 2000 listeners behind. **1975** *Globe & Mail* (Toronto) 26 May s5/1 England won the British soccer championship . . with Wales, once again the wooden spoonists. **1981** *Daily Mail* 25 Nov. 30 (*heading*) A flat rate from the wooden spoonists.

8. wooden walls (after *ξύλινον τεῖχος*, Herodotus vii. 141): ships or shipping as a defensive force. (Rarely in *sing.*)

1598 W. Phillip tr. *Linschoten* To Rdr., Our Wodden Walles (as Themistocles called the Ships of Athens). **1598** Stow *Surv.* 468 [484] Ships . . bee the wodden walles for defence of our Realme. **1625** Sanderson *Serm., Ad Mag.* iii. (1681) 129 Our carnal confidence and security in the strength of our wooden and watry walls. *c* **1645** in *Wood's Life*, etc. (O.H.S.) II. 55 Your stone and wooden wall Shall not defend you, but shall then Begin to sink and fall. **1750** Beawes *Lex Mercat.* (1752) 248 Our wooden walls are our bulwarks and redoubts, to which we owe our safety. **1849** Longf. *Building of Ship* 69 Every climate, every soil, Must bring its tribute, great or small, And help to build the wooden wall! **1862** Gen. P. Thompson in *Bradford Advertiser* 26 Apr. 6/1 Your wooden walls wherein was your trust, have become fit only for firewood, or at most for transports.

9. In various special collocations: †**wooden bridle**, a fanciful name for a rudder; †**wooden casement**, **cravat**, slang or jocular names for the pillory (cf. *hempen cravat* s.v. cravat *sb.* 1 b); **wooden cross** *Mil. slang*, a wooden cross on a serviceman's grave; hence, death in action regarded ironically as an award of merit; †**wooden dagger**, the dagger of lath worn by Vice in the old moralities; †**wooden doublet** *jocular*, a coffin; **wooden island** (see quot.); **wooden isle**, a rhetorical designation for a ship; **wooden kimono** *U.S. slang*, a coffin; **wooden leg**, an artificial leg made of wood; also *fig.*; **wooden mare** = *wooden horse*, 5 b; **wooden nickel** (or **money**) *U.S. slang*, a worthless or counterfeit coin; chiefly in *fig.* phr. ***to take a wooden nickel*** and varr., to be swindled or fooled; **wooden nutmeg**: see nutmeg 1 b; **wooden overcoat**: see overcoat; **wooden pear**, an Australian tree, *Xylomelum pyriforme*, bearing hard inversely pear-shaped seed-vessels; †**wooden ruff** = *wooden cravat* (see ruff *sb.*[2] 4); **wooden suit** *slang*, a coffin; **wooden surtout** *slang*, = *wooden doublet*; **wooden tongue**, an infectious disease of cattle and horses, in which the tongue is enlarged and hardened; **wooden ware**, articles, esp. household utensils, made of wood (sometimes written with hyphen or as one word; cf. *earthenware*); **wooden wedding** orig. *U.S.*, the fifth anniversary of one's wedding, on which it is appropriate to give presents made of wood; **wooden wedge** *Cambridge Univ.* (see quot. and wedge *sb.* 8).

1614 Sylvester *Parl. Vertues Royall* 705 A skilfull Pilot, . . Her winged manage rightly to command With hempen Rains, and *wooden Bridle. **1685** *Roxb. Ball.* (1885) V. 606 To be pelted with Eggs thro' a lewd *wooden-casement. **1676** *Poor Robin's Intell.* 4–11 Apr. 2/1 We hear of none this bout that are to wear the *Wooden Crevat. **1917** A. G. Empey *Over Top* 314 **Wooden Cross*, two pieces of wood in the form of a cross placed at the head of a Tommy's grave. **1919** in *Amer. Speech 1972* (1975) XLVII. 117 Seven of the 'Blue Tails' went down to get their Wooden Crosses. **1949** A. Murphy *To Hell & Back* xvi. 195 There is no other branch of the army that offers so many chances for the Purple Heart, the Distinguished Wooden Cross, the Royal Order of the Mattress Covers. **1589** Nashe *Martins Months Minde* Wks. (Grosart) I. 181 The *woodden dagger may not bee worne at the backe, where S. Paules sword, hangs by the side. **1599** Shaks. *Hen. V*, iv. iv. 77 This roaring diuell i'th olde play [*sc.* Pistol], that euerie one may payre his nayles with a woodden dagger. *a* **1625** Fletcher *Noble Gentl.* v. i, According to his merits he should wear, A guarded coat, and a great wooden dagger. **1761** [F. Forrest] *Ways to kill Care* Ded. p. ii, Where to find a guardian for the bawling brat, in case papa . . should suddenly tumble into his *wooden doublet. **1808** Ashe *Trav. Amer.* III. 310 *Wooden Islands, are places, where . . large quantities of drift-wood have . . been arrested and matted together in different parts of the river. **1603** Chettle *Eng. Mourn. Garm.* E 3, The inhabitants of those *wooden Iles, are worthy Sea-men. **1926** Maines & Grant *Wise-Crack Dict.* 15 **Wooden kimona*, case for cold storage. **1946** Mezzrow & Wolfe *Really Blues* ii. 19, I expected the man to turn up . . with his tape measure to outfit me with a wooden kimono. **1582** *Aldeburgh Rec.* in *N. & Q.* 12th Ser. VII. 366/2 P[d] to ye Joyner for a *wooden Legge . . xviii[d]. *a* **1663** Killigrew *Parson's Wedd.* i. iii. (1664) 81 She hates a man with all his Limbs; a Wooden-leg, a Crutch . . wins her heart. **1668** R. Steele *Husbandman's Calling* i. (1672) 7 Every man should be of some use in the body politick . . else he is but an artificial member, a meer wooden leg. **1709** Steele *Tatler* No. 48 ¶ 2, I was the old Soldier who . . pretended that I had broken my Wooden-Leg. **1887** Besant *The World went* ii, His right leg had been lost in action, and was replaced by a wooden leg. **1819** *Wooden mare [see mare[1] 2 b]. **1829** Scott *Old Mort.* ix. *note*, The punishment of riding the wooden mare was . . one of the . . cruel modes of enforcing military discipline. **1915** C. Mathewson *Catcher Craig* ii. 25 He was instructed . . not to take any *wooden money. **1922** S. Lewis *Babbitt* v. 67 S'long! Don't take any wooden money. **1971** F. P. Grove *Tales from Margin* 27 'Well,' said Walt, 'be good, fellah! Don't take any wooden money!' Even this cheap vulgarity irritated her now. **1927** *Amer. Speech* III. 132 [College slang.] Not to 'take any *wooden nickels', in other words, to be alert. **1937** L. Hellman *Diary* 23 Oct. in *Unfinished Woman* (1969) viii. 100 Luis and I got to Madrid. He said I was not to take any wooden nickels. **1964** in Hamblett & Deverson *Generation X* 90 Then one night I met Johnny, one of the biggest sharks in the Mayfair aquarium, and that was the end of that. Nobody ever sold Johnny a wooden nickel. **1971** M. Torrie *Bismarck Herrings* ii. 29 Having advised her . . not to accept any wooden nickels, [he] drove back. **1971** R. Dentry *Encounter at Kharmel* iii. 58 There hadn't been a tribal rising worth a wooden nickel since the Partition troubles died down. **1860** G. Bennett *Gatherings of Naturalist* 322 The *Wooden Pear-tree of the colonists . . is peculiar to Australia. **1889** Maiden *Usef. Pl. Australia* 615 *Xylomelum pyriforme* . . Native Pear. Wooden Pear. **1968** W. Garner *Deep, Deep, Freeze* xx. 188 Any mistake on his part could win him the prize of the *wooden suit. **1972** J. S. Hall *Sayings from Old Smoky* 42 When a guy comes and steals my stuff, he better be ready for a wooden suit or Boot Hill. **1865** *Slang Dict.*, **Wooden surtout*, a coffin, generally spoken of as a wooden surtout with nails for buttons. **1884** Klein *Micro-organisms & Dis.* xvi. 148 In cattle the disease [actinomycosis] mainifests itself by firm tumours in the jaw, . . and particularly by a great enlargement and induration of the tongue—*wooden tongue. **1914** *Christian World* 12 Mar. 3/2 A Haverfordwest saddler has died from the disease known as 'wooden tongue'. It occurs occasionally among horses, but is extremely rare in human beings. **1727** Earbery tr. *Burnet's St. Dead* 20 If a Man should build a fine and magnificent Seat, and fill the Inside thereof . . with . . *Wooden-ware and the most sordid Furniture. **1884** Sargent *Rep. Forests N. Amer.* 495 Large quantities of . . woodenware, handles, spools, bobbins, etc. **1870** D. MacRae *Americans at Home* II. 293 The fifth anniversary is called the *wooden wedding... The presents suitable to this anniversary are of wood. **1888** *Girl's Own Paper* 24 Mar. 407/3 In America, too, the fifth anniversary of the marriage ceremony is known as the 'wooden-wedding'. **1918** H. Barnett *Canon Barnett* I. xiv. 162 In 1893 we decided to commemorate our wooden wedding by a congregational party. **1860** *Slang Dict.* (ed. 2) **Wooden wedge*, the last name in the classical honours list at Cambridge.

III. 10. Combinations, as (in sense 1) ***wooden-barred, -hooped, -hulled, -legged, -pinned, -seated, -shoed, -soled, -walled***, adjs.; also (in sense 2 a) ***wooden-faced, -featured*** adjs.; also †**wooden-footed** *a.*, wooden-shoed; **woodenhead**, a stupid person, a blockhead; **wooden-headed** *a.*, having a 'wooden head', stupid (hence ***wooden-headedness***); **woodentop** *slang*, (*a*) a uniformed policeman; (*b*) a dim-wit; **wooden-weary** *a.*, stupefied with weariness.

1854 *Poultry Chron.* II. 23/1 Every one of our pens was made with an open *wooden-barred back. **1605** Camden *Rem.* 78 By this name [*sc.* Dorcas], the Amorous Knights were wont to salute freckled . . *wodden-faced wenches. **1863** Miss Braddon *Eleanor's Vict.* xxx, His nieces, . . whose wooden-faced stolidity had . . something . . suggestive of being listened to and stared at by two Dutch clocks. **1848** Dickens *Dombey* vii, A *wooden-featured . . Major. **1670** G. H. *Hist. Cardinals* i. i. 12, I heard a certain *wooden footed [orig. *zoccolante*] Frier Preach. **1831** Carlyle *Let. to Wife* 8 Sept., I . . saw the coronation procession, which seventy or eighty thousand *woodenheads besides were looking at. **1906** J. Oxenham *Giant Circumstance* x. 140 Is it true that that woodenhead placed you under arrest? **1865** *Sat. Rev.* 4 Feb. 143/1 That still more *wooden-headed creature, a man who fails to appreciate his value. **1850** Dickens *Let. to Mrs. Watson* 14 Dec., For which *wooden-headedness the Child shall be taken to task. **1906** *Macm. Mag.* Apr. 454 A large *wooden-hooped net. **1883** *Whitaker's Alm.* 445/1 Of the *wooden-hulled vessels the largest is the *Lissa*. **1840** Thackeray *Shabby-genteel Story* i, A stout old *wooden-legged Scotch regimental surgeon. **1895** Kipling *2nd Jungle Bk., Undertakers* 86 Square-sailed, *wooden-pinned barges. **1890** 'R. Boldrewood' *Col. Reformer* xxv, The *wooden-seated American chairs. **1800** *Wooden shoed [see sabot 1]. **1840** Thackeray *Paris Sk.-bk., Cartouche*, Virtue . . may exist among wooden-shoed Papists as well as honest Church-of-England men. **1810** Milman in *Biogr. Sk.* i. (1900) 18 *Wooden-soled shoes. **1910** Crockett *Dew of Youth* i. ii. 10 Tramp of wooden-soled clogs. **1981** J. Wainwright *All on Summer's Day* 96 I'm a copper. An ordinary flatfoot... A real old *woodentop. That's me. **1983** A. Beevor *Faustian Pact* v. 33 They've even got the bleeding Army out... Bunch of woodentops from Chelsea barracks. **1984** *Listener* 16 Feb. 24/3 A policeman who is called a 'butter boy' or a 'wolly' must be something like a 'woodentop'. **1891** C. James *Rom. Rigmarole* 23, I walked on between the tall, straight stems... A sudden turn in the *wooden-walled alley . . brought me face to face with a great, still lake. **1888** Doughty *Trav. Arabia Deserta* I. 427 Hounds . . *wooden-weary with long watch.

Hence (chiefly *fig.*) ˈ**wooden** *v. trans.*, (*a*) to render wooden; (*b*) *Austral.* and *N.Z. slang*, to render insensible; to knock unconscious; also const. *out*; ˈ**woodenize** *v.* (*nonce-wd.*) *trans.* = *wooden* (*a*); ˈ**woodenly** *adv.*, in a wooden manner; ˈ**woodenness**, wooden quality or style; ˈ**woodeny** *a.*, of a wooden quality.

1641 Milton *Animadv.* Wks. 1851 III. 239 How little wee neede feare that the unguilding of our Prelates will prove the *woodening of our Priests. **1904** 'G. B. Lancaster' *Sons o' Men* 252 He'll wooden more of you out if you scare him. *c* **1926** 'Mixer' *Transport Workers' Song Bk.* 126 It [*sc.* a block of ice] 'woodened' him out, and he lay there quite flat. **1952** M. Allingham *Tiger in Smoke* xi. 184 If you 'ad only woodened '*er*, we'd have 'ad all the time in the world. **1974** *Southerly* XXXIV. 145 If you can't wooden 'em [*sc.* kangaroos] at a 'undred yards with one I.C.I. bullet, you're not tryin'! **1877** SINCLAIR *Mount* 235 When the poetic vigour was enfeebled and *woodenised by age. **1653** DOROTHY OSBORNE *Lett.* (1888) 63 You would have both pitied and laughed at me if you could have seen how *woodenly I entertained the widow. *a* **1734** NORTH *Lives* (1826) I. 361 To have some sport in seeing how woodenly he would excuse himself. **1881** D. C. MURRAY *Joseph's Coat* I. xi. 262 Sitting by the fireside,..looking woodenly respectable as of old. **1894** W. C. RUSSELL *Good Ship 'Mohock'* i. 15 The mechanical hireling..who does his duty woodenly. **1854** H. D. THOREAU *Walden* 356 Many concentric layers of *woodenness in the dead dry leaf of society. **1860** F. W. FABER *Precious Blood* ii. 66 Considerable dryness, stiffness, woodenness,..would characterize this philanthropic city. **1872** *Daily News* 30 July, Woodenness.. cannot with truth be said to be banished from the handling of the Aldershot force. **1886** *Spectator* 6 Nov., Lit. Suppl. 1505 The book is..readable, notwithstanding faults of woodenness, which are inevitable whenever authors do not make their studies from life. **1888** SWEET *Hist. Eng. Sounds* p. xi, The 'woodenness' which then characterized German philology. **1864** *Morning Star* 19 Sept., Some of the horses ..are *woodeny old screws without a pace in them beyond the regulation amble. **1885** C. L. PIRKIS *Lady Lovelace* III. xxxviii. 19 Making..hard woodeny angles against the.. leaden sky. **1898** P. MANSON *Trop. Diseases* xii. 210 Woodeny hardness [of the heart-muscle]. **1905** *Sat. Rev.* 1 Apr. 415/2 The capercailzie..gives vent to..several hard woodeny clicks.

wood-end. *Shipbuilding.* = *hood-end* (HOOD *sb.*[1] 8). Cf. *whooding*, HOODING (sense 3, 1627).

1867 SMYTH *Sailor's Word-bk.*

†**wooder** (ˈwʊdə(r)). *Obs.* [OE. *wudere*, f. *wudian* to cut wood; later directly f. WOOD *v.*[2] or *sb.*[1] + -ER[1]. Cf. WOODYER.] = WOODMAN[1] 2.

c **1050** *Gloss.* in Wr.-Wülcker 371/5 *Calones*, wuderas. **1275** *Rot. Hundr.* II. 210 Andreas le Wodere. **1307** *Cal. Close Rolls 35 Edw. I* 484 Matthew le Woder. **1767** *Wallis's Voy.* in Hawkesworth *Voy.* (1773) I. 468, I ordered that no man, except the wooders and waterers, with their guard, should be permitted to go on shore. **1773** *Gentl. Mag.* XLIII. 419 They..sent wooders to fell timber.

ˈ**wood-ˌevil.** [? f. WOOD *a.* + EVIL *sb.*] Local name for dysentery or a similar disease in sheep and cattle; also called *moor-evil* or *black-legs*.

1523-34 FITZHERB. *Husb.* §50 A sickenes among shepe.. called the wode euyll..cometh in the sprynge of the yere,.. and maketh them to halt, and to holde theyr necke awry. **1614** MARKHAM *Cheap & Good Husb.* III. xix. 75 The wood-euill or Crampe..is a weakenesse or strayning of the sinewes got by colds and surfets. *a* **1722** LISLE *Husb.* (1757) 295 They have a distemper in Leicestershire frequent amongst the calves, which in that country they call the black-legs; but ..in Staffordshire..the wood-evil. **1741** *Compl. Fam. Piece* III. 495 The Wood-evil is seldom or never found among Sheep that have their Pasture in low Grounds. **1749** [see *moor-evil*, MOOR *sb.*[1] 6]. **1847** W. C. L. MARTIN *Ox* 151/2 Wood-evil, moor-ill, or pantas..is brought on in cattle by their devouring the acrid buds of trees, by bad winter provision, by impure water, and similar causes.

†ˈ**woodful,** *a. Obs. rare.* [irreg. f. WOOD *a.* + -FUL.] Mad, furious.

1582 STANYHURST *Æneis* II. (Arb.) 56 This sight foule freighted with woodful phrensye Chorœbus.

woodhack (ˈwʊdhæk). *Obs.* (or *dial.*) Forms: 5 wodehake, wodake, 6 wo(o)dhacke, 9 woodhack. [f. WOOD *sb.*[1] + stem of HACK *v.*[1] (Cf. *notehake*, NUTHATCH.)] A woodpecker.

c **1440** *Promp. Parv.* 531/2 Wodehake, or reyne fowle. *c* **1475** *Pict. Voc.* in Wr.-Wülcker 763/1 *Hic icter*, a wodake. *a* **1529** SKELTON *P. Sparowe* 418 The woodhacke, that syngeth chur Horsly, as he had the mur. **1530** PALSGR. 289/2 Wodhacke a byrde. **1885** SWAINSON *Prov. Names Birds* 100 Green woodpecker (*Gecinus viridis*)..Wood hack (Lincoln).

So †ˈ**woodˌhacker** (*rare*).

1548 THOMAS *Ital. Dict.* (1550), *Picchio*, a woodhacker or a woodwall.

†ˈ**woodhede.** *Obs.* Forms: 3 wod(h)ed, 4 wod(e)hede. [f. WOOD *a.* + *-hede*, -HEAD.] Madness, extreme folly.

c **1250** *Gen. & Ex.* 533 Wimmen..swilc woded wenten on, Golhed hunkinde he gunnen don. *Ibid.* 3539 Swilc wodhed ðis folc cam on, Ðat he seiden to aaraon, 'Mac vs godes foren us to gon'. **1303** R. BRUNNE *Handl. Synne* 9017 Twelue folys a karolle dyȝt; Yn wodehed, as hyt were yn cuntek. **1340** *Ayenb.* 18 Þe oþer ontreuþe þet comþ of prede is wodhede.

ˈ**wood-hen.** [f. WOOD *sb.*[1] + HEN *sb.*]

1. A female woodcock. Now *rare*.

Formerly, like the woodcock, often rendered as a tenant's due.

1281-2 *Yorkshire Inquis.* (Yorks. Rec. Soc. 1892) I. 248 [One fowl at Christmas, called] le Wodehen. **1343** in Blount *Fragm. Antiq.* (1815) 358 Reddendo..et unam Wed-henne. **1371** *Close Roll* m. 4 *dorso*, Tercia pars gallinarum illarum que erunt leuate infra dominium de Groby que vocantur le Wodehennes. *c* **1520** *Dial. Creatures Moralised* lxxi. A A iij, Ornix the wodehenne espyed the eggis of a Pecocke. **1612** *Reg. Mag. Sig. Scot.* 280/2 Cum silvarum gallinis lie wodehennis. **1836-48** B. D. WALSH *Aristoph., Clouds* IV. iv, I will not pay one groat to anyone, Who's ass enough to misname woodhens 'woodcocks'. **1901** RHYS *Celtic Folklore* i. 55 The wife then flew away like a wood-hen..into the lake.

2. Any flightless rail of the genus *Ocydromus*, of New Zealand and other Pacific islands: = WEKA.

1773 COOK *Voy. South Pole* I. iv. (1777) I. 73 In the bottom of this arm or cove [of Dusky Bay] we found many ducks, wood hens, and other wild fowl. **1845**, **1873** [see WEKA].

woodhenge (wʊdˈhɛndʒ). *Archæol.* [f. WOOD *sb.*[1], after STONEHENGE.] A henge (a prehistoric circular bank enclosing a circular ditch) believed to have contained a circular timber structure, as represented by a ring of post holes; *spec.* (with capital initial) and orig., the proper name of the first example of this kind to be discovered, near Stonehenge.

1927 M. E. CUNNINGTON in *Antiquity* Mar. (*caption to plate between pp. 92 and 93*) 'Woodhenge': oblique view from the south. **1927** *Times* 28 Nov. 17/5 Woodhenge is assigned to the Early Iron Age, say, 500 B.C., with a claim that the close correspondence in lay-out proves it to be a prototype in wood of Stonehenge. **1933** W. A. DUTT *Norfolk* (ed. 8) 60 One of the remarkable prehistoric circles known as 'Woodhenges'. **1935** *Nature* 7 Sept. 365/1 The generic term 'Woodhenge' was first used by Mrs. M. E. Cunnington to describe the circle near Amesbury with wooden uprights in place of stone, which she excavated in 1926 and 1928. The Norfolk Woodhenge, which was discovered from the air in 1929, was known from air photographs to be a striking example of the type. **1939** JOYCE *Finnegans Wake* 596 The Diggins, Woodhenge, as to hang out at. **1951** [see HENGE[2]]. **1970** *Sci. Amer.* May 58 The four largest henge monuments in England, each surrounded by earthworks measuring more than 1,000 feet in diameter, are Avebury and three woodhenges. **1977** *Griffith Observer* (Griffith Observatory, Los Angeles) May 14/2 The Cahotian circles bore a superficial resemblance to neolithic timber structures like Woodhenge, near Stonehenge... Wittry therefore dubbed Circle 2 as an 'American Woodhenge'.

wood-house (ˈwʊdhaʊs). [HOUSE *sb.*[1] 3.] A house, shed, or room in which wood is stored.

[**1274** *Close Roll 2 Edw. I* m. 10 De wodehusis videlicet Johanne Heruy pro quatuor acris & dimidis terre quatuor solid.] **1356-7** *Abingdon Rolls* (Camden) 13 In.. emendacione ostij de le Wodehous, vs. viij d. *c* **1450** *Godstow Reg.* 318 In the which mese is I-conteyned:—j halle, with ij. celers; j kechyn,..j doffe hous; j wodehous. **1570** LEVINS *Manip.* 225/16 A Wodehouse, *lignarium*. **1674** T. FLATMAN *Poems, To Mr. Austin* 14 Thus a black velvet Casket hides a Jewel; And a dark woodhouse, wholesome winter fuel. *a* **1721** PRIOR *Dial. Locke & Montaigne* Wks. 1907 II. 243 To the Coal hole or woodhouse? **1833** LOUDON *Encycl. Cottage Archit.* §721 The Coal-house and the Wood-house should always be adjoining the kitchen. **1856** MISS YONGE *Daisy Chain* I. viii, They claimed him for a good game at play in the wood-house.

woodhouse, var. WOODWOSE.

woodhouseite (ˈwʊdhaʊsaɪt). *Min.* [f. the name of C. D. *Woodhouse*, 20th-c. U.S. mineral collector + -ITE[1].] A hydrated sulphate and phosphate of calcium and aluminium, $CaAl_3(PO_4)(SO_4)(OH)_6$, found as colourless rhombohedral crystals and belonging to the beudantite group.

1937 D. M. LEMMON in *Amer. Mineralogist* XXII. 943 Woodhouseite is a late hydrothermal mineral lining vugs in quartz veins that cross the andalusite zones [in a Californian deposit]. **1980** *Mineral. Mag.* XXXI. 318/2 Heating such minerals as apatite..and woodhouseite to 600°–800° followed by quenching destabilizes these phosphates and allows more complete extraction of their uranium content.

woodie (ˈwʊdɪ). [-IE.] *colloq.* abbrev. of WOOD-PIGEON.

1947 *Contemp. Rev.* June 368 Their habits were not so regular as the woodies. **1960** *Farmer & Stockbreeder* 23 Feb. 57/3 These birds eat wood pigeons' eggs... Some keen observers estimate that something like 80 per cent of the 'woodies'' eggs that are laid are so destroyed. **1972** *Shooting Times & Country Mag.* 4 Mar. 17/3 There shouldn't be many woodies remaining in the area. **1980** G. HAMMOND *Reward Game* ix. 129 Do you want sixty-odd woodies for the freezer?

woodie, var. WIDDY; obs. f. WOODY *a.*

woodie, var. WOODY *sb.*

woodiness (ˈwʊdɪnɪs). [f. WOODY + -NESS.] The quality or condition of being woody.

1. Woody texture, consistence, or appearance.

1601 HOLLAND *Pliny* XV. xxviii. I. 450 Some fruits,.. neither without in shell, nor within-forth in kernell, have any of this woodinesse. **1670** EVELYN *Sylva* xxx. (ed. 2) 149 The Vatican Ilex, the Vine which was grown to that bulk and Woodinesse, as to make Columns in Juno's Temple. **1760** ELLIS in *Phil. Trans.* LI. 933 It promises, from the thickness and woodiness of its stem,..to become a shrub of six or seven feet high. **1850** NICHOL *Archit. Heavens* i. 17 Until individual trees could no longer be distinguished, and the view terminated in a..vague appearance, which I may be permitted to call a diffused woodiness. **1860** RUSKIN *Mod. Paint.* V. VI. viii. §10. 71 A very characteristic example of two faults in tree-drawing; namely, the loss not only of grace and spring, but of woodiness.

2. The condition of being full of woods or forests; prevalence or abundance of woodland; *concr.* woody growth.

1796 MARSHALL *Planting* I. 119 By Woody Waste [is meant] grass land over-run with rough woodiness. **1799** STUART in Owen *Wellesley's Desp.* (1877) 114 Their movements were so well concealed by the woodiness of the country. **1869** BLACKIE *Lett. to Wife* (1909) 180 The rich-sloping..woodiness that you remember on the Rhine.

wooding (ˈwʊdɪŋ), *vbl. sb.* [OE. *wudung*, f. *wudian*: see WOOD *v.*[2] and -ING[1].]

1. The action of procuring or taking in wood for fuel, esp. on board a vessel; also, feeding a fire with wood.

c **1000** ÆLFRIC *Hom.* II. 222 þæt Israhela folc ȝeðafode þæt sume ða hæðenan on heora ðeowte leofodon, to wudunge and to wæterunge. **1613** J. SARIS *Voy. Japan* (Hakl. Soc.) 69, I gaue leaue to as manye as would to goe ashoare, hauing done watring and wooding. **1745** P. THOMAS *Jrnl. Anson's Voy.* 116 Besides our constant Employment in Wooding and Watering. **1866** HOWELLS *Venetian Life* 35 By dint of constant wooding I contrived to warm mine [*sc.* stove]. **1875** BEDFORD *Sailor's Pocket Bk.* v. (ed. 2) 145 Notice any convenient creeks or rivers for wooding or watering.

attrib. **1789** PORTLOCK *Voy.* 314 At this island I would advise the watering and wooding business to be done. **1804** GILLESPIE in A. Duncan *Nelson* (1806) 222 The wooding and watering parties. **1863** RUSSELL *Diary North & South* I. 269 The scenery and the scenes were just the same as yesterday's—high banks, cotton-slides, wooding stations.

2. The action of planting ground with trees; *concr.* a plantation or collection of trees. *Sc.*

1788 PICKEN *Poems* 76 The mantlan ivy clings To wooding in the grove. **1790** A. WILSON IN *Poems & Lit. Prose* (1876) II. 106 Deep in lanely woodings lost. **1827** STEUART *Planter's G.* (1828) 355 The wooding of two acres of ground..as a Close Plantation. **1875** W. MCILWRAITH *Guide Wigtownshire* 103 Much of the wooding which gives variety..to the landscape.

woodish (ˈwʊdɪʃ), *a.* Now *rare.* Also 6 wodd-, 6-7 woodd-. [f. WOOD *sb.*[1] + -ISH[1].]

1. Having the nature, quality, or consistence of wood; (somewhat) woody.

1562 TURNER *Herbal* II. 40b, The braunches [of Lithospermon] are..strong..and woddishe. *Ibid.* 87 A.. woddish torche or fyrebrande. **1620** VENNER *Via Recta* vii. 115 Quince-Peares are of a verie hard and wooddish substance. **1721** MORTIMER *Husb.* II. 214 Bastard-bittany.. having many brown woodish Stalks.

†**2.** Belonging to or characteristic of the woods or wooded country; sylvan. *Obs.*

1588 T. THOMAS *Lat. Dict.* (1615), *Faunicus*..wilde, wooddish, rude. **1612** DRAYTON *Poly-olb.* xi. 116 Wanton woodish sports. **1630** CAPT. J. SMITH *Trav. & Adv.* 2 He retired himselfe into a little wooddie pasture... Here..he built a Pavillion of boughes... His friends perswaded one Seignior Theadora Polaloga..to insinuate into his wooddish acquaintances.

†ˈ**woodist.** *Obs. nonce-wd.* In 7 wooddist. [f. as prec. + -IST.] = WOODWOSE, WOODMAN[1] 4.

1613 T. CAMPION *Relat. Royal Entert.* B 1, Such musick as the wilde Wooddists shall bee ashamed to heare the report of it.

ˈ**wood-kern, -kerne.** *Hist.* Also 6 -karne, 7 -carne, -cerne. [tr. Ir. *ceithearnach coille* (*ceithearn* KERN *sb.*[1], *coill* wood).] An Irish outlaw or robber haunting woods or wild country; such outlaws collectively.

Used by Holland to render L. *latro*.

1548 *State Papers Irel., Edw. VI*, I. 84 (MS.) The kynd of peopull which we call outlawes & wodkerne. **1581** DERRICKE (*title*) The Image of Irelande, with a Discoverie of Woodkarne, wherein is..expressed, the Nature..of the.. Wilde Irishe Woodkarne, their notable aptnesse celeritie and pronesse to Rebellion. **1600** HOLLAND *Livy* XL. ix. 1065 The same is said unto me..which were more beseeming to speake unto a wood-kerne and robber by the high-way side. **1617** MORYSON *Itin.* II. 101 Cormacke O Neale..was of a mild honest disposition..yet..little lesse barberous then the better sort of wood kern. **1632** LITHGOW *Trav.* v. 210 The Lawlesse Wood Carnes in Ireland. **1656** in P. H. Hore *Hist. Wexford* (1911) VI. 516 Mount Leinster..which by reason of the great adjoining woods hath always beene haunted with Irish Toryes or Woodcernes. **1845** PETRIE *Eccl. Archit. Irel.* 96 At the close of the sixteenth century, these Towers became the receptacles of thieves and wood-kerne.

ˈ**wood-knife.**

1. A dagger of short sword (KNIFE *sb.* 1 b) used by huntsmen for cutting up the game, or generally as a weapon. *arch.* or *Hist.*

1426 *E.E. Wills* (1882) 76 A swerd harnesed, a wodeknyf harnesed, and a Dagger. **1470-85** MALORY *Arthur* XVIII. xxi. 764 They were shoters, and coude wel kylle a dere..and they dayly bare bowes and arowes, hornes & wood knyues. **1568** FULWELL *Like Will to Like* E ij b, Come no neer me you knaues for your life. Lest I stick you bothe with this woodknife. **1611** COTGR., *Malcus*, A Fauchion, Hangar, Wood-knife. *a* **1650** *Boy & Mantle* xxxviii. in Child *Ballads* I. 273/2 He pulld forth a wood kniffe,..He brought in the bores head. **1721** STRYPE *Eccl. Mem.* III. xxvi. 212 He drew his woodknife and hit the priest on the head. **1821** SCOTT *Kenilw.* xxxiv, The gay baldric, which sustained a bugle-horn, and a wood-knife instead of a sword. **1867** MORRIS *Jason* I. 83 The wood-knife at the side.

2. A large knife for cutting off branches or twigs.

1880 C. R. MARKHAM *Peruv. Bark* vii. 54 The *cateador*.. conducted the party for hours through the tangled brush-wood,..using the wood-knife at every step.

woodland (ˈwʊdlənd). Forms: see WOOD *sb.*[1] and LAND *sb.*[1] **1. a.** Land covered with wood, i.e. with trees; a wooded region or piece of ground.

869 in Birch *Cartul. Sax.* II. 141 Æȝþer ȝe etelond ȝe eyrð lond ȝe eac wudulond. *c* **1205** LAY. 1699 Wenne hundes hine bistondeð i þon wode-londe. *a* **1400** *Sir Perc.* 208 In that wodde land. **1456** SIR G. HAYE *Gov. Princes* Wks. (S.T.S.) II. 137 Cow or calf..in wodland upbrocht. **1536** BENESE

Meas. Land A ij, Woodlande and fyldelande be not measured with perches of lyke and equale length. **1573** TUSSER *Husb.* (1878) 31 What champion vseth, That woodland refuseth. **1610** HOLLAND *Camden's Brit.* 567 In the mids of this Woodland standeth Coventrey. **1622** SELDEN *Illustr. Drayton's Poly-olb.* xiii. 15 What is now the Woodland in Warwickshire, was heretofore part of a larger Weald or Forest, called Arden. **1669** WORLIDGE *Syst. Agric.* (1681) 88 There's no Field Champion-Land of that yearly value for either Corn or Pasture, as is the Wood-land. **1709** PRIOR *Henry & Emma* 307 She to the Wood-land with an Exile ran. **1763** W. ROBERTS *Nat. Hist. Florida* 34 The number of marshes and woodlands prevented the horse from pursuing them. **1793** M. CUTLER in *Life*, etc. (1888) II. 276 Tracts of woodland never yet cleared, but kept inclosed for a supply of fuel and timber. **1824** W. IRVING *T. Trav.* II. iv. I. 214 A hunting-seat of Queen Elizabeth,..when the neighbourhood was all woodland. **1867** 'OUIDA' *Cecil Castlemaine* i, The morning was fair and cloudless, its sunbeams piercing through the darkest glades in the woodlands.

b. *attrib.* Of or pertaining to woodland; used, situated, dwelling, or growing in woodland; consisting of or containing woodland; belonging to or characteristic of woodland; sylvan. **woodland caribou**, a northern caribou, *Rangifer tarandus*, found in forested areas of Canada.

† *woodland penny, silver* = *wood-penny, -silver*: see WOOD *sb.*[1] 10.

1351–2 *Durham Acc. Rolls* (Surtees) 552, vij li. iij s. i d. de Wodeland penys ad festum Nat. beati Joh. Bap. **1396–7** *Ibid.* 136 Ep'o pro Wodlandsiluer, vj d. **1536–7** *Ibid.* 674 Pro Wodlandpennez ejusdem ville. **1536** BENESE *Meas. Land* A ij, Two maner of perches, the woodlande perche and the fyldeland perche... The woodlande perche is communely .xviii. foote in length. But in some places it is longer. **1577** HARRISON *England* III. xii. 111 b/1 in *Holinshed*, Adders.. are found only in our woodland countryes and highest groundes. **1601** SHAKS. *All's Well* IV. v. 49, I am a woodland fellow sir, that alwaies loued a great fire. **1610** HOPTON *Baculum Geodæt.* VI. lii. 264 The woodland measure of 18 feete in the pole. **1697** DRYDEN *Virg. Georg.* IV. 783 Adore the Woodland Pow'rs with Pray'r. **1725** POPE *Odyss.* IX. 178 Rows'd by the woodland nymphs.. The mountain goats came bounding o'er the lawn. **1798** WORDSW. *Tables Turned* iii, Come, hear the woodland linnet. —— *We are Seven* iii, She had a rustic, woodland air. **1805** SCOTT *Last Minstrel* III. xiii, They came to a woodland brook. **1831** —— *Quentin D.* Introd., In the more woodland districts of Flanders. **1854** MAYNE REID *Young Voyageurs* 154 He had killed three caribou, of the large variety known as 'woodland caribou'. **1855** KINGSLEY *Westw. Ho!* xxv, Garments..rather the worse for a fortnight's woodland travel. **1855** TENNYSON *Maud* I. XII. ii, Gathering woodland lilies. **1877** BLACK *Green Past.* i, The secrecy and silence of the still woodland ways. **1879** *Cassell's Nat. Hist.* III. 68 The Woodland Caribou and the Barren-ground Caribou are the names given to a larger and a smaller breed in Canada. **1902** CORNISH *Naturalist Thames* 76 The [grey] partridge is becoming a woodland bird. **1921** *Daily Colonist* (Victoria, B.C.) 30 Oct. 21/1 The only caribou I've ever hunted were in the Kootenays, woodland caribou. **1965** F. SYMINGTON *Tuktu* 44 The woodland caribou eats about the same forage as the barren-ground caribou.

2. *Archæol.* (With capital initial.) The name of a culture that existed in eastern North America between approximately 1000 B.C. and A.D. 1000, characterized by agriculture, hunting, burial mounds, and a distinctive style of pottery.

1917 C. WISSLER *Amer. Indian* xiv. 219 We now come to the so-called Eastern Woodland area, the characterization of which is difficult. **1946** *Nature* 2 Nov. 615/2 A single mound-group belongs to a later phase, the Middle Mississippi, and the village site and one mound are ascribed to the Woodland-culture pattern, probably still later. **1967** *Listener* 2 Mar. 290/2 Most of the characteristic traits of the late, *i.e.*, the Woodland, period are found in incipient form in the late Archaic, and it is a period about which it is difficult to generalize. **1977** G. CLARK *World Prehistory* (ed. 3) ix. 408 Hunting and fishing continued to play significant roles..even during the terminal phase of the Woodland culture (A.D. 900–1300).

Hence **'woodlanded** *ppl. a.*, covered with woodland; **'woodlander**, an inhabitant of the woodland; *occas.* an animal that lives in woodland; also, a plant whose natural habitat is in woodland.

1774 T. WEST *Antiq. Furness* (1805) 40 The woodlanders of High Furness were charged with the care of the flocks and herds. **1810** WORDSW. *Prose Wks.* (1876) II. 259 A few vassals following the employment of shepherds or woodlanders. **1887** HARDY (*title*) The Woodlanders. **1889** F. A. KNIGHT *By Leafy Ways* 61 Another much calumniated woodlander, the badger. **1945** J. BETJEMAN *New Bats in Old Belfries* 6 By roads 'not adopted', by woodlanded ways She drove to the club in the late summer haze. **1948** W. ARNOLD-FORSTER *Shrubs for Milder Counties* iv. 113 *D[aphne] Blagayana*. A dwarf woodlander, evergreen. **1974** *Country Life* 12 Dec. 1896/1 American woodlanders, such as shortias and erythroniums revel in it [*sc* beech leaf-mould]. **1982** *Garden* CVII. 487/2 All [clintonias] are woodlanders or shade plants.

woodlark ('wʊdlɑːk). Forms and etym.: see WOOD *sb.*[1] and LARK *sb.*[1] A species of lark (*Alauda arborea*) which perches on trees; distinguished from the skylark by having a shorter tail, more variegated plumage, and a different song.

c **1325** *Gloss. W. de Bibbesw.* in Wright *Voc.* 164 La calaundre [*gloss* wode-larke]. *c* **1340** *Nominale* (Skeat) 808 Esperuer tele et chalaundre and wodelarke. **1544** TURNER *Avium Praecip.* E 1 b, Superset tertium galeritæ genus, Germanis copera. *Marg.* a uuodlerck. **1686** [see SKYLARK *sb.* 1]. **1769** G. WHITE *Selborne* (1789) 69 In hot summer nights woodlarks soar to a prodigious height and hang singing in the air. **1818** KEATS *Walking in Scotland* 14 Wood-lark may sing from sandy fern. **1868** MORRIS *Earthly Par., Man born to be King* 1496 Mid them [*sc.* yew-trees] did the woodlark flit, Or sang well sheltered from the wind.

woodless ('wʊdlɪs), *a.* [f. WOOD *sb.*[1] + -LESS.] Destitute of wood or woods; treeless.

1551 TURNER *Herbal* I. P ij, Our heth groweth in playnes ..and vpon sum wodles hylles. *a* **1661** FULLER *Worthies, Norfolk* (1662) 246 Here are Fens and Heaths,..and Meddows and Pasture, and Arable and Woody, and (generally) woodless land. **1796** MORSE *Amer. Geog.* I. 141 The coasts are..rocky..and woodless. **1835** J. DUNCAN *Beetles* (Nat. Lib.) 96 Travellers across the woodless pampas sometimes make their fire of a dead horse. **1881** MORGAN *Contrib. Amer. Ethnol.* 106 The woodless plains of the Sacramento.

woodlet ('wʊdlɪt). *rare.* [f. WOOD *sb.*[1] + -LET.] A little wood.

1821 FOSBROKE *Berkeley MSS.* 226 This elegant woodlet. **1890** *An Australian Girl* II. v. 57 Groves and woodlets.

wood-louse ('wʊdlaʊs). Pl. **wood-lice** (-laɪs). [f. WOOD *sb.*[1] + LOUSE *sb.*]

1. A small isopod crustacean of the genus *Oniscus* or family *Oniscidæ*; *esp.* the common species *O. asellus*, found in old wood, under stones, etc., and having the property of rolling itself up into a ball; also called †*cheeselip, hog-louse, slater, sow-bug*, etc.

1611 COTGR. s.v. *Anthoine*, The vermine called, a Cheslop, or Wood-louse. **1663** BOYLE *Usef. Exp. Nat. Philos.* II. 154 Those vile Insects commonly called in English, Wood-lice, or Sows. **1725** SWIFT *Wood an Insect* 3 An Insect they call a Wood-Louse, That folds up itself in itself for a House. **1844** HOOD *Haunted House* 177 The wood-louse dropped and rolled into a ball. **1869** MRS. I. L. BISHOP *Notes on Old Edinb.* 11 The walls were black and rotten, and alive with woodlice.

2. Locally or occas. applied to various other small invertebrates found in woodwork or in woods, or resembling the crustacean described in 1.

a. A white ant or termite. **b.** A species of infusorian. **c.** One or more species of mite or other parasite. **d.** Various insects of the family *Psocidæ*, as the book-louse and death-watch. **e.** A millepede of the family *Glomeridæ*; a pill-millepede.

1666 J. DAVIES *Hist. Caribby Isles* 149 A kind of Ant.. bred of rotten wood, and thence some call them Wood-lice. **1769** ELLIS in *Phil. Trans.* LIX. 150 The *volvox oniscus*, or wood-louse. **1770** J. R. FORSTER tr. *Kalm's Trav. N. Amer.* (1772) II. 133 Wood-lice (*Acarus Americanus*, Linn.) abound here. **1781** [see *wood-ant*, WOOD *sb.*[1] 10 b]. **1819** D. B. WARDEN *Acc. U.S.* I. 496 Musquitoes and wood-lice [note, *Acarus Americanus*] are most troublesome in thickly wooded vallies. *Ibid.* II. 525 The wood louse, or Chigo, or Bete Rouge (*Acarus sanguinis*). **1825** JAMIESON, *Wood-louse*, a book-worm. **1863** WOOD *Illustr. Nat. Hist.* III. 631 The Great Sea-slater or Sea-woodlouse. *Ibid.* 632 The well-known Pill-woodlouse.

3. *attrib.*

1796 STEDMAN *Surinam* II. xxv. 234 The..bird, which.. the negroes called *woodo-louso-fowlo*, from its feeding on wood-lice. *Ibid.* (Illustration), The Yellow Woodpecker or Wood-louse fowl. **1817** KIRBY & SP. *Entomol.* xxiii. (1818) II. 307 The woodlouse tribe (Oniscidæ). **1854** A. ADAMS, etc. *Man. Nat. Hist.* 267 Woodlouse-Millipedes (Glomeridæ). **1859** P. P. CARPENTER in *Rep. Smithsonian Instit.* (1860) 207 Chitonidæ or Woodlouse shells.

†**'woodly**, *a. Obs. rare.* [OE. *wódlic*: see WOOD *a.* and -LY[1].] Mad, frantic, furious.

c **1000** ÆLFRIC *Hom.* II. 182 Sa eadiȝa Benedictus.. manode þone reðan ehtere þæt he ðære wodlican reðnysse geswice. *c* **1422** HOCCLEVE *Learn to Die* 700 The fyry flaumbes..In which the soules brenne in woodly wyse. **1513** BRADSHAW *St. Werburge* II. 789 Roryng and yellyng his outragious trespase, [he] Tore his tonge a-sonder in wodely violence.

'woodly, *adv. Obs.* or *dial.* Forms: see WOOD *a.* [OE. *wódlíce*: see WOOD *a.* and -LY[2].] Madly, ferociously, furiously, wildly, passionately.

c **1000** ÆLFRIC *Hom.* II. 230 Hi wæron..mid deofle afyllede, ðaða hi swa wodlice to ðam welwillendan Hælende spræcon. *c* **1000** tr. *Basil's Admon.* vi. (Norman 1849) 46 Ðam wulfe ȝelic ðe wodlice abiteð ða..sceap. *c* **1000** in Assmann *Hom.* (1889) 6/145 þam unðeawfæstum, ðe wodlice drincað and heora ȝewitt amyrrað. *c* **1205** LAY. 3201 He mochul a þa wodeloker wilnede þeos mæidenes. *c* **1330** *Arth. & Merl.* 9426 King Margaras..Ban asailed wodeliche. *c* **1350** *Will. Palerne* 550 þat i wrouȝt so wodly & wold to him speke. *c* **1385** CHAUCER *L.G.W.* 1752 *Lucrece*, Desyr That in his herte brende as any fer So wodly that his wit is al forgetyn. ? *a* **1400** *Morte Arth.* 2827 Wyes..appone wyght horsez, Walopande wodely. *c* **1400** *Destr. Troy* 3694 The wyndes full wodely wackont anon. *a* **1500** *Hist. K. Boccus & Sydracke* (? 1510) P iv b, Yf he loue one wodly. **1556** OLDE *Antichrist* 163 Antichrist layeth about him so woodly. **1630** J. TAYLOR (Water P.) *Anagr. & Sonn.* Wks. II. 251/1 He rose..And frantickly ran woodly through the wood. **1725** RAMSAY *Gentle Sheph.* V. iii, They skelpit me when woodly fleid.

woodman[1] ('wʊdmən). Pl. **woodmen**. Forms and etym.: see WOOD *sb.*[1] and MAN *sb.*[1] (Cf. WOODSMAN.)

The meaning in the following is uncertain:—**972** in Birch *Cartul. Sax.* III. 603 Fram hwitingho to wudemannes tune. **1275** *Rot. Hundr.* II. 19 Johanni Wodeman.

1. One who hunts game in a wood or forest; a huntsman. *Obs.* or *arch.*

c **1410** *Master of Game* (MS. Digby 182) xxxiii, As of þe manere howe he shulde be vndo y passe ouere lightly, for þer is no wodemann nor good hunter in Inglonde, but þei cann do it wele ynowgh. **1555** *Instit. Gentl.* H v, Ther is a saying emonge hunters that he cannot be a gentleman which loueth not hawkyng and hunting, whiche I haue heard olde woodmen wel allowe. **1598** SHAKS. *Merry W.* V. v. 30 Am I a Woodman, ha? Speake I like Herne the Hunter? **1616** BOYS *Expos. Proper Ps.* xlvii. 9 Wks. (1629) 935 Woodmen say that Deere are most circumspect in fat pasture. **1676** SHADWELL *Virtuoso* III, I have taken more Pains to single you out, than ever Wood-man did for a Deer. **1805** SCOTT *Last Minstrel* VI. vii, Conrad..Was by a wood-man's lyme-dog found. [**1835** W. IRVING *Tour Prairies* xi. 85 He looked down with contempt upon the rangers, as..inexperienced woodmen, but little skilled in hunting lore.]

b. *fig.* or *allusively.*

1590 GREENE *Never too late* (1600) 47 He was not..so ill a Woodman to giue ouer the chace at the first default. **1603** SHAKS. *Meas. for M.* IV. iii. 170. **1618** FLETCHER *Chances* I. ix, I see ye are a wood-man, and can chuse Your dear. **1673** DRYDEN *Marr. à la Mode* II. i. 18 Has the old Cupid, your Father, chosen well for you? is he a good Woodman?

2. One who looks after the trees in a wood or forest; one who fells or lops trees for timber or fuel; also, one who provides or purveys wood.

1426 LYDG. *De Guil. Pilgr.* 17745 Her ys a woode off lytel prys, Wych a woodeman selleth me. **1530** PALSGR. 289/2 Wodman that lyveth by fellyng wode, *bocquillon*. **1585** HIGINS *Junius' Nomencl.* 519/2 *Dendrophori*,..woodemen or such as carrie wood about streetes to be sold. **1634** MILTON *Comus* 484 Either som one like us night-founder'd here, Or els som neighbour Wood-man. **1726** J. LAURENCE *New Syst. Agric.* 229 Of the Aspen Tree our Woodmen make Hoops, Firewood, and Coals. **1800** CAMPBELL *Beech-Tree's Petition* 2 Spare, woodman, spare the beechen tree. **1856** KANE *Arctic Expl.* II. vii. 83 Bonsall and Petersen are now woodmen, preparing our daily fuel. **1875** BEDFORD *Sailor's Pocket Bk.* vii. (ed. 2) 250 Each half company providing 2 woodmen, 2 watermen. **1903** MAUD S. RAWSON *Apprentice* 141 The oldest woodmen say that it takes a hundred years to grow a perfect oak for an English ship.

†**3.** A forester having charge of the king's woods.

1594 CROMPTON *Jurisd.* 146 b, Auant que sera perfect Forest, le Roy couient appointer certaine officers, come vn keeper, Forester, Woodmen, Regarders, Agistors. **1604** MANWOOD *Lawes Forest* xxi. (1615) 193 The foresters & woodmen did take no good regard to the forests.

†**4.** An inhabitant of the woods, a wild man, a savage; a person representing one in a pageant, or a figure of one in heraldry: = WOODWOSE. *Obs.*

1442 *Extr. Aberd. Reg.* (1844) I. 9 The fleschowares sal fynd [for a play], twa or four wodmen. **1566** in J. Nicholl *Comp. Ironmongers* (1866) 85 They shall fynde us two woodmen, w[t] clubbes, squibbes and powder. **1601** in Moryson *Itin.* II. (1617) 106 To march..into Colrane..to have brought into subjection all the woodmen. **1660** J. TATHAM *Royal Oake* 10 Several persons in the habit of Wood-men and Wood-Nymphs. **1780** EDMONDSON *Heraldry* II. Gloss., *Woodman*, a name given by several Writers to the wild man, or savage.

5. A workman who makes something of wood, esp. the woodwork of a carriage.

1879 *Cassell's Techn. Educ.* IV. 175/1 When the body is finished from the hands of the woodman, it passes into the hands of the currier. **1908** *Advt.*, Wanted Coach Builders and Wheelwrights.—Good woodman.

Hence **'woodman(s)craft, 'woodmanship**, the business or skill of a woodman; † **'woodmanlike**, † **'woodmanly** *advs.*, in the manner of or befitting a woodman.

c **1410** *Master of Game* (MS. Digby 182) xxxiii, If þe lorde will haue þe deere vndone, he þat he biddeth..shulde vndo hym þe moste wodemanly and clenly þat he cann. And wondreth ye nought, þough y say wodmanly, for it is a poynte of wodemancrafte. **1479** [see WOODSALE]. **1575** GASCOIGNE *Hearbes* 156 Gascoignes woodmanship written to the L. Grey of Wilton. **1627** J. TAYLOR (Water P.) *Armado* Ep. Ded. A 3 b, You know what belongs to the Wood-manship, the Wardship, and Stewardship. *a* **1650** *Marr. Sir Gawaine* in Furniv. & Hales *Percy Folio* I. 106 The kyng in hys hand toke a bowe, And woodmanly he stowpy'd lowe. **1831** SCOTT *Ct. Rob.* xxix, It were bad woodmanship to raise the hollo upon the game, ere it had been driven within compass of the nets. **1881** *Sat. Rev.* 23 July 122/1 Colonel Fraser's political sagacity hardly seems on a par with his woodmanscraft. **1911** A. C. BENSON *Ruskin* v. 180 He was fond of woodmanship. His..hedging-gloves and his chopper were very characteristic signs of his presence.

†**'woodman**[2]. *Obs.* Forms and etym.: see WOOD *a.* and MAN *sb.*[1] A madman, lunatic, maniac.

1297 R. GLOUC. (Rolls) 3338 Hii verde as wodemen; hii wende hii were ynome. *c* **1375** *Sc. Leg. Saints* xi. (*Symon & Iudas*) 412 Wodmen..In quhame þe feyndis þan can dwel. *Ibid.* xix. (*Cristofore*) 285 þe Iugis,..Fore a wodman demyt hym. *c* **1400** *Beryn* 1351 He trampelid fast with his feet, & al to-tare his ere And his visage both, ryȝt as a woodman. **1470–85** MALORY *Arthur* X. xii. 432 Cryenge and rateynge hym as a wood man. **1512** J. PARFRE *Candlemas-Day* in Marriott *Miracle-Plays* (1838) 200 Like as a wodman he gan to fray.

woodmonger ('wʊdˌmʌŋgə(r)). Now *rare* exc. *Hist.* Forms and etym.: see WOOD *sb.*[1] and MONGER *sb.* A dealer in wood; a timber-merchant, or (*esp.*) a seller of wood for fuel.

1260–1 *Cal. Wills Crt. Husting, Lond.* I. (1889) 8 Robert le Wudemongere. **1372** *Ibid.* II. 147 William Wodemongere. **1464** *Rolls of Parlt.* V. 567/2 Carpenters, Woodemongers and Colemakers. **1567** in *Archaeologia* XXXVI. 51 Paide to Mr. Fermer, wodemonger, for a M and iii qrs. of billetts, xviij s. viij d. **1599** SHAKS. *Hen. V*, V. i. 69. **1609** DEKKER *Ravens Alm.* Wks. (Grosart) IV. 186 Winter,..the friend to none but Colliers and Woodmongers. **1632** MASSINGER *City Madam* II. i, Though The dishes were raised one upon another, As woodmongers do billets. **1667** *Lond. Gaz.* No.

215/4 The many great abuses committed by the Company of Woodmongers in the Sale..of Fuel. **1720** STRYPE *Stow's Surv.* II. VI. v. 76/1 Two Woodmongers Wharfs for the Sale of Fuel. **1722** DE FOE *Plague* (1754) 254 Vessels, such as the Wood-mongers, that is the Wharf Keepers, or Coal-Sellers furnished. **1821** SCOTT *Kenilw.* iii, These sturdy oaks had long since become the property of some honest woodmonger. **1908** W. G. COLLINGWOOD *Scandinavian Britain* 111 'Six score to the hundred' is still familiar to Lake District gardeners and wood-mongers.

'woodness. *Obs.* exc. *dial.* or *arch.* Forms: see WOOD *a.* [OE. *wódnes*: see WOOD *a.* and -NESS.]

1. Mental derangement, insanity, mania, frenzy, lunacy, craziness: = MADNESS 1.

c **1000** ÆLFRIC *Hom.* I. 458 Þa ȝeaxode se cyning Polimius be ðam witseocum menn, hu se apostol hine fram ðære wodnysse ahredde. **1382** WYCLIF *Acts* xxvi. 24 Poul, thou maddist..; manye lettris turnen thee to woodnesse. **1493** H. PARKER *Dives & Pauper* v. xviii. (W. de W. 1496) 220/1 Yf a man in his woodness & rauynge slee man & woman or childe. **1565** GOLDING *Ovid's Met.* III. (1593) 72 Drunken woodnes wrought by wine. **1605** VERSTEGAN *Dec. Intell.* (1634) 238 Wee yet retayne in some parts of England the word *wodnes* for furiousnesse or madnesse. **1657** THORNLEY tr. *Longus Daphnis & Chloe* 60 Their minds were struck with a kind of Woodnesse. **1803** W. S. ROSE *Amadis* 128 Wrapt in imagin'd flames to woodness stung Deep in a roaring stream, she headlong sprung.

2. Extravagant folly or recklessness; vehemence of passion or desire; wildness, infatuation. Cf. MADNESS 2.

c **1000** in Assmann *Hom.* (1889) 60/212 Þa sæt he.. tælende þone hælend..His wodnys wearð ȝewrecen swa þurh god. *c* **1374** CHAUCER *Troylus* III. 1382 They callen loue a woodnesse or folye. **1387** [see WOOD *a.* 2 b]. *c* **1430** LYDG. *Min. Poems* (Percy Soc.) 76 A woode wisdom, and a wise woodenesse. **1435** MISYN *Fire of Love* II. viii. 90 Here is lufe with-outen meyknes, wodnes ful likynge. **1484** CAXTON *Fables of Auian* vi, Now perceyue I wel thy foly and grete wodenesse. **1588** A. KING tr. *Canisius' Catech.* II. i viij, It is extreme vodnes to doubt quhither thay ar to be kept haly or nocht. **1615** CROOKE *Body of Man* 284 When their genitalles are full of seede they grow into woodnesse and rage of lust.

3. Violent anger, wrath, fury, rage; extreme fierceness, ferocity, savageness, cruelty. Cf. MADNESS 3.

c **1000** ÆLFRIC *Hom.* II. 30 þæt earme wif ȝelyfde his waelhreowum ȝeðeahte, and wearð mid maran wodnysse astyrod. *a* **1340** HAMPOLE *Psalter* vi. 1 Lord in thi wodnes argu me noght. *Ibid.*, Wodness or ire is a stirynge of mannys will, excitand to vengaunce. *c* **1375** *Sc. Leg. Saints* ii. (*Paulus*) 704 Nero wes brocht In sa mekill wodnes of thocht, þat he his awne modir gert sla. *c* **1400** *St. Alexius* (Vernon) 474 Heo ter his cloþus al in sunder, in a gret woodnesse. **1460** CAPGRAVE *Chron.* (Rolls) 237 In her wodnes thei kyllid the bischop of Cauntirbiry. *a* **1533** LD. BERNERS *Gold. Bk. M. Aurel.* (1546) R viij, You haue chased the bulle, and scaped his woodnes. **1550** BALE *Engl. Votaries* II. Q j, He fretted for wodenes, and was angry with himselfe. **1577** HANMER *Anc. Eccl. Hist.* (1663) 166 He proceeding in cruelty, and daily increasing his savage woodness against the Saints of God. **1600** HOLLAND *Livy* XXVI. xiii. 593 Wild and savage beasts..madded..with blind rage and woodnesse against one. **1825** J. WILSON *Noct. Ambr.* Wks. 1856 I. 12 Whiles I just girn out-by yonner, wi' perfect wudness when I think o' you..rinning down me, and ither men of genius. **1906** DOUGHTY *Dawn in Britain* XIII. IV. 36 So woodness kindles his great heart, gainst Romans.

b. *fig.* Excessive violence or severity, 'fury' (of pain, or of inanimate things, as wind, fire, etc.).

a **1400** *Stockholm Med. MS.* II. 704 in *Anglia* XVIII. 324 It doth noth awey all þe pyne, But all þe wodnesse for þe tyme. *c* **1400** *Destr. Troy* 2008 þe fuerse wyndes, And the wodenes of waghes. *c* **1425** *Found. St. Bartholomew's* (E.E.T.S.) 21 His kechyn was a-fyre sodenly, and likely to perissh with wooddenes of fyre. **1450–1530** *Myrr. our Ladye* II. 189 Fayre flowres wherof the nynte parte faded by the wodnesse of the northe. **1508** DUNBAR *Gold. Targe* 229 The Lord of Wyndis, wyth wodenes, God Eolus, his bugill blew. **1557** *Tottel's Misc.* (Arb.) 127 No rage of drenching sea, nor woodenesse of the winde.

'wood-nymph.

1. A nymph of the woods; a superhuman being imagined as a beautiful maiden inhabiting woods; a dryad or hamadryad.

1577 GRANGE *Golden Aphrod.* M ij b, The Woodnymphes likewise followed moste nicely tripping. **1634** MILTON *Comus* 120 By dimpled Brook, and Fountain brim, The Wood-Nymphs deckt with Daisies trim, Their merry wakes and pastimes keep. **1667** —— *P.L.* IX. 386 She..like a Wood-Nymph light Oread or Dryad..Betook her to the Groves. **1794** MRS. RADCLIFFE *Myst. Udolpho* xxxvii, Marble statues of wood-nymphs. **1821** SCOTT *Kenilw.* xxvii, She possessed the form and hue of a wood-nymph, with the beauty of a sylph. **1867** MORRIS *Jason* I. 92 Then mayst thou find, In some fair grassy place, the wood-nymphs kind.

b. *transf.* (cf. DRYAD 2 a, NYMPH *sb.* 2).

1780 MRS. COWLEY *Belle's Stratagem* II. i, The maxims you learnt among the wood-nymphs, in Shropshire, won't pass current here.

2. a. Name for certain species of humming-bird, esp. of the genus *Thalurania* (Gould). **b.** Collector's name for moths of the genus *Eudryas.*

1861 GOULD *Trochilidæ* II. Plates 99–109. **1885** *Riverside Nat. Hist.* (1888) II. 462 The beautiful wood-nymph, *Eudryas grata.*

'wood-oil. A name for several oils or oily substances obtained from various trees: (*a*) from the East Indian *Dipterocarpus alatus* and other species (= GURJUN *balsam* or *oil*); (*b*) from the East Indian Satinwood, *Chloroxylon Swietenia*; (*c*) from the seeds of the Chinese Oil-tree or Varnish-tree, *Aleurites cordata* (also called *tung-oil*, from Chinese *yu-t'ung* or *t'ung-tzŭ-shu*, native names of the tree), used chiefly for varnishing woodwork. Also *attrib.*

1759 in A. Dalrymple *Oriental Repertory* (1793) I. 109 The Bûraghmah Dominions yield Gold,..Earth-Oil, and Wood-Oil. **1800** *Asiat. Ann. Reg., Misc. Tracts* 95/1. **1841** W. ROBINSON *Assam* 62 The Dipterocarpus levis..yields the thin liquid balsam commonly known by the name of 'wood oil', and which is much used in painting. **1857** HENFREY *Bot.* §438 *Chloroxylon Swietenia* furnishes East Indian Satin-wood, and an oil called Wood-oil is obtained from it. **1881** *Spons' Encycl. Manuf.* IV. 1411 Tung-, Tree-, or Wood-oil..is a product of the so-called 'oil-tree' of China, Cochin China, and Japan. **1890** HOSIE *Three Yrs. W. China* 18 The wood-oil tree..was scattered about among the fields.

‖**woodoo** (wu:'du:). Also 8 wodou, 9 wazzoo, wuzu. [Turkish *wazū.*] The minor ablution of the Muslims. Cf. ABDEST.

1794 P. RUSSELL *A. Russell's Hist. Aleppo* I. 194 The ordinary preparation for prayer, consists in washing the face, hands, and feet, and is termed Wodou. **1813** J. FORBES *Oriental Mem.* III. 124 Ablutions, called the wazzoo, preparatory to the namauz, or prayer. **1836** LANE *Mod. Egypt.* I. ii. 67 The father usually teaches his son to perform the *woodoo*' and other ablutions. **1855** BURTON *Meccah & Medinah* (1879) 56 The first thing on rising is to perform the Wuzu, or lesser ablution.

woodos(e, -owes, var. WOODWOSE.

†**'woodpeck.** *Obs.* Also 6 -pyke. [app. alteration of WOODSPECK after next.] = next, 1.

1552 HULOET, Woodepyke byrde, *picus.* **1555** EDEN *Decades* (Arb.) 224 Certeyne byrdes..lyke vnto those which we caule woodwaules or woodpeckes. **1601** HOLLAND *Pliny* x. xxix. I. 285 Men say that in the territorie of Tarentum there be no wood-pecks or tree-jobbers. **1694** ADDISON *Poems, Virgil's 4th Georg.* 19 Nor Wood-pecks, nor the Swallow harbour near. **1706** GARDINER tr. *Rapin's Gardens* (1728) 197 Wood-pecks, and various birds the trees invade.

woodpecker ('wʊdˌpɛkə(r)). Also 7 -picker. [f. WOOD *sb.*[1] + PECK *v.*[1] + -ER[1]. (Cf. the Gr. names δρυ(ο)κολάπτης, δρυοκόλαψ, δρυοκόπος, f. δρῦς tree + κολάπτειν to peck, κοπ- to strike.)]

1. a. A bird of the family *Picidæ*, esp. of the sub-family *Picinæ*, comprising very numerous genera and species found in most parts of the world; usually having variegated plumage of bright contrasted colours with various markings; characterized by their habit of pecking holes in the trunks and branches of trees.

1530 PALSGR. 289/2 Woodpecker a byrde, *espec.* **1591** SYLVESTER *Du Bartas* I. v. 228 As the Wood-pecker, his long tongue doth lill Out of the clov'n pipe of his horny bill, To catch the Emets. **1604** DRAYTON *Owle* 191 The Wood-pecker, whose hardned beake hath..pierc'd the heart of many a sollid Oke. **1624** CAPT. SMITH *Virginia* v. 171 Numbers of small Birds..Wood-pickers. **1778** J. CARVER *Trav. N. Amer.* xviii. 471 The Woodpecker..is a very beautiful bird; there is one sort whose feathers are a mixture of various colours; and another that is brown all over the body, except the head and neck, which are of a fine red. **1806** MOORE *Ballad Stanzas* ii, I heard not a sound But the woodpecker tapping the hollow beech-tree. **1859** DARWIN *Orig. Spec.* vi. (1860) 184 In North America there are woodpeckers which feed largely on fruit. **1862** —— *Orchids* iii. 127 As a woodpecker..climbs up a tree in search of insects. **1872** COUES *N. Amer. Birds* 191 Woodpeckers nest in holes in trees.

b. With defining words, denoting various species.

The three British species are the Green Woodpecker (*Gecinus viridis*), the Pied or Greater Spotted Woodpecker (*Dendrocopus major*), and the Barred or Lesser Spotted Woodpecker (*D. minor*). Others are the Great Black Woodpecker (*Picus* or *Dryocopus martius*) of the northern parts of Europe and Asia, and many N. American species, as the Downy W. (*Picus* or *Dendrocopus pubescens*), the Golden-winged W. (*Colaptes auratus*), the Hairy W. (*Picus* or *Dendrocopus villosus*), the Pileated W. (*Hylotomus* or *Dryotomus pileatus*) etc. Several of these are locally known by special names, as FLICKER, HICKWALL, IVORY-*bill*, LOG-*cock*, POPINJAY, SAP-*sucker*, WITWALL, WOODSPITE, YAFFLE, etc. (see these words).

1668 CHARLETON *Onomast.* 86 *Picus Martius*..the great Wood-pecker. **1731** CATESBY *Nat. Hist. Carolina* (1754) I. 21 *Picus varius minor, ventre luteo.* The yellow belly'd Wood-pecker. **1782** LATHAM *Gen. Syn. Birds* I. 558 Red-necked woodpecker. The whole head and neck..are crimson. *Ibid.* II. 591 Yellow Woodpecker..less than our green Woodpecker: being only nine inches in length..is common at Cayenne. **1782–1890** [see SPOTTED *ppl. a.* 4 b]. **1802** BINGLEY *Anim. Biog.* (1813) II. 129 The Black Wood-pecker subsists on insects, which it catches on the bark of trees... It is able to pierce..hard trees, as the oak and hornbeam. **1808** A. WILSON *Amer. Ornith.* I. 142 His tri-colored plumage..is so striking..that almost every child is acquainted with the Red-headed Woodpecker. **1884** *Harper's Mag.* Mar. 622/2 The golden-winged, and the yellow-bellied woodpeckers..are also with us. **1898** MARIA R. AUDUBON *Audubon & Jrnls.* II. 51 Harris and Bell had gone shooting and returned with several birds, among which was a female Red-patched Woodpecker.

†**2.** *Cant.* At gaming, a bystander who encourages novices by putting up small stakes. *Obs.*

1608 DEKKER *Lanth. & Candle Lt.* iii. D 2, He that winnes all, is the Eagle. He that stands by and Ventures, is the Woodpecker. *a* **1700** B. E. *Dict. Cant. Crew.*

3. *U.S.* and *Austral. Mil. slang.* A machine-gun.

1898 J. H. PARKER *Hist. Gatling Gun Detachment* vii. 127 Goin' to let the woodpeckers go off? **1932** J. DOS PASSOS *1919* 410 The shrill bullets combing the air and the sorehead woodpeckers the machineguns mud cooties gasmasks and the itch. **1945** BAKER *Austral. Lang.* viii. 157 *Woodpecker*, a Japanese .77 machine-gun. **1945** *Yank* 27 July 7 The Japs opened up with what sounded like dual-purpose 75s, 20-mm pompoms and woodpeckers. **1976** G. MARKHAM *Japanese Infantry Weapons World War Two* 41 The popular Taishō 3rd year type machine-gun..was introduced in 1914. Its peculiar stuttering fire earned the gun the Australian nickname of 'woodpecker' (or 'woodchopper').

'wood-ˌpigeon. Any of the species of pigeon that live in woods, as the stock-dove, *Columba œnas*, and (now esp.) the ring-dove, *C. palumbus.*

1668 CHARLETON *Onomast.* 77 *Columbæ Cavernalis*..the Stock-dove, or Wood Pigeon. **1743** SHENSTONE *Pastoral Ballad* II. v, I have found out a gift for my fair; I have found where the wood-pigeons breed. **1780** G. WHITE *Selborne, Let. to Pennant* 30 Nov., As to the wild wood-pigeon, the *oenas*, or *vinago*, of Ray, I..see no reason for making it the origin of the common house-dove; but suppose those that have advanced that opinion may have been misled by another appellation, often given to the *oenas*, which is that of stock-dove. **1837** P. KEITH *Bot. Lex.* 217 Knots or bunches ..formed by means of a plexus of young shoots,..apt to be mistaken..for a wood-pigeon's nest. *a* **1887** JEFFERIES *Field & Hedgerow* 303 The forest is not vacant... Wood-pigeons and turtle-doves abound.

'wood-quest, -quist, -queest. Now *dial.* Also 6–7 -quyst(e, -coyst, 7 -quiste, -coist. [f. WOOD *sb.*[1] + *quest, quist*, QUEEST.] = prec.

1543 TRAHERON *Vigo's Chirurg.* III. xvi. 109/2 Grated bread in the broth of a woodquyste. **1580** T. NEWTON *Approved Medicines* 85 b, Yᵉ stockdooue, or Woodquist. **1582** BATMAN *Trevisa's Barth. De P.R.* XII. vi. 181/1 The Stock-doue or Wood-coyst. **1623** tr. *Favine's Theat. Hon.* II. xiii. 231 Ring-doues, or Wood-coysts. **1761** *Jackson's Oxf. Jrnl.* 12 Dec. 2 Two Brothers being out a shooting Wood-quists. **1806** J. N. WHITE *Poems* 18 The wood-quest wild. **1825** JENNINGS *Obs. Dial. W. Eng.*, Wood-quist. **1877** *Hon. Miss Ferrard* II. ii. 173 The woodquests' cooing formed a melodious bass.

'wood-reeve. Also 6 -ryfe, 7 -reefe, 8 -reef. [f. WOOD *sb.*[1] 2 + REEVE *sb.*[1] 2.] The steward or overseer of a wood or forest.

1579 TWYNE *Phisicke agst. Fort.* I. xlvii. 70 What is he now other then a Woodryfe, or Woodman? **1643** *MS. Acc. St. John's Hosp., Canterb.*, Spent vpon our woodreefe for coming to giue vs notice of sume abuses done to our wood. **1795** *Trans. Soc. Arts* XIII. 218 Those [trees] that fail to form so desirable a shape as in the opinion of a judicious wood-reef is necessary. **1866** *Morn. Star* 6 Mar. 6/5 The case was proved by Wm. Goodhew, woodreeve to Miss Hayes. **1913** *Daily News* 15 Aug. 5 We are mostly shepherds and wood-reeves and thackers and foresters here.

†**'wood-ˌrowel.** *Obs.* [f. WOOD *sb.*[1] + ROWEL *sb.*, in reference to the whorled leaves.] = next.

1568 TURNER *Herbal* III. 24 Of wood rofe or wood rowell. **1579** LANGHAM *Gard. Health* 683 Woodrowell..is a good healer vp of wounds. **1905** *Engl. Dial. Dict.*, *Wood-rowell*, sb. Obsol. Yks. The sweet woodruff, *Asperula odorata.*

woodruff[1] ('wʊdrʌf). Forms: 1 wudu-, wuderofe, -rife, 3 wuderoue, 4 woderowe, 4–5 -rove, 5 -rofe, wodrove, -roffe, -ruffe, 5–6 -rofe, 6 woodroue, -rowe, -rofe, -roof(f)e, 7 -rof, -rough, 7- -roof, (8 -rooff), 9 woodruff, (*Sc.* -riff, *arch.* wooderoofe, wood-ruffe). [OE. *wudurofe*, f. *wudu* WOOD *sb.*[1] + **rofe*, **rife*, of unknown meaning.] A low-growing herb (*Asperula odorata*, N.O. *Rubiaceæ*) found in woods in Britain and Europe generally, with clusters of small white flowers, and strongly sweet-scented leaves in whorls; also descriptively or distinctively called ***sweet woodruff.*** Also *attrib.*

c **1000** *Sax. Leechd.* I. 18 Herba astula regia þæt is wudu rofe. *Ibid.* II. 64 Wiþ þære winestran sidan sare wudurifan ȝecnuwa on eced. *c* **1265** *Voc. Plants* in Wr.-Wülcker 558/10 *Hastula regia, i. muge de bois, i.* wuderoue. *a* **1310** in Wright *Lyric P.* xiii. 43 A-way is huere wynter wo, when woderove springeth. *a* **1400** *Stockholm Med. MS.* 191 Woderowe, *hastilogia.* **14..** in Wr.-Wülcker 566/20 *Astula regia*, woderofe. **1477–9** *Rec. St. Mary at Hill* (1905) 81 Rose-garlondis and wodrove-garlondis. **1525** *Grete Herbal* xli. (1529) C iv, De astula regia. Woodroue. **1597** GERARDE *Herbal* II. ccccxlvii. 966 In English Woodrooffe, Woodrowe, and Woodrowell. **1785** MARTYN *Lett. Bot.* xv. (1794) 164 Sherardia and woodroof have funnel-shaped corollas. **1824** HOGG *Tales & Sk., Priv. Mem. Fanatic* (1837) V. 83 Murder will out, though the Almighty should lend hearing to the ears of the willow, and speech to the seven tongues of the woodriff. **1872** BLACK *Adv. Phaeton* xix. 263 As a bunch of woodruff will sweeten a lumber-room.

b. Extended to other species of *Asperula.*

1597 GERARDE *Herbal* II. ccccxlvii. 965 There is another sort of Woodrooffe called *Asperula Cærulea*, or blew Woodrooffe. **1688** HOLME *Armoury* II. 98/2 Woodroof... Some have blew, others purple coloured flowers. **1841** CATLIN *N. Amer. Ind.* II. App. A. 260 Woodroof, a species of madder used as a red dye. **1865** *Sowerby's Engl. Bot.* (ed. 3) IV. 231 *Asperula Arvensis*... Blue Field Woodruff. **1866** *Treas. Bot.* 1236 Woodroof, or Woodruff.., Quinsy, *Asperula cynanchica.*

Woodruff[2] ('wʊdrʌf). *Mech.* [See quot. 1892.] ***Woodruff key***: a key whose cross-section is part circular (to fit into a curved keyway in a shaft) and part rectangular.

1892 P. BENJAMIN *Mod. Mechanism* 455 [The Woodruff System of Keying.—The Woodruff Manufacturing Co., of Hartford, Conn., has brought out a novel system of keying.] *Ibid.* 924 (Index), Woodruff keys. **1923** C. D. ALBERT *Machine Design Drawing Room Probl.* i. 63 Woodruff keys are quite extensively used in machine tools and in machine construction generally. **1976** *New Motorcycling Monthly* Oct. 34/1 Remove Woodruff key from its slot in magneto shaft.

woodruffite (ˈwʊdrʌfaɪt). *Min.* [See quot. 1953 and -ITE[1].] A hydrated oxide of zinc and manganese, $(Zn,Mn^{4+}{}_3)Mn^{4+}O_7.1\text{–}2H_2O$, found as black or grey monoclinic crystals.

1953 C. FRONDEL in *Amer. Mineralogist* XXXVIII. 769 The name woodruffite is proposed for this species after Samuel Woodruff (deceased), for many years employed as a miner by the New Jersey Zinc Company. **1979** *Ibid.* LXIV. 1214/1 The spectrum of woodruffite shows it to be a structural analog of todorokite, as has been assumed from the similarity of their X-ray powder patterns.

ˈwood-rush. [RUSH *sb.*[1]] Any plant of the genus *Luzula*, comprising grass-like herbs allied to the rushes, with clusters of chaffy brown flowers.

The name belongs properly to the sylvan species, as *L. sylvatica* (Great Wood-rush, also called *wood-grass*); the common species *L. campestris* (Field Wood-rush) is better called *field-rush*.

1776 WITHERING *Bot. Arrangem.* 213 Small hairy Wood-rush. **1857** MISS PRATT *Flower. Pl.* V. 299 *L[uzula] sylvatica* (Great Hairy Wood Rush). **1861** S. THOMSON *Wild Fl.* III. (ed. 4) 170 The broad-leaved wood-rush, with its hairy leaves, may..be gathered in woods. **1889** *Science-Gossip* XXV. 188 Luzula albida..is a very graceful woodrush of a peculiar shade of light green.

ˈwood-sage. [SAGE *sb.*[1]] A common name for Wood Germander (*Teucrium Scorodonia*), a labiate herb with dull greenish-yellow flowers, and leaves having a heavy aromatic smell like sage and a bitter flavour like hops.

1570 PENA & LOBEL *Stirp. Advers. nova* (1576) 210 Scordium alterum Plinij... Wood sage. **1597** [see SAGE *sb.*[1] 3]. **1758** BORLASE *Nat. Hist. Cornw.* 229 Wood-sage, *Salvia agrestis seu scorodonia*,..at St. Michael's Mount. **1796** WITHERING *Brit. Plants* (ed. 3) III. 519. **1880** JEFFERIES *Gt. Estate* 91.

†**ˈwoodsale.** *Obs.* [SALE *sb.*[2]] A periodical sale of wood or timber from an estate.

1479 in *Catal. Anc. Deeds* (1915) VI. 168 The said beches to be drawen on the saide grounde wodmanlyke after the custume of wodsale. **1540** *Act 32 Hen. VIII*, c. 46 §10 The said Maistre of the Wardes..shalhave auctoritie..to make wood sales to the Kinges use of al underwooddis. **1562** LEIGH *Surv.* (1577) D iv, Profites of woodsale, is where sometymes the Lord of a Mannour doeth make a yerely sale of his woodes. *c* **1617** BACON *Memorial* Wks. 1819 V. 485 What course shall be taken for the rest of the years with the wood sales for supply of this 25,000*l.* yearly. **1786** in *Jrnls. Ho. Comm.* XLIII. 622 Warrants for raising £2,000..by Wood Sales in Dean Forest.

attrib. **1605** SYLVESTER *Du Bartas* II. iii. IV. *Captains* 243 A sort of lusty bil-men set In wood-sale time to sell a cops.

wood-sear, -seer, -sere (ˈwʊdsɪə(r)). *Obs.* or *dial.* Also 9 *erron.* -sour. [? f. WOOD *sb.*[1] + SERE *a.*]

1. A frothy exudation on plants, produced by an insect: = CUCKOO-SPIT[2] 1; also, the insect itself.

1585 HIGINS *Junius' Nomencl.* 72/1 *Attelabus*,..the smallest sort of locustes that be wingless: ye woodseare. **1589** [? LYLY] *Pappe w. Hatchet* B ij, Such a warming, as shall make all his deuices as like wood, as his spittle is like wood-sere. **1600** SURFLET *Country Farm* I. viii. 39 Spiders, wormes, woodseere and other such like vermine. **1664** POWER *Exp. Philos.* I. 28 That spumeous froth or dew (which here in the North we call Cuckow-Spittle, and, in the South, Woodsear..) looks like a heap of glass-bubbles. **1821** CLARE *Vill. Minstrel* I. 135 Insects of mysterious birth.. Hid in knots of spittle white..'Wood seers' call'd, that wet declare, So the knowing shepherds say. **1825** HONE *Every-day Bk.* I. 535 The abundance of woodseare and honey dew on herbs indicates fine weather.

attrib. **1599** CUTWODE *Caltha Poet.* lviii. C 2 b, I will not (as the creeping canker) waste thee, nor as the worm in wodsear time bespew thee.

2. The season in which a tree or shrub will decay or die if its wood be cut.

Erroneously explained as 'the season for cutting wood'.

1573 TUSSER *Husb.* (1878) 111 From Maie til October leaue cropping, for why? In wood sere, whatsoeuer thou croppest wil dy. *Ibid.* 119 The bushes and thorne..In woodsere or sommer cut downe to destroy. **1603** SIR C. HEYDON *Jud. Astrol.* ii. 43 If wood be cutte after the sunne decline from vs till he come to the equinoctiall, (which time they call woodsere) it will neuer growe againe. **1610** FOLKINGHAM *Feudigr.* I. ix. 22 All sappie weedes cut downe in Wood-seare, and often mowne againe.., their roots will putrifie and rotte. **1851** *Gloss. Essex* 14 *Woodsere*, decayed or hollow pollard, also the season for felling wood.

3. *attrib.* or *adj.* Applied to 'loose, spungy ground' (Lisle). Hence **ˈwood-ˌseary** *a.*, in same sense.

1670 AUBREY in *Miscell. Cur. Subj.* (1714) 24 Let us imagine..what Kind of Country this was..by the Nature of the Soil, which is a Soure, Woodsere Land, very natural for the Production of Oaks especially. *a* **1722** LISLE *Husb.* (1757) 27 Chalk fills up the vacuities of sandy, or wood-seary ground. *Ibid.* 79 Cold, loose, hollow, wood-sear land. **1759** tr. *Duhamel's Husb.* I. viii. (1762) 37 Chalk laid on sandy or wood-seary ground. **1811** T. DAVIS *Agric. Wilts* 112 The red strong land on the high level parts of the Downs, which was once woodland, and sometimes expressly called 'wood-sour land'.

†**ˈwood-shaw.** *Obs.* Forms and etym.: see WOOD *sb.*[1] and SHAW *sb.*[1]; also with gen. 4 **wodesschawe**. A thicket: = SHAW *sb.*[1] 1 b.

c **1205** LAY. 21561 Halden ut of wude scaȝe scalkes swiðe kene. *a* **1300** *Thrush & Night.* 179 in Hazl. *E.P.P.* (1864) I. 57 Fowel, for thi false sawe, For bedd i the this wode shawe; Thou fare into the filde. **1390** GOWER *Conf.* II. 339 Whan sche under the wodesschawe Hire child behield. *a* **1400** *Isumbras* 73 And als he wente by a wodschawe [*v.r.* came by a lytell schawe] þare mett he with a lyttill knaue. *c* **1400** *Laud Troy Bk.* 7618 Then men myȝt se swordes drawe Thikkere then trees by wode-schawe. **1470–85** MALORY *Arthur* IX. xii. 356 Sir lamorak..rode vnto the forest, and there he mette with two knyghtes houynge vnder the wood shawe. **1513** DOUGLAS *Æneis* I. vi. 10 His navy derne amang the thik wod schaw.

woodshed (ˈwʊdʃɛd), *sb.* Also **wood shed, wood-shed.** [f. WOOD *sb.*[1] + SHED *sb.*[2]] **1.** A shed for storing wood, esp. for fuel. Also *euphem.*, a lavatory.

1844 LOUISA S. COSTELLO *Bearn & Pyrenees* I. 282 We were glad to take shelter in a wood-shed. **1854** H. D. THOREAU *Walden* 54, I have also a small wood-shed adjoining, made chiefly of the stuff which was left after building the house. **1868** N. HAWTHORNE *Passages from Amer. Notebks.* II. 9 We have been employed partly in an augean labor of clearing out a wood-shed. **1921** W. DE LA MARE *Mem. Midget* ii. 10 Pollie had gone to the wood-shed to fetch kindling. **1940** W. FAULKNER *Hamlet* II. ii. 129 Serve you right for keeping a mare like that in a woodshed. **1974** M. HOYT *Thirty Miles* i. 1 The plumbing wasn't. Its place was taken by a small building known by the somewhat less-than-frank title of 'woodshed'.

2. *fig.* **a.** Phr. ***to take into the woodshed*** and varr.: to reprimand or punish. *N. Amer. colloq.*

From the old tradition of giving a child a spanking in the woodshed, i.e. not in the presence of others.

1907 *St. Nicholas* July 826/2 He could save himself and most of his companions from unpleasant reckonings in various and sundry woodsheds. **1949** *Time* 18 Apr. 22/2 If you don't do what we tell you to do we are going to take you out into the woodshed. **1966** *Toronto Daily Star* 21 Dec. 14 (*heading*) Taking the Senator to the woodshed. **1983** *Chicago Sun-Times* 16 July 34 Assuming the Fed is traditionally pliant, why does not Reagan simply take Volcker to the woodshed and tell him to ease up?

b. Phr. ***something nasty in the woodshed***: see NASTY *a.* 7. Also in allusive varr.

1940 AUDEN *Another Time* 111 What was it, Ernst, that your shadow unwittingly said? O did the child see something horrid in the woodshed Long ago? **1958** *Times Lit. Suppl.* 17 Jan. 30/1 Mr Amis does not, however, present Garnet Bowen as a case-history, whose dislike of foreign parts could be explained on a woodshed basis. **1959** *Listener* 8 Jan. 78/3 As the leading Torquemada, Miss Margaret Lane clearly felt some obligation to strive to uncover something—well—interesting in the woodshed.

c. *Mus. slang.* As a place where a musician may, or should, practise in private (see also quot. 1937).

1937 *Printers' Ink Monthly* May 45/3 *Wood shed*, a severe rehearsal. **1946** *Hollywood Note* June 4 T.D. [*sc.* Tommy Dorsey] goes back to the woodshed. **1977** *Rolling Stone* 16 June 66/2 Leavell's playing won't scare many jazz pianists into the woodshed.

woodshed (ˈwʊdʃɛd), *v. Mus. slang.* [f. the sb.] *trans.* and *intr.* To practise or rehearse, esp. privately (see also quot. 1978).

1936 L. ARMSTRONG *Swing that Music* 71 We used to practice together, 'wood-shed' as we say (from the old-time way of going out into the wood-shed to practice a new song). **1946** MEZZROW & WOLFE *Really the Blues* viii. 108 I'll have to woodshed this thing awhile so I can get straight with you all. **1950** BLESH & JANIS *They all played Ragtime* (1958) x. 203, I would hear the tunes and, to make sure, go home and 'woodshed' them in every key, put them in major and minor and all the ninth chords. **1968** A. YOUNG in A. Chapman *New Black Voices* (1972) Drew's got an alto [horn]... Drew dont hardly touch it, he too busy woodsheddin his drums. **1978** *Amer. Speech* 1975 L. 302 [Jargon of barber-shop singing.] *Woodshed*, work out the harmony parts (to a known melody) by ear; sing as a group for the first time..; improvise (an interpretation).

Hence **ˈwoodshedding** *vbl. sb.*, (*a*) the dispensing of punishment; (*b*) the practice or rehearsal of music; (*c*) spontaneous or improvised barber-shop singing.

1940 *Amer. Speech* XV. 205 *Woodshedding*, disciplinary action. **1946** MEZZROW & WOLFE *Really the Blues* ix. 151 Instead of woodshedding, he went out after the big money with the primitive equipment he had when he started. **1955** SHAPIRO & HENTOFF *Hear me talkin' to Ya* xi. 190 It was here that the term 'woodshedding' originated. When one of the gang wanted to rehearse his part, he would go off into the woods and practice. **1956** S. LONGSTREET *Real Jazz* xiii. 101 Bix [Beiderbecke] did plenty of woodshedding, playing alone, to some recording on the family Victrola. **1973** T. PYNCHON *Gravity's Rainbow* I. 129 No head falsetto here but complete, out of the honest breast, a baritone voice brought over years of woodshedding up to this range. **1974** *Harmonizer* Jan.-Feb. 18/2 Woodshedding is not a 'spectator sport'—only participants can fully enjoy it. **1976** *Times* 27 Sept. 12/4 Spontaneous barbershopping is known as woodshedding, because a woodshed is as good a place as any to burst into sudden song.

†**ˈwoodship.** *Obs.* [OE. *wódscipe*: see WOOD *a.* and -SHIP.] Madness; = WOODNESS.

c **1000** *Ags. Gloss.* in Wr.-Wülcker 245/12 *Furia, insania, amentia*, wodscipe, reþnes. *a* **1225** *Ancr. R.* 120 *Ira furor brevis est*: wreððe is a wodschipe. *a* **1240** *Lofsong* in *O.E. Hom.* I. 211 Leste þu wreoke ham on me i wodschipe of þine wreððe. *a* **1325** *Prose Psalter* xxxvi[i]. 8 Ende fram ire, and forsak wodeship. *c* **1430** *Pilgr. Lyf Manhode* I. cxx. (1869) 62 Glotonye hath double woodshipe; woodshipe of savouring, and woodshipe of outrageous spekinge.

woodshock (ˈwʊdʃɒk). [app. popular alteration of a native form of WOODCHUCK (see WEJACK).] A North American species of marten or its fur: = FISHER[1] 2 b, PEKAN.

1829 J. RICHARDSON *Fauna Bor.-Amer.* I. 52 *Mustela Canadensis* (Lin.) The Pekan or Fisher..Its skins are.. imported into England..under the names of Woodshocks or Fishers.

Woodsia (ˈwʊdzɪə). *Bot.* Also **woodsia.** [mod.L., f. the name of Joseph *Woods* (1776–1864), architect and botanist + -IA[1].] A fern of the genus of this name (family Polypodiaceæ), comprising small, rock-loving, tufted plants found in mountainous parts of Britain and other temperate regions and in the Arctic.

1815 R. BROWN in *Trans. Linnean Soc.* XI. 171 This genus I have named in honour of my friend Mr. Joseph Woods... The character distinguishing *Woodsia*..consists in its involucrum being inserted under the group of capsules..the *sorus*, which it completely surrounds at the base; while it is in every stage open at top. **1848** T. MOORE *Handbk. Brit. Ferns* iii. 37 The Woodsias have no especial claim to be esteemed for their elegance. *a* **1894** W. FALCONER *Let.* in W. Robinson *Wild Garden* (ed. 4) viii. 83 Woodsias, tiny Aspleniums, and other Ferns. **1908** E. STEP *Wayside & Woodland Ferns* 55 Oblong Woodsia (*Woodsia ilvensis*). This species differs but slightly from the Alpine Woodsia, and some botanists deny its distinctness. **1961** R. W. BUTCHER *New Illustrated Brit. Flora* I. 176 *Woodsia alpina*. .. This Northern Woodsia occurs very rarely on mountain cliffs and rocks in a few places in Scotland and N. Wales.

woodside (ˈwʊdsaɪd). Forms and etym.: see WOOD *sb.*[1] and SIDE *sb.*; also with gen. 4 **wodessyde**, 6 **woodessyde**. The side or edge of a wood.

Chiefly in phr. with prep., as ***by*** or ***under the*** or ***a woodside*** = beside a wood; cf. BEDSIDE, ROADSIDE, WAYSIDE.

a **1300** *Cursor M.* 5734 Bi a wildrin wod side. *a* **1300** *K. Horn* 1024 (Camb.) His folk he dude abide Vnder wude side. **1375** BARBOUR *Bruce* IX. 139 Thai that in the wodsyde weir. *c* **1400** *Parce Michi* 181 in *26 Pol. Poems* 148 By dale, by doune, by wodes syde. *c* **1430** LYDG. *Min. Poems* (Percy Soc.) 110 So that ye wylle goo thys tyde Dowen to the chapylle under the wood syde. **1530** PALSGR. 290/1 Woodessyde, *oriere du boys*. *a* **1533** LD. BERNERS *Huon* vii. 18 They came to a lytyll woodsyde. **1658** CROMWELL *Sp.* 4 Feb. in *Carlyle*, I would have been glad to have lived under my woodside, to have kept a flock of sheep, rather than undertaken such a government as this. **1666** DRYDEN *Ann. Mirab.* ccxlviii, Thus to some desert Plain, or old Wood-side, Dire Night-hags come. **1774** GOLDSM. *Nat. Hist.* IV. 11 A buck, or male hare, is known by its..feeding farther from the wood-sides. **1818** HAZLITT *Eng. Poets* ii. (1870) 47 You see a little withered old man by a wood-side opening a wicket. **1853** G. JOHNSTON *Nat. Hist. E. Bord.* I. 253 The woodside on the south is very swampy. **1865** KINGSLEY *Herew.* xxxv, It will be as well for some of us to remain here; and, spreading our men along the wood-side, prevent the escape of the villains. **1895** *Atlantic Monthly* Mar. 425 The snow may be gone..except..along fences and woodsides.

attrib. **1863** COWDEN CLARKE *Shaks. Char.* xvi. 402 Like a babbling woodside brook. **1871** PALGRAVE *Lyr. Poems* 68 In the wood-side field.

woodsman (ˈwʊdzmən). Pl. **woodsmen.** (Chiefly *U.S.*) [f. *wood's* gen. sing. or *woods* pl. of WOOD *sb.*[1] + MAN *sb.*[1]; cf. BACKWOODSMAN.] A man who inhabits, frequents, or ranges the woods, as a huntsman, sportsman, wood-cutter, etc. (cf. WOODMAN[1] 1, 2, 4); one acquainted with or accustomed to the woods.

1688 CLAYTON *Virginia* in *Phil. Trans.* XVIII. 122 There are abundance of brave Red Deer, so that a good Woodsman, as they call them, will keep a House with Venison. **1699** DAMPIER *Voy.* II. II. 86 The Captain..told him..that he was but a sorry Woodsman, and that he would swing him but twice round and he should not guess the way out again. **1755** R. ROGERS *Jrnls.* (1769) 9 One company of woodsmen or rangers..to make excursions towards the enemy's forts. **1797** F. BAILY *Jrnl. Tour N. Amer.* (1856) 358 My companion..was an excellent woodsman; and I.. trusted myself to his guidance, well knowing that he would not easily mistake the track. **1817** SCOTT *Harold* II. xiv, A woodsman thou and hast a spear, And couldst thou such an insult bear? **1825** —— *Talism.* xxii, The low wail of a dog,.. which, as an experienced woodsman, he had no hesitation in recognising to be that of his own faithful hound. **1827** HOOD *Plea Mids. Fairies* xlvi, A merry Woodsman, clad in green, Stept vanward from his mates. **1875** WHYTE-MELVILLE *Katerfelto* xvi, Rube was far too practical a woodsman to pass such a slot without inquiry. **1896** *N. Y. Weekly Witness* 30 Dec. 13/1 The woodsmen were going for the opposite party. **1902** S. E. WHITE *Blazed Trail* vi, A veteran woodsman who had come to swamping in his old age.

ˈwood-ˌsorrel. [Englishing of *sorrel de boys*, superseding WOODSOUR: see WOOD *sb.*[1] and SORREL *sb.*[1] (3 a): so called from the sour taste of the leaves, resembling sorrel.] The common name of *Oxalis Acetosella*, a low-growing woodland plant having delicate trifoliate leaves and small white flowers streaked with purple, appearing in spring.

1525 *Grete Herball* I. (1529) C vj, Alleluya, wood sorell or cocowes meate. **1578** LYTE *Dodoens* IV. xliii. 502 Woode Sorrel is a lowe or base herbe, without stalkes. **1634–5**

BRERETON *Trav.* (Chetham Soc.) 192, I took a good quantity of mithridate and wood-sorrel. **1774** GOLDSM. *Nat. Hist.* III. 166 Wood sorrel,..being boiled up with [milk], and coagulating, the whole is put into casks..and kept under ground to be eaten in winter [in Lapland]. **1888** T. W. REID *Life W. E. Forster* (ed. 2) I. ii. 42 The first appearance of cuckoo or swallow, of wood sorrel or anemone. **1899** R. BRIDGES *Idle Flowers* vii, Woodsorrel's pencilled veil.

b. Applied with defining words to other species of *Oxalis*; also in the West Indies to species of *Begonia*.

1770 J. R. FORSTER tr. *Kalm's Trav. N. Amer.* I. 201 The yellow wood sorrel, or *Oxalis corniculata*. **1855** DELAMER *Kitch. Gard.* (1861) 49 The *Oxalis crenata*, or Notched Wood-sorrel, a tuberous-rooted esculent, cultivated in Peru under the name of Oca. **1858** A. IRVINE *Handbk. Brit. Plants* 754 *Oxalis stricta*,..Upright Yellow Wood-sorrel. **1864** GRISEBACH *Flora W. Ind. Isl.* 787/2 Sorrel, wood, *Begonia acutifolia*.

† **'wood-sour.** *Obs.* Forms: see WOOD *sb.*¹; 4–6 **-sour**, 5 **-sowr, -soure, -soour,** 6 **-sore, -sower.** [f. WOOD *sb.*¹ + SOUR *sb.*, corresp. to ON. *skógarsúra* (*skóg* SCOGH, wood, *súra* sorrel), Da. *skovsyre*. Cf. (= sorrel) MDu. *suerkruyd*, *suerick*, Du. *zuring*, WFris. *sûrblêdden* pl., G. *sauerampfer*, etc., and (= wood-sorrel) G. *sauerklee*, *saurekraut*, Da. *surklever*, etc.] = prec.

a **1387** *Sinon. Barthol.* (Anecd. Oxon.) 10 *Alleluia*, i. wodesour. *a* **1425** tr. *Arderne's Treat. Fistula* etc. 68 Panis cuculi alleluya, i. wodsour, is a treyfole growyng vnder buschez and bereþ white flourez, is a ful sour herbe. **1538** TURNER *Libellus, Oxys..a latinis dicitur trifolium acetosum, ab officinis Alleluya, uulgus etiam uocat Alleluya* wodsore, & cuckowes meat. **1562** —— *Herbal* II. 74 Oxys..shuld be called wod sour or sorell. **1578** LYTE *Dodoens* IV. xliii. 503 This herbe is called..in English Woodsorel..and Woodsower. **1597** GERARDE *Herbal* Suppl., Woodsower is *Oxys*.

wood-sour, erron. form of WOOD-SEAR.

woodspeck ('wʊdspɛk). *dial.* Also 6 **-spike**, 9 **-spack.** [See WOOD *sb.*¹ and SPECK *sb.*³ Cf. WOODSPITE.] A woodpecker.

15.. Woodspecke [see SPECK *sb.*³]. **1562** TURNER *Herbal* II. 25 Euery suche leafe or pricke [of Juniper] is very like vnto yᵉ ende of the tonge of an hueholl or wodspike. **1567** GOLDING *Ovid's Met.* XIV. (1593) 330 On the head thereof were garlands store, And eke a woodspecke. **1601** HOLLAND *Pliny* XXX. xvi. II. 399 As many as have about them the bill of a woodspeck when they come to take hony out of the hive, shall not be stung by bees. **1847** HALLIWELL, *Woodspack*, a woodpecker. **1885** [see WOODSPITE].

† **'wood-spell¹.** *Obs.* [f. WOOD *sb.*¹ + SPELL *sb.*¹ 3.] A spell or charm against danger in passing through a wood or forest.

1579 [see SPELL *sb.*¹ 3]. **1612** J. MASON *Anat. Sorc.* 63.

'wood-spell². *U.S.* [f. WOOD *sb.*¹ + SPELL *sb.*³ 2.] A spell or turn of work at piling or storing wood for fuel.

1864 WEBSTER, *Spell*..2. A gratuitious helping forward of another's work; as, a wood-*spell*. (U.S.) **1869** MRS. STOWE *Oldtown Folks* xxxvii, It was in the winter of this next year that the minister's 'wood-spell' was announced... There was a certain day set apart in the winter,..when every parishioner brought the minister a sled-load of wood. **1878** —— *Poganuc P.* ii. 12 The great wood-pile in the back yard, where, at the yearly 'wood-spell', the farmers deposited the fuel needed for the long..winters.

'wood-ˌspirit. [f. WOOD *sb.*¹ + SPIRIT *sb.* 3, 21.]

1. *Myth.* A spirit or imaginary being, fabled to dwell in or haunt woods.

1845 [C. H. J. ANDERSON] *Swedish Brothers* 4 The Nipen, or wood-spirit was..said to haunt these woods. **1877** J. E. CARPENTER tr. *Tiele's Hist. Relig.* 184 The wood-spirits, *Lyeshie*, bear most resemblance in conception and character to Pan and the Satyrs. **1911** W. W. FOWLER *Relig. Exper. Roman People* x. 235 Diana was a wood-spirit, a tree-spirit.

2. Crude methyl alcohol obtained from wood by destructive distillation.

1842 in Ure *Revenue in Jeopardy* (1843) 11 A sample of crude naphtha..the unrectified combustible liquid obtained from the distillation of wood,..imported from Scotland under the name of naphtha or wood-naphtha... It is named in Chemistry wood-spirit or pyroxylic spirit. **1854** RONALDS & RICHARDSON *Chem. Technol.* (ed. 2) I. 367 Wood-spirit is used to some extent..in place of alcohol, in spirit-lamps. **1887** *Buck's Handbk. Med. Sci.* IV. 751/1 Methylic alcohol,..more popularly known under the several names of pyroligneous spirit, pyroxylic spirit, wood spirit, wood alcohol, and wood naphtha.

woodspite ('wʊdspaɪt). Now *dial.* Also 6 **-specht**, 7 **-speight, -spight.** [f. WOOD *sb.*¹ + SPEIGHT.] A woodpecker; *esp.* the Green Woodpecker, *Gecinus viridis*.

1555 GESNER *Hist. Anim.* III. *Avium* 680 Primum pici genus Angli spechtam & wodspechtam..nominant. **1601** HOLLAND *Pliny* XXVII. x. II. 282 The roots must bee digged up in the night season, for feare that the Wood-speight or Hickway should see them: for in the day time the said bird would flie in their faces that carie it away, and be ready to job out their eyes. **1606** N. B[AXTER] *Sydney's Ourania* H 2, The coloured Woodspite runs along the trees. **1618** REYCE *Brev. Suffolk* (1902) 45 Others, whose notes I cannott commend .., as the Cookcow, the Jay, the wood spight, the owle. **1774** GOLDSM. *Nat. Hist.* V. 249 The Green Wood-spite or Wood-pecker is called the Rain-Fowl in some parts of the country. **1885** SWAINSON *Prov. Names Birds* 99 Green Woodpecker... Wood spite (Norfolk). Wood spack (Norfolk; Suffolk).

woodsy ('wʊdzɪ), *a.* orig. and chiefly *U.S.* Also **-ey.** [irreg. f. *woods*, pl. of WOOD *sb.*¹ (see 9 g) + -Y¹; formed thus for distinction from *woody*.] Of, pertaining to, characteristic or suggestive of the woods; sylvan.

1861 WHITTIER *Cobbler Keezar's Vision* vi, Woodsy and wild and lonesome, The swift stream wound away. **1869** MRS. STOWE *Oldtown Folks* xxxvii, [We] ran..about the piles of wood..with a joyous satisfaction. How fresh and spicy and woodsy it smelt! **1883** *Longm. Mag.* II. 78 Their songs have the delicacy and wildness of most woodsey forms. **1900** 'MARK TWAIN' *Man that corrupted* etc. 367 There was a deep, woodsy stillness everywhere. **1973** *Times Lit. Suppl.* 27 Apr. 472/5 The merely woodsy setting of the keeper's activities and of his meetings with Connie. **1977** *Daily Tel.* 9 Apr. 7/3 Scatter them on woodsy bits of the garden. **1981** 'D. JORDAN' *Double Red* xxi. 92 The same perfume, a cool tinge of something woodsy. **1985** *Dirt Bike* Mar. 44/2 Duane Summers powers the XC up a woodsy trail.

woodwall ('wʊdwɒl). Now *dial.* Forms: 3 **wude-**, 3–5 **wodewale**, 5 **-woll, wodwale**, 6 **wode-, woodw(h)ale, -waule, -weele**, 7 **-wal, woodhall**, 6– **woodwall.** See also *Eng. Dial. Dict.* [ME. *wodewale*, ad. or cogn. w. MLG. *wedewale* (early Flem. *widewael* 'oriolus') f. *wede* WOOD *sb.*¹ + **wale* of obscure origin. (Cf. WITWALL, and, for sense 2, HICKWALL.)]

† **1.** A singing bird: in early quots. of uncertain identity, but prob. (as later) the Golden Oriole, *Oriolus galbula*, which has a loud flute-like whistle: = WITWALL 1. *Obs.*

a **1250** *Owl & Night.* 1659 (Cott. MS.) þrusche & þrostle & wudewale [*Jesus MS.* wodewale] An fuheles boþe grete & smale. *a* **1310** in Wright *Lyric P.* v. 26 The wilde laveroc ant wolc ant the wodewale. *c* **1325** *Gloss. W. de Bibbesw.* in Wright *Voc.* 166 Escoter la note de l'oriol [*gloss* a wodewale]. ? *a* **1366** CHAUCER *Rom. Rose* 658 In many places were nyghtyngales, Alpes, fynches, and wodewales, That in her swete song deliten. *Ibid.* 914 With popyniay, with nyghtyngale, With Chalaundre, and with wodewale. *c* **1430** LYDG. *Min. Poems* (Percy Soc.) 23 On fresh braunches syngith the wodwale. *a* **1600** *Robin Hood* ii. in Child *Ballads* III. 91 The woodweele sang, and wold not cease, Amongst the leaues a lyne. *a* **1650** *Eger & Grine* 922 in Furniv. & Hales *Percy Folio* I. 383 The throstlecocke, the Nightingale, The laueracke & the wild woodhall. **1657** TOMLINSON *Renou's Disp.* 24 That Bird which Holerius calls Galbula, that is Woodwall. *a* **1667** SKINNER *Etymol. Ling. Angl.* (1671), Witwall vel Woodwall,..*galbula*.

2. A woodpecker; *esp.* the Green Woodpecker, *Gecinus viridis*: = WITWALL 2.

In quot. 1489 tr. OF. *bruhier* buzzard.

c **1489** CAXTON *Blanchardyn* xliv. 173 But men saye in a comyn langage that 'neuer noo wodewoll dyde brede a sperhawke'. **1555** EDEN *Decades* (Arb.) 224 Byrdes.. sumewhat lyke vnto those which we caule woodwaules, or woodpeckes. **1566** *Act 8 Eliz.* c. 15 §2 For the Head of everie Woodwall Pye Jaye Raven or Kyte, one peny. **1815** *Shaw's Gen. Zool.* IX. 185 [The Green Woodpecker] is called in different parts of England by the various names of Woodspite,..Woodwall, and Poppinjay. **1916** J. R. HARRIS in *Contemp. Rev.* Feb. 212 In Devonshire a common name for the bird is Woodall.

woodward ('wʊdwəd), *sb. Hist.* Forms: see WOOD *sb.*¹; also 6 **wodwarte**, 7 **wooddard.** [Late OE. *wuduweard*, f. WOOD *sb.*¹ + WARD *sb.*¹ Survives as a surname in the forms *Woodward* and *Woodard*.] The keeper of a wood; an officer of a wood or forest, having charge of the growing timber.

c **1050** *Rect. Sing. Pers.* §19 (Liebermann 452) Wuduwearde ȝebyreð ælc windfylled treow. **1290** *Rolls of Parlt.* I. 26/1 Wodewardos & proprios Forestar' ac Ministros Boscorum suorum predictorum. **1324–5** *Ibid.* 422/2 Le Wodeward Sire Johan de Brakenbery. *c* **1440** *Promp. Parv.* 531/2 Wodewarde, or walkare in a wode for kepynge, *lucarius*. **1495** *Rolls of Parlt.* VI. 466/1 The Office of Woodwarde within the Countie of Caernarvan. **1563** BP. SANDYS in Strype *Ann. Ref.* (1709) I. xxxv. 356 [He] is now my tenant and my bailiff and woodward of my manour. **1570** LEVINS *Manip.* 33/43 A Wodwarte, *saltuarius*. **1619** T. CLAY *Chorol. Disc.* 25 The Wood-ward is..an Officer of Charge, vnto whose care and trust, the custodie of the Lords Woods, and Receipt of the profits arising out of the same, are chiefly committed. **1638** WHITING *Albino & Bellama* 109 The wooddards greene with Tyrian dye was dight. *a* **1647** HABINGTON *Surv. Worc.* (Worc. Hist. Soc. Proc.) I. 454 Heerevppon dyd the Byshop of Worcester appoynt hys servant to bee hys woodward in Wenlond, and within the chase of Maluern. **1710** *Brit. Apollo* III. No. 119. 4/1 James Worseley, Esq.; is made Woodward of the New Forest. *a* **1722** LISLE *Husb.* (1757) 361 My woodward assures me, that windy weather makes the sap rise much sooner in trees than it would otherwise do. **1791** W. GILPIN *Forest Scenery* II. 20 The first officer [of the New Forest], under the lord-warden, is the woodward..Under the woodward are twelve regarders. **1871** *Daily News* 21 Sept., The under-keeper of the Loughton and Theydon Walks, gave evidence..that the ..Lord of the Manor of Loughton had enclosed a thousand acres of the public land,..and that his woodward..had cut down several thousand trees.

¶ Used for WOODWOSE.

1488 *Acc. Ld. H. Treas. Scot.* I. 82 A wodward of gold with a diamant. **1552** *Elyot's Dict., Cæpus*, a beast in face like a Satyre, or woodward. **1566** in J. Nicholl *Comp. Ironmongers* (1866) 90 Hewe Watts and Xpofer Beckes, Wadwardes, or Ivemen.

b. As the title of an officer of the 'Ancient Order of Foresters'.

1886 *Rules Court No. 2991 Foresters* No. 22 The Woodwards shall visit the sick members..once a week.

Hence † **'woodwardship**, the office of woodward.

1418 in *41st Dep. Kpr.'s Rep.* 700 [The] Wodewardships [of the commotes of Penthlyn and Thalepont, Merionethshire]. **1485** *Rolls of Parlt.* VI. 379/1 The Office of Keping of the Parke of Haseley, with the Wodewardship. **1586–7** in H. Hall *Soc. Eliz. Age* (1886) 242 Mr. Inkpen.. sold him the woodwardship of that manor for 33/4. **1640** in *Jrnls. Ho. Comm.* XLIII. 589/1 The..best Ship Timber there within the Wood-Wardship of Cesar Robert, Esquire.

woodward, -wards ('wʊdwəd(z), *adv. rare.* [f. WOOD *sb.*¹ + -WARDS(s.] Towards or to the wood. †*from the woodward*: away from the wood.

1621 LADY M. WROTH *Urania* 238 An other Lady.. running from the Wood-ward. *a* **1849** J. C. MANGAN *Poems* (1859) 371 Rury rode woodwards. **1893** N. GALE *Country Muse* Ser. II. 9 When the hush..brings the pigeons woodward.

'woodˌwarden. *rare.* [f. WOOD *sb.*¹ + WARDEN *sb.*¹] = WOODWARD *sb.*

1748 in *Trans. Cumb. & Westm. Archæol. Soc.* (1903) III. 205 That some of the Woodwardens go and view yᵉ wood blown down.

Woodward-Hoffmann ('wʊdwəd 'hɒfmən). *Chem.* The names of Robert Burns *Woodward* (1917–79), U.S. chemist, and Roald *Hoffmann* (b. 1937), Polish-born U.S. chemist, used *attrib.* with reference to a series of generalized symmetry selection rules first proposed by them in 1965 which predict whether a particular pericyclic reaction will be allowed under the given conditions.

1968 *Jrnl. Amer. Chem. Soc.* XC. 1920/2 A considerable amount of research has been directed toward exploring the validity and extent of applicability of the 'Woodward-Hoffman rules'. **1974** GILL & WILLIS *Pericyclic Reactions* iv. 100 (*heading*) The general Woodward-Hoffmann rule for pericyclic reactions. **1980** M. ORCHIN et al. *Vocab. Org. Chem.* x. 330 Sigmatropic shifts. Here the 'migrating bond' is treated as though it were heterolytically cleaved, then the Woodward-Hoffmann rules are applied.

woodware ('wʊdwɛə(r)). [f. WOOD *sb.*¹ + WARE *sb.*³] Articles made of wood, collectively.

1859 CORNWALLIS *New World* I. 326 Ironmongery, matches,..hatchets, woodware, and nails. **1894** J. DAVIDSON *Random Itin.* 49 'And what is there at Chesham?' 'Woodware. They make chairs, and bats, and..toy spades.'

woodwax ('wʊdwæks). ? *Obs.* Also 6 **wodwesse, -wosse**, 9 *dial.* **woodwish**, etc. [OE. *wuduweaxe*, f. *wudu* WOOD *sb.*¹ + **weaxe*, presumably f. Teut. *waχs-* to grow, WAX *v.*¹] = WOODWAXEN.

c **1000** *Sax. Leechd.* II. 66 Wudu weaxe & heȝerife ȝecnuwa þa togædere. **1570** LEVINS *Manip.* 85/35 Wodwesse, *glastum*. *Ibid.* 175/37 Wodwosse, *glastum*. *a* **1667** SIR W. PETTY in Sprat *Hist. Royal Soc.* 296 The Yellows are Weld, Wood-wax, and old Fustick. *a* **1691** AUBREY *Nat. Hist. Wilts* (1847) 49 In Bradon Forest growes very plentifully rank wood-wax. **1707** MORTIMER *Husb.* 241 Green-weed or Wood-wax. **1824** MACTAGGART *Gallovid. Encycl.* 486 *Wudwise*, a yellow flower, which grows on bad land, and has a bitter taste. **1845** *Jrnl. R. Agric. Soc.* V. II. 435 The wood-wax and gorse are very abundant.

Hence **'woodwaxer**, one who gathers woodwax.

1829 J. L. KNAPP *Jrnl. Nat.* 77 Our poorer people..used to collect it by cart loads..; and the season of 'woodwaxen' was a little harvest to them:..the old woodwaxers tell me that [etc.].

woodwaxen ('wʊdˌwæksən). Forms: 4–5 **wodewexen**, 6–9 **woodwaxen**, 9– **woad-waxen.** [app. oblique case of OE. form of WOODWAX (*wuduweaxan*) taken as nom. The form *woadwaxen* is due to association with WOAD.] The plant dyer's broom or greenweed, *Genista tinctoria*.

1367 *Close Roll 41 Edw. III*, m. 9 *dorso*, Tercia pars tocius comoditatis..tam in denariis quam de subbosco & wodewexen. *a* **1400** *Old Usages Winchester* in *Engl. Gilds* (1870) 358 Euerych a cart y-lade wᵗ mader, þᵗ comeþ to selle, twey pans;..Also, y cart y-lade wᵗ wodewexen to sale, fowre pans. **1567** MAPLET *Gr. Forest* 51 The Marigolde of Manardus is called Lysimachia... Woodwaxen [*glastum*].. growleth in Medowes and Pastures like to Brome. **1578** LYTE *Dodoens* VI. viii. 667 Of base Broome or Woodwaxen. **1650** [W. HOWE] *Phytol. Brit.* 46. **1829** [see WOODWAXER above]. **1861** S. THOMSON *Wild Fl.* III. (ed. 4) 236. **1946** G. STIMPSON *Thousand Things* 50 It is supposed that the original green cloth made at Kendal by the Flemish weavers was colored with a dye obtained from the plant known as woadwaxen.

woodwork, wood-work ('wʊdwɜːk).

1. † **a.** A piece of work in wood; an article made of wood, or such articles collectively. *Obs.*

1650 *Bury Wills* (Camden) 226, I give vnto my sonne Edmund Bacon all my plate,..hangings, wood worke, houshold stuffe, and furniture. **1681** GREW *Musæum* II. I. ii. 192 With these, all the turn'd Wood-Works in India and China are wrought and burnished. **1714** *Fr. Bk. of Rates* 57 Wood-works, such as Pater-Nosters, Button-Molds, Toys, &c. *c* **1792** *Encycl. Brit.* (ed. 3) IX. 342/2 The acknowledged skill of her ancient artizans in wood-works.

b. (without *pl.*) Work in wood; *esp.* those parts or details of a manufactured object or artificial structure which are made of wood; the wooden part *of* something.

1684 T. BURNET *Th. Earth* I. 205 If we could suppose this mill to have a power..of repairing all the parts that were worn away, whether of the wood-work or of the stone. **1725** *Fam. Dict.* s.v. *Plough*, This depends much upon the Truth of the Iron Work, and therefore it is best the Plough should rather be accommodated to the Irons,..the Wood-work being easily alter'd. **1837** *Civil Eng. & Arch. Jrnl.* I. 6/1 A groin is a frame of wood-work, constructed across a beach. **1852** THACKERAY *Esmond* III. vii, That long cupboard over the woodwork of the mantelpiece. **1880** MCCARTHY *Own Times* III. xxxviii. 178 Some of the woodwork of the benches was..torn from its place.

c. *Assoc. Football slang.* The frame of the goalposts.

1960 *Times* 21 Nov. 4/2 Three more times they hit Bonetti's woodwork. **1977** *Grimsby Even. Tel.* 5 May 18/6 Twice in the first half, Scunthorpe hit the Bradford woodwork.

d. Phr. ***to come*** or ***crawl out of the woodwork*** and varr., to come out of hiding; to emerge from obscurity. So ***to crawl (back) into the woodwork*** and varr., to disappear into obscurity.

1964 'E. LATHEN' *Accounting for Murder* (1965) vii. 59 These nutboys start crawling out of the woodwork. **1973** *Times Lit. Suppl.* 9 Feb. 154/4 The Nazi elite faded into the woodwork without waiting to be removed, making it tempting to say that denazification should have been left to the Germans. **1973** *Current Affairs Bull.* (Sydney) Aug. 31/1 They are the new Australian playwrights and they are coming out of the woodwork everywhere. **1974** 'M. INNES' *Appleby's Other Story* iv. 30 At least we can tell this bloody wog to crawl back into the woodwork. **1977** C. MCCULLOUGH *Thorn Birds* xii. 289 Funny how the men in my life all scuttle off into the woodwork, isn't it? **1979** 'J. LE CARRÉ' *Smiley's People* (1980) iii. 39 George Smiley, sometime Chief of the Secret Service..had one night come out of the woodwork to peer at some dead foreigner. **1984** *Broadcast* 7 Dec. 27/1 The imminence of a BBC licence increase application brings the advertising agencies out of the woodwork.

†**2.** A grove or plantation artificially laid out.

1712 J. JAMES tr. *Le Blond's Gardening* 28 A large Wood-work cut into a Star, with a circular Alley.

3. a. Work done at cutting wood. *nonce-use.*

a **1861** T. WINTHROP *Life in Open Air* xii. (1863) 94 We..chopped at the woods for fuel. Speaking for myself, I should say that our wood-work was ill done.

b. Work done in wood, as carpentry.

1913 *Board Educ. Rep. Pract. Work Secondary Sch.* 84 Syllabus of wood-work for country or small isolated Schools.

c. Forestry, work done in woods.

1738 W. ELLIS *Timber-Tree Improved* I. 24 There is in my Neighbourhood a Man that is..often imployed in Wood-Work. **1904** G. A. B. DEWAR *Glamour of Earth* x. 243 Making a good and sure living..and filling an honourable post in wood work, to our surprise he took one day a strange step: flung up his work and migrated..to the town.

4. *attrib.*

1959 I. & P. OPIE *Lore & Lang. Schoolch.* xvii. 362 The gardening master is commonly 'Spuds', the woodwork teacher is 'Chips'. **1980** E. BLISHEN *Nest of Teachers* I. iv. 22 The woodwork master..insisted that I come with him to his woodwork centre.

So **'wood,worker**, (*a*) a worker in wood, one who makes things of wood; (*b*) a machine for working in wood (= JOINER *sb.* 3); **'wood,working**, the action of working in wood, the manufacture of wooden articles (also *attrib.*); also, forestry. †**'wood,workman** = *woodworker* (*a*).

1659 in Marshall *Edwinstow Reg.* (1891) 32 Geo. Wightman..a woodworkman. **1872** J. RICHARDS *(title)* A Treatise on the construction..of Wood-working Machines. **1875** KNIGHT *Dict. Mech.* 418/1 *Cabinet-file*, a smooth, single-cut file, used in wood-working. *Ibid.* 2813/2 *Wood-worker*, a machine-tool having various attachments and adjustments for different kinds of work. **1890** W. J. GORDON *Foundry* 71 We stroll through the woodworking-shops, where nothing is done by hand that can be done by machine. **1892** *Labour Commission* Gloss. s.v., In the coach-making trade wood workers consist of wheel-makers, body-makers.., and carriage-makers. **1950** *New Yorker* 26 Aug. 71/1 Woodworking firms are making a candid twelve-per-cent profit. **1951** R. FIRTH *Elem. Social Organization* ii. 51 Their introduced steel tools must have materially lightened the labour of wood-working and clearing of brush-wood in agriculture.

†**'woodwose, 'woodhouse**, *sb. Obs.* (exc. *Hist.*). Forms: 1 **wudewasa**, 4 **wodwos**, (**-wysse**), 4–5 **wodewese**, 4–6 **wodewose**, 5 **wodwose**, (**-wous(e**, **-woys**, **-wosh(e**, **-wyssh(e**, **wodewyse**), 5–6 **woodwose**, **-wyss**, 6 **-woss**, *pl.* **wodys**, **vodys**. *β.* 5 **woodowes**, 6 **wodowes**, **woodos(e**, **wodehouse**, **-howse**, **wood(e)hous(e**. [Late OE. *wudewása*, f. *wudu* WOOD *sb.*[1] + **wása* (of obscure origin).] A wild man of the woods; a savage; a satyr, faun; a person dressed to represent such a being in a pageant.

Sometimes taken for or construed as *pl.*

a **1100** *Gloss.* in Wr.-Wülcker 108/22 *Satiri, uel fauni,.. uel fauni ficarii*, unfæle men, wudewasan, unfæle wihtu. **13..** *Gaw. & Gr. Knt.* 721 Sumwhyle wyth wormez he werrez,..Sumwhyle wyth wodwos, þat woned in þe knarrez. **13..** *Metr. Hom.* (Vernon MS.) in Herrig's *Archiv* LVII. 261 Þis Breusteres douhtur..tolde þe folk as wodewose wilde Who gat on hire þis forseyde childe. **1398** TREVISA *Barth. De P.R.* XV. xix. (Tollem. MS.) Þerin [*sc.* in Africa] ben satires, wodewoses, tigris, and oþer horrible bestes. ? *a* **1400** *Morte Arth.* 3817 Alls vnwyse wodewyse he wente at þe gayneste. *c* **1440** *Partonope* 7691 [4737] in *Anglia* XII. 616 Partanope hath now forsake The wodwous [*v. rr.* wodwoys, wodwose, wodwouse] lyfe. **1460** CAPGRAVE *Chron.* (Rolls) 257 The Kyng of Frauns daunsed in his halle with IIII knites, and was arayed lich a wodwous. **1484** CAXTON *Fables of Auian* xxii, A wodewose named Satyre. **1519** HORMAN *Vulg.* 109 Woode wosis be vpward nostrelde, *Satyri sunt sili.* **1555** MACHYN *Diary* (Camden) 96 Men lyke wodys alle in gren. **1556** WITHALS *Dict.* (1562) 15 A wodewose, *satyrus.*

β. *a* **1505** in Kingsford *Chron. Lond.* (1905) 251 Fourthly came..the Erle of Essex..wt a woodhous precedyng, and beryng a Sere tre. ? **1525** FITZHERB. *Husb.* Colophon, Emprynted at London in Southwarke, at the sygne of the wodowes. *a* **1548** HALL *Chron., Hen. VIII*, 9 b, These beastes were led with certayne men appareiled like wilde men, or woodhouses. **1553** T. WILSON *Rhet.* Pref. A iij, Some wente naked, some romed lyke woodoses, none did anye thing by reason. [**1832** ASPIN *Anc. Customs* etc. *English* 251 The savage men, or wodehouses, as they are sometimes called, frequently made their appearance in the public shows. **1866** J. NICHOLL *Comp. Ironmongers* 86 *note*, The engravings..represent ivy-men or wood-wards, characters introduced in the pageants..of that period [*c* 1515]. They were sometimes called woodhouses.]

b. A figure of such a being, as a decoration, a heraldic bearing or supporter, etc.

1355 in *Rep. MSS. Ld. Middleton* (1911) 465 Item j. botoner de roses, pris xl *s.* Item j. botoner de wodewoses, pris c *s.* **1381** *Test. Ebor.* (Surtees) I. 121 Lectum.. broudatum cum signis de wodewose. *a* **1400-50** *Wars Alex.* 1540 A vestoure..Wroȝt full of wodwose & oþer wild bestis. **1498** *Test. Ebor.* (Surtees) IV. 133 Sex cocliaria optima arg[entea] cum wodwoshes.

β. **1493** *Will of Feld* (Somerset Ho.), Dosen spones of siluer with woodowes on thende. **1513** in *Archaeologia* LXVI. 347 A Counterpoint of woodehouse lyned wt canvas. **1531** *Rec. St. Mary at Hill* (1905) 49, vj Sponys with woodos gylt. [**1910** F. BOND *Misericords* 16 The wodehouse is a very common supporter in heraldry. **1920** *Archaeologia* Ser. II. XIX. 81 Three woodhouses; between crosses.]

Hence †**'woodwose** *v. intr.*, to run wild.

13.. *Metr. Hom.* (Vernon MS.) in Herrig's *Archiv* LVII. 274 Ho is wodore þen þat mon þat muche skile and resun con..And goþ siþen wod wosande?

woody ('wʊdɪ), *a.* Forms: 4 **wodi**, 4, 6 **woddy**, 6 **woddye**, **wood(d)ye**, 6–7 **woddie**, **wood(d)ie**, 6–8 **wooddy**, 6– **woody**. [f. WOOD *sb.*[1] + -Y[1].]

I. 1. Covered or overgrown with wood; having a growth of trees or shrubs; full of or abounding in woods or forests; wooded.

1375 BARBOUR *Bruce* IV. 492 In a woddy glen. **1382** WYCLIF *Num.* xiii. 20 The erthe, fat, or bareyn, wodi, or with outen trees. **1545** BRINKLOW *Compl.* iv. (1874) 17 Such heathy, woddy, and moory ground, as is vnfruteful for corne or pasture. **1590** SPENSER *F.Q.* II. x. 33 Whence as he to those woodie hils did flie. *a* **1672** WOOD *Life* (O.H.S.) II. 134 The said mannour was in antient time, when 'twas wooddy, a stall or den for wild boares. **1788** GIBBON *Decl. & F.* xlii. IV. 250 A small woody island. **1796** [see WOODINESS 2]. **1835** THIRLWALL *Greece* viii. I. 305 The woody mountain tracts. **1842** HOWITT *Rur. & Dom. Life Germany* 251 As we approached, the hills..became wilder and woodier. **1867** MORRIS *Jason* XVII. 7 The rose-hung lanes of woody Kent.

¶**b.** Bushy.

1609 *Bible* (Douay) 2 Kings xvii. 10 They made them statues..under everie thicke woddie tree [Vulg. *omne lignum nemorosum*].

†**2.** Belonging to, inhabiting, or growing in woods or woodland; sylvan. *Obs.*

1590 SPENSER *F.Q.* I. vi. 18 The wooddy Nymphes, faire Hamadryades. **1599** T. M[OUFET] *Silkewormes* 14 The heards of woody outlawes fell. **1610** G. FLETCHER *Christ's Vict. Earth* vii, A grassie hillock..With woodie primroses befreckeled. **1655** J. S. *Bonarelli's Filli di Sciro* I. v. 20 Some woody Deity.

b. Of, pertaining to, or situated in a wood.

a **1721** PRIOR *Colin's Mistakes* i, To Wimpole's woody Shade his Way he sped. **1809** COLERIDGE *Three Graves* 495 Deep in a woody dell. *a* **1840** JOANNA BAILLIE *Verses Kirtled Spring* 17 The woody nook where bells of brighter blue Have clothed the ground. **1911** MRS. H. WARD *Case Rich. Meynell* xiv. 288 As they neared the end of the woody path, he looked up again.

II. †**3.** Made of wood, wooden. *Obs. rare.*

a **1540** BARNES *Images* Wks. (1573) 346/1 Stony & wooddy Images. **1563** *Mirr. Mag., Hastings* xx, In pryson pent, whose woddye walles to passe Of no less peryll than the dying was.

4. Of the nature of or consisting of wood; of or belonging to the wood as a constituent part of the plant; ligneous.

1597 GERARDE *Herbal* I. xvi. §2. 17 Salt Marsh Spike grasse hath a wooddie tough thicke roote. *a* **1704** LOCKE *Elem. Nat. Philos.* ix. (1754) 33 Herbs are those plants, whose stalks are soft, and have nothing woody in them. **1776** WITHERING *Bot. Arrangem.* 804 *Shrubby*, somewhat woody, as the stems of the Rose. **1846** *Zoologist* IV. 1282 The small roots of rose-bushes..sometimes produce rounded, warty, and woody knobs, inhabited by..gall-insects. **1859** DAWSON in *Q. Jrnl. Geol. Soc.* XV. 630 Leaves.. strengthened by nerves..composed of scalariform and woody tissue. **1908** *Animal Managem.* 87 Fibrous and woody elements..exist in varying proportions in all vegetable foods.

b. Of a plant: Of which wood is a constituent part; forming wood; having the stem and branches of wood; ***woody plant***, a tree or shrub, as distinguished from a *herb*; *spec.* in distinctive names of particular species, as ***woody nightshade***.

1578 LYTE *Dodoens* III. lvii. 398 Some Herboristes of Fraunce do cal it *Solanum lignosum*, that is to say, Wooddy Nightshade. **1796** WITHERING *Brit. Plants* (ed. 3) II. 48 Hardly to be called herbaceous; it is rather hard and wooddy. **1830** LINDLEY *Nat. Syst. Bot.* 99 The most northern woody plant..known is a kind of Willow, *Salix arctica.* **1883** *Longm. Mag.* July 307 Cinquefoil, grown woodier..from its..upland situation.

c. Resembling wood; having the texture or consistence of wood.

1791 W. BARTRAM *Carolina* 468 The fruit is a large, round, dry, woody apple..with dry woody cuneiform seed. **1840** *Civil Eng. & Arch. Jrnl.* III. 68/2 The coal is..rendered tougher, or, in the language of the colliers, more 'woody'. **1871** *Yng. Gentleman's Mag.* Mar. 132 An immense woody shell as large as a baby's head..hanging on one of the lower branches of the very tree on which I was sitting.

5. Pertaining to or characteristic of wood; resembling that of wood; having some quality (*e.g.* the smell) of wood.

1830 J. G. STRUTT *Sylva Brit.* 46 A piece of oak,..which, ..exposed to the sun and rains for a century,..yet smells woody. **1860** W. WHITE *Wrekin* xi. 100 Apples... Their substance is as hard as their flavour is woody and sour. **1876** MORRIS *Æneis* XII. 782 The gripping woody bite [of an arrow]. **1900** 'H. S. MERRIMAN' *Isle of Unrest* ix, Clean woody odours.

b. Having a dull sound like that of wood when struck.

1875 R. H. R. *Rambles in Istria* 50 A good campanile.. with two sweetly toned bells—why is it that ours are always so unmusical and woody? **1877** *Hon. Miss Ferrard* I. vii. 241 A little cottage piano, woody and dull of tone.

woody ('wʊdɪ), *sb. slang* (orig. *Surfing*). Chiefly *U.S.* Also **woodie**. [f. WOOD *sb.*[1] + -Y[6].] An estate car with timber-framed sides.

1961 *Surfer Q.* Winter 34 *(caption)* A 'woodie' piled high. Photographer Larry Stephens..challenges anyone to produce a picture of a surf car with more boards than his. **1969** *Surf Internat.* (Austral.) I. XI. 13 Nat and Paul push the woodie, it's stoked too, an' finally blows its gasket. **1973** J. MARKS *Mick Jagger* 87 Ramada Inn, the Yucca Hotel, Holiday Inn and the Seven Seas Hyatt Lodge—all in a row—saluting Dominique and the horde of military foundlings who plunge along Hotel Circle in borrowed *woodies*—those immaculate 1954 jobs by Ford: sturdy station wagons, armoured in wood. **1980** L. BIRNBACH et al. *Official Preppy Handbk.* 18/1 The other children were quite happy with their little red wagons; she would accept nothing but a woody.

woody, variant of WIDDY.

'wood-yard. Forms and etym.: see WOOD *sb.*[1] and YARD *sb.*[1] A yard or inclosure in which wood is chopped, sawn, or stored, esp. for use as fuel. Also *transf.* (quot. 1774).

1309-10 *Durham Acc. Rolls* (Surtees) 7 In j securi empt. pro le Wodyard, xj d. **1537-8** *Privy Purse Exp. P'cess Mary* (1831) 54 Item to the Squillary, vj s. Item to the Woodyerde, vij s. vj d. **1541-2** *Act 33 Hen. VIII*, c. 12 §3 The sergeant of the Woodyarde. **1627** CAPT. J. SMITH *Sea Gram.* i. 1 To those Docks..belongs their wood-yards, with saw-pits. *a* **1700** EVELYN *Diary* 12 Sept. 1676, Over against his Majesties wood yard. **1774** GOLDSM. *Nat. Hist.* IV. 166 Their wood-yards are larger or smaller, in proportion to the number in family; and..the usual stock of timber, for the accommodation of ten beavers, consists of about thirty feet in a square surface, and ten in depth. **1825** LONGF. in *Life* (1891) I. v. 62 There is no wood to be had from the College woodyard. **1859** JEPHSON & REEVE *Brittany* 268 We begged permission of the buxom proprietress of a woodyard, to pitch our tent among her heaps of timber.

†**woodyer.** *Obs.* In 5 **wodyere**. [OE. *wudi(ȝ)ere*, f. *wudian* to cut wood: see -IER. Cf. WOODER.] = WOODMAN[1] 2.

a **1100** *Gloss.* in Wr.-Wülcker 139/32 *Calones*, wudieras. *Ibid.* 150/31 *Calones*, wudiȝeras. *c* **1430** *Pilgr. Lyf Manhode* III. li. (1869) 146 A wodyere that solde me..wode in his foreste. **1802** *Sussex Weekly Advert.* 29 Nov. in *N. & Q.* (1910) 11th Ser. II. 529 To Be Sold Eight acres..of Underwood... Apply to James Wratton..the woodyer, who will shew the wood.

wooed (wu:d), *ppl. a.* [f. WOO *v.*[1] + -ED[1].] That is courted by a lover. Also *absol.*

1582 BENTLEY *Mon. Matrones* Pref. B i b, The wooed woman not to be by anie meanes cosined or abused in marriage. **1891** LE GALLIENNE *Retrosp. Rev.* (1896) I. 13 A wooer at a certain hot moment entreats the wooed: 'Will you, I ask once more, show your belief in me by letting me encircle you with my arm?'

wooer ('wu:ə(r)). Forms: 1 **woȝere**, 3, 5 **woware**, 4–5 **wowere** (4 **wouwere**), 4–6 **wower**, 5–6 *chiefly Sc.* **wowar**, 5 **woar**, *Sc.* **woweir**, 6 *Sc.* **wawar**, 6–8 **woer**, 6– **wooer**. [OE. *wóȝere*, f. WOO *v.*[1] + -ER[1].] One who woos a woman, esp. with a view to marriage, a suitor; *rarely* a woman who woos a man. Also in fig. context.

c **1000** ÆLFRIC *Saints' Lives* xvii. 157 Sume hi wyrcað heora woȝerum drencas..þæt hi hi to wife habbon. *c* **1025-50** *Rule of Chrodegang* lii. (1916) 64 Þonne wite þu þæt hi beoð woȝeras swiðor þonne preostas. *a* **1225** *Ancr. R.* 90 Ich am woware scheomeful. Ich nulle nouware bicluppe mine leofmon bute ine stude derne. **1377** LANGL. *P. Pl.* B. XI. 71 Ȝe faren lyke þise woweres, þat wedde none wydwes but forto welde here godis. *a* **1395** HYLTON *Scala Perf.* (W. de W. 1494) II. xliv, That it myghte come to theffecte of true spousage he hathe suche gracyous spekynges this maner of a wower to a chosen soule. **1513** DOUGLAS *Æneis* IV. Prol. 196 Traist nocht all talis that wantoun woweris tellis. **1546** J. HEYWOOD *Prov.* (1867) 73 He vnto hir a goodly tale began, More like a wooer, than a wedded man. **1635** A. STAFFORD *Fem. Glory* 88 He compares God to a Woer, the Angell to a sollicitour, and Mary to the beloved. **1724** RAMSAY *Tea-t. Misc.* (1733) I. 8 Now, Woer, quoth he, wou'd ye light down I'll gie ye my doghter's love to win. **1828** SCOTT *F.M. Perth* v, She were fittest Valentine in Perth for so craven a wooer. **1854** DICKENS *Hard T.* I. xvi, Mr. Bounderby went..to

Stone Lodge as an accepted wooer. **1869** SPURGEON *Treas. Dav.* Ps. xviii. 44 'Love at first sight' is no uncommon thing when Jesus is the wooer.

b. *transf.* of the lower animals.

1577 GOOGE *Heresbach's Husb.* 126 b, If shee haue not been horsed before, she wil so beate her woer, y[t] [etc.]. **1889** *Science-Gossip* XXV. 236 It is not always the males [*sc.* butterflies] who are the wooers.

c. *Comb.*

1513 DOUGLAS *Æneis* XII. Prol. 300 To crowd In amorus voce and wowar soundis lowd. **1785** BURNS *Halloween* iii, The lads sae trig, wi' wooer-babs. **1825** JAMIESON, *Wooer-bab*,..the garter knotted below the knee with a couple of loops, formerly worn by a young man who was too sheepish to announce in plain terms the purpose of his visit.

woof (wuːf), *sb.*[1] Forms: α. 1 owef, 3 of, 4–5 oof, 4, 6 ofe, 5 offe, 6 owfe, 7 oufe. β. 6–7 woofe, wouf(e, (6 wolfe, wowfe, 7 *pl.* woovis), 7–8 wooff, (8 wooft, whoof), 7– woof. [OE. *ówef* (later *áwef*), f. *ó-* + *wefan* to WEAVE. (Cf. the later parallel formation *óweb*, *áweb* ABB.) ME. **owf*, *oof* became *woof* partly by association with WARP *sb.* in *warp and (w)oof*, or with WEFT.]

1. The threads that cross from side to side of a web, at right angles to the warp: = WEFT *sb.*[1] 1.

α. *c* **725** *Corpus Gloss.* (Hessels) C 467 *Cladica*, wefl uel owef. *c* **1050** *Voc.* in Wr.-Wülcker 364/23 *Cladica*, wefl, oððe owef, oððe claudica. *c* **1200** *MS. Bodl. 730* lf. 145/1 *Subtemen*, of. **1382** WYCLIF *Lev.* xiii. 47 A wullun clooth, or lynnen, that hath a lepre in the oof, or in the werpe. **1398** TREVISA *Barth De P.R.* XVIII. xi. (1495) aa iv b/1 The spynner..begynnyth fro the mydyll poynt & gooth rounde abawte the ofe. **14..** *Metr. Voc.* in Wr.-Wülcker 628/1 *Subtegmen*, [*gloss* warpe], *sic quoque stamen*, [*gloss* offe]. *c* **1440** *Promp. Parv.* 362/1 Oof, threde for webbynge, *trama*. **1556** WITHALS *Dict.* (1562) 35 b/2 The warpe, *stamen*. The ofe, *subtegmen*. **1599** MINSHEU *Sp. Dict.* s.v. *Lizos*, The owfe or thread of linnen. **1603** HOLLAND *Plutarch's Mor.* 337 To spoole, winde quils, lay his warpe, shoot oufe.

β. **1530** TINDALE *Lev.* xiii. 48 Whether it be in the warpe or wolfe of the lynen or of the wollen. **1570** LEVINS *Manip.* 157/25 Y[e] Woofe of a web, *subtegmen*. **1626** BACON *Sylva* §846 As it is in the Warpe, and the Woofe, of Textiles. **1657** TRAPP *Comm. Ps.* xv. 2 Such, as through whose whole lives godliness runneth, as the Woof doth through the Warp. **1714** *Fr. Bk. Rates* 188 The Workmen shall not make Use, neither in the Warp or the Woof,..of any Yarn of a different Quality. **1780** A. YOUNG *Tour Irel.* I. 324 Threads thrown across by the shuttle are called the wooft. **1802** JOANNA BAILLIE *1st Pt. Ethwald* III. iv, But tell them, British matrons cross the woof With coarser hands than theirs. **1875** JOWETT *Plato* (ed. 2) V. 76 In a web the warp is stronger than the woof.

b. *fig.* and in fig. context, often in collocation with *warp*.

1583 MELBANCKE *Philotimus* I j, To..wrappe vp his life-warpes woofe with so euill a liste. **1596** NASHE *Saffron Walden* M 2, The process of that Oration, was of the same woofe and thrid with the beginning. **1627** W. HAWKINS *Apollo Shroving* I. i. 8 Where euery English thread is ouercast with a thicke woollen woofe of strange wordes. **1757** GRAY *Bard* II. i, Weave the warp, and weave the woof, The winding sheet of Edward's race. **1849** [see WARP *sb.*[1] 1 b]. **1863** GEO. ELIOT *Romola* xix, That commerce of feigned and preposterous admiration which..made the woof of all learned intercourse. **1882** MISS BRADDON *Mt. Royal* II. 19 The woof of self-interest is so cunningly interwoven with the warp of righteous feeling that very few of us can tell where the threads cross.

2. Thread used to make the woof; also in vague poetical use.

1540 HYRDE tr. *Vives' Instr. Chr. Wom.* I. iii. (1541) 3 b, To warpe, or els wynd spindels in a case, for to throw wofe of. **1598** R. BERNARD tr. *Terence, Heautontim.* II. iii, The old wife shee spun the woufe. **1634** MILTON *Comus* 83 First I must put off These my skie robes spun out of Iris Wooff. **1638** *Burgh Rec. Glasgow* (1876) 388 Thair suld be no woovis wovin of townis folkis thairin. **1667** MILTON *P.L.* XI. 244 Iris had dipt the wooff. **1892** RIDER HAGGARD *Nada* xi, Did I weave these visions from the woof of my madness?

3. A woven fabric, esp. as being of a particular texture: = WEFT *sb.*[1] 3; also, the texture of a fabric. Often *transf.* or *fig.*

1674 N. FAIRFAX *Bulk & Selv.* 74 That woof and plight that the whole ticklish frame of worldly beings are wheel'd into at such a tide of day [*viz.* dawn]. *Ibid.* 74 That we can sometimes force bodies to close with the woof or tenor of the whole. **1725** POPE *Odyss.* IV. 164 To spread the pall beneath the regal chair Of softest woof. **1757** DYER *Fleece* III. 40 Curious woofs of beauteous hue. **1790** COWPER *Odyss.* XIX. 173 A robe..of subtlest woof. **1811** SCOTT *Don Roderick* II. xxiv, Flames dart their glare o'er midnight's sable woof. **1820** KEATS *Lamia* II. 232 There was an awful rainbow once in heaven: We know her woof, her texture. **1826** JOANNA BAILLIE *Martyr* II. ii, The very spider through his circled cage Of wiry woof,..Scarce seems a lothly thing. **1838** LYTTON *Alice* V. v, That girl's thread of life has been the dark line in my woof. **1846** —— *Lucretia* II. xviii, The Parcæ closed the abrupt woof, and lifted the impending shears. **1866** —— *Lost Tales Miletus, Secret Way* 4 The woofs of Phrygian looms. **1871** BRYANT *Odyss.* V. 416 Receive this veil, and bind its heavenly woof Beneath thy breast.

†**4.** The action of weaving. *Obs. rare.*

1700 DRYDEN *Ceyx & Alc.* 237 Alcyone..hastens in the Woof the Robes he was to wear.

woof (wʊf), *int.* and *sb.*[2] Also wouf, wowff.

1. Imitation of a gruff abrupt bark of a dog; also *transf.* (Cf. WHOOF.)

1839 J. BALLANTINE in *Whistle-Binkie* Ser. II. 26 The wowff o' the colley. **1859** H. KINGSLEY *G. Hamlyn* xxv, Every now and then..he [*sc.* a dog] would discharge a 'Woof', like a minute-gun at sea. **1885** RIDER HAGGARD *K. Sol. Mines* iv, Presently.. came a loud 'woof, woof!' 'That's a lion', said I. **1918** B. CABLE *Air Men o' War* 14 The hoarse 'woof' of a bursting anti-aircraft shell.

2. Var. WHOOF *int.* (*sb.*)

3. Low-frequency sound of poor quality from a loudspeaker.

1961 in WEBSTER. **1962** *Listener* 22 Nov. 882/1 It isn't only technicians who can justifiably complain about too much tweet and woof. **1978** *Gramophone* Jan. 1298/3 They..are every bit the equal of the LPs, a beautifully warm and detailed orchestral tapestry, with..a richly resonant bass (without too much 'woof').

woof (wuːf), *v.*[1] *rare.* [f. WOOF *sb.*[1] Cf. WOOFED.] *trans.* To arrange (threads) so as to form a woof; to weave. Also *transf.*

1894 ALICE C. MACDONELL in *Lyra Celtica* (1896) 252 Woof well the cross threads, To make the colours shine. **1922** *Blackw. Mag.* July 6/2 The fearful tangle of vegetation, warped and woofed together by lianas and creeping plants.

woof, *v.*[2] Also wouff. **1.** (Of a dog) to utter a gruff abrupt bark.

1804 TARRAS *Poems* 59 (Jam.) Curs began to wouff an' bark. **1932** E. M. BRENT-DYER *Chalet Girls in Camp* vi. 97 Rufus..crossed the meadow at his best pace, woofing indignantly at intervals. **1955** V. NABOKOV *Lolita* II. xxviii. 171 A nondescript cur came out from behind the house, stopped in surprise, and started good-naturedly woof-woofing at me, his eyes slit, his shaggy belly all muddy, and then walked about a little and woofed once more. **1974** *Publishers Weekly* 5 Aug. 53/3 His attempt suggests a puppy woofing at a caterpillar—but keeping a safe distance.

2. *U.S. Blacks' slang.* **a.** *intr.* To talk (or, *trans.*, to say) in an ostentatious or aggressive manner.

1934 *Amer. Speech* IX. 290/1 [Negro slang.] *Woof*, to talk much and loudly and yet say little of consequence. **1935** Z. N. HURSTON *Mules & Men* I. iv. 86 The men would crowd in and buy soft drinks and woof at me, the stranger, but I knew I wasn't getting on. **1941** *Life* 27 Jan. 78 To reinforce a statement, a sub-deb says, *I ain't woofin'*..which means 'I'm not fooling'. **1941** *Direction* Summer 15/2 Stack got all big at the nose and woofed: 'All right, boss, you either fixes me up with that gin, or I pulls down this bar!' **1972** J. WAMBAUGH *Blue Knight* vi. 86 He was woofing me, because he winked at the blond kid. **1974** H. L. FOSTER *Ribbin', Jivin', & Playin' Dozens* iv. 140 A student might say, 'Mr. Foster, he's woofin' on me.' This may have meant anything from he is challenging me to a fight, to he is making fun of my clothing or my mother.

Hence **'woofing** *vbl. sb.* and *ppl. a.*

1942 *Amer. Mercury* July 96/2 *Woofing*, aimless talk, as a dog barks on a moonlight night. **1969** H. R. BROWN in H. L. Foster *Ribbin', Jivin', & Playin' Dozens* (1974) v. 179 Those young brothers came out of this woofing, diddy-bopping and raising hell period. **1973** B. G. COOKE in T. Kochman *Rappin' & Stylin' Out* 45 'Woofing' is a style of bragging and boasting about how 'bad' one is and is sometimes used by males and females when rapping to each other. **1975** *Today's Education* Sept./Oct. 54 Some of the woofin' has been precipitated by Whites trying to hustle Blacks out of goods and materials which have been promised or which are rightfully theirs. **1977** *Time* 14 Nov. 90/3 Cosby, who has one of the great faces of the Western world, is the best thing in this woofin', shuckin' film.

woof, obs. pa. t. of WEAVE *v.*

woofed (wuːft, *poet.* 'wuːfɪd), *ppl. a.* [f. WOOF *sb.*[1] + -ED. (Cf. WOOF *v.*[1])] Woven; *fig.* intricate.

1820 KEATS *Eve St. Agnes* xxxii, So mus'd awhile, entoil'd in woofed phantasies.

woofer ('wuːfə(r), 'wʊfə(r)). [f. WOOF *v.*[2] + -ER[1].]

1. *U.S. Blacks' slang.* (See quot. 1934.)

1934 *Amer. Speech* IX. 289/1 *Woofer*, applied to one who talks constantly, loudly, and in a convincing manner, but who says very little. **1935** Z. N. HURSTON *Mules & Men* I. iv. 88, I want outside to join the woofers, since I seemed to have no standing among the dancers. **1974** H. L. FOSTER *Ribbin', Jivin', & Playin' Dozens* v. 202 The woofer may also move his body in a menacing way to make his woof more threatening and intimidating.

2. A loudspeaker designed to reproduce accurately low-frequency sounds whilst being relatively unresponsive to those of higher frequency. Cf. SQUAWKER 3, TWEETER.

1935 K. HENNEY *Radio Engin. Handbk.* (ed. 2) xxiv. 830 Wide range of frequency response is sometimes secured by using as many as three groups of speakers: low ('woofers'), medium, and high ('tweeters'). **1959** *Consumer Rep.* Sept. 453/1 The Best Buy..is..much the better value of the two tweeters when coupled to a check-rated woofer. **1964** M. MCLUHAN *Understanding Media* (1967) xxxi. 348 It is like a badly wired woofer in a hi-fi circuit that produces a tremendous flutter in the bottom. **1979** *Arizona Daily Star* 5 Aug. I. 10/1 (Advt.), Big savings on a great sounding speaker. 8″ woofer for deep bass and 2½″ tweeter for clear highs.

woofits ('wuːfɪts). *slang.* [Origin unknown.] An unwell feeling, esp. in the head; moody depression.

1918 J. M. GRIDER *War Birds* (1927) 96 Curtis says he is suffering from the Woofits, that dread disease that comes from overeating and underdrinking. *Ibid.* 207, I drank too much coffee before getting up and I'm as nervous as a kitten now. Must be getting the Woofits. **1932** *Amer. Speech* VII. 338 [Johns Hopkins jargon.] *Woofits*, ailment that comes with 'the morning after the night before'. **1958** 'N. SHUTE' *Rainbow & Rose* 100 Getting the woofits now, because I don't sleep so good.

woofter ('wʊftə(r), 'wuːftə(r)). *slang.* Also wooftah. [Fanciful alteration of POOFTER.] = POOFTER.

1977 *Private Eye* 8 July 5/1 The headshrinker had been reduced to a nervous wreck, and was prepared to dismiss the rabidly heterosexual Tynan as a wooftah. **1980** A. N. WILSON *Healing Art* iv. 47 The two young woofters in the pub.

woofy ('wuːfɪ), *a.*[1] *rare.* [f. WOOF *sb.*[1] + -Y[1].] Resembling a woof or woven fabric; of dense texture. Also *transf.*

The sense of the 20th-c. quots. is unclear.

1826 JOANNA BAILLIE *Martyr* II. i, Close round us hung, the vapours of the night Had form'd a woofy curtain. **1976–7** *Art N.Z.* Dec./Jan. 15/1 She would have none of the delirious woofy mango-swamp muck of the then Auckland School. **1983** R. SUTCLIFF *Blue Remembered Hills* xvi. 124 A moustache..not of the woofy RAF variety but more akin to the kind worn by sergeant-majors.

woofy ('wʊfɪ), *a.*[2] [f. WOOF *int.*, *sb.*[2], and *v.*[2] + -Y[1].] Of reproduced sound: having too much bass, or bass that is indistinct.

1932 J. H. REYNER *Mod. Radio Communication* (ed. 4) xx. 204 We shall experience a loss of the upper frequencies, the reproduction lacking brilliance and sounding 'woofy'. **1975** *Gramophone* Nov. 819/2, I prefer the sound of the horns.. on the Decca Ace of Diamonds record, a much cleaner sound than the rather 'woofy' quality on the new record.

woofy, *a.*[3] *nonce-wd.* [Perh. f. WOOF *v.*[2]] ? Talkative.

1960 C. P. SNOW *Affair* xl. 371 The hairline which, when he was drunk, separated the diffuse and woofy benevolence from a suspicion of all mankind.

wooing ('wuːɪŋ), *vbl. sb.* Forms: 1 woȝung, 3 wouhinge, wowunge, 4–6 wowyng, -ing, 6 woynge, wooyng, 7–8 woing, 7– wooing. [f. WOO *v.*[1] + -ING[1].] The action of the verb woo; amorous solicitation, courtship: in ME. often with dyslogistic implication.

c **1000** ÆLFRIC *Saints' Lives* vii. 301 Wearð þa se casere for þære woȝunge astyrod. *a* **1225** *Ancr. R.* 204 Mid wouhinge, mid togginge, oðer mid eni tollunge. *a* **1310** in Wright *Lyric P.* vi. 28 Icham for wowyng al for-wake, wery so water in wore. **13..** *Gaw. & Gr. Knt.* 2361 Now know I wel þy cosses, & þy costes als, & þe wowyng of my wyf. *c* **1385** CHAUCER *L.G.W.* 1553 *Hypsip. & Medea*, As wolde god I leyser hadde & tyme By proces al his wowyng for to ryme. *c* **1440** *Jacob's Well* 164 Caste out..leccherous woordys, wowynges, leccherous syȝtes. *a* **1548** HALL *Chron., Edw. IV*, 195 Hys vnaduised wowyng, hasty louyng and to spedy mariage. **1588** SHAKS. *L.L.L.* v. ii. 884 Our woing doth not end like an old Play: Iacke hath not Gill. **1645** FULLER *Good Th. in Bad T.* (1646) 106, I do not like the wooing, that you should fetch a Bride with Fire and Sword. **1721** RAMSAY *'The Last Time I came o'er the Moor'* i, I met betimes my lovely Maid, In fit Retreats for wooing. **1792** BURNS *Song, Duncan Gray*, Duncan Gray cam'here to woo, Ha, ha, the wooing o't. **1867** TENNYSON *Window* 166 Here is the golden close of love, All my wooing is done. **1882** BESANT *All Sorts* xxvii, No girl likes to do her own wooing; she must be courted.

Proverbs. [**1596** SHAKS. *Tam. Shr.* II. i. 75 *Pet.* I would faine be doing. *Gre.* I doubt it not sir. But will curse Your wooing.] **1659** N. R. *Proverbs* 24 Courting and wooing brings dallying and doing. **1670** RAY *Prov.* 48 Happy is the woing, that is not long in doing.

b. freq. in *to go, come, ride a* (or †*on*) *wooing*.

c **1460** METHAM *Wks.* (1916) 150 Yt ys spedeful that day to go a wowyng. **1595** *Knaresb. Wills* (Surtees) I. 201 His short gowne..which he hath lente to Tho. Atkinson for iij dayes to ride on woweinge with. **1604** SHAKS. *Oth.* III. iii. 71 What? Michael Cassio, That came a woing with you? *a* **1611** in T. Ravenscroft *Melismata* F 1 b, The Frogge would a woing ride. **1690** LOCKE *Govt.* I. xi. §135 His Servant whom he sent a wooing for his Son. **1711** ADDISON *Spect.* No. 129 ¶10 When they go a wooing..they generally put on a red Coat. **1841** DICKENS *Barn. Rudge* iii, He went out to-day a wooing.

c. *fig.*

a **1225** *Ancr. R.* 116 Þis is wowunge efter Godes grome, & tollunge of his vuel. *a* **1240** *O.E. Hom.* I. 269 Her biginnes þe wohunge of ure lauerd. *c* **1440** *Promp. Parv.* 533/1 Wowynge, *procacio*. **1596** DRAYTON *Leg. Robt. Dk. Norm.* xxvi, Except in Perill, thou do'st not appeare; Yet scarcely then, but with Intreats and Wooing. **1613** W. BROWNE *Brit. Past.* I. ii. (1616) 41 My Maiden-Muse flies the lasciuious Swaines,..Will not dilate..His curious searches, his respectlesse wooings. **1856** GRINDON *Life* xviii. (1875) 218 Work is the wooing by which happiness is won.

d. *attrib.* and *Comb.*, as ***wooing act, dance, day, language, mind, suit***.

1704 *Phil. Trans.* XXIV. 1589 (2), I have plainly shewed their Ticking noise to be a *wooing Act. **1596** SHAKS. *Tam. Shr.* I. ii. 68 As wealth is burthen of my *wooing dance. **1562** J. HEYWOOD *Prov. & Epigr.* (1867) 130 In loue is no lacke, no in no *wooyng day. **1878** GIBBON *For the King* iii, The ardour of our wooing days. **1612** DRAYTON *Poly-olb.* To Rdr. (end), To Gentlewomen and their Loves is consecrated all the *Wooing Language..feigned by the Muse amongst Hills and Rivers. **1588** SHAKS. *L.L.L.* v. ii. 412 Henceforth my *woing minde shall be exprest In russet yeas, and honest kersie noes. **1622** *Buccleuch MSS.* (Hist. MSS. Comm.) I. 210 He comes upon a *wooing suit for the Infanta.

wooing ('wuːɪŋ), *ppl. a.* [f. WOO *v.*[1] + -ING[2].] That woos. **a.** That solicits in love; courting, as a lover; †wanton.

1382 WYCLIF *Prov.* vii. 13 The caȝte ȝunge man she kisseth; and with wowende [**1388** wowynge] chere she flatereth. **1387** TREVISA *Higden* (Rolls) VII. 409 [He] ordeyned wommen to serven hem..þat semede wowynge gigelottes in cloþing, face, and semblant. *c* **1440** *Jacob's Well* 163 Whan þou, wyth wowyng woordys, styrest oþere to þi lust, it is dedly synne. **1746** DUNKIN in Francis tr. *Hor.*, *Sat.*

II. v. 11 The wooing Tribe, in Revellings employ'd, My Stores have lavish'd.

b. *fig.* Alluring, enticing.

1549 COVERDALE, etc. *Erasm. Par. James* iv. 1–6 He maye not abyde the wowynge worlde to bee loued. *c* **1620** Z. BOYD *Zion's Flowers* (1855) 73 They..step back, or forward, in their wooeing wise. **1838** LYTTON *Alice* XI. iv, The letter was most courteous, most complimentary, most wooing. **1838** MANGAN *Poems* (1903) 204 Each wooing Zephyr that goes, At will from flower to flower a-maying. **1878** B. TAYLOR *Deukalion* II. iv, Be thou a wooing breeze.

Comb. *a* **1661** HOLYDAY *Juvenal* (1673) 95 No Hæmus or soft Carpophorus appears More wooing-voic'd.

wooingly ('wu:ɪŋlɪ), *adv.* [f. WOOING *ppl. a.* + -LY[2].] In a wooing manner.

†**1.** Wantonly, impudently. *Obs.*

1382 WYCLIF *Prov.* xxi. 29 The vnpitous man wowendeli [**1388** vnschamefastli, Vulg. *procaciter*] stablith his chere. **1552** HULOET, Wowingly, *procaciter*.

2. Enticingly, alluringly.

1605 SHAKS. *Macb.* I. vi. 6 The Heauens breath Smells wooingly here. **1824** MISS FERRIER *Inher.* lxxxi, I perhaps did not go so wooingly to work as some one more designing would have done. **1849** MISS MULOCK *Ogilvies* xl, It came over her senses wooingly. **1884** MRS. C. PRAED *Zero* viii, The air kissed wooingly.

3. Like a wooer; with amatory speeches.

1868 HOLME LEE *B. Godfrey* xvi, He was..whispering.. wooingly.

wook(e, obs. pa. t. of WAKE *v.*, obs. f. WEEK.

wool (wʊl), *sb.* Forms: 1, 5–6 **wul, wull,** 3–6 **woll,** 4–5 **wulle, wolle,** 4–6 **wole, woolle,** 5–6 *Sc.* **vol,** (1 **uul,** 3, 6 **wol,** 5 **who(o)ll, whowl,** *Sc.* **woyll, voyll, wo,** 6 **woull(e),** 5–7 *Sc.* **wow,** 6–8 **wooll,** (8 **owl,** 8– *dial.* **woo, oo', oo),** 6– **wool.** [Com. Teut. and Indo-Eur.: OE. *wull*, str. f. = OFris. *wolle, ulle*, (M)LG. *wulle*, MDu. *wolle, wulle* (Du. *wol*), OHG. *wolla* (MHG. *wolle, wulle*, G. *wolle*), ON. *ull* (Sw. *ull*, Da. *uld*), Goth. *wulla*:—OTeut. **wullō*:—pre-Teut. **wḷná*.

Cognate are Skr. *ū́rnā*, Zend *varənā-*, OSlav. *vlŭna*, Lith. *vìlna* thread of wool, pl. *vìlnos* wool, OPruss. *wilnis* coat, Russ. *vólna* fleece, wool, Gr. λῆνος (Dor. λᾶνος) wool, οὖλος (:—*ϝολνος) woolly, curly, Lat. *vellus* (:—**welnos*) fleece, *lāna* (:—**wlānā*) wool, Ir. *olann*, Welsh *gwlan*. The ultimate etymology is doubtful.]

1. a. The fine soft curly hair forming the fleecy coat of the domesticated sheep (and similar animals), characterized by its property of felting (due to the imbricated surface of the filaments) and used chiefly in a prepared state for making cloth; freq., the material in a prepared state as a commodity.

Spanish or ***oriental wool***, wool treated with a dye, used as a cosmetic.

c **725** *Corpus Gloss.* (Hessels) L 84 *Lana*, uul. *c* **1000** *Sax. Leechd.* I. 356 Blacu rammes wul on wætere ʒedyfed. *c* **1100** *Gloss.* in Wr.-Wülcker 190/25 Unawæscen wull. *c* **1290** *Kath.* 246 in *S. Eng. Leg.* 99 Also man draweth with combes wolle. **1297** R. GLOUC. (Rolls) 10033 Greye monekes þat newe come & pouere þo were, ȝeue al hor wolle þerto of one ȝere. **1338** R. BRUNNE *Chron.* (1810) 168 þe mene folk.. doand him seruise, þat bies woule & wyne. **1362** LANGL. *P. Pl.* A. XI. 18 Hit beo cardet with Couetise, as cloþers doþ heor wolle. *c* **1385** CHAUCER *L.G.W.* 1721 *Lucrece*, Softe wolle..she wroughte To kepe hire from slouthe & Idilnesse. **1436** *Libel Eng. Policy* in *Pol. Poems* (Rolls) II. 161 Oure Englysshe commodytees, Wolle and tynne. **1480** *Cely Papers* (Camden) 33 Howr father wyll schype the remanand of good whooll of thys sorte. **1506** *Acc. Ld. High Treas. Scot.* III. 249 Item, for woll to the schulderis of it [*sc.* a gown], xvj[d]. **1535** COVERDALE *2 Kings* iii. 4 Mesa y[e] kynge of the Moabites..payed tribute vnto the kynge of Israel with the woll of an hundreth thousande lambes. **1634** MILTON *Comus* 751 To teize the huswifes wooll. **1678** Spanish wool [see SPANISH *a.* 7]. **1712** J. MORTON *Northampt.* 451 Wool wrought together and compacted as closely, as Wool is by the Workman's Hands, in the making a Hat. **1755** *Connoisseur* No. 65 ¶2, I am ashamed to tell you that we are indebted to Spanish Wool for many of our masculine ruddy complexions. **1757** DYER *Fleece* II. 72 In the same Fleece diversity of wool Grows intermingled. **1826** J. RENNIE *New Suppl. Pharm.* 292 Oriental Wool. This coloured wool comes from China in large round loose cakes... The finest of these gives a most lovely and agreeable blush to the cheek. **1832** TENNYSON *Œnone* 246, I hear Dead sounds at night.. Like footsteps upon wool. **1871** W. REID *Sheep* 82 An increased supply of mutton and wool.

b. The fleece or complete woolly covering of a sheep, etc.; ***out of the wool***, shorn.

c **1400** *Destr. Troy* 161 This whethur and þe wole were wonderly keppit By..Mars. **1550** in Phillipps *Wills* (*c* 1830) 180 Threescore Sheep, to be delivered unto him out of their wool. **1572** *Satir. Poems Reform.* xxxii. 42 To bring the woll, the skin, and hyde To Edinburgh Towne. **1841** SARAH, LADY LYTTELTON in *Corr.* (1912) 310 Lord S... left town ..'to see the sheep just out of the wool after shearing.'

c. The short soft under-hair or down forming part of the coat of certain hairy or furry animals.

1605 SHAKS. *Macb.* IV. i. 15 Eye of Newt, and Toe of Frogge, Wooll of Bat, and Tongue of Dogge. **1607** TOPSELL *Four-f. Beasts* 274 The powder of the wooll of a Hare burned ..fasteneth the haire from falling off. **1615** MARKHAM *Country Contentm.* I. 103 After your dogge hath courst,.. first cleanse his mouth and chaps from the wool of the Hare. **1623** B. JONSON *Underwoods, Celebr. Charis* iv. 25 Ha' you felt the wooll of Bever? **1757** *Refl. Importation of Bar-Iron* 13 The American bought the Beaver Wool (the raw Material [of a hat]) at a much cheaper Rate. **1837** YOUATT *Sheep* iii. 57 The camel has, at the base of its long hair, a quantity of wool. **1870** YEATS *Nat. Hist. Comm.* 288.

†**d.** As the material of the thread spun and cut off by the Fates. *Obs.*

1608 B. JONSON *Hue & Cry after Cupid* Wks. (1616) 939 That was reseru'd, vntill the Parcæ spunne Their whitest wooll; and then, his thred begun. **1648** HERRICK *Hesper., Epithal.* 162 Let bounteous Fate your spindles full Fill, and winde up with whitest wool.

e. With qualifying word. See also *fell-wool* (FELL *sb.*[1] 4), *goat's-wool* (GOAT 4c), LAMB'S-WOOL, *skin-wool* (SKIN *sb.* 16), etc.

1495 *Nottingham Rec.* III. 42 Centum stones de flesse wolle et skyn wolle. **1498** HALYBURTON *Ledger* (1867) 219 A pok of lam vol. *c* **1541** *Tenours Indentures* 19 Cotiswold wolle of the growynge of this present yere. **1698–9** *Act 11 Will. III*, c. 20 §1 Manufactures..made of Sheeps Wooll or Coney Wooll.

f. In comparisons, e.g. *as soft, white as wool.*

c **825** *Vesp. Psalter* cxlvii. 16 Se seleð snawe swe swe wulle. *c* **1290** *S. Eng. Leg.* I. 265 Hire her was hor and swiþe ʒwijʒt as þei it were wolle. **1382** WYCLIF *Rev.* i. 14 The heed of him and heeres weren white, as whijt wulle. *c* **1386** CHAUCER *Miller's T.* 63 Softer than the wolle is of a wether. *c* **1480** HENRYSON *Two Mice* 359 Als warme as woll. **1533** GAU *Richt Vay* (S.T.S.) 63 Giff ȝour sinnis be.. reid as purpur neuthertheles yai sal be quhit as wow. **1742** R. FORBES *Ajax* etc. *Shop Bill* (1755) 38 Some are cotton, That's safter far na' ony woo, that grows on mutton. **1839** LONGF. *Wreck of Hesperus* xviii, She struck where the white and fleecy waves Looked soft as carded wool.

g. Phrases and proverbial sayings. (*a*) ***against the wool***: contrary to the direction in which wool naturally lies, the wrong way. (*b*) ***to draw*** (or ***pull,*** † ***spread***) ***the wool over*** (a person's) ***eyes***: to make blind to facts, to hoodwink, to deceive. orig. *U.S.* (*c*) ***to dye in the wool***: to dye the wool before spinning; *fig.* in *pass.* to be thoroughly imbued; ***dyed in the wool*** (chiefly *U.S.*), thoroughgoing, out-and-out (cf. *wool-dyed* in 5d). †(*d*) ***to gather wool***: see WOOL-GATHERING 2. (*e*) ***great*** (***much***) ***cry and little wool*** (etc.): much talk or clamour with insignificant results (see CRY *sb.* 16). (*f*) ***all wool and a yard wide*** and varr., of excellent quality; thoroughly sound or honourable. (*g*) ***wool away!*** (*Austral.* and *N.Z.*) (see quot. 1965). (*h*) ***to lose one's wool*** (slang), to lose one's temper; similarly ***to keep one's wool***, etc. (cf. HAIR *sb.* 8s and sense 2c below). (*i*) Miscellaneous.

(*a*) **1531** TINDALE *Expos. 1 John* iv. Wks. (1573) 415/1 He wresteth all the Scriptures & setteth them clean agaynst the woll, to destroy this article. **1546** J. HEYWOOD *Prov.* I. xi. (1867) 30 What should your face thus agayne the woll be shorne For one fall? **1599** BRETON *Wil of Wit* (Grosart) 60/2 But begging is a vile life in the meane time. *Patience.* Then worke. *Anger.* That goes against the wooll. *a* **1693** *Urquhart's Rabelais* III. xxxvi. 298 Let us..brush our former Words against the Wool.

(*b*) **1839** *Jamestown* (N.Y.) *Jrnl.* 24 Apr. 1/6 That lawyer has been trying to spread the wool over your eyes. **1842** *Spirit of Times* (Phila.) 29 Sept. (Th.), Look sharp, or they'll pull wool over your eyes. **1855** FRANCES M. WHITCHER *Widow Bedott* xv. (1883) 55 He ain't so big a fool as to have the wool drawd over his eyes in that way. *a* **1859** in Bartlett *Dict. Amer.* (ed. 2) 517 They think they find a prize, If they can only pull their wool o'er other people's eyes. **1884** HOWELLS *Silas Lapham* vii, I don't propose he shall pull the wool over my eyes.

(*c*) **1579–80, 1679** [see DYE *v.* 1c]. **1597** HOOKER *Eccl. Pol.* v. lxxii. §18 Children as it were in the Wooll of their infancie died with hardnesse may neuer afterwards change colour. **1830** D. WEBSTER *Sp.* in *Mass. Spy* 10 Feb. (Thornton) In half an hour [he can] come out an original democrat, dyed in the wool. **1840** J. P. KENNEDY *Quodlibet* ii. 52 As patent a dyed-in-the-wool Democrat as Theodore Fog himself. **1871** *College Courant* 21 Jan. (Schele de Vere *Amer.*) A drenching rain has washed the indigo from his new suit dyed in the wool at home, into his skin. **1885** HUMMEL *Dyeing Textile Fabrics* 289 If in any dyed woollen fabric the colour has been imparted to it while it was yet in the state of unspun wool, it is said to be wool-dyed, or to have been dyed in the wool. **1900** *Century Mag.* Feb. 503/2 Socialists dyed in the wool. **1903** *Smart Set* IX. 23/2 The governor of Alleghenia is a dyed-in-the-wool scoundrel.

(*d*) **1577** T. KENDALL *Flowers Epigr., Trifles* 15 The Papist praies with mouth, his minde on gathering woolle doeth goe. **1603** BRETON *Packet Mad Lett.* II. (1633) 83 For their wits, if they loose not their owne fleeces, let them gather Wool where they can.

(*e*) *c* **1460** FORTESCUE *Abs. & Lim. Mon.* x. (1885) 132 His hyghnes shall haue þeroff, but as hadd þe man þat sherid is hogge, muche crye and litil woll. **1579** GOSSON *Sch. Abuse* (Arb.) 28 Here is..as one said at the shearing of hogs, great cry and litle wool. **1644** PRYNNE *Falsities & Forgeries* 2 Here is a great cry indeed, but little wool. **1721** KELLY *Sc. Prov.* 165 Humph, quoth the Dee'l when he clip'd the Sow, A great cry, and little Woo. *a* **1734** NORTH *Life Ld. Kpr. North* (1742) 170 For Matter of Title he thought there was more Squeak than Wool. **1809** MALKIN *Gil Blas* v. i. (Rtldg.) 201 At first, there was much cry but little wool. **1862** HISLOP *Prov. Scot.* 142 'Mair whistle than woo', quo' the souter when he sheared the sow.

(*f*) **1882** G. W. PECK *Peck's Sunshine* 85 You want to pick out (as the 'boss combination girl' of Rock Co.) a thoroughbred, that is, all wool, a yard wide. **1909** [see LALLAPALOOSA]. **1913** J. LONDON *Valley of Moon* 60 You're a live one, all wool, a yard long and a yard wide. **1963** L. MEYNELL *Virgin Luck* v. 114 It didn't seem to matter so much with people as decent as that about. She was all wool and a yard wide, that one. **1974** 'A. GILBERT' *Nice Little Killing* iii. 40 No one will ever catch her..with an alibi all wool and a yard wide.

(*g*) *c* **1897** D. MCK. WRIGHT in A. E. Woodhouse *N.Z. Farm & Station Verse* (1950) 33 Wool away! Wool away is the cry And the merry game of busting is begun. **1949** P. NEWTON *High Country Days* v. 53 The call of 'wool away' had lagging fleecies dashing to rescue fleeces before the shearer would be out with his next sheep. **1965** J. S. GUNN *Terminol. Shearing Industry* II. 38 *Wool away*, the call of a shearer who wants the picker-up to carry away a fleece. This has to be done after each sheep, and fleeces are not left lying around on the floor while another sheep is being shorn.

(*h*) **1830** R. LOWER *Tom Cladpole's Jurn.* cxxxvi, Dat rais'd ma wool. **1890** BARRÈRE & LEYLAND *Dict. Slang* s.v., 'Keep your wool on,' don't get angry. **1926** 'A. BERKELEY' *Wychford Poisoning Case* v. 48 'All right,' Alec said soothingly. 'Keep your wool on.' **1944** D. WELCH *In Youth is Pleasure* v. 87 Dennis said a lot more, growing increasingly vicious with each new sentence... 'My dear, don't lose your wool,' she said, mimicking old-fashioned schoolboy slang. **1959** [see RAG *sb.*[1] 3c]. **1967** O. NORTON *Now lying Dead* vi. 108, I lost my wool then.

(*i*) **1393** LANGL. *P. Pl.* C. x. 264 Thyne sheep ar ner al shabbyd, þe wolf shiteþ woolle. **1583** HOWARD *Defensatiue* Ajb, Wooll driueth backe the Cannon shotte. **1620** SHELTON *Don Quix.* II. lxvii. 455, I would not haue her come for wooll, and returne shorne. **1680** C. BLOUNT tr. *Philostratus* 243 It is ill Wooll that will take no Dye. **1825** WATERTON *Wand. S. Amer.* iii. 242 Sancho Panza..says,.. many go for wool, and come home shorn. **1864** BROWNING *Mr. Sludge* 630 If such as came for wool, sir, went home shorn; Where is the wrong I did them?

2. Applied to substances resembling sheep's wool. **a.** A downy substance or fibre found on certain trees and plants; also, the thick furry hair of some insects or larvæ. Cf. COTTON-WOOL *sb.* 1.

c **1400** MAUNDEV. (1839) xxvi. 268 In that Lond ben Trees, that beren Wolle, as thogh it were of Scheep; where of men maken Clothes, and alle thing that may ben made of Wolle. **1567** MAPLET *Gr. Forest* 59b, His Apple or fruite is all ouer apparailed with a certaine kinde of wooll called Cotton. **1578** LYTE *Dodoens* I. lxxxi. 118 The other white Mulleyne..hath white leaues frysed with a soft wooll or Cotton. **1684** J. PETER *Siege Vienna* 108 Sacks of Wool made of Trees. **1731** MILLER *Gard. Dict.* s.v. *Xylon*, Seeds.. wrapped within that soft ductile Wool, commonly known by the Name of Cotton. **1827–8** R. SWEET *Flora Austral.* 15 Leaves..thickly clothed with white wool. **1831** DON *Dichlamydeous Pl.* I. 513 The wool contained in the fruit is called *Samauma* in Brazil, with which the natives stuff pillows and bolsters. **1840** *Cuvier's Anim. Kingd.* 611 The *Noctuælitese*... The body is generally clothed with scales rather than with wool. **1885** TENNYSON *Spinster's Sweet-Arts* xii, The wool of a thistle a-flyin'. **1895** OLIVER tr. *Kerner's Nat. Hist. Pl.* I. 354 Horse-chestnut leaves, when they make their way through the..bud-scales, are thickly covered with wool.

b. Any fine fibrous substance naturally or artificially produced. †Also (*poet.*) applied to ice.

philosophic(al, philosophers' wool, (L. *lana philosophica*), oxide of zinc, deposited as a fine flocculent powder, during the combustion of the metal.

[**1596** T. JOHNSON *Cornucopiæ* C3b, A stone named Abeston.., which hath..a kinde of Wooll growing about it.] **1599** M[OUFET] *Silkwormes* 74 The smel..of silken wool that's new. **1606** SYLVESTER *Du Bartas* II. iv. I. *Tropheis* 751 As the rigour of long Cold congeals To harsh hard Wool the running Water-Rils. **1758** REID tr. *Macquer's Chym.* I. 94 Into this form may the whole substance of the Zinc be converted. Several names have been given to these flowers, such as Pompholix, Philosophic Wool. **1850** C. J. HEMPEL *Homœopathic Pharm.* 275 Flowers of Zinc, Philosophical Wool. *c* **1865** J. WYLDE in *Circ. Sc.* I. 191/2 A flocky-white powder, which has been called 'philosophers' wool'. **1866** BRANDE & COX *Dict. Sc.*, etc. II. 886/1 *Philosophic Wool.* **1875** KNIGHT *Dict. Mech.*, *Wool*..a slag of iron blown by steam into a fibrous form. Known as slag-wool, or silicate cotton. **1884** LOCK *Workshop Rec.* Ser. III. 439/2 Slag-wool. .. The wool..is principally used for covering boilers or steam-pipes. **1885** [see GLASS *sb.*[1] 16].

c. The short, tightly-curled hair of Negroid peoples (*depreciating*). Also *gen.* (jocularly), the hair of the head.

1697 *Lond. Gaz.* No. 3256/4 Run away.., a Negro Boy.. the Wooll off the right side of his Head about the breadth of a Crown Piece. **1730** SOUTHALL *Bugs* 6 Meeting with an uncommon Negro, the Hair or (rather) Wooll on his Head, Beard, and Breast being as white as Snow. **1767** CARTERET in Hawkesw. *Voy.* (1773) I. 599 The people are..woolly-headed, like Negroes..the hair, or rather the wool upon their heads, was very abundantly powdered. *a* **1853** in 'C. Bede' *Verdant Green* I. ix, He'd got no wool on the top of his head,—just the place where the wool ought to grow, you know. **1884** SIR S. ST. JOHN *Hayti* iv. 146 The principal trouble to the female negro mind is her unfortunate wool.

3. a. Woollen clothing or material; a woollen garment. Sc. phr. ***amang the woo'***, in the blankets.

a **1300** *Cursor M.* 11112 He..Ne wered noþer wol ne line. **1534** MORE *Treat. Passion* Wks. 1272/2 How proude is many a man ouer his neighbour, because the wull of hys gowne is fyner? *a* **1625** FLETCHER *Noble Gentl.* I. i, A Countrey Fool, good to..eate course bread, weare the worst Wooll. **1818** J. KENNEDY *Poet. Wks.* 44 (E.D.D.) They..den amang the woo, Fu' quiet that night. **1882** EDITH A. BARNETT *Common-sense Clothing* 28 Wear wool in hot weather; do as you please in cold. **1933** H. ALLEN *Anthony Adverse* II. IV. xxv. 354 'I *am* a little cold after all,' said Father Xavier, looking at the fire regretfully. 'A second till I change into my wool.' **1952** M. LASKI *Village* v. 94 The beige silk frock could at last be discarded for a really not-too-bad navy blue wool. **1975** BYFIELD & TEDESCHI *Solemn High Murder* (1976) i. 10 Mueller had taken away his rumpled suit, leaving his heavier wools hanging in the open closet. **1978** S. BRILL *Teamsters* ix. 340 The custom-tailored wools that might..have made him look like a well-heeled Wall Street lawyer.

b. The nap of a woollen fabric.

1563 FULKE *Meteors* (1571) 14 Garmentes, whose woll is hyghe, as fryese mantels, and suche lyke. **1577** HARRISON *England* II. i. (1877) I. 34 Such patrons doo scrape the wooll from our [the parsons'] clokes. **1836** H. MANWARING *Tailors' New Guide* 16 First open the cloth with the wool to go with the back seam. **1892** N. Gale *Country Muse* 32 How his Pilot Jacket shows Ghosts of snowballs on the wool!

c. Twisted woollen yarn used for knitting and mending garments.

1840 Mrs. Gaugain *Lady's Assist. Knitting* I. 22 The Cap requires eight penny skeins of coloured Berlin wool, and six of white. *Ibid.* 27 Work..with white,..never breaking off the wools till the whole is finished. **1849** Esther Copley *Compr. Knitting-bk.* 4 Embroidery Wool is about the size of the thinnest Lady Betty. *Ibid.*, Shetland Wool..is in use for shawls, handkerchiefs, and scarfs. **1885** *Bazaar* 30 Mar. 332 Stocking..knitted with German fingering wool.

4. A quantity or supply, or a particular kind or class, of wool. Chiefly in *pl.*

1399 Langl. *Rich. Redeles* iv. 11 Whane þe countis were caste with þe custum of wullus. *c* **1400** *Contin. Brut* ccxxv. (1908) 293 Þe King askeþ þe vif part of alle þe meble goodez of Engelond, and þe wolles. **14..** *Chaucer's Pard. T.* 582 (Corp. MS.) Comeþ vp, ȝe wyues, offreþ ȝoure wulles. ?*c* **1470** in *Pol. Poems* (Rolls) II. 283 The marchauntes comme oure wollys for to bye. **1560** Daus tr. *Sleidane's Comm.* 118b, They followe..but one kynde of marchaundyse as Woulles or Sylkes. **1586** A. Day *Engl. Secretorie* ii. (1625) 61 Wools are as yet at high rate, but I thinke shortly they will fall. **1604** E. G[rimstone] *D'Acosta's Hist. Indies* iv. xxxiii. 299 If they could make profite of their woolls by sending them into Europe. **1706** *Lond. Gaz.* No. 4288/3 The Wools to be seen at Leathersellers Hall. **1835** Ure *Philos. Manuf.* 124 Wools have been distinguished in commerce into two classes; fleece wools and dead wools. **1859** E. B. Ramsay *Remin. Scott. Life & Char.* (ed. 5) 67 *Cus.* A' ae oo? *Shop.* Ay, a' ae oo [= Aye, all one wool].

5. *attrib.* and *Comb.*: **a.** simple attrib., as ***wool-bale***, ***basket***, ***bin***, ***-blanket***, ***-bob*** (bob *sb.*[1] 6), ***-clip***, ***-coat***, ***-crop***, ***-import***, ***-lock***, ***-mattress***, ***-produce***, ***-production***, ***-sheet***, ***shop***, ***-side***, ***-tax***, ***-top*** (top *sb.*[1] 2); = relating to or concerned with the manufacture, storage, transport, or commercial handling of wool or woollen goods, as ***wool-bill***, ***-boat***, †***chamber***, ***-dray***, ***duty***, ***-fair***, ***-hall***, ***-loft***, ***-market***, ***quay***, ***-room***, ***-sale***, †***-ship***, ***-store***, †***-tool***, ***trade***, ***-wain***, ***warehouse***, ***weight***, ***-wharf***. **b.** objective, etc. esp. in terms denoting operatives or machines concerned with the manufacture of wool or woollen goods, as ***wool-breaker*** (break *v.* 2c), †***-brogger***, ***-broker***, ***-burler***, ***-buyer***, †***-chapman***, ***-classer***, ***-cleaner***, ***-cutter***, ***-dealer***, ***-dresser***, ***-drier***, ***-duster***, ***-dyer***, ***-factor***, ***-farmer***, ***-gleaner***, ***-grower***, ***-holder***, ***-jobber***, ***-maker***, ***-merchant***, ***-monger***, ***-moter***, ***-oiler***, ***-picker***, ***-printer***, ***-puller***, ***-roller***, ***-scourer***, ***-scribbler*** (scribbler[2]), ***-scutcher***, ***-seller***, ***-slubber***, ***-washer***, ***-wearer***, ***-weaver***, †***-webster***, ***-weigher***; ***wool-bearing***, ***-broking***, ***-bundling***, ***-burring***, ***-classing***, ***-cleaning***, ***-growing***, ***-picking***, ***-printing***, ***-producing***, ***-rearing***, ***-scouring***, ***-washing*** sbs. and adjs. **c.** instrumental, similative, and parasynthetic, as ***wool-backed***, ***-fringed***, ***-laden***, ***-lined***, ***-o'erburdened***, ***-white***, ***-woofed***, ***-woven*** adjs.; also ***wool-like*** adj.

1907 *Westm. Gaz.* 26 Oct. 13/2 Soft *wool-backed satin. **1852** Mundy *Antipodes* (1857) 31 Long caravans of drays..laden with *wool-bales, hides, &c. *c* **1878** J. Albery *Dram. Wks.* (1939) II. 300 Fawley places a note in Haidee's *wool-basket. **1965** J. S. Gunn *Terminol. Shearing Industry* ii. 38 *Wool basket.* There are several of these containers into which various locks and bellies are thrown to be baled up separately. **1792** A. Young *Trav. France* I. 74 Our woollen manufacturers..when suing for their *wool-bill, of infamous memory, bringing one Thomas Wilkinson from Dunkirk quay..to swear that wool passes from Dunkirk without entry, duty, or any thing being required. **1933** *Press* (Christchurch, N.Z.) 30 Dec. 13/7 **Wool bins*, open compartments like stalls in a stable, where wool is stacked by classes until it is pressed. **1974** D. Stuart *Prince of My Country* i. 3 The woolbins loom broad and tall, the press towers above them, there are bales in squat heaps. **1519** *Registr. Aberdon.* (Maitl. Club) II. 174 Ane payr of dowbill *woll blankatis. **1897** Mary Kingsley *W. Africa* 570 It is not that wool-blanket, smothering affair that we were wrapped in down by Buana. **1898** *Dublin Rev.* July 171 The journey was continued in a flat-bottomed *wool-boat. **1891** Miss Dowie *Girl in Karp.* 101 The lads of the village had..coloured *wool-bobs..in their black felt hats. *a* **1691** Aubrey *Nat. Hist. Wilts* (1847) 110 Mr. Ludlowe..and his predecessours have been *wooll-breakers 80 or 90 yeares. *a* **1722** Lisle *Husb.* (1757) 427 Wool-breakers..separate the fleeces by themselves that run most of a sort. **1835** Ure *Philos. Manuf.* 219 Gill-machines of the ordinary construction as represented in the wool-breaker. **1714** [Blanch] *Beaux Merchant* iii. 42 The *Wooll-brogger buys his Wooll in the Summer, and sells out the greatest part in the Winter. **1852** T. Baines *Hist. Liverpool* 756 *note*, Mr. Thomas Southey, *wool-broker, London. **1871** W. Reid *Sheep* Contents p. vii, *Woolbroking advantageous to the Grower. **1875** Knight *Dict. Mech.*, *Wool-bundling Machine. **1858** Simmonds *Dict. Trade*, **Wool-burlers*, women who remove the little knots or extraneous matters from wool, and from the surface of woollen cloth. **1875** Knight *Dict. Mech.*, **Wool-burring Machine*, a machine for picking the burs from wool. **1641** *D. Fergusson's Scot. Prov.* (S.T.S.) 8 A woole seller kens a *woole buyer. **1775** W. Donaldson *Agric.* 110 The rich grazier, who can..compel the wool-buyers to his own terms. **1876** J. S. Blackie *Lett.* (1909) 245 We took dinner..with the big sheep lairds, the wool-buyers and wool-brokers. **1603** in Gage *Hengrave* (1822) 22 Y[e] graneries; y[e] *woole chamber. **1600** J. Pory tr. *Leo's Africa* iii. 157 The feete and the skin they sell vnto the *wool-chapmen. **1892** W. E. Swanton *Notes on N.Z.* ii. 96 There is the *wool classer with his assistant rollers. **1911** W. H. Koebel *In Maoriland Bush* viii. 122 The wool-classer takes his stand before the sorting table. **1968** *Guardian* 29 Feb. 14/3 Ian Redpath (Victoria), 26. Wool classer. Opening bat. **1890** 'R. Boldrewood' *Col. Reformer* xi, A natural aptitude for *wool-classing. **1875** Knight *Dict. Mech.*, **Wool-cleaner*, a machine for cleaning dust, burs, and other foreign matters from wool. *Ibid.*, Fig. 7345 *Wool-cleaning machine. **1904** M[c]Cabe *Haeckel's Evol. Man* I. 107 The embryonic *wool-coat usually, in the case of the human embryo, covers the whole body. **1884** Helen Jackson *Ramona* i, You could reckon up the *wool-crop to a pound while it was on the sheep's back. **1723** *Lond. Gaz.* No. 6192/9 Mary Louff.., Coney *Wooll-Cutter. **1819** Rees *Cycl.* s.v. *Wool*, The English *wool-dealers. **1845** D. Mackenzie *Emigr. Guide Australia* 91 Of these bales,..one of our ordinary *wool-drays, drawn by eight bullocks, will carry to Sydney from 15 to 20. **1727** Arbuthnot *Tables Anc. Coins* etc. 300 Struthium..is a Root us'd by the *Wool-dressers. **1867** Simmonds *Dict. Trade* Suppl., **Wool-drier*, a workman who dries wool after washing. **1875** Knight *Dict. Mech.*, *Wool-dryer*, a machine for removing the moisture from wool after washing, dyeing, or what not. *Ibid.*, **Wool-duster*, a machine for mechanically removing the coarser impurities from wool. **1673–4** Earl Essex *Papers* (Camden) I. 172, I cannot learn that any more then 1500[ld], or at most 2000[ld] a year, was ever made for *wooll dutys to y[e] chief Govern[r]. **1858** E. Baines in T. Baines *Yorks.* (1875) I. 648 *Wool dyers. **1801** T. Peck *Norwich Direct.* 10 Coulsen Ralph, *Wool-Factor. **1806** *Monthly Mag.* June 481/1 At a recent meeting of..wool growers of Glamorganshire, resolutions were adopted for establishing a *wool-fair in that county. **1742** Jarvis *2nd Pt. Quix.* iii. xvii. II. 258 Pedro Perez the *wool-farmer. **1834** M. Scott *Cruise Midge* xviii, The heavy clouds..had..settled down in a black, *wool-fringed bank. **1899** H. Johnston *Chron. Glenbuckie* xxii. 255 Her profession was that of a *wool-gleaner. **1806** *wool growers [see *wool-fair*]. **1921** *Daily Colonist* (Victoria, B.C.) 11 Oct. 6/3 Mr. Vernon, a wool-grower of Albert Head. **1962** *Economist* 31 Mar. 1275/1 Australian woolgrowers stand to earn £24 million more this season. **1971** *Sunday Australian* 8 Aug. 1/5 Half of Australia's 93,000 woolgrowers will get less than $600 each from the Federal Government's new wool subsidy. **1847–54** Webster, **Wool-growing, a.*, producing sheep and wool. **1868** *Rep. U.S. Comm. Agric.* (1869) 42 *Wool-growing would be profitable if it were not for ravenous dogs. **1751** *Engl. Gazetteer* I. s.v. *Buckingham*, This Town was many years a wool-staple, and many of its *wool-halls are yet standing. **1842** Bischoff *Woollen Manuf.* II. 57 Another meeting of foreign *wool holders. **1919** *Glasgow Herald* 27 June 7 A congestion of *wool imports at the docks. **1775** Ash, **Wool-jobber*, one who buys up small parcels of wool and sells them again. **1890** 'R. Boldrewood' *Col. Reformer* xii, The teams *wool-laden departed. **1796** Withering *Brit. Plants* (ed. 3) II. 159 The straight hairs on the leaves disappear by cultivation, but the *wool-like hairs continue on the stem. **1880** C. R. Markham *Peruv. Bark* 251 Dense bodies of white wool-like exhalations fill the deeper valleys. **1824** E. Weeton *Let.* 22 May (1969) II. 270 My *wool-lined beaver gloves. **1891** C. Roberts *Adrift Amer.* 43 He then told me to put on my wool-lined rubber boots. **1382** Wyclif *Wisd.* v. 15 The hope of the vnpitous is as a *wlle loke, or thistil-doun. *c* **1422** Hoccleve *Lerne to Dye* 219 Myn hope is as it were a wolle-loke Which the wynd vp reisith for his lightnesse. *c* **1440** *Promp. Parv.* 534/2 Wullok, *villus*. **1497** *Naval Acc. Hen. VII* (1896) 245, xix newe cabulles owte of the *Wollofte at Southampton. **1833** Loudon *Encycl. Archit.* §887 The wool-loft bears evidence that sheep form a part of the live stock. **1483** *Cath. Angl.* 423/1 A *Wolle maker, *lanifex*. **1886** C. Scott *Sheep-farming* 192 It will take a long time to cause such a demand for woollen goods as appreciably to affect the *wool-markets. **1899** *Daily News* 11 Sept. 2/6 A mattress invoiced as a '*wool mattress'. **1836** *Pigot & Co's Lond. Commerc. Direct.* ii. 315 *Wool merchants and warehouses. **1297** R. Glouc. (Rolls) 11173 [They] þe porters bede To late in tueie *wolmongers, hor chaffare in to lede. *a* **1400** *Old Usages Winch.* in *Engl. Gilds* (1870) 353 No wollemongere..ne may habbe no stal in þe heye-stret. **1697** *View Penal Laws* 257 Wool and Woolmongers. **1843** *Penny Cycl.* XXVII. 551/2 Impurities..are afterwards picked out by boys or women, called '*wool-moaters', or 'wool-pickers'. **1654** Blount *Acad. Eloq.* 47 The *Wool-ore-burthened sheep. **1875** Knight *Dict. Mech.*, **Wool-oiler*..a device for attachment to the first breaker over the feed-apron, and immediately in front of the feed-rolls of the carding-machine. **1536** *Act 28 Hen. VIII* c. 4 §1 Weauers, tuckers, spinners, diers, and *wulpikers..haue ben..without worke. **1843** [see *wool-moter*]. **1875** Knight *Dict. Mech.*, *Wool-picker*, a machine for burring wool. **1817** M. Birkbeck *Notes Journ. Amer.* (1818) 56 The wife was at a neighbour's on a '*wool-picking frolic,' which is a merry-meeting of gossips..to pick the year's wool and prepare it for carding. **1867** Simmonds *Dict. Trade* Suppl., *Wool-printer. **1852** Earp *Gold Col. Austr.* 3 The *wool produce of Australia. **1886** C. Scott *Sheep-farming* 186 A *wool-producing breed. **1903** Flemming *Pract. Tanning* 1 The first operation to which sheepskins are subjected by the tanner or *wool-puller is soaking. **1376** *Rolls of Parlt.* II. 351/1 Charges sur les Laynes..al *Wolkey en la Port de Londres. **1476** *Stonor Papers* (Camden) II. 5 The ij pokets woll, beynge at the Wollkey. **1721** *Act 8 Geo. I* c. 31 All that Piece or Parcel of Ground..called or known by the Name of Wooll Key, situate..in the Parish of All Saints Barking in the City of London. **1901** *Westm. Gaz.* 19 Feb. 10/1 A large *wool-rearing district. **1890** *Melbourne Argus* 20 Sept. 13/7 The fleece he carries to the 'skirting table,' where the '*wool roller' stands. **1833** Loudon *Encycl. Archit.* §779 The granary and the *wool-room are both seven feet high. **1858** Simmonds *Dict. Trade*, **Wool-sale*, a periodical public sale, in London or Liverpool, for the disposal of large quantities of wool. **1890** 'R. Boldrewood' *Col. Reformer* xii, The reputation of the Garrandilla clip in the forthcoming wool sales. **1858** E. Baines in T. Baines *Yorks.* (1875) I. 652 *Wool Scourers, Driers, &c. **1860** Jubb *Shoddy-trade* 60 *Wool-scouring..has become general, as regards fine foreign and colonial wools. *c* **1830** in Southey *Comm.-Pl. Bk.* (1851) IV. 491 Mr. Taylor, *wool-scribbler, ..City Road. **1858** Simmonds *Dict. Trade*, *Wool-scribblers*, machines for combing..wool into thin downy translucent layers. **1884** *Spectator* 26 Apr. 548 An ideal *wool-scutcher, with more tearing-power than any other combination of iron teeth. **1641** *woole seller [see *wool-buyer*]. **1858** Simmonds *Dict. Trade*, **Wool-sheet*, a packing-wrapper for bales of wool. **1481** *Cely Papers* (Camden) 80, I undyrstond be yowr letter that aull the *whowlschypys ar cwm to Calles. **1923** *Harmsworth's 'Best Way' Series No. 95* 15/1 Ask at any *wool shop for 'Beehive' Recipe Card No. 50 (price 2d.). **1943** A. Christie *Moving Finger* xiii. 147 She was knitting—ever so vexed she'd run out of wool... So I ran her in, dropped her at the wool shop. **1983** C. Bowder *Birth Rites* i. 38 The colour's a bit unusual. It was a discontinued line in my local wool-shop. **1903** Flemming *Pract. Tanning* 65 By which all fleshy particles are removed from the inner or flesh side and the loose dirt removed from the *wool side [of the pelt]. **1835** Ure *Philos. Manuf.* 9 The *wool slubber,..after a visit to the beer-shop, resumes his task with violence. **1828–43** Tytler *Hist. Scot.* (1864) I. 241 The *wool-tax fell heavily upon the inhabitants. **1842** Bischoff *Woollen Manuf.* II. 2 Deputies from the manufacturing districts, anxious for the repeal of the wool tax. **1578** *Richmond Wills* (Surtees) 282 Studills, wheles, card and all *wooll toiles. **14..** in Wr.-Wülcker 588/31 *Icarpa*, a *wolletoppe. **1775** Ash, **Wooltrade*, the trade of buying and selling wool. **1906** Kipling *Puck of Pook's Hill* viii. 242 They go over to Rye o' Thursday in the *wool-wains. **1808** W. Wilson *Hist. Diss. Ch.* I. 397 The meeting-house in Gravel-lane, was afterwards occupied as a *wool-warehouse. **1884** W. S. B. M[c]Laren *Spinning* (ed. 2) 51 No *wool-washer ought to allow his suds to run away in the form they leave the bowls. **1884** Knight *Dict. Mech.* Suppl. 955/2 'Smith's' wool washer. **1884** W. S. B. M[c]Laren *Spinning* (ed. 2) 38 So much has been heard..of the superior *wool-washing in Verviers. **1553** W. Turner in Strype *Eccl. Mem.* (1721) III. iv. 49 Whereas there sitteth but seven or eight linnen-wearing bishops..in the convocation-house, if there be threescore pastors and elders, they are *woolwearers. **1585** Higins *Junius' Nomencl.* 506/2 *Lanarius*,..a *wooll weauer. **1377** Langl. *P. Pl.* B. Prol. 219 *Wollewebsteres and weueres of lynnen. *a* **1661** Holyday *Juvenal* vi. (1673) 123 (Illustr.) The word..is by the Scholiast expounded so, by *Lani-pendia* (a *wool-weigher). **1858** Simmonds *Dict. Trade*, **Wool weight*. The following are the subdivisions used in weighing wool. **1326** *Cal. Wills Crt. Husting, Lond.* i. (1889) 319 Le *Wollewharf. **1423** *Ibid.* ii. (1890) 433. **1818** Shelley *Rosal. & Helen* 1092 The hissing frankincense, Whose smoke, *wool-white as ocean foam, Hung in dense flocks beneath the dome. **1848** Tennyson in *Mem.* (1897) I. 281 Thick wool-white fog. **1821** Keats *Lamia* ii. 179 A sacred tripod..Whose slender feet wide-swerv'd upon the soft *Wool-woofed carpets. **1888** G. M. Hopkins *Poems* (1967) 198 No more: off with—down he dings His bleachèd both and *wool-woven wear.

d. Special comb.: **wool alien**, a plant introduced into a country by means of imported wool containing its seed; **wool-ball** (see quot.); †**wool-battery**, a battery faced with wool-packs built up as a breast-work; **wool-bird** *slang*, a lamb; **wool-blind** *Austral.* and *N.Z.*, (of a sheep) having its sight obscured by its growth of wool; also *ellipt.*; hence **wool-blindness**; †**wool-bow** (see quot. and bow *sb.*[1] 13); †**wool-butter**, butter used to salve the wool of sheep; **wool church**, one of the English churches built or modified out of the wealth produced by the Tudor wool trade; **wool clip** = clip *sb.*[2] 2b; **wool-clipper**, a clipper for carrying wool; †**wool-craft**, wool manufacture; **wool-driver**, one who buys wool from a sheep-owner to sell it in the market or to manufacturers; **wool-dyed** *a.*, dyed 'in the wool' (see 1g(*c*)); **wool-fat**, (*a*) = suint; (*b*) = lanolin; **wool-flock**, coarse, inferior wool; †**wool-folder** = wool-winder; †**wool-gatherer**, one who collects wool from the flockmasters; †**wool-graither**, one who prepares wool for the manufacturer; **wool-grass**, name for various grasses or grass-like plants having woolly spikelets, as the American *Scirpus cyperinus* (*S. eriophorum*) and the European *Erianthus ravennæ*; **wool-grease** = suint; **wool hat**, (*a*) a hat made of coarse wool; †(*b*) *U.S.*, a supporter of the Democratic Party (*obs.*); (*c*) *U.S.*, a small farmer, or an unsophisticated or conservative countryman, from the South; also (senses (*b*) and (*c*)) ***wool hat boy***; **wool-hole** *Printing*, also *Printers' slang* (see quot.); †**wool-hurdle**, a sheep-fold; **wool king** *Austral.* and *N.Z. colloq.*, a wealthy or large-scale sheep farmer; **Woolmark** = sheep-mark; an international quality symbol for wool instituted by the International Wool Secretariat; also *transf.*; †**wool-master**, an owner of wool-producing sheep; a wool-producer; **wool-mill** = willy *sb.*[1] 3; **wool-moth**, the clothes-moth, *Tinea sarcitella*; **wool-needle**, a blunt needle used for wool-work; **wool-nipping**, a portion of wool nipped off a sheep in branding; **wool-oil**, †(*a*) oil used to salve the wool of sheep; (*b*) = lanolin; **wool-owner**, a sheep-owner; **wool-pated** *a.*, woolly-headed; **wool-plant**, ? = mullein; **wool-press**, a press used in packing wool; **wool presser**, one who operates a wool press; **wool-pulling** *vbl. sb.*, (*a*) the removal of wool from a sheepskin; (*b*) the act of pulling the wool over a person's eyes; deception; **wool-scour** *Austral.*, a large shed where wool is washed; **wool-screw**, a wool-press; **wool-shear**, now only *pl.* **-shears**, shears used for shearing sheep; also †***wool-shearers***; **wool-shed** *Austral.* and *N.Z.*, the large building at a sheep-station in which the shearing and wool-packing are done; **wool-sorter**, a sorter of wool; ***wool-sorters' disease***, anthrax, also known as *splenic fever*; so **wool-sorting**; **wool-spinner**, (*a*) a workman who spins wool; (*b*) a species of mussel (see quot. 1815); so **wool-spinning**; **wool-sponge** *U.S.*, a variety of bath-sponge; **wool-stock**, a heavy wooden hammer used in fulling cloth; **wool table** *Austral.* and *N.Z.* (see quot. 1965); **wool team** *Austral.* and *N.Z.*, a team of draught animals for transporting wool; **wool-thistle** = *woolly-headed thistle* (see WOOLLY-HEADED a); **wool-track** *Austral.*, a track along which wool was conveyed to a port; **wool-tree**, any species of *Eriodendron*; **wool-wax**, (*a*) = SUINT; (*b*) = LANOLIN; **wool-weed**, any species of *Eriocaulon* (pipewort); †**wool-weigh** *sb.* [WEIGH *sb.*[1] 2], scales for weighing wool; †**wool-weigh** *a.*, that weighs out wool for spinning; **wool-wheel**, a wheel for spinning wool; **wool-witted** *a.*, woolly-minded; **wool-yarn**, yarn spun from wool; *spec.* (see quot. 1863).

1919 HAYWARD & DRUCE *Adventive Flora Tweedside* p. xxi, It must not.. be assumed that all the *wool aliens will disappear. **1961** *Proc. Bot. Soc. Brit. Isles* IV. 221 The party visited a railway siding in the same county, and further wool aliens were found... On enquiry he found that wool waste ('shoddy') was unloaded at the sidings and delivered to local farmers for use as a manure, and when this was followed up foreign weeds were found to be plentiful in their fields. **1976** *B.S.B.I. News* Sept. 22 J. R. Palmer searched hop fields near Wateringbury (Kent) and also found wool aliens present although no 'shoddy' has been used here for at least four years. **1753** *Chambers' Cycl.* Suppl., **Wool-balls*,.. masses of Wool compacted into firm and hard balls, and found in the stomachs of sheep. **1852** COL. HAWKER *Diary* (1893) II. 341 A large model of my wheel-barrow stanchion gun artillery, with *wool battery, for raking a close column of infantry. **1825** C. M. WESTMACOTT *Engl. Spy* I. 156 The wing of a *wool bird [= shoulder of lamb]. **1933**, **1953** *Wool-blind [see *eye-clip* vb. s.v. EYE *sb.*[1] 28]. **1955** J. MORRISON in B. James *Austral. Short Stories* (1963) 158 Worse than pushing a mob of wool-blinds up the ramp of a shearing shed. **1965** J. S. GUNN *Terminol. Shearing Industry* II. 37 The wig is removed with all the wool during shearing ..because, if it is not done, the sheep may become 'wool-blind' before shearing time. **1950** *N.Z. Jrnl. Agric.* Oct. 349/3 Through eye clipping, *wool blindness is avoided. **1688** HOLME *Armoury* III. 291/1 **Wool-Bow*,..an Instrument by which Wool is rent and torn and beaten very fine,..before it can be worked into Hats. **1600** *Reg. Mag. Sig. Scot.* 352/2 Reddendo..barrellam butiri *lie *wollbutter*. **1936** M. ALLIS *Eng. Prelude* xxxiii. 252 Long Melford.. with the stately '*wool' church, a miracle of lace in stone and flint. **1950** H. J. MASSINGHAM *Curious Traveller* ix. 175 Wild nature is the architect in Pembrokeshire and the massive castles..bear the same architectural relation to cliff and mountain as..the wool-churches of the Cotswolds. **1976** *Cambridge Independent Press* 16 Dec. I. 3/5 An interesting talk, illustrated with coloured slides, on the wool churches of East Anglia was given. **1862** *Rep. Comm. Patents 1861: Agric.* 131 The *wool-clip of New England commands a ready cash market in Boston. **1893** *Times* 18 July 2/6 The wool-clip of the year throughout Australia. **1977** *Weekly Times* (Melbourne) 19 Jan. 3/4 The Corporation had put proposals to the Minister for Primary Industry..to acquire the export portion of the Australian wool clip. **1984** *N.Z. Farmer* 12 Apr. 12/1 The wool clip never strayed far from about 5kg per sheep wintered. **1984** *Oxf. Illustr. Hist. Brit.* iii. 160 Their reserves of liquid capital enabled Italian companies to offer attractive terms. They could not only buy an abbey's entire wool clip for the current year; they could also buy it for years in advance. **1903** C. PROTHEROE *Life in Mercantile Marine* 4 The *Chatto* was a full-rigged ship of a thousand odd tons, in reality a *wool-clipper, but being winter time, she was now loaded with tallow and grain. **1924** J. MASEFIELD *Sard Harker* 37 The wool-clippers and big four-masters were being squeezed out. **1387** TREVISA *Higden* (Rolls) II. 297 Pallas..fonde vp meny craftes, and specialliche *wolcraft [L. *lanificium*]. **1398** —— *Barth. De P.R.* xv. xliv. (1495) G iij, This londe [*sc.* Cos] was fyrste endowed wyth wolle crafte. **1555** *Act 2 & 3 Phil. & Mary* c. 13 Yf..the said *Wooll-dryver shall sell his sayd Woolles at any other place forthe..of Halyfaxe. **1775** W. DONALDSON *Agric.* 111 The wool-drivers, or owlers, are the only persons who profit by their necessities. **1832** *Niles' Weekly Reg.* XLIII. 65/2 Messrs. Randolf and Ritchie who are chiefs of the '*wool-dyed democrats' of the present day. **1844** G. DODD *Textile Manuf.* iii. 97 The distinction between 'wool-dyed' cloth and 'piece-dyed' cloth. **1904** *Charlotte* (N. Carolina) *Observer* 19 June 2 Higginson is one of the old abolition gang, is wool-dyed and blind. **1875** *Chem. News* 15 Jan. 26/2 The question as to the composition of the *wool-fat could not be fully solved. **1891** *Jrnl. Soc. Chem. Industry* X. 709/1 An Improved Manufacture of Saponifiable Fatty Matter from Wool-Fat. **1555** *Cal. Anc. Rec. Dublin* (1889) 451 A newe charter..by the whiche they have the forfaictures of *woll flocks. **1662** *Act 14 Charles II* c. 18 §1 Whereas..great quantities of Wooll Woolfels.. Yarn made of Wool Woolflocks..are secretly exported. **1904** *Daily Chron.* 27 Aug. 7/2 We would not object if Parliament forbade the sale of wool-flock as bedding material. **1550** *Proclam. Winding of Wools* 23 May 2 No grower..or gatherer of any wolles..shall..set a worke any *wollefolder, or wollewynder to folde or wynde his..wolle or wolles, vnlesse [etc.]. **1482** *Cely Papers* (Camden) 102 Aull *wholl getherars wher sent for be wryt. **1551–2** *Act 5 & 6 Edw. VI* c. 7 §1 The corrupt practises of diverse.. Woolgatherers and Regrators. *c* **1420** *Pref. Ep. Jerome* vi. in *Wycliffite Bible* (1850) I. 67 *Wulle graithers and fullers. **1854** THOREAU *Walden* xvii. (1863) 331 The arching and sheaf-like top of the *wool-grass. **1856** A. GRAY *Man. Bot. U.S.* (1860) 501 *Scirpus Eriphorum*, Michx. (Wool-Grass.) **1875** *Chem. News* 15 Jan. 26/2 We have examined two fresh kinds of *wool-grease. **1891** *Jrnl. Soc. Chem. Industry* X. 709/1 Acids generally used in the recovery of wool grease from the waste water from wool washing and combing factories. **1794** T. COXE *View U.S.* 314 *Wool hats, of Winchester make, are in much repute. **1828** *Western Intelligencer* (Hamilton, Ohio) 3 Oct. 3/1 Thus has Mr. Woods endeavored to gain the votes of the wool hats as he terms his Jackson friends in Washington. **1836** *Western Hemisphere* (Columbus, Ohio) 3 Aug. 1/7 The very men whom a few years ago they called the 'ragged wool hat boys' and 'Tories', they are now seeking to attach to their [Whig] party!! **1856** *Encycl. Brit.* (ed. 8) XI. 240/2 Wool hats are made entirely of coarse native wool and hair stiffened with glue. Before the emancipation act these hats were largely exported for negroes' wear. **1880** *Harper's Mag.* Dec. 159 An old 'wool-hat' came along with a cart drawn by a single ox. **1898** B. H. YOUNG *Hist. Jessamine County, Kentucky* 163 They made wool hats. **1927** K. EUBANK *Horse & Buggy Days* 170, I was a smart boy from town, and this particular guy thought I was a wool-hat boy. **1942** J. A. RICE *I came out of Eighteenth Cent.* ii. 95 South Carolinians liked their hatred to be personal, and the 'Wool Hat Boys' whooped with delight when Tillman ripped the hide off the 'Columbia Ring' and the Charlestonian gentlemen. **1942** *Time* 21 Sept. 19/3 Georgia's 'wool-hat' boys (small farmers). **1960** *Spectator* 2 Sept. 332 The 'wool-hats' (i.e. dyed-in-the-wool segregationists) of the rural Tobacco Roads who fear negro competition. **1980** *Washington Star* 29 Sept. A13/5 Carter knows that when..Eugene Talmadge shouted about 'state's rights', the 'woolhats' of Georgia knew what he was saying. **1841** SAVAGE *Dict. Printing* 814 **Wool hole*, a place boxed off sometimes under a stair case, or in any situation where the dust will not affect the press room,..in which the wool is carded wherewith to make the balls. *Ibid.*, *Wool hole*, the workhouse. When a compositor or pressman is reduced by age or illness to take refuge in the workhouse, it is said he is in the *Wool Hole*. **1586** [? J. CASE] *Praise Mus.* vi. 76 When he hears his maids either at y^e^ *woolhurdle, or the milking pail. **1889** G. R. HART *Stray Leaves from Early Hist. Canterbury* iii. 19 Founders of the present race of *wool kings in many parts of Canterbury. *a* **1922** H. LAWSON in *Penguin Bk. Austral. Ballads* (1964) 156 These are men who died to make the Wool-Kings rich. **1844** H. STEPHENS *Bk. Farm* II. 93 It is in your power to follow your strayed stock, and claim it any-where by the *wool-mark. **1964** *Wool Future* Sept. 1/1 Woolmark, the international quality symbol for pure new wool, will be seen in British and Irish shops for the first time this month. **1980** *Times* 8 July 10/5 To get the Woolmark seal of approval you can only have a minute percentage of gorse..or whatever still stuck on the yarn. **1983** D. DUNNETT *Dolly & Bird of Paradise* xi. 141 One or two sheep..with no barbed wire in sight to ruffle their gorgeous Woolmark. **1550–3** *Decay Eng.* in *Supplic.* (E.E.T.S. 1871) 101 Refusyng none, but only them that hath al this aboundance, that is to saye, shepe or *wollmasters, and inclosers. *a* **1691** AUBREY *Nat. Hist. Wilts* (1847) 110 Our cloathiers combine against the wooll-masters, and keep their spinners but just alive. **1905** *New Mills Cloth Manufactory* Introd. p. lxxx, The woolmasters secured a small advantage. **1819** REES *Cycl.* XXXVIII. 4 O 3 b, The wool for coarse goods is passed several times through the *wool-mill. **1830** BOUCHER *Analyt. Dict.* 176 The Woolmill, (commonly called the Devil). **1844** H. STEPHENS *Bk. Farm* III. 887 The *wool-moth then takes up its residence, in summer, amongst such fleeces. **1882** CAULFEILD & SAWARD *Dict. Needlework* 522 **Wool Needles* ..are short and thick, with blunt points, and long eyes, like those of darning needles. **1669** WORLIDGE *Syst. Agric.* (1681) 83 Course *Wool-nippings and Tarry Pitch-marks.. having great virtue in them. **1760** R. BROWN *Compl. Farmer* II. 68 Wool-nippings..are beneficial for lands. **1545** *Rates of Custome Ho.* d j, *Woll oyle called trane the tonne. *a* **1585** in *Engl. Hist. Rev.* (1914) XXIX. 519 All our wolle oyles and swete oyles. **1894** H. NISBET *Bush Girl's Rom.* 225 Wildrake came down with Mr. Craven and the other *wool owners. **1703** DAMPIER *Voy.* III. I. 27 The Inhabitants of this Island ..are all Negro's, *Wool-pated like their African neighbours. **1883** BROWNING *Joch. Hakkadosh* 18 Hairs silk-soft, silver-white, Such as the *wool-plant's. **1846** C. J. PHARAZYN *Jrnl.* 21 Dec. (MS., Turnbull Libr., Wellington, N.Z.) 67 Employed all day at Watarangi assisting in packing fleeces. George making *wool press. **1859** H. KINGSLEY *G. Hamlyn* xxxiv, I dreamed..that the devil had got me under the wool-press, screwing me down as hard as he could. **1892** W. E. SWANTON *Notes on N.Z.* ii. 96 There is..the *wool presser and his mate to bale up the wool. **1847** J. S. ROBB *Squatter Life* 16 In short I'm up to the whole '*wool pulling' system. **1885** *Harper's Mag.* Jan. 278/2 A high duty on wool makes it cheaper to have the 'wool-pulling' done in England, and let the skins come to us as our raw material. **1971** D. BAGLEY *Freedom Trap* iii. 59, I was given permission to start correspondence courses... It was all a bit of wool-pulling to make them think Rearden was reconciled to his fate. **1911** BEAN *'Dreadnought' of the Darling* xi. 101 The wool..goes on to be washed by machinery in a second big shed, the *wool-scour, so as to get the grease and dirt out of it. **1828** P. CUNNINGHAM *N.S. Wales* (ed. 3) II. 82 Wooden *wool-screw. **1643** *Orkney Witch Trial* in *Abbotsford Club Misc.* I. 184, I took ane seif and..set ane cogge full of water in the seive, and then laid ane *woll scheir on the coggis mouth. **1831** LOUDON *Encycl. Agric.* (ed. 2) 373 The wool-shears are ..worked with one hand. **1809** *Med. Jrnl.* XXI. 414 A Lad ..was wounded in the abdomen by a pair of *wool-shearers. **1846** C. J. PHARAZYN *Jrnl.* 11 Dec. (MS., Turnbull Libr., Wellington, N.Z.) 67 Counted rams after breakfast. George finished washing penn at river with Robin and Teddy and self to *wool shed at Watarangi and finished the same. **1850** CLUTTERBUCK *Port Phillip* II. 23 In some instances the flood has swept away the wool-sheds. **1859** H. KINGSLEY *G. Hamlyn* xxiii, Backed by huts, sheep-yards, a wool-shed, and the usual concomitants of a flourishing Australian sheep station. **1977** *N.Z. Herald* 8 Jan. 4–7/7 (Advt.), Four-brm home, 3-stand woolshed, barn, yards, airstrip. **1834** *Tait's Mag.* I. 411/2 Merchants in Sydney, some of whom employ *wool-sorters of their own to assort and repack it for the London market. **1844** G. DODD *Textile Manuf.* iii. 97 If the wool-sorter be out of practice for any considerable time, his fingers lose the delicacy of touch indispensable to his occupation. **1880** *Daily Tel.* 10 Dec. 3/8 Henry Slater has died here from 'woolsorter's disease'. **1858** E. BAINES in T. Baines *Yorks.* (1875) I. 653 The *wool sorting done by the proprietors themselves. **1815** S. BROOKES *Conchol.* 157 *Woolspinner, *Mytilus discors*. **1848** *Blackw. Mag.* Aug. 208 In proportion, however, to his taciturnity was the loquaciousness of a woolspinner. **1821** GALT *Ann. Parish* xii. (1895) 85 Superintending..a great *wool-spinning we then had. **1879** SIMMONDS *Commerc. Products Sea* 159 The [American] grades are glove sponge..*wool sponge..and yellow and hard head. **1858** —— *Dict. Trade*, **Wool-stocks*, heavy wooden hammers for milling cloth, or driving the threads of the web together. **1865** M. A. BARKER *Let.* 1 Dec. in *Station Life N.Z.* (1870) 32 We next inspected the *wool tables, to which two boys were incessantly bringing armfuls of rolled-up fleeces. **1950** *N.Z. Jrnl. Agric.* Oct. 310/2 The scrubbing of the shearing board and the wool table is an essential practice. **1965** J. S. GUNN *Terminol. Shearing Industry* II. 40 *Wool table*, a table of spaced ridged lateral slats on which the fleece is rolled and skirted and the pieces picked. Any loose locks fall through to be picked up. **1865** R. HENNING *Let.* 18 Feb. (1952) 82/3 Biddulph..has sent both the bullock-drivers to the Port with the *wool-teams. **1959** H. P. TRITTON *Time means Tucker* v. 41/2 Yarragrin.. was also famous as a camp for the wool-teams, coming in from the north-west. **1769** J. HILL *Herb. Brit.*, *Wool-thistle. **1903** 'T. COLLINS' *Such is Life* (1937) vi. 317 These *wool-tracks, that knew him so well, will know him no more again for ever. **1959** J. WRIGHT *Generations of Men* (1960) xvii. 217 They followed a line through the trees that led southward across the road, once an important wool-track to the coastal ports. **1831** DON *Dichlamydeous Pl.* I. 512 *Eriodendron leiantherum*..Smooth-anthered *Wool-tree. **1911** *Encycl. Brit.* XX. 51/2 An exceptional position [among animal waxes] is occupied by *wool wax, the main constituent of the natural wool fat which covers the hair of sheep... Wool fat is now being purified on a large scale and brought into commerce, under the name of lanolin, as an ointment. **1943** *Thorpe's Dict. Appl. Chem.* (ed. 4) VI. 135/2 Wool grease (wool fat..) is the crude mixture of wool wax and fatty acids recovered from the soapy liquor used for the scouring of raw wool. *Ibid.*, Crude wool grease is used as a lubricant..; some is refined for use as 'lanolin' (pure wool wax) in..cosmetics,..rust preventives, etc. **1954** [see DEGRAS, DÉGRAS b]. **1956** *Nature* 10 Mar. 470/1 Further work was carried out..on the formation of polyacrylonitrile in wool and on suint and wool wax. **1964** N. G. CLARK *Mod. Organic Chem.* xvii. 340 Wool wax occurs to the extent of 20 to 30 per cent in raw sheep's wool. **1966** GETTENS & STOUT *Painting Materials* 81 Wool Wax..is the natural grease from the fleece of sheep. **1772** J. HILL *Veg. Syst.* X. 26 *Woollweed. Eriocaulon. *c* **1100** *Gloss.* in Wr.-Wülcker 148/21 *Campana*, *wulwæȝa. **1533** *Extr. Aberd. Reg.* (1844) I. 451 Ane pair of woll weyiss, ane pair of ballendis of brass, [etc.]. *a* **1661** HOLYDAY *Juvenal* vi. (1673) 100 Illustr. 123 Wo to the *Wool-weigh-maide. **1630** in Ramsay *Bamff Charters* (1915) 223 Ane *woll qwheill. *a* **1806** JAS. THOMSON *Poems* (1894) 233 A gude woo' wheel, my wife to spin on. **1865** MRS. GASKELL *Sylvia's Lovers* iv, A woman stands at the great wool-wheel, one arm extended, the other holding the thread. **1905** A. T. SHEPPARD *Red Cravat* I. i. 12 A belated Mastodon, stumbling from some old German forest..would have caused little more sensation among the *wool-witted villagers. **1429** *Rolls of Parlt.* IV. 360/2 Grete quantite of fyne *Wolle yerne. **1556** *Richmond Wills* (Surtees) 88 To Jenet my doghter, all my wolle and wolle yarne. **1863** J. WATSON *Weaving* 39 Wool yarn is spun from the short fibres of the fleece.., and Worsted yarn from the long staple.

wool (wʊl), *v.* [f. WOOL *sb.* (Cf. OE. *wullian* to wipe with wool.)]

1. *trans.* †**a.** To coat or line with wool. *Obs.*

1660 in *N. & Q.* 7th Ser. XII. 67/2 One Richard Bailey, who..is also very skilfull in the Art of Oyling of Linnen Cloath or Taffaty, or Woolling of either, so as to make it Impenetrable.

b. To stuff *up* with wool.

1883 'OUIDA' *Wanda* viii, I feel as if some hand had woolled up my ears.

2. *U.S. slang.* **a.** To pull the 'wool' or hair of (a person) in sport or (esp.) in anger.

c **1831** A. LINCOLN in H. Binns *Life Lincoln* (1927) 34, I never use tussle and scuffle. I don't like this wooling and pulling. **1854** in *Congressional Globe* July 1690 (Thornton), I regret very much to see these two gentlemen from Illinois wooling each other in the most approved fashion. **1869** LE FANU *Wyvern Myst.* I. 163 The more you and the old boy wool each other the better for Hal. **1894** H. GARDENER *Unoff. Patriot* 315 Wool little Margaret's curly pate for me.

b. To 'pull the wool over the eyes of': see quot.

1890 BARRÈRE & LELAND *Dict. Slang*, *Wool*, to (common), to get the better of, to discomfit.

†ˈ**woolage.** *Obs. rare.* In 7 **wollage.** [f. WOOL *sb.* + -AGE, after obs. F. *lanage*.] (See quot.)

1611 COTGR., *Lanage*, wollage; the trade of wooll, or gaine thats made thereof.

woolant, obs. form of VOLANT *a.*[2]

1503 in Meyrick *Ant. Armour* (1824) III. 238 Woolant piece over the head.

wool-beard, -bed: see WOUBIT.

ˈ**wool-ˌbearer.** An animal that bears wool, *esp.* a sheep.

1483 *Cath. Angl.* 423/1 A Wolle berere, *laniger*. **1607** TOPSELL *Four-f. Beasts* 631 The Epithets of this beast are, horne-bearer,..wool-bearer [etc.]. *c* **1611** CHAPMAN *Iliad* XXIV. 134 A huge wooll-bearer, slaughtered there. **1651** BARKSDALE *Nympha Lib.* II. xlv. 45 The trembling Wool-bearer. **1837** YOUATT *Sheep* iii. 95 Many an animal that had not been dreamed of as a wool-bearer. **1891** C. ROBERTS *Adrift. Amer.* 245 To maunder on behind the slow and harmless wool-bearers.

So ˈ**wool-ˌbearing** *a.*

1830 BOOTH *Analyt. Dict.* 186 The Sheep, or Woolbearing animal (*Ovis aries*).

†ˈ**wool-blade.** *Obs.* [ad. MDu. *wolblad*, f. *wolle* WOOL *sb.* + *blad* BLADE *sb.*] Mullein.

1585 HIGINS *Junius' Nomencl.* 138/1 *Verbascum*,..wool-blade: loongwoort. **1606** *Holyoke's Rider's Dict.*, Etymol. II. K kk iij/3 *Candelaria*, torch-hearbe, wooll-blade, long-wort. **1858** LADY WILKINSON *Weeds & Wild Flowers* 59.

'wool-card. [Cf. LG. *wull(e)karten*, MDa. *uldkard*, etc.] An instrument (see CARD *sb.*[1] 2) used in carding wool. Also in comb.

1564 *Knaresb. Wills* (Surtees) I. 96, iij paire of woll cardes. **1587** MASCALL *Bk. Cattell* I. (1596) 71 Ye shall therefore vse to kembe them with wooll cards or horse combe, as some do. **1629** *Leather* 10 Woll-Card makers. **1630** *Proclam.* in Rymer *Foedera* (1732) XIX. 164 English Wyer..for the making of good Wooll Cardes. **1750** in *6th Rep. Dep. Kpr.* App. II. 125 For pricking the Leathers of Wool, Silk, Cotton, or any other Cards. **1833** J. HOLLAND *Manuf. Metal* II. 231 The works [at Barnsley] were long famous for the manufacture of wool-cards.

So **'wool-,carder**, one who cards wool; **'wool-,carding** *vbl. sb.* and *ppl. a.*

1580 HOLLYBAND *Treas. Fr. Tong, Cardeur de laine*, a wooll carder. **1806** *Balance* (Hudson, N.Y.) V. 288/2, I was, lately, much pleased with seeing a wool-carding machine in operation. **1835** URE *Philos. Manuf.* 166 The wool-carding engine. **1863** GEO. ELIOT *Romola* i, Streets..noisy with the ..broad jests of wool-carders in the cloth-producing quarters.

'wool-comb. [OE. *wullcamb* = OHG. *wollakampâ* (MHG. *wollechampe*, *wollekam*, G. *wollkamm*), ON. *ull(ar)kambr* (Sw. *ullkam*. Da. *uldkam*): see COMB *sb.*[1]] The toothed instrument used in carding wool by hand; later also, a machine to perform the same operation.

a **1100** *Gerefa* in *Anglia* (1886) IX. 263 Wulcamb, cip, amb. **1418** *Bury Wills* (Camden) 3, j. par de wollecombes. **1533** *Extr. Aberd. Reg.* (1844) I. 451 Ane par of wool camis. **1613** in *Trans. Soc. Antiq. Scot.* (1792) I. 173 An heckell with a pair of clatting wool cammis. **1780** EDMONDSON *Her.* II. Alph. Arms, *Bromley*, Sa. three wool-combs ar. **1797** W. TAYLOR in *Monthly Mag.* III. 125 Bishop Blaze, to whom their traditions ascribe the beneficial invention of the wool-comb. **1854** R. S. SURTEES *Handley Cr.* xv, Just as if I'd had it teased with a pair of wool-combs. **1870** MORRIS *Earthly Par.* III. IV. 111 Withal the wool-comb's sound within the fleece Began and grew.

'wool-,comber. [Cf. MLG. *wulkemmer*, (M)Du. *wolkammer*, G. *wollkämmer*.]

1. One who combs or cards wool.

1702 *Lond. Gaz.* No. 3820/4 Philip Adams,..aged 25, a Woollcomber. **1776** ADAM SMITH *W.N.* I. x. I. 156 Half a dozen wool-combers perhaps are necessary to keep a thousand spinners and weavers at work. **1835** URE *Philos. Manuf.* 144 The wool is not carded in the factory, but is given out to the wool-combers, who comb it by hand. **1889** J. BURNLEY *Hist. Wool* etc. 210 The term 'woolcomber' had completely changed its significance. In 1825 it indicated a member of the operative classes; in 1873 it was only used in regard to a class of employers. **1913** *Times* 9 Aug. 17/2 An outbreak [of fire] at a Bradford woolcomber's.

2. = WOOL-COMB. *rare.*

1854 R. S. SURTEES *Handley Cr.* l, I should sit on pins —on woolcombers—with nothin' but summer drawers on, till the account appeared.

So **'wool-,combing** *vbl. sb.* (also *attrib.*).

1723 *Abridg. Specif. Patents, Spinning* (1866) 3 Two instruments of iron, to be used in the said trade of wooll kembing and pressing. **1813** VANCOUVER *Agric. Devon* 387 The woolcombing business was formerly carried on..at Chumleigh. **1837** HEBERT *Engin. Encycl.* II. 913 Wool-combing by machinery has now almost superseded the work by hand. **1841** *Civil Eng. & Arch. Jrnl.* IV. 440/1 A new wool-combing apparatus.

woold (wu:ld), *sb.* Forms: 7 wolde, would, 9 woold. [Related to next.] **a.** *Naut.* = WOOLDING. **b.** *attrib.* in **woold cord, rope** (cf. WFlem. *oelkorde*): binding cord or rope.

1628 *Toke* (Kent) *Estate Accts.* lf. 115 (MS.) For making 16 lbs of hempe into a wolde rope. 4/-. **1639** *Ibid.* lf. 202 A payer of would ropps. **1688** HOLME *Armoury* III. xv. (Roxb.) 43/1 The Would or wouldings of the mast or yard: is the ropes about them to keep on a fish. **1805** R. W. DICKSON *Pract. Agric.* II. 775 [Bundles of weld plants] are tied up by a string made for the purpose, and sold under the title of woold cord.

woold (wu:ld), *v.* Forms: *α.* 7 woll (*pa. t.* and *pa. pple.* wolled, woolled), 9 wool; *β.* 7– would, 8– woold (9 wowld, wold). [The late appearance of this word suggests that it is a back-formation from WOOLDING (q.v.), but it was probably a late ME. adoption of MLG. *wolen*, *wölen* (LG. *wölen*, pa. pple. *wöld*), MDu. *woelen* 'premere.. constringere, torquere' (Kilian), Du. *woelen* to woold (whence G. *wuhlen*, *wulen*, Da. *vule*), also Du. *bewoelen* (G. *bewuhlen*), Flem. *woeln*, *oelin* to bind round with cord or rope, WFris. *woelje* to wind. (Further relations are uncertain.) The infinitive forms *would*, *woold* appear to be due to the influence of the pa. t. and pa. pple.] *trans.* (*Naut.*) To wind rope or chain round (a mast or the like) to strengthen it where it is broken or where (being made of two or more pieces) it is fished or scarfed. Also said of the rope.

α. **1616** R. COCKS *Diary* (Hakl. Soc.) I. 96 The master sent hym to tell me the mast was wolled. **1622** R. HAWKINS *Voy S. Sea* xxxvi. 88 Wee woolled the two byghtes to the shanke. *Ibid.* lxi. 147 In fishing and wolling our mastes and yards. **1674** JOSSELYN *Two Voy.* 5 We found the head of our mainmast..shivered and the fore-top-mast crackt; So they wolled them both.

β. *a* **1625** MANWAYRING *Sea-man's Dict.* (1644) 116 To *Would*: or *Woulding* is to bind Roapes about any Mast, yard, or the like, to keepe on a fish, or somewhat to strengthen it. **1691** T. H[ALE] *Acc. New Invent.* 35 With her whole Body woulded about with Hawsers for preventing her very sides falling out. **1730** W. WRIGLESWORTH *MS. Log-bk. of the 'Lyell'* 30 Oct., Yesterday in the afternoon stowed the Lazaretta, and this morning Woolded the Main Mast. **1750** [see WOOLDING 1 b]. **1804** NELSON 27 Aug. in Nicolas *Disp.* (1846) VI. 172 You will use every dispatch in woolding and securing the foremast. **1837** MARRYAT *Perc. Keene* xx, Our main-mast had received so many shots, that we were obliged to wold it for its support.

b. *gen.* To wrap or bind round.

1775 ROMANS *Florida* App. 65 Keeping your lead going, till you come on soundings so soft that the lead will bring none of the mud up, unless it be woolded with canvas. **1823** [see WOOLDER]. **1833** MARRYAT *Peter Simple* xliii, A carronade, well woulded up. **1837** E. HOWARD *Old Commodore* xiv, This love of a sail was woulded, with studied accuracy, by brilliant, black, and very narrow ribbon. **1847** HALLIWELL, *Wool*..(2) To twist a chain round a refractory horse to render him obedient. *Kent.* **1890** W. C. RUSSELL *Nelson* 62 Her hull was kept together by cables, which frapped or woolded the fabric from stem to stern.

woold, obs. form of WELD *sb.*[1]

woolder ('wu:ldə(r)). Also 6 woller, 8 wooler, 9 wolder, woulder. [f. WOOLD *v.* + -ER[1].]

†**a.** *Naut.* A woold rope. *Obs.* **b.** *Rope-making.* A stick used as a lever in woolding; also, a workman operating this. By extension applied also to other similar levers (see quots. 1863, 1875). **c.** *dial.* A rolled bandage.

1548 *Acts Privy Council* (1890) II. 177 Six coyle of rope for wollers. **1750** BLANCKLEY *Nav. Expositor* 190 *Woolers*, Double, Single, Hand—used at the Rope Yard, and the Men that work with them, are a great Help to those that heave at the Hooks in laying or closing Cables. **1794** *Rigging & Seamanship* I. 59 *Woolders*, single and double handed, are sticks about three feet long and four inches in circumference, with strops of rope-yarn made fast, to fix on the rope and assist the men at the hooks in closing the rope. **1797** *Encycl. Brit.* (ed. 3) XVI. 487/1 (Rope-making), The woolders should keep their eye on the men at the crank, and make their motion correspond with his. **1823** MOOR *Suffolk Words* 497 *Woulders*, bandages. 'Teent quite well, I'm forced to keep the woulders on.' Wowld is also used as a verb. *a* **1825** FORBY *Voc. E. Anglia*, *Wolder*, a rolled bandage. **1863** A. YOUNG *Naut. Dict.* (ed. 2) 360 *Spanish Windlass*, a wooden roller having a rope wound round it, through the bight of which rope an iron bolt called a woolder is inserted as a lever for heaving it round. **1875** KNIGHT *Dict. Mech.* 1981/1 The three [strands] are placed in the three groves of a conical wooden block termed a *top*, through which is passed a transverse stick forming the handles or *woolders*.

woolding ('wu:ldɪŋ), *vbl. sb.* Forms: *α.* 5 wolling, 5–6 wolyng(e, 6 wooling(e. *β.* 5 woldynge, 7 *pl.* wouldens, 7–8 woulding, 7– woolding (9 wolding). [late ME. *wol(l)ing*, prob. ad. MLG. **woling*, MDu. **woeling* (Du. *woeling*, whence G. *wuhling*, *wuling*, Da. *vuling*, cf. Sw. *vulning*), f. MLG. *wolen*, etc. WOOLD *v.*]

1. The action of binding an object tightly with cord; esp. *Naut.* the action of winding rope or chain round a mast or yard, to support it where it is fished or broken. Also *attrib.*

c **1440** *Promp. Parv.* 532/1 Wolynge, or stronge byyndynge (*K.* woldynge, *S.*, *W.* worlynge), *provolucio, prostriccio* (*perstrinctio*). **1495** *Naval Acc. Hen. VII* (1896) 207 A cabelette of cc weght occupied & spent Abought the wollyng of the mayne yerde. **15..** in Meyrick *Ant. Armour* (1824) III. 290 Ropis of hempe for wolyng and brechyng. **1548** *Acts Privy Council* (1890) II. 174 Wooling ropes, xij coyles. **1670** in *Cal. St. Pap., Col., Amer.* (1889) 50 It is a common thing amongst the [W. Indian] privateers,..to cut a man in pieces,..sometimes tying a cord about his head, and with a stick twisting it till the eyes start out, which is called 'woolding.' **1677** W. HUBBARD *Pres. St. New-Eng.* 59 He would owne nothing but what was forced out of his mouth, by the woolding of his head with a cord. **1750** BLANCKLEY *Nav. Expositor* 110 Nails, *Woolding*, drove through the Ropes that Woold the Ship's Masts. **1804** LARWOOD *No Gun Boats* 14 Such masts require no splicing, no wolding, no fishing. **1883** W. D. CURZON *Manuf. Industries Worcs.* 76 For Barge and Ship Builders, barge nails,..scupper and woolding and lap nails.

2. *concr.* **a.** A wrapping, swathing (in first quot. glossing L. *pero* a rustic boot); esp. *Naut.* (often *pl.*) the rope or chain used in woolding a band or wrapping of rope wound round a mast, spar, etc.

c **1425** *Voc.* in Wr.-Wülcker 656/9 *Hic pero, -ri*, wolyng. **1558** in Hakluyt *Voy.* (1589) 123 The Tyger sprong the woolings of her boltspreete. *a* **1625** MANWAYRING *Sea-man's Dict.* (1644) 117 Also those Roapes, which come from the beake-head, over the bolt-spritt, and Lashes it fast downe from rising off the pillow are called the Wouldings of the bolt-spritt. **1626** CAPT. J. SMITH *Accid. Yng. Seamen* 12 Coates and wouldings, for all masts and yeards. **1699** T. ALLISON *Voy. Archangel* 36 We..got two Wouldens on our Rudder Head. **1729** SHELVOCKE *Artillery* v. 388 Sew up your Cloth, and reinforce it throughout with a Woulding of Marline. **1748** *Anson's Voy.* I. v. 54 The main-mast was sprung at the upper woulding. **1769** FALCONER *Dict. Marine* (1780) s.v. *Yard*, They [*sc.* the lateen yards] are..composed of several pieces fastened together by wooldings. **1788** A. COCHRANE *Direct. Using Coal Tar* 11. **1837** E. HOWARD *Old Commodore* xiii, The immense wolding of flannel and swathing around his right leg.

woolf(e, obs. forms of WOLF *sb.*

'wool-fell. *Hist.* [FELL *sb.*[1]] = WOOL-SKIN.

1422 *Rolls of Parlt.* IV. 173/2 All sakkes of Wolle and Wolle felle yshipped by Marchants Englissh. **1543** tr. *Stat. Staple 27 Edw. III* c. 1 The staple of wolles, lether, wolfelles, and leade growynge and commyng forth within our sayd realme. **1612** DAVIES *Why Ireland*, etc. 41 Wooll and Wooll-fels were euer of little value in this Kingdome. **1675** HOBBES *Odyssey* XVI. 39 To which [seat] Eumæus a Wool-fell apply'd With Rushes under it. **1765** BLACKSTONE *Comm.* I. viii. 304 The duties on wool, sheep-skins, or wool-fells, and leather, exported, were called *custuma antiqua sive magna.* **1829** R. THOMSON *Magna Charta* 389 A half mark upon every 300 wool-fells, or undressed sheep-skins. **1888** DOWDEN *Transcripts* 196 Chaucer loved the woolfells and leather of the Petty Customs only because they helped to save his purse from getting light.

Woolfian ('wʊlfɪən), *a.* and *sb.* [f. the name *Woolf* + -IAN.] **A.** *adj.* Of, pertaining to, or characteristic of Virginia Woolf (1882–1941), English writer, or her work. **B.** *sb.* An admirer or devotee of Virginia Woolf. *rare.*

1936 *Scrutiny* V. 183 The more discerning might have noticed that it [*sc. A Note in Music*] was drawn not from life but from *Jacob's Room* and *Mrs. Dalloway*, a solemn exercise in Woolfian style and structure. **1944** E. H. W. MEYERSTEIN *Let.* 24 Nov. (1959) 296, I read the proofs of *Mrs. Dalloway* years ago which a Woolfian gave a friend of mine. **1977** W. HILDICK *Loop* viii. 40, I don't think I'd ever used the word 'lark' like that..before. It was..something I'd picked up in my Woolfian researches.

woolfist, var. WOLF'S-FIST.

'wool-,gathering, *vbl. sb.* and *gerund.*

1. The action of gathering fragments of wool torn from sheep by bushes, etc.

1581 J. BELL *Haddon's Answ. Osor.* 424 b, Your Diuinitie raungeth very much at randon, as if it were strayed and runnyng in some wildernes a wollgatheryng. **1878** E. PEACOCK in *Archaeologia* XLVI. 384 Wool-gathering yet goes on in many places even on enclosed lands. **1889** H. JOHNSTON *Chron. Glenbuckie* xxii. 261, I got it by working for it—hard 'oo'-gathering and hard spinning.

2. In fig. phr. *to go* (*run, be*) *wool-gathering*, formerly always *a* (or †*on*, †*of*) *wool-gathering*: to indulge in wandering fancies or purposeless thinking; to be in a dreamy or absent-minded state: said esp. of 'the wits', etc. Similarly, *to send* or *set* (*a*) *wool-gathering.*

1553 T. WILSON *Rhet.* II. 59 Hackyng & hemmyng as though our wittes and our senses were a woll gatheryng. **1577** tr. *Bullinger's Decades* (1592) 652 Their mindes goe a wool-gathering. **1579** GOSSON *Sch. Abuse* (Arb.) 42 To busy the wittes of his people, for running a woolgathering. **1601** W. PERCY *Cuckqueanes & Cuckolds Errants* IV. i. (Roxb.) 46 My Husband..[had] so drawne mee, after him, on woole-gathering, in search of him, as now you see mee. **1607** R. C[AREW] tr. *Estienne's World of Wonders* xxxix. 349 This gentle Frier (whose wit was not gone of wool-gathering). **1625** BP. MOUNTAGU *App. Cæsar* 23 If you read them, but marked them not, your wits went on wooll-gathering at that instant. **1652** GAULE *Magastrom.* 41 He..sends his father-in-law almost a wooll-gathering. **1748** RICHARDSON *Clarissa* VII. 326 That my wits may not be sent a wooll-gathering. **1796** *Girlh. M. J. Holroyd* (1896) 386, I suppose you thought my Brains were Wool gathering! **1845** CARLYLE *Cromwell* (1873) I. i. 7 Sacred Poets have..gone a woolgathering after 'Ideals' and suchlike. **1890** J. HATTON *By Order of Czar* II. xii, You are wool-gathering a little, eh?

b. Hence, Indulgence in idle imagining or aimless speculation.

1607 MIDDLETON *Fam. Love* v. iii, Ha' you summoned your wits from wool-gathering? **1824** LADY GRANVILLE *Lett.* (1894) I. 279 A great deal of wool-gathering about what it will bring. **1859** GEO. ELIOT *Adam Bede* xxvii, There never was such a chap for wool-gathering. **1893** PATMORE *Religio Poetæ* (1898) 90 The crazy wool-gathering which is ordinarily regarded as thought.

So **'wool-,gathering** *a.*, indulging in wandering thoughts or idle fancies.

1850 MRS. STOWE in *Life* (1889) 140 If my wits are somewhat wool-gathering and unsettled. **1859** GEO. ELIOT *Adam Bede* i, It was Seth Bede, as was allays a wool-gathering chap. **1893** E. H. BARKER *Wand. Southern Waters* 259 At those moments when the wool-gathering mind has to be hurried back and fixed upon the sacredness of the ritual.

'woolgathersome, *a.* *nonce-wd.* [-SOME[1].] Suggestive of wool-gathering.

1922 C. E. MONTAGUE *Disenchantment* vii. 91 The average German soldier, the docile blond with yellow hair, long skull, and blue, woolgathersome eyes.

†**'wool-house.** *Obs.* [HOUSE *sb.*[1] 3.] A building for the storage (or manufacture) of wool.

1295 *Cal. Wills Crt. Husting, Lond.* I. (1889) 122 [House called] Wolhous [in] Sporiereslane. **1340** *Durham Acc. Rolls* (Surtees) 540 Et in plankis sarrandis pro le Wollehous de Pytingdon, 6s. *c* **1475** *Pict. Voc.* in Wr.-Wülcker 804/12 *Hoc lanifisium*, a wulhowse. **1497** *Naval Acc. Hen. VII* (1896) 249 Havyng owte the cordage owte of the Wollehouse. **1541** *Lanc. Wills* (Chetham Soc. 1857) I. 81 In ye wullhouse a pyle of wole. **1646** *Inv.* in *Milton Papers* (Camden) 92 In the wooll-house, hoppes at 2 0 0. **1783** BERRIDGE *Wks.* (1864) 430 Mr. John Raymond's great house, with his wool-house ..and two thousand pounds worth of wool.

woolled (wʊld), *a.* Forms: 5–6 wolled, *Sc.* wollit (6 vollit), 6– woolled, 8– (now *U.S.*) wooled. [f. WOOL *sb.* + -ED[2].]

1. Bearing wool, covered with wool; having the wool still on, unshorn.

1425 *Rolls of Parlt.* IV. 292/2 Many..personnes leeden oute of the Royaume..grete nombre of Shepe wolled into Flaundres. **1489** *Acta Dom. Conc.* (1839) 117/1, v aulde wollit scheip. **1513** DOUGLAS *Æneis* III. x. 9 The wollit scheip him followand at the bak. **1550** *Rec. Elgin* (New Spald. Cl. 1903) I. 104 The said vollit skynnis. **1552** HULOET, Wolled or wrapped in wolle, *lanatus.* **1890** *Cornh. Mag.* Oct. 385 At times we find a 'woolled one' on the fell after a shepherds' meeting, then we just shear it. **1898** *Westm. Gaz.* 21 Sept. 6/3 Bales of woolled sheepskins.

2. Having wool of a specified kind.

1577 GOOGE *Heresbach's Husb.* 137b, Looke, that your Ewe haue a large body, deepe woolled. **1611** COTGR. s.v. *Houssu, Mouton houssu*, a sheepe well woolled. **1778** D. LOCH *Tour Scot.* 20 Well adapted for..feeding the best wooled sheep. **1797** *Encycl. Brit.* (ed. 3) XVIII. 883/2 The best breeds of fine-woolled sheep. **1801** *Farmer's Mag.* Jan. 74 A good long-wooled skin. **1886** C. SCOTT *Sheep-farming* 183 The original sheep in most countries where improved species are now found, were invariably fine wooled.

†**b.** Of cloth: Having a (good) nap. *Obs.*

1600 SURFLET *Country Farm* II. liii. 381 You must then couer such chafe with thicke new cloath being well woolled [Fr. *bien lainu*].

woollen ('wʊlɪn), *a.* and *sb.* Forms: 1, 5 **wullen**, 4–6 **wolen**, 4–7 **wollen**, (4 **-ene**, **wolyn**, **wullun**, 4–5 **wollin**, 5 **-yn**, **wolland**, **-on**, 6 **wolan**, **woulne**, *Sc.* **volene**, **woone**, 7 **wollan**, 8–9 *north.* **woon**, **woun**), 6– **woollen**, (now *U.S.*) **woolen**. [Late OE. *wullen*, f. *wull* WOOL *sb.* + -EN[4], replacing the mutated form *wyllen* (= OHG., MHG. *wullîn*). Cf. (M)LG. *wullen*, (M)Du. *wollen*, Fris., G. *wollen*.] **A.** *adj.*

1. Made of or manufactured from wool.

1046 in Kemble *Cod. Dipl.* IV. 107 Ic ȝe-an sancte Æðelðryðe anes wullenan kyrtles. **13..** *K. Alis.* 4445 (Laud MS.), Þe spere carf þorouȝ out As þorouȝ a wollene clout. **1376** *Rolls of Parlt.* II. 353/1 File de Layn appelle Wolyn-yerne. **1377** LANGL. *P. Pl.* B. v. 215 My wyf was a webbe and wollen cloth made. *c* **1430** *Two Cookery-bks.* I. 32 Þen take a quantyte of wollen cloþe. **1556** *Extr. Aberd. Regr.* (1844) I. 300 Scottis wairis, sic as claith, lynning and woone. **1575** A. FLEMING *Virg. Bucol.* III. 9 Nowe doth the Ram, and other sheepe theyr wollen garments drye. **1674** *Essex Papers* (Camden) I. 278 Woollen Yarne being within yᵉ prohibition of yᵉ aforsaid Acts. **1776** ADAM SMITH *W.N.* I. I. 13 The woollen coat..which covers the day-labourer. **1799** *Med. Jrnl.* I. 41 Coarse woollen stockings. **1815** ELPHINSTONE *Acc. Caubul* (1842) I. 183 In winter, the people are all clad in woollen garments. **1858** LARDNER *Hand-bk. Nat. Phil.* 403 A woollen carpet is a non-conductor of heat. **1884** W. S. B. MCLAREN *Spinning* 60 A woollen yarn..is a thread spun from wool in which the fibres are arranged so as to lie in every direction.

†**b.** Covered with (a fleece of) wool. *Obs. rare.*

1482 in *Charters &c. Edin.* (1871) 169 Of the hundreth skynnis, wollin, calfis, gaittis, [etc.]

†**c.** *fig.* Silent, as if padded with wool: said of the feet or footsteps. *Obs.*

After L. *pedes laneos* or *lanatos habere*, 'to have woollen feet', to walk silently, to move unperceived.

1597 J. KING *On Jonas* (1618) 173 Following with wollen feet, but smiting with an arme of iron. **1617** COLLINS *Def. Bp. Ely* II. ix. 362 You shall find..woollen pace and iron vengeance.

¶ The allusion in the foll. quot. is uncertain.

1596 SHAKS. *Merc. V.* IV. i. 56 There is no firme reason.. Why he cannot abide a gaping Pigge?.. Why he a woollen bag-pipe. [See **1876** STAINER & BARRETT *Dict. Mus. Terms* 43/2 s.v. *Bagpipe*.]

†**2.** Wearing woollen clothing, (*a*) as a mark of penance (cf. WOOLWARD *a.*), (*b*) as a mark of poor or lowly status. *Obs.*

1481 CAXTON *Godfrey* cci. 293 By comyn acord of the bisshoppes they cam wullen and barfote in the chirche of our lord. **1607** SHAKS. *Cor.* III. ii. 9, I muse my Mother Do's not approue me further, who was wont To call them Wollen Vassailes, things created To buy and sell with Groats.

B. *sb.* Cloth or other fabric made of wool or chiefly of wool. Now *rare*.

†*to lie in the woollen*: to sleep with a blanket next to one. *to be buried in woollen*: to have a woollen shroud, as required by the Act of 18 & 19 Chas. II for the encouragement of the woollen manufacture.

a **1300** *Fragm. 7 Sins* 16 in *E.E.P.* (1862) 19 Linin, wollin, glouis and schone. **1362** LANGL. *P. Pl.* A. I. 18 He hihte þe eorþe to seruen ow vchone Of wollene, Of linnene. *a* **1425** *Cursor M.* 11112 (Trin.) He wered nouþer wollen ny lynne. **1459** *Paston Lett.* I. 457 Vesselys or vestmentes of sylke, lynen, or wollyn. **1577** GOOGE *Heresbach's Husb.* 122 In Winter, they would be clothed with Wollen for taking of cold. **1599** SHAKS. *Much Ado* II. i. 33, I could not endure a husband with a beard on his face, I had rather lie in the woollen. **1663** BUTLER *Hud.* I. i. 309 His Breeches were of rugged Woollen. **1666** *Act 18 & 19 Chas. II* c. 4 (*title*) An Act for Burying in Woollen onely. **1719** D'URFEY *Pills* III. 187 Let 'em damn us to Woolen, I'll never repine At my Lodging when Dead. **1778** D. LOCH *Tour Scot.* 14 There are several looms employed here..for linens and coarse woolen, adapted for country use. **1791** A. MACAULAY *Hist. Claybrook* 116 An affidavit was sent..of the body having been buried in woolen in Saint Pancras church-yard. **1836** C. WORDSWORTH *Athens* v. (1855) 27 Over which is a shorter vest of woollen. **1885** ADA S. BALLIN *Sci. Dress* 128 Woollen should be worn not only in winter but in summer also. **1908** *Animal Managem.* 73 Knee caps..are made of stout woollen or kersey.

b. *pl.* Woollen cloths or clothes.

1800 STUART in Owen *Wellesley's Desp.* (1877) 577 A great quantity of English goods, particularly woollens, found their way into that country. **1816** TUCKEY *Narr. Exped. R. Zaire* ii. (1818) 52 Instead of melting under an equinoctial sun in the lightest cloathing,..they were glad to resume their woolens. **1823** J. BADCOCK *Dom. Amusem.* 53 They grew small sallad by means of woollens, in which the seeds were sown. **1876** BANCROFT *Hist. U.S.* III. iv. 358 The exportation of Irish woollens to the colonies and to foreign countries was prohibited.

¶A proposed name for the Mullein, *Verbascum Thapsus*, formed by substituting *wull*, *woll* WOOL *sb.* for the first syllable (but cf. MLG. *wullene* '? verbascum').

1578 [see WOLLEYN]. **1597** GERARDE *Herbal* II. cclvi. 630 Mullein is called..in English Mullein, or rather Woolen. **1866** *Treas. Bot.*, Woollen. *Verbascum Thapsus*.

C. *attrib.* and *Comb.* (chiefly of the sb.):

a. simple attrib., as ***woollen*** †***-card, district, -loom, manufacture, -mill, -trade, -weaving***; **b.** objective, as ***woollen-dyer, -manufacturer, scribbler*** (SCRIBBLER[2]), ***-spinner***, †***-webster, -worker***; **c.** instrumental and parasynthetic, as ***woollen-clad, -frocked, -stockinged*** adjs.; **d.** Special comb.: **Woollen Act**, the act of 18 & 19 Chas. II prescribing burial in woollen; †**woollen-going** *vbl. sb.* = *woolward going* (see WOOLWARD b); †**woollen-head**, a thick-headed or dull person (in quot. *attrib.*); †**woollen-witted** *a.*, = WOOLLY-HEADED c; **woollen-work**, †(*a*) woollen manufacture; (*b*) = *wool-work*. Also WOOLLEN-DRAPER.

1678 DRYDEN *Œdipus* Prol. 36 Record it,.. The first Play bury'd since the *Wollen Act. **1612** *Sc. Bk. Rates* in *Halyburton's Ledger* (1867) 294 Cardes called *wollen cardes. **1890** W. J. GORDON *Foundry* 162 The *woollen-clad soldiers of Alexander. *c* **1890** CASMEY *Ventilation* 14 In the *woollen districts. **1709** *Lond. Gaz.* No. 4611/4 James Ford of Bow,..*Woollen-dyer. **1864** BRYCE *Holy Rom. Emp.* x. (1866) 175 An imperial penitent, standing barefoot and *woollen-frocked on the snow. **1493** [H. PARKER] *Dives & Pauper* I. xxxvi. (W. de W. 1496) 76/1 All they that vse.. masses syngynge, fastynges,..*wullen goeynge, and such other in theyr wytchecrafte. **1756** TOLDERVY *Hist. 2 Orphans* III. 31 Proving to that *woollen-head justice, that we are neither felons nor vagrants, tho' he was disposed to call us so. **1538** *Nottingham Rec.* III. 200 Unum *wollenlome. **1565** *Burgh Rec. Prestwick* 15 Oct. (Maitl. Club) 69 Ane volene lwyme. **1666** *Act 18 & 19 Chas. II* c. 4 For the Encouragement of the *Woollen Manufactures of this Kingdom..Be it enacted [etc.]. **1726** SWIFT *Gulliver* I. viii. **1846** MCCULLOCH *Acc. Brit. Emp.* (1854) I. 277 Various branches of the woollen manufacture have been introduced into Roxburghshire. **1732** BERKELEY *Alciphr.* II. §2 Other manufacturers, as well as the *woollen. **1802** *Ann. Reg., Chron.* 67 The woollen-manufacturers are incensed at the introduction of new machinery. **1835** URE *Philos. Manuf.* 72 At Bannockburn and Stirling, are a few *woollen-mills. **1858** SIMMONDS *Dict. Trade*, **Woollen-scribblers*,.. machines for combing or preparing wool into thin downy translucent layers. **1884** W. S. B. MCLAREN *Spinning* (ed. 2) 61 The object of the *woollen-spinner will always be to have yarn in which [etc.]. **1907** *Daily Chron.* 7 Dec. 4/4 Women, thick-booted, *woollen-stockinged, flannel-petticoated. **1735** BERKELEY *Querist* §89 Our hankering after the *Woollen-Trade. **1842** BISCHOFF *Woollen Manuf.* II. 68 The wool and woollen trade. **1588** KYD *Househ. Phil.* Wks. (1901) 272 [A wife's] principall care should be of Lynnen or of *wollen weauing. **1630** tr. *Camden's Hist. Eliz.* I. 119 Other such like stuffes of linnen and woollen weauing. **1362** LANGL. *P. Pl.* A. Prol. 99 (MS. T.) *Wollene websteris and weueris of lynen. **1638** *Knaresb. Wills* (Surtees) II. 170, I, Richard Umpelbie of Linelandes, wollan webster. ? **1622** FLETCHER *Love's Cure* II. i, Thou *Woollen-witted Hose-heeler. **1635** SHIRLEY *Lady Pleas.* III. (1637) G 1, Course woollen witted fellowes. **1483** *Cath. Angl.* 423/1 *Wolland warke.., *lanificium*. **1866** *All Year Round* XV. 189/2 Four young ladies, carrying baskets of woollen-work. **1872** YEATS *Growth Comm.* 287 The arrival from the Spanish Netherlands of *woollen-workers.

'**woollen-ˌdraper**. Now *Hist.* [f. prec. sb. + DRAPER *sb.*] A dealer in woollen goods.

1554 *Act 1 & 2 Phil. & Mary* c. 7. §1 Lynnen Drapers, Woollen Drapers, Haberdashers and Grocers. **1619** PURCHAS *Microcosmus* lv. 521 The Woollen Draper hath belonging to him, the Dier, Cottoner, Sherman, Fuller [etc.]. **1641** EARL MONM. tr. *Biondi's Civil Wars* VI. 24 The Company of Wollen-drapers kept a Store-house in Calleis, from whence the Low-countries, and all Germany were furnished. **1749** FIELDING *Tom Jones* XI. v, I can neither live on Hopes or Promises, nor will my Woollen-draper take any such in Payment. **1815** JANE AUSTEN *Emma* xxi, Ford's was the principal woollen-draper, linen-draper, and haberdasher's shop united. **1890** GROSS *Gild Merch.* II. 55 The trades of clothiers, weavers, woollen-drapers.

So '**woollen-ˌdrapery**, woollen goods; also, a shop for the sale of these.

1688 *Lond. Gaz.* No. 2322/4 All sorts of Woollen Drapery. **1766** ENTICK *London* IV. 40 Dealers in upholstery,.. woollen drapery. **1919** *Jrnl. Friends Hist. Soc.* XVI. 141 Daniel Dunbabin, of Warrington, of a substantial woollen-drapery.

woollenette (wʊlɪ'nɛt). *U.S.* Also **woolenet**. [f. WOOLLEN *sb.* + -ETTE.] A thin woollen stuff.

1825 MOTLEY *Corr.* (1889) I. 3, I wish you would send me up some nankeen pantaloons, as my woolenet ones are so tight that they are uncomfortable. **1846** WORCESTER, *Woollenette*, a thin woollen stuff.

woollenize ('wʊlənaɪz), *v.* [f. WOOLLEN *a.* and *sb.* + -IZE.] *trans.* To impart to (vegetable fibres) the appearance and texture of wool. Hence '**woollenizing** *vbl. sb.*

1890 *Times* 19 Aug. 10/4 The various processes to be carried out at the model fibre factory..comprise.. cottonizing and woollenizing fibres to imitate fine cotton or wool. **1927** *Daily Tel.* 21 June 8 (Advt.), Successful fancy cloth effects have been attained by the application of mercerising and woollenising processes to these yarns.

woolleny ('wʊlɪnɪ), *a. rare.* [f. WOOLLEN *a.* and *sb.* + -Y[1].] Made of or resembling woollen cloth.

1863 'G. HAMILTON' *Gala-Days* 41, I have a veil—none of your woolleny gruff fabrics.

†'**wooller.** *Obs. rare.* Also 5 **woller**. [f. WOOL *sb.* + -ER[1].] A wool-carrying ship.

1482 *Cely Papers* (Camden) 111 Yowre oder stuffe I schall send..unto yowre masterschypp be on of the wollers. **1693** *Ho. Lords MSS.* (Hist. MSS. Comm.) 384 The Bill..gives but half to the privateers of all Owlers and Woollers.

Woollies ('wʊlɪz). Also **Wooleys**, **Woolies**, **Woollys**. *colloq.* name for a shop bearing the name of F. W. *Woolworth* PLC (cf. WOOLWORTH); occas. used for the company itself.

1939 *Airman's Gaz.* Dec., At Woollies store they congregate For powders, creams and lotions. **1957** R. HOGGART *Uses of Literacy* v. 120 Popular shops (with 'Wooley's'—Woolworth's—a clear favourite with working-class people). **1962** *Guardian* 24 Dec. 4/2 Some of them are shoplifting: not Woollies combs, but watches and rings. **1971** *Daily Tel.* 16 July 17 'Woolies' says that profits for the first half included a surplus of £261,000 on property sales. **1980** J. DITTON *Copley's Hunch* I. ii. 33 It's a good one. Not one of your Woollie's specials at a tanner a throw.

woollily ('wʊlɪlɪ), *adv.* Also **woolily**. [f. WOOLLY *a.* (*sb.*) + -LY[2].] In a way lacking in clarity or incisiveness.

1937 *Daily Express* 5 Feb. 13/2 Since nothing reads more woolily than descriptions of colours..I'll skip a list of new shades. **1979** *Guardian* 26 Oct. 2/8 Mr Atkins [was] saying a thing woollily not once..but twice.

woolliness ('wʊlɪnɪs). [f. WOOLLY *a.* + -NESS.] The quality or condition of being woolly, in various senses; also *concr.* a woolly substance.

1597 GERARDE *Herbal* II. cclix. 634 Leaues..like vnto those of Hygtaper, but far whiter, softer, thicker, & fuller of woollinesse, which wooll is so long, that one may with his fingers pull the same from the leaues. **1721** MORTIMER *Husb.* II. 210 The Seed with its Woolliness, beginning a little to rise of its self at the lower-end of the Head. **1785** MARTYN *Lett. Bot.* xiii. (1794) 142 The woollyness of the flowers in the Reed. **1824** *Examiner* 307/2 Mr. Fielding's execution is ..soft without woolliness. **1856** *Mem. W. Yarrell* p. xvii, He [*sc.* Yarrell] said that though pretty well he felt a 'woolliness' in the brain. **1859** GULLICK & TIMBS *Painting* 198 A 'muzzy', feeble, unpleasant appearance,..technically called 'woolliness'. **1862** M. HOPKINS *Hawaii* 344 The hair is black and waving... Its curl is perfectly free from the woolliness of the African. **1883** *Hardwich's Phot. Chem.* (ed. 9) 152 In attempting to coat a large plate, a wavy appearance, often known as woolliness of the film, is seen at the lower corner. **1883** MISS BROUGHTON *Belinda* IV. v, That state of numb woolliness to which yesterday a less portion of labour had brought her. **1894** H. O. FORBES *Primates* I. 204 The woolliness of their under-fur.

†'**woolling**, *vbl. sb. Obs.* [f. WOOL *sb.* + -ING[1].]

1. Combing wool; only in ***woolling comb***.

1599 in *Antiquary* XXXII. 243 One p' of woollinge combes.

2. Coating or lining with wool.

1660 [see WOOL *v.* 1 a].

3. Carrying of wool, esp. illicitly (= OWLING).

1665 SIR J. LAUDER *Jrnl.* (1900) 3 The great number we meit of souldiers all the way begat in us great fears of wooling, yet it pleased God to bring us most safely to Paris. **1764** A. ANDERSON *Hist. & Chron. Deduction* (1787) II. 480 The mischievous practice of wooling, as it is vulgarly termed, that is, the running of our English and Irish wool into France.

4. = WOOL-GATHERING 2.

1705 E. WARD *Hud. Rediv.* I. i. 6 When these the Sons of Knipperdoling, Let all their Senses run a wooling.

†'**woollish**, *a. Obs.* [f. WOOL *sb.* + -ISH[1].] Resembling wool, woolly.

1562 TURNER *Herbal* II. 65 The fruit [of oleander]..when as it openeth sheweth a wollyshe nature lyke an thystel down. **1578** LYTE *Dodoens* VI. lxxi. 750 The leaues..be neither white, smooth, nor wollish.

woolly ('wʊlɪ), *a.* (*sb.*) Also 6 **woolley**, 7 **wolly**, 7, 9 **wooly**, 8 *Sc.* **ooy**. [f. WOOL *sb.* + -Y[1]. Cf. (M)LG. *wullig*, Du., G. *wollig*.]

A. *adj.* **1.** Consisting of wool. Also *transf.* relating to wool; containing wool (or sheep).

1591 SPENSER *M. Hubberd* 302 Giuing accompt of th' annuall increace Both of their lambes, and of their woolley fleece. **1662** J. DAVIES tr. *Olearius' Voy. Ambass.* 165 He had upon his upper Garment, some black Sheep-skin, the woolly side out. **1697** DRYDEN *Virg. Georg.* IV. 493 Thus while she sings, the Sisters turn the Wheel, Empty the wooly Rock, and fill the Reel. **1700** —— *Ovid's Met.* XV. *Pythag. Phil.* 171 The Sheep..A patient, useful Creature, born to bear The warm and woolly Fleece, that cloath'd her Murderer. **1820** KEATS *Eve St. Agnes* i, Silent was the flock in woolly fold. **1891** M. MURIEL DOWIE *Girl in Karp.* 214 The high perfection of all woolly occupations.

2. a. Of the nature, texture, or appearance of wool; resembling wool; wool-like.

c **1586** C'TESS PEMBROKE *Ps.* CXLVII. v, Snowes woolly locks by him wide scatt'red are. **1588** SHAKS. *Tit. A.* II. iii. 34 My fleece of Woolly haire. **1597** GERARDE *Herbal* I. lxxiii. 106 Called..in Latine *Laniferus*, bicause of his abundance of woolly flockes, wherewith the whole plant is in euerie part full fraughted. **1652** BENLOWES *Theophila* III. iii, The woolly-curdled Clouds. *a* **1700** EVELYN *Diary* 18 June 1657, Its haire was woolly like a lamb. **1708** J. PHILIPS *Cyder* II. 186 O, may'st Thou often see Thy Furrows whiten'd by the woolly Rain [cf. ὕδωρ ἐριῶδες], Nutricious! **1726** POPE *Odyss.* XIX. 280 Short woolly curls o'erfleec'd his bending head. **1801** SHAW *Gen. Zool.* II. 91 Its fur..is of a woolly nature. **1840** R. H. DANA *Bef. the Mast* xiii. 31 Coarse black hair, but not wooly, like the negroes. **1856** GEO. ELIOT *Scenes Cler. Life, A. Barton* ii, The sky had the white woolly look that portends snow. **1902** *Words of Eye-witness* 53 A puff of woolly smoke in the air.

b. Having a soft and clinging texture; said esp. of edible things which are consequently unpleasant to the palate; also of the surface of a road.

1687 A. LOVELL tr. *Thevenot's Trav.* II. 117 The Fruit.. is pretty sweet but woolly [orig. *cotonneux*]. **1829** *Sporting Mag.* XXIII. 416 He..has a pair of leaders ready when the roads run woolly. **1849** D. J. BROWNE *Amer. Poultry Yd.* (1855) 207 Barley..is apt to render the flesh [of poultry] insipid, and woolly. **1854** *Poultry Chron.* I. 619 She has found the eggs of Spanish fowls eat woolly. **1862** WHYTE-MELVILLE *Inside Bar!* ix. 345 Time's short,..roads woolly, and whip-cord scarce. **1874** RAYMOND *Statist. Mines & Mining* 497 The pulp soon assumes a spongy appearance, technically known as 'woolly'. **1882** *Garden* 18 Mar. 176/2 Turnips have become all tops, and..are just getting into the woolly stage.

3. a. Having a natural covering of wool, wool-bearing.

1596 SHAKS. *Merch. V.* I. iii. 84 When the worke of generation was Betweene these woolly breeders in the act. **1697** DRYDEN *Æneis* III. 844 Like him in Caves they shut their woolly Sheep. **1725** POPE *Odyss.* XII. 319 Then suddenly was heard..To low the ox, to bleat the woolly train. **1788** PICKEN *Poems* 104 Twall score o' sheep..sal be thine, O' ooy sheep, the fattest o' the plain. **1860** G. H. KINGSLEY in Galton *Vac. Tour.* 139 [The colly dog] is jumping from one woolly back to another, intent on singling out the one which has been indicated to him.

b. Having hair resembling wool: applied esp. (*depreciatingly*) to Blacks of African origin or descent (= *woolly-haired* or *-headed*).

1767 CARTERET in Hawkesw. *Voy.* (1773) I. 568 Two of the natives..were black, with woolly heads. **1812** MRS. BARBAULD *1811*, 166 Streets, where the turban'd Moslem, bearded Jew, And woolly Afric, met the brown Hindu. **1881** MISS BRADDON *Asphodel* xxiv, He had eaten pemmican, and ridden a woolly horse. **1886** W. J. TUCKER *E. Europe* 351 It was a large, woolly poodle, snowy white.

c. In specific names of animals, often rendering L. *lanatus, laniger*.

woolly bear, (*a*) *colloq.* (esp. *children's*), also *dial.* a hairy caterpillar; also *spec.* the larva of the carpet beetle; freq. *attrib.*; (*b*) *Mil. slang* (see quots.); **woolly boy**, a large hairy caterpillar, esp. the larva of the tiger-moth. **woolly mammoth** = MAMMOTH *sb.* 1; **woolly worm** *U.S.*, a hairy caterpillar.

1781 PENNANT *Hist. Quadr.* I. 213 Woolly Maucauco. **1793** *Ibid.* (ed. 3) II. 196 Woolly Rat. **1805** DOROTHY WORDSWORTH *Jrnl.* 7 Nov., Like an immense caterpillar, such as, when we were children, we used to call *Woolly Boys*, from their hairy coat. **1842** LOUDON *Suburban Hort.* 551 The pear..is seldom affected with the woolly aphis. **1863** WOOD *Illustr. Nat. Hist.* III. 535 Its [*sc.* the Tiger-moth's] caterpillar is..familiar under the name of Woolly Bear. *Ibid.* 598 Fig., Woolly crab, *Dorippe lanata.* **1877** *Cassell's Nat. Hist.* I. 171 The Woolly Monkeys, *Lagothrix. Ibid.* 221 The Woolly Lemur—The Avahi. *Indris laniger.* **1878** *Ibid.* II. 333 *Rhinoceros trichorhinus*, or the Woolly Rhinoceros. **1909** WEBSTER, *Wooly worm*, the larva of any sawfly that covers itself with a white woolly secretion. **1911** E. FERBER *Dawn O'Hara* ii. 19 I'd eat wooly worms if I thought they might benefit me. **1915** *War Illustr.* 31 July 546/2 The German high-explosive shell, known to our men by the nickname of the 'Woolly Bear',..detonates with a cloud of thick white smoke. **1918** H. W. MCBRIDE *Emma Gees* 135 'Woolly Bear' is the name given to a large, high explosive shell, with a time fuse, which bursts overhead, giving out a dense black smoke. **1923** KIPLING *Irish Guards in Gt. War* II. 82 They were drenched with a five hours' bombardment of 4.2's and 'woolly bears'. **1933** A. S. ROMER *Vertebr. Paleontol.* xix. 376 The woolly mammoth was a form adapted to cold climates. **1940** R. G. RUSSELL *101st Field Artillery 1917–19* 94 A German 150-millimetre battery fired 'woolly bears', time-fuse shells, which burst too high to do any harm. **1950** *N.Z. Jrnl. Agric.* Nov. 478/3 The most common enemy of cinerarias in New Zealand is the 'woolly-bear' caterpillar, the larva of the magpie moth. **1951** *Good Housek. Home Encycl.* 324/2 *Woolly bear.* This is the grub of a small beetle which..congregates in hot airing cupboards. **1961** Woolly bear [see *carpet beetle* s.v. CARPET *sb.* 5]. **1969** BENNISON & WRIGHT *Geol. Hist. Brit. Isles* xvi. 359 The presence of either the woolly mammoth or the reindeer does not necessarily indicate an arctic climate. **1972** E. WIGGINTON *Foxfire Bk.* 209 The woolly worm tells of a bad winter if: there are a lot of them crawling about. **1974** A. DILLARD *Pilgrim at Tinker Creek* xiv. 247 Woolly bears, those orange-and-black-banded furry caterpillars of the Isabella moth, were on the move. **1976** *Islander* (Victoria, B.C.) 16 May 6/1 The woolly mammoth..roamed the tundra areas. **1980** *Blair & Ketchum's Country Jrnl.* Oct. 28/2 October is the month when the woolly bear caterpillar, sometimes called a fuzzy-wuzzy or woolly worm, can be seen crossing country roads. **1983** *Listener* 27 Oct. 16/3 Our wall-to wall carpets attract the 'woolly bear' grubs of the carpet beetle.

d. ***wild and woolly***, orig. applied to the Far West (WEST *sb.*[1] 3 b) of the United States of America on account of its rude and uncivilized character; hence *gen.* barbarous, lacking culture. Also *transf.*, and as *woolly* simply.

1884 A. J. SOWELL *Rangers & Pioneers of Texas* xi. 330 Occasionally, in some Western village, you will hear a voice ring out on the night air..'Wild and woolly',..and then you may expect a few shots from a revolver. It is a cowboy out on a little spree. **1891** A. WELCKER *Tales of the 'Wild & Woolly West'* Publishers' Note, Woolly..seems to refer to the uncivilized—untamed—hair outside—wool still in the sheepskin coat—condition of the Western Pioneers. **1891** M. E. RYAN *Told in Hills* III. iv. 191 Let us 'move our freight', 'hit the breeze', or any other term of the woolly West that means action. **1894** *Westm. Gaz.* 30 Aug. 2/1 How many Indians did you kill? Now, Cappen, I want something wild and woolly. **1907** S. E. WHITE *Arizona Nights* viii. 130 'Who's your woolly friend', the shiny Jew asks of the girls. **1940** R. S. LAMBERT *Ariel & All his Quality* viii. 197 [They] looked with scepticism upon a plan which they regarded as wild and woolly.

†**e.** = WOOLLEN *a.* 1 c. *Obs. rare.*

1631 DEKKER *Match Mee* II. D 1 b, Thankes vengeance; thou at last art come (Tho with wolly feet).

4. a. Of parts of plants: Covered with a pubescence resembling wool; downy, lanate, tomentose.

1578 LYTE *Dodoens* I. lxxiv. 124 Aethiopis hath great brode woolly leaues. **1616** B. JONSON *Forest* ii, The blushing Apricot, and woolly Peach. **1697** DRYDEN *Æneis* XII. 611 Rough is the Stem, which woolly Leafs surround. **1731** MILLER *Gard. Dict.* s.v. *Abutilon*, The large-leav'd American *Abutilon*, with woolly Stalks. **1845** BROWNING *Lost Mistr.* ii, The leaf-buds on the Vine are woolly. **1870** HOOKER *Stud. Flora* 53 Githago segetum..Calyx woolly.

b. In specific names of plants, often rendering L. *lanatus* or *tomentosus*.

woolly butt [BUTT *sb.*[3] 4], an Australian name for species of *Eucalyptus*, esp. *E. longifolia*.

1597 GERARDE *Herbal* I. lxxiii. 106 *Bulbus Eriophorus*, Woolly Iacint. *Ibid.* II. cclix. 634 We may call it Mullein of Æthiopia, or woolly Mullein. **1650** [W. HOWE] *Phytol. Brit.* 61 Hypericum tomentosum,..Lobells Woolly S. Iohns-wort. **1830** J. D. MAYCOCK *Flora Barbadensis* 294 *Phaseolus Mungo*..Woolly-Pyroe. **1857** ANNE PRATT *Flower. Pl.* V. 111 *Salix lanata*..Woolly Broad-leaved Willow. **1862** *Internat. Exhib., Catal. Products Queensld.* 25 Eucalyptus sp... Woolly Butt. **1889** J. H. MAIDEN *Usef. Pl. Australia* 524 'Woolly Gum' of Berrima..This is the smooth-barked variety of *Eucalyptus Stuartiana.* **1912** *Contemp. Rev.* Aug. 247 Giant woolly-butt forests.

5. *gen.* Having a wool-like texture, surface, or covering.

1796 KIRWAN *Elem. Min.* (ed. 2) II. 27 The nativo [nitre] is generally acicular or woolly. **1914** C. MACKENZIE *Sinister St.* III. xv, The golf-bag..woolly now with the accumulated mildew of neglect.

6. *transf.* and *fig.* Lacking in definiteness or incisiveness; 'muzzy'; (of the mind, etc.) confused and hazy; (of painting, etc.) lacking in clearness or definition; (of sound, etc.) dull and indistinct.

1815 *Sporting Mag.* XLVI. 54 It [*sc.* a picture] looks woolly, undecided in shapes. **1839** CHATTO & JACKSON *Wood Engraving* 711 Some of the chiaro-scuros..seem too soft and woolly. **1864** YATES *Broken to Harness* I. viii. 146 The daughter of old Dunkel..was a little woolly. **1865** HAWKER in *Life* (1905) 518 Pusey's woolly mind appears to cling to him [*sc.* Gladstone]. **1872** GEO. ELIOT *Middlem.* xxxv. II. 198, 'I suppose you know..' said Mrs. Waule, in she lowest of her woolly tones. **1874** LISLE CARR *Jud. Gwynne* v, The farm-servants..lost in woolly wonder. **1878** LOCKYER *Stargazing* 354 Except on the finest of nights the stars..appear woolly. **1879** G. MACDONALD *Sir Gibbie* xix, 'That is not a bad remark, Joseph,' replied the laird, with woolly condescension. **1881** STEVENSON *Virg. Puerisque, Some Portraits by Raeburn* (1905) 142 Dugald Stewart's woolly and evasive periods. **1884** *Bazaar* 26 Dec. 681/3 A drawing to look into, but rather woolly at a few paces off. **1895** MARY KINGSLEY *W. Africa* 572 The performance.. growing woollier and woollier in tone, and then dying out in sleep. **1897** *Graphic* Christmas No. 9 The stiff woolly piano.

7. *Comb.*, as ***woolly-butted*** (BUTT *sb.*[3] 4), ***-coated, -haired, -leaved, -looking, -minded*** (hence ***-mindedness***), ***-pated, -tailed, -witted*** adjs.

1843 J. BACKHOUSE *Narr. Visit Austral. Col.* 445 The Gum-trees..are of several species. One called here, the *Woolly-butted Gum, seems identical with the Black-butted Gum of Tasmania. **1852** R. S. SURTEES *Sponge's Sp. Tour* (1893) 341 A lank, *woolly-coated weed [*sc.* a horse]. **1791** BOSWELL *Johnson* 3 June an. 1781, Lord Monboddo's notion, that the ancient Egyptians..were not only black, but *woolly-haired. **1848** THACKERAY *Van. Fair* xii, Miss Swartz, the woolly-haired young heiress from St. Kitt's. **1868** LYELL *Princ. Geol.* III. xlvii. (ed. 10) II. 563 The.. woolly-haired rhinoceros. **1822** *Hortus Anglicus* II. 380 *Inula Suaveolens.* *Woolly-leaved Inula. **1859** W. S. COLEMAN *Woodlands* (1862) 128 The Woolly-leaved Rose (*Rosa tomentosa*). **1881** *Cassell's Encycl. Dict.*, *Breislakite*.., a *woolly-looking variety of aluminous pyroxene. **1898** *Daily News* 8 Nov. 5/4 There are plenty of such *woolly-minded men in high places. **1923** *Blackw. Mag.* May 598/2 The Don, with much alacrity and *woolly-mindedness,.. proceeded to ransack all the lockers. **1698** FRYER *Acc. E. India & P.* 18 A comely well Limb'd Person, though a *Woolly-pated Coffery. **1848** tr. *Hoffmeister's Trav. Ceylon* etc. x. 362 *Woolly-tailed Yak ox. **1927** *Observer* 6 Nov. 15/1 The managerial attitude towards producers is at present *woolly-witted. **1949** ST. J. ERVINE *Craigavon* II. lvii. 273 That woolly-witted insurrectionist.

B. *sb.* **1.** A woollen garment or covering; now esp. *pl.*, garments or wraps knitted of (fleecy) wool. ***winter woollies***, warm underwear (not necessarily of wool); freq. *joc.* Also *fig.*

1865 *Slang Dict.*, *Woolly*, a blanket. **1899** *19th Cent.* Aug. 283 'Granny the Thimbleman'..knits woollies for the 'quality'. **1916** *Contemp. Rev.* Oct. 514 *note*, Flannel shirts ..and woollies of all sorts for the wounded soldiers. **1919** *Blackw. Mag.* Feb. 148/2 Some thin underclothing and a 'woolley' in addition to the spare shirt and socks. **1926** WODEHOUSE *Heart of Goof* vi. 194 His mother had bought him a new set of winter woollies which felt like horsehair. **1933** DYLAN THOMAS *Sel. Lett.* (1966) 24 Catch him [*sc.* Wordsworth].. walking the hills with a daffodil pressed to his lips, and his winter woollies tickling his chest. **1964** *Observer* 13 Sept. 11/3 If we wear the winter woollies of traditional trade unionism against the hot sun of automation, we may sweat it out instead of thinking it out. **1974** *Nature* 18 Oct. 569/1 The dinosaurs' unsatisfied need was not so much for laxatives as for winter woollies!

2. A sheep; esp. (*Austral.* and *N.Z.*) one before shearing. *U.S.*, *Austral.*, and *N.Z. colloq.*

1910 J. G. NEIHARDT *River & I* iii. 92 In Scotland when a feller sees a sheepman coming down the road with his sheep, he says: 'Behold the gentle shepherd with his fleecy flock!'.. In Montana, that same feller says..'Look at that crazy blankety-blank with his woolies!' **1930** *Bulletin* (Sydney) 2 Apr. 23/1 We curse the stubborn woollies..as the sweating shearers tussle. **1935** H. DAVIS *Honey in Horn* xi. 162 She had a little short-bodied guitar of the kind that Mexican sheep herders used to carry around behind their saddles to entertain the woolies with. **1949** F. SARGESON *I saw It in my Dream* II. xiii. 111 White dots that you could tell were both sheep and lambs; and they were so white it was easy to tell that they weren't woollies any more. **1972** P. NEWTON *Sheep Thief* vi. 48 The biggest proportion proved to be Totara sheep of mixed ages, three of them woollies.

3. [Cf. WOLLY.] A uniformed policeman. *slang.*

1965 R. E. RIDGWAY in B. Wannan *Fair Go, Spinner* II. 66 Later on, as the station expanded and more 'woollies' were added, the shed grew accordingly. **1975** *Listener* 6 Feb. 163/2 Sir Robert Mark...saw its [*sc.* the CID's] members behaving as if they could walk on water, and looking down on the 'woollies' who had to plod the beat in uniform. **1978** 'B. GRAEME' *Double Trouble* xv. 191 One of the woollies blew his whistle. **1984** *Private Eye* 20 Apr. 6/2 A small army of 'Woollies'—CID slang for uniformed officers—were summoned.

woollyer, wooll(e)ying, var. forms of WILLYER, WILLYING *vbl. sb.* (s.v. WILLY *sb.*[1]).

1828 T. ALLEN *Co. York* II. 302 Teasing, or as it is sometimes called, woolleying, is done upon a large cylindrical machine. **1875** BAINES *Yorks.* I. 670 Woollyers.

'woolly-head. A person with woolly hair, *esp.* (*disparagingly*), a Black, a Negro; hence, a nickname for an abolitionist in America.

1859 BARTLETT *Dict. Amer.* (ed. 2), *Wooly-heads*, a term applied in the first place to negroes, and then to anti-slavery politicians. **1864** *Daily Tel.* 20 Sept., I must do the American press the justice to say that..I get it quite as hot from the Woollyheads as from the Copperheads. **1884** *19th Cent.* June 993 Our friends the 'woolly heads' [*sc.* Arabs] are peeping at us from amongst the bushes.

'woolly-'headed (stress variable), *a.* Having a woolly head: **a.** in specific names of plants; **b.** Woolly-haired; **c.** *fig.* Dull-witted.

a. 1650 [W. HOWE] *Phytol. Brit.* 22 *Carduus eriocephalus* ..Wolly-headed Thistle. **1796** WITHERING *Brit. Plants* (ed. 3) III. 701 *Carduus eriophorus*..Woolly-headed Thistle. **1857** ANNE PRATT *Flower. Pl.* III. 237 *Cnicus eriophorus* ..(Woolly-headed Plume-thistle). **1889** J. H. MAIDEN *Usef. Pl. Australia* 72 *Andropogon bombycinus*.. 'Woolly-headed Grass.'

b. 1708 *Brit. Apollo* No. 5. 2/1 The Blacks in Guinea are Woolly-headed. **1813** PRICHARD *Phys. Hist. Man* vi. §6. 307 Most of them resembled the woolly-headed Papuas. **1877** MISS A. B. EDWARDS *Up Nile* xvi. 435 Abyssinians and Nubians,..flat-nosed, and wooly-headed.

c. 1883 MISS BROUGHTON *Belinda* IV. iv, She has taken.. the Borrowdale road, walks along it for some distance confused and woolly-headed. **1883** *Harper's Mag.* Oct. 708/2 This, too, not by silly, woolly-headed people, but by practical, hard-headed men of business.

woollyish ('wʊlɪʃ), *a. rare.* [f. WOOLLY *a.* + -ISH[1].] Somewhat woolly.

1793 MARTYN *Lang. Bot.* (1796), Woollyish,..*sublanatus.*

'woolman. Now chiefly *Hist.* [f. WOOL *sb.* + MAN *sb.*[1]: cf. MDu. *wolman* 'lanarius'.] A dealer in wool, a wool-merchant.

1390 *York Memorandum Bd.* (Surtees) I. 43 John de Gysburn, wolleman. **1424** *Cov. Leet Bk.* 84 Joh. Deyster, woleman. **1458** in *Hearne's Collect.* (O.H.S.) V. 256 Hic jacent Johannes Townsende, quondam..Wolman istius villae [etc.]. **1550** *Proclam. Winding of Wools* 23 May 1 The Masters & wardens of the company, and felowshippe of the wolmen of the Cytie of London. **1641** BEST *Farm. Bks.* (Surtees) 27 Woolmen dislike and find greate falt with woll that hath much salve or tarre in it. *a* **1722** LISLE *Husb.* (1757) 425 When the wool-man was weighing my wool, he shewed me the difference of some fleeces in goodness. **1761** *Lond. & Environs* VI. 363 *Woolmen*, a company probably of great antiquity, though they have no charter, and are a community only by prescription. **1912** J. S. M. WARD *Brasses* 20 The brasses of the woolmen are the finest. **1920** *Glasgow Herald* 21 Oct. 7 Woolmen, bankers, and journalists were consulted.

†**'woolner.** *Obs. rare.* In 7 wollner. [f. WOOLLEN + -ER[1].] A dealer in woollen goods.

1619 in Foster *Engl. Factories India* (1906) 87 To publish unto the brokers and wollners of the towne your intente to sett them a worke in the makinge of broade baftaes.

'wool-pack. [f. WOOL *sb.* + PACK *sb.*[1]]

1. A large bag into which a quantity of wool or of fleeces is packed for carriage or sale.

1297 R. GLOUC. (Rolls) 11171 [They] Ride vpe tueye wol-pakces, chapmen as hii were. **14..** in Krapp *Leg. St. Patrick's Purg.* (1900) 65 Stoppeng and shovyng þe felthe downe into here bodies as þe wold stoppe a wullepak. **1600** *Maldon, Essex, Docts.* Bundle 162 lf. 3 (MS.), ii s. of Richard Studd, collector for the woolpacks, for the profitts of his office this yeare. **1601** WEEVER *Mirr. Mart.* D 1, In chaires of hardest oke they sate Insteede of wooll-packes. **1688** HOLME *Armoury* III. 285/1 A Wool Pack..is a great number of Fleeces made up together on a cloth tied at the four ends. **1726** SWIFT *Gulliver* II. iv, There was a Fellow with a Wen in his Neck, larger than five Woolpacks. **1758** *Hist. London-Bridge* 14 The Foundation of this Bridge is by the Vulgar generally believed to be laid upon Woolpacks; which Mistake probably arose from a Tax upon Wool towards its Construction. *a* **1763** SHENSTONE *Progr. Taste* I. 104 This wards the jokes of ev'ry kind,..As wool-packs quash the leaden ball. **1823** SCOTT *Quentin D.* xx, This coming Countess..hangs on our arms as dead a weight as a wool-pack. **1845** D. MACKENZIE *Emigr. Guide Australia* 91 One man is employed in gathering the fleeces as they are shorn

—another in folding them up, and handing them to a man who is pressing them into a large bag, called a wool pack, capable of containing..about 250 lbs. of wool, or about 100 average fleeces. **1866** ROGERS *Agric. & Prices* I. xxii. 568 Hempen fabrics were used for woolpacks.

†**b.** = WOOLSACK 2. *Obs.*

a **1658** CLEVELAND *Epig. on People* Wks. (1687) 254 We.. Call'd out a Parliament,.. Which being obtain'd at last, what did they do? Even squeeze the Wool-packs, and lye snorting too. **1660** PEPYS *Diary* 20 Aug., My Lord Chancellor being gone to the House of Lords, I went thither, and..there staid all the morning, seeing their manner of sitting on woolpacks, &c. which I never did before. *c* **1710** CELIA FIENNES *Diary* (1888) 261 These twelve judges sitt in the House of Lord[s] on wool packs.

2. *transf.* Something resembling a wool-pack.

†**a.** A large mass of white water. *Obs.*

1599 NASHE *Lenten Stuffe* Wks. (Grosart) V. 267 Boystrous woolpacks of ridged tides, came rowling in, and raught him from her. **1733** *Trav. J. Massey* 36 We spy'd that which Sailors call a Wool-Pack, seemingly as big as a great Cask, within Cannon-shot of our Ship.

b. orig. ***wool-pack cloud***: A fleecy cumulus cloud. Chiefly *pl.* (or *collect. sing.*).

1648 EARL WESTMLD. *Otia Sacra* (1879) 128 A day most clear;..wherein Some wool-pack Clouds in corner's bin. *a* **1722** LISLE *Husb.* (1757) 440 The sky full of light wool-pack clouds boding no rain. **1794** G. ADAMS *Nat. & Exp. Philos.* IV. lii. 483 In the north of England, such clouds are called woolpacks. **1869** *Daily News* 13 Feb., The ordinary cumulus or woolpack cloud. **1883** BURTON & CAMERON *Gold Coast* I. iii. 69 The bright blue air, flecked with wool-pack.

c. *pl.* Masses of Wenlock limestone. *local.*

1848 J. PHILLIPS in *Mem. Geol. Surv.* II. I. 185 The solid masses of limestone are locally termed 'Woolpacks'.

3. *attrib.*, as ***wool-pack cloud*** (see 2 b); in quot. *a* 1651, ? resembling a pack of sheep.

a **1651** CLEVELAND *Mixt Assembly* 4 Chaos of Presbyt'ry, where Lay-men guide With the tame Woolpack Clergy by their side.

'wool-,packer. One who makes up packages of wool for transport or sale. Also, later, a machine for packing wool. So **'wool-,packing.**

1376 *Durham Acc. Rolls* (Surtees) 584 In donis dat. Wolpakkers, 4*s.* ? **1480** *Cely Papers* (Camden) 30, xxvj sarplerys the weche ys fayre woll as the woll packar..saythe to me. **1543** tr. *Act 8 Hen. VI*, c. 22 That no wolpacker shal make within the realme but good and due packyng. **1604** *Proclam. Winding Wools* 18 June §1 All Wool-packers, and Winders of wools. **1633** *Stow's Surv.* 640 The Company of Wooll-packers. **1808** W. WILSON *Hist. Diss. Ch.* I. 330 [The old meeting-house] is at present occupied by a wool-packer. **1875** KNIGHT *Dict. Mech.*, *Wool-packer*, a machine for compressing and tying fleeces. *Ibid.*, Wool-packing table. **1894** H. NISBET *Bush Girl's Rom.* 33 The wool-packing season was at its busiest.

Woolpit ('wʊlpɪt). The name of a village in Suffolk, used *attrib.* in ***Woolpit brick***, a pale-coloured brick made from earth there.

1887 J. E. TAYLOR *Tourist's Guide Suffolk* 103 One of its chief industries is brickmaking, for the bed of brick-earth here makes a beautiful stone known everywhere as 'Woolpit Brick'. **1966** G. E. EVANS *Pattern under Plough* ii. 36 The Tudor front of the house was given a severe façade of Woolpit brick.

woolsack ('wʊlsæk). [f. WOOL *sb.* + SACK *sb.*[1] Cf. Du. *wolzak*, G. *wollsack.*]

1. A large package or bale of wool.

a **1300** *Sat. People Kildare* xi. in *E.E.P.* (1862) 154 Ȝe marchans wiþ ȝur gret packes of draperie..and ȝur wol sackes. **1390** GOWER *Conf.* I. 99 Bot lich unto the wollesak Sche proferth hire unto this knyht. *a* **1552** LELAND *Itin.* (1768) II. 32 Sum say..that Wollesakkes be yn Ewelm in token of Marchaundise. **1575** GASCOIGNE *Posies*, *Praise Mistr.* (1907) 55, I seeke to wey yᵉ woolsack down, with one poore pepper grain. **1611** BEAUM. & FL. *Knt. Burn. Pestle* Prol., The rearing of London bridge upon Woollsacks. **1657** TRAPP *Comm. Esther* i. 10. 107 Having farced his body with good chear like a wool-sack. **1715** *Lond. Gaz.* No. 5324/2 Woollsacks and other Materials of use in making a Siege. **1758** JOHNSON *Idler* No. 87 ⁋2 As woolsacks deaden arrows though they cannot repel them. **1879** FARRAR *St. Paul* (1883) 457 Old London Bridge was built not 'on woolsacks', but out of the proceeds of a tax on wool.

b. Applied jocularly to a corpulent person.

1596 SHAKS. *1 Hen. IV*, II. iv. 148.

2. A seat made of a bag of wool for the use of judges when summoned to attend the House of Lords (in recent practice only at the opening of Parliament); also, the usual seat of the Lord Chancellor in the House of Lords, made of a large square bag of wool without back or arms and covered with cloth. Often *allusively* with reference to the position of the Lord Chancellor as the highest judicial officer; hence, ***the woolsack***, the Lord-Chancellorship; ***on the woolsack***, in this office.

[**1539**: see SACK *sb.*[1] 1 d.]

a **1577** SIR T. SMITH *Commw. Eng.* II. iii. (1589) 49 In the middest thereof vpon woolsackes sitteth the Iudges of the realme, the maister of the roules, and the secretaries of estate. But these that sit on the woolsackes haue no voice in the house. **1586** J. HOOKER *Hist. Irel.* in *Holinshed* II. 123/2 In the middle roome beneath them sit the chiefe iustices and iudges of the realme, the barons of the excheker, the kings sergeants, and all such as be of the kings learned councell,.. and all these sit upon great woollsacks, couered with red cloth. **1647** CLARENDON *Hist. Reb.* III. §11 The Lord Keeper of the Great Seal, upon the Wooll-sack. **1710** J. CHAMBERLAYNE *St. Gt. Brit.* 95 The Lord Chancellor..sits on the first Wool-Sack... Upon other Wool-Sacks sit the Judges, the King's Council at Law, and the Masters of Chancery. **1737** *Gentl. Mag.* VII. 536/2 The noble Lord on the Wool-Sack. **1785** *Rolliad*, *Prob. Odes* xvi. 8 By G——d I swore, while George shall reign, The Seals, in spite of changes, to retain, Nor quit the Woolsack, till he quits the throne. **1796** T. MORTON *Way to get Married* I. i. (1800) 16 *Caust.* Pray stick to the law. *Tang.* And to the woolsack. Does not the hope of that..cram our courts full of barristers, with heads as empty as they leave their clients' pockets? **1817** EVANS *Parl. Deb.* 414 The Lord Chancellor took the Woolsack at one o'clock. **1842** J. WILSON *Chr. North* (1857) I. 108 What seated Thurlow, and Wedderburne,..and Brougham on the woolsack? Work. **1854** EMERSON *Lett. & Soc. Aims*, *Eloquence* Wks. (Bohn) III. 189 If the performance of the advocate reaches any high success, it is paid in England..with seats in the cabinet, earldoms, and wool-sacks. **1862** MISS BRADDON *Lady Audley* xxv, She drags her husband on to the woolsack, or pushes him into parliament. **1901** *Empire Rev.* I. 467 The woolsack is technically not in the House, a fact recognised by the Standing Orders which provide that when the Lord Chancellor wishes to speak he is 'to go to his own place as a Peer'.

attrib. **1633** DAVENANT *Cœlum Brit.* Wks. 1673 I. 362 Though I am but a Woollsack-god, and have no vote in the sanction of new Laws.

‖**woolsaw** ('wʊlsɔː). Also 8 **woolesaw**, 9 **oulasser.** [Mosquito *wulasha.*] Among people of African descent in Central America, an evil spirit or demon.

1757 R. HODGSON *Mosquito Territ.* (1822) 46 A kind of priests called Sookies, who..pretend to deal with an evil spirit called Woolesaw. **1827** O. W. ROBERTS *Voy. Centr. Amer.* 267 Their great evil spirit is the 'woolsaw' or devil. **1842** T. YOUNG *Residence on Mosquito Shore* vi. 72 After sun-set a Sambo will not venture out alone, lest the Oulasser should carry him away.

†**woolsey**, *sb. Obs. rare.* The second element of LINSEY-WOOLSEY used independently.

1737 BENTLEY *Rem. Disc. Free-Thinking* liv. III. 12 Unless he thought his Verses were to sell by the Foot, no matter for the Stuff whether Linsey or Woolsey.

woolsey ('wʊlzɪ), *a. rare.* [f. WOOL *sb.* + *-sey* derived from LINSEY-WOOLSEY.] Woolly; woollen.

1839 LANDOR *Andrea of Hungary* IV. iv, This woolsy race [*i.e.* sheep]. **1877** BLACKMORE *Cripps* i, The Carrier's mantle, or woolsey coat.

woolskin ('wʊlskɪn). Also 6 **wol-**, **volskyn(g.** [SKIN *sb.*] A sheepskin with the fleece on it.

c **1440** LYDG. *Hors, Shepe & G.* 361 The wolle skynnys makith men to rise To gret richesse in many sondry wise. **1482** *Acta Audit.* (1839) 103/1 þre hundretht & foure skore woll skynnes. **1531–2** *Durham Househ. Bk.* (Surtees) 109 Expenduntur 448 wolskyns. **1533–4** *Ibid.* 313 Vocatæ volskyngs. **1612** *Sc. Bk. Rates* in *Halyburton's Ledger* (1867) 340 Woll skins the hundreth, xx li. **1643** *Docq. Lett. Pat. at Oxf.* (1837) 370 Lettres Patentes..for the collectinge of the Custome of wooles hydes woolskinnes..in the Porte of.. Southampton. **1903** FLEMMING *Pract. Tanning* 64 Woolskins are also very cheaply tanned in the following manner.

'wool-,staple[1]. [STAPLE *sb.*[2]] A market appointed for the sale of wool.

1593 NORDEN *Spec. Brit.*, *M'sex* (Camden) Introd. p. xvii, Ther are within this cytie the longe Woulstaple and the rounde, both which take name of the Staple that ther was kepte for woules. *a* **1700** EVELYN *Diary* 8 July 1656, The pinnacle of one of their wool-staple houses. **1778** *Engl. Gaz.* (ed. 2) s.v. *Sandwich*, The wool-staple was removed hither from Queenborough, in the reign of Richard II.

So **'wool-,stapler** [STAPLER 2], a merchant who buys wool from the producer, grades it, and sells it to the manufacturer. Also **'wool-,stapling.**

1709 *Lond. Gaz.* No. 4529/3 Eden Hardy,.. Bermondsey, .. Woollstapler. **1835** URE *Philos. Manuf.* 160 The matted fleeces supplied by the wool-stapler. **1888** T. W. REID *W. E. Forster* I. 137 The wool-stapling business of James Fison and Son of Thetford. **1897** 'OUIDA' *Massarenes* xlviii, An Australian wool-stapler.

'wool-,staple[2]. [STAPLE *sb.*[3]] The staple of (a particular) wool.

1835 URE *Philos. Manuf.* 155 The distance between the first and last pair of rollers is much greater, on account of the greater length of the wool-staple.

woolsted, obs. for of WORSTED.

woolster ('wʊlstə(r)). *Sc.* [f. WOOL *sb.* + -STER.] A wool-stapler (Jam. 1825).

1577 in *Agric. Surv. Ayrs.* 99 (Jam.) All other art or trade viz. of shoemakers,..carpenters, and woolsters.

woolsy: see WOOLSEY.

Woolton ('wʊltən). The title of F. J. Marquis (1883–1964), 1st Earl of *Woolton*, used in (***Lord***) ***Woolton pie***, a vegetable pie publicized when he was wartime Minister of Food.

1941 *Food Facts for Kitchen Front* 44 *Lord Woolton Pie.* The ingredients of this pie can be varied according to the vegetables in season. Potato, swede, cauliflower and carrot make a good mixture. **1955** E. WAUGH *Officers & Gentlemen* II. vi. 291 The London crowd shuffled past, surfeited with tea and Woolton pies. *a* **1969** O. SITWELL *Queen Mary* (1974) 47 At luncheon..we found a new and rather horrible war-time dish had been prepared for us, called Lord Woolton Pie. **1981** *Times* 16 Mar. 12/7 A wartime diet of Woolton Pie and whalemeat.

wooluish, var. WOLVISH *a. Obs.*

†**'woolward**, *a. Obs.* Forms: see WOOL *sb.*; also 6 **woldward.** [ME. *wolleward*, prob. alteration of **wollewerd* (of which there is perh. a relic in the form *welleward*, for *wolleward*, of quot. 1480), from an unrecorded OE. **wullwerd*, f. *wull* WOOL *sb.* + *-werd*, *-wered* wearing, clothed (in), f. stem of *werian* WEAR *v.*[1] (cf. OE. *línenwerd* clothed in linen, and prob. *scírwered*, *sweȝlwered* 'clothed' or enveloped in brightness). The assimilation of *-werd* to -WARD, initiated by lack of stress, would be furthered by the prevalence of the word in the phr. *to go woolward* (cf. *to go heavenward*).] Wearing wool next the skin, esp. as a penance: chiefly in ***to go woolward.***

c **1315** SHOREHAM *Poems* I. 1024 Baruot go, Wolle-ward and wakynge. **1377** LANGL. *P. Pl.* B. XVIII. 1 Wolleward and wete-shoed went I forth after. *c* **1450** *Mirk's Festial* 43 Saynt Thomas, be come to Caunturbury, wolward and barfote. **1480** CAXTON *Chron. Eng.* xcix. f 1, Good men..that wenten baarfoot & wellewerd [*Brut* 99 wolward] for to haue mercy of the ij. kynges. *c* **1489** —— *Sonnes of Aymon* xxvii. 574 He is goon his wayes wulwarde & barefote wyth a sory staff in his hande. **1508** FISHER *7 Penit. Ps.* cii. Wks. (1876) 181 Truly it was a more glorious sight to se saynt Poule..in hungre, thurst, watchynge, in colde, goynge wol-ward. **1588** SHAKS. *L.L.L.* v. ii. 717 The naked truth of it is, I haue no shirt, I go woolward for penance. **1621** BURTON *Anat. Mel.* III. ii. v. i. 627 Poore people fare coursly, worke hard, goe wollward and bare. **1646** TRAPP *Comm. John* xvi. 2 If he thought his shirt were infected with that heresie, he would tear it from his own back, and rather goe woolward. **1822** SCOTT *Nigel* xvii, To walk wool-ward in winter.

b. in attrib. position or comb.

1493 [H. PARKER] *Dives & Pauper* IV. xxi. (W. de W. 1496) 186/2 Auowe that she hath made to god as of fastynge, of pylgremage, contynence, wolwarde goynge, and such other. **1531** TINDALE *Expos. 1 John* (1537) 23 His fastynge, his woldward goynge, bare foote goynge. **1628** BP. HALL *Serm.* 30 Mar., Wks. 1634 II. 327 Their woolward and barefoot walks. **1655** [G. HALL] *Tri. Rome* vi. 73 What woolward penances, what weary pilgrimages?

c. ***to lay woolward***: to bury in wool. *rare.*

1604 T. M. *Black Bk.* in *Middleton's Wks.* (Bullen) VIII. 25 The sexton..so laid the dead bodies wool-ward.

Woolwich ('wʊlɪdʒ). The name of a town in Greater London (formerly in Kent), used attrib., esp. to designate productions of its old dockyard and the Royal Arsenal, as ***Woolwich-gun***, ***-hulk***; also **Woolwich-beds** *Geol.* (see quot. 1859); **Woolwich infant**, a jocular name given to a class of heavy guns.

1794 BURNS *Epist. fr. Esopus* 40 The shrinking Bard.. dreads a meeting worse than Woolwich hulks. **1859** PAGE *Handbk. Geol. Terms*, *Woolwich-beds*, a name occasionally employed by English geologists to designate those beds of plastic and mottled clays, sands, and rolled flint-pebbles which lie between the 'Thanet Sands' and the 'London Clay'. **1871** RUSKIN *Fors Clavig.* ii. 21 The 35-ton gun called the 'Woolwich infant', which is fed with 700 pound shot and 130 pounds of gunpowder at one mouthful. **1875** W. T. VINCENT *Warlike Woolwich* 30 *note*, The name of the 'Woolwich Infant'..was suggested to the writer of these pages by Sergeant Major Adamson, of the Depot Brigade, Royal Artillery. **1876** VOYLE & STEVENSON *Milit. Dict.* (ed. 3) 472 *Woolwich Gun*, a gun rifled on the French system, with this modification, that the grooves are shallower, and have their corners rounded off.

'wool-,winder. [WINDER *sb.*[1] (WIND *v.*[1] 16, 23 b).] **1.** One who 'winds' or packs up fleeces for transport or sale.

1523–34 FITZHERB. *Husb.* §52 Let the wol be well folden or wounden with a woll-wynder, that can good skyll therof. **1550** *Proclam. Winding of Wools* 23 May 1 The feloweshippe of wole wynders, otherwyse called wollmen. **1657** HOWELL *Londinop.* 63 The residue of the Lofts were letten out to Marchants, the Wooll-winders and Packers therein, to winde and pack their Wools. **1727** BYROM *Rem.* (Chetham Soc.) I. 286 It was the feast day of the woolwinders. **1886** C. SCOTT *Sheep-farming* 138 Pick up the fleeces, and carry them to the wool-winders.

2. A frame on which wool is wound.

1969 *Canad. Antiques Collector* Aug. 20/2 An old wool-winder, still in its original state, stands to the left. **1976** *Evening Post* (Nottingham) 15 Dec. 20/6 (Advt.), Knitmaster 321 Punchcard Knitting machine, with worktable, woolwinder, punch etc.

'wool-work. [Cf. G. *wollwerk* woollen goods.]

†**1.** Working in wool; manufacture of woollen goods. *Obs.*

c **1475** *Cath. Angl.* 423/1 (Add. MS.) Wolle werke, *lanificium.* *a* **1513** FABYAN *Chron.* VI. clvi. (1811) 145 His doughter he set to spynnynge and woll warke. **1570** LEVINS *Manip.* 171/39 Wolworke, *lanificium.* **1630** BRATHWAIT *Engl. Gent.* 125 The Towne of Kendall, so famous for Wooll-worke.

2. Needlework executed in wool usually on a canvas foundation. Also, knitted wool fabric.

1871 *Cassell's Househ. Guide* IV. 5 Design for a fire-screen in wool-work. **1882** CAULFEILD & SAWARD *Dict. Needle-work* 465 Berlin woolwork. **1888** FERGUS HUME *Mme. Midas* Prol., A red cap of wool-work.

attrib. **1899** *Westm. Gaz.* 26 Mar. 3/2 The eye of a wool-work needle. **1905** MRS. BARNES-GRUNDY *Vacil. Hazel* 55 She placed a woolwork cushion at the back of my head.

So **'wool-worked** *a.*, worked in wool, consisting of wool-work.

1870 *Routledge's Ev. Boy's Ann.* Apr. Suppl. 8/2 A good wool-worked Cricket-belt. **1900** *Bookseller's Catalogue*, Magnificent Woolworked and Silk Picture.

'wool-ˌworker. [Cf. G. *wollwirker*.] One who works in wool.

1372 *Cal. Wills Crt. Husting, Lond.* II. (1890) 151 [The light of] Wolwyrchers [in the same church]. **1552** HULOET, Wolle worker, *lanifex*. **1903** A. ROBERTSON *R.C. Ch. in Italy* ix. 187 St. Blaise..was once venerated in Yorkshire as the patron of woolworkers.

Woolworth ('wʊlwɜːθ). The name of the retailing company (orig. sixpenny store) F. W. *Woolworth* PLC, used *attrib.* to designate low-priced goods regarded as typical of its merchandise.

1931 *Times Lit. Suppl.* 5 Nov. 862/3 Miss Helen Simpson is refreshingly modern with her 'Woolworth craze' at Oxford as the real villain. **1932** AUDEN in *Rev. Eng. Stud.* (1978) XXIX. 292 Moving woodenly like a woolworth doll, A lady came in clothes so ugly..that the eye was cruel. **1939** T. S. ELIOT *Old Possum's Bk. Pract. Cats* 22 One of the girls Suddenly missed her Woolworth pearls. **1948** 'J. TEY' *Franchise Affair* vii. 69 Some Woolworth plants in the gardens. **1974** *Guardian* 21 Mar. 10, I am never likely to be involved in a study of..Lehar and can only look on all of it as real Woolworth stuff (in contrast to, say, Mozart, who is vintage Fortnum and Mason). **1980** I. ST. JAMES *Money Stones* III. iii. 106 You couldn't swing a Woolworth watch on diamonds found here.

Hence **Wool'worthian** *a.*

1933 R. W. CHAMBERS *Whatever Love Is* xx. 286 A strange, stark, snowless, dingy Christmastide with a Woolworthian cheapness about it. **1937** P. THORNTON *Dead Puppets Dance* II. vii. 144 There were hundreds of people at Kučevište, and many of them wore..high-heeled shoes and Woolworthian stockings if their husbands could afford.. them. **1978** *Washington Post* 27 Aug. C-38/2 Nowadays the plates are chipped and the tables lit by Woolworthian gilded pierced tin lamps flickering with candles.

woom, var. VOME *Obs.*, vomit.

woomera ('wuːmərə). *Austral.* Forms: **wom(m)erah, womrah, wom(m)-, wummera, wommeira, womerar, wo-, wamara, woom-, wammera, wommora, -ala.** [Native name, given as *womar, womerra, wommerru*, etc. in various vocabularies.] A throwing-stick used by Australian aboriginals. = THROWING-STICK a. Also = next.

1817 OXLEY *Jrnls. Two Exped. N.S. Wales* (1820) 117 He [*sc.* the native] was quite naked, except the netted band round the waist, in which were womerahs. **1835** J. BATEMAN in Cornwallis *New World* (1859) I. 407 We..encountered six men, armed with spears fixed in their wommeras. **1845** J. O. BALFOUR *Sk. N.S. Wales* 17 A *whamera* whizzed past where I was standing, and with unerring aim struck Fighting Jemmy on the arm. **1907** *Macm. Mag.* Oct. 935 He,..with the aid of a favourite womerah, could send a long spear, tipped with palm-wood, through a deal plank an inch thick a hundred yards away.

woomerang ('wuːməræŋ). *Austral.* Also **wom-**. [Native name (*wo-mur-răng* in D. Collins *N.S. Wales*, 1798, I. 613).] A missile club used by Australian aboriginals. = THROWING-STICK b.

1849 J. C. PRICHARD *Ethnol.* in *Man. Sci. Enquiry* 433 The ancient Gauls were known by their gæsa or javelins... The Australians by their woomerangs or throwing-sticks. **1864** J. ROGERS *New Rush* II. 46 Next—high in air the womerang-spear he flings.

woomph (wuːmf, wʊmf), *int.* (*sb.*, *adv.*) *slang.* Also **woomf**. [Imitative.] (Expressing) a sound similar to a 'whoof' (WHOOF *int.* (*sb.*) 2) but with a deeper or more resonant component. Cf. the synonymous WHOOMPF *int.* (*sb.*).

1955 LD. WINTERTON *Fifty Tumultuous Years* 82 Two old gentlemen were dozing in their chairs when the 'Woomph', 'Boomph' of a bomb simultaneously woke them up. **1979** R. FIENNES *Hell on Ice* ix. 144 There was a sudden *woomf* as the fumes and the liquid ignited. **1982** S. BRETT *Murder Unprompted* xiv. 133 He threw a cushion, which went woomph into the side of Charles's head.

wooms. (See quot.)

1834 MCCULLOCH *Dict. Commerce* (ed. 2) 628 A mixture of *cheek* beaver, with white and brown stage beaver, or seasoned beaver, commonly called 'wooms'.

woon (wuːn). Also **wun**. [Burmese *wun*.] A Burmese administrative officer. Also **woondock, woongee**, names for different grades of this.

1800 M. SYMES *Acc. Embassy Ava* xiii. 308 To assist in the administration of affairs, four officers, called Woondocks, are associated with the Woongees. *Ibid.* 309 There are.. officers..who bear no ostensible share in the administration of public affairs, such as the Daywoon, or King's armour-bearer; the Chaingeewoon, or master of the elephants; also the Woons of the Queen's household. **1856** *Putnam's Monthly Mag.* June 561/1 A message came down from the Woon, or head man, of the friendly people who inhabited the interior town of Pegu. **1886** LD. R. CHURCHILL in *Daily News* 26 Jan. 2/4 Those [English] officers were supported by troops and were working through local woons. **1898** H. F. HALL *Soul of People* vii. 92 Outside Mandalay the country was governed by *wuns* or governors. **1972** A. T. Q. STEWART *Pagoda War* ix. 112 (*caption*) Thibaw's envoy, the *wun* with his golden umbrella, stands beside him.

woon, var. WONE, WOOLLEN.

woond(e, woonder, woone, woont: see WIND *v.*[1], WONDER, ONE, WONT.

woontak: see *womb-tack*, WOMB *sb.* 5.

†**woop.** [? var. of HOOP *sb.*[3] 2.] The bullfinch.

1668 CHARLETON *Onomast.* 91 *Rubicilla*, Pyrrhula, the Woop, or Bulfinch.

woop, variant of WOUP *Sc. Obs.*

woop woop ('wʊpwʊp). *Austral.* and *N.Z.* Also **woop-woop(s, wop-wop.** [Sham Aboriginal (but see below).] **a.** A jocular name for a remote rural town or district; also (without *the* and with capital initials) as the name of an imaginary place in a remote area.

One suggestion is that the term is derived from the 'geelorious town o' Whoop-Up' in E. L. Wheeler's *Deadwood Dick on Deck* (1878), where 'Whoop-Up' is the name of a back-country American goldmining town.

1926 'J. DOONE' *Timely Tips for New Australians* 23 *Woop Woop*, a humorous method of alluding to the country districts used most frequently in New South Wales. **1928** A. WRIGHT *Good Recovery* 34 They're chasin' Murraba out along the Woop Woop Road, or somewhere. **1930** *Bulletin* (Sydney) 1 Jan. 28/2 'Who on earth is she?' gasped the visitor from Woop-Woop. **1958** J. LINDSAY *Life Rarely Tells* 213 Next morning he'd rush away. 'Off to the Woop-woop!' Somewhere in the backblocks that meant. **1960** N. HILLIARD *Maori Girl* III. i. 174 'Where do you come from?' 'Up in the wilds—the woop-woops, Taranaki.' **1963** *Truth* (Wellington, N.Z.) 8 Oct., A job was found right out in the wop-wops. **1970** *N.Z. Listener* 21 Dec. 51/2 While you're out in the woop-woops next time, spare a thought for the local farmer. **1975** *Courier-Mail* (Brisbane) 26 Mar. 12/6 Police feared they would be transferred to 'Woop Woop'.

b. An inhabitant of such a place; a country bumpkin. *rare.*

1936 M. FRANKLIN *All that Swagger* 472 Adrienne was no blob or woop-woop. **1950** *Coast to Coast 1949–50* 201 I'll make a fair dinkum woop-woop out of you in no time.

woorali, wourali (wuː'rɑːliː). Also 8–9 **woorara**, 9 **woorrara, wooraly.** See also OORALI, URALI, URARI. [See CURARE.] A South American climbing plant, *Strychnos toxifera*, from the root of which one of the ingredients of the poison CURARE is obtained; also, the poison itself. Also *attrib.*, as ***woorali poison, vine.***

[**1596** L. KEYMIS *Relat. Second Voy. Guiana* G 2, Names of poysoned hearbes. Ourari.] **1769** E. BANCROFT *Ess. Nat. Hist. Guiana* 101 The Woorara, which is the principal ingredient in the composition of the fatal Indian arrow poison of that name. **1796** STEDMAN *Surinam* I. xv. 395 A few of the above arrows are frequently dipped in the woorara poison, which is instantaneously fatal. **1803** WINTERBOTTOM *Sierra Leone* I. xv. 271 A kind of dart,..dipped in a poison called woorrara. **1825** WATERTON *Wand. S. Amer.* 53 A vine grows in these wilds, which is called wourali. *Ibid.*, The wourali poison destroys life's action so gently, that the victim appears to be in no pain whatever. *Ibid.* 54 He scrapes the wourali vine and bitter root into thin shavings. **1842** *Penny Cycl.* XXIII. 152/2 Wooraly, Urari, or Poison-plant of Guiana. **1862** *N. Syd. Soc. Year-bk. Med.* 18 Nervous sensibility, after its suspension by woorara poisoning. **1902** P. FOUNTAIN *Mts. & For. S. Amer.* vii. 185 My mixture.. was, like the true wourali, innocuous if swallowed. *Ibid.* 189, I have..strong grounds for believing that it is snake-poison that is the active principle in the wourali paste.

woord, woorld, woory(e, etc., obs. ff. WORD, WORLD, WORRY *v.*, etc.

woos, obs. f. OOZE, WHOSE.

woosel(l, obs. ff. OUZEL.

woosh, var. WHOOSH *v.*, *sb.*

woost, obs. 2 sing. pres. ind. of WIT *v.*[1]

Wooster ('wuːstə(r)). The name of Bertie *Wooster*, an amiable, vacuous, young man about town in the novels of P. G. Wodehouse, used allusively. Also *attrib.*

1939 AUDEN & ISHERWOOD *Journey to a War* i. 44 He was so much more subtle, more intelligent than his cultivated Bertie Wooster drawl. **1960** *New Statesman* 24 Sept. 424/2 Very young men about town..quite amiable in a Bertie Wooster sort of way. **1963** R. H. MORRIESON *Scarecrow* (1964) xii. 135 Her husband, the aged Wooster type whom Angela and I had encountered.

Also as *v. intr.*, to behave in the manner of Bertie Wooster; **'Woosterish** *a.*; **'Woosterism**, a remark or action characteristic of Wooster.

1959 *Observer* 26 Apr. 23/5 Harold..lives in a pretty Woosterish way. **1964** *Punch* 17 June 906/3 Frolicsome nitwits woostering in well-heeled suburbia. **1969** *Times* 5 May 23/3 Dapper, cheerful young men without the disdain of the real Jeeves when provoked by inane Woosterisms. **1978** *Country Life* 14 Dec. 2103/1 A ridiculous pink velvet dog with inane Woosterish eyes. **1979** K. BONFIGLIOLI *After you with Pistol* xvii. 130 We Woostered away for a while, giggling slightly. *Ibid.*, While we idly bandied these Woosterisms..he slid a scribbling-pad across the desk. **1983** *Times* 17 Oct. 15/4 This show..reducing Olivia to a charm-school hostess, Andrew to a Woosterian silly ass and ..Toby to a bar-fly.

woosy(e, obs. ff. OOZY.

woot(e, obs. ind. pres. of WIT *v.*[1]

wootes, obs. pl. of OAT.

1559 in *15th Rep. Hist. MSS. Comm.* App. III. 74, ye peckes wootes.

wootz (wuːts). Also **wudz**. [app. orig. misprint for *wook*, repr. Canarese *ukku* (pronounced with initial *w*) steel.] A crucible steel made in southern India by fusing magnetic iron ore with carbonaceous matter. Also *attrib.* and *Comb.*

1795 *Phil. Trans.* LXXXV. 322 Doctor Scott..has sent over specimens of a substance known by the name of wootz; which is considered to be a kind of steel. **1824** *Encycl. Brit.* Suppl. III. 456/2 Wootz, a steel from India, has lately been most successfully employed [for cutlery]. **1839** URE *Dict. Arts* 1176 The wootz ore consists of the magnetic oxide of iron, united with quartz. **1869** BALDWIN *Preh. Nations* vi. (1877) 229 The celebrated India steel called wudz. **1881** *Blackw. Mag.* May 569/1 The Indian 'wootz' steel,..which possesses remarkable toughness and sharpness.

woo-woo. Imitative of the sound of wind.

1841 CARLYLE *Misc. Ess.*, *Baillie* (1872) VI. 215 The ever-moaning..unsyllabled *woo-woo* of wind in empty churches!

wooy, Sc. form of WOOLLY *a.*

wooze, var. OOZE.

woozy ('wuːzɪ), *a.* *colloq.* orig. *U.S.* Also **whoosy, whoozy, woozey.**

1. Dizzy or unsteady as when fuddled with drink; muzzy; 'dotty'.

1897 *Voice* (N.Y.) 22 Apr. 3/2 In the woozy lexicon of the voting church there is no such word as power. **1909** 'O. HENRY' *Roads of Destiny* iv. 64 A woman gets woozy on clothes. **1915** WODEHOUSE *Psmith, Journalist* xvi. 114 'He's still woozy,' said the Kid. 'Still—what exactly, Comrade Brady?' 'In the air,' explained the Kid. 'Bats in the belfry. Dizzy.' **1917** CONAN DOYLE *His Last Bow* viii. 292 The man was mad. Well, he went a bit woozy. **1929** KIPLING *Limits & Renewals* (1932) 356 He had kept himself going on rum sometimes, and was woozy when the pinch came. **1937** *Black Mask* Jan. 24/2, I got hit. It made me woozey for a minute. **1952** B. MALAMUD *Natural* 17 He got up whoozy and walked, finding it hard to believe his eyes. **1961** J. B. PRIESTLEY *Saturn over Water* iii. 29 The woozy state I was in. **1977** M. HINXMAN *One-Way Cemetery* xix. 139 He'd have phrased it more delicately if he hadn't felt quite so whoosy. **1978** *Daily Tel.* 17 Jan. 17/2 Liquid lunches can leave a man weak and woozy late in the afternoon, drinkers were told.

2. Representing or marked by muddled thinking or unclear expression; lacking rigour or discipline; sloppy.

1941 AUDEN *New Year Let.* II. 37 All vague idealistic art ..Is up his alley, and his pigeon The woozier species of religion. **1961** *Catholic Gaz.* May 129/2 To Dickens, Christmas meant a debauch of vague and woozy sentiment. **1970** AUDEN in *New Yorker* 21 Feb. 118/1 Like Ruskin, he can at times write sentences which I would call 'woozy'; that is to say, too dependent upon some private symbolism of his own to be altogether comprehensible to others. **1971** *Daily Tel.* 15 Mar. 13/4 One wonders if it is not simply the drink that has made so many Irish writers bury their poetic insights beneath so much that is garrulous, maudlin and whoozy. **1975** *New Yorker* 3 Feb. 84/2 There are gaps in the plot and woozy lapses in time. **1977** *Rolling Stone* 24 Mar. 41/2 She supports the old male stereotype of woman as overwhelmingly physical, instinctual, and her writing is too woozy for me. **1977** *N.Y. Rev. Bks.* 9 June 16/3 The other poem of 1939 [by Auden], with its 'affirming flame', is woozy too. **1980** *Times Lit. Suppl.* 25 Apr. 470/5 A level of woozy tautology.

Hence **'woozily** *adv.*, **'wooziness.**

a **1911** D. G. PHILLIPS *Susan Lenox* (1917) I. xxi. 395 'Shut up!' cried the drunken man... He caught them each by an arm, stared woozily at Etla. **1924** *Black Mask* Nov. 48/2 This thing had fallen on me while my nerves were ragged from three days of boozing... [Now] my wooziness had passed. **1937** *Ibid.* Jan. 23/2, I shook my head woozily. **1937** AUDEN *Let.* in Auden & MacNeice *Lett. from Iceland* 221 Landscape's so dull if you haven't Lawrence's wonderful wooziness. **1967** *Listener* 9 Feb. 193/2 Staring woozily at a wine flask. **1977** C. ISHERWOOD *Christopher & his Kind* xii. 181 Much of what Christopher called Wystan's wooziness was essentially religious in context. **1984** *Observer* 19 Feb. 25/5 Later in life she more stubbornly shut herself off from the world's demands behind the defences of deafness, bad English and Benedictine-fuelled wooziness.

†**wop**, *sb.*[1] *Obs.* [OE. *wóp*: see WEEP *v.* etym.] Weeping. Hence †**wopi** *a.*, tearful.

Beowulf 785 þara þe of wealle wop ȝehyrdon, gryreleoð galan godes andsacan. *c* **1000** *Ags. Gosp.* Matt. viii. 12 þær bið wop & toþa gristbitung. *c* **1175** *Lamb. Hom.* 157 Ure drihten..iturnd hore horte and heore wope to muchele blisse. *c* **1205** LAY. 5970 Wælle muchel wes þa wop [*c* 1275 wepinge]. *a* **1225** *Ancr. R.* 376 Iblesced beo þu, Louerd, þet ..efter wopie wateres ȝeldest blið muruhðes. **1297** R. GLOUC. (Rolls) 6912 Heo..bileuede þer al niȝt In wop & in orisons. **1340** *Ayenb.* 71 Oure blisse is ywent in-to wop.

wop (wɒp), *sb.*[2] and *a.* *slang* (orig. *U.S.*). Also **Wop.** [Origin uncertain; perh. ad. It. dial. *guappo* bold, showy, ruffian, f. Sp. *guapo* bold, dandy, f. L. *vappa* sour wine, worthless fellow.]

A. *sb.* **a.** An Italian or other southern European, esp. as an immigrant or foreign visitor (see also quot. 1914). Now considered *offensive.*

[**1912** A. TRAIN *Courts, Criminals & Camorra* ix. 232 There is a society of criminal young men in New York City. .. They are known by the euphonious name of 'Waps' or 'Jacks'. These are young Italian-Americans who allow themselves to be supported by one or two women... They form one variety of the many gangs that infest the city.] **1914** JACKSON & HELLYER *Vocab. Criminal Slang* 88 *Wop*, noun. Used principally in the east. An ignorant person; a foreigner; an impossible character... Example: 'You couldn't find a jitney with a search warrant in this bunch of wops.' **1915** WODEHOUSE *Psmith, Journalist* xix. 138 He's a wop, kid... A wop. A dago... An Italian. **1924** E. HEMINGWAY *In our Time* 17 Wops, said Boyle, I can tell wops a mile off. **1930** G. B. SHAW *Apple Cart* II. 78 *Lysistrata.* What they call an American is only a wop pretending to be a Pilgrim Father. He is no more Uncle Jonathan than you are John Bull. *Magnus*. Yes: we live in a world of wops, all melting into one another. **1940** N. MITFORD *Pigeon Pie* i. 7 Luke's Italian was far more affected than that of any native wop. **1942** *R.A.F. Jrnl.* 13 June 26 The pilots..suggested that the 'Wops were yellow' or that they could not 'take it through cloud'. **1952** E. F. DAVIES *Illyrian Venture* ii. 26 We had breakfast in the mess tent, waited on by a cheerful wop. **1973** 'I. DRUMMOND' *Jaws of Watchdog* ii. 26 Sandro dived into the pool... 'You great fat clumsy Wop,' said Jenny, 'you've put my cigarette out.'

b. The Italian language.

1937 [see *for all I know* s.v. KNOW *v.* 11 g]. **1938** E. POUND *Let.* 6 May (1971) 313 'Sardinia is Barbagia' don't seem either English or Wop. **1982** A. MELVILLE-ROSS *Trigger* xx. 225 There's a lot of chat in Wop which I doesn't understand.

B. *adj.* Italian.

1938 E. POUND *Let.* 8 Jan. (1971) 303 'Praedis': I don't care how you spell your wop painters. **1940** [see KIKE]. **1941** C. E. MILBURN *Diary* 15 Feb. (1979) 83 We have dropped parachutists in Italy... A very nice surprise for our 'Wop' enemy! **1955** E. WAUGH *Officers & Gentlemen* 326 You'll find her full of wop prisoners. **1983** S. F. X. DEAN *It can't be my Grave* iv. 64 Are you telling me, you Wop son of a bitch, that I can't get into my father's lift?

wop (wɒp), *sb.*^{3} *R.A.F. slang.* [Acronym from *w*(*ireless op*(*erator* (cf. OP^3 2 b).] A radio operator.

1939 *Airman's Gaz.* Dec., You have a choice of three.. trades—..W.O.M.,..W.E.M.,..and the W/Op. which rude people twist into Wop (most unfairly). **1957** R. BARKER *Ship-Busters* iv. 70 Wireless operator/air gunners..most of the wop/A.G.s..came straight from gunnery school.

wop, var. WHOP.

wopen, obs. f. WEAPON.

†**wopne, -one.** [?]

c **1440** *Promp. Parv.* 532/2 Wopne, or pysse (*S.* wopone of pis), *urina*.

wopnen, obs. form of WEAPON *v.*

wopper, var. WAPPER *a.*

a **1658** CLEVELAND *Old Man courting young Girl* 62 Perish'd Lungs and wopper Eyes.

wopper, var. WHOPPER.

wops, dial. and joc. var. WASP *sb.*

wor, var. WAR *a.* and *adv.*, worse.

†'**worble**, *v.* *Sc. Obs.* [var. WARBLE *v.*^{3}; cf. WRABBLE *v.*] *intr.* To wriggle, writhe; to wallow.

a **1598** ROLLOCK *Serm.* Wks. 1849 I. 444 We wer..then worbling [*ed.* 1616 warbling] and waltering in our awin sinne and filthinesse. *a* **1600** MONTGOMERIE *Sonn.* xlvii. 10 Vhy haif I not, O God, als blunt a [braine] As he that daylie worbleth in the wyne. **1808** JAMIESON s.v. *Wrabil*, S. *warble*, *wurble*: as to *wurble in* or *out*.

worble, variant of WARBLE *sb.*^{2}

Worcester ('wʊstə(r)). **1.** The name of the county town of Worcestershire, used *attrib.* to designate articles originating there, e.g. (formerly) a fine cloth, (now chiefly) a kind of China ware; also *ellipt.* = †Worcester cloth, Worcester porcelain, Worcester sauce, etc.

Worcester sauce = Worcestershire sauce (see WORCESTERSHIRE).

1551–2 *Act 5 & 6 Edw. VI*, c. 6 §5 All and everie white Clothe and Clothes whiche shalbe made within the Cittie of Worcester commonlye called Longe Worcesters. *Ibid.* §7 All and everie White Clothe and Clothes comonlye called Shorte Worcesters. **1802** R. WARNER *Tour Northern Counties* I. 47 That exquisite porcelain..known by the name of Worcester china. **1822** *Auction Catal. Fonthill Abbey* 45 A Worcester tea and coffee set. **1848** H. R. FORSTER *Stowe Catal.* 2 An oval sugar-basin, cover, and stand, of rare old Worcester. *Ibid.* 92 A pair of vases, or Worcester porcelain. **1863** MISS BRADDON *Aurora Floyd* xxxi, He poured Worcester sauce into his coffee, and cream over his devilled cutlets. **1885** *Encycl. Brit.* XIX. 642/1 Dr. Wall..started the Worcester Porcelain Company in 1751. **1889** J. K. JEROME *Three Men in Boat* ii. 22 If Harris's eyes fill with tears,..it is because Harris has been eating raw onions, or has put too much Worcester over his chop. **1897** *Daily News* 15 Nov. 8/6 Hops. Worcester..Trade in Worcesters keeps quiet. **1981** T. HEALD *Murder at Moose Jaw* ix. 103 A straight tomato juice with a liberal splashing of Worcester.

2. Used *attrib.* (with *Pearmain* or *apple*) and *absol.* to designate an early, slightly conical red-skinned eating apple belonging to a variety introduced to cultivation about 1875 by Richard Smith, a Worcester nurseryman.

1877 *Garden* 13 Oct. 344/1 Worcester Pearmain Apple.—Of this beautifully coloured, fully flavoured new Apple, Mr. Richard Smith, of Worcester, has sent us samples. **1929** E. A. BUNYARD *Anat. Dessert* 6 The really ripe Worcester has character..and the Raspberry flavour distinctive. **1958** *Listener* 27 Nov. 903/1 Four medium-sized Worcester Pearmain apples. **1936** H. V. TAYLOR *Apples of England* iii. 43 Worcester Pearmain..became the most important of the commercial early dessert apples. **1982** R. HOLLES *Sun Blight* i. 6 She walked along..inspecting the piles of Worcester apples. *Ibid.* ix. 98 In the Portobello Road..mounds of apples grinned at him, Worcesters, Granny Smiths, Golden Delicious.

Worcesterberry ('wʊstəbɛrɪ). Also **worcester-**. [f. prec. + BERRY *sb.*^{1}] A small black gooseberry of the North American species *Ribes divaricatum*, once believed to be a hybrid of the blackcurrant and the gooseberry and sold as such by a Worcester nurseryman.

1923 *Amat. Gardening* 27 Oct. p. ix/3 (Advt.), Worcesterberry. Cross between gooseberry and black currant. Fruiting trees. 3/- each. Richard Smith & Co... Worcester. **1926** *Observer* 5 Sept. 9/2 New fruits, such as the logan and most excellent worcesterberry, multiply almost yearly. **1969** *Oxf. Bk. Food Plants* 80/2 The so-called 'Worcesterberry'..seems first to have been sold by a nurseryman in Worcester who thought it was a black currant gooseberry hybrid. **1980** *Amat. Gardening* 25 Oct. 20/2 If spraying fails, or if you do not like doing it, why not try growing the Worcesterberry instead?

Worcestershire ('wʊstəʃə(r)). The name of an English county: *attrib.* in ***Worcestershire sauce***, which is made in Worcester (also *ellipt.* for this).

1686 PLOT *Staffordsh.* ii. §107 Worcestershire Salts. **1749** FIELDING *Tom Jones* x. iii, They found no fault with my Worcestershire Perry, which I sold them for champagne. **1843** *Naval & Military Gaz.* 1 Apr. 208/2 (Advt.), Lea and Perrin's 'Worcestershire Sauce', prepared from a recipe of a nobleman in the county. **1870** LOWELL *Study Wind.* (1886) 22 A bottle of Worcestershire. **1889** G. ALLEN *Falling in Love*, etc. 205 Mulligatawny soup, Worcestershire sauce, preserved ginger, hot pickles.

worch, worcher, worchip: see WORK, WORKER, WORSHIP.

word (wɜːd), *sb.* Forms: 1– **word**, 1–6 **wurd**, (3 **wored, woerd, weord, wuord, wort**), 3–6 **werd**, 3 (4–6 *Sc.*) **wourd**, (4 **wrd**, 4–6 **worde, wurde**, *Sc.* **vord(e, vourd**, 5 **worþ** (?)), 4–7 **woord** (6–7 **-e**), 5–6 *Sc.* **wird(e**. [OE. *word* str. n. = OFris., OS. *word*, MDu. *wort* (Du. *woord*), OHG., MHG., G. *wort*, ON. *orð* (Sw., Da. *ord*), Goth. *waurd*:—OTeut. **wurdom*:—pre-Teut. **wrdho-*; cf. Lith. *var̃das* name, Lett. *wàrds* word, forename, OPruss. *wirds* word, OIr. *fordat* 'inquiunt'.

Indo-Eur. *werdh-* is generally taken to be a deriv. of *wer-*, *werē-*, which appears in Gr. ϝερέω I shall say, ϝρήτωρ speaker, L. *verbum* word, Skr. *vratám* command, law, etc.]

I. Speech, utterance, verbal expression.

1. *collect. pl.* Things said, or something said; speech, talk, discourse, utterance; *esp.* with possessive, what the person mentioned says or said; (one's) form of expression or language. Often in such phrases as ***in these, other,*** etc. ***words***, in (such-and-such) language; ***many words, few words*** (see also 22, 26); ***to give words to, to put into words***, to express by means of language; ***beyond words***, incapable of being expressed in language, unutterable, unspeakable.

a **900** CYNEWULF *Juliana* 83 Ʒif þas word sind soþ. *a* **1000** *Cædmon's Gen.* 2389 Ne wile Sarran..ʒelyfan wordum minum. *c* **1200** *Trin. Coll. Hom.* 27 Ne mai no man þese word seggen..ȝief he haueð on his heorte onde. *Ibid.* 43 Vnderstonde we on ure heorte his holie wordes. *Ibid.* 217 On þesse fewe litele wored lotieð fele gode wored, ȝif hie weren wel ioponed. *c* **1205** LAY. 3606 Þe alde king..þas wuord seide. *Ibid.* 8835 Nu beoð his word [*c* **1275** wordes] gode. *a* **1300** *Cursor M.* 890 Til þat worm þan drightin spak Wordes bath o wrath and wrak. **1375** BARBOUR *Bruce* IX. 752 Sen thou spekis so ryaly, It is gret skill at men chasty Thi prowd vourdis. **1450–1530** *Myrr. Our Ladye* I. i. 11 These ar the wordes of the prophete Dauid. *Ibid.* II. 66 Youre holy rewle forbydeth you all vayne and ydel wordes. **1526** TINDALE *John* vi. 63 The wordes that I speake vnto you are sprete and lyfe. **1533** GAU *Richt Vay* (S.T.S.) 5 Ane prayer is noth the mair plesand to god for causz we wsz mony vordis in it. **1605** SHAKS. *Macb.* IV. iii. 209 Giue sorrow words; the griefe that do's not speake, Whispers the o're-fraught heart, and bids it breake. *Ibid.* v. viii. 6, I haue no words, My voice is in my Sword. **1638** JUNIUS *Paint. Ancients* 89 Seeing they cleare such a great point in a few words. **1667** MILTON *P.L.* x. 865 Soft words to his fierce passion she assay'd. **1709**, **1795** words of course [see COURSE *sb.* 37 a]. **1749** *Copy Let. Fr. Lady at Paris* 17 Not yet, answered Mr. de Vaudreuil, at which Words, the Prince darted a menancing Look at him. **1813** LADY BURGHERSH *Lett.* (1893) 61 Words can't describe the figures the women dress here. **1817** SHELLEY *Sonn., Ozymandias* 9 And on the pedestal these words appear. **1825** SCOTT *Betrothed* xvii, Forbear these wild and dangerous words!.. There may be here those who will pretend to track mischief from light words. **1847** HELPS *Friends in C.* I. viii. 124 All this is what I have often heard you say yourself in other words. **1848** THACKERAY *Van. Fair* xx, When he had a duty to perform, Captain Dobbin was accustomed to go through it without many words or much hesitation. **1850** TENNYSON *In Mem.* v. i, I sometimes hold it half a sin To put in words the grief I feel. **1878** BESANT & RICE *Celia's Arb.* xvii, I have no words..to express the very great thanks which I..owe you. **1882** BESANT *All Sorts* viii, At a loss to give indignation words. **1885** 'H. CONWAY' *Family Affair* xxvii, To use his own words, he was in a cleft stick. **1892** *Temple Bar* Dec. 541 She could not put her fear into words. **1905** ELIN. GLYN *Viciss. Evang.* 277 Her tact is beyond words.

b. In various obsolete or casual use (sometimes *spec.* speech as distinguished from writing).

Beowulf 612 Ðær wæs hæleþa hleahtor, hlyn swynsode, word wæron wynsume. *a* **940** in Kemble *Cod. Dipl.* V. 248 Ic Æðelstan..on ðisum ʒewrite mid wordum afæstniʒe, ðæt ic wille [etc.]. *c* **1000** ÆLFRIC *Hom.* (Th.) I. 24 Þa com se engel to hire and hi ʒegrette mid Godes wordum. *c* **1205** LAY. 51 Feþeren he nom mid fingren..& þa soþere word sette togadere & þa þre boc þrumde to are. *Ibid.* 6675 Mid wurden and mid writen he dude heom wel to witen þat [etc.]. *a* **1300** *Cursor M.* 12226 Fle for-soth fra him wil i, His wordes i mai noght vnderli. *c* **1386** CHAUCER *Prol.* 313 Discreet he was and of greet reuerence; He semed swich his wordes weren so wise. *a* **1450** *Knt. de la Tour* 18 We felle in wordes of prisoners. *Ibid.* 25 The wiff aught to..lete the husbonde haue the wordes, and to be maister. **1471** CAXTON *Recuyell* (Sommer) 542 Stameryng in his wordes. *c* **1489** —— *Blanchardyn* vii. 28 Wythout moo wordes the knyght mounted..on horsbake. **1500–20** DUNBAR *Poems* xlii. 47 Sayand till hir with wirdis still, Haif pety of ȝour presoneir. **1560** DAUS tr. *Sleidane's Comm.* 1 [They] affirmed their doynges to be good, bothe in wordes and writyng. **1563** FOXE *A. & M.* 1225/1 We had more woordes of thys matter. **1602** SHAKS. *Ham.* I. iii. 134, I would not..Haue you..giue words or talke with the Lord Hamlet. **1677–8** in *Jrnl. Friends Hist. Soc.* XIX. 61 Shee..was much runn into words. **1697** DRYDEN *Æneis* VI. 723 They..in Words and Tears had spent The little time of stay.

c. *spec.* The text of a song or other vocal composition, as distinguished from the music; also, the text of an actor's part.

In first quot. also *sing.*

1450–1530 *Myrr. Our Ladye* I. xxi. 56 Whyle there ys thre thynges in goddes seruyce..The sentence, the worde, and the songe, the notes and songe serue to the wordes, and the wordes serue to the inwarde sentence. **1605** SHAKS. *Macb.* I. iii. 88 To th' selfe-same tune and words. **1611** —— *Cymb.* IV. ii. 238. **1761** VICTOR *Theatres Lond. & Dublin* II. 5 The Rehearsals..begin to be of Use to the Actor: When he is quite perfect in the Words and Cues. **1774** [see SET *v.*^{1} 73]. **1847** TENNYSON *Princess* VII. 270 Till at the last she set herself to man, Like perfect music unto noble words. **1890** BARING-GOULD *Old Country Life* 279 A marvellous store of old words and tunes in her head.

d. *too* —— *for words*: —— to an extent that cannot adequately be described. *colloq.*

1913 *Vanity Fair* Nov. 65 New York is beginning to look too smart and clean for words. **1928** E. O'NEILL *Strange Interlude* VIII. 289 But for Gordon to..propose marriage —it's too idiotic for words! **1937** J. MERCER *Too Marvellous for Words* (song), You're just too marvellous, too marvellous for words.

2. a. *sing.* Something said (= sense 1); a speech or utterance; esp. defined by a possessive or demonstrative. *arch.*

c **1000** *Ags. Gosp.* Matt. iv. 4 Ne leofað se man be hlafe anum ac be ælcon worde þe of godes muðe gæð. *a* **1175** *Cott. Hom.* 235 He cweð a wunder word to þar sawle bi þa witie ysaiam. *c* **1200** ORMIN Ded. 45 Min word..Maȝȝ hellpenn þa þatt redenn itt to sen & tunnderrstanndenn. *Ibid.* 282 Swa wass filledd opennliȝ þatt word tatt ær wass cwiddedd. *a* **1300** *Cursor M.* 1600 Þis word out of his hert sprang..'Me reus þat euer made i man.' **1375** BARBOUR *Bruce* xv. 145 With that vorde assemblit thai. *c* **1400** *Anturs of Arth.* xvi, Ways me for thi wirde! *c* **1470** HENRY *Wallace* VI. 538 Wallace was blyth fra he had hard thair wourd. **1500–20** DUNBAR *Poems* xxxvii. 15 The wird of Jesew is fulfillit rycht, Surrexit sicut dixit. **1534** FEWTERER *Myrrour Christes Passion* 124 A contemplation of this seconde worde spoken by Christe vpon the crosse. *Ibid.*, This moste comfortable worde of our most swete sauyour Iesu spoken vnto the thefe. **1563** FOXE *A. & M.* 1258/1 At this worde which he coupled with an othe, came I in. **1781** COWPER *Conversat.* 533 He bless'd the bread, but vanish'd at the word. **1801** SCOTT *Eve St. John* xxviii, Yet hear but my word. **1831** JAMES *Philip Aug.* xxviii, We have striven..to draw some word from her; but she..sobs, and answers nothing. **1867** MORRIS *Jason* I. 217 So at this word the king along the shore Built many a tower. **1871** B. TAYLOR *Faust* (1875) I. iv. 69 The word, alas! dies even in the pen.

b. with negative expressed or implied, or with *every*: Any or the least utterance, statement, or fragment of speech; anything at all (said or written).

a **1000** *Riddles* xix. 1 Ic..ne mæʒ word sprecan. *c* **1200** ORMIN Ded. 70 Þatt upponn all þiss boc ne be Nan word ȝæn Cristess lare. *a* **1300** *K. Horn* 260 (Harl.) Þah hue ne dorste at bord Mid him speke ner a word [*v.r.* no worde]. *c* **1470** *Gol. & Gaw.* 1166 Thair wes na word muuand, Sa war thai all stil. *a* **1508** DUNBAR *Tua Mariit Wemen* 157, I sall say furth the south, dissymyland no word. **1581** J. HAMILTON *Cath. Traictise* V iv b, He sal not haif ane vourd to ansueir. **1611** *Bible* 2 Sam. xix. 10 Why speake ye not a word of bringing the king backe? **1667** EARL ORRERY *St. Lett.* (1742) 305 He..got an order..without so much as telling me one word of it. **1676** EARL ESSEX in *Essex Papers* (Camden) II. 83, I was above four months before I could gett one word of answer from him. **1720** DE FOE *Capt. Singleton* xi. (1840) 198 They never heard a word of English. **1753–4** RICHARDSON *Grandison* I. xlviii. 342 You undo me, if one word of this matter escape you. **1758** MRS. LENNOX *Henrietta* II. ii. (1761) I. 105 That..her every word and action [might] be under his direction. **1797** JANE AUSTEN *Sense & Sensib.* xxx, I would not mention a word about it to her. **1855** MACAULAY *Hist. Eng.* xi. III. 10 No word indicating that he took blame to himself. **1863** W. C. BALDWIN *Afr. Hunting* vii. 294 It is now eighteen months since I heard a word..from my friends. **1879** McCARTHY *Donna Q.* I. iii, Before she had time to put in a word. **1882** BESANT *All Sorts* xxi, Her ladyship held out her hands, without a word.

c. ***a word***: a (short or slight) utterance or statement; a brief speech or conversation; similarly ***a word or two***, †***a couple of words***; ***a word in your ear*** (*colloq.*): a brief message for you in confidence.

c **1485** *Digby Myst.* (1896) III. 1423 Master of þe shepe, a word with þe. **1526** *Pilgr. Perf.* (W. de W. 1531) 142 Than yf we be touched with a sharpe worde, we shal yelde a.. gentyll answere. **1581** T. WILCOX *Glass Gamesters* vi. c v b, Nowe a worde or two, out of the fathers,..for the ouerthrowyng of Dise and Cardes. **1589** PUTTENHAM *Engl. Poesie* III. xxv. (Arb.) 307 So occupied..in the Princes affaires, as it is a great matter to haue a couple of wordes with them. **1599** SHAKES. *Much Ado* IV. ii. 27 Come you hither, sirrah; a word in your ear, sir. **1611** *Bible* Isa. l. 4 To speake a worde in season [*Geneva* a worde in time] to him that is wearie. **1639** [see WISE *a.* 6 c]. **1726** SWIFT *Gulliver* II. iii, I entreated to be heard a Word or two. **1810** CRABBE *Borough* xxii. 5 Peter..had of all a civil word and wish. **1836** DICKENS

Sk. Boz, Visit to Newgate, Some ordinary word of recognition passed between her and her mother. **1837** —— *Pickw.* xxxiv, And now, gentlemen, but one word more. **1838** DICKENS *Let.* 25 Jan. (1965) I. 360 A word in your ear. Macready *objected* to Talfourd's play. **1842** TENNYSON *Dora* 42 If you speak with him .. Or change a word with her. **1855** BROWNING *Men & Women*, (*title*) One Word More. **1893** MAX PEMBERTON *Iron Pirate* iii, I leave in ten minutes and write you here my last word. **1980** *Daily Tel.* 9 May 18 Salome and Kumba [*sc.* two gorillas] would like a word in your ear.

d. *spec.* Something said on behalf of another; esp. in such phrases as ***to speak a (good) word for***: see also 23. †In quot. 1625, *pl.* votes.

1540, etc. [see 23]. **1617** MORYSON *Itin.* I. 197 A Gentleman .. understood that I had been robbed in France, where-upon hee gave his word for me unto the Maior. **1625** in *10th Rep. Hist. MSS. Comm.* App. v. 472 Whoesoever .. shall labour or practise to gaine woordes for to make a Mayor, Sheriffe, or any other officer. **1831** CARLYLE *Misc. Ess., Early Ger. Lit.* (1872) III. 196 The venerable man deserves a word from us. **1849** MACAULAY *Hist. Eng.* iii. I. 301 Any dissolute courtier for whom one of the king's mistresses would speak a word.

e. *spec.* A watchword or password.

to give the word: (*a*) to utter the password in answer to a sentinel's challenge; (*b*) to inform officers or men of the password to be used.

[*c* **1400**–: see WATCHWORD.]

a **1533** LD. BERNERS *Huon* lxvii. 230 When he sawe his tyme, he cryed his worde & token. **1605** SHAKS. *Lear* IV. vi. 93 *Lear*. Giue the word. *Edg.* Sweet Mariorum. *Lear*. Passe. **1667** DUCH. NEWC. *Life Dk. N.* (1886) II. 92 He offered my Lord the keys of the city, and desired him to give the word that night. **1847** MARRYAT *Childr. New Forest* v, He gave the word, and the gate was opened. **1849** MACAULAY *Hist. Eng.* v. I. 608 The word by which the insurgents were to recognise one another in the darkness was Soho. **1855** *Ibid.* xvi. III. 679 The first morning on which Marlborough had the command, he gave the word 'Wirtemberg.' **1868** *Queen's Reg. & Orders Army* ¶42 The Governor .. will give the Word or parole in all places within his government.

†**3.** *abstr.* or *collect. sing.* (without *a* or *pl.*) Speech, speaking: often as distinguished from writing, esp. in phr. ***by word***, now ***by word of mouth*** (see 19); also, the faculty of speech; occas. language, tongue. *Obs.* exc. as in 19.

a **1000** *Gloria Patri* 56 þu .. him .. sealdest word and ȝewitt. *c* **1200** ORMIN 3043 þatt Godess enngell seȝȝde þær Till Josæp þuss wiþþ worde. *a* **1300** *Cursor M.* 24074 Es na tung mai speke wit word, Ne writer write wit pens ord. **1390** GOWER *Conf.* I. 206 Couste in Saxoun is to sein Constance upon the word Romein. *Ibid.* III. 135 Above alle erthli creatures The hihe makere of natures The word to man hath yove alone. *c* **1400** *Rule St. Benet* (prose) 44 Sho sal be repreuid foure siþe with worde. *c* **1475** *Rauf Coilȝear* 100 The Carll was wantoun of word. **1491** *Acta Dom. Conc.* (1839) 185/2 Duncane laid in wedset a land and tenement in Linlithqw to Thomas Gudelad be word and but charter or possessioune. *a* **1553** UDALL *Royster D.* II. iii. (Arb.) 36 No man for despite, By worde or by write His felowe to twite. **1580** HAY in *Cath. Tractates* (S.T.S.) 39 The traditions quhilk ye have learned ather be wourd, or be our epistle. **1628** A. LEIGHTON *Appeal to Parlt.* 74 The Anti-episcopall government .. which by word and writ he had maintained. **1728** P. WALKER *Life Peden* To Rdr. (1827) p. xiii, It is .. maliciously spread, both by Word and Writ.

4. *sing.* and *pl.* Speech, verbal expression, in contrast with action or thought.

Beowulf 289 ðescad witan worda and worca. **971** *Blickl. Hom.* 35 We .. agyltaþ .. þurh ȝeþoht, & þurh word, & þurh weorc, & þurh willan. *c* **1175** *12th Cent. Hom.* 118 Mid worde, mid dæda, & mid alle heortæ. *c* **1200** *Trin. Coll. Hom.* 65 Ȝif man haueð wið us agilt, woerdes oðer wurkes. *a* **1300** *Cursor M.* 15263 For þat i sai yow here wit word, þar sal yee find in dede. **1338** R. BRUNNE *Chron.* (1725) 94 Ouþer in word or dede has þou greued him. **1390** GOWER *Conf.* I. 7 The word was lich to the conceite Withoute semblant of deceite. *c* **1400** in *26 Pol. Poems* xiii. 127 Wiþ word of wynd, mad neuere werre ende. **1471** CAXTON *Recuyell* (Sommer) 19 He was iust & trewe in dede & in word. **1500–20** DUNBAR *Poems* ix. 6 Baith in werk, in word, and eik intent. *c* **1560** A. SCOTT *Poems* (S.T.S.) i. 109 Wordis w[t]out werkis availȝeis nocht a cute. **1601** B. JONSON *Poetaster* III. v, Great Caesars warres cannot be fought with worde. **1602** SHAKS. *Ham.* III. iii. 97, 98 My words flye vp, my thoughts remain below, Words without thoughts, neuer to Heauen go. **1605** —— *Macb.* II. i. 61 Words, to the heat of deedes, too cold breath giues. **1605** BODLEY *Let. to James* 1 May, Wordes are women, and deedes are men. **1667** SPRAT *Hist. Royal-Soc.* 434 A Society that prefers Works before Words. **1671** MILTON *P.R.* III. 9 Thy actions to thy words accord. **1800** COLERIDGE *Piccol.* I. iii. 61 Men's words are ever bolder than their deeds. **1862** [see DEED *sb.* 5 b]. **1875** [see DEED *sb.* 1].

5. *pl.* orig. in various phr. denoting verbal contention or altercation, e.g. †***to be*** or ***fall at words*** (***into words***), †***to have some*** or ***many words***, †(***some***) ***words are between***..., etc., now chiefly ***to have words*** or ***a word*** (***with***); hence simply ***words*** = contentious or violent talk between persons, altercation; also with epithet, as *hard*, *high*, *sharp*.

†occas. Defamatory or libellous statement.

1462 *Paston Lett.* II. 105 Your brother and Debenham were at words. *c* **1489** CAXTON *Sonnes of Aymon* iii. 88 Whan we playd togyder, we hade some wordes. **1526** *Hundred Mery Talys* (1887) 8 The other agayn said he shuld not, & he agayn said he wold bryng them ouer spyte of his teth & so fell at wordys. *a* **1533** LD. BERNERS *Huon* lxv. 222 Whan I se that wordes [be] betwen you, I shall Issu out. **1565** COOPER *Thesaurus* s.v. *Altercor*, *Cum patre altercasti dudum*, thou wast at words. **1590** *Tarlton's News Purgat.* (1844) 82 Whereupon they grewe to woords, and from woords to blowes. **1591** SHAKS. *1 Hen. VI*, II. v. 46 In argument vpon a Case, Some words there grew 'twixt Somerset and me. **1663** BUTLER *Hud.* I. i. 3 When hard Words, Jealousies, and Fears Set Folks together by the Ears. **1684** LUTTRELL *Brief Rel.* (1857) I. 307 His royall highnesse has brought his action of scandalum magnatum against Dr. Titus Oates for words. **1753–4** RICHARDSON *Grandison* II. xii. 86 High words passed between them. They parted in passion. **1777** W. MAWHOOD *Diary* 24 Aug. in *Publ. Cath. Rec. Soc.* (1956) L. 117 Came to Town to breakfast had words with Mrs. Mawhood. **1815** *Sixteen & Sixty* II. iii, Propriety and myself have been at high words on your account. **1839** DICKENS *Nicholas Nickleby* xlviii. 480 'We were a very happy little company, Johnson,' said poor Crummles. 'You and I never had a word.' **1842** TENNYSON *Dora* 16 He and I Had once hard words, and parted. **1848** DICKENS *Dombey* xxxi, Words have arisen between the housemaid and Mr. Towlinson. **1862** MRS. CARLYLE *Lett.* III. 103 We had got into words about an invitation. **1901** 'ZACK' *White Cottage* 37 Have you and Mark had wuds? **1910** KING GEORGE V in H. Nicolson *George V* (1952) vii. 105, I have lost my best friend & the best of fathers. I never had a word with him in his life. **1913** M. ROBERTS *Salt of the Sea* vii. 182 My old man said he was a blood-sucker, and that led to words. **1935** Z. N. HURSTON *Mules & Men* II. vi. 287 Celestine is not mad any more about the word we had last week.

6. a. Report, tidings, news, information. (Always in *sing.* without article, in such phrases as ***to bring, send, write word***; ***to have word***; ***word came***, etc.)

971 *Blickl. Hom.* 173 Sona swa þæt word becom to Nerone. *a* **1122** *O.E. Chron.* an. 1046 þam cynge com word þæt unnfriðscipa læȝen be westan and herȝodon. *c* **1205** LAY. 3732 And Cordoille com þat wourd þat heo was iworðen widewe. *c* **1205** [see SEND *v.*[1] 6 b]. **1297** R. GLOUC. (Rolls) 826 He sende þe quene is doȝter word wuch is aunters were. *a* **1300** *Cursor M.* 11454 Word cum til herod þe kyng þat þar was suilk kynges cummun. *c* **1400** MAUNDEV. (Roxb.) xxv. 119 He schall hafe worde within a day and a nyght. **1415** SIR T. GREY in *43rd Rep. Dep. Kpr. Rec.* 583 He sende me no more worde of yat mater til I cam to Yorke. *c* **1440** *Alphabet of Tales* 102 Hur husband .. hard no tithandis nor wurd of his wyfe nor of his childer. *a* **1533** LD. BERNERS *Huon* lxv. 221 My brother Huon .. is now .. in the abbay of seint Mauryse, the abbot there hath sent me worde therof. **1598** SHAKS. *Merry W.* III. v. 48, I must carry her word quickely. **1606** —— *Ant. & Cl.* II. v. 118 Bid you Alexas Bring me word, how tall she is. **1662** STILLINGFL. *Orig. Sacræ* I. iv. §11 Alexander .. writ word to his Mother he had found out the head of Nilus in the East Indies. **1712** STEELE *Spect.* No. 284 ¶5 Send me Word .. whether he has so great an Estate. **1848** DICKENS *Dombey* xlvi, We had word this morning .. that Mr. Dombey was doing well. **1850** THACKERAY *Pendennis* lxx, A servant brought word that Major Pendennis had returned. **1853** LYTTON *My Novel* IV. xxiii, The Parson writes word that the lad will come to-day. **1948** 'H. GREEN' *Concluding* 205 Word had gone round that at last they were engaged. **1958** M. L. KING *Stride toward Freedom* iii. 45 The arrest .. was becoming public knowledge. Word of it spread around the community like uncontrolled fire. **1983** *Times* 16 Sept. 16/2 Word is the Government is offering a fixed price for small investors. **1984** *Times* 14 June 22/2 Word in the market suggests Mr Holmes a'Court may be prepared to sell on his stake.

b. Common report or statement, rumour. (Usually with *the*, *this*, etc.) Now usu. in phr. ***the word is that*** (..) (chiefly *U.S.*).

c **1000** *Ags. Gosp.* Matt. xxviii. 15 þis wurd wæs ȝewidmærsod mid iudeum. *c* **1205** LAY. 160 þa com þat word to him, þat was widene cuð, þat þe king Latin ȝef Lauine his douter Eneam to are brude. *a* **1300** *K. Horn* 1017 (Camb.) þe word bigan to springe Of Rymenhilde weddinge. **1375** BARBOUR *Bruce* II. 78 Our all the land the word gan spryng, That the Bruce the Cumyn had slayn. *a* **1578** [see SPRING *v.*[1] 2]. **1718** RAMSAY *Christ's Kirk Gr.* III. 38 Word gae'd me was nae canny. **1819** SHELLEY *Cenci* I. iii. 6 An evil word is gone abroad of me. **1819** SCOTT *Noble Moringer* xxi, Her husband died in distant land, such is the constant word. **1963** R. JESSUP *Cincinnati Kid* iv. 55 Money is beginning to show for you against The Man, Kid... The word is .. that you're good enough to take Lancey, if anybody can. **1965** P. O'DONNELL *Modesty Blaise* vii. 82, I know of him. The word is that he's good. **1982** P. LOVESEY *False Inspector Dew* IV. 153 The word is that the captain will be speaking to us.

†**c.** Common report in praise or celebration of a person or his actions; fame, renown, high repute.

c **1000** ÆLFRIC *Saints' Lives* vii. 388 þa asprang his word wide ȝ eond land. *c* **1200** *Trin. Coll. Hom.* 127 Ðo sprong þe word of his holi liflode wide into þe londe. *c* **1205** LAY. 6302 Of hire wisdome sprong þat word wide. *a* **1225** *Ancr. R.* 88 Wo is me þet he, oðer heo, habbeð swuch word ikeiht. **13..** *Gaw. & Gr. Knt.* 1521 Your worde & your worchip walkez ay quere. *c* **1400** *Destr. Troy* 295 The worde of his werkes thurghe þe worlde sprange. *c* **1470** HENRY *Wallace* III. 252 The worde of him walkit baith fer and ner.

d. Reputation, character (*of* being or having what is stated). *Sc.*

1722 RAMSAY *Three Bonnets* I. 89 Rosie had word o' meikle siller, Whilk brought a hantle o' wooers till her. **1825** JAMIESON s.v., 'She gets the word o' being a licht-headit queyn', i.e. it is generally said of her.

7. a. A command, order, bidding; a request. (See also 17.) Usually qualified by possessive or *the*.

to say the word: to give the order, say 'go' or the like. In phr. ***to send word*** sometimes combining senses 6 and 7.

873–89 *K. Ælfred's Will*, þa word ȝelæstan þe on mines fæder yrfewrite standað. *a* **900** CYNEWULF *Crist* 1630 Hy bræcon cyninges word. *c* **1220** *Bestiary* 51 Silden he us wille, If we heren to his word. *c* **1250** *Gen. & Ex.* 736 God seide wurd to abram: 'Abram, ðu fare ut of lond and kin.' *c* **1275** *Passion our Lord* 363 in *O.E. Misc.* 47 Alle þat beoþ in soþe i-hereþ myne word. *a* **1300** *Cursor M.* 18053 Quen i word herd þat he badd I quok for him. **1486** *Bk. St. Albans* e v b, The first worde to the houndis that the hunt shall owt pit. **1496** in Ellis *Orig. Lett.* Ser. I. I. 29 Please your Graice to send me wourd quhat serves .. I sall do. **1526** TINDALE *Luke* v. 5 Yet nowe at thy worde I wil loose forthe the net. *a* **1548** HALL *Chron., Hen. VI*, 164 His worde only ruled, & his voyce was only hearde. **1560** GOOGE tr. *Palingenius' Zodiac* III. (1561) E viij, If thou sayst the woord, we goe. **1594** SHAKS. *Hen. V*, IV. vi. 38 Then euery souldiour kill his Prisoners, Giue the word through. **1601** —— *Jul. C.* I. ii. 104 Vpon the word, Accoutred as I was, I plunged in. **1631** HEYWOOD *1st Pt. Fair Maid West* IV. i. 44 Shall I strike that Captaine? say the word, Ile have him by the eares. **1667** MILTON *P.L.* III. 708 When at his Word the formless Mass .. came to a heap: Confusion heard his voice, and wilde uproar Stool rul'd. **1753–4** RICHARDSON *Grandison* I. xxxvii. 270, I rang .. to beg my cousins' company. They wanted but the word: In they came. **1803** WORDSW. *Sonn. Pass Killicranky* 12 O for a single hour of that Dundee, Who on that day the word of onset gave! **1806** [see SPEAK *v.* 21]. **1842** TENNYSON *Dora* 25 In my time a father's word was law. **1856** DICKENS *Christmas Stories* (1874) 50, I gave Rames the word to lower the Longboat and the Surf-boat.

b. ***Ten Words***: the Ten Commandments, the Decalogue. *Obs.* or *arch.*

1382 WYCLIF *Deut.* iv. 13 The ten wordis, that he wroot in the two stonen tablis. **1650** TRAPP *Comm. Exod.* xx. 17 These ten words written by God himself. **1884** S. COX *Miracles* 18 The fundamental moralities of the 'Ten Words'.

8. A promise, undertaking. Almost always with possessive, as in ***to give*** (***pass, pledge***) ***one's word***, ***to keep*** (***hold*** *arch.*) ***one's word***, ***to break one's word***; ***to be as good as one's word***, to keep one's promise (so ***to be worse than one's word***, to break one's promise); ***a man of*** (†***master of***, etc.) ***his word***, one who keeps his promises; also ***on*** (†***in, under***) ***the word of*** (***a prince***, etc.). See also 15, 18, 28 b.

See also BOND *sb.*[1] 8, BREAK *v.* 15 c, PLEDGE *v.* 2 b, PLIGHT *v.*[1] 2, etc.

[**971** *Blickl. Hom.* 243 Hwær syndon þine word, Drihten. .. 'ðif ȝe me ȝehyrað and ȝe me beoð fylȝende, ne an loc of eowrum heafde forwyrð?' *a* **1122** *O.E. Chron.* an. 1014 (Laud MS.) Man .. freondscipe ȝefæstnode mid worde & mid wædde.] **1390** GOWER *Conf.* I. 67 It sit wel every wiht To kepe his word in trowthe upryht. **1474** CAXTON *Cheese* II. i. (1883) 22 That the symple parole or worde of a prynce ought to be more stable than the oth of a marchaunt. **1496** *Rolls of Parlt.* VI. 513/2 The said Kyng .. bound hym by his writyng, .. and also in the worde of a Kyng promysed to kepe the same. **1526** *Reg. Privy Seal Scot.* I. 527/2 Our soverane lord promittis fathfullye and on the word of ane kyng, that [etc.]. **1542** UDALL *Erasm. Apoph.* 304 Neither proued Marcus Tullius a false manne of his woorde. *a* **1548** HALL *Chron., Hen. VI*, 98 b, My Lorde of Winchester .. hath subscribed .. vnder the worde of priestehod, to stande at the aduise .. of the persones abouesaied. **1555** *Instit. Gentl.* E iij b, The seconde .. poynte in a Gentleman .. is promes kepyng, as to bee Mayster to hys woorde. **1580** T. FORREST *Perf. Looking Gl.* 5 b, Haue .. greater care in geuing thy worde, then in lending thy money. **1584** LODGE *Alarum* (Shaks. Soc.) 60 Promising .. (so his creditour woulde be his wordes master) to doo his indeavour to perfourme his will. **1590** SHAKS. *Mids. N.* I. i. 222 Keepe word Lysander. *Ibid.* III. ii. 266–8, *Lys.* I will keepe my word with thee. *Dem.* I would I had your bond: .. Ile not trust your word. **1593** NASHE *Christ's T.* To Rdr. *4 b, The deuill & he be no men of their words. **1598** SHAKS. *Merry W.* V. v. 258 To Master Broome, you yet shall hold your word. **1601** —— *Twel. N.* III. iv. 357 For that I promis'd you Ile be as good as my word. **1633** BP. HALL *Occas. Medit.* (ed. 3) 256 An honest mans word must be his maister. **1672** WYCHERLEY *Love in Wood* V. v, Will you be worse then your word? **1744** M. BISHOP *Life* 130 They .. did not fly from their Words but stood firmly to what they first proposed. **1813** SCOTT *Trierm.* III. xxii, I swore upon the rood, Neither to stop, nor turn, nor rest, .. In life or death I hold my word! **1849** MACAULAY *Hist. Eng.* v. I. 535 Having solemnly pledged his word .. not to attempt anything against the government. **1861** READE *Cloister & H.* lv, Give me your words to show her no countenance. **1886** RIDER HAGGARD *Jess* iii, No English government goes back on its word.

9. With possessive: Assertion, affirmation, declaration, assurance; esp. as involving the veracity or good faith of the person who makes it. See also 15, 18, 28 b.

1601 SHAKS. *Twel. N.* I. v. 87 Sir Toby will be sworn that I am no Fox, but he wil not passe his word for two pence that you are no Foole. **1610** —— *Temp.* II. i. 86 His word is more then the miraculous Harpe. **1730** *Lett. to Sir W. Strickland rel. to Coal Trade* 30 The Buyer .. must take his Goods unseen on the Seller's Word. **1736** AINSWORTH *Engl. Lat. Dict.*, To call back one's word, *recanto*, *retracto*, *denego*. **1744** M. BISHOP *Life* 211, I just saved my Word. **1850** THACKERAY *Pendennis* xi, I give you my word that my brother did not leave a shilling to his son. **1859** H. KINGSLEY *G. Hamlyn* vi, What surety had he that Lee would leave him in peace .. ? none but his word—the word of a villain like that. **1869** SPURGEON *Treas. David* Ps. vii. 3–6 If we cannot be believed on our word, we are surely not to be trusted on our oath.

10. a. An utterance or declaration in the form of a phrase or sentence. *arch.* (Cf. 25.)

c **1000** ÆLFRIC *Hom.* (Th.) II. 236 Ðæt word belimpð synderlice to Gode anum, Ic eom. **1593** SHAKS. *Rich. II*, I. iii. 152 The hopelesse word, of Neuer to returne, Breath I against thee. **1780** COWPER *Boadicea* 13 Rome shall perish —write that word In the blood that she has spilt. **1903** J. KEATINGE *Priest* iii. 46 We should put down the three words 'Peace', 'Perseverance', 'A worthy Communion to-day.'

b. A pithy or sententious utterance; a saying; a maxim; a proverb. Now *rare* or merged in 2, exc. in BYWORD 1, NAYWORD[1] 2 (*dial.*), *household word* (see HOUSEHOLD 8); †in first quot., a 'dark' saying, riddle.

c **1375** *Sc. Leg. Saints* iii. (*Andreas*) 1079 Gywe [= if] he cane vndo þat worde. *a* **1400** *Relig. Pieces fr. Thornton MS.* 49 Ife þou will be lufely, resayfe these thre wordes with-owtten forgetynge. **1599–1888** [see HOUSEHOLD 8]. **1645** BP. HALL *Rem. Discontents* 130 It is a true word of Saint Augustine, that every soul is either Christs Spouse, or the Devils Harlot. **1833** DE QUINCEY *Revol. Greece* Wks. (ed. Masson) VII. 317 It seemed likely .. that .. Shakspere's deep word would be realized, and 'darkness be the burier of the dead'. 1853 Trench *Prov.* 26 That well-known word which forbids the too accurate scanning of a present, 'One must not look a gift horse in the mouth'.

†**c.** A significant phrase or short sentence inscribed upon something; = Mot[1] 1, Motto 1. *Obs.*

1431 *E.E. Wills* (1882) 88 My creste, myn armes,..and my word 'mercy and ioie'. *a*1500 *Assemb. Ladies* 87 On her purfyl her word..*Bien et loyalment.* 1562 Legh *Armorie* (1568) 42 b, The armes of euerye gentleman..with the supporters helme, wreathe, and creast, with mantelles, and the woorde. 1589 *Pasquil's Ret.* D iij, The Painter..hath drawne him his word with a Text-pen. *Zelus domus tuæ comedit me.* 1590 Spenser *F.Q.* II. iv. 38 And round about the wreath this word was writ, *Burnt I do burne.* *c*1630 Risdon *Surv. Devon* § 144 (1810) 159 His word was *quid non.*

11. Religious and theological uses (in *sing.*, mostly with possessive or def. article); often in full, ***the word of God*** (***God's word***), ***the word of the Lord***, etc.

a. A divine communication, command, or proclamation, as one made to or through a prophet or inspired person; *esp.* the message of the gospel (also ***the word of Christ***, ***of grace***, ***of life***, etc.).

971 *Blickl. Hom.* 141 On þa ilcan stowe on þære þe we wæron ȝesamnode þær we ȝeherdan Godes word. *c*1000 *Ags. Gosp.* Matt. xiii. 19 Ælc þæra þe godes wurd ȝehyrð. —— Mark iv. 14. *c*1175 *Lamb. Hom.* 81 Þis monne me mei sermonen mid godes worde, for hwat he scal his sunne uorsaken. *a*1300 *Cursor M.* 19214 Vte o þair hali hertes hord Spedli þai speld godds word. *a*1340 Hampole *Psalter* cxviii[i]. 172 My tunge sall shew forth þi worde. 1382 Wyclif *2 Sam.* vii. 4 And loo! the word of the Lord to Nathan, seiynge, Go, and spek to my seruaunt Dauid, Thes thingis seith the Lord. —— *Col.* iii. 16 The word of Crist dwelle in ȝou plenteuously. 1450–1530 *Myrr. our Ladye* II. 145 As my sowlle suffereth pacyently wronges..in obedyence of his worde. So I hope to be rewarded after the trouthe of his worde. 1526 Tindale *Mark* iv. 17 As sone as eny trouble or persecucion ariseth for the wordes sake, anon they fall. 1526 —— *Acts* iv. 31 They spake the worde of god boldely. *Ibid.* xx. 32, I commende you to god and to the worde of his grace. 1564 Martiall *Treat. Crosse* 83 The lawes of the church (which lawes are the worde off god). 1601 Bp. W. Barlow *Defence* 181 The ministerie of the word is a coadiutor with the Spirite. 1648 T. Shepard *Clear Sunshine of Gosp.* 12 This old man hath much affection stirred up by the Word. 1758 Wesley *Hymn*, '*See how great a flame aspires*' iii, Sons of God, your Saviour praise!..He hath given the word of grace. 1859 Geo. Eliot *Adam Bede* xlix, Where I used to be blessed in carrying the word of life to the sinful and desolate. 1921 *Act 11 & 12 Geo. V*, c. 29 Sched. vii, To..promote union with other Churches in which it finds the Word to be purely preached. 1927 Abp. Davidson *Addr. Convoc.* 29 Mar. in *Church Times* 1 Apr. 392/1 Right Reverend and Reverend Brothers in the Sacred Ministry of Word and Sacrament.

b. The Bible, Scripture, or some part or passage of it, as embodying a divine communication.

1553 *Proclam.* 18 Aug. 1 Some euell disposed persons, whiche take vpon them..to interprete the worde of God, after theyr owne brayne. 1570 Foxe *A. & M.* (ed. 2) 2187/1 *Gage.* The worde sayth it is his body before it is eaten. *Wood.* Those words would I faine heare: but I am sure they be not in the Bible. 1567 Allen *Def. Priesthood* Pref., They remember well (such is theyr exercise in ye woord) how ye disdayne of Moyses & Aarons prelacy ouer ye people [etc.]. 1598 Shaks. *Merry W.* III. i. 44 What? the Sword, and the Word? Doe you study them both, Mr. Parson? 1781 Cowper *Hope* 659 Mighty to parry and push by God's word With senseless noise. 1859 H. Kingsley *G. Hamlyn* xl, Read us a chapter out of the Bible. I am very low in my mind, and at such times I like to hear the Word. 1875 Manning *Mission Holy Ghost* i. 7 The word of God declares, first of all, that the Son of God is 'The true Light'.

c. ***the Word*** (***of God, of the Father***), ***the Eternal Word***, etc., as a title of Christ: = Logos, q.v.

*c*950 *Lindisf. Gosp.* John i. 1 *In principio erat uerbum*, in fruma uæs uord. 1340–70 *Alex. & Dind.* 615 Godus worþliche word as we wel trowen, Is sone soþliche of man. *c*1400 *Sowdone Bab.* 3 God..That al thinge made in sapience By vertue of woorde and holy goost. 1450–1530 *Myrr. our Ladye* II. 103 The endelesse worde of the father that is oure lorde Iesu cryste. 1567 Allen *Def. Priesthood* 19 The seruile fourme of our owne nature, ioyned merueilously in one person, to the woorde and eternall Sonne of God the Father. 1667 Milton *P.L.* VII. 163 And thou my Word, begotten Son, by thee This I perform. 1784 Cowper *Task* v. 897 Thou art the source and centre of all minds..eternal Word! 1805–6 Cary *Dante, Parad.* VII. 29 Until it pleas'd the Word of God to come Amongst them down. 1850 Tennyson *In Mem.* xxxvi, And so the Word had breath, and wrought With human hands the creed of creeds. 1875 Lightfoot *Colossians* 221/2 The Eternal Word is the goal of the Universe, as He was the starting-point.

II. An element of speech.

12. a. A combination of vocal sounds, or one such sound, used in a language to express an idea (e.g. to denote a thing, attribute, or relation), and constituting an ultimate minimal element of speech having a meaning as such; a vocable. Also ***four-letter word***: see *four-letter* adj. s.v. Four C. 2.

Sometimes with reference to the writing of a word as an indivisible unity, e.g. *as one* or *a single word, as two words.*

*c*1000 Ælfric *Gram.* ii. (Z.) 5 Butan ðam stafum ne mæȝ nan word beon awriten. ?*a*1400 *Wyclif's Bible* Prol. 57 This word *autem*, either *vero*, mai stonde for *forsothe*, either for *but*. 1450–1530 *Myrr. Our Ladye* I. ii. 7 There ys many wordes in Latyn that we haue no propre englyssh accordynge therto. *Ibid.* II. 77 Thys worde Amen ys a worde of hebrew. 1581 Mulcaster *Positions* xli. (1888) 244 Wordes be names of thinges applyed and giuen according to their properties. 1598 Shaks. *Merry W.* IV. i. 68 You doe ill to teach the childe such words. 1651 Hobbes *Leviath.* II. xxxi. 192 Words..have their signification by agreement, and constitution of men. 1677 [see witticism]. 1694 Locke *Hum. Und.* III. ii. §1 (ed. 2) 223 *marg.*, Words are sensible Signs necessary for Communication. 1746 Francis tr. *Hor.*, *Epist.* II. ii. 170 Long darken'd Words he shall with Art refine. 1802 Wordsw. *Resolution & Indep.* xiv, Choice word and measured phrase, above the reach Of ordinary men. 1819 Shelley *Cenci* v. iv. 14 These three words..'They must die'. 1853 Trench *Prov.* 31 So long as a language is living, it will be appropriating foreign words, putting forth new words of its own. 1875 Jevons *Money* (1878) 250 We use a great many words with a total disregard of logical precision. 1884 J. A. H. Murray *N.E.D.* I. Gen. Explan. p. xxiii, There are necessarily many compounds as to which usage has not yet determined whether they are to be written with the hyphen or as single words.

b. †(*a*) As designating a thing or person: A name, title, appellation. *Obs.* (*b*) As expressing an idea: A term, expression.

*c*900 tr. *Bæda's Hist.* v. xi, On his mæran ceastre, seo ealde worde þare þeoda is nemned Wiltaburhȝ. 971 *Blickl. Hom.* 135, 'Ic eow sende frofre Gast.' þæs wordes andȝit is swa mon cweþe þingere oþ þe frefrend. 1533 Bellenden *Livy* v. xv. (S.T.S.) 200 Sa þir gaulis, following the werde of þe said place (quhare þai war cumin to), biggit ane toun namit millane. 1571 Ld. Burghley in E. Nares *Mem.* (1830) II. 544 *note*, Your assured loving friend, William Cecill. I forgot my new word, William Burleigh. 1596 *Edw. III*, II. i. 85 Deuise for faire a fairer word then faire. 1596 Harington *Metam. Ajax* H 4, I doe before hand gyue the worde of disgrace to any that shal so say. 1626 Bacon *Sylva* §354 Sulphureous and Mercuriall, which are the Chymists Words. 1668 Moxon *Dyalling* 48 An Explanation of some Words of Art used in this Book. 1848 Clough *Amours de Voy.* I. 10 *Rubbishy* seems the word that most exactly would suit it.

c. A written (engraved, printed, etc.) character or set of characters representing this.

*a*1000 *Riddles* xlvii[i], Moððe word fræt. 1521 [see write *v.* B. 2]. 1612, 1888 [see spell *v.*[2] 3]. 1725 Watts *Logic* I. iv. §1 We convey [our Ideas] to each other by the Means of certain Sounds, or written Marks, which we call Words. 1845 Maurice *Mor. Philos.* in *Encycl. Metrop.* II. 556/1 Betokening, as the words inscribed upon their foreheads implied, that they were a dedicated race. 1904 Budge *3rd & 4th Egypt. Rooms Brit. Mus.* 210 The common name for words of power of all kinds is 'heku', and whether they were inscribed upon amulets, or merely recited over them, the effect was the same.

d. In contrast with the thing or idea signified.

*c*1450 *Bk. Curtesy* (Oriel MS.) 343 His [*sc.* Chaucer's] longage was so feyre and pertinent, That semed vnto mennys heryng, Not only the worde, but verrely the thing. 1699 Bentley *Phal.* vii. 189 Wise men take Words for the shadow of Things. 1722 Wollaston *Relig. Nat.* v. 87 This word [*sc.* nature]..frequently..is used merely as a word.., they who use it not knowing themselves, what they mean by it. 1754 Gray *Poesy* 110 Thoughts that breath, and words that burn. 1782 Priestley *Corrupt. Chr.* I. I. 114 A business of words only, and ideas not concerned in it. 1822 *Examiner* 723/2 Men are apt to be led away by words. 1827–1876 [see thing *sb.*[1] 8 a]. 1867 Dk. Argyll *Reign of Law* ii. (ed. 4) 63 Words, which should be the servants of Thought, are too often its masters. 1898 'H. S. Merriman' *Roden's Corner* x. 106 'You don't take any interest in the Malgamite scheme?' 'No,..And I am weary of the very word.' 1912 *Times* 5 Aug. 7/3 A question of words.

e. ***the word*** (as predicate): the right word for the thing, the proper expression; hence contextually denoting or indicating the thing spoken of, esp. the business in hand or to be done. *colloq.*

1596 Shaks. *Merch. V.* III. v. 58 Bid them prepare dinner. *Clow.* That is done to sir, onely couer is the word. 1611 —— *Cymb.* v. iv. 155 Come Sir, are you ready for death?.. Hanging is the word, Sir. *Ibid.* v. 422 Pardon's the word to all. 1700 Congreve *Way of World* I. ix, If Throats are to be cut, let Swords clash; Snug's the Word, I shrug and am silent. *a*1704, 1852 [see mum *sb.*[1] B]. 1712 Addison *Spect.* No. 403 ¶5 Sharp's the Word. 1775 Sheridan *Duenna* II. ii, Trust me when tricking is the word. 1848 Dickens *Dombey* xlviii, Steady's the word, and steady it is. Keep her so! 1885 Howells *Ind. Summer* ii. 16 Lady-like was the word for Mrs. Bowen. 1885 W. S. Gilbert *Princess Ida* II, Contempt? Why, damsel, when I think of man, Contempt is not the word.

f. *Telegr.* Any of the sequences of a prescribed fixed number of characters (including a space) in a telegraphic message that has been coded or redivided for transmission.

1897 J. Nicolson *Telegraphic Signals* ii. 20 Artificial letter-grouping, mathematically called 'words', or permutations,..is referred to in a pamphlet by the French cryptographist, M. le Marquis de Viaris..as a substitute for telegraphic codes composed of dictionary words. 1911 *Encycl. Brit.* XXVI. 521/2 An experimental printer constructed about 1908 by the British Post Office, operated ..at the rate of 210 words (1260 letters) per minute. 1976 R. N. Renton *Telegraphy* i. 14/2 The 'telegraph word' is taken as an arbitrary 5-letter word with one letter-space, making six characters in all.

g. *Math.* An ordered sequence of generators of a group.

1952 S. C. Kleene *Introd. Metamath.* xiii. 382 A finite sequence of zero or more (occurrences of) the letters, we call a word. 1971 G. Higman in Powell & Higman *Finite Simple Groups* vi. 212 Any word in the n_i and their inverses determines a partial map of the set of equivalence classes into itself. 1972 M. Kline *Math. Thought* xlix. 1141 There may be relations among the generators, and these would be of the form $F_i (A_i) = 1$; that is, a word or combination of words equals the identity element of the group. 1981 *Sci. Amer.* Mar. 26/1 A lovely 'pretty pattern' called the 6-*U* state..can be reached from the start position by way of the word $L' R^2 F' L' B' U B L F R U' R L R_s F_s U_s R_s$.

h. *Computers.* A consecutive string of bits that can be transferred and stored as a unit (see quot. 1969); ***machine word***, a word of the length appropriate for a particular fixed word-length computer.

1946 [see write *v.* 3 h]. 1948 *Proc. R. Soc.* A. CXCV. 272 Certain of these numbers or 'words' are read, one after another, as orders. 1954 *Computers & Automation* Dec. 16/1 *Machine word*, a unit of information of a standard number of characters, which a machine regularly handles in each register. 1964 F. L. Westwater *Electronic Computers* ix. 140 The basic unit of internal storage is called a 'word', which may contain either instructions or data. 1969 P. B. Jordain *Condensed Computer Encycl.* 566 Computers with words less than 9 bits long call the words bytes, characters, or digits (decimal). 1970 A. Cameron et al. *Computers & O.E. Concordances* 58 It is heavily dependent upon fitting *x* number of characters into each machine word, a problem we cannot get around easily. 1980 C. S. French *Computer Sci.* vi. 24 The number of bits in each location (word), known as the word length will depend on the make and model of computer.

III. Phrases. (See also above senses.)

* with preposition.

13. a. at a or **one word**: (*a*) upon the utterance of a single word; as soon as a word is spoken; without further parley; without more ado; at once, forthwith; so †***at the first word***; (*b*) in short, briefly, in a word; so †***at wordes thre***, †***at fewe wordes***, †***at wordes short***, etc. ***to be at a*** or ***one word***: to be brief. *Obs.* exc. *arch.* or *dial.*

*a*1300 *K. Horn* 118 (Harl.) þe children ede to þe stronde ..Ant in to shipes borde At þe furste worde. 13.. *Gregorius* 618 in Herrig *Arch. Neu. Spr.* LV. 435 A Cardinal þer spac a mong, schortliche he seide at wordes þreo. 13.. *Coer de L.* 101 Seuene score, and moo j wene, Welcomyd hem alle at on wurd. *Ibid.* 2813 The Sarezynes..comen afftyr ffaste fflyngyng, At schorte wurdes a gret route. *c*1375 *Cursor M.* 7770 (Fairf.) þen drogh saule his awen squorde And slogh him-self atte a worde. *c*1386 Chaucer *Melib.* Prol. 11 Pleynly at a word, Thy drasty rymyng is nat worth a toord. 14.. *Seege of Troy* 1724 Alisaunder dyed at worddis short. *a*1400–50 *Bk. Curtasye* 764 in *Babees Bk.*, When þe sewer comys vnto þe borde, Alle þe mete he sayes at on bare worde. *c*1400 *Rom. Rose* 2129 Thou shalt be holpen at wordis fewe. *c*1420 *Liber Cocorum* (1862) 17 Hakke hom on a borde, As smalle as þou may, at a worde. *c*1430 *Syr Gener.* (Roxb.) 363 Thes vii sages..bad here lodesman at a word Shuld cast hem ouer the ship bord. 1483 *Vulgaria quedam abs Terentio* 2 b, Tell me att oon word [*vno verbo*] what thou woldist wyth me. 1597 Morley *Introd. Mus.* 123 At a word I would haue flung it awaie. 1597 Shaks. *2 Hen. IV*, III. ii. 319 Go-too: I haue spoke at a word. Fare you well. 1598 —— *Merry W.* I. i. 109 He hath wrong'd me, indeed he hath, at a word he hath. *Ibid.* iii. 15, I am at a word: follow. 1599 —— *Much Ado* II. i. 118 *Vrsula.* I know you well enough, you are Signior Anthonio. *Anth.* At a word, I am not. 1601 —— *Jul. C.* I. ii. 270 If I would not haue taken him at a word, I would I might goe to Hell. 1605 Camden *Rem., Surnames* 104 At a word, all [names] which in English had *Of* set before them, ..and all which in Latine..have had *De* præfixed,..were borrowed from places. 1609 Holland *Amm. Marcell.* 231 That I may speake fully at a word, it is the most plentifull habitation and seat of Kings. 1694 Penn *Rise & Progr. Quakers* ii. 45 They were at a Word in Dealing: Nor could their customers many Words tempt them from it. 1777 S. J. Pratt *Emma Corbett* i. 1 To be at a word, will you render it possible for me to call you my son? 1831 Scott *Ct. Rob.* xxvi, So you may at a word count upon remaining prisoner here until [etc.]. *a*1845 B'ness Nairne *Song, Caller Herrin'* vii, At ae word be in ye're dealin'.

†**b. *at one word***: of one mind. *Obs.*

1297 R. Glouc. (Rolls) 6812 Boþe hii were at one worde to libbe in clene liue, So þat hii were wiþoute eir.

c. *to take* a person ***at his word***: to assent to his statement, or agree to his proposal; to accept what he says and act accordingly.

1535 Coverdale *1 Kings* xx. 33 He sayde: yf he be yet alyue, he is my brother. And the men toke him shortly at his worde,..and sayde: Yee Benadab is thy brother. 1590 Shaks. *Com. Err.* I. ii. 17 *Ant.* Get thee away. *Dro.* Many a man would take you at your word And goe indeede. 1670 Dryden *Conq. Granada* II. i, Old as I am I take thee at thy word, And will tomorrow thank thee with my sword. 1742 Fielding *J. Andrews* III. xii, One of the servants whispered Joseph to take him at his word, and suffer the old put to walk if he would. 1800 Wordsw. *Idle Shepherd-Boys* v, 'Come on, and tread where I shall tread.' The other took him at his word, And followed as he led. 1884 *Manch. Exam.* 12 May 4/7 Our contemporaries must not be offended if we decline to take them quite at their word.

14. a. in a word: in a simple or short (esp. comprehensive) statement or phrase; briefly, in short. Now only introductory or parenthetical. Occas. ***in one word***; also †***with a word***.

1591 Shaks. *Two Gent.* II. iv. 71 His yeares but yong, but his experience old; His head vn-mellowed, but his Iudgement ripe; And in a word..He is compleat in feature, and in minde. 1596 —— *1 Hen. IV*, II. iv. 283 Then did we two, set on you foure, and with a word, outfac'd you from your prize. 1598 R. Bernard tr. *Terence, Andria* I. i, Tell me in a word what ist you would with me? 1665 Boyle *Occas. Refl.* II. xiv. 235 To return to my former Studies, and Recreations, and Dyet; and in a word, to my wonted course of Life. 1704 Norris *Ideal World* II. xii. 496 If you will have in one word a just distribution of each, it is this, that the Idea we see in God, but the sentiment we feel in ourselves. 1710 Berkeley *Princ. Hum. Knowl.* I. §4 Houses, Mountains, Rivers, and in a word all sensible Objects. 1855 *Orr's Circ. Sci., Inorg. Nat.* 236 Some natural exposure on a cliff, in a valley, by a stream, or wherever—in a word—the surface coating of soil being absent, the underlying rock can be seen. 1892 Westcott *Gospel of Life* 13 Man in a word is dependant on that which lies outside himself.

b. in so many words (tr. L. *totidem verbis*, cf. So 37 d): lit. in precisely that number of words; in those very words; also, †word for word.

1670 W. WALKER *Idiomat. Anglo-Lat.* 23, I rendred it even almost in so many words..*totidem fere verbis interpretatus sum.* **1720** DE FOE *Capt. Singleton* xv. (1840) 253 William told us in so many words, that it was impossible. **1836** DICKENS *Sk. Boz, Scotland-Yard*, That the Lord Mayor had threatened in so many words to pull down the old London Bridge, and build up a new one. **1881** W. COLLINS *Black Robe* I. 194 That the object was to bring Romayne and Stella together..was as plain to him as if he had heard it confessed in so many words.

15. a. on or **upon one's word**: (*a*) in const. with a verb, in sense 8 or 9: On the security of, or as bound by, one's promise or affirmation; hence (*b*) as an asseveration, ***on*** or ***upon*** (†*of*, †*a*) ***my word***: Assuredly, certainly, truly, indeed.

(*a*) **1598** R. BERNARD tr. *Terence, Andria* v. i, The good turne that..you promised me on your word. **1600** E. BLOUNT tr. *Conestaggio* 206 If he woulde assure him vpon his word, he would go to the campe. **1607** DEKKER & WEBSTER *Northw. Hoe* II. i, *Doll*... Tis but poore fifty pound. *Alla.* If that bee all, you shall vpon your worde take vp so much with me.

(*b*) **1588** SHAKS. *Tit. A.* IV. iii. 59 Of my word, I haue written to effect. **1592** —— *Rom. & Jul.* I. i. 1 A my word wee'l not carry coales. **1598** —— *Merry W.* IV. ii. 61 He will seeke there on my word. **1643** *Decl. Commons Rebell. Irel.* 52 Upon my word your Lordship is little beholding to him. **1646** in *Buccleuch MSS.* (Hist. MSS. Comm.) I. 308 But of my word she will not meet with the like proffer again. **1766** GOLDSM. *Vicar W.* xvii, A very good boy, Bill, upon my word. **1848** DICKENS *Dombey* xxxix, Upon my word and honour, Captain Gills, it would be a charity to give me the pleasure of your acquaintance. **1871** GEO. ELIOT *Middlem.* xxxviii. II. 295 Upon my word, I think the truth is the hardest missile one can be pelted with.

b. (with ellipsis of prep.) ***my word!*** as an ejaculation of surprise. *colloq.* (†*vulgar*).

1841 MRS. GASKELL *Lett.* (1966) 44 My word! authorship brings them in a pretty penny. **1857** LOCKER *Lond. Lyrics* 72 Half London was there, and, my word, there were few.. But envied Lord Nigel's felicity. **1890** 'R. BOLDREWOOD' *Col. Reformer* xix, My word!..that's something like a mob!

** with another sb.

16. a word and a blow: a brief utterance of anger or defiance, followed immediately by the delivery of a blow, as the beginning of a fight; hence in reference to prompt or sudden action of any kind; sometimes used predicatively of a person. Also (with hyphens) *attrib.*

1592 SHAKS. *Rom. & Jul.* III. i. 43 *Tyb*... Gentlemen, Good den, a word with one of you. *Mer.* And but one word with one of vs? couple it with something, make it a word and a blow. **1639** J. CLARKE *Parœm.* 178 He's but a word and a blowe. **1753** RICHARDSON *Grandison* (1811) IV. xxvi. 207 My cousins are grieved [at my going so soon]: they did not expect that I would be a word and a blow, as they phrase it. **1820** BYRON *Juan* III. xlviii, With him it never was a word and blow, His angry word once o'er, he shed no blood. **1840** MRS. TROLLOPE *M. Armstrong* iv, Mr. Joseph Parsons had a Napoleon-like promptitude of action, which the unlearned operatives described by calling him 'a word-and-a-blow man'. **1847** RUXTON *Adv. Mexico* xxvii. 242 Firm friends and bitter enemies, with them it is 'a word and a blow'.

17. word of command: a word or short phrase uttered by an officer to a body of soldiers as an order for some particular movement or evolution; also by a carter to a horse, etc.

1639 R. WARD *Animadv. War* I. 230 You are to use these words of Command following. **1684** R. H. *School Recr.* 45 Keep..your Musket hard against your Shoulder after you have fired, till the next Word of Command. **1726** SWIFT *Gulliver* II. vii, I have seen this whole Body of Horse upon a Word of Command draw their Swords at once. **1837** DICKENS *Pickw.* iv, The hoarse shout of the word of command ran along [the line]. **1853** [see COMMAND *sb.* 1 b]. **1898** [see GEE *int.*[1], def.].

18. word of honour: an affirmation or promise by which one pledges one's honour or good faith.

1814 D. H. O'BRIEN *Captiv. & Escape* 65 They suspected we were deserters..We assured them upon our word of honour, they were very much mistaken. **1896** EDITH THOMPSON in *Monthly Packet* Christmas No. 97 He had passed his word of honour..that he would report himself at the fort.

19. a. by word of mouth: by speaking, as distinguished from writing or other method of expression; orally. Also ***word of mouth*** sb. phr., oral communication, oral publicity; so ***word-of-mouth*** attrib., executed, done, given, etc. by speaking; oral.

a **1553** UDALL *Royster D.* III. ii. (Arb.) 40 A little message vnto hir by worde of mouth. **1598** R. BERNARD tr. *Terence, Hecyra* I. ii, It cannot be told by word of mouth, howe desirous I was to returne hither agaıne. **1601–1849** [see MOUTH *sb.* 3 c]. **1638** FEATLY *Strict. Lyndom.* II. 121 Pretending I know not what nuncupatory will by word of mouth. **1639** J. TAYLOR (Water P.) *Pt. Summers Trav.* 44 They can flatter..with Pen, Picture, and by word of mouth. **1752** BERKELEY *Th. Tar-water* Wks. 1871 III. 498 Of this I have been informed by letters, and by word of mouth. **1883** D. C. MURRAY *Hearts* xxxiv. (1885) 288 He would rather tell him of this by word of mouth than by letter. **1934** in WEBSTER. **1951** B. SCHULBERG *Disenchanted* vi. 67 He tells everyone..that you're one of his favorite American authors and..that kind of word of mouth ain't bad. **1967** B. WHITAKER *Of Mice & Murder* xiii. 147, 'I wonder how he heard it was for sale.' 'Word of mouth, I suppose.' **1980** 'D. KAVANAGH' *Duffy* iii. 43 The only way to get successful.. was to work at being really efficient and then hope for word-of-mouth to back you up. **1984** A. BROOKNER *Hotel du Lac* i. 14 The only publicity from which the hotel could not distance itself was the word of mouth recommendations of patrons of long standing.

1802–12 BENTHAM *Ration. Judic. Evid.* (1827) II. 562 Word-of-mouth wills are, in certain cases, allowed by the Statute of Frauds. **1829** —— *Justice & Cod. Petit., Abr. Petit. Justice* 6 The language..employed in word-of-mouth discussion. **1894** K. HEWAT *Little Scott. World* Pref. p. xii, The author has to acknowledge his indebtedness..for much word-of-mouth information.

b. *humorously* in reference to drinking.

1738 SWIFT *Pol. Conversat.* ii. 164 Come, Sir John, take it by Word of Mouth, and then give it the Colonel. (Sir John drinks.)

20. a. word for word: in the exact, or (in reference to translation) precisely corresponding, words: = VERBATIM A. 1 a, b. Also (with hyphens) *attrib.* = VERBATIM B. 1.

c **1385** CHAUCER *L.G.W.* 1002 *Dido*, I coude folwe word for word Virgile. **1474** CAXTON *Chesse* II. v. (1883) 61 He.. dyde do saye to hym word for worde lyke as the physicien had sayd. **1538** COVERDALE *N.T.* Ded. + ij b, We do not followe thys olde Latyn texte word for word. **1601** SHAKS. *Twel. N.* I. iii. 28 He..speaks three or four languages word for word without booke. **1656** COWLEY *Pindar. Odes* Pref., If a man should undertake to translate Pindar word for word. **1686** HORNECK *Crucif. Jesus* xxii. 741 Some..have been able to rehearse the whole New Testament word for word. **1746** FRANCIS tr. *Horace, Art of Poetry* 191 Dwell not on Incidents already known; Nor Word for Word translate with painful Care. **1862** MRS. H. WOOD *Mrs. Hallib.* I. viii, 'I will faithfully repeat it to you',..'Faithfully?—word for word?' **1878** W. T. THORNTON (*title*) Word for Word from Horace. **1891** *Law Times* XCII. 107/1 The 8th section of the Act of 1874 is word for word the same as the 40th section of the Act of 1833.

c **1611** CHAPMAN *Iliad* To Rdr. A 4 b, Those Translators ..that affect Their word-for-word traductions. **1858–9** G. P. MARSH *Engl. Lang.* xvii. (1860) 361 More closely literal, more exactly word-for-word translations.

b. So †***word after word*** (occas. †***after the word***), †***word in word***, †***fro word unto word***. ***word by word*** (also attrib.); also *spec.*, in alphabetization; opp. *letter by letter* (see LETTER *sb.* 1 c).

[*a* **1000** *Ælfred's Boeth.* Proem, Hwilum he sette word be worde, hwilum andgit of andgite.] *c* **1200** *Trin. Coll. Hom.* 17 Ich wille..segge ou þe erede word after word. **1379** *Glouc. Cath. MS.* 19 No. I. i. iii. lf. 7 All that I have sayde yn this chapitre Isaac techith word by word. ?*a* **1400** *Wyclif's Bible* Prol. xv. 57 This wole..make the sentence open, where to Englisshe it aftir the word, wolde be derk and douteful. *c* **1449** PECOCK *Repr.* II. ii. 144 The..late named psalmes..ben ouer long to be rehercid word bi word here. *c* **1475** *Partenay* 3187 Geffray the letters After breke and rayd, Fro wurde unto wurd. **1493** *Acta Dom. Conc.* (1839) 308/2 þe bill of Complaint..of þe quhilk þe tenour folowis word in word. *a* **1548** HALL *Chron., Hen. IV* 2 b, Then turnyng hymself to his accuser, [he] declared worde by worde what he had said. **1575** (*title*) A Commentarie of M. Doctor Martin Luther upon the Epistle of S. Paul to the Galathians first collected and gathered word by word out of his preaching. **1613** R. C. *Table Alph.* (ed. 3), *Verbatim*, word by word. **1865** RUSKIN *Sesame* i. §25 The kind of word-by-word examination of your author which is rightly called 'reading'. **1927** H. W. FOWLER *S.P.E. Tract No. XXVI* 193 And let me here accept my title word by word: I am a moralizer because I wish morals to be drawn [etc.]. **1938** L. M. HARROD *Librarians' Gloss.* 12 There are two methods [of alphabetization] in use: 1, 'letter by letter'; 2, 'word by word', or 'nothing before something'. In the former method 'Newton' *precedes*, in the latter it *follows*, 'New York'. **1951** *British Standard Alphabetical Arrangement* (B.S.I.) 6 Items having the same first word shall be arranged in the alphabetical order of the second word, those with no second word standing first. Similarly those having two words in common are arranged in the alphabetical order of their third word and so on. The whole group thus arranged shall precede any word alphabetically qualified to follow the first word of the group. (This is known as the 'word-by-word' or 'nothing-before-something' principle.) **1979** *Amer. Speech* 1976 LI. 149 This dictionary uses word-by-word rather than letter-by-letter alphabetizing.

*** with qualifying adj.

21. fair words (FAIR *a.* 5): pleasant or attractive speech (usually implying deceitfulness or insincerity).

a **1000** *Cædmon's Gen.* 899 Me nædre..to forsceape scyhte & to scyldfrece fah wyrm þurh fægir word. *c* **1200** *Vices & Virtues* (1888) 11 Ic habbe beswiken min emcristen mid faire wordes. **1538** STARKEY *England* II. ii. (1878) 191 By hys dyssymulatyon and fare wordys. **1546** J. HEYWOOD *Prov.* I. ix. (1867) 18 It hurteth not the tounge to geue fayre wurdis. **1639** [see PARSNIP 1 b]. **1676** WYCHERLEY *Plain Dealer* v, Fair words butter no cabbage. **1697** DAMPIER *Voy.* I. 282 The men began to murmur against Captain Swan..but he gave them fair words. **1897** *Pall Mall Mag.* Nov. 340 'Ho, ho! my masters', cried he; 'fair words break no bones'.

22. of few words: not given to much or lengthy speaking; taciturn; laconic.

c **1450** HOLLAND *Howlat* 175 Off fewe wordis, full wyss and worthy thai war. **1561** HOBY tr. *Castiglione's Courtyer* I. E iij, Of few wordes, and no bragger. **1599** SHAKS. *Hen. V*, III. ii. 38 That men of few Words are the best men. **1697** *Lond. Gaz.* No. 3260/4 Well set and middle sized, and of few Words. **1759** DILWORTH *Pope* 120[Gay] had always been a man of but few words. **1837** DICKENS *Pickw.* xxiv, Mr. Dubbley, who was a man of few words, nodded assent.

23. good word: a friendly, favourable, or laudatory utterance; something said on behalf of or in commendation of a person or thing. ***to give*** (one) ***a good word***, to speak well of. ***to say*** or ***speak a good word for***, (*spec.*) to recommend to the favour of another. †In *pl.* also (*a*) used *ellipt.* in deprecation of angry or violent speech (see GOOD *a.* 7 b, quot. *c* 1592); (*b*) in bad sense = *fair words* (21).

c **1205** LAY. 665 Heo hine gretten mid godene heore worden. [*a* **1300** *Cursor M.* 20095 þan spak ihesus words gode, Als he hang þar on þe rode.] **1540** PALSGR. *Acolastus* III. i. N iv, [Thou] dyddest speke a good word for me, and dydst tourne away..the.. strokes from me. **1548**, *a* **1632** [see GOOD *a.* 7 b]. **1562** J. HEYWOOD *Prov. & Epigr.* II. ix. (1867) 77 Good woordes bryng not euer of good deedes good hope. **1573** BARET *Alv.* W 352 That helpeth one with his good worde at a time, *suffragatorius.* **1607** SHAKS. *Timon* I. ii. 217 You gaue good words the other day of a Bay Courser I rod on. **1622** J. TAYLOR (Water P.) *Farew. Tower-bottles* A 7, False hearts can put on good wordes and lookes. **1698** FRYER *Acc. E. India & P.* 222 Only giving us good words instead of Payment. **1699** BENTLEY *Phal.* Pref. p. xlviii, The Good Word, that Mr. Grævius has been pleas'd publicly to give me. **1731–8** SWIFT *Pol. Conversat.* i. 71, I know I shall always have your good Word. **1852** C. B. MANSFIELD *Paraguay* etc. (1856) 364 My friend M. Cerruti..has diplomatic business here; and with his good words..I hope to be in clover. *a* **1859** MACAULAY *Hist. Eng.* xxiii. V. 78 It was..not in the character of tenant that the Czar was likely to gain the good word of civilised men. **1892** [see GOOD *a.* 7 b].

24. half a word (HALF *a.* 1 b): a very short utterance, a slight fragment of speech or conversation.

1700 T. BROWN tr. *Fresny's Amusem.* 19 Taking it for granted, that we two understand one another by half a Word. **1865** DICKENS *Mut. Fr.* I. vi, Might I have half a word with you?

25. last word (in special senses). **a.** The final utterance in a conversation or (esp.) dispute. **b.** *pl.* The latest utterance of a person before death. ***The Seven Last Words***, the seven utterances of Christ on the cross (also simply ***The Seven Words***). **c.** The final or conclusive statement, after which there is no more to be said; hence *transf.* (also ***latest word***) the final achievement, the latest thing.

a. 1563 FOXE *A. & M.* 1416/2 My lorde of Lincolne.. sayde that thou were a frantike felow, and a man that wyll haue the last worde. **1593** G. HARVEY *Pierce's Super.* Wks. (Grosart) II. 43 Come hee- and shee-scoldes, you that..will rather loose your liues, then the last word. **1875** LE FANU *Willing to Die* xxxvi, It was plain..she would have one last word more.

b. 1692 H. HARRISON (*title*) The Last Words of a Dying Penitent. **1808** SCOTT *Marm.* VI. xxxii, 'Charge, Chester, charge! On, Stanley, on!' Were the last words of Marmion. **1870** tr. *Bellarmino* (*title*) The Seven Words from the Cross. **1874** E. KING (*title*) Meditations on the last seven words of our Lord Jesus Christ. **1883** GROVE *Dict. Mus.* III. 476 *Seven Last Words, The*..a composition of Haydn's dating about 1785... The 'Seven Words' were for long a favourite in Vienna both in church and concert-room.

c. 1881, 1891 [see LAST *a.* 6]. **1888** *Daily News* 21 Sept. 5/6 The long mantles that are the latest 'word' of Paris fashions. **1901** 'L. MALET' *Sir Richard Calmady* V. vi, The clothes.. supposed..to present the last word of English fashion.

26. of many words: given to much or lengthy speaking, loquacious, talkative, verbose; also said of a statement, verbose.

c **1430** *How Good Wife taught Dau.* 43 in Hazl. *E.P.P.* I. 183 Be noght of many wordes. **1563** FOXE *A. & M.* 1438/1 Your diffinition is of many wordes to no purpose. **1599** SHAKS. *Much Ado* I. i. 158, I thanke you, I am not of many words, but I thanke you. **1797** JANE AUSTEN *Sense & Sensib.* xxxiv, She was not a woman of many words. **1854** R. S. SURTEES *Handley Cr.* iii. (1901) I. 18 Augustus Barnington, ..not being a man of many words, contented himself by stammering something about honour.

**** with verb.

27. make words. †**a.** ***to make few*** or ***many words***: to speak briefly or at great length. Also ***to make but one word.*** *Obs.*

1530 PALSGR. 843/1 To make fewe wordes, *a brief dire.* *a* **1634** CHAPMAN *Alphonsus* III. (1654) 38 Fall to thy business and make few words. **1677** MIÈGE *New Dict.*, To make many words about a small trifle, *barguigner, contester pour une chose de neant.* **1752** AINSWORTH *Engl.-Lat. Dict.* s.v., I will make but one word with you..*te absolvam brevi.*

b. with neg.: (Not) to say anything (more) about a matter; (not) to speak or make mention *of*.

1576 FLEMING *Panopl. Epist.* 67 To make no words of that which I have oftentimes read,..what harme can there be in death. **1579–80** NORTH *Plutarch* (1595) 50 Lycurgus neuer bashed or made worde at the matter. **1610** HOLLAND *Camden's Brit.* I. 259 Those Chronicles of the English Saxons..reported only their owne fortunate battailes, and victories but never made words of their foiles & overthrowes. **1749** FIELDING *Tom Jones* VII. xiv, I will be so far from making any Words with you, that I will give you a Shilling more than your Demand. **1773** GOLDSM. *Stoops to Conq.* IV, Bring me your bill, and let's make no more words about it. **1870** MORRIS *Earthly Par.* III. IV. 8 Then no more words the Strong Man made, but straight Caught up the elder in his arms.

†**c.** To make a proposal *of*. *Obs.*

1645 MILTON *Tetrach.* 43 Herod..cast his eye..upon Herodias..and durst make words of marrying her.

d. To speak at (too) great length *of*. *Sc.*

1823 SCOTT *Quentin D.* xxxvi, You make words of nothing. **1825** JAMIESON s.v., *To make words*, to talk more about any-thing than it deserves.

28. a. take (up) the word: to begin speaking, esp. immediately after or instead of some one else.

Partly after F. *prendre la parole*; partly from Gr. τὴν παραβολὴν ὑπολαβεῖν to take up one's 'parable' (PARABLE *sb.* d).

c **1489** CAXTON *Sonnes of Aymon* ix. 204 The kinge Yon toke the worde & sayd [etc.]. **1523** LD. BERNERS *Froiss.* I.

cccxliii. 219/1 Than the duke of Bretayne toke the wordes, & sayd [etc.]. **1557** N. T. (Genev.) *Luke* x. 30 Iesus taking his word said [etc.]. **1697** DRYDEN *Æneis* XI. 510 Then Drances took the word. **1808** SCOTT *Marm.* I. xxii, Young Selby.. reverently took up the word: 'Kind uncle, [etc.].' **1811** *Ora & Juliet* II. 192 Henry.. was going to address Mrs. Brewster; but lady Harriet took the word. **1823** SCOTT *Quentin D.* xxxv, There was a general murmur. 'My Lord Duke', said the Count of Crèvecœur, taking the word for the rest, 'this must be better thought on.' **1884** HOWELLS *Silas Lapham* x, The Colonel, left alone with his wife.., made haste to take the word. **1887** MORRIS *Odyssey* I. 32 The Father of Gods and of men.. took up the word.

b. *to take* (a person's) *word*: to accept (his) statement or assertion as true or trustworthy: usually with *for*, esp. in the phrase ***take my word for it*** used to emphasize an assertion = I can assure you, you may be sure, believe me. †Formerly also, to accept or trust (a person's) promise; to give (him) credit (*for* a debt).

1587 in W. M. Williams *Ann. Founders' Co.* (1867) 69 He givinge his fayth promyse to Mr Alderman.. Mr Alderman tooke his worde. **1597** SHAKS. *2 Hen. IV*, IV. ii. 66, I take your Princely word, for these redresses. **1597** E. S. *Discov. Knts. Poste* A 4, Will you take my word for two pence? Take thy word? Ile see thee hangd first (qd she) pay me my money. **1628** SHIRLEY *Witty Fair One* I. i. B 4, Saue your credit and let swearing alone, I dare take your word. **1672** WYCHERLEY *Love in a Wood* IV. i. 62 But may I take your word Jonas? **1693** *Humours Town* 38 Take my word for't. **1712** STEELE *Spect.* No. 284 ¶4 Take my Word for it, there is nothing in it. **1712** ARBUTHNOT *John Bull* II. iii, Nobody will take our words for sixpence. **1771** SMOLLETT *Humphry Cl.* 30 Sept., I took his word and honour that he would make an effort. **1864** WHATELY *Chr. Evid.* iii. 21 How can you know, except by taking the word of the learned for it? **1889** J. K. JEROME *Three Men in a Boat* 186 On a matter of this kind you can take Harris's word.

c. *to take* (a person) ***at his word***: see 13 c.

IV. 29. *attrib.* and *Comb.* **a.** Simple attrib. Of, pertaining or relating to, or consisting of a word or words, as ***word-accent, -boundary, -break, -combination, -division, -element, -end, -ending, -family, -form, -function, -game*** (also *fig.*), ***-group, -history, -idea, -memory, -music, -order, -pattern, -patterning, -position, -sound, -status, -stem, -store, -stress, -structure, -study, -taboo, -tone, -trap, -usage, -value, -weapon***; (with agent-n. or the like) dealing with or acting by means of words, as ***word-artist, -conjuror, -epicure, -juggler, -master, -merchant, -musician, -pirate, -smith,*** (also ***word-smithing***), ***-warrior***, etc.; (with n. of action or the like, in instrumental sense) done or carried on by means of words, as ***word-battle, -fence*** (FENCE *sb.* 2 b), ***-jugglery, -war, -wound, -wrangle***, etc.; also ***word-based, -like*** adjs. **b.** Instrumental, as ***word-beat, -drunk, -pity*** vbs.; ***word-charged, -clad,*** †***-strooken, -wounded*** adjs. **c.** Objective, as ***word-bearer, -breaker,*** †***-bridger*** (BRIDGE *v.*[2]), ***-coiner, -hunter, -spinner***, etc.; ***word-breaking, -building, -coining, -compelling, -finding, -juggling, -keeping, -making***, see also sense d below, ***-setting***, (SET *v.* 73), ***-spinning, -splitting, -twisting***, etc. sbs. and adjs.; also with pl., †***words-speaking***; ***word-choice, -coinage, -composition, -creation, -formation***, etc.; also ***word-formational, -formative*** adjs. **d.** Special comb.: **word association** *Psychol.*, a psycho-diagnostic technique based on analysis of a person's reactions to the presentation of stimulus words, esp. with regard to the (subconscious) contents and type of the immediate associations formed, reaction time, etc.; more generally, the associations connected with certain words; freq. *attrib.*; **word-base** *Philol.*, the simple word from which its derivatives and inflected forms arise; a root morpheme, etc.; †**word-bate** [BATE *sb.*[1]], contention about words; **word-blind** *a. Path.*, affected with **word-blindness**, *i.e.* inability to understand written or printed words when seen, owing to disease of the visual *word-centre*; **word-bound** *a.*, (*a*) restrained in speech, unable to use words freely or fluently; (*b*) bound by one's word or promise; †**word-braving**, boasting; **word-catcher**, (*a*) one who catches or cavils at words, a petty or carping critic; (*b*) one who catches and collects words: applied contemptuously to a lexicographer (quot. 1835); **word-catching**, catching at words, petty criticism; **word-category** *Linguistics* = *word-class*; **word-centre** *Anat.*, each of certain centres (CENTRE *sb.* 7 a) in the brain which govern the perception and use of words (spoken or written); **word-class** *Linguistics* [cf. G. *wortklasse*], a category of words of similar form or function; esp. applied to parts of speech; **word-count**, a statistical study of *word frequency* (see below); **word-craft**, the art of using words, oratorical or literary skill; **word-deaf** *a. Path.*, affected with **word-deafness**, *i.e.* inability to understand words when heard, owing to disease of the auditory *word-centre*; †**word-dearthing** *a.*, producing dearth of words, involving a great expenditure of words; **word-field** *Linguistics*, a group of lexical items seen as associated in meaning because occurring in similar contexts; **word-final** *a.*, occurring at the end of a word; also as *sb.*, a letter or sound occurring in this position; hence **word-finally** *adv.*; cf. *word-initial* adj. below; †**word-flowing** *a.*, fluent in speech; **word frequency**, the relative frequency with which a word is used in a given text or corpus; **word geography**, the study of the regional distribution of word and phrases, or a book treating of this; hence **word-geographical** *a.*; **word-hoard**, literal rendering of OE. *wordhord* treasure of speech; recently in general use, the words used by a person or group of people, vocabulary; also, a source or store of words; **word-index**, a list of the words used by a given author or in a given work (or corpus) with reference to the passages in which they occur, but without quotations (cf. CONCORDANCE *sb.* (6 b); **word-initial** *a.*, occurring at the beginning of a word; also as *sb.*, a letter or sound occurring in this position; hence **word-initially** *adv.*; **word-internally** *adv.*, = *word-medially* below; **word-ladder**, a puzzle in which a word has to be converted into another of equal length by being taken through a series of word-changes, each word differing by one letter from the last; also called *doublets*; **word length** *Computers*, the number of bits, digits, etc., in a word (sense 12 g above); **word-magic** *Anthropol.*, magic thought to be exerted by the knowledge or use of the proper name or term for something, or the supposed magical property residing in such a name; also *transf.*; **word-making and word-taking**, a game played with lettered cards, app. a forerunner of the modern Lexicon or Scrabble; **word mark**, (*a*) a real or invented word used as a trade mark; (*b*) *Computers*, a bit that takes a different value according as the character containing it does or does not begin (or end) a word; a character containing such a bit; **word-medial** *a.*, occurring in the middle of a word; hence **word-medially** *adv.*; **word method** *Educ.*, a method of teaching pupils to read in which they are taught to recognize words as complete units before learning the letters or syllables which compose them; the 'look-and-say' method (see LOOK *v.* 47); **word-paint** *v. trans.*, to 'paint' in words, describe vividly, make a *word-picture* of; so **word-painter, word-painting** *sb.* and *a.*; **word-painted** *a.*, (*a*) decorated or adorned with words; (*b*) 'painted' or described vividly in words; **word-pair**, a pair of words resembling each other in sound or form; **word-palatogram** (see quot. 1948); **word-perfect** *a.*, knowing perfectly every word of one's lesson, part, etc.; **word-picture**, a vivid description in words, presenting the object to the mind like a picture; **word-play** [cf. G. *wortspiel*], a play of or upon words (see PLAY *sb.* 7 b); **word problem** *Math.*, the problem of determining whether two different products are equal, or two sequences of operations are equivalent; **word processing** [cf. G. *textverarbeitung* text processing], the storing and organizing of texts by electronic means, *spec.* by a word processor; hence (as a back-formation) **word-process** *v. trans.* to edit, produce, etc., using a word processor; **word-processed** *ppl. a.*; **word processor**, a keyboard device incorporating a computer programmed to store, amend, and format text that is keyed in, a printer to print it automatically, and often also a screen to display it; **word recognition** *Educ.*, the process or faculty of perceiving words in reading and identifying them with the ideas they represent; **word-salad**, a type of speech indicative of advanced schizophrenia in which random words and phrases are mixed together unintelligibly; also *fig.*; **word-shot** *nonce-wd.* [after *earshot*], the distance within which one person can speak to another; **word-sign**, something used to represent a word; *spec.* a graphic character representing a complete word; esp., in Egyptian hieroglyphics, etc. = LOGOGRAM 2 b; **word-spite**, spite or ill-will expressed in words (in quot. *attrib.*); **word square**, a set of words of the same number of letters to be arranged in a square so as to read the same horizontally or vertically; a puzzle in which such a set of words has to be guessed (Webster Suppl. 1880); **word-stock**, the sum of words available to a language, dialect, etc.; vocabulary; also *fig.*; **word-strife**, a rendering of LOGOMACHY; **word-symbol**, a word used as a sign or symbol; *spec.* = LOGOGRAM 2 b; **word time** *Computers*, the time between the reading of the first bits of successive words; **word-type**, (*a*) a word used to symbolize or represent an idea; (*b*) *Philos.* (see quot. 1936); (*c*) a word forming a distinct item in a vocabulary; **word-vision**: see quot., and cf. *word-blindness*; **word-watch** *v. intr.*, to observe linguistic usage, esp. with regard to changes and innovations; also **word-watcher**; **word-watching** *vbl. sb.*; †**word-wood** *a.* [WOOD *a.*], 'mad', wild, or unrestrained in speech; **word-wrap** [cf. WRAP-AROUND *sb.* 3] (see quot. 1982); so **word-wrapping** *vbl. sb.*; **word-writing,** Bloomfield's term for ideographic writing. See also WORD-BOOK, etc.

1903 WINBOLT *Lat. Hexam. Verse* 75 Discrepancy.. between *word-accent and metrical stress. **1933** DYLAN THOMAS *Let.* Sept. (1966) 20 Mr. Neuburg has payed you a.. compliment. 'One of the most exquisite *word-artists of our day.' **1945** C. BAX *Vintage Verse* III. 95 This faultless word-artist [*sc.* Milton].. was buried in St. Giles's, Cripplegate. **1910** *Rev. Neurol. & Psychiatry* VIII. 641 (*title*) The practical value of the *word-association method in the treatment of the psycho-neuroses. **1918** M. D. EDER *Jung's Stud. in Word-Association* p. v, We owe to Dr. Jung ..the application of the association method to *unconscious* mental processes... These studies in word association have now acquired a permanent place in the historical development of this [*sc.* psychoanalytical] theory. **1946** A. CHRISTIE *Hollow* xxvi. 221 'What is there about that that interests you so, M. Poirot?..' 'Association—a point of the psychology.' 'Word association? Horse and cart. Rocking horse?' **1952** C. P. BLACKER *Eugenics: Galton & After* 52 Galton also tried out on himself an elaborate system of word-association tests. His method was different.. from that later popularized by C. G. Jung, but the underlying idea was the same. **1971** J. ELSOM *Theatre outside London* vii. 126 These discussions were linked with word-association games. **1977** *Canad. Jrnl. Linguistics* 1976 XXI. II. 200 'Navaho word associations', which examines the role of grammatical form-classes in word association tests, has no subject under the age of seventeen. **1931** C. L'E. EWEN *Hist. Surnames* xiv. 360 The root of Skr. and Pers. *yuvan* 'young' may well be one of the *word-bases of Ewan, Owen [etc.]. **1956** *Essays & Studies* IX. 98 The appearance of the same word-base in various forms (polyptoton): (al) ar knitt & onyd in this onyng, & made holy in this holyhede. **1964** J. VACHEK in D. Abercrombie et al. *Daniel Jones* 195 Some ModE affixes (especially the word-formative ones) are.. more easily separable from their word-bases than others. **1963** J. LYONS *Structural Semantics* ii. 11 A *word-based grammar seems to be more satisfactory than a morpheme-based grammar for the description of languages of the 'inflecting' type. *a* **1640** JACKSON *Creed* X. xxxvii. 3155 *Word-Bates, or Verbal Quarrels, arising from ambiguous ..expressions. **1853** KINGSLEY *Hypatia* xxvii, Not unwilling, like a philosopher and a Greek,.. to embark in anything like a *word-battle. **1846** TRENCH *Mirac.* xxxii. 442 The *word-bearer for the rest of the apostles proves also, when occasion requires, the sword-bearer. **1641** J. JACKSON *True Evang. T.* III. 197 They revile, and *word-beate our persons. **1890** W. JAMES *Princ. Psychol.* I. ii. 55 combines If this order of association be ingrained and habitual in that individual, injury to his *visual* centres will make him not only *word-blind, but aphasic as well. **1898** H. C. BASTIAN *Aphasia* etc. 329 The patient.. was neither word-deaf nor word-blind. **1881** J. ROSS in *Lancet* 26 Nov. 905/1 This particular variety of amnesic aphasia has been named '*word-blindness' by Kussmaul. **1644** W. NEWPORT *Fall of Man* 23 For a Christian to be absolutely *word-bound, to be tied so to anothers forme or his own, that he hath no liberty to vary in any expression, is a great bondage. **1714** *Spect.* No. 560 ¶2 If I appear a little word-bound in my first.. responses, I hope it will.. be imputed.. to the long disuse of speech. **1836** JOANNA BAILLIE *Separation* II. iii, Learn from him The story of the war. Word-bound he is not: He'll tell it willingly. **1933** L. BLOOMFIELD *Language* xxiii. 419 At the time of the loss of *-n*, the language did not distinguish *word-boundaries in the manner of present-day English. **1978** *Language* LIV. 21 The well-known word-boundary phenomena of French, such as liaison, elision, and *h*-aspiré. **1642** FULLER *Holy & Prof. St.* III. xvii. 195 A *word-braving, or scorning of all wealth in discourse. **1968** J. R. BIGGS *Basic Typogr.* 41/1 Spacing is consistent but the right-hand margin is left irregular. This does not always reduce *word breaks very much. **1980** B. CRUTCHLEY *To be a Printer* 55 Bad word-breaks at the end of lines and similar shoddiness. **1825** SCOTT *Betrothed* iii, The promiser.. escapes not the sin of a *word-breaker, because he hath been a drunken braggart. *Ibid.* vii, Better is an empty stomach.. with a clear conscience, than a fatted ox with iniquity and *word-breaking. *a* **1400** *Wyclif's Bible* Pref. Ep. vii. 72 Recapitulatour, *word bregger. **1862** W. BARNES *Tiw* p. v, The known course of Teutonic *word-building. **1894** (*title*) Word Building as a Guide to Spelling. **1735** POPE *Prol. Sat.* 166 Each *Word-catcher, that lives on syllables. **1835** R. GARNETT *Philol. Ess.* (1859) 8 Of this sort of knowledge—the very foundation of all rational etymology—our word-catchers do not seem to have had the smallest tincture. **1837** LOCKHART *Scott* I. x. 330 This narrow-minded, sour, and dogmatical little word-catcher. *a* **1743** SAVAGE *Wks.* (1775) II. 253 (Jod.) Is not *wordcatching more serviceable in splitting a cause than in explaining a fine poet? **1837** LOCKHART *Scott* IV. iv. 152 Sharp word-catchings,.. and all the quips and quibblets of bar pleading. **1938** B. L. WHORF in *Language* XIV. 275 **Word Category*; a category (overt or covert or mixed) which delimits one of a primary hierarchy of word classes each of limited membership (not coterminous with entire vocabulary), e.g. the familiar 'parts of speech' of Indo-European and many other languages, vs. *Modulus Category*; one which modifies, either any word of the vocabulary, or any word already allocated to a delimited class, e.g. voices, aspects, cases. **1964** J. VACHEK in D. Abercrombie et al. *Daniel Jones* 195 The comparative suffix *-er* does not imply the change of the word-category of the basic word, while the agentive *-er* necessarily does so. **1898** H. C. BASTIAN *Aphasia* etc. 14 It is permissible to speak of these portions as auditory and visual '*word centres' respectively. **1941** E. BLUNDEN *Thomas Hardy* xi. 236 An innovation of *word-choice. **1879** SPURGEON *Serm.* XXV. 328 He sought truth, not controversy and *word-chopping. **1812** W. TENNANT *Anster F.* VI. lxi, Sweet utterance of *word-clad breath. **1914** L. BLOOMFIELD *Introd. Study Lang.* iv. 108 (*title*) *Word-classes. *Ibid.* iv. 109 Other word classes which are not expressed by formational similarity. **1924** O. JESPERSEN *Philos. Gram.* iv. 61 We have a great many words which can belong to one word-class only: *admiration, society, life* can only be substantives [etc.]. **1953** C. E. BAZELL *Linguistic Form* vi. 76 The so-called parts of speech (still more inappropriately word-classes) are classes of stem-morpheme. **1973** *Computers & Humanities* VII. 159 Lyne's resolution of word class problems (is *y* an adverb or a pronoun?) uses a rather complex algorithm. **1865** *Reader* 4 Feb. 133/1 Largely drawn upon by our modern *word-coinage, more especially by the nomenclature of science. **1935** *Vanity Fair* Nov. 38/1 There appears to be little leakage of their vernacular into even so ambitious a *word-coiner as *Variety*. **1981** *Verbatim* Spring 14/2 Since I started publishing *Verbatim*, these and other word-coiners have been sending their creations to me, pressing for recognition. **1920** *19th Cent.* Mar. 482 *Word-coining was then a common industry. **1887** RIDER HAGGARD *Allan Quatermain* ix, A time-serving and *word-coining politician. **1864** W. D. WHITNEY in *Ann. Rep. Bd. Regents Smithsonian Inst. 1863* 108 The conditions of that ancient period, and the degree in which they could quicken the now sluggish processes of *word-combination and formation are beyond our ken. **1932** A. GARDINER *Theory of Speech & Lang.* iii. 158 Syntax..may be defined as the study of the forms both of the sentence itself and of all free word-combinations which enter into it. **1872** LOWELL *Dante* Prose Wks. 1890 IV. 139 The..*word-compelling Dante. **1904** H. BRADLEY *Making Engl.* 127 The copious *word-composition of Greek. **1845** MAURICE *Mor. Philos.* in *Encycl. Metrop.* II. 576/1 These..specimens of Greek subtlety..they would be inclined to denounce..as the exploits of a mere *word-conjuror. **1930** *Proc. Brit. Acad.* XVI. 147 There are prejudices, preferences, analyses, comparisons, statistics, verse-tests, *word-counts, sense of style, poetical feelings, intuitions—but we must not call all this evidence. **1937** PALMER & HORNBY *Thousand-Word Eng.* 11 The compiler has recourse to statistics of word-frequency; he organizes a 'word-count'. **1957** *Eng. Lang. Teaching* (British Council) XII. 1.10 There are valuable word-counts which give a clear picture of the relative importance of specific words in our total lexicon. **1980** *Amer. Speech* 1977 LII. 7 A computerized word count. *a* **900** CYNEWULF *Elene* 592 He is ..*wordcræftes wis. **1804** J. COLLINS *Scripscrap* A3, A Noviciate in the Science of Word-craft. **1894** *Athenæum* 22 Dec. 863/2 The French school of literary critics of life.. have been curious in their wordcraft. **1884** *Amer. Jrnl. Philol.* July 187 That species of *word-creation commonly designated as parasynthetic. **1952** W. D. JACOBS *William Barnes, Linguist* 7 Are there means of word-creation and actual words themselves in the writings of Barnes by which English might well profit? **1898** H. C. BASTIAN *Aphasia* etc. 329 Such individuals though *word-deaf have nevertheless preserved their voluntary speech. **1886** *Buck's Handbk. Med. Sci.* II. 329/1 The so-called *word-deafness, in which the patient hears but does not understand words, though he reads them understandingly and repeats them perfectly. **1593** NASHE *Christ's T.* Wks. (Grosart) IV. 102 Thys huge *word-dearthing taske. **1891** *Tablet* 29 Aug. 331 The science of *word-derivation is a growing one. **1914** L. BLOOMFIELD in *Trans. Amer. Philol. Assoc.* XLV. 66 We have many instances of the writing of uneducated people.. in which the *word-division is entirely wrong. **1929** K. SISAM in *S.P.E. Tract* XXXIII. 441 A respectably printed American book..is not noticeably different in [typographical] word-division from a contemporary English book. **1976** *Classical Q.* XXVI. 95 His word-divisions are probably his own and without any authority. **1912** KIPLING *Diversity of Creatures* (1917) 23 *Word-drunk people. **1964** *Punch* 15 Apr. 575/1 The word-drunk Don Adriano. **1928** O. JESPERSEN *Internat. Lang.* II. 121 In Novial the elements are separate words, in Esp[eranto]—Ido inseparable *word-elements. **1964** C. BARBER *Ling. Change Present-Day Eng.* iv. 78 These [new learned words] are usually formed from Latin or Greek word-elements. **1965** W. S. ALLEN *Vox Latina* i. 35 It [*s*] is not voiced between vowels or at word-end as in English *roses*. **1878** W. BARNES *Outl. Eng. Speechcraft* 83 (*heading*) The power of the *word-endings [*sc.* suffixes]. **1966** J. DERRICK *Teaching English to Immigrants* vi. 210 Meaning is conveyed..with a reduced form of grammar—word-endings are left off, structural words omitted, etc. **1926** FOWLER *Mod. Eng. Usage* 553/2 A phonetically consistent method is in English peculiarly hard to reconcile with the keeping together of *word families. **1978** *Language* LIV. 237/1 Finding translation equivalents and association of morphological word-families. **1862** MERIVALE *Rom. Emp.* lxvi. VII. 456 The vanity and frivolity of these masters of *word-fence. **1952** H. BASILIUS in *Word* VIII. 103 Jost Trier's study of the German *word-fields relating to the concept reason, its powers and qualities. **1965** *Amer. Speech* XL. 62 *Job* is not identical with *Arbeit*; it stands at the lowest level of this word-field. **1918** A. W. ARON in C. Hockett *Leonard Bloomfield Anthol.* (1970) 58 These variations in word-initial [in Irish] do depend on the phonetic character of the original preceding *word-final. **1949** E. A. NIDA *Morphology* (ed. 2) ii. 24 Only the word-final tones are indicated. **1977** G. P. DELAHUNTY in D. Ó Muirithe *Eng. Lang. in Ireland* 132 Devoicing of word-final voiced consonants. **1983** *Word* XXXIV. 149 We find that in modern Swabian they all occur in word-final position. **1965** *Canad. Jrnl. Linguistics* Fall 64 Those [vowel segments] which occur both before consonants and *word-finally. **1978** *Language* LIV. 443 High vowels are dropped after heavy stems word-finally. **1955** R. JAKOBSON in Saporta & Bastian *Psycholinguistics* (1961) 423/2 The more difficulties he has with *word-finding in the proper sense of this neuropsychiatric term; that is, difficulties with spontaneous selection of words. **1681** R. L'ESTRANGE *Tully's Offices* 66 Crassus..was a *word-flowing Speaker. **1897** MARY KINGSLEY *W. Africa* ii. 36 A perfect *word-fog of directions and advice. **1874** H. BENDALL tr. *A. Schleicher's Compar. Gram.* 3 The Semitic, which is not akin to the Indo-European, has more *word-forms. **1952** *Mind* LXI. 239 As society discovers..that judgments imputing responsibility ..are never justified, the word-form 'responsibility' comes to change its meaning. **1967** D. G. HAYS *Introd. Computational Linguistics* ii. 21 The plan is to record, before each word form, the number of cells it occupies. **1856** W. D. WHITNEY in *Jrnl. Amer. Oriental Soc.* V. 197 The work ..exhibits..the phenomena of the agreement and disagreement of the Greek and Sanskrit accentuation, throughout the departments of declension, conjugation and *word-formation. **1884** CUST in *13th Addr. Philol. Soc.* 77 The oldest phase of the Hæmitic Word-formation. **1948** L. SPITZER *Linguistics & Lit. Hist.* ii. 81 Thus Cervantes has expressed his perspectivistic vision in a *word-formational pattern of the Renaissance reserved for hybrids. **1979** *Dictionaries* I. 18 Lexicographers very often assume a kind of word-formational capacity or knowledge when they list derivatives as run-on entries. **1964** *Word-formative [see *word-base* above]. **1928** B. Q. MORGAN *German Frequency Word Bk.* p. ix, It was our original intention to publish the figures for *word frequency, group frequency, and basic frequency. **1951** *Archivum Linguisticum* III. II. 123 (*heading*) Word-frequency in Norwegian. **1974** BEDFORD & DILLIGAN *Concordance Poems Alexander Pope* II. 669/1 A six-page analytic table showing word-frequency distribution and the ratio between each word and the number of its occurrences. **1912** L. BLOOMFIELD in C. Hockett *Leonard Bloomfield Anthol.* (1970) 35 The relation of word-form to *word-function. **1910** R. B. STERN *Neighborhood Entertainments* vi. 263 (*heading*) Some *word games [describes anagrams, logomachy, etc.]. **1922** S. LEWIS *Babbitt* xviii. 227 Word-games in which you were an Adjective or a Quality. **1929** A. C. S. ASHMORE (*title*) Word games and word puzzles. **1934** *Mind* XLIII. 117 Those who are reluctant to regard philosophy as mere mystery-mongering or as an academic word-game. **1953** E. COXHEAD *Midlanders* vi. 143, I never could do word-games or crosswords. **1974** PASSMORE & ROBSON *Compan. Med. Stud.* III. xxxiv. 8/1 Wittgenstein described speech as a 'word game', implying that language follows defined rules similar to those which govern sports. **1975** R. LEWIS *Double Take* iv. 124 We aren't here to play word games... If this is the way you want to conduct the discussion we might as well call it off. **1962** A. MCINTOSH in Davis & Wrenn *Eng. & Medieval Stud.* 240 *Word-geographical criteria..may well therefore turn out to provide the only practicable line of attack. **1921** E. C. ROEDDER in *Jrnl. Eng. & Ger. Philol.* XX. 183 The finding and fixing of the isolectic lines is a task of *word geography. **1949** H. KURATH (*title*) A word geography of the Eastern United States. **1980** *Amer. Speech* LV. 195 Its lexicology is sketched here as a development of conventional word geography. **1884** H. SWEET *ibid.* 90 Concentrating his attention on the mere sounds of his *word-group. **1897** ANWYL *Welsh Gram.* §19 The unit of connected speech is.. the word-group; *e.g.* in English, 'what-do-you-want?' **1876** WHITNEY *Lang. Study* iii. 66 If English stood all alone among the other languages..but an insignificant part of its *word-history could be read. **1869** W. BARNES *Early England & Saxon-English* 130 A Hoard, as herd, is a kind of gathering of any kind of things, as..*Word-hoard—Vocabulary. **1892** BROOKE *E.E. Lit.* I. 1 Widsith told his tale, unlocked his wordhoard. **1961** WEBSTER *Pref.* 6a/1 Books consulted in the Springfield City Library whose librarians have..given the editorial staff..access to its large and valuable word-hoard. **1966** *Listener* 24 Nov. 779/2 Thomas was immensely proud of his bulging word-hoard. **1975** P. FUSSELL *Great War & Mod. Memory* (1977) ii. 49 *Lousy with*, meaning *full of*,.. entered the colloquial word-hoard around 1915. **1876** A. S. PALMER (*title*) Leaves from a *Word-hunter's Note-book. **1753** ARMSTRONG *Taste* 131 Those sacred groves where raptur'd spirits..in *word-hunting waste the live-long day. **1935** A. HUXLEY *Let.* 13 Jan. (1969) 389 Nothing is more inclined to keep me awake than *word-hunting. **1902** E. W. SCRIPTURE *Elem. Exper. Phonetics* x. 150 A *word-idea should be learned as parts of various courses of thought in order to form the necessary language associations. **1922** D. H. LAWRENCE *Aaron's Rod* xiii. 175 Even his deepest ideas were not word-ideas, his very thoughts were not composed of words and ideal concepts. **1899** *Allbutt's Syst. Med.* VII. 399 *Word-images as integral components of percepts and concepts. **1937** M. L. HANLEY (*title*) *Word index to James Joyce's *Ulysses*. *Ibid.* p. iii, In 1931..I had made a word index and partial concordance to the B-Text of *Piers Plowman*. **1960** *Amer. Speech* XXXV. 215 A lamentable deficiency is the lack of a full word index. **1918** *Word-initial [see *word-final* above]. **1926** L. BLOOMFIELD in Saporta & Bastian *Psycholinguistics* (1961) 29/2 English word-initial [st-]. **1949** E. A. NIDA *Morphology* (ed. 2) ii. 16 Word-initial prevowel glottal stops. **1981** *N. & Q.* Oct. 398/1 A large number of unexplained intersubstitutions of *c* and *g* in word-initial position. **1973** A. H. SOMMERSTEIN *Sound Pattern Anc. Gr.* iii. 103 Not all rules with left-hand environments can apply *word-initially. **1964** D. WARD in D. Abercrombie et al. *Daniel Jones* 385 The substitution of corresponding voiceless phonemes for all voiced phonemes except sonants in word-final position and *word-internally before voiceless consonants. **1876** EMERSON *Lett. & Soc. Aims, Poet. & Imag.* Wks. (Bohn) III. 160 Barbaric *word-jingle. **1901** *Month* Jan. 16 The greatest *word-juggler of all time. **1847** LEWES *Hist. Philos.* (1867) I. ii. 14 The *word-jugglery of mysticism. **1855** MILMAN *Lat. Christ.* XIV. iii. (1864) IX. 143 Bewildered by his own skilful *word-juggling. **1876** MRS. WHITNEY *Sights & Insights* xxxiv. 320 Very faith, deeper than mere *word-keeping. **1945** *N. & Q.* 6 Oct. 151/1 In the amusement sections of newspapers it [*sc.* the game or puzzle called 'Doublets'] is usually referred to as '*Word-Ladder'. **1958** *Birmingham Mail* 27 Jan. 6/7 Today's puzzle is for your shortest Word Ladder from *Head* to *Body*. It can be done in five easy steps without using any unusual words. **1982** D. PARLETT *Penguin Bk. Word Games* 98 Word Ladders. **1951** *Proc. IRE* XXXIX. 277/2 Digital computers commonly use a fixed *word length (that is, a fixed number of characters) which is a characteristic of each computer. **1970** O. DOPPING *Computers & Data Processing* vi. 98 The word length is usually chosen in such a way that a numeric operand or result in general can be stored in one memory cell with 'normal' precision. **1960** J. B. CARROLL in Saporta & Bastian *Psycholinguistics* (1961) 338/2 A single word or *word-like utterance. **1866** G. STEPHENS (*title*) The Old Northern Runic Monuments of Scandinavia and England, with Introductions, Appendices, *Word-Lists, Runic Alphabets, &c. **1923** OGDEN & RICHARDS *Meaning of Meaning* ii. 42 The earlier writers are full of the relics of primitive *word-magic. To classify things is to name them .. to know their names is to have power over their souls. **1938** S. CHASE *Tyranny of Words* iv. 37 Here, to follow Malinowski, we note the seeds of word magic, in which *the name gives power over the person or thing it signifies*. **1960** H. READ *Forms of Things Unknown* vii. 121 The name he chooses is magically apt, and in word-magic we must acknowledge the primordial intensive aspect of poetry. **1855** KINGSLEY *Glaucus* 69 What the long-*word-makers call an 'interosculant' group. *a* **1856** J. STODDART *Glossology* (1858) x. 231 *Onomatopoeia*. The literal signification of the term.. is nothing more than '*word-making'. **1867** W. D. WHITNEY *Lang. & Study of Lang.* 116 All word-making by combination..is closely analogous with phrase-making. **1876** GEO. ELIOT *Dan. Der.* lx, The order of word-making. **1935** *Encycl. Sports, Games & Pastimes* 396/1 The games played with these [cardboard] letters are very numerous. *Word making and word taking may be mentioned first. **1952** G. RAVERAT *Period Piece* xii. 243 Our chief intellectual exercise [*c.* 1900] was the Letter Game; Word-making and word-taking. **1980** L. LEWIS *Private Life of Country House* ii. 20 My mother..scattered on the floor the cardboard letter squares from a game called 'Wordmaking and Wordtaking'. **1902** *Encycl. Brit.* XXXIII. 387/1 The registration of '*word marks' was first provided for by the Trade Marks Act, 1883. In that statute, however, clause (d) read 'a fancy word or words not in common use'. **1964** T. W. MCRAE *Impact of Computers on Accounting* i. 11 The programmer then looks at the data..and divides up the storage locations as required by setting a 'wordmark' in the far right-hand position of each variable-length storage word. **1969** P. B. JORDAIN *Condensed Computer Encycl.* 567 Each instruction must begin with a word mark [in a variable word-length computer]. **1976** *Century of Trade Marks* (Patent Office) i. 1/2 These were early instances of word marks, though usually in conventional form—for example, CATIM (Cati manu: from the hand of Cato), and OFALBIN (officina Albini: the workshop of Albinus)—whereas earlier marks had been almost invariably devices or ideographic symbols. **1980** J. FRATES *Introd. Computer* vi. 165 The storage location of the last piece of data will store a word mark in addition to the character to indicate to the computer that it has reached the end of that particular item of data. **1884** H. SWEET in *13th Addr. Philol. Soc.* 89 This.. makes the colloquial language a far better medium of teaching *word-meanings. **1949** E. A. NIDA *Morphology* (ed. 2) 293 (*heading*) Reduction of *word-medial consonant clusters. **1963** J. LYONS *Structural Semantics* iv. 68 There is an opposition.., in word-initial and word-medial position, between the voiced and the voiceless plosives. **1968** *Language* XLIV. 532 A variety of further clusters occurred *word-medially. **1890** W. JAMES *Princ. Psychol.* I. xvi. 684 'Ataxic' and 'amnesic' aphasia, 'word-deafness', and 'associative aphasia' are all practical losses of *word-memory. **1899** *Allbutt's Syst. Med.* VII. 394 Forms of word memory. **1920** *Punch* 7 Jan. 9/2 The *word-merchant [*sc.* a journalist] was laughing at us all the time. **1977** *Grimsby Even. Tel.* 14 May 7/4 He [*sc.* Malcolm Muggeridge] is the best word merchant of our time. [**1879** *First Infant Reader* in *Mod. School Reader Series* p. 2 The experience of many years has convinced us that a judicious combination of the Word and Phonic methods of teaching Children to read is the best.] **1932** in E. Blyton *Mod. Teaching in Infant School* v. 62 The *Word Method, or the Look-and-say Method. **1981** D. ROWNTREE *Dict. Educ.* 350 *Word method*, teaching a pupil to read by getting him to recognize whole words right from the start. **1853** MRS. GORE *Dean's Dau.* xxiv, Do not give Miss Mordaunt reason to suppose me the only *word-mill in the family! **1855** GEO. ELIOT in *Westm. Rev.* Oct. 596 As long as the English language is spoken, the *word-music of Tennyson must charm the ear. **1895** G. B. SHAW *Our Theatres in Nineties* (1932) I. 77 M. Maeterlinck's fragile word-music. **1962** *Observer* 22 Apr. 23/4 The ailing cause of Shakespeare-designed-to-be-read-as-word-music. **1895** 'MARK TWAIN' in *N. Amer. Rev.* July 11 This is [James Fenimore] Cooper. He was not a *word-musician. His ear was satisfied with the *approximate* word. **1892** H. SWEET *New Eng. Gram.* I. §113. 42 We find the same grammatical relation expressed..sometimes by *word-order. **1898** SWEET *New Engl. Gram.* II. §1772 The original Arian word-order. **1958** *Aspects of Translation* 35 Inflexions and grammar impose a more rigorous word-order on the French language than on English. **1965** O. FUNKE in *English Studies* Feb. 58 The transition from paradigmatic to syntagmatic (prepositional or word-order) expression. **1973** *Archivum Linguisticum* IV. 28 The comparative fixity of word-order relative to grammatical function is the conditional par excellence for the supposed superfluity of gender distinctions. **1894** DYAN *Man's Keeping* vi, His mother ..*word-painted a picture to him. **1906** G. A. B. DEWAR *Faery Year* 57 We can no more word-paint the water than we can the sunbeam. **1870** J. G. WHITTIER in *Atlantic* Apr. 467 Not by the page *word-painted Let life be banned or sainted. **1937** 'C. CAUDWELL' *Illusion & Reality* v. 100 The word-painted lands of the nightingale, of the Grecian urn, of Baiae's isle. **1861** *Bentley's Misc.* XLIX. 169 Owen Meredith is another *word-painter, even luxuriant in power. **1866** (*title*) *Word Paintings: in Series. **1892** J. TAIT *Mind in Matter* (ed. 3) 296 Like a poem, a parable is a word-painting. **1882** *Archaeologia Cantiana* XIV. 3 The descriptive power of a *word-painting historian. **1936** G. K. ZIPF *Psycho-Biol. of Lang.* iv. 134 *Word-pairs like *submit* and *remit*, or *accuse* and *excuse*. **1964** J. VACHEK in D. Abercrombie et al. *Daniel Jones* 194 The ModE word-pair *longer* [lɒŋgə] (comparative of *long*): *longer* [lɒŋə] (the noun of agent derived from the verb *to long*). **1948** J. R. FIRTH *Papers in Linguistics 1934–51* (1957) xi. 150 Palatograms here presented..are *word-palatograms*. That is to say, they are used for the abstraction of articulatory contact and possibly also of movement from suitably selected words taken as whole utterances. **1957** Word-palatogram [see KYMOGRAPHY]. **1694** PEPYS *Let.* in *Academy* (1890) 9 Aug. 110/1 Your Specimen of Musick-Characters..must appeare Gracefull, when yᵉ *Word-Part shall bee added. **1912** M. BEERBOHM *Christmas Garland* 66 Intensive vision has this Mr. Hardy, With a dark skill in weaving *word-patterns. **1938** L. MACNEICE *Mod. Poetry* ii. 40 The normal business of poetry is the conveying of information through certain kinds of word-patterns. **1957** C. E. BAZELL in *Miscelanea Homenaje a André Martinet* I. 27 Some languages confer word-status by integrating a unit into the particular word-pattern. **1951** R. FIRTH *Elem. Social Organiz.* vii. 221 It does this..by response to the aesthetic qualities of the *word-patterning and imagery used. **1673** Marvell *Reh. Transp.* II. 255 You are..a meer *Word-pecker. *a* **1700** B. E. *Dict. Cant. Crew*, *Word-pecker*, one that play's with Words. **1894** 'J. S. Winter' *Red Coats* 104 [He] had gone over, with care and loving attention, every little trifling detail of this interview, until he might fairly have been described as '*word-perfect.' **1851** J. Brown *Let.* 23 June (1912) 119, I wish you would paint some *word pictures, some studies from Nature as you take your drives. **1858–61** J. Brown *Horæ Subs.* (1863) 284 Such word-pictures as you find in Dante. **1603** Dekker *Wonderful Year* To Rdr., Banish these *Word-pirates, (you sacred mistresses of learning) into the gulfe of Barbarisme. **1642** Fuller *Holy & Prof. St.* I. iii. 8 Not so much *word-pitying her, as providing necessaries for her. **1855** H. Martineau *Autobiogr.* (1877) I. 397 An opportunity..for paradox, and *word-play. **1896** J. Rendel Harris *Hermas in Arcadia* 74 To determine what the word-play consists in. **1911** H. M. R. Murray *Erthe upon Erthe* Introd. p. xxix, Word-plays of the kind..are..not common in Latin verse of the time. **1962** W. Nowottny *Lang. Poets Use* v. 99 The next [chapter] will discuss some aspects of conspicuous word-play—or, to use a more convenient term—of 'verbal schemes'. **1967** *Sci. Amer.* Sept. 268/1 The double acrostic..was..the most popular form of word-play in English-speaking countries throughout the last quarter of the 19th century and until the end of World War I. **1967** C. L. Wrenn *Word & Symbol* 13 The medieval love of riddling and word-play was occasionally displayed by Anglo-Saxon versifiers. **1982** I. Hamilton *Robert Lowell* (1983) ii. 18 Argument pursued for the sake of wit and wordplay rather than for any just or true solution. **1894** O. Jespersen *Progress in Lang.* iv. 99 Is it beneficial to a language to have a free *word-position? **1961** *Brno Studies* III. 46 The number of word-positions in which the correlation could be utilized. **1657** J. Watts *Scribe, Pharisee*, etc. I. 123 You cannot bring us of, from the *word-preaching. **1947** *Jrnl. Symbolic Logic* XII. 90 The *word problem for semigroups. **1972** M. Kline *Math. Thought* xlix. 1143 For one defining relation Wilhelm Magnus (1907–) showed that the word problem is solvable. but the general problem is not. **1984** *Which Micro* Dec. 73 (Advt.), For *word processing letters in professional type. **1985** *Daily Tel.* 10 June 11/1 To a newspaper reporter, the ability to wordprocess stories on aircraft and in hotel bedrooms must truly be a boon. **1984** *N. & Q.* Dec. 552/1 This text (excepting the chapter-notes and bibliographies) reproduces a *word-processed typescript. **1970** *Administrative Management* Nov. 36/3 '*Word processing', a concept that combines the dictating and typing functions into a centralized system. **1977** *Times* 12 Sept. 5 Word processing can already be seen to be at the forefront of the next revolution in the office... The keyboard of the word-processing typewriter..is standard but typing on it produces not only a paper copy but also a magnetic recording which can be automatically searched and edited. **1970** *Administrative Management* Nov. 37/1 In 1970..ITEL..introduced its '*Word Processor'. **1974** *Ibid.* Mar. 48/2 The multi-functional word processor can handle a whole range of text manipulations. **1977** *N.Y. Times* 1 Jan. 22 Word processors call up documents, page by page and line by line, on cathode ray screens for editing. They print out finished versions automatically or send them via telephone lines to distant points. **1979** *Daily Tel.* 24 Dec. 16/3 Word-processors show their greatest strengths when they are used to produce long reports which need to be constantly altered and with any typing which must be word perfect. **1981** *Times Lit. Suppl.* 22 May 588 (Advt.), Manuscripts typed, edited, corrected and indexed by word processor. **1984** D. Lodge *Small World* II. ii. 121 A roomful of secretaries..would wait patiently beside their word-processors, ready to type..his latest reflections. **1928** *Funk's New Stand. Dict.*, *Word recognition. **1956** T. W. Clymer in R. H. Beck *Three R's Plus* 139 Word-recognition skills have been mentioned... Context clues are the quickest and easiest of the word-recognition techniques. **1978** J. Baron in W. K. Estes *Handbk. Learning & Cognitive Processes* VI. iv. 159 Let us assume that one mechanism of word recognition in reading involves activation of a semantic code directly from a letter or spelling-pattern code. **1915** *Stedman's Med. Dict.* (ed. 3) 1034/2 **Word-salad*, a term applied by Forel to the jumble of meaningless words uttered by a patient suffering from catatonia. **1930** L. E. Hinsie *Schizophrenia* ii. 28 The symptomatology is ordinarily not at all bizarre; there is not the scattering of thought, nor the 'word-salad'. **1960** R. D. Laing *Divided Self* xi. 215 Her 'word-salad' seemed to be the result of a number of quasi-autonomous partial systems striving to give expression to themselves out of the same mouth at the same time. **1976** N. Postman *Crazy Talk* 228 The exorbitant fee one must pay..is made to seem plausible by a word salad of imposing proportions. **1736** *Gentl. Mag.* VI. 353/2 Dame Law.. call'd over her *Word-selling Crew. **1960** *Times* 18 Jan. 3/1 And so many composers have turned gratefully to *word-setting. **1985** *Times* 13 June 13/8 Why is word-setting generally so difficult for English composers? **1900** *Jrnl. Anthrop. Inst.* XXX. 156 As regards *word-signs, in general the connection of the meaning of the word with the picture is obvious enough once it is pointed out. *Ibid.*, The connecting link between the picture and its word-sign value. **1908** G. K. Chesterton *Man who was Thursday* ix. 165 It did not take him long to learn how he might convey simple messages by what would seem to be idle taps upon a table or knee... 'We must have several word-signs,..words that we are likely to want.' **1941** *Language* XVII. 149 In my opinion, *ideogram* and *word-sign* are not interchangeable terms, either in Egyptian or English. **1964** P. A. D. MacCarthy in D. Abercrombie et al. *Daniel Jones* 162 Four uniliteral 'word-signs' for *the*, *of*, *and*, *to*, are standard. **1872** *Yng. Gentleman's Mag.* 212 Little *word-sketches of those absurd scenes. **1896** *Literary World* 19 June 571/2 Stevenson, the soaring child of genius and the plodding *word-smith. **1961** *Observer* 23 July 19/3 Gunther has lost none of his old skill as a wordsmith: the adjectives come pouring out in a torrent of enthusiasm, bristling with brackets, dashes, afterthoughts, and statistics. **1968** *Daily Tel.* 7 Nov. 23/1 We already know John Updike as a resourceful wordsmith, a fine writer. **1976** *Bookseller* 4 Sept. 1645/1 That ubiquitous wordsmith A. J. P. Taylor. **1958** *Wordsmithing [see *copy-writing* vbl. sb. s.v. copy *sb.* C]. **1981** *Maledicta* V. 346 Enjoys word-smithing, learning languages, and the study of names. **1925** I. A. Richards *Princ. Lit. Criticism* xvi. 119 Many people are able to imagine *word-sounds with greater delicacy..than they can utter them. **1951** N. M. Gunn *Well at World's End* xxx. 295 She was making word-sounds, lapping him about. **1582** N. T. (Rhem.) *Acts* xvii. 18 What is it that this *wordsower would say? **1887** W. Morris in Mackail *Life* (1899) II. 187, I am an inveterate *word-spinner. **1872** Spurgeon *Treas. Dav.* III. Pref. p. v, Huge folios, full of dreary *wordspinning. **1857** Sir F. Palgrave *Norm. & Eng.* II. 561 A silly, yet ferocious, *wordspite quarrel between Otho and Hugh-le-Grand. **1861** J. Tulloch *Engl. Purit.* iv. 436 He had too large a soul to take delight in mere *word-splitting. **1890** *Little Folks* Jan. 68 Geographical *Word Square. *c* **1400** *Rom. Rose* 5451 They maken foolis glorifie Of her *wordis spekyng. *c* **1440** *Alphabet of Tales* 511 Þerfor is it not gretelie to charge of wurdis-spekyng and a man do wele. **1937** A. H. Gardiner in *Mélanges Ling. et Phil. offerts à J. van Ginneken* 310 It seems necessary, as between the different classes [of proper names], to assign independent *word-status further only to classes II and V. **1982** *Papers Dict. Soc. N. Amer. 1977* 67 In such cases the problem of word-status is involved. **1948** L. Spitzer *Linguistics & Lit. Hist.* i. 7 This French word-family..was a blend of at least two *word-stems. **1962** W. Nowottny *Lang. Poets Use* v. 100 Syntactical patterns and individual words (or word-stems). **1911** L. Bloomfield in C. Hockett *Bloomfield Anthol.* (1970) 29 The farther back we look into the history of any IE. language, the more diversified and concrete a *word stock do we find. **1926** Friedrichsen *Gothic Vers. Gosp.* 23 By skilfully grafting the vigorous scions of his own speech on to the exotic word-stock. **1940** J. H. Jagger *Eng. in Future* i. 25 About two per cent. of the word-stock consists of words of this sort [*sc.* slang words that have entered Standard English] made since the Norman conquest. **1973** *Computers & Humanities* VII. 195 Normal discourse draws upon a word-stock which in any theorizing must be treated as infinite. **1863** W. Barnes *Gram. & Gloss. Dorset Dial.* 9 In searching the *word-stores of the provincial speech-forms of English, we cannot but behold what a wealth of stems we have overlooked at home. **1971** J. Z. Young *Introd. Study Man* xxxv. 489 [The region behind the superior temporal gyrus] has also been called 'the area of ideational speech' or indeed 'word store'. **1924** H. E. Palmer *Gram. Spoken Eng.* I. 6 **Word-stress.* (In the opinion of the author the term *syllable-stress* would be more appropriate.) This term is used with reference to a syllable (in a word of more than one syllable) which is susceptible of receiving one of the four nucleus-tones. **1953** C. E. Bazell *Linguistic Form* viii. 100 Word-stress is therefore highly marginal in language. **1966** J. Derrick *Teaching Eng. to Immigrants* iii. 111 This distribution of stress in the individual word, 'word stress' as it is called, is a basic difficulty for the foreign learner. *a* **1670** Hacket *Abp. Williams* II. (1693) 107 The end of this λογομαχία, or *Word-strife. **1850** T. A. Trollope *Impress. Wand.* iv. 56 The emasculated tribe of *word stringers. **1622** Mabbe tr. *Aleman's Guzman d'Alf.* I. 263 Whilest he was hearing this sad storie..being so *word-strooken to the heart. **1951** *Essays & Studies* IV. 123 Alliteration, assonance..can be considered as markers or signals of *word-structure or of the word-process in the sentence. **1975** *Language for Life* (Dept. Educ. & Sci.) xi. 183 Their attention should constantly be drawn to details of word structure. **1940** *Amer. Speech* XV. 183 Mrs. Ernst presents for her pupils..the essentials of *word-study. **1979** *N. & Q.* June 245/2 The author of a word-study. **1904** *Word-symbol [see *ideogenetic* a. s.v. ideo-]. **1933** L. Bloomfield *Language* xvii. 287 In the writings of other languages, where words are of various lengths, we find word-symbols used for phonetically similar parts of longer words. **1955** G. A. Kelly *Psychol. Personal Constructs* 459 A pre-verbal construct is one which continues to be used even though it has no consistent word symbol. **1923** Ogden & Richards *Meaning of Meaning* ii. 37 In Fraser's *Golden Bough* numerous examples of *word taboos are collected. **1978** *Language* LIV. 217 The importance of word taboo on the basis of more recent linguistic-anthropological work. **1954** *Computers & Automation* May 22/1 *Word time. **1969** P. B. Jordain *Condensed Computer Encycl.* 567 All activities must be calculated in multiples or submultiples of word time or cycle time. **1894** O. Jespersen *Progress in Lang.* ix. 340 So much for *word-tones; now for the sentence melody. **1928** *Proc. Brit. Acad.* XIV. 354 The four word-tones used in the Mandarin language of Peking to keep otherwise identical words apart. **1964** *Archivum Linguisticum* XVI. 81 He gives some interesting examples of how word-tones and sentence intonation may combine. **1610** Holland *Camden's Brit.* I. 307 With a wily *word-trap, hee deceiued the Archbishop. **1820** T. Mitchell *Com. Aristoph.* I. 92 With silent glee his word-traps he lays deftly. **1920** D. H. Lawrence *Women in Love* xxiii. 339, I know your dodges. I am not taken in by your *word-twisting. **1959** I. & P. Opie *Lore & Lang. Schoolch.* xiv. 320 By using slang, local dialect,..word-twistings, codes and sign language, children communicate with each other in ways which outsiders are unable to understand. **1911** S. S. Colvin *Learning Process* (1931) vii. 108 The *word-types of images, as can be readily seen, are symbolic; they stand for concrete realities, which, however, generally are not revived in connection with the symbol. **1936** *Jrnl. Philos.* 17 Dec. 702 Let us call a 'word-type' a class or kind of defining character of a class of tokens which are similar to one another in certain essential aspects. **1961** *Brno Studies* III. 33 Mathesius laid special stress on the part played in English complex condensation cases by three types of nominal forms derived from verbal bases... The word-types will be referred to as..condensers. **1976** *Biometrika* LXIII. 435 How many word types did Shakespeare actually know? **1924** R. M. Ogden tr. *K. Koffka's Growth of Mind* v. 270 A difference in the serial order of the correct *word-usage must then depend..upon a difference in the colour-phenomenon itself. **1971** *Jrnl. Gen. Psychol.* Apr. 188 Creativity and originality were not measured by any of the three types of word-usage. **1932** Faucett & Maki (*title*) Study of English *word-values. *Ibid.* 8 This book will..be useful to those interested..in fixing a graded vocabulary scale for supplementary readers, ..in helping teachers and students to develop a sense of word-values [etc.]. **1938** I. Goldberg *Wonder of Words* xx. 438 For & has the phonetic value of *et*, but it has the word-value of *and*. **1899** *Allbutt's Syst. Med.* VII. 313 Visual ideation, more particularly in reference to the association of written symbols with their meaning—that is, *word-vision —is specially impaired by lesion of the left angular gyrus. **1647** Trapp *Comm. Jas.* ii. 14 (1656) 906 Livy telleth us of the Athenians, that they waged *Word-war against Philip. **1862** Merivale *Rom. Emp.* lxvi. VII. 460 The word-war of the dogmatists. **1856** R. A. Vaughan *Mystics* (1860) I. 123 He regarded with dislike the idle *word-warfare of scholastic ingenuity. **1600** Nashe *Summers Last Will* 1447 Those *word-warriers..Had their heads fild with coosning fantasies. **1866** Liddon *Bampton Lect.* i. (1867) 17 Professional word-warriors of the fourth and fifth centuries. **1968** *Listener* 25 Apr. 525/1 What happens if in turn we *word-watch on Mr. Davie? Could it be that to use the word 'histrionic' ten times in one short article is itself somewhat histrionic? **1973** *N.Y. Times* 7 May 39/1 *Word watchers introduce a note of good sense..to the action and passion of their times. **1980** *Amer. Speech* LV. 77, *-gate* has undergone some developments that should interest word-watchers. **1981** *Verbatim* VII. III. 20/2 Collectors are needed to find quotations for a new dictionary of American slang... The chief motivation for volunteering should be interest in specialized *word-watching. *a* **1555** Ridley *Cert. Godly Confer.* (1556) 34 b, Truste not..to these *worde weapons, for the kingdome of godde is not in wordes, but in power. **1849** Lytton *Caxtons* VIII. iii. (1874) 199 Trevanion was a terrible *word-weigher. *a* **1250** *Prov. Alfred* 281 in *O.E. Misc.* 118 Wymmon is *word-woþ [*v.r.* word-wod]. **1902** F. E. Hulme *Proverb-Lore* 114 Sword-wounds may be healed, *word-wounds are beyond healing. **1810** Crabbe *Borough* iv. 523 When the preacher..Dropp'd the new word,..we heard the cry Of the *word-wounded. **1643** Herle *Answ. Ferne* 11 Indisposed to this kind of *word wrangle. **1914** D. Crawford *Thirsting After God* III. i. 152 Mere windy *word-wrangling. **1977** *IEEE Trans. Professional Communication* June 14/2 One very useful feature..is called *word wrap. **1982** A. J. Meadows et al. *Dict. New Information Technol.* 193/1 *Word-wrap*, a word processing term. It refers to the way in which a partially typed word is moved to a new line if its length proves too much to fit into the existing line. **1983** *Austral. Personal Computer* Sept. 124/2 Automatic wordwrap operates at the end of a screen line (40 chars). **1984** *Computing Today* May 93 (*heading*) *Word-wrapping. **1985** *Listener* 25 Apr. 38/1 Word-wrapping, that puts in the ends of lines automatically on reaching the right-hand side of the screen, was another counter-creative feature. **1571** Golding *Calvin on Ps.* xii. 3 This dubblehartednesse..maketh men dubble-tunged & *woordwresters. **1933** L. Bloomfield *Language* xvii. 285 A better name [for ideographic writing]..would be *word-writing or logographic writing. **1942** —— in C. Hockett *Bloomfield Anthol.* (1970) 385 In word writing each word is represented by a conventional sign... Chinese writing is the most perfect system of this kind.

word (wɜːd), *v.* [f. word *sb.*; cf. OHG. *wortôn* in *spilewortôn* to jest, MHG. *worten* to converse, discourse, ON. *orða* to talk, Goth. *-waurdjan* to speak).]

1. a. *intr.* To utter words; to speak, talk, *Obs.* or *arch.*

c **1205** Lay. 18052 Þe king wordede þus. **1393** Langl. *P. Pl.* C. xiv. 246 Whi ȝe worden to me þus was for ich aresonede reson. ? *a* **1400** *Morte Arth.* 3393 And now wate thow my woo, worde as the lykes. *c* **1400** *Beryn* 3261 Al be that Geffrey wordit sotilly, The Steward & þe burgeysis held it for foly, Al that evir he seyd. **1690** C. Nesse *O. & N. Test.* I. 131 The judge..will not ask men..how they have worded, but how they have walked. **1819** Keats *Hyperion* II. 251 Thus wording timidly among the fierce. **1850** [see wording *vbl. sb.* 1].

b. *to word it*: to talk, esp. excessively or violently; to have (high) words *with*. *Obs.* or *dial.*

1612 Webster *White Devil* II. i. C 3 b, My Lords, you shall not word it any further Without a milder limit. **1613** Day *Dyall* vi. (1614) 102, I will not stand wording it with our Adversaries. **1643** Trapp *Comm. Gen.* xi. 7 Thus God words it with them. **1647** —— *Comm. Jas.* iii. 13 (1656) 909 [*Who is a Wise man.*] Not he that words it most; for *multiloquio stultiloquium*. **1692** L'Estrange *Fables* ccccxxiii. 399 He that..contemns a Shrew to the Degree of not Descending to Word it with her. *a* **1716** South *Serm.* (1744) X. 148 Men may snarl, and word it high against providence. *a* **1825** Forby *Voc. E. Anglia*, *Word*, to dispute; to wrangle. Ex. 'They *worded* it a long while'.

2. *trans.* To utter in words, say, speak (occas. as distinct from singing); †also, to speak of, mention. *Obs.* or *arch.*

13.. *E.E. Allit. P.* C. 421 When I hade worded quatsoeuer I cowþe, To manace alle þise mody men. **1606** Shaks. *Ant. Cl.* IV. xiii. 9 Say, that the last I spoke was Anthony, And word it (prythee) pitteously. **1611** —— *Cymb.* IV. ii. 240, I cannot sing: Ile weepe, and word it with thee. **1663** Waterhouse *Fortescutus Illustratus* 424 This way of Government being..changed,..it was made capitall (not onely to endeavour, but even to word the restitution thereof). **1849** [see wording *vbl. sb.* 1].

†3. a. To ply or urge with words. *Obs. rare.*

1606 Shaks. *Ant. & Cl.* V. ii. 191 He words me Gyrles, he words me, That I should not be Noble to my selfe.

†b. To bring by the use of words (into or out of a specified condition or course of action). *Obs.*

c **1645** Howell *Lett.* (1650) II. xix. 32 To have to doe with perverse irrationall half-witted men, and to be worded to death with nonsence. **1692** South *Serm.* I. Ep. Ded. A 3 b, Men are not to be Worded into new Tempers, or Constitutions. *a* **1716** *Ibid.*, *1 Peter ii. 23* (1744) VIII. 187 Not..to word away our souls, or declaim ourselves into perdition.

4. a. To express in or put into words; to compose, draw up. *Obs.* exc. as in b.

1613 (*title*) Songs of Mourning... Worded by Tho. Campion. And set forth to bee sung with one voyce to the Lute, or Violl: by John Coprario. **1623** Lisle *Ælfric on O. & N. Test.* To Rdr. 32 It would giue vs occasion either in wording or sentensing the principall parts thereof to looke back a little into this outworne dialect. **1654** Whitlock *Zootomia* 210 Before the first Logician ever worded a Proposition. **1658–9** *Burton's Diary* (1828) IV. 225, I would have the question worded, before you rise, lest to-morrow be spent in it. *a* **1700** Ken *Hymnotheo* Poet. Wks. 1721 III. 282 Love dictated, Love worded ev'ry Line. **1806** W. Taylor in *Ann. Rev.* IV. 604 Spreading languages..have flourished and have faded, without wording one eminent narrative poem. **1831** GEN. P. THOMPSON *Exerc.* (1842) I. 456 This statement of limits is found worded over again in the Protocol.

b. esp., and now only, with reference to the kind of language or form of words used; hence freq. with advb. qualification.

1619 MIDDLETON *Love & Antiq.* Wks. (Bullen) VII. 315 Triumphs, wherein Art hath been but weakly imitated and most beggarly worded. **1671** BAXTER *Holiness* lxiv. 18 They have not the skil to word and methodize their notions rightly. **1701** J. NORRIS *Ideal World* I. ii. 126 'Tis in reality one and the same question, only differently worded. **1713** POPE *Let. to Addison* 14 Dec., This little instant of our life, which (as Shakespear finely words it) is rounded with a sleep. **1836** THIRLWALL *Greece* xx. III. 153 Instructions angrily worded. **1883** MISS BROUGHTON *Belinda* I. viii, It is coarsely worded, I admit,.. but, believe me, the advice is sound. **1908** R. BAGOT *A. Cuthbert* xxii. 267 She kept repeating to herself various ways of wording her message; for it was.. no easy one to construct.

c. *nonce-uses.* To represent as in words; to pad *out* with (unnecessary) words.

1611 SHAKS. *Cymb.* I. iv. 16 This matter of marrying his Kings Daughter.. words him (I doubt not) a great deale from the matter. **1646** T. COLEMAN *Brotherly Exam. Re-ex.* Postscript 22 Pamphlets.. wherein six pages.. are worded out to thirty six.

d. *intr.* for *pass.* To admit translation into words. *poet.*⁻¹ (after WEAR *v.*[1] 15).

1935 L. MACNEICE *Poems* 26 My dream will word well —But will not wear well.

5. To speak to, accost; to tell, pass word to. Also to rebuke or tell off. *Austral. slang.*

1906 E. DYSON *Fact'ry 'Ands* i. 2 I'll word 'em [girls] when they pass again. **1916** C. J. DENNIS *Songs Sentimental Bloke* 50 I met 'im on the quite, An' worded 'im about a small affair. **1936** N. MARSH *Death in Ecstasy* vi. 79 He looks more like a regular dick. An' yet if I worded him maybe he'd talk back like a bud's guide to society stuff. **1945** BAKER *Austral. Lang.* vi. 121 He.. *words* him, rebukes him. **1967** K. S. PRITCHARD *Subtle Flame* 234 Ted worded a mate of his on the *Western Star.*

word, obs. (erron.) form of WEIRD *sb.*

14.. *Guy Warw.* (Camb.) 1155, 7416.

word: see ORD, WORLD, WORTH *v.*

wordage ('wɜːdɪdʒ). [f. WORD *sb.* + -AGE.] Words collectively; = VERBIAGE 1. In recent use also, an amount of words written or spoken; the number of words in a document.

1829 *Westm. Rev.* Apr. 417 The plates are.. sufficient without all the wordage. **1858** ARNOT *Laws from Heaven Ser.* II. 22 [The tongue] may revolve with the rapidity.. of.. machinery, throwing off.. a continuous web of wordage. **1926** *Glasgow Herald* 19 May 7/2 Managers of the great news agencies.. have never placed upon the cables so large a wordage concerning any British domestic event. **1958** *Times* 26 Aug. 5/7 Telegrams will carry a fixed charge irrespective of wordage. **1966** *Punch* 21 Sept. 455/2 Obviously he took his correspondence as seriously as he took his Journals and his daily wordage of publishable prose. **1975** G. HOWELL *In Vogue* 64/1 [Tallulah Bankhead] spoke seventy thousand words a day—the wordage of *War and Peace* over a weekend. **1985** *Univ. Cape Town Studies in English* Feb. 61 Scientists and scholars who have published in abundance are actively solicited by editors, bookmen, and publishers for still more wordage to be put into print.

word-book ('wɜːdbʊk). [f. WORD *sb.* + BOOK *sb.*; in sense 1 cf. G. *wörterbuch* (f. gen. pl. of *wort* word + *buch* book), Du. †*woordboek*, *woordenboek*, Icel. *orðabók*, Sw. *ordbok*, Da. *ordbog*.]

1. A book containing a list of words (as of the vocabulary of a language, a book, an art, or science) arranged in alphabetical or other systematic order.

The term is often used where it is desired to avoid the implication of completeness or elaboration of treatment characteristic of a dictionary or lexicon.

1598 FLORIO *Ital. Dict.* To Rdr. b 1, If no other bookes can be so well perfected, but still some thing may be added, how much lesse a Word-booke? **1730** BAILEY (fol.), *Vocabulary*, a Word-Book, a little Dictionary containing a Collection of Words. **1791** BOSWELL *Johnson* an. 1755 (1904) I. 197 Johnson's Dictionary.. a work of much greater mental labour than mere Lexicons, or Word-books, as the Dutch call them. **1867** SMYTH (*title*) The Sailor's Word-book: an Alphabetical Digest of Nautical Terms. **1879** MISS JACKSON (*title*) Shropshire Word-Book: a Glossary of Archaic and Provincial Words, etc. used in the County. **1882** (*title*) A Word-Book for Students of English History.

2. The 'book of the words' or libretto of a musical composition.

1878 J. MARSHALL in Grove *Dict. Mus.* I. 353 Besides translating many foreign libretti, [H. F. Chorley] wrote the original word-books of one version of the 'Amber Witch' (Wallace),.. of the 'May Queen' (Bennett), [etc.]. **1891** *Guardian* 23 Sept. 1531 Mr. Culwick's interesting summary of the word-book and its annotations.

worde: see ORD, WORD, WORLD, WORTH *v.*

worded ('wɜːdɪd), *ppl. a.* [f. WORD *sb.* or *v.* + -ED.]

1. Formed into words; expressed in or put into words. *rare.*

1606 CHAPMAN *Gentl. Usher* IV. i. 69 Away with this vnmedicinable balme Of worded breath. **1869** RUSKIN *Q. of Air* i. §42 Capable of interpretation only by the majesty of ordered, beautiful, and worded sound. **1880** 'MARK TWAIN' *Tramp Abr.* l. 516 No worded description of a moving spectacle is a hundredth part as moving as the same spectacle seen with one's own eyes.

b. Qualified by an adv.: Expressed in a particular kind of language or form or words; phrased in such-and-such a manner.

1848 W. K. KELLY tr. *L. Blanc's Hist. Ten Y.* II. 210 A cautiously worded, but firm answer. **1871** MISS BRADDON *Lovels* i, Every occasion brought.. the same coldly worded letter. **1899** MACKAIL *W. Morris* II. 270 His latest and most carefully-worded confession of faith.

2. Full of words: **a.** involving the use of many words, wordy; **b.** having a good stock of words at command. *nonce-uses.*

1638 WILKINS *New World* vi. 81 He was much opposed by Aristotle in some worded disputations, but never confuted by any solid reason. **1734** J. RICHARDSON *Milton's P.L.* p. lxxxiii, A Man of Learning indeed, and a Great Etymologist, but a Meer Scholar... Morus was also a Worded Man; and he was a Celebrated Preacher.

wordel, wordely, obs. ff. WORLD, WORLDLY.

worder ('wɜːdə(r)). *rare.* [f. WORD *v.* + -ER[1].]

†**a.** One who uses (many) words; a chatterer, prater. *Obs.* **b.** One who puts something into words; one who frames the words or terms of a subject.

1606 J. CARPENTER *Solomon's Solace* i. 3 They were neither worders, or giuen to high laughter. **1654** WHITLOCK *Zootomia* 206 Each good Action speaking more effectually.. Conviction to Spectators, than any (though the subtlest worder) could ever arrive to. *Ibid.* 359 It were to be wished, we cold not say as much of our high worders, of their Covetousnesse. **1683** E. HOOKER *Pref. Pordage's Mystic Div.* 36 Other worders as there are too mani, not to conceal som of our impertinently idl Pulpit-praters [etc.]. **1887** KNOLLYS *Sk. Life Japan* 267 The.. details belong to the worders of science.

wordeyn, obs. form of ORDAIN.

wordie, var. WORDY *sb. Sc.*; obs. f. WORDY *a.*, WORTHY.

wordily ('wɜːdɪlɪ), *adv.* [f. WORDY *a.* + -LY[2].] In a wordy manner or style; with excess or abundance of words; verbosely.

1522 *World & Child* 277 The kynge of Wrathe full wordely.. wyll me mayntayne. **1609** J. DAVIES (Heref.) *Hum. Heav. on Earth* II. lxviii, Some wordy-men.. raught at Rethorikes Rules to rule thereby:.. they rul'd wordily. **1702** CALAMY *Life R. Baxter* x. 564 This Article of the Controversie hath been manag'd very Wordily. **1873** SYMONDS *Grk. Poets* i. 32 Sophists and rhetoricians begin to flourish and everything that can be wordily elaborated, is grist for their mill. **1891** SMILES *Mem. J. Murray* I. ix. 198 Southey wrote so smoothly, so easily, so wordily.

wordine, obs. Sc. pa. pple. of WORTH *v.*

wordiness ('wɜːdɪnɪs). [f. as prec. + -NESS.] The quality of being wordy; excess or multiplicity of words; verbosity.

1727 BAILEY (vol. II), *Wordiness*,.. Talkativeness, &c. **1809** W. IRVING *Knickerb.* VII. xiii. 112 The empty wordiness of his factious subjects—their intemperate harangues. **1862** J. ANGUS *Handbk. Engl. Tongue* 373 A copious phraseology is one cure of wordiness, and is essential to effective writing.

wording ('wɜːdɪŋ), *vbl. sb.* [f. WORD *v.* (or *sb.*) + -ING[1].]

1. Speaking, talking, utterance. *Obs.* or *arch.*

1604 DEKKER *Honest Wh.* Wks. 1873 II. 62 The Senate will leave wording presently. **1625** MASSINGER *New Way* III. ii, *Marrall.* Pray you a word Sir. *Greed.* No wording now. **1819** KEATS *Otho* II. i, Fine wording, Duke! but words could never yet Forestall the fates. **1849** SEARS *Regenerations* III. i. (1859) 126 The wording and rewording of liturgies is not prayer. **1850** BUSHNELL *God in Christ* 159 They must have their reality to me in what they express when taken as the wording forth of God.

attrib. **1860** SWINBURNE *Queen-Mother* I. ii, All this wording-time I am not perfect where this wrong began.

†**b.** A saying, statement. *Obs. rare.*

1606 WARNER *Alb. Eng.* XIV. lxxxiii. 348 Old Wordings.. prouing trew.

†**2.** Angry or abusive speech; 'having words' (see WORD *sb.* 5). *Obs.*

1564 *Child-Marriages* 129 In wordinge betwixe the mother of the said Isabell & the said Rafe, the said Rafe said to her, that 'her doughter Isabell was a hoore and a thief'. **1594** O. B. *Quest. Profit. Concern.* 13 She termeth.. his outfacing & wording at me, audacitie and manly boldnesse. **1614** PURCHAS *Pilgrimage* VIII. viii. (ed. 2) 780 They are great gamsters, their play like that of Dice: in which they carrie themselues very patiently without swearing or wording.

3. The action of putting or condition of being put into words; composition or expression in language (spoken or written), esp. in reference to the words used; mode of speech, form of words, phrasing.

1649 MILTON *Eikon.* iv. 36 Tis beleev'd this wording was above his known stile and Orthographie. **1654** WHITLOCK *Zootomia* 364 If constancy may be tainted with this selfishnesse (to use our new Wordings of old and general Actings). **1657** HEYLIN *Ecclesia Vind.* Pref. c 1 b, The Directory which prescribes.. the sense and scope.. of the Prayers and other parts of publick Worship, doth in effect leave nothing to the Ministers spirit but the wording of it. **1687** LD. SUNDERLAND in *Magd. Coll.* (O.H.S.) 169 His Majesty leaves the wording of it to you. **1718** BREVAL *Play is the Plot* II. i. 18 Take me Pen, Ink, and Paper, and write him a Letter of my Wording. **1765** BLACKSTONE *Comm.* I. Introd. 7 Some forms necessary in the wording of last wills and testaments. *Ibid.* vi. 228 This is the form of the coronation oath, as it is now prescribed..: but the wording of it was changed at the revolution, because.. the oath itself had been framed in doubtful words and expressions. **1818** KEATS *Endym.* IV. 962 Things for which no wording can be found. **1837** DICKENS *Pickw.* xxxiv, I entreat the attention of the jury to the wording of this document. **1839** HALLAM *Lit. Eur.* IV. vii. §43 His plain and manly sentences often give us pleasure by the wording alone. **1865** M. ARNOLD *Ess. Crit.* x. (1875) 411 The clear thought which is.. at the bottom of that troubled wording. **1882** PROCTOR *Fam. Science Studies* 43, I have altered the wording.. in such a way as to avoid the use of technical expressions. **1913** *Spectator* 26 July 148/1 The meaning.. is plain, though the wording is, to say the least,.. involved.

4. A set of written words, an inscription. *rare.*

1908 *Times* 28 Jan. 4/6 A box.. with.. the well-known Havana indications, including the lock-label with the Spanish wording.

So †'**wording** *ppl. a.* (*a*) consisting in (mere) words, verbal; (*b*) using many or empty words, wordy; (*c*) characterized by angry words, contentious, quarrelsome.

1601 CORNWALLIS *Ess.* II. xxx. (1631) 48 Patrone of the vulgar whose wording favour.. hath such an operation with mans frailtie. **1615** J. STEPHENS *Satyr. Ess.* 315 It is probable she was begotten by some.. wording Poet, for she consists of as many fearefull sounds without science. **1682** BUNYAN *Holy War* To Rdr. (1684) A 3 b, In Parleys, or in wording Jars.

†'**wordish**, *a. Obs.* [f. WORD *sb.* + -ISH[1].]

1. Consisting in or concerned with words, esp. mere words (as opposed to realities); verbal: cf. WORDY *a.* 3.

a **1586** SIDNEY *Apol. Poetry* (Arb.) 33 A perfect picture I say, for hee yeeldeth to the powers of the minde, an image of that whereof the Philosopher bestoweth but a woordish description. *Ibid.* 69 Both [Poetry and Oratory] haue such an affinity in this wordish consideration. **1657** J. SERGEANT *Schism Dispach't* 36 Blundering the plainest truths with multitudes of wordish evasions. **1675** CROWNE *Calisto* v. 73 All wordish praise she is so much above That eloquence would prophanation prove. **1697** J. SERGEANT *Solid Philos.* 454 To make the Doctrine of Words to be a.. part of Philosophy, is to make Philosophy Wordish.

2. Using, or containing, an excess of words; verbose: = WORDY *a.* 1.

1604 SCOLOKER *Daiphantus* Argt., More desirous to be thought honest, then so to be wordish beyond discretion. *a* **1657** R. LOVEDAY *Lett.* (1663) 19, I have made my story too wordish;.. I should have pared much away.

Hence †'**wordishly** *adv.*, †'**wordishness**.

1657 J. SERGEANT *Schism Dispach't* 26 Loquacity, that is, voluntary talking wordishly without a syllable of sense. *Ibid.* 390 The emptie wordishnes in his 'Reply'. **1697** —— *Solid Philos.* 286 All the Wordishness, and empty Disputes among Trivial Philosophers.

wordle, obs. f. WORLD; var. WORTLE.

wordless ('wɜːdlɪs), *a.* [f. WORD *sb.* + -LESS.]

1. Inexpressible in words; unspeakable, unutterable. *Obs.* or merged in 2.

c **1200** *Trin. Coll. Hom.* 113 Wordles song is þe herte michele blisse, þe heo haueð of heuenliche ðinge, and ne mai þeroffe be stille ne mid worde hem atellen. **1647** TRAPP *Comm. 1 Cor.* xv. 51 (1656) 701 This, likely was one of those wordless words [ἄρρητα ῥήματα: 1611 unspeakable words] that Paul heard in his rapture, 2 Cor. 12. 4. **1683** E. HOOKER *Pref. Pordage's Mystic Div.* 66 Hee was caught up into the third Heaven.. where Hee heard wordless Words (so the Græc most emphaticly) Words unutterabl, unexpressibl.

2. Not expressed in words; unspoken, unuttered.

a **1500** *Chaucer's Dreme* 889 So thought I.. That word-lesse answere in no toun Was tane for obligacioun. **1633** P. FLETCHER *Elisa* II. iv, So sat she joylesse down in wordlesse grief complaining. **1820** BYRON *Juan* III. lviii, The stern,.. deep, and wordless ire Of a strong human heart. **1870** MORRIS *Earthly Par.* II. III. 189 Some wordless prayer of agony. **1871** TYLOR *Prim. Cult.* I. viii. 270 The deaf-and-dumb.. work out.. such analogies.. in their wordless thought. **1884** 'EDNA LYALL' *We Two* xix, Love of the deepest sort is wordless.

3. Not uttering a word; not speaking, silent, speechless. Also *transf.* of action or feeling (cf. 2).

a **1500** *Chaucer's Dreme* 516 Wordlesse he was, and semed sicke. **1593** SHAKS. *Lucr.* 112 Her ioie with heaued-vp hand she doth expresse, And wordlesse so greetes heauen for his successe. **1852** BAILEY *Festus* (ed. 5) 522 She, wordless, went, But looked her thanks. **1881** CHRISTINA ROSSETTI *Later Life* iii. Poems (1904) 298 Our wordless tearless numbness of distress. **1890** *Brit. Med. Jrnl.* 8 Feb. 300/2 The patient was quite speechless, or, at least, wordless. **1904** G. WATSON *Sunshine & Sentim.* 188, I was unable to follow her, and stood dumfounded and wordless.

b. Lacking the faculty or power of speech.

1648 J. QUARLES *Fons Lachrym.* 52 The wordless tongues of thirsty children cleave To their unliquid mouths. **1846** *Chambers's Jrnl.* 16 May 312 A Word for the Wordless.

c. Lacking words for expression.

1881 POYNTER *Among the Hills* I. 282 Her mind was too uncultivated, too wordless. **1896** HOWELLS *Impressions & Exp.* 104 The innocence of wordless infancy.

4. Not accompanied by words; (of a play) acted without words.

1598 SYLVESTER *Du Bartas* II. ii. II. *Babylon* 333 The winged quiers,.. Their sound want sense; their notes are word-lesse still. **1855** BAILEY *Mystic* 137 No wordless murmurs of expectant joy. **1882** J. HAWTHORNE *Fort. Fool* xxx, The little wordless song which his.. mother had sung. **1897** *Westm. Gaz.* 9 Jan. 3/2 The history of wordless plays on the modern London stage. **1922** G. K. CHESTERTON *Man* *who knew* 258 The man..cast it down with a wordless sound more shocking than a curse.

Hence **'wordlessly** *adv.*, **'wordlessness.**

1852 BAILEY *Festus* (ed. 5) 250 The eagle they petitioned to preside,..The bird of curvéd beak and radiant eye Bowed wordlessly, and swept down from the sky. **1891** M. MURIEL DOWIE *Girl in Karp.* xiii. 178 We were left..wordlessly grateful. **1895** *Westm. Gaz.* 8 June 3/1 The momentary wordlessness that is certain to fall occasionally to the lot of everyone.

wordli(e, -lich(e, wordling, obs. ff. WORLDLY, WORLDLING.

wordlore ('wɜːdlɔə(r)). [f. WORD *sb.* + LORE *sb.*[1] Cf. G. *wortlehre.*] **a.** The study of words and their history; the words collectively of a language and their history. **b.** (= G. *wortlehre.*) The doctrine of the forms and formation of words; morphology. Hence **'wordlorist.**

1861 *Trans. Philol. Soc. 1860–1* 154 A perfect Dictionary must not only be a complete Repertory, but also an available Directory within the whole province of word-lore (*wort-lehre* as distinguished from *satz-lehre*). **1870** *Dublin Univ. Mag.* Mar. 282 (*art.*) Word-lore. **1871** KENNEDY *Public Sch. Lat. Gram.* 5 Etymology comprises:—I. Phonology or Soundlore, the doctrine of Sounds. II. Morphology or Wordlore, the doctrine of Words. **1904** A. S. PALMER (*title*) The Folk and their Word-Lore: an Essay on Popular Etymologies. **1929** *N. & Q.* 15 June 419/2 No word-lorist who studies place-names.

'wordly, *a. rare.* [f. WORD *sb.* + -LY[1].] Dealing in, or consisting in, mere words; verbal.

1633 AMES *Fresh Suit agst. Cerem.* Pref. p. v, These wordly gospellers. *Ibid.* II. 36 A wordly distinction betwixt Doctrinall and Rituall Ceremonies. **1927** M. SADLEIR *Trollope* 370 This fact indicates..two of his personal qualities..his wordly proficiency and his good manners.

wordly, -lyche, obs. forms of WORLDLY.

wordman ('wɜːdmən). *rare.* [f. WORD *sb.* + MAN *sb.*[1]] A man who deals with or has command of words; a master of language. So **'wordmanship,** skill in the use of words.

1623 COCKERAM II, A great Word man, *grandiloquus.* **1654** J. WEBSTER *Acad. Exam.* 68 Men that..think themselves the most skilful wordmen or Logodædalists in the world. *a* **1721** PRIOR *Dial. betw. Charles & Clenard* Wks. 1907 II. 213, I will not shew my Anger against this Word-man. **1882** STEVENSON *Men & Bks.* Pref. p. xiii, The great contemporary master of wordmanship, and indeed of all literary arts.

wordmonger ('wɜːdˌmʌŋɡə(r)). [f. WORD *sb.* + MONGER.] One who deals in words, esp. in strange or pedantic words, or in empty words without sense or substance. Orig. *contemptuous.*

1590 *Tarlton's News Purgat.* Ep. Ded. A 2 b, The word-mongers of malice, that like the Vipers grew odious to their own kinde. **1628** SHIRLEY *Witty Fair One* v. iv, A pedantical, lousy wordmonger. **1749** LAVINGTON *Enthus. Meth. & Papists* (1820) 331 God hath cautioned me against these word-mongers. **1855** MOTLEY *Dutch Rep.* VI. iii. (1866) 813 The word-mongers who could clothe one shivering thought in a hundred thousand garments. **1884** TENNYSON *Becket* II. ii, Diagonalise! thou art a word-monger. **1916** *Daily News* 8 Nov. in E. Weekley *Etymol. Dict. Mod. Eng.* (1921) 944 Professor Weekley is well known to our readers as the most entertaining of living word-mongers. **1981** V. GLENDINNING *Edith Sitwell* 4 She is a poet of dream and vision, a musical wordmonger.

So **'wordˌmongering, -ˌmongery.**

1879 H. N. HUDSON *Hamlet* Pref. p. xiv, Too much time ..spent in mere word-mongering and lingual dissection. **1881** MAX MÜLLER tr. *Kant's Critique Pure Reason* II. ii. 223 There remains nothing but mere wordmongery. **1903** *Times Lit. Suppl.* 20 Mar. 87/3 Word-mongery has been overdone here and there.

wordre, obs. form of ORDER *sb.*

wordsman ('wɜːdzmən). = WORDMAN. So **'wordsmanship.**

1959 I. & P. OPIE *Lore & Lang. Schoolch.* iii. 50 Wordsmanship. It is common practice to snub a companion who makes irritating use of words such as 'Well!' 'What?' and 'Eh?' **1962** *Canadian Intelligence Service* XII. II. 3/1 The U.S. Senate Security Subcommittee recently issued a report entitled *Wordsmanship; Semantics as a Communist Weapon.* **1981** W. SAFIRE in *N.Y. Times Mag.* 27 Apr. 18/3 Robert Burchfield, chief editor of the Oxford Dictionaries, known to wordsmen as 'Superlex'. **1984** *N.Y. Times Mag.* 30 Dec. 6/2 The occasion was a gathering at the library of renowned scholars, including a babble of wordsmen, to mark the 200th anniversary of the death of Samuel Johnson.

wordster ('wɜːdstə(r)). *nonce-wd.* [f. WORD *sb.* + -STER.] One who deals in or handles words: (*a*) one who indulges in talk rather than action; (*b*) a skilful user of words; (*c*) a student of words and their meanings.

1917 H. A. JONES *Pacifists* [Dedication], *Dedicated* To the tribe of Wordsters, Pedants, Fanatics, and Impossibilists, who so rabidly pursued an ignoble peace, that they helped to provoke a disastrous war. **1965** *English Studies* XLVI. 465 [The suffix *-ster*] may serve the function of condensing long words such as 'philologist' and 'lexicographer' into short *wordster.* **1971** 'J. QUARTERMAIN' *Man who walked on Diamonds* ii. 14 The..brilliant wordster, always good for the *bon mot.* **1976** *Verbatim* Dec. 8/2 As an amateur wordster, my personal lexicon contains lengthy lists of various types of words.

Wordsworthian (wɜːdzˈwɜːθɪən), *sb.* and *a.* [f. the name of the English poet William *Wordsworth* (1770–1850) + -IAN.] **a.** *sb.* An admirer or imitator of Wordsworth, or a student of his works. **b.** *adj.* Of, belonging to, or characteristic of Wordsworth; (of a poem) composed by, or in the style of, Wordsworth.

1815 *Sporting Mag.* XLVI. 12, I am enough of a Wordsworthian not to confine my tastes to the received elegancies of society. **1817** W. WHEWELL *Let.* in M. Moorman *William Wordsworth* (1965) II. ix. 325 His [*sc.* Coleridge's] critique on the Daffodils might serve as a model for similar strictures on all Wordsworth's Wordsworthian poems. **1825** LOCKHART in *Scott's Fam. Lett.* (1894) II. 342 Miss Hume is an ecstatic Wordsworthian, and is to go to see him one of these days in the flesh. **1845** A. DE VERE *Let.* 28 Sept. in *Recoll.* (1897) x. 204 You are a greater admirer of the special Wordsworthian genius. **1856** RUSKIN *Mod. Painters* III. IV. xvii. §29. 304 'J'aime mieux ma mie', is..the first Wordsworthian poem brought forward on philosophical principles, to oppose the schools of art and affectation. **1874** BLACKIE *Self-Cult.* 44 Given to indulge in Wordsworthian musings. **1878** R. H. HUTTON *Scott* xvi. (1888) 162 Even Scott, who was so little of a Wordsworthian,..must have recurred that day..to that favourite Wordsworthian poem. **1921** *Spectator* 2 July 7/1 Imagine a poet whose mind was perfectly balanced between the desirability of gorgeous Swinburnesque ornament and Wordsworthian austerity.

Hence **ˌWordsworthiˈana** [-IANA suffix], things connected with Wordsworth, writings about Wordsworth; **Words'worthianism; Wordsworthy** *a. colloq.*, typical or suggestive of Wordsworth.

1881 *Sat. Rev.* 12 Feb. 215 There has been of late a recrudescence of Wordsworthianism. **1889** W. KNIGHT (*title*) Wordsworthiana: papers read to Wordsworth Society. **1938** S. BECKETT *Murphy* v. 106 They [*sc.* sheep] seemed in rather better form, less Wordsworthy. **1983** *London Rev. Bks.* 7–20 July 18/4 Recent items of Wordsworthiana include *The Visionary Company.*

wordy, wordie ('wɜːdɪ), *sb. Sc.* [f. WORD *sb.* + -Y[6].] A little or slight word.

1718 RAMSAY *Christ's Kirk Gr.* III. xx, She her man like a lammy led Hame, wi' a well-wail'd wordy. **1785** BURNS *To Rev. J. M'Math* iii, A pack..Wha..Can easy, wi' a single wordie, Lowse hell upon me. *a* **1840** JOANNA BAILLIE *Song, Woo'd & Married* 38 Weel waled were his wordies.

wordy ('wɜːdɪ), *a.* [Late OE. *wordiȝ*, f. WORD *sb.* + *-iȝ*, -Y[1].]

1. Full of or abounding in words. **a.** Of speech or writing: Consisting of or containing many words; = VERBOSE 1.

c **1100** *Aldhelm Gloss.* in Napier *O.E. Glosses* 38/1416 *Uerbosa*, wordiȝ. **1382** WYCLIF *1 Cor.* Prol., Wordy eloquence of philosophie. **1641** BP. HALL *Answ. Vind. Smect.* 103 In this their wordy, and wearisome Volume. **1713** ROWE *Jane Shore* III. i, To deal in wordy Compliment Is much against the Plainness of my Nature. **1778** BP. LOWTH *Transl. Isaiah* Prelim. Diss. p. lxviii, The Chaldee Paraphrase..often wanders from the Text in a wordy allegorical explanation. **1853** HALLAM *Mid. Ages* (ed. 10) ii. Note 5. I. 297 If the Franks scorned the complex and wordy jurisprudence of Rome. *a* **1873** LYTTON *Pausanias* i. (1876) 49 The Athenian fashion of wordy boasting. **1877** KINGLAKE *Crimea* (1880) VI. ix. 309 This despatch was beyond measure wordy.

b. Of a person: Using an excess of words; = VERBOSE 2; *occas.* garrulous, talkative.

1382 WYCLIF *Job* xvi. 21 My woordi frendis [1388 ful of wordis]. **1483** *Cath. Angl.* 423/2 Wordy, *verbosus, & cetera; vbi* Chaterer. **1636** SIR R. BAKER *Cato Variegatus* 9 Words against wordy men, thou must not vse. **1712** STEELE *Spect.* No. 448 ¶1 Phocion, beholding a wordy Orator, while he was making a magnificent Speech to the People. **1854** R. S. SURTEES *Handley Cr.* xiv. (1901) I. 106 The barber's pretty but rather wordy wife. **1881** STEVENSON *Virg. Puerisque* 80 A wordy, prolegomenous babbler.

†**2.** Skilled in the use of words. *Obs. rare.*

1603 J. DAVIES (Heref.) *Microcosmos* Wks. (Grosart) I. 80/1 Be he a Pleader, and a wordie Man. **1609** —— *Hum. Heav. on Earth* II. lxviii, Some wordy-men, by words, sought worthinesse. **1680** OTWAY *Orphan* IV. vii, You talk to me in Parables, Chamont; You may have known that I'm no wordy Man.

3. Consisting or expressed in words; of words; verbal. Now chiefly in phr. *wordy war.* (Often with mixture of sense 1 a.)

1627 W. SCLATER *Expos. 2 Thess.* (1629) 129 Intrusion on Gods Prerogatiues royall is rather in facts, then wordy profession. **1685** BAXTER *Paraphr. N.T.* James ii. 14 Is not a meer wordy Profession an unprofitable thing to your selves..? Will..saying you believe, profit to Salvation, if you..live not according to the Gospel? **1715** ROWE *Lady Jane Gray* I. i, These Clergy Quarrels, These wordy Wars of proud ill-manner'd Schoolmen. **1741** B. FRANKLIN *Poor Richard* (1890) 111 He that talks much, talks in vain; We from the wordy torrent fly. **1791** COWPER *Iliad* II. 463 All that wordy tempest for a girl. **1814** BYRON *Lara* I. xxiii, To mar The mirthful meeting with a wordy war. **1860** TENNYSON *Sea Dreams* 31 When the wordy storm Had ended.

wordy, -nesse, obs. ff. WORTHY, WORTHINESS.

†**wore,** *sb. Obs.* Of doubtful origin and meaning; perh. identical with WARE *sb.*[1], ORE[5] (OE. *wár*) seaweed, but possibly repr. OE. *wára, wárum,* glossing med.L. *sablonum, sablonibus* ?sandy or pebbly shore (see, however, note in Napier's *O.E. Glosses*, p. 49).

a **1310** *Alysoun* iv. in Wright *Lyric P.* 28 Icham for wowyng al forwake, wery so water in wore. **13..** *Maximon* in Böddeker *Altengl. Dicht.* 249 Y wake as water in wore; iesu crist, þin ore!

†**wore,** *v.*[1] *Obs. rare.* Also wori. [perh. to be referred to OE. *wórian* only intr. to wander, f. *wōr*, root of *wérig* WEARY *a.*, q.v.] *trans.* To trouble, disturb, confuse.

a **1225** *Ancr. R.* 386 þis mong woreð [*v.r.* weorreð] so þe eien of þe heorte þet heo ne mei iknowen God. *c* **1230** *Hali Meid.* (MS. Bodl.) 714 þet hare flesches eggunge, ne þe feondes fondunge..ne wori [*v.r.* weorri] hare heorte wit. *a* **1310** in Wright *Lyric P.* iv. 24 Ther afterward this worldes won with muchel unwynne us woren wolde.

†**wore,** *v.*[2] *Naut. Obs.* Pa. t. of WEAR *v.*[2] irreg. used for inf.

1744 J. PHILIPS *Jrnl. Exped. Anson* 8 At 8 made the Signal to wore Ship. *Ibid.* 41 Fresh Gales..which obliged most of the Ships to wore and bear down to the Leeward.

wore (wɔə(r)), pa. t. of WEAR *v.*[1]; pa. t. and pple. of WEAR *v.*[2]

wore, obs. pa. t. of BE *v.*; obs. f. ORE[2], ORE[5]; var. WARE *sb.*[6] *Obs.*

wored, obs. form of WORD.

'wori, *a. Obs.* [? f. stem of WORE *v.*[1] + *-i*, -Y[1]. (Connexion with OE. *wáriȝ* is improbable.)] 'Troubled', disturbed, turbid.

c **1175** *Lamb. Hom.* 29 Hu maht þu iseon þine sceadewe in worie watere. *a* **1200** *Moral Ode* 142 in *O.E. Hom.* I. 169 Betere is wori water drunch þen atter meind mid wine. *a* **1225** *Ancr. R.* 386 Haue euer schir heorte þus, & do al þet tu wilt. Haue wori heorte & al þe sit vuele. *c* **1290** *St. Brendan* 26 in *S. Eng. Leg.* 226 Twey faire wellene, þat on was suyþe cler, And sumdel wori..þat oþer was.

worie, obs. form of WORRY *v.*

work (wɜːk), *sb.* Forms: *α.* 1—4 weorc, 2-4 weork(e, (3 *Orm.* weorrc, weorrk-). *β.* 1-4 werc, (3 wærc, wærk, *Orm.* werrc), 3-6 werk(e, (4 -cke, -kke, 5 wherk, 6 *Sc.* verk); *Sc.* and *north.* 4 warc(ke, vark, 4-7 warke, 4- wark. *γ.* 1 wyrc, 1-2 wurc, 3 wurck, wurk, (5 wrke); 4 wirke. *δ.* 1-3 worc, 3-7 worke, (3, 6 worck, 4 vorke, 6 worke, wourke, 6-7 worcke), 6- work. *ε.* 2-3 werch, 3, 5-6 worch(e, wurch, 9 *dial.* wurtch; 3, 7- warch (see WARK *sb.*[1]). [OE. *weorc* = OFris., OS., (M)LG., (M)Du. *werk*, OHG. *werah, werc* (MHG. *werch, werc*, G. *werk*), ON. *verk* (Sw., Da. *verk*):—OTeut. **werkom* (see WORK *v.*); cognate are Gr. ἔργον, Arm. *gorc*, Zend *varəza-* activity. Forms *γ* and *ε* show partial assimilation to the forms of WORK *v.*; see also WARK, WARCH *sb.*[1] (in a specialized sense).]

I. 1. Something that is or was done; what a person does or did; an act, deed, proceeding, business; in *pl.* actions, doings (often collectively = 3). *arch.* or *literary* in gen. sense.

sing. **971** *Blickl. Hom.* 47 þis weorc biþ deoflum se mæsta teona. *c* **1000** *Ags. Gosp.* Matt. xxvi. 10 God weorc heo worhte on me. *c* **1000** ÆLFRIC *Hom.* I. 318 þæt weorc wæs begunnen onȝean Godes willan. *c* **1205** LAY. 2574 Menbriz dude an vuel weorc. *c* **1230** *Hali Meid.* (1922) 25 Halden ham i reste fram þat fleschliche werc. **1338** R. BRUNNE *Chron.* (1810) 80 Or it wer alle ent þe werke þat þei did wirke. *c* **1400** *Rule St. Benet* (verse) 446 Chaistese þam..Efter þe wark þat þai haue wroght. **1450–1530** *Myrr. our Ladye* III. 310 Whyle god fulfylleth thys daye the worke of nature. *c* **1470** HENRY *Wallace* I. 434 Quhen Wallas thus this worthi werk had wrocht. *a* **1529** SKELTON *P. Sparowe* 569 The kestrell in all this warke Shall be holy water clarke. *a* **1548** HALL *Chron., Edw. IV* 207 b, Se the worke of God,..ther rose suche a sodain wynde and a terrible tempest. **1595** SHAKS. *John* IV. iii. 57 It is a damned, and a bloody worke. **1599** PEELE *David & Bethsabe* E ij b, Is not the hand of Ioab in this worke? **1613** PURCHAS *Pilgrimage* III. xv. 272 A people of that beastly disposition, that they performed the most secret worke of Nature in publike view. **1679** SOUTH *Serm., Prov.* iii. 17 (1697) I. 28 After a long fatigue of Eating, and Drinking, and Babling, he concludes the great work of Dining Gentilely. **1848** THACKERAY *Van. Fair* lxvii, For almost the last time in which she shall be called upon to weep in this history, she commenced that work. **1859** H. KINGSLEY *G. Hamlyn* viii, All this doctor's stuff is no use, unless you can say a charm as will undo her devil's work.

pl. *Beowulf* 289 ðescad witan worda and worca. *c* **897** ÆLFRED *Gregory's Past. C.* xxxii. 210 ðif we hie myndgiað hiera godna weorca. *c* **1000** *Ags. Gosp.* Matt. xxiii. 3 Ne do ȝe na æfter heora worcum; Hiȝ secgeað & ne doð. *c* **1175** *Lamb. Hom.* 145 Alle we beoð in monifald wawe..hwat for ure eldere werkes, hwat for ure aȝene gultes. *c* **1250** *Hymn* 16 in *Trin. Coll. Hom.* App. 257 þat ic non þing mid unricht Wurche þe werches þe beoð towilde. *c* **1250** *Prayer to our Lady* 29 in *O.E. Misc.* 193 Ich habbe isuneȝet mid wurken and midd muðe. *a* **1300** *Cursor M.* 1983 Wit lele werks lok ȝee dele. **1362** LANGL. *P. Pl.* A. Prol. 3 In Habite of an Hermite vn-holy of werkes. **1471** CAXTON *Recuyell* (Sommer) 19 She was..wyse in her werkes honeste in conuersacion & flowryng in alle vertuys. **1526** TINDALE *Matt.* xi. 2 When Jhon beinge in preson herde the workes of Christ. **1560** *Bible* (Genev.) Isa. lix. 6 Their workes are workes of iniquitie. **1613** PURCHAS *Pilgrimage* I. viii. 119 Hypocrisie loues her workes should be seene, but not her humour. *a* **1763** SHENSTONE *Ess.* xxxi. Wks. 1765 II. 223 A Deity, whose very words are works, and all whose works are wonders. *a* **1863** WHATELY *Chr. Evid.* v, The works performed by Jesus and His disciples were beyond the unassisted powers of man.

b. *Theol.* (*pl.*) Moral actions considered in relation to justification: usually as contrasted with *faith* or *grace*. Rarely in *sing.* (See also 32.)

Covenant of Works: see COVENANT *sb.* 8a.

1362 LANGL. *P. Pl.* A. XI. 268 3if I shal werke be here werkis to wynne me heuene,..þanne wrouȝte I vnwisly. **1382** WYCLIF *Eph.* ii. 9 By grace ȝe ben saued bi feith,..it is the ȝifte of God, not of werkis, that no man glorie. *c* **1480** HENRYSON *Fox, Wolf & Husb.* 207 Warkis that fra ferme faith proceidis. **1526** TINDALE *Rom.* xi. 6 Yff hit be of grace then is it not by the deservynge of workes [1611 then is it no more of workes]. **1533** GAU *Richt Vay* (S.T.S.) 107 Faith causis hime to virk throw lwiff godlie and chrissine varkis. **1625** MOUNTAGU *App. Cæsar.* 164 The person with God must be made acceptable..before any work of his become approveable. **1635** D. DICKSON *Hebr.* vii. 19. 131 To seeke to bee..justified and saved, by workes, is to seeke that by the Lawe, which could never bee brought to passe, by it. **1739** J. WESLEY *Doctrine of Salvation* 5 Because all Men are Sinners against God, and Breakers of his Law, therefore can no Man by his Works be justified, and made righteous before God. **1883** W. C. DOWDING *Luther & his Work* 6 We are accounted righteous before God only for the merits of our Lord Jesus Christ, by faith; and not from our own works or deservings. **1906** W. WALKER *John Calvin* xv. 415 Calvin ..leaves room for a conception of 'works' as strenuous..as any claimed by the Roman communion. **1963** E. P. THOMPSON *Making of Eng. Working Class* xi. 364 How, then, to keep grace? Not by good works, since Wesley had elevated faith above works:..Works were the snares of pride and the best works were mingled with the dross of sin; although..works might be a *sign* of grace. **1972** Q. BELL *Virginia Woolf* I. i. 4 The Clapham Sect was concerned with works rather than with faith.

c. Qualified by phr. with *of* expressing the moral quality of the action, as *a work* or *works of charity*, *of darkness*, *of mercy*, etc.

c **1200** *Trin. Coll. Hom.* 11 Ðe werc of þesternesse þat ben alle heuie sennen. *a* **1300** *Cursor M.* 19764 Cristen sco was and euer fus Abute all werkes of almus. **1340–1824** [see MERCY *sb.* 7]. *c* **1380** WYCLIF *Sel. Wks.* II. 25 It is werk of mercy to birie dede men. *c* **1440** *Gesta Rom.* 341 It was a werke of charitee. **1526** TINDALE *Eph.* v. 11 Have no fellishippe with the vnfrutfull workes of derckness. **1560** DAUS tr. *Sleidane's Comm.* 18 Amonges other workes of Charitie..we shoulde..comforte the sicke. **1703** EARL ORRERY *As you find it* v. ii. 63, I have another Work of Charity upon my hands,..to reform an extravagant Husband. **1816** J. WILSON *City of Plague* III. ii, Even in her dreams Her soul is at some work of charity.

d. *the work of ...*: a proceeding occupying (a stated length of time). So *a work of time*: a proceeding which takes a long time.

1605 BACON *Adv. Learn.* I. vi. §2 The confused mass and matter of heaven and earth was made in a moment; and the ..disposition of that chaos or mass was the work of six days. **1749** J. CLELAND *Mem. Woman of Pleasure* II. 120 All this was not the work of the fourth part of a minute. **1813** SCOTT *Rokeby* II. xxi, To wrench the sword from Wilfrid's hand.. Was but one moment's work. **1818** —— *Hrt. Midl.* li, They had now only to double a small head-land..; but in the state of the weather, and the boat being heavy, this was like to be a work of time. **1819** —— *Ivanhoe* xxxi. **1834** MARRYAT *Peter Simple* xxxiii, All this was..but the work of a few minutes. **1871** HARDY *Desperate Remedies* II. ii. 74 To bring him out and lay him on a bank was the work of an instant. **1906** ALICE WERNER *Natives Brit. Central Africa* vi. 136 Once the water has been brought to the boil, which..is apt to be a work of time. **1927** C. ASQUITH *Black Cap* 73 To light his candle and put on his dressing-gown and slippers was the work of a moment.

e. *spec.* (see quots.).

1869 LANDRETH *Life Adam Thomson* i. 43 The services on such an occasion [*sc.* the communion] were..emphatically designated by devout people 'the work'. **1887** W. S. S. TYRWHITT *New Chum in Queensland Bush* viii. 147, I have found the Cape rifle..a very useful gun for Queensland work [*i.e.* kangaroo shooting]. **1888** BRYCE *Amer. Commw.* lvii. II. 395 The 'work' of politics means in America the business of winning nominations..and elections.

2. Something to be done, or something to do; what a person (or thing) has or had to do; occupation, employment, business, task, function.

Often only contextually distinguishable from 1; in later use viewed as a fig. or extended application of 4 or 5.

c **1000** *Ags. Gosp.* Mark xiii. 34 Se man [þe]..sealde his þeowum þæne anwald ȝehwylces weorces. *c* **1200** ORMIN 1833 Whatt weorrc himm iss þurrh Drihhtin sett To forþenn her onn eorþe. *c* **1489** CAXTON *Blanchardyn* x. 40 The werke that he hath vndertaken. **1596** SHAKS. *1 Hen. IV*, II. iv. 118 Fie vpon this quiet life, I want worke. **1602** —— *Ham.* v. ii. 333 The point envenom'd too, Then venome to thy worke. **1611** COTGR. s.v. *Ouvrage*, Euerie bodies worke is no bodies worke. **1643** BURROUGHES *Exp. 1st 3 ch. Hosea* ix. (1652) 302 It is not my worke to handle the point of the Sabbath-day or Lords-day now. **1786** BURNS *Twa Dogs* 206 Gentlemen, and Ladies..Wi' ev'n down want o' wark are curst. **1852** MRS. STOWE *Uncle Tom's C.* xxviii. 259 The Lord has a work for mas'r. **1862** RUSKIN *Unto this Last* iv. §82 The desert has its appointed place and work. **1865** TROLLOPE *Belton Est.* i. 9 To fight the devil was her work, —was the appointed work of every living soul.

b. *Cricket*, *Rowing*, etc. What a batsman, an oarsman, etc. has to do, esp. with reference to the points at which his force is to be applied.

1851 PYCROFT *Cr. Field* vii. 117 Be sure you stand up to your work, or close to your block-hole. **1856** 'STONEHENGE' *Brit. Rural Sports* II. VIII. iii. §2. 476/1 He [*sc.* a rower] sits quite square to his work. **1925** G. C. BOURNE *Oarsmanship* 32 Those theorists who would have us place oarsmen some three to six inches away from their work.

3. †**a.** Action (of a person) in general; doings, deeds; conduct. (Often conjoined with *word*.) *Obs.*

971 [see WORD *sb.* 4]. *a* **1200** *Moral Ode* 108 in *O.E. Hom.* I. 167 His aȝe werch and his þonc te witnesse he scal demen. *c* **1200** ORMIN 5426 Whase maȝȝ wiþþ word & weorrc Her fillenn Godess wille. *a* **1300** *Cursor M.* 8696 Bath warr and wis in all his werc. *c* **1400** *Rule St. Benet* (prose) 3 Wha sam heris my word and dos it in werke. *c* **1470** *Gol. & Gaw* 1244 Ilkane be werk and be will Is worth his rewarde. **1533** GAU *Richt Vay* (S.T.S.) 9 Inuertlie in thair hart and outuertlie in thair word and wark. **1564–78** BULLEIN *Dial. agst. Pest.* (1888) 34 The euill [man], whose woorke is either dronkennesse, adulterie, thefte. **1581** *Satir. Poems Reform.* xliv. 15 Maisters of ane euil steik of vark Sould ay detest the godlie, vpricht lyf. **1609** *Bible* (Douay) Deut. v. 1 Heare Israel the ceremonies & judgements..and fulfil them in worke.

b. Action (of a person or thing) of a particular kind; †doing, performance; working, operation. In various connexions; of a thing, often in reference to result; *to do its work*, to produce its effect (cf. 9b).

c **1440** *Gesta Rom.* 4 In werke of ony goode dede. *c* **1449** PECOCK *Repr.* I. xvi. 89 If the maner of outring which is sauory in a sermonyng schulde be sett..in the office of scole prouyng..al the werk ther of schulde be the vnsauerer and the vnspedier. **1480** *Cely Papers* (Camden) 58 Hys howsse.. schall come to be pluckyd schorttly down or elles burnyd for the schortter warke. *a* **1635** SIBBES *Confer. Christ & Mary* (1656) 92 The work of God's spirit in his children, is like fire. **1644** DIGBY *Nat. Bodies* v. 36 The composition or dissolution of mixed bodies..is the chiefe worke of Elements, and requireth an intime application of the Agents. **1731** *Art of Drawing & Paint.* 23 When the Spirit of Wine has done its Work, it must be pour'd off. **1763** *Museum Rust.* I. 348 It will be so steady that no unevenness of the ground will be able to throw it out of its work, as a clod or stone will a common harrow. **1819** BYRON *Juan* II. cii, Famine, despair, cold, thirst, and heat, had done Their work on them by turns. **1837** DICKENS *Pickw.* iii, The brandy-and-water had done its work.

c. *Cricket.* Deflection of the ball after touching the ground, resulting from the spin or twist imparted to it by the bowler.

1846 W. DENISON *Sk. Players* 12 His delivery is from over the wicket, so there is..scarcely any 'work' from it. **1882** *Evening News* 2 Sept. 1/6 The amount of work the bowlers could get on the ball.

4. Action involving effort or exertion directed to a definite end, esp. as a means of gaining one's livelihood; labour, toil; (one's) regular occupation or employment.

c **825** *Vesp. Ps.* ciii. 23 Utgaeð mon to werce his. *c* **1000** ÆLFRIC *Exod.* xx. 9 Wyrc six daȝas ealle ðine weorc. *c* **1000** *Rule of Chrodegang* xiv, Niht wæs ȝeworht to reste ealswa dæȝ to worce. *c* **1290** *S. Eng. Leg.* 61/248 An Asse..is i-harled here and þere and to file weorke i-do. *a* **1300** *Cursor M.* 5870 Þat..ned-wais suld þai Do tua dais werkes on a dai. *Ibid.* 21528 Of he kest al to his serk, To mak him nemel til his werk. *c* **1400** MAUNDEV. (1839) xxvi. 265 Thorghe werk of his men. **1557–8** in Feuillerat *Revels Q. Mary* (1914) 236 Doinge certen Iobbes of woorke. **1611** R. FENTON *Usurie* 29 A dayes worke is valuable at a certaine price. **1665** *Phil. Trans.* I. 88 In Carpentry and Joyners work. **1667** MILTON *P.L.* IV. 618 Man hath his daily work of body or mind Appointed. **1783** *Jrnl. Ho. Comm.* XLVII. 372/1 To leave off Work perhaps Half an Hour before Bell Ringing. **1840** DICKENS *Old Cur. Shop* xxxiv, I do all the work of the house. **1866** RUSKIN *Crown Wild Olive* i. 40 There must be work done by the arms, or none of us could live. There must be work done by the brains, or the life we get would not be worth having. **1871** SMILES *Charac.* iv. (1876) 98 Work—employment, useful occupation—is one of the great secrets of happiness. **1895** *Manch. Guardian* 14 Oct. 5/6 Half the workmen employed are Italians, who are said to do four times as much work as the Bulgarians. **1914** 'IAN HAY' *Knt. on Wheels* xiii. §3 Philip was a glutton for work.

b. Used *gen.* in reference to any action requiring effort or difficult to do. Often with epithet.

1518 *Star Chamber Cases* (Selden Soc.) II. 141, I had as myche worck as I cowde by ony meanys to pacyffye theyme. **1626** BACON *New Atl.* 20 Wee had Worke enough to get any of our Men to looke to our Shipp. **1806–7** J. BERESFORD *Miseries Hum. Life* (1826) ii. 8 Walking obliquely up a steep hill when the ground is what the vulgar call greasy. Sad work! **1832** HT. MARTINEAU *Life in Wilds* vi. 76 It..was weary work with any tool but the hatchet. **1864** BROWNING *Rabbi Ben Ezra* xviii, Here, work enough to watch The Master work, and catch Hints of the proper craft. **1902** BUCHAN *Watcher by Threshold* 127 It was hard work rowing, for the wind was against him.

c. *spec.* The labour done in making something, as distinguished from the material used (in reference to the cost); = WORKMANSHIP 1.

1737 W. SALMON *Country Builder's Estimator* (ed. 2) 25 Steps of common Stairs,..of Oak, 8*d.* per Foot; the Work only 1*d.*½ per Foot. *Ibid.* 26 Whole Deal-Doors..are allowed, work and half work, or double work, if of two-inch Stuff, in consideration of their being wrought on both sides.

d. Exercise or practice in a sport or game; also, exertion or movement proper to a particular sport, game, or exercise.

1856 'STONEHENGE' *Brit. Sports* I. III. vi. §2. 194 On all occasions after the day's work, the frictioning must be had recourse to. **1874** *Kennel Club Stud Bk.* 161 Lilly then made a good point, and the other backed very well, these two doing the prettiest work seen as yet. **1877** [see WORKER 2]. **1882** *Society* 7 Oct. 23/1 As a man he has done extraordinary work at long-jumping, sprinting, and hurdle-racing. **1895** foot work [see FOOT *sb.* 35].

5. A particular act or piece of labour; a task, job. Also *gen.* something difficult to do, a 'hard task' (cf. 4b); or in special connexions, e.g. a particular operation in some manufacture. *Obs.* exc. *Hist.*

c **960** ÆTHELWOLD *Rule St. Benet* (Schröer 1885) 65 ðif hy ut an æcere wurc [*v.r.* weorc] habben [L. *si opera in agris habuerint*]. *c* **1205** LAY. 8709 An are nihte firste þat worc [*c* **1275** worch] wes iforðed. *a* **1300** *Cursor M.* 5527 Wit herd werckes þai heild þam in. **13..** *E.E. Allit. P.* B. 136 A þral ..vnþryuandely cloþed, Ne no festiual frok, bot fyled with werkkez. **1382** WYCLIF *Gen.* iv. 22 Alle werkis of bras and of yrun. *c* **1450** *Godstow Reg.* 318 He ought to mowe the ladies corne ix. daies.., without other werkes that he shold do. **1513** DOUGLAS *Æneis* VIII. v. *heading*, In loving of the douchty Hercules The pepill singis his werkis. *c* **1520** SKELTON *Magnyf.* 1095 Cockys armys! this is a warke, I trowe. **1580** G. HARVEY *Let. to Spenser* Poet. Wks. (1912) 627/2 Vnlesse ye might..haue your meate, and drinke for your dayes workes. **1819** REES *Cycl.* s.v. *Foundery*, The ear of the bell requires a separate work, which is done during the drying of..the cement. **1894** MAITLAND in *Engl. Hist. Rev.* IX. 419 At the beginning of the fourteenth century we see that some of the 'works' were done in kind, while others were 'sold to the homage'.

†**b.** In early use applied *spec.* (in *sing.* or *pl.*) to the building or repair of a church. *Obs.*

Cf. *Beowulf* 74, *Crist* 3.

1387 *E.E. Wills* (1882) 1 To the werkes of our lady of Abbechirch xx s. **1398** *Munim. de Melros* (Bann.) 490, I..sal paye ilke wowke..halfe a marc..to þair new werke of Melros. **1428** *E.E. Wills* (1882) 81 Y be-quethe to the wherk of the Ill of the toon side of the Cloistere..vj s viij d. **1482** in *Charters &c. Edin.* (1871) 169 Of ilk schip in generale of gudis ii bollis..to sanct Gelis werk.

c. *slang.* A criminal act or activity. Cf. JOB *sb.*[2] 1 b.

1812 J. H. VAUX *Vocab. Flash. Lang.* in *Mem.* (1964) 279 An offender having been detected in the very fact..is..said to have been *grab'd at work*. **1865** in *Comments on Etym.* (1983) XIII. III.–IV. 17 We..surrounded her from observation while at 'work'. **1926** J. BLACK *You can't Win* xxi. 338 Coppers located 'work' for burglars and stalled for them while they worked. *Ibid.* xxiv. 379 That kind of 'work' is unprofessional, unnatural, and disgusting. **1963** T. TULLETT *Inside Interpol* xiv. 192 If he netted only about 200 guilders he would start 'work' again in a week.

6. a. Trouble, affliction; in later use in lighter sense: Disturbance, fuss, 'ferment'. (See also 31.) **b.** Pain, ache: see WARK *sb.*[1] *dial.*

a **900** CYNEWULF *Juliana* 569 Þæt þam weliȝan wæs weorc to þolianne. **1297** R. GLOUC. (Rolls) 9207 Holichirche He bigan to worri & made him þe worse wurche. **1473** *Paston Lett.* III. 92 He seyde that thys troble sholde begyn in Maye, ..that the Scotts sholde make us werke. **1676** EARL OF ANGLESEY in *Essex Papers* (Camden) 71 Philipsburgh and Mastrick are sore pressed, and there is hot worke at both. **1717** PRIOR *Alma* III. 250 Tokay and Coffee cause this Work, Between the German and the Turk. **1848** MRS. GASKELL *Mary Barton* ii, This work about Esther, and not knowing where she is, lies so heavy on my heart. **1896** *Warwicksh. Gloss.* s.v., There'll be nice work over this broken window.

7. *Math.* The process of or an operation in calculation; a process of calculation written out in full; = WORKING *vbl. sb.* 7, 7 b. Now *rare* or *Obs.*

1557 RECORDE *Whetst.* Cc ij, The totalle will bei (as here in worke appeareth) 335016. **1623** J. JOHNSON *Arith.* I. C 1, The proofe of Addition is made by Subtraction; for if you subtract the numbers which you added from the totall of the Addition, there will remaine nothing, if the worke be truly done. *a* **1675** COCKER *Arith.* (1688) 249 Reduce a fraction to its lowest terms at the first Work. *Ibid.* 270 Quest. 6. What is the Quote of 8 divided by $\frac{3}{5}$? Answ. $\frac{40}{3}$ which is equal to $13\frac{1}{3}$. .. See the work in the margent. **1709** J. WARD *Introd. Math.* (1734) 19 Take a few Examples without their Work at large. **1839** MAYNARD *Goodacre's Arith.* (ed. 9) 37 When..the remainder is more than the divisor, the quotient figure was too small, the work must be rubbed out, and a larger number supplied.

8. *Physics* and *Mech.* The operation of a force in producing movement or other physical change, esp. as a definitely measurable quantity: see quots.

1832 W. WHEWELL *First Princ. Mech.* iv. 52 The *work done* does not depend on the pressure alone. *Ibid.* 53 The work done by a machine may be represented as certain pressures exerted through certain spaces. **1855** RANKINE *Misc. Sci. Papers* (1881) 216 'Work' is the variation of an accident by an effort, and is a term comprehending all phenomena in which physical change takes place. Quantity of work is measured by the product of the variation of the passive accident by the magnitude of the effort, when this is constant; or by the integral of the effort, with respect to the passive accident, when the effort is variable. **1873** MAXWELL *Electr. & Magn.* (1881) I. 5 The unit of Work is the work done by the unit of force acting through the unit of length measured in its own direction. **1877** ATKINSON tr. *Ganot's Physics* (ed. 8) 42 When a force produces acceleration, or when it maintains motion unchanged in opposition to resistance, it is said to do work. **1879** THOMSON & TAIT *Nat. Phil.* I. I. §238 In lifting coals from a pit, the amount of work done is proportional to the weight of the coals lifted; that is, to the force overcome in raising them; and also to the height through which they are raised.

II. 9. With possessive: The product of the operation or labour *of* a person or other agent; the thing made, or things made collectively; creation, handiwork. Also vaguely, the result of one's labour, something accomplished.

c **825** *Vesp. Psalter* viii. 7 Ðesettes hine ofer werc honda ðinra. *Ibid.* cxliv. 10 Ondettað ðe, dryhten, all werc ðin. *c* **888** ÆLFRED *Boeth.* v. §3 Ic wat ðætte God rihtere is his aȝenes weorces. **971** *Blickl. Hom.* 207 Wæs þæt ilce hus eac hwem draȝen, nalas æfter ȝewunan mennisces weorces þæt þa waȝas wæron rihte. **1382** WYCLIF *2 Chron.* xx. 37 For thou haddist couenaunt of þese with Ochosia, the Lord smote thi werkes. —— *Jer.* i. 16 Hem, that..offreden to aliene goddis, and honoureden the werc of ther hondis. *c* **1400** *26 Pol. Poems* xxiv. 236 Lord, þou shalt clepe me, And I shal answere to þe, werk of þyn hande. **1535** COVERDALE *Isa.* lxiv. 8 We all are the worke of thy hondes. **1551** ROBINSON tr. *More's Utopia* II. (1895) 156 Thether the workes of euery familie be brought. *a* **1593** MARLOWE & NASHE *Dido* III. ii, Ile make the Clowdes dissolue their watrie workes. **1667**

MILTON *P.L.* III. 59 The Almighty Father..bent down his eye, His own works and their works at once to view. **1697** DRYDEN *Virg. Georg.* IV. 809 The waxen Work of lab'ring Bees. **1773** MONBODDO *Lang.* (1774) I. Pref. 1 Man in his natural state is the work of God. **1843** CARLYLE *Past & Pr.* III. iv, And now thy work, where is thy work? Swift, out with it; let us see thy work! **1847** TENNYSON *Princess* III. 281 Dare we dream of that..Which wrought us, as the workman and his work, That practice betters? **1875** JOWETT *Plato* (ed. 2) III. 298 Workmen and also their works are alike apt to degenerate. **1890** KIPLING *Departm. Ditties*, etc. (ed. 4) 102 Mine's work, good work that lives!

b. The result of the action or operation of some person or thing; 'effect, consequence of agency' (J.); (one's) 'doing'; the device or invention *of* some one.

1382 WYCLIF *Isa.* xxxii. 17 Ther shal be the werk of riȝtwisnesse pes. **1604** SHAKS. *Oth.* V. ii. 364 Looke on the Tragicke Loading of this bed: This is thy worke. **1667** MILTON *P.L.* V. 112 Mimic Fansie..misjoyning shapes, Wilde work produces oft, and most in dreams. **1707** *Curios. Husb. & Gard.* 35 This wonderful Œconomy for the Propagation..of Animals can not be the Work of the fortuitous meeting of Atoms. **1753** CHALLONER *Cath. Chr. Instr.* 171 Other Hereticks..condemned Marriage as the Work of the Devil. **1818** SCOTT *Br. Lamm.* iv, What has been between us has been the work of the law, not my doing. **1859** G. MEREDITH *R. Feverel* xxiii, This suggestion, the work of the pipe.

10. Without possessive: A thing made; a manufactured article or object; a structure or apparatus of some kind, esp. one forming part of a larger thing. Now chiefly in generalized sense with qualification, esp. in established compounds such as BRICKWORK, FIREWORK, FRAMEWORK, LATTICEWORK, WAX-WORK.

c **825** *Epinal Gloss.* 699 *Opere plumario*, bisiuuidi uuerci. **1382** WYCLIF *Isa.* xxix. 16 As if..the werk sey to his makere, Thou hast not mad me. *c* **1470** HENRY *Wallace* V. 1135 Tre wark thai brynt, that was in to tha wanys. **1535** COVERDALE *Ezek.* i. 15, I sawe a worke off wheles vpon the earth. **1591** RALEIGH *Last Fight of Revenge* (Arb.) 21 All her tackle cut a sunder, her vpper worke altogither rased. **1598** BARRET *Theor. Mod. Warres* 134 Eight men who haue in their charge the iron workes, cables, anchors, and grappling. **1621** *Abridgm. Specif. Patents, Iron & Steel* (1858) 1 The misterie and arte of meltinge iron ewre, and of making the same into cast workes or barrs. **1697** DRYDEN *Æneis* VIII. 825 The radiant Arms beneath an Oak she plac'd... He rowl'd his greedy sight Around the Work. **1706** PHILLIPS, *Pastry*, Work made of Paste or Dough. **1805** T. LINDLEY *Voy. Brazil* 45 A long arched vault, with a plank work on one side. **1819** REES *Cycl.* s.v. *Foundery*, Foundery of statues, great guns, and bells... The matter of these large works is.. commonly a mixture of several [metals].

†**11.** An architectural or engineering structure, as a house, bridge, pier, etc.; a building, edifice.

a **900** CYNEWULF *Crist* 3 Se weallstan þe ða wyrhtan iu wiðwurpon to weorce. *c* **1000** ÆLFRIC *Hom.* I. 368 Se ðe ne bytlað of ðam grundwealle, his weorc hryst to micclum lyre. **1076–85** *Westm. Abbey Domesday Book* lf. 463 De quadam mansione terre apud London quam Anglica lingua 'Vuerc' appellant. *c* **1205** LAY. 16951 He lette bulden halles & rihte al þa workes þe ær weore to-brosene. *a* **1300** *Cursor M.* 8780 Þe wrightes þat suld rais þe werck. *c* **1375** *Sc. Leg. Saints* i. (*Petrus*) 14 Þu art petir, at is, oure stane, to byg myn wark one haff I tane. *c* **1450** *Merlin* ii. 27 The mountayne that the werke was sette on gan to tremble. **1540** PALSGR. *Acolastus* II. i. I iij b, This warke that is in buyldynge. **1660** M. CARTER *Honor Rediv.* 248 Gresham Colledge... This famous work and most worthy Colledge. **1667** MILTON *P.L.* I. 731 The work some praise And some the Architect.

b. *pl.* Architectural or engineering operations. ***Clerk of the Works, Master of the Works***: see CLERK *sb.* 6 c, MASTER *sb.*¹ 19 a.

a **1700** EVELYN *Diary* 12 Sept. 1641, The New Citidall was advancing with innumerable hands,..I was permitted to walk the round and view the workes. **1907** J. H. PATTERSON *Man-Eaters of Tsavo* vi. 66, I had works in progress all up and down the line.

12. *spec.* (*Mil.*) A fortified building, fortress, fort; a defensive structure, fortification; any one of the several parts of such a structure (often in *pl.*). Also as second element of a compound, as *earth-work*, *field-work*, *hornwork*, *outwork*, etc.

The continental equivalent is found in BULWARK.

a **1000** *Daniel* 44 To ceastre..þær Israela æhta wæron bewriȝene mid weorcum. *c* **1470** HENRY *Wallace* XI. 19 Fortrace, and werk that was with out the toun, Thai brak, and brynt. **1560** DAUS tr. *Sleidane's Comm.* 137 b, He taketh Turrine,..and fortifieth it with workes and strength of men. **1604** SHAKS. *Oth.* III. ii. 3, I will be walking on the Workes. **1613** —— *Hen. VIII*, V. iv. 61, I was faine to..let 'em win the Worke. **1669** STAYURED *Fortification* 4 There may be.. occasion in Forts to raise..Platforms, or Batteries, to command all the other Works. **1755** R. ROGERS *Jrnls.* (1769) 6, I..sent out four men as spies, who..informed me, that the enemy had no works round them, but lay entirely open to an assault. **1826** J. F. COOPER *Last of Mohicans* xv, Some six or eight thousand men..whom their leader wisely judges to be safer in their works than in the field. **1834–47** J. S. MACAULAY *Field Fortif.* (1851) 87 If the ditches of a work can be filled with water, it is an excellent means of defence. **1879** TENNYSON *Defence of Lucknow* ii, Frail were the works that defended the hold that we held with our lives.

13. A literary or musical composition (viewed in relation to its author or composer); often *pl.* and *collect. sing.*, (a person's) writings or compositions as a whole.

a **1300** *Cursor M.* 112 In hir wirschip wald I bigyn A last-and warc apon to myn. *c* **1375** *Sc. Leg. Saints* v. (*Johannes*) 524 Als tellis elynandus Of sancte Johnnis varkis, sayand þus, Quhene he suld þe ewangel wryte [etc.]. *c* **1450** CAPGRAVE *Life St. Aug.* Prol. 1 Than wil I, in þe name of our Lord Ihesu, beginne þis werk. *c* **1520** SKELTON *Garl. Laurel* 381 Plutarke and Petrarke..With Vincencius..that wrote noble warkis. **1525** *Extr. Aberd. Reg.* (1844) I. 111 Ony bukys or verkys of the saide Lutheris. **1540–1** ELYOT *Image Gov.* 41 He made also a newe lybrary, garnyshyng it..with most principall warkes in euery science. **1555** *Instit. Gentl.* K vj b, Alexander Magnus..vsed alwayes to carrye wyth hym the woorkes of Homer. **1610** HOLLAND *Camden's Brit.* I. 681 When I was first writing this worke. **1711** ADDISON *Spect.* No. 124 ¶1 A Man who publishes his Works in a Volume. **1837** DICKENS *Pickw.* xv, The famous foreigner—gathering materials for his great work on England. **1848** THACKERAY *Van. Fair* i, A Johnson's Dictionary—the interesting work which she invariably presented to her scholars on their departure. **1865** MAX MÜLLER *Chips* (1880) I. i. 18 This title distinguishes the Vedic hymns..from all other works. **1879** *Grove Dict. Mus.* I. 116 Bach wrote unceasingly.., and the quantity of his works is enormous. **1885** *Manch. Exam.* 11 Nov. 3/3 It bears a stronger resemblance to the work of 'Ouida' than to that of any other English writer. **1900** W. P. KER *Ess. Dryden* Introd. p. xix, The history of Corneille's original work.

14. A product of any of the fine arts (in relation to the artist), as a painting, a statue, etc. In the phr. ***a work of art*** including, besides these, literary or musical works (13), and connoting high artistic quality. Also (without *pl.*), artistic production in the abstract, or artistic products collectively.

1531 ELYOT *Gov.* I. viii, Pandenus, a counnyng painter,.. required the craftis man to shewe him where he had the.. paterne of so noble a warke. **1539** *Bible* (Great) Ps. lxxiv. 6 They breake downe all yᵉ carued worcke therof. **1611** SHAKS. *Wint. T.* V. ii. 107 Her Mothers Statue..by that rare Italian Master, Iulio Romano, who (had he himselfe Eternitie, and could put Breath into his Worke) would beguile Nature of her Custome. **1611** COTGR., *Ouvrage de Marqueterie*, Checker-worke, or Inlaid worke, of sundrie colours. *a* **1721** PRIOR *Dial., Locke & Montaigne* Wks. 1907 II. 243 Your Work is meer Grotesque, half images of Centaures and Sphynxes trailing into Flowers and branches. **1736** T. ATKINSON *Conf. Painter & Engraver* 16 If the Engraver..with masterly shading Touches improve the Work. **1853** DICKENS *Bleak Ho.* vii, [The portrait] is considered a perfect likeness, and the best work of the master. **1877** S. REDGRAVE *Descr. Catal. Water-Col.* 22 Protect your drawings..from the utter destruction so many fine works have suffered from exposure to the direct rays of the sun. **1883** *Atlantic Monthly* Jan. 86 The homage of rapt appreciation due to a great work of art. **1884** W. C. SMITH *Kildrostan* 43 The carved work mouldered fast 'Neath the suns, and the frosts.

†**15.** Make, workmanship; *esp.* ornamental workmanship (phr. ***of work*** = ornamental). *Obs.*

1393 LANGL. *P. Pl.* C. I. 179 Colers of crafty werke. *c* **1400** MAUNDEV. (Roxb.) xi. 46 Ane ymage of stane of alde werk. **1424** *E.E. Wills* (1882) 56 Too fyne borde-clothes, þe one of werk, þe oþer playn. **1474** CAXTON *Chesse* III. vii. (1883) 140 A gate of marble of meruayllous werke. **1529** CROMWELL in Merriman *Life & Lett.* (1902) I. 57 My best ioyned bed of Flaunders wourke. **1603** in Gage *Hengrave* (1822) 26 One large coobard carpett..of Turkeye work. *a* **1700** EVELYN *Diary* 17 Nov. 1644, A rare clock of German worke. *Ibid.* 18 Jan. 1645, The walls..are incrusted with most precious marbles of various colours and workes. **1795** MRS. COWLEY *Town before you* I. iii. 9 Why did I never tell you before that she is a sculptor. She has a large room full of fine things of her own work.

b. *concr.* An ornamental pattern or figure, ornament, ornamentation, decoration. *Obs.* or merged in other senses.

c **1467** *Noble Bk. Cookry* (1882) 52 Mak gret coffynes with lowe liddes..and lay on the liddes wild werks. **1547** in Feuillerat *Revels Edw. VI* (1914) 11 Cootes..of clothe of golde with workes. **1622** *Mourt's Relat. Engl. Plant.* 12 Baskets..curiously wrought with blacke and white in pretie workes. *Ibid.* 38 Their faces..painted,..some with crosses, and other Antick works. *a* **1700** EVELYN *Diary* 23 Mar. 1646, The bed was dress'd up with flowers, and the counter-pan strewed in workes.

16. The operation of making a textile fabric or (more often) something consisting of such fabric, as weaving or (usually) sewing, knitting, or the like; *esp.* any of the lighter operations of this kind, as a distinctively feminine occupation; also *concr.* the fabric or the thing made of it, esp. while being made or operated upon; needlework, embroidery, or the like.

See also DRAWN-WORK, FANCY WORK, LACE-WORK, OPEN-WORK, etc.

1382– [see NEEDLEWORK]. [**1390** GOWER *Conf.* II. 41 Whan sche takth hir werk on honde Of wevinge or enbrouderie.] **1440** in Peacock *Eng. Ch. Furniture* (1866) App. 182 A vestment of baudekyn yᵉ ground black with grene Werk. **1530** PALSGR. 290/1 Worke made of woll, *œuure de layne, lanifice*. **1560** *Bible* (Genev.) Ezek. xvi. 10, I clothed thee also with broydred worke. **1604** E. G[RIMSTONE] *D'Acosta's Hist. Indies* IV. xli. 320 Their maner of weaving their workes, being both sides alike. **1783** JOHNSON *Let. to Miss Thrale* (1788) II. 290 Your time, my love, passes, I suppose, in devotion, reading, work, and company... Of work, unless I understood it better, it will be of no great use to say much. **1795** MRS. COWLEY *Town before you* I. i. 2 Mrs. Fancourt ..(rising and laying down her work). **1842** DICKENS *Amer. Notes* iii, The work she had knitted, lay beside her. **1862** LYTTON *Str. Story* xlviii, Taking pleasure..not in music, nor books, nor that tranquil pastime which women call work. **1882** BESANT *All Sorts* vii. (1898) 65 On the other side [sat] a girl, with work on her lap, sewing.

17. An excavation in the earth, made for the purpose of obtaining metals or minerals; a mine. *Obs.* exc. = WORKING *vbl. sb.* 16.

1475 tyn werk [see TIN *sb.* 5]. **1482** *Cely Papers* (Camden) 113 All the schoutes yn the colle warkys and abowte the marttes were schett for joye. **1540–1** ELYOT *Image Gov.* 46 He wolde haue them sent into..the iles called Cassiterides, to labour in tynne workes. **1565** *Reg. Privy Council Scot.* I. 400 Sauffand the werk and mynd of Glengonar and Wenlok. **1604** G. BOWES in Cochran-Patrick *Early Rec. Mining Scot.* (1878) 111 Clensing an ould worke..I found the same 13ᵗʰ feette deepe. *c* **1610** in G. C. Bond *Early Hist. Mining* (1924) 15 After..his collyers have wrought sixe dayes in the workes. **1665** cole-workes [see COAL-WORK 2]. **1769** *Ann. Reg., Chron.* 102 Four colliers at work in a pit near Whitehaven, were all suffocated by the foul air of an old adjoining work. **1883** GRESLEY *Gloss. Coal-m.*, *Work*, a stall or working place.

b. A kind of trench in draining. *local.*

1653 BLITH *Eng. Improver Impr.* vii. 93 Cut a good substantiall Trench about thy Bog..; And..make one work or two just overthwart it. **1794** T. DAVIS *Agric. Wilts* 31 That the disposition of the trenches (provincially 'the works of the meadow,') should be uniform. **1799** T. WRIGHT *Art of Floating Land* 60 That one feeder made diagonally, and two others in different directions..will..with the assistance of the smaller works..be competent to effect a regular distribution of the water.

18. *pl.* An establishment where some industrial labour, esp. manufacture, is carried on, including the whole of the buildings and machinery used; a factory, manufactory, etc. In later use commonly construed as sing., in earlier use (to *c* 1860) also in *sing.* form. Often as the second element of a compound; see references below.

1581 iron workes, **1634–5** iron-work [see IRONWORK 2]. **1617** allome workes [see ALUM *sb.* 5]. **1722** DE FOE *Col. Jack* (1840) 273 The servants,..in both the works, were upwards of three hundred. **1748** in *Jrnl. Friends Hist. Soc.* (1918) 24 At Liverpool. We went to see..silk works where one wheel works above 300 Twisting bobbins. **179.** BURNS *Verses on window at Carron*, We came na here to view your warks In hopes to be mair wise. **1819–** gas works [see GAS *sb.*¹ 7]. **1822** tan-work [see TAN *sb.*¹ C. 1]. **1848** MRS. GASKELL *Mary Barton* vii, During the half-hour allowed at the works for tea. **1882** *Daily News* 4 Mar., A new works for the manufacture of steel wire. **1898** MRS. H. WARD *Helbeck* III. i, On night-duty at a large engineering 'works'.

attrib. **1885** W. S. HUTTON (*title*) The Works Manager's Hand-Book. **1901** *Scotsman* 11 Mar. 8/7 The position of the directors.., of their consulting chemist, and of their works chemist.

b. Phr. ***in the works*** = ***in the pipeline*** s.v. PIPE-LINE *sb.* b. *N. Amer.*

1973 *Globe & Mail* (Toronto) 12 July 2/3 In his statement, Mr. Cote said he had been informed during the election campaign that a 'telegraph organization was in the works in certain ridings of the South Shore'. **1976** *National Observer* (U.S.) 16 Oct. 10/3 As might be expected, a movie deal is in the works. **1979** *Tucson Mag.* Jan. 10/3 Actually there is a sequel in the works and the project was begun as a two film package. **1984** *National Times* (Austral.) 2 Nov. 41/2 There are, of course, follow-up books in the works.

19. Something that is to be or is being operated upon: in various connexions (see quots.; cf. also 15).

1680 MOXON *Mech. Exerc.* x. 190 The Diameter of the Work they intend to Turn in the Lathe. **1799** G. SMITH *Laboratory* I. 104 Boil the work, either in alum-water, or aqua fortis. **1881** RAYMOND *Mining Gloss.*, *Work*. Ore not yet dressed.

20. A set of parts forming a machine or piece of mechanism: orig. *sing.*, esp. as the second element of compounds (see references below); as an independent word now only *pl.*, the internal mechanism of a clock or watch, which actuates the hands or the striking apparatus.

Also (*colloq.*) humorously applied to the internal organs or viscera of an animal, as in ***to take out the works*** = to 'draw' a fowl, etc., or of a person.

a **1628–** [see CLOCK-WORK]. **1667–** [see WATCHWORK]. **1670–** [see WHEELWORK]. **1766** A. CUMMING (*title*) Elements of Clock and Watch-work. **1769** W. EMERSON *Mechanics* 109 This work is within the watch between the two plates. **1773** T. MUDGE *Descr. Timekeeper* (1799) 40 The repeating work. *Ibid.*, The balance work. **1819** REES *Cycl.* s.v. *Watch*, The interior works of an ordinary watch. **1835** DICKENS *Sk. Boz*, *Parish* ii, He took to pieces the eight-day clock..under pretence of cleaning the works. **1884** 'MARK TWAIN' *Huck. Finn* xxxii. 333 Here we're a running on this way, and you hain't told me a word about Sis, nor any of them. Now I'll rest my works a little, and you start up yourn. **1885** —— in *Century Mag.* Dec. 196/1 Then it would bray—..spreading its jaws till you could see down to its works. It was a disagreeable animal. **1906** E. DYSON *Fact'ry 'Ands* xv. 197 'Ceptin fer er hun-expected wail he jerked out iv 'is works now 'n 'again, that cat was just er livin' silence.

b. *slang* (orig. *U.S.*). ***the (whole) works***, the whole lot, everything; *esp.* in phrases, ***to give*** (or ***tell***) ***the works***: to tell the whole story; ***to shoot the works***: see SHOOT *v.* 23 j; ***to give*** (someone) ***the works***: to give (him) a rough time, *spec.* to murder; also, to give (someone) the full treatment (not necessarily unpleasant); ***to get the works***: to receive severe punishment, reprimand, adverse criticism, etc.

1899 J. LONDON *Let.* 18 May (1966) 38, I..quite enjoyed the thought of saying good-bye to the whole works. **1920** *Collier's* 5 June 36/3 'I ain't trying to jimmy into your most intimate affairs, but is they—*is* they a girl?'.. He..sat down ..and gimme the works. **1927** *Vanity Fair* XXIX. 134/2 'Giving a guy the works' is handing someone a raw deal. **1928** *Amer. Mercury* Apr. 429/2 One-Lung here squealed, an' I got the works for two years—poundin' rocks wit' a sledge. **1929** C. F. COE *Hooch* vii. 156 This man never was bumped here at all. They gave him the works some place a long way off. **1930** *Daily Express* 23 May 11/3 Threatening that unless the money was produced somebody would 'get the works'. **1934** WODEHOUSE *Right Ho, Jeeves* ix. 111 Heave a couple of sighs. Grab her hand. And give her the works. **1936** J. Steinbeck *In Dubious Battle* iii. 35 Tell him the works. **1969** E. Bagnold *Autobiogr.* xii. 236 *The Chinese Prime Minister* is a better play than *The Chalk Garden* but it didn't get the works. **1979** L. Kallen *Introducing C. B. Greenfield* xiv. 193, I have uncovered a sensational story that is crying to be written... Best-seller list, movie, the works.

c. *pl.* A drug addict's equipment for taking drugs. *U.S. slang.*

1934 L. Berg *Revelations of Prison Doctor* iv. 42 All became adept in the use of 'the works'; this was a syringe and needle. **1951** *N.Y. Times* 15 June 14/3 Do they ask you if you want the 'works' when you're buying needles? **1953** W. Burroughs *Junkie* xiv. 140, I went into the bathroom to get my works. Needle, dropper, and a piece of cotton.

21. A froth produced by fermentation in the manufacture of vinegar: cf. work *v.* 33.

1839 Ure *Dict. Arts* 4 To..see if the fermentation [of the vinegar] has been complete..we plunge into the liquor a white stick or rod..: if it be covered with a white thick froth, to which is given the name of work (*travail*), we judge that the operation is terminated.

III. Phrases. (See also above senses.)

* with *work* as obj. of a preposition.

†**22. a work, awork** [A *prep.*[1]]: = *at, on, to work* (23, 26, 28, 29); esp. in ***to set a work***. *Obs.* exc. as in a-work (q.v.).

c **1380** Wyclif *Serm.* Sel. Wks. II. 16 Monkis and freris assenten to werris wiþouten cause, and bringen þes lordis awerke. *c* **1400** *Sowdone Bab.* 2599 Tho was Durnedale set a werke. **1450** *Paston Lett.* I. 167 Asay how ye can sett hem a werk in the Parlement. **1450–1530** *Myrr. our Ladye* II. 67 That your redyng & study be..pryncypally to enforme your selfe, & to set yt a warke in youre owne lyuynge. **1480** *Cov. Leet Bk.* 431 That they that set them awarke shuld pay for hym. **1530** Palsgr. 712/2 Sette hym nat a worke, he can do yvell ynoughe of hymselfe. **1556** in *Vicary's Anat.* (1888) App. iii. 4. 175 Beggers..to be sett a worke, & be compelled ..to gett their owne lyvinges. **1678** Cudworth *Intell. Syst.* I. iv. 437 The Gods and Demons being first made, by the Supreme God, were set a work..by him afterward in the making of man. **1694** W. Wotton *Anc. & Mod. Learn.* (1697) 371 To set their Members awork to collect a perfect History of Nature. *a* **1716** South *Serm.* (1823) I. 170 To move and set a work the great principles of actions.

23. at work.

Used predicatively with *set* (set *v.*[1] 25); *to work* is now more usual (see 29).

a. Occupied with labour; engaged in a task; working, esp. at one's regular occupation. (Of a person or animal; also of a machine.)

1613 Shaks. *Hen. VIII*, III. i. 74, I was set [= seated] at worke, Among my Maids. **1683** Moxon *Mech. Exerc., Printing* xvii. ¶1 That the Matrice fly or start not back when it is at Work. **1688** Holme *Armoury* III. 369/2 You may rest your right Hand or Arm upon it [*sc.* the maulstick],..whilst you are at work [*sc.* painting]. **1692** R. L'Estrange *Fables* ccccxl. 417 You [the Mole] have Nothing for Digging 'tis True; but pray who set you at Work? **1709** Strype in *Thoresby's Lett.* (1832) II. 235 The book will make one hundred sheets..there are three presses at work about it. **1765** Goldsm. *Ess.* Misc. Wks. 1837 I. 351 We may..set beggars at work. **1840** Dickens *Old Cur. Shop* x, The poor woman was still hard at work at an ironing-table. **1882** Besant *All Sorts* xxxii. (1898) 222 The street..was as quiet as on the Sunday, the children being at school and the men at work.

b. *gen.* Occupied in some action or process, esp. one directed to a definite end or result; actively engaged; operating. (Of persons or their faculties, or of animals; also of forces or influences.)

1655 *Clarke Papers* (Camden) III. 17 The Blades..who were att worke to have brought new troubles uppon us. *c* **1680** Beveridge *Serm.* (1729) I. 344 The Father is always at work in the government of the world. *a* **1700** Evelyn *Diary* 7 Oct. 1688, The Jesuites hard at worke to foment confusion among the Protestants. **1820** Southey *Wesley* I. 3 He has set mightier principles at work. **1862** *Cornh. Mag.* V. 35 The mare..continued her feeding. How she enjoyed this plashy young grass! She had been at work in this way for the last five or six hours. **1887** Lowell *Democracy* etc. 12 The little kernel of leaven that sets the gases at work. *a* **1890** Liddon *Life Pusey* (1893) II. 151 Newman..was at work on his article on 'The Catholicity of the English Church'. *Ibid.* 170 The same influence..was already at work.

c. in passive sense: In process of being worked.

1911 *Act 1 & 2 Geo. V* c. 50 §36 Two shafts..with which every seam for the time being at work in the mine shall have a communication.

24. in work. a. †(*a*) = *at work*, 23 a; (*b*) in regular occupation; also with qualifying adj., as ***in full work, in good work*** = working full time or remuneratively.

1535 Coverdale *1 Chron.* x. [ix.] 33 Daye and night were they in worke withall. **1568** Abp. Parker *Corr.* (Parker Soc.) 328, I am content to set some of my men in work. *c* **1610** in G. C. Bond *Early Hist. Mining* (1924) 15 It is mutche wished..that suche an ingein may be seene in worcke. **1842** W. C. Taylor *Notes Tour Lancs.* 39 When in good work the united earnings of both averaged about 30s. weekly.

†**b.** *to put in work*: (*a*) to make use of; (*b*) to put in operation: = *set to work*, 29. *Obs.*

c **1400** Maundev. (1839) xxviii. 288 In that Contree..men putten in werke the Sede of Cotoun. **1626** C. Potter tr. *Sarpi's Hist. Quarrels* 100 The Iesuites..put in worke all their artifices. **1653** Urquhart tr. *Rabelais* I. viii. 41 For his Gloves were put in work sixteen Otters skins,..for the bordering of them. **1664** J. Webb *Stone-Heng* (1725) 193 These rude Remains being put in Work, in his Judgment, before the Flood.

25. of work. a. ***piece of work***: see piece *sb.* 7. **b.** —— ***of all work*** (†***works***): employed in all kinds of work, esp. in a household: chiefly in ***maid-of-all-work*** (see maid *sb.*[1] 4 b); hence allusively.

1775 *Pennsylv. Even. Post* 30 Mar. 114/2 Advt., Wanted a complete Servant for a Place of all Work, in a middling Family. **1797** Jane Austen *Sense & Sensib.* xxxviii, Two maids and two men, indeed..! No, no; they must get a stout girl of all works. **1821** Scott *Mrs. Radcliffe* Biogr. Mem. (1834) I. 359 A garrulous waiting-maid;..a villain or two of all work. **1821** Byron *Reply to Southey* Wks. (1846) 513/1 This arrogant scribbler of all work. **1822** —— *Vis. Judgem.* c, Mine is a pen of all work. **1886** Ruskin *Præterita* I. iii. 97 The kitchen servant-of-all-work.

†**26. on work,** in ***to set*** (a person, etc.) ***on work*** = *to work* (29). *Obs.*

1549 Latimer *4th Serm. bef. Edw. VI* (Arb.) 40 To the setting his subiectes on worke, and kepyng them from idlenes. **1551** Robinson tr. *More's Utopia* Transl. Ep. (1895) 16 Hauing no profitable busines wherupon to sette himself on worke. *a* **1568** Ascham *Scholem.* II. Wks. (1904) 239 His witte shalbe new set on worke. **1576** Gascoigne *Droome of Doomesday* Wks. 1910 I. 224 They..buyld houses,..till feildes,..and set milles on worke. *a* **1645** Featly *Reynolds* in Fuller *Abel Rediv.* (1651) 487 It pleased his Majesty to set some learned men on worke, to translate the Bible. **1692** Norris *Pract. Disc. Div. Subj.* (1722) III. 134 When the Powers of the Soul shall be more awaken'd, and its thoughts more vehemently set on work. **1788** Priestley *Lect. Hist.* v. lii. 401 By setting on work such immense numbers of our manufacturers.

27. out of work (out of 11 b): having no work to do, unemployed, workless. Also (with hyphens) *attrib.*, or as *sb.*; hence ***out-of-worker***; ***out-of-workness***.

1599 Shaks. *Hen. V*, I. ii. 114 All out of worke, and cold for action. **1864** J. O'Neil *Diary* 10 Apr. in J. Burnett *Useful Toil* (1974) I. 85 One half of the time I was out of work and the other I had to work as hard as ever I wrought in my life. **1885** *Marine Engineer* 1 Sept. 157/2 'Out-of-work benefit' came to £57,000. **1886** *Daily News* 4 Feb. 5/7 The Amalgamated Engineers..had lost £40,000 last year in out-of-work pay. **1887** *Spectator* 4 June 763/2 Afraid of being out of work. **1888** [see out of III.]. **1894** A. Morrison *Tales of Mean Streets* 48 The advent of a flush sailor.., disposed to treat out-o'-workers. **1903** A. McNeill *Egregious Engl.* v. 49 Out-of-workness is..the most fearful thing in life that can happen to an Englishman. **1906** *Westm. Rev.* Jan. 39 The unemployed of all classes, including the genuine out-of-works. **1913** A. Spender in H. Barnett *Canon S. A. Barnett* (1918) II. xlvi. 273 How to tide over the winter for the out-of-work docker. **1939** 'G. Orwell' *Coming Up for Air* II. ix. 153 We'd suddenly changed from gentlemen..into miserable out-of-works whom nobody wanted. **1955** M. Gilbert *Sky High* viii. 105 He was an out-of-work actor. **1974** R. Butler *Buffalo Hook* v. 45 I'm just an out-of-work who wants to stay that way.

28. to go to work (go *v.* 34): to proceed to some action (expressed or implied); to begin doing something; to commence operations. So ***to fall to work*** (see fall *v.* 67 e).

1377 Langl. *P. Pl.* B. v. 347 Vche a mayde that he mette he made hir a signe Semynge to synne-ward..and to the werke ȝeden. **1393** *Ibid.* C. VII. 181 To werke we ȝeden. **1563–87** Foxe *A. & M.* (1596) 1811/1 Say your mind, & go briefly to worke: for I think it almost dinner time. *a* **1586** Sidney *Arcadia* II. ii. (1912) 152 Swearing he never knew man go more aukewardly to worke. **1601** Shaks. *Twel. N.* IV. i. 36 Ile go another way to worke with him: Ile haue an action of Battery against him. **1718** *Free-thinker* No. 20 ¶2, I shall go a shorter and a plainer way to work. **1771** Goldsm. *Hist. Eng.* I. 363 This parliament..went expeditiously to work upon the business of reformation. **1890** *Temple Bar* July 329 His wits went instantly to work.

29. to set to work (set *v.*[1] 112, 113). **a.** *trans.* (*a*) To set (a person, the faculties, etc.) to a task, or to do something; less commonly, to put (a thing) in action; *refl.* to apply oneself to labour, or to some occupation or undertaking; to set about doing something.

1497–8 in *Archæol. Jrnl.* (1886) XLIII. 168 A fyne..for werkyng by nyght & settyng to werk a child vnbound & vnablid. *c* **1520** Skelton *Magnyf.* 1246 A nysot..That wyll syt ydyll..And can not set herselfe to warke. **1719** De Foe *Crusoe* I. (Globe) 246, I set Friday to Work to boiling and stewing. **1749** Smollett *Gil Blas* XII. i. (1782) IV. 211 The time draws near when I shall set thy address to work. **1827** Faraday *Chem. Manip.* iv. (1842) 105 Such a lamp..is..soon set to work, and as soon extinguished. **1867** 'Ouida' *Cecil Castlemaine*, etc. 235 Somebody else daring him to go in for honours,..he set himself to work to show them all what he could do. **1879** Sala *Paris Herself Again* xxxi, The owners set their wits to work.

†(*b*) To begin working upon: cf. 23 c. *Obs.*

1694 T. Houghton *Royal Instit.* Ded. A 3 Which Veyns and Mines, if they was..Set to Work, by any that understands them, would..prove as Rich.

b. *intr.* for *refl.*: see a (*a*): = 28.

1691 W. Nicholls *Answ. Naked Gospel* 92 The Doctor sets to work to his exposition of the Trinity. **1782** R. Cumberland *Anecd. Emin. Painters* I. 147 The devout painter sate to work. **1825** *New Monthly Mag.* XVI. 353, I ..set to work at another two-act piece. **1889** H. D. Traill *Strafford* iv. 46 Charles..set seriously to work to govern alone.

** with *work* as obj. of a verb. (See also 3 b.)

30. to cut out work *for* a person: to prepare work to be done by him, to give him something to do; now only ***to have (all) one's work cut out (for one)*** (colloq.): to have enough, or as much as one can manage, to do.

1619, 1795 [see cut *v.* 57 l]. **1843** Dickens *Christmas Carol* ii. 61 Old Fezziwig stood out to dance with Mrs. Fezziwig. Top couple too; with a good stiff piece of work cut out for them. **1862** Trollope *Orley Farm* II. xxxi. 247 Then Mr. Chaffanbrass rose..and every one knew that his work was cut out for him. **1866** [see cut *v.* 57 l]. **1874** Hardy *Far from Madding Crowd* II. xxii. 276 What with one thing and another, I see that my work is well cut out for me. **1879** H. C. Powell *Amateur Athletic Ann.* 19 This [race] Crossley had all his work cut out to win. **1893** R. L. Stevenson *Catriona* vii. 71 'Ye'll find your work cut out for ye to establish that,' quoth she. **1899** E. W. Hornung *Amateur Cracksman* 43 'We shall have our work cut out,' was all I said. **1927** R. Austin Freeman *Magic Casket* vii. 222 'You will have your work cut out,' I remarked, 'to trace that man. The potter's description was pretty vague.' **1951** *Sport* 27 Jan.–2 Feb. 9/3 The Quakers will have their work cut out to keep the bigger clubs away.

31. to make work. a. (also ***to make a work***): To work havoc or confusion; hence, to make a to-do or fuss, to cause disturbance or trouble (cf. 6); †in quot. 1574, to trouble oneself *to do* something. *dial.*

1530 Palsgr. 616/2 He maketh suche a worke whan he cometh that all the house is wery of hym. **1574** *Satir. Poems Reform.* xlii. 234 Thay maid na werk To seek ony. **1581** Pettie *Guazzo's Civ. Conv.* III. (1586) 136 These women.. like some Phisitions, make work where all was well before. **1607** Shaks. *Cor.* I. iv. 20 There is Auffidious. List what worke he makes Among'st your cloven Army. **1678** *Lauderdale Papers* (Camden 1885) III. 102 It is a foolish thing for scots men to complain or make worke heir, or to endeavour a Rebellion in scotland. **1867** *E. B. Ramsay's Remin.* (ed. 15) 30 People make a work if a minister preach the same sermon over again. **1816** Scott *Antiq.* ix, Ou dear! Monkbarns, what's the use of making a wark? **1884** Walford *Baby's Grandmother* iv, Passing in and out and making no end of a work.

b. ***to make work for***: to give (a person, etc.) something to do.

1595 Shaks. *John* II. i. 303 Yong Arthur..Who..this day hath made Much worke for teares in many an English mother. **1622** Mabbe tr. *Aleman's Guzman d'Alf.* II. 238 Lest by sauing their workmanship, my selfe might haue made worke for the hang-man. **1706** E. Ward *Wooden World Diss.* (1708) 2 To make more Work for the Hempen Whores in London.

c. with qualifying adj., as ***to make good, short, sure*** (etc.) ***work*** (*of* or *with* a person or thing): to do the business, or deal with the person or thing, well, shortly, surely, etc.; often with special implication, as ***to make short work of*** or ***with***, to destroy or put an end to quickly; to settle and dismiss peremptorily; ***to make sure work with***, to secure, to get safely into one's possession or control.

1592 Shaks. *Rom. & Jul.* II. vi. 35 Come with me, & we will make short worke. **1607** —— *Cor.* IV. vi. 95, 100 You haue made good worke, You and your Apron men... You haue made faire worke. **1608** Topsell *Serpents* 265 Hauing made sure worke with one, she [*sc.* the spider] hyeth her to the Center of her Web, obseruing..whether any newe prey will come. **1706** M. Henry *Gen.* xxxviii. 7 Sometimes God makes quick work with sinners. *a* **1774** Goldsm. tr. *Scarron's Com. Romance* (1775) I. 164 Believing they would at last make shorter work with me, and dispatch me with pistols. **1789** Twining *Aristotle's Treat. Poetry* (1812) II. 52 Seeing what strange work Lord Shaftsbury has made with this passage in his..translation of it. **1824** Scott *Redgauntlet* let. xi, Wild wark they made of it; for the Whigs were as dour as the Cavaliers were fierce. **1826** Disraeli *Viv. Grey* VI. i, It is a very awful tale, sir, but I will make short work of it. **1859** H. Kingsley *G. Hamlyn* xli, The Doctor, on his..mare, was making good work of it across the plains. **1885** *Law Times* LXXIX. 169/2 A Lords Committee would probably make very short work of these precedents.

*** with qualifying adj. (or phr.: see also 1 c, d, 14, 31 c).

32. good work: a morally commendable or virtuous act; an act of kindness or good will; *esp.* (in religious and theological use) an act of piety; usually *pl.* such acts done in obedience to divine law, or as the fruits of faith or godliness (cf. 1 b).

c **1000** *Rule of Chrodegang* i, þurh soðe lufe & þurh hyrsumnesse & þurh oðre gode worc. *c* **1020** *Rule St. Benet* (Logeman) 14 Ðif beteran oðram on godum weorcum & eadmodren we beoð ȝemette. *c* **1175** *Lamb. Hom.* 9 Oðre godere werke þe nu were long eou to telle. *a* **1300** *Cursor M.* 26525 Es na god werc wit-vten mede, Ne na wick wit-vten wrak. **1340** *Ayenb.* 160 Zigge ich wel, þet in on wyt þise zeue uirtues be-uore yzed byeþ þe boȝes of riȝtuolnesse, and al þet frut of guod workes þet of ham wexeþ belongeþ to þise trawe. **1382** Wyclif *Matt.* xxvi. 10 What be ȝe heuy [*gloss* or sory] to this womman? sothely a good work she hath wrouȝt in me. *c* **1449** Pecock *Repr.* I. iii. 13 He ouȝte be douȝty and strong into gode werkis. **1516** *Kal. New Leg. Eng.* (Pynson) 2 He dyed in great Age full of good werkes & vertues. **1596** Harington *Metam. Ajax* 41 When a man hath done but two good workes in all his life. **1653** W. Ramesey *Astrol. Rest.* 183 Those times are to be shunned at the beginning of any good work. **1724** Erskine *Serm., Tit. iii. 8* Wks. (1791) 92 To make a work a good work, it must be done, by a good and holy person, renewed by the Spirit of Christ, and justified by his merit. *a* **1819** G. Hill *Lect. Div.* v. iii. (1850) 472 Good works are the fruits and evidences of a true and lively faith. **1887** J. Hutchison *Lect. Phil.* iii. 25 Every good work wrought within us and wrought by us.

b. In trivial sense, esp. in phrases ***carry on with, get on with, keep up,*** etc. ***the good work.***

1920 'Sapper' *Bull-Dog Drummond* xii. 309 Vallance Nestor carried the good work on. **1938** G. Greene *Brighton Rock* VII. ix. 347 Drink up. We better get on with the good work. *a* **1953** E. O'Neill *Long Day's Journey* (1956) I. 17 So keep up the good work, Mary.

**** **33.** Proverbs and proverbial sayings.

14.. [see hand *sb.* 62 e]. *c* **1530** R. Hilles *Comm.-pl. Bk.* (1858) 140 Meny hondys makyth lyght werke. **1670** Ray *Prov.* 158 All work and no play, makes Jack a dull boy. **1897** *Globe* 9 July 1/2 Heroic conduct of this type has to be, and is, regarded by British officers..as 'all in the day's work'.

IV. 34. *attrib.* and *Comb.* **a.** Simple attrib., as *work-boat, -chant, -hour, -life, light, -load* (LOAD *sb.* 4c), *-norm* (NORM 1c), *-pause, -place, -plan, -room, -site, -song, -thing, -time, -tool, -week, -yard* (see also WORK-DAY, etc.); (of persons) employed in manual, mechanical, or industrial labour, as *work-gang, -girl, -lass, -person, -servant* (see also WORK-FOLK, -MAN, etc.); (of animals) used for work on a farm or otherwise (= 'of burden' or 'of draught'), as *work-beast, -horse, -mare, -nag, -ox, -steer, -stock* (cf. OE. *weorcnieten*); (of clothes) worn for work, as *work boot, -clothes, pants, -shirt, -shoe, -wear*; pertaining to or used for needlework or the like (see 16), as *work-case, -desk, -drawer, -pattern, -stand* (see also *work-bag*, etc. in d). **b.** Objective, etc., as *work-seeker*; *work-producing* adj. **c.** Instrumental, as *work-driven, -gnarled, -hard, -hardened, -soiled, -stained, -thickened, -wan, -weary, -worn* adjs. **d.** Special comb.: **work-and-back** *Printing* = *sheet-work* s.v. SHEET *sb.*[1] 12b; **work and tumble, work and turn, work and twist,** methods of printing the second side of a sheet of paper from the same forme as the first (see quots.); **work-bag, -basket,** a bag, or basket, to contain implements and materials for needlework; **work-bench,** a bench, with accessories, at which mechanics work, esp. a carpenter's bench; **work-board,** a board upon which some kind of manual work is done; **work book,** (*a*) in a business firm etc., a book containing a record of daily duties, work (to be) done, etc.; (*b*) (chiefly *U.S.*), a book in which are set out problems to be worked out, questions to be answered, etc.; **work-box,** a box to contain instruments and materials for needlework; **work camp** orig. *U.S.*, (*a*) a camp organized for a work project, esp. by volunteers serving the community; (*b*) = *labour camp* s.v. LABOUR, LABOR *sb.* 8; **work card,** (*a*) a card issued by one's employer and serving as a kind of identity document; (*b*) a pupil's card on which are set out questions to be answered, problems to be worked, etc. (cf. *work-book* (*b*) above); **work-covenant** *Theol.* = *Covenant of Works* (see COVENANT *sb.* 8a, and cf. sense 1b above); **work ethic,** work seen as virtuous in itself, a term usu. connected with Protestant attitudes and deriving from Max Weber's thesis on the origins of modern capitalism (cf. *Protestant ethic* s.v. PROTESTANT *a.* 1b); **work experience,** work projects arranged for the purpose of providing experience of employment, esp. for school-leavers; **work-fellow** = *work-mate*; **work-field,** (*a*) a field or piece of ground used for training in farm-work; (*b*) a 'field' of work, region of activity; **work flow,** in an office or industrial organization, the sequence of processes through which a piece of work passes from initiation to completion; **work-force,** the workers or employees collectively, usu. of a particular firm or industry; **work furlough** *U.S.*, leave of absence from prison by day in order to continue in one's daily work; **work group,** (*a*) a group of people in a factory or the like who customarily work together; (*b*) = *work party* (*a*) below; **work-hand,** (*a*) [HAND *sb.* 8] a person employed by another to do work; (*b*) with defining adj. [HAND *sb.* 9], as *a good work-hand*, one who is a 'good hand' at work, a capable worker; **work-harden** *v. trans. Metallurgy*, to toughen (a metal) by cold-working; also *intr.*, to become tough as a result of cold-working; so **work-hardened** *ppl. a.*, **work-hardening** *vbl. sb.*; **work head,** (*a*) = HEADSTOCK 1b; (*b*) an interchangeable working attachment for a powered implement or tool; **work-holder,** a device in a sewing-machine for holding the work or fabric; †**work-holy** *a. Theol.*, aiming at or pretending to holiness on the ground of works (see 1b); **work-horse,** (*a*) a horse used for work on a farm; (*b*) *fig.*, a machine, person, etc., that dependably performs arduous labour; **work-in-progress,** work undertaken but not completed, esp. (*a*) in commerce (see quot. 1978); (*b*) in the arts; †**work-jail,** a penal workhouse; **work-lead,** †(*a*) a vat (LEAD *sb.*[1] 5a) used for fermentation; (*b*) = G. *werkblei*, lead as it comes from the smelting furnace, containing impurities; †**work-like** *a.*, inclined for work, industrious; **work-mate,** a fellow-labourer, one engaged in the same work with another or others; **work measurement** (see quot. 1979); **work-minded** *a.*, eager to work hard; eager to go out to work; hence **work-mindedness; workmonger,** a controversial term for one who expects to be justified by works (see 1b); **work name,** an alias used by someone engaged in secret intelligence work; **work party,** (*a*) a group of people who come together to carry out a piece of work of mutual or social benefit; (*b*) = *working party* s.v. WORKING *ppl. a.* 2c (*d*); **work permit,** a document representing official permission to take a job in a foreign country; **workpiece,** the object which is worked on with a machine or tool; **work point,** in the People's Republic of China, a unit used in calculating wages due, based on the quality and quantity of work done; **work rate** *Football*, the extent to which a player contributes towards the fatiguing running and chasing in a game; **work release** *U.S.* = *work furlough* above; **work-rule** *U.S.*, one of a set of regulations governing working procedures, conditions, etc., in a business or industry; **work-sharing,** short-time working by all employees within an industry intended to prevent redundancies when there is an excess of available man-power; **work-sheet,** (*a*) = *work-book* (*a*) above; also *fig.*; (*b*) *U.S.*, a questionnaire; (*c*) a paper on which are recorded notes, calculations, etc., relating to work in progress; (*d*) a list of exercises, problems, etc., to be worked by a student (cf. *work-book* (*b*) above); **work-shy** *a.*, shy of or disinclined for work, lazy; also *absol.* as *sb.*; hence *work-shyness*; **work-space,** (*a*) *Computers* = *working storage* s.v. WORKING *vbl. sb.* 16b; (*b*) space (for people) to work in; **work-stone,** a sloping cast-iron plate (? originally a stone) in the front of an ore-hearth, with a groove down which the melted metal flows; **work study,** (*a*) investigation of the methods of working in a business, etc., with the aim of increasing output and efficiency; (*b*) used *attrib.* with reference to schemes of combining work and study established in Communist China; **work surface** = *work-top* below; cf. *working surface* s.v. WORKING *vbl. sb.* 16b; **work-table,** a table for supporting working materials and tools; *esp.* a small table with compartments and drawers, and sometimes with a well for needlework; **work-team,** (*a*) a team of draught-horses, oxen, etc.; (*b*) a team of people who work together, a work group, *spec.* in Communist China any of the working units making up a commune; **work-top,** a table or other flat surface suitable for working on, *esp.* in a kitchen; **work-train,** a train of wagons or trucks for conveying materials for construction or repair of a railway, etc.

1959 L. M. HARROD *Librarians' Gloss.* (ed. 2) 249 *Sheet work*, printing one side of a sheet of paper from an 'inner forme' and the other from an 'outer forme'. Also called '*work and back'. **1967** E. CHAMBERS *Photolitho-Offset* ii. 18 Sheet work is the term used to indicate that two formes are used to print the sheet, sometimes called 'work and back'. **1931** H. JAHN *Hand Composition* xvi. 251 The *work-and-tumble method..in a broad sense is also a work-and-turn method. *Ibid.* 254 In the work-and-tumble form the pages are so imposed that the sheet must be 'tumbled' or turned on the 'long cross'. **1959** L. M. HARROD *Librarians' Gloss.* (ed. 2) 296 *Work and tumble*, the method of printing the second side of a sheet of paper by turning it over in its narrow direction and feeding it into a printing machine to print the reverse side. **1888** *Work and turn [see *sheet-work* s.v. SHEET *sb.* 12b]. **1919** V. POSSNETT *Stonework* 49/3 The sheet may be turned over after the first side has been printed, and the same edge of the sheet fed to the grippers for a second impression. This is termed 'work-and-turn'. **1931** H. JAHN *Hand Composition* xvi. 263 The Dexter standard jobbing folder..makes thirteen different folds adapted to work-and-turn and sheetwise forms. **1964** Work-and-turn [see *half-sheet* (*b*) s.v. HALF- II. n]. **1930** *20th Cent. Encycl. Printing* viii. 253 The *work and twist form is used for the printing of ruled work where the vertical and horizontal rules of a sheet are printed with one impression. **1968** *Gloss. Terms Offset Lithogr. Printing* (B.S.I.) 25 *Work and twist*, printing one side of the sheet, then reversing the sidelay edges and front and back edges of the sheet, and printing the same side again with the same printing plate. **1775** TWISS *Trav. Port. & Sp.* 36, I bought here several *work-bags made in the Brasils. **1853** DICKENS *Bleak Ho.* v, Some half-dozen reticules and work-bags, 'containing documents', as she informed us. **1743** BULKELEY & CUMMINS *Voy. S. Seas* 39 A small Basket..about the Size of the Womens *Work-baskets in England. **1897** VOYNICH *Gadfly* I. vii, His mother's work-basket stood in a little cupboard. **1380** *Lay Folks Catech.* (L.) 866 Thow schalt not coueyte þy neyȝborys wyf,..ne his oxe ne his *werk-best. **1782** T. JEFFERSON *Notes State Virginia* (1787) 275 While we have land to labour then, let us never wish to see our citizens occupied at a *work-bench, or twirling a distaff. **1864** R. KERR *Gentl. Ho.* 307 A Carpenter's Shop..will contain..the well-known work-bench of the trade, and perhaps a lathe. **1811** SUTCLIFF *Trav. N. Amer.* 58 A tailor..whose *work-board being at a front window, he had an opportunity of noticing the passengers in the street. **1885** C. G. W. LOCK *Workshop Rec.* Ser. IV. 325/1 The [watchmaker's] 'workboard' should be made of well-seasoned wood. **1941** H. I. CHAPELLE *Boatbuilding* v. 339 Lines of a 45-foot *workboat. **1977** *Washington Post* 4 Sept. A12/3 A fleet of workboats is continually dredging a passable channel. **1910** A. BENNETT *Clayhanger* III. vi. 371 Edwin was familiar with every detail of the printer's *work-book. **1932** W. D. LEWIS et al. (*title*) Practical workbook in English. **1959** HALAS & MANVELL *Technique Film Animation* xix. 171 The Work Book is derived directly from the final storyboard, and is an analysis of each shot and sequence on a frame-by-frame basis. **1960** G. E. EVANS *Horse in Furrow* ix. 115 Work Books offer us a great deal of information about farming methods at this time [*sc.* early nineteenth century]. **1975** *Publishers Weekly* 17 Nov. 98/1 With its workbook approach of charts, graphs, questionnaires and the like, this book will put some women off. **1976** *National Observer* (U.S.) 22 May 16/1 At first wearing a suit, then gradually assuming *work boots and old clothes. **1605** P. ERONDELL *French Garden* sig. E7 verso, I haue not my siluer thimble, it is within my *worke-boxe. **1790** F. BURNEY *Diary* Jan. (1940) 263 Everything..was spread about, as in any common day—work-boxes, netting-cases, etc. etc! **1811** MISS HAWKINS *Countess & Gertrude*, Workbox. **1848** DICKENS *Dombey* viii, Berry brought out a little work-box,..and fell to working busily. **1933** NICHOLS & GLASER *Work Camps for America* 13 The types of participants in *work camps vary according to the purpose of the camps and the organizations which control them. **1943** F. L. WRIGHT *Autobiogr.* (rev. ed.) IV. 309 Now by way of an architect's work-camp comes fresh adventures in the desert. **1964** M. BANTON *Policeman in Community* iii. 56 They stopped to talk with a youth they knew who was serving a sentence in a work camp. **1970** *Honey* June 106/3 International Work Camps are held in most countries. Some camps offer paid work in forestry or farming. Others have specific projects that are usually related to social service. **1981** 'W. HAGGARD' *Money Men* i. 18 The Gestapo ..had sent him back to Germany to a work camp where he'd been starved to death. **1984** *Listener* 11 Oct. 26/1 An elaborate process of deception was instituted, by which the evacuation of Jews to the death-camps was disguised as a 'resettlement' into 'work-camps'. **1959** M. LEVIN *Eva* 4, I managed to get a blank German *work card. **1966** J. DERRICK *Teaching Eng. to Immigrants* 239 The work cards, picture-cards, wall pictures and flashcards which accompany the course, are also recommended. **1975** A. WATSON *Living in China* iv. 99 The work card issued by the place of employment is an important means of social identification. **1980** *Daily Tel.* 12 Feb. 6/8 Instead of text books the scheme uses a series of work-cards... These..are distributed to the pupils according to their ability. **1879** MRS. A. E. JAMES *Ind. Househ. Managem.* 25 You must..have a *work-case with thread, cotton, needles, pins, thimble, scissors, knife, and pencil. **1946** R. BLESH *Shining Trumpets* I. iii. 57 Perhaps the most familiar form of *work-chant is the vendor's street cry. **1967** A. L. LLOYD *Folk Song in Eng.* i. 54 The work-chants of Portland quarrymen. **1901** 'MARK TWAIN' in *Century Mag.* Nov. 26/2 Tommy was..in his dreadful *work-clothes. **1978** F. WELDON *Praxis* xx. 170 She changed out of her work clothes. **1892** WESTCOTT *Gospel of Life* 260 The *work-covenant of Sinai brings to light the duty and the weakness of men. **1611** FLORIO, *Scrignetto*, a little shrine, chest, coffin, or deske... Also a womans *worke-deske. **1848** THACKERAY *Van. Fair* viii, She took from her *work-drawer an enormous..piece of knitting. **1880** E. H. ROLLINS *New Eng. Bygones* (1883) 42 These farmers..were almost always *work-driven and weary. **1959** *Past & Present* xv. 44 Weber also asserted that Calvinistic Protestantism was an indispensable precondition of the development of a capitalistic *work ethic. **1973** P. A. WHITNEY *Snowfire* vi. 112 The work ethic, you mean?..my little Puritan. **1980** *Jrnl. R. Soc. Arts* July 468/1 *They* are showing the way which we should follow—if only we were not 'locked on to' some puritanical work ethic. **1975** *Whitaker's Almanack 1976* 1041/2 In recent years there has been a marked growth in the provision of '*work-experience' schemes which involve the participation of pupils in the work of industrial, commercial and other firms. **1983** *Fortune* 16 May 112/3 CETA's primary approach, providing 'work experience' in temporary public service jobs, does no good at all, presumably because the jobs don't lead anywhere. Work experience has big payoffs, however, when it comes in the form of on-the-job training for a permanent position in the private sector. **1526** TINDALE *Rom.* xvi. 21 Thimotheus my *worke felow. **1564** *Brief Exam.* D ij b, We nede many workefelowes. *a* **1890** J. H. NEWMAN *Meditations* (1893) II. 289 We thus pray..for our associates and work-fellows. **1903** C. COLERIDGE *Charlotte M. Yonge* x. 276 She was the most delightful comrade, workfellow, or playfellow. **1888** *Times* (weekly ed.) 9 Nov. 9/3 A training-farm or '*workfield' managed by the poor-law authorities. **1918** ABP. DAVIDSON in *Times* 30 Dec. 6/3 Their activities are in His larger workfield now. **1950** I. A. HERRMAN *Office Methods, Systems, & Procedures* vii. 131 *Work flow diagrams are effective in solving various kinds of problems. **1976** *National Observer* (U.S.) 19 June 2/4 Byrd is a master of legislative detail with a reputation as a fair-minded manager who accelerates the work flow. **1961** *Times* 30 May 13/7 Books come off no assembly line. The raw material is provided by a notoriously undisciplined *work-force. **1982** *Daily Tel.* 18 Nov. 2/1 They were non-unionised because 'that is the wish of the majority of the work force'. **1957** *Statutes of California 1956 & 1957* II. MDLXXX. 2933 If the court so directs that the prisoner be permitted to continue in his regular employment, the *work furlough administrator shall arrange for a continuation of such employment so far as possible without interruption. *Ibid.* 2934 This section shall be known..as the 'Work Furlough Rehabilitation Law.' **1970** *Criminology* May 63 Work furlough has been used..for felons as well as misdemeanants. **1980** *New Age* (U.S.) Oct. 15/2 Both men received suspended jail sentences and three years probation; each will serve about a month in a work-furlough program or community service and must undergo psychiatric counselling. **1948** *Common Ground* Summer 41/2 Their pianos sound the *work-gang chorus. **1981** W. EBERSOHN *Divide Night* xii. 157 A work gang..cleaning up the litter along the road. **1848** MRS. GASKELL *Mary Barton* iv, The blooming young *work-girl. **1886** BESANT *Childr. Gibeon* I. vi, We're work-girls, and we've got to earn our living. **1913** D. H. LAWRENCE *Sons & Lovers* x. 256 She began to spare her hands. They, too, were *work-gnarled now. **1957** J. KEROUAC *On Road* vi. 216 A wiry..man..with work-gnarled hands. **1954** J. A. C. BROWN *Social Psychol. of Industry* iv. 114 A factory or a society is not ordinarily a mass of isolated individuals..; it is an integrated pattern of primary *work-groups. 1960 Ann. Reg. 1959 381 All of them [sc. sects] laid emphasis on activity: dancing, propagation of the faith, and free labour with work-groups building and cleaning temples. 1972 M. Argyle Social Psychol. of Work ix. 233 Many studies have shown that job satisfaction is affected by relationships in the work group. 1834 W. Sewall Diary (1930) 154 He was an excellent *work hand. 1866 Carlyle E. Irving in Remin. (1881) I. 129 Miller's assistant and work-hand for many years was John Bell, a joiner. 1893 T. N. Page Ole Virginia 173 He was a good work-hand, and a first-class boatman. 1932 W. Faulkner Light in August i. 14 The gray woman not plump and not thin, manhard, *workhard, in a serviceable gray garment. 1924 Engineer 7 Mar. 249/1 Metal rolled cold or drawn through dies may be *work-hardened to an extent rendering it quite unsuitable for further working. Ibid. 251/2 It may be that its [sc. 'browning''s] real function is to reduce the tendency of the steel to work-harden. 1961 New Scientist 16 Mar. 672/1 The ability of the material to work-harden by deformation more than compensates for the thermal weakening of the interatomic bonds. 1972 Mineral. Mag. XXXIII. 265/2 Naturally deformed galena has been 'work-hardened' by tectonic movement. 1984 E. P. DeGarmo et al. Materials & Processes in Manuf. (ed. 6) ii. 41 When most materials are plastically deformed, they work-harden; that is, they become harder and the yield-point stress is raised. 1859 Geo. Eliot Adam Bede iv, She stands knitting.. with her *work-hardened hands. 1924 Jrnl. Iron & Steel Inst. CX. 431 The abnormally low value of the limit of proportionality..is found in both quench-hardened and work-hardened steels. 1973 J. G. Tweeddale Materials Technol. II. iv. 102 Cold drawing can impart a good surface finish and accurate size to a product and leaves the material in a work-hardened condition which is often desirable. 1924 Engineer 7 Mar. 248/2 (heading) *Work-hardening of metals and the Herbert tester. 1973 J. G. Tweeddale Materials Technol. II. iv. 87 The work-hardening can be used to give enhanced strength. 1930 Engineering 25 Apr. 538/3 A pair of flat ways for the *work-head, tailstock and journal supports. 1960 Farmer & Stockbreeder 12 Jan. 121/1 (Advt.), Other workheads, quickly interchangeable without tools, include —12 and 17in. hedge-cutters, pruning saw,..etc. 1964 S. Crawford Basic Engin. Processes vii. 194 The workhead is ..a self-contained unit carried at the opposite end of the table to the tailstock. 1875 Knight Dict. Mech. 2120/2 The cylinder sewing-machine has a cylindrical *work-holder for sewing seams on sleeves, trousers,..and other tubular work. 1528 Tindale Obed. Chr. Man 42b, The sophistres, *werke-holy, & iustifiars,..which so magnifie their dedes. 1543 Richmond Wills (Surtees) 41 Inventarye..in ye stable ..Item iij^or *warke horses. 1812 Sir J. Sinclair Syst. Husb. Scot. I. 17 A pair of work-horses may be accommodated in a space of sixteen feet by eight. 1949 Sun (Baltimore) 3 Oct. 2/6 This caliber howitzer has gained the reputation of being the 'work horse' of the Army. 1966 Electronics 3 Oct. 54 The satellites will be launched on improved versions of the workhorse Delta vehicle. 1973 Listener 20 Dec. 841/2 Gerald Ford..has been known..as the most dependable of Republican work-horses. 1981 H. Engel Ransom Game (1982) xxii. 133 The big barn doors. The entrance is on the lower floor, where the cows and work horses used to be. 1982 Habitat Catal. 1982/83 56/2 A real workhorse of a table, with maple block top. 1985 A. Blond Book Book iii. 42 An admirable workhorse of a publisher. 1848 Mrs. Gaskell Mary Barton vii, To try and get a little sleep before *work-hour. Ibid., Unfettered by work-hours. 1930 Times 25 Mar. 24/5 '*Work in progress, less instalments thereon,' is £141,069, against £47,351 in the previous year. 1952 R. Giroux Let. 10 Mar. in Breit & Lowry Sel. Lett. M. Lowry (1967) 450 It is clear that the place of the finished book will be important in your long work-in-progress. 1976 P. Israel French Kiss (1977) ii. 24 The work-in-progress on one of the easels. 1978 J. Kellock Elements of Accounting x. 176 Work-in-progress, is the value of incomplete work in the factory and is usually computed on the following basis: the cost of materials and production labour plus the proportion of indirect expenses chargeable to the work up to its present stage of manufacture. 1618 Bolton Florus (1636) 233 Breaking up the *worke-jayles, or bridle-wels [L. refractis ergastulis] by right of Warre. 1834 Poulett Scrope in Hansard's Parl. Debates Ser. III. XXIII. 1326 The whole country must be studded with district workhouses, or rather work-gaols. 1920 D. H. Lawrence Lost Girl vi. 98 Yet it was always packed with colliers and *work-lasses. 1471–2 Durham Acc. Rolls (Surtees) 156 Pro operacione cc^a v^xx viij petr. plumbi in iiij *warkledes, brewledes, et j steplede. 1881 Raymond Mining Gloss., Work-lead. See Base bullion. 1946 J. W. Day Harvest Adventure vii. 112 The pond..is tenanted by tame decoy ducks, pinioned, whose *work-life is to lure the wild birds down. 1977 National Observer (U.S.) 1 Jan. 1/2 Men.. committed to serious and demanding work lives. 1947 J. Steinbeck Wayward Bus 13 Get the *work-light on the long cord connected. 1977 Chicago Tribune 2 Oct. I. 53 (Advt.), Self-cleaning oven..Fluorescent worklight. a1642 Bedell Erasmus in Fuller Abel Rediv. (1651) 57 Seaven Cities, no contemptible portion of witty and *work-like Greece. 1946 *Work-load [see load sb. 4c]. 1962 Listener 4 Jan. 4/1 The application of time study to speed and tighten up the work load. 1962 J. Glenn in Into Orbit 195, I pushed and pulled thirty times at the bungee cord which permitted me to exercise with a known workload. 1978 G. A. Sheehan Running & Being xv. 210, I shift to shorter steps..to maintain the same workload. 1985 Times 18 Jan. 5/1 He is one of more than 1,000 teachers whose workload is being analysed by the National Union of Teachers in a survey to be published next week. 1627 Drayton Agincourt lxxviii, A *Work-mayd in her Summers weed, With Sheafe and Sickle. 1587 Lanc. Wills (Chetham Soc.) 144 One *worke horse or maire. 1851 H. Mayhew Lond. Labour (1861) II. 95 The man accordingly got a boat, and was soon afloat among his old *workmates. 1948 (title) Manual of procedures: *work measurement in public works offices (U.S. Bureau of Yards & Docks). 1969 J. Argenti Managem. Techniques 271 The procedure used in Work Measurement to determine the amount of labour required to do a job is to time how long it takes the average man to perform each element of the job. 1979 Gloss. Terms Work Study (B.S.I.) 2 Work measurement, the application of techniques designed to establish the time for a qualified worker to carry out a task at a defined rate of working. 1954 Encounter Sept. 33/1 The Army requires ..*work-minded people who try to do a good job of whatever they're told to do. 1968 Economist 11 May 46/1 The more 'work-minded' a mum in her later years, the less available she is to look after her daughter's kids. 1960 Encounter Nov. 27/1 William H. Whyte, Jr.,..points out that some large corporations, worried about the decline in '*work-mindedness', are seeking to substitute an ideology of corporate loyalty. 1549 Allen Jude's Par. Rev. xii. 3–6 The truth of the christen faith..beyng persecuted..of Emperours and Kynges, of *workemongers. 1581 Marbeck Bk. Notes 882 The Harlots and Publicans repenting truly, and..submitting themselues to the mercie of God, are more acceptable vnto God, then ye proud workmongers, that trust in their owne righteousnesse. 1882 Mrs. Booth Addr. Crit. Salvation Army 7 One class of critics stigmatise us as being ..work-mongers. 1576 Wills & Inv. N.C. (Surtees 1835) I. 411, ij *woryke nagges. 1977 'J. le Carré' Hon. Schoolboy iii. 54 Karla..was the *workname of the Soviet case officer who had recruited Bill Haydon..and had the running of him. 1959 Encounter Feb. 14/2 At the local level, there must always be potential disputes between workers and management over redundancy, *work-norms, wage-differentials..and so on. 1980 Times 24 May 14/7 You can poke fun at life under Communism.. how to fiddle your work-norms. 1567 Richmond Wills (Surtees) 210, xxj *wark oxen. 1897 O. Wister in Harper's Mag. Mar. 534/2 He looked as wise as a work-ox. 1927 Amer. Speech II. 366/2 The man had on his *work pants this morning. 1978 H. C. Rae Sullivan i. ii. 19 Denim workpants slung low on his thick hips. 1957 R. Frankenberg Village on Border 20 They [sc. women] also work together in sewing groups and *work-parties preparing material for sales-of-work. 1957 V. W. Turner Schism & Continuity in an African Society i. 22 The cutting and clearing of bush..may involve a collective work-party..of kin and neighbours. 1981 I. Boland tr. Ginzburg's Within Whirlwind I. iii. 22 Many considered the shock of being drafted to a work party every bit as bad as being arrested. 1815 Scott Guy M. xxix, Miss Bertram's *work-patterns. 1894 A. S. Robertson Provost o' Glendookie 91 The Glendookian year contained two *work-pauses. 1965 Globe & Mail (Toronto) 26 June 13/3 The Union des Artistes will give endless *work permits, he points out, but is most cautious about applications for membership. 1971 Times 25 Feb. 4/1 A Commonwealth citizen wishing to work here in future will need a work permit issued for a specific job in a specific place for a fixed initial period. 1983 Daily Tel. 12 May 4/8 Work permit clamp. The Singapore Government has tightened up on employment permits for foreigners. 1807 Monthly Mag. I Feb. 67/1 The return of the carriage without any assistance from the *work-person. 1980 S. Brett Dead Side of Mike ii. 17 Even the most brilliant workperson in the world needs some sort of tools. 1934 Webster, *Workpiece. 1949 Tool Engineers Handbk. (Amer. Soc. Tool Engineers) xcviii. 1544 Improper workpiece locating can readily result in excessive troubles and spoilage. 1952 Economist 6 Dec. 721 The guiding wheel is charged negatively and the work-piece positively. 1978 Sci. Amer. Nov. 110/2 The surface of the workpiece undergoes much more heating in abrasive machining than in conventional machining. a1828 Bewick in Zoologist (1862) Ser. I. XX. 8150 He had it sent for to my *work-place. 1875 Act 38 & 39 Vict. c. 55 §91 Any factory, work-shop, or workplace..not kept in a cleanly state. 1957 J. Kerouac On Road II. ix. 170 A paper for the want ads and *workplans. 1976 Columbus (Montana) News 10 June 1/1 A district program and a work plan was written outlining the conditions and situations relating to soil and water conservation within the district. [1959 C. K. Yang Chinese Village in Early Communist Tradition xvii. 246 For most co-operatives the distribution of income was based neither on equal sharing nor on individual needs but on the quantity and quality of labor performed under the system of labor units or points.] 1964 Current Scene 15 Apr. 2/2 The use of *work points rather than absolute money terms to express wages..preserves Peking's control over the allocation of the harvest. 1969 [see Tachai]. 1979 China Now Jan.–Feb. 14/1 She cultivates vegetables..and earns nine workpoints a day. 1969 *Work-rate [see through ball s.v. through- 2]. 1976 South Notts. Echo 16 Dec. 7/5 In midfield J. Uren read the game well and with a higher work rate could be destined for higher things. 1957 Session Laws & Resolutions State of N. Carolina 489 The governing body of the State Prison System is authorized and directed to establish a *work release plan for those serving sentences for misdemeanors. 1981 C. Bartollas Introd. Corrections viii. 168 Objectives of work release. 1828 Scott F.M. Perth vii, The *work-room of Simon Glover was filled to crowding by personages of no little consequence. 1848 Mrs. Gaskell Mary Barton xiii, Thoughts..of the morrow..to be spent in that close monotonous work-room. 1963 Economist 16 Mar. 997/2 A committee made a two-year study of the railway dispute and recommended far-reaching changes in the *work-rules on the trains [in the U.S.], to try to eliminate the 'feather-bedding' which keeps unnecessary men on the job. 1979 Wall Street Jrnl. 20 Dec. 18/5 Mr. Church will be under considerable pressure to implement the [U.S. mineworkers'] convention's..work-rule demands. 1892 Daily News 18 May 6/1 There are no openings for *work-seekers. 1593 Lanc. Wills (1884) 155, I gyve..unto everye one of my *worke servants over and beside theire waigs x s. apeece. 1934 Planning II. xxxiv. 12 Another group of proposals look to *work-sharing as a method of adjusting labour to labour requirements. a1974 R. Crossman Diaries (1976) II. 56 They were entirely concerned about the problem of redundancy and in particular the impression created by Gunter's public statements that in principle the Government is opposed to work-sharing in the motor-car industry. 1925 S. Lewis Arrowsmith xxxix. 427 'I'll find out from my wife what dates we have already and telephone you tomorrow evening'. 'So you let the Old Woman keep the *work-sheet for you, huh?' 1930 Dialect Notes VI. 73 Professor Jud made a number of specific suggestions regarding mechanical features of the work-sheets. 1958 Listener 31 July 155/1 Sorted away in the stacks are some 5,000 sets of poets' worksheets, the notes, drafts, revisions. 1966 J. Derrick Teaching Eng. to Immigrants 238 A new type of course, designed for eight-year-old foreign learners, consisting of gramophone records, teacher's notes, and pupils' 'working scripts' which are work-sheets and meant to be expendable. 1967 R. Bregzis in Cox & Grose Organization & Handling Bibl. Rec. by Computer v. 118 NUC catalogues and other files or catalogues are checked as necessary, and all information [is] recorded on a catalogue worksheet. 1975 Language for Life (Dept. Educ. & Sci.) x. 145 It is even less likely to happen where children work individually through assignment cards or work sheets. 1976 P. Alexander Death of Thin-Skinned Animal xx. 206 Look, if you haven't done any maintenance there, boyo, how come I've got a work-sheet for renewing thirty foot of ogee guttering and repointing the bloody gable end? 1981 Amer. Speech 1977 LII. 167 He employed a variable questionnaire based upon the New England short worksheets. 1923 Dialect Notes V. 235 A *work shirt made of crossbarred cotton cloth. 1980 Daily Tel. 19 Nov. 15/8 (Advt.), Fisherman's smock. Original workshirt of local fishermen. 1965 H. I. Ansoff Corporate Strategy (1968) vi. 96 Royal Little has built the successful Textron Corp. composed of consumer electronics, textiles, helicopters, *work shoes, and satellite motors. 1980 D. E. Westlake Castle in Air vi. 63 Manuel was dressed in rough corduroy trousers,..heavy workshoes, and a coarse cotton shirt. 1904 H. Preston-Thomas Rep. Vagrancy Switz. 4 If the council..decide that (to use the expressive term officially employed) he is *work-shy (Arbeits-scheu). 1928 Daily Express 2 Apr. 7/4 To make the lot of the work-shy as favourable as that of the worker. 1983 Times 12 Oct. 14/5 The Gravediggers' Union, understandably affronted by having their members portrayed as drunken workshies. 1904 H. Preston-Thomas Rep. Vagrancy Switz. 9 The offence of most of them has been begging or '*work-shyness.' 1975 BP Shield Internat. May 5/4 Up to three teams of divers may be maintained under these conditions to permit a 24-hour per day diving operation at the *work-site. 1980 Daily Tel. 20 Mar. 28 (Advt.), He must be an engineer, between 30 and 50, perfectly fluent in French and English, with overseas experience in work-site construction. 1932 W. Faulkner Light in August ii. 28 The men in faded and *work-soiled overalls. 1911 Jrnl. Amer. Folk-lore XXIV. 379 Like the other songs, the *work-songs give a keen insight into the negro's real self. 1933 E. Caldwell God's Little Acre xiv. 205 The sound of the picks..rose and fell in their ears to the rhythm of Uncle Felix's work-song. 1977 Listener 25 Aug. 244/3 The persistent play with three for four notes suggests incantation or work-songs. 1959 New Scientist 25 June 1375/2 Such a code would mean building an automatic translating system into existing designs of computers, thereby reducing their '*work-space'. 1979 Kraft & Toy Mini/Microcomputer Hardware Design viii. 413 Its general register set is placed in main storage and realized as a 16-word area of memory that is considered a workspace. 1979 Tucson (Arizona) Citizen 20 Sept. 1C/1 Several high-rise government office buildings with a combined work space of perhaps 100,000 to 150,000 square feet. 1985 Which Computer? Apr. 53/2 Even on a fully configured IBM PC.. you can find yourself running out of workspace. 1892 Pall Mall Gaz. 15 Jan. 3/2 His rough and *work-stained hearers. 1901 Scotsman 8 Oct. 5/1 There are some of us who have learned to love that work-stained river. 1849 C. Bronte Shirley xxix, He placed another chair opposite that near the *work-stand. 1911 Blackw. Mag. Sept. 359/2 Setting him up with a *work-steer and a milk cow. 1877 Rep. Indian Affairs 22 Unprecedented storms and heavy roads had.. broken down our light Indian *work-stock. 1883 'Mark Twain' Life on Miss. 603 The people cared first for their work stock,..horses and mules were housed in a place of safety. 1911 Blackw. Mag. Sept. 360/2 Wheat..for his work-stock feed. 1667 in Pettus Fodinæ Reg. (1670) 35 Five Hearths with Backs, Cheeks, *Workstones, Iron Plates, and other necessaries. 1884 C. G. W. Lock Workshop Rec. Ser. III. 336/2 Extending forwards from the front of the hearth.. is an iron plate called the 'fore-stone' or 'work-stone'. c1951 (title) The implications of *work study (Imperial Chemical Industries Ltd.). 1962 E. Snow Other Side of River (1963) xxx. 227 Part-time and work-study middle schools are discussed in the next chapter. 1965 J. Ch'ên Mao & Chinese Revolution (1967) I. iii. 72 In August 1920 Mao and others founded a small Russian affairs study group as well as sponsoring a Work-study Scheme for students to go to Russia. Ibid. v. 95 Work-study students who had just returned from France or Russia. 1978 Cornish Guardian 27 Apr. 6/7 (Advt.), Applicants would be expected to have at least two years' practical experience in the Work Study and O & M field. 1971 House & Garden Dec. 76/2 Spotlights illuminating *work surfaces and dining-area. 1979 J. Barnett Backfire is Hostile! xii. 117 They were inside a kitchen, work surfaces, refrigerator, an electric cooker gleamed. 1790 F. Burney Diary Jan. (1905) IV. 348 Dr. Fisher says he hopes it was not a card-table, and rather believes it was only a Pembroke *work-table. 1800 S. & Ht. Lee Canterb. T. (ed. 2) III. 139 On one side stood an ornamental work-table. 1885 'Mrs. Alexander' At Bay i, A small basket work-table, overflowing with bright-colored wools and silk. 1885 Ann. Rep. U.S. Office Indian Affairs 41 There is a growing desire among these Indians to obtain and care for stock and work cattle... The desire to obtain *work-teams has been great. 1933 L. I. Wilder Farmer Boy xi. 75 He was old enough to..drive the old, gentle work-team... They were wise, sober mares. 1951 R. Firth Elem. Social Organization ii. 47 The clash between the values of..work-team and church which so often occurs in a highly differentiated larger community. 1965 New Statesman 3 Sept. 321/1 The giant communes were divided into smaller units. The basic unit is a work-team, generally about the size of an average village. 1972 M. Argyle Social Psychol. of Work x. 252 The construction of work-teams, introducing democratic supervision, participation in management, and arousal of intrinsic motivation all increase cooperation. 1978 China Now Mar./Apr. 18/2 Each family belongs to a work team,..a group of teams makes up a brigade, and..the brigades together make up the commune as a whole. 1931 W. Faulkner Sanctuary xvi. 146 Along the fence a row of heads hatted and bare above *work-thickened shoulders. 1970 L. Jeffers My Blackness is the Beauty of this Land 8 Work-thickened hand thoughtful and gentle on grandson's head. 1812 Miss Mitford in L'Estrange Life (1870) I. 168 The playthings and the *workthings, that this unlucky search discovered. 1882 Besant All Sorts xx. (1898) 143 During *work-time he planned amusements for Miss Kennedy and her girls. 1889 Browning Asolando, Epilogue iv, At noonday in the bustle of man's work-time. 1588 Lanc. Wills (Chetham Soc.) 151 Bellowes and other *work tooles. 1955 E. Pound Classic Anthol. I. 78 We have blunted our axes, We lack work-tools. 1953 Archit. Rev. CXIV. 127/1 Though not as highly resistant to abrasion as Formica it is considerably cheaper, and suitable for anything but *worktops where there is much cutting and sliding. 1967 Observer 21 May 30/5 A work-top bridging two drawer units makes a perfectly good dressing-table. 1978 Lancashire Life

Oct. 125/1 (Advt.), Now in our upstairs showroom shown in three displays of door and worktop colour—the kitchen of rounded edges—doors and worktops in a host of colours and textures. **1984** *Which?* Oct. 458/3 If you are going to use tiles for a worktop, check that they have good scratch resistance. **1884** *Lisbon* (Dakota) *Star* Oct. 10 The *work-train is again engaged in hauling gravel on the road. **1877** TENNYSON *Harold* I. i. 54 Look! am I not *Work-wan, flesh-fallen? **1967** *St. Andrews Citizen* 25 Feb. 5/4 Men's *workwear. Full range mens overalls..trousers, jackets, coats and boilersuits. **1981** *Daily Tel.* 22 Sept. 9 (Advt.), The workwear rental company. **1853** C. BRONTË *Villette* I. v. 82 A brief holiday, permitted for once to *work-weary faculties. **1865** MRS. L. L. CLARKE *Common Seaweeds* iv. 75 The man of business takes a ramble on the sea shore, work-weary. **1935** *Economist* 26 Oct. 802/1 Hourly wage rates are a little higher;..the *work-week is a little longer. **1980** *News & Observer* (Raleigh, N. Carolina) 28 Oct. 21/3 Layoffs in a local furniture plant and shortened workweeks at county textile mills. **1865** C. STANFORD *Symb. Christ* vi. (1878) 170 When for a few moments that *work-worn man takes up his Bible. **1614** T. GENTLEMAN *England's Way* 31 Houses, and *worke-yards erected for Coopers, and Rope-makers. **1864** R. KERR *Gentl. Ho.* 308 An enclosed Work-yard is.. required... The Workshops ought to face it.

35. *attrib.* and *Comb.* with *works* (sense 18), as ***works bus***, ***canteen***, ***club***, ***kitchen***, ***manager***, ***outing***; **works committee, council**, a committee of workers or their representatives, formed for joint discussions with employers.

1969 R. BLYTHE *Akenfield* iv. 80 Works-bus waiting to carry him from door to site. **1980** A. TOWNSIN *Blue Triangle* iii. 48/1 A second works bus. **1963** A. HOWARD in Sissons & French *Age of Austerity* i. 17 The Naafi and the works-canteen. **1978** J. B. HILTON *Some run Crooked* iii. 19 He ate his midday meal in a works canteen. **1908** *Mod. Business* Aug. 69/1 Any surplus is devoted to some charity or to some of the works clubs. **1917** *Interim Rep. on Joint Standing Industr. Councils* 4 in *Parl. Papers 1917–18* (Cd. 8606) XVIII. 415 We are of opinion that..Works Committees, representative of the management and of the workers employed, should be instituted..to act in close co-operation with the district and national machinery. **1966** T. LUPTON *Managem. & Social Sci.* iii. 63 In a small firm, Joint Consultation might take place in a Works Committee. **1925** *Glasgow Herald* 31 July 5 The most important is the Works Council Law of 1920, which requires a works council to be set up in each establishment employing 20 persons or more. **1977** *Times* 22 Sept. 2/8 The need to develop industrial democracy on the shop floor through works councils. **1908** *Mod. Business* Aug. 69/1 Another valuable outlet for its energies is the management of a Works Kitchen. **1918** A. BENNETT *Pretty Lady* xxvii. 177, I used to take their part against the works-manager. **1976** *Derbyshire Times* (Peak ed.) 3 Sept. 3/7 Mr..Marshall (26), works manager,.. escaped unhurt. **1943** J. B. PRIESTLEY *Daylight on Saturday* viii. 47 His bus ride to the factory..took on the air of a works outing. **1974** *Listener* 23 May 664/2 A works outing to Blackpool.

work (wɜːk), *v.* Pa. t. and pple. **worked** (wɜːkt), *arch.* and *techn.* **wrought** (rɔːt). Forms: see below. [(1) OE. *wyrcan*, pa. t. *worhte*, pa. pple. *ʒeworht*, = OS. *workian*, OHG. *wurchen*, *worhta*, *wurhta*, *giworht*, *gewurchet* (MHG. *wurken*, *würken*, *worhte*, *geworht*, *gewürket*), ON. *yrkja*, *orta*, *ortr*, Goth. *waurkjan*, *waurhta*, *-waurhts*:—OTeut. **wurkjan*, **wurχt-*; (2) OE. (Mercian) *wircan*, = OFris. *werkia*, *wirza*, *wrochte*, *wrocht*, OS. *wirkian*, *war(a)hta*, *war(a)ht*, OHG. *wirchen*, *warahta* (MHG. *wirken*, *warhte*, G. *wirken*; *wirkte*, *gewirkt*), ON. *verkja*, *virkja* to feel pain:—OTeut. **werkjan*, **warχt-* (**wurχt-*). A third OE. type represented by late *wercan*, *weorc(e)an* seems to point to early influence of the sb. *we(o)rc* (see WORK *sb.*) upon the vowel of the vb.

Other Teut. forms are OFris. *werka*, OS. *-werkon*, (*-werkot*), (M)Du., M(LG.) *werken*, (*wrochte*, etc.), OHG. *werchôn* (MHG. *werchen*, *werken*), ON. *verka* (*-að*) in certain technical uses, *orka* to manage, effect, contrive (Sw. *verka* to do, perform, *virka* to crochet, Da. *virke* to operate, act, weave, etc.).

The Indo-Eur. base *worg-*, *werg-*, *wrg-* is represented outside Germanic by Zend *vərəzyeiti* he works, Gr. ἔρδω (:—**wergjō*), ῥέζω (:—**wrgjō*) I do, perf. ἔοργα, ὄργανον ORGAN, ὄργιον ORGY, OIr. *fairged* they made, *do-fairci* prepares, and the forms s.v. WARK *sb.* and *v.*, and WORK *sb.*

The normal representative of OE. *wyrcan* would be **worch* (for the vocalism cf. *worm*, *worse*, *wort*); the substitution of *k* for *ch*, producing the modern standard form (wɜːk) instead of (wɜːtʃ), is shown in north-midland areas *c* 1200, and is due mainly to WORK *sb.*, though Scandinavian influence (see various forms above) is possible.

The new pa. t. and pa. pple. *worked*, formed directly on the inf. stem, became established in the 15th century; it is now the normal form except in archaic usage (in which the older form *wrought* may appear in any sense), and in senses which denote fashioning, shaping, or decorating with the hand or an implement: see WROUGHT.]

A. Illustration of Forms.

1. *Inf.* and *Pres.-stem.* α. 1 **wyrc(e)an**, (**wyricean**), 2–3 **wurchen**, (3 **wrchen**, **wuerche**, **wourche**), 3–6 **wurche**, 5–6 **wurch**. β. 1 **wirc(e)an**, 3–5 **wirche(n**, 4–6 **wyrche**, 5 **wyrch**, **wirch**, (**whirche**), 9 *dial.* **wirtch**. γ. 1 **weorcean**, **wercan**, (2 *imper.* **wrec**), 2–4 **werchen**, (3 **werechen**), 3–5 **werche**. δ. 3–6 **worch(e**, (4 **worsche**, 6 *arch.* **woorchen**).

α. *c* **950** *Lindisf. Gosp.* Matt. iii. 2 Hreonisse doas *vel* wyrcas. *Ibid.* xxi. 28 Wuirc in winʒeard minne. **971** *Blickl. Hom.* 75 þæt we sceolan god weorc wyricean. *c* **1000** *Sax. Leechd.* II. 264 Hu mon læcedomas wiþ þon wyrcean scyle. *c* **1175** *Lamb. Hom.* 109 On monie wisen mon mei wurchen elmessan. *c* **1200** wuerche [see B. 3 d]. *c* **1205** LAY. 1547 Scaðe werc wrchen. *a* **1250** *Owl & Night.* 408 (Jesus MS.) He wile of bore wurche [*Cott.* wrchen] bareh. *c* **1450** *Godstow Reg.* 24 With feyth truly for to wurch. **1538** BALE *Thre Lawes* 1382 In Gods seruyce they honourablye wurche.

β. *c* **825** *Vesp. Psalter* xiv. 2 Se..wirceð rehtwisnisse. *a* **1250** *Owl & Night.* 722 (Cott. MS.) Clerkes ginneþ songes wirche. **13..** *Northern Passion* 1354 Alle the bettyr þey myghte wyrche. *c* **1400** *Rom. Rose* 6659–65 He bad wirken whanne that neede is... Seynt Poule that loued al hooly chirche He bade thappostles forto wirche And wynnen her lyflode..And seide wirketh with youre honden. *c* **1420** *Chron. Vilod.* 344 Elburwe þat religyose house let after whirche. *a* **1425** tr. *Arderne's Treat. Fistula*, etc. 45 Þe place wher arsenek is putte in, if it wirch perfitely, shal bycome blo & bolned. *c* **1449** PECOCK *Repr.* II. xiii. 222 Forto..wirche holi deedis. **15..** *Merch. & Son* 200 in Hazl. *E.P.P.* I. 146 He made hym evyn with every man, as far as he cowde wyrche. **1847** HALLIWELL, *Wirtch*, to ache. *North.*

γ. **971** *Blickl. Hom.* 67 þæt þu scealt..Godes willan wercan. *c* **1000** *Rule of Chrodegang* xvii, Þonne hi ne þurfon ʒemæne worc weorcean, wirce ælc sum þing þæs þe his aʒen neod sy. *a* **1175** *Cott. Hom.* 225 Wrec þe me an arc. *c* **1200** wercheð [see B. 21]. *c* **1275** LAY. 12167 Ich wolle werechen after þine willen. *c* **1460** werche [see B. 1 c].

δ. *c* **1275** *XI Pains of Hell* 310 in *O.E. Misc.* 220 Wo-so-euer wil halou þis sunundаy Wele and worch it ful. **1362** LANGL. *P. Pl.* A. VIII. 84 Wymmen with childe þat worchen ne mowen. *c* **1380** WYCLIF *Wks.* (1880) 123 Þei wolen not.. worsche aftir good conscience. *c* **1400** *R. Glouc. Chron.* (Rolls) App. xx. 94 Hi þoute wourche wo. *c* **1450** *Godstow Reg.* 8 Crist grawnt us grace truly to worch. **1566** DRANT *Horace, Sat.* VIII. 6 To woorchen all our will. **1865** WAUGH *Lancs. Songs* 24 When a mon's honestly willin' To wortch.

ε. 3 (*Orm.*) **wirrkenn**, 4 **wirc**, **wirck(e**, **wirkke**, **wyrkke**, **wyrc**, (**wrick**, **wrik**, **wryk**, *Sc.* **vyrk**), 4–6 **wirke**, **wyrk(e**, *Sc.* **virk**, 4–6, 8 *Sc.* **wirk**, 5 **wirken**, 5–6 **wyrcke**. ζ. 3–6 **werke**, 4 **werc**, **werkke**, **werken**, 5–6 **werk**, (6 **weorke**). η. 4–7 **worke**, 6 **woorke**, **wurk**, *Sc.* **vurk**, 7 **worck**, 6– **work**. θ. 5–6 **warke**, 9 *dial.* **wark**.

ε. *c* **1200** ORMIN 10118 To wirrkenn allmess werrkess. *a* **1300** *Cursor M.* 1229 To wrik þare wik wil. *Ibid.* 2200 To wyrk wondres. *Ibid.* 25251 Þi will to wirc. *c* **1330** R. BRUNNE *Chron. Wace* (Rolls) 5001 How þey schuld wyrke. *c* **1375** *Lay Folks Mass Bk.* (MS. B.) 4 Þo bokes of holy kyrc, þat holy men..con wyrc. *c* **1375** *Sc. Leg. Saints* xix. (*Christopher*) 79 To wryk in ws his wekit pouste. **1375** BARBOUR *Bruce* v. 488 He thoucht to virk with slicht. *a* **1400** *Morte Arth.* 1468 Fulle graythelye he wyrkkes. *c* **1400** wirken [see 1 β]. **1530** PALSGR. 783/1, I wyrke... Declared in 'I worke'. **1549** *Compl. Scot.* i. 21 The iugement of gode (quhilk virkis al thyng). **1550** CROWLEY *Last Trumpet* 482 For to wyrcke. **1596** DALRYMPLE tr. *Leslie's Hist. Scot.* IX. (S.T.S.) II. 201 Feireng..that Angus suld wirk thame sum ..iniure.

ζ. *c* **1220** werkeð [see B. 10]. *a* **1300** *Cursor M.* 14704 Þe werckes þat i werc. *c* **1386** CHAUCER *Can. Yeom. T.* 1477 As for to werken any thyng in contrarie. *c* **1450** HOLLAND *Howlat* 785 He couth werk wounderis. **1526** *Pilgr. Perf.* (W. de W. 1531) 136 b, It can werke no effect. **1553** *Respublica* 86 Avaryce maie weorke factes.

η. **1340** *Ayenb.* 206 Alneway workinde. **14..** *Sir Beues* 1798 (Pynson) Lat god worke what his wol is. **1546** *St. Papers Hen. VIII* XI. 225, I will do what I can..then must Godd worcke. **1551** CROWLEY *Pleas. & Payne* Ded. 108 The Lorde work in the hertis of the rych. **1570** G. HARVEY *Letter-bk.* (Camden) 9 Matter..for them to wurk uppon. **1581** *Satir. Poems Reform.* xliv. 368 Destroy the block, That vurkis thir Turkis aganis the. **1596** SPENSER *State Irel.* Wks. (Globe) 634/1 Divine powers which should woorke vengeaunce on perjurours. **1625** in Foster *Eng. Factories Ind.* (1909) III. 52 Discharging our broadsides as fast as wee coulde laied them and worck them. **1645** in *N. & Q.* 12th Ser. IX. 223/2 Brick to worke up the wall.

θ. **1450–1530** *Myrr. our Ladye* I. xiii. 35 The handes warke. *a* **1529** SKELTON *P. Sparowe* 799 Whereat they barke, And mar all they warke. **1880** MRS. PARR *Adam & Eve* II. 143 If 'tis to be done, he'll wark the oracle for me.

2. *Pa. t.* α. 1–3 **worhte** (1 **worohte**, **uorhte**); 1–4 **wrohte**, (3 **wrocte**, *Orm.* **wrohhte**), 3–4 **wrouht(e**, 3–5 **wroȝt(e**, 3–6 **wrouȝt(e**, **wrout(e**, **wroght**, 4 **wroghte**, **wroht**, **wrowht**, (**wroth**), 4–5 **wroughte**, *Sc.* **wroucht**, 4–6 *Sc.* **wrocht**, (**vrocht**), 5 **wrowȝte**, **wrowt**, (**wrouth**), 6 **wrowght**, 5– **wrought**. β. 1–2 **warhte**; 3 **wrahte**, **wrauhte**, 3–4 **wraȝte**, 4 **wraht**, 5 *Sc.* **wraucht**, 6 **wraught**.

α. *c* **950** *Lindisf. Gosp.* John ix. 6 Uorhte lam of ðæm spadle. **971** *Blickl. Hom.* 19 Hælend..þæt wundor worhte. **1056–66** *Inscr. on Dial, Kirkdale Ch., Yks.*, Haward me wrohte. *c* **1200** ORMIN 2256 Godd..þatt alle shaffte wrohhte. *c* **1205** LAY. 12024 He harm worhte. *a* **1225** *Ancr. R.* 258 Þe þet wrouhte þe eorðe. *c* **1250** *Gen. & Ex.* 156 His miȝt..ðe wroutis [= wrought them] on ðe ferðe day! *Ibid.* 230 It ne wrocte him neuere a del. *a* **1300** in *Anecd. Lit.* (1844) 91 Thenk, mon, werof Crist the wroute. *a* **1300** *Cursor M.* 362 First þan wroght he angel kind. **13..** *Northern Passion* 1367 (MS. Camb. Gg.) Þei wrothin hit wit maistrie. *c* **1350** *Will. Palerne* 3694, I wrouȝt nouȝt þe best. **1375** BARBOUR *Bruce* XVIII. 158 Johne wroucht syne sa vittely. *c* **1386** CHAUCER *Monk's T.* 403 Ful many an hethen wroghtestow ful wo. *c* **1400** *Parce Michi* 53 in *26 Pol. Poems* 144 In youthe I wrought folyes fele. *c* **1400** *Apol. Loll.* 106 Þe apostil wrowt wiþ his handis þingis able to mannis vse. *c* **1425** *Cast. Persev.* 3277 in *Macro Plays* 174 Wheyþer he wrouth wel or wyckydnesse. *a* **1529** SKELTON *Woffully Araid* 49 Y wrouȝt the, I bowgȝt the frome eternal fyre. **1533** GAU *Richt Vay* (S.T.S.) 39 The halie spreit vrocht this conceptione. **1539** *Bible* (Great) Ruth ii. 19 Where wroughtest thou? **1572** in Feuillerat *Revels Q. Eliz.* (1908) 159 His servantes that attended and wroute at the Coorte. **1573** *Ibid.* 196 The wyerdrawer..that..wrowght upon sundry propertyes. **1596** DALRYMPLE tr. *Leslie's Hist. Scot.* III. (S.T.S.) I. 199 How..vnwislie thay wrocht.

β. *a* **1100** *Life S. Chad* in *Anglia* X. 64 He warhte eac deʒulran eardung stowe. *c* **1175** *Lamb. Hom.* 91 Þa warhte god feole tacne. *a* **1225** *Leg. Kath.* 1071 Þet he wrahte þulliche wundres. *a* **1250** *Owl & Night.* 106 He..of his eyre briddes wrauhte [*Cott.* wraȝte]. **13..** *E.E. Allit. P.* A. 56 My wreched wylle in wo ay wraȝte. *c* **1425** WYNTOUN *Cron.* v. xiii. 5314 Al þe wilis þat he wraucht [*rime* noucht]. **1667** MILTON *P.L.* IX. 70 Sin, not Time, first wraught the change.

γ. 1 **wyrcte**, 2 **wercte**; 5 **wyrkkyd**, 6– **worked** (7– **work'd**).

c **825** *Vesp. Hymns* i. 3 *Digiti mei aptaverunt psalterium*, fingras mine wyrctun hearpan. *a* **1175** *Cott. Hom.* 229 Þa wercte he fele wundra. *c* **1470** *Pol. Poems* (Rolls) II. 284 They that wyrkkyd soche wooll. **1523** LD. BERNERS *Froiss.* I. cccxlvi. (1530) 24/1 Vrbayne..waxed proude and worked all on heed. **1743** BULKELEY & CUMMINS *Voy. S. Seas* 106 It being smooth water, she work'd very well.

3. *Pa. pple.* α. 1 **ʒeworht**, etc.: see YWROUGHT. β. 4 **worȝt**, **worght**; 3 *Orm.* **wrohht**, 3–4 **wroȝt**, 4 **wroghte**, **wrouht(e**, **wrow(h)t**, (**wrohut**, **wroȝth**, **wrouth**), 4–5 **wroȝte**, **wrouȝt(e**, **wroht**, 4–6 **wroght**, *Sc.* **wrocht**, 4–7 **wroughte**, (5 **wrowgt**, **wrow(g)th**, **wrout**, **wrothte**, **wroth**, **wrht**), 5–6 **wrowght**, 6 (**wrowte**, **wrotte**, **rought**), *Sc.* **wroucht**, (**vrocht**, **rocht**), 7 **wrote**, 4– **wrought**. γ. [1 **ʒewarht**], 3 **wrauht**, 6 **wraught**.

β. [*a* **900** *Leiden Riddle* 3 Ni uuat ic mec biuorthæ uullan fliusum.] *c* **1200** ORMIN Ded. 153 Icc hafe hemm wrohht tiss boc. *c* **1250** *Gen. & Ex.* 40 Of noȝt Was heuene and erðe samen wroȝt. *a* **1300** *Cursor M.* 25914 (Cott.) Þerfor haf i worght þis bok. *c* **1300** *Havelok* 1352 Dwelling haueth ofte scaþe wrouth. *Ibid.* 2453 He haue[de] ful wo wrowht. **13..** *Cursor M.* 1564 (Gött.) Iesu þat all has wrohut. **13..** *Harrow. Hell* (E.) 167 Ȝif ich haue sinnes wrouȝt. **13..** *Pol. Rel. & L. Poems* (1903) 264 To his licnesse þou art wrout. **1375** BARBOUR *Bruce* I. 94 Ȝe had nocht wrocht on that maner. *a* **1400–50** *Wars Alex.* 3264 Had he worȝt ay to wees welth. *c* **1400** *Apol. Loll.* 16 Lord, þu hast wrout al our warkis in vs. *c* **1400** *Rule St. Benet* (prose) Prol. iii. 3 It was wrht o-pon þe harde stane. **1447** BOKENHAM *Seyntys* (Roxb.) 79 O juge thi decre Is..wroct ful unrychtfully. *c* **1460** *Promp. Parv.* 278 (Winch. MS.), Madde, or wroth be crafte or cunnyng, *factus*. *a* **1500** *Bernard. de Cura Rei Fam.* III. 81 Qwhat wonder sulde be wrothte. **1549** *Compl. Scot.* vii. 69 The..figuris that hed bene grauit, vrocht, and brodrut. **1556** *Chron. Grey Friars* (Camden) 36 A tylte..the wych was wrotte on Assencion day. **1581** N. BURNE *Disputation* in *Cath. Tractates* (S.T.S.) 119 The lyme.. could not be vrocht. **1585** DANIEL *Pref. & Ep. bef. Paulus Iouius* To Rdr., Wks. (Grosart) IV. 24 This [invention].. which time hath now at length perfited and rought into a more regulare order. **1635** *Maldon, Essex, Borough Deeds* Bundle 145, No. 2 b, The earth being lately by the tide wroughte.

γ. [*c* **725** *Corpus Gloss.* C 780 *Conderetur*, ʒewarht. *c* **893** ÆLFRED *Oros.* v. ii. 216 Mon hæt Corrinthisce fatu ealle þe þærof ʒewarhte wæron. *a* **1100** *Life S. Chad* in *Anglia* X. 230 Heo wes ʒewarht ufan on huses ʒelicnesse.]

c **1275** *Serving Christ* 7 in *O.E. Misc.* 90 Yef we habbeþ werkes yeynes þi wille wrauht. **1518** *Sel. Pleas Star Chamb.* (Selden) II. 135 To..cawse further myschefe to have byn wraught. *a* **1542** WYATT *Poems* (1908) 55 Gesse, frend, what I am, or how I am wraught.

δ. 5 **worched**. ε. 6 **workyd**, 6– **worked**.

1470–85 MALORY *Arthur* VI. xi. 199 We haue worched al maner of sylke werkes. **1538** workyd [see B. 8]. **1733** BUDGELL *Bee* No. 5. I. 180 In what an hurry a Weekly Pamphlet of three Sheets must be work'd off.

B. Signification.

I. Transitive senses.

* To perform, execute.

1. To do, perform, practise (a deed, course of action, labour, task, business, occupation, process, etc.). Now *arch.*; chiefly with cognate obj. *work* or *deed*, or in such phr. as ***to work a miracle***, ***to work wonders*** (pa. t. and pa. pple. freq. *wrought*), in which sense 10 is blended with this.

Beowulf 930 A mæʒ god wyrcan wunder æfter wundre. **971** *Blickl. Hom.* 21 Eal swa hwæt swa se ʒesenelica lichama deþ oþþe wyrceþ. *c* **1000** ÆLFRIC *Gen.* xlvii. 3 He axode hwæt hy wyrcean cuþon: hi andswarodon..: We synd scephyrdas. *c* **1000** *Ags. Gosp.* Matt. xxvi. 10 God weorc heo worhte on me. —— John iii. 2 Ne mæʒ nan man þas tacn wyrcan þe ðu wyrest, buton God beo mid him. *c* **1175** *Lamb. Hom.* 117 Leorniað god to wurchenne. *c* **1200** ORMIN 9988 Swillke sinndenn alle þa þatt wirrkenn gode werkess. *c* **1200** *Trin. Coll. Hom.* 59 Swich elmesse to wurchen. *c* **1200–** [see WONDER *sb.* 2, 3]. *a* **1225** *Leg. Kath.* 1053 Oðre..þurh wicchecreftes wurchið summe wundres. *a* **1225** *Ancr. R.* 424 Wurche þet me hat hire wiðuten grucchunge. *c* **1250** *Gen. & Ex.* 2218 Ðe breðere ne wisten it noȝt Hu ðis dede wurðe wroȝt. **1297** R. GLOUC. (Rolls) 2569 Seint germayn.. prechede,..& vair miracle wroȝte. *c* **1375** *Cursor M.* 5870 (Fairf.) Þai salle..wirk .ij. dayes werk a-pon a day. *c* **1386** CHAUCER *Merch. T.* 241 Wirk alle thyng by conseil. *c* **1449** PECOCK *Repr.* I. x. 50 And wolde..wirche sumwhile the oon craft and sumwhile the other craft. **1508** DUNBAR *Tua Mariit Wemen* 351, I maid that wif carll to werk all womenis werkis. **1594** HOOKER *Eccl. Pol.* I. ii. §3 God worketh nothing without cause. *c* **1600** in *Engl. Hist. Rev.* (1919) July 435 She worcketh knittinge of stockings. **1618** W. LAWSON *New Orch. & Garden* x. (1623) 27 Grafting..is thus wrought. **1649** BP. HALL *Cases Consc.* IV. viii. (1654) 361 A Sacrament, conferring Grace by the very work wrought. **1746** FRANCIS tr. *Horace, Art Poetry* 264 Let not such upon the Stage be brought, Which better should behind the Scenes be wrought. **1784** COWPER *Task* VI. 557 So God wrought double justice. **1821** JOANNA BAILLIE *Metr. Leg.*, *Wallace* xci, In Guienne right valiant deeds he wrought. **1851** DIXON *W. Penn* ii. (1872) 12 The miracles wrought by Spanish saints. **1863** STANLEY *Jew. Ch.* I. iii. 64 The twenty years of exile and servitude had wrought their work. **1904** Budge *3rd & 4th Egypt. Rooms Brit. Mus.* 181 Stone object, with twenty facets, .. probably used in working magic. **1920** *Engl. Hist. Rev.* Jan. 25 The special work which he undertook, and the rich ability with which he wrought it.

b. To do (something evil or harmful); to commit (a sin, wrong, or crime). *arch.*

c **825** *Vesp. Psalter* v. 7 Alle ða ðe wircað unrehtwisnisse. *c* **1220** *Bestiary* 569 Sipes ȝe sinkeð, and scaðe ðus werkeð. *a* **1300** *Cursor M.* 24158 Vn-reufulli yee wirc vnright. *c* **1325** *Spec. Gy Warw.* 759 Anon, so þu hast sinne wrouht, .. to shrifte þat þu gange. **1340–70** *Alex. & Dind.* 688 þe hete .. þat enforceþ þe flech folie to wirche! *a* **1352** Minot *Poems* (ed. Hall) vii. 62 Fals treson alway þai wroght. *c* **1449** Pecock *Repr.* III. xi. 342 The pseudo Apostilis wrouȝten persecucioun .. aȝens the trewe Apostlis. *c* **1450** *St. Cuthbert* (Surtees) 5638 When he had þis theft wrought. *c* **1470** Henry *Wallace* I. 161 Mony gret wrang thai wrocht. **1535** Coverdale *Ezek.* xxxiii. 26 Ye worke abhominacions, euery one defyleth his neghbours wife. **1611** *Bible* Matt. vii. 23 Depart from me, ye that worke iniquity. **1613** Purchas *Pilgrimage* (1614) 25 Working that malice on the creatures .. which he could not .. wrecke on their Creator. **1829** Hood *Eug. Aram* xiii, Methought, last night, I wrought A murder, in a dream!

c. To perform, observe (a ceremony, etc.). *Obs.* exc. in *Freemasonry.*

c **950** *Lindisf. Gosp.* Matt. xxvi. 18 Mið ðec ic wyrco eastro [*facio pascha*] mið ðeȝnum minum. *c* **1325** *Chron. Eng.* 311 in Ritson *Metr. Rom.* II. 283 Eleutherie, the pope of Rome, Stablede suithe sone Godes werkes wurche, Ant singe in holy Chirche. **1340** Hampole *Pr. Consc.* 3685 Goddes minister .. þat þe sacrament of þe auter wirkes. *c* **1460** *Play Sacram.* 325 Seyng hys evynsong as yt hys worshepe for to werche. **1884** W. J. Hughan *Origin Eng. Rite Freemasonry* i. 5 It seems difficult to understand how any one conversant with their noble Histories can cherish the fancy that the Craft .. and other degrees were worked by our ancient brethren during the seventeenth century. **1903** J. T. Lawrence *Masonic Jurisprudence & Symbolism* viii. 74 What generally takes place in a lodge of instruction is that the lectures, or sections of them, are worked, officers to conduct the same being appointed at a previous meeting. **1954** W. Hannah *Christian by Degrees* iv. 65 The 26th degree known as Prince of Mercy (not worked in England) also regards Hiram as a type of Christ in His death and resurrection. **1978** *Lochaber News* 31 Mar. 2/7 An EA Degree was worked and was well received by the Brethren present.

†**d.** To carry on, wage, make (war). *Obs.*

c **1250** *Gen. & Ex.* 3220 Ðat folc ebru to werchen wi. *a* **1352** Minot *Poems* (ed. Hall) vi. 31 A were es wroght .. ȝowre walles with to wrote. *c* **1374** Chaucer *Boeth.* IV. metr. vii. 114 (Camb. MS.) Agamenon, þat wrowhte and continuede the batayles by x. ȝer. *c* **1475** *Partenay* 4056 Where this Geant were procured and wrought.

2. To perform, carry out, execute (a person's will, advice, etc.). *Obs.* or *arch.* (in later use passing into sense 10).

971 *Blickl. Hom.* 67 þæt þu scealt on æȝhwylee tid Godes willan wercan. *c* **1000** *Ags. Gosp.* Matt. vii. 21 Se þe wyrcð mines fæder willan. *c* **1175** *Lamb. Hom.* 81 Hu me sulde godalmihti serue, and his wille wurche in orðe. *a* **1225** *Juliana* 35 (Bodl. MS.) Wurch eleusius wil for ich þe ȝeoue leaue. *c* **1350** *Will. Palerne* 307 He .. graunted him .. Forto worchen his wille as lord wiþ his owne. *a* **1375** *Joseph Arim.* 491 His riche men .. þat his red wrouȝten. *c* **1400** *Destr. Troy* 1881 All the soueranis .. assignet me hir, For to wirke with my wille, & weld as myn owne. **1500–20** Dunbar *Poems* lxix. 23 Lat Fortoun wirk furthe hir rage. **1595** Munday *John a Kent* (Shaks. Soc.) 12 Leave the God of heaven to woorke his will. **1700** Dryden *Cock & Fox* 589 The false loon, who could not work his will By open force, employ'd his flattering skill.

** To construct, produce, effect.

3. To produce by (or as by) labour or exertion; to make, construct, manufacture; to form, fashion, shape. *Obs.* or *arch.* in general sense; often, now usually, implying artistic or ornamental workmanship (most commonly in pa. pple. *wrought*; see also e). See also *work up*, 39 h.

Beowulf 1452 Swa hine fyrndaȝum worhte wæpna smið. *c* **1205** Lay. 22911 Ich þe wulle wurche a bord .. þat þer maȝen setten to sixtene hundred & ma. ? *a* **1366** Chaucer *Rom. Rose* 559 Of body ful wel wrought was she. *c* **1386** —— *Sqr.'s T.* 120 He þat it wroghte koude ful many a gyn. *c* **1420** *Pol. Rel. & L. Poems* (1903) 271 A bok .. þat men callyt an abece, Pratylych I-wrout. *Ibid.*, Wrout is on þe bok with-oute, V. paraffys [*Bodl. MS. 789* wrouȝt]. *c* **1420** Lydg. *Assembly of Gods* 1882 So curyously, in so lytell a compace, In all thys world was neuer thyng wrought. *c* **1475** *Rauf Coilȝear* 264 To ane preuie Chalmer .. thay him led, Quhair ane burely bed was wrocht. **1513** Douglas *Æneis* XII. Prol. 138 Quharof the beis wrocht thar hunny sweit. **1545** Ascham *Toxoph.* (Arb.) 115 Some of them, whych .. worke ye kinges Artillarie for war. **1584** Cogan *Haven Health* lxxxiii. (1636) 86 The liver .. is the place where all the humours of the body are first wrought. **1697** Dryden *Virg. Georg.* I. 267 The blind laborious Mole In winding Mazes works her hidden Hole. **1752** Hume *Ess. & Treat.* (1777) I. 103 A hundred cabinet-makers in London can work a table .. equally well. **1791** Cowper *Iliad* XVI. 272 A goblet exquisitely wrought. **1817** J. Evans *Excurs. Windsor*, etc. 258 A public road, beneath which is worked a path conducting to a fine lawn. **1850** Scoresby *Cheever's Whalem. Adv.* i. (1858) 4 Whether the first .. whaling harpoon used in America was wrought there. **1864** J. Hunt tr. *Vogt's Lect. Man* x. 269 The [flint] instruments of oval shape have been mostly worked by gentle blows.

(*b*) with immaterial object.

a **1300** *Cursor M.* 29326 All þaa þat wirkes Laus gain right of hali kirkes. **1721** Prior *Predestination* Wks. 1907 II. 351 Are not the Texture of our Actions wrought By something inward that directs our thought? **1752** Gray *Bentley* 7 Each dream, in fancy's airy colouring wrought.

b. Said of God: To create. Also in *pass.*, the pa. pple. sometimes becoming equivalent to 'born'. *Obs.* or *rare arch.* See also 7.

Beowulf 92 þæt se ælmihtiȝa eorðan worhte. *c* **950** *Lindisf. Gosp.* Matt. xix. 4 *Qui fecit ab initio masculum et feminam fecit eos*, seðe worohte from fruma woepen-monn & wifmonn ȝeworhte hia. *a* **1225** *Leg. Kath.* 369 Nis buten an godd, .. þet al þe world wrahte. *a* **1300** *Cursor M.* 373 He wroght apon þe toþer day þe firmament. *c* **1369** Chaucer *Dethe Blaunche* 90 Alas (quoth shee) that I was wrought. *c* **1441** in *Pol. Poems* (Rolls) II. 205 Alle women that in this world be wrowght. ? *a* **1550** *Freiris Berwik* 364 in *Dunbar's Poems* (1893) 297 Quhat sall I do? Allace, that I wes wrocht. *c* **1586** C'tess Pembroke *Ps.* CXLV. v, All creatures thou hast wrought .. shall their Creator sound. **1639** Mure *Ps.* VIII. iii, The moone, the twinckling starrs .. Works, by thy finger wroght. **1648** Bp. Hall *Breathings Devout Soul* § 19 The less I can satisfie my self with marvailing at thy works, the more let me adore the majesty and omnipotence of thee that wroughtest them.

c. To construct, build (a house, church, wall, bridge, etc.) *Obs.* or *rare arch.* See also 39 a.

c **1000** Ælfric *Hom.* I. 22 Ða cwædon hi betwux him þæt hi woldon wyrcan ane burh. **13..** *Leg. Gregory* 218 Chirches, chapels, boþe ysame Werche sche dede. **14..** *Sir Beues* (MS. M.) 3685 Beues dyd wyrke Abbeys, mynesters, and meny a kirke. *c* **1470** *Gol. & Gaw.* 64 Weill wroght wes the wall, And payntit with pride. **1667** Milton *P.L.* x. 300 They .. the Mole immense wraught on Over the foaming deep high Archt. *a* **1701** Maundrell *Journ. Jerus.* 7 Mar. (1707) 18 An old Bridge .. exceeding well wrought. **1735** J. Price *Stone-Br. Thames* 7 Scaffolds for working the said Piers from Bottom to Top. **1747** Gould *Engl. Ants* 12 Their [*sc.* ants'] double Saw, by means whereof they work their Apartments. **1876** Morris *Sigurd* I. 1 Earls were the wrights that wrought it [*sc.* a house].

†**d.** To 'make', obtain (a friend). *Obs. rare.*

c **888** Ælfred *Boeth.* xxiv. § 3 Mid þis and weardan welan mon wyrcð oftor fiond ðonne freond. *c* **1200** *Trin. Coll. Hom.* 41 Mid weldede of giue [man mai] frend wuerche.

e. const. *of*, rarely *out of* (the material or constituents); also *in* (some material), usually implying artistic or ornamental workmanship. (In later use almost always in pa. pple. *wrought*.)

c **888** Ælfred *Boeth.* xxxix. § 12 Hit is þæs godcundan anwealdes ȝewuna þæt he wircð of yfle good. *c* **1000** *Ags. Gosp.* John ii. 15 He worhte swipan of strengon. *c* **1000** Ælfric *Gen.* vi. 14 Wyrc ðe nu anne arc of aheawenum bordum. *c* **1000** —— *Hom.* I. 12 God .. cwæð þæt he wolde wyrcan mannan of eorðan. *c* **1200** Ormin 15182 Nollde nohht te Laferrd Crist .. Hemm wirrkenn win inoh off nohht, .. Acc wollde off waterr wirrkenn win. *a* **1300** *Cursor M.* 22804 He þat dos flexs worth in to lame, O lam mai wirc flessli licam. *a* **1375** *Joseph Arim.* 204 A newe chaumbre-wouh wrouȝt al of bordes. *c* **1400** Maundev. (1919) xxiv. 141 In the myddes of this palays is the mountour for the grete Cane þat is alle wrought of gold & precyous stones. **1567** *Gude & Godlie B.* (S.T.S.) 131 O Lord, quhilk wrocht all thingis of nocht. **1596** *Edw. III*, III. i. 68 Their streaming Ensignes, wrought of coulloured silke. **1610** Holland *Camden's Brit.* 681 Good milstones are wrought out of the rocke. **1709** A. Philips *To Earl of Dorset* 34 Every shrub, and every blade of grass, And every pointed thorn, seem'd wrought in glass. **1842** Lover *Handy Andy* xl, Various ornaments .. wrought in the purest gold. **1877** Huxley *Physiogr.* 206 Forty-six noble columns, some wrought in granite and some in marble.

†**4.** To compose (a book or writing), to write.

c **900** tr. *Bæda's Hist.* III. xvii, On þære bec, þe ic worhte. **971** *Blickl. Hom.* 169 Se ðe þas boc worhte. *c* **1200** Ormin Ded. 24 þatt icc þiss werrc þe shollde wirrkenn. *Ibid.* 14269 þatt boc, þatt Moysæs & tatt profetess wrohhtenn. *a* **1272** *Luue Ron* 2 in *O.E. Misc.* 93 A Mayde cristes me bit yorne þat ich hire wurche a luue ron. *c* **1330** R. Brunne *Chron. Wace* (Rolls) 14836 Of Ynge saw y neuere nought, Neyþer in boke write ne wrought. *c* **1385** Chaucer *L.G.W.* Prol. 372 As thogh that he of malice wolde endyten Despyt of love, and had him-self hit wroght. **1617** Woodall *Surg. Mate* Pref., Wks. (1653) 13 Who likes, approves, and usefull deems This work, for him 'tis wrought. **1746** Francis tr. *Hor., Sat.* I. iv. 60 Some therefore ask, can comedy be thought A real poem, since it may be wrought In style and subject without fire or force.

†**b.** To utter, speak, say. *Obs. rare.*

c **1350** in Horstmann *Altengl. Leg.* (1881) 30 þai ditted þaire eris, for þai suld noght Here þir wurdes þat þus war wroght. *a* **1352** Minot *Poems* (ed. Hall) i. 45 Philip Valays wordes wroght And said he suld þaire enmys sla.

5. To make (a 'web' or textile fabric), to weave; to make (something consisting of such fabric, as a garment, quilt, etc.) by means of needlework, to sew or knit; to ornament with a design, figure, or pattern in needlework, to embroider.

c **1250** *Gen. & Ex.* 377 Two pilches weren ðurȝ engeles wroȝt. *a* **1400** *Engl. Gilds* (1870) 350 Non of þe Citee ne shal don werche qwyltes ne chalouns by-þoute þe walles. *c* **1449** *Gesta Rom.* xliii. 171 A damisell .. þe whiche can wel werche your sherte. **1511–12** *Act 3 Hen. VIII* c. 6. § 1 The Walker and Fuller shall truely walke fulle thikke and werke every webbe of wollen yerne. **1592** Shaks. *Ven. & Ad.* 991 Now she vnweaues the web that she hath wrought. **1595** —— *John* IV. i. 43 My hand-kercher .. (The best I had, a Princesse wrought it me). **1651** Davenant *Gondibert* II. xxviii, These belts (wrought with their ladies' care). **1768** Sterne *Sent. Journ., Pulse*, She was working a pair of ruffles. **1784** Cowper *Task* I. 33 A splendid cover .. of tapestry richly wrought. **1833** Ht. Martineau *Loom & Lugger* I. ii. 21 You have wrought your web thinner and thinner. **1839** Ure *Dict. Arts* 654 In the weaving of ribbed hosiery, the plain rib courses are wrought alternately. **1849** Macaulay *Hist. Eng.* vii. II. 174 The princess, who had been educated only to work embroidery, to play on the spinet, [etc.]. **1868** Louisa M. Alcott *Little Women* vi, I'm going to work Mr. Laurence a pair of slippers.

b. const. *with* the design, figure, or pattern.

? *a* **1366** Chaucer *Rom. Rose* 897 His garnement was euerydell Portreied and wrought with floures. **1480** *Wardr. Acc. Edw. IV.* (1830) 115 An hoby harneis .. enbrowdered and wroght with ageletts of silver and gilt. **1575** in *Archaeologia* XXX. 12 Sixe quyshions, wrought withe my L. [= Lord's] armes. **1842** Tennyson *Audley Court* 20 A damask napkin wrought with horse and hound.

c. with the design, figure, or pattern as obj.

1610 Holland *Camden's Brit.* 207* The Danes bare in their Ensigne a Raven wrought .. in needle-worke. **1841** *Hart's Fancy-work Bk.* 18 To work patterns drawn on canvas. **1859** J. Brown *Horæ Subs.* Ser. I. (1861) 286 Working her name on the blankets. **1883** D. C. Murray *Hearts* ix. (1885) 65 The maxims you cherish would have served .. for your grandmother to work on samplers.

6. To make (an image or figure); to delineate, paint, or draw (a picture, ornamental design, etc.); to carve (a statue or piece of sculpture); also, to represent by an image, portray, picture. *Obs.* or *arch.* exc. in special connexions. See also 39 h.

a **1300** *Cursor M.* 23216 Painted fire .. þat apon a wagh war wroght. **1448–9** Metham *Amoryus & Cleopes* 60 Lettyrrys off gold, þat gay were wrowght to þe ye. **1597** W. Barlow *Navig. Supply* H 1, If these diuisions be wrought vpon Latten plates. **1680** Moxon *Mech. Exerc.* xii. 206, I shall proceed to the working a Pattern or two in Soft Wood. **1697** Dryden *Æneis* v. 328 There, Ganymede is wrought with living Art. *a* **1707** Prior *To the Hon. C. Montague* ii, Each, like the Graecian Artist, woo's The Image He himself has wrought. **1769** Sir J. Reynolds *Disc.* (1778) 19 The pictures, thus wrought with such pain, now appear like the effect of enchantment. **1780** *Mirror* No. 103 A large iron gate, at the top of which the family arms are worked. **1874** J. H. Pollen *Anc. & Mod. Furniture S. Kens. Mus.* 129 As the ornamental tooling is worked on leather by the book-binder.

†**7.** With complemental word or phrase: To cause to be ..., make, render; to change, convert, turn into something different; to bring into a specified state; also, to make or create in the form of. With simple compl. or const. *to*, *into*. *Obs.*

c **1000** *Ags. Gosp.* Matt. xxi. 13 Hyt ys awriten, min hus is ȝebedhus; witodlice ȝe worhton þæt to þeofa cote. *c* **1205** Lay. 18737 His lond þu forbernest, & hine blæð wurchest. *a* **1300** *Cursor M.* 8392 For þi luue was i widue wroght. *Ibid.* 12370 Ye þat he has wroght to men And þat efter his aun ymage. *Ibid.* 24088 (Edin.) þat wroht me out of wite. **13..** *Ibid.* 13824 (Gött.) He þat me hal has wroght. *c* **1400** *Destr. Troy* 9004 Mony woundet þat worthy & wroght vnto dethe. *c* **1410** *Sir Cleges* 336 Thys sawe I neuer .., Syn I was man wrowght! *c* **1480** Henryson *Want of Wyse Men* 6 Welth is away, wit is now wrochtin to wrinkis. **15..** Dunbar *Poems* lxxii. 115 Ordane for Him ane resting-place, That is so werie wrocht for the. **1613** Shaks. *Hen. VIII*, II. ii. 47 We had need pray .. for our deliuerance; Or this imperious man will worke vs all From Princes into Pages. **1639** Saltmarshe *Policy* 43 If you suspect the performance of a promise, worke them obliged by some speciall engagement and pawne.

8. To make, form, or fashion *into* something (formerly also †*in*); to make up; to compound (ingredients); to shape (material). See also 39 e.

In various connexions; cf. senses above. Often with special reference to the process or operation performed; thus passing into branch ***.

1538 Starkey *England* II. i. 173 Our marchantys cary them [*sc.* lead and tin] out .., and then bryng the same in workyd agayn, and made vessel therof. **1558** in Hakluyt *Voy.* (1599) I. 303 All our olde hempe is spunne and wrought in tenne cables .. and thirteene Hausers. **1669** Sturmy *Mariner's Mag.* v. xii. 65 Gun-powder of a .. Russet colour .. may be judged to have all its Receipts well wrought. **1677** Moxon *Mech. Exerc.* i. 9 When you joyn several Bars of Iron together .. and work them into one Bar. **1717** Prior *Alma* III. 461, I .. melted down my Plate, On Modern Models to be wrought. **1748** *Anson's Voy.* II. ii. 135 To unlay a cable to work into running rigging. **1820** *Q. Mus. Mag.* II. 17 The subject of the Fugata .. is a very good one. It were to be wished that it had been worked into a regular Fugue. **1882** Caulfeild & Saward *Dict. Needlework* 464 String Rugs .. are made from odds and ends of .. wool, which are .. worked into coarse canvas in loops.

†**b.** To inflict (wounds). *Obs.*

c **1400** *Melayne* 1522 We sall wirke þam wondis full wyde. *c* **1460** *Towneley Myst.* xxvi. 363 Anoyntmentys .. ffor to anoyntt his woundys sere, That Iues hym wroght. **1471** Caxton *Recuyell* (Sommer) 339 These theues and robeurs smote .. fiersly vpon philotes .., worchynge and gyuyng to him many woundes.

c. To produce or cause by continued application of physical force, e.g. friction; to 'wear' (a cavity, etc.) by attrition.

1836 C. Wordsworth *Athens* xxvi. (1855) 174 The wheels have worked deep grooves in the rock. *Mod.* He works holes in the seat of his trousers.

9. To put in, insert, incorporate, esp. in the way of construction or composition (cf. 3, 4): in various special connexions (see quots.). See also 36 a.

1663 Gerbier *Counsel* 83 Glasse wrought with good lead, .. Glass wrought with an Arch well leaded. **1707** *Curios. Husb. & Gard.* 262 We .. work into the Aperture, the Colours we would give the Flower. **1710** Steele *Tatler* No. 226 ¶ 1 Those occasional Dissertations, which he has wrought into the Body of his History. **1711** W. Sutherland *Shipbuild. Assist.* 48 To .. work 3 whole Plank between 2 Buts. **1753–4** Richardson *Grandison* II. vii. 42 The love of pleasure .. was wrought into his habit. He was a slave to it. **1868** *Rep. U.S. Comm. Agric.* (1869) 254 Such a hedge may be repaired by thrusting .. brush .. into the holes .. and .. working saplings through it obliquely. **1888** *Iron* 25 May 465 Heavy coils of iron .. have been wrought round the .. fore part of each gun.

b. *Hort.* To graft (*on* a stock): also *fig.*

1658 Sir T. Browne *Hydriot.* ii. 10 The Romanes early wrought so much civility upon the Brittish stock. **1715** De Foe *Fam. Instruct.* I. i. (1841) I. 28 Getting the word of life wrought in your heart. **1837** T. Rivers *Rose Amateur's Guide* 72 A collection of Chinese Roses worked on short stems. **1859** R. Thompson *Gard. Assist.* 387 The..portion cut off, is termed the scion, or graft, and the rooted plant, on which it is placed or worked, is called the stock. **1868** *Rep. U.S. Comm. Agric.* (1869) 203 [The Kilmarnock willow] is frequently worked on low stems, and in consequence much of its beauty is lost.

10. To effect, bring about, bring to pass; to accomplish, achieve; to cause, produce. (In early use often approaching sense 1.) Esp. in phr. ***to work havoc***, where the pa. t. *wrought* is common (though it is often interpreted as the pa. t. of *wreak*: cf. wreak *v.* 8 b). See also 38 f, 39 h.

c **1220** *Bestiary* 498 He him iuel werkeð. *c* **1250** *Gen. & Ex.* 850 He werken sckaðe and bale. *Ibid.* 1812 Ðe ne leate ic noȝt, Til ðin bliscing on me beð wroȝt. *c* **1315** Shoreham *Poems* I. 774 Sauuacion to werche. **1340–70** *Alisaunder* 412 With his ferefull folke to Phocus hee rides, And is wilfull in werk to wirchen hem care. **13..** *Cursor M.* 20926 (Edin.) To quilis he wroȝte þe cristin scam. *c* **1350** *Will. Palerne* 1173 Forto wirch me no wrong. **1382** Wyclif *2 Cor.* vii. 10 That sorwe that is aftir God, worchith penaunce..; forsoth sorwe of the world worchith deeth. *c* **1385** Chaucer *L.G.W.* 1696 *Lucretia*, Ful longe lay the sege & lytil wroughten. **1398** Trevisa *Barth. De P.R.* iv. i. (1495) e iv b/1 In dyuerse maters [heete] werkyth dyuerse effectes. *c* **1400** *Pety Job* 32 in *26 Pol. Poems* 122 So moche woo hit [*sc.* sin] hath vs wrought. **1500–20** Dunbar *Poems* xxxi. 5 He wirkis sorrow to him sell. **1549** *Compl. Scot.* xv. 135 Tariand quhil the tyme virk ane bettir chance. **1568** Grafton *Chron.* II. 110 They were confederated..to worke him an vtter mischiefe. **1576** Fleming *Panopl. Epist.* 39 Whose daggers dinte wrought his dolefull death. **1596** Bacon *Max. Com. Law* iii. (1636) 15 Words are so to be understood, that they worke somewhat, and be not idle and frivolous. **1601** Daniel *Civ. Wars* I. l, Who else..his safetie might haue wrought. **1648** Gage *West Ind.* 200 He replyed, that what Porke might work upon mans body in other Nations, it worked not there. **1724** Ramsay *Vision* xxiv, Lat them..stryve to wirk my fall. **1751** Johnson *Rambler* No. 87 ¶2 Though good advice was given, it has wrought no reformation. **1825** Jefferson *Autobiog.* Wks. 1859 I. 17 To wait the event of this campaign will certainly work delay. **1831** James *Philip Aug.* xxxi, The ravages that confinement and sorrow had worked upon him. **1840** Dickens *Old Cur. Shop* xxvi, The beer had wrought no bad effect upon his appetite. **1843** Macaulay *Lays Anc. Rome, Virginia* 78 Let him who works the client wrong beware the patron's ire! **1844** H. H. Wilson *Brit. India* I. 475 They were objects of general esteem and respect.., and wrought an impression favourable to the ultimate reception of the doctrines which they taught. **1877** Huxley *Physiogr.* 183 The destruction wrought by the sea. **1900, 1908** [see havoc *sb.* 2]. **1912** *Halsbury's Laws of England* XXIV. 250 An alienation by tenant in tail..worked a discontinuance. **1978** *Washington Post* 30 Nov. A-14/2 Settlers who are prone to California dreaming,..and on whom..the anything-goes atmosphere and the wide-open spaces work havoc. **1983** *National Law Jrnl.* (U.S.) 4 July 14/2 With hard disk technology..power failures can often work havoc. **1984** *Financial Times* 4 June III. p. vii, A decade of inflation had wrought havoc with its portfolio of fixed interest mortgages.

†**11.** To act in order to or so as to effect (something); to plan, devise, contrive; to put in practice, manage (a business or proceeding). *Obs.*

c **1300** *K. Horn* 288 (Laud) Wat reymnild wroute Mikel wonder him þoute. **1362** Langl. *P. Pl.* A. II. 85 Such Weddyng to worche to wraþþe with truþe. **1561** Hoby tr. *Castiglione's Courtyer* II. (1577) G viij, Hee ought to worke the matter wisely. **1621** J. Taylor (Water P.) *Unnat. Father* Wks. (1630) II. 137/2 He resolued to worke some meanes to take away their..liues. **1635** R. N. tr. *Camden's Hist. Eliz.* I. 78 The Conspiratours so wrought the matter, that very many of the Nobility assented to the marriage. **1647–8** Cottrell tr. *Davila's Hist. France* (1678) 19 The Cardinal ardently wrought the Prince's destruction by counseling the King. **1667** Milton *P.L.* I. 646 To work in close design, by fraud or guile What force effected not.

b. *colloq.* To arrange, engineer, or bring about. Usu. const. *it.*

1889 E. Dowson *Let.* 1 Mar. (1967) 42 If you can *possibly* work it meet me somewhere to-morrow. **1911** G. B. Shaw *Doctor's Dilemma* III. 57 The way to work it is this. I'll postdate the cheque next October. **1953** K. Tennant *Joyful Condemned* xxxi. 305 I'll get young Rene... I guess I can work it. **1962** Wodehouse *Service with Smile* xi. 177 Uncle Fred, did you work this? **1975** D. Lodge *Changing Places* i. 17 Masters (who was Chairman) was prepared to work it for Philip if he was interested.

*** To do something to an object (thing or person).

12. To bestow labour or effort upon; to operate upon: in various connexions and shades of meaning. **a.** To till, cultivate (land): = labour *v.* 1; *rarely*, to cultivate (a plant or crop).

c **1000** Ælfric *Gen.* ix. 20 Noe..began to wyrcenne ðæt land. *c* **1440** *Pallad. on Husb.* III. 589 Faat lond, ydonged, moyst, & well ywroght Oynons desire. **1526** *Pilgr. Perf.* (W. de W. 1531) 49 b, [God] dyd..set hym in paradyse..for that entent that he sholde worke and kepe it. **1573** Tusser *Husb.* (1878) 120 Choose soile for the hop of the rottenest mould, well doonged and wrought. **1622** in *10th Rep. Hist. MSS. Comm.* App. I. 107 The earth is soft and sandy, esy to bee wrought. **1744** in *6th Rep. Dep. Kpr.* App. II. 121 For the..raising, planting, and working a vegetable (called Sesamo) extraordinary productive of oyl. **1796** C. Marshall *Garden.* xx. (1813) 394 When the ground can be conveniently worked. **1799** J. Robertson *Agric. Perth* 263 The common of Rattry..is indeed very barren; but if it were wrought, it would produce turnips and then grass.

b. To get, 'win' (stone or slate from a quarry, ore or coal from a mine, etc.) by labour; also with the quarry, mine, etc. as obj.

1297 R. Glouc. (Rolls) 3069 Me wolde wene þat in þis lond no ston to worke nere. **1604** E. G[rimstone] *D'Acosta's Hist. Indies* IV. vii. 226 The silver that hath beene wrought in the country. **1618** Ralegh *Apol. Guiana* (1650) 54 It had been no lesse a breach of Peace to have wrought any Myne of his,..then it is now cald'd..a breach of peace to take a towne of his. **1709** T. Robinson *Nat. Hist. Westmld.* x. 62 We found the Vein wrought three Yards wide, and twenty Fathom deep. **1778** Pryce *Min. Cornub.* 21 Several parts of the Lode..have been indiscreetly hulked and worked. **1791** Smeaton *Edystone L.* §99, I..went to view the quarries where the flat paving and steps were wrought. **1839** De la Beche *Rep. Geol. Cornwall*, etc. iv. 124 Roofing-slates and flagstones have been worked in some places. **1844** J. Dunn *Oregon Terr.* 241 The natives were anxious that we should employ them to work the coal. **1879** *Cassell's Techn. Educ.* IV. 212/1 Several mines were worked for this metal.

c. with various objects: see quots.

c **1385** Chaucer *L.G.W.* 1721 *Lucretia*, Softe wolle..she wroughte. **1770** Luckombe *Hist. Printing* 360 When he worked White Paper, he caught the sheet by the upper further corner. **1839** Mrs. Kirkland *New Home* x. 60 The road had been but little 'worked'..and in some parts was almost in a state of nature. **1880** Carnegie *Pract. Trap.* 7 The heaps with the most distinct tracks and most worked (*i.e.*, continually used). **1883** *Chamb. Jrnl.* 15 Dec. 791 Produce of value, such as tea, coffee, indigo, drugs, etc., have to be 'worked' for sale purposes; and this term embraces the opening of the package, examination for sea-damage, sorting into qualities, and a host of other operations.

d. To manipulate (a substance) so as to bring it into the required condition; *esp.* to knead, press, stir, etc. (a plastic substance), or to mix or incorporate (such substances) together by this means; also, to spread (a colour or pigment) over a surface.

1417 *York Memorandum Bk.* (Surtees) I. 183 That he wyrk na lede amanges any other metall.., bot if it be in souldur. **1466** *Cal. Anc. Rec. Dublin* (1889) 326 That no tanner, ne glover,..wyrche harr leddyr at the ryver. **1494** *Act 11 Hen. VII*, c. 19 Cussions stuffed with..gotis here, which is wrought in lyme fattes. **1565–6** Blundevil *Horsemanship, Horses Dis.* liii. (1580) 22 Mingle them togither, & stirre them continuallie in a pot.., vntill the Quicksiluer be so wrought with the rest, as you shall perceiue no quicksiluer therein. **1575** Gascoigne *Glasse Govt.* Wks. 1910 II. 36 You shall see..how I will worke this geare lyke wax. **1653** Walton *Angler* viii. 172 Mix with it [*sc.* paste] Virgins-wax and clarified honey, and work them together with your hands before the fire. **1747–96** Mrs. Glasse *Cookery* xxi. 340 When they are wrought to a paste, roll them with the ends of your fingers. **1756** Mrs. Calderwood in *Coltness Collect.* (Maitl. Club) 147 This salt they work into the butter. **1852** *Jrnl. R. Agric. Soc.* XIII. I. 41 After the butter is taken from the churn it must first be well squeezed or 'worked' by the hand. **1853** Soyer *Pantroph.* 285 Some cooks..worked sesame flour..with honey and oil. **1885** C. Wallis *Dict. Water-colour Technique* 14 The first tone should be decidedly grey..; and on this may be worked Raw Sienna and Brown Madder.

e. To shape (stone, metal, or other hard substance) by cutting or other process; also, to beat out or shape (metal) by hammering (see wrought *ppl. a.* 4). Also with *down.* Also *transf.* to wear by friction or attrition. Also *fig.*

1665 *Phil. Trans.* I. 65 Before the Glass is wrought down to its true Figure. **1679** Moxon *Mech. Exerc.* ix. 157 A greater number of Boards to work to a Level. **1703** *Ibid.* 37 Till you have wrought [*ed.* 1677 filed] the Spindle from end to end. **1717** Berkeley *Tour in Italy* Wks. 1871 IV. 550 Stone easily wrought. **1781** Cowper *Flatting Mill* 2 When a bar of pure silver or ingot of gold Is sent to be flatted or wrought into length. **1844** Mrs. Browning *Lady Geraldine's Courtship* li, Little thinking if we work our souls as nobly as our iron. **1853** Kane *Grinnell Exp.* xlix. (1856) 465 It [*sc.* an iceberg] is an amorphous mass, so worn that it must have been sorely wrought before its release from the glacier. **1855** Squier *Adv. Mosquito Shore* ix. (1856) 146 The trunk of the ceiba..is invaluable... The wood is easily worked. **1885** *Athenæum* 21 Mar. 382/1 The facility of working it [*sc.* limestone] would lead one to expect that an arcuated architecture would have sprung up in Assyria.

f. To do artistic work upon; to decorate, inlay (*with* something). (Cf. inwrought 1.) *rare.*

1634 Sir T. Herbert *Trav.* 61 Two Pillars..couered and wrought with blue and Gold. *Ibid.*, Roofe and sides imbost and wrought with gold.

g. *Sporting* (with the game, or the scent, as obj.).

1568 in *Archaeologia* XXXV. 207 The Emperore and my Lord wente a hontynge of the hare..and worked xx. hares or theare aboutes. **1855** Smedley *H. Coverdale* iii. 13 He says we've worked them [*sc.* the rabbits] quite enough. **1888** *Times* 16 Oct. 10/5 When I tried to work the scent of a deer which had got away.., the hound proved quite useless.

h. ***to work one's passage*** (etc.): to pay for one's passage on board ship by working during the voyage. Also *fig.*

app. arising from ellipsis for *work for*; but cf. 38 e.

1727 'E. Dorrington' *Hermit* II. 121 He sees..Hay-makers, going to work,..and resolves to make one of their Number, and work his passage up to London. **1743** [see passage *sb.* 4 b]. [**1751** *Affect. Narr. Wager* 151 The Captain of this Vessel he prevail'd on to carry them..on Condition of..their Working the Voyage for their Passage.] **1803** D. Wordsworth *Jrnl.* 25 Aug. (1941) I. 257 He was just come from America... I do not think that he had brought much [money] back with him, for he had worked his passage over. **1836** Mrs. C. P. Traill *Backw. Canada* 8 A pretty yellow-haired lad,..who works his passage out. **1849** Thackeray *Pendennis* xxv, Some months afterwards Amory made his appearance at Calcutta, having worked his way out before the mast from the Cape. **1884** *Century Mag.* Jan. 365/1 An educated young Englishman..worked his passage as a coal-passer and ash-heaver. **1934** G. B. Shaw *Village Wooing* 113, I have no time for talk. I have to work my passage. **1958** *Oxf. Mag.* 15 May 448/2 Italy, liberated piecemeal and 'working her passage' to the improved status of the Hyde Park Declaration and the New Deal for Italy. **1973** *Times* 20 Mar. 13/2 One of the greatest bores in packing is choosing which shoes to take... They are heavy..and do not really work their passage.

i. *colloq.* or *slang.* To go through or about (a place) for the purposes of one's business or occupation; to carry on one's trade or business, or some operation, in.

spec. (*a*) of a hound, (*b*) of an itinerant vendor, beggar, etc.; (*c*) of a clergyman; (*d*) of a canvasser; (*e*) of a thief, esp. a pickpocket.

1834 Col. Hawker *Diary* (1893) II. 68, I gave up my bitch..to Joe, to work the enclosures, and he got 5 brace and 1 hare. **1851** Mayhew *Lond. Labour* II. 79 I've worked both town and country on gold fish. **1859** *Slang Dict.* 117 To work a street or neighbourhood, trying at each house to sell all one can. **1859** H. Kingsley *G. Hamlyn* xii, Frank Maberly [a parson] had been..as he expressed it, 'working the slums' at Exeter. **1865** *Leaves from Diary Celebrated Burglar & Pickpocket* xvi. 55/2 They agreed, upon their discharge, to 'work' together. *Ibid.* xvi. 53/1 Joe edged himself into the Scotch Boy's 'mob'..and 'worked' with them. **1882** J. D. McCabe *New York* 520 Even vessels lying at anchor in the harbor, are busily worked by [thieves]. *a* **1885** Sladen *Poetry of Exiles* (ed. 2) I. 24 You and I..Were working on this very Twelfth the old Dumfriesshire moor. **1893** *Daily News* 18 Feb. 3/5 To use an electioneering phrase, it is not easy to 'work' this hilly region. **1897** *Tit-Bits* 4 Dec. 186/2 A professional beggar who 'works' seventy or eighty streets in a few hours. **1905** E. Wallace *Four Just Men* viii. 153 The night being comparatively young, Billy decided to work the trams. **1930** —— *Lady of Ascot* I. 19 It's the same crowd that has been working country houses for weeks. **1938** F. D. Sharpe *Sharpe of Flying Squad* xvi. 181 They [*sc.* pickpockets] used to go off in busloads..to 'work' various districts of London. **1951** W. C. Williams *Autobiogr.* xlv. 299 He had been a fur thief working the big department stores. **1963** T. Tullett *Inside Interpol* xii. 171 A Pole..last caught in August, 1957, working a crowd in Geneva.

transf. **1883** *Century Mag.* XXVI. 393 He 'worked' the hunting-field largely. It constantly reappears in his novels.

j. *slang.* To deal with in some way; to get, or to get rid of, esp. by artifice; (of an itinerant vendor) to hawk, sell.

1839 *Dict. Flash or Cant. Lang.* 36 Work the Bulls, get rid of bad 5s. pieces. **1851** Mayhew *Lond. Labour* I. 84 They made more money 'working' these [*sc.* pine-apples] than any other article. **1890** 'R. Boldrewood' *Col. Reformer* x, Somebody might claim the colt..—say you'd worked him on the cross.

k. To investigate or study systematically. See also *work out* (38 k), *work up* (39 j).

1900 J. Shephard & W. Strickland in *Handbk. Austral. Assoc., Melbourne* 74 The aquatic worms are an untouched group. There are very many forms and when worked they will doubtless yield interesting results.

l. To operate upon so as to get into some state or convert into something else; to bring or reduce *to*; *refl.* with *compl. adj.* to go through some process so as to become... See also *work up*, 39 e.

1594 Plat *Jewell-ho.* 70 An English trauayler..aduised me to make the same [*sc.* Malmesey] alwaies about the middest of Maie, that it might haue 3. hot moneths togither to work it to his ful perfection. **1713** Addison *Cato* I. *ad fin.*, So the pure limpid Stream, when foul with Stains..Work's it self clear, and as it runs, refines. **1753–4** Richardson *Grandison* II. ix. 59 His estate would..work itself clear. **1879** Geo. Eliot *Theo. Such* v. 113 All human achievement must be wrought down to this spoon-meat. **1884** *Manch. Exam.* 20 Feb. 4/6 It would take some time for the trade to work itself right.

13. *Math.*, etc. = *work out*, 38 g; cf. 28.

1593 P. Fale *Horologiogr.* 25, I worke this altogether like to the South reclining 45.^{d}...untill I have found out the Elevation of the Meridian. **1623** J. Johnson *Arith.* II. 137 A second way more briefly to worke this question. *Ibid.* 291 The same example wrought another way. **1669** Sturmy *Mariner's Mag.* II. xiv. 86 English Navigators work their Observation by the Complement of the Sun's Altitude. **1794** J. H. Moore *Pract. Navig.* (1828) 40 In all proportions wrought by Gunter's Scale. **1803** Beddoes *Hygëia* IX. 72 To sit a horse and to work figures by head at the same time. **1852** Thackeray *Esmond* II. v, The sum comes to the same figures, worked either way. **1885** S. Laing *Mod. Sci. & Th.* 5 To calculate the distance..with as much ease..as if we were working a simple sum of rule of three.

14. (= *work on*, 30). **a.** To act upon the mind or will of; to influence, prevail upon, induce, persuade (esp. by subtle or insidious means); more widely, to bring into a particular mental state, disposition, etc. Also, in later use, to strive or take measures to induce or persuade; to urge. See also *work up*, 39 k.

1595 Daniel *Civ. Wars* v. lxxvii, For frends, opinion, & succeeding chaunce, Which wrought the weak to yeld, the strong to loue. **1605** Bacon *Adv. Learn.* II. xviii. §2 In Negotiation with others; men are wrought by cunning, by Importunitie, and by vehemencie. **1610** Holland *Camden's Brit.* 532 Yet could hee not bee wrought..to disclose his complices. **1642** Rogers *Naaman* 45 What doth the Lord? workes Peters heart from that objection, and so from unwillingnesse. **1713** Addison *Cato* II. i, Are your Hearts subdu'd..and wrought By Time and ill Success to a Submission? **1832** Tennyson *Miller's D.* xxx, God..who wrought Two spirits to one equal mind. **1858** G. Macdonald *Phantastes* iii, The house or the clothes..cannot be wrought into an equal power of utterance.

1819 SCOTT *Ivanhoe* xxxvi, I have been working him even now to abandon her. **1857** HUGHES *Tom Brown* I. iii, He was constantly working the Squire to send him..to a public school. **1880** BLACKMORE *Mary Anerley* liv, Sooner, or later, he must come round; and the only way to do it, is to work him slowly.

b. To act upon the feelings of; to affect, agitate, stir, move, excite, incite. Also *refl.* (occas. *intr.* for *refl.*). Now usually *work up*; see 39 k.

1605 SHAKS. *Macb.* I. iii. 149 My dull Braine was wrought with things forgotten. **1610** —— *Temp.* IV. i. 144 Your fathers in some passion That workes him strongly. **1697** DRYDEN *Æneis* x. 1247 Love, Anguish, Wrath, and Grief, to Madness wrought,..his lab'ring Soul oppress'd. **1732** BERKELEY *Alciphr.* I. §4 Sometimes they work themselves into high passions. **1809–11** COMBE *Syntax* xx. 21 The well-dress'd man now stopp'd, to know What work'd the angry Doctor so. **1838** DICKENS *O. Twist* iv, Grasping his cane tightly, as was his wont when working into a passion. **1838** —— *Nich. Nick.* xxxiv, 'Who has?' demanded Ralph, wrought by the intelligence.., and his clerk's provoking coolness, to an intense pitch of irritation. **1848** —— *Dombey* xxiii, Endeavouring to work herself into a state of resentment. **1854** MILMAN *Lat. Christ.* IX. ii. (1864) V. 210 Philip..wrought by indignation from his constitutional mildness. **1883** R. W. DIXON *Mano* I. v. 13 Which rigour wrought those children of the ground To that mad rising.

c. Of medicine: To take effect upon.

1712–13 SWIFT *Jrnl. to Stella* 25 Mar., I take a little physic over-night, which works me next day. **1771** SMOLLETT *Humphry Cl.* 26 Apr., Let. ii, It worked Mrs. Gwyllim a pennorth.

d. To practise on, hoax, cheat, 'do'. *U.S.*

1884 'MARK TWAIN' *Huck. Finn* xix. 183 Preachin's my line, too; and workin' camp-meetin's. **1892** *Boston* (Mass.) *Jrnl.* 21 Sept. 6/1 (*heading*) Waltham officers looking for a horse dealer who has been working that town. **1894** HOWELLS *Trav. fr. Altruria* 122, I might..suspect him..of ..working us, as my husband calls it.

**** To move, direct.

15. To move (something) into or out of some position, or with alternating movement (to and fro, up and down, etc.): usually with some implication of force exerted against resistance or impediment. Also *fig.*

1617 MORYSON *Itin.* I. 115 This little ditch is not alwaies in one place but in time workes it selfe from one place to another. **1691** T. H[ALE] *Acc. New Invent.* 49 Her Rudder wrought it self out of the Irons, hanging only by the uppermost Pintell. **1720** DE FOE *Capt. Singleton* ix. (1840) 166 The rage of the floods..works down a great deal of gold out of the hills. **1831** SCOTT *Cast. Dang.* xx, That secret charm, which, once impressed upon the human heart, is rarely wrought out of the remembrance by a long train of subsequent events. **1842** LOUDON *Suburban Hort.* 327 Water is poured into it, and soil stirred in till the pit is half full of mud... The roots of the tree are then inserted, and worked about. **1857** B. TAYLOR *Northern Trav.* xii. (1858) 127 In vain I shifted my aching legs and worked my benumbed hands. **1867** F. FRANCIS *Bk. Angling* v. 135 Some people work their flies. **1889** *Science-Gossip* XXV. 62 The tube..can be 'worked down' through the hyaline cap. **1902** *Brit. Med. Jrnl.* 12 Apr. 878 Loose body felt at inner side of knee and by working the knee he can make it evident to the touch. **1918** *Times Lit. Suppl.* 11 July 325/4 A neighbouring battery of guns..were being worked into position with a heaving-song.

16. To direct or manage the movement of; to guide or drive in a particular course; *spec.*, *Naut.* to direct the movement of (a ship) by management of the sails and rudder; to move and direct (a boat), as with oars; also in *Angling*, to 'play' (a fish). Also of a locomotive engine, to pull (a train).

1667 MILTON *P.L.* IX. 513 A Ship by skilful Steersman wrought Nigh Rivers mouth or Foreland. **1669** STURMY *Mariner's Mag.* I. ii. 15 The Practick Part of Navigation, in working of a Ship in all Weathers at Sea. **1719** DE FOE *Crusoe* II. (Globe) 336 Having no Sails to work the Ship with. **1762** MILLS *Syst. Pract. Husb.* I. 160 Make a dam.. and a sluice, and work the water upon it through the winter. **1807** P. GASS *Jrnl.* 193 Making the finest canoes,..and.. expert in working them when made. **1825** J. WILSON *Noctes Ambr.* Wks. 1855 I. 74 He worked a salmon to a miracle. **1857** HUGHES *Tom Brown* I. v, Getting on the box, and working the team down street. **1878** C. TUTTLE *Border Tales* 31 To work the ship out of danger. **1912** *Standard* 20 Sept. 7/2 Special trains..will be worked over the systems of the Great Northern [etc.] railways. **1982** *Railway Mag.* Nov. 508/1 A replacement..powered the train as far as Carnforth where another '47' was later provided to work it forward.

b. To herd (sheep, cattle, etc.). Also *intr.* for *pass.* Chiefly *Austral.* and *N.Z.*

1930 L. G. D. ACLAND *Early Canterbury Runs* 1st Ser. i. 5 The practice was for a shepherd to go round the boundary once or twice a day, and at night work the sheep below one of the river terraces to camp. **1946** F. DAVISON *Dusty* (Foreword), Sheep dogs..working lost flocks in the mountain gullies. **1950** *N.Z. Jrnl. Agric.* July 5/2 Sheep work and draft best on a slight up-grade. **1961** B. CRUMP *Hang on a Minute* 87 With Jack working along the top of the ridge and Sam half-way down the side they worked all the sheep off that side of the valley. **1976** *Evening Post* (Bristol) 23 Apr. 24/9 (Advt.), Border collie bitch starting to work cattle.

17. *refl.* To make one's (or its) way; = 18.

1576 TURBERV. *Venerie* 196 [The vermin] will..worke themselues further in, so that your Terriers shall not be able to find them. **1639** S. DU VERGER tr. *Camus' Admir. Events* 99 Octavian..wrought himselfe into her good will. **1655** MRQ. WORCESTER *Cent. Inv.* §15 How to make a Boat work it self against both Wind and Tide. **1711** ADDISON *Spect.* No. 121 ¶5 [The mole] so swiftly working her self under Ground, and making her way so fast in the Earth. **1838** DICKENS *O. Twist* l, The women worked themselves into the centre of the crowd. **1857** HUGHES *Tom Brown* I. iv, Tom.. worked himself into his shoes and his great coat. **1871** SMILES *Charac.* i. (1876) 21 The solitary thought of a great thinker will dwell in the minds of men for centuries, until at length it works itself into their daily life.

18. with *way*, etc. as obj., usually ***to work one's*** or ***its way***: = 33, 33 b; also *fig.*

1713 ADDISON *Cato* I. iii, Through Winds, and Waves, and Storms, he works his way. **1725** DE FOE *Voy. round World* (1840) 311 They worked their way down these streams. **1831** SCOTT *Cast. Dang.* ix, [A contagious disease] ravaged the English Borders, and made some incursions into Scotland where it afterwards worked a fearful progress. **1889** 'J. S. WINTER' *Mrs. Bob* ii. (1891) 20 Mrs. Trafford worked her way round to Major Lovelace. **1889** R. BRYDALL *Art Scot.* vi. 106 He gradually wrought his way against the usual obstacles which a poor artist must always encounter. **1908** [ELIZ. FOWLER] *Betw. Trent & Ancholme* 23 The fluffy golden kerria..having worked its way through the thick wall.

***** Causal senses.

19. To set or compel (a person, animal, etc.) to work; to exact labour from; to employ or use in work. *spec.* in *N.Z.*, to use (a dog) for the purpose of herding sheep or cattle. See also 40 i.

1445 *Cov. Leet Bk.* 225 What man that wurchithe ony man of the seide craft in contrarie-wyse he shall forfet..x s. to the Towne walle. **1607** MARKHAM *Cavel.* I. (1617) 50 Many good breeders..will let their Mares after they are quickned be moderately trauelled or wrought. **1707** SLOANE *Jamaica* I. p. xvii, Oxen..are reckoned the best meat, if not too much wrought. *Ibid.* clii, The Slaves are usually so well wrought in the day,..that they do not easily awake. **1798** J. NAISMITH *Agric. Clydesdale* 123 Some gentlemen have again begun to use oxen for all the purposes of draught. The Right Honourable Lord Douglas always works a few. **1841** R. OASTLER *Fleet Papers* I. 267 Whether it was right to work little boys and girls in the mills, longer than from six o'clock in the morning to six o'clock in the evening. **1878** E. S. ELWELL *Boy Colonists* 48 Fricker..[was] delighted to shew the 'new chum' how to work a cattle dog. **1888** *Times* 13 Oct. 7/6 The manner in which the hounds should be worked. **1912** SIR G. O. TREVELYAN *Geo. III & C. Fox* I. vii. 243 The occupants of the best-paid places for the most part were not worked at all. **1928** P. T. KENWAY *Pioneering in Poverty Bay* viii. 56 It was said of the Highland shepherd in New Zealand, that he would..work his dogs, getting in stray sheep, every day for a month.

b. To bring or get into some condition by labour or exertion.

1628 FOLKINGHAM *Panala Med.* 72 As Oxen wrought leane, regaine the flesh of young beefes by good pasturage. **1727** A. HAMILTON *New Acc. E. Ind.* II. li. 246 He.. protested that he would not be accessory to the Destruction of so many Innocents, whom he foresaw, would be wrought and starved to Death. **1834** G. THORBURN *Resid. Amer.* 224 When first I began to handle the hammer,..my hands blistered too; but I wrought the blister down. **1840** DICKENS *Old Cur. Shop* xliv, She worked herself to death. **1853** —— *Bleak Ho.* xiii, Richard said that he would work his fingers to the bone for Ada. **1908** H. WALES *Old Allegiance* viii. 134, I should think you were working the edge away by this time.

20. To set in action, cause to act; to direct the action of; to exercise (a faculty, etc.); to actuate, operate, manage: with various objects, as a machine or apparatus (passing into ****: cf. 16), an institution or scheme, etc.

c **1374** CHAUCER *Troylus* I. 63 The raueshyng to wreken of Eleyne..þei wroughten al hire peyne. *c* **1550** ROLLAND *Crt. Venus* I. 772 To mend the crime thai will wirk all thair mane. **1591** DRAYTON *Harmony Ch., Deborah's Song* 59 Her left hand to the naile she put, her right the hammer wrought. *c* **1610** in G. C. Bond *Early Hist. Mining* (1924) 15 A smale weight..will growe heavye before it be worked up and worke many wheeles. **1756** C. LUCAS *Ess. Waters* I. 128 Water is raised by a machine,..wrought by an horse. **1791** R. MYLNE *2nd Rep. Thames Navig.* 15 The Power of the Millers in working their Heads of Water. **1798** COLERIDGE *Anc. Mar.* v. xi, The mariners all 'gan work the ropes. **1832** BABBAGE *Econ. Manuf.* xxxi. (ed. 3) 312 The cabinet-makers ..combined against it, and the patent has consequently never been worked. **1853** KINGSLEY *Hypatia* xiii, They are ..dead dolls, wooden, worked with wires. **1860** MILL *Repr. Govt.* (1865) 1/2 No one believes that every people is capable of working every sort of institutions. **1877** *Daily News* 19 Oct. 5/6 The best way to 'work' the elections. **1885** 'MRS. ALEXANDER' *At Bay* ix, Always working her money and my own very cautiously. **1922** TREVELYAN *Brit. Hist. 19th Cent.* ix. 154 Great noblemen who were also great coalowners, working their own mines. *a* **1923** W. P. KER *Tasso* in *Ess.* (1925) I. 339 The best way of working figures on their stage.

b. In fig. or allusive phrases expressing cunning management or manœuvring, as ***to work the oracle*** (see ORACLE *sb.* 1 b), ***the ropes***, ***one's ticket*** (TICKET *sb.*[1] 6 b).

1859 *Slang Dict.* 117 Work the oracle, to succeed by manœuvering, to concert a wily plan, to victimize. **1884** RIDER HAGGARD *Dawn* xvii, How our mutual friend worked the ropes is more than I can tell you. **1919** *Athenæum* 15 Aug. 759/1 'Working one's ticket' means taking steps, such as feigning insanity or sickness, in order to get discharged from the army.

c. To cause to ferment.

[Cf. quot. 1594 in 12 l.] **1764** ELIZA MOXON *Engl. Housew.* (ed. 9) 140 To make Balm Wine... When it is cold put a little new yeast upon it, and beat it in every two hours,..so work it for two days.

II. Intransitive senses.

* To act; to perform work or labour.

21. Of a person: To do something, or to do things generally; to act, esp. in the particular way mentioned; to proceed; to conduct oneself, behave, 'do'. *Obs.* or *arch.*, or merged in other senses.

a **1000** *Soul & Body* 64 (Gr.) Swa þu worhtest to me. *c* **1200** *Vices & Virtues* 27 Hem ðe on him belieueð and ðar after wercheð. **1297** R. GLOUC. (Rolls) 5819 Wisemen he drou to him, & after hom he wroȝte. **1340–70** *Alisaunder* 517 In battail..bigly too wirch. *c* **1386** CHAUCER *Prol.* 497 This noble ensample to his sheepe he yaf That firste he wroghte, and afterward that he taughte. **1387** TREVISA *Higden* (Rolls) I. 7 þey schulleþ fonge her mede of hym þat rewardeþ..al þat wel worcheþ. *c* **1400** *26 Pol. Poems* v. 8 Gostly blynd ..þat leueþ wit, and worchiþ by wille. *c* **1430** LYDG. *Min. Poems* (Percy Soc.) 140 Wher God list werche may be noon obstacle. **1471** CAXTON *Recuyell* (Sommer) 340 [He] putte hym self in to the grettest prees of the bataylle wher he wrought mortally. *a* **1529** SKELTON *Dyuers Balettys* Wks. (Dyce) I. 24 Aduertysing you..to warke more secretly. **1550** CROWLEY *Last Trumpet* 1357 If he haue wrought against the lawes. **1568** GRAFTON *Chron.* II. 63 He, because he could not otherwise speake vnto him, wrought by signes. **1601** SHAKS. *All's Well* IV. ii. 29 This ha's no holding To sweare by him whom I protest to loue That I will worke against him.

† **b.** ***to let work***: to allow to act or proceed (***let God work*** = leave the rest to God). *Obs.*

c **1230** *Hali Meid.* (1922) 13 Ne þarf þe bute wilnen, & lete godd wurchen. **14..** *Sir Beues* (Pynson) 3372 Iosyan.. trauayled of chylde... She sayde,..'go hens away,..And late me worke and our lady'. **1546** [see A. 1 η].

22. To act for a purpose, or so as to gain an end; to plan, plot; to contrive, manage. *arch.*

a **1000** *Boeth. Metr.* xx. 87 þæt ðu mid ȝeþeahte þinum wyrcest þæt ðu þæm ȝesceaftum swa ȝescеadlice mearce ȝesettest. *c* **1386** CHAUCER *Merch. T.* 417 God..may so for yow wirche, That..Ye may repente of wedded mannes lyf. **1390** GOWER *Conf.* I. 63 How he can werche Among tho wyde furred hodes, To geten hem the worldes goodes. *c* **1470** HENRY *Wallace* II. 242 Thai wyrk ay to wayt ws with supprys. *a* **1548** HALL *Chron., Edw. IV* 239 Se how politikely the French kyng wrought for his aduantage. **1613** SHAKS. *Hen. VIII*, III. ii. 311 Without the Kings assent or knowledge, You wrought to be a Legate. *a* **1674** MILTON *Hist. Moscovia* v. Wks. 1851 VIII. 511 The Chancellor, with others of the great ones..so wrought, that a Creature of thir own was sent to meet Sir Jerom. **1887** MORRIS *Odyssey* XII. 445 So wrought the Father of Gods and of men that I was not seen.

23. Of a thing (abstr. or concr.): To do something; to perform a function, or produce an effect; to act, operate, take effect; *esp.* to act in the desired way, do what is required; to be practicable or effectual, to succeed. See also 33.

1340 HAMPOLE *Pr. Consc.* 3137 þat fire..wirkes on wonderful manere,..Thurgh wilk þe saule most clensed be In purgatory. *a* **1375** *Joseph Arim.* 49 Louse þi lippes a-twynne & let þe gost worche. *c* **1375** *Sc. Leg. Saints* xxxii. (*Justin*) 593 þi strinth sal nocht wyrke Agane þe treutht of haly kirke. **1379** *Glouc. Cath. MS.* No. 1. I. iii. lf. 3 b, As the sonne wirkyth in all creaturis her beneathe. *c* **1386** CHAUCER *Knt.'s T.* 1901 Ther Nature wol nat wirche, Fare wel Phisik; go ber the man to chirche. *c* **1400** tr. *Secr. Secr., Gov. Lordsh.* 71 Whanne þe wyt werketh and þe wyl ys trauaylled. **1422** YONGE tr. *Secr. Secr.* 206 Prayer,..out-sayd in erthe, worchyth in hevyn. **1471** CAXTON *Recuyell* (Sommer) 376 Thise wordes wroughte in the hertes of the calcedonyens and gaf to them corage. **1526** TINDALE *Rom.* viii. 28 All thynges worke for the best [1611 worke together for good] vnto them that love god. **1585** T. WASHINGTON tr. *Nicholay's Voy.* III. xi. 91 b, Opium..doth so worke with them.., that they loose both their wits and vnderstanding. **1602** MARSTON *Antonio's Rev.* IV. iii, My plot begins to worke. **1651** FRENCH *Distill.* i. 40 This Oil taken inwardly worketh upward and downward. **1667** MILTON *P.L.* VIII. 507 Nature her self..Wrought in her so, that seeing me, she turn'd. **1671** —— *Samson* 850 It was not gold..That wrought with me. **1784** TWAMLEY *Dairying* 30 This [salt] will..cause the Rennet to Work quick. **1832** *Edin. Rev.* Oct. 245 How will the Reform Bill work in the returns of members to Parliament? **1843** R. J. GRAVES *Syst. Clin. Med.* vi. 75 The stomach works well and performs its functions with vigour. **1846** TRENCH *Mirac.* xvi. 262 [He] left the difficulty ..to work in the minds of the apostles. **1861** TROLLOPE *Framley Parsonage* xxix, Lady Lufton was beginning to fear that her plan would not work. **1869** W. T. THORNTON *On Labour* IV. i. 357 The cases..showing how this arrangement works. **1891** SCRIVENER *Fields & Cities* 116 This is how private ownership of property works. **1892** MRS. CLIFFORD *Aunt Anne* I. ii. 40 Walter had tried sending Florence and the children and going down every week himself; but he found 'it didn't work'.

b. Of a machine or apparatus: To perform its proper function; to act, operate.

Sometimes felt as *intr.* for *pass.* from 20. In this and next sense passing into **.

c **1610** in G. C. Bond *Early Hist. Mining* (1924) 15 Smale modles often fayle..when they cume to worcke upon heavye ..weightes. **1702** *Post Man* 21–24 Feb. 2/2 Advt., There is a small Engine, that Raises Water..now set up at the Engine-House..in Dorset Garden, which will Work every Saturday and Wednesday. **1726** LEONI *Alberti's Archit.* II. 11 Cranes or Skrews, or any other Engine, working either by Leavers or Pullies. **1842** DICKENS *Amer. Notes* ii, Telegraphs working; flags hoisted. **1867** tr. *Clausius' Mech. Theory Heat* 198 A machine which works with expansion. **1889** GUNTER *That Frenchman* iv. 37 Maurice..closes the door..spring it to be sure the spring lock has worked. **1917** MISS M. T. JACKSON *Museum* ii. 67 Like all mechanical devices it [*sc.* the thermostat] does not always work.

c. Of a part of mechanism: To have its proper action or movement in relation to another part with which it is in contact.

1770 LUCKOMBE *Hist. Printing* 324 [He] besmears..so much of the Cheeks as the ends of the Head works against. *Ibid.* 366 The square holes the Hose works in. **1825** J. NICHOLSON *Oper. Mech.* 130 The four bevelled nuts work into the bevelled wheels..and so turn them. **1892** *Photogr. Ann.* II. 172 An index working over a scale.

d. ***to work like a charm***: see CHARM *sb.*[1] 1 c.

24. To do something involving effort (of body or mind); to exert oneself (physically or mentally) for a definite purpose, esp. in order to produce something or effect some useful result, to gain one's livelihood or some profit or advantage, or under compulsion; to do work, perform a task or tasks, to toil: = LABOUR *v.* 11. (Opposed to PLAY *v.* 10, or to REST *v.*[1] 2.)

to work like a beaver, horse, nigger: see these words. Similarly ***to work like a dog, to work one's tail off. to work double tides***: see TIDE *sb.* 14.

c **888** ÆLFRED *Boeth.* xli. §3 Hwy sceall þonne ænig mon bion idel, ðæt he ne wyrce? *c* **1000** *Ags. Gosp.* Matt. xxi. 28 Ga and wyrce to-dæg on minum wingearde. *a* **1225** *Ancr. R.* 44 Lokeð..þet ȝe ne beon neuer idel: auch wurcheð, oðer redeð, oðer beoð i beoden. *c* **1275** LAY. 8710–11 Þare wrohte þeines, þare wrohte sweines, and þe king mid his honde. *a* **1300** *Cursor M.* 6843 Sex dais sal yee wirc,..And yee sal rest þe seuend dai. **13..** *Sir Beues* (A.) 58 Me lord is olde & may nouȝt werche. **13..** *E.E. Allit. P.* A. 525 Þay wente in to þe vyne & wroȝte. *c* **1386** CHAUCER *Sec. Nun's T.* 14 Wel oghte vs werche, and ydelnesse withstonde. *c* **1449** PECOCK *Repr.* III. xi. 342 Poul..wrouȝte with hise hondis forto haue his lijflode to preche. **1513** BRADSHAW *St. Werburge* II. 880 A woman which..sabbot-day dyd violate Vn-laufully wurkynge. **1526** *Pilgr. Perf.* (W. de W. 1531) 72 b, We must worke and labour in goostly exercyse certayn dayes. **1546** J. HEYWOOD *Prov.* I. xi. (1867) 36 As good þonne for nought as woorke for nought. *c* **1595** CAPT. WYATT *R. Dudley's Voy. W. Ind.* (Hakl. Soc.) 50 Our men wrought dalie to hoyse aborde all such goodes. **1620** *Reg. Mag. Sig. Scot.* 784/1 At such one of the saidis mynes as they sall have last wrought into. **1621** T. GRANGER *Expos. Eccles.* xii. i. 315 We must worke with the Oare while we haue strength, and after sit at the sterne. *a* **1633** G. HERBERT *Jacula Prudentum* 178 Thinke of ease, but worke on. **1851** KINGSLEY *Three Fishers*, For men must work, and women must weep. **1861** GEN. P. THOMPSON *Audi Alt.* III. clxiii. 180 To have taxed his paper, or his ink, or the rush-lights that he wrought by. **1866** RUSKIN *Crown Wild Olive* i. 40 Our third condition of separation, between the men who work with the hand, and those who work with the head. **1926** [see PERISH *v.* 1 e]. **1969**, etc. [see TAIL *sb.*[1] 5 a]. **1976–7** *Sea Spray* (N.Z.) Dec./Jan. 95/2 These lads have worked like dogs all winter.

b. const. *at*, *on* or *upon*, †rarely *in*, *of* (a material object, esp. in making (cf. 14), a subject of study or literary treatment, an occupation, etc.).

1154 *O.E. Chron.* (Laud MS.) an. 1137 Martin abbot..wrohte on þe circe. *c* **1200** ORMIN 16283 Swa þeȝȝ stodenn ..To wirrkenn o þe temmple. **1375** in Horstm. *Altengl. Leg.* (1878) 137/1 [Solomon] þeron..Dede worchen foure & twenty ȝere. **1497** *Naval Acc. Hen. VII* (1896) 324 Certeyn Shipwryghtes that wrought of the seid Ship. **1569** *Aldeburgh Rec.* in *N. & Q.* 12th Ser. VII. 184/1 Pd to Rodger coke and his man for workynge in the seatts at Churche. **1612** J. DAVIES (Heref.) *Muse's Sacrifice* Wks. (Grosart) II. 6/2 That proud Pyramed..Whereon, three-hundred-three-score-thousand wrought full twenty Yeeres. **1623** LISLE *Ælfric on O. & N. Test.* Pref., A sentence of Hesiod so commendable, that..Livie in that [Oration] of Minutius hath it well and diversly wrought-on. **1687** PRIOR *Hind & P. Transv.* Wks. 1907 II. 15 Vulcan working at the Anvil. **1712** J. JAMES tr. *Le Blond's Gardening* 205 Some Basons have been worked upon several times, without being able almost to make them hold Water. **1840** G. GODWIN *Last Day* i. 5 How hard some folks do work at what they call pleasure. **1853** DICKENS *Bleak Ho.* xviii, The little [church-] porch, where a monotonous ringer was working at the bell. **1893** LIDDON, etc. *Pusey* I. v. 96 Pusey..spent from fourteen to sixteen hours a day working at Arabic. *a* **1923** W. P. KER *Tasso* in *Ess.* (1925) I. 342 Tasso had been working at his epic poem.

(*b*) In humorous or trivial use, implying vigorous action of some kind.

1840 THACKERAY *Barber Cox* Feb., The Duchess and the great ladies were all seated,..working away at the ices and macaroons.

25. To exert oneself in order to accomplish something or gain some end (expressed by context); to strive: = LABOUR *v.* 12.

c **1250** *Gen. & Ex.* 1470 He wrogten and figt, Queðer here sulde birðen bi-foren. *c* **1380** WYCLIF *Wks.* (1880) 352 He is frend to þe frere þat hatiþ þus his synne & worchiþ to distrie it. **1483** *Cath. Angl.* 420 To Wyrke, *aporiare & -ri, anxiari, conari, cooperari, conniti.* **1591** SHAKS. *1 Hen. VI*, III. iii. 27 Your Honors shall perceiue how I will worke, To bring this matter to the wished end. **1818** SCOTT *Rob Roy* xxxiv, Such a deed might make one forswear kin, clan, country, wife, and bairns! And yet the villain wrought long for it. **1873** BURTON *Hist. Scot.* V. lviii. 230 He was a refugee in England during the regency of Morton, who wrought hard to lay hands on him. **1891** FARRAR *Darkn. & Dawn* xvii, That guilty and intriguing minister of Tiberius..had for years worked on with the deliberate intention of clearing every one of them from his path, and climbing to that throne himself.

26. To do one's ordinary business; to pursue a regular occupation; to be regularly engaged or employed in some labour, trade, profession, etc. (*in* a place, *for* or *under* a master or superior). Said also of animals. Also more widely, to do something for a definite end, to engage in some systematic occupation. (Often coinciding with 24.) ***to work out of***, to use it as a base, office, etc., for work; *to* (a person), to be responsible to as one's immediate superior or supervisor.

1307 *York Memorandum Bk.* (Surtees) I. 181 Boclemakers ..to serve and to wyrk to pouer and to riche within this cite. *a* **1400** *Isumbras* 398 'For mete', he sayde, 'I wold wyrke fayne.' *c* **1450** CAPGRAVE *Life St. Aug.* xii. 17 Be-neth þat hous..was housyng be þe ground, in whech dwelt coynoures of siluyr, and wroute þere ful bisily. **1552–3** in Feuillerat *Revels Edw. VI* (1914) 130 Taylours woorking by greate or taske woork. **1590** SHAKS. *Mids. N.* III. ii. 10 Rude Mechanicals, That worke for bread vpon Athenian stals. **1612** S. RID *Art of Jugling* C 4, The..matters wherevpon Iuglers worke vpon, and shew their featès. **1676** MARVELL *Mr. Smirke* I 4 b, Did not St. Paul himself, being a Tent-maker,..work of his trade.. to get his living? **1702** *Lond. Gaz.* No. 3809/8 He [*sc.* a glover] wought in Colemans-alley. **1704** DE FOE *Giving Alms no Charity* (1859) 58 'Tis the men that wont work, not the men that can get no work, which makes the numbers of our poor. **1771** GOLDSM. *Hist. Eng.* III. 326 He wrought for some days in the habit of a peasant, cutting faggots in a wood. **1854** H. MILLER *Sch. & Schm.* ii. (1858) 35 The farmers for whom he wrought. **1866** GEO. ELIOT *F. Holt* xi, He's one of the Company you work under. **1879** LUBBOCK *Sci. Lect.* ii. 34 Ants work not only all day, but in warm weather often all night too. **1883** SWINBURNE *Misc.* (1886) 117 It was not the aim of Wordsworth to work on the same lines, to rule in the same province as do these. **1898** 'H. S. MERRIMAN' *Roden's Corner* iv. 40 It is he who has made the discovery upon which we are working. **1941** B. SCHULBERG *What makes Sammy Run?* xii. 300 She's turned pro... She's working out of Gladys'. **1961** B. FERGUSSON *Watery Maze* xiv. 360 The Forward Officer (Bombardment) working to H.M.S. *Roberts* was killed with his signaller. **1972** *Where* Sept. 263/1 Registration officers work to the Registrar General. **1975** I. MURDOCH *Word Child* 6, I worked to a man called Duncan, now briefly seconded to the Home Office. **1976** M. DELVING *China Expert* i. 12 He had no shop but worked out of the small, comfortable house he had bought. **1979** P. COSGRAVE *Three Colonels* viii. 174 They had all worked either to Davies..or Morgan... None had come in contact with the head of the department.

b. const. *in* (†*with*) the material upon which labour is expended in some business or manufacture.

1471 CAXTON *Recuyell* (Sommer) 54 Than Iupiter began to lerne spynne and to werke in the silke. **1474** —— *Chesse* III. iii. (1883) 93 Thise..ben named drapers..for so moche as they werke wyth wolle. **1538** ELYOT *Dict.*, *Plasma*, the warke of a potter, or of hym that worketh in erthe. **1539** *Bible* (Great) Isa. xix. 9 They that worke in flaxe. **1604** E. G[RIMSTONE] *D'Acosta's Hist. Indies* IV. vi. 223 The veine of Tinne..is..rough and very painfull to worke in. **1759** R. SMITH *Harmonics* (ed. 2) 176 Any man who works true in brass may easily apply it [*sc.* this mechanism]..to any harpsichord ready made. **1869** BOUTELL *Arms & Armour* ii. 38 The Greeks of that age..were able to temper it [*sc.* iron], and they had actually commenced working in it.

c. *spec.* of sporting dogs. (Cf. 12 g.)

1832 [see WORKING *vbl. sb.* 1]. **1874** *Kennel Club Stud Bk.* 165 Bruce and Rob Roy..both worked in good style. **1874** CARPENTER *Mental Phys.* I. ii. §3. (1879) 104 Young Pointers and Retrievers, when first taken into the field, will often 'work' as well as if they had been long well trained.

27. To perform the work proper or incidental to one's business or avocation; to operate or practise in a professional way. *Obs.* exc. in general sense.

1340 *Ayenb.* 174 Þe leche ne may naȝt werche mid þe zike bote-yef he yzi his wonde. *a* **1425** tr. *Arderne's Treat. Fistula*, etc. 45 Wiþ som men it is to wirche wiþ cauteries. **1471** CAXTON *Recuyell* (Sommer) 233 Iupiter..wrought in his science and made his charmes. *a* **1500** in Arnolde *Chron.* 63 b/2 Wan ye mone is..in cankro Leone or Libra it is good [to] wurch in trees that bethe newe sprongen.

b. Said esp. of the performance of artistic work or the practice of an artist. †***worked upon***, †***about***: decorated or ornamented, e.g. with embroidery, engraving, or the like; also *fig.* ***worked over***: having the surface remodelled or redecorated.

1539 *Bible* (Great) Ps. xlv. 10 A vesture of gold (wrought about with dyuerse colours). *a* **1586** SIDNEY *Arcadia* II. xxii. (1912) 291 Her apparrell of white, wrought upon with broken knots. **1607** SHAKS. *Timon* I. i. 200 How lik'st thou this picture?.. Wrought he not well that painted it? **1638** JUNIUS *Paint. Ancients* 102 Exercising his scholars..in the necessary rudiments..before he would suffer them..to worke in colours. **1706** tr. *De Piles' Art Painting* 336 He work'd also in Sculpture. **1733** *Sch. Miniature* 42 When you work after Prints. **1786** STRUTT *Biogr. Dict. Engravers* II. 422 This artist worked with the graver only. **1874** J. H. POLLEN *Anc. & Mod. Furniture S. Kens. Mus.* 131 The work is profusely gilt and worked over with tooling. **1875** FORTNUM *Maiolica* iv. 39 He worked about 1550. **1883** T. WESTWOOD & SATCHELL *Bibl. Piscat.* 219 The scroll has.. been 'worked over', much to its detriment. **1889** R. BEYDALL *Art in Scot.* vii. 125 The students wrought in the academy daily at painting.

fig. **1875** WHITNEY *Life Lang.* iii. 39 For a long time there has existed..a tendency to work over such verbs, abandoning their irregularly varying inflection, and reducing them to accordance with the more numerous class of the 'regularly' inflected.

c. *slang.* (See quot. 1839.) Cf. sense 12 i (*e*) above.

1839 H. BRANDON in W. A. Miles *Poverty, Mendicity & Crime* 166/1 *Work*, to rob, or act in any way according to the divers occupations of thieves, &c. **1882** *Sydney Slang Dict.* 10/2 We went to the gaff that night and tried to work. **1955** *Publ. Amer. Dial. Soc.* xxiv. 70 Some Americans [*sc.* pickpockets]..are front workers..; that is, they can and do work facing the victim. **1963** T. TULLETT *Inside Interpol* x. 150 Huffman 'worked' for a short time in Rome, where he defrauded several shopkeepers.

d. ***to work to rule***: to follow the rules of one's occupational duties punctiliously in order to reduce efficiency, usu. as a form of protest in an industrial dispute. So ***work-to-rule*** attrib. phr.; also as *sb.* Similarly, in the professions, ***work-to-contract***.

[**1940** *Ann. Reg. 1939* 310 A 'ca' canny' movement—called 'work to rules'—among the [railway] employees.] **1950** *Ann. Reg. 1949* 40 The delegates replied by ordering a general work-to-rule 44-hour week..unless claims were settled. **1952** *News Chron.* 13 Mar. 5/7 That conductor was working to rule... All passengers must be seated before moving off; no overtaking of other buses; and no efforts to make up lost time. **1958** *Times* 4 Aug. 6/4 A report that prison officers.. were working to rule in protest against the report..that prisoners there had been assaulted. **1959** *Daily Tel.* 21 Nov. 1/5 The work-to-rule and shut-down were expected to be carried out in Manchester, Birmingham, Liverpool and other provincial cities. **1960** *Guardian* 13 June 1/6 A 'work-to-rule' plan instituted by members of the Amalgamated Engineering Union after pay negotiations..had broken down. **1962** *Spectator* 26 Jan. 96 What about lesser sanctions—go-slows, work-to-rules and overtime bans? **1967** R. WHITEHEAD in Wills & Yearsley *Handbk. Managem. Technol.* 69 The system would fail even more often if the staff stuck rigidly to the rules. We see the results when they 'work to rule', as it is. **1969** *Daily Tel.* 19 Apr. 23/3 Members of the London Schoolmasters' Association will 'work to contract' next term because of the two weeks' suspension without pay earlier in the year of 22 teachers. **1972** 'M. SINCLAIR' *Norslag* x. 82 A work-to-rule among ground staff had led to some flights being delayed. **1975** *Times* 13 Jan. 15/1 Instead of wholesale industrial action by most of the [medical] profession, we are left with the consultants and their 'work-to-contract'.

28. *Math.*, etc. To proceed (in a particular way) in calculation; to perform a calculation; to go through the process of solving a problem.

c **1391** CHAUCER *Astrol.* II. §5 Whan þat the degree of thy sonne falleth by-twixe two Almykanteras.., thow Most werken in this wise. *c* **1425** *Crafte Nombrynge* (E.E.T.S.) 23 Here he teches how þou schalt wyrch in þis craft. Þou schalt multiplye þe last figure [etc.]. **1610** A. HOPTON *Baculum Geodæticum* 35 For the distance of sides of Triangles, worke thus. **1614** HANDSON tr. *Barth. Pitisco's Trigonom.* II. 20 If you worke by the table of latitudes..the difference of longitude will be 68 deg. **1669** STURMY *Mariner's Mag.* V. xii. 62 You must work as if the Piece were fortified no more than only so much as the thinnest part of the Metal is. **1766** *Complete Farmer* s.v. *Surveying* 7 G 2/1 If instead of squaring the half feet, you square the half yards.., and work with them, you will attain the same end without any regardable difference. **1823** J. GUY *Tutor's Assist.* 79 Work for the tare and trett as before.

29. Of a substance (corresp. to various senses in 12); usually with qualifying adv. or phr.: To behave in a particular way while being worked. See also 39 d.

c **1489** CAXTON *Sonnes of Aymon* vi. 136 Whan the yron is well hoote, hit werketh the better. **1662** GERBIER *Princ.* 24 Portland Stone works well. **1676** J. SMITH *Art of Painting* ii. 16 Vermillion... If it be ground fine..no Colour works better. **1764** *Museum Rust.* III. xlviii. 205 Whilst in the quarry, it works better than after it has been exposed to the sun. **1815** J. SMITH *Panorama Sci. & Art* II. 732 Yellow ochre..is..much used [*sc.* in painting], as it works very freely. **1877** *Paper hanger* etc. 68 Distemper mixed with jellied size will lay on better..than when the size is used hot. Colour mixed on the former plan works cool and floats nicely, while the latter works dry, and drags and gathers.

30. With *on* or *upon* (†*into*, †*of*, †*to*, *with* arch.): To operate upon, produce an effect upon, take effect on, affect, influence: **a.** physically or generally.

1375 BARBOUR *Bruce* IV. 700 Of the hevyn..How that the disposicioune Suld apon thingis virk heir doune. **1542** UDALL *Erasm. Apoph.* 219 He toke poison..but..it would not worke vpon hym. *c* **1560** A. SCOTT *Poems* (S.T.S.) iii. 55 As for a weddow, wirk weill on hir wame, I knaw no craft sall cause hir lufe ȝow bettir. **1587** GOLDING *De Mornay* xvii. 314 This fault cannot bee imputed to the body..: neither can it be imputed to any infection receiued first from the body; for the Soule could not be wrought into by the body. **1601** SHAKS. *Twel. N.* II. iii. 188, I know my Physicke will worke with him. **1627** HAKEWILL *Apol.* IV. xiv. §5 (1630) 514 The same [sun-] beams exhale both stinking vapours out of the dunghills and sweete savours out of flowres, the beame is every way the same which workes vpon them, only the difference of the subjects..is it that..diversifies the effects. **1730** W. BURDON *Gentl. Pocket-Farrier* 75 When a Purge works..too strong upon him..give him an Ounce of Venice Treacle. **1847** TENNYSON *Princess* IV. 137 Cyril, with whom the bell-mouth'd glass had wrought,..began To troll a..tavern-catch.

b. mentally or morally; sometimes, to do something in order to affect, strive to influence (with *to* = LABOUR *v.* 13); sometimes, to influence successfully, prevail upon, induce, persuade: = 14 a. (Often in indirect passive.)

1616 W. BROWNE *Brit. Past.* II. ii. 737 Which wrought so on the Swains, they could not smother Their sighes. **1632** LITHGOW *Trav.* IV. 140 Sir Thomas..seriously wrought with the Grand Signior and his Counsell, to haue had him restored againe to his Lands. **1647** in *Verney Mem.* (1907) I. 435 Shee cries and tackes on..but all we can doo will not worke of her. **1662** ATWELL *Faithf. Surveyor* 4 He works to the Lady [owner] to send another to measure it [*sc.* the farm]... He prevails with her, she sends another. **1669** PEPYS *Diary* 10 May (1879) VI. 79 The King may yet be wrought upon..to bring changes in our Office. *a* **1715** BURNET *Own Time* (1823) I. 339 But he would not be wrought on. **1799** WASHINGTON *Let.* Writ. 1893 XIV. 184 He was not to be worked upon by Intriguers. **1823** SCOTT *Quentin D.* xxviii, Sweetest Lady, work with thy child, that he will pardon all past sins. **1849** MACAULAY *Hist. Eng.* vi. II. 72 She..worked on his feelings by pretending to be ill. **1869** FREEMAN *Norm. Conq.* III. xiii. 266 He had many minds to work upon and to win over to his cause.

31. To ache, hurt: = WARK *v. Obs.* exc. *dial.*

a **1400** *Morte Arth.* 2688 Thoffe my schouldire be schrede, ..And the wielde of myne arme werkkes a littille. *a* **1400–50** *Wars Alex.* 531 Sa sare werkis hire þe wame..þat all scho dredis hire dede. *c* **1400** *Rom. Rose* 1814, I felte such wo, my wounde ay wrought. **1470–85** MALORY *Arthur* XXI. v. 848, I may not stonde, myn hede werches soo. **1808** JAMIESON, *To werk*, to ache.

32. Of liquor: To ferment.

1570 TIMME tr. *Marlorat's Expos. Matt.* ix. 17 When the newe wyne worketh or spourgeth, the vessels breake. **1577** GOOGE *Heresbach's Husb.* IV. 183 b, The Hony is..suffered to stand vncouered a fewe dayes tyll it haue wrought, and cast vp a loft all his drags. **1673** *Phil. Trans.* VIII. 6021 About 7 or 8 dayes after the Must hath been thus boyled it begins to work. **1715** Leoni *Palladio's Archit.* (1742) I. 57 The tubs wherein the Wine is working. **1857** Miller *Elem. Chem., Org.* (1862) ii. §5. 129 The liquid becomes turbid, and small bubbles rise to the surface; or in popular language, it begins to work or to ferment.

fig. **1602** *2nd Pt. Return fr. Parnass.* I. ii. (Arb.) 9 Such barmy heads wil alwaies be working. **1821** Scott *Kenilw.* xxxiv, Men's brains are working like yeast.

** To move in a particular way or direction.

33. To go or move along, or in a particular course; to make one's (or its) way, take one's (or its) course; now usually, to make way slowly, laboriously, with some exertion or difficulty, or in an indirect course. (Usually with adv. or phr. expressing the direction or course: see also 36 b, 38 b, 39 c.)

c **1400** *Treat. Astron.* 3 (MS. Add. Bodl. B. 17), Therbe ..vij. planetis that meuyn and werkyn in the .vij. heuenes. **1474** Caxton *Chesse* III. ii. (1883) 87 Fortune hath of no thinge so grete playsir as for to torne & werke all way. **1535** Coverdale *Jonah* i. 13 The see wrought [Luther *fuhr*, Vulg. *ivit*, LXX. ἐπορεύετο] so, & was so troublous agaynst them. **1697** Dryden *Æneis* v. 891 The raging Fires.. lurking in the Seams,.. Work on their way, amid the smouldring Tow. **1802** Colman *Broad Grins, Elder Bro.* (1819) 118 Being *Bacchi plenus*,—full of wine,—..He work'd, with sinuosities, along. **1848** Dickens *Dombey* l, [The dog] worked round and round him, as if..undecided at what particular point to go in for the assault. **1862** Pycroft *Cricket Tutor* 57 A ball working away only a little way to the leg. **1878** Lady Brassey *Voy. Sunbeam* i. 2 After midnight ..the wind worked gradually round..and blew directly in our teeth. **1898** G. A. B. Dewar *In Pursuit Trout* 26 The trout was working up stream, always keeping under the bank. **1912** *Times* 19 Oct. 7/3 The Russians..worked round to the rear of the Turkish army.

b. To make one's (or its) way slowly or with effort through something, as in penetrating gradually through a substance, burrowing in the ground, etc.

c **1400** Maundev. (Roxb.) xxix. 132 So lang sall þis fox wirk in þe erthe þat at þe last he schall comme oute amang þis folk. *c* **1400** *Destr. Troy* 12007 All the cite.. þai set vppon fyre,.. Wroght vnder walles, walt hom to ground. **1596** Dalrymple tr. *Leslie's Hist. Scot.* I. 47 Sum says it is a mater that wirkes out of the stanes. **1691** in *Archaeologia* XII. 189 Sometimes the coneys work under the wall into the garden. **1766** *Complete Farmer* s.v. *Walk* 7 Z 3/2 The bottom of the walks should be laid with rubbish, coarse gravel, &c.,..and beaten down close, to prevent the worms from working through it.

c. *Naut.* Of a sailing vessel: To sail in a particular course, to make sail; *esp.* to beat to windward, to tack. See also 39 c.

1633 T. Stafford *Pac. Hib.* II. xii. 204 The shipping.. had direction to worke about to another Creake. **1704** *Lond. Gaz.* No. 4054/1 Perceiving..that they wrought from us, we followed them..with all the Sail we could make. **1748** *Anson's Voy.* II. viii. 223 She had sprung her fore-top-mast, which had disabled her from working to windward. **1768** *Phil. Trans.* LX. 116 A little before noon we weighed, and worked up the river. **1823** Scoresby *Jrnl.* 2 We reached down the river, and, on the ebb, worked out of the Rock Channel. **1836** Marryat *Pirate* xvi, The Comus..worked, in short tacks, outside the reef. **1853** Kane *Grinnell Exp.* xxiii. (1856) 184 We are working, i.e., beating our way in the narrow leads..between the main ice and the drift.

d. To proceed in a particular direction in some operation.

1877 *Paper Hanger*, etc. 26 The paper hanger generally works from left to right. **1881** Raymond *Mining Gloss.*, *Working home*, working toward the main shaft in extracting ore or coal. **1910** F. Fawcett in *Folk-Lore* (1912) XXIII. 39 He is given several sharp blows on the ribs, beginning under the armpit and working downwards.

e. *transf.* and *fig.* in various connexions. See also 39 c.

1691 T. Tryon *Art Brewing* (ed. 3) 49 So soon as it [your Corn] begins to come, or as some calls it Work. **1848** Lytton *Harold* IX. iii, A silent war between the two for mastery was working on. **1857** Mrs. Gaskell *C. Brontë* I. ii. 27 Their religion did not work down into their lives. **1865** Dickens *Mut. Fr.* II. ix, Hoping as Our Johnny would work round [= recover]. **1883** Sidgwick *Fallacies* II. vi. 205 Hence..the name [*sc.* demonstration] often works round again, in popular usage, to mean proof which is 'sufficiently' or 'practically' conclusive. **1895** P. Hemingway *Out of Egypt* II. 158 A new conversation starts up every hour, and debateable points acquire a fresh interest because there is never time to work to a conclusion.

34. To move restlessly, violently, or convulsively; to be in a state of agitation or commotion; to toss, seethe, rage (as a stormy sea, etc.); to struggle; to twitch; *Naut.* of a ship, to strain or 'labour' so that the fastenings become slack (cf. 35); so of an engine or carriage (see quots. 1791, 1892 s.v. working *vbl. sb.* 12). Also *fig.* of thought or feeling; sometimes with allusion to 32.

1581, 1582 [see working *vbl. sb.* 10, *ppl. a.* 4]. **1608** Shaks. *Per.* III. i. 48 The sea workes hie. **1652** J. Taylor (Water P.) *Relat. Journ. Wales* (1859) 11 The well..doth continually work and bubble with extream violence. **1689** H. Pitman *Relat.* in Arb. *Garner* VII. 351 Our little vessel..wrought so exceedingly by reason of the great motion of the sea, that we could not possibly make her tight. **1769** Falconer *Dict. Marine* (1776) s.v., A ship is..said to work, when she strains and labours heavily in a tempestuous sea, so as to loosen her joints or timbers. **1770** Wesley *Jrnl.* 4 July, She..wrought, like one strangled, in her breast and throat. **1815** Jane Austen *Emma* I. xiii, With men he can be..unaffected, but when he has ladies to please, every feature works. **1840** Dickens *Old Cur. Shop* lviii, Shaking his head, and working with both his hands as if he were clearing away ten thousand cobwebs. **1840** R. H. Dana *Bef. Mast* xi. 25 While everything was working, and cracking, strained to the utmost. **1886** Stevenson *Kidnapped* 5 With his face all working with sorrow.

fig. **1849** Macaulay *Hist. Eng.* vii. II. 215 While thoughts like these were working in the minds of many Dissenters. **1859** Tennyson *Elaine* 1300 Sea was her wrath, yet working after storm. **1865** C. Stanford *Symb. Christ* vi. (1878) 161 Tempests of feeling often work beneath an unchanged face.

35. With complement: To move irregularly or unsteadily so as to become out of gear.

1770 Luckombe *Hist. Printing* 325 [To] hinder the Press from working into a twisting position. **1840** R. H. Dana *Bef. Mast* xxv. 83 The anchor on the lee bow had worked loose, and was thumping the side. **1874** J. D. Heath *Croquet-player* 26 If the handle [of the mallet] be properly wedged into the head, it ought never to work loose.

III. With adverbs, in special senses.

36. work in. **a.** *trans.* To insert, introduce, incorporate (in various connexions: see 9, 12 d).

1675 A. Browne *App. Art Paint.* 11 Working in, driving, and sweetening the same Colours one into another. **1728** E. Smith *Compl. Housew.* (ed. 2) 129 Work in three quarters of a pound of Sugar. **1826** M. Crosfield in *Jrnl. Friends Hist. Soc.* XX. 93 The 5 American Epistles..abound with choice passages of Scripture well wrought in. **1847** Helps *Friends in C.* I. viii. 124, I would try and work in the old good thing with the new. **1870** Freeman *Norm. Conq.* (ed. 2) II. App. 584 A..tale in which several particulars..are worked in with a lofty contempt for chronology.

b. *intr.* To make one's (or its) way in. *lit.* and *fig.* See 33.

1748 *Anson's Voy.* II. i. 116 These..sudden gusts make it difficult for ships to work in with the wind off shore. **1849** Helps *Friends in C.* II. i. 12 All he meets seems to work in with, and assimilate itself to, his own peculiar subject. **1918** *Westm. Gaz.* 29 Apr. 5/4 Yorkshire troops..threw the enemy out of the village..but the enemy again worked in.

c. To co-operate or get along *with*.

1915 E. Fenwick *Diary* 14 Oct. in *Elsie Fenwick in Flanders* (1981) 89, I had tried so hard to work in with her. **1960** M. Spark *Ballad Peckham Rye* viii. 181 If Mr. Druce thought I was working in with you, he'd kill me. **1974** O. Manning *Rain Forest* I. ix. 101, I am a very fast learner, and I work in well with Mr. Axelrod.

37. work off. * **a.** *trans.* To print off (as from a plate); esp. to print in final form, so as to be ready for publication or distribution.

1662 Evelyn *Sculptura* 36 The very first..who published any works of this kind under their names, wrought off by the Rolling-Presse. **1672** Wood *Life* (O.H.S.) II. 247 Wee were then looking over and correcting the story of John Wycleve in 'Hist. et Antiq. Univ. Oxon.' before it was to be wrought off from the press. *a* **1704** T. Brown *Laconics* Wks. 1711 IV. 7 That..execrable Dog of a Printer..has work'd off the last Sheet..without sending me a Proof. **1708** T. Hearne *Coll.* 11 Apr. (O.H.S.) II. 102 Mr. Thorpe gave but 10 pence per hundred for working off his Plates to Schutzer. **1754** *Gentl. Mag.* XXIV. 58/1 An accident..to the Plate prevented a sufficient number [of etchings] from being wrought off. **1868** E. Edwards *Ralegh* II. Introd. p. lxxxi, By an accident of a miscarriage of proofs in the Post Office, the three letters ..were worked off, prior to correction of the press. **1882** Pebody *Engl. Journalism* xv. (1883) 107 The printers..often found themselves working off papers half through the night and all through the day.

†**b.** To make and throw off. *Obs.*

1695–6 *Act 7 & 8 Will. III*, c. 20 §3 A..profitable Invention..for the..more speedy..knitting of..Stockings ..whereby great Quantities are wrought off in a little tyme. **1739** Melmoth *Fitzosb. Lett.* lxii. (1749) II. 118, I am willing enough to join with you in thinking, that [the souls of both sexes] may be wrought off from different models.

c. To get rid of, palm off, pass off; to perpetrate, 'play off'. Occas. *refl.*

1813 M. L. Weems *Wks. & Ways* (1929) III. 92 The Maps..may be work[ed] off and in time to give you bank interest. **1884** Kipling *Let.* 21 Nov. in C. Carrington *Rudyard Kipling* (1955) iv. 58 I've been writing a story... I'm trying to work it off on some alien paper to get myself pice thereby. **1891** Nat. Gould *Double Event* xvi, A nice little swindle you worked off on me that time. **1897** 'O. Thanet' *Missionary Sheriff* 7 The lightning-rods ain't in it with this last scheme—working his self off as a Methodist parson. **1900** 'Mark Twain' *Speeches* (1910) 164 He had not written as many plays as I have, but he has had that God-given talent, which I lack, of working them off on the manager. **1948** V. Palmer *Golconda* viii. 58 Corney had been skiting about his claim for months, and everyone knew it was a duffer, but he hung on in the hope of working it off on someone.

** **d.** To take off or away by a gradual process, effect a riddance of; to get rid of, disburden oneself of, free oneself from, by some continuous action or effort.

1678 Rymer *Trag. Last Age* 83 This Scene having wrought off the Remains of Phedra's frenzy, in the next she seems more calm. **1702** A. De la Pryme *Let.* 27 Mar. in *Diary* (Surtees) 251 Returning to his labour,..he sweat and wrought it [*sc.* canine madness] of [= off] without any physic. **1737** Bracken *Farriery Impr.* (1756) I. 216 Nature is working off some latent Enemy. **1836** Marryat *Midsh. Easy* xxv, You..take some of his quack medicine, and then he will allow you a run on shore to work it off. **1873** Symonds *Gk. Poets* vii. 194 Should a man arise capable of seeing rightly and living purely, he may work off the curse. **1880** Mrs. Lynn Linton *Rebel of Family* x, So full of thoughts and energies she does not know how to work them all off.

†**e.** To draw off or dissuade (a person) from a certain course. Cf. 14 a. *Obs.*

1655 Stanley *Hist. Philos.* I. III. xvi. (1687) 94/1 Glauco before he was 20. years old had..aimed at some great office in the Common-wealth, not to be wrought off from this fancy..untill addrest by some friends to Socrates, who made him acknowledge his own error.

†**f.** To take or tear off by continuous application of force. *Obs.*

1703 Parker *Eusebius* VIII. 146 When the Flesh of her Sides and Breasts had been wrought off with Pincers, she was Sentenc'd to the Sea.

g. To finish working at; to dispose of and get done with.

1800 J. Haigh *Dyer's Assist.* 33 When a vat has been heated two or three times, and a good part has been worked off. **1892** W. S. Gilbert *Mountebanks* I, Giuseppe, he's to be married tomorrow,..and so on until we are all worked off. **1920** *Westm. Gaz.* 2 Dec. 4/2 When the existing contracts for new steamships are worked off.

h. To put to death; to hang. *slang.*

1840 Dickens *Barn. Rudge* lxiii, He was ready for working off.

38. work out. * **a.** *trans.* To bring, fetch, or get out by some process or course of action; to get rid of, or effect a riddance of; to expel, deliver, efface, etc. Also *refl.*

1595 Daniel *Civ. Wars* v. lxxi, These people-minions they must fall To worke out vs, to worke themselues int' all. **1605** Bacon *Adv. Learn.* II. xxii. §10 That..you may worke out the knots and Stondes of the mind. **1607** Topsell *Four-f. Beasts* 226 If the Fox be in the earth,..they take this course to worke him out. **1648** Gage *West Ind.* 2 Such plenary Indulgences, which may..work that soul out, which lyeth..in the deepest pit of Purgatory. **1660** Dryden *Astræa Redux* 275 Tears of Joy..Work out and expiate our former Guilt. **1691** Hartcliffe *Virtues* p. x, Strong Bodies will work out the Poyson they take, by degrees. **1758** *Hist.* in *Ann. Reg.* 3/2 To work out the old servants of the Crown, in order to make way for a more uniform system. **1874** Willshire *Anc. Prints* iii. 91 The engraver of metal plates has not rested satisfied with the chafing-tool, [etc.]..in working out their substance, but has had recourse to corrosives..to bite..away the metal. **1906** *Jrnl. Abnormal Psychol.* I. 37 We might properly say that the 'uncompleted emotion'..could be given an opportunity to work itself out.

b. *intr.* To make its way out, esp. from being imbedded or inclosed in something; to become gradually loose and come out: cf. 33, 35.

In quot. 1698, to lose its effect gradually.

1601 Holland *Pliny* xxx. xiii. II. 394 To draw forth spils of bones, and make them to worke out. **1683** Moxon *Mech. Exerc., Printing* ii. ¶1 Underlays..are often apt to work out, and..subject it to an unstable and loose position. **1698** Fryer *Acc. E. India & P.* 127 The Liquor working out by his Walking, he began to grow weary. **1794** *Rigging & Seamanship* I. 151 *Forelock*, a small wedge of iron driven through a hole near the end of iron pins to keep them from working out. **1832** Marryat *N. Forster* iii, Fresh splinters of the bone continually worked out.

c. *trans.* To work (a mine, etc.) until it yields no more; to exhaust by 'working'.

1545 in G. C. Bond *Early Hist. Mining* (1924) 8 [The parties shall cause all such coalpits as shall hereafter be] clenewrought out and gettyn [to be] caste in and stopped. **1827** Scott *Chron. Canongate* vii, The Highlands *were* indeed a rich mine; but they have, I think, been fairly wrought out. **1857** Westgarth *Victoria & Gold Mines* 226 The diggings, the greater part of which..had been abandoned as ground 'worked out,' to use the digger's phrase. **1906** Hockaday in *Vict. County Hist., Cornwall* I. 520/1 As one part [of the rock] was worked out it was filled in with rubble from the new excavations.

d. To wear out, esp. by labour, or by continued application of force. *Obs.* or *rare.*

1611 Cotgr. s.v. *Ouvrer*, *Le temps ouvre.* Time workes (or weares) out euerie thing. **1848** Thackeray *Van. Fair* lvii, During what long thankless nights had she worked out her fingers for little Georgy.

e. To discharge (a debt or obligation) by labour instead of a money payment.

1670 Marvell *Corr.* Wks. (Grosart) II. 354 Who cannot pay his 5*s*...shall worke it out in the House of Correction. **1773** *Pennsylv. Gaz.* 28 Apr. 3/2 Whereas I..am indebted £28:7:6,..I am desirous to engage and work it out. **1828** Kennedy & Grainger *Tenancy of Land* 297 The highway-tax is most frequently worked out. **1840** Dickens *Old Cur. Shop* xiv, Mind you're here, my lad, to work it out.

** **f.** To bring about, effect, produce, or procure (a result) by labour or effort; to carry out, accomplish (a plan or purpose).

In quot. 1597, to preserve to the end.

1534 Tindale *Phil.* ii. 12 Worke out youre awne saluacion with feare and tremblynge. **1597** Shaks. *2 Hen. IV*, I. i. 182 We..Knew that we ventur'd on such dangerous Seas, That if we wrought out life, was ten to one. **1621** T. Granger *Expos. Eccles.* vi. II. 148 Doth he not most often by his wit worke out his woe? and by his strength procure his owne ruine? **1633** Bp. Hall *Hard Texts* Hosea x. 11, Hee loves to injoy blessings, but not to earne, and worke them out. **1641** J. Jackson *True Evang. T.* III. 225 To go about to work out true peace by..compliances with men, is an endlesse work. **1805** Wordsw. *Waggoner* IV. 118 When the malicious Fates are bent On working out an ill intent. **1847** Tennyson *Princess* II. 75 O lift your natures up:..work out your freedom. **1869** Tozer *Highl. Turkey* I. 141 The natural tendency of their mode of life..worked itself out as time went on. **1874** Green *Short Hist.* ii. §7. 95 The fortunes of England were being slowly wrought out in every incident.

g. To go through a process of calculation or consideration so as to arrive at the solution of (a problem or question), to solve; also, to reckon out, calculate. Cf. 13.

1848 Dickens *Dombey* xix, Day after day, Old Sol and Captain Cuttle kept her reckoning..and worked out her course, with the chart spread before them. **1849** C. Brontë *Shirley* vi, While she completed the exercise, or worked out the sum (for Mdlle. Moore taught her arithmetic, too). **1856** Miss Yonge *Daisy Chain* I. xviii, She tried to work out the question in her own mind, whether her eagerness for classical learning was a wrong sort of ambition. **1891** *Speaker* 2 May 533/1 A practised novel-reader could probably work out the problem and complete the plot.

h. *intr.* for *pass.*: (*a*) of a course of events, narrative, etc.: To proceed so as to issue in a particular result; (*b*) with *at*, of a quantity: To amount to (so much) when reckoned up, to 'come to'.

1885 LD. COLERIDGE in *Law Rep. 14 Q. Bench Div.* 826 The justice of that course, and how it works out is shewn.. by the late Lord Chief Justice. **1887** *Spectator* 3 Sept. 1173 It is.. impossible to tell.. how the situation in Ireland will work out. **1898** *Tit-Bits* 16 July 311/3 This [quantity of tea] when infused works out at about 4,000,000 gallons.

i. *trans.* To fashion by cutting out, excavation, or the like. ? *Obs.*

1719 DE FOE *Crusoe* I. (Globe) 68 When I had wrought out some Boards.., I made large Shelves. **1774** GOLDSM. *Nat. Hist.* (1776) VIII. 100 The old one then, with as much assiduity as it before worked out its hole, now closes the mouth of the passage.

j. To bring to a fuller or finished state; to produce or express in a complete form or in detail; to develop, elaborate.

1821 SCOTT *Kenilw.* xvii, To see how Marlow, Shakspeare, and other play artificers, work out their fanciful plots. **1861** WHYTE-MELVILLE *Good for Nothing* xxxix, A picture.. worked out with a skill and knowledge of light and shade. **1865** J. FERGUSSON *Hist. Archit.* II. I. ii. I. 380 [Italy] did not work out the Basilican type for herself. **1880** MCCARTHY *Own Times* IV. lxvii. 518 The theory [of the survival of the fittest].. was worked out with the most minute and elaborate care. **1882** BESANT *All Sorts* xxviii, An idea.. which.. works itself out in his brain. **1895** F. HARRISON in *19th Cent.* Aug. 217 This important and far-reaching truth is worked out by Mr. Mallock with much acuteness.

k. To study or investigate completely; to work through. *Obs.* or *rare.*

1830 H. N. COLERIDGE *Grk. Poets* (1846) 10 After a boy has worked out a book or given portion of a classic poem.

*** **l.** *Pugilism. intr.* To box for practice, as distinguished from engaging in a set contest. Also *gen.* to practise, take exercise, rehearse.

1927 *Daily Express* 27 May 13/7, I saw Barber work out in the gymnasium.. boxing four rounds with Young Johnny Brown. **1929** *Cosmopolitan* Aug. 72/2 Feet's feet take up so much room when he is on the floor that only two other dancers can work out at the same time. **1948** G. VIDAL *City & Pillar* II. ix. 264 Jim worked out in the YMCA. **1965** C. BROWN *Manchild in Promised Land* viii. 221 I'd go up to the gym and work out for a little while, and I wasn't tired any more. **1973** R. L. SIMON *Big Fix* (1974) xv. 110, I sat.. watching the members of the *Teatro Comunal* work out. **1980** J. BALL *Then came Violence* xiv. 117 He belonged to a health club where he worked out regularly. **1984** *Daily Tel.* 30 Apr. 15/7 He does not look his 59 years. Perhaps it helps that he had his face lifted twice, works out with weights and had synthetic implants in his jaw.

39. work over. *slang.* To beat up, thrash (a person).

1927 *Dialect Notes* V. 467 *Work one over*, to resort to violence in the third degree inquisition of the police. **1934** D. HAMMETT *Thin Man* viii. 37 Morelli's face was a mess: the coppers had worked him over a little just for the fun of it. **1947** *Partisan Rev.* XIV. 329 The crooked cop can't look at Marlowe without a self-revealing yen to 'work him over'. **1970** *Daily Tel.* 11 Dec. 1/1 An engineer was followed into a sub-station by two men who threatened to 'work him over'. **1978** R. PERRY *Dutch Courage* ii. 23 Alan held me and Bernard worked me over.

40. work up. * †**a.** *trans.* To build up, construct, 'raise' (a wall, etc.): usually with special reference to the actual process. Cf. 3 c. *Obs.*

Occas. to build up material around (quot. 1712).

c **1400** *Destr. Troy* 1542 The walles [were] vp wroght, wonder to se. *c* **1435** *Torr. Portugale* 1532 The Giaunt wrought vp his wall And laid stonys gret and small. **1703** MOXON *Mech. Exerc.* 259 In working up the Walls of a Building, do not work any Wall above 3 foot high before you work up the next adjoining Wall. **1712** J. JAMES tr. *Le Blond's Gardening* 119 Set this Pole very upright,.. and work up the Foot of it with Rubble.., for fear its own Weight, or the Wind, should throw it down. **1735** J. PRICE *Stone-Br. Thames* 8 Strong Cross-Walls.. must be work'd up to the Top of the Crown of the Arches.

†**b.** To lift or raise (a weight) by labour; to hoist. *Obs. rare.*

c **1610** [see 20].

c. *intr.* To make one's (or its) way up, esp. against impediment or indirectly; to ascend, advance; also *fig.* Cf. 33, 33 c, 33 e.

1667 MILTON *P.L.* v. 478 Till body up to spirit work. **1790** BEATSON *Nav. & Mil. Mem.* II. 194 He ordered the Queenborough ahead to observe their motions, and continued endeavouring to work up after them. **1865** KINGSLEY *Herew.* xxvi, Nearer and louder came the oar-roll, like thunder working up from the east. **1882** *Daily Tel.* 28 Oct. 2/4 The Torridge is in full flood, and plenty of salmon are working up to spawn. **1899** KIPLING *Stalky* i. 27 He was merely working up to a peroration. **1903** G. H. LORIMER *Lett. Self-made Merch.* viii. 109 He was.. drawing ten thousand a year, which was more than he could have worked up to in the leather business in a century. **1916** LD. E. HAMILTON *1st Seven Divisions* (1917) 41 An additional flanking corps that was said to be working up from the direction of Tournai.

** **d.** *trans.* To stir up, mix, or compound, as a plastic substance or substances: cf. 12 d. Also *intr.* for *pass.*: cf. 29.

c **1450** *M.E. Med. Bk.* (Heinrich) 127 Let hit stande nyne dayes & nyne nyȝtes, & þan go werche hit vp, & let frye hit in apanne. *c* **1550** LLOYD *Treas. Health* V 2, Take.. Frankencense, [and] as much oyle as shalbe thought sufficient, make it and worke it vp well. **1584** COGAN *Haven Health* (1636) 53, I advise all students that be troubled with wind.. to cause Fennell seeds, Anise or Careway to bee wrought up in their bread. **1840** DICKENS *Old Cur. Shop* xviii, A stew of tripe,.. and cow-heel,.. and bacon,.. and steak,.. and peas, cauliflowers, new potatoes, and sparrow-grass, all working up together in one delicious gravy. **1855** *Orr's Circ. Sci., Inorg. Nat.* 213 Any hard material, that does not soon work up into mud or grind into dust. **1868** LOUISA M. ALCOTT *Little Women* xi, Hannah had left a pan of bread to rise, Meg had worked it up early,.. and forgotten it.

e. To make up (material) *into* something by labour (cf. 8); also, to bring into some condition, esp. so as to be ready for use (cf. 12 l).

1591 in G. C. Bond *Early Hist. Mining* (1924) 11 The fyner and hammerman for working up the said 50 tonns of barr iron. **1698** *Acts Massachusetts* (1724) 116 No Person.. shall work up into Shoes.. any Leather that is not tanned and curried in Manner as aforesaid. **1739** LABELYE *Short Acc. Piers Westm. Bridge* 60 Fir.. Timber was chosen as being.. the easiest work'd up. **1768** TUCKER *Lt. Nat.* (1834) II. 325 Seneca.. starting a doubt whether God made His own materials, or only worked up such as He found already in being. **1797** BURKE *Regic. Peace* iii. Sel. Wks. (1892) 236 The raw and prepared material [*sc.* silk].. is worked up in various ways. **1844** G. DODD *Textile Manuf.* Introd. 7 The straw-plait.. is wrought up into hats and bonnets. **1869** W. T. THORNTON *On Labour* III. v. 323 A builder.. willing to keep his men employed during the bad weather.. allowed them to work up a quantity of stone to be ready for use in the spring. **1899** *Allbutt's Syst. Med.* VI. 106 Mediastinal sarcoma.. spreads in upon and works up the pulmonary tissue in an irregular and crab-like manner, simulating cancer.

f. *gen.*, or in reference to something immaterial: To make up, develop, expand, enlarge (*to* or *into* something).

1693 CREECH in *Dryden's Juvenal* xiii. (1697) 336 For he that but conceives a Crime in thought, Contracts the danger of an Actual Fault: Then what must he expect that still proceeds To finish Sin, and work up Thoughts to Deeds? **1712** BUDGELL *Spect.* No. 307 ¶2 Your agreeable manner of working up Trifles. **1820** W. IRVING *Sketch Bk., Rural Life* (1821) I. 112 A spray could not tremble in the breeze—a leaf could not rustle to the ground—..; but it has been noticed by these.. observers, and wrought up into some beautiful morality. **1869** FREEMAN *Norm. Conq.* III. xiii. 278 All this could easily be wrought up into a claim. **1907** MRS. C. KERNAHAN *Fraud* iv. 28 He had got a dramatic situation.. which he meant Danvers to work up.

g. To bring by labour or effort *to* or *into* a higher state or condition. Cf. k below.

1668 DRYDEN *Dram. Poesy* 66 This last is indeed the representation of Nature, but 'tis Nature wrought up to an higher pitch. **1760** D. WEBB *Inq. Beauties Painting* 158 The expression in this statue [Laocoon], is worked up to such a just extremity,.. that, as the least addition would be extravagance, so every diminution would be a defect. **1861** HUGHES *Tom Brown at Oxf.* i, The kitchen and buttery were worked up to a high state of perfection. **1875** E. WHITE *Life in Christ* III. xviii. (1878) 237 A man can work himself up into an immortal condition of 'equality with the angels'.. no more than an ox or an ass can work himself up into humanity.

h. To make up, form, construct, compose, produce (something material or immaterial): with special reference to the process, or to the labour, exertion, or care expended upon it. Cf. 3–6, 10.

1710 ADDISON *Tatler* No. 153 ¶1 An eminent artist, who wrought up his pictures with the greatest accuracy. **1713** —— *Cato* I. iv, The Sun.. Works up more fire and colour in their cheeks. **1820** *Q. Mus. Mag.* II. 60 Fugues wrought up with infinite art, and little effect. **1885** *Manch. Weekly Times* 7 Mar. 5/5, I have perhaps worked up this picture a little too elaborately. **1897** HENTY *On the Irrawaddy* 120 My uncle is working up a very good business. **1911** 'G. A. BIRMINGHAM' *Lighter Side Ir. Life* i. 9 He stood.. in front of the looking-glass working up appropriate gestures.

i. *Naut.* To set to or keep at needless and disagreeable hard work as a punishment. Cf. 19.

1840 R. H. DANA [see HAZE *v.*[1] 2]. **1841** —— *Seaman's Man.* Dict., *Work up*.., a phrase for keeping a crew constantly at work upon needless matters, and in all weathers, and beyond their usual hours, for punishment. **1897** F. T. BULLEN *Cruise of 'Cachalot'* 208 The hands no longer felt that they were continually being 'worked up' or 'hazed' for the sole, diabolical satisfaction of keeping them 'at it'.

j. To 'get up' (a subject) by mental labour; to study carefully and in detail; to master by research. Cf. 12 k.

Mod. I'm working up mathematics for my examination. He's working up the history of the period for his new book.

*** **k.** *trans.* To bring by effort, or by some influence, into a particular state of mind or feeling, esp. one of strong emotion; to stir up, arouse, excite, incite (the mind, imagination, etc., or the person) *to* or *into* a state or action; to induce or persuade by effort *to do* something; without const., to put into a state of excitement, excite, agitate. Also *refl.* Cf. 14 a, b.

1688–9 STILLINGFL. *Serm., 1 Pet. iv. 18* (1698) III. 120 It is no very hard Matter to work up a heated and devout Imagination to the Fancy of Raptures and Ecstasies. **1698** COLLIER *Immor. Stage* 25 To work up their Lewdness with Verse and Musick. **1710** STEELE *Tatler* No. 172 ¶2 We cannot but tremble to consider, what we are capable of being wrought up to. **1752** YOUNG *Brothers* IV. i, When I have work'd him up to violence. **1831** JAMES *Philip Aug.* xxx, His whole powers and energies had been wrought up to bear it firmly and calmly. **1842** LOVER *Handy Andy* x, Tell him magnificent lies—astonish him with grand materials for a note-book and work him up to publish. **1874** BURNAND *My Time* xxxi. 306 My father had tried to work himself up into a passion. **1906** BEATRICE HARRADEN *Scholar's Dau.* xiii, Every time I speak of it, I get fearfully worked up.

l. To put into commotion, stir up, agitate (physically). *rare.*

1705 ADDISON *Italy* 54 This Lake [Garda] perfectly resembles a Sea, when it is work'd up by Storms.

m. *intr.* To be gradually stirred up or excited; to proceed or advance to a state of agitation or commotion. Cf. 34, and c above.

1681 DRYDEN *Abs. & Achit.* 141 So, several Factions from this first Ferment, Work up to Foam. **1709** STEELE *Tatler* No. 36 ¶3 You know a premeditated Quarrel usually begins and works up with the words, *Some people.*

n. *U.S. Med.* (See quot.) Cf. WORK-UP 2.

1961 *Amer. Speech* XXXVI. 145 *Work up*, to perform a series of diagnostic procedures (X-rays, laboratory blood tests, electro-cardiograms, and so forth).

workability (wɜːkəˈbɪlɪtɪ). [f. next + -ITY.] The condition of being workable; capability of being worked.

1874 *Daily News* 17 July 5/5 The workability, to coin a word, of the Militia. **1876** in F. S. Williams *Midl. Railw.* 300 We must have the engineer before us to prove the workability of the line. **1892** *Solicitor's Jrnl.* 5 Nov. 4/2 We.. hope that the new rules will be drafted with a full regard to practical workability in detail.

workable (ˈwɜːkəb(ə)l), *a.* [f. WORK *v.* + -ABLE.]

1. Of substances or materials: That can be worked, fashioned, or manipulated for use; said also of the state in which they are capable of being worked.

1545 ASCHAM *Toxoph.* (Arb.) 139 As the potter most connyngly doth cast his pottes whan his claye is softe and workable. **1629** JACKSON *Creed* VI. II. ix. §1 Workable or fashionable unto any set forme. **1709** T. ROBINSON *Nat. Hist. Westmld.* ix. 55 It is but eight or nine Inches thick, but the Roof and Covers being strong, it is a workable Coal. **1853** *Pharmac. Jrnl.* XIII. 118 Coal and fireclay, of workable value. **1879** *Cassell's Techn. Educ.* v. 299 Many heavy clays.. might be made friable, and easily workable by a liberal application of lime. **1887** P. MCNEILL *Blawearie* 90 The 'ochre hole'.. had been found too wet to be workable.

2. That can be worked, managed, or conducted, as a contrivance, establishment, institution, etc.

1756 in *Naval Chron.* (1799) I. 267, I stood off.., to put the ship in a workable state. **1862** SMILES *Engineers* III. 367 Often making a circuit to secure good, workable gradients. **1859** W. CHADWICK *Life De Foe* v. 272 Each of those hands was well furnished with a good workable hedging-bill. **1881** *Daily Tel.* 29 Nov. 5 The only workable boat of the Lord Hood was manned. **1881** MISS BRADDON *Asphodel* xii, There's not one of 'em knows how to plan a good workable hot-house. **1901** *Daily News* 28 Feb. 9/1 To realise how much had been done to make the hospital a really workable place.

b. of a plan, system, scheme, or the like.

1865 MILL *Repr. Govt.* (ed. 3) 63/1 Assuming the plan to be workable. **1878** BAYNE *Purit. Rev.* xi. 445 A permanently workable, broadly comprehensive ecclesiastical scheme.

3. Capable of working. *rare.*

1851 MAYHEW *Lond. Labour* II. 358 Very nearly seven millions of wives and children of a workable age still unoccupied.

Hence **ˈworkableness**, workability.

1793 SMEATON *Edystone L.* Contents p. viii, Tried the workableness of the Rock. **1874** MORLEY *Compromise* i. 2 The immediate and universal workableness of a policy.

workably (ˈwɜːkəblɪ), *adv.* [f. WORK *v.* + -ABLY.] In a workable way; so as to be workable.

1943 NISSEN & BERGMANN *Cineplastic Operations on Stumps of Upper Extremity* iii. 36 Three sutures are placed, one in each of the free corners.. and one in the centre edge of the pediculated flap for the purpose of holding it workably tense. **1971** *Nature* 12 Mar. 69/2 Should there not.. be some kind of rebate for bulk delivery or, more workably, a charge for single delivery which is mitigated by bulk delivery?

workaday, work-a-day (ˈwɜːkədeɪ), *sb.* and *a.* Forms: α. 3 (*Orm.*) **werrkedaȝȝ**, **werkedei**, 4–5 **werkeday(e**. β. 6– **workyday**, 7– **worky-day** (6–7 **workie-**, 7 **worki-**, **workey-**). γ. 9 **workaday**, **work-a-day**. [ME. *werkeday* (3 syllables), of uncertain origin: possibly f. gen. pl. (OE. *weorca*) of WORK *sb.* + DAY *sb.*[1], but perh. more probably f. directly on these with assimilation to the trisyllabic *sunnedei* SUNDAY, *messedei* MASSDAY. The type *workyday* is due to the influence of HOLIDAY, and *workaday* presumably to that of NOWADAY(S.]

A. *sb.* A day on which work is ordinarily done (distinguished from *holiday*); a work-day, working-day. *Obs.* or *dial.*

α. *c* **1200** ORMIN 11315 Forr ȝure wuke gifeþþ ȝuw Aȝȝ sexe werrkedaȝȝess. *a* **1225** *Ancr. R.* 18 Valleð to þer eorðe ȝif hit is werke dei, mit te Gloria Patri. **1387–8** T. USK *Test. Love* I. v. (Skeat) l. 104 After the seven werkedays of travayle. *c* **1412** HOCCLEVE *De Reg. Princ.* 4971 In þe longe ȝere be werke daye[s] I-nowe. **1426** AUDELAY *Poems* 80 On the werkeday ȝif that thou be About thi labor treuly. *a* **1450** MYRC *Par. Pr.* (1902) 893 For, a-pon þe werkeday, Men be so bysy in vche way.

β. **1550** in Strype *Eccl. Mem.* (1721) II. I. xxvii. 218 That divers preachers within your diocess.. do preach as well the worky days as the holy days. **1566** DRANT *Horace, Sat.* II. F 5, On workyday I neuer coulde be taken With better meate.. then roots or chimnye bacon. **1598–9** B. JONSON *Case is Altered* IV. iii, Fellow Onion for thy sake I finish this workiday. **1603** in Willis & Clark *Cambridge* (1886) II. 700

Sondaies, Holydaies, and workie days. **1653** FLECKNOE *Misc.* 127 He is one that makes alwayes Holy day for others, and worky-day for himself by taking upon him all the businesse. **1725** BOURNE *Antiq. Vulg.* xii. 116 We find a great Deference paid to Saturday Afternoon, above the other worky Days of the Week. **1789** H. WALPOLE *Let. to Mrs. H. More* 20 July, What the common people call a worky-day. **1860** W. WHITE *Wrekin* xvii. 170 If our teacher ain't ashamed to stop and shake hands with us, o' worky-days.

γ. **1840** DICKENS *Old Cur. Shop* xlix, In the very clothes that he wore on work-a-days. **1883** *Harper's Mag.* Jan. 238/2 Life was an unbroken work-a-day.

B. *attrib.* passing into *adj.* (cf. WORKING DAY). Belonging to or characteristic of a work-day or its occupations; characterized by a regular succession or round of tasks and employments; of ordinary humdrum everyday life: freq. in phr. ***this workaday world.***

β. **1554** *Bury Wills* (Camden) 146 My worky day cassocke. **1606** SHAKS. *Ant. & Cl.* I. ii. 55 Prythee tel her but a worky day Fortune. **1672** DRYDEN *Assignation* III. i, With such a Workiday-rough-hewn face too! **1751** MISS TALBOT *Let. to Mrs. Carter* 27 Sept., Oh this nasty worky-day world! **1877** F. JACOX *Scripture Prov.* xlix. 545 In the common law of facts in this worky-day world.

γ. **1802** MRS. RADCLIFFE *Gaston de Blondeville* Posth. Wks. 1826 I. 6 The plain reality of this work-a-day world. **1838** DICKENS *Nich. Nick.* xviii, The less of real, hard, struggling work-a-day life there is in that romance, the better. **1857** MUSGRAVE *Pilgr. Dauphiné* I. i. 8 Their work-a-day dress is a coarse brown or blue serge surtout. **1859** JEPHSON *Brittany* xvii. 284 We cannot long indulge in day-dreams in this workaday world. **1874** P. RUSSELL *Leaves Journalist's Note-bk.* 53 Goswell-road is..one of the most work-a-day of London thoroughfares. **1898** 'H. S. MERRIMAN' *Roden's Corner* xii. 128 He did not attempt to understand the lighter side of life, but took it seriously as a work-a-day matter.

workaholic (ˈwɜːkəhɒlɪk). *colloq.* (orig. *U.S.*). [f. WORK *sb.*, after *alcoholic.*] One who is addicted to work, or who voluntarily works excessively hard and unusually long hours. Also *attrib.* or as *adj.*

1968 W. E. OATES in *Pastoral Psychology* Oct. 16 (*heading*) On being a 'workaholic'. **1971** —— (*title*) Confessions of a workaholic. **1973** *Bulletin* (Sydney) 25 Aug. 45/2 The workaholic, as an addict is called, neglects his family, withdraws from social life, and loses interest in sex. **1974** *Daily Colonist* (Victoria, B.C.) 17 July 18/8 Often the workaholic boss threatens the health and welfare of those unfortunate enough to work for him. **1976** *S. Wales Echo* 27 Nov. 6/9 At all costs you should avoid becoming a 'Workaholic'... You should leave your work behind with the office. **1981** *Time* 13 May 67/3 Unlike their workaholic American cousins Europeans tend to see lengthy vacations as somehow part of the natural order of things. **1984** *Guardian* 22 Oct. 11/4 They're concerned about the pressures of their jobs, which demand that they become workaholics.

Hence ˈ**workaholism**, the condition of being a workaholic.

1968 W. E. OATES in *Pastoral Psychol.* Oct. 16/2, I have dubbed this addiction of myself and my fellow ministers as 'workaholism'. **1971** —— *Confessions of a Workaholic* i. 1 Workaholism is a word which I have invented... It means addiction to work, the compulsion or the uncontrollable need to work incessantly. **1981** *Farmstead Mag.* Winter 23/2 For them it requires no effort of will to go off energy-saving appliances,..leave off gluttony on home-grown foods or security schemes, give up workaholism. **1983** *Sunday Tel.* (Colour Suppl.) 20 Feb. 14/4 We talked about.. workaholism, autobiography and Isaac Asimov.

workalike (ˈwɜːkəlaɪk), *a.* and *sb.* Also **work-alike.** [f. WORK *v.* + ALIKE *adv.*] **A.** *adj.* Of a computer: able to use the software of another machine and behaving in the same way when the software is used. **B.** *sb.* A workalike computer.

1981 *Infoworld* 13 Apr. 54 (*heading*) PMC-80: TRS-80 'workalike' computer. *Ibid.* 54/1 Personal Micro Computers has renamed the Video Genie PMC-80, and uses the phrase 'TRS-80 workalike' in some of its advertising. **1983** *Austral. Personal Computer* Aug. 90/2 Most software writers recognise the existence of IBM workalike machines and therefore attempt to avoid nucleus calls to direct device I/O. **1983** *Popular Computing* Dec. 83/2 The Ace is an Apple II workalike that accepts Apple II software, disk drives, and.. add-on cards. **1985** *Daily Tel.* 9 Sept. 2 (Advt.), A true, 16-bit, μPD8086 chip. (Not the humble 8088 of so many IBM work-alikes.)

workaway (ˈwɜːkəweɪ). *U.S.* [f. WORK *v.* + *-a-* + WAY *sb.*[1]] One who works his passage on a ship.

1906 *Federal Reporter* CXXXIX. 92 He authorized the mate to take four men as workaways to earn their passage from Nome to Tocoma. **1933** M. PELL *S.S. Utah* 58 The workaway, a quiet young Swede, also went. **1945** *Seafarers' Log* 20 July 3/3 From there [*sc.* from Honolulu] they were sent as workaways back to San Francisco. **1973** *Art Internat.* Mar. 100/2 If one didn't have the price, one could present one's self to a ship's purser and ask for a job as a workaway.

work-brittle, *a. dial.* Also **-brattle, -brackle,** etc. (see *Eng. Dial. Dict.* s.v. *Work-bracco*). [f. WORK *sb.* or *v.*; the second element appears to be BRITTLE *a.*, but the sense-development is obscure.] Eager to work, industrious.

1647 TRAPP *Marrow Gd. Authors* in *Comm. Ep.* 627 What need she [*sc.* Anne Bullen] be so work-brittle, being a Queen? **1691** RAY *N.C. Words*, *Worch-bracco*, i.e. work-brittle, very diligent; earnest or intent upon one's work. *a* **1800** PEGGE *Suppl. Grose*, *Warck-brattle*, fond of work. Lanc. **1881** *Oxfordsh. Gloss.* Suppl. (E.D.S.), *Work-brittle*, eager to work.

work-day (ˈwɜːkdeɪ), *sb.* and *a.* [OE. *weorcdæȝ* (= Du. *werkdag*, OHG., MHG. *werctac*, G. *werktag*, ON. *verkdagr*) does not seem to have survived; ME. *werkday* is prob. a new formation on WORK *sb.* + DAY *sb.*[1], or ad. ON.; cf. WORKADAY.]

A. *sb.* A day on which work is ordinarily performed; a week-day.

c **1430** *Freemasonry* (1847) 270 That the mason worche apon the werk day. *c* **1440** *Promp. Parv.* 522/2 Werkday, *feria.* **1488** *Somerset Med. Wills* (1901) 279, I wold my prest shuld sing in them the werke daies during the 12 monethis. **1535** COVERDALE *Ezek.* xlvi. 1 Y[e] dore of the ynnermer courte..shall be shut the vj. worke dayes. **1548–9** *Bk. Com. Prayer, Communion* rubric, When the holy Communion is celebrate, on the workeday. **1563** *Homilies* II. *Of Place & Time of Prayer* I. 139 They vse all dayes a lyke, workedayes and holydayes are all one. *a* **1639** HINDE *J. Bruen* xlvii. (1641) 153 Neither holy-day, nor work-day. **1706** MRS. CENTLIVRE *Platonic Lady* I. ii. Wks. 1760 II. 194 She..paid the Labourers their Wages on Work-days, and took a Jigg with them on Holy-days. **1824** MISS MITFORD *Village* Ser. I. *Hannah* 22 We (the privileged) see on a work-day the names which the sabbath announces to the generality.

¶ Used for DAYWORK 2.

1670 BLOUNT *Law Dict.* (1691), When they performed their Boons or Work-days to their Lord.

B. *attrib.* passing into *adj.* Belonging to or characteristic of a work-day; performed, worn, etc. on a work-day; also *fig.* = WORKADAY B.

c **1500** *Ely Episc. Rec.* (1891) 211, I give to Edmund Garred my worke day gown. **1540** *Test. Ebor.* (Surtees) VI. 103 My warkday gowne. **1563** in Strype *Ann. Ref.* (1709) I. xxxv. 357 My Visitation Sermons and Workday Sermons. **1622** *Knaresb. Wills* (Surtees) II. 77 My woorkday gowne.. thre woorkday aprens, one woorkday band. **1808** SCOTT *Marm.* VI. iii, Ne'er, in work-day world, was seen A form so witching fair. **1831** JAMES *Philip Aug.* xl, [It] relieves the mind from petty calculation and workday cares. **1849** MRS. CARLYLE *Lett.* II. 72, I saw him..after unloading the waggon, in his workday clothes. **1859** KINGSLEY *Misc.* I. 16 Unfit for this workday world. **1889** CORBETT *Monk* xiv. 195 This dull work-day soldier.

worked (wɜːkt), *ppl. a.* [f. WORK *v.* + -ED[1].]

1. Used for farm-work.

1707 MORTIMER *Husb.* 170 An old worked Ox fatting as well, and being as good Meat as a young one.

2. Executed or ornamented with needlework, engraving, or the like.

1740 MRS. E. MONTAGU *Corr.* (1906) I. 47, I desire you to send me up my worked facing and robing. **1746–7** MRS. DELANY *Autobiogr.* (1861) II. 447 In my Irish green damask and my worked head. **1816** SCOTT *Old Mort.* xl, The worked-worsted chairs. **1857** DICKENS *Dorrit* II. xxx, She turned the watch upon the table, and..looked at the worked letters within. **1884** E. YATES *Recoll.* I. 181 Elaborately dressed, with a worked shirt-front and huge white waistcoat.

3. Shaped, fashioned, or dressed for use or ornament.

1864 J. HUNT tr. *Vogt's Lect. Man* x. 288 He reports that he has found..worked flints at a depth of twelve feet in a stratified soil. **1892** *Archaeologia* LIV. 110 Many fragments of worked bone and horn were discovered.

4. In various senses: Contrived, managed, conducted, etc.; *Hort.* grafted.

1848 W. PAUL *Rose Gard.* 106 When potting worked plants, we should have an eye to suckers from the wild stock. **1882** F. E. HULME (*title*) Worked Examination Questions in Plane Geometrical Drawing. **1886** COL. MAURICE *Lett. fr. Donegal* 4 A cleverly-worked intrigue. **1904** *Westm. Gaz.* 1 June 12/1 'Leased' or 'worked' lines.

5. With advs., as ***worked-off, -out, -up*** (see the corresponding senses of the verb).

1770 LUCKOMBE *Hist. Printing* 360 He grasps off the Worked off Heap so much at once..as he can well govern. **1831** P. EGAN *Show Folks* 41 Like a well-worked up scene on the stage. **1864** 'MARK TWAIN' in *Californian* Nov. 5 We admire his mature judgment in selling out of a worked-out mine. **1882** *Rep. Ho. Repr. Prec. Met. U.S.* 641 The worked-out space becomes more or less filled with bowlders. **1893** *Helps to Study of Bible* 269 Some old worked-out mines. **1903** *Daily Chron.* 29 Oct. 3/3 The worked-up feelings of a personal witness of these scenes. **1908** *Stage Year Bk.* 21 An ingeniously conceived and vigorously worked-out spectacle play.

worker (ˈwɜːkə(r)). Forms: see WORK *v.* [f. WORK *v.* + -ER[1]. Cf. Du. *werker*, MHG. *wercker* (G. *werker*).]

1. One who makes, creates, produces, or contrives.

†**a.** Applied to God as maker or creator; sometimes *absol.* the Creator, (one's) Maker. *Obs.*

13.. *E.E. Allit. P.* B. 1501 Þe worcher of þis worlde. **1382** WYCLIF *Job* xxxvi. 3 My werkere I shal proue riȝtwis. **1500–20** DUNBAR *Poems* xlvi. 53 He, of natur that wirker wes and king. *Ibid.* 60 He, the wirker, that put in hir sic grace. **1557** *N.T.* (Genev.) Ep. *ij, God the Creatour, moste perfect and excellent worker of all thinges. **1594** HOOKER *Eccl. Pol.* I. ii. §2 Only the workes and operations of God haue him both or their worker, and for the lawe whereby they are wrought. *a* **1602** W. PERKINS *Cases Consc.* (1619) 4 He is the author and worker thereof [*i.e.* of goodness].

b. An author, producer, contriver, or doer; †also with epithet, as ***evil worker*** = evil doer. *arch.*

c **1374** CHAUCER *Compl. Mars* 261 And therfore in the worcher was the vice. *c* **1380** WYCLIF *Sel. Wks.* II. 266 Þus men mai have prophecie, and al þes habitis in þer soule, and be schrewid wirchirs. **1382** —— *Luke* xiii. 27 Alle worcheris of wickidnesse. **1387–8** T. USK *Test. Love* III. ii. (Skeat) l. 63 Al your werkes be cleped seconde, and moven in vertue of the firste wercher. *c* **1400** tr. *Secr. Secr., Gov. Lordsh.* 88 Þe werkere of meruaylles ys oon god. *c* **1449** PECOCK *Repr.* IV. ii. 427 God is the cheef and principal and veri worcher of the principal effect. *c* **1470** HENRY *Wallace* III. 344 Causer of wer, wyrkar of wykitnes. **1513** DOUGLAS *Æneis* XII. iii. 103, I sall the warrand, and the wirkar [orig. *auctor*] be To mak the baldly vndertak. **1526** TINDALE *Phil.* iii. 2 Beware of dogges, beware of evyll workers. **1549** COVERDALE, etc. *Erasm. Par. Rom.* iii. 5–8 They can not laye to goddes charge the synnes, wherof themself be wylful workers. **1598** R. BERNARD tr. *Terence, Andria* II. vi, If any thing happen otherwise then well, euen that same varlet is the worker of it. **1623** BINGHAM *Xenophon* 107 The workers of the common safetie. **1796** MORSE *Amer. Geog.* I. 286 They believe that the devil is the doer or worker of every thing that gives offence. **1843** *Tait's Mag.* X. 606 The worker of all this evil. **1867** MORRIS *Jason* XVII. 441 She grew to be the sorceress, Worker of fearful things.

c. *transf.* of things.

a **1340** HAMPOLE *Psalter* ii. 11 Dred is wirkere of vertus. **1604** JAS. I *Counterbl. to Tobacco* (Arb.) 106 The Tobacco.. was the worker of that miracle. **1612** BEAUM. & FL. *Coxcomb* IV. i, You can say well: if you be mine, wench, you must doe well too, for words are but slow workers. **1842** DICKENS *Amer. Notes* iii, What a worker of hypocrisy this sight.. would appear to be!

†**d.** ? A commercial agent. *Obs.*

1560 GRESHAM in Burgon *Life* (1839) I. 323 The cheiffe sercher (whome ys all my worcker, and conveyer of all my velvets).

2. a. One who works or does work of any kind (sometimes with adj. denoting the quality of the work); esp. one who works *in* a certain medium, *at* a specified trade or object of manufacture, or in a certain position or status (often denoted by prefixed sb., etc., as *boiler-worker*, *cloth-worker*, *iron-worker*, *metal-worker*; *co-worker*, *fellow-worker*; *brain-worker*, *hand-worker*); in early use also, †a maker or manufacturer (*of* a specified thing).

1382 WYCLIF *Ecclus.* xxxvii. 13, 14 With the werkere, of alle werk [Vulg. *cum operario agrario, de omni opere*]. **1388** —— *Acts* xix. 24 A man, Demetrie bi name, a worcher in siluer. *c* **1400** *Pilgr. Sowle* (Caxton 1483) V. vi. 98 Now haue we none instrumentes, ne here ben no werkers for to make them newe. *c* **1440** *Pallad. on Husb.* VI. 62 Oon of thi workers falle [the tree] That kunyngest is of his felous alle. **1474** CAXTON *Chesse* III. v. (1883) 119 The two laste that ben practisiens and werkers ben callyd phisicyens and cyrurgyens. **1487** *Rolls of Parlt.* VI. 404/2 Th' Offices of Maister and Werker of oure Money. **1530** TINDALE *Exod.* xxxv. 35 Broderers and workers with nedle. **1566** *Act 8 Eliz.* c. 11 §4 Every Hatmaker that is nowe a maker or worker of Hates. **1611** COTGR., *Ouvrier*, a workeman; an Artificer, or handi-craftsman..& generally, any worker. **1660** F. BROOKE tr. *Le Blanc's Trav.* 357 Lazy people, and no good workers. **1663** COWLEY *Ode upon Dr. Harvey* iii, He so exactly does the work survey, As if he hir'd the workers by the day. **1760** *Court & City Reg.* 224 His Majesty's Mint... Master and Worker. Hon. Wm. Chetwynd, Esq. **1765** *Museum Rust.* IV. 76 Mr. Naish, tin-plate-worker. **1767** *Phil. Trans.* LVIII. 41 Another worker in ivory cut through that tusk which Lord Shelburne gave me. **1838** DICKENS *Nich. Nick.* x, I spoke of you as an out-of-door worker. **1877** *Oxf. & Camb. Undergrad. Jrnl.* 25 Jan. 173/2 Cowles not only has the knack of getting work out of his men, but is a very hard worker himself, though not a pretty oar. **1882** BESANT *All Sorts* xxxv. (1898) 242 There are a great many workers—ladies, priests, clergymen—among them, trying to remove some of the suffering. **1887** RUSKIN *Præterita* II. 207 The full happiness of that time to me cannot be explained except to consistently hard workers.

b. In emphatic use, esp. as opposed to *idler*, or the like.

1628 C. LEVETT *Voy. N. Eng.* viii. in *Collect. Mass. Hist. Soc.* Ser. III. VIII. 190 Except for every three loiterers, he have one worker. **1852** MRS. STOWE *Uncle Tom's C.* xxviii, A dreamy, neutral spectator..when he should have been a worker. **1866** RUSKIN *Crown Wild Olive* i. 8 The distinction between workers and idlers, as between knaves and honest men. **1871** —— *Fors Clav.* ix. 4 *note*, Here and there we have a real worker among soldiers, or no soldiering would long be possible. **1889** G. B. SHAW in *Fabian Ess.* 6 Rent..paid..by a worker to a drone.

c. One who is employed for a wage, esp. in manual or industrial work; now often in the language of social economics, a 'producer of wealth', as opposed to *capitalist*.

1848 KINGSLEY in Benham *Cassell's Bk. Quot.* (1907) 185 Workers of England, be wise, and then you must be free. **1857** *Househ. Words* 27 June 603/1 The first great body of workers, namely the clerks [*i.e.* railway clerks]. **1862** SMILES *Engineers* III. 14 They belonged to the ancient and honourable family of Workers—that extensive family which constitutes the backbone of our country's greatness, the common working people of England. **1867** LEVI *Wages Working Classes* 6 Some have limited the meaning to such as are in receipt of weekly wages, and some would limit the term 'workers' to such as are employed in the production of wealth. It might seem also a condition of such appellation that the person should stand in the capacity of servant or worker for others... On the other hand, we must remember that in many occupations the workers are paid by the month or quarter. **1885** E. B. BAX *Relig. Socialism* (1886) 125 This, then, is the empire which the blood and sinew of you, workers, are squandered to maintain and extend. **1891** MORRIS *Poems by Way* 112 For that which the worker winneth shall then be his indeed, Nor shall half be reaped for nothing by him that sowed no seed.

d. Of animals: †(*a*) A draught animal. *Obs.*

1617 *Toke* (Kent) *Estate Acc.* (MS.) fol. 9 One payer workers at £15.

(*b*) A horse, dog, etc. that works (well).

1844 [J. W. CARLETON] *Hyde Marston* I. 74 It's not fair to keep the double thong always going with a free worker. **1874** *Kennel Club Stud Bk.* 161 Bell and Lilly..the latter being a small, mean-looking white bitch, but a very good worker. **1908** *Animal Managem.* 283 Geldings..were proved to be very good workers in Somaliland.

(*c*) The neuter or undeveloped female of certain social hymenopterous and other insects, as ants and bees, which supplies food and performs other services for the community.

1747 W. GOULD *Engl. Ants* 73 As soon as the Queen has deposited a Parcel of Eggs, the Workers take them under their Protection. **1816** KIRBY & SP. *Entomol.* xvii. (1817) II. 32 The *workers* or larvæ, answering to the hymenopterous neuters, are the most numerous and at the same time most active part of the community. **1855** *Poultry Chron.* III. 351 Fertile workers lay none but male eggs.

e. *U.S. Politics.* One of a class of political agents or partizans subordinate to a 'boss'.

1873 'MARK TWAIN' *Gilded Age* xliv. 399 In Washington he was..clerk of two house committees, a 'worker' in politics. **1888** BRYCE *Amer. Commw.* II. lxiii. 451 The large and active class called, technically, 'workers', or more affectionately, 'the Boys.'

3. Applied to apparatus or pieces of machinery.

†**a.** A vessel in which wine has 'worked'. *Obs.* **b.** One of the small card-covered cylinders or 'urchins' in a carding-machine. **c.** A leather-worker's two-handled knife (Knight *Dict. Mech., Suppl.* 1884). **d.** In pillow lace-making, *pl.* the bobbins that are worked across a pattern. **e.** = WASHER *sb.*[1] 5 b. **f.** With prefixed sb., applied to an apparatus for 'working' the material denoted by the sb., as *butter-worker*.

1594 PLAT *Jewell-ho.* III. 70 Let your vessel bee such as hath alreadie conteined some muste or other liquor that hath wrought therin, (for he that knoweth not the vse of a worker is but a slender artist). **1835** URE *Philos. Manuf.* 167 Each pair of cylinders consists of a worker and a cleaner somewhat less in size than its fellow, and turning in the reverse direction of the drum. **1853** —— *Dict. Arts* I. 766 The points of this roller (called a 'worker') are inclined in a direction opposed to the movement of the swift. **1853** *Beils' Technol. Wbch., Worker, Washer* in paper manufacture. **1878** *Technol. Dict., Worker, Stripper* of the scribbling-machine. **1885** J. J. MANLEY *Brit. Almanac Comp.* 18 The butter-milk and water are carefully pressed out in one of Bradford's butter workers.

4. With adverbs, as *worker-up* (see WORK *v.* 40).

1656 *Second Ed. New Almanack* 10 He be no very good worker up. **1698** *Acts Massachusetts* (1724) 116 Tanners, Curriers, and Dressers, or Workers up of Leather. **1848** *Sinks of Lond.* 3 The worker-up of novels.

5. *attrib.*, as (sense 2 d (*c*)) *worker ant, bee, cell, grub*; **worker bobbin** = 3 d; **worker card** = 3 b. **worker-director**, a worker who is also on the board of directors of a firm; **worker participation** [PARTICIPATION 2 b], participation of workers in the management of the firms or industries for which they work; **worker-peasant**, used *attrib.* with reference to co-operation between urban and rural communities in Communist China; similarly **worker-peasant-soldier**; **worker-priest**, orig. a Roman Catholic priest in post-war France who earned his living as a factory-worker or the like; now more widely, a priest who engages in secular work for part of his time.

1882 *Athenæum* 1 July 18/3 As in bees and wasps, worker ants occasionally produce fertile eggs. **1816** KIRBY & SP. *Entomol.* xix. (1817) II. 138 The instinct and industry of the worker-bees. *Ibid.* xxiv. 394 When all the worker-brood was removed from a hive, and only male brood left. **1894** VICKERMAN *Woollen Spinning* 159 We call one of each of the pairs of top rollers a 'worker' card, in distinction from the adjoining one, which is a stripper. **1816** KIRBY & SP. *Entomol.* xix. (1817) II. 161 The instinct of the queen invariably directs her to deposit worker eggs in worker cells. **1881** COWAN *Bee-keeper's Guide Bk.* vii. 20 If we examine a hive, we shall find that worker-comb is ⅘ths of an inch.. thick. **1968** *Economist* 3 Aug. 53 The proposal—that worker-directors should be put on the boards of a number of nationalised industries..—is a waste of time. **1980** *Whitaker's Almanack 1981* 583/2 Sir Keith Joseph announced the ending of the Post Office worker-director experiment. **1855** *Poultry Chron.* III. 561 It is not invariably found that the bees will at once convert a worker grub into a queen. **1973** *Guardian* 19 June 17/4 Mr Heath's..flourish of the worker participation banner. **1978** *Jrnl. R. Soc. Arts* CXXVI. 326/2 'Industrial democracy', probably better called 'worker participation'. [**1937** E. SNOW *Red Star over China* IV. vi. 173 The Chinese Workers' and Peasants' Revolutionary Committee was organized about this time.] **1962** —— *Other Side of River* (1963) xviii. 135 This he managed to do by means of postulating the existence of a 'rural proletariat' and a worker-peasant army under the leadership of the Communist party itself acting as the vanguard of the true (urban) proletariat. **1968** in Gray & Cavendish *Chinese Communism in Crisis* 210 All enterprises with suitable conditions should introduce in a big way the worker-peasant labour system. **1976** tr. Tuan Jui-hsia in *Yenan Seeds & Other Stories* 19 Spring was very much in the air in the Worker-Peasant-Soldier Theatre. **1949** *Commonweal* 29 July 385/2 We must bow our heads in deep humility before the heroism of the worker priest. **1959** *Manch. Guardian* 4 Aug. 3/3 Five worker-priests..believed to be the only ones in the Church of England..do manual work, live on their factory earnings and receive no ecclesiastical stipends. **1970** *Daily Tel.* 29 Dec. 11/3 The Anglican church makes a distinction between worker-priests, who exercise a priestly function at their workplace, and priest-workers, who do an ordinary job, then return to parish work, usually as curate, in their 'spare time'. **1984** *Times* 28 May 10/8, I could not help wondering how it would be received by the congregations of, say, a worker priest in Nicaragua.

6. *Comb.* with *workers'*, as (sense 2 c) *workers' committee, control, flat*; **workers' co-operative**, a business or industry owned and managed by those who work for it; **Workers' Educational Association**, the name of an organization founded in 1903 to provide evening classes and tutorials in economic, political, and liberal studies, originally for working people.

1965 J. KOLAJA *Workers' Councils* II. 28 The highly skilled workers' committee, and the apartments committee were considered temporary. **1972** M. ARGYLE *Social Psychol. of Work* viii. 217 The workers' committees have worked well, and members have acted responsibly on them. **1928** *Britain's Industrial Future* (Liberal Party) III. xviii. 228 Consultation with a body of workers will improve and strengthen it [*sc.* a business]; anything that can accurately be described as 'workers' control' will destroy it. **1974** *Times* 5 Apr. 16/5 As a trades unionist, I am in favour of workers' control. [**1923** in *Internat. Index to Periodicals* (1924) III. 1417/1 What is the United Workers' co-operative association?] **1937** *Commonweal* 3 Dec. 145 (*heading*) Workers' cooperatives. **1965** B. PEARCE tr. *Preobrazhensky's New Economics* 220 Workers' co-operatives..essentially do nothing more than rationalize the system of distribution *within the state sector*. **1981** J. TILLEY in J. Thornley *Workers' Co-operatives* p. vi, Workers' co-operatives are suddenly being hailed as panaceas for unemployment, alienation, inner city decay and industrial strife. **1903** (*title*) The Workers' Educational Association. **1936** *N. & Q.* 11 July 19/2 What is gained from the University Extension, the Workers' Educational Association, or a year of study at Ruskin College? **1980** J. L. THOMPSON *Adult Education for Change* 22 The Workers' Educational Association provision has in many respects become barely distinguishable from that promoted by the universities, despite its roots in workers' education and political and economic studies. **1932** S. JAMESON *Single Heart* v. 127 She was able..to buy a slum estate in Evan's constituency and build on it blocks of workers' flats. **1982** S. GRANT DUFF *Parting of Ways* vi. 54 The shelling of the workers' flats in Vienna in February 1934.

workerist ('wɜːkərɪst), *a.* and *sb.* [f. WORKER + -IST.] **A.** *adj.* Of, pertaining to, or characteristic of a worker-oriented view of society; (too) sympathetic to the role of labour in the class struggle. **B.** *sb.* One who adopts workerist values; *spec.* applied (somewhat *derog.*) to a member of the middle or upper classes who espouses the cause of the working class.

1959 W. BIRMINGHAM tr. J. Daniélou in *Cross Currents* Fall 381/2 The workerist conception locates poverty on the level of the standard of living. The 'collectivist' locates poverty on the level of private property. **1981** *Filmnews* (Austral.) May 6/2 The practice of Cinema Action was criticised as workerist for assuming that there was a unified working class. **1984** *Sunday Tel.* 2 Dec. 21/2 Oxford, long the home of what is now known as the 'workerist' (public school student turning very Left-wing). **1985** *Daily Tel.* 11 Feb. 12/2 The genuine proletarians of the hard Left who regard him [*sc.* Mr. Benn] as 'workerist'.

workfare ('wɜːkfɛə(r)). orig. and chiefly *U.S.* [f. WORK *sb.*, after *welfare*.] A policy of requiring recipients of welfare money to do some work in exchange for this benefit.

1968 *Harper's* July 71 One of Evers' programs is what he calls workfare; he has said that everybody ought to work for what he gets. **1969** R. NIXON in *Washington Post* 9 Aug. 1/2 What America needs now is not more welfare but more 'workfare'. **1978** *Globe & Mail* (Toronto) 28 Nov. 5/3 Mr. Walker, one of the most conservative politicians in the Legislature..thinks they would support a pilot project in an interested municipality, although he is not claiming Government support for workfare. **1981** *Daily Tel.* 26 May 5 Two California towns..are at the forefront of a movement to implement 'workfare'—projects aimed at forcing welfare recipients to do some labour in exchange for taxpayers' money. **1985** *Times* 12 Feb. 14/5 There must be a real inducement to work. In the US a number of states have introduced 'Workfare' to complement welfare.

workfolk ('wɜːkfəʊk). Also (now *rare*) -folks. [f. WORK *sb.* + FOLK *sb.* Cf. Du. *werkvolk.*] = WORKPEOPLE, *esp.* farm labourers.

c **1475** *Pol. Poems* (Rolls) II. 285 That syche wyrfolk be payd in good moné. **1566** *Engl. Ch. Furniture* (Peacock 1866) 114 One sacringe bell—wch Mr Edmond Haselwood ..vsed in his house (as he said) to call workfolke to dinner. **1572** in Feuillerat *Revels Q. Eliz.* (1908) 164 Wages by him payd to 214 woorkfolkes. **1578** *Bk. Chr. Prayers* 88 b, We beseech thee (O thou Lord of the haruest) send workfolks into thy haruest. **1600** SURFLET *Country Farm* II. l. 327 At the discretion of the gardener,..according as his number of workefolkes is more or lesse. **1612** *S'hampton Assembly Bks.* (1924) III. 40 Theis seargmakers..were..desiered to paie good English money to their worcke folkes. **1702** *Guide for Constables* 30 Clothiers must pay their..workfolks their wages in ready money. **1828** *Craven Gloss., Wark-folk*, labourers. **1849** ROCK *Ch. Fathers* II. vii. 411 The lowliest work-folk in the town. **1883** T. HARDY in *Longman's Mag.* July 255 The regular farmer's labourers—'workfolk' as they call themselves. **1891** *Daily News* 26 Aug. 6/4 A slight improvement in the conditions under which farm workfolks live. **1902** *Athenæum* 20 Dec. 831/3 The writer..had.. smoked with the workfolk in their public-houses.

workful ('wɜːkfʊl), *a.* [f. WORK *sb.* + -FUL. Cf. OE. *weorcfull* 'operosus'.]

†**1.** Active, operative. *Obs.*

1340 *Ayenb.* 199 Þe uirtues huerof we habbeþ y-speke aboue be-longeþ to þe uerste liue þet is ycleped workuol. **1552** HULOET, Warkefull, *operosus*. **1565** HARDING *Confut.* II. xiii. 97 Seest thou then how workefull is the word of Christ? **1587** GOLDING *De Mornay* v. 60 In the most single essence of God, there is a workfull power. **1674** N. FAIRFAX *Bulk & Selv.* To Rdr., The Philosophy of our day and Land being so much workful as the world knows it to be.

2. Full of (hard) work; hard-working.

1854 DICKENS *Hard T.* I. v, You saw nothing in Coketown but what was severely workful. **1875** HOLYOAKE *Hist. Coop.* I. 353 Being very watchful and workful as a secretary. **1891** *Review Rev.* 15 Oct. 352/2 Seven happy workful months spent in Paris.

Hence '**workfulness**, †activity; laborious activity.

1573 DAUS tr. *Bullinger on Apoc.* 17 In the meane tyme his workfulnesse perceth euen into yͤ uery Church. **1854** *Tait's Mag.* XXI. 459 He might have seen, in any Coketown of the manufacturing districts, an allowance of what is playful, to compensate for its workfulness. **1903** J. C. SMITH *Robt. Wallace* vi. 174 He resigned..a position of usefulness and workfulness.

work function. *Physics.* [f. WORK *sb.* + FUNCTION *sb.*] **1.** The minimum quantity of energy, characteristic of the material concerned, which is required to remove an electron to infinity from the surface of a solid (usu. a metal). Symbol: ϕ.

1923 *Proc. R. Soc.* A. CIV. 637 The estimations of the photo-electric work function..are in all cases a good deal greater than the corresponding values of the thermionic work function. **1950** A. KOLIN *Physics* xxxv. 715 The work function can be determined by finding the threshold frequency v_0 below which no photoelectrons are emitted. **1972** *Sci. Amer.* Mar. 53/1 When two metals are placed in contact, electrons pass from one to the other because of the difference in the metals' quantum-mechanical work functions. This process continues until an equilibrium is reached.

2. A thermodynamic property of a system: its internal energy minus the product of its temperature and entropy. Symbol: A.

1929 R. H. FOWLER *Statistical Mech.* iv. 96, *k*log K(T) for the crystal is the thermodynamic function known as Planck's characteristic function, and $-kT$ log K(T) is the more usual work function..A. **1937** P. S. EPSTEIN *Textbk. Thermodynamics* v. 92 When the temperature and the volume of a system are kept constant, its work function has a tendency to decrease. **1978** P. W. ATKINS *Physical Chem.* v. 139 If we know the value of ΔA for a change we can also state the maximum amount of work the system can do. This relation is the reason why A is sometimes called the maximum work function, or the work function.

workhouse ('wɜːkhaʊs). [OE. *weorchús*: f. WORK *sb.* + HOUSE *sb.*[1] Cf. MDu. *werchuus*, Du. *werkhuis*, MHG. *werchûs* (G. *werkhaus*), ON. *verkhús* (in comb.).]

1. a. A house, shop, or room in which work is regularly performed; a workshop or factory. *Obs.* or *Hist.*

a **1100** in Wr.-Wülcker *Voc.* 185/3 *Officina*, smiðþe uel weorchus. *Ibid.* 186/27 *Ergasterium uel operatorium*, weorchus. **1350** in Riley *Mem. London* (1868) 262 In the werkhous..12,000 of plaunche-nail..3000 of dornail. **1387** TREVISA *Higden* (Rolls) VII. 307 Þe werkhous þere þey dooþ here werkes. **1431-40** in Glasscock *Rec. St. Michael's, Bp.'s Stortford* (1882) 6 Le Werkhous latomorum juxta cimiterium. **1497** *Naval Acc. Hen. VII* (1896) 324 The Grounde wher as the seid Ship was made & the Workehouse Belongyng to the same. **1575** in Plomer *Abstr. Wills Engl. Printers* (1903) 23 My workehowse of printing. **1601** HOLLAND *Pliny* III. vi. I. 61 The worke houses and furnaces of potters. **1669** *Lond. Gaz.* No. 3260/3 There were taken with him several Pairs of Stockins wet, as if they had been taken out of a Dyers Work-House. **1752** HUME *Ess. & Treat.* (1777) I. 445 His workhouse, of 20 cabinet-makers, is said to be a very considerable manufactory. **1881** S. R. MACPHAIL *Hist. Pluscardyn* Introd. 7 The court by which we first entered is occupied with stables and work-houses.

b. *fig.*

1548 UDALL *Erasm. Par. Luke* i. 34-35 The holy ghoste.. in thy wombe, (as it wer in an heauenly workehouse) shall accomplishe the workyng of this holy babe. **1581** MULCASTER *Positions* vi. (1888) 48 The liuer..the workhouse of thicke and grosse blood. **1645** RUTHERFORD *Tryal & Tri. Faith* 125 Christ being the very worke-house, and shop of the Devil, in which he wrought. **1684** tr. *Bonet's Merc. Compit.* III. 112 The Heart is the Workhouse of life and heat. *a* **1761** W. LAW *Comf. Weary Pilgr.* (1809) 81 The works of the devil are all wrought in self, it is his peculiar workhouse.

2. *spec.* orig. A house established for the provision of work for the unemployed poor of a parish; later, an institution, administered by Guardians of the Poor, in which paupers were lodged and the able-bodied set to work. The official name in 1928 was *Poor-law Institution*.

Earlier (and obs.) names were †*house of work* (1552, see HOUSE *sb.*[1] 2), †WORKING-HOUSE (1597-8, etc.); names of later introduction are †*house of industry* (1771-2 Irish Act 11 & 12 Geo. III. c. 30, see INDUSTRY 4 b), POOR-HOUSE (1782); for *union workhouse*, abbreviated to *union*, see UNION *sb.*[1] 10 b, 12.

1652 in W. Cotton & H. Woollcombe *Glean. Munic. Rec. Exeter* (1877) 156 The said house to be converted for a workhouse for the poore of this cittye and also a house of correction for the vagrant and disorderly people within this cittye. **1653** *Act Commw.* c. 13 (1658) 259 If he hath not wherewith to satisfie such Fine, the said Judges may adjudge him to the Pillory or a Work-house, or both. **1670-1** *Act 22 & 23 Chas. II*, c. 18 (*title*) An Act for the better regulateing of Workehouses for setting the Poore on Worke. **1702** *Post Man* 10-13 Jan. 2/1 The President and Governours for the Poor of the City of London, having enlarged their Work-house without Bishops-gate. **1731** *Flying Post* 12 Aug. 2/2 His Mother, who was maintain'd by his Labour, being come upon the Parish, is sent to the Work-house at Wandsworth. **1782** *Act 22 Geo. III*, c. 83 § 18 The several Poor Houses or Workhouses to be built..under the Authority of this Act, shall be situate within the Parish or Township for which they shall be used. **1797** MRS. BERKELEY *Poems G. M.*

Berkeley Pref. p. cccx, Most well-regulated Bridewells are Paradises compared to the Oxford Work-house. **1836** DICKENS *Sk. Boz, First of May*, He believed he'd been born in the vurkis, but he'd never know'd his father. **1856** EMERSON *Engl. Traits, Wealth* Wks. (Bohn) II. 71 Hargreaves invented the spinning-jenny, and died in a work-house. **1922** J. J. CLARKE *Soc. Administr.* 83 The work-house or institution is the representative institution of the Union, and is the foundation of all indoor relief.

allusively. **1690** C. NESSE *O. & N. Test.* I. 58 Through Adams fall the world was become a work-house, an house of correction for mans sin.

3. A prison or house of correction for petty offenders. *U.S.*

1653 *Boston Rec.* (1886) X. 26 The setting up of a Bridewell or Workehouse for Prisoners Malefactors &.. poore people. **1772** A. G. WINSLOW *Diary* 25 Feb. (1895) 36 She.. soon got into the workhouse for new misdemeanours. **1870** 'MARK TWAIN' *Curious Dream* (1872) 83 Eggs.. so unwholesome that the city physician seldom or never orders them for the workhouse. **1888** *Cassell's Encycl. Dict.* **1964** *Federal Probation* Dec. 8/2 The Workhouse receives and releases the work-release prisoner any time during the day or night, depending on his working hours.

4. *attrib.* and *Comb.*: †**a.** in sense 1, as ***workhouse stable***.

1569 *Richmond Wills* (Surtees) 218 In the warkhouse stable, sadles, haltars.

b. in sense 2, as ***workhouse brat, cough, fever, inmate, master, system***; ***workhouse-bred, clearing*** adjs.; **workhouse sheeting**, strong twilled unbleached cotton material used for sheeting, curtains, etc.; **workhouse test**, the test of good faith put to an applicant for poor relief by which he was obliged to consent, as a condition of relief, to go to the workhouse if required.

1810 CRABBE *Borough* xxii. 60 Workhouse-clearing men, Who, undisturb'd by feelings just or kind, Would parish-boys to needy tradesmen bind. **1834** E. LYTTON BULWER in *Hansard's Parl. Debates* Ser. III. XXII. 891 In those states [of America] where a strict workhouse discipline was kept up. **1838** DICKENS *O. Twist* v, Then I'll whop yer when I get in,.. my work'us brat! *Ibid.* xxxvii, Admiration at the workhouse-master's humility. **1846** *Blackw. Mag.* Nov. 560/2 The Utopian expectations of many, that a strict workhouse-test would destroy pauperism. **1850** CARLYLE *Latter-day Pamph.* i. 49 This brutish Workhouse Scheme of ours. **1857** BORROW *Rom. Rye* xlii, He would rob.. a workhouse child of its breakfast, as the saying is. **1859** H. KINGSLEY *G. Hamlyn* xlii, Base-born, workhouse-bred! **1875** L. TROUBRIDGE *Life amongst Troubridges* (1966) 116 A Workhouse sheeting jacket, body and *tablier*.. to wear with dark blue frilled petticoat and sleeves. **1880** [see BOLTON]. **1889** CONAN DOYLE *Sign of Four* ix, You would have made an actor, and a rare one. You had the proper workhouse cough. **1891** C. CREIGHTON *Hist. Epidem. Brit.* 538 There was no gaol-fever, workhouse-fever, or domestic typhus in general. **1894** OAKESHOTT *Humanizing of Poor Law* 26 Nearly one-third of the workhouse inmates are sixty-five years old or over. **1925** J. J. CLARKE *Local Govt.* 316 Workhouse infirmaries.

Hence **'workhoused** *a.*, lodged in, or habituated to, a workhouse.

1837 *New Monthly Mag.* LI. 115 Poor, workhoused wretches! **1895** in Begbie *Life W. Booth* (1920) II. 204 The parishes can send people to us before they have become workhoused.

work-in ('wɜːkɪn). [f. WORK *v.* + -IN[3].] A form of protest, usu. against threatened closure of a factory, etc., in which workers occupy the work-place and continue working. Also *transf.*

1968 *Punch* 6 Mar. 327/1 Student protest reached an all-time high with Leicester University's plan to stage a '24-hour work-in'. **1973** *Times Lit. Suppl.* 30 Nov. 1469/1 The series of work-ins or sit-ins in the past two or three years in which workers have occupied factories in pursuit of wage claims or as a refusal to accept redundancy notices. **1976** [see SIT-IN *sb.* 1]. **1983** *Daily Tel.* 23 June 19/3 A judge strongly attacked the police for staging a dawn raid to break up the work-in.

working ('wɜːkɪŋ), *vbl. sb.* [f. WORK *v.* + -ING[1]. Cf. MDu., MLG. *werkinge*, OHG. *wer(a)chunga*, MHG. *werkunge*; MHG. *wurkung*; (MH)G. *wirkung*.] The action of WORK *v.*; the result of this.

I. 1. a. Performance of work or labour; †formerly also, that which is done, work.

a **1300** *Cursor M.* 11997 Qui dos þou men sli plaint to mak, For þi wircking on vr sabbat? **13..** *Ibid.* 5522 (Gött.) We sal find wirking for þair sake; Apon þair neckes sal þai bere Bollis wid stan and wid mortere. *c* **1450** *Godstow Reg.* 605 Coterellis, rentis, workyngis, helpis, wardis, relefis. **1494** *Acc. Ld. High Treas. Scot.* I. 245 For vj dayis wyrken, vj s. **1550** CROWLEY *Epigr.* 186 To se where the treasure will finde them workinge, To the profit of the Citye. **1579** RICE *Invect. Vices* B iij, Is Carde plaiyng woorkyng? Is the blasphemie of Goddes moste holie name a woorkynge? **1616** SIR E. MOUNTAGU in *Buccleuch MSS.* (Hist. MSS. Comm.) I. 249 He.. wondered at what you had told him of my mother's working, being stone blind. **1686** tr. *Chardin's Trav. Persia* 357 There has been no working in the Gold Mine for this long time. **1748** *Anson's Voy.* II. iii. 147 The working upon the wreck, and the securing the provisions. **1832** *P. Egan's Bk. Sports* 237/1, I like to see the working of the hounds; to see them in difficulty; to mark the threading; the stopping, the eagerness to find. **1842** DICKENS *Amer. Notes* iv, The laws of the State forbid their working more than nine months in the year. **1899** *Westm. Gaz.* 14 Apr. 2/3 Working is agreeable to my nature and to my health.

b. ***working to rule***, the action of strictly observing the limits of one's occupational duties; also = *work-to-rule* sb. (see WORK *v.* 27 d).

1927 W. E. COLLINSON *Contemp. Eng.* 84 The inconveniences of lightning-strikes, ca' canny policy (deliberate restriction of output) and working-to-rule. **1951** *Engineering* 2 Nov. 568/3 The overtime ban and working to rule have remained in force. *Ibid.*, Similar working-to-rule methods.. were put into operation by lightermen at the Port of London. **1958** *Times* 19 Aug. 8/3 To what extent the 'working to rule' will apply will depend on the attitude of individual busmen. **1964** M. ARGYLE *Psychol. & Social Probl.* xiv. 172 Anti-organization practices such as restriction of output, unofficial strikes and working to rule. *a* **1974** R. CROSSMAN *Diaries* (1976) II. 686, I tried to make them realize.. what I meant by quietism. I suggested that it meant a 'non-enthusiastic execution'—working to rule, shall we say?

†**2. a.** Performance, execution, achievement (of some particular work or action); procedure. *Obs.*

c **1375** *Sc. Leg. Saints* xiii. (*Marcus*) 50 Of þe virkine Of ferly werkis þat he wrocht. **1382** WYCLIF *1 Cor.* xii. 10 The worchinge of vertues. **1390** GOWER *Conf.* I. 276 To se the worchinge of the dede. **1422** YONGE tr. *Secr. Secr.* 136 In Suche shewynge and oppyne wyrchynge of good werkes. *a* **1425** tr. *Arderne's Treat. Fistula*, etc. 21 A maner of wirchyng in fistula in ano. *c* **1449** PECOCK *Repr.* II. xiii. 224 Bi her.. wirching of miraclis. **1526** *Pilgr. Perf.* (W. de W. 1531) 74 b, In declynynge from euyll, and in dylygent workynge of good. **1604** E. G[RIMSTONE] *D'Acosta's Hist. Indies* III. viii. 143 For the working whereof, the vapors and exhalations of the sea, are sufficient. **1611** in *10th Rep. Hist. MSS. Comm.* App. I. 530 For y[e] working of their other endes. **1675** A. BROWNE *Appendix Art Paint.* 10 Observe that you be not too Curious in the first Working, but rather make choice of a good Free and Bold Following of Nature. **1693** MOXON *Mech. Exerc.* (1703) 261 In which Fig. 1. is shewn the usual way of bad Working.

b. *spec.* in *Freemasonry*, (the performance of) a rite, a system of ritual.

1884 W. J. HUGHAN *Orig. Eng. Rite Freemasonry* p. iii, Although under various Grand Lodges the details of the working differ, the landmarks remain practically identical. **1903** J. T. LAWRENCE *Masonic Jurisprudence & Symbolism* viii. 75 The more important one [*sc.* duty] is to see that ceremonies are conducted in accordance with working sanctioned by the Grand Lodge of England. **1932** S. M. HILLS *Freemason's Craft* viii. 64 The Articles of the Union .. stipulated that there should henceforth be perfect unity of working, and the Lodge of Reconciliation was formed.. to agree upon a working.

†**3.** Making, manufacture, production, preparation, construction; also, the manner or style in which something is made, handiwork, workmanship. *Obs.*

1362 LANGL. *P. Pl.* A. III. 49 We han a wyndow in worching [C. IV. 51 a worchyng] wol stonden vs ful heiȝe. **1452** in Willis & Clark *Cambridge* (1886) I. 282, iij sengulere Principalls in werkyng in inbowyng and in Scantlyon accordyng to the Principalls. **1460–70** *Bk. Quinte Essence* 5 Anoþer maner worchinge of oure quinta essencia is þis. **1496** *Acc. Ld. High Treas. Scot.* I. 278 For werking of the irne werk to the samyn hous, vj li. xij d. **1535** in Gage *Hengrave* (1822) 51 For working of ij doores. **1538** STARKEY *England* I. iii. (1878) 94 A thousand such tryfelyng thyngys, wych other we myght wel lake, or els, at the lest, our owne pepul myght be occupyd wyth the workyng therof. **1601** *Act 43 Eliz.* c. 10 (*title*) An Acte for the true workinge and makinge of Wollen Clothe. **1633** P. FLETCHER *Purple Isl.* IV. xx, Two streets.. Of severall stuffe, and severall working fram'd. **1677** MOXON *Mech. Exerc.* ii. 21, I shall now shew you the working of a Spring-lock. **1726** LEONI *Alberti's Archit.* I. 55 The difference between the working of a Vault and a Wall.

4. a. The action of operating or performing work upon something; manipulation, management (of an apparatus, a vessel in navigation, etc.); exploitation (of a mine, etc.); also in *Angling* (see quot. 1880).

†***in (the) working***: being worked upon, when worked upon; in operation; in use.

1450 *Rolls of Parlt.* V. 202/1 No maner of Merchaundises .. of the growyng nor wurkyng of the Landes and parties that the seide Duke.. occupieth. **1545** ASCHAM *Toxoph.* II. (Arb.) 114 Whan the backe and the bellye [of the bow] in woorkynge, be muche what after one maner. **1577** HARRISON *England* III. i. 95 b/1 in *Holinshed*, Because it [*sc.* brown bread] is dry and brickle in the working.. some adde a portion of rye meale. **1618** RALEGH *Apol. Guiana* 57 The working of a Myne there. *a* **1642** SIR W. MONSON *Naval Tracts* I. (1704) 190/1 They could not discern the Lord General's Working, but stood their Course as before directed. **1680** MOXON *Mech. Exerc.* xi. 201 When the Treddle comes down in working. *Ibid.* xiii. 222 A piece of Ivory.. strong enough to bear working till they bring it to as small a Cilinder as they can. **1795** *Local Act 35 Geo. III*, c. 156 §30 Nothing in this Act.. shall.. prevent the working or scouring of the same.. Mines. **1831–3** P. BARLOW in *Encycl. Metrop.* (1845) VIII. 546/2 This scraping, or working, as it is termed,.. renders the skin soft and pliant. **1853** *Beil's Technol. Wbch.*, *Working* of a blast-furnace (the mode of action to which the quality of iron is subjected). **1880** F. FRANCIS *Bk. Angling* vi. (ed. 5) 225 You must.. flip your fly to and fro to shake the water out and so dry it for another cast. This sometimes will require seven or eight 'flips' or workings to effect. **1892** *Photogr. Ann.* II. 535 Should it be wished during the lecture to introduce a mechanical slide,.. the working of it is as follows. **1894** *Jrnl. Anthrop. Inst.* XXIII. 273 If they [*sc.* flints] possess definite characteristics of form, of wear, of weather, of material, of working.

b. The carrying on or putting into operation (of a scheme, system, legislation, etc.).

1832 *Edin. Rev.* Oct. 245 *heading*, Working and Prospects of the Reform. **1845** C. F. BARKER *Mem. on Syria* title-p., The Purchase and Tenure of Land, And the Working of the Old and New Tarif. **1847** *Edin. Rev.* Apr. 397 Exhibiting on that wide theatre the useful working of the fundamental institutions of the British monarchy. **1884** STOCKTON *Lady or Tiger* 14 His majesty.. was greatly interested in the workings and development of this trial. **1884** DILKE in A. Cawston *Street Improv. London* (1893) 101 The working of the byelaws in Birmingham under the 90th section of the Public Health Act. **1912** *Engl. Hist. Rev.* Jan. 43 Some changes in the working of the chancery.

5. Action, operation. **a.** Of a person; esp. *collect. sing.* and *pl.* actions, doings, deeds. †*good working* (*rare*): good works. *Obs.* or *arch.*

c **1380** WYCLIF *Wks.* (1880) 386 God is so parfyte in alle his worchynge þat [etc.]. *c* **1386** CHAUCER *Wife's Prol.* 698 The children of Mercurie and Venus Been in hir wirkyng ful contrarius. *c* **1400** *Cursor M.* 29441 (Cott. Galba) þou may with him comun in dede, Bot þe wers may þi wirking spede. *c* **1400** *Rom. Rose* 6123 Thou most discouere all thi wurchyng, How thou seruest, and of what thyng. *c* **1407** LYDG. *Reson & Sens.* 3169 Withoute engyn of fals werkyng. **1426** —— *De Guil. Pilgr.* 11511 They sholde ellys for hunger deye, Ne were I & my werchyng. *c* **1440** *Jacob's Well* 110 To wythstonde alle temptacyouns & to be perseueraunt in good werkyng. *c* **1449** PECOCK *Repr.* II. xviii. 258 That he was lijk in wirching to a vyne. *c* **1480** HENRYSON *Swallow* i, The hie prudence, and wirking meruelous,.. of god omnipotent. **1539** MORISON *Invect. agst. Treas.* title-p., Wherein the secrete practises, and traiterous workinges of theym that suffrid of late are disclosed. **1594** HOOKER *Eccl. Pol.* I. ii. §2 The being of God is a kind of Law to his working. **1692** L'ESTRANGE *Fables* cxlvii. 134 The Wayes and Workings of Providence are unsearchable. **1706** E. WARD *Wooden World Diss.* (1708) 21 Against Wind and Tide too, there's no Working. **1742** RICHARDSON *Pamela* (1785) IV. 146, I leave you to your own Workings. **1874** W. P. MACKAY *Grace & Truth* 220 In the twelfth chapter of Revelation we have depicted a remarkable series of Satan's workings. **1909** W. JAMES *Unveiled Heart* 70 Almighty and Everliving God,.. it is Thy glory to conceal Thy workings.

†**b.** Of a thing; sometimes *pl.*, functions. *Obs.* in general sense.

1340 HAMPOLE *Pr. Consc.* 4907 þe wirkyng of þe fire swa brinnand. **1398** TREVISA *Barth. De P.R.* XVIII. i. (1495) Y j b/2 Membres [of beestys] ben.. dyuers in werkynge, as it faryth in the eeres of the olyphaunt with the whyche he fyghteth. *c* **1400** tr. *Secr. Secr., Gov. Lordsh.* 80 Alle þe fyue wyttes þat sholde gouerne.. alle þe wyrkynges of þe body. *c* **1449** PECOCK *Repr.* II. xvi. 242 That the seid parties of heuen reuliden ful myche the worchingis of bodies here binethe in the louȝer world. *c* **1460** SIR R. ROS *La Belle Dame* 342 (Camb. MS.) Loue is sotyle,.. Scharpe in worchyng. *c* **1470** HENRY *Wallace* VI. 10 In Aperill quhen cleithit is.. The abill grounde be wyrking off natur.

c. Of a drug, medicine, etc.

a **1425** tr. *Arderne's Treat. Fistula*, etc. 45 þat worchyng shal better done and soner if þe secounde day after þe puttyng to of arsenek be putte to larde wiþ þe emplastre sanguiboetes. **1562** TURNER *Herbal* II. (1568) 96 The lesse kynde [of Poly] is.. more effectuus or stronger in working. **1567** MAPLET *Gr. Forest* 1 b, She shal whilest she is in sleepe imbrace hir husband through the working of this stone. **1580** T. B[EDFORD] *Treat. Med.* (1615) 17 These strange workings of these foreigne drugges in our bodies. **1631** WIDDOWES *Nat. Philos.* 39 His Rozen is in smell, taste, and working better than common Turpentine. **1648** GAGE *West Ind.* 79 After my physicks working. **1694** SALMON *Bate's Dispens.* (1713) 281/2 It is a good Medicine for the Purposes intended... In the working of it, you must be sure to provide two or three Quarts of Posset-drink.. aforehand.

d. Of the mind, conscience, etc. Often *pl.*

1588 SHAKS. *L.L.L.* IV. i. 33 Glory growes guiltie.. When for Fames sake.. We bend to that, the working of the hart. **1591** —— *1 Hen. VI*, V. v. 86, I am sicke with working of my thoughts. *c* **1600** —— *Sonn.* xciii, What ere thy thoughts, or thy hearts workings be. **1602** —— *Ham.* II. ii. 580. **1707** ROWE *Royal Convert* V. i, The secret workings of my Brain, Stand all reveal'd to thee. **1748** RICHARDSON *Clarissa* (1768) III. 310 Who can account for the workings of an apprehensive mind, when all that is dear and valuable to it is at stake? **1798** S. & HT. LEE *Cant. T.* II. 380 A friend.. would find a generous pleasure in aiding the workings of an ingenuous nature. **1801** SOUTHEY *Thalaba* XII. ii, His brain, with busier workings. *a* **1845** BARHAM *Ingol. Leg.* Ser. III. *Hermann.* Workings Of conscience. **1869** FREEMAN *Norm. Conq.* III. xii. 138 *note*, The Archdeacon now gets very eloquent, and gives us all the inner workings of the mind.

e. The conduct or operations collectively of a factory, vessel, or the like.

1873 *Act 36 & 37 Vict.* c. 71. §58 Any grating.. placed so as.. to interfere with the effective working of any mill. **1920** GOODE *Econ. Cond. Centr.-Europe* I. 12 In full working the cotton mills of Russia consumed about 1,500,000 bales of cotton per annum. **1920** *Act 10 & 11 Geo. V*, c. 30 Sch. I. II, The profits or the gross earnings of the working of the vessel.

f. Of a bus, train, etc.

1978 M. KEELEY et al. *Birmingham City Transport* 181 City—Bull Ring—Coventry Road—Lyndon End. Short working of 94. **1982** *Railway Mag.* Nov. 508/1 A reader who visited Scarborough.. noted a wide variety of locomotive classes in use on summer-holiday workings.

6. Influential operation; influence, effectiveness; also, the result or effect of operation or influence. Somewhat *arch.*

c **1374** CHAUCER *Boeth.* III. pr. xi. (1868) 95 Whan þei ben gadred to-gidre al in to a forme and in to oon wirchyng [orig. *in unam veluti formam atque efficientiam*]. **1414** BRAMPTON *Penit. Ps.* (Percy Soc.) 24 Thanne schal the werkyng be ful sene Of 'Ne reminiscaris, Domine!' **1450–1530** *Myrr. our Ladye* I. xii. 34 Whan they began to prayse god; god tornyd tho enemys eche of them agenste other... A maruelous werkyng of goddes seruyce. **1547** *Homilies* I. *Exhort. rdg. Holy Script.* ij b, [The words of Scripture] haue euer an heauenly spiritual workinge in them. **1567** *Gude & Godlie B.* (S.T.S.) 14 Throw wirking of the Spirite in til our hart. *a* **1586** SIDNEY *Arcadia* II. xxiii. (1912) 295 Her fayre colour decaied;.. and hastily grew into the very extreme working of sorowfulnesse. **1592** TIMME *Ten Engl. Lepers* E 2 b, There is as great defference betwene the working of hypocrisie and the working of grace, as betwene the working of arte, and the operation of nature. **1718** *Free-thinker* No. 96. 291 The Workings of Superstition are insinuating and slow. **1759**

STERNE *Tr. Shandy* I. xix, The workings of a parent's love upon the truth and conviction of this very hypothesis. **1861** BROUGHAM *Brit. Const.* xi. 150 *note*, The working of clerical prejudice in..a liberal mind. **1875** MANNING *Mission Holy Ghost* i. 10 Faith, hope, and charity, are the three primary workings of the Holy Ghost in the soul.

7. Mathematical calculation; the process of calculating, or performing the necessary mathematical operations for ascertaining, a quantity, etc. Now chiefly, the statement of the operations involved in solving a mathematical problem.

c **1386** CHAUCER *Frankl. T.* 552 By his .8. speere in his wirkyng He knew ful wel how fer Alnath was shoue. *c* **1391** —— *Astrol.* II. §35 This is the workinge of the conclusioun, to knowe yif þat any planete be directe or retrograde. *a* **1400** in Halliw. *Rara Mathem.* (1841) 61 þat leves after þi wirkyng es þe heght fro A poynte to þe heght of þe thyng. *c* **1425** *Crafte Nombrynge* 30 þou most know well þe craft of þe wyrchynge in þe tabulle. **1543** RECORDE *Gr. Artes* 123 Ye same yt appeareth of ye other working before. **1654** J. EYRE *Exact Surveyor* 75 Which by the working according to the former directions, will be found to be about 63 yards. **1842** DICKENS *Amer. Notes* xvi, The observation every day at noon, and the subsequent working of the ship's course. **1873** TODHUNTER *Confl. Studies* 74 That a knowledge of mathematics may be gained without the perpetual working of examples. **1883** *Pall Mall Gaz.* 8 Nov., No marks are to be allowed in the arithmetic paper unless the candidate shows up the 'working' of the sums as well as the final result.

†**8. a.** Aching; ache, pain. *Obs.*

a **1400** *Stockholm Med. MS.* 96 For werkyng of the hed. *Ibid.* 151 For wynd in þe hed, & werkyng in þe hed. *Ibid.* i. 11 in *Anglia* XVIII. 295 3if a man..In hys heed hath gret sekenesse, Or ony grewaunce or ony werkynge. *c* **1400** tr. *Secr. Secr., Gov. Lordsh.* 76 Corrupcioun of sight, werkynge of þe brayn. *Ibid.* 77 He felys his mete bitter in his brest, and werkyng of þe koghe.

†**b.** Stomachic or intestinal disturbance. *Obs.*

1577 STANYHURST *Descr. Irel.* ii. 4b/1 in *Holinshed*, Beyng moderately taken..it [*sc.* Aqua vitæ] kepeth..the belly from wirtchyng. **1650** VENNER *Via Recta, Tobacco* 407 So..as to cause a violent and sickly working both upward and downward. **1717** FLOYER *Asthma* i. 9 A loose Stool frequently happens from the great working in the Belly, occasion'd by the Fit.

9. Fermentation of liquor.

1565 COOPER *Thesaurus, Aestus mustulentus*, the fomyng or sprincling vp of newe wine, in ale we call it workyng. **1626** BACON *Sylva* §992 Staying the Working of Beere. **1662** CHARLETON *Myst. Vintners* (1675) 153 Sickly commotions, or (to speak in the dialect of Wine-coopers) Workings. **1707** MORTIMER *Husb.* 561 It will set your Wine in a gentle working, and purifie it in twenty four Hours. **1753** *Chambers' Cycl.* Suppl. s.v. *Wash*, With respect to the..workings of this liquor, great regard is to be had to the containing vessel. **1826** *Art Brewing* (ed. 2) 103 Conclude the fermentation in from 40 to 50 hours, and when it is cleansed do not fill up too frequently, for it will work off with great rapidity: rather, by moderate fillings, encourage its working. **1833** LOUDON *Encycl. Archit.* §1324 Unless the weather be very severe, the working (as it is called) proceeds equally well with that removed to the vaults or cellars.

10. a. Restless movement of water (esp. the sea); straining of a ship, a vehicle, etc. so as to loosen the fittings.

1582 N. LICHEFIELD tr. *Castanheda's Conq. E. Ind.* I. xxix. 73 The Seas went so high..they thought it unpossible for the shippes to escape;..by the working of them it was thought, that sometime they did hoyse up theyr shippes aboue the Element. **1662** R. VENABLES *Exper. Angler* iii. 34 The working of the Lough makes it sandy. **1748** *Anson's Voy.* II. iv. 157 The water the Pink had made by her working and straining in bad weather. **1793** SMEATON *Edystone L.* §301 By the continual working of the carriage [*sc.* a carrier's cart], two of them had been broken. **1892** *Lockwood's Dict. Terms Mech. Engin.* 414 The working of the frames of locomotives signifies the loosening of their joints, due to the strains communicated to them by the engines. **1901** *Scotsman* 6 Nov. 10/5 Owing to the working of the masts the deck was opening up.

b. Involuntary movement of the face or mouth, esp. due to emotion.

1800 WORDSW. *Pet Lamb* 18, I unobserved could see the workings of her face. **1818** SCOTT *Hrt. Midl.* xii, As if to prevent his seeing the working of his countenance. **1844** ELIZ. SEWELL *Amy Herbert* xi. I. 201 The working of her forehead showed the storm that was gathering. **1848** DICKENS *Dombey* lii, Lighting a candle, which displayed the workings of her mouth [*sc.* 'mumbling and munching'] to ugly advantage.

11. The proper action or movement of a piece of mechanism or the like.

c **1645** HOWELL *Lett.* I. II. xi. (1890) 110 To hinder the working of your Fire-works. **1727** [DORRINGTON] *Philip Quarll* (1816) 38 Quarll..was astride on the main yard, with a hatchet to cut down what stopped the working of it. **1827** *Ann. Reg., Chron.* 77/1 The only noise he heard..was the working of a neighbouring pump. **1851** KINGSLEY *Yeast* ix, The workings of his lungs pumped great jets of blood out.

12. Gradual movement or progress (as against resistance).

1683 MOXON *Mech. Exerc., Printing* xi. ¶23 It will so enrage the Oyl, and raise the Scum, that it might endanger the working over the top of the Kettle. **1802** PLAYFAIR *Illustr. Huttonian Theory* 401 The working of water collected from the rains and the snows.

II. *concr.* †**13.** Decorative work. *Obs.*

1536 in *Antiq. Sarisb.* (1771) 193 Curiously ornate with dyvers workings and chasings. **1707** *Lond. Gaz.* No. 4373/4 A..Purse, worked round with 3 distinct Rows of Gold Working.

14. A place in which mineral is or has been worked; a mining excavation.

1766 *Ann. Reg., Chron.* 86 The foul air in an old working took fire. **1839** URE *Dict. Arts* 969 Many water-logged fissures come to be cut by the workings. **1872** *Echo* 8 Oct. 3 An explosion..occurred in a part of the working which extends in a northerly direction beneath the town. **1912** *Times* 10 July 8/1 Another explosion..took place,..while a rescue party was below in the workings.

III. 15. With adverbs, as ***working-off, -together, -up*** (see WORK *v.* 40); also *attrib.*; ***working-out***: also spec. in *Mus.* = DEVELOPMENT 10; ***working-over*** (*slang*) = GOING OVER, GOING-OVER 2 b and c.

1662 EVELYN *Sculptura* iii. 33 They also engrave upon stone, and imprint with it; but with this difference in the *working-off; that the paper being black, the Sculpture remains white. **1836** *Penny Cycl.* V. 240 By being careful in the operation of working off, a thinner paper is employed. **1855** KINGSLEY *Westw. Ho!* xxxii, Let him have his humour. ..It may be the working off of his madness. **1842** MANNING *Serm.* i. (1848) 17 All the face of the world bespeaks the *working-out of the prophecy. **1862** MRS. H. WOOD *Mrs. Hallib.* III. xx, 'It will be the working-out of my visions', said Henry. **1889** GROVE *Dict. Mus.* IV. 486/2 *Working-out* (also called Free Fantasia; and Development; Durchführung), the central division of a movement in Binary form, such as commonly occupies the first place in a modern sonata or symphony. **1894** C. N. ROBINSON *Brit. Fleet* 215 The working out of Descharge's idea revolutionized sea warfare. **1914** *Brit. Mus. Return* 184 The determination and working out of the Tabanidæ of Tropical Africa. **1936** *Discovery* Apr. 124/1 The music of Bach, with its perfect counterpoint and logical working-out. **1948** *Penguin Music Mag.* VII. 43 The ..sleight-of-hand that Grieg saw fit to employ in a 'working-out'. **1960** C. HAMBLETT in J. Pudney *Pick of Today's Short Stories* XI. 143 The cops frisked him.. hoping he would put up a fight, so they could give him a *working-over first. **1964** L. DEIGHTON *Funeral in Berlin* viii. 55 A girl with too much make-up..gave her eyebrows a working over. **1623** COCKERAM II, A *working together, *cooperation.* **1678** RYMER *Trag. Last Age* 76 If the Poet observe not these measures, the *working up of a Scene, is plainly the tormenting of nature, and holding our ears to the Grindstone. **1817** J. SCOTT *Paris Revisit.* (ed. 4) 135 All..is done..under the force of artificial impulse, causing what is called a working-up. **1893** *Daily News* 6 Feb. 7/4 Best steel working-up sheets. **1913** *Athenæum* 10 May 528/1 A working-up to a strong climax.

IV. 16. *attrib.* and *Comb.* **a.** Simple attrib.: = of or for working or the performance of a certain work, as ***working arrangement, bee, hour(s, humour, life, light, method, part, rate, talent, time, -week*** (cf. WORKING-DAY 2), ***week-day, year***; = used or worn when one is working, as ***working apron, clothes, dress,*** †***gear, instrument, model,*** †***stole*** (STOOL *sb.* 6), ***stone, tool***; = pertaining or necessary to, involved in, the conduct of a business, etc., as ***working capital, costs, expenses, fund***; = belonging to or situated in or at a working (sense 14), as ***working breast, drift, face, floor, headway, pit.***

b. Special comb.: **working-arch**, a tymp-arch; **working-barrel**, the cylinder in which the piston of a pump works; **working-beam**, a walking beam; **working-big** *a.* (see quot.); **working-box**, = *work-box* (WORK *sb.* 34 d); †**working canvas**, canvas upon which embroidery is worked; **working card** *U.S. obs.* = *union-card* s.v. UNION *sb.*[1] 11 c; **working copy**, a copy of a book or other document used or annotated by someone working on its contents; **working cylinder** (see quots.); **working dinner**: see: *working lunch*; **working door** (see quots.); **working drawing**, usually pl., the drawings made of the plan, etc. of a building from which the workmen employed carry out the construction of the work; **working heat** (see quot.); **working-hole**, (*a*) the opening in a furnace at which the melted glass is drawn out; (*b*) any of the holes which bees use in working; **working load**, the maximum load that a member in a machine or other structure is designed to bear; **working lunch**, a lunch at which those present discuss business (so *working dinner*); **working order**, a condition in which a machine, system, etc. works (well, badly, etc.); **working outline**, an outline which forms the basis of a finished drawing; **working place**, †(*a*) a work-shop; (*b*) the place at which a worker executes his work, *spec.* that at which a miner is engaged in excavation; **working plan**, a plan serving as the basis for the construction of a building, management of a project, etc.; *spec.* in *Forestry* (see quots. 1895, 1926); **working point**, the 'point' in a machine at which the useful work is done; **working rate** (see quot.); **working room**, (*a*) space in which one may work, room for the performance of work; (*b*) a work-room; †**working school**, a kind of industrial school; †**working-shop**, = WORKSHOP 1; **working space** = *working storage*; cf. *work-space* (*b*) s.v. WORK *sb.* 34 d; **working storage**, part of a computer's memory that is used by a program for the storage of intermediate results or other temporary items; **working surface** = *work-top* s.v. WORK *sb.* 34 d; **working title**, a provisional title given to a book, film, or other work before the final title is settled; **working top** = *work top* s.v. WORK *sb.* 34 d; **working-tube**, a glass-worker's blowing-iron; **working-tun**, a vessel in which fermentation takes place.

1769 LADY MARY COKE *Jrnl.* 4 May (1892) III. 67, I had but just time to throw off my *Working Apron. **1853** *Beil's Technol. Wbch.*, **Working arches*.. of a blast furnace. **1854** *Household Narrative* Apr. 80/2 He stated..that the more complete fusion of capital into one company ought not to be sanctioned, but that sort of combination known as *working arrangements should be encouraged. **1904** *Windsor Mag.* June 16/1 A simple working arrangement is usual based on a percentage division of the gross receipts between the two. **1970** *New Yorker* 29 Aug. 45/1 Jews and pagans would never get to Heaven, with the exception of..Moses, who had a close working arrangement with Allah. **1797** *Encycl. Brit.* (ed. 3) XVII. 750/1 To return the pump pistons into their places at the bottom of their respective *working barrels, in order that they also may make a working stroke. *Ibid.* 751/1 The rod X of the piston P is suspended from the arch of the *working-beam. **1883** 'A LADY' *Facts: or, Exper. Recent Colonist in N.Z.* viii. 68 The ladies of the community..meet for a common cause..*Working bees are then got up. **1956** W. R. BIRD *Off-Trail in Nova Scotia* i. 23 We were told much of working bees, barn raisings, the making of maple sugar. **1849–50** *Weale's Dict. Terms*, **Working-big*, in mining, signifies sufficiently large for a man to work in. **1778** J. WOODFORDE *Diary* 9 Sept. (1924) I. 235 It..looks when covered like a *working Box for Ladies. **1838** in *N. & Q.* 11th Ser. I. 423 My small inlaid Working Box. **1881** RAYMOND *Mining Gloss., Put*, to convey coal from the *working breast to the tramway. **1612** *Sc. Bk. Rates* in *Halyburton's Ledger* (1867) 319 Linning cloth..*working canves for cusheonis. **1657** *Acts of Interregn.* (1911) II. 1213 Canvas called..Working Canvas for Cushions. **1912** *Pitman's Commerc. Encycl.* IV. 1690 The *working capital of a business is the amount available for conducting its operations after it has been equipped in such a manner as to be in the condition desired in regard to fixed assets. **1872** *Pacific States Enterprise* (San Francisco) 16 Mar. 3/1 They have adopted the '*working card' system. **1874** *Internat. Typogr. Union Proc.* 34 Subordinate Unions are recommended to..enforce the 'working-card' system. **1896** *Ibid.* 35/2 It was agreed to issue him a working card. **1923** *Proc. 43rd Convention Amer. Fed. of Labor* 324/2 This resolution..affects such other organizations as they seek to affect with an exchange of working cards and other courtesies. **1892** E. REEVES *Homeward Bound* 309 Dressed in ordinary *working clothes of varied colours. **1897** W. C. HAZLITT *Confessions of Collector* vi. 100, I would gladly pay him a guinea for it, and find him a *working copy into the bargain. **1967** E. R. LANNON in Cox & Grose *Organization & Handling Bibl. Rec. by Computer* IV. 95 We can..print the dictionary in two forms; one form is referred to as the 'Working Copy' edition, intended for the use of our own editorial staff. **1912** *Times* 19 Dec. 19/2 The *working costs, including the London expenses. **1815** J. SMITH *Panorama Sci. & Art* II. 143 Such low steam..being admitted into a steam-vessel.., or *working cylinder.., will there be expanded in any ratio required. **1853** *Beil's Technol. Wbch.*, *Working cylinder*, principal cylinder of a water-pressure engine. **1970** *Daily Tel.* 22 Sept. 1/8 Union chiefs and chairmen of five nationalised industries had a '*working dinner'..last night. **1853** *Beil's Technol. Wbch.*, **Working door* of a reverberatory furnace (that opening through which the crucible is brought). **1877** RAYMOND *Statist. Mines & Mining* 393 The furnace has a working door at the side, and a charging door at the end. **1832** BABBAGE *Econ. Manuf.* xxvii. (ed. 3) 262 The actual execution from *working drawings. **1887** D. A. LOW *Machine Draw.* Pref. p. iv, The illustrations for this work..have been specially prepared by the author from working drawings. **1853** MRS. S. MOODIE *Life Clearings* 59 Her coloured flannel *working-dress. **1882** *Rep. Ho. Repr. Prec. Met. U.S.* 639 Further connections between these cross-drifts are made by *working-drifts parallel to the central one. **1868** *N. Amer. Rev.* Jan. 46 Returns for *working expenses. **1886** J. BARROWMAN *Sc. Mining Terms* 73 **Working face*, the place where the miner is excavating the mineral. **1914** *Brit. Mus. Return* 90 An important series of implements and flakes from *working-floors in or below brick-earth at Round Green near Luton. **1905** 'G. THORNE' *Lost Cause* x, A contribution to the *working fund. **1638** *Knaresb. Wills* (Surtees) II. 170 All my loume, *working geare and my husbandrie geare. **1640** *Ibid.* 174 All my working geare which belong to my trade. **1790** *Act 30 Geo. III*, c. 21 §1 To make, erect,..Water Wheels, Fire Engines, Mills, Machinery, Working Gears,..for raising..Water from the said River Wenson. **1855** *Orr's Circ. Sci., Inorg. Nat.* 242 Running a gallery..above the *working headway to the highest place worked. **1782** *Phil. Trans.* LXXII. 320 The fire is afterwards increased, for working the glass, to what is called the *working heat; and this I found, in plate-glass, to be 57°. **1839** URE *Dict. Arts* 577 Semi-circular holes..a little above the top of each pot, called *working holes. **1868** *Rep. U.S. Comm. Agric.* (1869) 276, I pack them [*sc.* bees] closely on benches in the cellar, leaving the box and working-holes open. **1832** HT. MARTINEAU *Hill & Valley* vii, After *working hours the evening before. **1882** BESANT *All Sorts* xxi. (1898) 154 His pay by the piece..gave him, as already stated, tenpence for every working hour. **1840** DICKENS *Old Cur. Shop* xxxv, I'm in a *working humour now,..so don't disturb me, if you please. *c* **1440** *Promp. Parv.* 305/2 *Werkynge instrument for sylke women. **1864** C. KNIGHT (*title*) Passages of a *Working Life during half a century. **1892** *Photogr. Ann.* II. 459 A square of ruby fabric admits a safe *working light. **1891** KIPLING *Light that Failed* vi. 102 If there's a good working light to-morrow I lose a day. **1875** MARTIN tr. *Havrez's Winding Mach.* 19 A round steel rope would bear a *working load of 13·158 kilogs. **1964** *Guardian* 27 Oct. 18/6 After these meetings there was a '*working' lunch at the British Embassy. **1912** *Nature* 26 Dec. 460/1 Formulæ and tables selected from the *working methods of practical photographers. **1966** H. MOORE *On Sculpture* 247 The first maquette for the wood Interior Exterior Forms was produced in 1951, later the same year I made the *working model (24½ in. high), which was cast into bronze. **1982** *Sunday Tel.* (Colour Suppl.) 14 Nov. 33/1 Carvings were plastercast, moulds were taken and durable metal-alloy working models were made. **1845** *Knickerbocker* XXVI. 410 The use of steam-pumps is requisite night and day, to keep them [*sc.* mines] in *working order. **1872** *Chamb. Jrnl.* 29 June 410/2 To see that the [telegraph] line is in working order. **1875** HIGGINSON *Hist. U.S.* xviii. 178 They at once began to get the militia into good working order. **1883** D. C. MURRAY *Hearts* xiii, Mark took care that his appetite, usually in good working order, should be deranged by the emotions of the morning. **1859** GULLICK & TIMBS *Painting* 147 A finished drawing of the full size being ready, a part of this '*working' outline..is now nailed to the wall. **1703** T. N. *City & C. Purchaser* 84 The *working part [of architecture] may be helped by deliberation. **1719** DE FOE *Crusoe* I. (Globe) 72 The working Part of this Day. **1726** LEONI *Alberti's Archit.* I. 38 The whole Business of the working Part of building is this. **1773** *Gentl. Mag.* XLIII. 617 [The fire] breaking down the..partition between the waste and the *working pit, made the most terrible explosion ever beheld. **1554–5** in Feuillerat *Revels Q. Mary* (1914) 176, ij dozen of Russhes for the *working places of thoffice. **1580** HOLLYBAND *Treas. Fr. Tong, L'ouvroir d'vn chacun mestier, ou on besogne,* a working place, a shop. **1827** FARADAY *Chem. Manip.* xxi. (1842) 562 Besides the working-place.., another, unconnected with the busy part of the laboratory, should be appointed. **1839** URE *Dict. Arts* 960 Each miner continues to advance his room or working-place. **1880** 'MARK TWAIN' *Tramp Abroad* xxxiv. 370 The ghastly desolation of the place was as tremendously complete as if Doré had furnished the *working-plans for it. **1895** W. SCHLICH *Man. Forestry* III. III. 173 Forest working plans regulate, according to time and locality, the management of forests in such a manner, that the objects of the industry are as fully as possible realized. **1926** TANSLEY & CHIPP *Study of Vegetation* xi. 255 The Working Plan forms..a scheme for exploiting the forest whereby regeneration will keep pace with exploitation. **1983** *National Trust* Spring 10/1 Constructive, planned woodland management..only became possible after the war, and our oldest working plans are now barely thirty years old. **1825** J. NICHOLSON *Oper. Mech.* 51 All the motion which has been accumulated on the fly during the whole progress of its accumulation, is exerted in an instant at the *working point. **1886** J. BARROWMAN *Sc. Mining Terms* 73 *Working rate,* the rate per ton paid to a miner. **1775** ROMANS *Florida* App. 9 From Beak's-Key, to the Riding Rocks, and Roques, there is *working room plenty, and good anchorage. **1827** FARADAY *Chem. Manip.* i. (1842) 16 There is working room all round it. **1898** *Allbutt's Syst. Med.* V. 258 The atmosphere of their working-rooms is so poisonous that birds die after being exposed to it for a fort-night. **1787** HAWKINS *Life of Johnson* 391 Dr. Madden, so well-known by his premiums for the encouragement of Protestant *working-schools in Ireland. **1783** *Phil. Trans.* LXXIII. 450 The dust of a *working-shop. **1954** *Working space [see *surface sterilization* s.v. SURFACE *sb.* 6c]. **1973** M. WOODHOUSE *Blue Bone* vii. 63 The converted hold..had contained a full-sized billiards table. There was, at least, plenty of working space. *?c* **1475** *Promp. Parv.* 305/2 (Camb. MS.) Lyncet, a *werkynge stole. **1502** *Privy Purse Exp. Eliz. of York* (1830) 7 For the stuff and making of iiij working stoles for the Quene..vs. iiij d. **1530** PALSGR. 290/1 Workyng stole fore a sylkeman, *mettier.* **1585** HIGINS *Junius' Nomencl.* 410/1 A *working stone: a stone that serueth to worke withall, as the whetstone. **1954** *Computers & Automation* Dec. 23/1 *Working storage... Like a work-sheet in pencil and paper calculation. **1971** N. CHAPIN *Computers* xv. 445 In the operand data structures, programers commonly distinguish between constants that are not part of the program, working storage (for intermediate results and status or progress indicators), and input-output buffer areas. **1983** D. H. SANDARS *Computers Today* v. 113 This total earnings figure is copied (instruction, 08) in address 15, which is the working storage area. **1962** A. WISE *Death's-Head* iii. 23 The electric percolator standing on the formica *working-surface. **1970** *Which?* Sept. 279/1 Three of the small freezers..had laminated tops you could use as a working surface. **1863** P. BARRY *Dockyard Econ.* 218 The *working system of the Thames Company is contract between owner and ship-builder. **1870** EMERSON *Soc. & Solit.* iv. 66 The solid result depends on a few men with *working talent. **1783** *Jrnl. Ho. Comm.* XLVII. 372/2 The *Working Time that is now lost in making up the Bundles. **1940** R. CHANDLER *Let.* 27 June in Gardiner & Walker *Raymond Chandler Speaking* (1962) 211 The title of my book is not *The Second Murderer.* I used that for a while as a *working title, but I didn't like it. **1977** G. FISHER *Villain of Piece* iii. 32, I was now busy turning the whole caboodle into a series of four articles... I gave it a working title: 'My Life with Britain's Top Villain'. **1562** J. HEYWOOD *Prov. & Epigr.* (1867) 101 Thou handledst no caruyng nor *woorkyng toole. **1690** CHILD *Disc. Trade* (1698) 182 Not to hinder any man from keeping as many servants as he can, nor looms, working-tools, &c. *a* **1728** WOODWARD *Nat. Hist. Fossils* 30 A people so barbarous, and destitute of all Working-Tools. **1869** BOUTELL *Arms & Armour* i. 3 Employing a second stone as his working-tool, ..he struck off splinters from the first stone. **1959** *Housewife* June 70/2 Table-top refrigerators are popular because they give an additional *working top. **1980** D. CLARK *Golden Rain* v. 115 'Which cupboard please?' 'The last one under the working-top on the left.' **1845** G. DODD *Brit. Manuf.* IV. 63 After the *working-tube has collected nearly sufficient colourless glass from one pot. **1707** MORTIMER *Husb.* 572 Covering your Fat close, that it [*sc.* yeast] fall not in your *Working-Tun. **1890** J. E. C. MUNRO in *Rep. Brit. Assoc.* 472 If the *working week was reduced from 56½ to 48 hours. **1867** AUG. J. E. WILSON *Vashti* xiv, She remarked that your eyes were, in comparison with other folks', what Sabbath is to *working week-days. **1913** *Times* 13 Aug. 3/1 The *working years of life.

working ('wɜːkɪŋ), *ppl. a.* [f. WORK *v.* + -ING².
(In several uses formerly often hyphened to the sb.)] That works, in various senses.

1. a. Of a person, personal attribute, etc.: Active, operative; energetic. *Obs.* or *arch.*

1387–8 T. USK *Test. Love* II. v. (Skeat) l. 43 He..that neither han lyf ne soule, ne ordinaunce of werchinge limmes. *a* **1586** SIDNEY *Arcadia* I. iii. (1912) 20 A woman.. of so working a minde,..it was happie shee tooke a good course. **1635** F. WHITE *Sabbath* Ep. Ded. 9 They command whatsoever their own working-heads affect. **1646** J. WHITAKER *Uzziah* 14 He had a working head, and a dextrous hand. **1681** FLAVEL *Meth. Grace* xxviii. 476 The working-heads of the enemies of that State. **1706** ? PRIOR *Ep. Elector Bavaria* 58 Wks. 1907 II. 371 Preluding cannons tell th' approaching storm, And working armies take a dreadful form. **1820** KEATS *Ode to Psyche* 60 A rosy sanctuary will I dress With the wreath'd trellis of a working brain.

†**b.** Of a thing (concr. or abstr.): Operative, effective. *Obs.*

1586 MARLOWE *1st Pt. Tamburl.* II. iii, You see, my Lord, what woorking woordes he hath. **1613** SHAKS. *Hen. VIII,* Prol. 3 Things..Sad, high, and working, full of State and Woe. **1622** J. TAYLOR (Water P.) *Shilling* B4, A gentle working Potion. **1644** MILTON *Areop.* (Arb.) 49 Childish men, who have not the art to qualifie and prepare these working mineralls. **1654** E. JOHNSON *Wonder-wkg. Provid.* 16 This was the first working providence of Christ to stir up our English Nation. *a* **1709** J. LISTER *Autobiog.* (1842) 43 Some working physic that might be likely to..remove the distemper.

2. a. That works or labours; *esp.* that works for an employer in a manual or industrial occupation (see also WORKING-CLASS, -MAN). Also *spec.* of a girl or woman: that goes out to earn a living rather than remain at home, as; ***working girl***: also *euphem.*, a prostitute (*U.S. slang*).

1639 G. PLATTES *Discov. Infin. Treas.* Pref. C 4 b, How the working poore may be imployed in these new improvements. **1830** *Poor Man's Guardian* 31 Dec. 4/2 The evils that beset the working population. **1864** RAMSBOTTOM *Phases* 23 Honest wortchin' folks one sees By scores reawnd th' Poor-law Office dur. **1865** DICKENS *Mut. Fr.* II. IV. vi. 209, I am removed from you and your family by being a working girl. **1871** SMILES *Charac.* i. (1876) 25 The common body of working-people. **1889** [see SISTER *sb.* 2]. **1913** MACEWEN *Hist. Ch. Scot.* I. xviii. 388 There must have been innumerable parishes which had no working parish priests. **1913** J. VAIZEY *College Girl* ix. 119 'I shall have to earn money myself, so I want to pass all the exams. I can.' The Percivals stared... They had never met a prospective *working* girl before! **1922** W. P. KER *Coll. Ess., Molière* (1925) I. 352 Respectable advice to working playwrights. **1933** D. C. PEEL *Life's Enchanted Cup* xv. 183 It was, perhaps, because she had known what it was to study in the intervals of tending children..that she could sympathise with working mothers. **1963** *Times* 2 Jan. 10/3 Many Australians had to take two jobs to make ends meet, and 'there were any number of working wives'. **1970** O. NORTON *Dead on Prediction* i. 7 I'm going to be a working girl again now. Doing some articles for *Mercia,* for a start. **1978** F. WELDON *Praxis* xx. 174 Praxis gave up her job: Ivor did not want a working wife. **1979** *Arizona Daily Star* 5 Aug. J 3/2 There were studies showing juvenile delinquents springing from single-parent or working-mother homes.

1968 *Current Slang* (Univ. S. Dakota) Fall 52 *Working girl,* n., a prostitute. **1971** *N.Y. Times* 9 Aug. 33/5 They call themselves 'working girls'... Their work is a 'business', or even..a 'social service'... By the prostitute's code, prostitution is moral. **1984** *Chicago Sun-Times* 26 Mar. 12 U.S. Prostitutes has estimated that thousands of 'working girls' will travel to San Francisco for business generated by the convention.

b. In contrast with: (*a*) 'master', 'managing', etc., in designations of trade or occupation; (*b*) 'sleeping', in reference to partners in a firm. Also in designations of persons or animals that work or are active in a special way.

1708 *Lond. Gaz.* No. 4436/3 He is by Trade a Working-Goldsmith. **1793–4** *Matthews's Bristol Directory* 78 Tanner, George, Working-cutler, Maryport-street. **1809** MALKIN *Gil Blas* IV. vii. ¶2, I..became the working partner in a new firm. **1839** in *Orders of Council Naval Service* (1866) I. 478 The Working Petty Officers of the Royal Navy. **1855** *Poultry Chron.* II. 507 The working Committee of a show. **1865** DICKENS *Mut. Fr.* I. vii, A working-jeweller population. **1874** GREEN *Short Hist.* x. §2. 747 Benjamin Franklin, who had risen from his position of a working printer in Philadelphia to high repute among scientific discoverers. **1898** *Daily News* 5 Jan. 2/4 Working homers, wonderful for their speed, such as are used on Government ships. **1908** *Church Times* 20 Mar. 374/1 Working House-keeper,..required by gentleman, to work..small house.

c. ***working party***: (*a*) *Mil.* a party of men detailed for a special piece of work outside their ordinary duties; (*b*) a group of women, meeting to do work, esp. sewing, for a good cause; (*c*) a committee appointed to examine and report on a particular subject and to make recommendations based on its findings; (*d*) a group of prisoners engaged on outdoor work, freq. outside the perimeter of the prison.

1744 M. BISHOP *Life* 204, I mounted Guard as Sergeant upon a working Party, and took them to a Mine, in order to work at a Sap. **1834–47** J. S. MACAULAY *Field Fortif.* (1851) 171 The men who undertake a surprise may be divided into four parties: 1st, the guides and interpreters; 2nd, the combatants; 3rd, the troops to cover the retreat; 4th, the working party. **1876** C. M. YONGE *Three Brides* I. viii. 127 Cecil had offered to take Anne to see the working party, and let her assist thereat. **1900** —— *Modern Broods* vii. 72 The parish room, where the ladies were to hold a working party for the missions. **1946** *Times* 10 Jan. 2/3 The 'working party' is a device for securing the best possible guidance on the policies that should be adopted to bring an industry to the highest pitch of efficiency under private enterprise. **1948** *Hansard Commons: Written Answers* 8 Mar. 112 The Working Party on the Turn-Round of Shipping was set up to examine the causes of delay... Teams from the Working Party have visited the major ports. **1963** T. PARKER *Unknown Citizen* v. 136 Charlie was out of the prison that day, on a working party at a farm some miles away. **1976** L. KENNEDY *Presumption of Innocence* I. 46 One day at Parkhurst he walked away from an outside working-party. ..Although he was wearing prison overalls, no one paid any attention. **1981** E. LONGFORD *Queen Mother* v. 82 The Queen and her working party met twice a week to make surgical dressings and comforters for the troops. **1982** *Church Times* 12 Nov. 1/3 The General Synod's Board of Education has set up a working party on independent schools which will look at the Independent sector in education 'from a Christian perspective'.

d. Of horses and cattle: Employed in work, esp. in agricultural work. Also of dogs used for hunting, herding, guard duties, etc. Also *fig.*

1613 *Liber Deposit. infra Archidiacon. Colcestrensem* lf. 29 (MS.), The herbadg or pasture of anye workeing cattell. **1773** *Pennsylv. Gaz.* 21 Apr. Suppl. 1/2 To be sold..several pair of working oxen. **1801** *Farmer's Mag.* Apr. 224 Bean and pease-straw is the customary fodder of the working stock. *c* **1830** *Glouc. Farm Rep.* 19 in *Libr. Usef. Knowl., Husb.* III, Two colts are generally bred from the mares to keep up the stock of working-horses. **1890** 'R. BOLDREWOOD' *Col. Reformer* xiii, Like an old working bullock in a lucerne field. **1897** *Blackw. Mag.* June 744/1 Notwithstanding the care most people take to buy pups of 'good working parents', it is the blood that tells. **1908** *Animal Managem.* 124 A working horse..will..swallow an inordinate quantity of water very rapidly. **1936** *Times Lit. Suppl.* 25 Jan. 73/2 The American husband (in fiction) is losing his working-dog quality, his ambition to toil. **1947** C. L. B. HUBBARD (*title*) Working dogs of the world. **1982** G. HAMMOND *Fair Game* xi. 99 [The dog] went for the pigeon ..and fetched it back... Miss Wyper was overwhelmed. This was her first introduction to the truly fulfilled dog, the working dog doing the job for which it was bred.

e. Of a bee or ant: That is a 'worker'.

1766 *Compl. Farmer* s.v. *Queen-bee* 6 H 1/2 Not only these common or working bees, but also the drones, or male bees. **1816** KIRBY & SP. *Entomol.* xxvii. (1818) II. 513 If we suppose them to know that the queen and working-grubs are originally the same.

f. In comb.: Producing, creating.

1595 W. C. *Polimanteia* (1881) 82 Glittering hate-working gold.

†**3.** Aching, throbbing with pain. *Obs.*

c **1460** *Towneley Myst.* vi. 8 Sore bonys, & warkand feete. *c* **1470** HENRY *Wallace* III. 204 With mony werkand wound. **1535** STEWART *Cron. Scot.* (Rolls) I. 75 Ay quhair tha hit makand ane werkand wound.

4. Of the sea, etc.: Agitated, tossing. *poet.*

1581 A. HALL *Iliad* I. 6 The working sea I wil goe seeke in point of morning gray. *Ibid.* VII. 123 Much like the Ocean waue, Which working storme, not green, but black doth make yᵉ colour haue. **1621** W. MASON *Ess.* 23 The billowes of the working-sea that cannot rest. **1666** DRYDEN *Ann. Mirab.* clxxi, On Biscay's working-Bay. **1676** —— *Aurengz.* IV. i, A working Sea, remaining from a Storm. **1725** POPE *Odyss.* XII. 265 Oars they seize, Stretch to the stroke, and brush the working seas. **1934** DYLAN THOMAS in *New Verse* No. 9. 12 The dry Sargossa of the tomb Gives up its dust to such a working sea.

5. Of liquor: Fermenting.

1675 EVELYN in J. Rose *Engl. Vineyard* 44 Some replenish their working Wines with Water only.

6. Of the features of the face: Moving involuntarily or convulsively, esp. as the result of emotion.

1753–4 RICHARDSON *Grandison* II. xi. 75 That little witch, I have been watching her eyes, and every working muscle of her saucy face. **1838** LYTTON *Alice* IX. iii, The smile vanished at once, as her eyes met his changed and working countenance. **1848** DICKENS *Dombey* xi, The working lip was loosened; and the tears came streaming forth. **1865** —— *Mut. Fr.* IV. vii, 'I heard of the outrage,' said Bradley, trying to constrain his working mouth.

7. a. Of an organism, a piece of machinery, etc.: That performs its function (esp. in a specified manner); that 'goes' (as opposed to being stationary).

1608 SHAKS. *Per.* V. i. 155 But are you flesh and bloud? Haue you a working pulse, and are no Fairie? **1769** FALCONER *Dict. Marine* (1789), *Vaisseau qui se manie bien,* a good working ship; a ship that is easily managed and steered. **1770** J. FERGUSON *Introd. Electricity* 134 A working model of the great crane at *Bristol.* **1822** C. F. PARTINGTON *Hist. & Descr. Account Steam Engine* i. 13 In the following year a working model of the above engine was submitted to the Royal Society. **1859** *Newton's Lond. Jrnl. Arts* 1 Feb. 115 Mr. J. A. Haswell exhibited a large working model of the new [railway-]switch. **1874** RAYMOND *Statist. Mines & Mining* 393 A continuous-working reverberatory furnace.

b. *Naut.* applied to certain sails.

1882 *Standard* 11 Aug. 6/6 Lorna and Chittywee last, the latter with a large jackyardtopsail set, the others having working squareheaders. **1883** *Harper's Mag.* Aug. 450/2 Racing or working rigs. **1898** ANSTED *Dict. Sea Terms, Working foresail* (in fore-and-aft rig), a foresail which runs on a horse. *Working lug,* the same as a standing lug; and it often has a boom.

8. a. Of a majority: Sufficient to secure the passing of measures.

1858 *Penny Cycl.* 2nd Suppl. 495/2 With the command of a working majority of about a hundred in the House of Commons, Sir Robert Peel entered on the greatest period of his political career. *a* **1859** MACAULAY *Hist. Eng.* xxiv. (1861) V. 131 It was not impossible that the servants of the Crown might, by prudent management, succeed in obtaining a working majority.

b. Of a theory, etc.: That provides a basis upon which to work.

1849 GROTE *Greece* II. xlv. V. 399 The confederacy would never have become a working reality. **1871** R. H. HUTTON *Ess.* I. v. 112 If it be only a working hypothesis, to keep us, while confined in the human, from blindly and unconsciously dashing ourselves against the laws of the divine. **1875** MAINE *Hist. Instit.* xiii. 400 He wishes to alter ..them according to a working rule gathered from his reflections. **1894** H. DRUMMOND *Ascent of Man* 8 No one asks more of Evolution at present than permission to use it as a working theory. **1919** G. HUDDLESTON *Peacemaking at Paris* ii. 25 To make a temporary treaty which would give us a working relationship with Germany.

Hence ˈ**workingly** *adv.*, †effectively; industriously; ˈ**workingness**, †effectiveness.

1611 FLORIO, *Operosita*, workingnesse or operation. **1642** J. EATON *Honey-c. Free Justif.* 269 Christ..in the residue of his whole life, afterwards fulfilled the whole Law, actually, workingly and perfectly. **1859** ATKINSON *Walks & Talks* (1892) 291 Such pretty birds hammering away so cheerfully and workingly.

ˈ**working(-)**ˈ**class.** Chiefly *pl.* ˈworking ˈclasses. [WORKING *ppl. a.*, CLASS *sb.* 2.] The grade or grades of society comprising those who are employed to work for wages in manual or industrial occupations.

1789 J. GRAY in G. Dempster *Discourse containing a Summary of Proceedings of Soc. for extending Fisheries & improving Sea Coasts of Gt. Britain* 50 More spacious plots of ground..may be allowed to the clergyman and schoolmaster, and to other persons superior to the working class. **1795** J. AIKIN *Descr. Country 30–40 Miles round Manchester* 262 Houses for the working class are not procured without difficulty. **1813** R. OWEN *New View Soc.* 5 The poor and working classes of Great Britain and Ireland have been found to exceed twelve millions of persons. **1844** H. COCKBURN *Jrnl.* (1874) II. 83 What are termed *the* working-classes, as if the only workers were those who wrought with their hands. **1875** *Act 38 & 39 Vict.* c. 36 §5 The accommodation of..as many persons of the working class as may be displaced. **1890** *Act 53 & 54 Vict.* c. 69 §18 The provisions of section eleven of the Housing of the Working Classes Act, 1885,..shall have effect as if the expression 'working classes' included all classes of persons who earn their livelihood by wages or salaries.

b. *attrib.*, as ***working-class family, house, vote.***

1839 J. S. MILL in *Westm. Rev.* Apr. 497 The Working Men's Association..who represent the best and most enlightened aspect of working-class Radicalism. **1849** F. D. MAURICE *Let.* 3 Mar. in J. F. Maurice *Life F. D. Maurice* (1884) I. xxv. 513 Thank you very much for entering so heartily into my working class meetings. **1869** W. T. THORNTON *On Labour* III. v. 316 Leading unionists, and working-class leaders. **1884** in A. Cawston *Street Improv. London* (1893) 105 Those working-class houses that you have bought up and repaired. **1895** *Q. Rev.* Oct. 558 The working-class vote. **1913** *Times* 14 May 5/5 The 3,000 working class families which form the population.

ˈ**working(-)**ˌ**day.** (Also 6 warkynday, 6–7 workenday.) [f. WORKING *vbl. sb.* + DAY *sb.*[1]]

1. a. A work-day.

1478 *Paston Lett.* III. 237 A hose clothe, oone for the halydays..and a nothyr for the workyng days. **1538** in R. G. Marsden *Sel. Pleas Crt. Admiralty* (1894) I. 62 The said John Halmdry shalbe dyscharged and his shyp of the sayd salt..within vj lawfull workyng dayes. **1549** W. THOMAS *Hist. Italie* 79 Euerie holidaie, and many times the workendaies, the same sitteth from diner till nyght. **1561** BP. J. PARKHURST *Injunct.* A ij b, That they baptize not children on the wourking daies. **1626** in *Cheque-bk. Chapel Royal* (Camden) 71 That a competent number of the gentlemen be appointed to attend the service uppon the workinge dayes throughout the yeare. **1671–2** in C. Worthy *Devon. Wills* (1896) 27 My blew coat which I did weare worken dayes. **1725** DE FOE *Voy. round World* (1840) 340 They quite forgot the days, and knew not a Sunday from a working-day any longer. **1832** SIR F. PALGRAVE *Rise & Progr. Eng. Commw.* II. p. clii, The first open or working day after the two great weekly festivals of Sun-day and Moon-day. **1839** THACKERAY *Fatal Boots* Feb., Then comes dismal February, and the working-days with it,..after the Christmas and the New Year's heyday and merry-making are over. **1911** ONIONS *Shaks. Gloss.* p. vi, The compilation of which has occupied the full working-days of a year and a half.

b. *attrib.* or as *adj.* (= WORKADAY B.), as ***working-day clothes, dress, face, world.***

1533 in Weaver *Wells Wills* (1890) 26 A roond warkynday gownd. **1589** GREENE *Menaphon* (Arb.) 25 Our shepheard must put on his working day face, and frame nought but dolefull Madrigalls. **1594** GREENE & LODGE *Looking Gl.* (1598) C 4, If you heard her working-day words,..they be ratlers like thunder. **1600** SHAKS. *A.Y.L.* I. iii. 12 Oh how full of briers is this working day world. **1683** in *Bedfordshire N. & Q.* (1889) II. 237 All my working-day clothes of wollen or stuffe. **1835** LANDON *Misc. Poet. Wks.* 2 The working-day portion of life's wondrous whole. **1840** DICKENS *Old Cur. Shop* xliv, The working-day faces come nearer to the truth. **1872** GEO. ELIOT *Middlem.* lvi, The working-day world. **1873** NEWMAN *Serm. Var. Occas.* (1881) xiv. 275 The working-day dress.

2. The portion of a day devoted to work or allotted to labour as a day's work.

1853 *Hogg's Instructor* X. 282/2 To grant the Saturday afternoon holiday, and to limit the duration of every other working day within a certain definite period of time, not exceeding twelve hours, including the proper interval for meals. **1875** J. MACDONELL in *Fortn. Rev.* Mar. 389 Leaving the length of the working day unchanged. **1890** J. E. C. MUNRO in *Rep. Brit. Assoc.* 472 The more rational proposals to establish a short working day.

†ˈ**working-**ˌ**house.** *Obs.* [WORKING *vbl. sb.*] = WORKHOUSE 1, 2.

1487 in *Cal. Lett.-bk. L London* (1912) 242 [That no time-expired apprentice..set up shop or] wirkyng hous [within the City]. **1599** SHAKS. *Hen. V*, v. Chor. 23 In the quick Forge and working-house of Thought. **1711** *Act 10 Anne* c. 19. §55 Any such Goods, so made, printed, painted, or stained..in..their Ware-houses, Working-houses, or Places aforesaid.

1597–8 *Act 39 Eliz.* c. 5 (*title*) An Acte for erecting of Hospitalls or abiding and working Howses for the Poore. **1639** *Bury Wills* (Camden) 178 The common workinghouse of Bury.

ˈ**working-**ˈ**man. a.** A man of the working classes; a man employed to work for a wage, esp. in a manual or industrial occupation: a term inclusive of 'artisan', 'mechanic', and 'labourer'.

1816 T. WILLIAMS *Means Improv. Condit. Poor* 23 How much more pleasant is the occupation of a working-man than of a beggar, or a vagrant! **1830** *B'ham Petit. Rights* §6 in *Life T. Attwood* (1885) 154 That..all the taxes ought to be taken off from those articles necessary for the subsistence and comfort of working men. **1873** *Iron* 5 July 5/1 The..prevalence of what are called 'working-men's candidates'. **1896** *Westm. Gaz.* 4 Mar. 8/2 The word 'working-man' was here held to include a clerk or small shopkeeper, or anyone whose total income did not exceed £150 a year. **1901** W. R. H. TROWBRIDGE *Lett. her Mother to Eliz.* x. 43 Mr. Wertzelmann..held out a hand like a working-man's.

b. *Comb.* in the possessive, denoting institutions established for working men, as ***working man's*** (or ***men's***) ***association, club, college, institute.***

1839 Working men's association [see WORKING CLASS b]. **1844** *Lexington* (Ky.) *Observer* 2 Oct. 3/1 The Working Men's Clay Club of this city will hold an adjourned meeting. **1861** MRS. GASKELL *Let.* 16 Apr. (1966) 650 He has..established a small working man's Club, with the help of a *low* Church curate. **1961** *Economist* 30 Dec. 1270/1 The Working Men's Club and Institute Union achieves its centenary next year. **1976** *National Observer* (U.S.) 18 Dec. 18/3 It opens in a Manchester secondary-school classroom, where a sextet of aspiring stand-up comics has assembled for their Big Chance, an audition before a real..agent at a local working-man's club. **1856** C. FOX *Let.* 27 June in *Jrnls.* (1972) 223 Oxford... I was delighted to hear of their successful experiment to unite Town and Gown by a Working Man's College. **1921** G. B. SHAW *Back to Methuselah* II. 61, I was asked to deliver an address to the students at the Working Men's College. **1971** G. STEINER *Bluebeard's Castle* iii. 61 The categories of schooling and public enlightenment—the lyceum, the public library, the working men's college. **1882** F. A. KEMBLE *Records of Later Life* III. 293 A reading that I gave for the Working Men's Institute in Brighton. **1980** E. BLISHEN *Nest of Teachers* I. i. 4 A Working Men's Institute..established in the last century.

So ˈ**working-**ˈ**woman.**

1853 DICKENS *Bleak Ho.* xv, A child, playing at washing, and imitating a poor working-woman. **1918** *Current History* Feb. 200 Workingmen and workingwomen have raised the cry for bread, peace, and liberty in the street.

workless (ˈwɜːklɪs), *a.* [f. WORK *sb.* + -LESS.]

1. Doing no work; inactive, idle. *Obs.* or *arch.*

1484 CAXTON *Fables of Æsop* v. ix. (1889) 150 What doo ye here, why are yow werkless? **1493** [H. PARKER] *Dives & Pauper* I. xxx. (W. de W. 1496) 69/1 Nedy werkelesse men that go so gay & spende grete. **1571** GOLDING *Calvin on Ps.* lxxv. 8 Wee imagin I wote not what maner of worklesse and ydle sovereintie, as though he ruled not mankynd with his power and providence. **1629** C. POTTER *Consecration Serm. Mar. 15, 1628* 77 These verball Doctors, these worklesse talkers. **1881** 'VERNON LEE' *Belcaro* vii. 195 Inactive, with listless limbs and workless hands.

†**2.** Of faith: Without works. *Obs.*

1532 MORE *Confut. Tindale* Wks. 529/2 A manne maye..haue the righte faythe ydle and woorkelesse. **1653** MANTON *Exp. James* ii. 14 The apostle calleth a workless faith a dead or lifeless faith.

3. Unprovided with work; having no work to do; out of work, unemployed. Often *absol.* with *the*.

1848 *Tait's Mag.* XV. 356 The workless silence, wageless misery. **1887** *Pall Mall Gaz.* 22 Nov. 1/1 The bitter cold of the fireless room..will wring from the workless workers a still more piteous moan. *Ibid.* 7 Dec. 10/2 The Workless in the Country. **1892** MRS. G. A. SALA *Famous People I have met* 18 The..workless weavers of the East-end.

Hence ˈ**worklessness**, the condition of being workless; unemployment.

1883 G. MACDONALD *Donal Grant* xlii, Ye maun be growin' some short o' siller i' this time o' warklessness! **1892** *Toynbee Rec.* Dec. 29 We are confronted this Winter with a worklessness which approaches..that of 1886.

ˈ**work-loom.** *Sc.* and *north.* (now in form **wark-**). [f. WORK *sb.* + LOOM *sb.*[1]] A tool or implement, esp. one used in manual labour.

c **1425** *Noah's Ark* in *Non-Cycle Myst. Pl.* 22/82 Unlusty I am..Worklooms for to work and weeld. **1475–6** *Burgh Rec. Edin.* (1869) I. 33 Gude and sufficiand graith and werkloumys. **1513** DOUGLAS *Æneis* VII. xi. 82 The lust of all sic werklomis was adew. **1570** LEVINS *Manip.* 161/34 A Worke loome, *instrumentum*. *a* **1583** MONTGOMERIE *Flyting* 43 That warkloome quite [*sc.* a pen]. **1691** SIR J. FOULIS *Acc. Bk.* (S.H.S.) 140, 4 pund steell for yᵉ work loomes. **1785** BURNS *Addr. to Deil* xi, The best wark-lume i' the house. **1796** GALL *Tint Quey* 9 [He] gat his wark-looms a' in tune, To ca' some tackets in his shoon.

workman (ˈwɜːkmən). Pl. **workmen**. Forms: see WORK *sb.* and MAN *sb.*[1]; also 4 **werman**, *Sc.* **warman**. [OE. *weorcmann* = Du. *werkman*, OHG. *werahman* (MHG. *werch-*, *wercman*), ON. *verkmaðr*.]

1. a. A man engaged to do work or (usually) manual labour, esp. one employed upon some particular piece of work: an operative; often (contextually) a skilled worker; †occas. a worker (*in* a medium).

c **888** ÆLFRED *Boeth.* xvii, He sceal habban ȝebedmen & fyrdmen & weorcmen. *c* **950** *Lindisf. Gosp.* Matt. ix. 37 *Operarii*, wercmenn. *c* **1205** LAY. 22892 A crafti weorc-man. *a* **1225** *Ancr. R.* 404 Iðen euentid, hwon me ȝelt werc-men hore deies hure. **13..** *Sir Beues* (A.) 3230 A morwe þe barouns gonne arise Sum to honten and sum to cherche, And werk men gonne for to werche. **1362** LANGL. *P. Pl.* A. II. 91 *Dignus est operarius mercede sua*: Worþi is þe Werkmon his hure to haue. *c* **1375** *Sc. Leg. Saints* xxii. (*Laurentius*) 594 It mycht nocht suffice..at a met bred to be,..to warmen thre. *c* **1450** *Mirk's Festial* 39 He had so mony werkemen of dyuerse craftys, þat a man schuld not here his felow speke for dount of strokes. **1474** CAXTON *Chesse* II. i. (1883) 22 A werkman in metall. **1562** J. HEYWOOD *Prov. & Epigr.* II. ix. (1867) 77 What is a woorkman, without his tooles? **1651** HOBBES *Leviath.* III. xlii. 306 A man is obliged in conscience to set on work upon all occasions the best workman. *a* **1700** EVELYN *Diary* 21 May 1645, This place has also been famous for lutes made by the old masters..; the workmen were chiefly Germans. **1725** WATTS *Logic* I. vi. §8 If I would learn the Nature of a Watch, the Workman takes it to pieces. **1842** GWILT *Archit.* Gloss. s.v. *Beds of a Stone*, In arching the beds are called summerings by the workmen. **1883** W. D. CURZON *Manuf. Industries Worcs.* 48 There were under the hands of the workmen..some of the cylinders for the bridge across the Dubbo river.

b. Connoting a class or grade, or in correlation with 'employer', 'capitalist', or the like.

1704 DE FOE *Giving Alms no Charity* (1859) 38 The price of wages not only determines the difference between the employer and the work-man, but it rules the rates of every market. **1727** —— *Eng. Tradesman* I. Introd. 2 There are several degrees of people employ'd in trade below these, such as workmen, labourers, and servants. **1868** RONEY *Rambles on Rlwys.* 62 These companies issue what are called 'work-man's tickets.' **1872** RUSKIN *Fors Clav.* II. Index 27 By workmen I mean people who must use their heads as well as their hands for what they do; by labourers, those who use their hands only. **1875** *Act 38 & 39 Vict.* c. 90 §10 The expression 'workman' does not include a domestic or menial servant, but save as aforesaid, means any person who, being a labourer, servant in husbandry, journeyman, artificer, handicraftsman, miner, or otherwise engaged in manual labour,..has entered into or works under a contract with an employer. **1906** *Economist* 15 Dec. 2048/2 At the present time..there is a widespread tendency to consider that no one is a work-man unless he be engaged in manual labour. **1908** *Daily Chron.* 12 Sept. 5/4 It was declared that the term 'work-man' should include clerks.

c. Of ants or bees: = WORKER 2 d (*c*). *rare.*

1870 DUNCAN *Blanchard's Transf. Insects* 349 Besides the neuters, workmen, and soldiers, two sorts of nymphs.

2. a. A skilled or expert craftsman. *Obs.* exc. in *Glassmaking*, the first man of a 'chair'.

1478 *Acta Dom. Conc.* (1839) 4/2 þe lordis..causit þe chenȝe to be weyt and prisit be werkmen, quhilkis prisit it to v li Scottis. **1496** *Cov. Leet Bk.* 574 There shall no persone of þe Craft set no straunge Journeyman on warke without license of þe Maisters of þe Craft, and they to see that he be a warkman. **1530** PALSGR. 472/2 This kote was never made of a workeman, it is but boungled up. **1553** ASCHAM *Rep. Germany* A iij b, Here is stuffe plenty to furnish well vp a trimme history if a workeman had it in handlyng. **1597** MORLEY *Introd. Mus.* 88 By working we become workmen. **1657** WORTHINGTON *Diary* etc. (Chetham Soc.) I. 100 He was not satisfy'd in William Pope, because he was not a workman of his trade. **1706** E. WARD *Wooden World Diss.* (1708) 71 From whence one may reasonably infer, that he's himself no Work-man. **1721** PERRY *Daggenham Breach* 68, I had answer'd them like an Artist, and like a Workman. **1849** [see SERVITOR 5].

b. *transf.*; e.g. applied to a rider, esp. in hunting, who manages his horse well or is conversant with the technique of the field; also to a horse that takes its fences well, etc.

1832 *Q. Rev.* XLVII. 238 The Squire having hit off his fox like a workman. **1840** J. C. WHYTE *Hist. Turf* II. 577 Although so splendid a rider over a race-course, Old Chifney by no means shone as a workman across a country. **1868** WHYTE-MELVILLE *White Rose* I. xiv. 177 'I'm blessed if the young 'un isn't a workman!' he mutters, while he marks Gerard's easy seat. **1887** F. GALE *Game Cr.* 63 [Our opponents] were all 'workmen',..and a tough job, clearly, was cut out. **1891** 'R. BOLDREWOOD' *Sydney-side Sax.* xii, A fine, solid, but active-looking horse,..looking more of a workman over timber than the other.

†**3.** The Creator; = WORKER 1 a. *Obs.*

1551 T. WILSON *Logike* P j b, The greate workeman of thynges god almightie himselfe. **1560** B. GOOGE tr. *Palingenius' Zodiac* III. (1561) G j, That workman first, that made yᵉ skies the earth, and seas also. **1587** GOLDING *De Mornay* vi. (1592) 64 This Speech [= Logos] being the workeman of God the Lord of the whole World. **1616** T. SCOT *Philomythie* D 7 b, Darknes was not created; tis as old As that great workman which the whole doth mold.

4. One who works or practises his craft or art (in some specified manner).

1484 CAXTON *Fables of Alfonce* xiii, As good a workman of his craft as ony was at that tyme in alle the world. **1620** I. C. *Two Merry Milkmaids* IV. i. L 4 b, And thou beest so good a workeman, thou shalt draw my Picture. *a* **1633** G. HERBERT *Outl. Prov.* 67 Never had ill workeman good tooles. **1668** EVELYN tr. *Freart's Idea Perfect. Paint.* Advt. to Rdr. a 2, Albert Durer, a German Painter, and a most incomparable Workman. **1849** PARKER *Gothic Archit.* 88 It being one of the characteristics of a good workman not to waste his material. **1868** DARWIN in F. Darwin *Life & Lett.* (1887) III. 98 My health makes me a very slow workman.

5. *attrib.*

1549 *Compl. Scot.* vii. 69 Mony politic verkmanlumis for mecanyc craftis. **1803** HEBER *Palestine* 199 No workman steel, no ponderous axes rung. **1908** *Westm. Gaz.* 7 Feb. 5/2 The workmen-shareholders.

6. *Comb.* in the possessive, denoting things (esp. transport) provided for workmen (sense 1), as ***workman's*** (or ***workmen's***) ***bus, club, compensation, train, tram.***

1965 A. PRIOR *Interrogators* xi. 198 An early morning workman's bus roared and rumbled. **1980** 'D. GRANT' *Emerald Decision* i. 20 Workmen's bus, heading for the harbour. **1911** G. B. SHAW *Doctor's Dilemma* I. 22 Except for the workmen's clubs, my patients are all clerks and shopmen. **1921** *Daily Colonist* (Victoria, B.C.) 12 Mar. 6/4 Compensation was paid to him by the Workmen's Compensation Board and he was later discharged as having recovered. **1940** *Economist* 3 Feb. 198/2 An all-round increase in the rates payable for workmen's compensation.

1872 JERROLD *London* p. ix, The workman's train and the crowds pressing over London Bridge. **1975** P. MCCUTCHAN *Very Big Bang* xi. 105 'They'll call back when the current's off.' 'No more workmen's trains?'.. 'Not on this section.' **1906** *Jackson's Oxford Jrnl.* 8 Sept. 6/6 At 5.10 the workmen's tram joined in the procession. **1970** S. ALEXANDER *St. Giles's Fair* 19 The workman's tram passed through St. Giles at five ten a.m.

workmanlike ('wɜːkmənlaɪk), *adv.* and *a.* [See -LIKE.]

A. *adv.* In a manner or style characteristic of a good workman.

1447 *Hist. Dunelm. Scriptores Tres* (Surtees) App. p. cccxiii, The said..Alexander [etc.]..sall wirke the said myne werkmanlike. *c* **1565** J. SPARKE in Hakluyt *Voy.* (1600) III. 504 They..doe iagge their flesh,..as workemanlike, as a Ierkin maker with vs pinketh a ierkin. **1612** DRAYTON *Polyolb.* xviii. 691 The Gardiner..their selected plants doth workman-like bestowe. **1618–19** in Willis & Clark *Cambridge* (1886) III. 305 To be all plastered over with lyme and hayer workeman lyke. **1634** SIR T. HERBERT *Trav.* 20 Darts of blacke Ebony barbed strongly and workmanlike. **1897** 'O. RHOSCOMYL' *White Rose Arno* i, You do your work as workmanlike as ever.

B. *adj.*

1. Of or pertaining to a workman; characteristic of or suitable to a workman. *rare.*

1663 GERBIER *Counsel* 103 To write, in such workman-like termes, as may serve for a Clark of the works to speak unto them. **1857** DICKENS *Dorrit* I. xxvi, An old workmanlike habit of carrying his pocket-handkerchief in his hat.

2. Characteristic of or resembling (that of) a good workman; orig. said of the execution of a work; later applied also to persons or animals having an efficient, 'business-like', or 'smart' appearance or action.

1739 LABELYE *Short Acc. Piers Westm. Bridge* 66 To compleat the intended Bridge..in a compleat and workman-like Manner. **1758** *Extr. Crt. Rolls Wimbledon* (1866) 318 To cause the same [lane] to be restored..in a workmanlike manner. **1768** TUCKER *Lt. Nat.* (1834) I. 475 A clock of artificial and workman-like construction. **1837** DICKENS *Pickw.* xlv, [He] filled out three glasses of gin, which Job Trotter and Sam disposed of in a most workmanlike manner. **1842** LOUDON *Suburban Hort.* 365 In nailing in the young shoots, dispose them as straight and as regular as possible: it will look workmanlike. **1861** WHYTE-MELVILLE *Mkt. Harb.* 58 Never in his life had he seen such a thoroughly workmanlike exterior. **1874** *Fancier's Gaz.* 4 Dec. 618/1 [A dog] Nice and evenly-balanced all over, workman-like. **1878** LORD R. GOWER *Remin.* (1883) II. 207 Two very workman-like little horses. **1884** *Contemp. Rev.* July 98 There is very much..to be done that requires nothing more than good workmanlike ability.

Hence '**workmanlikeness**.

1890 DAY *Every-day Art* 90 Even the amateur should know something of the value of workmanlikeness in ornament.

workmanly ('wɜːkmənlɪ), *adv.* and *a.* [f. WORKMAN *sb.* + -LY.]

A. *adv.* = WORKMANLIKE A.; efficiently, skilfully.

1467 *York Memorandum Bk.* (Surtees) I. 185 Suche girdelles as be clerely and warkmanly made upp. **1523** [COVERDALE] *Old God* (1534) C j, An ymage of his father very cunnyngly and workemanly carued. **1543** BALE *Yet a Course* 27 That he hath not gone processyon vpon saturdayes at euensonge, nor workemanlye made hys holye water and holy breade. **1545** —— *Image Both Ch.* I. Pref. (1550) A vi b, The beastes head that was wounded, is now healed vp againe so workemanly. **1550** —— *Engl. Votaries* II. 104 Here was a gnat workemanly strayned out to swalowe in a camell for it. **1591** HARINGTON *Orl. Fur.* To Rdr. (1634) A 1, Some three or foure pretie pictures (in octavo) cut in brasse very workmanly. **1656** DUGDALE *Antiq. Warw.* 355/2 To make and set up, finely and workmanly, a parclose of timber. **1905** *Times Lit. Suppl.* 1 Sept. 278/2 The four famous folio volumes workmanly bound in grey boards and canvas.

B. *adj.* = WORKMANLIKE B. (esp. sense 2).

1545 BALE *Myst. Inq.* 43 Marke the good workemanlye handelynge..therof. **1570** LEVINS *Manip.* 100/47 Workemanly, *artificiosus*. **1582** MULCASTER *1st Pt. Elem.* (1925) 64 Whatsoeuer shall belong to coloring, to shadowing, and such more workmanlie points. **1590** WEBBE *Trav.* (Arb.) 33 The roofes are couered with fine gold, in a very workemanly sort. **1766** BLACKSTONE *Comm.* II. xxx. 452 He has it upon an implied contract to render it again when made, and that in a workmanly manner. **1860** RUSKIN *Mod. Paint.* V. IX. iii. §4 Rudders, and yards, and cables, all needing workmanly handling and workmanly knowledge. **1907** *Times* 22 May 3/2 Not only the best architectural, but the best workmanly, skill has been employed.

workmanship ('wɜːkmənʃɪp). [f. WORKMAN + -SHIP.]

†**1.** The performance or execution of work or a work; work, labour: in early use often, the labour or amount of labour performed on a particular task or piece of work. *Obs.*

c **1375** *Cursor M.* 1684 (Fairf.) Loke þi werk-monshepe be sleyghe. **1377** LANGL. *P. Pl.* B. x. 288 Þanne shal borel clerkes..drede to wratthe ȝow..ȝowre werkemanship to lette. **1390** GOWER *Conf.* I. 127 With gret sleihte Of werkmanschipe it was begrave. *c* **1407** LYDG. *Reson & Sens.* 6132 Nature..Passeth soothly werke-man-shepe. **1467–8** *Rolls Parlt.* V. 620/1 To oversee the werkemanship of the seid Craftymen. **1503** *Acc. Ld. High Treas. Scot.* II. 206 For making and werkmanship and inlayk of the samyn xx li. **1552** in Feuillerat *Revels Edw. VI* (1914) 124 The charges of garniture & workemanshipp with stuf & other prouisions bought & made of new this year. **1581** PETTIE tr. *Guazzo's Civ. Conv.* I. (1586) 9 b, The knowledge of..handycrafts, of workmanships. *c* **1586** C'TESS PEMBROKE *Ps.* XCIV. ii, Sight shall he want, From whose first workmanshipp the eye did grow? **1612** *Churchw. Acc. Pittington*, etc. (Surtees) 163 Paid for mendinge the bell ropes with leather and workmanshipp, x d. **1617** MORYSON *Itin.* I. 150 A table..the Jewels wherof they valued at fiftie thousand Crownes, and the workmanship at twelve thousand Crownes. **1686** PLOT *Staffordsh.* 297 In case they would be at the charge of bringing stone, he would find Workmanship, and build them a Tower. **1751** LABELYE *Westm. Bridge* 78 All Workmanship to be performed at a fixed Price. **1793** J. LODGE *Topogr. Hist. Heref.* 54 Second year's rent and workmanship 2 3 0. **1818** *Min. Evid. Committee Ribbon Weavers* 195 An instance..where a master took a man up to a magistrate for spoiling the work, and the man paid every penny of the workmanship of it.

†**2.** Action, agency, operation. *Obs.*

1534 MORE *Treat. Passion* Wks. 1343/2 By the woorkemanshippe of his heauenly mercy. **1545** BALE *Myst. Iniq.* 20 b, Eyther has prestes wyues of their owne in those dayes, or els there was some other good workemanshyp a brode. **1546** —— *Engl. Votaries* I. 4 b, The deceytfull workemanshyp of the instrumentes of Sathan. **1641** MILTON *Ch. Govt.* I. v. 19 Before his audacious workmanship the Churches were rul'd in common by the Presbyters.

†**b.** Creation, making, manufacture, production.

1578 TIMME *Calvin on Gen.* 49 After that the workmanshippe of the World was fully perfected. **1594** PLAT *Jewell-ho.* I. 70 That it might haue 3. hot moneths togither to work it to his ful perfection... I haue thought good..to set downe mine own fansie, for the easier stirring vppe of this Malmesey to his workmanship. **1695** WOODWARD *Nat. Hist. Earth* 259 'Tis a great Mystery.. how Tubal-Cain..could ever have taught the Workmanship and Use of them.

†**c.** Make, fashion. *Obs. rare.*

1578 BANISTER *Hist. Man* v. 80 b, As he varied from the workemanshyp of other bodyes, so had he one passage also of choler that visited the ventricle.

3. That which is wrought or made by a workman or craftsman; (a person's) work. Also *transf.* something produced: *arch.* exc. as in ***piece of workmanship***, which may properly belong to 1.

1523 *Act 13 & 14 Hen. VIII*, c. 2 A proper marke..by the which their wares, vessels, and workmanshippes..may be knowen. **1535** COVERDALE *2 Esdras* viii. 7 We all are one workmanshipe of thy handes. **1549** *Compl. Scot.* vii. 69 The pleisand verkmenschips that vas in the middis of hyr mantil. **1551** T. WILSON *Logic* L ij b, The daie..whiche is the effecte, or woorkemanship of the Sunne. **1570** DEE *Math. Pref.* a ij, Formally, Number, is the Vnion, and Vnitie of Vnits. Which vnyting and knitting, is the workemanship of our minde. **1632** LITHGOW *Trav.* I. 18 To worship..the workemanship of mens hands. **1641** J. JACKSON *True Evang. T.* III. 183 It was the onely quarrell he pickt with his workmanship, that man was alone. **1710** PRIOR *Examiner* No. 6 ⁋2 A curious Piece of poetical Workmanship. **1729** BUTLER *Serm.* Wks. 1874 II. 102 Human nature, considered as the divine workmanship. **1732** BERKELEY *Alciphr.* VII. §12 Inconsistent ideas which are often the workmanship of their own brains. **1751** *Affect. Narr. Wager* 28 A little Hut,..the Workmanship, I guess, of some Indian. **1796** H. HUNTER tr. *St. Pierre's Study Nat.* xi. III. 266 This ball is the workmanship of the ants. **1857** RUSKIN *Pol. Econ. Art* i. 63 A new piece of gold or silver..with noble workmanship on it. **1859** GEO. ELIOT *Adam Bede* xiv, There's no denying she's a rare bit o' workmanship. **1892** WESTCOTT *Gospel of Life* 200 As the world was His workmanship; so man was made in His image.

4. Skill or cunning as a workman; craftsmanship as exhibited in a piece of work.

1529 *Burgh Rec. Edin.* (1871) 6 Of gud and sufficient stuff ..and sufficient werkmanschip. **1541** COPLAND *Galyen's Terap.* 2 C iv, For to cut is a redy and easy thynge, but for to heale by medycamentes is a greater thynge and that requyreth workemanshyp. **1601** R. JOHNSON *Kingd. & Commw.* (1603) 68 The inhabitants..doe excell in curious woorkmanshippe and mechanicall inventions. **1663** BOYLE *Usef. Exp. Nat. Philos.* I. i. 17 Idiots admire in things the Beauty of their Materials, but Artists that of the Workmanship. **1678** MOXON *Mech. Exerc.* iv. 66 It is counted a piece of good workmanship in a Joyner, to have the craft of bearing his hand so curiously even. **1838** MISS MITFORD in L'Estrange *Life* (1870) III. vi. 93 Some rings of negro workmanship. **1889** *Contemp. Rev.* Dec. 911 It is subject..that makes plays enduring, *plus* of course the requisite dramatic workmanship. **1909** *Mem. W. E. H. Lecky* 48 He had a high ideal of literary workmanship.

'**work-,master**. Now *rare.* [Cf. MLG. *werkmêster*, ON. *verkmeistari* (MSw. *werkmestare*).] A master workman; an overseer or employer of workmen.

a **1533** FRITH *Disput. Purgat.* II. H vij b, Lyke a wyse workemaster haue I layed the fundacyon, for I fyrst beganne to preche you Christ. **1535** COVERDALE *Song Sol.* vii. 1 Like a fayre iewell, which is wrought by a connynge workmaster. *a* **1589** M. PHILIPS in Hakluyt *Voy.* 580, I came to Siuill, and sought me out a workemaster, that I might fall to my science, which was weauing of taffataes. **1617** WOODALL *Surg. Mate* Wks. (1639) 193 This medicine..to an Artist which is a true Preparer of medicines..is plaine and pleasant to be done, and..will doe the worke-master credit that useth it. **1632** in E. B. Jupp *Carpenters' Co.* (1887) 297 That the workmaster be left at Liberty to make choyce whether he will have a Carpenter or Joyner to lay the same. **1703** T. N. *City & C. Purchaser* Title-p., Contracts betwixt the Workmaster and Workman. **1816** COLERIDGE *Lay Serm.* (Bohn) 307 The contents of every work must correspond to the character and designs of the work-master. **1876** BANCROFT *Hist. U.S.* IV. xxiv. 492 Like a bravo who loves his trade, he set about the task of his work-masters.

b. *fig.*: esp. applied to God as creator and ruler; rarely of a thing.

1535 COVERDALE *Job* xiii. 4 Ye are workmasters of lyes. —— *Wisd.* vii. 22 The worckmaster of all thinges hath taught me wyszdome. *a* **1548** HALL *Chron., Hen. VIII*, 198 These moste solempne ordinaunces of ye most high workemaster God. **1605** *London Prodigal* III. ii. 93 Nature, in her building, is a most curious worke-maister. **1607** MARKHAM *Cavel.* I. xix. (1617) 79 The braine of a man being a busie and laborsome workmaister. **1630** LENNARD tr. *Charron's Wisd.* I. iii. 16 The armes and hands, the workemasters of all things. *Ibid.* lxi. 225 The greatnesse, goodnesse, wisdome, power of the chiefe work-master.

'**work-,mistress.** [f. WORK *sb.* + MISTRESS, after prec.] A woman who controls or superintends work: only *fig.*, chiefly of Nature (personified).

1568 HACKET tr. *Thevet's New found World* lxviii. 108 b, Nature the great workemistresse. **1603** HOLLAND *Plutarch's Mor.* 337, I assure you Venus is the work-mistresse of mutuall concord. *a* **1635** NAUNTON *Fragm. Reg.* (Arb.) 60 God,..by an evident manifestation, that the same work which she acted, was a well-pleasing service of his own..had decreed the protection of the work-Mistresse. **1675** A. BROWNE *Appendix Art Paint.* 22 Since Nature, that Cunning Work-Mistress, is so extremely Various in her Representations. **1877** CARPENTER tr. *Tiele's Outl. Hist. Relig.* 224 Athena, the goddess of art, the 'workmistress' (*Ergané*).

'**work-out.** [See WORK *v.* 38 l.] **a.** A boxing bout for practice; more widely, an exercise session, practice, or test.

1909 R. A. WASON *Happy Hawkins* 161, I expect to give it a fair good work-out before I'm through with it. **1923** H. C. WITWER *Fighting Blood* iii. 96, I ain't going to get no gym workout. **1927** *Daily Express* 27 May 13/7 Either in a work-out or in an actual contest. **1938** M. K. RAWLINGS *Yearling* ix. 98 'Will we take both dogs?' 'Nobody but old Julia. She ain't had a work-out since she was hurt. A slow hunt'll do her good.' **1952** *Sun* (Baltimore) 3 Mar. 28/3 The United States Air Force Filter Center here had its first surprise workout yesterday. **1960** *Sunday Express* 27 Nov. 14/3 Work-out gymnasia with..general slimming equipment. **1963** A. ROSS *Australia 63* vii. 128 Both teams had work-outs at the Oval, over-watered pitches making net practice impracticable. **1972** *Daily Tel.* 6 Sept. 6/8, I am not suggesting that old people should do strenuous physical work-outs, but stiff joints and muscles may be helped by properly supervised exercises. **1979** *Tucson Mag.* Apr. 56/1 (Advt.), A multitude of weight training systems designed to accommodate your kind of workout room. **1981** J. FONDA *Jane Fonda's Workout Bk.* (1982) 22 She took me to an exercise class that put me through the most vigorous and thorough workout I had ever had.

b. *fig.*

1934 J. O'HARA *Appointment in Samarra* i. 17 Four of the young men had had work-outs with her off the dance floor, and as a result Constance was not a virgin. **1941** *Punch* 10 Sept. 222 This passage of rich prose is designed as a sort of test or work-out for the new alphabet. **1958** B. HAMILTON *Too Much of Water* viii. 161 A public work-out would test audience reaction. **1967** *Melody Maker* 29 Apr. 10 (Advt.), The totally new snare drum. This one you must see! Get round to your dealer and give it a workout. **1977** *New Yorker* 24 Oct. 173/1 The Villa-Lobos provides a thorough workout for the bassoon.

'**workover.** [f. WORK *v.* + OVER *adv.*] The repair or maintenance of an oil well.

1976 *Offshore Platforms & Pipelining* 232/3 A conventional wellhead is installed, and the wells are completed by a workover rig. **1977** *Financial Times* 1 Apr. 11/5 Some have suggested a well work-over every three years; others say once every 15 years will be sufficient. **1977** *Offshore Engineer* Aug. 12/3 The workover programme on B-14 well is now complete. **1980** *Daily Tel.* 11 Sept. 29 (Advt.), Jack Up Rig in the Southern North Sea on Viking workovers and new developments. **1985** *New Yorker* 22 Apr. 51/1 The auction business thrived: deep rigs, workover rigs.

workpeople ('wɜːkˌpiːp(ə)l). [WORK *sb.*] People employed in manual or industrial labour for a wage; workmen and (or) workwomen.

1708 *Caldwell Papers* (Maitland Club) I. 216 You cannot imagine what a parcel of cheating brutes the work people here are. **1818** *Min. Evid. Committee Ribbon Weavers* 152 How many people do they employ, weavers, warpers, winders and work people, of every description? **1848** MILL *Pol. Econ.* I. iv. §1 (1865) I. 69 Each capitalist has money, which he pays to his workpeople, and so enables them to supply themselves. **1883** W. D. CURZON *Manuf. Industries Worcs.* 36 Mechanical skill on the part of the workpeople not being necessary—the machines in fact doing the most part of the work.

workshop ('wɜːkʃɒp). [f. WORK *sb.* + SHOP *sb.* 3.] **1. a.** A room, apartment, or building in which manual or industrial work is carried on.

1582 T. WATSON *Centurie of Love* Ep. Ded. (Arb.) 25 Alexander the Great, passing on a time by the workeshop of Apelles, curiouslie surueyed some of his doinges. **1775** JOHNSON *West. Isl.* 132 (*Ostig*) Supreme beauty is seldom found in cottages or work shops. **1813** CLARKSON *Mem. W. Penn* xviii. 335 All prisons were to be considered as workshops. **1865** DICKENS *Mut. Fr.* I. ii, What was observable in the furniture, was observable in the Veneerings—the surface smelt a little too much of the workshop and was a trifle sticky. **1901** *Act 1 Edw. VII*, c. 22 §149 The expression 'workshop' means..any premises, room or place, not being a factory, in which..or within the close or curtilage or precincts of which..any manual labour is exercised.

b. *transf.* and *fig.*

1562 T. NORTON *Calvin's Inst.* Table s.v. *Supper of Lord*, The constitution which toke away from lay men the cup of the Lorde, came out of the deuells workshop. **1781** GIBBON *Decl. & F.* xvii. II. 62 *note*, Two accurate treatises, which come from the workshop of the Benedictines. **1814** SCOTT *Wav.* lii, Fergus's brain was a perpetual workshop of scheme and intrigue. **1838** DISRAELI *Sp.* 15 Mar. in *Hansard's Parl. Debates* XLI. 939/2 To suppose that..the continent would suffer England to be the workshop for the world. **1878** GURNEY *Crystallogr.* 8 The workshop of Nature. **1900** W. P. KER *Ess. Dryden* Introd. p. xxi, If he cannot explain the secrets of the dramatic workshop.

c. *attrib.*

1869 J. G. WINTON (*title*) Modern Workshop Practice as applied to marine, land, and locomotive engines. **1873** SPON (*title*) Workshop Receipts, for the use of manufacturers, mechanics, and scientific amateurs. **1902** *Daily Chron.* 29 Apr. 3/5 The workshop system answers because the master works with his men, and gets the best out of them.

2. a. A meeting for discussion, study, experiment, etc., orig. in education or the arts, but now in any field; an organization or group established for this purpose.

1937 *N.Y. Times* 1 Aug. VI. 5/3 The major requirement for admission to this Summer workshop is an approved project for which the applicant seeks aid and advice. **1938** L. MACNEICE *Mod. Poetry* xi. 200 The communist poet, Maiakovski, established a 'word workshop'.. to supply all revolutionaries with 'any quantity of poetry desired'. **1952** L. ROSS *Picture* (1953) 21 The elder Reinhardt.. came to Hollywood in 1934... For the next five years, he ran a Hollywood school known as Max Reinhardt's Workshop. **1959** *Ottawa Citizen* 14 Sept. 6/1 At a conference or 'workshop' on road safety sponsored by the Ontario Department of Transport recently, there was general agreement that much more must be done to improve driving standards. **1961** in *B.B.C. Handbk.* (1962) 36, I want to see a Television Workshop—a regular period in which everyone feels he can have a go without having to mind too much whether he is successful straight off. **1967** P. MCGIRR *Murder is Absurd* ii. 33 In college Kenny joined the.. drama workshop and began work on a play. **1972** *Computers & Humanities* VII. 96 The participants then divided into four workshops and, after five intensive meetings, reconvened to present their findings at the fourth and final plenary session. **1984** *Times* 17 Mar. 15/8 Priority bookings for their tastings, wine workshops and special dinners.

b. *attrib.*

1937 *N.Y. Times* 1 Aug. VI. 5/4 The importance of the workshop idea to American education. **1968** *Globe & Mail* (Toronto) 3 Feb. B 2/3 Local residents considered.. 17 consumer protection items suggested by workshop groups conducted on Thursday. **1976** S. BRETT *So much Blood* ii. 25 The Masonic Hall was not free for Charles to rehearse in... Michael Vanderzee had just started a workshop session... Charles.. had no objection to.. workshop techniques. They were useful exercises for actors. **1983** *National Trust* Spring 24/1 In the morning, group discussions were led by the Company's seven actor/teachers in a 'workshop' atmosphere concentrating on the social history of the early eighteenth century.

†**ˈwork-ˌsilver.** *Obs.* [WORK *sb.* 5.] A customary money payment made in lieu of service.

1391 *Ancient Deed* A. 1413 (P.R.O.), Septemdecim solidis annuis vocatis Werkseluer. **1430** *Ibid.* A. 8351, xvijs annuis vocatis Werkseluer et quinque solidis annuis vocatis lesowseluer. **1544** *Patent Roll 36 Hen. VIII* p. 3. m. 4 (P.R.O.) Proficua nostra quecumque vocata le Custumary Worke Syluer in hemyngforde abbatis. [**1795** LYSONS *Environs Lond.* II. 564 The Tenants services due formerly in this manor [Sudbury] seem to have been commuted for certain sums of money called work-silver.]

ˈworksome, *a. nonce-wd.* [f. WORK *sb.* or *v.* + -SOME.] Explained in Dicts. as = Industrious, diligent; but perh. modelled on G. *wirksam* efficacious, operative.

1837 CARLYLE *Fr. Rev.* III. VI. vi, Equality, Frugality, worksome Blessedness.

work station. Also ˈworkstation. [f. WORK *sb.* + STATION *sb.*] **1.** A location at which one stage in the manufacture or assembly of a product is carried out before it is moved on for the next stage.

1950 T. M. LANDY *Production Planning & Control* vii. 161 The assigning of work stations by the planners is largely influenced by these considerations: costs, centralization of work within a section.. and existing labor load. **1980** M. P. GROOVER *Automation, Production Systems & Computer-Aided Manufacturing* iv. 66 An automated flow line consists of several machines or workstations which are linked together by work handling devices that transfer parts between the stations.

2. A desk with a computer terminal and keyboard; the terminal itself.

1977 *Which Computer?* Sept. 25 Another cavil on the workstation is the absence of a 'home' key to return the cursor to the head of a new page. **1981** *Office* June 23/1 Wordcom 70 can be used as a shared facility system with up to eight work-stations using the cartridge disk. In this way a number of departments can have access to a single database. **1983** *What's New in Computing* Jan. 53 (Advt.), Featured above in teak: printer stand, linking quadrant and 3′ by 2′ workstation with monitor shelf. **1985** *Which Computer?* Apr. 122/3 It can then be viewed by users at any workstation attached to the system.

work-to-contract, work-to-rule: see WORK *v.* 27 d.

ˈwork-up. [f. vbl. phr. to *work up*: see WORK *v.* 40.] **1.** *Printing.* A piece of spacing material that works loose in the forme and prints a smudge, or the mark so printed. Also, an instance of this.

1948 R. R. KARCH *Graphic Arts Procedures* x. 270 The pressfeeder watches the sheets carefully so that if *work-ups* appear he will not spoil the run. A work-up is spacing material that has risen in the form so that it prints on the sheet. **1950** D. G. HYMES *Production in Advertising* vii. 279 Alert pressmen can.. stop the press, and hammer down the workups after only a few sheets have been spoiled. **1967** KARCH & BUBER *Offset Processes* ii. 24 The letterpress printer may be plagued by 'work-up'.

2. *Med.* A diagnostic examination of a patient. orig. *U.S.*

1961 in WEBSTER. **1966** *Current Diagnosis* 206/2 (*heading*) Diagnostic work-up for patients with diastolic hypertension. **1972** *Sci. Amer.* Aug. 71/3 A mother who was told that her child would be 'admitted for a work-up' did not realise that he was to be hospitalized. **1977** *New Yorker* 12 Sept. 103/1 We gave him the usual workup, including neurological and ear-nose-and-throat evaluations. **1978** PARSONS & SOMMERS *Gynecol.* (ed. 2) xx. 313/2 A few cases where the borderline between virilism and hirsutism is hazy will benefit from an extensive work-up.

3. *Chem.* The experimental procedures followed to separate and purify substances for analysis or the products of a chemical reaction.

1967 *Chem. Abstr.* LXVII. 10187/2 (*heading*) Workup of chlorohydrin process waste products. **1971** *Canad. Jrnl. Chem.* XLIX. 2467/1 The resulting mixture was then heated to reflux for 1 h to complete the acetylation and gave after usual work-up a quantitative yield of [compound] 12. **1978** *Jrnl. Amer. Chem. Soc.* C. 3548 Water added during work-up serving as the proton source at C-1.

4. The process of bringing a ship into seaworthy condition.

1971 *Daily Colonist* (Victoria, B.C.) 27 May 35/4 Canadian forces ships work on a 20-month cycle basis containing four parts: refit, trials, workups, and operational. **1978** *Navy News* Oct. 2/6 After trials and work-up the Achilles will return to Chatham for Christmas.

workwise (ˈwɜːkwaɪz), *adv.* [f. WORK *sb.* + -WISE.] As far as work is concerned.

1962 *Punch* 6 June 864/1 Workwise, your future is clear. **1979** *Yale Alumni Mag.* Apr. (Suppl.) cn32/1 Although Carol has kept herself busy (workwise) she managed to spend Thanksgiving in Portugal. **1981** S. JACKMAN *Game of Soldiers* I. ii. 33 The unit ticks over well enough work-wise. .. Trouble is, there's not enough work.

workwoman (ˈwɜːkˌwʊmən). [f. WORK *sb.*, after *workman.*] A woman who works; a female worker or operative; †a woman who does needlework.

1530 PALSGR. 290/1 Workewoman, *ouueriere*. **1581** A. HALL *Iliad* VI. 119 That they good workewomen may bin. **1584** R. SCOT *Discov. Witchcr.* XIII. iv. 291 Wherein.. nature sheweth hir selfe a proper workwoman. **1591** SPENSER *Muiopotmos* 260 The most fine-fingred workwoman on ground. **1626** T. H[AWKINS] *Caussin's Holy Crt.* 5 Vertue is a merueylous worke-woman, who can make Mercury of any wood. **1675** HOBBES *Odyssey* (1677) 188 One of these merchants sooth'd her into sin: For good work-women may be made do that. **1755** JOHNSON, *Workwoman*.. 2. A woman that works for hire. **1843** *Penny Cycl.* XXVII. 180/1 While the work-woman produces a kind of chain-work on the surface of the muslin. **1865** ESQUIROS *Cornwall* 74 The work-women of the mines. **1882** BESANT *All Sorts* xxxix. (1898) 263 To live here as a workwoman among other workwomen.

Hence **ˈworkˌwomanlike** *a.* or *adv.*, **-ˌwomanly** *a.*

1641 C. VAN PAS *Les abus du Mariage* Pl. 4, I now am Mistris of my crafte, and can Worke-womanlike deale in it. **1894** *Westm. Gaz.* 14 Nov. 6/2 The silver spade, to which she put her foot in true workwomanly fashion.

worky (ˈwɜːkɪ). *U.S.* [f. WORK *sb.* + -Y⁶.] A worker or operative. Also *attrib.*

1833 T. HAMILTON *Men & Manners Amer.* (1843) 171 The operative class [of New York] have already formed themselves into a society, under the name of 'The Workies'. *Ibid.* 175 The *Worky* convention. **1855** HT. MARTINEAU *Autobiog.* (1877) II. 305 The reasons why no gentry were admitted were,.. because there was no room for more than the 'workies'. **1894** *Sunday Reform Leaflet* (Columbus, Ohio) Sept. 5 Take away this rest-day, and you.. turn us into a nation of mere 'workies'.

workyday, obs. var. WORKADAY.

†**worl,** *v. Obs.* prob. var. WHIRL *v.*

c **1530** *Songs, Carols*, etc. (E.E.T.S.) 126 All þat euer myght it here, They myght not them self asstere, But worled on a hepe. *c* **1600** CHALKHILL *Thealma* 1577 Why do you kneel?.. I know No worth in me to worl you down so low.

worlais, obs. pl. of WARLOCK.

a **1300** *Hayl Mari* 15 in *Minor Poems fr. Vernon MS.* 755 þe worlais, þai wil be her Fort take þair pray.

world (wɜːld), *sb.* Forms: α. 1 weorold, wuruld, worold, uorold, wiarald, 1–3 weoruld, woruld, -eld, -old, 2 wurold, 3 we(o)reld, wæruld, *Orm.* we(o)relld. β. 1– world; 1–3 weorld, 4–6 worlde (2 worlð, 3 wurld, 5 whorlld(e); 2–3 werlð, 3 *Orm.* werrld, 3–5 werld(e; *north.* and *Sc.* 3– warld, 5–6 warlde, varld, (5 warlede). γ. 4–6 wordle, 5 wordel, wordil; *north.* and *Sc.* 5–7 wardle, 6 wardill, vardil, wardel, vardel; 3 werdle. δ. 3–6 word, 4–5 worde (6 woaude); 3–5 werd, 4–5 werde; 4 wird; *north.* 4, 6 ward. ε. 3 worl, 3–5 worle, 5 worlle, orlle, 6 worell; 8 worl', *north.* and *Sc.* 5 warle, 8 warl', 9 warl. [Com. Teut. (wanting in Gothic): OE. *weorold, worold, world* str. f., rarely m., corresp. to OFris. *wrald, ruald, warld* (EFris. *warld*, WFris. *wrôd*), OS. *werold* (MLG. *werlt, warlt*, LG. *werld*, MDu. *werelt*, Du. *wereld*), OHG. *weralt* (MHG. *werelt, werlt, welt*, G. *welt*), ON. *veröld* (Sw. *verld*, Da. *verden*): a formation peculiar to Germanic, f. *wer-* man, WERE *sb.*¹ + *ald-* age (cf. OLD *a.*, ELD *sb.*²), the etymological meaning being, therefore, 'age' or 'life of man'.]

I. Human existence; a period of this.

1. a. Chiefly ***this world, the world***: the earthly state of human existence; this present life.

to (*unto*, OE. *oð*) *the world's end*: as long as human things shall last, to the end of time (with admixture of senses 7, 9). Similarly in phrases such as ***as long as the*** or ***this world lasts***, and ***in this world***.

832 *Charter* in Sweet *O.E. Texts* 447 Ðet he ðas god forðleste oð wiaralde ende. *c* **897** ÆLFRED *Gregory's Past. C.* xviii. 137 [Hi] ne dooð him nan oðer god ðisse weorolde. **971** *Blickl. Hom.* 57 We witon þæt ælc wlite.. to ende efsteþ & onetteþ þisse weorlde lifes. *c* **1200** *Vices & Virtues* 17 'Andswere me'.. he wile seggen, 'hwat hafst ðu swa lange idon on ðare woreld?' *c* **1205** LAY. 5028 þa wifmon þa þe a ðas weoreld ibær. *c* **1250** *Kent. Serm.* in *O.E. Misc.* 33 þet ha yef us swiche werkes to done in þise wordle þet þo saulen of us mote bien isauued a domes dai. *c* **1250** *Gen. & Ex.* 32 Fader.. ðu giue me seli timinge To thaunen ðis werdes biginninge. *a* **1300** *Cursor M.* 91 Quat bote is to sette traueil On thyng.. þat es bot fantum o þis warld? *c* **1300** *Havelok* 2335 Was neuere yete ioie more In al þis werd, þan þo was þore. *c* **1374** CHAUCER *Troylus* v. 1058 Allas of me vn-to þe worldis ende Schal noþer ben wretyn noþer I-songe No good word. *c* **1400** *26 Pol. Poems* i. 123 They han here heuene in this world here. **1426** AUDELAY *Poems* 12 Ale the wyt of this word fallus to foly. *c* **1450** HOLLAND *Howlat* 43 Wa is me, wretche in this warld, wilsome of wane! **1451** *Paston Lett.* I. 189 In this werd that now is. **1513** *Life Hen. V* (1911) 22 Yearelie to be distributed.. twenty pounds in pence to the poore people duringe the Worlde. **1570** *Satir. Poems Reform.* x. 36 He sall with vs rest, And we with him, sa lang as warld may lest. **1590** SHAKS. *Com. Err.* II. ii. 108 Time himselfe is bald, and therefore to the worlds end, will haue bald followers. **1597** —— *2 Hen. IV*, v. iii. 102, I prethee now deliuer them, like a man of this World. **1670** T. BLOUNT *Acad. Eloq.* (ed. 4) 230 The Heir of a Knight in the right line shall be an Esquire to the worlds end. **1794** PALEY *Evid.* II. ii. §8 A Christian's chief care being to pass quietly through this world to a better. **1797** JANE AUSTEN *Sense & Sensib.* xliv, 'As to that,' said he, 'I must rub through the world as well as I can.' **1856** DICKENS *Christmas Stories* (1874) 43 She was too good for this world and for me, and she died six weeks before our marriage-day.

b. With reference to birth or death; esp. ***to bring into the world***, to give birth to (see BRING *v.* 7 c); ***to come into*** (or ***to***) ***the world***, to be born (see COME *v.* 4 c); *fig.* (of a book) to be published; ***to go*** or ***depart out of this world***.

Beowulf 60 Ðæm feower bearn forð ȝerimed in worold wocun. *a* **1000** *Genesis* 2284 þu scealt, Agar, Abrahame sunu on woruld bringan. *a* **1000** *Epist. Alex.* in Cockayne *Narrat.* (1861) 31 Ðin modor ȝewiteð of weorulde þurh scondlicne deað. *c* **1205** LAY. 17235 He sæt stille alse þeh he wolde of worlden iwiten. *c* **1250** *Gen. & Ex.* 2389 Ic sal to min sune fare.. or ic of werlde chare. **1297** R. GLOUC. (Rolls) 5116 & þe nyenteþe day of aueryl out of þis worl he wende. [**1382**, *c* **1510**– [see COME *v.* 4 c]. *a* **1400–50** *Wars Alex.* 2653 (Dubl.) Qwen he went of þis warld. *c* **1420** *Chron. Vilod.* 3953 þaw y shulde now ouȝt of þis worde gone. **1579** RANDOLPH *Let.* in Buchanan *Wks.* (S.T.S.) 56 The last little Treatise.. that lately come into the World. *c* **1588** *Cath. Tractates* (S.T.S.) 250 Not doutand bot angels and sanctis depairted out of this wardle may and do pray for us. **1607** [see BRING *v.* 7 c]. **1784** BURNS *Addr. Illeg. Child* iv, My funny toil is now a' tint, Sin' thou came to the warl asklent. **1914** 'IAN HAY' *Knt. on Wheels* xiii. §3 Having been born into the world with a club foot.

c. without article (with blending of sense 7): †(*a*) ***on, o, in world***, in this life, on earth.

c **900** tr. *Bæda's Hist.* IV. xxiii. (1890) 332 Eal þæt heo for worulde [*v.r.* on weorulde] hæfde. *c* **1175** *Lamb. Hom.* 111 Vnclene wif þoleð scome on weorlde & unclene wif bið unwurð on liue. *c* **1205** LAY. 22069 þe king for-bæd heom .. þat na mon on worlde swa wod no iwurðe.. þat his grið bræke. *Ibid.* 23475 þat nuste he neuere on weorlde hu feole þusend þer weoren. *c* **1220** *Bestiary* 120 An wirm is o werlde, wel man it knoweð. *c* **1300** *Havelok* 1349 Hwore so he o worde aren. **13..** *Gaw. & Gr. Knt.* 871 Wheþen in worlde he were, Hit semed as he myȝt Be prynce. *c* **1320** *Sir Tristr.* 1270 In warld was non so wiis Of craft þat men knewe. **1457** HARDING *Chron.* i. in *Engl. Hist. Rev.* (1912) Oct. 740 This book.. Whiche no man hath in worlde bot oonly ye. *c* **1475** *Partenay* 3816 Pray for me All dais while lif in worle here haue ye.

†(*b*) in genitive = temporal, earthly, secular: freq. in ***world's*** (***worldes***) ***riches, wealth, win*** (WIN *sb.*² 2), and the like. *Obs.* (in later use *Sc.*)

Beowulf 2343 Ende ȝebidan worulde lifes. *c* **1175**, etc. [see WIN *sb.*² 2]. *c* **1200** *Trin. Coll. Hom.* 51 þe hie weren wuniende in ierusalem.. and hadden þe fulle of wurldes richeisse. *c* **1250** *Gen. & Ex.* 48 Hise wise sune, Ðe was of hin fer ear bi-foren Or ani werldes time boren. *a* **1300** *Cursor M.* 8314 Salamon.. sal be a man o pes, And mikel haf o werldes es. *Ibid.* 12416 To sett iesu to werld lar. **1390** GOWER *Conf.* I. 362 For coveitise and worldes pride. ? *a* **1400** *Morte Arth.* 674 Alle my werdez wele. *c* **1400** LOVE *Bonavent. Mirr.* xxxiii. (1908) 159 Forsakynge all worldes besynesse. **1508** DUNBAR *Poems* vi. 34 A barell bung ay at my bosum, Of varldis gud I bad na mair. **1611** J. DAVIES (Heref.) *Of Work of Sylvester* 52 S.'s Wks. 816 For whose deare birth, thou didst all ease refuse, Worlds-weal, and (being a Marchant) thy Receits. **1606** G. WOODCOCKE *Hist. Justine* 15 b, When he saw they would not sel their liberty for any worldes good. **1781** BURNS *My Nanie, O* vi, My riches a's my penny-fee..; But warl's gear ne'er troubles me. **1786** —— *To Mr. J. Kennedy* iv, Now if ye're ane o' warl's folk, Wha rate the wearer by the cloak. *a* **1796** —— *Now bank & brae* ii, The chield wha boasts o' warld's wealth. **1820** *Blackw. Mag.* May 165 Let warld's gear gang.

d. ***the other, another, the next, a better world, the world to come*** or ***to be***: the future state, the life after death. Sometimes viewed as the 'realm' of departed spirits.

c **1000** *Ags. Gosp.* Matt. xii. 32 Ne byð hyt hym forȝyfen, ne on þisse worulde, ne on þære toweardan [**1382** WYCLIF, nether in this world, ne in the tother; **1526** TINDALE, nether in this worlde, nether in the worlde to come]. *c* **1200** ORMIN 4192 Ressteda33..tacneþþ all þatt resste & ro þ att hallȝhe sawless brukenn Inn oþerr werelld. **1548–9** *Bk. Com. Prayer, Nicene Creed*, The lyfe of the worlde to come. **1581** HAMILTON in *Cath. Tractates* (S.T.S.) 73 The horribill tormentis preparit for thame in the varld to cum. **1611** BEAUM. & FL. *Philaster* IV. iii, Will there be no slanders, No jealousies in the other world? **1715** I. MATHER *Several Serm.* title-p., When Godly Men dye, Angels carry their Souls to another and a better World. **1738** WESLEY *Hymn, 'Attend while God's Eternal Son'* v, Far from..Sin, and Earth, and Hell, In the new World thy Grace hath made, May I for ever dwell! **1770** GOLDSM. *Des. Vill.* 170 He..Allured to brighter worlds, and led the way. *a* **1796** BURNS *Epit. on Friend* 7 If there's another world, he lives in bliss. **1809** MAGEE *Atonement* (1816) II. 107 The appellation, 'mighty dead',..becomes applicable to all the inhabitants of the invisible world. **1816** SHELLEY *Mont Blanc* 49 Some say that gleams of a remoter world Visit the soul in sleep,—that death is slumber. **1846** TENNYSON *Golden Year* 56 'Tis like the second world to us that live. **1864** —— *En. Ard.* 899 Who will embrace me in the world-to-be.

e. *gen.* A state of (present or future) existence.

c **1300** *Beket* 77 Heo..ȝeode aboute as a best..As heo were of another wordle. **1602** SHAKS. *Ham.* IV. v. 134 Both the worlds I giue to negligence, Let come what comes. **1807** WORDSW. *Ode Intim. Immortality* 149 Blank misgivings of a Creature Moving about in worlds not realised. **1859** FITZGERALD *Omar* xxv, All the Saints and Sages who discuss'd Of the Two Worlds so learnedly.

2. The pursuits and interests of this present life; *esp.*, in religious use, the least worthy of these; temporal or mundane affairs. † ***world's*** = worldly.

a **1000** *Guthlac* 399 [370] Ne won he æfter worulde ac he in wuldre ahof modes wynne. *a* **1300** *Cursor M.* 10103 Thrin fas..þis werld, my fleche, þe warlau als. **1340** *Ayenb.* 92 Þe more þet [me] lykeþ þe zuetnesse of þe wordle, þe lesse me wylneþ þe zuetnesse of god. *c* **1410** *Master of Game* (MS. Digby 182) Prol. lf. 4, Þe devel, þe worlde, ande the flessh. *c* **1425** *Cast. Persev.* 192 in *Macro Plays* 83 Who-so spekyth a-ȝeyn þe werd, In a presun he schal be sperd. *Ibid.* 1009, 107 Þe Werld, þe Flesch, & þe Devyl, are knowe grete lordis. **1540** PALSGR. *Acolastus* I. iii. F iv, Bycause he is so sore sette, or to gredy vpon the world, or his thrift. **1564** J. MARTIALL *Treat. Crosse* 17 Christ hath subdued sinne, conquered the worlde, discomfited the deuil. **1579** SPENSER *Sheph. Cal.* May 73 Ah Palinodie, thou art a worldes childe: Who touches Pitch mought needes be defilde. **1675** OWEN *Indwelling Sin* ii. (1732) 17 Whence is it, that Men follow and pursue the World with so much greediness? **1780** COWPER *Love of the World Reproved* 25 Renounce the world —the preacher cries. **1784** —— *Task* II. 389 Infidelity and love of world. **1807** WORDSW. *Misc. Sonn.* I. xxxiii. 1 The world is too much with us. **1843** J. MARTINEAU *Chr. Life* xvii. 255 The world..i.e. the opportunities of action with a view to temporal good. **1882** SEELEY *Nat. Relig.* II. i. 130 The World is the collective character of those who do not worship.

3. a. The affairs and conditions of life; chiefly in phr., esp. with the verb *go* (e.g. ***how the world goes***, how events shape themselves; ***how goes the world with*** (a person), how are his affairs; ***as the*** (or ***this***) ***world goes***, as things are, considering the state of affairs); also † ***to let the world slide***, to allow things to take their course, to leave matters alone; ***to let the world wag*** (see WAG *v.* 7 c).

Beowulf 1739 Ac him eal worold wendeð on willan. *c* **888** ÆLFRED *Boeth.* xxvi. §1 Ðeþenc þu nu..Boetius..hwæðer þin woruld þa eall wære æfter þinum willan. *a* **1000** *Cædmon's Gen.* 318 Hyra woruld wæs ʒehwyrfed. **1362** LANGL. *P. Pl.* A. Prol. 19 A Feir feld ful of folk fond I þer bi-twene,..Worchinge and wondringe as þe world askeþ. **13..** *Gaw. & Gr. Knt.* 530 & wynter wyndez agayn, as þe worlde askez. ? *c* **1460–5** *MS. Trin. Coll. Dubl.* D. 4, 18 in *Archaeologia* XXIX. 341 Trust not..youre foos, For þei be double in wirking, as þe worlde gos. **1478** *Paston Lett.* III. 232 William Paston..paid to the parson..xxiiij*li*... It is yerly worth, as the world goth now, x*li.* **1481** *Cely Papers* (Camden) 81 Howr father..thynkes the whorllde qwhessy ..and therfor he whowlde that ze gepart not yowrselfe to hofton to Bregys. *a* **1529–** [see WAG *v.* 7 c]. **1540** PALSGR. *Acolastus* IV. iv. T iij, What is the matter, or howe gothe the worlde with hym? **1564** BULLEIN *Dial. agst. Pest.* (1888) 26 Now let vs go..and see how the worlde goeth with Master Antonius. **1570** FOXE *A. & M.* (ed. 2) 1848/1 What a Gospeller [he]..was in King Edwardes tyme, which now turning with the world, sheweth him self such a bytter Persecuter..in Queene Maries time. **1596, 1611** [see SLIDE *v.* 5 b]. **1602** SHAKS. *Ham.* II. ii. 178 To be honest as this world goes, is to bee one man pick'd out of two thousand. *Ibid.* III. ii. 285 Some must watch, while some must sleepe; So runnes the world away. *a* **1677** BARROW *Serm.* Wks. 1686 III. 74 However the world goes, we may yet make a tolerable shift. **1713** POPE *Let. to Addison* Wks. 1737 VI. 32 And give me leave to tell you, that (as the world goes) this is no small assurance I repose in you. **1855** DICKENS etc. *Househ. Words* Christmas No. 23/1 How's the world used you since this morning? **1862** H. KINGSLEY *Ravenshoe* xviii, The world is out of joint. **1886** BARING-GOULD *Crt. Royal* iv, What was the world coming to, when the police poked their noses into his shop?

†**b.** State of human affairs, state of things; hence, season or time as marked by the state of affairs. *Obs.*

1456 *Paston Lett.* I. 402 And as for the iiij[xx] *li.* to be sette on Olivere is taile, I can not see it wole be, for there is noo suche worlde to bringe it abowte. **1479** *Cely Papers* (Camden) 19 Here ys but strange warlede..the sekenese raynyd sore at London. **1484** *Ibid.* 152 What world wee schall hawe w[t] Flaunders I can nott say, I feyr me they wyll breke w[t] us. ? **1503** in *Lett. Rich. III & Hen. VII* (Rolls) I. 232 Good yt is that we see to our owne surtie..wat world so euer shall hapen to fall here after. **1513** MORE *Rich. III* Wks. 70 If the worlde woold haue gone as I would haue wished, king Henryes sonne had had the crown. *Ibid.*, What nede in that grene world y[e] protector had of y[e] duke. *c* **1523** —— in Ellis *Orig. Lett.* Ser. II. I. 295 They do but seke delayes till they may se how the world is. **1530** PALSGR. 559/2 Let the place be well fumygate..it is a daungerous worlde [Fr. *temps*] nowe a dayes. *a* **1548** HALL *Chron., Edw. IV*, 195 b, Til he might spye a tyme conuenient, & a world after hys awn appetite. *c* **1555** HARPSFIELD *Divorce Hen. VIII* (Camden) 178 Others which foretold this dolorous doleful wretched world that followed upon this divorce. **1596** SHAKS. *1 Hen. IV*, II. iii. 94 This is no world To play with Mammets. **1614** CHAPMAN *Odyssey* XI. 602 But take close shore disguisde, nor let her know, For tis no world to trust a woman now.

†**c.** (One's) condition in life, (good) fortune. *Obs.*

1390 GOWER *Conf.* I. 16 Bot every clerk his herte leith To kepe his world in special. *Ibid.* 84, I not in what degree Thou schalt thi goode world achieve. *Ibid.* III. 170 Whan that he weneth best achieve His goode world.

4. a. Secular (or lay) life and interests, as distinguished from religious (or clerical); also (by association with III, as in b and d below), secular (or lay) people. ***of the world***, † ***world's***: secular; see also MAN OF THE WORLD a.

a **1030** *Rule St. Benet* (Logeman) 109 Oððe æfter gode oððe æfter wurulde he sy. *c* **1200** [see MAN OF THE WORLD a]. *a* **1225** *Ancr. R.* 24 Hwon þe preostes of ðe worlde singeð hore messen. *c* **1290** *Beket* 244 in *S. Eng. Leg.* 113 Þo þis holi Man was i-torned fram þe office of holi churche To a gret office of þe world. *a* **1300** *Cursor M.* 27172 Werlds man, or clerc, or closterer. **1340** *Ayenb.* 49 Þe enlefte [sin of adultery] is of man of þe wordle to wyfman of religioun. *c* **1400** *Rule St. Benet* (prose) 37 Bot bettir chepe sal ye selle þan þe men of þe werld dose. **1526** *Pilgr. Perf.* (W. de W. 1531) 1 That is to say, some chose to go by the worlde and some by religion. **1533** GAU *Richt Vay* (S.T.S.) 25 The oder varkis qvhilk ar techit in al the buikis of the wardel. **1610** HOLLAND *Camden's Brit.* I. 521 Hee taking a loathing to the world..retired into that hospitall..where with poore people hee lived to God. **1671** RAVENSCROFT *Mamamouchi* II. i. (1675) 24 I'l threaten to flee beyond Sea to a Nunnery, and for ever seclude my self from the World. *a* **1700** in *Cath. Rec. Soc. Publ.* IX. 337 In the 20th of her age, forsaking y[e] world she desired nothing more, then to dedicate herselfe to God, in a Religious estate. **1717** POPE *Eloisa* 208 How happy is the blameless Vestal's lot! The world forgetting, by the world forgot. **1808** SCOTT *Marmion* II. iii, The Abbess.. early took the veil and hood, Ere upon life she cast a look, Or knew the world that she forsook. **1845** M. PATTISON *Ess.* (1889) I. 12 A book which is not only esteemed in the Church, but has had the honour..of commanding the respect of the world. **1888** 'BERNARD' *Fr. World to Cloister* ii. 12 Having resigned the situation I held in the world.

b. In the Society of Friends applied to those outside their own body.

1648 G. FOX *Jrnl.* (1852) I. 70 The Lord commanded me to go abroad into the world. *c* **1680** in *Sussex Archaeol. Coll.* (1912) LV. 81 The Other Months Named after ye Manner of ye world. **1698–9** STORY & GILL in S. B. Weeks *Southern Quakers* (1896) 67 The displeasure of God..against mixed marriages between them [*sc.* Quakers] and the world. *a* **1713** THOMAS ELLWOOD *Hist. Life* (1714) 340 Thomas Dell and Edward Moor [were discharged] by other People of the World, paying their Fines and Fees for them. **1837** HT. MARTINEAU *Soc. Amer.* II. 57 They are receiving a perpetual accession to their numbers from among the 'world's people'. **1867** DIXON *New Amer.* II. x. 93 Some of these [Quaker] ladies..have husbands (as the world would call them).

c. † ***to go to the world, to be*** (a man, woman) ***of the world***: to be married.

1565 CALFHILL *Answ. Martiall* 109 b, Ye say when a man wyl marry, then be goeth to the world. **1579** TOMSON *Calvin's Serm. Tim.* 230/2 This man is of the worlde, that is to say, he is maried: This man is of the Churche, that is to say, Spirituall. **1599** SHAKS. *Much Ado* II. i. 331 Good Lord for alliance: thus goes euery one to the world but I. **1600** —— *A.Y.L.* v. iii. 5, I do desire it [marriage] with all my heart: and I hope it is no dishonest desire, to desire to be a woman of y[e] world? **1601** —— *All's Well* I. iii. 20 But if I may haue your Ladiships good will to goe to the world, Isbell the woman and we will doe as we may.

d. In biblical and religious use: Those who are concerned only with the interests and pleasures of this life or with temporal or mundane things; the worldly and irreligious.

1362 LANGL. *P. Pl.* A. I. 37 Leef not þi licam, for lyȝere him techeþ, Þat is þe Wikkede word þe to bi-traye. **1382** WYCLIF *John* xv. 19 But I chees ȝou fro the world, therfore the world hatith ȝou. **1540–7** COVERDALE *Fruitf. Less.* (1593) E 1 b, The world, that is to say, fleshly men and children of the world, receiue not this spirite. **1738** WESLEY *Ps.* IV. vi, The World with fruitless Pain Seek Happiness below.

†**5. a.** An age or (long) period of time in earthly or human existence or history; *pl.* ages. *Obs.*

Phrases. † ***by long worlds***: ages ago. ***in*** or ***to worlds long***: for ages. ***worlds of years***: ages, centuries. ***the world(s) to come***: future ages, posterity.

c **1175** *Lamb. Hom.* 81 Þis bitacneð þe world þet wes from biginnegge [etc.].. In þisse worlde nas na laȝe ne na larþeu. *c* **1205** LAY. 23425 A þere ilke worlde [*c* **1275** worle] þa þis wes iwurðen wes Francene lond Gualle ihaten. *a* **1300** *Cursor M.* 1491 Þe formast werld adam be-gan, Þar-of lameth þe last man. *Ibid.* 15128 Suilc a man was neuer yeitt Sin ani werldes ware. **1390** GOWER *Conf.* III. 176 These olde worldes with the newe Who that wol take in evidence, Ther mai he se [etc.]. *c* **1400** tr. *Secr. Secr., Gov. Lordsh.* 113 Þe olde philosophers vsyd it by longe werldes. *c* **1440** *Pallad. on Husb.* XI. 162 Who wol do puruyaunce in worldis longe, The palmes forto sette he must ha mynde. *Ibid.* 482 Tyl worldis longe This drynkis wole abide and ay be stronge. **1450–1530** *Myrr. Our Ladye* II. 115 All thys worlde ys departed in to thre tymes. The fyrst tyme was when men lyued after the lawe of nature [etc.]. **1549** RIDLEY in Potts *Liber Cantabr.* (1855) 245 *note*, A dangerouse example to the worlde to cum. **1567** *Gude & Godlie B.* (S.T.S.) 44 He that all warldis was beforne, Come downe of Marie to be borne. **1574** HELLOWES *Gueuara's Fam. Ep.* (1577) 18 For that in the worldes to come, it might be known who was the author therof. **1587** GOLDING *De Mornay* vii. (1592) 87 The Heauen goeth about continually, and in so many worlds and ages as haue beene, we perceiue no alteration at all. **1593** BILSON *Perpet. Govt. Ch.* 5 This was the blessing due to the elder Brother in the first world. **1596** HARINGTON *Metam. Ajax* D 7, Tarquinius..prouident in peace, & in that young world, a notable polititian. *a* **1600** HOOKER *Serm., Habak. ii. 4* Wks. 1874 III. 640 Adam and all the fathers before Christ, till Christ's coming, were for so many worlds together detained. **1603** KNOLLES *Hist. Turks* (1621) 2 Forgetfull of all other things in their ancient country, after so many worlds of yeeres. **1606** SHAKS. *Tr. & Cr.* III. ii. 180 True swaines in loue, shall in the world to come Approue their truths by Troylus. **1674** N. FAIRFAX *Bulk & Selv.* 202 [200] From all which 'tis as clear, that we meant in the dayes of yore by the word World, time, ages [etc.].

b. A period or age of human history characterized by certain conditions or indicated by the character of those living in it. *Obs.* exc. as coloured by 16 a.

1530–1600 Golden world [see GOLDEN *a.* 7]. **1630** *R. Johnson's Kingd. & Commw.* 160 It was used in that good old world, when men wiped their nose on their sleeve (as the French man sayes). **1781** BLAIR in *Sc. Transl. & Paraphr.* (1793) 12 All old things now are past away, and a new world begun. **1849** MACAULAY *Hist. Eng.* iii. I. 401 These were men whose minds had been trained in a world which had passed away. **1886** E. B. BAX *Relig. Socialism* 166 In Shakespeare's 'historical plays' the characters live and speak in the world of the sixteenth century.

6. In various phrases translating eccl. Latin *in secula seculorum, in seculum seculi* = for ever and ever, for all time, through eternity. †**a.** ***from world into world(s, in world of world(s, in to (the) world(s of world(s, through all worlds, world always.***

c **888** ÆLFRED *Boeth.* xxi, Þa nu sculon standan to worulde. *c* **1110** *Ælfred's Boeth.* Epil., Si þe lof & wylder nu & aaa to worulde buton æʒhwilcum ende. *c* **1175** *Lamb. Hom.* 25 Þe lauerd..wuniende and rixlende on worulde a buten ende. *c* **1230** *Hali Meid.* (1922) 39 Ah schal ifinden him ai swettere & sauurure, fram worlde in-to worlde. *a* **1300** *E.E. Psalter* lx. 9 Swa salme saie sal I þe same In werld of werld vnto þi name. **1382** WYCLIF *Isa.* xxxiv. 10 Desolat shal [his land] be in to worldus of worldis. *a* **1400** *Prymer* (1891) 34 As hit was in the bygynnynge and now and euere: in the worldes of worldles amen. *c* **1400** *Rule St. Benet* (verse) 331 Sche sal..loue god euer of al his lone And wirchip him werld alwais. *c* **1420** *Prymer* (1895) 16 Glorie be to þee, lord,..in euerlastynge worldis. *Ibid.* 74 He ordeynede þo þingis into þe world, & in to þe world of world [L. *in aeternum, et in saeculum saeculi*]. **1434** MISYN *Mending of Life* 131 To qwhome be wyrschip & ioy..in warld of warldys. Amen. **1551** RECORDE *Cast. Knowl.* (1556) I. 4 Thorough worlde of worldes: whiche signifieth for euer. **1584** R. SCOT *Discov. Witchcr.* XV. xii. 411 Eternall God, which liuest and reignest euer one God through all worlds, Amen. [**1842** TENNYSON *Gard. Dau.* 205, I heard his deep 'I will,' Breathed, like the covenant of a God, to hold From thence thro' all the worlds.]

b. ***world without*** (ME. ***abuten*** or ***buten***) ***end***; later used hyperbolically: Endlessly, eternally. Hence as *adj. phr.* = perpetual, everlasting, eternal; and as *subst. phr.* eternal existence, endlessness, eternity.

a **1225** *Ancr. R.* 182 Þeo þet hefden ofearned þe pinen of helle world a buten ende. *c* **1305** *St. Swithin* 109 in *E.E.P.* (1863) 46 Þat vuel..ne schal no leng ileste, Ac þu worst þerof hol and sound, wordle wiþouten ende. *c* **1460** *Towneley Myst.* ii. 465, I must nedis weynd, And to the dwill be thrall warld withoutten end. **1483** CAXTON *Gold. Leg.* 94/1 Many benefetes ben gyuen to thonour of our lord Jhū crist whiche is blessed world wythouten ende. Amen. **1548–9** *Bk. Com. Prayer, Matins*, As it was in the begynning, is now, and euer shalbe, world without ende. **1588** SHAKS. *L.L.L.* v. ii. 799 A time me thinkes too short, To make a world-without-end bargaine in. **1649** MILTON *Eikon.* xxi. Wks. 1851 III. 484 This man..thinks by talking world without end, to make good his integrity. **1753** in *Life Ld. Hardwicke* (1847) II. 499 L[d] Chesterfield writes Worlds without End. **1881** MORRIS *Mackail's W.M.* (1899) II. 34 This world-without-end-for-everlasting hole of a London. **1888** *Advance* (Chicago) 20 Dec. 831 A city pastor, with a world-without-end of things to be done. **1896** HOUSMAN *Shropsh. Lad* xiv, My heart and soul and senses, World without end, are drowned. **1905** F. YOUNG *Sands of Pleasure* I. v, Small wonder if the embodiment of the world-without-end should prove no encourager of man's happiness!

II. The earth or a region of it; the universe or a part of it.

7. a. The earth and all created things upon it; the terraqueous globe and its inhabitants. (See also 21 a, 22 a.)

citizen of the world: see CITIZEN 2 c. ***universal world***: see UNIVERSAL *a.* 8. ***wide world***: see WIDE *a.* 1 b.

c **888** ÆLFRED *Boeth.* xxxiii. §5 Þeah þu þa ealle ʒesceafta ane naman ʒenemnede, elle þu nemdest togedere & hete woruld. *c* **893** —— *Oros.* I. vi. §1 On þæs Ambictiones tide wurdon swa mycele wæterflod ʒeond ealle world. *a* **900** CYNEWULF *Crist* 659 Se þas world ʒescop, godes gæst-sunu. *c* **1175** *Lamb. Hom.* 19 We habbeð ihereden þurh wise witega hu he erest astalde þeos woreld al for ure neode. *c* **1200** ORMIN 15460 Godd shop all þe werrld off nohht. *c* **1205** LAY. 7206 He [Julius Cæsar] þohte to bi-winnen..al middel-eærdes lond and halde þat worlde in his hond. *c* **1250** *Gen. & Ex.* 901 Wiste no man of werlðe ðo, Quat kinde he was kumen fro. *a* **1300** *Cursor M.* 346 Bot he þat mad al thing o noght To-geder he al þis werld wroght. *c* **1330** R. BRUNNE *Chron. Wace* (Rolls) 222 Noe sones..departed al þys werd..in þre parties. **1393** LANGL. *P. Pl.* C. I. 4 Ich wente forth in þe worlde wonders to hure. *a* **1400–50** *Wars Alex.* 1502 He mon ride þus & regne ouire all þe ronde werde. *c* **1400** *Maundev.* (1839) 180 Men myghte go be Schippe alle aboute the World, and aboven and benethen. **14..** *Childh. Jesus* 111 in Horstm. *Altengl. Leg.* (1878) 113 Jhesu, þat alle þys orlle hath wrowt. **1539** *Bible* (Great) Psalms lxxxix. 12 Thou hast layed the foundacion of the rounde worlde, and all that therin is. **1555** EDEN *Decades* 214b, The vyage made by the Spanyardes rounde abowte the worlde. **1598** SYLVESTER *Du Bartas* II. ii. I. *Ark* 60 The World's-re-colonizing Boat [*viz.* Noah's ark]. **1602** SHAKS. *Ham.* III. ii. 168 And thirtie dozen Moones..About the World haue times twelue thirties beene. **1653** H. COGAN tr. *Pinto's Trav.* viii. 25 The Bisquayn Ship..wherein Magellan compassed the World. **1667** MILTON *P.L.* XII. 646 The World was all before them, where to choose Thir place of rest, and Providence thir guide. **1784** COWPER *Task* I. 372 Its own revolvency upholds the world. **1877** *Encycl. Brit.* VII. 390/1 (*Drake*) This voyage round the world, the first accomplished by an Englishman, was thus performed in two years and about ten months.

b. *transf.* and *fig.*

1556 in T. Sharp *Cov. Myst.* (1825) 73 Paid to Crowe for makyng of iij worldys..ij[s]. **1593** SHAKS. *Lucr.* 408 Her breasts like Iuory globes circled with blew, A pair of maiden worlds vnconquered. **1597** —— *Lover's Compl.* 7, I ..Ere long espied a fickle maid full pale..Storming her world with sorrows, wind and raine. **1746** FRANCIS tr. *Hor. Epist.* I. xix. 29 Through open Worlds of Rhime I dar'd to tread In Paths unknown. **1873** BROWNING *Red Cott. Nt.-cap* 706 See, the sun splits on yonder bauble world Of silvered glass.

c. In phr. with *go round*, orig. referring to the rotation of the earth, but used chiefly fig. with implication of other senses (e.g. 1 a, 3).

1782 BURNS *A Toast* 4 Their fame it shall last while the world goes round. **1788** HURDIS *Village Curate* (1797) 21 Tis drink, And only drink, that makes the world go round. **1882** W. S. GILBERT *Iolanthe* II, It's Love that makes the world go round!

d. ***the world's end***: the farthest limit of the earth. Chiefly used hyperbolically.

Used as the proper name of out-of-the-way localities or houses, esp. formerly, of certain inns kept for illicit purposes (cf. quot. 1695).

1599 SHAKS. *Much Ado* II. i. 272 Will your Grace command mee any seruice to the worlds end? I will goe on the slightest arrand now to the Antypodes. **1628** tr *Matthieu's Powerfull Favorite* 13 Is it for this (say they) that they haue sent him to the worlds end. **1695** CONGREVE *Love for L.* II. ix, Poor innocent! you don't know that there's a place call'd the *World's End*? **1727** BOYER *Dict. Royal* II. s.v. *World*, He lives at the World's end (or a great way off). **1863** W. C. BALDWIN *Afr. Hunting* vi. 216 We saw..the fresh footprints of a Kaffir, and resolved to follow that to the world's end.

attrib. **1839** BAILEY *Festus* 90 Now we stand On the world's-end-land!

e. In generalized sense, usually qualified by *a*.

1676 DRYDEN *Aurengz.* III. 33 Too truly Tamerlain's Successors they, Each thinks a World too little for his sway. **1713** DERHAM *Phys.-Theol.* II. i. (1720) 39 This [spherical figure] must be allowed to be the most commodious, apt Figure for a World on many Accounts. **1748** RICHARDSON *Clarissa* (1768) VIII. 190 They have great force upon me.. or one world would not have held Mr. Lovelace and me thus long. **1784** COWPER *Task* IV. 89 'Tis pleasant through the loop-holes of retreat To peep at such a world. **1865** SWINBURNE *Chastelard* v. ii. 189 Life is not worth a world That you should weep to take it.

f. *pl.* Used hyperbolically for: 'a great quantity'; often advb. 'a great deal', 'infinitely' (cf. 19 b). (*a*) pl. ***not*** (..) ***for worlds***: not for all the wealth in the world, not on any account.

a **1586** SIDNEY *Arcadia* III. (1912) 517 Like two contrarie tides, either of which are able to carry worldes of shippes, and men upon them. **1590** SHAKS. *Mids. N.* II. i. 223 Nor doth this wood lacke worlds of company. **1621** J. TAYLOR (Water P.) *Unnat. Father* Wks. 1630 I. 142 Through worlds of Deaths I'l breake to fly to him. [**1831** JAMES *Philip Aug.* xix, I would not part with this for worlds of ore.] *Ibid.* xxiv, Nor would he do one act for worlds, that could..cast a shade over the fame and honour of one ——. **1872** LOCKER *Lond. Lyrics* (ed. 5) 178 I'd give worlds to borrow Her yellow rose with russet leaves. **1874** W. S. GILBERT *Sweethearts* II, I'm sure I wouldn't stand in his way for worlds. **1891** FARRAR *Darkn. & Dawn* x, She seemed to be separated by whole worlds of difference from such ladies as his own mother. **1892** 'G. TRAVERS' *Mona Maclean* vi, I was worlds too shy. **1900** H. S. HOLLAND *Old & New* 33 They look to you worlds apart.

(*b*) sing., in negative context, e.g. ***not for the world, all the world***, †***half the world***.

1588 SHAKS. *L.L.L.* II. i. 99 *Prin.* He'll be forsworne. *Nau.* Not for the world faire Madam, by my will. **1604** —— *Oth.* IV. iii. 68 Would'st thou do such a deed for al the world? **1605** ERONDELLE *Fr. Gard.* N 6 b, I would not faile in it for any thing in the world. **1634** SIR T. HERBERT *Trav.* 32 Not for all the world, purposing any hurt vnto him. **1664** in *Trans. Cumbld. & Westmld. Antiq. Soc.* (N.S.) 178 A thing I would not have been guilty of for halfe the world. **1665** BOYLE *Occas. Refl.* IV. i. 6 He would not for all the World return again. **1731–8** SWIFT *Pol. Conversat.* 43, I wou'dn't be as sick as she's proud, for all the World. **1784** COWPER *Task* III. 807 He..Can dig, beg, rot,..but could not for a world Fish up his dirty and dependent bread, [etc.]. **1797** JANE AUSTEN *Sense & Sensib.* xxxviii, But I am sure I would not do such a thing for all the world. **1822** SCOTT *Nigel* viii, Not for the world..will I be a spy on my kind godfather's secrets. **1847** BUCKSTONE *Flowers of Forest* III. vii, No, no —not for the wide wide world. **1881** MISS BRADDON *Asphodel* I. iii. 62 Daphne, usually loquacious, felt as if she could not have spoken for the world.

g. ***broke to the world***: see BROKE *ppl. a.* 3; (***it's a***) ***small world***: see SMALL *a.* 3 b; (***on***) ***top of the world***: see TOP *sb.*[1] 16.

8. a. With qualification: Any part of the universe considered as an entity, as †MIDDLE WORLD (the earth), ***lower*** or ***nether world*** (Hades or hell, less freq. the earth), UNDERWORLD 1.

c **1200**, *c* **1250**, **1822** [see MIDDLE WORLD]. **1607** SHAKS. *Timon* I. i. 44 This beneath world. **1609-** [see UNDERWORLD 1]. **1720** [see NETHER *a.* 6]. **1784** COWPER *Task* VI. 729 The groans of nature in this nether world, Which Heav'n has heard for ages. **1786** BURNS *Nature's Law* ii, This lower world I you resign. **179.**—— *To Mr. Renton*, Though 'twere a trip to yon blue warl' [i.e. hell]. **1814** CARY *Dante, Parad.* XVII. 22, I..With Virgil..visited the nether world of woe.

b. A planet or other heavenly body, esp. one viewed as inhabited.

1713 ADDISON *Cato* v. i, But thou shalt flourish..Unhurt amidst..The Wrecks of Matter, and the Crush of Worlds. **1732** POPE *Ess. Man* I. 254 Being on Being wreck'd, and world on world. **1781** COWPER *Retirem.* 81 The sun, a world whence other worlds drink light. **1870** R. A. PROCTOR (*title*) Other Worlds than Ours. **1872** BLACK *Adv. Phaeton* xxxi. 419 Overhead the great worlds became more visible in the deep vault of blue.

9. The material universe as an ordered system; the system of created things; 'heaven and earth'; the cosmos. Also (rarely) a system of heavenly bodies. Also *fig.* †In early use chiefly in ***the greater*** or ***more world***, the macrocosm, and ***the less*** or ***little world***, the microcosm, man. Now *rare.*

c **1200** ORMIN 17597 Mycrocossmos, þatt nemmnedd iss Affterr Ennglisshe spæche þe little werelld. *a* **1300** *Cursor M.* 552 For þis resun þat ȝee haue hard, Man es clepid þe lesse werld. **1340–70** *Alex. & Dind.* 645 ȝe liknen a lud to a litil wordle. **1390** GOWER *Conf.* II. 71 A soubtil man,.. Which thurgh magique and sorcerie Couthe al the world of tricherie. **1450–1530** *Myrr. our Ladye* II. 181 No meruayle thoughe god had more delyte in the thow lesse worlde that were yet to be made, then of thys more worlde. **1481** CAXTON *Myrr.* I. xvi. 50 This clerenesse..enuyronneth al aboute the worlde the foure elementis whiche god created. **1519** *Interl. Four Elem.* A vj b, The yerth as a poynt or center is sytuate In the myddes of the worlde. **1526** *Pilgr. Perf.* (W. de W. 1531) 1 Lyke as the great worlde was made perfecte in vij dayes, so y[e] lesse worlde, that is man, is made.. perfecte by grace in these vij spirituall dayes. **1551** RECORDE *Cast. Knowl.* I. (1556) 4 The worlde is an apte frame of heauen and earthe, and all other naturall thinges contained in them. **1605** SHAKS. *Lear* III. i. 10 (Qo. 1) In his little world of man. **1633** HERBERT *Temple, Man* viii, Man is one world, and hath Another to attend him. *c* **1645** HOWELL *Lett.* II. l. (1890) 444 Surely the Astronomers had reason to term this Sphere..a thing of no dimension at all, being compar'd to the whole World. **1690** LOCKE *Hum. Und.* II. xxiv. §1 The great collective Idea of all Bodies whatsoever signified by the name World. **1709** SHAFTESB. *Moralists* III. i. 182 Thy Works apparent to us, the System of the bigger World! **1728** CHAMBERS *Cycl.* s.v. *University*, The four Faculties are supposed to make the World or Universe of Study. **1755** B. MARTIN *Mag. Arts & Sci.* 8 The Philosophers of the present Age teach us, that the Universe ..is replenished with Systems or Worlds of different Bodies. **1882** T. FOWLER *Shaftesbury & Hutcheson* 106 We may infer that Shaftesbury conceived the relation of God to the World as that of soul to the body. Nature is..the vesture of God, and God the soul of the Universe.

10. The sphere within which one's interests are bound up or one's activities find scope; (one's) sphere of action or thought; the 'realm' within which one moves or lives.

In the earliest instances with allusion to the microcosm of man (see 9).

a **1586** SIDNEY *Apol. Poetry* (Arb.) 31 How it [*sc.* virtue] extendeth it selfe out of the limits of a mans own little world, to the gouernment of families. *a* **1642** SUCKLING *Poems* (1648) 11 In each mans heart that doth begin To love, there's ever fram'd within A little world. **1642** H. MORE *Song of Soul* III. II. xv, She dwells in her own self, there doth reside, Is her own world, and more or lesse doth pen Her self. **1807** WORDSW. *Personal Talk* 23 Children are blest and powerful; their world lies More justly balanced; partly at their feet, And part far from them. **1837** DISRAELI *Venetia* II. ii, With no aspirations beyond the little world in which she moved. **1837** HT. MARTINEAU *Soc. Amer.* III. 28 The atmosphere of insolence in which he dwells;..the taint of contempt which infects all the intercourses of his world. **1853** T. T. LYNCH *Self-Improvem.* iii. 53 A man's world is not of the senses simply, but of the spirit too. **1898** 'H. S. MERRIMAN' *Roden's Corner* xvi. 168 [His] world was a narrow one, consisting as it did of himself and his bank-book.

11. A section or part of the earth at large, as a place of inhabitation or settlement; †a country or region.

New World, a continent or country discovered or colonized at a comparatively late period, esp. the continents of America (the Western Hemisphere) as distinguished from the ***Old World***, or the continents of the Eastern Hemisphere, esp. Europe and Asia, as being known before the discovery of America.

1555 EDEN *Decades* title-p., The Decades of the Newe Worlde or West India. **1581** PETTIE tr. *Guazzo's Civ. Conv.* Ep. Ded. A iij b, Some of them..seeke new Countries and new worlds to shew their valiancie in. **1589** HAKLUYT *Princ. Navig.* (title-p.), The English valiant attempts in searching almost all the corners of the vaste and new world of America. *a* **1593** MARLOWE & NASHE *Dido* I. i, Of Troy am I,..driuen by warre from forth my natiue world. **1593** SHAKS. *Rich. II*, II. i. 45 This little world, This precious stone, set in the siluer sea. **1600** HAKLUYT *Voy.* III. title-p., Voyages..to all parts of the Newfound world of America, or the West Indies. **1601** HOLLAND *Pliny* VI. i. I. 115 From the one side to the other [of the Bosphorus]..men out of these two worlds may parly one to another with audible voice. **1627** MAY *Lucan* III. E 2 b, Tanais..doth diuide Europe from Asia, giuing to each side The name of seuerall worlds. **1638** BROME *Antipodes* I. vi, No Isle nor Angle in that Neather world, But I have made discovery of. **1698** FRYER *Acc. E. India & P.* 183 This World produces two Harvests. **1709** POPE *Ess. Crit.* 711 Thence Arts o'er all the northern world advance. **1741** WATTS *Improv. Mind* i. (1801) 16 Alexander the Great..when he had conquered what was called the Eastern World..wept for want of more worlds to conquer. **1812** ROGERS *Voy. Columbus* ii. 39 From world to world their steady course they keep. **1842** TENNYSON *Ulysses* 57 Come, my friends, 'Tis not too late to seek a newer world. **1859** CORNWALLIS (*title*) A Panorama of the New World [Australia]. **1861** M. PATTISON *Ess.* (1889) I. 46 Before the New World poured in so many objects hitherto unknown to Europe. **1888** BRYCE *Amer. Commw.* I. 29 *note*, The influence which American freedom would exert upon the Old World.

12. A division of created things; *esp.* each of three primary divisions of natural objects (the animal, vegetable, and mineral kingdoms).

organic world, the animal and vegetable kingdoms; ***inorganic world***, the material world outside these.

1695 WOODWARD *Nat. Hist. Earth* I. (1723) 3 Nor..did I neglect..whatever either the Vegetable or Animal World afforded. **1727–46** THOMSON *Summer* 112 The vegetable world is also thine, Parent of Seasons! **1861** BUCKLE *Civiliz.* (1873) II. viii. 530 In the inorganic world, the magnificent discoveries of Newton were contumeliously rejected. **1875** JOWETT *Plato* (ed. 2) III. 70 As in the animal or vegetable world.

13. a. A group or system of things or beings associated by common characteristics (denoted by a qualifying word or phrase), or considered as constituting a unity.

1673 T. BLOUNT (*title*) A World of Errors discovered in the New World of Words. **1685** G. SINCLAIR (*title*) Satans Invisible World discovered. **1690** LOCKE *Hum. Und.* IV. iii. §27 (1695) 319 The whole intellectual World; a greater certainly, and more beautiful World, than the material. **1701** NORRIS *Ideal World* I. vi. 389 Truth is where the Divine Ideas are,..in the Intelligible World, that world of true light and glory. **1704** *Ibid.* II. iii. 253 Intellectual world means the world of spirits, whereas by intelligible world we mean the world of Ideas. **1781** COWPER *Retirem.* 536 Then, all the world of waters sleeps again. **1807** WORDSW. *Personal Talk* 33 Dreams, books, are each a world. **1821** LAMB *Elia* I. *Witches*, Dear little T. H...finds all this world of fear [*i.e.* night fears]..in his own 'thick-coming fancies'. **1842** DICKENS *Amer. Notes* xvi, We carried in the steerage nearly a hundred passengers: a little world of poverty. **1851** [see VISIBLE *a.* 1]. *a* **1862** BUCKLE *Misc. Wks.* (1872) I. 213 The external world is governed by acts, the internal world by opinions. **1874** MIVART *Contemp. Evol.* (1876) 199 The mingling of the hyperphysical world of rationality with the irrational creation. **1893** W. S. FURNEAUX (*title*) The Outdoor World; or, Young Collector's Handbook.

†**b.** ***world of words***: a dictionary. *Obs.*

1598 FLORIO (*title*) A Worlde of Wordes, Or Most copious, and exact Dictionarie in Italian and English. **1611** COTGR., *Vocabulaire*, a Vocabularie, Dictionarie, world of words. **1696** PHILLIPS (*title*) The Moderne World of Words, or A Vniversall English Dictionary,..*Novus Orbis Verborum.*

III. The inhabitants of the earth, or a section of them.

14. a. The human race; the whole of mankind; human society. (See also 21 b, 22 b.)

Sometimes passing into 15.

a **900** CYNEWULF *Crist* 1424 Hwæt! ic þæt for woruulde ȝeþolade. *c* **1200** ORMIN 17496 Swa lufede þe Laferrd Godd þe werelld, tatt he sennde Hiss aȝhenn Sune..to wurrþenn mann onn erþe. *c* **1205** LAY. 9072 Jesu Crist..alre woruulde wunne. *c* **1275** *XI Pains of Hell* 128 in *O.E. Misc.* 214 þe sun of god, þat aȝayn boȝt þe word. **1390** GOWER *Conf.* I. 1 So that it myhte in such a wyse, Whan we ben dede..Beleve to the worldes eere. *c* **1400** *Pety Job* 596 in *26 Pol. Poems* 140 And so shall I see my sauyour Deme the worlde. **1535** in *Lett. Suppr. Monast.* (Camden) 31, I suppose it wolbe hard for you to purge your selfe before God or the worle. **1567** JEWEL *Def. Apol.* VI. vi. § 2. 620 They make Decrees expressely againste Goddes Woorde, and that not.. couertly, but openly, and in the face of the worlde. **1662** STILLINGFL. *Orig. Sacræ* II. i. §2 It being impossible that persons employed by a God of truth should make it their design to impose upon the world. **1714** DERHAM *Astro-Theol.* (1769) 27 The condition, state and order of the world inhabiting the earth. **1733** POPE *Ess. Man* III. 307 In Faith and Hope the world will disagree, But all Mankind's concern is Charity. **1842** TENNYSON *Locksley Hall* 128 In the Parliament of man, the Federation of the world. **1842** —— *Walking to Mail* 69 You know That these two parties still divide the world—Of those that want, and those that have. **1866** LIDDON *Bampton Lect.* vi. (1875) 337 The whole world was redeemed by Christ.

†**b.** ***world's, worlde(s shame, shame of the world***: universal or public disgrace. *Obs.*

Replacing the OE. compound *woruldscamu* (ME. *weorldscome*): see 25 a.

1390 GOWER *Conf.* I. 353 He schal with worldes schame Himself and ek his love schame. **1483–4** *Act 1 Rich. III*, c. 4 Persones of noo substaunce ne havur, not dredyng God nor worldez shame. **1594** SHAKS. *Rich. III*, IV. iv. 27 Worlds shame. **1611** CHAPMAN *May Day* IV, Has not one of them [*sc.* disguises] kept you safe from the shame of the world? **1731–8** SWIFT *Pol. Conversat.* 32 Fie, fie, Miss! for Shame of the World, and Speech of good People. **1882** PUSEY *Par. & Cath. Serm.* xii. 164 One decided act of blind, obedient faith, ready..to bear what might bring the world's shame.

c. ***against the world***: in opposition to or in the face of all mankind; hence, against all opposition, †in preference to everything else. (See also 21 b.)

1601 SHAKS. *Jul. C.* III. ii. 124 But yesterday, the word of Cæsar might Haue stood against the World. **1690** W. WALKER *Idiomat. Anglo-Lat.* 531, I am for the woods against the World, i.e. before any thing. **1859** TENNYSON *Guinevere* 114 There will I..hold thee with my life against the world.

15. The body of living persons in general; society at large, 'people', the public; often with reference to its judgement or opinion.

1603 SHAKS. *Meas. for M.* I. ii. 120 Fellow, why do'st thou show me thus to th' world? Beare me to prison. **1616** R. COCKS *Diary* (Hakl. Soc.) I. 127 Yet let both hym and the world judg of me yf I dealt frendly with hym. **1693** *Humours Town* 29 To make the World think he has been at a good Meal. **1738** POPE *Epil. Sat.* i. 147 In golden Chains the willing World she [*sc.* Virtue] draws. **1762** CHURCHILL *Night* 351 You must be wrong, the World is in the right. **1784** COWPER *Task* VI. 681 He.. call'd the world to worship on the banks Of Avon, fam'd in song. **1828** LD. ELLENBOROUGH *Diary* (1881) I. 201 There are all sorts of stories of the Lord High Admiral, and the world says he is mad. **1833–5** NEWMAN *Hist. Sk.* Ser. III. x. (1873) 191 It is harder to resist the world's smiles than the world's frowns. **1858** MRS. CRAIK *Woman's Th.* ix. 230 How often do we hear the phrases,—'What will the world say?' **1859** TENNYSON *Elaine* 936 The world, the world, All ear and eye. **1893** *Bookman* June 85/1 From the world's point of view his unpopularity was richly deserved.

16. Usually with qualification: A particular division, section, or generation of the earth's inhabitants or human society. **a.** with reference to the place or time of their existence.

1382 WYCLIF *2 Pet.* ii. 5 If God.. sparide not to the first world, but kepte Noe [TINDALE the olde worlde but saved Noe]. **1601, 1704** Western world [see WESTERN *a.* 4]. **1615** G. SANDYS *Trav.* 76 The old world, as is thought, was ignorant of this sport. *c* **1670** A. WOOD *Life* (O.H.S.) I. 317 The world of England was perfectly mad. **1781** COWPER *Charity* 40 While Cook is lov'd for savage lives he sav'd, See Cortez odious for a world enslav'd. **1822** SHELLEY *Calderon's Magico Prodigioso* i. 126 The wisdom Of the old world masked with the names of Gods. **1890** WRIGHTSON *Sancta Respubl. Rom.* 4 Theodosius left the Roman world in peace. **1922** G. M. TREVELYAN *Brit. Hist. 19th Cent.* v. 91 To prevent the domination and exploitation of the European world by France.

b. with reference to their interests or pursuits.

1601 SHAKS. *All's Well* IV. iv. 2 One of the greatest in the Christian world Shall be my suretie. **1658** R. BAILLIE in *Durham's Comm. Rev.* (1660) To Rdr. B 1 b, The matter of it.. cannot but be very welcom and acceptable to the world of Believers. **1710** STEELE *Tatler* No. 195 ¶ 1 The Learned World are very much offended at many of my Ratiocinations. **1779** SHERIDAN *Critic* I. i, A gentleman well known in the theatrical world. **1796** NELSON 25 Nov. in Nicolas *Disp.* (1845) II. 305 The part allotted to me.. ended, as our world here, say, much to my credit. **1779** *Mirror* No. 38 The female world. **1798** CHARLOTTE SMITH *Yng. Philos.* III. 74 Satiated as I am, and as I suppose two thirds of the reading world have been with sonnets. **1807** T. THOMSON *Chem.* (ed. 3) II. 470 A fact now well known to the chemical world. **1810** *Sporting Mag.* XXXV. 304 An extraordinary circumstance is stated to have taken place in the musical world. **1854** *Poultry Chron.* II. 219 Two noblemen, whose names are as eminent in the poultry world as in rank. **1870** HUXLEY *Lay Serm.* iii. 48 The serene resting-place for worn human nature—the world of art. **1882** SALA *Amer. Revis.* viii. (1885) 160 The whole world of ruffiandom. **1886** RUSKIN *Præterita* II. 5 He brought us news from the mathematical and grammatical world. **1897** MARY KINGSLEY *W. Africa* 441 An old marine engineer.. who loves them [his engines] as living things,.. defending them .. against the aspersions of the silly, uninformed outside world.

17. a. Human society considered in relation to its activities, difficulties, temptations, and the like; hence, contextually, the ways, practices, or customs of the people among whom one lives; the occupations and interests of society at large.

to begin the world: to begin to take an active part in the affairs of life; to start one's career.

1449 *Paston Lett.* Suppl. (1901) 21 He seythe that he shall dwelle with his wyffes fader.. and he will no forther medill in the werde. **1556** in Feuillerat *Revels Q. Mary* (1914) 215 These two will attempt the worlde to seke theyr fortune. **1570** FOXE *A. & M.* (ed. 2) 2237/2 A stocke of money to begin the world withall. **1598** SHAKS. *Merry W.* II. ii. 136 Olde folkes you know, haue discretion, as they say, and know the world. **1704** M. HENRY *Church in House* 55 You are beginning the World (as you call it). **1712** STEELE *Spect.* No. 491 ¶ 2 However he had so much of the World, that he had a great share of the Language which usually prevails upon the weaker Part of that Sex. **1732** BERKELEY *Alciphr.* I. §1 That great Whirlpool of Business, Faction, and Pleasure, which is called the World. **1753–4** RICHARDSON *Grandison* II. xvi. 124 He will be still kinder to them, when they are old enough to be put into the world. **1796** (*title*) Address to a Young Lady on her entrance into the world. **1839** NEWMAN *Par. Serm.* IV. xii. 212 By the world, I mean all that meets a man in intercourse with his fellow men. **1853** DICKENS *Bleak Ho.* xiii, The world is before you; and it is most probable that as you enter it, so it will receive you. **1882** W. BALLANTINE *Exper.* I. ix. 115 He was a perfect child in the world's ways. **1882** BESANT *All Sorts* xxxii. (1898) 227 Two thousand pounds; that's a large sum to hand over... Upon my word,.. you will have to begin the world again. **1899** JESSE L. WILLIAMS *Stolen Story* etc. 186 Hamilton J. Knox had been one of the great men of his day.. when in college. He was in the World now.

b. with reference to social status or worldly fortune.

Phrr. ***to get up in the world, to go down in the world***; † ***to be beforehand*** or ***behindhand in*** (or ***with***) ***the world***: to be in prosperous or indigent circumstances.

1687 MIÈGE *Gt. Fr. Dict.* II. s.v. *World*, To be before hand in the World, *être à son aise*... To be behind hand in the World, *faire mal ses Affaires*. **1777** THICKNESSE *Journ. France* (1789) I. 10 My landlord, Monsieur Dessein, who was behind-hand with the world ten years ago, is now become one of the richest men in Calais. **1784** COWPER *Tiroc.* 672 Low in the world, because he scorns its arts. **1791** J. WOODFORDE *Diary* 20 Mar. (1927) III. 257 John Greaves, my Carpenter.. married about 2 Years or more ago, to a Servant Maid of Mrs. Lombe's.. and lived very happy together and daily getting up in the World. **1837** J. S. MILL *Let.* 6 Aug. in *Works* (1963) XII. 346 To alter their style of living and go (as the vulgar phrase is) down in the world. **1838** DICKENS *O. Twist* xxxix, Indications of the good gentleman's having gone down in the world of late. **1840** MARRYAT *Poor Jack* xxviii, His family is getting up in the world. **1883** D. C. MURRAY *Hearts* xiv. (1885) 112, I am getting on a little in the world, and am in the way to earn a little money. **1889** [see COME *v.* 60 e].

18. High or fashionable society. More explicitly ***the world of fashion, the fashionable world***; also ***the polite world, the great world***, †occas. ***the very first world***. (See also 21 c.)

half-world (= DEMI-MONDE): see HALF- II. n.

1673 DRYDEN *Marr. à la Mode* I. i, He talks too like a man that knew the world To have been long a Peasant. **1711** ADDISON *Spect.* No. 15 ¶ 7 She.. fancies herself out of the World, when she is not in the Ring, the Play-House, or the Drawing-Room. **1713** SWIFT *Cadenus & Vanessa* 430 To know the world! a modern phrase For visits, ombre, balls, and plays. **1726** LADY M. W. MONTAGU *Let. to C'tess Mar* Wks. 1837 II. 185, I leave the great world to girls that know no better. **1750** CHESTERFIELD *Let. to Son* 11 June, The court is called the world here, as well as at Paris; and nothing more is meant, by saying that a man knows the world, than that he knows courts. **1763** *Brit. Mag.* Jan. 14/2 The polite world. **1786** BURNS *Twa Dogs* 158 To mak a tour, an' tak a whirl, To learn *bon ton* an' see the worl'. **1791** BOSWELL *Johnson* 24 Apr. 1779 (1904) II. 292 Mr. Beauclerk.. told us a number of short stories in a lively elegant manner, and with that air of *the world* which has I know not what impressive effect. **1791** CHARLOTTE SMITH *Celestina* (ed. 2) I. 32 His solicitude to maintain his importance as a man of taste in the fashionable world. **1796** —— *Marchmont* IV. 280, I saw enough of the lives of people of the very first world. **1853** DICKENS *Bleak Ho.* ii, It is but a glimpse of the world of fashion that we want. **1889** 'J. S. WINTER' *Mrs. Bob* ix. (1891) 109, I must tell you that the Parish set comprised 'the world' of the ancient city.

IV. Idiomatic uses and phrases: see also above.

19. a world. a. A vast quantity, an 'infinity'; in early use, esp. a vast expanse (of land or water). ***a world of years, of time*** (obs. or dial.): a vast extent of time, an age, an eternity. (Sometimes more emphatically ***a whole world of***.)

c **1440** *Pallad. on Husb.* VII. 28 The playner part of ffraunce a craft hath fonde To repe in litel space a world of londe. **1423** JAS. I *Kingis Q.* lxxxii, Standing there I sawe A warld of folk. **1579–80** NORTH *Plutarch, Nicias* (1595) 589 A world of trumpets, howboyes, and such marine musicke. **1588** SHAKS. *L.L.L.* v. ii. 353 A world of torments though I should endure. **1589** WARNER *Alb. Eng., Æneidos* 151 My Father.. deliuered mee with a world of Treasure to Polymnestor. **1590** SPENSER *F.Q.* I. i. 39 He, making speedy way through spersed ayre, And through the world of waters wide and deepe. **1596** SHAKS. *1 Hen. IV*, III. i. 94 For there will be a World of Water shed, Vpon the parting of your Wiues and you. **1598** CHAPMAN *Blinde Beg. Alexandria* D 3 b, What a worlde of tyme Is it for me to lie as in a sounde, Without my life. **1601** HOLLAND *Pliny* XIV. i. I. 404 Yet continued it hath a world of yeares uncorrupt. **1620** QUARLES *Pentel.* N 4, Seruing a world of yeeres. **1632** LITHGOW *Trav.* I. 16, I beheld a world of old Bookes. **1662** EVELYN *Sculptura, Acc. Signor Favi* c 6, He had made provision of sundry huge Volumes,.. besides a world more which he had sent away. **1703** EARL ORRERY *As you find it* II. ii. 22, I have a World of Business to do this Afternoon. **1779** G. KEATE *Sketches fr. Nat.* (ed. 2) II. 78 A ship that hath traversed the globe, and cut her passage through a world of waters. **1791** F. BURNEY *Jrnl.* Sept. (1972) I. 57 The Water has done me a World of good—I drink it at morning & Noon regularly. **1804** SCOTT 19 Mar. in *Lockhart* I. xii. 412, I had a world of things to say to you. **1812** ROGERS *Voy. Columbus* v. 2 A world of waves, a sea without a shore. **1849** ROBERTSON *Serm.* Ser. I. v. (1866) 79 A whole world of passions. **1854** ANNE E. BAKER *Northampt. Gloss.* s.v., It'll take a world of time to do it. **1897** S. CRANE *Third Violet* iv. 22 These long walks in the clear mountain air are doing you a world of good.

b. Used advb.: Infinitely, vastly. (Cf. *worlds*, 7 f.) *arch.*

1600 SHAKS. *A.Y.L.* II. vii. 160 His youthfull hose well sau'd, a world too wide, For his shrunke shanke. **1879** 'HESBA STRETTON' *Needle's Eye* xxxiv, Her smile.. had a world more tenderness in it. **1887** *Pall Mall Gaz.* 22 June 5/2 The Venus Anadyomene is a fine thing, but the Statue of Liberty is a world finer.

†**c.** ***it is a world***: it is a great thing, it is a marvel. Similarly † ***it is a world and wonder***, † ***wonder a world***. *Obs.* or *dial.*

c **1440** *Generydes* 2205 Euerychone on other ferly they sette.. and trewly for to speke It was a world to here the sperys breke. **1519** *Interl. 4 Elem.* C v b, It is a worlde to se her whyrle Daunsynge in a rounde. *a* **1562** G. CAVENDISH *Wolsey* (1825) I. 145 It is not a world to consider the desire of wilful princes, when they fully be bent.. to fulfil their voluptuous appetites. **1596** SHAKS. *Tam. Shr.* II. i. 313. **1600** HOLLAND *Livy* III. xxvi. 105 A world and wonder it is to hear them speak. **1620** BP. ANDREWES *96 Serm., Holy Ghost* xiii. (1629) 738 But it were a world to rake up old errors. **1666** DUGDALE *Orig. Jurid.* 152/1 The Prince so served will tender meats,.. as it seemed wonder a world to observe the provision. **1881** *Leic. Gloss.* s.v., It's a woo'ld to see that theer little un order the big uns to the roight abaout!

20. the world (see also above senses). **a.** ***in the world***: on earth, in existence; (*a*) as an intensive phrase after a superlative or *all, no, not a, everything, nothing*, etc. Also occas. † ***in*** (***a***) ***world***; OE. ***on worulde***.

a **1070** *Laws Ethelred, Be griðe* §25 On hwam mæȝ huru æfre ænìȝ man on worolde swyðor God wurðian ðonne on cyrcan? **1297** R. GLOUC. (Rolls) 181 Þe veireste men in þe world þer inne [*sc.* in England] beþ ibore. **1375** BARBOUR *Bruce* I. 240 Mar to prys Than all the gold in warld that is. *a* **1400–50** *Wars Alex.* 5131 Thretti goblettis of gold, þe grattest in þe worde. *c* **1489** CAXTON *Sonnes of Aymon* ix. 224 He began to make the gretest sorow in the worlde. *c* **1500** *Melusine* v. 27 He had nat mow say one only word for all the gold in the world. **1588** SHAKS. *L.L.L.* v. i. 74 And I had but one penny in the world, thou shouldst haue it. *a* **1589** R. LANE in *Hakluyt's Voy.* 739 The Riuer of Choanoak, and all the other sounds,.. shewe no currant in the world in calme weather. **1606** SHAKS. *Ant. & Cl.* II. vii. 3 The least winde i' th' world wil blow them downe. **1606** —— *Tr. & Cr.* I. ii. 41 *Cre.* Hectors a gallant man. *Man.* As may be in the world Lady. **1694** ATTERBURY *Serm.* (Isa. lx. 22) (1726) I. 110 The Gospel of Christ, at its Earliest appearance, had all the Probabilities in the World against its Success. **1711** STEELE *Spect.* No. 142 ¶ 7 It is the hardest thing in the World to be in Love, and yet attend Business. **1716** WODROW *Corr.* (1843) II. 123 They would have given all they had in a world to have been off. **1790** MRS. WHEELER *Westmld. Dial.* (1821) 21 Thats aw spite, nowt ith warld else. **1826** DISRAELI *Viv. Grey* III. viii, Here is everybody in the world that I wish to see, except yourself. **1833** DICKENS *Sk. Boz, Mr. Minns*, He was.. the most retiring man in the world. **1890** 'R. BOLDREWOOD' *Col. Reformer* xxvi, Hartley enjoyed his dinner.. as if he had not a debt in the world.

(*b*) intensifying an interrogative.

1530 PALSGR. 467/2 He wyste nat in the worlde what to do. **1595** SHAKS. *John* v. iv. 26 What in the world should make me now deceiue..? **1600** J. PORY tr. *Leo's Africa* I. 11 He knew not what in the world to doe. **1614** DAY *Dyall* Ep. Ded. ¶ 2 b, Hee.. could not tell where in the world he had laid it. **1835** DICKENS *Sk. Boz, Private Theatres*, And if they don't know how to do this sort of thing, who in the world does? **1865** MRS. WHITNEY *Gayworthys* xxvi, How in the world did you persuade the captain?

†**b.** ***of the world*** [cf. F. *du monde*]: = *in the world* (20 a). *Obs.*

13.. *Gaw. & Gr. Knt.* 238 Al studied þat þer stod, & stalked hym nerre, Wyth al þe wonder of þe worlde, what he worch schulde. **1476** *Stonor Papers* (Camden) II. 7 Yff ye wold be a good etter off your mete.. ye shuld make me the gladdest man off the world. *c* **1477** CAXTON *Jason* 69 Wherfore they began to crye and demene the gretteste sorow of the worlde. **1589** PUTTENHAM *Engl. Poesie* III. xxiv. (Arb.) 300 The most gentle and affable Prince of the world. **1611** SHAKS. *Wint. T.* v. iii. 72 No setled Sences of the World can match The pleasure of that madnesse. **1620** SHELTON *Quix.* III. ix. 203 He began the most sadd and dolefull lamentation of the world.

c. ***of*** (all) ***the world***: out of the whole world, above all others in the world. *Obs.* or *arch.*

1760–72 H. BROOKE *Fool of Qual.* (1809) II. 150 The man of the world, excepting yourself.., for whom I have the dearest respect. *Ibid.* III. 3 You are the man of the world whom I would have chosen. **1781** COWPER *Hope* 427 The book of all the world that charm'd me most Was—well-a-day, the title page was lost!

†**d.** ***all to the world***: in every respect; = 21 e.

1749 FIELDING *Tom Jones* VIII. viii, There the Bastard was bred up,.. all to the World like any Gentleman.

e. ***to think the world of***: to have the highest possible opinion of or regard for.

[**1852** H. B. STOWE *Uncle Tom's Cabin* II. xxxiv. 206 He had a cousin come to New Orleans, who was his particular friend,—he thought all the world of him.] **1892** 'MARK TWAIN' *Amer. Claimant* iii. 24 They.. think the world of Mulberry. **1894** 'L. KEITH' *'Lisbeth* xvii, She thinks the world of 'Lisbeth. **1905** F. YOUNG *Sands of Pleasure* II. i, She was kept by a Russian Prince, who thought the world of her.

f. See MAN OF THE WORLD. Similarly ***woman of the world***, a woman who is experienced in the ways of life or the conventions of society.

1780 F. BURNEY *Diary* Apr. (1904) I. VII. 328 She is an easy, chatty, sensible woman of the world. **1822** M. EDGEWORTH *Let.* 10 Apr. (1971) 393 Lady Clare is a painted —made up—vulgar thorough going woman of the world. **1837** HT. MARTINEAU *Soc. Amer.* III. 132 Girls.. boldly staring at all that is going on, and serving themselves, like little women of the world. **1844** KINGLAKE *Eothen* viii, Presently (though with all the skill of a woman of the world) she shuffled away the subject.

21. all the world. a. The whole of the inhabited globe; the entire earth (or universe).

c **1175** *Lamb. Hom.* 35 Me were leofere þenne al world [etc.]. **1297** R. GLOUC. (Rolls) 705 Þei al þe world wer min & al þe richesse iwis. *Ibid.* 7551 Þer nas prince in al þe world of so noble fame. *c* **1300** *Havelok* 1290 It [*sc.* the hill] was so hey, þat y wel mouthe Al þe werd se, als me þouthe. **1382** WYCLIF *Mark* viii. 36 What profiteth it a man, if he wynne al the world, and do peyringe to his soule? *a* **1400–50** *Wars Alex.* 18 Þat was þe athill Alexsandire.. þat aȝte euyn as his awyn all the werd ouire. **1420** in Ellis *Orig. Lett.* Ser. III. I. 70 Aboue all erthely Princeps thorw all the word Christene and Hethene. *c* **1450** *Hymns Virgin* (1867) 122 Alle the worlle schalle to-dryve. **1567** *Gude & Godlie B.* (S.T.S.) 4 Go zour way into all the warld, and preiche the Euangell. **1600** SHAKS. *A.Y.L.* II. vii. 139 All the world's a stage, And all the men and women, meerely Players. **1713** DERHAM *Phys.-Theol.* II. v. (1720) 48 Every where all the World over. **1784** COWPER *Task* I. 698 Such London is, by taste and wealth proclaim'd The fairest capital of all the world. **1830** TENNYSON *Sea-Fairies* 41 Who can light on as happy a shore All the world o'er? **1833** —— *New Year's Eve* 24 In the early early morning.. Before the red cock crows.. When.. all the world is still.

b. Everybody in existence; in narrower sense, everybody in the community, the public. ***against all the world***: in opposition to or competition with everybody. (= F. *tout le monde*.)

all the world and his wife: see WIFE *sb.* 2 b.

a **1300** *Cursor M.* 14495 All þe werld mon wit him rijs. **1303** R. BRUNNE *Handl. Synne* 2386 Þou mayst nat excuse þe with rous [*v.r.* ros], And sey, 'al þe worlde so dous'. **1393** LANGL. *P. Pl.* C. XXII. 219 For antecrist and hise shal al þe worlde greue. **1426** AUDELAY *Poems* 2 That al the werd schal have wyttying. **1523** CROMWELL in Merriman *Life & Lett.* (1902) I. 33 Theire insaciable apetite.. ys so manyfest and notorys to all the word. **1588** in *Border Papers* (1894) I. 307 The Kinge.. will mayntaine it [*sc.* religion] to the uttermoste of his power against all the worlde. **1597** SHAKS. *2 Hen. IV*, IV. v. 225 Which I, with more, then with a Common paine, 'Gainst all the World, will rightfully maintaine. **1617** MORYSON *Itin.* II. 157, I will faithfully serve her against all the World. **1660** JER. TAYLOR *Ductor Dubit.* III. iv. rule 13. 284 The Rogation fast (all the world knows) was instituted by Mammercus Bishop of Vienna. **1768** GOLDSM. *Goodn. Man* I. i, All the world loves him. **1841** THACKERAY *Gt. Hoggarty Diam.* xii, A man has no business to place them on paper for all the world to read. **1854** TENNYSON *Charge of Light Brigade* iii, Charging an army, while All the world wonder'd. **1879** MCCARTHY *Donna Q.* I. 60 A woman can be handsome without all the world running after her.

c. Everybody in fashionable society; everybody of account.

1813 *Sk. Char.* (ed. 2) I. 39 Oh, all the world's here, the season was never so full. **1860** TROLLOPE *Castle Richmond* xxvii, All the world—her world and his world—would think it better that they should part. **1877** *Echo* 31 July 1/4 The London Season when 'everybody' goes out of town—all the world, indeed.

d. Everything in existence: often in intensive emotional use = All that is of value or account *to* a person, something supremely precious.

Cf. quot. 1382 in a above.

1595 SHAKS. *John* III. iv. 104 My life, my ioy, my food, my all the world. **1704** POPE *Autumn* 88, I may.. Forsake mankind, and all the world—but love! **1797** JANE AUSTEN *Sense & Sensib.* xlvi, You, my mother, and Margaret must henceforth be all the world to me. **1853** MRS. GASKELL *Ruth* iv, Happiest of all, there was the consciousness of his love, who was all the world to her.

e. ***for all the world***: in regard to, or taking into consideration, everything in the world; hence, in every respect, exactly (like, etc.). Also occas. †***for all this world***, † ***in all the world***. (See also 7 f (*b*).)

c **1330** R. BRUNNE *Chron. Wace* (Rolls) 16063 For al þe werd, so ferde he, On lyue wolde he non let be. *c* **1374** CHAUCER *Troylus* III. 1244 For alle þis world in swich present gladnesse Was Troilus and hath his lady swete. *c* **1386** —— *L.G.W.* Prol. 218 For al the world ryght as the dayseye I-corounede is with white leuys lite. **1513** DOUGLAS *Æneis* III. vii. 40 Sic ene had he, and sic fair handis tway, For all the warld, sic mouth and face, perfay. **1596** SHAKS. *1 Hen. IV*, III. ii. 93 For all the World, As thou art to this houre, was Richard then. **1596** —— *Merch. V.* v. i. 149 A paltry Ring.. whose Poesie was For all the world like Cutlers Poetry Vpon a knife. **1601** HOLLAND *Pliny* XI. xliv. I. 349 Thumbs and great toes they have moreover, with joints like (in all the world) to a man. **1609** DEKKER *Gull's Horn-bk.* iii. 15 Two narrow paire of staires, that for all the world haue crooked windings like those that lead to the top of Powles steeple. **1621** BP. MOUNTAGU *Diatribæ* 339 Iust, for all the world, as the Pharises are taxed by our Sauiour. **1775** SHERIDAN *Duenna* II. iii, As to her singing..she has a shrill, cracked pipe, that sounds for all the world like a child's trumpet. **1809** MALKIN *Gil Blas* IV. v. ¶3 She..dressed herself up in such a costume, as to look for all the world as if her sex were of a piece with her appearance. **1893** STEVENSON *Catriona* 3 This city..was for all the world like a rabbit warren.

22. the whole world. a. = 21 a.

1534 TINDALE *Luke* ix. 25 What avauntageth it a man, to wynne the whole worlde, yf he loose him sylfe? **1557** *Bible* (Geneva) 1 John v. 19 We knowe..that the whole worlde lyeth in wyckednes. *c* **1570** *Misogonus* III. iii. 72 (Bond) As any is ith whole woaude. **1596** DALRYMPLE tr. *Leslie's Hist. Scot.* (S.T.S.) I. 4 The vther parte..sa is situat, as frome the hail warlde it war diuidet. **1625** N. CARPENTER *Geogr. Delin.* II. i. 7 Man..had left him notwithstanding for his lot the whole world besides. **1759** STERNE *Tr. Shandy* I. x, It being just so long since he left his parish, and the whole world at the same time behind him. **1856** MISS YONGE *Daisy Chain* II. viii, Ethel [was] full of glee and wonder, for once beyond Whitford, the whole world was new to her.

b. = 21 b.

1560 DAUS tr. *Sleidane's Comm.* 62, I had the whole worlde against me with all their force and myght. **1569** J. ROGERS *Glasse Godly Love* in *Tell-trothes N. Yr.'s Gift* etc. (1876) 188 The amendment of all the whole world. **1570** BUCHANAN *Admonit.* Wks. (S.T.S.) 22 Ȝe haif obleist ȝour selffis befoir ye haill warld to continew in yatilk vertew of justice. **1606** SHAKS. *Tr. & Cr.* III. iii. 175 One touch of nature makes the whole world kin. **1773** FOOTE *Bankrupt* II. Wks. 1799 II. 112 The whole world concur in giving him sense. **1918** *Nation* (N.Y.) 7 Feb. 135/1 The whole world is beggaring itself by war.

23. this world. a. ***out of this world***: (i) superlatively good, fine beyond description; beautiful, delightful, wonderful. Also as adv. and attrib. phrases. *colloq.* and *slang* (orig. *U.S. Jazz*).

1928 R. FISHER *Walls of Jericho* 303 *Out (of) this world*, beyond mortal experience or belief. **1931** *Inter-State Tattler* 17 Dec. 12 Alberta Hunter.. warbles out of this world. **1935** *Swing Music* July 114/2 Benny's clarinet playing here is out-of-this-world for beauty of tone. **1946** *Sat. Rev. Lit.* (U.S.) 19 Oct. 25/3 Petarded on his own cliché And violently hurled, Should be the Joe whose one bon mot Is 'It's out of this world!' **1952** G. WILSON *Julien Ware* 36 A slender, graceful, out-of-this-world bridge Claud... had been. **1957** J. BRAINE *Room at Top* vi. 51 You've got a lovely part. Out of this world. **1972** J. ROSSITER *Rope for General Dietz* v. 61 She gave me the skinned fruit... With Cointreau poured on, mine tasted out of this world.

(ii) In neutral or derogatory contexts: unworldly; quite remarkable; also incredibly bad or repulsive.

1941 B. SCHULBERG *What makes Sammy Run?* vii. 149 The gallery was in a funny little bungalow with an easy-going, out-of-this-world atmosphere. **1951** 'A. GARVE' *Murder in Moscow* ii. 32 They hate our guts, and the way they behave is out of this world. **1958** *Oxford Mail* 27 Aug. 6/1 The worst part of a woman's magazine..is the fiction. Stories about quite impossible people in out-of-this-world situations. **1963** P. WILLMOTT *Evolution of Community* viii. 92 The L.C.C.'s wallpapers..are very antiquated, out of this world.

b. ***the*** (personal or other proper name, pl.) ***of this world***: people (countries, etc.) considered to represent the type specified; people, etc., like (sb. sing.). *colloq.* Freq. somewhat *derog.*

1960 J. STROUD *Shorn Lamb* iv. 44 He's settling... We're quite used to the Egberts of this world. **1969** M. PUGH *Last Place Left* xiv. 106 The Pardoes of this world would always brownnose to the landed gentry. **1972** *Observer* 20 Feb. 11/3 There is a limit on how far the Libyas of this world can bid up the price of oil.

V. *attrib.* and *Comb.*

24. a. Simple attrib. = 'of, pertaining to, or relating to the world' (in various senses), as ***world-age***, ***-architect***, ***area***, ***battle***, ***-construction***, ***craft***, ***cruise***, ***day***, ***egg***, ***-end*** (attrib.), ***era***, ***events***, ***field***, ***formation***, ***-formula***, ***government***, ***hero***, ***-image***, ***level***, ***love***, ***-model***, ***nausea***, ***noise***, ***ocean***, ***-outlook***, ***philosopher***, ***première***, ***principle***, ***record***, ***riddle***, ***sadness***, ***sect***, ***sorrow***, ***stratum***, ***-structure***, ***stuff***, ***-system***, ***-theory***, ***tour***, ***wilderness***, ***-will***, ***wisdom***, ***wreckage***, ***wright***; in certain cases with reference to early cosmogonies, as ***world-egg***, ***mill***, ***mother***, ***oak***, ***tortoise***, ***tree***.

Some of these are translated from or modelled on G. compounds, as *weltalter* world-age, *weltgeräusch* world-noise, *weltschmerz*, *weltsorge*, world-sadness, world-sorrow.

(Not clearly distinguishable from some of the examples in sense 25 b.)

1908 *Ch. Times* 5 June 761/4 Our Lord's teaching..was that the end of the present *world-age was at hand. **1877** E. CAIRD *Philos. Kant* II. xviii. 635 The idea..of a *world-architect, who is limited by the character of the material he uses. **1911** ZWEMER *Unocc. Mission Fields* Pref. p. vii, The entire *world-area has not yet been wholly covered by the tracks of the explorer. **1871** R. B. VAUGHAN *S. Thomas of Aquin* II. 295 He was a world-saint, for he had a *world-battle to fight and win. **1906** W. R. INGE *Truth & Falsehood in Relig.* 115 Science has no commission to produce an ideal *world-construction on a materialistic basis. **1840** STRICKLAND *Lives Queens Eng.* I. 87 William Rufus..had an abundant share of *world-craft, and well knew how to adapt himself to his father's humour. **1933** *World cruise [see CRUISE *sb.* 1 a]. **1977** A. C. H. SMITH *Jericho Gun* iv. 54 Let's take a world cruise. **1851** MRS. BROWNING *Casa Guidi Wind.* II. 758 The earliest *world-day light that ever flowed. **1848** BAILEY *Festus* (ed. 3) 108 The azure serpent..that sloughs its years And lays its *world-eggs in thy brightness. **1874** SAYCE *Compar. Philol.* iii. 99 The primeval world-egg of Egyptian philosophy, out of which all things have been generated. **1896** KIPLING *Seven Seas* p. vii, I was born in her gate... Where the *world-end steamers wait. **1858** J. MARTINEAU *Stud. Christ.* 139 The end of the great *world-era of the Lord. **1940** J. PEDERSEN *Israel* II. IV. 559 Like Isaiah he [*sc.* Jeremiah].. undertakes to interpret *world-events. **1840** S. WILBERFORCE *Sp. Missions* (1874) 72 How great a thing..it is to be entrusted with sowing the *world-field with the seed of man. **1884** *Century Mag.* XXVII. 916 A part of the *world-formation. **1888** J. ROYCE *Let.* 21 May in R. B. Perry *Thought & Char. W. James* (1935) I. 800, I have largely straightened out the big metaphysical tangle about continuity, freedom, and the *world-formula. **1907** W. JAMES *Pragmatism* ii. 50 The whole function of philosophy ought to be to find out what definite difference it will make to you and me, at definite instants of our life, if this world-formula or that world-formula be the true one. **1915** N. L. MCCLUNG *In Times like These* ix. 153 The problems of discovery have been solved; the problems of colonization are being solved. and when the war is over the problem of *world government will be solved. **1958** B. W. ALDISS *Non-Stop* IV. v. 241 The ship is in an orbit round Earth and there it must stay. That was the edict of the World Government. **1981** *Washington Post* 18 Mar. 1 He would never be part of an organization that advocated world government. **1844** MARG. FULLER *Wom. 19th C.* (1862) 27 To implore these '*world-heroes'..to beware of cant above all things. **1936** *Discovery* May 162/1 The Determinists have created for themselves an intellectual structure which represents a *world-image or rather a physical world-image. **1891** H. CROSBY *Conform. World* 10 Many an honest..Christian has unguardedly gone down to the *world-level. **1637** RUTHERFORD *Let. to Lady Robertland* 4 Jan. (1671) 205 Pride, & self love, & Idol-love, & *world-love. **1889** R. B. ANDERSON tr. *Rydberg's Teut. Mythol.* 118 That the *world-mill has a *möndull*, the mill-handle, which sweeps the uttermost rim of the earth. **1949** G. J. WHITROW *Structure of Universe* v. 75 In order to obtain some picture of the universe as a whole, we must construct a *world-model which will reproduce satisfactorily the properties of this observable (limited region of space and time). **1902** *19th Cent.* Dec. 991 The *World-Mother looked down through the ascending incense, as through the veil of centuries. **1876** GEO. ELIOT *Dan. Der.* xxiv, She had a *world-nausea upon her. **1916** S. BROOKE in *Life & Lett.* (1917) II. 663 You are in the roar and hustle of *world-noises and affairs which make history. **1904** *Folk-Lore* Sept. 295 The *world-oak or cloud-oak of Central and Southern Europe. **1877** J. E. CARPENTER tr. *Tiele's Outlines Hist. Relig.* 181 A sea-voyage over the *world-ocean. **1915** (*serial title*) *World outlook. **1929** *New Statesman* 31 Aug. 628/1 All poetic genius has always fumbled instinctively for a world-outlook in which everything has significance at all times. **1976** tr. Shih Min in *Yenan Seeds & Other Stories* 75 Remould your world-outlook and steel yourself into a self-aware revolutionary. **1853** THACKERAY *Engl. Hum.* iv. 160 Mat was a *world-philosopher of no small genius. **1934** WEBSTER, *World première. **1948** *Daily Ardmoreite* (Ardmore, Okla.) 7 July 1/5 'Return of the Bad Man' will open a three day engagement in Ardmore just one day after its world premier. **1981** LD. HAREWOOD *Tongs & Bones* ix. 150 He..put on several important world premières of British operas. **1854** GEO. ELIOT tr. *L. Feuerbach's Essence of Christianity* x. 101 Individual subjectivity..is regarded as the highest essence —the omnipotent *world-principle. **1912** W. TEMPLE in *Foundations* v. §iii. 243 A World-principle, the Logos of the Stoics. **1909** G. B. SHAW *Pen Portraits & Reviews* (1931) 236 In his stories of mystery and imagination Poe created a *world-record for the English language. **1976** *Daily Tel.* 20 July 1/5 Cornelia Ender won 100m women's freestyle gold model in world record 55.65 secs. **1909** *Hibbert Jrnl.* July 723 Science..knows that the pretence of solving the '*world-riddle' by her means alone is a mere echo of youthful enthusiasm. **1901** *Chamb. Encycl.* VIII. s.v. *Pessimism*, The same '*world-sadness' (*Weltschmerz*).. colours..the poetry of Omar Khayyam, Leopardi, Heine, and Byron. **1853** T. PARKER *Theism, Atheism* Introd. p. xlviii, All the *world-sects, as well as all the Christian sects. **1868** GEO. ELIOT *Spanish Gypsy* II. 173 Silva had thought To melt hard bitter grief by fellowship With the *world-sorrow trembling in his ear In Pablo's voice. **1896** *Sunday Mag.* Nov. 729 The World-Sorrow. **1868** M. COLLINS *Sweet Anne Page* I. 185 That *world-stratum called society. **1920** A. S. EDDINGTON *Space, Time & Gravit.* ix. 150 The *world-structure is not of a kind which can be traced in an exact way by mesh-systems, and in any large region the mesh-system drawn must be considered arbitrary. **1886** WINCHELL *Geol. Talks* 213 The background of the heavens is phosphorescent with the glow of these distant fields of *world-stuff. **1874** G. H. LEWES *Problems* I. 85 Our parochial system will sometimes be favourably contrasted with the results of their *world-system. **1977** P. JOHNSON *Enemies of Society* ii. 12 We have characterized its [*sc.* Freedom's] development into the Roman world-system as essentially a liberal economic process, presided over by a night-watchman state. **1834** J. S. MILL in *Monthly Repos.* VIII. 657 They are probably as sincere as they are capable of being, in any creed, or *world-theory, or abstract principle. **1960** W. V. O. QUINE *Word & Object* i. 24 The saving consideration is that we continue to take seriously our own..aggregate science, our own particular world-theory or loose total fabric of quasi-theories, whatever it may be. **1958** J. POPE-HENNESSY in P. Quennell *Lonely Business* (1981) III. 210 Maps of his *world-tours on the walls. **1971** 'G. BLACK' *Tome for Pirates* v. 84 A very slow world tour from which he returned with reluctance. **1858** CARLYLE *Fredk. Gt.* I. iv. I. 46 Scepticism, which is there beginning at the very top of the *world-tree. **1872** HARDWICK *Trad. Lanc.* 177 The great world-tree, *Yogdrasil*. **1848** BAILEY *Festus* (ed. 3) 108 The scape goat of this dark *world-wilderness. **1891** G. B. SHAW *Quintessence of Ibsenism* iv. 70 The *world-will shall answer for Julian's soul. **1892** J. ROYCE *Spirit Mod. Philos.* 239 We ourselves are embodiments of the world-will. **1742** YOUNG *Nt. Th.* VIII. 1410 *World-wisdom much has done, and more may do. **1899** WATTS-DUNTON *Aylwin* II. iv, The narrow world-wisdom of this Welsh aunt. **1837** CARLYLE *Fr. Rev.* I. VII. x, The Cimmerian *World-wreckage. *a* **1721** PRIOR *Cromwell & Porter* Wks. 1907 II. 267 Your System-Makers and *World-wrights.

b. Objective, as ***world-beater***, ***-betterer***, ***-builder***, ***-changer***, ***-controller***, ***-creator***, ***-destroyer***, ***-encircler***, ***-girdler***, ***-improver***, ***-lover***, ***-maker***, ***-monger***, ***-saver***, ***-sharer***, ***-stormer***, ***-teacher***, ***-watcher***, ***-wielder***, ***-worker***; ***world-building***, ***-conquering***, ***-embracing***, ***-fearing***, ***-forgetting***, ***-making***; ***world-adorning***, ***-alarming***, ***-beating***, ***-bettering***, ***-changing***, ***-cheering***, ***-creating***, ***-commanding***, ***-compassing***, ***-compelling***, ***-contemning***, ***-covering***, ***-despising***, ***-destroying***, ***-devouring***, ***-embracing***, ***-encircling***, ***-enfolding***, ***-forgetting***, ***-girdling***, ***-knowing***, ***-lifting***, ***-mothering***, ***-producing***, ***-rejoicing***, ***-renouncing***, ***-reviving***, ***-revolving***, ***-scorning***, ***-shaking***, ***-shattering***, †***-shogging***, ***-subduing***, ***-supporting***, ***-surrounding***, ***-swallowing***, ***-tossing***, ***-transforming***, ***-troubling***, ***-wasting***, ***-wielding***, ***-winning*** adjs.; ***world-despise*** vb. **c.** Instrumental, as ***world-adored***, ***-besotted***, ***-despised***, ***-entangled***, ***-forgotten***, ***-fretted***, ***-jewelled***, ***-read***, ***-ridden***, ***-studded***, ***-used***, ***wearied***, ***-worn*** adjs.; ***world-deep***, ***-great***, ***-high***, ***-like***, ***-long***, ***-old*** adjs.; see also WORLD-WIDE. **d.** In other adverbial uses: (*a*) 'from or to the world', 'in, about, or over the world', 'to the end of the world', as ***world-abiding***, ***-abstracted***, ***-bound***, ***-lost***, ***-minded*** (so ***-mindedness***) adjs.; ***-dweller***, ***-famed***, ***-famous*** [cf. G. *weltberühmt*] adjs., ***-flight***, ***-lasting***, ***roving***, ***-wandering*** adjs.; (*b*) 'over the whole world', 'to all the world', as ***world-famed***, ***-familiar***, ***-famous***, ***-known***, ***-noted***, ***-renowned***, ***-spread*** adjs.; (*c*) 'of or in regard to the world', as ***world-†rich***, †***-seely***, ***-sick***, ***-tired***, ***-wearied***, ***-weary*** (hence ***-weariness***); (*d*) with pl. in sense 7 e, as ***worlds-high*** adj.

1876 F. HARRISON *Choice of Bks.* (1886) 52 The world-wide and *world-abiding masterpieces. **1898** *Trans. Yorks. Dial. Soc.* I. 7 A *world-abstracted monk in his solitary cell. **1852** BAILEY *Festus* (ed. 5) 554 King, conqueror, and master, *world-adored! **1598** SYLVESTER *Du Bartas* II. i. I. *Eden* 231 Thy wondrous *World-adorning Fruit. *a* **1699** J. BEAUMONT *Psyche* XVI. xci, The *World-alarming Trumpets. **1893** *Outing* (U.S.) XXII. 103/1 The master of Palo Alto believed that the filly would prove to be a *world-beater. **1928** *Sunday Express* 24 June 20/4 The way he flashed the passing shot wide of Higgs..was *world-beating stuff. **1977** *Daily Mail* 24 Sept. 15/1 The BBC..never became the really 'world-beating station that I would like it to have been'. **1932** W. B. YEATS *Words for Music* 15 Imitate him if you dare, *World-besotted traveller; he Served human liberty. **1875** W. CORY *Lett. & Jrnls.* (1897) 376 One should..try to be an improver, a '*world-betterer' (Cambridge slang of my time). **1896** TOLLEMACHE *Jowett* 118 That ardent world-betterer T. H. Green. **1877** BAILEY *Festus* (ed. 10) 148 Great deeds, great thoughts, great schemes, *world-bettering. **1797** T. PARK *Sonn.* 9 My *world-bound bark must course an hardier way. **1884** J. PARKER *Apost. Life* II. 264 He saw us world-bound. **1884** J. TAIT *Mind in Matter* (1892) 158 Imaginary *world-builders, like Mr. Spencer, lay their foundations in shallows. **1920** A. S. EDDINGTON *Space, Time & Gravit.* x. 160 It might seem that this kind of fantastic *world-building can have little to do with practical problems. **1891** W. JAMES *Let.* 30 Jan. (1920) I. 305 Verily you are the stuff of which *world-changers are made! **1876** GEO. ELIOT *Dan. Der.* l, The *world-changing battle of Sadowa. **1603** CHETTLE *Eng.*

Mourn.-Garm., Sheph. Spring Song F 4 The Sun, which now doth gild the skie, With his light-giuing and *world-cheering eie. **1603** J. Davies (Heref.) *Extasie* Wks. (Grosart) I. 90/1 A Ladie..Cladd like a *World-commanding Potentate. **1861** Max Müller *Sci. Lang.* Ser. I. vi. (1864) 236 Their *world-compassing migrations. **1901** *Daily Chron.* 27 Dec. 5/4 Wartburg, whence Luther's song entered upon its *world-conquering career. **1603** J. Davies (Heref.) *Sonn. Ld. Kinlosse* Wks. (Grosart) I. 98/2 Thy *World-contemning Thoughts. **1823** Scott *Quentin D.* viii, How now!..our world contemning daughter—Are you robed for a hunting-party, or for the convent, this morning? Speak. *c* **1648–50** Brathwait *Barnabees Jrnl.* I. (1818) 33 Joviall, jocund, jolly bowlers, As they were the *world controulers. **1826** W. Elliott *Nun* 80 There lies a *world-corrupted friend. **1854** Geo. Eliot tr. *Feuerbach's Essence Chr.* xxii. 218 The *world-creating activity in itself negatives every determinate activity. **1877** Caird *Philos. Kant* II. xviii. 635 The idea of a *world-creator, for whom the means can have no existence apart from the end. *c* **1843** Carlyle *Hist. Sk.* (1898) 299 The grand interior tide-stream and *world-deep tendency. **1857** Hawthorne *Engl. Note-bks.* (1870) II. 272 Their world-wide, though not world-deep, experience. **1692** Evelyn *Let. to Pepys* Aug. P's Diary (1889) IX. 365, I have been philosophizing and *world-despising in the solitudes of this place. **1847** Helps *Friends in C.* I. vi. 91 How often has fiction made us sympathize..with the *world-despised. **1603** J. Davies (Heref.) *Extasie* Wks. (Grosart) I. 90/1, I tooke her for some *World-despising Dame. **1858** Gen. P. Thompson *Audi Alt.* xliv. I. 171 The tyrants and *world-destroyers of antiquity. **1909** G. K. Chesterton *Orthodoxy* (ed. 2) iv. 92 We count on the ordinary course of things... We risk the remote possibility of a miracle as we do that of a poisoned pancake or a *world-destroying comet. **1598** Sylvester *Du Bartas* II. i. II. *Ark* 449 These stormy Seas' deep *World-devouring waves. **1938** Dylan Thomas *Let.* 1 June (1966) 199 A world-devouring ghost creature bit out the horror of tomorrow from a gentleman's loins. **1900** *Daily News* 17 Jan. 5/1 The *world disturbing turmoil [in the days of the Reign of Terror]. *c* **1586** C'tess Pembroke *Ps.* XLIX. i, *World-dwellers all. **1807** J. Barlow *Columbiad* IV. 155 The *world-embracing scope That prompts his genius and expands his hope. **1848** R. I. Wilberforce *Doctr. Incarnation* ii. (1852) 18 The world-embracing benefits of his [Abraham's] seed. **1827** Keble *Chr. Y., 5th Sund. in Lent* xii, The *world-encircling sun. **1928** W. B. Yeats tr. *Sophocles' King Oedipus* 6 For all is *world-enfolding sea. **1609** J. Davies (Heref.) *Holy Rood* Wks. (Grosart) I. 8/2 Ye heau'ns weepe out your *world-enlight'ning eies. **1812** Crabbe *Tales* xix. 202 *World-entangled men! **1858** *World-famed [see *seven-cubit* s.v. seven *a.* and *sb.* C. 2]. **1866** Trevelyan in *Macm. Mag.* Mar. 411 The world famed Straits of Salamis. **1837** Carlyle *Fr. Rev.* I. IV. iv. 176 A cunningly devised Beheading Machine, which shall become famous and *world-famous. **1873** Symonds *Grk. Poets* xi. 373 One who made the insignificant place of his origin world-famous. **1841** Helps *Ess., Dom. Rule* (1842) 58 Ridicule..tends to make a poor and *world-fearing character. **1895** K. Grahame *Golden Age* 54 Rosa looked far away in a visionary, *world-forgetting sort of way. **1861** *Westm. Rev.* LXXVI. 281 Such a *world-forgotten village as Raveloe. **1941** I. L. Idriess *Great Boomerang* iv. 29 This man's dream was to become a peaceful and world-forgotten patriarch. **1813** L. Hunt in *Examiner* 15 Feb. 104/1 The charm that stillness has for a *world-fretted ear. **1892** *Outing* (U.S.) Mar. 447/1 They probably learned enough about it to make them treat the next *world-girdler with high respect. **1934** A. Woolcott *While Rome Burns* 93 Twenty such *world-girdling tales. **1978** H. Wouk *War & Remembrance* xxi. 209 All the members of a world-girdling alliance were attacking us. **1837** Carlyle *Fr. Rev.* I. I. ii, And so..did this of Royalty..grow mysteriously,..till it also had grown *world-great. **1853** T. T. Lynch *Self-Improvem.* 25 'Young men and others' as self-improvers are to become *world-improvers. **1839** Bailey *Festus* 243 Night comes, *world-jewelled. **1833** T. Hook *Parson's Dau.* I. vii, The..well-turned insinuations of his *world-knowing mother. **1845** Bailey *Festus* (ed. 2) 172 *World-known for strangest powers. **1851** Brimley *Ess.* 105 No marble of which *world-lasting statue..may be hewn. **1894** Kipling *Seven Seas* (1896) 45 O' that *warld-liftin' joy no after-fall could vex. **1839** Bailey *Festus* 274 It hath starlike beauty, And *worldlike might. **1842** Manning *Serm.* i. (1848) 18 Then shall..the *world-long growth and gathering of this awful mystery be accomplished. **1854** J. G. Whittier in *Nat. Era* 17 Aug. 130/4 New-born, the *world-lost anchorite A man became! **1941** T. Wolfe *Hills Beyond* iii. 235 He abandoned finally the world-lost fastnesses of Zebulon for the more urban settlement of Libya Hill. **1633** Earl Manch. *Al Mondo* (1636) 87 The *world-lover ends his hope and happinesse, when he dyes. **1674** N. Fairfax *Bulk & Selv.* 138, I can't find in my heart to deny that skill to a *World-maker, that I must needs give to a Watch-maker. **1871** R. B. Vaughan *S. Thomas of Aquin* II. 678 Plato..who admitted a world-maker, and a Providence. *a* **1776** Hume *Dialogues conc. Nat. Relig.* (1779) v. 61 A slow, but continued improvement carried on during infinite ages in the art of *world-making. **1884** *Century Mag.* XXVII. 914 World-making as practiced by the Astronomers. **1945** G. Murphy *Human Nature & Enduring Peace* xvi. 241 What we mean by *world-minded education. We mean education for intelligent world citizenship. **1979** *Amer. Speech 1976* LI. 79 Germans have traditionally been world-minded, receptive to foreign influences. **1926** *Religious Education* Apr. 190 Character is not a cause of world-mindedness, it is a result of *world-mindedness and many other attributes. **1960** A. Bjerstedt in *Jrnl. Conflict Resolution* IV. 185 (*title*) Ego-involved world-mindedness. **1682** Peden *Lord's Trumpet* (1739) 7 O..*World-monger that thou art, hath not Christ answered thee in that 6th of Matthew 33 Verse? **1883** G. M. Hopkins *Poems* (1967) 93 Wild air, *world-mothering air, Nestling me everywhere. **1615** T. Adams *Blacke Devill* 48 Monstrous and *world-noted wickednesse. **1858** M. C. Clarke (*title*) World-noted Women. **1727–46** Thomson *Summer* 1747 The *world-producing Essence, who alone Possesses being. **1912** Hardy *Jude the Obscure* p. x, An influential article..printed in a *world-read journal. *a* **1644** Quarles *Sol. Recant.* xi. 20 Every one Takes pleasure in the *world-rejoycing Sunne. **1910** W. Montgomery tr. *A. Schweitzer's Quest Hist. Jesus* xvi. 247 Inexhaustible reserves of *world-renouncing, world-contemning sayings. **1964** C. S. Lewis *Discarded Image* iii. 47 A world-renouncing, ascetic, and mystical character then marked the most eminent Pagans. **1831** Carlyle in *Foreign Q. Rev.* Oct. 372 The wild, deep, and now *world-renowned, *Legend of Faust*, belongs to a somewhat later date. **1854** tr. *Hettner's Athens & Peloponnese* 1 The world-renowned islands of Ægina and Salamis. **1728–46** Thomson *Spring* 51 Thou *world-reviving sun. **1727–46** —— *Summer* 32 With what an awful *world-revolving power Were first the unwieldy planets launched along The illimitable void! **1393** Langl. *P. Pl.* C. XVII. 16 þese *worlde-riche men. **1848** Eliza Cook *Dreamer* xxvii, The dense *world-ridden brain. **1757** Dyer *Fleece* I. 460 Inferior theirs to man's *world-roving frame. **1952** B. Wolfe *Limbo* IV. 214 A 'messianic complex', an urge to be a '*world-saver'. **1606** *Sir G. Goosecappe* II. i. in *Old Pl.* (1884) III. 29, I That have studied with *world-skorning thoughts The way of Heaven. *c* **1205** Lay. 11043 þa comen to-somne *weorld-seli men. **1598** Sylvester *Du Bartas* II. ii. I. *Ark* 444 *World-shaking Father. **1884** J. Parker *Apost. Life* II. 5 Christianity..was a world-shaking faith. **1893** *Harper's Mag.* Dec. 36/1 The..tragic and world-shaking events which are associated with the history of the.. Parliament of Great Britain. **1606** Shaks. *Ant. & Cl.* II. vii. 76 These three *World-sharers, these Competitors Are in thy vessell. **1974** M. Tippett *Moving into Aquarius* II. 155 During those years there have been huge and *world-shattering events in which I have been inevitably caught up. **1611** Cotgr., *Croule-vniuers*, *World-shogging, all-shaking. **1884** R. F. Burton *Bk. Sword* Introd. p. xiii, Their recklessness of all consequences soared *worlds-high above the various egotistic systems. **1836** Newman in *Lyra Apost.* (1849) 239 *World-sick, to turn within and image there Some idol dream. **1886** W. J. Tucker *E. Europe* 233 Your *world-spread language. **1878** Bosw. Smith *Carthage* 271 The man who, like one of the *world-stormers of more modern times..could carry everything before him. **1852** Bailey *Festus* (ed. 5) 12 The ætherial web, *world-studded, of the skies. **1851** Brimley *Ess.* 105 Iron, of which *world-subduing machines may be wrought. **1876** Geo. Eliot *Dan. Der.* lii, A *world-supporting elephant. **1817** Shelley *To Constantia Singing* in *Posthumous Poems* (1824) 144 Whilst, like the *world-surrounding air, thy song Flows on. **1820** Shelley *Prometh. Unb.* I. 661 World-surrounding aether. **1885** R. L. & F. Stevenson *Dynamiter* 166 At one *world-swallowing stride, the heart of the tornado reached the clearing. **1887** Haweis *Lt. Ages* viii. 211 The Jew never was to have an Empire. He was the *world-teacher not the world-ruler. **1608** Sylvester *Du Bartas* II. iv. IV. *Decay* 657 *World-tossing Tempest! **1935** W. B. Yeats *Full Moon in March* 68 What sacred drama through her body heaved When *world-transforming Charlemagne was conceived? **1895** —— *Poems* 259 And shook at Invar Amargin The hearts of the *world-troubling seamen. **1860** Trollope *Cas. Richmond* xxvi, That dry, time-worn *world-used London lawyer. **1612** Drayton *Poly-olb.* x. 292 Those poore *world-wandring men. **1820** Shelley *Prometh. Unb.* I. 325 Jove's world-wandering herald, Mercury. **1592** Shaks. *Rom. & Jul.* v. iii. 112 This *world-wearied flesh. **1838** Lytton *Alice* II. vi, It was..this singular purity of heart which made to the world-wearied man the chief charm in Evelyn Cameron. **1858** Faber *Spir. Confer.* (1870) 142 *World-weariness is a blessed thing in its way. **1768** Murphy *Zenobia* I. i. 16 This sad *world-weary spirit. **1876** Swinburne *Erechtheus* 1140 Night that lulls world-weary day. **1881** G. M. Hopkins in *Note-Bks. & Papers* (1937) 346 Satan..is the κοσμοκράτωρ, the *worldwielder. **1887** —— *Poems* (1967) 70 And the azurous hung hills are his world-wielding shoulder. **1822** Byron *Werner* IV. i. 410 A *world-winning battle. **1843** Carlyle *Past & Pr.* III. vi. (1872) 146 Giant Labour, truest emblem there is of God the *World-Worker. **1826** A. A. Watts *Richmond-Hill* ix, The *world-worn man may here repair. **1842** Manning *Serm.* xxi. (1848) I. 310 The wearied and world-worn spirit.

25. Passing into adj.: **a.** in comb. derived from OE. compounds of *woruld*, in which this is equivalent to 'of or pertaining to this world, earthly, mundane', as *woruldǽht*, *-god*, *-þing*, *-wela* worldly possessions or wealth, *woruldcyning* an earthly king, *woruldscamu* public disgrace (cf. 14 b above), *woruldwynn* earthly joy.

c **1175** *Lamb. Hom.* 143 þer scal beon worldwunne wiðuten pouerte. *c* **1200** Ormin 7513, & uss birrþ weorelldþingess lusst Forrbuȝhenn & forrwerrpenn. *Ibid.* 12079 Off þatt hemm weorelldahhtess spedd A33 waxeþþ mare & mare. *c* **1200** *Trin. Coll. Hom.* 29 Gef þu hauest woreld wele þu miht þarof wurðliche fare. *c* **1205** Lay. 7345 Freoliche we hit haldeð wið alle weoruld kingen. *Ibid.* 8323, & æfter muchel weorld-scome wurð-scipe wurhten. **12..** *Moral Ode* 365 (Egerton MS.) Ne scal þer beo sced ne scrud ne woruld wele none. *c* **1250** *Prov. Alfred* 382 in *O.E. Misc.* 124 Alle world-ayhte schulle bi-cumen to nouhte. *c* **1275** Lay. 28131 Nolleþ hii hit bi-gynne for none worle-þinge. *a* **1300** *Cursor M.* 13281 Petre and andreu..wit a word þai left þair scipps tuin, For þat was al þair werld win [*Gött.* worldis win]. **14..** *MS. Sloane 2593* xlii. 25 in *Herrig's Archiv* (1902) CIX. 60 If þu welde þi wordel goodes [etc.]. *Ibid.* 81 þis wordel good xuld incres.

b. With the meaning 'of or pertaining to the whole world, embracing the whole world, world-wide, universal'.

Orig. translating or modelled on G. compounds, as *welthandel* world-commerce, *weltkrieg* world-war, *weltmacht* world-power, *weltreich* world-empire.

(Not clearly distinguishable from some of the examples in sense 24 a.)

1833 J. S. Mill in *Monthly Repos.* VII. 510 The most stirring scenes of that mighty world-drama, under his pen turn flat, cold, and spiritless. **1839** Bailey *Festus* 53 [Immortality] That is the great world question. **1848** *Ibid.* (ed. 3) 172 Pride and World-Ambition. **1843** Carlyle *Past & Pr.* II. ii, The World-Dramaturgist has written: *Exeunt.* **1850** Blackie *Æschylus* II. 6 That primeval age of gigantic 'world-strife' (if we may be allowed to Anglicize a German compound). **1852** Tennyson *Ode Wellington* 42 The great World-victor's victor will be seen no more. *Ibid.* 133 In that world-earthquake, Waterloo! **1856** Grote *Greece* II. xciv. XII. 367 Alexander, had he lived, would..have multiplied ..the communications..between the various parts of his world-empire. **1858** Carlyle *Fredk. Gt.* I. i. I. 20 The huge world-conflagration. *Ibid.* v. vi. 594 The Second Act..of this foolish World-Drama of the Double-Marriage opens. **1860** Pusey *Min. Proph.* 553 Alexander's policy was essentially different from that of the world-monarchs before him. **1864** —— *Daniel* ii. 78 When He took away their world-rule, He left them in being as nations. **1864** Bryce *Holy Rom. Emp.* vii. (1866) 99 The two great ideas which expiring antiquity bequeathed to the ages that followed were those of a World-Monarchy and a World-Religion. **1879** G. H. Lewes *Stud. Psychol.* ix. 162 The World-process has been assigned to a Soul of the World. **1887** *Contemp. Rev.* May 699 With the world price of wheat so closely approximating to the cost of production. **1890** W. Morris *News from Nowhere* xv. 129 They had gradually created..a most elaborate system of buying and selling, which has been called The world-market. **1894** A. J. Balfour *Found. Belief* (1895) 3 Looking at the World-problems which..we are compelled to face. **1898** G. B. Shaw *Perfect Wagnerite* 14 He is trusting to another great world-force, the Lie. **1898** *Q. Rev.* July 264 In any serious world-struggle we should be certain to have each other's sympathy. **1899** *Daily Tel.* 21 Aug. 6/7 We have had thrust upon us a drama played upon a world-stage. **1904** W. James *Ess. Radical Empiricism* (1912) i. 8 Experience, at this rate, would be much like a paint of which the world pictures were made. **1904** *Westm. Gaz.* 14 Nov. 4/2 The great British World-Empire. **1905** *Ibid.* 21 Sept. 3/2 The great world-commerce, upon which the very existence of England will depend. **1906** *Ibid.* 26 Sept. 5/2 A world-parliament of the Universities. **1910** A. G. Spink *National Game* 309 (*heading*) World champions. **1914** G. Frankau *Poet. Wks.* (1923) I. 185 Battlers for world-peace, slaves of Honour's lamp. **1920** B. Russell *Pract. & Theory Bolshevism* IX. 109 The following passages [from article by Lenin] seemed to me illuminating:—The present world-situation in politics places on the order of the day the dictatorship of the proletariat. **1921** J. C. Maxwell Garnett (*title*) Education and world citizenship. **1921** D. H. Lawrence *Sea & Sardinia* v. 163 Will the last waves of enlightenment and world-unity break over them [*sc.* the Sardinians] and wash away the stocking-caps? **1923** —— *Fantasia of Unconscious* 15 No more little Excelsiors crying world-brotherhood. **1927** A. Cecil *Brit. Foreign Secretaries* vii. 353 Aberdeen would have felt all the talk about German world-domination too journalistically sensational to be politically probable. **1929** J. Buchan *Courts of Morning* 14 America... could not take a big hand in world affairs... She had too much to do at home. **1930** J. H. Randall (*title*) A world community. **1932** A. G. Herbert tr. *Nygren's Agape & Eros* I. vi. 146 For Plotinus the whole world process is summed up in the double conception of the out-going of all things from the One..and the return of all things to the One. **1936** *Mind* XLV. 460 It was left to the Stoics to elaborate the conception of the world-state and of the world-citizen. **1936** World-culture [see culture *sb.* 5 d]. **1937** 'G. Orwell' *Road to Wigan Pier* xii. 247 It is quite easy to imagine a world-society, economically collectivist. **1940** World opinion [see appease *v.* 2 c]. **1943** E. M. W. Tillyard (*title*) The Elizabethan world picture. **1945** Auden *For Time Being* 89 Instead of Country Fair, there is World Market. **1946** J. S. Huxley *Unesco* i. 17 The task of unifying the world mind. **1948** L. Spitzer *Linguistics & Literary History* 220 This is also the main idea of Claudel's Spanish Catholic world-drama *Le soulier de satin.* **1954** 'M. Cost' *Invitation from Minerva* 218 The world-press.. was hourly dominated by bulletins of their plight. **1959** *New Yorker* 24 Oct. 185/1 Joyce..gave her..world rights to publish and sell 'Ulysses'. **1962** *Listener* 22 Mar. 498/1 Goethe, it will be remembered, spoke of *Weltkultur*... The great Russian component of world culture is as individual as our own or the French. **1966** S. Beer *Decision & Control* xv. 391 As usual, the study begins with a..world situation. **1967** P. D. James *Unnatural Causes* I. xv. 116 He was completely unconcerned with world affairs. **1974** I. Wallerstein (*title*) The modern world system and the origins of the European world-economy in the 16th century. **1977** P. Johnson *Enemies of Society* v. 61 Britain expanded this initial overseas foothold by the Navigation Acts..which..constituted the beginning of an English-controlled world market. **1981** *Listener* 2 July 3/1 American columnists..are querying whether Reagan is not hazarding world peace. **1981** N. Tucker *Child & Book* iv. 108 In Enid Blyton's work, this excessively simple world picture is carried to extremes. **1983** *Times* 14 May 8/3 The power of world opinion is a vital adjunct to non-violence.

26. Special comb.: **world-all** [tr. G. *weltall*], the world considered as a unit; the universe; **world-auxiliary**, a language (esp. an invented one) which may be used as a standard means of communication between speakers from different language communities throughout the world; cf. *auxiliary language* s.v. auxiliary *a.* 2 a; **World Bank**, an international banking organization established to control the distribution of economic aid between member nations, *spec.*: †(*a*) the Bank for International Settlements, established through the League of Nations at Basle in 1930 (*obs.*); (*b*) the International Bank for Reconstruction and Development, affiliated to the United Nations and operational since 1946; **world-class** *a.*, applied to persons or things regarded as outstanding throughout the world; **World Court**, the International Court of Justice (formerly, the Permanent Court of International Justice, 1921–45), established in 1946 as the principal judicial arm of the United Nations; **World Cup**, in Assoc. Football, a quadrennial competition amongst national teams for the Jules Rimet trophy, first contested in 1930; also *transf.* in other sports; **world-divided** *a.*, (*a*) separated from the rest of the world; (*b*) 'worlds' apart or asunder; **world English** = *Standard English* s.v. standard *a.* 3 e; **world fair** = *world's fair*, sense 27 a below;

world ground, the reality, or principle, that underlies the world; **World Health Organization**, an international body established in 1948 to promote co-operation between nations to improve health conditions (abbrev. *W.H.O.*: see W 3); **world-history** [G. *weltgeschichte*], history embracing the events of the whole world; hence ***world-historic***, ***-historical*** adjs.; **world-language**, (*a*) a language universally read and spoken by educated people; (*b*) a language for international use; **world-life**, life in the world, earthly life; **world-line** *Physics* and *Philos.* [tr. G. *weltlinie* (H. Minkowski, as for *world-point*)], the succession of points in space-time that are occupied by a particle; **world-literature** [cf. G. *weltliteratur*], (*a*) a body of work drawn from many nations and recognized as literature throughout the world; (*b*) (the sum of) the literature of the world; **world-old** [G. *weltalt*], as old as the world; **world-order**, an organized state of existence in this or another world; **world-point** *Physics* and *Philos.* [tr. G. *weltpunkt* (H. Minkowski in H. A. Lorentz et al. *Das Relativitätsprinzip* (1913) 57)], a point in space-time; a particular point in space at a particular instant of time; **world-policy**, **-politics** [G. *weltpolitik*], a policy or politics based upon considerations affecting the world as a whole; hence ***world-politician***, ***world-political*** *a.*; **world-ranking** *a.*, that ranks among the best in the world; **world-revolution**, a world-wide revolution in the social order or in any sphere of activity; **world-ruler**, a ruler of the (known) world; **World Series**, a series of games contested annually as a play-off between the champions of the two major baseball leagues in the U.S.; also *transf.*; **World Service**, a B.B.C. radio service with a strong content of news and current affairs, broadcast principally for English-speaking listeners overseas (formerly called the *Overseas Service*); **world-soul** [G. *weltgeist*, *weltseele*], the animating principle which informs the physical world; **world-spirit**, (*a*) the spirit of the world in its mundane aspects and activities; (*b*) = *world-soul*; **world-state**, (*a*) a state comprising the whole world; (*b*) a state possessing world-power; **world-thane** *Hist.* [OE. *woruldþeȝn*], a secular 'thane'; **world-view** [G. *weltanschauung*], contemplation of the world, view of life; so ***world-viewer***; **world-wise** *a.*, wise in the things of the world, worldly-wise; **world-worm**, a low creature of earth; **world-year** (see quot.).

1847 J. D. Morell *Hist. Philos.* (ed. 2) I. II. 369 Fichte founded a subjective idealism in which the me was the **world-all.* **1925** R. M. Ogden tr. *Koffka's Growth of Mind* 347 For a child there is as yet no single world-all. **1927** E. S. Pankhurst *Delphos* v. 49 The *world-auxiliary, used by everyone as a second language, will obviate the need for any other language save the native one. **1930** *Business Week* 28 May 9/2 French shares for the *World Bank were offered publicly this week. **1943** *N.Y. Times* 5 Apr. 6/3 Senator Elmer Thomas said..that the establishment of a world bank founded on a standard international coin was inevitable. **1944** *St. Louis* (Missouri) *Post-Dispatch* 23 July 6A/3 (*heading*) Russia agrees to boost quota in World Bank. **1973** 'D. Jordan' *Nile Green* xi. 47 The statistical boys..had worked out all the flaws in the World Bank report. **1950** *Sport* 22–28 Sept. 14/2 Such is the magnetism of *world class heavyweight boxers! **1973** *Daily Express* 11 May 22/1 Keegan, looking every inch a world-class player..scored with a spectacular header. **1973** *Guardian* 22 Oct. 21/4 The timescale of astronomers is human and to those in world class research..too short to waste much time on bumbledom. **1979** *Beautiful British Columbia* Winter 40 A total of more than $100 million is expected to be spent at Whistler..to make the area competitive with world-class resorts in the United States and Europe. **1927** *New Republic* 21 Sept. 110/2 Our reservations to the resolution adhering to the *World Court were received with an apathy which was next door to hostility. **1946** *N.Y. Times* 7 Feb. 8/2 (*heading*) 15 Judges elected for World Court. **1984** *Times* 10 Apr. 1/6 The Reagan Administration said yesterday it believed the World Court in The Hague did not have jurisdiction. **1950** B. Wright *Captain of England* xvii. 154 For the first time in my experience the words '*World Cup' began to come into the discussions footballers have when they meet, and as the four British home associations had re-entered F.I.F.A., it was only to be expected that they would..enter this competition. **1954** *Times* 8 Nov. 10/1 (*heading*) Rugby League results..World Cup. **1967** *Times* 9 Nov. 16/4 (*heading*) World Cup golf. **1978** R. Westall *Devil on Road* xx. 185 An action-replay of a World Cup goal on telly. *a* **1618** Sylvester *Sonn.* Wks. (Grosart) II. 321 Our little *World-divided Ile. **1743** Francis tr. *Hor.*, *Odes* III. v. 3 Since world-divided Britain owns his sway. **1899** *Folk-Lore* Mar. 75 Races world-divided in their range and their social conceptions. **1927** K. Malone in *Amer. Speech* II. 323/2 He..warns against a slavish conformity to the dictionary, i.e., to the prescriptions of standard English, or *world-English, as some people call it. **1980** *English World-Wide* I. I. 80 The categories or types of AVE..can be seen as existing across a scale having 'World English' ('book English', 'standard English', 'teachers' preferred English', &c.), at one end, and a national variety most distinct from it at the other. **1899** C. Stumpf *Let.* 8 Sept. in R. B. Perry *Thought & Char. W. James* (1935) II. 193 The tumult of a *world fair—even the thought of it makes me nervous! **1978** P. Boardman *Worlds of Patrick Geddes* vi. 179 A brief..account of the city [*sc.* Paris]..from pre-Roman times up to the greatest of world fairs. **1898** W. James in *Psychol. Rev.* July 424 The world is evidently more complex than we are accustomed to think it, the 'absolute *world-ground', in particular, being farther off (as Mr. F. C. S. Schiller has well pointed out) than it is the wont either of the usual empiricisms or of the usual idealisms to think it. **1948** *Scot. Jrnl. Theol.* I. 121 The most that science, working with its concepts of causation on a different level, can offer is a world-ground, or mind-energy at work in the world. **1946** *N.Y. Times* 28 June 9/1 The vanquished nations..with their large health problems, have acute need of the *World Health Organization that the United Nations is creating. **1977** *New Scientist* 7 Apr. 3/2 All the more horrendous, then, are the statistics which the World Health Organisation has published to publicise World Health Day, which falls today (7 April). **1876** Geo. Eliot *Dan. Der.* lxiii, In this romantic *world-historic position of his. **1854** C. C. J. Bunsen *Outl. Philos. Universal Hist.* I. 64 Both these researches, the philosophical and the *world-historical, will be reserved for the second volume of our sketch. **1879** Geo. Eliot *Theo. Such* xiv. 255 Something truly Roman and world-historical. **1837** Carlyle *Fr. Rev.* I. I. ii, Of these ages *World-History can take no notice. **1902** *Fortn. Rev.* Dec. 1006 A philosophy of history and civilisation..which holds its ground as the basis both of World-history and Christian theology. **1867** W. D. Whitney *Lang. & Study Lang.* xii. 469 If we expect..that our tongue become one day a *world-language, understood and employed on every continent.., then it is our bounden duty [etc.]. **1889** *Athenæum* 24 Aug. 256/3 The two classical and four great modern 'world-languages'. **1899** *Daily News* 3 July, A German Professor has proposed English as a World-language. *c* **1000** *Ags. Ps.* (Th.) ciii. 33 [civ. 35] þæt hio ne wunian on *world-life. *c* **1200** Ormin 2980 All þiss weorelld-lif iss full Off sinness þeossterrnesse. *c* **1205** Lay. 32075 þu uindest ænne pape..he þe scal scriuen of þine weorld-lifen. **1848** Bailey *Festus* (ed. 3) 324 With the world thy part is now... Now behoves to live The worldlife of the future. **1916** *Monthly Notices R. Astron. Soc.* LXXVI. 700 The points of space occupied by a given material point at successive times form in the four-dimensional time-space a continuity of one dimension, which is called the *world-line of the point. **1946** *Mind* LV. 146 The intersection of the world-lines AM and TM. **1962** *Listener* 27 Dec. 1095/3 According to Einstein's General Theory of Relativity it seems that objects which appear to be responding to the pull of gravity..are simply following the shortest available world-line through the space-time continuum. **1976** *Nature* 1–8 Jan. 30/2 The collapsing star is represented by some of its (time-like) worldlines including the worldline of its centre. **1831** Carlyle in *Edin. Rev.* CV. 179 Instead of isolated, mutually repulsive National Literatures, a *World Literature may one day be looked for? **1908** P. E. More *Shelburne Essays* V. 140 Longfellow brought from Germany the ideal of a world literature which should absorb the best of all lands. **1949** Wellek & Warren *Theory of Lit.* v. 41 The term 'world literature', a translation of Goethe's Weltliteratur, is perhaps needlessly grandiose. **1963** *English Studies* XLIV. 148 He has noted the widespread occurrence of the bond-story of *The Merchant of Venice* in world-literature. **1840** T. Gordon tr. *W. Menzel's Ger. Lit.* I. 265 The *world-old Oriental idea of the mystic unity of those contrasts which..are all united in God. **1862** Stanley *Jew. Ch.* (1877) I. i. 7 No modern traveller..has left a written account of this world-old place. **1875** Lowell *Wordsw.* Prose Wks. 1890 IV. 357 The world-old question of matter and form. **1846** Trench *Mirac.* Introd. (1862) 72 There is a nobler *world-order than that in which we live and move. **1894** H. Drummond *Ascent of Man* 38 The Struggle for the Life of Others..[is] engrained in the world-order as profoundly as the Struggle for Life. **1923** Perret & Jeffery tr. H. Minkowski in *Lorentz's Princ. Relativity* v. 76 A point of space at a point of time, that is, a system of values x, y, z, t, I will call a *world-point. The multiplicity of all thinkable x, y, z, t systems of values we will christen the world. **1930** L. Silberstein *Size of Universe* I. 1 The event thus localized in space..and in time is called a worldpoint. **1967** R. A. George tr. *Carnap's Logical Structure of World* iv. 194 The points of n-dimensional, real-number space, we call *world points*. **1975** R. Adler et al. *Introd. Gen. Relativity* (ed. 2) iv. 122 An event is a point in four-space: a world-point. **1896** *Daily News* 10 Mar. 6/5 The Minister again declared that Germany did not think of inaugurating a '*world-policy'. **1905** *Westm. Gaz.* 24 Mar. 2/1 A world-policy alliance with Japan. **1936** *World-political [see *anti-Comintern* s.v. ANTI-[1] 3 a]. **1958** S. Spender *Engaged in Writing* vii. 133 He was the first world-political, international, intellectual man. **1905** *Daily Chron.* 27 May 3/2 Our Future is on the Sea? Critical Inquiries and Deductions by a German *World Politician. **1858** Carlyle *Fredk. Gt.* v. iv. I. 571 Papa [King George I.] and Husband [the King of Prussia] being so blessedly united in their *World-Politics. **1905** *Daily Chron.* 24 June 4/3 The considerable measure of success which the Kaiser's intervention in Morocco has attained is an instructive lesson in the solidarity of world-politics. **1970** *Daily Tel.* 19 Aug. 10/4 Here in Britain we have two *world-ranking centres of radio astronomy. **1832** Carlyle *Remin.* (1881) I. 60 The great *world-revolutions send in their disturbing billows to the remotest creek. **1911** G. Elliot Smith *Anc. Egyptians* i. 6 The great world-revolution inaugurated by the advent of the Age of Metals. **1874** W. P. Mackay *Grace & Truth* 160 We protest against the awful power that the *world-rulers used in former days. **1881** *N.T.* (R.V.) *Eph.* vi. 12 Our wrestling is not against flesh and blood, but..against the world-rulers [κοσμοκράτορας] of this darkness. **1918** *The Crime* II. 423 The bombastic..vision of the future as it appears to the German World-ruler. **1913** *Collier's* 4 Oct. 5/1 In this next impending *world-series carnival between Giants and Athletics we have had the hunch [etc.]. **1951** *Time* 12 Mar. 59 For Norwegians..the Holmenkollen is the World Series, and stars such as Hoel and Björnstad are Norway's Di Maggios and Musials. **1973** M. Woodhouse *Blue Bone* iii. 20 'We could have played half the World Series by now.'..'Yes, we take three days to play a game of cricket.' **1966** *B.B.C. Handbk.* 83 The **World Service* addresses itself to those who understand English, wherever they happen to be—listeners throughout the Commonwealth and English-speaking people in other countries. **1981** *Times* 22 Jan. 8/7 The embassy press officer ..was waiting for news from the World Service of the BBC. **1848** Bailey *Festus* (ed. 3) 202, I am the *world-soul, nature's spirit am I. **1856** R. A. Vaughan *Mystics* I. iii. 27 The philosophers who believe themselves organs of the world-soul. **1846** G. H. Lewes *Biogr. Hist. Philos.* IV. 212 The *World-Spirit (*Weltgeist*) has at last succeeded in freeing himself from all incumbrances. **1850** Robertson *Serm.* Ser. III. xxi, The world-spirit can rebuke as sharply as the Spirit which was in John. **1909** Inge *Faith* viii. 129 This World-Spirit was once incarnated in a human life. **1890** Costelloe *Ch. Cath.* (1892) 25 She prophesies of a *World-State, and laughs at the little fences statesmen draw upon the map. **1902** *Daily Chron.* 1 Nov. 3/1 However desirable may be the lot of a small State among small States, the conditions are changed in a world of world-States. **1614** Selden *Titles Hon.* 225 Ealdormen, Holdes, Hetgerefas, Messethegnes, and *Werldthegnes. **1839** Keightley *Hist. Eng.* I. 83 The mass-thane or clergyman stood on a par with the world-thane or gentleman. **1858** J. Martineau *Stud. Christ.* 321 The deep penetration of his [*sc.* Paul's] mistaken *world-view. **1906** D. S. Cairns *Christ. in Mod. World* v. 233 Christianity, alike in its Central Gospel, and in its World-view, must come to terms with Hellenism. **1862** Gen. P. Thompson in *Bradford Advertiser* 20 Dec. 6/1 More instances will occur to the thoughtful *world-viewer. *c* **1205** Lay. 13721 þa *weorldewis mon þa oðere children biwusten. **1845** Bailey *Festus* (ed. 2) 240 Was he world-wise? **1862** Lytton *Str. Story* lxvii. II. 192 Silently thinking, I walked by the side of the world-wise woman. **1617** Fletcher *Mad Lover* II. i, Away thou *World-worm, Thou win a matchless Beauty? **1826** E. Irving *Babylon* II. 429 Rear your children to be men, not to be world-worms; to be saints, not to be drudges. **1860** *Chamb. Encycl.* I. 76/1 These Ages were regarded as the divisions of the great *world-year, which would be completed when the stars and planets had preformed a revolution round the heavens.

27. In the possessive. **a.** In senses corresponding to those at 25 and 26, as ***world's championship***, ***record***, ***Series***; **world's fair** orig. *U.S.*, an international exposition of arts, science, industry, and agriculture.

1888 *Spaulding's Base-Ball Guide* 47 In 1887 the world's championship series had become an established supplementary series of contests. **1910** A. G. Spink *National Game* 312 The world's championship. **1850** *New-England Farmer* II. 413 The State Board of Agriculture are making up a collection of samples of Indian corn for the World's Fair. **1908** E. Terry *Story of my Life* xii. 280, I had loved the Chicago of the Lake with the white buildings of the World's Fair shining on it. **1982** J. S. Borthwick *Case of Hook-Billed Kites* iv. 193 Like those rides at world's fairs ..where you sit in a little car that draws you through different habitats. **1893** *Outing* (U.S.) XXII. 154/2 He has ..held the world's record in the pole vault for distance. **1905** *Sporting Life* 7 Oct. 3/1 Jack Sheridan and Hank O'Day have been appointed to umpire the world's series. **1925** F. Scott Fitzgerald *Great Gatsby* iv. 88 He's the man who fixed the World's Series back in 1919. **1965** F. O. Du Pre *U.S. Air Force Biogr. Dict.* 58/1 He won the Schneider Cup Race—the World's Series of seaplane racing—in 1925, with an average speed of 232 mph.

b. In hyperbolical phr. ***the world's worst*** (..), the very worst or most incompetent. *colloq.*

1921 T. Wolfe *Let.* 13 Nov. (1956) 22 'The Woman of Bronze', the world's worst play. **1929** J. B. Priestley *Good Companions* II. i. 248 She was easily the world's worst as a pianist. **1933** L. Einstein in O. W. Holmes *Holmes-Einstein Lett.* (1964) 352, I hasten to add that they are the world's most famous bridge players and she the world's worst! **1954** R. Bissell *High Water* i. 11 He shaved every other day and of all the Second Mates in the company they could have dumped on me he was the world's worst. **1962** C. Draper *Mad Major* iv. 88, I am probably the world's worst dancer.

c. In colloq. phr. ***one of the world's workers***, an industrious person. Freq. in neg. contexts.

1933 [see PULL *v.* 25 f]. **1964** D. Gray *Devil wore Scarlet* x. 91 'Mr. Weston isn't one of the world's workers, exactly,' said Mary. **1976** G. Moffat *Short Time to Live* ii. 20 Jackson..is *not* one of the world's workers, as you must have noticed.

†**world**, *v.* *Obs. rare.* [f. prec.] *trans.* **a.** To furnish with a world of people; to people. Also *intr.* with *it.* **b.** To bring (a child) into the world.

1589 Warner *Alb. Eng.* VI. xxxi. 140 Zamois, when Troy must perish, shall send downe her Floods a Fleete, And world it where our Father rulde... But long time hence,.. that World shall world an Ile. **1628** Feltham *Resolves* II. [I.] lix. 170 Like Lightening, it can strike the childe in the wombe, and kill it ere 'tis worlded.

'**worlded,** (*ppl.*) *a.* *rare* (chiefly *poet.*). [f. WORLD *sb.* or *v.* + -ED.] Containing worlds. Also with qualifying word.

1885 Tennyson *Tiresias* 167 The fires that arch this dusky dot—Yon myriad-worlded way. **1907** 'Mark Twain' in *Harper's Mag.* Dec. 44/2, I think there is such a planet..in one of the thinly worlded corners of the universe. **1934** Dylan Thomas *18 Poems* 31 How light the sleeping on this soily star, How deep the waking in the worlded clouds.

worldful ('wɜːldfʊl). Also **-full.** [f. WORLD *sb.* + -FUL.] As much or as many as would fill a world. Chiefly in hyperbolical use.

1846 Hare *Mission Comf.* (1850) 4 Spiritual food wherewith to feed the whole world through all the generations of mankind, and worldfuls over and above. **1879** P. Brooks *Influence of Jesus* ii. 81 That through His sonship this world-full of men is to learn that they are God's sons. **1879** Black *Macleod of D.* xxiii, The one small word filled with a whole worldful of light and joy.

†'**worldhood.** *Obs. rare.* [f. WORLD *sb.* + -HOOD.]

1. Worldly possessions.

15.. Hen. VIII in D'Israeli *Amen. Lit.* (1841) II. 136 Content yourselves with what you have already, or else seek honest means whereby to increase your worldhoods.

2. State or condition as a world.
1674 N. FAIRFAX *Bulk & Selv.* 183 Not in the world as now 'tis, but chang'd in its kind of worldhood.

'worldish, *a. rare.* [f. WORLD *sb.* + -ISH[1].] Of or belonging to this world; worldly.
13.. *Cursor M.* 22754 (Edin.) Al þinges þat ani werdische [*v.r.* werldis] hald wit hinges. **1340** HAMPOLE *Pr. Consc.* 951 Swilk men worldisshe men men calles þat þair luf mast on þe world settes. *Ibid.* 1065–6 þas men worldesshe men men calles, For about worldisshe þynges þai here travaile Ful bysily. **1827** CUNNINGHAM *Lass of Gleneslan-Mill* iv, Wert thou an idol all of gold, Had I the eye of worldish care, I could not..love thee mair.

'worldkin. *nonce-wd.* [f. WORLD *sb.* + -KIN.] A little world, microcosm.
1831 CARLYLE *Sart. Res.* II. ix, I too could now say to myself: Be no longer a Chaos, but a World, or even Worldkin.

worldless ('wɜːldlɪs), *a. rare.* [f. WORLD *sb.* + -LESS.]
1. Not having a world to live in.
1826? LAMB in *Wks.* (1909) II. 824 Can the houseless have a claim above the worldless?
2. Not containing a world or worlds.
1848 BAILEY *Festus* (ed. 3) 222, I have seen him seize upon an orb, And cast it careless into worldless space. **1856** AIRD *Tragic Poem of Wold* I. i, The timeless, worldless, infinite abyss.
3. Free from the world, unworldly.
1864 TENNYSON *Aylmer's F.* 471 He pluck'd her dagger forth From where his worldless heart had kept it warm.

worldliness ('wɜːldlɪnɪs). [f. WORLDLY *a.* + -NESS.]
1. The condition of being worldly; devotion to worldly affairs to the neglect of religious duties or spiritual needs; love of the world and its pleasures.
c **1380** WYCLIF *Wks.* (1880) 121 þes proude possessioners lien on seyntis & sclaundren hem wiþ worldly lif.. And þei bryngen forþ poyntis of here worldlynesse whanne þei diden aȝenst holy lif & techynge. *c* **1440** *Promp. Parv.* 522/1 Werdlynesse, *mundialitas*. *c* **1480** HENRYSON *Fables, Trial of Fox* 36 O fulische man! plungit in warldlines, To conqueis warldlie gude. *c* **1590** *Faire Em* I. ii. 41 Yet may our myndes as highly scorne to stoope To base desires of vulgars worldlynes. **1685** BAXTER *Paraphr. N.T.* Mark xii. 37 Hypocrites..who by their long Liturgies, and Ceremonies, ..do but cloak their Worldliness, Pride and Oppression. *a* **1768** SECKER *Serm., Haggai i. 5* (1771) VII. 12 But, supposing we are clear both of Worldliness and Vanity, still what can we answer with respect to Pleasure? **1845** S. AUSTIN *Ranke's Hist. Ref.* II. 163 The Latin church stood in need of reform. Its thorough worldliness..rendered this necessary in a religious view. **1884** PENNINGTON *Wiclif* viii. 266 The sight of the vice and worldliness of many of the bishops around him.
†2. Worldly affairs. *Obs. rare.*
a **1513** FABYAN *Chron.* v. lxxxiii. (1811) 61 The Saxons.. couenaunted wt. the Brytons, yt the Brytons shuld entende theyr worldlynes and other necessaries. And the Saxons as theyr Sowdiours shuld defende the lande.

worldling ('wɜːldlɪŋ). [f. WORLD *sb.* + -LING. Cf. G. *weltling*.]
1. One who is devoted to the interests and pleasures of the world; a worldly or worldly-minded person.
1549 COVERDALE, etc. *Erasm. Par. Jude* 23 b, They bee worldelinges, and geuyng them selues in to the seruice of worldly affectes. **1553** SAUNDERS in Coverdale *Lett. Martyrs* (1564) 214 You haue dronke of the holy spirite with other, vnto whom the knowledge hereof semeth not folyshnes (as it doth vnto worlynges). *a* **1614** J. MELVILL *Autob. & Diary* (Wodrow Soc.) 271 The godlie, for his..doctrine, lovit him; the warldlings, for his parentage and place, reverenced him. *a* **1659** BP. BROWNRIG *Serm.* (1674) I. xxvii. 350 A Worldlings thoughts, like a Fools, are all for the present. **1700** DRYDEN *Ceyx & Alcyone* 186 The covetous Worldling in his anxious Mind Thinks only on the Wealth he left behind. **1707** *Curios. in Husb. & Gard.* 19 Trifles, with which those Worldlings are taken up. **1821** BYRON *Mar. Fal.* II. i, The world will think with worldlings; but my heart Has still been in my duties. **1844** LINGARD *Anglo-Sax. Ch.* (1858) II. App. H. 369 The various pretexts under which Worldlings delude themselves and neglect the welfare of their Souls. **1912** LADY BURGHCLERE *Life James, 1st Dk. Ormonde* I. xv. 474 A gay worldling of no known occupation.
†2. a. A 'citizen of the world', cosmopolite. b. An inhabitant of the world. *Obs.*
1586 T. B. *La Primaud. Fr. Acad.* (1589) 329 Socrates said, that he tooke not himselfe to be either an Athenian or a Grecian, but a worldling. *c* **1600** *Timon* I. iv. (Shaks. Soc. 1842) 13 *Gelas.* What cuntreyman, I pray you, sir? *Pseud.* A Wordling. **1625** N. CARPENTER *Geogr. Del.* II. viii. 133 God revealed not this art [of navigation] to the old worldlings. **1687** A. LOVELL tr. *Bergerac's Com. Hist.* 26 Which our Worldlings call a Moon also. **1816** BYRON *Ch. Har.* III. liii, The heart must Leap kindly back to kindness, though disgust Hath wean'd it from all worldlings.
3. a. *Comb.*, as ***worldling-like*** adv.
a **1639** WOTTON *Poems, Descr. Countrey's Recreat.* v, The fond Credulity Of silly Fish, which worldling-like, still look Upon the bait, but never on the hook.
b. *attrib.* or *adj.* Worldly.
1720 WELTON *Suffer. Son of God* II. xiv. 377 Those.. conceal a Wicked and Worldling-heart, under the Garb..of Religion. **1845** MANGAN *German Anthol.* I. 74 That to which worldling natures are blind.

worldly ('wɜːldlɪ), *a.* Forms and etym.: see WORLD *sb.* and -LY[1]; also 3 worlich, 8 *Sc.* warly. [OE. *woruldlic*: cf. OFris. *wraldlik*, OS. *weroldlîk*, MLG. *wer(l)tlik*, MDu. *wereldlîk*, Du. *-lijk*, OHG. *weraltlîh* (MHG. *wer(e)ltlîch*, G. *weltlich*), ON. *veraldligr* (Sw. *verldslig*, Da. *verdslig*).]
1. Of or belonging to this world (as distinguished from the other world); pertaining to or connected with man's earthly existence; earthly, mundane.
c **888** ÆLFRED *Boeth.* viii, ðesege..hwæðer þe betere þince, nu nanwuht woruldlices fæstes & unhwearfiendes bion ne mæȝ? *c* **1000** ÆLFRIC *Hom.* I. 60 To forsewennysse woruldlicra æhta. *c* **1175** *Lamb. Hom.* 149 If he ne mei mid worldliche echte his neode ibete þet him sare roweþ. *c* **1200** ORMIN 1628 þatt tu þweorrt ut..forrwerrþe All weorelldlike lif & lusst. *a* **1225** *Ancr. R.* 94 þeos sihðe [of the bliss of heaven]..schal urouren ou more þene muhte eni worldlich sihðe. *Ibid.* 190 Euerich worlich wo is Godes sonde. *c* **1325** *Song of Yesterday* 29 in *E.E.P.* (1862) 134 þis eorþeli ioie þis worldly blis Is but a fykel fantasy. *c* **1374** CHAUCER *Troylus* III. 813 Worldly selynesse Which clerkes callen fals felicite. *c* **1380** WYCLIF *Wks.* (1880) 453 þis is þe freest vss þat men han off worldly godis. **1447** BOKENHAM *Seyntys* (Roxb.) 241 Alle fleshly lustys she dede despyse, No werdly wurshepe myht hyr supprise. *c* **1450** *Knt. de la Tour* 14 Humilite is the furst entre and wey of frenship and wordely loue. *c* **1475** *Partenay* 3838 Adieu, my plesaunce And gladnesse worly! **1500–20** DUNBAR *Poems* xii. 13 Welth, warldly gloir, and riche array. **1548–9** *Bk. Com. Prayer, Matrimony*, With al my worldly Goodes I thee endowe. **1556** J. HEYWOOD *Spider & Fly* ii. 94 Then doth all worldelie pleasure past apere..all vanitee. **1617** SIR W. MURE *Misc. Poems* xviii. 6 Too sone (alace!).. Thy pairt is acted on this wordlie stage. **1671** MILTON *P.R.* IV. 213 And thou thy self seem'st otherwise inclin'd Then to a worldly Crown. **1708** PRIOR *Turtle & Sparrow* 139 Exempt from worldly Hopes and Fears. **1742** FIELDING *J. Andrews* IV. viii, The parson..persisted in doing his duty without regarding the consequence it might have on his worldly interest. **1784** BURNS *'Green grow the Rashes'* iv, Warly cares, an' warly men, May a' gae tapsalteerie, O! **1848** DICKENS *Dombey* xlix, Too much a child in worldly matters. **1849** LEVER *Con Cregan* xviii, While I wander along,..my worldly substance a few dollars. **1856** FROUDE *Hist. Eng.* I. iii. 246 In point of worldly prudence, his conduct was unexceptionably wise. **1871** SMILES *Character* i. (1876) 8 Indeed, goodness in a measure implies wisdom—the highest wisdom—the union of the worldly with the spiritual.
†2. Of, belonging to, or connected with this world and its inhabitants; earthly, human, mortal.
c **1205** LAY. 6304 Heo wes swiðe wis of wordliche dome. **1340–70** *Alex. & Dind.* 58 þe weies þat were here wordliche makus. **1393** LANGL. *P. Pl.* C. IV. 371 Who so wol haue to wyue my worldliche daughter. *c* **1400** MAUNDEV. (Roxb.) Pref. 2 Wald Godd þat þir werldly lordes ware at gude accorde. **1423** JAS. I *Kingis Q.* xliv, Gif ȝe be warldly wight, that dooth me sike. *c* **1440** *York Myst.* xxvii. 128 No wordely drede schall me withdrawe, That I schall with þe leue and dye. **1528** TINDALE *Obed. Chr. Man* 55 Is it not..a monstrous thinge yt no man shulde be founde able to governe a worldly kingdome save Bisshopes and prelates that have forsaken the worlde. **1558** KNOX *First Blast* (Arb.) 6 Kinges, princes and worldlie rulers did conspire against God. **1583** STANYHURST *Æneis* III. (Arb.) 73 Too what soyle worldlye to iourney Thow doost commaund vs? **1593** SHAKS. *Rich. II*, III. ii. 56 The breath of worldly men cannot depose The Deputie elected by the Lord. **1601** W. PERCY *Cuckqueanes & Cuckolds Errants* IV. i. (Roxb.) 45 *Dou.* I had a husband once, but he has left mee. *Aru.* A worse then myne the wordly eye beholds not. *Dou.* A worse then myne the heauenly coupe enfolds not. **1614** J. DAVIES in W. Browne *Sheph. Pipe*, etc. G 4 b, Of world, ne worly men take thou no keepe. **1674** N. FAIRFAX *Bulk & Selv.* 193 God did not make the world or worldly beings, that the bigness..of them should set forth to us his alfillingness.
†b. Of the whole world, universal, general. *Obs.*
1538 CROMWELL in Merriman *Life & Lett.* (1902) II. 153 Ye do thus admonyshe them, to thintent they shuld.. eschewe..the wordely rebuke that they might incurre hereafter. *a* **1550** *Vox Populi* xi. 38 in *Skelton's Wks.* (1843) II. 410 There is no smale nombre That this faute dothe incombre: Yt is a wordly wondre.
c. Of the terrestrial globe. *rare.*
1812 CARY *Dante, Parad.* I. 40 [The sun] comes; and, to the worldly wax, best gives Its temper and impression.
†3. Of or belonging to the world (as distinguished from the church or the cloister); secular; *occas.* †lay. *Obs.*
a **900** *O.E. Martyrol.* 7 Mar. 36 He forlet þa wæpna ond þa woruldlican wisan ond eode on þæt mynster. *c* **1380** WYCLIF *Wks.* (1880) 121 Bi colour þat crist was þus worldly lord, þerfore þei schulden haue þus seculer lordischipis bi heritage of crist. *c* **1390** in *Wyclif's Wks.* (Wycl. Soc. 1910) 145 A curat and an officer in worldly seruise. *a* **1400** HYLTON *Scala Perf.* (W. de W. 1494) I. lxii, It may be that there is many a wyf and many worldlyche woman shall be nerer god than thou. *c* **1400** *Rom. Rose* 6230 It folowith not that they Shulde..her soules leese, That hem to worldly clothes chese;..Men may in seculer clothes see Florishen hooly religioun. *a* **1500** *Bernard de Cura rei fam.* I. 4 Sum [books] maide for law of god in document, And oþir sum for varldly regiment. *c* **1500** *Melusine* lvii. 336 There he herd the deuyne seruyse deuoutly but yet had he on hys worldly gownes. **1562** JEWEL *Apol. Ch. Eng.* 56 b, What other be the Abbots at this day in ye Popes kingdome, but worldly Princes? **1658** in Morris *Troubles Cath. Foref.* (1872) I. vi. 315 All this time [of the floods], Shrovetide, some worldly people came in to see the harm which the waters had done us.
4. Of persons, their actions or attributes: Devoted to the world and its pursuits.
c **1320** *Cast. Love* 983 þe worldlich mon euere i-liche Loueþ þing þat is worldliche. **1340** *Ayenb.* 210 Alle þoȝtes ulessliche and wordleliche me ssel diȝte uram þe herte. *c* **1380** WYCLIF *Wks.* (1880) 89 Worldly prelatis ful of coueitise symonye & heresie. *c* **1410** LOVE *Bonavent. Mirr.* xxxi. (1908) 153 Worldely men and fleschely. **1570** GOOGE *Pop. Kingd.* II. 20 Besides more worldly mindes they haue, and of more wanton chere, Than worldlymen. **1610** SHAKS. *Temp.* I. ii. 89, I thus neglecting worldly ends, all dedicated To closenes. **1667** MILTON *P.L.* XI. 803 The conquerd also ..Thenceforth shall practice how to live secure, Worldlie or dissolute. **1693** PRIOR *To C'tess of Exeter* 26 You far above Both these Your God did place; That Your high Pow'r might worldly Thoughts destroy. **1785** BURNS *Ep. Lapraik* xx, Awa, ye selfish, warly race. **1832** LYTTON *Eugene A.* I. xii, The worldlier passions are the growth of mature years. **1860** HAWTHORNE *Transformation* xii, It is the surest test of genuine love, that it brings back our early simplicity to the worldliest of us. **1875** MANNING *Mission H. Ghost* viii. 218 A man who is trying to serve two masters is a worldly man. **1902** VIOLET JACOB *Sheep-Stealers* xi, The 'Green Dragon' ..was the point of migration to the worldly part of the county, just as the Cathedral was the point of migration to the spiritual.
5. *Comb.*, as ***worldly-witted*** adj.; †**worldly-handed** *a.*, occupied in worldly or secular employment; **worldly-minded** *a.*, having a worldly mind, having the thoughts set upon the things of this world (hence **ˌworldly-mindedness**).
1657 J. WATTS *Vind. Ch. Eng.* 256 You have brought us to be *worldly-handed men, handy-crafts-men. **1601** *Song of Mary* in Farr *Sel. P., Eliz.* (Parker Soc.) II. 426 The world disdaines them; And why? because they are not *worldly-minded. **1611** *Bible* Luke xiv. (heading), Vnder the parable of the great supper, sheweth how worldly minded men.. shalbe shut out of heauen. *a* **1838** [see UNHUMBLED *ppl. a.*]. *a* **1628** PRESTON *Mt. Ebal* (1638) 36 **Worldly mindednesse*.. begets coldnesse of affection. **1748** HARTLEY *Observ. Man* II. iv. §4. 405 Men..carried from Worldly-mindedness to Heavenly-mindedness. **1849** LONGF. *Kavanagh* vii. Prose Wks. 1886 II. 313 Evil propensities, and self-seeking, and worldly-mindedness. **1563** *Homilies* II. *Inform. Places Script.* I. S ssj b, And some *worldlye witted men, thynke it a great decaye to..their common wealthes, to geue eare to the simple..preceptes of..Christ. **1845** MRS. NORTON *Child of Islands* (1846) 168 The shallow craft of worldly-witted fools.
Hence (chiefly *nonce-wds.*) **'worldlify** *v. trans.*, to render worldly; †**'worldlihood**, worldliness; **'worldlily** *adv.*, in a worldly manner; †**'worldlyship**, worldliness.
1612 T. JAMES *Jesuits' Downf.* 57 When religion was once *worldlefied in him, and that state-matters..had so great a part in his studies. *c* **1449** PECOCK *Repr.* III. vii. 319 Tho persoones..were religiose men, forsaking miche of *worldlihode and of fleischlihode. **1818** BENTHAM *Ch. Eng., Ch. Eng. Catech. Exam.* 122 Hired and *worldlily-interested advocates. **1825** T. HOOK *Sayings* Ser. II. *Doubts & F.* iv, He began to reconsider *worldlily* and suspiciously all the incidents. *c* **1380** WYCLIF *Serm.* Sel. Wks. II. 151 And þis *worldlyshipe shal laste as longe as prelatis ben þus worldli.

worldly ('wɜːldlɪ), *adv.* [f. after prec. with -LY[2]. Cf. OHG. *werltlîchi*.] In a worldly manner; with a worldly intent or disposition: freq. qualifying an adj. used attrib. (and hyphened). See also next.
a **1225** *Ancr. R.* 234 Alle þe haluwen weren worldliche itented. **1340–70** *Alex. & Dind.* 427 We ben busy of no swink nor no burn maken For to wirchen our wil & wordliche serue. *c* **1380** WYCLIF *Serm.* Sel. Wks. II. 151 Here is þe world taken for men þat lyven worldli. **1390** GOWER *Conf.* III. 162 It were als litel nede or lasse, That thou so worldly wolt compasse With flaterie forto serve. *c* **1400** *Apol. Loll.* 104 þei lifen worldly, & hidun þer vicis wiþ a veyn hiȝt of better lif. *c* **1485** *Wisdom* 405 Her is a man that levith wardly. **1526** *Pilgr. Perf.* (W. de W. 1531) 20 Worldly lyuynge chrysten people. **1534** MORE *Comf. agst. Trib.* III. xi. Pj b, Those worldly disposed people. **1667** MILTON *P.L.* XII. 568 By things deemed weak Subverting worldly strong, and worldly wise By simply meek. **1700** DRYDEN *Wife of Bath's Tale* 493 Since I see your Mind is Worldly bent. **1883** H. DRUMMOND *Nat. Law in Spir. W.* (ed. 2) 197[A] lowering of religious tone to the level of the worldly-religious world around. **1884** J. TAIT *Mind in Matter* (1892) 332 They embrace and sanctify every form of worldly-personal consequence. **1896** BLACK *Briseis* xvii, Worldly-pious waverings.

'worldly-'wise (stress variable), *a.* Wise in a worldly manner or in worldly affairs; *transf.* of actions or conduct. Also *absol.*
c **1400** *26 Pol. Poems* i. 45 Worldly wys is gostly nys. *c* **1415** *Crowned King* 85 þou most be worldly wys & ware þe be-tymes. **1540** COVERDALE *Fruitf. Less.* To Rdr. (1593) ¶3 b, This is peradeunture laughed to scorne of the vnexpert, proud, worldly wise. **1562** PILKINGTON *Expos. Abdyas* Ee ij, These Edomites..picked oute..the worldly wisest men, thei coulde finde to be their rulers. **1667** [see prec.]. **1753–4** RICHARDSON *Grandison* II. xiii. 97 It was now, in the worldly-wise way of thinking, become his interest to keep up the distance..between them. **1851** MRS. BROWNING *Casa Guidi Wind.* I. 485 The friars with worldly-wise Keen sidelong glances. **1865** KINGSLEY *Herew.* iv, The lads.. imposed on by the cynical and worldly-wise tone which their..uncle had assumed.
b. ***worldly wiseman*** (cf. WISE MAN): a worldly-wise man; now only with allusion to the character so named in Bunyan's *Pilgrim's Progress*. So †*worldly wiseling* [-LING].
1591 LODGE *Catharos* (Hunter. Club) 22 Oh worldy wiseman, you are still entring into the marrow of matters. **1620** DONNE *Serm., Ps. cxliv. 15* (1640) 749 Not onely a worldly wiseman, but a Christian wiseman may reach out both hands, to both kinds of blessings,..spirituall and temporall. **1681** H. MORE *Exp. Dan.* Pref. 30 The worldly Wiselings who for coarse carnal ends decry all pretence to the understanding of Prophecies. **1821** *Blackw. Mag.* VIII. 434 There worldly wisemen sold the damaged beast.

'world-man. [OE. *woruldman*, f. *woruld* WORLD *sb.* + MAN *sb.*¹]

1. A man of this world, a human being.

a **900** CYNEWULF *Crist* 1016 Woruldmonna seo unclæne ȝecynd. *a* **1000** *Boeth. Metr.* xxviii. 10 An þara tungla woruldmen hatað wænes þisla. *c* **1205** LAY. 28131 Nulleþ [hii] hit biginne for nane weorld-monne [*later text* worleþinge]. **1852** BAILEY *Festus* (ed. 5) 341 The hero is the world-man, in whose heart One passion stands for all, the most indulged.

†**2.** A man who is devoted to this world; a worldling. *Obs.*

a **1225** *Leg. Kath.* 881 Ichulle fordon þe wisdom of þeos wise world men. **1601** BP. W. BARLOW *Eagle & Body* (1609) E 2 b, An infallible note, he will not say of a reprobate, but certainly of a worldman, not yet regenerate.

'world-power. [After G. *weltmacht.*]

1. The power of 'this world' (as distinguished from the spiritual world); secular power.

1866 BARING-GOULD *Cur. Myths Mid. Ages, Antichr. & Pope Joan* 159 Christ will descend to avenge the blood of the saints, by destroying Antichrist and the world-power. **1884** *Expositor* Feb. 89 To crush the heathen world-power, and thereby abolish idolatry.

2. Any of the powers (nations, empires) that dominate the world. Also *transf.* of a person.

1860 PUSEY *Min. Proph.* 409 He has, like all great world-powers, a real dignity and majesty. **1900** *Congress Rec.* 29 Jan. 1259/1 We have become a 'world power'. **1901** B. HARRISON in *N. Amer. Rev.* Feb. 184 If the World Powers have any recognized creed, it is that it is their duty as 'trustees for humanity' to take over the territories of all the weak and decaying nations. **1904** J. GAIRDNER in *Camb. Mod. Hist.* II. xiii. 472 The foundation of England's greatness as a world-power.

†**world-riche.** *Obs.* Also 4 **worldesriche.** [OE. *woruldríce*: see WORLD *sb.* and RICHE *sb.*] 'The kingdom of the world', the world.

c **897** ÆLFRED *Gregory's Past. C.* iv. 38 Þa he hine asced of ðæm worldrice. *c* **1200** ORMIN 11800 Þurrh þatt te laþe gast himm bæd All weorelldriches ahhte. *c* **1205** LAY. 17182 Swa wid swa is weorlde-riche nis nan weorc his iliche. **1390** GOWER *Conf.* I. 366 To seche in al this worldesriche, Men schal noght finde upon his liche. *Ibid.* II. 130, I hadde hir levere than a Myn Of Gold; for al this worldesriche Ne mihte make me so riche As sche.

†**'worldship.** *Obs.* [OE. *woruldscipe*: see WORLD *sb.* and -SHIP.] Worldly things.

c **897** ÆLFRED *Gregory's Past. C.* xviii. 130 Nele nan Godes ðeow hiene selfne to unȝemetlice ȝebindan on worldscipum. *c* **1200** ORMIN 1633 Swillc lif iss all þwerrt ut dæd Fra weorelldshipess lusstess.

World War, world war. [f. WORLD *sb.* + WAR *sb.*¹; cf. G. *weltkrieg.*] **1.** A war involving many important nations; *spec.* that of 1914–18 or of 1939–45.

1909 *Westm. Gaz.* 8 Apr. 4/2 This..is the type of dirigible by which in a world-war..360,000 German troops could be transported from Calais to Dover in half an hour. **1914** B. VAUGHAN *What of To-Day?* xii. 103 What the South African War failed to teach I really believe this world-war will bring home to us. **1921** A. HUXLEY *Crome Yellow* ix. 82 Armageddon, that world war with which the Second Coming is to be so closely associated. **1949** G. A. BIRMINGHAM *Laura's Bishop* 171 To call this, when it comes, a world war is to minimize its importance. It will be worse than a world war. **1978** I. B. SINGER *Shosha* v. 90 Let's snatch a little peace before another world war breaks out.

2. In the designation of a particular (real or hypothetical) war, as ***First World War, World War* (*No.*) *I*** (or ***One***): see FIRST *a.* C. 2 a; ***Second World War, World War* (*No.*) *II*** (or ***Two***): a subsequent world war, *spec.* that of 1939–45: see SECOND *a.* 7 a; ***Third World War, World War* (*No.*) *III*** (or ***Three***): see THIRD *a.* 5. Also *transf.*

1919 *Manch. Guardian* 18 Feb. 10/2 (*heading*) World War No 2. **1939** *Time* 11 Sept. 38/1 Some of the diplomatic juggling which last week ended in World War II was old-fashioned international jockeying for power. *Ibid.* 18 Sept. 10/2 Exports of arms, munitions and related materials in World War I amounted..to only 25% of total exports to the Allies. **1945** DUKE OF BEDFORD *Let.* 16 Apr. in B. Russell *Autobiogr.* (1969) III. i. 44 You will have to postpone your visit until the brief interlude between this war & world-war no 3. **1947** *Time & Tide* 29 Nov. 1269/2 The despair and cynicism that followed what it has now become fashionable to call World War One. **1948** N. WIENER *Cybernetics* 7 When I came to the Institute after World War No. 1 [etc.]. **1959** *N.Z. Listener* 17 Apr. 6/1 Clearly the meaning of the treaties in case of wars which can be limited is somewhat different from the meaning they have in the event of World War III. **1963** D. BROUN *Egypt's Choice* i. 12 'During World War Deuce, sir,' the Colonel said. **1968** K. BIRD *Smash Glass Image* viii. 102 Rattling their rifles as if they were fighting World War Three. **1968** *Listener* 12 Dec. 787/3 When World War Two broke out on 3 September 1939, Monnet remembered his World War One experiences. **1976** P. R. WHITE *Planning for Public Transport* iv. 72 As early as World War One some minor stations and routes were closed.

worldward ('wɜːldwəd), *adv.* (*a.*) [f. WORLD *sb.* + -WARD.]

1. (orig. *to the worldward*) In regard to the world; in worldly respects.

1583 GOLDING *Calvin on Deut.* iv. 19 Although I be rich and honorable to the worldward. **1587** —— *De Mornay* xvi. (1617) 283 Considering man what hee is to Godward, to the Worldward, to Manward and to himselfe. *a* **1617** BAYNE *Lect.* (1634) 148 Such as live worldward just, but have no oare of religion. *a* **1639** W. WHATELEY *Prototypes* I. vi. (1640) 82 Be not Hypocrites, satisfied with some externall shew of religiousnesse, and orderly living to the world-ward. **1651** J. READING *Guide Holy City* xix. 215 Another man riseth in honours..another is many waies prosperous to the world-ward.

2. Towards or in the direction of the world.

1642 ROGERS *Naaman* 45 Thoughts that were roving helward, worldward, and sinward. **1865** LOWELL *Thoreau* Prose Wks. 1890 I. 368 Emerson..has drawn steadily manward and worldward.

B. *adj.* Directed towards or facing the world.

1857 J. HAMILTON *Lessons fr. Gt. Biog.* 261 Over his general and world-ward conduct his eye could glide with prevailing satisfaction. **1883** *Evang. Mag.* Oct. 464 Such vanities had a worldward tendency. **1900** *Longm. Mag.* May 26 They chose a beggar from the world outside To keep their worldward door for them.

So **'worldwards** *adv.*, in respect of the world.

1845 BAILEY *Festus* (ed. 2) 79 Thy church,—One, universal, and invisible World-wards, yet manifest unto itself.

worldwide (stress variable), *a.* Also **world-wide.** [f. WORLD *sb.* + WIDE *a.*]

a. 'As wide as the world'; extending over or covering the whole world.

1632 LITHGOW *Trav.* II. 71, I had the ground to be a pillow, and the world-wide-fields to be a chamber. **1842** TENNYSON *Locksley Hall* 125 The world-wide whisper of the south-wind rushing warm. **1851** MRS. BROWNING *Casa Guidi Wind.* I. 899 The world-wide throes Which went to make the popedom. **1860** WORCESTER, *World-wide*, coextensive with the world; as, 'World-wide fame'. **1877** C. GEIKIE *Christ* lvii. (1879) 693 The Jews thought Christ would raise Israel to world-wide supremacy. **1896** HOUSMAN *Shropshire Lad* xlii, The world-wide air was azure. **1912** *Athenæum* 24 Aug. 183/1 The problems he undertook to solve were worldwide.

b. as *adv.*

1892 E. REEVES *Homeward Bound* 294 Where in caves live the world-wide known gipsies. **1953** *Reader's Digest* July 27 World-wide, three million dogs have already safely got this ..vaccine. **1972** *Nature* 24 Mar. 184/3 Workers in the field number no more than about fifty, worldwide. **1980** *Bookseller* 14 June 2528/1 (Advt.), Subscriptions manager required for expanding publishing business trading worldwide.

Hence **worldwidely** *adv.*, **worldwideness.** *nonce-wds.*

1897 *Daily News* 25 Nov. 5/1 World-widely famous. **1920** *19th Cent.* July 37 Don Sturzo's ambitions are Caesarean in their world-wideness.

†**'worldy,** *a.* *Obs. rare.* [f. WORLD *sb.* + -Y¹. (The difficulty of writing *-ldl-* correctly makes it probable that some examples are errors for *worldly.*)] Worldly.

c **1380** *Sir Ferumbras* 5202 Þan scholdest þow of al þis lond be kyng, And y þy quene, my swete þyng, & þy worldy make. **1513** BRADSHAW *St. Werburge* I. 2539 Worldy desyres she clerely dyd subdue. **1526** TINDALE *Eph.* vi. 12 For we wrestle..agaynst power, and agaynst worldy ruelars of the darcknes of this worlde. **1552** ABP. HAMILTON *Catech.* (1884) 5 Nathing in this life apperis to warldy men mair facil.

worley, worlie, var. forms of WURLEY.

worling, var. WARLING *Obs.*

worm (wɜːm), *sb.* Forms: 1 wyrm, 3, 5–6 *Sc.* wirm(e, (3 wrim, 5 wyrme, 6 *Sc.* virme); 1–3 weorm, 3–5 werm, 4–5 werme; 1–4 wurm, (3 wurem, *Orm.* wurrm, 3, 5 wrm); 6 wourme, *Sc.* woirme, 6–7 woorme, 4–7 worme, 3– worm. [OE. *wyrm* (:—**wurmi-z*) = OFris. *wirm* (WFris. *wjirm*, NFris. *würm*, EFris. *wurm*), OS. *wurm* serpent (MLG., LG. *worm*, MDu., Du. *worm*), OHG., MHG., G. *wurm* †serpent, worm; also (with *a*-stem) ON. *ormr* (for **wormr*) serpent (Sw., Norw., Da. *orm*); the stem of Goth. *waurms* ὄφις is uncertain. Related to L. *vermis* worm, Gr. ῥόμος, ῥόμοξ wood-worm.

In this word, as in WORSE and WORT, the spelling *wo* is an early graphic substitution for *wu* (cf. ME. *wolf, wolle, wonder*, for OE. *wulf, wull, wunder*), and this again is a reversion from OE. *wy* (i.e. *wü*) to the unmutated vowel through the influence of the following *r*. More normal developments of OE. *wyrm* appear in the ME. (eastern and Sc.) *wirm* and (south-eastern) *werm.*]

I. 1. A serpent, snake, dragon. Now only *arch.*

Beowulf 2287 Þa se wyrm onwoc. *c* **1000** ÆLFRIC *Deut.* xxxii. 24 Ic sende wildeora teð on hi mid wurmum & nædrum. *c* **1250** *Gen. & Ex.* 321 He..Wente in to a wirme, and tolde eue a tale. *c* **1290** *St. James* 179 in *S. Eng. Leg.* 39 A fuyr Drake þar-opon a-ȝein heom cominde huy seiȝe.. Anon hadde þis luþere worm is pouwer al ilore. *a* **1300** *Cursor M.* 5896 Þan tok aaron þis ilk yeird, And on þe flore he kest it don, And it become a worme felon. **13..** *Gaw. & Gr. Knt.* 720 Sumwhyle wyth wormez he werrez, & with wolues als. **1362** LANGL. *P. Pl.* A. XI. 66 Whi wolde God vr saueour suffre such a worm In such a wrong wyse þe wommon to bi-gyle? *c* **1475** *Partenay* 5859 The serpent fill don dede..Which worme was ny ryght ten hole feete of lenght. **1526** TINDALE *Acts* xxviii. 4 When the men off the countree sawe the worme hange on hys honde. **1606** SHAKS. *Ant. & Cl.* v. ii. 243 Hast thou the pretty worme of Nylus there, That killes and paines not? **1667** MILTON *P.L.* IX. 1068 O Eve, in evil hour thou didst give eare To that false Worm. **1727** POPE *To Mr. John Moore* iii, That ancient Worm, the Devil. **1778** W. HUTCHINSON *View Northumb.* ii. 162 The Laidley Worm of Spindleston Heughs. **1784** COWPER *Task* VI. 780 The mother sees, And smiles to see, her infant's playful hand Stretch'd forth to dally with the crested worm. **1867** MORRIS *Jason* x. 258 Therewith began A fearful battle betwixt worm and man.

†**2. a.** Any animal that creeps or crawls; a reptile; an insect. *Obs.* In ME. often ***wild worm.***

Cf. *blind-worm, slow-worm* (a lizard); also *galleyworm, glow-worm.*

c **893** ÆLFRED *Oros.* I. vii, Froxas comon..swa fela þæt man ne mihte..nanne mete ȝegyrwan, þæt þara wyrma nære emfela þæm mete, ær he ȝeȝearwod wære. *c* **1000** ÆLFRIC *Deut.* iv. 18 Ne wyrce ȝe eow..nane anlicnyssa..ne fuȝeles, ne wyrmes [*reptilium*], ne fisces. *c* **1175** *Lamb. Hom.* 51 Þer wunieð fower cunnes wurmes inne [*viz.* adders, toads, frogs and crabs]. *a* **1225** *Ancr. R.* 206 Þe scorpiun is ones cunnes wurm. *c* **1250** *Gen. & Ex.* 2982 Ðis wirmes [frogs and toads] storuen in ðe stede. *c* **1325** *Sir Orfeo* 252 (Sisam) Now seþ he noþing þat him likeþ, Bot wilde wormes bi him strikeþ. **1377** LANGL. *P. Pl.* B. XIV. 112 Briddes and bestes..And wilde wormes in wodes. *c* **1386** CHAUCER *Pard. T.* 27 If Cow or Calf or Sheepe or Oxe swelle That any worm hath ete or worm ystonge. ?*c* **1400** LYDG. *Æsop's Fab.* v. 117 Thus were these wormes [the frog and mouse] contrary of livyng. **1535** COVERDALE *Exod.* viii. 21, I wil cause cruell wormes (or flyes) to come vpon the. **1561** HOLLYBUSH *Hom. Apoth.* 37 Cantarides..are grene wormes shewing with a glosse lyke golde. **1578** LYTE *Dodoens* II. xxxvii. 196 This herbe dryueth away..the stinking wormes or Mothes called Cimici. **1585** T. WASHINGTON tr. *Nicholay's Voy.* II. viii. 41 b, Certaine small flying wormes, which with their billes and stinges picking the other figs, sodaynely after they are picked, they come to a good and perfect ripenesse. **1587** TURBERV. *Trag. Tales* ix. 128 b, Vnderneath this bed of Sage, The fellow that did dig, Turnd vp a toade, a loathsome sight, A worme exceeding big. **1667** MILTON *P.L.* VII. 476 At once came forth whatever creeps the ground, Insect or Worme. **1805** WORDSW. *Prelude* XIV. 274 The meek worm that feeds her lonely lamp Couched in the dewy grass. **1820** SHELLEY *Prometheus Unb.* IV. 545 Ye beasts and birds, Ye worms, and fish.

†**b.** Applied (like *vermin*) to four-footed animals considered as noxious or objectionable. *Obs.*

c **1400** *Destr. Troy* 1573 Lions & Libardes & other laithe wormes. **1481** CAXTON *Reynard* xxxiv. (Arb.) 100 Alas me growleth of thyse fowle nyckers [*sc.* young marmosets]..I sawe neuer fowler wormes.

3. a. A member of the genus *Lumbricus*; a slender, creeping, naked, limbless animal, usually brown or reddish, with a soft body divided into a series of segments; an earthworm. More widely, any annelid, terrestrial, aquatic, or marine.

Also with defining term, as *dew, earth, ground, lug, mud, pipe, rag, rain, sand, sea, tag, tube, water*: see the words.

a **1100** *Voc.* in Wr.-Wülcker 320/31 *Uermis*, wyrm. **1398** TREVISA *Barth. De P.R.* XVIII. cxv. (1495) hh i b/1 Some ben water wormes and some ben londe wormes. *c* **1400** *Lanfranc's Cirurg.* 44 Maddockis, þat ben wormes of þe erþe. *c* **1440** *Promp. Parv.* 530/1 Wyrme, *vermis.* **1526** *Pilgr. Perf.* (W. de W. 1531) 234 b, Lyke as the worme yᵗ is crusshed or poysoned, may scantly crepe or lyfte vp her heed. **1530** PALSGR. 290/2 Worme in the erthe, *uers de terre.* **1577** B. GOOGE *Heresbach's Husb.* 149 A marrishe is to be preferred before a dry ground, that they [*viz.* swine] may..digge vp woormes. **1608** SHAKS. *Per.* IV. i. 79, I neuer..trode vpon a worme against my will, but I wept fort. **1731** in *10th Rep. Hist. MSS. Comm.* App. I. 269 The slimy tribe of Snails and Worms. **1774** GOLDSM. *Nat. Hist.* (1776) VII. 144 We now are in doubt whether he means a real worm, or a young animal of the lizard species. **1840** NEWMAN *Paroch. Serm.* V. viii. 128 Like worms working their way upwards through the dust of the earth. **1855** KINGSLEY *Glaucus* (1878) 166 Pectinaria Belgica..is an Annelid, or true worm. **1855** GOSSE *Mar. Zool.* I. 84 The Sea-mouse (*Aphrodita*) one of the most common as well as the largest of our Worms. **1881** DARWIN *Form. Veget. Mould* i. 13 Worms are nocturnal in their habits.

b. Prov. ***tread on a worm and it will turn***: i.e. even the humblest will resent extreme ill-treatment. Also in variant or abbreviated forms, e.g. ***even a worm will turn.***

Cf. F. *un ver se recoquille bien quand on marche dessus.*

1546 HEYWOOD *Prov.* (1867) 52 Tread a woorme on the tayle and it must turne agayne. *a* **1548, 1641** [see TURN *v.* 66 d]. **1593** SHAKS. *3 Hen. VI*, II. ii. 17 The smallest Worme will turne, being troden on. **1611, 1641** [see TURN *v.* 59 c]. **1691** S. SHAW *Diff. Humours Men* 18 He has scarce the courage of a Worm, to turn at him that treads upon him. **1818** [see WOUND *v.* 3]. **1857** G. A. LAWRENCE *Guy Liv.* xxv. 245 It exhausted the patience of the much-enduring Willis; so that the worm turned again—insolently. **1864** BROWNING *Mr. Sludge* 72 Tread on a worm, it turns, sir! If I turn, Your fault!

†**c.** ***naked as a worm***: entirely naked (= F. *nu comme un ver*), or in allusion to this. *Obs.*

?*a* **1366** CHAUCER *Rom. Rose* 454 Nakid as a worme was she. *c* **1386** —— *Clerk's T.* 824 Lat me nat lyk a worm go by the weye. *c* **1450** *Cov. Myst., Fall of Man* 291, I walke as werm with-outyn wede. *a* **1467** [see NAKED *a.* 1 b].

†**d.** ***to look worms***: ? to peer narrowly (*through*). *Obs.* (But perh. a corrupt reading.)

c **1600** *Timon* I. ii, I'le make the[e] looke wormes through the pryson grates, Vnlesse thou satisfie to me my debt.

e. transf. and fig. phr. ***worm's-eye view*** [after *bird's-eye view* (BIRD'S-EYE *a.* 3); see also EYE VIEW], a view taken as from the standpoint of a worm, i.e. from ground-level; a revealing or detailed perspective of a subject. Also ***worm's-eye map*** (Geol.) (see quot. 1972).

1908 [see EYE VIEW, EYE-VIEW]. **1933** *Archit. Rev.* LXXIII. 67/2 The illustration is a worm's-eye view of a corner of the building. **1945** A. HUXLEY *Time must have Stop* xiv. 145 He..looked..up at the statue above him. What a curious worm's-eye view of a goddess! **1951** KRUMBEIN & SLOSS *Stratigr. & Sedimentation* xiii. 421 Such paleogeologic maps, in which the observer looks upward at the base of a higher unit, have been called worm's eye maps. **1960** *John o' London's* 14 Apr. 428/3 His 'worm's eye view' of Dublin was beginning to give way to the great vision of a major artist. **1964** *Bull. Amer. Assoc. Petroleum Geologists* XLVIII. 1187/2 A lap-out map, commonly known as a 'worm's eye' map, is a special method of paleogeologic expression where post-unconformity geologic relations are portrayed. **1972** *Gloss. Geol.* (Amer. Geol. Inst.) 797/1 *Worm's-eye map*, (a) a term applied..in reference to the pattern of formations that would be visible to an observer looking upward at the bottom of the rocks overlying a given surface. (b) A map showing overlap of sediments. **1982** A. PRICE *Old Vengeful* ix. 147 This is the worm's-eye view of what you seek. If you wish for the eagle's-eye view, you must go to Paris.

4. Any endoparasitic helminth breeding in the living body of men and other animals. Usu. *pl.* (formerly often with *the*). Also, the disease or disorder constituted by the presence of these parasites.

The numerous kinds are indicated by a defining term, as *flat*, *gourd*, *Guinea*, *hair*, *maw*, *palisade*, *pin*, *round*, *tape*, *thread*: see these words.

c **1000** *Sax. Leechd.* II. 120 Wiþ þam wyrmum þe innan eȝlað þam men. *c* **1290** *Beket* 2213 in *S. Eng. Leg.* 170 Ful of wormes was is flesch. **1382** WYCLIF *Acts* xii. 23 And he waastid of wormes, deiede. *c* **1440** *Alphabet of Tales* 466 Als lang as he liffid after, wormes & mawkis bred in his flessh & eate it away. **1486** *Bk. St. Albans* c vij b, A medecyne for wormys called anguellis. **1523–34** FITZHERB. *Husb.* §103 The wormes is a lyght dysease, and they lye in the greatte paunche, in the belye of the horse, and they are shynynge, of colour lyke a snake, syxe inches in lengthe. *a* **1530** J. HEYWOOD *Play of Love* 676 (Brandl) Wherby loue is a drynk mete To gyue babes for wormes, for it drynketh bytter swete. **1630** RANDOLPH *Aristippus* 25 The King of Russia had died of the wormes, but for a powder I sent him. **1652** W. POOLE *Country Farrier* 33 To cure the Wormes, or Bottes that doe wring his belly. **1665** *Golden Coast, Guinney* 10 There is a kinde of long Worm, that ariseth in the Legs, Arms, and Thighs of some men that come hither. **1705** BOSMAN *Guinea* xiii. (1721) 94 The National Diseases here are the Small-Pox and Worms. **1732** ARBUTHNOT *Rules of Diet* (1736) 413 Children subject to Worms ought not to live much upon Milk, Cheese, or ripe Fruits. **1822** GOOD *Study Med.* (1829) I. 365 In an attack upon worms, brisk cathartics should always take the lead. **1826** J. EVANS *Brit. Herbal* 57 Germander, the juice of the leaves dropped in the ears killeth the worms in them. **1898** P. MANSON *Trop. Diseases* xxxvi. 534 A dose of santonin often produces results which will seem to justify a diagnosis of 'worms.'

5. a. The larva of an insect; a maggot, grub, or caterpillar, esp. one that feeds on and destroys flesh, fruit, leaves, cereals, textile fabrics, and the like. Also collect. ***the worm***, as a destructive pest.

With defining term prefixed, as *book*, *caddis*, *canker*, *case*, †*cawel*, *horn*, *measuring*, *palmer*, *red*, *rook*, *silk*, *slug*, *span*, *tobacco*, *whirl*, *white*, *wire*: see these words.

a **1000** *Riddles* xlviii. 3 Me þæt þuhte wrætlicu wyrd..þæt se wyrm forswealȝ wera ȝied sumes. *a* **1225** *Ancr. R.* 138 Wiðuten salt fleshs gedereð wurmes..& forroteð sone. **1297** R. GLOUC. (Rolls) 10045 Þo grene corn in somer ssolde curne, To foule wormes muchedel þe eres gonne turne. *a* **1300** *Cursor M.* 6612 Þai fand bot wormes creuland emid [*i.e.* in the manna]. **1398** TREVISA *Barth. De P.R.* XVII. cxiv. (Tollemache MS.) In somer þe tender leues þerof beþ eten with smal schagges, and with oþer wormes. **1415** HOCCLEVE *To Sir John Oldcastle* 466 The worm for to sleen in the pesecod. *c* **1440** *Palladius on Husb.* IV. 965 Now pike out moughthes, attercoppes, wormes, And butterflie whos thost engendring worm is. **1450–1530** *Myrr. our Ladye* p. xxv, The Chambres schal haue al the clothes in her warde,.. makyng, repayryng, and kepyng them from wormes. **1578** LYTE *Dodoens* IV. lx. 522 The small wormes that are found within the knoppes or heades of Teaselles. **1601** SHAKS. *Twel. N.* II. iv. 114 She..let concealment like a worme i'th budde Feede on her damaske cheeke. **1608** TOPSELL *Serpents* 78 The small Wormes of the Drones. *c* **1630** MILTON *Arcades* 53 Or what the cross dire-looking Planet smites, Or hurtfull Worm with canker'd venom bites. **1654** WHITLOCK *Zootomia* 230 Books are subject among other Chances to fire, and the Worme. **1677** *Rector's Bk. Clayworth* (1910) 35, I observed worms in wheat and Rye. **1718** PRIOR *Solomon* III. 132 The Worm that gnaws the ripening Fruit. **1797** in A. Young *Agric. Suffolk* 39 Wheat never plants kindly after a thin crop of clover; but is subject to the worm, and to be root fallen. **1807** CRABBE *Par. Reg.* III. 239 The crawling worm, that turns a summer-fly. **1847** EMERSON *Repr. Men, Shakesp.* Wks. (Bohn) I. 358 They have left..no file of old yellow accounts to decompose in damp and worms. **1848** THACKERAY *Van. Fair* xli, The worms have eaten the cloth a good deal. **1857** KINGSLEY *Lett.* (1877) II. 41 The office of worms in this world is to prevent, while they seem to accelerate, putrefaction. **1884** J. PHIN *Dict. Apicult.* 78 When worms are spoken of by the ordinary beekeeper, the larvæ of the bee-moth are almost always meant. **1886** *Tobacco* (ed. Lock) 55 Worms, in the American phraseology, here generally known as caterpillars, are the *bête noire* of the tobacco grower.

fig. **1557** R. EDGEWORTH *Serm.* 305 b, Pride, which is the moght, the worme that eateth vp the riche men. **1860** PUSEY *Min. Proph.* 287 Nothing can man have so pleasing, green, and, in appearance, so lasting, which has not its own worm prepared by God, whereby, in the dawn, it may be smitten and die.

b. The larva or grub of many kinds of beetles, destructive to trees, timber, furniture, etc. (Cf. 9 and *wood-worm* (WOOD *sb.*[1] 10 b).)

a **1100** *Gloss.* in Wr.-Wülcker 121/35 *Termes, uel teredo*, wyrm þe borað treow. *c* **1386** CHAUCER *Wife's Prol.* 376 Right as wormes shendeth a tree. *c* **1470** *E.E. Misc.* (Warton Club) 70 Iff wormys wex in a tre. **1531** ELYOT *Gov.* II. xiv. ¶1 As the wormes do brede moste gladly in softe wode and swete. **1567** *Satir. Poems Reform.* iv. 154 As the woirme that workis vnder cuire At lenth the tre consumis that is duire. **1601** HOLLAND *Pliny* XVII. xxiv. I. 539 As touching the Worme, some trees are more subject unto it than others. **1657** R. AUSTEN *Fruit Trees* I. (ed. 2) 72 Foure Diseases that sometimes happen to Fruit-trees. Mossinesse, Bark bound, Canker, and Wormes. **1733** W. ELLIS *Chiltern & Vale Farm.* 190 The Worm is very apt to get between the Bark of this Wood after it is fell'd. **1807** CRABBE *Par. Reg.* III. 236 Worms ate the floors, the tap'stry fled the wall. **1925** C. J. GAHAN *Furniture Beetles* 5 Furniture or..woodwork.. destroyed by what is commonly known as *the worm*—little six-legged, white grubs which live inside the wood, devouring it and turning it to powder.

c. *contextually*. A silkworm.

a **900** *Leiden Riddle* 9 Uyrmas mec ni auefun uyndicræftum. **1559** W. CUNINGHAM *Cosmogr. Glasse* 196 In this country breed the Wormes which make silk. **1599** T. M[OUFET] *Silkwormes* 53, I thinke that God and nature thought it meete, The noblest wormes on noblest tree to feede. **1604** SHAKS. *Oth.* III. iv. 73 The Wormes were hallowed, that did breede the Silke. **1626** MIDDLETON *Anything for Quiet Life* II. ii, An especial good piece of Silk; the Worm never spun a finer thread. **1634** MILTON *Comus* 715 Spinning Worms, That in their green shops weave the smooth-hair'd silk. **1707** MORTIMER *Husb.* 220 It is good to let the [Mulberry] Leaves be clear of Dew or Rain before you give them unto the Worms. **1887** *Encycl. Brit.* XXII. 59/1 As these moulting periods approach, the worms lose their appetite and cease eating.

6. a. A maggot, or, in popular belief, an earthworm, supposed to eat dead bodies in the grave.

a **900** *Juliana* 416 Þæs lichoman seþe on leȝ re sceal weorðan in worulde wyrme to hroþor. *a* **1000** *Soul & Body* 114 Rib reafiað reðe wyrmas. *c* **1200** *Vices & Virtues* 15 We beoð wiðuten al swa ðe deade mannes þruh, þe is wiðuten ihwited, and wiðinne stinkende and full of wermes. *c* **1250** *Death* 157 in *O.E. Misc.* 178 Nu þe sculen wormes [*Jesus MS.* wurmes] wunien wiðinne. *a* **1300** *Cursor M.* 14321 Wormes biginnes at ete him nu. *a* **1400** *Minor P. Vernon MS.* 661/114 Wormes blake wol vs enbrase. **1477** EARL RIVERS (Caxton) *Dictes* 37 b, Thou shalt haue no power to fele the stenche of thy body, nor howe the wormes shall suke thy roten kareyn. **1542** *Test. Ebor.* (Surtees) VI. 164 My soull to God my maker, and my bodie to the wormes. **1560** *Bible* (Geneva) Job xix. 26 Thogh after my skin wormes destroy this bodie. **1600** SHAKS. *A.Y.L.* IV. i. 108 Men haue died from time to time, and wormes haue eaten them. **1611** *Bible* Job xxiv. 20 The worme shall feed sweetly on him. *a* **1679** J. WARD *Diary* (1839) 274 Three months after, his bodie went to the wormes. **1795** M. G. LEWIS *Monk* (1796) III. 65 (*Alonzo the Brave* xii), The worms they crept in, and the worms they crept out, And sported his eyes and his temples about. **1815** SOUTHEY *Life & Corr.* (1850) IV. 135 Some of our party told me of a third [grave], in which the worms were at work, but I shrunk from the sight. **1892** W. WATSON *Great Misgiving* 4 in *Lachrymæ Musarum* 52 Life is a feast, and we have banqueted—Shall not the worms as well?

punningly. (Cf. SHAKS. *Ham.* IV. iii. 21–3.) **1785** GROSE *Dict. Vulgar T.* s.v., He is gone to the diet of worms, he is dead and buried, or gone to Rot-his-bone.

b. *fig.* as one of the pains of Hell (Mark ix. 48, Isa. lxvi. 24).

c **1000** *Ags. Gosp.* Mark ix. 48 Aworpen on helle fyr, þar hyra wyrm ne swylt. *c* **1275** *Sinners Beware* 53 in *O.E. Misc.* 73 Þe wurmes..þat doþ þe saule teone. *a* **1340** HAMPOLE *Psalter* i. 1 Þe saule thurgh assent gets þe worme þ[t] neuer sall dye. **1547** BECON *Agst. Whoredom* iii. in *Homilies* I. R iv b, The worme, that shall there gnawe the conscience of the dampned, shall neuer dye. **1654** WHITLOCK *Zootomia* 230 As to the other Fate of Books, it is to be feared these feed their Authors never dying Worme. **1667** MILTON *P.L.* VI. 739 Driven down To chains of Darkness, and th' undying Worm.

c. ***worm's*** or ***worms' meat***, said of a man's dead body, or of man as mortal. Also †***worms' food*** or ***ware***; ***food*** or ***meat for*** (or †*to*) ***worms***.

[*a* **1000** *Soul & Body* 127 Lic..bið þonne wyrmes ȝiefl. *a* **1023** WULFSTAN *Hom.* xxx. 145 We syndon deadlice menn and to duste sceolon on worulde wurðan wurmum to æte.]

a **1225** *Ancr. R.* 276 Ne schalt tu beon wurmes fode? *c* **1230** *Hali Meid.* (1922) 59 Þat lam & wurmene mete. **1340** *Ayenb.* 216 Saint bernard zayþ huet is man bote uelþe.. wermene mete [*esca vermium*]? *Ibid.*, He is..mete to wermes ine his dyaþe. *c* **1400** *Pety Job* 7 in *26 Pol. Poems* 121, I shalbe wormes ware. **1411–12** HOCCLEVE *De Reg. Princ.* 1087 It is to gret an abusioun, To seen a man, þat is but wormes mete, Desire riches. **1561** B. GOOGE tr. *Palingenius' Zodiac* VI. Q j b, To day with myrthe alyue, and foode to wormes within a whyle. **1592** SHAKS. *Rom. & Jul.* III. i. 112 They haue made wormes meat of me. **1637** RUTHERFORD *Lett.* (1671) 235 Fear not clay and worm's meat. **1675** COCKER *Morals* 45 Poor Worms-meat, Soar not to the hight of State. **1677** OTWAY *Cheats of Scapin* II, By Heaven, he shall be Worms-meat within these two hours.

7. †**a.** A tick or mite breeding in the hand, foot, or other part of the body. *Obs.*

See also HANDWORM, *nose-worm* (NOSE *sb.* 18), *wheal-worm* (WHEAL *sb.*[1] b), RING-WORM, DEW-WORM (etym. note).

c **1000** *Sax. Leechd.* II. 124 Ȝif wyrm hand ete. **1523–34** FITZHERB. *Husb.* §47 There be some shepe, that hath a worme in his foote, that maketh hym halte. **1530** PALSGR. 290/2 Worme in the hand, *ciron*. **1545** ASCHAM *Toxoph.* I. (Arb.) 49 A litle blayne, a small cutte, yea a silie poore worme in his finger, may kepe him from shoting wel ynough. **1592** SHAKS. *Rom. & Jul.* I. iv. 65 Her Waggoner, a small gray-coated Gnat, not halfe so bigge as a round little Worme, prickt from the Lazie-finger of a man [Qo. 1 maide]. **1605** ERONDELLE *Fr. Gard.* G 7 b, His knees are very round, he hath a worme at the right knee.

†**b.** *fig.* or *allusively*. *Obs.*

1577 GRANGE *Golden Aphrod.* K iv b, To picke a worme betweene two forked fingers [*i.e.* to make horns: cf. Cotgrave s.v. *Ciron*]. **1604** ? DEKKER *Newes fr. Grauesend* Ep. Ded. in *Plague Pamphlets* (1925) 67 Strange fashions did I pick (like wormes) out of the fingers of euery Nation.

c. *popularly* = COMEDO.

1730 SWIFT *Lady's Dressing Room* 64 A Glass that can to Sight disclose The smallest Worm in Cælia's Nose, And faithfully direct her Nail, To squeeze it out from Head to Tail. **1899** *Allbutt's Syst. Med.* VIII. 752 It is also known as grub, worm, black-head, or 'waster'.

8. An earthworm, or a larva (see 3, 5 above). **a.** as the food of birds.

a **1250** *Owl & Night.* 601 Ac wat etestu..Bute attercoppe and fule uliȝe, An wormes, ȝif þu miȝte finde Among þe uolde of harde rinde? *c* **1381** CHAUCER *Parl. Foules* 326 The foules smale That eten as that nature wolde enclyne, As worme, or thynge of whiche I tel no tale. *c* **1386** —— *Sqr.'s T.* 609 And to the wode he wole and wormes ete. *c* **1480** HENRYSON *Cock & Jewel* 94, I had leuer haif scrapit heir with my naillis Amangis this mow, and luke my lyfis fude, As draf, or corne, small wormis or snaillis. **1605** SHAKS. *Macb.* IV. ii. 32 How will you liue? *Son.* As Birds do Mother. *Wife.* What with Wormes, and Flyes? **1670** RAY *Prov.* 84 The early bird catcheth the worm. **1815** STEPHENS in *Shaw's Gen. Zool.* IX. I. 18 The old birds feed them with small worms, caterpillars and insects. **1836** [HOOTON] *Bilberry Thurland* III. 195 As brisk as a robin wi' worms. **1864** BROWNING *Dram. Pers., Caliban* 51 The pie with the long tongue That pricks deep into oakwarts for a worm. **1865** DICKENS *Mut. Fr.* I. vi, As the early bird catches the worm.

b. as bait for fish.

Also with defining term prefixed, as *caddis*, *dew*, *dug*, *lob*, *lug*, *red*, etc.: see these words.

c **1320** *Cast. Love* 1129 As fisch þat is w[t] hok inomen, Þat whon þe worm he swoleweþ alast, He is bi þe hok itiȝed fast. **1510** STANBRIDGE *Vocabula* (W. de W.) D j, *Lumbrex*, a worme or an angle twache. **1566** *Nottingham Rec.* IV. 130 Diggyng dovne the comon dycke..for gettyng of wormes. **1604** SHAKS. *Ham.* IV. iii. 28 (Qo. 2) A man may fish with the worme that hath eate of a King, and eate of the fish that hath fedde of that worme. **1622–34** PEACHAM *Compl. Gent.* xx. (1906) 258 For your live baits they are wormes of all kinds, especially the red worme. **1657** T. BARKER *Barker's Delight* (1659) 41 For the Barbell, I have taken great ones in Ware river with wormes, for I know no better bait than wormes. **1806** WOLCOT (P. Pindar) *Tristia, Elegy Donithorne* 6 Patient as men, upon the river's side, Who for a dinner throw the worm or fly.

collect. sing. **1909** W. C. PLATTS *Light Lines* 82 There may be no particular skill required in catching a few trout with worm in coloured water.

c. In colloq. phr. (***to open***) ***a can of worms***, (to address) a complex and largely unexamined problem or state of affairs the investigation of which is likely to cause much trouble or scandal.

1962 *Times* 21 Feb. 12/4 He..knew that he had opened the bidding on what is sometimes called 'a can of worms'. **1969** *N. Dakota Law Rev.* XLV. 215 Counsel can..better comprehend..the domestic can-of-worms that appears in so many delinquency and neglect cases. **1973** *Times* 22 May 16/5 Mr Berger has opened, in the old American phrase, a fine can of worms. He is suggesting that an impeached President, should he be found guilty, could appeal to the Supreme Court. **1976** L. BERNSTEIN *Unanswered Question* vi. 418 There are so many of those 'underlying strings'.. waiting to be tied up; so many cans of worms have been opened, and a lot of those slippery little beasts are still wriggling around. **1984** A. PRICE *Sion Crossing* vii. 137 Oliver isn't up to this sort of thing. And this is my can of worms.

9. A name for various long slender crustaceans and molluscs (e.g. *Teredo navalis*, the ship-worm) which destroy timber by boring. Also collect. ***the worm***, as a destructive pest.

Formerly supposed to be a grub or larva: cf. 5 b and TEREDO. See also *ship-worm* (SHIP *sb.*[1] 9 b), †TREE-WORM.

1621 in Foster *Eng. Factories Ind.* (1906) 314 She being a new shipp, onely spoyled with the worme. **1691** T. H[ALE] *Acc. New Invent.* 7 Securing the Hulls of his Majesties Ships against the Worm. **1774** E. LONG *Jamaica* III. 740 This tree ..having been found to stand the sea-water very well, uncorroded by..the worm, which is not able to penetrate it. **1864** BROWNING *James Lee's Wife* II. iii, Some ships, safe in port indeed, Rot and rust, Run to dust, All through worms i' the wood.

II. 10. *fig.* **a.** A human being likened to a worm or reptile as an object of contempt, scorn, or pity; an abject, miserable creature.

c **825** *Vesp. Psalter* xxi. 7 Ic soðlice eam wyrm [*vermis*] & nales mon. *c* **1200** ORMIN 4870 Icc amm an wurrm, & nohht nan mann. **1340** *Ayenb.* 215 Ich am, he zede, a lite werm, and no man. *c* **1400** MAUNDEV. (Roxb.) Pref. 1 In þat land he wald..suffer hard passioun and dede of þe Iews for vs synfull wormes. **1402** *Friar Daw* in *Pol. Poems* (Rolls) II. 45 Sith that wickide worme, Wiclyf be his name, began to sowe the seed of cisme in the erthe. *c* **1450** tr. *De Imitatione* III. iv. 67, I am þi most poure seruaunt, and an abiecte worme. *a* **1586** SIDNEY *Arcadia* III. xiii. §2 O Clinias,..the wickedest worme that euer went vpon two legges. **1598** SHAKS. *Merry W.* V. v. 87 *Pist.* Vilde worme, thou wast orelook'd euen in thy birth. **1623** MASSINGER *Dk. Millaine* III. ii. G 4 b, If I am dull now, may I liue and dye The scorne of wormes & slaues. *a* **1662** DUPPA *Rules & Helps Devot.* I. (1675) 26 A Dignity that raiseth us poor Worms of the Earth to a kind of equality with the Angels themselves. **1732** POPE *Ess. Man* I. 258 All this dread Order break—for whom? for thee? Vile worm! **1859** TENNYSON *Enid* 213 He, from his exceeding manfulness.., Wroth to be wroth at such a worm. **1864** TROLLOPE *Small Ho. Allington* xxvii, Poor reptile; wretched worm of a man! **1882** BESANT *All Sorts* vii. (1898) 67 The meanest amongst us poor worms of earth. **1926** *Introduction to Sally* iv. 51 In the presence of her loveliness, what a mere mincing worm he was.

b. Similarly ***the son of a worm*** (after Job xvii. 14).

1633 SHIRLEY *Gamester* II. (1637) D 1, He that affronts Me, is the sonne of a Worme, and his father a Whoore. **1872** MORLEY *Voltaire* (1886) 3 Man, who is a worm, and the son of a worm.

†**c.** With qualification expressing tenderness, playfulness, or commiseration: A human being, 'creature'. *Obs.* (In 16th c. esp. ***loving worm***.)

Cf. G. *das arme wurm*, applied to a child.

a **1553** UDALL *Royster D.* III. ii. (Arb.) 41 Yea and he is as louing a worme againe as a doue. **1561** HOBY tr. *Castiglione's*

Courtier II. R ij, Thus bicause they woulde bee counted to louynge woormes, they make menne counte them lyars, and fonde flatterers. **1568** FULWELL *Like will to Like* A ij b, Yet are women kinde wormes I dare wel say. **1593** G. HARVEY *Pierces Super*. Wks. (Grosart) II. 247 Apuleius Asse was.. a cunning Ape, a loouing worme. **1610** SHAKS. *Temp.* III. i. 31 Poore worme thou art infected. *a* **1625** FLETCHER *M. Thomas* I. i, *Val.* How does his father? *Hyl.* As mad a worm as e'er he was. **1626** B. JONSON *Staple of Newes* v. iii, There hee sits like an old worme of the peace.

†**d.** Used, like CATERPILLAR *sb.* 2, for: One who preys on society. *Obs.*

1591 GREENE *Notable Disc. Coosnage* Wks. (Grosart) X. 30 The seruing-man sent with his Lordes treasure, loseth ofttimes most part to these worms of the commonwelth. **1633** *Costlie Whore* v. i. in Bullen *O. Pl.* IV. 296 Lords, see these wormes of kingdomes be destroyed. [Cf. 295 *ante* the catterpillers of the state.]

e. *slang*. A policeman.

1865 *Slang Dict.* 272 *Worm*, the latest Slang term for a policeman.

11. *fig.* **a.** A grief or passion that preys stealthily on a man's heart or torments his conscience (like a worm in a dead body or a maggot in food); esp. the gnawing pain of remorse. Cf. CANKERWORM 2.

Sometimes 'the worm that never dies' (as in 6 b).

a **900** *Andreas* 769 Brandhata nið weoll on ʒewitte, weorm blædum faʒ. *c* **1386** CHAUCER *Doctor's T.* 280 The worm of conscience. **1560** *Nice Wanton* 281 (Manly) The worme of my conscience, that shall neuer dye, Accuseth me dayly more and more. **1578** H. WOTTON *Courtlie Controv.* 143 Euery man read easily in his face.. that some secret worme gnawed vpon his accustomed ioy. **1594** SHAKS. *Rich. III*, I. iii. 222 The Worme of Conscience still begnaw thy Soule. **1623–4** MIDDLETON & ROWLEY *Changeling* III. iv, 'Twil hardly buy a capcase for ones conscience tho To keep it from the worm. **1727** POPE *To Mr. John Moore* vii, Their Conscience is a Worm within, That gnaws them Night and Day. **1753** SMOLLETT *Ct. Fathom* xlv, While in this manner he secretly nursed the worm of grief that preyed upon his vitals. **1813** BYRON *Br. Abydos* II. xxvii, And, oh! that pang where more than madness lies! The worm that will not sleep —and never dies. **1826** HAZLITT *Plain Speaker* x. Wks. 1903 VII. 106 We secretly persuade ourselves that there is no such thing as excellence. It is that which we hate above all things. It is the worm that gnaws us, that never dies. *a* **1865** J. GIBSON in T. Matthews *Biog.* (1911) 56 Nor did I feel the worm of envy creeping round my heart whenever I saw.. a beautiful idea skilfully executed by any of my young rivals.

†**b.** A whim or 'maggot' in the brain; a perverse fancy or desire; a streak of madness or insanity. Often ***wild worm*** (cf. 2). *Obs.* (So G. *wurm.*)

a **1500** MEDWALL *Nature* II. 307 (Brandl) The wylde worm ys com into hys hed, So that by reason only he ys led. *a* **1530** J. HEYWOOD *Play of Love* 678 (Brandl) Our louer, in whose hed By a frantyke worm his opinion is bred. *a* **1548** HALL *Chron., Hen. V* 44 Some private Scorpion in your heartes or some wild worme in your heades hath caused you to conspire my death and confusion. *Ibid., 3 Rich. III* 42 The wilde worme of vengaunce wauerynge in his hed. **1606** CHAPMAN *Gent. Usher* v. iv. 50 But a father Would rather eate the brawne out of his armes Then glut the mad worme of his wilde desires With his deare issues entrailes. **1623** MASSINGER *Dk. Millaine* v. i. L 2 And if I now out-strip him not, and catch him,.. hereafter I'le sweare there are wormes in my braines. **1653** DOROTHY OSBORNE *Lett.* (1888) 84 Lest you should think I have as many worms in my head as he. **1674** RYMER *Rapin's Aristotle's Poesie* 47 The Emperor Nero who had the Worm in his Head, and conceited himself a Wit. **1678** RAY *Prov.* (ed. 2) 278 He has a worm in 's brain. **1705** HEARNE *Collect.* 26 Nov. (O.H.S.) I. 100 He presently after laid it aside, by reason the worm (wth wch he is possessed) mov'd in his head another way.

†**c.** ***greedy worm*** (cf. 13): avarice or greediness as an itching passion in the heart. *Obs.*

1430–40 LYDG. *Bochas* III. 4251 Auarise, to al vertu contraire, The gredi werm, the serpent vnstaunchable. **1587** HOLINSHED *Chron.* III. 137/1 Thus we see.. what occasion the emperour and duke did take, to inrich themselves by the meanes of the king, whome they forced not to impoverish, so their owne greedie worme were serued. **1607** BEAUM. & FL., *Woman-Hater* I. iii, He is of good wit, and sufficient understanding, when he is not troubled with this greedy worm.

12. ***the worm***: formerly a popular name for various ailments supposed to be caused by the working of a 'worm', or resulting in a worm-shaped tumour or growth. †**a.** Colic. *Sc. Obs.*

c **1500** *Roule's Cursing* 57 in *Maitland Fo.* (1919) 163 The worme, the wareit vedumfa [= wedenonfa']. *c* **1633** SIR A. JOHNSTON (Ld. Wariston) *Diary* (S.H.S.) I. 12 That Sunday ..schoe took the worme at midnight, begoud to cast, and so contineued al Mononday. **1654** *Ibid.* II. 275, I heard after sermon of M. W. G. haiving the worme, and not being able to com to the kirk al the Saboth.

b. Toothache. *Sc.* ? *Obs.*

Cf. SHAKS. *Much Ado* III. ii. 27.

a **1583** MONTGOMERIE *Flyting* 301 (Tullibard. MS.) The choikis, the charbunkill, with þe wormis in thy cheikis. **1673** WEDDERBURN *Vocab.* 20 (Jam.) *Laborat dolore dentium*, he hath the worm. **1881** W. GREGOR *Folk-Lore N.E. Scot.* x. 48 It was a common belief that toothache was caused by a worm at the root of the tooth, and toothache was often simply called 'the worm'. **1890** SERVICE *Thir Notandums* vii. 44 The auld man was girnin' wi' the worm.

†**c.** ? An abscess or swelling thought to resemble a worm in shape. *Obs.*

1607 TOPSELL *Four-f. Beasts* (1658) 336 If a Horse do labor in that kinde of impostume which they vulgarly call the Worm, either any where as well as in the nose, they do open the skin with a searing iron.

III. 13. a. A small vermiform ligament or tendon in a dog's tongue, often cut out when the animal is young, as a supposed safeguard against rabies; = LYTTA.

Also † ***greedy*** or † ***hungry worm***: see GREEDY 1 d, HUNGRY 4.

1530, **1585**, **1627** [see GREEDY 1 d]. **1538** ELYOT *Dict.*, *Lytta*, a worme in a dogges tongue. **1589** NASHE *Pasquil's Ret.* Wks. (Grosart) I. 113 Full of play like a wanton whelpe whose worme was not taken out of his tongue. **1654** C. WASE *Gratius' Cyneget.* B 8 b, Where the tongue is with fast tendons bound, The fury (call'd a worme) is thence convey'd. **1737** [see HUNGRY 4]. **1868** R. OWEN *Anat. Vertebr.* III. 197 The long cylindrical fibrous body.. called 'lytta', and in Dogs, where it attains its largest size, 'the worm'.

fig. **1599** *Broughton's Lett.* i. 6 Your worme from your youth hath been a proud conceit of your self, which, being nourished vnder your tongue so long, makes it now runne riot.

b. A tendon in a dog's tail, often cut or pulled out when the tail is being docked.

1877 STABLES *Pract. Kennel Guide* 141 There is no earthly occasion for pulling out the nerve or 'worm' as it is called.

14. Used to render L. anatomical terms. †**a.** The epididymis (see quot. and cf. WORMY *a.* 2). *Obs.*

1545 RAYNALDE *Byrth Mankynde* I. xi. (1552) 23 Thys parte of the sede cariars may be called the worme: in latyn, *Corpus lumbricosum*: for because that it hath many conuolutions as wormes lyinge togeather haue.

b. The median lobe of the cerebellum; the *vermis* or vermiform process.

1857 DUNGLISON *Med. Lex.* **1899** *Syd. Soc. Lex.*

15. a. An artificial or natural object resembling an earthworm.

1702 *Lond. Gaz.* No. 3858/4 A small Picture of a Man in Armour, set in Gold in a Shagrin Case, 2 little Gold Worms on each side the Picture. **1894** K. GRAHAME *Pagan Papers* 129 The drippings made worms of wet in the thick dust of the road. **1907** *Westm. Gaz.* 1 Jan. 7/2 The 'worm' of the Somerset Light Infantry.. is a black thread woven into the gold lace on the officers' sleeves.

b. *pl.* The coiled pods of *Astragalus hamosus*.

1849 *Gardeners' Chron.* 3 Feb. 96 Vegetable and Flower Seeds.. Hedgehogs per paper 0*s.* 3*d.*.. Snails 0*s.* 3*d.*.. Worms 0*s.* 3*d.* **1902** L. H. BAILEY *Cycl. Amer. Hort.* 1990 Under the name of 'Worms,' 'Snails' and 'Caterpillars,' various odd fruits of leguminous plants are grown as curiosities... *Astragalus hamosus*.. is the one usually known as 'Worms'.

16. Used as the name of various implements of spiral form. (Supposed to resemble the sinuous shape and movement of an earthworm.) †**a.** The screw of a screw-press. *Obs.*

1548 *Elyot's Dict.*, *Cochlea*,.. the vice or wourme of a presse. **1565** COOPER *Thesaurus*.

b. A double or single screw fixed on the end of a rod, used for withdrawing the charge or wad from a muzzle-loading gun.

1591 G. CLAYTON *Mart. Discipl.* 17 Euery Souldiour to haue a sufficient Caliuer,.. rammer, worme [etc.]. ? **1594** BARWICK *Disc. Weapons* 8 His scrues and wormes to serue all for his skowring sticke. **1600–1** *Churchw. Acc. E. Budleigh* (Brushfield 1894) 19 P^{d}.. the makinge cleane of the musketts and for a worme and scowerer. **1703** *La Hontan's Voy. N. Amer.* I. 132 My Men began.. to unload their Pieces with Worms, in order to charge 'em afresh. **1708** *Lond. Gaz.* No. 4455/4 Fine Triangle Worms.. experienc'd for drawing of Balls out of Pieces, with Scowerers and Washers to them, made either to screw upon the Rod with a Socket, or to pin on. **1774** *Pennsylv. Gaz.* 9 Feb. Suppl. 2/3 Best double worm, box handle, single worm, ash handle. *c* **1860** H. STUART *Seaman's Catech.* 4 What is the use of the worm? To draw the gun after loading.

c. A sharp-pointed spiral tool, used for boring wood or soft stone; an auger or gimlet, or the screw of such a tool. *local.*

1594 PLAT *Jewel-ho.* II. 28 If there happen to bee any quarrie of soft stone betweene him and the marle: he must firste make his entrance thorough the stone with a piercing worme. **1812** [see SCREW *sb.*^{1} 5]. **1875** KNIGHT *Dict. Mech.*, *Worm* 6. **1886** *Cheshire Gloss.*, *Worm*, a gimlet.

d. The thread or spiral ridge of a male screw.

1677 MOXON *Mech. Exerc.* ii. 31 The Rules and manner of cutting Worms upon great Screws. The Threds of Screws when they are bigger than can be made in Screw-plates are called Wormes. **1688** R. HOLME *Armoury* III. 321/2 The Screw-Pin (of a vice) is cut with a square strong Worm or Thred. **1726** LEONI *Alberti's Archit.* II. 12/2 If these Rings or this Worm be.. cut in too near to the centre of the Skrew, the weight will then be moved by shorter Leavers. **1750** BLANCKLEY *Nav. Expositor* 143 *Screws for Hatches*, are made with a very nice Worm, that works in a Nutt let into a Sort of Drum-head. **1773** W. EMERSON *Princ. Mech.* (ed. 3) 42 The endless or perpetual screw *AB*, having one worm, leaf, or tooth, which drives the teeth of the wheel *CD*. **1802** *Trans. Soc. Arts* XX. 254 He.. made the thread of the worm too fine. **1833** J. HOLLAND *Manuf. Metal* II. 152 Fly-screws and others having several worms. **1884** *Longm. Mag.* Mar. 488 The inner end of the spoke has a worm cut upon it and is screwed into a solid metal centre, or hub.

e. A spiral channel cut in a hollow cylinder to correspond to the ridge of a screw which turns in it; the spiral of a female or hollow screw.

1725 *Bradley's Fam. Dict.* s.v. *Reservatory*, Each Pipe is three foot and a half long, and there are Bridles at each end of them, which are join'd and closed together by Screws and Worms. **1835** *Brit. Cycl. Arts & Sci.* II. 357/1 In the head is fixed a metal nut, containing a worm or hollow screw. The worm is adapted to receive the screw by which the pressure is produced. **1875** FORTNUM *Maiolica* vi. 52 Some of these pieces have a stopper fitting into the neck by a screw, the worm of which is worked upon it by means of a piece of wood formed with projecting teeth, the interior of the neck being furnished with a corresponding worm. **1878** 'H. COLLINGWOOD' *Secr. Sands* iii, In either end of each length was inserted a narrow band of metal thick enough to allow of a worm and screw, so that all the lengths of each cylinder could be screwed together perfectly water-tight.

f. The spiral of a corkscrew; also, the corkscrew as a whole. *local.*

1681 GREW *Musæum* III. §i. v. 303 A Steel Worme used for the drawing of Corks out of Bottles. **1702** *Phil. Trans.* XXIII. 1367 A close spiral revolution like the Worm of a Bottle Screw. **1875** KNIGHT *Dict. Mech.*, *Worm*,.. The spiral of a cork-screw. **1887** *Kentish Gloss.*, *Worm*, a corkscrew.

g. An endless or tangent screw the thread of which gears with the teeth of a toothed wheel (or similar device).

1729 DESAGULIERS in *Phil. Trans.* XXXVI. 197 Where Goods are to be rais'd high,.. then an endless Screw turn'd by an Handle at each End.. leading an Axis in Peritrochio, or as it is commonly call'd, a Worm and Wheel applied to a Crane, with a Gibbet, is most useful. **1855** LARDNER *Handbk. Nat. Phil., Hydrostatics* etc. § 145 This wheel revolves on an axis, upon which there is a worm or endless screw. **1863** SMILES *Industr. Biogr.* xv. 293 The plan he adopted was to fix a worm-wheel on the side of the ladle, into which a worm was geared. **1904** MECREDY *Dict. Motoring* 129 Worms were formerly cut on a lathe, and the wheels in a gear-cutting machine in the usual way, the teeth being set diagonally to match the angle of the worm.

h. A long spiral or coiled tube connected with the head of a still, in which the vapour is condensed.

1641 FRENCH *Distill.* i. (1651) 25 Put it into a Copper Still with a worme. **1682** *Lond. Gaz.* No, 1686/4 Six Backs, several Stills and Worms. **1757** A. COOPER *Distiller* I. (1760) 2 A subsequent Treatment of the fermented Liquor by the Alembick, or hot Still, with its proper Worm and Refrigeratory. **1885** 'C. E. CRADDOCK' *Prophet Gt. Smoky Mts.* xv, They.. cut the tubs and still to pieces, destroyed the worm, demolished the furnace. **1887** *Manch. Exhib. Catal.* 239 Samples of Whisky. Model Still and Worm.

i. A spiral heating flue in a furnace or coiled steam pipe in a boiler.

1758 [DOSSIE] *Elaboratory Laid Open* 9 Another great error in the building furnaces, particularly those for harts-horn pots, or sand-pots, is the carrying the fire round the object, to be heated, in a vermicular flew, or worm (as it is commonly called);.. as the principal force of the fire is exercised on that great mass of brickwork, which forms the worm. **1766** *Museum Rust.* VI. 299 They [*sc.* two caldrons] may be set in the open fire, without any flew or worm round them, in an oven-like furnace. **1857** MILLER *Elem. Chem., Org.* 371 The steam is either admitted into the copper by a perforated pipe, or it is made to circulate within it through a closed coil or worm.

j. A spring or strip of metal of spiral shape.

1724 *Lond. Gaz.* No. 6318/2 A Steel Worm or Rowling Spring,.. to be used in hanging of Coaches. **1840** *Civil Engin. & Arch. Jrnl.* III. 172/2 The cutting instrument.. performs its operations with wonderful precision, frequently cutting a large and continuous shaving of thirty or forty feet in length.. which, curling up, forms a curious and perfect worm or screw.

IV. 17. *attrib.* and *Comb.* **a.** gen., as ***wormfinger***, ***-kind***, ***-tribe***; objective, as ***worm-breeding*** adj.; instrumental, as ***worm-cankered***, ***-chewed***, ***-consumed***, ***-gnawed***, ***-gnawn***, ***-laid***, ***-spun***, ***-worn*** adjs.; dative, as ***worm-reserved***, ***-ripe***; parasynthetic, as ***worm-faced***, ***-shaped*** adjs.

1611 FLORIO, *Vermifero*, *worme-breeding. **1830** TENNYSON *To J. M. K.* 6 Thou art no sabbath-drawler of old saws, Distill'd from some *worm-canker'd homily. **1927** D. H. LAWRENCE *Mornings in Mexico* 28 Rattling the *worm-chewed window-frames. **1612** J. DAVIES (Heref.) *Muses Sacrif.* Wks. (Grosart) II. 65/1 The *Worme-consumèd Corse. **1934** DYLAN THOMAS *Let.* 12 Apr. (1966) 105 Avaunt, you *worm-faced fellows of the night. **1922** JOYCE *Ulysses* 550 Jogging, mocks them with thumb and wriggling *wormfingers. **1793** WOLCOT (P. Pindar) *Epistle to the Pope* 76 The wise Parisians mock her *worm-gnaw'd shrine. **1598** SYLVESTER *Du Bartas* II. ii. II. *Babylon* 491 Th' old, rusty, mouldy, *worm-gnawn words of yore. **1774** GOLDSM. *Nat. Hist.* VIII. 166 Animals of the *worm kind.. being entirely destitute of feet. **1933** C. S. LEWIS *Pilgrim's Regress* 248 Once the *worm-laid egg broke the wood. **1611** COTGR., *Vermiformes*, two *worme-resembling parts of the *Cervelet*. **1593** NASHE *Christ's T.* Wks. (Grosart) IV. 176, I am the vnworthiest of all *worme-reserued wretches. **1893** 'Q' (Quiller Couch) *Delect. Duchy* 117 A glance up at the *worm-riddled rafters. **1893** J. STRONG *New Era* xi. 247 This morbid, *worm-ripe piety, once in favor. **1767** *Phil. Trans.* LVII. 430 When it is extended, it is of a *worm-shaped figure. **1870** P. M. DUNCAN *Blanchard's Transf. Insects* 384 The larvæ are worm-shaped. **1922** *The Enchanted April* ix. 138 Mrs. Fisher had never cared for maccaroni, especially not this long, worm-shaped variety. **1593** NASHE *Christ's T.* Wks. (Grosart) IV. 214 Though we glister it neuer so in our *worme-spunne robes. **1774** GOLDSM. *Nat. Hist.* VIII. 5 This may serve to distinguish them [*sc.* caterpillars] from the *worm tribe. **1820** PRAED *Eve of Battle* 119 Sleep, in Honour's *worm-worn bed. **1828** LYTTON *Pelham* lxiii, Worm-worn volumes.

b. In sense 8 b, as ***worm-bag***, ***-bait***, ***farm***, ***-hook***, †***-poke***, ***-tackle***, ***-tin***; ***worm-bobber***, ***-catcher***, ***-catching***, ***-fisher***, ***-fishing***, ***-hunter***, ***-hunting***; †***worm-embowelled*** adj.

1909 W. C. PLATTS *Light Lines* 83 Scudding across the meadows, with his rod and his *worm-bag, to the river. **1842** PULMAN *Rustic Sk.* 48 On the Axe the only kind of *worm-bait used is the blackhead or bluehead. **1844** J. T. HEWLETT *Parsons & Widows* i. 11 He is a mere *worm-bobber—cannot throw a fly or spin a minnow. **1880** F. BUCKLAND *Nat. Hist. Brit. Fishes* 11 A short gentleman, like you, sir,.. would never make a *worm-catcher. **1881** *Athenæum* 30 Apr. 594/2 Mr. Wells offered to back against Frank Buckland a long-legged and long-armed friend.. on any night at *worm-catching. **1608** DAY *Hum. out of Breath*

i. [ii.] B 3 b, And see if any siluer-coated fish Will nibble at your *worme-emboweld hooks. **1880** F. Buckland *Nat. Hist. Brit. Fishes* 10 A *worm farm at Nottingham. **1847** Stoddart *Angler's Comp.* 115 The *worm-fisher ought.. always to possess a stock of it [hart's-horn moss]. **1904** Gallichan *Fishing Spain* 64 The worm fisher has his opportunity when the streams are in spate. **1842** Pulman *Rustic Sk.* 48 *Worm-fishing is followed with greatest success.. during the season of mowing grass. **1857** W. C. Stewart *Pract. Angler* vii. (ed. 3) 133 Fly-fishers are apt to sneer at worm-fishing. **1747** Bowlker *Art Angling* 64 This is a very large Fly, and is to be made upon a small *Worm-hook. **1837** Kirkbride *North. Angler* 12 In Carlisle.. we speak of.. large worm, middle, and small worm hooks. **1865** A. S. Moffat *Secr. Angling* 165 If the *worm-hunter only takes care to tread softly upon the bosom of his mother earth. **1890** *Science-Gossip* XXVI. 159 The worm-hunter will turn over every likely stone or rubbish heap which comes in his path. **1852** *Zoologist* X. 3421 He employed himself in this *worm-hunting for a considerable time. ?**1630** W. Lauson *Comm.* on J. Dennys *Secr. Angling* Note 13 *Worme poake of cloath. **1835** *Chambers's Edin. Jrnl.* Jan. 390/3 First of all, the *worm-tackle. For this, sizeable hooks.. are generally preferred. **1847** Stoddart *Angler's Comp.* 108 In preparing worm-tackle. **1906** *Macm. Mag.* Apr. 417 The rod, basket, and.. the *worm-tin.

c. In sense 4, as ***worm-colic, -disease, -fever, -sickness***; also in names of remedies, as ***worm-cake, -lozenge, -medicine, -powder, -preventive, -syrup, -tea***; also ***worm-killing*** adj.

1773 *Pennsylv. Gaz.* 23 June, Suppl. 2/3 His never failing *worm cake, which destroys that vermin so pernicious to children. **1788** J. Hurdis *Village Curate* (1797) 102 His worm-cake and his pills. **1810** James *Milit. Dict.* (ed. 3), **Worm-cholic*, a distemper in horses, occasioned by broad, thick, and short worms or truncheons. **1848** Dunglison *Med. Lex.* (ed. 7), *Helminthiasis*, *worm disease. **1792** J. Townsend *Journ. Spain* II. Index, *Worm fever. **1899** *Syd. Soc. Lex.*, *Worm fever*, pyrexia consequent on the irritation set up by intestinal worms. **1763** Foote *Mayor of G.* i. Wks. 1799 I. 164 You.. *worm-killing, blistering, glistering ——. **1818** Susan Ferrier *Marriage* I. xxvii, If Mary had taken some of her nice *worm-lozenges. **1889** *Buck's Handbk. Med. Sci.* VIII. 2/1 The popular 'worm lozenges'. **1702** J. Purcell *Cholick* (1714) 177 Two Girls.. were seized with most violent Cholicks,.. which no Clysters, Purges or *Worm Medicines could appease. **1799** *Med. Jrnl.* II. 151 Recommenders of some newly-broached worm-medicines. **1727** Pope in *Miscellanies*, To Mr. John Moore, Author of the celebrated *Worm-Powder. **1880** Garrod & Baxter *Mat. Med.* 447 The *worm-preventives are medicines which give tone to the intestinal membrane. **1899** *Syd. Soc. Lex.*, **Worm-sickness*, a severe disease occurring among sheep in Holland, set up by the fly *Lucilia sericata*. **1773** *Pennsylv. Gaz.* 30 June 3/3 A new invented *Worm-Syrup. **1897** *Sears, Roebuck Catal.* 27/2 *Worm syrup*.. for expelling worms from children. **1972** E. Wigginton *Foxfire Bk.* 247 Take 'worm syrup' which is made by boiling Jerusalem oak and pine root together. **1850** Pereira *Elem. Mat. Med.* (ed. 3) II. 1478 A preparation kept in the shops of the United States, and much prescribed by physicians, under the name of **worm tea*, consists of spigelia root, senna, manna, and savine, mixed together.

d. In sense 16 g, as ***worm-drive, -gear, -gearing, -jack, -pinion, -rack, -screw, -shaft, -spindle, -thread, -wheel; worm-geared*** adj.

1907 *Westm. Gaz.* 19 Nov. 4/2 This machine.. retains.. the silent *worm-drive. **1884** *B'ham Daily Post* 24 Jan. 3/1 Wanted, 10 ton Foundry Ladle, extra strong, with *worm gear. **1936** *Discovery* Aug. 238/2 It [*sc.* the camera] is loaded into position on the plane with a *worm-geared winch and pulley system. **1973** *Gloss. Terms Materials Handling* (*B.S.I.*) VI. 16 *Worm geared chain pulley block*,.. mechanical advantage is obtained chiefly by.. use of a worm wheel and worm. **1884** Knight *Dict. Mech., Suppl.*, **Worm Gearing*.. has an arrangement for transmitting circular motion in either direction. **1904** Mecredy *Dict. Motoring* 128 Worm gearing is used in the steering apparatus for adjustments. **1677** Moxon *Mech. Exerc.* iii. 37 Fig. 1. is call'd a *Worm-Jack. **1913** F. Young & Aston *Complete Motorist* (ed. 8) 177 A worm-driven axle with the *worm pinion underneath. **1891** *Century Dict.*, **Worm-rack*, a rack gearing with a worm-wheel. **1677** Flamsteed in Rigaud *Corr. Sci. Men* (1841) II. 172 To this a toothed arch was fastened, by the help of which, and a *worm screw, the piece of wood.. might be raised or depressed easily. **1835** Ure *Philos. Manuf.* 228 The toothed wheel, acted on by the worm-screw. **1892** *Photogr. Ann.* II. 391 The mechanical power is a central worm screw working in four racks on pillars. **1839** Ure *Dict. Arts* 372 Screws or *worm-shafts, which are placed so as to keep the carriage parallel to the drawing rollers [in a spinning-mule]. **1677** Moxon *Mech. Exerc.* iii. 45 That the Teeth of the Worm wheel may gather themselves into the Grooves of the Worm in the *Worm-spindle. **1773** W. Emerson *Princ. Mech.* (ed. 3) 43 All things here laid down relating to the perpetual screw, do suppose that the axis of the worm-spindle lies in the plane of the wheel it works in. **1925** *Chamb. Jrnl.* May 332/2 The *worm-thread and the teeth in the strip are square and of great strength. **1677** *worm-wheel [see *worm-spindle*]. **1842** *Civil Engin. & Arch. Jrnl.* V. 73/1 A vertical shaft, on the bottom of which is a worm, taking into a worm-wheel. **1925** *Chamb. Jrnl.* May 332/1 An ideal clip for hose connections.. based on the worm and worm-wheel principle.

e. In sense 16 h and similar applications, as ***worm-cooler, -maker, -pipe, refrigeratory, -safe, -tank, -tub***.

1812 *Ann. Reg., Chron.* 35 A large *worm cooler, which contained nearly 60,000 gallons of water. **1793-4** *Matthews's Bristol Directory* 31 Pewterers, *Worm-makers, and Copper-smiths. **1850** *Patent* in *Law Times Rep.* X. 861/1 The coal is.. put into a common gas retort, to which is attached a *worm pipe passing through a refrigerator. **1839** Ure *Dict. Arts* 6 A clean copper still, furnished with a capital and *worm-refrigeratory. **1853** *Ibid.* (ed. 4) I. 594 The *worm-safe.. is a contrivance for permitting the distiller to observe and note at any period of the distillation the alcholic strength or specific gravity of his spirits, without access to the still. **1860** Gesner *Coal, Petrol.*, etc. (1865) 79 The worm is.. fastened securely by iron stays into the *worm tank. **1756** P. Browne *Jamaica* (1789) 158 Barbadoes Cedar.. is.. frequently made into *worm-tubs. **1757** A. Cooper *Distiller* I. xvi. (1760) 74 Another Requisite to be observed is that the Water in the Worm-tub be kept cold. **1880** *Act 43 & 44 Vict.* c. 24 §143 (1) An officer may require a distiller.. to cause the water in any worm tub.. to be drawn off.

f. Special combinations: **worm-bark**, the anthelmintic bark of the West Indian cabbage-tree, *Andira inermis*; **worm-burrow**, the hole made by a worm in the earth; a fossil perforation of this sort; **worm-cast**, the convoluted mass of mould thrown up by an earthworm on the surface of the soil after passing through the worm's body; so **worm-casting**; **worm-conveyor** (see quot. 1910 and conveyor 4 b); †**worm-earth** = *worm-cast*; **worm-fence** *U.S.* = snake-fence; †**worm-fowl**, *collect.* birds that feed on worms; †**worm-fret** *a.* [*fret*, obs. pa. pple. of fret *v.*[1]], worm-eaten; **worm-killer**, a preparation for destroying garden worms; †**worm line**, a spiral; **worm month** *Sc.* and *N. Ir.*, July (or the second half of July and first half of August); cf. Da. *ormemaaned*; **worm-oil** = *wormseed oil*; **worm pipe-fish**, *Syngnathus* (*Nerophis*) *lumbriciformis*; **worm red** *a.*, ? dull brownish red; also *sb.*; **worm-shell**, the twisted shell or tube of a marine annelid or mollusc, as *Serpula* and *Vermetus*; also applied to the animal itself; **worm-snake**, a name for various small harmless snakes, as *Typhlops nigrescens* and *Carphophis amoena*; **worm-spring**, a spiral spring; †**worm-state**, the larval stage in insect transformation; †**worm-stone**, a spirally-twisted fossil; †**worm-tongued** *a.* (see sense 10); **worm-track** = helminthite; **worm-tube** = *worm-shell*; **worm-web** *Sc.*, a cobweb; †**worm-work**, ? a winding earthwork.

c **1791** *Encycl. Brit.* (ed. 3) VII. 631/2 *Geoffræa*,.. also called the *worm-bark tree. **1860** Mayne *Expos. Lex.*, *Worm-Bark*,.. the bark of the *Geoffræa Surinamensis*. **1859** Page *Geol. Terms*, *Arenicolites*,.. those circular holes.. which appear.. on the upper surface of many sandstones, and which seem to have been *worm-burrows. **1883** *Science* I. 520/2 The more slender side-roots descend chiefly through worm-burrows. **1914** *Brit. Mus. Return* 213 One worm-burrow from the Cambrian of Bray Head. **1766** *Complete Farmers* s.v. *Walk*, Which will be of service to prevent weeds from growing through the gravel, and to hinder *worm-casts. **1862** *Chambers' Encycl.* III. 740/2 (*Earthworm*) Worm-casts gradually accumulate on the surface to form a layer of the very finest soil. **1881** Darwin *Veg. Mould* 10 On such grassy paths *worm-castings may often be seen. **1884** C. G. W. Lock *Workshop Rec.* Ser. iii. 439/1 From the stones it [*sc.* crushed slag] passes through a *worm conveyer to a brick-press. **1910** *Encycl. Brit.* VII. 53 The worm conveyor, also known as the Archimedean screw,.. consists of a continuous or broken blade screw set on a spindle. This spindle is made to revolve in a suitable trough, and as it revolves any material put in is propelled by the screw from one end of the trough to the other. *a* **1722** Lisle *Husb.* (1757) 2 *Worm-earths also abound most in the richest land. **1796** F. Baily *Jrnl. Tour N. Amer.* (1856) 111 They place split logs angular-wise on each other making what they call a '*worm-fence' and which is raised about five feet high. **1833** T. Hamilton *Men & Manners Amer.* (1843) 149 The worm fences and the freshness and regularity of the houses are sadly destructive of the picturesque. **1842** Dickens *Amer. Notes* xiv, The primitive worm-fence is universal, and an ugly thing it is. *c* **1381** Chaucer *Parl. Foules* 505, I.. wol sey my veyrdit.. For watir foule.. And I for *worme foule, seyde the foole cukkowe. **1430-40** Lydg. *Bochas* I. 6566 *Wermfrete stokkes. **1915** H. H. Thomas *Gardening for Amateurs* I. 22/1 Proprietary *worm-killers can also be obtained, and these must always be employed as directed. **1959** *Times* 7 Mar. 9/1 There are always the lead arsenate wormkillers. **1551** Recorde *Pathw. Knowl.* A iiij b, An other sorte of lines is there, that is called a spirall line, or a *worm line, whiche representeth an apparant forme of many circles, where there is not one in dede. **1782** J. Ramsay in Allardyce *Scot. & Scotsmen 18th C.* (1888) II. 256 It looked like February than the *worm month. **1825** Jamieson, *Worm-month*.. the month of July, Perths... from the hatching of many kinds of reptiles in this month. **1880** *Antrim & Down Gloss.*, *Worm month*,.. a fortnight before and a fortnight after Lammas. **1855** Ogilvie *Suppl.*, **Worm-oil*. **1835** Jenyns *Man. Brit. Vertebr. Anim.* 488 *Syngnathus lumbriciformis*, Nob. (*Worm Pipe-Fish). **1831** J. Holland *Manuf. Metal* I. 309 The files.. are then heated.. to a sort of *worm-red. **1833** *Ibid.* II. 80 The [sword-] blade is then hardened.. by the smith heating it in the fire until it becomes worm red. **1881** Greener *Gun* 252 The pot is then placed in a bright coal fire, where it remains till the whole is of a worm red. **1666** Merrett *Pinax* 194 *Tubuli in quibus vermes*, *Worm-shells. *c* **1711** Petiver *Gazophyl.* vi. liii, Great Indian furrowed Worm-shell. **1767** *Phil. Trans.* LVII. 432 The Serpula, or Worm-shell. **1776** Mendes da Costa *Elem. Conchol.* 148 The third family is the Vermiculi, or Worm Shells. **1860** P. P. Carpenter in *Rep. Smithsonian Instit.* 1859, 206 The Ivory Worm-shell (*Vermetus eburneus*). **1861** *Ibid.* 1860, 210 Family Vermetidæ. (Worm-Shells.) **1885** F. McCoy *Prodromus Zool. Victoria* xi. 7 *Typhlops nigrescens*... The Blackish Australian *Worm-Snake. **1885** [see *ground-snake*, ground *sb.* 18 b]. **1729** *Phil. Trans.* XXXVI. 133 The upper Wire or Point.. is by Means of the *Worm-spring EF.., made to push the said Beam upwards with the Force of the Spring. **1797** *Encycl. Brit.* (ed. 3) XIII. 488/1 There must be a worm-spring fastened to the key, and to the bar W.., to keep down the end of the key. **1752** J. Hill *Hist. Anim.* 64 This Insect, in the *worm-state, is about the bigness of a louse. **1677** Plot *Oxfordsh.* 126 At the same rubble Quarries we find also the *Lapides vermiculares*, or *Worm-stones. **1681** Grew *Musæum* iii. §i. v. 303 The Worme-Stone... Not much unlike a Steel Worme used for the drawing of Corks out of Bottles. **1593** G. Harvey *Pierce's Super.* 17 *Woorme-toungued Oratours, dust-footed Poets, and weatherwise historians. **1859** Page *Geol. Terms*, *Vermiculites*.. the smaller.. *worm-tracks which appear on the surfaces of many flaggy sandstones. **1776** Mendes da Costa *Elem. Conchol.* 285 A single Vermiculus, or *Worm-tube. **1883** *Science* II. 88 2 As the coral grows, it spreads round the worm-tube. **1914** *Brit. Mus. Return* 213 A supposed Worm-tube from the Chalk.. of Bridlington. *c* **1817** Hogg *Tales & Sk.* V. 214 My bed-cloth consisted of a single covering not thicker than a *wormweb. **1821** Galt *Sir A. Wylie* I. xxi. 178 Your Leddyship's character's no a gauze gown, or a worm web. **1643** *Lancash. Tracts Civil War* (Chetham Soc.) 179 They bringe up an open trench in a *worme work, the earth being indented or sawed, for the securitie of their myners.

worm (wɜːm), *v.* Forms: 3 wirme, 6–7 worme, 7 woorme, 7– worm. [f. the sb. Cf. Du., G. *wurmen* (in various senses).

In *Gen. & Ex.* 3342 'Quo so nome up forbone mor it [the manna] wirmede, bredde, and rotede ðor' read 'wirmes bredde' (cf. Petrus Comestor *scatebat vermibus*).]

I. 1. *intr.* To hunt for or catch worms.

1576 Turberv. *Venerie* li. 153 When he [the boar] feedeth on fearne or rootes, then is it called rowting or fearning, or (as some call it) worming: bycause when he doth but a little turne vp the grounde with his nose, he seeketh for wormes. *Ibid.* liii. 154 In soft places where he wormeth. **1611** Cotgr., *Vermiller*, to worme, to root for wormes. **1614** Markham *Cheap & Good Husb.* vi. i. 115 It is good to keepe Chickens one fortnight in the house, and after to suffer them to goe abroad with the Henne to worme. **1880** F. Buckland *Nat. Hist. Brit. Fishes* 11 Men, women, and children are employed in 'worming'. **1899** R. Haggard in *Longm. Mag.* Apr. 520 The old thrush goes on worming without even taking the trouble to look up.

2. a. *trans.* To cause to be eaten by worms; to devour, as a burrowing worm does. Chiefly *pass.*, to be eaten by worms. Also *fig.*

1604 Dekker *Honest Wh.* i. i. A 3, The body, as the Duke spake very wisely, is gone to be wormd. **1633** T. Adams *Exp. 2 Pet.* ii. 4. 530 The people called him [Herod] a god, but the wormes soone confuted their ridiculous deity, That.. when the Angell had worm'd that Idoll, he might say, Behold your king. **1784** Cowper *Task* ii. 816 Ev'ry plague that can infest Society, and that saps and worms the base Of th' edifice that policy has rais'd. **1821** Galt *Ann. Parish* xxvii. 235 The Manse had fallen into a sore state of decay—the doors were wormed on the hinges. **1864** T. S. Williams & Simmonds *Engl. Commerc. Corresp.* 285 Buffalo hides except rubbed, holed, or wormed, cannot be laid down at all near your limit. **1895** *Bookseller's Catal.*, Some few margins are wormed, but this can be repaired at a trifling cost. **1900** *Trans. Highland & Agric. Soc. Scot.* Ser. v. XII. 235 It might have been suspected that part of the thinness [of the oats] at one end of the plots was due to worming.

b. To eat (one's way) *through*. (Cf. 9 c.)

1858 Masson *Milton* I. 481 There were men who had wormed their way through libraries, and might be classified according to the colours left in them by the food they had devoured.

II. 3. a. To extract the 'worm' or lytta from the tongue of (a dog). (Supposed to be a safeguard against madness: see worm *sb.* 13.)

1575 Turberv. *Faulconrie* 369 It shall be good when spanell whelpes are one moneth olde.. to worme them vnder the toung. **1599** *Broughton's Lett.* i. 6 A dog not wormed while he is yong, will in time proue mad. **1632** B. Jonson *Magn. Lady* i. vii, *Int.*.. Hee Will screw you out a Secret from a Statist ——. *Com.* So easie, as some Cobler wormes a Dog. **1641** Peacham *Worth of Penny* 21 For a peny you may have your dog worm'd, and so be kept from running mad. **1743** H. Walpole *Let. to Mann* 3 Oct., Patapan is in my lap; I had him wormed lately, which he took heinously. **1815** Scott *Guy M.* vii, The men.. assisted the laird in his sporting parties, wormed his dogs, and cut the ears of his terrier puppies. **1855** Browning *Protus* 50 He wrote the little tract 'On worming dogs'.

b. *transf.* and *fig.* (as a remedy for madness, a ribald tongue, or greediness).

1564-78 Bullein *Dial. agst. Pest.* (1888) 62 You learned your Retorike in the vniuersitie of Bridewell; you were neuer well wormed when you were young. **1589** Nashe *Countercuffe* Wks. (Grosart) I. 77 The blood and the humors that were taken from him, by launcing and worming him at London vpon the common Stage. **1615** Day *Festivals* xii. 335 Abishai desiring leave.. to go and worme that unhappy Tongue of his [Shimei's]. **1619** R. Harris *Drunkard's Cup* 9 He bans, and cannot be quiet till his tongue be wormed. **1621** Fletcher *Pilgrim* iv. i, Is She grown mad now? Is her blood set so high? I'le have her madded, I'le have her worm'd. **1623** Massinger *Dk. Millaine* iii. ii. G 3 When I had worm'd his tongue, and trussed his hanches. **1676** Shadwell *Virtuoso* i. 12 He is such a froward testy old fellow, he should be Wormed like a mad Dog. *a* **1679** J. Ward *Diary* (1839) 137 A certaine woman that eat much before her husband, and hee complained of her to her mother, shee told him itt was her fault, for she had not wormd her.

†**c.** ***to worm a person in the nose***: to extract information from him by adroit questioning. *Obs.*

Cf. F. *tirer à quelqu'un les vers du nez.*

1613 *Treas. Aunc. & Mod. Times* ix. xxii. 953/2, I haue so cunningly wormed my husband in the nose; that he hath discouered vnto me, more Mony then hee acquainted you withall.

4. a. To rid (plants, esp. tobacco) of 'worms' or grubs.

1624 Capt. Smith *Virginia* v. 172 Wormes in the earth also there are but too many, so that to keepe them from destroying their Corne and Tobacco, they are forced to worme them euery morning,.. else all would be destroyed. **1641** [cf. worming *vbl. sb.* 2]. **1649** W. Bullock *Virginia* 11 The poore Servant goes daily through the rowes of Tobacco stooping to worme it. **1779** J. Carver *Treat. Culture Tobacco*

iv. 23 This is termed 'worming the tobacco'. **1864** De Coin *Cotton & Tobacco* 274 The plants ought to be wormed—which means searched and cleared of worms—at least once a week.

absol. **1886** C. G. W. Lock *Tobacco* 69 The usual practice is to worm and sucker while the dew is on in the morning.

b. To treat (an animal) with a preparation designed to free it of parasitic worms.

1932 N. Mitford *Christmas Pudding* xi. 179 Lady Bobbin spoke to those about her of horses, hounds, and such obscure eventualities as going to ground..and being thoroughly well wormed. **1940** W. Faulkner *Hamlet* iv. i 276 He drenched and wormed and..drew the teeth of horses and mules. **1961** C. H. D. Todd *Pop. Whippet* 69 Having decided upon your puppy..ask if it has been wormed. **1978** *Detroit Free Press* 5 Mar. c 20/3 (Advt.), Collie Pups..wormed, pet or show.

III. †**5.** To pry into the secrets of (a person); to play the spy upon. *Obs.*

1607 Beaum. & Fl. *Woman-Hater* iii. iii, O he is a very subtile and a dangerous knave, but if he deal a Gods name, we shall worm him. *a* **1616** —— *Wit without Money* iv. iv, I'le teach you to worm me, good Lady sister, and peep into my privacies to suspect me. **1648** *Hunting of Fox* 41 You have..a Lay-presbytery to worme your Purposes and Consciences. **1807** J. Barlow *Columb.* iv. 211 Spies with eye askance, Pretended heretics who worm the soul.

6. *to worm* (a person) *out of*: to deprive or dispossess of (property, etc.) by underhand dealing. ? *Obs.*

1617 W. Fennor *Compters Commw.* 10 It was onely a tricke to worme mee out of my money. **1649** G. Daniel *Trinarch., Hen. IV* xi, Richard (whom late wee left dethron'd) is not Worne from the Storye, though worm'd out of King. *a* **1700** B. E. *Dict. Cant. Crew, Worm'd out of*, Rookt, Cheated, Trickt. **1718** tr. *Tournefort's Voy. Levant* I. 58 This gave us a suspicion..that they jointly contriv'd to worm us out of this Mony. **1838** Lytton *Alice* iii. viii, We cannot wrestle against the world, but we may shake hands with it, and worm the miser out of its treasures.

7. *to worm out*: to thrust out, get rid of, expel, by subtle and persistent pressure or undermining.

1594 Lyly *Mother Bombie* ii. ii, I haue tied vp the louing worme my daughter, and will see whether fansie can worme fansie out of her head. **1643** Sir T. Browne *Relig. Med.* i. §30. 67 It is a riddle to me, how this story of Oracles hath not worm'd out of the World that doubtful conceit of Spirits and Witches. *a* **1662** Heylin *Laud* i. (1671) 46 He did not only stock his Colledge with such a generation of Non-conformists as could not be wormed out in many years after his decease; but [etc.]. **1665** *Surv. Aff. Netherl.* 127 The industrious Portugeze, whom they have wormed almost out of all their discoveries in Asia and Africa. **1683** in J. Wickham Legg *Eng. Ch. Life* (1914) 115 A Temper, which must Inevitably..Worme out once againe the Common Prayer. **1706** Phillips (ed. Kersey), To *Worm*, to work one out of a Place, &c. **1714** R. Fiddes *Pract. Disc.* ii. 271 He who has the handsomest address..in worming others out of business, and winding himself in. **1748** E. Erskine *Serm.* (1755) 332 The Venom of the Old Serpent has diffused itself through all the Powers and Faculties of the Soul and Body; and it is worming out your Life. **1760** *Ann. Reg., Chron.* 114/1 Such a body of troops as..in time might be able to worm out the English from the trade of Bengal. **1785** Grose *Dict. Vulgar T., Worm*, to worm out,..also to undermine, or supplant. **1811** Lamb *Elia* Ser. i. *Bachelor's Complaint*, Innumerable are the ways which they take to insult and worm you out of their husband's confidence.

8. *to worm out*: **a.** to extract (information, a secret, etc.) by insidious questioning. Similarly const. *out of* or *from* (a person).

1715 Addison *Drummer* ii. i, I fancy..thou could'st worm it [a secret] out of her. **1785** Grose *Dict. Vulgar T., Worm*, to worm out, to obtain the knowledge of a secret by craft. **1800** Mar. Edgeworth *Pop. T., The Will* iv, I do not want to worm your secret from you. **1807** Crabbe *Birth of Flattery* 56, I..Who've loosed a guinea from a miser's chest, And worm'd his secret from a traitor's breast. **1840** Thackeray *Catherine* xi, Old Wood knew all her history... He had wormed it out of her, day by day. **1844** A. Smith *Mr. Ledbury* xx. (1886) 60 He was able..to worm out a description of the locality. **1853** Lytton *My Novel* x. xx, By little and little our Juvenile Talleyrand..wormed out from Dick this grievance. **1863** Cowden Clarke *Shaks. Char.* iii. 68 He counsels his mother not to let the king worm from her his secret. **1865** Baring-Gould *Werewolves* v. 62 The judge ordered one of his peasants to visit the man, and to worm the truth out of him. **1900** 'Anthony Hope' *Quisanté* i. 14 She could not get much out of him, but she found herself trying to worm out all she could.

b. To extract (money, etc.) *out of* (a person) by pleading.

1851 Kingsley *Yeast* xiii, They make the labourer fancy that he is not to depend upon God and his own right hand, but on what his wife can worm out of the good nature of the rich.

9. a. *intr.* To move or progress sinuously like a worm; also *transf.* of things. Usually with adv., as *about, along, up, down*, or prep., as *in, into* (a confined space). Also, to move windingly *through*; to twine or twist *about* (something).

1610 G. Fletcher *Christ's Tri.* i. xxii, Thousand flaming serpents hissing flew..And woorming all about his soule they clung. **1802** G. Colman *Br. Grins, Elder Bro.* (1819) 118 He [a drunk man] work'd, with sinuosities, along, Like Monsieur Corkscrew worming thro' a Cork. **1826** J. F. Cooper *Last of Mohicans* xx, I little like that smoke which you may see worming up along the rock above the canoe. **1839** Bailey *Festus, The Centre*, Through seas and buried mountains..have we wormed Down to the ever burning forge of fire. **1884** *Century Mag.* XXIX. 139 They wormed through the grass to within forty or fifty feet of the rifle-pits. **1885** *Cyclist* 19 Aug. 1101/1 The procession..moved off in a straggling manner... Once in order, however, the riding was excellent, and a very presentable line wormed through the Newport Road. **1896** Baden-Powell *Matabele Campaign* xvi, The caves and their passages worm about inside the koppie.

b. *refl.* in same sense.

1865 Gosse *Land & Sea* 255 So, kneeling,..or fairly stretched at full-length supine.., we worm ourselves into the holes and crannies. **1899** D. C. Murray *Dangerous Catspaw* 200 Gale wormed himself into the little passage. **1927** Agatha Christie *Big Four* viii. 107, I crawled cautiously out of the bushes, and inch by inch..I wormed myself down the steep path.

c. With advb. acc., as *to worm one's way*. Also of figurative progress (cf. next).

1822 Good *Study Med.* (1829) I. 399 Fistulous ulcers..have sometimes..wormed a sinuous path, and opened into the vagina. **1845** Lingard *Hist. Anglo-Saxon Ch.* I. ii. 95 Through such intrigues it occasionally happened that men, in no wise qualified for the episcopal office, wormed their way to the episcopal bench. **1851** F. B. Head *Stokers & Pokers* iii. 39 A number of newspaper-vendors..are worming their way through the crowd. **1869** Trollope *He Knew*, etc. lxii. (1878) 348 That snake in the grass who wormed his way into my house. **1883** F. M. Crawford *Dr. Claudius* vii. 117 The screw..rushed round, worming its angry way through the long quiet waves.

10. *fig.* **a.** To make one's way insidiously like a worm *into* (a person's confidence, secret affairs, etc.); to burrow *in* so as to hurt or destroy. Also, to wriggle *out of* (a difficulty).

1627 P. Fletcher *Locusts* iv. xxi, To comply With that weake sexe, and by fine forgerie To worme in womens hearts, chiefly the rich and high. **1633** G. Herbert *Temple, Church-Rents* ii, But when debates and fretting jealousies Did worm and work within you more and more, Your colour faded. **1639** Saltmarshe *Policy* 231 Vse subtle and crafty men, they will search, and skrew, and worme into busines of difficulty. **1833** Ritchie *Wand. Loire* 138, I worm into their secrets like a being of supernatural power. **1868** *Cornh. Mag.* July 68 We cannot pause to tell how imposters..wormed into his confidence. **1881** Tennyson *Cup* i. i. 54 And once there I warrant I worm thro' all their windings. **1893** in J. H. Barrows *World's Parlt. Relig.* I. 618 These facts..are exceedingly embarrassing for the adherents of the evolutionary theory; but they worm out of the difficulty in a manner that provokes..a smile.

b. *refl.* To insinuate oneself *into* (a person's favour or confidence, a desirable position, etc.).

1711 Swift *Jrnl. to Stella* 1 Aug., I was endeavouring to settle some points of the greatest consequence, and had wormed myself pretty well into him, when his Under Secretary came in..and interrupted all my scheme. **1712** *Perquisite Monger* 10 One Zaraida..so worm'd herself into the Confidence of her Mistress, as to be in the highest Esteem with her. **1809** Malkin *Gil Blas* iii. iii. ¶4 If you have management enough to worm yourself into his confidence. **1840** Dickens *Old C. Shop* vi, Worm yourself into her secrets; I know you can. **1853** Reade *Chr. Johnstone* iii, Flucker,..with admirable smoothness and cunning, wormed himself into cabin-boy on board the yacht. **1871** Dixon *Tower* III. v. 45 He was to worm himself into the family councils. **1911** J. H. Rose *W. Pitt & Gt. War* x. 432 This was before Wedderburn had wormed himself into favour with Lord North.

11. *trans.* with predicate-extension: To move (an object) *off, down, through*, etc. by a gradual tortuous propulsion or dragging.

a **1861** T. Winthrop *Life in Open Air* (1863) 117 Aided by the urgent stream, we carefully and delicately..wormed our boat off the rock. **1873** J. T. Moggridge *Harv. Ants* i. 33 We measured a tunnel [formed by ants] by worming a straw down it. **1888** Stevenson *Black Arrow* 251 Dick had gradually wormed his right arm clear of its bonds. **1899** *Westm. Gaz.* 11 Dec. 2/1 To repel all attempts on the part of the enemy to worm his patrols through our advanced troops.

IV. 12. [See worm *sb.* 16 d, e.] To make a screw-thread on. † *to worm in*, to screw in; to insert and secure by screwing.

1598 Sylvester *Du Bartas* ii. i. iv. *Handie-Crafts* 523 He hatcheth files, and winding vices wormeth. **1683** Moxon *Mech. Exerc., Printing* xi. ¶18 It hath four Iron Hooks.., whose Shanks are Wormed in. **1868** Rogers *Pol. Econ.* x. (1876) 130 A smith may be engaged generally in forging or worming screws. **1884** M. Mackenzie *Dis. Throat & Nose* II. 271 Its outer surface is smooth for four inches from the distal end; but for the rest of its length it is wormed.

13. a. *Naut.* To wind spun-yarn or small rope spirally round (a rope or cable) so as to fill up the grooves between the strands and render the surface smooth for parcelling and serving.

1644 [implied in worming *vbl. sb.* 6]. **1706** Phillips (ed. Kersey), To *Worm a Cable*, or *Hawser*,..to succour or strengthen it, by winding a small Rope all along between the Strands. **1760** Capt. W. Wriglesworth *MS. Log-bk. of the 'Lyell'* 22 Sept., Got our Main Stay down, Wormed the lower end of it. **1769** Falconer *Dict. Marine* (1780) *Emmieller un êtai*, to worm a stay. **1799** *Hull Advertiser* 13 Apr. 2/2, 60 fathom of cable, part of which is wormed. **1860** H. Stuart *Seaman's Catech.* 28 It should be tarred and wormed with stout spunyarn. **1875** Bedford *Sailor's Pocket Bk.* x. 360 Three men can worm, parcel, and serve 2 fathoms of 12-inch in an hour.

b. *transf.* To wind packing strips between (the cores of a multicore electric cable) so as to give a more nearly circular cross-section; also, to wind (conductors) together to form such a cable.

1909 Coyle & Howe *Electric Cables* ii. 112 Prior to impregnating, the paper-insulated cores are laid up together and wormed with jute. **1953** C. C. Barnes *Power Cables* i. 6 The laid-up cores are wormed into circular formation and are armoured overall. **1982** King & Halfter *Undergound Power Cables* ii. 31 These solid-type multicore cables are of belted construction, in which the conductors are separately paper-insulated, 'wormed' together and the interstices filled with a packing or filling of fibrous material in order to obtain a circular section.

14. To remove the charge or wad from (a gun) by means of a worm (see worm *sb.* 16 b). Also *absol.*

1802 C. James *Milit. Dict.* s.v., *To worm a Gun*, to take out the charge of a fire-arm by means of a worm. **1859** F. A. Griffiths *Artil. Man.* 209 No. 4. Worms, sponges, rams home, runs out, and trains. **1873** *Routledge's Young Gentlm. Mag.* Jan. 79/1 The guns were 'wormed', 'sponged', loaded, and run out.

†**wor'matic**, *a. Obs.* [f. worm *sb.*, prob. after *rheumatic.*] Of, consisting of, or containing worms.

1665 Nedham *Med. Medicinæ* 177 The Wormatick Cadaverous Humor and Matter. *Ibid.* 511 It came from a Wormatick Cause in the Bowels... Salts might kill the Worms. **1690** R. Clark *Vermiculars Destroyed* 15 Slime and wormatick matter.

†**worm-eat**, *ppl. a. Obs.* = worm-eaten, *lit.* and *fig.*

1597 Bp. Hall *Sat.* i. iv. 6 Some brauer braine in high Heroick rimes Compileth worm-eate stories of olde tymes. **1601** *2nd Pt. Return fr. Parnass.* iv. iii. 1936 Spending the marrow of their flowring age, In fruitelesse poring on some worme eate leafe. **1607** R. Turner *Nosce Te* E 3, This worme-eate Churle.

†**worm-eat**, *v. Obs.* [Back-formation from next.]

1. *trans.* To eat into by, or as by, worms.

1598 Florio, *Tarmare*, to mothe-eate or worme-eate. **1653** Chisenhale *Catholike Hist.* 109 Should the gnawing rusty teeth of time worm-eat and rase all his Records. **1663** Head *Hic & Ubique* ii. i. 20 Let 'em rot with their cares And worldly affairs, And worm-eat their souls with their treasures. *a* **1739** Jarvis *Don Quix.* ii. iv. x, Leave off these vanities, which worm-eat your brain.

2. *intr.* To undergo being worm-eaten.

1641 Best *Farm. Bks.* (Surtees) 125 That they bee reade-deale, which are allmost as durable as oake, and will not worme-eate so soone as white deale.

'worm-,eaten, *pa. pple.* and *ppl. a.* Eaten into by a worm or worms.

1398 Trevisa *Barth. De P.R.* xvii. lxxiv. (1495) Q iij/1 Frute..yf it be not roten nother worme eten. *c* **1420** *Liber Cocorum* (1862) 45 Take white pese and wasshe hom wele;..Devoyde þo worme-etone alle bydene. **1493** *Festyvall* (W. de W. 1515) 139 An olde staffe of asshe that..was all worme eten. *c* **1570** *Misogonus* iii. iii. 84 A neighboure of yours wch is payned in hir mandible wth a wormetone toth. **1590** Spenser *F.Q.* ii. ix. 57 Some made in books, some in long parchment scrolles, That were all worme-eaten, and full of canker holes. **1599** Shaks. *Much Ado* iii. iii. 145 Smircht worm-eaten tapestrie. **1600** Abbot *On Jonah* xx. 434 The worke of wormes shall not be refused, to cloath a worme-eaten body. **1653** W. Ramesey *Astrol. Restored* 72 He found [it] in an old rotten worm-eaten book. **1679** *Rector's Bk. Clayworth* (1910) 45 Y^e^ beans were sound and ye pease wormeaten. *a* **1704** T. Brown *Walk Lond. & Westm.* Wks. 1720 III. 316 Old worm-eaten Presses, whose Doors flew open on our Approach. **1827** Clare *Sheph. Cal.* 148 Then, like worm-eaten fruit, it drops and dies. **1838** Dickens *O. Twist* xxxviii, Old worm-eaten ship timber. **1883** J. G. Wood in *Sunday Mag.* Oct. 628/2 No one ever yet found an unsound or worm-eaten nut in a squirrel's store.

b. *transf.* Applied to organic tissue which is indented with small holes.

In Elizabethan writers as a jocular description of a 'grog-blossom' nose.

1592 Nashe *P. Penilesse* Wks. (Grosart) II. 18 A huge woorme-eaten nose, like a cluster of grapes hanging downewards. **1603** Dekker *Wonderf. Yeare* F 1 An Antiquary might haue pickt rare matter out of his Nose, but that it was worme-eaten (yet that proued it to be an auncient Nose). **1897** *Allbutt's Syst. Med.* III. 966 The whole of the colon above the stricture was distended and worm-eaten by small ulcers. *Ibid.* IV. 746 A larger superficial ulcer..with irregular 'worm-eaten' or 'mouse-nibbled' margins. **1899** *Ibid.* VI. 550 The surface [of the bone] has a worm-eaten appearance.

c. *fig.* (of persons and things). Decayed, decrepit; antiquated, outworn.

c **1575** W. Wager *Longer thou livest* 329 (Brandl) You begin to be scabbie and worme eaten, It is time Salt vpon you to strow. **1589** R. Harvey *Pl. Perc.* (1590) 6 His worm-eaten Conscience. **1597** Morley *Introd. Mus.* 158 Your close in the treble part is so stale that it is almost worme eaten. **1604** ? Dekker *Newes fr. Grauesend* Ep. Ded. A 4 That worme-eaten name of Liberall... It's a name of the old fashion. **1614** Ralegh *Hist. World* i. vii. §4. 103 And therefore..were all thinges among the Greekes (which antiquitie had worne out of knowledge) called *Ogygia*, which we in English commonly call (worme-eaten) or of defaced date. **1637** Rutherford *Lett.* (1671) 187 O poor fools who are beguiled with painted things..and rotten worm-eaten hopes! **1721** Ramsay *Tartana* 362 These musty Fools Who only move by old worm-eaten Rules. **1888** *Pall Mall Gaz.* 13 Sept. 5/1 The worm-eaten bibliophile.

absol. **1730** Pope *Let. to Gay* 1 Oct., The employment I am fittest for—conversation with the dead, the old, and the worm-eaten.

Hence †**worm-eatenness**, worm-eaten condition.

1617 Rider *Bibl. Schol., Caries*..Rottennesse or worm-eatennesse in wood. **1617** Barbier *Janua Ling.* 94 The tops of chesnut trees rot with rustie wormeatennesse. **1666** J. Smith *Old Age* 85 By the ceasing of the teeth we must understand, all those infirmities that are incident to them by reason of age, whether looseness, hollowness, rottenness,..wormeatenness, [etc.]. **1730** Bailey (folio), *Verminousness*, Fulness of Worms, Worm-eatenness.

'worm-,eater.
1. A bird or other creature that feeds on worms; *spec.* the Worm-eating Warbler (see below).
1760 G. EDWARDS *Glean. Nat. Hist.* II. 200 The Worm-eater [of Pennsylvania]. **1831** SWAINSON & RICHARDSON *Fauna Bor.-Amer.* II. 221 *Sylvicola* (*Vermivora*) *peregrina*. .. Tennessee Worm-eater. **1878** J. BULLER *New Zealand* I. v. 39 A desperate gang headed by a chief called 'Kaitoke' (worm-eater).
2. [f. WORM-EATEN.] (See quots.)
1890 *Boston* (Mass.) *Jrnl.* 22 Apr. 2/3 A man..gave his occupation as that of a worm-eater... He said he was employed by a furniture manufacturer to fire shot at furniture so as to give it a worm-eaten appearance. **1900** *Daily Mail* 31 Oct., Worm-eaters..assist the makers of spurious oak furniture to deceive the public by drilling worm holes into the wood so as to give it an ancient appearance.

†**'worm-,eating,** *vbl. sb. Obs.* The eating of worms into fruit, timber, etc.
1594 PLAT *Jewell-ho.* I. 36 Steeping of seeds in the infusion of wormewood, centuary, coloquintida, and such like, will defende them from wormeating. **1600** SURFLET *Countrie Farme* I. x. 48 Hee shall cleanse them [*sc.* trees] from wormes, filthines, and worme eatings. **1677** N. COX *Gentl. Recreat.* IV. 15 To preserve these Stocks or Tops from rotting, or worm-eating, rub them over thrice a year with Sallet or Linseed-oyl. **1691** T. H[ALE] *Acc. New Invent.* 40 To make good the damage she brought home by Worm-eating.

'worm-,eating, *ppl. a.* That eats worms for food. ***worm-eating warbler***, the bird *Helminthotherus vermivorus* of the eastern U.S.
1817 STEPHENS in Shaw's *Gen. Zool.* X. 730 Worm-eating Warbler. *Sylvia vermivora*... Inhabits Pensylvania. **1831** SWAINSON & RICHARDSON *Fauna Bor.-Amer.* II. 204 The worm-eating Warblers (*Vermivoræ*). **1872** COUES *Key N. Amer. Birds* 93 *Helmi*[*ntho*]*therus vermivorus*. Worm-eating Warbler.

wormed (wɜːmd), *ppl. a.* [f. WORM *v.* and *sb.* + -ED.]
1. Eaten into or bored by worms; infested with worms.
1846 A. YOUNG *Naut. Dict.* 371 Wormed, the state of timber or plank when a number of internal cavities are made in it by a particular kind of worm, called the *Teredo navalis*, that abounds chiefly in tropical climates. **1853** G. JOHNSTON *Nat. Hist. E. Bord.* I. 96 Old bushes may generally be seen growing, all knaggy and wormed, about decaying onsteads. **1860** *Encycl. Brit.* (ed. 8) XXI. 976/1 There is great reason to believe that some inflammatory action of the liver, of the eye, and of other wormed viscus, precedes the evolution of parasites in them. **1883** R. BRIDGES *Prometheus* 102 Then in the ruined dwellings and old tombs He dug, unbedding from the wormèd ooze Vessels and tools of trade and husbandry. **1913** MASEFIELD *Daffodil Fields* III, Wormed hard-wood piles were driv'n in the river bank.
2. Formed with a screw-thread. Also in parasynthetic combinations = furnished with a (specified) number of screw-threads.
1683 MOXON *Printing* xi. ¶1. 62 A Three-Worm'd Spindle comes faster and lower down than a four-Worm'd Spindle. **1884** *Pall Mall Gaz.* 8 Aug. 11/1 Two perpendicular bars of iron are firmly fixed at B B, the upper portion of each of them deeply wormed for a screw. When the silo is full, planks are laid lengthwise over its whole surface, through which the wormed ends of the iron bars protrude.

wormer ('wɜːmə(r)). [f. WORM *v.* + -ER[1].]
1. One who pries into the affairs of others; one who 'worms out' (secrets).
The meaning in quot. 1602 is uncertain.
1602 CHETTLE *Hoffman* III. (1631) F 1 b, How say you, most valiant and reprobate Country men: haue ye not heard I haue bin a stinger, a tickler, a wormer. **1822** MRS. NATHAN *Langreath* III. 465 The insidious wormer of family secrets.
2. a. One who catches or collects worms for bait.
1880 F. BUCKLAND *Nat. Hist. Brit. Fishes* 11 It is a very interesting sight to see the lights of the numerous wormers when they are out with their lanterns collecting of a dark night. **1881** *Athenæum* 30 Apr. 594/2 A long reach is indispensable to a good wormer.
b. One who angles with a worm or worms as bait.
1891 A. LANG *Angling Sk.* 26 In a small burn a skilled wormer may almost depopulate the pools. **1909** W. C. PLATTS *Light Lines* 82 And how keen some of these old wormers are!
3. *U.S.* = WORM *sb.* 16 b.
1891 *Century Dict.* **1895** *Funk's Standard Dict.* **1911** WEBSTER.
4. A preparation used to rid animals of worm infestations.
1934 in WEBSTER. **1971** *Farmer & Stockbreeder* 23 Feb. 45 (Advt.), An ideal wormer. It is highly effective against all roundworms in the gut. **1980** *Kenya Veterinarian* June p.v (Advt.), There's only one total spectrum wormer for sheep and cattle.

wormery ('wɜːmərɪ). [f. WORM *sb.* + -ERY 2 b.] A place or container in which worms are kept.
1952 *Britannica Bk. Year* 667/1 *Wormery*, a place for breeding worms. **1972** *Daily Tel.* 10 July 14 We kept a wormery and during our observations we found the worms had pulled leaves down under the soil. **1980** M. DRABBLE *Middle Ground* 129 She complained about the smell of the hamster and rabbits, and thought the wormery disgusting.

†**wormete,** *a. Obs.* In 4 **wermethe.** [OE. *wyrmǽte*, f. *wyrm* WORM *sb.* + *ǽt-* pret. stem of *etan* EAT *v.* Cf. MHG. *wurmǣze*.] Worm-eaten.
c **1000** *Sax. Leechd.* II. 126 Wiþ wyrmætum lice. **1340** *Ayenb.* 229 Ase þet frut ne is naʒt guod, þaʒ hit by wel uayr wiþ-oute, huanne hit is uorroted and wermethe.

'worm-grass.
†1. A species of stonecrop, *Sedum album*, with worm-like leaves. *Obs.*
1578 LYTE *Dodoens* I. lxxvii. 114 Wilde Prickmadam, great Stone Croppe, or Worme grasse. **1597** GERARDE *Herbal* II. cxxxvi. 414. **1706** PHILLIPS (ed. Kersey), *Worm-Grass*, an Herb that kills Worms.
2. The Pinkroot, *Spigelia marilandica*, of the Southern U.S., the root and leaves of which are used as a vermifuge. Also applied to *S. Anthelmia.*
1756 P. BROWNE *Jamaica* 156 *Anthelmenthia*..*Spigelia*.. Worm-grass. **1786** ABERCROMBIE *Arrangem.* 66 in *Gard. Assist.*, *Spigelia marilandica*, or Mariland worm grass, or Carolina India pink. **1822** GOOD *Study Med.* (1829) I. 375 The Indian-pinks, or worm-grasses..*s*[*pigelia*] *anthelmia*, and *s. Marylandica.* **1864** GRISEBACH *Flora W. Ind. Isl.* 789 Worm-grass, *Spigelia Anthelmia.*

'worm-hole. Also **wormhole. 1.** A hole made by a burrowing worm or insect in wood, fruit, books, etc.
1593 SHAKS. *Lucr.* 946 To fill with worme-holes stately monuments. **1599** —— *Hen. V*, II. iv. 86 'Tis no sinister, nor no awk-ward Clayme, Pickt from the worme-holes of long-vanisht dayes. **1615** ROWLANDS *Melancholie Knt.* 33 Old bookes, wherein the worm-holes doe remaine. **1684** J. S. *Profit & Pleas. United* 167 As for your Float let it be of the lightest Cork you can get, clear from cracks or worme holes. **1774** GOLDSM. *Nat. Hist.* VIII. 23 Others, whose time of transformation is also near at hand, fasten their tails to a tree, or to the first worm-hole they meet, in a beam. **1858** O. W. HOLMES *Aut. Breakf.-T.* (1883) 261 An apple with a worm-hole. **1874** WILLSHIRE *Anc. Prints* iii. 79 The worm-holes so frequently to be met with in the old crab and pear-wood blocks of the early masters.
2. *Physics.* A hypothetical interconnection between widely separated regions of space-time.
1957 MISNER & WHEELER in *Ann. Physics* II. 532 This analysis forces one to consider situations..where there is a net flux of lines of force through what topologists would call a handle of the multiply-connected space and what physicists might perhaps be excused for more vividly terming a 'wormhole'. **1978** PASACHOFF & KUTNER *University Astron.* xii. 326 Thus, in principle, mass that disappears in a black hole may emerge somewhere else. If the somewhere else is a distinct region in our universe, the connection is called a wormhole. **1981** P. DAVIES *Edge of Infinity* ix. 179 The quantum disturbance will be so severe that even the topology of spacetime will alter. Instead of a 'bumpy sheet', it will display a foam-like structure, full of worm-holes and bridges.
Hence **'worm-holed,** *a.*, perforated with worm-holes.
1870 LOWELL *Among my Bks.* Ser. I. 202 The resolution and persistence of the one, like sound timber wormholed and made shaky, as it were, by the other's infirmity of will and discontinuity of purpose. **1875** 'S. BEAUCHAMP' *N. Hamilton* I. 166 'See, sir,' he would say as he turned the chairs over with a rap on the floor, to shake the sawdust out. 'There's the proof: worm-holed you see, sir, worm-holed'.

'wormhood. *nonce-wd.* [-HOOD.] The state or condition of being a worm.
1692 S. SHAW *Diff. Humours Men* 26, I doubt he will make a worse Beast of him than a Worm; if the company do not over-rule him, he'll make him that he cannot crawl, and then he will lose his worm-hood as well as his manhood. **1917** LD. BRAYE *Lines in Verse & Fable* 63 Extinction of all influence and fame, And abject knowledge of my wormhood.

wormian ('wɔːmɪən), *a. Anat.* [ad. mod.L. (*ossa*) *Wormiān-a*, f. the name of the Danish physician Olaus *Worm* (1588–1654).] The designation of small bones of irregular shape (otherwise styled *ossa triquetra*), frequently found in the sutures of the skull.
1831 R. KNOX *Cloquet's Anat.* 59 A wormian bone, which varies in size, and is frequently of an oval form. **1849–52** *Todd's Cycl. Anat.* IV. 960/1 An interval is formed, which is afterwards filled up with Wormian ossicles. **1866** HUXLEY *Prehist. Rem. Caithn.* 88 There is a large Wormian bone in the right crus of the lambdoid suture. **1884** J. G. GARSON in *Jrnl. Anthropol. Inst.* XIII. 391 The wormian bones are small in most instances.

'worming, *vbl. sb.* [f. WORM *v.* + -ING[1].]
1. a. Extraction of the 'worm' or lytta from a dog's tongue.
1575 TURBERV. *Faulconrie* 371 The worming doth discharge the Spanell of madnesse and frenesie. **1654** C. WASE *Gratius' Cyneget.* Illustr. 13 To prevent Madnesse by Worming. **1818** *Sporting Mag.* II. 31 Worming..is most efficacious.
b. *slang.* (See quot.)
1859 *Slang Dict.*, *Worming*, removing the beard of an oyster or muscle.
2. a. The action of ridding (plants, etc.) of 'worms' or grubs.
1641 MILTON *Animadv. Remonstr. Def.* 52 [He] challenges as his right..the clipping of every bush, the weeding and worming of every bed. **1864** DE COIN *Cotton & Tobacco* 274 The worming must continue, after the hoeing is done, until the plants are ripe for cutting.
b. Treatment administered to rid an animal of parasitic worms.
1936 J. Z. RINE *Dog Owner's Man.* vi. 99 All worming may prove more effective if preceded by a twenty-four-hour diet of buttermilk. **1947** *New Biol.* III. 69 The cost and labour of rounding them [*sc.* sheep] up for this periodical 'worming' may be..great. **1981** *Times* 22 May 3/2 Worker cats needed neutering, vaccinating, worming, regular feeding.
3. †a. The practice of a spy or informer. (In quot. *attrib.*) *Obs.*
1607 BEAUM. & FL. *Woman-Hater* III. iii, Has not many men been raised from this worming trade?
b. The use of insidious methods of progress or advancement.
1916 *Nineteenth Cent.* Nov. 1074 In the Two Americas,.. Deutschtum has, by silent worming, won enormous power all the way from Chicago to the Chilean coast.
4. Angling with worms as bait.
1842 PULMAN *Rustic Sk.* 48 Zo 't's all up wi' wormin', an' huomward da trot Th' angler, wull pleyz'd wi' th' spoort e've a-got. **1910** *Encycl. Brit.* II. 28/1 The other methods of taking trout..are spinning, live-baiting and worming. **1922** *Blackw. Mag.* Jan. 39/1 When I showed him how to cast the worm up-stream,..he was delighted with this, to him, novel method of worming.
5. The action of catching worms (for bait).
1881 *Athenæum* 30 Apr. 594/2 Worming is an art; the worms are very cunning, and apt to pop back into their holes if the hunter treads heavily.
6. a. *Naut.* The process of winding spun-yarn round a rope or cable, so as to fill up the spiral furrows between the strands (cf. WORM *v.* 13). Also *concr.*, the yarn or line thus used as a filling.
1644 MANWAYRING *Sea-mans Dict.* 116 Worming is the laying of a small-roape, or line alongst, betwixt the strands of a cabell or hawser. **1711** W. SUTHERLAND *Shipbuild. Assist.* 120 Lanyards, Ratling, Worming. **1791** SMEATON *Edystone L.* (1793) §137 Not only the service and worming were cut, but the cable itself was..injured by the sharpness of the rocks. **1794** *Rigging & Seamanship* I. 65 Worming is made of 2 or 3 strands. *c* **1860** H. STUART *Seaman's Catech.* 27 The worming is put in the lay. **1897** F. T. BULLEN *Cruise Cachalot* 84 A favourite design is to carve the bone into the similitude of a rope, with 'worming' of smaller line along its lays.
b. *transf.* The action of worming electric cables; also *concr.*, material used for this.
1909 COYLE & HOWE *Electric Cables* ii. 112 The specific gravity of the worming jute. **1949** *Proc. Inst. Electr. Engineers* XCVI. II. 633/1 Would the author indicate..in what sizes additional worming or padding is required to allow the inclusion of the 0.0225-in[2] conductor and yet produce a good cable design? **1962** P. DUNSHEATH *Hist. Elect. Engin.* xvi. 259 Much attention was given to such refinements as..construction of wormings.
7. A worm-like incrustation.
1903 CONRAD & HUEFFER *Romance* v. iii. 425, I knew the feel of every little worming of rust on the iron candlestick.
8. *Comb.* **worming machine** (for making screw-threads); **worming-pot,** a utensil for forming worm-like ornaments on stoneware.
1866 J. CHAMBERLAIN in *B'ham & Midl. Hardware Distr.* 607 They [*sc.* screw-blanks] are next carried to the *worming machine. **1839** URE *Dict. Arts* 1017 Common stoneware is coloured by means of two kinds of apparatus; the one called the blowing-pot, the other the *worming-pot.

'worming, *ppl. a.* [f. WORM *v.* + -ING[2].] Winding, twisting; *fig.* working or advancing insidiously or tortuously.
1626 B. JONSON *Staple of Newes* v. ii, I ha' you in a purse-net Good Master Picklocke, wi' your worming braine, And wrigling ingine-head of maintenance. **1650** FULLER *Pisgah* III. v. 369 But Saint Hierome will have them [*sc.* windows] lattised, *Lignis interrasilibus, et vermiculatis*, with worming or winding splinters of shaved wood. *a* **1764** LLOYD *Charity* Poet. Wks. 1774 II. 156 Your sly, sneaking, worming souls, Whom Friendship scorns, and Fear controuls. **1835** W. G. SIMMS *Yemassee* I. 14 (Funk) Around the fields the negro piles slowly the worming and ungraceful fence.

'wormish, *a. rare.* [-ISH.] Worm-like; as weak or despicable as a worm. Also **'wormishness,** wormish or craven behaviour.
a **1586** SIDNEY *Arcadia* v. (1922) 177 In such a shadowe, or rather pit of darkenes, the wormish mankinde lives, that neither they knowe how to foresee, nor what to feare. **1616** HAYWARD *Sanct. Troub. Soul* I. §3. 52 Be not angry with vs (wormish weakelings) although we offend; for thou knowest what we are and whereof we are made. **1632** LITHGOW *Trav.* I. 3, I haue a..iudgement to discerne such wormish waspes. **1923** V. WOOLF *Let.* 1 Apr. (1977) III. 26 Murry wrote me a wormish letter, by the way, about the differences between us, and our memories and so on. **1925** H. NICOLSON *Let.* 23 July in J. Lees-Milne *Harold Nicolson* (1980) I. xi. 239 My wormishness to Elizabeth.

†**worm-kin.** *Obs.* Forms: 1 **wyrmcyn(n,** 3 **wrimkin.** [OE. *wyrmcyn(n* = OHG. *wurmchunni, -khunni*, MHG. *-künne*, f. WORM *sb.* + KIN *sb.*[1]] The race of worms or serpents, or a species of these.
Beowulf 1425 ðesawon ða æfter wætere wyrmcynnes fela, sellice sædracan sund cunnian. *c* **893** ÆLFRED *Oros.* III. ix. (1883) 136 On westennum wildeora & wyrmcynna missenlicra. *c* **1000** *Ags. Gosp.* Luke xi. 12 Scorpionem, þæt is an wyrm-cynn. *c* **1250** *Gen. & Ex.* 3895 Ðor-fore hem cam wrim kin among, ðat hem wel bitterlike stong.

wormless ('wɜːmlɪs), *a. rare.* [-LESS.] Free from, destitute of, worms.
1837 DARLEY *Syren Songs* v. Poet. Wks. (1908) 441 In the wormless sands shall he Feast for no foul gluttons be. **1902** MABEL BARNES-GRUNDY *A Thames Camp* vii. 111, I was in a shocking bad temper owing to the absolutely wormless condition of our plot.

† **'wormlet.** *Obs.*$^{-0}$ [-LET.] A little worm.

1611 FLORIO, *Verminucci*,..wormelets. *Ibid.*, *Vermolini*, little wormes, grubs, or wormelets.

'worm-like, *a.* and *adv.*

A. *adj.* Resembling a worm in structure, form, movement, etc.; vermiform.

1721 BAILEY s.v. *Valvula major*,..the foremost Worm-like Process of the *Cerebellum*. **1774** GOLDSM. *Nat. Hist.* I. 173 The whole body of the water then is found replete with little worm-like insects. **1854** *Poultry Chron.* I. 77 A strange spiral, or worm-like, motion. **1868** W. CORY *Lett. & Jrnls.* (1897) 218 A dreadful fat worm-like black thing with onions..; it was lamprey. **1885** *Guide Mammalia Brit. Mus.* 50 The Ant-eaters have narrow heads with long snouts, to accommodate their enormously long worm-like tongues.

b. *fig.* (Cf. WORM *sb.* 13.)

1805 WORDSW. *Prelude* XI. 252, I..wished that Man Should start out of his earthy, worm-like state, And spread abroad the wings of Liberty. **1877** GLADSTONE *Diary* 7 May in Morley *Life* II. VII. iv. 565 Never did I feel weaker and more wormlike.

B. *adv.* After the manner of a worm.

1813 BYRON *Corsair* I. xiv, That heart hath long been changed; Worm-like 'twas trampled, adder-like avenged. **1841** BROWNING *Pippa Passes* III, A pale wretch..Who through some chink had pushed and pressed, On knees and elbows, belly and breast, Worm-like into the temple.

wormling ('wɜːmlɪŋ). Also 7 **wormeling**, **wormlin**. [f. WORM *sb.* + -LING. Cf. ON. *yrmlingr*.] A small worm; chiefly *fig.*, a poor despicable creature.

1598 SYLVESTER *Du Bartas* II. i. II. *Imposture* 498, O dusty wormling! dar'st thou strive and stand With Heav'ns high Monarch? **1612** SHELTON *Quix.* III. iv. (1620) 149 God.. doth not abandon the little flies of the aire, nor the wormelings of the earth, nor the spawnlings of the water. **1621** BRATHWAIT *Nat. Embassie* (1877) 14 Thou wormlin, how dar'st thou reuile his name? **1628** SIR W. MURE *Doomesday* 185 Vile wormeling, Thou whose tender pride The weakest sunshine scarce couldst byde. **1821** CLARE *Vill. Minstr.* etc. II. 129 The good and great, That lent a portion of their wealthy power, And sav'd a wormling from destruction's fate. **1858** E. CASWALL *Masque of Mary* etc. 179 The uncreated Word, who flesh became For us poor wormlings creeping on the ground. **1891** C. DAWSON *Avonmore* IV. 85 But if [there is] a God, what of the wormling man, Who madly dares impeach His awful will?

† **'wormly.** *Obs. rare.* [? Named from *Wormley* in Herts. or that in Surrey.] A horse.

1605 SYLVESTER *Du Bartas* II. iii. I. *Vocation* 852 Thy white Wormly brave [*ton blanc corserot*].

wormseed ('wɜːmsiːd). [WORM *sb.* 4.]

1. A name for various plants considered to have anthelmintic properties; as swine's fennel or sulphurwort, *Peucedanum officinale*; *Artemisia Santonica*, *A. Vahliana*, *A. judaica*, *A. maritima*; *Erysimum cheiranthoides* (Treacle or English Wormseed); *Chenopodium anthelminticum* and *Ambrina anthelmintica* (American Wormseed); *Halogeton tamariscifolium* (Spanish Wormseed).

a **1400-50** *Stockh. Med. MS.* 188 Swynys fenkel or wyrmsed: *feniculus porosus*. *c* **1400** [see *swynesfenel*, SWINE 5 b]. **1541** *Bk. Properties Herbs* D j, *Feniculus poeticus*..is called worme sede. It is good to destroy wormes in a mannes body. **1597** GERARDE *Herbal* II. xxii. 212 Cameline, or English Woormseed. *Ibid.* 213 Treacle Wormeseede riseth vp with tough and pliant braunches. *Ibid.* II. ccccxxxv. 942 The Latines name it *Sementina*: the seede is called *Semen sanctum*, Holie seede, and *Semen contra Lumbricos*: in English Wormseed; the herbe it selfe is also called Wormseed, or Wormseedwoort. **1640** PARKINSON *Theat. Bot.* VII. xxviii. 867 *Camelina*..English Wormeseede. **1686** RAY *Hist. Plant.* I. 368 Absinthium Santonicum Alexandrinum C.B...Semen Sanctum Park. Sementina Ger...Wormseed. **1760** J. LEE *Introd. Bot.* App. 332 Worm-seed, *Chenopodium*. **1770** J. R. FORSTER tr. *Kalm's Trav. N. Amer.* I. 163 *Chenopodium anthelminticum* is very plentiful on the road... The English who settled here, call it Worm-seed and Jerusalem Oak... In Pensylvania and New Jersey its seeds are given to children, against the worms. **1796** WITHERING *Brit. Plants* III. 585 *Erysimum cheiranthoides*..Treacle Wormseed. **1831** J. DAVIES *Mat. Med.* 418 Wormseed. Jerusalem Oak. *Chenopodium anthelminticum*,..growing all over America. **1866** *Treas. Bot.* s.v., Spanish Wormseed, *Halogeton tamariscifolium*.

2. The dried flower-heads of one or other of these plants, used as an anthelmintic. Formerly also in pl. ***Levant***, ***Alexandrian***, ***Barbary***, ***Tartarian wormseed***, that prepared from species of *Artemisia*.

1502 ARNOLDE *Chron.* (1811) 234 Worme sede, ij. s. vi. d. **1555** EDEN *Decades* (Arb.) 269 Woorme seede of the best kynde, cauled *Semenzina*. **1594** R. WILSON *Coblers Proph.* ii. 427 (Malone Soc.) *Sould.* I abhorre and defie thee. *Con.* Euen as the child doth wormeseed hid in Raisons. **1597** GERARDE *Herbal* II. ccccxxxv. 941 This Wormwood called *Sementina* and *Semen sanctum*..beareth that seede which we haue in vse, called Wormseede: in shoppes *Semen santolinum*. **1615** in W. Foster *Lett. recd. E. Ind. Co.* (1899) III. 177 Wormseeds likewise doth grow in Corosson. **1690** LOCKE *Hum. Und.* I. ii. §25 The Child certainly knows.. That the Wormseed or Mustard it refuses, is not the Apple or Sugar it cries for. **1704** *Lond. Gaz.* No. 3983/4 The Cargo of the Ship Hamstead Galley,..consisting of..Worm-seeds, Gum Arabeck [etc.]. **1727-51** CHAMBERS *Cycl.*, Wormseed, *Semen contra*, *semen sanctum*, or *semen santonicum*. **1731** MILLER *Gard. Dict.* s.v. *Chenopodium*, The fourth and fifth Sorts were brought from America, where the Seeds are call'd Worm-Seed. **1789** *Phil. Trans.* LXXIX. 82 The Chenopodium, producing the semen santonicum, or worm-seed, a medicine formerly in great character. **1866** *Treas. Bot.*, *Wormseed*... The name is applied in herb-shops to *Semen contra*, the produce of several species of *Artemisia*. **1867** WATTS *Dict. Chem.*, Wormseed. *Semen Cinæ. Semen Contra. Semen Santonici.*—The flower-buds of *Artemisia Vahliana*, *A. Sieberi*, and *A. inculta*. **1880** GARROD & BAXTER *Mat. Med.* 293 Santonica or worm-seed.

3. The eggs of the silkworm moth. Cf. SEED *sb.* 6 a.

1733 P. LINDSAY *Interest Scotl.* 133 By supplying the Planters in those Parts with small Quantities of Wormseed, of the best Breed.

4. *attrib.* in ***wormseed mustard***, ***oil***, † ***stone***, ***weed***, † ***wort*** (see quots.).

1856 A. GRAY *Man. Bot.* (1860) 35 *Erysimum cheiranthoides*. *Worm-seed Mustard. **1830** LINDLEY *Nat. Syst. Bot.* 167 The essential oil of Chenopodium anthelminticum, known in North America under the name of *Worm-seed Oil, is powerfully anthelmintic. **1868** WATTS *Dict. Chem.*, Wormseed-oil. *Oleum cinæ*. **1729** WOODWARD *Nat. Hist. Fossils* I. 65 A Stone..found in..Cornwall: and is called there, *Wormseed-Stone, being thick set with small Bodies, not unlike the *Semen Santonici*, or Wormseed. **1750** G. HUGHES *Barbados* 170 The *Worm-Seed Weed. **1830** J. D. MAYCOCK *Flora Barbadensis* 446 Worm Seed Weed. *Chenopodium anthelminticum*. **1597** *wormseedwoort [see 1].

'wormship. *nonce-wd.* [-SHIP.] The personality of a worm. (With possess. pron., as a mock-title.)

1648 J. BEAUMONT *Psyche* V. cxlix, Vain Son of Dust pull down thy foolish Crest, And in this Glasse thy feeble Wormship see. **1652** BENLOWES *Theophila* II. xviii, Now serves our Guiltiness, as winding sheet To wrap up Lepers; Cover meet; While thus stern vengeance does our Wormships sadly greet. **1775** S. J. PRATT *Liberal Opin.* cxxxiv. (1783) IV. 217 A dead man being..property *under the earth*; so that..as the property properly belonged only to the worms, the matter ought to be submitted to their worshipful wormships.

† **'wormstall.** *Obs.* [? Altered f. dial. *oumer*, UMBER *sb.*[1] + STALL *sb.*[1]] An outdoor shelter for cattle in warm weather.

1601 HOLLAND *Pliny* XVIII. xxxiii, Drive thy sheepe and cattaile out of the Sunne, into some worme-stall and place of shade. **1613** MARKHAM *Eng. Husb.* Former Pt. ii. A 4, The shelter will..be an excellent wormestall for cattell in the summer. **1703** THORESBY *Let. to Ray*, *Wormstall*, shelter for cattel in hot weather.

wormwood ('wɜːmwʊd). Forms: 5 **wyrmwode**, 5-6 **worm(e)wod(e**, 6 **wormwodd**, **worme-**, **woormewoodde**, **wourmewodde**, 6-7 **-wood(e**, 6- **wormwood**. [Altered f. WERMOD, as if f. WORM *sb.* + WOOD *sb.*[1]]

1. The plant *Artemisia Absinthium*, proverbial for its bitter taste. The leaves and tops are used in medicine as a tonic and vermifuge, and for making vermouth and absinthe; formerly also to protect clothes and bedding from moths and fleas, and in brewing ale. It yields a dark green oil.

a **1400-50** *Stockh. Med. MS.* 11 For to makyn surripe of violet; it. of wormwode. *c* **1440** *Promp. Parv.* 530/1 Wyrmwode, herbe, *absinthium*. **1486** *Bk. St. Albans*, *Hawking* c v, A medecyne for an hawke that hath mites. Take the Iuce of wormewode and put it ther thay be and thei shall dye. **1573** in Gage *Hengrave* (1822) 201 For wormewoode to lay amongst the bedding at Coleman Streete, xij *d*. **1573-80** TUSSER *Husb.* (1878) 123 Where chamber is sweeped, and wormwood is strowne, no flea for his life dare abide to be knowne. **1592** SHAKS. *Rom. & Jul.* I. iii. 30 When it did tast the Worme-wood on the nipple of my Dugge, and felt it bitter. **1610** BEAUM. & FL. *Faithf. Shepherdess* II. ii. D 1 b, These for frenzy be A speedy and a soueraigne remedie, The bitter Wormewood, Sage and Marigold. **1626** MIDDLETON *Anything for Quiet Life* II. i, He burnt wormwood in't, to kill the fleas i' the rushes. **1807** CRABBE *Par. Reg.* I. 628 And Artemisia grows, where Wormwood grew. **1855** DELAMER *Kitchen Garden* (1861) 140 Wormwood gives its flavour to the 'purl' of the English workman. **1899** BRIDGES *Idle Flowers* xv, Ragwort and stiff Wormwood And straggling Mignonette.

b. With qualifying word, designating species of *Artemisia* and some similar plants; as

† **French wormwood**, *A. gallica* or *A. Santonica*; † **holy w.**, *A. Santonica*; **Pontic**, **Roman w.**, *A. pontica* or *A. Absinthium*; **sea w.**, *A. maritima*; **tree w.**, *A. arborescens* of the Mediterranean. Also **Roman w.**, *Ambrosia artemisiæfolia*; **wild w.**, *Parthenium Hysterophorus*.

1548 TURNER *Names of Herbes* 7 Wormwod pontike..in englishe maye be also called wormwod gentle. *Ibid.* 8 Absinthium santonicum..may be called in englishe frenche wormwod. *Ibid.*, Frenche wormwod is weaker then Sea wormwod is. **1551-** *Herbal* I. A iiij, Ponticum absinthium.. maye be named in english, wormwode gentle or wormwode Romane, Wormwode pontyke. **1578** LYTE *Dodoens* I. ii. 5 The second kinde of Wormwood is called..in Latine *Seriphium*, and *Absynthium Marinum*... In English Sea wormwood. *Ibid.* 6 *Santoni* wormwood, or French wormwood. **1597** GERARDE *Herbal* II. ccccxxxiii. 940 It is called in English small leafed Wormwood, Romaine Wormwood, garden or Cypres Wormwood, and French Wormwood. *Ibid.* II. ccccxxxv. 941 Holie Wormwood.. called *Sementina* and *Semen sanctum*..beareth that seede which we haue in vse, called Wormseede. *Ibid.* II. ccccxxxvi. 943 *Absinthium arborescens*. Tree Wormwood. **1696** SLOANE *Catal. Plant. Jamaica* 127 Artemisia humilior flore majore albo... Wild Wormwood. **1721** *Queen's Closet* 10 To make Syrup of Wormwood. Take Roman Wormwood, or Pontick Wormwood, half a Pound. **1731** MILLER *Gard. Dict.* s.v. *Absinthium*, The Roman and Sea Wormwoods are great Creepers at the Root... The Tree Wormwood rises to be a Shrub five or six Foot high. **1760** J. LEE *Introd. Bot.* App. 332 Wormwood, Wild, *Parthenium*. **1854** THOREAU *Walden* xiv. (1886) 261 It was overrun with Roman wormwood and beggar-ticks. **1864** GRISEBACH *Flora W. Ind. Isl.* 789 Wormwood, wild, *Parthenium Hysterophorus*.

allusively. **1672** R. WILD *Poet. Licent.* 27 This bitter Cup hath Roman Wormwood in 't.

c. ***salt of wormwood***, an impure carbonate of potash, obtained from the ashes of wormwood.

1617 WOODALL *Surg. Mate* Wks. (1639) 209 The salt of wormwood is esteemed hot and dry like the hearb. **1666** WOOD *Life* (O.H.S.) II. 95 Salt of wormwood and juyce of lemmon. **1756** F. HOME *Exper. Bleaching* 277 To four pints of lime-water..I added 20 gr. of salt of wormwood. **1789** BUCHAN *Dom. Med.* xiv. (1790) 153 An ounce of the bark.. with an equal quantity of salt of wormwood. **1866** *Treas. Bot.* 95/1.

2. *fig.* An emblem or type of what is bitter and grievous to the soul.

1535 COVERDALE *Deut.* xxix. 18 Lest there be amonge you some rote, that beareth gall & wormwodd. —— *Amos* v. 7 Ye turne the lawe to wormwod. *Ibid.* vi. 12 Ye haue turned true iudgment in to bytternesse, and the frute of rightuousnesse in to wormwod. **1555** EDEN *Decades* (Arb.) 90 But..amonge his soo many prosperous, pleasaunte, and luckye affayres, fortune mengeled sume seedes of wormewoodde, and corrupted his pure corne with the malicious weedes of coccle. **1588** SHAKS. *L.L.L.* v. ii. 857 To weed this Wormewood from your fruitfull braine. **1593** G. HARVEY *New Let. Notable Cont.* Wks. (Grosart) I. 285 Conuerting the wormewood of iust offence into the angelica of pure attonement. **1594** NASHE *Unfort. Trav.* F 4 Too much gall dyd that wormwood of Gibeline wittes put in his inke. **1617** J. TAYLOR (Water P.) *London to Hamburgh* C 4 b, All his sugred sweet promises, were in the proofe but Gall and wormwood in the performance. **1622** BACON *Hen. VII* 209 These two Persons..turned Law and Iustice into Woormewood and Rapine. **1628** FORD *Lover's Mel.* II. ii. (1629) 33 *Mel.* Ha, ha, ha. *Rhe.* There's wormewood in that laughter. **1632** LITHGOW *Trav.* III. 107 Venemous also is the Wormewood of his braine. **1633** G. HERBERT *Temple*, *Repentance* iv, Sweeten at length this bitter bowl, Which thou hast pour'd into my soul; Thy wormwood turn to health. **1641** MILTON *Animadv.* Wks. 1851 III. 232 It had beene happy for this land, if your priests had beene but onely wooden; all England knowes they have been to this Iland not wood, but wormewood. **1691** HARTCLIFFE *Virtues* 239 Thus Judgment is turned into Wormwood: for it is embittered by injustice, and delays make it sour. **1852** MRS. STOWE *Uncle Tom's C.* iii. 13 My life is bitter as wormwood.

b. ***to be wormwood*** (or ***gall and wormwood***): to be acutely mortifying or vexing (*to* a person).

1809 MALKIN *Gil Blas* XII. x. (Rtldg.) 435 The accounts her ladyship brought from Madrid were wormwood to the duke. **1821** SCOTT *Kenilw.* xl, His presence and his communications were gall and wormwood to his once partial mistress. **1856** R. A. VAUGHAN *Mystics* (1860) II. VIII. iv. 51 It was wormwood to the proud spirit of Agrippa to be treated as a mere astrologer. **1898** F. T. BULLEN *Cruise Cachalot* 339 The sight of other people's good fortune is gall and wormwood to a vast number of people.

3. Used as a name or specific epithet for certain moths.

1832 J. RENNIE *Butterfl. & Moths* 91 The Wormwood (*Cucullia Absinthii*, Ochsenheimer). *Ibid.* 134 The Wormwood Pug (*Eupithecia Absinthiata*, Stephens). *Ibid.* 169 The Wormwood Eyelet (*Semasia pupillana*, Stephens). **1869** E. NEWMAN *Brit. Moths* 136, 434.

4. Short for ***wormwood ale*** (see 5).

a **1843** SOUTHEY *Comm.-pl. Bk.* IV. 425 Oxford, All Souls. .. Their silver cups..are called ox-eyes, and an ox-eye of wormwood was a favourite draught there. Beer with an infusion of wormwood was to be had nowhere else.

5. *attrib.* and *Comb.*, as ***wormwood-bush***, †***-cake***, ***-diet***, ***-draught***, ***-drink***; ***wormwood-coloured*** adj.; **wormwood-ale**, **-beer**, ale or beer in which wormwood is infused; **wormwood coal** (see quot.); **wormwood water**, **wine**, a cordial prepared (like absinthe or vermouth) from wormwood; also *fig.*

1603 *wormewoode ale [see *w. beer*]. **1665** in *Maitland Club Miscell.* (1840) II. 528 For wormewood aill and other aill in the morneing 000 03 00. **1603** F. HERING *Cert. Rules* B 1 b, You may vse a good draught of *wormewoode beare or ale. **1718** *Poor Robin* May A 8 b, Scurvy-grass Ale, clarified Whey, And Wormwood Beer are good they say. **1858** LADY WILKINSON *Weeds & Wild Flowers* 418 Purl, or wormwood-beer. **1851** MAYNE REID *Scalp Hunt.* v. 38, I came opposite to a small clump of *wormwood bushes. **1658** W. M. *Queens Closet Opened* (ed. 4) 15 *Wormwood Cakes good for a cold Stomach, and to help Digestion. **1858** LADY WILKINSON *Weeds & Wild Flowers* 353 An old belief continues to be connected with the circumstance of the dead roots of wormwood being black, and somewhat hard, and remaining for a long period undecayed beneath the living plant. They are then called '*wormwood coal'; and if placed under a lover's pillow they are believed to produce a dream of the person he loves. **1816** *Beckford's Vathek* (ed. Garnett) 72 He awoke..stung to the quick by *wormwood-coloured [1786 wormwood-colour] flies. **1655** VAUGHAN *Silex Scint.* II. *Providence* 46 Gladly will I, like Pontick sheep, Unto their *wormwood-diet keep. **1750** LADY LUXBOROUGH *Lett. to Shenstone* 9 Sept., I have a return of my fever to-day; and take *wormwood-draughts. **1658** in *12th Rep. Hist. MSS. Comm.* App. v. 6 [Let it] be celebrated with cow-heeles, and tripes, the keenest mustard, and the bitterest *wormewood drinke. **1612** WEBSTER *White Devil* v. vi. 5 *Vit.* Ha, are you drunke? *Flam.* Yes, yes, with *wormewood water; you shall tast Some of it presently. **1620** VENNER *Via Recta* ii. 45, I aduise them to take two or three parts of wormwood-water, and one of *Aqua vitæ*. **1725** G. SMITH *Distilling* 46 Wormwood-water is in good demand in the Country. **1832** G. DOWNES *Lett. Cont. Countries* I. 168, I was..attacked with a violent pain in my stomach, which yielded only to a strong dram of wormwood water (*Eau d' Absinthe*). **1565** COOPER *Thesaurus*, *Absynthites*..*wormewoodde wyne. **1587** HARRISON *England* II. vi. (1877) 150 Artificiall stuffe, as ypocras and wormewood wine. **1617** MORYSON *Itin.* III. 81 In upper Germany the first draught commonly is of wormewood wine. **1692** in *Earthquake at Lima* (1748) App. 328 This Gentleman..engaged me to take a Glass of

Wormwood Wine with him, as a Whet before Dinner. **1806** J. PINKERTON *Recoll. Paris* II. xv. 208 A decanter of Jamaica rum, Wormwood wine, or that of Vermouth. **1844** MANGAN *Love & Madness* Poems (1903) 323 Why must Medjnims evermore Drink their tears as wormwood wine?

b. *fig.* Attrib., passing into adj. = bitter, tart, unpleasant to experience. So also †**wormwood lecture**, a scolding or 'talking to'.

1593 SHAKS. *Lucr.* 893 Thy secret pleasure turnes to open shame,.. Thy sugred tongue to bitter wormwood tast. **1601** B. JONSON *Poetaster* I. ii, An honest decayed commander, cannot skelder, cheat, nor be seene in a bawdie house, but he shall be straight in one of their wormewood comœdies. **1608** DAY *Law Trickes* II. C 2 b, Trust me, loue hath kild That worme-wood humor. **1640** *Womens Sharpe Revenge* 5 And now lately one or two of the sonnes of Ignorance have pen'd three severall.. ill-favoured Pamphlets.. called Lectures, as the Juniper Lecture, the Crabtree Lecture, and the Wormwood Lecture, wherein they have laid most false aspersions upon all women generally. **1678** DRYDEN *Kind Keeper* II. i. (1680) 14, I shall read him a Worm-wood Lecture, when I see him. **1682** M. PARKER (*title*) A brief sum of certain wormwood lectures: Which women used to sing and say Unto their husbands every day. **1871** F. T. PALGRAVE *Lyr. Poems* 24 Clouding with wormwood drops the wine of life. **1895** G. P. LATHROP in *Month* (B.C.) Jan. 6 Notwithstanding the wormwood memories of wrongs in the past. **1897** HARDY *Poems of Pilgrimage, Lausanne*, Still rule those minds on earth At whom sage Milton's wormwood words were hurled.

wormy (ˈwɜːmɪ), *a.* [f. WORM *sb.* + -Y[1]. Cf. MHG. *wurmic, -ec*, G. *wurmig*, Du. *wormig*.]

1. Attacked, gnawed, or bored by worms or grubs; worm-eaten.

c **1430** *Pilgr. Lyf Manhode* II. cxxxiii. (1869) 128, I am a wormy wilowh; who so leneth to me is lost. **1562** LEGH *Armorie* (1568) 120 b, Studiously keping those monuments from wormie wemes. **1611** COTGR., *Vereux*, wormie, full of wormes. **1708** OZELL tr. *Boileau's Lutrin* 54 The wormy Boards, by Time's corroding Spight disjoin'd. **1756** MRS. CALDERWOOD in *Coltness Collect.* (Maitland Club) 213 All the fruit in that country is very wormy, and some of the finest nuts had a great worm in the kirnall. **1847** EMERSON *Poems, Woodnotes* II. 307 And thou,—go burn thy wormy pages. **1848** DICKENS *Dombey* lvii, An old brown, panelled, dusty vestry,.. where the wormy registers diffuse a smell like faded snuff. **1864** LOWELL *Fireside Trav.* 176 We have picked nearly every apple (wormy or otherwise).

transf. **1833** in *New Statist. Acc. Scotl.* (1845) III. *Selkirk* 41 The.. herbage on the hills.. was destroyed by a caterpillar in 1762, long called the *wormy* year.

b. *fig.* = WORM-EATEN c.

1611 *Coryate's Crudities, Panegyr. Verses* c 5 b, Old wormy age that in thy mustie writs Of former fooles records the present wits. **1908** HARDY *Dynasts* III. VII. viii. 343 Europe's wormy dynasties rerobe Themselves in their old gilt.

c. *Arch.* = VERMICULATED I c.

1823 [see VERMICULATED I c].

2. Of the body, its parts and secretions: Infested or affected with worms, itch-mites, etc. Of fish: Lousy (*U.S.*).

1599 A. M. tr. *Gabelhouer's Bk. Physicke* 362/1 An oyntment for the Wormye, and itchinge Handes. **1600** SURFLET *Countrie Farme* II. xlii. 255 The iuice thereof dropped into wormie eares, doth kill the wormes that is in them. **1625** HART *Anat. Ur.* II. viii. 105 What would.. he presage by such a wormie vrine? **1679** TRAPHAM *Disc. Health Jamaica* 103 Children the chief subjects of Worms and wormy Slime. **1707** SLOANE *Jamaica* I. 140 It is used by Chirurgeons in putrid and wormy ulcers. **1766** *Compl. Farmer* s.v. *Ascarides*, The horses that breed ascarides are, above all others, subject to slime and wormy matter. **1860** *Encycl. Brit.* (ed. 8) XXI. 974/2 The poor of Scotland.. are not more wormy than the better fed poor of England. **1884** *Springfield* (Mass.) *Wheelmen's Gaz.* Nov. 110/3 The stream was fairly alive with trout but the large ones were wormy.

3. Of earth, soil, the grave, etc.: Infested with worms, full of worms.

1590 SHAKS. *Mids. N.* III. ii. 384 Damned spirits all,.. Alreadie to their wormie beds are gone. **1625** MILTON *Death fair Infant* 31 Yet can I not perswade me thou are dead.. Or that thy beauties lie in wormie bed. **1631** W. LISLE *Faire Æthiopian* x. 176 The men of Sere, Who brought the King two silken robes to weare, Of daintie sleaue drawne from their wormie trees. **1686** PLOT *Staffordsh.* 345 Loose wormey ground. **1814** WORDSW. *Excurs.* III. 281 Feelingly sweet is stillness after storm, Though under covert of the wormy ground! **1838** DE QUINCEY *Shaks.* Wks. 1890 IV. 76 The wormy grave brought into antagonism with the scenting of the early dawn. **1852** HAWTHORNE *Blithedale Rom.* II. iv. 71 Birds.. busily scratched their food out of the wormy earth.

transf. **1820** KEATS *Isabella* xlix, Wherefore all this wormy circumstance? Why linger at the yawning tomb so long?

4. Resembling a worm; worm-like.

Formerly in techn. terms, esp. *Anat.*; as *wormy body* [tr. *corpus lumbricosum*: see WORM *sb.* II a], the epididymis; *wormy process* = vermiform process (VERMIFORM 3 b).

1545 RAYNALDE *Byrth Mankynde* I. xi. (1552) 23 b, When thys foresayd wormye body hath attayned to the myddle regyon.. of thee stone, it.. is no more.. thycke wrethed, but playne, smoth, and round. **1615** CROOKE *Body of Man* 477 The anterior and posterior processes of the braine, called vermi-formes or the wormy processes. **1634** T. JOHNSON *Parey's Wks.* VI. xxix. 222 The 4. other [muscles of the hand] are called, by reason of their figure, the *Lumbrici* or wormy muscles. *a* **1682** SIR T. BROWNE *Tracts* (1683) 60 Pliny.. calls it *Coccus Scolecius*, or the Wormy Berry.

1856 MRS. BROWNING *Aur. Leigh* I. 220 A weary, wormy darkness, spurred i' the flank With flame, that it should eat and end itself Like some tormented scorpion. **1876** MORRIS *Æneids* VII. 351 The dreadful wormy thing Seemed the wrought gold about her neck [*fit tortile collo aurum ingens coluber*]. **1888** *Harper's Mag.* Aug. 327 With fleshy, brilliant, long, wormy feelers instead of fins. **1895** MRS. CROKER *Village T.* (1896) 152 Lumps of sticky cocoanut and deliciously long, wormy native sweets.

b. *fig.* Grovelling; earthy; crooked, tortuous.

1640 BP. REYNOLDS *Passions* xxxvii. 459 Hereby wee are brought to a Just Contempt of sordid and wormie Affections. *Ibid.* xxxviii. 499 To be of a creeping and wormy disposition,.. to raise the Soule unto no higher Contemplations, than Base and Worldly. **1662** J. CHANDLER *Van Helmont's Oriat.* 353, I have constantly considered the light of the Sun married as a husband to the Splendour of the Glo-worm;.. one Heavenly and constant; but the other wormy or corruptible. **1868** BROWNING *Ring & Bk.* VII. 669 That is the fruit of all such wormy ways, The indirect, the unapproved of God: You cannot find their author's end and aim.

5. Of or pertaining to worms. *poet.*

1801 SOUTHEY *Thalaba* IX. xxiii, Next with naked hand, She pluck'd the boughs of the manchineel; And of the wormy wax she took, That, from the perforated tree forced out, Bewray'd its insect-parent's work within. **1842** HOOD *Elm Tree* III. 351 With sudden fear her wormy quest The Thrush abruptly quits.

†**worn**, *v. Obs. rare.* [? repr. OE. *weornian* to wither, fade.] *intr.* To waste *away*.

1538 STARKEY *England* 76 And so hyt fallyth into manyfest dekey, and by lytyl and lytyl wornyth away.

worn (wɔːn, wɔən), *ppl. a.* Forms: see WEAR *v.*[1]; also 7 wooren. [pa. pple. of WEAR *v.*[1]]

1. a. Impaired by wear or use, or by exposure; showing the results of use or attrition.

1508 FISHER 7 *Penit. Ps.* cii. Wks. (1876) 196 Heuen & erth shall perysshe.. theyr condycyons shall in maner be olde & worne. **1563** in *Inuentaires de la Royne Descosse* (Bannatyne Club) 57 Mair ane vther coitt of blew veluot weill auld and worne. **1573** BARET *Alv.* s.v., Old worne houses and rotten, *exesæ ædes.* **1575** A. FLEMING *Virg. Bucol.* VI. 17 The waightye pott of Bacchus with worne eares [*attrita ansa*]. **1576** TURBERV. *Venerie* xxii. 64 Whether it be a worne footing or a sharpe cuttying foote. **1817** KEATS *Spec. Induction* 15 From the worn top of some old battlement. **1840** DICKENS *Old C. Shop* iii, His dress consisted of.. a worn dark suit. **1847** A. GATTY *Bell* Pref., The worn pen of an habitual sermon writer. **1897** *Westm. Gaz.* 31 Mar. 8/1 By the new arrangement, bankers in the country are deprived of all excuse for not sending in their worn coins. **1913** EDITH WHARTON *Cust. Country* II. xv. 203 The curtains of worn damask.

b. *fig.* Of words or ideas: Hackneyed by use or repetition; trite.

1569 ROEST tr. *J. van der Noot's Theat. Worldlings* 37 Hys woren Romyshe trashe patched and newly redressed. **1642** R. CARPENTER *Experience* III. v. 47 According to the worne axiome of Divinity, Grace perfecteth nature. **1853** LANDOR *Imag. Conv., L. Philippe & Guizot* Wks. 1876 VI. 565 There you will see the most honourable men at the helm of government, who never thought their worn words worth keeping any more than their worn cloaths.

2. a. Of persons: Wasted, enfeebled, or exhausted by toil, exposure, age, anxiety, or ill-health; showing signs of such enfeeblement. (Cf. *care-worn.*) Also of animals. Also *Comb.*, as ***worn-looking*** adj.

1508 [see 1]. **1573** BARET *Alv.* s.v., An old worne souldiour. **1579** LYLY *Euphues* (Arb.) 64 Finding him so worne and wasted with continual mourning. **1581** A. HALL *Iliad* IX. 164 Though.. The hie and mightie gods should say they would againe renew To youth my worne corpse. **1587** FLEMING *Contn. Holinshed* III. 1368/1 To doctor Sanders a naturall borne subiect, but an vnnaturall worne priest. **1690** PEPYS *Mem. Navy* (1906) 85 A worn unassisted Secretary. **1697** DRYDEN *Æneis* XI. 400 So worn, so wretched, so despis'd a Crew. **1814** WORDSW. *Excurs.* VII. 906 To conceal Tender emotions spreading from the heart To his worn cheek. **1842** DICKENS *Amer. Notes* viii, The President.. looked somewhat worn and anxious, and well he might. **1853** —— *Bleak Ho.* xxiv, I.. was shocked to see the worn look of his handsome young face. **1870** HUXLEY *Lay Serm.* iii. 48 The serene resting-place for worn human nature—the world of art. *a* **1891** T. B. ALDRICH *Lander* (Cent.) Lead the worn war-horse by the plumèd bier. **1918** MRS. B. LOWNDES *Out of War?* 48 Stern worn-looking man. **1978** D. MURPHY *Place Apart* vi. 120 They seem so watchful and worn-looking.

b. Of land: Spent, exhausted, no longer fertile.

1681 R. KNOX *Hist. Ceylon* 20 Which Inclosures they will keep up for several years, until the Ground becomes so worn, that the Flowers will thrive there no longer. **1860** WORCESTER cites Gray.

†**3.** Of time, a period: Past, spent. *Obs.*

1611 SHAKS. *Wint. T.* v. i. 142 Infirmitie (Which waits vpon worne times).

4. With adv. (See also WORN-OUT.)

a. ***worn-down***: in senses 1, 2 above.

1814 *Sporting Mag.* XLIV. 147 The poor worn-down sort [of horses] are the most common victims of this barbarity. **1833** C. LYELL *Princ. Geol.* III. 265 A worn-down crater. **1845** DARWIN *Voy. Nat.* xix. (1873) 440 The worn-down sandstone. **1849–52** *Todd's Cycl. Anat.* IV. 876/2 The old worn-down tooth is shed.

b. ***worn-in***, ingrained by attrition or exposure to weather. (Cf. INWORN.)

1883 *Gd. Words* Aug. 543/2 Weather-stain and worn-in dirt.

†**c.** ***worn-up*** (WEAR *v.*[1] 10 b) = WORN-OUT 2.

1812 *Sporting Mag.* XXXIX. 209 A purchaser of worn-up horses.

Hence ˈ**wornness**, worn condition.

1873 MRS. WHITNEY *Other Girls* vi. 72 The first poetry, the first fresh touches [of her new life].. were passed into established use, and dulled into wornness and commonness.

worne, rare obs. form of WARN *v.*[2]

wornel, wornil, var. ff. WARNEL.

worn-out, *ppl. a.* [See WEAR *v.*[1] 9 b, 10 b, 11, 17. Cf. OUTWORN.]

1. Of material things: Injured, damaged, defaced by wear, usage, attrition, or exposure, esp. to such a degree as to be no longer of use or service. †Of graphic characters: Obliterated.

1612 SELDEN *Illustr. Drayton's Poly-olb.* iv. 72 The errour I imagine to be from restoring of wooren out times in Bede and others. **1615** SANDYS *Trav.* 40 The bases whereof did beare these now worne out characters. **1637** SPELMAN in *Lett. Lit. Men* (Camden) 153 A single letter in a worne-out worde, is a great help to revive what wanteth. *a* **1653** GOUGE *Comm. Heb.* xiii. 1 It is a very obscure and almost worn-out stamp of that glorious Image in which at first God made man. **1683** MOXON *Mech. Exerc., Printing* xiii. ¶2 For.. Triangular Punches, I commonly reserve my worn out three square Files. **1756** C. SMART tr. *Horace, Epist.* I. xix. 38 For the bribe of a worn-out coat. **1835** DICKENS *Sk. Boz, Pawnbroker's Shop*, The worn-out thin shoes. **1851** RICHARDSON *Geol.* (1855) 439 A worn-out vein of ironstone. **1865** TROLLOPE *Belton Est.* xxii. 259 The worn-out carpets and old-fashioned chairs. **1874** BURNAND *My Time* xxxiv. 372 There was a worn-out old safe in a corner.

b. Of a colour: Dull; not bright or vivid.

1731 MILLER *Gard. Dict.* s.v. *Apocynum*, Small Umbels of worn-out purple-colour'd Flowers. **1812** *New Bot. Garden* I. 6 These [flowers of Asclepias Syriaca] are of a worn-out purple colour.

2. Of persons, living things, etc.: Utterly exhausted and wasted in strength or vitality.

a **1700** EVELYN *Diary* 17 Feb. 1695 The Hospital design'd to be built at Greenwich for worn-out seamen. **1758** P. WILLIAMSON *Life* (1812) 49 They used all proper means to recover my worn-out spirits. **1789** WESLEY *Minutes* Wks. 1872 VIII. 327 Every worn-out Preacher shall receive, if he wants it, at least ten pounds a-year. **1793** COWPER *To Mary* 55 Thy worn-out heart will break at last. **1795–6** WORDSW. *Borderers* II. 927 We kill a worn-out horse, and who but women Sigh at the deed? **1796** MARSHALL *Planting* I. 93 The rough and the worn-out Hedges. **1851** D. JERROLD *St. Giles* xi. 105 Her father was a worn-out, broken merchant. **1852** HOSKYNS *Talpa* 78 The specific operation of lime upon a worn-out soil. **1854** *Poultry Chron.* I. 595 This practice of crossing with a Gamecock was much in vogue with the old breeders, to improve a worn-out stock. **1876** BANCROFT *Hist. U.S.* V. xiv. 496 There, in the woods, worn-out men sank down on the bare, frozen ground.

b. Of a smile: Faint, feeble, 'wan'.

1842 LOVER *Handy Andy* xiv, At last, with 'bated breath,' and a very worn-out smile, [she] faltered forth.

3. Of ideas, devices, etc.: Hackneyed by use, trite, stale, out of fashion. Of institutions: Effete.

1713 ADDISON *Cato* I. iii. 7 Your cold Hypocrisie's a stale Device, A worn-out Trick. **1782** COWPER *Mutual Forbearance* 5 Those hangings, with their worn-out graces. **1801** HT. LEE *Canterb. T.* IV. 5 Under the claims of a sort of antiquated and worn-out nobility. **1819** in *Croker Papers* 3 May, His speech.. treated a worn-out subject so as to make it appear a new one. **1841** W. SPALDING *Italy & It. Isl.* II. 23 This composition.. exhibits the worn-out Grecian mythology in an aspect of picturesque novelty. **1851** KINGSLEY *Yeast* xv, I am too old for that worn-out quibble. **1882** BESANT *All Sorts* xxviii. (1898) 194 The House of Lords.. was an effete and worn-out institution.

†**4.** Of time: Past, departed. *Obs.*

1593 SHAKS. *Lucr.* 1350 This patterne of the worne-out age.

Hence **worn-outness** (also *-outiness*).

1844 J. T. HEWLETT *Parsons & W.* ii, The worn-outiness of the old pony on which he used to ride. **1898** B. GREGORY *Side Lights* 434 Receiving allowances.. on the same plea of wornoutness.

worod, obs. pa. t. WORRY *v.*

worow(e, obs. forms of WORRY *v.*

worp, obs. form of WARP.

worple, var. of WARPLE *sb. dial.*

†**worral.** *Obs.* Also warral, waral, (woralla). [a. Arab. *waral*.] A monitor lizard; = VARAN.

1714 MAUNDRELL *Journ. Aleppo* Add. 3 Here is found a large Serpent which has legs and claws, called Woralla. **1738** T. SHAW *Trav.* 429 Of the Lizard Kind, the Warral is of so docible a Nature, and appears withal to be so affected with Musick, that I have seen several of them keep exact Time and Motion with the Dervishes, in their circulatory Dances. **1743** R. POCOCKE *Descr. East* I. 208 The Worral.. is.. four feet long,.. has a forked tongue. **1744** C. THOMPSON *Trav.* III. 326 The Worral is a Sort of Lizard, which sometimes is thirty or forty Inches in Length.

worre, obs. f. WAR *sb.*[1], *v.*[1], WAR *a.* and *adv.*

worret, worrey: see WORRIT, WORRY *v.*

worriable (ˈwʌrɪəb(ə)l), *a.* [f. WORRY *v.* + -ABLE.] That can be worried or roughly treated.

1882 C. LLOYD MORGAN in *Nature* XXVI. 524/2 A dog can call his companion's attention to a worriable cat.

worricow (ˈwʌrɪkaʊ). *Sc.* Forms: α. 8 wirrycow, -kow, 8–9 wirricow, -kow. β. 8–9 worry-, worricow (9 worriecow, warricoe). [f. WORRY *v.* + COW *sb.*[3] (as if 'a goblin apt to worry').] A scarecrow; a hobgoblin. Also *transf.* a person of frightful or unprepossessing appearance.

α. **1711** RAMSAY *On Maggy Johnstoun* xi, I hirsl'd up my dizzy Pow, Frae 'mang the Corn like Wirricow. **1728** ——

Gen. Mistake 181 Much hated Gowk, tho' vers'd in kittle Rules, To be a Wirry-kow to writing Fools. **1815** G. BEATTIE *John o' Arnha'* (1826) 41 Or yet wi' wirriekows to mingle, That brinstane belsh. **1894** CROCKETT *Raiders* vi, That's Yawkins and his crew..the ill-contriving wirricows. *β.* **1757** SMOLLETT *Reprisal* II. i, It canna be our commander Monsieur de Champignon, running about in the dark like a worricow. **1789** D. DAVIDSON *Seasons* 122 The worrycow gid sic a yell. **1809** T. DONALDSON *Poems* 37 Where harpie, imp, an' warricoe, An' goblins dwell. **1816** SCOTT *Bl. Dwarf* ii, They do say there's a sort o' worricows and lang-nebbit things about the land. **1818** —— *Hrt. Midl.* xxviii, It..keeps unceevil folk frae staring as if ane were a worrycow.

b. with *the* = the Devil.

1719 W. HAMILTON *3rd Ep. Ramsay* xiii, May thou..thro' thy creed, Be keeped frae the wirricow, After thou's dead. *a* **1774** FERGUSSON *Farmer's Ingle* vii, Auld warld tales..O' warlocks loupin' round the wirrikow.

worried ('wʌrɪd), *ppl. a.* [f. WORRY *v.* + -ED.] In senses of the vb.: Killed or mangled by biting, etc.; maltreated, harassed; troubled or distressed in mind. Also *Comb.*, as ***worried-looking*** adj.

1559 BP. COX in Strype *Ann. Ref.* (1709) I. vi. 99 God was mightily angred with his People, because they offered unto God the Blind, Lame and worried Sacrifice. **1624** QUARLES *Sion's Elegies* III. ii, Heauen's souldiers doe beleager My worried soule. **1646** —— *Judgem. & Mercy* Wks. (Grosart) I. 115/2 Can poore affrighted Lambs wanton, and frisk upon the pleasant plains, when as their worried Mothers tremble at the Quest of every Curre? *a* **1699** J. BEAUMONT *Psyche* XIV. lxx, His worryed limbs forthwith the Soldiers stretch To fit Him to His wide tormenting Tree. *Ibid.* XIX. xxxviii, Must thou Sail from thy quiet Home, and yield to be The worried Slave of all the Winds that blow. **1800** HURDIS *Fav. Village* 111 To the branch Which midway meets him in his worried flight. **1825** C. K. SHARPE *Corr.* (1888) II. 347, I am now better—but a good deal shaken, as they say of half-worried kittens. **1864** SIR F. PALGRAVE *Norm. & Eng.* IV. 194 A fagged, worried, hard-working, dusty-footed labouring man. **1865** DICKENS *Mut. Fr.* III. v, 'I don't mean that,' said Mrs. Boffin, with a worried look. **1887** MISS BRADDON *Like & Unlike* xxxviii, 'You look ill and worried', said the Colonel. **1903** BRIDGES *Wintry Delights* 248 And 'tis a far escape from wires, wheels and penny papers And the worried congestion of our Victorian era. **1942** 'N. SHUTE' *Pied Piper* 26 Howard saw him the first Saturday that he was there, a sandy-haired, worried-looking man of forty-five or so. **1982** T. HOLME *Devil & Dolce Vita* vii. 49 She's been a bit worried-looking... Distracted.

Hence **'worriedly** *adv.*, in a worried or distressed manner, concernedly.

1924 'L. MALET' *Dogs of Want* v. 125 She worriedly wondered whether green isn't a more trying colour than blue when you get hot. **1952** S. KAUFFMANN *Philanderer* (1953) xii. 195 'That's wonderful.' He looked at her worriedly. 'Only it's got to be your decision. Your responsibility.' **1976** 'R. GORDON' *Doctor on Job* iii. 18 'It won't take long, will it?' he asked worriedly.

worrier ('wʌrɪə(r)). Forms: 6 *Sc.* wirrear, -iare, 7 -ier; 6 wurrier, *Sc.* worriar, 7- worrier. [f. WORRY *v.* + -ER¹.]

1. An animal that kills or injures others by biting and rough treatment. Also *fig.*

c **1536** LYNDESAY *Compl. Bagsche* 26 For I haif bene, ay to this hour, Ane wirrear of lamb and hog. **1583** *Elgin Rec.* (New Spalding Club) I. 173 Calling him auld wouff facet theiff carle and worriar of scheip. **1606** BIRNIE *Kirk-Buriall* vi. (1833) B4b, Diogenes..being admonished that so he should be torne by birds and beasts, did reiyre a taunt, in requyring a cudgell to be coutched beside, whereby to weare his wirriers away. **1634** CANNE *Necess. Separ.* 35 Beeing doubtlesse very theeves, robbers, wolves, and worriers of the Flocks. **1663** J. SPENCER *Prodigies* iii. §4 (1665) 229 Κύνες χθόνιοι terrestrial Dogs (as they called their more material and coarser sort of Dæmons, conceived the Worriers of Souls). **1732** SWIFT *Exam. Abuses Dublin* 12 Tory Dogs; whereof great Numbers have since been so prudent, as intirely to change their Principles, and are now justly esteemed the best Worriers of their former Friends. **1839** HOOD *To Lady Dep. India* 31 Go where the fierce musquito is a worrier. **1862** CALVERLEY *Verses & Transl.* (ed. 2) 29 The Worrier-Dog—the Cow with Crumpled horn.

†**b.** *jocularly.* A swiller *of* (liquor). *Sc. Obs.*

1584 *Leg. Bp. St. Androis* 12 Still daylie drinckand or he dyne, A wirriare of the gude sweit wyne.

2. One who harasses or persecutes another.

1712 STEELE *Spect.* No. 304 ¶6 Certain Persons..who by the Strength of their Arms, and Loudness of their Throats, draw off the Regard of all Passengers from your said Petitioners; from which Violence they are distinguished by the Name of *the Worriers*. **1734** SWIFT *Yahoo's Overthrow* xi. Wks. 1765 XIII. 291 On this Worrier of Deans whene'er we can hit, We'll shew him the way how to crop and to slit.

3. One who causes distress of mind to another; also, one who gives way to anxiety or mental disquietude.

1891 *Cent. Dict.* **1897** *Voice* (N.Y.) 11 Feb. 3/1 'Worry' is from inside, and the fault of the 'worrier.' **1912** *Sat. Rev.* 28 Dec. 802/1 Both brothers write of their mother, an excellent woman but a worrier—of the son she was with and about the son she was absent from.

worriless ('wʌrɪlɪs), *a.* [f. WORRY *sb.* + -LESS.] Free from worry.

1889 *Science* 1 Feb. 88/2 The professor, leading a comparatively congenial and worriless life, is a deeper sleeper [than the teacher].

worriment ('wʌrɪmənt). Chiefly *U.S.* [f. WORRY *v.* + -MENT.] The act of worrying or causing anxiety; the state of being worried or troubled in mind. Also, something that harasses or causes worry.

1833 S. SMITH *Life & Writings Major J. Downing* 161 I've had a good many head-flaws and worriments in my life time. **1855** HALIBURTON *Nat. & Hum. Nature* I. v. 128 The worriment we have had about money lately has set you a dreaming. **1863** B. TAYLOR *H. Thurston* I. iv. 91 Over and over again he had been on the point of giving her up, out of sheer worriment and exhaustion of soul. **1866** 'G. F. HARRINGTON' *Inside* i. 9 It was a special weapon in her arsenal in the worriment of her husband. **1883** E. P. ROE in *Harper's Mag.* Dec. 46/1 Her slight tendency to worry saved others a world of worriment. **1886** B. ROOSEVELT *Copper Queen* I. x. 165 Ready with vinegar, hartshorn, and the usual worriments towards resuscitation. **1912** MRS. ALLEN HARKER *Mr. Wycherly's Wards* vii. 108, I don't know how they'll take this fresh worriment.

worrisome ('wʌrɪsəm), *a.* [f. WORRY *sb.* or *v.* + -SOME¹.] Apt to cause worry or distress; given to worrying.

1845 W. G. SIMMS *Wigwam & Cabin* 1st Ser. viii. 107, I ..followed the old man into the house, with my feelings getting more and more strange and worrisome at every moment. **1869** BLACKMORE *Lorna D.* xlv, I must give orders ..that you come in at once, with that worrisome cough of yours. **1882** H. C. MERIVALE *Faucit of B.* II. I. xix. 43 Which is likely..to become before long the highest good of these worrisome days. **1893** *Harper's Mag.* Dec. 61/1 The best an' the most worrisome woman thet God ever made.

So **'worrisomely** *adv.*

a **1699** J. BEAUMONT *Psyche* XIX. vii, How worrisomly cross and peevish were Thy feeble years. **1973** *Newsweek* 23 Apr. 22/1 Three simultaneous crises..that seemed worrisomely different from those of the past. **1981** G. MCDONALD *Fletch & Widow Bradley* xiii. 51 Charley is a worrisomely tight man... Anything out of the ordinary rattles him.

worrit ('wʌrɪt), *sb. colloq.* Also 9 -et. [f. the vb.] A state of worry or mental distress; a fretting care or anxiety. Also, a person that worries others or himself.

1838 DICKENS *O. Twist* xvii, 'A porochial life, ma'am,' continued Mr. Bumble,..'is a life of worrit, and vexation, and hardihood.' **1844** in Ashwell *Life Bp. Wilberforce* (1880) I. vi. 221 Assuaging any and every worret, temporal and spiritual. **1848** DICKENS *Dombey* xxiii, 'Mrs. Richards's eldest, Miss!' said Susan, 'and the worrit of Mrs. Richards's life!' **1861** CALVERLEY *Charades* I, Endless cares and endless worrits, well I knows it, has a wife. **1889** GRETTON *Memory's Harkback* 68 The young men did not mind strictness, but they would not stand worrying... B was as kindly and good-natured as possible, but he was a 'worrit.'

worrit ('wʌrɪt), *v. colloq.* Also 9 -et. [App. a vulgar alteration of WORRY *v.* Cf. WHERRIT, WERRIT.]

1. *trans.* To worry, distress, vex, pester.

1818 LAMB *Let. to Mrs. Wordsworth* 18 Feb., These pests worrit me at business. **1837** DICKENS *Pickw.* xxvi, 'Don't worrit your poor mother,' said Mrs. Sanders. **1848** THACKERAY *Van. Fair* lviii, Lord bless us, how she did use to worret us at Sunday-school. **1854** W. COLLINS *Hide & Seek* II. xiv. (1904) 313 Why worrit yourself about finding Arthur Carr at all? **1869** J. R. GREEN *Lett.* (1901) III. 235, I have been worriting myself these last days with those Welsh chaps and our early history.

b. with advb. extension.

1854 W. COLLINS *Hide & Seek* II. x. (1904) 259 It don't do me no good: it only worrits me into a perspiration. **1855** TROLLOPE *Warden* viii. 116 Sir Abraham won't get papa another income when he has been worreted out of the hospital. **1871** GEO. ELIOT *Middlemarch* xxvi. II. 66 It will worret you to death, Lucy; *that* I can see.

2. *intr.* To give way to worry; to experience or display mental disquietude, impatience, etc.

1854 W. COLLINS *Hide & Seek* II. xiv. (1904) 317 It was how to track the man as was Mary's death, that I puzzled and worrited about in my head, at that time. **1857** KINGSLEY *Two Y. Ago* viii. (1881) 127 He..snaps, and worrits, and won't speak to her sometimes for a whole morning. **1868** WHYTE MELVILLE *White Rose* vii, 'Look alive, girl! Come —bustle, bustle! It's gone six o'clock.' 'Why, father, how you keep on worriting!'

Hence **'worriting** *vbl. sb.* and *ppl. a.*

1857 DICKENS *Dorrit* I. xxiii, There would be none of this *worriting and wearing. **1845** GERALDINE JEWSBURY *Zoe* I. 33 [He] is just the naughtiest and most *worritting boy I ever saw. **1861** HUGHES *Tom Brown at Oxf.* I. xi. 194 Here and there some..worriting, energizing mortal..gets command of a boat. **1871** SMILES *Character* viii. 219 Worreting, petty, and self-tormenting cares.

worrow, obs. form of WORRY *v.*

worry ('wʌrɪ), *sb.* [f. the vb.]

1. a. A troubled state of mind arising from the frets and cares of life; harassing anxiety or solicitude.

1804 W. WILBERFORCE in *Life* (1838) III. 190 Broomfield ..is a scene of almost as much bustle as Old Palace Yard. So much so, that the incessant *worry* (it is an expressive word) of this house makes me think of quitting it. **1835** MARRYAT *Jac. Faithf.* xxv, It were better to know the worst at once, than to be kept on the worry all your days. **1838** BUCKSTONE *Our Mary Anne* 20 After all the worry of mind I have endured this day. **1844** DICKENS *Martin Chuz.* xxii, Martin felt, from pure fatigue, and heat, and worry, as if he could have fallen on the ground. **1862** MRS. H. WOOD *Mrs. Hallib.* II. xxvi. (1888) 290 The fact is..I have a good deal of worry upon me. **1871** SMILES *Character* viii. 219 Cheerfulness.. enables nature to recruit its strength; whereas worry and discontent debilitate it. **1879** MRS. CRAIK *Young Mrs. Jardine* III. ix. 227 It is not work that kills, but 'worry'.

transf. **1866** LONGF. *Flower-de-luce* ii, Thou laughest at the mill, the whir and worry Of spindle and of loom.

b. An instance or case of this; a cause of, or matter for, anxiety; *pl.* cares, solicitudes.

1813 *Sketches of Character* (ed. 2) I. 178 You may suppose what a worry Mrs. Mac. was in. **1852** MRS. STOWE *Uncle Tom's C.* v. 27 Eliza came in here..in a great worry, crying and taking on. **1861** FLOR. NIGHTINGALE *Nursing* 66 There is scarcely a greater worry which invalids have to endure than the incurable hopes of their friends. **1859** LEVER *Davenport Dunn* ix. 76 'Delicious spot to come and repose in from the cares and worries of life', said Lord Lackington. **1868** LOUISA M. ALCOTT *Little Women* ix, Rich people have about as many worries as poor ones, I think. **1899** *Allbutt's Syst. Med.* VIII. 25 To learn to write with the left hand is a labour and a worry. **1912** *Times* 1 May 10/2 His chief worry was that he was unable to be of any further use.

2. The act of biting and shaking an animal so as to injure or kill it. (Properly of hounds when they seize their quarry.)

1847 SURTEES *Hawbuck Grange* xii. 250 The whole pack flew from their noses to the worry, and rolled one over another with their victim into the river. **1859** G. A. LAWRENCE *Sword & Gown* iii. 28 They will..join in the 'worry' as eagerly as the youngest hound. **1882** C. LLOYD MORGAN in *Nature* XXVI. 524/2 But no dog could tell his companion of the successful 'worry' [*sc.* of a cat] he had just enjoyed. **1886** *Fores's Sporting Notes* III. 155 And then among the reeds is a rolling over, a confusion, and a worry. *transf.* **1901** 'LINESMAN' *Words by Eyewitness* (1902) 100 There is a brief and breathless 'worry' at the top, and the hill is ours. Few Boers have remained to face the bayonets.

3. Irritation or morbid stimulation (of bodily tissue).

1897 *Allbutt's Syst. Med.* III. 750 This form of looseness appears to be due to direct worry of the mucous membrane.

4. Special Combs. **worry beads**, a string of beads manipulated by the fingers as a means of occupying one's hands and calming the nerves; **worry lines**, lines or wrinkles on the forehead supposedly formed by a habitual expression of worry.

1964 in M. McLuhan *Understanding Media* viii. 78 You will notice that many Greek men..spend a lot of time counting the beads of what appear to be amber rosaries... They are *komboloia* or 'worry beads'. **1978** G. GREENE *Human Factor* v. i. 233 The man had a rosary in his lap and seemed to be using it like a chain of worry beads. **1985** *Observer* 3 Feb. 19/3 Sheikh Yamani, worry beads to hand, sums up the general feeling of unease as OPEC last week managed to preserve its fragile unity. **1972** 'J. QUARTERMAIN' *Rock of Diamond* xvi. 99 Worry lines creased his forehead. **1982** L. CODY *Bad Company* xiv. 102 There was grey in her hair and worry lines between her brows.

worry ('wʌrɪ), *v.* *Pa. t.* and *pple.* worried. Forms: *α.* 1 **wyrȝan**, 4 **wyryȝ(e**, 4–5 **wirwe, wirie, wiry(e, wyrie, wyry(e**, 5 **wyrwyn, wyrhy**, 5–7 **wirrie, wyrry**, 6 *Sc.* **wirrey, virry**, 5–6, 9 *Sc.* **wirry**. *β.* 4 **werew**, *Sc.* **ver(r)y**, 4–6 **wery(e**, (5 **were, werou-**), 5–7, 9 *dial.* **werry**, 6 **wearry**, 6–7 **wearie, weary**. *γ.* 4–6 **worow(e**, (4 *pa. pple.* **yworewid**, 5 *pa. t.* **worod**, 6 *3rd sing.* **woroeth**), 5 **worwyn**, 6–7 **worrow**, 7 **wurrow**; 4–7 **wory(e**, (5 **vory**), **worie**, 6 **worrye**, 6–7 **woorry(e**, 7 **woorie, worrey, whorry, worr'** (*in verse*), 6–8 **wurry**, 6– **worry**. [OE. *wyrȝan* = OFris. *wergia* to kill, MLG. *worgen*, MDu. *worghen* (Du. *worgen, wurgen*), to strangle, throttle, OHG. *wurgan, wurkjan* (MHG. *wurgen, würgen*, G. *würgen*), to strangle, worry, kill by violence:—OTeut. **wurgjan*, related to **werg-*, a strong vb. stem found in MHG. *irwergen* to throttle:—Indo-Eur. **wergh-*.

The *α-* and *β*-forms (*wirry* and *werry*) are normal ME. developments of OE. *wyrȝan*: cf. the forms of MERRY *a.* The *γ*-forms apparently represent a late WS. **wurȝan*, with later graphic substitution of *wo-* for *wu-*; see the note to WORM *sb.* The original *u*-sound of this form is indicated by the late spellings with *woo-*.]

†**1. a.** *trans.* To kill (a person or animal) by compressing the throat; to strangle. *Obs.*

α. *c* **725** *Corpus Gloss.* S 558 *St[r]angulat*, wyrȝeð *uel* smorað. *c* **1300** *Havelok* 1921 On þe morwen, hwan it was day, Ilc on other wirwed lay, Als it were dogges þat weren henged. **1387** TREVISA *Higden* VII. 534 (MS. *β*) Harald.. threwe hym to the grounde and had wyried [*MS. γ* ywyryed] hym with his hondes, nadde he be the rather delyvered out of his clowes. *c* **1440** *Promp. Parv.* 530/1 Wyrwyn', *strangulo, suffoco.* **1513** DOUGLAS *Æneis* VIII. v. 26 Tua gret serpentis..The quhilk he wyrreit wyth his handis tuay. *a* **1578** LINDESAY (Pitscottie) *Chron. Scot.* (S.T.S.) II. 191 Thay wirrit him to the deid. **1606** *Reg. Privy Counc. Scot.* (1885) VII. 185 He tuike the said compleiner be the throat and thought to have wirryed her or she had awaked.

β. *c* **1300** *Havelok* 1915 Weren he werewed. *c* **1375** *Sc. Leg. Saints* xxvi. (*Nycholas*) 994 He..weryt hyme [*eum strangulavit*]. **1456** SIR G. HAYE *Law Arms* (S.T.S.) 23 The fende weryit him in his bed. **14..** *Quatuor Serm.* (Caxton 1483) d4, I denounce..al tho that werye or slee theyr generacions. **1483** *Cath. Angl.* 414/2 To Wery, *strangulare, suffocare.*

γ. **13..** *St. Greg. Trental* 19 in *Min. Poems fr. Vernon MS.* 261 Anon as hire child I-boren was, þe Nekke heo nom, þe child heo woriede [*Cott. MS.* wyryede]. **14..** *Promp. Parv.* 532/2 (MS. K.) Worwyn, *supra in* wyrwyn. **1483** *Cath. Angl.* 423/2 To Worowe, *jugulare, suffocare.* **1558** KENNEDY *Compend. Tractive* ii. in *Wodrow Misc.* (1844) I. 104 That thay abstayne..fra it that is worreit [Acts xv. 20]. **1600** HAMILTON in *Cath. Tractates* (S.T.S.) 240/5 East Laudiane knawis the loue and fidelitie of ane of thair Ministers towards his wyf, wha worriet hir before he passit to his preaching.

†**b.** *fig. Obs.*

1387 TREVISA *Higden* VII. 465 þese..wexe so riche þat it semede þat þe douȝter passede and weried [*v.rr.* wyryȝede, wyryed, wyryde] þe moder [*ut filia ditata matrem supergredi videretur et suffocare*].

†**2. a.** To choke (a person or animal) with a mouthful of food. Used with the food as subj., or *refl.* and *pass.* Const. *on* (the food); hence ***to be worried***, or ***worry oneself***, ***on*** = to devour greedily. Also *fig. Obs.*

a **1300** *Cursor M.* 16929 Ai til iesus þe thrid dai had fughten gain sathan, And werid him on his aun bit, als hund es on a ban. **14..** WYNTOUN *Chron.* VII. 514 (Wemyss MS.) God lat neuer of it a crote, Till I be weryit [*v.rr.* wyrryd, wereyt], pass oure my throte. *c* **1520** SKELTON *Magnyf.* 1568 On suche a female my flesshe wolde be wroken...weryed I wolde be on suche a bayte. *a* **1529** —— *P. Sparowe* 29 Gib, I saye, our cat Worrowyd her on that Which I loued best. **1535** STEWART *Cron. Scot.* II. 663 How Godowyn worreit himself to Deid in Presence of Edward King. *Ibid.*, The breid..stak so fast..., it wirreit him to deid. **1536** BELLENDEN *Cron. Scot.* (1821) II. 276 'God gif that breid wory me, gif evir I wes othir art or part of Alarudis slauchter.' And incontinent, he fel doun weryit on the breid. **1674** RAY *N.C. Words* 55 To be *Worried*, to be choak't. *a* **1779** D. GRAHAM *Collect. Writ.* (1883) II. 39 She.. squattles up a mutchkin at a waught, which was like to wirry her.

†**b.** *intr.* (for *refl.*) To be choked, to choke. Const. *on* (as above). *Obs.*

c **1420** WYNTOUN *Chron.* VII. 504 Swa suddandly richt at þe burde He wereit. **1500–20** DUNBAR *Poems* xxxi. 24 Now quhill thair is gude wyne to sell, He that dois on dry breid virry [*v.r.* wirrie], I gif him to the Devill of hell. **1715** in Maidment *Old Ballads* (1844) 33 He..like a fool, did eat the cow, And worried on the tail. **1756** MRS. CALDERWOOD *Lett. & Jrnls.* (1884) v. 123 A great fat carle..so short necked that you would think he would worry [at] every word he spoke. **1721** KELLY *Scot. Prov.* 385 You fasted long, and worried on a Fly.

†**c.** Of smoke: To suffocate (a person). *Obs.*

1755 *Edom of Gordon* xv. in Child *Ballads* III. 434 Dear mother, gie owre your house,..For the reek it worries me.

3. a. *trans.* To seize by the throat with the teeth and tear or lacerate; to kill or injure by biting and shaking. Said e.g. of dogs or wolves attacking sheep, or of hounds when they seize their quarry.

α. *c* **1380** [see b]. **1393** LANGL. *P. Pl.* C. x. 226 Wolues þat wyryeþ men, wommen and children. *c* **1480** HENRYSON *Fox, Wolf & Cadger* 25 Mak ane suddand schow vpon ane scheip, Syne with thy wappinnis wirrie him to deid. **1549** *Compl. Scotl.* 156 There is ouer mony doggis in scotland that virreis there master as acteon vas virreit. **1606** *Wily beguiled* 71 My dog wirried my neighbours sow, and the sow died. **1623** *Extr. Aberd. Reg.* (1848) II. 383 Mastishe and cur doggis.. quha..wyrries and devouris thair sheip.

β. *c* **1375** *Sc. Leg. Saints* iii. (*Andreas*) 259 Sewine hundis com quhare he lay, and verrit hym sodanly. *c* **1400** *Rom. Rose* 6264 He wolde hem wery and drinke the bloode. *c* **1400** LOVE *Bonavent. Mirr.* xviii. 46 Þe prophete Abdo þat was weroude [*v.r.* wirwed] of þe lyoune. **1554** W. PRAT *Aphrique* K iv b, Manye other beastes whiche the dogges do werye & kyll. **1586** WHETSTONE *Engl. Mirror* 44 If a Beare appeare, ..they will all joyne to wearie him. **1599** PEELE *David & Bethsabe* B iv, The mastiues of our land shall werry ye. **1609** *Ev. Woman in Hum.* v. i. in Bullen *O. Pl.* IV, Acteon..was ..werried to death with his own dogs. *a* **1653** GOUGE *Comm. Hebr.* xi. 37 When he observeth that the Wolf hath wearied some sheep.

absol. **1638** BRATHWAIT *Barnabees Jrnl.* III. (1818) 141 Farre from home old foxes werry.

γ. **1340** HAMPOLE *Pr. Consc.* 1229 Lyons, libardes and wolwes kene, þat wald worow men bylyve, And rogg þam in sonder and ryve. **13..** *Gaw. & Gr. Knt.* 1905 Ryȝt bifore þe hors fete þay fel on hym alle, And woried me þis wyly wyth a wroth noyse. ? *a* **1400** *Morte Arth.* 958 Ȝone warlawe wyt, he worows vs alle! *c* **1400** *Laud Troy Bk.* 8777 To scle the Gregais wold he not ses, As hongre lyoun bestes vories. *c* **1440** *Alphabet of Tales* 421 And with þat he ran on þe selie lambe and worod itt. **1579** GOSSON *Sch. Abuse* (Arb.) 47 The men of Hyrcania, that keepe Mastiffes, to woorrye them selues. **1592** BACON *Observ. Libel* (end) Resuscit. (1657) 150 The persecutions of the Primitive Church... As that, of Worrowing Priests, under the Skins of Bears, by Doggs, and the like. **1620** QUARLES *Feast for Wormes* Med. iii. D 4, Alas! the rau'nous Wolues will worr' thy Sheepe. **1639** J. CLARKE *Parœm.* 56 Many dogs may easily woorie one. **1680** P. HENRY *Diar. & Lett.* (1882) 285 Ralph Nixon had three sheep worry'd to death in one night. **1795** *Life John Metcalf* 3 One of the young hounds happening to worry a couple of lambs. **1844** STEPHENS *Bk. Farm* II. 88 Many dogs..are in the habit of looking out for sheep to worry, at some distance from their homes. **1847** C. BRONTË *Jane Eyre* xx, She bit me. .. She worried me like a tigress. **1866** AUGUSTA WILSON *St. Elmo* v, Did not he worry down and mangle one of my best Southdowns? **1867** *Times* 8 May 13/2 Defendant's dog.. seized Mrs. Miller by the leg, and bit her several times, throwing her down, and worrying her very much.

absol. **1872** TENNYSON *Gareth & Lynette* 990 Such a dog am I, To worry, and not to flee. **1899** H. D. RAWNSLEY *Life & Nat. Eng. Lakes* 173 A dog that shows signs of worrying is 'put down' at once.

b. *fig.* (or in figurative context).

c **1380** WYCLIF *Wks.* (1880) 24 No warde to hem hou faste þe woluys of helle wirien cristen soulis. **1399** LANGL. *Rich. Redeles* III. 72 His owen kynde briddis, þat weren..well ny yworewid with a wronge leder. **1529** MORE *Dyaloge* IV. xi. 114 b/2 To play yᵉ wyly foxes & wyrry simple soules & pore lambes. **1549** [see 3 a]. **1560** DAUS tr. *Sleidane's Comm.* 318 That they..oversee that other Ministers do theyr dutye, that the wolues do not worrye the flocke. **1563** FOXE *A. & M.* 1442/2 My L. is it not enough for you to wery your own shepe, but ye must also meddle wᵗ other mens shepe? **1603** HOLLAND *Plutarch's Mor.* 238 Even so those parts of our life which are diseased, naught and ill affected,..these they seize upon, and are ready to worry and plucke in peeces. **1641** MILTON *Reform.* II. Wks. 1851 III. 67 To let them still hale us, and worrey us with their band-dogs, and Pursivants. **1690** C. NESSE *O. & N. Test.* I. 317 Herod pretended to worship Christ when he intended to worry him. **1863** R. F. BURTON *Wand. W. Africa* I. 1 White sea-dogs coursed and worried one another over Father Mersey's breadth of mud.

c. *transf.* To bite at or upon (an object); to kiss or hug vehemently; to utter (one's words) with the teeth nearly closed, as if biting or champing them.

1567 GOLDING *Ovid's Met.* XIII. 568 Queene Hecub ronning at a stone, with gnarring seazd theron, And wirryed it beetweene her teeth [*morsibus insequitur*]. **1611** SHAKS. *Wint. T.* v. ii. 58 Then againe worryes he his Daughter, with clipping her. **1678** DRYDEN *All for Love* IV. 54 And then he grew familiar with her hand, Squeez'd it, and worry'd it with ravenous kisses. **1905** L. J. VANCE *Ter. O'Rourke* I. xiv, As the Irishman entered, Prince Felix said a word, or two, low-toned and tense—worried them between his teeth, like an ill-dispositioned cur. **1914** A. N. LYONS *Simple Simon* I. i. 13 Their sons, late of the Great School, home from India on leave and unanimously worrying small moustaches of the tooth-brush pattern.

d. *intr.* To pull or tear *at* (an object) with the teeth.

1882 *Little Folks* Jan. 24/2 There was Floss, worrying at the parcel, which had only thin paper wrapped round it.

4. *trans.* To swallow greedily, devour. Also with *up*. Latterly *north.* and *Sc.*

a **1300** *Cursor M.* 5902 Bot aaron wand it wex sa kene þas oþer it wired [*Gött.* wirid, *Trin.* woryed] al bidene. **1619** A. GIL *Logon. Angl.* Pref. B 3 To worrow, *Voro.* **1634** SIR T. HERBERT *Trav.* 125 They had seene him weare many [jewels] and twas them, hee had woorried in his Ostrich appetite. **1643** HORN & ROB. *Gate Lang. Unl.* li. §568 Stout feeders..do nothing else but devour (never lin wurrowing). **1728** RAMSAY *Monk & Miller's Wife* 138 Think ye..his gentle stamock's master To worry up a pint of plaister. **1805** G. MᶜINDOE *Poems* 65 (E.D.D.) Great claggs o' meat they ne'er could worry. **1887** *Jamieson Suppl.*, *Wirry*, to worry, devour, eat ravenously.

5. a. To harass by rough or severe treatment, by repeated aggression or attack; to assail with hostile or menacing speech.

a **1553** UDALL *Royster D.* III. iii. (Arb.) 46 But in spite of Custance, which hath hym weried, Let vs see his mashyp solemnely buried. **1594** NASHE *Unfort. Trav.* 34, I thought verilie they woulde haue worried one another with wordes, they were so earnest and vehement. **1610** ROWLANDS *Martin Mark-all* 12 Hath your nightly watchings and continuall disorder of your braines so whorried your senses. **1652** PEYTON *Catastr. Ho. Stuarts* 74, I being a man can speak by experience, who hath beeen most justly worryed by the hand of the Almighty for sins. **1675–7** WARWICK *Mem. Chas. I* (1701) 321 Cromwell..marched forwards into Scotland, and left Lambert to worry Hamilton in England. *a* **1680** GLANVILL *Serm.* iv. (1681) 212 No mans Life or property will be safe; mankind would worry and prey upon one another. **1725** B. HIGGONS *Rem. Burnet* II. (1736) 177 He cruelly worries the Memory of a Daughter of England. **1729** GAY *Polly* I. xiv, In conniving at my escape, you save me from your husband's worrying me with threats and violence. **1852** ROCK *Ch. of Fathers* III. I. 302 They vowed they would give peace to the land they were then wasting and worrying by fire and sword. **1877** FREEMAN in *Brit. Q. Rev.* Jan. 182 He perhaps hardly brings out how thoroughly Edward the Third was worried into war by the aggression of Philip. **1885** *Manch. Exam.* 23 Feb. 5/3 Having found their range during daylight, they continued to worry our men all the night.

transf. *a* **1699** J. BEAUMONT *Psyche* XXII. x, Soil..if not duly worried, digg'd and plow'd, Harrow'd and torn. **1898** *Allbutt's Syst. Med.* V. 304 A repeated application to some of these drugs..by worrying the cardiac ganglia..tends to dilatation of the heart.

b. with advb. extension expressing result, as *away*, *in*, *to death*.

1565 COOPER *Thesaurus* s.v. *Abigo*, He chased or weried away his sonne to Rhodes. **1603** DEKKER *Wonderful Year* E 4 First to scratch out false Cressidaes eyes, and then (which was worse) to woorry her to death with scolding. **1659** MILTON *Civil Power* 74 If departed of his own accord, like that lost sheep..the true church either with her own or any borrowd force worries him not in again. **1678** *Poor Robin's True Char. Scold* 6 Thus she worries him out of his senses at home. **1711** in *10th Rep. Hist. MSS. Comm.* App. V. 184 He is wurryed to death by those ungrateful nations.

c. *transf.* With adv. (e.g. *out*, *down*) or advb. phr.: To get or bring into a specified condition by harassing treatment, persistent aggression, or dogged effort. Similarly ***to worry one's way***. Also without adv. (phr.), to worry about (a problem, etc.) (*U.S. colloq.*).

1727 E. LAURENCE *Duty of Steward* 55 The Tenants.. have been suffer'd to..worry out the strength of the Land by sowing Rape, &c. **1806–7** J. BERESFORD *Miseries Hum. Life* (1826) xx. xxx. 256 You at last worry out a solitary spark [from the flint]. **1811** JANE AUSTEN *Sense & S.* II. x. 186 She was sometimes worried down by officious condolence to rate good-breeding as more indispensable to comfort than good-nature. **1870** E. E. HALE *Ten Times One* iii. 61 While she 'worried down' the tea, and ate a slice of toast. **1890** *Nature* 4 Sept. 455/2 All such points he will delight to worry out for himself. **1894** CROCKETT *Play-actress* iv. 52 Worrying out a knotty point in the 'Original Hebrew'. **1898** L. STEPHEN *Stud. Biogr.* II. ii. 48 Scott..worried his way into some understanding of the language by main force. **1920** A. HOPE *Lucinda* ii. 24 Waldo was not quick-witted, but he had a good brain. If he got hold of a problem, he would worry it to a solution. **1959** N. MAILER *Advts. for Myself* (1961) 119 He had always asked too many questions, he had worried the task too severely. **1963** *N. & Q.* Dec. 443/1, I shall not worry the distinction between *alba* and *aube*. **1978** T. L. SMITH *Money War* I. 17 He had worried the chance meeting on the flight home.

d. To irritate (an animal) by a repetition of feigned attacks, etc.

1807–8 SYD. SMITH *Plymley's Lett.* iii. Wks. 1859 II. 146/2, I admit there is a vast luxury in selecting a particular set of Christians, and in worrying them as a boy worries a puppy dog. **1840** DICKENS *Old C. Shop* xxi, Hissing and worrying the animal [a chained dog] till he was nearly mad.

e. *U.S.* To afflict with physical fatigue or distress.

1828 WEBSTER, *Worry*..2. To fatigue; to harass with labor; a popular sense of the word. **1876** HOLLAND *Sevenoaks* v. 66 For three steady hours he went on, the horse no more worried than if he had been standing in the stable.

f. Fencing. ***to worry the sword***: 'to fret one's opponent by small movements in rapid succession which seem about to result in thrusts or feints' (*Century Dict.*).

6. a. In lighter sense: To vex, distress, or persecute by inconsiderate or importunate behaviour; to plague or pester with reiterated demands, requests, or the like.

1671 MILTON *Samson* 906 Witness when I was worried with thy peals. **1728** GAY *Begg. Op.* II. xiii, 'Tis barbarous in you to worry a Gentleman in his Circumstances. **1788** FRANKLIN *Autobiog.* Wks. 1840 I. 196 He had continually worried the Assembly with message after message. **1840** DICKENS *Old C. Shop* vii, You worry me to death with your chattering. **1846** LANDOR *Wks.* II. 9 (*Albani & Picture-dealers*), I am infested and persecuted and worried to death by duns. They belabor and martellate my ears. **1882** MISS BRADDON *Mt. Royal* II. v. 103 She will worry you till you give your consent. **1885** *Manch. Exam.* 15 July 5/3 The supply of ignorant *ciceroni* to worry visitors with their foolish babblement. **1889** JESSOPP *Coming of Friars* vi. 281 The scholars were not to be worried with everlasting ritual observances. **1927** J. B. PRIESTLEY *Adam in Moonshine* x. 203 They won't really do anything but worry you with questions.

b. with advb. extension as *out*, *out of* (something).

1729 SWIFT *Grand Question debated* (1732) 8 But, Madam, I beg, you'll contrive and invent, And worry him out, till he gives his Consent. **1853** WHYTE MELVILLE *Digby Grand* I. x. 269 Addressing 'dear Angelina' in an affectionate whisper that would never have led one to suppose she worried the poor girl's life out at home. **1876** HOLLAND *Sevenoaks* xv. 209 She..had worried him out of his life, and he had gone and left her childless. **1898** *Times* 18 Oct. 9/3 If by chance it [the French Government] imagines that this country is going to be worried out of the position taken up by Lord Salisbury, it is making a very grave mistake.

7. a. To cause distress of mind to; to afflict with mental trouble or agitation; to make anxious and ill at ease. Chiefly of a cause or circumstance, or *refl.* or *pass.*

1822 HAZLITT *Table-Talk* xxiii. (*On great and little Things*), Small pains are..more within our reach; we can fret and worry ourselves about them. **1822** W. IRVING *Bracebr. Hall*, *Bachelor's Conf.*, He had settled the point which had been worrying his mind. **1848** DICKENS *Dombey* v, I quite fret and worry myself about her. **1866** GEO. ELIOT *F. Holt* i. (1868) 21 Increasing anxieties about money had worried her. **1867** TROLLOPE *Last Chron. Barset* II. lvi. 121 Men when they are worried by fears..become suspicious. **1874** L. STEPHEN *Hours in Libr.* (1892) II. iii. 95 This self-plagiarism sometimes worries us. **1875** MRS. RANDOLPH *Wild Hyacinth* I. 74 Don't worry yourself about it, my love. **1889** 'J. S. WINTER' *Mrs. Bob* xxi. (1891) 238 It puzzles me and worries me to guess why Miss Lavinia always wanted to drop the subject.

b. in pa. pple., denoting a state of mind.

1863 PRINCESS ALICE *Mem.* (1884) 60, I am sure, dear Mama, you are worried to death about it. **1867** TROLLOPE *Last Chron. Barset* I. xxi. 179 The subject..was a sore one, and he was worried a little. **1871** GEO. ELIOT *Middlemarch* xxiii. II. 25 He felt a little worried and wearied, perhaps with mental debate. **1899** *Allbutt's Syst. Med.* VIII. 602 Some patients are attacked [by lichen] when worried or in low condition.

c. *intr.* (for *refl.*) To give way to anxiety or mental disquietude. Also in colloq. phrases, as ***I should worry***: see SHALL *v.* 18 d; ***not to worry***: see NOT *adv.* 4.

1860 WORCESTER, *Worry* v.n., to indulge in idle complaining; to fret; to be troubled. (Colloquial.) *Roget.* **1861** HOLLAND *Lessons in Life* xiii. 181 When she can find nothing to do, then she worries. **1874** LD. COLERIDGE in *Life* (1904) II. ix. 244 'Don't coddle and don't worry' is his recipe for longevity. **1879** H. GEORGE *Progr. & Pov.* IX. iv. (1881) 414 Men would no more worry about finding employment than they worry about finding air to breathe. **1901** ALDRIDGE *Sherbro* xx. 205 My head-man..begged me not to worry.

8. *intr.* with advb. extension (cf. the transf. uses 5 b, c, 6 b above): **a.** To advance or progress by a harassing or dogged effort; to force or work one's way *through*. Of the wind: To go *on* blowing in a harassing way.

a **1699** J. BEAUMONT *Psyche* IV. xcvii, Yet worying among the waves they spy'd A wracked Mortal. *Ibid.* XIII. iv, Winter..worries forward at his due Determin'd season, spight of all the Ice Which clogs his heels. **1820** W. IRVING *Sk. Bk.*, *Spectre Bridegroom* ¶ 11 He was naturally a fuming, bustling little man, and could not remain passive... He worried from top to bottom of the castle with an air of infinite anxiety. **1883** SYMONDS *Ital. Byways* i. 13 For the next three days the wind went worrying on. **1901** *Daily Express* 21 Mar. 7/1 In the end we worried through and.. anchored. **1903** KIPLING *5 Nations* 211 When the wind worries through the 'ills.

b. To get *through* (a business, piece of work) by persistent effort or struggle; so with *through* adv. ***to worry along***: to contrive to live, 'keep going', in the teeth of trials or difficulties (*U.S.*).

1871 'MARK TWAIN' *Screamers* xxix. 146 My friend, you seem to know pretty much all the tunes there are, and you worry along first rate. **1873** HOWELLS *Chance Acquaint.*

(1882) 299 She must . . try to worry along without him. **1876** Besant & Rice *Gold. Butterfly* xx, I worried through that war without a scratch. **1878** —— *Celia's Arb.* xii, Often on Saturday night I wonder how I have managed to worry through the work of the week. **1885** Howells *Silas Lapham* (1891) I. 269, I think I can manage to worry along. **1899** *Westm. Gaz.* 7 Oct. 2/2 The British farmer has . . much to contend with, but on the whole he worries through a great deal more successfully than could be expected.

9. *Comb.*: **worryguts** *dial.* and *colloq.* = *worry wart*; freq. as a term of address; † **worry pear** (*tree*) = CHOKE-PEAR; **worry wart** *colloq.* (chiefly *U.S.*), an inveterate worrier, one who frets unnecessarily.

1932 *Somerset Year Bk.* 83 The missis, who be a prapper worryguts. **1966** O. Norton *School of Liars* iv. 72 He laughed. 'Worryguts!' 'I wasn't worried. I was just trying to be efficient.' **1982** D. Phillips *Coconut Kiss* ix. 94 It's all right . . isn't it?' I asked. ''Course it is, Worryguts,' said Vera. **1562** Turner *Herbal* II. 108 The wyld Pere tre or chouke Pere tre or worry Pear tre. **1956** I. Belknap *Human Problems of State Mental Hospitals* x. 177 The persevering, nagging delusional group—who were termed 'worry warts', 'nuisances', 'bird dogs', in the attendants' slang. **1974** J. Heller *Something Happened* 445 'Don't be such a worry wart.' 'Don't use that phrase. It makes my skin prickle.'

worrying ('wʌrɪɪŋ), *vbl. sb.* [f. WORRY *v.* + -ING[1].]

1. The action of strangling or of biting and tearing by the throat.

In quot. 1621 'worrien' is perhaps this word, altered for the rhyme.

1483 *Cath. Angl.* 414/2 Werying, *jugulamen*, . . *suffocamen*. **1560** Daus tr. *Sleidane's Comm.* 422 The moste importune barkynge of Dogges, and werieng one an other. **1621** Brathwait *Nat. Embassie* etc. 194 How duely I did keepe My woollie store (as I had care) from worrien, Scab, sought, the rot or any kind of murren. **1859** H. Kingsley *G. Hamlyn* xii, Then the astounded Tom heard the worrying of a terrier, and the squeak of a dying rat.

2. The action of harassing, pestering, or distressing.

1848 Dickens *Dombey* lix, Worryings and quellings of young children. **1862** *Sat. Rev.* 8 Feb. 157 Amidst all this worrying and being worried. **1864** Carlyle *Fredk. Gt.* XVI. vii. (1872) VI. 218 Such worryings (*ces sortes de compromis*) leave their mark on a man.

'**worrying**, *ppl. a.* [f. WORRY *v.* + -ING[2].]

† **1.** Given to harrying or raiding. *Obs.*

1610 Holland *Camden's Brit.* 109 A greater rabble of worrying freebutters.

2. Harassing; distressing to the mind or spirits.

1826 F. Reynolds *Life* I. 212 Your whole conduct is literally worrying and annoying in the extreme. **1834** Hook *Gilbert Gurney* xi. *New Mo. Mag.* XLII. 470 Whether she would allow me to send her anything to cheer her up after her worrying journey. **1837** Dickens *Pickw.* xxxvi, There are few things more worrying than sitting up for somebody, especially if that somebody be at a party. **1853** —— *Bleak Ho.* vii, Whatever the sound is, it is a worrying sound.

Hence '**worryingly** *adv.*

1842 Moore *Mem.* VII. 311 The difficulty . . still haunts me most worryingly.

worsam, var. of WORSUM *Obs.*, pus.

worse (wɜːs), *a.* and *sb.* Forms: α. 1 **wiersa, wirsa**, 1–2 **wyrsa** (1 **wuyrsa**), 2 **wursa**, 2–6 **wurse**, 4 **wirse**, 3 **wrse**, 3–6 **wurs**; 3– **worse**, 3–6 **worsse**, 4 **worss**, 3–7 **wors**, 6 **woorse, wourse**, 7 **wours**, 9 *vulgar* **wuss**. β. 2 **wærsa, wersa**, 2–6 **werse** (3 *Orm.* **werrse**), 3 **weorse**, 4 **wersse**, 4–5 **vers**, 4–6 **wers**, 5 **werce**; 5–6 **wars, warsse**, 5–6, 8–9 *north.* **warse**. [OE. *wyrsa, wiersa* = OFris. *wirra, werra* (for **wirsa*, **wersa* by assimilation), OS. *wirsa*, OHG. *wirsiro, -ero, -oro* (MHG. *wirser*), ON. *verri* (for **wersi*; Sw. *värre*, Da. *værre*; see WAR *a.*), Goth. *wairsiza*:—OTeut. **wersizon-*, f. root **wers-*, found in OS., OHG. *werran*, G. (*ver-*)*wirren* to entangle, confound (see WAR *sb.*[1]) + *-izon-* compar. suffix.

For the graphic change of *wu-* to *wo-* see the notes to WORM *sb.* and WORRY *v.* The β-forms appear first in north-east midland texts and are app. due to Scandinavian.]

A. *adj.* Used as the comparative of BAD, EVIL, ILL, or as the opposite of BETTER.

1. a. More reprehensible morally; more wicked, depraved or vicious; more cruel, unkind, or ill-conditioned.

c **888** Ælfred *Boeth.* xiv. §3 Þi hi send wyrsan þonne nytenu þy hi nellað witan hwæt hi sint. *c* **1000** *Ags. Gosp.* Matt. xii. 45 Ðonne gæð he, and hym to ʒenimð seofun oþre gastas wyrsan þonne he. *a* **1122** *O.E. Chron.* an. 979 (Laud MS.) Ne wearð Angelcynne nan wærsa dæd ʒedon. **1154** *Ibid.* an. 1140 Oc æfre þe mare he iaf heom, þe wærse hi wæron him. *a* **1225** *Ancr. R.* 82 Idel speche is vuel; ful speche is wurse. *c* **1300** *Havelok* 1100 He werse was þan Sathanas. **1340** *Ayenb.* 64 Ine þise zenne [of swearing] byeþ þe cristene worse þanne þe sarasyn. *c* **1380** Wyclif *Sel. Wks.* III. 348 Þei stelen pore mennis children, þat is werse þan stele an oxe. *c* **1386** Chaucer *Nun's Priest's T.* 466 Now certes I were worse than a feend If I to yow wolde harm or vileynye. **1396** —— *Lenvoy a Bukton* 18 Bet ys to wedde than brenne in worse wise. *c* **1460** *Towneley Myst.* xxx. 195 It is saide in old sawes . . Wars pepill wars lawes. **1593** Shaks. *Rich. II*, III. ii. 132 Three Iudasses, each one thrice worse then Iudas. **1671** H. M. tr. *Erasm. Colloq.* 226 And didst thou return holy from thence? . . Nay somewhat worse than I went. **1718** Prior *An Epitaph* 26 So ev'ry Servant took his Course; And bad at First, They all grew worse. **1818** Wilberforce in *Life* (1838) IV. 395 Keswick worse now as to morals than thirty years ago. **1847** Tennyson *Princess* IV. 232 The song Might have been worse and sinn'd in grosser lips Beyond all pardon. **1848** Thackeray *Van. Fair* xi, 'He *be* a bad'n, sure enough,' Mr. Horrocks remarked; 'and his man Flethers is wuss.' **1863** W. C. Baldwin *Afr. Hunting* iii. 69 Considering it no worse to employ myself usefully than to pass the time loitering about.

b. qualifying an agent-noun.

1653 in *Verney Mem.* (1907) I. 547 Wors livers then my self have seen their errors. **1871** Geo. Eliot *Middlemarch* xxxv. II. 199, I only hope and trust he wasn't a worse liver than we think of.

c. ***worse and worse*** = worse in an increasing degree, progressively worse.

1535 Coverdale *Ecclus.* iii. [26] He that is frowarde of hert wyll euer be the worse and worse. **1567–9** Jewel *Def. Apol.* (1611) 151 That the Wicked and Wilfull . . should . . wax woorse and woorse. **1596** Spenser *F.Q.* v. Proem. i, The world . . being once amisse growes daily wourse and wourse. **1154** *O.E. Chron.* an. 1137 (Laud MS.) And ðæt lastede þa .xix. wintre wile Stephne was king & æure it was werse & werse. *c* **1522** Skelton *Why nat to Courte?* 132 Whyles he doth rule, All is warse and warse. *a* **1548** Hall *Chron., Hen. IV* 2 b, All thynges . . , as well in the realme as without, waxed worsse and worsse. **1596** Shaks. *Tam. Shr.* v. ii. 93 Worse and worse, she will not come: Oh vilde, intollerable, not to be indur'd. **1682** *Lond. Gaz.* No. 1760/2 The affairs of Hungary grow worse and worse. **1720** Lady B. Germaine in *Ctess. Suffolk's Lett.* (1824) I. 73 Worse and worse here every day—no soul left that we know but Lady Kit and Mrs. Coke. **1735** Pope *Donne Sat.* iv. 121 So when you plague a fool, 'tis still the curse, You only make the matter worse and worse. **1852** Mrs. Stowe *Uncle Tom's C.* iii. 13, I have been patient; but it's growing worse and worse—flesh and blood can't bear it any longer. **1885** 'Mrs. Alexander' *At Bay* iv, 'This is worse and worse,' said Lady Gethin, gravely.

2. a. More harmful, painful, grievous, regrettable, unpleasant, offensive, unfavourable, unlucky, etc.

Beowulf 2969 He . . forʒeald hraðe wyrsan wrixle wælhlem þone. *c* **888** Ælfred *Boeth.* xxix. §2 Hwylc is wirsa wol . . þonne he hæbbe on his ʒeferrædenne . . feond & freondes anlicnesse? *c* **897** —— *Gregory's Past C.* xvii. 122 Oft sio wund bið ðæs þe wierse & ðy mare, ʒif hio bið unwærlice ʒewriðen. **971** *Blickl. Hom.* 243 Þy læs wen sie þæt . . God . . us sende on wyrsan tintreʒo. *c* **1000** *Ags. Gosp.* Matt. ix. 16 Se slite byð þe wyrsa [*peior scissura fit*]. *c* **1200** Ormin 7395 Þa beþ hemm ȝarrkedd mare inoh & werrse pine inn helle, þann iff [etc.]. *c* **1230** *Hali Meid.* (1922) 19 Se herre degre, se þe fal is wurse. **1297** R. Glouc. (Rolls) 7691 Wo so come to esse him riȝt of eni trespas, Bote he payde him þe bet, þe wors is ende was. *c* **1386** Chaucer *Knt.'s T.* 366 Now is my prison worse than biforn. *a* **1440** *Sir Eglam.* 293 Yn werse tyme blewe he never hys horne. **1484** Caxton *Fables of Auian* xiii, Werse is the stroke of a tonge than the stroke of a spere. **1531** Elyot *Gov.* I. xiii. (1883) I. 116 Whiche nowe, beinge men, nat onely haue forgotten their congruite . . but, that wars is, hath all lernynge in derision. **1542** Udall *Erasm. Apoph.* II. 300 And to that horrible cruell dede he gaue no wurse name but vncomely demeanure. **1580** G. Harvey *Three Proper Lett.* 35 *Non omni dormio*, worse lucke. **1596** *Edward III*, II. i. 451 Lillies that fester smel far worse then weeds [= Shaks. *Sonn.* xciv. 14]. **1597** Middleton *Hist. Chinon* v. F 4, Closelie pent vp in delights, farre more worse vnto her than darke Dungeons. **1602–12**, **1693** [see REMEDY *sb.* 1 b]. **1634** A. Warwick *Spare Min.* I. (ed. 2) 14, I will either make my fortunes good, or bee content they are no worse. **1658** Style *Rep.* 23 Oftentimes dubious words shall be taken in the worse sense. **1685** Dryden *Sylvæ* Pref. a 3, But it will be ask'd why I turn'd him into this luscious English, (for I will not give it a worse word). **1697** —— *Æneis* IV. 526 What have I worse to fear? **1732** Pope *Ep. Bathurst* 319 Which of these is worse, Want with a full, or with an empty purse? **1775** Sheridan *St. Patrick's Day* I. i, I never see her but she puts me in mind of my poor dear wife. *O'Con.* Ay, faith; in my opinion she can't do a worse thing. **1834** Marryat *P. Simple* xxxviii, 'If the weather becomes worse—' 'It can't be worse,' interrupted O'Brien, 'it's impossible to blow harder.' **1835** T. Mitchell *Acharn. of Aristoph.* 584 *note*, This word [λιπαρός] bore two meanings; its better sense implying *brightness* and *splendour*, its worse betokening *fatness* and *grease*. **1840** Dickens *Old C. Shop* vi, Come, you drop that stick or it'll be worse for you. **1870** J. H. Newman *Gram. Assent* II. x. 398 If logic finds fault with it, so much the worse for logic. **1871** Geo. Eliot *Middlemarch* xxv. II. 56 No very good news; but then it might be worse. **1876** Q. Victoria *More Leaves* (1884) 333 The rain continued persistently, having got worse just as the prayer began. **1879** McCarthy *Donna Q.* I. 55 There are worse things to be endured in life than being thought too much of by one's husband. **1881** Miss Braddon *Asphodel* II. 6 If you have not profited by my outlay, so much the worse for you.

† **b.** Harder to deal with, more difficult. *Obs.*

a **1225** *Ancr. R.* 50 Þe blake cloð . . is þiccure aȝein þe wind, & wurse to þurhseon. **1297** R. Glouc. (Rolls) 1114 Vor ȝif hii adde o þing iwonne of castel oþer of toune, Wel þe worse it wolde be to bringe hom þer doune.

c. More unattractive; more unsuitable or unfitting; more faulty, incorrect, ill-conceived, etc.

1640 Hobbes *Hum. Nat.* Ep. Ded. (1650) A 7, For the Stile, it is therefore the worse, because, whilst I was writing, I consulted more with Logick then with Rhetorick. **1666** Earl Orrery *St. Lett.* (1742) 187 The argument was bad, the plot worse, the contempt of authority worst of all. **1741** Ctess. Pomfret in *Ctess. Hartford's Corr.* (1805) III. 85, I . . went to see the palace of prince Giustiniani. In my life I never saw a worse. *a* **1745** Swift *Story Injured Lady* (1746) 2 She has bad Features, and a worse Complexion. **1797** Ht. Lee *Canterb. T.* (1799) I. 338 Nothing makes a man worse company than being in love with his own thoughts. **1841** Spalding *Italy* I. 372 They were much given . . to fixing maximum prices on provisions of every sort, but in respect to corn they did what was even worse. **1841** Dickens *Barn. Rudge* lxv, 'Worse manners', said the hangman, . . 'I never see in this place afore.' **1847** Ruxton *Adv. Mexico* xxxiii. 306 Old manuscripts, written on bad paper, and with worse ink. **1868** A. L. Gordon in Turner & Sutherland *Developm. Austral. Lit.* (1898) 201 Mount . . has a head worse if possible for business than mine.

d. With agent-noun: More unskilful or inefficient; that does the work more badly. Also, more addicted to some (specified) bad habit.

1719 De Foe *Crusoe* I. (Globe) 136 If I was a bad Carpenter, I was a worse Taylor. **1827** Faraday *Chem. Manip.* xvii. (1842) 459 These remarks . . become more applicable, when the substance acted upon is a worse conductor of electricity. **1871** Geo. Eliot *Middlemarch* xxiii. II. 21, I never heard but one worse roarer in my life, and that was a roan. **1898** J. Arch *Story of Life* xii. 281 The more uneducated a man is the worse hand he is at waiting.

e. ***worse and worse***: cf. 1 c.

3. a. Less good, not so good, inferior; of lower quality or value.

Beowulf 1212 Wyrsan wiʒfrecan wæl reafedon æfter guðsceare. *c* **888** Ælfred *Boeth.* xxx. §1 Ic wat . . þæt mæniʒne mon sceamaþ þæt he wiorðe wyrsa þonne his eldran wæron. *c* **1000** *Ags. Gosp.* John ii. 10 Ælc man sylþ ærest god win & þonne hiʒ druncene beoð þæt þe wyrse byð. *c* **1200** *Vices & Virtues* 65 Þe þingð ðat þu naust naht to wurðin . . ane wurse mann ðane ðu art. *c* **1200** Ormin 14064 Siþþenn he biginneþþ To brinngenn forþ summ werrse win, Son summ þe follc iss drunnkenn. *c* **1205** Lay. 383 Heo wes a cheuese, hire cheap wes þe wrse. *a* **1300** *Cursor M.* 38 O gode pertre coms god peres, Wers tre, vers fruit it beres. *c* **1380** Wyclif *Wks.* (1880) 190 And so þei menen þat crist . . nedid alle prestis to leue þe betre and take the worse lif. *c* **1386** Chaucer *Reeve's Prol.* 18 That ilke fruyt [the medlar] is euer leng the wers Til it be roten. **1390** Gower *Conf.* I. 5 Men sein it [the world] is now lassed, In worse plit than it was tho. **1481** *Cely Papers* (Camden) 65, I saw newer Hollendars make whorsse payment in my dayys. **1573–80** Tusser *Husb.* (1878) 35 The soile and the seede, with the sheafe and the purse, the lighter in substance, for profite the wurse. **1594** *Knaresb. Wills* (Surtees) I. 200 My worse cloke. **1597** Hooker *Eccl. Pol.* v. lvii. §1 They which at all times haue opportunitie of vsing the better meane to that purpose, will surely hold the worse in lesse estimation. **1601** Shaks. *Jul. C.* III. i. 139 The Master is a Wise and Valiant Romane, I neuer thought him worse. **1606** —— *Ant. & Cl.* III. ii. 52 He ha's a cloud in 's face. *Eno.* He were the worse for that, were he a Horse. **1615** J. Taylor (Water P.) *Urania* xliii. B 8 b, Worse then the dust, that vnder-foot is trod. **1654** Gayton *Pleas. Notes* I. 2, I attribute this Costivenesse . . to his yeares, being on the worse side of forty. **1759** Brown *Compl. Farmer* 32 Sheep . . should be bought from a worse land to bring on to a better. **1776** Adam Smith *W.N.* IV. viii, Though it is acknowledged, that the commodity of the distant country is of a worse quality than that of the near one. **1770** *Cases temp. Hardwicke* 35 It can never be interpreted, that removing oneself from a worse prison to a better is a surrender of oneself into custody. **1820** Scott *Monast.* Introd. Ep., 'They are prime stanes' . . ; 'warse than the best wad never serve the monks, I'se warrant.' **1894** *Times* 10 July 11/3 [Tennis] Two fine chases—worse than a yard and better than half a yard.

† **b.** Of silver or coin: Of less value *than* (a specified standard). *Obs.*

1488–9, **1676**, **1681** [see STERLING B. 3]. **1549** Latimer *Ploughers* (Arb.) 27 The sayinge is, that since priests haue bene minters, money hath bene wourse then it was before. **1715** in *Lond. Gaz.* No. 5349/3 A certain Person was indicted for selling Silver Wares worse than Sterling. **1716** *Ibid.* No. 5404/4 Silver . . one third Part worse than the said Act directs. **1782** in *Phil. Trans.* (1803) XCIII. 135 The coins were worse than standard.

† **c.** In phrases implying loss or defeat, as ***the worse deal, end, part, side***. *Obs.*

a **900** Cynewulf *Crist* 1225 Ond þær womsceaþan on þone wyrsan dæl fore scyppende scyrede weorþað. *a* **1300** *Cursor M.* 21466 Þan said þat juu, bi sant drightin Mi thinc þe wers part es mine. **1387** Trevisa *Higden* II. 29 Þat ȝere men of þat side schal haue the worse ende and be ouercome. **14..** *Guy Warw.* (Cambr. MS.) 602 Wyth pryde he wolde juste wyth Gye: The worse parte come hym bye. *Ibid.* 3537 Yf he falle on þe warse syde. *a* **1530** J. Heywood *Play of Love* 1258 (Brandl) Then shall I shewe such a thyng in this purs As shortly shall shewe herein your part the wurs. **1583** Golding *Calvin on Deut.* lxxiii. 449/1 He shall obtayne no right in Law. And if he doe, yet shall he haue the worse end of the staffe.

d. ***to be worse than one's word***: to fail to carry out, or act up to, what one has promised.

1672 Wycherley *Love in a Wood* v. v. 89 Will you be worse then your word? **1715** De Foe *Fam. Instruct.* I. viii. (1841) I. 139, I will not be worse than my word to my lady. **1826** Galt *Last of Lairds* xxxix. 352 Mrs. Soorocks was not worse than her word, for [etc.].

e. ***worse half***: used jocularly to match *better half* (see BETTER A. 3 c).

1783 H. Walpole *Let. to Lady Browne* 19 Oct., It is not fit my better-half should be ignorant of the state of her worse-half. **1884** Flor. Marryat *Under Lilies & Roses* iv, The preparations would serve to occupy our time, whilst our worse halves are out shooting.

4. Predicatively (often with *the*: see THE *adv.*). **a.** Of persons: Less fortunate, less well off; in less favourable circumstances or position. Const. *for* (some person or thing that causes deterioration or loss).

a **1122** *O.E. Chron.* an. 1064 (Laud MS.) Swa þet seo scyre & þa oðra scyre þe þær neh sindon wurdon fela wintra þe wyrsan. *a* **1250** *Owl & Night.* 303 Wenestu þat haueck bo þe worse Þoȝ crowe bigrede him bi þe mershe? **1340–70** *Alex. & Dind.* 231 For þe wers is no weih, wis ȝif he seme, Þouh he finde oþur folk folewen his dedus. **1362** Langl. *P. Pl.* A. I. 26 And drink whon þou druiȝest, but do hit not out of Resun, Þat þou worþe þe worse whon þou worche scholdest. *c* **1520** Skelton *Magnyf.* 1761 To make fayre promyse, what are ye the worse? *a* **1542** Sir T. Wyatt *Poems* (1913) I. 150 A diligent knave that pikes his maisters purse May please him so that he withouten mo Executor is, and what is he the wourse? **1595** Shaks. *John* I. i. 183 A foot of Honor better then I was, But many a many foot of Land the worse. **1596** —— *Merch. V.* III. ii. 263 When I told you My state was nothing, I should then haue told you That I was worse then nothing. **1601** —— *Twel. N.* V. i. 30 Thou shalt not be the worse for me, there's gold. **1610** —— *Temp.* II. i. 261 Say, this were death That now hath seiz'd them, why they were no worse Then now they are. **1621** LADY M. WROTH *Urania* I. 1 Miserable Vrania, worse art thou now then these thy Lambs; for they know their dams, while thou dost liue vnknowne of any. *a* **1708** BEVERIDGE *Thes. Theol.* (1711) III. 203 Thou art never the worse, for others being better. **1777** SHERIDAN *Sch. Scand.* III. i, I hadn't the Pleasure of knowing his Distresses till he was some thousands worse than nothing. *a* **1784** JOHNSON in Mrs. Piozzi *Anecd.* (1925) 43 How would the world be worse for it, ..if all your relations were at once spitted like larks, and roasted for Presto's supper? **1840** BARHAM *Ingol. Leg.* Ser. I. *Jackdaw of Rheims*, Nobody seem'd one penny the worse!

b. Less well in health, physical condition, or spirits; less hale or strong.

the worse for (Sc. *of*): overcome or intoxicated by (liquor, drink). Also *transf.*

c **1000** *Ags. Gosp.* Mark v. 26 [Hire] hit naht ne fremode, ac wæs þe wyrse. **1388** WYCLIF *Mark* v. 26 [She] was nothing amendid, but was rather the wors. *c* **1440** *Partonope* 6402 (E.E.T.S.) Forthewyth was broghte hym hys hakeneye, Neyther better ne worse, but in þe same a-Raye As he hym fryste broȝte frome the foreste: He semyd no-þynge a lusty beste. **1508** KENNEDIE *Flyting* 464 And now thy wame is wers than ewir it was. **1540** PALSGR. *Acolastus* IV. vi. V iv b, It liketh me not to remember it .i. I am the worse whan I thynke on it. **1552** HULOET, Warsse to be for age, *vetutesco.* **1594** SHAKS. *Rich. III*, I. iii. 3 Ther's no doubt his Maiesty Will soone recouer his accustom'd health. *Gray.* In that you brooke it ill, it makes him worse. **1597** —— *2 Hen. IV*, II. iv. 113, I am the worse when one sayes, swagger. **1603** DEKKER *Wonderful Year* E 2 b, There was she worse then before. **1776** *Trial of Nundocomar* 23/1 He was at first very ill, then got better; he is now worse. **1837** LOCKHART *Scott* IV. viii. 261 He answered, that he had ridden more than forty [miles], a week before, ..and felt nothing the worse. **1856** MERIVALE *Rom. Emp.* (1871) V. xliii. 196 Germanicus grew rapidly worse. **1861** FLOR. NIGHTINGALE *Nursing* 10, I hope you were not the worse for my visit.

(*b*) **1835** MARRYAT *Jac. Faithf.* i, My mother had retired to her bed a little the worse for liquor. **1871** GEO. ELIOT *Middlemarch* xxxix. II. 316 When a man..has..made himself the worse for liquor, he's done enough mischief for one day. **1881** J. B. GOUGH *Sunlight & Shadow* 266 Who ever saw me the worse for drink? **1885** STEVENSON *Prince Otto* III. ii. 268 To tell you the open truth, your Highness, I was the worse of drink. **1913** *Spect.* 24 May 874/1 A learned judge said of Mr. Gladstone that he was often 'the worse' for flattery.

c. Of things: In less good condition; showing signs of damage, deterioration, or loss of quality. Const. *for* (see 4 a), obs. or dial. *of*.

it would be none the worse for: i.e. it would be all the better for, would be improved by. *colloq.*

c **1290** *St. Dominic* 64 in *S. Eng. Leg.* 279 Þat writ lay longue in þat fuyr, and neuere þe weorse it nas, Ne nouȝt i-wemned of one letter. *c* **1440** *Pallad. on Husb.* XI. 101 Let brede hem [*sc.* olives], lest they hete and be the wers. **1546**, **1706**, **1711** [see WEARING *vbl. sb.*[1] 3]. **1592** SHAKS. *Ven. & Ad.* 207 What were thy lips the worse for one poore kis? **1596** SPENSER *F.Q.* V. xii. 35 Euery matter worse was for her melling. **1753–4** RICHARDSON *Grandison* II. xviii. 129 Sir Charles answered..That he would take a survey of the timber upon his estate, and fell that which would be the worse for standing. **1782** COWPER *John Gilpin* 183 A hat not much the worse for wear. **1824** in *Spirit Public Jrnls.* (1825) 213 His face..rather the worse of the dirt by which it was encased. **1835** DICKENS *Sk. Boz*, *Greenwich Fair*, Blue satin shoes and sandals (a *leetle* the worse for wear). **1839** FR. A. KEMBLE *Resid. Georgia* (1863) 20 Their allowance of rice and Indian meal would not be the worse for such additions. **1883** D. C. MURRAY *Hearts* xvii. (1885) 137 Her finery was naturally all the worse for having been fine. **1911** *Athenæum* 19 Aug. 216/3 We do not know that his book is much the worse for this avowal of purpose. *Mod.* His coat would be none the worse for a good brushing.

d. ***worse and worse***: cf. 1 c, 2 e.

1471 CAXTON *Recuyell* (Sommer) 23 Saturne thus felyng hym in grete sorow & trowble and alwey wors and wors as a fore is sayd. **1553** *Respublica* IV. iii. 1019 Truelie, I fele miselfe hitherto wurse and wurse. **1605** SHAKS. *Macb.* III. iv. 117, I pray you speake not: he growes worse and worse. **1848** THACKERAY *Van. Fair* xiv, 'Well, Jane?' 'Wuss and wuss, Miss B.,' Firkin said, wagging her head. 'Is she not better then?'

5. *Comb.*, as ***worse-natured***, ***-tempered*** adjs.

1648 JENKYN *Blind Guide* Pref. A 3, His being badly nurtur'd formerly, and worse natur'd still. **1659** *Gentl. Calling* 446 These differ from the former..as a worse natured fool from a better. **1747** RICHARDSON *Clarissa* I. ii. 10 My poor sister is not naturally good-humoured... She must therefore have appeared to great disadvantages when she aim'd to be worse-temper'd than ordinary.

B. *absol.* or as *sb.* Chiefly ellipt. or absol. uses, with or without the def. or indef. article.

1. a. A person that is less good, virtuous, kindly, etc. As *pl.*, those that are worse.

c **1175** *Lamb. Hom.* 85 In halie chirche boð betere and wurse. **13..** *Cursor M.* 1057 (Gött.) Caym was þe feindes fode, was neuer wers of moder born. **13..** *E.E. Allit. P.* B. 80 Boþe burnes & burdez, þe better & þe wers, Laþez hem alle luflyly to lenge at my fest. *a* **1529** SKELTON *Agst. Garnesche* iv. 17 Beholde thi selfe, and thou mayst se; Thow xalte beholde no wher a warse. **1579** SPENSER *Sheph. Cal.* Envoy 12 The better please, the worse despise, I aske. nomore. **1601** SHAKS. *Jul. C.* III. ii. 116, I feare there will a worse come in his place. **1606** —— *Ant. & Cl.* I. ii. 68 And let her dye too, and giue him a worse, and let worse follow worse. **1667** MILTON *P.L.* x. 903 He..shall see her gaind By a farr worse. **1823** BYRON *Juan* x. lxvii, That worse than worst of foes, the once ador'd False friend. **1901** *Westm. Gaz.* 6 Nov. 2/4 Fool will take Fool, and Worse take Worse.

†**b.** ***the worse***: the Evil One, the Devil. *Obs.*

c **1200** *Trin. Coll. Hom.* 187 Iob..þe wan wið þe wurse. *Ibid.* 191 Neddre smuhgð diȝeliche. Swo doð þe werse. *c* **1205** LAY. 1140 Temple heo funden þar ane..þe wrse hit hafde to welden. *Ibid.* 11091 Þe wurse [*c* 1275 þe feond] hine luuede. *Ibid.* 29188 Crist seolue he forsoc and to þan wursen he tohc.

c. *sb. pl.* (***one's***) ***worses*** = inferiors. (Nonce-use, after *betters*.)

1873 RUSKIN *Fors Clav.* xxviii. 9 Speaking to you, then, as workers, and of myself as an idler, tell me honestly whether you consider me as addressing my betters or my worses? *Ibid.* 18 The question whether you are the betters or the worses of your masters.

2. a. Something worse; what is more evil, harmful, grievous, unlucky, etc.; a greater degree of badness.

Beowulf 1739 He þæt wyrse ne con. *c* **888** ÆLFRED *Boeth.* x, Hu meaht þu þonne mænan þæt wyrse & þæt laðre nu ðu ðæt leofre hæfst ȝehealden? *a* **900** CYNEWULF *Elene* 1039 He þæt betere ȝeceas..& þam wyrsan wiðsoc. *c* **1205** LAY. 3431 Ich wende swiðe wel to don ac wurse ich habbe vnderfon. *Ibid.* 24822 Ȝif þu swa nult don þu scalt wursen vnderfon. *c* **1330** R. BRUNNE *Chron. Wace* (Rolls) 2432 Alas! he seyde, y hider cam! Fro wycke vntil wors y nam. *c* **1374** CHAUCER *Troylus* III. 1074 Now is wykke i-turned vnto worse. *c* **1500** *Lancelot* 515 Wers than this can nat be said for me. **1581** A. HALL *Iliad* I. 10 This tyrant too, whose senses stil to worse and worse do runne. **1590** SPENSER *F.Q.* II. iii. 46 For feare of worse, that may betide. **1593** SHAKS. *Rich. II*, I. iii. 301 Oh no, the apprehension of the good Giues but the greater feeling to the worse. **1602** —— *Ham.* III. iv. 179 Thus bad begins, and worse remaines behinde. **1606** —— *Tr. & Cr.* III. ii. 79 To feare the worst, oft cures the worse. **1614** BP. HALL *Recoll. Treat.* 974 Weake and base mindes euer incline to the worse. **1667** MILTON *P.L.* IX. 128 Though thereby worse to me redound. *a* **1796** BURNS *Grace bef. Dinner*, And, if it please thee, Heavenly Guide, May never worse be sent. **1812** BYRON *Ch. Har.* I. iv, Worse than adversity the Childe befell. **1824** SCOTT *Redgauntlet* ch. xx, With fair warning not to come back on such an errand, lest worse come of it. **1864** TENNYSON *Enoch Arden* 742 That which he better might have shunn'd, if griefs Like his have worse or better. **1864** G. A. LAWRENCE *Maurice Dering* I. 132 You had better take yourself off peaceably, before worse comes of it. **1869** MORRIS *Earthly Par.* III. 423 (*Lovers of Gudrun*), Ah, farewell, Lest of mine eyes thou shouldst have worse to tell Than now thou hast! **1896** HOUSMAN *Shropshire Lad* xliv, Dust's your wages, son of sorrow, But men may come to worse than dust.

b. ***to do worse***: to behave more wickedly, badly, foolishly, etc.; also, with dative of person or *to*, to deal with or treat (a person) more harshly or unkindly.

Orig. const. with the adv.: see WORSE *adv.* 1, 1 b. In the early examples given here, the inflexion seems to indicate the neut. adj. or quasi-sb., and the word is perh. usually so apprehended in later use. Cf. *do good*, GOOD *sb.* 5 a.

1154 *O.E. Chron.* an. 1137 (Laud MS.) Næure hethen men werse ne diden þan hi diden. *Ibid.* 1140 He..dide þanne wærse þanne he hær sculde. *c* **1200** *Moral Ode* 223 (Trin. MS.) Werse he doð his gode wines þan his fiendes. *c* **1205** LAY. 3496 Nule heo me do na wurse þanne hire lond forwurnen. *Ibid.* 29186 Gurmunddes mon he bicom: ne mihte he na wurse don, for crist seolue he forsoc. *a* **1250** *Owl & Night.* 1408 Hweþer deþ wurse, flesch þe gost? *c* **1330** R. BRUNNE *Chron. Wace* (Rolls) 8696 Syn þey had mercy & pyte, Wirse þan þey schul nought do we. *c* **1380** WYCLIF *Sel. Wks.* III. 250 Why schulde noȝt men now reprove popes, ȝif þei don now wersse? *c* **1386** CHAUCER *Squire's T.* 592 Who kan sey bet than he, who kan do werse? **1396** —— *Lenvoy a Bukton* 17 But yet lest thow doo worse, take a wyfe. *c* **1500** MEDWALL *Nature* II. 245 In good fayth syr ye may do wurs. **1535** COVERDALE *Jer.* iii. 5 Thou speakest soch wordes, but thou art euer doinge worse, and worse. **1605** SHAKS. *Macb.* IV. ii. 71 To do worse to you were fell Cruelty.

c. What is less good or precious or valuable. (Cf. WORSE *a.* 3.)

a **1586** SIDNEY *Arcadia* III. Wks. 1922 II. 22 Never after to feede of worse then furmentie. **1596** SHAKS. *Merch. V.* II. vii. 55 Neuer so rich a Iem Was set in worse then gold. **1667** MILTON *P.L.* IX. 102 For what God after better worse would build? **1697** DRYDEN *Virg. Georg.* I. 289 All below, whether by Nature's Curse, Or Fate's Decree, degen'rate still to worse. **1876** GEO. ELIOT *Dan. Der.* lvi, That thorn-pressure which must come with the crowning of the sorrowful Better, suffering because of the Worse.

d. Used as an alternative or addition to an unfavourable epithet or characterization = something worse still. Usually ***or worse***, ***and worse***.

1393 LANGL. *P. Pl.* C. XVIII. 72 Men may lykne letterid men to a lussheborgh, oþer werse. **1513** BRADSHAW *St. Werburge* I. 1011 A vyllayne orels wers sothly thou was borne. **1653** WALTON *Angler* vii. 147, I might say more of this, but it might be thought curiosity or worse. *a* **1734** NORTH *Ld. Kpr. Guilford* (1742) 224 The Man's Wife was his Nurse, or worse. **1851** KINGSLEY *Yeast* xiii, They say, sir, he went up to court, and slandered the nuns there for drunkards and worse. **1898** 'H. S. MERRIMAN' *Roden's Corner* xxv. 269 Everybody knows that it is a disgrace or worse—perhaps a crime.

3. In phrases with a preposition. **a.** ***for better, for worse***, also ***for better or*** (***for***) ***worse***: used where an issue is doubtful or beyond human control.

to put to better and to worse: ? to subject to every kind of luck (quot. *c* 1430).

1390 GOWER *Conf.* II. 24 For bet, for wers, for oght, for noght, Sche passeth nevere fro my thoght. *c* **1430** *Chev. Assigne* 244, I wolle putte my body to better & to worse, To fyȝte for þe qwene. *a* **1500** *Sarum Manuale, In sponsalibus* (Rouen 1501) fo. xlvii, I N. take the N. to my wedded wif to haue and to holde fro this day forward for bettere for wers for richere for pouerer. *a* **1548** HALL *Chron., Hen. VIII* 59 b, And so for better or worse, the Frencheman called the Englisheman knaue and went away with the stockdoues. **1639** J. CLARKE *Parœm.* 122 For better for worse. **1848** DICKENS *Dombey* lix, Mr. Towlinson..informs the kitchen that him and Anne have now resolved to take one another for better for worse. **1871** SMILES *Charac.* i. (1876) 10 Character is undergoing constant change, for better or for worse. **1905** H. W. BOYNTON *Bret Harte* 85 He had also, for better or worse, a decided instinct to invest human nature..with certain attributes of ideal grace.

b. ***for*** (†***to***, †***into***) ***the worse***: chiefly used to indicate the result of a change in condition or quality, fortune, or circumstances.

c **1400** MAUNDEV. (Roxb.) xxiv. 113 Þe iournee chaunged efter to þe werse. **1548** FORREST *Pleas. Poesye* 352 The worlde is chaunged from that it hathe beene, Not to the bettre but to the warsse farre. **1620** [? G. BRYDGES] *Horæ Subs.* 319 Honor nourisheth in light and vain men a wrong opinion of their own worth, and consequently, often changeth their manners into the worse. **1668** DRYDEN *Maiden Q.* III. i, All we have done succeeds still to the worse. *a* **1712** W. KING *Letter* Wks. 1776 III. 272 It is thy curse Ever to change, and ever for the worse. **17..** [BURNS] *Carl, an the king come* ii, I trow we swapped for the warse. **1835** T. MITCHELL *Acharn. of Aristoph.* 263 *note*, The Doric character generally was undergoing a most important change for the worse.

c. ***from bad*** (†***evil***, †***ill***) ***to worse***.

1549 LATIMER *4th Serm. bef. Edw. VI* (Arb.) 121 He by vnrepentaunce fell frome euyll to worse, and frome worse, to worste of all. **1550** LEVER *Serm.* (Arb.) 32 You whych haue gotten these goodes into your own handes, to turne them from euyll to worse. **1562** J. HEYWOOD *Prov. & Epigr.* (1867) 73 Suche driftes draue he, from yll to wars and wars. **1579** SPENSER *Sheph. Cal.* Febr. 12 Must not the world wend in his commun course From good to badd, and from badde to worse, From worse vnto that is worst of all..? **1639** J. TAYLOR (Water P.) *Pt. Summers Travels* 43 You draw us from bad to worse, and from worse to worst. **1649** C. WASE *Sophocles, Electra* 38 See then lest Bad enough to Worse advance. **1667** MILTON *P.L.* XII. 106 Thus will this latter, as the former World, Still tend from bad to worse. **1739–40** RICHARDSON *Pamela* (1740) I. xxvii. 85 How easy it is to go from bad to worse, when once People give way to Vice. **1894** SOMERVILLE & 'ROSS' *Real Charlotte* I. vii. 87 The land went from bad to worse. [**1930** F. A. POTTLE *Stretchers* 64 The weather was warm, and if worse came to worst, we could encamp in our pup tents where we were.] **1961** NEW ENG. BIBLE *2 Tim.* iii. 13 Wicked men and charlatans will make progress from bad to worse.

†**d.** (***to judge***) ***to the worse***: disadvantageously, unfavourably. *Obs.*

1549 COVERDALE *Erasm. Par. Rom.* xiv. 39 Take heede that no man iudge others actes to the worse [*nec alius alium judicet in malum*].

e. (***to differ***) ***for the worse***: to one's disadvantage.

1855 MACAULAY *Hist. Eng.* III. xi. 83 The situation of the Quaker differed from that of other dissenters, and differed for the worse.

4. a. ***the worse***, the losing or less desirable part (in a contest, or the like); disadvantage. Cf. A. 3 c and WORST *sb.* 8. Chiefly in the phrases which follow (b, c, d).

c **1205** LAY. 26594 And ær heo to-tweinden þe wurse wes Rom-leoden. *Ibid.* 26997 Bruttes wokeden þa & heore wes þat wurse. **14..** *Guy Warw.* (Cambr. MS.) 11073 He þoght, þe warse went on hys syde. *a* **1425** *Cursor M.* 7760 (Trin.) Of þis batail þat was so snel þe wors [*Cott.* force, *Gött.* fors] on kyng saul fel. *c* **1489** CAXTON *Sonnes of Aymon* i. 39, I byleue, yf the kynge beseege the castelle that the worsse shalle retourne vnto hym.

b. ***to have the worse***: to be worsted or defeated in a contest. Also *gen.* to have the disadvantage in a comparison with another.

c **1205** LAY. 26712 Þa iwræð sone þat Bruttes hafden þat wurse. *c* **1330** R. BRUNNE *Chron. Wace* (Rolls) 16373 He þat hit gan, þe worse he hadde. **13..** *E.E. Allit. P.* C. 48 Þenne is me lyȝtloker hit lyke & her lotes prayse, Þenne wyþer wyth & be wroth & þe wers haue. *c* **1386** CHAUCER *Knt.'s T.* 490 Yow loueres axe I now this question, Who hath the worse [*v.r.* werse], Arcite or Palamon? **1390** GOWER *Conf.* II. 380 Wicke is to stryve and have the worse. *c* **1450** *Merlin* iii. 56 In that bataile was grete mortalite on bothe parties, but the hethen peple hadde moche the werse. **1470–85** MALORY *Arthur* VII. xxx. 261 Sir Gawayne and syr Trystram mette, and there syr Gawayne had the werse. **1567** PAINTER *Pal. Pleas.* II. xxx. 352 b, In the end, the Salimbenes had the worsse [in a skirmish with the Montanines]. **1590** SPENSER *F.Q.* II. v. 15 Was neuer man, who most conquestes atchieu'd, But sometimes had the worse, and lost by warre. **1860** EMILY EDEN *Semi-attached Couple* iv, Perhaps the instinct that always leads a man to foresee when an impending explanation is not likely to end in his favour, prompted him to divine that he should have the worse of this. **1888** OMAN *Hist. Greece* xv. (1901) 142 A running fight ensued, in which the invaders had greatly the worse.

†**c.** ***to go*** (***away***) ***with***, ***to go*** (or ***come***) ***to***, ***unto***, ***by the worse***: to be defeated or worsted, fail, miscarry.

(*a*) *c* **1374** CHAUCER *Troylus* IV. 49 The folk of Troye hem seluen so mysledden That with þe worse at nyght homward þey fledden. **1632** HOLLAND *Cyrupædia* I. 12 Went he any time away with the worse? very pleasant he was and laughed at himselfe most of all.

(*b*) **1470–85** MALORY *Arthur* I. ix. 46 Fyghte not with the swerde ye had by myracle, til that ye see ye go vnto the wers. **1532** TINDALE *Exp. v–vii Matt.* vii. (*c* 1550) 87 b, Which handes, if thou for werines once let fal, thou goest to the worse immediatly. **1591** SAVILE *Tacitus, Hist.* II. xi. 67 In those ordinary bickerings..he commonly went to the worse. *Ibid.*, *Agricola* 251 Now sommer and winter alike they went to the worse [*tum aestate atque hieme iuxta pellebantur*]. **1597** BEARD *Theatre God's Judgem.* (1612) 96 As Truth got euer the vpper hand, ..so the brochers and vpholders of falshood came euer to the worse.

(*c*) **1560** DAUS tr. *Sleidane's Comm.* 310 The beginning should procede of you, whiche in the cause are inferiours, and goe by the worse. **1565** GOLDING *Cæsar* I. 23 [c. 31] To whom the Heduanes and their confederates had diuerse tymes gyuen battell: wherin going by the wors, they had receyued great domage. 1641 C. BURGES *Serm.* 5 Nov. 55 Have they not miscarried, and gone by the worse all along? 1641 J. SHUTE *Sarah & Hagar* (1649) 34 Neither let us despair of them, because they have been foiled, that they will still hereafter go by the worse. 1671 MILTON *Samson* 904 In argument with men a woman ever Goes by the worse.

†**d.** ***to put to the*** (or ***one's***) ***worse***: to defeat, worst, discomfit, in a contest or conflict. *Obs.*

1470–85 MALORY *Arthur* x. lviii. 512 He put me to the werse or on foot or on horsbak. *c* 1482 J. KAY tr. *Caoursin's Siege of Rhodes* Ded. in Gibbon's *Crusades*, etc. (1870) 136 But ther [at Rhodes] he was put to hys worse and to shame. 1538 ELYOT *Dict.*, *Pessundo*, to cast vnder foote, to put to the warse. 1568 GRAFTON *Chron.* II. 78 For euer, if they chaunced to skirmishe, the Frenchmen were put vnto the worse. 1584 POWEL *Lloyd's Cambria* 9 When he had by the space of ten yeares warred with diuers Kings, and often put them to the woorse. 1606 G. WOODCOCK *Hist. Ivstine* IV. 22 He was twice put vnto the worse [IV. iv. 9 *duobus proeliis victus*]. 1611 *Bible* 2 Chron. vi. 24 If thy people Israel be put to the worse before the enemy. *a* 1641 BP. MOUNTAGU *Acts & Mon.* (1642) 265 Aretas..took the field againe, but was put to the worse.

†**e.** ***to wring to the worse***: to vex, distress. *Obs.*

1553 ASCHAM *Germany* Wks. (1904) 133 Octauio was euermore wrong to the worse by many and sundry spites.

worse (wɜːs), *v.* *Obs.* exc. in nonce-use. Forms: 1 **wyrsian, wyrsigan,** 2 **wursien,** 3 **wurse(n, wursi, wursin, werse(n,** *Orm.* **werrsenn,** 4 **worsi,** 4, 6–7, 9 **worse.** [OE. *wyrsian*, f. *wyrsa* WORSE *a.* Cf. OFris. *wersia* to resist, withstand, OHG. *wirsôn* (MHG. *wirsen, würsen*) to make worse.]

1. *intr.* To become or grow worse, deteriorate.

c 825 *Vesp. Ps.* xxxvii. 6 Fuladun & wyrsadon [*deteriora verunt*] wundsweðe mine. *c* 1000 ÆLFRIC *Hom.* I. 124 He sceolde beon ascyred fram manna neawiste, gif his hreofla wyrsigende wære. *a* 1023 WULFSTAN *Hom.* xxxiii. (1883) 158 Folclaga wyrsedan ealles to swyðe. *a* 1122 *O.E. Chron.* an. 1085 (Laud MS.) & aa hit wyrsode mid mannan swiðor & swiðor. *c* 1175 *Lamb. Hom.* 47 þa sende me claðes..for to biwinden þe rapes, þet his licome þe feble wes ne sceolde noht wursien. *c* 1205 LAY. 18931 ȝif ich wilne æhte, þenne wursede [*c* 1275 wersede] ich on crafte. *a* 1225 *Ancr. R.* 326 þe wunde þet euer wurseð an hond, & strengre is forte helen. *a* 1240 *Sawles Warde* in *O.E. Hom.* I. 265 Sikere ha beoð.. of þulli blisse, þat hit ne mei neauer mare lutlin ne wursin. 1340 *Ayenb.* 33 Efterward comþ werihede þet makeþ þane man weri and worsi uram daye to daye. 1854 SIR J. D. HOOKER in L. Huxley *Life* (1918) I. 352 Evil as our days are, whether they mended or worsed, it would [etc.].

2. *trans.* To make worse, impair, injure, blemish.

c 1200 ORMIN 11845 To werrsenn & to niþþrenn uss Biforenn Godess ehne. *a* 1225 *Ancr. R.* 428 ȝe muwen muchel þuruh ham beon i-goded, and i-wursed [*MS. T.* wursnet]. *a* 1225 *Leg. Kath.* 2165 þet tet wake ules ne wursi neauer mi mod. *a* 1240 *Ureisun* in *O.E. Hom.* I. 202 Mine sunnen habbeð grimliche iwursed me. *c* 1320 *Cast. Love* 811 Hire holy maidenhod þat neuer for no þing i-worsed nas. *c* 1380 WYCLIF *Sel. Wks.* II. 161 Oþer creaturis ben beterid, and noon ben worsid, bi þis ȝifte. *Ibid.* III. 349 Whan þei maken freris, þat ben worsid bi þis makyng, þei don hem a goostli harm. 1598 R. HAYDOCKE tr. *Lomazzo* To Rdr., Other Translators, who are reputed to haue taken great paines in worsing their authors. 1616 BRETON *Good & Bad* 39 His breeding may eyther better or worse him. 1621 QUARLES *Esther* Wks. (Grosart) II. 52/1 What's good, (like Iron) rusts for want of vse, And what is bad, is worsed with abuse. 1667 MILTON *P.L.* VI. 440 Perhaps more valid Armes,..when next we meet, May serve to better us, and worse our foes. 1867 A. TROLLOPE *Last Chron. Barset* (1869) I. xlii. 446 [Waiter at country inn *loq.*] Them as goes away to better themselves, often worses themselves, as I call it. 1886 *Referee* 21 Feb. 7/4 Instead of bettering it [*sc.* their condition] they have 'worsed' it.

worse (wɜːs), *adv.* Forms: α. 1 **wiers, wirs,** 1–2 **wyrs;** 2–6 **wurs,** 3 **wrs(e,** 3–6 **wurse;** 3–6 **wors,** 3– **worse,** 4 **worsse,** 6 **woorse.** β. 2–6 **wers,** 4–6 **werse,** 5 **werce;** 5–7 **wars,** 5, 8–9 *north.* **warse,** 5–6 **warsse.** [OE. *wyrs, wiers* = OS. *wirs*, OHG. *wirs* (MHG. *wirs, würs*), ON. *verr* (for **wers*; hence WAR *adv.*; SW. *värr*), Goth. *wairs*: see WORSE *a.*] Used as the comparative of the advs. *badly, ill, evil, evilly.*

1. More badly or wickedly; more censurably or foolishly in regard to conduct.

In *do worse*, the word is now perh. usually regarded as the neuter adj. or sb.: see WORSE *sb.* 2 b.

c 897 ÆLFRED *Gregory's Past. C.* xxviii. 189 Ða underðioddan ðæt hie wiers ne don ðonne him man bebeode. *a* 1000 *Sal. & Sat.* 181 Wyrs deð se ðe liehð oððe ðæs soðes ansæceð. *a* 1250 *Owl & Night.* 1416 Such heo mahte beo of golnesse, þat sunegeþ wurse in modinesse. *c* 1315 SHOREHAM III. 221 þou halst wel wors þane masseday þane man myd hys workynge. 1340–70 *Alex. & Dind.* 783 Wers wirchen no folk þan ȝe weiȝes alle. 1362 LANGL. *P. Pl.* A. III. 102 Unwittily, ywys, wrouht hastou ofte, Bote worse wrouhtest þou neuere þen whon þou fals toke. *Ibid.* A. XI. 279 þanne marie þe maudeleyn who miȝte do wers? *c* 1380 WYCLIF *Sel. Wks.* I. 44 But oure Pharisees to dai done wel wers. 1546 J. HEYWOOD *Prov.* I. xi. (1867) 32 We maie doo much ill, er we doo much wars. 1781 COWPER *Table Talk* 518, I judg'd a man of sense could scarce do worse Than caper in the morris-dance of verse.

b. More severely, hardly, harshly, unkindly, or unfavourably.

† *to do* (a person) *worse*, to treat more harshly or severely. Cf. WORSE *sb.* 2 b, and, for the use of the adv., WOE A. 6.

a 1200 *Moral Ode* 236 (Lambeth) Hi hem deð wa inoch.. Nute hi hweþer hom deþ wurs [*Trin. Coll.* doð wers]. *c* 1200 *Vices & Virtues* 57 Ðeih he betere do ðan an oðer, þeih hweðere he læte wers of him seluen, ðanne he do of oðre. *a* 1250 *Owl & Night.* 793 Telstu bi me þe wrs [*Cott.* wurs] for þan þat ic bute enne craft ne kan? *c* 1400 *26 Pol. Poems* ii. 66 Euel thou spekest, worse dost mene. *c* 1440 *Generydes* 1365 He hym reportid wers thanne euer he ment. 1471 CAXTON *Recuyell* (Sommer) 68 Her sone tytan gouerned hym so malicyously and allewey worse and worse with out ony compassion on the peple. 1535 COVERDALE *Gen.* xix. 9 We will deale worse with the then with them. 1553 *Respublica* 13 But let this be taken no wurse then yt ys mente. 1590 SHAKS. *Mids. N.* III. ii. 45 Now I but chide, but I should vse thee worse. 1598 —— *Merry W.* II. i. 56, I shall thinke the worse of fat men. 1605 —— *Lear* II. ii. 155 My Sister may recieue it much more worsse, To haue her Gentle-man abus'd, assaulted. 1667 in *Extr. St. Papers Friends* Ser. III. (1912) 271 They have used us worse then they did before. 1667 MILTON *P.L.* XII. 484 Will they not deale Wors with his followers then with him they dealt? 1802 WORDSW. *Stanzas Castle Indol.* 33 Some thought far worse of him, and judged him wrong. 1853 DICKENS *Bleak Ho.* xiv, I hope you won't think the worse of me for having made these little appointments at Miss Flite's. 1880 TENNYSON *Columbus* 106 Being but a Genovese, I am handled worse than had I been a Moor. 1881 W. COLLINS *Black Robe* I. 236 You are sure you won't think the worse of me, if I tell it?

c. More carelessly, faultily, unskilfully, imperfectly, etc.

c 1205 LAY. 28560 Mon i þan fihte non þer ne mihte ikenne nenne kempe, no wha dude wurse [*c* 1275 wors], no wha bet. *a* 1225 *Ancr. R.* 208 Oðer ȝif me ȝemeð wurse ei þing ileaned oðer biteih to witene, þen he wene þet hit ouh. *a* 1250 *Owl & Night.* 505 Yet þu singest wrse [*Cott.* worse] þan þe heysuhge. 1377 LANGL. *P. Pl.* B. XVII. 322 It doth hym worse þan his wyf or wete to slepe. *c* 1400 *26 Pol. Poems* ix. 51 Here waȝtes, þat þey waye þe wors. *Ibid.* x. 10 We fareþ as knaue þat takeþ his hyre byfore, Serue his mayster wel þe worse þerfore. 1442 *Rolls of Parlt.* V. 64/1 Your Souldeours .. the wers paied of theire wagees. 1538 STARKEY *England* 99 The ground also wors tyllyd and occupyd. 1546 HEYWOOD *Prov.* I. xi. (1867) 32 Who is wurs shod than the shoemakers wyfe? *Ibid.* 34 At end I might put my winnyng in mine eye, And see neuer the woorse. 1580 SIDNEY in A. Collins *Lett. & Mem.* (1746) I. 285, I would..your Worship would learne a better Hand, you write worse then I, and I write evell enough. 1611 SHAKS. *Wint. T.* IV. i. 30 If euer you haue spent time worse, ere now. 1709 POPE *Ess. Crit.* 35 There are who judge still worse than he can write. 1749 FIELDING *Tom Jones* VIII. vii, I may put all the good I have ever got by you in my eyes, and see never the worse. 1769 ROBERTSON *Chas. V*, III. XI. 368 Raw soldiers, ill-disciplined, and worse commanded. 1821 SOUTHEY *Lett.* (1856) III. 288 The prints are ill drawn and worse executed upon stone. 1849 MACAULAY *Hist. Eng.* I. iii. 394 The English women of that generation were decidedly worse educated than they have been at any other time since the revival of learning.

2. More unfortunately, unluckily, or unhappily. ***worse off***, in worse circumstances, less happily or fortunately situated: see OFF *adv.* 11.

In early use often with impers. vb. and dat. of person, e.g. (*it*) *is, cheves, limps him wors* (cf. WOE A. 3 and *Hêliand* 1347 'wirs is thêm ôðrun'); later, *it is, goes*, etc. *worse with him*.

Prov. ***to go further, and fare worse***: see FURTHER *adv.* 1 a.

c 897 ÆLFRED *Gregory's Past. C.* xxxvi. 247 Ðylæs him ðy wirs sie. *c* 1000 *Ags. Gosp.* John v. 14 Ne synga þu, þe-læs þe þe on sumon þingon wyrs getide. *c* 1100 *O.E. Chron.* an. 994 (MS. F) Ac hi þar..wyrs geferdan þonne hi æfre wendan. *c* 1205 LAY. 3453 Wel oft wes Leir wa and neuer wurs þanne þa. *a* 1250 *Owl & Night.* 34 Me is þe wurs þat ich þe iseo. *c* 1275 *Vox & Wolf* 202 in *Rel. Ant.* II. 276 Therfore ich fare the wors. *a* 1300 *K. Horn* 116 Ofte hadde horn beo wo Ac neure wurs þan him was þo. *a* 1300 *Cursor M.* 26784 And worthes þam wel wers þan ar, And quilum bettis neuer mare. *c* 1325 *Sir Orfeo* 98 (Sisam) When Orfeo herd þat tiding, Neuer him nas wers for no þing. 1377 LANGL. *P. Pl.* B. IX. 143 And alle for her forfadres þei ferden þe worse. *Ibid.* XIV. 226 And if he chyde or chatre, hym chieueth þe worse. *c* 1380 *Sir Ferumb.* 4550 þay awondrede of him ecchon, þat for al þe strokes þat þay gerde on, þat hym nas noȝt þe wers. *c* 1386 CHAUCER *Miller's T.* 547 And Absolon hym fil no bet ne wers. *c* 1400 *Gamelyn* 740 By god, for thi wordes he shal fare the wors. *c* 1400 *Destr. Troy* 5985 The Troiens full tyte were tyruit to ground: Thurghe Achilles chiualry hom cheuyt the worse. *c* 1400 *26 Pol. Poems* xiv. 51 Make oþere folk þe worse to lyue, For synguler profyt þou wolde haue. *c* 1420 *Anturs of Arth.* 615 But him lymped þe worse. *c* 1440 *Alphabet of Tales* 502 'Suster, how is it with the?' And sho ansswerd agayn & said; 'Nevur wars.' *c* 1460 *Towneley Myst.* iii. 191 God spede, dere wife, how fayre ye? *Vxor.* Now, as euer myght I thryfe, the wars I thee see. *c* 1500 *Melusine* xxix. 216 It is now with me wers than euer was. 1525 BP. J. CLERK in Ellis *Orig. Lett.* Ser. II. I. 316 He shall ryght well knowe that he farythe nothyng the wars for the Kynges Highnes and your Grace is recommendation. 1548 HALL *Chron., Hen. V* 67 But this mocion worse succeded then the entreators deuised. 1573–80 TUSSER *Husb.* (1878) 44 But worse shall he speed, that soweth ill seed. 1609 ROWLEY *Search for Money* (Percy) 12 Seeke him and finde him hee must, or it would goe worse with him. 1639 G. PLATTES *Discov. Subterr. Treas.* 21 But the more I tryed the worse I sped. 1667 MILTON *P.L.* II. 996 With ruin upon ruin, rout on rout, Confusion worse confounded. 1832 G. C. LEWIS *Lett.* (1870) 20 On the whole they are rather worse off than the convicts in the hulks. 1847 TENNYSON *Princess* IV. 467 A clamour grew As of a new-world Babel, woman-built, And worse-confounded.

b. ***worse and worse.*** Cf. WORSE *a.* 2 e.

1487 *Cely Papers* (Camden) 159 The exchaunge goyth ever the lenger warsse and wars. 1553 *Respublica* IV. ii. 990 And howe doo youe mend now in your thrifte & your purse? *People.* As zoure ale in sommer, that is still wurse & wurse. 1562 J. HEYWOOD *Prov. & Epigr.* (1867) 105 How dooth your eye syght? woorse and woorse (said he). 1639 J. CLARKE *Parœm.* 83 It mends like soure ale in summer worse and worse.

3. a. As an intensive, with verbs of hurting, harming, vexing, fearing, hating, etc.: More greatly, severely, or intensely; in a greater degree.

1596 SHAKS. *1 Hen. IV*, IV. ii. 21 Such as feare the report of a Caliuer, worse then..a hurt wilde-Ducke. 1599 —— *Much Ado* II. iii. 163 He would but make a sport of it, and torment the poore Lady worse. *a* 1600 DONNE *Sat.* iv. 90 As Itch Scratch'd into smart, and as blunt iron ground Into an edge, hurts worse. 1607 SHAKS. *Cor.* I. viii. 2, I do hate thee Worse then a Promise-breaker. 1613 —— *Hen. VIII* III. ii. 295 Ile startle you Worse then the Sacring Bell. 1667 MILTON *P.L.* II. 293 Such another Field They dreaded worse then Hell. *Ibid.* VI. 607 Back defeated to return They worse abhorr'd. 1676 HOBBES *Iliad* I. 312 Which, angry as he is, will vex him worse. *a* 1796 BURNS *Ep. from Esopus* 65 Thou know'st, the virtues cannot hate thee worse. 1819 KEATS *Cap & Bells* xviii, That fellow's voice, which plagues me worse than any. 1819 SHELLEY *Cenci* V. ii. 110 That stern yet piteous look, those solemn tones, Wound worse than torture.

b. As a diminuent, with verbs of liking, trusting, praising, pleasing, etc.: In a lesser or lower degree, less, less well. Similarly ***worse at ease***, less well at ease.

c 897 ÆLFRED *Gregory's Past. C.* xix. 143 Ðylæs hira lufu aslacige, & he him ðe wirs licige. *a* 1122 *O.E. Chron.* an. 1043 (Laud MS.) Se arcebiscop wende þæt hit sum oðer mann abiddan wolde..þe he his wyrs truwude and uðe. *a* 1300 *Cursor M.* 9035 þe wick er neuer þe worthier, þat man tell quat þe dughti er, Ne þe gode þe wers to prais, Quat-so men o þe wick sais. 1362 LANGL. *P. Pl.* A. III. 168 Nay, lord, quaþ þat ladi, leef him þe worse, Whon ȝe witen witerliche wher þe wrong lihþ. *c* 1530 REDFORD *Wyt & Sci.* 835 (Manly) Ye, and I lyke him never the wurs. 1592 SHAKS. *Ven. & Ad.* 774 Your treatise makes me like you worse and worse. 1600 —— *A.Y.L.* III. ii. 25 The more one sickens, the worse at ease he is. 1607 —— *Cor.* V. ii. 75 The glorious Gods..loue thee no worse then thy old Father Menenius do's. 1607 HARINGTON in *Nugæ Ant.* (1804) II. 250 Even Augustus was the worse beloved for appointing an ill man to his successor.

4. ***worse than*** used before an adj. (sb., vb.) as a form of pejorative comparison. Cf. MORE C. (*adv.*) 5.

13.. *Gosp. Nicod.* 741 (MS. G.) ȝe wers [*v.rr.* wors, wars] þan wode, how dar ȝe negh þis stede? 1588 SHAKS. *Tit. A.* II. iii. 175 Oh keepe me from their worse then killing lust. 1605 —— *Lear* I. ii. 82 Brutish Villaine; worse then brutish. 1607 —— *Timon* III. v. 106 I'm worse then mad. 1671 MILTON *P.R.* III. 419 Besides thir other worse then heathenish crimes. —— *Samson* 893 By worse than hostile deeds. 1799 WORDSW. *Ruth* 164 O Ruth! I have been worse than dead. 1810 —— *Sonn.*, '*Yet, yet, Biscayans*' 3 Else 'twere worse than vain To gather round the bier these festal shows. 1867 A. T. DRANE *Christian Schools* II. vi. 253 Among the scanty relics that escaped the hands of these worse than Vandals. 1867 AUGUSTA WILSON *Vashti* xx, To feed the worse-than-Ugolino hunger of never-satiated scandal and gossip. 1897 *Westm. Gaz.* 18 Jan. 3/2 He deliberately chose to worse than waste his opportunities and his talents.

5. Used parenthetically or conjunctionally to introduce an additional clause or sentence containing a further and stronger instance of action which incurs reprobation. Cf. MORE *adv.* 6.

1784 COWPER *Task* II. 21 Thus man devotes his brother, and destroys; And, worse than all, and most to be deplor'd, ..Chains him, and tasks him, and exacts his sweat With stripes. 1805 WORDSW. *Rob Roy's Grave* 24 They stir us up against our kind; And worse, against ourselves. 1913 G. MURRAY *Euripides* vii. 166 He had denied the gods; worse, he had denounced the doings of the gods as evil. 1926 H. E. ROLLINS *Gorgeous Gallery* p. xvi, Worse still, he has omitted one leaf.

6. *Comb.*, as ***worse-affected, -applied, -armed, -bodied, -born, -calculated, -disposed, -executed, -governed, -ordered*** adjs.; also †**worse-opinionated** *a.*, having a more unfavourable opinion (*of*); †**worse-willing** *a.*, less well-disposed; more unwilling.

1617 MORYSON *Itin.* II. 63 It was apparant that either he was growne weaker in iudgement or *worse affected to the Queenes seruice. 1591 SYLVESTER *Du Bartas* I. ii. 418 Before the rest of my deere Country-men, Of better wit, but *worse-applyed pen. 1829 SCOTT *Anne of G.* xxviii, If the Lord of Hosts should cast the balance in behalf of the fewer numbers and *worse-armed party. 1590 SHAKS. *Com. Err.* IV. ii. 20 Ill fac'd, *worse bodied, shapelesse euery where. 1834 H. LYTTON BULWER *France* I. 92 That 'great manner,' ..by which the old nobility strove to keep up the distinction between themselves and their *worse-born associates. 1817 JAS. MILL *Brit. India* III. VI. i. 50 Parliament was so completely an instrument of bad government, that it was *worse calculated to produce good results than the mere arbitrary will of a King. 1579 T. F. *Newes fr. North* D j b, I am very sure, that many are *wurse disposed, and much more vngodly in high and honorable calling. 1820 *Q. Mus. Mag.* II. 454 Irregular, ill-directed, and *worse-executed rehearsals. 1672 SIR W. TEMPLE *Ess. Govt.* Misc. (1680) 69 Fugitives out of some *worse governed Family. 1642 HEYLIN *Hist. Episc.* II. vi. 436 Confessors..who..having suffered much in testimonie of their perseverance, became the *worse-opinionated of those, who had not beene endued with an equall constancie. *a* 1715 SOUTH *Serm.* IV. 366 An ill-inclined Judgment, and *worse-ordered Morals. 1549 COVERDALE *Erasm. Par.* 1 Cor. ix. 20–3 That..I might, folowing their mindes, allure them either vnto Christ, or at the least, not make them thereunto *worse willing by displeasing their mindes. 1550 SOMERSET tr. *Calvin's Epistle* B ij b, But this muste not astonyshe vs, nor make vs wurse willynge or fearefull. 1584 R. SCOT *Discov. Witchcr.* II. ii. (1886) 15 The people would be woorse willing to accuse them; for feare least they worke revenge upon them.

worsement (ˈwɜːsmənt). [f. WORSE *v.* + -MENT, after *betterment*. Cf. WORSENMENT.] Deterioration and depreciation of real property caused by the action of persons outside without the owner's consent.

1884 LD. SALISBURY in *1st Rept. Royal Commiss. Housing Working Classes* Q. 13690 If you charge for betterment, do not you think you should pay for worsement? **1890** *Pall Mall Gaz.* 18 July 2/2 We doubt whether the abolition of the gates and bars will in fact conduce to the 'worsement' of the squares and streets in question. **1908** ARNOLD-FORSTER in *Mem.* (1910) xxii. 340 That the principle of betterment should only be adopted concurrently with the principle of worsement, or deterioration.

b. *transf.* and *gen.* (nonce-uses).

1893 *Westm. Gaz.* 30 May 1/1 This morning's batch contains 52 pages of 'amendments' (or worsements, ought not Mr. Plunket to call them?) on the Home Rule Bill. **1902** *Ibid.* 17 June 11/1 The 'Worsement' or 'Betterment' of Directors... Do the Directors stand to lose or gain.. by the consolidation of the companies and the enlargement of the capital?

worsen ('wɜːs(ə)n), *v.* [f. WORSE *a.* + -EN[5] 1. Cf. LESSEN *v.*

The word is common in dialect (see *Eng. Dial. Dict.*) and was reintroduced to literature *c* 1800–1830 (by writers like Southey and De Quincey) as a racy vernacular substitute for *deteriorate* and the like.]

1. *trans.* To make worse; to impair, vitiate, cause to deteriorate.

a **1225** [see WORSE *v.* 2]. *c* **1450** *Mirk's Festial* 112 Tymes byn changet, men byn worsont. **1533** tr. *Erasm. Com. Crede* 171 b, Such persons which by crafte done appayre and worsen the commune coyne. **1641** MILTON *Reform.* I. Wks. 1851 III. 10 It is still Episcopacie that.. worsens and sluggs the most learned, and seeming religious of our Ministers. **1644** DIGBY *Nat. Soul* x. §11. 432 A.. state, where she can neyther be bettered, or worsened. *c* **1647** FELTHAM *Resolves* II. xiii. (1661) 205 Life in it self is a Blessing: And it is not worsened by being long. **1670** BROOKS *Wks.* (1867) VI. 239 The righteous are signally sanctified by fiery dispensations, but the wicked are signally worsened by the same dispensations.

1806 W. TAYLOR in *Ann. Rev.* IV. 251 If effeminacy could become the attribute of a whole nation, it would be proper to institute societies for worsening the condition of the poor. **1807** SOUTHEY *Espriella's Lett.* (1808) II. 357 Methodism.. has worsened whatever it has altered. **1816** —— *Ess.* (1832) I. 172 The manufacturer worsened his wares, the landholder increased his rents. **1832** —— *Penins. War* III. 703 Men whose nature, originally bad, had been worsened by their way of life. **1835** CARLYLE in Froude *Life in London* (1884) I. i. 19 To ask able editors to employ you will not improve but worsen matters. **1853** DE QUINCEY *Autobiogr. Sk.* ii. Wks. 1862 XIV. 93 Their case was certainly not worsened by being booked for places in the grave. **1870** MORRIS *Earthly Par.* IV. 40 There sat a woman all alone Whom some ten years would make a crone, Yet would they little worsen her. **1906** *Spectator* 30 June 1043/2 Irrelevance and confusion are worsened, not bettered, when advanced under the cloak of a distinguished reputation.

b. *spec.* To inflict loss upon (a person, locality) in respect of real property (see WORSEMENT).

1894 *Times* 4 Apr. 6/2 Every man who was worsened having to be compensated before he was turned out. **1894** *Daily News* 21 June 2/3 The construction of these thoroughfares had worsened Wardour-street and other streets through diversion of the traffic.

c. To represent (a thing) as worse than it is; to depreciate.

1885 JEAN INGELOW *Perdita* 66, I have worsened life, I have wronged the world. **1885** GLADSTONE in *Times* 28 Apr. 7/4 The policy which is necessary in the existing circumstances, which I shall say nothing to exaggerate or worsen.

d. *refl.* To make oneself worse or (*dial.*) worse off.

1828 CARR *Craven Gloss.* s.v., I will not worsen mysell. **1860** PUSEY *Min. Proph.* 167 Moab and Ammon chose them gods like themselves, and worsened themselves by copying these idols of their sinful nature. **1864** KINGSLEY *Water of Life* (1879) iv. 51 They feel that they have weakened and worsened themselves thereby. **1866** GEO. ELIOT *F. Holt* v, That's how the working men are left to foolish devices, and keep worsening themselves.

2. *intr.* To become worse, deteriorate.

1795 WORDSW. in *Mem.* (1851) I. 86, I am still much engaged with my sick friend; and sorry am I to add that he worsens daily. **1823** DE QUINCEY *The Dice* Wks. 1862 X. 325 Next day Schroll was in a violent fever.... On hearing this report, Schroll rapidly worsened. **1829** SOUTHEY *Sir T. More* (1831) II. 183 It is the nature of man to worsen if he be left to himself. **1839** CARLYLE *Chartism* ii. (1858) 9 If life last longer.. the general condition of the poor must be bettering instead of worsening. **1861** BERESF. HOPE *Engl. Cathedral* v. 184 However the world may mend or worsen. **1880** MISS BROUGHTON *2nd Thoughts* II. III. vi. 226 The weather has again changed and worsened. **1882** MORRIS *Hopes & Fears for Art* iv. 119 Whether the times better or worsen.

Hence '**worsened** *ppl. a.*; '**worsening** *vbl. sb.* and *ppl. a.*

(*a*) **1830** SOUTHEY *Let. to Allan Cunningham* 4 Mar. in *Life* (1850) VI. 89 The portrait.. is a worsened copy of 'Fitzbust the Evangelical'. **1875** A. J. ELLIS tr. *Helmholtz' Sensat. Tone* 783 Skhismic Intonation exaggerates the errors of the Thirds in Bosanquet's, of which it is simply a worsened form. **1888** *Jewish Chron.* 17 Feb. 11/2 Even this worsened condition is disputed by some eminent authorities.

(*b*) **1831** SOUTHEY *Lett.* (1856) IV. 250 To the serious injury of his health, and even to the worsening of his temper. **1837** CARLYLE *Fr. Rev.* II. v. i, Such.. desperate hope that worsening of the bad might the sooner end it and bring back the good. **1876** GEO. ELIOT *Dan. Der.* xix, The ten or twelve years since the parting had been time enough for much worsening. **1887** *Athenæum* 29 Jan. 153/3 The steady worsening of social conditions.

(*c*) **1858** CARLYLE *Fredk. Gt.* IX. x. (1873) III. 173 Does not reach Potsdam till the 14th September, and then in a weak, worsening, and altogether dangerous condition. **1891** G. A. SMITH in *Robert W. Barbour* (1893) 425 A very large number of worsening or desperate cases [of drunkenness].

'**worsen**, dial. or illiterate alteration of WORSE *a.* and *adv.* (? arising from the colloq. *worse'n* = worse than).

1634 HEYWOOD & BROME *Lancash. Witches* v. i. L 1, It stinket.. worsen than ony brimstone. **1854** DICKENS *Hard T.* I. xi, From bad to worse, from worse to worsen. **1854** A. E. BAKER *Northampt. Gloss.* s.v., It's worsen than it was.

worseness ('wɜːsnɪs). [f. WORSE *a.* + -NESS. Cf. WORSERNESS.] The quality or state of being worse or inferior.

c **1380** WYCLIF *Sel. Wks.* I. 187 And siþ þe worsnesse of þing is matere of sorewe, man shulde have more sorewe for synne þan for ony oþer þing. **1845** SIR J. D. HOOKER in L. Huxley *Life* (1918) I. 207 The badness of the specimens, the worseness of the published descriptions. **1871** RUSKIN *Fors Clav.* v. 23 We will have.. no equality..; but recognition of every betterness that we can find, and reprobation of every worseness. **1913** J. HUNTER in L. S. Hunter *Mem.* (1921) 248 He said I was worse than when I came the first time —the worseness due, no doubt, to the strain and worry of last winter.

†**b.** *spec.* Quality below the standard for gold or silver. Cf. WORSE *a.* 3 b and BETTERNESS 1 b.

1782 in *Phil. Trans.* (1803) XCIII. 135 The accuracy of these assays was farther confirmed, by nearly the same average of worseness being found upon more than 170000 guineas.

'**worsenment.** [f. WORSEN *v.* + -MENT.] Occas. used in preference to WORSEMENT as a more analogical form.

1894 *Westm. Gaz.* 26 July 2/1 The word, we suppose, ought to be 'worsenment', for while the verb of better is 'to better', the verb of worse is 'to worsen'. **1905** J. M. ROBERTSON *Chamberlain* ix. 43 Whereafter his worsenment is swift indeed. **1906** *Pall Mall Gaz.* 10 Mar. 2 If 'betterment' is recognised, worsenment should be equally allowed for.

worser ('wɜːsə(r)), *a.* and *adv.* Also 6 wurser, woorser, 9 *vulgar* wusser. [A double comparative, f. WORSE *a.* and *adv.* + -ER[3]. Cf. *lesser.*

The word was common in the 16th–17th c. as a variant of 'worse', in all its applications. In modern use, it is partly a literary survival (esp. in phrases like *the worser part, sort, half*), partly dial. and vulgar.]

A. *adj.* = WORSE *a.*

1495 *Trevisa's Barth. De P.R.* XIX. cvi. ll viij/1 More-thrumbles egges ben lyke to Geys egges but they ben lesser ..and worser of smellynge. **1553** BRENDE tr. *Curtius* VII. 122 b, Fearing the sequel of worser inconueniences. **1553** T. WILSON *Rhet.* (1580) 127 If one should sett Lukes Veluet against Geane Veluette, the Lukes will appeare better, and the Geane will seeme worser. **1559** *Mirr. Mag., Duke of Suffolk* xxiii, To preserve me from a wurser yll. *c* **1566** *Merie Tales of Skelton* in *Wks.* (1843) I. lix, The one woulde call thother Swanborn, the whyche they dyd take for a worser woorde then knaue. **1572** R. T. *Discourse* 40 Vniuster then Pilate, worser then Lucifer. **1573–80** TUSSER *Husb.* (1878) 99 What worser for barlie than wetnes and cold? **1582** T. WATSON *Centurie of Love* xxx. (Arb.) 66 In harder case and worser plight am I. **1583** STUBBES *Anat. Abus.* II. (1882) 33 They are not onely not inferior to any nation in the world in the excesse of apparell, but are farre woorser, if woorser can be. **1591** SHAKS. *1 Hen. VI*, v. iii. 36 Chang'd to a worser shape thou canst not be. **1595** MARKHAM *Trag. Sir R. Grinuile* clxxi, His pure part, from worser parts refind. **1605** *London Prodigal* v. i. 68 (Brooke) Such bad beginnings oft haue worser ends. **1605** ROWLANDS *Hell's broke loose* To Rdr. (Hunterian Club) 7 All composed of the scumbe and waste worser-sort. **1633** FORD *Love's Sacrif.* v. i. K 2, I find she is A diuell, worser then the worst in hell. **1638** CHILLINGW. *Relig. Prot.* I. i. §8. 36 The conclusion alwaies followes the worser part, if there be any worse. *a* **1639** W. WHATELEY *Prototypes* I. iv. (1640) 15 We must speake of Caine, who being the elder brother was yet the worser man. **1643** TRAPP *Comm. Gen.* xxxviii. 26 The worser sort of Papists. **1667** *Termes de la Ley* 352 It is there taken in the worser sense. **1682** NORRIS *Hierocles* 88 Hence 'tis that the worser actions are accompany'd with the worser pleasures. **1713** DERHAM *Phys.-Theol.* III. iv. 83 Our own great infirmities and failings.. deserve a worser place, a more incommodious Habitation. **1742** *Lond. & Country Brewer* I. (ed. 4) 38 The worser earthy Part of the Hop is greatly the Cause of that rough, harsh, unpleasant Taste. **1783** BURNS *Remorse* 9 Or worser far, the pangs of keen Remorse. **1811** SOUTHEY in *Edinb. Ann. Reg.* II. I. 417 Upon the convention of Cintra ministers had chosen the worser part. **1827** [see HALF *sb.* 4 b]. **1829** SOUTHEY *Sir T. More* II. 208 Lawcraft, if not a twin-fiend with Priestcraft, is.. perhaps the worser devil of the two. **1854** S. AUSTIN *Germany* 312 The worser part of the press was timid, venal and obsequious. **1871** M. COLLINS *Inn Str. Meetings* 33 One might imagine it a worser Troy. **1876** FARRAR *Marlb. Serm.* xxvii. 272 He must break, if need be, his old life in two, and fling away the worser half. **1887** MORRIS *Odyss.* XI. 621 For I, e'en I, the bondsman of a worser man was made.

vulgar. **1837** DICKENS *Pickw.* xxii, You might ha' made a worser guess than that, old feller. **1845** DISRAELI *Sybil* III. i, 'It's the butties', said Nixon; 'they're wusser nor tommy.'

b. *absol.* and *ellipt.*

1586 WARNER *Alb. Eng.* I. iv. (1592) 13 He.. setteth Tenedos on fire, whose fearefull flames espide, Gaue Sommons vnto carelesse Troy for worser to prouide. **1587** GOLDING *De Mornay* ii. (1617) 22 [He] shall not bee able to discerne which is the worser. **1622** MABBE tr. *Aleman's Guzman d'Alf.* II. 269 If thou shalt reserue the better for thy selfe, and giue the worser vnto God. **1632** LITHGOW *Trav.* IX. 394 A worser neuer liued. **1635** HAYWARD tr. *Biondi's Banish'd Virg.* 58 If the change chance to be from a bad Prince to a worser. **1660** GAUDEN *God's Gt. Demonstr.* 50 There is no necessity.. to make evil deeds good by doing worser. **1680** W. ALLEN *Peace & Unity* 75 This was no call to the better sort of Christians to separate from the worser. **1840** G. GODWIN *Last Day* i. 5 Fanny, you are a hignorant creature, and Mr. Brisk's a worser. **1887** *Field* 19 Feb. 233/1, I hear it was a toss up which day was the better or 'wusser' of the two.

†**c.** *sb. pl.* (One's) inferiors. *Obs.*

1581 PETTIE tr. *Guazzo's Civ. Conv.* II. (1586) 91 b, They ought to beholde their inferiours with a more gratious eie,.. by meanes whereof they get the good will of their worsers.

B. *adv.* = WORSE *adv.*

1560 PILKINGTON *Expos. Aggeus* C iiii b, And the worser learned be preferred afore the better, to the ministery,.. let not the better disdayn him. **1573–80** TUSSER *Husb.* (1878) 90 There pasture and cattel.. worser do fare. **1584** LYLY *Campaspe* v. i, How like you this? doth he well? *Diog.* The better, the worser. *Ibid.* v. iv. I pray thee, what doost thou think of loue? *Diog.* A little worser then I can of hate. **1602** WARNER *Alb. Eng.* IX. li. 232 But thus do ye, nay worser. **1604** SHAKS. *Oth.* IV. i. 105 How do you Lieutenant? *Cas.* The worser, that you giue me the addition. **1606** —— *Ant. & Cl.* II. v. 90, I cannot hate thee worser then I do, If thou againe say yes. *a* **1625** FLETCHER *Woman's Prize* III. i, 'Twould make his head ake worser than his horns do. **1628** *Mad Pranks Robin Goodfellow* (Percy Soc.) 45 My hostesse asked me how I liked this tale? I said, it was.. good enough to passe time that might be worser spent. **1642** D. ROGERS *Naaman* 435 Where he does well, none does better, but where ill, none worser. **1664** J. WEBB *Stone-Heng* (1725) 21 His Draught.. I am confident you will like the worser, because he likes it so well. **1671** tr. *Palafox's Conq. China* xxiv. 429 The other Chinese Merchants.. were much worser used. **1700** T. BROWN *Amusem. Ser. Com.* 48 Persons ..that have a great deal of Idle Time lying upon their Hands, and can't tell how to employ it worser. **1835** DICKENS *Sk. Boz, Pawnbroker's Shop*, Your poor dear wife as you uses worser nor a dog.

worser ('wɜːsə(r)), *v. rare.* [f. WORSER *a.*, after BETTER *v.*] *trans.* To make worse; *refl.* to impair one's worldly position. Hence '**worsering** *vbl. sb.*

1842 *Collectanea Glocestr.* 283 Worsered, made worse. **1883** *Century Mag.* Oct. 827/2 This, be it for the bettering or the worsering of the type, is to our democratic.. civilization forbidden forever. **1906** *Macm. Mag.* Oct. 914 She says, 'Be going to better myself, Guv'nor.' I says, 'Take care you don't worser yourself.'

worserer ('wɜːsərə(r)), *a.* A further extension (jocular or vulgar) of WORSER *a.*

1752 FOOTE *Taste* I. (1781) 8, I have heard, good Sir, that every Body has a more betterer and more worserer Side of the Face than the other. **1842** *Collectanea Glocestr.* 283 *Worser, worserer*, worse.

'**worserment.** [f. WORSER *a.* or *v.* + -MENT, after *betterment.*] = WORSEMENT.

1890 *Daily News* 10 Feb. 5/5 What, if we may coin so barbarous a term, may be called the avoidance of 'worserment'. **1902** C. G. HARPER *Holyhead Road* I. 93 They received no compensation for this 'worserment' which must have practically ruined many of them.

†'**worserness.** *Obs. nonce-wd.* [f. WORSER *a.* + -NESS. Cf. WORSENESS.] The quality of being 'worser' or inferior.

1602 WARNER *Alb. Eng.* XIII. lxxviii. 322 In Heats and Colds Extremities is Worsernesse in neither: Nor, working in their Seasons, is a Betternesse of Either.

worsest ('wɜːsɪst), *a.* A jocular and dial. refashioning of WORST, as if f. WORSE *a.* + -EST. (See *Eng. Dial. Dict.*)

1838 *Bentley's Misc.* III. 104 But a laughing woman, with two bright eyes, Is the worsest devil of all.

worset(t, worssett, north. ff. WORSTED.

worship ('wɜːʃɪp), *sb.* Forms: α. 1 weorðscipe, -scype, *north.* worðscip, 3 worðscipe, -schipe, -schepe, 4 worþssipe, -schip, wortscip, -schyp; 3 worsipe, 4 -ssipe, 4–6 -schipe (4 -schupe, 5 -schype, whorshype); 4–5 worschepe, -shepe; 4 worchipe, -chepe; 4–5 worschippe (5 -schyppe), 4 -chippe, 5–6 worshyppe, 5–7 -shippe; 4 worscip (-sip), 4–6 worschip (4–5 -schipp, 4 -schyp); 4–5 worchip, -chyp, -chep; 4– worship (6–7 -shipp), 5–6 worshyp (5 -shypp); 6 *Sc.* wourship, 7 woorship; 9 *vulg.* wash-up. β. 1–3 wurð-, wurþscipe (1 -scype), 3 wurð-, wurþschipe, -shipe (*Orm.* wurrþshipe), -sipe, -sype, wurhscipe; 3 wrð-, wrþsipe, wrh-, wrscipe (-sipe), 4 wrshepe, -chepe; 3 wurschipe (*Orm.* wurrshipe), -sipe, 4 -shype, 5 -chipe; 4 wurshippe, 5 -chippe, 6 wushippe; 5 wurschip (-chip, -chyp, -chep), 5–6 wurship. γ. 1 wyrðscipe; (chiefly *north.* and *Sc.*) 4 wirscipe, -schepe, 5 -shipe, -chipe, -chepe, wyr-; 4 wirscippe, 5 -shippe, wyrschyppe, -chippe (vir-, vyrchippe); 4 wirscip(p, -scep(p, 4–6 wirschip (6 -schep, virschip), wirchip, -chep; 5 wir-, wyrship. [OE. *weorðscipe*, later *wurð-*, *wyrð-*, northern *worðscipe*, f. *weorð* WORTH *a.* + *-scipe* -SHIP. The formation is peculiar to English.]

I. 1. a. The condition (in a person) of deserving, or being held in, esteem or repute; honour, distinction, renown; good name, credit. *Obs.* exc. *arch.* (Common down to 16th c.)

c **888** ÆLFRED *Boeth.* xl. §4 Hi wunnon æfter weorðscipe on þisse woulde, & tiolodon goodes hlisan. *c* **950** *Lindisf. Gosp.* John iv. 44 Witȝa on his œðle worðscip ne hæfis. *c* **1000** *Ags. Gosp.* ibid., Nan witeȝa næfð nanne weorðscype on his aȝenum earde. *c* **1205** LAY. 3159 Worðschepe [*c* **1275** worsipe] haue þu. *Ibid.* 3291 Me þuncheð þat mi fæder nis no whit felle, no he wurh-scipe ne can. *a* **1250** *Owl & Night.* 1342 An maide mai luue cheose þat hire wurþschipe ne forleose. *c* **1330** *Arth. & Merl.* 8619 (Kölbing) On him y told hir wele bitowe: So ful y knawe him of worþschipe. *c* **1350** *Will. Palerne* 551 þat were semlyest to seye to saue my worchep. *c* **1386** CHAUCER *Frankl. T.* 83 To seke in Armes worshipe and honour. **1387** TREVISA *Higden* I. 155 To wynne þe maystrie of wommen þou getest but litel worschippe. *c* **1430** *Compleynt* 341 in Lydg. *Temple Glas* 63 Of worshepe, honour & mesure She is the welle. **1425** *Paston Lett.* I. 21 Because ye arn..of worshepe and cunnyng worthyly endowed. **1432** *Ibid.* 35 The said Erle..hath..desired..to kepe his trouthe and worship unblemysshed. **1485** CAXTON *Paris & V.* (1868) 9 Every man dyd hys best to gete worshyp there. **1530** PALSGR. 418/1 If he wyll say it of his worshyp [*sur son honneur*] I dare affyrme it. **1555** *Instit. Gentl.* Prol. *vj b, Thus most men desyre the title of wurship, but fewe doo worke the dedes that vnto worship apperteigne. *c* **1586** C'TESS PEMBROKE *Ps.* cxxx. ii, With thy justice mercy dwelleth, Whereby thy worshipp more excelleth. **1859** TENNYSON *Elaine* 1318 It will be to your worship, as my knight,..To see that she be buried worshipfully.

†**b.** A source or ground of honour or credit (to a person). *Obs.*

a **1240** *Ureisun* in *O.E. Hom.* I. 199 Nis hit ðe no wurðscipe þet þe deouel me to-drawe. *c* **1386** CHAUCER *Melib.* ¶2675 Salomon seith It is a greet worshipe to a man to kepen hym fro noyse and stryf. *c* **1400** *Gamelyn* 185 Moche worship it were..to vs alle Might I þe ram and þe rynge bryngen home to þis halle. *c* **1430** *Syr Gener.* (Roxb.) 7099 Litle worship had it been If ye my ladies clothes hed seen. **1470–85** MALORY *Arthur* IV. xxi. 146 Me semeth hit were your worship to helpe that dolorous knyghte. **1493** *Festivall* (W. de W. 1515) 3 b, The synnes that a man..is shryuen of..shall be moche worshypp to hym. **1535** COVERDALE *Prov.* xix. 22 It is a mans worshipe to do good.

†**c.** One who, or that which, constitutes a source or ground of honour. *Obs.*

c **1410** HOCCLEVE *Mother of God* 23 Thow art ensaumple of chastitee, And of virgynes worsship and honour. **1513** DOUGLAS *Æneis* X. xiv. 73 He bad ga fech Rhebus, hys ryall steyd, Quhilk was hys wirschyp and hys comfort hayll. **1535** COVERDALE *Ps.* iii. 3 But thou (o Lorde) art my defender, my worshipe, and the lifter vp of my heade. **1596** DALRYMPLE tr. *Leslie's Hist. Scot.* I. 345 Wallase, the cheife honour and Wirschep of the Weiris, drew him back to the Scotis partie.

†**d.** *spec.* Worthiness in battle; valour. *Obs.*

a **1300** *Cursor M.* 7022 After þam com Iedeon, þat wirscep in his time had don. **1375** BARBOUR *Bruce* III. 50 And throw his worschip sa wroucht he, That he reskewyt all the flearis. *Ibid.* XV. 154 Bot thar fell fayis sa can assaill, That thar mycht no worschip availl. *c* **1420** WYNTOUN *Cron.* II. xvi. 1521 Hir douchtyr..Tuk vp armys in hir stede, þat worschep pruffit in mony deide.

†**2.** In phrases: **a.** ***to win* (*one's*) *worship***: to gain honour or renown. *Obs.*

c **1200** ORMIN 12373 Forr þurrh þatt tatt teȝȝ wolldenn ba ȝæn Godd wurrshipe winnenn. *a* **1300** *Cursor M.* 2439 He luued hir wil mare þan are, For wirscipp þat sco did him win. **13..** *Guy Warw.* (A.) 818 Who þat þer be of mest miȝt, Grete worþschipe he winneþ. *c* **1350** *Will. Palerne* 618 Nis no man vpon mold þat more worchip winnes. *c* **1400** *26 Pol. Poems* iii. 57 A worþi knyȝt wol worchip wynne. *a* **1450** *Le Morte Arth.* 35 That Auntre shall by-gynne..That knightis shall there worship wynne. **1471** RIPLEY *Comp. Alch.* V. xxviii. in *Ashm.* (1652) 155 But wyll ye here what worshyp and avayle, They wyn in London. *a* **1513** FABYAN *Chron.* (1811) 574 Vpon yᵉ v. day played togyder an Henauder, and a squyre called John Stewarde, whiche daye also the Englyssheman wan yᵉ worshyp. **1572** *Satir. Poems Reform.* xxxvi. 157 Quha vantis be bluid thay all thair worschip wan. **1590** SPENSER *F.Q.* I. i. 3 Vpon a great aduenture he was bond,..To winne him worship. **1598** MARSTON *Sco. Villanie* I. iii. 184 That with industrious paines hath..wonne His true got worship.

†**b.** ***to get*, or *have*, *the worship of***: to gain the honour of overcoming or winning. *Obs.*

1481 CAXTON *Godfrey* lxxii. 116 Bawdwyn, and they that were with hym,..said that they ought to haue the worship of this toun. *a* **1502** ARNOLDE *Chron.* (1811) p. xxxv, A batell in Smytfeld, betwene the Lord Scales and the bastard of Burgoyne, and the Lord Scales had the worship of the felde. *a* **1513** FABYAN *Chron.* (1811) 574 An Englysshe esquyer..gatte suche worshyp of the same Henauder, that the kynge..made hym streyght knyght.

3. a. The condition (in a person) of holding a prominent place or rank; dignity, importance, high standing or degree. Now *arch.*

c **888** ÆLFRED *Boeth.* vii. §3 Swelce þu..sie ðines agnes benumen, ægþer ge þinra welona ge þines weorþscipes. *c* **1030** *Rule St. Benet* (Logeman) 105 Swa hwylcere ylde oððe wurðscipe [L. *dignitatis*] he si. *a* **1154** *O.E. Chron.* (Laud MS.) an. 1132, He com on s' Petres messe dei mid micel wurscipe into the minstre. *a* **1200** *Vices & Virtues* 55 Ðanne hie scolde forliesen ða michele wurðscipe mang ðo aingles. *c* **1205** LAY. 22452 Swa þu scalt wunien in wurðscipe þire. *a* **1225** *Ancr. R.* 278 Al so as prude is wilnunge of wurðschipe, riht al so..edmodnesse is forkesting of wurðschipe. *c* **1330** R. BRUNNE *Chron. Wace* (Rolls) 7099 Constant [a monk] þe coroune tok, &..þus to worschipe gan he lende. **1340** *Ayenb.* 18 Guodes of auenture, ase richesses, worssipe, and heȝnesse. *c* **1380** WYCLIF *Wks.* (1880) 13 For to haue lykynge of mete and drynk and cloþ and worldly worschipe. *c* **1435** *Chron. Lond.* (Kingsford 1905) 42 We pryve hym [Richard II] off alle kyngly dignyte, and worship. **1461** *Paston Lett.* II. 13 Ye ar inbylled to be made knygth at this Coronacion..but and it lyke you to take the worchip uppon you [etc.]. **1483** CAXTON *Golden Leg.* 409/2 There was a clerke moche renomed at rome whiche could not come to the worship that he desyred. **1535** COVERDALE *Job* xiv. 21 Whether his children come to worshipe or no, he can not tell: And yf they be men of lowe degre, he knoweth not. **1549** in Tytler *Eng. under Edw. VI* (1839) I. 219 And we..and others of worship in these countries..do incur by these means much infamy. **1573–80** TUSSER *Husb.* (1878) 208 Yet is it not to be forgot, In Court that some to worship come. **1597** HOOKER *Eccl. Pol.* V. lxxiii. §7 In professing that his intent was to adde by his person honour and worship vnto hers, he tooke her plainly and clearely to wife. **1607** *Stat.* in *Hist. Wakefield Gram. Sch.* (1892) 57 Savinge unto everye man his higher place of worshipp and degree. **1731–8** SWIFT *Polite Conv.* 194 She was as fine as Fi'pence; but truly, I thought there was more Cost than Worship. **1765** FOOTE *Commissary* I. Wks. 1799 II. 8 Indeed you labour..for little or nothing: only victuals and cloaths, more cost than worship. **1814** SCOTT *Lord of Isles* II. vii, Worship and birth to me are known By look, by bearing, and by tone.

†**b.** With *a* and pl.: A distinction or dignity; a position of honour or high place. *Obs.*

1340 *Ayenb.* 75 Al þe blisse of þise wordle him ssolde by drede and wo, rychesses dong, worþssipes uoulhede. **1340** HAMPOLE *Pr. Consc.* 1139 Pride of lyf þat some in hert kepes, Falles to honours and worshepes. **1387** TREVISA *Higden* II. 113 Offa..was wrooþ wiþ men of Caunterbury, and byname hem þat worschippe [*sc.* the archbishopric]. *a* **1395** HYLTON *Scala Perf.* II. xxvii. (W. de W. 1494), He þat hath forsake the loue of the worlde in worshyppes and riches. ?*a* **1400** *Morte Arth.* 22 How they whanne wyth were wyrchippis many. *c* **1400** *Cursor M.* 25368 (Cott. Galba MS.) He þat victori may gete sall be corond [with] wirschippes grete. *c* **1450** tr. *De Imitatione* I. xxiv. 35 If þou haddist lyued unto now in worshipes & lustes of þe worlde. *c* **1491** *Chast. Goddes Chyld.* 69 Riches and worshippes ben but lente to man for a tyme. **1605** SHAKS. *Lear* I. iv. 288 Men..That..in the most exact regard support The worships of their name. **1606** G. WOODCOCK *Hist. Ivstine* III. 19 That it should be lawfull for them..to possesse all their estates and worships whatsoeuer.

†**c.** An alleged name for a company *of* writers.

1486 *Bk. St. Albans* f. vij, A worship of writeris.

4. a. ***man*, *gentleman*,** etc., ***of worship***: a person of repute and standing. Now *arch.*

In quot. 1598 contrasted with *of honour* (= belonging to the nobility).

1340 *Ayenb.* 259 Hit becomþ wel to man of worssipe..þet he by..amesured ine alle his dedes. **1340–70** *Alex. & Dind.* 17 þanne weies of worschipe..Wiþ his lettres he let to þe lud sende. *c* **1386** CHAUCER *Frankl. T.* 234 He..was a man of worshipe and honour. **1463** *Bury Wills* (Camden) 18 With other folkes of wourshippe, preests, and good frendys. **1523** FITZHERB. *Surv.* Prol. b ij, Euery great estate, bothe men & women of worship, that haue great possessyons of landes and tenementes, shulde haue [etc.]. **1556** *Acts Privy Counc. Irel.* (Hist. MSS. Comm.) 21 They..shall examyne hym or them before the nexte gentilman of worshipe. **1577–87** STANYHURST *Descr. Irel.* 39/1 in *Holinshed*, There are besides these noble men, certeine gentlemen of woorship, commonlie called baronets. **1592** CHETTLE *Kind-harts Dr.* To Gentl. Rdrs. 3 Besides, diuers of worship haue reported, his vprightnes of dealing. **1598** STOW *Surv.* 265 In this Cloyster were buried many persons, some of worship, and others of honour. **1618** J. TAYLOR (Water P.) *Pennyles Pilgr.* C 2 b, Kinde Mr. Thomas Banister, the Mayor, Who is of worship and of good Respect. **1655** FULLER *Ch. Hist.* IX. 178 Our Author (though a person of witt and worship) deriveth his intelligence from a French writer disaffected in religion. **1693** CONGREVE *Old Bach.* V. vi, All the World know me to be a Knight, and a Man of Worship. **1820** SCOTT *Monast.* xix, 'This in our presence, and to a man of worship!' said the Abbot. **1837** BARHAM *Ingol. Leg.*, *Leech of Folkestone*, Which [mansion] bespoke the owner a man of worship, and one well to do in the world. **1889** GRETTON *Memory's Harkback* 295 His uncle and his grandfather were both men of worship in my boyish days.

†**b.** So ***of good*, or *great*, *worship***. *Obs.*

1555 J. PROCTOR *Wyat's Rebell.* 6 b, Christopher Roper (a man of good wurshippe, and so estemed of them). *Ibid.* 7 Maister Tucke..& maister Dorrel..gentlemen of good wurshyppe, and Iustices of peace. **1583** STUBBES *Anat. Abus.* I. (1879) 103 One dish or two of good wholsome meate was thought sufficient for a man of great worship to dyne withall. **1592** GREENE *Upst. Courtier* F 2, The other two..seemed meaner then himselfe, but yet Gentlemen of good worship. **1603** G. OWEN *Pembrokeshire* (1892) 12 It hath ben allwaies inhabited with diuerse Knights and gentlemen of greate worshippe.

†**c.** ***place of worship***: a 'good house'. ***town of worship***: an important town. *Obs.*

1484 MARG. PASTON in *P. Lett.* III. 314 Sweche dysports..as sche hadde seyn husyd in places of worschip ther as sche hathe beyn. **1494** in *Househ. Ord.* (1790) 130 The said lordes goeing on foote in everie towne of worshippe.

5. a. With *your* or *his*: A title of honour, used in addressing or speaking of a person of note. In later use *spec.* as the title of a magistrate.

1548 GESTE *Pr. Masse* Ded., I..doo offre yᵉ same..to your worshipful mastership, not that I adiudge it a present, worthy your worship, but that [etc.]. **1557** *Order of Hospitalls* B 6 b, Your worships..were then elected Governours of this said Hospitall. **1570** G. HARVEY *Letter-bk.* (Camden) 1 Your wurship is not ignorant that [etc.]. **1607** SHAKS. *Timon* III. iv. 61 What does his casheer'd Worship mutter? **1631** HEYWOOD *1st Pt. Fair Maid of West* III. i. 28 *Roughm.* Ha, what will you draw? *Clem.* The best wine in the house for your worship. **1693** DRYDEN *Persius* V. 111 Now Marcus Dama is his Worship's Name. **1722** DE FOE *Relig. Courtsh.* I. ii. (1807) 59 Indeed I did not know your worship at first; I am sorry to see you out so late, and 't please your worship, and all alone. **1742** FIELDING *J. Andrews* IV. v, He..arrived when the justice had almost finished his business. He..was acquainted that his worship would wait on him in a moment. **1768** *Complete Letter-Writer* (ed. 12) 45 To P.S. Esq; High Sheriff of the County of Y. *Sir, your Worship.* **1773** GOLDSM. *Stoops to Conq.* IV. i, *Dig.* I have got a letter for your worship. **1797** LAMB *Let. to Coleridge* 10 Jan., Is it a farm you have got? And what does your worship know about farming? **1837** DICKENS *Pickw.* xxv, 'This here's Pickvick, your wash-up,' said Grummer. *Ibid.*, 'Muzzle!' 'Your worship'. 'Open the front door'. 'Yes, your worship.' **1861** AGNES STRICKLAND *Old Friends* Ser. II. 73 For which I humbly hopes your worship will be pleased to send him to Botany Bay. **1861** *Hand-bk. Letter-writing* 63 To his Worship..E. C. Walton, Esq., Mayor of Manchester.

†**b.** Without personal pronoun. *Obs. rare.*

1606 WARNER *Alb. Eng.* XVI. cii. 404 If Variance hapt to fall, They went not to such Worships as like Tyrants men miscall. **1663** BARROW *Serm.* (1687) I. xii. 171 The next in dignity to himself..(Though such an alliance would perhaps be thought derogatory to the Worships of our days).

†**c.** ***my worship***: jocular for 'me', 'myself'. *Obs.*

1601 W. PERCY *Cuckqueanes* III. v. (Roxb.) 39 If I shewe you not such a peice of Hammer-craft,..neuer giue you my worship credit hencefurth. **1668** in *Verney Mem.* (1907) II. 223, I saw 3 good matches at Newmarket which pleased the king well, but not my worshippe, for I gott no money by them. **1728** [DE FOE] *Street-Robberies* 10 My Mother..got a Hand-Basket, into which..she put my Worship. *Ibid.* 26 She let him know that her Husband (meaning my Worship..) was out of town.

†**6.** Of things: Repute, worth, value. *Obs. rare.*

c **1200** *Trin. Coll. Hom.* 29 Wel wurð wunne be of wurðshipe swo hit be. *a* **1300** *Cursor M.* 8259 O wortscip was þis tre to wonder. **1398** TREVISA *Barth. De P.R.* XVI. xcix. (1495) M iiij b/1 Moost worshyp is in whyte glasse [Isidore XVI. xvi. 4 *maximus honor in candido vitro*].

II. †**7. a.** Respect or honour shown to a person or thing. *Obs.*

c **1000** ÆLFRIC *Hept.*, *On Old Test.* (1922) 28 He heold his fæder on fullum wurðscipe þær. *c* **1020** WULFSTAN *Hom.* xxxiii. (1883) 163 Ealne þæne bysmor..we gyldað mid weorðscype þam þe us scendað. *a* **1122** *O.E. Chron.* (Laud MS.) an. 1115, He his onfeng mid mycelan wurðscipe. *c* **1200** ORMIN 3925 Si Drihhtin..Wurrþshipe & loff & wullderr. *c* **1205** LAY. 1211 Ich þe wulle huren mid wrhscipe hæȝan. *a* **1225** *Ancr. R.* 68 Bereð wurðschipe þerto, uor þe holi sacrament þet ȝe iseoð þer þurh. *a* **1300** *Cursor M.* 12092 Til eldrin men wirscip to scau. *c* **1369** CHAUCER *Dethe Blaunche* 1032 That I may of yow here sayne Worshyp or that ye come agayne. **1389** *Eng. Gilds* (1870) 7 To bringe þe body in to þe place þider withe worschepe. *c* **1400** *Rule St. Benet* (Verse) 1950 A souerayn sal ger gestes kepe With honour & with gret wirchepe. *c* **1420** *Pol., Rel. & L. Poems* (1903) 241 He salutyd his moder with gret worchepe. **1422** YONGE tr. *Secreta Secret.* 181 And therfor grete honoure, glorie, and Perpetuel virchippe, is to the Prynce. **1480** *Cely Papers* (Camden) 54, I haue spokyn wᵗ Bongay and he spekys of yow myche whorschype. **1508** DUNBAR *Flyting* 103 Sen thow with wirschep wald sa fane be styld, Haill, souerane senȝeour! **1535** COVERDALE *Apoc. Esther* xiii. ¶2 Thou wotest that I loue not the glory and worshipe of the vnrighteous. **1576** FLEMING *Panopl. Epist.* 117, I pretermitted nothing, which might make for your aduauncement,..in respecte of the worship that might be ministred by wordes. *a* **1604** HANMER *Chron. Ireland* (1633) 70 So that they were then received with all worship.

†**b.** ***in*, *for* or *to* (one's) *worship***: in honour of. Also with dat. *Obs.*

c **1175** *Lamb. Hom.* 5 Heo..nomen þa..blostme and..bistreweden al þane weye him to wurþscipe. *a* **1225** *Ancr. R.* 30 Halewen þet ge luuieð best & mest, in hore wurðchipe siggeð oþer les, oþer mo. *c* **1290** *Magdalena* 338 in *S.E. Leg.* 472 þe Marie heo mauden wardein of heom.., þe swete holie Maudeleyne in cristes wurthschipe, For heo was þe kingue of heouene leof and deore. *a* **1300** *Cursor M.* 111 In hir wirschip wald i bigyn A lastand warc apon to myn. **1338** R. BRUNNE *Chron.* (1810) 17 In stede of kynge's banere he did him bere þe croice, In wirschip of Jhesu. **1387** TREVISA *Higden* I. 93 Medus..cleped þe citee Media also, in worschippe of his moder. **1389** *Eng. Gilds* (1870) 27 A bretherhode þer is ordened of barbres..in þe worschep of god and ys moder. *c* **1430** *Compleynt* 550 in Lydg. *Temple Glas* 66 In hir worshepe & memorye, Was mad a laumpe of this ston. *c* **1450** CAPGRAVE *St. Aug.* Prol. 1 Than wil I..beginne þis werk, to þe worchip of þis glorious doctour. **1465** *Paston Lett.* II. 235, I wold make my doblet all worsted for worship of Norffolk. **1494** *Cov. Leet Bk.* 558 Such Craftes..as bere ȝerely charge in þis Cite to þe worship of the same. **1526** R. WHYTFORD *Martiloge* 51 b, The dedicacyon of a chirche that saynt Bonyface yᵉ pope halowed in the worshyp of our lady & of all martyrs. **1568** GRAFTON *Chron.* II. 125 It is written at the length, and in most shewyng maner, to their honour and worship.

†**c.** ***to do* (one) *worship***: to show honour, pay respect or homage, to. *Obs.*

c **1205** LAY. 9828 Claudien..wes þi cudliche freond, þe dude þe þa wurhscipe. *c* **1250** *Gen. & Ex.* 2757 [Jethro's daughters] gunen him ðore tellen, Hu a ȝunge man..ðewe and wursipe hem dede. *c* **1375** *Cursor M.* 5290 (Fairf.) He has me cast of alle my care, and done me worshepe. **1357** *Lay Folks' Catech.* (T.) 206 Our gastly fadirs..techis us..til ilk man that worshipfull is, for to do worship aftir that it is. **14..** *Sir Beues* (C.) 1222 So moche worschypp he haþ for me ido. *c* **1450** *Life St. Cuthbert* (Surtees) 7090 Kyng william in his ȝere thryd Worschip to Robert comyn did. *c* **1489** CAXTON *Sonnes of Aymon* xiv. 329 Ye have doon to theim soo grete worship. **1526** TINDALE *Titus* ii. 10 That they maye do worshippe to the doctryne off god oure saveoure in all thynges. *a* **1553** UDALL *Royster D.* I. iv, Do your maister worship as ye haue done in time past. **1610** B. JONSON *Alchemist* III. iv, That shirt may doe you More worship then you thinke. [**1871** FREEMAN *Norm. Conq.* xvii. §3 IV. 78 To accompany the King on his voyage or simply to do him worship on his departure.]

†**d.** ***to have*, or *hold*, *in worship***: to hold in honour. *Obs.*

c **1380** WYCLIF *Serm.* Sel. Wks. II. 67 For þe puple hadde Crist in worship as a prophete. **1387** TREVISA *Higden* I. 429 Belles and staues [That] in worschippe men haues. *c* **1400** MAUNDEV. (Roxb.) ix. 34 þai hafe þat place in grete wirschippe. **1450–80** tr. *Secreta Secret.* iii. 6 That his philesofris..be had in worshipe and high recomendacioun. *Ibid.* xviii. 15 And euyrmore loke that thou holde alle thi lordis in gret worshipe as they ben of estate.

8. a. Reverence or veneration paid to a being or power regarded as supernatural or divine; the action or practice of displaying this by appropriate acts, rites, or ceremonies.

place of worship: see PLACE *sb.* 16.

a **1300** *Cursor M.* 5980 þe folk..of egypte..mas to beistes þair wirscipe. *Ibid.* 5985 Thre dais gang..We most weind in to wildirness To mak vr lauerd his wirscip to. *c* **1330** R.

BRUNNE *Chron. Wace* (Rolls) 7362 We [Saxons] haue Godes seeres, ffor whos wyrschip we make auteres. *c* **1350** *Leg. Rood* iii. 63 Oure angels went fra vs oway, Bifor god þaire wirschip to ma. *c* **1400** *Rule St. Benet* 1141 Þarfor þe rowle I wil reherce, How þai sal do wirchep alway, When þai to god sal sing or say. **1450–1530** *Myrr. Our Ladye* II. 208 Whan theyre ioye ys not else but that worshyp and glory be gyuen vnto god. **1550** CROWLEY *Way to Wealth* 215 Doinge them dayly worshipe and reuerence in the temples. **1567** *Gude & Godlie B.* (S.T.S.) 12 Lord, thow will haif.. Wirschip in Spirite and veritie. *Ibid.* 87 Quhilk is the trew wirschip and rychteousnes That God requyris of mankynd. **1596** BARLOW *Three Serm.* i. 3 His presence in that temple so holy, so glorious, and appointed for his woorship. **1641** J. BURROUGHS *Sions Joy* 53 The changers of Gods worship amongst the ten Tribes were wiser. **1644** (*title*) A Directory for The Publique Worship of God, Throughout the Three Kingdoms. **1662** STILLINGFL. *Orig. Sacræ* II. iv. §7 Which Pliny takes notice of as a great part of the Christians worship. **1680** BURNET *Rochester* 53 He believed there should be no other Religious worship, but a general Celebration of that Being in some short Hymn. **1711** STEELE *Spect.* No. 147 ¶4 As the matter of Worship is now managed, in Dissenting Congregations. **1759** ROBERTSON *Hist. Scot.* VII. Wks. 1813 I. 485 In some places scarce as many ministers remained as to perform the duties of religious worship. **1777** *Archaeologia* (1779) V. 197 The Church of Kirkdale was considered in Doomsday-Book as the place of worship belonging to that manor. **1820** HAZLITT *Lect. Dram. Lit.* 20 He redeemed man from the worship of that idol, self. **1838** LYTTON *Leila* I. iv, The attitude that Nature dedicates to the worship of a God. **1876** MOZLEY *Univ. Serm.* vi. 129 To think that we know everything about God is to benumb and deaden worship; but mystical thought quickens worship. **1883** C. D. WARNER *Roundabout Journ.* 45 Protestant worship was forbidden in this region, houses of worship were pulled down, meetings for worship were forbidden.

b. *transf.* Veneration similar to that paid to a deity. *Obs.*

1838 MRS. BROWNING *To Bettine* 3 Upturning worship and delight..To his grand face, as women will. **1851** RUSKIN *Stones Ven.* (1874) I. i. 25 The dying city..obtained wider worship in her decrepitude than in her youth. **1893** *Harper's Mag.* Dec. 13/1 The General Assembly addressed James in terms of worship extraordinary to a republican ear.

9. a. With *a* and pl. A form or type of veneration or adoration; †a single instance or occasion of performing the acts associated with this.

1604 E. G[RIMSTONE] *D' Acosta's Hist. Indies* v. iii. 334 Virachocha, which helde the chiefe place amongst the worships which the Kings Inguas made. **1643** TRAPP *Comm. Gen.* xxxv. 1 The Church, in her Worships, is terrible as an army with banners. **1657** J. WATTS *Scribe*, etc. III. To Rdr. *1 b, This Dipping of two new Sisters in a Pond of the Yard ..being in publick, upon the Lords-day, and betwixt the Morning and Evening Worships, drew away much people thither. **1669** W. PENN in *Extr. St. Papers rel. Friends* III. (1912) 282 The Phar[isees], Esseans, Saduces &c had the free exercise of their destinct worships. **1687** *Proclam.* in *Lond. Gaz.* No. 2221/5 And likewise Indemnifying fully and freely all Quakers, for their Meetings and Worships. **1835** T. MITCHELL *Acharn. of Aristoph.* Introd. p. xii, A faith, which..stood far indeed above the baser worships, which surrounded it. **1845–6** TRENCH *Huls. Lect.* Ser. II. v. 217 Free from the more debasing admixtures of most..worships of heathendom. **1859** I. TAYLOR *Logic in Theol.* etc. 210 Continuing..to dispense the customary gratuities among the ministers of worships, which were still adhered to by large masses of the Roman people. **1906** A. E. WHATHAM in *Amer. Jrnl. Relig. Psychol.* II. 56 Asherah worship was a combination of two separate worships.

b. *poet.* An object of worship. *rare.*

1621 FLETCHER *Isl. Princess* II. vi, By that brightness That gildes the world with light, by all our worships,.. I will not rest.

III. 10. *attrib.* and *Comb.*, as †*worship-deed*, †*-house*, *-music*, *service*, *-song*; *worship-worth*, *-worthy* adjs.; † **worship-willer**, one who desires to be worshipped.

c **1400** *Laud Troy Bk.* 12770 But wold ȝe, lord, do my rede, Ȝe scholde do a worschip-dede. **15..** *Plowman's T.* I. 228 (Urry), Soche worship-willers mote ill fele. **1570–6** LAMBARDE *Peramb. Kent* 364 Then were the wisest of the people woorship woorthie. **1794** in *Jrnl. Friends' Hist. Soc.* (1918) 9 The Castle..with their Worship House adjoining is a fine Object. **1871** FORMAN *Living Poets* 363 This..offers positive existences as worship-worthy in the room of those ideas. **1884** *Chr. World Pulpit* 12 Nov. 309/2 This passage ..indicates..the true nature of worship-song. **1884** PAYNE *1001 Nights* IX. 151 None is worshipworth save God alone. **1919** C. A. HARRIS *Brit. Music* 130 The Fathers of the Genevan School prohibited all worship-music except unisonous psalm-tunes. **1954** *Grove's Dict. Mus.* (ed. 5) VIII. 10/2 In the worship services of those groups among which the urban urge has been less evident, they [*sc.* gospel songs] have been immensely useful now for nearly a century. **1978** R. M. NIXON *Mem.* 538 On our first Sunday in the White House we held the first White House worship service in the East Room.

worship ('wɜːʃɪp), *v.* Forms: α. 4 worþ-, worssipie; 4–5 (6 *Sc.*) worschipe, 4 -schupe, 5–6 -schype (6 -schypen); 4–5 worshipe(n), -sshipe, -shepe(n), 4– shupe; 4–5 worschippe, 5 -shippe, 5–6 -shyppe; 4 worsip, 4–5 (6 *Sc.*) worschip (5 -schyp), 4–6 worshyp, 4– worship; 6 woorship, *Sc.* wourschip; 3–5 worchip (5 -chep, -chyp, -chyppyn), 4–5 worchipe (5 -chepe, -chepyn). β. 3 wurðsupen, wursipe, 5 wurshepe, -schip, -shup, -chippe, -chep, 6 wurship. γ. (Chiefly *north.* and *Sc.*) 4 wyr-, wirschipe, 5 wir-, virschepe; 4 wirsc(h)ippe, 5 -schuppe; 4 wirscip (-scep), 4–5 wirschip (6 -schep, virschip); 5 wirchip(e, -chep, wyrchip. [Early ME. *wurþ-*, *worþscipien*, f. *wurþ-*, *worþscipe* WORSHIP *sb.*]

1. a. *trans.* To honour or revere as a supernatural being or power, or as a holy thing; to regard or approach with veneration; to adore with appropriate acts, rites, or ceremonies.

c **1200** *Trin. Coll. Hom.* 5 We understonden ure louerd on ure eðele bede, and wurðsupen him on ure edie dede. *c* **1275** *XI Pains of Hell* 94 in *O.E. Misc.* 213 Hole cherche is a house of prayere, þe ȝat of heuen crist doþ hit calle, To worchip þer-in our saueour. *a* **1300** *Cursor M.* 1937 Noe.. did to rais an auter suyth; He ȝod to wirscippe godd als wis. *Ibid.* 22292 Þat hali trinite..aght ouer-all wirsceped be. **1340** *Ayenb.* 5 Þou ne sselt habbe god bote me ne worssipie ne serui. *Ibid.* 6 Zuiche byeþ þe ilke þet worssipeþ þe momenes. **1390** GOWER *Conf.* II. 170 The Cronique..Seith that the gentils most of alle Worschipen hire and to hire calle. **1412–20** LYDG. *Chron. Troy* II. 5796 And þei of Lewne worschip Wlcanus, þe god of fyre. **1447** BOKENAM *Seyntys, Marg.* 153 And for she dede wurshepe Crist and loue..Hyr fadyr hyr hatyd. *c* **1489** CAXTON *Sonnes of Aymon* xiv. 315, I come from Ierusalem, where I have worshypd the holy grave. **1529** MORE *Dyaloge* IV. Wks. 253/1 Euery man well woteth how reuerently hym selfe worshypped both our lady and all saintes. **1561** T. NORTON *Calvin's Inst.* I. v. 8 To driue farre away the true God whome we ought to feare and worshyp. **1599** NASHE *Lenten Stuffe* 53 The King was as superstitious in worshipping those miraculous herrings as the fisherman. **1639** J. CLARKE *Parœm.* 12 Men use to worship the rising sunne. **1647** COWLEY *Mistr., Leaving me* 6 They worshipt many a Beast, and many a Stone. **1680** MORDEN *Geog. Rect., Poland* (1685) 74 There is no City in the World where God is Worshipped after so many different Ways, unless in Amsterdam. **1743** J. MORRIS *Serm.* vii. 200 The true God, whom their fathers had worshiped. **1756–7** tr. *Keysler's Trav.* (1760) III. 328 The virgin Mary, with the infant Jesus, and St. Mary Magdalene worshipping him. **1774** GOLDSM. *Nat. Hist.* VII. 191 We may say..that the most frightful of reptiles is worshipped by the most.. barbarous of mankind. **1847** HELPS *Friends in C.* I. vii. 102 Men have worshipped some fantastic being for living alone in a wilderness. **1876** L. STEPHEN *Engl. Th. 18th Cent.* I. v. 293 The God whom Butler worships is, in fact, the human conscience deified.

b. *transf.* To regard with extreme respect or devotion; to 'adore'.

Phr. *to worship the ground* (one) *walks* or *treads on.*

1720 MRS. MANLEY *Power of Love* I. (1741) 126 Why may I not know and worship my Benefactor? **1749** FIELDING *Tom Jones* XI. ii, Men are strangely inclined to worship what they do not understand. **1837** LOCKHART *Scott* IV. ii. 63 Under the shadow of the genius that he had worshipped almost from boyhood. **1848** A. BRONTË *Tenant of Wildfell Hall* II. viii. 147 As to looking askance to another woman —he's safe enough for that..he worships the very ground I tread on. **1849** MACAULAY *Hist. Eng.* vii. II. 258 Lady Churchill was loved and even worshipped by Anne. **1851** KINGSLEY *Yeast* x, She had worshipped intellect, and now it had become her tyrant. **1854** DICKENS *Hard Times* III. iii. 287 There are ladies—born ladies..who next to worship the ground I walk on. **1856** DICKENS, etc. *Wreck Golden Mary* ii. 19, I worshipped the very ground she walked on! **1889** 'J. S. WINTER' *Mrs. Bob* iv, Our mother was the sweetest..of women—Maimie and I worshipped her. **1906** *Lit. World* 15 Nov. 508/2 His wife simply worshipped him.

c. *absol.* To engage in worship; to perform, or take part in, the act of worship.

a **1703** BURKITT *On N.T.* Matt. iv. 9 If to worship before the devil, be to worship the devil, then to worship before the image, is to worship the image. **1824** LAMB *Elia* Ser. II. *Blakesmoor*, I..knew every nook and corner, wondered and worshipped everywhere. **1860** WARTER *Seaboard* II. 462 It distresses me sadly to see the effect of not worshipping where good men of all ages have been used to worship. **1889** 'J. S. WINTER' *Mrs. Bob* ii, Ever since the first day..he had persistently and abjectly worshipped at the shrine of Mrs. Lovelace. **1908** R. BAGOT *A. Cuthbert* vi. 52 The parish church in which the Cuthbert family had worshipped.

†**2. a.** *trans.* To honour; to regard or treat with honour or respect. *Obs.*

c **1250** *Gen. & Ex.* 511 Siðen sal..chirches ben wursiped mor and mor. *a* **1300** *Cursor M.* 6474 Fader and moder þou wirschip ai. *Ibid.* 28141 Ic hafe coueitid in blis to be for-þi þat alle suld wirschippe me. **1338** R. BRUNNE *Chron.* (1810) 163 Richard curteise was,..Forgaf alle þe trespas, wirschipid himself aboue,..Wirschipped him at reson, right as himself was digne. **1362** LANGL. *P. Pl.* A. VII. 94, I wol Worschupe þer-Wiþ Treuþe in my lyue. **1390** GOWER *Conf.* I. 7 The privilege of regalie Was sauf, and al the baronie Worschiped was in his astat. *c* **1440** *Alphabet of Tales* 39 Þai war fayr yong men..and þai war wurshuppid & had in grete dayntie with evure man. *c* **1489** CAXTON *Sonnes of Aymon* xxv. 538 Worship your better, & love your neyghbour. **1530** PALSGR. 784/2, I worshyp a man, *Je honnore*... I have ever worshypped hym for his great vertues. **1561** T. HOBY tr. *Castiglione's Courtyer* III. (1577) Qivb, A womanne knowing hir selfe so muche beloued and worshipped many yeares togither..at length is brought to loue him. **1579** LYLY *Euphues* (Arb.) 120, I..will honour those alwayes that be honest, and worship them..whom I shall know to be worthy in their liuinge.

†**b.** To treat with signs of honour or respect; to salute, bow down to. *Obs.*

1362 LANGL. *P. Pl.* A. XI. 168, I grette þe goode mone as þe gode wyf me tauȝte, And afterward his wyf, I worschupet hem boþe. *c* **1440** *Alphabet of Tales* 62 And þis Putiphar & his wife come & mett hym, and wurschippid hym. *c* **1450** LOVELICH *Grail* lii. 480 Thanne his Meyne Aȝens hym gonne gon, and hym worschepid Everichon. **1523** BERNERS *Froiss.* I. cxlvi. 175 When he had thus sayde, euery man worshypped hym, and dyuers kneled downe at his fete. **1535** COVERDALE *1 Kings* ii. 19 The kynge stode vp, and wente to mete her, and worshipped her. *a* **1591** H. SMITH *Serm.* (1594) 228 If they doe so admire me in silkes, how would they cap me..and worship mee, if I were in veluets? **1737** WHISTON *Josephus, Antiq.* VII. ix. §5 When he had worshipped Absalom, he withal wished that his Kingdom might last a long time.

†**c.** To honour *with* gifts, etc. *Obs.*

1387 TREVISA *Higden* II. 113 Offa..worschipped [L. *insignivit*] Aldulf, bisshop of Lichefeld, wiþ þe archebisshoppes pal. *Ibid.* III. 69 Þe kyng of Babilon worschepede [L. *honoravit*] þis Ezechias wiþ ȝiftes. *c* **1450** *Lay-Folks Mass-Bk., Bidding Prayer* iii. 71 We sal pray specially for all þaes þat wirchips þis kirke owther with buke or bell, uestment or chales. **1475** *Bk. Noblesse* (Roxb.) 84 So that none of us reserve and kepe to his propre use but ringis and uouches for to worship his wiffe and children withalle. **1482** *Monk of Evesham* (Arb.) 87, I suppose..that oure lord dyd worschype hys seruante with seche benefettys to geue other example.

†**3.** To invest with, raise to, honour or repute; to confer honour or dignity upon. *Obs.*

1338 R. BRUNNE *Chron.* (1810) 330 At London is his heued, his quarters ere leued, in Scotland spred, To wirschip þer iles. *c* **1380** WYCLIF *Sel. Wks.* I. 286 Þe manheed of Crist is a margarite þat worshipiþ his Chirche and confortiþ mennis hertis. *a* **1425** tr. *Arderne's Treat. Fistula* 4 The excercyse of bokes worshippeþ a leche. *Ibid.* 38 Sich pronosticacion..shal worshipe þe bisynes of þe leche. *c* **1450** BURGH *Secrees* 2326 Lyke as a Robe fayr of greet Rychesse, Worshippeth the body of a mighty kyng, So fair language Worshippeth a lettir with good endityng. *c* **1530** *Songs, Carols*, etc. (E.E.T.S.) 111 She had a-went, she had worshipped all her kyn. *a* **1591** H. SMITH *Serm.* (1594) 337 He gapes for a phrase that..he may haue one figure more to grace and worship his tale. **1601** A. MUNDAY *Downf. Earl Huntington* I. iii. B 3, You haue dishonoured mee, I worshipt you, You..Unto a Iustice place I did preferre, Where you vniustly haue my tenants rackt.

ˌ**worshipa'bility.** *rare.* [f. next.] Capability of being worshipped.

1812 COLERIDGE *Lit. Rem.* (1836) I. 378, I commend the modern Unitarians for their candour in giving up the possible worshipability of Christ.

worshipable ('wɜːʃɪpəb(ə)l), *a.* [f. WORSHIP *v.* + -ABLE.]

†**1.** Entitled to honour or respect; honourable, worshipful. *Obs.*

c **1407** LYDG. *Reson & Sens.* 3511 Thy disposicion Ordeyned had the table By lyklyhede of high degre And of estate ful worshipable. *c* **1410** —— *Life Our Lady* (MS. Ashm. 39 lf. 94 b), Se howe lowely in a stall or stabill howe that she satte this lady worshipabill. **1426** —— *De Guil. Pilgr.* 7724 A Gorger off Sobyrnesse, The wych Armure ys profytable, To alle folkys worshepable.

2. Capable of being worshipped.

1840 CARLYLE *Heroes* i. (1858) 196 Nature is still divine,.. the Hero is still worshipable. **1857** P. FREEMAN *Princ. Div. Serv.* II. 173 A worshippable Presence of Christ, resulting from their consecration. **1883** *American* VI. 7 Woman's being is to him fairly worshipable.

worshipful ('wɜːʃɪpfʊl), *a.* (*sb.*, *adv.*). Forms: α. 4 worþssipuol; 4 worshup-, 4–5 worschip-, worschep- (4 worschipp-), 5 worchip-, 4– worship-, 5–6 worshypful, *Sc.* wourschip-, 6 woorshipfull, etc. β. 5 wurschip-, -chep-, 5–6 -shipful(l. γ. 5 wir-, wirschip-, etc. [f. WORSHIP *sb.*]

1. Of things: Notable or outstanding in respect of some (good) quality or property; distinguished, imposing; reputable, honourable. Now *arch.*

a **1300** *E.E. Psalter* lxxi. 14 Worschepfulle [L. *præclarum*] þe name of þa Bifore hime it sal be swa. **1340** *Ayenb.* 80 Vor uirtue is þing wel worþssipuol, lostuol and uremuol. **1357** *Lay-Folks Mass-Bk.* App. II. 119, I beleve that the moost worshipful sacrament of the auter is Crystis body in fourme of bred. **1388** WYCLIF *Gen.* xxviii. 17 Hou worschipful [L. *terribilis*] is this place! **1398** TREVISA *Barth. De P.R.* XIV. xliv. (Tollem. MS.) With his comynge þerto oure Lorde made þis Mountt [Tabor] worschipful [L. *commendabilem*]. *c* **1450** *Merlin* v. 85 He..seide that so high and wurschipful a-mendes dide neuer a lorde to his man. *c* **1450** LOVELICH *Merlin* 6815 In the most worschepful and reverent gyse they hym beryeden as they cowde devyse. **1479** *York Memo. Bk.* (Surtees) I. 171 The mare of this said wirshupfull cite for time beyng. **1508** FISHER *7 Penit. Ps.* cii. Wks. (1876) 189 He shall gyue vs power to preche..., whiche shall be a very worshypfull offyce. **1560** PILKINGTON *Expos. Aggeus* (1562) 182 They shall finde mo worshipfull names geven to the preachinge minister, then to any one sorte of men. **1575** LANEHAM *Lett.* (1871) 1, I am placed at Coourt heer (as yee wot) in a woorshipfull room. **1610** HOLLAND *Camden's Brit.* 175 When this right worshipful title [of knighthood] was by the Prince conferred upon one. *a* **1661** FULLER *Worthies, Suff.* (1662) 65 His Posterity still flourish in a Worshipful equipage at Nacton. **1687** *Reflect. on Hind & Panther* 34 No Romance can furnish us with such pleasant and worshipful Tales. **1826** SCOTT *Woodst.* ii, Will he give us the remains of his worshipful and economical house-keeping? **1871** FREEMAN *Norm. Conq.* xxi. IV. 626 Whether standing or sitting, his look was worshipful and kingly. **1876** GEO. ELIOT *Deronda* xxxvii, Isn't that better than painting a piece of staring immodesty and calling it by a worshipful name?

absol. *a* **1871** GROTE *Eth. Fragm.* v. (1876) 176 Aristotle distributes good things into three classes—the admirable or worshipful [τὰ τίμια]—the praiseworthy—the potential.

2. Of persons: Distinguished in respect of character or rank; entitled to honour or respect on this account. Now *arch.*

a **1340** HAMPOLE *Psalter* xxviii. 4 Konynge that makis men worschipful. **1357** *Lay Folks' Catech.* (T.) 205 Ilk man that worshipfull is. **1390** GOWER *Conf.* I. 182 And ek so worschipful a wif, The doughter of an Emperour, To wedde it schal be gret honour. *c* **1420** *Chron. Vilod.* 3147 A worshipfulle woman in þat contre þo dwelt. **1450–80** tr. *Secreta Secret.* lviii. 34 Þus shalt thou be holden wijs and worshipfulle for thi governance. **1470–85** MALORY *Arthur* X. viii. 425 Syr Tristram that is the worshipfullest knyght that now is lyuynge. *Ibid.* XVI. iii. 668 Of a moche more worshypfuller mans hand myghte I not dye. *c* **1530** *Prov.* in *Pol., Rel. & L. Poems* (1903) 58 A nobyll and a wurshipfull hert nevyr askyth of womens dedys. **1555** EDEN *Decades* (Arb.) 272 Wyse & woorshypful men experte in nauigations. **1579** W. WILKINSON *Confut. Fam. Love* To Rdr. ☛ i b, The answere..beyng intercepted by my worshypfull frend, came not into my handes. **1610** HOLLAND *Camden's Brit.* 199 Small townlets..which have given surnames to ancient and worshipfull families. **1632** LITHGOW *Trav.* IX. 396, I encountered with a Worshipfull English Gentleman Mr. Stydolffe Esquier of his Maiesties body. **1655** FULLER *Ch. Hist.* IX. 197 Edwin Sands, Arch-Bishop of Yorke, born in Lancashire of worshipfull Parentage. **1819** MISS MITFORD in L'Estrange *Life* II. 52 Oh! what a delicious painter of mind and body is that worshipful Master Aubrey! **1845** CARLYLE *Cromwell* Let. ccxvii. (1871) IV. 239 If not the noblest and worshipfulest of all Englishmen, at least the strongest and terriblest.

†**b.** Applied to Bede, = VENERABLE *a.* 1. *Obs.*

14.. ? LYDG. *Assembly of Gods* 1583 Behynde all these was worshipfull Beede. *c* **1450** *Compend. Olde Treat.* (Arb.) 175 Worshupfull Bede in his first booke telleth [etc.]. **1483** CAXTON *Golden Leg.* 411/1 He is not called of holy chyrche Saynt bede but worshypful bede.

3. a. As an honorific title for persons or bodies of distinguished rank or importance: formerly used very widely, but now restricted to the livery companies and freemasons' lodges and their masters. ***right worshipful*** is applied to mayors.

1398 *Test. Ebor.* (Surtees) III. 316 Y..by for yow hier, worshepful fader in God, and lord, Richard, by the grace of God erche bysshop of York,..make avowe [etc.]. **1405** *Rolls of Parlt.* III. 605/1 To comune..with the Wyrshipfull Prince Robert the King of Scotland, and his Conseil. **1426** in *Surtees Misc.* (1890) 10 Vnto his wirshipfull Mair,..and all þe wirshipfull Counsell of þe cite of York. **1473** *Rolls of Parlt.* VI. 79/1 The fundation of that worshipfull Fader William Wykeham, sumtyme Bisshop of Wynchestre. **1578** T. NICHOLAS tr. *Cortes' Conq. W. India* (1596) Ep. Ded., Whilest I abode..in the Isle of Palma, in affaires of merchandize for the worshipfull Thomas Lock deceased. **1605** CAMDEN *Rem.* Ded. 1 To the Right Worshipfvll, Worthy and Learned Sir Robert Cotton. **1615** R. COCKS *Diary* (Hakl. Soc.) I. 48 The Worshipfull Companys letters. **1639** J. TAYLOR (Water P.) *Part Summers Trav.* 20 The right worthy worshipfull Knight Sir Paul Neale. **1641** W. S. *More's Edw. V* Ded., To the Right Worshipfull Sir Iohn Lenthall Knight. **1720** A. PETRIE *Rules Deportm.* (1877) 79 The Manner of directing of your Letters... To the Right Worshipful Lady M.S... To the Worshipful Lady A.S. **1732** POPE *Hor. Satires* II. ii. 75 How pale, each Worshipful and Rev'rend guest Rise from a Clergy, or a City feast! **1756** C. LUCAS *Ess. Waters* III. 286, I thanked..his worshipful brethren of the Council. **1768** *Complete Letter-Writer* (ed. 12) 46 To the Master and Wardens of the Worshipful Company of Mercers. **1848** DICKENS *Dombey* lvii, A dusty old beadle..who has something to do with a Worshipful Company who have got a Hall in the next yard. **1849** JAMES *Woodman* ii, Sir Charles Weinants, a right worshipful gentleman also. **1876** *Law Rep. 2 Probate Div.* 382 A certain Cause now pending in our Consistory Court, before the Worshipful Thomas Hutchinson Tristram,..our Vicar General.

b. Used in forms of address, as ***worshipful sir***, (***right***) ***worshipful master***, etc.

1425 *Paston Lett.* I. 19 Right worthy and worshepefull Sir, I recommaunde me to yow, [etc.]. **1440** *Corr.* etc. *Coldingham Priory* (Surtees) 114 Wirshipfull sir I comend me to ȝowe. *c* **1440** MARG. PASTON in *P. Lett.* I. 42 Ryth reverent and worsepful husbon. *c* **1455** BEKYNTON *Corr.* (Rolls) II. 342 [To Henry, Duke of Somerset, begins] High mighti Prince and my right worshipful and good lord. **1473** *Paston Lett.* Suppl. (1901) 144 Ryght wyrshypfull and my ryght tendre modre, I recommaunde me to yow. **1542** UDALL in *Lett. Lit. Men* (Camden) 2 Right worshipfull and my singlar good Maister. *a* **1592** GREENE *Alcida* (1617) Ded. A 3, To the Right Worshipfull, Sir Charles Blount, Knight. *Ibid.*, So (right worshipfull) after your returne from the Low Countries, [etc.]. **1681** OTWAY *Soldier's Fort.* III. i, Her Ladyship, Right-worshipful, is pleas'd not to be at home. **1768** *Complete Letter-Writer* (ed. 12) 48 Justices of the Peace, and Mayors, are stiled Right Worshipful. **1818** SCOTT *Rob Roy* ix, 'Thanks, most worshipful,' returned Miss Vernon. **1843** LYTTON *Last Bar.* I. i, It shall not be my fault if I do not, though but a humble headman to your worshipful Mastership, help to make them so. **1861** *Dict. Daily Wants* s.v. *Addresses*, The Mayors of all Corporations, with the Sheriffs, Aldermen, and Recorder of London, are styled *Right Worshipful*; and the Aldermen and Recorder of other Corporations, as well as Justices of the Peace, *Worshipful*. **1906** *Complete Letter-writer* 21 A Mayor is addressed as The Worshipful the Mayor of—; in a few cities as 'Right Worshipful'.

c. *absol.* (chiefly pl.) or as *sb.* In later use *spec.* a magistrate.

c **1450** *MS. Trin. Coll. Camb. R. 3. 19* lf. 170b, Worshipfull and dyscrete that here present be, I wyll you tell a tale, two or thre. *c* **1460** J. RUSSELL *Bk. Nurture* 655 þan durst y do my devoire with any worshipfulle to be wonnynge. **1536** in *Lett. Suppress. Monasteries* (Camden) 129 As by the reporte of dyvers worshyppfulles..yt ys to us openly declared. **1565** *Child-Marriages* (1897) 49 As he hard it reportid by diuerse worshipfull and others. **1579** W. WILKINSON *Confut. Fam. Love* 30b, Hauyng..deceiued some Justices of Peace, and other worshypfull of countrey, where they dwel. **1595** *Churchw. Acc. St. Marg. Westm.* (Nichols 1797) 24 When the worshipfull of the parish.. went the perambulacion to Kensington. **1806** *Spirit Publ. Jrnls.* X. 213 Anon the day of trial comes, The Worshipfuls were on their bums, And all the court in solemn silence sat.

†**4.** Showing or bringing honour or distinction *to* a person; reputable or honourable *for* one. *Obs.*

c **1380** WYCLIF *Wks.* (1880) 14 And ȝif þei seyn þat grete chirchis ben worschipful to god [etc.]. *c* **1400** *Lanfranc's Cirurg.* 46 þer is no þing more worschipful to a leche..þan to kepe a lyme woundid fro swellynge. **1455** *Rolls of Parlt.* V. 325/1 Craftes which be convenient, wurshipfull and accordyng for Gentil wymmen, and oþer wymmen of wurship. ? **1472** *Paston Lett.* Suppl. (1901) 143 That shuld not be wurchepfull for you; for men shull not than set be you. **1474** CAXTON *Chesse* II. v. (1883) 63 For he had oppynyon that hit was as worshipfull and fittynge to a kynge to pardone as to punysshe.

5. Imbued with the spirit of worship or veneration.

1809 W. TAYLOR in Robberds *Mem.* II. 274, I should have been more humble, panegyrical, worshipful. **1840** *Tait's Mag.* VII. 3 The Whigs..are more worshipful of that perfection of wisdom, the glorious British constitution. *a* **1861** T. WOOLNER *My Beautiful Lady, Night* ix, Or kneels she worshipful beside her bed. **1891** HARDY *Tess* xxxi, He would sometimes catch her large, worshipful eyes..looking at him from their depths.

6. Deserving or capable of being worshipped; worshipable.

1872 BROWNING *Fifine* xxxii, Obey Implicitly, nor pause to question, to survey Even the worshipful! **1901** *Athenæum* 19 Jan. 72/3 The theory of transmigration of ancestral souls into worshipful plants and animals.

†**7.** *adv.* = next. *Obs. rare.*

1470 *Paston Lett.* Suppl. (1901) 135 It is a fowle slaunder that he was so wurchepful beried..and so litill do for hym sithen.

'worshipfully, *adv.* Now *rare.* Forms: α. 4–5 **worschip-**, 5 **worschyppe-**, **worsshep-**, **worshipp-**, 5–6 **worshyp-** (5 **warshyp-**), 6 **worshypp-**, **woorshipfully**, etc.; 4 **worchipfulli**, **worchepefulleke**. β. 4 **wurschyp-**, 5 **wurshepfully**. γ. 4 **wirship-**, **wirshep-**, 4–5 **wirschip-**, 5 **wirchip-**, **wyrschypfully**. [f. prec. + -LY^2.]

†**1.** With due honour; with words, acts, or attentions, expressive of esteem or regard. Now *arch.*

1303 R. BRUNNE *Handl. Synne* 9897 þat y þys wrþy sacrament mowe begynne, And wurschypfully þar-of to speke. **1357** *Lay Folks' Catech.* (T.) 186 That we neuen noght his name but worshipfully. **1389** *Eng. Gilds* (1870) 57 þan xal ilk a broþer..comyn and gon wit þe cors to cherche, worchepefulleke. *c* **1400** LOVE *Bonavent. Mirr.* (1907) 248 Oure lady and hir sustres and Maudeleyn resceyued hem worschipfully with knelynge and lowe bowynge to the erthe. **1447** BOKENAM *Seyntys, Marg.* 872 Fro whens..they come to..a relygyous place..wher wurshepfully Austyn was receyuyd. *c* **1500** *Melusine* i. 10 It is grett shame to me..that I ne doo you to be conueyed worshipfully thrugh my land. **1535** COVERDALE *Ecclus.* xlvii. 10 He ordeyned to kepe the holy daies worshipfully, and that the solempne feastes.. shulde be honorably holden. **1579** TWYNE *Phis. agst. Fortune* II. xliii. 219b, Thou oughtest eyther to speake worshypfully of thy father, or els to holde thy peace. **1859** TENNYSON *Elaine* 1319 It will be to thy worship, as my knight,..To see that she be buried worshipfully. **1872** —— *Gareth & L.* 809.

†**2.** In such a way as to confer honour or dignity, or to make a good appearance. *Obs.*

c **1330** R. BRUNNE *Chron. Wace* (Rolls) 12462 He schulde set hit most worschipfuly, ffor he wolde vrle his pane wyþal. *c* **1350** *Will. Palerne* 5157 God has þe nouȝt for-gete..for worchipfulli artou wedded to welde a kinges sone. *c* **1400** MAUNDEV. (Roxb.) vi. 20 He gers þam be keped honestly and wirschipfully,..þan sall scho be..bawmed and wirschipfuly cledd. **1448** HEN. VI *Will* in Willis & Clark *Cambridge* (1886) I. 378 To thentent that diuine seruice shal mowe be doon therin worshipfully vnto the honour of god. *a* **1450** *Le Morte Arth.* 1117 Worshippffully we shulle hyr lede Into the palys and bery her so. **1535** COVERDALE *Neh.* iii. 20 After him buylded Baruc the sonne of Sabai the other pece worshipfully & costly. **1577** tr. *Bullinger's Decades* (1592) 42 The wisedome of Salomon, is worshipfully thought of throughout the whole compasse of the world. **1606** DEKKER *Seven Deadly Sins* Wks. (Grosart) II. 38 Worshipfully is this Lord of Limbo attended, for Knights themselues follow close at his heeles.

†**3.** So as to obtain or deserve honour or praise; worthily. *Obs.* (or *arch.*)

1439 *E.E. Wills* (1882) 127 If she gouerne hir worshipfully. **1450–80** tr. *Secreta Secret.* iv. 8 If a kyng wolle regne worshipfully, it bihouyth him neyþer to haue..skarste ne fool large. **1470–85** MALORY *Arthur* IV. iv. 123 The thyrd ..is wel to be one of the knyghtes of the round table..for many tymes he hath done ful worshipfully. **1485** *Rolls of Parlt.* VI. 336/1 Charges, which must be kept and borne Worshipfully and Honourably. *a* **1500** *Bale's Chron.* in *Six Town Chron.* (1911) 141 They worshipfully ruled and governed. *a* **1529** SKELTON *Col. Cloute* 914 To take on hande Worsshepfully to withstande Such temporall warre and bate. **1545** in *Cal. St. Papers Irel.* Pref. 6 The said Wyllame fowght stylle manly and worshipfully. *a* **1661** FULLER *Worthies, Berks* (1662) 109 A family of his alliance is still worshipfully extant in this County. **1859** TENNYSON *Elaine* 490 Then Sir Lavaine did well and worshipfully.

†**4.** *Ironically.* Finely, properly. *Obs.*

1532 MORE *Confut. Tindale* III. Wks. 463/2 Is not this conclusion worshipfully deduced vpon scripture?

5. In a spirit of worship.

1886 RUSKIN *Præterita* I. i. 39 Gleaning worshipfully what fragmentary illustrations of the history..of the family might fall from their lips.

worshipfulness ('wɜːʃɪpfʊlnɪs). Also 4 **worschupefulnesse**, 5 **worschipfulnes**, 6 **woorship-**. [f. as prec. + -NESS.] The quality of being worshipful, in various senses.

a **1400** *Minor Poems fr. Vernon MS.* 501/292 Vppon a day for worschupefulnesse þe Pope wolde synge a Messe. **1482** *Monk of Evesham* (Arb.) 82 Y saw al seche [= such] with a special certen worschipfulnes put to ful softe and esy peynys. **1556** J. HEYWOOD *Spider & Fly* xxxix. 16 Honestnes is vertousnes, and woorshipfulnes Due where honestnes, or vertusnes, bearth rout. **1628** FORD *Lover's Mel.* v. i, I owe all Sir-Reuerence to your Right Worshipfulnesse. **1877** BLACKIE *Wise Men* 137 We may not confront the polished and blazoned worshipfulness of the Ten Hundred, with our blank smocks and uncurried roughness. **1887** FLOR. WARDEN *Scheherazade* III. 168 Distant awe and reverent worshipfulness.

†**'worshipfulty.** *Obs.* *nonce-wd.* [f. WORSHIPFUL *a.* + -TY^1.] Worshipfulness; in quot. as a title.

1589 NASHE *Countercuffe* A ij b, To be brefe with your worshipfultie, Pasquill hath posted very dilligently ouer all the Realme.

†**'worshiphead.** *Obs. rare.* In 4 **worþssiphede**. [f. WORSHIP *sb.* + -HEAD.] Dignity, rank.

1340 *Ayenb.* 49 þis zenne anheȝeþ and loȝeþ by the hodes and þe worþssiphede.

worshipless ('wɜːʃɪplɪs), *a.* [See -LESS.]

1. Not practising worship; unworshipping.

1765 J. BROWN *Chr. Jrnl.* 231 What mad-men are these, who thrust themselves..into wicked, worshipless families.

2. Destitute of worship; unworshipped.

1815 BYRON *Hebrew Mel., On Jordan's Banks* 12 How long by tyrants shall thy land be trod? How long thy temple worshipless, Oh God? **1839** BAILEY *Festus* xxxiii. (1848) 356 Who gave their names to stars which still roam round The skies, all worshipless. **1842** *Blackw. Mag.* LII. 455 Long has the god been worshipless!—To prayer! *c* **1914** H. S. HOLLAND in S. Paget *Mem.* (1921) 300 [He felt the Cathedral services] rather limp and worshipless.

†**worshiply**, *a.* *Obs. rare.* In 4 **worþssiplich**. [f. WORSHIP *sb.* + -LY^1.] Honourable.

1340 *Ayenb.* 80 Me can todele þri manere guodes, guod worþssiplich, guod lostuol, and guod uremuol.

†**'worshiply**, *adv.* *Obs.* Forms: α. 4 **worþschiplich(e**, **worschip-**, **worssip-**, **worshepliche**; 4 **worshepeli**, **-ly**, 4 **worschip-**, 5 **worshyp-**, **worshup-**, **worshep-**, 5– **worshiply** (**-lie**, etc.). β. 5 **wurchyply**, 7 **wurshiply**. γ. 4 **wirschiply**, 5 **wyrchiply**. [Irreg. f. WORSHIP *sb.* + -LY^2.]

= WORSHIPFULLY *adv.* (in various senses).

a **1300** *Cursor M.* 27498 Wirschiply, i thanc it þe, þat suilk a simple wroght als me Did be broght vnto preist-hade. **13..** *Guy Warw.* (A.) 131 His lordis honour he held worþschipliche, & defended it wele & hardiliche. *Ibid.* 5040 þan y-herberwed weren he Worþschipliche in þat cite. **1338** R. BRUNNE *Chron.* (1810) 81 To Ʒorke þe[i] com aȝeyn, & wrouht þer worschiply..a Kirk of our Lady. **1340** *Ayenb.* 54 þo þet libbeþ be hyre onestete: þe ilke..libbeþ worssipliche to þe wordle. *c* **1400** *Brut* xxii. 26 þis Belyn duellede þo in pees, and worshepliche him helde amonges his barons. **1459** *Paston Lett.* I. 494 My Lord Chanceler wold that my master schuld be beryed wurchyply. **1475** *Bk. Noblesse* (Roxb.) 69 The whiche king Cirus received the saide Lizander full worshiplie in his palais. *c* **1489** SKELTON *Death Earl Northumbld.* 186 Barons and those knygtes bold..Whom he as lord worshyply mainteyned. **1601** J. DEE *Diary* (Camden) 64 He used me and reported of me very freely and wurshiply.

worshipped ('wɜːʃɪpt), *ppl. a.* [f. WORSHIP *v.*] Regarded with worship; adored, venerated.

1757 DYER *Fleece* II. 361 To Agra, the proud throne Of India's worshipp'd prince, whose lust is law. **1803** VISCT. STRANGFORD *Poems of Camoens* Sonn. xviii. (1810) 104 Dear band, which once adorn'd my worshipp'd fair. **1867** AUG. J. E. WILSON *Vashti* xxviii, Heaven shield you, my worshipped one! **1871** SMILES *Charac.* ii. (1876) 49 The poet himself was..interred beside her worshipped grave.

absol. **1860** *N. Brit. Rev.* XXXII. 141 The Worshipped and the worshipper are there.

worshipper ('wɜːʃɪpə(r)). Also 4 **worschiper**, **wirshiper**, 5 **wor-**, 6 **woorshypper**, 7, 9 **worshiper**. [f. WORSHIP *v.* + -ER^1.]

1. One who worships. Freq. const. *of* (the deity or thing worshipped).

c **1380** WYCLIF *Wks.* (1880) 88 þes wickid ydolatrours, worschiperis of false goddis. **1382** —— *2 Macc.* i. 19 Prestis that thanne weren wirshipers of God. —— *Acts* xvii. 22 Men of Athenis, bi alle thingis I se ȝou as veyn worschiperis. **1526** *Pilgr. Perf.* (W. de W. 1531) 168 God..is a spiryte: and they that be his true worshyppers, must worshyp hym in spiryte. *a* **1533** BERNERS *Gold. Bk. M. Aurel.* (1546) P iij b, He was a greatte louer of his goddis, and woorshypper of theym. **1549** CHEKE *Hurt Sedit.* (1569) M j, Such fansies lighted nowe in Papistes, and irreligious mens heades,..delighteth in true worshippers hurt. **1612** *Two Noble K.* v. i. 41 True worshippers of Mars. **1631** GOUGE *God's Arrows* III. §3. 187 This immortall fewde against worshippers of the true God. **1756–7** tr. *Keysler's Trav.* (1760) I. 58 The ready imitation of his [Odin's] superstitious worshippers. **1794** R. J. SULIVAN *View Nat.* I. 141 Fire, being the purest body in nature, its worshippers supposed that it ought to be honoured with the purest kind of devotion. **1828** SCOTT *F.M. Perth* xxxii, The good father..is..already a worshipper of the Deity whom I have served. **1843** CARLYLE *Past & Pr.* II. iii, All men, especially all women, are born worshipers. **1868** FITZGERALD *Omar* ii, When all the Temple is prepared within, Why lags the drowsy Worshipper outside? **1876** J. PARKER *Paraclete* I. vii. 108 The worshippers of Intellect may not know that they are worshippers of God under another name.

b. One engaged in, or taking part in, divine worship.

1825 SCOTT *Talism.* ix, Did you, or did you not, know any lady amongst that band of worshippers? **1855** MACAULAY *Hist. Eng.* xiii. III. 252 The worshippers were dispersed, beaten, and pelted with snowballs. **1914** J. MACKAY *Ch. Highlands* v. 107 Few worshippers could be got together.

2. *transf.* One who regards a person or thing with feelings akin to worship; a devotee.

1647 COWLEY *Mistr., Her Unbelief* 10 Thou sit'st, and dost not see, nor smell, nor hear Thy constant zealous worshipper. **1694** tr. *Milton's Lett. State* 142 All your

Enterprizes .. in asserting the Liberty of the Gospel and the Worshippers of it. **1788** Crowe *Levesdon Hill* 3 And, vested so, Thou dost appear more gracefully array'd Than Fashion's worshippers. **1792** Almon *Anecd. W. Pitt* I. xx. 331 Notwithstanding the state of modern depravity, Truth will continue to have her worshippers. **1805** Scott *Last Minstrel* v. i, When the Poet dies, Mute Nature mourns her worshipper. **1829** Lytton *Devereux* II. v, A worshipper of the 'Glass of Fashion', rather than of 'the Mould of Form'. **1847** S. Hickson in *Westm. Rev.* XLVII. 60 We can only conclude, worshipper of Shakspere as he is, that he prejudged the question. **1855** Macaulay *Hist. Eng.* xvii. IV. 85 Sarsfield was .. too honourable a gentleman to abuse his immense power over the minds of his worshippers.

worshipping ('wɜːʃɪpɪŋ), *vbl. sb.* [f. WORSHIP *v.* + -ING^1.]

1. The action of offering worship (to a deity).

1303 R. Brunne *Handl. Synne* 9372 But yn alle here moste gladyng, To fals goddys þey made wurschypyng. *c* **1315** Shoreham II. 4 Þou opene myne lyppen, lord, .. And my mouþe .. Schel þyne worschypyng sende. **14..** *Pol., Rel. & L. Poems* (1903) 174 Angels alle in his presence Ar vndyr thyn obedyence, And do the worshippynge! **1450–1530** *Myrr. Our Ladye* II. 195 They felle .. by ydolatrye from the worshypynge of very god. **1526** *Pilgr. Perf.* (W. de W. 1531) 36 The abhominable synne of ydolatry, y^{t} is the worshyppyng of false goddes. **1535** Coverdale *Wisd.* Contents, The worshippinge of ymages. **1585** T. Washington tr. *Nicholay's Voy.* IV. xxxvi. 158 b, [They left] the woorshipping and calling on their false gods. **1623** Cockeram II, A worshipping of Idols, *Idolatrie*. **1851** Mrs. Browning *Casa Guidi Wind.* II. 375 For .. virtue, and God's better worshipping.

b. With *a* and pl. An instance of this; a form or variety of worship.

1450–1530 *Myrr. Our Ladye* II. 197 They .. were wretchedly ledde to the worshypynges of Idols. **1549** Olde *Erasm. Par. Ephes.* Prol. ¶ iij, To walke .. as it were before the porche of the temple, .. to expell and kepe out all false worshyppinges. **1587** Golding *De Mornay* xx. (1617) 348 What are all the worshippings of God which man hath ordained of his owne head, but childish imaginations. **1613** Purchas *Pilgrimage* V. vi. 406 To acknowledge one God, whome varietie of Sects and worshippings should best content. **1674** N. Fairfax *Bulk & Selv.* 193 That the thoughts .. should enkindle in us .. hearty worshippings, of a boundless goodness.

†**2.** The action of honouring, revering, or treating with profound respect. *Obs.*

13.. *Gosp. Nicod.* 993 Haue pese with wirschiping, iosep of Aramathy. *c* **1380** Wyclif *Sel. Wks.* III. 440 Too myche worshypyng of Antecristis lawe. **1423** Jas. I. *Kingis Q.* cxxxix, He that to hir worschipping Myght ought auaile. **1589** Puttenham *Eng. Poesie* I. xiii. (Arb.) 45 Some perchance would thinke that next after the praise and honoring of their gods, should commence the worshippings and praise of good men. **1645** Milton *Tetrach.* 77 For the dignities sake of religion, which cannot be liable to all base affronts, meerely for the worshiping of a civil mariage.

attrib. **1611** Tourneur *Ath. Trag.* I. ii, This worshipping kinde of entertainment is a superstitious vanitie.

'**worshipping**, *ppl. a.* [f. as prec. + -ING^2.] That worships; engaged in worship.

1760–72 H. Brooke *Fool of Qual.* (1809) IV. 116 Then will his cross be exalted for an ensign to the circling, bending, and worshipping universe. **1789–96** Morse *Amer. Geog.* I. 446 In 1738, there were seven worshipping assemblies in this town [Newport]. **1876** Blackie *Lett. to Wife* (1909) 240 Either I must speak the truth and offend the worshipping widow, or print lies and prostitute my own intellect. **1880** 'Mark Twain' *Tramp Abr.* xxxii. 308 She was a brand-new bride, .. happy in herself and her grave and worshipping stripling of a husband.

Hence '**worshippingly** *adv.*, adoringly.

1850 Miss Mulock *Olive* xxiii, Once again I will lie on the floor of the Sistine, and look up worshipingly to Michael the angel. **1891** D. Dormer *Steven Vigil* II. IV. x. 51 Mary's eyes were continually straying across to rest worshippingly on her sister's face.

ˌ**worsifi'cation.** *rare.* [Humorous corruption of *versification*, as if f. WORSE *a.* and -FICATION.]

The composition of bad verses; poor versification.

1849 J. R. Lowell in *Mass. Q. Rev.* Dec. 51 Since we have found fault with some of what we may be allowed to call the worsification, we should say that the prose work is done conscientiously and neatly. **1908** *Let. to F. J. Furnivall* 27 Nov., The worsification of the poetry written in younger days is far more complete and thorough in the Italian and French poets [*sc.* Tasso and Ronsard] than in the English one [*sc.* Langland].

† '**worsing**, *vbl. sb. Obs.* [f. WORSE *v.* + -ING^1.] Deterioration.

c **1575** *Balfour's Practicks* (1754) 195 He .. is haldin to restoir .. the wad [= pledge] to the debtour, without worsing or deterioratioun.

'**worsle**, *v. Sc.* and *north. dial.* Also 6 **worsill.** [var. of WARSLE *v.* Cf. MDu. and Du. *worstelen.*] *intr.* To wrestle. Hence '**worsler**; '**worsling** *vbl. sb.*

1513 Douglas *Æneis* III. iv. 138 Our fallowschip exerce palestrale play, .. Nakit worsling and strougling at nyse poynt. **1535** [see WARSLE *v.* 1]. **1571** *Satir. Poems Reform.* xxviii. 43 Be worsling first in faith the feild was myne. **1573** *Ibid.* xxxix. 350 Then wes he worsland our ane wondie swyre. **1629** Z. Boyd *Last Battell* 12 (Jam.), I cannot expresse what a worsling I finde within mee. *Ibid.* 1073 (Jam.) We shall worsle with God in prayer that your end may be peace. **1828** Carr *Craven Gloss.*, *Worsle*, to wrestle, to contend. *Worsler*, a wrestler. *Worsling*, wrestling.

worst (wɜːst), *a.* and *sb.* Forms: α. 1 **wyrresta, wyrsta, wirresta, wierresta,** (**wyrest**); 1 *Northumb.* **wurresta,** 2–6 **wurst,** 3–4 **wrst;** 3–6 **worste,** 3– **worst,** 6 **woorst,** 9 *vulgar* **wust.** β. 1 **werresta,** 1–2 **wersta,** 2–6 **werst(e,** 3 **wer(r)est,** 4 *Sc.* **verste,** 4, 6 *Sc.* **verst;** 4–6, 8–9 *north.* **warst,** 5–6 **warste.** [OE. *wyrresta, wyrsta, wierresta, werresta, wersta* = OFris. *wersta*, OS. *wirsista*, OHG. *wirsisto, -esto* (MHG. *wirseste, wirste, würste*), ON. and Icel. *verstr* (Norw. *verst*, Sw. *värst*, Da. *værst*):—OTeut. **wersistaz*, f. *wers-*: see WORSE *a.* and -EST.

The β-forms, which were local in OE., were reinforced in Anglian ME. by Scandinavian; cf. WORSE *a.*]

A. *adj.* Used as the superlative of the adjs. *bad*, *evil*, or *ill*.

1. a. Most bad or evil, in regard to moral character or behaviour; most vicious, wicked, cruel, etc.

c **888** Ælfred *Boeth.* xxxix. §11 He ne sceal lufian to unȝemetlice ðas woruldȝesælða, forðæm hie oft cumað to þæm wyrrestum monnum. *c* **897** —— *Gregory's Past. C.* xxi. 153 Ðeseoh ða scande & ða wierrestan ðing ðe ðas menn her doð. *c* **1000** *Ags. Gosp.* Matt. xii. 45 And swa byð þysse wyrrestan cneorysse. *c* **1200** *Vices & Virtues* 77 Gif ðu luuest ðo ilche ðe ðe luuiȝeð: ne don swa ðe werste menn of ðe woreld? *c* **1205** Lay. 29545 Þer he funde þa wurste men þa on londe wuneden. *a* **1225** *Ancr. R.* 82 Idel speche is vuel; ful speche is wurse; attri speche is þe wurste. **1297** R. Glouc. (Rolls) 8616 Þe worste men of þe lond, & mest cruel al so, He wolde make is conseilers. *a* **1300** *K. Horn* 648 Fikenhild, þat was þe wurste moder child. *a* **1310** in Wright *Lyric P.* 99 When y my self have thourh-soht, y knowe me for the wrst of alle. **1340** Hampole *Pr. C.* 4456 Gog and Magog .. þe werst folk þat in þe world duels. **13..** *Gaw. & Gr. Knt.* 2098 Þer wonez a wyȝe in þat waste, þe worst vpon erþe. *c* **1386** Chaucer *Shipman's T.* 161 Myn housbonde is to me the worste man That euere was. —— *Merch. Prol.* 6, I have a wyf, the worste that may be. **1390** Gower *Conf.* I. 145 Pride, Which is the werste vice of alle. *c* **1440** *Alphabet of Tales* 57 He .. went vnto a grete company of thevis; & he, þat was gude emang his brethir, was þer þe warste of all. *c* **1440** *Promp. Parv.* 523/1 Werst, or most badde, *pessimus*. *a* **1500** *Mankind* 297 in *Macro Pl.* 12 He ys worst of þem all. **1552** Huloet, Warste of all, *nequissimus*, *pessimus*. **1598** Shaks. *Merry W.* I. iv. 13 His worst fault is that he is giuen to prayer. **1607** —— *Timon* IV. ii. 39 Strange vnvsuall blood, When mans worst sinne is, He do's too much Good. **1709** Pope *Ess. Crit.* 579 The worst avarice is that of sense. **1737** —— *Hor. Epist.* II. i. 37 Chaucer's worst ribaldry is learn'd by rote. **1790** Burke *Fr. Rev.* 299 It will be impossible to keep the new tribunals clear of the worst spirit of faction. **1829** Lytton *Devereux* I. iii. 11 The worst passions are softened by triumph. **1918** *Cornhill Mag.* June 562 Able editors, who most often quoted what was worst and most Prussian in Carlyle.

b. Qualifying an agent-noun or the like.

c **1000** Ælfric *Hom.* I. 66 Þu ne cuðest ðone soðan freond; and for ði þu beurne on ðone wyrstan feond. *c* **1380** Wyclif *Sel. Wks.* I. 140 Homely enemyes ben þe worste. **1382** —— *Ephes.* vi. 16 The firy dartis of the worste enmye [*tela nequissimi ignea*]. **1435** Misyn *Fire of Love* 62 Þe fowlest worme, þe warst synner, þe lawest of men. **1675** Dryden *Aurengz.* I. (1676) 13 And yet believe your self, your own worst Foe. **1840** Dickens *Old C. Shop* lvi, My worst enemies .. never accused me of being meek. **1854** J. S. Mill *Lett.* (1910) II. App. A. 371 His worst flatterer is himself. **1862** H. Kingsley *Ravenshoe* xx, Lord Welter's worst enemies could not accuse him of driving slow. **1872** Morley *Voltaire* (1886) 12 The man of the world, that worst enemy of the world.

2. a. Most grievous, painful, unlucky, uncomfortable, unpleasant, unfavourable, etc.

c **825** *Vesp. Psalter* xxxiii. 22 *Mors peccatorum pessima*, deað synfulra se wyrresta. *c* **888** Ælfred *Boeth.* xxxviii. §2 Ðæt is þæt sweotoloste tacen þæs mæstan yfeles on þisse weorulde, & þæs wyrrestan edleanes æfter þisse worulde. **971** *Blickl. Hom.* 245 Ic wæs ȝetoȝen to þæm wyrstan tintreȝum. *a* **1122** *O.E. Chron.* an 1086 (Laud MS.) Swylc coðe com on mannum, þæt full neah æfre þe oðer man wearð on þam wyrrestan yfele, þet is on ðam drife. *a* **1200** *Moral Ode* 217 (Lamb. MS.) Þe þe deþ is wille mest, he haueð wurst mede. *a* **1300** *Cursor M.* 14555 Of all him fell þe werst lot. **1382** Wyclif *Rev.* xvi. 2 A wounde feers and worst [**1388** werst, Vulg. *vulnus saevum et pessimum*]. **1390** Gower *Conf.* I. 349 False Egiste .. Was demed to diverse peine, The worste that men cowthe ordeigne. *c* **1450** *Mirk's Festial* 145 Then come þay all wroþe and beten þys man on þe worst maner þat þay cowþe. *c* **1470** Henry *Wallace* IX. 174, I traist to God our werst dayis ar gane. **1484** Caxton *Fables of Auian* xxvii. (1889) 248 Of two euyls men ought euer to eschewe and flee the worst of bothe. **1552** Huloet, Worste tyme for a publycque weale, *alienissimum rei publice tempus*. **1577** B. Googe *Heresbach's Husb.* IV. 176 b, If he bee angry, and fierce, and round, he is worst of all. **1596** *Edw. III*, II. i. 449 Poyson shewes worst in a golden cup. **1604** Shaks. *Oth.* III. iii. 132 Giue thy worst of thoughts The worst of words. **1639** S. Du Verger tr. *Camus' Admir. Events* 123 He repaires to his owne house, meager, pale, and in the worst case that can be imagined. **1667** Milton *P.L.* VI. 462 But pain is perfet miserie, the worst Of evils. **1697** Dryden *Æneis* IX. 392 That hope alone will fortifie my Breast Against the worst of Fortunes and of Fears. **1719** De Foe *Crusoe* II. (Globe) 498 We thought they ought to be every one of them put to the worst of Deaths. **1765** Gray *Shakespeare* 8 What awaits me now is worst of all. **1803** *Med. Jrnl.* IX. 527 The worst cases were discharged cured .. in about an average period of twelve days. **1805** *Ibid.* XIV. 227 Bleeding had been attended with the worst consequences. **1809** *Ibid.* XXI. 410 The two worst wounds in the loins were foul and deep. **1866** Carlyle *Remin.* (1881) II. 240 It was by her address and invention that I got my sooterkin of a 'study' improved out of some of its worst blotches. **1881** W. Collins *Black Robe* I. 272 'How does Stella bear it?' 'In the worst possible way .. In silence.'

b. Hardest, most difficult to deal with. Const. *to* and inf.

c **1400** *King Solomon's Bk. Wisdom* 100 Þre þinges on erþe beþ þat men mowen nouȝth yknowe. .. þe werst is þe fierþe. **1526** *Pilgr. Perf.* (W. de W. 1531) 35 Moost perylous kynde of lepry & worst to be cured. **1639** J. Clarke *Parœm.* 87 The best things are worst to come by. **1860** Tyndall *Glac.* I. xiv. 98 Our worst piece of work was now before us.

c. U.S. colloq. phr. ***the worst kind***; also used adverbially = most severely, most thoroughly. Also, ***the worst way***.

1839 Marryat *Diary Amer.* Ser. I. II. 227 He loves Sal, the worst kind. **1859** Bartlett *Dict. Amer.* (ed. 2) 517 *Worst kind.* Used in such phrases as, 'I gave him the worst kind of a licking.' Also adverbially; as 'I licked him the worst kind,' i.e. in the worst manner possible, most severely. **1904** *N.Y. Tribune* 26 June (Illustr. Suppl.) 4/4 'So you want to go to Cuba, do you?' asked Colonel Roosevelt. 'I do, worst kind,' replied McShane. **1914** G. Atherton *Perch of Devil* I. 55, I need new duds the worst way.

d. ***worst-case*** adj. phr.: that is or pertains to the worst of a number of possibilities.

1964 R. F. Ficchi *Electrical Interference* ii. 18 It is first assumed, using a worst-case analysis technique, that the mean beam of the receiver and transmitter antenna are in direct line of sight. **1979** R. Littell *Debriefing* v. 88 Worst-case contingency planning is still the basis of scenario construction. **1980** *Times* 18 Jan. 14/1 Analysts believe that the Kremlin drew up a 'worst-case' scenario which took into account both an embargo on American grain and a threat to the Moscow Olympics. **1985** *Harper's Mag.* Jan. 68/2 Pickens could spin off a royalty trust, perhaps sell the downstream operations. .. Such a move had been possible all along, but it was obviously the worse-case method of going about the task.

3. a. Most wanting in the good qualities required or expected; least good, valuable, desirable, or successful; most inferior; meanest or poorest in quality; least considerable or important.

c **1325** *Sir Orfeo* (Sisam) 367 Þe werst piler on to biholde Was al of burnist gold. *c* **1400** *Destr. Troy* 1570 The werst walle for to wale .. Was faurty cubettes by coursse. *c* **1420** *Sir Amadas* (Weber) 345 The warst hors is worthe ten pownde Of hom all that here gon. **1470–85** Malory *Arthur* X. xvi. 439 The werst of them wille not be lyghtly matched of no knyghtes that I knowe lyuynge. **1493** *Bury Wills* (Camden) 82, iii syluer sponys of the werste sorte. **1540** *Test. Ebor.* VI. 113 To John Colson my worst chamlet dublet. **1542** Udall *Erasm. Apoph.* 38 marg., The more hast ye wurst speede. **1562** Winȝet *Wks.* (S.T.S.) I. 114 The best geris tane away and sauld, and the werst reseruit. **1573–80** Tusser *Husb.* (1878) 49 Graie wheat is the grosest, yet good for the clay, though woorst for the market, as fermer may say. **1644** Milton *Areop.* (Arb.) 33 Naturall endowments haply not the worst for two and fifty degrees of northern latitude. **1654** Gayton *Pleas. Notes* IV. 226 He was secure, being on the worst side of fifty. **1696** Prideaux *Lett.* (Camden) 182 For then ye University would have the disposall of their liveings, wch now they give to ye worst men they can find. **1732** Pope *Ep. Bathurst* 299 In the worst inn's worst room. **1740** Mrs. E. Montagu *Corr.* (1906) I. 42 Living in a cottage on love is certainly the worst diet and the worst habitation one can find out. **1749** Fielding *Tom Jones* VIII. vii, To charge the same for the very worst provisions, as if they were the best. **1786** Burns *Auld Farmer's Salut. Mare* xv, They drew me thretteen pund an' twa, The very warst. —— '*My Father was a Farmer*' ii, My talents they were not the worst. **1825** Lytton *Falkland* 10 He was one of that class .. who, with the best intentions, have made the worst citizens. **1836** Southey *Lett.* (1856) IV. 436 Burnaby Green was the worst of translators. **1839** Lane *Arab. Nts.* I. 127 One of the worst dogs is then slipped at the herd. **1855** *Poultry Chron.* III. 466 It was the worst [show] I ever saw, cattle included.

†**b.** Phr. ***at (the) worst hand***: (*a*) in a position of defeat; (*b*) most dearly or unprofitably; (*c*) on the lowest estimate. *Obs.*

c **1489** Caxton *Sonnes of Aymon* xiv. 352 He saw well that his folke was at the worste hande, soo made he to sowne the retrete. *a* **1604** Hanmer *Chron. Irel.* (1809) 380 They were driven at the worst hand to sell unto the mercilesse Merchants, their Cowes, Hackneyes [etc.]. **1621** Bp. Mountagu *Diatribæ* 421 More ignorant barbarisme here, than in Paulus, who at worst hand hath related it in good and true Latine.

†**c.** ***in worst part***: in the most unfavourable aspect or construction. *Obs.*

a **1530** J. Heywood *Play of Love* 1508 A louer best loued hath paynes in lyke wyse As here hath apered by sondry weys Which sheweth his case in wurst part to aryse. *c* **1611** Chapman *Iliad* XXIV. 124 Myself take that wrong he hath done To Hector in worst part of all.

†**d.** ***to have the worst end*** (***of the staff***, etc.): cf. WORSE *a.* 3 c. *Obs.*

1564 T. Dorman *Proof Cert. Articles Relig.* 92 Yow maie haue cause to thincke, that yow holde by the worst ende of the staffe. **1597** Montgomerie *Cherrie & Slae* 1204 Persave then, ȝe haif then The warst end of the trie.

4. *predicatively.* Most unfortunate or badly off.

1603 Shaks. *Meas. for M.* III. i. 126 Or to be worse then worst Of those, that lawlesse and incertaine thought Imagine howling. **1605** —— *Lear* IV. i. 2 To be worst, The lowest, and most deiected thing of Fortune.

5. *Comb.*, as ***worst-humoured***, ***-intentioned***, ***-natured***, ***-surfaced***, ***-willed*** adjs.

c **1400** *Apol. Loll.* 105 Warst willid traytoris [*malignissimi proditores*]. **1656** Harrington *Oceana* (1658) 103 When I consider that our Country-men are none of the worst natur'd. **1678** Otway *Friendship in F.* III. i. 25 Every body knows I am the worst natur'd fellow breathing. *a* **1680** Earl Rochester *Allus. Horace* 60 The best good Man with the worst natur'd Muse. **1774** *Goldsmith's Retal.* Postscript, Thou best humour'd man with the worst humour'd Muse. **1896** Crockett *Grey Man* xxxiv. 231 The greediest and worst-intentioned rascals in the world. **1906** *Westm. Gaz.* 3 Mar. 3/1 From Blois to Chartres was the worst-surfaced road we came across.

B. *sb.* (absol. uses of the adj.; usu. with *the.*)

1. ***the worst***: **a.** one who is, or those who are, most objectionable or least estimable in moral character, behaviour, accomplishments, etc.

1606 SHAKS. *Ant. & Cl.* I. ii. 68 And let worse follow worse, till the worst of all follow him laughing to his graue. **1633** G. HERBERT *Temple, Church-porch* st. 72 Judge not the preacher... The worst speak something good. **1757** W. WILKIE *Epigoniad* IX. 270 Favor, your sex and innocence will plead, Ev'n with the worst. **1827** POLLOK *Course T.* I. 435 Lovely to the worst she [Virtue] seems. **1880** TENNYSON *First Quarrel* xiii, An' *she* wasn't one o' the worst. **1898** KIPLING *Day's Work* (1923) 363 Mr. Pepper himself, beyond question a man of the worst.

†**b.** *spec.* The Devil. Cf. WORSE *sb.* 1 b. *Obs.*

1388 WYCLIF *Ephes.* vi. 16 The firy dartis of the worste [1382 the worste enmye]. *c* **1400** *Destr. Troy* 1961 Thou sot with vnsell, seruand of o þe werst!

2. a. What is most objectionable or deplorable in regard to morals, taste, etc.

1390 GOWER *Conf.* I. 174 How so his mouth be comely, His word sit evermore awry And seith the worste that he may. *a* **1400–50** *Wars Alex.* 4656 He þat wayues ay þe werst & wirkis þe bettir. *c* **1400** *Pilgr. Sowle* (Caxton 1483) I. xvii. 14 He is euermore redy to do and say the werst. *c* **1480** HENRYSON *Trial of Fox* 10 Of euill cummis war, of war cummis werst of all. *c* **1600** SHAKS. *Sonn.* cl. 8 In the very refuse of thy deeds, There is such strength and warrantise of skill, That in my minde thy worst all best exceeds. **1600** E. BLOUNT tr. *Conestaggio* 65 For that we easily encline to the woorst. **1855** LYNCH *Letters to the Scattered* vii. 95 Unchecked sin tending to the perfect worst in wretchedness because to the perfect worst in character.

b. With *of*: What is most reprehensible or faulty in a person's character.

1865 DICKENS *Mut. Fr.* I. vi, Do you know the worst of your father? **1871** GEO. ELIOT *Middlemarch* xxxviii. II. 284 He's Whiggish himself..; that's the worst I know of him. **1897** WATTS-DUNTON *Aylwin* VIII. ii, 'We's all so modest in Primrose Court, that's the wust on us,' replied the woman.

3. a. What is most grievous, unlucky, painful, hard to bear; a state of things that is most undesirable or most to be dreaded.

c **1374** CHAUCER *Troylus* II. 304 Beth nought agast.. For hardely þe werste of þis is do. **1390** GOWER *Conf.* I. 25 Bot yet the werste of everydel Is last. *a* **1400–50** *Wars Alex.* 532 All scho dredis hire dede & doute for þe werst. *c* **1440** *York Myst.* xxxv. 212 þe werste is paste. *c* **1470** HENRY *Wallace* XI. 1222 Off Wallace end my selff wald leiff, for dredis To say the werst. **1562** J. HEYWOOD *Prov. & Epigr.* (1867) 166 Prouyde for the woorst, the best wyll saue it selfe. **1577** GRANGE *Golden Aphrod.* I iv, N.O. (fearyng the worste). **1596** SHAKS. *Merch. V.* I. ii. 96 And the worst fall that euer fell. **1605** —— *Lear* IV. i. 8 The Wretch that thou hast blowne vnto the worst, Owes nothing to thy blasts. **1605** B. JONSON *Volpone* V. xii, Take good heart, the worst is past, sir. You are dis-possest. **1631** GOUGE *God's Arrows* V. §15. 428 Wisdome teacheth men to forecast the worst, that they may be provided against the worst. *c* **1660** J. GWYNNE *Milit. Mem.* (1822) 84 We were prepar'd, as knowing the worst, to receave our doome bravely. **1665** in *Verney Mem.* (1907) II. 251, I beleeve she conceales the worst from you. **1667** MILTON *P.L.* IX. 269 Her Husband.. Who guards her, or with her the worst endures. **1674** —— *Samson* 1570 Then take the worst in brief, Samson is dead. *a* **1796** BURNS '*In vain would Prudence*' 4 Above that world on wings of love I rise, I know its worst—and can that worst despise. **1794** MRS. RADCLIFFE *Myst. Udolpho* xxv, Tell me the worst at once. **1796** MME. D'ARBLAY *Camilla* IV. 220 The best thing we can do, is to get off as fast as we can, for fear of the worst. **1853** DICKENS *Bleak Ho.* xxxvi, I knew the worst now, and was composed to it. **1859** W. COLLINS *Q. of Hearts* ii, To face the worst that might happen. *a* **1873** LYTTON *Pausanias* II. i, I am prepared for the worst, even recall. **1893** ASHBY-STERRY *Naughty Girl* vii. 68 She turned pale.. and fancied the very worst.

b. A course of action ill-advised in the highest degree.

1568 GRAFTON *Chron.* II. 767 Wherefore me thinketh it were not the worst to send to the Quene some honourable and trustie personage. **1591** SAVILE *Tacitus Hist.* II. §39 Neither can it so easily be discerned what had beene best to haue done, as that it was the worst which they did.

c. The worst part, degree, or phase *of*.

1615 SANDYS *Trav.* 138 Hauing with two daies rest refreshed them, now to begin the worst of their journey. **1889** 'J. S. WINTER' *Mrs. Bob* xxii. (1891) 252 Miss Theodosia had already got the worst of her grief over. **1919** *Glasgow Herald* 8 Sept. 7 The confectioners.. have got over the worst of their sugar troubles.

d. ***the worst is***: the most painful or unfortunate thing or circumstance is (*that*...). Also ***the worst of*** (something), ***the worst of it, is***, etc.

1581 PETTIE *Guazzo's Civ. Conv.* I. (1586) A 6 b, The woorst is, they thinke that impossible to be done in our Tongue. **1585** T. WASHINGTON tr. *Nicholay's Voy.* II. xv. 50 The worst of all was that more then 13000 persons remayned dead. **1682** BUNYAN *Holy War* (1905) 379 Now the worst on't was, a Chirurgeon was scarce in Mansoul. **1711** ADDISON *Spect.* No. 184 ¶5 The worst of it is, that the drowsy Part of our Species is chiefly made up of very honest Gentlemen. **1762** STERNE *Tr. Shandy* VI. xviii, And 'twill be lucky, if that's the worst on't. **1809** MALKIN *Gil Blas* I. ii. (Rtldg.) 6 But paying through the nose was not the worst of it. **1835** DICKENS *Sk. Boz, Parish* ii, The worst of it is, that having a high regard for the old lady, he wants to make her a convert to his views. **1849** ROCK *Ch. of our Fathers* I. v. (1903) I. 293 But this is not the worst of having a church too near the houses of a small town. **1853** MRS. GASKELL *Cranford* xiv, Here I broke down utterly... The worst was, all the ladies cried in concert. **1873** MRS. WHITNEY *Other Girls* vi. 68 And she couldn't help it, poor lady, either; that is the worst of it; one gets so as not to be able to help things.

e. Phr. ***to come***, †***fall to the worst***; † ***to go all of the worst.***

1390 GOWER *Conf.* II. 237 Ful many a worthi kniht It hadde assaied,.. And evere it fell hem to the worste. *Ibid.* 380 Falle it to beste or to the werste. **1542** UDALL *Erasm. Apoph.* 212 b, And therefore the matter gooeth not all of the wurst, when the lighter maladie.. expelleth and drieueth out the greater. **1863** W. C. BALDWIN *Afr. Hunting* 253 Things never come to the worst but they mend.

f. ***if the worst come(s) to the worst***: if things fall out as badly as possible or conceivable.

1597 E. S. *Discov. Knts. Poste* C 3 b, If the worst come to the worst, it is but the hiering of a hackney to ryde to London. **1622** MABBE tr. *Aleman's Guzman d'Alf.* I. 28 Had the worst come to the worst, yet could we not haue wanted meate and drinke. **1667** DRYDEN & DK. NEWCASTLE *Sir M. Mar-all* II. (1668) 14 Why, if the worst come to the worst, he leaves you an honest woman. **1700** T. BROWN *Amusem. Ser. & Com.* 108 Let the Worst come to'th Worst. **1719** DE FOE *Crusoe* I. (Globe) 201 If the worse came to the worst, I could but die. **1821** GALT *Ann. Parish* xiii. (1895) 93 Which would have been a witness for the elders, had the worst come to the worst. **1904** WEYMAN *Abb. Vlaye* iii, If the worst comes to the worst, I can aid him.

†**g.** pl. ***worsts*** = the things that are worst (in phr. ***worst of worsts***). *poet. Obs.*

1609 JONSON *Epicoene* V. iv, This is worst of all worst worsts! that hell could haue deuis'd. **1624** QUARLES *Job Militant* xv. 37 But what is worst of worsts, (Lord) often I Haue cry'd to Thee, a stranger to my cry.

4. What is least good in quality or least valuable; the most inferior kind or lowest quality (of an article).

? *a* **1400** *Stanzaic Life of Christ* 2344 But Caynes cornes God forsok, that of the worst made his offryng. **1509** *Will* in *Archæol.* LXVI. 314 Item ij grayles oon of the best another of the worst. **1573–80** TUSSER *Husb.* (1878) 125 Paie Gods part furst, and not of the wurst. **1576** FLEMING *Panopl. Epist.* ¶iiij, The very woorst of all being of great vertue and value. **1587** HARRISON *England* II. vi. (1877) 149 Being sure that they [the clergy] would neither drinke nor be serued of the worst. **1615** SANDYS *Trav.* 136 The merchants brought with them many Negroes; not the worst of their merchandizes. **1637** RUTHERFORD *Lett.* (1671) 215 The worst of Christ, even his chaff, is better than the world's corn.

5. ***at (the) worst.*** **a.** In the most evil or undesirable state that can be; at the greatest disadvantage; fallen to the lowest degree of badness, illness, or misfortune. Similarly ***at one's worst.***

1532 MORE *Confut. Tyndale* Wks. 1557 fol. 611/2 That they shalbe no woorse, parde, not when they be at yᵉ very worst, then faithfull harlottes. *a* **1586** SIDNEY *Astr. & Stella* xcv. 2 Yet sighes, deare sighes, indeede true friends you are, That do not leaue your best friend at the wurst. **1599** SHAKS. *Hen. V*, V. ii. 250 Thou hast me, if thou hast me, at the worst. **1605** —— *Macb.* IV. ii. 24 Things at the worst will cease, or else climbe vpward, To what they were before. **1605** —— *Lear* IV. i. 27 Who is't can say I am at the worst? **1671** MILTON *P.R.* III. 209, I would be at the worst; worst is my Port. **1771** T. HULL *Sir W. Harrington* (1797) III. 122 Mrs. Stanhope was at the worst.

1605 BACON *Adv. Learn.* II. xxiii. §6 A man leaveth things at worst, and depriveth himself of means to make them better. **1639** J. CLARKE *Parœm.* 122 When the world is at worst it will mend.

1845 HT. MARTINEAU *Autobiog.* (1877) II. 362 Your people (never beginning to do their best till they are at their worst). **1846** LANDOR *Imag. Conv., Southey & Landor* Wks. 1853 II. 168/1 Unhappily Italian poetry in the age of Milton was almost at its worst. **1872** MORLEY *Voltaire* (1886) 12 A dark and tyrannical superstition at its worst. **1885** *Spectator* 30 May 716/1 No Dickens himself at his very worst has such tiresome repetition. **1887** SAINTSBURY *Hist. Eliz. Lit.* 284 Heywood, even at his worst, is a writer whom it is impossible not to like.

b. Even on the most unfavourable view or estimate or surmise.

c **1374** CHAUCER *Troylus* V. 96 Somwhat shal I seye; For at the worste it may yit shorte our weye. **1729** P. WALKDEN *Diary* (1866) 73 At the worst, I would subscribe to take half a quarter. **1771** *Junius Lett.* liv. 288 At the worst, what do they amount to. **1824** SOUTHEY *Let. to May* 29 Aug., He had seasons of good-nature, and at the worst was rather to be dreaded than disliked. **1840** DICKENS *Old C. Shop* ix, I thought.. that if a man played long enough he was sure to win at last, or, at the worst, not to come off a loser. **1871** THIRLWALL *Lett.* (1881) II. 267 Urban II pronounced that the killing of an excommunicated person was not a murder, but at the worst an offence to be expiated by a penance.

1598 FLORIO, *Alpeggio andare*, at woorst, if the woorst fall out. **1634** MILTON *Comus* 484 Or els som neighbour Woodman, or at worst, Som roaving Robber calling to his fellows. **1667** —— *P.L.* II. 100 If our substance.. cannot cease to be, we are at worst On this side nothing. **1670** DRYDEN *1st Pt. Conq. Granada* V. ii, But 'tis, at worst, but so consumed by fire, As cities are, that by their falls rise higher. **1758** J. BLAKE *Plan Mar. Syst.* 36 He is at worst sure of wholesome bread. **1778** SIR J. REYNOLDS 7 *Disc.* 215 So that not much harm will be done at worst. **1837** LANDOR *Pentam.* i. Wks. 1853 II. 308/1 Brutus and Cassius, at worst, but slew an atheist. **1881** MISS BRADDON *Asphodel* I. vii. 209 This kind of thing went on for another week of weather which at worst was showery.

6. (*to do*) ***the worst*** or ***one's worst***: the utmost evil or harm possible. Hence occas. ***one's worst***, without *do*.

c **1489** CAXTON *Blanchardyn* xiv. 48 Blanchardyn herkned the prouost, to whom boldly he answered that he shold doo the best and the worst that he coude [in the joust]. *c* **1489** —— *Sonnes of Aymon* iii. 78 It is the man among all oure enmyes, that worste dooth to vs. **1528** *Star Chamber Cases* (Selden) II. 177 [He] beds them to do to hym the best and the worst that they can For he setts not a Strawe by them all. **1553** ASCHAM *Germany* Wks. (1904) 133 Let his enemies do to him the worst they could. **1567** *Horestes* 385 (Brandl) Drawe thy sword, vylyne, yf thou be a man, And then do the worst, that euer thou can. **1568** NORTH *Gueuara's Diall Pr.* IV. xiv. 150 b, The woorst they can doo, they can but murmur. **1608** SHAKS. *Per.* III. i. 40, I do not feare the flaw, It hath done to me the worst. **1869** MORRIS *Earthly Par.* III. *Lov. Gudrun* (end), I did the worst to him I loved the most.

(*b*) **1390** GOWER *Conf.* III. 311 Ha, thou fortune, I thee deffie, Nou hast thou do to me thi werste. **1470–85** MALORY *Arthur* X. lvii. 511 Wete ye wel that I am sire Tristram de lyones, and now doo your werste. **1605** SHAKS. *Macb.* III. ii. 24 Treason ha's done his worst. **1616** T. DRAXE *Bibl. Scholast.* 30 A fig for him. Let him doe his worst. **1639** J. TAYLOR (Water P.) *Pt. Summers Travels* 43 And there-fore now you with all double diligence, doe endevour to doe your best to doe your worst. **1650** T. VAUGHAN *Anthroposophia* 27 When Death hath done her worst. **1653** WALTON *Angler* iv. 115 Let the winde sit in what corner it will, and do its worst. **1713** ADDISON *Guard.* No. 102 ¶8 To defie the Cold and Rain, and let the Weather do its worst. **1781** COWPER *Table Talk* 729 Satire has long since done his best; and curst And loathsome ribaldry has done his worst. **1842** BROWNING *Pied Piper* xi, You threaten us, fellow? Do your worst, Blow your pipe there till you burst! **1882** BESANT *All Sorts* xxxii. (1898) 226 Now you may go away and do your worst.

(*c*) **1599** SHAKS. *Hen. V*, III. iii. 5 Therefore to our best mercy giue your selues, Or like to men prowd of destruction, Defie vs to our worst. **1611** —— *Wint. T.* III. ii. 180 What old or newer Torture Must I receiue? whose euery word deserues To taste of thy most worst.

7. a. The harshest view or judgement; as ***to speak*** or ***think the worst*** (***of*** a person or thing).

c **1586** C'TESS PEMBROKE *Ps.* CXIX. C. iv, Let princes talk, And talk their worst of me. **1611** SHAKS. *Cymb.* II. iii. 159 She's my good Lady, and will concieue, I hope, But the worst of me. **1632** HAYWARD tr. *Biondi's Eromena* 63, I hold my selfe greatly injured of such as judge of me rather the worst than the best. **1871** RUSKIN *Fors Clav.* ix. 2 The worst he can venture to say is, that it is ridiculous.

†**b.** ***to take*** or ***wrest to the worst***, ***to take at worst***: to put the most unfavourable construction upon. *Obs.* Cf. WORSE *sb.* 3 d.

1535 COVERDALE *Prov.* x. 32 The lippes of the rightuous are occupied in acceptable thinges, but the mouth of the vngodly taketh them to the worst. **1593** G. HARVEY *Pierce's Superer.* Wks. (Grosart) II. 52 Let me not bee mistaken by sinister construction, that wreasteth and wrigleth euery sillable to the worst. **1607** SHAKS. *Timon* V. i. 181, I cannot choose but tell him that I care not, And let him tak't at worst.

c. ***to make the worst of***: to regard or represent in the most unfavourable light.

1796 MME. D'ARBLAY *Camilla* II. 162 But it's over, you know; so what signifies making the worst of it? **1853** DICKENS *Bleak Ho.* xxxvi, Now I was hot, and had made the worst of it, instead of the best. **1877** TRENCH *Lect. Med. Ch. Hist.* 115 Roman Catholic writers make no attempt to conceal the depth of desecration and dishonour which the Papacy then passed through; nay, they seem rather to take a pleasure in making the worst of this.

8. Defeat in a contest. (Cf. WORSE *sb.* 4.)

†**a.** ***to put to the worst***: to defeat, overcome. Also ***to put at***, ***drive to the worst***; ***to give*** (one) ***the worst on't.*** *Obs.*

c **1460** *Three 15th C. Chron.* (Camden) 59 She.. put him dyverse tymes at the worste. **1574** HELLOWES *Guevara's Ep.* (1584) 328 They liued by robbing and pilling one from another, euermore driuing the weakest to the worst. **1591** PERCIVALL *Sp. Dict.*, *Destroço*, putting to the woorst, putting to flight. **1598** R. BERNARD *Terence, Andria* I. iii. (1607) 20 *Me & illum herus pessundedit.* My master hath put him and me to the worst. **1644** VICARS *Jehovah-Jireh* 194 Our left wing being thus put to the worst. **1684** BUNYAN *Pilgr.* II. (1900) 229 Why, I would a fought as long as Breath had been in me; and had I so done, I am sure you could never have given me the worst on't. *a* **1700** EVELYN *Diary* 10 Mar. 1687 The party were exceedingly put to the worst by the preaching and writing of the Protestants. **1726** DE FOE *Hist. Devil* I. v. (1840) 69 Putting Michael and all the faithful army to the worst.

b. ***to have the worst***: to be defeated. †Similarly ***to go*** or ***come to***, ***come*** or ***go by***, ***come off by***, ***go away with***, ***come off with the worst.***

1529 *Morte Darthur* I. ix. (W. de W.) Fyghte not with the swerde.. til that ye see ye go to yᵉ worste [*Caxton* vnto the wers]. **1596** SHAKS. *Tam. Shrew* I. ii. 14, I should knocke you first, And then I know after who comes by the worst. **1597** BEARD *Theatre God's Judgem.* (1612) 90 His owne side came to the worst, doing more scath to themselues than to their enemies. **1605** *London Prodigal* I. i. 51 He is a mighty brawler, and comes commonly by the worst. **1613** SIR E. HOBY *Counter-snarle* 24 Hee which bringeth a great Armie into the field, without victuall or munition, is like to goe by the worste. **1639** [see GO *v.* 57 c]. *c* **1645** HOWELL *Lett.* (1650) I. II. 29 There was a shrewd brush lately twixt the young King and his Mother, who.. met him in open field..; but she went away with the worst. **1710** E. WARD *Brit. Hud.* 26 Those who laugh'd aloud at first, At last may chance to come by th' worst. *Ibid.* 116 Those who by reviling first Begot the Fray, came off by th' worst. **1834** GODWIN *Lives Necrom.* 184 In these wars, the Peris generally came off with the worst.

1598 R. BERNARD *Terence, Andria* II. v. (1607) 43 *Nostræ parti timeo.* I feare our side will haue the worst. **1670** G. H. *Hist. Cardinals* III. III. 300 There happen'd a fray betwixt the Souldiers.. and the Halberdiers.., the last of which had the worst of it. **1709** MRS. MANLEY *Secret Mem.* (1720) III. 166 The King of the Bulgari made a troublesome, uncertain War upon the Empire, which sometimes had the better, oftentimes the worst. **1848** THACKERAY *Van. Fair* xlvi, George.. bragged.. about his valour in the fight,.. in which he decidedly had the worst.

worst (wɜːst), *v.* [f. WORST *a.*]

†**1.** *trans.* To make worse, impair, damage, inflict loss upon: = WORSE *v.* 2, WORSEN *v.* 1. *Obs.*

1602 HARINGTON in *Nugæ Ant.* (1804) I. 321 Her betterring the state of my father's fortune (which I have, alass! so much worsted). **1648** Earl Westmoreland *Otia Sacra* (1879) 22 God makes all things for good; 'tis Man Sowers and worsts Creation. **1649** Jer. Taylor *Gt. Exemp.* Pref. ¶16 If I be intemperate I grow sick and worsted in some faculty. **1682** Penn in Clarkson *Mem.* (1849) xviii. 115 Thy father's public spirit had worsted his estate. **1728** W. Smith *Ann. Univ. Coll.* 88 By which the College may be said to be wosted [*sic*] above 3*l.* 10*s.* per Annum. *a* **1741** Tull *Horse-hoeing Husb.* ii. (1822) 26 A pear grafted upon a quince may be mended but if grafted upon a white thorn will be worsted. *Ibid.* xix. 274 *note*, But suppose I had worsted my substance, are there not many who..have lessened their estates, though they have never practised agriculture? **1742** Richardson *Pamela* III. 26 To better the Condition of the Tenants at the same time, at least not to worst them. **1748** —— *Clarissa* (1811) VII. 341 Suppose you kill one another, will the matter be bettered or worsted by that? **1745** tr. *Columella's Husb.* II. xiv, Nor is there any doubt but the land is annoyed and worsted [*infestetur*]..by these seeds. **1783** Pott *Chirurg. Wks.* II. 69 He may be much worsted by the experiment.

†**b.** *intr.* To grow worse, deteriorate. *Obs. rare.*

1781 P. Beckford *Th. Hunting* (1802) 314 We perceived that our scent worsted, and were going to stop the hounds. *c* **1815** Jane Austen *Persuasion* (1818) I. i. 10 Anne haggard, Mary coarse, every face in the neighbourhood worsting.

2. *trans.* To defeat, overcome, get the better of (an adversary) in a fight or battle.

1636 Brathwait *Rom. Emp.* 20 After many battailes Otho being worsted..slew himselfe. **1657** Earl Monm. tr. *Paruta's Pol. Disc.* 187 He got a notable Victory, worsting a great many of the Enemy with a much lesser number. **1663** Butler *Hud.* I. ii. 878 The Bear was in a greater fright, Beat down and worsted by the Knight. **1703** Earl Orrery *As you find it* II. ii. 27 There's no more believing him than the Paris-Gazette, when it relates a Battle where the French were worsted. **1772** Priestley *Inst. Relig.* (1782) II. 194 The Syrians having been worsted in the hilly country. **1849** Grote *Greece* II. liv. (1862) IV. 527 A battle ensued, in which that prince was completely worsted. **1856** Kane *Arct. Expl.* I. xxix. 391 He turned on them and worsted them badly before making his escape. **1886** Child *Eng. & Sc. Ballads* II. 441/2 The page worsts his accuser in a duel. **1889** Morris *Ho. Wolfings* 18 In forty fights hast thou foughten, and been worsted but in four. **1902** J. F. Rusling *European Days & Ways* 299 Blücher now took pleasure in getting even with Napoleon for worsting him at Ligny.

b. To defeat in argument, in a suit, attempt, etc.; to outdo, prove better than; to quell (an attack). Freq. in *pass.*

1651 Baxter *Inf. Bapt.* 209 Lest if you were silent the people should think you were worsted. **1654** Whitlock *Zootomia* 150 How are al Lyricks out-gon by Davids Harp and how do Salomons Proverbs (for contracted sense) worst Seneca? **1655** Fuller *Ch. Hist.* v. 229 And where His Highnesse was worsted or wearied, Arch-bishop Cranmer supplied His place. **1664** Butler *Hud.* II. ii. 520 Remember how in Arms and Politicks We still have worsted all your holy Tricks. **1693** *Humours Town* 20 If I must be worsted, it shall be in good Christian English. **1694** Kettlewell *Comp. for Persecuted* 69 Who art ofttimes pleased to permit a righteous Cause to be worsted. **1791** Boswell *Johnson* an. 1781 (Oxf. ed.) II. 414 Johnson could not brook appearing to be worsted in argument. **1802** Mar. Edgeworth *Irish Bulls* ix, I could not bear to go away worsted, and borne down as it were by the English faction. **1868** Milman *St. Paul's* iii. 70, He appealed to Rome, but was worsted in his appeal. **1881** Miss Braddon *Asphodel* I. v. 136 In any skirmish with this young lady he was likely to be worsted. **1887** Ruskin *Præterita* II. 273 [I was] in the habit of feeling worsted in everything I tried of original work. **1911** Rose *Pitt & Gt. War* x. 234 In this secret chaffering Pitt and Grenville were worsted.

Hence 'worsting *vbl. sb.*

1842 J. H. Newman *Ch. Fathers* 60 We might have conquered by a worsting which was honourable and dignified. **1883** Miss Broughton *Belinda* I. ix, The dispute ends in the worsting of the person to whom alone it is of any consequence to succeed.

worst (wɜːst), *adv.* Forms: α. 1 **wyrst, wyrrest, wierst,** 2–3 **wurst,** 4–5 **worste,** 6 **woorst,** 4– **worst.** β. 1–2 **wærst,** 3–6 **werst** (3, 6 *Sc.* **verst,** *Orm.* **werrst,** 4 **werist**), 4–5 **werste,** 6– *Sc.* **warst.** [OE. *wyrrest, wyrst, wierst* = ON. (Icel., Norw.) *verst* (Sw. *värst*, Da. *værst*). Cf. worst *a.*] **a.** In a manner, or to a degree, that is most (or extremely) bad or evil.

c **897** Ælfred *Gregory's Past. C.* xxxii. 209 Ðonne hie wenen ðæt hie hæbben betst ȝedon, ðæt we him ðonne secgen ðæt hie hæbben wierst [*Cott.* wyrst] ȝedon. *a* **1000** *Boeth. Metr.* xxxiv. 60 þa ofermodan oðre rican ðe þis weriȝe folc wyrst tuciað. *a* **1122** *O.E. Chron.* an. 1087 (Laud MS.) [He] dyde ȝit eallra wærst ofer eall þæt land. *a* **1200** *St. Marher.* 14 þis beoð þe wepnen þet me wurst wundeð. *c* **1200** Ormin 4250 Uss birrþ clippenn all aweȝȝ þe flæshess fule wille, þatt allre werrst & allre mast Werdeþþ þe wrecche sawle. *a* **1300** *K. Horn* 68 Of alle wymmanne Wurst was godhild þanne. *a* **1300** *Cursor M.* 21450 [I shall treat him] þe werst [*Gött.* werist] þat euer i can or mai. *c* **1380** *Sir Ferumb.* 2809 þat me greueþ werst. *c* **1380** Wyclif *Wks.* (1880) 370 As þe peple of israel wern werst gouernyd undir her prestis. **1390** Gower *Conf.* I. 121 Thus he, which love hadde in desdeign, Worste of all othre was besein. *Ibid.* II. 15 Whan that he worst ferde. **1549** *Compl. Scotl.* vii. 69 The thrid part of hyr mantil..vas verst grathit. *c* **1560** A. Scott *Poems* xvi. 46 Thay cary victuallis to þe toun That werst dois dyne. **1575** Gascoigne *Glasse Govt.* Wks. 1910 II. 11, I am not the worst furnished of a servaunt with this good fellow. **1601** Shaks. *Jul. C.* IV. iii. 106 When thou did'st hate him worst. **1629** N. Carpenter *Architophel* II. (1640) 66 Oftentimes he that can best act, can worst pen his own part. **1632** Lithgow *Trav.* iv. 142 The Turkes Sabboth is worst kept of all. **1786** Burns *Twa Dogs* 205 But Gentlemen, an' Ladies warst, Wi' ev'n down want o' wark are curst. **1787** —— *John Barleycorn* xi, But a miller us'd him worst of all, For he crush'd him between two stones. —— '*My Father was a Farmer*' iii, And when my hope was at the top, I still was worst mistaken. **1888** Saintsbury in *Encycl. Brit.* XXIV. 293/1 In this great mass [of correspondence] Voltaire's personality is of course best shown, and perhaps his literary qualities not worst.

b. With a vb. of liking, loving, allowing, pleasing, etc.: Least well, least.

971 *Blickl. Hom.* 195 Oft hit ȝesæleþ þæt his æhta weorþaþ on þæs onwealde þe he ær on his life wyrrest uþe. *c* **1375** *Cursor M.* 4386 (Fairf.), I salle þe make wiþ myne housbande þe werst loued [*Cott.* luue] of alle þis lande. *c* **1400** *Pilgr. Sowle* (Caxton 1483) IV. xxxvii. 84 Oftyme suche maystres as ben of lest reputacion ben mooste necessary, and worst mowe ben myssed. *a* **1568** Ascham *Scholem.* II. (Arb.) 153 Cæsar and Cicero, whose puritie was neuer foiled, no not by the sentence of those, that loued them worst. **1577** B. Googe *Heresbach's Husb.* III. (1586) 150 Swine of al other beastes can woorst away with hunger. **1608** Shaks. *Per.* IV. iii. 21 Of all the faults beneath the heauens, the Gods doe like this worst. **1613** —— *Hen. VIII*, v, iii. 78, I cry your Honour mercie; you may worst Of all this Table say so. **1634** J. Levett *Ordering Bees* 8 Bees of all other creatures can worst away with any great noyse. **1786** Burns '*What ails ye now*' xii, But, Sir, this pleas'd them warst ava.

c. *Comb.*, as ***worst-affected, -bred, -damaged, -deserving, -favoured*** (Sc. ***-faurd***), ***-formed, -governed, -looking, -managed, -manned, -paid, -used*** adjs. **worst-seller**, a book distinguished commercially by its low sales (opp. *best seller* s.v. best *adv.* 3 b); the writer of such a book; also **worst-selling** *a.*

1556 *Aurelio & Isab.* (1608) F 5 The pehenne (the whiche of price unto him without comparison is the worste faverdeste). **1701** Rowe *Amb. Step-Mother* II. i, What Titles had they had,..if Nature had not Strove hard to thrust the worst-deserving first? **1721** Amherst *Terræ Fil.* xxxii. 170 His majesty's worst-affected subjects. **1751** Chesterf. *Lett.* (1774) II. 103 The worst-bred man in Europe, if a lady let fall her fan, would certainly take it up and give it her. **1768–74** Tucker *Lt. Nat.* (1834) II, 283 In the worst-formed bodies..there lies an immortal spirit. **1813** Hogg *Queen's Wake* 74 The warst-faurd wyfe on the shoris of Fyfe Is cumlye comparet wi' thee. **1831** Scott *Ct. Rob.* xxiii, Waiting for the slowest and worst manned vessels. **1835** Dickens *Sk. Boz, Streets—Morning*, The hardest worked, the worst paid, and too often, the worst used class of the community. **1853** —— *Bleak Ho.* ix, I thought him the worst-looking dog I had ever beheld. **1857** Mrs. Carlyle *Lett.* II. 318 The worst-used woman I ever knew. **1871** Le Fanu *Checkmate* I. 276, I believe that we are the worst-governed and the worst-managed people on earth. **1890** W. J. Gordon *Foundry* 55 The worst-damaged plate was taken out, re-rolled, and replaced. **1924** O. Sitwell *Triple Fugue* 73 Could a written testimonial be obtained from the shades of..Dryden,..Gray, Keats..and from their heirs, the worst-sellers of to-day, it is probable that the purport.. would be found..to be remarkably alike in every case. **1925** V. Woolf *Common Reader* 262 There is..the best-seller public and the worst-seller public. **1933** T. E. Lawrence *Let.* 17 Dec. (1938) 783, I confess to a lively apprehension of that potential worst-seller of yours. **1956** A. Huxley *Adonis & Alphabet* 120 If there were no 'angels', there would be no worst-selling literature to leaven the enormous lump of intellectual and artistic conformity. **1980** 'J. Gash' *Spend Game* vi. 65 A tatty copy of the world's worst-seller like Dr Chase's book.

worsted ('wʊstɪd), *sb.* Forms: α. 3–4 **worth-,** 4 **wurthstede, worthested(e, wortestede;** 3 **wr-,** 4–5 **wurstede,** 6 **-steede,** 5–6 **wursted** (5 **-stet**); 4–5 **wirsted,** 6 **wyrsted,** 5 **werstede;** 4–6 **worstede** (5 **wore-**), 4– **worsted** (4 **-seted,** 6 **-stedd, -styd;** 5 **-stet,** 6 **-stett;** 6 **vorsted**), 5 **worsteyd,** 6 **-steid;** 6–8 **worstead;** 6 **woorstred,** 7 **-sted, -stead.** β. 5–6 **wolsted(e,** 6 **wullstid, ulsted,** 7 **wolsteed,** 6, 8 **woolsted.** γ. 5–6 **wusted,** 5–7 **wosted,** 6–8 **woosted.** δ. *Sc.* and *n. dial.* 4, 6–7, 9 **worset,** 4, 6–7 **worsett,** 7 **worssett;** 5–6 **worsat,** 6 **worsatt, -ait,** 9 **wurset, -it, wossat, wusset;** 4 **wirset,** 5 **wirssat,** 6 **wirsait;** 5 **wersed.** [From the name of a parish in Norfolk, north of Norwich, originally (OE.) *Wurðestede*, later *Wurthstede, Worthsted*, etc., and now written *Worstead.*]

†**1.** (Anglo-Latin) *pannus*, (Anglo-French) *drap, de Wurthstede*, etc.: = sense 2. *Obs.*

1296 *Cal. Close Rolls* (1904) 511 Pannum de Worthstede. **1301** *Let. Pat.* 4 Oct. in *Northampton Bor. Rec.* (1898) I. 59 De quolibet panno de wurthstede qui vocatur coverlit. **1328** *Rolls of Parlt.* II. 28/1 Ses poueres..Overours des Draps de Wurthstede en le Counte de Norff. **1347** *Ibid.* 168/2 Pur Draps de Worstede une novelle Custume levee. **1350** *Durham Acc. Rolls* (Surtees) 173 In 11 pannis de nigro worseto. **1402–3** *Ibid.* 182 In tribus pannis de wirsted. **1442–3** *Ibid.* 185 In 1 panno nigro de worestede.

2. a. A woollen fabric or stuff made from well-twisted yarn spun of long-staple wool combed to lay the fibres parallel.

α. **1293** in *Camden Misc.* II. 13 Pro xj. ulnis de wrstede ad caligas faciendas. **1345–9** in *Archaeologia* XXXI. 78 Eidem ad vnam aulam de worstede operatum cum papagailles. *c* **1386** Chaucer *Prol.* 262 Of double worstede was his semycope. **1393–4** *Act 17 Rich II*, c. 2 Les Marchants & overours de draps appelez sengle Worstede. **1411** *E.E. Wills* (1882) 19 Also y be-queythe to Robert, myn heldest son, a reed bedde of worsteyd. **1459** *Paston Lett.* I. 478 Item, j pece of grene wurstet xxx yards longe. **1465** *Ibid.* (1904) IV. 201 A coverlyte of whyte werstede longyng therto. **1535** in *Archaeologia* IX. 249 A dubblette of wursteede. *a* **1548** Hall *Chron., Hen. VIII*, 61 b, Within hys gate..dwelled dyuerse Frenchmen that Kalendred Worsted, contrary to the kynges lawes. **1610** Holland *Camden's Brit.* 475 They obtained..that the Worsted made there [at Norwich] might be transported. *a* **1661** Fuller *Worthies, Norf.* (1662) 247 It surpasseth my skill to name the several stuffs (being Worsted disguised with Weaving and Colouring) made thereof. **1728** Pope *Dunc.* II. 150 The very worstead still look'd black and blue. **1771** Mrs. Haywood *New Present for Maid* 258 Directions for cleaning of Worsted and other Sorts of Stuffs. **1886** Beck *Draper's Dict.* 373 *Worsted*, cloth of long stapled-wool, combed straightly and smoothly, as distinct from woollens, which are woven from short staple wool, crossed and roughed in spinning.

β. **1436** *Nottingham Rec.* II. 152 Unum cowle de nigro wolstede. **1551–2** *Act 5 & 6 Edw. VI*, c. 7 §1 Any kynde of Clothe Chamlettes Wolstede Sayes [etc.]. **1598** Stow *Surv.* 76 His guarde..all in a Liuery of Wolsted.

γ. **1440** in Peacock *Eng. Ch. Furniture* (1866) 182 A vestment of Black wosted. **1481–90** *Howard Househ. Bks.* (Roxb.) 38 A piece wusted iij. yerdes deppe, for stremers and standartes. **1537** in Glasscock *Rec. St. Michael's, Bp.'s Stortford* (1882) 126 Item a vestment of grene wusted w[t] an obe. **1556** *Towrson's 1st Voy.* in *Hakluyt* (1589) 108 They shewed vs a certaine course cloth,..it was course wooll, and a small threed, and as thicke as wosted. **1607** R. C[arew] tr. *Estienne's World Wond.* 235 Sleeues.., one halfe of woosted, the other of veluet.

δ. **1350** [see 1]. **1375** *Exch. Rolls Scot.* II. 505 Per empcionem de xij ulnis cum dimidio de wirset. **1436** *Registr. Aberdon.* (Maitl. Club) II. 148 Vnum vestimentum integrum de nigro wersed. **1483** *Acta Auditorum* (1839) *112/1 A couering of Inglis worsat. **1520–1** *Fabric Rolls York Minster* (Surtees) 305 One vestment of blacke worsett. **1565** in Hay Fleming *Reform. Scot.* (1910) 610 Ane baithky[t] [*sic*] of roich worsat, to ly under nobillis feit. **1612** *Sc. Bk. Rates* in *Halyburton's Ledger* (1867) 289 Beltis..of worsett the groce, viij li.

b. With *pl.* A particular variety of this fabric.

1314–5 *Rolls of Parlt.* I. 292/2 Draps qe homme appele Worthstedes & Aylehames. **1348** in Rymer *Fœdera* (1708) V. 618 Stapula..aliorum Pannorum de Worstedes. **1393** *Pat. Roll 16 Rich. II*, II. 28 Feb., Pro mercatoribus et operatoribus de worstedes. **1442** *Rolls of Parlt.* V. 60/2 Persones that maken untrewe ware of all maner Worstedes. **1471** *Paston Lett.* III. 14 A Worsted man of Norffolk, that solde worstedys at Wynchester. **1541–2** *Act 33 Hen. VIII*, c. 16 §2 The makinge and weavinge of worstedes and other clothes. **1573–80** Baret *Alv.* V 92 As if a man should carrie Mockadoes and woolsteds to be sold at Norwich. **1603** R. Johnson *Kingd. & Commw.* 27 They inuented..the making of tapestrie, saies, searges, wosteds, russets. **1853** Ure *Dict. Arts* II. 833 The class of goods technically distinguished as 'woollens' in distinction to 'worsteds.' **1895** *Daily News* 13 Sept. 5/3 The revival is more apparent in the production of the higher class of goods known as worsteds than in that known as woollens.

c. *ellipt.* for a garment made of worsted cloth; a worsted jacket or suit.

1962 L. Deighton *Ipcress File* i. 9, I struggled into the dark worsted and my only establishment tie. **1972** K. Bonfigioli *Don't point that Thing at Me* iii. 20, I put on a dashing little tropical-weight worsted, curly-brimmed coker and a pair of buckskins. **1975** *Times* 8 Jan. 12/7 Behaving in a manner more suited to the canvas jacket than the charcoal-grey worsted.

3. A closely twisted yarn made of long-staple wool in which the fibres are arranged to lie parallel to each other. Later, a fine and soft woollen yarn used for knitting and embroidery (cf. wool *sb.* 3 b).

1465 *Paston Lett.* II. 235, I pray yow ye woll send me hedir ij. clue of worsted for dobletts, to happe me thys cold wynter. **1546** *Extracts Aberd. Reg.* (1844) I. 236 Ane grit buyst, and certane kemmis, worsettis, spectikyllis, and wther small geir in it. **1612** *Sc. Bk. Rates* in *Halyburton's Ledger* (1867) 296 Sewing worssett. **1687** A. Lovell tr. *Thevenot's Trav.* I. 143 Their loom stands before them, and in their left hand they have several ends of round bottoms of Woorstead of many colours, which they place in their several places. **1709** *Phil. Trans.* XXVIII. 265 She being a Spinner of Yarn or Woosted. *a* **1745** Swift *Story Injured Lady* (1746) 7 If a Tenant carried but..an Inch of Worsted to mend his Stockings, he should forfeit his whole Parcel. **1784** Adam Smith *W.N.* IV. viii. (1793) II. 507 Woollen yarn and worsted are prohibited to be exported under the same penalties as wool. **1841** Barham *Ingol. Leg., Nell Cook* Scene, Mrs. John Ingoldsby at the table, busily employed in manufacturing a cabbage-rose..in many-coloured worsteds. **1854** Surtees *Handley Cr.* lx. (1901) II. 152 The young ones sought out their threads and their worsteds to work her a collar or a piece of crochet work each. **1889** *Hardwicke's Sci.-Gossip* XXV. 134 The syphon, which may consist of a single thread of wool or worsted.

4. *attrib.* or *adj.* Made of worsted or worsted yarn; said of cloth, thread, garments, etc.; also in specific names of fabrics or materials, as ***worsted braid, damask***, etc.

1410 *Rolls of Parlt.* III. 637/2 Les Worstedes appelez Worsted-beddes, doubles, & sengles. **1492** *Acc. Ld. High Treas. Scot.* I. 202 For ij dowbil wirssat beltis til him, price iij s. **1502** *Ibid.* II. 198 For iiij elne worsait ribane to cord the said goune. **1533** *Test. Ebor.* VI. 43 A wolsted dublet. **1566** in Peacock *Eng. Ch. Furniture* (1866) 67 Item iij worsted copes. **1589** Greene *Menaphon* (Arb.) 74 Spangled like to the woosted stockings of Saturne. **1605** Erondelle *Fr. Gard.* D 8 b, I will haue no woorsted hosen. **1647** Herrick *Noble Numb., Widow's Tears* iv, The woosted thred Is cut, that made us clothing. **1720** T. Gordon *Humourist* I. 45 Renouncing his Buckles and conforming to Woolsted-Tapes. **1748** Smollett *R. Random* xvii, His white silk stockings were converted into black worsted hose. **1828** Scott *F.M. Perth* vi, The thumb of his mother's worsted glove might hold the treasure of the whole clan. **1843** *Penny Cycl.* XXVII. 555/2 Worsted shag [is made] at Banbury and Coventry. **1858** Lytton *What will He do?* I. vi, Two small worsted rugs. **1878** Miss Braddon *Eleanor's Vict.* ii, Voluminous worsted curtains falling before the narrow windows. **1882** Caulfeild & Saward *Dict. Needlework* 524 Worsted Braids...Worsted Damasks.

Comb. **1767** *Ann. Reg.* 158 The looms of a worsted-lace-weaver.

5. Simple attrib. and adjective comb., as ***worsted-breaker, -comber, -dealer, -factory,***

machinery, -maker, -making, manufacture, -manufacturer, merchant, mill, repository, †*-shearing,* †*shearman, -spinner, -spinning, -throwster, trade, -weaver, -weaving*; **worsted work**, embroidery done with worsted yarn on canvas; an example of this; hence **worsted-worked** *a.*

1835 URE *Philos. Manuf.* 217 These two endless chains pass over fluted guide-rollers (like those more obviously seen in the *worsted-breaker). **1702** in P. Wright *New Bk. Martyrs* (1784) 808/1 William Hussey, a *worsted comber. **1830** PARSON & WHITE *Directory Leeds* etc. 426 *Worsted Dealers. **1843** *Penny Cycl.* XXVII. 554/1 A *worsted factory in the north. **1875** KNIGHT *Dict. Mech.* 2819 *Worsted machinery. **1538** STARKEY *England* I. iii. 95 Weuerys, *worstyd-makyrs, tukkarys and fullarys. **1534** *Act 26 Hen. VIII*, c. 16 §5 The said mysterie and occupacion of *Worsted makinge. **1805** LUCCOCK *Wool* 156 The state of the *worsted manufacture. **1736** in *Rec. Convent. Royal Burghs Scot.* (1885) V. 604 The case of the silk and *worset manufacturers. **1801** T. PECK *Norwich Directory* 11 Crowe William, Worsted-Manufacturer. **1481** *Paston Lett.* III. 278 One Bolt, a *worstede marchaunt. **1880** GOLDW. SMITH *Cowper* vii. 100 The letter slides from spiritual despair to the worsted-merchant. **1836** W. WHITE *Hist.* etc. *Norf.* 96 Two *worsted mills at Norwich. **1858** SIMMONDS *Dict. Trade*, **Worsted-repository*,.. a shop where fancy knitting-wools are sold. **1503-4** *Act 19 Hen. VII*, c. 17 §1 The *Worsted Sheremen wythin the seid Citie.. have chosen Wardens of *Worsted sheryng. **1830** PARSON & WHITE *Directory Leeds* 171 *Worsted spinners. **1895** *Daily News* 21 June 2/2 The *worsted-spinning business of Henry Pease and Company. **1716** *Lond. Gaz.* No. 5401/4 A *Worsted-Throwster by Trade. **1835** URE *Philos. Manuf.* 68 The *worsted trade of England. **1442** *Rolls of Parlt.* V. 60/2 The craft of *Worsted Wevers. **1707** *Lond. Gaz.* No. 4319/4 George Durant, of the City of Norwich, Worsted-Weaver. *c* **1702** C. FIENNES *Journeys* (1947) 277 One with a half bedstead as the new mode, dimity with fine shades of *worsted works well made up. **1826** M. WILMOT *Let.* 25 Sept. (1935) 250, I do *worsted work*.. but.. my eyes are too weak to count the threads of any but coarse canvas... What do you make of yours? Foot stools! cushions! bell pulls! **1888** MRS. H. WARD *Robert Elsmere* I. I. x. 280 His wife, whose head was bent close over her worsted work. **1853** MRS. GASKELL *Cranford* viii. 116 Carlo lay on the *worsted-worked rug.

worsted ('wɜːstɪd), *ppl. a.* [f. WORST *v.* + -ED.] Defeated.

1690 CHILD *Disc. Trade* (1698) 198 The worsted party, by the fate of war, being deprived of their estates. **1780** S. J. PRATT *Emma Corbett* (ed. 4) II. 52 The general on the worsted side affected to be dismayed. **1812** J. & H. SMITH *Rej. Addr.* i. (1873) 6 God bless the guards, though worsted Gallia scoff. **1869** GLADSTONE *Juventus Mundi* iii. 84 A place of refuge for fugitives, and for the worsted party expelled from other portions of Greece.

absol. **1855** BROWNING *Old Pict. Florence* xiv, To submit is the worsted's duty.

'**worstness.** *rare.* [f. WORST *a.* + -NESS.] The quality or state of being worst.

a **1665** J. GOODWIN *Filled w. the Spirit* (1867) 92 Lastness or worstness in estate or condition.

†'**worsum, 'wursum.** *Obs.* Forms: α. 1 **worsm** (**uuorsm**), **wursm**, 3 (9 *north. dial.*) **wursum** (**wrusum**), 4, *Sc.* 6–7, 9 **worsum**; *Sc.* 7 **worsam**, **-some**, 6 **woursome**, 9 **woursum**. β. 3, 6 *Sc.* **wirsum** (3 *Orm.* **wirrsenn**), 9 *north. dial.* **wirsom**. [OE. *worsm, wursm*, metathetic form of the more usual *worms, wurms* (also *wyrms*), app. related to *wyrm* WORM *sb.*] Purulent matter, pus.

α. *c* **825** *Epinal Gloss.* 777 *Pus*, uuorsm. *c* **1000** *Sax. Leechd.* I. 100 Heo.. þæt worsm [*v.r.* worms] ut atyhð. *Ibid.* II. 202 Oþ þæt he þæt wursm of muðe hræce. *a* **1225** *Ancr. R.* 274 Mine wunden.. gedereð neowe wrusum [*v.r.* wursum] & foð on eft uorte rotien. *a* **1300** *Cursor M.* 11835 Ouer-al wrang vte worsum and ware, And wormes creuld here and þare. **1513** DOUGLAS *Æneis* III. ix. 64 Thir wretchit mennis flesche, that is his fude, And drinkis worsum, and thair lopperit blude. **1595** DUNCAN *App. Etym.* (E.D.S.), *Pus, sanies*, worsum of a byle. **1610** in Pitcairn *Crim. Trials* III. 95 For Bewitching of ane kow, quhairthrow þe haill milk that scho þaireftir gaif was bluid and worsam. **1613** P. FORBES *On Rev.* iv. 15 It is not mixed with bloud.. much lesse with bloudy worsum. **1666** *Despaut. Gram.* D4a (Jam.), *Tabes*.. rotten and putrified blood and worsome. **1808** JAMIESON, *Woursum, Worsum*, purulent matter; S. pron. *wursum*. **1846** BROCKETT *N.C. Words* (ed. 3), *Wursum*, pus; particularly when foul.

β. *c* **1200** ORMIN 4782 War & wirrsenn toc anan Ut off hiss lic to flowenn. *a* **1250** *Ancr. R.* 322 (Titus MS.), Hwon.. al þe fulðe scheawes him & wringes ut tat wirsum. **1597** in *Misc. Spalding Club* (1841) I. 93 Thow.. keist witchecraft on the said cow,.. that scho gewe no milk, bot.. lyk wirsum or wenem. **1847** HALLIWELL, *Wirsom*, foul pus. *Yorksh.*

b. quasi-*adj.* Purulent.

a **1599** ROLLOCK *Serm.* Wks. 1849 I. 444 He hes not skunnert.. at thy worsum bylis, and botchis.

wort (wɜːt), *sb.*[1] Forms: 1 **wyrt**, 2 **wirte**, 6 *pl.* **wirtes**; 2 **wert**, 4 *pl.* **wertes**; 1, 3, 5–7 **wurt** (5 *pl.* **wurten**), 3 **wrt**, 3–7 **worte** (5 **wourte**), 4– **wort** (5 *pl.* **worttus**, 6 **woort**). [OE. *wyrt* root, plant = OS. *wurt*, OHG. (MHG. and G.) *wurz*, ON. (Icel., Norw., Sw., Da.) *urt*, Goth. *waurts*; the stem is related to those of ON. *rót* ROOT *sb.*, and of L. *rādix*, Gr. *ῥίζα*.

For the history of the spelling and pronunciation, see the note to WORM *sb.*]

1. A plant, herb, or vegetable, used for food or medicine; often = pot-herb.

Not in ordinary use after the middle of the 17th cent. and now *arch.* As a second element, however, retained in various plant-names, as *colewort, liverwort*.

c **825** *Vesp. Psalter* lxxxix. 6 On marne swe swe wyrt leoreð. *c* **897** ÆLFRED *Gregory's Past. C.* xxiii. 173 Maneȝra cynna wyrta & grasu. *c* **950** *Lindisf. Gosp.* Luke xi. 42 ðiæ teiȝðas meric & cunela & ælc wyrt. *c* **1000** *Sax. Leechd.* I. 70 Ðeos wyrt þe man betonicam nemneð. *c* **1250** LAY. 31884 Þat folc flah in to wudes.. heo luueden bi wurten. *c* **1250** *Gen. & Ex.* 119 Ilk gres, ilc wurt,.. His owen sed beren bad he. **1297** R. GLOUC. (Rolls) 6999 It wolde finde hom lec & worten inowe bi þe ȝere. **13..** *E.E. Allit. P.* A. 42 Schadowed þis wortez ful schyre & schene, Gilofre, gyngure, & gromylyoun, & pyonys. *c* **1386** CHAUCER *Clerk's T.* 170 Whan she homward cam she wolde brynge Wortes or othere herbes tymes ofte. *c* **1420** *Liber Cocorum* (1862) 46 Hakke smalle þy wortis and persyl. *c* **1475** *Macro Plays, Mankind* 265, I was neuer worth a pottfull a wortis, sythyn I was borne. **1531** ELYOT *Governor* III. xxii. (1883) II. 343 Wortes that the feldes do brynge furthe, for their potage. **1578** LYTE *Dodoens* V. lxxv. 642 Cyues.. is set in gardens amongst potte herbes, or wurtes. **1605** VERSTEGAN *Dec. Intell.* vii. 238 *Wirta* or *Wurta*. Woortes, for which wee now vse the French name of herbes. **1653** JER. TAYLOR *Serm. Yr., Winter* xvi. II. 204 It is an excellent pleasure to be able to take pleasure in worts and water, in bread and onions. **1755** JOHNSON, *Wort*. 1. Originally a general name for an herb; whence it still continues in many, as *liverwort, spleenwort*. **1864** COCKAYNE *Leechd.* (Rolls) I. Pref. p. liii, We find the healing power of worts spoken of as a thing of course. **1888** A. S. WILSON *Lyric Hopeless Love* cxv. 330 And worts and pansies there which grew Have secrets others wish they knew.

†**2.** A general name for any plant of the cabbage kind, genus *Brassica*; colewort. *Obs.*

c **1340** *Nominale* (Skeat) 190 Woman mylk and wortis soupith. *c* **1440** *Palladius on Husb.* I. 154 Saue wortis [*exceptis caulibus*] sowe in hem what euere hit be. *c* **1450** *Two Cookery-Bks.* 69 Hare in Wortes—Take Colys, and stripe hem faire from the stalkes. *a* **1500** *Mourn. Hare* in *E.E. Misc.* (Warton Club) 44 Yf I to the toune come or torne, Be hit in worttus or in leyke. **1538** TURNER *Libellus, Brassica.. anglice uocatur* wortes *aut* Cole *aut* Cole Wortes. [**1598** SHAKS. *Merry W.* I. i. 123 *Fal.* Good worts? good Cabidge.] **1601** HOLLAND *Pliny* XIX. iv. II. 11 Here is the stem of a woort so well growne, here is a cabbage so thriven and fed, that a poore mans boord will not hold it. **1617** FLETCHER *Valentinian* III. ii, I am poor,.. yet digging, pruning,.. Planting of Worts and Onions, any thing That's honest,.. I'll rather chuse. **1648** HERRICK *Hesper., To M. Jo. Wicks* 12 A Dish Of thrice-boyl'd-worts. **1755** JOHNSON, *Wort* 2. A plant of the cabbage kind.

†**3.** *pl.* **a.** = POTTAGE 1. *Obs.*

c **1400** *Master of Game* (MS. Digby 182, Prol. 231 He shall lat ordeynn wele his soper with wortis of the necke of the hert and of oþer good metes. **1545** RAYNOLD *Byrth Mankynde* 114 Wortes made of olde chese, cicer, cristall beaten to powder and taken with hony. **1547** BALDWIN *Mor. Philos.* 7 If thou, Diogenes, couldest flatter Dionise, thou shouldst not need to make woorts. **1556** WITHALS *Dict.* (1562) 51/2 *Pulmentum*, a meate made lyke grewell or wortes.

†**b.** With qualifying word: esp. ***long worts***.

c **1430** *Two Cookery-Bks.* 5 Lange Wortys de chare.—Take beeff and merybonys, and boyle yt in fayre water; þan take fayre wortys and.. parboyle hem in clene water [etc.]. *Ibid.*, Lange Wortes de pesoun. *c* **1460** J. RUSSELL *Bk. Nurture* 518 Frumenty with venesoun, pesyn with bakon, longe wortes not spare. *c* **1500** *Wyl Bucke's Test.* (Copland) B 1 b, For to make small wortes... then take herbes of the beste that thou can gete for wortes, and hewe them small.

4. *Comb.*, as †***wort blade***, †***-leaf***, †***-plant***, †***porridge***; ***wort-blue*** adj.; †**wort-cropper**, a name for the hare; **wort-cunning** (pseudo-*arch.*), the knowledge of herbs and plants; †**wort-stock**, a cabbage-stalk; †**wort-yard**, a herb-garden. Also WORTWORM.

14.. *Lat.-Eng. Voc.* (MS. Harl. 2257), *Caulis*,.. a *worte blade. **1933** AUDEN in *Rev. Eng. Stud.* (1978) Aug. 304 Wound round neck the *wort-blue tie. **13..** *Names of Hare* (MS. Digby 86 lf. 168b), þe cawelhert, þe *wort-croppere. **1864** COCKAYNE (*title*) Leechdoms, *Wortcunning, and Starcraft of Early England. **1579** LANGHAM *Gard. Health* 13 Rosted in a Docke or *Worte leafe. *c* **1475** *Pict. Voc.* in Wr.-Wülcker 786/37 *Hoc olusculum*, a *wurtplant. **1556** in W. H. Turner *Select. Rec. Oxford* (1880) 240 Item, *worte porrege,.. iij[d]. **14..** in Wr.-Wülcker 594/31 *Mandarus*,.. a *wortstoke. **1601** HOLLAND *Pliny* XX. ix. II. 50 Wort-stocks beeing dried and burnt into ashes. *c* **1000** *Cambr. Ps.* cxliii. 13 *Prumptuaria*, hordyrn *vel* *wyrt-ȝeardas. *c* **1380** WYCLIF *Serm.* Sel. Wks. I. 331 He.. suffrede not, for defaute of preching, Goddis vyneȝerde passe to a wortȝerd. **1382** —— *1 Kings* xxi. 2 Ȝif to me thi vyn ȝerd, that I make to me a wort ȝerd.

wort (wɜːt), *sb.*[2] Forms: 1 **wyrt**, 5 **wirt**; 4– **wort**, 4–7 **worte** (5 **wortte**), 4 **wourt**, 5 **wurt(e**, 5–7 **woort** (6 **woorte**). [OE. *wyrt* = OS. *wurtja* spicery, MHG. and G. *würze*, spice, brewer's wort), f. the stem *wurt-*; cf. *wyrt* WORT *sb.*[1]]

1. The infusion of malt or other grain which after fermentation becomes beer (or may be used for the distillation of spirits), unfermented beer. †Of beer: *(to be) in wort*, still unfermented. (See also SWEETWORT.)

c **1000** *Ags. Leechd.* II. 268 Bewylle þone þriddan dæl on hwætene wyrt. *c* **1325** *Gloss. W. de Bibbesw.* in Wright *Voc.* 158 Fro wort to ale. *a* **1387** *Sinon. Barthol.* (Anecd. Oxon.) 16 *Ciromellum*, worte. *c* **1450** *Two Cookery-Bks.* II. 107 Seth hem [*sc.* quinces] in goode wort til þey be soft. **1492** *Acta Dom. Concil.* (1839) 243/1 Þe spoliatioun.. of.. half a chalder of malt in ail and wort. **1574** R. SCOT *Hop Garden* (1578) 54 In the first Woorte.. there goeth out of these Hoppes almost no vertue at all. **1588** SHAKS. *L.L.L.* V. ii. 233 Nay then two treyes, an if you grow so nice Methegline, Wort, and Malmsey. **1602** ROWLANDS *Greenes Ghost* 8 They put in willowe leaues and broome buds into their woort in steed of hoppes. **1626** BACON *Sylva* §385 It were good also to try the Beere, when it is in Wort, that it may be seene, whether [etc.]. **1697** DAMPIER *Voy.* (1699) I. 314 This in 2 hours time will ferment and froth like Wort. **1731** P. SHAW *Three Ess. Artif. Philos.* 65 When a parcel of Wort, brewed in the common manner, is become fine by standing. **1738** *Gentl. Mag.* VIII. 140/1 An eighth Part of the Wort evaporated in three Hours boiling. **1837** *Penny Cycl.* IX. 24/1 By the excise rules, 100 gallons of such wort ought to yield one gallon of proof spirit for every five degrees of attenuation. **1868** SPENCER *Princ. Psych.* VI. vii. (1872) II. 71 Fermenting wort gives out carbonic acid. **1880** *Act 43 & 44 Vict.* c. 24 §5 (1) No person may, without being licensed.. Brew or make wort or wash.

†**b.** *Sc.* ***to play wort***: to work or stir the mash in the brewing vessel. *Obs.*

1644 *Markinch Kirk Sess. Rec.* 10 Jan., The collecteres.. delateth that Alex[r] Greig his wyff & his woman wer playing wort. *Ibid.* 12 May, James Robertson.. denyed that thair was any wort played in his hous the fasting Wednesday.

†**c.** *fig.* ***to cast in one's worts that***, etc.: to give one something to meditate upon or consider. *Obs.*

1539 CROMWELL *Let. to Hen. VIII*, 5 Feb. (1902) II. 176 And yet further I casted in his worttes that if they wold regarde them [*sc.* the Pope's censures] your highnes was and shuld be hable.. to defende.. yourself.. and that.. they shuld not fynde your grace unfournished of all thinges expedient.

2. An infusion or decoction of malt formerly used in treatment of ulcers, of scurvy, and other diseases.

1694 SALMON *Bate's Dispens.* (1713) 717/2 This medicine will do much better in a strong Decoction of Ground Malt, Anglice Wort. **1766** in Macbride *Th. & Pract. Physic* (1772) 642 The first day he took the wort, he had the following scorbutic symptoms. **1770** RUSH in *Med. Observ.* (1772) IV. 367 An Account of the Usefulness of Wort in some ill-conditioned Ulcers.

3. *attrib.* and *Comb.*, chiefly in names of utensils and materials used in brewing, as †***wort-cake***, ***-condenser***, ***-cooler***, ***copper***, †***dish***, †***-fat***, ***-filter***, †***-lead***, ***-refrigerator***, †***-stone***, †***-trough***, ***tub***, ***tun***; also ***worts-receiver***.

1795 SIR J. DALRYMPLE *Let. to Admiralty* 3 My Yeast-powder.. to set the first parcel of *Wort-cakes in fermentation. **1875** KNIGHT *Dict. Mech.*, **Wort-condenser*, one for condensing the vapor which rises from the wort in the process of boiling. *Ibid.*, **Wort-cooler*, usually a shallow vat of large area, in which the infusion of malt is placed to cool. **1838** *Civil Engin. & Arch. Jrnl.* I. 406/2 The consumption of fuel was much more considerable in the immense grate under the *wort copper. **1747** in *Nairne Peerage Evid.* (1874) 80 In the brewhouse.. a *wort dish, sixpence. **1367** *Priory of Finchale* (Surtees) p. lxxviii, iiij gilfatts sive *wourtfatts. **1583** *Rec. Elgin* (New Spald. Club 1903) I. 172 Ane masking fatt, ane wortfatt. **1875** KNIGHT *Dict. Mech.*, **Wort-filter*, one for extracting the clear liquor from the boiled mash. **1420** *Inventory* in *Lincoln Chapter Acc. Bk.* A. 2. 30. f. 69, 2 *wortleddes. *a* **1550** in Strutt *Horda* (1776) III. 65 Item 6 wort leeds, callyd coolars. **1893** NETTLETON *Manuf. Spirit* 103 They drain by several pipes.. into a *worts-receiver. **1875** KNIGHT *Dict. Mech.*, **Wort-refrigerator*, an apparatus for cooling wort after boiling with hops and previous to fermentation. **1529** *Reg. Mag. Sig. Scot.* (1883) 178 A mask fat, a *wort stane. **1542** *Richmond Wills* (Surtees) 30 A brown leed.. a maskefatt,.. and a worston. **1485** in *Ripon Ch. Acts* (Surtees) 371, j *wort trogh de lapide. **1660** *Melrose Regality Rec.* (S.H.S.) I. 295 Ane woorttroch. **1580** *Reg. Privy Council Scot.* III. 320 Foure gyle fattis and ane *wort tube. **1635** *Toke* (Kent) *Estate Accts.* (MS.) fol. 178 The great *worte tunne in bruhouse.

†**wort,** *sb.*[3] *Sc. Obs.* [Metathetic form of *wrot* WROOT *sb.*] The snout of a pig.

1507 *Extracts Aberd. Reg.* (1844) I. 436 That nay swyne be haldin withtin this toun, vtteuche band, or ane ring in thar wort,.. and gif thai be fundin vteuche band, and without ring in thar wort,.. thai salbe eshet, [etc.].

wort, variant of WHORT.

1796 WITHERING *Brit. Plants* (ed. 3) II. 370 Black Worts. Black Whortle-berries.

†**wort,** *v. Sc. Obs.* [Metathetic form of *wrot* WROOT *v.* Cf. WORT *sb.*[3]] *trans.* Of swine: To root or dig *up* (ground).

1536 BELLENDEN *Cron. Scot.* (1821) II. 164 Ane swine that.. wortis othir mennes landis, sal be slane. **1560** *Maitl. Club Misc.* III. 218 That odiouse Beast and lecherouse Swyne (quhai hais worted and ruted vp the Lordes wyne yard so far as in him wes). **1597** JAS. VI *Dæmonol.* III. i. 59 When as Swine wortes vppe the graues. **1808** JAMIESON, To *Wort, Wort-up*, v.a., to dig up.

wort, var. *vorte*, FORTE *conj.* (= until).

a **1400** *R. Glouc. Chron.* (Rolls) 4920 + 22 Vorte [MS. *a.* wort] God yt wolde amende.

‖**Wörter und Sachen** ('vœrtər ʊnt 'zaxən). [Ger., words and things (R. Meringer *Indogermanische Forschung* (1904) XVI. 101).] (See quot. 1964.) Freq. *attrib.*

1937 J. ORR tr. *Iordan's Introd. Romance Linguistics* i. 73 Their researchers imply the investigation of a variety of cultural influences and exchanges which entitles them to be associated.. with the Wörter und Sachen movement. **1957** *Language* XXXIII. 54 The twin methods of 'Wörter-und-Sachen' and 'Sachen-und-Wörter', devised half a century ago by.. Meringer and Schuchardt.. require no formal introduction at this late date. **1964** R. H. ROBINS *Gen. Linguistics* 79 A special aspect of dialect study is known as *Wörter und Sachen*... This involves the detailed study in different dialects of the forms of words relating to material objects and processes. **1976** *Amer. Speech 1973* XLVIII. 164 The Wörter-und-Sachen technique has been used for five decades by Swiss and German dialectologists to probe the relationship between words and the objects and processes they describe.

worth (wɜːθ), *sb.*[1] Forms: 1 **weorþ, weorð** (1–2 **weord**), **wurð** (2 **wurhðe**), **wyrþ**, 1, 3 **wurþ**, 2–3 **wurth** (5 **wurthe, wyrtht**); 1, 4 **worþ**, 3– **worth** (6 **wortht**), 4–7 **worthe**, 6 **woorth, wourth(e**. [OE. *weorþ* (*wurþ, worþ*) neut., = OFris. *werth*, OS. *werđ*, OHG. *werd* (MHG. *wert*, G. *werth, wert*), ON. *verð* (Norw. *verd*, Da. *værd*), Goth. *wairþ*. Cf. WORTH *a.*]

1. Pecuniary value; †price; †money.

c825 *Vesp. Psalter* xliii. 13 Ðu bibohtes folc ðin butan weorðe. c893 ÆLFRED *Oros.* IV. x. 198 Þeh þe he hie sume wið feo ȝesealde,.. he þæt weorð nolde aȝan. 971 *Blickling Hom.* 89 Hire innoþ þu ȝefyldest niȝon monaþ mid ealles middanȝeardes weorþe. c1000 *Ags. Gosp.* Matt. xxvi. 9 Þys mihte beon ȝeseald to miclum weorþe, and þearfum ȝedæled. c1175 *Lamb. Hom.* 31 Þet he nime þa ilke ehte oðer his wurð. a1225 *Ancr. R.* 150 Nis heo uniseli þet mit te wurð of heouene buð hire helle? 1297 R. GLOUC. (Rolls) 7674 Þe King Willam uorto wite þe wurþ of is londe Let enqueri streitliche [etc.]. a1300 *Cursor M.* 12390 Treen beddes for to make, Was he wont for worth to take. 1390 GOWER *Conf.* II. 46 That al the gold of Cresus halle The leste coronal of alle Ne mihte have boght after the worth. c1450 *Godstow Reg.* 539 He sholde yeve to them eschaunge to the worthe of the same acris. 1581 A. HALL *Iliad* I. 1 Chryses.. with things of price,.. His daughter captiue helde by Greekes by worth hir home to buy. 1642 D. ROGERS *Naaman* 133 A pearle.. makes all base, & to come under the worth thereof. 1695 LOCKE *Further Consid. Value Money* 27 Rising and falling of Commodities is always between several Commodities of distinct worths. 1781 COWPER *Charity* 133 The bark.. Charg'd with a freight transcending in its worth The gems of India. 1836 DICKENS *Sk. Boz, Doctors' Commons*, Some poverty-stricken legatee,.. selling his chance.. for a twelfth part of its worth. 1870 MORRIS *Earthly Par.* IV. 41 Of little worth Was all the gear that hall did hold.

b. The equivalent *of* a specified sum or amount.

For OE. examples see PENNYWORTH, and cf. HALFPENNYWORTH, *pounds' worth* (s.v. POUND *sb.*[1] 4), SHILLINGSWORTH.

1508 *Reg. Privy Seal Scot.* I. 258/1 The malis.. of the vi merkis worth of land of the Redecastell. 1583 STOCKER *Civ. Warres Lowe C.* IV. 55b, This victualler had about him in Gold to the Worth of 20. Florins. 1607 SHAKS. *Timon* III. iii. 22 I'de rather then the worth of thrice the summe, Had sent to me first. 1627 *Treasurer's Almanacke* (ed. 2) B6, The Operation of the worth of 30 *li.* Annuitie for 6 yeares. a1687 PETTY *Polit. Arith.* viii. (1691) 108 If the Tradesmen.. could do one Million worth of Work extra-ordinary. 1781 COWPER *Table-T.* 85 The worth of his three kingdoms I defy, To lure me to the baseness of a lie. 1859 TENNYSON *Geraint & Enid* 410 'Take Five horses and their armours;' ..'My lord, I scarce have spent the worth of one!' 1890 'R. BOLDREWOOD' *Col. Reformer* xxiii, He always gets the worth of his money.

†c. In allusive phr.: The amount or value *of* something small or insignificant. *Obs.*

13.. *Guy Warw.* (A.) 150 Þer nas man.. þat bireft him worþ of a slo. 1377 LANGL. *P. Pl.* B. IV. 170 ȝit ȝeue ȝe me neuere þe worthe of a russhe. 1546 J. HEYWOOD *Prov.* I. x. (1867) 24 Beggyng of hir booteth not the woorth of a beane.

†d. Money (in contrast to goods). *Obs. rare.*

a1300 *Cursor M.* 5393 Þai had noþer worth ne ware þat þai moght for þair mete spare.

2. The relative value of a thing in respect of its qualities or of the estimation in which it is held.

Freq. with implication of high value: cf. b.

1340 *Ayenb.* 82 Hit ssewеþ þet þe wordle is ydel, ine byinge vyl, in worþ biter. 1390 GOWER *Conf.* I. 25 Of Selver that was overforth Schal ben a world of lasse worth. 1570 LEVINS *Manip.* 174/2 Y[e] Worth of a thing, *precium, dignitas.* 1599 STORER *Life & D. Wolsey* C3, A man made old to teach the worth of age. 1605 CAMDEN *Rem., Epitaphs* 42 This bad inscription which I insert more for the honor of the name, then the worth of the verse. 1616 DRAXE *Bibl. Scholast.* 2 A man knoweth not the worth of a thing before that he wanteth it. 1663 BUTLER *Hud.* I. i. 880 Nor doth the bold'st attempts bring forth Events still equal to their worth. 1746 FRANCIS tr. *Horace, Art Poet.* 526 Let them not come forth, 'Till the ninth ripening Year mature their Worth. 1782 MISS BURNEY *Cecilia* VIII. ix, I knew not.. the full worth of steadiness and prudence till I knew this young man. 1857 MAURICE *Epist. St. John* i. 4 He made me see the worth of habits, the worth of acts, the worth of moral purposes. 1877 C. GEIKIE *Christ* xxxi. (1879) 370 The worth of man's homage to God does not depend on the place where it is paid.

b. High or outstanding value, excellence. *Obs.* or *arch.*

1617 J. TAYLOR (Water P.) *Three Weeks' Observ.* D2b, A paire of such Organs, which for worth and workemanship are vnparalelld in Christendome. 1659 *Gentl. Calling* VI. xvii. 435 Any thing that carries the stamp of ancient worth and nobility. 1678 WANLEY *Wond. Lit. World* V. ii. §16. 469/2 A covetous Pelagian, and one that had nothing of worth in him.

3. The character or standing of a person in respect of moral and intellectual qualities; *esp.* high personal merit or attainments.

In early use also comprising rank or dignity.

1591 SHAKS. *Two Gent.* II. iv. 102 His worth is warrant for his welcome hether. 1593 —— *Rich. II*, III. iii. 110 By the Worth and Honor of himselfe,.. His comming hither hath no further scope, Then for his Lineall Royalties. 1615 G. SANDYS *Trav.* 19 He was a iust Prince, full of worth and magnanimitie. 1621 BRAITHWAIT *Nat. Embassie* Ded. A2, The accomplished mirror of true worth, Sr. T. H. the elder. 1655 ASHE *Funeral Serm. Gataker* 46 To favour the Son very highly for his own worth and work in the Ministry. 1728 YOUNG *Love Fame* III. 265 How hard for real worth to gain its price? 1753–4 RICHARDSON *Grandison* I. xvi. 103, I regard him.. for his own worth's sake, and for his uncle's. 1788 J. HURDIS *Village Curate* (1797) 14 The down-cast eye of modest worth, Which shrinks at its own praise. 1827 SOUTHEY *Funeral Song, P'cess Charlotte of Wales* 21 Henry, thou of saintly worth. 1872 MORLEY *Voltaire* 3 Each did much to raise the measure of worth.. of mankind.

b. In *pl.*, †sometimes of one person.

a1586 SIDNEY *Arcadia* II. ii. §4 How can you him unworthy then decree, In whose chiefe parte your worthes implanted be? a1593 MARLOWE & NASHE *Dido* III. iv. 1037 If that you maiestie can looke so lowe, As my despised worths. 1616 T. SCOT *Philomythie* II. C3, If either of you, thinke you can Out of your owne worths, proue more fit. 1631 WEEVER *Anc. Funeral Mon.* 116 Honourably preferred, and prouided for according to their worthes.

4. In the phrases ***of great, little, no,*** etc., ***worth***.

1590 SPENSER *F.Q.* II. iii. 21 A goodlie Ladie.. That seemed to be a woman of great worth. 1597 HOOKER *Eccl. Pol.* v. lxii. §15 As the sacrament it selfe is a gift of no meane woorth. 1600 SHAKS. *A.Y.L.* v. iv. 161 Euerie day Men of great worth resorted to this forrest. 1634 SIR T. HERBERT *Trav.* 70 Seeing resistance of no worth, [they] fled. 1784 COWPER *Task* VI. 952 Forgive him, then, thou bustler in concerns Of little worth. 1820 SHELLEY *Hymn Merc.* xxx, Caldrons and tripods of great worth. 1847 TENNYSON *Princess* II. 397 And two dear things are one of double worth. 1846 LANDOR *Imag. Conv., Colonna & Buonarotti* Wks. II. 217/2 A man of highest worth.

b. ***of worth***: of high merit or excellence.

c1586 C'TESS PEMBROKE *Ps.* XLV. i, My harte endites an argument of worth. 1591 SHAKS. *Two Gent.* III. i. 107 She.. is promis'd by her friends Vnto a youthfull Gentleman of worth. 1634 SIR T. HERBERT *Trav.* 38 Rings and Iewels of Gold inammeld and set with stones of worth and lustre. 1686 tr. *Chardin's Coronat. Solyman* 84 All the Kaanas or Governments of Persia were likewise bestow'd upon persons of worth. 1766 FORDYCE *Serm. Yng. Wm.* (1767) I. Pref. p. vii, Women of worth and sense are to be found every-where. 1816 L. HUNT *Rimini* IV. 391 Her thin white hand, that wore a ring of worth. 1825 SCOTT *Betrothed* xxvii, The sordid wretches.. conceive those temptations too powerful for men of worth.

5. The position or standing of a person in respect of property; hence *concr.*, possessions, property, means. *Obs.* or *arch.*

1592 SHAKS. *Rom. & Jul.* II. vi. 32 They are but beggers that can count their worth. 1598 MANWOOD *Lawes Forest* xvi. (1615) 109 Euery Gentleman, Husbandman, Farmer and householder of any worth. 1634 SIR T. HERBERT *Trav.* 206 They.. generally loue play:.. so that.. they will hazard all their worth, themselues, wiues, children and other substance. 1753–4 RICHARDSON *Grandison* (1781) II. 227 She gave in an estimate of her worth, to what amount the Ladies knew not. 1812 CRABBE *Tales* xvii. 172 To legal claims he yielded all his worth.

†6. ***to take at, of,*** or ***to worth***; ***to take*** (***accept, bear, have***) ***in worth,*** or ***in good worth***; ***to take*** (or ***bear***) ***well in worth***: to take (something) at its true or proper value; to take in good part, to be content with. (See also AWORTH *adv.*) *Obs.*

(*a*) 1377 LANGL. *P. Pl.* B. XII. 125 Take we her wordes at worthe, for here witnesse be trewe. 1483 *Vulgaria abs Terentio* n ij, I thanke the that thou tokist it to worthe. *Ibid.* q ij b, Thi mynde or hert that shulde take it at worthe. c1520 *Everyman* 903 This memorayall men may haue in mynde, Ye herers take it of worth.

(*b*) c1481 *Paston Lett.* III. 278 Yf she be eny better than I wryght for, take it in woo[r]the, I shew the leeste. c1490 CAXTON *Rule St. Benet* (1902) 134 He that it was sent vnto shall take it in worthe & cherefully. c1520 SKELTON *Magnyf.* 1439 And so as ye se it wyll be no better, Take it in worthe suche as ye fynde. 1576 GASCOIGNE *Kenelw. Castle* Wks. 1910 II. 100 That you take in worth my will, which can but well deserve. 1636 SIR R. BAKER *Cato Variegatus* 16 When a poore friend, a small gift gives to thee: Take it in worth: and let it praysed be.

(*c*) c1500 *Yng. Child. Bk.* 114 in *Babees Bk.*, Be it gode or be it badde, Yn gud worth it muste be had. 1523 [COVERDALE] tr. *Dulichius' Old God* (1534) Oj, Yf greate abbottes wolde take my salutation in good worthe it sholde be redy for theym. 1549 LATIMER *3rd Serm. bef. Edw. VI* (Arb.) 82 It becommeth me to take it in good worthe, I am not better then he was. 1576 R. PETERSON *G. della Casa's Galateo* 26 Some.. neuer take in good worthe the honour and courtesie that men doe vnto them. 1609 HOLLAND *Amm. Marcell.* A ij b, Not doubting that you wil take this small gift in good worth. 1642 FULLER *Holy & Prof. St.* I. vi. 16 He compounds with his father to accept in good worth the utmost of his endeavour.

(*d*) a1542 WYATT *Poems, Lo! how I seek* 8 Hap evyll or good I shallbe glad To take that comes as well in worthe. 1564 *Brief Exam.* A iiij, I trust your most Reuerende fatherhood wyll beare all these thynges well in worth. 1592 TIMME *Ten Eng. Lepers* A2, Pardon my rudenesse herein, and take it well in woorth.

worth (wɜːθ), *sb.*[2] Now only *Hist.* Also 7 **woorth**. [OE. *worþ* (*weorþ*), *wurþ*, = OS. *wurđ*, MLG. *wurd, word*.] An enclosed place, a homestead.

Except in quot. 1649, only by inference from place-names in which it forms the second element.

1575 LANEHAM *Let.* (1871) 4 The name.. iz called Kenelvvorth. Syns most of the Worths in England stand ny vntoo like lakez [etc.]. 1628 COKE *On Litt.* 5b, Worth signifieth a watry place or water. 1649 *Deed of Conveyance, Windsor*, All those two closes.. one.. on y[e] Spittlehill and the other in the Woorth comonly called Margret Acre. 1917 *Q. Rev.* Oct. 338 Probably the 'worths' were farms on clearings made later than the original settlements.

†worth, *sb.*[3] *Obs. rare*$^{-1}$. [Perh. an error for WORTHING.] Manure.

1609–10 *Act 7 Jas. I*, c. 18 §1 The Counties of Devon and Cornewall, where the moste parte of the Inhabitantes have not commonly used any other Worth, for the bettringe of their Arrable Groundes and Pastures.

worth, *sb.*[4] error for ORD (beginning).

14.. *Sir Beues* (S) 293 [He] tolde [it] boþ worth and ende.

worth (wɜːθ), *a.* Forms: 1–2 **weorþ, weorð, weorðe**, 1–5 **worþ**, 3–5 **worþe**, 3–6 **worthe**, 3– **worth**; 1, 3 **wurð**, 1–5 **wurþ** (*Orm.* **wurrþ**, 3, 5 **wrþ**), 3–5 **wurth** (5 **wurght**), 4–5 **wurthe**; 5 **wourth**, 6–7 **woorth** (6 **-the**); 5 **werth**, 9 *dial.* **wirth**. [OE. *weorþ, worþ, wurþ*, = OFris. *werth*, OS. *werđ*, MDu. *wert, weert* (Flem. *weerd*), *waert* (Du. *waard*), OHG. *werd* (MHG., G. *wert*), ON. *verðr* (Icel. *verður*, Norw. *verd*, Sw. *värd*, Da. *værd*), Goth. *wairþs*; the relationships of the stem are obscure. OE. also had the derivative form *wierðe, wyrðe*, which is represented by *wurðe, wurthe*, in early southern texts; see WURTHE *a.* The Anglian form of this, *weorðe*, cannot in ME. be distinguished from *weorð*.]

Almost always (now only) in predicative use, or following the sb. as part of a qualifying phrase.

I. 1. a. Of the value of a specified amount or sum; equivalent to (something) in material value.

Also used indefinitely in direct or indirect questions; see group (*b*).

(*a*) a695 *Laws Ine* lv, Ewo bið mid hire ȝiunge sceape scill. weorð. *Ibid.* lviii, Oxan horn bið x. pæninga weorð. c1330 R. BRUNNE *Chron. Wace* (Rolls) 11416 Somme riche robes, wyþ [*v.r.* worth] many poundes. c1350 *Athelston* 391 Now is my goode hors forlorn,.. He was wurþ an hundryd pounde. c1435 *Torr. Portugal* 712 At the beddes hed he fond A swerd, worthe an Erllys lond. c1450 *Mirk's Festial* 86 ȝe haue a comyn sayng among you, and sayn þat Godys grace ys worth a new fayre. 1480 WARKWORTH *Chron.* (Camden) 25 Alle the good that was therin, whiche was worthe xx. ml. li. or more. c1530 [see MARCH *sb.*[2] 2]. 1544 tr. *Littleton's Tenures* 81 Though the horse.. be nat the .xx. part worth in value of the summe of money. 1573–80 TUSSER *Husb.* (1878) 44 A rottenly mould is land woorth gould. 1600 J. PORY tr. *Leo's Africa* VII. 289 An ell of the scarlet of Venice or of Turkie-cloath is here worth thirtie ducates. 1639 J. CLARKE *Parœm.* 45 A penny at a pinch is worth a pound. 1697 DRYDEN *Virg. Past.* v. 127 What Present worth thy Verse can Mopsus find! 1705 ADDISON *Italy, Pavia* 28 It [the statue] is esteem'd worth its weight in Gold. 1779 WARNER in Jesse *Selwyn & Contemp.* (1844) IV. 285 He would be worth a mint of money, and make one of the best hunters in the kingdom. 1839 LANE *Arab. Nts.* I. 80 It is worth ten pieces of gold. 1869 RUSKIN *Q. of Air* §122 The money of all nations is worth, at its maximum, the property of all nations, and no more.

(*b*) a1122 *O.E. Chron.* (Laud MS.) an. 1085 He lett ȝewritan.. hu mycel ælc mann hæfde.. & hu mycel feos hit wære wurð. c1400 *Rule St. Benet* lvii. 37 Loke what it is wrz [= wrþ], þat ye ne sette na felun price þar-on. 1528 *Sel. Cases Star Chamber* (Selden) II. 19 A Fyne.. whych amountyth nygh asmoche as the sayd landes.. be worth clyerly to be solde. 1605 ERONDELLE *Fr. Gard.* K5b, There is a fayre Diamond, what is it worth? 1795–6 WORDSW. *Borderers* III. 1278 Pray tell me what this land is worth by the acre. 1905 'G. THORNE' *Lost Cause* ii. 37 What'll it be worth when it is reaped?

ellipt. a1690–1874 [see CANDLE *sb.* 5f]. 1883 D. C. MURRAY *Hearts* xviii, The game didn't seem worth the candle.

b. Of (such-and-such) value *to* a person. Also with dative of person.

1484 CAXTON *Fables of Poge* xii, [The Dene sayd] I pray yow what is this benefyce worth to yow a yere. 1533 MORE *Apol.* x. Wks. 867/1 Al the landes and fees that I haue.. is not at this daye.. woorthe yearelye to my lyuynge, the summe of full fyftye pounde. 1560 DAUS tr. *Sleidane's Comm.* 303 Certenly that countrey is not so much worth vnto hym, but that, if he myght with his honour, he coulde be content to forgoe it. 1632 *Star Chamber Cases* (Camden) 160 He said the first oath should stand and that it should be worth her 100[li]. 1686 tr. *Chardin's Coronat. Solyman* 83 Which Employment was worth to him about fifteen thousand pounds yearly.

c. In contemptuous comparisons. Sometimes *ellipt.* after verbs of action: see (*b*).

For futher examples see BUTTON *sb.* 1b, CRESS 2, FAS 2, FIG *sb.*[1] 4, FLY *sb.*[1] 1d, HALFPENNY 1, HAW *sb.*[2] 2, LEEK 3, MITE[2] 1b, PEASE *sb.* 2b, PIN *sb.*[1] 3b, PREEN *sb.* 1b, STRAW *sb.*[1] 7, TURD 1b.

c1250 *Orison of Our Lady* 28 in *O.E. Misc.* 160 Þis liues blisse nis wurð a slo. a1272 *Luue Ron* 86 ibid. 95 Hit nere on ende wrþ on heryng. c1290 *St. James* 52 in *S. Eng. Leg.* 35 Ouwer power nis nouȝt wurth an hawe. a1300 *Cursor M.* 26991 Hop es god at hald wit houe, bot til vnskil noght worth a gloue. 1303 R. BRUNNE *Handl. Synne* 769 For euery gadlyng nat wurþ a pere Takyþ ensample at ȝow to swere. c1320 *Sir Tristr.* 3167 Þis lond nis worþ anay [= an egg], When þou darst do swiche adede. a1352 MINOT *Poems* i. 24 Þai fled,.. And all þaire fare noght wurth a flye. 1390 GOWER *Conf.* I. 334 To hasten is noght worth a kerse. 14.. ? LYDG. *Assembly of Gods* 597 For all the baytys that ye for hym haue leyde.. be nat worth a peere. 1542 UDALL *Erasm. Apoph.* 8 Whereas in maters not woorth a blewe point.. wee will spare for no cost. a1548 HALL *Chron., Hen. VII*, 7 She knewe it to be but a feigned & peinted mattre & not woorth two strawes. 1580 FULKE *Retentive, Discov. Dang. Rock* ii. 181 Therfore these three differences are not worth three chippes. 1600 W. WATSON *Decacordon* (1602) 72, I would say they [the Jesuits] had no scholerisme worth a blew button amongst them.

ellipt. 1776 FOOTE *Bankrupt* II. 36 Manufacturers, and meagre mechanicks? fellows not worth powder and shot.

(*b*) 1338 R. BRUNNE *Chron.* (1725) 204 Þou fisshes not worþe a leke, rise & go þi ways. 1362 LANGL. *P. Pl.* A. VIII. 54 Schal no deuel at his deþ-day deren him worþ a Myte. c1425 *Macro Plays, Castle Persev.* 2227 Go hens! ȝe do not worthe a tord!

2. a. Of material value; capable of being estimated in terms of money or some other material standard; valuable as a possession or property. Qualified by adv. of quantity, as *little*, *much*, †*nought*. †*well worth*: of full value. *arch.*

c **1200** *Trin. Coll. Hom.* 213 Þe sullere loueð his þing dere and seið þat it is wel wurð, oðer betere; þe beȝer.. seið þat hit nis noht wurð. *c* **1340** *Nominale* (Skeat) 306 Lityl is worth the reme of an ey. **1482** *Cely Papers* (Camden) 118 As for a gosse hawke I gett non here yett for..my lordd Chamberleyn beyth hem upp and [= if] they be any thyng wurth. **1558** T. Watson *Seven Sacr.* xviii. 113 Bye me one or twoo of the best of them and leaste woorthe. **1568** *Jacob & Esau* II. iv. C iv b, Ah sir, when one is hungry, good meat is much worth. **1581** Pettie tr. *Guazzo's Civ. Conv.* III. (1586) 138 It may rightly be saide..that the feathers are more worth then the byrde. **1615** W. Lawson *Country Housew. Garden* (1626) 6 Fruit blown vnripe, are small worth. **1718** *Entertainer* No. 19. 126 A Carbunkle is more worth than a Rock. **1719** De Foe *Crusoe* I. (Globe) 68 My Time or Labour was little worth, and so it was as well employ'd one way as another.

b. Of value in other than material respects. *arch.*

c **1200** Ormin 1156 Mare wass hiss bede wurrþ þann alle þeȝȝre lakess. *c* **1205** Lay. 26555 Nis noht wurð þratte buten þer beo dede æt. **1297** R. Glouc. (Rolls) 2318 His sacringe was lute worþ & naþeles it was ydo. **1390** Gower *Conf.* I. 25 That figure..Betokneth how the world schal change And waxe lasse worth and lasse. *c* **1430** *Freemasonry* (1840) 36 Hyt ys so muche worthe,..The vertu therof no mon telle may. **1484** Caxton *Fables of Æsop* I. xii, Better worthe is to lyue in pouerte surely, than to lyue rychely beyng euer in daunger. **1568** Cecil in *Cal. St. Papers Irel.* Pref. 8 Marry! an ounce of advise is more worth to be executed aforehand than in the sight of perrills. **1579** Googe *Lopez de Mendoza's Prov.* 32 That wisedome is more woorth then the weapons of the mightie. **1648** Gage *West Ind.* 37 Their prayers for them is more worth then the means of sustenance which they receive from them. **1672** Marvell *Reh. Transp.* I. 19, I do not think it so much worth to gain his approbation. **1781** C. Johnston *Hist. J. Juniper* II. 173 A blessing that is more worth than all the wealth of which the Jews have ever cheated honest men. **1834** Southey in *Corr. w. C. Bowles* (1881) 311 He will have..a living lesson, better worth than Divines could teach. **1871** B. Taylor *Faust* II. II. ii. 148 Little worth is woman's beauty, So oft an image dumb we see.

3. a. Of a specified or certain value in other than material respects.

1297 R. Glouc. (Rolls) 810 To soþ þou seidest me, þat as muche as ich hadde ich was worþ. **1303** R. Brunne *Handl. Synne* 8550 Þy lyfe hym þynkeþ ys wurþ no þyng. **1340–70** *Alex. & Dind.* 261 For riht wisdam is worþ al þe world riche. **1362** Langl. *P. Pl.* A. Prol. 75 Weore þe Bisschop..worþe boþe his Eres, Heo scholde not beo so hardi to deceyue þe peple. **1526** J. Rastell *Hundred Merry Tales* (1866) 93, I pray ye teche me my Pater noster, & by my trouth I shall therfore teche the a songe of Robyn hode that shall be worth .xx. of it. **1590** Spenser *F.Q.* I. iii. 30 A dram of sweet is worth a pound of sowre. **1617** Moryson *Itin.* I. 248, I thought an howers rest worth a Kings ransome. **1638** Chillingw. *Relig. Prot.* I. iii. §26. 139 Neither is this deduction worth any thing. **1713** Addison *Cato* II. i, A Day, an Hour of virtuous Liberty, Is worth a whole Eternity in Bondage. **1795–6** Wordsw. *Borderers* II. 1003 A thought that's worth a thousand worlds! **1818** Scott *Br. Lamm.* xxviii, A night-cowl of good claret is worth all the considering-caps in Europe. **1849** Lytton *K. Arthur* VI. lxxx, But one live dog is worth ten lions dead. **1867** Freeman *Norm. Conq.* I. vi. 574 The judgement of a competent tribunal is always worth something. **1894** *Solicitor's Jrnl.* XXXIX. 2/1 In a matter of this kind a grain of common sense is worth a peck of scientific hair-splitting.

b. In the phrase ***as much..is worth.***

1711 Steele *Spect.* No. 24 ¶4 It is as much as my Life is worth, if she should think we were intimate. **1849** Cupples *Green Hand* x, To haul on a wind was as much as her spars were worth.

c. ***for all (it, one) is, was worth***: to the fullest extent. Orig. *U.S.*

1875 'Mark Twain' *Sk. New & Old* 310 We shall fly our comet for all it is worth. **1883** *Mercury* (N.Y.) in Ware *Passing Engl.* 5 Scalchi, to use a side-walk phrase, played Siebel for all the character was worth. **1884** *Boston* (Mass.) *Jrnl.* 1 Oct. 2/4 The Boston Post, having worked the bogus ..letter for all that it was worth, now admits that it was a forgery. **1889** Gunter *That Frenchman* xxi. 298 [The steamer] is driving, for everything she is worth, down the waters of the Finnish Gulf. **1897** Mary Kingsley *W. Africa* 197 We spun round and round..I steering the whole time for all I was worth.

d. ***for what it is worth***, a dismissive phr. intimating that something (esp. an accompanying statement) is of uncertain or little value. Often *parenthetically*.

1888 J. Ross *Three Generations* 228 There is my opinion; I give it for what it is worth. **1922** F. Harris *My Life & Loves* I. xv. 327 However, the fact is so peculiar that I insert it here for what it may be worth. **1952** M. Norton *Borrowers* xx. 157 'Well,' she conceded at last. 'I'll tell you. For what it's worth.' **1962** A. Huxley *Let.* 19 Jan. (1969) 928 Laura brought up the idea suddenly and it fired my imagination. So here, for what it is worth, it is. **1979** J. Johnston *Old Jest* 152 You're going to have to decide which side you're on. Nancy, for what it's worth, seems to have made her decision.

†**4. a.** Valuable; of value or use (*to* some end); worthy. *Obs.*

1340 *Ayenb.* 90 Zaynte paul..heþ hyer ynemned þe meste gentile guodes þet man may do and þet mest were ywoned to by worþ and profiti. **1382** Wyclif *Matt.* v. 13 To no thing it [salt] is worth ouer, no bot that it be sent out, and defoulid of men. **1422** Yonge tr. *Secreta Secret.* 196 Hit is noȝt wourth, the Science and Iugementes of the Sterrys. **1449** Pecock *Repr.* III. viii. 325 And therfore this afore sett answere is not worth. *a* **1450** *Le Morte Arth.* 2545 To Ryde A-ȝeyne hem All by dene Or ther worthe walles holde.

†**b.** Worth while. *Obs.*

c **1386** Chaucer *Prol.* 785 Vs thoughte it was noght worth to make it wys..And bad him seye his voirdit as hym leste. **1449** Pecock *Repr.* II. i. 136, I wote not that it is worth forto talke in resonyng with eny persoon of the laife vpon eny mater of Goddis lawe, but if he be able [etc.].

5. Of standing in respect of possessions, property, or income; possessed of, owning. Usu. with specification of the sum.

1460 *Paston Lett.* III. 429 Enquere of hym wher his goode is, and what he is wurthe..; for I undre stande that he is wurthe in money v^c^ marke. **1497** *Plumpton Corr.* (Camden) 123 She is called worth m^li^ beside hir land. **1531–2** *Act 23 Hen. VIII*, c. 2 Euery suche person..beynge worthe in mouable substaunce the cleere value of .xx.li. or aboue. **1551** in Feuillerat *Revels Edw. VI* (1914) 59 Gentlemen that.. wolde not be seen in london so..disgysed for asmoche as they ar worthe or hope to be worthe. **1567** Harman *Caveat* 61 The troth is..she would wekely be worth vi. or seuen shyllinges with her begging. **1655** *Nicholas Papers* (Camden) II. 257 Sr Theodore Mayerne is dead and left his dawghter wourth a hundred thousand pounds in ready mony. **1676** Etheredge *Man of Mode* III. iii, You are for Masks, and Private Meetings; where Women engage For all they are worth I hear. **1711** Steele *Spect.* No. 260 ¶1 If.. all my Securities are good, I shall be worth Fifty thousand Pound. **1778** Miss Burney *Evelina* lxxxii, She assures me ..that I shall be sole heiress of all she is worth. **1821** Lamb *Elia* I. *Old Benchers Inner T.*, He was master of four or five hundred thousand pounds; nor did he look..worth a moidore less. **1878** G. Macdonald *Ann. Q. Neighb.* xxxii, She will be worth something when she is married.

†**6.** Of persons: of account or importance; entitled to respect or honour; worthy. *Obs.* (In OE. also of things.)

Beowulf 1902 He þæm batwearde..swurd ȝesealde, þæt he syðþan wæs..maþme þy weorðra. *c* **888** Ælfred *Boeth.* xxxix. §2 Weliȝ & weorð & rice & foremære on his aȝnum earde. *a* **1100** *Gerefa* in *Anglia* IX. 260 A swa he ȝecneordra, swa bið he weorðra. *a* **1122** *O.E. Chron.* (Laud MS.) an. 876 þa ȝislas þe on þam here weorþuste wæron. *c* **1200** Ormin 5020 & tu þe sellf narrt rihht nohht wurrþ Wiþþutenn Godess hellpe. *c* **1205** Lay. 30993 Þer neoren eorles no wurðer [*c* **1275** worþere] þene cheorles. *c* **1300** *Harrow. Hell* (E.) 172 Ʒa, leue lord, godes sone, welcom be þou & worþ come. **1340** *Ayenb.* 23 Þet byeþ þe heȝe men and þet byeþ mest worþ. *Ibid.* 90 Huo þet lest heþ, lest is worþ. *c* **1350** *Will. Palerne* 2498 He wan a-ȝen to william & to his worþ make. **1393** Langl. *P. Pl.* C. XI. 310 Fore þe more a man may do,..The more is he worth and worthi. **1535** Coverdale *Prov.* xvi. 32 He that can rule him selfe, is more worth then he y^t^ winneth a cite.

II. †**7. a.** Of sufficient merit, entitled by merit, deserving, *to* be or do something. *Obs.*

In OE. usually expressed by *wyrðe*: see wurthe *a.*

c **1000** Ælfric *Hom.* II. 316 We ðe næron wurðe beon his wealas ȝeciȝde. *c* **1200** Ormin 2357 Þærþurrh wass ȝho wel wurrþ to ben Swa wurrþedd her onn erþe. *Ibid.* 19875 Forrþi wass ȝho wurrþ att Godd,..To don þatt dede o Sannt Johan. *c* **1205** Lay. 2965 Hu mochel worȝ leste þu me [*c* **1275** hu mochel worþ holdist þou me] to walden kineriche. *a* **1300** *Cursor M.* 12822, I am noght worthe to lese þe thuanges of his sco. **1340** *Ayenb.* 231 Naȝt ne is worþ to habbe maidenhod of bodye þet heþ wyl to by y-spoused. *c* **1375** *Sc. Leg. Saints* i. (*Peter*) 332 He..mad hym byschope; for þat he ves worth to haf sic degre. **1390** Gower *Conf.* I. 107, I trowe ther be noman..That halt him lasse worth than I To be beloved. *c* **1420** Wyntoun *Cron.* v. 4502 He was worthe to wyn wictorys.

b. Deserving or worthy of (something). †In early use with genitive.

In OE. only in form *wyrðe*, Angl. *weorðe*.

c **833** *Will* in Birch *Cartul. Sax.* I. 575 Ða hwile þe God wille ðæt ðeara æniȝ sie þe londes weorðe sie. *c* **888** Ælfred *Boeth.* xvi. §1 For his cræftum he bið anwealdes weorðe, ȝif he his weorðe bið. **12..** in Bracton *De Leg. Angl.* IV. i. (Rolls) III. 184 He ne es othes worthe that es enes gylty of oth broken. *c* **1400** *Destr. Troy* 10353 Now, loke if þis lede soche longyng be worthe, As þou writis in þi wordes. *c* **1400** *Rule St. Benet* (verse) 922 Than es þer wark worth mikyl mede. *a* **1425** *Cursor M.* 12302 (Trin.) Þe childes frendes fro þat houre helde ihesu worþe honoure. *c* **1470** *Gol. & Gaw.* 1245 Ilkane be werk and be will Is worth his rewarde. **1615** W. Lawson *Country Housew. Garden* (1626) 18 And it is hardly possible to misse in graffing so often, if your Gardiner be worth his name. **1772** T. Mudge *Descr. Timekeeper* (1799) 19 It flatters me not a little that you should think any thing of mine so much worth your trouble. **1830** Marryat *King's Own* lii, The captain..is not worth his salt. **1873** Browning *Red Cott. Nt.-cap* 194 He will have recognized..How much that's good in man..makes Monsieur Léonce Miranda worth his help.

†**c.** Without const.: Of merit, deserving. *Obs.*

c **1380** Wyclif *Serm.* Sel. Wks. I. 358 Ʒour place is ordeyned in hevene after þat ȝe ben worþe.

†**d.** Deserving on account of demerit or fault. *Obs.*

c **1375** *Lay Folks Mass Bk.* (MS. B.) 72 In worde, & werk I am to wite and worth to blame. *c* **1375** *Cursor M.* 44 (Fairf.) Our dedis fra our hert takis rote, queþer þai be worþ bale or bote. *c* **1400** *Rom. Rose* 7104 Wel were it worth to bene brent.

8. a. Sufficiently valuable or important to be an equivalent or good return for (something). Also const. *of*. ***worth (the) while***: see while *sb.* 3 b.

1387 Trevisa *Higden* IV. 355 The queene..beet Iudas ful ofte, but al for nouȝt, ffor it was not worþ þe while. **1513** Douglas *Æneis* II. vii. 129 Thair with my handis wrocht I worth my deid. **1556** Huggard *Display. Protestants* 40 It shall be worth the traueill to say somwhat therein. **1642** C. Saltonstall *Navigator* 65 They [the Theorems] will give you so great a light..that it will be well worth your labour. **1667** Milton *P.L.* I. 262 To reign is worth ambition though in Hell. **1711** W. King tr. *Naude's Ref. Politics* iii. 107 That the crown of France was well worth the trouble of hearing one mass. **1866** Neale *Sequences & Hymns* 23 Ye, who sometimes think the glory Of the labour scantly worth.

b. With vbl. sb. (in early use with *the*, *one's*) as complement. †Also *to* with inf. (quot. 1559).

The const. also occurs with OE. *wyrðe*, *weorðe*.

In recent times the illogical use of *worth* for *worth while*, and vice versa, is frequent.

(*a*) **1540** Palsgr. *Acolastus* IV. vii. X ij b, My corne..was not worth the cuttyng downe. **1559** Clough in Burgon *Life Gresham* (1839) I. 255 It was sure a sight worth to go 100 myles to see it! **1582** N. Lichefield tr. *Castanheda's Conq. E. Ind.* I. v. 13 (*margin*) Three smal Ilands discouered not worth the entering. **1617** Moryson *Itin.* I. 32 A Tower.. worth the seeing, for the antiquity and building. **1630** *R. Johnson's Kingd. & Commw.* 112 All histories will tell you, it is a point worth the looking into. **1669** Earl Sandwich tr. *Barba's Art of Metals* I. (1674) 129 It is very well worth ones making a journey purposely to see them. **1692** L'Estrange *Fables* cccxliii. 300 Hang 'em All up..they are not Worth the Begging. **1798** Wordsw. *Peter Bell* III. 815 An Ass like this was worth the stealing! **1832** Lister *Arlington* II. 252 You may think it little worth the telling,..but you shall know every thing.

(*b*) **1591–5** Spenser *Col. Clout* 85 Well I weene it worth recounting was. **1638** Junius *Paint. Ancients* 28 Viewing round about all what was worth seeing in so famous a place. **1686** [Allix] *Dissert.* iii. in *Ratramnus' Body & Bl.* (1688) 54 It is worth observing..that the Adoration of the Sacrament sprang not up till some Ages after. **1751** Hume *Enq. Princ. Morals* vii. (1902) 256 [He] soon lost his iron lamp, the only furniture which he had worth taking. **1782** Miss Burney *Cecilia* VIII. iv, That the matter is somewhat spread..is now not to be helped, and therefore little worth thinking of. **1836** *Hints on Etiquette* (ed. 2) 15 If a man be worth knowing, he is surely worth the trouble to approach properly. **1877** Mallock in *19th Cent.* Sept. 251 (*article*) Is Life worth living? **1889** T. A. Trollope *What I remember* III. 285, I have then, as at all times, found life eminently 'worth living.' **1915** Sisam *Skeat's Havelok* p. xxxi, When a text has any claims to belong to the thirteenth century, it is worth noticing what evidence it contains for the lengthening of short vowels in open syllables.

c. With nouns having the force of vbl. sbs.

1660 *Nicholas Papers* (Camden) IV. 231 He is acquainted with diuers things worth the knowledge. **1744** M. Bishop *Life* 137, I..was very inquisitive in asking about every particular Thing that was worth my Observation. **1772** *Junius Lett.* lxviii. 338 It is worth the reader's attention to observe. **1837** Dickens *Pickw.* iii, 'They are not worth your notice,' said the dismal man. **1877** Huxley *Physiogr.* 76 The rusting of this particular metal is worth closer study.

†**9.** Fit, meet, proper. *Obs. rare.*

a **1300** *Cursor M.* 7515 It es noght worth, leif sir king, þat man in godd haue mistrouing. *a* **1400–50** *Wars Alexander* 3426, I maynly ȝow swere,..þe worthe wage þaim [to] wayue þat þai haue wele serued. *c* **1412** Hoccleve *De Reg. Princ.* 441 Certes to blame ben þe lordes grete,..þat hir men lete Vsurpe swiche a lordly apparaille; [It] Is not worþ.

worth (wɜːθ), *v.*[1] *Obs.* exc. *arch.* Forms: (see below). [Common Teut.: OE. *weorðan*, *wurðan* (*wearþ*, *wurdon*, *ȝeworden*) = OFris. *wertha*, *wirtha*, *wirda* (WFris. *wirde*), OS. *werdan* (MLG. and LG. *werden*; MDu. and Du. *worden*), OHG. *werdan*, *werthan* (MHG. and G. *werden*), ON. and Icel. *verða* (Norw. dial. *verda*, *verta*, MSw. *varþa*, *vardha*, Sw. *varda*, Da. *vorde*), Goth. *wairþan*. The stem is prob. the same as that of L. *vertĕre*, OSlav. *vrŭtěti*, *vratiti* (Russ. *vertjet'*), Lith. *versti* (stem *vert-*), Skr. *vrit* (*vártatē*, *vartti*) to turn, the sense in Germanic having developed into that of 'to turn into', 'to become'. Cf. -ward *suffix*.

OE. compounds are represented by the obsolete forworth and i-worth.]

A. Illustration of Forms.

1. a. *Inf.* α. 1 **weorðan, wurðan, wyrðan**, 2–3 **wurðen, wurþen** (3 *Orm.* **wurrþenn**), 3 **wrþan**, 4 **worþen, worthyn**. β. 2 **wurðe**, 4 **werþe**, 4–5 **worþe**, 4–6 **worthe**. γ. 4 **worþ**, 4–5 **worth**. δ. 4 **worde**, 5–7 *Sc.* **word**.

α. *Beowulf* 2526 Unc sceal weorðan..swa unc wyrd ȝeteoð. *a* **900** *Andreas* 182 (Gr.) Sceal feorhȝedal..æfter wyrðan. *c* **1000** *Daniel* 115 (Gr.) Þætte rices ȝehwæs.. sceolde..ende wurðan. *c* **1200** *Trin. Coll. Hom.* 147 He wiste..þat hit wurðen solde. *c* **1200** Ormin 492 Þatt nan ne shollde wurrþenn þa sett to wurrþenn prest. *c* **1205** Lay. 1234 Þar on þu scalt wrþan sæl. *c* **1275** *Prov. Ælfred* 200 in *O.E. Misc.* 115 It sollen wurþen to nout. *c* **1330** *Assump. Virg.* 262 (B.M. MS.), Ne schal me neuer worþen wel. *c* **1394** *P. Pl. Crede* 9 Schent mote y worþen. *a* **1400** in *Anglia* XVIII. 324 Ʒif on be in poynt to worthyn wod.

β. *c* **1200** *Trin. Coll. Hom.* 147 He spec of þat þe sholde wurðe. **13..** *Guy Warw.* 1171 Swiche no miȝt y neuer werþe. *c* **1350** *Will. Palerne* 327 God lene him grace to god man to worthe. *c* **1400** *Gamelyn* 491 Cursed mot he worthe. *a* **1450** *Le Morte Arth.* 1817 What shall worthe of vs twoo!

γ. *a* **1300** *Cursor M.* 930 To puder sal þou worth again. **1377** Langl. *P. Pl.* B. II. 47 Lat hem worth til lewte be iustice. *a* **1400–50** *Wars Alexander* 2878 He bad hym..on a blonk worth. **1549** Latimer *4th Serm. bef. Edw. VI* (Arb.) 120 What wyl worth..of thys man?

δ. *a* **1300** *Cursor M.* 22489 (Edinb.) Þe sternes..sal.. worde al blak sum ani col. *c* **1375** *Sc. Leg. Saints* xviii. (*Egipciane*) 1181 Now quhat sal word of me? **1533** Gau *Richt Vay* (S.T.S.) 30 He wald word man for our saluation. *a* **1665** W. Guthrie *Serm.* 14 (Jam.) What will word of my wife?

b. *Pres. Ind.* (*3rd sing.*) α. 1 **weorðeð**, (**uuiurthit**), **wyrðeþ**, 3 **wurðeð**, 4 **worþeþ** (*pl.* **worþen**); *north.* 1 **worðes**, 4 **worþez**, **-is** (*2nd* **worþest**), 5 **worthis**, *Sc.* **wordis**, **wourdis**. β. 1 **weorð**, **wierð**, **wyrð**, **wirð**, **wurð**, 2 **wrð**, 3 **wurþ**, 3–4 **worþ**, 4–6 **worth** (4 **worht**); *2nd* 1 **wyrst**, 3–5 **worst**.

In OE. and early ME. the present tense is sometimes used in place of the future.

α. **735** [see B. 2]. *a* **900** *Andreas* 483 (Gr.) ðif ðu..larna þinra este wyrðest. *c* **950** *Lindisf. Gosp.* Luke i. 34 Huu worðes ðis? *a* **1000** *Laws of Æthelbirht* xxxiv, ᵹif banes blice weorðeþ, III scillingum ᵹebete. *c* **1205** LAY. 8786 For ȝet heo wurððeð þe laðe. *c* **1290** *Beket* 998 in *S. Eng. Leg.* 135 Alle we worþez i-brouȝt to nouȝte. *a* **1310** in Wright *Lyric P.* ix. 36 Hit wortheth al to wyn. **13..** *Guy Warw.* 407 þou worþest to hewen. **13..** *Gaw. & Gr. Knt.* 1106 Hit worþez to yourez. **1398** TREVISA *Barth. De P.R.* VI. v. (Tollem. MS.), þe ouir party..worþeþ more lyȝte, and þe neþer parties..worþen more heuy. *a* **1450** *Le Morte Arth.* 782 Vp he worthis vppon his stede. *c* **1475** *Rauf Coilȝear* 706 Ȝone is Wymond, I wait, it worthis na weir. *c* **1480** HENRYSON *Cock & Jewel* 23 þe bow þat ay is bent Wordis vnsmart.

β. *c* **888** ÆLFRED *Boeth.* iv, þonne he betwux us & hire wyrð. *c* **897** —— *Gregory's Past. C.* xvii. 111 He wierð self to ðæs onlicnesse. *c* **900** *Bæda's Hist.* Pref. i. (1890) 2 Hu wurð he elles ᵹelæred? *a* **1000** *Laws Æthelbirht* lxv, ᵹif he healt weorð, þær motan freond seman. *c* **1000** ÆLFRIC *Gen.* iii. 19 Ðu..to duste ᵹewyrst [*v.r.* wyrst]. *Ibid., Exod.* vii. 9 Heo wyrð to næddran. *a* **1175** *Cott. Hom.* 235 Fram þa forme man to þa latst þe wrð et þes wrldes ende. *c* **1250** *Prov. Ælfred* 304 in *O.E. Misc.* 120 And selde wurþ he blyþe and gled. **1297** R. GLOUC. (Rolls) 1570 So is þe stude icluped nou & euere worþ. *c* **1325** *Spec. Gy Warw.* 128 Sauued worþ he neuere mo. *c* **1380** *Sir Ferumb.* 488 þyn auaunt worþ dere aboȝt. **1513** DOUGLAS *Æneis* XII. Prol. 187 Slekyt worth thir bestis skynnis.

1297 R. GLOUC. (Rolls) 2232 þou worst þer king anon. **1377** LANGL. *P. Pl.* B. XIX. 404 Ysaued worstow [*v.r.* worst þou] neure. *c* **1380** *Sir Ferumb.* 805 Elles þow worst beleyn. *c* **1425** *Seven Sag.* (P.) 1505 Certys, syre, thou worst schent.

c. *Pres. Subj.* 1 **weorðe**, (**uueorthae**), 2–3 **wurðe**, (*pl.* **wurðen**), **wurþe**, 3 **wurthe**, 4 **wurth**; 3–4 **worþe**, 4–6 **worthe**; 4 **worþ**, 4– **worth**, (4 **wortht**, 5 **vorth**); 6 *Sc.* **wirth**.

735 [see B. 2 b]. *c* **1000** *Saxon Leechd.* III. 58 ᵹif næᵹl of honda weorðe. *c* **1175** *Lamb. Hom.* 153 I þonked wurðe him. *c* **1200** *Trin. Coll. Hom.* 193 Ure fon..wulled swo don, bute we wurðen us warre. *c* **1250** *Prov. Ælfred* 633 Wel worþe þe wid. *c* **1300** *Havelok* 434 Waried wurthe he. *Ibid.* 2873 Blissed worþe his soule ay! *a* **1352** MINOT *Poems* ii. 11 Wele worth þe while. *a* **1375** *Joseph Arim.* 146 Mensked he worþe! *c* **1400** *Destr. Troy* 597 Till ye fay worthe. *c* **1440** *Generydes* 4871 Woo worth the tyme. **1500–20** DUNBAR *Poems* xliv. 9 Wo wirth the fruct..And wo wirth him. **1563** *Homilies* II. *Passion* II. 199 Wo worth the tyme that euer we synned. **1611** SPEED *Hist. Gt. Brit.* IX. xviii. 887 Ah woe worth him.

d. *Imper.* 4 **worth**, 5 **worthe**.

a **1330** *Otuel* 828 Worþ vp bi-hinden me her. *c* **1450** *Pol. Poems* (Rolls) II. 249 Thanne worthe upp, Walis.

2. *Past Tense.* (*1st* and *3rd sing.*) α. 1–3 **wearþ**, **wearð**, **warð**, 2, 4 **ward** (2 **uuard**), 3–4 **warþ** (3 *Orm.* **warrþ**); 2–3 **werð**, **werþ**, 4 **werþe**, **werth**; *pl.* 1 **wurdon**, 2 **wurðon**, **wurþen**, 5 **worden**. β. 3 **wurð**, **wurd**, **worþ**, (4 **worþe**), 4–6 **worth** (5 **worthe**). γ. *Sc.* and *north.* 5 **word**, 5–6 **worde**.

α. *a* **900** *Andreas* 1343 (Gr.) Hwæt wearð eow? *c* **1000** *Ags. Gosp.* Luke xxiii. 12 On ðam dæge wurdun herodes & pilatus ᵹefrynd. *a* **1154** *O.E. Chron.* an. 1135 Wurþen men suiðe of uundred. *c* **1160** *Hatton Gosp.* Matt. viii. 26 þær warð ȝeworðen mychel smoltnyss. *c* **1175** *Lamb. Hom.* 133 Sum [seed]..werð totreden. *c* **1200** *Trin. Coll. Hom.* 167 þe lichame warð bretful of wunden. *Ibid.* 181 He..wearð þar mide acheked. *c* **1200** ORMIN 10960 þæraffterr warrþ itt efft to nohht. **13..** *Guy Warw.* 4723 Opon a mule sche warþ anon. **1387** TREVISA *Higden* V. 277 At laste he werþe sike. *c* **1400** *Chron. R. Glouc.* (Rolls) App. G. 171 Noble he werþ & riche. *c* **1400** T. CHESTRE *Launfal* 131 He ward yn greet dette. **1481** CAXTON *Reynard* xvi. (Arb.) 34 Thus worden my teeth al blody.

β. *c* **1200** *Trin. Coll. Hom.* 99 þat bred wurð to fleis. *c* **1250** *Gen. & Ex.* 995 His name ðo wurð a lettre mor. *Ibid.* 1197 Ȝhe wurd wið child. *c* **1275** *Duty of Christians* 109 in *O.E. Misc.* 144 þat folk worþ eft wroþe i-spild. **1387** TREVISA *Higden* V. 195 Lowys..worþe sike. *c* **1440** *Gesta Rom.* xlvi. 186 What worthe of hit he ne knew. *c* **1470** HENRY *Wallace* III. 13 Wictaill worth scant. **1513** DOUGLAS *Æneis* V. xi. 86 The myndis worth agast.

γ. *c* **1375** *Sc. Leg. Saints* xii. (*Mathias*) 420 He worde stane-blynde. **1570** *Durham Depos.* (Surtees) 137 He knewe not..what worde of them.

3. *Past Participle.* α. 1 **ᵹeworden**, 2 **-ðen**, 3 **iwurðen**, 4 **iworþe**. β. 1 **worden**, 2 **wurðen**, 3 *Orm.* **wurrþenn**, 5 **wurthen**; 2–3 **worðen**, 4 **worþen**, 4–5 **worthen**; *Sc.* 4–5 **worthyn**, **-ine**, 5–6 **worthin** (6 **-ing**), 6 **wordine**. γ. 2 **wurþe**, 5 **worthe**.

α. **971** *Blickl. Hom.* 223 He..sona wearð hal ᵹeworden. *c* **1160** *Hatton Gosp.* Matt. viii. 26 þær warð ȝeworðen mychel smoltnyss. *c* **1230** *Hali Meid.* 9 And is þat..iwurðen to meastling. **1387** TREVISA *Higden* IV. 187 þe Parthes þat were i-worþe rebel.

β. *c* **1000** *Daniel* 124 (Gr.) Wearð he..acol worden. *c* **1200** *Trin. Coll. Hom.* 147 He spec of þat..alse þehȝ hit wurðen were. *c* **1200** ORMIN 3873 Godess Sune..Wass wurrþenn mann. *c* **1375** *Sc. Leg. Saints* iv. (*James*) 198 Herrod..wes worthine þe devilis lyme. *c* **1400** *Destr. Troy* 9691 To frete hom with fyre, þat were fey worthen. **14..** WYNTOUN *Cron.* (W.) IV. 1654 Thai had sene The wethere worthing brycht and schene. *c* **1430** *Pilgr. Lyf Manhode* II. cxli. (1869) 131 On horse he is wurthen vp. *c* **1480** HENRYSON *Want of Wyse Men* 6 Wit is worthin wrynkis. **1513** DOUGLAS *Æneis* III. Prol. 26 Wenis thou..the craw be worthin quhite. **1533** GAU *Richt Vay* (S.T.S.) 29 That God is wordine mane.

γ. *c* **1200** *Trin. Coll. Hom.* 219 Also suteliche swo it wurþe were. *c* **1449** PECOCK *Repr.* V. vi. 516 Lete se what schulde haue worthe of the men.

4. *Weak forms.* **a.** *Pa. t.* 3 **wurðede**, 5 **wurthed**; 4–5 **worthed(e**, **-id** (*Sc.* **-yd**); *Sc.* and *north.* **worthit**, **-yt** (5 **wourthit**). **b.** *Pa. pple.* 4 **worþed**, **worthed**, *Sc.* 7 **worde**, 9 **wort**.

c **1250** *Gen. & Ex.* 2946 Ðe fisses..wurðeden dead. **13..** *Gaw. & Gr. Knt.* 485 Til worþed an ende. *Ibid.* 678 A duk to haue worþed. **1375** BARBOUR *Bruce* XIII. 354 Thame worthit..abyde. *c* **1400** MAUNDEV. (Roxb.) xxiv. 112 þe whilk..worthed till a worthy and a..Cristen man. *c* **1440** *Alphabet of Tales* 307 What at wurthed of þe bodie cuthe neuer man tell. *c* **1470** *Gol. & Gaw.* 973 Thus wourthit schir Gawyne wraith. *a* **1500** *Hist. K. Boccus & Sydracke* (? 1510) *S* iij, The kyng..worthed there vpon. **1570** *Durham Depos.* (Surtees) 149 He knoweth not what is woorde of the graill. **1629** Z. BOYD *Last Battell* 425 (Jam.) What can bee worde of such a..professor. **1818** HOGG *Brownie of Bodsbeck* I. 38 What could be wort of a' the sheep.

B. Signification.

1. *intr.* To come to be, come to pass, come about, happen, take place.

c **950** *Lindisf. Gosp.* Luke i. 34 Cuoeð..[Maria] to ðæm engel, huu worðes ðis? *c* **1000** *Ags. Gosp.* Matt. viii. 26 He bebead þam winde & þare sæ, & þær wearð ᵹeworðen mycel smyltness. *c* **1200** *Trin. Coll. Hom.* 147 He spec of þat þe sholde wurðe. *Ibid.* 197 Hit is worðen alse ure louerd wolde. **13..** *Northern Passion* H 410 Or þe kok haue krawin thrise Sall it worth opon þis wise. **13..** *Gaw. & Gr. Knt.* 485 Wyth wele walt þay þat day, til worþed an ende, in londe. *c* **1400** *Leg. Rood* iv. 127 And so it wurthed at þe last þe cros al out of minde was past. *c* **1425** *Eng. Conq. Ireland* xvi. 38 Aftyr this, worth gret spech yn-to all þe lond.

b. In the subjunctive mood, expressing a wish for something to happen to one, usually with dat. of person.

13.. *Cursor M.* 25633 (Gött.) Gabriel..said, 'leuedi! ful of blis, ai worth þe wel!' *c* **1300** *Havelok* 2221 He let his oth al ouer-go, Euere wurþe him yuel and wo! *c* **1350** *Will. Palerne* 2567, I ne wot in wat wise to worche be best,..but worþe god wiþ alle. *c* **1394** *P. Pl. Crede* 493 Eft he seyde to hem-selfe wo mote ȝou worþen. *c* **1400** *Gamelyn* 482 But ever worthe hem wel that doth thee moche sorwe. *c* **1450** *Mirk's Festial* 295 þe dor tyneth on hym for euermore and so eurelasting farewel worthe hym and hys werkys.

c. In the phrases ***woe worth*** (now arch.), and ***well worth*** (obs.) followed by noun or pronoun. (Cf. WOE A. 4, WELL *a.* 1.)

(*a*) *c* **1205** LAY. 3359 Wa worðe þan monne þe lond haueðe mid menske. **13..** *Cursor M.* 21992 (Edin.) Antecriste..wa worþe his wit! *c* **1350** *Will. Palerne* 4118 Ȝif i wrong seie any word, wo worþ me euer. **1390** GOWER *Conf.* III. 320 Wo worthe evere fals envie! *c* **1440** *Gesta Rom.* lxi. 260 Woo worthe the oure that euer I was made in! **1470–85** MALORY *Arthur* IV. xi. 132 Wo worth this swerd, for by hit haue I geten my dethe. *a* **1542** SIR. T. WYATT *Poems* (1913) I. 76 Thou toke her streight from me: that wo worth thee! **1600** HOLLAND *Livy* V. xlviii. 211 Wo worth men conquered, and downe with them still. **1647** HERRICK *Noble Numb., Widow's T.* 21 Woe worth the Time, woe worth the day, That reav'd us of thee, Tabitha. *a* **1801** R. GALL *Poems & Songs* (1819) 30 Wae worth ye, sir! it sets ye ill To talk to me in sic a style. **1810**, **1870** [see WOE A. 4].

(*b*) *c* **1205** LAY. 13079 Wel wurðe þe Vortiger þat þu ært icumen her. *c* **1250** *Gen. & Ex.* 155 Wel wurðe his miȝt.., ðe wrout is on ðe ferðe day! **13..** *Gaw. & Gr. Knt.* 2127 Wel worth þe, wyȝe, þat woldez my gode. *a* **1352** MINOT *Poems* ii. 5 It es wrokin, I wene, wele wurth þe while. *c* **1374** CHAUCER *Troylus* v. 379 Wel worth of dremes ay þese olde wyues. *c* **1480** HENRYSON *Fox & Wolf* 35 Weill worth my Father, that send me to the lair.

2. To become, come to be (something): **a.** With sb. or adj. as complement.

735 *Bæda's Death-verse* 1 Fore there neidfaerae naeniᵹ uuiurthit thoncsnotturra than him tharf sie. **971** *Blickl. Hom.* 175 þa hwile þe he þær stod, he wearþ færinga ᵹeong cniht. *a* **1154** *O.E. Chron.* an. 1135, And uuard þe sunne suilc als it uuare thre niht ald mone. *Ibid.* an. 1154, þat ilce dæi..þa sæclede he & ward ded. *c* **1200** ORMIN 160 Oþre unnfæwe shulenn ec Full glade & bliþe wurrþenn. *c* **1205** LAY. 32107 þenne scullen i[n] Bruttene blissen wurðen riue. *c* **1250** *Gen. & Ex.* 1175 Abimalech wurð sek on-on. **1297** R. GLOUC. (Rolls) 2806 Louerd he worþ of france. *c* **1320** *Sir. Tristr.* 836 Til y tristrem se, No worþ y neuer bliþe. **1340–70** *Alex. & Dind.* 265 Bute þe loweste þat liuede his lord mihte worþe. **1387** TREVISA *Higden* I. 189 Scheepe þat drynkeþ of þat oon [river] schulle worþe blak, and schepe þat drynkeþ of þat oþer schul worþe whyte. *a* **1400** *Stockh. Med. MS.* 699 in *Anglia* XVIII. 324 Ȝif on be in poynt to worthyn wood For peyne of teth, dragance is good. *c* **1425** WYNTOUN *Cron.* VIII. iii. 145 He suld hawe worthyd rede for schame A fre kynryk swa til defame. **1456** SIR G. HAYE *Law Arms* (S.T.S.) 45 For dout that thai worth proude and hautayn of thair office. **1513** DOUGLAS *Æneis* IV. Prol. 245 O lust,.. Thyself consumyng worthis insaciable.

b. With past participles.

735 *Bæda's Death-verse* 5 Hwæt his gastae..æfter deothdaeᵹe doemid uueorthae. *a* **1154** *O.E. Chron.* an. 1135, Wurþen men suiðe of uundred & of dred. *c* **1175** *Lamb. Hom.* 133 Sum of þe sede feol..bi þe weie and werð totreden. *c* **1200** ORMIN 347 þatt streon þatt wass..lac to wurrþenn offredd her O rodetreowwess allterr. *c* **1250** *Gen. & Ex.* 1943 In ðis ðisternisse,..Ȝet wurðe [he] worpen naked and cold. **1297** R. GLOUC. (Rolls) 2801 Cristendom worþ icast adoun. *c* **1350** *Will. Palerne* 2291 But god now hem help, slayn worþ þei slepend. **1377** LANGL. *P. Pl.* B. XIX. 404 But þow lyue by lore of *spiritus iusticie*,..ysaued worstow neure. *c* **1380** *Sir Ferumb.* 1871 If þou tarie longe her-wyþ þou worst y-schent Heȝe þow worst an honge. *c* **1425** *Eng. Conq. Ireland* xlix. 124 Al the contrey forth ther-aftyr worth so I-storbet, that [etc.].

3. With prepositional or adverbial complements: **a.** To come to be, attain to being (in a particular place or condition).

c **888** ÆLFRED *Boeth.* iv, Swa deð eac se mona..þonne he betwux us & hire [the sun] wyrð. *a* **900** CYNEWULF *Crist* 1028 þonne..Adames cynn..weorþeð foldræste eardes æt ende. **1297** R. GLOUC. (Rolls) 327 þo he adde is bone ido he werþ aslepe riȝt þere. *c* **1374** CHAUCER *Compl. Mars* 248 He wend anon to worthe out of his mynde. *c* **1400** TREVISA *Higden* VII. 505 The strete werth a fuyre. *c* **1400** T. CHESTRE *Launfal* 131 So savagelych hys good he besette, That he ward yn greet deete. *c* **1470** *Gol. & Gaw.* 1096 Lat it worth at my wil the wourschip to wale.

b. To turn or be converted *to* something; to change in status *to*.

Beowulf 2203 Heardrede hildemeceas..to bonan wurdon. *a* **1122** *O.E. Chron.* (Laud MS.) an. 870, Hit þa þæt ær wæs ful rice, þa hit wearð to nan þing. *a* **1023** WULFSTAN *Hom.* xxx. 145 We..sceolon on woruIde wurðan wurmum to æte. *c* **1200** ORMIN 6976 þatt steorrne..Warrþ all to nohht.. Affterr þatt Crist wass fundenn. *c* **1200** *Trin. Coll. Hom.* 99 þat bred wurð to fleis and þe drinke to blod. *c* **1230** *Hali Meid.* 9 And is þat tu wendest gold, iwurðen to meastling. *c* **1300** *K. Horn* (Laud) 467 þou art so fayr and briycte, þou schalt worþe to knyte. **13..** *Gaw. & Gr. Knt.* 1106 Quat-so-euer I wynne in þe wod, hit worþez to yourez. *c* **1394** *P. Pl. Crede* 746 And ich a beggers brol.. worþ to a writere. **1456** SIR G. HAYE *Law Arms* (S.T.S.) 211 Sa that, bot gif thare war a soverane..all the world wald worth to nocht.

c. To get *up*, *on* or *upon*, a horse, etc.

c **1290** *Beket* 1164 in *S. Eng. Leg.* 139 þe holi Man..werth op..and rod him forth wel faste. **13..** *Guy Warw.* 4723 Opon a mule sche warþ anon. *c* **1330** *Arth. & Merl.* 5053 (Kölbing) A destrer þo ladde Agreuein..& seyd, 'Worþ her on hastiliche!' *c* **1374** CHAUCER *Boeth.* II. pr. ii. (1868) 35 Worþe vp [L. *ascende*] yif þou wilt. *c* **1400** *Master of Game* (MS. Digby 182) xxxiii, þe horsmen þat beth þere at þe deth, shulde worthe vppe on horse. *c* **1450** LOVELICH *Merlin* 11398 Kyng Arthewr be þe Reyne his hors took son,..'My leve frend,' he seide, 'worth vp jn haste.' *a* **1500** *Hist. K. Boccus & Sydracke* (? 1510) *S* iij, For thy the kyng Boccus anon Toke hors and worthed there vpon.

d. To become *of* (= happen to, betide). Also with *on*.

c **1380** WYCLIF *Serm.* Sel. Wks. II. 277 God behiȝt hem Isaac, and tolde what shulde worþe of him. *c* **1400** MAUNDEV. (Roxb.) xxxi. 139 We wist neuere what worthed of þe remenaunt. *c* **1449** PECOCK *Repr.* V. vi. 516 Lete se what schulde haue worthe of the man in these ȝeeris, if thei hadden not be mad religiose. **1549** LATIMER *4th Serm. bef. Edw. VI* (Arb.) 120 What wyl worth, what wyl be the ende of thys man? *c* **1570** *Durham Depos.* (Surtees) 150 He knew not from whence they came, or what worde of them. **1629** Z. BOYD *Last Battell* 425 (Jam.) Then many shall wonder what can bee worde of such a blazing professor. *a* **1665** W. GUTHRIE *Serm.* 14 (Jam.) What will word of my house? And, What will word of my goods and gear? **1818** HOGG *Brownie of Bodsbeck* I. 38, I was..considering what could be wort of a' the sheep.

e. To pass *away*, go *hence*, remain *after* (= behind).

13.. *Cursor M.* 19110 (Edin.) þe lastand dede sal worþe awai. *c* **1350** *Will. Palerne* 2355 Wende listly hennes & late me worþ after. *c* **1400** *Destr. Troy* 1975 þou shalt haue þat I hete & þou hence worth. *a* **1425** *Cursor M.* 22588 (Trin.) Lord god þat lasteþ ay þou shal vs do to worþe away.

4. ***to let*** (one) ***worth***: to let alone; = I-WORTH 6.

1297 R. GLOUC. (Rolls) 2330 þer fore he was so prout & þe king nas him sulf bote as a ssade, & let im worþe al out. *c* **1350** *Will. Palerne* 3597 'Lat me worþ', quaþ william, 'þat schal i wite sone'. **1377** LANGL. *P. Pl.* B. Prol. 187 For-þi I conseille alle þe comune to lat þe catte worthe. *c* **1400** *Rom. Rose* 6037 Late ladies worthe with her thyngis. *c* **1450** *Merlin* iii. 58 Than seide Merlyn, 'Let me worthen ther-with, and I shall a-quyte me of the couenaunt that I made'.

5. To behove, need, be necessary. Usu. impersonal with dative preceding (*him worthit*, etc.). *Sc.*

1375 BARBOUR *Bruce* IV. 194 Him worthit, magre his, abyde In till ane hamelat neir thair-by. *c* **1375** *Sc. Leg. Saints* ii. (*Paul*) 651 þis Nero worthit ay of ned..ryse aye quhene his master come nere. *c* **1425** WYNTOUN *Cron.* VI. 333 þis Pyppyne þan..Werthit til tak til hym..Off Frawns þat tyme þe gouernaylle. *c* **1470** HENRY *Wallace* III. 271 Schir Amar said; 'Trewis it wordis tak'. *Ibid.* VIII. 1616 Off this sayn[g] me worthis for to ces.

†**worth**, *v.*[2] *Obs.* Forms: 1 **weorðian**, **wurðian**, **wyrðian**, *north.* **worðiᵹan**, 2–3 **wurðien**, **-in**, **wurðen** (3 *Orm.* **wurrþenn**), **wurðgin** (*pa. pple.* 2 **iwurðeȝed**, 3 **iwur(d)get**), **wurðie**, 3 **wurrþe**, **worþi**, 5 **worth(e**. [OE. *weorðian*, *wurðian*, f. *weorþ* WORTH *sb.*[1]]

1. *trans.* To honour (a person or thing); to treat with honour or respect.

c **897** ÆLFRED *Gregory's Past. C.* xvii. 123 Ðu weorðasð ðine suna ma ðonne me. **971** *Blickl. Hom.* 11 Weorþian we eac þa claþas his hades. *c* **1000** *Ags. Gosp.* Matt. xv. 8 þis folc me mid welerum wurþað [*v.r.* weorþað]. *c* **1175** *Lamb. Hom.* 45 We aȝen þene sunne dei swiþeliche wel to wurþien. *c* **1200** ORMIN 2358 þærþurrh wass ȝho wel wurrþ to ben Swa wurrþedd her onn erþe. *c* **1205** LAY. 13422 þas cnihtes weoren an hirede hæhliche iwurðed. *c* **1250** *Gen. & Ex.* 262 Ihesus..Ros fro ded on ðe sunenday, ðat is forð siðen worðed ay. *Ibid.* 3503 Wurð ðin fader and moder so, ðat ðu hem drede. *a* **1400–50** *Wars Alexander* 2124, I wald more worth..a wyse man disciple, þan þe honour þat Acheles aȝt.

b. To pay divine honours to (a deity); to worship.

c **893** ÆLFRED *Oros.* IV. iv. 162 þa diofla þe hie an simbel weorþedon. **971** *Blickl. Hom.* 27 ᵹif þu feallest to me & me weorþast. *c* **975** *Rushw. Gosp.* John iv. 22 ᵹie worðiᵹas þte ᵹe ne wutun, we worðiᵹað þte we wutun. *c* **1175** *Lamb. Hom.* 11 Hine ȝe scule wurþian and hersumen and luuian mid al euwer heorte. *c* **1200** *Trin. Coll. Hom.* 45 Ure hlouerd ihesu crist..heȝed and wurðed bie he. *c* **1205** LAY. 1162 Heo wurðeden þæt anlicnes: þe scucke hit on-feng. *c* **1250** *Gen. & Ex.* 1845 Wið newe alter wurðed he wel ðe strong god of ysrael.

2. To raise to honour; to distinguish.

a **900** CYNEWULF *Elene* 1195 (Gr.) Bið..se hwæteadiᵹ wiᵹᵹe weorðod, se þæt wicg byrð. *a* **1000** *Waldere* i. 22 (Gr.) Weorða ðe selfne godum dædum. *c* **1205** LAY. 2614 Al his cun he wurðede, richen & wrecchen. *c* **1400** *Chron. R. Glouc.* (Rolls) App. G. 154 þeos foure weyes on þis lond, king belin ..Made & worþede ham wiþ gr[et] franchise.

ˈ**worthen**, *v.* *nonce-wd.* [f. WORTH *a.* + -EN.] *trans.* To raise in worth.

1894 'G. EGERTON' *Discords* 241 Woman has cheapened herself..through ignorant innocence, she must learn to worthen herself by all-seeing knowledge.

worthethy, obs. form of WORTHY.

worthful (ˈwɜːθfʊl), *a.* Forms: 1 **weorðful**, 1–3 **wurð-**, **wurþful** (3 *Orm.* **wurrþfull**), 3 **wurthful**; 4

worþuol, 7 **worthful(l**; 6 **wyrthfull**. [OE. *weorþ-, wurþful*, f. *weorþ, wurþ*, WORTH *sb.*[1] In later use app. re-formed (partly to match *worthless*) in 16–17th and again in 19th cent., perhaps on the model of G. *wertvoll*.]

1. Of persons: Honourable; deserving of honour; meriting respect or reverence; full of worth or merit. Also *absol.*

Beowulf 3099 Swa he manna wæs wiȝend weorðfullost wide ȝeond eorðan. *c* **1000** *Ags. Gosp.* Luke xiv. 8 Ne site þu on þam fyrmestan setle, þe-læs..sum weorðfulra siȝ inȝelaðod fram hym. *a* **1122** *O.E. Chron.* (Laud MS.) an. 1086. §8 Se cyng Willelm..wæs..swiðe rice & wurðfulre ..þonne ænig his fore-genga wære. *c* **1200** ORMIN 5195 Helyas wass..an wurrþfull prophete. *a* **1250** *Owl & Night.* 1481 Ȝef he is wurþful and aht man. **1340** *Ayenb.* 16 Þe heȝe men..and þe hardi and þe worþuolle. **1536** in *Lett. Suppr. Monast.* (Camden) 126 Ryght wyrthfull sir, with due reverens my duty remembred [etc.]. **1607** ROWLANDS *Guy Warw.* Ep. Ded., Disdain not therefore (most worthful and precious spirit)..to vouchsafe the view of these Artless Lines. **1647** TRAPP *Comm. 2 Cor.* x. 13 (1656) 728 As any man is more worthful, he is more modest. **1849** ROCK *Ch. Fathers* II. 272 Those high-born dames and worthful females whom Margaret the queen had drawn about her. *a* **1909** G. TYRRELL *Autob.* (1912) I. 238 The more worthful have to repair the defective training of the noviceship.

†**2.** Respectful, reverent; loyal. *Obs.*

c **1000** *Sax. Leechd.* III. 440 Munecas ȝestaþolode to weorþfulre þenunge hælendes cristes. *c* **1250** *Gen. & Ex.* 2678 Or [= before] haue he hire pliȝt & sworen, ðat him sal feið wurðful ben boren.

3. Having worth or value; valuable; precious.

a **1225** *Ancr. R.* 140 Þet heo..strenðeð & deð menske hire wurðfule soule. *a* **1225** *Leg. Kath.* 1017 His wundri werkes & wurðful in eorðe. *a* **1240** *Lofsong* in *O.E. Hom.* I. 211 Turn to þe worlde þi wurðful rode þet þu spreddest þe on. **1599** MARSTON *Antonio's Rev.* II. ii, That prince that worthfull praise aspires, From hearts, and not from lips, applause desires. **1879** PENTECOST *In Vol. Bk.* vi. (1882) 43 Just as a man's note is only current and worthful because the man is good. **1888** FURNIVALL *E.E.T.S., Texts preparing, Gen. Notices* 3 Some [Lives of Saints] are dull..But..all are worthful for the history of our language. **1893** UPTON *Hibbert Lect.* (1894) 298 The presence of absolutely worthful ideas in our consciousness.

Hence †ˈ**worthfulhead**, honour, dignity; ˈ**worthfulness**, value.

c **1250** *Gen. & Ex.* 3499 Ne let ðu nogt min wurð-ful-hed forfaren in ðe fendes red. **1894** PENTECOST in *Brit. Weekly* 20 Sept. 338 Make this the touchstone of worthfulness in selecting the books.

†ˈ**worthihead, -hood.** *Obs.* [f. WORTHY *a.*] Honour; distinction; worthiness.

1375 BARBOUR *Bruce* VI. 333 Thar may no man haf worthyhede, Bot he haf wit to steir his stede [*v.r.* deid]. *c* **1470** HARDING *Chron.* Ed. Pref. (1812) p. x, He was a knyght, electe for worthihode.

worthiless, obs. var. WORTHLESS *a.*

a **1542** WYATT *Ps. cii.* Proem. 15 The Justice yͭ so his promesse complyshythe For his wordes sake to worthilesse desert. **1590** J. PROCTOR in C.S. *Right Relig.* A iij, I will leaue you, loth to keep you too long, perusing a worthilesse pamphlet.

†ˈ**worthily**, *a. Obs.* Forms: 4 **worþiliche, -lych, worthilyche**; 4 **worþili, worthily, -yly**, 5 **wurthyly, wordyly**. [var. of WORTHLY *a.*, after *worthy*.] Worthy, honourable.

13.. *Gaw. & Gr. Knt.* 343 Wolde ȝe, worþilych lorde,.. Bid me boȝe fro þis benche. **13..** *E.E. Allit. P.* A. 846 For-þy vche saule þat hade neuer teche, Is to þat lombe a worthyly wyf. *c* **1350** *Will. Palerne* 1642 A! worþiliche wiȝt, wel wo is me nouþe! ? *a* **1400** *Morte Arth.* 695 Seyne that worthilyche wy went vn-to chambyre. *c* **1400** *Anturs of Arth.* 365 (Thornton MS.) Scho was the worthilieste wyghte, þat any wy myghte welde.

worthily (ˈwɜːðɪlɪ), *adv.* Forms: α. 4 **worþ-, worthilych**, 5 **wurthilyche**; 4 **worþili, -ily, -yly**, 4–5 **worthili**, 4–6 **worthyly** (4 **-ylye**, 5 **-ylie, wurthyly**), 4– **worthily** (5 **worththily**, 7 **worthilie**); 5 **wordyly(e**, 6 *Sc.* **vordily**. β. 4 **wortheliche, -eli**, 4–7 **worthely** (6 **-elie, woorthely**). [f. WORTHY *a.* + -LY[2]. The β-forms are not always distinguishable from variants of WORTHLY *adv.*]

†**1.** With due dignity, pomp, or splendour. *Obs.* (Passing into sense 3.)

13.. *Gaw. & Gr. Knt.* 72 When þay had waschen, worthyly þay wenten to sete. *c* **1350** *Will. Palerne* 4290 With a real route he rod hire a-ȝens, & worþili hire he wolcomed. **1377** LANGL. *P. Pl.* B. II. 8, I..was war of a womman wortheli yclothed. *c* **1400** *Destr. Troy* 1632 Priam..a pales gert make,..Full worthely wroght & by wit caste. *c* **1440** *Gesta Rom.* iv. 12 Thei buryed the body of the knyȝt, worthely among hem in a newe sepulcre. *a* **1450** *Contin. Brut* 461 This coronacion was worthely doon. *Ibid.* 486 Lordes and ladyes were worthely served thurgh all the Court. **1522** *World & Child* (facs.) A ij, I am not worthely wrapped nor went But powerly prycked in pouerte.

†**b.** Becomingly, elegantly. *Obs. rare.*

13.. *Gaw. & Gr. Knt.* 144 Bot his wombe & his wast were worthily smale.

2. In a manner befitting one of high standing or character; in accordance with one's own dignity or personal worth; honourably, nobly.

c **1374** CHAUCER *Troylus* II. 186 Men tellen þat he doth In armes day by day so worþily..þat alle prys hath he. **1382** WYCLIF *Ephes.* iv. 1 So I..byseche, that ȝe walke worthily in the clepinge, in which ȝe ben clepid. *a* **1400–50** *Wars Alexander* 1405 Þai within on þe wall worthili with-stude. **1450–1530** *Myrr. Our Ladye* II. 259 Al this sayde worshyp was done vnto oure lady..by cause she had worthyly ouercome the fende. **1471** CAXTON *Recuyell* (Sommer) 462 Hercules and theseus did worthyly and digne of memorye. **1569** J. ROGERS *Glasse Godly Love* (1876) 188 This blessed state of Matrimony..I exhort you..that you walke worthely therin. **1596** SPENSER *F.Q.* VI. ii. 25 Well may I certes such an one there read, As by thy worth thou worthily hast wonne. **1606** SHAKS. *Ant. & Cl.* II. ii. 102 Worthily spoken Mecenas. *a* **1629** HINDE *J. Bruen* xxxi. (1641) 97 He that had done so worthily at Ephrata, became famous in Bethlehem. **1658–9** *Burton's Diary* (1828) IV. 2 The gentleman has moved worthily, and like a gentleman. **1784** COWPER *Task* v. 807 The soul that sees Him,..learns at least t' employ More worthily the pow'rs she own'd before. **1807** G. CHALMERS *Caledonia* I. III. vii. 380 He worthily fell, in fighting for his people. **1858** J. G. HOLLAND *Titcomb's Lett.* vii. 157 An incident of a life worthily spent. **1886** *Manch. Exam.* 8 Feb. 5/5 The office he has long worthily held as parliamentary secretary to the Trades' Union Congress.

b. Const. *of*, or ellipt. for this.

1841 W. L. GARRISON *Life* iii. 15 There are..some..who do not walk worthily of their profession. **1881** F. T. PALGRAVE *Visions Eng.* 237 Oft hast thou acted thy part, My country, worthily thee!

3. According to desert or merit; as one (or it) is deserving or worthy; deservedly, justly, rightly.

The attribution of desert may be either to the subject or object of the sentence.

a **1340** HAMPOLE *Psalter* Prol. 3 We menge wordis of louynge sa þat worthily he may trow him. **1447** BOKENAM *Seyntys, Marg.* 86 This blyssyd mayde Margrete wurthyly Be these sexe vertuhs to heuene dede stye. **1535** COVERDALE *1 Chron.* xvi. 25 For the Lorde is greate and can not worthely be praysed. **1548** PATTEN (*title*) The Expedicion into Scotlande of the most woorthely fortunate prince Edward. **1591–5** SPENSER *Col. Clout* 375 Or be their pipes vntunable and craesie, That they cannot her honour worthylie? **1617** MORYSON *Itin.* I. 109 The other wines of this Country..and all the other fruits cannot be worthily praised. **1642** D. ROGERS *Naaman* Ep. Ded. 1 For all men to cast their eyes upon, and that worthily; for most costly and pretious was their matter. **1695** LD. PRESTON *Boethius* II. 62 That which cannot be taken away is worthily esteemed the most excellent. **1825** J. NEAL *Bro. Jonathan* II. 2 We know of no case..wherein he [the Wild Man] is worthily represented. **1844** H. G. ROBINSON *Odes of Horace* I. vi, Who worthily of Mars shall write In adamantine Tunic bound? **1865** KINGSLEY *Herew.* ix, His father..promised him the succession—which indeed he had worthily deserved.

b. Used with reference to demerit or the punishment for this.

1398 TREVISA *Barth. De P.R.* VI. xvii. (Bodl. MS.), Dauid blamed worthilich þe seruantes of king saule þat were sleping. **1509** BARCLAY *Ship of Fools* (1874) I. 247 But suche youth..worthely lyue in brawlynge stryfe and payne. **1550** CROWLEY *Last Trumpet* 175 But if thou wilt be styl sturdy.. The Lord shall plage the worthely. **1592** GREENE *Repentance* Wks. (Grosart) XII. 187, I haue so often offended thee that I haue worthely deserued death. **1624** HEYWOOD *Gunaik.* IV. 188 As the processe of her life was in many passages therof worthily infamous. *a* **1678** T. STANLEY *Hist. Philos.* XIII. xxix. (1687) 933/2 Ingratitude is worthily hateful to all men. **1784** COWPER *Tiroc.* 404 Egregious purpose! worthily begun In barb'rous prostitution of your son.

c. Fittingly, in respect of subject or matter.

1553 EDEN *Treat. New Ind.* (Arb.) 6 My trauayl herein coulde no wayes be more worthely bestowed. **1565** T. STAPLETON *Fortr. Faith* 14 Here a man not knowing the mistery, might worthely be astonned. **1642** J. EATON *Honey-c. Free Justif.* 68 That new distinction..is the more worthily to be suspected for a corrupter of the Gospel.

4. With due devotion or reverence; in a fitting spirit; reverently, devoutly; also, with real desert by reason of faith or good life.

a **1340** HAMPOLE *Psalter* xiv. 1 Lord wha sall won in þi tabernakile, þat is wha worthily lufis þe here. *c* **1386** CHAUCER *Pars. T.* ¶ 385 Men may also refreyne venial synne by receyuynge worthily of the precious body of Ihesu crist. *c* **1430** *Pilgr. Lyf Manhode* I. lxxiii. (1869) 42 And if this bred thou wolt nempne and clepe wel and wurthilyche, j sey it is bred of lyf. *a* **1500** *Hist. K. Boccus & Sydracke* (? 1510) F iv b, Yf this word be worthely spoken It shalbe hard fro erth to heuen. **1526** *Pilgr. Perf.* (W. de W. 1531) 171 b, Clennesse of hert, wherby they may worthyly laude and prayse god. **1565** HARDING *Answ. Jewel* 132 By the vertue and efficacie of this Sacrament duely and worthely receiued. **1610** HEALEY *St. Aug. Citie of God* xv. xxiii. 563 Wee do worthily beleeue that the 70. had the spirit of prophecy. **1755** YOUNG *Centaur* i. 11 As to God, they say, 'The natural religion commands us to think worthily, and speak reverently, of Him'. **1770** *Sacraments Explain'd* (ed. 2) 54 A second Thing required, is the State of Grace, without which, no one can worthily receive this Sacrament.

†**5.** At a proper rate or value. *to take worthily*: to accept graciously. *Obs.*

c **1380** WYCLIF *Wks.* (1880) 381 Heliye left þe grete richesse..& tooke worþili þe þore ordenance..þat a goode man & his wyfe proferid to hym. **1390** GOWER *Conf.* I. 180 As thei come To hire..To schewen such thing as thei broghte, Whiche worthili of hem sche boghte.

†ˈ**worthine.** *Obs.* [OE. **worðiȝn*, var. of *worðiȝ*, f. *worþ* WORTH *sb.*[2] Survives in place-names as *-wardine.*] An enclosure, close; see also quot. 1701.

12.. *Reg. Prior. B. M. Wigorn.* (Camd.) 95 b, W. persona de Wittun pro j Wrthin: In festo viij. d. **1701** *Cowel's Interpr.* (ed. Kennett), *Worthinus*, a Worthine of Land, a certain quantity or dimension of Ground so call'd in the Mannor of Kingsland, Com. Hereford.

worthiness (ˈwɜːðɪnɪs). Forms: α. 4 **worþi-, worþynes(s(e**, 4–7 **worthi-, worthynes**, 5–6 **worthy-**, 5– **worthiness**; 4 **wurþy-**, 5 **wurthyness(e, wurthines (wurghtinesse)**; 6 **woorthi-, woorthyness(e, wourthines.** β. 5 **wordynesse**, 6 *Sc.* **wirdines.** [f. WORTHY *a.* + -NESS.]

1. The character or quality of being worthy, in various senses: **a.** Of persons.

α. **1340** HAMPOLE *Pr. C.* 3757 Þe help..Availles til þe saules in purgatory,..Aftir þai er of worthynes. *c* **1374** CHAUCER *Troylus* II. 178 In al þis world þer nys a bettre knyght Than he þat is of worthinesse welle. **1390** GOWER *Conf.* I. 90 Remembrance That thei toke of his worthinesse Of knyhthod and of gentilesse. **1447** BOKENAM *Seyntys, Anna* 607 This lady to preysen..Aftyr þe meryte of hyr worthynesse, Fer pasyth my wyt. *c* **1489** CAXTON *Blanchardyn* xliii. 167 By the hyghe prouesse & grete worthynes of blanchardyn. *a* **1533** BERNERS *Gold. Bk. M. Aurel.* (1546) L vj b, All the world feared Rome onely, for her worthynes in armes. **1550** CROWLEY *Inform.* Sel. Wks. (1872) 163 Stand not to much in your own conceyte, gloriynge in the worthyness of your bloude. *c* **1590** *Faire Em.* I. iv. 35 Such costly robes As may become her beauties worthynes. **1604** SHAKS. *Oth.* II. i. 212 He is a good one, and his worthynesse Do's challenge much respect. **1651** HOBBES *Leviath.* I. x. 46 Worthinesse, is a thing different from the worth, or value of a man; and also from his merit, or desert; and consisteth in a particular power, or ability for that, whereof he is said to be worthy. *a* **1676** HALE *Common Law* (1713) 239 They are in Law in the same Right of Worthiness and Proximity of Blood, as their Root..was. **1741** RICHARDSON *Pamela* I. 104, I am awaken'd to see more Worthiness in you, than ever I saw in any Lady in the Land. **1801** WORDSW. *Prioress' T.* I. 30 My knowledge is so weak, ..To tell abroad thy mighty worthiness. **1879** FARRAR *St. Paul* (1883) 173 A Divine Charity not only perceives real worth, but even creates worthiness where it did not before exist.

β. *c* **1450** *Merlin* xiv. 203 Thei semede to be of grete wordynesse. *c* **1489** CAXTON *Blanchardyn* xiv. 49 O thou free knyght, replenysshed wyth prowesse & of grete wordynesse.

b. Of things or qualities.

1398 TREVISA *Barth. De P.R.* XVI. vii. (1495) 556 Siluer.. bereþ þe prise after golde in worþines and valow. *c* **1400** *Rom. Rose* 5536 For ther may be no Richesse Ageyns frendshipp of worthynesse. **1426** LYDG. *De Guil. Pilgr.* 17383 For love excellyth in worthynesse Euery tresour and rychesse. **1450–1530** *Myrr. Our Ladye* II. 288 All erthly creatures restored ageyne in maner to the worthynesse of effecte that they were made for. **1541** *Act 33 Hen. VIII*, c. 37 ¶ 1 Suche..hereditamentes shoulde be knytt unyted and annexed,..agreable to the worthinesse and dignitye thereof. **1577** B. GOOGE *Heresbach's Husb.* II. 67 Next vnto the Rose in woorthynesse, for his Sauour and beautifull whitenesse is the Lillye. **1638** JUNIUS *Paint. Ancients* 47 Art can doe nothing without the materiall; whereas the materiall without Art hath her own worthinesse. **1675** BAXTER *Cath. Theol.* II. I. 235 Is there ever the less worthiness in it, because God causeth it? *a* **1768** SECKER *Serm.* (1771) VI. 132 Convinced of their Mission from Heaven by..the singular Worthiness of their Conduct. **1850** CLOUGH *Poems*, etc. (1869) I. 167 Say, if you can,..when was there most real worthiness of existence.

c. With *a* (and plural), *that*, or *this*.

13.. tr. Ælred in *Engl. Stud.* VII. 328 Now, suster,..go nyer and chalange sum partye of alle þis swete wurþynesse. *c* **1449** PECOCK *Repr.* II. xv. 235 Forto be..deuoutli remembrid..upon Goddis worthinessis. **1450–1530** *Myrr. Our Ladye* II. 91 A prerogatyue is an excellente worthynes. **1590** STOCKWOOD *Rules Construct.* 8 This woorthiness of one person aboue another, is not of birth or blood. **1657** JER. TAYLOR *Disc. Friendship* 39, I may take in also the accidental and extrinsick worthinesses. **1685** BAXTER *Paraphr. N.T.* Matt. x. 11 There is a worthiness consistent with free Grace. **1753** RICHARDSON *Grandison* (1781) I. xxxvi. 256 My Brother is valued by those who know him best, not..for this or that single worthiness [etc.]. **1803** SOUTHEY *Lett.* (1856) I. 243, I could make a swelling..passage about the old gentlemen and their worthinesses. **1860** TRENCH *Serm. Westm. Abbey* xxxiii. 382 There is a worthiness in God's saints,..though that worthiness is itself of God's free giving.

†**2.** With possessive pron., as a title. *Obs.*

1390 GOWER *Conf.* Prol. 50* He..bad me doo my besynesse That to his hihe worthinesse Som newe thing I scholde boke. *a* **1400–50** *Wars Alexander* 1938 Sire, wetis it wele, ȝoure worthines [etc.]. *Ibid.* 3163 First wrate I to ȝour worthines. **1455** *Rolls of Parlt.* V. 287/1 The grete and outrageouse costes and expenses not unknowen unto your wurthynesses, which..I bare, in execution of the said charge. **1564** *Brief Exam.* B j, Your worthynesse may knowe what my iudgement is. **1602** CHETTLE *Hoffman* I. (1631) C 1, We know your worthinesse is experienc't in all true wisedome. **1608** HEYWOOD *Sallust, Hist.* Ded., Your worthinesse.

†**3.** Ceremony, pomp. *Obs.*[−1]

a **1450** *Contin. Brut* 428 The Quene was dellyuyryd of a feyre sone,..whiche with high and grete worthynesse was brought forthe, and cristenyd.

†**4.** The quality of deserving *to* be treated in a specified manner. *Obs.*[−1]

1396–7 in *Eng. Hist. Rev.* (1907) XXII. 303 Ȝet [this sin] ..passith in worthinesse to ben punischid in peynis of helle.

†ˈ**worthing**[1]. *Obs.* Forms: 1 **weorðung**, 1–2 **wurðung**, 1–3 **wurðing**; 1 **worðung**, 3–4 **worþing** (4 **worþynge**). [OE. *weorðung, wurðung*, f. *weorð-, wurðian* WORTH *v.*[2]] Honour; respect; worship.

c **897** ÆLFRED *Gregory's Past. C.* iii. 35 For ðære weorðunge ðæs folces he bið on ofermettu awended. *c* **950** *Lindisf. Gosp.* Mark vi. 4 Ne is witȝe buta worðung. *c* **1000** ÆLFRIC *Lev.* ii. 2 Lecge uppan þæt weofod Drihtne to wurþunga. *c* **1175** *Lamb. Hom.* 59 Þencheð nu men hwilch wurðin(g) eow haueð idon þe heouenking. *Ibid.* 109 Godes laȝe bit ec mon wurðie efre his feder and his moder mid muchelere wurþunge. *c* **1250** *Gen. & Ex.* 33 Ðu giue me seli timinge To thaunen ðis werdes biginninge, Ðe, leuerd god, to wurðinge. *Ibid.* 3787 Of ðo Reklefates for wurðing, Woren mad..Corunes. *a* **1300** *Fall & Passion* 5 in *E.E.P.* (1862) 13 Þat ic mote wiþ moch worþing..to ȝov schow is vp-rising. c1315 Shoreham iii. 182 As al holy cherche þe tekþ, þou make þyne worþynge.

b. *worthing day*, Sunday; *worthing-night*, ? Sunday night.

c1175 *Lamb. Hom.* 9 þat wes heore sunedei and bet heo heolden heore wurðing dei þene we doð. a1327 *Adam Davy's Dreams* 87 Me met a sweuene, on worþing-niȝth Of þat ilche derworþe kniȝth.

† **'worthing**[2]. *Obs.* [app. f. ME. *wurþ* worth *a.* Cf. gooding *vbl. sb.*] Dung; manure. Also *fig.*, moral corruption or filth.

c1175 *Lamb. Hom.* 85 þet smal chef þet flid ford mid þe winde bicumeð wurþinge. a1200 *St. Marher.* 3 Ne lettu neauer þe unhwiht warpen hire i wurðinge. c1230 *Hali Meid.* 13 þe ilke sari wrecches þe i þe fule wurðinge vnwedde waleweð..þeos walewið i wurðinge, & forrotieð þrin.

c1582 in T. West *Antiq. Furness* (1774) App. viii. 3 D 4, Five hundred fudder, or wayne load, alias coupe load, of wurthinge or dung. 1591 *Broomfleet Manor Roll* (MS.), Item, that Thomas Waile remove his swynestye..that the worthing or fylth theirof do not corrupt the water. 1592 in *Lancs. Q. Sess. Rec.* (Chetham Soc.) I. 54 Eighte wayne lodes of worthinge or dounge. 1605 *Shuttleworths' Acc.* (Chetham Soc.) 161, xxj lood of worthing for barlye..; xv loodes of worthinge, with good store of lyme in yt.

attrib. 1688 Holme *Armoury* iii. 337/1 A Worthing Forke, or a Dung Fork. 1876 E. Leigh *Cheshire Gloss.*, *Wording hook*, dungfork.

worthless ('wɜːθlɪs), *a.* [f. worth *sb.*[1] + -less.]

1. Of things, etc.: Destitute of (material) worth; having no intrinsic value.

1588 Shaks. *Tit. A.* v. iii. 117 Me thinkes I do digresse too much, Cyting my worthlesse praise. 1591 —— *Two Gent.* iv. ii. 6 But Siluia is..too holy, To be corrupted with my worthlesse guifts. 1664 Dryden *Rival Ladies* Ep. Ded., My Lord, this worthless Present was design'd you, long before it was a Play. 1693 Prior *To Hon. C. Montague* vii, Scorning at Night the worthless Prey, We find the Labour gave the Joy. 1726 Pope *Odyss.* xviii. 435 A worthless triumph o'er a worthless foe! 1784 Cowper *Epist. J. Hill* 18 Can gold grow worthless that has stood the touch? 1823 Scott *Quentin D.* xxiii, Why should I occasion more bloodshed than has already taken place on so worthless an account? 1849 Macaulay *Hist. Eng.* vii. II. 208 The indulgence..was clogged by conditions which made it almost worthless. 1885 *Manch. Exam.* 11 Nov. 3/1 The book seems to us about as worthless as a book can be without being morally offensive.

2. Of persons: Lacking worth or merit; destitute of moral character; contemptible, despicable.

1591 Shaks. *1 Hen. VI*, v. v. 53 So worthlesse Pezants bargaine for their Wiues, As Market men for Oxen, Sheepe, or Horse. 1611 Beaum. & Fl. *Maid's Trag.* ii. *Asp.*.. Perhaps he found me worthless. 1619 J. Taylor (Water P.) *Kicksey Winsey* B 5 b, Seuenthly, and last's a worthy worthlesse crew, Such as heau'n hates. 1671 Milton *Samson* 1020 The Timnian bride Had not so soon preferr'd Thy Paranymph, worthless to thee compar'd. 1713 Addison *Cato* iv. ii, Am I then doom'd to fall By a boy's hand?..and for a worthless woman? 1771 Franklin *Autobiog.* Wks. 1840 I. 68 He was a worthless fellow, though an excellent workman. 1852 Mrs. Stowe *Uncle Tom's C.* xxix. 275 They get lazy..and take to drinking, and go all down to be mean, worthless fellows. 1855 Macaulay *Hist. Eng.* xx. IV. 384 A worthless adventurer, whose only recommendation was that he was a Papist. 1881 Miss Braddon *Asphodel* III. 300, I am very sorry that an honest man..should have been fooled by a worthless girl.

absol. a1768 Secker *Serm.* (1770) III. 192 If it brings the Worthless and the Wicked into Credit and Familiarity with their Betters. 1890 W. James *Princ. Psychol.* I. 552 The mode of genesis of the worthy and the worthless seems the same.

†**3.** Unworthy (in various senses) *of* something, or *of* a person. *Obs.*

1592 Greene *Philomela* Wks. (Grosart) XI. 176 But now thou art valued worthlesse of all thy former honours. 1601 Shaks. *Jul. C.* v. i. 61 A peeuish School-boy, worthles of such Honor. 1602 Chettle *Hoffman* iv. (1631) H 2, The worthy Dutchesse, worthles of this death, Was murder'd. 1639 G. Daniel *Ecclus.* xxi. 79 But the wise Man will scorne soe poore An Act, soe worthles of him.

Hence **'worthlessly** *adv.*

1847 C. Bronte *Jane Eyre* xxxii, Miss Oliver..was..exacting, but not worthlessly selfish. 1883 Whitelaw *Sophocles, Ajax* 1162 Me too it shames to hear Words of a babbler, prating worthlessly.

worthlessness ('wɜːθlɪsnɪs). [f. prec. + -ness.] The character or quality of being worthless.

1611 Cotgr., *Vileté*, vilenesse, basenesse, worthlesnesse. 1642 Fuller *Holy & Prof. St.* ii. ix. 87 That his people may find his worth by the worthlesnesse of him that succeeds. 1662 H. Stubbe *Indian Nectar* Pref. 12 Man ought to entertain other despair, then what his own Worthlessness creates in him. 1703 J. Savage *Lett. Antients* liv. 139, I am heartily glad that other Ladies besides me have discovered thy Worthlesness. 1771 *Junius Lett.* lvii. 297 The meanness and intrinsic worthlessness of the object (supposing he could attain it) would fill him with shame..and disgust. 1817 J. Scott *Paris Revisit.* (ed. 4) 313 A cold cruelty of practice, quite equal to the worthlessness of her principles. 1852 Grote *Greece* ii. lxxi. IX. 247 He proclaimed that..he was ashamed of the worthlessness of his countrymen. 1884 R. W. Church *Bacon* v. 102 The many extravagant tributes paid..to high-handed worthlessness.

† **'worthly**, *a. Obs.* Forms: 1 weorðlic, wurðlic, 2 wurdlich (*comp.* wuredluker), 3 wurð-, wurþlich (*sup.* wurðlukest), 4 wurthli; 3–4 worþlich (3 *sup.* -lokest, 4 *comp.* -loker), 4 wortlich, -lych, worþelych, 5 worþeliche; 4 worþ-, worthli, -ly, worþe-, worthely. [OE. *weorðlic, wurðlic*, f. *weorð* worth *sb.*[1] + -ly[1].]

1. Of things: Having great value or importance; noble, fine, excellent, worthy.

c893 Ælfred *Oros.* iii. x. 140 Papirius..weorþlicne siȝe hæfde. a900 *Juliana* 9 Wæs his rice brad, wid & weorðlic. c1000 Ælfric *Saints' Lives* xix. 143 Hi worhton eac þa wurðlice cyrcan. c1100 *O.E. Chron.* (MS.D.) an. 1058, He ..wurðlic lac ȝeoffrode. c1175 *Lamb. Hom.* 47 Heo hafð mid hire þreo wurdliche mihte. c1205 Lay. 11772 Ah loke wulche..wunliche londes, whulche wurðliche wude. *Ibid.* 28923 He..bad alle þe ȝeonglinges..þat heo heom biȝeten wurðliche wepnen. a1240 *Ureisun* in *O.E. Hom.* I. 187 Hwi nis me unwurhþ elc wurþliche þing aȝein þe muchel delit of þi swetnesse. c1320 *Sir Tristr.* 1029 Swiche meting nas neuer non made Wiþ worþli wepen wiȝt. 13.. *E.E. Allit. P.* C. 464, I wysse a worþloker won to welde I neuer keped. 1340–70 *Alisaunder* 1024 Hee aboute hath ibene..And iwonne at his will þe wortlych places. c1350 *Libeaus Desc.* (Kaluza) 761 Her wer a worþly won For man, þat wer in doute. 1422 Yonge tr. *Secreta Secret.* 146 Riches of golde, syluer, yowelis, and othyr worthely possessionys. 14.. in *Hist. Coll. Citizen London* (Camden) 126 The cyttezyns.. shall have alle ande every franches..þe whiche of worthely mynde be progenys of oure lorde the kynge,..to hem and to hys sayde cytte were grauntyde.

2. Of persons: Estimable, honourable, worthy.

c888 Ælfred *Boeth.* xxxiii. §1 ðeþenc hu weorðlic and hu foremærlic þe wolde se mon þincan. c1100 *O.E. Chron.* (MS. D.) an. 1023, Hi þa mid weorðlicum weorode..hine.. feredan. c1200 *Trin. Coll. Hom.* 29 Ðu ert wel don man and þarto wurðlich. c1205 Lay. 25496 Wenhauer his quene, wurðlukest [c1275 worþlokest] wiuen. c1275 *Ibid.* 26459 Hii þanne gonne go and leope to horse, worþliche kempes. c1320 *Sir Tristr.* 1687 Play miri he may Wiþ þat worþli wiȝt. a1352 Minot *Poems* v. 38 Als wise man of wordes and worthli in wede. c1394 *P. Pl. Crede* 233 Canstou me graiþ tellen To any worþely wiȝt. c1467 in *Excerpta Hist.* (1831) 188 That no man thenk that I..undirtake the thynges abovesaide by any arrogance..to be callid worthly.

† **'worthly**, *adv. Obs.* Forms: 3 wurðeliche, -like, wurðliche (wirdliche, *Orm.* wurrþlike), -lich, -lic; 3–5 worþliche, 3–4 worþ-, worthli, 5 worthely, wordly, 4–6 worthly. [f. worth *a.* + -ly[2].] **1.** = worthily *adv.* 1.

c1200 Ormin 8177 All he wass wurrþlike shridd, Alls iff he wære o life. c1205 Lay. 14164 Þu sca[l]t habben gærsume hæhliche heom to ueden & wurðliche scruden. a1225 *Ancr. R.* 174 Heo schulen beon ine heouene, ouer oðer kunnes folke, wurðliche iheied. c1250 *Gen. & Ex.* 1518 Ðor he was for his fadres luuen Holden wurðelike a wel a-buuen. c1350 *Will. Palerne* 673 He..welcomes hir worþli. *Ibid.* 3202 Whan þei were cloþed worþli in here wedes. c1400 *Ywaine & Gaw.* 184 When we war in that fayre palays, It was ful worthly wroght always.

2. = worthily *adv.* 2.

c1205 Lay. 5770 þe sculleð eow wurðliche wreken. a1400–50 *Wars Alexander* 1428 þan Alexander..Wynnes worthly ouer þe wallis with-in to þe cite.

3. = worthily *adv.* 4.

c1200 *Vices & Virtues* 21 His flesc and his blod,..ȝif ic hit swa wurðliche underfenge, swa hit wurðe wære. c1200 Ormin 1033 þatt follkess haliȝdomess, þatt wærenn inn an arrke þær Wel & wurrþlike ȝemmde. a1300 *Cursor M.* 11618 þe lauerd agh yee worthli to lufe. 1551 S. Gardiner *Expl. Cath. Fayth* 18 For such as receaue Christes most precious body and bloud in the Sacrament worthly, they haue Christ dwellyng in them.

4. = worthily *adv.* 3 c.

1482 *Monk of Evesham* (Arb.) 43 Hyt was so gret and ynestymable that y can not remembre..how y myght wordly speke of hyt.

† **'worthmint**. *Obs.* Forms: 3 wurðmunt, -mund, worðmunt. [OE. *weorð-, wurð-, wyrðmynt* (also *-mynd, -myndu*), f. *weorþ, etc.*, worth *sb.*[1]] Honour; worship.

c1205 Lay. 18851 þe wile þe þis world stænt ilæsten scal is worðmunt. a1225 *Leg. Kath.* 1455 O witti wummon! wurðmunt & alle wurðschipe ware! a1225 *Juliana* 65 (Bodl. MS.) þu art wurðe wurðmunt from worlde into worlde.

† **'worthness**. *Obs.* [OE. *weorð-, wurð-, wyrþnes* (north. *worðnis*), f. *weorþ*, worth *a.*] **a.** Honour. **b.** Worthiness.

1258 *Proclam. Hen. III*, §2 þæt vre rædesmen..habbeþ idon and schullen don in þe worþnesse of gode and on vre treowþe for þe freme of þe loande. 1486 *Bk. St. Albans, Her.* aj, Beyng in worthenes aarmes for to bere by the Royall blode in ordynance.

'worthship. [f. worth *sb.*[1] + -ship.] The condition of being of worth.

1843 Carlyle *Past & Pr.* i. vi, It is the summary..of all manner of 'worship', and true worthships and noblenesses whatsoever. 1851 —— *Sterling* i. v, The world..its worthships and worships unworshipful.

worth-while, *sb. rare.* [See while *sb.* 3 b, and worth *a.* 8.] The quality of being, or that which is, worth while.

1867 Mrs. Whitney *Leslie Goldthwaite* ii, How did the world seem to such a person, and where was the *worth-while* of it? 1899 *Westm. Gaz.* 3 Aug. 2/1 The pursuit of the worth-while.

worth-while, *a.* Also worthwhile. [Cf. prec.] That is worth while; of sufficient value or importance.

Common in recent use.

1884, 1904 [see next]. 1912 *World* 7 May 677/1 He has.. scarcely any worthwhile reversionary interests. 1927 *Publishers' Circular* 30 Apr. 487/3 Each book is offered as a book particularly worth-while in the judgment of the Board of Editors.

Hence **worth-whileness**, the quality of being worth while.

1884 *B'ham Weekly Post* 18 Oct. 5/1 The worth-whileness of forming a local portrait gallery. 1904 B'ness v. Hutten *Pam* 128 If something does present itself to you in the light of worth-whileness, nothing can stop you.

worthy ('wɜːðɪ), *a.*, *adv.*, *sb.* Forms: α. 3 wurði (wrþi), 4 wurþy (wrþy), 4–5 wurthi, -thy (5 whurthy); 5 *Sc.* wirþy, 6 *Sc.* wirthie, -thy; 3–5 worþi (4 wortþi), 4–5 worþy, 3–6 worthi (4 worthti, 6 *Sc.* vorthi), 3–7 worthye, 4–7 worthie (4–5 worthé), 3– worthy (4 worthethy, 5 whorthy; *Sc.* 5 vorthy, 6 vorthty); 5 wourthy, 6 wourthie, -thye, 6–7 woorthy. β. *Sc.* (and *north.*) 5–6, 8– wordy, 6 vordy, wirdy, -die, worde. [ME. *wurði, worði*, etc., f. worth *sb.*[1] + -y, replacing OE. *wyrðe, weorðe*, wurthe *a.*, and in some senses OE. *weorð, wurð*, worth *a.*

The following are illustrations of the β-forms:

c1375 *Sc. Leg. Saints* xl. (*Ninian*) 224 Sa..[he] made feil wordy goddis burde. 14.. *Pol. Rel. & L. Poems* (1903) 114 Alle men helde her wordy heuen. c1460 *Merita Missæ* 71 in *Lay Folks Mass Bk.* 150 Pray..That thow be wordy to see that syght. 1513 Douglas *Æneis* i. vii. 137 Ane wordy weriour..thai mycht hir ken. 1533 Gau *Richt Vay* (S.T.S.) 64 It is ane trew vord and aluay wordy to be resauit. 1583 *Extracts Burgh Rec. Lanark* (1893) 89 Quharfor..I am nocht wirdie..to be ballie [bailie]. 1721 [see 1 b]. 1724, 1725 [see 8]. 1804 R. Anderson *Cumbld. Ball.* 114 It's for auld Kit Craffet, our wordy wise neybor. 1872 J. Young *Lochlomond* 49 (E.D.D.) Cottars puir, wha ne'er had daurk Wordy the name o' honest wark.]

A. *adj.* **I. 1. a.** Of things: Having worth; possessed of value or importance; good; excellent. Now *arch.*

c1250 *Gen. & Ex.* 1501 Firme birðe was wurði wune. c1380 Wyclif *Serm.* Sel. Wks. II. 226 Cristene men shulden þenke shame to..foule þe worþi suyt of Crist. 1393 Langl. *P. Pl.* C. xiv. 28 Thauh ich preise pouerte þus and preoue hit by ensamples Worthiour. c1440 *Jacob's Well* 190 Prayere is more worthy to god, þan almes or fastyng. c1450 *Mirk's Festial* 86 þus ȝe may se by veray reson þat Godys grace ys more worþy þen any fayre. c1450 *Cursor M.* 10160 (Laud) Of hym we wille our story rede, For worthyest yt is in-dede. 1557 Seager *Sch. Vert.* 513 in *Babees Bk.*, Aristotle the Philosopher this worthy sayinge writ. 1577 B. Googe *Heresbach's Husb.* ii. 108 The Date (a woorthy tree) bendeth vp agaynst his burden. 1593 *Bacchus Bountie* B 1 b, The pots feet finely roasted In a worthie fire. 1628 R. Hayman in *Eng. Hist. Rev.* (1918) Jan. 31 Vnlesse your maiestie suddainely assist, this worthie busines is like to vanish Lamentablely. 1669 Worlidge *Syst. Agric.* (1681) 171 Cows and Oxen are worthy Beasts, and in great request with the Husbandman. 1674 Playford *Skill Mus.* i. xi. 55 All the most passionate Graces used in this most worthy manner of singing. 1774 Pennant *Tour Scot. in 1772*, 303 According to the worthy custom of these islands.

†**b.** Of the value of, worth (so much). *Obs.*

1303 R. Brunne *Handl. Synne* 6323 Hys vessel was ten mark wurþy [*v.r.* wrþy]. ?a1500 *Chester Pl., Nativ.* 592 Thyrd parte the worlde, as reade wee, that temple was worthye. 1569 J. Sanford tr. *Agrippa's Van. Artes* 160 The thinge is so muche worthy as it maye be solde for. 1577 Kendall *Flowers Epigr.* 36 b, If thou saie they are no gifts, but trifles worthie nought. 1604 E. G[rimstone] *Acosta's Hist. Indies* iii. xx. 185 The traffike they make of it, is worthy much mony. 1721 Ramsay *Rise & Fall Stocks* 124 We thought that dealer's stock an ill ane, That was not wordy haff a million.

c. Capable of justifying (expense).

1785 J. Phillips *Treat. Inland Nav.* 44 It would be found worthy the expence to carry the navigation..to Braintree.

2. a. Of persons: Distinguished by good qualities; entitled to honour or respect on this account; estimable.

13.. *K. Horn* (Harl.) 1222 For þer bueþ myne knyhte worþi men & lyhte. 1338 R. Brunne *Chron.* (1810) 162 Of his men most worþi, at þam conseile gan [he] take. c1385 Chaucer *L.G.W.* 597 *Cleopatra*, This ilke senatour Was a ful worthy gentyl werriour. c1400 Maundev. (Roxb.) xv. 67 Criste es þe best, þe worthiest and next to Godd. 1422 Yonge tr. *Secreta Secret.* 197 Iosue the Wourthy and wyse weryor. 1489 Caxton *Faytes of A.* i. xxi. 36 The good.. admonestyng of the worthy duc encreaceth in an oost hardynes..and vertue. 1548–9 (Mar.) *Bk. Com. Prayer, Offices* 24 Thou moste worthy iudge eternal. 1581 A. Hall *Iliad* ii. 20 He callde the auntients of the host, they that most worthy were. 1594 Shaks. *Rich. III*, iii. vii. 239 Long liue King Richard, Englands worthie King. 1639 W. C. *Italian Convert* xxx. 222 But especially his worthy wife did then shew her selfe most loving and loyall. 1663 Jer. Taylor *Funeral Serm. Abp. Armagh* 20 He was bred in Cambridge, ..under Mr. Hulet, a grave and a worthy Man. 1711 Addison *Spect.* No. 106 ¶4 My worthy Friend has put me under the particular Care of his Butler. 1758 *S. Hayward's Serm.* Introd. p. iii, A small collection of your late dear and worthy Pastor's sermons. 1806 H. Siddons *Maid, Wife, & Widow* III. 211 That worthy man could read hearts with great perspicuity. 1848 Lytton *Harold* iii. ii, Slowly then rose Alred, Bishop of Winchester, the worthiest prelate in all the land. 1885 'Mrs. Alexander' *At Bay* vii, She would like her to be..married to some worthy person.

b. *absol.* in sing. or plural sense.

1377 Langl. *P. Pl.* B. xiii. 33 þis maister was made sitte as for þe moste worthy. 1390 Gower *Conf.* II. 196 That he be [= by] worthi and be wise..was conseiled. c1412–20 Lydg. *Chron. Troy* iv. 342–3 Howe Kynge Pryamus, with al the worthy of Troyans partye, kame to the felde. 1490 *Acta Dom. Concil.* (1839) 149/2 To tak a deligent inquesicioune.. of þe best and wordiast of þe said burghe. 1535 Coverdale *Gen.* xlix. 10 The cepter shal not be remoued from Iuda.. tyll the Worthye come. 1845 J. C. Mangan *German Anthol.* I. 76 The Worthy possess not the earth.

c. ***worthy of blood*** in *Eng. Law*: see quots.

1544 tr. *Littleton's Tenures* 2 b, The elder brother shall haue the lande by discent,..for that, that the eldest brother is more worthy of blod. **1628** COKE *On Litt.* 12 b, The bloud of the part of the father is more worthy..in iudgement of law, than the bloud of the part of the mother. *a* **1676** HALE *Common Law* (1713) 230 In the Case of Purchasers,..it resorted to the Line of the Mother, and the nearer and more worthy of Blood were preferred. **1766** BLACKSTONE *Comm.* II. 213 The worthiest of blood shall be preferred. **1841** STEPHEN *Comm. Law Eng.* I. 382 All the female ancestors.. were equally worthy of blood.

d. Of mind or character: Having a high moral standard.

1753-4 RICHARDSON *Grandison* IV. 12 But all three are men of worthy minds, and deserve better fortune. **1788** WESLEY *Wks.* (1872) VI. 469 Such as are styled, in the cant term of the day, men of worthy characters;—one of the most silly, insignificant words, that ever came into fashion. **1843** MIALL in *Nonconformist* III. 1 An act of homage done to great and worthy principles.

Comb. **1590** SIR J. SMYTH *Disc. Conc. Weapons* 50 b *marg.*, No honorable nor worthie minded men. **1760-72** H. BROOKE *Fool of Qual.* (1809) II. 153 He is a worthy-hearted child. **1856** *N. Brit. Rev.* XXVI. 227 A worthy-minded parson of the old school.

†**3. a.** Of persons: Holding a prominent place in the community; of rank or standing. *Obs.*

c **1386** CHAUCER *Cant. T.*, Prol. 217 Famulier was he With frankeleyns..And [eek] with worthy wommen of the toun. *c* **1400** *Destr. Troy* 7607 There was Ecuba þe honerable.. With women of worship, the worthiest of Troy. *c* **1460** *Urbanitatis* 45 in *Babees Bk.*, If þou sytte be a worthyor man Then þy self thow art on, Suffre hym fyrste to towche þe mete.

†**b.** ***worthy man*** (also as one word): a man of note or standing. *Obs.*

1427 in *Cov. Leet Bk.* (1907) 111 The seyd meir..made com afore hym thes wurthymen foloweng. **1435** *Ibid.* 182 The whiche bille the seid meyre..send to all the wurthymen of the seyd lete. *c* **1440** *Promp. Parv.* 537/2 3erde, borne a-forne a worthyman, *Quiris*. **1485** *Rolls of Parlt.* VI. 338/1 Burgeis and Worthymen, Cominaltie and their Successours. *a* **1500** *Bale's Chron.* in *Six Town Chron.* (1911) 133 To have ..had diverse worthymen and their goodes of the citee.

†**4.** Of things: **a.** Strong, powerful. *Obs.*⁻¹

a **1300** *E.E. Psalter* xlix. 3 Fire in his sight sal brenne sothli And in his vmgange storme worthi [L. *valida*].

†**b.** Honourable; held in honour or esteem. *Obs.*

1377 LANGL. *P. Pl.* B. xix. 24 Is cryst more of my3te & more worthy name Than ihesu or ihesus? *c* **1380** WYCLIF *Wks.* (1880) 98 þis stat is most worþi in þe chirche. **1557** N.T. (Geneva) *Matt.* xxiii. 6 They..loue to syt in the worthiest place at feastes. **1586** MARLOWE *1st Pt. Tamburl.* I. i. 191 We knew..The Lords would not be too exasperate, To iniure or suppresse your woorthy tytle. **1597** A. M. tr. *Guillemeau's Fr. Chirurg.* 5 b/2 The worthyest partes of the bodye, as the Braynes, Harte, Liver, or throte. **1623** J. TAYLOR (Water P.) *New Discov. by Sea* Ep. Ded., All which ..I humbly Dedicate to your Noble, Worshipfull and worthy Acceptances. *a* **1721** PRIOR *Down-Hall* ix, He is a Lawyer of worthy Renown.

5. a. Of sufficient worth or value; sufficiently good; appropriate, fitting, suitable.

a **1300** *Cursor M.* 11492 Ilkan him gaf worþi offrand. *a* **1440** *Found. St. Bartholomew's* xviii. (1886) p. lxvii, God, that is mervelous in his seyntes he..with worthy preysyng magnyfied. **1563** *Homilies* II. *Sacram.* I. 214 A right & a worthy estimation, and vnderstanding of this mistery. **1594** in Brydges *Restituta* (1815) III. 298 You that..sought for matter in a forraine soyle, As worthie subjects of your silver pen. **1738** GRAY *Statius* I. 19 Ye Argive flower..Receive a worthier load; yon puny ball Let youngsters toss. **1808** SCOTT *Marmion* I. xii, We saw the victor win the crest He wears with worthy pride. **1870** F. R. WILSON *Ch. Lindisf.* 64 It was improved by the insertion of worthy windows.

†**b.** Sufficiently heavy or severe; deserved, merited by default or wrong-doing, condign. *Obs.*

1551 CROWLEY *Pleas. & Payne* 197 No hell can be worthy payne For your offence, it is so greate. **1574** *Homilies* II. *Wilful Rebell.* IV. 586 A woorthy end of al false rebelles, who ..become hangmen vnto them selues. *c* **1586** C'TESS PEMBROKE *Ps.* CVI. xv, Often he freed them..But..Left them at length in worthy plagues to pine. **1601** SHAKS. *All's Well* IV. iii. 7 He has much worthy blame laid vpon him. **1622** J. TAYLOR (Water P.) *Merry Wherry Voy.* Wks. 1630 II. 10/1 They..did as much as lay in them to doe,..to giue them worthy punishment.

6. a. Of persons: Possessed of sufficient worth, desert, or merit.

1552 *2nd Prayer-Bk. Edw. VI, Commun.*, rubric, The humble..acknowledgyng of the benefites of Chryst, geuen vnto the woorthye receyuer. **1788** PICKEN *Poems* 86 A wordy frien' is e'en right rare, An' virtue ill to hit on. **1818** BYRON *Ch. Har.* IV. clv, Thou Shalt one day, if found worthy,..See thy God face to face. **1832** *Edin. Rev.* Oct. 146 No worthy successor of Richard Turpin arises to 'murder sleep'. **1885** *Manch. Even. News* 6 July 2/1 Mr. Phelps..is bent on proving that he is a worthy successor to Mr. Russell Lowell.

b. Of actions, etc.: Adequate or suitable in respect of moral excellence or noble aims.

1563 *Homilies* II. 444 (*title*) An Homely of the worthy receauing..of the Sacrament of the body and bloud of Christ. **1609** DEKKER *Gull's Hornbk.* iv, Your next worthy worke is, to repaire to my Lord Chancellors Tomb. **1619** J. TAYLOR (Water P.) *Kicksey Winsey* C 3, I know there's many worthy proiects done, The which more credit..hath won. **1675** COMBER (*title*) A Companion to the Altar. Or, an Help to the worthy receiving of the Lords Supper. **1851** MRS. BROWNING *Casa Guidi Wind.* I. 223 Before the eyes of men, awake at last, Who..turn to wakeful prayer and worthy act.

II. With various constructions.

Freq. intensified by *well*: see WELL *adv.* 16 b.

7. a. Of sufficient merit, excellence, or desert *to* be or have something. †Also with *that*.

c **1220** *Bestiary* 186 in *O.E. Misc.* 6 Ne deme ðe no3t wurdi, Ðat tu dure loken up to ðe heueneward. *c* **1250** *Gen. & Ex.* 1012 Of ðe ðre he wurðede ðe ton,..Ðe was wurði wurðed to ben. *Ibid.* 3753 He seiden he weren wurði bet To ðat seruise to ben set. *a* **1300** *Cursor M.* 4056 Ioseph he sagh a night in sueuen, þe quilk es worþie for to neuen. **1362** LANGL. *P. Pl.* A. II. 91 Worþi is þe Werkmon his hure to haue. **1377** *Ibid.* B. III. 228 Mede is wel worthi þe maistrye to haue! *c* **1400** *Rule St. Benet* 228 Þat we may fle fro paines of hell And be worthi in blis to dwell. **1450-1530** *Myrr. Our Ladye* II. 97 O mayden worthy to be loued of god. **1526** *Pilgr. Perf.* (W. de W. 1531) 2, I requyre you all in the moost worthy to be loued woundes & passyon of Chryst. **1596** DALRYMPLE tr. *Leslie's Hist. Scot.* (S.T.S.) II. 11 He will, perchance, be fund worthie to be counted amang the maist wirthie vndir the sone in his tyme. **1642** D. ROGERS *Naaman* 139 Not worthy to be named the same day..with God. **1651** HOBBES *Leviath.* I. x. 46 He is Worthiest to be a Commander ..that is best fitted with the qualities required to the well discharging of it. **1708** ATTERBURY *Serm.* (Job xxii. 21) 24 That we may be found worthy to be admitted into the Blessed Vision of him in the next [life]. **1781** COWPER *Retirement* 700 All such as manly and great souls produce, Worthy to live, and of eternal use. **1799-1805** WORDSW. *Prelude* IV. 131 Those walks well worthy to be prized and loved. **1816** J. WILSON *City of Plague* II. iv. 53 One hand alone on all the earth was worthy To place these flowers. **1875** JOWETT *Plato* (ed. 2) III. 307 The only knowledge worthy to be called knowledge.

ellipt. *c* **1420** *Sir Amadace* (Camden) xxxi, 3e mone haue maystURS euyrqware As wele wurthi 3e ar soe.

b. With ellipsis of *to*.

a **1300** *Cursor M.* 1148 It es nogtht worþi forgiuen be. **1390** GOWER *Conf.* II. 46 As hire thoghte..Sche was noght worthi axen there, Fro when they come. *c* **1400** *26 Pol. Poems* xx. 120 He is worþy be loued.

†**c.** Const. *for* (some purpose). *Obs.*

1591 SHAKS. *Two Gent.* II. iv. 76 He is as worthy for an Empresse loue, As meet to be an Emperors Councellor. **1658** EARL MONM. tr. *Paruta's Wars Cyprus* 65 Doria refused to fall upon any petty businesse, as not worthy for his Kings Fleet, to run any hazard in.

8. a. Deserving *of* something, by reason of merit or excellence.

a **1300** *Cursor M.* 10350 Berns..oft er for þair dughtihede Selcuth worþi mikel of mede. **1471** CAXTON *Recuyell* (Sommer) 492 Your labours shall neuer be dygne ne worthy of preysyng. *c* **1534** TINDALE *Prol. Mark*, Ye see..of what authoritie his writing is, and how worthy of credence. **1565** STAPLETON tr. *Bede's Hist. Ch. Eng.* 177 He was founde.. best worthy of that bishopprick. **1605** CAMDEN *Rem., Wise Sp.* 186 No mortall man doubtlesse is woorthy of such an high name. **1650** *Nicholas Papers* (Camden) 181, I thinke him worthy of much greater trust and favor. **1724** RAMSAY *Tea-t. Misc.* (1733) I. 68 For now she's..wordy of my hand. **1725** —— *Gent. Sheph.* I. i, Weel are ye wordy o't. **1737** *Gentl. Mag.* VII. 596/1 The only Service..worthy of Preferment in the Army. **1798** FERRIAR *Illustr. Sterne* iv. 137 It contains nothing worthy of attention. **1848** L. HUNT *Jar of Honey* Pref. 16 French has lately been thought worthy of cultivation. **1860** TYNDALL *Glac.* I. xxvi. 192, I thought such services worthy of some recognition. **1874** GREEN *Short Hist.* iii. §4. 128 Abelard was a foe worthy of the menaces of councils.

b. With ellipsis of *of*: Deserving, meriting.

a **1300** *Cursor M.* 19362 (Edin.) Þa wente ioifuler þan are, ..þat tai for him war worthi grame. *c* **1400** *26 Pol. Poems* ii. 40 The trewe seruant is worthy hys mede. **1494** FABYAN *Chron.* lxxxiii. (1811) 62 That thou..resygne..the Rule of thy lande to hym yᵗ is more worthy this rome than thou art. **1550** CROWLEY *Inform.* Sel. Wks. (1872) 162 Your owne conscience shall iudge you worthye no mercye. **1563** *Homilies* II. *Martrimony* 540 This man is worthye much commendation. *c* **1600** SHAKS. *Sonn.* xxxviii, Oh giue thy selfe the thankes if ought in me, Worthy perusal stand against thy sight. **1639** in *Verney Mem.* (1904) I. 94 There is no newes worth your acceptance or worthy my labour. **1648** WINYARD *Midsummer Moon* 3 Good ingenious soules ..are thought worthy heaven because they boast no merit. **1675** DRYDEN *Aurengz.* I. (1676) 14 Be worthy me, as I am worthy you. **1727** SWITZER *Pract. Gard.* I. v. 38 And it is worthy remark, that he waters [etc.]. **1743** FRANCIS tr. *Hor., Odes* IV. ix. 30 Greece had with Heroes fill'd th' embattled Plain, Worthy the Muse in her sublimest Strain. **1777** W. DALRYMPLE *Trav. Sp. & Port.* cxxxii, It was worthy notice, I was informed. **1813** J. C. HOBHOUSE *Journ.* (ed. 2) 509 Whatever was worthy imitation was imitated by the Turks. **1864** TENNYSON *Aylmer's F.* 712 Him too you loved, for he was worthy love. **1889** SWINBURNE *Stud. B. Jonson* 83 Dame Polish is a figure well worthy the cordial and lavish commendation of Gifford.

c. With verbal sbs. (Cf. WORTH *a.* 8 b.)

c **1440** *Alphabet of Tales* 90 Þan þe grete devull..sayde þat he was wurthi lovyng. **1548** UDALL *Erasm. Par. Matt.* iii. 1 Nowe is it worthy the hearyng to knowe how our Lorde Iesus Christ began & entred with the matter, that he came for. **1581** PETTIE tr. *Guazzo's Civ. Conv.* I. (1586) A 6 b, Either to doe thinges worth the writing, or to write things worthy the reading. **1613** PURCHAS *Pilgrimage* (1614) 152 The wordes of Beniamin are worthy the inserting. **1685** *Caldwell Papers* (Maitl. Club) I. 145, I took boat from Middleburgh to Dort; nothing occurred worthie noticeing. **1718** *Entertainer* No. 27. 179 He is not worthy regarding who has not some Spice of this Ambition. **1795-6** WORDSW. *Borderers* III. 1179 'Twere matter Worthy the hearing. **1879** MORLEY *Burke* iii. 40 A time..when England would not be worthy living in.

9. Deserving or meriting by fault or wrong-doing. Const. as in senses 7 and 8.

(*a*) *c* **1220** *Bestiary* 447 in *O.E. Misc.* 14 Man al so ðe foxes name Arn wurði to hauen same. *c* **1366** CHAUCER *A.B.C.* 123 And þat my soule is wurthi for to sinke. **1377** LANGL. *P. Pl.* B. v. 236 Þow haddest [be] better worthy be hanged þerfore. *c* **1440** *Alphabet of Tales* 155 He said his head war wurthi to be smetyn off. *c* **1449** PECOCK *Repr.* IV. iii. 435 Mannys lawe ..is leeful and not worthi be vndirnome and blamed. *c* **1460** *Contin. Brut* 517 Þei said playnly þat þe Lorde Say,..& many mo, wer traytoures, & worthy to be dede. **1508** STANBRIDGE *Vulgaria* (W. de W.) B v, Thou arte worthy to be hanged. **1561** T. NORTON tr. *Calvin's Inst.* I. ix. 20 Then suche carelesnesse is woorthye to be laughed at. **1584** R. SCOT *Discov. Witchcr.* III. xix. (1886) 56 Whereby it is inferred that they are worthie to die. **1632** *Star Chamber Cases* (Camden) 171, I think, therefore, he is worthie to paie 500ˡⁱ dammage.

ellipt. **1297** R. GLOUC. (Rolls) 1417 Pilatus he sende.. Vorto holde hom harde inou, as hii wel wrþi were. **1556** *Chron. Gr. Friars* (Camden) 41 To be hongyd and heddyd.. and there sufferde as they ware wordy.

(*b*) **1340-70** *Alex. & Dind.* 746 As 3e ben worþi of wo whan þe word failus. *c* **1350** *Will. Palerne* 4788 Þat we ar worþi to þe deth, wel we be a-knowe. **1505** *Presentm. Juries* in *Surtees Misc.* (1890) 31 Yowr wyff hays had hyll wordes for me, qwylk yᵗ I was never worde off. **1583** STUBBES *Anat. Abus.* II. (1882) 84 There are manie woorthie of great blame in this respect.

(*c*) *a* **1340** HAMPOLE *Psalter* vi. 1 Sett noght swilk skilles agayns me þat i be conuycte & worþi dampnacioun. *c* **1400** *Pilgr. Sowle* (Caxton 1483) III. ix. 56 In this fyre haue they theyr sepulture, none other be they worthy. **1542** UDALL *Erasm. Apoph.* 10 b, Idlenes euermore [is] worthie blame. **1581** A. HALL *Iliad* II. 28 Oh hatefull case, worthy reproche. **1615** BRATHWAIT *Strappado* 193 O I were worthy death, Not to loue them.

10. Appropriate, suitable, becoming, fit: †**a.** In the phrase ***it is worthy that***.., or variations of this. *Obs.*

a **1300** *Cursor M.* 7311 It es wel worthye þat qua Mai bere no wel ne thole na wa. **13..** *Ibid.* 6508 (Gött.) Þis ilk es he þat broght vs thoru þe rede se,..Þar-for es worthi he honurd be. *c* **1400** *Rom. Rose* 7573 It were worthy To putte thee out of this baily. *c* **1400** *Pilgr. Sowle* (Caxton) v. xiv. (1859) 79 Now for this feste shalle we seyen the graces, as worthy is, with all oure dylygence. **1450-1530** *Myrr. Our Ladye* II. 288 Yt is worthy that man shulde calle..all the workes of god to prayse hym. *c* **1480** HENRYSON *Fox, Wolf & Cadger* 149 'It is weill worthie', quod he, 'I want 3one tyke, [etc.].'

b. Const. with noun as object. In later use = of sufficient excellence, etc., to be appropriate for (one). Now *arch.* and *rare.*

c **1440** *Jacob's Well* 267 Þe glose..seyth, þat it is no3t worthy god to be mercyfull to hym þat is cruel & vnmercyfull. *c* **1513** MORE *Hist. Edw. V* Wks. 35/1 Katheryne..is..in verye prosperous estate, and woorthye her birth and vertue. **1639** DU VERGER tr. *Camus' Admir. Events* 40 Her lookes..did but seeke to find a Rocke worthy her ship-wracke. **1697** DRYDEN *Æneis* VI. 1178 These are Imperial Arts, and worthy thee. **1718** POPE *Iliad* XVIII. 166 The host to succour, and thy friends to save Is worthy thee. *a* **1774** GOLDSM. *Hist. Greece* II. 130 To teach him all such arts and sciences as are worthy the heir to a great Kingdom. **1833** TENNYSON *Dream Fair Women* 164 A name for ever!.. Worthy a Roman spouse. **1852** J. H. NEWMAN *Idea University* viii. (1873) 186 It is the drawing the mind off.. to subjects which are worthy a rational being.

c. Const. *of*.

1576 FLEMING *Panopl. Epist.* 219 Mine *Aeneas*, which if it were worthy of your person, I wold most willingly present it to your highnesse. **1591** SPENSER *Ruins Time* 287 Treasure passing all this worldes worth, Worthie of heauen it selfe, which brought it forth. **1637** RUTHERFORD *Lett.* xci. *To J. Kennedy* (1671) 186 That our little inch of time-suffering is not worthy of our first night's welcome-home to heaven. **1667** MILTON *P.L.* IV. 241 Nectar, visiting each plant,..fed Flours worthy of Paradise. **1697** DRYDEN *Æneis* XI. 633 Let that vile Soul in that vile Body rest; The Lodging is well worthy of the Guest. **1795** *Gentl. Mag.* LXV. 542/2 His charities..were truly splendid, worthy of the son of the celebrated Bishop of Cloyne. **1810** SCOTT *Lady of L.* v. x, The stern joy which warriors feel In foemen worthy of their steel. **1829** SCOTT *Anne of G.* xxxv, Your sentiments and conduct are worthy of the noble house you descend from. **1864** BYRCE *Holy Rom. Emp.* xv. (1875) 244 There had been pontiffs whose fearlessness and justice were worthy of their exalted office.

†**11.** Under an obligation *to* do something. *Obs.*⁻¹

1469 *Paston Lett.* Suppl. (1901) 128 Wheche wele considered, she were wurthy to recompense you.

B. *adv.* or quasi-*adv.* **a.** Worthily; in a manner worthy *of* (something). *Obs.* or only *poet.*

13.. *Gaw. & Gr. Knt.* 1477 Sir Wawen her welcumed worþy on fyrst. *c* **1475** *Rauf Coilȝear* 360 Thay callit it the best ȝule than, And maist worthie began, Sen euer King Charlis was man. **1526** TINDALE *Ephes.* iv. 1, I..exhorte you thatt ye walke worthy [Gr. ἀξίως] off the vocation wher with ye are called. **1577** B. GOOGE *Heresbach's Husb.* III. 114 Among all other creatures..the Horse may worthiest challenge the chiefest place. **1806** H. SIDDONS *Maid, Wife, & Widow* II. 67 It is a prouder triumph to found a race by living worthy, than to receive the greatest honours from the records of the dead. **1815** MRS. PILKINGTON *Celebrity* III. 47 Satisfaction which arises from a conviction of having acted worthy of ourselves.

b. In comb. with adjs. or verbs, as ***worthy-sing*** vb. (= to sing worthily), ***worthy-sweet*** adj.

1606 SYLVESTER *Du Bartas* II. iv. *Tropheis* 34 Let me his Harp-strings..haue; His Lute, and not his Launce, to worthie-sing Thy glorie. **1844** MRS. BROWNING *Lady Geraldine's Courtship* xlv, The leafy sounds of woodlands.. Brought interposition worthy-sweet.

C. *sb.* **1. a.** A distinguished or eminent person; a famous or renowned man or woman; esp. a man of courage or of noble character.

13.. *Gaw. & Gr. Knt.* 1508, 'I woled wyt at yow, wy3e,' þat worþy þer sayde,..'what were [etc.].' *c* **1350** *Will. Palerne* 755 A sete þat was..vnder a windowe of þat worþeis chaumber. *c* **1400** *Destr. Troy* 9481 He woundit þat worthy in his wide þrote. **1412-20** LYDG. *Chron. Troy* I. 4103 Vp-on þe whiche..many worþi loste þer his lif. *c* **1450** HOLLAND *Houlate* 849 The Pape..Wosche with thir worthyis, and went to counsall. **1535** COVERDALE *2 Sam.* i. 21 There is the shylde of the Worthies smytten downe. —— *1 Macc.* ix. 21 Alas, that this worthy shulde be slayne. **1582** STANYHURST *Æneis* II. (Arb.) 46 Too serue this woorthy,..My father vnwelthy mee sent. **1605** *1st Part Jeronimo* III. ii. 30 This fierce, couragious Prince, a noble worthy. **1628** A. LEIGHTON *Appeal to Parlt.* 126 Sundry worthies of the Scottish nation. **1654** WHITLOCK *Zootomia* 322 Rule to trye the reall worth of Feminine worthies by. **1664** BUTLER *Hud.* II. ii. 149 Did not our Worthies of the House, Before they broke the Peace, break Vows? **1706** E. WARD *Wooden World Diss.* (1708) Ded. A 6 b, To excite some renown'd Worthy to do you Justice. **1784** COWPER *Tiroc.* 647 With commendation due, To set some living worthy in his view. **1805** SOUTHEY *Madoc* I. xviii, The Bard of years to come.. Shall with the Worthies of his country rank Llewelyn's name. **1866** J. MARTINEAU *Ess.* I. 1 Before he can be.. registered among the worthies of humanity. **1868** FREEMAN *Norm. Conq.* II. vii. 81 In the course of the next year England lost one of her truest worthies.

b. *spec.* A hero of antiquity.

1552-3 in Feuillerat *Revels Edw. VI* (1914) 133 A maske of greate personages representinge the woorthyes of the greekes. **16..** ROWLEY *Birth of Merlin* IV. v. 119 He to the world shall add another Worthy. **1638** JUNIUS *Paint. Ancients* 51 Hercules among all the other Worthies was most frequently made in a Lions skinne. **1711** POPE *Temple Fame* 65 *note*, The western front is of Grecian architecture: The Doric order was peculiarly sacred to Heroes and Worthies. **1762** HURD *Lett. Chivalry* 32 Do not you remember that the Grecian worthies were.. as famous for encountering Dragons.. as for suppressing Giants?

c. ***the nine worthies***: nine famous personages of ancient and mediæval history and legend, also called †*the nine nobles* (see NOBLE *sb.*[1] 1 b).

The number is composed of three Jews (Joshua, David, and Judas Maccabæus), three Gentiles (Hector, Alexander, and Julius Cæsar), and three Christians (Arthur, Charlemagne, and Godfrey of Bouillon).

c **1417** *Agincourt* 13 Though thou be not set amonge ye worthyes nyne, Yet wast thou a conqueroure in thy tyme. **1454** *E.E. Wills* (1882) 133, I bequeth to my brother.. the hallyng with the ix wurthy. **1550** J. COKE *Eng. & Fr. Heralds* § 11 (1877) 61 Charlemayne.. for his valyauntnesse is of the nombre of the nyne worthyes. [**1589** WARNER *Alb. Eng.* VI. xxix. 128 For well this Subiect might increase the Worthies vnto ten.] **1610** TOFTE *Honours Acad.* II. 3 That famous Iosuah, one of the nine Worthies. **1619** J. TAYLOR (Water P.) *Kicksey Winsey* C 1 b, Forgot had bin the thrice three worthies names, If thrice three Muses had not writ their fames.

transf. **1586** FERNE *Blaz. Gentrie* 156 Semyramis.. is one of the nine worthies of that sexe. **1906** G. B. SHAW *Let.* 29 Sept. (1972) II. 657 The points we cannot accept. These are .2. The triumvirates, on the ground that the nine worthies cannot be found to take the responsibility.

†**d.** A prominent scholar or theologian. *Obs.*

1605 HIERON *Short Dial.* A iij b, Popish grounds, which our owne worthyes, long since haue razed and overthrowne. **1607** —— *Defence* I. Pref. *3 b, Is not this,.. to make voyd all the writings of our worthyes written in condemnation of those corrupt translations? **1611** *Bible* Transl. Pref. ¶ 13 So many of their Worthies disclaiming the now receiued conceit.

e. Applied colloquially or facetiously to any person, esp. one having a marked personality. (Common in 19th cent.)

1751 WARBURTON *Pope's Wks.* III. 69 Thus it fared with our two Worthies. **1821** SCOTT *Kenilw.* iii, Tressilian acquiesced, and the two worthies left the apartment together. **1836** DICKENS *Sk. Boz, Streets—Night*, Stirring the taproom fire and.. taking part in the conversation of the worthies assembled round it. **1850** 'SYLVANUS' *Bye-lanes & Downs* i. 13 Another worthy of York appertaining to the turf about this period. **1880** BROWNING *Dram. Idyls* Ser. II. *Pietro* 351 Ho, my knaves without there! Lead this worthy downstairs!

2. A thing of worth or value. *rare.*

1588 SHAKS. *L.L.L.* IV. iii. 236 In her faire cheeke, Where seuerall Worthies make one dignity.

†**worthy**, *v. Obs.* [f. WORTHY *a.*]

1. *trans.* To render, or hold, worthy (*of* something); to raise to honour or distinction.

1387-8 T. USK *Test. Love* I. ii. 109 Who hath worthyed kinges in the felde? **1549** COVERDALE etc. *Erasm. Par. Jas.* i. 13-21 This is the honoure that the heauenly father worthyed vs withal. **1565** CALFHILL *Answ. Martiall* 128 b, To make hir wel apayde, that she should be worthied to haue a God to talk to hir. *Ibid.* 170 b, Sith the Scripture is worthyed of these titles. **1601** W. WATSON *Import. Consid.* (1831) 4 By how much I might be worthied with a favourable conceit had of you all. **1605** SHAKS. *Lear* II. ii. 128 When he.. put vpon him such a deale of Man, That worthied him, got praises of the King. **1624** QUARLES *Job Militant* Med. xvi. N 1, So wisedome be the message; Embassadours are worthyed in th' Embassage.

2. To hold in honour, pay respect to.

c **1425** *Eng. Conq. Ireland* 93 The Pepil of the londe manshiply hym sholde vp-take, and worthy as lorde.

-worthy, the adjective employed as a second element in a number of compounds, of which only a few have come into regular use, as *blame-*, *note-*, *praise-*, *sea-worthy*. The earliest instances, occurring in the 13th century, are later variants of forms in *-wurthe* (OE. *-wyrðe*), as *dere-*, *luve-*, *stalworthi* for earlier *derewurthe*, etc., = OE. *déor-* and *stælwyrðe*. Other OE. examples, as *nytwyrðe*, are not represented in ME., and there is app. no direct connexion between OE. *þancwyrðe* and the late ME. *thankworthy*. Of new formations the 13th cent. affords *deathworthy*, the 14th *blame-* and *thankworthy*, and the 15th *sale-worthy*; the 16th adds *faith-*, *honour-*, *praise-*, *note-*, *fault-*, and *name-worthy*, and the 17th *worship-*, *wonder-*, *scorn-*, *fame-*, *laugh-*, and *labour-worthy*. The common *sea-worthy* is not recorded before 1807, and more recent formations include *mark-*, *song-*, *battle-worthy*, and irregularly from verb-stems, *teach-* and *paint-worthy*.

wortle ('wɜːt(ə)l). Forms: α. 5 **wirtil**, **writel**, 9 **whirtle**, **wortle**. β. 7 **wurdle**, 9 **wordle**. [Of obscure origin.] An implement used in the drawing of wire or lead-pipe (see quots. 1875). Also *Comb.*, as ***wortle-maker***, ***-plate***.

1430 *Cov. Leet-bk.* 142 Joh. Smyth, wirtilmaker. *Ibid.* 160 Tho. Smyth, writelmaker. **1664** H. POWER *Exp. Philos.* 56 Your Wire-drawers know, that if they take a short piece of Wire,.. and drill it through, that then though they draw it out to the smalness of a hair, yet will it still remain hollow quite through in despite of their Wurdle. **1819** REES *Cycl.* XXVII. 3 M 2, The workmen are provided with a great number of these plates..; they are called whirtles. *Ibid.*, This winds up the double chains, drawing the pipe through the whirtle, by which it diminishes its size and lengthens it out. **1875** KNIGHT *Dict. Mech.*, *Whirtle*, a perforated steel plate through which pipe or wire is drawn to reduce its diameter. *Ibid.*, *Wordle*, one of the pivoted cams in a draw-head,.. capable of simultaneous adjustment.. to regulate the size of the throat through which the tube or wire is drawn. **1888** *Science* 14 Dec. 286/1 The wire.. breaking into short lengths when being pulled through the wortles. **1913** *Engineering* 18 Apr. 541/3 It is also probable that the earliest wortles were hard stones. *Ibid.* 542/1 The wortle-plates required by those engaged in drawing wire by hand.

wortle(berry, obs. ff. WHORTLE(BERRY.

†'**wortling.** *Obs. rare.* [f. WORT *sb.*[1] + -LING.] A young vine-plant.

1691 Y-WORTH *New Art Making Wines* 9 But if thou wilt repair an old Vine, these [roots] are taken out, and are now call'd Wortlings. *Ibid.*, These our Wortlings.. are the better able to defend against the Frost.

wortwale, var. WARTWALE *Obs.*

†'**wortworm.** *Obs.* Forms: 4-5 **worte worm** (6 **worme**), 5 **wortworme**, **-wyrme**, **wurtwurme.** [f. WORT *sb.* + WORM *sb.*] A caterpillar that feeds on worts or cabbages.

1388 WYCLIF *Joel* i. 4 A locuste eet the residue of a worte worm [L. *residuum erucæ*]. *c* **1440** *Promp. Parv.* 532/2 Wort wyrme, þat etythe wortys, *eruca*. *c* **1440** *Palladius on Husb.* I. 880 Tak Iuce of hennebane With sour aysel,.. Ereither wol be wortewormys bane. **1496** *Bk. St. Albans, Fishing* i j b, In August take wortwormes & magotes. **1530** PALSGR. 290/2 Worte worme.

worwyn, **wory(e**, obs. forms of WORRY *v.*

wos, obs. and vulgar f. *was*, pa. t. of BE *v.*

wos, **wose**, obs. forms of WHOSE.

wosbird, dial. var. *whore's bird* (WHORE *sb.* 3).

wose, obs. of OOZE.

wosen, obs. f. WEASAND.

wosie, obs. f. OOZY *a.*

wosing, obs. f. OOZING *vbl. sb.*

†**wosith.** *Obs.* Also 3 **wasið**, [**wei-sið**]. [f. WOE *sb.* + SITHE *sb.*[1]] Trouble, affliction.

c **1200** *Trin. Coll. Hom.* 209 ȝif he seð his emcristene þolien wosið. [*c* **1205** LAY. 25846 þa fond he þer ane quene.. weop for hire wei-sið.] *c* **1230** *Hali Meid.* (Titus) 51 Alle þe alde wiues schome craft, þat cunnen of þat wasið. *Ibid.* 53 Lutel wat meiden.. of hire wasiðes of þat fode fostringe. *c* **1330** R. BRUNNE *Chron. Wace* (Rolls) 15712 Manie oþere sore hit ment,.. þat wyth hym byde many wo sith.

wosse, **wosshe**, obs. ff. WISH. *v.*

wosseyle, obs. f. WASSAIL *v.*

wost, obs. f. VOUST *sb.*

wost(e, **wostow(e**, **wostu:** see WIT *v.*[1]

wostour, obs. f. VOUSTER.

wosy(e, obs. ff. OOZY.

wot (wɒt), *v. arch.* Forms: (see below). [var. of WIT *v.*[1], due to the carrying over of the preterite-present stem *wǭt* (earlier and northern *wāt*) into other parts of the verb. The substitution occurs first in the 2nd pers. sing. (*wāt*, *wǭt* for *wāst*, *wǭst*) and the plur. (for *witen*) of the present tense, and appears in northern texts from the end of the 13th century. In the 14th cent. the new forms *wotest* and *woteth* (*wotis*) appear. The infin. *woten* occurs early in the 15th cent., and *wotte*, *wote*, *wot* in the 16th, together with the pres. pple. *wotting*. The pa. t. *wotted* is an archaism of the 19th cent.] *trans.* and *intr.* To know. Freq. const. with *of*. (See WIT *v.*[1])

1. *2nd sing. pres. indic.* α. *north.* and *Sc.* 4-5 **wat**, 4-6 **wate**, (4 **whate**, **quat**, **vat**), 6 **wait**, (**vait**). β. 4 **whote**, 5 **woot**, **wot**.

α. *a* **1300** *Cursor M.* 766 Wat þou [*Gött.* quat. *Fairf.* wate] quarfor? **1340** HAMPOLE *Pr. Consc.* 2666 Ne þou whate never in what stede þou sal dyghe. **1375** BARBOUR *Bruce* v. 241 Thou vat nocht quha is thi frend. **1423** JAS. I *Kingis Q.* cxxix, Lo, wate thou quhy? *c* **1425** WYNTOUN *Cron.* v. xiii. 5247 (Cott.) Quhar was God, wat þou oucht, Befor þat hewyn and erde was wroucht? **1549** *Compl. Scot.* xv. 126 Thou vait that ane man vil haue childir of deferent conditionis. *c* **1550** ROLLAND *Crt. Venus* I. 404 Thryis als mekle scho reuis, That thou not wait. *a* **1568** in *Bannatyne MS.* (Hunter, Club) 133 Thow wate nocht quhen that it will licht.

β. *a* **1352** MINOT *Poems* (ed. Hall) xi. 4 þou whote wham I mene. *c* **1400** *Non-Cycle Myst. Plays* iii. 40 Now wot þou wele of all oure wo. *a* **1425** *Cursor M.* 3231 (Trin.) Wende in hye vnto mesopothanye, þere þou woot oure frendes wone.

2. *Pres. indic. plural.* α. *north.* and *Sc.* 4-6, 8 **wat** (4 **quat**, 5 **vat**), **wate** (5 **quate**), 5-6 **wait** (6 **vait**, **waite**). β. 4-6 **wote** (4 **woteþ**, **wotin**, 5 *north.* **woteys**), 5 **woote**, 5-6 **woot**, **wott(e**, 5-9 **wot** (5 **whot**).

α. *a* **1300** *Cursor M.* 4729 Wel wat [*Fairf.* wate] yee Mi stiward ioseph al fedes me. *Ibid.* 14571 We wat [*Gött.* quat] mast quat er þai þar. **1340** HAMPOLE *Pr. Consc.* 1432 Ofte chaunges þe tymes here, als men wele wate. *c* **1375** *Sc. Leg. Saints* vi. (*Thomas*) 172 Of pollucione of flesche grovis, as ve vat, giltines. *c* **1425** WYNTOUN *Cron.* v. xi. 2931 (Cott.) As ȝhe wate and has herde tel. **1456** SIR G. HAYE *Law Arms* (S.T.S.) 151 Changeing of men that wate the kingis secretis .. may do grete scathe. **1513** DOUGLAS *Æneis* x. Prol. 66 Lik as the sawle of man is ane, we wait, Havand thre poweris distinct and separate. **1549** *Compl. Scot.* v. 32 Thai vait nocht quhat thing is the varld. **1596** DALRYMPLE tr. *Leslie's Hist. Scot.* I. 58 Quhilkes to cal scheip or gait.. we knawe nocht, nor wat we neil. **1720** RAMSAY *Prosp. Plenty* 171 Right wiel they wate That truth and honesty hauds lang the gate. **1724** —— *Tea-t. Misc.* (1733) I. 66 Now wat ye wha I met yestreen?

β. **1303** R. BRUNNE *Handl. Synne* 39 þys clerkys.. wote þat ys to wetyn. *c* **1400** tr. *Secreta Secret., Gov. Lordsh.* 51 We woot wel þat þe kepynge of largesse ys right herd. **1426** LYDG. *De Guil. Pilgr.* 2432 They.. wot nat wher to saue or lese. *c* **1460** *Play Sacr.* 334 Ye wott what I haue sayd. **1521** FISHER *Serm.* Wks. (1876) 315 We woot that that people of the Iewes was a shadow of the chrysten people. *c* **1530** LATIMER in Strype *Eccl. Mem.* (1721) I. App. xliii. 119 Ye call the Scripture the new Lerninge; which.. is eldre than any lerninge, that ye wote to be the old. **1598** SHAKS. *Merry W.* II. ii. 90 Then you may come and see the picture.. that you wot of. **16..** MIDDLETON etc. *Old Law* III. i, I have found out the true age.. of the party you wot on. **1657** TRAPP *Comm. Ps.* xxxii. 5 Wot you what?.. he hath confessed himself as guilty.. as his man. **1753-4** RICHARDSON *Grandison* (1810) IV. xvii. 141 Wot ye not the indelicacy of an early present, which you are not obliged to make? **1841** JAMES *Brigand* iv, There are more dangers around than you wot of. **1874** MOTLEY *John of Barneveld* xi. II. 30 'Don't forget to caress the old gentleman you wot of,' said the Advocate frequently.

3. a. *2nd sing. pres. indic.* 5 **wotest**, **-ist**, **-ys(t**, 6- **wottest**, 6 **wottst**, **wotste**, *Sc.* **wattis.**

1387-8 T. USK *Test. Love* I. ii. 74 Wottest thou not wel.. that every shepherde ought.. to seke his sperkelande sheep. *c* **1400** *Beryn* 45, I myȝte nat lyve els, þowe wotist. **1448-9** METHAM *Amoryus & Cleopes* 360 Wotys thow qwat me thynkyth best? **1470-85** MALORY *Arthur* I. xxiv. 72 This knyght is a man of more worship than thou wotest of. **1549** COVERDALE *Erasm. Par. Rom.* Prol. ✠ iv b, Thou woteste not what thou teachest. **1579** HAKE *Newes out of Powles* (1872) A vij, For well thou wotste, if thyrsty were my minde.. Then would I [etc.]. *a* **1585** MONTGOMERIE *Cherrie & Slae* 426 Thou wattis not quhat thou wald. **1819** SCOTT *Ivanhoe* xxxvi, Wottest thou that Lucas de Beaumanoir.. is now himself at Templestowe? **1844** MRS. BROWNING *Crowned & Buried* xv, I would have The dead whereof thou wottest, from that grave.

b. *3rd sing. pres. indic.* 4 **wotis**, 6 **woteth**, **-ith**, 6 **wottyth**, 6- **wotteth**, 9 **wots**; *Sc.* 6 **wattis**, 7 **waits**, 9 **wats**.

13.. *Cursor M.* 10506 (Gött.) He wotis þis haue i ȝernid ay. **1523** SKELTON *Garl. Laurel* 1431 Lytill wotith the goslyng what the gose thynkith. *Ibid.* 1438 Wele wotith the cat whos berde she likkith. **1531** *Dial. Laws Eng.* II. liii. 44 It is therefore no synne to say he wottyth not where he is. **1535** COVERDALE *Baruch* iii. 32 He that woteth all thynges, knoweth her. **1577** *St. Aug. Man.* (Longman) 27 O kyngdome without ende;.. where the day.. woteth not what time meaneth. **1602** J. DAVIES (Heref.) *Mirum in Modum* (Grosart) 6/1 Through which she wots what works hir woe or weale. **1633** SIR A. JOHNSTON (Wariston) *Diary* (S.H.S.) 81 Quho waits bot the Lord wil deal bountifully with his servant once this weak as he did [etc.]. **1818** SCOTT *Hrt. Midl.* xi, Let her know that he she wots of remained here.. expecting to see her. **1879** E. ARNOLD *Lt. Asia* VIII. 22 The ant wots of its ways, The white doves know them well.

4. *Infin.* 5 **woten**, 7 **wote**; 6 **wotte**, 6- **wot.** Also *subj.* 6 **wote**; *imper.* 6 **wot**, **wat**, 7 **wote**.

1414 *Rolls of Parlt.* IV. 59/1 Which is gret doel to alle the Kynges trewe lieges.. to woten of swiche meschiefs done and used withinne the Rewme. **1509** FISHER *Ps.* cxlii. Wks. (1876) 253 No meruayle it is yf than the sely soule.. wote not what to saye. **1530** PALSGR. Ep. Ded. p. iij, So that we myght wotte for the kepynge of trewe congruite in that tonge.. how [etc.]. **1575** A. FLEMING *Virg. Bucol.* III. 8 If so much thou know not, then, well wot, the goate is mine. **1601** HOLLAND *Pliny* XXX. iii. II. 406 Wote well, that ordinarily the water thereof is not good. **1605** CAMDEN *Rem.*, *Lang.* 19 Conscience, they called Inwit, as that which they did inwardly wit and wote, that is, know certainely. **1813** SCOTT *Trierm.* I. xi, The.. Monarch full little did wot That she smiled, in his absence, on brave Lancelot. **1875** MORRIS *Æneids* III. 379 The other things the Parcæ still ban Helenus to wot.

5. *Pres. pple.* (and *verbal sb.*). 6 **wottyng**, 6- **wotting.**

1523 CROMWELL in Merriman *Life & Lett.* (1902) I. 42 People browght to extreme distresse and not wottyng how to lyue. **1562** J. HEYWOOD *Prov. & Epigr.* (1867) 120 Wottyng and weenyng, were those two thingis one. **1574** A. L. *Calvin's Four Serm.* ii, He stammered, not wotting what to say. **1624** GATAKER *Transubst.* 60 Well wotting that there was no such thing. **1817** SCOTT *Harold* III. iii, Hardly wotting why, He doff'd his helmet's gloomy pride. **1887**

MORRIS *Odyss.* XIV. 451 And neither the Queen nor Laertes the Elder were wotting of this.

6. *Past tense.* 9– **wotted.**

1818 SCOTT *Rob Roy* viii, That honest gentleman's terror communicated itself to him, though he wotted not why. **1853** HUXLEY in *Life & Lett.* (1900) I. 114 Having rushed into more responsibility than I wotted of. **1901** 'LINESMAN' *Words by Eyewitness* (1902) 217 He will see many things he wotted nothing of.

wot (wɒt), non-standard written form of WHAT *pron.*, *a.*[1], etc.

1829 [see SLAP-UP *a.* b]. **1865** [see WATER *sb.* 6 f]. **1898** [see CHIVVY *sb.*]. **1925** [see GARDEN *sb.* 1 f]. **1949** E. POUND *Pisan Cantos* lxxvii. 50 I'll tell you wot izza comin'. **1972** 'H. CARMICHAEL' *Naked to Grave* v. 60 He's going to have a tough job convincing the police he wasn't the one wot done it.

b. In phr. *wot, no* ——?: orig. (in the war of 1939–45) a catchphrase protesting against shortages, written as the caption accompanying a Chad (see CHAD); now also in extended humorous use.

1945 *Sunday Express* 2 Dec. 2/3 Chad is the Watcher... He peers over walls and asks, 'Wot, no...?' **1946**, **1950** [see CHAD, CHAD]. **1958** J. TOWNSEND *Young Devils* ii. 16 A rusty drawing-pin supported an old Teachers' Union notice. It had scribbled across it 'Wot, no money?' **1979** K. CONLON *Move in Game* I. v. 64 Joanna sent a postcard which said, 'Wot no tulle and confetti?'

wot(e, obs. forms of OAT.

wotcher (ˈwɒtʃə(r)), *int.* Also **watcha.** Colloq. corruption of 'what cheer?' (CHEER *sb.* 3 b), a familiar greeting.

1894 A. CHEVALIER *Humorous Songs* 4 'Wot cher!' all the neighbours cried, 'Who're yer goin' to meet, Bill?' **1899** *North-China Herald* 13 Nov. 962/3 (Advt.), 'Wot Cher, Mate?' may be a rough form of salutation. **1928** *Granta* 2 Nov. 71 (*caption*) Wotcher! **1954** J. MASTERS *Bhowani Junction* xxxii. 279 Howland waved violently to Victoria.. and shouted, 'Wotcher, Vicky!' **1977** 'J. GASH' *Judas Pair* iii. 38 'Watcha, Lovejoy.' 'Come in, Tinker.' **1980** 'J. GASH' *Spend Game* xvi. 162 'Hello, Lovejoy.' 'Wotcher, love.'

wote, obs. Sc. form of VOTE *sb.*

wote: see WIT *v.*[1], WOT *v.*

woth, obs. ind. pres. of WIT *v.*[1]

†**wothe**, *sb.* and *a.* *Obs.* Forms: α. 4 **waþe** (**quaþe**), 4–5 **wathe** (5 **waghe**, ? **wauhte**, *Sc.* **vathe**); 4 **wath** (**quat**, 5 *Sc.* **vath**); 4 **wayth**, 5 *Sc.* **waith.** β. 4–5 **wothe**, 5 **woth.** [a. ON. **wāðe* (ONorw. and Icel. *váðe*, *váði*, Norw. *vaade*, *vaae*; MSw. *vaþe*, *vadhe*, Sw. *våde*, Da. *vaade*), perh. f. **wā* (ONorw. and Icel. *vá*), harm, disaster.]

A. *sb.* The condition of being exposed to or liable to injury or harm; danger, peril; hurt or harm; a cause of harm or injury. Also const. *of.*

α. *a* **1300** *E.E. Psalter* cxiv. 3 Sorwes ofe dede vmgafe me ai, And wathes ofe helle me fand þai. *a* **1300** *Cursor M.* 1846 þe stormes starked wit þe wind, Wath vas bifor and sua bihind. *Ibid.* 29362 Quen man es in wath o ded. **1338** R. BRUNNE *Chron.* (1725) 293 If him com any scaþe, tinselle of seignorie, Tille ȝow it wille be waþe. *c* **1440** *York Myst.* v. 65 Nay, certis it is no wathe, Ete it safely ye maye. *c* **1470** HENRY *Wallace* IX. 1737 Fast south thai went; to bid it was gret waith.

β. **13..** *E.E. Allit. P.* A. 375 Bot much þe bygger ȝet was my mon, Fro þou was wroken fro vch a woþe. **13..** *S. Erkenwolde* 233 in Horstm. *Altengl. Leg.* (1881) 271 Bot for wothe ne wele, ne wrathe ne drede.. I remewit neuer fro þe riȝt. *c* **1400** *Destr. Troy* 6050 For to wacche and to wake for wothis of harme. *c* **1400** *26 Pol. Poems* xx. 143 She seyþ, þey go to helle woþes. *c* **1460** *Towneley Myst.* iii. 416 Ye shuld not be so spitus standyng in sich a woth.

B. *adj.* Dangerous.

a **1300** *Cursor M.* 4213 Alla! þat i him [Joseph] ouþer outesent, þat wai þat was so wath to wend. *Ibid.* 28687 To fall in syn hu gret foly,—hu quat [*Cotton Galba* wathe] it es þar-in to ly.

Hence †**wothely** *adv.* [Icel. *váðaliga*, MSw. *vadhelika*, *vadelige*], dangerously, perilously.

? *a* **1400** *Morte Arth.* 2090 This gentille.. wondes alle wathely, that in the wayе stondez! *Ibid.* 2186, I am wathely woundide, waresche mone I neuer! *c* **1400** *Destr. Troy* 8827 Achilles woundit full wothely in were of his lyffe. *c* **1420** *Anturs of Arth.* 303 (Thornton) Arthure.. Salle be wondede, I wysse, fulle wathely [*Douce* woþely; *Irel.* wothelik], I wene.

wothe, var. of *woghe* WOUGH *sb.*[2]

wother, obs. form of OTHER.

wother, woþer, obs. forms of WHETHER.

wother-weight (Sc.); see WITHER-[1], 2.

†ˈ**wotless**, *a.* *Obs. rare.* [irreg. f. WOT *v.*] Unknowing, ignorant.

1594 H. CONSTABLE *Diana* VI. x, Whose hands I kisse.. when she stands wotlesse whom so much she blisseth.

wot-save, obs. form of VOUCHSAFE *v.*

wott, obs. Sc. form of WIT *sb.*

wott(e, obs. ind. pres. of WIT *v.*[1]

†ˈ**wottingly**, *adv.* *Obs.* [f. *wotting*, pres. pple. of WOT *v.*] Wittingly, knowingly.

1530 PALSGR. 846/2 Wottyngly, *a escient.* **1851** *Gloss. Cumberld.*, *Wittenly*, wottenly; designedly.

†**wottoo** = wilt thou: see WILL *v.*[1] A. 3 a. δ.

1701 STEELE *Funeral* III. (1702) 42 Wottoo, Wottoo Fright thy own Trembling shivering Wife.

wou, obs. f. HOW *adv.*; obs. Sc. f. VOW *sb.* and *v.*[1]

ˈ**woubit**, ˈ**oobit.** *dial.* Forms: α. 5 **wolbode** (**welbode**), **wolle bode**; 5 **welbede**, 6 **wolbede**, 7 **wolbet**, **volbet**; 7 **wool-beard**, **woollbed**, 8 **wool bed.** β. *Sc.* 6 **wowbat**, **woubet** (**voubet**), **wobat**, 9 **vowbet**, **woubit.** γ. *north.* and *Sc.* 7 **oubut**, 9 **oubit**, **oobit**, **ubit**, **yeubit**, **hoobit**, **hubert**; **obeed.** [ME. *wolbode* and *wolbede*, app. f. *wol* WOOL *sb.* with obscure second element; the form *-bode* may be connected with BOUD or BUDDE.] A hairy caterpillar, esp. the larva of the tiger-moth; a 'woolly bear'. Also *transf.* (and *attrib.*) applied contemptuously to a person.

α. **14..** *Nom.* in Wr.-Wü lcker 706/15 *Hic multipes*, a welbode. **1483** *Cath. Angl.* 423/1 A wolle bode (*A.* Wolbode), *multipes.* **1496** *Treat. Fishing w. Angle* (1883) 24 Bynde it on your hoke with fletchers sylke and make it rough lyke a welbede. **15..** *Ortus Vocab.* (Shrewbury MS.) Wolbede. **1601** HOLLAND *Pliny* XXIX. v. II. 369 The Woollbeads or Caterpillers,.. which are a kind of earth-wormes.., all hairie, having many feet, and courbing arch-wise as they creepe. **1662** R. VENABLES *Exper. Angler* iii. 27 Those rough insects (which some call Wooll-beds, because of their woollike outside, and rings of divers colours). **1681** CHETHAM *Angler's Vade-m.* iv. §8 (1700) 35 Palmer-worm, Palmer-fly, Wooll-bed, and Cankers, Are all one Worm. **1787** BEST *Angling* (ed. 2) 18.

β. **1508** DUNBAR *Tua Mariit Wemen* 89 Ane wallidrag, ane wowrme, ane auld wobat carle. *c* **1560** A. SCOTT *Poems* (S.T.S.) xxxiv. 94 Swa ladeis will nocht sounȝe With waistit wowbattis rottin. *a* **1585** MONTGOMERIE *Flyting* 268 Wanshapen woubet [*v.r* wowbat, wolbet], of the weirds invyit. *Ibid.* 614 An warloch, an warwolfe, an voubet but haire. **1802** SIBBALD *Chron. S.P.* Gloss., *Woubit, Oubit*, one of those worms which appear as if covered with wool. **1809** *Edin. Rev.* XIV. 143 The *hairy vowbet*, or *yeubit*,.. is the name given by boys [in Berwickshire] to the caterpillar of the tiger-moth.

γ. **1608** TOPSELL *Serpents* 103 The English-Northrenmen call the hairie Catterpillers, Oubuts. *c* **1800** *Ayrs. Gl. Surv.* 693 (Jam.) *Ubit*, dwarfish. **1825** JAMIESON, *Oobit*, a hairy worm, with alternate rings of black and dark yellow. **1851** KINGSLEY *Poems*, *The Oubit*, It was an hairy oubit, sae proud he crept alang. **1861** J. BROWN *Horæ Subs.* Ser. II. 117 Very like a huge caterpillar or hairy *oobit*. **1865–** in dialect glossaries, etc. (see *Eng. Dial. Dict.*).

wouch(e, var. forms of WOUGH *sb.*[2] *Obs.*

wouchaif(f)e, wouchesafe, etc., obs. forms of VOUCHSAFE *v.*

woud, obs. Sc. f. VOID *v.*, obs. f. WOOD *sb.*[1] and *a.*

wouf, var. WOOF *int.*

wouf(e, obs. form of WOOF *sb.*[1]

wough (waʊ, wɔː), *sb.*[1] *Obs.* exc. *dial.* Forms: α. 1–4 **wah** (5 *Sc.* **wacht**). β. 1 **waȝ**, 4 **wagh**, **wau**; 1 (*dat.*) **waȝe**, 3 **waȝhe**, **wauȝe**, 4 **waghe**, **wawe**; *pl.* 1 **waȝas**, 3 **waȝes**, 4 **waghis**, 5 **wawis**, **-es.** γ. 4 **woȝ** (*dat.* **woȝe**, *pl.* **woȝes**), 4, 7–9 **wogh**, 5 **woch**, 8 **woagh**; 3–4 **wouh**, 4 **wouȝ**, **woughe**, 5, 8–9 **wough.** δ. 4–5 **wowe**, 4 **wow**; *pl.* 3–5 **wowes** (3 **woawes**), 5 **wowen.** [OE. *wáȝ* (also *wǽȝ*), *wáh*, = OFris. *wâch* (W.Fris. *weach*, EFris. *wôch*, NFris. *woch*, *wuch*, *ûch*, etc.), related to Goth. *waddjus*, ON. *veggr* (see WIG *sb.*[2]).

The later Sc. *waw*, *wa'*, and northern dial. *waw*, *woa*, *wo'*, are normal phonetic developments of *wall*, and their wide currency indicates that they represent that word rather than this.]

1. A wall of a house; a partition.

α. *c* **888** ÆLFRED *Boeth.* xxxvi. §7 Swa swa ælces huses wah bið fæst ægðer ȝe on ðære flore ȝe on ðæm hrofe. *c* **1000** ÆLFRIC *Hom.* I. 288 Him ne wiðstent nan ðing, naðer ne stænen weall ne bryden wah. *c* **1200** ORMIN 1015 An waȝheriftt Wass spredd fra wah to waȝhe. *c* **1205** LAY. 25887 He nom þare halle wah [*v.r.* wað] and helden hine to grunde. *a* **1240** *Sawles Warde* in *O.E. Hom.* I. 247 Is eauer hire unþeaw forte sechen in-ȝong abute þe wahes to a murðrin hire þrinne. **13..** *Cursor M.* 23216 (Edin.) Paintid fire.. þat apon a wah war wroht. *a* **1500** *Bernardus de cura rei fam.* (E.E.T.S.) 7 Quhile þa ly by þe wacht.

β. *Beowulf* 1662 þæt ic on waȝe ȝeseah wlitiȝ hangian eald sweord eacen. *c* **893** ÆLFRED *Oros.* v. xv. 250 He oft.. sloȝ mid his heafde on þone waȝ. **971** *Blickl. Hom.* 151 Hie þa wurdon sona ablinde.. & heora heafdu sloȝan on þa waȝas. *c* **1200** ORMIN 6815 An waȝhe off Cristess kirrke. *Ibid.* 6825 þatt hirnestan þatt band ta tweȝȝen waȝhess. *c* **1205** LAY. 10182 Heo letten alle þa scrud at þere dure werpen vt, wascen þe waȝes [*c* 1275 wowes]. *a* **1300** *Cursor M.* 7667 þe king þan hent a sper scarp To stair him thoru vnto þe wau [*Gott.* wawe; *Fairf.* wagh]. **1340** HAMPOLE *Pr. Consc.* 6619 A purtrayd fire on a waghe, þat es paynted outher heghe or laghe. *a* **1400–50** *Wars Alex.* 3222 3it ware þe wawes of þe wanes.. Polischid all of pure gold.

γ. *c* **1200** *Vices & Virtues* 95 Careteð arist up fram ðe grundwalle, and beclepð all ðe wouh. *c* **1290** *St. Dunstan* 132 in *S. Eng. Leg.* 23 þe harpe he heng vp bi þe wouh. *a* **1300** *K. Horn* 970 (Camb.) þe se bigan to þroȝe Vnder hir woȝe. **1303** R. BRUNNE *Handl. Synne* 1144 þys olde man was broght so logh þat he lay ful colde besyde a wogh. **1340** *Ayenb.* 72 Betuene ham and paradys ne is bote a lyte woȝ. **1382** WYCLIF *Ps.* lxi. 4 As to a boowid woughe, and to a ston wal put doun. *c* **1400** *Destr. Troy* 4773 In the castell.. all was bare as a bast, to þe bigge woghes. *c* **1440** *Pallad. on Husb.* I. 785 Hym liketh best a daubed wough, and he Wol haue a wal of cley and stoon. *a* **1450** *Mirk's Festial* 181 An adyrcope.. come of þe woch. **1674** RAY *N.C. Words* 54 A *Wogh*, a Wall, Lanc. **1703** THORESBY *Let. to Ray*, A *Wogh*, any Partition, whether of Boards or mud Walls, or Laths and Lime; as a Boardshed-woagh, studded wogh. *c* **1746** J. COLLIER (Tim Bobbin) *View Lancs. Dial.* Wks. (1862) 69, I crope under a Wough. **1847** LYTTON *Lucretia* II. xix, She lived agin the wogh yonder, where you see that gent coming out.

δ. *a* **1225** *Ancr. R.* 172 þauh hire licome beo wiðinnen þe uour woawes. *a* **1250** *Owl & Night.* 1528 Wowes west and lere huse. **1303** R. BRUNNE *Handl. Synne* 4272 Here mayst thou bettyr slepe a throwe Than sytte and loke vppon a wowe. **13..** *E.E. Allit. P.* B. 1531 In þe palays pryncipale vpon þe playn wowe. **1390** GOWER *Conf.* I. 324 Ther was nothing hem betwene, Bot wow to wow and wall to wall. *c* **1400** *Laud Troy Bk.* 18388 Troye is doune & ouerthrowen, Tour & bour, walle & wowen. *c* **1440** *Promp. Parv.* 533/1 Wowe, wal [*v.rr.* wowe or wall], *paries, murus.* *c* **1450** *Godstow Reg.* 551, j. yerde bitwene the wowes. *a* **1470** H. PARKER *Dives & Pauper* (W. de W. 1496) v. iii. 198/1 God lykeneth flaterers to theym that playstren & paynten walles and wowes without.

2. *Mining.* The side of a vein.

1653 MANLOVE *Liberties of Lead-Mines* 234 If.. woughs be strete, the Miner then may fire. *Ibid.* 259 Water holes, Wind holes, Veyns, Coe-shafts and Woughs. **1681** T. HOUGHTON *Rara Avis* (E.D.S.) 44 *Woughs*, the walls or sides, sometimes of hard stone, and sometimes soft. **1836** R. FURNESS *Astrologer* I. Wks. (1858) 135 Where wough or rider, twitch'd a leading fast, There he was matchless at a tearing blast.

3. *Comb.*: †**wough-nail**, wall-nail (WALL *sb.*[1] 25).

OE. *wáȝryft*, *-rift* occurs in the Ormulum as *waȝheriftt*.

1331 in Topham *Colleg. Chap. St. Stephen* (1834) 67 Eidem pro 1000 de Wounail empt' pro quadam interclus' in dicta domo faciend'. *c* **1300** in Rogers *Agric. & Prices* I. 498 [On the Irish estates we find a kind of nail called] 'woh' or 'wouwe-nails'. **1411** *Ibid.* III. 447 Wogh prig nails.

†**wough**, *sb.*[2] *Obs.* Forms: α. 1–4 **woh**, 3 **woch**, 3 (5 *Sc.*) **wocht**, 4 **woht.** β. 1 (3) *dat.* **wo** (**woo**), 3–4 **woȝ** (4 **woȝh**), 3–5 **wogh**, 1 *dat.* **woȝe**, 3–4 **woȝe** (4 **woȝhe**), 3–5 **woghe**, 5 **wothe.** γ. 3 **wou**, 3–5 **wow**; 3–4 **wouh** (3 *pl.* **wouhwes**), **wouȝ** (5 **wouȝh**, **wowȝ**), 4 **wough**, 5 **wugh**, *Sc.* **weuch**; 5 **wouche**, **wou-**, **wowȝe**, **woughe.** [OE. *wóh* (inflected *wó-*, *wóȝ-*), neut. of *wóh* WOUGH *a.* used as *sb.*]

1. Wrong, evil; injury, harm.

α. *c* **893** ÆLFRED *Oros.* VI. x. 264 þa sæde him hiora an, .. þæt he woh bude. *c* **1000** *Ags. Ps.* (Th.) xciii. 4 Hi.. woh meldiað. *c* **1205** LAY. 11589 þat wes swiðe muchel woh. *c* **1250** *Death* 261 in *O.E. Misc.* 184 Lete us hatie þat woh and luuie þat riȝte. *c* **1250** *Orison* 16 ibid. 160 þu brohtest dai and eve niȝt, Heo broȝte woht, þu broȝtest riȝt. *c* **1300** *Harrow. Hell* (Harl.) 52 Mon haþ do me shome ynoh wyþ word ant dede in heore woh.

β. *c* **888** ÆLFRED *Boeth.* xl. §7 Englas.. nanes wos [*v.r.* woȝes] ne wilniað. *c* **897** —— *Gregory's Past. C.* xlv. 343 Hie .. nyllað wietan mid hwelcum woo [*v.r.* wo] hie hit ȝestriendon. *c* **924** *Let.* in Birch *Cartul.* II. 236 Ic him wolde fylstan to ryhte and næfre to nanan wo. *c* **1200** *Trin. Coll. Hom.* 165 Al riht is leid and wogh arered. **13..** *Gaw. & Gr. Knt.* 1550 þus hym frayned þat fre, and fondet hym ofte, For to haf wonnen hym to woȝe. *c* **1350** *Will. Palerne* 554 For þat were swiche a woȝh þat neuer wolde be mended. *a* **1400–50** *Wars Alex.* 2812 As me is wa for þi woȝe & þi wrange bathe.

γ. *a* **1225** *Ancr. R.* 126 Wouh þet me mis-deð us, oðer of word oðer of werc. *Ibid.* 190 Wel is us nu, Louerd, uor þe dawes þet tu lowudest us mide oðre monnes wouhwes. *c* **1330** R. BRUNNE *Chron. Wace* (Rolls) 7279 Of two þynges wakned hys wough. *c* **1320** *Cast. Love* 1117 3if þou wole amenden his wouȝ, þou most deþ þolen þorw strong pyne I-nouȝ. *a* **1450** *Le Morte Arth.* 1333 Her hertes was full of sorow and woughe.

2. In phrases: **a.** *to do* or *work wough.* Also const. *to*, *on* (a person) or with dat.

(*a*) *c* **1205** LAY. 22456 þat ne scal þe king woh don. *a* **1225** *Ancr. R.* 158 Vor þolemod is þe þet þuldeliche abereð wouh þet me deð him. *a* **1300** *Cursor M.* 15828 Wit þair bastons bete þai him And did him mikel wogh. **1338** R. BRUNNE *Chron.* (1810) 119 To William did he wouh, He did brenne Helwelle, & William broþer slouh. *c* **1400** *Rowland & O.* 119 For here schall no man do the woghe, till aughte dayes ben a-goo.

(*b*) **1297** R. GLOUC. (Rolls) 7687 Vor no mon ne durste him wiþsegge, he wroȝte muche wou. *a* **1300** *Cursor M.* 24340 (Edin.) To me his moder did þai þat mis, þat wroht on him þis woh. **13..** *E.E. Allit. P.* A. 622 þay laften ryȝt & wroȝten woghe. *c* **1470** *Gol. & Gaw.* 700 The wyis wrought vthir grete wandreth and weuch. *Ibid.* 1199 To wirk him wandreth or wough. *c* **1550** *Hunt. Cheviot* xxvi. in Child *Ballads* III. 308/2 He wrought hom both woo and wouche.

b. *to have wough*: to be in the wrong.

c **1205** LAY. 3327 Leiuedi þu haues mochel wouh. *Ibid.* 5043 þu hauest woh & [he] haued riht. *a* **1225** *Ancr. R.* 54 Me leoue sire, þu hauest wouh. *c* **1275** *Passion of Our Lord* 332 in *O.E. Misc.* 46 Seye þu me soþ, Yf þu ert gywene kyng oþer hi habbeþ woh. *c* **1320** *Sir Tristr.* 1531 þai seiȝen he hadde þe riȝt, þe steward hadde þe wouȝ. *c* **1400** *Solomon's Bk. Wisd.* 284 Ac so wys clerk ne worþ þer non, þat ne schal haue to don ynouȝ, fforto disputen aȝeins hym þeiȝ he haue þe wouȝ.

c. *mid* or *with wough*: wrongfully. (OE. also *on wóh.*)

c **885** *Ælfred's Will* in Birch *Cartul.* II. 177 þæt ic mine mæȝecild oððe yldran oððe ȝingran mid woh fordemde. *c* **960** *Laws Edgar* II. iv, & se þe oðerne mid woȝe forseggan wile, þæt he [etc.]. *c* **1175** *Lamb. Hom.* 29 þas ruperes and þas reueres þet nemeð oðres monnes eahte mid wohe. *c* **1205** LAY. 24811 Of Frolle þan kinge, þat þu mid woȝe at Paris asloȝe. *a* **1240** *Lofsong* in *O.E. Hom.* I. 205 Summe tide ich habbe iheued of oðer monnes mid woh. *c* **1290** *Beket* 1239 in *S. Eng. Leg.* 142 [They] tolden þe kinge of al þe wo þat seint thomas hadde with wouȝ. *a* **1300** *Cursor M.* 161 Herode kyng wit wogh For crist sak þe childer slogh. **13..** *Guy*

Warw. 5080 Ich on of hem þat he toke, he slouȝ, Were it wiþ riȝt, were it wiþ wouȝ. [*c* **1300** *Arth. & Merl.* 4806 Wiþ gode riȝt & no wouȝ.]

d. ***without(en) wough***: truly.

13.. *Guy Warw.* 6876 Ich it seye, wiþouten wouȝ. *c* **1400** *Merlin* 1415 (Kölbing) Herkneþ alle, wiþ owte wouȝh, Y schal ȝow telle, why y louȝh. **14..** *Sir Beues* (S.) 2135 Certes, madame, with our wowȝ. *c* **1420** *Chron. Vilod.* 1172 Suche virtuose werkus he wolde welle do Fulle sotelyche wᵗ-owte ony wothe [*rime* bothe]. *Ibid.* 2100. *c* **1450** *Le Morte Arth.* 1638 Withe Syr mador, with-outen woughe, Full sone acordement gon they make.

wough (wʊf), *sb.*³ Also *Sc.* wouch. [Imitative. Cf. WUFF.] The bark of a dog or other animal.

1824 MACTAGGART *Gallovid. Encycl.* 481 *Wouch*, the same with *bouch*, a dog's bark. **1850** MAYNE REID *Rifle Rangers* II. xxii. 200 The hound, with a short 'wough' dropped in upon his head. **1898** *Longm. Mag.* May 67 Little squirrels..have quite a large vocabulary,..a bark or wough when suddenly alarmed.

†**wough**, *a. Obs.* (or *dial.*) Forms: 1-4 woh (3 woþ), 4 wouȝ, 9 *dial.* oogh; *pl.* (etc.) 3 woȝe, woȝhe, wowe. [OE. *wóh* (inflected *wó-*, *wóᵹ-*), of obscure origin. Hence WOUGH *sb.*²]

1. Crooked, bent.

862 *Grant* in Birch *Cartul.* II. 114 Ðanne fram langan leaᵹe to ðam won stocce. *c* **897** ÆLFRED *Gregory's Past C.* xi. 67 Sio micle nosu & sio woo. *a* **1000** *Laws Æthelb* xliv, Ꝥif muð oþþe eaᵹe woh weorðeþ. *a* **1100** *Gloss.* in Wr.-Wülcker 146/38 *Diuortia, diuerticula*, mistlice woᵹe weᵹas. *a* **1250** *Owl & Night.* 813 Þe fox..can paþes riȝte & woȝe.

1866 BROGDEN *Prov. Words Lincs.* 141 The woodman said that the stuff was kind, but all I've seen was oogh inclined.

2. Wrong, evil, bad. Also *absol.*

Beowulf 1747 Wom wundorbebodum werᵹan gastes. *c* **888** ÆLFRED *Boeth.* xxxviii. §3 Hit is woᵹ þæt hi mon læte unwitnode. *a* **1000** *Riddles* xl. 24 (Gr.) Woh wyrda ᵹesceapu. *c* **1200** ORMIN 1375 Þær Cristess mennisscnesse Drannc dæþess drinnch o rodetreo forr ure woȝhe dedess. *c* **1205** LAY. 4333 Þat is woh & na wiht riht. *a* **1225** *Ancr. R.* 2 Wiðute knotte & dolke of woh inwit & of wreinde. *c* **1250** *Owl & Night.* 164 Schild þine svikeldom vram þe liȝte, & hud þat woȝe [*v.r.* wowe] among þe riȝte. *c* **1320** *Sir Tristr.* 1730 Her wening was al wouȝ, Vntroweand til hem to. *a* **1400** *Octouian* (Weber) 1050 Florentyn naȝt forsok hyt, Þey hyt wer woȝ.

†**wough**, *int. Obs.*⁻¹ = WAUGH, WOW.

a **1553** UDALL *Royster D.* III. iv. (Arb.) 52 Wough, she is gone for euer, I shall hir no more see.

wouȝ, var. HOW *adv.*

c **1394** *P. Pl. Crede* 356 Wiþ hertes of heynesse wouȝ halwen þei chirches.

†**wouhleche.** *Obs.*⁻¹ [f. *wouh-*, repr. OE. *wóᵹ-*, stem of *wóᵹian* to WOO + *-lēche* -LEDGE.] Wooing, courtship. So also † **wouhlechung**.

a **1225** *Ancr. R.* 96 No wouhleche nis so culuert ase is o pleinte wis. *Ibid.* 388 He uor wouhlecchunge sende hire his sonden.

wouke, obs. form of WEEK *sb.*

†**woul**, *v. Obs. rare.* [Imitative. Cf. WAWL *v.*] *intr.* To howl, cry, wail.

c **1340** *Nominale* (Skeat) 748 *Tesson craile*, Brok woulith. **1382** WYCLIF *Hosea* v. 8 Woule ȝe in Bethauen. *Ibid.* vii. 14 Thei crieden not to me in her herte, but thei wouliden in her couchis.

would (wʊd). [The subj. of WILL *v.*¹ used substantively.] The feeling or expression of a conditional or undecided desire or intention.

1390 GOWER *Conf.* III. 32 Bot yit is noght mi feste al plein, Bot al of woldes and of wisshes, Therof have I my fulle disshes. **1626** FENNER *Hid. Manna* (1656) 58 Thou hast a setled will to sinne, but a sorry would, or a months minde to repent. *a* **1653** BINNING *Serm.* (1735) 559/2 Your Woulds and Wishes after Christ and Salvation..are not the real Exercises of your Soul's flying unto him for Salvation. **1864** TREVELYAN *Compet. Wallah* (1866) 131 If all my 'woulds', dear Jones, were changed to 'coulds', I'd deck thy bungalow with Europe goods. **1876** EMERSON *Lett. & Soc. Aims, Poet. & Imag.* Wks. (Bohn) III. 151 All writings must be in a degree exoteric, written to a human *should* or *would* instead of to the fatal *is*.

b. With *the*, denoting desire or intention in contrast to duty or necessity.

1753-4 RICHARDSON *Grandison* II. xvii. 127 But so it will always be with silly girls, that distinguish not between the *would* and the *should*. **1831** CARLYLE *Misc. Ess., Early Ger. Lit.* (1872) III. 188 When man, hemmed-in between the Would and the Should, or the Must, painfully hesitates.

would, pa. t. of WILL *v.*¹

would, obs. f. HOLD *v.*, OLD *a.*, WELD *sb.*¹, WOLD; var. WOOLD *sb.* and *v.*

woulda ('wʊdə), repr. U.S. dial. pronounc. of 'would have'.

1913 *Dialect Notes* IV. 6 *Would a went*, would have gone. **1925** T. DREISER *Amer. Trag.* (1926) I. I. xii. 83, I coulda chucked my job, and I woulda. **1952** B. MALAMUD *Natural* 103 If it was something serious you woulda been caught long ago. **1978** G. VAUGHAN *Belgrade Drop* x. 63 Security woulda got her. She'd never have the chance to tell DI.

would-be ('wʊdbiː), *a.* and *sb.* [The phrase *would be* (see WILL *v.*¹ 40) used attributively and absolutely.]

A. *adj.* **a.** Of persons: That would be; wishing to be; posing as.

In the earliest examples used as a mock addition to a designation or title: cf. B.

1300 GRAYSTANES in *Hist. Dunelm. Script. Tres* (Surtees) 77 Eum [*sc.* Henry de Luceby] contempserunt, vocantes eum H. walde be Priur. **1642** KYNASTON *Leoline* etc. 138 By the skill of Marquis would-be Iones, 'Tis found the smoakes salt did corrupt the stones.

1647 TRAPP *Comm. Matt.* v. 21. 286 Epictetus complained that there were many would be Philosophers, as far as a few good words would goe. **1691** *Rabshakeh Vapulans* 2 The Wou'd-be-Wits, and wou'd-be-Wise, The witty Fool must have the foremost place. **1708** *Brit. Apollo* No. 73. 2/2 The next a Proctor's Clerk, a Would-be Beau. **1750** *Student or Oxf. Misc.* I. 23 None but Academical Pedants and would-be-wits. **1794** JEFFERSON *Writ.* (1859) IV. 112 We shall see what the court lawyers..and would-be ambassadors will make of it. **1832** LYTTON *Eugene A.* IV. ii, They are not rascals—they are would-be men of the world. **1864** PUSEY *Lect. Daniel* ii. 91 Antiochus was a propagator of false religions, a would-be destroyer of the true. **1889** GRETTON *Memory's Harkback* 307 Napoleon I..actually bequeathed a legacy..to Cantillon, the would-be assassin of Wellington.

b. *transf.* Of things: Intended as.

a **1839** PRAED *Poems* (1864) II. 54 The burnished plate That decks the would-be rustic gate. **1856** MISS YONGE *Daisy Chain* II. xxvi, Speaking with a would-be tone of congratulation. **1869** TROLLOPE *He Knew* etc. xcii. (1878) 513 He had continued to speak with the same fluent would-be cynicism. **1901** H. SUTCLIFFE *B. Cunliffe* v. 75 His usual stilted gait softened to a would-be airiness.

c. With following adj., forming a hyphened phrase.

1813 JANE AUSTEN *Let.* 11 Oct. (1952) 343 A large, ungenteel Woman, with self-satisfied & would-be elegant manners. **1826** GALT *Last of Lairds* xxvii. 238 The would-be-genteel coxcombs of Calcutta. **1840** T. GORDON tr. *W. Menzel's Ger. Lit.* II. 80 Books..are filled with Philistinism and would-be-wise morality. **1865** ANNIE THOMAS *On Guard* II. 90 A sayer of would-be-sensible things. **1883** MISS BROUGHTON *Belinda* I. iii, With a would-be-valedictory wave of the hand.

d. ***would-be-thought***: wishing to be considered as.

1805 T. HARRAL *Scenes of Life* II. 67 The wits, and would-be-thought wits, of the day. **1815** MRS. PILKINGTON *Celebrity* II. 148 'Perhaps I might', rejoined the would-be-thought cynic.

e. Used *predicatively*: mannered, pretentious. (App. restricted to the works of D. H. Lawrence.)

1922 D. H. LAWRENCE *Lett.* (1932) 556 These drawings are so completely without irony, so crass, so strained and so would-be. **1928** *Ibid.* 751 James Joyce bores me stiff—too terribly would-be and done-on-purpose, utterly without spontaneity or real life. **1932** A. HUXLEY in *Lett. D. H. Lawrence* p. xvii, The symphony oppressed him; it was too big, too elaborate, too carefully and consciously worked out, too 'would-be'—to use a characteristic Lawrencian expression. He was quite determined that none of his writings should be 'would-be'. He allowed them to flower as they liked from the depths of his being.

B. *sb.* One who fain would be (something specified or implied).

Sometimes used as a fictitious surname.

(*a*) **1605** B. JONSON *Volpone* Dram. Pers. (1607), Politique Would-bee, a Knight..Fine Mada. Would-bee, the Knights wife. **1706** MRS. CENTLIVRE *Love at Venture* I. i. 5 *Enter a Servant. Ser.* Sir, here is Mr. Wou'dbe to wait on you.

(*b*) **1672** MARVELL *Reh. Transp.* I. 238 They are the Politick would-be's of the Clergy. *c* **1730** RAMSAY *To his Son* vi, Yet, this let little would-be's know. **1732** *London Mag.* I. 240 Of all the Fops in Nature, none are so ridiculously contemptible as the Wouldbees. **1781** COWPER *Conversat.* 612 A man that would have foiled, at their own play, A dozen would-be's of the modern day.

†'**woulder.** *Obs.* [irreg. f. *would*, pa. t. of WILL *v.*¹ + -ER¹.] In the proverbial phrase ***wishers and woulders***: those given to saying 'I wish...' and 'I would...', i.e. indulging idle wishes instead of making active efforts.

The proverb in which the word rimes with *householders* is freq. quoted (with slight variations) down to the 18th cent.

1508 STANBRIDGE *Vulgaria* (W. de W.) C vj, Wysshers and wolders be small housholders. **1546** J. HEYWOOD *Prov.* I. xi. (1867) 26 Wishers and wolders be no good householders. *a* **1617** BAYNE *Lect.* (1634) 140 A man may bee a wisher and woulder with Balaam, but misse of his desires. **1623** R. CARPENTER *Consc. Christian* 18 The imperfect Essayes..of lazie languishing wishers and woulders. **1646** HAMMOND *Tracts, Consc.* 36 The hypocrisie of the wisher and woulder, that could wish he were better then he is. **1670** RAY *Prov.* 295 (Scot. Prov.) Wishers and walders are poor househalders. [**1870** SCHAFF *Comm. Prov.* xxi. 25-6 Wishers and woulders are neither good householders nor long livers.]

†**b.** In ***well-woulder***: well-wisher. *Obs.*⁻¹

1643 *Plaine English* 28 These are well-woulders to the Parliament.

would-have-been, *a.* [The verbal phrase used attributively.] That would have liked to be, that aimed at being, (something specified).

1744 ELIZA HEYWOOD *Female Spect.* v. (1748) I. 233 Her penetrating eyes immediately discovered her would-have-been gallant. *Ibid.* VII. II. 29 The would-have-been member was ready to burst with inward rage at this sneer. **1844** ALB. SMITH *Adv. Mr. Ledbury* xxxiv, The would-have-been assassin of Louis the Fifteenth. **1901** *Westm. Gaz.* 16 Nov. 7/1 The hunt goes forward after the would-have-been invaders of Natal.

†'**woulding**, *vbl. sb. Obs.* [irreg. f. *would* pa. t. of WILL *v.*¹] The action or fact of desiring. Usually coupled with *wishing*.

1549 CHALONER *Erasm. on Folly* K iii, There be some who onely with wishyng and wouldyng are riche in their owne fantasie. **1620** SANDERSON *Serm. ad Clerum* iii. (1681) I. 51 You may call it wishing and woulding, (and we have Proverbs against wishers and woulders;) rather than Praying. **1655** GURNALL *Chr. in Arm.* I. (1656) 314 If woulding and wishing will bring them to heaven, then they may come thither. *a* **1714** M. HENRY *Wks.* (1835) I. 113 Wishing and woulding is but trifling.

b. *pl.* Desires, inclinations.

a **1640** FENNER *Sacrif. Faithfull* (1648) 38 Many a poore soule, that hath forcible wouldings, and wracked desires after grace and holinesse. **1661** GURNALL *Chr. in Arm.* III. (1662) 554 Some lazy wouldings or wishings, or weak vellieties. **1710** J. NORRIS *Chr. Prud.* 217 They have a great many imperfect Motions, Inclinations, Half Consents, and Velleities or Wouldings to do so. *a* **1758** JON. EDWARDS in *Life Brainerd* (1845) 368 His desires were not idle wishings and wouldings.

†'**wouldingness.** *Obs. nonce-wd.* [f. as prec. + -NESS.] Desire, inclination.

a **1660** HAMMOND *Pract. Catech.* I. iii. Wks. 1674 I. 31 And 2. whatsoever you do, you do, first against one velleity (or wouldingness) or other; and secondly, with some mixture of the contrary.

Woulfe (wʊlf). Also Woulf. [The surname of Peter Woulfe (? 1727–1803), a London chemist.] ***Woulfe's apparatus***, a series of glass receivers (***Woulfe's bottles***) formerly used in distillation.

1800 tr. *Lagrange's Chem.* I. 109 A bent tube immersed to the bottom of the water, contained in one of Woulf's bottles. **1815** J. SMITH *Panorama Sci. & Art* II. 311 Woulfe's apparatus evolved so large a quantity of subtile, elastic, and often incondensable vapours. **1827** FARADAY *Chem. Manip.* xv. (1842) 369 An arrangement of vessels first devised by Glauber, but which with some modifications, has since received the name of Woulfe's apparatus. **1855** SCOFFERN *Elem. Chem.* 358 The..Woulfes bottles are about two-thirds filled with water.

woulk, obs. Sc. form of WEEK *sb.*

woult, obs. Sc. var. VAULT *sb.*¹

wouman, obs. form of WOMAN.

wound (wuːnd), *sb.* Forms: *α.* 1-3 **wund**, 3 **wunde (wnde)**; 3-5 **wonde**, 4-6 **wond** (6 *Sc.* **vond**), 5 **woynd**, 6 *Sc.* **wind.** *β.* 3-7 **wounde**, 3- **wound** (5 **wownd**, *Sc.* **vound**); 8 *pl.* **wawnds.** [Common Teutonic: OE. *wund* = OFris. *wunde*, *wund* (WFris. *woune*, EFris. *wûn*), MDu. *wonde* (Du. *wond*), OS. *wunda* (LG. *wunde*, *wunne*, *wunn*), OHG. *wunta*, *wunda* (MHG. *wunte*, *wunde*, G. *wunde*), ON. (Icel., MSw.) *und* (Da. *vunde* from LG.), of uncertain relationship.

The original *ŭ* was normally lengthened before *nd*, but in the standard pronunc. has been prevented from developing into *ou* (as in *bound*, *hound*, *ground*, etc.) by the influence of the *w* (in contrast to *wound*, pa. t. of WIND *v.*¹). The pronunc. (waund) is however given by some dictionaries of the 18th century (Kenrick, 1733; Jones, 1798), is widely current in dialects, is implied in various forms of WOUNDS and ZOUNDS, and was common in the adv. WOUNDY.]

1. a. A hurt caused by the laceration or separation of the tissues of the body by a hard or sharp instrument, a bullet, etc.; an external injury.

† *death's wound*: see DEATH-WOUND.

α. Beowulf 2711 Ða sio wund ongon, þe him se eorðdraca ær ᵹeworhte, swelan and swellan. *c* **900** *Bæda's Hist.* II. ix. (1890) 124 Eac wæs se cyning ᵹehæled from þære wunde, þe him ær ᵹedon wæs. *c* **1000** *Sax. Leechd.* I. 180 Wið wunda, ..ᵹenim þas wyrte þe we senecio nemdun. *c* **1175** *Lamb. Hom.* 79 Þa com þer an helendis Mon and heuede rouþe of him and wesch his wunden mid wine. *c* **1205** LAY. 23969 He wunde afeng feouwer unchene long. *c* **1275** *Passion of Our Lord* 187 in *O.E. Misc.* 42 Ne schullen hi nouht yete þolie none wnde. *c* **1300** *Havelok* 1980 He haues a wunde in the side. **1340** HAMPOLE *Pr. Consc.* 5337 Byhalde þe wondes þat yhe styked. *c* **1380** *Sir Ferumb.* 501 Þan he askede of Olyuere ..If þat he any wonde bere in ys body þat tyde. *c* **1400** *Destr. Troy* 6316 Achylles..hymselfe fore to no fyght for hys fel wondys. **1422** YONGE tr. *Secreta Secret.* 181 The bee is a Passynge wrathfull beste..and for vengeaunce they lewyth thar Styngill in the wonde. **1526** TINDALE *Acts* xvi. 33 He toke them..and Wasshed their wondes. **1549** *Compl. Scot.* xiv. 121 The mortal vondis that he hed resauit fra bessus his seruituir.

β. *c* **1290** *Sancta Crux* 438 in *S. Eng. Leg.* I. 14 To-gadere huy smiten to grounde..and maden heom wel bitere woundes. **1297** R. GLOUC. (Rolls) 11397 He hadde mo þan tuenti wounde ar he were inome. *c* **1325** *Spec. Gy Warw.* 442 And þere þeih sholen se soþliche, His grisli wounden openliche. **1390** GOWER *Conf.* III. 137 Of word among the men of Armes Ben woundes heeled with the charmes, Wher lacketh other medicine. *c* **1400** MAUNDEV. (Roxb.) xix. 87 Þe blude rynnez doun fra þer woundes. *c* **1440** *Promp. Parv.* 533/1 Wownde, festryd, *cicatrix.* Wownde, made wythe swerde or other wepne, *stigma.* *c* **1489** CAXTON *Sonnes of Aymon* xv. 356 He..cast hym doun to the grounde with a wounde mortall. **1547** BOORDE *Brev. Health* I. ccclxxvii. (1557) 120 b, There be dyuers sortes of woundes, some be newe and freshe woundes and some be olde woundes, some be depe woundes, [etc.]. **1594** SHAKS. *Rich. III*, I. ii. 55 Dead Henries wounds, Open their congeal'd mouthes, and bleed afresh. **1611** MIDDLETON & DEKKER *Roaring Girl* L 3, Wounds should be drest and heal'd, not vext, or left Wide open, to the anguish of the patient. **1665** MANLEY *Grotius' Low C. Wars* 271 Octavius..was shortly after shot by the Besieged, and dyed of the Wound. **1679** OLDHAM *Sat. Jesuits* III. (1681) 70 A Wound though cur'd, yet leaves behind a Scar. **1732** LEDIARD *Sethos* II. VIII. 222, I receiv'd a wound with a sword which laid me on the ground. **1744** J. ARMSTRONG *Art Preserv. Health* III. 516 For want of timely care Millions have died of medicable wounds. **1770**

GOLDSM. *Des. Vill.* 157 The broken soldier.. Wept o'er his wounds. **1804** *Naval Chron.* XII. 387 Having..several sabre and pike wounds. **1841** LEVER *O'Malley* lxxi, 'And his wound? Is it a serious one?' said a..voice, as the doctor left my room. **1866** G. MACDONALD *Ann. Q. Neighb.* xxvi, The blood flowed from a wound on the head. **1907** J. H. PATTERSON *Man-eaters of Tsavo* vii. 78, I..bathed and dressed his wounds.

b. Esp. in *the* (*Five*) *Wounds* of Christ.

c **1175** *Lamb. Hom.* 75 Ac he hom helde mid his halie fif wunden. *a* **1225** *Ancr. R.* 292 Nem ofte Jesu.. Vlih into his wunden, creop in ham mid þine þouhte. *a* **1300** *Leg. Rood* ii. 258 He aros to lyue From deþe þen þridde dai myd is wounden viue. **13..** *Gaw. & Gr. Knt.* 642 Alle his afyaunce vpon folde was in þe fyue woundez þat Crist kaȝt on þe croys. **1450–1530** *Myrr. Our Ladye* II. 155 By meryte of our lordes fyue woundes. **1526** *Pilgr. Perf.* (W. de W. 1531) 2 The moost worthy to be loued woundes & passyon of Chryst. **1533** in *Linc. Dioc. Docum.* (1914) 157 The ij. cunstabelles.. shall deyll v[d] in honor and worship of the v. wondes of our lord to the v. porest folkes in the towne. **1625** tr. *Camden's Hist. Eliz.* 220 They..brought into the field many men, vnder flying colours, wherein were painted in some, the fiue wounds of our Lord. **1660** F. BROOKE tr. *Le Blanc's Trav.* 53 The Church of the five wounds of our Saviour. **1807** WORDSW. *White Doe* II. 21 And figured there The five dear wounds our Lord did bear. **1845** PUSEY tr. *Horst's Parad. Soul* (1847) II. VI. 81 Salutations to the Five Wounds of Christ. **1887** *Encycl. Brit.* XXII. 549/2 As regards full stigmatization, with the visible production of the five wounds,..the oldest case, after St. Francis, is that of Ida of Louvain.

c. Used as an oath or strong exclamation, as ***by Christ's,*** or ***His, wounds, His arms and wounds, Wounds of God,*** etc. (Cf. WOUNDS *int.*)

See also BLOOD *sb.* 1 e, GAD *sb.*[5] 3, GOD *sb.* 14 a, GOG[1] 2, and OONS, SWOUNDS, ZOUNDS.

c **1350** *Athelston* 144 Sodaynly þan schalt þou dy, Be Cristes woundys fyue. *c* **1480** HENRYSON *Wolf & Lamb* 2689 Be his woundis, fals tratour, thow sall de. *a* **1533** BERNERS *Huon* clxxxix. 762 Than the maister ruffian began to swere bloode & woundes that thei shulde plei at the dyse. **1550** LATIMER *Serm.* G ii b, He cried oute, what, shall I dye (quod he) woundes, sydes, hart, shal I dye,..woundes and sydes shal I thus dye? **1560** *Nice Wanton* 215 It is lost, by His woundes! and ten to one! **1568** FULWELL *Like will to Like* B 1 b, Gogs hart.., Blood, wounds and nailes, it wil make a man mad. **1589** *Rare Tri. Love & Fort.* (Roxb.) 143 By his wounds I would never lin [etc.]. **1602** CHETTLE *Hoffman* IV. (1631) H 2 b, S'wounds ile confound her, and she linger thus. **1728** CIBBER & VANBR. *Provok'd Husb.* I. 14 Ad's waunds, and heart!.. I'm glad I ha' fun ye. **1748** SMOLLETT *Rod. Random* xi, 'Blood and wounds! (cried Weazel) d'ye question the honour of my wife, madam!' [**1869** BLACKMORE *Lorna D.* xxv, Wounds of God! In what way thought you that a lawyer listened to your rigmarole?]

d. *fig.* or in fig. context.

a **900** *Cynewulf's Crist* 1314 Eala! þær we nu maȝon wraþe firene ȝeseon on ussum sawlum synna wunde. *c* **1000** *Rule St. Benet* (Logeman) 80 Ælfremeda wunda na abarian [L. *aliena vulnera non detegere*]. *c* **1200** *Trin. Coll. Hom.* 41 Ure helende com to helen þe wundes þe þe deuel hadde on mancun broht. *a* **1240** *Ureisun* in *O.E. Hom.* I. 189 þine wunden healen þe wunden of mi saule. *c* **1374** CHAUCER *Anel. & Arc.* 239 My foo that gave myn herte A wounde. **14..** HOCCLEVE *Virg. & Christ* 62 Vn-to the souerain leche, preye of grace, þat he my wowndes vouchesauf to cure. **1530** TINDALE *Answ. More* I. Wks. (1572) 261/1 The wound of temptation beyng greater then that it could bee healed with the preaching of a woman. **1560** DAUS tr. *Sleidane's Comm.* 231 That the woundes of the Church might be healed. **1592** TIMME *Ten Eng. Lepers* L 3 b, Who falleth from patience by the wounds of evill tongues. **1621** ELSING *Debates Ho. Lords* (Camden) 59 The wounde of the priviledge of the House not soe greate, as that his Majestie shoulde conceave a suspicion of our zeale to his honor. *a* **1683** SIDNEY *Disc. Govt.* i. xi. 24 This Wound is not cured by saying, that he first conquers one, and then more. **1708** POPE *Ode St. Cecilia* 29 She.. Pours balm into the bleeding lover's wounds. **1744** H. BROOKE in E. Moore *Fables* xv. 14 The wounds of honour never close. **1823** SCOTT *Quentin D.* xvi, Louis, who searched the wounds of the land with steel and cautery. **1862** MRS. BROWNING *De Profundis* v, And tender friends go sighing round, 'What love can ever cure this wound?' **1885** 'MRS. ALEXANDER' *At Bay* xi, My jewel will always believe the best of me; time will heal up her wounds.

2. *transf.* **a.** An incision, abrasion, or other injury due to external violence, in any part of a tree or plant.

1574 T. HYLL *Ordering Bees* etc. 77 Then the barke of him [an Apple tree] is sicke: then cut it with a knife,..and when the humour thereof is somwhat flowen ouer,..stoppe diligently his wounde with clay. **1658** EVELYN *Fr. Gard.* (1675) 33 Make as few wounds in a Tree as possibly you can. **1707** MORTIMER *Husb.* 397 If you have occasion to make any great Wounds, cover them over with Clay. **1799** H. ROOKE *Sk. Sherwood Forest* 15 Where the Bark has been stript off for cutting the letters, the wood which grows over the wound never adheres to that part. **1837** P. KEITH *Bot. Lex.* 73 If the cortical layers, while yet young, are accidentally injured, the part destroyed is again regenerated, and the wound healed up without a scar. **1897** W. G. SMITH tr. *Tubeuf's Dis. Plants* 79 Wounds to the wood are also frequently produced during the felling of neighbouring Trees.

b. In other transf. uses.

1667 MILTON *P.L.* I. 689 Soon has his crew Op'nd into the Hill a spacious wound And dig'd out ribs of Gold. *Ibid.* IX. 782 Her rash hand..Forth reaching to the Fruit, she pluck'd, she eat: Earth felt the wound. **1792** PAKENHAM in *Trans. Soc. Arts* X. 210 Fifty-eight lower masts were wounded,..thirty-two of which had their wounds in the upper third.

3. *Surgery.* An incision or opening made by a surgical operator.

1668 CULPEPPER & COLE *Barthol. Anat.* III. vi. 143 If.. you..then by a Wound made in an Artery shall put in a crooked hollow probe. **1805** *Med. Jrnl.* XIV. 522 The wound of the integuments was contracted with strips of adhesive plaster. **1884** THOMPSON *Tumours of Bladder* 37 At the operation no tumour was found,..on Feb. 20, the wound was quite healed.

4. Something which causes a wound (lit. or fig.).

1715 POPE *Iliad* IV. 225 My varied belt repell'd the flying wound. **1844** MRS. BROWNING *Drama of Exile* 667 Let thy words be wounds..For, so, I shall not fear thy power to hurt.

†**5.** (= L. *plaga.*) **a.** A blow, a stroke. (Cf. PLAGUE *sb.* 1.) *Obs.*

1382 WYCLIF *Luke* xii. 47 Thilke seruaunt that knew the wille of his lord, and made not him redy, and dide not vp his wille, schal be betun with many woundis. **1398** TREVISA *Barth. De P.R.* VI. xvi. (1495) n ij/1 The seruaunt that is not chastysed with wordes muste be chastysyd with woundes. **1450–1530** *Myrr. Our Ladye* II. 68.

†**b.** A plague. *Obs.*

c **1369** CHAUCER *Dethe Blaunche* 1207 That was the ten woundes of Egypte.

†**6.** An imperfection, a flaw. *Obs.*

1646 SIR T. BROWNE *Pseud. Ep.* I. i. 1 Our first and ingenerated forefathers, from whom..we derive our being, and the severall wounds of constitution.

7. *Her.* (See quot.)

1572 BOSSEWELL *Armorie* 10 Seuen signes, or tokens whiche are figured in Armes round..7. Is of Purpre, and is to be called a Wounde.

8. *attrib.* and *Comb.* **a.** simple attributive, as ***wound-complication, -fever, -mark, -print, -secretion, -surface, -typhoid***; with meaning 'used for the healing of wounds', as ***wound balsam, -dressing*** (concr.: cf. 8 b), ***-oil, -ointment, -paste***; **b.** objective and instrumental, as ***wound-dilator, -dressing, explorer***; ***wound-healing, -inflicting, -plowed, -producing, -scarred, -worn*** adjs.

1658 A. FOX tr. *Wurtz' Surg.* IV. i. 300, I like and approve better of Wound Oyles, and of Wound Ointments, than of *Wound Balsams. **1850** PEREIRA *Elem. Mat. Med.* (ed. 3) II. 1525 Wound Balsam. **1899** *Allbutt's Syst. Med.* VI. 213 A common and formidable *wound-complication. **1846** JAMES *Heidelberg* III. 141 In every country town,..the latter [*sc.* the barber] exercised the craft of bone-setting and *wound-dressing. **1887** T. LONGMORE in J. B. Hamilton *Trans. Internat. Med. Congress, 9th Session* II. III. 117 Primary wound dressings shall be available at all times and in all places. **1959** *First-Aid Boxes in Factories Order* 21 May in *Stat. Instruments 1959* (1960) I. 1266 A sufficient number (not less than twelve) of adhesive wound dressings of an approved type and of assorted sizes. **1976** D. FRANCIS *In Frame* xi. 159 The outer bandages proved to be large strong pieces of linen..just below my shoulder blade, a large padded wound dressing. **1884** KNIGHT *Dict. Mech.*, **Wound explorer*, an electric sound used in searching for bullets. **1863** L. M. ALCOTT *Hospital Sk.* iv. 51, I..recognized a certain Pennsylvania gentleman, whose *wound-fever had taken a turn for the worse. **1888** FAGGE & PYE-SMITH *Princ. & Pract. Med.* (ed. 2) I. 70 Pyæmia (wound-fever, surgical infection). **1949** M. MEAD *Male & Female* x. 216 The resistance against certain diseases, the *wound-healing capacities of a whole people, may depend upon the meticulousness with which they use learned, not specific inherent, capacities. **1964** *Oceanogr. & Marine Biol.* II. 409 Under conditions of wound-healing and repair the normal inhibitor of melanogenesis present in the rest of the animal is overcome or absent. **1866** J. B. ROSE tr. *Ovid's Met.* 229 So did the *wound inflicting brute rush on. **1892** J. A. HENDERSON *Ann. Lower Deeside* 114 One of the survivors of the gang used to exhibit..the *wound-mark of a dagger. **1658** *wound-oil, *-ointment (see *wound balsam* above). **1753** J. BARTLET *Gentl. Farriery* xxv. 224 Pledgits of tow spread with black or yellow basilicon (or the wound ointment). **1902** *Brit. Med. Jrnl.* 12 Apr. 907 Herr König did not approve of *wound-paste. *c* **1600** J. DAY *Begg. Bednall Gr.* I. i. (1881) 10 Thou art a Souldier, and thy *wound-plow'd face Hath every furrow fill'd with falling tears. **1862** J. M. NEALE *Hymns East. Church* 88 In His Feet and Hands are *Wound-prints, And His Side. **1897** *Westm. Gaz.* 9 Oct. 5/3 One of the most terrible *wound-producing bullets with which our military could be armed. **1888** GUNTER *Mr. Potter* xii. 144 The weather-beaten, *wound-scarred veteran of the plains. **1880** BARWELL *Aneurism* 2 This cord..was saturated in *wound-secretion. **1884** BOWER & SCOTT *De Bary's Phaner.* 108 *Wound-surfaces, of whatever sort, are closed and healed by it. **1896** *Allbutt's Syst. Med.* I. 611 Pyæmia has been called *wound-typhoid. **1820** SHELLEY *Prometh. Unb.* II. i. 62 His pale *wound-worn limbs.

9. Special comb.: **wound-cork**, a protective layer formed on a damaged trunk or branch of a plant or tree; † **wound-drink** (see quot. 1694); **wound-free** *adj.*, free from wounds; invulnerable; **wound-fungus**, a fungus which grows on the injured part of a plant; **wound-herb**, a plant used in the healing of wounds; = WOUNDWORT; **wound hormone** [tr. G. *wundhormon* (G. Haberlandt 1921, in *Sitzungsber. d. Preuss. Akad. d. Wissensch.* 222)], a substance that is produced in a plant in response to a wound and stimulates healing; cf. *traumatic acid* s.v. TRAUMATIC *a.* 3; **wound-parasite**, a parasite infesting damaged plants; **wound-rocket** (see quot.); † **wound-shrub**, a shrub having healing properties; **wound-stripe** *Hist.*, a strip of gold braid worn by a wounded soldier on the left sleeve, vertically, above the cuff; **wound stump** = CICATRIX 2; † **wound-tree** (see quots. and cf. *wound-shrub*); **wound-tumour disease**, a plant disease marked by tumours on roots, stems, or leaves and enlargement of veins and caused by the ***wound-tumour virus***, *Aureogenus magnivena*, which is transmitted by leafhoppers; **wound-weed** = WOUNDWORT; **wound-wood**, wood formed over an injured part.

1897 W. G. SMITH tr. *Tubeuf's Dis. Plants* 76 A corky tissue—*wound-cork—may be formed in consequence of wounds to the bark. **1657** W. COLES *Adam in Eden* cccxxxv. 614 Of Bugle..The decoction..is an especial helpe in all *Wound-drinkes. **1694** W. SALMON *Pharm. Bate* 757/1 A *Wound Drink, or Drink for wounded People. **1609** HEYWOOD *Brit. Troy* XII. xciii. 263 Nor scapt the Troian *wound-free. **1613** —— *Silver Age* III. i, When we prou'd his skin To be wound-free, not to be pierc'd with steele. **1624** —— *Gunaik.* VI. 280 An hearbe with whose juice if he would annointe any part of his bodie it should preserve it wound-free. **1897** W. G. SMITH tr. *Tubeuf's Dis. Plants* 77 They are less suited for the entrance of *wound-fungi than wounds on the living branch. **1597** GERARDE *Herbal* II. cxci. 508 In the world there are not two better *wound herbes. **1640** PARKINSON *Theat. Bot.* 543 Golden Rodde..is the most soveraigne woundherbe of many. **1671** SALMON *Syn. Med.* III. xxii. 416 Clowns-woundwort an excellent woundherb. **1955** A. L. ROWSE *Expansion of Elizabethan England* i. 6 Scottish practitioners flocked..to gather simples and wound-herbs. **1977** *Irish Press* 29 Sept. 10/1 The Yarrow was principally used by herbalists as a wound-herb. **1921** *Chem. Abstr.* XV. 2914 Exptl. evidence exists that the action of a wound as a stimulus in exciting cell division is due to decompn. products of the mechanically injured or dead cells. These products function as *wound hormones. **1966** R. M. DEVLIN *Plant Physiol.* xvii. 427 Most plant tissues do not respond to traumatic acid, suggesting that it may be a specific wound hormone for bean-pod tissue. **1897** W. G. SMITH tr. *Tubeuf's Dis. Plants* 76 The normal duramen is preyed on for nutriment by many *wound-parasites. **1548** TURNER *Names of Herbes* (E.D.S.) 82 Barbara herba..maye be called in englishe *wound-rocket, for it is good for a wounde. **1659** LOVELL *Herball* 542 *Wound-shrub, *Izontecpatlis, Vulnerum medicina.* **1919** *Chamb. Jrnl.* Feb. 82/2 A young fellow with *wound-stripes on his arm. **1923** D. H. LAWRENCE *Birds, Beasts & Flowers* 52 Yet see him fling himself abroad in fresh abandon From the small *wound-stump. **1640** PARKINSON *Theat. Bot.* 1650 *Negundo mas & fœmina.* The male and female *wound tree. *Ibid., Nimbo.* Another healing or wound tree. **1945** L. M. BLACK in *Amer. Jrnl. Bot.* XXXII. 408/1 It now seems that the terms '*wound-tumor virus' and 'wound-tumor disease' may be more appropriate and distinctive. **1967** K. M. SMITH *Insect Virol.* xi. 219 A quick method of detecting the wound-tumor virus in the leafhopper is by staining the hemolymph smears of the insect with the D (dialysis) conjugates. **1857** ANNE PRATT *Flower. Pl.* III. 288 *Solidago Virgaurea*..This Golden Rod..was called *Wound-weed. **1897** W. G. SMITH tr. *Tubeuf's Dis. Plants* 77 These reagents ..even replace the formation of protective *wound-wood.

wound (wuːnd), *v.* Forms: 1 **wundian**, 2 **wundie**, 3 **wunden** (4 **wnden**); 3–5 **wonde**, 5–6 **wond**; 3–6 **wounde** (4 **wownde**, 5 **wowndyn**, 6 *arch.* **wounden**), 4– **wound** (5 *Sc.* **vound**). *Pa. t.* 5 (9 *arch.*) **wound**. [OE. *wundian* (f. *wund* WOUND *sb.*) = OFris. (*w*)*undia* (WFris. *wounje*), MDu. and Du. *wonden*, OHG. *wuntôn* (MHG. *wunden*, G. *verwunden*), OIcel. *undaðr* pa. pple.; also OE. *ȝewundian* = Goth. *gawundôn*.]

1. *trans.* To inflict a wound on (a person, the body, etc.) by means of a weapon; to injure intentionally in such a way as to cut or tear the flesh.

c **760** *Pœnit. Abp. Ecgbert* IV. xxii. in Thorpe *Laws* II. 210 Ȝif hwylc læwede man oðerne wundiȝe, ȝebete wid hine ða wunde. *c* **897** ÆLFRED *Gregory's Past. C.* xxxviii. 277 Swelce he..sua nacodne hine selfne eowiȝe to wundiȝeanne [*v.r.* wundianne] his feondum. *c* **1000** ÆLFRIC *Exod.* xxi. 12 Se ðe man wundað & wile hine ofslean, swelte he deaðe. *c* **1175** *Lamb. Hom.* 15 Ȝif þu me wundedest, ic sculde wundie þe þer on-ȝein. *c* **1200** *Trin. Coll. Hom.* 33 Hie him bireueden alle hise riche weden and wundeden him swiðe. *c* **1205** LAY. 1724 Heo..mid wepnen hine wundeden [*c* **1275** wondede] & seoððen hine slewen. *c* **1290** *Beket* 2101 in *S.E. Leg.* 166 He woundede is Arm swyþe sore, þat blod orn faste a-doun. **1338** R. BRUNNE *Chron.* (1810) 330 Come Roberde's squiere, & wonded him wele more. *c* **1380** WYCLIF *Wks.* (1880) 421 Crist..koude not ordeyne siche buschementis to robbe men & to wounde hem. **1412–20** LYDG. *Chron. Troy* I. 3403 Eueryche gan oþer for to hurte and wounde, Til eche his felawe hath cruelly y-slawe. **1503–4** *Act 19 Hen. VII*, c. 36 Preamble, Stanhop..lay in wayte uppon the seid sir William and hym grevously wouneded and maymed. **1556** *Chron. Gr. Friars* (Camden) 17 Brake owte of the kynges jayle of Newgatte Owyn..& wondyd hys keper. **1651** HOBBES *Leviath.* II. xxvii. 155 If he wound him to death, this is no Crime. **1704** POPE *Windsor For.* 180 With her dart the flying deer she wounds. *c* **1800** *Young Hunting* iv. in Child *Ballads* II. 148/1 He..little thocht o that penknife Wherewith she wound him deep. **1839** LANE *Arab. Nts.* I. 110 From the day on which I had wounded him, he had never spoken. **1887** RIDER HAGGARD *A. Quatermain* xxii. 254 They hacked and hewed at him with swords and spears, wounding him in a dozen places.

refl. *c* **1400** MAUNDEV. (Roxb.) xix. 87 Þai wound þam self in þe legges and þe armes. *a* **1450** *Mirk's Festial* 136 He wondyd hymselfe in þe honde wyth his nalle grevesly.

b. Said of the weapon, etc.

c **1000** *Ags. Ps.* (Th.) lvi. 5 Wæpen-strælas þa me wundedon. **1303** R. BRUNNE *Handl. Synne* 1374 One of þe arwys wounded [*v.r.* wndede] a knyȝt. **1581** A. HALL *Iliad* IV. 75 His cruell darte did Pirus wounde. **1593** SHAKS. *Lucr.* 1185 My Honor ile bequeath vnto the knife That wounds my bodie so dishonored. **1727** DE FOE *Hist. Appar.* iv. (1840) 31 No engine or human art can wound him. **1735** JOHNSON *Lobo's Abyssinia, Voy.* v. 29 One [of the muskets] ..flew out of the Soldier's Hand, and falling against my Leg wounded it very much.

c. Freq. in passive.

c **900** *O.E. Chron.* (Parker MS.) an. 894, Hiora cyning wæs ȝewundod on þæm ȝefeohte, þæt hi hine ne mehton ferian. *c* **1200** ORMIN 17431 Aȝȝ þan aniȝ wundedd wass þurrh þa firene neddress. *c* **1250** *Gen. & Ex.* 853 Wunded ðor was gret folc and slaȝen. **1297** R. GLOUC. (Rolls) 2974 Þe king let ..do vnder lechcraft hom þat iwounded were. *a* **1300** *Cursor M.* 7762 Þe king saul was wonded sare. *c* **1350** *Will. Palerne* 1377 Wel weldes he nouȝt his hele, for wonded was he sore. **1382** WYCLIF *Zech.* xiii. 6 With these Y was woundid in the hous of hem that loueden me. *c* **1450** LOVELICH *Grail* xliii. 283 Of a wilde swyn thow were wondid sore thoruh thin hype. **1538** in P. H. Hore *Hist. Wexford* (1900) I. 237 The residue being wondide to death flede away. **1610** HOLLAND *Camden's Brit.* (1637) 453 Hee was deadly wounded in the head. **1672** WISEMAN *Wounds* I. 88 In a wound in the right Temporal Muscle, where the Artery was wounded. **1712** ADDISON *Spect.* No. 383. ¶2 An honest Man that has been wounded in the Queen's Service. **1794** MRS. RADCLIFFE *Myst. Udolpho* xxv, Count Morano was wounded as bad as he. **1836** DICKENS *Sk. Boz, Tuggs's at Ramsgate*, All the coaches had been upset,..each coach had averaged two passengers killed, and six wounded. **1891** FARRAR *Darkn. & Dawn* lxv, For nearly three centuries the legend lingered on ..that Nero was the wild beast, wounded to death, but whose deadly wound had been healed.

2. *fig.* To injure, inflict pain or hurt upon, in a manner comparable to the infliction of a wound; in later use *esp.* to pain or grieve deeply.

a **1200** *Vices & Virtues* 71 Ðar ðu art ðurh hem [*sc.* sins] ȝewunded, ðat ðu cunne hes halen. *c* **1200** ORMIN 12484 Þe deofell comm to wundenn Crist þurrh gluternessess wæpenn. *c* **1230** *Hali Meid.* 15 He..schoteð niht & dai hise earewen..to wundi þe wið wac wil & makien to fallen. *a* **1340** HAMPOLE *Psalter* vii. 14 Thai may say we ere woundid with charite. *c* **1374** CHAUCER *Troylus* II. 533 So sore hath she me wounded That stod in blak wyth lokyng of her eyen. **1435** MISYN *Fire of Love* II. v. 78 Nedy I am & hongry,..wonedyd & ill-colorde for absens of my lufe. **1531** ELYOT *Gov.* II. xii. (1883) II. 155 Wherwith Gysippus was so wounded to the harte,..that oppressed with mortall heuynes he fell in a sowne. **1600** SHAKS. *A.Y.L.* v. ii. 25, I thought thy heart had beene wounded with the clawes of a Lion. *Orl.* Wounded it is, but with the eyes of a Lady. **1667** PEPYS *Diary* 6 May, He has said that he would wound me with the person where my greatest interest is. **1675** DRYDEN *Aurengz.* II. (1676) 16 Oh! Indamora, hide those fatal Eyes; Too deep they wound, whom they too soon surprise. **1738** JOHNSON *Lond.* 168 Fate never wounds more deep the gen'rous Heart, Than when a Blockhead's Insult points the Dart. **1797** JANE AUSTEN *Sense & Sensib.* xxix, She dared not trust herself to speak, lest she might wound Marianne still deeper. **1814** SCOTT *Ld. of Isles* v. xviii, And many a word, at random spoken, May soothe or wound a heart that's broken! **1873** BLACK *Pr. Thule* xxiv. 402 If he says something careless she is sensitive to it, and it wounds her. **1905** 'G. THORNE' *Lost Cause* viii, It does wound one deeply to hear the Highest and Holiest things spoken of in this way.

b. With immaterial objects.

1340 HAMPOLE *Pr. Consc.* 1702 When þe saule es wounded with syn. **1526** *Pilgr. Perf.* (W. de W. 1531) 43b, The mynde is so wounded with ignoraunce..that [etc.]. **1526** TINDALE *1 Cor.* viii. 12 When we synne so agaynst the brethren and wounde their weake consciences. **1609** B. JONSON *Sil. Wom.* v. i, We must not wound reputation. **16..** *Lust's Domin.* II. v, It wounds my soul, To see the miserablest wretch to bleed. **1631** HEYWOOD *1st Pt. Fair Maid of West* III. i. 31 To spare my flesh And wound my fame, what is't? **1713** ADDISON *Cato* I. iv, Better to die ten thousand thousand deaths, Than wound my honour. **1753–4** RICHARDSON *Grandison* II. xviii. 128, I come to attend you as a duty which I owe to my mother's memory; and I hope this may be done without wounding that of my father. **1832** J. AUSTIN *Jurispr.* (1879) I. 342 The execution would wound the sovereignty of the foreign supreme government. **1859** KINGSLEY *Misc.* I. 92 You have undone me, wounded my credit with the King, past recovery. **1884** L. J. JENNINGS *Croker Papers* I. 51 Moore's vanity was easily wounded at any time.

c. Used to express the effect of harsh or disagreeable sounds upon the ear.

1669 DRYDEN *Tyrannic Love* I. i, [*A Dead March within, and Trumpets.*] *Max.* Somewhat of mournful, sure, my Ears does wound. *a* **1675** TRAHERNE *Poems of Felicity* (1910) 52 The Bells do ring,..Their shriller Sound doth wound the Air. **1766** FORDYCE *Serm. Yng. Wm.* (1767) I. iii. 94 Their ears are wounded by the language of vice. **1866** TROLLOPE *Claverings* i, I shall be away from Clavering, so that the marriage-bells may not wound my ears.

3. *absol.* or *intr.* To inflict a wound or wounds; to do harm, hurt, or injury (physically or otherwise); to impair in any way. Freq. *fig.*

c **897** ÆLFRED *Gregory's Past. C.* xi. 71 Se cleweþa.. wundað & sio wund sarað. **1426** LYDG. *De Guil. Pilgr.* 2540 The swerd, Wych ys sharp..To wounde, & hurte, & parte atwene. **1591** DRAYTON *Harmony Ch., Song Moses* xx, I kil, giue life, I wound, make whole againe. ?**1622** FLETCHER *Love's Cure* v. 1 This curtesie Wounds deeper than your Sword can, or mine own. **1668** J. WILSON tr. *Erasm. Praise of Folly* (1913) 137 Sometimes also they use somewhat of a sting, but so nevertheless that they rather tickle than wound. **1692** PRIOR *Ode Imit. Hor.* xi, He Wounds, to Cure; and Conquers, to Forgive. **1735** POPE *Prol. Sat.* 203 Willing to wound, and yet afraid to strike, Just hint a fault, and hesitate dislike. **1744** E. MOORE *Fables* x. 30 From the hoop's bewitching round, Her very shoe has pow'r to wound. **1818** SHELLEY *Julian & Maddalo* 413 Even the instinctive worm on which we tread Turns, though it wound not. **1829** *Chapters Phys. Sci.* 272 Its strokes are so fine and delicate, that while it wounds it pleases. **1860** THACKERAY *Roundabout P., Thorns in Cushion*, Ah me! we wound where we never intended to strike.

4. *transf.* To pierce or cut as with a wound; to damage in this way.

a **1225** *Ancr. R.* 124, & te ilke wind ne wundeð nout bute þe eare one. *c* **1374** CHAUCER *Former Age* 9 Yit nas the grownd nat wownded with þe plowh. **1387** TREVISA *Higden* III. 459 Hit is unlaweful among us to woundy þe hilles wiþ culter and wiþ schare. **1553** EDEN *Treat. New Ind.* (Arb.) 14 The anuyl and hammer shall soner be wounded and leape away. **1592** SHAKS. *Ven. & Ad.* 267 His wouen girthes he [the steed] breakes asunder, The bearing earth with his hard hoofe he wounds. **1608** —— *Per.* IV. Prol. 23 When she would with sharpe needle wound The Cambricke which she made more sound By hurting it. **1697** DRYDEN *Æneis* x. 412 Force on the Vessel that her Keel may wound This hated Soil. **1743** R. BLAIR *Grave* 192 The tapering Pyramid!.. whose spiky Top Has wounded the thick Cloud. *a* **1766** J. W. BAKER in *Complete Farmer* s.v. *Turnep*, Some [turnips], which had been accidentally wounded by cows. **1833** *Penny Cycl.* I. 446/1 (*America*), The American aloe..yields, when wounded, an abundance of sweet fluid. **1886** *Encycl. Brit.* XXI. 820/1 s.v. *Shipbuilding*, For the sake of avoiding unnecessarily wounding the timbers.

†**b.** *spec.* To damage (a mast), esp. in a naval action. *Obs.* (freq. in 18th cent.)

1743–4 in *10th Rep. Hist. MSS. Comm.* App. I. 211 The Namure being in a shattered Condition,..all the Topmasts wounded. **1758** *Ann. Reg.* I. 100/2 The Orpheus..is peppered very well too, her masts very much wounded. **1798** *Hull Advertiser* 16 June 1/3 Her rigging was much cut, and her mainmast wounded.

c. *fig.* Of wine: To overpower.

1613 T. MILLES tr. *Mexia's Treas. Anc. & Mod. T.* I. 610/1 Vpon the left hand..lay the bodies of beasts stretched out along, sleeping verie soundly... All were wounded with Wine. **1819** SHELLEY *Cyclops* 416, I..filled Another cup, well knowing that the wine Would wound him soon.

wound (waʊnd), *ppl. a.* [Pa. pple. of WIND *v.*[1]] Subjected to winding, in various senses of the verb.

1382 WYCLIF *Isaiah* xxvii. 1 An eddere,..a crookid wounde serpent. **1583** *Durham Wills* (Surtees) II. 78, ij pair of bownd wheales..j paire of wounde wheales. **1865** SWINBURNE *Chastelard* III. i. 88 Soft as the loosening of wound arms in sleep.

wound, pa. t. and pple. of WIND *v.*[1]

woundable ('wu:ndəb(ə)l), *a. rare.* [f. WOUND *v.* + -ABLE.] Capable of being wounded; vulnerable.

1611 COTGR., *Blessable*, Woundable. **1650** FULLER *Pisgah* III. iii. 414 Power and Profit are the two apples of Princes eyes, woundable with the least touch thereof. **1655** —— *Ch. Hist.* IV. xiv. 130 So woundable is the dragon, under the left wing, when pinched in point of profit. **1975** *Times Lit. Suppl.* 21 Mar. 293/1 When trauma appears on the scene.. Scully shows that he is as woundable as the next boy. **1976** *Sunday Times* (Colour Suppl.) 22 Feb. 39/1 He is also shy, loyal and surprisingly woundable.

'wound-down, *a.* [f. *wound*, pa. pple. of WIND *v.*[1] + DOWN *adv.*] That has undergone winding down (see WIND *v.*[1] 21); that has been lowered by winding.

1939 DYLAN THOMAS *Map of Love* 20 The wound-down cough of the blood-counting clock. **1974** P. MCCUTCHAN *Call for Simon Shard* xii. 110 He sniffed through the wound-down window. **1984** W. GARNER *Rats' Alley* xi. 218 He could hear its [*sc.* the helicopter's] racket through the wound-down window of the car.

wounded ('wu:ndɪd), *ppl. a.* [f. WOUND *v.* + -ED[1].]

1. Subjected to, injured or impaired by, wounding; suffering from a wound or wounds; **a.** Of persons or animals.

1382 WYCLIF *Ps.* lxxxvii. 6 As woundid men slepende in sepulcris. *c* **1400** *Destr. Troy* 7238 Mony woundit wegh fro his wepyn past. **1412–20** LYDG. *Chron. Troy* III. 5410 Þere I leue þis dedly wounded man, Ful sore seke. **1600** SHAKS. *A.Y.L.* III. ii. 254 There lay hee stretch'd along like a Wounded knight. **1672** WISEMAN *Wounds* I. 74 All these wounded Patients. **1709** POPE *Ess. Crit.* 357 A needless Alexandrine ends the song That, like a wounded snake, drags its slow length along. **1771** *Junius Lett.* liv. 283 It is the wounded soldier who deserves the reward. **1795–6** WORDSW. *Borderers* v. 2152 The wounded deer retires to solitude. **1805** SCOTT *Last Minstrel* III. x, It stretch'd him on the plain, Beside the wounded Deloraine. **1846** MRS. A. MARSH *Father Darcy* II. xi. 205 Like some poor wounded bird that steals into a thicket to die. **1872** TENNYSON *Gareth & Lyn.* 633 Kay near him groaning like a wounded bull.

b. Of parts of the body.

1597 A. M. tr. *Guillemeau's Fr. Chirurg.* 5 b/2 We can not, without dilaniatione of the wounded parte, drawe forth the bullet. **1599** SHAKS. *Hen. V*, IV. vi. 25 Ouer Suffolkes necke He threw his wounded arme. **1697** DRYDEN *Æneis* XII. 946 Fix'd on his wounded Face a Shaft he bore. **1769** E. BANCROFT *Ess. Nat. Hist. Guiana* 399 A cataplasm..applied to the wounded part, is the general remedy for venomous Bites. **1826** S. COOPER *First Lines Surg.* (ed. 5) 101 A stratum of coagulated blood..extending from a few inches below the wounded part.

c. *fig.* Impaired, attainted.

1692 PRIOR *Ode Imit. Hor.* xiii, Tell 'em howe're, the King can yet Forgive Their guilty Sloth,..And let their wounded Honour live.

2. *absol.* Those who have received wounds.

c **1000** *Rule of Chrodegang* l, þam ȝemete þe gode læcas doð ymbe ȝewundode. *c* **1300** *E.E. Psalter* lxxxviii. 5 Als wounded, slepand þat are In throghes. **1672** WISEMAN *Wounds* II. 67 From the defeat of the Scotch-army near Dunbar, there came many of the wounded to St. Johnstons. **1813** SCOTT *Rokeby* IV. xxiii, The yellow moon her lustre shed Upon the wounded and the dead. **1845** C. SUMNER *True Grandeur Nations* (1846) 15 A little cheese and a few vegetables are all that can be afforded to the sick and wounded. **1894** in W. W. Tomlinson *Songs & Ballads Sport* (1895) 260 Round the goals the wounded sit.

3. *fig.* Deeply pained or grieved.

1390 GOWER *Conf.* III. 370 Sche hath my wounded herte enoignt. **1613** SHAKS. *Hen. VIII*, II. ii. 75 The quiet of my wounded Conscience. **1647** FULLER (*title*) The Cause and Cure of a wounded Conscience. **1781** COWPER *Retirem.* 341 No wounds like those a wounded spirit feels. **1848** DICKENS *Dombey* xlix, The wounded heart of Florence. **1884** FLOR. MARRYAT *Under Lilies* ii, The only person in the room who pours oil upon his wounded sensibility. **1891** FARRAR *Darkn. & Dawn* lix, If there were anyone who could bring healing to her wounded soul.

4. Of inanimate objects: Marked or injured by cutting or piercing.

c **1586** C'TESS PEMBROKE *Ps.* LV. v, Their speach..softer flowes then balme from wounded rind. *a* **1717** PARNELL *Song* Poems (1737) 20 No more he..with a True-love Knot and Name Engraves a wounded Tree. **1718** PRIOR *Solomon* III. 229 Whom the cut Brass, or wounded Marble shows Victor o'er Life. **1801** NELSON in Nicolas *Disp.* (1845) IV. 384 The greatest quantity of rope has been made from the wounded cables of the prizes. **1812** BYRON *Ch. Har.* I. xlix, Wide scatter'd hoof-marks dint the wounded ground. **1846** DICKENS *Battle of Life* i, For a long time, there were wounded trees upon the battle-ground. **1897** W. G. SMITH tr. *Tubeuf's Dis. Plants* 75 A healing tissue immediately begins to form on wounded surfaces.

†**5.** = WOUNDY *adv. Obs.*

1753 A. MURPHY *Gray's Inn Jrnl.* No. 28 ¶2 A wounded sharp Boy he is.

'woundedly, *adv.* [f. WOUNDED *a.* + -LY[2].]

†**1.** = WOUNDILY. *Obs.*

1794 WALDRON *Heigho for Husb.* III. ii. 33 Are you certain sure..it was only a leady I met?—it look'd woundedly like an angel!

2. In a wounded manner; as though wounded.

1802 COLERIDGE in Mrs. Sandford *T. Poole & Friends* (1888) II. 100 It does a friendship no good for a man to have felt resentfully, and woundedly, towards his friend. **1925** A. S. ALEXANDER *Tramps* 95 [The grey hen] rises, fluttering broken-wingedly or woundedly.

'woundedness. [as prec. + -NESS.] The state of being wounded.

a **1640** FENNER *Serm.* (1657) 223 The Patients here are felt and discerned to have two wounds or maladies; First, brokenness in heart, Secondly, woundednesse.

†**'wounden**, *ppl. a. Obs.* [pa. pple. of WIND *v.*[1]] Twisted, twined.

Beowulf 1193 Him wæs..wunden gold estum ȝeeawed, earmhreade twa. **13..** *Evang. Nicod.* 65 in *Archiv Stud. neu. Spr.* LIII. 392 A wonden wrethe þat his heued hyd Spred he all furth on brede. **1602** W. BASSE *Three Past. Elegies* ii. (1893) 61 A wounden wreathe she had of Baies and Firre.

wounder ('wu:ndə(r)). [f. WOUND *v.* + -ER.] One who or that which wounds.

1483 *Cath. Angl.* 424/1 A Wounder, *plagarius.* **1573–80** TUSSER *Husb.* (1878) 7 Your father was my founder, till death became his wounder. **1584** R. SCOT *Discov. Witchcr.* XVI. x. (1886) 410 The blood of him that is wounded, reboundeth and slippeth into the wounder. **1621** G. SANDYS *Ovid's Met.* IX. (1626) 179 Like a Bull, that beares A wounding iauelin; whom the wounder feares. **1818** TODD. **1877** MRS. OLIPHANT *Makers Flor.* i. 23 He was one of the *feditori* or wounders, i.e., one of the band of volunteers who ..made the assault upon the enemy. **1901** 'LINESMAN' *Words by Eyewitness* (1902) 57 Shells are unlovely killers and wounders.

wounder, obs. form of WONDER *sb.* and *v.*

wounderus, obs. form of WONDROUS.

woundikins, *int.* [f. WOUND *sb.* 1 c: see -KIN.] A variant (with dim. ending) of WOUNDS *int.*

1836 E. HOWARD *R. Reefer* xxxii, Woundikins! if there bean't feyther.

woundily ('waʊndɪlɪ), *adv. Obs.* exc. *arch.* [f. WOUNDY *a.*[2] + -LY[2].] Excessively, extremely, dreadfully.

1706 FARQUHAR *Recruit. Officer* I. i, It smells woundily of Sweat and Brimstone. **1710** in Wilkins *Pol. Ballads* (1860) II. 90 Sir Peter..pour'd such charges that wounded much deeper, But yet he was woundily beat. **1749** SMOLLETT *Gil Blas* x. x. ¶28, I..got off in a twinkling; being woundily afraid that he would strip me of my clothes. **1796** *Hist. Ned Evans* I. 17, I own I's woundily afraid of dead men. **1818** SCOTT *Rob Roy* xxxviii, The butler observed, 'it was burning clear now, but had smoked woundily in the morning.' **1850** THACKERAY *Pendennis* lii, Pen..suffered woundily when called on to pay his share. **1880** L. WINGFIELD *In H.M. Keeping* II. 248 You convicts are woundily crooked cattle.

wounding ('wu:ndɪŋ), *vbl. sb.* [f. WOUND *v.* + -ING[1].]

1. The action of the verb; the fact of being wounded. Also *fig.*

13.. *K. Alis.* 3737 (Laud MS.), Riȝth also he was arise, Of his woundyng he was agrise. *a* **1400–50** *Wars Alexander* 4795 Þare was hurling on hiȝe,..Quat of wrestling of wormes, & wonding of kniȝtis. *a* **1425** tr. *Arderne's Treat. Fistula* 52 If any man..be smyten in any party of þe legge violently and without wondyng of þe skynne. **1518** *Sel. Cases Star Chamber* (Selden) II. 140, I ame Indytyd thear for beatyng and wondyng of one John Holtt. **1581** A. HALL *Iliad* I. 2 Nine dayes Apollo bent, and shot, and them with wounding sped. **1633** P. FLETCHER *Piscat. Eclog.* v. xvi, How can thy eye most sharp in wounding be, In seeing dull? **1749** FIELDING *Tom Jones* III. iv, An Indictment of Assault, Battery, and Wounding, was instantly prefered against Tom. **1799** W. NICOL *Pract. Planter* 225 All wounding, in pruning, should be performed on, or towards the extremities of boughs which [etc.]. **1842** MANNING *Serm.* xviii. (1848) 267 The sharp inward wounding of the soul. **1890** *Retrospect. Med.* CII. 275 All kinds of head injury from slight concussion to compound comminuted fractures of the skull with wounding of the brain substance.

2. = WOUND *sb.* 1.

1581 A. HALL *Iliad* IV. 65 That this your wounding got, Which irkes you so, he should delay. **1595** MARKHAM *Sir R.*

Grinvile (Arb.) 78 At length, the Maister..hath procurd The Knight discend, to haue his woundings curd. **1760–72** H. BROOKE *Fool of Qual.* (1809) III. 7 The great physician of sin-sick souls..had healed my own woundings.

wounding (ˈwuːndɪŋ), *ppl. a.* [f. as prec. + -ING².] That wounds or injures; capable of causing hurt or pain. *lit.* and *fig.*

a **1225** *Ancr. R.* 60 Mid spere of wundinde word.. weorreð lecherie..wið þe lefdi of chastete. *c* **1586** C'TESS PEMBROKE *Ps.* LXIV. iv, Their own tongues to their own woe Shall all their wounding sharpnes bend. **1596** *Edward III*, v. 138 Crosbowes and deadly wounding darts. ? **1638** WOTTON in L. P. Smith *Life & Lett.* (1907) II. 384 You have left in him *illos aculeos*,..for you are indeed a wounding man, as my servant Nicholas saith. **1648** J. QUARLES *Fons Lachrym.* 13 Oh what a wounding sorrow 'tis to think How all will be destroyd. **1718** PRIOR *Solomon* III. 360 His Journey to pursue, Where wounding Thorns, and cursed Thistles grew. **1820** SHELLEY *Prometh. Unb.* I. i. 271 Forms Of furies, driving by upon the wounding storms. **1825** T. HOOK *Sayings* Ser. II. *Passion & Princ.* ix. III. 176 To a simple unsophisticated girl, this must surely have been cutting and wounding. **1915** F. S. OLIVER *Ordeal by Battle* III. i. 181 The result must necessarily be wounding to the credit of popular institutions all the world over.

Hence **ˈwoundingly** *adv.*

1887 *Temple Bar* May 144 What she had said to him gently, was said now roughly, woundingly. **1919** J. D. BERESFORD *Jervaise Comedy* xv. 272 What she implied was woundingly true of that old self of mine which had so recently come under my observation and censure.

woundir, obs. form of WONDER *sb.* and *v.*

woundit, obs. Sc. pa. pple. of WIND *v.*¹

woundless (ˈwuːndlɪs), *a.* [f. WOUND *sb.* + -LESS.]

1. Free from a wound or wounds; unwounded.

1579 SPENSER *Sheph. Cal.* Oct. 41 Doubted Knights, whose woundlesse armour rusts. **1591** SYLVESTER *Du Bartas* I. vii. 353 He that steals home wound-less from the Wars, Is held a Coward. **1635** J. HAYWARD tr. *Biondi's Banish'd Virg.* 216 Undertaking to deliver them you in a short time woundlesse and friends. *c* **1650** *Don Bellianis* 42 So many sluggard knights lying in field, for all I see your person woundlesse. **1755** JOHNSON. **1817** MOORE *Lalla R.*, *Fireworshippers* IV. 565 And some who, grasp'd by those that die, Sink woundless with them. **1855** M. ARNOLD *Balder Dead* ii. 18 All at night return to Odin's hall Woundless and fresh. **1891** MEREDITH *One of our Conq.* I. xii. 226 His pride in appearing woundless and scarless.

†**2.** That cannot be wounded; invulnerable. *Obs.*

1604 SHAKS. *Ham.* IV. i. 44 (Qo. 2) Whose whisper..may misse our Name, And hit the woundlesse ayre. *a* **1618** SYLVESTER *Maiden's Blush* 338 Th' Angell..through the woundless Welkin swifter glides Then Zephyrus.

3. Inflicting no wound, unwounding, harmless.

1795 SOUTHEY *Joan of Arc* VIII. 346 And not a dart fell woundless there.

woundly (ˈwaʊndlɪ), *adv.* ? *Obs.* [f. WOUNDS *int.* + -LY².] = WOUNDILY *adv.*

1646 QUARLES *Judgem. & Mercy* Wks. (Grosart) I. 80/1 One thing hee told me, now I think on't, troubles me woundly. *a* **1661** FULLER *Worthies, Suffolk* (1662) 72 Wat [Tyler] was woundly angry with Sir John Newton. **1719** D'URFEY *Pills* III. 41 Andrew..talk'd woundly wittily to them all. **1839** C. CLARK *J. Noakes* xxxiii, A woundly larned man was he.

woundrous, obs. form of WONDROUS.

wounds (waʊndz), *int. Obs.* exc. *arch.* Also 9 wouns; 7–8 **wauns**, 8 **waund(s**; *dial.* 8–9 **wuns**. [pl. of *wound*: see WOUND *sb.* 1 c.] = God's wounds; used as an oath or asseveration.

α. **1610** DEKKER *Shoemaker's Holiday* D 1, Wounds then farewell. **1753** FOOTE *Englishm. Paris* I. 14 But Wounds how the Powder flew about. **1801** G. COLMAN *Poor Gentl.* I. i. 4 Wouns! let me come at him. **1820** KEATS *Cap & Bells* lxii, 'Wounds! how they shout!' said Hum. **1822** SCOTT *Nigel* ix, Wouns! man, we'll stuff his stomach with English land.

β. **1694** ECHARD *Plautus* 14 Waunds! I ha'nt let fly sure. **1706** FARQUHAR *Recruit. Officer* I. i, Wauns! I wish again that my Wife lay there. **1728** CIBBER & VANBR. *Provok'd Husb.* IV. 65 Waund, he'll storm any thing. *Ibid.* 68 Waunds! you have had one hundred this Morning. **1796** T. MORTON *Way to get Married* II. ii. (1800) 33 *Clem.* Who's at the door? *Serv.* Wauns I forgot. It be maister Dashall fra Lunnon.

γ. *c* **1746** J. COLLIER (Tim Bobbin) *View Lanc. Dial.* Reader, Wks. (1862) p. xxxiv, Wuns eigh; theawrt likt' strowll ogen. **1843** T. WILSON *Pitman's Pay* 57 'Wuns', says aw, 'this rough beginnin'..freightens me'.

ˈwound-up, *a.* [f. *wound*, pa. pple. of WIND *v.*¹ + UP *adv.*] That has undergone winding up (see WIND *v.*¹ 20 and 24).

1788 J. WOODFORDE *Diary* 27 Nov. (1927) III. 68 Ben returned about 4 o'clock this Aft. completely wound up, eat no Dinner but went directly to sleep in a Chair. **1837** LEVER *H. Lorrequer* i, All were breathless in their wound-up anxiety to hear of their countryman. **1853** DICKENS *Bleak Ho.* xxxix, That..old gentleman is still murmuring, like some wound-up instrument running down. **1973** A. GREY *Some put their Trust in Chariots* v. 22 The wound-up windows of the car.

woundward (ˈwuːndwəd), *a. nonce-wd.* [f. WOUND *sb.*: see -WARD.] Towards wounds or wounding.

1946 DYLAN THOMAS *Deaths & Entrances* 48 The woundward flight of the ancient Young from the canyons of oblivion!

woundwort (ˈwuːndwɜːt). [f. WOUND *sb.* + WORT *sb.*¹, after Du. *wondkruid*, G. *wundkraut*.] A popular name given to various plants from their use in healing wounds, *esp.* (*a*) one of the species of *Stachys*, often more fully as Clown's w., Downy w., Marsh w., etc.; (*b*) the golden-rod (*Solidago Virgaurea*); (*c*) the kidney-vetch (*Anthyllis vulneraria*); (*d*) the comfrey (*Symphytum officinale*); †(*e*) Saracen's w. (*Senecio saracenicus*); (*f*) Hercules' all-heal (*Opopanax Chironium*); (*g*) Knight's pondwort (*Stratiotes aloides*).

1548 TURNER *Names of Herbes* (E.D.S.) 87 Solidago seracenica..is called in duch Heidnishe wuntkraut... It may be called in english Woundewurte. **1597** GERARDE *Herbal* II. xcvii. 347 Saracenes Consounde is called in Latine *Solidago Saracenica*,..in English..Saracenes Woundwoort. *Ibid.* xcix. 349 Of captaine Doreas his Woundwoort. *Ibid.* cclxxxv. 677 It seemeth to be *Stratiotes aquatilis* or *Stratiotes potamios*, or Knights water Woundwoort. *Ibid.* ccclxxiv. 851 Of Clownes Woundwoort or Alheale. *Ibid.* 852 Where-upon I haue named it Clounes Woundwoort. **1640** PARKINSON *Theat. Bot.* 693 *Achillea Sideritis lutea*. Achilles yellow Woundwort. **1657** W. COLES *Adam in Eden* ccxli. 381 Allheale..is called in English Hercules Allheale, and Hercules Woundwort. **1718** ROWE *Lucan* IX. 1566 Woundwort and Maiden-weed perfume the Air. **1756** P. BROWNE *Jamaica* 320 The downy Woundworth [*sic*]..is a native of..Jamaica. It should be a fine vulnerary. **1796** BURNEY *Mem. Metastasio* I. 364 You speak to me of dittany and wound-wort. **1796** WITHERING *Brit. Pl.* III. 531 *Stachys sylvatica*,..Hedge Nettle Woundwort. *Ibid.* 728 Common Goldenrod. Woundwort. *Solidago Virga-aurea*. **1819** REES *Cycl.*, *Wound-Wort*, Hercules's, or All-heal, the *laserpitium chironium* of Linnæus. **1852** *G. W. Johnson's Cottage Gard. Dict.*, *Anthyllis vulneraria* (common woundwort). **1857** ANNE PRATT *Flower. Pl.* IV. 190 *Stachys sylvatica* (Hedge Woundwort). *Ibid.* 191 *Stachys palustris* (Marsh Woundwort). *Ibid.* 192 *Stachys Germanica* (Downy Woundwort). *Ibid.* 193 *Stachys arvensis* (Corn Woundwort).

woundy (ˈwuːndɪ), *a.*¹ *rare.* [f. WOUND *sb.* + -Y¹.] **a.** Characterized by wounds. **b.** Causing wounds.

1660 WATERHOUSE *Discourse Arms* 30 Like Sicinius Dentatus who served his Country one hundred and twenty battayles, and brought from them woundy Testimonies of valour. **1826** HOOD *Love* 5 What art thou, Love?..a boy that shoots, From ladies' eyes, such mortal woundy darts.

woundy (ˈwaʊndɪ), *adv.* and *a.*² *Obs.* exc. *arch.* Also 8 **waundy**. [f. WOUNDS *int.* + -Y¹.

The pronunc. (ˈwaʊndɪ) is given by Sheridan (1789) and Smart (1846) in contrast with the noun (wuːnd).]

A. *adv.* Very; extremely; excessively.

α. *c* **1621** ROWLEY etc. *Witch Edmonton* II. i, 'Tis woundy cold, sure! **1660** *Dial. betw. Tom & Dick* 1/2 And yet the Thief is woundy Close. **1695** CONGREVE *Love for L.* IV. xiii, He was woundy angry when I gav'n that wipe. **1706** E. WARD *Wooden World Diss.* (1708) 79 His drinking much Flip, makes him woundy subject to the Vapours. **1774** C. DIBDIN *Waterman* i, She keeps her a-bed woundy late of a morning. **1824** SCOTT *Redgauntlet* ch. xv, His orders are woundy particular. **1829** —— *Jrnl.* 19 Apr., We smoked and I became woundy sleepy. **1864** LE FANU *Uncle Silas* II. 237 He was 'a woundy ugly customer in a wax, she could tell me.'

β. **1718** BREVAL *Play is the Plot* II. i. 19 And the Jade's a great Fortune, and waundy handsom too into the Bargain. **1791** O'KEEFE *Mod. Antiques* I. (1792) 16, I was waundy hungry.

B. *adj.* Very great; extreme.

1681 *Plain Dealing, Dial. Humphrey & Roger* 1/1 By the Mass, Hodge, thou say'st well, I have a woundy mind to do as thou say'st, but [etc.]. **1702** FARQUHAR *Twin-Rivals* V. iii, You must know Sir, there is a Neighbour's Daughter that I had a woundy Kindness for. **1718** BREVAL *Play is the Plot* II. i. 11 And has she such a waundy deal of Wit, do you say Sir? **1794** GODWIN *Caleb Williams* 37 So he flew into a woundy passion and threatened to horsewhip me. **1836** T. HOOK *G. Gurney* I. 213 You'll kill a woundy sight on 'em, I think, at that distance. **1888** F. COWPER *Capt. Wight* 218 They castle folk be a woundy lot of gallants.

woundyr, obs. f. WONDER *sb.*

wouned, wount(e, obs. ff. WONT *ppl. a.*

wounty, obs. f. WANTY.

†**woup.** *Sc. Obs.* Forms: 6 **wowp, wop**, 6–8 **woup**, 7 **woupe**, 8 **woop**. [Of obscure origin; the related verb is now represented by WUP.] A hoop or ring, esp. a finger-ring of plain metal as distinguished from one set with stones.

1511 *Acc. Ld. High Treas. Scot.* IV. 310 For outquitting of Wille Wodis wowp at lay in wed..xxviij s. **1535** in Ramsay *Bamff Charters* (1915) 70 Ane woup of gold. **1542** *Acts & Decreets* I. f. 140 Ane woup of gold about his arme of ane pund weycht. **1633** SIR A. JOHNSTON (Wariston) *Diary* (S.H.S.) 31 Thy uyfs woupe brak on thy finger in two halfs. **1691** in *Proc. Soc. Antiq. Scot.* (1919) LIII. 54 Two stoned ringes,..with five gold woupes and ane gold lockit. **1720** in *Fraser Papers* (S.H.S.) 164 Three woups and a pearl necklace... A small diamond ring, three woops and a pair of gold lockets.

wourali, var. WOORALI.

wourd, obs. form of WORD.

wourne, var. *worne*, *wurne*, WARN *v.*²

1568 *Jacob & Esau* I. iv. B iij, But wife Rebecca, I woulde not haue you to mourne, As though I did your honest petition wourne.

wourt(e, obs. forms of WORT *sb.*¹, ².

wous, southern form of FOUS *a. Obs.*

13.. *Vox & Wolf* 12 in *Rel. Antiq.* II. 272 Withinne the walle wes on hous, The wox wes thider swithe wous.

†**wous**, var. of VOUS *int. Obs.*

1674 J. HOWARD *Engl. Mounsieur* V. ii. 62 *French.* Make way English Clown. *Wil.* Wous, but we won't.

woushesauff, obs. f. VOUCHSAFE.

woust, obs. f. VOUST.

woustour, var. VOUSTER *Sc.*

wout, var. VULT *Obs.*

wout(e, obs. varr. VAULT *sb.*¹ and *v.*¹

wou-wou, var. WOW-WOW.

wouyn, obs. pa. pple. of WEAVE *v.*¹

wove (wəʊv), *ppl. a.* and *sb.* [var. of WOVEN: see forms of WEAVE *v.*¹]

1. a. = WOVEN *ppl. a.* 1, 2, 3.

1710 SHAFTESB. *Soliloquy* III. ii. 147, I can't conceive.. how a Writer changes his Capacity, by this new Dress, any more than by the wear of Wove Stockins, after having worn no other Manufacture than the Knit. **1817** JAS. MILL *Brit. India* I. I. ii. 37 Opening a trade for wove goods on the coast. **1831** SCOTT *Ct. Robt.* xii, The chairs and couches were covered with Eastern wove mats. **1840** MRS. GAUGAIN *Lady's Assist. Knitting* I. 57 If a wove stocking, open up the seam. **1903** KIPLING *Five Nations* 15 'Mid bergs about the Ice-cap Or wove Sargasso weed.

b. *wove mould*, the particular kind of mould used in making wove paper (see quot. 1854).

1806 H. FOURDRINIER *Brit. Patent 2951* 4 A number of moulds of the description called laid or wove, any number of which..are capable of forming one long mould. **1839** URE *Dict. Arts* 927 The frame-work of a *wove* mould is nearly the same. **1854** C. TOMLINSON *Obj. Art-Manuf., Paper* 20 In wove moulds, as their name implies, the wire is woven into wire cloth.

2. *techn.* **a.** Of paper: Made on a mould of closely woven wire. (See 1 b, and cf. WOVEN *ppl. a.* 4.)

1809 R. LANGFORD *Introd. Trade* 63 Wove Foolscap. **1815** *Ann. Reg., Chron.* 86 It is printed on the most splendid wove paper. **1879** *Print. Trades Jrnl.* XXIX. 43 A hand-made, blue wove Foolscap paper.

b. *absol.* or as *sb.*

1859 *Stationers' Handbk.* 12 In woven papers may be mentioned *Blue Wove*..; then comes another, which..is termed *Yellow Wove*. **1880** J. DUNBAR *Pract. Papermaker* 56 That warm cream colour..so much desired in high-class cream wove and laid post.

wove, pa. t. and pple. of WEAVE *v.*¹

woved, obs. pa. pple. of WEAVE *v.*¹

woven (ˈwəʊv(ə)n), *ppl. a.* Also 6 **wouen, wovyn**; *Sc.* 5 **wowen**, 6 **wolvin**, 7 **wolfin**. [pa. pple. of WEAVE *v.*¹]

1. That has undergone the process of weaving; formed or fabricated by weaving.

c **1470** HENRY *Wallace* I. 242 A wowen quhyt hatt scho brassit on with all. **1560** B. GOOGE tr. *Palingenius' Zodiac* II. (1561) C iij, The wouen webbe of flaxe. **1575** in *Archaeologia* XXX. 19 Item v pairs of woven shets. **1612** *Sc. Bk. Rates* in *Halyburton's Ledger* (1867) 293 Busteanis or woven tweill stuffe. **1727** DE FOE *Eng. Tradesm.* (1732) I. 332 Her Stockings from Tewksbury, if ordinary; from Leicester, if woven. **1758** WHITEHEAD *Verses to People Eng.* 4 And Navies powerful to display Their woven wings to every wind. **1819** SHELLEY *Cenci* V. ii. 27 You clothed me in a robe of woven gold. **1833** MRS. BROWNING *Prometh. Bound* 834 Where Scythia's shepherd peoples dwell aloft, Perched in wheeled wagons under woven roofs. **1883** W. D. CURZON *Manuf. Industries Worcs.* 80 Travelling endless woven wire sieves.

fig. **1894** J. DAVIDSON *Ballads & Songs* 33 We set about To bring the world within the woven spell.

2. Formed by interlacing or intertwining after the manner of weaving.

1590 SPENSER *F.Q.* I. v. 4 Soone after comes the cruell Sarazin, In wouen maile all armed warily. **1596** *Edw. III*, III. v. 31 Whilst he, Lion like, Intangled in the net of their assaults, Frantiquely wrends, and byt(e)s the wouen toyle. **1628** MAY *Virg. Georg.* II. 49 Take a thick-woven Osiar colander, Through which the pressed wines are strained clear. **1658** ROWLAND tr. *Moufet's Theat. Ins.* 901 They live here longer..then in their artificial woven Hives. **1793** WORDSW. *Evening Walk* 240 Long grass and willows form the woven wall. **1820** SHELLEY *Witch Atl.* xxxiii, Woven tracery ran..o'er The solid rind. **1892** W. B. YEATS in *1st Bk. Rhymers' Club* 7 Under the woven roofs of..boughs.

fig. **1644** VICARS *God in Mount* 6 A pernicious woven-knot of malignant active spirits. **1815** SHELLEY *Alastor* 48 Voice of living beings, and woven hymns Of night and day. **1891** CAYLEY *Math. Papers* (1897) XIII. 121 The groups thus obtained, with substitutions which interchange the two sets of letters, are said to be 'woven' groups.

Comb. **1885** MRS. CADDY *Footsteps Jeanne D'Arc* 12 Horses feed in the wide, woven-fenced fields. **1904** HARDY *Dynasts* I. 5 O woven-winged squadrons of Toulon..draw westward Ere Nelson be near!

3. Interlaced, intertwined; wreathed.

1815 SHELLEY *Alastor* 459 A well..Images all the woven boughs above. **1833** TENNYSON *Miller's Dau.* 232 The kiss, The woven arms, seem but to be Weak symbols of the settled bliss..I have found in thee. **1849** LYTTON *K. Arthur* III. cx, Fair was her prison, walled with woven flowers.

†**4.** Of paper: = WOVE *ppl. a.* 2. *Obs.*

1797 *Brit. Critic* IX. 72 We have volumes every day, on woven-paper,..in which war is execrated.

woves, obs. form of VOWESS.

a **1550** LELAND *Itin.* (1768) II. 33 An Image in the Habite of a Woves.

wow (waʊ), *sb.*^{1} [Imitative: cf. WOUGH *sb.*, and BOW-WOW.] **1. a.** A bark or similar sound. **b.** A waul.

1811 *Sporting Mag.* XXXVII. 131 Johnson with a surly wow, wow. **1862** HISLOP *Prov. Scot.* 125 It's weak i' the wow, like Barr's cat. **1913** *Blackw. Mag.* Mar. 452/2 A barking deer explodes in an unexpected 'wow' ten yards off.

2. Fluctuations in pitch in reproduced sound that are sufficiently slow to be heard as such in long notes; a property in a reproducer that gives rise to this, esp. uneven speed.

1932 *Wireless World* 16 Mar. 277/2 Wobble or 'wow'—to use the expressive American term..is not so troublesome nowadays, most modern sound cameras having anti-wow mechanism. **1942** *Electronic Engin.* XIV. 640/1 The principal snag of sub-standard projectors, that of speed variations, is well cared for in so far as relates to low-frequency variations, which are known as 'wow' and not, as stated, warble. **1960** K. AMIS *Take Girl like You* xxiii. 271 Every couple of weeks Graham found out some new way of reducing distortion or filtering off surface noise or eliminating wow. **1968** *New Scientist* 20 June 615/1 The Lick Observatory conclusion was entirely spurious, the result of undetected 'wow' in the tape recorder used. **1971** *Wireless World* Oct. 478/1 Wow can be caused by a badly eccentric or warped record. **1982** *Listener* 16 Dec. 34/2 Insist on listening to some music, preferably piano music that shows up wow and flutter especially well.

wow (waʊ), *sb.*^{2} and *a. slang* (orig. *U.S.*). [f. WOW *int.*] **A.** *sb.* A sensational success. Freq. const. *of*.

1920 *Collier's* 11 Dec. 21/1 In Round Five they stalled some more... The sixth innin' was a wow! **1926** [see STOP *v.* 21 c]. **1927** WODEHOUSE *Small Bachelor* vi. 94 'A friend of mine tipped me off that this company was a wow'. 'A what?' 'A winner. He said it was going to be big and advised me to come in on the ground floor.' **1944** S. BELLOW *Dangling Man* 54 What a wow of a finish. **1954** C. CHURCHILL *Let.* 1 Sept. in M. Soames *Clementine Churchill* (1979) xxvi. 445 Mr Graham Sutherland is a 'Wow'. He really is a most attractive man. **1962** V. CONNAUGHT *Secret Heart of Princess Alexandra* vii. 73 From that moment forward, she was a wow with every Australian in the land. **1983** D. FRANCIS *Danger* xvii. 236 Chattering guests all having a wow of a time.

B. *adj.* Exciting or expressing admiration and delight.

1921 *Variety* 9 Dec. 31 The *wow* comedy song... '*Say It With Liquor*'. **1962** *John o' London's* 1 Mar. 211/2 A chorus of wow reviews from international critics. **1972** *Daily Colonist* (Victoria, B.C.) 13 Feb. 27/4 Two-foot-high letters inviting you to buy Vitamin E capsules, often at wow potencies, plaster the fronts of drug stores.

wow (waʊ), *v.*^{1} [Imitative: cf. WOW *sb.*^{1}] *intr.* To howl, to waul.

1806 R. JAMIESON *Pop. Ballads* I. 234 The wolf wow'd hideous on the hill. **1824** CARR *Craven Gloss.*, *Wow*, to howl. **1900** C. LEE *Cynthia in West* v. 69 You should hear her wow, just like an owld cat!

wow (waʊ), *v.*^{2} *slang* (orig. *U.S.*). [f. WOW *int.*, *sb.*^{2}] *trans.* To make enthusiastic, to impress or excite greatly (esp. an audience).

1924 *Variety* 24 Dec. 14/5 He doesn't wow 'em at any time and seems misplaced in the show. **1938** E. B. WHITE *Let.* 20 Dec. (1976) 191 Your Hollywood visit piece (which I had never read) wowed me. **1949** *Time* 19 Sept. 45/3 She wowed them with a dramatic reading of the death scene from *Romeo and Juliet*. **1950** BLESH & JANIS *They all played Ragtime* ii. 44 The ragtime pianists were already 'wowing' their audiences with syncopated renderings of the classics. **1961** *Sunday Express* 12 Mar. 14/5 Yet *another* new look..wowed London last week. **1980** *Times* 17 June 13/3 They are unlikely to wow anybody who does not already respond to Burne-Jones's rather wan charms. **1984** *Daily Tel.* 25 Sept. 11/4 Mr Macdonald, who supplied the off-screen commentary for this year's Channel 4 coverage of the SDP conference, had the bright notion of training up a novice speaker who would wow them at Buxton.

wow (waʊ), *int.* [Of exclamatory origin: cf. VOW *int.*]

1. Chiefly *Sc.* **a.** An exclamation, variously expressing aversion, surprise or admiration, sorrow or commiseration, or mere asseveration.

1513 DOUGLAS *Æneis* VI. Prol. 19 Out on thir wanderand spiritis, wow! thow cryis. **15..** *Peblis to Play* 74 (Maitl. fol. 178) Ane winklot fell and hir taill vp; wow, quod malkin, hyd ȝow. **1721** RAMSAY *Prosp. Plenty* 74 Wow! that's braw news. **1789** BURNS *Grose's Peregr.* 11 And wow! he has an unco sleight O' cauk and keel. **1815** SCOTT *Guy M.* xi, Wow, woman, the Bertrams of Ellangowan are the auld Dingawaies lang syne. *a* **1840** JOANNA BAILLIE *Poems, Fy, let us a'* 16 But wow! he looks dowie and cow'd. **1892** LUMSDEN *Sheep-head* 36 As below the brig we turn—Oh, Wow! the deavin' din there!

b. Followed by *but* or *gin*.

1715 RAMSAY *Christ's Kirk Gr.* II. 40 And wow gin she was skeigh And mim that Day. **1724** —— *Tea-t. Misc.* (1733) I. 8 The woer he step'd up the house, And wow but he was wond'rous crouse. *a* **1800** *K. Henry* x. in Child *Ballads* I. 299/1 O whan he slew his good gray-hounds, Wow but his heart was sair! **1843** J. BALLANTINE *Gaberlunzie's Wallet* vi. 151 My auld uncle Willie cam doun..An' wow but he was a braw man.

2. In general use. Now chiefly expressing astonishment or admiration.

1892 RIDER HAGGARD *Nada* v. 35 Wow! my father, of those two regiments not one escaped. **1896** ADE *Artie* 8 'The girls—wow!' 'Beauties, eh?' 'Lollypaloozers!' **1916** J. J. BELL *Little Grey Ships* 17 'Wow!' exclaimed the young seaman..'Wish I was in Egypt. How's this for cold, old Bill?' **1931** R. CAMPBELL *Georgiad* i. 11 Bang on your nose my spectacles appear And (Wow!) an earring slits my tender ear. **1941** J. D. CARR *Case of Constant Suicides* i. 17 A brown-haired girl..straightened up to stare at him. 'Wow!' said Alan inaudibly. **1962** E. CLEAVER in A. Dundes *Mother Wit* (1973) 20/1 Wow, what a sight that would be! **1980** 'R. B. DOMINIC' *Attending Physician* xxiv. 217 'Wow!' Mike Isham whistled reverently. 'No wonder she was willing to murder.'

Also **wow'ee** († **wowey**) *int.*, = sense 2.

1921 S. FORD *Inez & Trilby May* xvi. 279 Think of the row that will start when it comes out that this is an inside job, with a princess playing the star part. Wowey! **1963** *Mad Mag.* July 23/2 Boy! Wow-wee! That's quite an exciting evening line-up! **1975** R. H. RIMMER *Premar Experiments* (1976) iii. 216 Bren was jubilant. 'My big sister is pregnant. Wow-ee! Unbelievable! Fantastic!' **1981** R. BARNARD *Sheer Torture* iii. 29 He had served on the Arts Council Music Panel, 1958–60. Wowee!

wow, obs. Sc. f. VOW *sb.* and *v.*^{1}, *v.*^{2}; obs. f. WOO *v.*^{1}, var. WOUGH *sb.*^{2}

woward(e, var. ff. VAWARD. *Obs.*

wowbat, obs. var. WOUBIT.

wowchaife, wowchesaf, obs. ff. VOUCHSAFE *v.*

†**wowe.** *Obs.* Forms: 1 **wawa**, 2–4 **wawe**, 3–4 **wowe**, 3 **wou**. [OE. *wáwa* = OHG. *wêwe*, ON. *vá*:—OTeut. **waiwan-*, f. the root **wai-*, repr. by OE. *wá* WOE.] Misery, distress, trouble, sorrow.

α. a **1000** *Genesis* 466 (Gr.) þæt þær yldo bearn moste onceosan godes & yfeles,..welan & wawan. *c* **1000** ÆLFRIC *Gram.* xlviii. (Z.) 279 On ðære wæron awritene heofunga.. and wawa... Se wawa ȝetacnað þone ecan wawan, ðe ða habbað on hellewite. *c* **1175** *Lamb. Hom.* 73 He wurð idemed to þolien wawe mid douelen in helle. *a* **1200** *Moral Ode* 151 in *O.E. Hom.* I. 169 Eure he walde her inne wawe and ine wene wunien. *c* **1200** ORMIN 13349 þatt he shollde wurrþenn harrd To þolenn alle wawenn.

β. c **1200** *Trin. Coll. Hom.* 165 Here is..smertinge, sorinesse, werinesse, and oðre wowe muchel. *c* **1205** LAY. 27560 þar was wowe and sorinisse inowe. *c* **1250** *Owl & Night.* 414 Al þat ho singeþ hit is for wowe. *a* **1300** *Fragm. Seven Sins* I. iii. in *E.E.P.* (1862) 17 þis worldis wel nis bot wowe. *c* **1315** SHOREHAM VII. 858 þanne falþ ous rewelyche by kende To soffry wowe.

wowe, var. WOUGH *sb.*^{1} and *a.*; obs. form of WOO *v.*^{1}

†**wowell.** *Obs. rare.* [Of obscure origin; perh. connected with *uouelle* in *Saxon Leechd.* II. 266.] Coltsfoot.

c **1450** *Alphita* (Anecd. Oxon.) 140 *Pes pulli, herba terrestris*,..donnhoue uel wowell uel feldhoue.

wowen, obs. f. WOO *v.*^{1}; obs. Sc. f. WOVEN *ppl. a.*

wowf (waʊf), *a. Sc.* [Of obscure origin.] Crazed, daft, mad.

1802 SIBBALD *Chron. S.P.* IV. Gloss., *Wowf*, mad. **1819** SCOTT *Leg. Montrose* vi, It is very odd how Allan, who, between ourselves,..is a little wowf, seems at times to have more sense than us all put together. **1824** —— *Redgauntlet* ch. vii, 'What d'ye mean by deft [= daft]—eh?' 'Just Fifish', replied Peter; 'wowf'. **1897** SNAITH *Fierceheart* ix. 101 Is yer honour gane clean wowf?

wowing, obs. form of WOOING *vbl. sb.*

wowl (waʊl), *v.* [Imitative.] *intr.* and *trans.* To howl.

1757 [E. PERRONET] *Mitre* I. xxviii, A second blinks and wowls his dread. *a* **1825** FORBY *Voc. E. Anglia*, *Wowl*, *v.* to howl, to wail vociferously.

wowld, obs. f. WOLD.

wown, obs. pa. pple. of WIND *v.*^{1}

wownd(e, obs. ff. WOUND *sb.* and *v.*

wowp, obs. var. WUP *v. Sc.*

wowser ('waʊzə(r)). Also **wowzer**. orig. *Austral.* (now chiefly *Austral.* and *N.Z.*). [Of obscure origin.] **a.** A Puritanical enthusiast or fanatic; *esp.* a fanatical or determined opponent of intoxicating drink.

1899 *Truth* 8 Oct. 5 Willoughby 'Wowsers' Worried. The 'Talent' get a 'Turn'... Ten young men were fined..for having behaved in a riotous manner on the Military Rd. **1909** *Daily News* 1 Apr. 4 'Wowser' is a term applied by certain portions of the Australian Press to parsons of all denominations, more particularly to those who are fanatical on temperance and social evils. **1912** *Nation* 11 May 214/2 A wowser is one who wants to compel everybody else..to do whatever he thinks right, and abstain from everything he thinks wrong. **1918** *Chrons. N.Z.E.F.* 79/2 The Wowzers look with disdain upon the 'Come and have a spot, old boy' kind of welcome. **1937** R. A. KNOX *Double Cross Purposes* ii. 40, I hope to God the old wowzer didn't see we'd been at it. He's as sharp as a weasel. **1939** R. CAMPBELL *Flowering Rifle* I. 18 Where wowsers may discharge their wondrous lore Who'll 'fight for peace', and yet disarm for war. **1939** X. HERBERT *Capricornia* xviii. 233 Only ones't got a victory outer that flamin' war was the blasted wowsers! **1941** C. BARRETT *Coast of Adventure* iii. 56 Men without vision or liberal views. We might call them 'wowsers' today. **1949** D. M. DAVIN *Roads from Home* I. v. 72 The good old days were gone. And it wasn't only the wowsers that had spoilt everything. **1961** *N.Y. Times* 12 Feb. 36/1 A relentless wowser (prohibitionist)..banned saloons. **1963** *Economist* 3 Aug. 422/2 Some alien wowser such as Senator Goldwater. **1970** *N.Z. Listener* 12 Oct. 13/2 A bit late to find that out, you snobbish ratbag wowser. **1975** D. STUART *Walk, Trot, Canter & Die* xxiii. 137 But now in me old age I'm a wowser an' I don't have to worry about anything. I'd have a bottle of whisky in the packs... but most trips it wouldn't even get opened, so you can't say I was a drunkard. **1977** *Times* 18 Mar. 18/7 This country's pattern of..licensing hours..is the work of wowzers of every description. **1981** M. GEE *Meg* xiv. 142 You won't drink with me, will you? Didn't think so. I'm stuck in a family of wowsers. **1982** *Times* 7 Dec. 12/6 These authoritarian wowsers would like to see a law forbidding anybody to watch any programme they disapprove of.

b. *attrib.* and *Comb.*

1934 *Bulletin* (Sydney) 12 Sept. 11/4 That morbid sex curiosity which is the curse of wowser-ridden communities. **1936** R. CAMPBELL *Mithraic Emblems* 125 Let Spender over wowser-problems fret. **1966** G. W. TURNER *Eng. Lang. Austral. & N.Z.* i. 22 The wowser tradition is stronger in New Zealand, where there is less of the bush tradition; it usually takes the form of a cautious anxiety about life rather than open Puritanism. **1969** *Age* (Melbourne) 24 May 2/5 Sir Henry, while making his attack on NSW and its poker machines, maintained that Victoria was not a 'wowser' State. **1978** P. H. JOHNSON *Good Husband* xxii. 190 There were 'no smoking' notices, at which Maisie demurred... 'I find this wowser activity uncomfortable.'

Hence **'wowserish** *a.*, of the nature of a wowser; puritanical; **'wowserism**, the practice or beliefs of a wowser or wowsers; **wowserite** a supporter of wowserism.

1909 *Daily News* 1 Apr. 4 Their followers are called 'Wowserites', and their propaganda 'Wowserism'. **1933** F. CLUNE *Try Anything Once* 122 They had lost their dash and grown wowserish. **1936** M. FRANKLIN *All that Swagger* l. 377 Novels which..provoked attention by their unreticent details of bodily functionings and provided capital sport when flung in the face of *fin de siècle* wowserism. **1966** *New Statesman* 4 Mar. 289/2 After a time, I warmed even to Stennis and Morse; though the first was narrow and wowserish. **1966** G. W. TURNER *Eng. Lang. Austral. & N.Z.* i. 21 Wowserism is prohibition elevated into a philosophy. **1971** *Observer* 14 Mar. 15/2 Australia's peculiar 'wowserism', the often unpredictable censorship of films, books and shows by the authorities, is largely a function of older Australia. **1983** *Age* (Melbourne) 3 Dec. 11/2 Coming hard on the heels of the casino inquiry, which also recommended in the negative, the Government's decision on poker machines may give it a puritanical or wowserish image. **1984** *Daily Tel.* 24 Aug. 10/4 When Pierre Trudeau visited Australia in 1970 he told the natives: 'You have wowserism; we have Toronto.'

wowt(e, obs. var. ff. VAULT *sb.*^{1} and *v.*^{1}

‖**wow-wow**^{1} ('waʊwaʊ). Also **wou-wou, wau-wau, wawou, wa-wa, wawah, wah-wah.** [a. Malay *wauwau*, Javanese *wawa* (whence also Du. *wouwouw*, *wawwaw*), imitative of the animal's cry.] The silver gibbon of Java, *Hylobates leuciscus*. Also applied to *H. agilis*.

α. **1827** GRIFFITH tr. *Cuvier* I. 209 The Ash-coloured or Silvery Gibbon, also called the Wou Wou. **1838** *Libr. Entert. Knowl., Menageries, Monkeys* etc. I. 183 The wou-wou (*Hylobates Leuciscus*) is covered with a very fine long fur of a woolly texture. **1885** H. O. FORBES *Wand. Eastern Archip.* 70 The loud plaintive wailings of a colony of Wau-waus.

attrib. **1894** H. O. FORBES *Handbk. Primates* II. 154 The Wau-Wau Gibbon. *Hylobates leuciscus*.

β. **1882** DE WINDT *Equator* 102 Monkeys of every description, from the hideous proboscis to the pretty wa-wa. **1883** ISAB. L. BIRD *Golden Chersonese* 297 A little wah-wah, the most delightful of apes. **1939** A. KEITH *Land below Wind* xvii. 291 *Wah wah* was the native name for gibbon ape. **1959** 'M. DERBY' *Tigress* iii. 145 The birds and the *wah-wahs*.. woke. **1975** *Blackw. Mag.* June 542/1 The only members of the ape family found in Malaya are the gibbons, the commonest of which is locally known as the *wah-wah*.

attrib. **1891** E. ARNOLD *Seas & Lands* xl. 520 A 'wah-wah' monkey..was a delightful little creature, with very long silky arms. **1964** J. POPE-HENNESSY *Verandah* II. ii. 78 He [*sc.* Hugh Low] once wrote to his daughter Kitty that he loved only two creatures in the world—his wah-wah monkey, Eblis, and herself.

wow-wow^2. [Imitative.] A bird of Guyana.

1855 H. G. DALTON *Hist. Brit. Guiana* II. 413 The 'boclora', or wow-wow (*Trogon melanopterus*), so named from the noise it makes, is about the size of a small pigeon.

wow-wow^3. ? *Obs.* [Of obscure origin.] Only in ***wow-wow sauce***, a fanciful name for a preparation used with stewed beef.

1822 MAY *Cook's Oracle* (ed. 4) 325 Wow Wow Sauce for Stewed or Bouilli Beef. **1868** *Enquire Within* (ed. 35) 285.

wowyn, obs. f. WOO *v.*^{1}

wox, obs. Sc. f. VOICE *sb.*

wox, woxe(n, obs. pa. t. and pa. pples. of WAX *v.*

woxin, woxsen, etc., obs. pa. pple. of WAX *v.*

woy, *int.* Also **woyh**. [Exclamatory.] A call to a horse to stop. (Cf. WAY, WO, WHOA *int.*)

1797 T. MORTON *Cure for Heart-ache* I. i, *Frank* (*with-out*) Woyh! whoh! Smiler! **1809** R. KERR *Agric. Berw.* 503 Formerly, in speaking to their horses, carters..in calling to stop used the incommunicable sound of *prroo*, now *wo*, or *woy*. **1828** CARR *Craven Gloss.*, *Who*, *Woy*, a word used to stop horses in a team.

woyage, obs. Sc. f. VOYAGE.

woyce, obs. Sc. f. VOICE *sb.*

woyd, obs. f. WOOD *sb.*[1]

woyd(e, obs. Sc. and north. ff. VOID *a.*, *sb.*, and *v.*

woye, var. VOYE *Obs.*, way.

woyid, obs. Sc. f. VOID *v.*

woys(e, obs. ff. VOICE *sb.*

woyse, obs. f. OOZE *sb.*

woywod, var. VOIVODE.

woze, obs. f. OOZE *sb.*[2]

wozen, obs. f. WEASAND.

wp(e, **wpone**, etc., obs. ff. UP, UPON, etc.

W particle: see W 4 b.

wr, obs. var. OUR *pron.*

wr- (r), a consonantal combination occurring initially in a number of words (frequently implying twisting or distortion), the earlier of which usually have cognates with the same initial sounds in the older Germanic languages. The combination is regularly preserved in Gothic, OS., OFris., and OE., but in OHG. is reduced to *r*. In ON. the *w* was lost before *rŏ*, *rŭ*, at an early date over the whole Scandinavian area; at a later period in all other words in ONorw. and OIcel. In the modern Germanic tongues *wr-* remains in Du., Flem., LG., and Fris., and is represented by *vr-* in Da., Sw., and some Norw. dialects.

Some 130 words in *wr-* are recorded from the OE. period, and a number of these survive in the later language, while others have been added from Du. and LG. Early difficulty in pronouncing the combination may be indicated by the Old Northumbrian spellings with *wur-*, and by the 14–15th cent. *weritt* 'writ', *werangus* 'wrongous'. The *r* is sometimes separated from the *w* by metathesis, as in ME. *wærð* for *wræð* 'wroth', *werch* for *wrech* 'wretch', *wirten* for *written*; but conversely *wr-* may arise from the same cause, as in OE. *wryhta* 'wright', for *wyrhta*. Signs of the dropping of the *w* begin to appear about the middle of the 15th cent. in such spellings as *ringe* for *wring* v., *rong* for *wrong* adj.; these become common in the 16th cent. (for examples see WRANGLE, WRAP, WREAK, WRECK, WRENCH, WREST, etc.). Reduction of the sound is also indicated by the converse practice of writing *wr-* for *r-*, which similarly appears in the 15th cent. (in *wrath* for *rathe*), and becomes common in the 16th; for examples see the subordinate entries under WRACK, WRACKED, WRAGGED, WRAP, WRAPE, WRETCHLESS, etc. In standard English the *w* was finally dropped in the 17th century; it has remained (though now obsolescent) in Scottish, and in some south-western English dialects is represented by *v*, which is also regular in north-eastern Scottish.

The phonetists Bullokar (*Amendment of Ortographie*, 1580) and Gill (*Logonomia*, 1621) have *wr-* throughout, and no doubt pronounced the *w*. Later authorities, e.g. R. Hodges (*English Primrose*, 1644), mark the *w* in this combination as silent.

wra, ME. var. WRO.

wraak, var. WRAKE *sb.*[1] *Obs.*

wraaste, obs. var. WREST *sb.*[1]

wrabbe, var. WROB *v. Obs.*

†**wrabbed**, *a. Obs. rare.* [Of obscure origin. Cf. WRAWED *a.*] Perverse; difficult to manage.

1540 J. HEYWOOD *Four P.P.* 986 By theyr condicions so croked and crabbed, Frowardly fashonde, so waywarde and wrabbed. **1568** *Jacob & Esau* II. ii, Haue any mo maisters suche a man as I haue?..so eluishe, so frowarde? So crabbed, so wrabbed, so stiffe, so vntowarde?

†'**wrabble**, *v. Obs. rare.* In 6 wrable-, *Sc.* wrabill. [Of obscure origin. Cf. WARBLE *v.*[3], WORBLE *v.*] *intr.* To wriggle.

1513 DOUGLAS *Æneid* VIII. x. 84 About hir palpis..The tua twynnis..Sportand full tyte gan to wrabill and hing. **1534** MORE *Answ. Poysoned Bk.* I. iii. 7 The hote fyre of hell shalbe so fast tayed in all theyr tayles wrabelynge there together, y[t] neuer shall they gete ye fyre fro theyr taylys.

wrable, obs. Sc. variant of WARBLE *sb.*[1]

1513 DOUGLAS *Æneid* XII. Prol. 245 In wrablis [*ed.* 1553 werblis] dulce of hevynly armonyis The larkis..Lovys thar lege with tonys curyus. [Cf. WRIBLE.]

W.R.A.C. Also **WRAC** and (*colloq.*) **Wrac** (ræk). [f. initial letters of its name.] The Women's Royal Army Corps, formed as the women's corps of the British Army in 1949 to replace the A.T.S.; also, a member of this corps.

1949 *Times* 1 Feb. 2/3 (*heading*) Inauguration of W.R.A.C. and W.R.A.F. *Ibid.*, The King has given orders for the following appointments in the W.R.A.C.:—The Queen to be Commandant-in-Chief the Women's Royal Army Corps. **1950** *R.A.F. Rev.* Sept. 7/2 They have defeated the W.R.A.C. in every championship shoot since the women's inter-Services championships were started in 1947. **1956** R. MACAULAY *Towers of Trebizond* xv. 179 Now the women who go with armies are not encouraged to be so useful to them, they are called Ats and Wrens and Waafs and Wracs and are kept behind the battle lines and are only a small consolation to the troops. **1982** *Whitaker's Almanack 1983* 482 Retirement Benefits... The annual rates for W.R.A.C. were given; these apply to equivalent ranks in all Services. **1984** *Daily Tel.* 7 Apr. 8/1 'You are following in the footsteps of great men,' said the Duchess, Controller-Commandant of the WRAC.

wrache, obs. Sc. var. WRETCH *sb.*

wrachit(ness, obs. Sc. ff. WRETCHED(NESS.

wrack (ræk), *sb.*[1] Forms: 1 **wræc**, 3–5, *Sc.* 6 **wrak**, 4 **wrac**, 4– **wrack**, 6–7 **wracke**. [OE. *wræc* neut., f. pret. stem of *wrecan* to drive, etc., WREAK *v.* Cf. WRACK *sb.*[2], by which the later senses (esp. sense 5) may partly have been influenced; in writers of the 16–17th cent. it is sometimes uncertain which word is intended.

The evidence of rhymes shows that early northern ME. instances of the spelling *wrak* usually have a long vowel, and belong to WRAKE *sb.*[1]]

I. 1. Retributive punishment; vengeance, revenge; in later use also, hostile action, active enmity, persecution. *Obs.* exc. *arch.* or *poet.*

Freq. coupled with words of similar meaning, as *war*, *wrath*, *wreak*, and tending to pass into sense 2.

c **900** tr. *Baeda's Hist.* IV. xxv. (1890) 356 Hi..mid þy wiite ðæs foresprecenan wræces slæȝene wæron. **971** *Blickl. Hom.* 25 Þæt unasecgenlice wræc & þæt unȝeendode wite, þæt þon unlædon þær ȝeteohhod biþ. **13..** *Cursor M.* 890 (Gött.), Til þat worm vr lauerd þan spack wordis bath of wreth and wrack. **1535** STEWART *Cron. Scot.* (Rolls) I. 24 Sic diuisioun may nocht lest rycht lang, But weir and wrak and mekle opin wrang. **1575** TURBERV. *Venerie* 177 And yet can man..Use wracke for rewth! can murder like him best? *c* **1586** C'TESS PEMBROKE *Psalms* LXXVIII. xix, Now pine and paine conspire With angry angells wreak and wrack to frame. **1596** SPENSER *F.Q.* VI. ii. 21 There gan he..with bitter wracke To wreake on me the guilt of his owne wrong. **1863** LONGF. *Wayside Inn, K. Olaf* II. v, Strange memories crowded back Of Queen Gunhild's wrath and wrack. **1870** MORRIS *Earthly Par.* II. III. 516 Will it bring him back To let loose on the country war and wrack?

fig. **1590** SHAKS. *Com. Err.* V. i. 49 Hath he not lost much wealth by wrack of sea?

†**b.** In the phr. *to do* or *take wrack* (*on* one).

12.. *Mem. Ripon* (Surtees) I. 91 Tol Tem Sok et Sak with yryn' and with water deme and do wrak. **1426** LYDG. *De Guil. Pilgr.* 1585 Myn hornys [are made] for to take wrak On shrewes, & to putte abak.

2. Damage, disaster, or injury to a person, state, etc., by reason of force, outrage, or violence; devastation, destruction.

In very frequent use from *c* 1580 to *c* 1640.

c **1407** LYDG. *Reson & Sens.* 5426 The tother [bow], hydouse and ryght blak, Wrought al oonly for the wrak, Ful of knottys. **1412–20** —— *Chron. Troy* I. 2184 For lak of manhod drawiþ hym euer a-bak; He is so dredful and ferful of þe wrak. **1557** *Tottel's Misc.* (Arb.) 188 The golden apple that the Troyan boy Gaue to Venus.., Which was the cause of all the wrack of Troy. **1561** NORTON & SACKV. *Gorboduc* V. ii, Loe, here..the wofull wracke And vtter ruine of this noble realme! **1581** A. HALL *Iliad* VI. 120 On this odde knight alacke We neuer shall set eyes againe, this day wil be his wracke. **1596** SPENSER *F.Q.* IV. ix. 25 Eftsoones the others..on their foes did worke full cruell wracke. **1634** *Malory's Arthur* I. cxxxix. Ff2, If he be angry he wil.. worke you much wrack in this countrey. **1640** T. CAREW *Perswasions to love* 69 Time and age will worke that wrack Which time or age shall ne'er call back. **1659** *Bibliotheca Regia* (title-p.), Such of the Papers..as have escaped the wrack and ruines of these times. **1817** SCOTT *Harold* I. i, When he hoisted his standard black, Before him was battle, behind him wrack. **1853** M. ARNOLD *Sohrab & Rustum* 414 The wind in winter-time Has made in Himalayan forests wrack. **1873** DIXON *Two Queens* I. 122 While the country was a prey to fire and sword, the Church stood high above the wrack and waste.

b. In the phr. *to bring, go, put, run to wrack* (*and ruin*). Also *fig.* Cf. RACK *sb.*[5] 1.

In freq. use, esp. with *go* (*went*), *c* 1560–*c* 1680.

1412 LYDG. *Chron. Troy* Prol. 161 For nere writers, al wer out of mynde, Nat story only, but of nature and kynde The trewe knowyng schulde haue gon to wrak. **1420–2** —— *Thebes* II. 2215 Vpon his foon he rolled it [*sc.* a huge stone] at onys, That ten of hem wenten vnto wrak. **1528** ROY *Rede Me* (Arb.) 41 What dido monkes and fryeres thanne, When masse went thus to wracke? **1540** PALSGR. *Acolastus* III. iii. P iij b, He whose shyppe is gone to wracke. **1581** MARBECK *Bk. of Notes* 70 This Arke..by diuine prouidence..was gouerned from running to wracke. **1591** SPENSER *Tears of Muses* 400 Thy scepter rent, and power put to wrack. **1601** R. JOHNSON *Kingd. & Commw.* (1603) 111 Arezzo beeing by long dissention amongest themselues almost brought to wracke. **1606** G. WOODCOCK *Hist. Ivstine* XVI. 67 The greater part of his army..were all put to wrack. **1667** MILTON *P.L.* VI. 670 And now all Heav'n Had gone to wrack, with ruin overspred. **1692** R. L'ESTRANGE *Josephus, Antiq.* V. ii. (1733) 115 All their Affairs went to wrack upon it. **1757** HUME *Ess. & Treat.* (1777) II. 421 All nature was going to wrack... Gods and men were perishing in one common ruin. **1864** KINGSLEY *Roman & T.* ii. (1875) 31 All things were going to wrack. **1876** BROWNING *Pacchiarotto*, etc. 129 The man but for whom had gone to wrack All that France saved from the fight.

(*b*) **1577** HANMER *Anc. Eccl. Hist.* I. ix. 12 Herod.. supposing..his rule to goe to wracke, and ruine. **1577** H. BULL tr. *Luther's Comm. Ps.* (1615) 287 Whiles all things seeme to fall to wracke and ruine. **1585** ABP. SANDYS *Serm.* 196 Gods familie and the common wealth goe to wracke and ruine.

c. In other phrases, as †*at*, *in wrack*. *rare.*

1592 A. DAY *Eng. Secretorie* I. (1595) 51 When Rome was now at wracke, her Nobilitie spoyled, and her glorie trode vnder foote. **1901** J. BARLOW *Ghost-bereft* 113 Round his gang crashed roof and wall in wrack.

d. *dial.* The brunt or consequences *of* some action. (Cf. RACKET *sb.*[3] 4.)

1844 W. BARNES *Dorset Gloss.* s.v., 'Mind you'll stan' the wrack o't'. **1871–** in south. dial. use (Oxf., Berks., Devon): *Eng. Dial. Dict.* s.v.

3. A disastrous change in a state or condition of affairs; wreck, ruin, subversion. ? *Obs.*

c **1400** *Found. St. Bartholomew's* 49 Where oure dede and purpos ys of the wracke of chastite. **1557** *Tottel's Misc.* (Arb.) 256 A frend no wracke of wealth, no cruell cause of wo, Can force his frendly faith vnfrendly to forgo. **1588** GREENE *Metam.* Wks. (Grosart) IX. 87 Wit oft hath wracke by selfe-conceit of pride. **1591** *2nd Pt. Troubl. Raigne K. John* (1611) 108 What haue I lou'd but wracke of others weale? **1595** MARKHAM *Sir R. Grinvile* (Arb.) 42 The wet worlds sacke Swells in my song, the Dirge for glories wracke. **1601** SHAKS. *All's Well* III. v. 24 The miserie is example, that so terrible shewes in the wracke of maiden-hood. **1692** LOCKE *3rd Let. Toleration* x. 281 Toleration then does not..make that woful wrack on True Religion which you talk of. **1823** SCOTT *Peveril* xxvii, He that serves Peveril munna be slack, Neither for weather, nor yet for wrack. **1862** LYTTON *Strange Story* II. 159 Have all those sound resolutions..melted away in the wrack of haggard dissolving fancies!

†**b.** The ruin, downfall, or overthrow of a person or persons; adversity, misfortune. *Obs.*

1426 LYDG. *De Guil. Pilgr.* 7727 Lat no man..with hys wordys falsly smyte, Malycyously to make wrak Off hys neyhebour. *a* **1578** LINDESAY (Pitscottie) *Chron. Scot.* (S.T.S.) I. 21 Tyrantis settand thair haill purpois and intent vpone mischeiff and wrack of vtheris. *a* **1586** SIDNEY *Astr. & Stella* Sonn. xix, On Cupids bowe, how are my hart strings bent, That see my wracke, and yet imbrace the same? **1595** MARKHAM *Sir R. Grinvile* lvii, To flye from them.. Were to..crush my selfe with shame and seruile wrack. **1625** A. GIL *Sacred Philos.* i. 119 By sinne there was a generall wrack of mankinde. **1667** DENHAM *Direct. Painter* 55 Presuming of his certain wrack, To help him late, they send for Rupert back. *a* **1699** J. BEAUMONT *Psyche* II. cxxxvii, That smooth-tongu'd Gale whose whispers woke That Wrack which stole on me.

II. †**4.** An instance of suffering or causing wreck, ruin, destruction, etc. *Obs.*

1594 KYD *Cornelia* V. i, Amongst so many wracks As I haue suffred both by Land and Sea. **1613** PURCHAS *Pilgrimage* 609 The new Conquerours..by wrackes testified to the earth, that they had wrecked themselues on her and their enemies. **1630** LORD *Banians* 33 Thunder and lightning..such as seemed to threaten a finall wracke to the earth. **1632** HEYWOOD *1st Pt. Iron Age* I. i, Troy was twice rac't, and Troy deseru'd that wracke.

†**b.** A means or cause of subversion, overthrow, or downfall. *Obs.*

1579 GOSSON *Sch. Abuse* (Arb.) 20 The Syrens song is the Saylers wrack. **1593** SHAKS. *2 Hen. VI*, I. ii. 105 And thus I feare at last, Humes Knauerie will be the Duchesse Wracke. *c* **1611** CHAPMAN *Iliad* II. 781 The fool Amphimachus, to field, brought gold to be his wrack. **1613** DAY *Festivals* (1615) ix. 248 How at length might it haue prooved a wrack to his owne Person. **1650** W. BROUGH *Sacr. Princ.* (1659) 183 When shall I be delivered from thee, gaol of my soul, and wrack of my salvation. **1682** COCHRAN in Howie *Cloud of Witnesses* (1778) 199 Jugling with the Lord ..hath been our ruin and wrack.

5. A thing or person in an impaired, wrecked, or shattered condition. (Cf. WRACK *sb.*[2])

a **1586** SIDNEY *Psalms* XXXVII. xv, The mann whom God directs,..Though he doth fall, no wrack he proveth. **1611** SHAKS. *Cymb.* IV. ii. 366 Young one,..who is this Thou mak'st thy bloody Pillow?.. What's thy interest in this sad wracke? *a* **1803** in Child *Ballads* IV. 187/2 O spare me, Clyde's water,..Mak me your wrack as I come back, But spare me as I gae. **1866** GREGOR *Banffshire Gloss.* 204 *Vrack*, ..a broken down person. **1888** *Scot. Sermons* in *Brit. Workman* May, Doon gaed the biggin', and unco wrack.

b. That which remains after the operation of any destructive action or agency; a vestige or trace left by some subversive cause. Also *fig.*

In later use, esp. with *leave*, freq. by misapprehension of Shaks. *Temp.* IV. i. 156, where the reading (altered by Malone to *wrack*) is *racke*: see RACK *sb.*[1] 3 b.

1602 MARSTON *Antonio's Rev.* IV. iv, I am a poore, poore orphant—a weake, weake childe, The wrack of splitted fortune. **1656** COWLEY *Pindar. Odes, Muse* iii. note, Poetry ..makes what Choice it pleases out of the Wrack of Time of things that it will save from Oblivion. **1793** WORDSW. *Evening Walk* 360 No wrack of all the pageant scene remains. **1813** BYRON *Giaour* 1237 The wither'd frame, the ruin'd mind, The wrack by passion left behind. **1878** BOSW. SMITH *Carthage* 406 An ancient seat of civilisation..was swept away at a single stroke, leaving hardly a wrack behind.

†**c.** A damaged or injured part; damage, impairment. Also *fig. Obs.*

1601 DONNE *Progr. Soul* I. vii, This soule which oft did teare And men the wracks of th' Empire. **1610** GUILLIM *Heraldry* III. xvii. 151 With the threeds..[the spider] repaireth all rents and wracks of the same [web]. *Ibid.*, A man carefull of his priuate estate, and of good foresight, in repairing of small decaies and preuenting of wracks. *a* **1631** DONNE *Paradoxes* (1652) 9 We mend the wrack and stains of our apparel.

wrack (ræk), *sb.*[2] Forms: 4–5, *Sc.* 6–7 **wrak**, 5 *Sc.* **wrac**, 6–7 **wracke**, 6– **wrack** (9 *Sc.* **vrack**). [a. MDu. (also mod.Du.) *wrak* neut. (older Flem. *wracke*, Kilian), or MLG. *wrak*, *wrack* (whence G. *wrack*), = MDa. *vrak* (Da. *vrag*) neut., MSw. *vrak* (*wrack*, *wragh*; Sw. *vrak*) neut., Norw. dial. *rak* neut., wreck, wrecked vessel, a parallel formation to OE. *wræc* WRACK *sb.*[1]

Except for its frequent use by southern writers between 1508 and 1690 (cf. the note to WRACK *sb.*[1]), the form is predominantly northern and Scottish.]

1. A wrecked ship or other vessel; a vessel ruined or crippled by wreck. Now *dial.*

c **1386** CHAUCER *Man of Law's T.* 513 The Constable of the Castel down is fare To seen this wrak and al the shipe he soghte. **1626** CAPT. SMITH *Accid. Yng. Seamen* 29 She will ..split or billage on a Rocke, a wracke. **1636** G. SANDYS *Paraphr. Ps.* xlviii. 76 Blacke Eurus roars, And spreads his wracks on Tharsian shores. **1687** A. LOVELL tr. *Thevenot's Trav.* I. 126 Close by shoar we saw the wrack of that Saique, which stranded the same day. **1692** in *Rec. Convent. Burghs Scot.* (1880) IV. 594 His ship become a wrak. **1756** in *Hist. Coll. Essex Inst.* (U.S.A.) V. 158/1 Drowned from the wrack of the sch[ooner]. *Ibid.*, The sea came and washed them over from the said wrack. **1772** ANNE LINDSAY *Auld Robin Gray* v, But hard blew the winds, and his ship was a wrack. **1862** LONGF. *Birds of Passage* II. *The Cumberland* vi, Down went the Cumberland all a wrack. **1905** *Cornh. Mag.* Feb. 209 'Wracks, man,' he shouted,..pointing to the double light-house,..'there is no chance of wracks for a puir fisherbody noo'.

transf. (of persons). **1589** GREENE *Menaphon* (Arb.) 27 Menaphon..espied certain fragments of a broken ship floating vpon the waues, and sundrie persons driuen vpon the shore... These three (as distressed wrackes) preserued by some further forepoynting fate [etc.]. **1594** SHAKS. *Rich III*, I. iv. 24 Me thoughts, I saw a thousand fearfull wrackes: A thousand men that Fishes gnaw'd vpon. **1601** —— *Twel. N.* v. i. 82 That most ingratefull boy.. From the rude seas.. Did I redeeme: a wracke past hope he was.

b. Remnants of, or goods from, a wrecked vessel, esp. as driven or cast ashore; shipwrecked effects or property, wreckage; also in earlier use, the right to have such. Now *arch.*

1428 *Excheq. Rolls Scotl.* IV. 439 Le wrak cujusdam navis combuste infra portum de Leth. **1452** *Reg. Mag. Sig. Scot.* 125/1 Invenerunt dictum forestarium custodem de *Wrac* et *Waif* infra dictum dominium de Coldingham. **1501** *Extr. Aberd. Reg.* (1844) I. 428 Ane brokin schip,..quhilk, throw storme of sey, happin to brek, and the wrak of hir come in on the cost of Croudane. **1584** GREENE *Morando* Wks. (Grosart) III. 84 Tis an ill flaw that bringeth vp no wracke. **1599** SHAKS. *Hen. V*, I. ii. 165 As rich..As is the Owse and bottome of the Sea With sunken Wrack. **1639** in Maitland *Hist. Edinburgh* (1753) II. 151/1 All their antient Rights,.. with Pit and Gallows, Sack and Soke, Thole, Theam, Vert, Wrack, Waifs [etc.]. *a* **1662** HEYLIN *Cosmogr.* I. (1669) 71 Charybdis is a Gulf..which violently attracting all Vessels that come too nigh it, devoureth them, and casteth up their wracks [*ed.* 1652 wrecks]. **1670** DRYDEN *Conq. Granada* IV. i, My own lost Wealth thou giv'st not only back, But driv'st upon my Coast my Pyrat's Wrack. **1759** PHILIPOTT *Villare Cant.* 11 Witsom were goods driven to the shore, when there had not been for some space any wrack visible. **1883** WHITELAW *Sophocles, Antigone* 591 Casting up mire and blackness and storm-vext wrack of the sea. **1897** *Longm. Mag.* Feb. 333 Through the heaped mysteries of waith and wrack, When the long wave from the long beach draws back.

†**c.** *pl.* Fragments of wreckage. Also *fig.* *Obs.*

a **1586** SIDNEY *Arcadia* II. (1912) 350 Who then myselfe should flie So close unto my selfe my wrackes doo lie.

2. The total or partial disablement or destruction of a vessel by any disaster or accident of navigation; = SHIPWRECK *sb.* 2. Now *rare.*

1579 GOSSON *Sch. Abuse* (Arb.) 41, I haue in my voyage suffred wrack with Vlisses. **1590** SPENSER *F.Q.* I. vi. 1 As when a ship..An hidden rocke escaped hath vnwares, That lay in waite her wrack for to bewaile. **1615** G. SANDYS *Trav.* 2 Glad that with wracke of ship, and losse of goods they may prolong a despised life. **1648** G. DANIEL *Eclog* v. 331 In a wracke, wee trust A Sayle-yard, or a Planke of broken Chest, To carrie vs. **1673** DRYDEN *2 Pt. Conq. Granada* (ed. 2) III. 105 As Seamen, parting in a gen'ral wrack, When first the loosening Planks begin to crack Each catches one. **1706** PHILLIPS (ed. Kersey) s.v. *Flotson*, Jetson, or Goods cast out of the Ship, being in danger of Wrack. *a* **1879** H. DEWAR in *Poems of Places, Brit. Amer.* 35 In the wrack tall masts would crack.

b. *fig.* and in fig. context.

1580 H. GIFFORD *Posie of Gilloflowers* (1870) 52 Fell Sathan is chiefe rular of these seas: Hee seekes our wracke, he doth these tempestes rayse. *a* **1586** SIDNEY *Arcadia* v. Wks. 1922 II. 150 Yet being imbarqued in the same ship, the finall wrack must needs be common to them all. **1600** DEKKER *Fortunatus* Wks. 1873 I. 114 Ryot sets up sayles, And..Drives your unsteddie fortunes on the point of wracke inevitable. **1611** SPEED *Hist. Gt. Brit.* VI. lii. §7 When Seas did foame..His force effecting with his cares preuented still my wracke. **1628** FELTHAM *Resolves* II. ii. 5 Hee that steeres by that gale, is euer in danger of wracke. **1649** G. DANIEL *Trinarch., Rich. II*, vii, The greater winds of Faction broke in here, To make a wracke. *a* **1699** J. BEAUMONT *Psyche* I. ccxxxiv, That venturing any longer stay to make, Was but to run upon a certain wrack.

3. Marine vegetation, seaweed or the like, cast ashore by the waves or growing on the tidal seashore. (Cf. WRECK *sb.*[1] 2, VAREC I.)

Also *cart-*, *grass-*, *kelp-*, *lady-*, *sea-wrack*.

In first quot. the precise sense is not quite clear.

1513 DOUGLAS *Æneid* III. ix. 34 Rent me in pecis, and in the fludis swak, Or droun law vndir the large seis wrak. **1551**– [see SEA-WRACK 2]. **1650** [HOWE] *Phytol. Brit.* 101 Divers sorts of Sea-Oake, or Wrack. **1668** WILKINS *Real Char.* 71 Herbs..growing commonly upon Stones and Rocks in the Sea: 14. Wrack. **1700** WALLACE *Descr. Orkney* (1883) 42 *note*, When the sea-weed is driven in greater plenty, all the people..divide the wrack according to the proportion of land they have. **1716** *Petiveriana* I. 159 Full of small seedy Warts as in our common Wrach or *Quercus maritima*. **1785** MARTYN *Lett. Bot.* xxxii. 500 Fucus, Wrack, or Sea-weed properly so called, has two kinds of bladders. **1849** H. MILLER *Footpr. Creat.* i. 10 The shores.. of the lake were strewed..by a line of *wrack*, consisting..of marine plants [etc.]. **1855** KINGSLEY *Glaucus* 57 The purple and olive wreaths of wrack, and bladder-weed, and tangle. **1880** *Antrim & Down Gloss.* 78 The farmers grow sea-weed for manure, cutting the wrack periodically... Stones are placed for the wrack to grow on.

b. Weeds, rubbish, waste, etc., floating on, or washed down or ashore by, a river, pond, or the like; = WRECK *sb.*[1] 2 b.

1598– water-wrack [see WATER *sb.* 29]. **1851** H. STEPHENS *Bk. Farm* (ed. 2) I. 396/2 To prevent the *wrack* floating on the surface of the water finding its way into the sluice. **1865** LIVINGSTONE *Zambesi* i. 14 When we came within five or six miles of the land, the yellowish-green tinge of the sea..was suddenly succeeded by muddy water with wrack, as of a river in flood. *Ibid.*, The wrack, consisting of reeds, sticks and leaves. **1877** V. L. CAMERON *Across Africa* I. 63, I observed wrack of grass and twigs in the branches of small trees.., showing how high the floods..must be at times.

c. Field-weeds, roots of couch-grass or the like, esp. as loosened from the soil to be collected for burning; vegetable rubbish or refuse found on agricultural lands; = WRECK *sb.*[1] 2 c.

1715 PENNECUIK *Tweeddale* 6 [They] will not suffer the *Wrack* to be taken of their Land, because (say they) it keeps the Corn warm. **1825** JAMIESON, *Wrack*, Dog's grass, ..*Triticum repens*, Linn.; Roxb. Perhaps denominated *Wrack*, because..it is harrowed out in the fall, and burnt. **1883** *Longm. Mag.* April 658 Seed has to be sown, turnips have to be thinned and hoed..and 'wrack' gathered. **1894** HESLOP *Northumb. Gloss.* 799 *Wrack*, weeds; especially 'whickens' and sea-weed.

4. *attrib.* and *Comb.*, as †***wrack-ship*** (= sense 1); †***wrack-rich***; ***wrack-threatened***, ***-threatening***; also †**wrackfree**, = WRECKFREE *a.*; †**wrack-goods** [cf. Du. *wrakgoederen*, G. *wrackgut*] *Scots Law*, = sense 1 b; **wrack-spangle** *local* (see quot. 1856).

1570 in W. Boys *Hist. Sandwich* (1792) 775 Savyng that we shalbe wrakfree of oure owne goodes whatsoever. **1594** SHAKS. *Lucr.* 590 All which together like a troubled Ocean, Beat at thy rockie, and wracke-threatning heart. **1598** J. DICKENSON *Greene in Conc.* (1878) 138 More deafe..then are the wrack-rich Libique rocks. **1603** J. DAVIES (Heref.) *Microcosmos* Wks. (Grosart) I. 38/2 A Sternelesse Shippe.. On mightiest Seas, wrack-threatn'd on each syde. **1671** *Shetland Docum.* in *Proc. Soc. Ant. Scot.* (1892) XXVI. 194 To..secure all wrack and waith goods. **1681** STAIR *Instit.* vii. 76 Our Custome agrees with..other Nations, except in the Matter of waith and wrack Goods. **1693** *Ibid.* (ed. 2) III. iii. 420 Where the Wrack ship is, the Owner may be known by Writs in the Ship. **1706** PHILLIPS (ed. Kersey), *Wrecfry*, ..wrack-free, exempt or freed from the forfeiture of Shipwracked Goods and Vessels to the King. **1856** *Househ. Words* 8 Nov. 391/1 Wrack-spangle, the popular name of these things, implies that they deck the sea-weeds as spangles adorn robes. The savans call them Serpulæ.

wrack (ræk), *sb.*[3] Also 5, 6 *Sc.* **wrak**, 6 **wracke**, 9 *Sc.* **vrack**. [a. (M)LG. or Du. *wrak* (whence MHG. and G. dial. *wrack* refuse, rubbish, Da. *vrag*, Sw. *vrak*, refuse); see also WRAKE *sb.*[3], WRECK *sb.*[2], and cf. WRACK *a.*]

1. That which is of an inferior, poor, or worthless quality; waste material; rubbish. Now *rare.*

1472–5 *Rolls of Parlt.* VI. 156/1 Such [bowstaves] as were called the wrak, not goode ne able to make of but Childern' Bowes. **1492–3** *Durham Acc. Rolls* (Surtees) 249 Reparaciones [on a mill];..pro cariagio le remell et wrak a scaccario usque Viram. **1542–3** *Act 34 & 35 Hen. VIII*, c. 9 §4 That no persone or persones doo caste or unlade out of any maner of Ship..any maner of Balaste rubbishe gravell or any other wracke or filthe, but oonelie upon the Lande. **1866** GREGOR *Banffshire Gloss.* 204 *Vrack*, anything worthless. *Ibid.*, 'His nout's jist mere vrack.' **1885** *Pall Mall G.* 27 March 4 They send anything—the very wrack of towns—instead of the valuable agricultural labourer which we want.

†**b.** *Sc.* ***world's wrack***, earthly 'pelf' or 'dross'; worldly possessions, goods, or gear. *Obs.*

c **1480** HENRYSON *Swallow & Birds* 307 (Bann.), Our wickit ennemye..evir is reddye, Quhen wretchis in þis warldis wrak do scraip, To draw his nett. **1500–20** DUNBAR *Poems* xxiii. 10 For warldis wrak but weilfair nocht awailis. *a* **1568** in *Bannatyne MS.* (Hunter. Cl.) 223 Quhill..stuffit weill with warldis wrak, Amang my freindis I wes weill kend. *a* **1586** in *Maitland Fol. MS.* (S.T.S.) 241 Now he hes gold and warldis wrak lyand him besyd. **1792** BURNS *My Wife's a winsome wee thing* iv, The warld's wrack we share o't, The warstle and the care o't.

2. An inferior grade of flax. Also *attrib.*

1879 J. PATON in *Encycl. Brit.* IX. 298/1 Of the lower qualities of Riga flax the following may be named:—Wrack flax, White picked wrack,..Picked wrack flax. *Ibid.*, The lowest quality of Riga flax is..Dreiband Wrack.

wrack, freq. erron. f. RACK *sb.*[1] 3, 3 b.

1794 MRS. PIOZZI *Synon.* II. 397 Observing how the wrack rides before the wind. **1848** LYTTON *Harold* v. i, The smoke rises..to join the wrack of clouds. **1878** H. S. WILSON *Alpine Ascents* ii. 57 A filmy wrack wreathes round and upward.

wrack, erron. f. RACK *sb.*[3] 1, 1 b, 1 c.

1591 SHAKS. *1 Hen. VI*, II. v. 3 Euen like a man new haled from the Wrack, So fare my Limbes with long Imprisonment. **1666** *Boyle's Orig. Forms & Qual.* a 2 Mystical Notions, which put the Understanding upon the Wrack. **1866** SWINBURNE *Poems & Ballads* 306 For the pure sharpness of her miseries She had no heart's pain, but mere body's wrack.

wrack, erron. f. RACK *sb.*[6]

1829 H. MURRAY *N. America* II. III. iv. 442 They abhor a trot, and instruct the animal only in a pace and a wrack.

†**wrack**, *a.* *Obs. rare.* Also 4 **wrac**, 6 *Sc.* **wrak**. [a. MLG. *wrak*, *wrack*, LG. *wrak* (whence G. dial. *wrack* worthless, Sw. *vrak-*, Da. *vrag-*), or MDu. *wrac*, *wrak* (Kilian *wrack*, *wraeck*, Du. *wrak*), OFris. *wrak*, *wrac* base (WFris. *wrak* shaky): cf. WRACK *sb.*[3]]

1. Of persons: Worthless, base, evil.

c **1375** *Kindheit Iesu* 315 in Horstm. *Altengl. Leg.* (1875) 12 Bote a giw of heorte wrac Alle hise lawes þare he to brac.

2. Damaged, impaired, injured; unsound.

1487 *Cely Papers* (Camden) 164, iiij last heryng, iij wrack & on rooue; the wrack cost viij[li] & the roue ix[li]. **1496–7** *Rec. St. Mary at Hill* (1905) 32 Item, a diaper clothe, wrack, content in lengthe iij yardes di. **1584** *Burgh Rec. Edinb.* (1882) IV. 343 To devyde the guid and sufficient fische fra the wrak and evill.

†**wrack**, *v.*[1] *Obs.* Forms: 3 **wracken**, 4–5 **wrak**, 6 **wracke**. [Irreg. var. of WREAK *v.* Cf. *brack*, *brak*, for BREAK *v.*]

1. *trans.* To avenge or revenge (a person, deed, etc.); to punish. Also const. *on.*

c **1205** LAY. 20256 Baldulf..þencheð in þissere nihte to slæn þe..to wracken his broðer. *a* **1300** *Body & Soul* in *Map's Poems* (Camden) 338 Merci criende lutel availede, ȝwan Crist it wolde so harde wrac. [**1871** WADDELL *Psalm* xviii. 47 The God wha wracks a' right for me.]

2. To give vent to or wreak (spite, malice, etc.).

1635 J. HAYWARD tr. *Biondi's Banish'd Virg.* 199 The King went to wrack his spite on their corpes. **1644** J. FARY *Gods Severity* (1645) 21 You..must needs wrack your malice by revenge. **1720** PRIOR *Cupid Mistaken* iii, Couldst thou find none other, To wrack [*ed.* 1709 wreck] thy spleen on?

wrack (ræk), *v.*[2] Now *arch.* or *dial.* Also 5–7 **wracke**, 6–7 *Sc.* **wrak**, 9 **rack**. [f. WRACK *sb.*[2] Cf. WRECK *v.*[1]]

†**1.** *intr.* To suffer or undergo shipwreck. *Obs.*

1470–85 MALORY *Arthur* VIII. xxxviii. 331 One told hym there was a knyghte of kyng Arthur þ[a]t had wrackyd on the rockes. **1596** [A. MUNDAY] tr. *Sylvain's Orator* 333 The ship happened to wracke, so that the poore man and his daughter saued themselues in a little Island. *a* **1620** J. DYKE *Sel. Serm.* (1640) 146 When a Shippe wrackes at Sea, the goods are utterly lost. **1632** SANDERSON *Serm.* 56 We may..cast our wares into the Sea, to lighten the ship that it wracke not.

fig. and in fig. context. *a* **1592** GREENE *Alcida* (1617) C 1 b, Thus selfe-loue..Makes beautie wracke against an ebbing tide. **1596** BP. ANDREWES *Serm.* (1629) 327 Their Love hath wracked, and from kind love, beene turned to deadly hate. **1616** B. JONSON *Forrest* iii. 95 God wisheth none should wracke on a strange shelfe. **1622** BACON *Hen. VII*, 223 Sir, you haue beene saued vpon my coast, I hope you will not suffer mee to wrack vpon yours.

2. *trans.* To wreck (a vessel, mariners, etc.); to ruin or cast ashore by shipwreck. Chiefly *pass.*

1562 A. BROOKE *Romeus & Jul.* 1368 Driuen hard vpon the bare and wrackfull shore, In greater daunger to be wract, then he had been before. **1593** MARLOWE *Edw. II*, II. ii, I feare me he is wrackt vpon the sea. **1596** BACON *Max. & Use Com. Law* I. (1636) 44 Goods wrackt..shall be preserved to the use of the owner. **1614** RALEIGH *Hist-World* III. (1634) 86 They pursuing the victorie, had left part of the fleet..to save those that were wrackt. **1683** *Brit. Spec.* 86 Most of the Fleet, wrackt that Night by a sudden Tempest, lay split on the Shore. **1699** T. ALLISON *Voy. Archangel* 22 Putting provision therein for subsistance, in case we should be forced ashore and wracked. **1755** JOHNSON. **1838** J. F. COOPER *Homeward Bound* xxiv, I esteem it a great privilege ..to have the honour of being *wracked*..in such company. *Ibid.*, If she [the ship] had been honorably and fairly wracked. **1871** PALGRAVE *Lyr. Poems* 19 The seas..With outstretch'd angry arms..Wracking whole fleets in pride like riven toys.

fig. and in fig. context. **1583** GREENE *Mamillia* Wks (Grosart) II. 193 A professed Curtizan, whose honestie and credit is so wracked in the waues of wantonnesse. *Ibid.* 242 No..tempests of aduersitie shal..wracke my fancie against the slipperie rockes of inconstancie. **1594** *Selimus* G 3 b, My feeble barke,..while thy foamie floud doth it immure, Shall soon be wrackt vpon the sandie shallowes. **1598–9** B. JONSON *Case Altered* II. vii, O! in what tempests do my fortunes saile, Still wrackt with winds more foule and contrary, Then any other northern guest. **1670** DRYDEN *1st Pt. Conq. Granada* III. (1672) 23 Though wrack'd and lost, My Ruines stand to warn you from the Coast. *a* **1699** J. BEAUMONT *Psyche* I. ccxvii, Till miserably wrack'd, most woful she Quite sinks in this self-torments monstrous Sea. [**1897** W. BEATTY *Secretar* x. 77 The wind that drave them ..was the same that had wracked..Darnley, and Bodwell.]

3. To cause the ruin, downfall, or subversion of (a person, etc.); to ruin, overthrow. Also *refl.*

1564 QUEEN MARY in *Reg. Privy Council Scot.* XIV. 201 Seing the puir men, awnaris of the saidis ship and guidis, ar ..uterlie heriit and wrakkit. **1567** *Gude & Godlie B.* (S.T.S.) 186 Suppose we suld wrack [**1621** wrake] our self, and tyne The feild, and all our kin be hangit syne. *a* **1586** SIDNEY *Ps.* XLI. iv, Now he is wrackt, say they, loe their he lies. **1604** A. CRAIG *Poet. Ess.* A 4, When Troy was wrackt, ..He came... Yet sayd he nought. **1628** PRYNNE *Love-lockes* 59 Externall Beautie..betrays and wrackes the Soules of many. **1792** BURNS '*What can a young lassie*' iv, I'll cross him, and wrack him, until I heart-break him. **1810** in R. H. Cromek *Remains* 27 He'll dance wi' ye, 'O'er Bogie', Maiden, and wrack ye.

refl. **1595** DANIEL *Civ. Wars* III. xvi. 47 b, That weake, and enuied if they should conspire They wracke themselues, and he hath his desire.

b. To render useless by breaking, shattering, etc.; to injure or spoil severely; to destroy.

1587 FLEMING *Contn. Holinshed* III. 1310/2 In the towne of Bedford the water came vp to the market place..; their fewell, corne and haie was wrackt & borne awaie. *a* **1593** MARLOWE *Dido* I. i, Of them all scarce seuen [ships] doe anchor safe, And they so wrackt and weltred by the waues [etc.]. *a* **1678** MARVELL *Bermudas* 9 Where he the huge Sea-Monsters wracks, That lift the Deep upon their Backs. **1817** SHELLEY *Rev. Islam* VII. xxxviii, As if the world's wide continent Had fallen in universal ruin wracked. **1845** MRS. S. C. HALL *Whiteboy* vi. 56 The [castle]..is wracked by the Saxon's breath. **1899** S. MACMANUS *Chimney Corners* 252 His queeny bee..was wrackin' an' ruinin' all afore her.

transf. *a* **1586** SIDNEY *Astr. & Stella* Sonn. lxvii, Doth Stella now beginne with pitteous eye The raigne of this her conquest to espie? Will she take time before all wracked be? **1594** SHAKS. *Rich. III*, IV. i. 97 Eightie odde yeeres of sorrow haue I seene, And each howres ioy wrackt with a weeke of teene. **1648** J. BEAUMONT *Psyche* III. cxxxii, The Precedent may dangerous prove, and wrack Thy Throne and Kingdome.

4. *intr.* To undergo ruin or subversion.

a **1586** SIDNEY *Ps.* XXXVII. xviii, [Those] who be swarved To ill, both they and theirs shall wrack. **1599** SANDYS *Europæ Spec.* (1632) 191 Ayde..without which the whole Empire were in daunger of wracking. *a* **1600** MONTGOMERIE *Misc. Poems* xlvi. 56, I smore if I conceill, I wrak if I reveill, My hurt. **1607** J. CARPENTER *Plaine Mans Plough* 89 What gaine these..when they..themselves remaine castawayes, wracking in the depth of hell.

Hence **'wracking** *vbl. sb.* and *ppl. a.*

1611 COTGR., *Ruinement*, a ruining, *wracking, spoyling. **1642** VICARS *God in Mount* 13 The utter wracking and worrying of the..holy lambes of Christ. **1611** COTGR., *Naufrageux*, *wracking, shipwrack-bringing.

†**wrack**, *v.*[3] *Sc. Obs.* [ad. MLG. *wracken* (whence G. *wracken* to sort), to reject, refuse, var. of *wraken*, WRAKE *v.*[3]] *trans.* = WRAKE *v.*[3]

1609 in *Rec. Convent. Burghs Scot.* (1870) II. 284 Ilk last vesetit urackit, jadget and brunt be thame [*sc.* inspectors]. **1611** *Ibid.* 326 Anent the mater of the hering and barrells thairof, sufficiencie of pakking and wrakking of the same.

†**wrack**, *v.*[4] *Obs.*$^{-1}$ (? ad. Du. *wraken* to make leeway. Cf. G. *wrak, waking*, leeway.)

1635 L. FOXE in *North-West Fox* 180 In that distance holding the same course, I had 2 deg. 14 min. to wracke upon, and within one point at most of my paralell.

wrack, freq. erron. f. RACK *v.*[3]

1553-5 LATIMER in Strype *Eccl. Mem.* (1721) III. App. xxxv. 98 The Martyrs in the old Time were wracked. **1622** FLETCHER *Sea Voy.* I. i, The Money I ha wrackt by usury. *a* **1637** B. JONSON *Discov.* Wks. (1641) 118 Doubtfull writing hath wrackt mee beyond my patience. **1674** N. FAIRFAX *Bulk & Selv.* To Rdr., As the one had wrackt and limm'd my thoughts, with endless tenters. **1683** CAVE *Ecclesiastici, Eusebius* 33 The Church rather expounds the Opinion..into a favourable sence, than nicely weighs and wracks their words. **1720** WELTON *Suffer. Son of God* II. xiv. 370 What great Concern wracks the Spirit of a faithful Servant of God. **1721** STRYPE *Eccl. Mem.* II. II. xiv. 353 Landlords had now so wracked their rents. **1756** *Monitor* No. 72 II. 197 If they wrack their brains..to find out [etc.]. **1785** BURNS *Scotch Drink* i, Let..Crabbit names an' stories wrack us, An' grate our lug. **1895** PARKHURST in *Advance* (Chicago) 7 Mar. 808/2 Sin..wracks the machinery of the mind. **1898** *Daily News* 31 Aug. 5/3 They themselves are wracking their busy brains.

absol. **1607** SHAKS. *Cor.* V. i. 16 A paire of Tribunes, that haue wrack'd for Rome, To make Coales cheape.

wracked (rækt), *ppl. a.* [f. WRACK *v.*[2] + -ED[1].] That has undergone or suffered wreck, esp. shipwreck; ruined, destroyed.

1581 A. HALL *Iliad* I. 15 Yeelding the Greekes a thorough feare, the Troyans courage hie, So that the wracked Campe restore his credite worthilie. **1608** SYLVESTER *Du Bartas* II. iv. *Schisme* 371 A hundred Prophets..from sad drowning keep The wracked planks on th' Idol-Ocean deep. **1648** J. BEAUMONT *Psyche* IV. lxxxv, When Ioe an angry Sea..on its proud waves bears In dreadfull triumph a wrack'd Man. **1652** NEEDHAM tr. *Selden's Mare Cl.* 157 Those wrack't goods that had been seized by the Receivers of his Customs. **1747** *New Canto Spenser's F.Q.* xxiii, The wrack'd Merchant, now secure, from Shore Looks back with Dread on all his Perils past. **1864** MRS. LLOYD *Ladies Polc.* 17 Every body's troubles is her troubles, from a wracked boat to a broken putcher! **1875** MORRIS *Æneid* IX. 263 Two cups ..which my father took from wracked Arisbe's hold.

wracked, erron. f. RACKED *ppl. a.*[3]

1606 SYLVESTER *Du Bartas* II. iv. *Tropheis* 823 Hee makes th' whole Kingdom's wracked ribs to meet. **1656** COWLEY *Davideis* III. 683 Merab rejoyc'd in her wrackt Lovers pain. *a* **1699** J. BEAUMONT *Psyche* X. ccxxxiv, New fear Stormed their wracked Souls. **1974** *Times Lit. Suppl.* 19 Apr. 417/4 Lowry could be sodden, sullen, wracked with shame and remorse: a figure of total anguish. **1974** A. DAVIS *Autobiography* IV. 279 During the few months of our friendship, I don't think I realized how wracked he must have been by that decade of accumulated frustrations, by that terrible sense of impotence.

wracker[1] ('rækə(r)). *rare.* [f. WRACK *v.*[2] + -ER[1].] One who wrecks, ruins, or subverts.

1611 COTGR., *Ruineur*, a ruiner, wracker, spoyler.

†**wracker**[2]. *Obs. rare.* [f. WRACK *v.*[3] + -ER[1], or ad. MLG. *wraker* (whence Da. *vrager* sorter).] = WRAKER.

1584 [see WRAKER]. **1719** in *Rec. Convent. Royal Burghs Scot.* (1885) V. 217 By means of wrackers of herrings to be imported there. *Ibid.*, To appoint..ane overseer of these wrackers.

wracker[3] ('rækə(r)). *rare.* [f. WRACK *sb.*[2] 3 + -ER[1] 1. Cf. VRAICKER.] One who collects wrack, vraic, or seaweed.

1833 *Fraser's Mag.* VII. 293 The Norman wrackers, as they gathered sea-weed on the beach.

wracker, obs. var. RACKER[1].

1736 AINSWORTH I, *Contortor*,..a wracker, or wrester.

†**'wrackful**, *a.*[1] *Obs.* Also 3 wracful, 4 wrakful, 5 -fulle. [f. WRACK *sb.*[1] + -FUL.] Characterized by resentment or anger; vengeful, angry.

c **1230** [implied in next]. **13..** *E.E. Allit. P.* B. 302 Now God in nwy to Noe con speke Wylde wrakful wordez. *Ibid.* 541 Suche a wrakful wo for wlatsum dedez Parformed þe hyȝe fader. ? *a* **1400** *Morte Arth.* 3818 He wente at the gayneste, Wondis of thas wedirwyns with wrakfulle dynttys.

Hence †**'wrackfully** *adv.*, vengefully. *Obs.*

c **1230** *Hali Meid.* 41 Hwen godd se wracfulliche fordemde his heh engel.

†**'wrackful**, *a.*[2] *Obs. rare.* In 4 wrecful. [OE. *wræcful*, f. *wræc* WRACK *sb.*[1] + -FUL.] Full of misery; wretched.

c **1311** in Wright *Pol. Songs* (Camden) 256 For wille is red, the lond is wrecful; For wit is qued, the lond is wrongful.

'wrackful, *a.*[3] Now *arch.* and *rare.* [f. WRACK *sb.*[2] + -FUL.]

1. Causing shipwreck; wreckful.

1558 PHAER *Æneid* II. 64 To Syllas wrackfull shore with shypps approche we nye. **1583** MELBANCKE *Philotimus* T iv b, That..shears the fruitles sande with wrakfull waues. **1591** SYLVESTER *Du Bartas* I. ii. 353 To stand still firm against the roaring noise Of wrackfull Neptune. **1612** DRAYTON *Poly-olb.* i. 326 Where king Latinus lent safe harbor for his Ships, with wrackfull tempests rent. **1623** DRUMM. OF HAWTH. *Flowres of Sion* xii. 6 These Lockes, of blushing deedes the gilt attire, Waues curling, wrackfull shelfes to shadow deepe. **1633** T. BANCROFT *Gluttons Feauer* F 2 b, A Vessell, neare some wrackfull strand.

2. Causing destruction or devastation; effecting damage or harm; destructive.

1578 *Mirr. Mag.* 23 b, Then my delight was in the diery dent Of wrackful warre. **1594** CAREW *Tasso* (1881) 24 Eu'n so the king of streames..Beyond his banckes abroad all wrackfull goes. *c* **1600** SHAKS. *Sonn.* lxv. 6 O how shall summers hunny breath hold out Against the wrackfull siedge of battring dayes? **1633** T. BANCROFT *Gluttons Feauer* B 6 Cracke all mine arteries with tortures tride, Yet must more stormes, more wrackfull woes abide? **1921** *Chambers's Jrnl.* Jan. 50/1 A people that..has not had its mind and feelings warped by that wrackful war.

3. Subject to, attended by, injury, harm, etc.

1581 T. HOWELL *Deuises* B iv, To shunne the sheete of shame, Which had bewrapt her wrackfull blemisht name. **1612** J. DAVIES (Heref.) *Muses Sacr.* Wks. (Grosart) II. 82/1 This Life, a Way; (a wrackfull way) that Wisedome lothes to proue. **1811** SCOTT *Don Roderick* III. vi, What wanton horrors marked their wrackful path!

wracking, erron. f. RACKING *vbl. sb.*[3] (also *attrib.*).

1676 *Lond. Gaz.* No. 1083/1 Certain Instruments..made use of for the wracking of Criminals. **1688** HOLME *Armory* III. 311/1 A Wracking Plank, with a Rowling Wheel of so many Spokes. **1803** W. BLAKE *'I saw a Monk'* ii, Voltaire [arose] with a wracking wheel.

wracking, erron. f. RACKING *ppl. a.*[1] 2.

1749 *Milton's P.L.* (ed. Newton) II. 182 We perhaps.. shall be hurl'd Each on his rock transfix'd, the sport and prey Of wracking whirlwinds. **1837** CARLYLE *Misc. Ess.*, *Mirabeau*, The sport of wracking winds.

wrack-rider. *north. dial.* Also rack-. (See quots.)

1794 HUTCHINSON *Hist. Cumbld.* I. 460 [The] Brandling ..is the Rackrider of the county of Durham, and the Samlet. **1825** BROCKETT *N.C. Words*, *Wrack*, or *Wrackrider*,..the same species of trout as the brandling.

†**'wracksome**, *a. Obs. rare*$^{-1}$. [f. WRACK *v.*[2] + -SOME[1].] Destructive.

1584 HUDSON *Du Bartas' Judith* II. 361 Then mine not you their towers and tourets tall, Nor bring the wracksom engine to their wall.

wrackstaff, obs. erron. form of RACK-STAFF.

1706 E. WARD *Hud. Rediv.* I. xii. 6 If he eat Nothing but Wrack-staves for his Meat.

wrae, Sc. var. WRO *sb.*

wræcche, obs. var. WRETCH.

wræstlen, obs. f. WRESTLE *v.*

wræð, obs. pa. t. of WRITHE; obs. var. WROTH *a.*

W.R.A.F. Also **WRAF** and (*colloq.*) **Waf** (ræf). [f. initial letters of its name.] The Women's Royal Air Force (1918–20, reformed 1949), the women's corps of the Royal Air Force; also, a member of this.

1918 *Times* 3 Apr. 4/4 No women for the 'mobile' branch will be enrolled at present. Candidates for posts as officers should apply to the W.R.A.F. Inquiry Office,..Strand. **1921** *Spectator* 4 June 719/2 Sketches with pen and pencil of the duties of the 'Wrafs'. **1955** *Times* 23 May 6/6 Five women holding W.R.A.F. commissions, all with university degrees, are serving as technical officers in the R.A.F. **1977** *R.A.F. News* 11–24 May 2/5 A charity disco at Newton enabled the WRAF girls there to raise £58. **1983** *Daily Tel.* 22 Aug. 8/5 Dame Felicity Peake was director of the WRAF from its inception in 1949.

wrag, obs. erron. f. RAG *sb.*[2] 2.

1844 *Civil Eng. & Arch. Jrnl.* VII. 63/1 Two stone offices ..formed of Kentish wrag ashlar.

†**wrag**, *v. Obs. rare*$^{-1}$. [Of imitative origin. Cf. WRAGGLE *v.*[1]] *intr.* To struggle or strive; to resist. Hence **wragging** *vbl. sb.*

a **1275** *Ancr. R.* (MS. Cleopatra C. VI) fol. 173 b, For þeo ȝet [*sic*] fondunges..waggeð oðer hwiles, & [heo] mote wresten aȝein wið strong wraggunge.

wrag, erron. f. RAG *v.*[2]

1841 J. BLACKWOOD in Mrs. Oliphant *Blackwood & Sons* (1898) II. 261, I do not forget to wrag the Doctor on this subject.

†**wragged**, obs. erron. f. RAGGED (rough).

c **1600** SHAKS. *Sonn.* vi, Then let not winters wragged hand deface, In thee thy summer ere thou be distil'd.

†**'wragger.** *Obs.* Also **wrager.** [Cf. WRAG *v.*] One who wrangles.

c **1460** *Towneley Myst.* xii. 58 Both bosters and bragers god kepe vs fro;..Sich wryers and wragers gose to and fro For to crak. *Ibid.* xxx. 143 A bag full..Of Wraggers and wrears, a bag full of brefes, Of carpars and cryars [etc.].

†**'wraggle**, *v.*[1] *Obs. rare.* In 3 wragel-, 6 *Sc.* **wraggil, wraigle,** 7 **wragle.** [See WRAG *v.* and -LE, and cf. WFris. *wraggelje* to waddle, LG. dial. *wraggeln* to wiggle, to wriggle.]

1. *intr.* To struggle or strive; to resist. Hence **'wraggling** *vbl. sb.*

a **1225** *Ancr. R.* 374 þe oðer bitternesse is bitternesse in wrastlunge, & in wragelunge aȝean uondunges. *Ibid.*, For þe ȝet [*sic*] fondunges, þet beoð þe deofles swenges, waggeð oðer hwules, & [heo] moten wresten aȝean mid stronge wragelunge.

2. To wriggle. Hence **'wraggling** *ppl. a.*

1508 DUNBAR *Flyting* 195 Wan wraiglane [*Maitl.* wraggilland] wasp! **1602** MIDDLETON *Blurt, Master Constable* C 2, I strugled and stragled, and wrigled and wragled.

'wraggle, *v.*[2] (See quot. and cf. RAGGLE *v.*)

1875 GILLIES in *Trans. N.Z. Inst.* (1876) VIII. 246, I could make out two or three holes..where the silk lining.. was raised and wraggled.

wraggle-taggle, var. RAGGLE-TAGGLE *a.* and *sb.*

wragh, obs. var. WRATH *sb.*; var. WRAW *a.*

Freq. in the Egerton and Harleian copies of the *E.E. Psalter*, e.g. ii. 13, xvii. 9, lix. 1, lxxiii. 1.

†**wragland.** *Obs. rare.* [Of obscure origin. Perh. merely a var. of the erroneous form *wranglan(d)* cited s.v. WRANLONS; but cf. WRAGGLE *v.*[1]]

1. (See quot. and cf. WRANLONS.)

1611 COTGR., *Raboudris*, wraglands; crooked, or misgrowne trees which will neuer proue timber.

2. (See quot. and cf. WRECKLING.)

1611 COTGR., *Rabougrir*,..to wax mishapen, or imperfect of shape; to become a wragland, or grub.

wrah, variant of WRAW *a. Obs.*

wraht, var. *wrought*: see WORK *v.*

wrai(e, wraier, varr. WRAY(ER *Obs.*

†**wrain-bolt**, variant of RING-BOLT. Also †**wrain-stave**, a staff for inserting in an eye of this.

1750 BLANCKLEY *Naval Expos.* 17 *Wrain Bolts.* [Each] has a ring at one End for a Staff to go through, [etc.]. *Ibid.* 190 *Wrain Staves* are a Sort of thick Billets, tapered so at each End that they may go into the Ring of the Wrain Bolt. [Hence in Rees' *Cycl.* (1819), Young *Naut. Dict.* (1846), Smyth *Sailor's Word-bk.* (1867), etc.]

Hence †**'wraining-bolt, -staff.** *Obs.*$^{-1}$

1769 FALCONER *Dict. Marine* (1776), *Antoit*, a crooked instrument of iron, used to bind the side-planks round the timbers in ship-building. The English artificers perform this operation by wraining-bolts and staffs.

wraist(e, obs. variants of WREST *sb.*[1], *a.*, and *v.*

wrait, obs. or Sc. pa. t. of WRITE *v.*

wraith (reɪθ), *sb.* Orig. (and chiefly) *Sc.* Also 6 **wrath, wrayth, wraithe,** 7 **wreath.** [Of obscure origin.]

1. a. An apparition or spectre of a dead person; a phantom or ghost.

1513 DOUGLAS *Æneid* X. x. 112 Nor ȝit na vane wrathis nor gaistis quent Thi char constrenyt for to went. *Ibid.* xi. 93 In diuers placis The wraithis walkis of goistis that ar deyd. *a* **1585** POLWART *Flyting w. Montgomerie* 658 Thy speach.. is espyed, That wrytes of witches, warlocks, wraiths, and wratches. **1786** BURNS *'When Guilford good'* viii, Chatham's wraith, in heavenly graith,..cry'd, 'Willie, rise!' **1808** SCOTT *Marm.* VI. Introd. 146 In realms of death Ulysses meets Alcides' wraith. **1861** E. S. KENNEDY in *Peaks, Passes & Glaciers* Ser. II. I. 170 She..died broken-hearted... Afterwards, in the still of the evening,..the damsel's wraith would enter the dairy department. **1866** ALGER *Solit. Nat. & Man* IV. 288 While Winander, Fairfield and Rydal remain, to all visionary minds his [*sc.* Wordsworth's] wraith will haunt them. **1893** T. E. BROWN *Old John*, etc. 44 While I.. Drift vaporous to the ancient sea, A wraith, a film, a memory. **1900** A. UPWARD *E. Lobb* 226 Tall, pale and hollow-eyed, with gaunt cheek-bones, .. like a wraith from an extinct world.

fig. **1880** G. MACDONALD *Diary Old Soul* Feb. ix, Duty's firm shape thins to a misty wraith.

b. An immaterial or spectral appearance of a living being, freq. regarded as portending that person's death; a fetch.

1513 DOUGLAS *Æneid* x. xi. 127 Thydder went this wrath or schaddo of Ene. **1597** JAS. VI *Dæmonol.* III. i. 60 These kindes of spirites, when they appeare in the shaddow of a person .. to die, to his friendes, .. are called Wraithes in our language. **1691** R. KIRK *Secr. Commonwealth* i. §7. 18 What the Low-countrey Scotts calls a Wreath, and the Irish *Taibhshe* or Death's Messenger. **1772–3** R. FERGUSSON *To Mem. Dr. W. Wilkie* 35, I dream't yestreen his deadly wraith I saw Gang by my ein as white's the driven snaw... I kent that it forespak approachin' wae. **1802** SCOTT *Minstr. Scott. Bord.* I. p. cxxxvi, The wraith .. of a person shortly to die, is a firm article in the creed of Scotish superstition. **1824** MRS. GRANT in *Mem. & Corr.* (1844) III. 66 A wraith .. is the shadowy likeness of an absent living person. **1838** LYTTON *Alice* XI. ii, As the shape of the warning wraith haunts the mountaineer. **1870** MYERS *Poems* 92 She and her love,—how dimly has she seen him Dark in a dream and windy in a wraith! **1871** TYLOR *Prim. Cult.* I. 404 This is well-shown by the reception not only of a theory of ghosts, but of a special doctrine of 'wraiths' or 'fetches'.

transf. **1849** C. BRONTE *Shirley* xvii, An opposition procession was there entering, headed also by men in black. .. 'Is it our double?' asked Shirley: 'our manifold wraith?'

fig. **1850** TENNYSON *In Mem.* lxxii. 13 O hollow wraith of dying fame, Fade wholly, while the soul exults.

c. Without article.

1884 E. GURNEY in *19th Cent.* 796 The coincidences of death and wraith are due to chance. **1898** H. NEWBOLT *Island Race* p. x, O Strength divine of Roman days, O Spirit of the Age of Faith, Go with our sons on all their ways When we long since are dust and wraith.

2. A water-spirit.

1742, etc. [see WATER *sb.* 24q]. **1801** M. G. LEWIS *Bothwell's Bonny Jane* ii, I hear, with mournful yell, The wraiths of angry Clyde complain. **1832** J. BREE *St. Herbert's Isle* 132 Wraiths and warlocks by the rush-grown mere. **1854** H. MILLER *Sch. & Schm.* x. (1858) 203 Highlanders .. cutting down their corn, when the boding voice of the wraith was heard.

3. An appearance or configuration suggestive of a wraith or spectre.

1882 WHITTIER *Storm on Lake Asquam* iii, A fire-veined darkness swept Over the .. range; A wraith of tempest, .. From peak to peak the cloudy giant stepped. **1912** L. TRACY *Mirabel's Isl.* i, Through the wraiths of scud he thought he had seen something.

4. *attrib.* and *Comb.*, as ***wraith-land***, ***-seeing***, ***-ship***, ***-spell***; ***wraith-like*** adj.

1756 *Yorkshire diary* in *N. & Q.* (1922) 390/2 For the warding off of all things whatsoever from the dead—be they imps, wraithspells, wick things and the like ket. **1865** J. YOUNG *Homely Pictures* 126 Their leggies gat wraith-like, their cheekies gat death-like. **1871** TYLOR *Prim. Cult.* I. 405 In Silesia and the Tyrol the gift of wraith-seeing still flourishes. **1893** *Columbus* (Ohio) *Dispatch* 27 Apr., What challenges are prompted to the great .. to come from their wraithlands! **1924** V. F. BOYSON *Falkland Islands* viii. 181 Dimly as she came, so she passed away, as though in very truth the wraithship said to appear at every British naval fight.

wraith, obs. Sc. var. WRATH *sb.*, *v.*, WROTH *a.*

wraith(e, erron. varr. RATHE *sb.*[2]

1824 CARR *Craven Gloss.*, *Wraiths*, shafts of a cart. **1851** L. D. B. GORDON *Art Jrnl. Illustr. Cat.* p. vii**, The 'wraithe' is for the purpose of keeping the threads separate. **1897** *Westm. Gaz.* 2 Feb. 7/2 He got a rope, fastened it .. to the cart wraiths, and .. strangled himself.

wraithly ('reɪθlɪ), *a. rare.* [f. WRAITH *sb.* + -LY[1].] Resembling a wraith, wraith-like.

1909 M. B. SAUNDERS *Litany Lane* I. iv. 41 The tinkle-tinkle of a wraithly Tom Moore singing flowery lovesongs at fluted-silked pianos.

wraithly, etc., obs. Sc. varr. WROTHLY, etc.

wrak: see WRACK *sbs.*, WRAKE *sb.*[1], *sb.*[3]

†**wrake**, *sb.*[1] *Obs.* Forms: 1 **wracu**, 3–5 **wrak**, 4 *north.* **wrac**, 5 **wraak**, *Sc.* **vrak**; 2– **wrake**, 5–6 *Sc.* **wraik**. [OE. *wracu* (oblique cases *wrace*, *wræce*), f., revenge, vengeance, etc., = Goth. *wraka* persecution, f. the same stem as OE. *wræc* neut., WRACK *sb.*[1] For the related OS. *wrâka*, OHG. *râhha*, see WRECHE *sb.*]

1. Suffering that comes or is inflicted as a retribution or penalty; retributive punishment, vengeance, revenge. Also (*b*) coupled with cognate terms.

Beowulf 2336 Him ðæs guðkyning, wedera þioden, wræce leornode. *c* **825** *Vesp. Psalter* lvii. 11 Bið ʒeblissad se rehtwisa ðonne he ʒesið wrece ðeara arleasra. *c* **1050** tr. *Bæda's Hist.* I. xv. §2 (MS. Corpus Camb.), Ne wæs unʒelic wracu þam ðe iu Caldeas bærndon Hierusaleme weallas. *c* **1200** *Trin. Coll. Hom.* 61 Bute we turnen to gode anradliche, he wile his swerd draȝen, þat is his wrake. *a* **1225** *Juliana* 50 Ah we schulen sechen efter wrake on alle þat we biwiteð. *a* **1300** *Cursor M.* 13055, I dred bot þou ne bete þi sake, þou sal noght dei wit-vten wrake. **13..** *E.E. Allit. P.* B. 386 [On] þe moste mountaynez .. flokked þe folke, for ferde of þe wrake. *c* **1375** *Sc. Leg. Saints* xii. (*Matthias*) 179 At þe laste Iudas for wrake Rubene in þe nek .. strake. *c* **1430** *Chev. Assigne* 72 Wolt þou werne wrake to hem þat hit deseruethe? *a* **1500** *Hist. K. Boccus & Sydracke* (? 1510) U j b, That scourge is a swerd of wrake That one shal agayne a nother take. **1513** DOUGLAS *Æneid* II. ii. 120 The cruell wraik of that dissaitfull slycht.

(*b*) *c* **1175** *Lamb. Hom.* 13 3if ȝe .. to-brecað mine lare .., þenne scal eou sone ȝewaxen muchele wrake and sake, here and hunger. *a* **1250** *Owl & Night.* 1194 Ic wot hwar sal beo niþ & wrake. *c* **1250** *Gen. & Ex.* 552 So cam on werlde wreche and wrake. *a* **1300** *Cursor M.* 890 Til þat worm þan drightin spak wordes bath o wrath and wrak [*Trin.* wrake]. **1303** R. BRUNNE *Handl. Synne* 3389 Þer shewed God weyl by þat kas þat þe kote a-cursed was, And tokened wel sorowe and wrake. **1382** *Pol. Poems* (Rolls) I. 252 The grete vengaunce and wrake That schulde falle for synnes sake. *c* **1400** *Sowdone Bab.* 2446 Vengeaunce shalle than on you come, With sorowe, woo and wrake! *a* **1450** *Le Morte Arth.* 1451 The knyghtis answerd with wo and wrake. **1513** DOUGLAS *Æneid* VII. x. 117 Hevy wraik And sorofull vengence ȝit sall the ourtak.

b. In the phr. ***to do, have, nim*** (= take), ***ta***, or ***take wrake*** (*of*, *on*, or *upon* a person or thing, or with indirect object).

In freq. use *c* 1375–*c* 1480, esp. with *take*.

? *a* **900** *Laws of Ine* ix, Ʒif hwa wrace do, ærðon he him ryhtes bidde. *c* **1000** *Ags. Gosp.* Luke xviii. 7 Ne deð god his ʒecorenra wrace .. ? *c* **1175** *Lamb. Hom.* 9 Þa ilke wrake þe ic dude þe, þu scoldest don me. *a* **1200** *Moral Ode* 205 God nom .. muchele wrake for are misdede. *a* **1275** *Prov. Alfred* 647 in *O.E. Misc.* 136 For he þe wile wrake don. *a* **1300** *Cursor M.* 11554 On þe sakles he suld ta wrake. **1357** *Lay Folks' Catech.* (T.) 485 For to take wrake Or wickedly to venge him opon his euen-cristen. *c* **1450** *Ludus Cov.* 375 Mercy nay nay they xul haue wrake. *c* **1489** CAXTON *Blanch.* xxvi. 95 To be pressented .. to the kynge of salamandrye, .. for to haue wrake vpon hym. *a* **1500** *Hist. K. Boccus & Sydracke* (? 1510) E j, On thy goddes we shall do wrake. **1513** DOUGLAS *Æneid* XI. vi. 80 The montane Caphareus, .. That vengeans tuke and wraik apon our floit. **1533** BELLENDEN *Livy* III. xxiii. (S.T.S.) II. 40 We desire nowther þe goddis nor men to tak ony wraik or punyssement on ȝow. **1613** CHAPMAN *Hymn to Hymen* Plays 1873 III. 122 Let Peace grow cruell, and take wrake of all.

c. ***in wrake of***, in revenge or punishment for. *Sc.*

c **1375** *Sc. Leg. Saints* xxx. (*Theodera*) 799 In wrak of hyr fals plicht [the accuser] deit sodanely in þare sicht. **1513** DOUGLAS *Æneid* III. iv. 91 For strang hunger sall ȝe stand in sic state, In wraik of our iniuris and bestis slane.

2. Adverse action; active enmity; hostility; mischief.

a **1023** WULFSTAN *Hom.* (1883) 106 His sunu hatte Mars, se macode æfre ʒewinn, and wrohte, and saca and wraca he styrede ʒelome. *c* **1205** LAY. 4040 Wrake wes on londe; wa wes þone vnstronge. *a* **1327** *Metr. Treat. Dreams* in *Rel. Ant.* I. 262 Armes y-sen ant eke bataille, Hit is strif ant wrake withoute faille. *c* **1330** *Amis & Amil.* 397 All thus the wrake gan biginne, And with wrethe thai went atvinne, Tho bold bernes to. **1393** LANGL. *P. Pl.* C. XVIII. 85 What þorw werre and wrake and wycked hyfdes, May no preiour pees make in no place. *c* **1430** LYDG. *Min. Poems* (Percy Soc.) 125 Hertis devided have caused mochel wrake. *a* **1450** *Le Morte Arth.* 1675 Syr gawayne And mordreite that mykelle couthe of wrake. **1470–85** MALORY *Arthur* XX. i. 797 For and there ryse warre and wrake betwyx syr launcelot and vs, wete you wel [etc.].

3. Distress of body or mind; pain, suffering, misery.

a **1000** *Phœnix* 51 (Gr.), Nis þær on þam londe .. ne wop ne wracu, weatacen nan. *c* **1320** *Bonaventura's Medit.* 366 My breþren also, kepe hem fro wrake. **13..** *Sir Beues* (A.) 328 A was ibrouȝt in tene & wrake Ofte for þat childes sake. **13..** *Leg. St. Gregory* 338 He tok þat child wiþouten hete and bar it hom wiþouten wrake. *c* **1440** CAPGRAVE *St. Kath.* 866 Þis wille turne vs all to wrake & to dole. *c* **1450** *Ludus Coventriæ* 189 He xall suffer for mannys sake .. moch gret sorow and wrake.

4. Destructive harm or injury; wrecked, ruined, or impaired state or condition; ruin, destruction, wreck.

a **1275** *Prov. Alfred* 142 in *O.E. Misc.* 111 For God may giuen wanne he wele goed after yuil, wele after wrake. *c* **1380** *Sir Ferumb.* 1815 He wol þe chacy as ys fo & werche þe sorwe & wrake. *a* **1400** *R. Gloucester's Chron.* (Rolls) II. 786 Her was muche manqualm, wrake was in londe. *c* **1400** *Anturs of Arth.* xvii, These wrechut wurmus .. wurchen me this wrake. Thus to wrake am I wroȝte, Waynor, i-wis. *c* **1450** *Guy Warw.* (C.) 1158 For thy sake To vs ys comen moche wrake, And all for the loue of the. **1470–85** MALORY *Arth.* VII. xx. 244 He wil doo moche harme .., and worche you wrake in this countray. *a* **1586** MONTGOMERIE *Banks Helicon* 47 Fals Helene .. causd King Priamus wraik [*v.r.* wrake] In Troy. **1596** DALRYMPLE tr. *Leslie's Hist. Scot.* (S.T.S.) II. 178 That sik hatred war nocht the occasioun of the wrake of the hail Realme. **1602** CHETTLE *Hoffman* I. (1631) B 4 b, Newes .. more welcome then the sad discourse Of Leninberg our nephewes timeles wrake.

b. In the phr. ***to bring unto, to fall into, to go, put***, or ***work to wrake***.

a **1425** *Cursor M.* 9204 (Trin.), Ierusalem was stroyed & take; þat kyngdome fel in to wrake. *c* **1425** *Non-Cycle Myst. Pl.* 35 Alas, all þen had gone to wrake; Wold ye haue slayne my son Isaac! *c* **1435** *Chron. London* (Kingsford, 1905) 15 Jurrours went also to Wrake, wher that they myht be ffounde. **1513** DOUGLAS *Æneid* II. vii. 110 By multitude and nomer on ws set All ȝeid to wraik. *c* **1550** R. BIESTON *Bayte Fortune* A ij b, Displeasure and thought doth bring him vnto wrake. **1565** *Satir. Poems Reform.* i. 107 W[hi]ch made muche myserye, and wrought this realme to wrake. **1596** DALRYMPLE tr. *Leslie's Hist. Scot.* (S.T.S.) I. 158 Quhen his armie was al put to wrake.

5. An instance or occasion of suffering or inflicting vengeance, harm, injury, or the like.

c **1300** *Cursor M.* 4950 Now es vs comen our ald sakes In to wandret new, and wrakes. **13..** *E.E. Allit. P.* B. 235 Þat oþer wrake þat wex on wyȝez. **13..** *Coer de L.* 1562 Kyng Rychard hys hostel gan take, Thar he gan hys fyrste wrak. *c* **1425** WYNTOUN *Chron.* I. 1361, V. wrakys syndry has our tane .. þis Brettane. *Ibid.* II. 533 The wrakys ten in Egipte rasse. *c* **1440** *Bone Florence* 1977 God had sende on hym a wrake, That in the palsye can he schake. *a* **1450** *Le Morte Arth.* 948 The quene .. swore to venge hyr of that wrake. *a* **1578** LINDESAY (Pitscottie) *Chron. Scot.* (S.T.S.) I. 125 Seand nathing bot wraikis to come to hir pretendit husband.

Hence †'**wrakedom**, revenge. *Obs. rare*[-1].

c **1205** LAY. 76 For þe wrake-dome of Menelaus quene, .. for hire weoren on ane daȝe hund þousunt deade.

†**wrake**, *sb.*[2] Chiefly *Sc. Obs.* Also 6–7 *Sc.* **wraik** (6 **vraik**), 7 **wraick**. [var. of WRACK *sb.*[2]; the form may be due to the influence of the preceding word.]

1. Shipwreck; = WRACK *sb.*[2] 2.

1513 DOUGLAS *Æneid* I. iii. *heading*, How that Enee wes witht the tempest schaik, And how Neptune his navy saifit fra wraik. **1530** PALSGR. 290/2 Wrake of a shippe, *naufraige*.

2. Wreck, wreckage; = WRACK *sb.*[2] 1 b.

1544 *Aberdeen Reg.* (1844) I. 205 Ane schip of fyr, quhilk wes storit as vraik in hir cumin in the havyn. **1581** *Sc. Acts Parlt., Jas. VI* (1814) III. 255/2 The haill wraik and wayth that sal happin to be fund .. within the boundis of the saidis landis or sie cost thairoff. **1610** *Reg. Mag. Sig. Scot.* 146/1 Cum lie wraik et wair, piscaria de lie yair de Avach, silvis lie scroggis et bussis. **1615** [see WAITH *sb.*[2]]. **1632** *Extracts Burgh Rec. Lanark* (1893) 327 With furk, fork, .. vert, vair, wraik, vennysone.

3. Sea-wrack; = WRACK *sb.*[2] 3.

1547 SALESBURY *Welsh Dict.*, *Brock mor*, Wrake of the sea. **1597**, **1657** [see SEA-OAK]. *c* **1690** KENNETT in *Promp. Parv.* (1865) 533 Reits, sea-weed, of some .. called reits, of others wrack or wraick.

4. *Sc.* A wrecked edifice, etc. *rare*[-1].

c **1625** A. CRAIG in H. Bisset *Rolment* (S.T.S.) I. 23 One man .. consecratis religius workis to Gods: ane Other leavs sad wrakis, and Ruynis now.

†**wrake**, *sb.*[3] *Obs. rare.* Also 6 *Sc.* **wraik**. [var. of WRACK *sb.*[3]; for the long vowel cf. WRAKE *v.*[3]] Refuse, rubbish; something worthless.

a **1350** *Northern Passion* (G.) 1372 Þe met of þat oþir [tree] ne wol it notht del. Hit was schortir þan þe make. Awei þei slongen hit alle for wrake. *a* **1586** *Maitland Quarto MS.* (S.T.S.) 111 Sum houpe is ȝit that my seruice sall speid, Without ye quhilk I wait I am bot wraik. **1604** A. CRAIG *Poet. Ess.* C 3, Then shuld we not bin poynted at for wrake, scorne, and disgrace.

†**wrake**, *v.*[1] *Obs.* Also 4 *north.*, 5 *Sc.* **wrak**, 8 **rake**; 6 *pa. pple.* **ywrake**. [Irreg. var. of *wreke* WREAK *v.*, prob. influenced by WRAKE *sb.*[1] Cf. MDu. *wraken*, var. of *wreken*; MLG. *wraken* to torture.

OE. *wraciende* occurs as var. of *wrecende* (= carrying on) in *Oros* I. xi.]

1. *trans.* = WRACK *v.*[1] 1. Occas. *refl.* Also *fig.*

c **1205** LAY. 6015 Wrake we us on Bruttes & in to þan londen we sullen faren. *a* **1300** *Cursor M.* 6256 Bot þan i sal me on him wrake. *Ibid.* 6597 Drightin sal me on yow wrak [*v.r.* wrake], To sauue þaa men þat has na sak. *c* **1400** *Pride of Life* 88 in *Non-Cycle Myst. Plays* 90 Deth & Life .. striuith a sterne strife King of Life to wrake.

2. *intr.* To execute vengeance (*on* a person).

a **1300** *Cursor M.* 25458 O mans-slaghter had I na mak, Ne nan sa wild in wa to wrak [*Fairf.* wrake], To riue þe grene and gra. *Ibid.* 27459 Quare euer he mai þat man ouer-tak, He sal wit suerd apon him wrak [*Fairf.* wrake].

3. a. To be wroth or angry. *rare*[-1].

a **1300** *E.E. Psalter* vii. 12 (E.), God demer riht, þoland, and strang, Nou wrakes [*v.r.* wrathes] be daies alle lang?

b. To wax violent or furious; to rage.

c **1330** *King of Tars* 148 Gret werre tho bigon to wrake, For the mariage ne moste be take Of that mayden heende.

4. *trans.* To vent (one's wrath); = WREAK *v.* 3.

1596 SPENSER *F.Q.* IV. viii. 14 Ah wofull man, what .. wrath of cruell wight on thee ywrake .. doth thee thus wretched make?

b. To take (vengeance) *on* some one.

1755 *Mem. Capt. Peter Drake* I. xiii. 102 In the End, I sufficiently raked my Vengeance on Mrs. Dickering.

†**wrake**, *v.*[2] *Sc. Obs.* Also **wraik(e**. [var. of WRACK *v.*[2] Cf. WRAKE *sb.*[2]]

1. *trans.* To bring (a person) to ruin; = WRACK *v.*[2] 3. Also *refl.*

1571 *Satir. Poems Reform.* xxviii. 141 And scho wer wrakit, all the warld may wene, Than sould the Duke but dout ressaif ye croun. *a* **1578** LINDESAY (Pitscottie) *Chron. Scot.* (S.T.S.) I. 71 They thocht no thing better nor to wraike them and that witht extreme weiris. **1599** ALEX. HUME *Poems* (S.T.S.) 41 The Lord the wicked wraikes. **1603** *Philotus* liii, Quhome haue ȝe wraikit bot ȝour awin. **1621** [see WRACK *v.*[2] 3, quot. 1567].

b. To subvert or overthrow.

1570 *Satir. Poems Reform.* xii. 74 Apperandly thir plaigis ar powrit out To wraik this warld, and wait ȝe quhair about? **1574** *Ibid.* xlii. 447 Quhen the Kirk sa ȝe haue wrakit, Ʒit all the Kirkis sall not be stakit. *a* **1614** J. MELVILL *Diary* (Wodrow Soc.) 246 The presuming .. of the cheiff corrupt members .. had vitiat and wrakit the esteat of the Kirk.

2. To hurt, harm, or injure severely; to damage, wreck, or ruin materially.

1570 *Satir. Poems Reform.* xxiv. 8 Quhair furious Fleming schot his Ordinance, Willing to wraik him wantit na gude will. **1578** *Sc. Acts, Jas. VI* (1814) III. 113/2 Sum of thair housiss wyiffis and bairnis being thairin wer alluterlie wraikit and brount. **1596** in *Spalding Club Misc.* (1841) I. 88 His haill geir surmounting to mair nor thrie thowsand lib. .. ar altogidder wrakit and away. **1607** *Extr. Aberd. Reg.* (1848) II. 295 Dumbartane .. is liklie to be wrakit be the inundatioun of the watter of Clyde. **1692** in *Rec. Convent. Burghs Scot.* (1880) IV. 595 Ane bush .. named the Generall, was wraked in this harbour.

3. *intr.* = WRACK *v.*[2] 4. *rare*[-1].

1570 *Satir. Poems Reform.* xii. 67, I dout not, in our dayis, Hepburnis will wraik for wyrrying of the King.

Hence †'**wraking** *vbl. sb. Obs.*

1569 *Diurn. Occurr.* (Bann. Cl.) 147 The wraiking of James erle of Mortoun and his assistaris.

†**wrake**, *v.*[3] *Sc. Obs.* Also 7 wraik. [a. (M)LG. *wrâken* (whence Sw. *vraka*, Da. *vrage*), older Du. *wraaken*, Du. *wraken*, older Flem. *wraecken* (Kilian), to reject, etc. Cf. WRACK *v.*[3]] *trans.* To examine (goods, etc.) with a view to rejecting or destroying the unsound, faulty, or damaged. Hence **wraking** *vbl. sb.*

1584 *Burgh Rec. Edinb.* (1882) IV. 343 All the heiring and quhyte fische that sall cum within the said port..to be strukin vp, visitet and wraket. **1599** in *Rec. Convent. Burghs Scot.* (1870) II. 60 Anent the office of jedgerie wraking and burneing of all hoghedis and barrellis of herings. **1609** *Ibid.* 284 Nane to be transportit furth of the realm quhill thai [*sc.* herring-barrels] be packit, wraikit and merkett as followis.

ˈ**wrakeful**, *a. Obs.* [f. WRAKE *sb.*[1] + -FUL. Cf. WRACKFUL *a.*[1], WREAKFUL *a.*]

1. Vengeful; = WRACKFUL *a.*[1]

a **1225** [implied in WRAKEFULLY]. *c* **1480** HENRYSON *Test. Cres.* 329 Ane wraikfull sentence geuin on fair Cresseid.

2. Of persons: Revengeful, vindictive.

a **1300** *E.E. Psalter* xvii. 51 (E.), Leser min be niht and dai Fra mi faes wrakeful [*v.r.* wrathful] are.

3. ? Wicked; sinful.

c **1310** in Wright *Lyric P.* iv. 23 This wrakeful werkes under wede in soule soteleth sone.

4. *Sc.* Destructive.

c **1625** *Bisset's Rolment* (S.T.S.) I. 22 Evin in this act, thow rearest a Monument That all the spyte of wraikfull tyme out faces.

Hence †ˈ**wrakefully** *adv.*, vengefully. *Obs.*

a **1225** *Ancr. R.* 364 Wule God so wrakefuliche awreken him upon sunne? *a* **1225** *Leg. Kath.* 2047 (Royal MS.), Hu wrakefulliche [*Cott. MS.* wrakeliche] wenestu wule he ant wreððe uppon þe, wrecche!

†ˈ**wraker**. *Sc. Obs.* [f. WRAKE *v.*[3] + -ER[1] or a. (M)LG. *wraker*. Cf. WRACKER[2].] One who inspects goods and rejects or destroys the faulty.

1584 *Sc. Acts, Jas. VI*, III. (1814) 302 [To] appoint ane discrete man to be visitour, wraker [*v.r.* wracker], gager, and birnar of the saidis treis. **1584** *Burgh Rec. Edinb.* (1882) IV. 343 Jadgeares, wrakeris, visitouris and markeris of the haill hering and quhyte fishe that sall cum within the port. **1598** in *Rec. Convent. Burghs Scot.* (1870) I. 31 Iadger burnear, or wraker of all barrellis and hogheidis of salmond and hering.

†**wrakling**. *Sc. Obs.* Also -lin, -lyne, -lene. [ad. MLG. *wrakelinge*, MDu. *wrakelinc* (whence also Fris. *wrakling* plank-nail, Da. dial. *vrækling*).] A large make of nail, esp. used in shipbuilding. Also *collect.*

1494 *Acc. Ld. High Treas. Scot.* I. 250 The expensis..for the macken of the erne grathe of the barge [include]..for wraklynys bocht, xvj[d]. *Ibid.* 253, vij stane and xij pundis of boltis and wrakling. **1496** *Ibid.* 310 Ane thousand of singil bowssleit, and iiij[m] wraklene.

attrib. **1497** *Acc. Ld. High Treas. Scot.* I. 334, iij[c] gret wraklin nalis.

†**wrall**, *sb. Obs. rare.* Also wrawl. [f. next.]

1. A winding or twisting; a twist or coil.

1398 TREVISA *Barth. De P.R.* XVIII. ix. (Camb. MS.), þe eddir amphibena..wigleþ wiþ wralles [*ed.* 1495 wrynkles] corckles & drauȝtis of þe bodi.

2. A wreathed decoration or ornamentation.

1540 in V. Green *Hist. Worcs.* (1796) II. App. p. iii, Item, vj spones with wrawles. *Ibid.* p. iv, vj spones with wralls.

†**wrall**, *v. Obs.* [Of obscure origin; cf. UNWRALL *v.*] *trans.* To wreathe, wind, or twist; to convolve.

1398 TREVISA *Barth. De P.R.* v. xii. (Tollem. MS.), These holes ben set in þe stony bon [of the ear]..and ben wrallid and wounde as a spyndel of a presse. *Ibid.* XVII. lxxx, Genista] haþ..ȝelow floures in somer, þikke and wrallid [L. *involutos*]. *Ibid.* XVIII. ix. (Bodl. MS.), Serpentes and addres þat may binde and wralle and folde is owne bodie.

fig. *c* **1395** *Plowman's Tale* I. 370 Such successours [of Peter] ben to bold, In winning al their wit they wral.

Hence †ˈ**wralling** *vbl. sb. Obs.*

1398 TREVISA *Barth. De P.R.* XVII. clxxiv. (Bodl. MS.), Smellinge smoke..croked wiþ many bendinges and wrallinges.

wrall, etc.: see WRAWL, etc.

wramp (ræmp), *sb. north. dial.* and †*Sc.* Also 9 ramp. [Of obscure origin. Cf. MLG. *wrampachtich*, Da. *vrampet* warped, twisted.] A twist or sprain. Chiefly *fig.*

1669 FLEMING *Fulfilling of Scripture* (1671) 99 How dreadful it is to give the conscience a wramp which is more easily hurt then healed. **1690** D. WILLIAMSON *Serm. bef. King's Commissioner* 17 Young ones may get a wramp, and a wrong set by bad Masters. *a* **1706** in J. Watson *Coll. Poems* I. 60 It will be better than Swine Seam, For any Wramp or Minzie. **1724** M. SHIELDS *J. Renwick* in *Biogr. Presbyt.* (1827) II. 138 Grieved for the Wounds and Wramps, Stabs and Strokes his Mother Church of Scotland hath received. **1747** RELPH *Misc. Poems* 17 Oft wittingly..I fell, Pretendin some unlucky wramp or strean. **1846** BROCKETT *N.C. Words* (ed. 3). **1878-** in Cumb. and Northumb. glossaries (s.v. *Ramp*).

wramp (ræmp), *v. north. dial.* and *Sc.* [Related to prec.] *trans.* To twist or sprain (the ankle, etc.); to rick or wrench.

1808 JAMIESON s.v. *Ibid.*, Cumb., I've wrampit my kute. **1878-** in Cumb. and Northumb. glossaries (s.v. *Ramp*). **1897** LD. E. HAMILTON *Outlaws* ix. 101 He's wrampit his ankle.

wran, Sc. or dial. var. WREN[1].

†**wranchevel**. *Obs.*$^{-1}$ (Meaning obscure.)

c **1315** SHOREHAM *Poems* I. 1608 þe fend hyt was þat schente hyt [*sc.* spousing] al Myd gyle and hys abette, Wrancheuel.

wrancke, obs. erron. f. RANK *a.*

wranckle, obs. erron. f. RANKLE *v.*

wrang, obs. or dial. pa. t. of WRING *v.*: obs., dial., or Sc. var. WRONG.

†**wrangel**. *Obs.* [Cf. WRONG *sb.*[1]] The rib of a boat. Also *attrib.* in ***wrangel-nail***.

1355 *Pipe Roll 32 Edw. III*, m. 33 Computat in..[3,900] de Wrangelnaille et .xlvij. doleis vacuis emptis. **1511** *Nottingham Rec.* III. 331 Reparacions of makyng and amendyng the Boote belongyng to the Bridge... Peyd..for v wrangells, xviij d. Item..for ij wrangells, viij d.

wranglan(d)s: see WRANLONS, WRAGLAND, and WRONG *a.* I.

wrangle (ˈræŋg(ə)l), *sb.* [f. next.]

1. An angry dispute or noisy quarrel; an altercation or bitter disputation. Also *fig.*

1547 LATIMER in Foxe *A. & M.* (1563) 1350/2 Or els he had neuer come into this wrangle for his own goods with your brother. **1611** COTGR., *Noise*, brabble,..wrangle, squabble. **1673** *Essex Papers* (Camden) I. 92 [This] animated all those persons who were mutinous & discontented..to raise wrangles & cavills at what ever I did. **1732** SWIFT *Consid. Two Bills* Wks. 1841 II. 225/1 An infinite number of wrangles and litigious suits in the spiritual courts. **1779** G. KEATE *Sketches fr. Nat.* (ed. 2) II. 72 When discord agitated the assembly of the gods, and their wrangles had made a bear-garden of Olympus. **1787** JEFFERSON *Writ.* (1859) II. 335 The complicated wrangles of this continent. **1839** T. MITCHELL *Frogs of Aristoph.* p. cvi, Preferring the songs of Colonean nightingales to the wrangles of the stage. **1859** HOLLAND *Gold Foil* xxiv. 279 The disgraceful wrangles of the religious newspapers. **1874** GREEN *Short Hist.* iv. §2 (1882) 171 Each..had to be extorted after a long wrangle between the borough and the officers.

attrib. **1602** PARSONS *Warn-word to Sir F. Hastings* 22 The arrival of O.E., his wrangle-word. *Ibid.* 26 This pedling marchant comming later to the faire with his wrangle-word.

transf. and *fig.* **1866** G. A. LAWRENCE *Sans Merci* II. 235 There are days when [the horse]..will jump only on compulsion; but he has to deal with sharp spurs and hands of iron; and he has never once got much the best of a wrangle. **1931** BLUNDEN *To Themis* 22 Rumour multiplies the wrangle of wheels and clash of hoofs abroad.

†**2. a.** A disputatious answer or argument. **b.** A controversy. *Obs.*

1579 W. WILKINSON *Confut. Fam. Love* 21 b, To the fourme of wordes he hath formed a wrangle, the matter he graunteth belike to be true. **1752** LAW *Spirit of Love* I. (1766) 1 Your Objections rather tend to stir up the Powers of Love, than the Wrangle of a rational Debate.

3. Without article: The action of wrangling; angry altercation or argument; noisy dispute or contention.

a **1797** H. WALPOLE *Mem. Geo. III* (1845) III. iii. 81 From this dialogue the assembly fell to wrangle, and broke up quarrelling. **1824** BYRON *Juan* XV. xci, None can hate So much as I do any kind of wrangle. **1834** LADY GRANVILLE *Lett.* (1894) II. 159 They are just well and ill enough together to turn the stream of wrangle into a new channel. **1877** TALMAGE *Serm.* 255 The Book of Job has been the subject of unbounded theological wrangle.

wrangle (ˈræŋg(ə)l), *v.* Also 7-8 rangle. [Cf. LG. *wrangeln*, MHG. *rangelen*, frequentative f. *rangen* (= MLG. and LG. *wrangen*) to struggle, wrestle, make uproar, related to *ringen*: see WRING *v.*]

1. a. *intr.* To dispute angrily; to argue noisily or vehemently; to altercate, contend; to bicker.

1377 [see WRANGLING *vbl. sb.*]. **1552** ELYOT, *Altercor*, to contende with wordes,..to wrangle. **1582** N.T. (Rhem.) *2 Tim.* ii. 24 The servant of the Lord must not wrangle. **1582** MULCASTER *Elementarie* I. (1925) 83 The contrarie to right wold be soon espied, howsoeuer it [*sc.* the tongue] wrangle. **1633** G. HERBERT *Temple, Humility* iv, Here it is For which ye wrangle. **1653** WALTON *Angler* 211 None do here Use to swear, Oathes do fray Fish away,..Fishes must not rangle. **1704** PRIOR *Let. to M. Boileau Despreaux* 192 With too much Heat, We sometimes wrangle, when We should debate. **1743** FIELDING *J. Wild* I. viii, First secure what share you can before you wrangle for the rest. **1774** GOLDSM. *Retal.* 55 Now wrangling and grumbling to keep up the ball. **1847** JAMES *Convict* iii, Sometimes they laughed and wrangled good-humouredly enough. **1867** [T. WRIGHT] *Some Habits Working Classes* 124 Even in cases in which no premeditated resolve to wrangle exists, wrangles often occur. **1879** DIXON *Windsor* I. iii. 22 While his Norman lords were wrangling.

b. Const. *about*, *against*, *anent*, *over*, and esp. *with* (a person).

c **1395** *Plowman's Tale* II. 526 Why cleimen they wholy his powere, And wranglen ayenst al his hests? *c* **1400** *Langland's P. Pl.* C. XVII. 80 þaugh couetyce wolde with þe poure wraxle [*Camb. MS.* wrangle] þei mai nat come togederis. *a* **1553** UDALL *Royster D.* v. ii. (Arb.) 80 Certaine men with you haue wrangled About the promise of mariage by you to them made. **1596** BELL *Surv. Popery* II. ii. 194 Howsoeuer you wrangle about your formall succession. **1609** DEKKER *Gull's Horn-bk.* i. 6 Did man..come wrangling into the world, about no better matters? **1650** W. D. tr. *Comenius' Gate Lang. Unl.* §795 They wrangle anent..that universal and present remedie, whether it bee to bee had or no. **1725** DE FOE *Voy. round World* (1840) 353 Quarrelling and wrangling about their wealth. **1746** LD. HARDWICKE in Harris *Life* (1847) II. 290 Wrangling about trifles, they lose great objects. **1816** SCOTT *Antiq.* xi, They sometimes wrangle with her for an hour together under my study window. **1859** JEPHSON *Brittany* i. 3 While rival farmers wrangle over rates and road-making. **1904** *Verney Memoirs* II. 135 [They] were still wrangling with his mother and his many creditors.

fig. **1604** SHAKS. *Oth.* III. iv. 144 Mens Natures wrangle with inferiour things. **1614** J. COOKE *Greene's Tu Quoque* K 2 b, Let vs no longer wrangle with our Wittes, Or dally with our Fortunes. **1615** G. SANDYS *Trav.* 207 The windes favorable, and the seas composed; but anon they began to wrangle and we to suffer.

transf. **1648** CRASHAW *Delights Muses, Musicks Duell* 43 A nightingale..In controverting warbles evenly shar'd, With her sweet selfe shee wrangles.

c. To make a noise suggestive of or comparable to wrangling; to jangle.

1816 L. HUNT *Rimini* I. 178 The golden bits keep wrangling as they go. **1873** LONGF. *M. Angelo* I. ii. ad fin., Low and loud the bells..Jangle and wrangle in their airy towers.

2. To argue or debate; to engage in controversy; formerly also, to dispute or discuss publicly as at a university, for or against a thesis, etc. Freq. const. *about*, *over*, *upon*, *with*. Also with clause (quots. *a* 1586, 1586).

1570 DRANT *Serm.* C iij b, Hence wrangle the Iesuistes, hence wrastle the Sorbonistes. *a* **1586** SIDNEY *Apol. Poetrie* (Arb.) 41 So must they bee content little to mooue: sauing wrangling, whether Vertue bee the chiefe, or the onely good. **1586** A. DAY *Eng. Secretorie* II. (1595) 46, I must wrangle whie you stole awaie Toms bread and butter. **1612** BRINSLEY *Lud. Lit.* xvii. (1627) 208 In wrangling about words, not disputing to the purpose, and to the point. **1638** R. BAKER tr. *Balzac's Lett.* (vol. II) 182 Being resolved..to forsake my own [opinion], if any man will wrangle with me for it. **1665** J. BUCK in Peacock *Stat. Cambridge* (1841) App. B. p. lxxii, The Commencers and their Sophisters are disputing and wrangling there until the clock strikes 5. **1732** POPE *Ess. Man* I. 49 All the question (wrangle e'er so long) Is only this, if God has plac'd him wrong? **1773** LD. MONBODDO *Language* (1774) I. I. viii. 108 About which we see men wrangle and dispute without end. **1807** CRABBE *Par. Reg.* III. 4 When..few [were ready] to write or wrangle for their creed. **1855** MACAULAY *Hist. Eng.* xiii. III. 365 The factions of the Parliament House, awe-struck by the common danger, forgot to wrangle. **1877** FIELD *Lakes of Killarney to Golden Horn* 75 For this reason..the Assembly wrangles over unimportant matters.

transf. *a* **1608** in Davison *Poet. Rhapsody* (1621) 102 Tell wit how much it wrangles In tickle points of nicenesse. **1858** H. BUSHNELL *Serm. for New Life* vii. (1861) 93 The mind that judges God..stumbles, complains, wrangles, and finds no issue to its labour.

3. *trans.* †**a.** With *out*: To argue out (a case, dispute, etc.); to contest or dispute contentiously to an end or issue. *Obs.*

1609 B. JONSON *Sil. Wom.* IV. vi, If I make 'hem not wrangle out this case to his no comfort. **1632** BROME *North. Lass* V. ix, While they wrangle out their cause, let vs agree. **1664** POWER *Exp. Philos.* III. 184 If he could but stiffly wrangle out a vexatious dispute. **1728** [DE FOE] *Street-Robberies* 42 The poor Captain was left to wrangle it out with the People of the House.

b. In *pass.* To be argued or debated.

c **1734** NORTH *Ld. Kpr. Guilford* (1742) 165 And so it was wrangled off and on till the Session ended.

c. To utter wranglingly. *rare*$^{-1}$.

1760 STERNE *Tr. Shandy* III. xxxviii, All that had been wrote or wrangled thereupon in the schools and porticoes of the learned.

4. To get (something) *out of* a person by bargaining; to obtain by wrangling.

1624 CAPT. SMITH *Virginia* III. 75 We wrangled out of the King ten quarters of Corne for a copper Kettell. **1934** in WEBSTER. **1976** *National Observer* (U.S.) 31 Jan. 1/3 The pall of snowdrifts and ice would have impeded reinforcements' marching even if Arnold had been able to wrangle help from American Brig. Gen. David Wooster, a procrastinator who then occupied Montreal.

5. a. To influence or persuade (a person) by wrangling or contention; to argue *out of* a possession, etc., or *in* to some state.

1633 BURROUGHS *Sov. Brit. Seas* (1651) 4 Princes..disdaining to bee wrangled out of the ancient rights and regalities. **1658** BRAMHALL *Consecr. Bps.* viii. 182 To wrangle the Church of England out of a good possession. *a* **1659** BP. BROWNING *Serm.* (1674) I. xii. 165 Will a man..be wrangled out of his Evidences? **1675** BROOKS *Gold. Key* Wks. 1867 V. 525 All the devils in hell shall never wrangle a believer out of his heavenly inheritance. **1705** HEARNE *Collect.* (O.H.S.) I. 70 The Latter would have wrangled 'em out of it. **1847** MRS. GORE *Castles in Air* viii, Moral philosophy [has] wrangled the world in and out of its senses.

b. To force or drive *out of* a place by wrangling.

1693 C. MATHER *Wond. Inv. World* 26 To wrangle the Devil out of the Country, will be truly a new Experiment.

†**c.** *refl.* To harass (oneself) by altercation. *Obs.*

1649 BP. SANDERSON in D'Oyly *Life Sancroft* II. 442 When we have wrangled ourselves as long as our wits and strengths will serve us. **1721** AMHERST *Terræ Fil.* No. 8 (1726) 37 In this..mischievous course have these our reverend old mothers continued for several centuries, wrangling themselves about trifles.

6. With *away*, *out*. To consume, spend, or pass away (time) in wrangling. *rare.*

1794 MRS. A. M. BENNETT *Ellen* IV. 230 They..may at last possibly agree to wrangle out the evening of their lives together. **1905** R. GARNETT *W. Shakespeare* 53 Do I weakly Wrangle away my precious moments?

7. *Western U.S.* To take charge of (horses); to herd.

1899 F. REMINGTON *Sundown Leflare* 11 De herd, which was more horses..dan ten men kin wrangle. **1903** A. ADAMS

Log Cowboy xiii. 197 Forrest detailed Rod Wheat to wrangle the horses, for we intended to take Honey-man with us. **1952** H. INNES *Campbell's Kingdom* I. ii. 38 He wrangles a bunch of horses and acts as packer for the visitors in the summer.

wrangled ('ræŋg(ə)ld), *ppl. a.* [f. WRANGLE *v.* + -ED[1].] Disputed, contested.

1876 MISS BROUGHTON *Joan* II. ix, The children returning ..to ask loudly for arbitration on some wrangled point.

'wrangled, var. RANGLED *ppl. a.*[1]

wrangler ('ræŋglə(r)). [f. as prec. + -ER[1].]

1. a. One who wrangles or quarrels; an angry or noisy disputer or arguer.

c **1515** *Cocke Lorell's B.* 4 Here is gylys Fogeler of ayebery, ..With wallys the wrangler. *c* **1520** *Dial. Creatures Mor.* v. B ij b, Many one..ageynst Lawe and Reason somtyme wyll stryue and..be full of questyons, wherfore they be takyn for wrangelers and euyll people. **1579** LYLY *Euphues* (Arb.) 106 Lucilla..will either shut mee out for a Wrangler, or cast mee off for a Wiredrawer. **1619** in Foster *Eng. Factories Ind.* (1906) I. 68 Giles James, a swaggerer and wrangler, much discommended. **1654** WHITLOCK *Zootomia* 159 Convinced gainesayers and wranglers they are, in stead of convincers. **1741** WATTS *Improv. Mind* I. xiii. §20 Rather like well-bred gentlemen in polite conversation, than like noisy and contentious wranglers. **1790** COWPER *Iliad* I. 360 But this wrangler here—Nought will suffice him but the highest place. **1809** IRVING *Knickerb.* IV. i, His name..was a corruption of *Kyver*, that is to say, a *wrangler* or *scolder*. *a* **1901** STUBBS *Germany in Early Mid. Ages* (1908) 107 Henry the Wrangler conspired with the Czechs of Bohemia.

fig. and *transf.* **1578** H. WOTTON *Courtlie Control.* 129 Where so the wofull Louer is, euen there also is he [*sc.* Cupid], In bedde the wrangler will not misse his pillowbeare to be. **1606** SHAKS. *Tr. & Cr.* II. ii. 75 The Seas and Windes (old Wranglers) tooke a Truce. **1633** G. HERBERT *Temple, Family* ii, What doth this noise of thoughts within my heart? ..Lord,..Turn out these wranglers, which defile thy seat.

Prov. **1616** DRAXE *Bibl. Scholast.* 244 A wrangler neuer wanteth words. **1671** T. HUNT *Abeced. Scholast.* 18 Many Lawyers, many Wranglers.

b. One who engages in argument, debate, or controversy; a debater, disputant, or controversialist.

1561 T. N[ORTON] *Calvin's Inst.* IV. xviii. 145 b, Nowe least any wrangler shoulde stirre vs vp strife by reason of the names of sacrifice and sacrificing prest. **1597** MORLEY *Introd. Mus.* 90, I set downe the proportions..to content wranglers, who..will..take occasion to..detract from that which they cannot disproue. *c* **1643** LD. HERBERT *Autobiog.* (1824) 42 Teaching them the subtilities of Logic, which as it is usually practised, enables them for little more than to be excellent wranglers. **1690** LOCKE *Hum. Und.* IV. viii. §11 These general Maxims..are of great Use in Disputes, to stop the Mouths of Wranglers. **1741** WARBURTON *Div. Legat.* II. II. Append. 23 There is indeed a Time when a serious Writer would not trouble himself to confute or set a Wrangler right. **1774** REID *Aristotle's Logic* vi. § I (1788) 127 A man who has studied logic all his life may be, after all, only a petulant wrangler. **1842** I. TAYLOR *Enthus.* iv. 79 The argumentative resources of the modern..wrangler [*earlier edd.* stoic]. **1881** PAXTON HOOD *Christmas Evans* 162 He was not a wrangler, not disposed to maintain debates as to his rights.

c. The name for each of the candidates who have been placed in the first class in the mathematical tripos at Cambridge University. See TRIPOS 2, and cf. SENIOR *a.* 3.

1750 *Friendly Adv. Old Tory to Vice-C. Cambr.* (1751) 26 The Wranglers..have usually expected, that all the young Ladies of their Acquaintance..should wish them Joy of their Honours. **1791** in C. Wordsworth *Schol. Acad.* (1877) 323, I did above three times as much as the Sen[io]r Wrangler last year. **1812** *Examiner* 7 Sept. 571/2 These two drivellers are respresented as having been fellow-wranglers at College! **1831-** [see SENIOR *a.* 3]. **1859** H. KINGSLEY *G. Hamlyn* xii, He took up his books once more, and came forth third wrangler. **1874** C. WORDSWORTH *Soc. Life Eng. Univ.* 232 The set for Com. Priora, Feb. 9, 1748-9,..being the earliest which bears on its back a list of the Wranglers and Senior Optimes.

fig. *c* **1820** BYRON *Diary* Wks. (1846) 630/2 Lady B. would have made an excellent wrangler at Cambridge.

2. *Western U.S.* One who is in charge of a string of horses or ponies on a stock-farm; a herder.

1888 ROOSEVELT in *Cent. Mag.* April 851/2 There are two herders, always known as 'horse-wranglers'—one for the day and one for the night. **1901** *Munsey's Mag.* XXV. 405/2 One of them would..overpower the 'wrangler' in the darkness, and turn the horses loose.

3. Also **Wrangler.** A proprietary name for jeans. Freq. *pl.* orig. *U.S.*

1947 *Official Gaz.* (U.S. Patent Office) 16 Dec. 395/2 Blue Bell, Inc., Greensboro, N.C... *Wrangler*. For Western style dungarees and pants. Claims use since Jan. 19, 1929. **1963** *Trade Marks Jrnl.* 16 Oct. 1478/1 *Wrangler*... Articles of protective clothing..and articles of sports clothing... Kilgour & Walker Limited.., Aberdeen; manufacturers. **1966** *Ibid.* 7 Sept. 1313/2 *Wrangler*... Articles of protective clothing..; trousers, jeans [etc.]. Blue Bell, Inc., Greensboro, State of North Carolina. **1972** *New Society* 13 Apr. 68/2, I suggested..that..the girls..might like to travel in jeans and change into their best gear when we stopped for lunch. My idea..produced..a unanimous decision..that they were going in their wranglers anyway. **1978** D. BLOODWORTH *Crosstalk* xxvii. 211 A tall blond youth in wranglers and ringlets. **1981** C. WATSON *Bishop in Back Seat* xxi. 131 He was in his regulation costume: Wrangler jeans, soiled Stetson.

'wranglership. [f. prec. 1 c + -SHIP.] The position or rank of a wrangler of Cambridge University.

1791 in Wordsworth *Schol. Acad.* (1877) 323 I'm perfectly satisfied that the Senior Wranglership is Peacock's due. **1843** R. J. GRAVES *Syst. Clin. Med.* xxx. 397 Obtaining the senior moderatorship [in Dublin university] (analogous to the wranglership of the English universities). **1882** *Standard* 30 Jan. 3 To witness the last conferment of degrees under the old system of Wranglership. **1883** MISS M. BETHAM-EDWARDS *Disarmed* xxx, Those young ladies as yet outside the intellectual region of Wranglerships and the Classical Tripos.

attrib. **1872** *Daily News* 25 Mar., Men break down under a wranglership competition.

wranglesome ('ræŋg(ə)lsəm), *a. colloq.* or *dial.* [f. WRANGLE *sb.* + -SOME.] Given to wrangling; quarrelsome; contentious, peevish.

1817 *Ann. Reg., Chron.* App. 215/1 Why do you flurry yourself so much: the child is only a little wranglesome and cross. **1847** HALLIWELL. **1869-** in dialect use (Yks., Lanc., and Chesh.).

'wrangling, *vbl. sb.* [f. WRANGLE *v.* + -ING[1].]

1. The action of the verb; noisy quarrelling.

1377 LANGL. *P. Pl.* B. IV. 34 There as wratthe and wranglyng is þere wynne þei siluer. **1551** GARDNER *Explic. Christ's Presence* 14 As for such other wranglyng..shall after be spoken of by further occasion. **1598** FLORIO, *Contèsa*,.. a strife, a debate or wrangling. **1653** W. RAMESEY *Astrol. Restored* 137 Mars..causes discord and wrangling. **1722** RAMSAY *Three Bonnets* IV. 137 The king of brutes..wad.. rage Wi' bootless wrangling in his cage. **1813** SCOTT *Rokeby* III. xii, Though wild debate And wrangling rend our infant state. **1882** SIR C. DILKE in Gwynn *Life* (1917) I. 426 Much unseemly wrangling would be prevented for many years.

fig. **1609** ARMIN *Maids of More-cl.* C 2 b, 'Twill become ye, well, when wrangling wrestles with such violent iniurie.

b. Controversial argument or debate; contentious disputation.

1612 BRINSLEY *Lud. Lit.* 219 There falleth out amongst them oft-times..much wrangling about the questions. **1641** MILTON *Reformation* 25 What wrangling the Bishops and Monks had about the reading, or not reading of Origen. **1679** PENN *Addr. Prot.* II. ii. (1692) 71 Philosophy..became little else than an Art of Rangling upon a multitude of Idle Questions. **1720** S. PAYNE *Bp. R. Cumberland's Sanchon.* p. xxvii, His Averseness to any thing like Wrangling made him ..leave his Book to shift for it self. **1768-74** TUCKER *Lt. Nat.* (1834) II. 334 All that wrangling and witticism wherewith the prophecies..have been pelted by freethinkers. **1827** WHATELEY *Logic* 26 A system of such rules..must, instead of deserving to be called the art of wrangling, be [etc.]. **1879** FROUDE *Cæsar* xxv. 436 A refuge from platform oratory and senatorial wrangling.

attrib. *c* **1700** POMFRET *Strephon's Love* 10 Those dull, pedantic rules, They had collected from the wrangling schools. **1708** ROWE *Royal Convert* I. i, Unpractis'd in Disputes, and wrangling Schools.

2. A wrangle; a noisy quarrel.

1580 LYLY *Euphues* (Arb.) 472 They that can-not suffer the wranglyngs of young marryed women. **1605** SYLVESTER *Du Bartas* II. iii. *Vocation* 1152 He heard amid the street A wrangling, jangling, and a murmur rude. **1668** GLANVILL *Plus Ultra* Pref., Consider me as a Person that contemns all Wranglings. **1727** SWIFT *To Stella* 7 Not in Wranglings to engage With such a stupid vicious Age. **1788** V. KNOX *Winter Even.* lxx. (1790) II. 530 The wranglings of Cambridge, and the disputations at Oxford, are apt to give young men a controversial turn, which [etc.]. **1821** BYRON *Sardanap.* II. i, Truce with these wranglings, and but hear me! **1890** TALMAGE *Fr. Manger to Throne* 562 Unseemly wranglings concerning who should be greatest in the kingdom of Christ.

'wrangling, *ppl. a.* [f. as prec. + -ING[2].]

1. That wrangles, quarrels, or disputes; engaged or embroiled in, given or addicted to, noisy altercation or dispute; contentious.

1487 *Cely Papers* (Camden) 161 Hys atorney ys a wranglyng felow, he wold non odyr mony but nemyng grotes. *a* **1529** SKELTON *Agst. Garnesche* ii. 40 Thow manytycore, ye marmoset,..Wranglyngе, waywyrde, wytles, wraw, and no-thyng meke. **1581** A. HALL *Iliad* v. 100 Mars is a wrangling craking wretche. **1633** P. FLETCHER *Purple Isl.* VII. xxxiv, The third Hæreticus, a wrangling carle. **1656** EARL MONM. tr. *Boccalini's Advts. fr. Parnass.* I. xxxi. (1674) 36 It might serve..for a Lesson to wrangling Courtiers. **1718** POPE *Let. to Caryll* 18 Jan., The unrighteous labours of wrangling statesmen, and the quarrelsome ones of uncharitable divines. **1759** DILWORTH *Pope* 39 After the death of poor wrangling Dennis. **1820** WORDSW. '*Dogmatic Teachers*' 2 Ye wrangling Schoolmen, of the scarlet hood! **1825** SCOTT *Betrothed* Concl., For wrangling curs will fight over a banquet as fiercely as over a bare bone. **1846** MRS. A. MARSH *Father Darcy* II. v. 112 The wrangling nobles of Philistia.

transf. and *fig.* **1583** MELBANCKE *Philotimus* Dd iv, A wrangling tongue is the best language thou hast. *a* **1721** SHEFFIELD (Dk. Buckhm.) *Wks.* (1753) I. 15 Thy happy stroke can into softness bring Reason, that rough and wrangling thing. **1898** MEREDITH *Odes Fr. Hist., Revolution* xiii, And he, the bright day's husband,..Beheld a wrangling heart, as 'twere her soul On eddies of wild waters cast. **1899** SWINBURNE *Rosamund* I. 18 Let no wrangling breath distune the peace That shines..about us.

b. Noisy; clamorous; also *transf.*, jangling.

1608 MACHIN *Dumb Knt.* III. E 3 b, When the sad nurse to still the wrangling babe, Shall sing the carefull story of my death. **1845** LONGF. *Belfry of Bruges, Carillon* ii, When the wrangling bells had ended. **1856** MRS. GORE *Life's Lessons* II. 227 Her remote Dale, with its wrangling beck. **1891** *Athenæum* 15 Aug. 214/1 So has it fared with the marshlands ..with their wrangling sea-fowl.

2. Of the nature of wrangling; contentious, noisy, clamorous.

1551 GARDNER *Explic. Christ's Presence* 43 Wherof this auctor may not thinke nowe as vpon a wranglyng argument, to satisfie a coniecture diuised. **1614** RALEIGH *Hist. World* III. vi. §6 To finde him busie in wrangling altercation. **1641** MILTON *Animadv.* 57 Because hee may not as a Judge sit out the wrangling noyse of litigious Courts. **1663** BP. PATRICK *Parab. Pilgr.* xix, This wrangling piece of Learning. **1722** HORROBIN in Keble *Life Bp. Wilson* (1863) 507 The wrangling, jangling disputes about the Divinity of our Saviour. **1753** MISS COLLIER *Art Torment.* (1811) 216 Some wrangling dispute or other that shall sour the whole company.

3. Marked or characterized by noisy or contentious disputation or altercation.

1576 WHETSTONE *Rock of Regard* I. 97 A wrangling hate, where once was passing loue. **1594** SHAKS. *Rich. III*, II. iv. 55 Accursed, and vnquiet wrangling dayes. **1603** HOLLAND *Plutarch's Mor.* 251 Our wrangling humour and desire to be cavilling about questions disputable. **1628** MAY *Virg. Georg.* II. 61 He sees no wrangling courts, no lawes undone By sword. **1656** COWLEY *Pindar. Odes, Destinie* iii, Thou neither great at Court,..Nor at th' Exchange shalt be, nor at the wrangling Bar. **1715** POPE *Iliad* II. 307 Peace, factious monster, born to vex the state, With wrangling talents form'd for foul debate. **1851** MAYNE REID *Scalp Hunt.* xxxiv. 262 It is hard to behold the worshipped men of our wrangling days become degraded under modern light. **1883** WHITELAW *Sophocles, Antigone* 111 At call of Polyneices, stirred By bitter heat of wrangling claims, Against our land they gathered.

Hence **'wranglingly** *adv.*

1611 COTGR., *Tempestativement*,..contentiously, seditiously, wranglingly. **1698** NORRIS *Pract. Disc.* IV. 65 We should..discourse of it not..Wranglingly and Contentiously,..but Cordially and Spiritually.

†**wrang-nail.** *Obs. rare.* [var. of ME. *angnail* (OE. *angnægel*), perh. by confusion with *warnail* (OE. *wernægel*) WARNEL.] A corn on the foot or hand; = AGNAIL I.

? *c* **1530** *Pol., Rel., & L. Poems* (1903) 64 For to Dystroy a Wrang Nayle, othe[r]wyse callyd a Corne. **1556** WITHALS *Dict.* Xj, An agnayle or wrangnayle [**1562** wragnayle], *clauus.*

wrang-nail, -rope: see WRONG *sb.*[1]

wrangous(lie, -uis(lie, -us(lie, etc., obs. varr. WRONGOUS(LY.

wrangwis(e, -ly, -ness, obs. ff. WRONGOUS, -LY, -NESS.

wrankle, obs. erron. f. RANKLE *v.*

†**wranlons.** *Obs. rare*[−1]. [Of obscure origin. Cf. WRAGLAND I.] *pl.* Unthriving trees that will never become timber.

1432-3 MARTIN in *Year-Book 11 Hen. VI* (1567) 1 b, Querkes qe sont appelles wranlons quel ne voet estre meresme, mes est suable bois, il nest aiuge wast. [Hence in Kitchin *Crt. Leet* (1580) *wranglans*, in translation (1651) *wrang-lands*, whence in Blount (1656), Skinner (1671), Coles (1677), etc.; also Bailey (1721) *wranglings*.]

wrap (ræp), *sb.* Also 5 **wrappe.** [f. the vb. Not usual before the 19th cent.]

1. a. A wrapper or covering. Also *fig.*

c **1460** J. RUSSELL *Bk. Nurture* 212 Thow must square & proporcioun þy bred..and so shaltow make þy wrappe [*v.r.* wrapper] for þy master manerly. **1589** HAKLUYT *Voy.* 216 In Goa they vse not to abate any tare of any goods, except of sacks or wraps. **1873** M. ARNOLD *Lit. & Dogma* (1876) 100 That want of power to penetrate through wraps and appearances to the essence of things.

b. A cover, blanket, rug, or the like for laying over or drawing about the person when travelling, reposing, etc. (Cf. 2 b.)

1861 *Daily Chron.* 12 Sept., We have heard.. Livingstone, the African explorer, and many other travellers, say that at night no wrap could equal the beard. **1863** DICEY *Federal St.* I. 54, I had..two large carpet-bags, a bundle of heavy wraps, and an umbrella, to transport with me. **1869** TOZER *Highl. Turkey* II. 15 A few wraps in case of a night bivouac.

c. Material used for wrapping, esp. very thin plastic film.

1930 *Food Industries* Jan. 13/1 [Cellophane] was first introduced into this country from France as a wrap for candy. *Ibid.*, The transparent type of wrap proved decidedly popular. **1958** *Chain Store Age* Apr. 168/3 The Aluminum Company of America is now packaging Alcoa wrap in a 'flat pak'. **1976** 'O. JACKS' *Assassination Day* v. 81 He bundled the notes up into foil wrap, put two in..his refrigerator. **1977** *Time* 14 Mar. 39/3 The thin sail (ordinary plastic kitchen wrap is five times thicker) would be coated with an aluminum reflecting layer on the side that will face the sun. **1979** *Sci. Amer.* Jan. 131/1 You could also build up layers of stretched plastic food wrap. **1980** *Outdoor Life* (U.S.) (Northeast ed.) Oct. 126/2 Cover an exposed drain valve with plastic wrap to prevent road slush from accumulating.

2. a. A loose garment or article of feminine dress used or designed to envelop or fold about the person; a shawl, scarf, or the like.

1827 *Lady's Mag.* June 342/1 The Circassian wrap is much worn for half-dress;..it well sets off the fine bust of a well-made female. **1840** *Ladies' Cabinet* Mar. 201 This is not however the case with the cloaks or shawls adopted as wraps for evening parties. **1885** MABEL COLLINS *Prettiest Woman* x, Arthur..had the delight of putting Zadwidga's wrap around her shoulders. **1894** MRS. DYAN *Man's Keeping* (1899) 222 Her face..was close to his shoulder; a light wrap of lace framed it.

b. An additional outer garment used or intended to be worn as a defence against wind or weather when driving, travelling, etc. Usu. *pl.* (Cf. 1 b.)

a **1817** JANE AUSTEN *Watsons* (1879) 353 Tom Musgrave in the wrap of a traveller. **1855** A. MANNING *O. Chelsea Bun-h.* xiv. 229, I was taking off my wraps, and making ready to go up stairs. **1861** J. H. BENNET *Winter Medit.* (1875) I. x. 303 A bitter cold north-west wind..had been blowing, which obliged us to use all our wraps. **1898** J. B. WOLLOCOMBE *Morn till Eve* i. 2 After unrolling and unbuttoning his outer wraps, the doctor..ascended the stairs.

3. a. *spec.* A single convolution, twist, or winding of a thread in fastening an object.

1879 OGDEN in J. H. Keene *Fishing Tackle* (1886) 172 Secure it with one wrap and two hitches before taking the tweezers off, cut off silk [etc.].

b. *techn.* (See quots.)

1888 C. P. BROWN *Cotton Manuf.* 28 A complete revolution of the latter [worm-wheel] means 3564 yards—technically called a wrap. *Ibid.*, If a warp contains 4 wraps and 7 teeth, it is 14,445 yards long.

4. *pl.* In *fig.* phrases referring to concealment or disuse, as ***under*** or ***in wraps***, concealed; in abeyance; ***to take*** or ***pull the wraps off***, to disclose; to bring back into use.

1939 *Sun* (Baltimore) 18 Dec. 3/6 The fact that the belligerents have kept their air power under wraps almost from the beginning reveals more than meets the eye. **1950** 'S. RANSOME' *Deadly Miss Ashley* xv. 178 You grabbed his notebooks and tried..to keep them under wraps. **1956** A. H. COMPTON *Atomic Quest* 49 Some members of the committee were insistent that the entire uranium project should be put in wraps for the duration. **1964** *New Society* 15 Feb. 21/2 The Government took the wraps off its plan for regenerating the Northeast. **1965** MRS. L. B. JOHNSON *White House Diary* 20 Jan. (1970) 226 Next Hubert [Humphrey] stepped forward—for once his exuberance was under wraps. **1973** *Times* 4 Oct. 4/3 Only now was the truth about battered wives being revealed 'because the wraps have just been pulled off a taboo subject'. **1978** *Dumfries Courier* 20 Oct. 11/1 Show visitors will see numerous others which are still under wraps until nearer the Show. **1984** *Times* 14 May 7/2 This week will see the wraps coming off another popular project, where Britain wants to be seen leading the way.

5. *Cinemat.* and *Television.* The end of a session of filming or recording.

1974 M. AYRTON *Midas Consequence* I. 63 Other cars are heard starting up out of shot and the lights on the pergola go off so I assume it's a wrap and the crew is listening to the director saying something consequential and busy about tomorrow's call. **1980** J. KRANTZ *Princess Daisy* xii. 191 'Right, it's a wrap.'.. The large lights, cameras, sound equipment and other tools of the trade were quickly stowed away. **1983** *Listener* 23 June 18/2 The director says: 'Cut! Thank you, Ben, that's a wrap—there is no more filming.'

6. Special Combs. (see also WRAP-): **wrap party** *Cinemat.*, a party held to celebrate the completion of filming; **wrap reel, wheel**, a large revolving framework on which yarn can be wound and measured.

1978 J. KRANTZ *Scruples* xiii. 388 Work on *Mirrors* finished on schedule, on Friday, August 23rd, and the wrap party was scheduled for the next night. **1978** *Morning Bulletin* (Rockhampton, Queensland) 3 Apr. 6/4 At the wrap party..Syl played host in a three-piece white suit. **1889** G. E. DAVIS *Sizing & Mildew in Cotton Goods* ii. 20 In order to test the fineness of yarn a wrap reel is used, measuring 54 inches in circumference, which is so arranged that by a single turn of a handle two complete revolutions are given to the reel itself. **1928** W. L. BALLS *Studies of Quality in Cotton* xii. 235 The lea was wound upon wrap-reels of varying diameter. **1956** S. E. ELLACOTT *Spinning & Weaving* 36/2 Arkwright's wrap reel for measuring hanks of yarn (840 yards) was a six-armed revolving star with a winch handle. **1953** Wrap wheel [see RICE *sb.*[1] 4]. **1969** E. H. PINTO *Treen* 318 After yarn had been spun on a spindle or spinning wheel, it was transferred on to a wrap or clock wheel, a rotary instrument which skeined and measured it. The original wrap wheel is always said to have been invented by Richard Arkwright.

wrap, obs. erron. f. RAP *sb.*[1]

wrap (ræp), *v.* Also 4–7 **wrappe** (6 *arch.* **wrappen**), 6 **warppe**, 6, 9 *dial.* **warp**, 7–8 **rap**, 9 *dial.* **wrop**. [Of obscure origin. Cf. the earlier BEWRAP *v.* (also BELAP *v.*, LAP *v.*[2] with the variant WLAPPE, and WAP *v.*[2]), and NFris. *wrappe* to press into, stop up, Da. dial. *vrappe* to stuff.

The dialect var. *wrop* had formerly greater currency. 'This word is often pronounced *rop*, rhyming with *top*, even by speakers much above the vulgar' (Walker, 1791). 'The same pronunciation is not uncommon in some parts of the United States' (Worcester, 1858).]

I. 1. a. To cover, enwrap, or swathe (a person or part of the body) by enfolding in a cloth or the like; in later use esp., to envelop or enshroud with a garment; to attire, garb, clothe in an enfolding garment. Occas. *refl.* Also with advs., as *about, around, round.*

c **1320** R. BRUNNE *Medit.* 975 Sone, y was wunt þe swetly to wrappe, Now swaþe y þe dede. **13..** *Coer de L.* 3094 Hys chamberlayn hym wrappyd warm. He lay and slepte. *c* **1400** *Pilgr. Sowle* (Caxton, 1483) IV. xx. 64 When thou bytoke hym me to clothe and wrappe. *c* **1450** *Myrr. our Ladye* II. 245 The vyrgyn wrappynge and gatherynge togyther the handes and fete of her lytel sonne..in a bande. **1560** BIBLE (Genev.) *Gen.* xxxviii. 14 She..coured hir with a vaile, and wrapped her selfe. —— *Isaiah* xxviii. 20 For the bed is streict.., and the couering narowe that one can not wrap him self. **1629** MILTON *Hymn Nativ.* i, The Heav'n-born-childe, All meanly wrapt in the rude manger lies. **1688** R. HOLME *Armoury* II. 477 Some term Beasts thus wrapped about the Body [*ante* 'with a Towel'] charged with a pale. **1791** COWPER *Iliad* III. 495 Helen..in her lucid veil close wrapt around, Silent retired. **1805** SCOTT *Last Minstrel* VI. xxvi, A shape with amice wrapp'd around. **1859** DICKENS *T. Two Cities* I. ii, All three were wrapped to the cheek-bones and over the ears. **1909** J. L. ALLEN *Bride of Mistletoe* vi. 159 Coarsely wrapped and carrying some bundle.., [she] opened her front door.

b. Const. *in* (†*on*) or *with*. Also *refl.*

c **1350** *Will. Palerne* 745 He gript his mantel; as a weiȝh woful he wrapped him þer-inne. *Ibid.* 2609 þei..wist wel þat þei went wrapped in þe skinnes. *c* **1375** *Pol., Rel., & L. Poems* (1903) 255/10 Iesu, swete, beo noth wroþ þou ich nabbe clout ne cloþ..þe on to folde ne to wrappe. **1382** WYCLIF *Isaiah* xxxvii. 1 King Ezechie..kutte his clothis, and wrappid is with a sac. *c* **1410** LOVE *Bonavent. Mirr.* vi. (1908) 47 Sche..wrapped hym in the keuerchiefes of hir heued. **1430–40** LYDG. *Bochas* I. 6169 Pouert eek liggith the colde wyntris nyht Wrappid in strauh, withoute compleynynge. **1526** TINDALE *Matt.* xxvii. 59 Joseph toke the body, and wrapped it in a clene lynnyne clooth. **1547** *Bk. Marchauntes* c v b, Thus coyffed and wrapped with their read hattes of this..capper, they go from town to town. **1590** SPENSER *F.Q.* II. i. 52 Weake wretch I wrapt my selfe in Palmers weed. **1617** MORYSON *Itin.* III. 171 Married women..wrap their heads and mouthes with a narrow long piece of linnen. *a* **1680** BUTLER *Charac.*, *Corrupt Judge* (1908) 68 He wraps himself warm in Furs. **1755** J. SHEBBEARE *Matrimony* (1766) I. 186 With his Legs wrapt close in a Pair of good Hay-Boots. **1784** COWPER *Task* VI. 675 Some noble lord Shall..wrap himself in Hamlet's inky cloak. **1825** SCOTT *Talism.* xxii, Sir Kenneth..then wrapped him in the haik, or Arab cloak. **1831** —— *Ct. Rob.* xxviii, Let me wrap my head round with my mantle..to dispel this dizziness. **1871** CARLYLE in *Mrs. Carlyle's Lett.* III. 247 We had to wrap our invalid in quite a heap of rugs and shawls.

transf. and *fig.* **1382** WYCLIF *Job* xxxviii. 9 Whan I shuld setten the cloude his clothing, and with dercnesse it..I wrappide aboute. *c* **1391** CHAUCER *Astrol.* Prol., He wrappeth him in his frend, þat condescendith to the rihtful preiers of his frend. *c* **1412** HOCCLEVE *De Reg. Princ.* 1036 So lewdly in my termes I me wrappe. *c* **1550** in *Gamm. Gurton* II, I am so wrapt, and throwly lapt Of ioly good ale. **1575** VAUTROLLIER *Luther on Ep. Gal.* 136 As he [*sc.* Christ] is wrapped in our flesh and in our bloud. *c* **1640** WALLER *Apol. Sleep* 28 Where Phoebus never shrouds His golden beams, nor wraps his face in clouds. **1675** T. BROOKS *Gold. Key* 359 Faith wraps it self in the righteousness of Christ. **1697** DRYDEN *Æneis* VIII. 953 Sad Nilus..spreads his Mantle o're the winding Coast; In which he wraps his Queen. **1753** RICHARDSON *Grandison* II. xli. 313, I was resolved, if I were applied to, to wrap myself close about in a general denial. **1759** MASON *Caractacus* 75 Silent, as night, that wrapt us in her veil, We pac'd up yonder hill. **1850** TENNYSON *In Mem.* v. iii, In words, like weeds, I'll wrap me o'er. **1866** *Reader* 2 June 533 Francis II, wrapping the imperial phantom on its fall as decently as he could. **1880** MEREDITH *Tragic Com.* (1881) 143 She had to wrap her shivering spirit in a blind reliance..on him.

c. Freq. with *up*; esp. in later use *passive*, = attired in warmer or protective clothing. Also, *refl.*

c **1645** HOWELL *Lett.* II. lxix. (1892) 495 If you continue to wrap up our young acquaintance..in such warm choice swadlings, it will quickly grow up to maturity. **1652** BENLOWES *Theoph.* II. xviii, Now serves our guiltiness as winding sheet, To wrap up lepers; cover meet. **1662** J. DAVIES tr. *Olearius' Voy. Ambass.* 10 In the night time they are forc'd to wrap themselves up in certain linnen cloaths. **1756** C. LUCAS *Ess. Waters* I. 196, I know a gentleman ..[whose] servant wraps him up in a sheet dipped in cold water. **1774** GOLDSM. *Nat. Hist.* (1776) I. 148 The former thinks the cold so severe, that he wraps himself up in all the garments he can procure. **1853** DICKENS *Bleak Ho.* lvii, Are you well wrapped up?.. It's a desperate sharp night for a young lady to be out in. **1862** KINGSTON *Three Midshipmen* x, Their blankets..quickly dried, and the poor fellows were then wrapped up in them again. **1885** 'MRS. ALEXANDER' *Valerie's Fate* v, He had to be wrapped up against the cold and further fortified by a cup of black coffee.

d. *absol.* for *refl.*

1848 DICKENS *Dombey* xl, She never wrapped up enough. If a man don't wrap up..he has nothing to fall back upon. **1872** MARCH. DUFFERIN *Canad. Jrnl.* (1891) 52 The governess..won't wrap up..: nothing but a frost-bite will make her careful. **1885** 'MRS. ALEXANDER' *Valerie's Fate* ii, I advise you to take that delightful shawl of yours to wrap up in on your return.

2. a. To cover or envelop (an object) by winding or folding something round or about it; to surround *with* or enwrap *in* a covering, wrapper, or the like, esp. so as to protect from injury, damage, loss, etc. Also *transf.* (Cf. LAP *v.*[2] 3.)

1382 WYCLIF *1 Sam.* xxi. 9 The swerd..is wrappid with a pal after the preestis coope. *c* **1386** CHAUCER *Sqr.'s T.* 628 Canacee..softely in plastres gan hire [*sc.* an injured falcon] wrappe. **1398** TREVISA *Barth. De P.R.* x. iv. (Bodl. MS.), Briȝte bemes of stronge fuyre schyneþ but þei beþ wrapped. **1471** CAXTON *Recuyell* 121 b, Hercules..brak the bondes in whiche he was wrapped and swaded in. **1484** *Cely Papers* (Camden) 149, iij Angelettes wrappyd yn paper. **1508** *Bk. Keruynge* in *Babees Bk.* 269 Yf ye wyll wrappe your soueraynes brede stately. *c* **1550** H. LLOYD *Treas. Health* K j, Dyp wool in the decoction.., and let thy syde be wrapped often therewyth. **1585** HIGINS *Junius' Nomencl.* 110/2 The cod, or coate wherewith any kind of pulse is wrapped or couered. **1602** *2nd Pt. Return Parnass.* I. iii. 352 He..furnishes the Chaundlers with wast papers to wrap candles in. **1647** J. TAYLOR (Water P.) *Kings Welcome to Hampton Court* 3 Thou hast not wrap'd thy Talent in a Clout. **1676** COTTON *Angler* II. vii. 57 A great Hackle, the body black, and wrapped with a red feather. **1762** COWPER *To Miss Macartney* 33 Some Alpine mountain, wrapt in snow, Thus braves the whirling blast. **1812** BYRON *Ch. Har.* I. l, Subtle poniards, wrapt beneath the cloke. *c* **1890** BP. SELWYN in F. D. How *Life* (1899) 260 We can't be kept in bandboxes and wrapped in cotton wool all our lives. **1893** HODGES *Elem. Photogr.* (1907) 49 Wrap the tube in a piece of clean white paper.

fig. **1399** LANGL. *Rich. Redeles* III. 122 For all his witte in his wede ys wrappid ffor sothe. **1545** BALE *Myst. Iniq.* 67 For that shall they be wrapped in the cheanes of longe darkenesse. *a* **1586** SIDNEY *Apol. Poetrie* (Arb.) 27 Because thys second sorte is wrapped within the folde of the proposed subiect.

refl. **1526** TINDALE *Gal.* v. 1 Stond fast therfore.., and wrappe nott youre selves agayne in the yoke of bondage.

b. Freq. with advs., as *about, down, round, together*, and esp. *up*.

1382 WYCLIF *Isaiah* xiv. 19 Thou forsothe art cast aferr fro thi sepulcre..; and aboute wrappid with hem that ben slayn with swerd. **1577** HARRISON *England* III. i. (1878) II. 11 When the Bore is..cut out, ech peece is wrapped vp..with bulrushes, ozier peeles, packethreed, or such like. **1588** SHAKS. *Tit. A.* IV. ii. 27 The old man..sends the weapons wrapt about with lines, That wound..to the quick. **1662** EVELYN *Chalcogr.* II. (1906) 13 When he has quite don with his plates..see that he..cleanse them very perfectly, wrapping them up in papers. **1676** COTTON *Angler* II. viii. 78 A white Hackle, the body of white Mo-hair, and wrapped about with a white Hackle Feather. **1726** SWIFT *Adv. Grub-st. Writers* 8 Your still-born Poems shall revive, And scorn to wrap up Spice. **1799** G. SMITH *Laboratory* I. 35 When you see them, wrap them up in tow. **1827** FARADAY *Chem. Manip.* xxiii. 566 Waxed paper is very useful..for wrapping up deliquescent or changeable substances. **1846** TRENCH *Mirac.* xxix. (1862) 418 Every limb was wrapped round with these stripes by itself.

ellipt. **1879** OGDEN in J. H. Keene *Fishing Tackle* (1886) 170 Take a length of gut,..test it,..lay it underneath the hook, and wrap down with the waxed silk close and even.

†**c.** *Prov.* (See quot., and cf. LAP *v.*[2] 3 d.) *Obs.*[−0]

1677 MIÈGE *Fr. Dict.* II, Wrapped up in his mothers smock, *aimé des femmes.*

3. a. To envelop or enclose *in* a surrounding medium, as flames, water, etc. Freq. in *passive.* (Cf. 6 d.) Also *refl.*

1382 WYCLIF *Exod.* xiv. 27 The Egipciens fleynge,..the Lord wrapte hem with ynne in the myddel floodes. —— *Judith* xiv. 4 The dukis of hem..finden hym heded, in his blod wrappid. *c* **1510** *Gesta Rom.* (W. de Worde) A v, In his blode the bone was wrapped. **1590** SPENSER *F.Q.* III. xi. 55 Sad shadowes gan the world to hyde From mortall vew, and wrap in darkenesse dreare. *c* **1659** *Roxb. Ball.* (1888) VI. 326 A Man..Whose Father is wrapped in mould. **1667** MILTON *P.L.* IX. 158 Of these the vigilance I dread, and to elude, thus wrapt in mist Of midnight vapor glide obscure. **1715** POPE *Iliad* IV. 54 Fulfil thy stern desire, Burst all her gates, and wrap her walls in fire! **1761** GRAY *Odin* 93 Till wrap'd in flames, in ruin hurl'd, Sinks the fabric of the world. **1785** COWPER *Task* IV. 124 Oh Winter,..Thy forehead wrapt in clouds, A leafless branch thy sceptre. **1814** SCOTT *Wav.* i, The baron who wrapped the castle of his competitor in flames. **1908** G. CORMACK *Egypt in Asia* ii. 18 The loftier summits are wrapped in clouds.

fig. and in fig. context. **1382** WYCLIF *Job* xxxvii. 19 Wee forsothe ben wrappid in dercnessis. **1508** FISHER *7 Penit. Ps.* vi. Wks. (1876) 18 The fylthy voluptuousnes of the body, wherin the synner waltereth and wrappeth hymselfe lyke as a sowe waloweth..in the puddell. **1604** SHAKS. *Ham.* v. ii. 128 (Q. 2), Why doe we wrap the gentleman in our more rawer breath? **1896** MRS. CAFFYN *Quaker Grandmother* 176 Wrapping sin in clouds won't alter its character, my girl.

ellipt. **1382** WYCLIF *Judg.* v. 27 And he was wrappid bifore the feet of hir.

†**b.** To involve, environ, or entangle (a person, etc.) in something that impedes movement or restricts liberty; to catch in this way. Chiefly in *passive*. Also with *in*. *Obs.*

c **1412** HOCCLEVE *De Reg. Princ.* 1686 Be war of þencombraunce Of þe feend, which..him castiþ þe wrappe in & wrye. **1560** A. L. tr. *Calvin's Foure Serm. Songe Ezech.* (1574) D vij, When we shall mourne so that we should be so wrapped in and tangled. **1562** A. BROOKE *Romeus & Jul.* 220 How surely are the wareles wrapt by those that lye in wayte? **1569** BLAGUE *Sch. Conceytes* 268 The Hart..being entred into a thick wood, his horns were wrapped faste in the boughes. **1577** tr. *Bullinger's Decades* 158/1 Absalom.. beeing wrapped by the haire to a tree.

fig. **1591** GREENE *2nd Pt. Conny Catching* (1592) B 4 These moathes of the Common-wealth, apply their wits to wrappe in wealthy farmers with strange and vncoth conceits. **1594** SHAKS. *Lucr.* 636 O how are they wrapt in with infamies, That from their own misdeeds askaunce their eyes?

c. To clasp, embrace. Also in fig. context. (Cf. LAP *v.*[2] 3 c.)

1588 SHAKS. *Titus A.* IV. ii. 58 What dost thou wrap and fumble in thine armes? *a* **1600** DELONEY *Gentle Craft* II. vii, To perswade our great Grandmother the earth to wrap his cold body in her warme bosome. **1716** GAY *Trivia* I. 192 Others you'll see..Wrapt in th'embraces of a kersey coat. **1797** COLERIDGE *Melancholy* 3 Her folded arms wrapping her tatter'd pall.

4. a. To envelop, entangle, or implicate (a person, etc.) *in* (†*into*), to surround, encompass, or beset *with*, some (esp. prejudicial) condition of things, as sin, trouble, sorrow, etc. (Cf. ENWRAP *v.* 2 c.) Also occas. with *up*.

Freq. in *passive*, not always distinguishable from 6.

1380 *Lay Folks Catech.* (Lamb. MS.) 81 We be..wrappid with many myscheuys. *a* **1400** *Relig. Lyrics 14th C.* (1924) 234 Mannes soule was wrapped in wo. *c* **1412** HOCCLEVE *De Reg. Princ.* 959 My goost is wrapped in an heuy drede. *c* **1450** tr. *De Imitatione* III. v. 68 A synner þou art & encombred and wrapped in many passions. **1525** LD. BERNERS *Froiss.* II. vii. 16 Suche as than bare moost rule in the towne, were so wrapped with treason, y[t] [etc.]. **1526** TINDALE *Rom.* xi. 32 God hath wrapped all nacions in vnbeleve. **1560** DAUS tr. *Sleidane's Comm.* 37 b, The deuill is disposed to wrap vs in sondry calamities at one time. **1624** CARLETON *Thankf. Remembr.* ix. 95 They..stirred vp new troubles..by wrapping them in new garboiles against the King. *c* **1659** *Roxb. Ball.* (1886) VI. 326 It is a Man wrapped in woe. *a* **1839** PRAED *Poems* (1864) II. 40, I see him brood, Wrapt in his mental solitude. **1859** TENNYSON *Guinevere* 147 So the stately Queen abode.., Wrapt in her grief. **1899** G. WYNDHAM in *Westm. Gaz.* 15 Dec. 5/3 We were living from day to day wrapped in anxiety.

refl. *c* **1386** CHAUCER *Pars. T.* ¶ 586 Alle this manere of folk ..wrappen hem in hir synnes. *c* **1430** in *Pol., Rel., & L. Poems* (1903) 217 þou wrappist þee wiþ vanytees. *a* **1548** HALL *Chron., Hen. VII*, 49 He brought him selfe into a streyghter custody..and wrapped him selfe into tortures and punyshmentes. **1565** COOPER *Thesaurus* s.v. *Induco*, To wrappe or intangle him selfe in captious questions. **1675** DRYDEN *Aurengz.* I. (1676) 13 Though in one Fate I wrap my self and you.

transf. *c* **1611** CHAPMAN *Iliad* III. 418 Unhappy Deity! Why lov'st thou still in these deceits to wrap my fantasy?

b. To involve, enfold, or enwrap (a person, etc.) *in* some soothing or tranquillizing state or influence. Freq. in *passive*, = sunk *in* slumber, rest, etc. Also with *up*.

1399 LANGL. *Rich. Redeles* III. 291 Ho so þus leued his lyff to the ende, Euere wrappid in welle,.. Myȝte seie [etc.]. **1414** BRAMPTON *Penit. Ps.* (Percy Soc.) 10 Whan I am wrappyd in wele. **1590** SPENSER *F.Q.* I. i. 41 Carelesse Quiet lyes, Wrapt in eternall silence farre from enemyes. **1598** *Mucedorus* IV. i. 42 Musicke speake loudly now, the season's apt, For former dolours are in pleasure wrapt. **1717** POPE *Eloïsa* 302 Enter, each mild, each amicable guest; Receive, and wrap me in eternal rest! **1730** THOMSON *Autumn* 1202 He..hears, At distance safe, the human tempest roar, Wrapt close in conscious peace. **1798** COLERIDGE *Fears in Solitude* 25 His senses gradually wrapt In a half sleep, he dreams of better worlds. **1841** DICKENS *Barn. Rudge* ix, The house is wrapped in slumbers. **1857** HOLLAND *Bay Path* xxx. 371 Wrapped in ineffable repose, lay her child. **1872** *Punch* 2 March 95/2 They were soon wrapped in sound and healthy slumbers.

fig. **1791** COLERIDGE *Happiness* 79 Where far from splendour, far from riot, In silence wrapt sleeps careless Quiet.

5. a. To involve or enfold (a subject or matter) so as to obscure or disguise the true or full nature of it; to conceal or hide by enveloping *in* a mass of different character. Cf. 3.

1382 WYCLIF *Job* xxxviii. 2 Who is this, wrappende in sentencis with woordis vnwise? *c* **1386** CHAUCER *Sqr.'s T.* 507 Al were he ful of treson and falsnesse It was so wrapped vnder humble cheere And vnder hewe of trouthe. *c* **1400** *Destr. Troy* 1426 A word þat is wrappid, and in wrath holdyn. **1565** COOPER *Thesaurus*, *Implicata res controversiis*, a mattier wrapped and incombred with many controuersies. *a* **1586** SIDNEY *Arcadia* III. iv, He dispatched privat letters to al those principall Lords.., wrapping their hopes with such cunning, as they rather [etc.]. *a* **1639** T. CAREW *Ingrateful Beauty Threatened* iii, Wise poets, that wrapt Truth in tales. **1712–4** POPE *Rape Lock* II. 104 Some dire disaster..; But what, or where, the fates have wrapt in night. **1759** MASON *Caractacus* 41 Heard'st thou the awful invocation, Youth, Wrapt in those holy harpings? *a* **1770** JORTIN *Serm.* (1771) I. v. 85 The religion of the Egyptians..was all mystery, wrapt in obscurity. **1825** SCOTT *Talism.* xviii, I have no objection that leeches should wrap their words in mist. **1833** MRS. BROWNING *Prometh. Bound* Poems (1850) I. 184 Zeus requires Thy declaration..Do not wrap thy speech..but speak clearly! **1865** R. W. DALE *Jew. Temp.* iii. (1877) 35 The image wrapped in the word..is a very impressive and instructive one. **1869** FREEMAN *Norm. Conq.* (1875) III. xii. 253, I found the question wrapped in darkness.

b. Freq. with *up*. Also *transf.*

1560 BIBLE (Genev.) *Micah* vii. 3 Therefore the great man he speaketh out the corruption of his soule: so they wrap it vp. **1601** DANIEL *To Egerton* vi, If it be wisedome..Which so imbroyles the state of truth with brawles, And wrappes it vp in strange confusednesse. **1619** VISCT. DONCASTER *Let.* in *Eng. & Germ.* (Camden) 119 Sum more bitternes then her Highnes had wrapped up in sweet termes. **1669** STILLINGFL. *Serm.* 125 Here is no wrapping up Religion in strange figures and mysterious non-sense, which the Ægyptians were so much given to. **1712** ADDISON *Spect.* No. 271 ¶4 If it had been proper for them [*sc.* ladies] to hear,..the Author would not have wrapp'd it up in Greek. **1779** *Mirror* No. 22, It was some error in education which had wrapt up Cleone's character in so much obscurity. **1830** GEN. P. THOMPSON *Exerc.* (1842) I. 228 Their best..plan for seizing on the savings of other men's industry in the funds, is only spoliation wrapped up. **1897** P. WARUNG *Tales Old Régime* 14 Without troubling to wrap up his resolve in smooth-sounding words.

6. a. Of qualities, etc.: To invest, environ, or beset (a person, etc.); to encompass *in* some condition. Also with *up*. (Cf. 4.)

1382 WYCLIF *Job* xviii. 11 Al aboute feris shul gasten hym, and withinne wrappen his feet. **1549** COVERDALE, etc. *Erasm. Par. 1 Cor.* 18 Albeit matrimonie be a holy thyng, yet it wrappeth a man..in worldlye care. **1560** DAUS tr. *Sleidane's Comm.* 358 b, The self same cause..wyl shortly after wrap vp them also in great distresse. **1591** SPENSER *M. Hubberd* 602 Ay me..whom euill hap Vnworthy in such wretchednes doth wrap. **1608** SHAKS. *Lear* IV. iii. 54 (Q. 1) Some deere cause Will in concealement wrap me vp awhile. **1650** EARL MONM. tr. *Senault's Man bec. Guilty* 388 Humane Justice..wraps up the innocent and the guilty in the same punishment. **1665** SIR R. HOWARD & DRYDEN *Ind. Queen* II. i, Guilty rage, Which..wrapt all things in one cruel fate. **1734** WATTS *Reliq. Juv.* 122 Thy power, thy fulness of blessing, wrap my soul up in astonishment and devout silence. **1737** POPE *Hor., Ep.* II. i. 401 O'er the land and deep, Peace stole her wing, and wrapt the world in sleep. **1784** COWPER *Task* III. 146 They disentangle from the puzzled skein, In which obscurity has wrapp'd them up, The threads of..shrewd design. **1817** SHELLEY *Rev. Islam* VI. xxx, Oblivion wrapped Our spirits.

transf. *a* **1542** WYAT in *Tottel's Misc.* (Arb.) 73 Some pleasant hower thy wo may wrappe, and thee defend, and couer.

b. Of mould, etc.: To contain, cover (the dead).

1602 MARSTON *Antonio's Rev.* IV. v, By the fresh turned up mould that wraps my sonne. **1745** COLLINS *Ode on Death of Col. Ross* vii, Every sod, which wraps the dead. **1792** BURNS *Highland Mary* iii, Cauld's the clay, That wraps my Highland Mary! **1794** —— *Sonn. Death R. Riddel* ii, The sod that wraps my friend.

c. To form a wrap or covering for (a person or thing); to cover, clothe. Also with *round*.

c **1611** CHAPMAN *Iliad* x. 122 About him a mandilion,..A garment that 'gainst cold in nights, did soldiers use to wrap. **1732** POPE *Ep. to Cobham* 249 Let a charming Chintz, and Brussels lace Wrap my cold limbs, and shade my lifeless face. **1805** SCOTT *Last Minstrel* II. xix, A palmer's amice wrapp'd him round. **1871** *Amer. Encycl. Printing* 504/1 Wrappers..differ from them [*sc.* labels] in having larger margins, so that they can inclose or wrap up a bottle of patent medicine, a bar of soap, etc.

fig. **1842** TENNYSON *Vis. Sin* IV. v, Wine is good for shrivell'd lips, When a blanket wraps the day.

d. Of flames, etc.: To spread or extend around, about, or over (something); to surround, encompass. (Cf. 3.) Also with advs., as *round*, *up*.

1656 COWLEY *Davideis* II. 534 [A] sudden cloud..all his fame benights, and all his store, Wrapping him round, and now he's seen no more. **1699** GARTH *Dispens.* II. 13 Night had wrap'd in Shades the Mountain Heads. **1716** GAY *Trivia* III. 385 Flames sudden wrap the walls. **1774** GOLDSM. *Nat. Hist.* (1776) I. 357 Our own muddy atmosphere, that wraps us round in obscurity. **1810** SCOTT *Lady of Lake* III. xxiv, Not faster..speeds the midnight blaze,..Wrapping thy cliffs in purple glow. **1860** TYNDALL *Glac.* I. xviii. 133 A thick fog..wrapped the mountain quite closely. **1899** CROCKETT *Kit Kennedy* 337 The snow had wrapped all the city in a white clinging mystery.

fig. **1794** MRS. RADCLIFFE *Myst. Udolpho* xv, How beautiful was the tranquility that wrapped the scene. **1813** SHELLEY *Q. Mab* IV. 4 The speaking quietude That wraps this moveless scene.

e. To veil or conceal *from* a person, etc.

1817 SHELLEY *Rev. Islam* Ded. xiv, While clouds are passing by Which wrap them [*sc.* stars] from the foundering seaman's sight. **1867** MORRIS *Jason* II. 105 A cloud..That wrapt the Goddess from him.

7. *to wrap up* (*fig.*) **a.** *trans.* To put an end to, bring to completion; also, to defeat; *to wrap it up*, to stop doing something. *slang.*

1926 T. E. LAWRENCE *Seven Pillars* (1935) III. xxxvi. 213 The British were wrapping up the Arabs on all sides—at Aden, at Gaza, at Bagdad. **1937** *Amer. Legion Monthly* May 9/1 Only one shot to finish before midnight and we'd wrap it up in thirteen days. **1949** A. MILLER *Death of Salesman* II. 128 To hell with whose fault it is... Let's just wrap it up, heh? **1957** J. OSBORNE *Look back in Anger* I. 25 Wrap it up, will you? Stop ringing those bells! **1957** P. FRANK *Seven Days to Never* II. vii. 80, I guess that wraps it up for tonight. .. I don't know of anything else we can do. **1960** G. SANDERS *Mem. Professional Cad* II. iii. 127 'Wrap it up,' he would shout. **1976** *Billings* (Montana) *Gaz.* 2 July 1-c/1 Nastase wrapped up Ramirez, 6-2, 9-7, 6-3. **1984** *Times* 14 Mar. 2/1 (*heading*) Labour MPs advised to wrap up their muck raking.

b. *intr.* To stop talking. Freq. as imp. *slang.*

1943 HUNT & PRINGLE *Service Slang* 70 *Wrap up*, stop talking. Or, get ready to go home. **1945** C. H. WARD-JACKSON *Piece of Cake* (ed. 2) 63 *Wrap up!*, Be quiet! Pipe down! **1958** F. NORMAN *Bang to Rights* I. 49 Why dont you rap up. **1959** 'O. MILLS' *Stairway to Murder* iv. 44 'Geoff, wrap up about the jigsaws,' Charles entreated him.

8. *intr. Cinemat.* and *Television.* To finish filming or recording.

1976 in B. Armstrong *Gloss. TV Terms* 94. **1983** *London Mag.* Aug./Sept. 30 We wrapped on schedule, three days later.. The movie got terrible reviews.

II. 9. To wind or fold up or together, as a pliant or flexible object; to roll or gather up in successive layers; = LAP *v.*² 2. Occas. with *up* or *together*. Also *transf.*

c **1350** *Will. Palerne* 2421 As bliue þe bere schinnes from here bodi þei hent, & wiȝtly wrapped hem to-gadere. **14..** *Trevisa's Barth. De P.R.* XVIII. ix. (B.M. Add. MS.) fol. 266 b/2 Alle kynde of serpentes and addres þat by kynde may wrappe and folde his owne body. **1535** COVERDALE *2 Kings* ii. 8 Then toke Elias his cloke, and wrapped it together. **1555** WATREMAN *Fardle Facions* I. ii. B v, For saie thei, the begynner of thinges visible, wrapped vp bothe heauen and earth..together in one paterne. **1590** SPENSER *F.Q.* I. i. 18 The vgly monster.., wrapping vp her wrethed sterne arownd, Lept fierce vpon her shield. **1600** in *Lyly's Wks.* (1902) I. 416 Can there be miste or darkenes where you are, whose beames wrappes up cloudes as whirlewindes dust? **1608** *Great Frost* in Arber *Garner* I. 87 The western barges might now wrap up their smoky sails; for..their voyage was spoiled. **1653** W. RAMESEY *Astrol. Restored* 304 Thunder is ..an exhalation..thickened and wraped into a cloud. **1662** R. VENABLES *Experienc'd Angler* v. 61 Bream loveth red worms, especially those that [lie]..wrapped up in a knot or round Clue.

fig. *c* **1374** CHAUCER *Boeth.* II. met. vii. (1868) 60 Deep wrappeþ to gidre þe heye heuedes and þe lowe. **1382** WYCLIF *Lam.* i. 14 Wakide the ȝoc of my wickenesses in his hond, wrappid thei ben togidere, and leid on my necke. **1399** LANGL. *Rich. Redeles* I. 82 Wayte well my wordis, and wrappe hem togedir. *a* **1568** ASCHAM *Scholem.* I. (Arb.) 27 In these fewe lines, I haue wrapped vp the most tedious part of Grammer. **1576** FLEMING *Panopl. Epist.* 337 For end, he wisheth malicious..persons a better spirit..and so wrappeth vp all with commendations. **1618** DONNE *Serm.* (1661) III. 173 In all this, thou dost but wrap up a snow-ball upon a coal of fire. **1625** BACON *Ess., Cunning* (Arb.) 441 Some haue in readinesse so many Tales and Stories, as there is Nothing, they would insinuate, but they can wrap it into a Tale.

refl. **1565** COOPER *Thesaurus* s.v. *Torqueo*, The scalie serpent wrappeth himselfe in rounde rundels.

10. a. To fold, wind, or roll (a covering, garment, or the like) about a person, etc.; to arrange or dispose (a wrapping, etc.) so as to cover or envelop; = LAP *v.*² 1. Usu. with advs. or preps., esp. *about*, *around*, *round*.

Somewhat rare before *c* 1790.

c **1400** *Rom. Rose* 7368 A large couerechief of threde She wrapped all aboute hir heede. **1565** COOPER *Thesaurus* s.v. *Intortus*, His garment wrapped rounde about his lefte arme. **1590** SPENSER *F.Q.* I. ix. 36 His garment.., The which his naked sides he wrapt abouts. **1636** SIR H. BLOUNT *Voy.* 19 The Levantines used to wrap white linnen about their heads. **1773** GRAVES *Spiritual Quixote* XI. iv, Unto the old Incumbent at his gate.., His banyan, with silver clasp, wrapt round His shrinking paunch. **1796** COLERIDGE *'Away, those cloudy looks'* vi, There shiv'ring sad,..Round his tir'd limbs to wrap the purple vest. **1813** SCOTT *Rokeby* I. i, The warder..wraps his shaggy mantle round. **1860** TYNDALL *Glac.* I. vi. 45 Wrapping my plaid around me, I wandered up towards Charmoz. **1882** *Blackw. Mag.* March 309/1 Dick..wrapped the heavy coat around her and held her in his arms.

fig. and *transf.* *a* **1814** WORDSW. *Excurs.* IV. 83 Thou, who didst wrap the cloud Of infancy around us. **1820** SHELLEY *Hymn Merc.* xxxvi, The God wraps a purple atmosphere Around his shoulders. **1865** BARING-GOULD *Werewolves* x. 160 Among many..people, the body is regarded as a mere garment wrapped around the soul.

b. To twist or coil (a pliable or flexible substance, etc.) *round*, *about*, or *on* something; to twine. Also *refl.*

1523 FITZHERB. *Husb.* §127 Cutte the settes..the more halue a-sonder;..and wrappe and wynde theym together. **1535** COVERDALE *Jonah* ii. 5 The depe laye aboute me, and the wedes were wrapte aboute myne heade. **1560** BIBLE *Job* viii. 17 The rotes thereof are wrapped about the fountaine. **1578** LYTE *Dodoens* 390 Woodbine hath many small branches, whereby it windeth and wrappeth itself about trees. **1728** CHAMBERS *Cycl.* (1738) s.v. *Turban*, About this [cap] is wrapped a long piece of fine thin linnen or cotton. **1753–4** RICHARDSON *Grandison* II. xxxix. 310 Again she wrapped her arms about me. **1815** J. SMITH *Panorama Sci. & Art* II. 119 The Screw of Archimedes..is formed by wrapping a tube round a cylinder. **1852** MRS. STOWE *Uncle Tom's C.* xxviii, 'What did you wrap this round the book for?' said St. Clare, holding up the crape. **1854** R. BLAKEY *Angling* 60 A strong peg..on which..the line can be wrapped.

11. a. *intr.* (for *refl.*). To twine, encircle, or wreathe *round* or *about* something as or in the manner of a wrapper or cover; = LAP *v.*² 1 b. Also *transf.*

1608 *Relat. Trav. W. Bush* D j b, The Vyne so loueth the Elme by nature that it wrappeth more kindely about it. **1680** MOXON *Mech. Exerc.* xiii. 223 A Flat Leather Thong, which wrapping close and tight about the Rowler..commands it the easier. **1681** T. FLATMAN *Heraclitus Ridens* No. 35 (1713) I. 228 Well; and Conscience,..when you have once boil'd it tender in the Pipkin of Reformation, it will wrap about your Finger like a Glove. **1838** *Civil Eng. & Arch. Jrnl.* I. 272/1 [With] the formation of the extreme end of the breakwater..it would be next to impossible for a sea to warp or wrap around it. **1855** *Orr's Circ. Sci., Inorg. Nat.* 55 Gneiss is often found wrapping round the central granitic axis of mountain chains.

b. Of a garment: To extend *over* the figure, etc., so as to cover it, or form a lap. (Cf. LAP *v.*² 8.)

1798 *Lady's Monthly Mus.* Nov. I. 397 The gown, wrapping over one side,..drawn up a little with white cord. **1827** *Lady's Mag.* Nov. 621/1 Mantles..well wadded, capacious, and wrapping well over the form, are much in request.

12. *to wrap oneself (a)round* (an item of food or drink): to eat or drink it. Occas. with non-*refl.* direct obj., to make (another) eat or drink. *colloq.*

1880 J. C. HARRIS *Uncle Remus* xv. 219 She cut me off er slishe..an' I sot down on de steps an' wrop myse'f roun' de whole blessid chunk. **1927** D. L. SAYERS *Unnatural Death* xii. 136 Lord Peter, having wrapped himself affectionately round an abnormal quantity of bacon and eggs, strolled out. **1946** K. TENNANT *Lost Haven* (1947) xviii. 305, I bet they had to wrap Alec round a few beers before they got him up to the mark. **1959** G. ENDORE *Detour through Devon* 3 Wrap yourself around a cup of coffee. **1962** A. LEJEUNE *Duel in Shadows* ii. 25, I shall be glad to get indoors and wrap myself round a large drink.

13. To crash (a vehicle) into a stationary object. Const. *around*, *round*. *slang.*

1950 J. D. MACDONALD *Brass Cupcake* (1955) x. 105, I took a car off the street and wrapped it around an oak tree. **1958** 'J. BROGAN' *Cummings Report* xvii. 183 Steady, or you'll have us both wrapped round a telegraph pole if you're not careful. **1969** L. G. ARTHUR in A. E. Wilkerson *Rights of Children* (1973) 132 If a child wraps a stolen car around a telephone pole, is $2,000.00 restitution..an excessive fine? **1984** *Times* 19 May 8/1 The men towing the boat from one training venue to another wrapped it round a traffic light.

wrap, erron. f. (freq. *c* 1600–1680) of RAP *v.*³

1561 NORTON & SACKV. *Gorboduc* IV. ii. 239 His noble limmes in such proportion cast As would have wrapt a sillie womans thought. **1592** *No-body & Some-b.* in Simpson *Sch. Shaks.* (1878) 317 Your kinglie presence wraps my soule to heaven. **1615** DAY *Festivals* 295 Al they can wrap and rend is little enough for Wife and Children. **1622** PEACHAM *Compl. Gent.* xvi. 206 Whatsoeuer he could wrap or wring. **1641** SYMONDS *Serm. bef. Ho. Comm.* C, The command must needs come with much evidence when it wrappeth the will into such an height. **1653** HOLCROFT *Procopius, Vandal Wars* II. 55 Artabanes..[fell] into a deep musing,..seeming wrapt with the greatness of the action. **1679** C. NESSE *Antid. agst. Popery* 193 The Apostle..[was] wrap'd up to the third heaven. **1854** MISS BAKER *Northampt. Gloss.* II. 408 He wraps and wrings all he can. **1922** E. PHILLPOTTS *Grey Room* iv. 106 He was wrapt from this life to the next.

wrap-, **1.** the verb stem in comb. with a sb. or adv., in sense of 'that which wraps or is wrapped about', as **wrap reel** (see quot.), **wrap tobacco** (also *ellipt.*), = WRAPPER *sb.* 4. Also WRAP-RASCAL.

1888 *Pall Mall G.* 2 Oct. 11/1 What is known as 'wrap' tobacco is the special kind which it is sought to cultivate. *Ibid.*, 'Wrap' fetches from 2*s.* to 3*s.* 6*d.* [per lb.]. **1890** NASMITH *Mod. Cotton Spinning Machinery* xiv. 291 In order to ascertain the counts of yarn, a machine known as a 'wrap reel' is employed. This consists of a small fly or swift.

2. *spec.* Designating a garment to be wrapped about the body for warmth, or a wraparound garment (see WRAPAROUND *a.* 1 a).

1845 *Ainsworth's Mag.* VII. 499 A wrap-cloak, or sheet, being thrown penance-ways over the head and shoulders. **1887** *Manch. Exhib. Catal.* 64 Warm Wrap Shawls. **1928** *Daily Mail* 9 Aug. 3/4 A..bathing dress worn under a well cut wrap-coat of crêpe de Chine. **1976** *New Yorker* 8 Mar. 1 (Advt.), Reversible wrap skirt lined in red and white. **1980** L. BIRNBACH et al. *Official Preppy Handbk.* 131/1 Diane von Furstenburg wrap dress. **1982** BARR & YORK *Official Sloane Ranger Handbk.* 30/1 A belted wool wrap coat: this can be tweedy, checked or camel. **1984** *Chicago Sun-Times* 25 Jan. 33/1 By 1976 she had designed the wrap dress, which became an overnight success.

wraparound ('ræpəraʊnd), *sb.* and *a.* Also **wrap-around, wrapround, wrap-round.** [f. WRAP *v.* + AROUND *adv.* and *prep.*]

A. *sb.* **1.** A garment that is thrown or wrapped round the body; a wraparound garment (see sense B. 1 a below).

1877 BROWNING *Agamemnon* 120 A wrap-round [Gr. ἀμφίβληστρον] with no outlet..I fence about him—the rich woe of the garment. **1959** *Vogue Pattern Bk.* June–July 25 A wrap-around that buttons into place... The sort of comfort-with-elegance dress. **1973** *Harrods Christmas Catal.* 27 Casual wrap-around in figured polyester.

2. A fastening or label that wraps round a bottle.

1953 *Federal Suppl.* CXVIII. 182/2 The Guardian Seal, made of aluminum, attached to the bottle and requiring no secondary closure;..wrap arounds, a laminated foil attached to a paper with an adhesive on the inside giving the same decorative features as a cellulose band; [etc.]. **1966** J. AIKEN *Trouble with Product X* iii. 43, I switched over to copy for a counter-card, window bill and wrap-around for Bom, the Meat'n Milk Drink. **1970** K. PLATT *Pushbutton Butterfly* (1971) xiii. 149 He..came back with a bottle. He unfurled the plastic wraparound and broke it open.

3. *Computers.* The procedure or facility by which a linear sequence of memory locations or positions on a screen is treated cyclically, so that when the last has been counted or occupied the first is returned to automatically (on the line below in the case of screen displays). Also *transf.*

1965 E. A. WEISS *Programming the IBM 1620* ii. 21 This wrap-around feature does not apply to addresses used in commands. **1970** O. DOPPING *Computers & Data Processing* vi. 101 Even when the index register has no room for sign, subtraction can be done by utilizing the cyclic character of the addressing system ('wraparound'). **1979** J. E. ROWLEY *Mechanised In-House Information Syst.* I. 76 Display can be improved by..contextual wrap-around, or bringing the end of the title to the left hand side of a keyword and then marking the end of the title with a display device.

B. *adj.* **1.** *Fashion.* **a.** Of a garment: that is open all the way down, wraps around the body, and is fastened usu. by tying. Also, of a belt.

1937 M. LEVIN *Old Bunch* 13 She dressed spiffy with wrap-around sport skirts. **1938** 'E. QUEEN' *Four of Hearts* (1939) x. 143 A silver lamé hostess-gown with a trailing wrap-around skirt over Turkish trousers. **1945** [see POP-OVER 2]. **1951** *Rep. Patent, Design & Trade Mark Cases* (U.S.) LXVIII. 256 Mr. Percival contended that the Applicants' skirt was a novel 'wrap round' skirt. **1957** *U.S. Supreme Court Rep.* 2nd Ser. I. 880/1, 1 Purple wool imitation lambskin wrap around short coat. **1972** J. GODEY *Three Worlds* ii. 19 The man was wearing a wraparound coat of some synthetic fur. **1976** *Scotsman* 20 Nov. (Weekend Suppl.) 4/3 (Advt.), Right: The unlined, hooded style of winter coat with wrap-around belt. **1976** T. STOPPARD *Dirty Linen* 9 Maddie is..wearing..a wrap-round skirt, quite short. **1982** BARR & YORK *Official Sloane Ranger Handbk.* 42/1 There are a few basic lines that continue practically for ever, like the pre-war wraparound double-breasted and the basic City three-piece.

b. Of sunglasses, goggles, etc.: that have lenses which extend around the side of the head.

1966 T. PYNCHON *Crying of Lot 49* iii. 57 There stood Di Presso, in a skin-diving suit and wraparound shades. **1968** A. WILLIAMS *Brotherhood* I. iv. 50 He was no longer wearing his wrap-around dark glasses. **1976** *National Observer* (U.S.) 27 Mar. 15 (Advt.), Space-age wraparound sunglasses make all others obsolete!

2. a. That extends round a corner, esp. of parts of a building or parts of a motor vehicle.

1954 *Archit. Rev.* CXVI. 92/1 The wrap-round cornices are used to tie it back to the side façade. **1957** H. ROTH *Shadow of Lady* xiv. 103 A sturdy little car..even if without American flourishes, like 'wrap-around' wind-screens. **1959** *Motor* 21 Jan. 951/1 Protective wrap-around bumpers. **1966** *Daily Tel.* 9 Nov. 12/5 Recent years' flirtation with vestigial fins, wrap-round rear windows and other gimmicks. **1972** [see *wet-suited* adj. s.v. WET *a.* 21]. **1972** *Village Voice* (N.Y.) 1 June 87/4 (Advt.), Huge liv rm & wraparound sundeck. **1976** *Glasgow Herald* 26 Nov. 19/5 Visibility from the reclining driver's seat is outstanding, with a very wide and deep 'wrap around' rear window. **1980** J. STROUSE *Alice James* (1981) xiii. 221 The buildings..are..ornamented with scrollwork, wraparound porches, archways.

b. Of a cinema screen: having a greater sideways extent than normal; subtending a large angle at the audience. Similarly of a view. Also *fig.*

1950 *Pop. Sci. Monthly* Aug. 75 You're not just looking *at* this 'wrap-around' movie show—you're in it! **1968** *Globe & Mail* (Toronto) 17 Feb. 25 (Advt.), Look down on the world from Stop. 33. The room with the wrap-around view. **1968** *Tel.* (Brisbane) 18 Sept. 34/5 His book is entitled *The Invasion*... Hay contents himself with a brief, wraparound picture of the real invasion. **1972** J. MCCLURE *Caterpillar Cop* i. 7 The Big Romance soon to be filmed in fabulous Technicolor on a wrap-round screen.

3. *gen.* That surrounds or encompasses.

1957 *Times Survey Brit. Aviation* Sept. 2/4 The missile has a two-stage propulsion system, consisting of wrap-around boosts and a sustainer rocket motor. **1964** M. MCLUHAN *Understanding Media* (1967) xxviii. 300 Stereo sound..is 'all-around' or 'wrap-around' sound. **1967** *Maclean's Mag.* Sept. 14 The Volkswagen is the German's ideal image of space: it's a wraparound, secure little thing. **1970** *Gloss. Aeronaut. & Astronaut. Terms* (*B.S.I.*) VI. 3 *Wrap-round boost*, a number of boost rocket motor assemblies located externally along the sides of the missile body. **1978** *Detroit Free Press* 5 Mar. A10 (Advt.), Wrap-around heat encircles the sides of the crockware. **1979** *Jrnl. R. Soc. Arts* CXXVII. 655/2 The 21 new rooms and the lower gallery..provide a more than adequate wrap-around environment for the works on display. **1981** *Times* 27 Jan. 1/8 His wrap-around bodyguards leapt from the flower-beds.., shouldering reporters and Saudi policemen from his path so that..it was simply not possible to see more than his eyebrows and hair.

4. *Printing.* Designating a flexible relief printing plate which is wrapped round the cylinder of a rotary press, and machines or methods which employ one.

1959 *Brit. Printer* Dec. 116/3 (Index), Wrap-around, Harris letterpress rotary. **1962** [see ROTARY *a.* 2 b]. **1963** *Publishers' Weekly* 5 Aug. 87/1 Wrap-around relief printing —direct and indirect—is..being used increasingly... Most of the printing is for labels and packaging materials. **1972** A. TYRRELL *Basics of Reprography* xiv. 216 In this way curved or wrap-around printing formes can be prepared by reprographic methods, from relief surfaces in the flat. **1983** A. CAMPBELL *Designer's Handbk.* viii. 128 A modern development of letterpress printing is the wrap-around rotary press, which prints from a one-piece shallow relief plate fastened around a press cylinder.

5. *Publishing.* Designating (*a*) a book cover made from a single sheet of material; (*b*) a jacket whose design extends from front to back without being divided by the spine.

1968 G. A. STEVENSON *Graphic Arts Encycl.* 418 *Wrap-around cover*, soft cover used to bind or hold a booklet, brochure, etc. It consists of one sheet or stock that forms both front and back covers. Any type of mechanical binding may be used. **1972** *N.Y. Law Jrnl.* 24 Oct. 4/2 It must have a wrap-around cover page containing the usual information. **1979** *Bookseller* 23 June 2829/2 Mr. Paton thought that designers did not give nearly enough consideration to the potential of the spine. In this respect he was suspicious of the wrapround jacket.

6. *U.S. Finance.* Used with reference to (*a*) a mortgage which continues when the mortgaged property is sold, the repayments to the original lender being made by a new lender who also provides the additional funds needed for the purchase; (*b*) a tax-deferral scheme in which the interest on certain investments goes into paying the premiums for an annuity.

1968 *Federal Suppl.* CCXCII. 594 Midwestern would exchange a $2·2 million wrap around note, secured by certain hotel properties. **1971** *Legal Bull.* (U.S.) Sept. 185 Wrap-around mortgage financing. **1977** *National Observer* (U.S.) 22 Jan. 8/2 The days may be numbered for a popular tax shelter known as the investment, or 'wrap-around', annuity. **1979** *Arizona Daily Star* 5 Aug. (Advt. Section) 17/8 Priced below appraisal. Will consider a wrap-around deed or trust. **1981** *U.S. Federal Reg.* 7 Apr. 20875/1 Official Staff Interpretation FC-0146..treats 'wrap-around' loans as the equivalent of refinancings.

wrape, obs. erron. f. RAPE *v.*[2] 4.

1584 PEELE *Arraignm. Paris* II. ii, The least of these delights,..Able to wrape and dazle humaine eyes.

wrap-over ('ræpəʊvə(r)), *sb.* and *a.* Also **wrap over, wrapover.** [f. WRAP *v.* + OVER *adv.*]

A. *sb.* Part of something, usu. a garment, that overlaps another part of itself.

1935 *Times* 21 Oct. 11/3 There is a good wrapover on the skirt of the coat. **1960** *Vogue Pattern Bk.* Early Autumn 37 Divided skirt..concealed by a wrap-over at front and back.

B. *adj.* **a.** Of a garment: having a wrap-over. **b.** Overlapping.

1960 *Guardian* 19 Feb. 8/7 A wrap-over petal skirt. **1973** *Harrods Christmas Catal.* 24/1 Wrap-over coat from Italy. **1979** *Nature* 19 Apr. p. xvii/3 The simple laboratory stirrer ..has a wrapover top to provide spillage protection. **1979** *Homes & Gardens* June 103/1 The wrapover skirt, very fashionable this summer, is made of four flared panels, lightly gathered at the waist.

wrappage ('ræpɪdʒ). [f. WRAP *v.* + -AGE.]

I. 1. That which wraps, enfolds, or covers; a wrap or outer covering; a wrapper of a parcel, packet, or the like.

In freq. use, esp. *fig.*, from *c* 1860.

fig. **1827** CARLYLE *Ess.*, *Richter* (1840) I. 15 Every work, be it fiction or serious treatise, is embaled in some fantastic wrappage, some mad narrative accounting for its appearance. **1842** SARA COLERIDGE in Coleridge *Aids Refl.* (1843) II. 445 To consider the words of Scripture as mere wrap-pages for some more definite revelation out of Scripture. **1851** CARLYLE *Sterling* II. iii, Not till..he had unwinded from him the wrappages of it [*ante* the conscious life ecclesiastical], could he become clear about himself. **1859** HELPS *Friends in C.* Ser. II. II. iii. 68 All these things, dress, fortune, etc. are mere wrappages compared with the substantial ground of a man's character. **1881** A. C. BRADLEY in *Macm. Mag.* XLIV. 36 The words of the *Prometheus*, however insignificant their historical wrappage may have seemed to him.

lit. **1846–8** LOWELL *Biglow P.* Ser. I. vi. ad fin., Tomorrow this sheet..shall be the wrappage to a bar of soap. **1871** W. COLLINS *Marq. & Merchant* I. 232 No possible wrappages can keep that poison from operating. **1886** D. C. MURRAY *First Person Sing.* xxii, The knots were conquered, the paper wrappages removed.

b. Without article. Material used for covering or enveloping; wrapping material. Also *fig.*

a **1876** M. COLLINS *Th. in Garden* (1880) I. 187 Odd things are met with in the papers used by shopkeepers for wrappage. **1881** E. DOWDEN in *Academy* 12 Feb. 118 Nothing should be lost, except what is unvital, mere wrappage and encumbrance of history.

2. A loose garment for enveloping the person; a wrapper. Also in fig. context.

1831 CARLYLE *Sart. Res.* I. i, The vestural Tissue..which Man's Soul wears as its outmost wrappage and overall. **1837** —— *Fr. Rev.* II. III. iv, Figure under what thousand-fold wrappages and cloaks of darkness Royalty, meditating these things, must involve itself. **1863** D. WILSON in *Edin. New Phil. Jrnl.* XVIII. 79 The constant laying of the infant to rest on its side,..along with the fashion of cap, hat, or wrappage, may [etc.]. **1868** BROWNING *Ring & Bk.* III. 446 Another wrappage, namely one thick veil That hid her, matron-wise, from head to foot.

3. Something wrapped up; a package, parcel.

1883 *Daily Tel.* 19 Nov. 5/3 This paper wrappage was taken on by train to Stalybridge.

II. 4. The action of wrapping. *rare*—[0].

1846 WORCESTER (citing *Ec. Rev.*). [Hence in later Dicts.]

wrappe, obs. var. (and pa. t.) of WARP *v.* 1.

1303 R. BRUNNE *Handl. Synne* 7517 Alle naked hym-self he wrappe Among þe þornes þat were sharpe. **1426** LYDG. *De Guil. Pilgr.* 21932 Yiff I hadde wrappyd the, Nakyd, cast the vp and doun In thornys for thy savacioun. **15..** *Henryson's Paddock & Mouse* 171 (Harl. MS.), Now hie, now law,..Now on the quheill, now wrappit [*Bann. MS.* wappit] to the ground.

wrapped (ræpt), *ppl. a.* and *pa. pple.* Also 7– wrapt. [f. WRAP *v.* + -ED[1].]

I. 1. Concealed, covered, hidden.

1398 TREVISA *Barth. De P.R.* x. iv. (Bodl. MS.), Fuyre.. beschyneþ alle þinges wiþ his..wrapped [L. *circumvelatus*] briȝtenes. **1601** CHESTER *Love's Mart.*, etc. (1878) 125 Ile be partener Of thy harts wrapped sorrow more hereafter.

2. With *up*: **a.** Involved, complicated; couched in complex, covert, or vague terms.

1787 JEFFERSON *Writ.* (1853) II. 304, I have analyzed these declarations, because being somewhat wrapped up in their expressions, their full import might escape, on a transient reading. **1896** *Daily News* 13 Jan. 7/1 It is the way of the 'Temps' to speak in wrapped-up language, but throughout ..the crisis its utterances have been even more than usually enigmatical. **1898** *Ibid.* 14 Nov. 5/2 The beauty of the Fashoda Blue Book was the absence..of wrapped up phrases.

b. Muffled *up* in, covered *up* with, a wrap or enveloping garment.

1793 F. BURNEY *Let.* 24 Feb. (1972) II. 26, I live a Wrapt up Invalide, close to the Fire side. **1852** DICKENS *Bleak Ho.* ii, The shining figure of a wrapped-up man. **1901** *Westm. Gaz.* 8 June 1/3 The wrapped-up figure on a pedestal.

c. Marked or characterized by absorbed attention. (Cf. 6.)

1884 *Pall Mall G.* 8 Nov. 4/1 His incapacity to hear.. gives him a more wrapped up air than the brother. **1893** *Daily News* 27 June 6/3 Faces wore a 'wrapped up' expression, and voices were hard and tuneless.

3. Drawn together, fashioned, made, or constructed by wrapping or twining.

1820 KEATS *Cap and Bells* xxv, With hasty steps, wrapp'd cloak, and solemn looks..[he] upon his errand sallies. **1837** KIRKBRIDE *Northern Angler* 2 The wrapt hackle flies are generally most esteemed in this part of the country. **1907** C. HILL-TOUT *Brit. N. Amer.*, *Far West* vi. 109 Woven basketry..embraces by far the greater number of basket forms, and includes..such [kinds] as wicker-work, wrapped-work, twilled-work.

4. Enclosed in a wrapping; *spec.* prepackaged.

1957 M. SUMMERTON *Sunset Hour* xiii. 186 The loaf of wrapped bread. **1963** L. DEIGHTON *Horse under Water* vi. 31 Plastic spoons and large wrapped sugar segments. **1976** *Times* 13 Aug. 2/6 The familiar wrapped and sliced white loaf still accounts for more than half of bread sales. **1984** C. CURZON *Masks & Faces* viii. 90 He fetched the wrapped loaf and filled the toaster.

II. In predicative use. **5. a.** Deeply interested, centred or absorbed, *in* a person or thing.

a **1548** HALL *Chron.*, *Hen. V*, 34 b, Benedict the .xiii... was wrapped in his owne folishe and fantastical opinion. **1581** MARBECK *Bk. of Notes* 599 Him that is wrapped in the businesse of this world. **1816** BYRON *Ch. Har.* III. cxv, My daughter!.. I see thee not, I hear thee not, but none Can be so wrapt in thee. **1848** DICKENS *Dombey* xxxv, Whether Mr. Dombey, wrapped in his own greatness, was at all aware of this or no.

b. Freq. with *up*. †Also const. *with* (= *in*).

In very frequent use from *c* 1820.

(*a*) **1699** BOYER *Fr. Dict.* II, I am so wrapt up with him, *je l'aime si éperdûment*. **1704** F. FULLER *Med. Gymn.* (1705) 142 How much soever some People may be Rapt up with their *Sal Volatile*. **1784** P. WRIGHT *New Bk. Martyrs* 794/2 King James was..so wrapt up with a conceit, that he had now conquered the whole nation.

(*b*) **1709** STEELE *Tatler* No. 139 ¶5 Being wrapped up in the safety of my old age. **1711** ADDISON *Spect.* No. 105 ¶6 The State-Pedant is wrapt up in News. **1776** FOOTE *Bankrupt* I. 3 His whole soul is wrapt up in Miss Lydia. **1784** P. WRIGHT *New Bk. Martyrs* 805/1, I want words to express it, he was like one wrapped up in heaven. **1806–7** J. BERESFORD *Miseries Hum. Life* (1826) XVI. iii, Before you are yet sufficiently wrapped up in the study. **1851** BRIMLEY *Ess., Wordsw.* 166 His heart was wrapped up in his wife and sister. **1880** J. PAYN *Confid. Agent* I. 31, I like a man to be wrapped up in his own calling.

c. *wrapped* (*up*) *in*, entirely associated or bound up with; quite dependent on; involved in.

1648 J. BEAUMONT *Psyche* v. 131 O then, first for your own illustrious sake, And next, for Us wrapp'd up in you, beware Of his Designs in time. **1711** ADDISON *Spect.* No. 123 ¶4 His young Wife (in whom all his Happiness was wrapt up) died. **1760–72** H. BROOKE *Fool of Qual.* (1809) II. 157 He was the only child.., and..the lives of his parents were wrapt up in him. **1847** JAMES *Convict* I. 108, I put mine [*sc.* happiness] under your guardianship also, for mine is wrapped up in yours. **1859** MISS PIDDINGTON *Last of Cavaliers* II. 69 My mother's whole life is wrapped in him. **1892** J. TAIT *Mind in Matter* (ed. 3) 167 Wrapped up in the mysterious nature of Self-existence, is the equally mysterious power of communicating existence.

6. Absorbed or engrossed *in* thought, contemplation, etc. Also in earlier use with *up*.

Perhaps partly suggested by RAPT *pa. pple.* 4.

1601 SHAKS. *All's Well* v. iii. 128, I am wrap'd in dismall thinkings. **1634** MILTON *Comus* 546, I..began Wrapt in a pleasing fit of melancholy To meditate my rural minstrelsie. **1726** SWIFT *Gulliver* III. ii, He is always..wrapped up in cogitation. **1751** SMOLLETT *Per. Pic.* xiii, He seemed to be wrapped up in profound contemplation. **1771** BEATTIE *Minstrel* I. xix. 1 Where the stripling, wrapt in wonder, roves. **1809** MALKIN *Gil Blas* VII. i. ¶2, I found..Don Cæsar just as much wrapped up..in the contemplation of the happy couple. **1859** GEO. ELIOT *A. Bede* ii, Some..were resting..with their eyes closed, as if wrapt in prayer or meditation. **1894** BARING-GOULD *Kitty Alone* II. 162 The girl stood wrapped in delight.

Hence †'**wrappedly** *adv.* intricately. *Obs.*$^{-0}$

1589 RIDER *Bibl. Scholast.* 1685 Wrappedly, *contorte.* **1647** HEXHAM I. s.v.

wrapper ('ræpə(r)), *sb.* Also 6 wraper, 8 rapper, 9 *dial.* wropper. [f. WRAP *v.* + -ER[1].]

I. 1. a. That in which anything is wrapped, enveloped, or enclosed; a piece of fabric or other material forming a wrapping; esp. in later use, a protective covering for a parcel or the like.

c **1460** J. RUSSELL *Bk. Nurture* 224 Take boþe endis of þe towelle,..and wrythe an handfulle..next þe bred myghtily, and se þat thy wrappere be made strayt. *c* **1500** *Melusine* xxiii. 153 His wounde opend, and out of it ranne blood thrugh the wraper. **1580** HOLLYBAND *Treas. Fr. Tong*, *Vne envelope & couverture*, a wrapper. **1611** COTGR., *Envelope*,.. a wrapper; a peece of wast paper for that purpose. **1662** *Act 14 Chas. II*, c. 18 §6 Woolflocks..pressed togeather with Scrues..into Sacks Baggs and other Wrappers made of Wool or Linnen. **1711** ADDISON *Spect.* No. 90 ¶7 My legs [were] closed together by so many Wrappers one over another, that I looked like an Ægyptian Mummy. **1727** BAILEY (vol. II), *Wrapper*, a coarse Cloth in which Bale-Goods are wrapped, &c. **1785** W. TOOKE in Ellis *Lit. Lett.* (Camden) 430 As soon as such a number of books are perfected, the surplus of the various signatures are thrown aside for wrappers and other official uses. **1802** G. V. SAMPSON *Statist. Surv. Londonderry* 354 The fabric..is of two characters: 1st, Narrow, or 27 inches wide, called wrappers, and made of tow-yarn...2d. Wide;..made of lint yarn. **1827** FARADAY *Chem. Manip.* xxiii. 574 The object would often be attainable by a wrapper of tin foil. **1844** KINGLAKE *Eothen* xvi, I saw the burial of a pilgrim,.. miserably poor... There was no coffin, nor wrapper. **1901** *Wide World Mag.* VI. 442 The assassin..had torn open the wrapper of the package.

transf. **1552** RAYNALD *Byrth Mankynde* 35 b, The thyrde wrapper of the [fœtus]. *Ibid.* 36 These iii. wrappers or caules.

fig. **1859** DICKENS *T. Two Cities* I. ii, Each was hidden under almost as many wrappers from the eyes of the mind.

b. A detachable outer paper cover of a book, published part, etc., intended to protect the print, boards, or binding.

1806 *Med. Jrnl.* XV. 334 Any publication, calling itself a Review,..used as the means of circulating the celebrity of such remedies,..on their wrappers, covers, or a few leaves tacked at the beginning and end. **1825** HONE *Every-day Bk.* I. 597 The wrappers to the parts of this work. **1891** *Athenæum* 3 Oct. 448/2 Books..notable for the sylvan colour of the wrappers, their large print and liberal margin.

c. A covering to protect and compact a newspaper, magazine, etc., when sending by post or delivery.

1846–8 LOWELL *Biglow P.* Ser. I. vi. ad fin., Tearing off the wrapper of my newspaper. **1871** *British P.O. Guide* 1 Jan. 10 The postage must be prepaid..by the use of a stamped wrapper. **1898** 'H. S. MERRIMAN' *Roden's Corner* ii, A large table littered with newspaper wrappers.

d. *pl.* = WRAP *sb.* 1 b. ? *Obs.*

1853 *Heal & Son Catal.: Illustr. Catal. Bedsteads* 5 The plain Quilts..are applicable wherever extra warmth is required, either as a wrapper in the carriage, or as an extra covering on the bed. **1858** SIMMONDS *Dict. Trade* 312 *Railway blanket*,..a traveller's warm wrapper. **1865** MRS. L. L. CLARKE *Common Seaweeds* i. 18 A double strap such as we use for a rolled railway wrapper. *Ibid.* vii. 137.

e. A sheet put over furniture, shop-goods, etc., to protect from dust or fading.

1848 DICKENS *Dombey* xxiii, The tarnished paws of gilded lions, stealthily put out from beneath their wrappers. **1905** H. G. WELLS *Kipps* I. ii. §2 At half-past six in the morning ..he would..dust boxes and yawn, and take down wrappers and clean the windows. *Ibid.*, Hanging wrappers over the fixtures and over the piles of wares upon the counters.

2. a. An article of apparel for wrapping, rolling, or coiling from the head. *rare.*

a **1548** HALL *Chron., Hen. VIII*, 7 Other two ladyes.., and on theyr heades skayns and wrappers of Damaske golde with flatte pypes. **1789–96** MORSE *Amer. Geog.* II. 264 The women of the lower class wear on their heads a wrapper of white linen.

b. A shawl, mantle, etc., for wearing about the person.

1782 J. WARTON *Ess. Pope* II. 330 Pope was so..infirm, and his body required so many wrappers and coverings, that it was hardly possible for him to be neat. **1838** DICKENS *O. Twist* xxv, A man..pulled off a large wrapper which had concealed the lower portion of his face... 'Pop that shawl away' [he said]. **1885** MABEL COLLINS *Prettiest Woman* i, She had thrown a loose white wrapper round her shoulders. **1897** *Daily News* 25 Dec. 2/3 The silk wrapper that he was wearing was stolen from off his neck.

3. a. An outer garment, esp. for indoor wear or use in household work, designed for loosely enveloping the whole (or nearly the whole) figure; a loose robe or gown. In later use chiefly *U.S.*

1734 in *Trans. Roy. Hist. Soc.* Ser. IV. VI. 42 The [Indian] Queen's [garment] was a sort of scarlet rosetti in the make of our English wrappers. **1740** H. WALPOLE *Lett.* (1903) I. 84 Her dress, her avarice, and her impudence must amaze any one that never heard her name. She wears..an old mazarine blue wrapper, that gapes open and discovers a canvas petticoat. **1745** *De Foe's Eng. Tradesman* xxvi. (1841) I. 265 Her wrapper, or morning-gown, a piece of Irish linen, printed at London. **1782** *Jrnl. Yng. Lady of Virginia* (1871) 42 We got up [from bed], put on our rappers, and went down in the Seller. **1839** DICKENS *Nickleby* xxiv, Mrs. Curdle was dressed in a morning wrapper. **1862** [see MORNING *sb.* 7 b]. **1883** MISS C. F. WOOLSON *For the Major* vii, His wife..had just risen—or so it seemed, for she wore a rose-colored wrapper. **1886** A. G. MURDOCH *Scotch Readings* (ed. 2) 15 She got on a working wrapper, and sat herself down. **1905** *Outlook* 11 Nov. 663/2 The English-woman..scorns the hideous 'wrapper' which so many French and Americans wear in the bosom of their family.

b. An article of dress, esp. for masculine wear, intended to wrap about or fit loosely over the person; a wrap. Now *dial.*

1799 *Hull Advertiser* 30 Nov. 2/3 Tandy was clad in a white serge wrapper, resembling a friar's gown. **1832** LYTTON *Eugene A.* II. vi, A shower of rain now began to fall. Sir Peter,..turning to Walter,..said to him, 'What! no cloak, sir? no wrapper even?' **1842** E. FITZGERALD *Lett.* (1889) I. 86 Just the same price as I gave for a Chesterfield wrapper (as it is called). **1844** STOCQUELER *Handbk. Brit. India* (1854) 411 The dress of the people, both male and female, commonly consists of a large loose wrapper and trousers. **1888** T. HARDY *Wessex Tales* I. 58 An old milk-man near, in a long white pinafore or 'wropper'. **1891** —— *Tess* xiv, The brown rough 'wropper' or over-all—the old-established..dress of the [harvesting] field-woman.

4. a. Also *wrapper leaf*. Tobacco-leaf of a superior grade prepared and used for the outer cover of cigars or of plug-tobacco; a covering made of this. Chiefly *U.S.*

1688 R. HOLME *Armoury* III. xxii. (Roxb.) 274/2 Filler, is the inside of the Roll [of tobacco]: which is any sorts of Leaves and Stalks. Wrapper, the out side of the roll, which are good leaves. **1839** LOWELL *Lett.* (1894) I. 48 The filling of cigars now belies the wrapper. **1864** R. L. DE COIN *Hist. & Cult. Cotton & Tobacco* 301 The best leaves..are required by the twisters for wrappers around twists or plugs. **1884** *Pall Mall G.* 17 May 4 A cigar consists of three parts, the wrapper, the bunch, and the filler. **1944** [see RUN *sb.*[1] 20 e]. **1978** D. WILLIAMS *Treasure up in Smoke* v. 50 All hand-made cigars consist of a thick core of compressed tobacco leaf, a binder.., and finally a wrapper leaf.

b. *U.S.* A cigar.

1849 HAWTHORNE *Twice-told T.* 60 Our friend.. expending a whole bunch of Spanish wrappers among.. horrified audiences.

5. *Bot.* †**a.** (See quots.) *Obs.*

1718 tr. *Tournefort's Voy. Levant* I. 256 The Wrapper of the Acorn..is a sort of Box set off with several Scales pale green. *c* **1789** *Encycl. Brit.* (ed. 3) III. 446/1 *Calyx*, the cup. .. *Involucrum*, or wrapper, a cup remote from a flower. **1793** MARTYN *Lang. Bot.* s.v. *Corolla*, The envelope, cover, or wrapper of the stamens and pistils.

b. In Fungi, = VOLVA[1].

1796 WITHERING *Brit. Plants* (ed. 3) III. 286 *Agaricus volvaceus*... Wrapper at the root, grey or greenish. *Ibid.* 373 Lycoperdon... Wrapper many-cleft, expanding. **1807** JAS. E. SMITH *Introd. Botany* 253 *Volva*, Wrapper, or covering, of the Fungus tribe. **1860** MAYNE *Expos. Lex.* 1337/1 *Volva*, ..the membranous covering, curtain, or wrapper of the fungus tribe, hiding the parts of fructification, till bursting all round it forms a ring on the stalk.

6. *Amer.* **a.** (See quot.)

1792 G. CARTWRIGHT *Jrnl. Labrador* III. p. x, *Wrappers*, loose sleeve-pieces to button round the wrists, to defend them from the frost.

b. A make of leather boot adapted for fastening round the leg (also called *wrapping-boot*).

1808 PIKE *Sources Mississ.* (1810) III. App. 36 A kind of leather boot or wrapper. *Ibid.*, In the eastern provinces the dragoons wear, over this wrapper or boot, a sort of jack-boot made of sole-leather.

c. An undershirt.

1891 *Cent. Dict.*

7. *Lumbering.* A chain for binding logs on a skid.

1901 *Munsey's Mag.* XXV. 391/2 The load is stopped exactly opposite long parallel skids. Two men cautiously unhook the 'wrappers'.

II. 8. One who wraps or packs up anything; *spec.* one whose occupation consists in wrapping parcels. Also with *up*.

1591 PERCIVALL, *Embolvedor*, a roller, a wrapper vp. **1755** JOHNSON. **1866** in S. Timmins *Resources*, etc. *B'ham* 356 Women & Girls as Lacquerers: Chargers of Tubes, Press Women, & Wrappers-up. **1881** *Instr. Census Clerks* 45 Cutlery:..Wiper,..Getter up, Wrapper up. *Ibid.* 99 Factory Labourer..: Storeman, Wrapper, Slinger. **1883** *B'ham Daily Post* 11 Oct., Grocery and Provisions.—Junior ..wanted... Good flat wrapper and correct accountant preferred.

III. 9. *attrib.* and *Comb.*, as *wrapper-apron*, *-brat*; *wrapper-addresser*, *-writer*.

1876 MRS. G. L. BANKS *Manchester Man* ii, She..had taken off her wrapper-brat [*footnote* A sort of close pinafore]. **1893** *Pall Mall G.* 23 June 11/1 They were..mostly clerks and..wrapper addressers. *Ibid.*, Some half-dozen wrapper-writers,..each..copying with lightning-like rapidity from a directory page before him. **1896** M. QUILLER-COUCH *Jane Vercoe*, etc. 145 Enveloped in what was commonly called a 'wrapper-apern'.

wrapper ('ræpə(r)), *v.* [f. prec.]

1. *trans.* To cover with, enclose or envelop in, a wrapper.

1885 C. G. W. LOCK *Workshop Receipts* Ser. IV. 263/1 Vegetable parchment..is used very extensively..for wrappering the better class of literature. **1890** W. J. GORDON *Foundry* 209 Delivering the papers folded and wrappered ready for post. **1893** *Sat. Rev.* 7 Jan. 24/2 A volume in quarto, handsomely, but alas! very loosely, wrappered.

2. To cover *up* in or as in a wrapper. Also *absol.* or *intr.*

1905 H. G. WELLS *Kipps* II. ix, All the stalls were wrappered up, and all the minor exhibitions locked and barred. **1934** H. G. WELLS *Exper. Autobiogr.* I. iv. 151 Half an hour before closing time we began to put away for the last time and 'wrapper up'.

Hence '**wrappered** (**-up**), *ppl. a.* Also '**wrapperer**, one who covers (esp. magazines or books) with wrappers.

1896 H. G. WELLS *Wheels of Chance* iv, A cheerless, shutter-darkened, wrappered-up shop. **1906** —— *Days of Comet* I. v, Two other wrappered figures came out of the bungalows. **1908** *Daily Chron.* 24 April 11/3 Girls wanted as book wrapperers (magazine).

wrappering ('ræpərɪŋ). [f. as prec. + -ING[1] 1 d.]

1. Coarse fabric or material used or designed for wrapping or covering.

1844 *Civil Eng. & Arch. Jrnl.* VII. 88/2 Upon the bricks is placed a quantity of..gravel, and a piece of fabric, such as common wrappering. **1864** MRS. H. WOOD *Oswald Cray* xlv, Her apron is a piece of wrappering off a bale of goods. **1867** *Morn. Star* 17 Sept. 6 Calverley..tied round his neck a piece of linen wrappering.

2. A loose outer garment; a wrap or wrapper.

1862 MRS. H. WOOD *Mrs. Hallib.* I. x, Mrs. Dare was silently removing some of her outer wrapperings. **1900** F. S. ELLIS *Rom. Rose* I. 406 A great fur cloak for wrappering She wore.

†'**wrappery.** *Obs. rare*$^{-1}$. [f. as prec. + -Y[3].] A wrap or covering.

1662 J. CHANDLER *Van Helmont's Oriat.* 354 The hand or arm of the Young is cut off..; neither is it found among the wrapperies [L. *involucra*], even as the head is.

wrapping ('ræpɪŋ), *vbl. sb.* [f. WRAP *v.* + -ING[1]. App. rare between the 16th and 19th cent.]

1. a. The action of covering with or enveloping in a wrap or wrapper. Occas. with advs., as *round*, *up*. Also *fig.*

c **1440** *Promp. Parv.* 533/1 Wrappynge, or hyllynge, *coopercio, involucio.* **1553** BRENDE *Q. Curtius* 170 Which [arrow] he pulled out and without wrappinge of his wound called for his horse. **1611** COTGR., *Emmaillotement*, a swadling, or a wrapping in swathe bands. **1837** HT. MARTINEAU *Soc. Amer.* III. 73 A wrapping round of inconvenient considerations with an inpenetrable cloud of the plainest-seeming words. **1872** MARCH. DUFFERIN *Canad. Jrnl.* (1891) 52 The children play in the snow... Their nurse, Mrs. Hall, dislikes the wrapping up.

b. The action of interlacing or intertwining; the fact of being interwoven. Also *fig.*

1553 BRENDE *Q. Curtius* 105 By reason that the wreathing and wrappinge togither of the bowes kept them of from the bodies of the tres. **1565** COOPER *Thesaurus* s.v. *Implexus*, A wrappyng of armes crosse one within an other. **1836** J. GILBERT *Chr. Atonem.* iii. (1852) 70 Yet this artful wrapping together of the one with the other, this blending of things so dissimilar, will not accomplish the object designed.

2. a. Something used or designed for enveloping or wrapping up; a wrap or covering. Also in fig. context.

1387 TREVISA *Higden* I. 9 My witt is ful luyte to un-wralle þe wrappyinges of so wonder werkes. **1388** WYCLIF *Wisd.* vii. 4 Y was nurschid in wrappyngis, and is greet bisynesses. **1855** [G. R. LEIFCHILD] *Cornwall* 298 The wearing of thin shoes and stockings during unsuitable weather, being a dangerous transition from the thick shoes and wrapping worn by the same persons in daily work. **1876** *Encycl. Brit.* V. 775/2 Broken leaf tobacco..firmly wrapped round with one or two wrappings of whole leaf tobacco. **1883** GILMOUR *Among Mongols* xvii. 201 The volumes are..carefully swathed up in their yellow wrappings. **1894** 'J. S. WINTER' *Red Coats* 78 Dolly was eagerly tearing the paper wrappings off the big box of sweeties.

fig. **1836** ARNOLD in Stanley *Life* (1844) II. 28 Having been enabled to receive Scripture truth in spite of the wrapping which has been put round it. **1901** F. CAMPBELL *Love* 319 Hidebound in a wrapping of utter selfishness.

b. An article of dress used or intended for enveloping the figure; a loose covering or upper garment; a wrap, wrappage, or wrapper.

1635 RAINBOW *Serm.* 15 The sheepe..gives us shelter enough from the cold, why should we hunt after more costly furres and wrappings? **1853** DICKENS *Bleak Ho.* iii, A gentleman in the coach who..looked very large in a quantity of wrappings. **1882** T. COAN *Hawaii* 35, I..preached in wet clothes, continuing my..labors until night, when in dry wrappings I slept well. **1899** RODWAY *Guiana Wilds* 30 No stiff wooden figure made up of corset and wrappings, but a woman of flesh and blood.

3. a. *attrib.* in sense of 'used or designed for wrapping or covering', as ***wrapping-cloth, -silk, -wire***; †**wrapping boot** *U.S.*, form of boot adapted for wrapping about the ankle and calf; **wrapping-paper**, a special make of strong paper for packing or wrapping up parcels.

1566 *Eng. Ch. Furniture* (Peacock, 1866) 75 A cup of sylver for the communion with ij wrappinge clothes for yt. **1648** HEXHAM II, *Een Windel*.., a Wrapping-cloath. ?**1715** POPE *Let.* in *Corr.* (1956) I. 317 If the Fruit is not so good as I wish, let the Gallantry of this Wrapping-paper make up for it. **1768** J. LYNDON *Let.* 17 June in *Rec. Colony of Rhode Island* (1861) VI. 548 One paper mill, at which is manufactured wrapping, package and other coarse paper. **1789** *Deb. Congr. U.S.* (1834) 1st Congress 1 Sess. App. 2130 The several duties shall be aid on the following goods. .. On all writing, printing and wrapping paper. **1808** PIKE *Sources of the Mississippi* (1810) III. App. 41 Their dress is.. the wrapping boot with the jack boot, and permanent spur over it. **1828–32** WEBSTER, Wrapping paper. **1842** FARADAY *Chem. Manip.* (ed. 3) 470 Strong common brown wrapping paper. **1860** RIMBAULT *Pianoforte* 183 Modern pianofortes have steel wire throughout, with about one octave in the bass closely lapped. The wrapping wire is of soft iron for the upper part of the octave, and of copper for the lower. **1883** *Daily News* 24 Apr. 5/8 The four main cables are 15⅜ inches in diameter... There are 243 miles 493 feet of wrapping wire on each. **1883** W. D. CURZON *Manuf. Industries Worcs.* 80 The manufacture of the heavy and coarse sorts of wrapping paper. **1890** *Cent. Dict.* s.v. *Silk*, *Wrapping-silk*, a fine strong floss employed in the manufacture of artificial flies.

b. In sense of 'used or worn as a wrapper or enveloping outer garment', as ***wrapping cloak, coat, mantle, pelisse, robe***. Also WRAPPING-GOWN.

1787 MME. D'ARBLAY *Diary* 8 Nov., What was my surprise to see a large man, in an immense wrapping greatcoat, buttoned up round his chin! **1800** *Lady's Monthly Museum* Nov. V. 408 White muslin wrapping robe, with full sleeves. **1818** SCOTT *Rob Roy* xxi, His dress [was] a horseman's wrapping coat. **1824** MEYRICK *Ant. Armour* II. 11 The birrus or large wrapping cloak. **1842** BORROW *Bible in Spain* x, The large wrapping man's cloak which she wore. **1870** MORRIS *Earthly Par.* III. IV. 198 He came, and to the floor he cast His wrapping mantle.

c. With advs., as ***wrapping up department***.

1883 W. D. CURZON *Manuf. Industries Worcs.* 101 [In] the wrapping up department..girls are busily engaged wrapping goods of all kinds.

'wrapping, *ppl. a.* [f. WRAP *v.* + -ING².] That wraps, covers, or envelops. Also *fig.*

1582 STANYHURST *Æneis* II. (Arb.) 50 In vayne Laocoon.. Is to sone embayed with wrapping girdle y coompast. *a* **1586** SIDNEY *Ps.* XXXI. ii, Preserve me from the wyly wrapping nett, Which they for me..have sett. **1813** [LEIGH HUNT] in *Examiner* 31 May 351/1 Give me..a small wrapping silence about me. **1869** *Daily News* 13 Oct., The necessity of plunging through a deep gulph of air before one meets the wrapping and oblivious wave.

Hence †**'wrappingly** *adv.*, disguisedly. *Obs.*⁻¹

1649 CANNE *Snare Broken* 12 It would not have been so ambiguously, darkly, wrappingly given forth.

†**'wrapping-gown**. *Obs.* [f. WRAPPING *vbl. sb.* 3 b + GOWN *sb.*] A night-gown.

1709 S. WESLEY in Quiller Couch *Hetty Wesley* (1903) I. viii, She had nothing on but her shoes and a wrapping-gown. **1709** STEELE *Tatler* No. 139 ¶7 She rush'd out of bed in her wrapping gown, and consulted her glass. **1777** SHERIDAN *Trip Scarb.* I. ii, I shall never be reconciled to this nauseous wrapping-gown. **1809** MALKIN *Gil Blas* VII. x. ¶5 What was my surprise at meeting him in his wrapping-gown and night-cap. **1827** SCOTT *Chron. Canongate* i, The wide wrapping-gown and night-cap. **1877** MISS YONGE *Cameos* III. i. 8 The King..was soon standing before the fire in his wrapping-gown.

wrap-rascal ('ræprɑːskəl, -æ-). Now *arch.* or *dial.* [f. WRAP *v.* + RASCAL *sb.*³ Cf. *hap-harlot*.] A loose overcoat or great-coat, esp. worn in the 18th century; a surtout.

1716 GAY *Trivia* I. 58 The true Surtout. *marg.*, A Joseph, a Wrap-rascal, etc. **1738** in W. C. Sydney *Eng. & Engl. 18th C.* (1891) I. 121 Those loose kinds of great-coats..which I have heard called 'wraprascals'. **1802** BENTHAM *Ration. Judic. Evid.* (1827) II. 191 A sort of knave's coat; or (to use an appellative not many years ago applied in vulgar language to a particular sort of surtout) a wrap-rascal. **1845** *Punch* VIII. 87 The shapeless articles which, under the various names of Taglionis, Wrap-rascals,..are now placed on the human form. **1884** SALA *Journ. due South* I. i, Muffled up in these hirsute wrap-rascals, and with wide-awake hats slouched over our eyes. **1893** STEVENSON *Catriona* xxv, On the threshold, in a rough wraprascal,..stood James More.
fig. **1812** J. O. in *Examiner* 23 Nov. 750/1 The specious cloak of Prudence,—that wraprascal of the worldy-minded. **1862** THACKERAY *Round. Papers, Letts's Diary*, There is the cozy wraprascal, self-indulgence—how easy it is!
attrib. **1898** WEYMAN *Castle Inn* 192 A big dingy man in a wrap-rascal coat.

†**b.** (See quot.) *Obs.*

1796 GROSE *Dict. Vulg. Tongue* (ed. 3), *Wrap Rascal*, a red cloak, called also a roquelaire.

wrap-round: see WRAPAROUND *sb.* and *a.*

wrapt, obs. erron. f. RAPT *ppl. a.* 2.

1796 MME. D'ARBLAY *Camilla* IV. 337 [She] was absorbed in..wrapt expectation. **1809** MALKIN *Gil Blas* VII. xiii. ¶16 He will hear it read with so grave and wrapt a silence.

wrapture, obs. erron. form of RAPTURE.

wrap-up ('ræpʌp), *sb.* and *a.* [f. vbl. phr. *to wrap up*: see WRAP *v.* 7 a.]

A. *sb.* **1. a.** An easily satisfied customer; an easy sale. **b.** Any easy task.

1938 *Amer. Speech* XIII. 150/2 *Wrap-up*, an easy sale. Also a customer easily satisfied. **1940** 'E. QUEEN' *New Adventures* 284 Not too tough. A wrap-up. **1952** *N.Y. Times Mag.* 21 Sept. 58/3 The ideal customer is known as a 'wrap-up', which is self-explanatory.

2. A summary or résumé, esp. of news; a conclusion.

1960 WENTWORTH & FLEXNER *Dict. Amer. Slang* 588/2 *Wrap-up*,..a conclusion, an ending; a summary and conclusion. **1961** *Times Lit. Suppl.* 13 Oct. 677/4 Finally, Mr. Kalb gives us what he calls the wrap-up [of a book]. **1969** *New Yorker* 30 Aug. 20 (*caption*) Suddenly..a wrap-up of the highlights of my life flashed before my eyes. **1973** H. GRUPPE *Truxton Cipher* xv. 155 'I have no further questions for you.'.. This was the wrap-up. Harry knew.. he would be handed over for court-martial. **1975** *New Yorker* 5 May 128/2 NBC presented a thirty-minute 'special report' on Cambodia, which consisted mainly of a wrapup of NBC's regular news footage of the previous week. **1980** U. CURTISS *Poisoned Orchard* ix. 97 The wrap-up of a job I've been working on will have to be done tonight. **1981** *Daily Mail* 18 May 19/4 Last night's wrap-up saw the old soldier with the black eye-patch welcomed by desert Bedouins. **1985** *Village Voice* (N.Y.) 8 Jan. 39/2 Only in his final wrap-up does he concede that power can also take the form of creative 'attention, or love'.

B. *adj.* That concludes or sums up.

1968 MRS. L. B. JOHNSON *White House Diary* 9 Apr. (1970) 658 Here on the courthouse square at Gonzales was the wrap-up scene, an official good-by for our five-day adventure. **1976** *Publishers Weekly* 27 Sept. 82/2 A long wrap-up section amplifies this practical aspect of their book. **1977** *Church Times* 7 Apr. 2/4 A two-day centennial programme... The Archbishop will..address the wrap-up banquet. **1980** *Jewish Chron.* 21 Mar. 23/3 This is what is described as a 'wrap-up' volume, summarising, in non-technical language, what has been learned. **1980** *Quilt World* Sept./Oct. 16/3 The group session wound down with a light monologue..on 'Fifty Ways to Lose Business', and then small group discussions were held, followed by a wrap-up session.

†**wrase**. *Obs. rare.* Also 5 **warse**. [OE. *wrásen* band, tie. Cf. also LG. *wrasen* stuffed pad for the head.]

1. A small bundle.

c **1275** *Passion of our Lord* 383 in *O.E. Misc.* 48 Of one wrase of þornes he wryþen hym one crune. *c* **1470** *Cath. Angl.* 425/1 (A.), A Warse, [*sic*], *fasciculus*.

2. = WASE 2. (Cf. WREATH 5 a, WRITH.)

1565 COOPER *Thesaurus*, *Arculum*,..a roll that women weare on their heads to beare water: a wrase [*Elyot* wase].

wraskle, obs. var. WRAXLE *v.*

wrasle, wrassil, Sc. varr. WRESTLE.

wrasse (ræs). Also 8 **wraws**, 8–9 **wrass**. [ad. Cornish *wrach*, mutated form of *gwrach* = Welsh *gwrach* wrasse, also old woman (cf. OLD WIFE 3). Mod. Cornish dial. has also the form *wrath*, and *wrasse* may be an E. plural in -*s*.]

1. One or other species belonging to the acanthopterygian family *Labridæ* or esp. the genus *Labrus* of bony, thick-lipped, marine fishes; esp. the ballan (the 'old wife', *Labrus maculatus*) or the striped, red, or cook species (*L. mixtus*), found on the British coasts.

a **1672** WILLUGHBY *Hist. Pisc.* (1686) 319 *Turdus vulgatissimus, Tincti marini* Venetis: Cornub. *Wrasse. Ibid.* 320 *Cornubiensibus* Wrasse *dicitur*. *a* **1705** RAY *Syn. Pisc.* (1713) 136 *Turdus vulgatissimus*,..the Wrasse, or Old Wife. **1752** J. HILL *Hist. Anim.* 249 The Wrasse, or Old-wife,..is frequent in the Mediterranean. **1774** GOLDSM. *Nat. Hist.* VI. 307 The Labrus or Wrasse [has] the body oval; the head middling; the lips doubled inward. **1860** GOSSE *Rom. Nat. Hist.* 295 The brilliant wrasses dart out and in, decked in scarlet and green. **1888** *Encycl. Brit.* XXIV. 686/2 Some 450 species of wrasses..are known.

b. With distinguishing epithet.

comber, cook, cuckoo, rainbow, red, small-mouthed, striped wrasse: see these words.

1769 PENNANT *Brit. Zool.* III. 203–8 Ballan Wrasse... Bimaculated Wrasse, *L. bimaculata*. Trimaculated Wrasse. .. Striped Wrasse... Gibbous Wrasse. **1776** *Ibid.* (ed. 4) pl. xlvii, Comber Wrasse. Antient Wrasse. **1836** YARRELL *Brit. Fishes* I. 279–291 The Green-streaked Wrasse... Red Wrasse, Three-spotted Wrasse [etc.]. **1840** *Cuvier's Anim. Kingd.* 310 *L. Lineatus*, the Lineal-streaked,..*L. variegatus*, the Blue-streaked,..*L. carneus*, the Three-spotted Wrasse. **1848** *Maunder's Treas. Nat. Hist.* s.v., Several species of this Acanthopterygious fish, viz...the Cook Wrasse or Blue-striped Wrasse (*L. variegatus*), the Comber Wrasse (*L. comber*). **1874** COUCH *Brit. Fishes* III. 30–41 Green Wrass. .. Scale-rayed Wrasse... Small-mouthed wrass. [etc.].

c. *New Zealand.* (See quots.)

1872 J. HECTOR *Fishes N. Zealand* 108 A small Wrasse,.. called the Spotty or Poddly. **1898** MORRIS *Austral Eng.* 518/2 *Wrasse*, this English name..is given, in New Zealand, to *Labrichthys bothryocosmus*, Richards. Called also Poddly, Spotty, and Kelp-fish.

2. Without article: Wrasses collectively.

1750 HEATH *Acc. Isl. Scilly* 45 The Fish are..Pilchards, Hake, Wrass, Whistlers. **1763** in Pennant *Brit. Zool.* (1776) I. 143 Where the whistling fish, wraws, and polacks resort. **1878** P. THOMSON in *Trans. N. Zealand Institute* XI. 384 Wrasse, Parrotfish, and Spotties are often in the market. **1883** *All Year Round* 16 June 16/1 The bill of fare of a family of the neolithic period... They had mullet and wrasse, dogfish and skate.

3. *attrib.*, as ***wrasse family, -fish***.

1840 tr. *Cuvier's Anim. Kingd.* 309 *Labridæ* (the Wrasse, or Rock-fish Family). **1890** *Cent. Dict.* s.v. *Labrus*, Wrasse-fish (*Labrus maculatus*).

wrassle, U.S. dial var. WRESTLE *v.*

†**wrast**, ? *sb. Obs.*⁻¹ (Meaning obscure.)

Perhaps *to-wrast* pa. pple., 'wrested away' (from what is right): but cf. next.

13.. *Gaw. & Gr. Knt.* 1663 He..dalt with hir al in daynte, how-se-euer þe dede turned to wrast.

†**wrast**, *a. Obs.*⁻¹ [OE. *wrǽst*, *wrást* elegant, noble, excellent. In ME. perh. a back-formation from UNWRAST *a.*] **a.** Of sound: Loud, strong. **b.** Of persons: Stout, active.

13.. *Gaw. & Gr. Knt.* 1423 Wylde wordez hym warp wyth a wrast noyce. **1338** R. BRUNNE *Chron.* (1725) 170 Wilde fire þei kast, þe kyng to confound, His schipmen were fulle wrast [*printed* wrask], els had he gon to ground.

wrast, etc.: see WREST, etc.

wrat (ræt). Now *dial.* or *Obs.* Also 6 **wratte**, 9 **wraught**. [a. (M)LG. *wratte* (LG. *wratt*, Du. *wrat*), or metathetic var. WART *sb.*] = WART *sb.* 1.

1527 ANDREW *Brunswyke's Distyll. Waters* II. ccxix. Pj/1 The syck wrattes in the foundament. **1562, 1629** [see WART *sb.* 1]. **1768** ROSS *Helenore* I. 30 Black hairy wrats..Outthrow her fiz were like mustaches seen. **1808** JAMIESON. **1825** BROCKETT *N.C. Words* s.v.

wrat(e, obs. or Sc. pa. t. of WRITE *v.*

†**wratbyhe**. *Obs.*⁻¹ [Of obscure origin; perh. f. Cornish *wrath* WRASSE + *bihan* small.] (See quot.)

1443 in *Bekynton's Corr.* (Rolls) II. 238 Magister Tregoran dedit piscem vocatum base et le wratbyhe alias a tenche of the see.

wratch, etc.: see WRETCH, etc.

wrath (rɔːθ, rɒθ, *U.S.* ræːθ), *sb.* Forms: *α.* 1 **wræððu, -o**, 3 **wreððe**, 2 **wredða**, 3 **wredðe** (**wreadðe**), 2–3 **wreððe**, 3–4 **wreþþe**, 4–5 **wrethe**. *β.* 1 **wraððo**, 3 **wraððe** (**wraððhe**), **wraðþe**, 3 *Orm.*, 4–5 **wraþþe**, 4–5 **wratthe**. *γ.* 3 **wraðe**, 4–5 **wraþe**, 4–6 **wrathe**; 3 **wrað**, 4– **wrath** (4 **wragh**, 5 **wraaþ**, **wraugth**, 7 **wrauth**). *δ.* *Sc.* 5–7 **wraith**, 6 -**the**, 6 **vraith**, **vr-**, **wrayth** (**wrayith**). [OE. *wrǽððu*, -*o*, = *wrǽþþu*, f. *wráþ* WROTH *a.* + -*þu*:—Teut. -*iþō*: see -TH¹. Cf. WRETHE *sb.*

The original long vowel (*ǽ*) was shortened before the double consonant, and gave the two ME. types *wreþþe* and *wraþþe*. From the latter comes the mod. *wrath*, with later lengthening of the *a*, as in *path*, *lath*. The pronunc. (rɑːθ), regarded by Walker (1791) as 'more analogical', and formerly common in Eng. use but now displaced by that with the rounded vowel (rɔːθ), and later by (rɒθ), is still given as the standard by American dictionaries.]

1. Vehement or violent anger; intense exasperation or resentment; deep indignation:

a. In the phrases ***for***, †***o***, †***on***, ***of***, ***with*** (†***mid***), or esp. ***in wrath***.

c **950** *Lindisf. Gosp.* Mark iii. 5 [Jesus] ymb-sceawde hia mið wræððo..cueð to ðæm menn, aðen hond ðin. *c* **1175** *Lamb. Hom.* 113 Þe lauerd [scal] do hit for rihtwisnesse.. and noht for wreððe. *a* **1200** *Vices & Virtues* 121 Ne he ðe ðurhwuneð on wraðþe, ne he ðe wuneliche lið on hordome. *a* **1225** *Leg. Kath.* 1361 Þe Keiser kaste his heaued, as wod mon, of wraððe. *Ibid.* 2048 Hu wrakeliche, wenestu, wule he, al o wraððe, wreken on þe, wrecche! **13..** *Guy Warw.* (C.) 3326 It is Guy, That in wrath from the woll departi truly. **1382** WYCLIF *Mark* iii. 5 He biholdynge hem aboute with wrathe..seith [etc.]. *c* **1400** *Destr. Troy* 6697 Then for wrath of his wound..He gird to a greke. *c* **1450** *Myrr. our Ladye* II. 79 Some vse when they here the fende named in play or in wrathe to saye Aue Maria. **1586** MARLOWE *1st Pt. Tamburl.* II. ii, My heart is swolne with wrath, on this.. villaine Tamburlaine and of that false Cosroe. **1590** SPENSER *F.Q.* II. xii. 86 Yet being men they..stared ghastly,..some for wrath, to see their captiue Dame. **1663** DRYDEN *Wild Gallant* II. (1669) 24 Come not near me to night, while I'm in wrath. *c* **1743** SIR C. H. WILLIAMS *Wks.* (1822) I. 203 Great Earl of Bath, Be not in wrath, At what the people say. **1798** WORDSW. *Peter Bell* 348 On he drives with cheeks that burn In downright fury and in wrath. **1882** 'OUIDA' *Maremma* I. 243 But we may go in wrath.

b. In general use. Occas. *personif.*

c **1175** *Lamb. Hom.* 105 Wreððe hafð wununge on þes dusian bosme. *a* **1200** *Vices & Virtues* 41 All ðare hwile ðe ðu wraððe oðer nið hauest mid te. *c* **1250** *Gen. & Ex.* 3863 Ðer ros wreððe and strif a-non Aȝen moysen and aaron. **1338** R. BRUNNE *Chron.* (1810) 6 He ne suffred neuere wrath to be aboue. **1362** LANGL. *P. Pl.* A. VI. 98 Beo wel i-war of wraþþe þat wykkide Schrewe. *c* **1412** HOCCLEVE *De Reg. Princ.* 3872 Wratthe, þe body of man inward fretith. *c* **1425** *Cast. Persev.* 210 in *Macro Plays* 83 Wretthe, þis wrecche, with me schal wawe. *c* **1450** *Cov. Myst.* (Shaks. Soc.) 214 Ageyn hym wrathe if thou accende The same in happ wylle falle on the. **1526** TINDALE *Ephes.* iv. 31 Let all bitternes, fearsnes and wrath..be put awaye from you. **1590** SPENSER *F.Q.* I. iv. 35 Such one was Wrath, the last of this vngodly tire. **1640** G. SANDYS *Christ's Passion* II. 201 Wrath, the

Nurse of War. **1691** HARTCLIFFE *Virtues* 125 Upon every triffle they shall be provoked to Wrath. **1781** COWPER *Expost.* 132 He judg'd them with as terrible a frown As if not love, but wrath, had brought him down. **1839** J. H. NEWMAN *Par. Serm.* IV. ii. 40 Wrath was abroad and in his path. **1848** DICKENS *Dombey* xlvi, Mrs. Brown's daughter looked out..; and there were wrath and vengeance in her face. **1885** *10th Rep. Hist. MSS. Comm.* App. I. 143 He was now full of wrath and resentment against them.

transf. **1827** POLLOK *Course T.* v. 595 He..heard the weltering of the waves of wrath. **1848** O. W. HOLMES *Battle of Lexington* iii, Fast on the soldier's path Darken the waves of wrath.

c. With qualification (adj. or poss. pron.).

α. *c* **900** *Rituale Eccl. Dunelm.* (Surtees) 12 Ælc bitternesse & irra & wræððo..sie ȝ invmmen from ivh. *c* **1175** *Lamb. Hom.* 67 For-ȝif þi wreððe and þi mod, for þenne is þi bode god. *c* **1205** LAY. 1441 Corineus..seide þas ilke word mid muchelere wredðe. **1387** TREVISA *Higden* IV. 163 þe way was y-opened forto take wreche of al olde wreþþe. *a* **1400** *R. Gloucester's Chron.* (Rolls) II. 857 þis spousing was enchesen of gret hate & wreþþe. *c* **1440** *York Myst.* xxvi. 154 Of my wretthe wreke me I will.

β. *a* **1200** *St. Marher.* 18 þa warð þe reue woð and beð..o great wraððe bringen forð a uet. *c* **1205** LAY. 6379 Ah hit wes muchel hærme..þat þurh his wraððe his wit wes awemmed. *a* **1250** *Owl & Night.* 941 þe wraþþe binymeþ monnes red. *c* **1350** *Will. Palerne* 728 Ȝif þemperour were wiþ me wroþ his wraþþe forto slake. **1390** GOWER *Conf.* I. 154 The king.. Was..so wel paid That al his wraththe is overgo. *c* **1425** *Cursor M.* 5085 (Trin.), Mi wraþþe is clene fro me goon.

γ. *c* **1300** *Havelok* 2719 Do nu wel with-uten fiht, Yeld hire þe lond... Wile ich forgiue þe þe lathe, Al mi dede and al mi wrathe. *c* **1374** CHAUCER *Anel. & Arc.* 51 Mars which..The old wrath of Juno to fulfille Hath sette the peoplis hertis.. on fyre Of Thebes [etc.]. *c* **1440** *Generydes* 1373 Yet in his wraugth this thought he euer among, If he shuld avenge hym sodenly [etc.]. **1484** CAXTON *Fables of Æsop* II. vii, His mayster..by grete wrathe beganne to bete gym. **1526** TINDALE *Ephes.* iv. 26 Lett nott the sonne goo doune apon youre wrathe. **1594** SHAKS. *Rich. III*, II. i. 106 Who sued to me for him? Who (in my wrath)..bid me be aduis'd? **1616** T. SCOT *Philomythie* II. C 3, Ech roreth out his wrath, Nor other need of drums or trumpets hath. **1697** DRYDEN *Virg. Georg.* IV. 651 The Seer..could not yet his Wrath asswage. **1735** POPE *Prol. Sat.* 30 Which must end me, a Fool's wrath or love? **1796** MME. D'ARBLAY *Camilla* I. 339 When he had respectfully suffered her wrath to vent itself, he made apologies. **1862** THACKERAY *Philip* xxvii, His chafing, bleeding temper is one raw; his whole soule one rage, and wrath, and fever. **1871** B. TAYLOR *Faust* (1875) I. xxv. 209 The evil one with terrible wrath Seeketh a path His prey to discover.

δ. *c* **1480** HENRYSON *Fox, Wolf, & Cadger* 7 In his wraith he werryit thame to deid. *c* **1520** M. NISBET *N. Test.* (S.T.S.) II. 238 *marg.*, As for malice or vnlawful wraith, it is vtirly forbiddin. *c* **1614** SIR W. MURE *Dido & Æneas* I. 296 His hoarie head he reares Above the waters, toss'd by Juno's wraith.

d. Righteous indignation on the part of the Deity.

c **900** *Rituale Eccl. Dunelm.* (Surtees) 8 God,..beado folces ðines biddendes rvmmodlice biseh, & sv'oppa ðines vraððo..ymbwoend. *a* **1200** *Vices & Virtues* 21 Fondie we te kelien godes wraððe mid teares. *a* **1300** *E.E. Psalter* xciv. 11 (E.), Als in mi wrath swore I best, If þai sal in-ga in mi rest. **1303** R. BRUNNE *Handl. Synne* 780 He takyþ more to wraþþe þat synne þan [etc.]. **1382** WYCLIF *Ezek.* xxxviii. 19 Saith the Lord God, myn indignacioun shal styre vp..in my wrath. *a* **1450** *Knt. de la Tour* 13 Forto apese the wrathe of God..thei..fasted. **1535** COVERDALE *Hosea* xiii. 11, I gaue the a kinge in my wrath. **1562** WINȜET *Wks.* (S.T.S.) I. 30 For the abusing of thir dayis..God is at wrayith with vs. **1634** MILTON *Comus* 803 As when the wrath of Jove Speaks thunder. **1667** —— *P.L.* III. 406 To appease thy wrauth ..[thy Son] offerd himself to die For mans offence. **1827** POLLOK *Course T.* x. 556 The native fires, which God awoke, And kindled with the fury of His wrath. **1853** T. PARKER *Theism, Atheism*, etc. p. li, To appease the wrath of God, or purchase his favour.

e. *transf.* Violence or extreme force of a natural agency, regarded as hostile to mankind or growth.

1579 SPENSER *Sheph. Cal.* Jan. 19 Thou barrein ground, whome winters wrath hath wasted. **1608** *The Great Frost* in Arber *Garner* (1895) I. 86 [This] may teach them..in summer to make a provision against the wrath of winter. **1648** J. BEAUMONT *Psyche* II. xvi, Stern bristles hedg'd up high His back, which did all wrath of thorns defie. **1810** SCOTT *Lady of Lake* IV. xxi, A wasted female form, Blighted by wrath of sun and storm. **1813** —— *Rokeby* VI. xxi, Mine be the eve of tropic sun!.. No twilight dews his wrath allay. **1833** WORDSW. *'If Life were slumber'* 34 She knelt in prayer —the waves their wrath appease. **1876** SWINBURNE *Erechtheus* 588 All her flower of body..With the might of the wind's wrath wrenched.

2. An instance of deep or violent anger; a fit or spell of ire or fierce indignation.

a **1200** *Vices & Virtues* 41 Ðe dieule..ararð upp ðe wraððhes and þe cheastes and te bitere wordes. **1338** R. BRUNNE *Chron.* (1810) 294 Bituex þe kyng of France & þe erle..Was þat tyme a distance, a wrath bituex þam nam. *c* **1375** *Cursor M.* 27671 (Fairf.), To deme a man til ille for a wraþ he has him tille. *a* **1400–50** *Wars Alex.* 2310 In a wrath, þe wale kyng swyth Him of his principalete priued. **1474** CAXTON *Chesse* II. v. (1883) 68 Hit is better to leue a gylty man vnpunysshyd than to punyshe hym in a wrath or yre. **1535** COVERDALE *2 Cor.* xii. 20 Lest there be amonge you, debates, envyenges, wrathes, stryuynges. **1596** SPENSER *F.Q.* IV. vi. 8 So both to wreake their wrathes on Britomart agreed. **1610** SHAKS. *Temp.* III. iii. 79 Lingring perdition..shall step by step attend You, and your wayes, whose wraths to guard you from [etc.]. **1855** M. ARNOLD *Balder Dead* III. 79 For haughty spirits and high wraths are rife Among the Gods. **1864** TENNYSON *Aylmer's F.* 706 When some heat of difference sparkled out, How sweetly would she glide between your wraths.

†**3. a.** Impetuous ardour, rage, or fury. *Obs.*

c **1489** CAXTON *Sonnes of Aymon* iii. 78 [They] go vpon the oost..by soo grete wrathe that it was merueyll. **1539** BIBLE (Great) *2 Macc.* iv. 25 Bearynge the stomack of a cruel tyraunt, & y[e] wrath of a wylde brute beest. **1597** SHAKS. *2 Hen. IV*, I. i. 109 Henrie Monmouth, whose swift wrath beate downe The neuer-daunted Percie to the earth. **1601** —— *Twel. N.* III. iv. 257 Your opposite hath in him what youth, strength, skill, and wrath, can furnish man withall.

†**b.** The ardour *of* passion, love, etc. *Obs.*$^{-1}$

1600 SHAKS. *A.Y.L.* v. ii. 44 They are in the verie wrath of loue, and they will together.

4. Anger displayed in action; the manifestation of anger or fury, esp. by way of retributory punishment; vengeance: **a.** Of the Deity, etc. Freq. in ***wrath of God***, ***day of wrath***; also *fig.* in phr. ***like the wrath of God***, dreadful, terrible; dreadfully, terribly.

c **950** *Lindisf. Gosp.* Luke xxi. 23 Bið forðon ofer-suiðnisso micelo on-ufa eorðo & wræððo folce ðissum. **1050–72** in *Leofric Missal* (1883) 1/1 Hæbbe he godes curs and wræð e ealra halȝena. *c* **1200** *Trin. Coll. Hom.* 27 He..biddeð þat godes wraððe cume uppen his oȝen heued. **1382** WYCLIF *1 Thess.* i. 10 Jhesu, that delyuerede vs fro wraththe to comynge. *c* **1375** *Cursor M.* 27362 (Fairf.), þe day of wraþ & wrake & sorou. *c* **1440** *Jacob's Well* 107 Sodeynly þanne þe wretthe & þe wreche of god schal fallyn on þe. **1482** *Monk of Evesham* (Arb.) 61 The whyche..tresur to hem fro daye to daye the wrathe of owre sauyur ihesu cryste in the daye of hys wrathe. **1535** COVERDALE *Ecclus.* vii. 16 Remembre that the wrath shall not be longe in tarienge. **1583** W. HUNNIS *Ps.* vi. 11 If into heauen I might ascend,..O Lord, thy wrath would thrust me forth downe to the earthe againe. **1624** QUARLES *Job* IX. 46 The smoothest pleader hath No power in his lips, to slake his [*sc.* God's] Wrath. **1682** PEDEN *Lord's Trumpet* (1739) 13 When Wrath is so near, I pray You to take notice what Ye are doing, for..[soon] Ye shall..be overthrown with the Wrath of God. **1758** S. HAYWARD *Serm.* i. 7 Sin brings us under the wrath and curse of God. **1793** R. GRAY *Poems* 133 To redeem [him] from wrath, His Saviour once did bleed and die. **1820** SHELLEY *Fragm.*, *Satire upon Satire* 14 Then send the priests..To preach the burning wrath which is to come. **1846** MRS. A. MARSH *Father Darcy* II. v. 107, I have dedicated myself to..the god of wrath and vengeance. **1936** J. BUCHAN *Island of Sheep* xii. 224 The winds..in the Norlands can blow like the wrath of God. **1955** M. ALLINGHAM *Beckoning Lady* xiii. 178 Fancy coming home like the wrath of God and starting a fight. **1967** 'R. FOLEY' *Fear of Stranger* (1968) v. 56 You look like the wrath of God, Kay... No flesh on you to speak of. **1982** 'W. R. DUNCAN' *Queen's Messenger* ii. 19 Are you ill? You look like the wrath of God.

b. Of persons.

a **1500** *Songs & Carols* (Warton Cl.) 98 The chylderyng ȝyng, With Herowdes wretthe to deth were wrong. **1533** BELLENDEN *Livy* IV. (S.T.S.) II. 94 The wraith and Ire of romanis aganis þe veanis war defferrit to þe nixt ȝere. **1602** CHETTLE *Hoffman* III. (1631) F 3, The Dukes squadrons arm'd with wrath and death, Watch but the signall when to ceaze on you. **1667** MILTON *P.L.* IX. 14 The wrauth Of stern Achilles on his Foe. **1781** COWPER *Table-T.* 597 Man lavish'd all his thoughts on human things—The feats of heroes, and the wrath of kings. **1805** WORDSW. *Prelude* x. 26 Avengers, from whose wrath they fled In terror. **1836** J. GILBERT *Chr. Atonem.* (1852) 339 Legal wrath is nothing else than the just award of crime. **1868** HEAVYSEGE *Jezebel* I. 130 My red wrath shall fall like yon bright bolt.

5. An act done in anger or indignation.

c **1440** *Jacob's Well* 42 Ȝif ȝe wyl fle fro þe iiij wrettys [*sic*] of god. **1525** LD. BERNERS *Froiss.* II. ccvi. [ccii.] 633 To make amendes for all wrathes, forfaytes, and dommages that euer they dyde to hym. **1611** BIBLE *Zech.* vii. 12 There-fore came a great wrath from the Lord of hostes. *a* **1754** E. ERSKINE *Serm.* (1755) 200 No Man can read his Bible..but he must hear of a wrath to come from God upon Impenitent Sinners.

6. *attrib.* and *Comb.*, as ***wrath-bearing***, ***-fire***, ***-storm***; objective, as ***wrath-provoking***, †***-venger***; similative, as ***wrath-faced***, ***-like***; instrumental, as ***wrath-bewildered***, ***-consume*** v., ***-kindled***, ***-swollen***.

a **1593** MARLOWE *Ovid's Elegies* II. v. 52 She..kissed so sweetely as might make Wrath-kindled Ioue away his thunder shake. **1593** SHAKS. *Rich. II*, I. i. 152 Wrath-kindled Gentlemen be rul'd by me. **1600** ROWLANDS *Lett. Humours Blood* iv. D 8 b, [To] Threaten to drawe his wrath-venger, his sworde. **1644** VICARS *God in Mount* 42 The guilt of such a wrath-provoking sin. **1656** SPARROW tr. *Boehme's Aurora* xix. 434 When thou fightest against him, thou stirrest up his wrath-fire. **1718** WODROW *Corr.* (1843) II. 356 The extraordinary stirrings of the Jacobites, and their elevation, especially since our wrath-like divisions at Court. **1757** W. WILKIE *Epigoniad* III. 66 They fly dispers'd, nor tempt..His wrath-swoln neck and eyes of living fire. **1798** SOTHEBY tr. *Wieland's Oberon* (1826) I. 27 His sov'reign's wrath-bewilder'd brain. **1859** FITZGERALD *Omar K.* lvi, Whether the one True Light Kindle to Love, or Wrathconsume me quite. **1886** J. PULSFORD *Infoldings* v. 63 The wrath-storm which our sins have created. **1892** G. MEREDITH *Poems* 81 It surges like the wrath-faced father Sea To countering winds. **1920** T. S. ELIOT *Ara Vos Prec* 12 These tears are shaken from the wrath-bearing tree.

Hence †'**wrathhead**, wrath; deep anger. *Obs.*$^{-1}$

1303 R. BRUNNE *Handl. Synne* 12460 God..Oþer forȝyueþ..alle with gladehede, Or alle abydeþ to hys wraþhede.

wrath, ME. var. WROTH *a.*

wrath (rɔːθ), *a.* [var. of WROTH *a.*, prob. by association with WRATH *sb.*] Wroth, angry, irate; deeply resentful.

Somewhat rare; but occuring in various passages of the Douay Bible (1609) where earlier versions and the Authorized have *wroth.*

1535 *Trevisa's Barth. De P.R.* XVIII. xii. 316/2 No creature is..more feruente to take wreche than is the bee whan he is wrathe. **1590** SHAKS. *Mids. N.* II. i. 20 Oberon is passing fell and wrath [*rime* hath]. **1596** SPENSER *F.Q.* IV. viii. 43 Whereat the Prince full wrath, his strong right hand.. heaued vp on hie. **1609** BIBLE (Douay) *Gen.* xl. 2 Pharao being wrath against them..sent them into the prison. **1629** MILTON *Hymn Nativ.* xviii, Th'old Dragon under ground.. wrath to see his Kingdom fail. [**1847** MADDEN *Laȝamon* I. 271 When he was wrath with any man.] **1860** THACKERAY *Lovel* iv, Lovel, seldom angry, was violently wrath with his brother-in-law. **1862** BULWER *Strange Story* II. 229, I saw the child..looking towards us, and..she seemed near. I felt wrath with her.

†**wrath**, *v.* *Obs.* Forms: *α.* 3 **wreððen, wreþþen,** 4 **wreþþe, wretþe,** 4–5 **wretthe.** *β.* 3 **wraððen (wraðhin),** 3–4 **wraþþen** (3 *Orm.* -enn), 4–5 **wraþþe,** 5 **wraþþi, wrathþe;** 3 **wratþen,** 4–5 **wratthen, wratthe.** *γ.* 3 **wraðen, wraþen (wrahþen),** 4 **wrathen,** 4–5 **wraþe, wrathe, wraþ** (4 **wragh**), 4–6, *arch.* 9 **wrath.** *δ.* 5, *Sc.* 6 **wraith.** [Early ME. *wreþþen*, *wraþþen*, f. the sb. (see WRATH *sb.*), taking the place of the earlier *wrēðen* WRETHE *v.* Cf. AWRATH, IWRATHE, and WROTH *vbs.*]

1. *intr.* To be or become angry, wrathful, or wroth; to feel, manifest, or exhibit anger; to rage.

c **1205** LAY. 1450 þa iwredðede [*v.r.* iwreððede] Numbert. *a* **1225** *Leg. Kath.* 746 þe king bigon to wreððen [*Cott. MS.* wraððen]. *a* **1300** *E.E. Psalter* cxi. 10 Sinful sal se, and wrath he sal. **13..** *E.E. Allit. P.* B. 230 Ȝet wrathed not þe wyȝ, ne þe wrech saȝtled. **1393** LANGL. *P. Pl.* C. I. 189 Yf he wratthe, we mowe be war. **14..** *Sir Beues* (C.) 632 He wrathed sore yn is hertte. *c* **1450** *Merlin* i. 3 Whan the gode man herde this he gan to wratthe.

transf. *c* **1275** LAY. 4577 þe wind com on wiþere, And þe see wreþþede. *Ibid.* 12006 þe see was wonderliche wod; and þe see wraþþede.

b. Const. *against*, *at*, *in*, *with* (a person or thing).

1338 R. BRUNNE *Chron.* (1810) 111 Whan wrathed Steuen with Dauid of Scotland. *c* **1400** *Destr. Troy* 8442 The worthy at his wife wrathet a litle. *a* **1450** *Knt. de la Tour* (1868) 20 A gentille knightes doughter that wratthed atte the tables with a gentille man.

transf. *a* **1300** *E.E. Psalter* cxxiii. 3 When wrathed [*Harl.* wraghed] breth of þa in us þus. **1382** WYCLIF *Ps.* cxxiii. 3 Whan shulde wrathen the wodnesse of hem in to vs.

c. Of the Deity: To be or grow righteously angry or wroth (*against* or *with* a person or thing).

a **1300** *E.E. Psalter* vii. 12 (H.), God demer rith,..Nou wrathes be alle daies in land? **1377** LANGL. *P. Pl.* B. IX. 128 Caymes kynde & his kynde coupled togideres, Tyl god wratthed for her werkis. **1382** WYCLIF *Lam.* v. 22 Lord,.. thou wrathedist aȝen vs hugely. *a* **1450** *Knt. de la Tour* (1868) 77 And God wratthed therwith, and bade Moyses [etc.].

2. *trans.* To make (a person, etc.) irate, angry, or wroth; to move to wrath, ire, or deep resentment; to anger, enrage; to annoy, vex.

In very frequent use from *c* 1350 to *c* 1450.

α. *c* **1205** LAY. 3771 Heo werðede [*c* **1275** Hii wreþþede] heore moddri mare þene heo sulden. *a* **1225** *Ancr. R.* 426 On alle wise uorberen to wreððen hore dame. *a* **1250** *Prov. Ælfred* (A.) 276 And þu hi myd worde iwreþþed heuedest. **1340** *Ayenb.* 8 þet we ous loky þet we ne wreþþi uader ne moder wytindeliche. *c* **1380** *Sir Ferumb.* 4045 þenk eftsones to auenged be of þe Amyral þat haþ y-wreþþed þe. *a* **1450** *Northern Passion* (D) 727 Petir stod wretthid ful sore.

β. *a* **1200** *Vices & Virtues* 99 Se ðe hafð ðese eadi mihte, him ne mai no mann wraðhin. *c* **1205** LAY. 7200 þe feond wes iwraððed. **1297** R. GLOUC. (Rolls) 7721 Ȝif þat eni him [= William] wraþþede, adoun he was anon. **13..** *K. Alis.* 3369 (Laud MS.), Ne shaltou wraþþe þi lorde gent. **1303** R. BRUNNE *Handl. Synne* 8584 Of þese dedly synnes seuene, þat we wraþþe with God of heuene. **1362** LANGL. *P. Pl.* A. II. 85 Serwe on þi lokkes, Such weddyng to worche to wraþþe with truþe. **1398** TREVISA *Barth. De P.R.* XVIII. xii. (Bodl. MS.), þe bee whan he is ywraþþed. *a* **1450** MYRC *Par. Pr.* 1142 Hast þou..Wrathþed þy neȝbore in any þynge? **1480** CAXTON *Cron. Eng.* ccxxx. 244 The kyng was gretely meuid and wratthed.

transf. *c* **1205** LAY. 12006 þe sæ wes wunder ane wod, and ladliche iwraððed.

absol. **13..** *Pol., Rel., & L. Poems* (1903) 260 Lechery.. wasteþ.., hit wraþþeþ, hit bigileþ.

γ. *a* **1275** *Prov. Ælfred* (B.) 276 If..þu hire mid worde wraþed hauedest. *a* **1300** *Cursor M.* 16427 Pilate forthoght þaim bath to wrath. *c* **1350** *Will. Palerne* 981, I wraþed him neuer..in word ne in dede. *c* **1369** CHAUCER *Dethe Blaunche* 1151 Ne I wolde haue wrathed her truly. *c* **1450** *Mirk's Festial* 29 But yn a myshappe..þay wraþeden hor modyr. **1486** *Bk. St. Albans* f v b, Wrath not thy neighborys next the. [**1866** MORRIS *Ayenb.* 8 *marg.*, Wrath not thy Father or Mother.]

transf. *c* **1205** LAY. 4577 þe wind com on weðere, and þa sæ he wraðede [*c* **1275** þe see wreþþede].

δ. *c* **1400** *Brut.* II. 310 Wherfore þe King was gretly.. wraithed. *c* **1480** HENRYSON *Fables, Wolf & Lamb* 43 He wraithit me, and than I culd him warne Within ane ȝeir.

b. Predicated of things. Somewhat *rare.*

a **1225** *Leg. Kath.* 238 Ne nis na þing hwerþurh monnes muchele madschipe wreððeð [*Cott. MS.* wraððeð] him wið mare [etc.]. *c* **1230** *Hali Meid.* 27 Moni þing schal ham wraððen & gremen. **1472** *Paston Lett.* III. 57 Sir Jamys is evyr choppyng at me..with syche wordys as he thynkys wrathe me.

c. To provoke or incite (the Deity) to righteous anger or wrath; to move to displeasure. Also const. *to*, *with.*

In frequent use from *c* 1325 to *c* 1425.

c **1200** ORMIN 5615 þu Ne darrst nohht Drihhtin wraþþenn. *a* **1225** *Ancr. R.* 138 Monnes soule..geð ut of hire heie heouenliche cunde, & forte paien hire, wreððet hire schuppare. **1297** R. GLOUC. (Rolls) 8813 þo þou.. wraþþedest so muche god. *c* **1330** *Amis & Amil.* 606 Al our ioie..We schuld lese, and, for that sinne, Wretthi God therto. *c* **1375** *Cursor M.* 1227 (Fairf.), Vn-sely cayme..and alle his osspringe..wraþet him wiþ wikked rede. *c* **1430** *Hymns Virg.* (1867) 16 Ihesu, for them y þe biseche þat wraþþen þee in ony wise. *a* **1450** MYRC *Par. Pr.* 978 Hast þou.. I-wrathþad þy god greuowsly? **1485** CAXTON *St. Wenefr.* 3 Thou hast gretely wrathed oure lorde.

3. *refl.* To wax, become, or grow angry.

c **1205** LAY. 20345 Arður..þis gomen isæh and wraðde hine sulfne. *a* **1225** *Juliana* 10 (Royal MS.), þa þe reue iherde þis, he wreððede him swiðe. *c* **1290** *Beket* 972 þo þe king i-saiȝ him so come he wrathþede him a-non. *c* **1320** *Sir Tristr.* 661 Fader, no wretþe þe nouȝt. **1362** LANGL. *P. Pl.* A. III. 176 Whi þou wraþþest þe now, wonder me þinkeþ. *c* **1420** *Chron. Vilod.* 4125 Hurre brother wratthede hym þo at þe last. *c* **1450** LOVELICH *Grail* xxxvii. 644 Anon to wraththen sche gan hire there. [**1822** SCOTT *Peveril* xxii, 'Nay, wrath thee not, Will,' said Ganlesse.]

4. *trans.* To be or become angry with (a person); to treat with anger, ire, or deep resentment.

c **1374** CHAUCER *Troylus* III. 174 Ne I nyl forbere, yf þat ye don a-mys, To wrathen [*Harl. MS.* wreth] yow, and whil þat ye me serue, Cherycen yow right after ye deserue. **1375** *Cantic. de Creatione* 288 ȝut bad me Michel with word od Worschipen þe, or elles god Wolde wrathen me. *c* **1430** in *Pol., Rel., & L. Poems* (1903) 191/11 Whi wraþþist þou me? y greue þee nouȝt. **1567** TURBERV. *Ovid's Ep.* 73 b, A cruell stepdame will my children wrath [L. *saeviet in partus meos*].

5. To afflict, harm, or injure; to bring to grief or disaster.

13.. *Guy Warw.* (A.) 1529 Gwichard, who haþ wretþed þe, & where hastow in bateyle be? **13..** *Gaw. & Gr. Knt.* 726 For werre wrathed hym not so much, þat wynter was wors. *Ibid.* 2420 Adam,..Salamon..and Samson..were wrathed wyth her [*sc.* woman's] wyles. **14..** *Guy Warw.* 1123 (Camb. MS.) 3252 Or they be passyd the hyllys hye, We schall þem wrath.

Hence †'**wrather**, one who excites, or moves to, wrath; †'**wrathing** *vbl. sb. Obs.*

1382 WYCLIF *Ezek.* ii. 7 Therfor thou shalt speke my wordis to hem,..for thei ben *wraththers. *c* **1370** *Stacions of Rome* 107 (Vernon MS.), *Wraþþing of Fader or Moder ȝif hit be In godes nome he forȝiueþ þe. *c* **1400** *Cato's Morales* 296 in *Cursor M.* 1673 For nane alde wraþþing hate noȝt þi frende if he chaunge his manere. *c* **1440** *Jacob's Well* 241 Princepally for dreed of god, for dreed of his wretthyng. *a* **1450** *Knt. de la Tour* (1868) 24 For drede of sclaunder and wratthinge of her.

wrath, obs. erron. f. RATHE *adv.*

c **1400** *Arth. & Merl.* 2145 (Linc. Inn MS.), King Anguis ..Did arme his men wrath & prest.

wrathe, obs. pa. t. of WRITHE *v.*

wrather-hail, -heal, -hele, varr. WROTHER-HEAL *Obs.*

wrathful ('rɒθfʊl, 'rɔːθ-), *a.* [f. WRATH *sb.* + -FUL. Cf. WRETHFUL *a.*, WROTHFUL *a.*]

1. Of persons, etc.: Harbouring wrath; full of anger; enraged, incensed.

a **1300** *E.E. Psalter* xvii. 51 Mi leser artou..Fra mi faes ben wrathful ai. *c* **1330** *Spec. Gy de Warw.* 262 þeder he wole lihten adoun Wraþful..as a lioun. **1388** WYCLIF *Prov.* xv. 18 A wrathful man reisith chidyngis. **1398** TREVISA *Barth. De P.R.* XVIII. xii. (Bodl. MS.), Some [bees] beþ..foule to siȝt and more wraþfulle þanne oþer. *c* **1430** in *Babees Bk.* 12 [Do not be] to wielde, ne to wraþful, neiþer waaste. **1568** GRAFTON *Chron.* II. 758 He was malicious, wrathfull, enuyous. **1582** STANYHURST *Æneis* I. (Arb.) 18 Al the frushe and leauings of Greeks, of wrathful Achilles. **1624** MILTON *Ps.* cxxxvi. 10 O let us his praises tell, That doth the wrathfull tyrants quell. **1697** DRYDEN *Virg. Georg.* IV. 344 The Bees, a wrathful Race. **1697** —— *Æneis* VIII. 81 With sacrifice the wrathful queen appease. *a* **1718** PRIOR *2nd Hymn of Callimachus* 22 Lest wrathful the far-shooting God emitt His fatal Arrows. **1775** ADAIR *Amer. Ind.* 303 They hung down their heads, and looked gloomy and wrathful. **1846** W. H. MILL *Five Serm.* (1848) 116 Describing Himself as wrathful against the determined sinner. **1877** 'RITA' *Vivienne* I. viii, Her heart was wrathful and indignant. **1892** A. E. LEE *Hist. Columbus, Ohio* I. 315 The tollgates..were torn away by wrathful citizens.

b. *transf.* Of things.

1563 SACKVILLE *Induct. Mirr. Mag.* i, The wrathful winter prochinge on a-pace. **1590** SPENSER *F.Q.* II. ii. 30 Thousand furies wait on wrathfull sword. **1591** SYLVESTER *Du Bartas* I. ii. 902 Thou hast felt the rod Of the revenging wrathfull hand of God. **1605** SHAKS. *Lear* III. ii. 43 The wrathfull Skies Gallow the very wanderers of the darke. **1697** DRYDEN *Æneis* IX. 461 Nor with less Rage Euryalus employs The wrathful Sword, or fewer Foes destroys. **1709** STEELE *Tatler* No 38 ¶3 They stripp'd and..fought full fairly with their wrathful Hands. **1727** THOMSON *Summer* 741 Unusual Darkness..gains The whole Possession of the Air, sur-charg'd With wrathful Vapour. *a* **1835** MRS. HEMANS *Treasures of Deep* ii, Sweep o'er thy spoils, thou wild and wrathful main. **1841** DICKENS *Barn. Rudge* lvi, A threatening light..which showed like a wrathful sunset.

2. Marked or characterized by, expressive of, of the nature of, wrath or anger.

1390 GOWER *Conf.* III. 98 Full of ymaginacion Of dredes and of wrathful thoghtes, He fret himselven al to noghtes. *c* **1400** *26 Pol. Poems* xx. 77 þan comeþ she hom in wraþþeful hete. **14..** *Of Manners* 8 in *Babees-bk.* 34 Of wraþful wordis euermore be ware. **1514** BARCLAY *Egloges* (1570) Biv/1 Better is..a small handfull with rest and sure pleasaunce, Then twenty dishes with wrathfull countenaunce. **1535** COVERDALE *1 Macc.* ii. 49 Now is the tyme of destruccion and wrathfull displeasure. **1610** *Mirr. for Mag.* 630 Ioue in the tempest of his wrathfull mood Powr'd downe his wreake vpon my wretched hed. **1631** GOUGE *God's Arrows* III. §3. 186 Wrathfull and revengefull affections. **1716** POPE *Iliad* V. 1092 Him.. with a wrathful Look The Lord of Thunders view'd. **1834** PRINGLE *Afr. Sh.* vii. 252 The tremendous screams of their wrathful voices. **1900** *Longm. Mag.* March 452 His accelerated and somewhat wrathful departure from Brackenhurst.

Comb. **1885** C. J. LYALL *Anc. Arab. Poet.* 5 A lion wrathful-eyed.

'**wrathfully**, *adv.* [f. prec. + -LY². Cf. WRETHFULLY *adv.*] In a wrathful manner; angrily, wrothfully.

c **1330** *Arth. & Merl.* 1362 þe king for þis was swiþe wroþ, wraþfulliche swore his oþ. **1390** GOWER *Conf.* II. 375 Bot he hem wrathfulli congeide. **1596** SPENSER *F.Q.* V. i. 18 His sword he drew all wrathfully. **1601** SHAKS. *Jul. C.* II. i. 172 Let's kill him Boldly, but not Wrathfully. **1740** RICHARDSON *Pamela* II. 281 He..said wrathfully, Begone, rageful Woman! **1833** MRS. BROWNING *Prometh. Bound* 189 Zeus.. Right wrathfully Bears on his sceptral soul unbent. **1839** DICKENS *Nickleby* xii, 'Hold your tongue,' replied Miss Squeers wrathfully. **1885** *L'pool Daily Post* 7 March 4/8 The recollections of our correspondent have apparently been wrathfully awakened.

'**wrathfulness.** [f. as prec. + -NESS.] The state, condition, or quality of being wrathful; wrath, ire.

1382 WYCLIF *Ecclus.* i. 28 Wrathefulnesse forsothe of wilfulnesse..is his turnyng vp so doun. **1546** *Wycklyffes Wycket* (1828) 3 He shalbe raysed tyll the wrathfulness before determyned is perfectilye made. **1583** GOLDING *Calvin on Deut.* xxxii. 189 There is no wrathfulnesse in God. **1591** HARINGTON *Orl. Fur.* XLII. i, What iron band, or what sharp hard mouth'd bit..Can bridle wrathfulness and conquer it? **1683** J. PORDAGE *Mystic Div.* 118 To the Fire-essence do belong, Fierceness, Fieriness, Wrathfulness. **1727** BAILEY (vol. II), *Irefulness*, wrathfulness. **1859** GEO. ELIOT *Adam Bede* l, Adam..was afraid she had thought him serious about his wrathfulness.

†'**wrathless**, *a.* Also 4 **wraþþelees**. [f. WRATH *sb.* + -LESS.] Free from, devoid of, wrath.

c **1310** in Wright *Lyric P.* xii. 42 To alle that ever hider eode, To do to day my neode, ichulle be wraththe-lees. **1598** SYLVESTER *Du Bartas* II. i. *Handycrafts* 635 Tost by the Fiend that fiercely tortures them, With wrathlesse wounds their senselesse members wounding. *c* **1636** WALLER *On C'tess Carlisle's Chamber* 14 Before his feet so sheep and lions lay, Fearless and wrathless, while they heard him play.

wrathli, wraðliche, etc., varr. WROTHLY *adv.*

† **wrath money.** *local.* [var. of *warth-money*: cf. *ward-silver* WARD *sb.*² 25 b and WARDPENNY.] = WROTH MONEY.

1730 THOMAS *Dugdale's Warwick* I. 4/2 The party paying it must go thrice about the cross, and say The *Wrath* money, and then lay it in the hole of the said cross before good witness.

† **wrathness.** *Obs.*⁻¹ In 5 **wrathenesse.** [f. ME. *wrath* WROTH *a.* + -NESS.] Anger.

c **1440** *York Myst.* xxxi. 12 Dragons..schall derke in þer denne In wrathe when we writhe, or in wrathenesse ar wapped.

wrathy ('rɒθɪ, 'rɔːθɪ, *U.S.* 'rɑːθɪ), *a.* Orig. (and chiefly) *U.S.* [f. WRATH *sb.* + -Y¹. Cf. WROTHY *a.*]

1. Of persons: Feeling, or inclined to, wrath; wrathful, very angry, incensed.

1828 J. F. COOPER *Red Rover* viii, You are wrathy, friend, without reason. **1828** WEBSTER, *Wrathy*, very angry; a colloquial word. **1833** [S. SMITH] *Lett. J. Downing* viii. (1835) 66 When things don't go right, and the Gineral gits a little wrathy. **1859** TROLLOPE *West Indies* (1860) xiii. 198 They are wrathy men, and have rough sides to their tongues. **1887** MRS. D. DALY *S. Australia* 307 The wrathy owner of the missing horses.

absol. **1902** C. G. HARPER *Holyhead Road* II. 185 But the habitations of wrathy and peaceable are alike overthrown.

b. Marked or characterized by, expressing or evincing, deep anger or indignation.

1873 MISS BROUGHTON *Nancy* II. 112 A wrathy red light has come into his deep eyes. **1890** *Big Game N. Amer.* 352 He was in a decidedly wrathy mood. **1897** H. G. WELLS *Certain Matters* (1898) 131 Coming back to wrathy swearing,..I am sorry to see it decay.

2. *transf.* Of the elements, etc.: Fierce, violent, tempestuous.

1872 TALMAGE *Serm.* 100 The shrill blast of the wrathiest tempest that ever blackened the sky or shook the ocean. **1876** MISS BROUGHTON *Joan* I. xxxi, The wrathy, masterful, winter sea.

Hence '**wrathily** *adv.*, wrathfully. *U.S.*

1847 WEBSTER. **1879** G. W. CABLE *Old Creole Days* (1883) 235 The negro begged; the master wrathily insisted.

†'**wratling**, *a. Obs. rare*⁻¹. [Imitative. Cf. RATTLING *ppl. a.*] (See quot.)

a **1661** FULLER *Worthies, Leics.* II. 126 [They] have an harsh and wratling kind of Speech, uttering their words with much difficulty and wharling in the Throat, and cannot well pronounce the Letter R.

wraught, obs. f. *wrought*, pa. t. of WORK *v.*

wraw, *a. Obs.* exc. *dial.* Forms: α. 3 **wrah**, 4 **wragh**, 5 **wraȝe**; 4 **wrau**, 4–5 (9 *north. dial.*) **wraw**, 4–6 **wraw**, 9 *dial.* **raw**. β. 4 **wrowe, wroȝ**, 5 **wrow**. [Of obscure origin; the forms indicate an unrecorded OE. **wrāh*, **wrāȝ*.]

1. Of persons: Angry, wrathful, wroth.

c **1205** LAY. 3354 þis iherde Leir king; þar fore he wes swuþe wrah. *a* **1275** *Ancr. R.* 416 (Cott. Cleop. MS.), þe nan from ow ne parti wið scandle, ne wrah, ne mispaiet. *a* **1300** *Thrush & Night.* in Hazl. *E.P.P.* I. 51 Hy gladieth hem that beth wrowe. *c* **1315** SHOREHAM IV. 139 Wat helpþe hyt so wrau to be, Wanne þou wyþ gode chyst? *c* **1386** CHAUCER *Manc. Prol.* 46 With this speche the Cook wax wrooth & wraw. *c* **1400** *Rule St. Benet* (Prose) 8 Wisit þat er seke;.. Sahtil þat ere wraȝe. *c* **1500** *Blowbol's Test.* in Halliw. *Nugæ P.* 9 They be than so angry and so wraw. *a* **1529** SKELTON *Agst. Garnesche* ii. 40 Thow mantycore,..Wranglynge, waywyrde, wytles, wraw, and nothyng meke. **1811** WILLAN in *Archaeol.* (1814) XVII. 163 *Wrawe*, angry. **1887** *Kentish Gloss.* 126 *Raw*, angry.—Sittingbourne.

b. Marked or characterized by anger or ire.

c **1475** *Promp. Parv.* (K.) 80/2 Clenchyn a-ȝen in wraw speche,..*obgarrio*.

2. Peevish, crabbed; perverse, contrarious.

c **1386** CHAUCER *Pars. T.* ¶677 Accidie maketh hym heuy thoughtfull & wrawe [*v.rr.* wrowe, *Ellesm. MS.* wrawful]. *c* **1440** *Promp. Parv.* 99/2 Crabbyd, awke, or wrawe.., *ceronicus, bilosus. Ibid.* 533/1 Wraw, froward, ongoodly, ..*protervus, exasperans.*

Hence †'**wrawful** *a.*, = WRAW *a.* 2; †'**wrawly** *adv.*, perversely; †'**wrawness**, perverseness.

c **1386** CHAUCER *Pars. T.* ¶680 He dooth alle thyng with anoy and with wrawnesse, slaknesse, and excusacion. *c* **1400** wrawful [see prec. 2]. *c* **1440** *Promp. Parv.* 18/2 Awkely, or wrawely, *perverse, contrarie. Ibid.* 533/1 Wrawnesse, *protervia*,..*bilositas, perversitas.*

† **wraw**, *v. Obs. rare.* Also 5 **wrawen.** [ad. MDu. *wrauwen*, of imitative origin.] *intr.* To miaul, as a cat; to mew.

1481 CAXTON *Reynard* x. (Arb.) 22 Thenne..began he [*sc.* Tybert the cat] to wrawen for he was almost ystranglyd. **1662** in Pitcairn *Crim. Trials* III. 611 Quhan we vold [= would] be in the shap of cattis, we did nothing but cry and wraw.

† **wrawed**, *a. Obs.* 5–6 **wrawd.** [f. WRAW *a.* + -ED¹.] Angry, wroth; perverse.

a **1400–50** *Wars Alex.* 3167 For he..Is wrawid & wrathfull of will, & wode as a lyon. *c* **1460** J. RUSSELL *Bk. Nurture* 590 Crabbe is a slutt to kerve & a wrawd wight. **1582** STANYHURST *Æneis* IV. (Arb.) 116 O forlorne Dido, now now wrawd destenye grubs the.

wrawl, *v. Obs.* exc. *north. dial.* Also 4 **wral**, 6 **wrall**, 7 **wralle**; 5, 7 **wrawle**, 6, 8 **wraul**, 7 **wraule**, 6– **wrawl** (9 *dial.* **rawwl**); also 4 (9 *dial.*) **warl**. [Imitative. Cf. Norw. *vraula*, *raula*; also Da. *vraale*, *vræle*, Sw. *vråla*, LG. *wrâlen*, to squall, bellow, scream.]

1. *intr.* To utter an inarticulate noise or sound; to bawl, squall.

c **1440** *Ipomydon* 1835 Thus he wrawled & wroth a way, One word to hyr he nolde not say. **1573** TUSSER *Husb.* (1878) 191 Bralling fooles that wrall for euerie wrong. **1601** HOLLAND *Pliny* I. 152 Man alone..she hath laid all naked upon the bare earth,..to cry and wraule presently from the very first houre that he is borne into this world. **1606** BRYSKETT *Civ. Life* 53 Euer crying and wrawling for they wote not what. *c* **1780** M. LONSDALE in S. Gilpin *Songs Cumbld.* (1866) 276 Guidman stuid wraulin at her lug, An' ca'd her many a garrick. **1811** WILLAN in *Archaeol.* (1814) XVII. 163 *Wrawling*, quarrelling, or contending with a loud voice. **1859** B. BRIERLY *Daisy Nook* 49 A lot o' dhrunken chaps rawlin' wi' one another.

†**2.** Of cat: = WRAW *v. Obs.*⁻¹

1596 SPENSER *F.Q.* VI. xii. 27 Some were..of cats, that wrawling still did cry.

Hence '**wrawler**, one who brawls or squalls; '**wrawling** *vbl. sb.* and *ppl. a.*

c **1440** *Promp. Parv.* 37/2 Blaffoorde or *warlare [*Winch. MS.* wrawlere].., *traulus.* **1579–80** NORTH *Plutarch* (1595) 55 Neither were..[the children] cryers, wrallers, or vnhappy children. *a* **1530** HEYWOOD *Johan & Tyb.* (Brandl.) 365 She wyll neuer leue her *wrawlyng. **1570** GOOGE *Popish Kingd.* II. (1880) 21 b, Children there that lye, And fill their eares with wrawling all the night. **1603** HOLLAND *Plutarch's Mor.* 1219 Cries and wrawlings of an infinite number of children. **1623** *New & Merry Prognost.* E 2, Beggars loue brawling, And wretches loue wrawling. **1573** A. ANDERSON *Expos. of Benedict.* 30 To quiet & make stil his wanton and *wrauling cryes. **1619** R. WEST *Bk. Demeanor* 60 in *Babees Bk.*, Nor practize snuffingly to speake, for that doth imitate The brutish Storke..and the wralling cat. *c* **1620** *Welsh Embass.* IV. 1510 [The women] to still their wrawlinge bastards cry out, husht [etc.].

wrax, erron. f. RAX *v. Sc.* and *north. dial.*

'**wraxle**, *v. Obs.* exc. *s.w. dial.* Forms: 1 **wraxlian**, 3–4 **wraxli**, 4–5, 9 *dial.* **wraxle** (5 **wracsle, wraskle**, 9 *dial.* **wroxle, roxle**). [OE. *wraxlian* = OFris. *wraxlia* (WFris. *wrakselje*, *wrokselje*). The orig. form of the stem may have been *wrasc-*; cf. OE. *wræstlian* WRESTLE *v.*] *intr.* To wrestle; to contend, strive. Also *fig.*

c **1000** ÆLFRIC *Gen.* xxxii. 24 Ða wraxlode an engel wið hyne on merigen. *c* **1000** —— *Saint's Lives* xxiii. 578 Ic wæs ..on unmætum costnungum winnende and wraxligende. *c* **1275** LAY. 1858 Brutus hine lette witie..fort lete fondien of his main stronge, to wraxli to vore Brutus. *Ibid.* 24699 Somme þar wraxlede and wiþer-game makede. *c* **1305** *St. Swithin* in *E.E.P.* (1862) 45 þe baldelikere hi miȝte Huppe ouer diches wher hi wolde, boþe wraxli and fiȝte. **1393** LANGL. *P. Pl.* C. XVII. 67 Yf wratthe wraxle with þe poure he hath þe worsse ende. *Ibid.* 80 þaugh couetyce wolde with þe poure wraxle þei mai nat come to-gederis. **14..** *Voc.* in Wr.-Wülcker 593 *Luctor*, to wraxle. **1746** *Exmoor Scolding* (E.D.S.) 217 [Though he] wriggled, and pawed, and wraxled, and twined. **1851, 1886** in Devon and Isle of Wight glossaries. **1854** *N. & Q.* 16 Dec. 479 (Cornish dialect), *Wroxle*,..to wrestle.

Hence '**wraxling** *vbl. sb.* (also *attrib.*) and *ppl. a.*

c **1000** ÆLFRIC *Voc.* in Wr.-Wülcker 150 *Luctatio*, wraxlung. *c* **1275** LAY. 1871 þar was mochel folk at þare wraxlinge. **1746** *Exmoor Scolding* Gloss., *Wraxling*, wrestling. **1837** [Mrs. Palmer] *Dial. Devon. Dialect* 9 Wot'n go..to rail and zee the wraxlin? **1855** Kingsley *Westw. Ho!* xxx, I'll..buy me a pair of horn-tips to my shoes, like a wraxling-man. **1867** Rock *Jim an' Nell* cxxi. (E.D.S.), Jan's wraxling ginged tha wildego. **1892** Sarah Hewett *Peasant Speech Devon* 150 A wraxling match between Joe Gooding and Dick Gollop.

wray, ME. or dial. var. wro.

†**wray**, *v.*[1] *Obs.* Forms: *α.* 1 **wrœȝan, wreȝan,** 2 **wreiȝen,** 3 **wreȝen, wreiȝen** (*Orm.* **wreȝ(h)enn**); 2 **uureien,** 2–3 **wreien,** 3 **wreyen,** 5 **wreyyn;** 3 **wreiȝe,** 3–4 **wreie,** 3–5 **wreye,** 4–5 **wreȝe** (5 **wreythe**), **wregh(e,** 4 **wreȝ, wrei,** 4–6 **wrey;** 4 **wroie, wroye,** 4–5 **wraie,** 5–6 **wray** (6 *Sc.* **vray**). *β.* 3–4 **wryghe,** 5 **wrigh,** 4–5 **wryen, wrye,** 4–6 **wrie,** 5–6 **wry.** *γ.* 5 *Sc.* **wre,** 8 *north. dial.* **wree.** [Comm. Teut.: OE. *wrǽȝan, wréȝan,* = OFris. *wrôgia, wrêia* (WFris. *wroegje,* EFris. *wrögje, wrög,* NFris. *wröge*), MDu. *wroeghen* (Du. *wroegen*), OS. *wrögjan* (MLG. *wrogen, wrugen, rogen,* LG. *wrogen, wragen, wrögen, rögen*), OHG. *ruogen* (MHG. *rüegen,* G. *rügen*), ON. *rǿgja* (Icel. *rægja*; Norw. *røgja,* Sw. *röja*), f. the stem *wrōȝ-* (ON. *róg* slander, strife), with a variant *wrōh-* which appears in Goth. *wrôhs* accusation, *wrôhjan* to accuse.

By normal dialectal developments, three main forms of the stem appear in ME., viz. *wrey* or *wray, wry,* and northern *wrē*.]

I. 1. To accuse, denounce, or inform on (a person); to expose (one) by revealing or divulging information, etc., to one's harm, prejudice, or discredit; to charge with a crime, offence, fault, etc.; = bewray *v.* 2.

c **725** *Corpus Gloss.* (Hessels) D 74 *Defferuntur,* meldadun *uel* wroegdum. *a* **900** *O.E. Martyrol.* 10 Dec. 216 Ic cume eft on domes dæȝ ond þe þonne wreȝe beforan Crystes þrymsetle. *c* **1000** Ælfric *Saints' Lives* ii. 184 Færde þa ardlice..to þam heah-ȝeræfan..and begann hi to wræȝenne. *a* **1122** *O.E. Chron.* (Laud MS.) an. 1069, Her man wræȝde ðone biscop Æȝelric on Burh, & sense hine to West mynstre. *c* **1175** *Lamb. Hom.* 29 Ne mei þe deofel þe wreien on þan oðre liue. *c* **1200** Ormin 2889 He [*sc.* Joseph] wass ædmod & milde, I þatt tatt he ne wollde nohht Unnshaþiȝ wimmann wreȝhenn. *c* **1275** *Passion of our Lord* 84 in *O.E. Misc.* 39 Þe maystres of þe temple..For to vndernyme vre louerd..were euer abute..þet heo hynemyhte wreye and don of lyf-daye. *c* **1330** *Amis & Amil.* 1090 Than told Sir Amis al that cas..And hou the steward gan hem wrain. **13..** *Gosp. Nicodemus* (G.) 204 Pilat..seþin to þe iewes..sayd: 'Ȝe wrigh him wrangwisly'. *c* **1400** *Ywaine & Gaw.* 2859 Sho hyr talde..How wikkedly that sho was wreghed, And how that traytyrs on hir leghed. *c* **1450** *Northern Passion* (MS. Ad.) 609 Þe Iewes..ledde hym..vn to..cayphase And by fore hyme þay gune hym wrye. **1480** Caxton *Trevisa's Higden* (1482) 167 b, Cithero ..borwede of one scilla, but he was wryed er þe bargayne was made.

refl. *c* **1100** *O.E. Chron.* (MS. D) an. 1076, Walþeof eorl ferde ofer sæ & wreide hine sylfne & bæd forȝyfenysse. *c* **1175** *Lamb. Hom.* 27 Ȝif þu wreiest þe seolfen to þine scrifte. *a* **1225** *Ancr. R.* 304 Mon schal wreien him suluen ine schrifte. *a* **1300** *Cursor M.* 26706 Qua wil noght him-seluen wrei..nu ar he dei. *Ibid.* 16466, 26701, 26716, 26967.

fig. *a* **1225** *Ancr. R.* 306 Let..þouhtes munegunge wreie him, & bicleope him of misliche sunnen. *a* **1400** in *Minor Poems fr. Vernon MS.* 741 In bremful bale he schal hit by, When concience his werk schal wrye.

b. Const. *to* (another), *of* (a thing).

a **900** *O.E. Martyrol.* 8 Nov. 202 Þa wreȝdon þa oðre cræftiȝan hy to þam casere. *c* **1000** *Ags. Gosp.* Luke xxiii. 14 Ic nanne intingan findan ne mæȝ on þisum men of þam þe ȝe hine wreȝað. *c* **1132** *O.E. Chron.* (Laud MS.) an. 1132, Þa com Henri abbot & uureide þe muneces of Burch to þe king. *a* **1225** *Ancr. R.* 172 He was sone iwreied to þe kinge Salomon. *c* **1308** *Pol. Songs* (Camden) 200 Ic am i-wreiid, Sire, to the, For that ilk gilt. **13..** *Guy Warw.* (A.) 3303 Here wil we no longer duelle: To þemperour y-wraid we beþ. *c* **1400** *Pepysian Gosp. Harmony* 95 Þe Jewes euerichon bigonnen hyn to wryen of many þinges. *c* **1450** *Mirour Saluacioun* (Roxb.) 134 Antipater..was wryed to the Emperoure Julian.

fig. *a* **1200** *Vices & Virtues* 141 Ȝif ure hierte..us ne undernemeð naht ne ne wreihð of nane senne.

refl. *a* **1300** *Cursor M.* 26668 Þat þou..wrei þi-self and oþer noght O þi wicked werkes wroght.

2. To declare or assert (something about another) by way of accusation or denunciation; to bring forward as a charge.

a **900** *O.E. Martyrol.* 25 Aug. 152 Þa foron þa hæðnan bisceopas ond þæt wreȝdon to þæs kyninges breðer. *c* **1000** Ælfric *Hom.* I. 478 Þæt folc wrehton his modiȝnysse to ðam casere. *c* **1200** Ormin 416 Þatt fand mann nan þing upponn hemm To wreȝenn, ne to tælenn. *c* **1350** *Northern Passion* (1916) II. 128 Somme..folwede [Jesus] þinges to here; Wat þey miȝte on him leye To þe Iuws vorto wrey.

3. To reveal or disclose (something secret) perfidiously or prejudicially; to divulge with breach of trust; to betray; = bewray *v.* 3.

a **1300** *Cursor M.* 26690 Þat þou sa wrei aun dede, þat na soigne be for þe lede. *c* **1330** *Arth. & Merl.* 3656 Non com oȝain..To wray þe kinges parlement. **1387** Trevisa *Higden* VI. 281 But his counsaile was i-wried, and he was..i-closed in an abbay. **1398** —— *Barth. De P.R.* xvi. lxxxiii. (Tollem. MS.), Quyrin..; þis ston wryeþ and discouereþ in slep counsel and priuite. *c* **1400** *Laud Troy Bk.* 3546 Priamus has ..spies That ȝoure consayl to him wries. *c* **1465** *Eng. Chron.* (Camden, 1856) 21 As sone as the said lordez wiste that thair counselle was discovered and wraid, they fledde. **1563** *Mirr. Mag., Lord Hastings* xlvii, Alas, are counsels wryed to catch the goode? **1576** Gascoigne *Steele Glas* 128 Cut out my tong,..Least I should wraye this bloudy deede of his.

4. *gen.* To reveal, disclose, or divulge (some fact, etc.); to declare, communicate, or make known; = bewray *v.* 4.

a **1300** *Floriz & Bl.* 533 (Camb. MS.), Hele ihc wulle, and noþing wreie, Ower beire cumpaignie. *c* **1375** *Sc. Leg. Saints* xviii. (*Egiptian*) 1446 Ilke ȝere solempnyt fest..þai mad, one þat day scho deyt, fra þat he hyre lyf had wreyt. *c* **1386** Chaucer *Frankl. T.* 216 In his songes somwhat wolde he wreye His wo as in a general compleynyng. **1513** Douglas *Æneid* ix. iii. 5 The deid is auld for to beleif or wry, Bot the memor remanis perpetually. *a* **1542** Wyatt in *Tottel's Misc.* (Arb.) 57 Your sighes yow fet from farre, And all to wry your wo. **1587** Turberv. *Trag. T.* R viij b, Then gan hee wrie his former loue, And all his flame vnfolde.

transf. *c* **1374** Chaucer *Compl. Mars* 91 Alas I dye; the torche is come that al this world wol wrie. **1398** Trevisa *Barth. De P.R.* x. v. (Tollem. MS.), Leye bischineþ derke þinges, and wryeþ þinges þat ben hidde, and makeþ hem knowe.

b. Const. with clause. *rare*$^{-1}$.

1575 *Gascoigne's Poesies* Wks. 1907 I. 23 In thundring verse he wrayes, where highest mindes be thrall.

5. To reveal or make known the presence of (a person); to expose; = bewray *v.* 5.

c **1290** *Beket* 1214 in *S. Eng. Leg.* I. 141 With him a-morewe he nam His oste, þat he ne scholde him wreiȝe forto he aftur weie cam. **13..** *Sir Beues* (A.) 1675 And for þai scholde him nouȝt wrain, Vnder his hond he made him pai. **13..** *Gaw. & Gr. Knt.* 1706 Þa sued hym fast, Wreȝande hym ful weterly with a wroth noyse. *c* **1400** *Laud Troy Bk.* 18341 To an..old tour..He hyed hem with mechel hast For drede lest thei were y-wraied.

b. To put (a person) in the power of an enemy or opponent by disloyalty or treachery; to betray.

c **1275** *XI Pains of Hell* 111 in *O.E. Misc.* 150 He..þat wreyeþ his sibbe oþer him fled Abuuen his eyen þe flod geþ. **1387** Trevisa *Higden* V. 117 He was i-wreyed by þe same douȝter Fausta..and fliȝ to Marcil. *Ibid.* 157 Þere he was i-wreyed wiþ [= by] a wenche.

c. To expose (a person) by revealing some hidden fact or private matter.

c **1340** Hampole *Pr. Consc.* 5460–2 Als stolne thyng wreghes a thefe funden, When it es obout his neke.. bounden, Right swa þair syns sal wreghe þam þar. *c* **1400** T. Chestre *Launfal* 147 Thane seyde syr Launfal.., Tell ye no man of my poverte... The knyghtes answerede and seyde tho, That they nolde him wreye never mo. *c* **1400** *Rule St. Benet* (Prose) 36 Wreȝ hir noht þat te þing es sent to. *a* **1450** *Knt. de la Tour* (1868) 62 As a theef wol be gladde there as he ys hidde, and not be wrayed of his thefte. *a* **1500** *Hist. K. Boccus & Sydracke* (? 1510) G j, Yf thou thy frende it sey, And wenyst he shal the not wrey.

6. To reveal, disclose, or discover the true character of; to show or expose the existence or presence of (something desired to be concealed); to betray; = bewray *v.* 6.

1576 Whetstone *Rock of Regard* I. 38 Thou mayst (God wot) thy visard vaile, thy wanton maskes are wrayd. *Ibid.* 65 The colours which I wore, my secrete mourning wrayde. **1587** *Mirr. Mag., Stater* iii, The werke wrayes the man, seeme he neuer so fine.

7. To expose to view; to exhibit, show.

1587 Turberv. *Trag. Tales* M iiij, He wried his wounds, he shewde the shameful blows, He told the trayters treason.

8. *intr.* or *absol.* **a.** To denounce or slander a person; to make accusations, cast aspersions.

c **1320** *Sir Tristr.* 2179 Meriadok wrayeþ ay, To þe king þus seyd he. **1399** Langl. *Rich. Redeles* ii. 84 Þat no manere mede shulde make him wrye. **14..** *Wheatley MS.* (1921) 8 First ye gloþered, now ye wrye.

b. To make disclosures or statements.

c **1425** *Thomas of Erceld.* (1875) 2 If j solde sytt to domesdaye, with my tonge, to wrobbe and wrye. *c* **1440** *York Myst.* xxi. 25 They askid yf I a prophete ware, And I saide 'nay'; but sone I wreyede high aperte.

c. *north. dial.* (See quot.)

1781 J. Hutton *Tour to Caves* (ed. 2) Gloss., *To wree against a person,* to insinuate to his disadvantage.

Hence **wraying** *vbl. sb.* and *ppl. a.*

c **1000** Ælfric *Gram.* (Z.) 317 *Accusatio,* *wreȝing. *a* **1225** *Ancr. R.* 200 Þe vifte [vice] is Wreiunge. *Ibid.* 304 We schulen beon cwite of wreiunge ette muchele dome. *c* **1330** *King of Tar* 739 The ladi bad hire maydens anon, Out of hire chaumbre forte gon, For drede of wriyying sake. *c* **1400** *Cursor M.* 27671 (Cott. Galba MS.), Þai wil of deme a man with ill, And has bot a wreghing þar-till. *c* **1425** *Eng. Conq. Ireland* 102 He beleued þe fals mannys talys & wryynge. *a* **1225** *Ancr. R.* 2 Þe on [rule] riwleð þe heort, þe makeð hire efne & smeðe, wiðute knotte & dolke of woh inwit & of *wreinde. *c* **1300** *Cursor M.* 26350 [One should be] Wreiand [in confession].

†**wray**, *v.*[2] *Obs.*$^{-1}$ [See ray *v.*[2] 5.] *intr.* To evacuate.

1620 I. C. *Two Merry Milk-maids* iv. i. M 1, I thinke some Bird was wraid in my eye.

†**'wrayer.** *Obs.* In 1 **wreȝere,** 2 **wreiere,** 4 **-er, wraier,** 4–5 **wreyer** (4 **wroyer**), 5 **-are;** 5 **wryer;** 5 *north.* **wrear.** [OE. *wréȝere* (f. *wréȝan* wray *v.*[1] + -er[1]), = OFris. *wreiere, wrôger* (NFris. *wröger*), MDu. and older Flem. (Kilian) *wroegher.*] One who denounces, discloses, or betrays; an accuser or betrayer.

c **1000** Ælfric *Hom.* II. 336 Se ealda wreȝere cwæð, Buton ȝe forȝifon [etc.]. *c* **1175** *Lamb. Hom.* 57 Prud ne wreiere ne beo þu noht. *a* **1300** *Cursor M.* 26709 He sal for-soth on domes-dai Haue wreiers [*Fairf.* wroyers]. *c* **1320** *Sir Tristr.* 3288 Þe wraiers þat weren in halle, Schamly were þai schende. *c* **1425** *Eng. Conq. Ireland* 102 He was onful & bakbyter, wreyer, false & traytur. *c* **1440** *Promp. Parv.* 37/2 Blabbe or labbe, wreyare of cownselle,..*futilis.* *c* **1460** [see wragger].

†**'wrayful,** *a.* *Obs. rare.* In 3 **wreiful.** [f. wray *v.*[1] + -ful.] Containing or involving an accusation; accusatory.

a **1225** *Ancr. R.* 302 Schrift schal beon wreiful, bitter, mid seoruwe. *Ibid.* 304.

wrayst(e, obs. f. wrest *sb.*[1] and *v.*

wrayt, obs. pa. t. of write *v.*

wraythe, obs. pa. t. of writhe *v.*[1]

†**'wrayward,** *a.* *Obs. rare.* [Prob. an alteration of wayward *a.*] Perverse, froward.

1516 *Promp. Parv.* (W. de W.) C iij, Crabbyd or wraywarde, *aceronicus, bilosus.* *c* **1520** *Dial. Creatures Mor.* v. B ij b, A wrayward man cawseth stryues. *Ibid.* xii. D ij b, A sertayne lorde somtyme had a wraywarde seruant and iuylwyllyd.

wrd, obs. form of word.

wre, obs. Sc. variant of ore[2].

1633 *Reg. Mag. Sig. Scot.* 44/2 Reservand to ws yron wre and all other kynd of minerallis.

wre, Sc. var. wray *v.*[1] *Obs.*; obs. var. wry *v.*[1]

wreachednes(s, obs. ff. wretchedness.

wreade, obs. var. wreathe *v.*

1584 Twyne *Æneid* xi. S i, The snake about him wrigling winding wreades with griefe of wound.

wreak (riːk), *sb.* Now *arch.* or *Obs.* Forms: 4–7 **wreke** (4, 6 **wrek**), 6–7 **wreake,** 6– **wreak.** [In early Northern texts a normal variant of wreche *sb.*; in later use prob. substituted for this, or for wrake *sb.*, under the influence of the verb.]

1. Pain or punishment inflicted in return for an injury, wrong, offence, etc.; hurt or harm done from vindictive motives; vengeance, revenge.

In frequent use from *c* 1540 to *c* 1620.

a **1300** *Cursor M.* 22604 (Edin.), Saint peter sal be domb þat dai,.. For doubt of demsteris wrek [*Cott.* wreke]. *c* **1340** Hampole *Pr. Consc.* 5338 Howe suld þai þan in þe tyme of wreke Bestille? *Ibid.* 6101 Þe day of wreke and of vengeaunce. *c* **1400** *Destr. Troy* 12072 Þe sayntis of hell Were wode in hor werkis for wreke of Achilles. *c* **1420** *Prose Life Alex.* 76 Þe wrethe & þe wreke of oure goddez..fallez apon vs. ? *a* **1500** *Chester Pl.* x. 120 [On] all knaves childer in this Countrey..shall fall the wreake. **1526** Tindale *Prol. Romans* Wks. (1572) 49/1 He describeth the outward conuersation of Christen men, how they ought..to commit wreake and vengeaunce to God. **1559** *Myrr. Mag.* 63 But wrath of man his rancour to requite, Forgets all reason... I mean by rancour the parentall wreke. **1587** Turberv. *Trag. T.* (1837) 158 Such flames of wreake withyn her bowels fride. **1629** Sir W. Mure *True Crucifixe* 2610 Thee carying headlongs to eternall wreake. **16..** *Faithful Friends* ii. iii, Nor shall the life or goods Of thee, or any thy assistants, feel The wreak of his just anger. **1865** *Reader* No. 142. 309/2 Pride and haughty wreak From irreverence begin. **1899** Swinburne *Rosamund* ii. 32, I would.. the wreak of wrath were wroken, and I Dead.

b. In the phr. *to perform, seek, spend, work,* and esp. *take* (...) *wreak.*

c **1330** R. Brunne *Chron. Wace* Prol. 202 (Petyt MS.), When god toke wreke of Caym synne. *c* **1375** *Cursor M.* 1156 (Fairf.) Þat I sal take wreke on þe. *c* **1440** Capgrave *St. Kath.* v. 61 God..on the puple tho took ful grete wreke. *c* **1460** *Towneley Myst.* xxv. 191, I saide that he shuld..of youre warkys take wreke. **1525** Tindale *Wks.* (Parker Soc. 1849) 229 No man should avenge himself, or seek wreak, no, not by the law. **1576** Whetstone *Rock of Regard* I. 72 Sith fortune threates, to woorke our wreake of ioy, By sowsing of our ship in seas of yre. **1582** Batman *Barth. De P.R.* xviii. xi. 349/1 No creature is more wreakful, nor more feruent to take wreak than is the Bee when he is wrath. **1607** R. C[arew] tr. *Estienne's World Wond.* 162 A huswife of Millan ..wrought her wreake vpon the fruite of her womb. **1613** Chapman *Rev. Bussy D'Ambois* iii. i. E 4 Dull and drossie in performing Wreake of the deare bloud of my matchless Brother. **1855** Singleton *Virgil* II. 308 Enough of wreak is spent; A passage hath been made among the foes. **1886** Burton *Arab. Nts.* (abr. ed.) I. 167 None murdered the damsel but I; take her wreak on me this moment.

†**c.** *in* (or *for*) *wreak of,* in revenge of, in return or repayment for. *Obs.*

1599 B. Jonson *Ev. Man out of Hum.* ii. iv, Would to heaven (In wreak of my misfortunes,) I were turn'd To some faire water-Nymph. **1599** Peele *David & B.* E ij, They with him conspire, And kill thy sonne in wreake of Thamars wrong. **1606** Chapman *Gentl. Usher* v. i. 123 Death..he shall indure For wreake of that joyes exile I sustaine.

d. The avenging of a person.

1613 Chapman *Rev. Bussy d'Ambois* iii. i, Your defect of spirit and valour, First showne in lingring my deare Brothers wreake.

†**2.** An instance of taking vengeance or exacting retribution. *Obs.*

a **1300** *E.E. Psalter* xvii. 51 God þat giues wrekes me to. *a* **1547** Surrey *Æneid* ii. 750 Of the Grekes the cruel wrekes. *c* **1586** C'tess Pembroke *Ps.* lxxi. xiii, My tongue..[shall] Tell thy wreakes and their disgraces, Who this ill to me procure. **1591** Spenser *Ruins of Time* 397 Where mortall wreakes their blis may not remoue. *a* **1626** Bp. Andrewes 96 *Serm., Passion* xvi. (1661) 224 To take a wreak or revenge upon sin.

†**3.** Harm, injury; damage. *Obs.*

15.. *Parl. Byrdes* 24 in Hazl. *E.P.P.* III. 168 All the byrdes..Said, the Hauke doth vs great wreake. *a* **1542** Wyatt in *Tottel's Misc.* (Arb.) 38 Vnkind tongue, to yll hast thou me rendred, For such desert to do me wreke and shame. **1591** Spenser *Ruins Rome* 33 These same olde walls ..is that which Rome men call. Behold what wreake, what ruine, and what wast. *a* **1600** Montgomerie *Mindes Melodie*

vi. 44 My foes.. would rejoise To see my wreak, and would my soule subuert.

wreak (ri:k), *v.* Forms: 1–2 wrecan, 2 wrecon, 2–4 wreken (3 wræken, wærken, wreoken, *Orm.* wrekenn), 5 wrekene, wrekyn; 3–7 wreke (4 wrekke), 4–5 wrek (4 wreck), wreek, 5 wreeke, wreike, 5–6 *Sc.* wreik, 6–7 wreake, 6– wreak (7–8 reak); *Sc.* 5 wryk(e, 6 wrik. *Pa. t.* 1 wræc (uuraec, *pl.* wræcon), 2–3 wrac, 3 *pl.* wrake, 4–5 wrake, 5 wrak, 6–7, 8–9 *arch.* wroke (9 wrok); 4 wrek. *Weak*: 4–5 wreked, 4 -id, 5 -yd, *Sc.* -yt, 6– wreaked (8 raked, 9 wreak'd, *Sc.* wreakit). *Pa. pple.* 1 wrecen (ȝewrecen), 3–4 wreken (iwreken), 3–5 wreke (4 y-, 4–5 iwreke); 3–7, 9 *arch.* wroken (4–6 y-, 5 iwroken), 4, 5–6 *Sc.* wrokin, 4–5 wrokyn, 5 -yne, 6 wrokne, *Sc.* wrokkin, wrockin, 6–7 wrocken; 4–5, 9 *arch.* wroke (4–5, 6 *arch.* ywroke, 5 iwroke), 6 wrooke, *Sc.* wrok. *Weak*: 6, 9 wreaked, 6 wrekte, wreackt, 7 wreakt, 9 *U.S.* reeked. [Common Teut.: OE. *wrecan* str. v. (*wræc*, *wrǽcon*, *wrecen*), = OFris. *wreka* (WFris. *wrekke*), OS. *wrekan* (MLG. and LG., MDu. and Du. *wreken*; also LG. *wräken*), OHG. *rëchan*, *rëhhan* (MHG. *rechen*, G. *rächen*), ON. and Icel. *reka* (Norw. *reka*; Sw. *vräka*), Goth. *wrikan* (to persecute), f. the Teut. stem *wrek-*, pre-Teut. **wreg-*, cognate with that of L. *urgēre*. Cf. WRACK *v.*[1], WRECHE *v.*, WRECK *v.*[2], also A-, BEWREAK *vbs.*]

I. † 1. *trans.* **a.** To drive, press, force to move. *Obs.* (OE. only.)

c 725 *Corpus Gloss.* (Hessels) T 213 *Torquet*, uuraec. *a* 1000 *Riddles* I. 1 (Gr.), Hwylc is hæleþa þæs horsc.. þæt þæt mæȝe asecgan, hwa mec on sið wræce? *Ibid.* XXI. 11 Me þurh hrycg wrecen hongaþ under an orþonc pil.

† b. To cast or throw *out* of a place. *Obs.*

c 1250 *Gen. & Ex.* 3148 Ilc folc is to fode framen,.. And noȝt ðor-of [*sc.* of a kid] vt huse wreken. *Ibid.* 3191 Ðor he doluen,.. and hauen up-broȝt ðe bones ut of ðe erðe wroken.

† c. *transf.* With *out*. To pass or spend (time). Cf. DRIVE *v.* 21. *Obs.*[−1]

a 1300 *Cursor M.* 1547 Quen sa fele yeier ar wroken oute, þe mikel spere es rune aboute.

† 2. To banish or expel, to drive out or away. *Obs.*

c 1100 *O.E. Chron.* (MS. D.) an. 1076, Sume hi wurdon ȝeblende, & sume wrecen of lande. ?*a* 1300 *Gregory* 216 Sche halpe þe pouer and þe lame, þe deuel fram hir for to wreke. 1340 *Ayenb.* 215 Huerout he wrek þo þe zyalde and boȝte ine þe temple.

fig. and *transf.* 1340 *Ayenb.* 189 Huanne he his ssel wreke out of his uelaȝrede. *a* 1400–50 *Wars Alex.* 4428 For all ȝoure wisdom, I-wis, is wroken to ȝour tongis.

II. 3. a. To give vent or expression to, to exercise or gratify (wrath, anger, etc.); to vent.

a 900 *Genesis* 2508 þas folc slean, cynn on ceastrum mid cwealmþrea, & his torn wrecan. *c* 1000 *Ags. Ps.* (Thorpe) lxxxiv. 5 Ne wrec þu þine yrre, wraðe mode, of cynne on cynn. *c* 1200 ORMIN 19606 Forrþ i let he takenn himm To wrekenn hise tene. *c* 1385 CHAUCER *L.G.W.* 324 He schal nat ryghtfully his yre wreke. 1421 *26 Pol. Poems* 83 Lete not vengeance þy wraþþe wreke. Vengeance is goddis. *c* 1430 *Syr. Gener.* (Roxb.) 4674 Darel roode wel wrothe and yll, For he had not wroken his fill. 1530 PALSGR. 785/1, I wreake myne anger. 1577 HOLINSHED *Chron., Hist. Eng.* I. 231/1 The more to wreake his wrath, the King spoyled many Religious houses of their goodes. 1596 SPENSER *F.Q.* IV. ix. 23 As when Dan Æolus.. Sends forth the winds.. Vpon the sea to wreake his fell intent. 1600 HOLLAND *Livy* 323 They were staied.. in this sweetnesse of wreaking their anger, and satiating their revenge. 1648 *Hunting of Fox* 10 [The] heart-breaking stile of Enemies: and such Enemies too, as to wreake their malice. 1819 SHELLEY *Cenci* IV. ii. 23 'Tis my hate and the deferred desire To wreak it, which extinguishes their blood. 1870 BRYANT *Iliad* IV. I. 113 So in time to come May Agamemnon wreak his wrath. 1878 SEELEY *Stein* III. 315 Stein wreaked his disappointment in unsparing criticism.

transf. 1794 WORDSW. *Guilt & Sorrow* 103 The only creature.. On whom the elements their rage might wreak. 1817 SHELLEY *Rev. Islam* III. vii, Beneath most calm resolve did agony wreak Its whirlwind rage.

b. More usu. const. *on* (†*in*, *against*) or *upon* a person. (Freq. from *c* 1560.)

c 1200 ORMIN 19866 3ho.. þohhte þatt ȝho shollde onn himm Wel wrekenn hire tene. *c* 1374 CHAUCER *Troylus* v. 589 Wel hastow lord y-wroke on me þin Ire. *c* 1375 *Sc. Leg. Saints* vii. (*James Minor*) 133 þar-fore þai wrekyt þar wodnes In þis Iamis, callit þe les. 1470–85 MALORY *Arthur* III. vii. 107 Leuer I had ye had wroken your angre vpon me. 1556 PHAER *Æneid*, IV. (1558) L iij, On my brother fals I wroke my tene. 1588 GREENE *Pandosto* (1607) 9 Pandosto.. determined to wreake all his wrath on poore Bellaria. 1627 DRAYTON *Agincourt* ccvi, I neuer will retire, Vntill our Teene vpon the French we wreake. 1697 BURGHOPE *Disc. Relig. Assemb.* 180 As tho' they wou'd reak their Malice upon God. 1697 DRYDEN *Æneis* XII. 1233 The moody Sire, to wreak his Hate On Realms. 1749 SMOLLETT *Regicide* Pref., I wreaked my Resentment upon the innocent Cause of my Disgraces. 1761 HUME *Hist. Eng.* lxiv. (1806) IV. 732 The church.. persevered in the project of wreaking her own enmity against the nonconformists. 1818 MRS. SHELLEY *Frankenstein* viii. (1865) 119 That I might wreak the utmost extent of my anger on his head. 1840 DICKENS *Old C. Shop* xiii, The dwarf.. wanting somebody to wreak his ill-humour upon. 1871 FREEMAN *Norm. Conq.* IV. 112 To wreak a coward's spite on the corpse of the dead Harold.

c. *refl.* Of a passion, feeling, etc.: To give expression to (itself); to find utterance or free course.

1590 SPENSER *F.Q.* II. v. 5 Disleall knight, whose coward courage chose To wreake it selfe on beast all innocent. 1839 DE QUINCEY *Recoll. Lakes* Wks. 1862 II. 186 That the indignation of mankind should have wreaked itself upon the chief monsters. 1850 HAWTHORNE *Scarlet L.* xiii, In the education of her child, the mother's enthusiasm of thought had something to wreak itself upon. 1887 R. S. STORRS in *Libr. Mag.* Aug. 106 The Hellenic spirit.. wreaked itself in immortal expressions on the choicest marbles and temples in the world.

d. To bestow or spend *on* a person, etc.; to expend.

a 1586 SIDNEY *Sonn.* Wks. 1922 II. 303 She hath no other cause of anguish But Thereus love, on her by strong hand wrokne. 1819 WIFFEN *Aonian Hours* 107 To wreak Such love upon the task as [etc.]. 1871 BROWNING *Pr. Hohenst.* 174 God.. Grants each new man.. Intercommunication with Himself, Wreaking on finiteness infinitude. 1871 B. TAYLOR *Faust* (1875) I. iv. 76 *Mephis.* Here is the genuine path for you; Yet strict attention must be given. *Stud.* Body and soul thereon I'll wreak.

† 4. a. To punish or chastise (a person); to visit with retributive punishment. Also *refl.* *Obs.*

c 888 ÆLFRED *Boeth.* xli. § 3 þæt wæs þæt mon wræce & witnode hwone for his yfle. *a* 1122 *O.E. Chron.* (Laud MS.) an. 1090, Se cyng wæs smæȝende hu he mihte wrecon his broðer Rodbeard, swiðost swencean. *a* 1300 *Cursor M.* 11773 For to wreke þam was he bun þat þus did cast þair goddes dun. *c* 1460 *Towneley Myst.* xxviii. 186 With the Iues he [*sc.* Jesus] was so stad, to ded they can hym wreke. *a* 1626 BP. ANDREWES *96 Serm.* (1661) 165 To wreak our-selves for so often offering so foul indignities to Heaven.

transf. *a* 1658 LOVELACE *Poems* (1904) 134 The desp'rate Heron.. turns his last to wreak The palizadoes of his [*sc.* a falcon's] Beak.

† b. To injure, hurt, or harm (a person). *Obs.*

c 1440 *Bone Florence* 104 He was.. all to-brokyn, Ferre travelde in harnes, and of warre wrokyn. 1572 *Satir. Poems Reform.* xxxii. 124 Lat neuer thair micht.. Haue strenth or power thame for to hurt or wreik. *a* 1593 MARLOWE tr. *Ovid's Elegies* II. xi. 22 What each one speakes Beleeue, no tempest the beleeuer wreakes [L. *credenti nulla procella nocet*]. 1683 W. WALKER *Phraseol. Gen.* 1351 In labour the stronger wreaks the weaker. *In opere firmior* (*bos*) *imbecilliorem conficit.*

III. 5. a. To avenge (a person).

In senses 5, 5 b, very frequent *c* 1200–*c* 1600. The passive construction, *to be wreaked* (†*wroken*), freq. implies that the revenge is taken by the injured party, and is thus equivalent to the reflexive use.

Beowulf 1385 Selre bið æȝ-hwæm þæt he his freond wrece þonne he fela murne. *c* 950 *Lindisf. Gosp.* Luke xviii. 5 Forðon woedo *uel* hefiȝ wæs me.. ðas widiua ic wræco ða ilco. *a* 1122 *O.E. Chron.* (Laud MS.) an. 979, Hine nolden his eorðlican maȝas wrecan. *c* 1205 LAY. 27612 Cumeð hidere to me, and wreke we Beduer min æm. *c* 1250 *Gen. & Ex.* 1856 Symeon and leui it bi-speken, And hauen here sister ðor i-wreken. *c* 1320 *Sir Tristr.* 3295 Mani on slain þer lay... Ful wele wreken er þay. 13.. *Sir Beues* (A.) 4466 Wrekeþ ȝour fader wiþ ȝour miȝtes. *a* 1400–50 *Wars Alex.* 855 þe wee in his wreth wrekis his modire. *c* 1450 *Merlin* xxv. 451 Thei thought well to be wroken whan thei saugh tyme. ?*a* 1500 *Chester Pl.* v. 101 Therfore how will I wroken be? 1530 PALSGR. 454/1 He wyll be wroken whan you shall thynke lest. 1586 J. HOOKER *Hist. Irel.* in *Holinshed* II. 13/1 He counteth it for a sufficient reuenge, that he can reuenge and be wreaked. 1765 in Percy *Reliques* I. 106 And soon i' the Gordon's foul hartis bluid He's wroken his dear ladie. 1872 TENNYSON *Gareth & Lynette* 355 Grant me some knight to.. Kill the foul thief, and wreak me for my son.

refl. *c* 1200 *Trin. Coll. Hom.* 179 Ne wrec þu þe mid wussinge ne mid warienge. *a* 1225 *Ancr. R.* 186 Ne wrekie ȝe nout ou suluen, ne ne grucche ȝe nout. 1377 LANGL. *P. Pl.* B. v. 85 To wreke hymself he þouȝte With werkes or with wordes whan he seighe his tyme. *c* 1407 LYDG. *Reson & Sens.* 369 Antropos, hir self to wreke, Doth ful many thredes breke. *c* 1470 HENRY *Wallace* I. 310 Will God I leiffe, we sall ws wreke on part. ?*a* 1500 *Chester Pl.* XIV. 267, I am as wroth as I may be, And some way I will wreak me. 1530 PALSGR. 785/1 If thou cannest nat wreake the, byte the poste. 1596 SPENSER *F.Q.* v. viii. 44 How worthily.. Iustice that day of wrong her selfe had wroken. 1606 BRYSKETT *Civ. Life* 70 They that by combat seeke to wreake themselues. 1659 SOMNER *Dict.* s.v. *Wræcan*, *Vulgo dicimus*: to wreke ones selfe, or take revenge.

b. Const. *of*, *on* (†*o*, *in*), or *upon* (†*up*) one who has done harm, etc.

c 950 *Lindisf. Gosp.* Luke xviii. 3 Widiua.. cuoeð wræc ðu mec of wiðerworde minum. 993 *Battle of Maldon* 279 He his sincȝyfan on þam sæmannum wurðlice wrec. *a* 1200 *Vices & Virtues* 5 Ðanne ȝelpð he ðat he is wel iwreken of his unwine. *c* 1205 LAY. 12210 [To] wreken uppen [*c* 1275 vppe] Maximien Valentin & Gratien. *c* 1250 *Gen. & Ex.* 2028 3he ðhenkeð on him for to ben wreken. *c* 1330 *Arth. & Merl.* 5962 (Kölbing), þe king.. Wele him wrake of his foman. 1362 LANGL. *P. Pl.* A. II. 169, I wolde be wreken on þis [B. II. 194 wroke of þo] wrecches. *a* 1400 *Prymer* (1891) 31 In oure lordes name, y am wroken in hem. *c* 1450 *Mirk's Festial* I. 88 Lorde,.. þou wreke me apon þis man. 1480 CAXTON *Trevisa's Higden* (1482) 358 b, He wold be wroken vpon kyng rychard. 1575 GASCOIGNE *Dan Barth., Dol. Disc.* 50 The Goddesse of revenge devisde So to bee wreackt on my rebelling wyll. 1596 SPENSER *F.Q.* IV. ii. 21 Both greedie fiers on other to be wroken. *Ibid.* IV. vi. 23 She.. vpheld her wrathfull hand, With fell intent, on him to bene ywroke.

transf. 1390 GOWER *Conf.* II. 148 Be war forthi thou be noght sik Of thilke fievere [*sc.* jealousy].. For it wol in him-self be wroke. *c* 1520 SKELTON *Magnyf.* 1566 That on suche a female my flesshe wolde be wroken. 1561 NORTON & SACKV. *Gorboduc* IV. i, Canst thou hope.. that these handes will not be wrooke on thee? 1592 SHAKS. *Rom. & Jul.* III. v. 102 To wreake the Loue I bore my Cozin, Vpon his body that hath slaughter'd him.

refl. *c* 1200 ORMIN 914 God wollde himm wrekenn o þe preost. *c* 1205 LAY. 15052 Wrekeð eow ȝif ȝe cunnen of Sexisce monnen. *a* 1300 *Cursor M.* 11963 Vr neghburs mai þam on vs wreke. 1338 R. BRUNNE *Chron.* (1810) 46 Of fals Edrik fayn wild he him wreke. *c* 1385 CHAUCER *L.G.W.* 395 *Balade*, Hym deynyth nat to wreke hym on a flye. *c* 1450 *Crt. of Love* 702 She saw an egle wreke him on a fly. *a* 1542 WYATT *Poet. Wks.* (1913) I. 131 Comfort thy self my wofull hert, Or shortly on thy self the wreke. 1561 NORTON & SACKV. *Gorboduc* II. i, Attempt redresse by armes, and wreake your-self Upon his life. 1604 PARSONS *3rd Pt. Three Convers. Eng.* 192 The Duke thought best to vse this mans meanes, to wreake himselfe of the said Bishops. 1611 CHAPMAN *Widowes T.* III. i, That I may wreake my selfe vpon my selfe. 1730 T. BOSTON *Mem.* x. (1899) 292 They usually wreaking themselves on the ministers as the cause of all public evils. *c* 1830 in Child *Ball* III. 438/1 He micht hae spared my lady's life, And wreakit himsell on me! 1872 TENNYSON *Gareth & Lynette* 800 Well that ye came, or else these caitiff rogues Had wreak'd themselves on me.

† c. To revenge (a person) *of* (*on*) a wrong, injury, etc. *Obs.*

1340–70 *Alisaunder* 76 þe King was carefull in hert, Till hee were wroken of þe wrong. *c* 1386 CHAUCER *Frankl. T.* 56 On euery wrong a man may nat be wreken. *a* 1400–50 *Wars Alex.* 3199 He will me wreke on ȝoure werke wers þan of thefes. *c* 1430 *Syr Gener.* (Roxb.) 4634 Be wroke he wold of sum thing. *c* 1450 *Erle Tolous* 1028 Syth hyt ys soo, Cryste wreke hur of hur woo. *a* 1529 SKELTON *Col. Cloute* 600 Then ye wyll be wroken Of euery lyght quarell. 1535 STEWART *Cron. Scot.* (Rolls) I. 34 To find ane way of Pechtis to be wrok Of thair injure. 1590 SPENSER *F.Q.* II. v. 21 Stirring to be wroke Of his late wrongs. 1591 *2nd Pt. Troub. Raigne K. John* (1611) 73 Tis Gods decree to wreake us of these harmes.

refl. *c* 1386 CHAUCER *Can. Yeom. Prol. & T.* 620 On his falshede fayn wolde I me wreke, If I wiste how. *c* 1470 HENRY *Wallace* v. 22 About the park thai set.. With vi hundreth.., All likly men, to wrek thaim of thar harmes. 1577 HOLINSHED *Chron.* II. 606/2 The man.. wanted nothing but faithful subiectes to haue wroken himselfe of such wrongs. 1578 T. PROCTER *Gorg. Gallery* B iv, That thou and I shall ioyne in ioy, and wreake vs of our wrong.

† d. To deliver or rescue (a person) *from* or *out of* woe, etc. *Obs. rare.*

13.. *E.E. Allit. P.* A. 375 Much þe bygger ȝet was my mon, Fro þou was wroken fro vch a woþe. *c* 1450 *Cov. Myst.* (Shaks. Soc.) 29 Out of whoo ȝet art not wrokyn, In helle logge þou xalt be lokyn. *Ibid.* 330, I xal delyvere mannys kynne,—From wo I wole hem wreke!

† e. *refl.* To satisfy or gratify (oneself). *Obs.*[−1]

1377 LANGL. *P. Pl.* B. IX. 181 Whiles þow art ȝonge, and þi wepne kene, Wreke þe with wyuynge, ȝif þow wilt ben excused.

6. a. To take vengeance or inflict retributive punishment for, to avenge or revenge (some wrong, harm, or injury).

Beowulf 1670 Ic.. fyren-dæda wræc, deað-cwealm deniȝea. *c* 825 *Vesp. Psalter* lxxviii. 10 Wrec blod ðiowa ðinra ðæt agoten is. *c* 1205 LAY. 19365 He þohten hider wenden & wræken his fader wunden. *a* 1300 *Cursor M.* 17332 Mi-self es sett to wrek þe wrang. *c* 1300 *Havelok* 327 þat non ne mihte comen hire to.. with hir to speken, þat euere mihte hire bale wreken. 1382 WYCLIF *Deut.* xxxii. 43 For the blood of his seruauntis he shal wreek. *c* 1400 *Destr. Troy* 1750 Now [is] tyme.. To mene vs with manhode & our mys wreke. 1471 RIPLEY *Comp. Alch.* Ep. ii. in Ashm. (1652) 109 Of your great fortune ye be not presumptuous, Nor vengeable of my rode to wreke every wrong. *a* 1525 *Vergilius* in Thoms *E.E. Prose Rom.* (1858) II. 23 When wyll you wreke your faders dethe? 1581 A. HALL *Iliad* IX. 169 Yet list he not their wretched woe to wreake. 1587 TURBERV. *Trag. T.* (1837) 141 The dome divine.. Yet strikes at last, and surely wreakes the wrong. 1596 SPENSER *F.Q.* IV. xi. 5 For of a womans hand it was ywroke, That of the wound he yet in languor lyes. 1622 FLETCHER *Prophetess* II. ii, Lend me your helping hands To wreak the Parricide. 1700 DRYDEN *Ovid's Met.* XII. 338 Arms, Arms, the double-form'd with Fury call; To wreak their Brother's Death. 1813 SCOTT *Trierm.* II. xxvii, Vanoc's death must now be wroken. 1814– *Lord of Isles* IV. xxx, O Scotland! shall it e'er be mine To wreak thy wrongs in battle-line. 1887 SWINBURNE *Locrine* IV. ii. 56 My will It is that holds me yet alive.. Till all my wrong be wroken.

b. Const. *on* or *upon* (a person or persons).

a 900 *Juliana* 204 þonne ic nyde sceal.. on þære grimmestan godscyld wrecan. *a* 1300 *Cursor M.* 2586 Wroken on þaim sal be þat wrang. 1375 BARBOUR *Bruce* XII. 227 Wreik on thame the mekill ill That thai and tharis has done vs till. 1423 JAS. I *Kingis Q.* lxix, On my-self bene al my harmys wrokin. 1577 HOLINSHED *Chron., Hist. Scot.* I. 390/1 That he might haue wroken his grief vpon him. 1590 SPENSER *F.Q.* III. xi. 15 Perhaps this hand may.. wreake your sorrow on your cruell foe. 1717 POPE *Iliad* IX. 684 She.. call'd the powers beneath On her own son to wreak her brother's death. 1882 TENNYSON *Promise of May* I. 507 Why then the crowd May wreak my wrongs upon my wrongers. 1883 R. W. DIXON *Mano* I. xii. 37 On him, [I] beseech thee, wreak my wrongs amain.

† c. To vindicate (something). *Obs.*

c 1400 *26 Pol. Poems* 18 God biddeþ vengeaunce hiȝe, And helpe trouþe be wel wroken. 1589 R. ROBINSON *Gold. Mirr.* (1851) 10 Poore clout-shooes gate their clubs, and willingly attend, To wreke there mistris cause.

† 7. To visit (a fault, misdeed, evil action) with punishment; to punish (wrong-doing). *Obs.*

c 888 ÆLFRED *Boeth.* xxxviii. §7 þæt is þonne hiora mildsung þæt mon wrece hiora unðeawas be hiora ȝewyrhtum. *c* 897 —— *Gregory's Past. C.* xlix. 383 Ðæt he ða gyltas.. wrece on scyldeȝum monnum. 971 *Blickl. Hom.* 185 Swa se wer hit wreceþ ȝif his wif hie forhealdeþ. *c* 1200 *Trin. Coll. Hom.* 161 Godes wrake cumeð on þis woreld to wrekende on sun-fulle men here gultes. *a* 1240 *Lofsong* in *O.E. Hom.* I. 209 Ne bi-hold þu ham [*sc.* sins] nout leste þu wreoke ham on me. *c* 1250 *Gen. & Ex.* 3067 So sal ðin hardnesse ben wreken, ðat men sulen longe ðor-after speken. 1338 R. BRUNNE *Chron.* (1810) 77 þat wikkednes, þat men suld haf wroken. *a* 1375 *Lay Folks Mass Bk.* App. iv. 395 þat god may wreke Euerich a word þat we speke. 1481 CAXTON *Reynard* xix. (Arb.) 46 A! reynart that ye now al thus haue your wyl I pray god to wreke it. 1596 SPENSER *F.Q.* VI. ii. 22 There gan he.. with bitter wracke To wreake on me the guilt of his owne wrong. 1610 BEAUM. & FL. *Faithf. Sheph.* v. i, Else Pan wreak, With double vengeance, my disloyalty.

8. a. To inflict or take (vengeance, etc.) *on* or *upon* a person; to execute or carry out by way of punishment or revenge.

In frequent use from *c* 1830.

c **1489** CAXTON *Sonnes of Aymon* i. 30 That ye make punyssyon thereof and wrek on hym grete vengaunce. **1700** DRYDEN *Sigism. & Guisc.* 589 He left the Dame, Resolv'd.. To wreak his Vengeance, and to cure her Love. **1758** P. WILLIAMSON *Life & Adventures* (1812) 39 So desirous was every man to have a share in wreaking his revenge on them [*sc.* dead Indians]. **1772** PRIESTLEY *Inst. Relig.* (1782) I. 412 Xerxes..wreaked his vengeance upon Babylon. **1809** W. IRVING *Knickerb.* IV. vii, An historian springs up, who wreaks ample chastisement on it [*sc.* a nation] in return. **1855** PALEY *Æschylus* Pref. (1861) p. xxv, Till vengeance had been wreaked for the wrongs suffered in life. **1872** TENNYSON *Gareth & Lynette* 1236 Thou hast wreak'd his justice on his foes. **1899** SWINBURNE *Rosamund* II. 32/2, I would the deed Were done, the wreak of wrath were wroken, and I Dead.

b. To cause or effect (harm, damage, etc.), esp. in phr. ***to wreak havoc***. (For *wrought havoc* see WORK *v.* 10.)

1817 SHELLEY *Rev. Islam* II. xxxix, With thee..will I seek Through their array of banded slaves to wreak Ruin upon the tyrants. **1818** —— *Rosal. & Helen* 670 That poor and hungry men should break The laws which wreak them toil and scorn, We understand. **1865** DICKENS *Mut. Fr.* III. ii, [In] the fog..the unpopular steamer..always was.. wreaking destruction upon somebody or something. **1880** *Daily News* 22 Sept., Landslips..are looked for and wreak but little harm. **1926** A. CHRISTIE *Murder of R. Ackroyd* xx. 239 Annie is not allowed to wreak havoc with a dustpan and brush. **1976** B. FELL *America B.C.* viii. 101 The storm waves could surely wreak more havoc upon the timbered hulls of Phoenician galleys than on the steel plates of modern ships. **1978** C. RAYNER *Long Acre* vii. 70 Fenton, well aware of the havoc he was wreaking in poor Miss Emma's heart, wickedly fed her passion for him. **1983** *Times* 21 Nov. 7/7 Moko, the banana disease, has already wreaked havoc on the trade. **1984** *Daily Tel.* 5 Nov. 20/2 The feared shake-out in microcomputer manufacturing..will wreak havoc in the industry.

c. To inflict or deliver (a blow, etc.); to deal.

1817 SHELLEY *Rev. Islam* I. x, The wreathed Serpent.. did ever seek Upon his enemy's heart a mortal wound to wreak. **1849** MEREDITH in *Chambers' Edin. Mag.* July 16/2 There the murder-mouthed artillery..Wrok the thunder of its treachery On the skeleton brigade. **1897** F. THOMPSON *New Poems* 55 Though they wreak Upon me stroke and again stroke.

9. With *out*. To exact by way of punishment.

1879 MOMERIE *Origin Evil* i. 16 Justice, which can only be appeased by wreaking out a certain quantity of agony as an equivalent for a certain quantity of sin.

IV. †**10.** *intr.* To take vengeance; to inflict punishment. Also const. *on*. *Obs.*

c **825** *Vesp. Psalter* cxvii. 12 In noman dryhtnes ic wreocu in him. *c* **897** ÆLFRED *Gregory's Past. C.* lvi. 435 Ic wrice on eow æfter eowrum ȝeðeahte. *c* **1000** *Ags. Ps.* (Thorpe) cxlix. 7 Mid þy hi wrecan þenceað wraðum cynnum. *a* **1200** *Vices & Virtues* 77 Lat him wreke ðe is riht deme ouer ðe liuiende. *a* **1225** *Leg. Kath.* 2049 Hu wrakeliche, wenestu, wule he, al o wraððe, wreken on þe, wrecche! *a* **1325** *Prose Psalter* xcviii. 9 Our God, þou herd hem; þou, God, was mercyful to hem and byginnand to wreke in alle her fyndeynges. **13..** *E.E. Allit. P.* B. 198 Bot neuer ȝet..I herde þat euer he wrek so wyþerly on werk þat he made. *a* **1500** *Ratis Raving* 2786 Thai here glaidly, and lytill spekis, Laith for to crab and seldin wrekis. *c* **1614** SIR W. MURE *Dido & Æneas* III. 252 Fy, now ȝowr oares employ, Sack, wreak, revenge, demolish and destroy!

Hence ˈ**wreaking** *vbl. sb.*

a **1300** *Cursor M.* 19336 (Edin.), Queþir ȝie wil driue on us þe blame Of ani wreking of [*Fairf.* on] þis name. *c* **1374** CHAUCER *Boeth.* IV. met. vii. (1868) 147 Agamenon..purged in wrekyng by þe destruccioun of troie þe loste chambres of mariage of hys broþer. *c* **1440** *York Myst.* xxix. 323 Thy wordis and werkis will haue a wrekyng. *a* **1638** MEDE *Wks.* (1672) 298 When our hearts..tell us it is but the wreaking of our Malice. **1692** R. L'ESTRANGE *Fables* xxxviii. 41 The Wreaking of a Malice, and..the gratifying of a Revenge.

wreak, erron. f. *reak*, obs. var. RECK *v.*

1579 SPENSER *Sheph. Cal.* Dec. 29 What wreaked I of wintrye ages waste. **1592** R. JOHNSON *Nine Worthies* F j, He layde him downe like one that wreaked no guerdon to this grace. **1594** *Selimus* 200, I wreake not of their foolish ceremonies. **1600** [see RECK *v.* 3 a]. **1683** G. MERITON *Yorks. Dialogue* 661 Better's a comming; pray thee, do not wreak [*rime* break].

wreak, obs. erron. f. REEK *sb.*[1] and *v.*[1]

wreake, ? variant of WRECK *sb.*[1] 5.

1627 DRAYTON *Agincourt* 41 The French lye yonder like to wreakes of sand.

†**wreake**, obs. var. WRECK *v.*[1]

1599 T. M[OUFET] *Silkwormes* 49 Huge whales in Seas that mighty carricks wreake.

wreaker (ˈriːkə(r)). Now *arch.* and *rare.* Also 4–5 wreker(e, 5 -ar, 6 *Sc.* wrekar. [f. WREAK *v.* + -ER[1]. Cf. OHG. *rechâri* (MHG. *-ære*, *-er*, G. *rächer*), MLG. *wreker*, *wrecher*, (M)Du. *wreker*, and WRECHER.] One who takes vengeance; an avenger.

a **1300** *E.E. Psalter* viii. 3 þat þou for-do þe faa, þe wreker him vnto. *c* **1374** CHAUCER *Boeth.* IV. pr. iv. (1868) 128 Ne seek no foreyn wrekere [*ed.* 1560 wreckerie] out of þi self, for þou þi self hast prest þe in to wicked þinges. *c* **1381** —— *Parl. Foules* 361 The stork the wrekere of a-vouterye. *a* **1400** *Prymer* (1891) 18 That thow destroye the enemy and the wrekere. **1483** CAXTON *Gold. Leg.* 201 b/2 This holy man was a grete wreker and auenger on hymself. **1513** DOUGLAS *Æneid* VI. ix. 81 Tysyphone, the wrekar of misdedis. **1557** PHAER *Æneid.* VI. (1558) S j, Brutus, mischief wreaker. [**1599** THYNNE *Animadv.* (1875) 68 The storke..ys a greater wreaker of the adulterye of hys owne kynde.] **1887** MORRIS *Odyssey* XI. 280 For him she left indeed All woes that a mother's wreakers to dreadful end may speed.

wreakful (ˈriːkfʊl), *a.* Also 6 wreke-, 6–7 wreakeful(l. [f. WREAK *sb.* + -FUL. Cf. WRACKFUL, WRAKEFUL, WRECHEFUL *adjs.*]

Freq. from *c* 1560 to *c* 1610. Now *rare* or *Obs.*

1. Of persons, etc.: Given or addicted to revenge; vengeful.

1531 TINDALE *Wks.* (1572) 24/2 They also fayne y[e] saintes ..more wreakeful, and vengeable, then the Poetes fayne their goddes. **1562** A. BROOKE *Romeus & Jul.* 2116 Not helping to do any sinne that wrekefull Ioue forbode. **1570** T. NORTON tr. *Nowel's Catech.* (1853) 201 A wreakful mind and revengeful of injuries. **1582** [see WREAK *sb.* 1 b]. *c* **1611** CHAPMAN *Iliad* XIV. 119 Atrides, this, doth passing fitly stand With sterne Achilles wreakfull spirit. **1653** H. COGAN tr. *Scarlet Gown* 80 Knowing well, that Antonio was wreakful, and vindicative. **1801** W. RICHARDSON *Maid of Lochlin* 111, Of their own renown Wreakful assassins are those shallow rulers. **1805–6** CARY *Dante, Inf.* XI. 91 Less wreakful pours Justice divine on them its vengeance down.

b. *transf.* Of natural agencies.

1561 NORTON & SACKV. *Gorboduc* III. i, Destroy, I say, with flash of wreakefull fier The traitour sonne. **1594** WILLOBIE *Avisa* 7 b, Was earth consumde with wreakful waues? **1598** SYLVESTER *Du Bartas* II. i. *Eden* 197 The wreakfull nature-drowning Flood Spar'd not this beauteous place. **1616** W. BROWNE *Brit. Past.* II. v. 344 Unsuccoured ..From wreakefull stormes' impetuous tyranny. **1838** S. BELLAMY *Betrayal* 18 Summoning..From earth, and air, and their more proper hell, All wreakful influences.

2. Marked or characterized by desire for revenge; of the nature of vengeance or retribution.

1532 *Henryson's Test. Cresseid* 329 (Thynne), So scheweth through thy dede, A wrekeful sentence gyuen on Creseyde. **1581** A. HALL *Iliad* IX. 166 This short discourse..is onely you to pray..to put this wreakful wrath away. **1593** NASHE *Christ's T.* (1613) 153 He will (in wreakfull recompence that thou hast so disgrac't him)..deforme thee. **1610** NICCOLS *Eng. Eliza* Induct. 9 In top of heau'n he tooke his wreakfull stand Ore that great Towne. **1616** W. BROWNE *Brit. Past.* II. ii. 592 Cold winter's stormes and wreakfull teene. **1751** MENDEZ *Seasons, Spring* 11 The cuckoo..with his wreakful tale the spouse doth fray. **1757** MICKLE *Concub.* I. xxiv, Left to your Aunts fell Spight and wreakfull Crueltie.

wreakless (ˈriːklɪs), *a.*[1] *rare.* [f. WREAK *sb.* + -LESS.] **a.** Unpunished. **b.** Unavenged.

1613 CHAPMAN *Rev. Bussy d' Ambois* III. i, Nought that is Approu'd by Reason, can be Cowardise. *Charl.* Dispute when you should fight. Wrong wreaklesse sleeping, Makes men dye honorlesse. **1615** —— *Odyssey* II. 223 You still wreaklesse liue: Gnaw (vermine-like) things sacred: no lawes giue To your deuouring. **1880** SWINBURNE *Birthday Ode* 142 Under these the watch of wreakless wrong With fire of eyes anhungered.

†ˈ**wreakless**, *a.*[2] *Obs.*[−1] [Cf. WREAK *v.*, obs. var. RECK *v.*] = RECKLESS *a.*

1593 SHAKS. *3 Hen. VI*, V. vi. 7 So flies the wreaklesse shepherd from y[e] Wolfe.

†**wreaks**, erron. f. REAKS (pranks) *Obs.*

1653 MORE *Antid. agst. Atheism* III. vi. 125 A very perfidious Master, who plays wreaks..on purpose to betray them.

wrear, var. WRAYER *Obs.*

wreast, obs. f. WREST *v.*, WRIST.

wreastlen, obs. f. WRESTLE *v.*

wreat, Sc. var. WRITE *sb.* and *v.*

wreat(t, obs. Sc. forms of WRITE *sb.*[1]

wreatch, obs. f. WRETCH *sb.*

wreath (riːθ). Pl. **wreaths** (riːðz). Forms: 1 wriða, wriþa, 4–5 wreþe, 4–6 wrethe, 5 *Sc.* wreth, 6 wreith, wrayth, 6–7, 9 wreathe, 6– wreath (9 *north. dial.* wreeath). [OE. *wriða*, *wriþa*, f. the weak grade of the stem of *wriþan* WRITHE *v.*[1] Cf. WRITH *sb.*

The alleged OE. *wræð* as a variant of *wræd* rests only on a transcript by Junius.

Walker (1791) gives the pronunciations (riːθ) and (riːð), preferring the former on grounds of analogy, though he thinks it 'the least usual mode'. Occasional rimes of that period (e.g. Roscoe, Shelley) attest the currency of the latter pronunciation.]

I. 1. Something wound, wreathed, or coiled into a circular shape or form; a twisted or wreathed band, fillet, or the like.

c **1000** ÆLFRIC *Saints' Lives* xxiii. 608 Hi..becnytton anne wriþan eall onbutan his swuran. *a* **1050** *Liber Scint.* (1889) 200 Mid wriþan treowenum [L. *loramento ligneo*] ȝewriþen grundweall..na byþ toslopen. **13..** *Gosp. Nicod.* 65 A wonden wrethe þat his heued hyd Spred he all furth on brede. *c* **1410** *Master of Game* (MS. Digby 182) xxiii, For sometyme þei croiteth in wrethes and sometyme flatte. **1495** *Trevisa's Barth. De P.R.* XVII. clii, The sowles & stakes be pyghte in the grounde, & there abowte ben wrethes wouen & wounden of thornes & roddes. **1530** PALSGR. 290/2 Wrethe of olde cordes dypped in grece and pytche,..*tourbiginaulx*. **1552** in Feuillerat *Revels Edw. VI* (1914) 120 White taffata for wreathes abowte their hattes. **1634** SIR T. HERBERT *Trav.* 187 A low Tulipant (or wreath of silke and gold). **1642** FULLER *Holy & Prof. St.* V. xv. 420 Where one gaineth a garland of bayes, hundreds have had a wreath of hemp. **1656** J. SMITH *Pract. Physick* 162 Let them be thicker, by wispes or wreathes of small sticks—wrapt up in linnen. **1769** FALCONER *Dict. Marine* (1780) s.v. *Rigging*, A circular wreath or rope, called the grommet, or collar. *c* **1850** *Rudim. Navig.* (Weale) 122 *Grommets*,..wreaths of rope which confine the oars. **1868** ATKINSON *Cleveland Gloss.*, *Garlands*, wreaths of ribbon enclosing a white glove. **1883** GRESLEY *Gloss. Coal-mining* 295 *Wreaths*, four short pieces of hemp rope placed round the legs of a horse.

b. A ring, band, or circlet of (usu. precious) metal, etc., esp. for wearing as an ornament; a torque.

a **1000** *Riddles* lix. [lx.] 5 Friþospede bæd God nerȝende gæste sinum se þe wende wriþan. *c* **1000** ÆLFRIC *Hom.* I. 568 Ic ȝeslea ænne wriðan on his nosu, and ænne bridel on his weleras. **13..** *K. Alis.* 5723 (Laud MS.), A griselich best..; Teeþ he had so wreþen wriþen. *c* **1375** *Sc. Leg. Saints* xlvii. (*Euphemia*) 196 To quham þe lug..gef a kirtil & of fyne gold a wrethe þar-til. *c* **1386** CHAUCER *Knt.'s T.* 1287 A wrethe of gold..Vpon his heed, set ful of stones brighte. **1456** SIR G. HAYE *Law Arms* (S.T.S.) 46 [He] tuke..a grete wreth of golde..and put it about his hals. **1443** in *Rep. MSS. Ld. Middleton* (1911) 111 The scheriffez of Coventre hath..a salt seller, the wrethis gilt. **1521** *Test. Ebor.* (Surtees) V. 203 Cum uno flore argenti in fundo, cum uno wreith deaurato circa florem. *c* **1530** *Hickscorner* 587 They be yemen of the wrethe that be shakled in gyues. [**1855** THORPE tr. *Beowulf* 4041 Oft she a ringed wreath [OE. *beah-wriðan*] to the warrior gave.]

c. *Her.* A representation of a ring or circlet used as a bearing; *spec.* the circular fillet or twisted band by which the crest is joined to the helmet; = ORLE 1 c. Also *fig.* (quot. 1622).

1478, etc. [see TIMBRE *sb.*[2]] **1513** in *Glover's Hist. Derby* (1829) I. App. 61 Robert Darley baryth..3 barrs upon his nek, sabul unde or wave, issant owt of a wrayth goulls and sylver. **1572** BOSSEWELL *Armorie* 105 He beareth on a wreathe 'Topaze' and 'Saphiere' an Alcian. **1622** BACON *Hen. VII* (1876) 15 The wreath of three, was made a wreath of five; for to the three first titles of the two houses..were added two more. **1688** HOLME *Armoury* II. 393/2 A Sarazens Face..environed about the Temples with a Wreath or Torce. **1780** *Encycl. Brit.* (ed. 2) V. 3608 The Wreath is a kind of roll..which ancient knights wore as a head-dress when equipped for tournaments. **1864** BOUTELL *Her. Hist. & Pop.* xvii. 265 The Crest was worn supported by a Chapeau or Wreath. **1869** CUSSANS *Her.* 172 A Coronet, or a Wreath,..was composed of two strands of twisted silk, on which the Crest appeared to be supported. *Ibid.*, The Wreath, Bandeau, or Torse (sometimes, though improperly, styled a Chaplet).

†**d.** A metal ring forming a holder for a spindle.

1733 TULL *Horse-Hoeing Husb.* xxii. 335 The Spindle is kept from moving end-ways, by Wreaths, in the same Manner as the Axis of a Wheel-Barrow is. *Ibid.* xxiii. 377 The Hopper and Spindle are..kept in their Place..by two Wreaths screw'd on to the Spindle.

2. Something resembling or comparable to a twisted or circular band; *esp.* a coil of a spiral column of smoke, steam, or the like.

Before *c* 1790 *rare*; freq. from *c* 1820: cf. next.

1667 MILTON *P.L.* VI. 58 So spake the Sovran voice, and Clouds began To darken all the Hill, and smoak to rowl In duskie wreathes. **1836** [HOOTON] *Bilberry Thurland* I. ix. 181 Having lit her pipe, to add a few more wreathes to the general volume. **1866** *All Year Round* XV. 189/1 Certain misty wreaths—the skirts..of an adjacent sea-fog—kept sweeping up the valley. **1899** GUNTER *M. S. Bradford* xvi, 210 As he puffs the wreaths out of his complacent lips.

b. Freq. const. *of* (smoke, etc.).

1789 WORDSW. *Evening Walk* 112 As the sun declines.. The shepherd, all involved in wreaths of fire,..shows a shadowy speck. **1794** —— *Guilt & Sorrow* lviii, Where wreaths of vapour tracked a winding brook. **1797** SCOTT *Erl-King* ii, It is but a dark wreath of the cloud. **1859** DICKENS *T. Two Cities* II. v, Wreaths of dust were spinning round.. before the morning blast. **1875** BUCKLAND *Log-bk.* 365 Wreaths of sea came rolling in. **1894** HALL CAINE *Manxman* V. iii. 288 The homes of the fishermen were putting out curling wreaths of smoke.

c. A bank or drift of snow; a snow-wreath, snowdrift. Freq. ***wreath of snow***. Orig. (and chiefly) *Sc.*

1725 RAMSAY *Gentle Sheph.* I. ii, The thick blawn Wreaths of Snaw..May smoor your Wathers. **1744** THOMSON *Winter* 828 Scarce his Head Rais'd o'er the heapy Wreath, the branching Elk Lies slumbering sullen in the white Abyss. *c* **1790** in Burns *Wks.* (1800) IV. 177 Weeping at the eye o' life, I wander through a wreath o' snaw. **1806** J. GRAHAME *Birds of Scot.* 13 While yet in mountain cleughs Lingers the frozen wreath. **1843** PRESCOTT *Mexico* V. ii. (1864) 284 [He] lived to see his empire melt away like the winter's wreath. **1855** KINGSLEY *Glaucus* 26 Those wild gardens amid the wreaths of the untrodden snow.

d. *transf.* A bank of sand.

1892 STEVENSON *Across the Plains* 207 Endless links and sand wreaths.

3. Each of the turns, convolutions, or coils of a ringed or spiral structure, spiral shell, etc.; a whirl, whorl.

1641 BEST *Farm. Bks.* (Surtees) 61 There is in most hives 17 or 18 wreathes. *Ibid.*, 4 wreathes from the bottome. **1650** FULLER *Pisgah* V. vii. 155 The four first wreaths of my scrue are undoubtedly..true. **1669** *Phil. Trans.* IV. 1012 The open of the shell is pretty sound, the second turn or wreath is very large for the proportion. **1712** J. MORTON *Nat. Hist. Northampt.* 416 A small Brown Buccinum.., with a roundish Mouth of six Wreaths. **1753** *Chambers' Cycl.* Suppl. s.v. *Scalare*, A peculiar species of..screw shell, the several wreaths of which [etc.]. **1778** [W. MARSHALL] *Minutes Agric., Observ.* 58 Let the wreaths (or twists) of the [sheaf] bands be turned upward, toward the ears. **1818** *Gleaner's Port-folio* Sept. 68 The wreaths being ornamented with transverse undulating costæ.

b. *Conch.* The genus *Turbo* (TURBO 2); a turbinated or wreathed shell; a turbinate.

1777 PENNANT *Brit. Zool.* (ed. 4) IV. 128 *Turbo.* Wreath. .. Its animal [is] a Slug. **1797** *Encycl. Brit.* (ed. 3) XVIII. 595/2 The clathrus, or barbed wreath, has a taper shell of eight spires. **1815** BURROW *Elem. Conchol.* 203 *Turbo*, Whorl or Wreath.

†**c.** *Bot.* = COROLLA 2. *Obs.*

1760 J. LEE *Introd. Bot.* I. iii. (1765) 7 The Petal .. encloses and protects it [*sc.* the flower] in the manner of a Corolla, or Wreath.

4. A fold, crease, or wrinkle.

?*a* **1400** *Morte Arth.* 1093 Alle falterde þe flesche in his foule lyppys, Ilke wrethe as a wolfe-heuede, it wraythe owtt at ones! **1600** SURFLET *Countrie Farme* III. xxvii. 484 As it [*sc.* the fig] is verie fat the iuice doth constraine the skin to fall into wreathes. **1610** MARKHAM *Masterp.* II. v. 225 If he haue a short chub neck, with a thicke skin, and many wreathes, or rolles, about the setting on of his chaps. **1677** N. COX *Gentl. Recreat.* I. 126 The Wild-Goat is as big as a Hart... They have Wreaths and Wrinkles on their Horns. **1737** BRACKEN *Farriery Impr.* (1740) II. 71 You will know whether it [*sc.* the horny part of the hoof] be smooth and even, or, otherwise, in Wreathes or Wrinkles.

b. A raised band or string-course. *rare*$^{-1}$.

1677 MIÉGE *Fr. Dict.* I, *Cordon de muraille*, an outstanding wreath or edge of stone on the out-side of a building, commonly distinguishing the several Stories.

c. *north. dial.* (See quot.)

1828 CARR *Craven Gloss.* 271 *Wreath*, the mark and swelling on the skin occasioned by a blow.

5. a. = ROLL *sb.*^{1} 8 c. Now *dial.*

1556 WITHALS *Dict.* (1562) 43 b/1 A wase or wreath to be layed vnder the vessell, that is borne vpon the head. **1570** LEVINS *Manip.* 213 A Wreath, *cirrus, cesticillus.* **1687** MIÉGE *Gt. Fr. Dict.* I, *Tortillon*, .. a Wreath of Cloth which Women lay upon their heads when they carry a Pail or Basket. **1706** PHILLIPS (ed. Kersey). **1855–76** in Yorks. glossaries. **1876** *Whitby Gloss.* 172 The *skeel* .. is carried on a 'wreath' or pad.

†**b.** A roll of bread. (Cf. TORTE.) *Obs.*

1600 HAKLUYT *Voy.* III. 220 They beat their corne to powder: then they make paste of it, and of the paste, cakes or wreathes. **1615** R. COCKS *Diary* (Hakl. Soc.) I. 47 A present of .. 10 wreathes of bread, and a basket of grapes.

†**c.** (See quot.) *Obs. rare.*

1611 COTGR., *Penide*, a Pennet; the little wreath of sugar taken in a cold.

6. a. A twist, coil, or winding (of some material thing or natural growth); a sinuosity; a winding motion.

1589 ? LYLY *Pappe w. Hatchet* D iv, The Cedar .. knitteth it selfe with such wreaths into the earth, that it cannot be remooued. *a* **1600** HOOKER *Eccl. Pol.* VII. xviii. (1662) 53 The second wreath of that Cable. **1617** MORYSON *Itin.* I. 242 The very tailes of them [*sc.* large sheep] hanging in many wreathes to the ground. **1667** MILTON *P.L.* IX. 517 Of his tortuous Traine [the serpent] Curld many a wanton wreath in sight of Eve. **1702** POPE *Sappho* 149 Round your neck in wanton wreaths I twine. **1762** FALCONER *Shipwr.* II. 213 A troop of porpoises .. In curling wreaths .. gambol on the tide. **1810** SHELLEY *Posth. Fragm. M. Nicholson, Spectral Horseman* 50 Then does the dragon .. twine his vast wreaths round the forms of the daemons. **1815** —— *Alastor* 338 Twilight .. Entwined in duskier wreaths her braided locks O'er the fair front .. of day. **1898** MEREDITH *Odes Fr. Hist.* 72 A lowly look on .. twisted wreaths of the worm in dirt.

†**b.** *Venery.* The tail of a boar. *Obs.*

1576 TURBERV. *Venerie* 241 The tayle of a Bore is to be termed his wreath. **1598** MANWOOD *Lawes Forest* iv. 27 b. **1616** BULLOKAR *Eng. Expos.* [Hence in some later Dicts.] **1627** J. TAYLOR (Water P.) *Navy Landships* D 2, A Deere, Bore, a Hare, .. haue no more tayles then a Iack-an-Apes, for it is a Deeres Single, a Bores Wreath, a Hare or Connyes Scut. [**1817** PUCKLE *Club* 90 [The flatterer's] next discourse was of the tail or single of a deer, the wreath of a boar.]

7. Something formed by twisting; yarn of a specified texture.

1757 DYER *Fleece* III. 61 A diff'rent spinning ev'ry diff'rent web Asks from your glowing fingers: some require The more compact, and some the looser wreath.

8. A curve in the handrail or string of a geometrical stair; that part of the handrail which bends round such curve.

1814 P. NICHOLSON in *Trans. Soc. Arts* XXXII. 134 The Plank, out of which the Wreath is to be cut. **1820** —— *Staircases*, etc. p. iii, Squaring the wreath upon geometrical principles. **1871** R. RIDDELL *Carp. & Joiner* 68 In this case the wreath must be in two pieces. **1881** *Dict. Architecture* s.v., A wreath of a staircase handrail is continuous in a circular or elliptic staircase.

9. *south. dial.* (See quots.)

1813 DAVIS *Agric. Wilts.* 268 *Wreaths*, the long rods of hurdles used for sheep-folding. **1856** *Morton's Cycle. Agric.* II. 727 *Wreathes*, (Dorset.), withes to keep hurdles and sowels together.

10. *techn.* A defect in glass (esp. flint glass), consisting in almost imperceptible striæ producing certain optical aberrations. ? *Obs.*

1839 URE *Dict. Arts* 584 An uniform flint-glass, free from striæ, or wreath, is much in demand for the optician. *Ibid.*, Glass allowed to cool slowly in mass in the pot is particularly full of wreath.

II. 11. A chaplet or garland of flowers, leaves, or the like, esp. worn or awarded as a mark of distinction, honour, etc. Also rarely without article.

1563 SHUTE *Archit.* D iv b, The whiche Astragalus shalbe as it were certaine round beryes and the other Astragalus .. shalbe wrothonne [*sic*] like a wreath. **1589** WARNER *Alb. Eng.* I. iii. 7 Apollos sonne perceauing him with Garland on his head, .. caused him to cast the wreath away. **1596** DRAYTON *Legends* iii. (1605) Gg 8, Goddesse of Artes and Armes, .. Be thou assisting to this Poet of mine, With funerall wreathes incompassing his browes. **1628**, etc. [see LAUREATE *a.* 1 b]. **1694** PRIOR *Hymn to Sun* ii, As His Infant Months bestow Springing Wreaths for William's Brow. **1737** GLOVER *Leonidas* I. 196 He the wreath Pontific bore amid the Spartan camp. **1784** COWPER *Task* v. 712 But fairer wreaths are due .. To those who, posted at the shrine of truth, Have fall'n in her defence. **1821** BYRON *Sardanap.* I. ii, The shepherd kings of patriarchal times, Who knew no brighter gems than summer wreaths. **1839** DICKENS *Nickleby* xxiv, Mrs. Borum and the governess cast wreaths upon the stage. **1842** TENNYSON *Talking Oak* 288 She .. shall wear Alternate leaf and acorn-ball In wreath about her hair. **1891** *Science-Gossip* XXVII. 29/2 He is ready to resign his victor's wreath to Darwin.

fig. and *transf.* **1593** MARLOWE *Edw. II*, v. i, [May] this crowne, .. like the snakie wreathe of Tisiphon, Engirt the temples of his hatefull head. **1612** DRAYTON *Poly-olb.* v. 61 Hee .. gained The Stewards nobler name: and .. attain'd The royal Scottish wreath, upholding it in state. **1613** BROWNE *Brit. Past.* I. iv. 73 Sow-thistle .., whose downy wreath If any one can blow off at a breath, We deeme her for a maide. **1784** COWPER *Task* VI. 938 There he .. obtains fresh triumphs o'er himself, And never with'ring wreaths. **1799** CAMPBELL *Pleas. Hope* I. 46 Auspicious Hope! in thy sweet garden grow Wreaths for each toil. **1817** SHELLEY *Rev. Islam* VI. xvii, Twilight o'er the east wove her serenest wreath. **1835** WORDSW. *Death Jas. Hogg* 30 Our haughty life is crowned with darkness. Like London with its own black wreath.

b. Const. *of.*

c **1450** *Mirk's Festial* I. 113, I for þe on my hed suffyr a wreþe of stynkyng þornes. **1595** SPENSER *Epith.* 256 Hymen also crowne with wreathes of vine. **1671** MILTON *P.R.* II. 459 A Crown, Golden in shew, is but a wreath of thorns, Brings dangers. **1697** DRYDEN *Æneis* v. 177 The common Crew, with Wreaths of Poplar Boughs, Their Temples crown. **1704** POPE *Summer* 10 The Muse .. adds this wreath of Ivy to thy Bays. **1800** WORDSW. *Ellen Irwin* 4 A Grecian maid Adorned with wreaths of myrtle.

fig. and *transf.* **1605** SHAKS. *Lear* II. ii. 113 The wreath of radiant fire On flicking Phœbus front. **1812** J. WILSON *Isle of Palms* II. 397 The glory .. That plays like a wreath of halo-light Around his Mary's head. **1841** EMERSON *Ess.*, *Love* §5 The remembrance of these visions .. is a wreath of flowers on the oldest brows. **1868** FARRAR *Silence & V.* iii. (1875) 60 The power and splendour of her literature, conferred upon her [*sc.* Greece] a wreath of unfading admiration.

c. A trailing cluster of flowers, tendrils, etc.

1610 HOLLAND *Camden's Brit.* 631 A poore Chappel .. adorned onlie with wilde mosse, and wreathes of clasping Ivie. **1784** COWPER *Task* v. 158 Long wavy wreaths Of flow'rs .. Blush'd on the panels. **1798** WORDSW. *Lines in Early Spring* 10 Through primrose tufts .. The periwinkle trailed its wreaths. **1881** E. WAUGH *Lancs. Songs* (ed. 5) 84 Wreaths of fairy frost-work hung Where grew last summer's leaves.

d. ***purple wreath***: (see PURPLE *a.* C 2 c).

1864 GRISEBACH *Flora W. Ind.* 789. **1890** *Cent. Dict.*, *Petrea volubilis*, the purple wreath, .. is a native of the West India islands and of the mainland from Vera Cruz southward.

e. As the title of a book comprising a collection of short literary pieces: = GARLAND *sb.* 4.

In frequent use from *c* 1825.

1753 (*title*), The Wreath: a Curious Collection of New Songs. **1799** E. DUBOIS (*title*), The Wreath; composed of Selections from Sappho [etc.] .. accompanied by a prose Translation and Notes. **1843** (*title*), The Ayrshire Wreath: a Collection of Original Pieces, in Prose and Verse. **1881** 'A.L.O.E.' (*title*), A Wreath of Indian Stories.

f. A representation of a wreath in decorative work, metal, stone, etc.

1847 C. BRONTE *J. Eyre* iii, A certain brightly painted china plate, whose bird of paradise, nestling in a wreath of convolvuli and rosebuds, had [etc.]. **1890** YOUNG *Ann. Barber-Surg. Lond.* 506 Four .. wrought silver garlands or wreaths for crowning the Master and Wardens on Election Day.

†**12.** A twisted mass (*of* something). *Obs.*$^{-0}$

1648 HEXHAM II, *Een Wrongel van Pieren ofte Wormen*, a Wreath of Wormes for bobbing.

III. 13. *attrib.* and *Comb.*, as ***wreath hurdle***, ***line***, ***-offering***, ***part***, ***rail***, ***work***; ***wreath-drifted***, ***maker***, ***-wise***; **wreath animalcule** (see quot. and cf. PERIDINIAL *a.*); **wreath shell**, = sense 3 b; **wreath-wort**, the early purple orchis, *O. mascula.*

1854 A. ADAMS, etc. *Man. Nat. Hist.* 370 *Wreath-Animalcules (*Peridiniidæ*). **1832** MOTHERWELL *Poet. Wks.* 76 More dazzlingly white Than the *wreath-drifted snows. **1818** *Sporting Mag.* II. 181 The making of *wreath hurdles is a profitable business. **1825** J. NICHOLSON *Operat. Mechanic* 597 Draw a line, which will give the *wreath line formed by the nosings of the winders. **1881** *Instr. Census Clerks* 55 Artificial Flower Maker: .. Shell Flower Maker. *Wreath Maker. *a* **1835** MRS. HEMANS *Korner & Sister* Poems (1875) 425 With his *wreath-offering silently to stand In the hush'd presence of the glorious dead. **1825** J. NICHOLSON *Operat. Mechanic* 597 In preparing the string for the *wreath part, a cylinder should be made. **1820** P. NICHOLSON *Staircases*, etc. 17 Getting a *wreath rail out of the least quantity of stuff. **1825** W. HAMILTON *Hand-book* 423 *Turbo*, the *wreath shell. **1845** J. C. MANGAN *German Anthol.* II. 105 Hand-with-hand, linked *wreathwise round, The virgins dance in order. **1686** PLOT *Staffordsh.* 384 The same person .. hath contrived an Engine to turne *wreath work. **1730** W. GEORGE in *Mem. W. Stukeley* (Surtees) III. 255 Another large partition, encompassed with plaited wreath-work. **1884** W. MILLER *Plant-n.* 148 Purple *Wreath-wort.

Hence **'wreathage**, wreaths collectively. *rare*$^{-1}$.

1883 W. ALLINGHAM in *Athenæum* July 79 Then one sees .. In their hedgerow wreathage manifold Clustering.

wreathe (riːð), *v.* Also 6–7 **wreth(e**, 6–9 **wreath**, 7 **wreeth**, **wreith**, 9 *Sc.* **wraithe**. [Early mod.Eng. *wrethe*, partly a back-formation from *wrethen* (see WREATHEN *ppl. a.*), pa. pple. of WRITHE *v.*^{1}, and partly f. WREATH *sb.* Senses 6–7 clearly show the influence of WRITHE *v.*]

I. 1. *trans.* To twist or coil (something); to form or fashion into a coil or coils. Occas. in fig. context. Also with *about*, *up*.

1535 *Trevisa's Barth. De P.R.* v. xii, These hooles bene wrethed and wounde as a spyndle of a presse. **1555** EDEN *Decades* (Arb.) 327 Longe heare which they wreath on both sydes theyr eares. **1592** SHAKS. *Ven. & Ad.* 879 An adder Wreathed up in fatal folds. **1617** MORYSON *Itin.* I. 246 These parts yeeld sheepe, whereof the taile of one wreathed to the ground, doth [etc.]. **1667** MILTON *P.L.* IV. 346 Th' unwieldy Elephant .. us'd all his might, and wreathd His Lithe Proboscis. **1668** CULPEPPER & COLE *Barthol. Anat.* I. x. 22 The Guts are oblong, round, hollow bodies variously wreathed about. **1738** THOMSON *Agamemnon* I. vii. 26 Troy .. yet wreathing smoke to heaven. **1750** GRAY *Elegy* 102 Yonder nodding beech That wreathes its old fantastic roots so high. **1810** SCOTT *Lady of L.* v. xviii, Fitz-James .. wreath'd his left hand in the mane. **1818** KEATS *Endym.* I. 6 Therefore .. we are wreathing A flowery band to bind us to the earth. **1826** SHERER *Notes & Refl. Ramble Germany* 126 A large hollow spire of open stone-work, wreathed and twisted as fancifully as an elegant toy might be. **1835** I. TAYLOR *Spir. Despot.* vi. 246 The chain of spiritual despotism had been beaten and wreathed upon the anvil .. of the .. afflicted Church.

refl. **1603** G. OWEN *Pembrokeshire* (1892) 68 To ymagine that the coale should wreth or turne it self in some place to the one [vein]. **1660** BOYLE *New Exp. Phys. Mech.* Digress. 379 The Beards of wilde Oats .. continually wreath and unwreath themselves according to .. the temperature of the ambient Air. **1753** *Adventurer* No. 31 ¶10 Wreathing themselves in various contortions, a new brood of serpents hissed round her head. **1758** *Phil. Trans.* L. 585 Like the slugs, they wreath themselves up, and when touched make themselves quite round. *a* **1853** ROBERTSON *Lect.* i. (1858) 20 The clouds wreathing themselves in that strange wild way.

b. To wind or turn (some flexile object) about or over something; to form or adjust as a wreath or encircling coil. Freq. with *round* or *about*. Also *transf.*

1530 PALSGR. 785/1 He had a kercher wreathed about his heed. **1583** tr. *Maison Neuve's Gerileon* I. 80 b, [This] dismeasured Crocodile .. wreathyng his Tayle .. all aboute his [*sc.* a horse's] Feete afore. **1585** T. WASHINGTON tr. *Nicholay's Voy.* IV. xii. 125 They .. weare on their heads a cloth wreathed. **1603** B. JONSON *Sejanus* v. K 4 b, A new Head being set vpon your Statue, A Rope is since found wreath'd about it. **1622** PEACHAM *Compl. Gentl.* v. 42 A Serpent wreathed about a Sword, placed vpright. **1687** A. LOVELL tr. *Thevenot's Trav.* I. 30 Round that, they wreath a white or red Turban. **1777** POTTER *Æschylus* 11 Ye waves That o'er th' interminable ocean wreath Your crisped smiles. *a* **1814** WORDSW. *Excurs.* VIII. 352 An ill-adjusted turban .. wreathed around their sunburnt brows. **1845** J. C. MANGAN *German Anthol.* II. 62 The white flowers wreathed Around my temples by thy whiter hand. **1877** TENNYSON *Achilles over the T.* 5 Around his head The glorious goddess wreath'd a golden cloud.

refl. **1600** SHAKS. *A.Y.L.* IV. iii. 109 About his necke A greene and guilded snake had wreath'd it selfe. **1631** BRATHWAIT *Eng. Gentlewoman* 122 The Iuye windes and wreathes it selfe about the Plant. **1866** BRYCE *Holy Rom. Emp.* v. 83 The gorgeous drapery of romance gradually wreathed itself round his name.

c. *Sc.* To fasten or secure (a yoke) upon a draught-animal. Only in fig. context.

Perhaps partly by influence of *Lam.* i. 14 (see 3 b. *fig.*).

1650 J. NICOLL *Diary* (Bann. Cl.) 17 These men .. labour to wreith the yok of thair oppressiounes upon thair bodyes and soules. *a* **1732** T. BOSTON *Crook in Lot* (1805) 46 A yoke, which the wretched sufferers can neither bear, nor yet shake off, is wreathed about their necks. **1759** ROBERTSON *Hist. Scot.* II. (1817) I. 399 Troops .. employed as instruments for subduing the Scots, and wreathing the yoke about their neck. **1777** WATSON *Philip II*, I. 92 Till, the yoke being wreathed about their necks, the most secret murmurings became .. fatal to those who uttered them. **1827** POLLOK *Course T.* VII. 509 Not those who .. sailed To purchase human flesh, or wreath the yoke Of vassalage on savage liberty.

transf. **1852** J. JARVIE *Disc.* 108 The burden of man's guilt is wreathed to the neck of the Only Begotten.

2. To surround or invest with or as with something twisted or turned; to enwreathe. Also with advs., as *about*, *in*.

1558 in Feuillerat *Revels Q. Eliz.* (1908) 41, vj Corled hed Sculles .. wrethen abowte with redd golde sarsnett and sylver Lawne. **1631** T. HEYWOOD *2nd Pt. Fair Maid of West* I. B j b, I for this Will wreathe thee in a glorious arch of gold, stuck full of Indian gemmes. **1671** MILTON *P.R.* IV. 76 Dusk faces with white silken Turbants wreath'd. **1769** SIR W. JONES *Palace Fortune* Poems (1777) 7 With stings of asps the leafless plants were wreath'd. **1832** SCOTT *Betrothed* Note D, Three hundred of the British, who fell there, had their necks wreathed with the Eudorchawg. **1833** WORDSW. *In Frith of Clyde* 4 Ne'er did morn .. more gracefully .. wreathe with mist his [*sc.* a crag's] forehead high. **1854** F. W. MANT *Midshipman* 90 Like some huge baronial castle wreathed in with smoke. **1879** BARTLETT *Egypt to Pal.* i. 18 Wreathed with fresh Sculpturings of forgotten warfare.

fig. **1842** J. WILSON *Chr. North* (1857) I. 243 Contentment wreathes with silk and velvet the prisoner's chains.

b. To encircle or surround with a wreath or garland; to bedeck or adorn with or as with a wreath; to garland.

1634 MILTON *Comus* 55 This Nymph .. gaz'd upon his clustring locks, With Ivy berries wreath'd. **1678** DRYDEN *All for Love* I. 5 With Laurels wreath your posts, And strow with Flow'rs the Pavement. **1702** POPE *Sappho* 25 Would you with ivy wreath your flowing hair. **1796** COLERIDGE *To a beautiful Spring* 6 With one fresh garland of Pierian flowers .. My languid hand shall wreath thy mossy urn. **1810** SCOTT *Lady of L.* II. xxi, To wreathe a victor's brow. **1848** LYTTON *Harold* I. i, Doors and windows were .. wreathed with garlands. **1887** BOWEN *Æneid* v. 73 Then with the myrtle of Venus the chieftain wreathes him.

c. Of flowers, etc.: To encompass or enclose (an object) as or after the manner of a wreath; to form a wreath about (something).

1718 PRIOR *Solomon* II. 140 In the Flow'rs that wreath the sparkling Bowl, Fell Adders hiss. **1796** COLERIDGE *On Autumnal Evening* 10 Each flower that wreath'd the dewy locks of Spring. **1908** *Westm. Gaz.* 10 Dec. 2/3 Flowers of heaven!..wreathing The God-centred vision of all coming years!

3. To unite (two or more things) by twining or twisting together; to entwine, intertwine; also, to fold (the arms).

1553 BRENDE *Q. Curtius* 13 A rope folded and knit with many knots, one so wrethed within an othir, that [etc.]. **1577** B. GOOGE *Heresbach's Husb.* II. 61 You shall wynde and wreathe the greene blades [of the garlic] togeather, and treade them to the grounde. **1591** SHAKS. *Two Gent.* II. i. 19 You haue learn'd..to wreath your Armes like a Male-content. **1596** MASCALL *Cattle* 275 To ring hogges.., some put a red paste wyar vnder the skinne of his snout,..then wreath it altogether. **1602** MARSTON *Ant. & Mel.* IV. Wks. 1856 I. 53 Enter Andrugio and Antonio wreathed together. **1808** WORDSW. *White Doe* 1724 If she too passionately wreathed Her arms. **1817** SHELLEY *Rev. Islam* I. viii, I behold..An Eagle and a Serpent wreathed in fight. **1847** MADDEN *Laȝamon* III. 31 Twelve swine, tied together, with withies exceeding great wreathed altogether.

b. To combine (several things into one structure) by interweaving; to twine together; to form or make by intertwining.

a **1547** SURREY *Par. Eccl.* iv. 34 Cables brayded thre fould.., to gether wrethed swer [= sure]. **1579** E. K. *Gloss. to Spenser's Sheph. Cal.* Dec. 81 A kind of woodde..fit to wreath and bynde in leapes to catch fish withall. **1604** E. G[RIMSTONE] *D'Acosta's Hist. Indies* v. xxix. 420 A great cord wreathed of chaines of roasted mays. **1767** GRAY *Death of Hoel* 15 Chains..Wreath'd in many a golden link. **1788** COWPER *Gratitude* 7 She gave..me beside, Wreath'd into an elegant bow, The ribbon. **1811** T. DAVIS *Agric. Wilts* 263 Hurdles..made of hazel rods closely wreathed. **1844** W. BARNES *Poems Rural Life* 289 *Bliake*, a bar of wood..with holes to take the soles of a hurdle while the maker wreaths it.

refl. **1555** EDEN *Decades* (Arb.) 225 The leaues of this *Cocus*..wreathynge them selues one within an other.

fig. **1597** HOOKER *Eccl. Pol.* v. lxxvi. §8 When..heauenly and earthly happines are wreathed in one crowne. **1611** BIBLE *Lam.* i. 14 The yoke of my transgressions is bound by his hand: they are wreathed, and come vp vpon my necke. *a* **1716** SOUTH *Serm.* (J.), In such base noisome hearts you shall ever see pride and ingratitude indivisibly wreathed and twisted together.

†**c.** *local.* To support, maintain, or hold up (a bank, etc.) by or as by wattled work. *Obs.*

1569 *Surrey & Kent Sewers Comm.* (L.C.C., 1909) 34 That he stake wreth & lande vppe so mutche earth as neade ys. **1572** *Ibid.* 120 To stake walle or wreath his banke against the riuer of thames. **1576** *Ibid.* 252 To scale watle and wretche [*sic*] the outer side of the saied shewer.

4. To arrange or dispose flowers, etc., as (a wreath); in later use *esp.* to adjust or fashion (flowers, etc.) into a garland or chaplet.

1595 *Locrine* II. vi. 14 A flowring garland wreath'd of bay. **1667** MILTON *P.L.* IX. 892 From his slack hand the Garland wreath'd for Eve Down drop'd. **1828** *Lady's Mag.* Aug. 446/1 A very beautiful chintz, with flowers, delicately wreathed..on a striped ground of yellow muslin. **1849** RUSKIN *Sev. Lamps* iv. §2 His next step was to gather the flowers themselves, and wreathe them in his capitals. **1892** TENNYSON *Akbar's Dream* 23 Gathering..From each fair plant the blossom choicest-grown To wreathe a crown..for the king.

†**5.** To make (a bow) by a supple bending of the body. *Obs. rare*$^{-1}$.

1730 THOMSON *Autumn* 1197 Let..those of fairer front.. Wreathe the deep bow, diffuse the lying smile.

II. †**6.** To strain or turn forcibly round or to a side; to wring, wrench, or wrest. *Obs.*

1590 SPENSER *F.Q.* II. i. 56 Sir Guyon..from so heauie sight his head did wreath. **1592** A. DAY *Eng. Secretorie* I. (1595) 23 Statelie trees (some tops wherof the wind seemeth to wreath and turne at one side). **1606** HOLLAND *Sueton.* 25 By wreathing their [*sc.* fugitives] throats he turned them againe vpon the enemies. **1617** PURCHAS *Pilgrimage* (ed. 3) 139 They killed a man which was a first-borne, wreathing his head from his body. **1662** EVELYN *Chalcogr.* II. (1906) 15 To wreath, rub, slap and smooth them [*sc.* blankets] till you have rendred them very soft and gentle. **1674** HOOKE *Animadv.* 52 This Plate..must be wrenched or wreithed, so that the Plain thereof must stand parallel to the Plain of the Index-Frame. **1712–4** POPE *Rape Lock* IV. 100 Was it for this you..your locks..with tort'ring irons wreath'd around? **1737** WHISTON *Josephus, Antiq.* II. ix. §7 Moses threw it [*sc.* a diadem] down to the ground, and..wreathed it round, and trod upon it.

fig. **1580** LYLY *Euphues* (Arb.) 344 To wrest the will of man, or to wreath his heart to our humours.

†**b.** *fig.* To extend unduly the application or meaning of (a writer or writing); to 'wrest', stretch, strain. *Obs. rare.*

1566 STAPYLTON *Ret. Untr. Jewel* IV. 62 b, To wreste and wrethe Scriptures at his pleasure. **1583** FOXE *A. & M.* (ed. 4) II. 1820 It is shame for you to wrast and wreath the Doctors as you do. **1656** J. HAMMOND *Leah & R.* (1844) 23 They were resolved to wreth and stretch their commission to the prejudice of Mary-land.

†**c.** *refl.* To worm (oneself) *in*; to insinuate.

a **1571** JEWEL *On 2 Thess.* ii. 1, 2 [Antichrist] shall shew forth himself at the first with countenance of deuotion and holinesse, that hee may..secretly wreath in himselfe.

d. To twist, turn, or contort (the body, limbs, etc.); to writhe.

1642 MILTON *Apol. agst. Smect.* Wks. (1697) 334 When in the Colleges..young Divines..have been seen so oft upon the Stage wreething and unboning their Clergy-limbs. **1695** BLACKMORE *Pr. Arth.* VIII. 171 Octa his wounded Body wreaths in Pain. **1697** R. PEIRCE *Bath. Mem.* II. v. 318 He was suddenly seized with a violent Convulsion Fit, which wreathed him every way. **1711** GAY *Rural Sports* I. 236 Impatient of the wound, He rolls and wreaths his shining body round. **1787** *Minor* III. ix. 187 My mother..wreathed her body,..and cried. **1817** SHELLEY *Rev. Islam* XI. xi, Even in death their lips are wreathed with fear. **1855** MRS. GASKELL *North & South* ix, Margaret wreathed her throat in a scornful curve.

e. To alter (the features, etc.) *in, into*, or *to* a smile, etc. (Cf. WREATHED *ppl. a.* 1 c.)

1813 SCOTT *Rokeby* I. xxiii, Contempt kept Bertram's anger down, And wreathed to savage smile his frown. **1865** KINGSLEY *Herew.* xvi, Gilbert..walked up to the pair, his weather-beaten countenance wreathed into..paternal smiles. **1877** MISS A. B. EDWARDS *Up Nile* x. 286 [They] wreathed their countenances in ghastly smiles.

refl. **1868** MISS BRADDON *Dead-Sea Fruit* i, The mobile mouth..will wreathe itself into such a smile that [etc.].

†**7. a.** To take (something) by force; to wrest or seize. *Obs. rare.*

1590 C. S. *Right Relig.* 11 To wreath from Princes their crownes is more impossible. *Ibid.* 15 Authoritie to wreath from kinges their crownes.

†**b.** To rend or tear. *Obs.*

1598 HAKLUYT *Voy.* II. I. 104 If it should happen to haue lighted on any part of the shippe,..it would rent and wreth sayles, mast, shroudes and shippe and all in manner like a wyth. **1606** N. B[AXTER] *Sydney's Ourania* E j, The stemme of an Oke in peeces they wreath. **1607** TOPSELL *Four-f. Beasts* 487 Lyons..doe not onely bite, but also wreath and teare the wounds.

III. *intr.* **8.** To undergo writhing, twisting, or deviation; to diverge or swerve; to bend, turn, or coil. Also with *round.*

1584 R. SCOT *Discov. Witchcr.* XII. vii. 225 From their course the starres doo wreath, And soules she coniure can. **1599** T. CUTWODE *Caltha Poet.* (Roxb.) xxxi, The Bay tree ..seems to sigh..And with the wanton wind to wrig & wreath, against the god. **1603** G. OWEN *Pembrokeshire* (1892) 64 Sometymes the same [vein of limestone] is found to wreath to the northe and southe. *c* **1611** CHAPMAN *Iliad* VII. 236 Aiax a farre greater stone lift up, and, wreathing round, With all his body layd to it, he sent it forth. **1821** CLARE *Vill. Minstr.* II. 190 Downy bents, that to the air did wreathe. **1878** SUSAN PHILLIPS *On Seaboard* 60 Where..the lithe brown sea-flowers wreathe and sway.

fig. **1849** C. BRONTE *Shirley* III. 151 Beauty is never so beautiful as when, if I teaze it, it wreathes back on me with spirit. **1850** TENNYSON *In Mem.* xlix, The lightest wave of thought shall lisp, The fancy's tenderest eddy wreathe.

†**b.** To become involved or intertwined. *Obs.*

1631 BRATHWAIT *Eng. Gentlew.* Table †2, The Iuie while it is winding, decayes the plant, with which it is wreathing.

9. To assume the form of, circle in the manner of, a wreath. Also *fig.*

1776 J. BARCLAY *Par. Psalms* 88 The flames of fire shall round him wreathe. **1814** BYRON *To Belshazzar* ii, Go! dash the roses from thy brow—Gray hairs but poorly wreathe with them. **1853** KANE *Grinnell Exp.* (1856) 444 A strange, palpable obscurity, wreathing up in long strata to the northward. **1867** MORRIS *Jason* VII. 395 Real fire of pinewood..Wreathing around my body greedily. **1875** STEDMAN *Vict. Poets* iii. (1887) 81 The weary penman who could send a smile wreathing from Land's End to John o' Groats.

b. *Sc.* To form into, assume the shape of, a snowdrift or snow-wreath.

1861 R. QUINN *Heather Lintie* (1863) 43 We'd na be rad o' scath fra wather, Though snaw was wreathin'. **1887** *Suppl. Jamieson* 280/1 The snaw was wraithin' in the glen.

10. Of flour or meal, in milling: To hug the eye of the millstone so closely as to hinder its descent.

1891 *Cent. Dict.* s.v.

wreathed (riːðd), *ppl. a.* [f. WREATHE *v.* + -ED[1]. Cf. next and WRITHED *ppl. a.*]

1. Formed by or as by wreathing, wrying, twisting, or twining; arranged or disposed in coils, curves, or twists; contorted, twisted.

In frequent use from *c* 1590 to *c* 1630.

c **1530** TINDALE *Exod.* xxviii. 14 Thou shalt make.. cheynes off fine golde: lynkeworke and wrethed, and fasten the wrethed cheynes to the hokes. **1535** in *Bury Wills* (Camden) 127 My ij wrethed rynges of gold. **1587** A. DAY *Daphnis & Chloe* (1890) 14 Yong rammes..with their wreathed hornes. **1605** B. JONSON *Masque Blackness* ⁋1 Musique made out of wreathed shells. **1608** SIR H. PLAT *Garden of Eden* (1653) 142 Winding the young stock about the stick,..it will grow in a wreathed form. **1665** G. HAVERS *P. della Valle's Trav. E. India* 114 [The] Diadem..might have been of wreath'd Linnen, or Gold, or other solid matter. *a* **1711** KEN *Psyche* Poet. Wks. 1721 IV. 273 Unicorns..with their terrible wreath'd Hornes. **1743** DAVIDSON *Virgil, Aeneid* VII. 351 A chain of wreathed gold. **1817** SHELLEY *Rev. Islam* I. x, The Eagle..unremittingly assailed The wreathed Serpent. **1820** P. NICHOLSON *Staircases* p. iv, The geometrical construction of the wreathed part of the Rail. **1844** KINGLAKE *Eothen* xx, The short and proudly wreathed lip. **1908** [MISS FOWLER] *Betw. Trent & Ancholme* 362 The fog at times lies wreathed, white and still.

fig. *c* **1586** C'TESS PEMBROKE *Ps.* CXIX. D iii, From falshoods wreathed way, O save me, Lord. **1846** J. C. MANGAN *Poems* (1903) 95 Whence flowed the tones Of silver lyres, And many voices in wreathed swell.

†**b.** Corrugated; wrinkled. *Obs.*

1567 MAPLET *Gr. Forest* 42 The Fig tree;..all his Wood not so plaine, as wrethed & wrinckled. **1656** BEALE *Heref. Orchards* (1657) 12 You shall find the better-tasted fruit to be more wrethed or wrinckled.

c. Formed by wreathing the countenance.

1633 MILTON *L'Allegro* 28 Nods, and Becks, and Wreathed Smiles.

†**2.** Crossed, folded; also, having the arms folded.

1588 SHAKS. *L.L.L.* IV. iii. 135 Longauile Did..neuer lay his wreathed armes athwart His louing bosome, to keepe downe his heart. **1595** MARKHAM *Sir R. Grinvile* iv, Thetis ..with wreath's armes. **1599** B. JONSON *Cynthia's Rev.* III. ii, Another..walks off melancholic, and stands wreath'd As he were pinn'd up to the arras.

3. a. Of columns, etc.: Twisted or shaped in a screw-like form; contorted.

1624 WOTTON *Elem. Archit.* 31 Wreathed, and Vined, and Figured Columnes, which our Author himselfe condemneth. *a* **1700** EVELYN *Diary* 25 Mar. 1644, Some of the columns wreathed, others spiral. **1823** P. NICHOLSON *Pract. Build.* 596 Wreathed columns; such as are twisted in the form of a screw. **1842** GWILT *Archit.* 1053 *Wreathed columns*..are..very appropriately called contorted columns.

†**b.** Having a spirally-grooved bore; rifled. *Obs.*

1681 R. CROMWELL *Let.* in *Eng. Hist. Rev.* (1898) XIII. 96 The little gun..is not so propper for shott it being a wreathed barrell.

4. Formed or combined by twining or interweaving; entwined, intertwined.

1578 H. WOTTON *Courtlie Controv.* 8 A banquet..vnder a wreathed arbor of Laurell, Iessemen, Holly, and Iuy. *Ibid.*, A banke of wrethed boughes. **1633** T. ADAMS *Exp. 2 Pet* ii. 4. 524 These chaines,..were they of cords, of wreathed trees, of iron,..might bee burst asunder. **1633** G. HERBERT *Temple, Wreath* 1 A Wreathed garland of deserved praise. **1688** HOLME *Armoury* II. 468/2 Two Serpents in Fesse to the sinister; wreathed, respecting. *Ibid.*, Two Snakes wreathed in pale. **1795** H. TOOKE *Purley* II. 256 A *raddle* hedge, is a hedge of..twisted or wreathed twigs or boughs. **1817** *Dugdale's Monasticon* I. 1 Here St. Joseph..erected,..of wreathed twigs, the first Christian oratory in England. **1828** TENNYSON *Lover's Tale* II. 43 They vanish'd..Beneath the bower of wreathed eglantines.

transf. **1782** WARTON *On Sir J. Reynolds's Painted Window* 24 Where Superstition with capricious hand In many a maze the wreathed window plann'd.

fig. **1820** KEATS *Ode to Psyche* 60 A rosy sanctuary will I dress With the wreath'd trellis of a working brain.

5. Covered, decked, or encompassed by a wreath or wreaths; garlanded.

1819 KEATS *Lamia* I. 38 When from this wreathed tomb shall I awake? **1847** LONGF. in *Life* (1891) II. 76 Byron's wild and wicked travesty..hits the Laureate [*sc.* Southey] hard on his wreathed head. **1897** *Daily News* 30 June 6/2 The wreathed coffin was conveyed..to the burial ground.

b. *Her.* Encircled with a twisted band or wreath.

1688 HOLME *Armoury* II. 473/2 A Flower de Lis Wreathed, or in the middle Wreathed. *Ibid.* 393/2 A Sarazens Head..wreathed about the temples. **1838** *Penny Cycl.* XII. 143/2 Heads are also blazoned wreathed or banded, as the case may be.

c. In the specific names of birds (see quots.).

Frequently used by Latham.

1781 LATHAM *Gen. Synop. Birds* I. 358 Wreathed Hornbill;..on the top of the upper mandible is an appendage..rounded at top. **1785** *Ibid.* V. 216 Wreathed Plover;..round the crown runs a list of white, encircling the head like a wreath. **1819** STEPHENS in Shaw's *Gen. Zool.* XI. 488 Wreathed Pluvian. *Pluvianus coronatus*,..[= Latham's] Wreathed Plover. **1823** LATHAM *Gen. Hist. Birds* VII. 140 Wreathed Warbler... From the eye round to the nape a white line, passing backwards, and surrounding it as a wreath at the back part.

Hence **'wreathedness.** *rare*$^{-0}$.

1730 BAILEY (fol.), *Contorteousness*, wreathedness.

wreathen (riːð(ə)n), *ppl. a.* Also 4–6 **wrethen**, 5 **-yne**, **-in**, (?) **wrethe**. [ME. *wrēðen*, normal variant of *wriðen*, pa. pple. of *wrīðen* WRITHE *v.* Cf. WRITHEN *ppl. a.*]

1. = WREATHED *ppl. a.* 1.

α. *a* **1400–50** *Wars Alex.* 5526 All þe watir of þe werd [to him seemed] bot as a wrethen neddire. **1401–2** *Durham Acc. Rolls* (Surtees) 393, vj libr. de wrethyn candell, *xs.* *a* **1450** *Songs & Carols 15th C.* (Warton Club) 85 My baselard haȝt a wrethin hafte. **1465** *Will of Pachett* (Somerset Ho.), A wrethyne rynge of golde. *c* **1530** in Gutch *Coll. Cur.* II. 310 Great gilte Candilsteks costid withe wrethin shanks. *a* **1548** HALL *Chron., Hen. VIII*, 207 b, Veluet..fret with flowers of Siluer, and small twigges of wrethen worke. *a* **1600** MONTGOMERIE *Misc. Poems* iv. 5 Mercure with his wrethin wand. **1887** *Suppl. Jamieson* 280 Wrethin' strae-rapes.

β. **1568** BIBLE (Bishops') *Exod.* xxviii. 22 Chaynes of pure golde and wreathen worke. **1598** DELONEY *Jacke Newb.* i. Wks. (1912) 7 The Bel-weather..by the force of his wreathen hornes..slew him. **1608** TOPSELL *Serpents* 245 Many..are the Epithets which are giuen to Snakes,..as.. Gorgonean, wreathen, slyding. **1611** BIBLE *Exod.* xxviii. 14 Thou shalt make..two chaines of pure gold..; of wreathen worke shalt thou make them. **1792** *Mass. Mag.* Nov., Imagination very easily giving them [*sc.* stalactites] pedestals and chapiters, and even wreathen-work. **1871** J. HAY *Pike County Ball.* (1880) 154 Wreathen amulet Forged against sword-stroke. **1872** RUSKIN *Aratra Pentelici* 51 The wreathen work of its doors,..the foliage of its capitals. **1875** —— *Fors Clav.* lviii. 288 The pierced fractional coins will only bear a chased wreathen fillet. **1877** BLACKMORE *Erema* li, The glorious woods of wreathen gold..all were mine.

Comb. **1796** WITHERING *Brit. Plants* (ed. 3) III. 566 Wreathen-podded Whitlowgrass. [Grows in] Fissures of limestone rocks.

2. Formed or arranged by or as by twining or interweaving; entwined, intertwined.

1611 SPEED *Hist. Gt. Brit.* VI. ix. §21. 81 Their Oratory, built onely of wrethen wands. **1631** WEEVER *Anc. Funeral Mon.* 58 To build a Church or Oratorie of wreathen wands. **1713** C'TESS WINCHELSEA *Misc. Poems* 39 The Flowers..In wreathen Garlands dropt agen On Lucullus. *a* **1850** in Mrs. Jameson *Leg. Monast. Orders* (1852) 45 A church of wreathen wands.

wreather ('riːðə(r)). [f. WREATHE *v.* + -ER[1].] One who or that which wreathes, twists, or twines. Also *transf.*

1566 STAPLETON *Ret. Untr. Jewel* IV. 62 To proue you wresters and wrethers of Gods holy worde. **1579–80** NORTH *Plutarch* (1595) 5 Pityocamtes, that is to say, a wreather or bower of pine apple trees. **1648** HEXHAM II, *Een Wrijter*, an Extorter, a Wreather, or a Wrester. **1817** KEATS *Sleep & Poetry* 14 Sleep,.. Soft closer of our eyes!.. Wreather of poppy buds, and weeping willows!

wreathing ('riːðɪŋ), *vbl. sb.* [f. as prec. + -ING[1].] **1.** The action of twisting or contorting; the fact of writhing; an instance of this.

1580 HOLLYBAND *Treas. Fr. Tong*, *Torsement*, a wreathing. **1587** GOLDING *De Mornay* xiii. 223 Leauing their mouings free; which yet..shall come to the end which God hath listed to appoint vnto them, whatsoeuer windings and wreathings they seeme to themselues to make. **1615** G. SANDYS *Trav.* 34 By the wreathing of their bodies..they seek to avoid the pursuer. **1668** CULPEPPER & COLE *Barthol. Anat.* I. v. 8 Touching the Contorsion or Wreathing of the recurrent Nerve. **1721** BRADLEY *Philos. Acc. Wks. Nat.* 130 The Earth-Worm..by a sort of wreathing..takes hold of the Ground with its small Feet. **1794** R. J. SULIVAN *View Nat.* II. 456 The sun,..whose oblique course is not unaptly represented by the wreathings of a snake. **1800** *Med. Jrnl.* III. 451 The attendants told me, from the wreathing of her body.., that she would soon have another fit. **1823** JOANNA BAILLIE *Poems* 260 [Steam] With tressy wreathings playing in the air. **1885** R. BRIDGES *Eros & Psyche* Oct. 23 Mid the wreathings of the vapour dim The goddess grew in glory visible.

fig. **1612** SHELTON *Quix.* I. IV. vi. (1620) 345 His Friend did notable injurie to their amitie in searching out wreathings and ambages in the discovery of his most hidden thoughts to him. **1641** FANNANT *True Relat. Parl. Rich. II*, 37 Those infinit wreathings of contention.

b. *concr.* That which is wreathed or twisted.

1600 SURFLET *Countrie Farme* III. xiii. 449 And for these grafts it is ynough, if euerie one of them, haue one good eielet or two aboue the wreathing. **1634** PEACHAM *Compl. Gentl.* (ed. 2) xii. 110 To Painters, for the picturing of some exquisit arme, leg, torse or wreathing of the body.

†**2.** A wresting of the sense or meaning of something. *Obs.*

1628 PRYNNE *Cens. Cozens* 67 Which is a grosse abuse, a wreathing, a peruerting of the Scriptures.

3. The action or fact of entwining or intertwining; an instance of this.

1533 [see WRAPPING *vbl. sb.* 1 b]. **1590** SPENSER *F.Q.* II. xii. 53 Boughes and braunches..did..dilate Their clasping armes, in wanton wreathings intricate. **1661** BOYLE *Spring of Air* II. ii. (1682) 32 In strings there is required either wreathing or some..texture of component parts. **1844** MRS. BROWNING *Cry of Children* viii, Let them touch each other's hands, in a fresh wreathing Of their tender human youth! *a* **1901** W. BRIGHT *Age of Fathers* (1903) II. 23 The wreathing of a garland for the Penates.

4. The action of investing with a wreath.

1852 GROTE *Greece* II. lxx. IX. 137 The operations of wreathing and unwreathing must here have been performed by the soldiers symbolically.

'**wreathing**, *ppl. a.* [f. as prec. + -ING[2].] **1.** That wreathes, twists, or twines; enwreathing.

1677 DRYDEN *State Innoc.* III. 16 When your kind Eyes look'd languishing on mine, And wreathing Arms did soft embraces joyn. **1697** —— *Virg. Past.* IV. 22 Unbidden Earth shall wreathing Ivy bring. **1718** ROWE tr. *Lucan* 180 To cast from off her Brow the wreathing Green. **1816** BYRON *Siege Cor.* vi, In red and wreathing columns flash'd The flame. **1842** DICKENS *Amer. Notes* xiv, [To] see the wreathing water in the rapids hurrying on to take its fearful plunge. **1887** HISSEY *Holiday on Road* 327 The wreathing mists and wandering clouds of such a day.

†**2.** *wreathing-team*, part of the gear of a plough.

Perhaps an error for *wrethen* WREATHEN *ppl. a.*

1523 FITZHERB. *Husb.* §5 He muste haue his ploughe and his..horses, and the geare that belongeth to them;..bowes, yokes, landes, stylkynges, wrethynge-temes.

Hence '**wreathingly** *adv.*

1845 J. C. MANGAN *German Anthol.* II. 59 That lone Gate which the tall wild weeds encircle wreathingly. **1891** *Temple Bar Mag.* Aug. 542 [The smoke] falls wreathingly upon the face of the sleeping child.

wreathless ('riːθlɪs), *a.* [f. WREATH *sb.* + -LESS.] Having no wreath; destitute or devoid of a wreath or wreaths.

1825 COLERIDGE *Work without Hope* 11 With lips unbrightened, wreathless brow, I stroll. **1878** SWINBURNE *Poems & Ball.* 139 While youth with burning lips and wreathless hair Sang toward the sun. **1903** *Daily Chron.* 30 March 5/7 The almost clandestine removal of the coffin.. wreathless and flowerless to the numbered luggage-van.

wreathlet ('riːθlɪt). [f. as prec. + -LET.] A small wreath.

1833 *Blackw. Mag.* XXXIV. 258 From that Wreath he has woven wreathlets. **1857** *Fraser's Mag.* LVI. 491 These tiny wreathlets wandered hither and thither. **1887** [C. MACKAY] *Twin Soul* I. xxii. 235 The blue smoke curled in beautiful wreathlets to the sky.

wreathy ('riːθɪ), *a.* [f. as prec. + -Y[1].] **1.** Of the form of a wreath, coil, or twisted band; marked or characterized by convolution, twisting, or twining; wreathing, curling.

1644 DIGBY *Nat. Bodies* xxiii. §1. 203 A vast multitude of seuerall little ioyntes, and wreathy labyrinthes of nature. **1658** SIR T. BROWNE *Pseud. Ep.* (ed. 3) III. xxiii. 135 That famous one [*sc.* horn] which is preserved at St. Dennis near Paris, hath wreathy spires, and cochleary turnings about it. **1798** JOANNA BAILLIE *Fugitive Verses* (1840) 3 Slowly mounts the smoke in wreathy clouds. *Ibid.* 110 Wreathy folds. **1817** MOORE *Lalla R.*, *Nourmahal* 411 Those wreathy, Red Sea shells, Where Love himself, of old, lay sleeping. *a* **1851** MOIR *Evening Tranquillity* vi, Above yon cottage..The wreathy smoke ascends. **1853** KANE *Grinnell Exp.* xxxvi. (1856) 332 The long, wreathy brown clouds.

transf. **1784–5** *Ann. Reg., Poetry* 137 Wreathy smiles, and roseate pleasures, Are thy richest, sweetest treasures. **1853** *Fraser's Mag.* XLVII. 513 The very foam of the sea, flung in all its wreathy airiness from the crest of a wave.

2. Decked with a wreath or wreathing.

1697 DRYDEN *Æneis* IV. 438 The Bacchanalian Dames.. houl about the Hills, and shake the wreathy Spear.

b. *Her.* (See quot.) *rare*[−0].

1894 *Parker's Gloss. Her.*, *Tortilly*,..a term applied to Ordinaries which are wreathed; the term *wreathy* is also found.

3. Of the nature of, forming or constituting, a wreath or garland. Also *transf.*

1718 ROWE tr. *Lucan* 181 Her bristling Locks the wreathy Fillet scorn. **1725** POPE *Odyssey* VI. 152 Around his loins the verdant cincture spreads A wreathy foilage. *c* **1750** R. CUMBERLAND in *Mem.* (1806) 62 The victim beast,..With all its wreathy honours on its head. **1818** *Blackw. Mag.* III. 90 On Carmel's brow the wreathy vine Had all its honours shed. **1828** MISS MITFORD *Village* Ser. III. 146 A wilderness of blossom, interwoven, intertwined, wreathy, garlandy. **1830** [see GARLANDY *a.*]. **1845** BROWNING *Flight of Duchess* xvii. 59 His forehead chapleted green with wreathy hop.

†**wrecche**, *v. Obs.* [OE. *wreccan* (*wreahte*, *wrehte*; *wreaht*, *wreht*) to arouse, undertake, raise. Cf. MDu. *wrecken*, NFris. *wräki* to waken, *wräken* (adj.) awake.] *trans.* To rouse, arouse; to bring to life.

c **897** ÆLFRED *Gregory's Past. C.* xxviii. 193 Ne sceal he no ðæt an don ðæt he ana wacige, ac he sceal eac his friend wreccean [*v.r.* wreccan]. *c* **1000** ÆLFRIC *Saints' Lives* xi. 241 We feollan on slæpe.., ac he læg þurh-wacol.., and wræhte us siððan. *a* **1250** *Owl & Night.* 106 Þo hit bycom þat he hayhte [= hatched] & of his eyre briddes wrauhte [*Cott.* wraȝte].

wrecche, wreche, etc.: see WRETCH, etc.

wrecful, variant of WRACKFUL *a.*[2] *Obs.*

†**wreche**, *sb. Obs.* Forms: *α.* 3 **wræche**, 3–6 **wreche**, 4–6 **wrech**, 4 **wrieche**, 4–5 **wreeche**, 5 **wreach.** *β.* 3–4 **wrache**, 5 **wrach.** *γ.* 4–5 **wrecche** (4 **vrecche**), 5–6 **wretche.** [The normal representative of an OE. *wrǣc* (with palatal *c*) fem., of which however the existing texts present no example which can be definitely distinguished from *wrǣc* neut., WRACK *sb.*[1] (A possible instance occurs in *Riddles* ii. 4, if the reading *wræce* is correct.) The vowel of *wrǣc* (:—earlier **wrāk-jō*) corresponds to that of OFris. *wrêke*, *wrêtse* (NFris. *wrêk*, *wräk*), OS. *wrâka*, *wrêka* (MLG. *wrâke*; MDu. *wrâke*, Du. *wraak*), OHG. *râhha* (MHG. *râche*, G. *rache*), Goth. *wrêkei*.

The *β*-forms partly represent a south-eastern variant of *wræche*, and are partly due to confusion with *wrake* WRAKE *sb.*; the *γ*-forms show assimilation (in some instances merely graphic) to *wrecche* WRETCH *sb.* The normal spelling, if the word had survived into modern English, would have been *wreach* or *wreech*.]

1. Retributive punishment; vengeance; = WREAK *sb.* 1.

In very frequent use from *c* 1290 to *c* 1450.

α. *c* **1200** ORMIN Introd. 19 Forr þatt wass mikell wræche wiss þatt all follc for till helle. *c* **1205** LAY. 29581 Vre drihte ..his wreche sende an wræstliche þan folke. *c* **1250** *Gen. & Ex.* 552 So cam on werlde wreche and wrake. *a* **1333** W. HEREBERT in *Relig. Lyrics 14th C.* (1924) 20 Nou, dame, ich þe byseche At þylke day of wreche..spek uor me. **13..** *E.E. Allit. P.* B. 230 Ȝet wrathed not þe wyȝ, ne þe wrech saȝtled. *c* **1386** CHAUCER *Monk's T.* 625 The wreche of god hym smoot so cruelly, That thurgh his body wikked wormes crepte. *c* **1400** *Pilgr. Sowle* (Caxton, 1483) III. viii. 55 Euer haue they in theyr hertes holden wreeche and rancour. **1477** NORTON *Ord. Alch.* i. in Ashm. (1652) 15 For doubt of such pride and wreach, He must be ware that will this Science teach. *c* **1485** *Digby Myst.* (1882) III. 469 To kepe þis place from wreche.

Personif. **1413** *26 Pol. Poems* 53 Euere by trouþe stondes wreche, For wreche is goddis champioun. *c* **1460** *Wisdom* 698 in *Macro Plays* 58 Let se: cum in, Indignacion & Sturdynes,.. Wreche, & Dyscorde expres.

β. *c* **1200** [see 1 b *β*]. *c* **1320** *Cast. Love* (H.) 1560 The eyȝhte day betokynth gret wrache. **13..** *E.E. Allit.* P. B. 204 He forȝet alle his fre þewes, & wex wod to þe wrache, for wrath at his hert. *c* **1450** *Mirk's Festial.* I. 36 And for wrach schuld falle on hymselfe yn party, þerfor [etc.]. **1535** *Trevisa's Barth. De P.R.* XVIII. xii. 315 b/1 Some [bees] for grete wrath and desyre of wrache stingethe soo depe, that [etc.].

γ. **1297** R. GLOUC. (Rolls) 1585 Þus him vel vrecche of god, vor he þe apostles slou. *c* **1330** *King of Tars* 658 Leef on hym that strengor is, For doute of more wrecche [*rimes* teche, leche]. **1387** TREVISA *Hidgen* I. 253 Anon þe pride of Romaynes,..oþer som oþer wrecche of God all myȝti falleþ vppon hem. *a* **1470** H. PARKER *Dives & Pauper* (W. de W. 1496) I. xxix. 67/2 Harde wretche was comyng but yf they wolde amende them of her falshode. *a* **1513** FABYAN *Chron.* VI. (1811) 147 Hir eyen dystylled dropes of blode,..the which, in token of Goddes wretche, in yᵗ boke remayne at this day.

b. In the phr. *to do, have, make, nim, seek,* and esp. *take wreche.* (Cf. WREAK *sb.* 1 b.)

α. *c* **1200** *Trin. Coll. Hom.* 29 Ȝef þu wreche ne secst hwanne þu time siest. *a* **1240** *Ureisun* 107 in *O.E. Hom.* I. 197 Ȝif þu heuedest wreche inumen of mine luðernesse. *c* **1275** *Duty of Christians* 56 in *O.E. Misc.* 143 Elles vre louerd god on vs wulle don wreche. **1297** R. GLOUC. (Rolls) 1334 Ichabbe of him wreche inou, wanne he bisecþ min ore. *a* **1300** in *E.E.P.* (1862) 4 Tak wrech of sinful man. **13..** *K. Horn* 1292 (Harl. MS.), Þat lond ichulle þorhreche & do mi fader wreche. **1340** *Ayenb.* 45 He heþ ynome to lite wreche. *c* **1350** *Will. Palerne* 3404 [They] þouȝt manli to make wreche here lorde to queme. *c* **1425** *Eng. Conq. Ireland* 120 Yn hope þat god shold take wrech of ham. *c* **1430** *Syr. Gener.* (Roxb.) 6396 Generides, youre lord, now besech On this mater to doo som wrech. *c* **1450** LOVELICH *Grail* xii. 244 Be war lest god wele taken wreche. *a* **1513** FABYAN *Chron.* II. (1811) 24 This Appolyn toke wreche of theim that spoyled the goddes & theyr Temples. **1529** RASTELL *Pastyme* (1811) 138 To take wrech for the cruell murder of his nevew.

β. *c* **1200** *Trin. Coll. Hom.* 51 He nam stronge wrache þerof. *c* **1325** *Chron. Eng.* 724 in Ritson *Metr. Rom.* II. 300 Hou schulde he speren eni mon Wen he of bestes wrache nom?

2. An act or instance of vengeance; = WREAK *sb.* 2.

c **1250** *Gen. & Ex.* 641 On wreche ðat sal ȝet wurðen sent, wan al ðis werld wurðe brent. *Ibid.* 2985 Ðe ðridde wreche dede aaron Bi-foren ðe king pharaon. **13..** *E.E. Allit. P.* B. 229 Fro heuen to helle þat hatel schor laste... Þis hit was a brem brest & a byge wrache. **1387** TREVISA *Higden* II. 329 Egipte was i-smyte wiþ ten grete wreches. **1398** —— *Barth. De P.R.* IX. xxi. (Tollem. MS.), God sente mo wreches upon þe Egyptians þan ten. *a* **1425** *Cursor M.* 5943 (Trin.), Fast on god þo gon þei cal To delyuer þe folke of þat wreche. *a* **1513** FABYAN *Chron.* VII. (1811) 241 By reason of a wreche done..vpon one of Kynge Wyllyams knyghtes.

3. Affliction or calamity; deep distress, misery.

c **1250** *Gen. & Ex.* 3396 Ȝet sal ðe kinde of amalech Ben al fled dun in deades wrech. **1387–8** T. USK *Test. Love* I. i. (Skeat) l. 60 Thinke on your wreche and your daunger. *a* **1400** *Leg. Rood* (1871) 138 Lord of loue..For þe was set sely sacrynge, To winne þe world þat was in wreche. *c* **1450** *Ludus Coventriæ* 327 Cryst..hath us wonnyn owt of wreche. **1460–70** *Bk. Quintessence* 19 Siþ þat deuelis be dampned, & ful of wreche of helle.

b. *to go to wreche*, to go to wrack. *rare*[−1].

13.. *Body & Soul* 242 in *Map's Poems* (Camden) 343 Thyn other thing, nou thou art ded, Al schal geynliche gon to wreche.

†**wreche**, *v. Obs. rare.* [f. prec.]

1. *trans.* To rescue or deliver; = WREAK *v.* 5 d.

c **1330** R. BRUNNE *Chron. Wace* (Rolls) 16076 Þat bischop cam, his folk to preche, Þer Cristendam fro Paen wreche [*v.r.* to reche].

2. *refl.* To avenge (oneself).

1398 TREVISA *Glanvil De P.R.* XVIII. vii. (Bodl. MS.), Þe bore..takeþ herte and strengþe to wreche hym of his adversarye wiþ his tuskes.

3. To give effect to (wrath, etc.); = WREAK *v.* 3.

c **1420** LYDG. *Ballad Commend. Our Lady* 41 Or þe wycked fend his wrath up on us wreche [*rime* leche].

Hence †'**wrecher**, an avenger (*of* some wrong).

a **1325** *Prose Psalter* viii. 3 Þat þou destruye þe enemy and þe wrecher [L. *ultorem*] of Adam sinne.

†'**wrecheful**, *a. Obs.* Also 3–4 **wrech-**; 4 **wrac(c)h-**, 5 **wreechful.** [f. WRECHE *sb.* + -FUL. Cf. WREAKFUL *a.*] Vengeful; revengeful.

c **1290** *St. Edmund* 333 in *S. Eng. Leg.* I. 309 God..nis nouȝt so wrechful ase men weneth. **1387** TREVISA *Higden* I. 377 Seyntes and halowes of þis lond beeþ more wrecheful þan seyntes of oþer londes. **1398** —— *Barth. De P.R.* XVIII. xii. (B.M. Add. MS.), No creature is more wrecheful..þan is þe bee whanne he is ywraþþed. *a* **1400** *New Test.* (Paues) 1 Thess. iv. 6 God is wrachful of alle suche men. *c* **1410** *Lantern of Light* 99 He smytiþ not to venge is owene wreechful herte but to do þe wille of God & saue his neibours soule.

wrecht, obs. Sc. form of WRIGHT *sb.*[1]

wreck (rɛk), *sb.*[1] Forms: [1–3 **wrec** (1 **werec, waerece, warec**), 2 **wrech**, 3–4 **wrek**, 3 **wreck-**, 4 **wreck**,] 3, 5–6 **wrek**, 5–7 **wrekke, wrecke**, 6– **wreck.** [a. AF. *wrec*, *wrech*, *wrek* (also *werec*, *waerec*, *warec*, whence F. *varech*, *varec* VAREC), a. ON. **wrec*, **wrek* (Norw. and Icel. *rek* n.), f. the stem of *wrekan* to drive: see WREAK *v.*, and cf. WRACK *sb.*[2] The AF. word is also the source of med.L. *wreccum*, *warectum*. The ON. variant **wreke* (Icel. *reki*) is represented in English by the obsolete WREKE. Another French form appears in VRAIC.]

I. 1. *Law.* That which is cast ashore by the sea in tidal waters; esp. goods or cargo as thrown on land by the sea from a wrecked, stranded, or foundered vessel. Occas. *wreck of the sea* (med.L. *wreccum maris*, AF. *wrec* or *wreck de mer*), †*wreck of the king* (med.L. *wrech regis*). Cf. SHIPWRECK *sb.* 1, SHIPBRECHE.

[**1077** WM. I in *Chron. Abb. Ramsey* (Rolls) 201 Bramcestre..cum omni maris ejectu quod nos *wrec* [*v.r. waerec*] nominamus. **1175–6** *Pipe Roll Hen. II* (1904) 83 Quia accepit wrech regis. **1200** K. JOHN *Charter to Dunwich* in *Rotuli Chart.* (1837) 51/2 De ewagio de wrec et lagan et de omnibus aliis consuetudinibus. *a* **1268** BRACTON *De Leg.* I. xii. (Rolls) I. 60 Item ubi non apparet dominus rei, sicut est de wrecco maris. **1292** BRITTON I. 216 Par fraunchises de aver wrek de mer trové en soen soil. **1343** in *Rymer's Fœdera* (Rolls) II. II. 1225 Wreccum maris..tam de piscibus regalibus, quam de aliis rebus quibuscumque, ad terram ibidem projectis. **1600**: see JETSAM 1.]

1228 in *Mem. Ripon* (Surtees) I. 52 Wrek, weyf, stray, merchet, lecherwyt, blodewyt. *Ibid.* 57 Wrek et weyf, stray. **1455** *Rolls of Parlt.* V. 311/2 Wrecke of the Sea, Weyves, Estrayes. **1477** *Paston Lett.* III. 211 Mastras Clere hath sen down hyr men, and with set alle the stuff and wrekke. **1482**

Rolls of Parlt. VI. 205/1 The same Duc shall have .. Wrekke of the See, Tresour founde. **1570** LAMBARDE *Peramb. Kent* (1576) 229 If a ship were cast on shoare .. and were not repaired by suche as escaped on liue within a certaine time, .. this was taken for Wreck. *Ibid.*, If from thencefoorth any one thing (being within the vessell) arriued on liue, then the ship and goods should not be seised for wrecke. **1630** *Aldeburgh Rec.* in *N. & Q.* May (1921) 427/2 Burying a man that came ashore when the Kings wreck came ashore. **1651** tr. *Kitchin's Courts Leet* (1657) 24 The Kings Prerogative, chap. 11. the King shall have Wreck of the Sea throughout the whole Realm. **1666** *N. Riding Rec.* VI. 101 A warrant against 11 Britton men for riotously taking a whale and other wrecke. **1728** CHAMBERS *Cycl.* (1738) s.v., Wreck, antiently, not only comprehended goods .. from a perishing ship, but whatever else the sea cast upon land; whether it were precious stones, fishes, .. or the like. **1765** BLACKSTONE *Comm.* I. 283 If any persons .. take any goods so cast on shore, which are not legal wreck. **1768** *Ibid.* III. 106 The court of the admiral [had] .. no manner of cognizance .. of any wreck of the sea: for that must be cast on land before it becomes a wreck. **1800** ADDISON *Amer. Law Rep.* 63 *Wreck*, in its legal signification, is confined to such goods as, after shipwreck at sea, are by the sea cast upon the land. **1822** *Act 1–2 Geo. IV*, c. 75 §26 That no .. person who may be entitled .. to Wreck of the Sea .. shall be entitled to appropriate such Wreck or Goods .. until he [etc.]. **1866** *Daily Tel.* 3 Nov., The more scrupulous deliver up their spoil to the receiver of wreck. **1888** J. WILLIAMS in *Encycl. Brit.* XXIV. 687/1 As wreck in the last resort became crown property, it was never subject to forfeiture. *Ibid.*, Wreck was frequently granted to subjects as a franchise.

2. a. = WRACK *sb.*[2] 3, SEA-WRACK 2 a, VAREC 1. Latterly *Sc.* and *north. dial.*

Cf. *tangle-wreck* TANGLE *sb.*[1] 3, *sea-wreck* s.v. SEA-WRACK. **1499** *Promp. Parv.* (Pynson) s v b, Wrek of the see, *alga, norga.* **1500** *Ortus Vocab.* B iij, *Alga, .. herba marina*, i.e. *illud quod mare projicit*, wrekke or frothe of the see. **1634–5** BRERETON *Trav.* (Chetham Soc.) 97 The grass, weeds and wreck, brought by the sea .. and left upon the sands. **1728** CHAMBERS *Cycl.* (1738) s.v., Wreck .. in some places .. is used to manure the ground. **1752** in *Scots Mag.* (1753) July 335/2 He was then employed in gathering wreck. **1791** *Statist. Acc. Scotl.* I. 113 The shores [of Ayrshire] abound with .. rich sea-weed or wreck for manure. **1806** FORSYTH *Beauties Scotl.* III. 351 Sea-ware .. driven upon the shore by the tides .. is commonly called *blown wreck.* **1876** in *Cleveland Gloss.* Suppl. **1894** K. HEWAT *Little Scottish World* vii. 112 The 'Wreck Brethren' .. annually .. raised funds for their purposes and regulated the carting of the wreck.

b. = WRACK *sb.*[2] 3 b. Now *dial.*

c **1440** *Promp. Parv.* 533/2 Wrek, of a dyke, or a fenne, or stondynge watyr, *ulva.* **1742** *N. Riding Rec.* VIII. 242 The Treasurer to pay £1 for clearing away the wreck from How and Kirby Misperton Bridges. **1851** MAYNE REID *Scalp Hunt.* II. 298 Our faces were concealed by the 'wreck' that covered the stones. **1877–86** in Lincoln and Chesh. glossaries. **1884** G. S. STREATFIELD *Lincoln. & Danes* 376 Wreck, weeds and other rubbish floating down streams or on ditch water.

c. *Sc.* and *dial.* = WRACK *sb.*[2] 3 c.

1743 R. MAXWELL *Sel. Trans. Soc. Improv. Agric. Scot.* 11 Cause pull up and gather carefully the Wreck, or Roots of Weeds and Grass, into Heaps. **1787** W. H. MARSHALL *Norfolk* II. 392 *Wreck*, dead undigested roots and stems of grasses and weeds in plowland. **1801** *Farmer's Mag.* Jan. 59 A field .. where dung was applied amid mountains of wreck, or couch grass.

3. a. A vessel broken, ruined, or totally disabled by being driven on rocks, cast ashore, or stranded; a wrecked or helpless ship; the ruins or hulk of such. Occas. also ***wreck of a ship.***

[*c* **1290** *Fleta* I. xliv. (1647) 61 Item dicitur wreckum navis vel batellus fractus, de quibus nihil vivum evaserit.] ? *a* **1500** *Chaucer's Man of Law's T.* 415 Wks. (1532) 24 b, The constable of the castel downe is fare To seen this wrecke, & al the shyp he sought. **1611** COTGR., *Vuaresque*, a wrecke, or ship cast away. **1652** HEYLIN *Cosmogr.* I. 67 Charybdis is a Gulf .. which violently attracting all Vessells that come too nigh it, devoureth them, and casteth up their wrecks. **1698** FRYER *Acc. E. India & P.* 80 He shall restore whatever Wrecks may happen on his Coasts. **1719** DE FOE *Crusoe* I. (Globe) 189, I could plainly see .. the Wreck of a Ship cast away in the Night. **1743** BULKELEY & CUMMINS *Voy. S. Seas* 14 The Ship is a perfect Wreck. **1762** FALCONER *Shipwr.* III. 669 Three .. from the wreck on oars and rafts descend. **1805** J. TURNBULL *Voy. World* (1813) 391 The ship .. struck upon a reef of rocks .., and shortly became a total wreck. **1812** J. WILSON *Isle of Palms* I. 32 Fast the miserable Ship Becomes a lifeless wreck. **1865** H. KINGSLEY *Hillyars & Burtons* lxxix, The wreck of a little coasting craft still lay about two hundred yards to sea.

fig. and in fig. context. **1781** COWPER *Retirem.* 386 To the fair haven of my native home, The wreck of what I was, fatigu'd, I come. **1796** BURKE *Corr.* (1844) IV. 350 Such is the person you come to see, or rather the wreck of what was never a first-rate vessel. **1883** S. C. HALL *Retrospect* I. 322 All of manhood in him .. had given way and left him a stranded wreck. **1885** TENNYSON *The Wreck* 5 My life itself is a wreck, .. I am flung from the rushing tide of the world as a waif of shame.

b. An unserviceable or crazy old vessel.

1896 *Westm. Gaz.* 5 Dec. 5/1 There are too many of these old wrecks [= barges] on the river.

4. a. *Law.* A piece or article of wreckage; a fragment of a wrecked vessel or its cargo. Freq. *pl.*

1570 in Boys *Sandwich* (1792) 775 Wrecks and fyndalls floating, and the half of all wrecks and fyndalls jottsome. **1577** HOLINSHED *Chron.* II. 489/2 [Richard I] pardoned al wreckes by sea .., releasing for euer al his right to the same. **1579** [RASTELL] *Termes Lawes* 187 b, The Lorde shall haue that as a wreck of y[e] sea. **1652** NEEDHAM *Selden's Mare Cl.* I. xxv. (1663) 167 The Question is, whether the Goods bee .. called Spoils or Wrecks. **1729** JACOB *Law Dict.* s.v. *Lagan*, [If] these Goods .. are cast away upon the Land, they are then a Wreck. *Ibid.* s.v., It was usual to seise and forfeit Wrecks to the King, only when no Owner could be found. **1768** [see 1].

b. Without article. = WRECKAGE 2.

1744 *Gentl. Mag.* 616/2 Several chests, broken masts, and other pieces of wreck floating in the sea. **1796** CHARLOTTE SMITH *Narr. Loss Transports* 34 The Chissel-bank .. was strewn .. with pieces of wreck, and piles of plundered goods. **1815** *Ann. Reg., Chron.* 42 Six men reached the shore .. upon planks, being much bruised by the surf and wreck. **1833** REDDING *Shipwrecks* I. 194 All the crew believed the ship was crushed to pieces, but no wreck floated up. **1865** SWINBURNE *Felise* 80 [Such things] As the sea feeds on, wreck and stray and castaway.

5. A drifted or tossed-up mass; a large heap; a great quantity; an abundance. Now *north. dial.*

1612 DRAYTON *Poly-olb.* II. 34 Where Chesill lifts Her ridged snake-like sands, in wrecks and smouldring drifts. **1683** G. M[ERITON] *Yorks. Dial.* 15 There's sike a wreck, it [*sc.* corn] liggs all down o'th Land. **1846** BROCKETT *N.C. Words* (ed. 3), *Wreck*, a great quantity .. as a confused heap. **1876** *Whitby Gloss.* 224/1, I saw wrecks on 't.

6. a. That which remains *of* something that has suffered ruin, demolishment, waste, etc.; the dilapidated, disorganized, or disordered residue or remainder *of* anything. Also (*a*) with *a* and pl.

(*a*) **1713** ADDISON *Cato* V. i, But thou shalt flourish .. Unhurt amidst .. The Wrecks of Matter, and the Crush of Worlds. **1756** MRS. CALDERWOOD in *Coltness Collect.* (Maitl. Cl.) 250 His friends .. got him, out of the wrecks of his estate, betwixt L. 30 or L. 40 *per annum.* **1780** *Westm. Mag.* 371 He continued obstinate and mad, going .. over the wrecks of the house. **1821** SHELLEY *Epipsych.* 493 An envy of the isles, a pleasure-house .., It scarce seems now a wreck of human art. **1888** BRYCE *Amer. Commw.* II. lv. 335 The Republican party was formed .. out of the wrecks of the Whig party.

(*b*) **1743** R. BLAIR *Grave* 30 Names once famed, now dubious or forgot, And buried 'midst the wreck of things which were. **1751** SMOLLETT *Per. Pic.* ix, From the wreck of the hammock [she] made an occasional bed for herself on the floor. **1794** MRS. RADCLIFFE *Myst. Udolpho* xxviii, Assisted with suggestions which they had since executed with the wreck of their fortunes. **1804** W. L. BOWLES *Spir. Discov.* III. 46 My destined voyage, by the shores Of Asia, and the wreck of cities old. **1840** ARNOLD *Hist. Rome* II. xxxi. 255 There he was joined by the wreck of the consul's army. **1854** R. S. SURTEES *Handley Cr.* lxxvi, As Mamma surveyed the wreck of luncheon.

transf. and *fig.* **1791** BURNS *Song of Death* iii, Thou strik'st the dull peasant—he sinks in the dark, Nor saves e'en the wreck of a name. **1813** SHELLEY *Q. Mab* v. 109 He sheds A passing tear perchance upon the wreck Of earthly peace.

b. The broken-down, debilitated, or emaciated form *of* a person. (Cf. 7 b.)

1820 W. IRVING *Sketch Bk.* I. 225 It was, indeed, the wreck of her once noble lad. **1836** LYTTON *Duchess de La Vallière* v. iii, These wrecks of man Worn to decay. **1893** SELOUS *Trav. S.E. Africa* 62 All the Portuguese here were mere wrecks of men—frail, yellow, and fever-stricken.

7. a. That which is in a state of ruin; anything that is broken down or has undergone wrecking, shattering, or dilapidation.

1814 SOUTHEY *Roderick* XVI. 62 Amid heaps Of mountain wreck, on either side thrown high, .. The tortuous channel wound. **1816** SCOTT *Antiq.* iii, This wreck of ancient books and utensils. **1842** MACAULAY *Horatius* lv, Like a dam, the mighty wreck [*sc.* of a bridge] Lay right athwart the stream. **1855** KINGSLEY *Westw. Ho!* xx, Alas! a crack, a flap, a rattle, .. and all forward was a mass of dangling wreck. **1889** MRS. E. KENNARD *Landing a Prize* i. (1891) 4 What was left of the wreck had to be given up to creditors.

fig. **1849** ROBERTSON *Serm.* Ser. I. viii. (1866) 145 The life-hopes have become a wreck.

b. A person of undermined, shattered, or ruined constitution; one who is debilitated by ill-health, hardship, etc. (Cf. 6 b.)

1795–6 WORDSW. *Borderers* I. 336 *Osw.* But how fare you? *Her.* Well as the wreck I am permits. **1828** LYTTON *Pelham* I. xxxi, 'Yes,' continued the venerable wreck, after a short pause. **1857** MRS. CARLYLE *Lett.* (1883) II. 335 It is easy to see you have suffered! an entire wreck, like myself. **1899** E. W. HORNUNG *Dead Men* xii, I was slowly dying of insomnia. I was a nervous wreck. **1901** W. R. H. TROWBRIDGE *Lett. of her Mother to Eliz.* xxxi. 154, I think I am in for influenza. I feel a perfect wreck.

8. [By misapprehension.] = WRACK *sb.*[1] 5 b.

1787–9 WORDSW. *Evening Walk* 306 No wreck of all the pageantry remains. **1813** SHELLEY *Q. Mab* IX. 130 These ruins soon left not a wreck behind. **1835** I. TAYLOR *Spir. Despot.* v. 185 Other systems have .. been swept away, leaving hardly a wreck behind.

II. 9. a. The disabling or destruction of a vessel by any disaster or accident of navigation; loss of a ship by striking on a rock, stranding, or foundering; an instance of this; = SHIPWRECK *sb.* 2. ***to make wreck***: cf. MAKE *v.*[1] 64.

1463–4 *Rolls of Parlt.* V. 507/1 Yf eny of the forseid Wares or Chaffares .. come into this Reame or Wales by wey of wrek. **1477** *Paston Lett.* III. 211 There is a grete chyppe go to wrekke be for Wynterton. **1568** GRAFTON *Chron.* I. 4 This Arke .. by diuine prouidence .. was gouerned from running to wreck. **1577** HOLINSHED *Chron.* II. 490/1 That euery person makyng wrecke by sea, and comming aliue to lande, shoulde haue all his goodes free. **1590** SPENSER *F.Q.* II. x. 6 Learning his ship from those white rocks to saue, .. Threatning vnheedie wrecke and rash decay. **1607** COWELL *Interpr.* s.v. *Flotsen*, Jetson is a thing cast out of the shippe being in danger of wrecke. **1672** DRYDEN *2nd Pt. Conq. Granada* III. 107 As Seamen, parting in a gen'ral wreck, When first the loosening planks begin to crack, Each catches one. **1749** *Gentl. Mag.* 396/1 The ill behaviour of his crew, and the bad condition of the ship occasioned its wreck. **1795** BURNS *O Mally's meek* iii, Her two eyes .. Would keep a sinking ship frae wreck. **1809** R. WARNER *Tour Cornwall* 158 A range of rocks, the terrible scene of many a disastrous wreck. **1845** C. WILKES *Narr. U.S. Explor. Exped.* II. 91 In leaving the harbour we had a narrow escape from wreck. **1888** F. HUME *Mme. Midas* I. Prol., We are .. shipwrecked sailors; and I will tell the story of the wreck.

fig. and in fig. context. **1564** BULLEIN *Dial. agst. Pest* (1888) 93 The ship of fooles .. wanteth a good Pilot, the storme, the rocke, and the wrecke at hand. **1770** COWPER *Let.* 25 Sept., The storm of sixty-three made a wreck of the friendships I had contracted.

b. *Stock Exchange.* (See first quot.)

1876 'E. PINTO' *Ye outside Fools!* 360 A *Corner, Pool, Clique, Ring* are all terms equivalent to a *Rig* or *Wreck. Ibid.* 408 The seductive interest of Rigs and Wrecks.

c. *N. Amer.* A road or railway accident.

1912 J. SANDILANDS *Western Canad. Dict. & Phrase-Bk.*, *Wreck*, the word to apply to a railway accident; or, more correctly, train wreck. **1974** *Evening Herald* (Rock Hill, S. Carolina) 19 Apr. 11/4 In spite of the reduction in accidents, the sergeant said, 'We still have too many wrecks.' **1979** N. MAILER *Executioner's Song* (1980) I. xviii. 304 On the drive back to Springville, she was dreaming away and got in a wreck. Nobody was hurt but the car.

d. The death of a large number of pelagic birds, usually as the result of a storm.

1936 *Brit. Birds* XXIX. 327 In January, 1915, there was a great oil 'wreck' of Scoters. **1971** *New Scientist* 8 Apr. 69/1 There have been similar wrecks in the past, and the report mentions 11 for guillemots and the auks in the last century.

10. a. The action of subverting or overthrowing an established order of things, etc.; the fact of being brought to disaster; downfall, overthrow, ruin.

1577 HANMER *Anc. Eccl. Hist.* 494 He came into Mesopotamia, not without plaine daunger and wrecke to the state. **1594** SPENSER *Amoretti* xxv, Then all the woes and wrecks which I abide, as meanes of blisse I gladly wil embrace. **1608** *Great Frost* ad fin., Being .. thus round beset with the horrors of so present a wreck, he fell down on his knees. **1763** J. BROWN *Poetry & Music* v. 78 The most celebrated bards of ancient Greece, whose songs have perished in the wreck of time. **1775** SHERIDAN *Rivals* III. iii, Proud of calamity, we will enjoy the wreck of wealth. **1838** PRESCOTT *Ferd. & Is.* Introd. (1846) I. 23 The wreck of their ancient liberties. **1839** TALFOURD *Glencoe* I. i, You come To share the wreck of the Macdonalds. **1885** J. PAYN *Talk of Town* I. 182 It was not that she feared to risk the wreck of her own happiness.

fig. **1793** BURNS '*Where are the joys*' iv, A' that has caused this wreck in my bosom, Is Jenny.

b. The action of wrecking or breaking apart; the fact of being materially wrecked or ruined; destruction or demolition.

1711 ADDISON *Spect.* No. 166 ¶2 Books, which .. may last as long as the Sun and Moon, and perish only in the general Wreck of Nature. **1774** GOLDSM. *Nat. Hist.* (1776) I. 25 The manner in which he relieves the earth from this universal wreck. **1839** MURCHISON *Silur. Syst.* I. xxix. 376 In accounting for these extraordinary accumulations of broken coal we may undoubtedly refer their origin to the wreck of the regular seams. **1864** LOWELL *Fireside Trav.* 31 Dealing thunderous wreck to the two hostile vessels. **1886** J. BARROWMAN *Sc. Mining Terms* 73 *Wreck*, a break-down, as in a shaft or on an incline.

c. In the phr. ***to go to wreck (and ruin).***

a **1547** SURREY *Æneid* II. 542 Our fained shields and wepons then they found, And .. our discording voice they knew. We went to wreck, with nomber ouerlayd. **1548** UDALL, etc. *Erasm. Par. Mark* v. 11–17 The flocke goeth to wrecke and vtterly perisheth. **1600** HOLLAND *Livy* 676 All things els about him went to wreck. **1721** DE FOE *Mem. Cavalier* (1840) 65, I saw our men go to wreck. **1789** BURNS *Elegy on Year 1788* 4 A Towmont, sirs, is gane to wreck! ? **1834** DE QUINCEY *Autob. Sk.* Wks. 1858 I. 126 To wreck goes every notion or feeling that divides .. the brave man from the brave. **1877** BLACK *Green Past.* i, The whole estate is going to wreck and ruin. **1883** STEVENSON *Treas. Isl.* xxviii, Here you are in a bad way: ship lost, .. your whole business gone to wreck.

ellipt. **1782** BURNS '*No Churchman am I*' v, A letter inform'd me that all was to wreck.

III. 11. a. *attrib.* and *Comb.*, as ***wreck buoy, case, chart, flag***; objective and instrumental, as ***wreck-finder, raiser, -seeker***; †***wreck-fishing, -raising, -threatening***; also ***wreck-devoted, -strewn.***

1874 BEDFORD *Sailor's Pocket-bk.* v. 109 *Wreck buoys are painted green. **1892** MARSDEN *Sel. Pleas* p. lxiv, In 1377 a *wreck case was tried before justices. **1862** *Catal. Internat. Exhib., Brit.* No. 2747, Large *wreck chart of the British Isles for 1861. **1819** SHELLEY *Cenci* V. iv. 42 A *wreck-devoted seaman thus might pray To the deaf sea. **1902** *Daily Chron.* 29 Oct. 7/1 (citing *N.Y. Tribune*), The wreck of a coal barge was first located... Two boats, termed '*wreck-finders', then .. by means of derricks or suction pumps raise the coal to the surface. **1674** TEMPLE *Let.* Wks. 1720 II. 310 This Invention of *Wreck-fishing [by Sir Edmund Curtis], for the Recovery of His Majesty's Tin, cast away before Ostend. **1897** *Daily News* 15 Sept. 8/4 The Thames Conservancy have hoisted their green '*wreck flag', warning all craft to steer clear of the debris. **1881** *Instr. Census Clerks* (1885) 36 Wharfinger, Wharf Agent, .. *Wreck Raiser. **1898** *Westm. Gaz.* 14 July 5/2 The *wreck-raising vessels that are to make an attempt to save some of Admiral Cervera's unfortunate squadron. **1843** CAPT. MARRYAT *M. Violet* xxviii, The unconscientious *wreck-seeker of a captain. **1821** SHELLEY *The Fugitives* 21 The Earth is like Ocean, *Wreck-strewn and in motion. **1757** DYER *Fleece* IV. 620 Inaccessible *Wreck-threatening Staten Land's o'erhanging shore.

b. Attrib. in names of persons having, or appointed to take, charge of wreck or wreckage, as **wreck commissioner, -master.**

1846 WORCESTER (citing *Lee*), *Wreck-Master*, a master of a wreck. *a* **1868** in Grant *Rep. Wrecking Bahamas* 77 The first-licensed wreck-master boarding a vessel wrecked, stranded, or in distress .. shall .. become the master of all wreckers employed on such vessel, and shall be styled the '*wreck-master'. **1876** *Act 39–40 Vict.* c. 80 §29 It shall be the duty of a wreck commissioner..to hold any formal investigation into a loss. **1891** *Cent. Dict.* s.v., *Receivers of wrecks* (in Great Britain), *wreck-masters* (in New York and Texas), officers whose duty [etc.]. **1898** *Engineering Mag.* XVI. 70 Instructions for the handling of explosives..should be placed in the hands of the railroad staff, including wreckmasters.

c. Special Combs., as **wreck-fish**, the stone-bass; † **wreck-goods** *Sc.*, goods cast ashore from a wreck; † **wreck-make**, *poet.* that which causes wrecks; **wreck-ware** *Sc.*, **-weed**, = sense 2; **wreck-wood**, wood washed up or ashore from a wreck; also *attrib.*; **wreck-works**, salvage-works for raising a wreck or wrecks.

1880 DAY *Fishes Gt. Brit.* I. 18 This fish..is called in Devonshire, *Wreck fish, because it follows floating timbers. **1883** *Fisheries Exhib. Catal.* 270 Special Line, furnished with all accessories, used in fishing for Stone Bass or Wreck-fish. **1693** STAIR *Instit.* (ed. 2) Alph. Index K 2, *Wreck-goods..become Escheat as Publick. **1765–8** ERSKINE *Inst. Law Scot.* II. i. §13 Wreck-goods..were not claimed as escheat, but secured for the owners. **1582** STANYHURST *Æneis* III. (Arb.) 88 And Caulons castels we doe spy, with Scylla the *wreckmake. **1865** WAY *Promp. Parv.* 533 *note*, On the coasts of Scotland sea-weed is called '*wreck-ware'. **1821** SCOTT *Pirate* x, One whom the sea flung forth as *wreck-weed. *Ibid.* v, The *wreck-wood that the callants brought in yesterday. **1843** *Times* 25 July 3/2 The mast is still standing, and very little wreck-wood has driven from her. **1895** QUILLER COUCH *Wandering Heath* 5 The rain drove..aslant like threads of gold silk in the shine of the wreckwood fire. **1903** E. CHILDERS *Riddle of Sands* xx, The *wreck-works were evidently what they purported to be.

† **wreck**, *sb.*[2] *Sc. Obs.* [var. of WRACK *sb.*[3], after prec.] 'Pelf'; 'dross'; = WRACK *sb.*[3] 1 b.

1562 WIN3ET *Cert. Tractatis* Wks. (S.T.S.) I. 8 Hauand regarde to the wrek of this warld or lustis of thair bodyis. *a* **1568** BLYTH in *Bannatyne MS.* (Hunt. Club) 321/11 Ane wreche sall haif no mair, Bot ane schort scheit at heid and feit, For all his wrek and wair.

† **wreck**, *sb.*[3] *Obs. rare.* [Alteration of WREAK *sb.*: cf. WRECK *v.*[2]] Vengeance; revenge.

1591 *Legh's Armory* 96 b, His irefull heart straight braided out wrothfull wordes of wreeke [**1562** wreke] and reuenge. **1596** SPENSER *F.Q.* IV. vi. 16 Ah cruell hand, and..hart That workst such wrecke on her.

wreck, obs. erron. var. RACK *sb.*[1] 3.

1707 E. SMITH *Phædra & Hipp.* III. 30 Why did you raise me to the heighth of Joy, Above the wreck of Clouds and Storms below?

wreck, var. RECK *sb.*[2] (= RACK *sb.*[2] 5 d).

1674 RAY *Coll. Words, Smelting Tin* 122 The head tin passes to the *wreck*, where they work it with a wooden rake in Vessels. **1800** MISS EDGEWORTH *Lame Jervas* ii, I had new models made of the sieves for lueing, the box and trough, the buddle, wreck, and tool.

wreck (rɛk), *v.*[1] Also 5–6 **wrek-**. [f. WRECK *sb.*[1] Cf. med.L. *wrecare* (12th cent.).]

In various senses common only in passive use.

† **1.** *trans.* To cast on shore. *Obs.*

c **1420** *Sir Amadas* (W.) 475 Folke fordryvon in the schores,..Brone stedes,..All maner of ryches,..Wrekkyd with the water lay. [= xliv. (Camden), He fond wrekun a-mung the stones Kny3tes in meneuere.] *a* **1440** *Sir Eglam.* 894 He say that lady whyte as flowre, Was wrekyd on the sonde. *a* **1509** in *Rep. Hist. MSS. Comm.* Var. Coll. (1907) IV. 87 [Seizing them] as goodes wrekked, which neither can ne may soo bee taken as long as the veray owners thereof be certainly knowen. **1596** SPENSER *F.Q.* v. iv. 5 A Coffer strong,..seeming to haue suffred mickle wrong by being wreckt vppon the sands. **1729** JACOB *Law Dict.* s.v., If Goods wreck'd are seised by Persons having no Authority. **1821** *Act 1–2 Geo. IV*, c. 75 §26 That Part of the Coast where the same [goods] shall have been stranded, wrecked or found.

2. To cause the wreck of (a vessel); to wreck (a ship); = SHIPWRECK *v.* 1 b. Chiefly *passive.* Also *fig.* and in fig. context.

1570 LAMBARDE *Peramb. Kent.* (1576) 228 A shippe laden with the Kings owne goods was wrecked within the precinct of this libertie. **1590** SPENSER *F.Q.* II. xii. 7 The ribs of vessels broke, And shiuered ships, which had bene wrecked late. **1732** *Gentl. Mag.* 976 A great Number of Ships were wrecked..by stormy Weather. **1774** GOLDSM. *Nat. Hist.* (1776) VI. 395 Brought into the European seas, in some India ship that might be wrecked upon her return. **1845** J. C. MANGAN *German Anthol.* II. 100 The shallop of my peace is wrecked on Beauty's shore. **1846** MRS. A. MARSH *Father Darcy* II. ii. 60 So bravely as we have struggled against the overwhelming waters! The vessel is finally wrecked! **1865** H. KINGSLEY *Hillyars & Burtons* lxxvii, If the *Wainoora* has sailed,..she is wrecked somewhere on the coast.

refl. **1864** TENNYSON *Aylmer's F.* 716 This frail bark of ours, when sorely tried, May wreck itself without the pilot's guilt.

b. To make or cause (a person) to suffer or undergo shipwreck; to involve in wreck; also, to cause the loss of (goods or cargo) by shipwreck; = SHIPWRECK *v.* 1. Chiefly *passive.*

1617 MORYSON *Itin.* II. 8 The..Spaniards, last yeere wrecked on the Coasts of Connaght,..had left..great store of treasure. **1796** CHARLOTTE SMITH *Narr. Loss Transports* 14 A young Gentleman,..wrecked himself, and wandering along the unhospitable shore. **1836** MARRYAT *Midsh. Easy* xx, We were wrecked in our boat last night. **1877** TENNYSON *Harold* II. i, Thy villains with their lying lights have wreck'd us! **1903** S. E. WHITE *Forest* vii, A big roller rips along your gunwale [of a canoe]. You are wrecked.

fig. **1821** SHELLEY *Epipsych.* 148 The rocks on which high hearts are wrecked. **1845** BAILEY *Festus* (ed. 2) 323 Bound to earth, Wrecked in the deeps of Heaven, in Death's expiring birth! **1880** W. H. D. ADAMS *Wrecked Lives* Ser. I. p. vi, If he would not wreck his life amid the rocks and quicksands of worldly lusts.

absol. **1881** H. D. RAWNSLEY *Sonn. Eng. Lakes* 115 So may it be when storms my life shall strand On treacherous shoal, ..May..waves that wrecked reach out a pitying hand To gulf my sorrow.

c. *transf.* (See quot.)

1617 MORYSON *Itin.* III. 144 There be some quicksands, wherein footemen are in danger to be wrecked.

3. To cause or bring about the ruin or destruction of (a structure, etc.) as by violence or misuse; to reduce to a ruinous condition in this way; to shatter, ruin, destroy.

1510 in Leadam *Star Chamber Cases* (Selden) II. 70 [He] maketh Fysch garthes & weeres..by reason wherof the seid porte is so wrekked & shallowed, that [etc.]. **1594** SPENSER *Amoretti* lvi, That tree..am I, whom ye do wreck, do ruine, and destroy. **1821** SHELLEY *Epipsych.* 370 Thou too, O Comet.., Who drew the heart of this frail Universe Towards thine own; till, wrecked in that convulsion,.. Thine went astray. **1865** *Pall Mall G.* 14 July 9/2 The mob ..commenced 'wrecking' Conservative houses, stoning one sick old gentleman as he lay in his bed. **1878** BROWNING *La Saisiaz* 34 The everyway external stream..leaves it [*sc.* a rush]..wrecked at last. **1899** *Allbutt's Syst. Med.* VII. 123 The joint is found to be completely wrecked.

transf. **1878** BROWNING *Poets Croisic* xli, How now? My Duke's crown wrecked?

b. To cause or bring about the subversion or overthrow of (some condition or order of things); to shatter, ruin.

1749 SMOLLETT *Regicide* I. vi, O recal Those flatt'ring arts thy own deceit employ'd To wreck my peace! **1791** BURNS *Fair Eliza* ii, Can'st thou wreck his peace for ever? **1826** in *Sheridaniana* 334 Their want of tact and judgment has wrecked the party. **1858** CARLYLE *Fredk. Gt.* VII. iv, Do not wreck, upon trifles, a noble interest we have in common. **1883** SIR C. S. C. BOWEN in *Law Times Rep.* XLIX. 251/2 We hear of abuse of different kinds of process..which amounts to wrecking credit. **1884** *St. James's Gaz.* 11 Jan. 6/1 His Administration was very nearly wrecked at the outset.

c. To frustrate or thwart; to prevent the passing of (a measure, etc.).

1855 MOTLEY *Dutch Rep.* v. v, Every fresh attempt at an amicable compromise was wrecked upon the obstinate bigotry of the leading civic authorities. **1901** *Scotsman* 28 Feb. 7/2 The measure will, it is pretty certain, be wrecked before it gets out of committee.

4. To bring (a person) to ruin or disaster; to subvert, ruin. Also *refl.*

1590 SPENSER *F.Q.* III. ix. 4 All his mind is set on mucky pelfe, To hoord vp heapes of evill gotten masse, For which he others wrongs, and wreckes himselfe. **1594** [see 3]. **1644** *Raleigh's Remains* 48 If he resolve..to wreck him, and to have his life. **1732** POPE *Ess. Man* I. 254 Let ruling Angels from their spheres be hurl'd, Being on Being wreck'd, and world on world. **1782** WOLCOT (P. Pindar) *Ode R.A.'s* iii. Wks. 1812 I. 20 Despising Pride, whose wish it is to wreck 'em.

b. To shatter (a person's health, constitution, or nerves) by sickness, hardship, or the like; to destroy the quality or tone of. Usu. in *passive.*

1850 ROBERTSON *Serm.* Ser. III. (1857) 125 The drunkard ..discovers that he is unexpectedly degraded, his health wrecked. **1897** KIPLING *Capt. Cour.* 213, I wonder your nervous system isn't completely wrecked.

5. *intr.* **a.** To suffer or undergo shipwreck; = SHIPWRECK *v.* 2. Also *fig.* and in fig. context.

1671 MILTON *P.R.* II. 228 Honour, glory, and popular praise; Rocks whereon greatest men have oftest wreck'd. **1671** —— *Samson* 1044 What Pilot so expert but needs must wreck Embarqu'd with such a Stears-mate at the Helm? **1729** BERKELEY *Lett.* Wks. 1871 IV. 161 My letters were in one of the vessels that wreck'd. **1860** MRS. C. CLIVE *Why Paul Ferroll* iv, With all her early impressions wrecking around her, she did not know to what to cling. **1864** LOWELL *Fireside Trav.* 172 The *montagna bruna* on which Ulysses wrecked. **1884** TENNYSON *Becket* II. ii, Holy Church May rock, but will not wreck, nor our Archbishop Stagger on the slope decks for any rough sea.

b. To break down in health.

1876 R. BRIDGES *Growth of Love* xiv, What is this wreck of all he hath in fief, When he that hath is wrecking?

6. a. To cause damage by washing *up.*

1634 *Rotherham* (Yorks.) *Feoffees Accounts* (MS.), P[ai]d to Tho. Sandall..for paveing at the bridge where the water had wreckt up.

b. To silt *up*, as with tide-driven sand, etc.

1786 in *Trans. Soc. Arts* (1789) VII. 56 By a gradual, continual loss of out-fall amongst the sands, and by the sluice on the marsh and other parts wrecking up.

7. To seize or collect wreck or wreckage; to search *for* wreck. Also *transf.*

1843 *Times* 28 Mar. 7/1 The news of the wreck spread rapidly.., and in the evening a large mob assembled with a view of 'wrecking'. **1897** *Westm. Gaz.* 2 Oct. 3/1 [Your job,] perhaps, is to go 'wrecking' for firewood. Down upon the rocks the friendly tide casts many a spar and log.

† **wreck** (rɛk), *v.*[2] *Obs.* Also 6–7 **wrecke**, 6–7, 9 **reck**, 7 **recke**. [Late variant of WREAK *v.*; the exact reason for the shortening of the vowel is not clear, but cf. dial. *breck* for BREAK *v.*]

1. *trans.* = WREAK *v.* 5, 5 b. Chiefly *refl.*

1570 LEVINS *Manip.* 54 To Wreck, *vindicare.* **1583** BABINGTON *Commandm.* (1590) 331 Any larger commission granted to vs to wreck our selues vpon our brethren. **1612** T. TAYLOR *Comm. Titus* i. 10 The minde and intention of the Apostle here..was not..to wrecke himselfe vpon them. **1622** P. HANNAY *Philomela* lxxxiv, The world shall know I was not slow To wreck a wronged maid. **1670** MILTON *Hist. Eng.* VI. Wks. 1851 V. 242 They wreck'd themselves on the Countries roundabout, wasting..all Essex, Kent, and Sussex.

2. = WREAK *v.* 3.

1658 *Whole Duty Man* xv. §31 It is a kind desire of his amendment (and not a willingness to wreck his own rage) which [etc.]. **1672** MARVELL *Reh. Transp.* I. 11 Being ready at once to asswage his Concupiscence, and wreck his Malice. **1681** *Character Ill-Court-Favourite* 5 These Insufferable Grandees, who reck their Private Spleens.

b. With preps., as *on, upon, against* (a person, etc.); = WREAK *v.* 3 b. Also with *out.*

1577 GRANGE *Golden Aphrod.*, etc. Q ij b, She sought on me to wrecke hir spight. **1583** GREENE *Mamillia* II. Wks. (Grosart) II. 151 With what greater plague..can..the vniust gods..wreck their wrath and extreme rigour vppon any man. **1613** PURCHAS *Pilgrimage* (1614) 25 That malice.. which he could not there so easily wrecke on their Creator. **1649** MILTON *Eikon.* xxvi, To wreck his spleen, or ease his mind upon the Parlament. **1702** ROWE *Tamerl.* IV. i, Give him Pow'r to wreck his Hatred Upon his greatest Foe? **1712** ADDISON *Spect.* No. 439 ¶3 [They] often wreck their particular Spite or Malice against the person whom they are set to watch. **1777** WATSON *Philip II*, I. 191 The king..was determined to wreck his resentment on all concerned. **1793** R. GRAY *Poems* 25 Some in the fray wreckt out his spleen On some sly pate or sawney.

3. = WREAK *v.* 6, 7.

1593 MARLOWE *Edw. II*, IV. iv, For the open wronges and iniuries Edward hath done to vs,..We come in armes to wrecke it with the swords. **1596** SPENSER *F.Q.* v. iv. 24 He Talus sent To wrecke on them their follies hardyment. **1667** MILTON *P.L.* IV. 11 Satan..came down..To wrecke on innocent frail man his loss Of that first Battel.

4. = WREAK *v.* 8.

1764 GOLDSM. *Hist. Eng. in Lett.* (1772) II. 231 There was no object on whom to wreck their vengeance. *a* **1790** HENRY *Britain* (1793) VI. 419 They not only wrecked their vengeance on the living, but on the ashes of dead heretics.

wreck, obs. erron. var. RACK *v.*[3] 2 c.

1776 G. SEMPLE *Building in Water* 101 Splicing the long Sides of the Belts, so as they may not wreck in dropping them down. [Cf. WRECKING.]

wreck, obs. erron. form of RECK *v.*

wreckage ('rɛkɪdʒ). [f. WRECK *v.*[1] + -AGE 3.]

1. The action or process of wrecking; the fact of being wrecked. Also *fig.*

1837 CARLYLE *Fr. Rev.* II. v. ii, Wreckage and dissolution are the appointed issue for both [*sc.* wisdom and folly]. **1890** GASQUET & BISHOP *Edw. VI & Bk. Com. Prayer* 272 A lively picture of the wreckage of ecclesiastical structures at that time [1548–9]. **1899** MACKAIL *Life Morris* II. 291 There had been much wreckage of unverified beliefs and extravagant hopes.

2. Fragments or remains of a shattered or wrecked vessel; wreck.

1846 WORCESTER (citing *Times*). **1867** *Morn. Star* 4 Feb., A large quantity of timber, ship's spars, &c...The wreckage appeared to be that of a large ship. **1885** T. P. BATTERSBY *Elf Island* 36 The deck was..covered with wreckage. **1899** DOYLE *Duet* (1909) 119/2 Some of the wreckage from those vanished vessels.

attrib. **1898** MEREDITH *Odes Fr. Hist.* 23 His wreckage-spars, His harried ships.

b. *pl.* Pieces or fragments of wreck. *rare.*

1864 CARLYLE *Fredk. Gt.* XVII. vii, A bolt shot into the storm-tost Sea and its wreckages.

3. Material of or from a wrecked or shattered structure; a ruined fabric, building, etc.

1874 J. GEIKIE *Gt. Ice Age* xvi. 208 The ice-current.. would leave upon their frozen shores the wreckage of the distant mountains. **1891** BARING-GOULD *In Troubadour-Land* viii. 112 They form the wreckage of a palace for princes. **1894** DOYLE *Mem. Sherlock Holmes* 103 The venerable wreckage of a feudal keep.

b. *fig.* Persons whose lives have been wrecked, who have failed to maintain a position in society.

1883 F. PEEK (*title*) Social Wreckage; a Review of the Laws of England as they affect the Poor. **1888** *Pall Mall G.* 26 Nov. 6/1 Twenty beds..are nightly filled by wreckage, more or less battered, from the stress of life. **1898** *Daily News* 18 Apr. 5/1 What a line of flotsam and jetsam it is!.. that mass of human wreckage.

wrecked (rɛkt), *ppl. a.* [f. WRECK *v.*[1] + -ED[1].]

1. That has undergone or suffered shipwreck; destroyed, lost, or cast ashore by shipwreck; = SHIPWRECKED *ppl. a.*

1729 WOODWARD *Fossils* I. 116 The Coral found affix'd and growing upon wreck'd Ships. **1795** W. LEE *Hist. Lewes* 547 It has..been the practice of many lords to keep the wrecked goods. **1818** SHELLEY *Rosal. & Helen* 394 Wrecked mariners, Who cling to the rock of a wintry sea. **1821** SCOTT *Pirate* vii, One wave..made the wrecked vessel completely manifest in her whole bulk. **1850** W. IRVING *Mahomet* II. 483 Whether the old man..was one of the wrecked cruisers, or a wrecker,..is not specified. **1869** *Daily News* 11 Aug., Throwing upon the holders of wrecked goods the burden of accounting for their possession.

2. a. Damaged or destroyed by wreck, violence, or disaster; shattered, ruined.

1818 SHELLEY *Julian* 224 Like weeds on a wrecked palace growing. **1818** —— *Marenghi* vii, Thou shadowest forth that mighty shape in story, As ocean its wrecked fanes, severe yet tender. **1867** SMILES *Huguenots Eng.* ix. (1880) 150 Amidst the ruins of a wrecked church. **1875** KNIGHT *Dict. Mech.* 2821/1 Removing obstructions from the track, such as wrecked cars or locomotives.

b. *fig.* That has suffered wreck; brought to ruin or disaster.

1819 KEATS *Lines to Fanny* 33 That most hateful land, [where]..my friends..live a wrecked life. **1855** G. BRIMLEY *Ess.* (1858) 84 The incipient stage of madness, springing from the wrecked affections. **1879** FROUDE *Cæsar* xviii. 301

He flung into bribery what was left of his wrecked credit. **1901** *Munsey's Mag.* XXIV. 470/2 He was thinking of the old king with the wrecked mind.

c. Intoxicated; under the influence of drugs. *U.S. slang.*

1968–70 *Current Slang* (Univ. S. Dakota) III–IV. 139 *Wrecked*, intoxicated. **1973** D. LANG *Freaks* 63, I could not get it on, could not get it *on*, not unless I was, one: totally wrecked; and, two: had to have a gun in my hand.

wrecker[1] (ˈrɛkə(r)). [f. WRECK *v.*[1] + -ER[1].]

1. a. One who causes shipwreck, exp. for purposes of plunder by showing luring lights or false signals; a person who makes a business of watching for and plundering wrecked vessels; also, one who wrongfully seizes or appropriates wreck washed ashore.

1820 W. IRVING *Sketch Bk.* (1821) I. 27 The good people ..thronged like wreckers to get some part of the noble vessel ..driven on shore. **1843** *Times* 20 Jan. 3/6 Although the officers of the coast-guard keep a sharp look-out, considerable depredation was carried on by the wreckers. **1882** FARRAR *Early Chr.* xxii, Cornish wreckers went straight from church to light their beacon-fires.

fig. **1865** THOREAU *Cape Cod* vi. 105 Are we not all wreckers contriving that some treasure may be washed up on our beach?

b. One who wrecks or ruins a structure, institution, concern, etc.

1882 C. G. WALPOLE *Short Hist. Irel.* 441 The Defenders especially had begun to turn the tables upon the 'wreckers', and were the terror of the country side. **1889** GASQUET *Hen. VIII & Eng. Monast.* II. 426 Like a swarm of locusts the royal wreckers went forth over the land.

fig. **1883** *American* VI. 37 Lawyers and agents, who might be described with fairness as 'wreckers' and who generally manage to absorb the assets. **1903** *Westm. Gaz.* 28 Feb. 10/1 As a wrecker of Cabinets Ireland holds a proud position.

c. *fig.* One who wrecks, or successfully obstructs the passing of a measure, etc.

1892 *Pall Mall G.* 12 July 1/2 If..they are not able to reckon more than 8 Parnellite 'wreckers'. **1901** *Scotsman* 20 Nov. 8/4 The wreckers in the Senate claimed for America the right of fortifying the Canal.

2. *Stock Exchange.* (See first quot.)

1876 'E. PINTO' *Ye Outside Fools!* 359 *Wreckers*,..those who make a similarly-organized attack as bears upon some stock, rotten or good,..and force down the price by large and successive sudden sales. **1884** *American* VIII. 84 The clamor of contending inflaters and wreckers at the stock exchange.

3. A demolition worker.

1958 J. THURBER in *Atlantic Monthly* Feb. 52/1 Jacob Volk, a building wrecker..who tore down two hundred and fifty big structures in Manhattan. **1968** *Globe & Mail* (Toronto) 17 Feb. 6/3, I was saddened to discover wreckers' hoardings surrounding the Royal Bank building at 10-12 King Street East. **1977** H. FAST *Immigrants* VI. 352 He stood on the corner of California Street on Nob Hill watching the wreckers take the Seldon mansion apart, stone by stone.

wrecker[2] (ˈrɛkə(r)). Orig. (and chiefly) *Amer.* [f. WRECK *sb.*[1] + -ER[1].]

1. A person engaged in salving wrecked or endangered vessels or cargo; a salvager, salvor.

1804 M'KINNON *Tour West Indies* ix. 137 Those persons called wreckers, who are licensed by the Governor of the Bahamas, and cruise amongst these islands for the benefit of salvage. **1819** *Edwards' Hist. W. Indies* (ed. 5) IV. 225 The business of wreckers..consists in giving assistance to those who are wrecked, or in danger of being so, upon the almost endless rocks and shoals [of the Bahamas]. **1851** *Rovings in Pacific* I. 173 Our own vessel..had heeled on to a sunken patch in the offing... It gave us wreckers a tremendous fright. **1875** TALMAGE *Old Wells* 273 The wreckers shoot a rope out to the suffering men.

2. a. A ship or vessel employed in salvaging sunk, wrecked, or stranded vessels.

1789 O. EQUIANO *Life* II. viii. 57 They met with this little sloop, called a wrecker; their employment in those seas being to look after wrecks. **1864** WEBSTER. **1868** [see WRECKING *vbl. sb.*[2] 2]. **1898** *Westm. Gaz.* 14 July 5/2 The Wreckers and Admiral Cervera's Vessels.

b. A railway vehicle with a crane or hoist for removing crashed trains or similar obstructions; also, a breakdown truck. Also *attrib.*

1904 *Booklovers' Mag.* May 663 This special train has been dubbed the 'Wrecker'. Really it is a relief train, ready to respond to any call for aid in case of accident. **1955** V. NABOKOV *Lolita* II. xxx. 188 Around midnight, a wrecker dragged my car out. **1970** *Globe & Mail* (Toronto) 28 Sept. 31/6 (*caption*) Ward has picked Maggie up..in a wrecker! **1973** *Amer. Speech* 1969 XLIV. 257 The wrecker train..has a flatcar with a crane. **1978** *Detroit Free Press* 16 Apr. F8/10 (Advt.), Business offered... Car wash, wrecker service and ..service station. **1980** R. L. DUNCAN *Brimstone* vi. 126 A couple of police cars and a wrecker pulling apart three cars that had tailgated.

†**wreck-free**, *a. Obs.* [Early ME. *wrec-frī*, f. WRECK *sb.*[1] 1 + FREE *a.*] Exempted or free from the forfeiture of wrecked vessels and goods.

1205 *Rot. Chart.* (1837) 153/2 Cum socca & sacca & thol & theam & infangeneth[ef] & wrecfri & witefri & lestagefri & locofri. **1278** *Charter to Cinque Ports* in *Rymer's Fœdera* (1816) I. II. 558/1 Et quod habeant infangenethef; & quod sint wrecfry, & wytefry & lestagefry. **1598** HAKLUYT *Voy.* I. 117 (tr. quot. 1278), That they shall be wreckefree, lastagefree, and louecopfree. [**1706** PHILLIPS (*Wrec-fry*); and in later Dicts.]

wreckful (ˈrɛkfʊl), *a.*[1] [f. WRECK *sb.*[1] + -FUL.] Causing shipwreck, ruin, or disaster; dangerous, destructive.

1596 SPENSER *F.Q.* VI. viii. 36 Straungers..which on their border Were brought..by wreckfull wynde. **1810** SCOTT *Lady of L.* v. i, The wreckful storms that cloud the brow of War. **1848** MANGAN *Poems* (1903) 106 This dull world still slumbers... In a midnight dream, Drifts it down Time's wreckful stream. **1876** TENNYSON *Harold* III. i. 51 A summer mere with sudden wreckful gusts From a side-gorge.

†ˈ**wreckful**, *a.*[2] *Obs.* [f. WRECK *sb.*[3] + -FUL. Cf. WRACKFUL *a.*[1], WRAKEFUL *a.*, WREAKFUL *a.*] Full of, manifesting or taking, revenge; marked or characterized by vengeance.

1557 NORTH *Gueuara's Diall Pr.* IV. xvii. (1568) 158 Per force my self dooth straine the wreckfull gods, vouch saue it doo not so. **1601** W. T. *Ld. Remy's Civ. Consid.* 36 If a man haue to deale with some manner of men which are wreckfull, of a strange nature, hard to please. **1610** HOLLAND *Camden's Brit.* I. 709 The Earle in wreckfull displeasure..laid his Castle even with the ground.

ˈ**wrecking**, *vbl. sb.*[1] [f. WRECK *v.*[1] + -ING[1].]

1. The action of destroying by shipwreck or causing wreck; the fact of having suffered wreck; demolition.

1775 ASH, *Wrecking*,..the act of destroying by dashing against rocks or sands at sea; the act of destroying by violent means. **1851** W. COLLINS *Rambles beyond Railw.* v. (1852) 108 'Wrecking' is a crime unknown in the Cornwall of our day. **1868** M. PATTISON *Academ. Org.* 3 Wrecking was no longer permitted by public morality. **1891** C. DAWSON *Avonmore* 46 Till drunk with wrecking's awful toil, Havoc will laugh and Ruin smile! **1940** *Construction Methods* Apr. 110/2 Wrecking is, in reality, construction in reverse gear... At the Louisville, Ky. East End slum clearance project.. there were approximately 480 buildings to wreck... The Cleveland Wrecking Co. has had many large contracts of this type. **1972** *Times* 10 Mar. (Suppl.) p. ii/1 (Advt.), The most experienced firm in the U.K. in the wrecking of blast furnaces.

attrib. **1885** *N. & Q.* 6th Ser. XI. 428/1 The Wrecking system once practised on the English coasts.

2. *concr.* That which is wrecked; *pl.* wrecked remains.

1855 SINGLETON *Virgil* I. 200 The more vigorously all will toil To mend the wreckings of a fallen race.

3. *attrib.*, as ***wrecking company***; **wrecking ball**, a large, heavy metal ball which, hung from a crane, may be swung into a building to demolish it; **wrecking bar**, an iron bar with one end chisel-shaped for prising and the other bent and split to form a claw.

1952 *Business Week* 19 July 33/2 Instead of using a one-ton wrecking ball at the end of a 60-ft. beam, the building must be knocked down..with a 16-lb. sledge hammer. **1977** *Rolling Stone* 21 Apr. 34/4 It's the laugh of a man who just watched a wrecking ball smash his house to splinters so a new freeway could go through. **1984** *New Yorker* 20 Feb. 50/2 The wrecking ball bursts through the wall with the bookshelves, scattering the works of famous authors. **1924** *Sears, Roebuck Catal.* No. 148. 866/3 Wrecking Bars. Forged steel 24-inch, 30c. **1947** *Construction Methods* Mar. 88/2 To minimize damage to material during removal, the contractor developed his own tools as supplements to the standard wrecking bar and claw hammer. **1940** Wrecking company [see sense 1 above]. **1976** *National Observer* (U.S.) 3 Apr. 7/1 A wrecking company recently signed a contract to level all 30 of the remaining 11-story buildings.

ˈ**wrecking**, *vbl. sb.*[2] *Amer.* [f. WRECK *sb.*[1] 3.]

1. The action or business of salvaging a wreck or wrecks.

1804 [see 2]. **1868** H. D. GRANT *Rep. Wrecking in Bahamas* 35 Wrecking has become a regular vocation for considerable portion of the population. **1969** *Sydney Morning Herald* 24 May 63/2 (Advt.), Jaguars, wrecking now. Continually dismantling 2·4, 3·4 and 3·8.

2. a. *attrib.*, esp. in sense 'used for, or in connexion with, relating to, salvaging wreck', as ***wrecking car, crane, outfit, pump, train***; also ***wrecking law, operation.***

1804 M'KINNON *Tour West Indies* ix. 144 Effecting an immediate escape in a wrecking-vessel from this wild and inhospitable spot. **1868** H. D. GRANT *Rep. Wrecking in Bahamas* 36 Copies of abstract of the wrecking laws. *Ibid.* 62 The harbour-master.., who formerly commanded a wrecker and now owns licensed wrecking vessels. **1875** KNIGHT *Dict. Mech.* 644/1 Fairbairn's traveling-crane..is adapted for a wrecking-crane for railroad use. *Ibid.* 2821/1 *Wrecking-car*, one carrying devices for removing obstructions from the track, such as wrecked cars or locomotives. *Ibid.*, 2821/2 *Wrecking-pump*, a steam-pump specially designed for pumping the water out of bilged or sunken vessels, in order to raise them. **1891** *Harper's Weekly* 19 Sept. 914/2 A wrecking train soon removed the débris. **1898** *Engineering Mag.* XVI. 68 The wrecking outfit should be immediately available. *Ibid.*, Wrecking operations.

b. In sense 'engaged in salvaging wreck or wrecks', as ***wrecking company, crew, expedition.***

1851 *Rovings in Pacific* I. 149 Bound on a wrecking Expedition. **1878** B. HARTE *Man on Beach* 33 A wrecking crew of curlew hastily manned the uprooted tree that tossed wearily beyond the bar. **1891** in *Leeds Mercury* 19 Sept. 12 Captain Merritt, of the Merritt Wrecking Company. **1939** [see OUT-CITY *a.*]. **1968** *Globe & Mail* (Toronto) 13 Feb. 32/2 (Advt.), Well established wrecking business with living quarters on large lot fronting on Napanee River.

wrecking, obs. erron. var. RACKING *vbl. sb.*[3] 1.

1776 G. SEMPLE *Building in Water* 128 That the Timber ..be both firmly spliced and bolted together, to prevent their wrecking, swagging or dislocating.

ˈ**wrecking**, *ppl. a.* [f. WRECK *v.*[1] + -ING[2].]

1. That wrecks; causing wreck, ruin, or destruction; destructive. ***wrecking amendment*** (Pol.), one designed to defeat the purpose of the bill concerned.

a **1677** BARROW *Serm.* Wks. 1686 III. 228 [Industry] is in itself..satisfactory; as freeing our mind from distraction, and wrecking irresolution. **1809** MALKIN *Gil Blas* XII. ix. ¶4 The wrecking fury of the storm. **1880** R. BRIDGES *Shorter Poems* Wks. (1912) 275 The moon, That poured her midnight noon Upon his wrecking sea. **1893** *Westm. Gaz.* 9 Feb. 7/2 Playing a wrecking game towards the present Government. **1967** M. PINTO-DUSCHINSKY *Polit. Thought of Lord Salisbury* vii. 145 Its very moderation led directly to the passing of a wrecking amendment by Lord John Russell, who favoured a different and much more far-reaching measure. **1979** H. WILSON *Final Term* ix. 189 Again the Conservatives, with considerable Labour support, moved 'wrecking' or near-wrecking amendments.

2. Going to wreck; becoming wrecked.

1903 S. E. WHITE *Forest* viii, A man..scaled the face of the moving jam, and reached the top just as the two sections ground together with the brutish noise of wrecking timbers.

wreckle, variant of WRIGGLE *sb.* 3.

1816 BINGLEY *Usef. Knowl.* III. 225 Sand-launce, Sand Eel, or Wreckle (*Ammodytes tobianus*) is a small fish distinguished by its eel-shape.

ˈ**wreckless** (ˈrɛklɪs), *a. rare.* [f. WRECK *v.*[1] + -LESS.] That cannot be wrecked.

1821 BYRON *Heaven & Earth* iii. 753 Hence to where our all-hallow'd ark uprears Its safe and wreckless sides!

wreckless, obs. erron. f. RECKLESS *a.*

ˈ**wreckling.** Now *dial.* [var. of RECKLING. Cf. WREGLING.] A weak, puny, or dwarfish animal (or plant); *spec.* the smallest and weakest of a litter.

1601 HOLLAND *Pliny* I. 530 It causeth it [*sc.* the vine] to seeme scortched and full of knots, yea and to grow like a dwarfe or wreckling. **1607** MARKHAM *Cavel.* I. 48 When shee shoulde come to foale, shee would bring foorth nought but a wreckling. **1614** —— *Cheap Husb.*, *Swine* xi. 94 Take the wreckling, or worst Pigge, and annoint it all ouer. **1781** [see RECKLING]. **1825-** in dialect glossaries, etc. (N. Cy.; Nhb. to Warw.).

attrib. **1602** tr. *Pastor Fido* IV. viii. M 2 b, Too much I honour thee, poore weake and wreckling child.

wrecky (ˈrɛkɪ), *a.* [f. WRECK *sb.*[1] + -Y[1].] Broken-down; debilitated.

1925 *Brit. Weekly* 17 Sept. 541/1 After which you are left a wreck and probably remain wrecky next day. **1973** M. AMIS *Rachel Papers* 15, I had a well-earned-half at the pub and chatted with the landlord and his wrecky wife.

wree, Sc. variant of WRY *v.*[2]

†**wreekes**, erron. f. REAKS (pranks) *Obs.*

1628 BURTON *Anat. Mel.* (ed. 3) III. ii. VI. iii. 515 Fawnes and Satyrs will certainely play wreekes.

wreest(e, obs. or dial. varr. WREST *sb.*

†ˈ**wregling.** *Sc. Obs.* = WRECKLING.

1679 in Wodrow *Ch. Hist.* (1828) IV. 501 What through grace he will make such a weak wregling able to endure.

wrehche, obs. f. WRETCH *sb.*

wrei, etc.: see WRAY *v.*, etc.

wreicht, wreight, obs. ff. WRIGHT *sb.*[1]

wreist, obs. Sc. var. WREST.

wreithe, obs. f. WREATHE *v.*

wreitt, wreitten, obs. Sc. pa. t. and pa. pple. of WRITE *v.*

wrek, alteration of WRACK *v.*[4]

a **1635** L. FOXE *North-West Fox* in *Voy.* (Hakl. Soc. 1894) II. 280 In that distance holding the same course, I was 1 d. 17 m. wrekt from my true course.

†**wreke.** *Obs.* Also 6 reke. [a. early ON. **wreke* m. (Icel. *reki*, Norw. *reke*), from the same stem as **wrek* neut.: see WRECK *sb.*[1]]

1. = WRECK *sb.*[1] 1.

1420 *Stonor Papers* (Camden) I. 32 Every man here knoweth wel þat þe wreke is parcel of þe enheritance of Ermyngton. **1477** *Paston Lett.* III. 213 Remembir your ryth of your wreke at Wynterton. *Ibid.*, Gret plante of wreke of the schyppe..worth meche mony. **1495** *Act 11 Hen. VII*, c. 34 *Preamble*, With wreke of the Sea and all other forfaitures. [**1535** *Act 27 Hen. VIII*, c. 26 §23 Lordes marchers..shall have, hold, and kepe within..the precincte of their said Lordeshipps..wreke de mere, wharfage.]

2. = WRECK *sb.*[1] 2.

c **1440** *Promp. Parv.* 553/2 Wreke, of þe see, *alga, norga.* **1500** *Ortus Vocab.* BB viij b/1 *Norga, fex maris*,..wreke. **1545** ELYOT, *Vlua*, reke or wiedes of the sea.

wreke, etc., obs. ff. WREAK *sb.* and *v.*

†**wrele**, *v. Sc. Obs.* [? Of imitative origin.] *intr.* To struggle or move about writhingly

1513 DOUGLAS *Æneid* I. Prol. 298 Quha is attachit on till a staik..Ma go no ferrar, but wrele about that tre. *Ibid.* v.

iv. 114 First Sergest behind sone left hes he, Wreland [L. *luctantem*] on skelleis and wndepis of the see.

wren[1] (rɛn). Forms: α. 1 wrenna (werna), 3–7 wrenne, 5 wrenn, 5–6 wrene (6 *pl.* wreneys), 5– wren. β. 1 wrænna (wærna), 3, *Sc.* 6–7 wranne, 5 *Sc.*, 9 *Sc.* and *dial.* wran (7 wrane, 9 ran), *Sc.* 6, 9 vran (9 vraun). [OE. *wrenna* (also with metathesis *werna*), *wrænna* (*wærna*), obscurely related to OHG. *wrendo, wrendilo*, Icel. *rindill*.]

1. *Ornith.* **a.** One or other species of small dentirostral passerine birds belonging to the genus *Troglodites*, esp. the common wren (jenny- or kitty-wren), *T. parvulus*, native to Europe.

In quot. *c* 1450 used in some allusive sense.

α. *c* **725** *Corpus Gloss.* (Hessels) B 136 *Birbicariolus*, werna. *a* **1100** *Gloss.* in Wr.-Wülcker 132 *Parrax*, wrenna, *uel* hicemase. *a* **1250** *Owl & Night.* 564 (Jesus Coll. MS), Hwat dostu godes among monne? Na mo þene doþ a wrecche wrenne [*Cotton MS.* wranne]. *Ibid.* 1717 Þe wrenne [*Cotton MS.* wranne] for heo cuþe singe þar com.. To helpe þare nyhtegale. **13..** in *Rel. Ant.* II. 107 Levere is the wrenne, Abouten the schowe renne, Than the fithel draut, Other the floute craf. **1390** GOWER *Conf.* III. 349 So that the litel wrenne in his mesure Hath yit of kinde a love under his cure. *c* **1401** LYDG. *Flour of Curtesye* 57 The sely wrenne, the titmose also,.. have free eleccioun To flyen.. Wher-as hem liste. *c* **1450** *Merlin* xxviii. 573 Thus shull the knyghtes of the rounde table go to a-venge the deth of the wrenne. *a* **1529** SKELTON *P. Sparowe* 600 The prety wren, That is our Ladyes hen. **1593** MARLOWE *Edw. II*, v. iii, The Wrenne may striue against the Lions strength, But all in vaine. **1613** W. BROWNE *Brit. Past.* I. iv. 13 As little wrens, but newly fledge, First by their nests hop up and downe the hedge. **1652** BENLOWES *Theoph.* I. xcviii, Shrubs cannot cedars, nor wrens eagles praise. **1710** ADDISON *Tatler* No. 224 ¶2 Thus the fable tells us, that the wren mounted as high as the eagle, by getting upon his back. **1750** C. SMITH *State Co. Cork* II 334 The Wren makes but short flights..; to hunt and kill him is an antient custom of the Irish on St. Stephen's day. **1768** PENNANT *Brit. Zool.* II. 268 The wren may be placed among the finest of our singing birds. **1825** WORDSW. *The Contrast* 30 This moss-lined shed, green, soft, and dry, Harbours a self-contented Wren. **1864** BRYANT *Little People of Snow* 21 A pleasant spot in spring, where first the wren Was heard to chatter. **1888** NEWTON in *Encycl. Brit.* XXIV. 688/2 The range of the Wren in Europe is very extensive.

β. *c* **1050** *Voc.* in Wr.-Wülcker 260 *Litorius*,wærna. *a* **1100** *Voc.* Ibid. 286 *Bitorius*, wrænna, *uel pintorus*. *a* **1250** [see α]. *c* **1450** HOLLAND *Houlate* 649 The litill we Wran, That wretchit dorche was. **1549** *Compl. Scot.* vi. 39 Robeen and the litil vran var hamely in vyntir. **1823** JENNINGS *Observ. Dial. W. Eng.* 128 Wrans an robin-riddicks. *a* **1842** in Halliwell *Nursery Rhymes* 184 We'll hunt the wran, says Robin to Bobbin. *a* **1859** in *N. & Q.* 2nd Ser. VIII. 209/1 The wran, the king of all birds. **1880–91** in Antrim, Cornwall, and Devon glossaries. **1899** SOMERVILLE & ROSS *Some Exper. Irish R.M.* i, The carpenter.. wished the divil might run the plumber through a wran's quill.

Phrases. *a* **1550** *Image Hypocr.* III. 105 in *Skelton's Wks.* (1843) II. 434 As wise as any wrenne And holy as an henne. *a* **1598** FERGUSSON *Prov.* (S.T.S.) 10 As sair fights wranes as cranes.

transf. **1601** SHAKS. *Twel. N.* III. ii. 70 [Stage direction] Enter Maria. *Toby.* Looke where the youngest Wren of mine comes.

b. With distinguishing epithets.

1638 W. LISLE *Heliodorus* VI. 87 A bird no bigger then.. the Iynny Wren. **1648–** [see JENNY WREN]. **1808–14** A. WILSON *Amer. Ornith.* (1831) II. 188 *Sylvia troglodytes*, Winter Wren. **1825–** [see KITTY[1] 2]. **1831** J. RENNIE *Montagu's Ornith. Dict.* 570 Wren... Provincial[ly called] Vraun, or Ran. Cutty, Katy, or Kitty Wren. **1848** *Maunder's Treas. Nat. Hist.* s.v., The American House Wren (*Troglodytes domestica*).. inhabits the whole of the United States. **1884** *Harper's Mag.* March 616/1 The winter wren [*T. hyemalis*].. is a saucy little atom. **1914** *Brit. Mus. Return* 157 An example of the St. Kilda Wren (*Troglodytes hirtensis*).

2. a. Applied, esp. with distinguishing term, to various other small birds of the family *Trogloditidæ* or *Sylviidæ*, resembling the common wren in appearance or habits; esp. the gold-crest (*Regulus cristatus*).

Also *hill-, marsh-, reed-, rock-, sedge-, willow-, wood-wren*: see HILL *sb.* 4f, MARSH[1] 4b, REED-WREN, ROCK *sb.*[1] 9c, SEDGE *sb.*[1] 6, WILLOW *sb.* 6, WOOD *sb.*[1] Some provincial names are recorded by Swainson (1885), pp. 25–27.

1868 *Chambers's Encycl.* X. 287/1 The *Carolina wren ..(*Thryophorus Ludovicanus*) and the Marsh Wren ..(*Cistophorus palustris*).. are found chiefly in the vicinity of water. **1674** RAY *Coll. Words* Eng. Birds 87 The *copped Wren: *Regulus cristatus*. **1700–** [see COPPED *ppl. a.* 3]. **1750** C. SMITH *State Co. Cork* II. 335 The *Regulus* or *crested wren..is a smaller bird. **1843** *Penny Cycl.* XXVII. 583/2 [The] Golden-crested Wren.. must not be confounded with the rarer *Fire-crested Wren,.. also to be seen in Britain. *Ibid.* 583/1 This species is the..*Gold crested Wren.. and Kinglet of the modern British. **1867** H. MACMILLAN *Bible Teach.* iv. (1870) 67 The twitter of the *golden wren. **1768** PENNANT *Brit. Zool.* II. 511 The small and delicate *golden Crested-wren. **1797** BEWICK *Brit. Birds* I. 170 The Golden-crested Wren is diffused throughout Europe. **1830** BOOTH *Analyt. Dict.* I. 98 The smallest of all the British birds, is called the Golden-crested Wren. **1678** RAY *Willughby's Ornith.* 227 The *golden-crown'd Wren: *Regulus cristatus*. **1774** G. WHITE *Selborne* xli, The feeble little golden-crowned wren, that shadow of a bird, braves our severest frosts. **1823** LATHAM *Gen. Hist. Birds* VII. 205 *Gold-naped Wren, *Sylvia elata*,.. inhabits Cayenne in the Winter. **1802** MONTAGU *Ornith. Dict.* s.v., Yellow Wren... Provincial[ly called] Willow Wren. *Ground Wren. **1758** G. EDWARDS *Glean. Nat. Hist.* I. 95 The *Ruby-crowned Wren. **1760** *Ibid.* II. 143 The *Yellow Wren hath.. been figured and described by different authors under various names. **1776** PENNANT *Brit. Zool.* (ed. 4) II. 378 The yellow wren [*Sylvia trochilus*] frequents.. places where willow trees abound from which it takes one of its names.

b. Applied to various Australasian species of wren-like birds (see quots.).

Also *emu-, rock-wren* (see EMU 4, ROCK *sb.*[1] 9c).

1848 GOULD *Birds Australia* III. 18 *Malurus Cyaneus*,.. Superb Warbler, Blue Wren, etc., of the colonists. *Ibid.* 29 The Striated Wren [*Amytis striatus*] ran with amazing rapidity. *Ibid.* 19–31, 39–40 [many species of *Malurus, Amytis*, and *Hylacola*].

3. A woman, esp. a young woman. *U.S. slang.*

1920 S. LEWIS *Main Street* 388 Some tank, that wren! Ha, ha, ha! **1927** *Amer. Speech* III. 167/1 *Dame, frail, skirt, Jane, wren, broad*, girl. **1929** A. CONAN DOYLE *Maracot Deep* 198 Scanlan has.. married his wren in Philadelphia. **1946** B. TREADWELL *Big. Bk. Swing* 125/2 *Wren*, small, fickle young girl. **1982** M. MCMULLEN *Until Death do us Part* (1983) 9 Midge was, in her quiet unobtrusive way, a perfect marvel of efficiency, 'My dear wren,' Jane sometimes called her.

4. *attrib.* and *Comb.*, as ***wren-hunting, -king***; ***wren-like, -nested*** adjs.; **wren-box**, a collecting-box used by 'wren-boys'; **wren-boys**, in Ireland, a party of boys or young men, carrying a decorated holly-bush with a wren or wrens hanging from it, who go about on St. Stephen's Day singing verses; **wren-bush**, a bush used for this; †**wren creeper**, a variety of tree-creeper (see quots.); **wren song**, the song carolled by the wren-boys; **wren-tail, wren's-tail**, an artificial fly for trout-fishing; **wren-tit** *U.S.* (see quot.); **wren-warbler**, any of several warblers of the genus *Primia*, found in tropical Africa or Asia; also, a brightly coloured wren of the subfamily Malurinæ, found in Australasia.

1901 *Folk-Lore* June 131 A *wren-box from the Pitt Rivers Museum at Farnham. ? *a* **1800** in Croker *Researches in S. Ireland* (1824) 233 It won't agree with the *Wren boys at all. **1824** CROKER *Ibid.*, A holly bush.. having many wrens depending from it.. is carried from house to house with some ceremony, the 'Wren boys' chaunting several verses. *a* **1855** in *N. & Q.* 1st Ser. XII. 489 Song of the Youghal Wren-boys. **1871** *Yarrell's Brit. Birds* (ed. 4) I. 465 The dead bird, hung by the leg between two hoops,.. was carried about by the 'Wren-boys' [of Cork]. **1901** *Folk-Lore* June 131 [He] exhibited a *Wren-bush from co. Wicklow. **1904** *Longm. Mag.* Oct. 537 The practice of carrying about 'the wren-bush' on St. Stephen's Day. **1811** SHAW *Gen. Zool.* VIII. 268 *Wren Creeper,.. Size of the.. Willow Wren. **1822** LATHAM *Gen. Hist. Birds* IV. 271 Wren Creeper, *Certhia trochilea*,.. inhabits America. **1696** AUBREY *Misc.* iv. 44 A whole Parish running like madmen from Hedg to Hedg a *Wren-hunting. **1885** SWAINSON *Prov. Names Birds* 36 Wren-hunting. [Particulars follow.] **1900** *Westm. Gaz.* 15 Jan. 10/1 It used to be a common custom.. to make wren-hunting parties a feature of the season from Christmas to New Year. **1965** AUDEN *About House* (1966) 13 From gallery-grave and the hunt of a *wren-king to Low Mass and trailer camp is hardly a tick by the carbon clock. **1641** *True Char. of Untrue Bishop* 4 Witnesse his many Sparrowish, *Wrenlike wanton extravagances. **1805** WORDSW. *Prelude* v. 207 From those loftiest notes Down to the low and wren-like warblings. **1878** BROWNING *Poets Croisic* cxxxi, I'm nobody —a wren-like journalist. **1925** BLUNDEN *Eng. Poems* 104 *Wren-nested hedges. **1855** *N. & Q.* 1st Ser. XII. 489 The *Wren Song in Ireland. **1837** KIRKBRIDE *Northern Angler* 40 The *Wren's Tail,.. an excellent summer fly. **1856** 'STONEHENGE' *Brit. Sports* 245/2 The Wren's Tail..; legs of a wren's tail-feather, used as a hackle. **1867** F. FRANCIS *Angling* vi. 204 The *Wrentail, Brown Bent, Froghopper. **1875** *Encycl. Brit.* II. 38/1 Among the best of these are.. the wren-tail, the grouse and partridge hackles. **1872** COUES *N. Amer. Birds* 79 *Chamæidæ*; *Wren-tits.. much like a titmouse in general appearance,.. with the general habits of wrens. **1924** E. C. S. BAKER *Fauna Brit. India: Birds* (ed. 2) II. 530 The Ashy *Wren-Warbler breeds from March to September. **1931** *Discovery* May 141/2 The tiny new wren warbler.. a wee mite of a bird with a tail almost as long as its body. **1955** MACKWORTH-PRAED & GRANT *Birds E. & N.E. Afr.* 392 Wren-warblers.. occur in both woodland and thorn-scrub. **1974** I. ROWLEY *Bird Life* vi. 68 Most *Malurus* have distinctive and attractive songs so that the name 'wren-warbler' is an apt one.

Wren[2] (rɛn). Also wren. [f. three of the initial letters of the name of the Service, made into a singular noun.] A member of the Women's Royal Naval Service, formed in 1917; also (*pl.*), the Service itself.

1918 [see PENGUIN 2b]. **1927** *Glasgow Herald* 15 Apr. 7 The war years with all their Waacs and Wrens and Wrafs, seem now to be immeasurably far off. **1940** *War Illustr.* 5 Jan. 558 At all Naval depots 'Wrens' are now doing work as clerks, cooks and in many other capacities, thus relieving men for more active work. **1946** 'TACKLINE' (*title*) You met such nice girls in the Wrens. **1956** [see W.R.A.C.]. **1979** D. GURR *Troika* xi. 75, I.. reported to the Admiralty... 'Captain Jackson's office, please?' 'Second floor, sir.' A good bust and a smile on the duty wren cheered me up.

Hence **'Wrennery** *joc.*, a building used to accommodate Wrens.

1943 HUNT & PRINGLE *Service Slang* 70 *Wrennery*, billets of the 'Jenny Wrens'. **1945** 'N. SHUTE' *Most Secret* 124, I shall be living in the Wrennery and coming out to Dittisham every day. **1959** P. MCCUTCHAN *Storm South* ii. 41 Where did you pick up all this insight into human nature—in the Navy? Serve in a Wrennery or something, did you? **1964** *Navy News* July 5/4 The work included.. the building of a Wrennery to accommodate 200 Wrens.

Wrenaissance (rɛ'neɪsəns, -ɑːs). *Archit.* [f. the name of Sir Christopher *Wren* (see WRENEAN *a.*) after RENAISSANCE.] An architectural style modelled on or influenced by that of Wren, esp. as represented by some of the work of Sir Edwin Lutyens.

1942 R. LUTYENS *Sir Edwin Lutyens* iii. 40 Gothic and Renaissance ('Wrenaissance'! as father has punned..) are both architectures of meaning. **1944** *Archit. Rev.* XCV. p. xlvi/1 We cannot.. allow ourselves, out of affection for a great man [*sc.* Lutyens] and out of admiration for his highly personal style, to be saddled with a Wrenaissance London as a monument to a period which the first world war brought to a murderous close. **1967** *Time* (Atlantic ed.) 26 May 45/1 Frederick Gibberd.. extended a piazza to roof over an English Wrenaissance crypt built in the 1930s. **1980** M. LUTYENS *Edwin Lutyens* iv. 62 In 1906, with the building of Heathcote at Ilkley, Yorkshire, for Mr Ernest Hemingway ..he reached what he called his 'Wrenaissance'; Wren thereafter became his lodestar. **1981** *Times* 12 Feb. 17/4 That heavy, florid.. brick and stone style christened 'Wrenaissance'.

†**wrench**, *sb.*[1] *Obs.* Forms: α. 1–2 wrenc; 2–6 wrench, 3–6 wrenche. β. 6 wrinch(e. [OE. *wrenc*, corresponding in form to OHG. *renki* twist, sprain (G. *ränke* bend, hollow), and in sense to MHG. and G. *rank* bending, turning, trick, artifice. Cf. WRENK *sb.* and WRENCH *v.*]

1. A crooked, cunning, or wily action or device; a trick, wile, or artifice. Freq. coupled with *wile*.

α. *c* **888** ÆLFRED *Boeth.* iv. §1 Nauht ne deregað monnum mane aþas, ne þæt lease lot þe beoð mid þam wrencum bewrigen. *a* **1050** *Liber Scintill.* xxxvii. (1889) 136 On swa hwylcum wrence worda ænig swerige. *a* **1122** *O.E. Chron.* (Laud MS.) an. 1003, Ða sceolde.. Ælfric lædan þa fyrde ac he teah forð þa his ealdan wrenceas. *c* **1175** *Lamb. Hom.* 67 He fondede god solf mid his wrenche. *a* **1225** *Ancr. R.* 270 Auh þis heie sacrament.. ouer alle oðer þinges unwrihð his wrenches, & brekeð his strencðes. *a* **1250** *Prov. Ælfred* 163 Monymon weneþ þat he wene ne þarf, longes lyues, ac him lyeþ þe wrench. **1303** R. BRUNNE *Handl. Synne* 7711 He dredde hym of sum wykked wrenche. **1387** TREVISA *Higden* I. 347 At þe laste Turgesius deide by gileful wyles and wrenches. **14..** *Sir Beues* (E.) 2753 + 32 Þe dragoun cowde soo many a wrenche. *a* **1450** *Medit. Life & Passion of Christ* 1650 Þere ne shal.. No wrenches ne no fendes wyle Make þat swetnesse away to gon. **1519** HORMAN *Vulg.* 23b, All those thynges were wroughte by wrenches of wyked spyrittis. **1579** HAKE *Newes out of Powles* (1872) To Rdr. A iiij b, The wrenches and wyles.. that the lewde sorte of this people.. doe vse to gette money with.

β. **1530** PALSGR. 290/2 Wrinches or wyles, *chariuaris*. **1534** LD. BERNERS *Gold. Bk. M. Aurel.* (1546) A a vij, If we take not hede to prepare against his wrinches, it wyll ouerthrow vs. **1547** *Bk. Marchauntes* e ij, God knoweth what wily wrinches.. they do commit fro day to day.

2. Without article: Trickery, deceit, guile; fraud.

1297 R. GLOUC. (Rolls) 2924 Of is luþer wrenche.. Four hondred & four score mid treson he slou þere. *c* **1300** *Beket* (Percy Soc.) 44 He was stronge adrad ȝut of wommanes wrenche. **13..** *Seuyn Sages* (W.) 438 She schette the dore, and set him on benche. Wil ye nou i-here of wommannes wrenche? **1566** STERNHOLD & H. *Ps.* xxvi. 10 Their right hand with wrenche and wile for bribes doth plucke and pull.

wrench (rɛn(t)ʃ), *sb.*[2] Also 5 wrynche, 6–7, *dial.* 9 wrinch (9 *dial.* wringe, rinse); 6 wren(t)che, 9 *Sc.* wrunch, runch. [App. not a continuation of the prec. word, but directly based upon the verb.]

† **1.** *on wrench*, crosswise. *Obs. rare*[−1].

? *c* **1460** *MS. Porkington 10* fol. 58 (Halliwell), The vij. wyffe sat one the bynche, And sche caste her legge one wrynche.

2. a. An act of wrenching, or the fact of being wrenched; a twisting or pulling aside, awry, or out of shape; a violent twist or turn.

1530 PALSGR. 290/2 Wrenche, *torche*. **1618** BP. HALL *Contempl., O.T.* XII. i, Gods iudgements are the racke of godlesse men: If one straine make them not confesse, let them bee stretched but one wrench higher, and they cannot be silent. **1755** JOHNSON, *Wrench*,.. a violent pull or twist. **1771** LONNERGAN *Fencer's Guide* 87 A Wrench is thus formed. *Ibid.* 88 Retire a little upon the second wrench. **1837** DICKENS *Pickw.* xi, The little stone having been raised with one wrench of a spade. **1855** MRS. GASKELL *North & S.* xxii, They all could hear.. the creak of wood slowly yielding; the wrench of iron; the mighty fall of the ponderous gates. **1861** READE *Cloister & H.* lii, [She] gave a contemptuous wrench of her shoulder. **1893** MAX PEMBERTON *Iron Pirate* iv, [The yacht] jibbed round of a sudden, with an appalling wrench at the horse.

fig. and in fig. context. **1533** MORE *Apol.* xxii. 128 The same reason wold.. serue with one lytell wrenche ferther, to take in lyke wyse a waye from euery other man. **1607** SHAKS. *Timon* II. ii. 218 A Noble Nature May catch a wrench. **1854** B'NESS BUNSEN in Hare *Life* (1879) II. 167 Quite conscious that it is a strong wrench that drags him out of so large a part of the habits of life. *a* **1865** MRS. GASKELL *Wives & Daughters* (1866) I. 247 Then, with a wrench, changing the subject,.. he broke out [etc.]. **1878** BROWNING *La Saisiaz* 51, I shall.. bless each kindly wrench that wrung From life's tree its inmost virtue.

b. A sudden or sharp twist or jerk causing pain or injury to a limb, person, etc.; a sprain, strain. Also in fig. context.

1530 PALSGR. 290/2 Wrenche out of joynt, *deboytement, dejoincture*. **1545** ASCHAM *Toxoph.* (Arb.) 49 If he haue a wrentche, or haue taken colde in his arme. **1578** H. WOTTON *Courtlie Controv.* 28 If.. a wrenche breake a bone without perishing the fleshe or skinne whiche couereth it. **1655** FULLER *Ch. Hist.* II. 69 Every small Wrinch, or stepping awrie, is enough to put an ill-set Bone out of joynt. **1665** EARL ORRERY *St. Lett.* (1742) 100, I have got such a wrench in my ancle. **1748** *Anson's Voy.* II. ix. 226 They haled him into the ship, without.. any other injury than a wrench in his arm. **1802** PALEY *Nat. Theol.* viii. §1 The contortions and wrenches to which the limbs of animals are continually subject. **1860** Tyndall *Glac.* i. xix. 134 They compelled the arms to take a position which, if the footing gave way, would necessitate a wrench. **1879** Meredith *Egoist* iv, She quietly gave a wrench to the neck of the young hope in her breast.

c. An instance of this in horses; also with *the*, as the specific name of an ailment.

1578 H. Wotton *Courtlie Controv.* 301 Claribel supposing it hadde bin some wrench, commaunded his man to bathe the horse leg. **1580** Blundevil *Horsemanship* 59 The Curbe..commeth..by some straine or wrinch wherebie the tender sinewes are grieued. **1627** J. Taylor (Water P.) *Navy Land Ships* C6b, The shedding of the haire, the Horse-hipped, the Wrench, the Neckecricke. **1639** T. de Gray *Expert Farrier* 306 A horse that hath gotten a wrench in his shoulder. **1695** *Lond. Gaz.* No. 3105/4 A dark brown gelding,..goes wadling behind, as if he had a Wrench in his Back. **1727** Bailey (vol. II), *Entorses*, Wrenches of the Pasterns in Horses.

d. *fig.* A parting or separation causing painful or violent emotion; pain or anguish resulting from leave-taking.

In frequent use from *c* 1875.

1849 Robertson *Serm.* Ser. i. xii. (1855) 202 The misery of the wrench from all that is dear and bright. **1874** Green *Short Hist.* viii. §4 It was not without a wrench that they tore themselves from their English homes. **1889** 'J. S. Winter' *Mrs. Bob* x, Now that it had come to parting with the last of them [*sc.* daughters] it was an undeniable wrench.

e. *Mathematical Physics.* (See first quot.)

1876 Ball *Theory of Screws* 4 We now introduce the word *wrench*, to denote a force *and* a couple in a plane perpendicular to the force. *Ibid.* 5 These wrenches could be replaced by one wrench which is called the resultant wrench.

†**3. a.** A sharp turn, bend, or deflection; an abrupt turning movement. *Obs. rare.*

1549 Coverdale, etc. *Erasm. Par. Rom.* Argt. ad fin., The reader wandering vppe and downe, as it wer in wrenches, or ..in a mismase diuersly tournyng and wyndyng. **1596** Sir J. Davies *Orchestra* liii, I loue Meanders path,..Such winding sleights, such turnes and tricks he hath, Such Creekes, such wrenches, and such daliaunce.

fig. **1654** I. Ambrose *Ultima* 203 Austin after some turns and wrenches concludeth thus.

b. *Coursing.* A turning or bringing round of the hare or rabbit at less than a right angle.

1615 Markham *Country Content.* i. viii. 105 That Dogge which giueth the first turne, if after the turnes be giuen and neither coat, slip, nor wrench extraordinary, then he [etc.]. **1686** [see wrench *v.* 2]. **1688** Holme *Armoury* ii. ix. 189/1 A Wrench, is not a turn, but as it were, a half turn. **1840** Blaine *Encycl. Rural Sports* 598/1 A cote is when..one [dog] outruns the other, and gives the hare a turn or wrench. **1856** 'Stonehenge' *Brit. Rural Sports* 212/1 Working Power is evinced by the Wrench and the Turn. **1887** *Field* 19 Feb. 235/3 The brindled [greyhound] eventually finishing the course with a couple of wrenches and a kill.

4. Change from the original purport or signification; a strained or wrested meaning; a forced or false interpretation. (Cf. wrest *sb.* 3.)

1603 J. Davies (Heref.) *Microcosmos* Wks. (Grosart) I. 55/2 If there be wrench in this Paralell, It is in that [etc.]. **1701** Strype *Life Aylmer* 265 Whence..the Popish Bishops might see their Wrenches and Cavillations..to be maintained thereby. **1864** Lowell *Black Preacher* 11 But since I might chance give his meaning a wrench,..I'll put what he told me..In a rhymed prose.

5. a. One or other form of mechanical screw.

1552 *Acts Hen. VIII* (ed. Berthelet) 40 The Bier [= buyer]..shall not..straine..the same clothes..by teintour or wrinche [**1514** wynche]. **1598** Florio, *Storta*,..a wrench or wrest that ioyners vse. **1600** Hakluyt *Voy.* III. 810 Hee was faine to cause them to bee tormented with their thumbes in a wrinch. **1618** Dalton *Country Justice* 34 Any teynters, wrinches or other engines whatsoeuer, wherby any deceipt may be vsed in..the stretching of any wollen Cloth. [**1702** *Guide for Constables* 31 Tenters,..headwrinches, or other engines for stretching of cloth.] **1825** Jamieson, *Wrunch*, a winch or windlass. *Lanarks[hire]*.

†**b.** *fig.* A means of compulsion or constraint. *Obs. rare.*

1622 Bacon *Hen. VII*, 90 He.. resolued to make this profit of this businesse..as a Wrench and meane for Peace.

c. A tool or implement of various forms, consisting essentially of a metal bar with (freq. adjustable) jaws adapted for catching or gripping a bolt-head, nut, etc., to turn it; a screw-key, screw-wrench, or spanner.

Also *bed-, monkey-, pipe-, screw-, tap-, tube-wrench*: see those words.

1794 W. Felton *Carriages* (1801) I. 78 A spindle that is turned with a wrench upon the outside. *Ibid.* 223 Tool-budget..[for carrying] the few requisites for the coachman's use—such as a wrench, a hammer, a chissel. **1834** Marryat *P. Simple* xxi, We worked very hard until the hole was large enough, using the crow-bar..and a little wrench. **1862** *Catal. Internat. Exhib., Brit.* II. No. 6111, Patent wrench and mallet to save all taps from damage. **1879** *Cassell's Techn. Educ.* IV. 199/2 The wrench or spanner..is used for fastening the headstock or poppet down on the bed.

d. *Surg.* Applied to various makes of instruments having adjustable jaws, spec. for gripping a deformed foot to be rectified by torsion.

1895 *Arnold's Catal. Surg. Instruments* 774 Wrenches for bending Thomas's Splints. **1896** Tubby *Deformities* 416 Some wrenches are formidable and powerful instruments. *Ibid.* 418 Holding the foot in the bite of the wrench too long.

6. *attrib.* and *Comb.*, as ***wrench finisher, forger***; ***wrench hammer, handle***; **wrench fault** *Geol.* = *strike-slip fault* s.v. strike *sb.* 20.

1875 Knight *Dict. Mech.* 2822/1 *Wrench-hammer*, a hammer having a movable member to form a spanner. **1880** Blackmore *Mary Anerley* lv, Mr. Mordacks..holding him, as in a wrench-hammer, all the way, silencing his squeaks, with another turn of screw. **1881** *Instr. Census Clerks* (1885) 44 Wrench Finisher and Forger. **1884** Knight *Dict. Mech.* Suppl. 957/1 *Wrench Handle*, a double-arm wrench for use with dies for cutting threads, and other purposes. **1951** E. M. Anderson *Dynamics of Faulting* (ed. 2) i. 2 The term 'Blatt' will be translated as wrench fault. **1977** A. Hallam *Planet Earth* 61/1 Major wrench faults (e.g., the Great Glen Fault of Scotland) exhibit displacements of 100km..or more.

wrench (rɛn(t)ʃ), *v.* Forms: *α.* 1 wrencan, 2–4 wrenchen, 4, 6 wrenche, 5– wrench, 6 wrensh (7–8 rench, 8 *arch.* wranch). *β.* 4 wrynch, 5 wrynche, 6 wrinche, 6–7 wrinch. [OE. *wrencan* to twist, turn (also *fig.* to practise wiles), = OHG. *renchan* (MHG. and G. *renken*) to twist; of obscure relationship. Cf. wrenk *v.*]

I. †**1.** *intr.* **a.** To perform or undergo a quick or forcible turning or twisting motion; to turn or writhe (*about* or *aside*). Also *fig. Obs.*

α. *c* **1050** *Indicia Monast.* (MS. Cott. Tib. A III) fol. 97, Is þæs horderes tacen, þæt mon wrænce mid is hande, swilce he wille loc hunlucan. *c* **1200** *Trin. Coll. Hom.* 211 At pleȝe ..þih and shonkes and fet oppieð, wombe gosshieð, and shuldres wrenchieð. *a* **1240** *Wohunge* in *O.E. Hom.* I. 281 Hu þu was naket bunden faste to þe piler, þat tu ne mihtes now-hwider wrenche fra þa duntes. *c* **1375** [see wrenk *v.* 1]. **1387** Trevisa *Higden* VII. 538 Anoon his knyȝtes come to Venus to have the ryng, but heo wrenchide [*MS. α.* wrynchede] and blenchide and strof longe tyme, but [etc.]. *c* **1500** *New Notbr. Mayd* 152 in Hazl. *E.P.P.* III. 7 To fulfyll His wanton wyll, Wrenchynge from me alway. *c* **1530** Tindale *Num.* xxii. 25 The asse..wrenshed vnto the walle and thrust Balams fote vnto the wall. **1591** Sylvester *Du Bartas* i. v. 258 This Torpedo..Doth not as other Fish, that wrench and wriggle When they be prickt. **1625** Bp. Mountagu *App. Cæsarem* 319 Setting some rigorous Puritans aside, that like no Religion but one of their owne making,..there are few Calvinists..that will wrench at this. **1716** Gay *Trivia* iii. 123 Should thy shoe wrench aside, down, down you fall.

β. *c* **1340** Hampole *Pr. Consc.* 1538 Some gase wrynchand to and fra, And some gas hypand. **1509** Hawes *Past. Pleas.* xviii. (1845) 84, I can not wrynche by no wyle nor croke, My heart is fast upon so sure a hoke. *a* **1632** T. Taylor *God's Judgem.* i. i. xxii. (1642) 84 A charet.., wherein were certain yron-works, which with wrinching about gave an horrible sound. *a* **1641** Bp. Mountagu *Acts & Mon.* (1642) 497 Rather then goe to law, to sit down by losse; and without wrinching forgo what was his due.

†**b.** *Fencing.* (See quots. and cf. whirl *v.* 3.)

1771 Lonnergan *Fencer's Guide* Index, *Wrenching*, is to disarm, by whirling off your adversary's blade, without setting any bounds to it, or whirling to any certain parade. *Ibid.* 88 When you parry with a Prime, wrench round into a Tierce.

2. *Coursing.* Of a hare, etc.: To veer or come round at less than a right angle; to rick.

1576 Turberv. *Venerie* 244 A deare..will holde on the same waye, and neuer turneth and wrencheth as a Hare will do before the Greyhounds. **1686** R. Blome *Gentl. Recreat.* ii. 98/1 Sometimes the Hare doth not Turn, but Wrench; for she is not properly said to Turn, except she Turn as it were round, and two Wrenches stand for a Turn. **1753** *Chambers' Cycl.* Suppl. s.v. *Coursing*, If the hare turns not quite about, she only *wrencheth*, in the sportsman's phrase. **1839** *Laws of Coursing* in Youatt *Dog* (1845) 261 If a dog draws the fleck from the hare, and causes her to wrench or rick only.

II. 3. *trans.* To twist or turn (a thing) forcibly or with effort; to jerk or pull with a violent twist; = wrest *v.* 1. Also with advs., as *about, round.*

a **1225** *Ancr. R.* 210 Summe iuglurs beoð þet ne kunnen seruen of non oðer gleo, buten makien cheres, & wrenchen mis hore muð. *Ibid.* 222 Ich chulle wrenchen hire þiderward ase heo mest dredeð. **1545** Ascham *Toxoph.* (Arb.) 146 Some will take theyr bowe and writhe and wrinche it. **1578** Lyte *Dodoens* 41 Small seedes, whiche be as they were wrenched or writhen about. **1590** Tarlton *News Purgat.* 22 Though shee coulde not treade right, yet wrincht her shoue inward. **1600** Surflet *Countrie Farme* iii. xi. 444 The wood of such great plants, doth pinch and wrinche the graft mightily. **1674** [see wreathe *v.* 6]. **1718** Bp. Hutchinson *Witchcraft* 146 One [cart carrying corn] wrench'd Amy Duny's House, upon which she came out in a Rage. **1819** Scott *Leg. Montrose* xiii, If you venture to call for assistance, I will wrench round your neck. **1825** —— *Talism.* xxviii, Each strange and disproportioned feature wrenched by horror into still more extravagant ugliness. **1839** Murchison *Silur. Syst.* i. xxxi. 422 The limestone of the principal branch is suddenly wrenched round. **1863** B. Taylor *Poets Jrnl.* iii. *Watch of Night* 7 Blow, winds..And wrench the trees forlorn That struggle where they stand. **1876** Swinburne *Erechtheus* 588 All her flower of body,.. With the might of the wind's wrath wrenched and torn.

b. To tighten with or as with a wrest or wrench; †to tune (a harp, etc.) in this way. Also with *up.*

1577 Grange *Golden Aphrod.* H iij b, Orpheus with thy Harpe in hande, Arion also.., Wrinche vp your strings. *Ibid.* M ij b, Playing..vppon their Harpes, wrinched and set to the highest note of Diatesseron. **1875** Knight *Dict. Mech.* 2253/1 The eye [of the spanner] is caught over the stud on the collar, so as to wrench it fast.

fig. **1607** Shaks. *Cor.* i. viii. 11 For thy Reuenge Wrench vp thy power to th' highest.

†**4.** *fig.* **a.** To draw or turn (a person) aside; to force *out of* the right way. *Obs.*

a **1200** *St. Marher.* 4 þæt tu ne maht nanes weies.. wenden me ne wrenchen ut of þe weie. *a* **1225** *Leg. Kath.* 124 Nes þer nan þet mahte neauer eanes wrenchen hire..ut of þe weie. *c* **1230** *Hali Meid.* 47 Ihesu crist..leue swa hare heorte halden to him, þat hare flesches eggunge..ne weorri hare heorte wit, ne wrenche ham ut of þe wei þat ha beoð in gongen.

†**b.** To draw *out* or expel (temptations); to withdraw or shelter (oneself); to divert or deflect towards another. (Cf. wrenk *v.* 2.) *Obs.*

a **1225** *Ancr. R.* 244 Swuche þouhtes ofte, i vlesliche soulen, wrencheð ut sonre vlesliche tentaciuns þeone summe of þe uorme. *Ibid.* 294 þet tu ne meiht þis scheld holden o þine heorte, ne wrenchen þe þerunder frommard þe deofles eare-wen. *Ibid.* 304 ȝif þu seist þet þin unstrencðe ne muhte nout elles, þu wrenchest þine sunne o God.

†**c.** To misrepresent or slander (a person).

c **1300** *Pol. Songs* (Camden) 157 ȝef y am wreint in heore write, Thenne am y bac-bite.

5. To injure or pain (a person, the limbs, etc.) by undue straining or stretching; to rick, sprain, strain.

α. **1530** Palsgr. 785/1, I wrenche my foote, or any lymme, I put it out of joynt. **1578** Lyte *Dodoens* 235 A playster.. upon places that be out of ioynt or wrenched. **1611** Florio, *Storcersi le membra*, to straine or wrench ones limmes out of ioint. **1638** W. Lisle *Heliodorus* viii. 141 Bagoas..with a fall Had wrench'd his leg. **1729** Swift *Direct. Serv.* Rules, You wrenched your foot against a stone, and were forced to stay. **1835** T. Mitchell *Acharn. of Aristoph.* 1064 *note*, To wrench the ankle. **1854** Thackeray *Newcomes* xxii, He.. came down on the pavement and wrenched his leg.

fig. **1642** Fuller *Holy & Prof. St.* iii. xix. 204 Would it not have wrench'd and sprain'd his soul?

β. **1578** H. Wotton *Courtlie Controv.* 259 By wrinching their foote in drawing on their hose. **1583** tr. *Maison Neuve's Gerileon* 54 b, His fistes..so were wrinched that he felt them not. **1607** Topsell *Four-f. Beasts* 78 If an Ox be wrinched and strayned in his sinewes. **1684** J. S. *Profit & Pleas. United* 204 Leg out of Joynt or Wrinched.

b. To affect with severe pain, suffering, or anguish; to distress or pain greatly; to rack.

1798 Coleridge *Anc. Mar.* vii. xv, Forthwith this frame of mine was wrenched With a woful agony. *a* **1814** Wordsw. *Excurs.* vii. 872 Through the space Of twelve ensuing days his frame was wrenched. **1821** Shelley *Hellas* 456 A spirit not my own wrenched me within.

transf. **1805** Wordsw. *Prelude* v. 31 Should the whole frame of earth by inward throes Be wrenched.

6. To pull or draw with a wrench or twist; to twist or wrest out; to force, turn, etc., by a twisting movement: **a.** With preps., as *from, into, out of, to.*

1582 Stanyhurst *Æneis* iii. (Arb.) 72 Swiftlye they determind..too wrinche thee nauye too southward. **1604** Shaks. *Oth.* v. ii. 288 Wrench his Sword from him. **1697** Dryden *Æneis* xii. 534 Turnus..Wrenched from his feeble hold the shining sword. **1730** Thomson *Winter* (ed. 3) 360 When Justice..Wrench'd from their hand Oppression's iron rod. **1748** *Anson's Voy.* ii. vi. 201 Seizing his pistol, [he] wrenched it out of his hand. **1820** Shelley *Prometh. Unb.* i. 39 To wrench the rivets from my quivering wounds. **1882** B. D. W. Ramsay *Recoll. Mil. Serv.* I. i. 25 We wrenched out of the wall an iron hook.

fig. and in fig. context. **1603** Shaks. *Meas. for M.* ii. iv. 14 How often dost thou..Wrench awe from fooles? **1605** —— *Lear* i. iv. 290 O most small fault,..Which like an Engine, wrencht my frame of Nature From the fixt place. **1790** Burns '*What needs this din*' 20 Bruce..Wrench'd his dear country from the jaws of ruin. **1820** Hazlitt *Lect. Dram. Lit.* 13 Nor could he [*sc.* Shakspere] have been wrenched from his place in the edifice..without equal injury to himself and it. **1851** Hawthorne *Ho. Sev. Gables* xvi, To wrench it [*sc.* a fixed opinion] out of their minds. **1879** McCarthy *Own Times* xlii. III. 283 His gift was that which wrenches success out of the very jaws of failure.

refl. **1834** Sir F. B. Head *Bubbles fr. Brunnen* 129 As if the corpse..had wrenched himself once again into daylight.

b. With advs., as *away, off, out, outward, up*; *asunder, open.*

1607 Topsell *Four-f. Beasts* 364 Staying the midst of your toole vpon the horses neather iaw, wrinch the tooth outward. **1608** Shaks. *Per.* iii. ii. 53 *Sec. Gent.* 'Tis like a coffin... *Cerimon.* Wrench it open straight. **1639** G. Plattes *Discov. Infin. Treas.* xii. 84 In a quarter of an houre the whole bush is wrenched up by the rootes. **1726** Swift *Gulliver* i. i, I had the fortune to..wrench out the pegs. **1796** Boys *Agric. Kent* (ed. 2) 120 A hop-dog, to wrench up the poles. **1819** Shelley *Peter Bell 3rd* i. x, As he was speaking came a spasm, And wrenched his gnashing teeth asunder. **1825** J. Neal *Bro. Jonathan* I. 251 He went up to the door, wrenched off the fastenings. **1863** Geo. Eliot *Romola* xxiv, Like a harp of which all the strings had been wrenched away except one. **1884** *Manch. Exam.* 11 Oct. 5/1 They wrench off cupboard doors to spare themselves the trouble of closing them.

fig. **1821** Hazlitt *Winterslow* x. (1850) 174 The revolutionary wheel which has of late wrenched men's understandings almost asunder. **1848** Mrs. Gaskell *Mary Barton* x, Wrenching up her natural feelings of home. **1868** Tennyson *Lucretius* 218 It seems some unseen monster lays His..filthy hands upon my will, Wrenching it backward into his.

refl. **1865** Dickens *Mut. Fr.* i. i, What he had in tow.. sometimes seemed to try to wrench itself away.

absol. (for *refl.*) **1912** P. A. Talbot *In Shadow of Bush* xxv. 277 At sight of us she wrenched free.

c. Without const. Also *fig.*

1655 Vaughan *Silex Scint.* ii. *Starre* v, Desire that never will be quench'd, Nor can be writh'd, nor wrench'd. **1697** Dryden *Æneis* x. 1273 To wrench the Darts which in his Buckler light. **1713** [Croxall] *Orig. Canto Spenser* xx. (1714) 17 Those honest Hounds..Striving..to wrench the Chain, Which did her tender Limbs to th' rock upty. **1879** R. Bridges *Shorter Poems* (1912) 248 The lazy cows wrench many a scented flower.

d. To seize or take forcibly; = wrest *v.* 4.

1605 Shaks. *Macb.* iii. i. 63 They..put a barren Scepter in my Gripe, Thence to be wrencht with an vnlineall Hand. **1796** Southey *Joan of Arc* v. 474 If the iron rod Should one day from Oppression's hand be wrench'd By everlasting Justice! **1810** Scott *Lady of Lake* v. vi, Wrenching from ruin'd Lowland swain His herds and harvest. **1832** Ht. Martineau *Ireland* vi. 92 Those from whose hands he had wrenched the means of subsistence. **1851** Gallenga *Italy*

13 To wrench from the reluctant hands of diplomacy exceptional modifications of those fatal treaties. **1868** E. Edwards *Ralegh* I. ix. 143 Spoils had been wrenched from Spain such as hitherto were almost unexampled.

e. To deprive (a person) *of* something by wrenching or wresting.

1786 Burns *To Mountain Daisy* viii, Till wrench'd of ev'ry stay but Heav'n, He, ruin'd, sink!

7. To twist, alter, or change from the right or true form, application, or import; to wrest, pervert, distort. Cf. wrest *v.* 5.

1549 Latimer *1st Serm. bef. Edw. VI* (Arb.) 29 Wrenching thys text of scrypture..after their owne phantasie. *Ibid.*, Thei wrench these wordes a wrye. **1589** Puttenham *Eng. Poesie* ii. iv. (Arb.) 89 Let his ryme and concordes be true,..and not darke or wrenched by wrong writing. **1593** Harvey *Pierce's Super.* 100 Should impertinent secrecies be reuealed;..euery proposition wrinched to the harshest sense? **1641** Milton *Reform.* ii. Wks. 1851 III. 51 These devout Prelates..for these many years have not ceas't in their Pulpits wrinching, and spraining the text. *c* **1655** —— *Sonn.*, *'Cyriack, whose Grandsire'* 4 [He] in his volumes taught our Lawes, Which others at their Barr so often wrench. **1863** Cowden Clarke *Shaks. Char.* viii. 211 They proceeded to wrench that power to the restraining of all dissentients. **1877** Winchell *Reconcil. Sci. & Relig.* xii. 325 It is infinitely better to learn how God really did proceed, than to..wrench our Bible to make it fit a misconception of facts.

†**b.** To derive (a word) by alteration *from* another. *Obs.*

1623 Camden *Rem.* (ed. 3) 70 *Lewis*, wrenched from *Lodowick*, which Tilius interpreteth, Refuge of the people.

8. *Coursing.* To divert, turn, or bring round (a hare, etc.) at less than a right angle; to rick.

1622 Drayton *Poly-olb.* xxiii. 345 When each man..notes Which Dog first turnes the Hare, which first the other coats, They wrench her once or twice, ere she a turne will take. **1839** *Laws of Coursing* in Youatt *Dog* (1845) 262 When a dog wrenches or ricks a hare twice following, without losing the lead, it is equal to a turn. **1840** *Sportsman* II. 216 Wrenched by the one or the other of her pursuers, she seemed every moment almost in the jaws of one of them. **1865** *Field* 4 Mar. 151/3 Rebe wrenched her hare half a dozen lengths in advance of Master Sweeney.

absol. **1876** *Coursing Calendar* 10 Gardenia shot in front, and..turned; she then wrenched and killed. **1886** *Field* 20 Feb. 227/2 Mr. Dent's dog went up for the kill after wrenching once.

†**9.** To drive, impel, or thrust (a weapon) with a twisting movement. *Obs. rare.*

1594 Kyd *Cornelia* iv. i. 23 Scipio hath wrencht a sword into hys brest. *Ibid.* v. 322 He wrencht it to the pommel through his sides.

†**b.** *refl.* To force (oneself) *in* among others. *Sc. Obs.*$^{-1}$

1729 Wodrow *Corr.* (1843) III. 454 [Such] persons..in a time of party and division, get in where they ought not to be, and when they have wrenched themselves in, talk [etc.].

10. *absol.* To pull or tug (*at* something) with a turn or twist. Also *fig.* and *transf.*

1697 Dryden *Æneis* xii. 1132 Th' incumbent Heroe wrench'd and pull'd and strain'd; But still the stubborn Earth the Steel detain'd. **1858** Carlyle *Fredk. Gt.* ix. ix. ⁋3 France has been wrenching and screwing at this Lorraine, wriggling it off bit by bit. **1865** Dickens *Mut. Fr.* ii. xv, He ..again grasped the stone..and wrenched at it. **1891** Kipling *Life's Handicap* 245 The water snarled and wrenched and worried at the timber.

b. To come *out* by or as by wrenching.

1903 E. Childers *Riddle of Sands* viii, The lower screw-plate on the stern post had wrenched out.

wrench, obs. or dial. erron. f. rinse *v.*

wrenched (rɛn(t)ʃt, *poet.* ˈrɛn(t)ʃɪd), *ppl. a.* [f. wrench *v.* + -ed[1].]

1. Sprained, strained; dislocated.

1556 Withals *Dict.* (1562) 77 b/2 Wrenched or hurte in the iointes, *distortus.* **1567** Gresham in Burgon *Life* (1839) II. 212, I wolde have waited upon you.., but that my wrenched legge would not suffer me. **1684** J. S. *Profit & Pleas. United* 73 Foot out of Joynt or wrinched Foot. **1872** Tennyson *Gareth & Lynette* 87 Who never knewest..pang Of wrench'd or broken limb. **1897** Anne Page *Afternoon Ride* 89 Brierly loosed the wrenched wrist.

b. Twisted, wrung. Also with *off.* Occas. *fig.*

1894 A. Morrison *M. Hewitt Investigator* 245 A trap-door..six or eight inches open, the edge resting on the half-wrenched-off bolt. **1908** A. Noyes *W. Morris* 63 There are wrenched hands and writhen lips in it. **1915** A. Reade *Poems Love & War* 78 From our tears..and wrenchèd hearts, Let some fair harvest spring.

2. *Pros.* (See quot.)

1891 J. C. Parsons *Engl. Versif.* 144 Wrenched Accent.—This term is used when the metrical stress is thrown upon a syllable which would not ordinarily be accented.

wrencher (ˈrɛn(t)ʃə(r)). [f. wrench *v.* + -er[1].]

1. A machine or instrument for wrenching or wringing. *rare.*

1495 *Trevisa's Barth. De P.R.* xix. l. 892 Sourysshe thynges..bere downe the meete as it were a pressour other a wrencher [*MSS.* wrynge]. **1832** S. Warren *Diary Late Physician* I. 380 Before proceeding to use our screws, or wrenchers, we once more looked and listened.

2. One who or that which wrenches or twists. Also *fig.*

1847 in *Home Life Sir D. Brewster* (1869) 190 [Thou wert] The pillar of thine own beloved fane; The wrencher of its chill and crushing chain. **1863** Cowden Clarke *Shaks. Char.* xvii. 415 The wrencher of a civil institution to his own individual aggrandisement.

†**ˈwrenchful**, *a. Obs. rare.* [f. wrench *sb.*[1] + -ful.] Artful, crafty, deceitful.

a **1225** *Ancr. R.* 268 His wihtful crokes, & his wrenchfule wicchecreftes. *c* **1225** *Leg. Kath.* 890 þe wrenchfule feont.. wið his wiles weorp ham ut sone of paraises selhðen. *c* **1230** *Hali Meid.* (1922) 64 þu wrenchfule [*Titus MS.* wrech-wile] ful wiht! al for nawt þu prokest me to for-gulten.

wrenching (ˈrɛn(t)ʃɪŋ), *vbl. sb.* [f. wrench *v.* + -ing[1].]

1. The action of the verb in various senses; an instance of this.

1398 Trevisa *Barth. De P.R.* v. xxviii. (Addit. MS.), þe hond is greued..by wrastinge and wrenching of ioyntes. *c* **1430** *Lanfranc's Cirurg.* 5 (Addit. MS.), þe secunde techynge a comyn word off wrenchynges out of Ioynte. **1545** Ascham *Toxoph.* (Arb.) 145 An other maketh a wrynchinge with hys backe. **1580** Blundevil *Horsemanship* 51 b, Of the wrinching of the shoulder. **1674** *Barbette's Chirurg.* (ed. 2) 17 Sometimes the Bone is..forced out of its place..but a little, or half, which is called Sub-luxation, or Wrenching. **1733** Tull *Horse-Hoeing Husb.* xxii. 338 By the Twisting (or Renching) of the Wheels. **1821** Byron *Two Foscari* i. i. 160 My curdling limbs Quiver with the anticipated wrenching. **1861** Dickens *All Year Round* 13 July 365 The sudden wrenching of him out of our boat. **1884** E. Yates *Recoll.* I. 159 The charioteers..declined to submit them to the unavoidable twists and wrenchings.

fig. **1555** Latimer in Foxe *A. & M.* (1583) 1724/2 Their racking, writhing, wrinching, and monstrously iniuryng of Gods holy scripture. **1583** Melbancke *Philotimus* Cc iij, Whose loue hath eased the wrenching of my heart. **1863** Cowden Clarke *Shaks. Char.* xvi. 391 No tyranny being equal to the wrenching of law for penal purposes.

b. *spec.* The action of rectifying a deformed foot, esp. by a foot-wrench.

1896 Tubby *Deformities* 415 Wrenching..may be effected more especially in this degree by manual force, and in the severer degrees by special apparatus. *Ibid.*, When wrenching is carried out with the hands.

c. *N.Z.* = *root-pruning* s.v. root *sb.*[1] 23.

1950 *N.Z. Jrnl. Agric.* July 55/1 Toward the end of August root crops..tend to run to seed. This growth can be retarded considerably by wrenching..pushing a fork or spade into the soil..and..levering the roots up slightly. This breaks the extreme end of the taproot.

†**2.** A griping pain in the bowels. *Obs.*

1607 Walkington *Opt. Glass* 124 Vexed much with wrinching and griping in the bowels. **1607** Topsell *Four-f. Beasts* 442 The wringings and wrinchings..in the guts or belly of a man or woman.

3. *attrib.* in *wrenching-iron.*

1592 Shaks. *Rom. & Jul.* v. iii. 22 Giue me that Mattocke, & the wrenching Iron. **1769** *Public Advertiser* 6 June 3/2 The Thieves left behind them a Wrenching Iron, about two Feet long.

ˈwrenching, *ppl. a.* [f. as prec. + -ing[2].] That wrenches or twists; of the nature of a wrench. Also *fig.*

1618 Gainsford *Glory Eng.* ii. xxv. 315 Yet we haue still gone forward, and could not bee pull'd backe by any wrenching arme whatsoeuer. **1889** Welch *Text Bk. Naval Archit.* vii. 99 The stem must be..strengthened to resist the wrenching stresses. **1889** Gunter *That Frenchman* xix. 248 He..gives this wrist..a wrenching twist. **1894** T. Pinkerton *Blizzard* 105 The thought..gave him a wrenching pang.

Hence **ˈwrenchingly** *adv.*

1884 L. Macbean tr. *Buchanan's Spir. Songs* 28 He was stripped and wrenchingly Stretched out with cruel strain.

†**wrench-milk.** *Obs. rare.* Also 6 **wrynche, urynche.** [f. the stem of wrench *v.* Cf. OE. *wringhwæʒ* curd.] Curd.

1510 Stanbridge *Vocabula* (W. de W.) C v, *Oxigulum*, wrenche mylke. [**1525** *Oxigala*, wrynche mylke.] **1530** Palsgr. 285/2 Urynche mylke, *maigre* [read *maigve*].

†**wrene**, *a. Obs. rare.* [OE. *wrǽne* lascivious, libidinous.] Wanton.

c **1400** *Laud Troy Bk.* 6600, I schal the teche bothe burdoun and mene, Ne be thow neuere so wroth ne wrene.

wrene, ME. var. wry *v.*[1]

Wrenean (rɛˈniːən), *a.* [f. the name of the architect Sir Christopher *Wren* (1632–1723) + -ean.] Of or pertaining to, following or consonant with the architectural theories or practices of, Sir C. Wren; built by Wren. See also Wrenian *a.*

1813 *Gentl. Mag.* Feb. 132 The decorations of the Wrenean school of architecture. *Ibid.* 133 Topped with Wrenean pedestals and balls. *Ibid.*, Whether at the Wrenean, or any subsequent period. **1896** *Westm. Gaz.* 11 Sept. 3/1 The exquisite gates which adorn the Wrenean terraces of Chelsea.

Hence **Wreˈneanize** *v. trans.*, to make Wrenean in character.

1813 *Gentl. Mag.* Feb. 133/1 The lanthern is wholly Wreneanised, in two tiers with lights to each.

wreng, obs. var. wring *v.*

†**wrength.** *Obs. rare*$^{-1}$. [repr. OE. type **wręngðu*, f. *wrang* wrong *a.* For the formation cf. *length*, *strength*.] Crookedness; distortion.

c **1220** *Bestiary* 85 in *O.E. Misc.* 3 Ðanne goð he to a ston, & he billeð ðer-on, Billeð til his bec biforn haueð ðe wrengðe forloren.

Wrenian (ˈrɛnɪən), *a.* Also **Wrennian.** [f. as Wrenean *a.* + -ian] Built by, or in the style of, Sir C. Wren.

1853 *Ecclesiologist* XIV. 393 The gallery front of a Wrennian church of two orders, such as S. James's Piccadilly. **1944** *Burlington Mag.* Oct. 260/1 The complete reinstatement of a destroyed Wrenian interior. **1973** *Country Life* 13 Dec. 2017/3 The style is about half correct Classical or Wrenian and half Victorian Italianate.

†**wrenk**, *sb. Sc.* and *north. Obs.* Forms: α. 4–5 **wrenk(e.** β. 5–6 **wrink(e, wrynk.** [Northern var. of wrench *sb.*[1] Cf. next.]

1. = wrench *sb.*[1] 1. Freq. coupled with *wile.*

c **1325** *Metr. Hom.* Prol. 2 Thou filde this gaste sa full of witte..That al bestes er red for man, Sa mani wyle and wrenk he can. *c* **1340** Hampole *Pr. Consc.* 1360 þe world.. ledes a man with wrenkes and wyles. **13..** *Cursor M.* 13336 (Gött.), Na wrenkes [*other MSS.* wrenches] of þe maledight Againes hir sal haue no might. *c* **1440** *York Myst.* xxx. 67 With wrynkis and with wiles to wend me my weys. *c* **1480** Henryson *Fox, Wolf & Cadger* 37 For euerie wrink, forsuith, thow hes ane wyle. *a* **1500** in *Ratis Raving*, etc. 3 the deuill wyll cast mony wrenkis of falsait. **1500–20** Dunbar *Poems* xxx. 42 In me..wes mony wrink and wyle. *a* **1508** Mersar in *Bannatyne MS.* (Hunter. Club) 808/19 For every wrynk luk that ye haif a wyle.

2. Trickery, deception; = wrench *sb.*[1] 2.

1338 R. Brunne *Chron.* (1810) 246 For falshed & for wrenk he forsuore þe land.

†**wrenk**, *v. Obs. rare.* Also 4 **wrenke, wrinck.** [Northern var. of wrench *v.* Cf. prec.]

1. *intr.* To writhe; to turn *away.*

a **1300** *Cursor M.* 17458 Bot iesu crist þat rightwis es,..A-wai to wrenk he dos þe wrang. *Ibid.* 19353 Þan be-gan þai wrenk [*Gött.* wrinck, *Fairf.* wrenche] and wrest, And for tene þair tethe to gnast.

2. *trans.* To turn aside, to divert from oneself. (Cf. wrench *v.* 4 b.)

a **1300** *Cursor M.* 26385 Þis ypocrites..wald ai wrenk þair aun wites, For to sem þam-self god and lele.

wrenlet (ˈrɛnlɪt). [f. wren[1] + -let.] A young wren.

1858 *Chambers's Jrnl.* Aug. 82/2 It affords a cradle to near a score of wrenlets. **1927** *Observer* 22 May 23/2 In a knot in the rope was a wren's nest, with two or three wrenlets visible inside.

wreoen, wreoðien: see wry *v.*, wrethe *v.*[2]

wrest (rɛst), *sb.*[1] Forms: α. 3–6 **wreste,** 5– **wrest** (7–9 **rest**), 5 **wreeste,** 6 **wreast,** *Sc.* **wreist,** 7 *Sc.* **wriest,** 8 **rist.** β. 4–5 **wrayst(e,** 5 **wraist(e.** γ. 5 **wraaste, wrastt,** 5–6 **wrast(e.** [f. the verb.]

I. 1. The action of twisting, wrenching, or writhing; a twist, wrench; a tug or violent pull; †a turn of a tuning-peg (quot. 1501).

a **1300** *Cursor M.* 3462 Þair strut it was vn-stern stith, Wit wrathli wrestes [*Gött.* wraystes] aiþer writh. *a* **1400–50** *Bk. Curtasye* 26 in *Babees Bk.* 300 First to the ryȝht honde þou shalle go, Sitthen to þo left honde þy neghe þou cast; To hom þou boghe withouten wrast. *c* **1500** *Proverbis* in *Antiq. Rep.* (1809) IV. 406 Stoppide in the freytes they [*sc.* lute-strings] abydeth the pynnes wrest. **1501** Douglas *Pal. Hon.* ii. iv, Thair instrumentis all maist war fidillis lang, But with a string quhilk neuer a wreist ȝeid wrang. **1575** Laneham *Let.* (1871) 53 With the wreast of a Cok [he] was sure of a coolar: water spurting vpward. **1611** Cotgr., *Torse*,..a wrest, wrinch; wrythe, wrying.

1883 A. Herschel in *Nature* March 458 The time-rates of each of these momenta..are respectively angular moment or twirl (of a force-couple) and tractive moment or wrest (of a motor-couple).

fig. *c* **1430** Lydg. *Lyfe of our Lady* (Caxton, ? 1484) I viii b, It causeth hertes no lenger to debate That partyd ben with the wreste of hate. *a* **1590** Greene *Orpharion* Wks. (Grosart) XII. 31 Loue,..if it be ouerstrained, cracketh at the first wrest. **1838** S. Bellamy *Betrayal* 126 In the strong wrest of supplication, then, sole travailing.

b. Extent of wresting; hence, reach of capacity; stretch, strain. *rare*$^{-1}$.

1593 Nashe *Christ's T.* L ij b, Thou wert chosen to make an Oration.., in which (hauing toyled thy wits to theyr highest wrest) thou [etc.].

†**c.** Without article. Twist or coil. *Obs.*$^{-1}$

a **1575** tr. *Pol. Verg. Eng. Hist.* (Camden No. 36) 49 Thei hade for the moste parte long heare, withowte wrest or curle.

†**d.** *Sc.* A wrenching or spraining of the muscles; a sprain or strain. *Obs.*

1616 *Orkney Witch Trial* in Dalyell *Darker Superstit. Scotl.* (1834) 118 [To make] a wresting thread, and give it in the name of the Father, Sone, and the Holie Gaist,..it wald mak ony wrest of man or beast haill. *c* **1700** in Jas. Watson *Coll. Sc. Poems* (1706) I. 60 It will be good against the Pine Of any Wriest or Strienzie. **1881** Paul *Past & Pres. Aberdeen.* 15 Mr. Thomson then [= in 1698] being bed-rid by reason of a wrest in his ankle.

†**2.** *fig.* An ill or evil turn; a trick. *Obs.*

14.. *Sir Beues* (E.) 1930 A made hire alway to ete ferst, Lest þey deden him ony wrest. *c* **1440** *York Myst.* xvii. 187 Than shall we wayte þam with a wrest, And make all wast þat þei haue wroght.

†**3.** The action of wresting, forcing, or straining the meaning or purport of words, etc.; an instance of this. *Obs.*

1581 J. Bell *Haddon's Answ. Osor.* 169 b, By what wrest of Logicke doth Osorius gather habilitie of Freewill out of the holy ordinaunces. **1597** J. Payne *Royal Exch.* 22 They seke fauls armure by wrest of scripture. *a* **1603** T. Cartwright *Confut. Rhem. N.T.* (1618) 467 Where the witnesse of the other hath often a wrest and tacke of her corruption. *Ibid.* 716 It is..partly falsification, partly a wrest of the Scripture. **1609** [Bp. W. Barlow] *Answ. Nameless Cath.* 38 To picke quarels at words, by wrests and streines, neither to purpose nor to sense.

II. *techn.* †**4.** *Surg.* A peg for tightening a ligature by twisting. *Obs.*

c **1370** ARDERNE *Practica* (MS. Ashm. 1434) fol. 4 In quo foramine vnum vertile, anglice *wrayst*, imponatur. *a* **1425** tr. *Arderne* 9 By middez of whiche wraiste in þe ouer ende shal be a litel hole.

5. An implement for tuning certain wire-stringed instruments, as the harp or spinet; a tuning-key. Now *arch.*

In ME. sometimes erron. used to render L. *plectrum*.

1398 TREVISA *Barth. De P.R.* v. xxi. (Bodl. MS.), þe sowne of speking byndeþ wordes; as wreste [**1495** wraste].. temperith þe strenges, so þe tonge smyteþ þe teeþ. *c* **1425** in *Anglia* VIII. 109/31 þis newe tymbrer settiþ.. hir handys and fyngers for a wrast, þat is an instrument of organ-songe. *c* **1440** *Promp. Parv.* 533/2 Wreste of an harpe or other lyke, *plectrum*. *c* **1460** *Liber Pluscardensis* (1877) I. 392 Sal we the menstral wyt? Yha, bot he bent and pruf thaim [*sc.* the strings] with his wraist. **1504** CORNISHE in *Skelton's Wks.* (1568) Z vij, A harper wt his wrest maye tune the harpe wrong. **1575** LANEHAM *Let.* (1871) 38 Hiz harp in good grace dependaunt before him: hiz wreast tyed to a green lace, and hanging by. **1612** in *Halyburton's Ledger* (1867) 333 Wrests for virginals the groce, vi li. **1663** PEPYS *Diary* 1 April, Calling on the virginall maker, buying a rest for myself to tune my tryangle. **1668** *Ibid.* 20 July, To buy a rest for my espinette at the ironmonger's.

1793 *Minstrel* I. 91 Beside it, suspended by a green lace, he hung the wrest, or key, by which it is tuned. [Cf. quot. 1575.] **1819** SCOTT *Ivanhoe* xliii, A silver chain, by which hung the wrest, or key, with which he tuned his harp. **1831** H. NEELE *Rom. Hist.* I. 201 Trying his harp strings, and with his wrest or screw tuning them to the proper pitch. **1861** W. F. COLLIER *Hist. Eng. Lit.* 36 The distinctive badge of the [minstrel's] profession was the wrest or tuning-key.

transf. **1398** TREVISA *Barth. De P.R.* v. xxiii. (Bodl. MS.), Soune is.. yschape with þe wraaste [L. *plectrum*] of þe tunge.

b. *fig.* and in fig. context.

a **1548** HALL *Chron., Hen. VII*, 3 There lacked a wrest to the harpe to set all the strynges in a monacorde and tune, which was the matrimony.. betwene the kynge and.. Elizabeth. **1603** J. DAVIES (Heref.) *Microcosmos* Wks. (Grosart) I. 81/1 O let the longest Largs be shortest Briefes In this discordant Note, and turne the Wrest. **1613** JAS. I *Edict agst. Private Combats* 45 This small instrument the Tongue.. being kept in tune by the wrest of awe.

c. *Her.* The figure of a 'wrest' used as a charge.

1572 BOSSEWELL *Armorie* II. 87 b, His crest a wrest in crosse, Sol. **1688** HOLME *Armoury* III. xvi. (Roxb.) 59/2 He beareth Argent, a Virginall Wrest sable.

†**6. a.** An implement for wresting; a tool for turning bolts, nuts, etc.; a screw-key. Also *fig.*

1589 in *Trans. Shropsh. Archæol. Soc.* (1878) I. 12, iiij vice pynnes with a wrest for a field bedde. **1593** *Rites & Mon. Ch. Durham* (Surtees) 8 Two silver.. Candlesticks for two tapers.. to be taken in sunder with wrests. **1598** [see WRENCH *sb.*[2] 5]. **1603** HOLLAND *Plutarch's Mor.* 4 Thie fellowship in feeding together is.. a wrest that straineth and stretcheth benevolence to the uttmost.

fig. *a* **1592** GREENE *Alcida* (1617) E 4, Faith is the key that shuts the spring of loue, Lightnesse a wrest, that wringeth all awry.

†**b.** A machine for hoisting or hauling weights. *Obs. rare.*

1584 B. R. tr. *Herodotus* II. 104 They deuised certayne engines or wrestes [Gr. μηχαναί] to heaue vp stones from the grounde,.. hauyng vppon each stayre a wreast.

†**c.** (See quot.) *Obs. rare*[−0].

1688 HOLME *Armoury* III. 102/1 Wrest, is that by which Saw Teeth are set.

7. Special Combs., as **wrest block**, = *wrest plank*; **wrest-pin**, the peg or pin round which the ends of the wires or strings of certain musical instruments are coiled; a tuning-pin (also *attrib.*); **wrest-plank**, the board in a piano in which the wrest-pins are fixed (also *attrib.* and *Comb.*).

1787 H. WALTON *Specif. of Patent* No. 1607, The *rest block,.. the damper.., and the rest pin.. are made the same as they always are made in Grand Piano Fortes. **1783** J. BROADWOOD *Specif. of Patent* No. 1379. 3 The *rist pins to which the strings are fixt. **1802** T. LOUD *Specif. of Patent* No. 2591. 2 The rest pin block. **1825** P. ERARD *Specif. of Patent* No. 5065. 2 The want of stability in the wrest pin plank. **1880** A. J. HIPKINS in Grove *Dict. Mus.* II. 722/1 The tuning-pin screws.. into the thick metal wrestpin-piece. **1799** J. SMITH *Specif. of Patent* No. 2345. 2 The Drawing.. shows the *rest plank, trussed with wood. **1846** BURKINYOUNG in *Repert. Patent Invent.* (1847) IX. 78 The rest plank bridge. **1881** *Instr. Census Clerks* (1885) 50 Piano Manufacturing:.. Tuner. Turner. Wire Maker. Wrest Plank Maker.

wrest, *sb.*[2] *Agric.* Now *dial.* Also 9 **wreest, wrist.** [Incorrect spelling of *rest*, var. REEST *sb.*, by association with prec. and WREST *v.*] A piece of iron (†or wood) fastened beneath the mould-board in certain ploughs. **b.** A mould-board.

1653 BLITHE *Eng. Improv. Impr.* xxviii. 190 The Plough-sheath, Wrest, Beam, Share, and Coulter.. retain these names clearly in most parts. **1669** WORLIDGE *Syst. Agricult.* 207 Any Plough.. having its true Pitch, with its true cast on the Sheild-board and short Wrest. **1765** A. DICKSON *Treat. Agric.* (ed. 2) 165 The earth of the furrow, in rising up from the fore part of the wrest, is soon resisted by the mold-board, and turned over suddenly. **1778** [W. H. MARSHALL] *Minutes Agriculture* 6 March 1776 *note*, The wrest is.. the piece of wood, or iron,.. which is meant to *wrest* open and clear effectually the bottom of the plow-furrow. **1796** BOYS *Agric. Kent* (1813) 64 The furrows.. are opened with an old plough, with a wrest at each side. **1844** H. STEPHENS *Bk. Farm* I. 408 The wrest or mould-board. **1887** PARISH & SHAW *Kentish Dial.* 191 *Wreest*,.. that part of a Kentish plough.. on which it rests against the land ploughed up. **1893** *S.E. Worc. Words* 49 *Wrist* (*Wrest* or *Rest*) of a plough, a piece of wood below the shield-board, which wrests the earth aside from the plough.

wrest, obs. var. WRIST *sb.*

wrest (rɛst), *v.* Forms: *α.* 1 **wræstan**, 3–4 **wresten**, 5 **-yn, -on**, 4–6 **wreste**, 4– **wrest** (7 **rest**); 6–7 **wreast(e**, 6 *Sc.* **wreist** (9 **reist**), 6 **wryst(e**, *Sc.* **wrist.** *β.* *north.* 4 **wraist(e**, 5–6 **wrayste.** *γ.* 4–6 **wrast, wraste.** *Pa. t.* 3–5 **wraste**; (also *pa. pple.*) 4–5 **wrast,** 5 **wraiste, wrest**; 4 **wraisted, wrastid** (etc.), 6– **wrested.** [OE. *wrǽstan*, = ON. **wreista* (ONorw. and Icel. *reista*; MDa. *vreste*, Da. *vriste*):—**wraistjan*, related to WRIST.

The northern forms with *ai*, *ay*, are directly ad. ON. **wreista*.]

I. 1. *trans.* To subject (something) to a twisting movement; to turn or twist. Also with advs., as *about*, *away*, *round*.

α. *a* **1000** *Sal. & Sat.* 95 (Gr.), T.. hine.. on ðа tungan sticað, wræsteð him ðæt woddor, and him ða wongan brieceð. *c* **1205** LAY. 7532 Julius hit wraste & þat sweord stike feste. *c* **1330** R. BRUNNE *Chron. Wace* 3194 Hur fyngres sche wrast, þe blod out brak. Sche tremblede. **1398** TREVISA *Barth. De P.R.* XVIII. ix. (Bodl. MS.) fol. 248/2 þe poette seiþ þat serpente wraste his owne white heed backeward. *a* **1425** *Cursor M.* 7510 (Trin.), I shook hem bi þe berdes so þat her chaules I wraste in two. *c* **1440** *Promp. Parv.* 533/2 Wrestyn, and wrythyn a-ȝen, *reflecto*. **1548** ELYOT, *Intorquere mentum*, to writhe or wreste the chynne. **1599** HAKLUYT *Voy.* II. I. 272 A small rod of siluer.. which is wrested, so that the two ends meet. **1603** HOLLAND *Plutarch's Mor.* 148 A shoe is wrested and turned according to the fashion of a crooked or splay-foot. **1676** MARVELL *Gen. Councils* Wks. (Grosart) III. 153 The heliotrope flower.. wrests its neck in turning after the warm sun. **1733** TULL *Horse-Hoeing Husb.* xiv. 193 A Rope.. which they bring over the Top of all the loaded Sheets, and wrest it at the Tail [of each waggon]. **1893** F. THOMPSON *Poems* 59 He wrested o'er the rhymer's head that garmenting which wrought him wrong.

transf. **1601** HOLLAND *Pliny* I. 105 Notwithstanding all these barres, within which he [*sc.* a mountain-range] is pent, twined, and wrested.

β, γ. *a* **1425** tr. *Arderne's Treat. Fistula*, etc. 9 Wraistyng þe skynne atuyx þe tewel & þe fistule. ? *a* **1500** *Chester Pl.* xvi. 547 This Caytyfe.. shall be wronge wrast, or I wend away. **1570** LEVINS *Manip.* 203 To wrayste, *torquere*.

†**b.** To screw or turn (the pin or pins of a musical instrument) so as to tighten or tune the strings; to tune or tighten (a stringed instrument, its wires, etc.) by means of a wrest. Also with *up*. Occas. in fig. context.

a **1000** *Bi Manna Wyrdum* 82 (Gr.), Sum sceal mid hearpan æt his hlafordes fotum sittan,.. & a snellice snere wræstan, lætan scralletan. *c* **1380** WYCLIF *Wks.* (1880) 340 An harpe haþe þre partis,.. þe ouermost in which ben stringis wrastid. *Ibid.* 341 And sorowe of trespasse aȝeyns hem ten [*sc.* strings] shal wraste þis harpe to a-corde welle. *c* **1440** *Promp. Parv.* 533 Wreston, *plecto*. **1504** CORNISHE in *Skelton's Wks.* (1568) Z vj, The claricord hath a tunely kynde As the wyre is wrested hye and lowe. **1581** PETTIE *Guazzo's Civ. Conv.* II. (1586) 117 Our lyfe is like to instruments of Musicke, which sometime wresting vp the strings and sometime by loosing them, become more melodious. **1587** GREENE *Tritam.* II, Siluestro.. had almost made Lacena peeuish, fearing if he wrested not the pin to a right key, his melody would be marred. **1615** SWETNAM *Arraignm. Wom.* 19 As fidlers do their strings, who wrest them so high [etc.].

fig. **13..** *E.E. Allit. P.* B. 1166 Þat wakned his wrath & wrast hit so hyȝe, þat [etc.]. **1430-40** LYDG. *Bochas* VI. 423 Of an harpe he herde the sueete soun. Which instrument.. Wrestid hym ageyn to al gladnesse. **1584** GREENE *Mirr. Modestie* (1866) 19 The Judges.. by the power of the law thought to wrest hir vpon a higher pin. **1599** NASHE *Lenten Stuffe* Wks. (Grosart) V. 232 Rouze thy spirites.. and wrest them vp to the most outstretched ayry straine of elocution.

†**c.** To put or set *in* with a twisting or tortuous movement; to insert or introduce in this manner. Chiefly *fig.* *Obs.*

1597 MORLEY *Introd. Mus.* 120 He can do nothing else in musik but wrest & wring in hard points vpon a plainsong. **1606** CHAPMAN *Gentl. Usher* III. ii. 450 Theres a fine word now; wrest in that if you can by any meanes. **1690** C. NESSE *O. & N. Test.* I. 109 If the subtle serpent can but see a hole to wrest in his head.

2. To pull, pluck, drag away, or detach (a person or thing) with a wrench or twist; to twist, tear, or wrench out, etc. Also with advs., as *aside*, *forth*, *off*, *out*, *whence*, or preps., as *off*, *out of*, and esp. *from*.

α. **1297** R. GLOUC. (Rolls) 4309 Bineþe þe nekke he him nom, & wraste him adoun of is hors. **1303** R. BRUNNE *Handl. Synne* 6195 Þe lyd vp sone þey wraste. **1387** TREVISA *Higden* V. 181 Fyve knyȝtes myȝte not wreste the rope out of his hond. **14..** *Sir Beues* (M.) 190 Wyth that syr Guy his swerde out wrasted. *c* **1450** LOVELICH *Grail* xiv. 670 Hym from his hors anon he wraste. **1590** SPENSER *F.Q.* III. xii. 33 From her.. The wicked weapon rashly he did wrest. *a* **1661** FULLER *Worthies* III. (1662) 197 He also then assisted Henry Bull.. to wrest.. out of the hands of the Choristers, the Censer. **1698** T. FROGER *Voy.* 33 Young girls.. could not be wrested from them [*sc.* apes] without a great deal of difficulty. **1724** C. L. *St. Taffy's Day* 37 Brass Knockers strong, from Doors fierce wresting. **1778**, etc. [see WREST *sb.*[2]]. **1821** SCOTT *Kenilw.* xxii, Foster.. wrested the flask from her hand. **1871** R. ELLIS tr. *Catullus* lxii. 21 Thou from a mother's arms canst wrest her daughter asunder.

transf. **13..** *E.E. Allit. P.* B. 1802 He was corsed for his vn-clannes,.. & of pyse worldes worchyp wrast out for euer. **1886** FLOR. MARRYAT *Tom Tiddler's G.* 173, I procured a bed, whence I was wrested at an unearthly hour the next morning.

refl. **1686** tr. *Chardin's Trav. Persia* 163 In another Condition, I should.. have wrested my self out of their Clutches Scotfree.

β, γ. *a* **1300** *Cursor M.* 3466 He þat on þe right side lai þe toþer him wraisted oft away. **13..** *E.E. Allit. P.* C. 80 Þay.. Wryþe me in a warlok, wrast out myn yȝen. *c* **1400** *St. Alexius* (Cotton) 316 He hyllde his hand so faste, That owte he myght hit [*sc.* a leaf] natt wrast. **1596** SPENSER *F.Q.* v. xii. 21 His yron axe.. by no meanes.. backe againe he forth could wrast.

b. *fig.* and in fig. context.

1513 MORE *Rich. III* (1883) 24 Suche euyll oppinyon once fastened in mennes hartes hard it is to wraste oute, and maye growe [etc.]. **1526** *Pilgr. Perf.* (W. de W. 1531) 88 b, That our holynes, deuocyon, & good religyon.. wrast vs not from the fauour of God. **1587** HARRISON *England* II. ii. (1877) I. 53 Being sore grieued, that she had.. wrested out such a verdict against him. **1693** PRIOR *To Dr. Sherlock* 44 You wrest the Bolt from Heav'ns avenging Hand. **1769** ROBERTSON *Chas. V*, XI. Wks. 1813 III. 350 Unfortunate Princes from whose hands some strong rival had wrested their sceptre. **1796** WORDSW. *Borderers* 1617, I yielded up those precious hopes, which nought On earth could else have wrested from me. **1825** MACAULAY *Ess., Milton* ¶81 He had been wrested by no common deliverer from the grasp of no common foe. **1846** LANDOR *Imag. Conv.* Wks. II. 47 Single states are poor props: but who can wrest out Germany?

†**c.** To force (a person) out *of* something. *Obs.*[−1]

c **1440** *York Myst.* xxxi. 261 He is wraiste of his witte or will of his wone.

†**d.** *transf.* To press or force *out* (sounds, etc.); to emit or utter, esp. with difficulty. *Obs.*

c **1402** LYDG. *Compl. Bl. Knight* 48 The nyghtyngale.. her voys gan oute wrest. *c* **1502** *Joseph Arim.* 388 In May, whan the nightyngale Wrestes out her notes musycall. **1576** WHETSTONE *Rocke of Regard* II. 116 To wreast out this following complaint. **1583** MELBANCKE *Philotimus* H j, The poore gentlewoman not able to wreste out one worde for weepinge.

†**e.** With *forth*. To pass or spend (time) in pain or distress. *Obs. rare*[−1].

1577 GRANGE *Golden Aphrod.* D iij, With many a sobbing sighe.. he wrested foorth the tedious night.

†**3.** To turn or dispose (some one, his heart) to a person or thing; to incline or influence (a person, etc.) *to* do something. *Obs.*

13.. *Gaw. & Gr. Knt.* 1482 Wyȝe þat is so wel wrast alway to god. *c* **1374** CHAUCER *Troylus* IV. 1427 Fynally he gan his herte wreste To trusten here. **1426** LYDG. *De Guil. Pilgr.* 7739 He brydlede hem, & dyde hem wreste, Whateuere they herde, to sey the beste. *c* **1440** *York Myst.* xi. 137 If thai with wrang ought walde þe wrayste Owte of all wothis I sall þe were. **1579** HAKE *Newes out of Powles* (1872) B ij, Ofte tymes by force they wrest and wring him to their handes. **1592** GREENE *Repentance* Wks. (Grosart) XII. 157 A yong man is like a tender plant, apt to be wrested by nurture either to good or euill. **1603** J. DAVIES (Heref.) *Microcosmos* Wks. (Grosart) I. 51/2 A sweete-sowre thing (Which may the Sov'raign wrest, the subiect wring) Call'd Lieges'-loue abus'd. *a* **1618** RALEIGH *Prerog. Parlt.* (1628) 23 To wrest the King, and to draw the inheritance vpon himselfe, hee perswaded his Majestie to relinquish his enterest.

†**b.** To move (the mind, attention, etc.) from a settled state or an object; to unsettle, unfix; to divert *to* something else. *Obs.*

a **1400-50** *Wars Alex.* 4622 Ouir wild [= will] is many ways wraiste, as þe wedire skiftis. **1423** JAS. I *Kingis Q.* x, Langer slepe ne rest Ne myght I nat, so were my wittis wrest. **1567** *Gude & Godlie B.* (S.T.S.) 70 We gloir for to speik of Christ:.. Bot far fra him our hartis we wreist. **1570** GOOGE *Pop. Kingd.* Pref. B ij b, They.. carefully wrest their mind hither and thither, to obtaine the forgiuenesse of their sinnes. **1609** LD. BROOKE *Mustapha* III. i, Who wrests his princes mind Presents his faith vpon the stage of chance. **1646** J. HALL *Horæ Vac.* 188 Whereas Ariosto will.. wrest his [*sc.* a reader's] Attention to a new businesse.

c. *poet.* To draw aside, divert (a look).

1738 J. G. COOPER *Father's Advice to his Son* iii, The father's eyes no object wrested, But on the smiling prattler hung.

4. To usurp, arrogate, or take by force (power, a right, etc.); to assume forcibly (a dignity or office); to seize, capture, or take (lands, dominion, etc.) from another or others:

a. Const. *away*, *from* (also in early use with dative), *out of*, †*into*, *upon*.

In very frequent use (esp. with *from*) since *c* 1820.

1426 AUDELAY *Poems* 23 He syȝ the Trinyte apere within his body clere, then enterd in hym envy, Whan he hade seyne this gloryis syȝt, He wolde wrast hym his myȝt. **1576** FLEMING *Panopl. Epist.* 15, I was very muche grieued.. that the triumphe which most iustly you did deserue, was so wrongfully wrested from you. **1609** BIBLE (Douay) *2 Macc.* iv. 24 He.. wrested the high priesthood upon him self. **1660** T. M. *Hist. Independ.* IV. 13 The English affairs and Government being thus wrested into the hands of a few desperate persons. **1682** BURNET *Rights Princes* iii. 96 The Popes had so strugled to wrest the Investitures out of the hands of the Princes of the West. **1702** ROWE *Tamerl.* IV. i, Oh! teach my Power To cure those Ills,.. Lest Heav'n should wrest it from my idle Hand. **1769** ROBERTSON *Chas. V*, II. Wks. 1813 V. 261 The emperors, too feeble to wrest them out of their hands, were obliged to grant the clergy fiefs of those ample territories. **1838** PRESCOTT *Ferd. & Is.* (1846) I. vi. 294 The rights, thus wrested from the grasp of Rome. **1879** FROUDE *Cæsar* xxii. 384 They had gradually wrested his authority out of his hands.

fig. and in fig. context. **1549** COVERDALE, etc. *Erasm. Par. Rom.* 32 They.. through their strength in faith.. wreste out with strong hande the benediccion of God. **1671** MILTON *P.R.* I. 470 Thou hast.. urg'd me hard with doings, which not will But misery hath rested from me. **1830** HERSCHEL *Study Nat. Philosophy* I. i. 3 The spoils of all nature are.. wrested with reluctance, from the mine, the forest, the ocean, and the air. **1834** L. RITCHIE *Wand. by Seine* 5 To wrest a territory from the sea. **1890** 'R. BOLDREWOOD' *Miner's Right* (1899) 163/2, I had wrested from fortune her favours and smiles.

b. Rarely without const.

1535 COVERDALE *Prol.* ¶24 Lest thou.. wrest the righte of the straunger. **1624** QUARLES *Job Militant* Wks. (Grosart) II. 87/1 He shall returne, what he did wrest. **1642** FULLER *Holy & Prof. St.* III. xxv. 230 The great means of the Clergie in time of Popery was rather wrested then given.

absol. **1582** C. FETHERSTONE *Dial. agst. Dancing* A 4, The extorcioner wresteth and wringeth, to the ende he may augment his gaines. *a* **1618** RALEIGH *Prerog. Parlt.* (1628) 19 The Lords being to strong for the King, forced his consent... They wrested too much beyond the bounds of reason.

c. To obtain or gain (money, information, etc.) by extortion, persistency, or strong persuasion; to wring; = SCREW *v.* 5. Also with advs., as *out*, or preps., as *from, out of*.

1565 COOPER *Thesaurus* s.v. *Extorqueo*, Thou diddest wreste..from Ceasar, 50. talentes. *Ibid.*, *Veritatem extorquere*,..to wreste out the truth. **1592** GREENE *Disput.* 12 Boon Companions, that by their wittes can wrest mony from a Churle. **1601** MOUNTJOY in Moryson *Itin.* (1617) III. 149, I should have wrested out of him [*sc.* a prisoner] the certainty of all things. **1624** *Termes de la Ley* 185 b, Exaction is where an Officer or other man demandeth and wresteth a fee..where no fee..is due at all. **1655** FULLER *Ch. Hist.* II. 91 At last she wrested leave from her Husband to live a Nun. **1671** MILTON *Samson* 384 Did not she..reveal The secret wrested from me? **1797** MRS. RADCLIFFE *Italian* xvii, Your obstinacy can neither wrest from us the truth nor pervert it. **1848** DICKENS *Dombey* xlii, She battled with herself.., but he wrested the answer from her. **1856** EMERSON *Eng. Traits, Truth* ad fin., Tortures..could never wrest from an Egyptian the confession of a secret.

transf. **1591** SPENSER *Ruines of Time* 486 Deepelie muzing at her doubtfull speach, Whose meaning much I labored foorth to wreste.

5. To strain or overstrain the meaning or bearing of (a writing, passage, word, etc.); to deflect or turn from the true or proper signification; to twist, pervert; = WRENCH *v.* 7, SCREW *v.* 3 c.

In very freq. use *c* 1575–*c* 1700. An earlier example is implied under WRESTING *vbl. sb.* 2.

α. *a* **1533** FRITH *Boke* (1548) C iiij b, Sophisters wolde wrest their sayinges, and expounde them after their fantasy. **1581** MULCASTER *Positions* iii. 12 Is it not he which wringeth the writer, and wreasteth his meaning? **1626** GOUGE *Serm. Dignity Chivalry* §1 The forenamed point, 'The Dignity of Chivalry', is not violently wrested. *a* **1674** CLARENDON *Surv. Leviath.* (1676) 287 To wrest and torture words to comply with his extravagant Wit. **1708** O. DYKES *Eng. Proverbs* 120 Are not the holy Scriptures good, because they are wrested? **1738** JURIN in *Keill's Anim. Oecon.* 98 See also how that can be done, which my learned Antagonist seems most to have wrested. **1814** SCOTT *Wav.* xxxi, You appear convinced of my guilt, and wrest every reply I have made. **1884** W. C. SMITH *Kildrostan* 52 Nay, do not wrest my words. **1909** T. R. GLOVER *Confl. Relig. in Early Rom. Emp.* x. 309 He can quibble and wrest the obvious meaning of a document to perfection.

absol. **1564** MARTIALL *Treat. Crosse* 84 Lett hereticks wringe and wrest as longe as they list, to wise men they shal neuer be hable to persuade the contrarie. **1592** GREENE *Upst. Courtier* C 3, The end of all being, is to knowe God, And not as your worshippe..wrests to creep into acquaintance.

transf. and *fig.* **1549** COVERDALE, etc. *Erasm. Par. Gal.* 4 This submyssion of myne is by them wrest into a wronge meanyng. **1581** HOWELL *Devises* G j, For Golde who shunnes to wrest a wrong And make it seeme as right and strong? **1599** SHAKS. *Hen. V*, I. ii. 14 God forbid..That you should fashion, wrest, or bow your reading. **1617** CAMPION *4th Bk. Ayres* xx, Wrest euery word and looke, Racke euery hidden thought. **1665** HOOKE *Microgr.* 28 Nor wrest I any experiment to make it *quadrare* with any preconceiv'd Notion. **1768** WALPOLE *Hist. Doubts* 94, I have thus, without straining or wresting probability, proved all I pretended to prove.

γ. **1538** BALE *Thre Lawes* 1126 By wrastynge the text, to the scriptures sore decay. **1561** T. N[ORTON] *Calvin's Inst.* III. 201 Diuines, that..violently wrasted..many places of Scripture. **1563** *Homilies* II. *Repentance* II. ¶6 The aduersaries go about to wrast this place for to maintaine their auricular confession withall.

b. Const. *against, from, †into, to, unto*.

1536 *Act 28 Hen. VIII*, c. 10 ¶1 The Pope..did obfuscate and wreste Goddis holy worde..from the spirituall and trew meanyng therof. **1550** LEVER *Serm.* (Arb.) 138 They wrest the saying of Paule vnto a wrong meanynge. **1560** DAUS tr. *Sleidane's Comm.* 9 What places of scripture the Papistes do depraue and wraste into a wronge sense. **1612** T. TAYLOR *Titus* i. 6 They are glad to snatch here and there a word, to wrest against the Author's meaning. **1665** GLANVILL *Scepsis Sci.* xviii. 116 To wrest names from their known meaning to senses most alien. **1683** KENNETT tr. *Erasm. on Folly* 135 St. Paul himself..mangles some citations..and seems to wrest them to a different sense. **1820** *Q. Mus. Mag.* II. 260 *note*, This word has been wrested from its pristine and legitimate signification. **1851** KINGSLEY *Lett.* (1878) I. 272 When you try to wrest Scripture and history to your own use. **1904** S. H. BUTCHER *Harvard Lect.* 184 If their utterances could not be wrested to the desired end.

absol. **1540** COVERDALE *Confut. Standish* (1547) d vij b, Thus make ye of gods holy scripture a shipmans hose, wresting and wringing to what purpose ye will.

c. To put a wrong construction on the words or purport of (a writer); to misinterpret.

1555 PHILPOT in Foxe *A. & M.* (1563) 1429/2 It is shame for you to wrast and wrieth the doctors as you do. **1579** GOSSON *Sch. Abuse* To Rdr. (Arb.) 18 His schollers were woont,..howe right soeuer hee wrote, to wrest him. **1604** *Supplic. Masse Priests, Answer* L 4 b, They haue no reason to quarrell with any of vs for wresting, or mistaking, or misalledging Fathers. **1656** BRAMHALL *Replic.* vi. 273 A confused companie of Authors..of little knowledge in our English affairs, tentered and wrested from their genuine sense. **1687** PRIOR *Hind & P. Transv.* Pref., Those Authors are wrested from their true Sense.

†d. To derive or deduce (a name, etc.) irregularly *from* something; to change improperly. *Obs.*

1596 SPENSER *State Irel.* Wks. (Globe) 628/1 The Irish thinke to ennoble themselves by wresting theyr auncientrye from the Spaynyarde. **1605** CAMDEN *Rem.* 59 *Gerusius* in Latine..may signifie..honourable, as wrested from *Gerousius*. *Ibid. James*, Wrested from *Iacob*. **1711** *Brightland's Gram. Eng. Tongue* 137 Asparagus, Sparagus, ..which the Vulgar wrest to..Sparrowgrass.

6. To turn or deflect (a matter, etc.); to divert to (*unto*, *†into*) some different (esp. undue or improper) purpose, end, etc.; to distort or pervert.

1524 SIR T. MORE in Ellis *Orig. Lett.* Ser. I. I. 256 To use th'erle of Angwish for an instrument to wryng and wreste the maters in to bettre trayne. **1535** COVERDALE *Exod.* xxiii. 8 Giftes blinde euen them y^t are sharpe of sight & wraist the righteous causes. **1598** ROWLANDS *Betraying Christ* 3 The art of Poesie..being..wrested and turned to the fooleries of Loue. **1620** E. BLOUNT *Horæ Subs.* 148 Let not the parties ielousie..wrest or wry his iudgement in the least degree to preiudice. **1651** HOBBES *Leviath.* III. 225 One casuall event that may bee but wrested to their purpose. **1721** BERKELEY *Prev. Ruin Gt. Brit.* Wks. III. 208 Cunning men, who bend and wrest the public interest to their own private ends. **1802** MAR. EDGEWORTH *Moral T.*, *Forester* xv, By wresting to the prisoner's disadvantage every circumstance. **1861** LD. BROUGHAM *British Const.* xvi. 247 A Pemberton wresting the rules of evidence, to the sacrifice of innocent persons. **1878** STUBBS *Const. Hist.* III. xviii. 281 The forms of government..might be overborne and perverted; and the charge of thus wresting and warping them is shared[etc.].

b. To deflect (the law, etc.) from its proper course or interpretation; to turn from the right application; to misapply, pervert.

α. *c* **1530** TINDALE *Deut.* xvi. 19 Wrest not the lawe.. nether take any rewarde. **1575** GASCOIGNE *Glasse of Govt.* v. ix, Where no mediacions..may wrest the sentence of the Lawe. **1596** SPENSER *State Irel.* Wks. (Globe) 622/2 The same Statutes are..very easely wrested to the fraud of the subject. **1611** BIBLE *Exod.* xxiii. 6 Thou shalt not wrest the iudgement of thy poore in his cause. **1683** BURNET tr. *More's Utopia* 149 A sort of People, whose Profession it is..to wrest Laws. **1761** HUME *Hist. Eng.* (1806) IV. li. 75 The law was generally supposed to be wrested, in order to prolong their imprisonment. **1885** LD. FITZGERALD in *Law Times' Rep.* LIII. 477/2 He would..have been wresting one of the rules.

β, γ. **1535** COVERDALE *1 Sam.* viii. 3 His sonnes..toke giftes, & wraysted the lawe. **1549** LATIMER *2nd Serm. bef. Edw. VI* (Arb.) 53 To wrast the wayes of iudgement.

†c. To divert or deflect unjustly *upon* some one. *Obs.*

1609 BIBLE (Douay) *Ps.* liv. 4 They have wrested iniquities upon me. **1632** LITHGOW *Trav.* x. 476 The Gouernour had wrested the Inquisition vpon mee.

7. a. To overstrain the muscles of (a joint, etc.); to sprain, strain, or rick (the foot, ankle, etc.). Chiefly *Sc.*

c **1550** LYNDESAY *Play* 742, I haif wreistit my schank. **1567** J. SANFORD *Epictetus* 29 Take heede..that thou wreaste not thy foote. **1649** T. WODENOTE *Hermes Theol.* 147 He.. stumbled, and wrested his foot. *a* **1670** SPALDING *Troub. Chas. I* (1850) I. 375 He, vnhappellie going throw Abirdein .., wrestit his cute or leg. **1904** in *Eng. Dial. Dict.* V. 84 s. *Sc.* I have reisted my wrist, by using a hammer.

b. To affect with griping pain; to rack, wring.

c **1520** SKELTON *Magnyf.* 2302 *Cou. Cou.* Ye shall be clappyd with a coloppe That wyll make you to halt and to hoppe. *Cra. Con.* Som be wrestyd there that they thynke on it forty dayes. **1700** BLACKMORE *Deborah's Song* 202 The earth with dreadful gripes was sore opprest, Which did its twisted bowels wrest.

II. †8. *intr.* To struggle or contend; to strive or wrestle *against* something. *Obs.*

a **1225** *Ancr. R.* 374 [Heo] moten wresten ajean [fondunges] mid stronge wragelunge. *a* **1300** *Cursor M.* 19353 (Edinb. MS.), þan bigan þai [*sc.* the Jews] wrenke and wraiste [*v.rr.* wraist, wrest], And for tene þair teþþe to gnaiste. *c* **1400** *Laud Troy Bk.* 3554 Thei holde 3ow so sore agast, That 3e dar not with hem wrast. **1548** P. NICHOLS *Godly New Story* E iij b, For some wring & wrest to go backe agayn into Egypt. *a* **1585** MONTGOMERIE *Cherrie & Slae* 277 Ane fische..in the nette,..Ay wristing and thristing, the faster still is scho. **1590** LODGE *Rosalind* P 2 b, He that wrests against the will of Venus. **1594** NASHE *Unfort. Trav.* I j b, She strugled, she wrested, but all was in vaine.

transf. **1577** FULKE *Confut. Purg.* 447 The blessed state of them that dye in the Lord, in the meaning of which you wrest and wrigle, like a snake.

†9. To force a way, make way with effort, find egress. Also with *through, out. Obs.*

c **1450** *Mirk's Festial* I. 9 þay bonden hym to þe crosse.. so hard..þat þe blod wrast apon yche a knot. *c* **1475** *Partenay* 1377 The timbre and yre thorugh hys body wraste. **1590** SPENSER *F.Q.* II. xii. 81 The faire Enchauntresse.. Tryde all her arts..thence out to wrest.

†10. Of sound: To break forth. *Obs.*[−1]

13.. *E.E. Allit. P.* B. 1403 Sturnen trumpen strake steuen in halle, Aywhere by þe wowes wrasten krakkes.

'wrestable, *a. rare*[−0]. [f. WREST *v.* + -ABLE.] Capable of being wrested.

1611 FLORIO, *Torceuole*, wrestable, to be wrested.

wrest-balk, obs. erron. f. REST-BALK *v.*

1807 VANCOUVER *Agric. Devon* (1813) 158 Another practice here, is to vell or wrest-balk at Midsummer.

†wrest-beer. *Obs. rare*[−1]. (See quot.)

Perh. for *rest-beer*, from the time it was allowed to lie before being used.

a **1654** SELDEN *Table-T., Parlt.* (Arb.) 81 Just as in brewing of Wrest-Beer, there's a great deal of business in grinding the Mault;..then it must be mash'd,..then they keep a huge quarter when they carry it into the Cellar, and a twelve month after 'tis delicate fine Beer.

wrested ('rɛstɪd), *ppl. a.* [f. WREST *v.* + -ED[1].]

1. That has undergone wresting or wringing; twisted. Also *transf.*

1609 HOLLAND *Ammianus Marcell.* 50 Bolts and darts discharged violently from the writhed and wrested strings of a brake or such like engine. **1616** W. BROWNE *Brit. Past.* II. v. 440 A wrested Bryre Onely kept close the gate which led unto it. *a* **1617** BAYNE *On Eph.* (1658) 72 The ache of a wrested joynt. **1656** J. SMITH *Pract. Physick* 320 The Bone may alwaies remain wrested.

2. *fig.* Deflected or turned from the true meaning or natural application; strained, perverted.

1551 ROBINSON tr. *More's Utopia* (Arb.) 60 The bare wordes of the lawe, or a wrythen and wrested vnderstandinge of the same. *c* **1554** HOOPER in Coverdale *Lett. Mart.* (1564) 160 This iudgement of Paul is more to be followed, then al your own fayned and wrested defences. **1559** T. BRICE *Reg. Martyrs* July 1557 D ij, When wrested law put him to deth. **1589** COOPER *Admon.* 32 So many wrested Scriptures, so many false conclusions. **1615** J. STEPHENS *Satyr. Ess.* 175 For he, wanting the humor of his wrested observance, falles away into ignorant silence. **1687** ATTERBURY *Answ. Consid. Spirit Luther* 46 Little wrested sentences of authors. **1729** T. INNES *Crit. Essay* I. 330 Wrested texts of the Old Testament. *a* **1743** SAVAGE *To Sir R. Walpole* 133 New courts of censure..Explain'd, at will, each statute's wrested aim. **1868** J. BRUCE *Digby's Voy. Medit.* Pref. p. xv, Opinions..raised upon wrested inferences.

3. Drawn out, taken or acquired, by force.

1565 COOPER s.v. *Cado, Non sponte cadentes lachrymae*, wrested teares. **1590** SPENSER *F.Q.* III. i. 24 Death me liefer were, then such despight, So vnto wrong to yield my wrested right. **1595** SHAKS. *John* IV. iii. 154 Vast confusion waites As doth a Rauen on a sicke-falne beast, The iminent decay of wrested pompe.

wrester ('rɛstə(r)). [f. as prec. + -ER[1].]

1. One who wrests or wrenches; a twister; †one who tunes with a wrest.

1504 CORNISHE in *Skelton's Wks.* (1568) Z vj, Any Instrument mystunyd shall hurt a trew song; Yet blame not the claricord ye wrester doth wrong. **1552** HULOET s.v., Wryste or wrythe, *extorqueo*. Wryster and wrynger, *idem*. **1611** COTGR., *Retordeur*,..a wrester, a retorter, a wrier backe.

†b. An implement for picking locks. *Obs.*[−1]

1591 GREENE *2nd Pt. Conny-Catch.* Wks. (Grosart) X. 86 The Picklocke is called a Charme. He that watcheth, a Stond. Their engins, Wresters.

2. One who wrests, strains, or deflects the meaning or application of words, etc.; a perverter, distorter.

1533 MORE *Conf. Tindale* Wks. 524/1 A false wryther and wrester of holy scripture. **1560** JEWELL *Answ. to Cole* I vi, A falsarie, a wrester, a corrupter of the Doctoures. **1598** R. BERNARD tr. *Terence, Phormio* II. ii, A troubler of good men, and a wrester of lawes. **1629** H. BURTON *Truth's Triumph* 348 All such wresters and peruerters of the truth. **1673** HICKERINGILL *Greg. F. Greyb.* 310 Antick foppish jugglers, and wresters of Holy Writ. **1711** ATTERBURY *Serm.* (1734) III. 287 In the first of these Senses,..these Wresters of it Bent and Warped the streight Line and Measure of their Duty. **1891** W. C. WILKINSON *Epic of Saul* I. 21 Those wresters of the law must feel the law.

transf. **1589** PUTTENHAM *Eng. Poesie* III. vii. (Arb.) 166 To forbid all manner of figuratiue speaches..as meere illusions to the minde, and wresters of vpright iudgement.

wresting ('rɛstɪŋ), *vbl. sb.* [f. as prec. + -ING[1].]

1. The action of twisting, or turning awry; the fact of being wrested. Also with *off*.

1398 [see WRENCHING *vbl. sb.* 1]. **1548** ELYOT, *Torsio*,..a writhyng, a wrestyng. **1578** LYTE *Dodoens* 367 Branches which will not easily breake with wresting or playing. ? *a* **1600** *Montgomerie's Cherrie & Slae* 276 (Laing MS.), Ane fysche fanggit in þe net,.. With wreisting and thrysting, The faster stykis scho. *a* **1610** HEALEY *Epictetus* (1636) 79 In thy walkes thou hast a care to avoide..the wresting of thy feete. **1706** PHILLIPS (ed. Kersey), *Distorsion*,..a wresting or wringing several Ways. **1730** BAILEY (fol.), *Sprain*,..a violent Contorsion or Wresting of the Tendons of the Muscles. **1892** ZANGWILL *Bow Mystery* x. 135 Never dreaming the wresting off [*sc.* of a staple] had been done beforehand.

transf. **1632** LITHGOW *Trav.* x. 480 The wresting of the Inquisition vpon me.

†b. Adjustment of the strings of a musical instrument by tightening with a wrest; tuning in this way. Also in fig. context. *Obs.*

c **1380** WYCLIF *Wks.* (1880) 341 Many men failen in þis wrastyng [of a harp] & in goostly syngyng aftur. *c* **1440** *Promp. Parv.* 533/2 Wrestynge, *plectura, plexura*. *c* **1500** *Proverbis in Antiq. Rep.* (1809) IV. 407 A slac strynge in a Virgynall..dothe abyde no wrestinge, it is so louse and light. **1530** RASTELL *Bk. Purgat.* II. xviii. e 1 b, A harper.. occupyed about ye wrastynge of his harpe strynges. **1579** W. WILKINSON *Confut. Fam. Love* 26 b, When he..with writhyng and wrestyng had brought his heresie into tune. **1627** HAKEWILL *Apol.* II. i. §4 The wresting of a string too high marres the musick.

c. *fig.* The action of taking away or obtaining by force; exaction; extortion.

1611 COTGR., *Extorsion*,..a violent wringing, or wresting of things from others. **1694** tr. *Milton's Lett. State* Wks. 1851 VIII. 339 The wresting of the Kingdom of Poland from Papal Subjection. **1721** BAILEY, *Extortion*, an unlawful and violent wresting of Money, &c. from any Man. **1853** KINGSLEY *Misc.* (1859) I. 289 His wresting from her the secret which had been locked for ages in the ice caves.

†d. With *in*: (see WREST *v.* 1 c). *Obs.*

1597 Morley *Introd. Mus.* 124 The vnpleasantnesse of it commeth of the wresting in of the point.

2. Perversion, distortion, or deflection of the meaning, interpretation, or application; misinterpretation; an instance of this.

c **1444** Pecock *Donet* 140 Prechers ben woned to wrynge oute of a worde alle maters whiche to hem liken, bi wrasting of sillablis and of lettris. *Ibid.* 142. **1550** Bale *Eng. Votaries* II. 66 Blasphemouse bablynges and abhomynable wrastynges of the scriptures. **1579** Fulke *Heskins' Parl.* 473 He hath nothing that may not bee reasonably construed on our side without any wresting. **1587** Golding *De Mornay* xxix. 528 It were an vtter wresting of the Text, to conuey it any other way. **1610** Healey *Theophrastus* (1636) 4 A wresting of actions and wordes to the worse or sadder part. **1641** Milton *Reform.* I. Wks. 1851 III. 19 The ridiculous wresting of Scripture. **1690** Locke *Govt.* II. iii. §20 A manifest perverting of Justice, and a barefac'd wresting of the Laws. **1711** Atterbury *Serm.* (1734) I. 267 Expressions ..so bright and clear, as should prevent all possible Wrestings and Misconstructions. *a* **1774** Tucker *Lt. Nat.* (1777) III. II. 61 Aiming to find out such a sense of them [*sc.* principles of human reason], without violence or wresting, as may coincide or prove reconcileable therewith. **1864** Pusey *Lect. Daniel* i. (1876) 5 If a prophecy .. admitted of no wresting.

†**3.** The action of contending or struggling; an instance of this. *Obs.*

1573 Tusser *Husb.* (1878) 180 Be lowly not sollen, if ought go amisse, What wresting may loose thee, that winne with a kisse. **1581** J. Bell *Haddon's Answ. Osor.* 355 Their dayly exercise then was a continuall wresting agaynst the world, and the Devill. **1613–8** Daniel *Coll. Hist. Eng.* (1626) 140 Discontentment still goes on, and neither side get any thing but by hard wrestings.

†**4.** Griping or wringing pain. *Obs.*$^{-1}$

1546 Phaer *Regim. Life* 59 In suche a disease, the glystre muste be greate in quantitie, or els ye shulde make wrestynge & roumblynge in yᵉ bellye.

5. *Comb.*, as †**wresting-vice**, **stick**, one suitable for or used in wresting or twisting; **wresting thread**, *Shetland dial.*, a thread wound or tied round a sprained or injured limb as a charm to effect a cure.

1568 W. Skinner tr. *Montanus Inquis.* (1569) 26 b, Hys armes .. are bound with very stiffe and small cordes .. which afterwards they straine with certaine stiffe wresting stickes or troncheons. **1609** Holland *Amm. Marcell.* 9 The hang-man prepared both hookes and wresting-vices. **1616** [see wrest *sb.* 1 c]. **1840** *New Statist. Acc.* (1845) XV. 141 The 'wresting thread' .. is a thread spun from black wool, on which are cast nine knots, and tied round a sprained leg or arm. **1883** R. M. Fergusson *Rambling Sk.* 122 When a person received a sprain the Wrestin Thread was cast.

ˈ**wresting**, *ppl. a. rare.* [f. as prec. + -ing².] That wrests or twists; in quot. *fig.*

c **1520** Skelton *Magnyf.* 1608 Let your Lust and Lykynge stande for a lawe. Be wrastynge and wrythynge, and away drawe.

Hence ˈ**wrestingly** *adv.*

1613 R. Yong in Zouch *Dove* A 3 b, But Love breaks forth,.. And wrestingly, out of my wonted lynes, It makes me shuffle in these hobling rymes.

wrestle (ˈrɛs(ə)l), *sb.* [f. next. Cf. warsle *sb.*]

1. Without article. The action of wrestling or struggling; the fact of having wrestled. Also *fig.*

1593 Q. Eliz. *Boeth.* IV. pr. vii. 99 So ought not a wise man beare with greefe, fortunes wrestell [L. *certamen fortunæ*]. **1796** Burns *Poem on Life* vii, His pangs, And murd'ring wrestle, As .. he hangs A gibbet's tassel. **1858** Carlyle *Fredk. Gt.* VI. ix. II. 118 War in Italy, universal spasm of wrestle there, being now the expectation of foolish mankind. **1883** *Century Mag.* Oct. 819/1 Their limbs gnarled and twisted as if they had won their places by splendid wrestle. **1915** 'Q' *Nicky-Nan, Reservist* xvii, He paused, seemingly in wrestle with an inward reluctance.

2. A struggle between two persons, each trying to throw the other by grasping his body or limbs; also, a wrestling-bout according to rules; a wrestling-match. Also with *over*, *up*.

1670 Milton *Hist. Eng.* I. 13 Corineus,.. Whom in a Wrestle the Giant catching aloft, with a terrible hugg broke three of his Ribs. **1849** Lytton *K. Arthur* I. lxxvi, Beyond the tilt-yard spread the larger space, For the strong wrestle and the breathless race. **1854** W. Waterworth *Orig. Anglicanism* 196 Fondness for the wrestle and the race prevailed. **1893** Robinson & Gilpin *Wrestling* 54 On the following day, the loser in the wrestle up proved victorious. *Ibid.* 85 Owing to some oversight on the part of the umpires, they decided it must be a wrestle over.

b. *fig.* A struggle or contest.

1850 Carlyle *Latter-d. Pamph.* iii. 4 Both parties in the wrestle professing earnest wishes of peace to us. **1855** Macaulay *Hist. Eng.* xi. III. 62 The body politic.. straining every nerve in a wrestle for life or death. **1893** Horton *Gospel Entering Europe* 27 [Paul's] long wrestle with spiritual realities in the desert of Arabia.

wrestle (ˈrɛs(ə)l), *v.* Forms: α. (1 **wræstlian**), 3 **wræstlen**, **wreastlen**, **wreastlin**, **wrestilen**, 3–4 **wrestlen**, 5 **-lyn**, **wrestelon**, 4–6 **wrestel**, **wrestil**, 5 **wrestele**, **wrestell**, **-tyll**, 5– **wrestle** (6 **wressell**). β. 3 **wrastlen**, 3, 5 **wrastelen**, 5 **wrastel(l)yn**, **-tlyn**, 4–6 **wrastel**, 4–5 **-tele**, **-til**, 5 **-till**, **-tule**, **-tyl**, 6 **-tyll(e**, **-tell**, 4– (latterly *Sc.*, *Eng. dial.*, or *U.S. dial.*) **wrastle** (6 **wrasle**, 8– **rassle**, chiefly *U.S. dial.* **rastle**, **wrassle**, 9 *dial.* **wrostle**, **wros(s)le**); 4 **wrastli**, **-tly**, 9 *s.w. dial.* **wrastly**, **wrassly**. γ. 4–5 **wristele**, **-tle**, **wrystille**, **-tel**, 9 *dial.* **wrustle**, **wrus(s)le**, **russel**. [OE. **wrǽstlian*, frequentative of *wrǽstan* to wrest, represented in the cognate languages by NFris. *wrassele*, *wrûstle*, MLG. *worstelen*, *wrostelen*, LG. *wrösseln*, *frösseln*, MDu. *worstelen* (also Du.), *werstelen*, *wrastelen*. Cf. warsle *v.*, wraxle *v.*]

I. 1. a. *intr.* To strive with strength and skill to throw a person to the ground by grappling with him; to endeavour to overpower and lay down another, esp. in a contest governed by fixed rules, by embracing his body and limbs and tripping or overbalancing him. Also with †*samen*, †*yfere*, *together*.

α. *a* **1100** [see wrestling *vbl. sb.* 1]. *c* **1205** Lay. 1858 Brutus hine lette witen .. to wreastlene bi-foren Brutus, Geomagog and Corineus. *Ibid.* 24699 Summe heo wræstleden And wiðer-gome makeden. **13..**, *c* **1375** [see β, γ]. *c* **1440** *Promp. Parv.* 533/2 Wrestelon, *luctor*, *palestriso*. **1480** Caxton *Chron. Eng.* iv. 14 So to gedre they wrestled longe tyme. **1503** in Meyrick *Ant. Armour* (1824) III. 238 To wrestle all manner of ways, at the pleasure of the commers. **1580** Lyly *Euphues* (Arb.) 447 To wrestle in the games of Olympia. **1603** Holland *Plutarch's Mor.* 229 With professours of wrestling, to bestrew his bodie with dust .. for to wrestle. **1718** A. Thompson tr. *Geoffrey of Monm.* IV. viii. 107 Two noble Youths .. wrestled together, and afterwards had a Dispute about the Victory. **1791** Cowper *Iliad* XXIII. 915 Arising to a third essay, They should have wrestled yet again. **1811** *Sporting Mag.* XXXVIII. 290 A handsome sum of money has been subscribed to be wrestled for. **1889** W. Armstrong *Wrestling* 183 The platforms at rural fairs where local champions wrestled for a fall.

β. *a* **1250** *Ancr. R.* 318 (MS. Titus D. XVIII), Ich .. biheold oðe wrastling, oðer me self wrastlede. **1297** R. Glouc. (Rolls) 7439 Ac he ouercom þe deuel, & adoun him caste, To gadere as hii wrastlede, & bond is honden vaste. *a* **1300** *Cursor M.* 3939 Sa lang þai wrasteld [*Gött.* wrestild, *Fairf.* wresteled] samen þare þat iacob was þan hurt wel sare. *c* **1386** Chaucer *Reeve's T.* 8 Pipen he koude,.. and wel wrastle and sheete. *c* **1440** *Alph. Tales* 164 þus þai wrasteld togedyr, & þis man fell. *c* **1489** Caxton *Sonnes of Aymon* xiv. 320 He .. toke the kynge wyth both his armes by the waste, & wrastled togyder a longe whyle. **1548** Forrest *Pleas. Poesye* xix. 61 b, To shoote, to wrastle, to dooe anye mannys feate. **1585** T. Washington tr. *Nicholay's Voy.* III. x. 86 [They] do wrastle .. two and two with force of armes. **1606** Sylvester *Du Bartas* II. iv. II. *Tropheis* 268 Wee wrastle not .. For painted sheep-hooks, or such pettie Prize. **1671** H. M. tr. *Erasm. Colloq.* 288, I am now a laying in the fourth week; and I am strong enough even to wrastle. **1758** L. Lyon in *Mil. Jrnls.* (1855) 33 [They] hopt and rassled together to see which would beat and our men Beat. **1795** Macneill *Scotland's Scaith* ii, Wha wi' Will cou'd rin or wrastle, Throw the sledge, or toss the bar? **1876–** in dialect glossaries (Sc., Yks., Lanc., Som.). **1896** P. Graham *Red Scaur* vi, Learnin' her son to box .. and wrastle. **1974** *Black World* Jan. 56/2 He might be stronger'n me and he might wrassle the best, but I got his waters on, all right.

γ. *a* **1300** *Cursor M.* 3933 Sammen handlinges wristeld [*Fairf.* wresteled] þai Al þe night, til it was dai. ? *a* **1400** *Morte Arth.* 1141 Wrothely þai wrythyne and wrystille togederz. **1535** Coverdale *2 Macc.* iv. 14 To lerne to fight, to wristle,.. & to put at yᵉ stone. **1869–** in *Eng. Dial. Dict.* (*wrustle*, *wrussle*, *russle*, etc.).

b. Const. *with* or †*mid* (a person, etc.).

α. *c* **1250** *Gen. & Ex.* 1804 Iacob .. bi-lef ðor on ðe niȝt,.. And ðor wrestelede an engel wið. *c* **1425** Wyntoun *Cron.* II. iii. 225 Wiþe hym wrestlyt þe angel. **1480** Caxton *Chron. Eng.* iv. 14 That he shold wrestell with Coryn. **1530** Palsgr. 756/1 Wrestell nat with me, for I wyll throwe the on thy backe. **1555** Eden *Decades* (Arb.) 171 She woolde oftentymes play and wrestle .. with the kynges chamberlens. **1712** Steele *Spect.* No. 502 ¶5 Were there a Scene written, wherein Penkethman should break his Leg by wrestling with Bullock. **1790** Burke *Fr. Rev.* 246 He that wrestles with us strengthens our nerves. **1856** Kingsley *Heroes* 169 He challenges all comers to wrestle with him. **1889** W. Armstrong *Wrestling* 229 Sam Rundle .. recently wrestled with Carkeck the American.

β. *a* **1225** *Ancr. R.* 280 þe ȝeape wrastlare nimeð ȝeme hwat turn his fere ne cunne nout, þet he mid wrastleð. **1297** R. Glouc. (Rolls) 515 Vor he ssolde mid corineus wrastli he adde iþoȝt. *c* **1330** R. Brunne *Chron. Wace* (Rolls) 1798 A place to pleye, ordeyned Brutus,.. [for Corineus] For to wrastle wyþ þat geaunt. *c* **1386** Chaucer *Monk's T.* 276 Sche couþe eke Wrastel .. Wiþ any ȝonge man, were he neuere so whight. *c* **1440** *Gesta Rom.* lvii. 373 Darste thou wrastill with me? *c* **1489** Caxton *Sonnes of Aymon* xxvi. 565 He .. toke aymonet by the wast for to wrastle wyth hym. **1530** Palsgr. 785/1, I dare nat wrastell with hym, leste he gyve me a fall. **1612** J. Davies (Heref.) *Muses Sacr.* Wks. (Grosart) II. 41/2 O thou, whom Iacob wrastled with a space. **1668** H. More *Div. Dial.* I. xxiii. 93 Consider .. how many Spectres have been seen or felt to wrastle, pull or tug with a man. **1940** L. I. Wilder *Long Winter* xvi. 150 I've spent this whole morning rasseling with that dumb horse. **1941** *Harper's* Feb. 329/2 Leaving .. us to rassle with the bear. **1962** W. Faulkner *Reivers* v. 101 'What you been doing? wrassling. with hogs?' 'We got in a mudhole.'

γ. **1382** Wyclif *Gen.* xxxii. 24 And loo ! a man wristlide with hym vnto the morwe.

c. To struggle physically (*with* something) after the manner of wrestling.

1589 Greene *Menaphon* (Arb.) 56 This infant .. wrastling with snakes in his swadling cloutes. **1613** Heywood *Silver Age* III. i. Wks. 1874 III. 129 It fits Ioues sonne Wrastle with Lyons, and to tugge with Beares. **1623** J. Taylor (Water P.) *Discov. by Sea* A 6, Against the rugged waues, we tugge and wrastle. **1643** Howell *Twelve Treat.* (1661) 94 She tugs and wrastles with the foamie waves. **1821** Joanna Baillie *Metr. Leg.*, *Lady G.B.* xxxii, With her in mimick war they wrestle; Beneath her twisted robe they nestle. **1844** Kinglake *Eothen* ii, Thames, the 'old Eton fellow' that wrestled with us in our boyhood. **1893** Robinson & Gilpin *Wrestling* 77 The boat .. upset, and the strong man went down, unable to wrestle with his remorseless foe. **1936** in P. Oliver *Screening Blues* (1968) vi. 189 If you keep on rasslin' you gonna make me break my needle off.

fig. and *transf.* **1398** Trevisa *Barth. De P.R.* XVIII. xv. (1495) v vj, [Mercury] is callyd the god of wrastlyng,.. for he [= the planet] wrastlyth wᵗ the sonne as he wold ouercome hym. **1539** Bible (Great) *Ecclus.* li. 19 My soule hath wrestled with her [*sc.* wisdom]. *a* **1600** Montgomerie *Misc. Poems* xvi. 4, I wrassill with the wind. **1610** Holland *Camden's Brit.* II. 233, I have in this worke wrastled with that envious and ravenous enemy Time. **1611** Cotgr., *Luicter contre les ombres*, to wrastle with shadowes; to be angrie without cause. **1844** A. B. Welby *Poems* (1867) 89 In bondage I must wrestle here with death. **1893** Robinson & Gilpin *Wrestling* 41 When lying on his death bed, while wrestling with a foe sure to triumph in the end.

d. With complement.

1893 Robinson & Gilpin *Wrestling* p. xliv, If Best did wrestle second,.. it must have been for some minor prize. *Ibid.* 26 Morton threw Halliwell of Penrith, and .. Anthony McDonald .. wrestled up with him.

2. a. To contend or struggle in hostility or opposition (*with* or *against* another or others).

a **1200** *St. Marherete* 14 Wrestlin ha moten ant wiðerin wið ham seoluen. *a* **1225** *Leg. Kath.* 2035 Wrecche mon ..! hwerto wultu wreastlin wið þe worldes wealdent? **1377** Langl. *P. Pl.* B. XIV. 224 If wratthe wrastel [*v.r.* wrystel] with þe pore. **1388–9** in *Wyclif's Sel. Wks.* III. 471 Prelatis, here deme ȝee and wrastulis ȝee who schal be mayster. **1390** Gower *Conf.* III. 350 Pan, which is the god of kinde, With Love wrastlede and was overcome. **1526** Tindale *Eph.* vi. 12 We wrestle not agaynst flesshe and bloud: but .. agaynst worldy ruelars. *a* **1548** Hall *Chron.*, *Hen. VI*, 167 For Kyng Henry .. and Richard .. wresteled for the game, and stroue for the wager. *a* **1575** Pilkington *Nehemiah* iii. 5 (1585) 41 b, Men .. that dare and wil wrastle with the rich in correction. **1601** R. Johnson *Kingd. & Commw.* (1603) 116 Wrastling with the venetians they had almost bereaued them of their estate and taken their city. *c* **1645** Howell *Lett.* (1688) III. 396 Venice wrastleth with the Turk.

b. *fig.* To strive or labour (esp. to obtain the mastery, superiority, or advantage) *with* or *against* difficulties, circumstances, forces, personal feelings, etc. Also (*b*) without const.

a **1225** *Ancr. R.* 80 To wrastlen stalewardliche aȝein þes deofles swenges. *a* **1340** Hampole *Psalter* xiii. 11 All þat wrestils agayns vices in actif lif. *c* **1386** Chaucer *Pars. T.* ¶655 This vertu is so .. vigerous that it dar .. wrastle agayn the assautes of the deuel. **1426** Lydg. *De Guil. Pilgr.* 1571 Who that .. Wyl wrastle ageyn yt [*sc.* vengeance]. **1489** Skelton *On Death Erle Northumbld.* 82 They buskt them .. Againe the kyngs plesure to wrestle or to wring. *c* **1534** T. Starkey *Let. to Cromwell* in Collier 9 *Hist. Lett.* (1871) 48 In such tyme as I was wrastelyng wyth my fevur. **1553** Wood tr. *Gardiner's De Vera Obed.* 5 b, Thei .. haue wrestled against the truth of a long time. **1610** Holland *Camden's Brit.* I. 79 Iewes who wrestled in vaine against the decree of God. **1663** Bp. Patrick *Parab. Pilgr.* ix, You must wrastle stoutly with the difficulties. **1742** Young *Nt. Th.* II. 167 We rave, we wrestle with Great Nature's Plan. *a* **1770** Jortin *Serm.* (1771) I. iv. 79 Strive to .. wrestle against principalities and powers. **1827** Keble *Chr. Y.*, *Tuesday bef. Easter*, Rather wouldst Thou wrestle with strong pain, Than overcloud Thy soul. **1865** Dickens *Mut. Fr.* II. xv, I had to wrestle with my self-respect.

transf. **1592** *Soliman & Pers.* I. v. 52 Were it not thou art my fathers sonne, And striuing kindnes wrestled not with ire.

(*b*) *a* **1340** Hampole *Psalter* cxviii. 170 Of corupcioun of my body, for it is heuy to wrestil here sa lange. **1449** Pecock *Repr.* II. xi. 214 His witt schal be dressid and lad forthe .. with myche lasse peyne and labour, than forto wrastle withinneforth in his owne ymaginaciouns. **1526** *Pilgr. Perf.* (W. de W. 1531) 118 b, The more that ony persone relucketh, wrestleth, or stryues to ouercome these manyfolde temptacyons. **1565** *Satir. Poems Reform.* i. 21 Who dothe wrest his will to wrastle in eche wronge. **1654** E. Johnson *Wonder-wrkg. Provid.* *104 For the which all the Israel of God fight, wrastle, pray.

c. To strive earnestly (*with* God) in prayer.

With allusion to Gen. xxxii. 24–26.

1612 T. Taylor *Comm. Titus* i. 180 The Lord .. whom we must wrastle withall by our praiers. **1638** [see 11]. **1652** Benlowes *Theoph.* VIII. lxxiv, By pray'r God's serv'd betimes; remember who The blessing got by wrestling so. **1677** W. Hubbard *Narrative* II. 57 [They] wrestled with God in their daily Prayers for his Release. **1816** Scott *Old Mort.* xxxiii, We have prayed, and wrestled, and petitioned, for an offering. **1849** C. Bronte *Shirley* xxiv, The mother .. wrestled with God in earnest prayer.

3. a. To labour, toil, or exert oneself; to strive (*for* something); to tussle.

1382 Wyclif *Ecclus.* li. 25 My soule wrastled in it; and in doing it I am confermed. **1549** Latimer *4th Serm. bef. Edw. VI* (Arb.) 107 Thus go these prelates aboute to wreastle for honoure. **1558** Phaer *Æneid.* VII. S ij b, They their ships in marble seas with ores dyd wrastlyng towe. **1603** Knolles *Hist. Turks* (1621) 469 Whilest Hysmaell was thus wrestling for the Persian kingdome. **1620–6** Quarles *Feast Worms* 1493 They rebell, and wrastle, And neuer cease, till they subdue the Castle. **1831** Carlyle *Misc.* (1872) IV. 28 How many a poor Hazlitt must .. believe that he is seeking Truth, yet only wrestle among endless Sophisms. **1873** Gosse *On Viol & Flute* 55 Two of us swam out to it... And as I strove and wrestled in the race, I turned and saw [etc.].

fig. **1633** Shirley *Bird in Cage* I. i, Like errand Knights, our valiant wits must wrastle To free our ladyes from the inchanted Castle.

b. Of natural agencies, etc.: To engage in conflict or strife; to act against each other.

13.. *Gaw. & Gr. Knt.* 525 Wroþe wynde of þe welkyn wrastelez with þe sunne. *a* **1400–50** *Wars Alex.* 784 As þe erth & all þe elementis at anes had wrestild. **1865** S. Bowles *Across the Continent* xviii. 185 River and rock have striven together, wrestling in close and doubtful embrace.

c. To engage in argument, debate, or controversy; to debate, dispute.

c **1450** Capgrave *St. Augustine* 53 A-geyn all þese þis souereyn maystir .. stood as a strong geaunt, wrestiling with argumentis for þe clennesse of þe feith. **1521** Fisher *Serm. agst. Luther* iii. Wks. (1876) 337 Here Martin luther for his shrewed brayne wyll some thyng wrastell agaynst vs. **1565** CALFHILL *Answ. Martiall* 105 Hosius doth wrestle maruelously about the word. **1626** DONNE *Serm.* 783 They were loath to wrastle with the people, or force them from dangerous customes.

d. To busy, occupy, or concern oneself closely or earnestly *with* a subject, etc.; to deal *with* something as a task or troublesome duty.

c **1454** PECOCK *Folewer* 7 Summe..wrastlen so long þerwith til þei gete competent vndirstondyng þerof. *Ibid.* 15 Eny oþir hard writyng with which þei schulen wrastle. **1582** MULCASTER *Elementarie* I. (1925) 43 The other..will rather cast awaie their armor, then wrastle with the difficulties of vnknown and vneasie passages. **1628** COKE *On Litt.* Pref., The yong student..wrastling with..difficult termes. **1638** R. BAKER tr. *Balzac's Lett.* (vol. III) 14, I am wrestling still with —— and preparing you an after-dinners Recreation. **1881** JOWETT *Thucyd.* I. Introd. 13 Wrestling with language and logic. **1905** R. BAGOT *Passport* ix. 80 After wrestling with French history or German poetry.

4. a. To twist or writhe about; to wriggle, move sinuously; to work backwards and forwards.

?*a* **1400** *Morte Arth.* 890 He welterys, he wristeles, he wryngez hys handez. *c* **1450** *Merlin* iii. 655 Petrius peyned hym sore to a-rise and turned wrastelinge. **1481** CAXTON *Reynard* viii. (Arb.) 15 He wrange, he wrastled, and cryed, ..he wiste not how he myght gete out. **1513** DOUGLAS *Æneid* XIII. iv. 82 The snaill..Fleand the birnand heit..A lang tyme gan do wrassill and to wreill. *a* **1618** SYLVESTER *Paradox agst. Libertie* 659 When Eole doth unlock Sterne Auster's stormie gate, making the waters wrastle, And rush ..against the sturdy Castle. *a* **1628** PRESTON *New Covt.* (1630) 154 Fire if it be out of its place, water, if it be out of its place, it is still wrastling..till it returne to its owne place. *c* **1870** B. HARTE *Fr. Pedro's Ride* in *Fiddletown*, etc. (1873) 108 He saw the wild oats wrestle on the hill.

b. To move or proceed with effort or toil; to struggle *out* (*of*) or *through* some place or condition. Also *fig.*

1591 SAVILE *Tacitus, Hist.* III. lix. 150 The armie..could hardly wrestle out of the snowe. **1614** LITHGOW *Trav.* L j b, Wrestling amongst intricate pathes of rockes: two of our Asses fell ouer a banke. **1634** SIR T. HERBERT *Trav.* 93 Wee ..lost our way,..and at length wrastled to Geer. **1648** J. BEAUMONT *Psyche* XVII. clxxi, Breath..forced is to goe about, And through the Noses Sluces wrestle out. **1728** RAMSAY *Robt., Richy & Sandy* 70 A squirrel wi' his bells Ay wrestling up. **1853** W. CADENHEAD *Flights of Fancy* 255 (E.D.D.), When we've wrastled thro' the warl', as wrastle we maun a'. **1879** JEFFERIES *Wild Life* 83 The flames running from thatch to thatch, and, as they express it, 'wrastling' across the intervening spaces. **1899** E. F. HEDDLE *Marget* 151 Once he said he would like to live to hear how Christian 'wrastled through'.

II. 5. *trans.* To engage in (a wrestling-bout or match). Also in fig. context.

a **1400–50** *Wars Alex.* 2276 If it ȝoure mekill maieste miȝt any thinge plese, I wald to wacken ȝoure welth now wirstill a turne. *c* **1412** HOCCLEVE *De Reg. Princ.* 5232 Þer-with þis land hath wrastled many a pul. **1588** DRAKE *Let.* 31 July in Barrow *Life* (1843) 304 We have the armey of Spayne before us, and mynd with the Grace of God to wressell a poull with hym. **1639** FULLER *Holy War* IV. xxxiii. 226 Now Ptolemais being to wrestle her last fall, stripped her self of all cumbersome clothes. **1645** [see FALL *sb.*[1] 13]. **1672** R. WILD *Declar. Lib. Consc.* 13 And for their Seditions and Treasons, let us leave Tyburn and them to wrastle a fair fall about them. **1816** SCOTT *Old Mort.* iv, Hark thee, friend,..wilt thou wrestle a fall with me? **1825** —— *Betrothed* Conclusion, Have we not wrestled a turn before now? **1843** in Robinson & Gilpin *Wrestling* (1893) 58 Charles Lowden..would wrestle a match with any individual of the same age. **1855**, **1883** [see FALL *sb.*[1] 13].

6. a. To contend with (a person) in wrestling; to overcome by, throw in, wrestling. Also with *down*.

Cf. the earlier *over-wrestle* OVER- 21, and WARSLE *v.* 1 c.

1818 in Robinson & Gilpin *Wrestling* (1893) 164 He now challenges his opponent..to wrestle him for ten guineas. **1843** *Ibid.* 58 The veteran..will be happy to accept the challenge, and wrestle Mr. Lowden..for £5 or £10 a side. **1881** DU CHAILLU *Land Midn. Sun* II. 51 A stout girl of twenty, strong enough to wrestle any man. **1903** S. E. WHITE *Forest* xv, [He] is not a mighty man physically... I think I could have wrestled Peter down. **1940** *Sat. Even. Post* 22 June 39/2 He could rassle any three men. **1968** *Listener* 30 May 702/3 In this picture he rides horses, climbs mountains and wrassles Indian chiefs. **1976** *Ibid.* 24 June 817/1 Thrown to the ground and wrastled by the brutally handsome Provo.

b. *Western U.S.* To throw (a calf) for branding.

1888 ROOSEVELT in *Century Mag.* April 861/2 A fire is built, the irons heated, and a dozen men dismount to, as it is called, 'wrestle' the calves. **1893** N. K. GRIGGS *Lyrics of Lariat* 46 A Maverick daisy he saw—..And so He rastled it low And gave it a touch of his brand.

7. To push or thrust *into* something with a wrestling motion. More widely, to move (something inanimate or inert) with physical force. Const. various preps. and advbs.

1820 BYRON *Juan* v. lxxviii, Wrestling both his arms into a gown, He paused. **1970** J. DICKEY *Deliverance* 186, I..dropped down on one knee and wrestled him across my shoulders in the fireman's carry from boy scout days. **1973** M. AMIS *Rachel Papers* 38 Eventually he wrestled all the string and paper into an armful-sized bundle and forced it down the Aga. **1973** M. WOODHOUSE *Blue Bone* vii. 63 We wrestled the crates down through the forward hatch. **1975** *Globe & Mail* (Toronto) 11 Sept. 2/7 Agents wrestled a ·45 calibre automatic pistol out of her hands. **1976** A. PRICE *War Game* I. viii. 142 The same hand, strong and supple.., had once wrestled a bomb-laden Lancaster into the air. **1976** SCOTT & KOSKI *Walk-In* x. 53 He wrestled one of the line of overhead doors up. **1981** J. D. MACDONALD *Free Fall in Crimson* xiv. 159 A truck pulled up... Two men hopped out and started to wrestle the wicker basket out of the back.

III. With adverbs. **8.** *to wrestle down*, to put down by wrestling or striving; to suppress, quell.

c **1611** CHAPMAN *Iliad* XX. 31 These his words did such a warre excite, As no mans powre could wrastle downe. **1808** SCOTT *Marm.* II. xxiv, If..they wrestled down Feelings their nature strove to own. **1816** —— *Bl. Dwarf* vi, I will wrestle down my feelings of rebellious humanity.

†**9.** *to wrestle off*, to set aside by argument; to controvert, rebut. *Obs. rare*$^{-1}$.

1639 LAUD *Confer. w. Fisher* 241 Where is then the Scriptures Prerogative? I know there is much shifting about this Place [*marg.* Num. 2], but it cannot be wrastled off.

10. *to wrestle out*: †**a.** To struggle through (a period of time) in discourse, etc. *Obs.*

a **1756** *Pennecuik's Collect. Scots Poems* 120 When Mess John has wrestl'd out the [hour] glass.

b. To go through, to perform or execute, to carry out, with struggle or effort.

1823 SCOTT *Quentin D.* xxii, In a moment the wretch wrestled out his last agonies. **1842** LOVER *Handy Andy* xxxiii, I would rather *wrastle* out a logical dispute any day. **1842** MANNING *Serm.* (1843) I. 312 They have wrestled out the strife with the unseen powers of the wicked one.

11. To drive or force *out of* something (as) by wrestling. Also *fig.*

1638 A. HENDERSON *Serm.* (1867) 279 If so be that we will wrestle with God for a blessing, and prevail with him, then ..we sall wrestle the enemies out of it also. **1858** R. CHAMBERS *Domest. Ann. Scotl.* I. 9 How to wrestle the people out of their love of the May-games.

wrestler ('rɛslə(r)). Forms: α. 1 **wræstlere**, 4 **wrestlere**, 5 **-telare**, **-teler**, 5– **wrestler**, 6 **wreastler**. β. 3 **wrastlare**, 4–5 **-t(e)lere**, 5 **-teler**, **-tyller**, 6 **-tlear**, **-tleer**, 6–7, *Sc.* and *dial.* 9 **wrastler**, 9 *dial.* **wrossler**, 20– *U.S.* **rassler**, **wrassler**. γ. 4–5 **wristeler(e**, 4 **-tilere**, 9 *dial.* **russ(e)ler**. [OE. *wræstlere*, agent-noun f. **wrǽstlian* WRESTLE *v.* + -ER[1]. Cf. older Flem. *worsteler*, Du. *worstelaar*.]

1. One who wrestles; esp. one who practises or is skilled in the art of wrestling, as an athlete.

c **1050** *Voc.* in Wr.-Wülcker 431 *Luctatur* [*sic*], wræstlere. *a* **1225** [see WRESTLE *v.* 1 bβ]. **1382** WYCLIF *Bible* Pref. Ep. vii. (1850) 70/1 Abacuc, a strong wristeler [**1388** wrastelere] and a sharp, stondith vpon his waard. **1387** TREVISA *Higden* II. 383 Minotaurus was a grete man and huge,..and a wiȝt wrastlere. *c* **1450** *Mirk's Festial* I. 94 By Iacob ys vndyrstond a wrasteler. **1497** BP. ALCOK *Mons Perfect.* C iij 14 A wrasteler..intendeth to haue ye vyctory of hym y^t he wrestled w^t. **1542** UDALL *Erasm. Apoph.* Table, Diogenes mocked a wrastlear. **1579** W. WILKINSON *Confut. Fam. Love* B ij b, One listed to see wrestlers bestirre them in their play. **1615–6** BOYS *Wks.* (1622) 190 Runners and wrastlers contend for a crowne that shall perish. *a* **1680** BUTLER *Rem.* (1759) II. 444 He embraces him and..lifts him above Ground, as Wrestlers do, to throw him down again. **1711** BUDGELL *Spect.* No. 161 ¶3 She was over-looking a Ring of Wrestlers. **1785** *Lond. Chron.* Mar. 262/3 He was celebrated as a prize fighter, a wrestler, and a cricketer. **1821** CLARE *Vill. Minstr.* I. 44 When wrestlers join to tug each other down. **1876** GLADSTONE *Glean.* (1879) II. 351 As a Cumbrian wrestler struggles..to get a good grip of his antagonist. **1900** F. P. DUNNE *Mr. Dooley's Philos.* 207 He was a gr-reat rassler an' whin he had a full Nelson on th' foolish man that wint again him, he used to say, 'Dear me, am I breakin' ye'er neck, I hope so.' **1901** N. LLOYD *Chronic Loafer* vi, I was the best wrastler in the walley. **1941** J. THURBER in *Sat. Even. Post* 5 Apr. 10/3 'Wrasslers,' says Magrew, cold-like, 'that's what I've got for a ball club, Mr. Du Monville, wrasslers—and not very good wrasslers at that.'

fig. **1681** FLAVEL *Meth. Grace* xvii. 317 The prayers of Mr. Knox..were mighty wrestlers with God. **1721** WODROW *Corr.* (1843) II. 596 He is..a great favourite, and mighty wrestler in prayer. **1814** CARY *Dante, Parad.* XII. 52 The hallow'd wrestler [St. Dominic], gentle to his own, And to his enemies terrible.

2. *fig.* One who strives or contends with difficulties, against adverse conditions, etc.

a **1340** HAMPOLE *Psalter* xiii. 11 For iacob is als mykill at say as wrestlere or supplantere of syn. —— *Cant.* 514 Iacob, ..þat is, writilere agayns vicys. *c* **1454** PECOCK *Folewer* 114 In hem þat ben with passions bisi wrastlers. **1577** HANMER *Eccl. Hist.* To Rdr., The valiant wrastlers, and inuincible champions of Christ Iesu. **1842** DICKENS *Amer. Notes* xv, He shall see in those young things..little wrestlers with him for his daily bread. **1873** HAMERTON *Intell. Life* II. iv. 72 Experienced wrestlers with fate and fortune. **1964** N. MAILER in *Esquire* Nov. 170/4 He was just another hog-wrassler of rhetoric.

3. *Western U.S.* One who throws cattle for the purpose of branding.

1888 ROOSEVELT in *Century Mag.* April 861/2 The calf-wrestlers, grimy with blood, dust, and sweat, work like beavers.

4. *Comb.*, as **wrestler-like**; **wrestler frog**, the S. American 'wrestling' frog, *Rana luctator*.

1594 CAREW *Huarte's Exam. Wits* xv. 329 He will prooue faire, fat, ful of bloud, & b[l]ockish, which habit Hippocrates called wrestler-like. **1616** CHAPMAN tr. *Musæus* G 6, Notus and Boreas wrastler like imbrace. **1892** W. H. HUDSON *Naturalist in La Plata* iv. 77 Plate, Wrestler frog. [*Ibid.* 76 The frog,..catching two of my fingers round with its fore legs, administered a hug.]

wrestless, ? erron. f. RESTLESS *a.*

Perh. associated with WREST *v.*, and intended to mean 'not admitting of being turned aside'.

1621 LADY M. WROTH *Urania* 368 He with sad thoughts ..and wrestlesse passions spent the time till his returne. **1648** J. QUARLES *Fons Lachrym.* 38 His wrestless arm hath bent his yeelding bow.

wrestling ('rɛslɪŋ), *vbl. sb.* [f. WRESTLE *v.* + -ING[1].]

1. a. The action or exercise of two persons grappling or gripping in a contest of strength and adroitness, the one endeavouring to throw the other by tripping or overbalancing him; the fact of contending or throwing in this manner. Also in fig. context.

a **1100** in Napier *O.E. Glosses* 122/1 *Palestram*, wræstlunge. *c* **1205** LAY. 1871 Þer wes muchel folc at þere wrastlinge. *a* **1250** *Owl & Night.* 795 ȝif tueie men goþ to wraslinge. *a* **1300** *Cursor M.* 28526 At wrestelyng, at wake, rengd haf i. *c* **1330** *Arth. & Merl.* 8873 What wiþ wristling, wat wiþ togging. *c* **1386** CHAUCER *Prol.* 548 Ouer al ther he cam, At wrastlynge he wolde haue alwey the Ram. *c* **1425** WYNTOUN *Cron.* I. vi. 356 To se how þat this Coryne Wald deil wiþ him in wresslyne. *c* **1489** CAXTON *Sonnes of Aymon* xiv. 350 He..caught the kynge..by the waast in maner of wrastelynge. **1539** ELYOT *Cast. Helthe* 50 b, Wrastlyng also with the armes and legges..dothe exercise the one and the other. **1562** J. HEYWOOD *Prov. & Epigr.* (1867) 152 The weaker hath the woorse, in wrestlyng alway. **1613** DEKKER *Strange Horse Race* Wks. (Grosart) III. 325 There could I describe what warlike Races the Winds held with the Waters: their Wrastling, Running, Retiring. **1644** MILTON *Educ.* 7 They must be also practiz'd in all the locks and gripes of wrastling. **1701** COLLIER *M. Aurel.* 125 The right Knack of Living resembles Wrastling more than Dancing. **1789** W. BUCHAN *Dom. Med.* (1790) 41 The fatal effects of carrying great weights, running, wrestling, and the like. **1801** STRUTT *Sports & Past.* II. 64 The wrestling is only practised on the afternoon of St. Bartholomew's day. **1850** MAURICE *Mor. & Met. Philos.* (ed. 2) I. 126 Some say that Plato..gained a prize for wrestling at the Isthmian games. **1901** W. CHURCHILL *Crisis* II. vi. 162 He an' de Colonel done commence wrastlin' 'bout a man name o' Linkum [*sc.* Lincoln]. **1930** *Amer. Speech* V. 494 Did any boy of the latter part of the last century ever *wrestle*? Ozarkers are not peculiar in their *rasseling*. **1975** *New Yorker* 1 Sept. 21/3 Mr. Hayes betrayed this when he mispronounced 'wrestling'; he called it 'wrestling'. Most self-respecting promoters, like Sid Morse, of Saginaw, Michigan, know that the correct pronunciation is 'rasslin'. **1976** L. DEIGHTON *Twinkle, twinkle, Little Spy* xiii. 133 Crude Yankee wrassling, was it? Not the kind of cricket you play at Lord's?

b. With *the*. The sport of grappling and throwing; a contest in wrestling; a wrestling-match.

a **1225** *Ancr. R.* 318 Ich..biheold hit, & oðe wrastlinge & oðer fol gomenes. **1297** R. GLOUC. (Rolls) 517 Þe wrastlinge bitvene hom was somdel toȝt. *c* **1330** R. BRUNNE *Chron. Wace* (Rolls) 1800 On a clyf faste by þe se Þe wrastlyng was ordeyned to be. *c* **1400** *Gamelyn* 190 Towardes þe wrasteling þe yong childe rode. *c* **1430** *How the Good Wijf* 81 in *Babees Bk.* 40 Go not to þe wrastelinge, ne to schotynge at cok. **1518** in Leadam *Star Chamber Cases* (Selden) II. 154 The wrestlyng at Seynt Jamys tide. **1598** STOW *Surv.* (1603) 524 This yeare was a great fray at the wrastling. **1661** PEPYS *Diary* 28 June, Went to Moorefields..and saw the wrestling ..between the north and west countrymen. **1725** POPE *Odyssey* VIII. 104 None in the leap spring with so strong a bound, Or firmer, in the wrestling, press the ground. **1843** *Penny Cycl.* XXVII. 588/1 Leaping and running..generally accompany the wrestling as prize games. **1893** ROBINSON & GILPIN *Wrestling & Wrestlers* 189 He went..to Newcastle, and won the wrestling there.

c. With *a* and pl. A wrestling-bout or match.

1303 R. BRUNNE *Handl. Synne* 992 ȝyf þou euer settyst swerde eyþer ryng For to gadyr a wrastlyng. *Ibid.* 8987 Karolles, wrastlynges, or somour games. *c* **1400** *Gamelyn* 171 Ther was ther be siden cried a wrastelynge. *c* **1440** *Jacob's Well* 291 Leuyth ȝoure rennyng on holy-dayes to wrestelynges, markettys, & feyris. *c* **1450** CAPGRAVE *St. Gilbert* 65 Thei..vsed not to renne to wrastillingis, berbaytingis and swech oþir onthrifty occupaciones. **1556** *Chron. Gr. Friars* (Camden) 6 Thys yere was one John Norwelde..slayne at Blackehethe at a wrestlynge. **1578** H. WOTTON *Courtlie Controv.* 37 Great preparation was made of stage playes,..wrastlings, and other infinite pastymes. *c* **1611** CHAPMAN *Iliad* XXIII. 610 Pelides then set forth Prize for a wrastling. **1683** in *Verney Mem.* (1904) II. 339 Where the wrestlings are used to be in Lincoln's Inn fields. **1893** ROBINSON & GILPIN *Wrestling* 11 [He] stood unrivalled in all the wrestlings.

2. a. The action of striving or contending, maintenance of resistance, opposition, or strife, on the part of persons.

c **890** WÆRFERTH tr. *Gregory's Dial.* 320 Swa wæs þær þa seo wræstlung ymb Stephanum. *Ibid.* 321 He þa..ut ferde of lichaman to gewinne & to wræstlunge lifes & deaðes. *a* **1400** *New Test.* (Paues) Ephes. vi. 12 For ȝoure wrastlynge ..is..aȝeyn princes. **1523** LD. BERNERS *Froiss.* I. xxxix. 54 So this wrastlyng endured a long space; but fynally the knyght was rescued. **1548** UDALL, etc. *Erasm. Par. Matt.* v. 19 b, [To] make ye redy to this wrastling, if ye esteme the blessed rewardes of the gospell. **1632** LITHGOW *Trav.* VI. 294 With sore Wrestling agaynst the parching Sun. **1642** *Declar. Lords & Comm.* 23 Sept. 9 Our wrastling, and striving with that fierce and peremptory opposition. *a* **1844** in Stanley *Arnold* I. ii. 31 His absolute wrestling with evil. **1883** *Knowledge* June 334/1 That heavy and subtle wrestling for position which distinguishes the first-class player [of chess].

transf. **1610** HOLLAND *Camden's Brit.* I. 279 The river having with a great turning compasse after much wrestling, gotten out towards the North. **1654** R. CODRINGTON tr. *Iustine* IV. 74 This concurse and wrastling of the water.

fig. **1534** MORE *Treat. Passion* Wks. 1347/1 Hys catholike faythe..euer continue shal whyle this worlde last, what wrestlyng soeuer the infideles shall make with it. **1639** S. DU VERGER tr. *Camus' Admir. Events* 227 How unequall is the wrastling between reason and passion in a weake spirit. **1849** ROBERTSON *Serm.* I. iii. (1866) 45 Language which describes the wrestling of the soul. **1872** MORLEY *Voltaire* (1886) 2 Life as a long wrestling with unseen and invisible forces of grace.

b. The action of struggling or labouring.

a1225 *Ancr. R.* 238 Al þus,..iðe wrastlunge [*printed* winstlunge] of tentaciun, ariseð þe biȝeate. a1225 [see WRAGGLE *v.* 1]. c1450 *Mirk's Festial* I. 61 And so yn wrastelyng, scho woke of hyr slepe. 1563 PILKINGTON *Burnynge of Paules Ch.* M iiij, Saint Willyams horse,..wyth wrastlynge and sparringe vppe, saued himselfe and his master from drowninge.

fig. 1599 NASHE *Lenten Stuff* Wks. (Grosart) V. 252 Which it will be no impeachment for the wisest to turne loose for a trueth, without any diffident wrastling with it.

c. The action of striving earnestly in prayer; an instance of this.

1722 WODROW *Corr.* (1843) II. 664 You have our prayers here, and..the Church of Scotland has a share in your wrestlings. 1818 J. PYE SMITH *Script. Test. to Messiah* I. 96 The 'wrestlings' of holy prayer. 1902 A. McILROY *Druid's Island* viii, After deep conseederation, an' sore wrastlin' wi' the Almichty in prayer.

3. *attrib.* and *Comb.*, as ***wrestling article, bout,*** †***game, -house, -master, -match, ring***; **wrestling place**, a place where wrestling is practised or held; †**wrestling pull**, a bout of wrestling; = PULL *sb.*² 3; **wrestling school** *Gr. Antiq.*, = PALÆSTRA a.

1714 PARKYNS *Inn-Play* 62 To make these *Wrestling Articles yet more stronge they may be with a Noverint Universi. 1869 TOZER *Highl. Turkey* II. 237 [The ballads] treat..of *wrestling bouts with Charon. 1596 SPENSER *F.Q.* VI. ix. 43 Coridon..Did chalenge Calidore to *wrestling game. 1874 SYMONDS *Sk. Italy & Greece* 8 The olives here tell more to us of Olivet..than of..the wrestling-ground. 1848 B. D. WALSH *Aristoph., Clouds* III. iii, This is the talk which daily..crowds the Bagnios, and drains the *Wrestling-houses! 1714 PARKYNS *Inn-Play* 15 Since the Diluvians..have been celebrated *Wrestling Masters. 1820 T. MITCHELL *Aristoph.* I. 272 Say further what the wrestling-master Instructed you. a1700 EVELYN *Diary* 19 Feb. 1667, A *wrestling-match for £1000..before his Ma[jes]ty. 1889 W. ARMSTRONG *Wrestling* 233 What a Lancashire wrestling-match is like. 1974 *Plain Dealer* (Cleveland, Ohio) 27 Oct. 2-C/1 Even the second Ali-Frazier fight became a financial success for the promoters after Ali put on his rassling match with Frazier during that TV interview. c1440 *Promp. Parv.* 533/2 *Wrestelynge place, *palestra*. 1556 *Chron. Gr. Friars* (Camden) 42 At Clarkenwell at the wrestlynge place. a1592 GREENE *Deb. betw. Follie & Love* Wks. (Grosart) IV. 218 Hath not Follie inuented a thousand deuices to drawe a man from idlenesse, as..Dancing schooles, Fencing houses, wrastling places? 1610 HEALEY *Theophrastus* (1636) 23, I pray you whose wrestling place is this? 1602 CAREW *Cornwall* 2 This *wrastling pull betweene Corineus and Gogmagog. 1695 LUTTRELL *Brief Rel.* (1857) III. 461 The *wrestling ring in Lincolns Inn Feilds. 1893 ROBINSON & GILPIN *Wrestling & Wrestlers* 52 [He] would not be quick enough in his movements in the wrestling ring. 1835 THIRLWALL *Greece* vii. I. 290 The exercises of the troop in..the *wrestling-school. 1623 COCKERAM, *Gymnasticke*, a teacher of the *Wrastling Science. 1893 ROBINSON & GILPIN *Wrestling & Wrestlers* 9 Old and young regarded wrestling science..with keen relish. 1869 BLACKMORE *Lorna D.* xxvi, When I be in *wrestling trim.

'wrestling, *ppl. a.* [f. as prec. + -ING².]

1. That wrestles or contends, in various senses. Also *transf.*

a1547 SURREY *Æneid* II. 531 As wrastling windes, out of dispersed whirl Befight themselues. 1593 NASHE *Christ's T.* Wks. (Grosart) IV. 156 Your paine shalbe..wrastling, tearing, and intollerable. 1597 C. MIDDLETON *Fam. Hist. Chinon* vi. 38 His Father.., whome wrestling age had almost now layed along in hys graue. 1605 Z. JONES tr. *Loyer's Specters* 12 There was amongst the Greeks, a Diuell.. named..the wrastling Diuell. c1611 CHAPMAN *Iliad* XIX. 361 All their stall flies up in wrastling flame. 1632 LITHGOW *Trav.* x. 465 The thundring noyse of my wrestling voyce. 1738 WESLEY *Ps.* XXIV. vii, Thou the true wrestling Jacob art. 1847 TENNYSON *Princ.* VII. 266 The wrestling thews that throw the world. 1889 W. ARMSTRONG *Wrestling* 232 Wrestling men are impulsive beings. 1892 W. H. HUDSON *Naturalist in La Plata* 366 How I saw and lost the noble wrestling frog [= wrestler frog].

2. Marked or characterized by strife or contention, or by earnest striving.

a1593 MARLOWE tr. *Lucan* 299 His graue looke appeasd The wrastling tumult. 1620 T. PEYTON *Glasse of Time* I. 50 That none by wrong oppression might Be crost, by cunning, wringing, wrestling guile. 1854 H. MILLER *Sch. & Schm.* v. (1857) 98 It was impossible to avoid being struck with its wrestling earnestness and fervour. 1859 GEO. ELIOT *A. Bede* xlvii, She poured forth her soul with the wrestling intensity of a last pleading.

†**wresty**, obs. erron. f. RESTY *a.*¹

1697 VANBRUGH *Relapse* Prol. i, Wresty Nature's Spight. 1702 —— *False Friend* v. i, I was at first, a little wresty, and stood off.

wret, obs. or dial. var. WART *sb.*; obs. Sc. f. WRIT *sb.*; obs. pa. pple. or Sc. pa. t. of WRITE *v.*

wretar, obs. Sc. f. WRITER.

wretch (rɛtʃ), *sb.* and *a.* Forms: α. 1 wrecca, wræcca, 2-5 wrecche, 2-3 wræcche, 3-4 wrehche, 3-5 wrechche, 4-5 wrechhe, wrechch, 5 wrecch, 3-6 wreche (5 *Sc.* werche), 4-5 wrech (5 *Sc.* werch), 4-6 wretche, 5- wretch (6 wreatch); 4 wroche, 8 *dial.* wrotch. β. 4-5 wrich, wriche (wirche), wryche, 5 wrycche, 6 wrytche. γ. *Sc.* 5-6 wrache (5 warche), 6 wratche, *Sc.* and *dial.* 9 wratch. [OE. *wrecca, wræcca*, = OS. *wrekkio, -eo* (applied to the Magi), OHG. *reccheo, reccho*, etc., exile, adventurer, knight errant (MHG. and G. *recke* warrior, hero):—OTeut. **wrakja(n)-*, f. the stem *wrak-, wrek-*: see WREAK *v.* The contrast in the development of the meaning in Eng. and German is remarkable.]

A. *sb.* †**1.** One driven out of or away from his native country; a banished person; an exile.

The ME. instances are doubtful; they may be contextual uses of sense 2.

Beowulf 1137 Ða wæs winter scacen, fæger foldan bearm; fundode wrecca, gist of ȝeardum. c888 ÆLFRED *Boeth.* ii, Ða lioð þe ic wrecca ȝeo lustbærlice song ic sceal nu heofiende singan. a1122 *O.E. Chron.* (Laud MS.) an. 722, Ealdbriht wrecca ȝewat on Suðreȝe & on Suð Seaxe. c1386 CHAUCER *Sec. Nun's Prol.* 58 Now help thow..Me flemed wrecche in this desert of galle. c1450 *Ludus Coventriæ* 26 Goo naked vngry and bare foot.., as wrecch in werlde þou wende. *Ibid.* 27, I wende as wrecch in welsom way.

2. One who is sunk in deep distress, sorrow, misfortune, or poverty; a miserable, unhappy, or unfortunate person; a poor or hapless being.

α. c1000 *Boeth. Metr.* x. 38 Ne mæȝ mon æfre þy eð ænne wræccan his cræftes beniman. a1023 WULFSTAN *Hom.* vi. (1883) 45 Wræccena reaflac is on heora hamum. c1175 *Lamb. Hom.* 109 3if þe cristene mon bið sacful, and 3if þe wrecche bið modi. a1225 *Ancr. R.* 388 So heih ȝeoue nes neuer iȝiuen to so louwe wrecches. c1275 *Sinners beware* 103 in *O.E. Misc.* 75 Nv weneþ ek þes wrecche þat he ne þurue recche. c1330 R. BRUNNE *Chron. Wace* (Rolls) 13564 Cowardie halp þer no wrecche. 1380 WYCLIF *Wks.* (1880) 385 Mercy or almes is a wille of relevynge of a wreche oute of his mysese. c1410 HOCCLEVE *Mother of God* 15 Modir of mercy,..Benigne confort of vs wrecches all! a1513 FABYAN *Chron.* clvi. (1811) 145 He was..mylde and gracious to the poore, and marcyfull to wretchis and nedy. 1577 tr. *Bullinger's Decades* 125/1 Solomon the..happy king of Juda, bycause of his Idolatrie..is of a soudeine made a wretch of all other. 1623 J. TAYLOR (Water P.) *Discov. by Sea* B3b, Poore wretches, which (were it not for your charity) would perish in your streetes. 1671 T. HUNT *Abeced. Scholast.* 140 If money do fail a wretch thou art. a1721 PRIOR *24 Songs* iii. 8 She scorns to hear, or see, The wretch that lies so low as me. 1754 GRAY *Pleasure* 49 The Wretch, that long has tost On the thorny bed of Pain. 1810 SOUTHEY *Kehama* IV. v, Even in the grave there is no rest for me, Cut off from that last hope, the wretch's joy. 1855 LD. GRANVILLE in *Life* (1905) I. 106 Being a bed-ridden wretch I do not venture to disobey you. 1868 MORRIS *Earthly Par.* I. I. 349 O King, whom all the world henceforth shall know As wretched among wretches.

β. a1300 *Cursor M.* 23104 (Edinb.), þar sal stand on his left side, Wrichis stad in waful wide. *Ibid.* 23236 þe v. [pine of hell] es vndemenes of dint, þat þa wriches þar sal hint. 1570 LEVINS *Manip.* 150 A Wrytche, *miser*.

γ. c1375 *Sc. Leg. Saints* xxvii. (*Machar*) 1010 þan was þat wratche wondir wa.

b. Without article. (Freq. in apposition to a personal pronoun.)

c1200 ORMIN 10140 þatt te birrþ forr þe lufe off Godd Wiþþ usell wrecche dælenn. 13.. *Guy Warw.* (A.) 294 Allas, wreche, hou may i duelle? c1350 in *Relig. Lyrics 14th C.* (1924) 63 God & man my spouse is—Wele aght me, wryche, to luf him dere. c1400 *26 Pol. Poems* 112/163, I, wreche, whyder shal y fle. 1509 HAWES *Past. Pleas.* XVI. (Percy Soc.) 65 Alas! I wretche and yet unhappy peke Into..trouble. 1526 *Pilgr. Perf.* (W. de W. 1531) 2 Fynally I beseche all.. to praye for me wretche. 1653 H. COGAN tr. *Pinto's Trav.* i. 2 For myself, poor wretch, I went..in my misery to Setuval. 1743 YOUNG *Nt. Th.* IV. 14 Imagination's fool, and error's wretch, Man makes a death, which nature never made. 1790 COWPER *On Receipt Mother's Picture* 24 Hover'd thy spirit o'er thy sorrowing son, Wretch even then? 1821 SHELLEY *Hellas* 909 Fond wretch! He leans upon his crutch, and talks of years To come. 1886 W. J. TUCKER *E. Europe* 36, I, poor wretch, in possession of nothing.

c. Used as a term of address.

c1175 *Lamb. Hom.* 29 Weilawei wrecche,..al swa eða þu mihtest..smiten of þin aȝen heaueð. a1225 *Leg. Kath.* 2049 Hu wrakeliche, wenestu, wule he, al o wraððe, wreken on þe, wrecche! c1230 *Hali Meid.* 37 Ah, wrecche! þe care aȝain þi pinunge þrahen binimeð þe nihtes slepes. c1400 *Destr. Troy* 7178 A! wrecches vnwar, woo ys in our hond! a1550 *Image Hypocr.* III. 331 in *Skelton's Wks.* (1843) II. 437 Ye call that poore man wretch, As thoughe ye hadd no retche. 1615 CHAPMAN *Odyss.* XIV. 503 O wretch of Guests..thy Tale hath stirr'd My minde to much ruth. 1819 SHELLEY *Cenci* v. ii. 34 Poor wretch, I pity thee.

d. Applied to animals, birds, or insects.

a1300 *Fox & Wolf* in Hazl. *E.P.P.* I. 66 The wrecche binethe nothing ne vind, Bote cold water. c1480 HENRYSON *Swallow* 1908 Thir hungrie birdis wretchis we may call. 1600 SURFLET *Countrie Farme* 628 Vpon them shall be fastened manie boordes or hurdles..for to pleasure this small wretch [*sc.* a silkworm] withall. 1602 *Ld. Cromwell* IV. i. 47 Who sees the Cob-web intangle the poore Flie, May boldlie say the wretches death is nigh. 1627 DRAYTON *Nymphidia* xxvii, Soone away the Waspe doth goe, Poore wretch was neuer frighted so. 1742 FIELDING *J. Andrews* III. iv, This was the second time this squire had endeavoured to kill the little wretch [= a favourite dog]. *Ibid.* vi, The hare was no sooner on shore than it..listened to the sound of the pursuers. Fanny was wonderfully pleased with the little wretch. 1744 THOMSON *Summer* 273 The villain Spider.., fixing in the Wretch his cruel Fangs, Strikes backward. 1802 G. V. SAMPSON *Statist. Surv. Londonderry* 210 As to the rearing of calves, there is a [cruel] superstition... As soon as the wretch is produced,..two persons..pull it most forcibly.

e. A person or little creature. (Used as a term of playful depreciation, or to denote slight commiseration or pity.)

c1450 *Merlin* xxxiii. 683 He that was full fierce and prowde hadde shame to iuste with so litill a wrecche. 1592 SHAKS. *Rom. & Jul.* I. iii. 44 The pretty wretch lefte crying, & said I. 1599 BRETON *Miseries Mauillia* ii, With these last words, Farewell good mistresse, the good poore wretch.. gave up the ghost. —— *Scholler & Souldiour* 30 Oh 'tis a heavenly noise to heare the sweete wretch [= the nightingale]. 1604 SHAKS. *Oth.* III. iii. 90 Excellent wretch: Perdition catch my Soule But I do loue thee. 1663 PEPYS *Diary* 25 May, She being a good-natured and painful wretch. 1749 FIELDING *Tom Jones* I. vii, Had you exposed the little wretch in the manner of some inhuman mothers. 1784 COWPER *Task* IV. 12 He whistles as he goes, light-hearted wretch, Cold and yet cheerful. 1821 SHELLEY *Hellas* 227 Swift as the radiant shapes of sleep From one whose dreams are Paradise Fly, when the fond wretch wakes to weep. 1850 KINGSLEY *A. Locke* xxviii, Two little boys hailed us..—two little wretches with blue noses and white cheeks. 1891 'S. MOSTYN' *Curatica* 85, I see my wife wants me. The poor wretch is terribly jealous.

3. A vile, sorry, or despicable person; one of opprobrious or reprehensible character; a mean or contemptible creature. Also without article.

In very frequent use from *c* 1300.

α. a1000 *Juliana* 351 Hyre se feond oncwæð, wræcca wærleas wordum mælde. c1230 *Hali Meid.* 47 þu prokest me to forgulten,..& waldes warpe me as wrecche i þi leirwite. c1250 *Gen. & Ex.* 1074 Ðat folc vn-seli,..ðo sori wrecches of yuel blod. 1340 *Ayenb.* 25 þus him ioisseþ and him glorifieþ þe wreche ine his herte. 1362 LANGL. *P. Pl.* A. II. 169, I wolde be wreken on þis wrecches þat worchen so ille. 1402 HOCCLEVE *Let. Cupid* 310 The feythles wrechch how hath he him for-swore. a1450 *Medit. Life & Pass. Christ* 1139 Wiþ rugged nayles þe wrecches wode Nailed him hard to þe rode. 1555 PHILPOT in Coverdale *Lett. Martyrs* (1564) 230 Vnto me moste vile, sinnefull, wicked and vnworthy wretch. 1568 GRAFTON *Chron.* II. 337 These wretches entred into the Princesse Chamber, and brake her head. 1617 J. TAYLOR (Water P.) *Observ. & Trav. fr. London to Hamburgh* C4b, [They] were amazed at the ingratitude of the wretch. 1687 A. LOVELL tr. *Thevenot's Trav.* I. 104 The perfidious wretch Theseus abandoned the poor Ariadne. 1715 DE FOE *Fam. Instruct.* I. i, Wretch that I am, how have I lived, as without God in the world. 1781 COWPER *Table-T.* 30 Let eternal infamy pursue The wretch to nought but his ambition true. 1805 J. TURNBULL *Voy.* xvii. (1813) 212 The wickedness of the wretch who would import a cargo of spirituous liquors into the..Society Islands. 1855 KINGSLEY *Westw. Ho!* xxix, If I be wretch enough to give place to the devil. 1883 D. C. MURRAY *Hearts* xi, What wretches men were, to be sure!

β. 1377 LANGL. *P. Pl.* B. x. 78 þe wrecches [*Camb. MS.* wrycches] of þis worlde is none ywar bi other. c1440 *York Myst.* xxxi. 360 If any wight with þis wriche any werse wate werkis. c1450 *Mirk's Festial* I. 2 He ys not but a wryche and slyme of erth.

γ. 1572 *Satir. Poems Reform.* xxxii. 118 Consume this wratche with Brinstane. 1866- in Scottish glossaries, etc.

b. Used as a term of opprobrious address.

13.. *Sir Beues* (A.) 1033 Brademond, olde wreche,.. Ertow come Iosiane to feche? a1400-50 *Wars Alex.* 4005 'A! wriches!' quod þe wale kyng,..'Eftir þe deth of ȝour duke quat deynes ȝowe to stryue?' c1430 *Chev. Assigne* 71 A, kowarde of kynde,..& combred wreeche! 1540 PALSGR. *Acolastus* IV. v. Vjb, Thou wretched person,..thou wretche that thou art. 1605 SHAKS. *Lear* III. ii. 53 Tremble thou Wretch. 1719 DE FOE *Crusoe* I. (Globe) 93 Wretch!..look back upon a mis-spent Life. 1810 CRABBE *Borough* xxii. 248 Wretch, dost thou repent? 1819 SHELLEY *Cenci* I. iii. 90 Thou wretch! Will none among this noble company Check the abandoned villain?

c. Used without serious imputation of bad qualities.

1688 PRIOR *Ode* vii, Levelling at God his wand'ring Guess ..Laws to his Maker the learn'd Wretch can give. 1834 DICKENS *Sk. Boz, Boarding-ho.* i, Her 'wretch of a husband', as she inwardly called him. 1847 HELPS *Friends in C.* I. viii. 159 A wretch of a pedant who knows all about tetrameters.

†**4.** A niggardly or parsimonious person; a miser. *Obs.* (In later use chiefly *Sc.*)

1303 R. BRUNNE *Handl. Synne* 6203 þe wrecche saw hys tresoure sperd, And sette hym up yn hys bedde. 1340 *Ayenb.* 188 Uor to ssette þe porses of þe wrechchen þet hi ne ssolle by open to do elmesse. c1386 CHAUCER *Melib.* ¶634 Vse..thy richesses..that men haue no..cause to calle thee neiþer wrecche ne chynche. 1500-20 DUNBAR *Poems* xli. 5 Be nocht a wreche, nor skerche in ȝour spending. 1513 DOUGLAS *Æneid* VIII. Prol. 53 The wrache walis and wringis for this warldis wrak. 1540 PALSGR. *Acolastus* II. i. Hiijb, Snayles..all the wynter season kepe theym within their shelles, lyuynge lyke a wretche. a1578 LINDESAY (Pitscottie) *Chron. Scot.* (S.T.S.) II. 318 All wratchis may tak example be this man nocht to hurd vp thair siluir. 1673 WEDDERBURN *Voc.* 23 (Jam.), *Est valde avarus*, he is a great wretch.

†**5.** A poor or paltry thing. *Obs. rare*$^{-1}$.

?a1300 *Prov. Hendyng* 202 þis worldes loue ys a wrecche.

6. *Comb.*, as ***wretch-like***.

1615 CHAPMAN *Odyss.* IV. 961 Th' abiect threshold [she] chose Of her faire chamber, for her loth'd repose; And mournd most wretch-like.

B. *adj.* †**1.** Of persons: Poor; miserable; deeply afflicted; = WRETCHED *a.* 1. *Obs.*

a1122 *O.E. Chron.* an. 1083, þa wreccan munecas laȝon onbuton þam weofode. 1154 *Ibid.* an. 1137, Wrecce men sturuen of hungær. c1175 *Lamb. Hom.* 125 Alswa baldeliche mei þe wrechesta mon clepian drihtan him to federe. c1205 LAY. 6556 Wha se hæfde richedom, he hine makede wræcche mon. 1297 R. GLOUC. (Rolls) 4187 Alas þou wrecche mon, woch mesaunture Aþ þe ybroȝt in to þis stede. 13.. *Guy Warw.* (A.) 4811 Sche was a wriche wiman þat michel sorwe so was an. 1398 TREVISA *Barth De P.R.* VI. xiii. (Addit. MS.), No man is more wrecche noþir haþ more woo ..þan he þat hath an yuel wif. 1412-20 LYDG. *Chron. Troy* III. 4151 Allas! I, woful creature,..I, wreche woman. c1450 *Mirk's Festial* I. 47 þenke how febull and how wrecche he ys, when he ys bore. 1556 OLDE *Antichrist* 158 The wretche people thinks they haue holpen a soule. 1596 SPENSER *F.Q.* VI. ix. 30 It is the mynd..That maketh wretch or happie.

†**2.** Of conditions, etc.: = WRETCHED *a.* 2. *Obs.*

1131 *O.E. Chron.* an. 1131, Crist ræde for þa wrecce muneces of Burch & for þæt wrecce stede. a1200 in *Fragm. Ælfric's Gram.*, etc. (1838) 5 þonne biþ þet wræcche lif iended. 1297 R. GLOUC. (Rolls) 4094 þat we after hor wrecche deþ hor londes auonge. c1375 *Cursor M.* 949 (Fairf.), Wende out of þis louesom lande, in-to þe wrecche werlde þou gange. 1583 G. BABINGTON *Commandm.* (1590) 60 Yet see, ah wretch, and woful plight,..Thy goodnesse to mee farre passeth all masters to their seruants.

†3. Despicable; vile; reprehensible. *Obs.*

a **1200** *Vices & Virtues* 103 Kiel mine wreche herte, þe is iattred of his manifealde fondinges. *c* **1290** *Beket* 1406 in *S. Eng. Leg.* I. 146 Ich drede for mine wrechche gultes þat worse worth þe ende. **1297** R. GLOUC. (Rolls) 9913 þe wrecche luþer giwes. *c* **1350** in *Relig. Lyrics 14th C.* (1924) 50 To holi chirche . . pes þou sende, And to vs wreche sinful, lif wyt-outen ende. **1387** TREVISA *Higden* III. 33 Sardanapallus was a man more wrecche þan eny womman.

†4. Of a paltry character; = WRETCHED *a.* 3 b.

a **1250** *Owl & Night.* 335 Euer croweþ þi wrecche crey þat he ne swikeþ nyht ne day.

†**wretch**, *v. Obs.* Also 5 **wrecche**, *Sc.* 7 **wreche**, 8–9 **wratch**. [f. the sb.]

1. *trans.* To render miserable.

a **1513** FABYAN *Chron.* VII. (1811) 302 Y^e^ fore namyd bisshop . . contynuynge his tyrannyes, . . greued ye bisshop of Wynchester, and wretchyd nygh all ye londe.

2. *intr.* To be or become niggardly or parsimonious. *Sc.*

a **1598** D. FERGUSSON *Sc. Prov.* (S.T.S.) 10 As the carle riches he wretches [Kelly (1721) wratches]. **1633** W. STRUTHER *True Happiness* 139 As the wretch wretcheth, the more he is enriched. [**1853** TRENCH *Proverbs* 104 The more the carle riches he wretches.]

†ˈ**wretchcock**. *Obs.* [Alteration of WRETCHOCK, prob. by misprint in the text of Jonson, and adopted from this by Gifford.] = WRETCHOCK.

1641 *B. Jonson's Gipsies Metam.* Wks. 50 The famous impe yet grew a wretchcocke [**1692** wretchcock]. **1816** GIFFORD *B. Jonson's Wks., Masque* VII. 371 *note*, In every large breed of domestic fowls, there is usually a miserable little stunted creature. . . . This unfortunate abortive, the good-wives . . call a wret[c]hcock. **1817** —— *Persius* ii. 55 *note*, The poor puny wretchcock in whom the good old grand-mother sees the future son-in-law of kings.

†ˈ**wretchdom**. *Obs.* In 3–4 **wrecche-**, **wrechedom**, 3 **-dome**, 4 **-dom**, **-dam**. [f. WRETCH *sb.* + -DOM.] Misery; distress; baseness.

a **1225** *Ancr. R.* 232 Muchel godnesse hit is uorto icnowen wel his owune wrecchedom, & his wocnesse. *a* **1275** *Prov. Ælfred* 705 in *O.E. Misc.* 138 þe rede mon he is . . scolde, of wrechedome he is king. *a* **1300** *Cursor M.* 3113 In wrechedom er now all went. **13 . .** [see WRETCHEDDOM].

wretche, var. WRECHE *sb. Obs.*

wretched (ˈrɛtʃɪd), *a.* Forms: α. 3–5 **wrecched** (**-ede**, 4–5 **-id**, 4 **-ide**, 5 **-yd**, **-et**), 5 **wrechched** (**-id**, **-yd**); 3–5 **wreched** (3–4 **-ede**, 3–5 **-id**, 4 **-yde**, 5–6 **-yd**, *Sc.* **-it**, **-yt**), 5 **vrechid**, **wreached**, 6 **wreiched**; 5– **wretched** (5–6 **-id**, **-yd**, *Sc.* **-it**, 6 **wreteched**). β. 3–4 **wrichede** (4 **-ed**, 5 **-id**), 4 **wryched**, 4–5 **wricched**, **-id**, 5 **wrycched**. γ. *Sc.* 5–6 **wrachit** (5 **wrochit**), 6 **wratchet**, **-eit**, **-it**, **ratchit**. [Irreg. f. WRETCH *a.* + -ED[1]. Cf. WICKED *a.*[1]]

1. a. Of persons, etc.: Living in a state of misery, poverty, or degradation; sunk in distress or dejection; very miserable or unhappy.

α. *a* **1200** *Vices & Virtues* 9 Ðanne ic wolde ðe wrecchede saule sa rewliche acwellan. *a* **1240** *Wohunge* in *O.E. Hom.* I. 277 Ihesu . . riche ar tu . . , and tah poure þu bicom for me, westi and wrecched. *a* **1300** *Cursor M.* 24517 Allas! quat es me nu to red, I wrechidest of all! *c* **1340** HAMPOLE *Pr. Consc.* 2426 Wreched saul, . . what may thou say When þou partes fra þe body away? *c* **1374** CHAUCER *Anel. & Arc.* 60 þe wrechid Thebans bretheren two Were slayne. *c* **1450** *Myrr. our Ladye* 7 So ye vouchsafe of youre tender charyte . . to praye for oure right poure & full wretched soulle. **1482** [see WRETCHEDFUL *a.*]. **1538** STARKEY *England* II. i. 173 Pepul, wych now lyue in idulnes, wrechyd and pore. *a* **1592** GREENE *Alphonsus* IV. iii, I am . . the wretchedst man aliue. **1622** FLETCHER *Prophetess* III. i, We are no Spinsters; nor, if you look upon us, So wretched as you take us. **1647** COWLEY *Mistr., My Heart Discovered* 37 What should the wretched Widow do? ?**1705** BERKELEY in Fraser *Life* (1871) 475 Man without God wretcheder than a stone or tree. **1795** SOUTHEY *Vis. Maid Orleans* II. 238 A most wretched band Groan'd underneath the bitter tyranny Of a fierce dæmon. **1829** HOOD *Dream Eugene Aram* xix, My wretched, wretched soul . . Was at the Devil's price. **1858** CARLYLE *Fredk. Gt.* V. i, The poor exasperated Mother, wretchedest and angriest of women. **1882** J. HAWTHORNE *Fort. Fool* I. xxiv, A mountain of it can't make you one hair's breadth the happier or the wretcheder.

β. *a* **1340** HAMPOLE *Psalter* ii. 2 þa ere fendis, þat bigiles wricched saules.

γ. **1567** *Gude & Godlie B.* (S.T.S.) 24 We wratcheit sinnaris pure, Our sin hes vs forlorne.

b. *absol.*, in sing. or plural sense.

1388 WYCLIF *Isaiah* xvi. 4 For whi dust is endid, the wretchid [1382 the wrecche] is wastid; he that defoulide the lond failude. **1576** WHETSTONE *Rocke of Regard* I. 41 *marg.*, Others pleasures a griefe to the wretched. **1600** SHAKS. *A.Y.L.* III. v. 37 Who might be your mother That you insult, exult, . . Ouer the wretched? **1730** THOMSON *Autumn* 1192 Let These Insnare the wretched in the toils of law. **1794** MRS. RADCLIFFE *Myst. Udolpho* liv, The delight of having made the wretched happy. *a* **1806** H. K. WHITE *Remains* (1825) 306, I heard the wretched's groan, and mourn'd the wretched's doom. **1844** KINGLAKE *Eothen* ii, The wretched look often more picturesque than their betters.

(*b*) *spec.* in phr. ***wretched of the earth*** [tr. F. *damnés de la terre* (F. Fanon 1961, as book title)].

1965 C. FARRINGTON tr. F. Fanon (*title*) The wretched of the earth. **1970** *Guardian* 21 Aug. 11/3 Are the refugees, the most wretched of the earth, fertile ground for revolutionary activity on a mass scale? **1979** *Country Life* 11 Oct. 1236/3 Our own native 'wretched of the earth', the alcoholics, the inadequates, the very poor. **1983** C. DRIVER *British at Table* viii. 140 Protein alone cannot rescue the wretched of the earth.

2. a. Of conditions, etc.: Marked or distinguished by misery or unhappiness; attended by distress, discomfort, or sorrow.

α. *c* **1200** *Trin. Coll. Hom.* 141 Hwu wunderlich was his hider-cume and hwu wrecchede his her-biwist. *a* **1300** *Cursor M.* 949 ȝee most leue þis lufsum land, Vnto þe wreched werld to gang. *c* **1340** HAMPOLE *Pr. Consc.* 557 þe bygynnyng of man . . Es vile and wreched to behalde. **1377** LANGL. *P. Pl.* B. xv. 138 A wrecched hous he helde al his lyf tyme. *c* **1450** *Cursor M.* 9573 (Laud MS.), Here now my prayere Of this wrecchid preson. **1538** STARKEY *England* I. ii. 47 Myserabul penury and wrechyd pouerty. **1581** A. HALL *Iliad* I. 3 You see howe in this wretched warre our people doe decay. **1602** SHAKS. *Ham.* III. iii. 67 Oh wretched state! Oh bosome, blacke as death! **1697** DRYDEN *Virg. Past.* I. 15 The raging Sword and wastful Fire Destroy the wretched Neighbourhood around. **1719** DE FOE *Crusoe* II. (Globe) 402 The Savages . . killed them over again in a wretched Manner, breaking their Arms. **1785** BURNS *Winter Night* ix, Think, for a moment, on his wretched fate! **1847** M^c^CULLOCH *Acc. Brit. Empire* (ed. 3) II. 511 The disorderly and wretched state of the population. **1855** TENNYSON *Maud* II. v. ii, Wretchedest age, since Time began, They cannot even bury a man.

β. *c* **1400** MAUNDEV. (Roxb.) vi. 21 It es lang sen any durst come nere þat wricched place.

γ. *c* **1480** HENRYSON *Prais of Aige* 25 This wrachit warld may na man trow. **1552** LYNDESAY *Monarche* Prol. 209 In this wracheit vaill of sorrow. **1567** *Gude & Godlie B.* (S.T.S.) 57 Quhen fra this wratcheit lyfe we wend.

b. Of weather, etc.: Causing discomfort; very unpleasant or uncomfortable.

1711 SWIFT *Jrnl. to Stella* 27 March, A rainy wretched scurvy day from morning till night. **1836** DICKENS *Sk. Boz, Streets—Night*, It was such a wretched night out o' doors. **1888** *Encycl. Dict.* s.v., Wretched weather.

3. a. Distinguished by base, vile, or unworthy character or quality; contemptible.

c **1250** *Kent. Serm.* in *O.E. Misc.* 28 þo ilke þinges so bieth bitere to þo wrichede flessce. *c* **1290** *Codicem MS. Digby 86* (1871) 99 Weilawei, wrecchede bali, nou þou shalt to bere. *a* **1333** W. HEREBERT in *Relig. Lyrics 14th C.* (1924) 19 Dame, help at þe noede . . þat uor no wreched gult Ich boe to helle y-pult. *c* **1375** *Lay Folks Mass Bk.* (MS. B.) 80 þat god haue merci . . of my wreched synfulnes. **1456** SIR G. HAYE *Law Arms* (S.T.S.) 172 Of this wrechit disobeysaunce cummys untreuth. **1495** *Rolls of Parlt.* VI. 502/2 Their cursed, myschevous and wreched purpose. **1529** MORE *Dyaloge* III. xi. Wks. 226 We take suche a wretched pleasure in the hearing of their sin. **1568** GRAFTON *Chron.* II. 776 *margin*, Oh depe and wretched dissimulation! **1608** TOPSELL *Serpents* 278 The wretched nature of the young man, and his extreame impietie. **1652** URQUHART *Jewel* Wks. (1834) 213 Compatriots infected with the same leprosy of a wretched peevishness whereof those . . rapacious varlets have given such cannibal-like proofs. **1720** T. INNES *Crit. Essay* (1879) 311 Knox himself . . led on the furious mob in this wretched expedition. **1754** SHERLOCK *Disc.* (1759) I. iii. 109 The wretched Circumstances which put an end to our Lord's life. **1835** DICKENS *Sk. Boz, Pawn. Shop*, Where the practised smile is a wretched mockery of the misery of the heart. **1868** FREEMAN *Norm. Conq.* (1876) II. ix. 421 The thing was clearly some wretched court intrigue.

b. Of a poor, mean, or paltry character; mean, worthless; sorry, trifling.

1375 BARBOUR *Bruce* IX. 403 Quhen sic a knycht, sa richt vorthy As this is . . , In-to sic perill has hym set To vyn ane vrechit hamlet. *c* **1450** CAPGRAVE *St. Augustine* 46 His cloþis . . wer not ouyr costful, ne ouyr wrecched. **1450** *Lincoln Diocese Doc.* 45, I gyff . . my wrechid body to be Beryd in a chitte with-owte any kyste. **1561** T. NORTON *Calvin's Inst.* III. 265 This wretched victory they shall obteine, where . . the Lord shal suffer them to ouerspreade the darknes of lyes. **1637** MILTON *Lycidas* 124 Their lean and flashy songs Grate on their scrannel Pipes of wretched straw. **1662** J. DAVIES tr. *Olearius' Voy. Ambass.* 274 He who play'd upon the Timbrel accompany'd with a wretched inharmonious Voice. *Ibid.* 406 A wretched coarse Cloth. **1711** ADDISON *Spect.* No. 13 ⁋6 The wretched Taste of his Audience. **1726** SHELVOCKE *Voy. round World* (1757) 297 A paper written in such wretched Spanish as we could muster up amongst us. **1778** E. HARWOOD *Eds. Classics* (ed. 2) 5 Editions . . printed on wretched paper. **1824** MISS MITFORD *Village* Ser. I. 189 That still wretcheder apology for a coat. **1855** MACAULAY *Hist. Eng.* xix. IV. 263 So wretched had his education been. **1891** FARRAR *Darkn. & Dawn* xxx, The wretched little islets of Gyara and Tremerus.

4. Of persons, etc.: Contemptible in character or quality; despicable, reprehensible; hateful.

c **1430** LYDG. *Min. Poems* (Percy Soc.) 79 There stode a dragon, . . Wretched and skaled al wyth asure. *c* **1440** *Alph. Tales* 82 [When] he hard þis clauce red, . . þis wrichid clerk made a skorn þerat & sayd þat it was fals. **1460** CAPGRAVE *Chron.* (Rolls) 62 Nero . . , of alle men wrecchidhest, redy to alle maner vices. *c* **1470** HENRY *Wallace* VII. 400 Had he the warld, and be wrachit off hart, He is no lord as to the worthines. **1526** *Pilgr. Perf.* (W. de W. 1531) 37 b, Al though they be wretched lyuers & noughty packes. **1560** tr. *Fisher's Godly Treat. Prayer* C j b, Euery man, be he neuer so extreme and wretched a synner. *c* **1585** [R. BROWNE] *Answ. Cartwright* 68 To eate the Lordes supper with open vnrepentant & wretched persons is not lawfull. **1710** BERKELEY *Princ. Hum. Knowl.* §92 The absurdities of every wretched sect of Atheists. **1809–10** COLERIDGE *Friend* (1865) 107 The wretched tyrant . . had exhausted the whole magazine of animal terror. **1855** TENNYSON *Maud* x. ii, At war with myself and a wretched race, Sick, sick to the heart of life, am I.

transf. **1853** KANE *Grinnell Exp.* xxxi. (1856) 266 The icebergs are wretched enemies in the dark.

5. Of persons or animals: Poor in ability, capacity, character, etc.

c **1482** *Monk of Evesham* (Arb.) 85 On spurre with the whiche he was compellid to stere his wrechid hors to renne. **1577** B. GOOGE *Heresbach's Husb.* III. 150 Such as are farrowed in winter are commonly poore and wretched. **1668** EVELYN tr. *Freart's Idea Perf. Paint.* 16 By the hand of some wretched Dauber. **1860** SALA *Lady Chesterfield* 31 The women who make the wretchedest wives in the world. **1864** PUSEY *Lect. Daniel* (1876) 363 Daniel's omission of the wretched kings between Nebuchadnezzar and Belshazzar.

†**6.** Niggardly; miserly. (Cf. WRETCH *v.*[2]) *Obs.*

1652 URQUHART *Jewel* Wks. (1834) 280 That the minister is the greediest man in the parish, . . and that the richer they become . . the more wretched they are.

7. *Comb.*, as †***wretched-fated***, ***-witched***, and esp. ***wretched-looking***.

1591 SYLVESTER *Ivry* 425 People . . Pleas'd with the blaze, do, wretched-witched Elves, For fuell (fooles) cast-in their willing Selves. **1615** CHAPMAN *Odyss.* XX. 50 Thou most sowre, and wretched-fated man Of all that breath! **1817** J. SCOTT *Paris Revisit.* (ed. 4) 74 The single wretched-looking horse of each, half drowned in the torrent. **1839** *Penny Cycl.* XIII. 383/2 The cattle of the district are in general wretched-looking. **1864** A. MCKAY *Hist. Kilmarnock* 295 The wretched-looking farm-houses of former years.

Hence †ˈ**wretcheddom**, misery. *Obs.*

c **1320** *Cast. Love* 408 He . . tyed hym . . To wreccheddam [*v.r.* wrecchedam] and serwe i-nouȝ.

†ˈ**wretchedful**, *a. Obs.* [var. of WRETCHFUL *a.*, after prec.] Full of misery; miserable, wretched.

1382 WYCLIF *Judg.* v. 27 Cisaram . . was wrappid bifore the feet of hir, and he lay out of lijf, and wretchidful. *c* **1420** *Prymer* 69 What schal y þanne, most wrechidful, þenke? *c* **1425** in *Anglia* X. 343/1 Wrecthedefulle & sorowfulle þou schalt abyde þe grace of þe hye iustyse. **1482** *Monk of Evesham* (Arb.) 36, I herde and sawe . . the wrechid companyes of men and women ouer wrechidful bounden to gedyr.

†ˈ**wretchedhede**. *Obs.* In 3–4 **wrecched-** (4 **wrocched-**), 4 **wrecchid-**, 3–4 **wrechid-**, 3–5 **wrechedhede** (4 **-hed**, 5 **-heed**). [f. WRETCHED *a.* + *-hede* HEDE 2. Cf. WRETCHHEAD.] The state or condition of being a wretch or wretched person; wretchedness, misery.

a **1300** *E.E. Psalter* cvi. 41 [God] helped poure fra wrecched-hede. *c* **1325** *Metr. Hom.* 23 Crist . . us teches For to forsak this werdes winne Ful of wrechedhed and sinne. **13 . .** *Cursor M.* 1141 (Gött), For þi ill wreched-hede [*Trin.* wrecched hede] þu sal lede euer þi liif in nede. *a* **1400** in *Relig. Lyrics 14th C.* (1924) 240 Whan y þenk vp-on my dede . . , Dede torneþ into wrecchidhede.

wretchedly (ˈrɛtʃɪdlɪ), *adv.* [f. as prec. + -LY[2].] In a wretched manner.

1. In a miserable or unhappy fashion; with great misery, discomfort, distress, or unhappiness; miserably.

a **1300** *Cursor M.* 9459 Quen he sa wrechedli had tint His heritage. *c* **1340** HAMPOLE *Pr. Consc.* 842 þus wrechedly endes þe lyf of man. *c* **1400** MAUNDEV. (1839) xxiii. 251 Thei lyven fulle wrecched-liche; and thei eten but ones in the day. *c* **1410** *Lanterne of Liȝt* 51 Art þou not þanne wrechidli diuidid in þi silf? *c* **1450** *Myrr. our Ladye* 5 Adam . . fel so wretchydly in to synne. **1538** STARKEY *England* 74 For lake therof [*sc.* food] many . . lyue veray wrechydly. **1562** J. HEYWOOD *Prov. & Epigr.* (1867) 82 Tyll death from this lyfe, did hir wretchedly fetche. **1652** BENLOWES *Theoph.* I. lxxxvi, Crest-fall'n by sin, how wretchedly I stray. *a* **1667** COWLEY *Ess., Liberty* ⁋7 Thus wretchedly the precious day is lost. **1765** *Museum Rust.* IV. 403 It is our lots to be so wretchedly situated . . as to be content with forty shillings *per* cow *per annum*, nett profit. **1817** BYRON *Manfred* II. i. 77, I can bear—However wretchedly . . —In life what others could not brook to dream. **1867** MORRIS *Jason* IX. 76 This body . . In thy despite here mangled wretchedly. **1868** FREEMAN *Norm. Conq.* (1877) II. viii. 187 Arnulf . . drove him out to die wretchedly in exile.

b. In a way suggestive of indisposition or bad health.

1728 YOUNG *Love of Fame* VI. 232 Methinks I look so wretchedly to-day! **1797** JANE AUSTEN *Sense & Sens.* xxx, Though looking most wretchedly, she ate more.

2. So as to cause, or involve in, misery, distress, or discomfort.

1297 R. GLOUC. (Rolls) 5049 þe wreche . . þat þus wrecched-liche vs drifþ out of vre kunde londe. *c* **1450** *Myrr. our Ladye* II. 190 Wretchedly caste oute from the glory of paradyse. *a* **1548** HALL *Chron., Edw. IV*, 223 b, The hepyng of synne vpon synne, wretchedly by his aunceters. *a* **1700** EVELYN *Diary* 8 July 1656, A faire towne, but now wretchedly demolished by the late siege. **1828–32** WEBSTER s.v., The prisoners were wretchedly lodged.

†**3.** *Sc.* In a miserly or niggardly manner. *Obs.*

1500–20 DUNBAR *Poems* xvi. 21 Sum gevis to littill full wretchitly, That his giftis ar not set by.

4. Qualifying adjs. (or advs.): To a distressing, vexing, or unsatisfactory degree; deplorably, very badly; = MISERABLY *adv.* 5.

In the trivial use frequent from *c* 1830.

1546 BALE *Eng. Votaries* I. 76 They are wretchedlye blynde, for want of lyuelye knowlege in the sacred scriptures. *a* **1677** BARROW *Serm.* xix. Wks. 1686 III. 219 Sloth is a base quality, the argument of a mind wretchedly degenerate and mean. **1696** STANHOPE *Chr. Pattern* I. iii. (1700) 8 Both Error and Vice do . . so wretchedly abound. *a* **1700** EVELYN *Diary* 23 July 1679, The land all about wretchedly barren. **1810** LADY GRANVILLE *Lett.* (1894) I. 4 Miss Berry . . looking wretchedly ill. **1830** GREVILLE *Mem.* 5 Feb. (1875) I. 275 They are wretchedly off for speakers. **1858** DICKENS *Lett.* (1880) II. 65 You will find it a wretchedly stupid letter. **1879** M^c^CARTHY *Own Times* xxvii. II. 306 The hospitals were in a wretchedly disorganised condition.

5. In an inexpert, unsatisfactory, or crude manner; inefficiently, unskilfully, very poorly.

1677 MIÉGE *Fr. Dict.* II. s.v., To do a thing wretchedly, . . *faire mal quelque chose.* *a* **1700** EVELYN *Diary* 8 July 1656, A statue of Coilus in wood, wretchedly carved. **1719** DE FOE *Crusoe* I. (Globe) 136, I made me a Suit of Cloaths wholly of these Skins; . . they were wretchedly made. **1757** [BURKE] *Europ. Settlem. Amer.* VII. xxvii. II. 269 The capital . . was a small place wretchedly fortified. **1778** E. HARWOOD *Eds. Classics* (ed. 2) 59 This Edition wretchedly reprinted, Francof. 1690. **1856** KANE *Arct. Expl.* I. xxvi. 349 We are wretchedly prepared for another winter on board. **1881** MISS BRADDON *Asphodel* II. 16 Lina, dearest, . . you were playing [billiards] almost as wretchedly as I.

wretchedness (ˈrɛtʃɪdnɪs). [f. as prec. + -NESS.] The state or quality of being wretched.

1. A condition of discomfort or distress caused by privation, poverty, misfortune, adversity, or the like; great misery or unhappiness.

In very frequent use from *c* 1375.

α. *a* **1340** HAMPOLE *Pr. Consc.* 6102 þe day of wrethe and of wrechednes. *c* **1386** CHAUCER *Manciple's T.* 67 Yet hath this brid . . Leuere in a fforest that is rude and coold Goon ete wormes, and swich wrecchednesse. *c* **1440** *Gesta Rom.* vii. 19 Thenne . . comyth aȝen . . our lord, whenne þat he hath pyte of our wretchidnesse. **1471** CAXTON *Recuyell* (Sommer) 448 Yf thou were in the abysmes of wrecchidnes and myseryes. **1526** *Pilgr. Perf.* (W. de W. 1531) 37 He cast hym out into this vale of mysery and wretchednes. **1596** SPENSER *State Irel.* Wks. (Globe) 614/1 When they are weary of warres, and brought downe to extreeme wretchednesse. **1605** SHAKS. *Lear* IV. vi. 61 Is wretchednesse depriu'd that benefit To end it selfe by death? **1679** DRYDEN *Pref. to Troil. & Cress.* ad fin., Consider the wretchedness of his condition. **1742** YOUNG *Nt. Th.* i. 229 Thought, busy thought! . . Strays (wretched rover!) o'er the pleasing Past: In quest of wretchedness perversely strays. **1760** D. WEBB *Inq. Beauties Painting* 161 A fine image of hopeless wretchedness, of consuming grief. **1820** SYD. SMITH *Wks.* (1850) 302 The manifold wretchedness to which the poor Irish tenant is liable. **1840** DICKENS *Old C. Shop* xlv, The great manufacturing town reeking with lean misery and hungry wretchedness. **1887** BRUCE SMITH *Liberty & Liberalism* 615 What we call 'wretchedness, unhappiness, and sin' are the inevitable results of the gap which does . . exist between our powers and our aspirations.

β. *a* **1340** HAMPOLE *Psalter* ii. 11 þe dred of god is noght of wricchidnes bot of ioy. *c* **1400** MAUNDEV. (Roxb.) xxvi. 124 þai liffe with grete wricchedness and scantness.

γ. *c* **1480** HENRYSON *Prais of Aige* 12 Wrachitness his [= has] turnyt al fra weil to vo.

b. A cause or occasion of misery.

1382 WYCLIF *James* v. 1 Do now, ȝe riche men, wepe ȝe, ȝoulynge in ȝoure wrecchidnessis that shulen come to ȝou. *c* **1410** *Lanterne of Liȝt* 49 þis a sorowful vanite & a greete wrecchidnes. *c* **1450** *Myrr. our Ladye* II. 242 How grete tormentes & how grete wretchednesses they gather and hepe to theyr owne sowles. **1837** CARLYLE *Fr. Rev.* I. I. ii, Call not the Past Time, with all its confused wretchednesses, a lost one. **1893** *Amer. Mission.* (N.Y.) Dec. 436 To these vices . . is added now a new wretchedness, . . the vice of drunkenness.

2. The condition or character of being base or vile, odious or contemptible; despicableness, meanness, badness.

13.. *Cursor M.* 10887 (Gött.), Widuten sinne and wrecchednes Sal þu be mayden as þu es. *Ibid.* 17288 + 273 Als mikel os scho loued bifore þe dele & wricchednes, Als mikel . . loued scho crist thoru hir grete godenes. **1389** in *Eng. Gilds* (1870) 7 ȝif it so befalle þat any of þe bretherhede falle in pouerte . . so it be nat on hymselue along, thorwȝ his owne wrecchednesse. *c* **1450** LOVELICH *Grail* xliii. 413 For more they loven wrechchednesse Thanne hevenely thing. *c* **1475** *Bk. Noblesse* (Roxb.) 51 Therfor ye oughte . . conceyve the gret adversite that fallithe to us is . . only for synne and wrecchidnes. **1513** BRADSHAW *St. Werburge* II. 2010 For baudy balades full of wretchednes. **1546** LANGLEY tr. *Pol. Verg. de Invent.* IV. i. 81 b, They . . returned to their old wretchednes and sinful abhominacions. **1617** WOODALL *Surg. Mate* Pref., Wks. (1639) C j, Censuring other men in many things, but not perceiving their own wretchednesse at all. **1645** MILTON *Colast.* Wks. 1851 IV. 345 The guilt of his own wretchednes. **1649** —— *Eikon.* Pref., [Their] Pulpit-stuffe . . hath bin the . . perpetuall infusion of servility and wretchedness to all thir hearers. **1755** JOHNSON, *Wretchedness*, . . despicableness.

†**b.** A base or reprehensible action; a vicious trait, deed, etc. *Obs.*

c **1380** WYCLIF *Wks.* (1880) 171 þei . . tellen lesyngis & wrecchidnessis of synnis. *c* **1386** CHAUCER *Frankl. T.* 795 [To] doon so heigh a cherlyssh wrecchednesse Agayns franchise and alle gentillesse.

†**3.** *Sc.* The state or condition of being miserly or parsimonious; niggardliness, miserliness. *Obs.*

c **1470** HENRY *Wallace* VIII. 526 Thai sawft na Sotheroun for thair gret riches; Off sic koffre he callit bot wretchitnes. *c* **1500** *Lancelot* 1857 Wrechitnes richt so . . Haith Realmys maid ful desolat & barre. **1500–20** DUNBAR *Poems* xxxi. 4 He that hes gold and grit richess, . . And levis in to wrechitness, He wirkis sorrow to him sell.

4. The state or condition of being mean, sorry, or paltry; inferiority, worthlessness.

1810 *Naval Chron.* XXIII. 39 His seventh assertion . . is . . a curious specimen of the wretchedness of his information. **1828–32** WEBSTER s.v., The wretchedness of a performance.

5. The fact or character of being uncomfortable or unpleasant; discomfort.

1836 DICKENS *Sk. Boz, Streets—Night*, After a little conversation about the wretchedness of the weather. **1888** *Harper's Mag.* Oct. 782 The gray wretchedness of the afternoon was a fit prelude to Barra.

†**wretchful**, *a.* *Obs.* Forms: (see quots.). [Irreg. f. WRETCH *sb.* and *a.* + -FUL. Cf. WRETCHEDFUL *a.*] Wretched; miserable; unhappy.

1382 WYCLIF *Eccl.* v. 15 Wreccheful forsothe infirmyte; what maner he cam, so he shal turne aȝeen. —— *Rev.* iii. 17 Thou art a wrecche, and wrechful [**1388** wretcheful], and pore, and blynd, and nakid.

†**wretchhead.** *Obs.* In 2 wreccehed, 2–4 wrec-, 3–4 wrecc-, wrechhede, 3 wrecchehed, wrecchade, 5 wrecheheed. [f. as prec. + -HEAD. Cf. WRETCHEDHEDE.] = WRETCHEDNESS 1.

Frequent in Robert of Gloucester's *Chronicle*.

1154 *O.E. Chron.* an. 1137, Wes næure gæt mare wreccehed on land. *c* **1175** *Lamb. Hom.* 79 þas þeues . . boð þo þet weren imakede engles in houene, and fellen ut for hore wrechede. *a* **1200** *Vices & Virtues* 21 We ðankieð gode . . ðe ȝew haueð of ðessere michele wrecchade ibroht. *Ibid.* 95 þurh hwam ic am . . on maniȝes kennes wrecchades, sori and sorhfull. *a* **1250** *Owl & Night.* 1219 Hwanne ic iseo þer sum wrecchede Is cumynde neyh inoh ic grede. *c* **1290** *S. Eng. Leg.* I. 292/133 þench nouþe, louerd, on mine wrechhede! **13..** *Chron. R. Glouc.* (MS. Digby 205) 5053 Nowe we ben . . Dryuen oute clene . . with sorwe & wrechehede [*v.rr.* wrechede, wrechhede, wrecheheed].

wretchless (ˈrɛtʃlɪs), *a.* ? *Obs.* [Erron. form of *retchless*, obs. var. of RECKLESS *a.*]

Also **1609** Daniel *Compl. Rosamond* lii, **1617** Hooker *Eccl. Pol.* v. 385, **1662** —— *Serm.* vi. §33 (in *Eccl. Pol.* 302), **1669** Heylyn *Cosmogr.* II. 200, **1689** Sanderson *Serm.* 389, **1710** Cowley *Cutter Colman St.* Pref., **1714** Quarles *Feast for Worms* Med. i, where however the earlier edd. have *rech-, retch(e)lesse, retchless.*

1. Of persons: Heedless, careless, imprudent; = RECKLESS *a.* 1.

1598 TOFTE *Alba* (1880) 85 Thus (carefull I) doe care for careless thee, Whilst wretchles thou, makst no account of mee. **1617** *Greene's Arbasto* v. D 3, A fit reuenge for so wretchlesse an enemy. **1643** PRYNNE *Sov. Power Parl.* IV. App. 20 The people fell away from their wretchlesse and lascivious king. **1666** [see RECKLESS *a.* 1]. **1681** *Gesta Rom.* v. B 3, This young Lord . . sought many Realms, and found many wretchless fools. **1853** TRENCH *Prov.* (ed. 2) 136 The motto of some, who . . become utterly wretchless, caring not . . how much further they advance.

2. Heedless *of* something; = RECKLESS *a.* 2.

1661 RUST *Origen's Opin.* 37 Some in their charge, who . . are . . wretchless and insensible of all wholesome counsels.

3. Marked or characterized by heedlessness or carelessness; = RECKLESS *a.* 3.

1607 TOPSELL *Four-f. Beasts* 473 The vnmercifull regard which wretchlesse and childish mindes beare towardes the greatest labors and deserts of the best men. **1633** [see RECKLESS *a.* 3]. **1656** OSBORNE *Observ. Turks* §15 This . . doth often hurry such as have had their hopes deluded . . into wretchlesse Infidelity. **1673** ALLESTREE *Lady's Calling* I. v. §26 The comprehensive description of the most wretchless profligated state of sin.

Hence †ˈ**wretchlessly** *adv.* *Obs.*

1615 DOD & CLEAVER *Expos. Prov.* 87 Hee doth vpbraid him with . . folly, which would so wretchlesly, and sinfully depart with that. ? **16..** in *Strype's Eccl. Mem.* III. App. 124 Cursed are al they that do the Lord's busines wretchlesly.

wretchlessness (ˈrɛtʃlɪsnɪs). Now only *arch.* [Erron. form of *retchlesnes*, obs. var. of RECKLESSNESS. Cf. RECKLESS *a.*]

Also **1634** Raleigh *Hist. World* IV. iii. §5, **1718** Daniel *Civ. Wars* v. xxi, where however the earlier edd. have *retchlesnes(se*, etc.

1. The condition or quality of being reckless or heedless; recklessness.

1625 PURCHAS *Pilgrims* II. 1304 [A language] corrupted not so much by the mixture of other Tongues, as through a supine wretchlesnesse. **1647** HAMMOND *Power of Keys* IV. 113 The pride and self-conceit of some, the wretchlesnes of others. **1673** HICKMAN *Quinquart. Hist.* II. 455 For any men to have the Doctor's . . sentence of Predestination alway before them, is no way . . apt to beget either despair or wretchlessness.

1855 KINGSLEY *Westw. Ho!* vii, Till lately, from my youth up, I was given over to all wretchlessness and unclean living. **1860** A. L. WINDSOR *Ethica* iv. 209 To the wretchlessness of human nature his mind . . must have been peculiarly sensitive.

2. Disregard or neglect *of* something.

Frequent in echoes of quot. 1630.

1630 *Articles Ch. England* xvii. C 2, Whereby the Devil doth thrust them either into desperation, or into wretchlesness [*earlier edd.* rech(e)lesnesse] of most unclean living. [**1819** G. S. FABER *Dispensations* (1823) I. 171 To drive man to absolute despair and thence (as our Church expresses it) to complete wretchlessness of unclean living.] **1882** FARRAR *Early Chr.* I. 377 What a rare insolence and wretchlessness of sin must be involved in such expressions. **1892** *Sat. Rev.* 17 Dec. 719/2 His fault-finding is due to wretchlessness of most unclean desperation in him.

†**wretchly**, *a.* *Obs. rare.* In 2–3 wrechelich. [f. WRETCH *sb.* + -LY[1].] Wretched, miserable.

c **1200** *Trin. Coll. Hom.* 33 Adam . . ferde ut fram þe fulle edinesse of paradis in to þesse wrecheliche hateringe of þisse worelde.

†ˈ**wretchly**, *adv.* *Obs.* Forms: 3 wræccheliche, wrecchelïȝ, 3–4 -lyche, 4 wrecheli, 5 *Sc.* wrechly. [f. WRETCH *a.* + -LY[2].] In a wretched or distressing manner; miserably.

c **1200** ORMIN 3326 And tohh þatt Godd wass . . wundenn þær swa wrecchelïȝ Wiþþ clutess inn an cribbe. *c* **1205** LAY. 12096 Ne miðte hit na mon telle þet weoren æi wimman Swa wræcchelichen atoȝene. *Ibid.* 30554 þa wes he wræccheliche of-lust after deores flæsce. **1340–70** *Alex. & Dind.* 88, I wrouthe wrecheli now & wraþede drihten. **13..** *Chron. R. Glouc.* (Hearne) 9157 Ac [þe] kyng . . nom hym vaste, And in prison hym huld, & wrecchelyche he deyde atte laste. *c* **1375** *Sc. Leg. Saints* xxiii. (*Seven Sleepers*) 161 Sa þat þai suld . . for hungyre de wrechly.

So †ˈ**wretchlike** *adv.* *Obs. rare*[−1].

c **1200** ORMIN 3708 To libbenn her onn eorþe Full wrecche-like inn uselldom Off metess & off claþess.

†ˈ**wretchness.** *Obs. rare.* In 4–5 wrechenesse, 5 -nys, wrachenes. [f. WRETCH *a.* + -NESS.] Wretchedness; misery; a cause or source of distress.

a **1330** W. HEREBERT in *Rel. Ant.* II. 227 What! ich vol of wrechenesse, hou shal ich take opon, When ich no god ne bringe to-vore the domes mon? **1382** WYCLIF *Job* xxx. 12 At the riȝt of the est my wrecchenesses anoon risen. **14..** in *Walter of Henley's Husb.* (1890) 42 The hard change off fortune . . discendithe . . to myche vnease or wrechenys. **1483** *Act 1 Rich. III*, c. 2 Mony worshipfull men . . were compelled . . to lyff in greate penurie and wrechenesse.

wretchock (ˈrɛtʃək). Now *dial.* Also 6 wretchocke, -ecke, 7 -ocke. [f. WRETCH *sb.* + -OCK. Cf. WRETCHCOCK.] The smallest or weakest of a brood, etc.; a puny fowl; a diminutive person, little wretch.

a **1529** SKELTON *E. Rummyng* 465 The goslenges were untyde; Elynour began to chyde, They be wretchockes [*v. rr.* wrethocke(s] thou hast brought, They are shyre shakyng nought! **1579** G. HARVEY *Letter-bk.* (Camden) 87 Lerned philosophers . . are the dryest, leanist, ill-favoriddist, abiectist, base-mind[e]dist carrions and wretcheckes that ever you sett your eie on. **1621** B. JONSON *Gypsies Metam.* in *Horatius*, etc. (1640) 48 The famous Impe yet grew a wretchocke [*Heber MS.* wretchock], and . . for seven years together he was carefully carried at his Mothers back. **1903** R. M. GILCHRIST *Beggar's Manor* 223 She can't have gone of her own account; the poor wretchock dotes on you. **1905** *Eng. Dial. Dict.*, *Wretchock*, . . the smallest pig of a litter. s. Wor[cester].

wrete, obs. var. WART *sb.*; obs. pa. t. and pa. pple. of WRITE *v.*

wreten, obs. f. *written*, pa. pple. of WRITE *v.*

wreth, obs. f. WREATH, WREATHE *v.*; obs. Sc. f. WROTH *a.*

†**wrethe**, *sb.* *Obs.* Forms: α. 1 wræðo, -u, wræþu, 2 wræþe, 3 wreðe, 3–5 wreth, 4–6 wrethe, 6 *Sc.* wreath. β. *north.* 4–5 wrythe, 5 writh(e, *Sc.* wryth. [OE. *wrǽðo* (also *wráðo*), *wrǽþu* (f. *wráþ* WROTH *a.*), = MLG. *wrêde*. ON. **wreiði* (Norw. *vreide*; MSw. *wredhe*, *vredhe*, Sw. and Da. *vrede*), *reiði* (Icel. *reiði*, Norw. *reide*). A different OE. formation is represented by WRATH *sb.*]

1. Violent anger; = WRATH *sb.* 1. Also in the phr. ***be*** **(= by),** ***but, for, of, in, on, through, with wrethe.***

c **950** *Lindisf. Gosp.* Mark iii. 21 And miððy ȝeherdon his eodon to haldanne hine, cuoedon forðon þætte on wræðo [L. *in furorem*] ȝecerred wæs. *c* **1100** *O.E. Chron.* (MS. F.) an. 1051, Forþan hi wæran intinga þare wræðe ðe was betwyx him & ðan cinge. *c* **1250** *Kent. Serm.* in *O.E. Misc.* 33 Yef se deuel us wille a-cumbri þurch senne . . oþer þurh wreþe. *c* **1250** *Gen. & Ex.* 482 Lamech wið wreðe is knape nam. *a* **1300** *Cursor M.* 10049 Moght in hir noþer be wreth ne het, Hir tholmodenes it was sa gret. *c* **1330** *Amis & Amil.* 830 Lete thi wrethe first ouergon, Y pray the. *c* **1375** *Sc. Leg. Saints* xlii. (*Agatha*) 121 In wryth quyncyane bad gef hire buffetis. *a* **1400** *Sir Degrev.* (Thornton MS.) 299 (Halliwell), Thus thay fighte in the frythe, With waa wreke thay thaire wrythe. **1422** YONG tr. *Secreta Secret.* 135 Hatredyn engendryth wronge and wrethe. *c* **1440** *Eng. Conq. Ireland* 75 But in nothynge thay myght acorde, & begon to de-pert, as in wrethe. **1530** PALSGR. 290/2 Wrethe, angre, *courroux, maltalent.* **1587** W. FOWLER *Wks.* (S.T.S.) I. 53 Sometymes through wreath, I forced was . . To teare them all in peaces small.

Personif. *c* **1420** LYDG. *Assembly of Gods* 624 Wrethe bestrode a wylde bore, and next hem gan ryde.

transf. *c* **1475** *Partenay* 231 An huge bore of meruelous wreth.

2. A fit or display of wrath; = WRATH *sb.* 2.

a **1400–50** *Wars Alex.* 865 (Dubl. MS.), Sir, lat þi wrethes all wende. **1434** MISYN *Mending Life* 117 Wrethis, hatredis, detraccions mekely suffyr.

3. Of the Deity: = WRATH *sb.* 4 a.

c **900** *Rituale Eccl. Dunelm.* (Surtees) 11 In alle soðfæst[nis] ðin se ymbvoended [L. *avertatur*] . . wræðo ðin. *a* **1023** WULFSTAN *Hom.* (1883) 174 Hæfþ eal folc . . micele wræþe æt gode þurh his ænne gilt. *a* **1300** *Cursor M.* 27362 O þat soruful dai o pain, . . þe dai o wreth, o quak and soru. *c* **1340** HAMPOLE *Pr. Consc.* 1552 þarewyth þai wreth God þat sese all; And his wreth at þe last sall with þam mete. **1387** TREVISA *Higden* I. 191 þat tyme þat Egipt was i-smyte wiþ God all myȝties wrethe. *c* **1420** [see WREAK *sb.* 1].

4. Injury, hurt, harm. *rare.*

c **1400** *Melayne* 96 Wende thy waye . . To Charles . . & he sall wreke thy wrethis alle. *c* **1440** *Bone Florence* 1613 Hys mowthe, hys nose, braste owt on blood, Forthe at the chaumbur dore he yode, For drede of more wrethe.

wrethe: see WREATH, WREATHE *v.*, WRIT *sb.*

†**wrethe**, *v.*[1] *Obs.* Forms: α. 1 *Northumb.* wræðan (wuræðan), 2–3 wreðen (3 werðen), 5 wrethyn; 4 wreþi, 4–5 wreþe, wreth(e, 5 *Sc.* wreyth. β. 5 *north.* writhe. [OE. *wrǽðan*, causative verb f. *wráþ* WROTH *a.* Cf. WROTH *v.*]

1. *trans.* Of persons (or things): To make angry; to vex, anger, irritate. = WRATH *v.* 2.

In frequent use from *c* 1300 to *c* 1400.

c **900** *Rituale Eccl. Dunelm.* (Surtees) 107 Se cyng . . mið ðy ȝiherde wræðde & sende hergvm sinvm. *c* **950** *Lindisf. Gosp.* Matt. xviii. 34 And wuraeðde [L. *iratus*] hlaferd his ȝesalde hine ðæm pinerum. *c* **1175** *Lamb. Hom.* 39 Bute we inwarliche imilcien and forȝeuen þan monne þe us wreðeð and sceandet. *c* **1230** *Hali Meid.* (1922) 38 For moni þing schal ham wreaðen & gremien. *a* **1240** *Ureisun* in *O.E. Hom.*

197 þet ich ðe wreðede sume siðe hit me reoweð sore. **13..** *Seuyn Sages* (W.) 3461 Sir, ye er wrethed wrang; That sal ye wit wele or I gang. **1375** BARBOUR *Bruce* XVII. 45 Gif he tuk till his helping, Ane or othir suld wrethit be. **1422** YONG tr. *Secreta Secret.* 199 God.. no man refusyth, haue he neuer so myche hym wrethyd. *c* **1475** *Partenay* 2856 More neuer ne was woer.. Then off that he hade wrethed so Raymounde.

b. *refl.* To wax angry; = WRATH *v.* 3.

c **1205** LAY. 9214 Þe kæisere hine wrædde, þe wurs him wes on heorte. *a* **1300** *Cursor M.* 18221 Wit þis can iesus him to wreth. *a* **1340** HAMPOLE *Psalter* vii. 12 God is rightwis iuge;.. he wrethis him noght ilk day. *c* **1400** *Ywaine & Gaw.* 995 For na thing that thou mai sayn, Wil i me wreth. *c* **1430** *Pilgr. Lyf Manhode* III. xxxii. (1869) 153 Nature wolde wretthe hire if man [etc.].

c. *impers.* = ANGER *v.* 2 b.

a **1400-50** *Wars Alex.* 4639 Or ellis ȝow writhis with ȝour wele, for ȝe na welth haue!

2. *intr.* To become or be angry; = WRATH *v.* 1.

c **900** *Rituale Eccl. Dunelm.* (Surtees) 197 Wræððe.. diwl [L. *fremuit diabulus*]. *c* **950** *Lindisf. Gosp.* Matt. v. 22 Eghuelc seðe uraeðes broðere his. *c* **1175** *Lamb. Hom.* 33 Tobreoke anes eorðliches monnes heste, he wile wreðe wið þe. *a* **1225** *Juliana* 13 (Bodl. MS.), Affrican wreaðede & swor swiðe deopliche. *c* **1250** *Gen. & Ex.* 1584 Be ðu ðer.. til esau Eðe moðed be, ðe wreðed nu. *a* **1340** HAMPOLE *Psalter* ii. 12 Gripes disciplyne, leswhen lord wreth: and ȝe perisch fra rightwis way. **1387** TREVISA *Higden* V. 207 Þat he schulde whanne he gan to wreþe seie ofte and by ordre foure and twenty lettres of Grewe. *a* **1400-50** *Wars Alex.* 2593 Þen þe berne writhis, Fandis him first on be-fore, & all foloȝes eftir. **14..** *Titus & Vesp.* (Roxb.) 1404 (Addit. MS. 10036), Thei wreþed with him for his sawe. *c* **1475** *Partenay* 4853 It was for his syne That his fader had wrethed heuyly so.

3. *trans.* To be angry with (a person); = WRATH *v.* 4.

c **1420** *Chaucer's Troylus* III. 174 (Harl. MS. 2280), Ny nyl [I] forbere if þat ȝe don amys To wreth ȝow. *c* **1500** *Poems Gray MS.* (S.T.S.) 46 Quhy wrethis þou me? I greif þe nocht.

Hence †ˈ**wrethed** *ppl. a.*; †ˈ**wrething** *vbl. sb.*

a **1340** HAMPOLE *Psalter* vi. 1 He sall be seen til ill men as *wrethid and as wode. **1567** *Satir. Poems Reform.* iv. 136 The crewell work of wretheit womanheid. *a* **1300** *Cursor M.* 29511 Quen man.. wit *wrething wode, Gis his sentence on ani man. *a* **1400-50** *Wars Alex.* 5036 Lefe of þi wordis, For writhing of þir wale treeis, & willne þaim na mare. **1423** JAS. I *Kingis Q.* cxlvi, By quhois effectis grete ȝe movit are to wrething.

†**wrethe**, *v.*[2] *Obs.* In 1 wreþian, wreðian (wræð-), 3 wreoðien. [OE. *wreðian* (also *a-*, *ȝe-*, *under-wreðian*), f. *wraðu* support, etc., = OS. *wređian*, *giwređian*.]

1. *trans.* To prop or hold up; to support or sustain. Also in fig. context. (Only OE.)

c **888** ÆLFRED *Boeth.* xxi, Heora ælc [*sc.* creature] winð wið oðer, & þeah wræðeð oðer, þæt hie ne moton toslupan. *c* **890** WÆRFERTH tr. *Gregory's Dial.* 175 Wreþiende [L. *sustenans*] þa tydran limu betwyh his ȝingrena handum. *a* **1000** *Andreas* 523 (Gr.), Se ðe rodor ahof & ȝefæstnode folmum sinum, worhte & wreðede.

2. *refl.* To support (oneself) by leaning upon another; = LEAN *v.*[1] 2 b. Also *fig.*

a **1225** *Ancr. R.* 252 3if þet heo wergeð, euerichon wreoðeð him bi oðer. *a* **1225** *Leg. Kath.* 857 Alle þeos writeres writes þet ȝe wreoðieð ow on.

3. *intr.* To rely *on*, depend *upon*, a person.

a **1225** *Ancr. R.* 142 þet heo owun to beon of so holi liue þet.. al Cristene uolc leonie & wreoðie upon ham. *a* **1225** *Leg. Kath.* 1327 We ne cunnen.. warpen na word aȝein to weorrin ne to wreððen him þet ha wreoðeð on.

wrethen, -in, obs. or Sc. varr. WREATHEN *ppl. a.*

wrether hail, var. WROTHER-HEAL *Obs.*

†ˈ**wrethful**, *a. Obs.* [Early ME. *wreðful*, f. *wreðe* WRETHE *sb.* + -FUL. Cf. WRATHFUL *a.*, WROTHFUL *a.*]

1. Of persons: Angry, irate; = WRATHFUL *a.* 1.

c **1175** *Lamb. Hom.* 43 Heo wes.. liȝere and swikel, and wreðful and ontful. *a* **1225** *Ancr. R.* 118 Pellican is a leane fowel, so weamod & so wreðful þet [etc.]. *c* **1340** HAMPOLE *Pr. Consc.* 5107 Ihesu Crist, þat til þam swa wrethful sal seme þan. **1387** TREVISA *Higden* IV. 297 For he was.. wreþful, and priveliche envious and opounliche disceyvable. **1422** YONGE tr. *Secreta Secret.* 233 He that hath a sharpe noose and smale, he is wrethfull.

absol. *a* **1225** *Ancr. R.* 212 þe wreðfule biuoren þe ueonde skirmeð mid kniues. **1340** *Ayenb.* 30 Þe þridde werre þet þe wreþuolle heþ is to þan þet byeþ onder him.

2. Marked or characterized by wrath.

c **1325** *Metr. Hom.* 141 The bischop sau that Godd wald tak Of this man sin wrethful wrac. **1513** DOUGLAS *Æneid* XI. viii. 163 Quhidder this turn to Goddis wrethful wraik, Or hardyment and honour.

Hence †ˈ**wrethfully** *adv.*; ˈ**wrethfulness**. *Obs.*

c **1400** *Apol. Loll.* 58 Þe hound of wrethfulnes [*text* wrechfulnes; L. *iracundiæ*] grenniþ wiþ his teþ. *c* **1475** *Partenay* 2218 Then thes paynymes wrethfully ther-thens Whent.

†**wrethly**, var. of WROTHLY *a.* and *adv. Obs.*

13.. *Cursor M.* 3462 (Gött.), Þair strut it was vnsterne stithe, wid wrethly [*Cott.* wrathli] wraystes oþer wreche. *c* **1480** HENRYSON *Age & Youth* 66 (Bann. MS.), He on his wayis wrethly went but wene.

wreþþe, etc., obs. variants of WRATH, etc.

wreton, -yn, obs. ff. *written*, pa. ppl. of WRITE *v.*

wrett, etc.: see WRIT *sb.*, WRITE *v.*

wrett(e, obs. or dial. varr. WART *sb.*

†**wrethy**, *a. Obs.*[−1] [f. *wreth*, ME. var. of WRATH *sb.*] = WROTHY *a.*

14.. *Latin-Eng. Voc.* (MS. Harl. 2257), *Fervidus, id est, calidus, iracundus, Anglice* hot, wretthy.

†**wrewche**, ? error for *wewch* WOUGH *a.*

c **1480** HENRYSON *Robene & Makyne* 125 Malkyne went hame blyth annewche,.. And so left him, bayth wo & wrewche, In dolour & in cair.

wrey, etc., varr. WRAY *v.*[1] *Obs.*; obs. f. WRY *v.*[2]

wrible, obs. Sc. var. WARBLE *sb.*[1]

1513 DOUGLAS *Æneid* VII. ii. 18 The birdis.. Wyth wriblis [*ed.* 1553 werblis] sweit.. Gan meis and glaid the hevynis. *Ibid.* VII. xii. 147. [Cf. WRABLE.]

wricched, -id, etc., obs. varr. WRETCHED *a.*

wrich, obs. var. WORK *v.*

wrich(e, obs. varr. WRETCH *sb.* and *a.*

wricht, Sc. var. WRIGHT *sb.*[1]

wrick (rɪk), *sb.* Also *dial.* vrick. [f. WRICK *v.*[2] Cf. RICK *sb.*[2]] A sprain or strain.

1831 YOUATT *Horse* 254 This wrick, or sprain of the coffin-joint. **1886** *W. Somerset Word-bk.* 841 A vrick in my back.

†**wrick**, *v.*[1] *Obs. rare.* In 4 wricke, wrikke. [ad. MLG. **wricken* (in *vorwricken*, *-wrycken*; LG. *wrikken*) to move here and there, to sprain; or Du. *wrikken* to move jerkily, to scull (whence G. *wricken*, Da. *vrikke*, Sw. *vricka*). Cf. WRIG *v.*] *intr.* To move (jerkily or unsteadily) from side to side.

c **1305** *St. Dunstan* 82 in *E.E.P.* (1862) 36 Þe deuel he hente bi þe nose.. þe deuel wrickede her and þer. **1308-30** *Erthe upon Erthe* 2 Erþ geþ on erþ wrikkend in weden.

wrick (rɪk), *v.*[2] [Perh. the same as prec., but recorded earlier as RICK *v.*[2] Cf. however WRICK *sb.*] *trans.* To sprain or strain.

1886-93 in Somerset, Berkshire, and Wiltshire glossaries. **1904** *County Gentleman* June 1963 [The race-horse] having wricked his back badly.

wride (raɪd), *sb.* Now *dial.* Also 1 wrid, wryd, 7- ride. [OE. *wrid*, f. *wrídan*, *wridian* to put forth shoots, grow. Cf. Yks. *writh*, *rithe*.] A shoot, stalk, or stem; a group or bush of stalks, etc., growing from one root.

c **725** *Corpus Gloss.*, *Culmus*, wyrð [*Erfurt* wryd]. **944** in Birch *Cartul.* II. 542 Þurh þone lea to þam miclan hæsl-wride. *c* **1000** *Sax. Leechd.* I. 216 Ðenim æscþrote ænne wrid. *c* **1440** *Pallad. on Husb.* Tab. 223 Letuce with other herbis in a wride. *Ibid.* II. 207 Heere is an helful thyng, a wondir wride. **1578** LYTE *Dodoens* 743 The Franke Ozier hath no great stemme, but only a great wride or head neare the ground. **1669-** [see RIDE *sb.*[3]]. **1790** *Oxford Jrnl.* 21 Aug. 3/2 From a single oat.—One hundred, and thirty three wrides, or stalks. **1848** W. BARNES *Dorset Gloss.* 370 A wride of hazel or ash. **1862** *Q. Rev.* Apr. 313 (Dorset), A hazel-bush may contain many wrides.

wride (raɪd), *v. s.w. dial.* [f. prec., or perh. a survival of OE. *wridan*, *wrídian*. Cf. WRITHE *v.*[2]] *intr.* To put forth shoots; to spread out.

1825 JENNINGS *Obs. Dial. W. Eng.* s.v. **1848** W. BARNES *Dorset Gloss.* s.v., The wheat da wride out well. **1873-** in s.w. dial. use (Som., Dorset, Devon).

wrie, etc.: see WRAY *v.*[1], WRY *v.* and *a.*

wried (raɪd), *ppl. a.* [f. WRY *v.*[2] + -ED[1].]

1. Turned aside; deflected, diverted.

c **1586** C'TESS PEMBROKE *Ps.* cxxv. iv, A vaine deceiver, Whose wryed footing not aright directed Wandreth in error.

2. That has undergone contortion or twisting; writhed, contorted.

1576 A. HALL *Acc. Quarrel*, etc. (1816) I. 100 His colour ..crymson, his eyes fyry, his visage wryed unnaturally. **1598-9** B. JONSON *Case is Altered* II. iv, Vsing their wryed countenances in stead of a vice, to turn [etc.]. **1638** MAYNE *Lucian* (1664) 342 The Quoiter.. who stands wryed in a Gesture ready to deliver. **1676** HOBBES *Iliad* XXIII. 656 A silver cup That crookt and wryed was about the brim. **1887** MORRIS *Odyss.* IX. 372 His thick neck [was] wryed and twisted. **1891** KIPLING *Life's Handicap* 106 His mouth was wried with agony.

transf. **1599** B. JONSON *Ev. Man out of Hum.* Prol. 178 Vsing his wryed lookes (In nature of a vice) to wrest and turne The good aspect of those that shall sit neere him.

†**wriels**. *Obs.* Forms: 1 wriȝels (wyrȝels), -ils, wriils, 3 wrieles, wriheles, 4 wrielys, 5 wriels (weryels). [OE. *wriȝels*, etc., f. *wriȝ-*, ppl. stem of *wríon*, *wréon* WRY *v.*[1] + -ELS.] A covering; a veil. Also *fig.*

In quots. *a* 1225 and *c* 1400 taken as a plural; see -ELS.

c **825** *Vesp. Psalter* ci. 27 Swe swe wriȝels onwendes hie, & hie bioð onwende. *c* **1000** in Assmann *Ags. Hom.* (1889) 196 He þa his wriȝels ȝeopenode. *a* **1225** *Ancr. R.* 320 Of þeos six wrieles despoile þine sunne. *a* **1275** *Ibid.* 420 (MS. Cott. Cleopatra), Wimpel ne hefde, nouðer ne nemned hali write, ah wriheles of heuet. **1382** WYCLIF *Job* xxiv. 8 Nakid thei leue men,.. whom wederes of hillis moisten, and not hauende wrielys [L. *velamen*] clippe stones. *c* **1400** *Pilgr. Sowle* (Caxton, 1483) IV. xxix. 61 They faren right as done weryels of ymages made of clothe, stopped with strawe.

†**wrien**, *ppl. a. Obs. rare.* In 3 iwrien, 4 wreyen. [pa. pple. of WRY *v.*[1]]

1. Hidden; covered.

a **1225** *Ancr. R.* 388 Herto ualleð a tale, and on iwrien [*v.r.* hulet] uorbisne.

2. Accoutred; equipped.

c **1330** *Arth. & Merl.* 7555 (Kölbing), He cleped an amirail,.. Wiþ fiften þousand wreyen kniȝtes, & bad him, þe cuntre sle doun riȝtes.

ˈ**wrier**. *rare.* [f. WRY *v.*[2]] One who twists.

1611 COTGR., *Retordeur*, a twister,.. a wrier backe.

wrieson(e, -oun(e, -own, obs. Sc. ff. ORISON.

†**wrig**, *sb.*[1] *Obs.*[−1] [Cf. WERG.] The willow-tree.

1564 *Brasenose Coll. Munim.* 19 (Berks.), [The tenant may take] boowes of the wrigges to make stakes.. for the mentayning of the mowndes.

wrig (rɪg), *sb.*[2] *Sc.* [Cf. WREGLING, WRECKLING.] The smallest or weakest of a litter, brood, or family.

1805 G. MCINDOE *Poems* 67 Tho' [I am] the wrig In a' the nest there's nane sae big, Excepting Jock. **1844** H. STEPHENS *Bk. Farm* II. 700 The small weak pigs are usually nicknamed *wrigs*, or pock-shakings. **1899** J. COLVILLE *Scot. Vernacular* 15 The wee wrig, or *puis-né* member of the litter [of pigs].

†**wrig**, obs. erron. f. RIG *sb.*[4]

1638 N. WHITING *Il Insonio Inson.* 139, I have espied a plump-cheek'd bonny lass. She is a wrig, I warrant.

wrig (rɪg), *v.* Now *dial.* [? ad. LG. *wriggen* to twist or turn, an imitative word of the same type as *wrikken*; see WRICK *v.*[1]]

†**1.** *trans.* To twist or bend (some flexible object) about; to cause to writhe or wriggle. *Obs.*

a **1529** SKELTON *E. Rummyng* 177 The bore his tayle wrygges.. Agaynst the hye benche. **1642** H. MORE *Song of Soul* II. II. ii. 37 Thus worms in sturdie pride Do wrigge and wrest their parts divorc'd by knife.

†**2.** To turn aside; to divert. *Obs.*[−1]

1582 STANYHURST *Æneis* III. (Arb.) 88 First thee pilot Palinure thee steerd ship wrigs to the lifthand.

3. *intr.* To move sinuously or writhingly; to wriggle, writhe. Now *dial.*

1599 T. CUTWODE *Caltha Poet.* xxxi. B 6, The Bay tree.. seems to sigh.. And with the wanton wind to wrig & wreath, against the god. **1854** MISS BAKER *Northampton Gloss.* 408 The child's allus wrigging about. **1881** *Leicester Gloss.* s.v.

wriggle (ˈrɪg(ə)l), *sb.* Also 8-9 riggle, 9 wreckle. [f. next. Cf. LG. *wriggel* wilfulness.]

†**1.** A piece of sophistry; a shift. *Obs.*[−1]

1675 T. TULLY *Let. Baxter* 14 To think such little wriggles and Evasions will pass for rational Discourse.

2. A quick writhing movement or flexion of the body, etc. Also *fig.*

1709 STEELE *Tatler* No. 85 ¶ 5 They have always a peculiar Spring in their Arms, a Riggle in their Bodies. **1768-74** TUCKER *Lt. Nat.* (1834) I. 481 Such length as they [*sc.* animalcules] can throw themselves forward by one wriggle of the tail. **1829** *Loudon's Mag. Nat. Hist.* II. 220 [The water-shrew] swims very rapidly;.. his very nimble wriggle is clearly discernible. **1862** TROLLOPE *N. Amer.* I. 37 Fishes ..assist.. their motion with no dorsal riggle. **1899** J. VINCENT *1st Bp. Bath & Wells* 11 To kill a story that has.. got into print, and to leave it dead, and without a wriggle.

transf. **1899** A. LANG in *Contemp. Rev.* March 403 There the line gives a wriggle, suggesting that the circle was evolved out of a spiral.

b. A sinuous or tortuous formation, marking, etc.; a wriggling or meandering course.

1825 JENNINGS *Obs. Dial. W. Eng.* 84 *Wriggle*, any narrow sinuous hole. **1833** T. HOOK *Parson's Dau.* I. i, The serpentine walks were mere wriggles. **1881** RUSKIN *Bible Amiens* ii. §24 A few careful pen-strokes, or wriggles, of your own off-hand writing. **1899** [see WRIGGLED *ppl. a.*].

c. A turn or sinuosity. *rare*[−1].

1853 HAWTHORNE *Tanglewood T.*, *Minotaur*, At every new zigzag and wriggle of the path.

3. *local.* The sand-eel or sand-launce.

1816 [see WRECKLE]. **1876** T. HARDY *Ethelberta* xxxiii, We dug wriggles out of the sand. **1885** *Field* 26 Dec. 895/3 Sand-eels are known.. along the Sussex coast as 'riggles or wriggles', from their action of burrowing into the sand.

wriggle (ˈrɪg(ə)l), *v.* Also 5 wryggle, 6-7 wrigle, 7-9 riggle. [a. (M)LG. *wriggeln* (LG. dial. also *friggeln*, *vriggeln*, = Du. *wriggelen*, WFris. *wriggelje*, Norw. *vrigla*, *rigla*), frequentative of *wriggen*: see WRIG *v.*, and cf. WIGGLE *v.*]

1. *intr.* To twist or turn the body about with short writhing movements; to move sinuously; to writhe, squirm, wiggle: **a.** Of reptiles, etc.

1495 *Trevisa's Barth. De P.R.* XVIII. ix. 758 The adder Alphibena.. glydeth and wryggleth [*MSS.* wigleth, -eþ] wyth wrynkles. **1558** PHAER *Æneid* v. M iv b, As whan some serpent.. wrigling wreathes his limmes about. **1591** [see WRENCH *v.* 1]. **1606** MARSTON *Parasit.* II. i. C j b, How the poore snake wriggles with this suddain warmth. **1665** *Phil. Trans.* I. 43 The Snake.. by turning and wriggling laboured ..to avoid it. **1821** *Q. Rev.* XXIV. 490 As clearly as you may see.. a serpent wriggle in the grass. **1882** BESANT *All Sorts* xx, Eels.. are used to being skinned. Yet they wriggle a bit.

b. Of things.

1567 GOLDING *Ovid's Met.* VI. 77 The tip of Philomelaas tongue did wriggle to and fro. **1583** MELBANCKE *Philotimus* Bb j b, Philomelaes tongue, which being cutte of, wrigled vp and downe a longe season. **1639** FULLER *Holy War* IV. xxxiii. 227 The severall parts of Insecta being cut asunder, may wriggle and stirre for a while. **1768-74** TUCKER *Lt. Nat.* (1834) I. 471 The pieces of an eel cut asunder continue to wriggle. **1831** JAMES *Phil. Augustus* III. v, His nose at the same time wriggling with most portentous agitation. **1867**

F. FRANCIS *Angling* iii. 65 The float will often bob and wriggle about.. before the bite is confirmed.

fig. **1611** TOURNEUR *Ath. Trag.* IV. i, [It] makes the spirit of the flesh begin to wriggle in my bloud.

c. Of persons (or animals): To twist, turn, or move uneasily. Also with quasi-obj. ***to wriggle it***, to move with a wriggling motion.

1573 TUSSER *Husb.* (1878) 111 If sheepe or thy lambe fall a wrigling with taile. **1602** [see WRAGGLE *v.*[1] 2]. **1610** B. JONSON *Alchemist* v. iv, Here shee is come. Downe o' your knees, and wriggle. **1657** THORNLEY tr. *Longus' Daphnis & Chloe* 125 The Lambs came under the damms, to riggle and nussle at their dugs. **1732** SWIFT *To a Lady* 90 Then apply Alecto's whip Till they [*sc.* villains] wriggle, howl, and skip. **1735** SOMERVILLE *Chase* IV. 460 On pointed Spears they lift him [*sc.* an otter] high in Air; Wriggling he hangs. **1856** MISS YONGE *Daisy Chain* I. i, Ethel.. wriggling fearfully on the wide window-seat. **1895** S. CRANE *Red Badge* vi, He wriggled in his jacket to make a more comfortable fit. **1922** JOYCE *Ulysses* 477 Come on, boys! Wriggle it, girls!

transf. and *fig.* **1577** [see WREST *v.* 8]. **1787** BEST *Angling* (ed. 2) 10 Observe that.. when put together they may not wriggle in the least. **1825** CARLYLE *Love-Lett.* (1909) II. 159 Self is a foundation of sand... Fools writhe and wriggle and rebel at this.

2. a. To move, proceed, or go with a writhing or worming movement. Const. with advs., as *along*, *away*, *in*, *out*, or preps., as *from*, *into*, *through*, *up*.

1602 MARSTON *Antonio's Rev.* IV. ii, These vinegar tart spirits are too pearcing... Finde they a chinke, they'l wriggle in and in. **1630** J. TAYLOR (Water P.) *Jack a Lent* Wks. 117/2 The Eele.. would wriggle vp and downe in his muddy habitation. **1647** TRAPP *Comm. Mark* ix. 25 Devils run and wriggle into their holes, as worms use to do in time of thunder. **1709** T. ROBINSON *Vind. Mosaick Syst.* 67 Talons fit to hold fast the Live Prey that it wriggle not from them. **1830** W. TAYLOR *Hist. Surv. Germ. Poetry* II. 375 No lizard wriggles through the brake. **1857** MRS. GATTY *Parab. fr. Nat.* Ser. II. (1868) 129 The eels wriggled away in the mud. **1891** C. L. MORGAN *Anim. Sk.* 235 Wriggling and squirming up a dark geen vertical wall.

fig. and in fig. context. **1734** SWIFT *Let. to Faulkner* Wks. 1841 II. 726/1 Is it not sufficient to see with what pain and shame he wriggles along. **1762** WARBURTON *Doctr. Grace* Pref., Truth.. forbids us to riggle into her sacred presence through by-paths. **1840** HARE *Mission Comf.* (1846) 47 That the Understanding is over-ready to.. riggle along the crooked paths of evil. **1859** *Habits Gd. Society* vii. 246 His words come cautiously and suspiciously wriggling up to you.

b. To flow or run sinuously; to meander.

1640 [see WRIGGLING *ppl. a.* 3]. **1682** W. RICHARDS *Wallogr.* 34 A Rivulet which wrigled along with a crooked current. **1760** H. WALPOLE *Let. to G. Montagu* 1 Sept., The Trent wriggles through a lovely meadow. **1861** READE *Cloister & H.* lxxiv, Little paths wriggling among the antiquities. **1894** EVANS *Freeman's Hist. Sicily* IV. 388 The southern Himeras, whose salt waters wriggle to and fro in the broad dale.

3. a. To insinuate oneself *into* favour, place, etc.; to advance, 'creep' or get *in* by wheedling or ingratiation.

(*a*) **1598** B. JONSON *Ev. Man in Hum.* I. iv, Now dos he creepe, and wriggle into acquaintance with all the braue gallants. **1633** SHIRLEY *Gamester* I. (1637) B3b, The Courtiers make Us cuckolds; marke, we wriggle into their Estates. *a* **1680** BUTLER *Rem.* (1759) I. 235 By low ignoble Offices.. To wriggle into Trust and Grace. **1745** YOUNG *Nt. Th.* VIII. 457 Earth's subtile serpents.. Which wriggle into wealth, or climb renown. *c* **1853** KINGSLEY *Misc.* (1859) I. 39 A scheme by which to wriggle into Court favour. **1871** DIXON *Tower* III. iv. 29 Lake had crept and wriggled into place and pay.

(*b*) **1636** MASSINGER *Gt. Dk. Flor.* II. ii, This courtier.. perhaps, by his place, Expects to wriggle further: if he does, I shall deceive his hopes. *a* **1652** BROME *Queenes Exch.* I. i, He's the King's Favourite;.. we may fear he'l wrigle in Twixt him and us. **1691** *Satyr agst. French* 9 If they but wriggle in his Lordship's Ear,.. they learn to domineer. **1789** WOLCOT (P. Pindar) *Imit. Horace* I. xii, He.. Who, wriggling to the Hanoverian Guards, Kept the poor Prince of Brunswick out.

b. To make use of shuffling or sinuous means; to get *out of*, escape *from*, a condition or position by evasion, mean artifice or contrivance.

a **1646** BURROUGHES *Exp. Hosea* v. (1652) 240 This affliction that thou doest so riggle to get out of. **1690** T. BURNET *Theory Earth* III. 29 Men will wriggle any way to get from under the force of a text. **1848** W. H. KELLY tr. *L. Blanc's Hist. Ten Y.* II. 223 Certain to.. wriggle out of its inevitable results by.. dangerous artifices. **1858** DORAN *Court Fools* 315 He wriggled out of his bargain. **1871** BLACKIE *Four Phases* I. 114 You are wriggling cunningly out of the position.

4. a. *trans.* To cause to writhe, twist, or bend tortuously; to move or turn writhingly or with quick jerks. Also with advs., as *aloft*, *away*, *down*, *out*, *up*, or preps., as *from*, *into*.

1573 TUSSER *Husb.* l. (1878) 109 Sheepe wrigling taile hath mads without faile. **1582** STANYHURST *Æneis* ii. (Arb.) 50 Their tayls.. they [*sc.* two serpents] wrigle. **1648** GAGE *West Ind.* 97 Wrigling his elbowes and shoulders scornfully from me. **1684** tr. *Bonet's Merc. Compit.* x. 365 The wretched Patient cannot lie down,.. wrigling his body all manner of ways. **1729** SWIFT *Direct. Serv.* ii, Make room for the sauce-pan by wriggling it on the coals. **1806** SOUTHEY *Lett.* (1856) I. 381 If you can conceive a blue-bottle fly wriggling his tail. **1862** MISS YONGE *C'tess Kate* ii, She wriggled her legs away from that of the chair. **1887** EGGLESTON *Graysons* xv, He tried to pull and wriggle his trousers-legs down to their normal place.

refl. **1665** *Phil. Trans.* I. 35 These [insects] would.. wrigle themselves up to the top of the water again. **1739** MRS. DELANY *Life & Corr.* (1861) I. 45 With violent squeezing.. we riggled ourselves into seats. **1837** CARLYLE *Fr. Rev.* I. v. iv, Besenval is painfully wriggling himself out, to the Champ-de-Mars.

fig. **1712** *Odes of Horace* II. 12/2 *Et* might easily riggle it self into the place of *ut*.

b. To bring into a specified state, form, etc., by writhing or twisting. Const. with advs., as *asunder*, *off*, or preps., as *into*, *to*. Occas. *refl.* Also *fig.*

1677 MOXON *Mech. Exerc.* ii. 18 With your Fingers and Thumb.. wriggle it quite asunder. **1857** W. C. STEWART *Pract. Angler* vii. (ed. 3) 138 The worm.. being free to wriggle itself into any shape. **1858** [see WRENCH *v.* 10]. **1878** O. W. HOLMES *Motley* xvii. 115 Slavery is wriggling itself to death.

5. a. To introduce, insert, or bring *in* (something) by wriggling; to insinuate (*into* something).

1599 NASHE *Lenten Stuffe* E4b, A snaile coulde not wriggle in her hornes betwixt them. **1692** R. L'ESTRANGE *Fables* I. lv. 55 A Slam, Thin-Gutted Fox made a Hard Shift to Wriggle his Body into a Hen-Roost. **1766** *Museum Rust.* VI. 374 As to the width of the gates,.. the men.. could.. easily incline the roller on one side, and.. wriggle it in. **1828** LYTTON *Pelham* II. 313 Power.. is a snake that when it once finds a hole into which it can introduce its head, soon manages to wriggle in the rest of its body.

fig. **1702** VANBRUGH *False Friend* I. i, I'm afraid.. they'll riggle you into some ill-favour'd affair. **1767** A. CAMPBELL *Lexiph.* (1774) 71 When you have wriggled in.. a new-fashioned long-tailed word.

b. To insinuate or introduce (a person) gradually (*into* favour, office, etc.), esp. by subtle or shifty means. Also with *in*. Chiefly *refl.*

1670 COTTON *Espernon* I. IV. 180 He by the means of the Mistriss.. wriggles himself into the company of the Duke's Baker. **1677** GILPIN *Demonol.* (1867) 355 By these arts doth Satan, like a cunning serpent, wriggle himself into the affections of men. **1710** SWIFT *Jrnl. to Stella* 5 Dec., While he was wriggling himself into my favour. **1754** H. WALPOLE *Let. to Mann* 28 March, She would have wriggled herself into the best clause in the will. **1766** —— *Let. to Mann* 18 July, He might have wriggled his brother in [= into office] afterwards. **1847** ALB. SMITH *Chr. Tadpole* xvi, He wriggled himself into the good opinion of the coachman. **1874** L. STEPHEN *Hours in Library* (1892) I. x. 359 [He] wriggled himself into a peerage.

c. To make (one's way) by sinuous motion. Also in fig. context.

1863 W. PHILLIPS *Speeches* viii. 214 Cunning statesmen who have wriggled their slimy way to wealth. **1891** *Century Mag.* March 649/1 The Pi-Utes.. wriggled their way out through the passages in the rocks. **1899** E. CALLOW *Old Lond. Tav.* I. 119 Whitebait seem to have wriggled their way higher up the river.

6. †**a.** To cut or carve (something) with a wriggly or sinuous pattern; to slash. *Obs.*

1610 B. JONSON *Alch.* IV. iii. 274 A collar of brawne, cut downe Beneath the souse, and wriggled with a knife. **1654** GAYTON *Pleas. Notes* I. i. 4 Many more.. by prowesse of the Captaine Joneses of our times.. have been hackt, hew'd, wriggled and utterly confounded.

b. To form in a tortuous or sinuous manner.

1760 H. WALPOLE *Let. to Mann* 20 June, Stanhope.. has.. wriggled a winding-gravel walk through [the groves]. **1896** *Voice* (N.Y.) 8 Oct. 2 Be content to wriggle pretty patterns on the mud of spoils!

†**7.** To twist, pervert. Cf. WREST *v.* 5. *Obs.*

1593 HARVEY *Pierce's Super.* Wks. (Grosart) II. 52 Sinister construction, that wreasteth and wrigleth euery sillable to the worst. **1637** J. WILLIAMS *Holy Table* 2 Which when it is in writing,.. is no more by a disputant indeed to be wrigled and wrested.

Hence **wriggled** ('rɪg(ə)ld) *ppl. a.*; ***wriggled work*** = ***wriggle-work*** s.v. WRIGGLE-.

1572 BOSSEWELL *Armorie* II. 100 They haue.. a wrigled tayle, and croked tethe like to a Bore. **1611** COTGR., *Fringotteries*, frets; cranklings, wrigled flourishings, in caruings, &c. *a* **1643** CARTWRIGHT *Ordinary* II. iii, Your hollow thumb join'd with your wriggled [dice] box. **1899** A. LANG *Contemp. Rev.* March 403 At each side are two-circled and one-circled specimens with the wriggled line, and two cups and circles with no wriggle. **1906** N. H. MOORE *Old Pewter* i. 22 The tool which makes the wriggled work is of the nature of a chisel. **1955** R. F. MICHAELIS *Antique Pewter* ix. 86 English pewter from the best period, i.e. the 17th century,.. displays remarkably fine applied decoration.. in the form of 'wriggled-work' engraving.

wriggle- (rɪg(ə)l), the verb-stem used attrib. in a few combs., in the sense 'undergoing or characterized by wriggling', as †**wriggle-eye**, **-tail**, etc.; **wriggle-work** (see quot. 1960); cf. *wriggled work*.

In quots. 1579, 1620, app. from *wriggled tail*.

1579 SPENSER *Sheph. Cal.* Feb. 7 They wont in the wind wagge their wrigle tailes, Perke as Peacock. **1604** T. M. *Black Bk.* E2b, Let no yong rigle-eyde Damosell.. be left vnassaulted. **1620** MIDDLETON *Chaste Maid* III. ii, Short rigle-tayle-Comfits, not worth mouthing. **1897** MARY KINGSLEY *W. Africa* 473 A dance of women.., the usual wriggle and stamp affair. **1960** *Connoisseur's Handbk. Antique Collecting* 312/2 *Wrigglework*, a form of engraved decoration on pewter and silver, employing a zig-zag line cut by rocking a gouge from side to side in its progress. Used in conjunction with line engraving at certain periods, principally late in 17th cent. **1975** *Oxf. Compan. Decorative Arts* 616/2 The flat-lid tankard shows the pewterer's craft at its best. The plain drum.. was sometimes decorated with 'wriggle-work' designs of symbolic or commemorative significance. **1982** 'J. GASH' *Firefly Gadroon* v. 62 The plate .. was wriggle-work... This was a William III plate, with.. a rim decorated by engraved wriggles.

wriggler ('rɪglə(r)). [f. WRIGGLE *v.* + -ER[1].]

1. One who or that which wriggles; *esp.* a wriggling fish, animalcule, etc.

1674 N. FAIRFAX *Bulk & Selv.* Ep. Ded., The Fryes of Wrigglers.. peep out of their Graves and Dungeons. **1694** MOTTEUX *Rabelais* v. Progn. v. 237 Drabs, Trulls, Light-skirts, Wrigglers, Misses. *a* **1825** FORBY *Voc. E. Anglia* II. 381 *Wrigglers*, small fish, of which commoner names are sand-eels or lance-fish. **1896** in *Advance* (Chicago) 18 June 897/2 To make the little wriggler [= a child] sit still. **1914** *Melbourne Argus* 17 March 13 Mosquitoes.. in the larval state.. are known as wrigglers.

2. *fig.* One who makes his way by subtle, ingratiating, or underhand means.

1631 A. WILSON *Swisser* II. i. 163 To obserue the tyme, yee wriglers. There is an ytching height that all do ayme at, But diuers wayes to come to 't. **1785** COWPER *Tiroc.* 432 Providence,.. In spite of all the wrigglers into place, Still keeps a seat or two for worth and grace.

3. (See quot.)

1900 *Daily Mail* 31 Oct., Wrigglers are engravers who devote their working hours to the tracing of those zig-zag lines which are so often a feature of cheap Britannia metal teapots.

'**wrigglesome**, *a. rare*[−1]. [f. WRIGGLE *sb.* + -SOME.] Wriggling.

1891 G. MACDONALD *There & Back* xxii, The wrigglesome, slimy things [*sc.* water-snakes].

wriggling ('rɪglɪŋ), *vbl. sb.* [f. WRIGGLE *v.* + -ING[1].]

1. The action of the verb in various physical senses; an instance of this.

1580 TUSSER *Husb.* 1 b, How to cure the wrigling of yͤ taile in a sheepe or a lambe. **1601** HOLLAND *Pliny* II. 427 The Lampreis.. get betwene the very mashes [of a net], which with their much winding and wrigling they will wrest wider and wider. **1665** *Phil. Trans.* I. 67 The wrigling and playing of the Mandril. **1711** SWIFT *Jrnl. to Stella* 2 Oct., Lovet, towards the end of dinner, after twenty wrigglings, said [etc.]. **1843** LE FEVRE *Life Trav. Phys.* III. III. viii. 189 Appetite.. is not sharpened by the wriggling of the locomotives. **1866** GEO. ELIOT *F. Holt* i, The wrigglings of a worm.

2. *fig.* Evasion; equivocation; shuffling.

1866 DARWIN in *Life & Lett.* (1887) III. 56 He is.. my superior, even in the master art of wriggling. **1895** *Advance* (Chicago) 7 Feb. 652/2 There is a wriggling that is wrong, as when Peter wriggled from the questioning accusations of the servant girl.

3. *attrib.* in allusive use, as †***wriggling disease***, ***mordicancy***, ***trade***.

1690 D'URFEY *Collin's Walk Lond.* I. 17 If any of his Flock were seiz'd By heat, with wrigling Disease. *a* **1693** URQUHART *Rabelais* III. xxxii. 271 Their.. figging Itch, wrigling Mordicancy. **1719** D'URFEY *Pills* VI. 91, I am a Baker, And.. have.. a Wrigling-Pole. **1765** [E. THOMPSON] *Meretriciad* 40 The fam'd itinerant lass.. by her motions in the wriggling trade, Two sterling thousands.. made.

'**wriggling**, *ppl. a.* [f. as prec. + -ING[2].]

1. That wriggles or squirms; writhing.

1565 GOLDING *Ovid's Met.* v. 63b, A wrigling taile streight to his limmes was added more beside. **1587** FLEMING *Contn. Holinshed* III. 1292/1 Two wrigling or scralling serpents. **1613** W. BROWNE *Brit. Past.* I. v. 102 As an Angler.. A wrigling yealow worme thrust on his hooke. **1690** C. NESSE *O. & N. Test.* I. 42 He assumes.. the shape of a wriggling crooked serpent. **1748** RICHARDSON *Clarissa* (1811) III. 363, I must take care.. the little wriggling rogue does not slip through my fingers. **1865** LIVINGSTONE *Zambesi* vii. 167 A native emerges out of the moving mass of dead elephant and wriggling humanity. **1888** J. INGLIS *Tent Life* 296 A great wriggling iguana.

transf. *c* **1590** J. STEWART *Poems* (S.T.S.) II. 71 Thir vrigling werse than plaine sall pass perfyt.

2. Characterized or distinguished by wriggling or writhing.

1608 SYLVESTER *Du Bartas* II. iv. *Decay* 887 As a fell Serpent.. With wriggling pase doth still approach his Foe. **1663** BOYLE *Usef. Exp. Nat. Philos.* I. ii. 42 A wrigling motion, like that of eels. **1783** WOLCOT (P. Pindar) *Odes to R.A.'s* I. viii, Won with such wry mouths and wriggling pain. **1799** SOUTHEY *Nondescript, Filbert*, Watching two maggots run their wriggling race. **1859** MURCHISON *Siluria* (ed. 3) xii. 303 Wriggling movements of a Salamandroid quadruped. **1888** GUNTER *Mr. Potter* xxii. 259 [A dog] with tail and ears and body all wriggling ecstasy.

fig. **1688** MIÉGE *Gt. Fr. Dict.* II. s.v., He took a wriggling byas in his Letter, which I am not pleased with. *c* **1869** SWINBURNE *Ess. & Stud.* (1875) 289 The wriggling prurience of such lackey's literature as is handed round.

3. Meandering; tortuous; winding.

1640 J. GOWER *Ovid's Festiv.* III. 48 [Sylvia] came unto the wriggling brook. *Ibid.* 62 His flow'ry green, Which wriggling Tyber laves. **1698** FRYER *Acc. E. India & P.* 5 It is not unlike the crawling of a Snake, it's various Hills and Vallies.. seem to borrow that riggling Shape.

Hence '**wrigglingly** *adv.*

1601 DEACON & WALKER *Answ. to Darel* To Rdr. 4 They ..do rather *incedere tortuosè*, goe wrigglinglie to worke. **1866** HOWELLS *Venet. Life* v. 73 [He spoke] wrigglingly, and with.. gesticulations towards the pit.

wriggly ('rɪglɪ), *a.* [f. WRIGGLE *v.* + -Y[1]. Cf. LG. dial. *wriggelig* wilful.]

1. Given to wriggling; squirming, writhing.

1866 EDMONDSTON *Gloss. Shetl. Dial.* 92 *Rigly* [sic], unsteady, rickety. **1906** *Westm. Gaz.* 30 Dec. 2/1 The thrush.. twice.. found a wriggly creature, and these he carried off to his family.

2. Winding; sinuous; tortuous.

1901 C. G. HARPER *Gt. North Road* II. 257 One leaves Dunbar by wriggly and exiguous streets.

wright (raɪt), *sb.*[1] Forms: α. 1 wyrhta, *Northumb.* wyrihta, -te, wyrchta, 1–2 *Kent.* werhta; 2 wirhta, 3 wurhte, wuruhte. β. 1 wryhta,

3 **wruhte**, **wrihhte**, 3–4 **wriht(e**, 5 **wrihte**, 3–5 **wryhte**, **wryht**, (3, 5 **wryth**, 5 **wrythe**), 4 **wryȝt(e**, 4–5 **wriȝt**, 4–6 **wrighte** (4 **whright**, **wrigth**, **writh**), 5–6 **wryght(e**, 4– **wright**; 2 **wrichte**, 5–6 *Sc.* **wrycht** (6 **vrycht**), 5–7, 9 *Sc.* **wricht** (5, 9 **vricht**, 9 **wiricht**); 4 **wreght**, 5 *Sc.* **wrecht**, 6 *Sc.* **wreicht**, 7 **wreight**, 9 *dial.* **wreeght**. *γ.* 5 **wryte**, *north.* **write**, 9 *north. dial.* **wreet** (**whreet**), **reet**. [OE. *wyrhta*, *wryhta*, etc. (also *ȝewyrhta*), = OFris. *wrichta*, OS. *wurhtio*, *-eo*, OHG. *wurhto* (MHG. (in combs.) *wurhte*, *würhte*, *worhte*), f. *wurh-*:—OTeut. **wurχ-*, variant stem of **wurk-*: see WORK *v.*]

1. An artificer or handicraftsman; *esp.* a constructive workman. Now *arch.* or *dial.*

eye-, glassen-, mill-, tile-wright: see those words.

α. ? *a* **695** *Laws of Ine* lix. (*Liebermann* I. 116) Mon sceal simle to beregafole aȝifan æt anum wyrhtan vi pund-wæȝa. *c* **950** *Lindisf. Gosp.* Mark vi. 3 Ahne ðis is smið *uel* wyrihte, sunu Maries? *c* **1000** ÆLFRIC *Hom.* I. 318 God eac forði hi to-stencte, swa þæt he forȝeaf ælcum ðæra wyrhtena seltcuð ȝereord. *c* **1205** LAY. 21134 On aluisc smið..; he wes ihaten Wygar, þe witeȝe wurhte. *a* **1225** *Ancr. R.* 284 Þe caliz þet was imelt iðe fure.. wolde he, ȝif he kuðe speken, awarien.. his wuruhte honden?

β. *γ* *c* **950** *Lindisf. Gosp.* Mark, Introd. 3 Wundrande þæt lar & mæhto ðæs wrihtes sunu *vel* smiðes sunu. *c* **1030** *Rule St. Benet* (Logeman) 2 Þam he.. clypað his wryhtan [L. *operarium*]. *a* **1200** in Kemble *Cod. Dipl.* IV. 204 And ic.. bebeode ðat paðu mi meodes [*sic*] wrichte and Wlnoð min huscarl.. on ðam minstre hersumian. *a* **1300** *Cursor M.* 325 Þis drithin.. in his witte.. all purueid His werc, als dos þe sotill wright. **1393** LANGL. *P. Pl.* C. xx. 137 Þe fyngres is ful hand, for failled thei here þombe,.. Sholde no wryȝt [*Ilchester MS.* write] worche. **1412–20** LYDG. *Chron. Troy* II. 497 He made seke in euery regioun.. For euery wriȝt and passyng carpenter. **1715** CHEYNE *Philos. Princ. Relig.* vi. 324 Being rapt into admiration of the infinite Wisdom of the Divine Architect, and contemning the arrogant Pretences of the World and Animal Wrights. **1848** BAILEY *Festus* (ed. 3) 207 Upon that central shrine.. Laid down.. The scribe, and the physician, and the wright His several offering. **1876** *Whitby Gloss.* 224/1 *Wreeghts*, or *Wrights*,.. work-people in general.

†**b.** Applied to the Deity, = CREATOR 1. *Obs.*

c **888** ÆLFRED *Boeth.* ad fin., Drihten ælmihtiga God, wyrhta & wealdend ealra ȝesceafta. *a* **1000** *Phœnix* 9 Wlitiȝ is se wong eall,.. æþele se wyrhta.. se þa moldan ȝesette. *a* **1200** *St. Marher.* 20 Þu wisest wruhte of alle, markedest eorðe. *c* **1200** ORMIN 18780 Þatt all þatt shaffte þat wass wrohht Wass lif inn himm þe wrihhte. *a* **1300** *Cursor M.* 331 Þis wright þat I spek of here.. wroght bath erth and heuen.

†**2.** One who does or performs something; a doer or worker. *Obs.*

971 *Blickl. Hom.* 111 Forðon þe nan wyrhta ne mæȝ god weorc wyrcean for Gode buton lufon & ȝeleafan. *a* **1000** *Genesis* 1004 Him ða se cystleasa cwalmes wyrhta ædre æfter þon andswarode. *c* **1200** *Trin. Coll. Hom.* 191 At tese fif gaten fareð in deaðes wrihte, and þerinne doð. *a* **1300** [see BATTLE *sb.* 14].

3. One who works in wood; a carpenter, a joiner.

From *c* 1470 to *c* 1655 chiefly *Sc.* and *north.*; in later use only *Sc.* and *north. dial.* (or *arch.*). The Sc. pron. is ((w)rɪxt, north-eastern vrɪxt).

cart-, house-, plough-, ship-, timber-, wagon-, wain-, wheel-wright: see those words.

α. *c* **1205** LAY. 16969 He lette axien anan.. gode wurhten þe mid æxe cuðe wurchen.

β. *a* **1200** *Vices & Virtues* 27 Wið-uten.. ðe wrihte his timber to keruen after ðare mone. *a* **1300** *Cursor M.* 1666 A schippe be-houes þe to dight, Þi self sal be þe maister wright. **1303** R. BRUNNE *Handl. Synne* 9163 He ded come wryȝtes [*gloss.* carponters] for to make Coueryng ouer hem. *c* **1380** WYCLIF *Sel. Wks.* II. 19 Joseph was a forgere of trees, þat is to seie a wriȝte. *c* **1450** *Northern Passion* 161/461 Than wantide the wryghtis a tre. **1464** *Nottingham Rec.* (1883) II. 372 To the wright.. to make the Pillorye, v s. **1566** DRANT *Horace, Sat.* viii. D 8 The wryghte uncertaine what to make, a stoole or God of me. **1577** HOLINSHED *Chron.* I. 41/1 He sawe yet howe the rest [of the ships].. might bee repaired: wherefore he chose forth wrightes among the Legions. *a* **1619** FOTHERBY *Atheom.* II. i. §8 (1622) 193 As we may.. see, in Platoes fore-named instances of his Smithes, and his Wrights. **1654** Z. COKE *Logick* 64 This Ship-wright.. makes the Ship, not as he is a man or good, but as he is a Wreight or Artizen. **1725** RAMSAY *Gentle Sheph.* v. iii, Masons and wrights shall soon my house repair. **1782** SIR J. SINCLAIR *Observ. Scot. Dial.* 198 *Wright*, at present, is a general name for timber workmen;.. but the Scots, by *wrights*, mean *carpenters*. **1829** CARLYLE *Misc.*, *German Playwrights* ¶1 The millwright, or cartwright, or any other wright whatever. **1858** *Times* 6 March 12/3 At Hull.. about 500 wrights are on strike. **1887** MORRIS *Odyss.* IX. 129 Nor yet among them ever ship-making wrights there are.

fig. *a* **1200** *Vices & Virtues* 91 Hier is igadered swilch timber ðe næure rotien ne mai, and þis derewurðe mihte is wrihte ðerover.

Sc. Prov. **1670** RAY *Prov.* 227 He is not the best wright that hewes the maniest speals.

γ. *c* **1440** *York Myst.* xxxvii. 230 Thy fadir knewe I wele be sight, He was a write his mette to wynne. *c* **1460** *Promp. Parv.* (Winch. MS.), Wryte, or carpentare, *carpentarius*. **1463** *Mann. & Househ. Exp.* (Roxb.) 230 A wryte that mayd my mastyrys stabyle. **1824–** in N. Cy., Nhb., Dur., Yks., and Lanc. glossaries (*reet*). **1841** HARTSHORNE *Salop. Ant.* 618 *Wreet's shop* a carpenter's, or more frequently a Wheelwright's shop. **1877–90** in Yks. glossaries (*wreet*).

4. *attrib.* and *Comb.*, as ***wright-craft***, †***-house***, ***-smith***; †**wright-garth**, a joiner's yard; **wright-work**, work performed or done by a joiner.

1385–6 *Durham Acc. Rolls* (Surtees) 391 [Le] Wrigthous et le Plomberhous. **1474–5** *Ibid.* 94 Le Wrightgarth et Swynegarth. *a* **1619** M. FOTHERBY *Atheom.* II. i. §8 (1622) 193 One Arte, of Wright-Craft; and one Arte, of Smiths-Craft. **1630** *Ann. Banff* (New Spald. Cl.) I. 64 Ane load of wricht wark 2 s. **1671** in Holmes *Pontefract Bk. Entries* (1882) 103 Item, for wrightworke, [£5]. **1881** *Instr. Census Clerks* (1885) 56 Wheelwright. Wrightsmith.

Hence †**ˈwrightry**, = WRIGHTING. *Obs.* *rare*$^{-1}$.

c **1460** *Towneley Myst.* iii. (*Noah & Ark*) 250 Now assay will I how I can of wrightry.

†**wright**, *sb.*^{2} *Obs.* In 2–3 **wriht**, 3 *Orm.* **wrihht**. [ME. reduction of **i-wriht*, OE. *ȝewyrht*: see I-WURHT.] Desert, what one has deserved; hence, blame, fault.

c **1175** *Lamb. Hom.* 69 Crist us ȝeue of him mihte; betere þenne we habbeð wrihte. *c* **1200** *Trin. Coll. Hom.* 217 Ich triste þat he [*sc.* God] nele neng [don ?] bi mine wrihte. *c* **1200** ORMIN Ded. 202 To þolenn dæþþ o rodetre Sacclæs wiþþ-utenn wrihhte. *Ibid.* 8240 He wass flemmd & drifenn ut All affterr hise wrihhte.

Hence †**ˈwrightful** *a.*, having deserved something; †**ˈwrightlesslike** *adv.*, undeservedly.

c **1250** *Gen. & Ex.* 2076 Ic am stolen of kinde lond, and her wriȝteleslike holden in bond. *Ibid.* 2204 Wriȝtful we in sorwe ben, for we siniȝeden quilum.

wright (raɪt), *v.* Also 4 **wrihte**, 9 *n. e. Sc.* **vricht**. [f. WRIGHT *sb.*^{1}, or WRIGHTING.]

†**1.** *trans.* To build, construct. *Obs. rare.*

1338 R. BRUNNE *Chron.* (1810) 88 At London, a haule he did vp wright. *Ibid.* 321 A brigge he suld do wrihte.

†**2.** To repair (a ship); to renovate, mend.

Perh. erron. for *righted*: see RIGHT *v.* 11 c.

a **1656** USSHER *Ann.* (1658) 391 Having there new wrighted up such ships of his as had been.. bruised in the fight.

3. *intr.* To pursue the occupation of a wright. *Sc.*

1886 GREGOR *Banffsh. Gloss.* 204.

wright(e, obs. varr. WRITE *sb.* and *v.*

wrighting (ˈraɪtɪŋ). Now *Sc.* and *dial.* Forms: (see quots.). [f. WRIGHT *sb.*^{1} + -ING^1.] The occupation, business, or craft of a wright or carpenter.

a **1500** *Hist. K. Boccus & Sydracke* (? 1510) *H* iij, Wryghtyng is also a conyng That myght not be foreborne be my iugyng. **1828** [CARR] *Craven Gloss.*, *Whreeting*, carpentry. **1866** GREGOR *Banffsh. Gloss.* 204 A've been a' simmer at the vrichtan. **1900** O. AGNUS *Jan Oxber* iv. 96, I zhall follow my wrighten agen.

†**wriguldy-wrag.** *Obs.* *rare*$^{-1}$. [Cf. next.] Mischief; harm.

1519 RASTELL *Interl. Four Elem.* E 2, Jak boy, is thy bowe i-broke? Or hath any man done the wryguldy wrage?

†**wrig-wrag.** *Obs. rare.* [Cf. WRIG *v.*]

1. *Sir Wrig-wrag*, ? a contentious person.

a **1529** SKELTON *Agst. Garnesche* iv. 149 The follest slouen ondyr heuen,.. Wytles, wayward, Syr Wryg wrag. *a* **1529** —— *Sp. Parrot* 91 Let syr Wrig wrag wrastell with syr Delarag.

2. ***at wrig-wrag***, at daggers-drawn; at enmity or variance.

1599 NASHE *Lenten Stuffe* G j b, Their townes.. were stil at wrig wrag, & suckt from their mothers teates serpentine hatred one against each other.

wriht, obs. form of WRIGHT, WRIT *sbs.*

†**wrike nail.** *Obs. rare.* [Origin obscure: cf. WRICK *v.*^{1}] ? A screw-nail.

1496 *Naval Acc. Hen. VII* (1896) 183 Prouision of Stuff for the Cokkebote aforesayd:.. ffor c wryke nayles vj^d.

wrily, var. WRYLY *adv.*

wrim, obs. var. WORM *sb.*

†**ˈwrimple**, *sb.* *Obs.* Also 5 **wrympyl**. [Cf. RIMPLE *sb.* (also RUMPLE *sb.*^{2}), and WRIMPLED *a.*] A crease or fold; a rimple, wrinkle.

1499 *Promp. Parv.* (Pynson) s v b, Wrympyl, or rympyl, *ruga*. *Ibid.*, Wrympyl, or pleyt of cloth, *plica*. **1578** FLORIO *1st Fruites* 88 b, The smooth throate maketh foldes with wrimples. **1603** —— *Montaigne* I. xxii. 51 The hoarie head and frowning wrimples of custome. **1611** COTGR., *Gelasin*, a wrimple in the face.

†**wrimple**, *v.* *Obs. rare.* [Probably a back-formation from WRIMPLED *a.* Cf. the later RIMPLE *v.*]

1. *trans.* (See quots. and cf. JAG *v.*^{1} 2.)

1611 COTGR., *Franger*, to fringe;.. also, to.. wrimple, iag, or snip on th' edges. *Ibid.*, *Rider*, to wrinkle, or to wrimple.

2. *intr.* To pucker the face or countenance.

1657 REEVE *God's Plea* 88 Alas we do but only.. wrimple at a Pulpit-launcing,.. sing a Penitentiall Psalm.

Hence †**ˈwrimpling** *vbl. sb.* *Obs.*

1611 COTGR., *Ridement*, a wrinkling, wrimpling, crumping. *Ibid.*, *Rugosité*,.. a crumpling, wrimpling, furrowing.

†**ˈwrimpled**, *a.* *Obs.* Also 5 **wrymplyd**. [f. MDu. or MLG. **wrimpelen* (older Flem. *wrempelen* 'to drawe the mouth awry', Hexham), frequentative of MLG. *wrempen*, *wrimpen* to wrinkle, bend, turn. Cf. the earlier RIMPLED *a.*] Wrinkled, rimpled, or puckered; creased.

c **1430** LYDG. *Min. Poems* (Percy Soc.) 203, I can not armys blase, Nor to the fulle rynge hire belle, That is so wrymplyd as a mase. **1553** EDEN *Treat. New Ind.* (Arb.) 37 Neyther haue they theyr bellies wrimpeled or loose. **1577** WHETSTONE *Gascoigne* B j, I holde a forme, within a wrimpled skin. **1592** R. D[ALLINGTON] *Hypnerotomachia* 28 b, A Dragon['s].. wrimpled backe. **1611** COTGR., *Renfrongué*,.. wrimpled, crumpled, puckered. **1642** H. MORE *Song of Soul* I. I. xlvii, Wafts of winds centrall That ruffle.. Psyche's wrimpled veil. **1657** REEVE *God's Plea* 23 The wrimpled skin.. of that old man. **1672** tr. *Hurtado's Lazarillo* II. O 4, Seeing me so bleak, and wrimpled, like an old Wives belly.

wrinch, erron. f. *rinch*, var. RINSE *v.*

1612 *Two Noble K.* I. i. 171 We stand before your puissance Wrinching our holy begging in our eyes To make petition cleere.

†**wrinch**, var. of (or error for) *winch* WINCE *v.*^{1} I.

1589 ? LYLY *Pappe w. Hatchet* E j b, Rub no more, the curtall wrinches.

wrinch, wrine, obs. varr. WRENCH, WRY *v.*^{1}

†**wrine**, *v.* *Obs.*$^{-1}$ [a. ON. **wrína* (ENorw. and Sw. dial. *vrina*, Norw. *rina*). Cf. WHRINE *v.*] *intr.* To squeal, as a pig.

1570 LEVINS *Manip.* 139 To Wrine, *vociferare, vt porcus.*

wring (rɪŋ), *sb.*^{1} Also 1, 5 **wringe**, 4–6 **wrynge**, 9 **ring**. [OE. *wringe*, f. *wringan* WRING *v.* Cf. OE. *wín-wringe*.]

1. A cider-press or wine-press.

c **890** WÆRFERTH tr. *Gregory's Dial.* 250 Sanctulus.. brohte æmtiȝe cyllan þyder to þære wringan. *a* **1350** in *Relig. Lyrics 14th C.* (1924) 28 Þy schroud red wyth blod.. Ase troddares in wrynge. *Ibid.*, Þe wrynge ich habbe y-trodded al mysulf on. **1398** TREVISA *Barth. De P.R.* XIX. xxxviii. (B.M. Add. MS. 27944), Sourisshe þinges.. bereþ doun þe mete as it were a pressoure oþer a wrynge. *c* **1440** *Pallad. on Husb.* I. 495 (Colchester MS.), Oilmylles, wheeles, wrynges, ..I nyl not speke of nowe. *Ibid.* XI. 107 Erly sette on werkyng hem [*sc.* olives] the wrynge. **1532–3** in Weaver *Wells Wills* (1890) 155 The dragge, and the wrynge, and the vate. **1664** NEWBURGH in Evelyn *Pomona* 42 The Cider, bottled immediately from the wring. **1844** W. BARNES *Dorset Gloss.* 370 *Wring*, a press, as a cider-wring. *a* **1906** in *Eng. Dial. Dict.* s.v., Cider from the wring.

2. A cheese-press.

[**1670** in C. Worthy *Devon. Wills* (1896) 27 A cheese wring.] **1891** T. HARDY *Tess* I. 226 The measured dripping of the whey from the wrings downstairs.

3. ***wring-house***, the house or shed where a cider- or cheese-wring is kept.

1807 VANCOUVER *Agric. Devon* (1813) 472 Wring-house for making cider. **1842** G. PULMAN *Rustic Sketches* 52 In th' ringhouse hard to work, Th' mill da grind. **1886** T. HARDY *Woodlanders* xiii, His dwelling, cider-cellar, wring-house.

wring (rɪŋ), *sb.*^{2} [f. WRING *v.*]

1. **a.** The act of wringing, twisting, or writhing; an instance of this. Also *fig.*

c **1460** *Towneley Myst.* xxi. 237 Bot he that forsake I shall gyf hym a wryng that his nek shall crak. **1611** COTGR., *Garrot*,.. a wring, or pinch in the wythers. **1634** BP. HALL *Contempl.*, *N.T.* IV. xxiv. ¶1 The sighs, and tears, and blubbers, and wrings of a disconsolate mourner. **1697** VANBRUGH *Relapse* III. i, My brother has given it a wring by the nose. **1789** T. RAWLINS *Fam. Archit.* 17 Arch-Stones, if any Wring or unequal Pressure happen,.. will naturally settle close to each other. **1889** *Century Mag.* May 85/1 She gave the shirt.. a vicious wring.

fig. **1602** MARSTON *Antonio's Rev.* I. i, Have I not crush't them with a cruell wring? **1628** FELTHAM *Resolves* II. xxii. 72 We sinke vnder the wring of sorrow.

b. The action of squeezing, pressing, or clasping; a squeeze or clasp of the hand.

1599 B. JONSON *Cynthia's Rev.* v. iii, A Wring by the hand, with a Banquet in a corner. *Ibid.* v. iv, The Wring by the hand, and the Banquet is ours. **1605** CHAPMAN *All Fools* II. i. D 4 b, Yet do I vnderstand.. your secret iogges and wringes; Your entercourse of glaunces. **1621** BRATHWAIT *Time's Curtain drawn* M 8, A winke, a nodd,.. a wringe, a kisse, Sent by some Childe. **1856** MISS YONGE *Daisy Chain* II. xvii, James, with one wring of the hand, retreated. **1894** J. A. STEUART *In Day of Battle* xvii, I gave the good soul's hand a hearty Christian wring.

2. A sharp or griping pain, esp. in the intestines.

c **1500** *Roulis Cursing* 61 Ane of thir infirmiteis.., The stany wring, the stane and sand blind. **1600** SURFLET *Countrie Farme* I. xxviii. 195 Hens dung swallowed by hap, bringeth frets and wrings in the bellie. **1609** HOLLAND *Amm. Marcell.* 220 An horse.. sore vexed with a suddaine gripe or wring in his belly, fell down. **1611** COTGR., *Trenchaison*, a gripe, or a wring, as of the Chollicke, &c.

3. With *down*. That which is obtained by wringing.

1874 T. HARDY *Far fr. Madding Crowd* lii, To look at the last wring-down of cider.

4. Comb.: ***wring-world***.

1885 G. M. HOPKINS *Poems* (1967) 99 But ah, but O thou terrible, why wouldst thou rude on me Thy wring-world right foot rock?

wring (rɪŋ), *v.* Pa. t. and pa. pple. **wrung** (rʌŋ). Forms: *Inf.* 1 **wringan**, 2–4 **wringen**, 4 **wryngen**, 5 **-ene**, **-yn**, **wringin**; 3–7 **wringe** (5 **ringe**), 4–6 **wrynge**, **wryng**, 4–5 **wreng**, 4– **wring** (6 *Sc.* **wrink-**, 7–8, 9 *dial.* **ring**). *Pa. t.* 1–9 (now *dial.*) **wrang**, 4–6 **wrange** (*pl.* 1 **wrungon**, 3–4 **-en**); 3–7 **wrong**, 3–6 **wronge**, 6 **wroong**, **wroung** (*pl.* 4 **wrongen**, 5 **-on**); 4– **wrung** (6 **wrunge**). *Pa. pple.* 1, 4 **wrungen**, 6 **wrunge**, 6– **wrung** (8 **rung**); 5–7 **wrong**, 5–6 **wronge** (4–6 **ywrong**, 4–5 **y-**, iwronge), wrongen, 5 wrounge, 6 wroung, wroong(e. *Weak pa. t.* 5–8 wringed; *pa. pple.* 6–7 wringed. [OE. *wringan* (*wrang, wrungon; wrungen*), = OFris. **wringa* (WFris. *wringe*), OS. **wringan* (in *ûtwringan*; MLG. *wringen*, LG. *wringen, ringen*), MDu. and Du. *wringen*, OHG. *rinkan, ringan, ringen* (MHG., G. *ringen*). Other grades of the stem *wring-* are represented by *wrang* WRONG *a.* and Goth. *wruggō* snare.]

I. 1. a. *trans.* To press, squeeze, or twist (a moist substance, juicy fruit, etc.), esp. so as to drain or make dry. Also *transf.* and in fig. context. (Cf. 14 b.)

c **890** WÆRFERTH tr. *Gregory's Dial.* 250 Witodlice hit ȝelamp..þa þa Langbeardisce mæn wrungon eleberȝan on þære treddan. *c* **1000** ÆLFRIC *Gen.* xl. 11 Ic nam þa winberian & wrang on þæt fæt. *c* **1250** *Gen. & Ex.* 2064 Ðe beries ðor-inne [*sc.* a cup] me ðhuȝte ic wrong. **13..** *K. Alis.* (W.) 333 Herbes he tok..And stamped heom in a morter; And wrong hit [*Laud MS.* wronge it out] in a box. *c* **1386** CHAUCER *Sir Thopas* 65 His faire steede..So swatte, þat men myghte him wrynge, His sydes were al blood. *c* **1430** *Two Cookery-Bks.* 28 Take Molberys, and wrynge a gode hepe of hem þorw a cloþe. *c* **1485** *E.E. Misc.* (Warton Cl.) 75 Wrynge hit [*sc.* turnsole with glair] into a schelle. **1508** DUNBAR *Tua Mariit Wemen* 438, I haif a water spunge for wa,..Than wring I it full wylely. **1580** LYLY *Euphues* (Arb.) 325 Protagenes portraied Venus with a sponge;..if once she wrong it, it would drop bloud. **1637** RUTHERFORD *Lett.* (1671) 147 God is wringing grapes of red wine for Scotland. **1662** R. VENABLES *Exper. Angler* vi. 65 Wash it [*sc.* moss] well,..wring it very dry. **1747** MRS. GLASSE *Cookery* xvii. 147 Strain them [*sc.* elderberries] through a coarse Cloth, wringing the Berries. **1799** G. SMITH *Laboratory* I. 263 Pour the rest of the milk to it,..then wring it through a cloth. **1865** SWINBURNE *Chastelard* III. i. 97 That your face Seen through my sleep has wrung mine eyes to tears For pure delight in you.

absol. *c* **1050** in Techmer *Zeitschrift* (1885) II. 123 Donne þu cyse habban wille, sete þonne þine twa handa togæþere bra[d]linga, swilce þu wringan wille.

b. To strain (juice, moisture, etc.) from a moist or wet substance by squeezing or torsion; to extract (fluid) *from* or *out of* something by pressure, etc. Occas. in fig. context. Also with advs., as *forth, out* (sense 14 a).

c **888** ÆLFRED *Boeth.* v. §2 Ne meaht þu win wringan on mide winter. *c* **1000** *Sax. Leechd.* I. 72 Ðenim þære ylcan wyrte leaf,..wyl on wætere, & wring þæt wos. **1398** TREVISA *Barth. De P.R.* XVII. clxxxviii. (Bodl. MS.), Newe wyne þat is newe take oute of þe presse and wrong. *a* **1400** *Leg. Rood* (1871) 138 Cristes Cros ȝit spac þis speche: Furst was I presse wyn to wringe. **1535** COVERDALE *Judges* vi. 38 He wrange yᵉ dew out of the flese. **1576** G. BAKER tr. *Gesner's Jewell of Health* 11 b, We..distill the lycour wrynged forth. **1631** ANCHORAN *Comenius' Gate Tongues* 69 Oyle is wringed and strained out of olives. *a* **1700** EVELYN *Diary* 21 May 1645, A laundress wringing water out of a piece of linen. **1746** HERVEY *Medit.* 42 The intolerable Pressure wrung Blood, instead of Sweat, from every Pore. **1857** RUSKIN *Pol. Econ.* i. 17 You have to..wring the honey and oil out of the rock. **1888** F. HUME *Mme. Midas* I. Prol., Wringing the water from his coarse clothing.

transf. **1652** BELL tr. *Luther's Table Talk* xxxv. 381 He wringeth from me a bitter sweat.

c. *transf.* To force (tears) *out of* the eye, *from* a person, etc.; to squeeze out.

a **1395** HYLTON *Scala Perf.* I. lix. (W. de W. 1494), He..somtyme wryngeth a tere oute of his eye. **1592** KYD *Sp. Trag.* III. xiii. 135 Art thou come..To wring more teares from Isabellas eies? **1602** MARSTON *Antonio's Rev.* I. v, The gripe of chaunce is weake to wring a teare From him. **1683** DRYDEN & LEE *Dk. Guise* III. i, It wrings the Tears from Grillon's Iron Heart. **1766** GOLDSM. *Vicar* xvii, It is not a small distress that can wring tears from these old eyes. **1815** MILMAN *Fazio* I. i, 'Twere sin to charity To wring one drop of brine upon thy corpse. **1819** KEATS *Otho* III. ii. 221 A foolish dream that from my brow hath wrung A wrathful dew.

2. a. To twist, writhe, or wrest (a person or thing); to force (a limb, etc.) *round* or *about* so as to cause a sprain or pain.

c **1000** *Sax. Leechd.* II. 196 Teoh him þa loccas, & wringe þa earan & þone wangbeard twiccige. **1362** LANGL. *P. Pl.* A. VII. 162 Hongur..hente wastor bi þe mawe, And wrong him ..be þe wombe. *c* **1435** *Torr. Portugal* 1014 By the nose I schall the wryng, Thow berdles gadlyng. **1481** CAXTON *Reynard* xl. (Arb.) 111 The foxe..grepe the wulf fast by the colyons. And he wronge hem so sore that [etc.]. *c* **1520** SKELTON *Magnyf.* 2196 Iche shall wrynge the..on the wryst. **1578** H. WOTTON *Courtlie Controv.* 114 After they had chaffed his temples.., wrong hys little finger [etc.]. **1612** SHELTON *Quix.* I. IV. v. 338 He wrung her throat so straitly betweene both his armes, that [etc.]. **1633** G. HERBERT *Temple, Agonie* ii, There shall he see a man..wrung with pains. **1709** STEELE *Tatler* No. 137 ¶3 Let me wring your Neck round your Shoulders. **1727–41** [see TWIST *v.* 9 b]. **1815** BURNEY *Dict. Marine, To Wring a Mast*, is to bend or strain it out of its natural position by setting the shrouds up too taught. **1816** SCOTT *Bl. Dwarf* viii, It's but wringing the head o' him about at last. **1839** LANE *Arab. Nts.* I. 64 The memlook..began to wring it [*sc.* another's ear] by little and little. **1881** 'RITA' *My Lady Coquette* xix, I shall wring that Budd's neck if he comes in my way.

refl. *a* **1548** HALL *Chron., Hen. VIII*, 171 The common people..wrong them selfes by the berdes.

fig. **1900** J. L. ALLEN *Incr. Purpose* iv. 39 His heart-strings were twisted tight and wrung sore this day.

b. To contract or contort (the features, etc.); to screw, distort, turn awry.

a **1300** *K. Horn* 1062 (Camb.), Horn tok burdon & scrippe, & wrong his lippe. **1576** WHETSTONE *Rocke of Regard* I. 83 She wroung her mouth awry. **1602** MARSTON *Antonio's Rev.* I. v, Would'st have me..wring my face with mimic action? **1607** TOPSELL *Four-f. Beasts* 141 When he fauneth vpon a man he [*sc.* a dog] wringeth his skinne in the forehead. **1665** J. WILSON *Projectors* I. i. 8 Do you not observe Sir, how hard he wrings his brows? **1808** SCOTT *Marm.* VI. xxx. 5 When pain and anguish wring the brow. **1885** R. L. & F. STEVENSON *Dynamiter* 184 The white face ..wrung with unspoken thoughts.

c. To twist or force (the features) *into* or *to* a smile, etc.

1806 J. BERESFORD *Miseries Hum. Life* (ed. 4) VII. xxxv, The necessity..of wringing your features into a smirk, in addressing a poltroon. **1827** HOOD *Mids. Fairies* xciv, To hope my solemn countenance to wring To idiot smiles!

3. a. To twist (a wet garment, cloth, etc.) in the hands, so as to force out water; also in modern use, to pass through a wringer. Occas. in fig. context. Also with *away* (quot. 1728).

c **1300** *Havelok* 1233 He sholen hire cloþen washen and wringen. **1377** LANGL. *P. Pl.* B. XIV. 18 Dowel shal wasshen it [*sc.* a coat] and wryngen it þorw a wys confessour. *c* **1425** *MS. Sloane* 73 fol. 201, [When] þat þou moystist it þus..loke þat þou wrynge it clene. **1471** CAXTON *Recuyell* (Sommer) 494 After she toke oute the sherte appertly and wronge hit. **1530** PALSGR. 785/2, I wringe..a clothe that is wete. **1598** GRENEWEY *Tacitus, Ann.* XI. x. 152 The presses were wrung, the vessels flowed with wine. **1633** FORD *'Tis Pity* III. vii, My whole body is in a sweat, that you may wring my shirt; feel here. **1684** BOYLE *Porousn. Bod.* iii. 11 To purify Quicksilver by tying it up strictly in a piece of kids.. leather, and then wringing it hard to force it out. **1728** RAMSAY *Last Sp. Miser* vii, I never..wrung away my sarks with washing. **1732** SWIFT *Let. to J. Brandreth* 30 June, Take care of damps;..if a stocking happens to fall off a chair, you may wring it next morning. **1812** J. WILSON *Isle of Palms* II. 283 Weeping, she wrings his dripping hair. **1874** BLACKIE *Self-Cult.* 51 A wet sheet, dipped in water, and well wrung.

absol. *c* **1425** in *Rel. Ant.* I. 275 A woman ys a worthy thyng: They dothe washe and dothe wrynge. **1573** TUSSER *Husb.* (1878) 173 Maids, wash well and wring well. **1635** *Life & Death Long Meg Westm.* ii. 5 She had been..used..to hard labour, as to wash, to wring.

b. To clasp and twist (the hands or fingers) together, esp. in token or by reason of distress or pain.

In very frequent use from *c* 1300.

c **1290** *S. Eng. Leg.* I. 43/303 He weop and criede and wrong is hondene. *a* **1300** *K. Horn* 980 (Camb. MS.), Hire fingres [*Harl.* hondes] he gan wringe. **1362** LANGL. *P. Pl.* A. v. 68 Wroþliche he wrong his fust. *c* **1375** *Cursor M.* 23960 (Fairf.), Hir louelie fingris ho did wringe. *a* **1440** *Sir Eglam.* 815 They weptyn faste and wrang ther hande. *c* **1489** CAXTON *Sonnes of Aymon* i. 37 There had you seen..many a hande wrongen. **1523** LD. BERNERS *Froiss.* I. cclxx. 165/1 They wronge their handes and tare their heeres. **1611** BEAUM. & FL. *Knt. Burn. Pestle* IV. i. Song, Come you whose loves are dead,..Weep and wring Every hand and every head. **1659** W. CHAMBERLAYNE *Pharon.* III. II. 105 Her hands Wringing each other's ivory joints. **1749** SMOLLETT *Regicide* IV. v, Wherefore dost thou wring thy tender hands? **1798** EDGEWORTH *Pract. Educ.* (1811) I. 104 Persons in violent grief wring their hands and convulse their countenances. **1845** MANGAN *German Anthol.* I. 162 She wrang her hands till blood gushed forth. **1884** F. M. CRAWFORD *Rom. Singer* I. 89 He wrung his fingers together and breathed hard.

transf. **1865** DICKENS *Mut. Fr.* I. xii, The wind sawed... The shrubs wrung their many hands.

absol. *a* **1300** *Cursor M.* 23960, I se him hang, I se hir wring. *c* **1386** CHAUCER *Clerk's T.* 1212 Lat hym care and wepe and wryng and waille. *c* **1430** *Pol., Rel. & L. Poems* (1903) 236, I wringe & wepe as þing for-lorn. **1587** TURBERV. *Trag. T.* (1837) 251 She wrong and wept a pace.

4. a. Of a tight shoe or boot: To press painfully upon (the foot, toe, etc.); to hurt (a person) in this way; = PINCH *v.* 1 b.

c **1449** PECOCK *Repr.* III. xi. 347 The schoon schulden be so narowe, that thei schulden needis wringe his sones feet into greet peyne. **1540** PALSGR. *Acolastus* IV. vii. X iij, Doth thy shoe wrynge the? **1580** NORTH *Plutarch, P. Æmylius* (1595) 262 Is not this a goodly shooe?..yet..neuer a one of you can tell where it wringeth me. **1581** PETTIE tr. *Guazzo's Civ. Conv.* I. 11 Hee bought a paire of Bootes, whereof the one was so straite that it wrong his legge and foote verie sore. **1612** SHELTON *Quix.* II. (1620) 223, I know where my shoo wrings me. **1678** OTWAY *Friendship in F.* IV, Quit her! as chearfully, as I would a Shooe that wrings me. **1770** LANGHORNE *Plutarch* (1879) I. 297/2 None knows where it [a shoe] wrings him but he that wears it. **1831** R. LOWER *Tom Cladpole* xxiv, I gun to feel..De haboot ring ma toe.

b. In figurative contexts; esp. in the proverbial phrase ***to know where the shoe wrings one***, or variants of this: cf. PINCH *v.* 1 b.

c **1386** CHAUCER *Merch. T.* 341, I woot best wher wryngeth me my sho. —— *Wife's Prol.* 492 He sat ful ofte and song Whan þat his shoo ful bitterly hym wrong. **1546** J. HEYWOOD *Prov.* II. v. (1867) 57 My selfe can tell best, where my shooe doth wryng mee. **1584** LODGE *Alarm* E iij b, We shall finde whereas their shooe wringeth them. **1602** MIDDLETON *Blurt, Master-Constable* A 4 b, I haue a shooe wrings me to th' heart. **1654** EARL MONM. tr. *Bentivoglio's Wars Flanders* 253 Here it is that the King of Spains shoe wrings him. **1672** MARVELL *Reh. Transp.* I. 314 They see where the shoo wrings him.

c. *absol.*, esp. in fig. or proverbial use.

1580 LYLY *Euphues* (Arb.) 413, I see that others maye gesse where the shooe wringes, besides him that weares it. **1589** GREENE *Menaphon* (Arb.) 54 As he were a Coblers eldest sonne, [he] would by the laste tell where anothers shooe wrings. **1609** ROWLANDS *Crew Kind Gossips* 4 Little do you know where my shoo wrings. **1658** A. FOX tr. *Würtz' Surg.* II. xxv. 149 He that weareth the shooes knoweth where they wring. **1887** *Brighouse News* 23 July (E.D.D.), Every man knows best where his shoe wrings.

5. a. To cause anguish or distress to (a person, his heart, etc.); to vex, distress, rack.

In freq. use from *c* 1780, esp. with *heart*.

c **1374** CHAUCER *Troylus* III. 1531 So hard hym wrong of sharp desir þe peyne. **1390** GOWER *Conf.* I. 91 If that thou fiele That love wringe thee to sore, Behold Ovide and take his lore. *a* **1535** FISHER *Serm.* Wks. (1876) 419 A penitent soule, that is sore prest and wrong with vtter shame. **1575** GASCOIGNE *Dan Barth., Reporter* vi, In deede the rage which wrong him there, was rathe. **1614** WITHER *Juvenil., Epigr.* v. 6 Where only thine own guiltinesse doth wring thee. **1648** *Hunting of Fox* 32 Every word hath its weight, and secretly wrings those lay-Levites. **1746** FRANCIS tr. *Horace, Art of Poetry* 158 For Nature..Wrings the sad Soul, and bends it down to Earth. **1766** GOLDSM. *Vicar* xxviii, Though he has wrung my heart,..that shall never inspire me with vengeance. **1831** JAMES *Phil. Aug.* III. ii, Even the sunbeam ..seemed but given to wring him [*sc.* a prisoner] with the memory of sweets he could not taste. **1845** MANGAN *German Anthol.* I. 161 Remorse may wring thy soul too late! **1884** W. C. SMITH *Kildrostan* 79, I must tell you all, Howe'er it wring my heart.

absol. **1553** ASCHAM *Germany* 23 His talke is alwayes so accompanied with discression.., as he neither biteth with wordes, nor wringeth with deedes. *a* **1893** CHR. G. ROSSETTI *Poems* (1904) 215/1 O faces unforgotten! if to part Wrung sore, what will it be to re-embrace?

b. To affect (a person, etc.) with bodily pain, hurt, or damage (sometimes *spec.* by torsion or pressure); to hurt, harm, or injure. Now *dial.* or *arch.* (after Shakespeare).

c **1520** SKELTON *Magnyf.* 2047 Howe the gowte wryngeth me by the too! **1565** COOPER *Thesaurus* s.v. *Constrictus*, The mouthe wrounge with the bytte. **1580** LYLY *Euphues* (Arb.) 249 Wring not a horse on the withers, with a false saddle. **1617** MORYSON *Itin.* I. 55 After they had first wrung their foreheads with twisted ropes. **1623** *St. Papers, Col.* 217 [Stale cider] doth extraordinarily wring the belly. **1698** FRYER *Acc. E. India & P.* 176 Being wrung by her Pain. **1711** *Lond. Gaz.* No. 4886/4 Rung with the Fetters on the white Foot, and rung a little on the Shoulders. **1718** POPE *Iliad* XVI. 195 When scalding Thirst their burning Bowels wrings. **1882** *N. & Q.* 29 July 94/1 My clothes wring me. **1887** *Kentish Gloss.* 192, I wrung my shoulder with carrying a twenty-stale ladder.

absol. **1575** GASCOIGNE *Weedes, Compl. Gr. Knt.*, A peece which shot..so streight, It neyther bruzed with recule, nor wroong with overweight.

fig. or in fig. context. **1580** LYLY *Euphues* (Arb.) 387 For deny I wil not that I am wroung on the withers. **1596** SHAKS. *1 Hen. IV.* II. i. 7 The poore Iade is wrung in the withers. [Cf. UNWRUNG *ppl. a.*] **1888** E. GOSSE *Congreve* 3 It wrung the withers of the poets of Collier's day.

c. To distress or afflict (a person) by exaction, severity, etc.; to oppress, keep down.

1550 BECON *Fortr. Faithful* C iiij, Thus yᵉ pore people be so wrounge of these ungentle gentlemen, yᵗ the selye soules are lyke unto dry haddockes. **1599** in Fowler *Hist. C.C.C.* (O.H.S.) 352 So as you [do not]..wring your Tenants in such sort for your private gain. **1613** P'CESS ELIZ. in Ellis *Orig. Lett.* Ser. II. III. 232 My Lorde, I have not bin forward to wringe you with requests. **1615** SYLVESTER *Job Triumph.* III. 537 The meanest Groom I saw, I feared so, I durst not wring, nor wrong, nor wrangle with. **1742** YOUNG *Nt. Th.* II. 152 Bare existence, man, to live ordain'd, Wrings, and oppresses with enormous weight.

†d. To press or ply (a person) with argument or confutation. *Obs. rare.*

1567 HARDING in Jewel *Def. Apol.* 2 What doo Heretikes when they are vrged and wroonge, when by force of arguments they are straighted. **1646** TRAPP *Comm. John* viii. 7 Thus our Saviour wrings those supercilious and censorious hypocrites.

6. a. To wrench or wrest out of position or relation; to cause to change place by turning or twisting. Const. with advs., as *apart, asunder*, or preps., as *from, off, out of*.

c **1320** *Sir Tristrem* 3262 His strirops he made him tine, To grounde he him wrong. **1495** *Trevisa's Barth. De P.R.* XI. xiii. (W. de W.) 9 vi b, Thonder dystroyeth hye trees and wryngyth [*MSS.* roteþ] theym out of the grounde. **1535** COVERDALE *Lev.* i. 15 The prest shal..wrynge the neck of it a sunder. *a* **1553** UDALL *Roister D.* I. iv, He wrong a club.. out of the hande of Belzebub. **1587** GOLDING *De Mornay* xxv. (1592) 386, I will..wring a sunder the yron barres [= Isaiah xlv. 2]. **1635** *Long Meg Westm.* xx, Meg..did wring the stick out of his hands. **1699** T. ALLISON *Voy. Archangel* 18 Our Rudder Head was wrung in peices. *a* **1784** in Child *Ballads* III. 480/1 His neck in twa I wat they hae wrung. **1857** BORROW *Romany Rye* xli. (1903) 257 My mouth being slightly wrung aside, and my complexion rather swarthy. **1883** STEVENSON *Treas. Isl.* xi, I'll wring his calf's head off his body.

fig. and in fig. context. **1548** UDALL *Erasm. Par.* Pref. B j, Godly Counsaillours, whom..this wicked rable found meanes to wryng out of fauour. **1580** LYLY *Euphues* (Arb.) 295 Now you haue my opinion, you must not think to wring me from it. *a* **1592** [see WREST *sb.* 5 b]. **1817** SHELLEY *Rev. Islam* x. xli, Who the life from both their hearts can wring. ?*c* **1830** BRYANT *The Past* v, My spirit..struggles hard to wring Thy bolts apart. **1878** BROWNING *La Saisiaz* 51 Each kindly wrench that wrung From life's tree its inmost virtue.

refl. *a* **1716** SOUTH *Serm.* (1744) VIII. 127 To wring themselves out of God's hand by annihilation.

b. To bring out (words, etc.) with effort.

a **1350** in *Relig. Lyrics 14th C.* (1924) 34 Þou wringest mani wrang word Wiþ wanges ful wete. **1633** G. HERBERT *Temple, Praise* (No. 3) i, Lord, I will..speak thy praise,.. Then will I wring it with a sigh or grone. **1820** KEATS *Ode to Psyche* 1 Hear these tuneless numbers, wrung By sweet enforcement and remembrance dear.

7. a. To acquire or gain (money, property, a right, etc.) by exaction or extortion; to wrest or wrench *from* or *out of* a person, etc.

a **1300** *Sarmun* in *E.E.P.* (1862) 3 Þe wrecchis wringit þe mok so fast; up ham silf hi nul noȝt spend. **14..** *Voc.* in Wr.-Wülcker 583 *Flecto*, to wrynge mony. **1576** FLEMING *Panopl. Epist.* 113 All which priuileges..they..do what they can to wrest and wring from us. **1594** WEST *2nd Pt. Symbol.* §215 Those offences..are committed when any.. wringeth money or other things from another man. **1630** *R.*

Johnson's Kingd. & Commw. 367 That Marquisate of Saluzzes..which Henry the fourth of France wrung from him. **1730** BAILEY (fol.), *Extort*, to wrest, wring or get out of one by force, threat or authority. **1819** SCOTT *Ivanhoe* vi, Hard hands have wrung from me my goods, my money, my ships. **1855** MACAULAY *Hist. Eng.* xxii. IV. 727 To wring taxes out of the distressed population. **1868** FARRAR *Silence & V.* i. (1875) 15 The fields which the usurer has wrung from the orphan.

absol. **1582** [see WREST *v.* 4 b].

fig. and *transf.* **1596** SPENSER *State Irel.* Wks. (Globe) 620 How hardly that Act of Parliament was wronge out of them. **1608–11** BP. HALL *Epist.* I. Ep. Ded., It were well..if I could wring ought from my selfe not vnworthie of a iudicious Reader. **1828** CARLYLE *Misc.*, *Burns* ¶31 They will wring from Fate another hour of wassail and good cheer. **1842** J. WILSON *Chr. North* (1857) I. 160 To wring from the very soil more than it could produce. **1849** MACAULAY *Hist. Eng.* ix. II. 464 The pressure which had wrung from him the only good acts of his whole reign.

b. To exact, extort, or draw (an admission, consent, etc.) *from* or *out of* a person, etc.

In frequent use from *c* 1830.

c **1444** [see WRESTING *vbl. sb.* 2.] **1581** LAMBARDE *Eiren.* II. vii. (1588) 213 At the common Law, *Nemo tenebatur prodere seipsum*, and then his fault was not to be wrung out of himselfe, but [etc.]. **1642** D. ROGERS *Naaman* 41 The Lord doth not so..to wring from him some tearmes of homage. **1671** MILTON *Samson* 1199 [They] constrain'd the bride To wring from me..my secret. **1721** YOUNG *Revenge* II. i, I wrung a promise from him he would try. **1792** ROGERS *Pleas. Mem.* I. 352 To wring the slow surrender from his tongue. **1833** HT. MARTINEAU *Brooke Farm* vi. 79, I was determined no enemy should wring a complaint out of me. **1864** G. A. LAWRENCE *M. Dering* II. 83 The gay dare-devilry of the man wrung from both..admiration. **1892** *Speaker* 3 Sept. 293 These are not admissions wrung by the energy of his opponents from Mr. Huxley.

transf. *a* **1813** SHELLEY *Falsehood & Vice* 73 The stifled moan Wrung from a nation's miseries.

fig. **1853** MAURICE *Proph. & Kings* xxv. 441 Wringing out of texts or symbols..the proof of some New Testament revelation.

8. a. To press, clasp, or shake (a person's hand); to press (a person) *by* the hand; to shake hands with.

1534 MORE *Comf. agst. Trib.* II. Wks. 1170/1 The one toke the other by the tip of the finger, for hand would there none be wrongen thorow the grate. **1580** LYLY *Euphues* (Arb.) 333 So wringing hir by the hand, he ended. **1601** [? MARSTON] *Pasquil & Kath.* III. (1878) 137 I'le..wring thy fingers with an ardent gripe. *a* **1700** EVELYN *Diary* 18 Aug. 1673, He wrung me by the hand. **1713** ADDISON *Cato* I. iv, The good old King at parting wrung my hand. **1816** SCOTT *Bl. Dwarf* xvii, Langley took his hand, and..wrung it hard. **1848** DICKENS *Dombey* l, Mr. Toots..wringing Walter by the hand. **1883** D. C. MURRAY *Hearts* iii, He shook hands with Tom, wringing his hand harder than he knew.

b. To squeeze or compress *together*. *rare*$^{-1}$.

1603 G. OWEN *Pembrokeshire* i. (1891) 3 He Joyned in on Mappe..the [four] greate sheeres [= shires]..by reason whereof he was forced to wringe them..neere together.

9. a. To subject (something) to a writhing, wresting, or turning movement; to press, drive, or impel in this way. Occas. *fig.* or in fig. context. Also with preps., as *in*, *into*, *upon*.

13.. *K. Alis.* 2383 (Laud MS.), His spores he gynneþ in horse wrynge. *a* **1489** CAXTON *Blanchardyn* xlix. 190 He wrang his fystes and brake the cordes al a sonder. **1565** J. HALL *Crt. Vertue* 73 b, Of wexe they make scripture a nose, To turne and wryng it evry way. **1582** MULCASTER *Elementarie* Peroration (1925) 252 In tormenting the minde, and wringing it to the worst. **1584** R. SCOT *Discov. Witchcr.* XIII. xxv. (1886) 270 If you wring a testor upon ones forehead, it will seeme to sticke, when it is taken awaie. *a* **1586** SIDNEY *Arcadia* II. ii, Wringing [*folios* wrieng] her waste, and thrusting out her chinne. **1610** SHAKS. *Temp.* I. ii. 135 It is a hint That wrings mine eyes too 't. **1648** HEXHAM, *Wringh-aersen*, to Wringe or Friggle the taile. **1760–2** GOLDSM. *Cit. W.* lxxix, They must..wring their figures into every shape of distress. **1818** SCOTT *Br. Lamm.* xxxv, And is it true, then,..that the bridegroom's face was wrung round ahint him? **1862** MRS. BROWNING *Little Mattie* iii, Her lips you cannot wring Into saying a word more.

transf. *c* **1489** CAXTON *Blanchardyn* vii. 28 [He] wringed his strock atte the pullyng out ayen, that he made of his swerde.

b. To wrest or twist (a writing, words, etc.); to strain the purport or meaning of; to deflect, pevert; = WREST *v.* 5.

[**1393** LANGL. *P. Pl.* C. v. 31 Wily-man and wittiman and waryn wrynge-lawe.] **1546** *Supplic. of Poore Commons* (E.E.T.S.) 77 Wryngyng & wrestynge the Scriptures. **1581** [see WREST *v.* 5]. **1606** S. GARDINER *Bk. Angling* 109 By this wringing the Scripture and causing it to bleede. **1641** MILTON *Ch. Govt.* v, By wringing the collective allegory of those seven Angels into seven single Rochets. **1645** —— *Tetrarch.* 8 [God's] commands and words..are not to be so strictly wrung, as [etc.].

absol. **1540** COVERDALE *Confut. Standish* (1547) d vij b, Thus make ye of gods holy scripture a shipmans hose, wresting and wringing to what purpose ye will. **1564** [see WREST *v.* 5].

c. To turn or deflect (a matter) *into* or *to* something; to convert. ? *Obs.*

1524 *State Papers Hen. VIII*, I. 152 To wryng and wreste the maters in to bettre trayne, if they walke a wrye. **1848** L. HUNT *Jar Honey* p. xvii. (tr. Bacon), So are those doctrines best and sweetest which..are not wrung into controversies and common-places.

†**d.** To incline or dispose (a person); to bend or divert *to* something. *Obs.*

1528 MORE *Dyaloge* III. Wks. 210/1 Our harte euer thinketh the iudgement wrong, that wringeth us to the worse. **1553** ASCHAM *Germany* 6 b, Octauio was euermore wrong to the worse by many and sundry spites. **1579** [see WREST *v.* 3].

e. To wreathe, twist, or coil (something flexible); to wind or dispose in coils.

1585 T. WASHINGTON tr. *Nicholay's Voy.* II. xvi. 50 b, Another great columne..in forme of three serpents, wrong one within another. **1597** A. M. tr. *Guillemeau's Fr. Chirurg.* 29 b/1 Cause the patient gentlye to wring about his neck a table naptkinne or a towell. **1623** tr. *Favine's Theat. Hon.* IV. iii. 3 That is to say, a Serpent writhed or wrung together. **1837** A. TENNENT *Vis. Glencoe* 49 Some in coils their forms did wring, As when the deadly serpent's spring Insures its victim's doom. **1896** 'M. FIELD' *Attila* IV. 107 She catches hold of her own veil and wrings it round her head.

†**10.** *refl.* To wriggle or insinuate (oneself) *into* a place, favour, etc. *Obs.*

a **1525** *Vergilius* in Thoms *E.E. Prose Rom.* II. 27 The deuyll wrange hym selfe into the lytell hole ayen. **1592** NASHE *P. Penilesse* B 4 b, They wring themselues into his good opinion ere he be aware. **1602** MARSTON *Ant. & Mel.* III, Niggard life Hath but one little, little wicket through. We wring our selves into this wretched world..to curse and raile. **1621** J. TAYLOR (Water P.) *Superbiæ Flagellum* D 7 b, These vipers..proudly make humility a screw, To wring themselues into opinions view.

II. With adverbs.

11. wring down: To force, squeeze, or press down; *spec.* to force down the throat.

1633 *Swedish Intelligencer* III. 23 [They] will eate you whole handfulls of raw Onyons..as familiarly as an Italian wrings downe sallets, or we apples. **1874** T. HARDY *Far fr. Mad. Crowd* lii, There were the fellers round her wringing down the cheese [in the press].

12. wring in: To insert, insinuate, or bring in with or as with a twisting movement. Chiefly *fig.*

1579 FULKE *Heskins Parl.* 227 Maister Hesk. wold fain make Euthymius to speak for him, if he could tell how to wring him in. **1597** [see WREST *v.* 1 c]. **1599** B. JONSON *Cynthia's Rev.* II. iv, Who when they haue got acquainted with a strange word, neuer rest till they haue wroong it in. **1622** DRAYTON *Poly-olb.* XXI. 187 Giue me those Lines..In which things naturall be, and not in falsely wrong.

13. wring off: To wrest or force off by twisting or turning round.

c **1520** SKELTON *Magnyf.* 1909 Of some I wrynge of the necke lyke a wyre. **1611** BIBLE *Lev.* i. 15 The Priest shall bring it vnto the altar, and wring off his head. **1726** SWIFT *Gulliver* II. v, One of our servants..wrung off the bird's neck. **1865** SWINBURNE *Chastelard* IV. i. 167 Let one..Wring my crown off and cast it underfoot.

14. wring out: **a.** To force out (moisture) by or as by twisting; to squeeze out. Also *fig.* and *transf.* Cf. OUTWRING *v.*

1340–70 *Alisaunder* 712 Hee wringes oute þe wet wus. *c* **1385** CHAUCER *L.G.W.* 2527 *Phillis*, To meche truste wel may I pleyne..on ȝoure teris falsely out i-wronge. **1388** WYCLIF *Isaiah* xvi. 10 He that was wont to wringe out, schal not wrynge out wyn in a pressour. *c* **1420** *Liber Cocorum* (1862) 50 þen grynde tansy, þo iuse owte wrynge. *c* **1450** *Mirour Saluacioun* (Roxb.) 33 Gedeon wronge out the dewe. **1560** DAUS tr. *Sleidane's Comm.* 40 b, He that bloweth his nose ouermuche, shall wringe out bloude. *a* **1586** SIDNEY *Arcadia* II. xxvii, With that the fellow..wrang out teares. **1612** S. RID *Art of Jugling* E 3 b, So (with a little sponge in your hand) you may wringe out blood or wine. **1624** WOTTON *Archit.* 111 A sturdie woman, washing and winding of linnen clothes,..wrings out the water. **1743** BLAIR *Grave* 328 From stubborn shrubs Thou wrung'st their shy retiring virtues out. **1816** J. WILSON *City of Plague* II. i. 196 Such return Wrings out the tears from my old wither'd heart.

transf. **1398** TREVISA *Barth. De P.R.* v. xxxvi. (Bodl. MS.), Colde aier..is ywronge oute [L. *exprimitur*] and idrawe to þe vtter parties.

b. To strain (a wet fabric, etc.) with a twisting motion, so as to press out most of the moisture. Also const. *of* (the liquid in which the thing has been wetted).

13.. [see 1]. **1388** WYCLIF *Judges* vi. 38 Whanne the flees was wrongun out, he fillide a pot with deew. *c* **1440** *Pallad. on Husb.* II. 417 [After it has been] so steped xix dayes, Wrynge out the mirte [= myrtle berries] & clense hit. **1561** HOLLYBUSH *Hom. Apoth.* 23 Wet a long cloth,..wringe it well oute. **1576** G. BAKER tr. *Gesner's Jewell of Health* 11 b, We wring out..the thyngs infused. **1676** WISEMAN *Surg.* II. ix. 191 With a Compress wrung out as is prescribed. **1771** MRS. HAYWOOD *New Present for Maid* 268 Then wring them out of those suds. **1848** MRS. GASKELL *M. Barton* viii, Just help me wring these out, and then I'll take 'em to the mangle. **1896** *Allbutt's Syst. Med.* I. 419 A large towel wrung out of cold water.

c. To get or fetch out (something) with a wrenching movement; to wrench or wrest out.

c **1420** *Wycliffite Bible* 2 Sam. xxiii. 21 (MS. Bodl. 296), He wrong out þe spere fro þe hond.

d. To express or bring out with effort. (Cf. 6 b.)

1402 *Pol. Poems* (Rolls) II. 106 Oft, Dawe, in thi writtyng, thou wryngist out contradiccion. **1831** LAMB *Elia* II. *Newspapers 35 Years ago*, We were wringing out coy sprightliness for the [Morning] Post.

e. To obtain or draw (something) from another by pressure, application, or art; to extract, elicit, bring out.

1560 DAUS tr. *Sleidane's Comm.* 118 b, Of all these thynges can they [*sc.* merchants] wrynge out [L. *elicere*] golde and syluer, to the wonderfull losse of people. **1591** LYLY *Endym.* v. iii, Marking..my sighes,..by questions [he] wrunge out that, which was readie to burst out. **1598** GRENEWEY *Tacitus, Ann.* XV. v. 228 Let false praise, and wroong out by praiers be restrained. **1602** MARSTON *Antonio's Rev.* II. v, Present thy guilt, As if twere wrung out with thy conscience gripe. **1674** N. FAIRFAX *Bulk & Selv.* 90 That which claws away world from about them, would, 'tis like, wring out their Planethood from within them. **1833** I. TAYLOR *Fanat.* ii. 38 The gratification..is wrung out from the very torments of the heart. **1855** MACAULAY *Hist. Eng.* xix. IV. 287 In order to wring out from them the names of their employers. **1879** BROWNING *Martin Relph* 121 He wrung their pardon out.

†**f.** To expel or depose (a person) from position or office; to thrust out. *Obs.*

1560 DAUS tr. *Sleidane's Comm.* 174 b, After he had wronge oute [L. *eliserat*] Mathew Helde..he..placed [another]..in his rome. **1631** WEEVER *Anc. Funeral Mon.* 232 In which office he continued, vntill hee was wrung out by Wolsey.

15. wring up: **a.** To pull up with a twist; to wrench up.

c **1440** *Pallad. on Husb.* II. 185 The wedis with an hond most vp be wronge. [Cf. *upwring*, UP- 4 a].

b. To squeeze, press, or compact by torsion; to twist or screw up.

c **1420** *Liber Cocorum* (1862) 14 Take almondes, bray hem, wryng hom up. *c* **1440** in *Househ. Ord.* (1790) 442 Take parsel, and grinde hit, and wringe hit up with egges thrugh a streynour. **1885** C. G. W. LOCK *Workshop Receipts* Ser. IV. 244 Wring the book up tightly in the press. **1891** T. HARDY *Tess* iii, The very white frock..which had been wrung up and ironed by her mother's own hands.

c. *Mining.* In passive. Of a lode: To become diminished or dwindled.

1839 DE LA BECHE *Rep. Geol. Cornwall*, etc. xi. 343 By continuing the workings through the space so wrung-up. **1855** [J. R. LEIFCHILD] *Cornwall* 143 Sometimes the lode..becomes 'wrung up', or impoverished.

III. *intr.* †**16. a.** To flow or run *out* under pressure; to issue. *Obs.*

a **1225** *Ancr. R.* 322 Al þet fule wrusum scheaweð him, & wringeð ut biuoren al þe wide worlde. *a* **1240** *Wohunge* in *O.E. Hom.* I. 281 þat te blod wrang ut at tine finger neiles. *a* **1300** *Cursor M.* 11700, I wil þat vte þe water wring. ? *c* **1400** *Emare* 881 The teres out of hys yen gan wryng. *a* **1450** *Northern Passion* (D) 1880 þe bloode a non began out to springe And þan þe watir after to wringe.

†**b.** To struggle or force a way *out*. Also *fig.*

c **1384** CHAUCER *H. Fame* 2110 Thus oute at holes gunne wringe Euery tydynge streght to Fame. *a* **1525** *Vergilius* in Thoms *E.E. Prose Rom.* II. 26 There was a lytell hole, and therat wrange the deuyll out like a yeel. **1584** R. SCOT *Discov. Witchcr.* III. xvi. 51 Little holes where a flie can scarselie wring out.

c. *Mining.* With *out*. (See quot. and 15 c.)

1855 [J. R. LEIFCHILD] *Cornwall* 91 Sometimes the schist so abounds in the lode, that the quartzose part disappears altogether, or is only continued in minute strings. In such a case, the lode is said to have dwindled away, or to have *wrung out*.

†**17. a.** To suffer or sustain twisting, wrenching, or turning. *Obs.*

a **1225** *Leg. Kath.* 1368 þe keiser..bed..ba binden ham swa, þe fet & te honden, þet ha wrungen aȝein.

b. To be engaged in, to perform the action of, writhing or twisting; *esp.* of the hands.

1377 LANGL. *P. Pl.* B. v. 85 His body was to-bolle for wratthe,..And wryngynge he ȝede with þe fiste. *c* **1435** *Torr. Portugal* 1690 Fore his men pursued a dere, To his castell,..That doth my hondys wring, This Giaunt hym toke. *a* **1450** MYRC *Par. Pr.* 780 Koghe þow not þenne, þy þonkes, Ny wrynge þou not wyth þy schonkes. ? *a* **1480** *Piers of Fulham* 143 in Hazl. *E.P.P.* II. 7 A gentyll byrd takyn can no defense, Save wrastyll and wrynge with the tale a lyte. **1546** *Supplic. Poore Commons* (E.E.T.S.) 69 When they sawe the worlde som what lyke to wrynge on the other syde, they denyed it. **1604** E. T. *Case is altered* C ij b, His wife with her handes wringing entertaines him with a weeping. **1682** BUNYAN *Holy War* 153 Mr. Weteyes went with hands wringing together. **183.** J. EDMESTON in *Sacred Poetry* (1868) 243 The hands I love dearly are wringing.

†**18.** To fling *away*; to rush precipitately. *Obs.*

c **1400** *Sowodne Bab.* 2557 Richard the whiles away he wronge, Thile thai were alle dismayede.

19. a. To twist the body in struggling or striving; to struggle *with* or strive *against* something; to contend, labour, or endeavour earnestly.

1470–85 MALORY *Arthur* v. v. 168 Arthur weltred and wrong that he was other whyle vnder and another tyme aboue. **1489** [see WRESTLE *v.* 2 b]. **1548** P. NICOLS *Godly New Story* E iij b, Some wring & wrest to go backe agayn into Egypt. **1556** J. HEYWOOD *Spider & Fly* i. 59 The more he [*sc.* a fly] wrange, the faster was he wrapt [in the web]. **1570** DRANT *Two Serm.* K vj, Iannes and Mambres wrong and shouldered at the truth. **1791** [W. BECKFORD] *Pop. Tales of Germans* II. 123 Violent convulsion fits shewed that they were wringing with death. **1837** CARLYLE *Misc.* (1857) IV. 114 With the many-headed coil of Lernean serpents..[Hercules] wrestled and wrang..for life or death.

b. To twist, turn, or struggle in pain or anguish; to writhe.

c **1485** *Digby Myst.* (1882) III. 1409 Swyche a cramp on me sett is,..I ly and wryng. **1596** HARINGTON *Metam. Ajax* (1814) 45 He..looked as if he had been wringing hard on a close-stool. **1611** SHAKS. *Cymb.* III. vi. 79 He wrings at some distresse. **1633** BP. HALL *Occas. Medit.* lxix. 167 How is it [*sc.* a worm] vexed with the scorching beames, and wrings up and down! **1789** [see WRINGLE *v.* 2]. **1843** CARLYLE *Past & Pr.* III. i, In hydra-wrestle, giant 'Millocracy'..wrestles and wrings in choking nightmare.

c. To suffer or undergo grief, pain, punishment, etc. (*for* something).

1565 J. HALL *Crt. Vertue* 134 b, None but the poore Doth wrynge therfore, And suffer the distres. **1586** FERNE *Blaz. Gentrie* 22 The shoemaker..hath so scanted his shoe that his foote wringeth therewith. **1608** CHAPMAN *Byron's Conspiracy* I. i, Such as are impatient of rest; And wring beneath some priuate discontent. **1760–72** H. BROOKE *Fool of Qual.* (1809) III. 28 My heart wrings with regret. **1831** R. LOWER *Tom Cladpole* cxlvi, My toe did ring full sore. **1882** *N. & Q.* 17 June 468/2, I took it [*sc.* a feather bed] away,..because he would not wring so [*i.e.* have such bed-sores].

20. †**a.** To set *upon* a person with hostile language. *Obs.*

1581 J. BELL *Haddon's Answ. Osor.* 334 Whereunto tendeth all the endeuour of those men, whome Osorius here wringeth vpon [L. *oppugnat*] so sharpely.

b. To carry *on* wringing or torture. *rare*⁻¹.

1821 BYRON *Two Foscari* I. i, Let them wring on; I am strong yet. *Guard.* Confess, And the rack will be spared you.

†**21.** To associate, or join hands, *with* another. *Obs. rare.*

1580 LUPTON *Sivqila* 109 Which [bribe] belyke you thought that my handes did so tickle to touche, that I would wring with the wrong and flee from the truth.

IV. 22. Comb.: †**wring-jaw** *U.S. slang*, rough cider.

a **1775** [see 'SIMMON *sb.*³]. **1845** J. F. COOPER *Chain-bearer* I. iii. 46 'To get a sup of cider for old Jaap.'.. His weakness in favour of wring-jaw being a well-established failing.

Hence †**wringed** *ppl. a.*, wrung; squeezed (out).

1582 STANYHURST *Æneis* II. (Arb.) 50 Wee wer al inueigled, with wringd tears nicetye blended. ? *a* **1600** *Roman Charity* in A. Philips *Coll. Old Ball.* II. 142 With wringed Hands, and bitter Tears, These Words pronounced she. *a* **1680** CHARNOCK *Attrib. God* (1682) 637 'Tis as if Divine Goodness did kneel down to a Sinner with wringed Hands.

wring, obs. erron. f. RING *v.*²

†**wring-bolt**, obs. erron. f. RING-BOLT.

1815 BURNEY *Dict. Marine, Wring-bolts*,..in ship-building, are bolts used to bend and secure the planks against the timbers. [Hence in Crabb (1823) and later Dicts. Cf. WRAIN-BOLT.]

†**wringe**, obs. variant of *wrinch* WRENCH *sb.*¹

1632 LITHGOW *Trav.* I. 3 A Dame..Whose wringes, winks, whose curious smiles and words, And scraping feete, lost blandement affoords.

wringer ('rɪŋə(r)). Also 6–7 ringer. [f. prec. + -ER¹. Cf. OHG. *ringari* (MHG., G. *ringer*) wrestler.]

I. 1. An exactor, extortioner; an oppressor.

a **1300** *Sarmun* xxi. in *E.E.P.* (1862) 3 Such a wringer goþ to helle for litil gode þat nis noȝt his. **1562** J. HEYWOOD *Prov. & Epigr.* (1867) 206 How lost you your welth?.. Who was your welthes wringer? **1578** T. WILCOCKS *Serm. Pawles* 56 Masters detayning seruaunts wages; a roring sinne, whiche shall make the wringers houle for it. *a* **1618** SYLVESTER *Sec. Sess. Parlt.* Wks. (Grosart) II. 141 An Act against all greedy Wringers, Wrongers, Usurers, and Oppressors. **1857** DICKENS *Dorrit* II. xxxii, You're..a screwer by deputy, a wringer, and squeezer, and a shaver by substitute.

2. a. One who presses *out* juice or moisture. *rare*⁻¹.

1388 WYCLIF *Isaiah* xvi. 10 Y haue take awei the vois of wryngeris out [L. *calcantium*].

b. One who wrings clothes or the like after washing; one whose occupation consists in wringing.

1598 SHAKS. *Merry W.* I. ii. 5 There dwels..his Laundry; his Washer, and his Ringer. **1618** REYCE *Brev. Suffolk* (1902) 22 Wringers, spinners, weavers, burlers. **1831** CARLYLE *Sart. Res.* I. iii, Old Lieschen,..who was..his washer and wringer. **1881** *Instr. Census Clerks* (1885) 59 Gun Cotton Manufacture: Beater. Dipper. Wringer.

transf. **1573** HARVEY *Letter-Bk.* (Camden) 102 Her waste so laste; her fingers sutch wringers.

†**3. a.** One who twists or distorts. *rare*⁻¹.

1552 HULOET, Wringer or wryster of a thinge out of ordre, *elico.*

†**b.** = WRESTER 2. *Obs. rare*⁻¹.

c **1560** *Godly & Fruteful Treatise*, Wresters and wringers of thy holy scripture.

†**4.** One who causes pain, suffering, etc.

1602 *Contention betw. Liberality & Prodigality* IV. ii, Thistles, and nettles most horrible stingers, Rauens, grypes, and gryphons, oh vengible wringers.

II. †**5.** A crow-bar. (Cf. RINGER *sb.*¹ 3.) *Obs.*

1703 [R. NEVE] *City & C. Purchaser* 48 They..united into one intire Body, so that they are forced to get them out with Wringers (or Iron-bars).

6. a. A wringing-machine.

1799 *Hull Advert.* 15 June 2/4 Mr. Beetham's..patent wringer. **1875** KNIGHT *Dict. Mech.* 2822/1 Palmer's Combined Wringer and Mangle. **1891** *Anthony's Photogr. Bull.* IV. 298 Passing it between the rollers of the wringer.

b. Fig. phr. ***to put through the wringer*** and varr.: to try or test (a person or, *rarely*, a thing); *esp.* to subject to severe questioning. *slang* (orig. *U.S.*).

1942 *Sun* (Baltimore) 20 June 15/1 With its capitalization put through the wringer through reorganization..the Erie board voted a payment of 550 cents a share. **1950** T. STERLING *House without Door* (1951) xviii. 196 Every one of them was being blackmailed..except one woman, and she was put through the wringer another way. **1965** J. PHILIPS *Twisted People* iv. 56 We felt..that there had been sabotage... Everybody..was put through a wringer by the CIA. **1972** L. LAMB *Picture Frame* xv. 133 Do you think we had better pick him up and put him through the wringer? **1977** D. FRANCIS *Risk* xiv. 184 If I hadn't recently been through so many wringers..I wouldn't have given it another thought. **1984** *Times* 3 July 12/6 Not since the controversial Bishop of Durham..has an episcopal appointee been put through the wringer in this fashion.

7. A device for wringing hot fomentations before application.

1884 EVA LÜCKES *Lect. Nursing* vii. 135 You will require new fomentation flannels and wringers. **1896** *Allbutt's Syst. Med.* I. 435 A good wringer is made by a strip of ticking.

'**wringing**, *vbl. sb.* [f. WRING *v.* + -ING¹.]

1. The action of the verb, in various senses; the fact of being wrung.

c **1350** *Will. Palerne* 5452 þer was siking.., weping & wringinge for wo at here hertes. **1398** TREVISA *Barth. De P.R.* XVII. cxii. (Bodl. MS.), Oile..renneþ þe better and þe clenner oute of þe draffe in the wringinge and pressinge. **1481** [see WRING *v.* 9 a]. **1548** PATTEN *Exped. Scotl.* Pref. c iij, The peynfull wringing of so vneasie a yok. **1593** NASHE *Christ's T.* To Rdr., He hath but a slight wringing by the eares. **1606** J. CARPENTER *Solomon's Solace* xiv. 57 The wringing of the shoo being knowne to him only which weareth it. **1611** BIBLE *Prov.* xxx. 33 The wringing of the nose bringeth forth bloud. **1656** JEANES *Mixt. Schol. Div.* 156 With..wringing of hands, knocking of breasts, tearing of haire. **1706** [see WRESTING *vbl. sb.* 1]. **1718** CHAMBERLAYNE *Relig. Philos.* I. 54 In this great Length of the Tube of the Bowels..no Body can encrease or diminish the Contractions or Wringings of the same. **1782** V. KNOX *Ess.* clxiv. (1819) III. 224 That wringing of the hands, beating of the breast. **1853** DICKENS *Bleak Ho.* lv, Her broken words, and her wringing of her hands. **1854** R. S. SURTEES *Handley Cr.* iv, The wringing of turkeys' necks.

b. *fig.* The action of wresting or taking forcefully; extortion.

1589 *Pasquil's Ret.* C ij, Ready to suffer wrong without wringing of reuenge out of Gods hand. **1607** COWELL *Interpr., Extortion*,..an vnlawfull..wringing of mony or mony worth from any man. **1611** [see WRESTING *vbl. sb.* 1 c].

c. With advs., as *out*, *up*.

1613 PURCHAS *Pilgrimage* (1614) 19 The wringing out of grapes to her husband. **1730** BAILEY (fol.), *Extortion*, an unlawful..wringing out of money..from any person. **1839** DE LA BECHE *Rep. Geol. Cornwall*, etc. xi. 343 The miner..terms such points..of contact a nipping-in or wringing-up of the lode.

2. The action of squeezing or pressing water or moisture out of clothes, etc.; †the personal service of doing such. Also in fig. context.

1560 *Wills & Invent. N.C.* (Surtees, 1835) 191 To find hym fyre and a chamber with all wessyng wry[n]ginge and one to help hym one with his clothes and of. **1587** *Sc. Acts, Jas. VI* (1814) III. 508/1 Meit drink clething bedding wesching and wringing. **1626–7** *Knaresb. Wills* (Surtees) II. 92 My keepinge with..washinge, wringinge and other necessaryes during my life. **1633** G. HERBERT *Temple, Love Unknown* 16 My heart..in a font..was dipt and di'd, And washt, and wrung: the very wringing yet Enforceth tears. **1821** SCOTT *Kenilw.* ix, Breakfast shall be on the board in the wringing of a dishclout. **1845** G. DODD *Brit. Manuf.* IV. 96 The wringing [of wool]..is..effected thus. **1875** KNIGHT *Dict. Mech.* 2822/1 The ordinary wringing injures fine apparel.

†**3.** A griping or wringing pain, esp. in the intestines. *Obs.*

c **1550** H. LLOYD *Treas. Health* L iv, The rynde of the pyne apple tree..doth..take awaye the wryngyng of the bely. **1578** LYTE *Dodoens* 235 The gryping paynes and wringings of the bellie. **1601** HOLLAND *Pliny* I. 445 The torments and wringing of the cholique. **1607** [see WRESTING *vbl. sb.* 2]. **1671** SALMON *Syn. Med.* I. 83 The wringing of the Guts. **1721** BAILEY, To *Verminate*,..to have a griping or wringing in the Belly.

†**b.** The action or fact of feeling remorse, apprehension, or mistrust; an instance of this. *Obs.*

1613 SHAKS. *Hen. VIII*, II. ii. 28 Doubts, wringing of the Conscience, Feares and despaires. **1633** FLETCHER & SHIRLEY *Nt. Walker* I. i, No wringings in your mind now, as you love me. **1760–72** H. BROOKE *Fool of Qual.* (1809) IV. 36 He beheld her, in the wringings of penitential desolation. *Ibid.* 41 The weight and wringing that was then at his heart.

4. Perversion; = WRESTING *vbl. sb.* 2. ? *Obs.*

1565 CALFHILL *Answ. Martiall* v. 127 Hys wordes without wringing or wresting at all, be taken..to importe much lesse. **1581** J. BELL *Haddon's Answ. Osor.* 279 Wordes in the Gospell, which (by wryngyng and wrestyng) you doe accustome to force to your purpose. *a* **1614** D. DYKE *Myst. Selfe-Deceiuing* (1630) 222 Diuers such like wringings of Scripture. **1852** MRS. JAMESON *Leg. Madonna* 325 Without any wringing of the text for an especial purpose.

5. *concr.* In *pl.*, that which is wrung out. Also *fig.*

1867 DENISON *Astron. without Math.* 168 That great law ..prevents the whole earth and the sea..from flying in pieces like the wringings of a mop. **1886** BROWNING in *Maggs' Catal.* March (1897) 48 The 'quality of lying is not strained' in this particular case, but droppeth 'as should the wringings of a felon brain for the sake of a dollar'.

6. *attrib.*, as †***wringing point***; **wringing-machine**, a machine for wringing clothes, etc., after washing; a wringer.

1637 WALTON in Wotton *Reliq.* (1651) 166 Then was Stigand, the Metropolitan,..fairly deposed, being too stiffe for the times: which was indeed the wringing point. **1833** LOUDON *Encycl. Archit.* §698 A washing and wringing machine. **1858** SIMMONDS *Dict. Trade* 417 Wringing-machine Maker.

'**wringing**, *ppl. a.* [f. as prec. + -ING².]

1. †**a.** Of hands: That undergo wringing, squeezing, or pressing; wrung under distress. *Obs.*

a **1225** *Leg. Kath.* 2324 Heo..seh..wepmen & wummen, mid wringinde honden wepinde sare. **1579** HAKE *Newes out of Powles* (1872) B vj, Another cryes with wringing handes. **1596** *Roman Charity* in *Roxb. Ball.* VIII. 6 With wringing hands and bitter teares, these words pronounced she. **1705** STANHOPE *Paraphr.* I. 73 Wringing Hands and Gnashing Teeth thenceforth and for ever.

b. Quasi-*adv.* in ***wringing-wet***, very wet; so wet that moisture may be wrung out.

a **1500** *Flower & Leaf* 406 To drie here clothes that were wringing wete. **1570** B. GOOGE *Pop. Kingd.* 49 b, Maydens ..dabbled all with durt, and wringing wette. *a* **1614** *Serm. Jude* i, in *Hooker's Wks.* (1888) III. 665 A poor fisherman.. with his clothes wringing wet. **1686** GOAD *Celest. Bodies* III. i. 377 The wringing-wet Influence (as Houswives call it) of ♂ and ♀. **1847** *Illustr. Lond. News* 21 Aug. 128/2 Their handkerchiefs are 'wringing-wet'. **1897** MARY KINGSLEY *W. Africa* 387 Then I clutch..a wringing wet blanket. **1901** ALLDRIDGE *Sherbro* xxiii, Foot-sore, utterly exhausted, and wringing wet with perspiration.

2. That writhes or twists.

1597 DELONEY *Gentle Craft* ii. Wks. (1912) 81 The wrathfull Dragon with his long, wringing taile.

3. Causing pain, distress, or anguish; racking, distressing.

1576 FLEMING tr. *Caius' Dogs* (1880) 27 Nipping neede & wringing want. **1601** HOLLAND *Pliny* II. 250 The wringing pains in the bellie. **1653** R. SANDERS *Physiogn.* 188 A painfull wringing grief in the body after food. **1831** JAMES *Phil. Augustus* II. viii, One task..which, however wringing to my heart, must be completed. **1891** H. LYNCH *G. Meredith* 88 The wringing sorrows brought about by his own baseness.

b. Characterized by oppression or extortion.

1620 [see WRESTLING *ppl. a.* 2]. **1814** BYRON *Lara* II. viii, Many a wringing despot..Who work'd his wantonness in form of law.

c. Causing straining or stretching (of the fingers).

1676 MACE *Musick's Mon.* 41 Therefore were they constrain'd to extreme hard, cross, and wringing Stops.. upon the Finger-board.

†**wringle**, *sb. Sc.* [f. next.] (See quot.)

1808 JAMIESON, *Wringle*, a writhing motion.

†**wringle** ('rɪŋg(ə)l), *v. Obs.* Also 7 ringle. [Corresponds in sense 1 to Da. *vringle*, Sw. and Norw. *vringla*, to twist, entwine, and in sense 2 to Flem. *wringelen* to squirm, writhe. The precise source is not clear.]

1. *trans.* To entwine or twist together; to wreathe.

1572 BOSSEWELL *Armorie* II. 63 b, This Serpente I haue descried as wringled into a wreathe.

2. *intr.* To move sinuously; to writhe.

1596 [see next]. **1643** '*Powers to be resisted*' 12 A poore worme..will wringle away from the foot, and earth it selfe. **1648** HEXHAM II, *Ringen*, to Ringle, or to Wrestle. **1789** *Shepherd's Wedding* 12 (E.D.D.), She threw and she drew, she wringl'd and wrang.

Hence '**wringling** *ppl. a.*

1596 DAVIES *Orchestra* liii, I loue Meanders path;..In his indented course and wringling play He seemes to daunce a perfect cunning Hay.

wringle- ('rɪŋg(ə)l), the verb-stem used attrib. in **wringle-gut**, **-straw** *dial.*, †**-tail**: (see quots.).

1658 ROWLAND tr. *Moufet's Theat. Ins.* 937 There is another Fly..which Pennius cals *Curvicaudem* [= curved tail], very well in English a Wringle-tail, in regard that..he bends his tail towards him with his sting started. **1691** RAY *N. Co. Words* (ed. 2) 84 *Wringle-streas*, or *Straws*,..Windle-Straws. **1777** in *Eng. Dial. Dict.* s.v., *Wringle-gut*, one who frets his guts to fiddle-strings by twisting and turning his body. **1877** *Holderness Gloss.* 160 *Wringlesthreea*,..a coarse grass.

†**wringleather**, obs. erron. f. RINGLEADER.

1525 WARHAM in Ellis *Orig. Lett.* Ser. III. I. 366 Some of the chief wringleathars.

wringle-wrangle. *rare*⁻¹. [Reduplication of WRANGLE *sb.* with change of vowel as in *jingle-jangle*, *tingle-tangle*, etc.] Controversial argument; wordy disputation.

[Cf. **1832** LYTTON *Eugene A.* II. viii, They be so.. quarrelsome..; wringle, wrangle, wrongle, snap, growl, scratch.]

1882 BESANT *All Sorts* xlv, The House was not sitting, and there was no wringle-wrangle of debates to furnish material for the columns.

†'**wringly**, *adv. Obs.* [Cf. WRINGLE *v.* 1.] In a wrung or twisted manner; twistedly.

1582 STANYHURST *Æneis* (Arb.) 137 Three showrs wringlye wrythen glimring, and forceblye sowcing.

'**wring-staff**, **-stave.** *rare*⁻⁰. [Cf. WRING-BOLT, WRAIN-STAVE.] A staff for inserting in an eye of a ring-bolt.

1815 BURNEY *Dict. Marine, Wring-staves*..are strong pieces of wood used with the Wring-Bolts. [Hence in Crabb (1823) and some later Dicts.] **1884** *Imp. Dict.* s.v., *Wring-staff*;..called also Wrain-staff.

wrink, var. WRENK *sb. Obs.*

wrink (rɪŋk), *v.* ? *Obs.* [Cf. WRINKLE *v.* and ME. *forwrynkked* (FOR-¹ 8).] = WRINKLE *v.* 3 b.

1821 CLARE *Vill. Minstr.* II. 11 Grief and age had wrink'd her brow.

wrinkle ('rɪŋk(ə)l), *sb.*¹ Also 5–6 wryncle, -kle, -kel, -kul, -kyl(le, 6 wrynckle, wrinkel(l, -kyll, -ckel, 6–7 wrinc(k)le (6 rinkle, 7 rinckle, -el). [Of obscure origin; possibly a back-formation from WRINKLED *a.*

Somner's OE. '*wrincle*, ruga, a wrincle' is not otherwise known. Kilian's '*wrinckel*, ruga' is also uncertified, and is rendered suspicious by his citing the English word.]

I. †**1.** A sinuous or tortuous movement, formation, etc.; a winding or curving; a sinuosity. *Obs.*

1430–40 LYDG. *Bochas* I. 2683 An hous..Callid Laboryntus,..Ful of wrynkles. **1480** CAXTON *Trevisa's*

Higden (1482) 40 b, Laborintus . . is an hous . . wrought with . . windynges so diuersly by wonderful wayes and wrynclis, that [etc.]. **1513** Douglas *Æneid* v. v. 62 The eddir . . Lang wrinklis makis oft with hir body. *Ibid.* xii. viii. 69 Als feill wrynklis and turnis can scho mak As dois the swallow.

2. a. A crease, fold, or ridge caused by the folding, puckering, or contraction of a fabric, cloth, or other pliant substance. Occas. in fig. context. Also without article.

In quots. 1676, 1869 with allusion to sense 4 b.

a **1420** *Wycliffite Bible* Gen. xxxviii. 14 (MS. Cotton Claudius E ii), She took a roket cloþ wiþ many wrynclis. *c* **1440** *Promp. Parv.* 534/1 Wrynkyl, or plate yn clothe, . . *plica.* **1514** Barclay *Cyt. & Uplondyshman* (Percy Soc.) 1 Nor of his clothynge one wryncle stode a wrye. **1537** Latimer *Serm. bef. Convoc.* A iij b, These wordis are so spoken in parabole, and ar so wrapped in wrinkels. **1594** Carew *Huarte's Exam. Wits* xiii. 212 With their hosen hanging about their heels, ful of wrinckles. *Ibid.* xv. 312 He takes it at heart, to haue a wrinckle in his pumpe. **1617** Woodall *Surg. Mate* Wks. (1639) 150 That there be no wrinckles in the clouts applied. **1676** W. Hubbard *Happiness of People* 54 Cause . . for that virgin . . Church to condemn themselves for some spots or wrincles in their garment. **1758** Johnson *Idler* No. 16 ⁋2 His stockings [were] without a wrinkle. **1842** Loudon *Suburban Hort.* 175 The roll of canvass . . winds up and lets down without a single wrinkle. **1869** Mrs. Stowe *Oldtown Folks* v, Her Sunday bonnet was without spot, her Sunday gown without wrinkle.

fig. **1624** Heywood *Gunaik.* iv. 191 She so farre insinuated into the King's breast, that the wrinckles of all suggestions were cleared.

b. A slight narrow ridge or depression on a surface; a longitudinal mark; a corrugation.

1523 Fitzherb. *Husb.* §100 The wryncles on the houe. **1601** *2nd Pt. Return fr. Parnass.* iii. iv. 1409 One that . . admires the good wrinckle of a boote. **1677** N. Cox *Gentl. Recreat.* i. 126 The Wild-Goat[s] . . have Wreaths and Wrinkles on their Horns. **1683** Moxon *Mech. Exerc., Printing* xxii. ⁋1 He leaves no wrinckles in the turnings up [of the paper lining]. **1737** Bracken *Farriery Impr.* (1740) II. 71 Whether it [*sc.* the horny part of the hoof] be smooth and even, or . . in Wreathes or Wrinkles. **1742** H. Baker *Microsc.* (1743) 224 The little Wrinkles, Hollows, or Crevices of the Corn. **1838** T. Thomson *Chem. Org. Bodies* 850 Wrinkles arising from the desiccation of the tube. **1839** *Civil Eng. & Arch. Jrnl.* II. 154/1 When . . docked she did not show a wrinkle in her copper.

fig. and in fig. context. **1719–20** Swift *Stella's Birthday* 54 The Cracks and Wrinkles of your Mind. **1822** Hazlitt *Table-T.* Ser. ii. vi. (1869) 127 They cause a wrinkle in the clear and polished surface of their existence.

c. *transf.* of physiographical features.

1805 Wordsw. *Prelude* viii. 583 Here is shadowed forth From the projections, wrinkles, cavities, A variegated landscape. **1849** Cupples *Green Hand* xiv, Every point and wrinkle in the headland. **1900** Le Gallienne *Trav.* xv. 234 Northleach, lying in 'a wrinkle' of the still dreary hills.

3. a. A small fold or crease of the skin, esp. due to age, care, displeasure, etc.

In frequent use from *c* 1590.

c **1425** *Cursor M.* 18840 (Trin.), His forhede feir wemles in siȝt wiþouten wrynkul [*earlier MSS.* runkel, -il, ronclis] hit was sliȝt. **1530** Palsgr. 290/2 Wrinkell in ones face, *raiere.* **1586–90** Greene *Metam.* Wks. (Grosart) IX. 30 Venus frowned on the smith with a rinkle on her forhead. **1617** Moryson *Itin.* iii. 169 Fier . . causeth wrinckles and spots on their bodies. **1673** [R. Leigh] *Transp. Reh.* 52 There are many wrinckles and chaps we will not fill up with the paint of art. *c* **1788** W. Blake *Tiriel* 108 To count the wrinkles in thy face. **1837** R. M. Bird *Nick of the Woods* III. 71 Though the wrinkles of forty winters furrowed deeply in his brows. **1877** Black *Green Past.* ii, The calm and thoughtful forehead that had as yet no wrinkle of age or care.

b. *transf.*, *fig.* and in fig. context. *spec.* a minor difficulty or irregularity; a snag; freq. in phr. ***to iron out the wrinkles.***

a **1586** Sidney *Arcadia* i. 1, Their bloud had (as it were) filled the wrinckles of the seas visage. **1643** Caryl *Expos. Job* I. 519 A perfect soul-state, and a perfect state of body, hath no wrinkle in it. **1692** Bentley *Boyle Lect.* 22 No wrinkles in the face, no gray hairs on the head of eternity! **1818** Byron *Ch. Har.* iv. clxxxii, Roll on, thou . . Ocean! . . Time writes no wrinkle on thine azure brow. **1855** *Whitby Gloss.* 199 *Wreeangs*, . . wrinkles of dust or dirt upon the skin. **1865** Carlyle *Fredk. Gt.* xx. v, [They] have contributed a wrinkle of human Fun to the earnest face of Life. **1966** D. F. Jones *Colossus* i. 15 As a project it's practically finished, we can't find any more wrinkles to iron out; we've checked and checked again. **1975** *Economist* 22 Feb. 92 The way for the east Europeans to reach western markets without accumulating further huge trade deficits is to import skills which can be exported in hardware. This also enables them to iron out wrinkles in their own system without having to embark on risky economic reforms. **1979** *Guardian* 30 Aug. 3/6 The BBC wanted to make certain advances in technical practices . . . Wrinkles still remained. **1984** *New Yorker* 14 May 43 Willa had sold her story to Universal Pictures and was in California ironing out some wrinkles in the deal.

c. A ripple or ruffle on the surface of water; a wavelet. Chiefly *poet.*

1633 P. Fletcher *Purple Isl.* v. xlvii, As when a stone . . Prints in the angry stream a wrinkle round. **1665** Sir T. Herbert *Trav.* (1677) 39 The Sea . . was as smooth as Glass, not the least curl or wrinkle discernable. **1821** Clare *Vill. Minstrel* II. 180 Nor faintest wrinkles o'er the waters creep. **1878** Browning *La Saisiaz* 17 Where the blue lake's wrinkle marks the river's inrush pale.

4. *fig.* A moral stain or blemish.

Freq. coupled (as in next) with *spot*, after Eph. v. 27.

a **1400** *Pauline Ep.* (Powell) Eph. v. 27 þe kyrke . . not hafande a spot or a wrynkylle. **1408** *Wycliffite Bible* Eph. v. 27 (MS. Fairfax 2), [That] þe chirche . . hadde noo wem ne ryueling eþer wrynkele. **1530** R. Whytford *Werke for Householders* A ij, Our owne conscyence . . shall clerely confesse al our hole lyfe, and euery wryncle & parte therof. **1569** Roest tr. *J. van der Noot's Theat.* 97 A glorious Church, without any spot or wrinckle. **1643** Caryl *Expos. Job* I. 519 Poverty is the wrinkle of riches, and disgrace is the wrinkle of honour. *Ibid.*, In the state of glory . . we shall not have . . one spot or one wrinkle.

b. Without article; chiefly in ***without (spot or) wrinkle.***

1526 Tindale *Eph.* v. 27 A glorious congregacion with oute spot or wrynckle. [Hence in later versions.] **1643** Caryl *Expos. Job* I. 519 Believers have now a righteousness in Christ without spot or wrinkle. **1651** N. Bacon *Disc. Govt. Eng.* ii. xxvii. 205 Henry . . continued in that condition eighteen years without wrinkle of Fame. **1675** T. Brooks *Gold. Key* 325 In this Robe of Righteousness . . we are without spot or wrinkle.

5. *Anat.*, *Zool.*, *Bot.* = ruga.

1545 Raynald *Byrth Mankynde* 11 Though that the matrix . . be full of ryuelles or wrinkles. **1577** B. Googe *Heresbach's Husb.* iii. (1586) 117 The skinne of their [*sc.* quadrupeds'] jawes . . , if it lie in wrinkles, . . sheweth he is olde. **1639** T. de Gray *Expert Farrier* 352 A wrinckle . . in the shoulder or in any other joynt. **1657** Tomlinson *Renou's Disp.* 275 It is a . . root, which by exsiccation hath contracted wrinkles and lineations. **1732** Monro *Anat.* 12 When they [*sc. laminæ*] make the first Turn or Wrinkle, he stiles them *Cancelli corrugati.* **1774** Goldsmith *Nat. Hist.* (1776) IV. 214 The muzzle [of the mandril] is . . strongly marked with wrinkles. **1775** [see ruga]. **1842** A. Combe *Physiol. Digestion* (ed. 4) 176 The numerous folds or wrinkles which line the inner surface of the duodenum. **1849** Cupples *Green Hand* xiii, Like the wrinkles on a nutmeg.

6. A section of a calcining furnace.

1884 C. G. W. Lock *Workshop Receipts* Ser. iii. 448 The ore . . is there thrust out of the furnace into the 'wrinkle'.

II. †**7.** A crooked or tortuous action; a crafty device; a trick or wile. *Obs.*

1402 in *Pol. Poems* (Rolls) II. 45 A! for-writhen serpent, thi wyles ben aspied, with a thousand wrynkels thou vexed many soules. **1547** Latimer in Foxe *A. & M.* (1563) 1350/2 When you note me to be so muche abused by so ignorante a manne, so simple, so playne, and so farre without all wrincles. *c* **1550** *Dice-Play* B v b, Euery wrynkel they haue to couer and worke disceit with al. **1579** Lyly *Euphues* (Arb.) 54 Euery wile and . . euery wrinkle of womens disposition.

8. *colloq.* **a.** A clever or adroit expedient or trick; a happy device; a 'dodge'. Esp. (*U.S.*) in phr. ***a new wrinkle.***

Freq. from *c* 1840 in phr. ***to put one up to a wrinkle*** (***or two***).

Perh. a development from the following, or some similar piece of repartee:

1731–8 Swift *Polite Conv.* i. 74 They say, mocking is catching. *Miss.* I never heard that. *Nev.* Why, then, . . you have a wrinkle more than ever you had before.

1817 Lady Granville *Lett.* (1894) I. 111 He could put her up to a wrinkle or two. **1848** *Punch* July 19 He . . knows 'a wrinkle' of everything. **1875** 'S. Beauchamp' *N. Hamilton* II. 155 'You surely don't mean to say you are going to fish with blue-bottles?' 'Yes, I do . . . It's a wrinkle.' **1882** *Cassell's Bk. Sports* 40 Such wrinkles experience alone will teach. **1941** W. C. Handy *Father of Blues* iv. 35 In addition to twirling their batons, they added the new wrinkle of tossing them back and forth to each other as they marched. **1969** *Wall St. Jrnl.* 12 Aug. 3/3 The idea for the briefings, a new wrinkle in selling Presidential policy, came from White House communications director Herbert Klein. **1978** *New York* 3 Apr. 37/3 In his budget proposals, the president came up with an investment tax credit with a new wrinkle: If passed by Congress, it will apply to structures as well as to capital equipment. **1984** *Gainesville* (Florida) *Sun* 29 Mar. 4A (*cartoon*) This guy Chernenko should put a new wrinkle in Russian politics.

transf. **1832** Col. Hawker *Diary* (1893) II. 44, I was . . among the workmen, getting some *ne plus ultra* wrinkles done for the great gun, covers, etc.

b. A piece or item of useful information, knowledge, or advice; a helpful or valuable hint; a 'tip'.

1818 *Sporting Mag.* II. 232 On that most auspicious day, I acquired two additional wrinkles. **1862** Ld. W. Lennox *Recreat. Sportsm.* I. 277 While upon the subject of yachting, we would venture to offer . . a 'wrinkle' as to coppering them. **1894** Hall Caine *Manxman* vi. xii. 402 [That] news . . hasn't got into the papers yet, but I've had the official wrinkle.

9. *Cant.* An untruth, fib, lie.

1812 J. H. Vaux *Flash Dict.*, *Wrinkle*, an untruth.

III. 10. *attrib.* and *Comb.*, as ***wrinkle-filling***, †***-wizard***; ***wrinkle-coated***, ***-faced***, ***-free***, †***fronted***, ***-furrowed***, ***-proof***, ***-resistant***, ***-scaled*** adjs.; ***wrinkle maker***; **wrinkle ridge** *Astr.*, one of the long, irregular ridges that can be seen on the maria of the moon and Mars.

1784 Twamley *Dairying* 55 Curdly or wrinkle-coated Cheese. **1591** Sylvester *Du Bartas* i. iv. 380 Ingenious Saturn, . . bald, hoary, wrinkle-faced. **1907** J. London *Before Adam* xii, A little . . fellow, wrinkle-faced. **1613** Dekker *Devils Last Will* Wks. (Grosart) III. 351 The Founder and Vpholder of Paintings, . . Wrinkle-fillings, and Botchings vp of old . . Faces. **1963** *New Yorker* 8 June 74 (Advt.), Stay neat and wrinkle-free all day. **1978** *Detroit Free Press* 16 Apr. 9A (Advt.), Sheets in wrinkle-free and easy-care cotton/polyester percale. **1567** Turberv. *Epit.*, etc. 70 Was neuer Bull so fell with wrinckle fronted face. **1744** Akenside *Pleas. Imag.* iii. 129 A female old and gray, With . . wrinkle-furrow'd brow. **1836** E. Howard *R. Reefer* lxvii, Thought is a sad wrinkle maker. **1957** *Economist* 31 Aug. 685/2 The steady introduction of new fibres . . new chemicals . . to render cloth . . wrinkle-proof. **1957** M. B. Picken *Fashion Dict.* 382/2 Wrinkle-resistant. **1969** *Sears Catal.* Spring/Summer 20 Perma Prest for great no-iron, wrinkle-resistant performance. **1944** J. E. Spurr *Geol. applied to Selenology* I. viii. 60 The wrinkle-ridges are distinct from faults in appearance . . . The ridges on the surface of the mare are not straight; they are curving, branching, imbricating, plaited. **1971** I. G. Gass et al. *Understanding Earth* vii. 106 (*caption*) The wrinkle ridges on the surface of Mare Tranquilitatis. **1978** *Sci. Amer.* Mar. 81/1 The Viking orbiter photographs show that much of the surface of Mars retains crisp topographic detail: lava flows, wrinkle ridges and crater ejecta stand out in sharp relief. **1829** Loudon *Encycl. Plants* (1836) 716 *Podolepis rugata*, wrinkle-scaled Podolepis. **1594** Nashe *Terrors of Night* F j b, So Socrates . . was censured by a wrinckle-wyzard.

Hence **'wrinkleful** *a.*, full of wrinkles or creases; **'wrinklet**, a small wrinkle.

1608 Sylvester *Du Bartas* ii. iv. *Decay* 121 With her best complexions, She mends her faces wrinklefull defections. **1848** Bailey *Festus* (ed. 3) 224 The lake smoothed down Each shining wrinklet.

wrinkle ('rɪŋk(ə)l), *sb.*[2] Also 7 **wrinckle.** Now *s.w. dial.* and *local U.S.* [Alteration of winkle *sb.*, after prec.] The periwinkle or whelk. Also *transf.*

1589 Rider *Bibl. Scholast.* 1724 A walke, or wrinkle, *turbo.* **1602** Carew *Cornwall* 30 b, Wrinckles, . . and Muscles, are gathered by hand upon the rockes. **1616** W. Browne *Brit. Past.* ii. i. 454 Oysters and small Wrinckles. **1750** Heath *Acc. Isl. Scilly* 46 Of Shell-fish are denominated . . Shrimps, Limpets, Wrinkles. **1795** Wolcot (P. Pindar) *Royal Tour* Proem. 24 She swears I'm . . Rather a wrinkle, limpet, paltry muscle. *a* **1870** J. Couch *Polperro* (1871) 153 A journey to the sea-coast . . to pick 'wrinkles'. **1880–2** in Cornwall glossaries.

wrinkle ('rɪŋk(ə)l), *v.* Forms: 5–6 **wrynkle,** 6 **wrynkel, wrynckle,** 6 **wrinkel(l, -kill, wrinkyl,** 6–7 **wrincle,** 6–8 **wrinckle;** 6– **wrinkle** (7 **wringkle).** [app. a back-formation from wrinkled *a.* or wrinkling *vbl. sb.*

Somner's OE. '*wrinclian*, rugare, crispare, . . to wrinkle' occurs in no known text, and was prob. inferred from *ȝewrinclod.* Kilian's *wrinckelen* 'rugare' is also uncertified and rendered suspicious by his citation of the English word.]

1. *intr.* To suffer or undergo contraction or puckering into wrinkles or small folds; to become corrugated. Also with †*together*, *up.*

1528 Paynell *Salerne's Regim.* C iij, This crampe . . wherby the membre is made shorte and great, and wrynkelynge to gether as lether. **1530** Palsgr. 785/2, I wrinkell, as a kercher or a garment dothe, *Je plionne.* **1594** Plat *Jewell-ho.* ii. (1596) 47 If yᵉ kernel do wrinkle or run together. **1719** London & Wise *Compl. Gard.* 90 [This] Apple . . is apt to wrinkle and wither. **1788** G. Parker & Stalker *Japaning* 30 Suffer [your print] . . not to cockle, wrinkle, or rise up in little bladders. **1825** T. Hook *Sayings* Ser. ii. I. 62 The neckcloth, after four vain attempts, wrinkled round his neck in folds. **1860** Tyndall *Glac.* i. 147 The ice . . seemed to wrinkle up in obedience to the pressure.

transf. **1653** Walton *Angler* v. 127 If he sees the water but wrinkle or move in one of these dead holes. **1864** Buchanan *Undertones, Proteus* iii, A trackless Ocean wrinkling tempest-wing'd.

b. Of persons, the face, etc.: To become creased or puckered; to assume or undergo marking with wrinkles, creases, or lines; to crease.

1530 Palsgr. 785/2 Your face begynneth to wrinkell. **1606** Marston *Parasit.* ii. C 3, What are you fleering at? ther's some weakenes in your brother you wrinkle at thus. **1684** *Contempl. St. Man* i. iv. (1699) 35 If he reach old Age . . his Face wrinkles. **1706** *Lond. Gaz.* No. 4252/4 When he Smiles both corners of his Mouth wrinkle. **1711** Addison *Spect.* No. 89 ⁋5 The finest Skin wrinkles in a few Years. **1819** Keats *Fall of Hyperion* i. 225 This old image here, Whose carved features wrinkled as he fell. **1890** *Nature* 20 Feb. 378 Its body began to wrinkle and to plump up.

c. To contract *into* smiles, etc., by puckering.

1853 J. B. Mozley *Lett.* (1885) 221 His face wrinkles into countless smiles. **1854** R. S. Surtees *Handley Cr.* x, Doleful's face wrinkled into half its usual size with delight.

†**2.** To move sinuously; to wriggle. *Obs.*

1565 Cooper *Thesaurus*, *Piscis tortilis*, a fish that writheth and wrinkleth. **1653** [see wrinkling *ppl. a.* 3].

3. *trans.* To form or cause corrugations, wrinkles, or folds in or on (a surface, etc.); to corrugate. Occas. in fig. context. Also with *over.*

1611 Cotgr., *Fronser*, to . . wrinkle, crumple, frumple. **1670** Milton *Hist. Eng.* Wks. 1851 V. 178 Neither do I care to wrincle the smoothness of History with rugged names of places unknown. **1766** *Compl. Farmer* s.v. *Madder*, Too hasty a drying wrinkles and splits the bark. **1796** Coleridge *To Young Friend* 38 A beauteous spring . . scarce wrinkled by the gale! **1818** Shelley *Rosal. & Helen* 542 The flood of cloud, Which sunrise from its eastern caves Drives, wrinkling into golden waves. **1820** —— *Prometh. Unb.* ii. i. 137 A wind swept forth wrinkling the Earth with frost. *a* **1825** Forby *Voc. E. Anglia*, *Crinkle*, . . to wrinkle, twist, plait, or rumple irregularly. *a* **1856** T. Seddon in *Mem. & Lett.* (1858) 205 A wilderness of mountain tops, in some places . . wrinkled over with ravines.

absol. **1543** Traheron *Vigo's Chirurg.* ii. 75 b, This pouldre . . draweth together the loosed parte, it dryeth, riueleth, or wrynkleth.

b. To contract or draw (the skin, countenance, etc.) into creases or wrinkles; to pucker, crease. Also *refl.*

1566 Painter *Pal. Pleas.* (1569) I. F iv, That the swelling of their body, might not irrugate and wrinckle their faces. **1602** *2nd Pt. Return Parnass.* iii. iii. 1324 My master will . . looke on the title and wrinckle his browe. *a* **1661** Holyday *Persius* (1673) 298 He . . ne're wrinkled his nose. **1721** Bailey, *Frown*, to . . wrinkle the Forehead. **1798** Southey *Surg. Warning* vi, He wrinkled his black eye-brow. **1858** Carlyle *Fredk. Gt.* v. vii, As if the face of the Sphynx were to wrinkle itself in laughter. **1865** Dickens *Mut. Fr.* iii. xv, Wrinkling his face into a very map of curves and corners.

fig. and in fig. context. **1606** Shaks. *Tr. & Cr.* ii. ii. 79 A Grecian Queen, whose youth & freshnesse Wrinkles Apolloes. **1647** T. Calvert *Heart Salve* To Rdr. 3 The other carries with it a decor and beautie that no old age . . can wrinkle or furrow with uncomelinesse. **1667** MILTON *P.L.* XI. 839 A keen North-winde..Wrinkl'd the face of Deluge, as decai'd. **1789** BURNEY *Hist. Mus.* III. 463 What is the secular Music that thirty years have not wrinkled, withered, and rendered superannuated! **1848** BAILEY *Festus* (ed. 3) 242 One..Whose heart was wrinkled long before his brow?

absol. c **1779** CRABBE *Midnight* 438 The Brow of State, On which Distraction..helps the Scythe of Time to wrinkle there.

c. With *up*.

?*c* **1590** *Sir T. More* III. ii. 205 For know,..Mirth wrinckls vpp my face. **1700** T. BROWN *Amusem. Ser. & Com.* 3 Wrinkling up his nostrils. **1746** FRANCIS tr. *Horace, Epist.* I. v. 33 That no foul Linen wrinkle up the Nose. **1819** SHELLEY *Cenci* I. iii. 38, I fear that wicked laughter round his eye, Which wrinkles up the skin even to the hair. **1865** SWINBURNE *Chastelard* V. ii. 186 Sad at her mouth a little, with drawn cheeks And eyelids wrinkled up.

d. To screw up (the eyes). Also with *up*.

1840 DICKENS *Old C. Shop* vi. Quilp, wrinkling up his eyes and luring her towards him with his bent forefinger. **1901** W. R. H. TROWBRIDGE *Lett. to Eliz.* x. 43 Blanche wrinkled her eyes at him in the prettiest way.

4. To manifest (something) in or by facial wrinkles. Also *refl.*

a **1586** SIDNEY *Arcadia* II. xix, Some ill-favoured cheerefulnesse..began to wrinckle it selfe in his face. **1852** THACKERAY *Esmond* II. xiii, Only crows' feet were wrinkled round them [*sc.* eyes]—marks of black old Time.

5. *intr. Cant.* (See quot.)

1812 J. H. VAUX *Flash Dict.*, *Wrinkle*, to lie, or utter a falsehood.

Hence **'wrinkler**. *Cant.* (See quot.)

1812 J. H. VAUX *Flash Dict.*, *Wrinkler*, a person prone to lying; such a character is called also a *gully*.

wrinkled ('rɪŋk(ə)ld), *a.* [f. WRINKLE *sb.*[1] + -ED[2], or in early use representing the rare OE. ppl. form *ȝewrinclod* winding (of a ditch), serrated: cf. WRINKLE *v.*]

†**1.** Formed or disposed in convolutions, sinuosities, or windings; twisted, curled, coiled. *Obs.*

c **1403** LYDG. *Temple Glas* 84 þe hous, That was forwrynkked [*v.r.* so wrynkled] bi craft of Dedalus. *c* **1407** —— *Reson & Sens.* 3607 The house of Dedalus..is so wrynkled to and froo That man not, how he shal goo. **1412–20** —— *Chron. Troy* II. 2512 þe serpent..Whiche wrinkled is, as ȝe may beholde, Vp-on þe ȝerde [= Mercury's wand]. **1513** DOUGLAS *Æneid* V. x. 79 The hous..Hait Laborynthus, with mony went and streit, Had wrinkillit wallis. *Ibid.* VI. i. 60 Laborinthus..Full of wrinkillit vnreturnable dissait. **1578** LYTE *Dodoens* 554 The fourth kind of red cole is called..in Englishe Wrinckled or ruffed Cole. **1587** MASCALL *Bk. Cattell* III. (1596) 283 The wrinckled tailes of hogs.

2. Having, distinguished by, or formed into wrinkles, corrugations, or creases; contracted or puckered into small furrows and ridges; corrugated; also, pleated.

1523 FITZHERB. *Husb.* §34 Peeke wheate..oft tymes..is flyntered, that is to saye, small corne wrynkeled and dryed. **1530** PALSGR. 785/2 Where have you ben, your kercher is wrinkled. **1567** MAPLET *Gr. Forest* 31 b, The Apple tree is..of wrinckled barck. **1612** *Two Noble K.* I. i. 122 Like wrinckled peobles in a glassie streame. **1617** MORYSON *Itin.* III. 160 The wild Irish used to weare 30 or 40 elles [of linen cloth] in a shirt, al gathered and wrinckled. **1711** ADDISON *Spect.* No. 129 ¶5 Every Ribbon was wrinkled, and every Part of her Garments in Curl. **1753** *Chambers' Cycl. Suppl.* s.v. *Leaf*, So as to give upon the whole [leaf] a wrinkled surface. **1841** *Penny Cycl.* XX. 461/2 The smooth and polished enamel..[of the tooth] presents a finely wrinkled appearance. **1861** HOLLAND *Less. Life* v. 70 Objects..distorted by reaching the eye through wrinkled window-glass. **1890** *Science-Gossip* XXVI. 8/1 A large, wrinkled lump of chalk.

fig. **1599** B. JONSON *Ev. Man out of Hum.* v. vii, The wrinckled fortunes of this poore spinster. **1643** CARYL *Expos. Job* I. 1519 His wealth and honour were extreamly wrinkled.

b. *poet.* Formed by, due to, swelling or surging.

c **1611** CHAPMAN *Iliad* VII. 49 Fresh horror..driven through the wrinkled waves By rising Zephyr. **1616** J. LANE *Contn. Sqr.'s T.* 193 Now Titan, in th'oriental, wrinckled wave, had filld his lavor.

3. Of persons, the face, etc.: Marked with small folds, wrinkles, or furrows; creased, lined, furrowed.

a **1529** SKELTON *El. Rumminge* 17 Her face..Woundersly wrynkled. **1596** SHAKS. *Merch. V.* IV. i. 270 To view with..wrinkled brow An age of pouerty. **1616** R. C. *Times' Whistle*, etc. (1871) 123, I am..crabbed, wringkled, olde. **1651** BARKSDALE *Nympha Lib.* II. ix. 32 With wrinckled face, thou cry'st out, Vanitie! *a* **1683** OLDHAM *Rem.* (1684) 114 An old wrinkled Baboon. **1718** POPE *Iliad* XV. 112 On her wrinkled front..Sat steadfast care. **1786** *Beckford's Vathek* (1883) 93 A wrinkled old eunuch. **1808** SCOTT *Marm.* VI. xi, His large and wrinkled hand. **1860** EMERSON *Cond. Life, Beauty*, Character gives splendour to youth, and awe to wrinkled skin.

transf. **1603** SHAKS. *Meas. for M.* I. iii. 5 A purpose More graue, and wrinkled, then the aimes..Of burning youth. **1817** SHELLEY *Rev. Islam* II. xxxiii, Old age, with its gray hair, And wrinkled legends of unworthy things. **1817** WORDSW. *Pass of Kirkstone* 17 Wrinkled Egyptian monument; Green moss-grown tower.

b. *fig.* and in fig. context.

1594 SHAKS. *Rich. III*, I. i. 9 Grim-visag'd Warre, hath smooth'd his wrinkled Front. **1599** B. JONSON *Ev. Man out of Hum.* I. iii. Dj, Or lies he hid Within the wrinckled bosome of the world? **1644** MILTON *Areop.* (Arb.) 71 Casting off the old and wrincl'd skin of corruption to..wax young again. **1660** R. COKE *Power & Subj.* Pref. 2 The frowns of perverse and wrinckled fortune. **1670** CLARENDON *Ess.* Tracts (1727) 197 The wrinkled face of antiquity. **1821** SHELLEY *Hellas* 139 The hoary mountains and the wrinkled ocean Seem younger still than he. **1871** E. F. BURR *Ad Fidem* xvi. 351 The fresh present, and wrinkled antiquity.

c. Marked or characterized by wrinkles.

1576 FLEMING *Panopl. Epist.* 154, I am entred into my wrinkled and withered age. **1581** A. HALL *Iliad* IV. 69 After our vnbrideled youth coms sage and wrinckled yeares. **1607** A. BREWER *Lingua* IV. ii, These two my lord Comedus and Tragedus,..This grave.., That light and quick, with wrinkled laughter painted. **1634** MILTON *Comus* 871 Listen and appear to us.., By hoary Nereus wrincled look. **1753** *Adventurer* No. 74, The lectures of wrinkled wisdom. **1792** BURNS '*In Simmer when*' ii, A dame in wrinkled eild.

4. *Bot., Anat., Zool.* Marked by rugæ or wrinkles; rugose, corrugated.

1563 HYLL *Art Garden.* (1574) 117 Those Nauews be the better, which be long and in a manner wrinckled. **1577** B. GOOGE *Heresbach's Husb.* IV. 167 The headdes and the neckes of [peahens]..couered with a wrinckled skinne. **1613** PURCHAS *Pilgrimage* (1614) 472 The skinne vpon the vpper part of this beast, is all wrinckled. **1638** JUNIUS *Paint. Ancients* 267 Their [*sc.* horses'] wrinkled and round nostrills. **1727** BAILEY, *Rugosus*,..(in Botan. Writers,) wrinkled. **1796** WITHERING *Brit. Plants* (ed. 3) II. 49 Leaves on leaf-stalks,..wrinkled and shining. **1854** MURCHISON *Siluria* ix. 233 Wrinkled tubes of these [annelids]. **1855** KINGSLEY *Glaucus* 83 The Spoonworm..with a strange scalloped and wrinkled proboscis. **1873** DAWSON *Earth & Man* iv. 65 The rugose or wrinkled corals.

b. In specific names (see quots.).

1681 GREW *Musæum* I. 127 The Wrinkled-Snail. *Cochlea rugosa.* **1770** PENNANT *Brit. Zool.* (1777) IV. 95 Wrinkled V[enus] with thick shells, marked with rugose concentric *striæ*. **1800** SHAW *Gen. Zool.* I. 33 Wrinkled Baboon,..with ..large blood-red wrinkled callosities behind. **1801** PENNANT *Tour* 114 *Salix reticulata*, or Wrinkled Willow. **1802** SHAW *Gen. Zool.* III. 28 Wrinkled Tortoise, *Testudo rugosa*...Tortoise with black wrinkled shell. *c* **1880** *Cassell's Nat. Hist.* III. 353 A curious envelope..thrown by a Wrinkled Hornbill (*Anorrhinus corrugatus*).

5. *Comb.*, as ***wrinkled-old***, ***-leaved***, ***-visaged***.

1592 SHAKS. *Ven. & Ad.* 133 Were I hard-favour'd, foul, or wrinkled-old. **1822** *Hortus Anglicus* II. 195 G[*eranium*] *Lividum*. Wrinkled-leaved Crane's Bill. **1838** HAWTHORNE *Amer. Note-bks.* (1868) I. 171 A grey,..wrinkled-visaged figure.

Hence **'wrinkledness**.

1552 HULOET, Wrinckelenesse [*sic*], or ruggednes of the skynne, *scabredo*. **1611** COTGR. s.v. *Rugosité*. **1727** BAILEY (vol. II), *Tortness*,..writhenness, wrinkledness. **1889** E. W. BENSON in *Life* (1899) II. 262 The Shah has a..nearness and wrinkledness of eyes.

'wrinkled, *ppl. a.* [f. WRINKLE *v.*] Subjected to wrinkling. In quot. with *up*.

1859 MEREDITH *R. Feverel* xxiii, Putting the mouth of the pipe to his wrinkled-up temples.

'wrinkleless, *a.* Also 8 wrinkless. [f. WRINKLE *sb.*[1] + -LESS.] Destitute of or free from wrinkles.

1793 HOLCROFT tr. *Lavater's Physiog.* xliv. 225 The wrinkless, compressed, yet open forehead. **1880** 'MARK TWAIN' *Tramp Abr.* xxvii. 245 He wore..wrinkleless kids. **1881** C. GIBBON *Heart's Problem* iii, His sallow and almost wrinkleless face.

wrinkling ('rɪŋklɪŋ), *vbl. sb.* [f. the stem of OE. *ȝewrinclod* (see WRINKLED *a.*) + -ING[1].]

†**1.** A twisting or coiling; a sinuosity. *Obs.*

1387 TREVISA *Higden* I. 9 As laborintus..haþ many..wyndynges and wrynkelynges, þat wil nouȝt be vnwarled. **1535** *Trevisa's Barth. De P.R.* XVII. clxxiii, A good smellynge smoke,..full meuable, and tornynge, and crokyd with many bendynges and wrynklynges.

2. The action of creasing, puckering, or contracting into wrinkles; the fact of becoming corrugated or rivelled.

1528 PAYNELL *Salerne's Regim.* Ciij, Retraction and wrynkelynge together of the veynes. **1594** T. B. *La Primaud. Fr. Acad.* II. 346 A certaine contraction and wrinckling..of the orifice. **1617** MORYSON *Itin.* III. 173 The Curtizans make all the forepart of their gownes in like manner open, to avoid wrinckling. **1693** tr. *Blancard's Phys. Dict.* (ed. 2) 111/2 The wrinkling of the lower part of the Vagina. **1698** *Phil. Trans.* XX. 174 If the Fly had been Dead for some while..I could have observed none of this Wrinkling. **1859** *Habits of Gd. Society* iii. 149 A peculiar wrinkling [of the trousers] from the foot to the knee. **1885** *Riverside Nat. Hist.* (1888) II. 268 [The] degree of wrinkling of the back of the mesothorax. **1888** *Cornh. Mag.* Jan. 40 Wrinklings of the crust..gave rise at first to baby mountain ranges.

transf. **1875** BROWNING *Aristoph. Apol.* 120 The olive-leaves curl, violets crisp and close Like a nymph's wrinkling at the bath's first splash.

attrib. **1875** KNIGHT *Dict. Mech.* 2822 *Wrinkling-machine*, ..one to wrinkle transversely the upper leathers of boots and shoes.

3. *concr.* A series or collection of wrinkles; a puckered surface, formation, etc.

1495 *Trevisa's Barth. De P.R.* v. lxiii. (W. de W.) l viij, Yᵉ fatnes..stretchyth oute the wrynkelynge of the skynne. **1579** LANGHAM *Gard. Health* 379 The shriueled wrincklings yᵗ appeare on womens bellies after their deliuerance. **1628** FOLKINGHAM *Panala Med.* 66 It clenses the Ventricle from ..Crudities sticking to its rugosities and wrinklings. **1857** P. P. CARPENTER *Cat. Mazatlan Shells* 225 The first whirl..is characterized by extremely minute wrinkling over the whole surface, only discernible..when quite fresh. **1905** H. G. WELLS *Kipps* III. iii. §6 Such wrinkling of brow and mouth as only an experienced actor can produce.

b. *spec.* (See quot.)

1894 *Amer. Dict. Printing* 588/1 *Wrinkling*, an uneven surface in a book, caused by not being properly backed or pressed, or occasioned by dampness.

'wrinkling, *ppl. a.* [f. as prec. + -ING[2].]

1. Causing or forming creases or wrinkles.

1601 [? MARSTON] *Pasquil & Kath.* II. 69 The wrinkling print of Time err'd when it seal'd my forehead vp with age. **1756** MASON *Odes* 16 To thee, whose..polish'd brow The wrinkling hand of Sorrow spares. **1820** SHELLEY *Prometh. Unb.* I. i. 62 Ye icy Springs, stagnant with wrinkling frost. **1834** AINSWORTH *Rookwood* I. i, A wrinkling smile crossed the sexton's brow. **1851** MRS. BROWNING *Casa Guidi Wind.* II. 49 We..took thy wrinkling cares For ruffling hopes, and called thee weak.

2. Undergoing marking with, characterized by, wrinkles or creases.

1791 E. DARWIN *Bot. Gard.* I. 113 Glad Echo..Her wrinkling founts with soft vibration shakes. **1820** KEATS *Hyperion* I. 100 This wrinkling brow, Naked and bare of its great diadem. **1839** BAILEY *Festus* 27 The wrinkling stalk of Time. **1881** CABLE *Mme. Delphine* iv. 13 Furniture..carved just enough to give the notion of wrinkling pleasantry.

†**3.** Wriggling, writhing. *Obs. rare*$^{-1}$.

1653 LAUSON *Dennys' Secr. Angling* 21 There be divers wayes to catch the wrinkling Eele.

†**'wrinklingly**, *adv. Obs. rare.* [f. as WRINKLING *vbl. sb.* + -ING[2] + -LY[2].] In a tortuous or turning manner; sinuously.

1387 TREVISA *Higden* I. xxx. (MS. Tiberius D. VII) fol. 29 Laborintus ys an hous..wiþ turnynges & wyndynges so dyuerslych & so wrynklynglych [*Rolls ed.* I. 313: wrynkyngliche] ywroȝt [etc.]. **1615** CROOKE *Body of Man* III. 157 In olde women..sometimes,..they [*sc.* breasts] are knit wrink[l]ingly vpward.

wrinkly ('rɪŋklɪ), *a.* and *sb.* [f. WRINKLE *sb.* + -Y[1].]

A. *adj.* Full of, marked with, wrinkles; creased; puckered; crumpled.

1573 TWYNE *Æneid* x. Dd iv b, Him Tryton..blew with whelked shell, Whose wrinckly wreathed flue, did fearful shril in seas outyell. **1687** A. LOVELL tr. *Thevenot's Trav.* II. 117 The Fruit being ripe is wrinkly. **1742** SHENSTONE *School-mistr.* xxix, Sour'd by age,..he..furls his wrinkly front. **1793** HOLCROFT tr. *Lavater's Physiog.* vii. 46 Foreheads..which are wrinkly, short and shining. **1854** R. S. SURTEES *Handley Cr.* lxxv, The Captain older and more wrinkly than she expected. **1882** SLADEN in *Jrnl. Linn. Soc.* XVI. 197 The whole membrane becomes very thick and wrinkly.

transf. **1872** GEO. ELIOT *Middlem.* xxxii, Mrs. Waule..giving occasional dry wrinkly indications of crying.

B. *sb.* Also **wrinklie**. An old or middle-aged person. *slang.*

1972 A. BIRCHALL *Living in Landscape* 51 (*heading*) What do we do with the Wrinklies? **1976** *Times* 31 Aug. 10/8 A Henley reader..says that her teenage daughter reserves 'wrinklie' for the 60-year-old generation. The reader and her husband..are known as 'oldies'. **1980** *Times* 28 Oct. 12/6 It's pointless to go on a CND march. They're all wrinklies. **1982** BARR & YORK *Official Sloane Ranger Hankbk.* 159/3 *Wrinkly* n., middle-aged Sloane—between 40 and 50. **1983** *Church Times* 11 Mar. 13/2, I am a wrinkly whose monthly cheque from the Church Commissioners is labelled 'Diocesan Dignitary'.

wrinse, erron. f. RINSE *v.*

1584 B. R. tr. *Herodotus* I. 63 b, They wash and wrinse themselues very cleane.

wrisled, obs. f. WRIZZLED *a.*

wrisoun(e, obs. Sc. ff. ORISON.

wrist (rɪst). Forms: α. 1– **wrist**, 5–6 **wriste**, 4–5 **wryste**, 5–6 **wryst**; 4 **virste**, 5 **wirste**, 5–6 **wyrste**, 9 *dial.* **wurst**. β. 4–7 **wrest** (5 **wrost**?), 5–6 **wreste**, 6 **wreast** (**wrast**, 8 *dial.* **wraste**), 9 *Sc.* **reist**. [OE. *wrist*, = OFris. *wrist*, *-wirst* (in *hand-*, *fôt-wirst*), *-werst* (in *fôt-werst*), *-riust* (NFris. *wrast*, *werst*), MLG. *wrist* (LG. *wrist*, *wirst*, *rüst*), MDu. *wrist*, MHG. *rist* m., *riste* f. (G. *rist* m., instep, wrist), ON. *rist* f., instep (Da., Sw. *vrist*, Norw. *vrist*, *rist*), prob. f. *wriþ-*, weak grade of the stem of *wrīðan* WRITHE *v.*]

1. a. *Anat.* That part of the human frame between the fore-arm and the metacarpus; the joint by which the hand is united to the fore-arm; the carpus, or radio-carpal joint, of primates.

Cf. *arm-wrist* (ARM *sb.*[1] III), HAND-WRIST.

α. ?*a* **940** *Laws Athelstan* in *Liebermann* I. 386/1 Ȝif hit anfeald tyhtle sy, dufe seo hand æfter þam stane oð þa wriste. *c* **1325** in *Rel. Ant.* II. 78 The virste, *la coude de la mein*. **13..** *E.E. Allit. P.* B. 1535 Non oþer forme bot a fust faylande þe wryste. **1430–40** LYDG. *Bochas* IX. 2258 He heeld..Hand and fyngres aboue the coles briht, Til the ioyntes faillyng heer & yonder, From the wirste [*v.rr.* wrest, wrost, wristis] departid wer assonder. *c* **1440** *Promp. Parv.* 534 Wryst, or wyrste of an hande, *fragus*. **1530** PALSGR. 290 Wrist of ones hande, *poignet*. **1574** SACKVILLE *Induct. Mirr. Mag.* lxvii, Cassandra..they haled From Pallas house,..Her wrists fast bound. **1600** HAKLUYT *Voy.* III. 49 An eare as bigge as the wrist of a mans arme. **1655** FULLER *Ch. Hist.* IX. 204 The Doctor fairly twisted his wrists. **1712** STEELE *Spect.* No. 515 ¶3 The fan can play without any force..but just of the wrist. **1774** GOLDSM. *Nat. Hist.* (1776) VII. 37 A substance ..as thick as one's wrist. **1813** J. THOMSON *Lect. Inflam.* 211 The pulse in the wrist was scarcely to be felt. **1868** MORRIS *Earthly Par.* I. I. 433 [Taking] her dear hands..about each little wrist. **1875** *Encycl. Brit.* I. 828 The wrist of the orang, gibbon, the tailed apes.

β. **13..** *Sir Beues* (A.) 1769 Beues smot..is left hande be þe wrest. **14..** [see α]. *a* **1513** FABYAN *Chron.* VII. (1811) 393 The whiche..had theyr ryght handes smyten of by the wrestes. **1548** PATTEN *Exped. Scotl.* K vj, Both his handes cut of by the wreasts. **1622** MABBE tr. *Aleman's Guzman d' Alf.* II. 354 Fastening Cords to the wrests of mine arme. **1646** SIR T. BROWNE *Pseud. Ep.* 184 The axillary artery..

passing by the wrest or place of the pulse. **1788** VALLANCEY *Voc. Bargie* in *Trans. R. Irish Acad.* II. 34 *Wraste*, the wrist.

b. Without article.

1686 in *Verney Mem.* (1907) II. 422, 3 Payres of black Buttons for wrist and neck. **1821** SCOTT *Kenilw.* xvi, I'll bracelet him with iron both on wrist and ankle.

c. *transf.* That part of a garment, sleeve, or glove, which covers the wrist.

1803 D. WORDSWORTH *Jrnl.* 10 Jan. (1941) I. 188 Worked all day—petticoats—Mrs. C.'s wrists. **1828** *Lady's Mag.* Aug. 446/1 The cuffs at the wrists of all gowns. **1873** SUSAN COOLIDGE *What Katy did* iii. 44 She .. adjusted her veil and the wrists of her three-buttoned gloves.

2. † **a.** The joint of the thigh or knee. (Cf. OE. *cnéow-wyrst.*) *Obs.*$^{-1}$

c **1450** *St. Cuthbert* (Surtees) 5850 Men wend his the [= thigh] bane had bryst; He had na harme in bane ne wrist.

b. The ankle; the instep. Usu. *wrist of the foot.* Now *dial.*

c **1530** *Hickscorner* (*c* 1550) B ij, *Frewyll.* But can they go no more. *Imag.* O no man, the wrest is twyst so sore. **1547** in Leland *Collectanea* (1774) IV. 321 He .. tyed himselfe .. a little beneath the Wrist of the Foot. **1563** T. GALE *Antidot.* II. 22 Thys vnguent must be applyed vppon .. the wreste of the handes, the wreste of the foote [etc.]. **1612** SHELTON *Quix.* (1620) II. 169 About the Wrists of her Legs .. she wore two .. Bracelets. **1615** CROOKE *Body of Man* (1631) 1005 The *Tarsus* or wrest of the Foot. **1658** A. FOX *Würtz' Surg.* II. xxv. 152 The bone of the Foots wrist. **1825** JAMIESON *Suppl.*, *Reist*, the instep. Upp[er] Clydes[dale]. **1894** *Northumbld. Gloss.* 799 *Wrist-o'-the-foot*, the ankle.

3. *Comp. Anat.* A part or joint analogous or answering to the wrist in man: **a.** The carpus or carpal joint in birds. **b.** The knee or knee-joint in the fore-legs of animals. **c.** *Ichth.* (See first quot.)

a. *a* **1843** *Encycl. Metrop.* (1845) VII. 327 The Wrist of Birds consists of but two bones.

b. *a* **1843** *Ibid.* 315 The Wrist [in reptiles], *carpus*, consists of numerous small bones. **1854** OWEN in *Orr's Circ. Sci.*, *Org. Nat.* I. 211 That [carpal bone] on the radial side of the wrist [in *Crocodilia*] is the largest. **1890** MIVART *Dogs, Jackals*, etc. 6 Vertically from the wrist up the front of the [wolf's] leg.

c. **1840** *Cuvier's Anim. Kingd.* 308 [In] some spinous fishes the carpal bones are so elongated as to form a sort of arm or wrist, to the extremity of which the pectoral fin is articulated. *Ibid.*, Fishes with Wrists to the Pectoral Fins. **1854** OWEN in *Orr's Circ. Sci.*, *Org. Nat.* I. 176 The carpal bones of these fins .. increasing in length from the ulnar to the radial side of the wrist.

4. a. *Mech.* One of the partitions of the bucket of an overshot water-wheel. ? *Obs.*

1797 *Encycl. Brit.* (ed. 3) XVIII. 903/2 We have heard them named the Start or Shoulder, the Arm, and the Wrest (probably for wrist, on account of a resemblance of the whole line to the human arm). **1829** *Nat. Philos.*, *Mechanics* v. 20 (L.U.K.), This bucket is formed of three planes; .. BC is called the arm, and CH the wrist.

b. A pin or stud, projecting from the side of a wheel, crank, etc., to which a connecting rod is attached; a wrist-pin.

1864 WEBSTER. **1875** KNIGHT *Dict. Mech.* 1720/1 *Pitman-box*, the stirrup and brasses which embrace the wrist of the driving-wheel. **1884** *Ibid.* Suppl. 229/2 A wrist on a crank wheel.

c. *Naut.* (See quot.)

1863 A. YOUNG *Naut. Dict.* (ed. 2) 450 *Wrist of an anchor*, the continuation of the arm in a square or rounded form towards the palm or fluke.

5. *attrib.*, as ***wrist connection, end, power***; freq. in sense 'worn about or depending from the wrist', as ***wrist-bag, -bangle, -cord,*** †***favour, -iron, -plaster***, etc.; in the names of devices worn on the wrist, as ***wrist compass, radio***, etc.

1904 *Daily Chron.* 28 Jan. 6/5 The sums stolen out of the '*wrist-bag' purses. **1922** JOYCE *Ulysses* 432 Fiercely she slaps his haunch, her goldcurb *wristbangles angriling. **1983** D. HART-DAVIS *Fire Falcon* xxiii. 272 His only means of steering was his *wrist compass. **1875** KNIGHT *Dict. Mech.* 2822/2 A pin passing through the axis of a *wrist-connection. **1865** TYLOR *Early Hist. Man.* viii. 201 A well-known New Zealand weapon .. is an edged club of bone or stone... Through the neck it has a hole for a *wrist-cord. **1899** *Allbutt's Syst. Med.* VI. 521 The *wrist end of the ulna. **1626** MIDDLETON *Anything for Quiet Life* III. i, A fine *wrist-favour of this gold. **1871** *Archaeologia* XLIII. 426 Stone *Wrist-guards... Those [plates] of finely-grained green stone .. appear to be intended to be worn on the wrist. **1885** RUNCIMAN *Skippers & Sh.* 83 We divides the sets of *wrist-irons. **1725** *Fam. Dict.* s.v. *Eye*, Mix all these together .. to a Consistence fit for a *Wrist-plaister. **1897** RANJITSINHJI *Cricket* 165 Every player who has much *wrist-power. **1972** *Times* 3 Nov. 33/3 It is a world first, it enables the memorable '*wrist radio' label of the Dick Tracy strip cartoons to become reality. **1984** *Listener* 17 May 36/3 You have the Snoop-Mobile, a wrist-radio, a list of suspects and information about each of them. **1901** *Scribner's Mag.* April 408/1 Big policemen, swinging their clubs by the *wrist-straps. **1984** *Tampa* (Florida) *Tribune* 5 Apr. 6B/4 Cellular mobile radio telephone service .. could be the forerunner of Dick Tracy-like *wrist telephones. **1972** D. BLOODWORTH *Any Number can Play* x. 81 I'm going to grow up into a millionaire cowboy with a two-way *wrist-television and a formula car.

b. In sense 'of or pertaining to a wrist-band or sleeve-cuff', as ***wrist-button, -link, -stud.***

1856 LEVER *Martins of Cro' M.* xxx. 315 His wrist-buttons, his shirt-studs, the camelia in his coat. **1859** *Habits of Good Society* iii. 142 Elaborate studs .. and wrist-links, are all abominable. **1865** LE FANU *Guy Dev.* II. 38 Having buttoned his jewelled wrist-studs in. **1875** KNIGHT *Dict. Mech.* 2822/2 *Wrist-link*, a link with connected buttons for the wristband or cuff.

c. In Cricket, etc., in the sense 'effected or directed by means of wrist-work,' as ***wrist hit, -play*** (hence ***wrist-player, -playing***), ***shot, stroke.***

1851 J. PYCROFT *Cricket Field* vii. 141 All that is required is, straight play and a free wrist... Without wrist play there can be no good style of batting. **1862** PYCROFT *Cricket Tutor* 19 Throwing back the bat to the bails .. necessitates good wrist-play. **1867** *J. Lillywhite's Cricketer's Comp.* 105 A. G. Lee, capital wrist player. **1888** STEEL & LYTTELTON *Cricket* 42 Players are not equally good both at the forward driving and the wrist-playing games. **1888** R. H. LYTTELTON in Steel & Lyttelton *Cricket* ii. 61 The cut .. requires a very strong use of the wrist, and, like all wrist strokes, charms the spectator by accomplishing great results at the expense of apparently little effort. **1895** KIPLING *Day's Work, Maltese Cat*, Hughes made some sort of quick wrist-stroke [in polo]. **1900** *Westm. Gaz.* 16 April 2/1 The cut was not a wrist hit, but a vehement exhibition of energy. **1906** *Ibid.* 21 March 10/1 A wrist shot that was remarkable.

d. Special Combs., as †**wrist-bender**, a muscle which bends or controls the wrist; **wrist-bone**, any one of the small bones of the wrist; a carpal bone; **wrist clonus** *Path.*, spasmodic contraction of the muscles of the hand, produced by sudden backward pressure; **wrist-drop** *Path.*, an affection marked by inability to extend the hand and fingers, resulting from paralysis of the forearm extensor muscles; also *attrib.*; **wrist-fall**, a drooping ruff or band (cf. FALL *sb.*[1] 23 c) formerly worn about the wrist; **wrist-guide** (see quots.); **wrist jerk** *Path.*, wrist clonus; **wrist-length** *a.*, (*a*) (of a glove) reaching as far as the wrist; (*b*) (see quot. 1957); **wrist-pin** *Mech.*, = WRIST 4 b; also *Comb.*; **wrist-plate** *Mech.*, an oscillating plate bearing one or more crank-pins or wrists on its face (*Cent. Dict.*); **wrist-slap** *slang*, a mild rebuke; so **wrist-slapping**; **wrist-spin** *Cricket*, spin imparted to a ball by the wrist; cf. *finger-spin* s.v. FINGER *sb.* 15; so **wrist-spinner, wrist-spinning** *vbl. sb.*; **wrist-watch**, a small watch worn in a wristlet or strap around the wrist; **wrist-work**, flexure of the wrist, as in batting; **wrist-wrestling**, a contest of strength between two people, each trying to force the arm of the other person backwards (strictly by interlocking thumbs instead of gripping hands); arm-wrestling; so **wrist-wrestler**.

1634 T. JOHNSON *Parey's Chirurg. Wks.* 222 Both the *Carpiflexores*, or *Wrest-benders, arise from the .. inner processe. **1552** HULOET, *Wreast bone of the hand, or arme, *brachiale.* **1612** PEACHAM *Gentl. Exerc.* ix. 29 The brawne of the arme must appeare full, shadowed on one side, then shew the wrist bone therof. **1825** SCOTT *Talism.* ii, The wrist-bones peculiarly large and strong. **1872** COUES *N. Amer. Birds* 42 Two little carpal bones, or wrist-bones. **1889** *Buck's Handbk. Med. Sci.* VIII. 33/2 Odd cases of supernumerary wrist-bones. **1888** *Ibid.* VI. 771/2 A *wrist clonus may be produced by a .. forcible hyperextension of the wrist. *a* **1841** *Encycl. Metrop.* (1845) VII. 522 One of these consequences [of the use of lead] is .. *wrist-drop. **1899** *Allbutt's Syst. Med.* VI. 693 The two commonest varieties—the wrist-drop type and the upper arm type. **1890** MRS. A. E. BARR *Friend Olivia* iii, The lace *wrist-falls and neck-bands. **1861** J. S. ADAMS *5000 Mus. Terms* 108 **Wrist Guide*, that part of Logier's Chiroplast which guides the wrist. **1876** STAINER & BARRETT *Dict. Mus. Terms* 90 The wrist-guide, by which the position of the wrist was preserved [in piano-playing] from inclination outwards. **1899** *Allbutt's Syst. Med.* VI. 700 The *wrist and elbow jerks. *Ibid.* VII. 191. **1935** E. FARJEON *Nursery in Nineties* IV. iii. 172 Long evening gloves and *wrist-length, kid and suède gloves! **1957** M. B. PICKEN *Fashion Dict.* 382/2 *Wrist length*, length of coat or other garment, taken with arms hanging at sides, which reaches to wrist. **1963** *Guardian* 1 Feb. 9/7 Jackets are either straight and short to the hips or straight to wrist-length. **1875** KNIGHT *Dict. Mech.* 2822 The *wrist-pin is a truncate, conical, tubular piece attached to the crank-wheel by a bolt. *Ibid.*, *Wrist-pin Turner*, a machine for turning wrist-pins .. or [for] the turning of journals. **1977** M. EDELMAN *Political Lang.* viii. 148 Antitrust laws similarly sanction mergers and pricing agreements, with occasional token *wrist slaps to keep the symbolism pure. **1979** *Time* 13 Aug. 36/3 Critical as the investigators may have been of the utility, the NRC itself got a wrist slap from Congress. **1958** *Times* 24 May 4/2 This unusual example of mass *wrist-slapping has been going on for a week. **1979** N. SLATER *Falcon* viii. 141 There was no sherry decanter in evidence, no coffee... This was turning out to be a right old wrist-slapping session. **1960** E. W. SWANTON *West Indies Revisited* iii. 49 He is reputedly unhappy against *wrist-spin. **1977** *New Society* 3 Feb. 246/2 Raffles was a leg-break bowler: can wrist-spin ever be *really* kosher? **1957** T. BAILEY *Cricket Bk.* vi. 66/1 Bruce Dooland .. clearly showed what destruction a top-class *wrist-spinner can achieve in Championship cricket. **1977** *Listener* 5 May 588/1 Garfield Sobers—finger-spinner, wrist-spinner, seam-bowler. **1963** T. E. BAILEY *Improve your Cricket* i. 31 Slow bowlers [from overseas] are more frequently of the *wrist-spinning variety. **1896** BADEN-POWELL *Matabele Campaign* iv, Field-glasses, *wrist-watch, buckles, and buttons should be dulled. **1898** RANJITSINHJI *With Stoddart's Team* vii. 103 His cutting was hard and full of *wrist work. **1902** *Westm. Gaz.* 3 June 3/2 There was any amount of wrist-work in his cutting. **1978** *Detroit Free Press* 16 Apr. 1A/1 My uncle Gerald is a pretty good *wrist wrestler. **1973** *N.Y. Times* 29 July x. 4/5 *Wrist wrestling, also known as arm wrestling, has its real roots in Petaluma, Calif., where the world championship matches have been televised on ABC's Wide World of Sports for the past four years. **1978** *Maclean's Mag.* 12 June 62 It seems perfectly natural for a wristwrestling championship to be held in Timmins.

wrist: see WREST *sb.* and *v.*

wristband ('rɪstbænd, †'rɪzbənd). [f. WRIST + BAND *sb.*[1]]

1. a. The band or part of a sleeve (esp. of a shirt-sleeve) which covers or fastens about the wrist; a cuff or sleeve-band.

1571 in Feuillerat *Revels Q. Eliz.* (1908) 146 Skarfes, ffawchions, buskins, wrestbandes. **1611** COTGR., *Poignet de la chemise*, the wrist-band, or gathering at the sleeue-hand, of a shirt. *a* **1625** BEAUM. & FL. *Bloody Brother* IV. ii, You'l .. dip your wrist-bands, (For Cuffs y' have none) as comely in the sauce As any Courtier. **1697** VANBRUGH *Æsop* II. i, With that the Hands to pocket went, Full Wrist-band deep. **1752** BERKELEY *Th. Tar-water* Wks. 1871 III. 500 Unbuttoning the neck and wristbands of his shirt. **1837** DICKENS *Pickw.* xxx, Although his coat was short in the sleeves, it disclosed no vestige of a linen wrist-band. **1886** *Tip Cat* XVI. 208 He was keenly conscious of his old boots and crumpled wristbands.

b. A band worn as a protector on the wrist. *rare.*

1882 *Imp. Dict.*, *Muffettee*, .. a wristband of fur or worsted worn by ladies.

2. a. A bracelet or wristlet.

1585 HIGINS *Junius' Nomencl.* 252 *Armilla*, .. a bracelet or wrist band. **1697** DAMPIER *Voy.* (1729) I. 365 A Silver Wrist-band, or Hoop to come about their Arms. **1706** PHILLIPS (ed. Kersey), *Brachiale* (Lat.), .. a Bracelet, .. a Wrist-band. **1909** *Westm. Gaz.* 28 June 5/2 Wrist-bands, which are a revival of the beaded bracelets worn in early Victorian days, have been introduced.

b. A band for shackling the wrist.

1884 THOMPSON *Tumours of Bladder* 17 The feet and hands [of the patient] are attached by anklets and wristbands. **1897** *Allbutt's Syst. Med.* II. 870 Strait-jackets are a survival of the dark ages, and leather wrist-bands and bandages abrade the skin.

3. A bandage for fastening round the wrist; also, a wrist-plaster.

1663 BOYLE *Usef. Exp. Nat. Philos.* I. v. 94 The *ligamentum latum*, or wrist-band, that keeps the tendons .. from inconveniently starting up. **1684** —— *Porousn. Bodies* iv. 32 Those [plasters] that Physicians call *Pericarpia*, or Wrist-bands.

4. In sport, a strip of material worn round the wrist to absorb perspiration.

1969 *New Yorker* 14 June 68/3 Ashe wipes his forehead with his wristband. **1984** *Oxford Times* 29 Feb. 3/7 (Advt.), Headband and wristband pack—£1.79.

wristed ('rɪstɪd), *a.* [f. as prec. + -ED[2].]

1. Having a (specified kind of) wrist.

c **1611** CHAPMAN *Iliad* XXIV. 61 White-wristed Juno .. Being much incensed. **1888** STEEL & LYTTELTON *Cricket* 53 Strong-wristed players play more back [etc.]. **1905** H. G. WELLS *Kipps* II. vii. §4 A thin wristed hand.

2. Carried on the wrist.

1899 *Daily News* 28 Oct. 7/5 A green parrot, 'wristed', like a falcon, but not hooded.

wrister ('rɪstə(r)). *U.S.* [f. as prec. + -ER[1].] A knitted covering for the wrist; a muffetee.

1879 WEBSTER *Suppl.* **1883** *Century Mag.* Aug. 624 A neighbor, come to tea, was crocheting wristers for her grandson.

†'**wristikin.** ? *nonce-wd. Obs.* [f. as prec.: see -KIN.] A muffetee.

1826 CARLYLE *Love Lett.* (1909) II. 257 She has manufactured two pairs of wristikins. **1851** MRS. CARLYLE in *Mem.* (1903) II. 35 A pair of woollen wristikins.

wrist-joint ('rɪstdʒɔɪnt). [f. as prec. + JOINT *sb.*] The joint of the wrist; the radio-carpal articulation or joint: **a.** In man.

1634-5 BRERETON *Trav.* (Chetham Soc.) 47 The obstruction, which perhaps occasioned .. that swelling in the wrist-joints. **1831** R. KNOX *Cloquet's Anat.* 209 Wrist joint. This articulation .. is formed by the junction of the hand and fore-arm. **1852** *Todd's Cycl. Anat.* IV. 1507 The wrist-joint enjoys every [such] variety of motion. **1873** T. H. GREEN *Introd. Pathol.* (ed. 2) 54 The extensors of the wrist-joint.

b. In birds.

a **1843** *Encycl. Metrop.* (1845) VII. 327/1 The Radio-carpal bone .. forms .. a cap to the front of the Wrist-joint. **1872** COUES *N. Amer. Birds* 31 Extension of the hand upon the wrist-joint increases and completes the unfolding of the wing.

wristle, etc., obs. varr. WRESTLE *v.*

wristled, obs. f. WRIZZLED *a.*

wristlet ('rɪstlɪt). [f. as prec. + -LET.]

1. a. (See quot.)

1847 WEBSTER, *Wristlet*, an elastic band worn by ladies around the wrist, to confine the upper part of a glove. [Hence in some later Dicts.]

b. A bracelet; = WRISTBAND 2.

1851 *Catal. Gt. Exhib.* 862 Articles for the Modea, Djedda, and Mecca Markets: .. Armlets and wristlets. **1863** SPEKE *Discov. Nile* viii. 203 The king .. wore, for ornament, neatly-worked wristlets of copper. **1889** *Daily News* 8 June 5/4 The poor little creature .. had been decorated with a pair of silver wristlets.

c. A handcuff, a wrist-iron.

1881 *Daily Tel.* 31 Dec. 6/1 Wearing black dresses instead of grey, with leg irons as well as wristlets, to show that they were bad-conduct men. **1901** *Daily News* 1 Feb. 7/5 The illegal use .. of belts, anklets, and wristlets, in restraining violent lunatics.

d. A small strap for wearing on the wrist. Also *attrib.*

1891 *Times* 16 Oct. 4/6 Blue gauntlet gloves, and watch in wristlet. **1914** *Ibid.* 24 Aug. 9/4 Stealing a wristlet watch.. from a dressing-box at the baths.

2. An ornamental band or covering for the wrist.

1851 *Illustr. Lond. News* 19 July 86/1 Wrought muslin wristlets about two inches in width. **1861** T. B. Aldrich *Pampina* Poems (1875) 90 A siren lithe.. With wristlets woven of scarlet weeds.

b. A muffetee. Cf. wristband 1 b, wrister.

1869 *Eng. Mechanic* 26 Nov. 264/1 Wristlets, muffs, collarettes,.. in different patterns,.. are knitted on the LK knitter. **1888** *Century Mag.* XXXVI. 771/1 Knitted gloves, suspenders, comforters, wristlets.

† **'wristling,** *vbl. sb. Obs.*⁻¹ [Of obscure origin.] The action of, or fact of undergoing, curling, coiling, or twisting.

1577 B. Googe *Heresbach's Husb.* III. 151 The wrystling and turnyng vp of the tayle [L. *cauda contorta*], is a signe of a sound Hogge.

wristy ('rɪstɪ), *a.* [f. wrist + -y¹.] Performed by flexure of the wrist; marked by or clever in wrist-work.

1867 *Australasian* 9 Mar. 300/2 Fowler, pretty wristy style, but not a very safe one. **1888** *Longm. Mag.* May 47 He was a good bat, noted for his 'wristy' play, as some critic termed it. **1893** W. L. Murdoch *Cricket* 54 A quick, wristy throw. **1936** Wodehouse *Laughing Gas* xxii. 242, I remember.. wondering how the dickens a female of her slight build and apparently fragile physique could possibly get that wristy follow-through into her shots. **1955** *Times* 18 July 12/3 With the deftest turn to leg and wristy punches through the covers he seemed set for an imposing score. **1959** *Times* 26 June 4/2 Krishnan's forte lay in his lovely wristy stop volleys. **1977** *World of Cricket Monthly* June 41/2 There was no prodding or pushing but a free swing on wristy cut. **1980** R. Hill *Spy's Wife* xix. 148 He downed his pale spirit in one quick wristy movement.

Hence **'wristily** *adv.*

1963 A. Ross *Australia 63* iii. 82 Barrington cut wristily to beat third man. **1972** P. Brent *Godmen of India* ii. 33 Women polish the earthen floors, bending straight-legged as they work wristily away with a flat stone.

writ (rɪt), *sb.* Forms: 1- writ (1 *north.* u(u)rit, *pl.* writto, wriot(t)o, 3-4 wriht, 5 wrethe, *Sc.* wirt, 6 wret), 3-8 writt (4 weritt), 3-7 writte; 3-7 wryt (5 *Sc.* wryte, wyrt), 4-6 wrytt (6 whrytt), 3-7 wrytte. [OE. *writ* (also *ȝewrit* i-writ), = ON. and Icel. *rit* writing (Norw. *rit* drawing), Goth. *writs* pen-stroke, OHG. *riz* m., stroke, character (MHG. *riz*, G. *ritz* m., *ritze* f.), f. the weak grade of *wrītan* to write. Cf. handwrit, and write *sb.*¹]

1. Something written, penned, or recorded in writing; a writing. Now *rare.*

a **900**, *c* **950** [implied in sense 1 c]. *a* **1122** *O.E. Chron.* (Laud MS.) an. 963, [He] fand þa hidde in þa ealde wealle writes þet Headda abb[od] heafde ær ȝewriton. *a* **1200** *Moral Ode* 100 Al ho habbeð in hore write þet we mis-duden here. *a* **1300** *Cursor M.* 8495 Þis writte wit fele was red and sene, Bot fa it wist quat it wald mene. *c* **1300** *Havelok* 2486 Þis writ shal henge bi him þare. **1338** R. Brunne *Chron.* (1810) 154 Sir haf here þis writ, & schewe him alle newe. **1412-20** Lydg. *Chron. Troy* I. 3290 Ful oft sythe þe writ he dide rede. **1488-92** *Acc. Ld. High Treas. Scot.* I. 87 There was a writ fund.. sayand: In hac boxa [etc.]. **1560** Daus tr. *Sleidane's Comm.* 151 b, He couered his mynde craftely, that his writte myght haue some shewe. **1586** Whitney *Emblems* 143 Th' Emperor.. tooke his penne, for to confirme the cause. But all in vayne:.. he rente the writte in twaine. **1762** Ld. Talbot in *Wilkes' Lett.* (1769) I. 10 A person who hath been the object of the writ of any paper. **1891** Walsham How in *Life* (1898) 323 You have a writ given you, which is like a small cake. **1905** *Westm. Gaz.* 7 Oct. 4/2 The writs of the insane are generally distinguished by great length.

transf. *c* **1250** *Gen. & Ex.* 1974 Ðo iacob saȝ dat sori writ [*sc.* the bloody coat], He gret.

†**b.** A written work, a book; also *pl.*, the writings or works of an author or authors. *Obs.*

a **1000** *Phœnix* 425 Þæs þe us leorneras wordum secgaþ, & writu cyþað. *a* **1200** *Vices & Virtues* 35 He wisseð ðes mannes iðangc.. ðurh haliȝe writes. *c* **1230** *Hali Meid.* 9 And tat schal forðre i þis writ beon openliche ischeawet. *Ibid.* 39 Hercne his read, þat he i þe frumðe of þis writ readde. *c* **1330** *Arth. & Merl.* 9655 Her after sone in þis write, Whi he it dede, ȝe schul it wite. *a* **1400-50** *Wars Alex.* 608 He walde-eȝed was, as þe writt schewys. *c* **1400** *Apol. Loll.* 63 Woo to hem þat.. writun writtis of vnritfulnes. **1456** Haye *Law Arms* (S.T.S.) 15 Sanct Paule in his wryttis, sayand [etc.]. **1508** Kennedy *Flyting w. Dunbar* 258 How thy for-bearis come.. the writ makis me war. **1590** Greene *Mourn. Garment* (1616) C 3 b, The Authors.. in their writtes plaine discusse, Fairer was not Tytirvs. **1646** R. Baillie *Anabaptism* (1647) Epist., In the following writ I point at the danger. **1681** Dryden *Abs. & Achit.* I. 665 Let Israels foes.. rashly judge his Writ Apocryphal. **1687** —— *Hind & P.* III. 2 Much malice.. Perhaps may censure this mysterious writ.

c. *spec.* Sacred writings collectively, the Bible or holy Scriptures, = scripture *sb.* 1; †a single passage in these. Freq. without article (cf. 2), in *Holy* or *Sacred Writ.* †Also *pl.*

a **900** *Rituale Eccl. Dunelm.* (Surtees) 79 Cwoeð forðon ðio writ, eȝhwoelc se ðe ȝilefeð on hine ne bið sceomiende. *c* **900-** [see Holy Writ]. *c* **950** *Lindisf. Gosp.* Matt. xxvi. 54 Ah huu forðon biðð ȝefylled wuriotto? *Ibid.* Mark xii. 10 Ne writ ðius leornada ȝie. *a* **1200** *Vices & Virtues* 67 Þenc ðat ðe writt seið þat æure bie ðe mildce ouer ðe rihte dome. *c* **1410** *Lantern of Light* 132 Alle þoo þat trowen þat helþe may cum of vsing Goddis word þat we clepen writtes. ? *c* **1490** in *Asloan MS.* (S.T.S.) I. 57 He vsit euer mercy and euer will ffor the writ sayis In eternum [etc.]. **1593** Shaks *2 Hen. VI*, I. iii. 61 His Weapons [are] holy Sawes of sacred Writ. **1685** Waller *Div. Love* I. 44 Sacred Writ our reason does exceed. **1745** Pococke *Descr. East* II. i. 60 Cæsarea.. is remarkable in sacred writ upon several accounts.

transf. **1608** Shaks. *Per.* II. Prol. 12 At Tarsus, where each man Thinks all is writ he speken can.

†**d.** A written communication; a missive, letter.

c **1200** *Trin. Coll. Hom.* 7 Sainte powel.. wrot þo a writ and sende hit synfulle men. *c* **1225** *Leg. Kath.* 407 He.. sende iseelede writes.. to alle þe icudde clerkes. *a* **1300** *K. Horn* 930 (Camb. MS.), A writ he dude deuise; Aþulf hit dude write. **13..** *K. Alis.* 4502 (Laud MS.), He.. sent to Alisaunder a wrytt. *c* **1380** *Sir Ferumb.* 1774 Delyuerieþ me þe wryt, þat Charles sente to sir Balanne. *c* **1470** Henry *Wallace* III. 425 The knycht Schew him the wryt lord Persie had him sent. **1588** Shaks. *Titus A.* II. iii. 264 All too late I bring this fatall writ. **1592** Kyd *Sp. Trag.* III. ii. 26 A letter written to Hieronimo... 'For want of incke receiue this bloudie writ'.

2. a. Without article (cf. 1 c). That which is written; written record.

c **1205** Lay. 25005 Nu ȝe habbeoð iherd.. wulc word heo sendeð us here into vre londe mid write [*c* **1275** writ] & mid worde. **13..** *K. Alis.* 7137 (Laud MS.), Þe kynge.. tolde hem by wrytt his damage. *c* **1375** in *Anglia* I. 315/507 Ȝut after he [= Adam] gat þretty sones mo,.. þus in writ fynde y. *a* **1400-50** *Wars Alex.* 24 As I in writt fynd. **1622** J. Mayer *Treas. Eccles. Expos.* 266 Barnabas cured the sick with the touch of euangelicall writ. **1671** Milton *P.R.* III. 184 If of my raign Prophetic Writ hath told That it shall never end. **1704** Pope *Windsor For.* 247 He.. Of ancient writ unlocks the learned store. *a* **1732** T. Boston *View Covt. Grace* (1734) 266 A Will declared, testified, and signified by Word or Writ. **1844** Kinglake *Eothen* iv, The mere human surmises and doubts which clash with Homeric writ!

†**b.** = writing *vbl. sb.* 9. Also *fig. Obs.*

a **1300** *Cursor M.* 8495 Þis writte [on a marble stone] wit fele was red and sene. **1340-70** *Alex. & Dind.* 1136 He bad bulden of marbre A piler..; & þat þei wrouhten a wrytte. *c* **1440** *Promp. Parv.* 534/1 Wrytte, vpone a grave stone, ..*epitaphium.* *c* **1450** Holland *Houlate* 395 Reid the writ of thar werk, to ȝour witness. **1600** Fairfax *Tasso* XII. xxxix, This found he grauen in the tender rinde;.. he mused on this vncouth writ. **1645** Rutherford *Tryal & Tri. Faith* 203 There is writ remaining after sin is acted... Writ written with a pen of iron, and diamond.

c. Written command, order, or authority.

In later use generalized from the senses under 3.

a **1400** in *Eng. Gilds* (1870) 360 Ȝif hit ne be pley of lond by wryt. *c* **1480** Henryson *Fox, Wolf, & Husb.* 48 Haif ȝe writ or witnes for to schaw? *c* **1520** *Vox populi* 328 in Hazl. *E.P.P.* III. 279 Lysens to compownde.. By fyne or wrytte of post. **1538** Starkey *England* I. iv. 117 Touchyng appellatyonys in causys and remouyng by wrytt. **1705** *Lond. Gaz.* No. 4103/3 Her Majesty hath been.. pleased, by Writ, to Call [him] to the House of Lords. **1765** Blackstone *Comm.* I. 148 The convention in 1688.. did not assemble without writ. **1808** W. Selwyn *Law Nisi Prius* II. 1020 [When] the proceedings .. have been instituted in the county court by plaint, and not by writ.

3. A formal writing or paper of any kind; a legal document or instrument. (Passing into next.)

a **1122** *O.E. Chron.* (Laud MS.) an. 963, Hu se papa Agatho hit feostnode mid his write. *a* **1200** in Kemble *Cod. Dipl.* IV. 203 Ich mid ðusen write ȝelde and ȝeue.. ðen broðren on Chertseye ðo .x. hyden lond. **1258** Hen. III *Proclamation*, We senden ȝew þis writ open, iseined wiþ vre seel. *c* **1300** *Havelok* 136 He sende writes sone on-on After his erles. **1362** Langl. *P. Pl.* A. II. 49 Alle to witnesse wel what þe writ wolde, In what manere that Meede in mariage was i-feffed. **1454** *Rolls of Parlt.* V. 257/1 Writtes executories under the Kynges grete Seale. **1467** *Mann. & Househ. Exp.* (Roxb.) 402 [Paid] for a nother wrytte uppon the patent of lyvelode, ij.s. iiij.d. **1538** Wriothesley *Chron.* (Camden) I. 91 [He] was made a baron by the Kinges wryt. **1562-3** *Reg. Privy Council Scot.* I. 231 That he may haif inspectioun of the saidis writtis producit. **1601** Weever *Mirr. Mart.* D vj, The Bishop.. Caus'd writs be set on Rochesters great Church.. commaunding me remember To appeare. **1672** *Sc. Acts* (1820) VIII. 87 The Writers to the signet.. are heirby discharged, to forme or write writts of any kind.., unles [etc.]. **1729** T. Innes *Crit. Ess.* Pref. (1879) 12 A writ under his great seal. **1809** Bawdwen *Domesday Bk.* 239 Witnessing the King's writ for that purpose. **1892** Tennyson *Foresters* IV. 48 Lawful King, Whose writ will run thro' all the range of life.

b. *Law.* A written command, precept, or formal order issued by a court in the name of the sovereign, state, or other competent legal authority, directing or enjoining the person or persons to whom it is addressed to do or refrain from doing some act specified therein.

a **1400** in *Eng. Gilds* (1870) 361 Þe wryt þat me pledeth in þe Citee, by-fore Justyces. *c* **1450** *Godstow Reg.* 206 [To] come fully to the strengthe of the courte for the kyngis breef or writte. *a* **1513** Fabyan *Chron.* VII. (1516) 33/1 A wryt was directed vnto the Mayre and Aldermen, chargynge theym that [etc.]. *a* **1596** *Sir T. More* III. i. 29 Bring them away to execution: The writt is come abooue two houres since. **1602** *2nd Pt. Return fr. Parnass.* V. iii. 2104 To be briefe Academico, writts are out for me, to apprehend me. **1659** Hammond *On Ps.* lxxiii. 4 There are no writts signed for their execution. **1717** Prior *Dove* xviii, This cruel Writ, wherein you stand Indicted. **1810** W. Selwyn *Law Nisi Prius* (ed. 2) II. 779 After possession has been given under the writ. **1874** Ld. W. P. Lennox *Recoll.* I. 281 A brother of an M.P., finding sundry writs out against him.

c. With *of* (the specific designation).

writ of aiel, certiorari, cessavit, distringas, ease, elegit, entry, error, execution, formedon, habeas corpus, injunction, inquiry, manumission, mesne, mort d'ancestor, non est inventus, privilege, prohibition, ravishment, rebellion, right, summons, venire facias, waste, etc.: see these words.

a **1400** in *Eng. Gilds* (1870) 360 Ȝif he is y-pleted by wryt of plee of londe. **1481** *Stonor Papers* (Camden) II. 134 My wrethe of subpena. **1568-9** in Bolton *Stat. Irel.* (1621) 325 Any writt of dower. **1643** Caryl *Expos. Job* I. 967 A writ or patent of protection. **1706** Phillips (ed. Kersey) s.v., Writ of Assistance,.. of Privelege,.. of Rebellion. **1833** *Act 3-4 Will. IV*, c. 27 §36 [lists many writs thereby abolished]. **1865** *Act 28 & 29 Vict.* c. 104 §47 A Writ of Diem clausit extremum may be issued.

d. *spec.* A document issued by the crown conveying a summons to a spiritual or temporal lord to attend Parliament, or directing a sheriff to hold an election of a member or members of Parliament.

c **1400** *Contin. Brut* 324 To þe parlement was sompned by wryt.. iiij bisshopes & iiij abbotes. **1455** *Rolls of Parlt.* V. 335 He was elect Abbot.. after the seid Parlement somond, and hadde never Writte of Parlement. **1573** *Nottingham Rec.* IV. 147 The whrytt for reioynyng ye Parlament. **1610** Holland *Camden's Brit.* (1637) 636 Then was Edward Nevill by the King's Writ called unto the Parliament. **1659** Peynne (*title*), A Brief Register, Kalendar, and Survey of the several Kinds and Forms of Parliamentary Writs. *a* **1700** Evelyn *Diary* 18 Sept. 1688, Writs were issued in order to a Parliament. **1729** Jacob *Law Dict.* s.v. *Parliament*, Among the Parliament Writs 14 Eliz. **1761** Hume *Hist. Eng.* III. lx. 292 They issued some writs for new elections. **1861** Buckle *Civiliz.* (1869) II. 117 In 1264 [the Earl of Leicester] set the first example of issuing writs to cities and boroughs. **1888** J. Williams in *Encycl. Brit.* XXIV. 697/1 The writ is to be returned by the returning officer.. with the name of the member elected endorsed on the writ.

†**4.** = writing *vbl. sb.* 5. Freq. ***in writ.*** *Obs.* (latterly *Sc.*).

c **1160** *Ælfric's Hom.* (MS. Bodl. 343) fol. 63 b, Felæ wundræ.. þe we her nyllæð on write setten. *c* **1175** *Lamb. Hom.* 75 Þet rihte ileue setten þe twelue apostles on write. *c* **1200** Ormin 3282 He badd settenn upp o writt All mannkinn, forr to lokenn [etc.]. *a* **1300** in *E.E.P.* (1862) 154 Sleiȝ he was.. þat þis lore put in writte. **1375** Barbour *Bruce* I. 13 To put in wryt a suthfast story. *c* **1460** *Towneley Myst.* VII. 106 Loke ye do it well in wrytt. **1585** Jas. I *Ess. Poesie* (Arb.) 14 When in writ I do theirof reherse. **1651** Calderwood *Hist. Kirk* (Wodrow Soc.) II. 446 The Bishop of Rosse his memorialls, left in writt. **1684** Sir G. Mackenzie *Inst. Law Scot.* (1694) 212 A Testament.. does require to be in Writ.

5. *attrib.* and *Comb.*, as ***writ-charter***; ***writ-proof*** adj., ***-reader***, ***-reading***; † **writ-rune**, a written character; hence in *pl.*, a document or letter.

c **1205** Lay. 5750 Þa com þer a mon irnen.. þe brohte writ-runen. **1781** *Reading not preaching* II. 5 To apply this to our writ-reading clergy. *Ibid.* 7 All that writ-readers can read. **1841** Lever *C. O'Malley* lxxxviii, Our family have been writ-proof for centuries. **1906** *Eng. Hist. Rev.* July 506 The writ-charter addressed to the shire-moot.

writ, dial. variant of wart *sb.*

writ (rɪt), *v. Anglo-Irish.* [f. prec.] *trans.* To serve (a person) with a writ or summons. Also *refl.*

1888 *Pall Mall G.* 14 Nov. 8/1 Pat Horty [interjected].. 'I was writted myself, and sold out'. **1894** Somerville & Ross *Real Charlotte* xxviii, Why don't ye writ her for the money?

writa'bility. *rare.* [Cf. next and ability.] Capability, readiness, or disposition to write.

1770 H. Walpole *Let. to Lady Ossory* 15 Sept., Having recovered my write-ability enough to thank your ladyship.. for your kind intentions. **1788** —— *Let. to Mrs. H. More* 22 Sept., My writability in pressing my letters on you.

writable ('raɪtəb(ə)l), *a.* Also **writeable.** [f. write *v.* + -able.]

1. That may be written; capable of being reduced to or set down in writing.

1782 Mme. D'Arblay *Diary* 30 Oct., The talk was by no means writable; but very pleasant. **1799** Coleridge in Sandford *T. Poole* (1888) I. 300, I go to the famous Harz Mountains.. to see the mines... On my return I will write you all that is writable. **1853** Ruskin *Stones Ven.* III. ii. 97 All written or writable law respecting the arts is for the childish and ignorant. **1913** G. B. Shaw *Let.* 26 Mar. (1952) 104, I have written everything that is writeable: The rest must be viva voce. **1926** B. Karlgren *Philol. & Anc. China* vii. 159 If the literary language is based on the modern colloquial language, it should.. also be writable phonetically. **1970** *IEEE Trans. Computers* XIX. 710/2 The control memory of LX-1 is read-only with respect to the microprogram, but is externally writeable. **1983** *Sci. Amer.* Mar. 43/2 Endowing a computer with a writable control store is a way of removing the hardware barrier from user microprogramming.

2. Suitable for writing with.

1844 Mrs. Browning *Lett. Horne* (1877) I. 267, I am turning this pen round and round to find a writable side to it.

† **wri'tation.** *Obs. rare.* [Irreg. f. as prec. + -ation.] Poor or insipid writing.

1778 Miss Carter *Lett. to Mrs. Montagu* (1817) III. 95 What writing, as somebody used to say, what writation it all is! **1787** Bentham *Wks.* (1843) X. 174 Nine-tenths of it is bad writation about the origin of society.

writative ('raɪtətɪv), *a.* [f. as prec. + -ative.]

1. Disposed to write; given or addicted to writing. Now *rare.*

1736 Pope *Let. to Swift* 17 Aug., Increase of years makes men more talkative but less writative. **1755** Chesterf. *Let.* 19 Dec., Deaf people are commonly as frivolously writative. **1920** *Sat. Rev.* 17 Jan. 55 Our 'writative' contemporaries.

2. Marked by inclination or addiction to writing.

1746 BURKE in *Leadbeater Papers* (1862) II. 72, I always distinguish between a man's talkative and writative character. **1768** *Woman of Honor* III. 102, I was in a fine writative vein.

write (raɪt), *sb.* Chiefly *Sc.* Also 5–7 **wryte** (5 **vryte,** 6 *Sc.* **vryit, wryt),** 4 **wriȝt,** 5 **wryȝt,** 6 *north.* **wrighte;** *Sc.* 6–7 **wreit** (6 **vr-, ur-**), 7 **wreitte,** 6–9 **wreat,** 7 **wreatt, wrait,** 9 **wraet, vreet.** [var. of WRIT *sb.* after WRITE *v.*, or directly f. the latter.

Examples earlier than the 16th century are prob. mere graphic variants of *writ* (as sometimes shown by the rime), but may have helped to introduce the new form.]

†**1.** That which is written; a written record or work; a writ, writing, letter, document, etc. *Obs.*

Latterly, and from *c* 1465 to *c* 1630 chiefly, *Sc.*

c **1375** *Cursor M.* 8495 (Fairf.), Þis write wiþ many was rede and sene. **14..** *Sir Beues* (C.) 1260 Forþe he goth with þat wryte. **1466** *Reg. Mag. Sig. Scot.* 214/2 Made the day of this present write be us and our counsale. **1500** *Caldwell Papers* (Maitl. Cl.) I. 52 We haiff subscriwit þis wryte wyth our handes. **1566** STAPLETON *Ret. Untr. Jewel* IV. 32 The.. Legat brought forth a write from Zosimus. **1568** T. HOWELL *Newe Sonets* (1879) 114 Thes my triflyng toyes, and far vnconning writes. **1633** *Costlie Whore* IV. ii, Let's read these writes. What's here? complaints against my worthy brothers. **1678** SIR G. MACKENZIE *Crim. Laws Scot.* (1699) 261 A Write that is null. **1705** DALRYMPLE *Coll. Sc. Hist.* 267, I have neither seen Writes nor Chartularies, only a Copy of the Charter. **1762** in *Nairne Peerage Evidence* (1874) 98 His own proper writes and evidents.

†**2. a.** *Holy* (or *the*) *Write*, = WRIT *sb.* 1 c.

1303 R. BRUNNE *Handl. Synne* 4845 Holy wryte swyche men holdes As wylde wulues brekyng foldes. *c* **1375** *Sc. Leg. Saints* v. (*John*) 184 Þe fyrste skil.. he tuk vt of haly wryte [*rime* it]. **14..** *Arth. & Merl.* 686 (Douce MS.), Þus holy wryȝt wetnessyþ hyt. **1551** CROWLEY *Pleas. & Pain* 537 Holy wryte teacheth you so. **1567** *Gude & Godlie B.* (S.T.S.) 113 Thow.. hes promittit in the write.. Of all thair Sin to mak thame quyte.

†**b.** Written record; writing; = WRIT *sb.* 2. Chiefly *Sc. Obs.*

1483 in *Acts Lords of Council* (1918) II. p. cxxvi, Ane act of the Lordis.. gevin thairupon be.. actentik write and document. **1552** LYNDESAY *Monarche* 5319 He hes red, in Hebrew wryte, Off fyftene signis. *a* **1553** UDALL *Royster D.* II. iii. (Arb.) 36 No man for despite, By worde or by write His felowe to twite. *a* **1578** LINDESAY (Pitscottie) *Chron. Scot.* (S.T.S.) I. 366 Of the quhilk.. the nobillis.. hard tell alsweill be write as be toung. *c* **1657** SIR W. MURE *Wks.* (S.T.S.) II. 238 The monuments of wryte of the greatest antiquitie. **1681** STAIR *Instit.* I. 345 Private Ways are Constitute.. by going and coming that way uninterrupted.. fourty years without Write, or any other Right. **1825** JAMIESON *Suppl., Write*,.. writing, as contrasted with verbal communication.

†**3.** *Law.* = WRIT *sb.* 3 b, c. *Obs.*

a **1400** in *Eng. Gilds* (1870) 361 Wrytes of newe disseysyne,.. And wriȝt of ryȝt of dowaryе. **1477** *Paston Lett.* III. 212 Ye must have a meen be sum wryte of trespas for them. **1489–90** *Plumpton Corr.* (Camden) 92 Afore Easter, send upp your pardons, wrytes of dedimus. **1516** in *Test. Ebor.* (Surtees) VI. 2 By wright of entre. **1538** STARKEY *England* I. iv. 117 He wyl by wryte remoue hys cause to the court at Westmynstur. **1550** CROWLEY *Epigr.* 249 A Baylife.. serued with one wryte an whole score or tweyne.

4. *Sc.* = WRIT *sb.* 4. Only in phr. ***in write***.

1535 STEWART *Cron. Scot.* (Rolls) III. 127 The king.. All his desyr in wryte syne to him send. **1609** SKENE *Reg. Maj., Stat. David II*, 47 The summonds.. sall be put in write. *a* **1645** LD. NAPIER *Mem.* (1793) 49 To set downe there.. informations in wreat under there hand. **1717** WODROW *Corr.* (1843) II. 270 They behoved to set them [*sc.* answers] down in write.

5. a. *Sc.* Handwriting; manner or style of calligraphy.

hand of write: see HAND *sb.* 16 b.

a **1614** J. MELVILL *Diary* (Wodrow Soc.) 185 He causit wryt a copie in guid wrait. **1678** SIR G. MACKENZIE *Laws Scot.* II. 525 One mans write will differ from it self at several occasions. **1814** *Galt's New Brit. Theatre* I. 351 Whose write is it? not Henry's, sure, no—yes! **1825** JAMIESON *Suppl.* s.v., *Sma' write*, small text; *Grit, Big*, or *Muckle write*, round text. **1887** SERVICE *Life Dr. Duguid* 190 My write being noo very crabbit.

b. ***write-of-hand***, the art or method of writing. *dial.*

1863 MRS. GASKELL *Sylvia's L.* xliii, A could wish as a'd learned write-of-hand,.. for a've that for to tell Christopher as might set his mind at ease.

write, obs. var. WRIGHT *sb.*[1]

write (raɪt), *v.* Forms: (see below). [OE. *wrítan*, = OFris. *wrîta* to score, write (Fris. *write* to wear by rubbing, etc.), OS. *wrîtan* to cut, write (MLG. *wrîten*), OHG. *rîzan* to tear, draw (MHG. *rîzen*, G. *reissen*), ON. *ríta* to score, write (Norw. *rita, vrita*, Sw. *rita* to draw); cf. ON. and Icel. *rita* (wk. v.), to write. The relationship of the stem *wrīt-* to Du. and LG. forms without *w* (MDu. and MLG. *rîten*, etc.) is doubtful.]

A. Illustration of Forms.

1. a. *Inf.* (and *Pres. stem*). α. 1–2 **writan,** 2–4 (6 *arch.*) **writen** (3 *Orm.* **writenn, wríttenn**), 4 **wryten,** 5 **-yn, writon;** 4– **write** (5 **wrijte,** 9 *dial.* **wroite**), 4–6 **wryte** (5 **wreyte, whryte, wryth(e,** 9 *north. dial.* **wreyt**), 5 **wrytt(e,** 5–7 **wryt,** 6 **vryt;** 5 **wrighte,** 6–7 **wright,** 6 *Sc.* **vriht,** 5 **wrygth, wryȝt(e,** 5–6 **wryght,** 6 **wryghte.** β. 4–5, *Sc.* 6 **writte,** 5–6 *Sc.*, 8 **writt,** 4, *Sc.* 5–7 **writ,** *Sc.* 5–7 **vrit.** γ. 5–7, 9 *Sc.* **wret** (7 *Sc.* **vret**), 6 **wrett, wrete,** *Sc.* **wreit, ureit,** 7–9 **wreat** (9 **vreet, wireete**). δ. *Sc.* 6 **wraite,** 9 **vrait.**

α. **831** in *O.E. Texts* 445 Þis mid episcopus rodetacne [ic] festnie & write. **835** *Ibid.* 447 Ic abba ȝeroefa cyðe & writan hate hu min willa is. *c* **1100** *O.E. Chron.* (MS. F.) an. 40, Matheus.. agan his godspell to writen. **13..** *Cursor M.* 648 [None] mai write.. þe mikel ioy. **14..** *Chaucer's Anel. & Arc.* 209 (Harl. MS.), Sheo gane hit wreyte. *c* **1440** *Promp. Parv.* 534 Wrytyn, *scribo.* **1449** *Paston Lett.* I. 87 [He prayeth] me to wrythe to ȝow. ? *a* **1450** tr. *Higden* V. 359 Orator.. did wryȝte the Actes of thapostles. **1480** in *Cely Papers* (Camden) 52 As of any tydynges her y con none wrytt yow as ȝett. **1503** DUNBAR *Thistle & Rose* 23 In my honour sum thing thow go wryt [*rime* delyt]. **1589** PEELE *Eglogue* B j b, To writen sike praise. ? **1616** SIR W. MURE *Misc. Poems* xvi. 3 My barren muse.. to wryt forbears. **1673** in *Jrnl. Friends' Hist. Soc.* July (1914) 98 Thou should wright to her. **1864** TENNYSON *North. Farmer* xv, Summun I reckons 'ull 'a to wroite.

β. **13..** *Cursor M.* 5323 Þe king þan did his lettres writte [*rime* lite]. *Ibid.* 9898 Fairer.. þan.. ani clerc mai writ wit inc. **1423** JAS. I *Kingis Q.* clxxxii, Quhat nedis me.. To writt all this? **1533** GAU *Richt Vay* 25 Al the buikis.. quhilk.. oders cane writ. *a* **1700** in *Cath. Rec. Soc. Publ.* IX. 365 To writt her life. **1704** ATHOLL in *Seafield's Lett.* (1915) 137, I did myself the honour to writte.. last week.

γ. **1477** in *Makculloch MS.* (S.T.S.) 28 *Sarffo*,.. to wret. **1536** BOORDE in *Introd.*, etc. (1870) 52 To wrett att theyr request. *a* **1547** in *Anglia* XII. 260 Off hur goodnese then wolde I wrete. **1573** TYRIE in *Cath. Tractates* (S.T.S.) 11, I haif thocht.. to wreit this writting amanges the rest. **1603** in *10th Rep. Hist. MSS. Comm.* App. I. 31 The man that teichis me to vret. **1640** SIR W. MURE *Covnter-Buff* 52 A schollar.. A pasquill did against his Countrey wreat. **1699** *Seafield's Lett.* (1912) 256, I have.. litell to wret. **1705** *Ibid.* (1915) 46 He layes it on me to wreat. **1859** E. B. RAMSAY *Remin.* v. (ed. 5) 99 To write.., in old-fashioned Scotch pronunciation.. [is] to wireete. **1871** W. ALEXANDER *Johnny Gibb* xlix, Ye'll jist vreet aff at ance. **1914** ANGUS *Shetland Gloss.* 158 *Wret*,.. to write; *p.t.* and *pa.p.* wret.

δ. **1564** Q. MARY in *Reg. Privy Council Scot.* XIV. 201 We ar movit.. to wrait this present unto you. **1580** HAY in *Cath. Tractates* (S.T.S.) 68 That quhilk Ihone Caluin wraites in the fourt buik. **1866** GREGOR *Banffsh. Gloss.* 204 *Vrait*,.. to write.

b. *3rd pers. sing.* 1–4 **writ,** 3 **wryt.**

c **1000** ÆLFRIC *Hom.* II. 2 Mycel yfel deð se ðe leas writ. *c* **1175** *Lamb. Hom.* 21 Þe deofel.. writ heo [*sc.* a sin] in his tables. **1390** GOWER *Conf.* III. 245 The Philosophre.. Writ and conseileth to a king.

2. *Pa. t.* **a.** *Sing.* (latterly also *pl.*). α. 1–6, 9 *north. dial.* **wrat** (3 *pl.* **wratenn,** 5 **whrat,** *Sc.* **vrat, wart**), 4, 6 **wratte;** 2, 4– **wrate,** 5 **wraite,** *Sc.* 5–7 **wrait,** 5 **wrayt(e,** 6 **wraitt, vrait,** 9 *dial.* **wraat, wreat.**

Since *c* 1300 chiefly *north.* and *Sc.*, but also in southern use *c* 1540–*c* 1620.

743–5 in Earle *Land Charters* (1888) 42 Wilfrið bisceop he hit wrat. *c* **1175** *Cott. Hom.* 235 God þas laȝe.. wrate his him self. *c* **1200** [see B. 4 b]. **13..** *Cursor M.* 21243 Þe godspel in itali he wratte [*Fairf.* wrate, *rime* smate]. *c* **1375** *Ibid.* 1470 (Fairf.), Ennoc.. wrate [*Gött.* wrat] sum bokis wiþ his hande. *c* **1425** WYNTOUN *Cron.* VII. 1854 Þis Alexander.. Wart [*v.r.* wrait] til Schir Mathow. **1481** *Cely Papers* (Camden) 76 The clawys that ȝe whrat of Laysetter. **1585** WHITNEY *Choice Embl.* (1586) *4 b, Seneca.. wratte lamentable Tragedies. *a* **1586** SIDNEY *Arcadia* III. (1922) 25 Upon a roote of the tree.. she wrat this couplet. **1620** T. PEYTON *Glasse Time* I. 51 That sweete Disciple which the Gospell wrate. **1708** FALCONER in Hearne *Collect.* (O.H.S.) II. 130, I wrate once and again. **1824** [CARR] *Craven Gloss.* 124 *Wraat*,.. wrote. **1828–** in Yorks. and Linc. glossaries (*wrate*). **1894** HESLOP *Northumbld. Gloss.* 799 He wrat him a letter.

β. 3–8 **wrot,** 5–6 **wrotte, wrott;** 4 **wrote,** 5 *pl.* **wroten,** 6 **wroate (wroght);** 4–5 **wroot,** 6 **wroott, wrout(e.**

c **1200** *Trin. Coll. Hom.* 17 Elch of hem wrot [= *Lamb. Hom.* 75 wrat] his uers. **1303** R. BRUNNE *Handl. Synne* 9281 A fende.. wrote alle þat euer þey spake. **13..** *K. Alis.* 4778 (Laud MS.), He.. wroot Alle þise wondres. **1377** LANGL. *P. Pl.* B. XIX. 478, I.. wrote [*v.rr.* wroot, wrouȝte, wroȝt] as me mette. *c* **1420** *Wycliffite Bible* Acts xv. 23 The apostlis.. wroten.. greting. ? **1481** *Cely Papers* (Camden) 202 A letter from you wherin ȝe wrotte for your mone. **1513** in Ellis *Orig. Lett.* Ser. II. I. 212 A letter the Swyssers wroott unto me. *a* **1529** SKELTON *Ware Hauke* 223, I wroute a verse. ? *c* **1530** in Ellis *Orig. Lett.* Ser. III. III. 189 Sythe I last wroght to you. **1557** in Foxe *A. & M.* (1576) 1891/1 Whether thou wrotest it not. **1590** TARLTON *News Purgat.* A 2 Virgill after he wrot his *Aeneidos*, wrote his *Culex*. **1709** STRYPE *Ann. Ref.* I. 246 He wrot to.. Cecil to release him. **1748** RICHARDSON *Clarissa* (1768) VI. 299 A Letter.. which thou wrotest.

γ. 5–9 (now *dial.*) **writ** (6 *Sc.* **vrit**), 5–7 **writt,** (7 **ritt**), 6–7 **writte;** 5 **wryt,** 6 **wrytte.**

c **1400** *Rom. Rose* 6585 There as he writ of these worchynges. **1479** *Cely Papers* (Camden) 15 Ȝe wryt to me a clawys in your letter. **1539** in Ellis *Orig. Lett.* Ser. II. II. 152 Yowr Kyng wrytte agaynste Lwtther. **1561** T. Hoby tr. *Castiglione* II. (1900) 144 A letter which [she] writt unto her lover. **1600** W. WATSON *Decacordon* (1602) 226 They writ to all their brethren. **1648–63** [see B. 23 b]. **1666** in *11th Rep. Hist. MSS. Comm.* App. V. 14, I ritt wonce to you. *a* **1699** LADY HALKETT *Autobiog.* (Camden) 9 My Lord H. writt to my mother. *a* **1774** GOLDSM. tr. *Scarron's Com. Romance* (1775) I. 313, I writ to her, she received my letter. **1788** *Trifler* No. 12. 156 Authors (who writ in the Latin tongue). **1852** THACKERAY *Esmond* II. i, He writ back a letter.

δ. 5–7 **write.**

c **1454** PECOCK *Folewer* 7 Þe book which y write in englisch. **1582** R. ROBINSON tr. *Leland's Assertion* iii. 5 That Iohn which concerning Arthure write the golden historie. *a* **1700** [see B. 17].

ε. *Sc.* 6–7 **wreit (vreit),** 7 **wreitt, wreat,** 6 **wrett,** 6, 9 **wret.**

1549 *Compl. Scot.* 116 Also he vreit ane lettir. *c* **1560** [see B. 7 b]. *a* **1568** *Henryson's Sum Practysis* 9 (Bann. MS.), The quhilk.. ȝe nocht vnderstude, Bot wrett on as ȝe culd. *a* **1585** MONTGOMERIE *Flyting* (T.) 645 Witness sum vers he wreit [*Harl. MS.* wreat]. *a* **1600** —— *Poems* (1910) 240 Sant peter wrett ane vþair quhair. **1652** in *Spalding Club Misc.* I. 45, I wreitt lykewayes to my sone in law to assist him. **1914** [see A. 1 γ].

b. *Pl.* α. 1 **writon,** 3–5 **writen** (3 *Orm.* **-enn**), 4–5 **wryten,** 5 **writun, wrytyn** (9 *dial.* **rit'n**); 4 **write,** 5 **whryte,** *Sc.* **wryt.**

c **888** ÆLFRED *Boeth.* xviii. § 3 Eac þa ðe hi ymb writon. *a* **1200** *Vices & V.* 27 Ðat ðe ure hali faderes.. writen. **1390** GOWER *Conf.* III. 85 Yit of that Calistre And Aristotle whylom write To Alisandre, thou schalt wite. *c* **1450** CAPGRAVE *St. Gilbert* 95 Þei.. mor-ouyr wrytyn and sent on-to þe Pope, compleynyng. **14..** *Wycliffite Bible* Acts xv. 23 The apostlis.. wroten [*v.rr.* wryten, writen, writun].. to hem.. greting. **1480** *Cely Papers* (Camden) 55 Ȝe whryte to howr father that [etc.]. **1887** *S. Chesh. Gloss.* 86 Wey rit·n,.. Yai rit·n,.. Dhai rit·n.

β. 1 **wreotan, -on,** 4–5 **wreten, wrete.**

852 in Birch *Cartul.* II. 58 Her sindan ða naman ðere monna þe þis wreotan & festnedan. *c* **900** tr. *Bæda's Hist.* (1890) 346 Þætte seolfan þa his lareowas æt his muðe wreoton. **1340–70** *Alex. & Dind.* 24 Þe gentil genosophistiens.. To þe emperour alixandre here answerus wreten. **1387** TREVISA *Higden* V. 147 Athanasius.. and oþer bisshoppes.. wrete for seventy chapitres. *c* **1440** *Wycliffite Bible* Acts xv. 23 (MS. Bodl. 277), Þe apostlis.. wreten bi þe hondis of hem.. greetyng. **1449** *Paston Lett.* I. 76 Your eronds that ye wrete to me fore.

c. *Weak forms.* 5 **wrytted,** *pl.* **writide(n.**

c **1420** *Wycliffite Bible* 1 Esdr. iv. 6 Thei writiden accusing aȝens the dwellers. *Ibid.* 8 [They] writen [*v.r.* writede].. oon epistil. **1449** *Paston Lett.* I. 88 My cosyn Cler wrytted to me that sche spake with Schrowpe.

3. *Pa. pple.* **a.** α. (*a*) 1 **ȝewriten,** 2–3 **ȝewriten,** 3–5 **i-,** 4–5 **ywriten,** 4 **ywriton, -ein,** 3–4 **i-,** 5 **ywryten,** 5–6 **-yn.** (*b*) 1–7 **writen** (1 **uuriten,** 3 *Orm.* **writenn,** 5–6 **wirten,** 5 **-in**), 4–5 **writene,** 4–5, *Sc.* 6 **-in,** 5 **-yn, -on, -un,** 6 *Sc.* **vrityn(e;** 4–6 **wryten,** 4–5 **-yn (wyrtyn,** 5 *Sc.* **vyrtyn**), 5 **-un, -on, -ine,** *Sc.* **vrytin;** 6 **wryghten,** 6–7 **wrighten.**

(*a*) *c* **880** in *O.E. Texts* 452 Ond sio ðis lond ȝewriten & unbefliten [etc.]. *c* **1175** *Lamb. Hom.* 11 [It] wes iwriten inne þa table. *Ibid.*, Nu weren þas þreo laȝe ȝe-writen. **13..** *K. Alis.* 4042 Hit is y-writein. **1362** LANGL. *P. Pl.* A. I. 174 Wordes i-writen in þe Ewangelye. ? *c* **1530** in Ellis *Orig. Lett.* Ser. III. II. 221 Y wrytyn at Godolphyn.

(*b*) *Beowulf* 1688 On ðæm wæs or writen fyrn-ȝewinnes. *a* **1200** *Moral Ode* 224 A boken hit [is] writen þer me mei hit reden. *a* **1400** in *Relig. Lyrics 14th C.* (1924) 157 Tyl a lettre of loue me lede, þat was wyrtyn on a wall. *a* **1447** in Ellis *Orig. Lett.* Ser. I. I. 8 Wrytyn.. the xij. day of Marche. **1517** *Lincoln Wills* (Linc. Rec. Soc.) V. 75 The last will.. wirten the day a bovesaid. **1552** *Office of Augm., Misc. Bk. XLV*, No. 147 The daye.. aboue wryghten. **1693** *Seafield's Lett.* (1912) 127 This is wryten in my bed. **1703** *Ibid.* (1915) 8, I have writen to the Earle.

β. 4–5 **iwritten,** 5 **ywrytten,** 6 **ywritten;** 4– **written** (5–6 **writtyn,** 5–6, *Sc.* 7 **-in,** 7 **writt'n**), 4–6 **wrytten,** 5 **wryttyn (whryttyn),** 5–6 **-yne,** 9 *Sc.* **vrutten.**

13.. *Cursor M.* 6995 In his time war þe fabu[l]s written. **1387** TREVISA *Higden* VIII. 41 As it is i-written in his lyf. *c* **1425** WYNTOUN *Chron.* II. 225 As in þe Bibil wryttyn [*v.r.* writtin] is. **1481** *Cely Papers* (Camden) 78, I have whryttyn to yow dyvarys lettyrs. **1562** A. BROOKE *Romeus & Jul.* 711 Ywritten haue I red.. There is no better way to fishe. **1644** MILTON *Areop.* (Arb.) 71 Things not before discourst or writt'n of. **1871** W. ALEXANDER *Johnny Gibb* xlviii, [How] hisna he vrutten to you?

γ. 4–5 **iwreten,** 5 **-yn, ywreten;** 4–7 **wreten,** 4–6 **-yn,** 5–6 **-in,** 5 **-yne, -on,** *Sc.* 6–7 **wreittin** (6 **vreittin**), 7 **wreaten,** 6 **wraitten.**

1387 TREVISA *Higden* VII. 79 As þere is wreten in lettres. *Ibid.* 441 Emerus.. had i-wreten and descryved Anselms lyf. **14..** *Chaucer's Sec. Nun's T.* 91 (Lansd. MS.), Euery where þis wordes al wiþ golde wreten [*Camb. MS.* i-wretyn] were. **1476** in *Cely Papers* (Camden) 4 That Thomas Kesten hat ywreten unto me. **1534** CROMWELL in *Life & Lett.* (1902) I. 385 Wretyn at my house. **1581** *Excheq. Rolls Scotl.* XXI. 421 The landis aboune wreittin. **1664** J. CARSTAIRS *Lett.* (1846) 109, I have wreaten ane other lyne to the Lord Chancellor. **1685** *Seafield's Lett.* (1912) 10, I would have wreiten to you. **1693** *Ibid.* 109 [A letter] wreitten to him.

δ. 5, *Sc.* 6 **wrettyn,** 6 **wretten** (**-on,** *Sc.* **-in**).

1445 *Paston Lett.* I. 59 Wrettyn in haste, at Norwich. *a* **1533** LD. BERNERS *Huon* cxvi. 407 Letters.. wretten on the pament. *a* **1578** LINDESAY (Pitscottie) *Chron. Scot.* (S.T.S.) II. 50 This letter.. [was] wrettin be thir thrie foirsaid personis in all heist.

ε. 7 *Sc.* **wraitten.**

a **1614** J. MELVILL *Diary* (Wodrow Soc.) 367, I have wraitten a special treatise thairof.

b. α. 3–5 **i-, ywrite, ywryte;** 3–7, *Sc.* 8 **write** (7 **wright**), 4–6 **wryte.**

c **1175** *Cott. Hom.* 241 Hit is iwrite Nemo [etc.]. *c* **1200**, etc. [see YWRIT *pa. pple.*]. *c* **1200** *Moral Ode* 228 (Trin.), A boc hit is write. **13..** *Chron. R. Glouc.* (Rolls) 1901 Ywrite [*v.r.* wryte] was lo þis. *c* **1420** *Chron. Vilod.* cccxvi, þe sothe as y fynd yn story y wryte. **1480** *Cely Papers* (Camden) 43 Wryte at London. **1678** in *12th Rep. Hist. MSS. Comm.* App. V. 53 Hee has wright my Lord all perticulars. **1682** [see B. 16 a]. **1705** SEAFIELD *Lett.* (1915) 61 It is write by one I can trust.

β. 5 **i-, ywritte,** 5, 6–7 *arch.* **ywrit;** 5–6 **writte** (5 **whritte**), 5 **wrytte,** 5–6 **wryt,** 6– (now *dial.* or *arch.*) **writ,** 6–7 **writt.**

1422 YONGE tr. *Secreta Secret.* 122 As y fynde writte. **1424** *Stonor Papers* (Camden) I. 39 I-wrytte at London. **1457** *Paston Lett.* I. 417 Wryt hastly at London. *a* **1542** WYATT in *Anglia* XVIII. 273 As it is writt. **1590** SPENSER *F.Q.* I. x. 19 Her sacred Booke, with bloud ywrit. **1642** H. MORE *Song of Soul* I. III. xxvi, On which.. be ywrit These words. **1681** PENN in *Pennsylv. Hist. Soc. Mem.* (1864) I. 210, I have..

writt truth. 1859 TENNYSON *Elaine* 1103 The letter..being writ And folded.

γ. 3–5 **iwrete**, 4–5 **ywrete**; 4–6 **wrete**, 7 *Sc.* **wreat(e, wreitt.**

c 1275 LAY. 22981 þat soþe his iwrete. 1303 R. BRUNNE *Handl. Synne* 2179 Hyt ys seyde þurgh lawe wrete, þat [etc.]. 1426 LYDG. *De Guil. Pilgr.* 10008 The word ywrete in sapyence. a 1529 SKELTON *Bouge of Court* 438 On that sleue these wordes were wrete. 1662 J. CARSTAIRS *Lett.* (1846) 97, I have wreate a lyne to the Provost in that matter. 1694 *Seafield's Lett.* (1912) 144 The Secretarys are wreitt to anent it.

δ. 5 **ywret**; 5 **wrette**, 5, *Sc.* 9 **wret**, 5, 7 **wrett.**

1423 in *Rep. Hist. MSS. Comm.* Var. Coll. IV. 83 Y wret at Exeter the day..a bove y sayd. ? 1460 *Paston Lett.* I. 539 Wret the v. day of Decembre. 1646 *Hamilton Papers* (Camden) 126 The other was wrett yesternight. 1914 [see A. 1 γ].

ε. 6–8, 9 *dial.* or *illit.* **wrote** (6 **roten**), 7 **wroate**; 6 **wrotte**, 7 **wrott**, 7–8 **wrot.**

1565 STAPLETON tr. *Bede* 12 Such thinges as I haue wrote of the most holy father. c 1572 GASCOIGNE *Fruites* xcii, When workes of warre are wrotte by such as I. 1637 J. TAYLOR (Water P.) *Drinke* D j b, So I..Have wroate a hotchpotch. 1693 PEPYS in *Lett. Lit. Men* (Camden) 212 As had they been wrott on purpose. 1710 PRIDEAUX *Orig. Tithes* iii. 154 An exhortatory Epistle wrot to him. 1728 CHAMBERS *Cycl.* s.v. *Verse*, The Books themselves were wrote [1738 written] all running. 1848 DICKENS *Dombey* xxxiv, Has she wrote to me? 1879- in dial. glossaries (Shropsh., Warw., etc.).

B. Signification.

I. *trans.* **1.** †**a.** To score, outline, or draw the figure of (something); to incise. *Obs.*

Beowulf 1688 Hroðgar..hylt sceawode, ealde lafe, on ðæm wæs or writen fyrn-ȝewinnes. c 897 ÆLFRED *Gregory's Past. C.* xxi. 160 Nim sume tiȝlan..& writ on hiere ða burȝ Hierusalem. c 1000 *Sax. Leechd.* II. 290 Writ þonne þam horse on þam heafde foran cristes mæl. c 1225 *Leg. Kath.* 190 [She] wrat on hire breoste..þe hali rode taken. c 1366 CHAUCER *Rom. Rose* 413 Another thing was don there write That semede lyk an Ipocrite. a 1450 *Medit. Life & Passion of Christ* 1350 Loue þat art so mykel of myȝt, Writ in myn herte þat reuful syȝt. 1579 SPENSER *Sheph. Cal.* Dec. 136 By myne eie the Crow his clawe dooth wright. 1590 —— *F.Q.* II. viii. 43 Guyons shield..Whereon the Faery Queenes pourtract was writ.

b. To form (letters, symbols, words, etc.) by carving, engraving, or incision; to trace in or on a hard or plastic surface, esp. with a sharp instrument; to record in this way.

In later use not clearly distinguished from sense 2.

a 1000 *Gnomic Verses* 139 Ræd sceal mon secgan, rune writan. c 1000 ÆLFRIC *Deut.* x. 2 Ic write on ðam bredum ða word ðe wæron on ðam ðe ðu ær bræce. c 1175, c 1250 [see TABLE *sb.* 2 a]. 1377 LANGL. *P. Pl.* B. XII. 80 Þorw carectus þat cryst wrot þe iewes knewe hemseluen Gultier..Þan þe woman. c 1400 MAUNDEV. (1839) iii. 17 In the Dust and in the Powder..thei wroot Lettres and Figures with hire Fingres. c 1450 CAPGRAVE *St. Augustine* 25 He took a peyre tables, and wroot in þe wax al his desir. 1535 COVERDALE *Deut.* xxvii. 3 Thou shalt set vp greate stones,..and wryte vpon them all the wordes of this lawe. 1599 HAKLUYT *Voy.* II. I. 117 Men being first inforced to write their actes..in barkes of trees. 1649 OGILBY tr. *Virg., Bucolicks* v. 13 I'll try that Song on the green Beech I writ. 1697 J. LEWIS *Mem. Dk. Glocester* (1789) 77 He made an Epitaph..to be wrote on a stone. 1728 POPE *Dunc.* III. 325 On Poets' Tombs see Benson's titles writ. 1781 COWPER *Hope* 588 Blush, calumny! and write upon his tomb..Thy deep repentance of thy thousand lies. 1831 SIR F. PALGRAVE *Hist. Anglo-Sax.* vii. 153 The slips of bamboo upon which the inhabitants..write or scratch their compositions with a bodkin. 1857 LOCKER *Lond. Lyrics* 51 It was I wrote her name on the sand.

fig. and in fig. context. c 1175 *Cott. Hom.* 235 [Jesus Christ] þe sceolde his aȝen wille..in ure heorte write. a 1300 *Cursor M.* 25586 Suete iesu!..þi pines in vr hertes write. c 1400 *26 Pol. Poems* 102 Þy countretayle þey wil shewe, þe skore, In helle or in heuene, wreten trewe. 1599, 1622 [see TABLE *sb.* 2 c]. a 1628 PRESTON *Effectual Faith* (1631) 49 It is the Holy Ghost that must write them in your hearts; wee can but write them in your heads. 1653 H. MORE *Antid. Ath.* I. ix. 27 When we see writ in our Souls..the Name or rather the Nature and Idea of God. 1877 MRS. OLIPHANT *Makers Flor.* i. 2 The names of the older generations are writ in brass on the glowing walls of the Inferno.

transf. 1588 SHAKS. *Titus A.* III. i. 170 Which of your hands hath not..rear'd aloft the bloody Battleaxe, Writing destruction on the enemies Castle? a 1623 FLETCHER *Love's Cure* I. i, Useless are all words Till you have writ performance with your swords. 1818 BYRON *Ch. Har.* IV. clxxxii, Roll on, thou..dark blue Ocean!.. Time writes no wrinkle on thy azure brow.

c. fig. ***to write in the dust, in*** or ***on sand, water, the wind***, etc., with reference to absence of abiding record. (See WATER *sb.* 1 f, and cf. SAND *sb.*[2] 2 c.)

1513 MORE *Edw. V* (1641) 130 For men use to write an evill turne in marble stone, but a good turne in the dust. 1611–3 [see WATER *sb.* 1 f]. a 1634 CHAPMAN *Revenge for Honour* V. ii, Words writ in waters, have more lasting Essence, then our determinations. a 1658 LOVELACE *Poems* (1904) 203 But what women say to kind Lovers, we write in rapid streams and wind. 1795 J. NOTT tr. *Catullus* lxvii. II. 113 What..are woman's vows? Fit to be written but on air, Or on the stream! 1821 KEATS in *Poet. Wks.* (1876) p. xxx, Here lies one whose name was writ in water. 1846 MRS. BROWNING *Lett.* (1899) I. 433, I may say of Henrietta that her only fault is, her virtues being written in water. 1847 MANGAN *Poems* (1903) 99 Oh! let not your vow Have been written in sand!

d. *transf.* To impress or stamp marks indicating (some condition or quality) *on*, *in*, or *over* a person, etc. Freq. in phr. ***to be*** (or ***have***) ***written all over*** a person.

1603 SHAKS. *Meas. for M.* IV. ii. 162 There is written in your brow Prouost, honesty and constancie. a 1653 H. BINNING *Sermon* Wks. (1845) 648 Insobriety is written upon many passages of your behaviour. 1682 DRYDEN *Mac Flecknoe* 195 A Tun of Man in thy large Bulk is writ. 1854 THACKERAY *Newcomes* xxv, Cook and housekeeper is written on her round face. 1866 LEVER *Sir B. Fossbrooke* I. 78 One on whom Nature had written gentleman. a 1899 in *Westm. Gaz.* 30 Dec. 1/2 Duty is written all over him. 1914 'I. HAY' *Knight on Wheels* (ed. 2) xxix. 292 It must be written all over me if you can spot it... Yes, you are right... I'm in love. 1967 G. F. FIENNES *I tried to run Railway* iii. 28 He had horse written all over him. 1979 J. GARDNER *Nostradamus Traitor* vi. 20 One was with her... Had DDR written all over him.

2. a. To form or delineate (a letter, symbol, ideogram, etc.) on paper or the like with a pen, pencil, etc.; to trace (significant characters) in this manner.

743–5 [see A. 2 α]. c 1000 *Ags. Gosp.* Luke xvi. 6 Nim þine feðere..& writ fiftiȝ. c 1200 ORMIN Ded. 104 Þatt he An bocstaff write twiȝȝess. c 1250 *Gen. & Ex.* 2527 And he ðat ðise lettres wrot, God him helpe weli mot. c 1300 *Havelok* 2481 We deme, þat..þare be writen þise leteres: 'þis is þe swike' [etc.]. 1387 TREVISA *Higden* VI. 221 He fonde þre R and þre F i-write. c 1425 *Crafte Nombrynge* 16 Þat digit þat þou hast y-write. 1521 BARCLAY *Introductory* B j, Whan .P. is wryten in the ende of a worde in frenche. 1590 SPENSER *F.Q.* III. xii. 31 And her before the vile Enchaunter sate, Figuring straunge characters of his art, With liuing bloud he those characters wrate. 1614 RALEIGH *Hist. World* III. 12 It was as easie..to erre in writing two for sixe and twentie, as for three and twentie. 1647 T. HILL *Paul* (1648) 15 Some tell us Jeremiah and Zachary written contractively in the Hebrew are the same. 1735 JOHNSON *Lobo's Abyssinia, Voy.* i. 4 Unhappily, the Secretary wrote Zeila for Dancala. 1845 *Kitto's Cycl. Bibl. Lit.* (1849) I. 601 At other times they [*sc.* hieroglyphics] are phonetic, and written by an alphabet of about 140 letters. 1887 A. J. ELLIS in *Encycl. Brit.* XXII. 381 Some system of writing speech-sounds.

b. To enter or record (a name) with a pen, etc.; to mention (a person) in this way. Also in fig. context.

c 1200 ORMIN 3554 He shall writenn alle þa Þatt cwemmdenn himm o life Onn eche lifess bokess writt. a 1300 *Cursor M.* 6889 He..wrat þe nam, and sett to sele. 1387 TREVISA *Higden* VII. 31 Otho..heet take hym þe names i-wrete of hem þat were gilty. a 1400 in Heath *Grocer's Comp.* (1869) 41 Plate, Alle these xxij personis before wretyn. a 1450 *Medit. Life & Passion of Christ* 884 To writon vs in bok þat neuere failes. 1472 in *Surtees Misc.* (1890) 25 We ordeyn that all vacabondes, bifore writen, kepe gode reule. 1535 COVERDALE *Isaiah* iv. 3 Al soch as are written amonge the lyuynge at Ierusalem. 1565 COOPER *Thesaurus* s.v. *Inscribo*, They write their owne names in the titles of their bookes. 1623 COCKERAM II. s.v., To Write his name to a Band. 1714 ADDISON *Spect.*, No. 568 ¶ 3 [He] had written the Names of several Persons..at the Side of every Sin..mentioned by that excellent Author. 1772 R. FERGUSSON *Braid Claith* i, To hae your name Wrote in the bonny book of fame. 1827 KEBLE *Chr. Y., St. Barnabas* v, Never so blest, as when in Jesus' roll They write some hero-soul. 1885 'MRS. ALEXANDER' *At Bay* v, Glynn took her programme and wrote his own name for several waltzes.

fig. 1594 SPENSER *Amoretti* lxxv, My verse..shall..in the heuens wryte your glorious name. 1860 *Slang Dict.* (ed. 2) 248 *To write one's name on a joint*, to have the first cut at anything,—leaving sensible traces of one's presence on it.

3. a. (*a*) To set down in writing; to express or present (words, etc.) in written form; to pen. Also (*b*) said of the pen, etc. Occas. in fig. context.

In frequent use from c 1380.

832 in *O.E. Texts* 446 Ic..mid cristes rodetacne ðis festnie & write. 971 *Blickl. Hom.* 133 Se Halȝa Gast dihtode ealle þa þing þe haliȝe men writon. c 1000 ÆLFRIC *Deut.* xxxi. 24 Æfter ðam ðe Moyses wrat ðisse æ bebodu. a 1200 *St. Marher.* 23 Hire bone wes þet ich hit write on bocfelle. c 1275 *Passion of our Lord* 467 in *O.E. Misc.* 50 Pilates wrot him seolf a writ al on hying. c 1290 *Beket* 222 in *S. Eng. Leg.* I. 113 Þis child..Seruede A borgeys of þe toun, and his a-countes wrot. 1303 [see A. 2 β]. 1362 LANGL. *P. Pl.* A. I. 174 Þeos beþ wordes i-writen in þe Ewangelye. c 1400 *Pety Job* 566 in *26 Pol. Poems* 139 Who may graunte me thys boone, That my wordes wreten were. 1473 WARKW. *Chron.* (Camden) 11 He..wrott in alle his lettres..the yere of his regne. 1526 *Pilgr. Perf.* (W. de W. 1531) 2 These instruccyons y^{t} I haue gathered & wryten for you. 1595 SHAKS. *John* IV. i. 37 Can you not reade it? Is it not faire writ? 1667 MILTON *P.L.* XII. 489 A Comforter..the Law of Faith..upon thir hearts shall write. 1681 in *Jrnl. Friends' Hist. Soc.* July (1912) 136 At leasure it may bee written faire in the Booke. 1751 LAVINGTON *Enthus. Meth. & Papists* III. (1754) 163 His Hand had wrote what was directly contrary to the Dictates of his malicious Mind. 1788 CLARA REEVE *Exiles* III. 191, I will get these instructions wrote in a proper form. 1825 J. F. COOPER *L. Lincoln* III. 258 At the close of his long life, he wrote Gen., Bart., and M.P. after his name.

(*b*) 1883 J. G. PETRIE *Man. for Type-Writer* 4 Machines..which write capitals and small letters. 1897 *Strand. Mag.* May 593/2 No pen can write, no song sing, and no story tell of half their happiness.

fig. 1605 SHAKS. *Lear* V. iii. 35 About it, and write happy when th'hast done. 1637 RUTHERFORD *Lett.* (1671) 134, I painted a providence of my own, and wrote ease for my self and a peaceable ministery. 1888 RUSKIN *Præterita* III. iv. 159 Mozart's birth wrote the laws of melody for all the world ..irrevocably.

b. To form by painting or the like; to paint.

a 1400 [see A. 3 a α]. 1556 *Chron. Gr. Friars* (Camden) 54 Alle churches new whytte-lymed, with the commandmenttes wryttyne on the walles. 1561 in *Archaeol.* (1770) I. 16 To the peynter for wrighting the scripture. 1714 SWIFT tr. *Hor., Sat.* II. 92 The lines Writ underneath the Country Signs. 1837 WHITTOCK *Bk. Trades* (1842) 358 Most mere house-painters undertake to paint sign boards.. and..write them tolerably well. 1889 SUTHERLAND *Sign-Writing* i. 1 A man might set out and write a sign in the time.

†**c.** To translate *into* another language. *Obs.*

c 1475 *Babees Bk.* 1 This tretys the whiche I thenke to wryte Out of latyn in-to my comvne langage.

d. ***writ*** (***written***) ***large***, penned, recorded, or exhibited in large or prominent characters. Chiefly in fig. use. Also in analogous *fig.* phrases, as ***writ double, small***, etc.

c 1645 MILTON *Sonn., On new Forcers of Conscience* 20 *New Presbyter* is but *Old Priest* writ Large. 1866 'GEO. ELIOT' *F. Holt* viii, The man was no more than the boy writ large, with an extensive commentary. 1868 FARRAR *Silence & V.* iii. (1875) 56 Let us look beyond them, and see it writ large upon the history of nations. 1877 L. MORRIS *Epic Hades* II. 117 That my life..Was but a tale Writ large by Zeus. 1951 E. BARKER *Princ. Social & Political Theory* I. 39 Corporativism may be defined as syndicalism writ double. 1959 *Times* 25 Feb. 11/2 This year's Defence White Paper.. is last year's writ quietly. 1961 *Observer* 23 Apr. 5/2 In a curious way he's [*sc.* Sir Isaac Hayward's] an amalgam, writ small, of Attlee, Morrison and Bevin. 1967 *Listener* 8 June 762/1 J. P. Donleavy's *The Saddest Summer of Samuel S.* is just *The Ginger Man* writ smaller and smaller.

e. Of a manuscript, etc.: To bear or exhibit in writing.

1607 SHAKS. *Cor.* V. iii. 145 Whose Chronicle thus writ, The man was Noble. 1712 ADDISON *Spect.* No. 470 ¶ 1, I have..been informed, that such or such Ancient Manuscripts for an *et* write an *ac*.

†**f.** To employ in dating. *Obs.*

1651 MARIUS *Adv. Bills of Exchange* (1700) 13 At Hamborough and Strasburg..they do write the same stile with us here in England, namely old stile; but in all other parts beyond the Seas..they do generally write new stile.

g. To print by means of a typewriter; to typewrite; = TYPE *v.* 4.

1883 J. G. PETRIE *Man. for Type-Writer* 3 Writing and re-writing familiar words until the fingers run easily.

h. *Computers.* To enter (an item of data) *in*, *into*, *on*, or *to* a storage medium (esp. a disc or tape) or a location in store; to enter data in or on (a storage medium). Also *absol.* Cf. *to read in* s.v. READ *v.* 6 f.

1946 GOLDSTINE & VON NEUMANN in J. von Neumann *Coll. Wks.* (1963) V. 28 In 'writing' a word into the memory, it is similarly not only the time effectively consumed in 'writing' which matters, but also the time needed to 'find' the specified location in the memory. *Ibid.*, A number that is to be written, i.e. stored, has to be placed at a definite, possibly inconvenient place in the memory. 1948 *Math. Tables & Other Aids to Computation* III. 123 The machines will be able to read from, or write on, the tapes. 1953 B. V. BOWDEN *Faster than Thought* iv. 95 He proposed to make it impossible to write into a store unless it contained zero. 1966 *McGraw-Hill Encycl. Sci. & Technol.* IV. 188/1 The store instruction selects an address through the selection circuit for writing the contents of the accumulator in the memory location specified. 1970 [see READ *v.* 5 h]. 1973 C. W. GEAR *Introd. Computer Sci.* iv. 161 A typical large computer system has many readers and printers... Usually several different jobs are being read and several different outputs are being written at the same time. 1980 *Sci. Amer.* Aug. 114/1 The head that writes the data can also be used to read it. 1980 S. HOCKEY *Guide Computer Applications in Humanities* ii. 28 Information can only be written to the tape when this ring is in place.

i. Of a recording device: to produce (a graphical record).

1949 [see MAREOGRAM]. 1975 *Nature* 6 Feb. 423/1 Our predicted signals do not resemble those of typical creep events as written by creepmeters.

j. To sit or take (a written examination). Chiefly *S. Afr.*

1958 *Cape Argus* 7 Nov. 3/3 Several women attended the course but Miss——was the only one to write the course examinations. 1971 *Sunday Express* (Johannesburg) 28 Mar. (Home Jrnl.) 14/2 My daughter is writing Matric this year. 1974 *Advocate-News* (Barbados) 19 Feb. 1/1 Students from Government primary schools will now write the Common Entrance Examination at their respective schools.

4. a. To state or relate in writing; to draw up or frame a written statement of (circumstances, events, etc.); to chronicle or make a record of. Also with *to*, *unto* (a person), or indirect personal object.

In very frequent use from c 1300.

c 900 *Bæda's Hist.* Pref. (1890) 4 Þæt ic be ðam halȝan fæder Cuðbyrhte wrat oððe on þysse bec oððe on oðre. a 1122 *O.E. Chron.* (Laud MS.) an. 1086, Fela þinga we maȝon writan þe on ðam ilcan ȝeare ȝewordene wæron. c 1175 [see A. 1 b]. c 1220 *Bestiary* 695 In boke is ðe turtres lif writen o rime. 1297 R. GLOUC. (Rolls) 6793 As it is of hire iwrite, & of ire holi fame. a 1300 *Cursor M.* 17843 We sal yow write..All þat we herd and sagh. 1303 R. BRUNNE *Handl. Synne* 8970 Þere..Þey dede to wryte yn boke þys chaunce. 1387, 1423 [see A. 3 a, γ, 1 β]. 1448 *Paston Lett.* I. 71, I wrythe to ȝow the very cause why. 1497 BP. ALCOK *Mons Perfect.* C j b/2 Cryst cam into ye worlde, as it is wryte. 1559 in T. Wright *Q. Eliz.* (1838) I. 17 We woll not write it for gospell that their power is so greate. 1568 HACKET tr. *Thevet's New found World* xxvii. 42 b, There resteth nowe to wright that, the which we haue learned. 1643 DIGBY *Observ. Relig. Med.* (1644) 44 To peruse what I have written at full upon this point. 1671 J. WEBSTER *Metallogr.* i. 12 The *Collegium Conimbricense* are perswaded that he writ the truth. a 1715 BURNET *Own Time* (1766) I. 18 Whose life is so curiously writ by Thomas Hubert. 1794 *J. H. Moore's Pract. Navig.* (ed. 10) 169 Occurrences which are written on the log-board. 1833 TENNYSON *Dream Fair Wom.* lx, It is written that my race Hew'd Ammon, hip and thigh. 1865 SWINBURNE *Chastelard* II. i. 55 Which alms (Remembering what was writ of Magdalen) I gave not grudging.

fig. and *transf.* a 1225 *Ancr. R.* 388 He..wrote mid his owune blode saluz to his leofmon. c 1400 *26 Pol. Poems* xvii. 181 His herte blod wrot oure hele, And Ihesus body, þe parchemyn is. a 1586 SIDNEY *De Mornay* v. ¶ 9 We haue read in nature that there is but one God, as a thing which we finde written euen in the least creatures. 1606 SHAKS. *Ant. & Cl.* V. i. 22 That selfe-hand Which writ his Honor in the Acts it did. a 1680 CHARNOCK *Attrib. God* (1682) 814 Those

Testimonies of it [*sc.* God's patience], which were written in showers, and fruitful seasons. **1781** Cowper *Expost.* 311 Is adverse providence, when ponder'd well, So dimly writ, or difficult to spell. **1869** Freeman *Norm. Conq.* III. xiv. 355 The great tale of which it became the theatre is legibly written on its natural features.

b. With clause as object, either introduced by *that*, etc., or directly quoted.

(*a*) **835** [see A. 1 *a*]. *c* **900** tr. *Bæda's Hist.* (1890) 42 Writeð Eutropius þæt Constantinus se casere wære on Breotone acenned. *Ibid.* 460 Hi on heora sinoðȝewrit onȝeþeoddon, & þus writon betwyh him: Wilfrið [etc.]. *c* **1200** Ormin (1878) II. 354 Acc hallȝhe weress wratenn uss,.. þatt [etc.]. *a* **1225** *Ancr. R.* 42 Leteð writen on one scrowe hwat se ȝe ne kunneð nout. **1390** Gower *Conf.* I. 4 If noman write hou that it stode. **1455** *Paston Lett.* I. 348 As ye wrygth they sey now. **1471** Caxton *Recuyell* (Sommer) 397 A table wherin was wreton wyth letters of gold Passe no further [etc.]. **1542** Udall *Erasm. Apoph.* 230 Of Pompeius it is writen, that [etc.]. **1596** Dalrymple tr. *Leslie's Hist. Scot.* (S.T.S.) I. 99 Sum wrytes scottis to eit menis flesche. **1686** *Seafield Lett.* (1912) 25 They write that.. their fleet sailed from the Texel. **1761** L. Morris in *Cambrian Reg.* (1796) I. 368 The bad sign-painter.. was obliged to write over his drawings, this is a horse, this is a cock, &c. **1848** Thackeray *Van. Fair* xxiv, 'I shall expect you at half-past five,' Captain Dobbin wrote. **1850** Tennyson *In Mem.* vi. 1 One writes, that 'Other friends remain'.

transf. *c* **1386** Chaucer *Man of Law's T.* 191 Parauenture in thilke large book Which þat men clipe the heuene ywriten was With sterres.. That he for loue sholde han his deeth allas! **1616** T. Scot *Philomythie* K 8, The stiffe-vdder'd Cow [missing].. the merry milke-maide.. by chance, wrot on the ground With milk-white letters where shee would be found.

c. To convey (tidings, information, etc.) by letter; to send (a message) in writing. Freq. with *to* or *unto*, or with dative of person; also with *how*, *that*, etc., and clause.

(*a*) ? *a* **1400** *Morte Arth.* 3904 He.. wraite vn-to Waynor how the werlde chaungede. **1449** [see A. 2 c]. **1561** T. Hoby tr. *Castiglione's Courtyer* II. (1900) 164 He wrott unto the Duke,.. he would [etc.]. **1596** Shaks. *1 Hen. IV*, IV. i. 31 He writes me here, that [etc.]. **1616** R. Cocks *Diary* (Halk. Soc.) I. 150 They wrot me how the Portingals had 4 gallions. **1685** Evelyn *Mrs. Godolphin* (1847) 92 She writes me.. what conflicts she had endur'd. **1763** Scrofton *Indostan* (1770) 77 The Colonel.. wrote the Soubah, 'That.. their enemies' [etc.]. **1833** J. H. Newman *Lett.* (1891) I. 434, I had.. written to Rose how we had best start agitating. **1875** B. Meadows *Clin. Observ.* 69 [She] writes me that she is very much better.

(*b*) **1607** Shaks. *Cor.* v. vi. 63 Haue you with heede perused What I haue written to you? **1662** Stillingfl. *Orig. Sacr.* I. iv. § 11 Alexander.. writ word to his Mother he had found out [etc.]. **1676** Essex in *E. Papers* (Camden, 1913) 59 What you say.. hath bin writt over hither by divers. **1678** [see A. 3 b *a*]. **1757** Mrs. Griffith *Lett. Henry & Frances* (1767) I. 179, I beg you will write me word.. whether [etc.]. **1760–72** H. Brooke *Fool of Qual.* (1792) III. 159 Your brother writ me an account of your fatal falling away. **1843** Lowe *Fishes Madeira* I. 101 Mr. Yarrell writes me word that [etc.]. **1850** Miss Mulock *Olive* xxv, You will .. write me word how it looks.

d. To decree, ordain, or enjoin in writing. Chiefly *fig.* (of fate).

1560 Bible (Genev.) *1 Esdr.* vi. 17 King Cyrus wrote that this House shulde be buylt vp. **1675** Dryden *Aurengz.* I. (1676) 14 'Tis writ in Fate, I can be onely yours. **1842** Borrow *Bible in Spain* xxxv, 'It was not so written,' said Antonio, who.. was a fatalist. **1902** 'Roma White' *Backsheesh* xvii. 280 That which is written is written. It is stronger than I. So let it be.

5. a. To give a written account or enumeration of; to describe or depict in writing.

c **1000** *Three O.E. Prose Texts* 2 Ac þa ðing þe me nu in ȝemynd cumað ærest þa ic þe write. *c* **1200** *Vices & Virtues* 19 Ne mai ic þenchen,.. ne on boke write, alle ðo pinen of helle. *a* **1225** *Ancr. R.* 240 Efter þe urouren þet beoð her iwritene. *a* **1300** *Cursor M.* 648 Ne writer nan mai write wit inc þe mikel ioy þat þam es lent. **13..** [see A. 2 β]. **1382** Wyclif *Ecclus.* xlii. 7 The ȝyuen thing.., and the taken, al diskryue, or wryte. *c* **1449** Pecock *Repr.* I. xi. 55 [= Rev. xxii. 18] Putte God upon him the veniauncis writun in this book. *c* **1600** Shaks. *Sonn.* xvii, If I could write the beauty of your eyes. **1608** Topsell *Serpents* 131 When the Egyptians will write a man eating or at dinner, they paynt a Crocodile gaping. **1636** E. Dacres *Machiavel's Disc. Livy* II. 545 Things which they have done, that lived in the manner above written.

b. To treat of (a subject, theme, etc.) in writing.

c **1000** *Ags. Gosp.* John i. 45 We ȝemetton ðone hælend .. þone wrat moyses & þa witeȝan on ðære æ. **1597** Morley *Introd. Mus.* 152 Those who haue of late daies written the art of musicke. **1711** Felton *Dissert. Classics* (1718) a 4 b, The Difficulties of writing History. **1737** Pope tr. *Hor., Ep.* II. i. 146 Ev'ry flow'ry Courtier writ Romance. **1821** Byron *Diary* 29 Jan., They talk Dante—write Dante.

c. To give expression to (one's feelings, thoughts, etc.) by means of writing; to express in written form.

a **1250** *Owl & Night.* 1756 Þar he demeþ mony riht dom & diht & wryt [*v.r.* writ] mony wisdom. **1382** Wyclif *Job* xiii. 26 Thou writist aȝen me bitternessis. *c* **1400** *26 Pol. Poems* xxiv. 146 Lord,.. aȝens me þou doest wryte Bitternesse, bote swete is past. **1524** Q. Margaret in Green *Lett.* (1846) I. 319, I did write my mind plainly to you. **1653** Walton *Angler* i. 29 God.. [allowed] those.. to write his holy will in holy writ. **1705** *Seafield Lett.* (1915) 34, I shall write my thoughts with all freedome. **1748** Richardson *Clarissa* (1768) VII. 76 My heart is full, and I can't help writing my mind. **1798** Nelson in A. Duncan *Life* (1806) 96 Buonaparte writes his distress for stores.

6. a. To compose and set down on paper (a literary composition, narrative, verse, etc.); to put into or produce in literary form, to bring out (a book or literary work) as an author; to indite.

In very frequent use from *c* 1570.

? *a* **900** *O.E. Chron.* (Parker MS.) an. 84, Her Iohannes.. wrat þa boc Apocalipsis. *c* **1175** *Lamb. Hom.* 55 For alswa god hit bit, and inne þe godspelle þe he writ. *c* **1200** *Vices & Virtues* 85 Ðis ic habbe iwriten for ðe te frieurien ðanne ðu niede hafst. *c* **1250** *Gen. & Ex.* 4124 He [*sc.* Moses].. wrot an canticle on ðat booc. *a* **1272** *Luue Ron* 210 in *O.E. Misc.* 99 And yeue him god endynge þat haueþ iwryten þis ilke wryt. *a* **1300** *Cursor M.* 14399 Vr for-eldres þe bible wrat. *c* **1330**, *c* **1386** [see style *sb.* 13]. **1390** Gower *Conf.* Prol. 6 Good is that we also.. Do wryte of newe som matiere. *c* **1450** *Myrr. our Ladye* I. v. 18 To him that writeth my songe & my praysynge. **1533** Gau *Richt Vay* 25 Al the buikis.. qvhilk.. oders cane writ. **1585** [see A. 2 *a*]. *a* **1586** Sidney *Astr. & Stella* Sonn. lviii, In pearcing phrases late The Anatomie of all my woes I wrate. **1608** Willet *Hexapla Exod.* 257 When Moses writte that storie. **1652** *Nicholas Papers* (Camden) 311 Pamphlets which.. he wrote to persuade those [etc.]. **1702** Addison *Dial. Medals* (1727) 50 They writ the whole Poem on purpose to abuse some one. **1781** Cowper *Let.* 12 July, I have writ Charity.. as well as I could. **1819** Scott *Ivanhoe* xxxiii, [If] the monks.. take not to writing chronicles. **1895** *Bookman* Oct. 11/2 He is.. busy writing the new novel.

fig. and *transf.* *c* **1600** Shaks. *Sonn.* xciii, The falce hearts history Is writ in moods and frounes and wrinckles strange. **1853** Bagehot *Lit. Stud.* (1879) I. 142 Marmion was 'written' while he [*sc.* Scott] was galloping on horseback.

b. With various preps., as *against*, *for* or *to* (or with indirect personal object), *of*, *on*, or *upon* (a subject, person, etc.).

c **1200** Ormin 5810 [They] writenn off þe Laferrd Crist Goddspell o fowwre bokess. **1377** Langl. *P. Pl.* B. x. 169, I wrote hir many bokes. **1481** in W. Blades *Caxton* (1882) 231 The polytyque book.. whiche that Tullius wrote vpon the disputacons. *c* **1520** M. Nisbet *N.T.* (S.T.S.) I. 17 It was niedful that it [*ante* the euangel] war writin alsa aganis heretikis. **1585** Whitney *Choice Emblems* (1586) Ep. Ded. *4 His priuate bookes he wratte to Traian, of counsell and gouernement. **1685** Waller *Div. Poesy* I. 17 Verse so designed, on that high subject wrote. **1714** Addison *Spect.* No. 568 ¶3 Some-body had written a Book against the 'Squire. **1794** Mrs. A. M. Bennett *Ellen* II. 47 Volumes wrote on the subject could not do it away. **1820** *Q. Mus. Mag.* II. 68 The character of the Count [in the opera] has been obviously written for Signor Garcia. **1888** Barrie *When a Man's Single* xi. 180 Mary Abinger.. read them [*sc.* books] proudly, knowing that they were all written for her.

c. To compose and set down (music, a melody, etc.) in notes.

1672 T. Salmon *Ess. Adv. Music* Contents, Chap. iv, One who can Sing a Treble part, can immediately Sing that which is written for the Base. **1782** Burney *Hist. Mus.* II. 566 Such keys as these pieces are written in. **1837** *Penny Cycl.* VIII. 108/1 Airs.. written in two parts. **1885** *Dict. Nat. Biog.* II. 105 [Arne] wrote new music for Addison's opera 'Rosamond'.

7. a. To pen (a document, writing, etc.); to put into proper written form; to draft or draw up. Also, to insert (provisions, etc.) *into* a law, agreement, etc. Also in fig. context.

831 [see A. 1 *a*]. *c* **1000** *Ags. Gosp.* John xix. 19 Witodlice pilatus wrat ofer-ȝewrit. *c* **1200**, etc. [see writ *sb.* 1 b, 1 c]. *a* **1333** W. Herebert in *Relig. Lyrics 14th C.* (1924) 19 And helpe he wole ich wot, Vor loue þe chartre wrot, þe enke orn of hys wounde. *c* **1400** *Ploughman's Tale* III. 1367 This writing writeth the pellican. **1455** *Rolls of Parlt.* V. 324/1 The said Officers woll write newe distressez ayenst your Commissioners. **1476** *Acta Auditorum* (1839) 42/1 þe hande þat wrate þe said write. **1573** [see A. 1 γ]. **1659** W. Chamberlayne *Pharon.* III. i. 252 Where Loves fair hand hath Valours passport wright. *a* **1703** Burkitt *On N.T.* Mark xv. 37 The inscription wrote by Pilate over our suffering Saviour. **1751** Smollett *Per. Pic.* vii, A lawyer.. to write her last will. **1876** Swinburne *Erechtheus* 517, I had made no question of thine eyes or heart, Nor spared to read the scriptures in them writ, Wert thou my son. **1962** *Listener* 25 Jan. 155/1 All sorts of safeguards have been written into the agreements. **1962** *Rep. Comm. Broadcasting 1960* 138 in *Parl. Papers 1961–2* (Cmnd. 1753) IX. 259 A suitable form of words to this effect should be written into the new Charter. **1967** *N.Y. Herald Tribune* (International ed.) 11–12 Feb. 3 The 25th Amendment to the Constitution, spelling out procedure for the vice-president to serve as acting president when the president is disabled, was written into law to-day.

b. To pen (a letter, missive, note, etc.); to communicate with a person by (letter, etc.). Freq. const. *to*, †*unto*, or *till* (now *Sc.* and *north. dial.*), or with indirect personal object (cf. 23 b).

Freq. from *c* 1450. See also billet-doux, chit *sb.*[5], letter *sb.*[1] 4, love-letter, note *sb.*[2] 16, pistle *sb.* 1.

c **1000** *Three O.E. Prose Texts* 1 Alexandres epistoles .. þone he wrat & sende to aristotile. *a* **1300** *Cursor M.* 5323 þe king þan did his lettres write To somond al. *c* **1374** Chaucer *Troylus* v. 1293 My rede is þis.. þat hastily a letre thow hire write. *c* **1380** *Sir Ferumb.* 1782 þe lettre þat ys til hym wryte. *c* **1420** *Prose Life Alex.* 66 He garte writte anoþer lettre, and sent it to Talyfride. **1513** [see A. 2 *a* β]. *c* **1560** A. Scott *Poems* (S.T.S.) ix. 17 It is þe hairt to quhome ȝe wret The misseif. **1613** J. Saris *Voy. Japan* (Hakl. Soc.) 94 This daye Mr. Cocks writt me a letter. **1662** [see A. 3 b γ]. **1710** Steele *Tatler* No. 4 ¶2 Another hath just now writ three Lines to Clarissa. **1802** Marian Moore *Lascelles* II. 126 The young man.. writ her a polite note. **1848** Thackeray *Van. Fair* xlix, I want you.. to write a card for Colonel and Mrs. Crawley. **1891** 'J. S. Winter' *Lumley* iv, I've got.. a dozen letters to write for you.

fig. **1382** Wyclif *2 Cor.* iii. 2 ȝe ben oure pistle, writun in oure hertis.

c. To fill in (a cheque, etc.) with writing.

1837 Dickens *Pickw.* liii, Perker wrote a cheque for the whole amount.

8. a. To describe or designate (a person) by writing *to* be something; to style, call, or term in writing; to set down in a particular class. Also *transf.*

1382 Wyclif *Jer.* xxii. 30 Writ this man a bareyn man. —— *1 Macc.* viii. 20 For togidre write vs ȝoure felawis and freendis. **1535** Coverdale *1 Macc.* x. 65 The kynge.. wrote him amonge his chefe frendes. **1565** Cooper s.v. *Ascribo*, Write or adde me also to be of my brothers opinion. *a* **1577** Sir T. Smith *Commw. Eng.* (1640) 61 If one were a Knight, they would write him.. Sir John Finch, Knight. **1605** Shaks. *Macb.* III. i. 101 Whereby he does receiue Particular addition, from the Bill, That writes them all alike. **1605** B. Jonson *Volpone* I. i,[That] you will vouchsafe To write me, i' your family. **1611** Bible *Jer.* xxii. 30 Thus saith the Lord, Write ye this man childlesse. **1633** G. Herbert *Temple, Church, Vanitie* 6 Heark and beware, lest what you now do measure And write for sweet, prove a most sowre displeasure. **1687** R. L'Estrange *Answ. to Dissenter* 47 The Author Writes himself a Church-of-England-Man.

fig. **1654** Whitlock *Zootomia* 186 The Invention or Advance of most Arts write [*sic*] the despised Scholler Creditor. **1667** Milton *P.L.* IV. 758 Haile wedded Love.. Farr be it, that I should write thee sin or blame. **1820** Scott *Abbot* i, One whom Heaven had written childless. **1856–9** Dickens *Novels & Tales* VI. 59 (Fl.), Nature had writ him villain on his face.

b. *refl.* To designate (oneself) by a particular title in documents, letters, etc. Also *fig.*

1533 Bellenden *Livy* (S.T.S.) II. 81 He.. wrate himself consul. *a* **1548** Hall *Chron., Edw. IV*, 193 Duke Reiner.. writyng hymself kyng of Naples, Scicile, and Jerusalem. **1570** Googe *Pop. Kingd.* I. (1880) 4 Therefore doth he wright Himselfe as heyre apparent to the Empire. **1648** Milton *Observ. Art. Peace* Wks. 1851 IV. 567 These write themselves the Presbytery of Belfast. **1678** *Black Prince* in *Harl. Misc.* (1809) III. 151 John, duke of Lancaster.. wrote himself king of Castile and Leon. **1771** Luckombe *Hist. Print.* 94 St. Giles's, Cripplegate,.. of which church he wrote himself vicar in 1566. **1818** Scott *Hrt. Midl.* viii, A man of law, Nichil Novit, writing himself procurator before the Sheriff-court. **1857** Trollope *Barchester T.* xx, In due process of time he took his degree, and wrote himself B.A. **1880** Ruskin *Bible Amiens* i. (1884) 3 Why should.. a little Frankish maid [*sc.* Amiens] write herself the sister of Venice?

ellipt. **1678** Godolphin *Repert. Canon.* (1681) 13 The Arch-bishop of Canterbury.. writes himself *Divina Providentia*.

c. ***to write oneself man***, etc.: To arrive at man's (or woman's) estate; to attain manhood, or a specified age. (Cf. 11 b.)

1660 Fell *Hammond* (1661) 3 He grew the Tutor of those who begun to write themselves men. **1663** Head *Hic & Ubique* IV. ii. 45 Now since I write my self Man, go thy way. **1823** Scott *Quentin D.* xxiv, Thou wilt be mad with vanity ere thou writest thyself man. **1831** —— *Cast. Dang.* v, The governor had attained his thirtieth year.. and his lieutenant did not yet write himself one-and-twenty.

d. *refl.* To name (oneself) in writing; to sign.

1821 Scott *Kenilw.* ix, This same Demetrius, for so he wrote himself when in foreign parts. **1911** Barrie *Peter & Wendy* v. 80 James Hook, or as he wrote himself, Jas. Hook.

e. To bring or reduce (a person, etc.) to a specified state by writing. Chiefly *refl.*

1735 Pope *Prol. Sat.* 32 A dire dilemma! either way I'm sped, If foes, they write, if friends, they read me dead. **1736** *Gentl. Mag.* VI. 662 The Craftsman hath seen better Days; but he has wrote himself into Contempt. **1751** Warburton in *Porson's Tracts* (1815) 345 *note*, That no man was ever written out of reputation, but by himself. **1768** Sterne *Sent. Journ., Calais*, I had wrote myself pretty well out of conceit with the *Desobligeant*. **1841** Thackeray *Gt. Hoggarty Diam.* xi, You have.. written yourself out of five hundred a-year. **1852** Thorpe *Northern Mythol.* III. 15 Another, whose cabbages were constantly stolen from his garden, wrote the thief fast from Saturday night till Sunday. **1871** Lytton *Coming Race* xvii, If we wrote our fingers to the bone, we could not throw any light [etc.].

f. To make (one's way) by literary work.

1890 T. F. Tout *Hist. Eng.* 111 Addison wrote his way with his Whig pamphlets to a secretaryship of state.

9. To spell (a word, name, etc.) in a specified or particular manner in writing.

c **1200** Ormin Ded. 109 Forr he ne maȝȝ nohht elless Onn Ennglissh writtenn rihht te word. *c* **1205** Lay. 28869 On feole bocken his nome me swa writeð. **1375** Barbour *Bruce* x. 748 And for this word scho gert vrit swa, Men wend the Franch-men suld it ta. *c* **1620** A. Hume *Brit. Tongue* (1865) 9 And Varro.. wrytes domineis and serveis, for dominis and servis. **1659** Philipott *Kent* 395/2 Blackmanstone, written Bleachmanstone, that is, Man's bleak Town. **1747** Johnson *Plan Eng. Dict.*, Many words written alike are differently pronounced. **1828** Duppa *Trav. Italy*, etc. 8 In this MS... Virgil is uniformly written Vergil. **1865** Way *Promp. Parv.* p. lxxiii, The word written according to the orthography of the period.

10. a. To carve, grave, or trace letters or words on (a hard or plastic surface). Also *fig.*

c **1250** *Gen. & Ex.* 3613 Oðere tables he broȝte eft writen. *c* **1320** *Sir Tristr.* 2040 Bi water he sent adoun Liȝt linden spon. He wrot hem al wiþ roun. **1382** Wyclif *Exod.* xxxi. 18 The Lord ȝaf to Moyses.. two stonen tablis of witnessyng, writun with the fyngre of God. *a* **1450** *Medit. Life & Passion of Christ* 883 He wrot his body wiþ harde nailes. *Ibid.* 1190 Strong was þy pyne þe to wyte His fayre forhed with þornes wryte. *c* **1822** Beddoes *Poems, Pygmalion* 157 Writing the sand Idly, he paused.

b. To cover, fill, or mark (a paper, etc.) with writing; to trace significant characters on (a surface, etc.).

a **1240** in *O.E. Hom.* I. 249 Euch an [*sc.* devil] bereð a gret boc al of sunnen iwriten wið swarte smeale leattres. **1382** Wyclif *Ezek.* ii. 9 A boke.., the which was writen withinforth and withoutforth. *c* **1394** *P. Pl. Crede* 175 Wyde wyndowes y-wrouȝt y-written full þikke, Schynen wiþ schapen scheldes to schewen aboute. **1468** *Anc. Deed C.* 5103 in *Catal.* VI. 173 A large roll of parchemyn wretyn and lympned with certeyn maters. **1471** Caxton *Recuyell*

(Sommer) 5 Aftyr that y had made and wretyn a fyve or six quayers. **1530** Palsgr. 499/1 Correcte this boke, it is falce written. **1599** Shaks. *Much Ado* II. iii. 138 Till she haue writ a sheet of paper. **1739** *Wks. Learned* I. 103 That the Leaves of these two great Poets were wrote at Random. **1833** Mrs. Stowe in *Life* (1889) 70 The envelope was written in a scrawny, scrawly, gentleman's hand. **1853** Rock *Ch. of Fathers* (1903) IV. 87 A small strip of vellum written with the following translation.

11. a. To employ, or be able to employ, (a particular language) in writing.

c **1320** *Cast. Love* 24 Ne mowe we alle Latin wite, Ne Ebreu ne Gru þat beþ i-write. **1521** A. Barclay (*title*), The Introductory to wryte, and to pronounce Frenche. **1582** Mulcaster *Elementarie* (1925) 59 Such people, as teach childern to read and write English. **1664** Dryden *Rival Ladies* Ep. Ded. ¶4, I have endeavoured to write English, as near [etc.]. **1757** tr. *Keysler's Trav.* (ed. 2) IV. 28 Charles VI ..speaks and writes Latin, Italian, Spanish, and French. **1845** M. Pattison *Ess.* (1889) I. 13 The Latin which Gregory writes is..his native tongue.

b. To employ (a name, word, etc.) in designating oneself; esp. †*to write man*, = 8 c.

(*a*) **1591** Shaks. *1 Hen. VI*, IV. vii. 74 The Turke, that two and fifty kingdoms hath, Writes not so tedious a Stile as this. **1599** —— *Much Ado* V. i. 37 How euer they haue writ the stile of gods.

(*b*) **1597** Shaks. *2 Hen. IV*, I. ii. 30 As if he had writ man euer since his Father was a Batchellour. **1601** etc. [see MAN *sb.*[1] 4 c]. **1616** B. Jonson *Underw., Celebr. Charis* I. 3 Though I now write fifty years, I have had, and have my peers. **1672** M. Locke *Obs. on Ess. Adv. Mus.* 2 When I began to write Man, and had convers'd in the world. *a* **1766** in Fordyce *Serm. Yng. Wom.* (ed. 3) I. 38 All mankind is the pupil..of female institution: the daughters till they write women. **1781** C. Johnston *Hist. J. Juniper* II. 219 Just as I had written man; or..was of age. **1829** Scott *Anne of G.* xiv, The elder, well-sized, and dark-visaged, may write fifty and five years.

c. To employ (a particular literary style) in written compositions.

1772 R. Fergusson *To Mr. R. Fergusson* ii, You write sic easy stile and plain,..Nae suth'ron lown dare you disdain.

12. To execute (a particular style of handwriting).

1390– [see HAND *sb.* 16]. **1593** Shaks. *2 Hen. VI*, IV. ii. 100 Nay, he can..write Court hand. **1631** Lenton *Charac.* C 9, Hee writes a faire hand. **1702** *Lond. Gaz.* No. 3865/4 Writing a tolerable Clerk's-Hand. **1716** [see Roman *a.*[1] 5 b]. **1738** Swift *Pol. Conversation* 28 Whoe'er writ it, writes a Hand like a Foot. **1766** [see ROUND HAND 1]. **1851** H. Mayhew *Lond. Labour* I. 313/1 He writes a good hand. **1865** Le Fanu *Guy Dev.* II. 73 What a hand he writes!

13. = UNDERWRITE *v.*[1] 2 b.

1882 'F. Anstey' *Vice Versâ* xvi. 298 They talked of 'risks', of someone who had only been 'writing' a year and was doing seven thousand a week,..and of the uselessness of 'writing five hundred on everything'. **1931** *Times* 14 Mar. 12/6 Not all insurance companies have felt justified in writing the risks. **1967** *Listener* 6 July 14/3 The company was still writing insurance in eleven American states. **1976** *Daily Tel.* 1 Nov. 16/2 Settlement of any claims will cost up to 50 p.c. more than had been expected when the risk was written.

II. With advs. **14. write down. a.** To put or set down in writing; to commit to, describe or record in, written form; to note or jot down.

1588 Shaks. *Titus A.* II. iv. 3 Write downe thy mind, bewray thy meaning so. **1611** —— *Wint. T.* IV. iv. 571 Things knowne betwixt vs three, Ile write you downe. **1682** *Rec. Scott. Cloth Manuf. New Mills* (S.H.S.) 40 He gives out wool to scrubleing and writes itt down. **1711** Steele *Spect.* No. 155 ¶2, I will..write down all they say to me. **1751** R. Paltock *P. Wilkins* I. p. xi, For the Purpose of writing down his Life from his own Mouth. **1853** Dickens *Bleak Ho.* xvii, I write down these opinions, not because I believe that [etc.]. **1891** W. Briggs & Bryan *Geometry* 143 This enables us to write down at once the equation.

b. With complement. Also *fig.*, and *refl.*

1599 Shaks. *Much Ado* IV. ii. 78 O that hee were heere to write mee downe an asse! **1602** —— *Ham.* I. ii. 222 We did thinke it writ downe in our duty To let you know of it. **1854** Lever *Dodd Family Abroad* xvi. 138 It's like writing yourself down Goth at once to oppose these. **1856** Mrs. Gore *Life's Lessons* III. 70 Why does not E. H. write himself down M.P. in the new House?

c. To overcome or suppress, to disparage or depreciate, by writing; to condemn or decry in writing; to write in disparagement of.

1726 Swift *Let. to Mrs. Howard* 17 Nov., However, one thing I was pleased with, that after you had writ [me] down you repented, and writ me up again. **1773** Johnson in Boswell *Hebrides* 1st Oct., It was said to old Bentley, upon the attacks against him, 'Why, they'll write you down.' 'No, sir,..no man was ever written down but by himself.' **1798** *Monthly Mag.* Jan. 49 [Wilkes] actually *wrote down* at least one administration. **1850** H. Walter *Tindale's Answ. More* Introd. Notice 2 This effort to write down Tyndale and his labours. **1851** [see 18 e]. **1902** A. Machen in *Among my Books* 103 That his only object is to write down those tedious romances of chivalry.

absol. **1877** Stubbs *Med. & Mod. Hist.* v. (1886) 110 It seems..that no man's zeal is roused to write unless it is moved by the desire to write down.

d. *refl.* To diminish or destroy one's literary reputation by inferior writing.

1716 Addison *Free-holder* No. 40 ¶3 There is not a more melancholy object in the learned world, than a man who has written himself down. **1773** [see prec.]. **1809** Malkin *Gil Blas* II. vii. ¶4 He has written himself down at a terrible rate by his last publication.

e. To reduce (an account, total, assets, etc.) to a lower amount in writing.

1894 *Westm. Gaz.* 27 June 6/1 That this, as well as all other similar accounts, should be steadily written down, and finally out of the balance-sheet. **1897** *Ibid.* 8 Sept. 6/1 The assets have been written down in a drastic manner.

f. To write (a literary work) in a style adapted to the level of readers of supposedly inferior intelligence or taste. Cf. sense 22 c below.

1876 C. M. Yonge *Womankind* xxviii. 243 Books..which do not dwarf the mind as a series of books written *down* are apt to do.

15. write in. To insert (a fact, statement, etc.) in writing; †to inscribe.

1382 Wyclif *Rev.* xxi. 12 It hadde a wal..and in the ȝatis of it twelue aungels, and names writun in. *c* **1425** Wyntoun *Cron.* II. xi. 1060 Oþir fenȝheide fabillis sere I wil forber to wryt in heyre. **1463** *Bury Wills* (Camden) 42 A book of papyr to wryte in expensis. **1863** Miss Braddon *Eleanor's Vict.* I. 108 All the great scenes have been written in by him. **1895** Crockett *Men of Moss-hags* liv. 390 It was a moment's work to write in the other name [on a pardon]. **1903** *Athenæum* 3 Jan. 10/2 The date is written in by the rubricator.

b. To send (suggestions, etc.) in written form to an organization. Cf. sense 23 c below.

1928 *Publishers' Weekly* 14 July 183 The customers.. were not slow about writing in their suggestions. *a* **1961** J. Britton in Webster, Teachers are encouraged to write in their requests.

c. To insert (the name of an unlisted person) on a ballot-paper or the like, as the candidate of one's choice. *U.S.*

1932 *Sun* (Baltimore) 23 Aug. 2/2 He knew nothing of the circulation of cards in the Middle West urging voters to write in Smith's name on the Presidential ballot. **1944** *Greeley* (Colorado) *Daily Tribune* 16 Sept. 2/2, I greatly appreciate the good will expressed and effort expended by the friends who wrote in my name as candidate for County Judge on the Republican primary ballot. **1957** *Ann. Reg. 1956* 174 Democratic voters 'wrote in' their preference for Mr. Stevenson over Senator Kefauver in the proportions of 8 to 5. **1968** *New Yorker* 9 Mar. 32 You know who I wrote in? You, Earl.

16. write off. a. To note the deduction of (money) in an account or financial statement; now *spec.* to record the cancelling of (a sum, as a bad debt, depreciated stock, etc.). Freq. *fig.*, to dismiss from consideration as insignificant or irrelevant.

1682 Scarlett *Exchanges* 107 To send the..Bill to the House of the Acceptant, and desire him to order that the Value be write of in Bank. **1752** Beawes *Lex Merc. Rediv.* 363 Write off from my Bank Book, one hundred and fifty-seven Pounds. **1819** *Mortimer's Commerc. Dict.* (ed. 2) 87 One of the clerks..writes off the sum required. **1891** *Law Times* XC. 283/2 The company wrote off the loss as a bad debt.

fig. **1889** *Spectator* 21 Sept., China and India being written-off as full of people. **1957** P. Lafitte *Person in Psychol.* 44 The psychologist..can write off the difficulty as not falling within the scope of scientific method. **1963** L. MacNeice *Var Parable* (1965) i. 21 A suspension of antipathy towards its author's attitude will give weight to what otherwise might be written off as whimsical. **1973** *Times* 20 Oct. 18/6 He is part of me and I of him. I find that painful. Perhaps he does too. But we cannot write each other off. **1984** A. Smith *Mind* v. xv. 297 To cover all possibilities so that the seemingly dead are not written off medically and therefore legally, before their time. **1985** *Times* 11 Jan. 12/6 All this is part of an exercise..to help girls be more assertive and self-confident about their educational potential: to stop writing themselves off as mere future wives and mothers.

b. To compose (a letter, etc.) with facility or expedition.

1848 Thackeray *Van. Fair* lxvii, She wrote off a letter to a friend. **1862** —— *Philip* xxviii, Philip was writing off..one of his grand tirades. **1871** [see A. 1 γ].

c. *slang* (orig. *Air Force*). To damage beyond repair, wreck (an aeroplane, motor vehicle, etc.).

[**1922** *Flight* 27 July 423/1 In another way, it may be stated that, should the work of the Committee lead to a reduction by one of the aeroplanes written off per year as a result of crashes, [etc.].] **1931** *Ibid.* 23 Jan. 80/1 The D.H.37..got down without much damage. The D.H.9.C..was less fortunate, and was written off in a forced landing. **1942** N. Balchin *Darkness falls from Air* ii. 44 They seemed to be dropping a hell of a lot of stuff... I saw next morning that they'd written off a pub in Notting Hill. **1973** C. Bonington *Next Horizon* xi. 166 She had crashed the car twice, writing it off completely on the second occasion. **1982** *Daily Tel.* 27 Oct. 3/6 He..wrecked his lorry and two cars; pulled out in front of a van and wrote that off too.

17. write out. a. To make a (fair or perfect) transcription or written copy of (something, a rough draft, etc.); to copy out; also, to transcribe in full or detail, as from brief notes or shorthand.

to write out fair, to make a fair copy of.

1548 Elyot s.v. *Describo*, To write out a boke by an other mans copie. **1565** Cooper, *Exscribere alicui*, to write out the copie of a thyng to one. **1611** Cotgr. s.vv. *Copier*, *Transcrit.* *a* **1700** in *Cath. Rec. Soc. Publ.* IX. 336 His Bookes, w[hi]ch she write out and faithfully practised. **1776** *Trial Nundocomar* 41/1 The writer wrote out a Persian bond. **1809** Malkin *Gil Blas* VII. xii. ¶5, I..offered to write his memorials out fair. **1877** *Smith & Wace's Dict. Chr. Biog.* I. 208 Atticus..wrote out his sermons and learnt them by heart.

b. *refl.* To exhaust one's resources or stock of ideas by excessive writing; = OUTWRITE *v.* 3.

1817 *Blackw. Mag.* L. 519/2 We have heard fears expressed, that Miss Edgeworth might have written herself out. **1832** Scott *St. Ronan's* Introd., The Author had exhausted himself, or, as the technical phrase expresses it, written himself out. **1905** *Author* 1 Feb. 152 He has written himself out.

c. To eliminate or contrive the temporary absence of (a character, etc., in a long-running radio or television serial), with the story-line written so as to account for it.

1967 *Listener* 13 Apr. 503/2 That [*sc.* the *Forsyte*] *Saga* is now more than half way through (Saturdays, BBC-2)... Some of the old characters have been written out. **1969** *Photoplay* Jan. 64/2 Being 'written out' of 'Peyton Place' is no disgrace. It has happened to other fine players. **1971** O. Norton *Corpse-Bird Cries* i. 2 You got them to write you out for a bit. **1982** A. Road *Dr. Who: Making of TV Series* 16/1 Eric Saward was asked..in the course of his story..to 'write out' the Doctor's sonic screwdriver. **1984** 'M. Innes' *Carson's Conspiracy* xiv. 149 Appleby took a searching look at her and—as it might be expressed—wrote her out of the story.

18. write over. a. To write (something) anew or again; to rewrite; = OVERWRITE *v.* 3, RESCRIBE *v.* 2.

1588 Shaks. *L.L.L.* I. ii. 120, I will haue that subiect newly writ ore. **1594** —— *Rich. III*, III. vi. 5 Here is the Indictment...; Eleuen houres I haue spent to write it ouer. *a* **1645** Ld. Napier *Mem.* (1793) 51 They might gaine some tyme in wreating them [*sc.* articles of accusation] over to consult vpon the mater. **1711** R. Martin in Burton *Life Challoner* (1909) I. 32 They spent..two dayes in..writeing over fair all ye answers. **1751** Chatham *Lett. Nephew* i. 1, I am extremely pleased with your translation now it is writ over fair.

b. To cover the whole or remaining surface of (a book, etc.) with writing; = OVERWRITE *v.* 1 b.

1828 Duppa *Trav. Italy*, etc. 9, I saw MSS. of some of the Codes..written over with monkish commentaries.

19. write up. a. To put in writing a full account, statement, or record of (something); to give an elaborate description of, describe fully; to pen or write in full or detail.

c **1425** Wyntoun *Cron.* IX. ix. 117 (Royal MS.), I wyll noucht wryt wp all That I hawe sene in my tyme fall. **1535** Coverdale *Esther* xii. 4 Mardocheus wrote vp the same matter. **1592** Timme *Ten Eng. Lepers* G 3 b, The Divell that playeth host in this worlde..writeth up all in his booke. **1860** *Cornh. Mag.* II. 750 You will be waited for..by a few of the discontented, and asked to 'write up' certain parts, without any reference to your story. **1887** J. Hawthorne *Tragic Myst.* ii, After interviewing the sentry..they departed to write up the tragedy.

†**b.** To enter (a person, his name) in a roll, list, etc.; to enroll; = INSCRIBE *v.* 1 b. *Obs.*

c **1500** *Priests of Peebles* 277 Thai wryt wp leile and falss, ..And dytis þaim vnder a perdoun. **1535** Coverdale *1 Macc.* x. 36 There shall xxx. M. also of the Iewes be written vp in the kynges hoost. **1539** Bible (Great) *Ps.* lxxxvii. 6 The Lorde shall rehearse it, whan he wryteth vp the people. **1666** P. Gordon *Diary* (Spald. Club) 72 Haveing told where wee were to lodge, they..sent a writer to write up our names.

c. To form, trace, or place (something) in writing in an elevated position.

1535 Coverdale *Dan.* v. 25 This is the scripture, that is written vp. **1593** Shaks. *3 Hen. VI*, I. i. 169, I will.., ouer the Chayre of State,..Write vp his Title. **1837** Dickens *Pickw.* xxxv, Not content vith writin' up 'Pickwick' [on the coach-door]. *Ibid.* lii, I call it a dispensary, and it's alvays writ up so.

d. To raise or elevate by writing.

1751 Warburton *Pope's Wks.* III. 68 Writers..writing themselves up into the same delusion with their Readers.

e. To commend (something) to notice or favour by appreciative writing; to laud by way of advertisement.

1726 [see sense 14 c]. **1824** *Blackw. Mag.* XVI. 165 She was never written up, to use the modern technical expression, in the Reviews. **1851** De Quincey *Wks.* (1863) XII. 21 Byron..wished to write up Pope by way of writing down others. **1893** 'Q.' [Quiller Couch] *Delect. Duchy* 7 I'll go in presently and write up this place.

f. To bring (a journal, report, etc.) up to date, or to the latest event, fact, or transaction; to complete (some record) in writing.

1839 Longf. *Hyperion* III. v, He..writes up the journal neglected for a week or two. **1848** Hannay *Biscuits & Grog* 19 Now that we..have little to do, suppose we write up our logs? **1900–1** *Proc. Univ. Durh. Phil. Soc.* II. 3 Even the minutes of the Curators cease to be written up.

III. *intr.* **20.** To inscribe letters *in*, *on*, or *upon* a hard or plastic surface by scoring, tracing, engraving, etc. Also *transf.* and in fig. context.

Differing from next chiefly in the specification of the material written on.

c **1000** *Ags. Gosp.* John viii. 6 Se hælend abeah nyþer & wrat mid his fingre on þære eorþan. *c* **1000** Ælfric *Hom.* II. 434 Swilce anes mannes hand writende on ðære healle waȝe. *a* **1300** *Cursor M.* 13729 He stuped dun, and wit his hand He wrat a quil in to þe sand. **1362** Langl. *P. Pl.* A. III. 62, I lere ȝou,..such writynge ȝe leue, To writen in Wyndouwes of ȝoure wel dedes. **1382**, **1387** [see TABLE *sb.* 2 b]. *a* **1450** *Medit. Life & Passion of Christ* 842 On þi forhed so whit so snow Thow writest with a thorny bow. *c* **1450** Holland *Houlate* 206 He couth wryte..With his neb for mistar, Apon the se sand. **1513** Douglas *Æneid* I. vii. 111 The speir ourturnit in the dust did write. **1535** Coverdale *Ezek.* xxxvii. 16 Take a sticke and wryte vpon it. **1585**, **1621** [see STYLE *sb.* 1]. **1674** C. F. *Wit at Venture* 85 They write in sand when they make oaths. **1706** Stevens *Sp. Dict.* I. s.v. *Escrivir*, To write on the Sand, or Water, is to do things to no purpose, as that Writing is immediatly effac'd. **1797** *Encycl. Brit.* (ed. 3) XVIII. 917/2 The Chinese..wrote or engraved with an iron tool upon thin boards or on bamboo. **1818** [S. Weston] *La Scava* 31 A great quantity of styles to write with on wax-tablets. **1878** [see STYLE *sb.* 5].

fig. *a* **1400** *Relig. Lyrics 14th C.* (1924) 114 Þogh my hert be hard as stone, ȝit maist þou gostly write þer-on. *a* **1653** [see WRITING *vbl. sb.* 7 b].

21. a. To engage in, perform the action of, writing (esp. with pen and ink); to produce (a specified kind of) writing.

to write and read: see READ *v.* 15 b.

c **825** *Vesp. Psalter* xliv. 2 Hreod writ[eres] hreðlice writendes. *a* **1225** *Juliana* 79 He þat her least on wrat swa as he cuðe. *a* **1300** *E.E. Psalter* xliv. 2 Mi tunge rede-pipe maister-writer, Of swiftlike writande be þer. **1382** WYCLIF *Isaiah* viii. 1 Tac to thee a gret boc, and writ it with the poyntel of a man. ? *a* **1400** *R. Gloucester's Chron.* (Rolls) II. 828 He bad & wrot & radde & huld godes seruise. **1500–20** DUNBAR *Poems* xxxiii. 12 He cowth wryte and reid. *c* **1524** R. CROKE in Ellis *Orig. Lett.* Ser. III. I. 336 Provided that no man may force hym [*sc.* a pupil] to wryte oonles I be there presente, to dyrecte.. his said hande and stile. **1590** P. BALES *Writing Schoolemaster* (title-p.), The Arte of Brachygraphie: that is, to write as fast as a man speaketh treatably. **1623** COCKERAM II, To Write after a strange manner, in so much as no man can reade it, *decipher*. **1661** BOYLE *Style of Script.* (1675) 159 We think they write backwards, and they, that we do. **1738** POPE *Epil. Sat.* ii. 186 Chartres scarce could write or read. **1775** C. JOHNSTON *Pilgrim* 73 Any one.. may write away, without restraint,.. whether they can even so much as spell. **1828** SCOTT *F.M. Perth* xxx, 'Do thou write.' 'Your Royal Highness forgets,' said Ramorny, pointing to his mutilated arm. **1864** BURTON *Scot Abr.* I. iii. 148 A fat philosopher sitting writing.. with a goose quill. **1874** SYMONDS *Sk. Italy & Greece* 18 Then would they [*i.e.* the monks] read or write, what long melodious hours!

transf. **1482** *Monk of Evesham* (Arb.) 54 The crystyn pepulle wolde wryte dayly.. aboute the placys of her herte wyth her fyngur. **1859** FITZGERALD *Omar* li The Moving Finger writes; and, having writ, Moves on.

b. Said of the writing-pen.

1588 SHAKS. *L.L.L.* I. ii. 191 Deuise Wit, write Pen, for I am for whole volumes in folio. **1733** POPE *Hor. Sat.* II. i. 98 Whether the.. whiten'd wall provoke the skew'r to write. **1742** GRAY *Lett.* (1900) I. 112 My having at last found a Pen that writes. **1786** S. TAYLOR *Shorthand Writing* 98 A steel or a silver one [*sc.* pen] that will write fine.

c. To depict on glass, etc.; to paint.

1854 SUTHERLAND *Sign Writer's Assistant* 24 To write, gild and ornament on glass. **1889** —— *Sign Writing* viii. 10/1 Writing upon the glass.

d. To print by means of a typewriting machine or the like; to typewrite.

1875 KNIGHT *Dict. Mech.* 2677/1 Johnston's apparatus for the blind is to enable them to write by pressure upon letters in the required order. **1883** J. G. PETRIE *Man. for Type-Writer* 3 The learner must be content to write slowly and deliberately at the commencement.

22. a. To perform the action of composing and putting on paper; to practise literary composition; to engage in authorship or literary work.

In very frequent use from *c* 1600.

a **1122** *O.E. Chron.* (Laud MS.) an. 963, Ic write & feostniȝe mid Cristes rodetacne. *c* **1205** LAY. 41 þa makede a Frenchis clerc Wace wes ihoten, þe wel couþe writen. *a* **1300** *Cursor M.* 17846 Sundri þai þam fra oþer saite, And aiþer be himseluen wrate. **1387** [see A. 2 b β]. **14..** *Wheatley MS.* (1921) i. 59 If I write al my lyue I schuld neuer here woo dyscryue. *c* **1445** PECOCK *Donet* 6 It is honest ynouȝ a man to speke and write aftir oon of þo opyniouns. **1526** *Pilgr. Perf.* (W. de W. 1531) 1 b, Therupon I begon after my poore maner to wryte in latyn. **1575** GASCOIGNE *Glasse Govt.* III. ii, To conceive that he spake or wrot like olde Duns or Scotus. **1609** BIBLE (Douay) *Ecclus.* xxxviii. comm., S. Paul not only preached, but also writte. **1689** PRIOR *Ep. Fleetw. Shephard* 38 He writes well, who writes with Ease. **1749** SMOLLETT *Regicide* Pref., A gentleman who had wrote for the stage. **1849** MACAULAY *Hist. Eng.* iii. I. 332 Halifax.., from whom Dryden was not ashamed to own that he had learned to write. **1890** *Science-Gossip* XXVI. 177/1, I am not writing in the dark.

fig. **1649** LOVELACE *Poems* (1904) 62 He fights now with her Penne, And she writes with his Sword.

b. With preps., as *about*, †*be*, †*o*, *of* (= on), *on*, *upon*, †*ymb* (a matter, subject, etc.); or *against*, †*contrary*, *to* (a person, etc.).

In very frequent use from *c* 1390.

c **888** ÆLFRED *Boeth.* xviii. §3, Swa some swa þa writeras dydon, & eac þa ðe hi ymb writon. **971** *Blickl. Hom.* 161 Se halȝa godspellere swa be him wrat. *a* **1225** *Ancr. R.* 410 ȝe habbeð of þeos blissen i-writen on oðer stude. *a* **1300** *Cursor M.* 21324 Matheu.. o crist manhedes wratte. **1390** GOWER *Conf.* II. 90 Thilke time at Rome also Was Tullius with Cithero, That writen upon Rethorike. *Ibid.* 91 Among the whiche in Poesie To the lovers Ovide wrot. **1448–9** METHAM *Amoryus & Cl.* 524 Qwere he off constellacionnys doth wryght. **1500–20** DUNBAR *Poems* lxxxiv. 22 Sen thir clarkis hes writtin in thair stylis To ȝoungar folk. **1565** COOPER s.v *Rescribo*, To write contrarie or agaynst olde orations. **1644** [see A. 3 a β]. **1698** FLOYER *Asthma* (1717) p. i, All the Moderns that have Writ on that Subject. **1737** *Gentl. Mag.* VII. 499/2 Had they wrote against the Ministry, we could have borne it. **1742** POPE *Dunc.* IV. 252 For thee we.. explain a thing till all men doubt it, And write about it, Goddess, and about it. **1819** S. ROGERS *Human Life* Poems (1856) 138 Once in thy mirth thou bad'st me write on thee. **1883** TYLOR in *Encycl. Brit.* XV. 199/1 Cicero writes of them as wise men, augurs, and diviners.

c. With various qualifications. Esp. as ***to write down***, to adapt one's literary style to the level of readers of supposedly inferior intelligence or taste; freq. const. *to*. Cf. sense 14 f above.

c **1600** SHAKS. *Sonn.* lxxxvi, By spirits taught to write, Aboue a mortall pitch. **1672** MARVELL *Reh. Transp.* I. 114 The fault is most his own who should have writ to the capacity of vulgar Readers. **1692** DRYDEN *St. Euremont's Ess.* Pref. iii, His subjects are often great and noble, and then he never fails to write up to them. **1711** FELTON *Dissert. Classics* (1718) 91 It must be our Care to think and write up to the Dignity.. of the Things we presume to treat of. **1809** MALKIN *Gil Blas* XI. vii. ¶5, I should be sorry to write down to their comprehension. **1851** *Househ. Words* 11 Jan. 372/2 Mr. Blackbrook and his disciples are hapless materialists, verse-makers without a sense of the beautiful. They are patronised by those to whom they write down. **1861** J. PYCROFT *Ways & Words* 33 Authors will learn to write down to the lowest standard. **1903** A. BENNETT *Truth about Author* xii. 150, I had entered into a compact with myself that I would never 'write down' to the public in a long fiction. **1921** *Sci. Amer.* Nov. 20/1 The Editor both 'writes down' and 'writes up'... He may translate the Einstein theories into the nontechnical phrases of everyday life. **1944** L. MACNEICE *Christopher Columbus* 9 The inference that to hold the attention.. a writer has got to 'write down'. (By writing down I mean pandering—writing by standards which the writer considers low.) **1960** *Guardian* 25 Feb. 6/4 English writers seem to write down to their readers and American writers write as if addressing their equals.

d. To compose music, a melody, etc.

1672 M. LOCKE *Obs. Ess. Adv. Mus.* 14 Our certain Method of the Scale; which never gives.. occasion for.. writing in improper Keys. **1782** BURNEY *Hist. Mus.* II. 556 The custom.. of writing upon a Plain-Song. **1789** *Ibid.* III. 109 Tallis and Bird had.. long accustomed themselves to write for voices.

23. a. To compose a letter, note, etc.; to communicate information, etc., send word, by writing; to conduct epistolary correspondence. Also with *for* (a person or thing) or *to* (do something).

1340–70 *Alex. & Dind.* 244 Whan dereworþe dindimus þe enditinge hurde Of alixandre askinge as he write hadde. *c* **1374** CHAUCER *Troylus* v. 1298, I kan not trowen þat she wol write a-yen. *a* **1400–50** *Wars Alexander* 2431, I wrate to ȝow at me to wayue [*v.r.* wafe] be ten wyse clerkis. ? **1481** [see A. 2 a β]. **1552** in Feuillerat *Revels Edw. VI* (1914) 89 Sir wheras you required me to write, for that [etc.]. **1586** RALEIGH *Let.* 29 May, The sider which I wrat to you for. **1626** BP. MOUNTAGU in *Corr. J. Cosin* (Surtees) I. 104, I haue no[t] much newes, nor occasion to write. **1692** PRIDEAUX *Lett.* (Camden) 158, I have expressly wrot to be informed of it. **1719** DE FOE *Crusoe* I. (Globe) 36 Goods, such as the Captain had writ for. **1751** JOHNSON *Rambler* No. 171 ¶6, I applied to him by letter, but had no answer. I writ in terms more pressing. *a* **1842** in Bischoff *Woollen Manuf.* II. 318 He wrote to request my aid. **1890** R. C. LEHMANN *H. Fludyer* 31 Tell Mary she hasn't written for an age.

b. With preps., as *to* (also *unto*, *till*), or indirect personal object (cf. 7 b). Also const. *of*.

In group (*a*), freq. from *c* 1560. In group (*b*), rare until *c* 1770; freq. from *c* 1790; often regarded as commercial or colloquial in U.K.; standard in U.S.

(*a*) *c* **1000** *Three O.E. Prose Texts* 1 þa ȝeþohte ic for þon to þe to writanne. **1382** WYCLIF *Jude* i. 3 Makinge al bisynesse of writinge to ȝou of ȝoure comoun helthe. **1434** *Acts Privy Counc.* IV. 351 The King hath wirten to þerle of Northumber[land]. *c* **1470** HENRY *Wallace* XI. 945 Than Eduuard wrayt till Menteth prewalie. **1534** CROMWELL in *Life & Lett.* (1902) I. 394 Wherefore.. I.. am bold to wryght vnto you. **1648** GAGE *West Ind.* 163, I writ unto my friends. **1663** CHAS. II in Cartwright *Madame* (1894) 136, I writt to you yesterday. **1751** ELIZA HEYWOOD *Betsy Thoughtless* IV. 191 The abbess was wrote to concerning me. **1814** WELLINGTON in Gurw. *Desp.* (1838) XII. 7 Write to me to General Colville's quarters. **1888** 'J. S. WINTER' *Bootle's Childr.* viii, Ferrers wrote to a friend of his at Chertsey.

(*b*) *c* **1374** CHAUCER *Troylus* v. 1303 Thow hast not wreten here syn þat she wente... Now write here þanne [*MS. Gg.* to hire]. **1611** USSHER *Lett.* (1686) 15 Together with.. Mr. Cook's Books you wrote me of. **1672** in *Camden Soc. Misc.* (1881) 13 Being in hast, have not tyme to wright any body else. **1763** ELIZ. CARTER in *Mem.* (1808) I. 356, I writ you from Amsterdam. **1795** NELSON in Nicolas *Disp.* (1845) II. 32 As I write you,.. I shall not write Mrs. Nelson this day. *a* **1800** PEGGE *Anecd.* (1814) 246 *Wrote* me, and *write* you, (merchant's language). **1854** THACKERAY *Newcomes* xxxi, Clive.. wrote me about the transmogrification of our school-fellow. **1864** NEWMAN *Apologia* VI. 346 When friends wrote me on the subject, I either did not deny or I confessed it. **1891** *Harper's Mag.* Nov. 840/1 Mr. Adams was another character of whom my host had written me. **1892** G. & W. GROSSMITH *Diary of Nobody* iii. 41, I wrote Merton to that effect. **1900** [see PHONE *sb.*[2] and *v.*]. **1905** HAVELOCK ELLIS *Stud. Psychol. Sex* IV. 239 She wrote me saying that she could not see me any more. **1922** C. MACKENZIE *Altar Steps* xxiii. 263, I will write you again when I have seen Father Burrowes. **1924** —— *Old Men of Sea* xi. 175, I shall write Mr. Hibben about that little joke. **1928** D. L. SAYERS *Ld. Peter views Body* iv. 74 He wrote me yesterday and said he'd accidentally left a bag in the cloakroom. **1953** WOODHOUSE *Performing Flea* 69 She is going to find out about quarantine and then write me. **1955** J. P. DONLEAVY *Ginger Man* xi. 104, I haven't. You can't blame me. I'm sorry I wrote your father. I'm sorry for it. **1968** *Globe & Mail* (Toronto) 17 Feb. B3 (Advt.), For free literature describing the.. accommodation.. write [*address given*]. **1973** *Black Panther* 17 Nov 10/2 It is circulating an impeachment petition nation-wide while encouraging all citizens to write their congressmen. **1974** I. MURDOCH *Sacred & Profane Love Machine* 35, I wrote you all about California—quite long letters—about the animals and so on. **1977** I. SHAW *Beggarman, Thief* I. i. 2 He lives in Chicago now and writes me often.

c. With advs., as *off*, *over*. Also, ***to write in***: (*a*) *Theatr.*, to send in notice in writing; (*b*) in gen. use, to send a written comment, request, etc., to an organization. Cf. sense 15 b above.

1577 HARRISON *England* III. i. (1878) II. 10 He wrote ouer for more of the same fish. **1849** *Theatrical Programme & Entr' Acte* 23 July 59/2 The time that elapsed between his last application to Drury-lane and his appearance was many months, for he 'wrote in', as it is termed from Exeter about the early part of the summer of 1813, acted first in London, January 26th 1814. **1855** KINGSLEY *Westw. Ho!* xv, He wrote off to Frank at Whitehall. **1866** LEVER *Sir B. Fossbrooke* II. 283, I.. have written off to Tom Lendrick to come over here with his sister. **1900** *Westm. Gaz.* 22 Nov. 9/2 The plaintiffs did not 'write in' or give notice that they were coming. **1931** *Publishers' Weekly* 5 Dec. 2471/2 The 'Brooklyn Eagle', however, complains bitterly about distribution: 'About seven hundred readers have written in —ever since that squib of ours appeared.. asking where they can put their hands on one.' **1949** N. MARSH *Swing, Brother, Swing* ix. 209 It's a mystery, that paper... The types that write in are amazing. **1957** M. MCCARTHY in *New Yorker* 23 Mar. 76/2, I wrote in for a Vogue pattern to make a tennis dress. **1972** *Listener* 28 Dec. 904/3 If anyone else doesn't know.... write in and I'll explain. **1977** *Broadcast* 13 June 10/1 The chap who writes in about a programme.

d. ***to write home about***: see HOME *adv.* 7 d.

24. In clauses introduced by *as*, or with advs., as *so*, *thus*.

11.. in *Eng. Misc. to Furnivall* (1901) 91 Swa swa Lycas wrat on his godspelle. *a* **1300** *Cursor M.* 11467 For þe prophet had written sua, And said [etc.]. **1375** BARBOUR *Bruce* I. 525 Then slayn wes mone thowsand.., As Dares in his buk he wrate. *c* **1380** WYCLIF *Sel. Wks.* II. 356 þis Poul .., whan he wroot þus in prisoun to folk to turne hem to Crist. *c* **1450** CAPGRAVE *St. Augustine* 60 Rith þus he wrot in Latin. **1483** CAXTON *G. de la Tour* G iv, It was done as the kynge had wreton. **1538** STARKEY *England* I. iii. 83 Thys hath destroyd more then any pestylens, as Lyuius wrytyth. **1594** H. WILLOBIE *Avisa* 57 b, He wrate againe so as followeth. **1605** CAMDEN *Rem.* (Epigr.) 11 To one.. he wrighteth thus: Discendi [etc.]. **1696** *Seafield's Corr.* (1912) 176 For newes, as Sr. James wreits to your Lo[rdshi]pe, ther is non. **1730** A. GORDON *Maffei's Amphith.* 95 Thus has one of those foul-mouth'd Poets wrote. **1770** [DALRYMPLE] *Anc. Sc. Poems* 310 The Cardinal.. writes thus to Cardinal Borromeo, 24th November 1561. **1874** SYMONDS *Sk. Italy & Greece* 121 While I am writing thus about the production .. of these love-songs.

25. To follow or practise writing as a profession or occupation; to work as a clerk, amanuensis, or journalist; †*Sc.* to act as a 'writer'.

c **1380** *Antecrist* in Todd *Three Treat. Wyclif* (1851) 138 To write to þe kynges seel and hold seculer courtes to byȝe & to selle. **1650** J. NICOLL *Diary* (Bann. Cl.) 2 Thomas Hunter, wryter,.. wes fund giltie of perjurie; and thairfoir wes declaired incapable of wryting or agenting ony bussines. **1853** DICKENS *Bleak Ho.* xx, You might live through it on much worse terms than by writing for Snagsby. **1895** ESCOTT *Platform, Press*, etc. 281 The *Daily News*, on which Pigott once wrote.

26. To spell words in writing; to represent words, etc., orthographically.

c **1620** A. HUME *Brit. Tongue* (1865) 7 To wryte orthographicallie ther are to be considered the symbol, the thing symbolized, and their congruence. *Ibid.* 21, I wald understand quhy they wryte not as they speak. **1704** J. PITTS *Acc. Moham.* A 4 b, I.. writ as near, as I could, to their way of speaking it.

IV. *intr.* for *passive*.

27. a. To be described in writing. *rare*$^{-1}$.

1827 LADY MORGAN *Mem.* (1862) II. 247 The comfortless, unaccommodating reality of those times which paint and write so well.

b. To be penned or written. *rare*$^{-1}$.

1862 O. COCKAYNE *St. Marher.* (1866) p. v, The manuscripts.. write straight away from end to end of the ruled lines.

V. 28. *Computers.* The infin. used *attrib.* and in *Comb.* with the sense 'writing': **write-permit ring** ('pɜːmɪt), a ring which has to be inserted in the hub of a tape reel before the tape can be written to or erased; **write-protect** *v. trans.*, to protect (a disc) from accidental writing or erasure, as by removing the cover from a notch in its envelope; also as *sb. attrib.*, designating such a notch, etc.

1951 *Proc. Inst. Electr. Engineers* XCVIII. II. 15/2 A number can be.. written in via the 'write' terminal. **1958** *Communications Assoc. Computing Machinery* Feb. 30 In each track, and separated by ·005" from the associated read head, is the 'write head'. **1961** L. W. HEIN *Electronic Data Processing for Business* v. 77 The reflective spot activates the switch only if the tape unit is in write status, that is, information is being written on the tape. **1964** F. L. WESTWATER *Electronic Computers* iv. 78 In the early applications valves were used to supply the relatively large read and write currents. **1965**, etc. [see READ *v.* 22]. **1970** A. CHANDOR *Dict. Computers* 402 Write permit ring. **1980** C. S. FRENCH *Computer Sci.* xii. 62 Each record is written onto tape in response to a 'write instruction'. **1980** S. HOCKEY *Guide Computer Applications in Humanities* ii. 27 One way of ensuring that this does not happen is to use.. a write permit ring, a plastic ring which can be inserted in the back of a tape reel. **1981** *Your Computer* May-June 100/3 *Write protect*, to remove the cover from the notch in a floppy disk so that it cannot be written on. **1983** *Austral. Personal Computer* Aug. 104/2 The only other hole in the disk envelope of importance to the user is the write protect notch... This notch must be covered up by an opaque material to write protect the disk.

writeable, var. WRITABLE *a.*

ˈ**write-back.** [f. the vbl. phr. *to write back*.] The process of restoring to profit a provision for bad or doubtful debts previously made against profits and no longer required.

1979 *Financial Times* 24 Jan. 21/5 In future the clearers.. will only make provision for the taxes actually expected to become payable in the forseeable future. This will result in the write-back into shareholders' funds of substantial amounts. **1980** *Times* 5 Aug. 17/7 Only then will it emerge whether there are any writebacks to profits arising from the results of the first six months of this year. **1983** *Times* 14 Mar. 14/6 Large write-backs of provisions made in earlier years and no longer needed kept the total [of provisions for bad and doubtful debts] to only £42m in 1981.

'write-down. [f. the vbl. phr. *to write down*: see WRITE *v.* 14e.] A reduction in the estimated or book value of assets.

1932 *Daily Express* 28 Jan. 10/7 This has involved a write-down of securities. **1955** *Times* 10 May 19/2 Consequent write-downs which, with the higher prices now ruling for footwear, are necessarily more severe than in the past. **1972** *Accountant* 23 Mar. 383/2 A large part of AEI's profit shortfall was attributable to stock and work-in-progress write-downs. **1978** S. BRILL *Teamsters* vi. 253 Executive Director Shannon, while only conceding 'possible write-downs', said it would take $10,000,000 just to appraise all the properties involved in the loans. **1979** *N.Y. Times* 13 Sept. D1/2 The Polaroid Corporation.. would take a $68 million write-down in the third quarter.

writee (raɪ'tiː). *rare*. [f. WRITE *v.* + -EE.] One to or for whom something is written; a reader.

c **1611** CHAPMAN *Iliad* XIV. Comm., Where a man is vnderstood, there is euer a proportion betwixt the writers wit and the writees. **1885** *Punch* May 243 The 'Writer' and the 'Writee', the 'Joker' and the 'Jokee'.

'write-in. [f. the vbl. phr. *to write in*: see WRITE *v.* 15c, 23c. For sense 2 (first part of def.), cf. also -IN[3].]

1. The name of an unlisted candidate inserted by a voter on a ballot-paper, etc., as the candidate of his choice; a vote cast for such a candidate, or the act of voting in this way. Freq. *attrib.* orig. and chiefly *U.S.*

1932 *Sun* (Baltimore) 23 Aug. 2/2 (*heading*) Smith's office denies all knowledge of write-in cards being circulated. **1933** *Ibid.* 4 May 2/2 In that election McKee, although not even a candidate, received a 'write-in' vote of nearly a quarter of a million. **1937** *Ibid.* 18 Sept. 10/3 The really significant item in the returns from New York.. is the extraordinary number of 'write-ins' for Mayor La Guardia on Democratic ballots. **1950** *Chicago Tribune* 2 Apr. 40/1 Such an attempted write-in for any candidate might result in many spoiled ballots. **1959** *Listener* 10 Dec. 1022/1 Stevenson got a tremendous write-in vote in one famous primary. **1964** MRS. L. B. JOHNSON *White House Diary* 10 Mar. (1970) 84 There was a creditable number of write-in votes for Attorney General Kennedy for Vice President. **1971** *Daily Colonist* (Victoria, B.C.) 2 Nov. 1/8 Another man who was out of town when filing closed says he'll gladly be a write-in candidate for councilman. **1982** *Daily Tel.* 13 Aug. 2/1 Three other spaces will be left for 'write-ins'.

2. A protest in the form of mass letters of complaint; also, an invitation from a radio broadcast to its listeners to write in and express their views. Cf. PHONE-IN.

1972 *Listener* 15 June 780/3 I'm proposing a mass write-in to request reassessment of most of the rates. **1981** MARSH & CHAMBERS *Abortion Politics* i. 27 Both organizations lobbied in Parliament and both organized meetings and write-in campaigns in the constituencies. **1981** *Church Times* 7 Aug. 16/5 In 1978, when the BBC's *Sunday* programme ran a write-in on the subject of a Graham mission, 15,000 listeners replied. **1984** *Times* 10 Nov. 1/4 There has been a 'strong response' to a direct-mail campaign asking pitmen to complete a write-in slip.

† **'writeling,** *vbl. sb. Obs. rare.* [Cf. OE. *wrítian*, to chirp, chatter, etc., and -LE 3.] Trilling or warbling (of the nightingale).

a **1250** *Owl & Night.* 48 West þu þat ich ne cunne singe, þeȝ ich ne cunne of writelinge? *Ibid.* 914 Wi nultu þare preoste singe, An teche of thire writelinge?

'write-off. [f. the vbl. phr. *to write off*: see WRITE *v.* 16.]

† **1.** A printed form with blanks for filling in with writing. *Obs.*

1752 BEAWES *Lex Merc. Rediv.* 363 No Money will be paid ..without such a Draught, or what is called, a Write off. **1826** in P. Auber *Analysis, Suppl.* (1828) 56 For every sum drawn out of the Bank of England, a write-off, or draft, shall be signed.

2. The cancellation from an account of a bad debt, worthless asset, etc.; an asset so treated; an amount cancelled or lost.

1905 *Daily Chron.* 22 July 2/6 The write-off in respect of the short weight was inevitable. **1957** *Times Lit. Suppl.* 20 Dec. 766/5 It is the point made earlier about the need for resources wherewith to make and replace the automation machines, the need for more rapid write-offs of those machines once installed, and the parallel need to 'pay' the machines more than normal machines have hitherto been 'paid'. **1970** K. PLATT *Pushbutton Butterfly* vii. 72, I understand you are behind a movement called World Peace. .. A foundation... Good tax write-off. **1971** *Daily Tel.* 26 Apr. 15/4 Above all, can share-holders.. be given an analysis of write-offs and a pre-tax comparison for the two halves? **1978** S. SHELDON *Bloodline* xxi. 243 The write-offs in our experimental laboratory. **1982** S. BELLOW *Dean's December* iv. 96 'Have you ever gotten a penny out of it?' 'I got tax write-offs.' **1984** *Times* 23 May 20/8 In competitor countries the comparison varies between one sort of asset and another but, in general, our write-off periods will be comparable with those overseas.

3. a. An aeroplane, motor vehicle, etc., so badly damaged as to be not worth repair; a wreck; an act of irreparably damaging. orig. *Air Force*.

1918 J. M. GRIDER *War Birds* (1927) 89 He wasn't hurt but the Spad [*sc.* an aeroplane] was a write-off. **1927** E. W. SPRINGS *Nocturne Militaire* 250 Both machines were complete write-offs and the only things they salvaged were the magnetos. **1944** [see OVERSHOOT *sb.*]. **1953** J. TRENCH *Docken Dead* xiii. 199 'What have you done to my car?' 'I'm afraid it's rather a write-off, sir, as far as immediate use goes, anyway.' **1963** N. MARSH *Dead Water* (1964) ix. 249 The hotel launch was still jammed... A complete write-off, it was thought. **1971** *E. Afr. Standard* (Nairobi) 10 Apr. 8/3 The car I tried was well run in and had in fact been rebuilt from a write-off condition. **1977** *Offshore Engineer* June 13/1 The Ekofisk incident has served to sharpen the risk potential of something more serious—like a major explosion, causing a platform write-off, and pollution seepage.

b. Something or someone dismissed as worthless or ineffectual; a failure.

1960 *Guardian* 26 Sept. 7/5 On English television this [film] would have been a write-off. **1966** *Listener* 17 Feb. 257/3, I find the new record of Rossini's *Stabat Mater*.. an almost complete write-off, because this New York performance.. is.. vulgarly and insensitively sung. **1974** J. COOPER *Women & Super Women* 20 In fact she's [*sc.* the pregnant woman's] a write-off from the sex appeal point of view after the fourth month. **1982** M. RUSSELL *All Part of Service* ii. 15 If it involves such an effort, I think it might well prove to be a write-off from the start. **1984** A. BROOKNER *Hotel du Lac* v. 65 The day would be a write-off.

writer ('raɪtə(r)). Forms: 1–5 **writere**, 3– **writer**, 6–7 **wrighter**, *Sc.* **writter** (6 **writare, -air**, 6–7 **writtar, -are**); 4–7 **wryter**, 5 **-ere, -are**, 5, *Sc.* 6 **-ar**, *Sc.* 6 **wrytear, vryter, wryttar**; *Sc.* 6 **wreter, -ar, wrettar**. [OE. *wrítere*, f. *wrítan* WRITE *v.* + -ER[1]. Cf. ON. *ritari* writer, Sw. *ritare*, OHG. *rizari*, etc., painter (G. *reisser* tracer).]

I. 1. a. A person who can write; one who practises or performs writing; occas., one who writes in a specified manner; = PENMAN 2. Also with advs., as *down*, *out*, *up*.

c **897** ÆLFRED *Gregory's Past. C.* liv. 423 Swa se writere, ȝif he ne dileȝað ðæt he ær wrat [etc.]. *c* **1000** ÆLFRIC *Hom.* I. 186 Oft ȝehwa ȝesihð fæȝre stafas awritene, þonne herað he ðone writere. *a* **1250** *Ancr. R.* in *Mod. Lang. Rev.* (1914) 331 I þench o þi writere i þine beoden sumchearre. *a* **1300** *Cursor M.* 24075 Es na.. writer [mai] write wit pens ord, Hu þat vr stur was strang. *c* **1450** *Mirk's Festial* I. 301 Þys monke was þe feyrest wryter þat was knowen in all þe world. *c* **1450** *Lay Folks Mass Bk.* (F.) 354 Whoso wol vse this deuocioun, I pray him.. Sey a pater-noster for the writere. **1529** MORE *Dyaloge* xl. Bj, Some fawte eyther in the translatour, or in the wryter, or nowe a dayes in the prynter. **1585** HIGINS *Junius' Nomencl.* 501 *Eclogarius*,.. a gatherer or writer down of such things in a summarie. **1639** S. DU VERGER tr. *Camus' Admir. Events* 145 This disease, much resembling that of writers, to wit, the itch of the fingers ends. **1727** BAILEY (vol. II), *Transcriber*,.. a Writer out, or Copier. **1850** GROTE *Greece* II. lxvi. (1862) VI. 15 His duty of Anagrapheus or 'Writer-up' of all the old laws of Athens. **1888** F. HUME *Mme. Midas* I. ii, Wishing his long fingers were round the writer's throat.

b. One who paints words, etc.; a sign-writer.

1837 WHITTOCK *Bk. Trades* (1842) 360 The Sign Painter, however, or writer, is a journeyman or master solus. **1861** *Internat. Exhib., Lists Trades U.K.* 80 Writers and Gilders on Glass. **1871** CALLINGHAM *Sign Writing* 98 In order to imitate raised letters.. the young writer should have some idea of.. the elements of linear perspective.

c. ***writer's cramp*** (***palsy***, ***paralysis***), a form of cramp or spasm affecting certain muscles of the hand and fingers essential to writing, and resulting from excessive use of these.

1853 SIEVEKING tr. *Romberg's Nerv. Diseases* I. 320 A peculiar form of local spasm in these parts has.. recently been made known under the name of the Writer's Cramp. **1885** H. A. REEVES *Bodily Deformities* 351 Writer's or Scrivener's Palsy. **1888** *Cassell's Encycl. Dict.*, *Scrivener's palsy*,.. a spasm or cramp.., called also Writer's Paralysis.

2. a. One whose business or occupation consists in writing; a functionary, officer, etc., who performs clerical or secretarial duties; a scribe, clerk, or law-writer.

ship's writer: see SHIP *sb.*[1] 9c.

c **890** WÆFERTH tr. *Gregory's Dial.* 52 [He] wæs writere [L. *notarius*] in þissere halȝan Romane cyrican. *c* **897** ÆLFRED *Gregory's Past. C.* Pref., Siððan min on Englisc Ælfred kyning awende worda ȝehwelc, & me his writerum sende suð & norð. **1382** WYCLIF *Ezek.* ix. 2 O man.. with.. an ynkhorn of a wryter [L. *scriptoris*] in his reynes. *c* **1450** *Godstow Register* 141 Walter scriptor oþerwise writer of þe abbei of Gloucetur. *Ibid.*, Scriptor or wryter. **1463** *Bury Wills* (Camden) 42, I beqwethe to.. John Elys, wrytere,.. a gowune of blak. **1526** *Reg. Privy Seal Scotl.* I. 512 Mak-and him directour of the chancellary.. with power.. to make deputis, clerkis, wrytaris. **1607** COWELL s.v., Writer of the talies.. is an officer in the Exchequer. **1660** BOYLE *New Exp. Phys. Mech.* p. vii, A very unskilful Writer (whom I was often times by haste reduc'd.. to imploy). **1708** J. CHAMBERLAYNE *St. Gt. Brit.* 586 Writer and Embellisher of the Queen's Letters to the Eastern Princes. *Ibid.* 734 William Douglass.., Writer to the Privy Seal. **1755** MAGENS *Insurances* II. 239 The Writer, or the Person who officiates in his Place, is carefully to note the Circumstances of the Danger. **1853** DICKENS *Bleak Ho.* x, This [affidavit] was given out, sir, to a Writer. **1873** W. STOKES *Rapid Writing* 104 Ready Writers, or persons prepared to write at a moment's notice.

† **b.** *Jewish Hist.* = SCRIBE *sb.*[1] 1. *Obs.*

c **1000** ÆLFRIC *Hept.* (1922) 46/1 Esdras se writere awrat ane boc. *c* **1000** *Ags. Gosp.* Matt. ii. 4 Þa ȝegaderode herodes ealle.. þæra.. folces writeras. **1387** TREVISA *Higden* III. 247 Esdras, the writere, come doun wiþ þe kynges lettres. **1388** WYCLIF *Jer.* xxxvi. 32 Jeremye.. ȝaf it to Baruc, the writer.

c. *Sc.* ***Writer to*** (†***of***) ***the Signet*** (abbrev. *W.S.*), originally, a clerk in the Secretary of State's office, who prepared writs to pass the royal signet; in later use, one of an ancient society of law-agents who conduct cases before the Court of Session, and have the exclusive privilege of preparing crown writs, charters, precepts, etc.

1488 *Acc. Ld. High Treas. Scotl.* I. 89 Item, to the writaris of the singnet, at the Kingis commande, ij vnicornis, xxxvj *s.* **1585** *Sc. Acts* (1814) III. 377 That the secretair admonishe all his deputis and writtairis to the signet That [etc.]. **1672** [see WRIT *sb.* 3]. **1708** J. CHAMBERLAYNE *St. Gt. Brit.* 501 There is at present about One hundred ordinary Writers to the Signet. *Ibid.* 734 Writers to the Queen's Signet. **1789** BURNS *Let. to Ainslie* 6 Jan., I do not know if passing a 'writer to the signet' be a trial of scientific merit. **1855** MACAULAY *Hist. Eng.* xiii. III. 252 The College of Justice, a ..society composed of judges, advocates, writers to the signet, and solicitors. **1881** *Daily News* 29 Dec. 2/1 A writer to the signet.. is the highest grade and finest flower of the profession of solicitor, as practised in Scotland.

ellipt. **1594** in *Hist. Writers to Signet* (1890) 230 Quhatsumevir writtare obeyis nocht his lordschipis depute keipare of the signet. **1695** *Ibid.* p. xliv, Ane convenient house, where.. the wryters may meet upon all occasions. **1837** LOCKHART *Scott* v. (1845) 36/2 In the discharge of his functions as a Writer's Apprentice.

d. *Sc.* An attorney or law-agent; an ordinary legal practitioner in country towns; a law-clerk.

1540 *Sc. Acts* (1814) II. 359 Except þame þat ar writtaris notaris and scribis in our souerane lordis courtis of Justice. **1565–6** *Reg. Privy Council Scot.* I. 417 We haif subscrivit thir presentis.. befoir thir witnessis, Alexander Hay, writtar, [and] Williame Dowglas. *c* **1610** SIR J. MELVIL *Mem.* (Bann. Cl.) 324 He maid the haill subiectis to trimble vnder him,.. vexing the haill wreters and lawers to mak sur his giftis and conkissis. **1658** J. NICOLL *Diary* (Bann. Cl.) 210 A long call.. maid be the Judges of the Court of Sessioun, and of the laweiris, clerkis, and writeris. **1773** R. FERGUSSON *Rising of the Session* i, Tir'd o' the law,.. The wylie writers.. Hurl frae the town in hackney chaises. **1826** GALT *Last of Lairds* xxv. 216 The fees both of advocate and writer. **1888** D. GRANT *Sc. Stories* 153 He had put him into the office of a 'writer' in the county town.

e. A clerk in the service of the former East India Company. Now *Hist.*

1676 in Wheeler *Madras* (1861) 64 Some of the Writers.. by their lives are not a little scandalous. **1747** in Yule & Burnell *Anglo-Ind. Gloss.* (1886) 742/2 Mr. Robert Clive, Writer in the Service, being of a Martial Disposition. **1775** CARACCIOLI *Life Clive* I. 14 Mr. Clive.. had served the East India company seven years, as a writer. **1809** *Cobbett's Pol. Reg.* 22 Apr. 578 These Writers are clerks, sent out to India, ..where they collect taxes from the people. **1891** KIPLING *Life's Handicap* 345 Writer to the Most Honourable the East India Company.

3. a. One who writes, compiles, or produces a literary composition; the composer *of* a book or treatise; a literary man or author; = PENMAN 3, 3b. Also with *on* (†*of*) or *upon* (a subject).

In very frequent use from *c* 1560. Also ***book-***, ***comedy-***, ***essay-***, ***history-***, ***letter-***, ***news-***, ***pamphlet-***, ***play-***, ***prose-***, ***story-***, ***tragedy-writer***, etc.: see these words.

c **888** ÆLFRED *Boeth.* xviii. §3 Hu ne forealdodon þa ȝewritu þeah & losodon þonecan þe hit wære, swa some swa þa writeras dydon. *c* **1055** *Byrhtferth's Handboc* in *Anglia* VIII. 327 Nu toȝeare þa Brihtferð writere þis awrat synd feowertyne epactas. *a* **1200** *St. Marher.* 2 Ant ich biȝet hit iwriten of þe writere þa, al hire passiun. *c* **1225** *Leg. Kath.* 856 Philistiones flites, & Platunes bokes; & alle þeos writeres writes þet ȝe wreoðieð ow on. *a* **1300** *Cursor M.* 21196 Lucas was.. O þe apostols dedis writer. **1390** GOWER *Conf.* II. 90 Many an other writere.. the bokes wise Translateden. *c* **1410** LOVE *Bonavent. Mirr.* (1908) 8 As it semeth to the writere here of most spedeful and edifienge to hem. **1538** STARKEY *England* 137 Prouysyon to stoppe folysch wrytarys and lyght bokys of the gospel. *a* **1586** SIDNEY *Apol. Poetry* (Arb.) 27 Such were.. Moses and Debora in theyr Hymnes, and the writer of *Iob*. *c* **1611** [see WRITEE]. **1660** STANLEY *Hist. Philos.* XIII. (1687) 841/2 A great Writer,.. and exceeding for multitude of Books. **1728** CHAMBERS *Cycl.* (1738) s.v. *Music*, The most antient writer of [= on] musick ..was Lasus Hermionensis. **1752** A. MURPHY *Gray's-Inn Jrnl.* No. 5, A cold, trifling, frothy Writer. **1834** DICKENS *Sk. Boz*, *Hor. Sparkins*, A writer of fashionable novels. **1861** LD. BROUGHAM *Brit. Const.* xv. 219 It has been remarked by writers on our Constitutional History. **1886** C. E. PASCOE *Lond. of To-day* xl. (ed. 3) 334 Women dress for each other, says one writer.

b. One who is writing. ***the*** (***present***) ***writer***, the writer hereof.

a **1578** LINDESAY (Pitscottie) *Chron. Scot.* (S.T.S.) I. 4, I the wrettar that dois considdar weill The sindrie myndis of men. **1623** JOBSON *Golden Trade* 8 It pleased them to imploy mee the present wrighter. **1784** COWPER *Table-t.* IV. 18 Tears.. trickled down the writer's cheeks Fast as the periods from his fluent quill. **1857** W. C. STEWART *Pract. Angler* vii. (ed. 3) 139 A brother of the writer made the same trial with the same result. **1895** ARBER *Sk. Marprel. Controv.* 193 The present Writer's belief on this subject.

c. A composer of music.

1688 T. SALMON *Prop. Perform Music* 19 That the Writers of Musick may more certainly know where to fix their Flats and Sharps. **1782** BURNEY *Hist. Mus.* II. 567 Written Discant, which is.. practised in Italy, by all writers for the Church. **1889** RUSKIN *Præterita* III. iv. 161 [Corelli] the simplest and purest writer of Italian melody.

d. ***writer-up***: see WRITE *v.* 19.

1841 *Tait's Mag.* VIII. 80, I had been misled by those writers-up of this country. **1904** *Times* 1 June 14 He carried on business as a writer-up of advertisements.

e. ***writer's block*** [BLOCK *sb.* 19e], a periodic lack of inspiration afflicting creative writers; ***writer's writer***: a writer whose appeal is primarily to his fellow writers (cf. *poet's poet* s.v. POET 1c).

1950 E. BERGLER *Writer & Psychoanal.* vi. 113 Writer's block sets in the moment the inner conscience rejects the alibi and substitute alibi. **1966** G. BAXT *Queer Kind of Death* xi. 150 Seth has had a *serious* writer's block for almost two *years* now. **1975** M. BRADBURY *History Man* x. 169 This book.. has decidedly not gone well. I've had what they call writer's block. The words won't come. **1983** *Listener* 13 Jan. 12/3 Graham Greene relies heavily on the unconscious to get round 'writer's block' as he revealed in an interview with Nigel Lewis.

1941 'G. Orwell' in *Listener* 12 June 841/1 Hopkins is what people call a writer's writer. He..appeals to people who are professionally interested in points of technique. **1951** *Sunday Times* 15 Apr. 3/2 She [*sc.* Ivy Compton-Burnett] is in the first place 'a writers' writer', because she is fascinated by words and phrases as such. **1980** *Times Lit. Suppl.* 12 Sept. 992/1 Nigel Williams is a writer's writer.

f. ***writer-in-residence***: a writer given a residential post in a university, etc., in order to share his professional insights. Cf. *poet-in-residence* s.v. poet 1 e; residence *sb.*[1] 2 b.

1957 J. D. Salinger *Zooey* in *New Yorker* 4 May 33/3 The second-eldest child, Buddy, was what is known in campus-catalog parlance as 'writer-in-residence' at a girls' junior college in upper New York State. **1972** [see residence 2 b]. **1980** *Times Lit. Suppl.* 2 May 496/3 The initiative to hold a poetry festival to celebrate..his [*sc.* Basil Bunting's] birthday came from Tom Pickard, writer-in-residence for this year at the University of Warwick.

4. *ellipt.* The writings of an author.

1605 Camden *Rem.* 2 Let therefore these few lines.. suffice, out of an antient Writer. **1676** Ray *Corr.* (1848) 122 [This] history makes me suspect he transcribed what he hath out of some writer. **1768–74** Tucker *Lt. Nat.* (1834) II. 465 In some of the classic writers it is said [etc.]. **1820** Hazlitt *Lect. Dram. Lit.* 11 A whole host of able writers.. are suffered to moulder in obscurity on the shelves of our libraries. **1859** Helps *Friends in C.* Ser. II. II. 96, I saw the other day in an American writer a humorous account.

5. ***writer's sand*** (see quot. and sand *sb.*[2] 8).

1899 *Allbutt's Syst. Med.* VII. 479 Such granulations vary in size from the finest 'writer's sand' ('tuberculous dust') to [etc.].

6. One who typewrites; a typist.

1883 J. G. Petrie *Man. for Type-Writer* 15 Unless the printers are accustomed to the writer's style of shortening words.

II. 7. A make of paint-brush.

1884 R. Leslie in Ruskin *Dilecta* (1900) 6 Turner..used short brushes, some of them like the writers used by house decorators. **1889** Sutherland *Sign Writing* iv. 4/4 A few sable and camels-hair pencils... There are what are called 'writers'.

8. A pen, etc., that writes in a specified manner.

1907 *Westm. Gaz.* 10 Dec. 12/2 These pens..are certainly excellent writers.

III. 9. *attrib.* (chiefly appositive), as ***writer body, chiel, -lad; writer-type, word.***

1686 Sir J. Lauder *Decis.* (1759) I. 401 Some Writer lads were also accessory. **1717** Ramsay *Elegy on Lucky Wood* ix, The writer lads fu' well may mind her. **1785** Burns *To W. Simpson* iii, Ferguson, the writer-chiel. **1818** Scott *Rob Roy* xviii, I have just arrested her *jurisdictiones fandandy causey*. Thae are bonny writer words. **1869** A. Macdonald *Clerical Intrigue* 108 A miserable writer body frae Glasgow. **1891** Kipling *Light that Failed* (1900) 169 That's the writer-type. He has the same modelling of the forehead as Torp.

Hence **'writeress**, a female writer or author; an authoress; **'writerling**, a petty writer; a sorry or indifferent author.

1822 *Blackw. Mag.* XII. 656 Our rhyming *writeresses are frequently single gentlewomen. **1855** Thackeray *Char. Sk.* Wks. 1898 III. 517 Remember it henceforth, ye writeresses—there is no such word as authoress. **1802** W. Taylor in Robberds *Mem.* (1843) I. 420 Every writer and *writerling of name has a salary from the government.

writerly ('raɪtəlɪ), *a.* [f. writer + -ly[1], after *painterly*.] Appropriate to, characteristic or worthy of a professional writer or literary man; consciously literary.

1957 *Times Lit. Suppl.* 16 Aug. p. xxxvii/2 Serious Canadian writers at present are firmly resolved to concentrate upon the writerly virtues. **1958** *Spectator* 24 Jan. 114/1 A clever and writerly book. **1977** M. Cohen *Sensible Words* i. 25 Dryden..sees his writerly obligations in new terms. **1982** *Listener* 23/30 Dec. 56/3 James Saunders dissecting writerly old age and the onset of what appears to be terminal cynicism.

writership ('raɪtəʃɪp). [f. writer + -ship 3.]

1. The office or position of a writer in the service of the former East India Company. Now *Hist.*

1763 in *10th Rep. Hist. MSS. Comm.* App. I. 358 The surprising applications made by the top familys for writerships..confounded him. **1800** *Asiat. Ann. Reg., Proc.* 98 The motives that influenced..their nominations to writerships. **1854** Thackeray *Newcomes* I. 21 Being offered a writership, he scouted the idea of a civil appointment.

2. The office or employment of a clerk; a clerkship.

1884 *Public Opinion* 5 Sept. 304 Officers..who are thoroughly competent for writerships in dockyard[s] and victualling yards at home.

'write-up. [f. the vbl. phr. *to write up*: see write *v.* 19.]

A written account or description commending or praising a person or thing. Now often more loosely, any journalistic account or review, whether favourable or not. Orig. *U.S.*

1885 *Weekly New Mexican Rev.* 19 Feb. 4/1, I have prepared quite an extensive 'write-up' of the resources of this country. **1887** *Aberdeen* (Dakota) *Republican* 31 Dec. 2/2 The LaMoure Progress..has an elaborate write-up of its city and county. **1902** Eliz. Banks *Newspaper Girl* 22 What 'write-ups' they gave me, to be sure! **1910** *Chambers's Jrnl.* July 431/1 The 'write-up' and the interviews are prominent features. **1919** Wodehouse *Damsel in Distress* ii. 28 My missus says she ain't seen a livelier show for a long time... *The Morning Leader* gave it a fine write-up. **1933** P. Godfrey *Back-Stage* viii. 102 In so far as a play is sensitively conceived..the newspaper write-ups of its story may be..extremely misleading. **1948** *Penguin Music Mag.* Oct. 29 He (or rather she) studies music with an eye sooner or later to engagement, a photograph in the 'press', and a 'write-up', as they call all criticism appearing in print. **1951** *Sport* 30 Mar.–5 Apr. 15/1 The critics..dismissed him in pre-fight write-ups as 'another Phil Scott'. **1965** *New Statesman* 14 May 753/2 The *Stern* reporter..gave [Prince] Philip one of the worst write-ups of his career. **1973** P. Evans *Bodyguard Man* xviii. 117 He..never gives me a good write-up unless I've played really well. **1985** *Contact* (Pre-School Playgroups Assoc.) Feb. 14/2 They prepared a paper summarising their findings... This was circulated to the press, who gave a good write-up.

writh (rɪθ). Now *dial.* [Cf. Da. *vrid*, Norw. *(v)rid*, turning, evasion, etc.; ON. *rið* winding staircase.] = writhe *sb.* 1, 1 b.

14.. *Latin-Eng. Voc.* (MS. Harl. 2257), *Grani*, a writh. **1570** Levins *Manip.* 150 A Writh, *cesticillus*. **1844** W. Barnes *Dorset Gloss.* 370 *Writh*, the bond of a faggot.

writh, southern dial. var. frith *sb.*[2] 3.

writhable ('raɪðəb(ə)l), *a. rare*$^{-1}$. [f. writhe *v.* + -able.] Capable of being writhed.

c **1425** *St. Christina* in *Anglia* VIII. 126 She..croked hir armes & fyngers as if þey were wryþabil for softenesse.

writhe (raɪð), *sb.* Also 6–7 **wrythe**. [f. next. Cf. wreath *sb.*, and OHG. *rida* 'tensio'.]

†**1.** Something twisted, wreathed, or formed into a circular shape; a twisted band; a wreath. *Obs.*

1513 Douglas *Æneid* v. x. 25 The writhe of gold, or chane lowpit in ringis. **1548** Udall, etc. *Erasm. Par. Luke* vii. 74 To brede [her hair] with wrythes of golde enterlaced emong it. **1569** Underdowne *Heliodorus* ix. 127 [Each] hathe a round Wrythe vpon his head, in which their Arrowes are set in order.

†**b.** (See quot. and cf. writhe.) *Obs.*$^{-0}$

1552 Huloet, Wrythes, or any thing that may be wrythed about like a willow or osier, *vitilia, ium*.

c. A curled or twisted formation; a wreath or twist.

1857 Ruskin *Arrows of Chace* (1880) I. 219 The castle sate its rock as a strong rider sits his horse,—fitting its limbs to every writhe of the flint beneath it. **1874** R. Tyrwhitt *Sketching Club* 164 The writhe in his mustache.

2. An act of writhing; a twisting or writhing movement of the body, countenance, etc.; a contortion.

1611 Cotgr., *Torse*,..a wrest, wrinch; wrythe. **1767** S. Paterson *Another Trav.* I. 185 Men who..could watch the excruciating writhes..of others. **1796** *Instr. & Reg. Cavalry* (1813) 29 The head or leading flank..whose writhes and turnings are followed by every other part of the body [of troops]. **1812** Chalmers *Biogr. Dict.* V. 312 He..expired.. without a writhe in his countenance. **1890** Miss Broughton *Alas!* xvi, The silent writhe with which Jim receives this piece of information.

†**b.** A twinge *of* pain, etc. *Obs.*$^{-1}$

1792 A. Young *Trav. France* 133, I had some writhes of it [*sc.* rheumatism] before I entered Champagne.

3. Degree of tautness; tension. *rare*$^{-1}$.

1879 *Grove's Dict. Mus.* I. 135 A body..of parchment, strained upon a hoop to the required writhe or degree of stiffness for resonance.

writhe (raɪð), *v.*[1] Forms: 1 **wriðan**, 3 **wriðen**, 4 **wryþen**, 4–5 **wrythen**, 5 **wrythyn**, **writhyn**; 4–5 **wriþe**, 4– **writhe** (6 **wriethe**), 4–7 **writh** (6 **wrieth**); 4–5 **wryþe**, 4–7 **wrythe**, **wryth**. *Pa. t.* 1 **wraþ**, 3 **wræð**, 5 **wraythe**, **wrathe**; 3 **wreoð**, 4–5 **wroþ**, **wroth**, 5 **wrothe**, **wrooth**. *Pl.* 1 **wriþon**, 2 **uurythen**, 3 **wryþen**, 4 **writhen** (7 **writhe**), 5–6 **wrythen** (6 **wrethen**). *Pa. pple.* 1 **ʒewriðen**, 3 **ywriðen**, 4–5 **iwriþen**, **ywrithen**, **ywryþe**, **y-**, **iwrithe**; 1, 4 **wriþen**, 4– **writhen** (4 **-un**, 5 **-yn**, 6 **-in**), 5–7 **wrythen** (5 **-yn**); 4 **writhe**, 5 **wrythe**; 4 **wreþen**, 4–6 **wrethen** (5 **-yn**), 5 **ywrethe**; 6 **wrothonne**. *Weak pa. t.* and *pa. pple.* 5– **writhed**, 4–6 **wrythed**. [OE. *wríðan* str. v. (pa. t. *wráþ*, pl. *wriðon*; pa. pple. *ʒewriðen*), also *ʒewríðan*, = OFris. **wrîða* (NFris. *wriir*, *wrial*), OHG. *rîdan* (in *ga-*, *kirîdan*; MHG. *rîden*), ON. *ríða*, MSw. *vriþa* (Sw. *vrida*), MDa. and Da. *vride*, related to *wriða* wreath. Cf. wreathe *v.*

The northern ME. pa. t. *wraythe* may represent ON. **wreið* pa. t. of **wríða* (later *ríða*).]

I. *trans.* **1.** To twist or coil (something); to fashion into coils or folds; to dispose or arrange in a coiled or sinuous form; to bend or distort by twisting. Freq. with *about*, *over*, *round* preps., *up* adv. Also *refl.*

c **1000** Ælfric *Gram.* xxvi. (Z.) 155 *Torqueo*, ic wriðe. **1154** *O.E. Chron.* (Laud MS.) an. 1137, Me dide cnotted stranges abuton here hæued & uurythen to ðæt it ʒæde to þe hærnes. **1362** Langl. *P. Pl.* A. vi. 9 He bar a bordun i-bounde wiþ a brod lyste, In a weþe-bondes wyse i-wriþen aboute. *c* **1380** Wyclif *Serm.* Sel. Wks. I. 278 A ȝerde mai growe so greet..þat men shal not wriþe it. *c* **1440** *Pallad. on Husb.* iii. 118 Writhe not the hed of thy sarment. *a* **1450** *Knt. de La Tour* (1868) 21 He brought..a litell wipse of strawe. *c* **1460** [see wrapper *sb.* 1]. *a* **1500** *Hist. K. Boccus & Sydracke* (? 1510) *A* ij b, A grene wand..may be wrethen whyle it is grene. **1568** Turner *Herbal* ii. 128 The floures grew very thyck together as they were writhen about the stalcke. **1614** D. Dyke *Myst. Selfe-Deceiuing* (1630) 279 Correcting the crookedness of a twig hee writhes it too much the other way. **1635** J. Hayward tr. *Biondi's Banish'd Virg.* 149 Never was there..serpent wrythen up so suddenly. **1643** in Sir J. Temple *Irish Rebell.* (1646) 117 They would take and writh wyths about their heads. **1658** tr. *Porta's Nat. Magic* i. viii. 12 The pulse called Lupines, still looks after the Sun, that it may not writhe his stalk. **1745** tr. *Columella's Husb.* iii. xviii, Twisting and writhing the head of a shoot. ? *c* **1745** Shenstone *Elegies* xx. 39 Here the dry dipsa writhes his sinuous mail. **1827** Pollok *Course T.* v. 597 The Worm ..writhing its folds In hideous sort. **1832** Motherwell *Poems* 45 This leafless tree, That's writhen o'er the linn. **1866** Chr. Rossetti *Prince's Progr.* 6 Who twisted her hair ..And writhed it shining in serpent-coils. **1901** Weyman *Ct. Hannibal* vi, The tiring-maid..flung herself..at Mademoiselle's knees,..writhing herself about them.

†**b.** To force in wreaths. *Obs.*

c **1374** Chaucer *Boeth.* i. met. iv. 7 (Camb. MS.), Veseuus ..writ[h]ith [L. *torquet*] owtthorw his brokene chymynees smokynge fyres.

c. To change or fashion *into* (†*to*) some form, etc., by wreathing or twisting.

1582 Mulcaster *Elementarie* i. (1925) 25 If the pliable mind be vnwiselie writhen to a disfigured shape. **1828** Scott *F.M. Perth* xxxiv, Their countenances seemed fiercely writhen into the wildest expression of pride. **1851** Ruskin *Stones Ven.* I. i. §26 The Arab..points the arch and writhes it into extravagant foliations. **1879** Symonds *Sk. Italy & Greece* (ed. 2) 291 Snow lies..writhed into loveliest wreaths.

†**2.** To unite, combine, or make compact, by twisting, entwining, or interweaving; to join *with* something, twine together; to intertwine. Freq. with *together*. *Obs.*

c **1205** Lay. 25974 Þat weore twælf swine..mid wiðen.. y-wriðen al to-gadere. **1388** Wyclif *Judges* xvi. 9 As if a man brekith a threed of herdis, writhun with spotle. **1398** Trevisa *Barth. De P.R.* xvii. cl. (Bodl. MS.), Al schrubbes and treen wiþ prickes..beþ ywounde and ywrethe togedres, and biclippiþ..euriche oþer. *a* **1400–50** *Bk. Curtasye* 440 in *Babees Bk.* 313 Litere..Wele watered, i-wrythen, be craft y-trode. *Ibid.* 442 Wyspes..Wele wrethyn and turnyd a-ȝayne þat tyde. *c* **1425** *Seven Sag.* (P.) 1792 The wyf fast hyre keyes wrothe In the end of the borde clothe. *a* **1500** *Flower & Leaf* viii, The hegge also..With sicamour was set and eglantere, Writhen in-fere so wel. **1565** Cooper *Thesaurus*, *Nerui tortiles*,..stringes writhed together. **1600** Surflet *Countrie Farme* i. xiii. 86 Let them rub them..with a wispe of strawe harde writhen together. **1654** Whitelocke *Jrnl. Swed. Emb.* (1772) I. 179 Their stirrup [is] a withe writhed togither. **1671** J. Webster *Metallogr.* xiii. 209 Thick truncks, which were writhen variously amongst themselves.

†**3.** To form or fashion (a wreath, etc.) by plaiting, entwining, or twisting; to plait. Also with *together*. *Obs.*

c **1275** [see wrase 1]. **1388** Wyclif *John* xix. 2 Kniȝtis writhen a coroun of thornes. *c* **1450** *Mirk's Festial* i. 121 Þay wrythen a crowne of þornys and setten on his hed. **1520** *Treat. Galaunt* 191 Theyr typpettes be wrythen lyke to a chayne. *c* **1550** Cheke *Matt.* xxvii. 29 Writhing together a crown of thistels. **1563** Shute *Archit.* D iv b, The other Astragalus..shalbe wrothonne like a wreath.

†**4.** To turn or wrench round or to a side; to twist about; to wring. *Obs.*

a **1300** *Cursor M.* 3462 Þair strut it was vn-stern stith, Wit wrathli wrestes aiþer writh. **1388** Wyclif *Lev.* i. 15 Whanne the heed is writhun to the necke. **1513** Douglas *Æneid* i. iii. 19 Ane blusterand bub..The schippis stewyn frawart hir went can writhe. **1584** Bedingfield tr. *Corte's Art Riding* 101 An angrie horsse..that dooth wryth his head from one side to the other. **1607** Markham *Cavel.* ii. (1617) 80 To carrie your cudgell in his eye of that side which he most writheth. **1697** Dryden *Æneis* x. 448 Æneas writh'd his Dart, and stopp'd his bawling Breath. **1713** Steele *Englishm.* No. 1. 5 There may be a Way of appearing Wise by writhing the Head.

fig. and in fig. context. **1513** Douglas *Æneid* iv. xi. 95 Hir faynt spreit in all partis writhis [L. *versabat*] sche. *a* **1547** Surrey *Æneid* iv. 282 [He] writhed his loke toward the royal walls. **1603** Holland *Plutarch's Mor.* 141 A yoong wench hath him sure enough by the necke, and doth writhe him which way she list! **1684** H. More *Answer* Pref. b j b, The Remarker..has writhen and forced his Wit and Invention to personate [etc.].

†**b.** *fig.* To divert or deflect from or to a person, course, etc.; to cause to turn away, bend, or incline towards another. Cf. wrench *v.* 4 b.

a **1300** *Cursor M.* 15569 For þai wald writ [*vrr.* writh, wriþe] on me..al þair aun wijt. *Ibid.* 28101. *c* **1375** *Sc. Leg. Saints* xxxi. (*Eugenia*) 361 Þar-for scho thocht wele to wricht [*read* writhe] in hyme hir wikitnes alsuyth. *Ibid.* xlii. (*Agatha*) 97 For to wryth agathis wil fra cryst. **1412–20** Lydg. *Chron. Troy* ii. 2011 Whan þat he his aspectis glade Fro a man listeth for to writhe. **1534** Whitinton *Tullyes Offices* ii. (1540) 87 Pleasures fayre..ofte tymes wrythe the bygger partes of the soule fro vertue. **1561** Norton & Sackv. *Gorboduc* i. ii, Lest the fraude..Of flattering tongues ..wrythe them to the wayes of youthfull lust. **1642** Chas. I *Let. to Mayor of Bristol* 2 The rebellious instigation..to writhe and bend your inclinations to oppose Me. **1655** [see wrench *v.* 6 c].

†**c.** With advs., as *about*, *aside*, *away*, *back*. Occas. *fig.* and in fig. context. *Obs.*

c **1400** *Rom. Rose* 4359 Fortune..can writhe hir heed awey. *c* **1480** Henryson *Bludy Serk* 107 Sa suld we wryth all syn away. *c* **1550** H. Lloyd *Treas. Health* A j, If the eyes be wrythen asyde. *a* **1564** Becon *Treat. Fasting* iv, To wryth his head about lyke an hope. **1609** Bible (Douay) *Lev.* v. 8 He..shal wryth backe the heade therof.

5. To subject (the body, limbs, etc.) to a contorting or twisting movement; to twist, contort; to wring or wreathe. Also with advs., as *around*, *round*, *together*, *up*, and absol.

1393 Langl. *P. Pl.* C. vii. 66 He wroth his fust vp-on wratthe. *c* **1425** Wyntoun *Cron.* vi. xviii. 1975 Þan spak Makbeth dispytusly,..Lyk al wrethyn [*v.r.* wrythin] in his skyn. *c* **1450** *Ludus Coventriæ* 28 Wryhte on to my necke bon with hardnesse of þin honde. **1565** Cooper *Thesaurus* s.v.

Torqueo, To writhe one's necke. **1633** G. Herbert *Temple, Constancie* vii, He..Whom nothing can procure..To writhe his limbes. **1691** Baxter *Certainty Worlds Spirits* 166 Some Reapers..were hurt, writhen, and one killed with a Whirlwind. **1711** Budgell *Spect.* No. 161 ¶3 A Country Girl..writhing and distorting her whole Body. **1791** E. Darwin *Bot. Gard.* I. 75 The alarmed Goddess..Writhes her fair limbs. **1814** W. Brown *Hist. Propag. Chr.* II. 434 In the fall, his hip was writhed. **1865** B. Brierley *Irkdale* I. 143 Aw'll wrythe thy neck reawnd. **1884** *Pall Mall G.* 14 March 1/1 The Arabs..writhed their bodies under guns, Gatlings, and muskets.

refl. **1667** Milton *P.L.* vi. 328 Then Satan first knew pain, And writh'd him to and fro convolv'd. **1814** Scott *Lord of Isles* vi. xxxii, The mountaineer Yet writhed him up against the spear. **1895** Crockett *Men of Moss-hags* xxiii. 169 The creature writhed himself in glee.

b. To distort (the face, etc.); to draw awry; = wring *v.* 2b.

c **1480** Henryson *Test. Cres.* 189 The God of Ire.. Wrything his face with mony angrie word. **1545** Ascham *Toxoph.* (Arb.) 145 Some make a face with writhing theyr mouthe. **1548** Elyot, *Intorquere mentum*, to writhe or wreste the chynne. **1609** Bible (Douay) *Prov.* xix. 1 Better is a poore man..then a rich writhing his lippes. **1667** Milton *P.L.* x. 569 They..writh'd thir jaws. **1755** Johnson, *Distortion*,..irregular motion by which the face is writhed. **1864** Tennyson *Boadicea* 74 [They] Madly dash'd the darts together, writhing barbarous lineaments.

c. To utter, speak *out*, with a writhe.

1889 Gunter *That Frenchman* xxi. 290, As they drag her back..she writhes out to Ora..: 'They'll do the same to you'. **1902** Snaith *Wayfarers* xii, Sir Thomas would grunt and wriggle and writhe his tipsy protests.

d. To make or pursue (its way) by writhing.

1867 J. G. Wood *Illustr. Nat. Hist.* 326 The snake which has writhed its way to the Mocking Bird's nest.

6. To twist or wrench (something) out of place, position, or relation; = wring *v.* 6. Const. with advs., as *asunder*, †*atwo*, *off*, *out*, or preps., as *from*, *off*, *out of*. Also *refl.* Occas. *fig.*

1388 Wyclif *2 Sam.* xxiii. 21 Bi miȝt he wrooth out the spere fro the hond of the man. **1390** Gower *Conf.* III. 271 He his necke hath writhe atuo. *c* **1420** *Liber Cocorum* (1862) 48 Sethe þy capone,..brisse hom in hast And wrythe itwen. **1490** Caxton *Eneydos* x. 39 There myghte ye see.. crampons of yron wrythen a sondre. **1554–9** *Songs & Ball. Phil. & Mary* (Roxb.) 12, I wolde God in sondare I myght wrythe his necke boune. ? *a* **1600** in Child *Ballads* III. 413/34 Then he writhe the gold ring of his ffingar. **1606** Marston *Parasit.* v. H4b, Cupid.., Whose force writh'd lightning from Ioues shaking hand. **1684** H. More *Answer* 224 Before their heads be writhen off. **1859** H. Kingsley *G. Hamlyn* ix, She writhed herself free. **1887** D. C. Murray *One Trav. Returns* xvii, Writhing the water from their auburn hair.

fig. *c* **1400** *Destr. Troy* 11616 But god..wrangis in his wrathe writhis to ground. **1570** Foxe *A. & M.* (ed. 2) I. 5/2 Here the Bishops began first to writhe out theyr elections and theyr neckes a litle from the Emperours subiection.

†**b.** To insert (something) *in* or *into* a space by insinuation or twisting. Also *transf.* and *refl.* *Obs.*

1590 Barrough *Meth. Physick* I. xliv. (1596) 67 You may writh a linnen cloth..in the nosthrils. **1593** Nashe *Christ's T.* G2b, This desolatiue-Trumpet of Ierusalem; a weake breath or two I will writhe into it. **1598** B. Jonson *Every Man in Humour* III. v, He had so writhen himselfe, into the habit of one of your poore *Infanterie*.

†**7.** To wrest, strain, or pervert the meaning of (a writing, passage, word, etc.); to deflect, misapply; = wrench *v.* 7, wrest *v.* 5, 6, wring *v.* 9b. *Obs.*

In frequent use from *c* 1555 to *c* 1600.

a **1533** Ld. Berners *Gold. Bk. M. Aurel.* (1546) Hhiv, They haue..writhen and enlarged the discipline of Justyce. **1546** Gardiner *Declar. Joye* 43 The pelagians..searched out places of scripture, and writhed them violently..to their purpose. **1565** Cooper *Thesaurus* s.v. *Torqueo*, To wreste & writhe the law. **1624** Bedell *Lett.* vi. 106 The *Ladies Psalter*, wherein that which is spoken of God by the Spirit of God is writhed to her. **1662** Hibbert *Body Divinity* I. 199 Wresting and writhing mens writings to another meaning.

†**b.** To misinterpret (a writer); = wrest *v.* 5c.

1555 [see wrest *v.* 5c]. **1561** T. Norton *Calvin's Inst.* I. xiv. 47 Stephen and Paule.., howe soeuer they be writhed, yet must..so be vnderstanded.

II. †**8.** To envelop, enfold, or swathe (something) by winding or folding. *Obs.*

a **1000** *Egbert's Penit.* III. xvi. in Thorpe *Laws* II. 202 Þa ðe forbrocene wæron, þa ȝe ne wriþon [L. *ligavistis*]. *c* **1000** *Ags. Gosp.* Luke x. 34 Þa ȝenealæhte he, & wrað his wunda. *c* **1205** Lay. 17762 Wreoð nu wel þene king þæt he ligge a swæting. *c* **1366** Chaucer *Rom. Rose* 160 Hir heed writhen was..with a greet towayle. **1398** Trevisa *Barth. De P.R.* XII. v. (Bodl. MS.), Been..makeþ honye combesse ywounde and writhe wiþ waxe. *a* **1400–50** *Bk. Curtasye* 685 in *Babees Bk.*, Þen brede he brynges, in towelle wrythyn. *c* **1440** *Promp. Parv.* 534/1 Wrythyn, *idem quod* hyllyn.

†**b.** To confine or fasten with a cord, bond, etc.; to bind, fetter. *Obs.*

Beowulf 964 Ic hine hrædlice heardan clammum on wælbedde wriþan þohte. [*c* **1175** *Lamb. Hom.* 123 Crist..ferde to helle and iwrað þene alde deouel.] *c* **1205** Lay. 17394 Ȝe mote uaste heom wriðen mid strongen sæil-rapen. **13..** *E.E. Allit. P.* C. 80 Þay..Wryþe me in a warlok, wrast out myn yȝen. *a* **1400** *Prymer* (1891) 98 Coordes of synful men ha a bouten writhe me.

fig. *c* **1400** *Laud Troy Bk.* 9088 In hir loue was he so writhen, That he myght not his wille refrayn.

†**c.** To secure or fix (something) *with* a pin, etc. *Obs.*[−1]

1683 Pettus *Fleta Min.* I. 12 Assay Ovens made..of strong Armor-plate, and writhen with Ironpins.

†**9.** To surround or invest *with* something; to wreathe, enwreathe. Also with *about*. *Obs.*

1513 Douglas *Æneid* v. v. 12 Ane mantill brusit with gold, With purpour selvage writhin mony fold. *a* **1727** Newton *Chronol. Amended* ii. (1728) 227 A Caduceus writhen about with two serpents.

III. *intr.* **10.** To move or stir in a turning or sinuous manner; to change posture by twisting; to twist about.

a **1300** in *Maps' Poems* (Camden) 336 Thi wretche with [= wit] so thunne, That ay was writhinde as a wond. **1303** R. Brunne *Handl. Synne* 5471 Þey..sawe hys coloure ofte ouer caste; And wroth a-boute, to and fro. **13..** *Gaw. & Gr. Knt.* 1200 Þen he wakenede, & wroth, & to hir warde torned. **13..** *E.E. Allit. P.* A. 510 For a pene on a day..forth þay gos, Wryþen & worchen & don gret pyne. ? *a* **1400** *Morte Arth.* 1141 Wrothely thai wrythyne and wrystille to-gederz. **1545** Ascham *Toxoph.* (Arb.) 111 Elles the one ende [of a bow-string] shall wriethe contrary to the other. **1588** Greene *Pandosto* (1843) 26 The babe..wrythed with the head to seeke for the pap. **1611** Cotgr., *Serpeger*, to.. wrigle, writhe, or goe waiuing, &c., like a serpent. **1809–14** Wordsw. *Excurs.* vi. 291 The Indian bird That writhes and chatters in her wiry cage. **1820** Southey *Lodore* 61 Flying and flinging, Writhing and ringing,..this way the Water comes down at Lodore. **1893** Mary Cholmondeley *Diana Tempest* xvi, [He] lit the paper, and..watched it writhe under the little chuckling flame.

fig. *c* **1460** *Towneley Myst.* xiii. 126 This warld fowre neuer so,..Now in weyll, now in wo, And all thyng wrythys.

b. To contort the body, limbs, etc., as from agony, emotion, or stimulation; to twist *under* or *with* pain, distress, etc.; to wring, turn. Also with *about*.

In frequent use from *c* 1800.

? *a* **1400** *Morte Arth.* 1920 Thane the worthy kynge [Arthur] wrythes, and wepede with his eghne. *a* **1400–50** *Wars Alex.* 1189 (Ashm. MS.), Þe wale kyng..writhis him vnfaire [*Dubl. MS.* wex wode wroth]. *Ibid.* 1409. *c* **1425** Wyntoun *Chron.* VIII. xi. 1776 Al brym he belyt in to brethe, And wrythit al in wedand wrethe. **1470–85** Malory *Arthur* I. cxxxvi. 242 Beaumayns..walowed and wrythed for the loue of the lady. **1713** Addison *Cato* III. v, Let them ..be..empal'd, and left To writhe at leisure round the bloody stake. **1798** S. & Ht. Lee *Canterb. T.* II. 431 [She was] writhing under the wound. **1840** Dickens *Old C. Shop* xiii, Mr. Brass, after writhing about,..was by this time awake also. **1848** Edmeston *Sacred Poetry* 171 Though the nerves may writhe with pain. **1890** W. Booth *In Darkest Eng.* 280 That dark ocean, full of human wrecks, writhing in anguish.

fig. **1846** Mrs. A. Marsh *Father Darcy* II. iii. 74 His heart writhing with hatred. **1893** Mary Cholmondeley *Diana Tempest* xxxiv, Passion, writhing in torment,..seized him in a Titan grip.

c. *poet.* To twine or coil (*round* something).

1795 Southey *Joan of Arc* III. (1853) 33, I saw The pictured flames writhe round a penanced soul.

11. To change place or position, to turn, move, or go, with a writhing or twisting motion. Usu. with preps., as *about*, *down*, *from*, †*of*, *to*, *up*, or advs., as *apart*, *away*, *back*, *out*.

c **1205** Lay. 6729 Þe king..him wræð [*c* 1275 leop] to, ase he hine wolde anho. **13..** *E.E. Allit. P.* A. 350 Of þe way a fote ne wyl he wryþe. *Ibid.* B. 533 Wylde wormez to her won wryþez in þe erþe. ? *a* **1400** *Morte Arth.* 1093 Ilke wrethe as a wolfe-heuede, it wraythe owtt at ones! **14..** *Chaucer's Miller's T.* 97 (Camb. MS.), With here hed sche wrythed faste a-wey. *c* **1440** *Ipomydon* 1835 Thus he wrawled & wroth a-way. **1540** Hyrde tr. *Vines' Introd. Chr. Wom.* II. xii. 122 Whan thou wrythest awaye from thy steppe chyldren, callynge the mother. **1565** Golding *Ovid's Met.* I. (1593) 18 He proffered kisses too the tree, the tree did from him wryth. **1849** Lytton *K. Arthur* XI. clii, Struggling for speech, the pale lips writhed apart. **1859** Tennyson *Merlin & V.* 237 Vivien..Writhed toward him, slided up his knee [etc.]. **1891** F. Tennyson *Poems* 369 Snakes writhed to their holes.

b. *fig.* and in fig. context.

c **1374** Chaucer *Troylus* IV. 986 If ther myght ben a variaunce, To wrythen out fro goddes purueynge. **1402** *Pol. Poems* (Rolls) II. 90 Thei ben bastard braunches that.. writhyn wrongli away from holy chirche techinge. *a* **1425** *Cursor M.* 4276 (Trin.), At þe ende wol priue loue out wriþe. *c* **1425** Wyntoun *Chron.* I. ix. 621 Fra his will quhen þat we writh. **1560** Becon *New Catech.* III. Wks. 1564 I. 337b, He writhed with his hande from doyinge wrong. **1601** [see wreathe *v.* 8].

†**c.** To turn, be converted, *to* something. *Obs.*

1303 R. Brunne *Handl. Synne* 130 To many maner synnes hyt [*sc.* handling] wryþys. **13..** *St. Alexius* 571 in Horstm. *Altengl. Leg.* (1881) 187 His wife kome þan..wiþ rewfull grate Als sche wold wiþ to watir writhe.

†**writhe**, *v.*[2] *Obs.* [OE. *wriðan*, *wrīðian*, var. of *wrīdan*, *wrīdian*: see wride *sb.* and *v.*] *intr.* To sprout, to flourish.

? *a* **1400** *Morte Arth.* 4322 Latt no wykkyde wede waxe, ne wrythe one this erthe.

writh(e), varr. wrethe *sb.* and *v.* *Obs.*

writhed (raɪðd), *ppl. a.* [f. writhe *v.*[1] + -ed[1]. Cf. wreathed *ppl. a.*]

1. That has undergone writhing, contortion, or twisting; twisted.

1578 Lyte *Dodoens* VI. lxxxiii. 764 The stem [of the smaller cedar] is croked or writhed. **1581** T. Howell *Deuises* Hij, Wrythed wrinckles [shall] peere on blemisht browe. **1590** Barrough *Meth. Physick* I. xliv. (1596) 67 A writhed linnen cloth. **1609** Holland *Amm. Marcell.* 50 The writhed and wrested strings of a brake. **1756** P. Browne *Jamaica* (1789) 396 The angular and variously writhed Worm-tube.

transf. **1562** Cooper *Answ. Defence Truth* 84 All, that here you haue vttered, be nothinge but wrythed coniectures.

b. Of the features, etc.: Subjected to contortion or writhing; contorted, wry.

1580 Hollyband *Treas. Fr. Tong*, *Laide grimace*, a writhed mouth. **1605** Sylvester *Du Bartas* II. iii. *Law* 96 Snuffing with a wrythed nose the Amber. **1650** Bulwer *Anthropomet.* 150 They have a black and wrythed Face. **1802** Joanna Baillie *2nd Pt. Ethwald* II. ii, There be some Whose writhed features..do stare upon you. **1830** Tennyson '*Clear-headed friend*' iii, Those writhed limbs of lightning speed. **1868** Kinglake *Crimea* IV. 292 A breed of the human race whose numberless cages of teeth stared out ..from between the writhed lips.

2. Fashioned by or as by twisting or convolution.

1552 Huloet, Writhed, or wynded one in another as a cord or rope is lincke to lincke, *versatilis*. **1565** Cooper *Thesaurus*, *Funes intorti*, writhed cordes. **1802** Leyden *Mermaid* i, How softly mourns the writhed shell Of Jura's shore, its parent sea! **1858** Skyring *Builders' Prices* 55 Every inch opening in the writhed rails.

b. Of pillars, etc.: = wreathed *ppl. a.* 3a.

1825 Scott *Talism.* xxvii, The fantastic forms of writhed pillars. **1849** Ruskin *Sev. Lamps* iii. 92 The dark..porches and writhed pillars of Verona.

Hence ˈ**writhedly** *adv.*, **-ness.** *rare.*

1565 Cooper *Thesaurus*, *Contorte*,..frowardly: obscurely: intricately: writhedly. **1755** Scott, *Contorteousness*, writhedness.

†**wriðel.** *Obs.* [Of obscure origin.] ? Wild lettuce.

c **1250** *Gen. & Ex.* 3153 Ilc man after his owen fond, Heued and fet, and in-rew meten, Lesen fro ðe bones and eten, Wið wriðel and vn-lif bread. [Cf. Exodus xii. 8 'Et edent carnes..et azymos panes cum lactucis agrestibus'.]

writhen (ˈrɪð(ə)n), *ppl. a.* Also 4 **writhun**, 6 **-yne**, 4– **wrythen**. [pa. pple. of writhe *v.*[1] Cf. wreathen *ppl. a.*]

1. Subjected to writhing, twisting, or turning; twisted out of regular shape or form; contorted; †also, closed, clenched (quot. 1377).

a. Of things.

13.. *K. Alis.* 5723 (Laud MS.), A griselich best..; Teeþ he had so wreþen wriþen. **1377** Langl. *P. Pl.* B. XVII. 174 Þe wrythen fuste, or the werkmanschip of fyngres. **1483** in *Arnold's Chron.* (1811) 116 Item a peir of coral beedis, the gawdies gilt wrythen. **1520** in *Archaeologia* LIII. 14 One playn paten chased yn the foote w[t] a wrythen knope. **1564** Bullein *Dial. agst. Pest.* 44b, A writhen arme of the tree. **1597** Bp. Hall *Sat.* IV. iv. 33 Some smoked beeve, Hang'd on a writhen wythe. **1611** Cotgr., *Grugeons*, the..most writhen fruit on a tree. **1668** Culpepper & Cole *Barthol. Anat.* I. xx. 53 In Men this Neck is more long-round, narrow, and a little writhen. **1689** Moyle *Sea Chyrurg.* II. xiii. 61 The Muscles bruised and writhen. **1725** Pope *Odyss.* VIII. 506 Dread Jove (whose arm in vengeance forms The writhen bolt). **1747** Hooson *Miner's Dict.* Ujb, Curl'd Stone..has..writhen Lumps in it. **1850** Allingham *Poems, Music-master* II. xv, The writhen elder spreads its creamy bloom. **1865** Swinburne *Poems & Ball.*, *At Eleusis* 72 That lame wisdom that has writhen feet.

fig. **1894** Stevenson & L. Osbourne *Ebb Tide* ii, 'I'll give my father up,' returned Herrick, with a writhen smile.

b. Of persons, their features, etc.

1579–80 North *Plutarch* (1595) 1111 A bauld writhen man. **1598** Hakluyt *Voy.* I. 21 Their countenances [were] writhen and terrible. **1635** R. Johnson *Hist. Tom a Lincolne* II. iii. (1682) G3b, Her cheeks..now appeared old and writhen. **1708** J. Philips *Cyder* I. 447 'Till, with a writhen Mouth,..He tastes the bitter Morsel. **1825** Scott *Talism.* xiv, My choice were rather..that my writhen features should blacken..in this evening's setting sun. **1888** Henley *Bk. Verses* 23 Her lip was gray and writhen.

c. *spec.* Of antique glass or silver: having spirally twisted ornamentation.

1919 M. Percival *Glass Collector* viii. 115 The..writhen glasses of funnel shapes are survivors of the old Venetian tradition. **1935** *Burlington Mag.* Oct. 150/1 Light vertical flutings, matching the bowl and wrythen in delivery. **1960** *Times* 9 Feb. 20/7 A Henry VIII spoon with writhen finial. **1970** *Canad. Antiques Collector* Oct. 17 The jugs and bowls are decorated with writhen ornament. **1981** *Times* 31 Oct. 8/6 An Edward IV wrythen-knop spoon made in London about 1463.

2. Combined or made by, subjected to, twining or plaiting; intertwined, entwined, or plaited. Cf. wreathen *ppl. a.* 2.

a **900** Cynewulf *Elene* 24 Garas lixtan, wriðene wælhlencan; wordum & bordum hofon herecombol. **1382** Wyclif *1 Tim.* ii. 9 Wymmen..ournynge hem silf, not in writhun heeris, ethir in gold,..but [etc.]. **1388** —— *Ecclus.* xlv. 12 Writhun reed threed. *c* **1430** *Pilgr. Lyf Manhode* I. v. (1869) 3 A corde wel wrythen, þat bi places was knet. **1523** Fitzherb. *Husb.* §31 Pees and beanes..set..thre sheues together, the toppes vpwarde, and wrythen together. **1535** Coverdale *Exod.* xxxix. 15 Wrythen cheynes of pure golde. **1585** Higins *Junius' Nomencl.* 113/2 *Corona pactilis*,..a writhen garland. **1609** Holland *Amm. Marcell.* 221 Many cords of wrythen and twisted sinewes. **1671** J. Webster *Metallogr.* xiii. 212 A capillary or hairy piece..crisped and writhen together. **1733** T. Gent *Hist. Rippon* 57 They built an House..with Wrythen Wands or Boughs. **1876** *Whitby Gloss.* 224 *Wrythen*, pp...; intertwined.

3. Disposed or arranged in coils, folds, or windings; formed or fashioned by or as by coiling, convolution, etc.

Cf. the earlier *forwrithen* ppl. a. (for- *pref.*[1] 8).

c **1542** *Test. Ebor.* (Surtees) VI. 172 A writhyne rynge of golde. **1559** Morwyng *Evonym.* 77 Destilled in serpentins, or writhen, or crouked vessels. **1585** Higins *Junius' Nomencl.* 263/2 *Linamentum tortile*,..a rolled or writhen tent. *a* **1608** Dee *Relat. Spir.* I. (1659) 115 A Serpent.. leaned upon her twice writhen taile. **1603** Knolles *Hist. Turks* (1621) 961 The wrythen rolls of the turbant. **1693** Dryden *Ovid's Met.* I. 454 His writhen Shell he takes. **1868** Morris *Earthly Par.* I. 258 [Full] of intertwining writhen snakes.

†**4.** *fig.* Wrested; perverted; deflected. *Obs.*

1551 ROBINSON tr. *More's Utopia* I. (1895) 91 A wrythen and wrested vnderstandynge of the same. **1561** T. NORTON *Calvin's Inst.* I. xiii. 31 b, To fense themselues againste the crooked writhen suttleties with plaine and simple truthe.

5. *Comb.*, as ***writhen-faced***, ***-formed***.

1594 NASHE *Unfort. Trav.* L 4 b, A wearish dwarfish writhen facde cobler. *c* **1861** J. T. STATON *Rays fro' Loominary* 115 A thing that's writhen-formt.

Hence **'writhenness** *rare*$^{-0}$; **'wrythening** *vbl. sb.* (see quot. 1960.)

1727 BAILEY, *Tortness*,..writhenness, wrinkledness. **1960** H. HAYWARD *Antique Coll.* 313/2 *Wrythening*, diagonally twisted or swirled ribbing or fluting on the bowl or stem of a glass vessel. **1967** S. CROMPTON *Eng. Glass* II. 209 (*caption*) Jug in bottle-green glass with white wrythening.

'writheneck. [f. WRITHE *v.*^{1}] = WRYNECK I.

1885 SWAINSON *Prov. Names Birds* 103 Wryneck (*Jynx torquilla*). So called from the extraordinary pliancy of its neck; whence also Writhe neck.

writher ('raɪðə(r)). Also 5–6 **wryther.** [f. WRITHE *v.*^{1} + -ER^1.] One who writhes or twists; †one who perverts.

c **1420** LYDG. *Assembly of Gods* 674 Ther were bosters,.. Praters, fasers, strechers, & wrythers. **1533** [see WRESTER 2]. **1545** BRINKLOW *Lament.* 25 Ye wresters and wrythers of Goddes holy worde.

writhing ('raɪðɪŋ), *vbl. sb.* [f. as prec. + -ING^1.]

1. The action of the verb in various senses; an instance of this. Also with *away*. Occas. *fig.*

c **1386** CHAUCER *Sqr.'s T.* 119 With writhyng of a pyn. *c* **1420** LYDG. *Ballad Commend. Our Lady* 96 ȝif ony offence or writhyng in hem be, þu art ay redy up-on her woo for to rewe. *c* **1520** SKELTON *Magnyf.* 136 Yf Lyberte lacked a reyne Where with to rule hym with the wrythyng of a rest. **1577** tr. *Bullinger's Decades* (1592) 241 Let..thy laughter [be] without vnseemely writhing of thy mouth and visage. **1603** HOLLAND *Plutarch's Mor.* 60 A writhing away or turning about of the bodie. **1634** SIR T. HERBERT *Trav.* 189 Ill-fauoured gestures, and writhing of their mouth and eyes. **1688** HOLME *Armoury* II. 84 The Writhing [of a tree] is the turning of branches. **1743** FRANCIS tr. *Hor., Odes* I. xxxvii. 34 The Writhings of the wrathful Asp. **1827** KEBLE *Chr. Year, Wedn. before Easter*, The writhings of a wounded heart. **1835** R. M. BIRD *Hawks* (1856) 134 Sterling..could not trace a single writhing or quivering of limb. **1889** CLARK RUSSELL *Marooned* xii, A slow writhing..of the shadowy substance of the brig's sails, masts, and hull, into determinable forms.

b. *spec.* in old glass: cf. WRITHEN *ppl. a.* 1 c.

1926 G. R. FRANCIS *Old Eng. Drinking Glasses* p. xxxi, Wrythen, external decoration of the bowl by twisting or wrything while still hot. **1929** W. A. THORPE *Hist. Eng. & Irish Glass* v. 166 The wrything was done by twisting the paraison while it was being blown.

†**2.** = WRESTING *vbl. sb.* 2, WRINGING *vbl. sb.* 4.

1555 TRAVERS in Strype *Eccl. Mem.* (1721) III. App. 87 Without wrythyng, wrastyng, or doubtyng of his promis. **1562** COOPER *Answ. Defence Truth* 78 All the argumentes that you haue brought are nothing but writhinges of extraordinary cases. **1662** HIBBERT *Body Divinity* I. 189 What wrything and wringing the Protestants make to shift off this place.

'writhing, *ppl. a.* [f. as prec. + -ING^2.]

†**1.** That wrings or extorts; practising extortion.

c **1520** [see WRESTING *ppl. a.*].

2. That writhes; twisting or turning to and fro.

1798 R. BLOOMFIELD *Farmer's Boy* 76 Where writhing earth-worms meet th' unwelcome day. **1812** BYRON *Ch. Har.* II. xcvii, Smiles..raise the writhing lip with ill-dissembled sneer. **1865** BARING-GOULD *Werewolves* x. 170 The forked and writhing lightning. **1882** T. S. HUDSON *Scamper through Amer.* 171 Our driver adroitly left one [rattlesnake] a writhing corpse.

transf. **1897** HOWELLS *Landlord at Lion's Head* 3 The children whose faces watched them through the writhing window panes.

3. Marked or characterized by sinuous or tortuous movement.

1808 JAMIESON, *Wringle*, a writhing motion. **1818** HAZLITT *Lect. Poets* iii. 128 The writhing agonies within. **1848** LYTTON *Harold* v, A writhing attempt to smile.

Hence **'writhingly** *adv.*, in a writhing manner.

1611 COTGR., *Tortuément*,..wryingly, writhingly. **1822** *New Monthly Mag.* IV. 524 The monster..turned writhingly. **1883** MISS BROUGHTON *Belinda* III. vii, Turning over writhingly in her chair.

writhled ('rɪð(ə)ld), *a.* [app. f. the stem of WRITHE *v.*^{1} (see -LE 3); but perh. an alteration of RIVELLED *a.*]

1. Of persons, the skin, etc.: Wrinkled; shrivelled, withered. Now *Obs.* exc. *arch.*

1565 COOPER *Thesaurus* s.v. *Vultus*, To make the face writheled and wrinkled. **1591** SHAKS. *1 Hen. VI*, II. iii. 23 This weake and writhled shrimpe. **1599** MARSTON *Sco. Villanie* I. iii. 187 Cold, writhled Eld. **1649** LOVELACE *Poems* (1904) 100 Cynthia spotted, she impure; Her body writheld. **1693** J. H. tr. *Juv. Sat.* x. 11 A writhled and discouler'd skin. **1865** SWINBURNE *Poems & Ball., St. Dorothy* 445 This makes him sad and writhled in his face.

Comb. *a* **1656** R. COX *Actæon & Diana* 4 A writhled fac'd companion.

†**2.** Rough; shaggy. *Obs. rare*$^{-1}$.

c **1600** *Timon* v. iv. (1842) 86 An vnshorne heade, a writhled beard, beetle browed.

writhy ('raɪðɪ), *a.* [f. WRITHE *v.*^{1} + -Y^1. Cf. Da. *vridig* flexible.] Moving sinuously; writhing.

1742 BLAIR *Grave* 330 Nor Fly, nor Insect, Nor writhy Snake, escap'd thy deep Research.

writing ('raɪtɪŋ), *vbl. sb.* [f. WRITE *v.* + -ING^1.]

I. 1. a. The action of one who writes, in various senses; the penning or forming of letters or words; the using of written characters for purposes of record, transmission of ideas, etc. Also with *out*.

a **1225** *Ancr. R.* 80 Of silence & of speche nis bute a lore; & forði, ine writunge, heo eorneð boðe togederes. **1362** LANGL. *P. Pl.* A. III. 61 For-þi I lere ȝou, lordynges such writynge ȝe leue, To writen in Wyndouwes of ȝoure wel dedes. **1377** *Ibid.* B. XII. 84 þe clergye..conforted þe womman. Holykirke knoweth þis þat crystes writyng saued. **1487–8** *Rec. St. Mary at Hill* 132 For the wrytyng of the names of the ffounnderes. **1513** MORE *Rich. III*, Wks. 56 For al yᵉ time..could scant haue suffised vnto yᵉ bare wryting alone. **1549** in Feuillerat *Revels Edw. VI* (1914) 42 To waplett the payntour..ffor the wryting of ix peces of Canvas. **1631** T. POWELL *Tom All Trades* (1876) 141 The Scriveners..had no imployment, but writing of blanke Bonds. **1671** *Buccleuch MSS.* (Hist. MSS. Comm.) I. 508 This way that I propose of the King's writing himself, is the only way to effect it. **1719** DE FOE *Crusoe* I. (Globe) 288 He directed me to send it with a Letter of his Writing. **1797** *Encycl. Brit.* (ed. 3) XVIII. 917/2 The bark of trees was also used for writing by the ancients. **1827** FARADAY *Chem. Manip.* xvi. 423 The diamond should be held in a vertical position during the writing. **1849** MRS. MERRIFIELD *Orig. Treat.* I. p. xxix, The two branches were frequently practised by the same person, whence the term 'writing'.. was applied to painting on glass, which was also called 'writing on glass'. **1882** *N. & Q.* 30 Dec. 542/2, I believe Lancaster first suggested writing on sand with the finger. **1898** J. TAYLOR tr. *Kautzsch's Hist. Lit. O.T.* 10 The writing out of the products of those earlier days.

fig. **1532** MORE *Confut. Tindale* 413 He that hath yt [*sc.* faith] in his herte of goddes own wrytynge.

b. ***at this*** (***present***) ***writing***, at the time of writing this. Also ***up to this*** (..) ***writing***.

1718 LADY M. W. MONTAGU *Let. to Mrs. Thistlethwayte* 4 Jan., I am, at this present writing, not very much turned for the recollection of what is diverting. **1832** J. P. KENNEDY *Swallow B.* (1860) 13 An account of all my doings up to this present writing. **1846** C. MITCHELL *Newsp. Press Direct.* 77 The critical (musical) department..is at 'this present writing', to use an Irishism, nothing if not meagre. **1884** *Cent. Mag.* Jan. 433/2 It is at this writing given out that [etc.].

c. = TYPEWRITING *vbl. sb.*

1883 J. G. PETRIE *Man. for Type-Writer* 5 While the writing is being done by the fingers of the right hand. **1899** WARDLE *Univ. Typewriter Man.* 10 It also keeps the paper in position for writing.

d. *Computers.* The process of causing an item of data to be entered into a store or recorded in or on a storage medium.

1946 [see WRITE *v.* 3 h]. **1970** O. DOPPING *Computers & Data Processing* xv. 244 Most writing errors on tape, like most reading errors, are caused by small particles of dust between tape and magnetic head, and in most cases the dust particle is removed..if the writing is repeated. **1973** C. W. GEAR *Introd. Computer Sci.* iv. 164 A computer input/output controller..sequences the reading and writing of characters.

2. a. The art or practice of penmanship or handwriting.

c **1440** LYDG. *Hors, Shepe & G.* 187 Yiff pennys & writyng were a-way, Off remembraunce we had lost the kay. *c* **1440** *Jacob's Well* 278 Johun enformyd hym in wrytyng, & in endyȝtyng. **1604** E. G[RIMSTONE] *D'Acosta's Hist. Indies* I. xxv. 80 They having no vse of bookes, or writing. **1638** JUNIUS *Paint. Ancients* 126 Before the invention of letters and writing. **1728** CHAMBERS *Cycl.* (1738) s.v., Writing is now chiefly practised among us by means of pen, ink, and paper. **1742** FIELDING *J. Andrews* II. xvii, The poor people ..bred their son to writing and accounts, and other learning. **1784** T. ASTLE (*title*), The Origin and Progress of Writing, as well hieroglyphic as elementary. **1828** *Mirror* V. 75/1 The three R's—Reading, Writing, and Rithmetic. **1892** *Pop. Sci. Monthly* XLII. 244 Writing..is the art of fixing speech by conventional signs.

b. Style, form, or method of fashioning letters or other conventional signs (esp. in handwriting or penmanship); the 'hand' of a particular person.

c **1440** *Jacob's Well* 278 þat his voys, his wrytynge,..was lych þe voys, lyche þe hand,.. of Johun his mayster. *c* **1440** *Promp. Parv.* 148/2 False wrytynge, *plastographia*. **1476** *Acta Auditorum* (1839) 42/1 It wes his awne propir hand and writting. **1560** BIBLE *Ezra* (Genev.) iv. 7 The writing of the letter was the Aramites writing. **1590** P. BALES *Writing Schoolem.* Q 2 The Arte and knowledge of faire writing. **1602** [J. WILLIS] *Art Stenogr.* (title-p.), A very easie direction for Steganographie, or Secret Writing. **1620**, etc. [see SHORT-WRITING, SHORTHAND c]. **1658** PHILLIPS, *Calligraphy*, fair, or handsome writing. **1728** CHAMBERS *Cycl.* (1738) s.v. *Gothic*, Gothic character, or writing, is a character, or manner of writing, which [etc.]. **1748** [see HIEROGLYPHICAL *a.* 1]. **1784** T. ASTLE *Orig. & Progr. Writing* 7 This..produced a further change in writing. **1819** SHELLEY *Cenci* IV. iv. 95 *Savella.* Knowest thou this writing, Lady?.. *Lucretia.* It should be Orsino's hand! **1883** *Stationer & Bookseller* 8 May 10/1 Best finished round-hand writing. **1892** ZANGWILL *Bow Mystery* 80 The landlady knew his writing.

c. The occupation of a (professional) writer.

1594 *Hist. Writers to Signet* (1890) 230 To be suspendit fra all writting quhill the payment of the foirsaid pane. **1681** *Sc. Acts* (1820) VIII. 244/1 All writers to the Signet, All publict Notars and other persons imployed in writeing or Agenting.

3. a. The action of composing and committing to manuscript; expression of thoughts or ideas in written words; literary composition or production.

c **1386** CHAUCER *Prol.* 326 Ther-to he koude endite and make a thyng, Ther koude no wight pynchen at his writyng. **1430–40** LYDG. *Bochas* I. 2677 As the poete bi wrytyng techith vs. **1485** CAXTON *Chas. Gt.* 1 Al thynges that ben reduced by wrytyng ben wryton to our doctryne. **15..** in *Dunbar's Poems* (S.T.S.) II. 311 Gif lytil rewarde be in wryting, Bettir war leif my paper quhyte. **1597–8** BACON *Ess., Studies* (Arb.) 10 Reading maketh a full man,..and writing an exacte man. **1639** *Hamilton Papers* (Camden) 89 Efter the wrytinge of this other the Lord Oboyne.. delyuered me your Ma[jes]ties of the 13. **1664** *Extr. St. Papers Friends* Ser. III. (1912) 213 Hee..is..not of parts for the writeing of such a Letter. **1759** STERNE *Tr. Shandy* II. xi, Writing..is but a different name for conversation. **1835** MARRYAT *Olla Podr.* xxx, Magazine writing..is the most difficult of all writing. **1885** 'MRS. ALEXANDER' *Valerie's Fate* iii, Though all three..could talk French fast enough, the writing of it was another matter.

b. Style or manner of composition or literary expression.

1509 HAWES *Past. Pleas.* xx. (Percy Soc.) 98 Besechyng you..to pardon me of my rude wrytyng, For with woful herte was myne endytyng. *c* **1530** L. COX *Rhet.* (1899) 84 Doubtful wrytynge..is whan the wordes may be expounded dyuers wayes. *a* **1626** BACON *Ch. Controv.* Wks. 1879 I. 344 Bitter and earnest writing must not hastily be condemned. **1664** DRYDEN *Rival Ladies* Ep. Ded., Supposing our countrymen had not received this writing [of scenes in verse] till of late. **1712** ADDISON *Spect.* No. 409 ¶10 A finished Taste of good Writing. **1760** D. WEBB *Inq. Beauties Painting* vii. 199 It is the character of fine writing..that the thoughts should be natural. **1819** KEATS in Forman *Wks.* (1883) III. 320 Fine writing is, next to fine doing, the top thing in the world. **1884** CHURCH *Bacon* ix. 220 Easy and unstudied as his writing seems.

c. The composition of music.

1782 BURNEY *Hist. Music* 490 The most subtle and elaborate productions [*sc.* masses] that I have ever seen in this kind of writing. **1837** *Penny Cycl.* VIII. 109/1 The art of writing in parts. **1889** PROUT *Harmony* (ed. 3) 245 Four-part writing is justly considered the foundation of harmony.

d. With advs., as *down* (WRITE *v.* 22 c), *in*, *off*, *up*. (Cf. 12 g.)

1897 *Westm. Gaz.* 28 Dec. 6/3 Some scheme for the writing down of capital. **1900** *Ibid.* 22 Nov. 9/2 [The] music-hall agents..said that due notice of 'writing in' was given. **1912** *Times* 19 Dec. 18/5 The scheme provided for the writing off of capital liabilities. **1951** E. E. EVANS-PRITCHARD *Social Anthropol.* v. 88 In this writing-up side of his work the social anthropologist faces a serious difficulty. **1960** *Guardian* 24 June 10/7 Simplification without 'writing down' can serve a good purpose. **1972** *Listener* 9 Nov. 644 The slick writing-down that many professional children's writers indulge in.

†**4.** Manner of setting down in written form; spelling, orthography. *Obs.*

1521 A. BARCLAY *Introd.* A v b, Whiche is contrary bothe in the true wrytynge, & also to the true pronuncyacion of perfyte frenche. **1582** [see WRITING-MASTER]. *c* **1620** A. HUME *Brit. Tongue* (1865) 1, I..seeing sik uncertentie in our men's wryting, as if a man wald indyte one letter to tuentie of our best wryteres, nae tuae..wald agree. **1636** B. JONSON *Eng. Gram.* iii, The unsteadfastness of our tongue, or incertainty of our writing. **1728** CHAMBERS *Cycl.* (1738) s.v. *Orthography*, Attempts have been since made to reduce the writing to the pronunciation.

5. The state or condition of having been written or penned; written form. Freq. ***in writing***.

See COMMIT *v.* 1 e, PUT *v.*^{1} 16 b, REDUCE *v.* 15 b.

1425 *Rolls of Parlt.* IV. 268/2 Yeving in a Peedegree in writyng. **1462** *Paston Lett.* II. 122 Let them..send ther excuse to me in wrytyng. **1560** DAUS tr. *Sleidane's Comm.* Pref. 2 Thei..commit to wrytinge, stories. **1611** COTGR., *Mettre par escrit*, to..set downe in, commit vnto, writing. **1657** tr. *Perkins' Profit. Bk.* vii. 179 Another will..by him put in writing. **1753** *Act 26 Geo. II*, c. 19 §15 Which Examination the said Justices are hereby required to take down in Writing. **1831** PALGRAVE *Hist. Anglo-Saxons* vii. 151 Many matters now consigned to writing. *Ibid.* 152 Some little was reduced into writing. **1887** BIRRELL *Obiter Dicta* Ser. II. 42 The author's agreement..is in writing.

II. 6. That which is in a written (now also typewritten) state or form; something penned or recorded; written information, composition, or production; literary work or compilation.

† ***the*** or ***Sacred Writing*** (quots. 1340, 1797), Scripture. Phr. ***the writing on the wall*** (with allusion to *Daniel* v. 5 and 25–28): warning signs of impending disaster, misfortune, etc.

1303 R. BRUNNE *Handl. Synne* 4671 Seynt Ysodre seyþ yn hys wrytyng, 'Alle þo' [etc.]. **1340** *Ayenb.* 71 Zuyche byeþ þo ȝonges of helle ase þe writinge ous telþ. **1382** WYCLIF *Dan.* v. 7 Who euere shal reede this wrytyng. *c* **1444** PECOCK *Donet* 156 Alle suche men..I remitte into þe writing and witnessing of seynt Austyn. **1451** *Paston Lett.* I. 208 The Shereffe..hath writyng from the Kyng that he shall make such a panell. *a* **1513** FABYAN *Chron.* lxvi. (1811) 45 That sayinge disagreeth to the wrytynge of Eutropius. **1537** *Coventry Leet Bk.* 726 Which was latelie surrendered & given vpp by wrytyng to theme. **1596** SHAKS. *Merch. V.* II. vii. 64 A carrion death, Within whose emptie eye there is a written scroule; Ile reade the writing. **1611** BIBLE *1 Esdras* ii. 2 He made proclamation..by writing. **1797** *Monthly Mag.* III. 529/1 A passage in sacred writing, where the Philistines..sent back the ark of God. **1808** W. SELWYN *Law Nisi Prius* II. 755 Neither the 4th nor 17th sections of this statute require, that the agent should be authorized by writing. **1837** LOCKHART *Scott* xxvii. (1845) 256/1 He pointed out to me this hand which, like the writing on Belshazzar's wall, disturbed his hour of hilarity. **1887** *Cornh. Mag.* Jan. 65 The laundress..denied all knowledge of the type-writer or the writing.

allusively. ? **1720** SWIFT *Poet. Wks.* (1736) 93 A baited Banker thus desponds, From his own Hand foresees his Fall; They have his Soul who have his Bonds; 'Tis like the Writing on the Wall. **1884** RIDER HAGGARD *Dawn* xxii, Cut it down, and you will have no more writing upon your wall. **1906** (*title*) The writing on the wall. **1949** E. COXHEAD *Wind in West* viii. 211 Just try to see the thing with..your famous detachment, and you'll soon recognise the writing on the wall. You've had your fling. **1965** *Listener* 2 Dec. 925/3 The 'eighties and 'nineties were the Golden Age [of music hall]; and in 1905 the writing was on the wall... Musical comedy, the cinema, television all hastened the decline. **1978** *Lancashire Life* Mar. 50/1, I was a fool not to see the writing on the wall when textile machinery manufacturers were rushing all over the world erecting spinning and weaving machinery.

transf. **1894** H. DRUMMOND *Ascent Man* 427 Nature is God's writing, and can only tell the truth.

7. a. A written composition; freq. *pl.*, the work or works of an author or group of authors; literary productions.

In frequent use from *c* 1560.

1340 *Ayenb.* 46 Þis boc is more ymad uor þe leawede, þanne uor þe clerkes þet conneþ þe writinges. **1382** WYCLIF *2 Macc.* ii. 1 It is founden in dyscryuyngis, or wrytyngis, of Jeremye, the prophete. *c* **1449** PECOCK *Repr.* I. xv. 81 Holi Writt in this wise takun, is not holier neither better than eny other writing is. **1526** *Pilgr. Perf.* (W. de W. 1531) 38 That suche wrytynges be approued by.. discrete goostly fathers. **1638** JUNIUS *Paint. Ancients* 105 Famous men have studied to illustrate these Arts.. by their writings and disputations. **1711** STEELE *Spect.* No. 4 ¶8 The present Writing is only to admonish the World. *a* **1720** SEWEL *Hist. Quakers* (1722) Pref., The said Bishop.. hath obtained such an high Esteem by his Writings. **1818** SHELLEY *Julian & M.* 340 If this sad writing thou shouldst ever see. **1849** MACAULAY *Hist. Eng.* vi. II. 108 The writings of the fathers. **1859** JEPHSON *Brittany* xiv. 233 A writing to the effect that..it [*sc.* a museum] was closed altogether.

b. *the* (*sacred* or *holy*) *writings*, the Scriptures. Also *spec.* = HAGIOGRAPHA *sb. pl.*

1340 *Ayenb.* 13 Þanne þridde day.., uor to uoluelle þe writeinges, he aros uram dyaþe to liue. *a* **1653** BINNING *Wks.* (1735) 20/2 The Hand of God must first write on their Heart, ere they understand the Writings of the Scriptures. **1663** BP. PATRICK *Parab. Pilgr.* (1687) 327 The truth of the holy Writings. **1711** FELTON *Dissert. Classics* (1718) 94 The Sacred Writings, even in our Translation, preserve their Majesty. **1837** *Penny Cycl.* IX. 438/1 Mention is made of the use of signets in the sacred writings. *a* **1909** [*N.E.D.*, in note s.v. Prophet *sb.* 3]. **1941** R. H. PFEIFFER *Introd. to O.T.* (ed. 5) iv. 61 The third division of the Hebrew Bible, following the Law and the Prophets, is simply called the 'Writings' (Hebrew, *Ketûbîm*) or 'Hagiographa' (sacred writings), because it consists of a miscellany of independent books. **1976** *Church Times* 30 Jan. 6/1 He begins with Ecclesiastes and some of the other books from the Writings—namely, Proverbs, Job and the Psalms.

c. A musical composition.

1789 BURNEY *Hist. Mus.* III. 197 It appears from the writings of this.. exquisite harmonist, that he had.. studied the greatest masters of his own time.

8. a. A written document, note, etc.; a letter or missive.

1456 *Paston Lett.* Suppl. (1901) 58 All though my wrytyngges put yow many tymes to gret labour. **1513** Q. CATH. in Ellis *Orig. Lett.* Ser. I. I. 90 Came a Post from my lord Howard with a writing at length of every thing as it was. **1555** *Instit. Gentl.* Lv, Yᵉ childe brought the same wryghting to the handes of Mertia. **1629** HOBBES *Thucyd.* (1822) 256 These were the contents of the writing. **1653** MILTON *Hirelings* Wks. 1851 V. 353 Without another clear and express Donation, wherof they shew no Evidence or Writing. **1890** GIRDLESTONE *Found. Bible* 21 There are frequent references in the Book of Ezra to writings, such as proclamations, genealogies, decrees, letters, copies.

b. A written paper or instrument, having force in law; a deed, bond agreement, or the like; a document relative to a marriage contract or settlement.

In very frequent use from *c* 1500.

1448 SHILLINGFORD *Lett.* (Camden) 66 If any suche writyng were knowe and proved by my seide Lorde and the other arbitrous. *c* **1450** *Godstow Reg.* 530 Into witnesse they put to theire seales, euerych to others writyng. **1520** in Glass-cock *Rec. St. Michael's, Bp.'s Stortford* (1882) 37 P[ai]d for makyng the wrytynges bytwene the parisshe and the bel-founder. **1592–3** in Barfield *Thatcham* (1901) II. 103 Pd. for two locks for the chest wher the wrightings are kept. **1631** HEYWOOD *Fair Maid of West* III. i. 40 These writings are the evidence of Lands. **1668** SEDLEY *Mulberry Gard.* II. ii. 27 You do not lay the necessity of marrying Home enough to her:..our Counsel [might] Have been drawing the Writings. **1710** STEELE *Tatler* No. 231 ¶2 The Lawyers finished the Writings (in which..there was no Pin-Money) and they were married. **1754** J. SHEBBEARE *Matrimony* (1766) I. 71 Perhaps your Lordship's Writings [= property-deeds] are in the Hands of those two Fellows. **1818** CRUISE *Digest* (ed. 2) I. 235 The Court ordered all deeds and writings..to be delivered up. **1840** THACKERAY *Shabby-genteel Story* ix, No writings at all were made, and the ceremony merely read through. **1893** SIR J. W. CHITTY in *Law Times Rep.* LXVIII. 430/1 The statute..requires a deed in cases where formerly a mere writing would have sufficed.

† **c.** A writ *of* divorce, etc. *Obs. rare.*

1382 WYCLIF *Col.* ii. 14 Doynge awey that wryting of decree, or dom, that was aȝens ȝou. **1568** BIBLE (Bishop's) *Matt.* v. 31 Whosoeuer putteth away his wyfe, let hym geue her a wrytyng of diuorcement.

9. Wording or lettering scored, engraved, or impressed on a surface; an inscription.

1382 WYCLIF *Exod.* xxxii. 16 The wrytyng forsothe of God was grauen in the tables. **1387** TREVISA *Higden* VII. 149 His epithaphy—þat is, writynge on his grave. **1388** WYCLIF *Mark* xii. 16 Brynge ȝe to me a peny... Whos is this ymage, and the writyng? **1471** CAXTON *Recuyell* (Sommer) 397 He shewid the wrytyng that that other ymage helde. **1530** PALSGR. 675/1 There was a writynge upon his grave, but the weather hath put it out. **1560** BIBLE (Genev.) *Ecclus.* xlv. 11 Precious stones.. set in golde..with a writing grauen after the nomber of the tribes of Israel. **1611** BIBLE *Exod.* xxxix. 30 They made the plate..of pure gold, and wrote vpon it a writing, like to the engrauings of a signet. **1623** COCKERAM II, Writings on Tombes, *epitaphes*. **1706** [see WRITE *v.* 20]. **1797** *Encycl. Brit.* (ed. 3) XVIII. 917/1 The most ancient remains of writing..are upon hard substances, such as stones and metals.

10. Words, letters, etc., embodied in written (or typewritten) form; written lettering.

1303 R. BRUNNE *Handl. Synne* 9294 He so moche sorow hadde, As hys wrytyng was alle to-fade. **1728** CHAMBERS *Cycl.* (1738) s.v., J. Ravenau..shews how to revive, and restore old writings almost effaced. **1787** *Phil. Trans.* LXXVII. 451 A new Method of recovering the Legibility of decayed Writings. **1834** DICKENS *Sk. Boz, Boarding-ho.* ii, The writing looked like a skein of thread in a tangle. **1884** KNIGHT *Dict. Mech.* Suppl. 957 For restoring faded writing. Brush it over with a solution of ammonium sulphide. **1899** WARDLE *Univ. Typewriter Man.* 14 Regulating the width between the lines of writing.

11. *Printing.* (See NEWS *sb.* 5 b.)

III. *attrib.* and *Comb.* **12. a.** Simple attrib., as ***writing chair, course, day, exercise,*** †***glove, hand, lesson, night, -speed, -system, terms, -time.***

1483 *Cath. Angl.* 425/2 A wrytynge chare. **1582** MULCASTER *Elementarie* (1925) 255 The platting of this my writing course. **1663** WOOD *Life* (O.H.S.) I. 501 A pair of writing gloves, 1*s*. **1675** MARVELL *Corr.* Wks. (Grosart) II. 450 Having been always on writing nights in an hurry. **1768** GOLDSM. *Good-n. Man* Epilogue, My writing days are over. **1788** COWPER *Wks.* (1837) XV. 205 My writing-time is expended. **1805** SCOTT *Let.* in *Lockhart* (1837) II. ii. 44, I shall hold myself well paid on the *writing* hand. **1840** DICKENS *Old C. Shop* iii, Preparations for giving Kit a writing lesson. **1857** W. COLLINS *Dead Secret* iv, The two were not..on speaking, or even on writing terms. **1875** DAVIDSON *House Painting* 206 What is called the Script or writing character, the most elegant of all. **1906** P. MACQUOID *Hist. Eng. Furnit.* III. iv. 139 (*caption*) Mahogany writing-chair. **1946** H. P. MAYNARD in W. S. Knickerbocker *20th-Cent. Eng.* 188 One of the most important skills is that of writing-speed. **1953** C. F. HOCKETT in Saporta & Bastian *Psycholinguistics* (1961) 58/1 In devising a writing-system one can..eliminate a symbol needed earlier. **1979** *Country Life* 14 June 1910/3 Corner chair appears to be the usual description nowadays: they used to be known as writing chairs. **1980** *English World-Wide* I. 1. 20 Almost all Native American writing systems developed..for bilingual education purposes utilize writing systems similar to English.

b. In sense 'used for writing with', as ***writing apparatus, -brush, cane, fluid, implement, tool, wire,*** etc. Also WRITING-INK, -PEN.

Cf. OE. *writing-feþer* 'a pen'.

1585 HIGINS *Junius' Nomencl.* 7/2 *Graphium*, a writing wyer. **1606** HOLLAND *Sueton.* 261 The sharp point of a bodkin or writing steele. **1800** M. KOOPS *Hist. Acc. Inv. Paper* 37 *Charta Augusta*..being too thin for the writing-cane. **1809** MALKIN *Gil Blas* VIII. vi. ¶1 That minister..made me take my writing apparatus. **1825** SCOTT *Talism.* xxi, Give him writing-tools. **1840** *Patents* (1869) 56 Ink or writing fluids. **1854** DICKENS *Hard Times* II. i. 134 Mrs. Sparsit was conscious that by coming in the evening-tide among the desks and writing implements, she shed a feminine..grace. **1866** *Patents* (1869) 388 Articles commonly called 'writing' or 'library' sets. **1873** W. STOKES *Rapid Writing* 78 The formidable iron Writing implement bearing the name of Style. **1921** H. E. PALMER *Princ. Language-Study* vii. 85 Suppose we wish to make Chinese characters with a native writing-brush. **1978** *China Now* Mar./Apr. 34/3 The following suggested items can be obtained from shops which cater for local Chinese communities: wok (a deep frying pan), abacus, Chinese writing brush.

c. In names of devices for performing or executing writing, as ***writing automaton, -ball,*** †***engine, machine, telegraph.***

1695 *Athenian Merc.* 9 April, The Writing Engine, for taking several Copies of the same thing at once. **1705** J. DUNTON *Life & Errors* 239 [Ridpath] invented The Polygraphy, or Writing Engin. **1799** *Patents* (1869) 8 A certain..writing and drawing machine. **1819** *Ibid.* 21 A machine..which I denominate the penographic or writing instrument. **1868** *Chambers's Jrnl.* 136/2 [A] Writing-machine for the Blind. **1875** KNIGHT *Dict. Mech.* 2823/2 *Writing-telegraph*, one which sends autographic messages. **1888** *Cassell's Encycl. Dict.*, *Writing-ball*, an electric printing apparatus. **1904** STANDEN & TAYLOR *Typing* i, Manipulating the writing machine [= typewriter].

d. In sense 'used or designed for writing upon', as ***writing cloth, material, slate, surface.*** Also WRITING-BOOK, -PAPER.

1800 M. KOOPS *Hist. Acc. Inv. Paper* 33 These writing-materials were not in general use. **1809** R. LANGFORD *Introd. Trade* 63, 2 [Reams] Writing Royal. **1851** *Catal. Gt. Exhib.* 540 Dowse's patent tracing and writing cloth. **1875** KNIGHT *Dict. Mech.* 2477/2 *Table*, a tablet..[or] writing-surface. **1888** BURGON *12 Good Men* II. v. 36 To get out his writing materials, and to scribble.

e. In sense 'forming a support or surface for writing on', as ***writing ledge, slope.*** Also WRITING-BOARD, -DESK, -TABLE 3.

1855 *Patents* (1869) 179 [The cover] which forms the continuation of the writing slope. **1902** *How to Make Things* 53/1 The construction of the writing ledge.

f. In sense 'engaged for or employed in writing', as ***writing class, clerk, hand.***

1772 J. WEDGWOOD *Let.* 28 Sept. (1965) 136 What were all the rest of the Writing Clerks doing not to observe this. **1815** SCOTT *Antiq.* vi, My lawyer['s]..writing-clerk (habited as a sharp-shooter) walked to and fro before his door. **1862** *Catal. Internat. Exhib., Brit.* II. No. 2867, Saving the cost of a writing clerk. **1896** *Harper's Mag.* XCIII. 17 If he ever puts me into one of his books I'll..amputate his writing-hand. **1899** CROCKETT *Kit Kennedy* 79 The writing-classes joggled each others' arms and elbows.

g. With advs., as ***writing-off, -out.*** (Cf. 3 d.)

1901 *Westm. Gaz.* 28 June 11/1 Its sister in misfortune..dare not face the writing-off stage yet. **1904** *Ibid.* 9 Feb. 4/2 The 'writing-out' process from which most popular authors suffer.

13. Special Combs.: **writing bed**, a board or level surface for writing on; **writing block**, (*a*) [BLOCK *sb.* 10 c], a pad of writing-paper; (*b*) [BLOCK *sb.* 19 e] = *writer's block* s.v. WRITER 3; **writing booth**, †(*a*) *Sc.* a writing-chamber; (*b*) a booth or stall where writing is transacted; **writing cabinet**, an article of furniture in which a writing-desk is combined with drawers, shelves, and other facilities for writing; **writing-case**, a portable case for holding writing requisites, and providing a desk or surface to write upon; also *Comb.*; **writing centre**, a physical centre which controls the action of writing; **writing-chamber**, a room or chamber where writing is transacted; freq. *pl.*, a lawyer's offices; **writing diamond**, = DIAMOND *sb.* 4; †**writing dust**, = *writing sand*; **writing-frame**, a frame with guides designed to help the blind in writing; **writing hand**, the peculiar position assumed by the hand in shaking palsy (*Syd. Soc. Lex.*); †**writing house**, a writing-chamber; **writing-pad**, (*a*) a blotter serving as a surface for writing on, sometimes (quot. 1895) furnished with writing materials, etc.; (*b*) a pad (PAD *sb.*[3] 4) of notepaper; **writing-room**, a writing-chamber; †**writing-sand**, a kind of sand used to dry wet ink after writing; **writing slider** (see quot. 1969); **writing speed**, (*a*) *Electronics*, the maximum speed at which the electron beam can scan the screen of a cathode-ray tube and its path still be recorded by the excitation of phosphors or on photographic film; (*b*) the effective speed of videotape past a head when the rotation of the head is taken into account; †**writing-standish** = STANDISH; †**writing type**, script type.

1911 *Daily Colonist* (Victoria, B.C.) 14 Apr. 3/5 (Advt.), Writing Desks. Just the thing for the home, nicely finished in Imperial Golden Oak, large *writing bed with enclosed pigeon holes for papers. **1971** *New Yorker* 8 May 3 Open, it's a sewing table. Closed, it's a writing bed..a fine mahogany Sheraton. **1913** 'S. ROHMER' *Mystery of Dr Fu-Manchu* xxix. 294 For this dreary vigil I had come prepared with a bunch of rough notes, a *writing-block, and a fountain pen. **1950** E. BERGLER *Writer & Psychoanal.* p. ix, They came with only one purpose in mind—to be cured of their 'writing block' (a euphemism for sterility of productivity). **1977** *N.Y. Rev. Bks.* 15 Sept. 36/3 This connection would also help to explain Darwin's long delay in publishing his theory (certainly he had no 'writing block'). **1983** T. ALLBEURY *Pay Any Price* xvii. 179 As Randall sat down the consultant took out a pen and reached for a writing block. **1597** *Extr. Aberdeen Reg.* (1848) II. 121 Ane hous..to be ane *vreting buyth to..thair servitour and clerk. **1609** in *Hist. Writers to Signet* (1890) p. xlvii, All wrytteris to the signet are..bothe..in the streittis and in thair wreitting boathe, to wear..a gowne. **1898** *Wide World Mag.* July 448 Public writing booths in Barcelona. **1851** *Catal. Gt. Exhib.* 758 Monocleid *writing cabinet... The whole of the drawers, closets, and partitions may be opened by one lock. **1813** M. EDGEWORTH *Let.* 19 Apr. (1971) 25 Mrs. Sneyd and Emma have given me a most convenient red morocco *writing case. **1853** *Arab. Nts.* (Rtldg.) 253 He drew from a little writing-case..some paper, a cut cane, and an ink-horn. **1858** CARLYLE *Fredk. Gt.* VII. iv. ad fin., Crown-Prince has given him in keeping a writing-case with private letters. **1899** *Allbutt's Syst. Med.* VII. 655 If the tumour should happen to produce complete destruction of the auditory nerve-centre..or the *writing centre. **1618** in *Hist. Writers to Signet* (1890) p. xliii, The *wryting chalmer of Adame Lawtie. **1708** J. SPOTTISWOODE *Introd. Stile* Pref., I did draw out of my Collections I had made, while in a Writing-Chamber,..such [etc.]. **1875** SCRIVENER *Lect. Text N. Test.* 4 In the scriptorium or writing-chamber of their convents. **1827** FARADAY *Chem. Manip.* iii. 71 Fragments of diamond..set in handles..are called scratching or *writing diamonds. **1646** SIR T. BROWNE *Pseud. Ep.* 69 The shining or glassie powder..usually implyed in *writing dust. **1875** KNIGHT *Dict. Mech.* 2823 *Writing-frames for the blind. **1597** *Extr. Aberdeen Reg.* (1848) II. 153 The *wreitting hous for the clerk of this burght. **1598** FLORIO, *Scrittoio*,..a counting house or writing house. **1865** *Writing-pad [s.v. PAD *sb.*[3] 4]. **1895** *Army & Navy Co-op Soc. Price List* 598 The 'York' Knee Writing pad. Contains Safety Ink, Scissors, Paper Knife,..pockets filled with Note Paper and Envelopes [etc.]. **1906** E. JOHNSTON *Writing & Illuminating* ii. 50 Under the writing-paper there should be a '*writing-pad*', consisting of one or two sheets of blotting-paper. **1917** *Harrods General Catal.* 297/2 Harrods Writing Pads. 100 Sheets. No. 1. Large 8vo., Thick Cream Wove, Plain, 8 × 5. 0/6. **1972** 'W. HAGGARD' *Protectors* i. 3 Scobell had risen behind his desk. There was a writing-pad on it, a pen—nothing more. **1825** FOSBROKE *Encycl. Antiq.* 108 Monasteries had..Museums, Scriptoria, or *writing-rooms. **1850** THACKERAY *Pendennis* i, The adjoining writing-room. **1750** HEATH *Acc. Scilly* 57 [A bay] where the Beach..is covered with an exceeding fine *Writing Sand. **1803** HATCHETT in *Phil. Trans.* XCIII. 174 Fine white writing-sand. **1803** T. SHERATON *Cabinet Dict.* 261 The top drawer [of a lobby chest] is usually divided into two; and sometimes there is a *writing slider which draws out under the top. **1969** J. GLOAG *Short Dict. Furnit.* (rev. ed.) 731 *Writing slider*, a sliding shelf, made to draw out beneath the top of a chest of drawers. **1933** R. A. W. WATT et al. *Applic. Cathode Ray Oscillograph* II. 37 This statement should not..be read as indicating the limiting '*writing speed' of the oscillograph used. **1954** LEWIS & WELLS *Millimicrosecond Pulse Techniques* vi. 196 A small spot size is required in order that the deflection sensitivity [of the cathode ray tube] may be high, but if the size is reduced too much there will not be sufficient brightness to give the necessary writing speed. **1981** I. Hickman *Oscilloscopes* vii. 95 Writing speed is defined as the maximum speed at which a spot, passing once across the tube face, can be photographed under specified conditions. **1983** E. Trundle *Beginner's Guide Videocassette Recorders* i. 3 This was simply the idea of moving the record or replay heads rapidly over the surface of a slowly-moving tape to achieve the necessary high 'writing' speed. **1984** *What Video?* Aug. 24/1 The soundtrack was being recorded at a writing speed of 580 cm per second—that's over 15 times the speed of professional studio recordings. **1773** Boswell *Let. to Johnson* 2 Dec. in *Life*, You may..have a little *writing-standish made of it. **1815** J. Scott *Vis. Paris* 313 *Writing types,..a kind of letter..much used in France.

writing ('raɪtɪŋ), *ppl. a.* [f. as prec. + -ing^2.] That writes; engaged in, addicted to, writing.

1592 Shaks. *Rom. & Jul.* i. ii. 44 What names the writing person hath here writ. **1711** Shaftesb. *Charac.* III. 246 A Rank superiour to the Writing Worthys. **1728** Ramsay *General Mistake* 181 To be a wirrykow to writing fools. **1848** Dickens *Dombey* xxiv, Do you take any interest in writing people? **1893** *Athenæum* 24 June 802/3 A great mistake,..to which one writing architect at least is liable.

'writing-board. [writing *vbl. sb.* 12e + board *sb.*] A board on which to rest the paper while writing.

c **1440** *Promp. Parv.* 534 Wrytynge borde, *pluteum.* **1648** Hexham ii, *Een Schrijf-berdt*, a Writing board. **1773** J. Noorthouck *Hist. London* 619 The writing school.. contains long writing boards..to sit and write upon. **1833** Loudon *Encycl. Archit.* §630 Underneath this writing-board is a space for papers.

'writing-book. [writing *vbl. sb.* 12d + book *sb.*]

1. A blank book in which to write for purposes of record, etc.; a book containing or consisting of writing-paper.

1580 Hollyband *Treas. Fr. Tong, Cayer*, a quier of any written paper, when a whole writing booke is deuided into equall partes. **1645** *Papers rel. Scots Army* (S.H.S.) 506 Payed for 3 wreattinge books, £0 14. 6. **1701** *Maryland Laws* v. (1723) 16 Substantial Writing Books..for registring such Proceedings in. **1848** Thackeray *Van. Fair* xxv, Poor Briggs went and placed herself obediently at the writing-book. **1865** *Enquire Within* (ed. 27) 93 Buy coarse white paper,..ready to be made into writing-books.

2. An exercise book in which to practise penmanship or handwriting; a copy-book.

1612 Brinsley *Lud. Lit.* iv. (1627) 30 A little copie booke fastened to the top of his writing booke. **1775** Ash. **1850** C'tess Ossoli *Woman in 19th Cent.* (1862) 333 Having the youngest daughter set..copies in the writing book. **1878** B. Harte *Man on Beach* 64 Guiding her hand over the writing book.

'writing-box. [writing *vbl. sb.* 13 + box *sb.*^{2}] A small box for containing paper and other writing requisites. Also, a small portable writing-desk; cf. writing-desk 2.

1474 *Paston Lett.* III. 110 My wryghtyng box of syprese. **1757** R. Bentley tr. *Hentzner's Trav.* 31 Two little silver cabinets..which she uses for writing boxes. **1779** Johnson *L.P., Pope* (1868) 416 That his writing-box should be set upon his bed before he rose. **1817** J. Evans *Excurs. Windsor*, etc. 164 A writing-box of sandal wood, inlaid with ivory. **1837** Lockhart *Scott* II. ii. 63 The..business which must be despatched before he had a right to close his writing-box. **1960** H. Hayward *Antique Coll.* 312/2 *Writing-box stands*: the post-Restoration writing-box might be placed on a stand instead of a table. This had gate-legs and the fall-down flap of the box opened on to them for writing. **1971** *Country Life* 1 July 22/1 Portable table-desks or writing-boxes were recorded in the 15th century.

'writing-desk. [writing *vbl. sb.* 12e + desk *sb.*]

1. A desk used or designed for writing on; such a desk fitted with conveniences for holding writing materials, papers, etc. Also *transf.*

1611 Florio, *Scrittoio*,..a writing deske. **1688** Holme *Armoury* iii. 370/2 He beareth Argent, a Writing Desk, proper. *c* **1732** Savage *Wks.* (1775) II. 263 The advertisement of the Lady's writing-desk. **1829** Scott *Wav.* Gen. Pref. ¶11 The drawers of an old writing desk. **1840** Thackeray *Shabby-genteel Story* i, A number of..bills, neatly docketed in his writing desk.

attrib. **1807** Jane Austen *Let.* 8 Feb. (1952) 178 She is now talking away..& examining the Treasures of my Writing-desk drawer. **1891** C. Nisbet & D. Lemon (*title*), Everybody's Writing-Desk Book.

2. A make of portable writing-case or box which on being opened forms or provides a desk or surface for writing on.

1862 *Catal. Internat. Exhib., Brit.* II. No. 6939, Despatch boxes, writing desks, and dressing cases. **1865** *Patents* (1869) 370 Improvements in portfolios, writing desks, writing cases.

'writinger. *nonce-word.* [f. writing *vbl. sb.* + -er^1.] An expert in handwriting.

1868 Furnivall in *Percy's Folio MS.* I. p. xiii, The change of the shape of the c..may help some future and more learned writinger to settle the date.

'writing ink. Also **writing-ink.** [writing *vbl. sb.* 12b + ink *sb.*^{1} 1.] A make of ink or writing-fluid prepared or suitable for writing with the pen.

1548 Elyot, *Atramentum scriptorium*, writyng ynke. **1663** Boyle *Usef. Exp. Nat. Philos.* ii. 127, I have presently made a Mixture..to serve for Writing Ink. **1688** *Patents* (1869) 2 A certaine powder..doth imediately turne the same [water] into very good black writing ink. **1728** Chambers *Cycl.* (1738) s.v. *Ink*, Chinese Ink is..not fluid, like our writing Inks. **1838** *Penny Cycl.* XII. 478/2 A blue writing ink has been lately introduced. **1887** D. A. Low *Machine Draw.* (1892) 2 For inking in drawings the best Indian ink should be used, and not common writing ink.

Comb. **1858** Simmonds *Dict. Trade* 417 *Writing-ink Maker*, a manufacturer of fluid inks for writing with.

'writing-master. [writing *vbl. sb.* 13 + master *sb.*^{1} 11.]

1. A teacher of or instructor in writing, penmanship, or calligraphy. Also *transf.*

1582 Mulcaster *Elementarie* i. (1925) 62 The hole ortografie, which concerneth the right writing of our tung, will..help the writing master. **1646** in Roberts *Soc. Hist. Eng.* (1856) 407 Given to the writing mr., 2s 6d. **1678** Danson in Marvell *Def. John Howe* 126 With a Writing-Master's directing his Scholars hand. **1710** Swift *Jrnl. to Stella* 12 Nov., That is a common caution that writing-masters give their scholars. **1754** G. Bickham (*title*), The English Monarchical Writing-Master. A new county copy-book. **1812** Miss Mitford in L'Estrange *Life* (1870) I. vi. 182 'Patience is a virtue,' was my writing-master's favourite copy. **1862** Mrs. H. Wood *Mrs. Hallib. Troub.* ii. xi, In the college school. There certainly was a writing-master.

2. The yellow-hammer, *Emberiza citrinella.*

1875 G. C. Davies *Rambles* xxxii. 231 Yellowhammers or 'writing masters', as the country lads sometimes call them, from the scribblings on the egg shells.

'writing-paper. [writing *vbl. sb.* 12d + paper *sb.*]

1. A special make of paper, usu. with a smooth surface and sized, for writing upon; now *esp.*, notepaper.

1548 Elyot, *Epistolaris charta*, writyng paper. **1596** *Edward III*, ii. ii, Go, breake the thundring parchment bottome out,..I will vse it as my writing paper. **1600** J. Lane *Tom Tel-troth* (1876) 113 If all the earth were writing paper made. **1686** *Lond. Gaz.* No. 2179/4 All sorts of Writing and Printing Paper. **1770** *Phil. Trans.* LX. 391 The film was not thicker than common writing-paper. **1809** Malkin *Gil Blas* vi. i. ¶4 Writing paper such as a secretary of state need not be ashamed of. **1879** *Cassell's Techn. Educ.* III. 110/2 Strong and tough writing-papers for account-books.

attrib. **1827** Faraday *Chem. Manip.* i. 23 A blank writing paper book..with pen and ink.

2. A sheet of this. *rare*$^{-1}$.

a **1777** in Evans *Old Ball.* I. 255 A writing-paper..Upon his head he had to wear, which did his treason show.

'writing-pen. [writing *vbl. sb.* 12b + pen *sb.*^{2} 4.] A pen suitable or adapted for writing.

1398 Trevisa *Barth. De P.R.* xvii. xxxi. (Addit. MS.), A wrytinge penne hatte *Calamus scripturalis.* **1535** Coverdale *Judges* v. 14 Out of Zabulon are there become gouernours thorow the wrytinge penne [Luther *Schreibfeder*]. **1656** Earl Monm. tr. *Boccalini, Pol. Touchstone* 410 He bore in his chief Standard..a writing Pen. **1688** Holme *Armoury* (Roxb.) iii. xv. 20/1 The Pen Knife is that with which we make the Pen, or writting Pen. **1831** *Patents* (1869) 30 Certain improvements in the construction of writing pens. **1866** *Ibid.* 390 To utilize writing pens which are..worn out.

'writing-school. [writing *vbl. sb.* 13 + school *sb.*^{1} 1, 9.]

†**1.** A school in which writing or calligraphy is taught. *Obs.*

1530 Palsgr. 433/1 He goeth to the writyng scole. **1607** *Extr. Aberd. Reg.* (1848) II. 294 A writting schoole..for instructing of the youth in writing and arithmetik allanerlie. **1691** *Athenian Mercury* 30 May, Advert., Young Gentlemen ..may be faithfully Taught by the Author,..at his Writing-School. **1721** W. Webster *Attempt* (title-p.), The Education of Youth..especially with Regard to their Studies at the Writing-School. **1773** [see writing-board]. **1780** *Mirror* No. 81, Going along with a set of other girls..to..a public writing-school.

2. At Oxford University: A room used or set apart for written examinations.

1876 T. G. Jackson *New Exam. Schools Univ. Oxf.* 3 The three Writing Schools..occupy..the first floor. *Ibid.*, The large crowded Writing Schools. *Ibid.* 6 For occasional use as a Writing School..I have arranged two of the Vivâ Voce Schools.

So †**writing-schoolmaster.** *Obs.*

1590 P. Bales (*title*), The Writing Schoolemaster: Conteining three Bookes in one;..teaching Swift.., True .., Faire writing. **1631** J. Davies (Heref.) *Lively Portraiture* (title-p.), The Writing Schoolemaster: The Anatomy of Faire Writing.

'writing-table. [writing *vbl. sb.* 12e + table *sb.*]

†**1.** A small thin tablet, sheet, or plate of wood, ivory, or other material for writing (esp. notes or memoranda) upon; a writing-tablet; = table *sb.* 2b. Cf. tablet *sb.* 1c. Usu. *pl. Obs.*

1526 Tindale *Luke* i. 63 Zacari..axed for wrytynge tables and wroote. **1589** Nashe *Pasquill's Counter-C.* A ij b, A newe paire of Writing-tables with profitable Notes for that quarter. **1625** K. Long tr. *Barclay's Argenis* iv. iii. 242 She taketh up her Writing-Tables, in which she writeth these lynes. **1696** in *Harl. Misc.* (1744) I. 512 Writing-tables Paper's Place supply'd. **1829** J. Murray *Pract. Rem. Mod. Paper* 15 The use of lead as the material of the writing table.

†**2.** = escritoire. *Obs.*

1712 Swift *Jrnl. to Stella* 30 Oct., Lady Orkney is making me a writing-table. **1722** *Lond. Gaz.* No. 6119/3 [He] took with him a Writing Table, containing 15 Drawers.

3. A table used, suitable, or adapted for writing on, having usu. drawers and other accessories or conveniences.

1833 Loudon *Encycl. Archit.* §2096 A handsome writing-table, with numerous drawers and divisions for containing papers, money, &c. **1862**- [see knee-hole]. **1891** Kipling *Light that Failed* (1900) 227 Torpenhow brought him the money..and carefully put it away in the writing-table.

attrib. **1893** Mary Cholmondeley *Diana Tempest* xi, The little pile..that you wound up, and put in your writing-table drawer.

b. = writing-board.

1875 Knight *Dict. Mech.* 2823 The writing table lets down, exposing a number of drawers, shelves, and pigeon-holes.

So **writing-tablet,** = sense 1 above; also, a pad (pad *sb.*^{3} 4) of paper for making notes, etc.; = tablet *sb.* 1e.

1829 J. Murray *Pract. Rem. Mod. Paper* 17 There are writing tablets of ivory, and of wax. **1831** *Patents* (1869) 31 A durable copy book or writing tablet. **1891** *Smith's Dict. Antiq.* II. 753 Ordinary Greek writing tablets. **1895** *Army & Navy Co-op. Soc. Price List* 619 Writing Tablets. 'The Remember.' Bound in long-grained, polished French Morocco. The Refills are made to slip in and out of case. **1917** *Harrods General Catal.* 296/2 Writing tablets. For Scribbling Memoranda and for School Purposes.

†**writling,** early f. ritling (var. reckling).

1611 Cotgr., *Coät*, the vnderling, starueling, or writling of a beast. *Ibid.*, *Grugeons*, the smallest, or most writhen fruit on a tree, writlings. *Ibid.* s.vv. *Couät, Regrouvi.*

†**writrix.** *nonce-word.* [f. writer, after L. fem. agent-nouns in *-trix.*] A female writer; an authoress.

1772 Nugent *Hist. Fr. Gerund* I. 145 Why should it not be said, she was not a common woman, but a geniusess, and an elegant writrix?

written ('rɪt(ə)n), *ppl. a.* Forms: 4-6 **writen** (5 *Sc.* -in, 5 ywriton), 4 **wreten** (5 -on, 6 -yn, *Sc.* -in); 5 **writtin, wryttin, -yn,** 6- **written** (6 **whrythyn**), 7 **writt'n.** [pa. pple. of write *v.*]

1. a. That is composed, recorded, preserved, or mentioned in writing; committed to writing; also, that is in writing (as opposed to oral or printed); manuscript.

In very frequent use from *c* 1570.

a **1300**, etc. [see 1 b]. **1485** in *10th Rep. Hist. MSS. Comm.* App. V. 385 The above wryttin Perse Lynche, Mayor. *c* **1511** *First Eng. Bk. Amer.* Introd. (Arb.) p. xxxi, In the lande of Armeneten..is whrythyn seruyce of the masses. **1565** Harding *Answ. Ivelles Challenge* 30b, Thinges.. either declared by written scriptures, or taught by the holy ghost. **1589** Hakluyt *Voy.* Ep. Ded. ¶2 Printed or written discoueries and voyages. **1617-20** Moryson *Itin.* (1903) 139 The written Relations of this tyme testifye that..they mantayned..600th men at Armes. **1669** Holder *Elem. Speech* 9 Written Language..is permanent. **1738** C'tess Pomfret in *C'tess Hartford's Corr.* (1805) I. 24, I make the tour of the world in Gemelli's written one. **1782** [see writer 3. c] **1837** Dickens *Pickw.* ii, He will consent to accept a written apology. **1865** *Patents* (1869) 365 Letters and other written documents. **1899** Wardle *Univ. Typewriter Man.* 6 The Bell gives the operator warning when the written line is about to be completed.

fig. **1605** Shaks. *Macb.* v. iii. 42 Can'st thou not..Raze out the written troubles of the Braine? *a* **1658** Lovelace *Poems* (1904) 168 O sacred Peincture!..Thou..art a written and a body'd mind. **1801** Southey *Thalaba* xii. vii, Bitter penitence, That gives no respite night nor day from grief, To abide the written hour. **1821** Shelley *Hellas* 809 Thou wouldst ask that giant spirit The written fortunes of thy house.

transf. **1889** Sutherland *Sign-Writing* ii. 2/1 The consideration of what a written sign ought to be. **1902** C. R. Conder *First Bible* 62 To assign dates to the written monuments on stone.

b. Of laws: Reduced to, established by, writing; formulated in documents, codes, or printed works. (Cf. unwritten *ppl. a.* 1b.)

a **1300** *Cursor M.* 14843 We sari men, quat mai wee sai, Ne knau we noght þe writen lai. *c* **1425** Wyntoun *Cron.* iii. Prol. 2 Moysses..Broucht to þe Iowis þar wryttyn lawys. **1471** Caxton *Recuyell* (Sommer) 146 Alle lawe posityf and alle lawe wreton condempne the vnto the deth. **1684** Sir G. Mackenzie *Inst. Law Scot.* (1694) 4 Our written Law comprehends, First, our Statutory Law [etc.]. **1728** Chambers *Cycl.* (1738) s.v. *Writing*, We also say, *written law, lex scripta*, in opposition to common law. **1853** [see writable *a.* 1]. **1882** *Encycl. Brit.* XIV. 365 The question whether a written law comes relatively early or late in the history of a nation.

c. Expressed in due literary form.

1909 J. R. Ware *Passing Eng.* 183/2 *Not enough written* (Authors', 1870), not sufficiently corrected for style. **1922** F. M. Ford *Let.* 14 Aug. (1965) 141 *Felicity Chimney* is a much more ambitious matter. The only thing that is wrong with it is that it is too written. **1963** *Times Lit. Suppl.* 1 Mar. 154/1 The writing is slipshod and frequently repetitive; in fact, as Henry James would say, it is not 'written' at all.

2. a. That is inscribed or carved upon; bearing engraving or inscription.

c **1440** *Pallad. on Husb.* xii. 114 Grekis sayn that pechis we may make Ywriton [L. *scripta*] growe. *c* **1793** *Encycl. Brit.* XII. 433 Written Mountain, Mountain of Inscriptions,..a supposed mountain..in the wilderness of Sinai. **1794** W. Hutchinson *Hist. Cumbld.* I. 138 Written Rocks on Gelt. **1861** Reade *Cloister & H.* lv, Presently we did pass a narrow lane, and..espied a written stone.

b. Bearing, inscribed or covered with, writing. Also with *on.*

1580 [see writing-book 1]. **1596** Shaks. *Merch. V.* ii. vii. 64 A carrion death, Within whose emptie eye there is a written scroule. **1656** T. Violet *Proposals* 19 A written parchment, and a written sheet of paper annexed thereunto. **1692** *Athenian Merc.* 24 Dec., A flat bundle of written Papers. **1831** James *Phil. Augustus* II. ii, Treaties which in all ages have been but written parchments. **1869** *Patents* 6 The written paper and the copying paper are laid on a board.

1948 A. N. Keith *Three came Home* vii. 124 They were constantly looking for my papers, written-on or otherwise. **1955** E. Bowen *World of Love* iv. 77 The written-on blue envelope.

fig. **1820** Shelley *Prometh. Unb.* II. i. 110 Oh, lift Thine eyes, that I may read his written soul!

†**3.** ***written hand***, cursive form of writing; a form of running hand. *Obs.*

1531 *Rec. St. Mary at Hill* 45 A prymmer lymmed with gold and with Imagery, wretyn hond. **1582** T. Watson *Centurie of Love* Ep. Ded., This worke.. being as yet but in written hand. **1617** Moryson *Itin.* I. 86 An old breviary of written hand and much esteemed. *a* **1700** Evelyn *Diary* 27 Jan. 1658, He had.. skill to reade most written hands. **1764** Foote *Mayor of G.* II. i, We appoint him our Secretary for he can read written hand. **1849** *Chambers's Jrnl.* 13 Oct. 239/1 Here, Theresa, see what it [*sc.* a paper] says: you can read written hand better than I.

4. Of letters, etc.: Traced or formed with the pen.

1582 Mulcaster *Elementarie* (1925) 60 Som writen figure or accent. *c* **1620** A. Hume *Brit. Tongue* (1865) 7 The symbol, then, I cal the written letter. **1861** Paley *Æschylus* (ed. 2), *Persians* 351 The vestiges of the written digamma. **1877** *N. & Q.* 31 March 246 Origin of written characters. **1881** *Lancet* 26 Nov. 904/2 As he wrote each letter he named one aloud, but the written and spoken letter never corresponded with one another.

5. a. That has been written to. Also with *to*. In quots. *absol.*

1748 Richardson *Clarissa* (1768) I. 206, I command thee to be pleased: If not for the writer's, or written's sake, for thy word's sake. *Ibid.* II. 121 [The letter] was written.. on one knee, kneeling with the other. Not from reverence to the written to, however.

b. With *advs.* That has been written *about*, *down*, *off*, *out*, or *up*.

1754 Richardson *Corr.* (1804) II. 198 Your capital men.. with their short written-down speeches. **1890** G. B. Shaw in *Star* 7 Mar. 2/3 The imagination of the public has undoubtedly been strongly seized by the spectacle of the much-written-up Tosca at the height of its prosperity. **1893** *Harper's Mag.* Dec. 59/1 Not thet I'd b'lieve any written-out foolishness. **1897** P. Warung *Tales Old Regime* 149 Negligently-written-up records. **1897** Mary Kingsley *W. Africa* 205 Using the native languages in his phonetically written-down form. **1899** *Daily News* 22 June 8/1 The best written about poet of modern times. **1961** *Sunday Express* 12 Feb. 9/2 He accuses them of.. selling 'written off' car wrecks. **1964** *Times Rev. Industry & Technol.* Feb. 9/1 The old British Lion Corporation.. was.. wound up in 1954 with a written-off loss of £2,969,000. **1972** *Listener* 6 July 3/2 *Catch 44*.. is becoming one of the most written-up television projects in America.

c. ***written out***: *spec.* of a writer, that has exhausted his creative capacity. Cf. WRITE *v.* 17 b.

a **1911** D. G. Phillips *Susan Lenox* (1917) II. xii. 355 He's had several failures... They say he's written out. **1959** C. Williams *Man in Motion* ii. 21 Suzy Patton, the has-been. The written-out writer. **1978** A. Powell *Messengers of Day* vii. 108 After a lifetime of work a novelist can possibly be 'written out'.

writter ('rɪtə(r)). [f. WRIT *sb.* + -ER[1].] One who serves a writ or process.

1882 *Punch* 4 Nov. 215/2 There was a regular army of writters to meet me. **1887** Black *Sabina Zembra* xxxi, The writters would be after him like a pack of wolves.

†**wrive**, *v. Obs.* In 5 **wryve**. [ad. MDu. *wrîven* (Du. and Flem. *wrijven*; MLG. and LG. *wrîven*, *wrîfen*; WFris. *wriuwie*, NFris. *wriwe*), = OHG. *rîban* (MHG. *rîben*, G. *reiben*).] *trans.* To rub.

1481 Caxton *Reynard* xliii. (Arb.) 116 They rubbed and wryued hym vnder his temples and eyen. [Hence **1894** F. T. Ellis *Reynard the Fox* 328 They.. wryved his eye.]

†**wrixle**, *v. Obs.* Also **wrixel**, **wryxle**. [OE. *wrixlian*, *-an* to alter, change, exchange, etc., also *ȝewrixlian*, altered form of *ȝewixlian*, = OFris. *wixlia*, OS. *wehsalon*, OHG. *wehsalon* (G. *wechseln*), etc.]

1. *trans.* To alter, change, confound.

c **1400** *Destr. Troy* 9327 What whylenes, or wanspede, wryxles our mynd? *Ibid.* 10328 Wodenes þe wrixlet, & þi wit failet.

2. To exchange.

c **1400** *Destr. Troy* 3120 Þai hade laisure.. þere likyng to say, And wrixle þere wit & þere wille shewe.

†**wrixling**, *vbl. sb. Obs.*[−1] [OE. *wrixlung* 'mutuum', f. *wrixlian*: see prec.] The action of changing, or the fact of being changed.

a **1240** *Lofsong* in *O.E. Hom.* I. 207 Ich bide þe.. bi his cloðes wrixlunge, Nu red nu hwit, him on hokerunge.

wrizzled ('rɪz(ə)ld), *a.* Now *dial.* Also **wrizled** (7 **wristled**, 8 **wrisled**). [? var. of WRITHLED *a.*] Marked with creases, wrinkles, or corrugations; wrinkled, shrivelled.

The reading *wrizled* in Shaks. *1 Hen. VI*, II. iii. 23 (where the authoritative texts have *writhled*) is due to Hanmer, 1744.

1590 Spenser *F.Q.* I. viii. 47 Her wrizled skin as rough, as maple rind, So scabby was, that [etc.]. *c* **1656** Sir H. Cholmley *Mem.* (1870) 32 A wristled [finger] nail, as if it had been crushed. **1705** tr. *Bosman's Guinea* 49 They look as awkward and wrisled as an old Company of Spaniards. **1708** Gay *Wine* 9 Youthful fires.. paint with ruddy hue His wrizzled Visage. **1777** in *Eng. Dial. Dict.* s.v., A wrizled apple, a wrizled old woman. **1873–1898** in Somerset and n. Yorks. glossaries.

wro. Now *north. dial.* Forms: α. *north.* and *Sc.* 3–6 **wra**, 5 **wraa**, 5, 9 **wray** (9 **ray**), 9 **wrae** (**rae**), **wraie**. β. 4–5 **wro**, 5 **rowe**. [a. ON. **wrá*, later *rá*, *ró* nook, cabin (whence MSw. *vraa*, *vra*, Sw. *vrå*, Da. *vraa*, Norw. *raa*, *ro*).]

1. A nook or corner; a retired or sheltered spot.

α. *a* **1300** *Cursor M.* 18155 Þaa waful wras sa dedli dim, All lighted þe lem þat come wit him. *c* **1375** *Sc. Leg. Saints* xliii. (*Cecilia*) 495, I.. giffis bot a lytil wra, a vyd merkat þare-for I ta. *a* **1400–50** *Wars Alex.* 4190 Quare þre wees in a wraa welk þaim allane. **1513** Douglas *Æneid* VI. Prol. 158 Sum blind Ciclopes of thi laithlie wra. **1840** De Quincey *Wks.* (1889) II. 365 The Dalesman.. selects a sheltered spot (a *wray*, for instance), which protects him from the wind altogether. **1891** in *Eng. Dial. Dict.* s.v. *Ray* sb.[2]

β. *a* **1300** *Havelok* 68 He made hem lurken, and crepen in wros. *c* **1395** *Plowman's Tale* I. 81 As I wandred in a wro, In a wode besyde a wall. *a* **1400** *Stac. Rome* 181 A lutel be-hynde.. þer stont a Chapel in a wro. *c* **1425** *Thomas of Erceld.* (1875) 43 Nere þat wro is a well.

transf. **13..** *E.E. Allit. P.* A. 866 In appocalyppce is wryten in wro, I seghe, says Iohan, þe loumbe.

2. *Sc.* An enclosure or shelter for cattle. ? *Obs.*

1808 Jamieson s.v. *Rae.*

wroath, obs. var. RUTH *sb.*[1] 4 b.

1596 Shaks. *Merch. V.* II. ix. 78 Ile keepe my oath, Patiently to bear my wroath.

†**wrob**, *v. Obs.*[−1] In 5 **wrobbe**, **wrabbe**. [Of obscure origin.] *intr.* To speak of a matter; to give information.

c **1425** *Thomas of Erceld.* (1875) 2/1 If j solde sytt to domesdaye, With my tonge to wrobbe [*v.r.* wrabbe] and wrye, Certanely þat lady gaye, Neuer bese scho askryede for mee.

†'**wrobber**. *Obs.*[−1] [f. prec.] An informer.

c **1300** *Havelok* 39 Wreieres and wrobberes made he falle.

wroche, etc., obs. forms of WRETCH *sb.*, etc.

wrocht(in, **wrocte**, **wroght(e**, etc.: see WORK *v.*

wrog, southern ME. var. FROG[1].

wroght, obs. var. WROTH *a.*

wrohte, var. WROUGHT *sb. Obs.*

wroie, obs. var. WRAY *v.*[1]

wroith, obs. Sc. f. WROTH *a.*

†**wroke**, *sb. Sc. Obs. rare.* Also **wroik**. [a. MLG. *wrok*, *wruk* (LG., Du. *wrok*) enmity, hatred, spite.] Active ill-will or hatred; spite, malice.

a **1500** *Bernard. de cura rei fam.* (E.E.T.S.) 23 All þar wroke sall ende wyght þam selwne. **1513** Douglas *Æneid* V. xi. 11 Juno.., Not satyfyit of hir auld fury nor wroik.

wroke, **wroken**, etc.: see WREAK *v.*

wrong, *sb.*[1] Now *dial.* Also 2 **wranga**, 3–4 **wrange**, 3–5, 6 *Sc.* **wrang**, 6 *Sc.* **wraing**, **wrayng**; 4–5 **wronge**. [a. ON. **wrǫng*, *rǫng* (gen. *rangar*), rib of a ship (Norw. *rong*, *raang*, *vrong*, *vraang*, Sw. dial. *vrang*), f. **wrangr* curved, bent: see WRONG *a.* Hence also MLG. *wrange*, Du. *wrang*, F. *varengue* (14th c.), *varangue*, Sp. *varenga*, floor-timber of a ship.]

†**1.** A rib of a ship or other vessel; also, a floor-timber of a ship. (Cf. RUNG *sb.* 4.) *Obs.*

(The sense of the OE. instances is not clear.)

c **1000** *Gloss.* in Wr.-Wülcker 201 *Cauernamen*, wrong. *c* **1100** *Ibid.* 182 *Nomina nauium, et instrumenta earum*: ..*cauernamen*, wranga.

1295 *Acc. Excheq. K.R.* 5/8 m. 3, Et xv.*d.* in .j. Wrange empt'... Et .v.*s.* j.*d.* in .v. Wranges emptis. **1296** *Ibid.* 5/20 m. 1 *dorso*, In .lx. arboribus emptis de Priore de Tynemue ..ad Wrangas faciendas in Galea, xxv.*s.* **1336** *Ibid.* 19/31 m. 6 In xl. lignis emptis in grosso pro Wronges faciendis, xv.*s.* **1352** *Exchеq. Acc. Q.R.* 20/27 (P.R.O.), Pro fotynges et wrongs inde confectis in naue predicta. **1407** *Acc. Exchеq. K.R.* 44/11 (1) m. 6 In xxiiij. Wronges.. infra paruam batellam expenditis. *c* **1435** *Ibid.* 53/3 m. 9 Pro lx peciis maeremii.. pro Wrangys.. dicte balingere Regis inde faciendis. **1513** Douglas *Æneid* V. xii. 164 Thai.. gan to forge newlie wrayngis and airis. *Ibid.* IX. ii. 98 Vpblesis ourloft, hechis, wrangis, and how.

2. A large crooked branch or bough of a tree, esp. one cut off and lopped for timber. Latterly *dial.*

1764 *Ann. Reg.*, *Chron.* 88 An oak.. which.. contained 13 loads 35 feet of timber, 5 loads of wrongs (pieces not less than six inches girt) [etc.]. **1787** W. H. Marshall *Norfolk* II. 392 *Wrongs*, crooked arms.. of trees. **1823** E. Moore *Suffolk Words* 498 The wrongs of oaks.. are as valuable nearly as the body or right up timber. *a* **1825** Forby *Voc. E. Anglia*, *Wrong*, a crooked bough.

3. *attrib.* (in sense 1), as †***wrong-nail***, †***-rope***; †**wrong-head**, = RUNG-HEAD (cf. *wrung-head*).

1296 *Acc. Exchеq. K.R.* 5/20 m. 3 *dorso*, M. C. clauis s[c]ilicet Wrangnayl emptis, iij.*d.* *c* **1340** in Nicolas *Hist. Navy* (1847) II. 477 [Two ropes called] wrangropes, ijs. **1352** *Acc. Exchеq. K.R.* 20/27 (P.R.O.), Pro mmccc. wrong-naill' emptis pro reparatione navis. **1356** in *Pipe Roll 32 Edw. III*, m. 33/1, ij. wrangeropes.. et .xxj. basteropes. **1633** *Admiralty Crt. Exam.* 50, 6 Nov. (MS.), She was sheathed from her bende to the wrong head.

wrong (rɒŋ), *sb.*[2] Forms: α. 1–5, *Sc.* and *north. dial.* 6– **wrang** (4 **vrang**, 9 *north. dial.* **wrank**), 4–5, *Sc.* 6 **wrange**. β. 3– **wrong** (5 **worng**), 4–6 **wronge** (5 **wronke**, 6 **wrongue**, 7 **ronge**), 5 **wrunge**. [Substantival use of WRONG *a.*]

I. 1. That which is morally unjust, unfair, amiss, or improper; the opposite of right or justice; the negation of equity, goodness, or rectitude. (Freq. contrasted with *right.*)

a **1100** *Wulfstan's Hom.* xlii. 203 Þa unrihtdeman, ðe.. wendaþ wrang to rihte and riht to wrange. *c* **1200** *Trin. Coll. Hom.* 193 Talewise men þe.. maken wrong to rihte, and riht to wronge. *a* **1250** *Owl & Night.* 877 If riht goþ forþ & a back wrong. **1303** R. Brunne *Handl. Synne* 4381 For wrong ne lefte he nyȝt ne day. **1375** Barbour *Bruce* I. 177 Degradyt syne wes he Off honour.. Quhethir it wes throuch wrang or rycht, God wat it. *c* **1430** *Chev. Assigne* 245, I wolle.. fyȝte for þe qwene with whome þat wronge seythe. *c* **1480** Henryson *Wolf & Lamb* 79 Quhar wrang and reif suld dwell in propertie. *a* **1578** Lindesay (Pitscottie) *Chron. Scot.* (S.T.S.) I. 65 They put no difference betuix wrang and right. **1596** Spenser *F.Q.* V. iv. 1 For to maister wrong and puissant pride. **1606** Shaks. *Tr. & Cr.* I. iii. 116 Right and wrong, (Betweene whose endlesse iarre, Iustice recides). **1667** Milton *P.L.* XI. 662 One,.. eminent In wise deport, spake much of Right and Wrong. **1737** [see RIGHT *sb.*[1] 3]. **1781** Cowper *Conversat.* 149 Without the means of knowing right from wrong. **1809–10** Coleridge *Friend* (1865) 72 The abandonment of all principle of right enables the soul to choose and act upon a principle of wrong. **1878** Browning *La Saisiaz* 35 Why are right and wrong at strife?

Personif. **1362** Langl. *P. Pl.* A. I. 61 A wiht þat wrong is i-hote, Fader of Falsness. *c* **1460** *Wisdom* 728 in *Macro Plays* 59 Let se fyrst, Wronge & Sleyght! Dobullnes & Falsnes, schew yowur myght! **1581** A. Hall *Iliad* IX. 166 But Wrong a mightie monster is. *a* **1586** Sidney *Sonn.* Wks. 1922 II. 321 For Love is dead: Sir wrong his tombe ordaineth. **1847** Mangan *Poems* (1903) 84 It foretold fair Freedom's triumph, and the doom of Wrong.

†**b.** The fact or position of being in the wrong (cf. 8 a). Chiefly in the phr. ***to have wrong*** (cf. Fr. *avoir tort*). *Obs.*

a **1300** in *Map's Poems* (Camden) 335 Ic seyȝe, gas[t], thouȝ hast wrong.. Al þe wyt on me to leye. *c* **1369** Chaucer *Dethe Blaunche* 1282 Whan I had wrong and she ryght She wolde.. For-yeve me. **1420–2** Lydg. *Thebes* II. 1811 But he hadde wronge, Which thoght.. the ȝeer was wonder longe Of his Exil. **1484** Caxton *Fables of Alfonse* xii, I.. thanke yow gretely. For ryght ye haue and I grete wronge. **1587** Golding *De Mornay* xv. (1592) 241 But let Aristotle alone (for he hath wrong). **1596** Dalrymple tr. *Leslie's Hist. Scot.* (S.T.S.) I. 121 Sche wil be in wrang to her housband, gif that he knaweng, sche offend. **1604** T. Wright *Passions* (1620) 117 Whether you have right or wrong, I knowe you must have the last word.

c. Deviation from fact, accuracy, or correct standard; incorrectness, error.

c **1620** A. Hume *Brit. Tongue* 2 To command.. the schooles to teach the future age right and wrang. **1796** Burke *Regic. Peace* ii. (1892) 126 Whether.. there was some mixture of right and wrong in their reasoning.

2. Unjust action or conduct; evil or damage inflicted or received; unfair or inequitable treatment of another or others; injustice, unfairness.

α. **12..** [see β]. *c* **1460** *Towneley Myst.* xxv. 279 *Ihesus.* I wyrk no wrang, that shall thou wytt. *c* **1470** Henry *Wallace* VI. 224 It slakis ire off wrang thai suld radres. *c* **1520** M. Nisbet *N. Test.* (S.T.S.) II. 71 Christ heir, in repreifing wrange, did nocht resist it with wyolence. **1570** *Satir. Poems Reform.* xiii. 71 Wickit men delytis ay in to wrang. *a* **1598** Fergusson *Sc. Prov.* (S.T.S.) 108 Wrang hes nea warrand. **17..** Ramsay *Address to Town Council* i, I've suffer'd muckle wrang.

β. *a* **1200** *Moral Ode* 168 (Lamb. MS.), Ne scal him [*sc.* God] na mon mene þer of strengþe ne of wronge [*Egerton MS.* wrange]. *c* **1300** *Havelok* 72 To wronge micht him no man bringe, Ne for siluer, ne for gold. *c* **1310** in Wright *Lyric P.* xxv. 68 Ihesu, for love thou tholedest wrong. **1362** Langl. *P. Pl.* A. I. 117 Alle þat wrong worchen, wende þei schulen After heore deþ-day [etc.]. *a* **1425** *Cursor M.* 15922 (Trin.), Ȝe bere me wrong on honde. *c* **1440** *Promp. Parv.* 534 Wronge, a-ȝen truthe and ryghtewysnesse,.. *injuria.* *a* **1500** *Gest Robin Hood* xciv. in Child *Ball.* III. 61 The hye iustyce and many mo Had take in to theyr honde Holy all the knyghtes det, To put that knyght to wronge. **1526** *Pilgr. Perf.* (W. de W. 1531) 301 The false accusacyon & testimonyes of yᵉ iewes was so euydent & playne wronge. **1590** Spenser *F.Q.* II. ii. 18 Ne ought he car'd, whom he endamaged By tortious wrong. **1611** Bible *Job* xix. 7 Behold, I cry out of wrong [*marg.* or, violence], but I am not heard. **1624** Wotton *Archit.* 111 Which mention.. I haue willingly made of his Name,.. with much wrong to his other vertues. **1671** Milton *Samson* 76 Expos'd To daily fraud, contempt, abuse and wrong. **1749** Melmoth *Fitzosb. Lett.* lxxii, Ye plaintive crew, that suffer wrong. **1793** R. Gray *Poems* 126 He doth conceive.. of high affront And mighty wrong committed. **1846** Mrs. A. Marsh *Father Darcy* II. vii. 131 One who never sees wrong, without the noble resolution to revenge it. **1874** J. Sully *Sensation & Intuition* 154 A man who never knows the deep anguish of conscious wrong until [etc.].

b. *Law.* Violation, transgression, or infringement of law; invasion of right to the damage or prejudice of another or others: injury, harm, mischief. In early use *Sc.*

12.. [see THWERT-NAY]. **1318** in *Acts Parlt. Scotl.* I. (1844) 471/1 Torth & noun raysoun quod dicitur wrang & unlaw. *a* **1400** *Ibid.* 647/1 Quoniam attachiamenta sunt principia et origo placitorum de wrang et unlaw. **1538** Starkey *England* I. iv. 117 So justyce ys oppressyd.. and wrong takyth place. **1609** Skene *Reg. Maj.*, etc. I. 95 b, Vnjustlie, and against the law, with wouch, wrang, and vnlaw. **1670** Blount *Law Dict.*, *Tort-feasor*, a Doer of wrong, a Trespasser. **1875** Maine *Hist. Inst.* ii. 45 The ancient Irish Law of Civil Wrong.

c. *to do* (. . .) ***wrong***, to act unjustly or unfairly (*to* a person or thing, or with dative).

c 1220 *Bestiary* 798 Bimene we us, we hauen don wrong. **c 1250** *Gen. & Ex.* 2683 He..bro3te vn-warnede on hem fi3t; He hadden don egipte wrong. **a 1300** *Cursor M.* 29084 Man dos to fasting mikel wrang. **c 1330** *Spec. Gy Warw.* 222 If man wole chese to don wrong. **1372** in *Relig. Lyrics 14th C.* (1924) 71 þe child þouthte sche dide him wrong. **c 1440** *Promp. Parv.* 126/2 Do wronge a-3ene resone (*P.* ayenst reason or lawe), *injurior, prejudico.* **1481** Caxton *Reynard* xxvii. (Arb.) 71 The lawe and right doth noman wrong. **1540–1** Elyot *Image Gov.* 28 That he whiche hath done wrong, be compelled to make restitution. **1573** Tusser *Husb.* (1878) 87 Place doong heape a low..Where water all winter time did it such wrong. **1610** Shaks. *Temp.* I. ii. 440, I feare you haue done your selfe some wrong. **1649** Milton *Eikon.* 102 As the King of England can doe no wrong, so neither can he doe right but..by his Courts. **1737** Pope *Hor., Ep.* II. ii. 12 To say too much, might do my honour wrong. **1831** Scott *Cast. Dang.* xiii, By which she has done me great wrong. **1850** Tennyson *In Mem.* LII. ii, Thou canst not move me from thy side, Nor human frailty do me wrong.

†d. *to have* (. . .) ***wrong***, to suffer injustice, prejudice, or harm; to receive injury. *Obs.*

c 1250 *Gen. & Ex.* 3077 'Hu! haue 3e wrong,' quad pharaon, '3u wapmen giue Ic leue to gon'. **1303** R. Brunne *Handl. Synne* 9582 Quyte þe weyl oute of borghgang, þat þou ne haue for hyt no wrang. **c 1410** *Lantern of Light* 45 Glotenye..drowneþ þe wittis of þe peple, til þat þei be vnresonable & kunnen not knowe whanne þei han wrong. **c 1450** *Mirk's Festial* I. 5 þogh þay haue moche wrong, þay may not gete amendes. **1509** *Coventry Leet Bk.* 626 He had grete wrong in certeyn ffyldes..by the comens of Couentre. **1560** Daus tr. *Sleidane's Comm.* 10 Suche as thinke they haue wronge at his hande. **1617** Moryson *Itin.* II. 12 In their opinion he had wrong to be so charged. [**1821** Scott *Kenilw.* v, He thinks he hath wrong, and is not the mean hind that will sit down with it. **1828** —— *F.M. Perth* x, I own you have had some wrong.]

3. In various prepositional phrases: †a. ***with*** or ***mid*** (. . .) ***wrong***, wrongly, wrongfully, unjustly. (Cf. 4.) *Obs.* [Cf. ON. *með röngu* wrongly.]

1124 *O.E. Chron.* an. 1124, [They] sæidon þet se king heold his broðer Rotbert mid wrange on heftnunge. **a 1200** *Moral Ode* 209 (Lamb. MS.), þa þe ledden hore lif mid unriht and mid wrange. **c 1290** *Beket* 839 in *S. Eng. Leg.* I. 130 Me þinchez with gret wrong þe chalangez þe king. **1338** R. Brunne *Chron.* (1810) 110 Steuen..suore, þat..þe kyng, no non of his, suld chalange þat of fe, With wrong no with right. **c 1400** *Brut* 257 þe Kyngus person bare..þe blame, wiþ wrong. **1481** Caxton *Reynard* xlii. (Arb.) 115 Suche false extorcionners..oppresse the poure peple wyth grete wronge. **a 1500** *Gest Robin Hood* cclxviii. in Child *Ball.* III. 69 There I holpe a pore yeman, With wronge was put behynde. **1598** Yong *Diana* 27 Rather then blame discredit me,..Let me with wrong forgotten be.

b. ***in*** or ***by wrong***. (Cf. 4 b.)

a 1400 *Sir Degrev.* 542 That y shalle faythly fyeght, Both in worng and in ryght. **1548** Udall, etc. *Erasm. Par. Matt.* v. 18 For mekenesse obteyneth more..than violence..can purchase or obtayne by right or wronge. **1590** Spenser *F.Q.* II. iv. 42 His am I Atin, his in wrong and right. *Ibid.* vii. 30 None could weene Them to efforce by violence or wrong. **1611** Bible *Jer.* xxii. 13 Woe vnto him that buildeth..his chambers by wrong. **1855** Tennyson *The Letters* 11 Then we met in wrath and wrong.

†4. Claim, possession, or seizure that is unjustifiable or unwarranted on legal or moral grounds. Esp. in phr. ***with*** or †***mid*** (. . .) ***wrong***. *Obs.*

c 1205 Lay. 27300 For heo al mid wronge wilneden of ure londe. **c 1300** *Havelok* 2806 þat þe swike Haues it [*sc.* the kingdom] halden with mikel wronge. **a 1325** *MS. Rawl. B.* 520 fol. 56b, 3if þe Eir mid wronge vsurped þe seisine of Eldere þoru deseisine. **1375** Barbour *Bruce* I. 209 And gyff that ony man thaim by Had ony thing that wes worthy,..With rycht or wrang it have wald thai. **c 1410** *Lantern of Light* 45 Couetise of hem þat purchasen wiþ wrong her nei3 boris ground & her catel. **c 1450** *Godstow Reg.* II. 540 That ..none other for hym or in his right, myght neuer clayme.. ony thyng of right, or of clayme, or of wronge, in the forsaid acre of lond. **1590** Spenser *F.Q.* I. iv. 12 Proud Lucifera.. did vsurpe with wrong and tyrannie Vpon the scepter.

b. In the phr. ***by, in,*** †***o,*** or †***of*** (. . .) ***wrong***.

a 1300 *Cursor M.* 28795 Vr lauerd..receues..nan Almus þat o [*v.r.* of] wrang es tan. **1528** in *Star Chamber Cases* (Selden) II. 23 [He] hathe of his owne auctoryte and wronge enteryd into the premissis. **1548** Elyot, *Iure uel iniuria*, by right or wronge. **1588** Kyd *Househ. Philos.* Wks. (1901) 278 Riches, either miserably gotten or encreased by wrong. **1594** —— *Cornelia* v. 439 Must I liue to see great Pompeys house ..Vsurpt in wrong by lawlesse Anthony? **1628** Coke *On Litt.* 181 Therefore no relation of an estate by wrong can helpe him. **1729** Jacob *Law Dict.* s.v. *Right*, An Estate gain'd by Wrong. **1818** Cruise *Digest* (ed. 2) V. 141 The defendants had done nothing to vest the freehold in them, either by right or by wrong.

5. With possessive pron. or genitive:

†a. Injustice, harm, or evil inflicted upon another or others; wrong-doing. *Obs.*

c 1275 *Duty of Christians* 59 in *O.E. Misc.* 143 We schule to criste grede, And bidde mylce of vre wrong. **1303** R. Brunne *Handl. Synne* 6430 Now we þe executore haue mysseyd, And of hys wrong he haþ vpbreyd. **13..** *E.E. Allit. P.* B. 76 More to wyte is her wrange, þen any wylle gentyl. **14..** in *Acts Parlt. Scot.* I. (1844) 352/2 Of a man grantand his awne wrang. **c 1440** *Pallad. on Husb.* XIII. 84 Gramerci, Lord, that list eek mortifie My wronge. **1513** Douglas *Æneid* I. i. 63 Sen Pallas mocht on Grekis tak sic wraik..for Aiax Oilus wrang? **c 1600** Shaks. *Sonn.* xl, Loue knowes it is a greater griefe To beare loues wrong, then hates knowne iniury. **1631–2** *Star Chamb. Cases* (Camden) 168 He shall therefore pay 500li..and make recognition of his fault and wrong. **1642** J. M[arsh] *Argt. conc. Militia* 17 It is against the rule of Law, that any man should take advantage of his owne wrong.

b. Injury, hurt, harm, or prejudice received or sustained by a person or persons. Also in phr. *to* or †***in one's (own) wrong***.

13.. *E.E. Allit. P.* A. 15 Ofte haf I wayted wyschande þat wele, þat wont was whyle deuoyde my wrange. **1399** Langl. *Rich. Redeles* Prol. 13 Whom all þe londe loued,..And ros with him rapely to ri3tyn his wronge. **a 1400–50** *Wars Alex.* 2812 As me is wa for þi wo3e, & þi wrange bathe. **1560** Daus tr. *Sleidane's Comm.* 57 b, It is not lawfull for anye Christian to reuenge his owne wronge. **1596** Spenser *F.Q.* v. viii. 11 What meane ye thus vnwise Vpon your selues anothers wrong to wreake? **1612** Drayton *Poly-olb.* II. 229 That she, to her own wrong, and every other's grief, Would needs be telling things exceeding all belief. **1656** H. Phillips *Purch. Patt.* (1676) 93 He will rebate in his own wrong. **1660** Waller *To King on his Return* 62 Armies and fleets.. redressed his wrong. **a 1740** Spotswood in W. S. Perry *Hist. Coll. Amer. Col. Ch.* I. 204 Be cautious how you dispose of the profits of your parish; least you pay it in your own wrong. **a 1768** Secker *Serm.* (1770) II. 364 The Abilities of the Man, that uses them to his Neighbour's Wrong. **1822** Shelley *Dirge* 8 Wail, for the world's wrong! —— *Calderon's Mag. Prodig.* II. 139 My words..shook Heaven, Proclaiming vengeance, public as my wrong.

fig. **1633** G. Herbert *Temple, Storm* iii, There it stands knocking, to thy musicks wrong, And drowns the song.

6. Physical hurt or harm caused to or sustained by some thing or person; treatment causing material injury or damage. (Cf. 11.) Now *rare.*

1382 Wyclif *Acts* xxvii. 10 With wrong and harm..of charge and schipp..bygynneth seiling for to be. **1398** Trevisa *Barth. De P.R.* v. xxxii. (Bodl. MS.), For þe more ese withstonding and putting of wronge and of hurting [of the marrow]. **c 1440** *Pallad. on Husb.* x. 12 In wanyng of Phebes be they toflonge, So may hit meest auayle and do leest wronge. **1573** Tusser *Husb.* (1878) 32 Light ladder and long doth tree least wrong. **1577** B. Googe *Heresbach's Husb.* 39 Flaxe..the more wrong it suffereth, the better doth it prooue. **1596** Spenser *F.Q.* v. iv. 5 There before them stood a Coffer strong,..But seeming to have suffred mickle wrong. **1602** Chettle *Hoffman* IV. (1631) H 2 b, A powder ..Being set on fire to suffocate each sence Without the sight of wound, or shew of wrong. **c 1660** in *Verney Mem.* (1907) II. 262 Small forts..to defend the merchants and their goods from wrong. **1726** Pope *Odyss.* XXI. 429 Lest time or worms had done the weapon [*sc.* a bow] wrong. **1873** A. G. Murdoch *Lilts* 44 Dinna dae the door-boards wrang, An absent tenant canna see ye.

7. ***the wrong***, that which is wrong; the opposite of justice or equity; absence of right or fairness; unjust or wrongful action.

a 1300 *Cursor M.* 17458 þof it neuer haf lasted sua lang, A-wai to wrenk he dos þe wrang. **c 1330** *Spec. Gy de Warw.* 749 Here 3e muwen se þe wrong. **1388** Wyclif *Acts* vii. 24 Moises..dide veniaunce for hym that suffride the wronge. **1411** *26 Pol. Poems* 44 My swerd..Shal shede þe ri3t fro þe wrong. **1513** Douglas *Æneid* VI. xiv. 25 Brutus..can revenge the wrang in his cuntre. **1556** Lauder *Tractate* 131 And 3our fals glosing of the wrang, Sall nocht mak 3ow to rax heir lang. **1671** Milton *Samson* 1030 Capacity not rais'd to apprehend Or value what is best In choice, but oftest to affect the wrong. **1831** Scott *Cast. Dang.* iv, If the Scottish have not had the right upon their side, they have..defended the wrong with the efforts of brave men. **1861** Paley *Æscylus* (ed. 2) *Supplices* 337 *note*, If the wrong has been wholly on one side.

8. The fact or position of acting unjustly or indefensibly; the state of being wrong in respect of attitude, procedure, or belief. (Cf. 1 b.)

†a. In the phr. ***to have the wrong***. *Obs.*

a 1300 *Cursor M.* 6029, I haue þe wrang, And al þis wrak on me es lang. **c 1330** *Amis & Amil.* 908 The steward was so strong, And hadde the right and he [= Amis] the wrong. **13..** *Seuyn Sages* (W.) 2900 Than sal thou thiseluen se Wha haue the wrang, the wife or he. **c 1430, 1828** [see right *sb.* 6 b].

b. In the phr. ***to be*** or ***put in the wrong***.

a 1400 *Chron. R. Glouc.* (Rolls) II. 795 þou wolt..þi soule to helle bringe, Vor þou ert in þe wronke [*v.r.* wronge]. **1489** Caxton *Sonnes of Aymon* xvii. 390 Ye knowe ye were in the wronge. **1513** West in Ellis *Orig. Lett.* Ser. I. I. 74 Your Grace was in the right and he in the wronge. **1561** T. Hoby tr. *Castiglione's Courtier* II. (1900) 186 Thinking that he himselfe had bine in the wronge. **1603** Shaks. *Meas. for M.* v. i. 86 You are i' the wrong To speake before your time. **1700** T. Brown *Amusem. Ser. & Com.* Wks. 1720 III. 91, I am in the wrong, I own it. **1795** Hutton *Hist. Birmingham* (ed. 3) 223 The authors I have seen are all in the wrong. **1849** Macaulay *Hist. Eng.* vii. II. 266 He had now put himself in the wrong. **1859** H. Kingsley *G. Hamlyn* xi, I quarrelled with her last night. I was quite in the wrong. **1895** *Cornh. Mag.* Oct. 380 It puts Lord Tennyson so brutally in the wrong.

†c. ***to give the wrong to***, to regard as being in the wrong. *Obs.*[−1]

1471 Caxton *Recuyell* (Sommer) 558 They shall gyue the wronge and blame to the Troians, And to vs the loose.

II. 9. A wrongful, unjust, or unfair action; a violation or infringement of one's rights; an injury received or inflicted; a mischief. a. With *any, no, that, this,* etc.

1067–77 *Ags. Laws* (Liebermann) I. 486/1 Ic nelle 3eþolian, þæt ænig man eow æni3 wrang beode. **c 1290** *Beket* 230 in *S. Eng. Leg.* I. 113 þar-of nolde he þolien no wrong. **c 1330** *Arth. & Merl.* 1363 (Kölbing), 3if y may atake þis wrong, He worþ to drawe & to hong. **c 1374** Chaucer *Troylus* III. 1008 þer-with mene I fynally þe peyne..Fully to slen and euery wrong redresse. **c 1470** *Golagros & Gaw.* 90 That sege wald sit with none wrang, Of berne that wes borne. **1481** Caxton *Reynard* ix. (Arb.) 19 That he myght auenge this ouer grete wronge. **1502** Atkynson tr. *De Imitatione* III. li. (1893) 239 If any wronge be layde vnto hym. **a 1586** Sidney *Arcadia* II. xxii, She resolved to spende all her yeares..in bewayling the wrong, and yet praying for the wrong-dooer. **1611** Bible *Ecclus.* x. 6 Beare not hatred to thy neighbour for euery wrong. **1667** Milton *P.L.* IX. 300 Thou thy self with scorne..wouldst resent the offer'd wrong. **1715** Pope *Iliad* II. 300 Durst he, as he ought, resent that wrong, This mighty tyrant were no tyrant long. **1781** Cowper *Conversat.* 25 All shall give account of ev'ry wrong, Who dare dishonour or defile the tongue! **1795–6** [see wrong-doer 1]. **1859** Tennyson *Geraint & Enid* 36 That each had suffer'd some exceeding wrong. **1862** Shirley (J. Skelton) *Nugæ Crit.* x. 444 The wrong indeed was redressed, as far as redress was possible.

b. With *a* and pl.

α. **a 1300** *Cursor M.* 6447 Quar thoru in right þai suld be gett, In smale wranges þat þar war. **c 1340** Hampole *Pr. Consc.* 5541 Alle þas þat has tholed here Falshedes and wrangs. **c 1400** *Destr. Troy* 11616 God, þat..wrangis in his wrathe writhis to ground. **1500–20** Dunbar *Poems* xc. 70 Quhen thow art ald, and ma na wrangis wyrke. **1596** Dalrymple tr. *Leslie's Hist. Scot.* II. 302 Quha war woundet or had gottin vtheris wrangis. **1786** Burns *Author's Cry & Prayer* xii, Then echo thro' Saint Stephen's wa's Auld Scotland's wrangs. **1818** Scott *Hrt. Midl.* xxxvii, We are for righting our ain wrangs.

β. **1303** R. Brunne *Handl. Synne* 11154 God..late hem neuer here soules lese For no wronges þat þey chese! **1362** Langl. *P. Pl.* A. XI. 19 As cloþers..þat Conterfeteþ disseites and Conspiret wronges. **1422–** [see redress *v.*[1] 11]. **c 1450** *Myrr. our Ladye* II. 145 My sowlle suffereth pacyently wronges and contraryous thynges. **a 1547** Surrey *Æneid* II. 867 May such a wrong passe from a father's mouth? **1612**, etc. [see redresser]. **1697** Dryden *Virg. Georg.* IV. 740 Trees bent their Heads to hear him sing his Wrongs. **1794–6** Coleridge *Relig. Musings* 306 The innumerable multitude of wrongs By man on man inflicted. **1811** W. R. Spencer *Poems* 11 Thy wrongs his guilty soul shall sting. **1874** Green *Short Hist.* iv. §4. 191 A wrong of brother against brother was also a wrong against the general body of the gild.

c. *Law.* An invasion of right, to the damage, harm, or prejudice of another or others; a violation of law or statute; a tort or trespass.

1386 *Rolls of Parlt.* III. 225/1 The folk of the Merceryе of London [compleynen]..of many wronges subtiles, and also open oppressions. **c 1400** *Brut* I. 265 He was at þe parlement at Wynchestre forto haue amendede þe wronges and trespasses þat were done amongus þe peple. **14..** in *Acts Parlt. Scotl.* I. (1844) 337/2 þe quhilk wrang was amuffyt betuen þaim in þe lande. **1518** in Leadam *Star Chamber Cases* (Selden) II. 128 They came to make their humble peticion..and sewed their grevys and wronges afforseid. **1588** Jas. VI in *3rd Rep. Hist. MSS. Comm.* 419/2 A puir man that dar nocht seik redres of this wrang be the ordinar course of iustice. **1617** —— in Halliwell *Lett. Kings Eng.* (1846) II. 143 Every wrong must be judged by the first violent and wrongous ground whereupon it proceeds. **1671** F. Phillips *Reg. Necess.* 259 The parties..endeavouring such breaches of Priviledge, should not take advantage..of their own wrongs or tortious doings. **1768** Blackstone *Comm.* III. 2 Wrongs are divisible into two sorts or species; private wrongs, and public wrongs. **1770** *Cases temp. Hardwicke* 35 The declarations must fall likewise as grafted on a wrong. **1838** W. Bell *Dict. Law Scot.* 498 Where there is reparation due on account of wrongs suffered through gross carelessness. **1888** Pollock in *Encycl. Brit.* XXIII. 454 Civil wrongs..for which there is a remedy by action in courts of common law jurisdiction. *Ibid.* 454/2 An actionable wrong.

d. In the phr. ***to do the*** (. . .) ***wrong*** (***to*** or ***unto*** a person, or with dative).

c 1330 *Spec. Gy de Warw.* 602 þenk..Off þe wrong and þe vilte, þat men to Iesu Crist dede. **c 1375** *Sc. Leg. Saints* vi. (*Thomas*) 666 þe wrange þat to myn god is done. **a 1400** *Pauline Ep.* (Powell) *2 Cor.* vii. 12 Not for hym þat has don þe wrong, nor for hym þat is suffryd. **1556** J. Heywood *Spider & Fly* 4 The wrong that I have done the flies here among. **1585** T. Washington tr. *Nicholay's Voy.* I. vii, The great wrong & iniurie that was done vnto him. **1643** Caryl *Expos. Job* I. 663 Only the creditor can remit the debt, and he the offence to whom we have done the wrong. **1671** *Acts Privy Council Scotl.* III. 345 She was the person who did the wrong. **1828** Scott *F.M. Perth* ix, The Earl deeply resented the wrong done to himself. **1883** D. C. Murray *Hearts* xxviii, In spite of the wrong he had done and the wrong he meant to do him.

e. Similarly with *a, any,* etc., or pl.

1382 Wyclif *Matt.* xx. 13 Frend, I do thee no wronge [**1388** noon wrong]. **c 1386** Chaucer *Melib.* ¶845 That ye causelees..han doon grete Iniuries and wronges to me. **c 1400** *Rule St. Benet* (Prose) vii. 13 Yef man dos yu ani wrang. **1479** *Paston Lett.* III. 267 Th' enjuryes and wrongys done..to John Paston. **1560** Bible (Genev.) *2 Macc.* iii. 12 That it were altogether vnpossible to do this wrong to them. **1591** Shaks. *Two Gent.* II. vii. 80 As thou lou'st me, do him not that wrong. **1638** R. Baker tr. *Balzac's Lett.* (vol. III) 28, I do not think I shall do you any wrong to send you a better companion. **1676** in *12th Rep. Hist. MSS. Comm.* App. V. 30 The wrongs Lord Marshall doth him, and all the younger children. **1813** *Nat. Intelligencer* (Washington, D.C.) 29 July 1/3 The wrongs done us by the British government. **1855** Tennyson *Maud* I. x. iv, I might persuade myself then She would not do herself this great wrong. **1861** Mill *Utilit.* (1863) 73 In each case the supposition implies two things—a wrong done, and some assignable person who is wronged.

†10. An incorrect or improper procedure. *Obs.*

c 1440 *Pallad. on Husb.* VIII. 53 The figtre now teneye [L. *inoculare*] hit is no wronge In weet lond. *Ibid.* x. 3 The same ek is no wronge Rather to do.

†11. A physical or material injury, hurt, or damage. (Cf. 6.) *Obs.*

1398 Trevisa *Barth. De P.R.* XVII. cxvii. (Tollem. MS.), By þe leues þe spray is defendid..a3ens colde and hete, and a3ens all wronges of frostes and snowe. **c 1440** *Pallad. on Husb.* I. 339 Yf me ferne hit wel..That in the tre the morter do no wronge.

†12. Something obtained or held wrongfully. *rare.*

c 1440 *Jacob's Well* 133 þerfore, restoryth 3oure wrongys, & caste out þe wose of false coueytise! *Ibid.* 136 3oure nede þanne excusyth 3ou nou3t fro dedly synne, but 3e 3erne 3elde to hem 3oure dette & 3oure wrong!

III. 13. *Comb.* (chiefly objective), as ***wrong-repressing***, ***righting***; ***wrong-redresser***, ***-righter***; also ***wrong-caused***, ***incensed***, ***-vexed***; ***wrong-proof*** adj.

a **1586** SIDNEY *Ps.* xxxv. i, Speake thou for me against wrong speaking foes. *a* **1586** —— *Arcadia* I. ii, Striving.. which coulde..recount their wrong-caused sorow. **1594** SHAKS. *Rich. III*, II. i. 51 These swelling wrong incensed Peeres. **1595** DANIEL *Civ. Wars* I. lxxxi, Wrong-worker Riot. **1608** SYLVESTER *Du Bartas* 210 Long wrong-vext, in a not-Need-less Cause. *a* **1816** BENTHAM *Offic. Apt. Maximized, Introd. View* (1830) 17 A penal, or say a wrong-repressing code. **1831** WORDSW. *Highland Hut* 12 Some gentle heart wrong-proof, Meek, patient, kind. **1849** LYTTON *K. Arthur* v. lxxxiii, The great Wrong-Redresser. **1869** KINGSLEY in *Life & Lett.* (1877) II. 296 The most unexpected forms of actual wrong-saying and doing. **1889** J. K. STEPHEN *Lapsus Calami* (1891) 51 A nursery of wrong-righters.

†**wrong**, *sb.*[3] *Obs. rare.* = LEAF *sb.*[1] 13.

1688 HOLME *Armoury* III. 374/1 All the Nicks or Notches in the [watch] Wheels are termed Teeth, and those in the Pinions are called Wrongs.

†**wrong**, obs. variant of WRING *sb.*[1] 1.

c **1440** *Pallad. on Husb.* I. 495 Oilmilles, whelis, wrongis [L. *prelum*], not bigonne Of new.

wrong (rɒŋ), *a.* and *adv.* Forms: α. 1–5, 6– *Sc.* and *north. dial.* **wrang** (6, 9 **vrang**, 9 *north. dial.* **wrank**), 4–5 **wrange**. β. 3– **wrong** (3 **wronk**, 5 **rong**), 3– 6 **wronge**; 9 *north. dial.* **wrung**, **wrunk**. [Late OE. *wrang*, a. ON. **wrangr*, *rangr* awry, unjust (Norw. *vrang*, *rang*, MSw. *vranger* (Sw. *vrång*), (M)Da. *vrang*), = MLG. *wrange*, *wrangh* sour, bitter, MDu. *wrangh*, *wranc* bitter, unpleasant, hostile (Du. *wrang* acid, tart; whence WFris. *wrang*); related to WRING *v.*

The adoption of the word in the OE. period is shown by its use as a sb. (see WRONG *sb.*[2]), but examples of the adj. are lacking, unless *on wrangan hylle* in a Berkshire document of 944, preserved only in a 13th century copy (Birch *Cartul.* II. 557), is accepted as original, and as representing this word. Early ME. instances may occur in the following place-names:—

a **1153** in *Coucher Bk. Kirkstall Abbey* (1904) 52 Confirmo donacionem terre quam eis fecerunt Rogerus de Wrangebroc et Henricus Walensis. **1167–8** *Pipe Rolls Hen. II*, 56 Pro murdro in Wrongedichhundred [in Rutland]. **1198** *Pipe Rolls Rich. I*, 23 Terra in eadem uilla [in Suffolk] s. ad Wrangaker i acr'. et i rodam.]

A. *adj.* **I.** †**1. a.** Having a crooked or curved course, form, or direction; twisted or bent in shape or contour; wry.

c **1200** ORMIN 9207 All þatt ohht iss wrang & crumb Shall effnedd beon & rihhtedd. *Ibid.* 9653. *c* **1220** *Bestiary* 78 His [*sc.* the eagle's] bec is ȝet biforn wrong. [*a* **1252** in *Cartul. Mon. Rameseia* (Rolls) I. 353 Fulbrocfurlange; Wrongelande; Wylokescroft.] **1388** WYCLIF *Lev.* xxi. 19 A man..[that] is ether of litil, ether of greet, and wrong [L. *tortus*] nose. **1426** LYDG. *De Guil. Pilgr.* 19656 The crookydnesse..off my crok, Wrong at the ende, as ys an hook. *a* **1470** H. PARKER *Dives & Pauper* VIII. xv. (1493) F ii, The bowe is made of ii. thynges, Of a wronge tree, and a right strynge. *a* **1500** *Hist. K. Boccus & Sydracke* (? 1510) Pj, A cocatryce..hath..many teth crokyd and wronge. **1611** COTGR., *Gauche*, left, left-handed;..wrong, sinister, awry. **1613** in *North Riding Records* IV. 143 Thone acre a brode wrangland, stinting att the strete, lying between six narrow wranglandes, towards the north, and one narrow wrangland..towardes the south.

fig. **1340** *Ayenb.* 159 Yef þe onderstondingge is wrong, oþer yef he tuysteþ oþer wyþwent.., al þe inwyt ssel by þiestre and þe hieap of uirtues.

†**b.** Marked by deviation; deflected. *Obs.*

c **1440** *Promp. Parv.* 197/1 Glacynge, or wronge glydynge of boltys or arowys,..*devolatus*.

†**c.** Of an oblong shape. *Obs.*

c **1440** *Promp. Parv.* 517/1 Warpyn, or wex wronge or avelonge, as vesselle, *oblongo*. *Ibid.* 534/1 Wronge, or avelonge.., *oblongus*.

2. Of persons: Mis-shapen; deformed. Latterly *dial.*

c **1430** *Pilgr. Lyf Manhode* III. xxx. (1869) 152 Boistows j am, and haltinge, and wronge. To the virly j go hippinge. **1787** GROSE *Prov. Gloss.*, *Wrong*, crooked. A wrong man or woman. *Norf.* *a* **1825** FORBY *Voc. E. Anglia*, *Wrong*,.. deformed; mishapen in person.

II. 3. a. Of actions, etc.: Deviating from equity, justice, or goodness; not morally right or equitable; unjust, perverse. Also *absol.*

α. *a* **1300** *Cursor M.* 16498, I sal me-seluen on me wreck For þis marchandis wrang. **13..** *E.E. Allit. P.* C. 384 Wepande ful wonderly alle his wrange dedes. *c* **1340** HAMPOLE *Pr. Consc.* 5994 Alle wrang haldyngs of gudes sere. *c* **1400** *Rule St. Benet* (Verse) 2248 For wit þai wele þat þai sal cum To reknyng on þe day of dome..Als sche sal for hir warkes wrang. *c* **1420** *Anturs of Arth.* 421 (Douce MS.), þou has wonene hem in werre, with a wrange wille. **1500–20** DUNBAR *Poems* ix. 11 The wrang spending of my wittis fyve. **1786** *Har'st Rig* cix, The beding time does now begin... Now, tho' they're a' together mixt, There's naething wrang. **1822** SCOTT *Nigel* ii, I hope there was naething wrang in standing up for ane's ain country's credit.

β. *a* **1275** *Prov. Ælfred* B. 596 þe woke ginne þu coueren, þe wronke ginne þu rihten mid alle þine mihten. *c* **1350** *Will. Palerne* 4582 Alle þe werre & þis wo is our wronge dedes. **1382** WYCLIF *Lev.* xix. 13 Thow shalt not doo wronge chalenge to thi neiȝbore. *c* **1425** *Cursor M.* 22276 (Trin.), Anticrist..shal him shewe in þo d[a]yes..his werkes wronge to fulfille. *c* **1440** *York Myst.* xxxv. 26 So þat oure wirkyng be noght wronge. **1535** COVERDALE *Hab.* i. 4 This is the cause, y[t] wronge iudgment procedeth. **1579** SPENSER *Sheph. Kal.* May 102 So often times, when as good is meant, Euil ensueth of wrong entent. **1620** T. PEYTON *Glasse of Time* I. 50 That none by wrong oppression might Be crost, by..wrestling guile. **1651** HOBBES *Leviath.* II. xxvi. 144 A wrong Sentence given by authority of the Soveraign. **1704** SWIFT *T. Tub* Auth. Apol. ¶13 One of the wrongest attempts in nature to turn into ridicule..a work which had cost so much time. **1728** VANBRUGH & CIB. *Prov. Husb.* III, When a sad wrong word is rising just to one's tongue's end, I..swallow it. **1763** TUCKER *Lt. Nat.* (1834) I. 211 If the finger rest against the trigger of a loaded musket, and a man stand just before, you cannot do a wronger thing. **1853** MISS YONGE *Heir of Redclyffe* ix, She did not awaken her mind to consider that anything could be wrong that Philip desired. **1861** MILL *Utilit.* (1863) 9 [That] creed holds that actions are wrong..[in proportion] as they tend to produce the reverse of happiness. **1878** JEVONS *Pol. Econ.* 65 There is nothing..morally wrong in a strike..when properly conducted.

b. In the phrase ***it is*** (***would be***, etc.) ***wrong to*** (do some thing).

1596 SPENSER *Hymn Heav. Love* 180 Had he required life of vs againe, Had it beene wrong to aske his owne with gaine? **1781** COWPER *Conv.* 291 'Tis wrong to bring into a mixt resort What makes some sick. **1857** BORROW *Romany Rye* xlii, I confess it was wrong in me to interrupt you. **1879** M[c]CARTHY *Donna Q.* I. iv. 87 It was very wrong of him to make such a request. **1881** W. H. MALLOCK *Rom. 19th C.* II. 93 It would be indeed wrong..to say he was making love at all.

4. a. Of persons: Deviating from integrity, rectitude, or probity; doing or prone to do that which is evil, noxious, or unjust; opprobrious, vicious.

a **1300** *Cursor M.* 29 þe wrang to here o right is lath. **13..** *Ibid.* 2204 (Gött.), þis nembrot..was wrang werour, Reuer and manqueller grett. **1382** WYCLIF *Isaiah* iii. 12 My puple his pleteres, or wrong axers [L. *exactores*], spoileden. *a* **1470** H. PARKER *Dives & Pauper* VIII. xv. (1493) F ii, Of them y[t] ben wronge throughe synne. *Ibid.* F ii b, So Crist at the doome shal sett the wrong lyuers on his left honde. **1715** DE FOE *Fam. Instruct.* I. iv. (1841) I. 78 For I think..we have all been wrong, and..it is my part to submit. **1784** COWPER *Tiroc.* 780 Th' incorrigibly wrong, the deaf, the dead! *a* **1845** BARHAM *Ingol. Leg.* Ser. III. *Truants* 58 Queer little devils were they! Cob was the strongest, Mob was the wrongest.

b. Actively opposed (†*to* another); antagonistic.

1340 *Ayenb.* 204 Ssarpnesse of liue to do his uless onderuot þet is wrang to þe goste. **1780** COWPER *Rep. Adjudged Case* 2 Between Nose and Eyes a strange contest arose,—The spectacles set them unhappily wrong.

c. *Criminals' slang.* Untrustworthy, unreliable; not sympathetic to or co-operative with criminals. Cf. RIGHT *a.* 8 e.

1908 J. M. SULLIVAN *Criminal Slang* 27 *Wrong*, man too familiar with police; not to be trusted. **1928** E. BOOTH in *Amer. Mercury* May 81/2 Aw, don't rap [i.e. speak indiscreetly] to that guy; he's wrong. **1953** W. BURROUGHS *Junkie* (1972) vi. 58 By and large, the reason a man can't score is because he is known to be 'wrong'. **1955** D. W. MAURER *Whiz Mob* ix. 130 He [*sc.* a pickpocket] tries to avoid those cities or those districts which are known to be *wrong*, or where the police will not have any part of protecting him. *Ibid.* 140 He was what thieves call a *wrong copper*; that is, he did not take the *fix*.

5. a. Not in conformity with some standard, rule, or principle; deviating from that which is correct or proper; contrary to, at variance with, what one approves or regards as right.

a **1310** in Wright *Lyric P.* viii. 31 Y-wis hit is al wrong. Al wrong y wrohte for a wyf, that made us wo in world ful wyde. **1362** LANGL. *P. Pl.* A. XI. 67 Whi wolde God..suffre such a worm In such a wrong wyse þe wommon to bi-gyle? **1390** GOWER *Conf.* I. 169 Of here wrong condicion To do justificacion. *c* **1459** in *Plumpton Corr.* (Camden) p. xxxix, Her hosband cometh..and seyeth the feyrest langwage that ever ye hard. But all is rong; he is ever in trouble. **1550** CROWLEY *Epigrams* 916 Ye must saye as they saye, Be it wrounge or ryght. **1591** SPENSER *Daphn.* 243 She fell away in her first ages spring;..For age to dye is right, but youth is wrong. **1676** HALE *Medit. Lord's Pr.* 183 When I look into my Conscience, I find her easily bribed, and brought over to the wrong party. **1690** LOCKE *Hum. Und.* IV. xxi. §16 The foundation of vice in wrong measures of good. **1709** POPE *Ess. Crit.* 338 But most by Numbers judge a Poet's song; And smooth or rough, with them is right or wrong. **1732** BERKELEY *Alciphr.* II. §19 Revenues that in ignorant times were applied to a wrong use. **1753–4** RICHARDSON *Grandison* (1781) III. xxviii. 333 Permitting the interview, which they suppose the wrongest step that could have been taken.

b. Not in consonance with facts or truth; incorrect, false, mistaken.

c **1420** *Prose Life Alex.* 34 And ȝe haffand in vs a wrange consayte, blamez vs. **1528** MORE *Dyaloge* III. Wks. 210/1 Our hart euer thinketh the iudgement wrong, that wringeth us to the worse. **1594** SHAKS. *Rich. III*, II. i. 54 If any heere By false intelligence, or wrong surmize Hold me a Foe. **1611** BIBLE *Deut.* xix. 16 If a false witnes..testifie against him that which is wrong. **1670** in *Buccleuch MSS.* (Hist. MSS. Comm.) I. 475, I do not use to be found in a wrong story. **1690** LOCKE *Hum. Und.* II. xi. §13 Mad Men put wrong Ideas together, and so make wrong Propositions. *Ibid.* §69 Fashion and the common Opinion having settled wrong Notions. **1728** CHAMBERS *Cycl.* (1751) s.v. *Errour*, Some philosophers define error [as]..a wrong judgment, disagreeing with the things whereon it is passed. **1730** BAILEY (fol.), *Misacceptation*, a wrong understanding or apprehending of any thing. **1865** WILLIAMS *Mem. M. Henry* 304 A wrong date is assigned to the delivery of this Sermon. **1871** LE FANU *Rose & Key* II. 27 Her watch..being seldom more than twenty minutes wrong, either way. **1884** tr. *Lotze's Logic* 370 An allegation..if wrong..deviates more or less from the truth. **1891** C. ROBERTS *Adrift Amer.* 111 There is something wrong in this, deer do not stand up..to be shot down that way.

c. Of belief, etc.: Partaking of or based on error; erroneous.

c **1400** *Rule St. Benet* (Prose) 42 þat þai ne falle in wrang trouȝ. **1591** SHAKS. *1 Hen. VI*, II. iii. 31 Marry, for that shee's in a wrong beleefe, I goe to certifie her Talbot's here. **1656** COWLEY *On Death of Crashaw* 56 His Faith perhaps in some nice Tenents might Be wrong; his Life..was in the right. **1733** POPE *Ess. Man* III. 306 For Modes of Faith let graceless zealots fight; His can't be wrong whose life is in the right. **1755** JOHNSON, *Misbelief*,..false religion; a wrong belief.

d. Of a painting: having an erroneous attribution.

1969 C. IRVING *Fake!* (1970) xiv. 173 It's an ugly thing.. when you have to tell a client he's bought a fake. Of all things in this business..the thing I dislike most is being called in to tell if a painting is right or wrong... Fernand.. brazenly offered Juviler a genuine Roualt in exchange for the 'wrong' Dufy. **1979** *Daily Tel.* 28 Feb. 10/2 There are huge numbers of 'wrong' paintings and other works on the market, not strictly fakes, although they often become fakes when resold with the intention to deceive. 'Forty per cent. of the pictures we see are wrong,' said Mr Peter Nahum, the Victorian paintings expert at Sotheby's Belgravia. 'They are wrongly attributed, have a false signature or are genuine contemporary copies.' **1983** *Sunday Times* 10 July 2/3 They invited Ronald Alley, deputy director of the Tate to inspect the pictures. He pronounced them 'wrong'—in art world parlance, fakes.

6. Not right or satisfactory in state or order; in unsatisfactory or bad condition; amiss.

what's wrong with (mod. colloq.), what is the matter with (see MATTER *sb.*[1] 25 b), what objection is there to, why not have (etc.)?

a **1425** tr. *Arderne's Treat. Fistula*, etc. 58 Also flowyng emoroydez somtyme ar hidde.., þat of som þai ar demed to be dissenterikez and yuelz wrong. *a* **1450** *Knt. de la Tour* (1868) 80 What aylithe you? y trow there be sum thinge wronge with you. *c* **1460** *Towneley Myst.* iii. 188 If any thyng wrang be, Soyne is she wroth. **1567** *Satir. Poems Reform.* vi. 131 In thy default se that na thing be wrang. *a* **1568** *Wyfe of Auchtermuchty* 103 (Bann. MS.), Scho fand all wrang that sowld bene richt. **1781** COWPER *Expost.* 301 Policy is busied all night long In setting right what faction has set wrong. **1793** [EARL DUNDONALD] *Descr. Estate of Culross* 56 We shall never get right till we get as far wrong as we can. **1824** SCOTT *St. Ronan's* xv, 'Something wrong here,'..said the traveller, pointing to his own forehead significantly. **1835–** [see PUT *v.* 25 b]. **1857** DICKENS *Dorrit* II. ix, You see,..it might put us wrong with our son-in-law. **1860** A. LEIGHTON *Trad. Sc. Life* 52 Nothing wrong with Mrs. Græme, I hope? **1925** R. A. KNOX *Viaduct Murder* ix. 90, I want to know what's wrong with a game of bridge?

7. a. Not adapted, according, or answering to intention, requirement, or purpose; not proper, fitting, or appropriate; unsuitable. †Also const. *to*.

a **1400** *Bk. Curtasye* 99 in *Babees Bk.* 302 Yf hit go þy wrang throte into, And stoppe þy wynde. *c* **1440** *Pallad. on Husb.* XII. 109 Kitte of euery roten thyng or drie, For grene yf that me kitte of, that is wronge. **1514** BARCLAY *Cit. & Uplondyshman* (Percy Soc.) 11 Than was no cocko..To laye wronge egges within a straunge nest! **1549** *Compl. Scotl.* x. 83 The iueis interpret it to the vrang sens. **1550**, **1560** [see WREST *v.* 5 b]. **1598** SHAKS. *Merry W.* III. i. 110, I haue directed you to wrong places. **1598** B. JONSON *Ev. Man in Hum.* II. i, He..claps his dish at the wrong mans dore. **1673** *Essex Papers* (Camden) I. 63 Of which if he thinks to make me y[e] first example he will find he has fixed upon a wrong man. **1698** FRYER *Acc. E. India & P.* 126 They brought me to the wrong side of a pretty Square Tank, or Well. **1706** PHILLIPS (ed. Kersey), To *Misrepresent*, not to represent fairly, to give a wrong or false Character of. **1727** BAILEY (vol. II), *Misplace*, to put in a wrong Place. **1736** [see WRONGNESS 2]. *a* **1778** TOP-LADY *Anecd.* Wks. 1794 IV. 152 To put your hand into the wrong pocket. **1793** W. ROBERTS *Looker-on* No. 38 (1794) II. 60 This was the wrongest time that could be chosen. **1821** LAMB *Elia* I. *Mrs. Battle*, An adversary, who has slipt a wrong [playing] card. **1836–7** DICKENS *Sk. Boz*, *Scenes* xvii, Shoving the old and helpless, into the wrong buss. **1871** GEO. ELIOT *Middlemarch* xl, The fatal step of choosing the wrong profession. **1884** E. YATES *Recoll.* II. 67 Never did a man so persistently..do the wrong thing in the wrong place.

b. In various allusive phrases: (see quots. and BARK *v.*[1] 2, BOX *sb.*[2] 21, SHOP *sb.* 8 b, SOW *sb.*[1] 3). ***to catch*** (a person) ***on the wrong foot***, ***to get off***, etc., ***on the wrong foot***: see FOOT *sb.* 29.

1554 RIDLEY in Foxe *A. & M.* (1563) 931/1 If you wil heare how Saint Augustine expoundeth that place, ye shal perceaue that ye are in a wronge boxe. **1562** J. HEYWOOD *Prov. & Epigr.* II. ix. (1867) 75 Ye tooke..the wrong sow by theare. **1616** *Withals' Dict.* 584 *Vlulas Athenas*, you bring your Corne to a wrong market. **1639** J. CLARKE *Parœm.* 7 You bring your hogs to a wrong market. **1761** *Brit. Mag.* II. 440 You'd have sworn he had got the wrong pig by the ear. **1833** JAS. HALL *Leg. West* 46 You are barking up the wrong tree, Johnson. **1836** DICKENS *Sk. Boz*, *Tales* xii, Does he want..money? meat? drink? He's come to the wrong shop for that, if he does. **1877** 'SAXON' (Mrs. Trotter) *Gall. Gossip* 190 Ye've got the wrang soo by the lug this time. **1897** *Daily News* 4 March 6/1 The now well-quoted phrase of Lord Salisbury's, 'we put all our money upon the wrong horse'. **1907** *N. & Q.* 19 Jan. 46/2 'You will find yourself in the wrong shop!' is a vague threat.

c. ***the wrong end***, the end, extremity, or limit less adapted, suitable, or proper for a required or particular purpose. Occas. *fig.* Also quasi-*adv.* (quot. 1897).

1587 UNDERDOWNE tr. *Heliodorus* VI. (1895) 166 Calasiris carried Cariclias quiver.., the wrong ende downeward on his shoulders. **1602** *2nd Pt. Return Parnass.* III. iii. 1323 My master..then turning..the wrong end of the booke vpward. **1690** LOCKE *Hum. Und.* III. xi. §24 They..begin at the wrong end, learning Words first. **1692** R. L'ESTRANGE *Fables* clxxv. 147 Till a Vain Repentance Minds us of it at the Wrong End on't. **1737** [see GO *v.* 1 c]. **1809** MALKIN *Gil Blas* VI. iii. ¶5 This was setting up the trade of a steward, but beginning at the wrong end. **1836** [HOOTON] *Bilberry Thurland* III. 252 He looked prodigiously cruel, having, as our country folks term it, got out of bed the wrong end first. **1878** [see END *sb.* 24]. **1886** KINGTON OLIPHANT *New English* I. 491 We talk of the wrong end of the stick. **1890-** [see STICK *sb.*¹ 15 e]. **1897** KIPLING *Capt. Cour.* 125 Patent rockets that went off wrong-end-first. **1902** S. E. WHITE *Blazed Trail* xxxii, Daly knew men. He was at the wrong end of the whip.

d. *Typog.* Not of the proper size, character, or face. Freq. in ***wrong fount*** (abbrev. *w.f.*); also *attrib.*

1771 LUCKOMBE *Hist. Printing* 444 Letters that..are of a wrong Fount. **1808** STOWER *Printer's Gram.* 216 Plate, The Exemplification of Typographical Marks... Stet. Ital... w.f. **1896** *Moxon's Mech. Exerc., Printing* p. xviii, Wrong-font characters, broken space-lines, and bent rules.

e. Not of requisite social standing.

1859 LEVER *D. Dunn* xxxii, She is 'tres grande dame',.. and never knows wrong people,..such as are to be met with in society; not by claim of birth and standing, but because they are very rich, or very clever, in some way or other.

f. *Mus.* ***wrong note***: a note such as one would not expect in a given key, a discordant note. Freq. *attrib.*

1934 C. LAMBERT *Music Ho!* II. 127 The spicing up of a simple harmonic basis by the addition of what are popularly—and rightly— known as 'wrong notes', such as we find in Auric. **1946** C. MASON in A. L. Bacharach *Brit. Music* x. 139 The 'wrong-note lyricism' of Prokofiev's Third Piano Concerto is as vulgar as the street tunes it distorts. **1958** *Listener* 16 Oct. 623/3 The fierce new musical idioms that had been developed by those whom he [*sc.* Vaughan Williams] called 'wrong-note' composers. **1979** *Oxf. Jun. Compan. Mus.* (ed. 2) 269/2 His [*sc.* Poulenc's] style was neo-classical, full of unexpected twists and delightful 'wrong-note' harmonies.

8. a. Of a way, course, etc.: Leading in, having a trend or aspect to, a direction other than one intends, desires, or expects.

to go the wrong way, of food, etc.: see WAY *sb.*¹ 4 e.

c **1440** *Promp. Parv.* 527/2 Wylgate, or wronge gate, *deviacio.* **1568** GRAFTON *Chron.* II. 765 Some brekyng downe the walles to bring in the next way, and some yet drew to them that holpe to carye a wrong way. **1572** GASCOIGNE *Hearbes* Wks. 1907 I. 349 He much mistooke and shot the wronger way. **1601** R. JOHNSON *Kingd. & Commw.* (1603) 158 The Russe Emperor..leading foorth his armie to incounter him marched a wrong way. **1632** HOLLAND *Cyrupædia* 94 They chaunced upon a wrong by-lane. **1778** MISS BURNEY *Evelina* xxi, That he had himself ordered the man to go a wrong way. **1787** 'G. GAMBADO' *Acad. Horsem.* 39 Only take care to point his head the wrong way. **1833** REDDING *Shipwrecks* I. 71 They were steering a wrong course. **1835** MACAULAY *Mackintosh* Ess. (1897) 324 Were their faces set in the right or in the wrong direction? **1856** SARA ROBINSON *Kansas* (ed. 3) 40 We..took the wrong road when nearly there. **1883** STEVENSON *Treas. Isl.* xxxii, This here crew is on a wrong tack, I do believe.

b. *fig.* and in fig. context.

1412-20 LYDG. *Chron. Troy* II. 1818 þoruȝ myst of errour falsely to forveye By pathis wrong from þe riȝte weye. **1526** *Pilgr. Perf.* (W. de W. 1531) 18 Takynge the wronge waye, they liue here a whyle in worldly pleasure. **1562** J. HEYWOOD *Prov. & Epigr.* II. ix. (1867) 75 Ye may see, ye tooke The wrong way to wood. *a* **1613** OVERBURY *Countrey Newes* Wks. (1890) 174 That the allegory of justice drawne blind, is turned the wrong way. **1698** COLLIER *Short View* 210, I observe the Moral is vitious: It points the wrong way. **1781** COWPER *Truth* 17 Grace leads the right way: if you choose the wrong, Take it, and perish. **1809** MALKIN *Gil Blas* VII. i. ¶6, I..muttered blessings on them the wrong way, and swore outright. **1856** OLMSTED *Mech. Heavens* 133 Because all the inquirers into Nature were upon a wrong road, groping their way through the labyrinth of error. **1901** *Scotsman* 8 March 6/5 The bill..seemed to proceed upon the wrong tack.

9. a. ***the*** (or ***a***) ***wrong way***, the way or method least conducive to a desired end or purpose; the (or an) incorrect manner.

c **1489** CAXTON *Sonnes of Aymon* xxvi. 546 Rohars..sayd, 'Sire,..here is my gage'. 'Rohars,' sayd Charlemagne, 'here ye take a wronge waye'. **1639** J. CLARKE *Parœm.* 8 You go the wrong way to worke. **1651** in *Verney Mem.* (1907) I. 518 Hee tooke the wrong way to right himself. **1727** [see GO *v.* 4]. **1884** *Times* (weekly ed.) 31 Oct. 14/3 They went the wrong way to work to gain the ear of the House.

b. (***the***) ***wrong way*** (†***wrong-way***, Sc. ***wrang-gates***), in adverbial use, = in a contrary or opposite direction or position to the proper or usual one.

1693 CONGREVE *Old Bach.* IV. viii, You wou'd have taken 'em for Friezland Hens, with their Feathers growing the wrong way. **1697** *Lond. Gaz.* No. 3325/4 The S stands the wrong way. **1700** T. BROWN *Amusem. Ser. & Com.* 157 A Band, or a Cravat put the wrong way. **1733** TULL *Horse-Hoeing Husb.* xxiii. 360 Being wrong-way upwards, the Seed is apt to arch in them. **1750** BLANCKLEY *Nav. Expos.* 103 *Marking-Yarn*,..is white Yarn spun the wrong Way. **1806** R. JAMIESON *Pop. Ballads* I. 210 Syne wrang-gaites round the kirk gaed he. **1840** HOOD *Kilmansegg, Dream* xiv, At night..He lies like a hedgehog rolled up the wrong way, Tormenting himself with his prickles. **1862-** [see RUB *v.*¹ 3 a, 13 e]. **1886** BESANT *Childr. Gibeon* II. ix, All three [had] got out of bed the wrong way that morning.

10. ***wrong side*** (†***wrong-side, wrongside***).

Cf. Da. *vrangside*, Norw. *rangsida*.

a. That side of some thing, a fabric, etc., which lies or is normally turned inward, downward, or away from one; the side opposite to the usual, or principal; the lower or under, the back or reverse, of two surfaces.

1511-2 *Act 3 Hen. VIII*, c. 6 §1 The Walker..shall not rowe..Clothe..on the right side nor of the wrong side. **1562** J. HEYWOOD *Prov. & Epigr.* (1867) 137 He hath turnd his typpet twyse..: Fyrst on the wronge syde and last on the right. **1596** SPENSER *State Irel.* Wks. (Globe) 635/2 The manner of theyr womens riding on the wrong side of theyr horse, I meane with theyr faces towardes the right side. **1601** SHAKS. *Twel. N.* III. i. 14 How quickely the wrong side [of a glove] may be turn'd outward. **1631** T. HEYWOOD *1st Pt. Fair Maid of West* IV. i. 42 The three sheep-skins with the wrong side outward. **1715** *Lond. Gaz.* No. 5353/12 A jet black Mare,..a thick Mane lying on the wrong side. **1771** MRS. HAYWOOD *New Present* 98 Slit the leg of lamb down on the wrong-side. **1890** L. C. D'OYLE *Notches* 92 He jumped hastily on to his pony (from the wrong side, after the Indian fashion).

fig. and in fig. context. **1553** ASCHAM *Germany* Wks. (1904) 147 Homer..: whose saying in Greeke is excellent, but beyng turned in the wrong side into English, it shall lesse delight you. **1605** SHAKS. *Lear* IV. ii. 9 Of Glosters Treachery..When I inform'd him, then he call'd me Sot, And told me I had turn'd the wrong side out. **1637** RUTHERFORD *Let. to J. Meine* 7 Sept., Christ's..winds turn not when he seemeth to change, it is but we who turn our wrong side to him. **1687** DRYDEN *Hind & P.* III. 438 Till frowning skys began to change their chear, And time turn'd up the wrong side of the year. **1831** CARLYLE *Sart. Res.* I. x, In looking at the fair tapestry of human Life,..he dwells.. chiefly on the reverse; and indeed turns out the rough seams, tatters, and manifold thrums of that unsightly wrong-side, with..indifference.

b. In the advb. phr. (***the***) ***wrong side out*** (†***outwards***), ***before***. In later use freq. without article.

1599 SHAKS. *Much Ado* III. i. 68 So turnes she euery man the wrong side out. **1604** —— *Oth.* II. iii. 54 My sicke Foole Rodorigo, Whom Loue hath turn'd almost the wrong side out. **1663** SOUTH *Serm.* (1717) V. 100 He will find, that if ever another Turn befals the Nation, it will be the Wrongside outwards, the Lowest Uppermost. **1859** H. KINGSLEY *G. Hamlyn* xxxiv, His hat was on wrong-side before. **1883** 'MARK TWAIN' *Life on Mississippi* liv. 481 We all struggled frantically into our clothes,..getting them wrong-side-out and upside-down, as a rule. **1888** 'J. S. WINTER' *Bootle's Childr.* ix, Trying hard to twist into its proper place a finger of the glove which would go on wrong side out.

c. Phrases: ***to laugh on the wrong side of one's mouth*** (see LAUGH *v.* 1 b); ***on the wrong side of the blanket*** Sc. (see BLANKET *sb.* 3).

1714 LUCAS *Gamesters* 65 But tho' he laugh'd, 'twas on the wrong side of his Mouth. **1771**, etc. [see BLANKET *sb.* 3]. **1809** MALKIN *Gil Blas* I. vii. §1, I..began to laugh and sing, though it was sometimes on the wrong side of my mouth. **1820** SCOTT *Monast.* xxxvii, Shafton.., men say, was a-kin to the Piercie on the wrong side of the blanket. **1837** CARLYLE *Diamond Necklace* iii, By and by thou wilt laugh on the wrong side of thy face mainly. **1889** [see LAUGH *v.* 1 b].

d. The side, party, or principle of which one disapproves.

1649 [see RIGHT *a.* 10 b]. **1784** COWPER *Tiroc.* 740 Because forsooth thy courage has been tried And stood the test, perhaps on the wrong side. **1857** W. COLLINS *Dead Secret* III. i, He could argue on the wrong side of any question with an acuteness [etc.].

e. ***on the wrong side of***, older than (a specified age); upwards of. (Cf. SHADY *a.* 2 b.)

a **1663** KILLIGREW *Parson's Wedd.* V. ii. (1664) 140 She is smitten in years o'th wrong side of forty. **1692** L'ESTRANGE *Fables* cccl. 306 An Old Man on the Wrong-side of Four-score. **1712** STEELE *Spect.* No. 282 ¶3 They had..passed their Prime, and got on the wrongside of Thirty. **1773** MME. D'ARBLAY *Early Diary* (1889) I. 220 He is on the wrong side of an elderly man, but seems to have good health. **1828** LYTTON *Pelham* III. xx, Am I..to look like a methodist parson on the wrong side of forty! **1895** *Pall Mall Mag.* Nov. 394 A good-looking woman, a little on the wrong side of thirty, perhaps.

f. The disadvantageous, undesirable, or unsafe side of some place, object, etc.

1719 DE FOE *Crusoe* II. (Globe) 521 We were on the wrong side of the Straits of Malacca. **1728** VANBRUGH & CIB. *Prov. Husb.* IV. i, He..takes me..into the lobby [to vote];..but.. I was got o' the wrong side the post. **1791-** [see POST *sb.*¹ 8 i]. **1791** 'G. GAMBADO' *Ann. Horsem.* (1809) vi. 91 [The horse] has got an awkward trick..of leaving the other two on the wrong side of the fence. **1814** SCOTT *Wav.* x, His grandsire was from the wrong side of the Border. **1893** MISS CHOLMONDELEY *Diana Tempest* i, The poor meagre home in a dingy street; the wrong side of Oxford Street.

fig. **1728** VANBRUGH & CIB. *Prov. Husb.* I. 10 We are got a little on the wrong side of the Question. **1783** COWPER *Ode to Apollo* 2 Patron of all those luckless brains, That, to the wrong side leaning, Indite much metre. **1861** A. LEIGHTON *Trad. Scot. Life* Ser. II. 65 That he would not speak to his wife on this the wrong side of eternity. **1865** SWINBURNE *Chastelard* I. ii. 38 For love, I think of that as dead men of good days Ere the wrong side of death was theirs.

g. ***to get up*** or ***out of bed*** (***on***) ***the wrong side***, with allusion to the supposed disturbing effect on one's temper. (Cf. RIGHT *a.* 20 c.) *colloq.*

1801 *Marvellous Love-Story* I. 167 You have got up on the wrong side, this morning, George. **1867** H. KINGSLEY *Silcote of S.* xi, Miss had got out of bed the wrong side. **1887** [see GET *v.* 73 a].

h. The side (of a highway) reserved for oncoming traffic (in Great Britain the right-hand side, in most other countries the left). Also *joc.* with reference to roads in countries having the opposite system to one's own.

1838 DICKENS *O. Twist* xxi, Keeping on the wrong side of the road. **1914** M. BEERBOHM in *Eng. Rev.* Dec. 19 Our car ..*was*, for an instant, full on the wrong side of the road. **1933** A. G. MACDONNELL *England, their England* xv. 264 A motor-bicycle..had been taking the natural advantage of its speed ..to pass the limousine at fifty-five miles an hour on the wrong side at a blind corner. **1965** L. SANDS *Something to Hide* ii. 31 'We..usually winter abroad.' 'Very nice too! If you can get used to driving on the wrong side.' **1972** *Guardian* 27 Nov. 12/7, 750,000 British drivers took their cars abroad last year... Many..accidents..[were] possibly caused by confusion over driving on the 'wrong' side of the road.

11. Of persons, etc.: **a.** Judging, believing, or acting contrary to the facts of the case; incorrect in judgement, assertion, or action; mistaken, in error.

1693 LOCKE *Educ.* Wks. 1714 III. 35 His Practice must by no means cross his Precepts, unless he intend to set him wrong. **1735** POPE *Prol. to Sat.* 158 Did some more sober Critic come abroad; If wrong, I smil'd; if right, I kiss'd the rod. **1748** RICHARDSON *Clarissa* (1768) III. 270, And I own I am wrong. **1797** S. & HT. LEE *Canterb. T.* (1799) I. 93 Though my head was wrong, my heart was right. **1806-7** J. BERESFORD *Miseries Hum. Life* (1826) v. Concl., If I am wrong in this. **1836** LYTTON *Duchess de La Vallière* III. iii, I was not wrong to feel remorse, But wrong to give it utterance! **1875** JOWETT *Plato* (ed. 2) I. 37, I should be very wrong not to obey you.

b. Not normal or sound *in* the senses, etc.; not sane.

1765 SIR J. PORTER in *10th Rep. Hist. MSS. Comm.* App. I. 381 Any suspicion that he was wrong in his senses. **1835** D. WEBSTER *Orig. Sc. Rhymes* 13 (E.D.D.), This maid that was wrang in the mind. **1881** D. THOMSON *Musings* 44 Lasses will laugh at yer havers, An' think ye are wrang in the head.

III. †**12. a.** That has no legal right, title, or claim; not legitimate; unlawful; = WRONGFUL *a.* 3 b. *Obs.*

1303 R. BRUNNE *Handl. Synne* 2026 Ȝyf a womman yn hordam do swyche outrage þat a wrong eyre bere herytage. *c* **1420** LYDG. *Assembly of Gods* 682 There were..Wrong vsurpers, with gret extorcioners. **1456** SIR G. HAYE *Law Arms* (S.T.S.) 23 In the quhilk tyme the traytrous Romayns maid thre wrang papis. **1460** CAPGRAVE *Chron.* (Rolls) 225 Herry the wrong Kyng of Spayn. *a* **1586** MAITLAND in *M. Folio MS.* (S.T.S.) 428 Fray god degressouris and vrang possessouris, repent sall ȝe.

†**b.** ***wrong-heir***, the hermit-crab. *Obs.*

1730 S. DALE *Taylor's Hist. Harwich* 436 The Wrong-Heire or Bernard the Hermit. **1854** MAYNE *Expos. Lex.* 155 The hermit crab..takes up its abode in univalve shells which it finds empty; hence has been named *Wrong heir.*

13. a. Marked or characterized by illegality; not legally valid.

1480 *Coventry Leet Bk.* 459 þe chirchewardens kepen hit still be wronge possession and sett hit to ferme yerely. **1593** SHAKS. *3 Hen. VI*, I. i. 159 Be thy Title right or wrong, Lord Clifford vowes to fight in thy defence.

†**b.** Obtained unjustly; held unlawfully. *Obs.*

1563 *Homilies* II. *Rogation Week* 524 God neuer suffereth the thirde heyre to enioye his fathers wrong possessions.

†**14.** False; fictitious; unreal. *Obs. rare*⁻¹.

c **1350** *Will. Palerne* 706 For soþe, ich am a mad man now, wel ich may knowe, Forto wene in þis wise þis wrong metyng soþe.

†**15.** Belonging to, situated on, the left side. *Obs. rare.*

? *a* **1400** *Morte Arth.* 1480 Wrothely one the wrange hande sir Gawayne he strykkes. **1533** BELLENDEN *Livy* (S.T.S.) I. 38 Becaus the Rivere of tyber severit þame fra þe romane landis on þare richt handis, þai turnit þame on þare wrang handis.

IV. *Comb.* **16.** Parasynthetic, as ***wrong-ended*** (see 7 c; hence ***wrong-endedness***), ***-hearted*** (hence ***wrong-heartedness***), ***-heired, -jawed, -minded, -principled.***

a **1400** *Octavian* (Camb. MS.) 107 Moche sorowe deryth mee, That Rome schalle wrong-heyred [*v.r.* wrange-ayerde] bee In vnkynde honde. **1552** HULOET s.v., Wronge iawed, or hauinge the neither longer then the vpper iaw, *bronchus.* **1805** JAMES *Milit. Dict.* (ed. 2) s.v., The inhabitants of England and Ireland are seldom wrong-hearted. **1835** GEN. P. THOMPSON *Exerc.* (1842) III. 275 Evidences of the wrong-endedness of a property-qualification, with which the British people are unhappily familiar. *a* **1849** H. COLERIDGE *Ess.* (1851) II. 88 His judgment of books is not so much superficial..as it is wrong-principled. **1883** *Imp. Dict.* IV. 669 *Wrongminded*, having a mind wrongly inclined; entertaining erroneous or distorted views. **1885** *Century Mag.* XXIX. 910 Wrong-headedness may be as fatal now as wrong-heartedness.

B. *adv.* **1. a.** In a direction differing from the right or true one; by an erroneous course or way; astray.

13.. *Cursor M.* 5760 (Gött.), Mi folk of ysrael es in wa; þai haue ben led wrang alsua. *c* **1330** R. BRUNNE *Chron. Wace* (Rolls) 15720 He sailed al day, & on þe nyght, Vmwhile boþe wrong & ryght, Til he com in-til an ilde. *c* **1386** CHAUCER *Reeve's T.* 332 By God, thoughte he, al wrang I haue mysgon. **1572** GASCOIGNE *Gascoigne's Woodmanship* 31 He winked wrong, and so let slippe the [bow-]string, Which cast him wide. **1614** SYLVESTER *Parl. Vertues Royall* 706 A fair Ship..wants..A skilfull Pilot,..That never wry shee sail, nor wrong shee row. **1715** *Lond. Gaz.* No. 5295/11 Lost or carried wrong.., several Parcels of Goods. **1773** GOLDSM. *Stoops to Conq.* I. ii, Lock-a-daisy, my masters, you're come a deadly deal wrong! **1824** MACTAGGART *Gallov. Encycl.* (1876) 293 We may wander even on kend grun; so I may run myself wrong in Gallowa, a land I weel ken. **1869** W. S. GILBERT *'Bab' Ballads, Peter the Wag* 15 He loved to send old ladies wrong, And teach their feet to stray. **1875** MISS BIRD *Hawaiian Archip.* 403 Our guide took us a little wrong once... 'Wrong' on Mauna Loa means being arrested by an impassable *a-a* stream.

fig. **1399** LANGL. *R. Redeles* III. 80 Thus lafte þey [*sc.* the young eagles] þe leder þat hem wrong ladde. **1729** BUTLER *Serm.* Wks. 1874 II. 167 How liable we are to be led wrong by passion and private interest. **1755** *Man* xxxvii. 4 When the powers of the soul are wrong directed. **1786** BURNS *Prayer in Prospect of Death* iii, List'ning to their [*sc.* passions'] witching voice Has often led me wrong. **1859** RUSKIN *Two Paths* App. i. (1891) 251 Tintoret..may lead you wrong if you don't understand him.

†**b.** In an oblique or deflected line or position; obliquely, askew. *Obs.*

c **1440** *Pallad. on Husb.* IV. 312 Sette hit [*sc.* a bough] in the delf so lenyng wronge [L. *oblique*]. *c* **1440** *York Myst.* xxxv. 182 We twoo schall see tille aythir side, For ellis þis werke wille wrie all wrang. ? *a* **1500** *Chester Pl.* xvi. 547 This Caytyfe I have cast, shall be wronge wrast, or I wend away.

2. *to go wrong.* **a.** To take a wrong way, road, or course; to go astray. Also in fig. context; and *fig.*, to make a mistake; to fall into error; to err.

a **1300** *Cursor M.* 15448 A taken þan i sal youu giue, þat yee sal noght ga wrang. **13..** *Ibid.* 25681 (Gött.), All þat singes þis sang..þu lede þaim right þar þai ga wrang. *c* **1340** HAMPOLE *Pr. Consc.* 193 Na wonder es, yf þai ga wrang, For in myrknes of unknawyng þai gang. *c* **1400** *26 Pol. Poems* 120 Whenne he wolde noȝt folwe hym [*sc.* the angel],..Out of the waye he wente wronge. *c* **1440** *Promp. Parv.* 202 Goo wronge, *devio, deliro.* **1513** DOUGLAS *Æneid* VI. Prol. 8 To follow Virgile in this dirk poese, Convey me, Sibill, that I ga nocht wrang. **1526** *Pilgr. Perf.* (W. de W. 1531) 71 b, Whan this sterre was hyd..they went wronge to theyr great peryll. **1606** SHAKS. *Tr. & Cr.* V. i. 74 *Aga*[*memnon*]. We go wrong, we go wrong. *Aiax.* No yonder 'tis. **1709** POPE *Ess. Crit.* 427 The Learn'd..So much..scorn the crowd, that if the throng By chance go right, they purposely go wrong. **1712** J. JAMES tr. *Le Blond's Gardening* 1 It being easy to go wrong where no-body has beaten the Way. **1793** R. GRAY *Poems* 10 There's mony a ane..That far frae gude's way hath gane wrang. **1849** *Tait's Mag.* XVI. 188/1 We went wrong in making any active intervention. **1873** H. SPENCER *Stud. Sociol.* xiv. 337 There are more ways of going wrong than of going right.

b. To deviate or depart from moral rectitude or integrity; to take to evil courses; also, to fall from virtue.

1500–20 DUNBAR *Poems* v. 33 Sanct Petir hat hir with a club,..becaus the wif ȝeid wrang. **1535** COVERDALE *Ecclus.* iv. 19 But yf he go wronge, she shall forsake him. **1780** COWPER *Progr. Err.* 556 Thus men go wrong..; Bend the straight rule to their own crooked will. **1848** DICKENS *Dombey* lviii, That when ladies had bad homes and mothers, they went wrong in their way too. **1888** H. S. MERRIMAN *Phantom Future* viii, I tried..to show you that I was not quite a blackguard. But it was useless; I went wrong again.

(*b*) **1837** LYTTON *E. Maltrav.* 21 She had a vague idea about girls going wrong. **1888** MCCARTHY & PRAED *Ladies' Gallery* III. viii. 169 A home..for poor girls who had gone wrong.

c. Of events, etc.: To happen amiss or unfortunately; to issue or result unsuccessfully or unprosperously.

1592 *Arden of Feversham* II. ii, Should you deceiue vs, twould go wrong with you. **1595** SHAKS. *John* I. i. 41 Your strong possession much more then your right, Or else it must go wrong with you and me. **1711** SWIFT *Jrnl. to Stella* 9 Oct., This day has gone all wrong, by sitting up so late last night. **1820** W. IRVING *Sketch-Bk., Rip van Winkle*, Everything about it went wrong, and would go wrong, in spite of him. **1857** BORROW *Romany Rye* xlii, Everything seemed to go wrong with me—horses became sick [etc.]. **1885** G. R. SIMS in *Pall Mall G.* 7 April 19/2 A thick slime of what looks like toffee gone wrong. **1891** E. KINGLAKE *Australian at Home* 114 A pal or two..ready to help a chap if things go wrong.

d. Of things: To get out of gear or working order; to fail to work, run, etc., by reason of friction, trouble, or break-down. Of a clock or watch: To fail to keep correct time.

1809 W. IRVING *Knickerb.* v. i, While others [*sc.* clocks] may keep going continually, and continually be going wrong. **1861** DICKENS *Gt. Expect.* v, We have had an accident with these [handcuffs], and I find the lock of one of 'em goes wrong. **1871** LYTTON *Coming Race* xxii, That watch..has never gone wrong since I had it. **1885** *Law Reports* 10 P.D. 100 The machinery had gone wrong. **1898** *Tit-Bits* 29 Jan. 342/2 The water supply has gone wrong.

e. Of persons: To fail in some undertaking or enterprise, or in the general conduct of life.

1819 W. TENNANT *Papistry Storm'd* (1827) 203 Seein' Papists' side gae wrang, Out at the Chanc'llor's-door he flang. **1848** THACKERAY *Van. Fair* xvii, He was a very kind old man... I'm really sorry he's gone wrong.

f. Of food, etc.: To get into bad or unsound condition; to become unwholesome.

1882 *Imp. Dict.* II. 403 *To go wrong*, to become unsound, as meat, fruit.

3. Not in accordance with good morals or a just standard of actions; in a manner contrary to equity or uprightness; unjustly, unfairly; = WRONGFULLY *adv.* 1, WRONGLY *adv.* 2.

a **1250** *Owl & Night.* 1362 Heo may do bi myne songe, hweþer heo wile wel þe wronge. **1303** R. BRUNNE *Handl. Synne* 12180 Þys erymyte..beheld..whyche come with gode deuocyoun, And whyche for ouþer encheсoun: Alle sagh þys ermyte euerydeyl, Who come wrong, and who come weyl. *c* **1350** *Will. Palerne* 1176 þer-for þe wyseman þe wirches, al þe world may know. *c* **1400** *Rule St. Benet* (Verse) 1608 Wyne þat es myghty & strang Mase witty men forto wirk wrang. *c* **1430** *Chev. Assigne* 170 Hit is þorowe þe werke of god or þey [*sc.* gold chains] be wronge wonnen. **15..** in *Dunbar's Poems* (S.T.S.) 322 The regeand tirrant..is exilit and his ofspring The land of Juda, that josit wrang. **1606** SHAKS. *Ant. & Cl.* III. vi. 80 We perceiu'd both how you were wrong led, And we in negligent danger. **1728** POPE *Dunc.* IV. 188 The Right Divine of Kings to govern wrong. **1801** *Farmer's Mag.* Apr. 191 The tithes..were gifted away to others (right or wrong, I do not presume to enquire). **1848** DICKENS *Dombey* lxi, I do conjure my relative..to set right ..whatever she has done wrong,..because it *is* wrong, and not right. **1865** GROTE *Plato* I. vii. 299 We ought not..to act wrong or unjustly.

4. a. Out of accordance or consistence with facts or the truth of the case; mistakenly, erroneously; incorrectly; = WRONGFULLY *adv.* 2 b.

c **1200** ORMIN 10020 Swillke sinndenn alle þa þatt spellenn wrang & leȝhenn. *Ibid.* 18312 Acc þatt niss nohht; ȝe wenenn wrang Off me. *a* **1300** *Cursor M.* 13906 Qua will þe sla? qui sais þou wrang? **13..** *Gosp. Nicodemus* 110 Me think in thoght þe bedell wrang ȝe blame. *c* **1350** *Will. Palerne* 4118 3if i wrong seie any word, wo worþ me euer. *c* **1400** *Rule St. Benet* (Prose) 14 Ofte speke þai wrang. *c* **1470** HENRY *Wallace* IX. 780 To Fyfe he past, to wesy that cuntre, Bot wrang warnyt off Inglismen was he. **1548** TURNER *Names Herbes* (E.D.S.) 13 Anethum is wronge englished, of some anise. **1593** G. FLETCHER *Licia* B 3 b, Wrong they doe esteeme She hath no heat. **1681** W. ROBERTSON *Phraseol. Gen.* 1355 You took my meaning wrong. **1690** LOCKE *Hum. Und.* IV. xvi. §11 A thousand odd Reasons..may make one Man quote another Man's Words or Meaning wrong. **1703** N. ROWE *Ulysses* IV. i, Whoe'er Brought you the Message.. Mistook the Queen, and has inform'd you wrong. **1711** SHAFTESB. *Charac.* III. 204 Thus at last a Mind..sees its Hindrances and Obstructions, and finds they are wholly from it-self, and from Opinions wrong-conceiv'd. **1791** COWPER *Judgm. Poets* 19 To poets..The nymphs referr'd the cause, Who..all judg'd it wrong. **1847** TENNYSON *Princ.* v. 278, I take her for the flower of womankind, And so I often told her, right or wrong. **1848** THACKERAY *Van. Fair* lxiii, In spite of her care and assiduity she guessed wrong. **1864** LATTO *Tam. Bodkin* xxiii, Ye maun hae been wrang informed.

b. *to get* (someone) *wrong*: to misunderstand a person's meaning or intentions, to misinterpret someone. *slang* (orig. *U.S.*).

1927 DUNNING & ABBOTT *Broadway* (1928) xix. 196 'Ever been accused of murder?'..'Don't get me wrong—that stuff ain't in my line.' **1934** T. WILDER *Heaven's my Destination* ii. 39 Don't get her wrong. **1942** WODEHOUSE *Money in Bank* (1946) xii. 91 We got Soapy all wrong, Chimp. He's explained everything. **1966** *Listener* 20 Oct. 561/1 Old L. B. J. is riddled with anxiety over the thought that we shall go to our graves having got him all wrong. **1968** *Ibid.* 5 Sept. 308/2 Stuart Hood's review of Harold Nicolson's last volume of *Diaries*..ends sympathetically, but begins with a devastating attack on my father's 'snobbishness'... I think, not merely as his son and editor, that they have got him wrong, and are a little uncertain what snobbishness really means. **1974** N. FREELING *Dressing of Diamond* 200 Don't get me wrong; there's no offence meant.

5. a. Not in the right or proper way; in an improper or unfitting manner; improperly, unduly, amiss.

c **1200** ORMIN 10030 Whatt teȝȝ don þe læwedd follc O Drihhtin wrang to trowwenn, & wrang to ledenn þeȝȝre lif, & Drihhtin wrang to þeowwtenn. *a* **1250** *Owl & Night* 196 He wot insyht in euche songe, huo singeþ wel huo singeþ wronge. *a* **1300** *Cursor M.* 12480 Quen þat þai wrang wit iesu delt. *c* **1340** HAMPOLE *Pr. Consc.* 2487 Our gude dedys er ofte done wrang. *c* **1400** *26 Pol. Poems* 107 My wittes on nyȝtes wrong y ware. *c* **1440** *York Myst.* xxxvii. 264 Here workis þou all wrang. **1504** CORNISHE in *Skelton's Wks.* (1568) z v b, If he [*sc.* the harper] play wrong. **1531** TINDALE *Expos. 1st Ep. John* Prol. (1538) 7 b, Because we be wronge taught. *c* **1620** A. HUME *Brit. Tongue* (1865) 11 The south.. pronounces eu, we ou, both, in my simple judgement, wrang. **1755** *Man* xlv. 5 Methods..extremely wrong calculated for promoting the real perfection..of individuals. **1787** JEFFERSON *Writ.* (1859) II. 332 They will amend it whenever they find it works wrong. **1828** *Life Planter Jamaica* 96 The estate was wrong managed. **1881** MISS BRADDON *Asphodel* I. x. 298, I asked him to come on with me... I hope I did not do very wrong. **1897** O. WISTER *Lin M'Lean* 164 Every guest's uneasiness lest he drink his coffee wrong.

b. Out of proper order or due place.

1573 BARET *Alv.* s.v., To put on his shoes Wrong, *inducere calceos alicui præpostere.* **1732** POPE *Ess. Man* I. 50 All the question..Is only this, if God has plac'd him wrong?

c. Clumsily; inelegantly; badly. *rare*$^{-1}$.

1727 BAILEY (vol. II), *Misfashioned*, shapen wrong or illy.

6. *Comb.* **a.** With pa. pples., as ***wrong-directed***, †***-feigned***, ***-grounded***, ***-ordered***, ***-screwed***, ***-timed***.

1768–74 TUCKER *Lt. Nat.* (1834) II. 371 A dull, or careless, or *wrong-directed application. **1513** BRADSHAW *St. Werburge* II. 1852 Subtell policy and *wrong-feyned euidens. **1768–74** TUCKER *Lt. Nat.* (1834) II. 80 *Wrong-grounded piety and obstinacy. *a* **1586** *Sidney's Arcadia* Wks. 1922 II. 214 To heare The poore-clad truth of loves *wrong-ordred lot. **1849** CUPPLES *Green Hand* xiii. (1856) 122 As if one saw through a *wrong-screwed glass. **1740** RICHARDSON *Pamela* II. 111 Don't let a little *wrong-timed Bashfulness take place.

b. With strong pa. pples., as †***wrong-take***(***n***; †**wrong-gotten** *a.*, unjustly obtained; ill-gotten.

a **1300** *Cursor M.* 27867 Til wrang takin [þ]yng [*v.rr.* wrang(e) þing] be quite again. **1388** *Wyclif's Sel. Wks.* III. 472 If he..make restitucioone of wrong-goten godis. *c* **1400** *26 Pol. Poems* 97 He þat ful is fylde Wiþ wrong take pore mennys thrift. *c* **1425** in *Anglia* VIII. 156/10 Summe men ..þat hadde mykel spendid..of wrange-goten goodes. *c* **1440** *Alph. Tales* 202 It was all of robbery & of wrong-getten gudis.

c. With vbl. sbs. and pres. pples., as ***wrong-believing***, ***-going***, ***-thinking***, ***-voting***; also †***wrong-wresting***, = turning aside; **wrong-reading** *a.*, such as can only be read after being first reversed by a mirror.

a **1560** PHAER *Æneid* IX. Cc iv, The winds vpcaught that stroke, and Iuno Queene the daunger brake Wrongwresting as it went. **1652** H. BELL *Luther's Colloq.* iv. 90 Superstitions and wrong-believings. **1850** J. BROWN *Disc. our Lord* I. 367 Our short-comings and wrong-goings. **1857** GEN. P. THOMPSON *Audi Alt.* I. xlvi. 184 Depriving wrong-voting officers of their commissions. **1877** HUXLEY *Techn. Educ., Sci. & Cult.* (1881) 66 Clear and consecutive wrong-thinking is the next best thing to right-thinking. **1955**, **1967** [see *right-reading* s.v. RIGHT *adv.* 16 b].

wrong (rɒŋ), *v.* Also *α.* 5 **wronge**, 6 *arch.* **wrongen**; *β.* 4– (latterly *Sc.* and *north. dial.*) **wrang**, 9 *n.e. Sc.* **vrang**. [f. WRONG *a.*]

I. *trans.* **1.** To do wrong or injury to (a person); to treat with injustice, prejudice, or harshness; to deal unfairly with, withhold some act of justice from (some one).

In frequent use from *c* 1600.

α. *c* **1330** R. BRUNNE *Chron. Wace* (Rolls) 11868 Þen schul we ryghte, þat now vs wranges. *c* **1400** *Apol. Lollards* 64 Now are iust men oft wrongid, and schrewis vnpunischid. **1479** *Paston Lett.* III. 266 He wyll be with me ayenst myn oncle in iche mater..that he entendyth to wrong me in. **1496–7** *Act 12 Hen. VII*, c. 12 §4 At the complaynte of the Constable..in the name of any party so hurted or wronged. **1526** *Pilgr. Perf.* (W. de W. 1531) 38 Shewynge hymselfe to be rather glad to be so despysed & wronged. **1596** SPENSER *State Irel.* Wks. (Globe) 623 By this Statute the sayd Irish Lord is wronged, for that he is cutt of from his customarye services. **1611** BIBLE *Prov.* viii. 36 Hee that sinneth against me, wrongeth his owne soule. **1654** BRAMHALL *Just Vind.* iv. (1661) 73 Why should it be in the power of a subject..to wrong his Prince and his Country? **1697** DRYDEN *Æneis* VII. 515 To this false Foreigner you give your Throne, And wrong a Friend, a Kinsman, and a Son. **1720**, etc. [see RIGHT *v.* 7]. **1748** RICHARDSON *Clarissa* (1768) I. 172 Vilely suspicious of..[his servants] wronging him..he is always changing. **1792** *Anecd. W. Pitt* II. xxix. 141 The Americans have been wronged. They have been driven to madness by injustice. **1839** DICKENS *Nickleby* xx, [That] day of reckoning..will be a heavy one for you if they are wronged. **1881** *Act 44–45 Vict.* c. 58 §180 (2 *d*), An officer..who thinks himself wronged by his commanding officer.

refl. **1598** SHAKS. *Merry W.* III. iii. 178 Good master Ford, be contented: You wrong your selfe too much. **1683** D. A. *Art Converse* 88 We wrong ourselves if we oppose their Sentiments. **1860** TENNYSON *Sea Dreams* 168 His gain is loss; for he that wrongs his friend Wrongs himself more.

β. **1423** JAS. I *Kingis Q.* xcii, Thus were thai wrangit that did no forfet. *c* **1459** *Reg. Aberbrothoc* (Bann. Cl.) II. 105 Ewyl myndit personis..wrangis and tribulis ws. *c* **1540** *Dr. Doubble Ale* a iv b, Some wolde he shuld be hanged Or els he shulde be wranged. **1596** DALRYMPLE tr. *Leslie's Hist. Scot.* (S.T.S.) II. 182 J suffirit him nocht in ane iot to be wrangte. **1784** COWPER *Task* III. 101 Hypocrisy, detest her as we may, (And no man's hatred ever wrong'd her yet) May claim this merit. **1792** BURNS *Bonie Lesley* iv, He'd look into thy bonie face, And say, 'I canna wrang thee'. **1793** R. GRAY *Poems* 27 Some silent sang, And glow'rt as they were wranged. **1825** JAMIESON *Suppl.* s.v.

b. To violate or do violence to; to treat unfairly or without due respect.

c **1449** PECOCK *Repr.* I. xiii. 70 So that he not wrongee [*sic*] the lawe of kinde..neither therbi wrongee Holi Scripture. **1592** *Soliman & Pers.* III. i, Spare me not, for then thou wrongst my honour. **1602** SHAKS. *Ham.* V. ii. 263, I do receiue your offer'd loue like loue And wil not wrong it. **1670** DRYDEN *Conq. Granada* III. i, You wrong our Friendship when your Right you name. **1706** E. WARD *Wooden World Diss.* (1708) 45 Without wronging the Rule of the Gospel. **1775** SHERIDAN *Duenna* III. vi, I would return it, but that I must touch it that way, and so wrong my oath. **1784** BURNS *1st Epist. to Davie* viii, To say aught less wad wrang the cartes, And flatt'ry I detest. **1808** SCOTT *Marm.* III. Introd. 111 The friendship thus thy judgment wronging With praises not to me belonging. **1847** TENNYSON *Princ.* VII. 221 She pray'd me not to judge their cause from her That wrong'd it. **1848** DICKENS *Dombey* xix, Rely on my not wronging your forbearance and consideration. **1855** TENNYSON *Maud* IV. iii, You wrong your beauty..in being so proud. **1861** READE *Cloister & H.* xlvii, Well then, mother, she is comely, and wrongs her picture but little.

2. To deprive or dispossess (a person) wrongfully *of* something; to cheat, defraud.

c **1484** *Plumpton Corr.* (Camden) 64 [He] is injuried & wronged of his tennor in Arkenden, contrarie to right and concience. **1594** KYD *Cornelia* IV. 208 A Cittizen so wrong'd Of the honor him belong'd. **1660** *Myst. Good old Cause* 13 He hath wrong'd him of a great estate. **1730** SWIFT *Let. to Esquire* 3 Jan., You wronged me of half my due. **1773** R. FERGUSSON *Ghaists* 98 The succeeding generations [to] wrang O' braw bien maintenance. **1839** THACKERAY *Fatal Boots* Jan., I never wronged any man of a shilling. **1840** DICKENS *Old C. Shop* lx, Ask anybody..whether I have ever wronged them of a farthing. **1871** W. ALEXANDER *Johnny Gibb* xlv, [He wants] to vrang no man o' 's money.

ellipt. **1607** ROWLANDS *Diog. Lanth.* (Hunter. Cl.) 34 Haue I wrong'd thee in all my life, Mouthfull of Hay or Grasse?

3. To do injustice to (a person) by statement, imputation, opinion, etc.; to impute evil to, asperse or calumniate undeservedly; to discredit or dishonour by word or thought.

1594 SHAKS. *Rich. III*, IV. iv. 421 *Queene.* Shall I forget my selfe, to be my selfe? *Rich.* I, if your selfes remembrance wrong your selfe. **1599** PEELE *David & Bethsabe* B ij b, Woman thou wrongst the King, & doubtst his honour. **1620** *Jrnls. Ho. Comm.* I. 535 His first Speech should be, to clear himself from Suspicion of wronging this House. **1634** W. TIRWHYT tr. *Balzac's Lett.* (vol. I) 120 Nor will I believe he was made after the image of God, lest therein I should wrong so excellent a nature. **1667** PEPYS *Diary* 27 July, He says that the Duke of York is suspected..; but that he do know that he is wronged therein. **1713** ADDISON *Cato* III. i, Thou wrong'st me, if thou think'st Ever was love..like mine. **1782** COWPER tr. *Mme. Guion, Happy Solitude* 9 Thy creatures wrong thee, O thou sov'reign Good! Thou art not lov'd, because not understood. **1795–6** WORDSW. *Borderers* I. 167, I wot not what ill tongue has wronged him with you. **1823** SCOTT *Quentin D.* vi, He wronged his uncle, however, in supposing [etc.]. **1836** LYTTON *Duchess de La Vallière* III. v, My foolish fancies wronged him! **1861** TENNYSON *In Mem.* l, I wrong the grave with fears untrue.

4. To cause undeserved physical harm or injury to (a person, etc.); to affect harmfully or injuriously; to hurt or damage. Now *Sc.*

1595 SPENSER *Epithal.* 49 For feare the stones her tender foot should wrong. **1617** MORYSON *Itin.* I. 37 The people after dinner, warmed with drinke, are apt to wrong any stranger. **1634** SIR T. HERBERT *Trav.* 211 One [fruit] out of curiositie I tasted of, which . . malignantly bit and wronged my mouth and lips. **1683** MOXON *Mech. Exerc., Printing* xiii. ¶5 The edges of his Graver . . may, in a slip, touch upon the Side and Face of the next Stroak, and wrong that more or less. **1712** J. JAMES tr. *Le Blond's Gardening* 151 Without breaking or wronging the greater Roots. *a* **1722** LISLE *Husb.* (1757) 376 Those boughs also . . draw all the sap to them and wrong the rest that are weaker. **1793** R. GRAY *Poems* 54 A gude man loves his beast, And will not wrange him. **1826** R. HETRICK *Poems* 92 Is't 'cause some farmer's wranged his pechan At some drunk frolic.

refl. **1620** VENNER *Via Recta* viii. 190 They . . greatly erre and wrong themselues, that . . surcharge their bodies with ouer-much meat. **1899** J. B. SALMOND *Man Sandy* xiii. 93 Blair leuch till I thocht he wudda wranged himsel'.

†**b.** To impair or injure the quality or substance of (something); to affect detrimentally or harmfully; to mar, spoil. *Obs.*

1592 KYD *Sp. Trag.* II. iii. 46 If she . . forgoe his loue, She both will wrong her owne estate and ours. **1630** in *Smith's Wks.* (Arb.) II. 898 All authoritie being dissolved, want of government did more wrong their proceedings, than [etc.]. **1638** W. M. *Garcia's Sonne Rogue* 149, I was constrained . . with the force of my sneezing to wrong my breeches. **1639** S. DU VERGER tr. *Camus' Admir. Events* Pref., Do not scoffe at the Histories, being good in themselves, though wronged by my want of language. **1661** PEPYS *Diary* 8 Jan., 'The Widdow', an indifferent good play, but wronged by the women being to seek in their parts. *a* **1700** EVELYN *Diary* 30 May 1662, Her teeth wronging her mouth by sticking a little too far out. **1784** COWPER *Task* VI. 748 Sweet is the harp of prophecy; too sweet Not to be wrong'd by a mere mortal touch.

5. *Naut.* To outsail (another vessel); to outdo or surpass in sailing; also = BLANKET *v.* 2. ? *Obs.*

1685 T. PHELPS *Captiv.* 2 We had try'd his sailing all ways, but found we could not wrong him any way. **1691** T. H[ALE] *Acc. New Invent.* p. vi, One Ship is said to wrong another, that exceeds it in swiftness of sailing. **1727** S. BRUNT *Voy. to Cacklogallinia* 21 Our Sloop wrong'd 'em so much, that we soon came up with, and took them. **1748** SMOLLETT *R. Random* lxv, We were very much wronged by the ship that had us in chase. **1760** C. JOHNSTON *Chrysal* I. I. x. 73 The officers [of an English man-of-war] . . observed they wronged her so much, they could go round her if they pleased. **1867** SMYTH *Sailors' Word-bk.* 739 To outsail a vessel by becalming her sails is said to wrong her.

II. *intr.* †**6.** To act wrongly, harmfully, or injuriously; to do wrong (*to* a person, etc.). *Obs.*

1390 GOWER *Conf.* I. 262 For whan that holi cherche wrongeth, I not what other thing schal rihte. *Ibid.* II. 389 God and . . the world . . Largesse awaiteth as belongeth, To neither part that he ne wrongeth. *c* **1460** *Oseney Reg.* 61 Our beloued sonnys Abbot and Couent . . shewed þat Richard Clerke and summe oþer . ., vppon tithis possessions and oþer thynges . ., wronge to þe same. **1540** *Rec. Elgin* (New Spald. Cl.) I. 49 The assise deliuerit that Angnes Baldon wrangit in the . . breking of Katerine Falconeris heid. **1613** W. BROWNE *Brit. Past.* I. i. 119, I wrong to say so. *a* **1676** HALE (J. s.v. *Higgle*), It argues an ignoble mind, where we have wronged, to higgle and dodge in the amends.

7. To heel over. (Cf. RIGHT *v.* 6 c.) *nonce-use.*

1842 DICKENS *Amer. Notes* ii, The ship rights. Before one can say 'Thank Heaven!' she wrongs again.

Hence '**wronging** *ppl. a.*

1845 J. C. MANGAN *German Anthol.* II. 60 That strong . . devotion which . . saved from wronging stain the sacred garland of Homage.

wrong-doer ('rɒŋ,du:ə(r)). Also **wrongdoer**. [f. WRONG *sb.*^{2} + DOER.] One who does wrong.

1. One who commits wrongful, unjust, or blameworthy acts; one who transgresses or offends against the moral law.

1387-8 T. USK *Test. Love* II. xiii. (Skeat) l. 18 Suche maner badnesse, whiche is used to purifye wrong-doers, is som-what. *c* **1450** tr. *De Imitatione* III. li. 123, I knowe hov all þinge is doon, I knowe þe wronge doer & suffrer. *c* **1460** FORTESCUE *Abs. & Lim. Mon.* iv. (1885) 116 That he defende his peple ayenst wronge doers inwarde bi justice. *Ibid.*, All the wronge doers of þe reaume. *a* **1513** FABYAN *Chron.* (1811) 307 Wyllyam, which was . . a defendor of ye pore people agayne extorcioners & wronge doers, was by them put wrongfully to deth. *a* **1586** SIDNEY *Arcadia* II. xxii, She resolved to spende all her yeares . . in . . praying for the wrong-dooer. **1612** BP. HALL *Contempl., O.T.* IV. ii. ¶11 Who is so ready to except and exclaim as the wrong doer? **1660** R. COKE *Power & Subj.* 183 [That] the King . . may both govern and rule . . the Holy Church, and that he defend the same from wrong-doers. **1703** ROWE *Ulysses* III. i, Vindictive Jove prepares his Thunder. Let the Wrong-doer and the Tyrant tremble. **1795-6** WORDSW. *Borderers* v. 2071 He forgave The wrong and the wrong-doer. **1849** MACAULAY *Hist. Eng.* v. I. 646 They were . . men of blameless life, and . . were regarded . . not as wrongdoers, but as martyrs. **1880** W. H. D. ADAMS *Wrecked Lives* Ser. I. p. iv, The unerring Nemesis of Failure dogs the footsteps of the wrongdoers.

2. *Law.* One who is guilty of a wrong, tort, or trespass; a trespasser, tort-feasor; a law-breaker.

1501 *Nottingham Rec.* (1885) III. 306 The seid Mayrez and brethern . . shall . . punysshe the wrongdoers therin in such maner as they may lawfully do. **1628** COKE *On Litt.* 181 For that [action] maketh him a wrong doer. **1642** —— *Inst.* II. 168 If the goods or merchandises . . be . . taken away by certaine wrong doers not knowne. **1726** AYLIFFE *Parergon* 171 If any Seat . . be taken away by a Stranger, the Church-warden . . may have their Action against the Wrong-doer. **1768** BLACKSTONE *Comm.* III. 182 A writ of entry in the post . . only alleges the injury of the wrong-doer. **1818** CRUISE *Digest* (ed. 2) V. 142 For the same acts that are good, when done by the person who has right, are not sufficient in the case of a wrong-doer. **1856** *N. Brit. Rev.* XXVI. 271 Shall the master . . be answerable pecuniarily to the dead man's widow, or shall it be the wrong-doer? **1911** *Times* 17 May 3/4 He . . denied that the mere fact . . relieved a wrongdoer from paying damages.

wrong-doing ('rɒŋ,du:ɪŋ), *vbl. sb.* Also **wrongdoing**. [f. as prec. + DOING *vbl. sb.*] The action of doing wrong or amiss, or the fact of wrong being done.

1. Transgression of or offence against the moral or established law; reprehensible action or behaviour; evil-doing, misdoing; misconduct.

Rare before 19th c. In frequent use from *c* 1860.

1480 *Coventry Leet Bk.* 444 The Priour & Couent . . desiren restitucion of such wrongedoyng. **1547** LATIMER in Foxe *A. & M.* (1563) 1352 He that is so obstacle and vntractable in wickednes and wronge doing. **1681** ROBERTSON *Phraseol. Gen.* 1355 To withstand the doing of wrong; to be against wrong doing, *obsistere injuriæ*. **1828-32** WEBSTER. **1837** HT. MARTINEAU *Soc. Amer.* III. 10 The idea of honour is such as to exclude all fear, except of wrong-doing. **1858** GEN. P. THOMPSON *Audi Alt.* lxxv. II. 25 It is the rule of heaven, that wrong-doing shall bring sorrow. **1891** FARRAR *Darkn. & Dawn* xxii, To act [thus] . . would have been to betray uneasiness and confess wrongdoing.

2. A wrongful or blameworthy action.

1874 M. CREIGHTON *Hist. Ess.* i. (1902) 21 A wrong-doing of which it felt no guilt. **1899** CROCKETT *Kit Kennedy* 245 [She] seemed to have suffered for every body else's wrong-doings.

wrong-doing, *ppl. a. rare.* [f. as prec. + *doing*, pr. pple. of DO *v.*] That does wrong, harm, or ill; prone to or committing wrongful actions.

c **1400** *Rule St. Benet* (Prose) xxxi. 23 Þat te celeresse sal . . be meke, and sobur, and noht . . noius, ne wrangdoande [L. *injuriosus*]. **1718** PRIOR *Solomon* III. 205 The . . violent Will of the wrong-doing Great. **1901** *Daily News* 3 Jan. 6/1 The populations of wrong-doing cities must pay.

wronge, etc., obs. pa. t. and pple. of WRING *v.*

wronged (rɒŋd), *ppl. a.* [f. WRONG *v.* + -ED^{1}.]

1. Of persons, etc.: Wrongfully, unfairly, or unjustly treated; affected harmfully or prejudicially; injured.

a **1547** SURREY *Æneid* IV. 462 The wronged hed by me of my deare sonne, Whom I defraud of the Hisperian crown. **1561** NORTON & SACKV. *Gorboduc* I. ii, The smaller compasse that the realme doth holde, . . The nearer [is] justice to the wronged poore. **1593** SHAKS. *Rich. III*, v. iii. 121 The wronged Soules Of butcher'd Princes. **1622** MABBE tr. *Aleman's Guzman d'Alf.* II. 178 A wronged womans reuenge. **1681** OTWAY *Soldier's Fort.* v. (1735) 111 Take this wrong'd Lady home and use her handsomely. **1709** ATTERBURY *Serm.* (1726) II. 221 He resolves to make Personal Restitution, where the Wrong can be discover'd and the wrong'd Person reach'd. **1806** SURR *Winter in Lond.* II. 104 Some wronged female orphan of this old Abbey. **1848** DICKENS *Dombey* xxiii, Two dragon sentries . . on duty over the wronged innocence imprisoned. **1891** FARRAR *Darkn. & Dawn* viii, The knight . . was charged with favour towards the wronged Britannicus.

absol. **1582** MULCASTER *Elementarie* (1925) 264 The name of Christians, which verie title enioyneth a serch to avoyd contention, euen by submission of the wronged. **1691** MAYDMAN *Nav. Spec.* 187 That the strong Man be . . made to restore the Wronged to his Right. **1864** [see WRONGER]. **1891** J. K. STEPHEN *Quo Musa Tendis?* 35 When the wronger falls and the wronged wins bays.

2. Of things: Subjected to detriment, prejudice, or unfavourable bias.

1632 J. HAYWARD tr. *Biondi's Eromena* 25 The vengeance of my wronged honour. **1644** MILTON *Divorce* (ed. 2) 4 He therefore . . shall restore the much wrong'd and over-sorrow'd state of matrimony. **1652** BENLOWES *Theoph.* II. lxi, She sees defamed Glory, wronged Right. **1849** LYTTON *K. Arthur* v. viii, On thy wronged grave one hand appeasing lays The humble flower. **1875** BROWNING *Aristoph. Apol.* 125 Strain a point the other way, And handsomely exaggerate wronged truth!

†**b.** Perverted. *Obs. rare*$^{-1}$.

1619 A. NEWMAN *Pleas. Vis.* C 3 b, Besides, preferments would attend On me that I might be the end, Whereat Mens wronged thoughts might aime.

3. Diseased; having the normal functions disordered.

1634 T. JOHNSON *Parey's Chirurg. Wks.* XV. ii. 562 Great paine in the interim torments the patient by reason of the wronged periostium. *Mod. Sc.* A wranged stomach.

†**wrongeld.** *Obs. rare.* Also **wrongeyeld**. [? f. WRONG *sb.*^{1} + *yeld* YIELD *sb.*] A form of tallage.

1340 in *Cal. Rotulorum Patent.* (1802) 137/2 Rex confirmavit relaxacionem Thomæ Comitis Norff[olk] . . concessam tenentibus suis . . manerij de Lopham . . de quodam tallagio vocato Wrongelde. [Cf. *Ibid.* (1898) 545 Le Wrongeyeld.]

wrongen, obs. var. WRUNG *ppl. a.*

wronger ('rɒŋə(r)). Also 4 **wrongar**. [f. WRONG *v.* + -ER^{1}. Cf. LG. *wranger* distorter.]

1. One who wrongs another; a person who does wrong or amiss; an inflicter of wrong, harm, or injury; a wrong-doer.

Freq. from *c* 1840 (often contrasted with *wronged*).

c **1449** PECOCK *Repr.* v. xiii. 549 Defenders aȝens wrongers and diffamers of the . . wickid world. **1591** SPENSER *M. Hubberd* 1098 That he should warne the wronger to appeare . . at Court, it to defend. **1594** BARNFIELD *Sheph. Content* xxv, If any by his fellowes be opprest, The wronger . . Shall be well bangd. *a* **1618** [see WRINGER]. **1667** *Phil. Trans.* II. 457 A great Wronger of our Nation. **182.** E. ELLIOT *Corn Law Rhymes* (1904) 23 In our prayers, If we forget our wrongers, may we be Vile as their virtues. **1864** TREVELYAN *Compet. Wallah* (1866) 228 Utterly unable to make out whether his client was the wronged or the wronger, guilty or not guilty. **1895** W. WATSON *Purple East* (1896) 16 A charge from Him Who watches . . To smite the wronger with thy destined rod.

2. An injurer or misuser *of* something.

1591 *Troub. Raigne K. John* ii. 152 Arme thee, traytor, wronger of renowne. **1610** BEAUM. & FL. *Faithf. Sheph.* IV. i, Learn not to be a wronger Of your word; was not your promise laid. *a* **1625** —— *Noble Gent.* I. i, Do not give thy self . . so open vile, So great a wronger of thy worth, so low. **1727** BAILEY (vol. II), *Wranglands* (old Records), misgrown Trees that will never prove Timber, q.d. Wrongers of Land.

wrong-foot (stress variable), *v. trans.* [f. WRONG *a.* + FOOT *sb.*] **1.** In tennis, football, etc.: (by deceptive play) to cause (an opponent) to have his balance on the wrong foot.

1928 [implied at the vbl. sb. below]. **1959** *Times* 7 Sept. 15/5 Viney and Hasty caught the defence wrong-footed. **1960** E. S. & W. J. HIGHAM *High Speed Rugby* xi. 136 You could pick up the ball as though to go one side, and then, having picked up the ball, swing to the other side. . . It will wrong-foot the attackers, thereby giving you more time for your kick. **1960** *Times* 29 Nov. 17/4 Truman found himself being wrong-footed by masked drop-shots [in squash rackets]. **1967** J. POTTER *Foul Play* (1968) ii. 28 The younger Fitch was holding forth about his patent method of wrong-footing full backs. **1976** DEXTER & MAKINS *Testkill* 21 Abbott, playing back instinctively, was wrong-footed, bat adrift in his hands.

2. *fig.* To disconcert by an unexpected move; to catch unprepared.

1957 F. HOYLE *Black Cloud* iv. 79 'Let me tell you . . that the Government has made enquiries and we are not at all satisfied with the accuracy of your report.' Kingsley was wrong-footed. **1963** 'W. HAGGARD' *High Wire* xii. 130 The tall man's technique was precisely calculated to put him at a disadvantage. . . Somehow they could always wrong-foot you. **1971** A. HUNTER *Gently at Gallop* xii. 128 They sensed he was close, and they were trying to wrong-foot him. **1983** *Listener* 6 Jan. 5/1 What happens in Washington, Moscow and Geneva will leave British political leaders moving quickly in order not to be wrong-footed. **1984** *Daily Tel.* 5 July 1/2 A walk-out would wrong-foot the union in its endeavour to appear ready for negotiations at all times.

Hence **wrong-footing** *vbl. sb.* and *ppl. a.*

1928 *Daily Tel.* 7 Aug. 12/3 His ground strokes had not the same speed and polish as Austin's, nor could he steer all his volleys into the same wrong-footing area. **1971** LAVER & COLLINS *Educ. of Tennis Player* xvi. 216 Wrong-footing is hitting to the place your opponent has just vacated. **1980** *Sunday Times* 17 Apr. 42/5 They emerge as wry, reflective, deliberately wrong-footing to outsiders.

wrongful ('rɒŋfʊl), *a.* Also 5 **wrangful**. [f. WRONG *sb.* + -FUL.]

1. Full of wrong, injustice, or injury; marked or characterized by wrong, unfairness, or violation of equity; unfair.

c **1311** [see WRACKFUL *a.*^{2}]. **1338** R. BRUNNE *Chron.* (1810) 211 Pandolf proued þe kyng, in his disputeson, He mayntend wrongfulle þing, & wild to no reson. **1390** GOWER *Conf.* I. 358 Of his wrongful herte he demeth That al is wel. *c* **1445** PECOCK *Donet* 94 Þouȝ al þis lijf be foule, peynful, . . vnkynde, wrongful. ? **1520** LD. J. BUTLER in Ellis *Orig. Lett.* Ser. II. II. 51 There is noo thinge so unjuste or so wrongfull but our Deputie here . . wolde . . suffer . . the same. **1553** ASCHAM *Germany* 10 This fact was very wrongfull of the Pope for the deede. **1608** *Yorksh. Trag.* I. ii, Heape not wrongfull shame On her. **1697** DRYDEN *Æneis* VI. 581 Nor want they lots, nor judges to review The wrongful sentence. **1810** SOUTHEY *Kehama* II. iv, In that wrongful and upbraiding tone Kehama found relief. **1859** I. TAYLOR *Logic in Theol.* 261 A wrongful policy may be maintained. **1879** TOURGEE *Fool's Err.* xl. 301 He regarded slavery simply as an unnatural and wrongful accident.

b. Of actions: Performed, executed, or done unjustly, unfairly, or harmfully; injurious, harmful; unjust.

c **1325** *Spec. Gy Warw.* 618 Þe kinde of þi manhede Wolde haue wreche of wrongful dede. **1390** GOWER *Conf.* I. 358 Thei wrongfull werres usen. *c* **1400** LOVE *Bonavent. Mirr.* (1908) 186 Ȝeuynge occasioun of offence . . by envie, false couetise, and wrongful demynge. **1502** *Ord. Crysten Men* (W. de W. 1506) IV. viii. Q iv b, In suche maner that the stroke or the betynge after ye ryght may be sayd cruell & wrongfull. *a* **1586** SIDNEY *Arcadia* II. vi, Where daunger would offer to make any wrongfull threatning upon him. *a* **1667** JER. TAYLOR (J.), He . . must redeem his fault by alms, according to the value of his wrongful dealing. **1727** BAILEY (vol. II), *Usurping*, a wrongful taking that which is another's Right. **1839-40** WORDSW. *Sonn.*, '*Fit retribution*' 5 She plants well-measured terrors in the road Of wrongful acts. **1877** E. R. CONDER *Basis of Faith* v. 203 Passion, prejudice, and corrupt self-interest make wrongful entrance.

†**2.** Of persons: That commits wrong; that does wrong or injustice *to* (or *against*) another. Cf. WRONG *a.* 4. *Obs.*

1382 WYCLIF *Luke* xii. 58 Lest perauenture . . the domesman bitake thee to the wrongful axere, and the wrongful axere sende thee in to prisoun. *a* **1425** *Cursor M.* 2204 (Trin.), Þis nembrot [was] . . wrongful emperour, Robber & monqueller greet. *Ibid.* 11539 Wrooþ wex þat wrongful [*v.r.* wrangwis] kyng [= Herod]. **1549** COVERDALE, etc. *Erasm. Par. Rom.* 25 It foloweth not that God is to any man wrongfull. *Ibid. 1 Cor.* 40 Yf we ryse not, . . bothe you and I . . are also founde wrongful agaynst god. *a* **1586** SIDNEY *Ps.* XXXVIII. x, Mighty wrongfull foes, Who do evill for good. **1614** R. HARRIS *Samuels Funerall* (1618) 22, I shall be wrongfull to conceale the other.

3. a. That is contrary to law, statute, or established rule; unlawful, illegal, tortious.

c **1386** CHAUCER *Pars. T.* ¶567 To yeuen conseil to areysen wrongful custumes and taillages. **1459** *Paston Lett.* I. 454 The wrongfull entre . . made upon serteyn personys feffyd to myn use. **1483** *Nottingham Rec.* (1883) II. 395 þe seid forcible & wrongfulle entree punysshable grevously by your lawes. **1596** SPENSER *State Irel.* Wks. (Globe) 622/2 The wrongfull distrayning of any mans goodes. **1628** COKE *On Litt.* 277 b, When an estranger that no right hath presenteth to a Church, . . the wrongfull act . . is called an Usurpation. **1729** JACOB *Law Dict.* s.v. *Trespass*, They were the Goods of the Plaintiff, when the Taking will be wrongful. **1766** BLACKSTONE *Comm.* II. ix. 150 Unless the owner . . will declare his continuance to be tortious, or, in common language, wrongful. **1844** MACAULAY *Sp.* 6 June (1854) 327 All the statutes of limitation . . sanction possession which was originally wrongful. **1862** *Chambers' Encycl.* III. 462/1 It was regarded as treason to the king, inasmuch as it was a wrongful detaining of his free liegeman. **1871** FREEMAN *Norm. Conq.* (1876) IV. xvii. 36 To charge Godric with wrongful occupation of the King's land.

b. Of persons: That is such without legitimacy or right; holding office, possession, etc., unlawfully or illegally; having no legal right or claim; = WRONG *a.* 12.

1567 GOLDING *Ovid's Met.* v. 60 In reuengement of the right against the wrongfull heyre. **1597** HOOKER *Eccl. Pol.* v. lxii. § 19 Charge them we cannot as . . wrongfull possessors of that whereunto they haue right. **1612** DRAYTON *Poly-olb.* xii. 359 His . . son . . to death was lastly done, To set his rightful Crown upon a wrongful head. **1768** BLACKSTONE *Comm.* III. 263 Seizing the franchise, or ousting the wrongful possessor. **1835** DICKENS *Sk. Boz, Greenwich Fair*, There is a rightful heir . . ; and a wrongful heir, who loves her too.

†**c.** Unjustly detained. *Obs. rare*$^{-1}$.

1596 SPENSER *F.Q.* v. viii. 27 The Prince . . did of him requere That Damzell, whom he held as wrongfull prisonere.

†**4.** Of the nature of error; mistaken, incorrect, erroneous. *Obs. rare.*

c **1470** *Cath. Angl.* 424/2 (A.), Wrongfulle, *erroneus.* **1562** COOPER *Answ. Priv. Masse* 113 To depende vpon your wrongefull interpretacion of Christes wordes.

wrongfully ('rɒŋfʊlɪ), *adv.* [f. prec. + -LY².] In a wrong or wrongful manner; wrongly.

1. In a manner contrary to the principles of justice or equity; unjustly, unfairly.

In very frequent use from *c* 1400 to *c* 1600.

c **1374** CHAUCER *Troylus* I. 414 If þat I consente, I wrongfully Compleyne i-wys. **1382** WYCLIF *Luke* iii. 14 He seith to hem, Smyte ȝe wrongfulli no man. *c* **1440** *Jacob's Well* 275 þou seest oftyn tyme goode lyuerys suffere wrongefully. **1474** CAXTON *Chesse* I. ii. (1883) 12 He was dampned to deth wrongfully. *a* **1513** [see WRONG-DOER 1]. *a* **1586** SIDNEY *Arcadia* III. xiv, Not to suffer such treasures to be wrongfully hidden. **1634** W. TIRWHYT tr. *Balzac's Lett.* (vol. I) 121 Justice so exact . . that they will not condemn the Devil himself wrongfully. **1697** DRYDEN *Æneis* v. 447 Salius . . pleads the prize is wrongfully conferred. **1759** STERNE *Tr. Shandy* I. xix, When once a vile name was wrongfully or injudiciously given. **1823** SCOTT *Quentin D.* xxvi, If he acted wrongfully, it was in no shape by any precept or example. **1893** MISS CHOLMONDELEY *Diana Tempest* iv, When a man was wrongfully keeping possession of many thousands.

b. In an illegal or unlawful manner; contrary to the law; unlawfully, illegally, tortiously.

1439 *E.E. Wills* (1882) 119 All maner land that is holden by me or yn my name wrongfully. **1480** *Coventry Leet Bk.* 446 Also the people . . hurten the ffysshe in Swanneswelpole be þeir wasshyng ther, which they don wrongfully. **1554** tr. *Littleton's Tenures* III. 115 b, Yf a man wrongfully take my goodes. *a* **1548** HALL *Chron., Edw. IV*, 231 b, Possessions, which wer from you bothe torciously and wrong-fully with holden. **1583** STUBBES *Anat. Abus.* II. (1882) 30 If they possess them [*sc.* their lands] wrongfully, then ought they to surrender their tytle. **1651** HOBBES *Leviath.* II. xxi. 113 A man might enter in to his own Land, (and dispossesse such as wrongfully possessed it,) by force. **1752–3** *Act 26 Geo. II*, c. 19 § 5 Where any such Goods . . are wrongfully bought, sold, or concealed. **1768** BLACKSTONE *Comm.* III. 4 When [another] . . wrongfully detains one's wife, child, or servant. **1810** W. SELWYN *Law Nisi Prius* (ed. 2) II. 1249 Plea, that . . because the gate was wrongfully erected across the same, the defendant pulled it down. **1885** SIR N. LINDLEY in *Law Rep.* 14 *Q.B.D.* 816 The sons' goods were in this case wrongfully seized.

†**2.** In an improper fashion; incorrectly. *Obs.*

1549–50 in Pettus *Fodinæ Reg.* (1670) 91 Where they find any Ground wrought wrongfully by any man, contrary to the right and custom of the Mine. **1551** T. WILSON *Logike* B ij b, Knotty Subtiltees that are bothe false, and wrongfully framed together.

b. Mistakenly; erroneously; falsely.

1743 BULKELEY & CUMMINS *Voy. S. Seas* 180 The Governor was right in his Conjecture, and did not suspect them wrongfully. **1896** *Allbutt's Syst. Med.* I. 123, I am forced to assume, perhaps wrongfully, that [etc.].

wrongfulness ('rɒŋfʊlnɪs). [f. as prec. + -NESS.] The state, quality, or character of being wrong or wrongful; absence of right, equity, or justice; wrongness.

a **1425** *Cursor M.* 7546 (Trin.), Nouþer may iren nor stele were monnes wrongfulnes wele. **1583** GOLDING *Calvin on Deut.* xxxvii. 222/2 To abstaine from anoyance, wrongfulnesse, and violence. **1587** —— *De Mornay* xvi. (1592) 264 Wit is maimed with ignorance, Will with wrongfulnesse. **1647** SPRIGGE *Anglia Rediviva* II. iv. 98 The right or wrongfulness of this that hath been said. **1856** R. A. VAUGHAN *Mystics* (1860) I. I. ii. 13 The summary expulsion of all superstition, wrongfulness, and ill-will. **1866** *Sat. Rev.* 28 Apr. 488/2 [To] allege the wrongfulness of his own acquisition. **1880** MATTHEW *Wyclif's Wks.* 393 On the Wrongfulness of the Clergy holding Secular Office.

†**wrong-half,** *v. Obs. rare.* Also 4 **wrang-halue,** 5 **-half.** [f. WRONG *a.* 10 + HALF *sb.* 1.] *trans.* In fulling: To dress the reverse side of (cloth) in some manner.

a **1400** *Little Red Bk. Bristol* (1900) II. 8 Qe nul folour face amesner . . nul drap al molyn auant qil soit lauee et apparaillee en manere qe home appele *Wranghalued.* **1514** *Coventry Leet Bk.* 640 þat non of the occupacion . . wronghalf no cloth but only vse dobyns or smoth tesyls. **1518** *Ibid.* 659 That no man . . put no cloth to ony walker to full but if he will burle it & wranghalf it within the Cite. *Ibid.*, That hytt be well byrled & . . truly wranghalft.

'**wronghead,** *sb.* and *a.* Also **wrong-head.** [f. WRONG *a.* + HEAD *sb.*¹]

A. *sb.* A perverse or wrong-headed person; one who displays perversity of judgement.

1729 MANDEVILLE *Fab. Bees* II. p. v, There really are such Wrongheads in the World, as will fancy Vices to be encouraged, when they see them expos'd. **1737** BRACKEN *Farriery Impr.* (1756) I. 168 The Family of the Wrong-Heads is . . a very numerous one. **1753** tr. *Genard's School of Man* 189 The part of . . a wronghead acted to perfection. **1822** *Blackw. Mag.* XII. 630 There is another point on which 'the Wrongheads' are equally mistaken. **1853** TRENCH *Proverbs* 57 Obstinate wrongheads, who will take no counsel except from calamities.

B. *adj.* = WRONG-HEADED *a.*

1732 POPE *Hor. Sat.* II. ii. 148 This jealous, waspish, wrong-head, rhyming race. **1850** LEVER *R. Cashel* liii, Tiernay is in one of his wrong-head humours.

wrong head: see WRONG *sb.*¹ 4.

wrong-headed, *a.* (stress variable). Also **wrongheaded.** [f. WRONG *a.*: cf. WRONGHEAD *sb.* and *a.*]

1. Having a perverse judgement or intellect; persistent or obstinate in erroneous opinion; perversely or obstinately wrong.

In frequent use from *c* 1750.

1732 BERKELEY *Alciphr.* VI. § 26 The pious fraud of some wrong-headed Christian. **1751** SMOLLETT *Per. Pic.* xxi, The characters of these wrong-headed enthusiasts. **1809** MALKIN *Gil Blas* VI. i. ⁋5 The most wrong-headed retail dealer in the town. **1848** THACKERAY *Van. Fair* xx, There's no reason she should die or live miserably because you are wrong-headed. **1883** *Daily Tel.* 10 Nov. 5/1 The furious zeal of wrong-headed bigots.

2. Marked or characterized by perversity of judgement.

1735 BERKELEY *Querist* § 436 So long as we entertain a wrongheaded distrust of England. **1753** MISS COLLIER *Art Torment.* I. iv, The wrong-headed anger of her master. **1809** W. IRVING *Knickerb.* IV. i. (1861) 116 Carts that went before the horses; weather-cocks that turned against the wind; and other wrong-headed contrivances. **1838** DICKENS *O. Twist* xviii, Wrong-headed and treacherous behaviour. **1912** *Times* 19 Oct. 5/3 Had her Southern Slav policy been less persistently wrong-headed.

Hence **wrong-'headedly** *adv.*

1737 *Hervey's Mem.* (1848) II. 398 [He] insisted, very wrongheadedly, that he would have his directions in writing. *a* **1776** JOHNSON in Boswell *Life* (1904) I. 30 [The headmaster] was very severe, and wrongheadedly severe. **1866** *Athenæum* 31 Mar. 427/3 The man . . would act very wrongheadedly. **1906** *Daily Chron.* 23 Aug. 3/1 This was to make, wrong-headedly, a toil of pleasure.

wrong-'headedness. Also **wrongheadedness.** [f. prec. + -NESS.]

1. The quality or character of being wrong-headed; perversity of judgement or intellect.

In frequent use from *c* 1850.

1740 CHEYNE *Regimen* p. xii, The Limits that separat Wisdom from Folly, Wrong-headedness from intellectual Sanity. **1752** H. WALPOLE *Lett. to Mann* (1834) III. 5 There is no end of his misfortunes and wrong-headedness. **1792** *Ann. Reg., Hist.* 8 The wrongheadedness and insanity of Mr. Godwin's publication must be admitted. **1834** H. MILLER *Scenes & Leg.* xxiv. (1857) 341 The wrongheadedness of a jury. **1860** GOSSE *Rom. Nat. Hist.* 299 [It] is enough with many to convict the inquirer of wrong-headedness and credulity. **1889** BARING-GOULD *Arminell* xli, Through youthful impetuosity and wrongheadedness I have jumped out of my social world.

2. With *pl.* A perverse or untoward act.

1748 CHESTERF. *Let.* 18 Nov., He was enabled . . to carry them [*sc.* the Powers] on to the main object of the war, notwithstanding their . . separate views, jealousies, and wrongheadednesses.

wronging ('rɒŋɪŋ), *vbl. sb.* [f. WRONG *v.* + -ING¹.] The action of doing wrong or acting wrongfully; an instance of this.

c **1449** PECOCK *Repr.* III. xvii. 395 If remedie of this wronging schulde be do in this wey. *c* **1450** *Godstow Reg.* 416 Without ony wrongyng of the heires . . of the forsaid Thomas. **1549** COVERDALE, etc. *Erasm. Par. 1 John* iv. 51 The man of a worldely spirite prouideth for his owne commoditie at al handes, yea euen with wronging of his brother. **1604** *Ho. Comm. Jrnl.* I. 218/2 [They] were Instruments of . . much wronging and oppressing the People. **1624** *Admiralty Crt. Exam.* 28 April (MS.), That their shippe might . . not bee overpressed with saile to the wrongeinge of her. **1659** *Gentl. Call.* (1696) 7 A wronging, a calumniating even of the very Devil. **1720** A. PETRIE *Rules Good Deportm.* (1877) 116 This not only is a wronging of the Magistrate of his Right, but it wrongs all fair Traders. **1867** A. L. GORDON *Ashtaroth* Wks. (1912) 253 Yet I forgive your wronging, . . I call your bitters sweet.

wrongish ('rɒŋɪʃ), *a.* [f. WRONG *a.* + -ISH.] Somewhat wrong.

1849 CARLYLE in Froude *Life in Lond.* (1884) II. 22 All these paper bundles were written last summer, and are wrongish, every word of them.

wrongless ('rɒŋlɪs). *rare*$^{-0}$. [f. WRONG *sb.*² + -LESS.] Devoid of, free from, wrong.

1755 JOHNSON, *Wronglessly*, adv. (from *wrongless*). [Hence in Ash (1775) and later Dicts.]

wronglessly ('rɒŋlɪslɪ), *adv. rare.* [Cf. prec. and -LY².] Without doing wrong or inflicting injury; harmlessly.

a **1586** SIDNEY *Arcadia* I. xv, He was . . deerly esteemed of her for his exceeding good parts, being honorablie courteous, and wronglesly valiaunt. **1868** G. MACDONALD *R. Falconer* II. 95 Some woman . . may have darkened his story —darkened it wronglessly, it may be with coldness, or only with death.

wrongly ('rɒŋlɪ), *adv.* Also 4 **wrongli, -liche;** 5 *north.* **wrangeli,** 9 *Sc.* and *north. dial.* **wrangly.** [f. WRONG *a.* + -LY². Cf. ON. *rangliga*, Norw. *ranglege*; MSw. *vranglika*, Da. *vrangelig.*]

1. In a wrong, undue, or inappropriate fashion; unfittingly, improperly. Also *Comb.*

1303 R. BRUNNE *Handl. Synne* 11069 Aȝens God, he ys nat quyte þat suffreþ for hys owne profyte Holy cherche wrongly be ȝyue To þo men þat wykkedly lyue. *a* **1586** SIDNEY *Arcadia* III. vii, So wrongly-consorted a power could not resist the ready minded force of Amphialus. *a* **1830** SIR T. LAWRENCE in Williams *Life & Corr.* (1831) I. 131, I began life wrongly, I spent more money than I earned, and accumulated debts. **1848** MRS. GASKELL *Mary Barton* ix, She . . was so afraid of speaking wrongly, that she was silent. **1904** *Daily Chron.* 2 May 5/6 A wrongly-set switch.

b. Inaccurately; incorrectly. Cf. WRONGFULLY *adv.* 2.

1633 [? WARE] *Spenser's State Irel.* Pref. ¶3 b, He deceased at Westminster in the year 1599. (others have it wrongly 1598.) **1690** LOCKE *Hum. Und.* II. xi. § 13. 71 Mad Men, . . having joined together some Ideas very wrongly, . . mistake them for Truths. **1818** CRUISE *Digest* (ed. 2) III. 414 The judgement is evidently misstated, or wrongly printed. **1858** [see URINOMETER]. **1892** *Photogr. Ann.* II. 735 If any houses have been omitted, or wrongly included under any heading.

c. In an erroneous manner; by mistake or misapprehension; erroneously, mistakenly; = WRONGFULLY *adv.* 2 b.

1755 JOHNSON, *Misbeliever*, . . one who holds a false religion, or believes wrongly. **1809–14** WORDSW. *Excurs.* v. 508 What sees he but a creature . . that yearns, Regrets or trembles, wrongly, or too much; Hopes rashly. **1838** JAMES *Robber* iv, You construe what I have said very wrongly. **1884** tr. *Lotze's Logic* 407 To us, rightly or wrongly, general principles appear rather as [etc.]. **1918** *Times Lit. Suppl.* 28 Mar. 147/1 The methods . . have, rightly or wrongly, largely fallen into discredit.

2. In an unfair, unjust, or inequitable manner; unjustly, unfairly; = WRONGFULLY *adv.* 1.

1340 *Ayenb.* 8 And yet zeneȝeþ he more þet deþ oþer porchaceþ ssame oþer harm to oþren wrongliche. **1393** LANGL. *P. Pl.* C. IV. 92 False puple, That by-gylen good men and greueþ hem wrongliche. *c* **1400** *Cato's Morals* in *Cursor M.* App. 1672 A-gaine man riȝtwise striue þou in na wise, ne wrangeli him greue. **1419** *26 Pol. Poems* 69 To wynne wrongly wele, wod þey gan wede. *c* **1450** *Myrr. our Ladye* II. 249 Many of them wrongly wandrynge from the ryghtnes of faythe. *c* **1586** C'TESS PEMBROKE *Ps.* LXIX. ii, Wrongly sett to worke my woe. **1605** SHAKS. *Macb.* I. v. 23 Thou . . would'st not play false, And yet would'st wrongly winne. **1609** DANIEL *Civ. Wars* v. ci, There he had his rightfull punishment, Though wrongly done; and there he lost his head. **1839–40** WORDSW. '*The Roman Consul*' 10 When they by wilful act A single human life have wrongly taken. **1847** C. BRONTE *J. Eyre* viii, I have been wrongly accused.

wrongness ('rɒŋnɪs). [f. as prec. + -NESS.]

†**1.** The state or condition of being curved or crooked; crookedness, wryness. *Obs. rare.*

c **1440** *Promp. Parv.* 534/2 Wrongnesse, of werke, . . *curvitas.* *c* **1475** *Ibid.* 433/2 (K.), Ryth, with owtyn wrongnesse, *rectus.*

2. Want of correctness or exactness; unsuitability or inappropriateness to a desired purpose or end; faultiness, error.

1726 BUTLER *Serm.* 306 There was a Probability, if he could see the whole Reference of the Parts appearing wrong to the general Design, that this would destroy the Appearance of Wrongness and Disproportion. **1796** COLERIDGE *Biog. Lit.* (1847) II. 365 Though not right in itself, it may become right by the greater wrongness of the only alternative—the remaining in neediness and uncertainty. **1831** CARLYLE *Sart. Res.* II. iii, This is indeed a time when right Education is, as nearly as may be, impossible: however, in degrees of wrongness there is no limit. **1871** RUSKIN *Fors Clav.* v. 10 The Botanical lecturer was, to the extremity of wrongness, wrong. **1897** *Westm. Gaz.* 4 Sept. 2/1 Her gown, even her gloves—everything that could be wrong was wrong, with the worst of all wrongness.

3. The character or quality of being morally wrong or wrongful; injustice, wrongfulness.

In frequent use from *c* 1870.

1833 CHALMERS *Const. Man* (1834) I. ii. 100 Malice, envy, falsehood, injustice, irrespective of their wrongness [etc.]. **1843** MIALL in *Nonconf.* III. 1 As if a man's sense of rightness and wrongness were nothing. **1851** H. SPENCER *Soc. Statics* x. § 1. 128 To determine the rightness or wrongness of certain actions. **1881** *Gentl. Mag.* CCL. 164 When nature . . is . . chastising us right and left for our wrongness, it is no time to sit at ease.

4. a. A wrong bent, tendency, or inclination. *rare.*

1736 BUTLER *Anal.* II. v. 203 The Wrongnesses within themselves which the best complain of, and endeavour to amend. **1799** W. GILPIN *Serm.* x. 119 What wrongnesses do such thoughts produce . . in our tempers, in our behaviour!

b. A wrongful, unfair, or faulty act or action; a wrong, injustice.

1856 FABER *Creator & Creature* III. iv. (1858) 457 All our wants..and all our wrongnesses carry their manifold burdens to God's fidelity.

wrongo (ˈrɒŋəʊ, ˈrɒŋgəʊ). *slang* (chiefly *U.S.*). Also **wronggo**. [f. WRONG *a.* + -O².] A bad, dishonest, or untrustworthy person; a 'wrong 'un'. Also, a counterfeit coin.

1937 'J. CURTIS' *You're in Racket Too* xxvi. 264 'Sure it ain't duff?' 'Never brought you nothing that was a wrongo yet, did I?' **1938** J. H. O'HARA *Hope of Heaven* x. 139 If I ever saw a wronggo, that Henderson is it. **1953** T. RUNYON *In for Life* v. 87 Tailoring skill was never called on more than in the case of wrongos. A well-known and disliked phony was likely to get a specially made suit not designed to please. **1968** L. W. ROBINSON *Assassin* vii. 78 Phyllis Carr was a wrongo from the beginning. **1985** 'D. RAYMOND' *Devil's Home* xxxiv. 163 I've had my eye on both of you..and you look like a couple of wrongos to me.

wrongous (ˈrɒŋəs), *a.* Latterly *Sc.* (and *north.*). Forms: *α.* 2–6 **wrangwis** (5 **-wiss(e, -uiss**, 6 **-uis**), 2–5 **wrangwise** (3 **wranc-**), 5 **-uise**, 4–5 **-wys(e**, 4 **wrangewis, -wys**, 5 **vrangwis (-ways, wranwos)**, 6 **wrangwus**; 3 **wrongwise**, 4–5 **-wis, -wys** (5 **-wes, -wos**). *β.* 5– **wrangous** (6 **-eous**), 5–7 **wrangus** (5 **-ws, werangus**, 5–6 **vrangus**, 9 *dial.* **wrangush**), 5 **wrangis**; 5– **wrongous** (5–6, 9 **-eus**, 6, 9 **-eous**, 5 **-ys, -os**, 5–6 **-us**). [Early ME. *wrangwīs*, f. *wrang* WRONG *a.* + *-wīs*, after *rihtwīs* RIGHTEOUS *a.* Cf. MSw. and older Da. *vrangvis*, Sw. *vrångvis* iniquitous, Da. *vrangvis*, Norw. *rangvis*, self-conceited.

The orig. spelling *wrangwis*, *-wise*, survived until the 16th c.; the obscured endings *-wes*, *-wos*, *-wus*, *-os*, etc., appear in the 15–16th c., and *wrangous*, *wrongous*, about the end of the 15th c. Cf. RIGHTEOUS *a.*]

The exact sense is doubtful in the following early example:—? *a* **1200** in Napier *O.E. Glosses* 47/2 *Salebrosos .i. asperos*,..wiþerwyrde, wrangwise, woȝe.

†**1.** Of persons: Acting wrongfully, inequitably, or unjustly; rascally, iniquitous, unjust. *Obs.*

a **1200** *Moral Ode* 256 Þer inne boð..Med-ierne domes men, and wrongwise [*Egerton MS.* wrancwise] reuen. *a* **1300** *Cursor M.* 11539 Ful wrath he wex, þat wrangwis king. *a* **1340** HAMPOLE *Psalter* lxxii. 12 Wrongwis men & couatous. *c* **1400** tr. *Secreta Secret.*, *Gov. Lordsh.* 116 He þat hauys right a longe vysage, ys wrongwys. *c* **1480** HENRYSON *Wolf & Lamb* 157 Wrangous men of fals Intent. **1535** COVERDALE *Ps.* lxxi. 4 He shal..punysh the wrongeous doer. **1567** *Gude & Godlie B.* (S.T.S.) 99 For wrangus men sall end mischeuouslie. *a* **1599** ROLLOCK *On 2 Thess.* (1606) 19 (Jam.) So man by nature is a wrangous and vnjust judge. *c* **1625** BISSET *Rolment* (S.T.S.) II. 162 Princes of Scotland, that war..wrangous usurperis of the crown.

absol. *a* **1300** *Cursor M.* 837 Þe wrangwis wit þar waful wrak þar þai biginning gan to tak.

2. Marked or characterized by wrong, injustice, or unfairness; = WRONGFUL *a.* 1.

a **1200** *Moral Ode* 48 Þer ne scal me us naut binimen mid wrangwise dome. *a* **1300** *Cursor M.* 7548 Godd es euer on rightwis side, Werraiand again wrangwis pride. *c* **1400** *Rule St. Benet* lxv. 43 Thoro þat er raysid..dissensiones, and werangus ordinansis. *c* **1450** *Mirour Saluacioun* (Roxb.) 149 Thi sharppest byndyngs and wrongwys Captivitee. *c* **1470** HENRY *Wallace* IX. 919 Off crystin blud to se it was gret syn, For wrangwis caus. **1535** COVERDALE *Ecclus.* xxxv. 12 Bewarre of wrongeous offeringes, for yᵉ Lorde..regardeth no mans personne. *c* **1550** ROLLAND *Crt. Venus* I. 583 Lufe is wrangous, and lufe is variable. *a* **1578** LINDESAY (Pitscottie) *Chron. Scot.* (S.T.S.) I. 74 It is nocht for no wrangous quarrell that we haue assembellit our selffis. **1617** JAS. I in Halliwell *Lett. Kings Eng.* (1846) II. 143 Every wrong must be judged by the first violent and wrongous ground whereupon it proceeds. *a* **1639** SPOTTISWOOD *Hist. Ch. Scot.* II. (1655) 51 The wrongous judgement and sentence given against them. **1826** GALT *Last of Lairds* xxvi, The wrongeous mischief ye would noo do to the sweet girl. **1830** —— *Lawrie T.* IV. vi, The issues of his wrongous suspicions.

b. Of actions, etc.; = WRONGFUL *a.* 1 b.

a **1300** *Cursor M.* 22276 Þan sal..sone þe anticrist come, ..his werkes wrangwis to fulfill. **1357** *Lay Folks Catech.* (T.) 222 Wrangwise takyng..of othir men godes. *a* **1400** *Relig. Pieces fr. Thornton MS.* 12 A wrangwise wylnynge or ȝernynge to haue any maner of gude that vs awe noghte. *c* **1425** WYNTOUN *Cron.* I. ix. 626 Na war his mercy grete excede Our gilt and our wranguise deid. **1483** in *Acta Dom. Conc.* II. Introd. 102 The actioun..anent the wrangwise occupacioun of the landis. **1517** *Reg. Privy Seal Scotl.* I. 448/1 The wranguis taking or steling of certane money. **1523** CROMWELL in Merriman *Life & Lett.* (1902) I. 31 In wrongus withholding of her Dowre. **1568** in Calderwood *Hist. Kirk* (Wodrow Soc.) II. 444 The alledged investing, and wrongous electioun of the said regent. *c* **1625** BISSET *Rolment* (S.T.S.) I. 8 Pilate beand..vexit in his spreit for..his wrangus doingis. **1907** *Times* 17 April 10/5 A Court of Session action for damages for alleged wrongous certification of lunacy.

3. Not right or justifiable in nature or application; not applicable or proper; unfitting, unsuitable.

a **1350** in Horstm. *Altengl. Leg.* (1881) 29 Ȝe suld haue schame On me to put swilk wrangwys blame. *c* **1460** *Towneley Myst.* xxiii. 551 Yonder is a fals tabyll,.. It is falsly writen, Iwys, This is a wrangwys thyng. *c* **1470** HENRY *Wallace* VIII. 649 Othir sum said, it was the wrangwis place. **1533** BELLENDEN *Livy* (S.T.S.) II. 81 He tuke litil fere how beit he war honorit with wrangwis stile. **1567** *Gude & Godlie B.* (S.T.S.) 174 Allace! this is ane wrangous way. ? *a* **1800** *Lord Ingram* xxv. in Child *Ballads* II. 129/2, I will not father my bairn on you, Nor on no wrongeous man. **1821** *Joseph the Book-Man* 52 Perchance I've play'd some very wrongous prance.

b. Wrongly directed or constituted.

1768 ROSS *Helenore* 17 If Lindy chanc'd..To play a feckless or a wrangous shot. **1845** R. W. HAMILTON *Pop. Educ.* iv. 77 In their improvement, if the State be wrongous and defective, you must raise the State to the people.

4. †**a.** Obtained by illegal, wrongful, or unfair means; ill-gotten. *Obs.*

c **1425** WYNTOUN *Cron.* VI. xiii. 1130 Be thyft, Oppyn refe, or wrangwys gyft,..all I wan The gud. *c* **1480** HENRYSON *Trial Fox* 11 (Bann. MS.), Off wrangus get [*v.r.* geir] cummys wrang successioun. **1533** GAU *Richt Vay* (S.T.S.) 16 Thay that haldis wrangus guidis of thair nichtburs or takis wp wrangus rentis. **1600** HAMILTON in *Cath. Tractates* (S.T.S.) 234 The Ministers dar not teache this restitution of wrangous geir. *a* **1750** in Walker *Bards Bon-Accord* (1887) 180 Wrangous gear can never thrive.

b. *Scots Law.* Contrary to law; unlawful, illegal.

1671 *Reg. Privy Council Scot.* III. 275 Manifest oppression and wrongous imprisonment committed upon the said compleaner. **1700** *Sc. Acts Parlt.* (1823) XI. 213/1 The draught of the Act..for preventing wrongous imprisonments and against undue delayes in tryalls. **1701** *Ibid.* 272–275. **1753** *Scots Mag.* Aug. 420/2 Under the pain of wrongous imprisonment. **1818** SCOTT *Rob Roy* xxx, Dougal will have a good action of wrongous imprisonment and damages agane him. **1854** H. MILLER *Sch. & Schm.* xxii. 473 The pedlar..raised an action for wrongous imprisonment. **1901** *Scotsman* 29 March 6/8 Pursuer claimed..damages for wrongous dismissal.

wrongously (ˈrɒŋəslɪ), *adv.* In later use chiefly *Sc.* Forms: 4–6 **wrangwis-**, 4–5 **-wys-**, 5– **wrongously**, etc. (see WRONGOUS *a.*); also 4–7 **-lie**, 4 **-li**; 5–6 **-le**. [f. prec. + -LY².]

1. In a wrongful, unjust, or evil manner; wrongfully, unfairly, inequitably.

In very freq. (esp. *Sc.*) use from *c* 1425 to *c* 1650.

c **1325** *Metr. Hom.* 32 It schawed..That I led mi lif wrangwislie. *a* **1340** HAMPOLE *Psalter* ix. 12 [People] wrangwisly slane or harmed. *c* **1400** *Relig. Pieces fr. Thornton MS.* 13 Noghte anely he þat wrangwysely getes, bot he þat wrangwysly haldes. **14..** *Guy Warw.* 6500 (Camb. MS.), Þou doyst vncurteslye For to smyte me wrongeuslye. *c* **1440** *Alph. Tales* 48 To pray for me, at I be nott wrongoslie putt to dead. *c* **1460** *Towneley Myst.* vii. 58 If thou swere wrongwosly,.. Thou art worthi grete blame. **1468** in *Surtees Misc.* (1890) 19 Ye tennauntes..have wrangwisly halden & occupies xviij poules feet of ye grounde. **1533** BELLENDEN *Livy* IV. xx. (S.T.S.) II. 123 For þe said law put þe faderis fra þe public landis quhilkis þai wrangwislie possedit. **1535** COVERDALE *Job* xxxiv. 12 God condemneth no man wrongeously. *a* **1615** *Brieue Cron. Erlis Ross* (1850) 17 He was sinistruously and wrongously put out of the Abbay. **1680** ALISON in Thomson *Cloud of Witnesses* (1871) 62 They have..assized and sentenced me wrongously. **1756** BYNG in Beatson *Nav. & Mil. Mem.* (1790) II. 81 The injury done to our characters..which ..[have] been most injuriously and wrongously attacked. **1833** CHALMERS *Const. Man* (1834) I. vi. 242 If one [child] ..on returning..shall find the chair in the possession of another occupier..it has the sense of being wrongously dispossessed. **1862** *Chambers's Encycl.* III. 462 Where a free man is wrongously captured or detained. **1894** HALL CAINE *Manxman* 340 She..slapped the schoolmaster for bating me wrongously.

2. Without good ground or justification; for no sufficient cause or reason; undeservedly.

a **1300** *Cursor M.* 27695 If þou..ever thoro envie Has ani man wreid wrangwisly. *c* **1350** *Relig. Lyrics 14th C.* (1924) 94 My well of my wele sa wrangwysly wryed. *a* **1400** *Gosp. Nicodemus* (G.) 204 Ȝe wrigh [*v.r.* blame] him wrangwisly. **1483** in *Acta Dom. Conc.* II. Introd. 103 The malis of the landis..excepand xli...quhilk it is allegit..that he is wrangwisly chargit with. **1563** WINȜET *Wks.* (S.T.S.) I. 53 Paull at that tyme wes..maist wranguslie persuadit, that all that he did wes..pleasand to God. **1574** in *Maitl. Club Misc.* I. 102 David..declarit that..the kirk wes wranguslie and sinesterlye informit of him. **1639** *Large Declar. Late Tumults Scotl.* 377 Wherein..wee are heavily and wrongously blamed and taxed of many great offences. **1828** E. IRVING *Last Days* 323 To endure reproof wrongously, for Christ's sake. **1885** BURTON *Arab. Nts.* (abr. ed.) III. 115 Let these folk go, for they are wrongously accused.

†**b.** Without due title, claim, or warrant.

14.. in *Anglia* VIII. 164 Hee wrangusly toke to hym þe name of an hirde-man. **1456** SIR G. HAYE *Law Arms* (S.T.S.) 23 Ane othir callit Damas was put in the sege wrangwisly.

†**3.** Incorrectly; = WRONGLY *adv.* 1 b. *Obs.*

1597 SKENE *De Verb. Sign.*, *Bovata Terræ*,..quhilk in sum buikes, is wrangeouslie writtin, *Davata terræ*. **1732** MONRO *Anat. Bones* (ed. 2) 191 A small Cavity..where the *Recti interni minores*, commonly (tho' wrongously) ascribed to Cowper, take their Rise. **1740** in Heslop *Northumbld. Wds.* (1894) 799 Pay'd by..one of ye late stewards, his fourth part of ye money—wrongously given to Ralph Smith.

ˈ**wrongousness.** *Obs.* exc. as *nonce-wd.* In 4 **wrangwisnes**; in 20 **wrongeousness** (after *righteousness*). [f. as prec. + -NESS.] The state or condition of being wrong; wrongfulness.

a **1300** *Cursor M.* 7543 Qua-sa fightes in wrangwisnes, Him helpes noght his Irinnes. *c* **1325** *Metr. Hom.* 136 Sua stroies mare men the lesse, Wit wa and werldes wrangwisnes. **1923** D. H. LAWRENCE *Kangaroo* xvi. 333 The heroic effort to carry out the old righteousness becomes at last sheer wrongeousness.

wrong-slot (stress variable), *v.* [WRONG *adv.* + SLOT *v.*²] In rally driving: to take the wrong road.

1961 *Motoring News* 23 Nov. 10/3 This was a special stage and..Walter had, in effect, only wrong-slotted. **1963** P. DRACKETT *Motor Rallying* iii. 36 We wrong-slotted just before the Gavia and dropped three. **1968** [see ROLL *v.*² 19 a].

Hence **wrong-slotting** *vbl. sb.*

1963 P. DRACKETT *Motor Rallying* iii. 45 Amazing the number of competitors who lose marks because they fail to take into account the extra miles they accrued after wrong-slotting.

wrong 'un (ˈrɒŋ(ə)n). *slang.* Also occas. in standard form **wrong one**. [f. WRONG *a.* + UN, 'UN².] **1.** *Horseracing.* Of a horse: Held in check so as to cause him to lose the race. Also *fig.*

1889 *Sporting Times* 29 June (Farmer), Isabel and Maudie knew the Turf and all its arts—They had often blewed a dollar on a wrong 'un. **1895** BREWER *Dict. Phrase & Fable* 1315 *A Wrong 'un*, a horse which has run at any flat-race meeting not recognised by the Jockey Club. **1935** H. SPRING *Rachel Rosing* xxv. 301 Hansford had never been known to tip a wrong 'un.

2. A bad, dishonest, or untrustworthy person, a rogue or crook; one who has gone wrong (see WRONG *adv.* 2 b).

1892 I. ZANGWILL *Childr. Ghetto* I. xi. 243 'What! aren't you *froom*?' she said... 'No, I'm a regular wrong 'un,' he replied. 'As for phylacteries, I almost forget how to lay them.' **1896** B. L. FARJEON *Betrayal J. Fordham* iv. 299 It don't make black white, 'cause I'm a wrong 'un. **1902** *Daily Tel.* 11 Feb. 10/7 A welsher can be had up for fraud, and anyone who is known as a wrong one is excluded from the racecourse. **1908** A. BENNETT *Old Wives' Tale* III. ii. 295 She was a tremendous—er—wrong 'un here in the forties. Made a lot of money. **1920** D. H. LAWRENCE *Lost Girl* vi. 107 The policeman was now convinced the man was a wrong-'un. **1925** E. WALLACE *King by Night* xiii. 63, I don't suppose there's a 'wrong one' in London that you don't know. **1951** L. P. HARTLEY *My Fellow Devils* 194 She could not..expect him to confess in so many words that he was a wrong 'un. **1978** J. B. HILTON *Some run Crooked* ii. 15 It seemed quite a hobby with her—Teds, and drop-outs and wrong 'uns.

3. *Cricket.* **a.** A ball that calls for defensive play on the part of the batsman. **b.** *spec.* = GOOGLY *sb.*

1897 K. S. RANJITSINHJI *Jubilee Bk. Cricket* iii. 118 Stockwell steadies himself after this, and will not pick another 'wrong 'un'. **1911** E. W. BALLANTINE in *Even. News* 18 Dec. 1/3, I see Hordern got Woolley with a 'wrong 'un'. For the benefit of those who may not grasp what a 'wrong 'un' is, it may here be stated that the 'wrong 'un' is the ball which breaks the opposite way to that indicated by the bowler's action. **1931** *Daily Tel.* 31 July 17/2 Weir deserved better of fate than to be bowled by Peebles' wrong 'un in the last over of the day. **1956** N. CARDUS *Close of Play* 142 These devices were of no use against the mysterious and seemingly illogical spin of the 'wrong 'un'. **1977** *World of Cricket Monthly* June 42/2 Neil showed who was the boss by repeatedly stepping out and driving Gupte's wrong 'uns to the fence.

4. A counterfeit coin.

1899 C. ROOK *Hooligan Nights* iv. 58 Billy the Snide produced a wrong 'un, and bade young Alf plant it at a big house near the Walk.

wrongways (ˈrɒŋweɪz), *adv.* *nonce-wd.* [f. WRONG *sb.*² + -WAYS.] In the direction of wrong-doing.

1922 JOYCE *Ulysses* 389 She beguiled him wrongways from the true path by her flatteries.

†**wrongwende**, *a.* *Obs.*⁻¹ [f. WRONG *a.* + *-wende*, as in *hálwende*, etc. Cf. Norw. *rangvend*.] Distorted, turned aside.

a **1225** *Ancr. R.* 254 Þeo..habbeð þe nebbes wrongwende euerichon frommard oðer, hwon non ne luueð oðer.

wrong-wise, *adv.* [f. WRONG *a.* + WISE *sb.*¹ II.] In a wrong or reverse manner.

1849 ROCK *Ch. of Fathers* IV. xi. 99 The illuminations, that they might be seen in their true position by the people, had to be limned wrong-wise up with regard to the writing. **1903** A. H. LEWIS *Boss* i. 6, I found such stimulus [*sc.* beatings with hickory] to go much against the grain and to grievously rub wrong-wise the fur of my fancy.

†**wroot**, *sb.* *Obs.* In 1 **wrot, urot, uurot**, 4–5 **wrot**, 5 **wrotte, wroughte**. [OE. *wrót*, = MLG. *wrote* (a mole), LG. *wrote*, *wröte*, WFlem. *wroete* (snout). Cf. next and WORT *sb.*³] The snout of a swine, etc.; a proboscis.

c **725** *Corpus Gloss.* (Hessels) B 188 *Bruncus*, wrot. *a* **1100** *Gloss.* in Wr.-Wülcker 118 *Promuscida*, ylpes bile, *uel* wrot. *a* **1325** *Old Age* ii. in *E.E.P.* (1862) 149 Moch me anueþ þat mi dribil druiþ and mi wrot wet. *c* **1375** in Horstm. *Altengl. Leg.* (1875) 43 Þis bestes heore wrot to him gonne beode. **1398** TREVISA *Barth. De P.R.* XIII. xxix. (Tollem. MS.), The sea swyne..piccheþ þe wrot [**1535** snowte] in grauel. *Ibid.* XVIII. xlii. (Bodl. MS.), With his wrotte and snowte he wroteþ vp treen. **14..** *Voc.* in Wr.-Wülcker 587 *Grunnus*,.. a gruyn, or a wrot.

†**wroot**, *v.* *Obs.* Forms: 1 **wrotan**, 2–4 **wroten** (5 **-yn**), 4–7 **wrote** (5 **wroth-**), 4–6 **wroote**, 6–7 **wroot** (5 *Sc.* **wrotte**, 6 **wrutt**). [OE. *wrótan*, = OFris. **wrôta* (WFris. *wrotte*, NFris. *wrote*, *wröte*, *wrät*), MLG. *wroten* (LG. *wröten*), MDu. and Du. *wroeten* (Antwerp dial. *wruten*), OHG. **wrôzian*, *ruozian* to plough up, ON. and Icel. *róta*, (M)Sw. and Norw. *rota*, Da. *rode*), f. *wrót* WROOT *sb.* Cf. ROOT *v.*², WORT *v.*, WROUT *v.*]

1. *intr.* To turn up soil with the snout, as swine in search of food; to dig up the earth by grubbing; = ROOT *v.*² 1. Also in fig. context.

c **725** *Corpus Gloss.* (Hessels) S 689 *Subigo*, wrotu. *a* **1000** *Riddles* XL[I]. 107 Swin, bearȝ bellende on bocwuda won wrotende wynnum lifde. *c* **1200** *Trin. Coll. Hom.* 37 Alse swin, þe uulieð and wroteð and sneuieð aure fule. *c* **1205** LAY. 469 Wilde swin þat wroteð ȝeond þan grouen. *c* **1386** CHAUCER *Pars. T.* ¶83 (Ellesm.), Right as a soughe wroteth in euerich ordure; so wroteth [*other MSS. add* sche, she] hire beautee in stynkynge ordure of synne. *c* **1410** *Master of Game* (MS. Digby 182) v, [Wild boars] wrote in þe grounde with þe rowell of hir snowte. *c* **1420** *Avow. Arth.* xii, The bore..be-gynnus to wrote, He ruskes vppe mony a rote. **1526** *Pilgr. Perf.* (W. de W. 1531) 20 In the wyldernesse of this worlde where they labour & wroote in the erth. *a* **1586** SIDNEY *De Mornay* Pref. ¶2 We..preach the kingdome of heauen, and haue our groynes euer wrooting in the ground. **1587** HARRISON *England* III. viii. (1878) II. 52 Some [sheep] also will wroot for them [*sc.* saffron-bulbs] in verie eger maner. **1612** DRAYTON *Poly-olb.* ii. 320 That cruell Boare, whose tusks turn'd up whole fields of graine, And wrooting, raised hills upon the leuell Plaine. **1641** BEST *Farm. Bks.* (Surtees) 144 To lye it wheare it may bee well wroten amongst with swine and beasts. *Ibid.* 148 Rye-strawe, well wrote amongst.

b. *transf.* Of worms.

c **1308** *Erthe upon Erthe* 2 þan schullen an hundred wormes wroten on þe skin. **13..** *E.E. Allit. P.* C. 467 God wayned a worme þat wrot vpe þe rote. *a* **1425** *Cursor M.* 23281 (Trin.), þo wormes euer shul on hem wrote. **1430-40** LYDG. *Bochas* I. 6435 Lik a werm that wrotith on a tre.

c. Of persons: To turn up the ground. *rare*$^{-1}$.

c **1325** *Orfeo* 239 Now he most bothe digge and wrote, Er he have his fille of rote.

2. *trans.* To turn over, dig or tear up, with the snout, as in grubbing or burrowing; = ROOT *v.*^{2} 2. Occas. with *up*. Also in fig. context.

c **1000** *Ags. Ps.* (Thorpe) lxxix. 13 Hine utan of wuda eoferas wrotað. *a* **1352** MINOT *Poems* vi. 32-33 A were es wroght,..ȝowre walles with to wrote. Wrote þai sal ȝowre dene. *c* **1380** WYCLIF *Sel. Wks.* I. 406 Molde-worpis þat wroten þe erþe. **1398** [see WROOT *sb.*]. *c* **1410** *Master of Game* (MS. Digby 182) xxiv, Rootes þat þei [*sc.* boars] wrote oute of þe erthe. *c* **1440** *Gesta Rom.* 148 (Addit. MS.), There entred a swyne, and the newe plantes..he wroted. **1567** MAPLET *Gr. Forest* 102 The Sow..wrooting vp the clots of the yearth. **1581** J. BELL *Haddon's Answ. Osor.* 29 Cursed be those Swynishe senses, whiche can wroote together all rootes of wickednesse. [**1601** *2nd Pt. Return fr. Parnass.* III. iv. 1390 If his earth wroting snout shall gin to scorne.]

transf. **1535** COVERDALE *Prov.* xv. 27 The couetous man wrutteth vp his owne house.

b. To draw or cast (earth, etc.) by grubbing.

c **1440** *Pallad. on Husb.* I. 802 Light molde aboute and on, anoon let wroote. *Ibid.* III. 445 More [mould] a litel herre vppon hit wrote. *Ibid.* XII. 469 But wete hym ofte, and donge aboute hym wrote.

Hence † **'wrooting** *ppl. a. Obs.*

c **1400** *Lanfranc's Cirurg.* 79 A wroting vlcus [L. *vlcus corosiuum*] is þat of his malice fretiþ [*B.M. Addit. MS.* wroteþ]. **1562** J. HEYWOOD *Prov. & Epigr.* (1867) 132 The wrotyng hogge. **1600** THYNNE *Emblems* (1876) xxiii. 5 With wrootinge groyne..[the] warlike bore Turnes vp and betters that bad lande.

wroot, obs. erron. form of ROOT *v.*^{1}

† **'wrooter.** *Obs.*$^{-0}$ [f. WROOT *v.* + -ER^1. Cf. Du. and older Flem. *wroeter*; WFlem. *wroeter* (snout), also WFris. *wrotter* field-worker.] An animal that roots.

c **1440** *Promp. Parv.* 534 Wrotare, *versor* (K. *verror*).

† **'wrooter**, obs. erron. f. ROOTER^1 I.

1599 NASHE *Lenten Stuffe* Wks. (Grosart) V. 229 Mollyfying the..homely crucifier of Iesus Christ crucifyde & wrooter vp of Pallestine.

wroothe, obs. form of WROTH *a.*

† **'wrooting**, *vbl. sb. Obs.* [f. WROOT *v.* + -ING^1.] The action of grubbing or rooting; the result of this, the furrow made by a pig rooting.

c **1380** WYCLIF *Wks.* (1880) 147 Curatis..resten as mold-warpis in wrotynge of worldly worschipe & erþely goodis. **1379** *Glouc. Cath. MS. 19* No. 1, I. iii. fol. 6 b, Scrophula ys a sore that is lyke a swynes wrotynge. *c* **1440** *Promp. Parv.* 534/2 Wrotynge, of bestys, *versio.* Wrotynge, of a swyne, *scrobs.* **1491** *Cal. Anc. Rec. Dublin* (1889) 333 Whate with wrotyng and tredyng of the saide bestes [*sc.* swine]. **1532** MORE *Confut. Tindale* Wks. 586/1 We must yoke them for breking hedges, and ringe them for wroting.

wropper, dial. f. WRAPPER *sb.*

wros(se, obs. varr. WORSE *a.*

wrot, obs. metathetic var. WART *sb.*

wrotch, etc.: see WRETCH, etc.

wrote, pa. t. and pa. pple. (now *illit.*) of WRITE *v.*

† **wroth**, *sb.*^{1} *Obs.* Also 5 **wrooþ**, **wrooth**, 5, *Sc.* 6 **wrothe**, 6 **wroath**. [f. WROTH *a.*, replacing WRATH *sb.* or WRETHE *sb.*] Deep anger or resentment; wrath, rage, or fury; ire.

The earlier examples are doubtful. The first may be a miswriting for *wrethe* or *wrothe*, and the second may be adjectival, as in Gower *Conf.* VI. 1696 (see FOR-^{1} *pref.* 10).

a **1400-50** *Wars Alex.* 2077 All þe werd [*v.r.* werld] war to waike his wrothe to with-stand. *a* **1425** *Cursor M.* 12183 (Trin.), Leuy for wrooþ..smot him on þe heed a dint. **1513** DOUGLAS *Æneid* II. x. 24 Sair pwnitioun of Greikis dred scho, als Hir husbandis wroth. **1581** A. HALL *Iliad* VI. 109 Thus sets the trayterous iade the king with griefe and wroth a fire. **1606** SHAKS. *Tr. & Cr.* II. iii. 182 Imagin'd wroth Holds in hir bloud..swolne and hot discourse. **1663** BUTLER *Hud.* I. i. 892 The objects of our Wroth. *Ibid.* ii. 737 At this the Knight grew high in wroth.

wroth (rəʊθ), *sb.*^{2} *Cornish dial.* [Cf. WRASSE.] One or other species of wrasse.

1750 HEATH *Acc. Isl. Scilly* 317 The Coast is plentifully stored..with Sea Round Fish; as..Cunner, Rockling, Cod, Wroth, Becket. **1882** JAGO *Anc. Lang. Cornwall* 314 *Wroth*, a fish known as Conner, or sea Carp.

wroth (rəʊθ, rɒθ), *a.* Forms: α. 1 **wrað** (*Northumb.* **urað, wurað**), 2-3 **wrað** (5 **wrad**), 3-4 **wraþ**, 4 **wraþe**, 4-5, *Sc.* 6 **wrathe** (4 **wrahte**), 4-5 **wrath** (4 **wragh**, 5 *Sc.* **vrath**, 6 **wraath**, **wraathe**), *Sc.* 5-6, 8 **wraith** (6 **wreith**); 3 **wræð** (**wærð**), 6 *Sc.* **wreth.** β. 3 **wroð**, 3-5 **wroþ** (3-4 **vroþ**), 3-5 **wroþe**, 4-6 **wrothe**, 4- **wroth** (4 **wrogh**, **wroght**, **wroþt**, 4-5 **wroht**, **worth**, 5 **wrought**, **wroghth**, **wourthe**); 4-5 **wrooþ**, **wrooth**, 5 **wrooþe**, 5 **rowthe**, 6 **wrouthe.** [OE. *wráþ*, = OFris. *wrêth* evil, OS. *wrêd* (MLG. *wrede, wrêt*, LG. *wrêd*), MDu. *wrêt, wreet* (Du. and Flem. *wreed* cruel), OHG. *reid, reidi* (MHG. *reit, reide* curled, twisted), ON. **wreiðr, reiðr* (Norw. *vreid, reid*, Da. and Sw. *vred*) angry, offended, f. the pa. t. of *wríðan* to WRITHE. Cf. WRATH *a.*]

In very freq. use *c* 1250-*c* 1450. Rare (exc. in or after Biblical usage), *c* 1530-*c* 1850, being regarded as 'out of use' by Johnson, 'nearly obsolete' by Ash, but as 'an excellent word and not obsolete' by Webster (1828-32). Revived in sense 1, esp. in formal or dignified style, *c* 1800.

1. Stirred to wrath; very angry or indignant; wrathful, incensed, irate.

Rarely *attrib.*, as in quots. *a* 1225, 1375, *c* 1400.

α. *c* **950** *Lindisf. Gosp.* Matt. xxii. 7 Ðe cyniȝ uutedlice mið ðy ȝeherde wurað wæs. *a* **1000** *Genesis* 2260 Ða wearð unbliðe Abrahames cwen, hire worcþeowe wrað on mode. *a* **1122** *O.E. Chron.* (Laud MS.) an. 1066, þa þe cyng Willelm ȝeherde þæt secgen þa wearð he swiðe wrað. *c* **1175** *Lamb. Hom.* 15 Ne beo þu nefre ene wrað þer fore. *c* **1200** ORMIN 19603 And ta warrþ wraþ Herode. *c* **1205** LAY. 8268 þa wes he wræð ful iwis. *Ibid.* 28723 þus þe king wordede, wræð on his þonke. *a* **1300** *Cursor M.* 1599 þof he was wrath it was na wrang. **1375** BARBOUR *Bruce* XVI. 245 Micht no man se ane vrathar man. *c* **1400** *Rule St. Benet* (Prose) 1 He, as a wrath fader,..deseret vs os not hys sons. *c* **1450** *Merlin* i. 18 Tho gan the Iuge to be right wrath. *c* **1475** *Rauf Coilȝear* 100 The Carll..wox wonder wraith. *c* **1520** M. NISBET *Ephes.* iv. 26 Be ye wrathe, and will ye nocht do synn. *c* **1560** A. SCOTT *Poems* (S.T.S.) vi. 38 For be scho wreth I will not wow it. **1590** BUREL in Watson *Coll.* II. (1709) 2 Anna, wondrous wraith, Deplors hir sister Didos daith. *a* **1776** *Lord Ingram* in Child *Ballads* II. 131/2 A' was blyth at Auld Ingram's cuming, But Lady Maisdrey was wraith.

β. *c* **1200** *Trin. Coll. Hom.* 183 Al þat me was leof, hit was þe loð; þu ware a sele ȝief ich was wroð. *a* **1225** *Ancr. R.* 120 Wroð mon is he wod? *c* **1290** *Becket* 413 þo was þe king wel of i-nouȝ, wroþere þane he was er. **13..** *Cursor M.* 4889 (Gött.), If he it wit he wil be wroght [*Trin.* wrooþ]. **1398** TREVISA *Barth. De P.R.* v. xli. (BM. Addit. MS.), By þe galle we ben wrooþ, by þe herte we ben wys. *c* **1450** *Knt. de la Tour* (1906) 22 Thanne she was wrother thanne afore. *c* **1489** CAXTON *Sonnes of Aymon* iii. 113 Sire,..ye be wroth of som other thyng. **1526** TINDAL *Matt.* xxii. 7 When the kyng hearde that, he was wroth. **1548** UDALL, etc. *Erasm. Par. Mark* x. 65 For he was nether wroth, nor murmured against Christ. *a* **1599** SPENSER *F.Q.* VII. vi. 35 There-at Ioue wexed wroth. **1611** BIBLE *1 Sam.* xx. 7 If he be very wroth,..euill is determined by him. **1656** BLOUNT *Glossogr.* **1716** M. DAVIES *Athen. Brit.* III. 25 Our modern Dissenters seem wroth, when they are deem'd a vulgar..kind of People. **1749** FIELDING *Tom Jones* VI. ix, The parson..saying, 'You behold, Sir, how he waxeth wroth at your abode here'. **1820** WORDSW. '*A Book came forth*' 7 But some..Waxed wroth, and with foul claws..On Bard and Hero clamorously fell. **1842** TENNYSON *Dora* 23 Then the old man Was wroth, and doubled up his hands. **1852** DICKENS *Bleak Ho.* xl, Sir Leicester is majestically wroth. **1880** BLACKMORE *Mary Anerley* xxxiii, 'I know it,' said Carroway, too wroth to swear.

absol. *a* **1250** *Owl & Night.* 944 Selde endeþ wel þe loþe & selde playdeþ wel þe wroþe.

transf. *c* **1386** CHAUCER *Cook's T.* 34 Reuel and trouthe.. been ful wrothe al day as men may see.

b. Said of the Deity.

a **1100** in Earle *Land-Charters* (1888) 253 Crist..him wurðe wrað þe hi hæfre ȝeþywie. *a* **1300** *Cursor M.* 959 Wa es me! lauerd,..þat euer i mad þe wrath. *c* **1340** HAMPOLE *Pr. Consc.* 5479 When he es wrathe þat es maker of alle. *c* **1386** CHAUCER *Pars. T.* ¶96 Ther shal the..wrothe Iuge sitte aboue. **1393** LANGL. *P. Pl.* C. I. 117 God was wel þe wroþer. *a* **1450** *Mirk's Festial* I. 4 Aboue hym schall be Crist his domes-man so wroþe, pat [etc.]. **1533** BELLENDEN *Livy* (S.T.S.) I. 106 The goddis war sa commovit and wraith, þat [etc.]. **1611** BIBLE *Isaiah* lxiv. 9 Be not wroth very sore, O Lord. **1697** DRYDEN *Æneis* v. 1110 The God was wroth. **1820** KEATS *Hyperion* II. 351 He saw full many a God Wroth as himself. **1877** TENNYSON *Harold* I. i. 28 Why should not Heaven be wroth?

c. With dative, or const. with preps., as *against, at, on*, †*to*, †*toward*, †*upon*, or esp. *with*.

(*a*) *a* **1000** *Genesis* 405 þonne weorð he him wrað on mode. *c* **1000** *Ags. Ps.* (Thorpe) lxxxiv. 4 þæt ðu us ne weorðe wrað on mode. *c* **1200** ORMIN 4814 Forr whatt iss Drihhtin me þuss wraþ? *c* **1230** *Hali Meid.* 31 Beo hit nu, þat..ti were beo þe wrað.

(*b*) *c* **1175** *Lamb. Hom.* 117 þi les ðe god iwurðe wrað wið eou. *c* **1205** LAY. 6369 A-nan se he wes wrað wid eni. **1297** R. GLOUC. (Rolls) 570 Corineus..wroþ inou was Toward þe king lotrin. **1303** R. BRUNNE *Handl. Synne* 12293 Al tymes ys God more wroþer with þys þan [etc.]. *a* **1352** MINOT *Poems* iii. 5 For mani men to him er wroth. **1375** BARBOUR *Bruce* I. 201 Gyff ony thar-at war wrath. **1388** WYCLIF *Num.* xxiv. 10 Balaach was wrooth aȝens Balaam. **1412** *26 Pol. Poems* 47 First whan god wiþ man was wroþ. **1471** CAXTON *Recuyell* (Sommer) 535 Dyane..was wrothe and angry vpon them. *c* **1489** —— *Sonnes of Aymon* i. 50 Charlemayne..was wrothe to theym. **1535** COVERDALE *2 Chron.* xxviii. 9 The Lorde God..is wroth at Iuda. **1590** SPENSER *F.Q.* III. vi. 19 She..woxe halfe wroth against her damzels slacke. *Ibid.* vii. 8 Be not wroth With silly Virgin. **1611** BIBLE *Ps.* lxxxix. 38 Thou hast bene wroth with thine anointed. **1794** MRS. RADCLIFFE *Myst. Udolpho* xxv, The signor, it seems, had lately been very wroth against her. **1859** TENNYSON *Elaine* 160 Then got Sir Lancelot suddenly to horse, Wroth at himself. **1873** 'OUIDA' *Pascarel* I. 39 She, dear soul, was very wroth against him always. **1883** WHITELAW *Sophocles, Antigone* 1177 Wroth with his pitiless sire, he slew himself.

fig. *a* **1300** *Cursor M.* 30 þe wrang to here o right is lath, And pride wyt buxsumnes is wrath.

† **2.** Marked or characterized by anger or wrath; indicative of ire or indignation. *Obs.*

c **1000** *Ags. Ps.* (Thorpe) lxiii. 4 Hi..hi mid wraðum wordum trymmað. *a* **1300** *E.E. Psalter* lxxiii. 1 Wrathe es þi breth, ouer schepe of þi fode. *a* **1325** *Prose Psalter* cxxiii. 3 Her wodeship was wroþe oȝains us. **13..** *Gaw. & Gr. Knt.* 1706 þay sued hym [*sc.* a fox] fast, Wreȝande hym ful weterly with a wroth noyse. *c* **1375** *Cursor M.* 828 (Fairf.), Sone bigan veniaunce to kithe, al was wraþ þat er was blithe. **1582** STANYHURST *Æneis* I. (Arb.) 22 Wroth woords stately thus [he] vsed. **1648** J. BEAUMONT *Psyche* XII. xxxiii, Wroth fiery Knots are marshalled upon Her Forehead.

† **3.** Of a fierce, savage, or violent disposition or character; stern, truculent. *Obs.*

Beowulf 319 Ic to sæ wille wið wrað werod wearde healdan. *c* **893** ÆLFRED *Oros.* VI. ii. 254 þa wearð Tiberius Romanum swa wrað & swa heard swa he him ær wæs milde & ieþe. *c* **1000** *Ags. Ps.* (Thorpe) lxvii. 5 þa þe wydewum syn wraðe æt dome. *c* **1205** LAY. 18583 þis iherde Gorlois..& he andsware ȝaf, eorlene wraðest. *Ibid.* 28503 Arður þat iherde, wraðest kinge. *c* **1275** *Ibid.* 6402 þar was mani bold Brut, and mani cnihtes wroþe [*c* **1205** bisi kempen].

† **b.** In the phrase ***as wroth as (the) wind.*** *Obs.*

13.. *Gaw. & Gr. Knt.* 319 He wex as wroth as wynde. **1377** LANGL. *P. Pl.* B. III. 328 Also wroth as þe wynde Wex Mede in a while. *c* **1400** *Destr. Troy* 13091 And he [was] wrothe as the wynde to his wale eme. **14..** *Erthe upon Erthe* 33/48 Erthe is as sone wroth as is the wynde. *c* **1470** *Gol. & Gaw.* 770 Golograse.., Wod wraith as the wynd, his handis can wryng.

† **4.** Of animals: Of a violent or fierce nature; irritated, enraged. *Obs.*

a **900** CYNEWULF *Crist* 1548 Se deopa seað..æleð hy mid þy ealdan lige.., wraþum wyrmum. *a* **1250** *Owl & Night.* 1043 þe vle wes wroþ, to cheste rad, Mid þisse worde hire eyen abraid. **13..** *E.E. Allit. P.* B. 1676 þou..on mor most abide..With wroþe wolfes to won. *c* **1375** *Sc. Leg. Saints* i. (*Peter*) 523 þan wes þe hound na thing wrath, Na schup to do na man schath. *a* **1400-50** *Wars Alex.* 738 As wrath as a waspe. **1526** TINDALE *Rev.* xii. 17 The dragon was wroth with the woman.

b. *transf.* Of the wind, sea, etc.: Moved to a state of turmoil or commotion; violent, stormy.

13.. *E.E. Allit. P.* C. 162 Euer was ilyche loud þe lot of þe wyndes, & euer wroþer þe water, & wodder þe stremes. **13..** *Gaw. & Gr. Knt.* 525 Wroþe wynde of þe welkyn wrastelez with þe sunne. **13..**, etc. [see 3 b]. **1426** AUDELAY *Poems* 47 Wry not fro Godis word as the wroth wynd. **1590** SPENSER *F.Q.* II. xi. 19 When the wroth Western wind does reaue their locks. **1835** BROWNING *Paracelsus* v. 661 The wroth sea's waves are edged With foam. **1852** C. B. MANSFIELD *Paraguay*, etc. (1856) 123 It rained heavily... So I was wroth, and the weather too. **1876** SWINBURNE *Erechtheus* 1649 The most holy heart of the deep sea, Late wroth, now full of quiet.

† **5.** Bad, evil; grievous, perverse. *Obs.*

In later use in ***to wrothe hele, -haile*** (see WROTHER-HEAL).

c **1000** *Ags. Ps.* (Thorpe) cxviii. 101 Ic minum fotum fæcne siðas, þa wraþan weȝas, werede ȝeorne. *a* **1023** WULFSTAN *Hom.* l. (1883) 273 Hu læne and hu lyðre þis lif is,..hu tealt and hu wrað. *a* **1225** *Juliana* 57 Weila as þu were iboren wrecche o wraðe [*v.r.* wraðer] time. *a* **1225** *Leg. Kath.* 171 þe wrecches þet ha seh..wraðe werkes wurchen. *a* **1250** *Prov. Alfred* 115 þenne beoþ his wene ful wroþe isene. **1297** R. GLOUC. (Rolls) 3019 To wroþe hele al þis lond was he so milde þo. *c* **1330** *King of Tars* 131 To wrothe hele that he was bore. *c* **1400** *Laud Troy Bk.* 7872 That was him to wrothe-haile: For thei of Grece opon him throng.

† **6.** Displeased, grieved; sorrowful, sad. *Obs.*

13.. *K. Alis.* 4528 (Laud MS.), Alisaunder haþ vnderstonde þe lettre þat com from darries sonde. Wroþ he was, & hadde pyte. **13..** *Gaw. & Gr. Knt.* 70 Ladies laȝed ful loude, þoȝ þay lost haden, And he þat wan was not wrothe. *c* **1450** *Ludus Coventriæ* 329 Lombe of love with-owt loth, I ffynde þe not, myn hert is wroth.

† **b.** Fearful, apprehensive, afraid. *Obs. rare*$^{-1}$.

13.. *K. Alis.* 544 (Laud MS.), Vche of hem so bycom wroþ: For a dragon þer com in fleen.

† **wroth**, *v. Obs.* Also 1 **wraðian**, 5 **wrothyn**, **wrothe.** [OE. *wráðian* (= OS. *wrêðian*, ON. **wreiða, reiða*, refl. *reiðask* (Norw. *vreidast*, MSw. *vreþas*, Sw. *vredgas*, Da. *vredes*) to get angry, f. *wráð* WROTH *a.* Cf. *awroth* (s.v. AWRATH), WRATH, WRETHE *vbs.*]

1. *intr.* To become wrathful or angry; to manifest anger.

c **975** *Rushw. Gosp.* Mark x. 41 Ða tenu ongunnun wraðiȝa of iacobe & iohanne. **14..** *Wars Alex.* 2593 (Dubl. MS.), ȝitt wer hys baratours abaist & þen þe bern wrothed. *c* **1435** *Torr. Portugal* 1196 Lo, sir kyng, hold this,..or ellis wroth we anon. *c* **1475** *Partenay* 1254 Again melusine wrothed he ful sore.

2. *trans.* To make wroth or angry; to enrage.

c **1450** *Mirk's Festial* I. 66 Adam loued hyr and wold not wroth hur. **1499** *Promp. Parv.* (Pynson), Wrothyn or maken wrothe, *irrito.* **1611** FLORIO, *Adirare*, to anger, to wroth.

b. *refl.* To become wrathful or angry.

c **1425** *Seven Sages* (P.) 1780 Bot thau he wrothe hym never so sore, For sothe I nylle prove hym no more.

wroth, obs. var. *wrought*, pa. pple. of WORK *v.*

wrothe, obs. metathetic var. *wort*, WART *sb.*

† **wrothe**, *adv. Obs.* Forms: α. 1 wraðe, 3 wraþe, 5 wrath. β. 3 wroðe, 3–4 wroþe, 5 wrothe, wroth. [OE. *wráðe*, f. *wráð* WROTH *a.*]

1. Wrathfully, angrily, severely; = WROTHLY *adv.* 1.

c **950** *Lindisf. Gosp.* Luke xiii. 14 Ondsuarade ða ðæs folces aldormon wraððe [*Rushw.* wraðe]. *a* **1000** *Guthlac* 638 Eow se waldend wraðe bisencte. *a* **1250** *Owl & Night.* (C.) 972 þu canst ȝolle wroþe & stronge. *c* **1275** in *O.E. Misc.* 144/109 þat folk worþ eft wroþe i-spild, þe nule to hire [*sc.* true love] turne. **1338** R. BRUNNE *Chron.* (1810) 265 Was neuer in þam both [*sc.* Wales and Scotland] terme set ne stounde, þat þei [ne] discorded wroth. *c* **1400** *Arth. & Merl.* 824 Heo..beot hire boþe eouele and wroþ. *c* **1430** *Syr. Gener.* (Roxb.) 2917 The Sowdon wrothe answerd ageyn. *Ibid.* 9229 The lord he smote than so wrothe That shelde to-rofe.

2. Evilly; badly; ill; = WROTHLY *adv.* 2.

c **888** ÆLFRED *Boeth.* i, He þa ȝehat swiðe yfele ȝelæste, & swiðe wraðe ȝeendode mid maneȝum mane. *a* **1000** *Ags. Ps.* (Thorpe) lvii. 2 Eft ȝe on heortan hoȝedon inwit, worhton wraðe. *c* **1200** *Trin. Coll. Hom.* 193 þese þreo þing noteð ech man on two wise, wel, and wroðe. *a* **1250** *Owl & Night.* 1360 Wymmon may pleye vnder cloþe hweþer heo wile wel þe wroþe. **1297** R. GLOUC. (Rolls) 729 Vor þou art mi doȝter.. I loued þe one; þou ȝelst nou my loue wroþe. **1340** *Ayenb.* 20 þet þou hest oft ziþes euele and wroþe y-loked hire festes. *c* **1400** *Gamelyn* 73 He clothed him and fedde hym yuel and eke wrothe.

3. Sorrowfully; sadly; = WROTHLY *adv.* 3.

a **1250** *Owl & Night.* (J.) 415 A wintre þu singest wroþe & yomere. *c* **1275** *Sinners Beware* 96 in *O.E. Misc.* 75 þer-fore heo schule siche And in helle smyche Acoryen hit ful wraþe.

† **wrother-heal**, *sb.* and *adv. Obs.* Forms: 3 wraðer-, 3–4 wraþer- (4 wreþer-), 3 wroðer-, 3–5 wrother-hele (5 wrothir-, wrothher-); also 3 -heale, 4 -hale, -haylle, 4–5 -hail(e, -hayl. [= OE. *(*tó*) *wráþre hǽle* (*hǽlu, -o*): see WROTH *a.* and HEAL *sb.* 2 b (HELE, HAIL *sb.*², HALE *sb.*¹). Cf. GODER-HEAL.]

A. *sb.* **a.** ***to wrother heal*** (*hele*, also *hail, hale*), with evil fate or fortune; with or to misfortune, injury, calamity, or destruction.

c **1205** LAY. 29556 þer heo iwurðen to, to wraðere hele. *a* **1225** *Ancr. R.* 102 Go ut ase dude Dina,..to wrother hele. *c* **1275** *xi Pains of Hell* 27 in *O.E. Misc.* 148 To wroþere hele he wes ibore. *c* **1305** *Pilate* 187 in *E.E.P.* (1862) 116 He swor his more oþ anon þat he to wroþere hele þer com. **1377** LANGL. *P. Pl.* B. XIV. 120 For to wrotherhele was he wrouȝte þat neuere was ioye shaped. *a* **1400** *Sqr. lowe Degre* 299 Alas! it tourned to wroth-her-heyle. *a* **1425** *Cursor M.* 21923 (Trin.), To wroþerhele he ȝaf vs wit.

b. With dative (noun or pronoun) of person, etc.

a **1200** *St. Marher.* 10 Ah crist to wurðmunt, ant him to wraðerheale, þe rode taken arudde hire readliche. *a* **1225** *Juliana* 43 þe ich font & habbe ifolhet me to wraðer heale. **1297** R. GLOUC. (Rolls) 7282 So þat harald was king to wroþerhele þe kinedom. **13..** *Gosp. Nicod.* 695 What raue þe vayle, þat in yhour temple hang? vs all to wrotherhail. **1362** LANGL. *P. Pl.* A. II. 20 Out of wrong heo wox to wroþerhele monye. *c* **1400** *Laud Troy Bk.* 4260 He sayled in with a feble sayl And þat was him to wrotherhayl.

c. With genitive pronoun. *rare*⁻¹.

c **1205** LAY. 490 Mid þræte he spilede: To wroþer heore hele habbeð heo such werc idon.

B. *adv.* Unfortunately; disastrously.

a **1300** *Cursor M.* 16477 Ful wrather-hail to min bihoue haf i tan þis mone. *c* **1325** *Spec. Gy Warw.* 129 Wroþer hele was Iudas born, For þurw þat sinne he was lorn. *a* **1330** *Otuel* 208 Wroþer hele come þou her, I rede þou ȝeld op þi brond. *a* **1400–50** *Wars Alex.* 1759 þou sekis fraward Sichim þi-selfe wrothir-haile.

ˈ**wrothful**, *a. Obs.* or *arch.* [var. of WRATHFUL *a.*, after WROTH *sb.* or *a.*]

An app. early example in R. Brunne *Chron.* (1810) 37 is prob. an error for *wrathful* or *wrethful.*

1. Of persons: Full of wrath; angry; = WRATHFUL *a.* 1.

c **1500** *Communycacyon* (W. de W.) C j, Alas why haue I wrothfull ben? **1535** COVERDALE *Nahum* i. 2 A taker of vengeaunce is yᵉ Lorde, and wrothfull. **1546** *Gasser's Prognost.* d ij b, The warrier & wrothful Mars, Lord of this yere. **1590** SPENSER *F.Q.* II. xi. 34 The knight yet wrothfull for his late disgrace,..him..sore smote. **1810** SCOTT *Lady of L.* v. vi, Wrothful at such arraignment foul, Dark lower'd the clansman's sable scowl.

b. Prone to wrath.

1535 COVERDALE *2 Sam.* vii. 8 His men..are stronge and of a wrothfull stomack.

2. Proceeding or arising from wrath; characterized by or expressive of anger.

1535 COVERDALE *Ps.* lxviii. 24 Let thy wrothfull displeasure take holde of them. **1562** LEGH *Armory* 165 b, His irefull hart straight braided out wrothful wordes of wreke and reuenge.

Hence ˈ**wrothfully** *adv.*, ˈ**wrothfulness**.

a **1500** *Hist. K. Boccus & Sydracke* (? 1510) P ij, He styreth and quakyth *wrothfully. **1535** COVERDALE *Ps.* cxxiii. 3 When they were so wrothfully displeased at vs. **1596** SPENSER *F.Q.* VI. vii. 16 But..(quoth he halfe wrothfully) Where is the bootie? **1855** THORPE tr. *Beowulf* 6116 Then was the quarrel wrothfully avenged. **1535** COVERDALE *Ecclus.* x. 22 Pryde was not made for man, nether *wrothfulness for mens children.

† **wrothly**, *a. Obs.* In 4 wrathli. [repr. OE. *wráðlic*, f. *wráþ* WROTH *a.*] Angry, violent.

a **1300** *Cursor M.* 3462 Wit wrathli [*Gött.* wrethly] wrestes aiþer writh.

† ˈ**wrothly**, *adv. Obs.* Forms: α. 1 wraðlice, 3 wraðliche, *Orm.* wraþeliȝ, 4 wrathli, -ly, 5 *Sc.* wraithly. β. 3 wroð-, wroðeliche, 4 wroþeliche, -lich, wroþlich, wroþli, -ly, 4–5 wroþely, wrothely, 5 wroothly. [OE. *wráðlice* (= MLG. *wretliken*, MDu. *wreedelick*, Du. *-lijk*), f. *wráð* WROTH *a.* + -LY².]

1. In a wrathful, bitter, or cruel manner; wrathfully, angrily, furiously.

α. *Beowulf* 3062 þa sio fæhð ȝeweard ȝewrecen wraðlice. *c* **1200** ORMIN 15832 ȝiff þatt Crist swa wraþeliȝ Draf menn ..Ut off þatt temmple. *c* **1205** LAY. 7379 Cezar iseh þis writ, and he hit wrað liche bi-heold. *a* **1300** *Cursor M.* 3958 Quen he of his cuming herd Ful wrathli gains him he ferd. *a* **1340** HAMPOLE *Psalter* i. 3 It is wiþ swa mykil delaiynge & swa wrathly, þat it is noght worth þat þai doe. *c* **1375** *Sc. Leg. Saints* xxix. (*Placidas*) 303 Forton..turnyt hyr bak one hym wrathly. *c* **1470** HENRY *Wallace* IV. 237 Wallace,..Sumpart amowet, wraithly till it..went. *c* **1470** *Golagros & Gaw.* 162 Wondirly wraithly he wroght, and all as of were.

β. *c* **1205** LAY. 485 þe king nom þat writ on hond & he hit wroðliche bi-heold. *c* **1330** *Amis & Amil.* 1166 The leuedi loked opon him tho Wrothlich. **13..** *E.E. Allit. P.* C. 132 þay wakened wel þe wroþeloker, for wroþely he cleped. **1362** LANGL. *P. Pl.* A. v. 68 Wroþliche he wrong his fust. **1421** HOCCLEVE *Min. Poems* 151 He wroothly wente out of hir conpaignie. *c* **1450** *Mirour Saluacioun* (Roxb.) 9 Oure Lord ..shoke thre speres wrothly.

2. Badly; ill. *rare.*

c **1200** *Trin. Coll. Hom.* 193 Man hit noteð wroðeliche, þe mid ȝepshipe bicherð his emcristen. *c* **1230** *Hali Meid.* 33 (Cott. MS.), ȝif þu art unwurðliche & wraðeliche ilatet.

3. Sadly; sorrowfully. *rare*⁻¹.

c **1374** CHAUCER *Boeth.* I. prose i. (1868) 7 þus þis compagnye of muses i-blamed casten wroþely [L. *mœstior*] þe chere adounward to þe erþe.

wroth money. *local.* [variant of WRATH MONEY.] (See quots.)

1730 THOMAS *Dugdale's Warwick.* I. 4/2 A certain rent due unto the Lord of this Hundred [of Knightlow], called Wroth money, or Warth money,..probably the same with Ward penny. **1864** CHAMBERS *Bk. of Days* II. 571/2 The payment..of Wroth or Ward money for protection, and probably also in lieu of military service. **1892** *Pall Mall G.* 12 Nov. 5/3 The [annual] custom of paying 'wroth money' ..at Knightlow Cross.

So **wroth silver** (also **wroth penny**). *local.*

1864 CHAMBERS *Bk. of Days* II. 571/2 The payment of this Wroth Silver. **1893** in *N. & Q.* 8th Ser. IV. 497 The Duke of Buccleuch..observed..the curious custom of collecting ..'Wroth Silver', or 'Wroth Penny', from various parishes. **1896** *Westm. Gaz.* 11 Nov. 10/1 The Duke.. demands 'wroth silver'..from some thirty parishes, and the nominal amounts are..placed in a stone trough on Knightlow Hill. **1900** *Ibid.* 12 Nov. 10/1 The Duke['s]..annual collection of 'Wroth silver'..is a curious old custom, carried on for centuries, and observed each year, on November 11.

† ˈ**wrothsome**, *a. Obs. rare*⁻¹. [f. WROTH *a.* + -SOME.] = WROTHFUL *a.* 1.

c **1518** SKELTON *Magnyf.* 2293 Thou hast bene so waywarde, so wranglyng, and so wrothsome.

wrothy (ˈrəʊθɪ, ˈrɒθɪ), *a.* [f. WROTH *a.* + -Y¹. Cf. MDu. *wrêdich* (Du. *wreedig*) cruel.] Wrathful, angry.

In 19th c., revived under the influence of WRATHY *a.*

1422 YONGE tr. *Secreta Secret.* 157 Mowrnynge and wrothi thow shalte reme. *Ibid.* 229 Tho men..bene wrothy and hugely angry. **14..** *Wheatley MS.* (1921) 28 In my flesche ther is no hele In presence of thi worthi [? *read* wrothi] face [L. *a facie ire tue*]. **1839** LEVER *H. Lorrequer* v, A more wrothy gentleman..it having rarely been my evil fortune to forgather with. **1869** TROLLOPE *Vicar Bullhampton* xvii, Gilmore..was waxing wrothy. **1902** RODKINSON *Talmud* VIII. p. xiii, Ezra was wrothy that the Torah should be given through him.

Hence ˈ**wrothily** *adv.*; ˈ**wrothiness**.

1422 YONGE tr. *Secreta Secret.* 227 A grete fleshy shorte neke tokenyth wrothynesse like as a bull is. **1898** N. MUNRO *J. Splendid* xxv. 257 [He] would ruffle up wrothily with blame for my harping on that incident.

wrotte, obs. var. WART *sb.*

wrough, *int. rare*⁻¹. [Imitative.] Used to represent the snort or grunt of a hog or pig.

1589 [? NASHE] *Almond for Parrat* F j b, A hogge..lifts vp his snoute into the ayre, and cryes wrough, wrough.

† **wrought**, *sb. Obs. rare.* In 3 wrohte, 4 w(h)rouhte. [Early ME. var. of *wruhte* (OE. *wryhta*), WRIGHT *sb.*¹] = WRIGHT *sb.*¹ 1, 1 b.

c **1275** LAY. 16969 Wrohtes, þat mid axe couþen weorche. *Ibid.* 21134 Wigar þe wittye wrohte. *a* **1333** W. HEREBERT in *Relig. Lyrics 14th C.* (1924) 22 Holy wrouhte of sterres bryht. *Ibid.* 27 Louerd god almyhti, Whrouhte of alle þinge.

wrought (rɔːt), *ppl. a.* Forms: 3–4 wroȝt, 5–6 wroght, 5– wrought (6 *arch.* wroughten), 5 wrout, 7 wrote. [ME. *wroȝt*, var. of *worht*, pa. pple. of *wirchen, wurchen*: see WORK *v.*] Worked into shape (or condition).

Freq. as the second element of combs., as *fine-, finely-, gold-, hammer-, hand-, hard-, high-, highly-, machine-, thick-, thin-, well-wrought*: see these words, and cf. IN-, FOR-, OVER-, UNWROUGHT *ppl. adjs.*

I. † **1. a.** Created; shaped, moulded. *Obs.*

c **1250** *Gen. & Ex.* 2606 Teremuth..bad it ben to hire broȝt, And saȝ ðis child wol faire wroȝt. *c* **1400** [see WELL-WROUGHT *ppl. a.* 1]. **1434** MISYN *Mending Life* 126 God truly is infinit of gretnes,..of all wroght kyndes vnconsauyd.

b. That is made or constructed by means of labour or art; fashioned, formed.

Cf. OE. *hand-worht*, = mod. E. 'hand-wrought'.

13.. *E.E. Allit. P.* B. 1381 With a wonder wroȝt walle wruxeled ful hiȝe. **1338**, *c* **1400**, etc. [see WELL-WROUGHT *ppl. a.* 1]. **1624** in *Archaeol.* (1806) XV. 161, 3 pare of wrote boote hose. **1660** R. READ *Wecker's Secr. Art* 220 Lay with every bed of your wrought and drawn Glass one of the said pieces of Glass. **1676** LADY FANSHAWE *Mem.* (1830) 189 A rich curious-wrought gold chain. **1696** DERHAM *Clock-maker* 4 The wrought piece which covers the Balance..is the Cock. **1700–1** *Act 12–13 William* c. 4 §1 For want of Assayers..to assay and touch their wrought Plate. **1739** *Act 12 Geo. II*, c. 26 §6 Any wrought Seal or Seals with Cornelian or other Stones set therein. **1818** KEATS *Endym.* I. 165 After them appear'd..a fair wrought car. **1850** ROSSETTI *Blessed Damozel* ii, Her robe..No wrought flowers did adorn. **1875** FORTNUM *Maiolica* 107 Most elegantly wrought earthen vases. **1890** YOUNG *Ann. Barber-Surg. Lond.* 506 Handsomely chased and wrought silver garlands.

c. Shaped, fashioned, or finished from the rough or crude material; cut.

1560 BIBLE (Bishops') *Numb.* xxxi. 51 Moses & Eleazar.. toke the golde of them, and all wroght iewels. **1579** SPENSER *Sheph. Cal.* Aug. 134 To him be the wroughten mazer alone. **1611** BIBLE *1 Chron.* xxii. 2 Hee set masons to hew wrought stones. **1652** BENLOWES *Theoph.* III. xxvi, Her lips rock-rubies, and her veins wrought sapphires show. **1818** KEATS *Endym.* II. 623 The water..mimick'd the wrought oaken beams. **1841** SPALDING *Italy & It. Isl.* III. 355 The country exports..the marble of Carrara, both wrought and unwrought. **1854** S. G. MORTON *Types Mankind* 357 Large quantities of wrought bones, human and animal.

† **2.** Artificial; specially prepared. *Obs.*

c **1400** tr. *Secreta Secret., Govt. Lordsh.* 83 He sholde.. caste vp-on his heued wroght waters attempred. *Ibid.* 85 Thre Rotes of wroght hony. [tr. L. *artificialis.*]

3. a. Of textile materials, esp. silk: Manufactured; spun. (Cf. RAW *a.* 2 a.)

1463–4 *Rolls of Parlt.* V. 506/1 Wrought Silke, throwen Rybans and Laces, falsely..wrought. **1503–4** *Act 19 Hen. VII*, c. 21, All other maner of Sylkes, aswell wrought as rawe or unwrought. **1630** *R. Johnson's Kingd. & Commw.* 336 The riches of the Kingdome are especially silkes, wrought and unwrought. **1694** E. CHAMBERLAYNE *Pres. St. Eng.* (ed. 18) I. 37 Merionethshire..abounds with Sheep, Fish, Fowl, and wrought Cottons. **1728** CHAMBERS *Cycl.* (1738) s.v. *Silk*, The silks brought from Italy are partly wrought, and partly raw, and unwrought. **1841** HAYDN *Dict. Dates* 472 Wrought silk was brought from Persia to Greece 325 B.C.

b. Decorated or ornamented, as with needlework; elaborated, embellished, embroidered.

1455 *Lincoln Diocese Doc.* 67 [A] Wrought bordcloth cum j. pari towalles de eadem. **1475** *Stonor Papers* (Camden) I. 155 Item..j. large wrought Bordeclothe. **1552–3** in Feuillerat *Revels Edw. VI* (1914) 104 Purple wrought vellet. *a* **1586** SIDNEY *Arcadia* I. xiii, A light taffeta garment, so cut, as the wrought smocke came through it in many places. **1598** B. JONSON *Ev. Man in Hum.* I. iii, As a Millaners wife [conceals] her wrought stomacher with a smokie lawne. **1599** —— *Ev. Man out of Hum.* IV. iv, A piece of my wrought shirt. **1614** BOYLE in *Lismore Papers* (1886) I. 50 A veary fair wrought purse. *a* **1680** CHARNOCK *Attrib. God* (1682) 609 A curious wrought Tapestry. **1686** *Lond. Gaz.* No. 2152/4 A green wrought Sattin Ribon. **1709** STEELE *Tatler* No. 91 ¶5 My Mistress presented me with a Wrought Nightcap. **1711** *Hermit* 25 Aug. 2/1 The old Tapestry Hangings and Wrought Bed [must be] pulled down. **1805** SCOTT *Last Minstrel* II. xix, A wrought Spanish baldric. *c* **1816** MRS. SHERWOOD *Stories Ch. Catech.* vii. 45 [She] had on a wrought muslin frock. **1847** C. BRONTË *J. Eyre* xi, Beds.. with wrought old English hangings crusted with thick work. **1851** [see WRISTLET 2].

transf. **1662** J. DAVIES tr. *Olearius' Voy. Ambass.* 310 A third sort of Melons..are wrought or embroider'd, having amidst the embroidery red, yellow, and green spots.

c. Of leather, etc.: Prepared by dressing; dressed.

1541 *Extr. Aberd. Reg.* (1844) I. 454 Quhat craftisman that braks the samyn [act], the rest of his wrought ledder to be escheitt. **1585** HIGINS *Junius' Nomencl.* 130/1 *Linum factum*,..wrought or hitchild flax.

d. Of articles: Made, manufactured, or prepared for use or commerce.

c **1580** in *Eng. Hist. Rev.* July (1914) 518 Pilchars and Red herringe, wrought Lime. **1584–5** *Act 27 Eliz.* c. 16 §1 Any Artificer using to work Leather into wrought Wares. *a* **1700** EVELYN *Diary* 17 Sept. 1657, Some habits of curiously-colour'd and wrought feathers. **1757** *Refl. Importation Bar Iron* 19 The Americans..would..take more wrought Goods from the British Manufacturers. **1803** MALTHUS *Popul.* III. x. 459 The whole value of the wrought commodity. **1807** T. THOMSON *Chem.* (ed. 3) II. 444 Wrought rosin, or shoe-maker's rosin. **1851** *Catal. Gt. Exhib.* 865 The traders..purchase the wrought articles from the heads of the lapidary workmen.

4. a. Of metals: Beaten out or shaped with the hammer or other tools.

1535 COVERDALE *Ps.* xliv. 13 Hir clothinge is of wrought golde. **1585** HIGINS *Junius' Nomencl.* 403/1 *Argentum factum*,..wrought siluer, as plate, coyne, &c. **1687** MIÈGE *Gt. Fr. Dict.* II. s.v. *Ouvré*, Wrought Silver,..wrought Brass. **1696–7** *Act 8–9 William III*, c. 34 §1 Evrey Hundred weight of Tin wrought commonly called Pewter. **1717** BERKELEY *Jrnl. Tour Italy* Wks. 1871 IV. 555 Gold and silver, wrought and unwrought, found along the side of the little sea. **1819** SHELLEY *Fragm., Tale Untold* 3 Empty cups of wrought and daedal gold. **1885** *Mag. Art* Sept. 459/1 A circular plate of thin wrought bronze.

Comb. **1893** *Outing* XXII. 111/1 A wrought-gold bracelet.

b. ***wrought iron***, slag-bearing malleable iron (see IRON *sb.*¹ 1 and MALLEABLE *a.* 1).

1703 *Act 2–3 Anne* c. 18 §12 Wares made of Wrought Iron. **1747** *Phil. Trans.* XLIV. II. 371 Cannon..cast so soft as to bear Turning like wrought Iron. **1837** *Civil Eng. & Arch. Jrnl.* I. 1/1 The rails are of wrought-iron,..fixed in cast-iron chairs. **1876** VOYLE & STEVENSON *Milit. Dict.* 473/2 Wrought iron is valuable as a gun material. **1881** [see IRON *sb.*¹ 2 a].

Comb. **1829** W. Ellis *Polyn. Res.* II. 298 A wrought-iron nail..four inches long. **1875** Knight *Dict. Mech.* 2823/2 *Wrought-iron Furnace*, ..[a] puddling-furnace. **1885** 'Mrs. Alexander' *At Bay* xi, Great old wrought-iron gates.

c. Of metal-work: Made by hammering or hand-work (in contrast to *cast*).

1807 W. Irving *Salmag.* xii, His learned distinctions between wrought scissors and those of cast-steel. **1810** in Ure *Dict. Arts* (1839) 875 Cut nails are full as good as wrought nails. **1849** Ruskin *Sev. Lamps* ii. §20 Ornaments ..of cast-iron..are always distinguishable, at a glance, from wrought and hammered work. **1883** W. D. Curzon *Manuf. Worcs.* 2 The wrought work of ploughs and..blacksmiths' work of all kinds.

†**5.** *transf.* Worked up; rough; agitated. *Obs.*

1585 T. Washington tr. *Nicholay's Voy.* II. iii. 33 The wind still continuyng.., and the seas sore wrought. **1603** Knolles *Hist. Turks* (1621) 368 The billowes of a wrought sea. **1604**, **1702** [see high-wrought *a.* 1].

6. a. Of coal: Hewn from the bed or seam; won.

1708 J. C. *Compl. Collier* (1845) 28 The Horse Engin.. serves..to draw up the Wrought Coals. **1883** Gresley *Gloss. Coal-mining* 295 *Wrought coal*, etc., worked or *gotten*.

b. Dug; moved by digging, etc.

1903 *Blackw. Mag.* Feb. 222/1 As the shelving banks close in there is a smell of the wrought earth.

7. Of animals: Employed in labour; worked.

1725 *Fam. Dict.* s.v. *Ox*, Wrought Oxen in the Seasons they are put to labour, ought to be fed with Care.

II. With adverbs. **8.** ***wrought-off***, worked off; printed.

1683 Moxon *Mech. Exerc., Printing* xxii. ¶7 He uses one of the Wrought-off Forms. **1771** Luckombe *Hist. Print.* 409 Then we impose from wrought-off Forms. **1838** Timperley *Printers' Man.* 114 Wrought-off heaps [of paper].

9. ***wrought-up***, stirred up; excited or stimulated; enlivened.

1810 Crabbe *Borough* xv. 67 He knew..How to make all the passions his allies, And..To watch the wrought-up heart, and conquer by surprise. **1823** Mrs. Hemans *Siege of Valencia* i, The deep..feelings wakening at their voice, Claim all the wrought-up spirit to themselves. **1828** Lytton *Pelham* III. xi, Excited as I had been by my painful and wrought-up interest in his recital. **1962** Auden *Dyer's Hand* (1963) 508 Whereupon we are shown Antony talking to his friends in a wrought-up state of self-dramatization and self-pity.

wrought, pa. t. and pa. pple. of work *v.*

wrought(e, erron. ff. *rought*, obs. pa. t. of reach *v.*[1]

wroughte, var. wroot *sb. Obs.*

wrouȝt(e), wrouht(e), wrout, etc.: see work *v.*

'wroughter. *Cant.* (See quot.)

1870 B. Hemyng *Out of the Ring* 31 The Welshers' Vocabulary... *Broad pitcher*, a man playing the three cards. *Wroughter*, the man who plays them. *Ibid.* 33, 35.

wrout, *v.* Now *dial.* [var. of wroot *v.*: cf. rout *v.*[8]] *intr.* = wroot *v.* 1.

1530 in *Ancestor* XI. (1904) 183 Crest a boore silver wrouting in a bushe of nettelles vert. **1530** Palsgr. 786/1, I wroote, or wroute, as a swyne dothe, *je fouille du museau*. **1565** *Satir. Poems Reform.* i. 355 Ledd with th' affection, th' onlie Springe and Roote, that all godlie Goverment clerelie wroutethe owte. **1624** Sanderson *Two Serm.* (1628) 46 Like Swine.., we grouze vp the ake-cornes, and..lie wrouting & thrusting our noses in the earth for more. **1825–63** in dial. glossaries (N. Cy., Nhp., Dorset) s.v.

wrow(e, obs. varr. wraw *a.*

wrox (rɒks), *v.* Now *dial.* Also 7 **wroxe**, 9 *dial.* rox. [Of obscure origin.]

1. *trans.* To cause to decay or rot.

1649 Blithe *Eng. Improver* vi. 34 So cut the Turfe, that the Soard may have all the Winters frost to wroxe, and moulder it. *Ibid.* xx. 119 For your Horse Dung..let it be but well Wroxed or Roten.

2. *intr.* To decay, rot. *dial.*

1847 Halliwell, *Wrox*, to begin to decay. *Warw.* **1854–1890** in dial. glossaries (Nhp., Leics., Warw., Gloucs.) s.v. *Rox*.

wroye(r, varr. wray *v.*[1], wrayer *Obs.*

†**wruck**, *v. Obs. rare*$^{-1}$. [Of obscure relationship. Cf. ruck *v.*[3]] *trans.* To throw *up* on shore; to cast ashore.

? *a* **1600** *Arthur & King of Cornwall* 187 (Percy Fol. MS.), One litle booke He found..at the sea-side, Wrucked upp in a floode.

wruȝen, wruhen, obs. pa. t. pl. of wry *v.*[1]

wruhte, obs. f. wright *sb.*[1]

†**wrung**, *sb. Obs.*$^{-1}$ [f. *wrung*, pa. pple. of wring *v.*] An affection in horses caused by straining of the withers.

1627 J. Taylor (Water P.) *Navy Land Ships* C6b, The Blood-shot, the Wrung in the Withers, the straine.

wrung: see rung *sb.*, wring *v.*, wrong.

wrung (rʌŋ), *ppl. a.* Also 4–5 **wrongun, -en**, 5 **wronge**, 6 **wrong**. [pa. pple. of wring *v.*]

1. a. Subjected to wringing, twisting, or squeezing; pressed, squeezed.

1382 Wyclif *Num.* xxiv. 10 Balac wrooth aȝen Balaam, with wrongun hoondis seith [etc.]. *a* **1548** Hall *Chron., Hen. VIII*, 51 The handes of the sayd Hun were wrong in the wristes, wherby we perceyued that his handes had been bounde. **1611** Florio, *Torcifecciole*, the dregges of wrung Grapes. **1678** Rymer *Trag. Last Age* 82 The Nurse with wrung hands lies at Phedra's feet.

(*b*) With *out*.

1976 *Times* 26 Jan. 12/4 Feeling like 60 wrung-out dishrags we stumbled out. **1979** P. Wallage *Restoration Post-War Cars* ii. 26/2 Wiping it off with a wrung-out cloth.

b. *transf.* Of fabrics: (see quot. 1904).

1902 *Westm. Gaz.* 12 March 2/2 An overdress of green wrung chiffon. **1904** *County Gentleman* 25 June 1966/3 Wrung muslin is the smartest fabric for tea-gowns... [It] looks as if it had been washed and had been wrung through the hands.

†**2.** Of a towel. *Obs.*$^{-1}$

Meaning not clear; app. opposed to *plain*.

1475 *Stonor Papers* (Camden) I. 155, ij schorte Wronge Towellys. It[em], ij longe Playne Towellys.

3. a. That has suffered or undergone distress, grief, or pain; racked, distressed.

1730 Thomson *Winter* (ed. 2) 289 The tender anguish nature shoots Thro' the wrung bosom of the dying man. **1817** Moore *Lalla R.* III. 365 Death had..taken thy wrung spirit home. **1841** James *Brigand* xxv, The refuge of many a wrung and broken heart.

b. Marked by distress, worry, or pain.

1862 Mrs. H. Wood *Mrs. Hallib. Troub.* III. xix, His face ..wore a wrung expression. **1882** *Mrs. Raven's Temptation* II. 188 Her nervous and wrung appearance.

c. ***wrung out***: completely exhausted.

1962 A. Lurie *Love & Friendship* iv. 68 Say, you do look kinda peaked... Not real bad, just kinda wrung out. **1975** *New Yorker* 29 Dec. 15/2 Although she caromed around her office there at enormous speed, she claimed to be 'wrung out'.

Hence **'wrungness.**

a **1875** J. Hinton in Hopkins *Life & Lett.* (1878) 273 There are two things awry;..the acting for self (a distinct tension and wrungness); and [etc.].

†**wrung-head**, erron. f. rung-head. *Obs.*

1711 W. Sutherland *Shipbuild. Assist.* 165 *Wrung-heads*, that part between the Floor-timber Head and second Foot-hook Heel, which, if a Ship lies on the Ground, bears the greatest Strain. [Hence in *Rees' Cycl.*, Smyth *Sailor's Word-bk.*, etc.]

†**wrung-staff**, obs. var. wring-staff.

1846 Young *Naut. Dict.* 372 Wrain-Staff, Wrung-Staff.

wrusum, wrutt, obs. varr. worsum, wroot *v.*

†**'wruxled**, *pa. pple. Obs. rare.* [Obscure: relationship to wrixle *v.* is not clear.]

13.. *E.E. Allit. P.* B. 1381 A wonder wroȝt walle wruxeled ful hiȝe. **13..** *Gaw. & Gr. Knt.* 2191 Wel bisemez þe wyȝe wruxled in grene Dele here his deuocioun.

wry (raɪ), *sb.* Also 5–6 **wrye**. [f. wry *v.*[2] or *a.*]

†**1.** ***on*** or ***upon wry***, = awry *adv. Sc. Obs.*

1375 Barbour *Bruce* iv. 705 Thair bemys strekit air, Owthir all evin, or on wry. **1423** Jas. I *Kingis Q.* lxxiii, To the colde stone my hede on wrye I laid. **1508** Dunbar *Flyting* 175 (Maitland Fol. MS.), With hingit luik ay wallowand vpone wry. **1535** Stewart *Cron. Scot.* (Rolls) III. 482 Scho..turnis hir face and luikis vpoune wry.

2. A twisting or tortuous movement.

1616 Surfl. & Markh. *Country Farme* vii. xxii. 674 The bitch being much lesse than the dogge..may haue some aduantage.., and so in turnes, slips, and wries, may get much ground. **1654** Vilvain *Epit. Ess.* v. xliii, The Sea flows and ebbs with crooked wry.

3. Distortion caused by refraction. *rare*$^{-1}$.

1869 Blackmore *Lorna D.* vii, You make full sure to prog him [*sc.* a loach] well, in spite of the wry of the water.

wry (raɪ), *a.* and *adv.* Also 6 **wrye**, 6–7 **wrie**, 6 **wrey**. [f. wry *v.*[2] Cf. prec. and awry *adv.* and *a.*]

A. *adj.* **1. a.** Of the features, neck, etc.: Abnormally deflected, bent, or turned to one side; in a contorted state or form; distorted.

1523 Ld. Berners *Froiss.* I. xi. 4b/2 Henry Erle of Lancastre with the wrye necke, called Torte colle. *c* **1530** *Crt. of Love* 1162 For they their members lakked, fote and hand, With visage wry and blind. **1542** Elyot, *Miriones*, men hauynge wry mouthes. *a* **1613** Overbury *Characters, Flatterer*, Hee will halt or weare a wrie necke. *a* **1637** B. Jonson *Horace, Art Poet.* 52 With faire black eyes and haire, and a wry nose. **1663** *Unfort. Usurper* I. iii. 6 In wry-neck'd Nero's Court, a wry-neck was the mode. **1705** *Lond. Gaz.* No. 4097/4 He likewise cures Hair Lips and Wry Necks. **1798** Ferriar *Illustr. Sterne*, etc. 138 Some of the disqualifications for priest's orders were..wry-noses [etc.]. **1819** *Rees' Cycl.* XXXVIII. s.v., A remedy for wry-necks. **1860** A. Leighton *Trad. Scot. Life* 224 The round cheek and wry lip, betokening his love of fun. **1861** Geo. Eliot *Silas M.* i, Their dreadful stare could dart cramp, or rickets, or a wry mouth at any boy.

b. Temporarily twisted, contorted, or writhed by reason or in manifestation of disrelish, disgust, or the like. Freq. in the phr. ***to make*** (***draw, pull***) ***a wry face*** or ***mouth*** (***wry faces*** or ***mouths***).

1598 R. Bernard tr. *Terence, Eunuch* iv. iv, Howe the hangman makes a wrie mouth. **1599** B. Jonson *Cynthia's Rev.* v. ii, The bitter bob in wit; the Reuerse in face or wry-mouth. **1611** [see wry-faced *a.*]. **1662** J. Davies tr. *Olearius' Voy. Ambass.* 208 Causing..a certain Buffoon..to make wry-faces and shew a thousand postures. **1697** Vanbrugh *Relapse* (1708) Pref., Saints..with screw'd Faces and wry Mouths. **1712** Swift *Jrnl. to Stella* 17 June, Flap your hand, and make wry mouths yourself. **1760** Sterne *Tr. Shandy* III. x, With a wry face..[he] read aloud, as follows. **1782** Miss Burney *Cecilia* v. i, [He] made a wry face, and returned it. **1783** [see wriggling *ppl. a.* 2]. **1802** Beddoes *Hygëia* III. 55 Hardly daring to draw a wry face at any thing offered them. **1839** Dickens *Nickleby* viii, Making a variety of wry mouths indicative of anything but satisfaction. **1876** Miss Broughton *Joan* I. i, Physic to be quickly swallowed with wry face. **1884** Mrs. C. Praed *Zéro* xiii, Each guest drank, made a wry face.

c. Of a smile, etc.: Made with a twisting of the features expressing dislike or distaste; 'twisted'.

1883 D. C. Murray *Hearts* xxvi, He only shook his head with a wry smile and declined a verbal answer. **1899** E. W. Hornung *Dead Men* xviii, He turned to me with a wry smile.

2. a. That has undergone twisting, contortion, or deflexion; wrung out of shape; twisted, crooked, bent.

1552 Huloet, Wrye, or disfourmed, or out of fashion, *distortus*. **1561** Hollybush *Hom. Apoth.* 6b, The membre becommeth lame and wrye. **1594** Carew *Huarte's Exam. Wits* viii. (1596) 113 Such..men..take dislike at any one wry plait of their garment. *a* **1613** Overbury *Characters* Wks. (1890) 50 Her wrie little finger bewraies carving. **1622** R. Preston *Godly Man's Inquis.* 47 Peter was shent for walking with a wry foote to the Gospell. **1751** F. Coventry *Pompey the Little* II. xiii. 241 A wry Plait in the Sleeve of his Shirt. **1851** *London Phil. Mag.* Feb. 133 The two pairs of planes, into which the wry quadrilateral was divisible. **1880** Meredith *Tragic Com.* (1881) 79 The timbers of their huts lean to an upright in wry splinters.

transf. **1579** Spenser *Sheph. Cal.* Feb. 28 For Age and Winter accord full nie, This chill, that cold; this crooked that wrye. **1776** Da Costa *Elem. Conchol.* 211 The gutter or beak..bends or falls on the back, in a wry manner. **1895** *Pall Mall G.* 25 Oct. 5/1 Their chanting in church is so wry that it makes you start.

b. Deflected from a straight course; inclined or turned to one side. Also in fig. context. ***wry look***, one expressive of displeasure or dislike. So ***wry twist*** (of the features).

1587 Golding *De Mornay* xviii. 330, I take to witnesse the happiest Courtiers that are, whether one wrye looke of their Prince do not sting them more at the heart, than [etc.]. **1613** W. Browne *Brit. Past.* I. ii. 712 As Tavy..among the woods doth wander, Losing himselfe in many a wry meander. **1615–6** Boys *Wks.* (1630) 183 If he run in wrie-wayes and bye-wayes, the more his labour. **1719** Atterbury *Serm.* (1734) II. 77 Every wry Step, by which he imagines himself to have declined from the Path of Duty. **1748** Cowper *Verses written at Bath* 28 Flatt'ning the stubborn clod, till cruel time,..on a wry step, Sever'd the strict cohesion. **1755** Johnson, *Contortion*,..twist; wry motion; flexure. **1857** Dickens *Dorrit* I. xxx, Here he..said to the stranger with his wryest twist upon him, 'Your commands'. **1864** C. Geikie *Life in Woods* v. 75 My eldest brother..had cast many wry looks at the thick logs. **1872** Gibbon *For the King* xxii, His features gave a wry twist.

fig. a **1586** Sidney *Arcadia* Wks. 1922 II. 226 Sometimes to her newes of my selfe to tell I go about, but then is all my best Wry words, and stam'ring, or els doltishe dombe.

3. a. Of words, thoughts, etc.: Contrary to that which is right, fitting, or just; aberrant, wrong; cross, ill-natured.

1599 B. Jonson *Cynthia's Rev.* II. iii, He's one, I would not haue a wry thought darted against. **1643–5** Milton *Divorce* II. iii, Thus were [they]..wont to thinke, without any wry thoughts cast upon divine governance. **1692** R. L'Estrange *Josephus, Antiq.* VIII. v. (1733) 220 All this together, might have aton'd for a wry word or two. **1759** Sterne *Tr. Shandy* I. iv, Which strange combination of ideas..produced more wry actions than all other sources of prejudice. **1821** Scott *Kenilw.* xv, Art thou not a hasty coxcomb, to pick up a wry word so wrathfully? **1856** G. H. Boker *Betrothal* I. i, Why this argument? I have heard ten thousand,..yet never Knew one wry notion straightened by them all. **1886** Spurgeon *Treas. Dav.* Ps. cxxxiii. Introd., In this psalm there is no wry word.

†**b.** Of persons: Perverse, cross. *Obs.*$^{-1}$

1649 Roberts *Clavis Bibl.* 190 With pure, thy self-thou-pure-wilt-show; And with the froward, wilt-be-wry.

c. Wrested; perverted; distorted.

1663 Butler *Hud.* I. ii. 431 He was..Next Rectifier of wry Law. *a* **1732** Atterbury (J.), He mangles and puts a wry sense upon protestant writers. **1896** Mrs. Caffyn *Quaker Grandmother* 290 Poor boy, he meant, what seemed to his wry mind, honestly towards you!

4. Marked or characterized by perversion, unfairness, or injustice.

1561 Norton & Sackv. *Gorboduc* I. i, My lordes, be playne, without all wrie respect Or poysonous craft to speake in pleasyng wise. **1593** Q. Eliz. *Boeth.* IV. pr. v. 89 When cheefely geayle, lawe & other tormentes..be turnd in wry sorte, & wickedest payne doo presse good men. **1851** Gladstone *Glean.* (1879) VI. xlii. 29 By influence individuals of a class will be powerful here and there, under any system, however cross and wry.

B. *adv.* In an oblique manner, course, or direction; awry.

1575 A. Fleming *Virg. Bucol.* IV. 12 Vnto thee, O childe, yᵉ ground..First offringes yuie wandring wrye [L. *errantes hederas*], in euerye place shall yeald. **1591** Sylvester *Du Bartas* I. ii. 1070 In these doubts much rather rest had I, Then with mine error draw my Reader 'wry. **1614** —— *Parl. Vertues Royall* 706 A fair Ship..wants..A skilfull Pilot,..That never wry shee sail. **1721** Bailey, *Wry*,.. on one side, not straight. **1886** *S.W. Linc. Gloss.* 169 It's not very pleasant, when things all go wry.

C. *Comb.*, as ***wry-angled, -eyed, -guided, -legged, -looked, -toothed; wry-blown; wry-formed, -set.***

1593 in Tytler *Hist. Scot.* (1864) IV. 212 A seduced king, ..and wry-guided kingdom. **1602** *Withals' Dict.* 286/2 That is crooke-footed, or wry-legged. **1604** F. T. *Case is Altered* C ij b, There was an old man,..stumpe-footed, wry-bodied, gagge-toothed, slandering-tongue. **1648** J. Quarles *Fons Lachrym.* 34 There is no..wry-look'd enemy T'upbraid thy actions. **1845** Youatt *Dog* iv. 103 A small breed of wry-legged terriers. **1883** *Longm. Mag.* Aug. 381 The wry-eyed, spectacled schoolmaster. **1883** Stallybrass tr. *Grimm's*

Teutonic Myth. III. 1075 Wry-toothed..beldams. **1897** H. N. HOWARD *Footsteps Proserpine* 16 The sea-brine beats on the wry-blown toft. **1905** A. T. SHEPPARD *Red Cravat* II. vii. 120 Their outlines..of twisted chimneys, wry-set doors. **1906** HARDY *Dynasts* II. v. vi. 781 What lewdness lip those wry-formed phantoms there? **1937** Wry-angled [see *mountain-roofed a.* s.v. MOUNTAIN 7 e].

b. Special combs.: **wry-bill**, the wry-billed plover (*Anarhynchus frontalis*), native to New Zealand; **wry-billed** *a.*, having a bill deflected to one side (see prec.); †**wry-neb**, a curvirostral fossil animal; †**wry-stroke** *fig.* (see quot.); **wry-tail**, a deformity in poultry, characterized by deflexion of the tail to one side.

1896 NEWTON *Dict. Birds* 1053 *Wrybill, *Anarhynchus frontalis*, [is] one of the most singular birds known, peculiar to New Zealand. **1873** SIR W. L. BULLER *Birds N.Z.* 216 *Anarhynchus frontalis*, *Wry-billed Plover. **1889** PARKER *Catal. N.Z. Exhib.* 116 (Morris), The curious wry-billed plover..[is] the only bird..in which the bill is turned..to one side—the right. **1708** *Phil. Trans.* XXVI. 78 *Curvirostra*, the *Wry-neb. **1655** FULLER *Ch. Hist.* VI. vi. §4 A Prior without a Posterior having none..after him to succeed in his place. We behold him only as the *wry-stroak given in by us out of courtesie, when the game was up before. **1880** L. WRIGHT *Illustr. Bk. Poultry* 201 *Wry-tail ..is in many cases owing to spinal causes, and in all such should be ruthlessly stamped out.

wry (raɪ), *v.*[1] *Obs.* exc. *dial.* Forms: *Inf.* (and *Pres. stem*). 1 **wreon**, 3 **wreoen**, 5 **wrene**, **wre**; 1 **wryon**, 3 **wri(h)en**, 4 **wryen**, 5 **wrine**, **wryne**, **wryyn**; 3 **wreie**, **wrihe**, 4 **wriȝ-**, 4–5 **wrye**, **wrie**, **wri**, 4–9 **wry**. *Pa. t.* 1 **wrah**, **wreah**, 3 **wreȝe**, 3–4 **wreih**, 4 **wreyh**, **wreighe**, **wreygh**, **wrei**, **wrey**, **wray**; *pl.* 1 **wriȝon**, **wruȝon**, 2–3 **wruȝen**, 3 **wruhen**, 3 **wriȝen**, **wrien**, 4 **wreȝen**, **wreghen**. *Pa. pple.* 1 **wriȝen**, **wroȝen**, 4 **wrien**, **wryen**, **wrin**; 3 **iwriȝen**, 3–4 **i-**, 4 **ywrien**, **ywryen**; 3–5 **i-**, 4–5 **ywrie**, **ywry(e**, 3 **iwroȝe**, 4 **ywryȝe**, 4–5 **ywriȝe**; 4 **wriȝe**, 4–5 **wrye**, 5 **wrie**; 3–4 **wreon**, 4 **wreiȝen**, 3 **wreȝe**, 4 **y-**, **iwreȝe**; 4–5 **wreygh**, **wreighe**, **wreye**. *Weak pa. t.* and *pple.* 4–5 **wryed**, **wried**, 4 **wryde**, 6 **wride**. [OE. *wréon* (pa. t. *wráh*, *wréah*, pl. *wriȝon*, *wruȝon*, pa. pple. *wriȝen*, *wroȝen*), *wríon*, **wríhan* (ONorthumb. *wríȝa*), = NFris. *wreye*, OHG. **rîhan* (in *intrîhan*, *inrîhan*, 'revelare'). Cf. BEWRY *v.*[1], OVERWRY *v.*, UNWRY *v.*]

†**1.** *trans.* To lay, place, or spread a cover over (something); to overlay with some covering; to cover up or over. *Obs.*

c **950** *Lindisf. Gosp.* Mark xiv. 65 Ongunnun summe efneȝespitta..hine &..wriȝa onsione his. *c* **1205** LAY. 27859 Þe while he wurchen lette..ane cheste longe And wreon heo al mid golde. *a* **1225** *Ancr. R.* 58 Uorþi was ihoten a Godes half..þet put were euer iwrien. *c* **1275** LAY. 7781 Þe toppe [of a tower] mihte wreie on cniht mid his cope. *c* **1366** CHAUCER *Rom. Rose* 56 Ther is neither busk nor hay In May that it nyl shrouded bene And it with newe leues wrene. *c* **1386** —— *Knt.'s T.* 2046 The maister strete That sprad was al with blak and wonder hye Right of the same is the strete ywrye. *c* **1440** *Pallad. on Husb.* I. 348 With marbil or with tile thy floryng wrie. *Ibid.* XIII. 47 The vessel fild be closid clene or wrie. **1499** *Promp. Parv.* (Pynson) t i b/2, Wryyn or hyllyn, *tego*. *a* **1825** FORBY *Voc. E. Anglia*, *Wry*, to cover close.

fig. *c* **1412** HOCCLEVE *De Reg. Princ.* 1686 Þe feend,..with many a circumstaunce Ful sly, him castiþ þe wrappe in & wrye.

b. To cover or rake up (a fire) so as to keep it alive. (Cf. RAKE *v.*[1] 5.) Now *dial.*

Cf. Ovid *Met.* IV. 64 'Quoque magis tegitur, tanto magis aestuat ignis'; also Fr. 'Le feu plus couvert est le plus ardant' (Cotgr. s.v. *Feu*).

c **1374** CHAUCER *Troylus* II. 539 Wel þe hottere ben þe gledes rede, That men hym wrien with asshe pale and dede. *c* **1385** —— *L.G.W.* 735 *Thisbe*, As wry the glede & hettere is the fyr; Forbede a loue and it is ten so wod. *a* **1895** in Rye *E. Angl. Gloss.* 251.

†**2.** To cover (a person) with a garment (or armour); to clothe, attire. Also *refl.* Occas. in fig. context. *Obs.*

a **901** ÆLFRED in Thorpe *Laws* I. 52 Ȝif mon næbbe buton anfeald hræȝl hine mid to wreonne oþþe to werianne. *c* **950** *Lindisf. Gosp.* Matt. xxv. 36 Ic wæs..nacod & ȝie clæðdon *uel* ȝie wriȝon meh. *a* **1000** *Genesis* 1572 Þæt he ne mihte.. hine handum self mid hræȝle wryon. **1297** R. GLOUC. (Rolls) 2246 Tuo hondred kniȝtes al so, Wel ywrie wiþ þe atyl. **1303** R. BRUNNE *Handl. Synne* 1148 Wrye me with sum cloþe. *c* **1374** CHAUCER *Troylus* II. 380 Swych loue of frendes regneth al þis town, And wre yow in þat mantel euere mo. *c* **1385** —— *L.G.W.* 1201 *Dido*, Dido al in gold & perre wrye. *c* **1400** *Rom. Rose* 6684 Of his hondwerk wolde he gete Clothes to wryne hym.

†**b.** To put trappings or armour on (a horse); to caparison, trap, harness. *Obs.*

1297 R. GLOUC. (Rolls) 1281 Mid vif hondred hors iwrie ..þe erl of kent was in a wode him vor to awreke. *Ibid.* 2052, 4076, 4096, etc. **13..** *Sir Beues* (A.) 3761 Beues..seȝ þe strete ful aboute Of stedes wrien [*v.r.* ytrapped] and armes briȝt. **13..** *K. Alis.* 1606 (Laud MS.), Þer men miȝtten quyk yseen Many hors wiþ trappen wryen. **14..** *Sir Beues* (C.) 4145 + 13 Þauȝe þat hors were with yren wrye Syr Befyse smote clene a way.

†**3.** To cover (a thing, or person) so as to protect, keep warm, or conceal. *Obs.*

a **1000** *Genesis* 2170 Ic þe..wið weana ȝehwam wreo & scylde folmum minum. *a* **1000** *Riddles* xxvi[i]. 12 Mec [= a book] siþþan wrah hæleð hleobordum. *a* **1225** *Ancr. R.* 84 Þes fikelares mester is to wrien, & te helien þet gong þurl. *a* **1240** *Wohunge* in *O.E. Hom.* I. 279 Alle gate þu hafdes hwer þu mihtes wrihe þine banes. **1340** *Ayenb.* 66 Þe þornhog þet ys al ywryȝe myd prikyinde eles. *c* **1369** CHAUCER *Dethe Blaunche* 627 She is the monstres heed ywryen, As filth over ystrowed with floures. *c* **1386** —— *Sompn. T.* 119 Though I him wrye a-nyght and make hym warm. *c* **1440** *Pallad. on Husb.* XIII. 34 From the wynd hem wrie With donge.

refl. *c* **1230** *Hali Meid.* (1922) 66 Ȝef þu wel wrist te under godes wengen. **13..** *K. Alis.* 2786 With targes, and hurdices, Theo Gregeis heom wryed als the wise. *c* **1330** *Amis & Amil.* 2333 He..in a bed him dight, And wreighe him wel warm aplight, With clothes. *c* **1400** *Rom. Rose* 6795, I haue..wel leuer..wrie me in my foxerie Vnder a cope of paperlardie. *c* **1440** *Jacob's Well* 265 He leyd hym in his bed, ..he wryed hym. **1447** BOKENHAM *Seyntys* (Roxb.) 175 Wyth hir mantyl he [*sc.* a child] dede hym wrye.

absol. *c* **1440** *Jacob's Well* 140 Þe chylderyn of mannys gettyng vnder þi weengys, god, wrying, In hope schul be gyed.

†**b.** To conceal or hide (a matter, etc.); to keep secret or unrevealed. *Obs.*

a **1000** *Genesis* 876 For hwon wast þu wean & wrihst sceome. *a* **1200** *Moral Ode* 160 in *O.E. Hom.* I. 169 Al scal þer bon þanne unwron, þet men wruȝen her and helen. *a* **1225** *Ancr. R.* 84 Mid his preisunge [he] heleð & wrihð mon his sunne. *a* **1275** *Ibid.* 420 (MS. Cott. Cleop.), Wrihen ha schal hire scheome, as sunfule Eue dohter. *c* **1320** *Cast. Love* 918 God..nom of hire his monhede þorw whom he wrey his Godhede. **1340** *Ayenb.* 61 Huanne þe blondere.. excuseþ and wryeþ þe kueades and þe zennes of ham. *c* **1374** CHAUCER *Troylus* IV. 1654 God, to whom þer nys no cause y-wrye. **1387–8** T. USK *Test. Love* II. v. (Skeat) l. 102 He wryeth moche venim with moche welth. **1412–20** LYDG. *Chron. Troy* I. 1813 For al þe foule schal couertly be wried, þat no defaute outward be espied. *c* **1460** *Wisdom* 862 in *Macro Plays* 63 With þe crose & þe pyll I xall wrye yt. *a* **1500** *Ragman Roll* 157 (MS. Bodl. 638, fol. 217 b), Though they her malice inwarde keuyr & wrye.

refl. *c* **1374** CHAUCER *Troylus* I. 329 And ay of loues seruantz euery while, Hym-self to wre, at hem he gan to smyle.

†**c.** To disguise (a person). *Obs. rare*[−1].

1567 GOLDING *Ovid's Met.* v. 61 b, The Gods..were faine themselues to hide In forged shapes... Ioue the Prince of Gods was wride In shape of Ram.

†**4.** Of things: To serve as a covering to (a person or thing); to be spread or extended over.

a **1000** *Genesis* 1386 Flod ealle wreah..hea beorgas. *c* **1000** *Sax. Leechd.* II. 242 Sio filmen biþ þeccende & wreonde þa wambe & þa innofaran. *a* **1200** *Vices & Virtues* 95 Ðe faste hope hafð hire stede up an heih, for ði hie is rof and wrikð alle ðe hire bieð beneðen. *a* **1225** *Ancr. R.* 150 Þe rinde, þet wrih [*v.r.* wrið] hit, þet is þe treouwes warde. *Ibid.* 390 Þis scheld þet wreih his Godhed was his leoue licome. **1340** *Ayenb.* 167 Vor þet is þe sseld of gold..þet him wriȝþ of eche half ase zayþ þe sauter. **1447** BOKENHAM *Seyntys* (Roxb.) 143 In.. Februarye..Whan frost & cold þe erthe doth wrye. **1642** D. ROGERS *Naaman* 581 Even as the bed..that is so narrow, that it will not wry them warme.

†**b.** To cover or stretch over (an expanse of ground). *Obs.*

c **1205** LAY. 5192 Weoren þa hulles and þa dæles iwriȝen mid þan dæden. *Ibid.* 17349 Þa Irisce fullen & wriȝen al þa feldes. **13..** *Guy Warw.* (A.) 4049 Of Sarrazins..was wrin al þe feld. *c* **1330** *Arth. & Merl.* 1764 (Kölbing), To Winchester þai gun spede Wiþ so michel pople of men, þat þai wreȝen doun & den. **13..** *K. Alis.* 1992 (Laud MS.), Alisaunder þi foo..Liggeþ now, wiþ swiche preye, þat he wriȝeþ [*v.r.* wrieth] al þe contreye.

wry (raɪ), *v.*[2] Forms: 1 **wriȝian**, 3–5 **wrien**, 4–5 **wryen** (5 **wryn**), 4–7 **wrie**, 4–6 **wrye**, 5– **wry**; 5 **wrey(e**, *Sc.* 6 **vrey** (8 **wray**), 9 **wree**. [OE. *wríȝian* to strive, move or go forward, tend, wend (= OFris. *wrigia* to bend, stoop), perh. related to LG. *wriggen* (see WRIG *v.*, and cf. BEWRY *v.*[2]).]

I. *intr.* †**1. a.** To move, proceed, or go; to turn, wend. (Only OE.) *Obs.*

c **888** ÆLFRED *Boeth.* xxv. §1 Þeah þu teo hwelcne boh ofdune to þære eorðan..swa þu hine alætst, swa sprincð he up & wriȝað wið his ȝecyndes. *a* **1000** *Riddles* xxi[i]. 5 Hlaford min [= master of the plough] on woh færeð, weard æt steorte, wriȝað on wonge.

†**b.** To have a particular or specified tendency, disposition, or inclination; to incline. *Obs.*

c **888** ÆLFRED *Boeth.* xxv. §1 Swa deð ælc ȝesceaft; wriȝað wið his ȝecyndes. *c* **1250** *Will & Wit* 7 in *O.E. Misc.* 192 Hwenne so wil to wene wrieð. **13..** *Erthe upon Erthe* 42 Wanne..eorþe toward eorþe þorw coueytise wryeþ. *c* **1400** *Pilgr. Sowle* (Caxton, 1483) IV. xxx. 78 He wylle cheuysse hym suche counceylle as he troweth wylle wryen to his purpoos. *c* **1430** *Pilgr. Lyf Manhode* II. (1869) 114 For j wole þat þe tale be turned ooþer weys,..þat it turne..wryinge to my wurshipes. **1549** COVERDALE *Erasm. Par. James* v. 39 b, The fore tokens of a mynde that wryeth downe vnto desperacyon. **1581** PETTIE tr. *Guazzo's Civ. Conv.* I. (1586) 23, I mean those, who though sprinkled with some imperfections, yet wrie rather to the good, then the euill.

†**2.** Of persons: To move or go, to swerve or turn, *aside*, *away*, or *awayward*. Also in fig. context.

c **1310** in Wright *Lyric P.* xv. 48 Þat feyre..wrieþ awey as hue were wroht. *c* **1386** CHAUCER *Miller's T.* 97 With hir heed sche wryed fast awey. **1426** AUDELAY *Poems* 18 To the worchip of this world thai wryn fro me away. *c* **1450** *Mirk's Festial* I. 112 Ȝet ȝe wryeth away and grucched to come to me. **1523** LD. BERNERS *Froiss.* I. cxlvi. 176 Than the kyng wryed away fro hym, and commaunded to sende for yᵉ hangman. **1534** MORE *Comf. agst. Trib.* I. Wks. 1162/1 Of wickednes thei wrie awaye and..turne to theyr fleshe for helpe.

†**b.** In similar use without adverb. *Obs.*

c **1400** *26 Pol. Poems* 26 Ȝif she grucche wiþ þe to rage, And alway fro the wole wrye. *c* **1430** *Syr Gener.* (Roxb.) 1352 The steward saw that, and did wry, And drew him som dele aside. *c* **1440** *York Myst.* xxx. 7 That wrecche may not wrye fro my wrekis. *a* **1500** *Hist. K. Boccus & Sydracke* (? 1510) S iij, He that clymeth ouer hye May happe somtyme to wrye. **1581** A. HALL *Iliad* III. 56 Paris wried at last, and so the blowe did shunne. **1596** DAVIES *Orchestra* lxiii, As when a Nimph..Leadeth a daunce.., she wries to euery hand And euery way doth crosse the fertile plaine. **1621** SANDERSON *Serm. ad Pop.* iv. ¶3 Like a young unbroken thing that hath metal, and is free, but is ever wrying the wrong way.

fig. **1581** T. HOWELL *Deuises* G ij b, How fayned friends do fayle, if fate doe wrye. **1593** Q. ELIZ. *Boeth.* I. met. i. 2 O with how defe eare she from wretched wries.

†**c.** *fig.* To deviate or swerve from the right or proper course; to go wrong, to err. Also with advs., as *amiss*, *aside*. *Obs.*

c **1369** CHAUCER *Dethe Blaunche* 627 An ydole of false purtraiture Is she, for she woll sone wrien [*v.r.* varien]. **1399** LANGL. *Rich. Redeles* II. 84 Þat no manere mede shulde make him wrye, For to trien a trouthe be-twynne two sidis. **1426** AUDELAY *Poems* 47 He..wrys away fro Godys word to his wyckydnes. *Ibid.* 50 Wry not fro Godis word. **1548** PATTEN *Exped. Scotl.* Pref. c v, If ye..wilfully wrye so far from hys truth. *a* **1557** MRS. M. BASSET tr. *More's Treat. Passion* M.'s Wks. 1365/2 Yf we of oure owne frowardnes wrye not a contrary way, but be readye..to folowe hys most blessed will. **1568** T. HOWELL *Arb. Amitie* (1879) 40 How much a man the greater is, By his Offence that wries amisse. **1611** SHAKS. *Cymb.* v. i. 5 How many Must murther Wiues much better then themselues For wrying but a little? **1632** SANDERSON *Serm.* II. 27 By wrying aside in some one or a few particulars, he may..offend the Lord. **1634** *Ibid.* I. 63 These wry too much on the right hand, ascribing to the holy scripture such a kind of perfection as it cannot have.

†**3.** Of things: To turn aside or obliquely; to undergo deflexion, twisting, or bending; to bend, wind; to turn from side to side.

c **1374** CHAUCER *Troylus* II. 906 Þe sonne Gan..downward for to wrye. *c* **1400** *Beryn* 2791 Then shalt þowe se an entre, ..Thouȝe it be streyt to-fore,..It growith more & more, & as a dentour wriythe. *c* **1440** *Pallad. on Husb.* I. 347 Thi somer hous northest & west let wrie. *c* **1450** *Ludus Coventriæ* 229 Þe patthe be-twyn bothyn þat may not wry Schal be hope and drede to walke in perfectly. **1553** M. WOOD tr. *Gardiner's True Obedience* 49 b, The decaied partes of their power (whose building..hath wried on the one side long ago). **1565** B. GOOGE tr. *Palingenius' Zodiac* VII. Y v b, Perchaunce..The liuely spirite enclosde..doth wrye as best it may, And striuing long through passage smal doth get at length away. **1633** P. FLETCHER *Purple Isl.* v. xii, The first [part of the brain] with divers crooks and turnings wries.

†**b.** Of a horse: To hold the head or neck to one side. *Obs.*[−1]

1610 MARKHAM *Masterp.* I. xxxvi. 70 Holding his necke awry;..The cure is to let him bloud..on the contrary side to that way he wryeth.

4. To contort the limbs, features, etc., as from pain or agony; to wriggle; to undergo twisting or turning; = WRITHE *v.*[1] 10 b.

1340–70 *Alex. & Dind.* 660 He was wraþ ful i-wrouht & wried in angur. *a* **1400** *Minor Poems fr. Vernon MS.* 338/381 On þe hed þonne [him] hard, þat he go wryȝinge þenneward. *Ibid.* 477/46 Þe ffisch..wroþly wrieþ on þe Crok. **1493** *Festyvall, Four Sermons* 21/2 As a galled horse that is touched on the sore wyncheth & wryeth. **1580** BLUNDEVIL *Art of Riding* III. xxii. 50 b, How to correct that Horse, which will mowe or wrie with his mouth. *c* **1590** J. STEWART *Roland Furious* VI, *Poems* (S.T.S.) II. 54 Scho schrinks, Scho vreyis, Scho vips for vo. *a* **1625** FLETCHER *Woman's Prize* III. i, She..wryes, and wriggles, As though she had the Itch. **1819** W. TENNANT *Papistry Storm'd* (1827) 34 He saw the wretchit men Wreein' and wreethin' wi' the pain. **1893** *National Observer* 30 Dec. 165/2 His mouth kept wrying from side to side.

II. *trans.* †**5.** To deflect or divert (a person or thing) from some course or in some direction; to cause to turn aside, away, or back. Also *refl.* *Obs.*

a **1400** *Partonope* 6865 Of hym they had the victory [in the lists], So sore hir aduersaries dyd they wrey. **1513** DOUGLAS *Æneid* v. xiv. 9 Baith to and fra al did thar nokkis wry [L. *torquent*]. *Ibid.* XI. xiv. 50 Latynis all thar ene about did wry [L. *convertere*]. **1555** PHAER *Æneid* II. 65 His tacle to the left hand set, and sterne to left hand wried. **1582** STANYHURST *Æneis* III. (Arb.) 88 Right so to thee same boord thee maysters al wrye the vessels.

fig. *c* **1425** *Cast. Persev.* 1675 in *Macro Plays* 127, I wyl me wryen ffro wyckyd wreche. **1549** CHALONER *Erasm. on Folly* O ij, If he [*sc.* a prince] wrie himselfe never so little from that becometh hym. *a* **1586** SIDNEY *Arcadia* I. xviii, Our mindes ..from the right line of vertue, are wryed to these crooked shifts. **1620** [G. BRYDGES] *Horæ Subs.* 148 Let not the parties ielousie..wrest or wry his iudgement in the least degree to preiudice. **1635** PEMBLE *Wks.* 6 Ambition and tyrannie in Churchmen wryed their thoughts..to the advancement of their owne greatnesse. **1650** TRAPP *Comm. Deut.* xxxiii. 9 Not to be wryed or biassed by respect to carnal friends, is a high..point of self-denial.

†**b.** To avert (the head, face, etc.); to turn aside or *away*. *Obs.*

c **1400** *Pilgr. Sowle* (Caxton, 1483) I. xv. 11 Hit sytteth the nought to wrye awey thy face. *c* **1407** LYDG. *Reson & Sens.* 1413 She gan ay hir hede to wrye. *a* **1450** MYRC *Par. Pr.* 776 Sum-what þy face from hyre þou wry. **1513** MORE *Rich. III*, Wks. 70/1 The duke..wried hys hed an other way. **1560** ROLLAND *Seven Sages* 35 He wryit his face away and his visage. **1581** A. HALL *Iliad* III. 55 Hector from his helmet then his countnance hauing wried,..the lots did turne. **1611** SPEED *Hist. Gt. Brit.* IX. xix. §22 Buckingham..wried his face another way. **1655** J. COTGRAVE *Wits Interpr.* (1662) 276 When [he was] pressing for a kiss her head she wried.

†**c.** To change or alter (one's course). *Obs.*[−1]

1598 Q. ELIZ. *Plutarch* i. 13 His course..wryed was to east, the sons arising place.

†**6.** To curve, inflect, bend. *Obs.*[−1]

c **1450** *Hymns Virg.* (1867) 122 The rayn bowe iwryyd schalle be.

7. To twist or turn (the body, neck, etc.) round or about; to contort, wring, wrench; to writhe. Also with advs., as †*a-doyle*.

c **1460** J. RUSSELL *Bk. Nurture* 285 Wrye not youre nek a doyle as hit were a dawe. **1593** [see WRING *v.* 2, quot. *a* 1586]. **1598** Q. ELIZ. *Plutarch* xii. 14 Diogines..bak wrying and turning nek in casting on her Looke. **1607** MARKHAM *Cavel.* I. (1617) 39 If you see her wrie her taile. **1656** EARL MONM. tr. *Boccalini's Advts. fr. Parnass.* I. (1674) 132 Wrying his Body twenty several waies. **1676** HOBBES *Iliad* XVI. 248 Jove .. granted him to save the ships from fire; But at returning safe his neck he wri'd. **1725** *Fam. Dict.* s.v. *Palsey*, Let him be blooded in his Neck-Vein..on the contrary Side to the Way he wryes his Neck. **1800** LAMB *Let.* in *Final Mem.* vi. 51 Without much wrying my neck I can see the white sails.

b. To twist out of shape, form, or relationship; to give a twist to; to pull, contort, make wry. Also *fig.* and in fig. context.

a **1586** SIDNEY *Ps.* XXII. viii, [My] loosed bones quite out of joynt be wried. **1594** DANIEL *Cleopatra* V. ii, In her sinking downe shee wryes The Diadem which..shee wore. **1594** CAREW *Huarte's Exam. Wits* 281 The heat..wrieth the proportion of the face. **1665** J. SPENCER *Prodigies* 254 They are a Nose of Wax which may be wry'd to what figure.. Fancy shall impose upon them. **1679** HOBBES *Behemoth* (1840) 217 They are, for the most part, Latin and Greek words, wryed a little at the point, towards the native language. **1686** G. STUART *Joco-ser. Disc.* 41 The Todd will ..wry about the Neck o' th' Cock. **1727** SWIFT *God's Revenge agst. Punning*, The Lord mercifully spared his neck, but as a mark of reprobation wryed his nose. **1842** BROWNING *In a Gondola* 47 Guests by hundreds—not one caring If the dear host's neck were wried. **1855** BAILEY *Mystic*, etc. 69 Some Titanian arm, Whose elbow, jogged by earthquakes, wryed the pole. **1861** SWINBURNE *Queen-Mother* I. i, I know him by the setting of his neck, The mask is wried there. **1883** R. W. DIXON *Mano* II. iv. 78, I put on those arms which he..From the dead body had begun to wry.

†**c.** *fig.* To wrest the meaning of; = WRITHE *v.*[1] 7. *Obs.*

1521 FISHER *Sermon agst. Luther* iv. Dv, Men of fell wyttes..[who] had the propre fayth to wrye & to torcasse the scryptures. **1548** UDALL, etc. *Erasm. Par. Matt.* xiii. 59b, False Apostles..whyche wresteth and wryeth by subtyll interpretacion, the heauenly doctrine after their lustes. **1564** *Brief Exam.* ***ij, You do wrye this place from his naturall sense. **1631** R. BYFIELD *Doctr. Sabb.* 156 This Alleager..wryeth the sense. **1649** BP. REYNOLDS *Hosea* vii. 136 Take heed of wresting and wrying that to the corrupt fancies of our owne evill hearts.

†**d.** To pervert. *Obs.*

1563 *Mirr. Mag., Hastings* xlvii, Alas, are counsels wryed to catch the goode. *a* **1585** MONTGOMERIE *Flyting* 754 The thingis I said, gif þow wald now deny, Weining to wry þe veritie with wylis. *a* **1586** SIDNEY *Arcadia* II. vi, Publique defences neglected; and in summe..all awrie, and (which wried it to the most wrie course of all) witte abused. **1620** E. BLOUNT *Horæ Subs.* 148 Let not the parties ielousie..wrest or wry his iudgement in the least degree to preiudice.

e. *poet.* To distort the judgement of; to warp.

1861 SWINBURNE *Queen-Mother* I. ii, *Hen.* This fool is wried with wine. *Mar.* French air hath nipped his brains.

f. *poet.* To turn, change, or alter (a colour).

1865 SWINBURNE *Poems & Ball., At Eleusis* 181 Ill slant eyes interpret the straight sun, But in their scope its white is wried to black.

†**8.** *absol.* = WRING *v.* 4c. *Obs. rare*$^{-1}$.

14.. *Chaucer's Merch. T.* 341 (Petw. MS.), But I woote best wher wrieþ my shoo.

9. To twist or distort (the face or mouth), esp. so as to manifest disgust or distaste; = WRITHE *v.* 5b. Also *refl.*

a **1510** DOUGLAS *K. Hart* II. 96 Her face scho wryit about for propir teyne. **1552** HULOET, Wrynge the mouth in waye of derision, *valgulatio.* ? **1554** COVERDALE *Hope of Faithful* (1574) 150 Though ye wry your mouthes at it. **1633** BP. HALL *Hard Texts* 173 Winking with their eyes and wrying their faces at me. **1681** COLVIL *Whigs Supplic.* (1751) 81 He wry'd his mouth, and knit his brows. **1691** MRS. D'ANVERS *Academia* 56 He dare not wry his Mouth to laugh. *a* **1779** D. GRAHAM *Writ.* (1883) II. 92, I made my eyes to roll, and wrayed my face in a frightful manner. **1857** HEAVYSEGE *Saul* (1869) 291 Bitter is bitter, though the lips be not Allowed to wry themselves thereat. **1888** *Sat. Rev.* 1 Dec. 650/1 The tonics..were bitter enough to wry the palate. **1898** M. HEWLETT *Forest Lovers* xv, She wried her mouth to a smile.

†**10.** To roll, wrap, or wind *up*. *Obs.*$^{-1}$

1674 N. FAIRFAX *Bulk & Selv.* 128, I take the seed..to be a cluster of bubbles wryed up snug.

wry, etc., varr. WRAY *v.*[1] *Obs.*

wrycche(d, wryche, etc., obs. ff. WRETCH(ED.

wryed, var. WRIED *ppl. a.*

wryer, var. WRAYER *Obs.*

wry-faced, *a.* (stress variable). [f. WRY *a.* 2.] Having the face out of line with the neck and chest; also, that has or makes a wry face.

1607 TOPSELL *Four-f. Beasts* 14 Antiphilus made a very noble one [*i.e.* picture of a satyr] in a Panthers skin, calling it *Aposcopon*, that is, Wri-faced. **1611** COTGR., *Caravirée*, a wry-mouthed, or wry-faced wench; or one that often makes wry mouthes, or ill fauoured wry faces. **1684** *Lond. Gaz.* No. 1990/4 One of the Robbers was..Wrifaced and Pock-broken. **1803** FESSENDEN *Poet. Petit.* 87 Each wry-fac'd rogue, and dirty trollop. **1837** DICKENS *Pickw.* xvii, You snivelling, wry-faced, puny villain. **1898** *Westm. Gaz.* 17 Feb. 9/3 A slim, wry-faced man.

transf. **1687** SETTLE *Refl. Dryden* 83 What a wry faced contradiction is here?

wryghe, obs. variant of WRAY *v.*[1]

wryght(e, obs. forms of WRIGHT *sb.*, WRITE *v.*

'**wrying**, *vbl. sb.*[1] *dial.* [f. WRY *v.*[1] + -ING[1].] (See quot.)

a **1825** FORBY *Voc. E. Anglia, Wrying*, covering, of bed-clothes, &c., not of apparel.

wrying ('raɪɪŋ), *vbl. sb.*[2] [f. WRY *v.*[2] + -ING[1].]

1. The action of twisting, wringing, or writhing; an instance of this.

1580 BLUNDEVIL *Horsemanship, Diseases* clix. 68b, The taint being made somwhat full, with continuall turning and wrieng of it. *a* **1586** SIDNEY *Arcadia* II. xiv, A certaine wrying I had of my necke. *c* **1595** CAPT. WYATT *Dudley's Voy.* (Hakl. Soc.) 42 The motion and wrynge of his mouth. **1611** COTGR., *Tortuement*, a crooking,..wrying, writhing. **1888** G. GISSING *Life's Morning* III. xx. 161 Wilfrid [spoke] with a little wrying of the lips.

†**2.** The action of wresting or perverting. *Obs.*

1562 WINȜET *Wks.* (S.T.S.) I. 20 We allegeit na thing.. bot sinceirlie the expres Word of God, but wrysting, wrying, gloissing, or cloking. *a* **1598** ROLLOCK *Passion* xxv. (1616) 237 We must not thinke, Brethren, that this is any wrying and wresting of the old Scripture.

†**3.** The action of deviating or turning from a course, etc.; straying. *Obs.*

1592 BABINGTON *Notes on Gen.* iii. 10 Wryings and turnings from the matter will not serue, minsings and shiftings before hym were neuer currant. **1604** —— *Notes on Exod.* iii. §18 How hard it is to leaue a wonted wrying from the right way. **1879** G. M. HOPKINS *Let.* 9 Apr. (1935) 78 It seems to me to hit the mark it aims at without any wrying.

'**wryingly**, *adv. rare.* [f. *wrying*, pres. pple. of WRY *v.*[2]] In a twisting or writhing manner.

1611 COTGR., *Tortuément*, wryly,..crookingly, wryingly. *Ibid.*, *Tortueusement*,..wryingly.

wryly ('raɪlɪ), *adv.* Also 6–7 **wrily**. [f. WRY *a.* + -LY[2].] In a wry, oblique, or distorted manner.

Frequent in recent use.

1580 HOLLYBAND *Treas. Fr. Tong, Tortuement*,..wrily, crookedly. **1611** COTGR., *Obliquement*, obliquely, wrily. **1736** AINSWORTH *Lat. Dict.* s.v. *Contorte.* **1848** LANDOR *Imag. Conv.* Wks. I. 16/2 Most of these..have chewed upon it harshly and wryly. **1893** *Chambers's Jrnl.* 18 March 164/2 Mr. Jones smiled wryly.

wry-mouth ('raɪmaʊθ). [f. WRY *a.* 1, 1b + MOUTH *sb.*]

†**1.** (See quot. 1859.) *Obs.*

1661 LOVELL *Hist. Anim. & Min.* 29 The gall of a wild Cat is very good against the wry mouth. **1859** MAYNE *Expos. Lex.* 1283 *Tortura*,..formerly used for *Spasmus*, chiefly of a part, as of the face or the mouth; wry-mouth.

2. a. *attrib.* = WRY-MOUTHED *a.* 1. Also *ellipt.*

1652 BENLOWES *Theoph.* VIII. lxxxiv, No wry-mouth squint-ey'd scoff can stay Their swift progression. **1655** GAYTON *Bagnal's Ghost* 3 Thick Ling and wry mouth Plaise. **1881** E. P. HOOD *Christmas Evans* iv. 120 Of wry-mouth fiends a wrathful brood.

b. One who has a distorted mouth.

1840 *Penny Cycl.* XVIII. 316/1 [It] had fallen into disuse since the death of Boleslav the Wry-mouth.

3. *U.S.* **a.** One or other fish belonging to the genus *Cryptacanthodes* of blennioid fishes, and native to the north-western Atlantic. **b.** The electric ray or torpedo (*Cent. Dict.* 1891).

1844 *Amer. Jrnl. Sci.* XLVII. 60 *Cryptacanthodes maculatus*, Storer, Spotted Wry-mouth. **1890** *Science* April 212/1 The sea-raven, the rock-eel, and the wry-mouth, which inhabit these brilliant groves, are all colored to match their surroundings.

wry-mouthed, *a.* (stress variable). [f. WRY *a.* 1. Cf. prec.]

1. Having a wry mouth.

1552 HULOET, Wrye mouthed men, *miriones.* **1604** F. T. *Case is Altered* Cijb, There was an old man..bleer-eied, wry-mouthed, botle nosed, lame-legged. **1616** T. SCOT *Philomythie* A6b, They..wrie-mouth'd Plaice..did eate. **1618** FLETCHER *Women Pleased* III. ii, A pack of wry-mouth'd mackrel Ladies. **1653** R. SANDERS *Physiogn.* 152 Looking asquint, wry-mouth'd, wry-neck'd. **1776** DA COSTA *Elem. Conchol.* 210 *Buccina Recurvirostra*,.. Wry-mouthed Whelks. **1870** ROSSETTI *Poems, Guido Cavalcanti* xxii, That wry-mouthed minx.

fig. **1614** J. TAYLOR (Water-P.) *Nipping Abuses* L4, The wri-mouth'd Crittick. **1620** QUARLES *Jonah* 1487 Daring Presumption, wry-mouth'd Derision, Damned Apostacie.

2. Marked or characterized by contortion of the mouth. Also *transf.*

1624 QUARLES *Sion's Elegies* iii. 21 What flout, what wry-mouth'd scoffe,..Hath scap'd the furie of my Foemans tongue To doe my simple Innocencie wrong? **1635** —— *Embl.* V. v. 34 What soul would not be proud Of wry-mouth'd scorns? *a* **1699** J. BEAUMONT *Psyche* XIII. ccxxviii, What wry-mouth'd play They us'd, their gentle Savior to flout. **1728** POPE *Dunc.* II. 145 A shaggy Tap'stry,.. Instructive work! whose wry-mouth'd portraiture Display'd the fates her confessors endure. **1748** RICHARDSON *Clarissa* (1768) VIII. 59 Lifting up her rolling eyes,..with a wry-mouthed earnestness.

wryneck ('raɪnɛk). Also **wry-neck**. [f. WRY *a.* 1 + NECK *sb.*]

1. One or other species of the genus *Iynx* of small migratory scansorial picoid birds; esp. the common species, *Iynx torquilla*, distinguished by its habit of writhing the neck and head.

1585 HIGINS *Junius' Nomencl.* 59/2 *Iynx torquilla*,..a wrynecke. **1611** COTGR., *Turcot*,..the little ash-coloured and long-tongued bird, called a Wrynecke. **1676** GREW *Museum, Anat. Stomach* viii. 38 A Young Wryneck..hath no Crop, and but a small Gulet. **1752** J. HILL *Hist. Anim.* 402 *Jynx*, the wry-neck,..has a very singular way of twisting it's head about, and bending it's neck; it thence obtained.. the name..of the Wry-neck. **1768** PENNANT *Brit. Zool.* I. 181 The Wryneck we believe to be a bird of passage... It takes its name from a manner it has of turning its head back to the shoulders. **1815** KIRBY & SP. *Entomol.* ix. (1816) I. 288 The wryneck and the woodpeckers..live entirely upon insects. **1839–43** YARRELL *Brit. Birds* II. 152 As the Wryneck makes its appearance here about the same time as the Cuckoo, it has..acquired the names of Cuckoo's Mate, and Cuckoo's Maid. **1888** NEWTON in *Encycl. Brit.* XXIV. 652/2 The *Picidæ* [include]..at least three Sub-families.. The Woodpeckers proper,..the Piculets,..and the Wrynecks.

†**b.** An infusorian (see quot.). *Obs.*$^{-1}$

1769 *Phil. Trans.* LIX. 149 The *Volvox torquilla*, or wry-neck.

2. a. One who has a wry neck.

Earlier versions of quot. 1879 have the form *wrynot*.

1607 R. [CAREW] tr. *Estienne's World Wond.* 300 They learne..to looke downe to the ground, to counterfet wry-necks. **1653** R. SANDERS *Physiogn.* 172 Of them is the Proverb, Never trust a wry Neck. **1656** FLECKNOE *Diarium* 2 And wry-neck they would ask with laughter, What newes 'twas he was hearkning after? **1879** W. HENDERSON *Folk-Lore N.C.* vii. 254 He caps Wryneck, and Wryneck caps the Dule [= Devil].

b. *attrib.* = WRY-NECKED *a.* 2.

1586 FERNE *Blaz. Gentrie* 129 The wrynecke Earle of Lancaster. **1615** BRATHWAIT *Strappado* (1878) To Rdr., Th' art no wri-neck critick. **1882** *Encycl. Brit.* XIV. 255/2 A son ..known as Henry Tort-Col or Wryneck... This Henry Wryneck died in 1361.

†**c.** *Cant.* (See quot.) *Obs. rare*$^{-0}$.

1796 GROSE *Dict. Vulg. T.*, *Wry Neck Day*, hanging day.

3. *Path.* A deformity characterized by contortion of the neck and face, and lateral inclination of the head; stiff-neck; = TORTICOLLIS.

1753 *Chambers' Cycl.* Suppl. s.v. *Wry-Necked*, If the Wry-neck proceeds from a contraction of one of the mastoide muscles. **1822–7** GOOD *Study Med.* (1829) IV. 334 This species, therefore, offers us the three following varieties:..Natural wry-neck... Spastic wry-neck... Atonic wry-neck. **1872** T. BRYANT *Pract. Surg.* (1884) II. 345 Wry-neck is an example of this affection [*sc.* rigid atrophy] due to a contracted sterno-mastoid muscle. **1881** W. RIVINGTON in *Brain* IV. 257 The ordinary form of spasmodic wry-neck.

b. (See quot.) *rare*$^{-0}$.

1819 REES *Cycl.*, *Wry-neck*, a disease of the spasmodic kind in sheep, in which the head is drawn forcibly to one side. [Hence in WEBSTER (1828–32), and later Dicts.]

wry-necked, *a.* (stress variable). [f. WRY *a.* 1. Cf. prec.]

1. Having a wry or crooked neck.

1596 SHAKS. *Merch. V.* II. v. 30 The vile squealing of the wry-neckt Fife. **1842** BARHAM *Ingol. Leg.* Ser. II. *Netley Abbey*, A squeaking fiddle and 'wry-neck'd fife'. **1870** ENGEL *Catal. Mus. Instr.* 62 The wry-necked Fife... The Italians call it *cornetto curvo*.

2. Of persons or animals: Affected with distortion of the neck; having wryneck.

1608 DEKKER *Dead Term* Wks. (Grosart) IV. 39 That aged and reuerend (but wry-necked) sonne of thine. **1653** [see WRY-MOUTHED *a.* 1]. *a* **1679** J. WARD *Diary* (1839) 273 Some are wry neckt from the womb. **1705** HICKERINGILL *Priest-cr.* II. Pref. A4 Great Alexander..(being blind) did love that Wry-neck'd Fool. **1753** *Chambers' Cycl.* Suppl., *Wry-Necked*, a term applied to persons affected with a distortion of the neck. **1844** H. STEPHENS *Bk. Farm* II. 608 It is almost impossible to bring the head of a wry-necked lamb into the passage of the womb. **1860** GEO. ELIOT *Mill on Fl.* II. v, She preferred the wry-necked lambs.

fig. **1624** HEYWOOD *Captives* III. iii. in Bullen *O. Pl.* IV, This same wryneckt death..still spoyles all drinkinge, 'tis a thinge I never coold indure. **1647** N. WARD *Simple Cobler* 20 All the squint-ey'd, wry-necked, and brasen-faced Errors that are or ever were of that litter.

Hence **wry-'neckedness**. *rare*$^{-1}$.

1881 TAIT in *Nature* XXV. 90 The wry-neckedness of the protecting shell.

wryness ('raɪnɪs). Also 6 **wrines**, 7 **-ness(e, wrynesse**. [f. WRY *a.* + -NESS.]

1. The fact or condition of being wry or distorted; distortion, twisting.

1591 PERCIVALL *Sp. Dict.*, *Tortedad*, crookednes, wrines, *obliquitas.* **1607** TOPSELL *Four-f. Beasts* 107 The waight of a groate thereof..helpeth the conuulsion and wrynesse of the mouth. **1616** DONNE *Serm.* Wks. 1839 V. 463 This is (*tortuositas serpentis*) the Wryness, the Knottiness, the Entangling of the Serpent. *a* **1693** *Urquhart's Rabelais* III. xxxi. 256 A perversive Wriness and Convulsion of the Muscles. **1693** EVELYN *De la Quint. Compl. Gard.* I. 35 A large Garden would..be less pleasing..if it had..some visible wriness to disfigure it. **1855** BAIN *Senses & Int.* II. iv. §4 A bitter taste produces wryness and contortion of the mouth. **1857** DICKENS *Dorrit* II. xxvi, The wryness of his face and the uneasiness of his limbs. **1898** MEREDITH *Later Alexandrian* Poems I. 200 An inspiration caught from dubious hues, Filled him, and mystic wrynesses he chased.

2. *fig.* Deviation from what is regular or normal; obliquity, wrongness.

1633 AMES *Agst. Cerem.* II. 498 Notwithstanding all this weaknesse, and wrinesse of these instances, the Rej. doth so triumph in them. **1648** W. MOUNTAGUE *Devout Ess.* I. xii. 143 An exploring the rectitude or wrynesse of their behaviours in this particular. **1906** HARDY *Dynasts* II. IV. v, The wryness of the times.

wrypick, erron. f. RYEPECK.

1881 G. D. LESLIE *Our River* 112 The boat is moored by short stout wrypicks. [*Ibid.* 230 A couple of ripicks.]

wrytche, obs. var. WRETCH *sb.*

wrythe, var. WRETHE *sb. Obs.*; obs. f. WRITHE *v.*

Wu (wu:). [Chinese *wú*.] Used *attrib.* of a group of Chinese dialects spoken in Shanghai, the south of Jiangsu province, and most parts of Zhejiang province, China. Also *absol.*
1908 M. KENNELLY tr. *Richard's Comprehensive Geogr. Chinese Empire* v. 348 The Ngeu..or Wu Dialects, comprising: 1—The Wênchow dialect. 2—The Ningpo dialect. 3—The Sungkiang or Shanghai dialect. **1943** *China Handbk.* i. 30 The Wu group is spoken south of the Yangtze in Kiangsu... It is characterized by the preservation of the ancient voiced stops as aspirated voiced consonants. **1948** R. A. D. FORREST *Chinese Lang.* xi. 224 The Wu language has in modern times a greater than average hostility to final consonants... Where palatalisation occurs in Wu before a.. we regularly find the occlusive beside the fricative. **1964** [see MIN *a.* and *sb.*[4]]. **1977** 'S. LEYS' *Chinese Shadows* (1978) ii. 95 The gracious Wu dialect used in south Kiansu and north Chekiang. **1978** *Whitaker's Almanack 1979* 838/1 The Chinese language has many dialects, Cantonese, Hakka,.. Wu (Shanghai) and the northern dialect.

wu, wuas, obs. varr. HOW *adv.*, WHOSE.

wucche, var. WHITCH *Obs.*

wuch(e, obs. varr. WHICH.

wud, obs. or dial. f. *would*, pa. t. of WILL *v.*[1]

wud(d, wude, obs. or Sc. and dial. ff. WOOD *sb.*[1] and *a.*

wuddie, -y, wuddle, var. WIDDY, WIDDLE.

wudz, obs. f. WOOTZ.

wueke, ME. var. WICK *sb.*[1]

‖**Wufan** ('wufan). Also **wu-fan.** [Chinese *wŭfăn*, f. *wŭ* five + *făn* anti-, against.] Used *attrib.* to designate an official campaign launched in China in 1952 against bribery, tax evasion, theft of state property, skimping on work and cheating on materials, and theft of state economic information.
1956 *Contemporary China 1955* I. 63 The *wu-fan* movement against the 'five vices' in the private sector: bribing, tax evasion, theft of government property, cheating on government contracts, and stealing economic information from government sources for private speculation. **1966** D. WILSON *Quarter of Mankind* iii. 35 Within a few months the second campaign followed, this time the *wufan* or 'five-antis' movement to root out bribery, tax evasion, theft of state property, theft of state economic secrets and embezzlement in carrying out state contracts. **1966, 1971** [see SANFAN].

wuff (wʌf), *sb.* [Echoic. Cf. WOOF *sb.*[2], WOUGH *sb.*, and next.] A low, suppressed bark of a dog.
1824 [CARR] *Craven Gloss.* s.v. **1888** 'J. S. WINTER' *Bootle's Childr.* ii, The 'wuff-wuff' of one or other of the dogs breaking the silence.

wuff (wʌf), *v.* [Echoic. Cf. WAFF *v.*, WOOF *v.*] *intr.* To bark in a low, suppressed manner.
1851 G. H. KINGSLEY *Sp. & Trav.* v. (1900) 143 That dog, now growling and 'wuffing' in his dreams. **1928** D. H. LAWRENCE *Lady Chatterley's Lover* xii. 197 The dog wuffed softly, slowly wagging her tail. **1932** E. M. BRENT-DYER *Chalet Girls in Camp* vi. 84 'That dog just worships you, Jo.' .. Rufus 'wuffed' joyfully.

wuffer ('wʌfə(r)). *rare*⁻¹. [f. WUFF *v.* + -ER[1].] A dog with a loud, deep bark.
1923 D. H. LAWRENCE *Ladybird* 245 The white cool monster was a Siberian steppe-dog. Alexander wondered what the steppes made of such a wuffer.

wugg (wʌg), *v. south. dial.* [dial. *wug, wugg, wo(a)g*, etc., a call to a horse.] *intr.* Of a horse: To move forward; to go on.
1876 BLACKMORE *Cripps* iv, Wugg then, Dobbin! Wun'not go home to-night? **1881** —— *Christowell* iii, No man as ever I see yet..hath received the power to make Teddy wugg, when a' hath his nosebag on.

wuke, wulc(h, obs. ff. WEEK *sb.*, WHICH.

wulde, obs. Sc. form of WILD *a.*

†**wulder.** *Obs.* Also 1 wuldor, -ur, -er, 3 *Orm.* wullderr. [OE. *wuldor, -ur, -er*, a derivative (with *r* suffix) from the stem of Goth. *wulþus*.] Glory; honour.
c **825** *Vesp. Psalter* xx. 6 Micel is wuldur his in haelu ðinre. *c* **888** ÆLFRED *Boeth.* xxx. §1 Is þæt unȝerisenlic wuldor þisse worulde & swiðe leas. *a* **1200** *Fragm. Ælfric's Gram.*, etc. (1838) 7 þin wombe was þin God, & þin wulder. *c* **1200** ORMIN 3379 Si Drihhtin upp inn heoffness ærd Wurrþminnt & loff & wullderr. *Ibid.* 7630 Crist..ȝarrkedd iss..till þiss Judewisshe follc Wurrþshipe & eche wullderr.

wulderne, var. WILDERN *Obs.*

wule, obs. f. WHILE, WILL.

wulf, obs. f. WOLF.

wulfenite ('wʊlfənaɪt). *Min.* [a. G. *wulfenit* (1845), f. the name F. X. von *Wulfen* (1728–1805), Austrian scientist, + -ITE[1] 2 b.] 'Molybdate of lead, found in brilliant crystals' (Chester).
1849 J. NICOL *Man. Min.* 385 Wulfenite, *Haidinger*; Molybdate of Lead, *Phillips* [etc.]. **1858** GREG & LETTSOM *Man. Min.* 411 Wulfenite..decrepitates when heated. **1883** *Science* I. 609/1 The red varieties of wulfenite.

Wulfilian (wʊl'fɪlɪən), *a.* [f. Gothic *Wulfila* Ulfilas (see below) + -IAN.] Of or pertaining to Ulfilas (311–382), missionary, translator of the Bible into Gothic, and inventor of the Gothic alphabet.
1926 G. W. S. FRIEDRICHSEN *Gothic Version Gospels* 144 It is quite clear, however, that this is no Wulfilian text. **1968** *Language* XLIV. 731 Thus there was no confusion between the two graphemes in Wulfilian orthography.

Wulfrunian (wʊl'frunɪən). [f. the name of *Wulfrun*, the 10th-century lady of the manor from whose name *Wolverhampton* is derived + -IAN.] An inhabitant of Wolverhampton (see also quot. 1959).
1959 J. W. GODSELL *I was no Lady* iii. 50 My English husband had attended the ancient and exclusive Gothic-arched Wolverhampton Grammar School, thereby becoming a Wulfrunian. **1974** *Times* 12 Nov. 15/7 There are 'self-made' Wulfrunians of many centuries on our roll. **1979** *Times* 26 Nov. 4/6 'Are you proud to live in Wolverhampton? Or do you, when asked where you come from,.. try to change the subject?' Those are the searching questions that Wulfrunians are being asked by their borough council.

wull, obs. f. WOOL *sb.*; Sc. var. WILL *sb.* and *v.*

wullcat, Sc. var. WILD CAT.

wullee, var. WELI.

wullen, obs. f. WOOLLEN *a.*

wulpere, var. VOLUPER *Obs.*

wult, Sc. var. VULT *Obs.*

wultre, obs. f. VULTURE.

†**wumme**, *int. Obs.* Also 2 wumē (3 wummen). [App. repr. OE. *wá mé*, f. *wá* WOE *int.* 5 + *mé* ME *pers. pron.* For the vowel cf. *nummor* s.v. NO MORE.] Woe is me!
c **1175** *Lamb. Hom.* 157 Wume [L. *heu michi*] nu þet min utbiwiste is her swa longe ituþed. *a* **1200** *St. Marher.* 13 Wumme lefdi qð he þa: wa is me mine liues. *a* **1225** *Ancr. R.* 158 Wummen [*v.r.* wumme] wo is me, he seið, þe holi prophete.

wummera, var. WOOMERA.

wummle, dial. f. WIMBLE *sb.*

wummon, obs. f. WOMAN *sb.*

wump (wʌmp). *slang* (somewhat *rare*). [Origin unknown.] A foolish or feeble person.
1908 [see *motor-bicyclist* s.v. MOTOR A. *sb.* 6]. **1934** R. NICHOLS *Fisbo* 31 Hail to thee, thou much sniffed at by superior Persons and all wowsers, wumps and knock-knees.

wump, var. WHUMP *v.*, WHUMP *sb.* (and *int.*).

wumph (wʌmf, wʊmf). [Echoic; cf. WOOMPH *int.* and WHUMP *sb.* (and *int.*).] A sudden deep sound, as of the impact of a soft, heavy object.
1913 *Daily News & Leader* 15 Aug. 5, I was ashamed of the heavy 'wumph' with which I landed on the other side amid the nettles. **1924** *Glasgow Herald* 20 Dec. 4/2 The female [bittern]..sometimes answers back with a subdued but exciting 'wumph'. **1967** *Punch* 3 May 640/1 The whiplash crack from the shock wave of the small fighters we were flying is no guide to the wumph of an airliner weighing up to 300 tons. **1971** 'A. DIMENT' *Think Inc.* viii. 141 A deep wumph as the fuel oil..caught fire.

wun, wun', wund, Sc. varr. WIN *v.*, WIND *sb.*

wun, var. WOON

wunde, obs. f. WOUND *sb.*

wunder, obs. f. WONDER *sb.* and *v.*

wunderelle, var. WONDEREL *Obs.*

‖**Wunderkind** ('vʊndərkɪnt). Also **wunder-kind.** Pl. **Wunderkinder, wunderkinds.** [Ger., lit. = wonder child.] **a.** A highly talented child, a child prodigy, esp. in music.
1891 G. B. SHAW in *World* 23 Dec. 15/2 Every generation produces its infant Raphaels and infant Rosciuses, and *Wunderkinder* who can perform all the childish feats of Mozart. **1913** W. J. LOCKE *Stella Maris* iii. 28 You call her Ariel, or Syrinx, or a Sprite of the Sea, or a Wunder-kind whose original trail of glory-cloud has not faded into the light of common day. **1923** D. H. LAWRENCE *Stud. Classic Amer. Lit.* (1924) 102 The absolute duplicity of that blue-eyed *Wunderkind* of a Nathaniel. **1931** *N. & Q.* 3 Jan. 16/1 A great many instances of *Wunderkinder* were brought together by the late Dr. Leonard George Guthrie, in his Fitzpatrick Lectures to the Royal College of Physicians (1907), entitled 'Contributions to the study of Precocity in Children', privately printed, 1921. **1947** A. EINSTEIN *Music in Romantic Era* xv. 213 Chopin was a *wunderkind*, both as virtuoso and composer. **1973** L. HEREN *Growing up Poor in London* iii. 65 Again I suppose that the [school] orchestra was better than most of its kind because of the Jews. Some took private lessons, and were regarded as *Wunderkinder* by their parents. **1984** P. ROSE *Parallel Lives* (1985) 81 His career at the Royal Academy school was impressive; indeed he was something of a *wunderkind* in the art world.

b. A talented or successful young man, a 'whizz-kid'. Also *transf.*
1930 E. CULBERTSON *Contract Bridge Blue Bk.* xvii. 227 He [*sc.* a bridge player] may belong to a proud class of *wunderkinder* who 'never need a book' or who 'have no system'. **1940** H. G. WELLS *Babes in Darkling Wood* I. i. 31 He was in the habit of calling his host and hostess 'The ultimate generation, the last and so far the best'. They were, he said, his '*Wunderkinds*'. **1972** [see KAPUT *a.*]. **1975** *New Yorker* 25 Aug. 50/3 Zen, the colt by Damacus that horsemen say will be the *Wunderkind* of the season, ran a temperature before the Sanford Stakes and was scratched. **1982** R. LUDLUM *Parsifal Mosaic* xx. 320 He's received a fair amount of media exposure—the thirty-year old *wunderkind*.

wundi, var. WINDI *a. Obs.*

Wundtian ('vʊntɪən), *a.* and *sb. Psychol.* [f. the name of the German psychologist Wilhelm *Wundt* (1832–1920), + -IAN.] **A.** *adj.* Of or pertaining to the school of experimental and physiological psychology founded in Leipzig by Wundt or to his ideas or methods. **B.** *sb.* A follower of Wundt, one who adopts his ideas or methods.
1890 W. JAMES *Princ. Psychol.* I. iii. 93 The facts, however, do not seem to me to warrant even this amount of fidelity to the original Wundtian position. **1932**, etc. [see HERBARTIAN *a.* and *sb.*]. **1945** *Mind* LIV. 215 The later Wundtians, particularly and most ingeniously E. B. Titchener, tried to save sensationism. **1972** H. J. EYSENCK *Encycl. Psychol.* II. 61/1 Külpe..and his students..used a more molar type of introspection, believing that the Wundtian approach was too atomistic.

wune: see WONE *sb.*[1] and *v.*[1]

wunna, *Sc.* = 'will not': see WILL *v.*[1] A. 6 b β.

wunner, obs. f. ONER *sb.* 1; Sc. f. WONDER.

wunnerful ('wʌnəfʊl). Also **wonnerful, wunnaful.** Repr. *dial.* or *U.S.* pronunc. of WONDERFUL *a.*, (*sb.*), and *adv.*
1924 H. DE SELINCOURT *Cricket Match* vi. 190 Wonnerful wholesome stuff celery, they say. **1930** M. ALLINGHAM *Mystery Mile* xiii. 122, I be a wunnerful smart old man. **1945** A. KOBER *Parm Me* 16 Certainly sounds like a wunnaful pickcha, Jen. **1977** *Sounds* 9 July 8/1 Mink's main claim for the credibility stakes is that he's been produced by Jack Nitzche, who scores pretty high in the living legend section of this wunnerful business.

†'**wunsele.** *Obs.* [f. *wune*, WON *v.* + SELE.] A dwelling-place.
c **1205** LAY 15703 þa wunede ich on bure, on wunsele mine. *Ibid.* 17602 Her wit scullen..biwinnen his wunseles.

wunsome, -sum, obs. or north. dial. forms of WINSOME *a.*

wunst: see ONCE *adv.* A. δ.

wunt, dial. f. WANT *sb.*[1] (mole).

wunt(e, etc.: see WONT.

wun tun, var. WON TON.

wuo, ME. var. WOE.

wuord, obs. form of WORD *sb.*

wup (wʌp), *v. Sc.* Forms: 6 **woup, wowp (wolp, wewp)**; 9 **wop, wup (oup, oop).** [Of obscure origin. Cf. WOOP *sb.* and WHIP *v.* 19.]
1. *trans.* To bind (something) round with cord, thread, etc.
1512–3 *Acc. Ld. High Treas. Scot.* IV. 464 Smale towis to wowp the Margrettis mast with. **1567** *Reg. Privy Council Scot.* I. 360 Two barrell cordis..to woup brokin stokis and quheillis. *a* **1586** *Dunbar's Goldin Targe* 62 (Maitland Fol. MS.), Tressis cleir wouppit [*v.r.* wypit] with goldin threidis. **1802** SIBBALD *Chron. S.P.* Gloss., *Oop, Oup*, to join by hooping. **1808** JAMIESON s.v. *Oop, Wup*,..to bind with a thread or cord; to splice.
2. a. To unite or join (thread, yarn, etc.). **b.** To secure or fasten by tying.
1815 SCOTT *Guy M.* iv, A hank [of yarn], but not a haill ane—the full years o' three score and ten, but thrice broken, and thrice to oop. **1871** W. ALEXANDER *Johnny Gibb* i, Tak the aul' pleuch ryn [= rein] there, and wup it ticht atween the stays.

wur-, var. (esp. ME.) spelling of WOR-.

wurble, dial. var. WARBLE *sb.*[2]

wurch(en, obs. ff. WORK *v.*

wurd, obs. form of WORD.

wurdle, obs. f. *wordle*, WORTLE.

wurhte, obs. var. WRIGHT *sb.*[1]

wurley ('wɜːlɪ). *Austr.* Also 9 **worley, worlie,** 20 **whirlie**; in *pl.* **wurlies.** [Native word 'from the language of the Adelaide tribe' (G. Taplin *Native Tribes S. Australia* 12).] An aboriginal's hut. Also *attrib.*
1847 G. F. ANGAS *Savage Life* I. 105 Two men.. approached one of the *wurlies*. **1848** G. B. WILKINSON *S. Australia* 323 The men break down branches of trees and strip bark to make themselves a worley or shelter. **1887** MRS. DALY *Digging* etc. *S. Australia* 31 The body of an

unfortunate Chinaman was found half-roasted on a wurley fire. *Ibid.* 67 They lived in wurleys... These miserable substitutes for houses are 'lean-to's', made of sheets of bark propped up by saplings. **1934** A. RUSSELL *Tramp Royal in Wild Austral.* x. 78 The camp was made up of a cluster of spinifex-covered wurlies. **1936** I. L. IDRIESS *Cattle King* vi. 51 A hundred warriors were lazing about their wurlies, sleeping the midday peace away. **1954** B. MILES *Stars my Blanket* xi. 76 A huddle of wurlies and a yapping throng of lean kangaroo dogs..told us the blacks were camped. **1959** A. UPFIELD *Bony & Black Virgin* x. 80 Several whirlies of bark and odd sheets of corrugated iron and hessian bags, inhabited by aborigines. **1961** *Times* 19 July 12/6 We found them [*sc.* aborigines]..sitting outside their whirlies.

Wurlitzer ('wɜːlɪtsə(r)). The proprietary name of various musical instruments made by the Rudolf Wurlitzer Company, *spec.* a type of large electric organ, or a player-piano. Freq. *attrib.*
1925 T. DREISER *Amer. Trag.* I. I. xvii. 124 A Victrola and Wurlitzer player-piano furnished the necessary music. **1926** *Official Gaz.* (U.S. Patent Office) 23 Mar. 840/2 *Wurlitzer.* Particular description of goods.—pianos, player pianos,.. organs,..banjos,..bassoons..and parts of such musical instruments. Claims use since Jan. 1, 1857. **1926** *Trade Marks Jrnl.* 12 May 1108 *Wurlitzer...* Musical instruments. The Rudolf Wurlitzer Company.., Cincinnati, State of Ohio, United States of America; manufacturers. **1930** C. BEATON *Diary* Dec. in *Wandering Years* (1961) IX. 200 Religious jazz played through a Wurlitzer. **1956** A. HUXLEY *Adonis & Alphabet* 231 The tail-coated organist at the console of his Wurlitzer. **1975** *Guardian* 20 Jan. 9/6 They play Wurlitzer music not inspiring to skate to. **1980** *Times* 1 Oct. 12/6 The daily organ recital on what must be the world's best known Mighty Wurlitzer.

wurlyon, obs. Sc. form of WIRLING.

Würm (vʊəm). *Geol.* The former name of a lake (the Starnberger See) in Bavaria, adopted by A. Penck (in Penck & Brückner *Die Alpen im Eiszeitalter* (1909) I. I. 110) and used *attrib.* to designate the fourth and final Pleistocene glaciation in the Alps; also *absol.* Cf. RISS.
1910, etc. [see RISS]. **1968** [see WEICHSEL]. **1972** *Sci. Amer.* Mar. 60/2 The very numerous remains found in the Dragon's Lair were evidently deposited there during the final Pleistocene ice advance, the 60,000-year Würm glaciation that ended some 12,000 years ago. **1977** G. CLARK *World Prehistory* (ed. 3) xi. 455 Access was easier during the last glaciation, but only noticably so during its colder phases, that is during the Early and Main Würm, to use designations taken from the Swiss Alpine sequence.
Hence 'Würmian *a.* (also *absol.*).
1927 PEAKE & FLEURE *Hunters & Artists* iv. 40 It is.. possible that the Capsian industry had passed from Tunis through Sicily to Italy during, or even before, the Würmian glaciation. **1967** *Oceanogr. & Marine Biol.* V. 453 One may conclude that the cooling of the water during the Würmian was very slight in the Eastern Basin [of the Mediterranean]. *Ibid.*, The shallow-water Würmian beds.

wurne, var. WARN *v.*[2] *Obs.*

†**wurp.** *Obs. rare.* In 1 wyrp, werp, 3 wrp. [OE. *wyrp* (= LG. *wurp*, MLG. and (M)Du. *worp*, a cast, throw, OHG. *wurf, wurph*, MHG., G. *wurf*), f. the weak grade of *werþ-* WARP *v.*] A (stone's) throw. Also *fig.* in *eie wurþ*, a glance of the eye.
c **950** *Lindisf. Gosp.* Luke xxii. 41 He ȝefearrad wæs from him sua micle woerp *vel* wyrp is stanes [*Rushw.* wyrp stanes is; *Ags. Gosp.* anes stanes wyrp; *Hatton Gosp.* werp]. *a* **1225** *Ancr. R.* 56 Dauid..þurh on eie wurp to one wummon.. lette vt his heorte. *c* **1275** *Passion of our Lord* 155 in *O.E. Misc.* 41 Iesus from heom iwende þe wrp of o ston.

wurra ('wʌrə), *int. Anglo-Ir.* [Ir. (*a*) *Mhuire* (O) Mary.] An exclamation of grief or despair.
1898 J. D. BRAYSHAW *Slum Silhouettes* 21 Oh! wurra, wurra, that I should live to see him stiff and cowld. **1936** M. MITCHELL *Gone with Wind* x. 206 He groaned. 'Wurra the day!' **1952** E. O'NEILL *Moon for Misbegotten* II. 91 I'm not like you, owning up I'm beaten and crying wurra wurra like a coward.

wurrow, wurry, obs. varr. WORRY *v.*

wurset, -it, Sc. ff. WORSTED *sb.*

wurst (wɜːst, v-). Also **worsht, wourst.** [a. Ger.] Sausage, esp. of the German type; a German sausage. Also *transf.*
1855 [see KRAUT 1]. **1868** *Amer. Odd Fellow* VII. 403/1 Sausages, or 'wourst', as they call them, are made in links. **1892** I. ZANGWILL *Childr. Ghetto* I. xvii. 59 Mrs. Hyams fried a piece of *Worsht* for Miriam's supper and put it into the oven to keep hot. **1939** C. ISHERWOOD *Goodbye to Berlin* 221 There were plates of ham and cold cut wurst. **1955** T. H. PEAR *Eng. Social Differences* 181 Liver-sausage and similar 'wursts'. **1966** L. DAVIDSON *Long Way to Shiloh* x. 142 We finished the *wurst* sandwiches. **1967** *New Scientist* 10 Aug. 281/2 The name given to the dam was apparently chosen because of the obliging way in which this huge water-filled wurst..returns to its original unostentatious shape when deflated. **1977** *Drive* May-June 124/2 In the South, one shop had invented its own delicacy: Satan's Sizzlers, 'the great curry wurst'.

wurst, obs. f. VERST, WORST *a.*; dial. f. WRIST.

wursum, var. WORSUM *Obs.*

Würtemberg siphon. (See quots.)
1829 *Nat. Philos., Pneumatics* vi. 27 (L.U.K.), A syphon, in which the extremities of the legs are turned upwards, called the Wirtemburg syphon. **1850** OGILVIE s.v. *Siphon*, *Würtemberg siphon*,..a siphon with both legs equal [etc.].

wurtewale, obs. var. WARTWALE.
c **1450** METHAM *Wks.* 138 Naylys the qwyche..that.. hath no wurtewalys..be most repreuabyl.

†**wurthe**, *a. Obs.* Forms: 1 **wierðe, wyrðe, wyrþe, wirðe,** 1-4 **wurðe, wurþe** (3 **wrþe**), 3-4 **worþe.** [OE. *wierðe, wyrðe*, etc., a derivative from *weorþ* WORTH *sb.*[1] or *a.* In OE. and early southern ME. texts distinguishable from WORTH *a.*, but subsequently merged with it.]
1. Worthy. (Freq. const. with inf.)
c **897** ÆLFRED *Gregory's Past. C.* xxxiii. 227 He..bit ðære tide hwonne he ðæs wierðe sie ðæt he hine besuican mote. **971** *Blickl. Hom.* 47 þa lareowas beoþ syþþan domes wyrþe. *c* **1000** *Ags. Gosp.* Matt. iii. 11 He ys strengra þonne ic, ðæs ȝescy ne eom ic wyrþe to beranne. *a* **1122** *O.E. Chron.* (Laud MS.) an. 1046, Behet man him þæt he moste wurðe beon ælc ðæra þinga þe he ær ahte. *a* **1200** *Vices & Virtues* 59 Ic am wel wurðe ðat and more to þolien. *c* **1205** LAY. 13445 Swa þat heo al speken..þat Uortiger weoren wurðe to walden þas þeode. *a* **1225** *Ancr. R.* 38 ȝif ich nam wurðe for to beon iblesced. *c* **1275** *Passion of our Lord* 320 in *O.E. Misc.* 46 Alle hi onswerede, he is wrþe to beo ded. **1297** R. GLOUC. (Rolls) 890 þe stude..me clupeþ..after him, vor he was so worþe man. *Ibid.* 3466 Wel aȝte þat be a wurþe stude wanne þer such sepulture ys. *c* **1325** *Chron. Eng.* 741 in Ritson *Metr. Rom.* II. 301 Afterward, ase he wes wurthe,..An abbot him remue wolde.
2. Deserved, merited.
a **1225** *Ancr. R.* 138 We moten þauh don him wo, ase hit is ofte wel wurðe.

wurðscipe, etc., obs. ff. WORSHIP.

Württemberger ('vɜːtəmbɜːgə(r)). Also **Würtemberger, -burger, Wur-.** [a. Ger., f. *Württemberg*, the name of a former state in S.W. Germany (now part of the *Land* of Baden-Württemberg) + -ER[1].] A native or inhabitant of Württemberg.
1896 G. A. HENTY *Through Russian Snows* x. 190 The seven battalions of Spaniards, Wurtembergers, and men from the Duchy of Baden. **1926** F. M. FORD *Man could stand Up* II. i. 78 Those blessed Wurtembergers would never that day get out of their trenches. **1934** W. S. CHURCHILL *Marlborough* II. xxiv. 539 The Würtembergers and Westphalians were only now approaching. **1938** C. V. WEDGWOOD *Thirty Years War* viii. 384 Of two thousand Württembergers who joined Horn in 1632 at least half deserted in less than a month. *a* **1974** J. POPE-HENNESSY in *Lonely Business* (1981) III. 267 To meet young Württembergers. **1977** N. FREELING *Gadget* IV. 182 'You're a Wurtemburger aren't you?' 'Badener, from Karlsruhe.' **1978** L. DEIGHTON *SS-GB* xxxviii. 333 We should have polished off all you bloody Württembergers in 1918.

wurtzilite ('vɜːtsɪlaɪt). *Min.* [f. the name of Henry *Wurtz* (1828-1910), U.S. mineralogist + *-i-* + -LITE.] A black, massive, sectile, asphaltic pyrobitumen produced by the metamorphosis of petroleum.
1889 W. P. BLAKE in *Engin. & Mining Jrnl.* XLVIII. 542/2 In now proposing for it the name *Wurtzilite* I desire to compliment my friend, Dr. Henry Wurtz, of New York who in 1865 described the mineral to which he gave the name grahamite. **1918** [see *pyrobituminous* adj. s.v. PYRO- 2]. **1965** [see IMPSONITE]. **1979** J. M. HUNT *Petroleum Geochem. & Geol.* viii. 403 Wurtzilite appears to be a more indurated polymer with an origin similar to elaterite.

wurtzite ('wʊə-, 'wɜːtsaɪt). *Min.* [f. the name Prof. C. A. *Wurtz*, a French chemist (1817-84), + -ITE[1] 2 b.] 'Zinc sulphide, crystallizing in the hexagonal system' (Chester).
1868 DANA *Min.* (ed. 5) 60 Wurtzite and sphalerite are the same compound under distinct crystalline forms. **1897** L. FLETCHER *Introd. Study Min.* 81 Wurtzite is interesting as crystallising in the Rhombohedral system.

wuruhte, obs. var. WRIGHT *sb.*[1]

wurzel, short for MANGEL-WURZEL.
1888 *Encycl. Dict.* **1898** JEROME *Second Thoughts* 305 An atmosphere of wurzels was the thing that somehow he [*sc.* a farmer] suggested.

wus, obs. var. OOZE *sb.*[1]

wusbard, dial. f. *whore's bird* WHORE *sb.* 3.

wusche, wuss, wuss(c)he: see WISH.

‖**wushu** ('wuːʃuː). Also **wu shu** and with capital initial. [Chinese *wǔshù*, f. *wǔ* military + *shù* technique, art.] The Chinese martial arts.
1973 P. J. SEYBOLT *Revolutionary Educ. in China* xxii. 252 In the gymnasium,..others, wielding swords and spears, were practicing the traditional Chinese *wushu*. **1975** *Times* 27 June 5/5 Some energetic youngsters are practising *wushu* (military art). **1977** O. SCHELL *China* (1978) III. 241 He has just come from *wu shu* practice (martial arts). **1978** CHOW & SPANGLER *Kung Fu* p. xii, Today Wu Shu remains the official term for martial arts in the People's Republic of China, although the emphasis is on its use as a national sport 'to serve the people' in the promotion of health. **1979** *Tel.* (Brisbane) 31 May 2/3 A few lessons in Wushu.

wuss (wʌs). Repr. *colloq.* or *dial.* pronunc. of WORSE *a.* and *sb.*, or *adv.*
1862 A. J. MUNBY *Diary* 22 Mar. in D. Hudson *Munby* (1972) 117 That's wuss than a day's work, that is. **1869** J. GREENWOOD *Seven Curses of London* vi. 91 She'll tell you that, wuss luck, I've got in co. with some bad uns. **1894** [see STRAIGHT *adv.* 6]. **1896** A. MORRISON *Child of Jago* vi. 61 Nobody's none the wuss for me knowin' about 'em. **1936** M. MITCHELL *Gone with Wind* lix. 994 It been awful! An' it's gwine be wuss. **1945** J. RHYS-WILLIAMS *Stern Daughter* xv. 97 Lucky if it aint no wuss, Sister.

wusse, var. WIS *adv. Obs.*

wust(e, obs. pa. t. of WIT *v.*[1]

wüstite ('vʊstaɪt). *Chem.* Also **wustite.** [ad. G. *wüstit* (R. Schenck et al. 1927, in *Zeitschr. f. anorg. Chemie* CLXVI. 141), f. the name of F. *Wüst*, German metallurgist: see -ITE[1].] An isometric solid solution of magnetite (Fe_3O_4) in iron oxide (FeO).
1928 *Chem. Abstr.* XXII. 566 The existence of 2 solid solns. is shown: (1) a soln. of small quantities of Fe_3O_4 in FeO for which the name '*Wüstite*' is coined, [etc.]. **1957** *Jrnl. Iron & Steel Inst.* CLXXXVII. 78/1 The gradient of the iron content of these layers was determined, and the wüstite composition at the iron-wüstite and wüstite-magnetite phase boundaries was used to define the wüstite area. **1977** *Nature* 6 Oct. 500/1 There are few reports on the direct reduction of wustite by carbon according to an autocatalytic mechanism. **1980** *Ibid.* 30 Oct. 778/1 The extraterrestrial nature of a specific spherule can be confirmed if it contains wüstite—a metastable iron oxide formed at high temperatures and low oxygen partial pressures. Wüstite slowly decomposes into α-iron and magnetite..and is thus almost unknown in nature.

wut, dial. variant of OAT.
1818 WILBRAHAM *Chesh. Gloss.* 31 *Wuts*,..oats. **1865-** in various dial. glossaries, etc. (Yks. to Devon). **1880** JEFFERIES *Gt. Estate* i. 8, I met Hilary..and listened to a long tirade which he delivered against 'wuts'.

wute(þ, etc.: see WIT *v.*[1]

wuther, var. WHITHER *sb.* and *v. dial.*

‖**wu ts'ai** (wu tsai). Also **wucai, Wu ts'ai.** [Chinese *wǔcǎi*, f. *wǔ* five + *cǎi* colour.] Polychrome; polychrome decoration in enamels applied to porcelain; porcelain with polychrome decoration esp. of the Ming and Qing dynasties.
1904 E. DILLON *Porcelain* vii. 101 We come again to a pentad of colour—not, however, quite the same as the *wu-tsai* of Wan-li times. **1906** S. W. BUSHELL *Chinese Art* II. viii. 32 The ordinary class of polychrome (*wu ts'ai*) decoration of the Ming period. **1915** R. L. HOBSON *Chinese Pott. & Porc.* II. ii. 8 There are the beautiful barrel-shaped seats, some with openwork ground, the designs filled in with colours (*wu ts'ai*). **1964** M. MEDLEY *Handbk. Chinese Art* 88/1 *Wu-ts'ai*.., a term applied to porcelains of the Ming and Ch'ing Dynasties decorated in overglaze enamel colours, and often with coarsely-handled under-glaze blue. **1971** L. A. BOGER *Dict. World Pott. & Porc.* 115/1 Wu ts'ai, which is practically a Chinese way of saying polychrome, is most commonly applied to a decoration comprising designs painted in enamel colors. **1980** *Catal. Fine Chinese Ceramics* (Sotheby, Hong Kong) 62 A fine pair of wucai (wu ts'ai) square Dishes of shallow flared form with brown-edged rims.

wutter, var. WITTER *sb.*[1], *sb.*[2]

‖**wu-wei** ('wu'wei). Also **Woo-wei, wu wei.** [Chinese *wúwéi*, f. *wú* no, without + *wei* doing, action.] **a.** The Taoist doctrine of letting things follow their own course. **b.** *Hist.* In China, the name of a minor sect.
1859 J. EDKINS *Relig. Condition of Chinese* xiv. 260 One of the most interesting among the minor sects in China is that called the Woo-wei-keaon. It is an off-shoot from Buddhism. The words Woo-wei, mean non-action. These words are, in China, a favourite philosophical phrase, used by all schools of a contemplative or mystic tendency. The Taouists, who spoke of the Eternal Reason which underlies all existences, held that it could be understood, and the perfection of our nature reached only by rest, by stillness physical and mental, by abstaining from external methods of improvement, and by disbelief in their efficacy. This they called Woo-wei, 'to do nothing'. **1917** *Encycl. Sinica* 545/1 Confucius believed in the power of human nature to remain upright *if properly taught*; Lao Tzû believed it would keep straight *if left to itself*. This is his famous doctrine of *Wu-wei*, (Inaction or Nonassertion). *Ibid.* 609/2 *Wu Wei* or Non-Action Society. A secret sect, variously stated as having been founded by disciples of Lao Tzû towards the end of the Chou dynasty, by Lo Huai, the originator of the Lung Hua and Hsien T'ien sects, who lived in the 15th and 16th centuries, and to have been begun three hundred years ago... Its members are described by Edkins as 'a kind of reformed Buddhists'. **1934** A. D. WALEY *Way & its Power* iii. 145 He slips in..*wu-wei*, 'non-activity', *i.e.* rule through *tê* ('virtue', 'power') acquired in trance. **1965** C. & W. CHAI *Humanist Way in Ancient China* 56 To govern by *Wu-wei* (inaction or noninterference), Shun was the one! **1970** H. G. CREEL *What is Taoism?* i. 9 The mere idea of all this toiling for immortality is repugnant to that of *wu wei*, not striving. **1975** C.-Y. CHANG *Tao* lxxiii. 194 *Wu-wei* does not mean that one does not act. It means that one acts but is free from ulterior motives.

wuz (wʌz). Also **wus.** Repr. *colloq.*, *dial.*, or *vulg.* pronunc. of *was.*
1886 F. H. BURNETT *Little Lord Fauntleroy* xi. 222 The rooms wus locked up 'n' empty. **1901** M. FRANKLIN *My Brilliant Career* iii. 16 Some of us wuz always good fer a toon on the concertina. **1945** J. RHYS-WILLIAMS *Stern Daughter* xv. 97 Sister wuz wunnerful good to me back at Wipers in 1917. **1966** *Listener* 15 Sept. 397/2 We were promised a discussion about the programme on BBC-2's *Late Night Line-Up*; we wuz robbed, the discussion hardly mentioned the programme at all. **1973** C. HIMES *Black on Black* 168

Mah belly feels lak mah throat wus cut. **1976** *Observer* 22 Aug. 5 (Advt.), Wor lad wuz in a reet steeut.

wuzeer(at, varr. WAZIR(ATE.

Wuzeerá, var. WAZIR².

wuzzent, Sc. var. WIZENED *a.*

wuzzy (ˈwʌzɪ), *a. colloq.* Confused, fuddled, vague. Cf. WOOZY, MUZZY, *adjs.*

1896 *Dialect Notes* I. 427 *Wuzzy*,..confused. **1921** E. A. J. B. LYTTON *Let.* 10 Mar. in Ld. Lytton *Antony* (1935) iii. 74, I am very nearly mad, I am quite slowly turning wuzzy. **1937** J. B. PRIESTLEY *Two Time Plays* 79, I can't remember. .. I'm—a bit—wuzzy.

wy, northern var. QUEY; obs. f. WEIGH, WHY.

wy-, freq. ME. variant of WI-.

wyage, wyayge, obs. varr. VOYAGE *sb.*

Wyandot (ˈwaɪəndɒt). Also †**Wayandott, Wyandot(t)e.** [ad. F. *Ouendat*, ad. Huron *Wendat*.]

1. (A member of) a North American Indian people belonging to the Huron nation and originally living in Ontario; the language of this people. Also *attrib.* or as *adj.*

1749 J. HAMILTON *Let.* 2 Oct. in *Documents Colonial Hist. New-York* (1855) VI. 531 The Twitchwees & Wayandotts ..for two or three years past have dealt largely with our Traders. **1785** T. JEFFERSON *Notes Virginia* xi. 187 Tribes.. Wyandots..Near Fort St. Joseph's and Detroit. **1786** [see HURON]. **1789** [see SAUK]. **1804** *Maryland Hist. Mag.* IV. 6 The Indian chief, Tarhie, a Wyandote..[was] hunting bears. **1826** J. F. COOPER *Last of Mohicans* III. ii. 46 What will our fathers think the tribes of the Wyandots have become? **1837** [see SHAWNEE *sb.* 1]. **1913** A. S. PALMER *Samson-Saga* xiv. 167 The Wyandot Indians have a like myth. **1965** *Canad. Jrnl. Linguistics* Spring 105 He [*sc.* Sapir] knew something about Wyandotte. **1979** B. A. LEITCH *Conc. Dict. Indian Tribes N. Amer.* 189 By the 1970s Wyandot were among the leading citizens of Ottawa County, Oklahoma, numbering about 1,000.

2. (Usu. with spelling **Wyandotte**.) One of a breed of medium-sized domestic fowls, of American origin.

1884 *Bazaar* 12 Sept. 866/1 Wyandottes. Wanted a few early pullets, pure bred. **1897** K. DE LA BERE *Poultry Guide* 1. 21 He has..reared 1,000 head of Black Minorcas,..and Wyandottes. **1906** *Westm. Gaz.* 24 Dec. 2/2 Time was when the world knew no Wyandotte fowl at all; but the ingenuity of the fancier has now given it White, Silver,..Partridge, Silver-pencilled, and Blue-laced Wyandottes.

wyandoure, Sc. var. VIANDER¹ *Obs.*

Wyatt (ˈwaɪət). The name of the architect and designer James *Wyatt* (1746–1813), used *attrib.* to designate buildings or architectural features designed by him or characteristic of his Gothic Revival style.

1819 M. EDGEWORTH *Let.* 4 May (1971) 206 A most comfortable sitting room (scarlet cloth and black furniture —Large Wyatt window plate glass—tables most comfortable). **1936** A. DALE *James Wyatt* vi. 32 The Wyatt window, a tripartite aperture similar to the Venetian window. **1962** *House & Garden* Dec. 63/2 Sienna marble columns (..from a Wyatt house in Somerset). **1973** *Country Life* 18 Jan. 152/3 It is unusual for a Philadelphia house... There is a vaguely Wyatt feeling about the whole concept.

Hence **Wyaˈttesque, ˈWyattish** *adjs.*

1942 J. LEES-MILNE *Jrnl.* 18 Jan. in *Ancestral Voices* (1975) 10 A terrible house.., with only a vestige of the eighteenth century in the central stairwell, where there is a trace of Wyattesque or Adamesque treatment, a frieze with ram's skulls. **1946** —— *Diary* 23 Nov. (1983) 108, I found the stairwell actually more Wyattish than Adamatic. **1973** *Country Life* 20 Sept. 776/3 Wyattesque decoration.

wyc, obs. f. WICK *a.*

wycch(e, obs. ff. WHICH, WITCH.

wyce, obs. f. VICE *sb.*¹, *v.*², VOICE; obs. Sc. var. WISE *a.*

wych(e: see WHICH, WHITCH, WICH, WITCH *sb.*

wych elm, witch elm (wɪtʃ ɛlm). Forms: α. 7 **weech**, 7–8 **wich**, 7–9 **witch elm.** β. 8– **wych elm.** (Also hyphened.) [f. WITCH *sb.*³ + ELM. Cf. the slightly earlier *witchen elm*.] A species of elm, *Ulmus montana*, having broader leaves and more spreading branches than the Common elm; the witch hazel or Scots elm; also, the wood of this.

α. **1626** BACON *Sylva* §475 A Cions of a Weech-Elme, grafted vpon the Stocke of an Ordinary Elme, will put forth Leaues, almost as broad as the Brimme of ones Hat. **1633** T. JOHNSON *Gerarde's Herbal* 1482 *Vlmus folio glabro*, Witch Elme, or smooth leaued Elme. *a* **1691** AUBREY *Nat. Hist. Wilts.* (1847) 54 Wich-hazells, as we call them in Wilts (in some counties wich-elmes). **1715** ADDISON *Drummer* II. i, There's a good deal of Virtue in that [Conjurer's] Wand—I fancy 'tis made out of Witch-Elm. **1733** W. ELLIS *Chiltern & Vale Farm.* 115, I here write of..the common Elm, and the witch Elm. **1810** SCOTT *Lady of L.* I. Introd. 2 The witch-elm that shades Saint Fillan's spring. **1850** TENNYSON *In Mem.* lxxxvii, Witch-elms that counterchange the floor Of this flat lawn with dusk and bright.

β. **1769** BARRINGTON in *Phil. Trans.* LIX. 34 The Wych (or broad-leaved) elm. **1778** LIGHTFOOT *Flora Scot.* I. 152 The variety with a smooth bark and leaf, commonly called the Wych-Elm. **1845** FABER *Rosary*, etc. 86 Many a bay, By ..a drooping wychelm fanned. **1866** *Treas. Bot.* 1189 Forked branches of Wych Elm,..were used as divining-rods. **1875** *Encycl. Brit.* II. 317 The Wych elm is a hardy tree, of rapid growth.

b. *attrib.*, as ***wych-elm faggot, foliage, tree.***

1763 *Museum Rust.* I. 28 To fill up the drains with witch-elm faggots. **1862** LYTTON *Str. Story* II. 11 In this yard there stood an old wych-elm tree. **1897** *Daily News* 12 Nov. 8/3 Bunches of wych-elm foliage.

wych(e)safe, obs. varr. VOUCHSAFE.

wycht, obs. Sc. f. WIGHT *a.*

wycke, obs. var. WEEK *sb.*

†**Wyclifan.** *Obs. rare*⁻¹. [f. as next + -AN.] A Wycliffite.

1402 *Pol. Poems* (Rolls) II. 92 He is callid an heretike that heresies sowith, as Arrians, Wyclyfanes, Sabellyanes, and other.

Wycliffian, -ifian (wɪˈklɪfɪən), *sb.* and *a. Church Hist.* Forms: (see quots.). [ad. med.L. *Wyclyvian-us*, or directly f. *Wycliffe, -clif*, etc.: see WYCLIFFITE.]

†**A.** *sb.* = WYCLIFFITE *sb. Obs.*

[*c* **1400** *Knighton's Chron.* (Rolls) II. 184 Sicque a vulgo Wyclyff discipuli et Wyclyviani sive Lollardi vocati sunt. *Ibid.* 312 Idem archiepiscopus firmavit sententiam excommunicationis super Lollardos sive Wyclyvianos.] **1570** FOXE *A. & M.* (ed. 2) II. 965/2 Chaucer..semeth to bee a right Wicleuian. **1621** BP. MOUNTAGU *Diatribæ* 100 It had been easily answered, in that poynt, by the Wickleuians. **1654** H. TURBERVILL *Man. Controv.* 47 Let him not cite the Wicklefians, for they held, That [etc.]. **1717** EARBERY *Pref. Varillas' Pretended Reformers* p. vi, Our new Allies the Lutherans, Calvinists, and Wickliffians.

B. *adj.* Of or pertaining to, characterizing the teaching of, Wycliffe or his followers.

1720 LEWIS *Life Wyclif* 114 The Wicliffian Superstition which obliges the Ministers of the Church to be Beggars. **1889** *Q. Rev.* April 510 Some of the sentiments are exclusively Wiclifian.

Hence †**Wycliffianism**, = next. *Obs.*⁻¹

1668 H. MORE *Div. Dial.* II. 90 That Principle of Wickleffianism,..which the Jesuites themselves so loudly hoot at.

Wycliffism, -ifism (ˈwɪklɪfɪz(ə)m). *Church Hist.* Forms: (see quots.). [f. as next + -ISM.] The religious doctrines or tenets advocated or propagated by Wycliffe, or held by his followers.

1675 in S. Knight *Life J. Colet* (1724) 267 To prevent the Growth of Wicklivism. **1732** NEAL *Hist. Purit.* I. 4 Urban.. writ to young King Richard II,..to put a stop to the progress of Wickliffism. **1796** MORSE *Amer. Geog.* II. 145 Wickliffism took shelter in Wales, when it was persecuted in England. **1814** W. WILSON *Hist. Dissent. Churches* IV. 487 He passed a law, making the profession of Wickliffism a capital offence. **1861** GOLDW. SMITH *Inaugural Lect.* 37 England..has not been the parent of great religious movements, excepting Wycliffism. **1884** *Brit. & For. Evang. Rev.* Oct. 620 John Stokes pronounced Hus's doctrines to be pure Wyclifism.

Wycliffist, -ifist (ˈwɪklɪfɪst), *sb.* and *a. Church Hist.* Forms: (see quots.). [f. as next + -IST. Cf. med.L. *Wiclefistæ* (Du Cange).]

A. *sb.* = WYCLIFFITE *sb.* ? *Obs.*

c **1449** PECOCK *Repr.* v. iii. 501 The sect of Wiclifistis, whiche aȝens the vij. principal gouernauncis..rehercid bi the proces of this present book holden [etc.]. **1460** CAPGRAVE *Chron.* (Rolls) 244 A Frere Augustyn..felle in the secte of Wiclefistis. **1532** MORE *Confut. Tindale* Wks. 352/2 In Boheme the Hussites, in England the wicliffystes. **1565** SHACKLOCK tr. *Hosius* 14 Whiche couet rather to be counted Carolstadians then Lutherans & other new Wicleffistes. **1631** WEEVER *Anc. Funeral Mon.* 807 Frater Robertus Rose ..writ much, yet neuer offended the VVickleuists. **1655** FULLER *Hist. Cambr.* 57 Iohn Bromiard..came to Cambridge,..sent thither..to ferret out the Wicklivists. **1673** HICKMAN *Hist. Quinquart.* 443 Wickliffists did maugre all the malice of their Adversaries increase. **1716** in M. Davies *Athen. Brit.* III. 27 The Wicklefists and Waldensians were against Episcopacy as being against the Pope. **1758** LOWTH *Life William of Wykeham* 207 The Wickliffists were persecuted and dispersed. **1819** *Rees' Cycl.* s.v. *Wicliff*, An account of his distinguishing tenets, and those of his followers,..Wickliffists and Lollards.

transf. **1679** OLDHAM *Sat. Jesuits* III. (1681) 65 The dangerous Works of that old Lollard, Paul; That arrant Wickliffist.

B. *adj.* = WYCLIFFITE *a.*

1725 LEWIS *Life Pecock* (1744) 320 In much the same manner does the bishop recommend these books to the Wiclifist laity.

Wycliffite, -ifite (ˈwɪklɪfaɪt), *sb.* and *a. Church Hist.* Forms: 6 *Sc.* **Wiclefit**, 7 **Wickliv-** (7–8 **-lev-**), 8 **Wicliv-**, 8–9 **Wicliff-** (9 **Wiclif-, Wiklif-**), **Wickliff-**, 9 **Wycliff-, Wyclifite.** [ad. med. or early mod.L. *Wiclefita*, etc., f. the name of John *Wycliffe* or *Wyclif* (*c* 1320–1384; also spelt *Wiclif*, etc.), English theologian, writer, and religious reformer, + -ITE¹ 1 b.]

A. *sb.* One who held or propagated the religious tenets or doctrines of Wycliffe; a follower of Wycliffe; = WYCLIFFIAN, WYCLIFFIST *sbs.*

1580 J. HAY in *Cath. Tract.* (S.T.S.) 54 Heresies, of the Albigenses, Waldenses, Wiclefits, Hussits. **1661** BLOUNT *Glossogr.* (ed. 2), *Wicklivites*, the followers of Wicklif. **1684** S. G. *Anglorum Spec.* 796 Eleanor Cobham was persecuted for being a Wicklevite. **1720** LEWIS *Life Wyclif* 108 A most effectual Way to ruine the poor Wicliffites. **1778** WARTON *Hist. Eng. Poetry* II. 390 The Wickliffites entirely grounded their ideas..on scriptural proofs. **1813** T. D. WHITAKER *Visio P. Pl.* p. xviii, That he..taught almost all the fundamental doctrines of Christianity has no tendency to prove him a Wickliffite or Lollard. **1850** FORSHALL & MADDEN *Holy Bible* I. p. xxxiii. *note*, The Wycliffites..were not backward to defend their right to have the Scriptures in their own language. **1870** ROGERS *Hist. Glean.* Ser. II. 57 [Bishop] Richard Fleming had also been a Wiklifite.

B. *adj.* **1.** Of or pertaining to, written or made by, Wycliffe or his followers.

1843 WAY *Promp. Parv.* 316 *note*, In the earlier Wicliffite version. **1880** F. D. MATTHEW *Wyclif's Wks.* p. xxviii, That he really held Wyclifite opinions. **1884** J. R. THOMSON *Life Wiclif* 86/1 The Wiclifite tenets spread most rapidly. **1896** SKEAT in *Trans. Philol. Soc.* 219 A diligent student of Wycliffite literature.

2. Of persons: That is a follower of Wycliffe; holding, advocating, or propagating the religious views of Wycliffe and his school.

1875 STUBBS *Const. Hist.* II. xvi. 450 The Wycliffite or Lollard preachers had raised a cry against the clergy. **1880** F. D. MATTHEW *Wyclif's Wks.* p. xxix. (*heading*), Wyclifite Party crushed.

†**Wycliffize**, *v. Obs. rare*⁻¹. In 7 **Wicclifize.** [f. as prec. + -IZE.] *intr.* To espouse or advocate the views of Wycliffe (esp. as to Church property).

1655 FULLER *Ch. Hist.* VI. 302 The Lay Parliament,.. which did wholly Wicclifize, kept in the twelfth year of King Henry the fourth.

ˈ**Wycliffry, -fry.** [f. as prec. + -RY. Cf. LOLLARDRY.] = WYCLIFFISM.

1896 J. H. WYLIE *Hist. Eng. Hen. IV*, III. 457 The very treatise on the Church..[by] Hus, is nothing but Wiclifry transplanted word for word into Bohemia. **1900** —— *Council Constance* 147 Wenzel gave no support to Wycliffry.

wycre, obs. f. WICKER.

wyd(e, obs. ff. WIDE *adv.*

wydder(e, obs. ff. *wider* (see WIDE), WHITHER *adv.*

wyddie, obs. f. WIDDY.

wyddo, -ow(e, wydew, etc., obs. ff. WIDOW, etc.

†**wyde.** *Obs.*⁻¹ A variety of apple-tree.

1525 FITZHERBERT *Husb.* 42 Dyuers apple trees that haue knottes in the bowes, as casses or wydes, and suche other that wyll growe on slauynges.

wyder, obs. f. WHITHER *adv.*

wydraught, etc., obs. ff. WITHDRAUGHT.

wydue, etc., obs. ff. WIDOW *sb.*¹

wydur, -yr, obs. ff. WHITHER *adv.*

†**wye**¹. Latterly *Sc.* and *north. Obs.* Forms: α. 1 **wiȝa**, 4 **wiȝe, wihe (whi, whie, whiȝ) wyȝe, wyȝ (wiȝh), wieȝ**, 5 **wiȝ**, 4–5 **wyghe**, 4–6 **wye**, 4–5, 6 *Sc.* **wy**, 4, 6 **wie.** β. 4 **weiȝ, weiȝh, weih (wehy)**, 4–5 **weiȝe, weie (4 waie), weye**, 5 **wey, wegh (whegh, whe), we**, 5–6 **wee.** [OE. *wiȝa*, f. the weak grade of the stem repr. by *wīȝ* WI *sb.* Cf. OHG. *widerwigo* 'rebellis', and *Wigo* as a proper name.]

In OE. chiefly, and in later use only, in poetic use.

1. One who fights; a fighting man; a warrior or soldier.

α. *Beowulf* 629 He þæt ful ȝeþeah, wælreow wiȝa, æt Wealhþeon. *c* **900** tr. *Baeda's Hist.* I. xv. (1890) 50 And hi þa sona hider sendon maran sciphere strengran wiȝhena. **993** *Battle of Maldon* 210 Swa hi bylde forð bearn Ælfrices, wiȝa wintrum ȝeong. **13..** *Gaw. & Gr. Knt.* 581 Syþen þe brawden bryne of bryȝt stel ryngez Vmbeweued þat wyȝ vpon wlonk stuffe. *c* **1350** *Will. Palerne* 3787 William & his wiȝes were armed wel sone. ? *a* **1400** *Morte Arth.* 56 [He] wente in-to Wales with his wyes alle. *c* **1450** HOLLAND *Howlat* 499 The wyis quhar the wicht went war in wa wellit. **1535** STEWART *Cron. Scot.* (Rolls) II. 505 With mony wy that worthie war and wycht, [he] Appeirit thair richt sone. **15..** [see β].

β. *a* **1400–50** *Wars Alex.* 1030 (Ashm. MS.), Bot wees wiȝtly with-in þe wallis ascendid, Freschely fendid of. *c* **1400** *Destr. Troy* 1212 Mony woundit we from his weppont paste. *c* **1420** *Anturs of Arth.* liv. (Douce MS.), þe wees, þat werene wounded so woþely.., Surgenes sone saued. **1515** *Scottish Field* 493 in *Chetham Misc.* (1856), A yong knight, ..Sir William Warkehoppe..was the wees [*Percy MS.* wyes] name. *Ibid.* 637 Now is this fuirse feilde foughten to an ende; Many a wee wanted his horse, and wandered home on fote.

2. A noble, vigorous man; hence *gen.*, a man, a person.

In very freq. use from *c* 1340 to *c* 1420, esp. in *α*-form.

α. *a* **900** *Andreas* 1711 (Gr.), Hie ða ȝebrohton æt brimes næsse on wæȝþele wiȝan unslawne. *a* **1000** *Menologium* 160 Se þe fæȝere iu mid wætere oferwearp wuldres cynebearn, wiȝa weorðlice. **13..** *E.E. Allit. P.* A. 579 Þen alle þe wyȝez in þe worlde myȝt wynne By þe way of ryȝt to aske dome. **1340–70** *Alex. & Dind.* 571 Wis holde ȝe no whi but ȝif he wel conne Faire tempren his tonge. **1377** LANGL. *P. Pl.* B. XVII. 98 Went neuere wy in this worlde thorw that wildernesse, That he ne was robbed. *a* **1400–50** *Wars Alex.* 1628 In þe same wedes, For all þis werld as þis wy wendes now attyred. *c* **1420** *Anturs of Arth.* xxix, Scho was the worthilieste wyghte, þat any wy myghte welde. *c* **1480** HENRYSON *Lion & Mouse* xxxii, Thair is na wy that will my harmis wreik. **1500–20** DUNBAR *Poems* xxx. 50, I awoik as wy that wes in weir. **1513** DOUGLAS *Æneid* v. xi. 19 Sone slaid scho down wnsene of ony wy. *a* **1568** in *Bannatyne MS.* (Hunter. Club) 739 Sen ye ar pleisit to pleiss ane vthir wy.

β. **1340–70** *Alex. & Dind.* 17 Þanne weies of worschipe, wittie & quainte, Wiþ his lettres he let to þe lud sende. *c* **1350** *Will. Palerne* 281 'Sertes,' þan seide þemperour,..'y am þat ilk weiȝh'. **1377** LANGL. *P. Pl.* B. xi. 374 'Holy writt,' quod that weye, 'wisseth men to suffre'. *a* **1400–50** *Wars Alex.* 134 He passis his way, Vn-wetandly to any wee. *Ibid.* 383 His liknes he changis, Worthis agayn to a wee, fra a worme turnys.

b. Used as a form of address.

13.. *Gaw. & Gr. Knt.* 1508, 'I woled wyt at yow, wyȝe, þat worþy þer sayde. **1340–70** *Alex. & Dind.* 69 Wordlich weiȝ, we wische of þi ȝifte Ai-lastinge lif. *a* **1400–50** *Wars Alex.* 2302 Welcom we [*Dubl.* wye], at all þe werd sall wyn with þi handis. *c* **1470** *Golagros & Gaw.* 57 Sen thy will is to wend, wy, now in weir, Luke that wisly thow wirk. **1515** *Scottish Field* 257 in *Chetham Misc.* (1856), I will wynde you to wreke, wees, I you heete.

c. Without article. (Cf. MAN *sb.*[1] 2.)

13.. *Gaw. & Gr. Knt.* 1039, I am wyȝe at your wylle to worch youre hest. **1377** LANGL. *P. Pl.* B. xi. 337 Hadde neuere wye witte to worche þe leest. **1399** —— *Rich. Redeles* III. 288 Þis warmnesse in welth with wy vppon erthe My3te not longe dure. *c* **1560** A. SCOTT *Poems* (S.T.S.) x. 51 Thair is nocht wie Can estimie My sorrow.

d. Applied to the Deity. *rare.*

13.. *Gaw. & Gr. Knt.* 2441 Þe wyȝe hit yow ȝelde þat vp-haldez þe heuen and on hyȝ sittez. *c* **1560** A. SCOTT *Poems* iii. 39 Be the wy that all the warld wrocht.

3. *transf.* A woman; a lady. *rare.*

c **1400** *Destr. Troy* 3356 Thou shalt haue riches more Rife ..þan any lady in þi land,..And more likandly lyf..as a wee noble. *c* **1560** A. SCOTT *Poems* xxxi. 34, I lufe þe wy Will nocht apply, Nor grant to giffe me grace agane.

wye[2] (waɪ). *techn.* [The name of the letter Y.]

a. (See quots. and cf. Y 3.)

1857 DAVIES & PECK *Math. Dict.*, *Wyes*, the supports of the telescope in the theodolite and level. **1875** KNIGHT *Dict. Mech.* 2823/2 *Wye*, a Y or crotch. Used in many ways as a temporary shore or brace. **1883** GRESLEY *Gloss. Coal-mining* 295 *Wye* (C[umb.]), the beam-end connection above the pump-rods of a winding and pumping engine.

b. *spec.* (*a*) *Plumbing.* A short pipe with a branch joining it at an acute angle. (*b*) *Electr. Engin.* = STAR *sb.*[1] 12 i.

a **1877** KNIGHT *Dict. Mech.* III. 2823 *Wye*... A name applied to a stem or pipe with branches. **1916** C. E. MAGNUSSON *Alternating Currents* ix. 97 If the three circuits be connected as shown..it is called a Star or Wye connection. **1964** R. F. FICCHI *Electr. Interference* x. 200 With a source that is wye-connected, the system neutral is readily available. **1978** K. W. SESSIONS *Homeowner's Handbk. Plumbing & Repair* iv. 145 (*caption*) Some cast-iron soil-pipe 90° wye branches. **1980** SLEMON & STRAUGHEN *Electric Machines* ii. 143 Three similar single-phase transformers may be connected to give 3-phase transformation, and since the primary and secondary windings may be connected either in delta or in wye, there are four possible combinations of connections.

wye, north. dial. var. QUEY; obs. var. WEIGH *sb.*[1] and *v.*[1]

wye byt, var. WAY-BIT *Obs.*

wyefde, var. WEVED *Obs.*

wyefe, obs. f. WIFE.

wyel, wyelde, wyeldeware, wyele, wyelfoyle, wyell, obs. ff. WHILE, WIELD, WILD-FOWL, WILDWARE, WEEL[2], WILE.

wyer, obs. f. WEIR, WIRE *sb.* and *v.*

wyes, wyese, etc., obs. forms of WISE *sb.* and *a.*

wyet, wyete, wyeued, wyeve, wyeygt, obs. ff. WHITE *a.*, WIT *v.*[1], WEVED, WEAVE *v.*, WEIGHT *sb.*[2]

wyf, wyfe, wyff(e, obs. ff. WIFE *sb.*

wyfyne, Sc. var. WIVEN *a. Obs.*

wygeon, wyghe, obs. ff. WIDGEON, WITH *prep.*, WYE[1].

wyghte, obs. f. WEIGHT *sb.*[1], WHITE *a.*

wyȝtsave, obs. var. VOUCHSAFE *v.*

wygorusly, obs. Sc. f. VIGOROUSLY *adv.*

wyhee, var. WEHEE *v.*

wyhylle, obs. f. WILE *sb.*

wyice, obs. Sc. f. WISE *a.*

wyif, obs. f. WIFE.

wyill, obs. Sc. f. WILE.

wyir, Sc. var. VIRE *sb.*[1] *Obs.*

wyis, etc., obs. Sc. ff. WISE.

wyk(e: see WEEK *sb.*, WICK, and WIKE *Obs.*

†**wyke**, *v.*[1] *Obs.* (Of obscure origin and meaning: not obviously connected with OE. *wícan.*)

a **1310** in Wright *Lyric P.* xxix. 87 Ofte when y syke, with care y am thourh-soht, When y wake y wyke, of serewe is al mi thoht.

†**wyke**, *v.*[2] *Obs. rare.* [ad. MDu. *wijcken* (Du. *wijken*) to give way, depart, etc.] *intr.* To give way, to withdraw.

1481 CAXTON *Reynard* xxviii. (Arb.) 67 In nede alwey [I] haue byden by yow where other beestis haue wyked and goon theyr way [Du. *ontweecken*]. *Ibid.* 71 It is better that we wyke [Du. *wijcken*] and departe, than we sholde..fyghte with hym.

wyked, obs. form of WICKED *a.*

†**Wykehamic** (-ˈkæm-), *a. Obs.*[−1] In 8 Wickhamick. [See WYKEHAMIST and -IC.] = WYKEHAMICAL *a.* 1.

a **1711** KEN *Edmund* Poet. Wks. 1721 II. 69 Thus from the two Wickhamick Springs shall rise Diffusive streams the Church to fertilise.

Wykehamical (wɪˈkæmɪkəl), *a.* Also 8–9 Wiccam-, 9 Wycchamical. [f. as prec. + -AL[1]. The form *Wiccamical* is ad. mod.L. *Wiccamic-us.*]

1. Of or pertaining to Winchester College, or the pupils or staff of this; = WYKEHAMIST *a.*

1758 C. GOLDING *Def. Cond. Warden Winchester Coll.* 38 He hath given the Electors Liberty to take a Person..from within the Wykehamical Societies. **1791** HUDDESFORD *Salmag.* 101 William of Wickham, a Song for the Wiccamical Anniversary. **1830** W. L. BOWLES *Life Ken* I. 18 Dulce Domum, the old Wykehamical song. *Ibid.* 23 The great object of Wykehamical hopes, New College. **1878** H. C. ADAMS *Wykehamica* xxii. 397 In Wykehamical phrase, the Præfect..would..have 'broken their necks'. **1901** *Athenæum* 26 Jan. 105/3 If we were asked to select the typical Wykehamical epitaph.

2. That is or has been a pupil of, or connected with, Winchester College.

1844 R. PALMER in *Mem.* (1896) I. 364, I printed them for private and anonymous circulation among my Wykehamical friends. **1878** H. C. ADAMS *Wykehamica* xvii. 320 This oath is one of the things which the Wykehamical body ought to have abolished long ago. **1903** FEARON in C. E. Osborne *Fr. Dolling* ix, He was rapidly adopted within the Wykehamical family, and was what the school would have called 'a most patriotic Wykehamist'.

Hence **Wykehamically** *adv.*

1878 H. C. ADAMS *Wykehamica* xxiii. 418 *Chouse*, 'a shame'... Here the word has been Wykehamically diverted from its original meaning, viz. 'to cheat'.

Wykehamist (ˈwɪkəmɪst), *sb.* and *a.* Also 8 Wykhamist, Wiccamist. [ad. mod.L. *Wykehamista* (16th c.), f. the name William of *Wykeham* (1324–1404), Bishop of Winchester, and founder of Winchester College (1382) and New College, Oxford (1379).]

A. *sb.* One who is or has been a pupil at Winchester College.

1758 C. GOLDING *Def. Cond.* 51 Lest any Wykhamist should be offended. **1773** *Hist. & Antiq. Winchester* I. 147 Andrew Phillips..shared the piety and doctrine of the Wiccamists. **1782** J. NICHOLS *Sel. Collect. Poems* VIII. 75 Young Cibber, being likewise a Wykehamist, called on Dr. Ridley. **1860** WALCOTT *Cathedrals* 251 That most characteristic gathering of Wykehamists old and young. **1885** *Athenæum* 4 July 14/3 The governors of Harrow have successively appointed the most learned and single-minded of Wykehamists. **1903** [see WYKEHAMICAL *a.* 2].

B. *adj.* = WYKEHAMICAL *a.* 1.

1865 (*title*), Wykehamist Meeting. The anniversary festival will be holden..May 17, 1865. **1867** AUG. G. DRANE *Chr. Schools* II. vii. 260 The Wykehamist Colleges..opened the way to other foundations of a similar description. **1891** *Athenæum* 14 Feb. 212/1 It may reasonably be hoped that this is not Wykehamist Greek.

wyker, -ir, wykker, wykur, etc., obs. ff. WICKER.

wyket(t, wykket(t, obs. ff. WICKET.

Wykhamite (ˈwɪkəmaɪt). [f. the name William of *Wykeham* (see WYKEHAMIST *sb.* and *a.*] = WYKEHAMIST *sb.*

1828 M. R. MITFORD *Our Village* III. 203 Two or three more of our young Etonians and Wykhamites. **1972** *Daily Tel.* 1 June 21/3 He is a Wykehamite and Balliol man who was originally destined for the Civil Service.

wykit, wykked, -id, etc., obs. ff. WICKED *a.*

wykke, obs. f. WICK *a.*

wyl, obs. f. VILE *a.*, WHILE *sb.*, WILE, WILL *sb.*

wylage, obs. f. VILLAGE *sb.*

wylanlyche, obs. f. VILLAINLY *adv.*

wyld(e, obs. ff. WEALD, WILD.

wylde, obs. f. WIELD.

wyldren, var. WILDERN.

wyldrenes(se, obs. ff. WILDERNESS.

wyldyng, obs. var. WIELDING *ppl. a.*

wyle, obs. Sc. f. VILE; var. WALE *v.*[1]; obs. f. WEEL[2], WHEEL, WHILE, WILE.

wyled, wylem, obs. ff. WILD, WHILOM.

wyliecoat (ˈweilɪkot, -kɔt). *Sc.* (and *north.*). Forms: 5–6, 9 wyle-, 6 vyle-, vile-, wile-, wele-; 5–7 wyly-, 6 vily-, veli-, 6–7 weyli- (8 weily-), 6- wylie-, 8- wylicoat (9 wili-, wilie-); 7 wylli(e)-, 9 willy-, willey-, welli-; 7 waly-, vali-, 7, 9 walli-, 9 walacoat; also 5 -coyt, 5–8 -cot, 5–7 -cott, -cote, -coit, 5, 7- -coat. (Occas. as two words, or with hyphen.) [Of obscure origin: the forms of the second element agree throughout with those of COAT *sb.*, but the first has not been identified, and may be an alteration of some foreign term.]

1. An under-waistcoat, in earlier use esp. one worn under a doublet; an under-vest, woollen or flannel under-garment. ? *Obs.*

In latest quots. applied to some kind of outer garment.

1478 *Acta Auditorum* (1839) 83/1 A doublat of Bukkessy with a wyle cot of quhit in It. **1494** *Acc. Ld. High Treas. Scot.* I. 225, v quarteris of Inglis quhit, to be the King ane wyly coit. **1505** *Ibid.* III. 109 For ane wyly cote undir his cote,..v s. vj d. **1513** DOUGLAS *Æneid* VII. Prol. 90 In double garmont cled and wyly coyt. **1561** in *Inv. de la Royne Descosse* (Bann. Cl.) 23 Foure wylie coittis of quhite lambskynnis. **1645** *Rec. Elgin* (New Spald. Cl.) I. 179 To delywer to James Walker ane wylliecote worthe thrie poundis four shillingis. **1786** BURNS *To a Louse* vi, I wad na been surpris'd to spy You on..some bit duddie boy On 's wyliecoat. **1820** SCOTT *Abbot* i, A hardy little boy..did not hesitate a moment to strip off his *wylie-coat*, [and] plunge into the water. **1823** *Mirror* I. 285/2 A wallicoat of white drugget, deep blue inexpressibles.

Prov. **1737** RAMSAY *Sc. Prov.* (1750) 107 We can shape their wylie-coat, but no their wierd.

2. An under-petticoat.

1544 *Acc. Ld. High Treas. Scot.* VIII. 326 Tua elnis and ane half scarlot to be hir ane wyle cote. **1551** *Ibid.* X. 33 Arche Clerk, send..with ane furrit vylecoit to my Lady Gordoun. *a* **1586** SIR R. MAITLAND in *M. Quarto MS.* (S.T.S.) 2 Sumtyme thay will beir vp their goun, to schaw thair wylicot hingand doun. **1604** *Compt Bk. D. Wedderburne* (S.H.S.) 45 Ane narrow pece quhyt clayth..to be my lassis weylecottis. **1686** G. STUART *Joco-ser. Disc.* 31 The Sisters skewed their Wylycoats. **1715** RAMSAY *Christ's Kirk Gr.* II. xxii, The bride she made a fen, To sit in wylicoat sae braw. *a* **1725** *Cock-laird* in *Orpheus Caled.* 26, I man' ha'e a Silk Hood,..wylie coat, And a Silk snood. **1797** PINKERTON *Hist. Scot.* I. 154 The kirtle, or close gown, was rarely accompanied..with the wylicot or under petticoat. **1895** CROCKETT *Men of Moss-Hags* xxxii. 235 We are a pack o' silly craiturs. A' thing that wears willy-coats; no yin muckle to better anither! **1895** —— *Grey Man* iii. 23 Nell Kennedy with her wylicoats kilted.

Prov. **1721** KELLY *Scot. Prov.* 54 A Wife knows enough, who knows the good Man's Breeks from Weilycoat.

b. A feminine (or esp. in later use, a child's) night-dress.

c **1634** in C. K. Sharpe *Pref. to Law's Mem.* (1818) p. lviii, She was seen..standing bare-legged and in hir sark valicot ..conferring with the devill. *a* **1670** SPALDING *Troub. Chas. I* (1851) II. 233 Scho gettis wp out of hir naiked bed in hir night walycot, bairfut and bairleg. **1894–9** in Northumb. and Cumb. glossaries.

wylk(e, wyll, obs. ff. WHICH, WEEL[2].

wyll, wylle, obs. ff. WHILE, WILE.

wyllanye, wylly, wylst, obs. ff. VILLAINY, WILY, WHILST.

wylt, obs. f. QUILT *sb.*

wyly(e, wylys, obs. ff. WILY, WHILES.

†**wymalve.** *Obs. rare.* Also 3 ymalue. [a. AF. *wimave, widmalve* (12th c.), = OF. *vi-, vismauve, vismalve*, etc. (F. *guimauve*):—pop.L. **viscomalva*, for **hibiscomalva*: see HIBISCUS and MALLOW.] = WYMOTE. (Cf. VIMAUE.)

c **1265** *Voc. Names Plants* in Wr.-Wülcker 556 *Althea*, i. ymalue, i. holihoc. *c* **1450** *Alphita* (Anecd. Oxon.) 22/2 *Bismalua, alta malua, altea idem*,..a[*ngli*]*ce*, wymalue *uel* marshmalue.

wyme, obs. form of WAME.

wymmen, obs. pl. form of WOMAN.

wymote (ˈwaɪməʊt). Now *local.* Also 9 **wymote, wimot(e.** [Unexplained var. of WYMALVE.] The marsh-mallow, *Althea officinalis.*

1597 GERARDE *Herbal* Suppl., Wymot is *Ibiscus.* **1665** LOVELL *Herball* (ed. 2) 479 Wymot, see Marsh mallow. **1796** WITHERING *Brit. Pl.* (ed. 3) III. 612 Marsh Mallow. Wymote. [Found in] salt marshes and banks of rivers. **1821** S. F. GRAY *Brit. Plants* II. 639 *Althæa officinalis.* Shop marsh-mallow... Wymote. **1879** MISS JACKSON *Shropsh. Word-bk.* 482 *Wimote*,..common Marsh Mallow.

wyn, wynn (wɪn). Formerly also **wen** (wɛn). [a. OE. *wyn* (also *wen*) WIN *sb.*[2]] The name of the Old English runic letter ᚹ (= w) and of the manuscript form of this (Ƿ ƿ) in Old and early Middle English.

a. *c* **1300** *M'Clean MS.* in *Mod. Lang. Rev.* (1911) VI. 442 Wen . Þ. Þimman . Þepman . Þonie. **1705** WANLEY *Antiq. Lit. Septentr.* Pref. †b 2, Quod a Runicis Thorn and Wen clauditur. **1758** WISE *Some Enq. Europe* 145 Ð þ, Th or Thorn, and Ƿ ƿ, W or Wen, are of Northern growth. **1884** EINENKEL *Life St. Kath.* 125 The scribe took the *wên* of his original for a *þorn*. **1907** J. E. WELLS *Owl & Nightingale* 3 In a number of places *thorn* is dotted, and so is like *wen*.

β. [**1892** S. A. BROOKE *Hist. Early Eng. Lit.* II. xxiii. 201 W. was sometimes taken to mean *Wyn, joy*, and sometimes *Wen, hope*. **1910** F. TUPPER *Riddles of Exeter Bk.* 234 W always demands the interpretation *Wyn*, a rendering of the rune sustained by the Anglo Saxon alphabet in the Salzburg MS.] **1912** A. J. WYATT *Old Eng. Riddles* p. xxxix, The commoner Anglian runes..þ w wynn (joy). **1955** *Jrnl. Eng. & Gmc. Philol.* LIV. 6 In later Old English *fuþorcs, wyn* and *wen* are generally confused, owing to some extent..to the semantic link existing between the two words, although the name of the W-rune was unquestionably *wyn*. **1965** C. BARBER *Flux of Lang.* vii. 129 The runic symbol 'wynn' was used for the Old English *w* sound. **1978** *Norfolk Archaeol.* XXXVII. 56, G offers one or two forms hardly explicable except as corruptions of original spellings with *wynn* for *w*.

wyn, obs. f. WEEN *v.*, WIN *v.*

wynakar, -ir, obs. Sc. f. VINEGAR.

wynbeme, obs. f. WINDBEAM.

wyncouth, wyncus, obs. Sc. ff. UNCOUTH, VANQUISH.

wynd, obs. f. WIND.

wynd (weind). Chiefly *Sc.* (and *north. dial.*). Also 5, 8 **wynde** (6 **vynd, wyne,** 9 *north. dial.* **wynnd**), 5 **winde**, 8–9 **wind** (9 **weind**). [App. f. the stem of WIND *v.*[1] (cf. OE. *ȝewind* winding ascent, spiral, etc.); the long vowel indicates an OE. disyllabic form **winde* or **wynde*.]

1. A narrow street or passage turning off from a main thoroughfare; a narrow cross-street; a lane or alley: **a.** In Scotland (and northern England).

c **1425** WYNTOUN *Cron.* VIII. xxvii. 4490 þai til Edynburgh helde þe way, And at þe Freyr Wynde enteryt þai. **1439** *Charters*, etc. *of Edinb.* (1871) 64 The comon venale callit Sanct Leonardis wynde. **1506** *Reg. Mag. Sig. Scot.* 617/1 Le Nudryis Vynd infra burgum de Edinburgh. **1596** DALRYMPLE tr. *Leslie's Hist. Scot.* (S.T.S.) II. 174 Seing a possest persone with the deuil..rinn throuch gaites, houses, close, wynes, straits and streits frilie. **1612** in *Halyburton's Ledger* (1867) 336 Bonnetts maid in Leith wynd. **1695** SIBBALD *Autobiog.* (1834) 127 A house neer to the head of Blackfriers Wynd. **1727** DE FOE *Tour Gt. Brit.* III. 30 Those Side Lanes which they call Wynds. *c* **1730** BURT *Lett. N. Scotl.* (1818) I. 18 Being in my retreat to pass through a long narrow wynde or alley,..a guide was assigned me. **1782** SIR J. SINCLAIR *Observ. Scot. Dial.* 165 Many narrow lanes, leading..down the sides of the hills; which lanes, from their being generally winding,..are called *winds*. **1822** SCOTT *Nigel* ii, A sma' house at the fit of ane of the wynds. **1860** SIR J. B. BURKE *Viciss. Families* Ser. II. 153 The site of Appleby is exceedingly beautiful... From this main street are narrow lanes, called *weinds*, jutting out towards the river Eden. **1886** MASSON *Edinb. Sketches* (1892) 11 A multiplicity of narrow foot-passages called closes, with a few wider and more street-like cuttings called wynds.

b. Applied to similar lanes, etc., in other parts.

1863 SIR R. ALCOCK *Capital of Tycoon* I. 255 Black-teethed women..rush down the wynds and passages [in Yeddo] which lead to the great thoroughfare. **1871** KINGSLEY *At Last* ii, Fresh from the cities of the Old World, and the short and stunted figures..which crowd our alleys and back wynds. **1894** WEYMAN *Man in Black* viii. 168 The priest passed unharmed through the lowest wynds of Paris.

c. Without article.

1812 W. TENNANT *Anster F.* VI. xxi, From lane and wynd the sounds of gladness peal. **1856** W. E. AYTOUN *Bothwell* 145 That cry..rung through street, and pealed through wynd.

d. *transf.*

1952 DYLAN THOMAS *Coll. Poems* 170 Small fishes glide Through wynds and shells of drowned Ship towns to pastures of otters.

2. *attrib.*, as *wynd house*; **wynd head**, the higher end of a narrow street.

1530 *Abstr. Protocols Town Clerks Glasgow* (1897) IV. 34 Fra the Wyndheid of Glasgw to the Grayfreris. **1665** J. NICOLL *Diary* (Bann. Cl.) 443 [He] errectit ane staige betwixt Niddries and Black Friers wynd head. **1888** BARRIE *When a Man's Single* i, The windows of the wynd houses.

wyndak, -ok, obs. ff. WINNOCK *Sc.*

wynde, wyndel, -ille, etc., obs. ff. WIND, WINDLE *sb.*[1]

wyndi, var. OUNDY *Obs.* (Cf. UNDY.)

1486 *Bk. St. Albans, Coat-arm.* b v, The secunde [coat-armour] is calde wyndi, that is to say whan the felde is made like wawis of oon coloure or of diuerse colouris.

wyndlas(e, -lasse, etc., obs. ff. WINDLASS.

†**wyndre**, *v. Obs. rare.* [ad. OF. *guingnier, guignier*, etc., to deck, trick out.] *trans.* To trim, deck, or embellish (oneself, the brows, etc.).

? *a* **1366** CHAUCER *Rom. Rose* 1018–1020 Fetys she was..; No wyntred [*sic*] browis had she [F. *ne fu fardee ne guignie*] Ne popped hir for it neded nought To wyndre hir [F. *de soi tifer*] or to peynte hir ought.

wyndyrtak, wyne-ȝarde, -yaird, obs. Sc. ff. UNDERTAKE *v.*, VINEYARD.

wynfall, obs. f. WINDFALL.

†**wyning.** *Obs.* Also 3 **wynyng**; 4 *pl.* **wyn(e)wes, wynwys.** [repr. OE. *wining* 'leg-band', of obscure formation.

For the later plural forms cf. *penewes*, for the earlier *peneȝas*, var. of *peningas*, pl. of *pening* PENNY.]

A small strong rope for tying a sail; = GASKET I.

1295 *Acc. Exch. K.R.* 5/8 m. 13 Et iiij. s. in xij. duodenis de Wyninges emptis..ad velum. **1296** *Ibid.* 5/20 m. 5 In filo empto ad velum et vna pecia de Wynyng emptis de eodem. **1304** *Acc. Exch. K.R.* 12/6 m. 3 In .ij. velis, et Wynwes, et minutis cordellis. **1336** *Ibid.* 19/31 m. 5 Computat..in CC. xx. vlnis de Beluere emptis pro Wynewes inde faciendis ad dictum velum cum eisdem ligandum. **1420** in *For. Acc. 3 Hen. VI*, G/2 In..sepo Towe Wynwys et aliis diuersis ferramentis.

wynk(e, obs. ff. WING, WINK.

wynland, obs. Sc. pr. pple. of WINDLE *v.*[1]

wynlas, -ase, -asse, obs. ff. WINDLASS.

wynn[1]. (See quot.)

1863 SIMMONDS *Dict. Trade* Suppl., *Wynn*, a kind of timber truck or carriage. [**1875** KNIGHT *Dict. Mech.* 2823/2 *Wynd*, a truck or low carriage.]

wynn[2]: see WYN.

wynscott, obs. Sc. f. WAINSCOT.

wyntermyte: see VITREMYTE.

wynwes, pl.: see WYNING.

wyolence, -ent, obs. Sc. ff. VIOLENCE, VIOLENT.

wyolet, obs. f. VIOLET.

wype (waɪp). Now *dial.* Also 7, 9 **wipe**. [Of doubtful etymology; perh. echoic, from its call. Cf. (M)Sw. and Norw. *vipa*, Sw. *tofsvipa*, Da. *vibe*, also PEESWEEP, PEEWEEP.] The lapwing.

c **1325** *Gloss. W. de Bibbesw.* in Wright *Voc.* 165 [La vanele e le pounzot; *gloss*] a wype and waschere. *c* **1425** *Voc.* in Wr.-Wülcker 640 *Hec vpipa*, wype. **1512** in *Earl Northumb. Househ. Bk.* (1770) 104 It is thought goode that Wypes be hade for my Lordes own Mees onely. **15..** *Parlt. Byrdes* 305 Thowgh thou be hasty, as the wype, And thy feders, flyght rype. **1579** HAKE *Newes out of Powles* D ij b, Right Plouer, Snype, and Woodcock fine with Curlew, Wype and Rayle. **1825** J. MACKINNON *Messingham* (1881) 18 Plover are here called Wipes, or Pywipes. **1895** *E. Angl. Gloss.* 251 *Wypes*, ..the lapwing or plover.

wyp(p)e, obs. ff. WHIP.

wyppit, wypt, obs. pa. t. and pple. of WIPE *v.*

wyr, Sc. var. VIRE *sb.*[1] *Obs.*

wyrall, obs. f. VIRL.

wyrch, obs. var. WORK *v.*

wyrckyn, wyrkyn, obs. ff. FIRKIN.

1480 *Cely Papers* (Camden) 54 Yowr ij wyrkyns whon of samon and the tothyr of tony. *Ibid.* 177 A wyrckyn with gonstonys.

wyrd(e, obs. variant of WEIRD *sb.*

wyre, Sc. var. VIRE *v.*[1] *Obs.*

wyrfolk, obs. variant of WORKFOLK.

wyrgyne, obs. Sc. f. VIRGIN.

wyrie, wyry(e, etc., obs. varr. WORRY *v.*

wyris land: see URE *sb.*[4]

wyrk, wyrle, wyrne, wyroa(u)nce, etc., obs. ff. WORK *v.*, WHIRL *v.*, QUERN, WEROWANCE.

wyrok, Sc. var. WIRROCK.

wyrstylle, obs. f. WARSLE *v.*

wyrt, obs. Sc. f. WRIT *sb.*

wys: see BE *v.* A. 6, VICE *sb.*, VISE *v.*[1], WIS, WISE.

wysage, obs. Sc. f. VISAGE.

wysar, etc., obs. ff. VISOR, WIZARD *sb.*

wyse, var. VISE *v.*[1] *Obs.*; obs. f. WISE.

wysh, var. WIS *v.*[1] *Obs.*

wysiwyg ('wɪzɪwɪg). Also **WYSIWYG**. [Acronym (see quots. 1984).] (See quots.)

1982 *Byte* Apr. 264/2 'What you see is what you get' (or WYSIWYG) refers to the situation in which the display screen portrays an accurate rendition of the printed page. **1982** *Economist* 1 May 8 If he wishes to converse with computer buffs, he will have to cope with neologisms such as 'wysiwyg' (what you see is what you get), pronounced 'whizziwig'. **1984** *Sci. Amer.* Sept. 54/3 Perhaps the most important principle is WYSIWYG ('What you see is what you get'): the image on the screen is always a faithful representation of the user's illusion. *Ibid.* 135/1 The resulting interface between the computer and the user would then fall into the class of interfaces known as WYSIWYG, which stands for 'What you see is what you get'.

wysk, obs. Sc. var. WHISK *sb.*

wysle, var. WIZLE *dial.*

wysment, Sc. var. VISEMENT *Obs.*

wysnit, -yt, obs. Sc. ff. WIZENED *a.*

wyson, Sc. or north. f. WEASAND.

wyss(e, etc., varr. WIS *adv.* and *v.*[1] *Obs.*; obs. ff. WISE.

wyssel, obs. f. WHISTLE *v.*

wysshe, etc., obs. pa. t. of WASH *v.*

wysshene, obs. f. CUSHION *sb.*

wyst(e, obs. pa. t. and pple. of WIT *v.*[1]

wyste, southern ME. var. FIST *sb.*[1]

1422 YONGE tr. *Secreta Secret.* 156 The honde..that nowe in leynthe othyre in Palme hym streythyth, agayn into a wyste hym closyth.

wystel, wystyll: see WHISTLE, WISSEL.

wyt, obs. f. WHIT, WHITE, WIGHT, WIT.

wytale, wytch(e, obs. ff. VICTUAL, WITCH.

wytch(e, obs. ff. WHITCH (a chest).

1558–9 *Will A. Cole* (Somerset Ho.), A wytche in the universitie of Oxforde called Cista Antiqua universitatis.

wyte, obs. f. WHITE, WIGHT, WIT; var. WITE.

wyte-, wythsave, obs. varr. VOUCHSAFE *v.*

wytel(e, obs. ff. WHITTLE *sb.*[1]

wytenge, obs. f. WHITING *sb.*

wytenonfa, var. WEDENONFA' *Sc. Obs.*

wyth(e, obs. ff. WHITE, WIGHT, WITH, WITHE.

wythen(n)e, varr. WHETHEN *Obs.*

wyther, -yr(e, obs. Sc. ff. OTHER.

Wyth-sounday, obs. form of WHIT SUNDAY.

wytht(e, obs. ff. WHITE, WIGHT.

wyþy, contr. f. *with thi*: see WITH *prep.* 6.

wytsaffe, -saue, etc., obs. varr. VOUCHSAFE *v.*

Wytson(e, obs. ff. WHITSUN.

wytstare, obs. f. WHITSTER.

wytt(e, obs. ff. WEIGHT *sb.*, WHITE, WIT *sb.* and *v.*

wyttail(e, obs. varr. VICTUAL.

wytyng, obs. f. WHITING *vbl. sb.*

wyue, wyve, obs. ff. WIFE *sb.*, WIVE *v.*

wyvel, etc., obs. ff. WEEVIL.

wyver, obs. Sc. var. WEAVER[1].

†**wyver.** *Obs.* Forms: 4 **guiure**, 5 **gwyuer** (**gwuer**), 4–5 **wiuere**, 5 **wiver**, 6–7 **wiuer**; 4–5 **wyuere**, 5–7 **wyuer**, 7 **wyver**. [a. OF. *wyvre, wivre, guivre* (F. *guivre, givre*), etc., varr. *vivre* serpent: see VIVER[2].]

1. A viper. Also *fig.* and in fig. context.

13.. *K. Alis.* 5609 (Laud MS.), Addres, guiures, & dragouns, Wolden þis folk..Envenymen & abite. *c* **1374** CHAUCER *Troylus* III. 1010 Ialousye..þat wikkede wyuere. **1387–8** T. USK *Test. Love* III. v. (Skeat) l. 34 Wherfore..ye ne ought..accompte thilke thing [*sc.* jealousy] among these other welked wivers and venomous serpentes, as envy, mistrust, and yvel speche. *c* **1400** *Partonope* 7079 Now is he allone in þe wildernesse Amonge wyuerse and serpentes. *Ibid.* 7254 Maruk shewed hir grete lyons,..Dragons, Wyuers, and eke serpentes.

2. *Her.* = WYVERN I.

1599 THYNNE *Animadv.* (1875) 41 A Wyuer is a kynde of serpent of good Bulke, not vnlyke vnto a dragon, of whose kinde he is, a thinge well knowen vnto the Heroldes, vsinge the same for armes, and crestes, & supporters. *Ibid.* 42 The erle of Kent bearethe a wiuer for his Creste and supporters; the erle of Penbroke, a wiuer vert for his Creste. **1631** WEEVER *Anc. Funeral Mon.* 293 A wiuer volant. *Ibid.* 294 A Wyuer being the Armes of Hugh Brent Esquire. **1678** PHILLIPS (ed. 4), *Wyver*, the name of an Animal, little known otherwise than as it is depicted in Blazonry.

3. *wyver-fish*, some chimerical fish. *nonce-use.*

1857 MEREDITH *Farina* ix. 153 Upon that he [*sc.* the Demon] shot out his wings, that were like the fins of the wyver-fish, sharpened in venomous points.

wyvern ('waɪvən). Also 7 **wiu-, wiverne**, 8–9 **wivern** (8 **wefforne**). [f. prec., with excrescent *-n* (see note on BITTERN[1]).]

1. *Her.* A representation of a chimerical animal imagined as a winged dragon with two feet like those of an eagle, and a serpent-like, barbed tail.

1610 GUILLIM *Heraldry* III. xxvi. 182 So doth the Wiuerne partake of a Fowle in the Wings and Legs,..and doth resemble a Serpent in the Taile. **1682** J. GIBBON *Introd. ad Lat. Blazoniam* 123 This Dragon hath but two Legs, and so is the same with our Wiverne. **1716** S. KENT

Gramm. Her. s.v. *Drake*, He beareth Argent, a Wivern, his Wings displaid and Tail nowed Gules. **1780** *Encycl. Brit.* (ed. 2) V. 3605/2 A Wivern volant Bendways Sable. *Ibid.*, A Wyvern with a human Face. **1822** GAGE *Hengrave* 38 A squirrel..impaling a coat argent, on a chevron, between three wyvern's heads. **1864** BOUTELL *Her. Hist. & Pop.* x. 68 Two Wyverns also support the shield of the Duke of Rutland. **1882** CUSSANS *Her.* (1893) 100 The wings of the Dragon..and Wyvern are always represented as addorsed.
attrib. **1688** HOLME *Armoury* II. 214/1 He beareth Vert,.. a Wivern-Wolf. *Ibid.*, He beareth Azure, a Wivern-Serpent, Or.

b. An image or figure of this monster.

1863 *Chr. Remembrancer* Oct. 436 The name of S. Romanus..is still dear to the boys and girls of Norman villages by sundry processions of dragons, wyverns,..made of combustibles. **1864** TENNYSON *Aylmer's F.* 17 Sir Aylmer Aylmer, that almighty man..Whose blazing wyvern weathercock'd the spire. *Ibid.* 516 The manorial lord.. Burst his own wyvern on the seal, and read..a letter from his child.

2. Such a monster conceived as having a real existence.

? *a* **1700** in Surtees *Hist. Durham* (1823) III. 243 Sir John Conyers, Knt., slew y[t] monstrous, and poysonous vermine or wyverne, an aske or werme, wh[ich] overthrew and devoured many people in fight. **1820** SURTEES *Ibid.* II. 172 [He] goes forth to slay wolf, bear, or wivern. **1835** BROWNING *Paracelsus* II. 454 Lakes which..Blaze like a wyvern flying round the sun. **1869** *Tales fr. Blackwood* XV. 74 As if she had been a Wyvern or a Gorgon.

wyvoll, wyvyl, obs. ff. WEEVIL.

wywe, obs. f. WEAVE *v.*

wywere, obs. var. VIVER[1].

wyyfe, wyȝffe, obs. ff. WIFE.

wyys, obs. f. WISE *a.*

wyzen, Sc. or north. f. WEASAND.

X

X (ɛks), pl. X's, *X*s (ˈɛksɪz), the twenty-fourth letter of the modern and the twenty-first of the ancient Roman alphabet, corresponding in form and position to the Greek *X*. The early Greek forms + X represented the aspirated voiceless velar (kh) in the Ionian alphabet, and (ks) in the Chalcidian alphabet. (In the former, (ks) was denoted by Ξ, in the latter, (kh) was denoted by ᛘ.) *X* was adopted by the Latins with the value (ks) from the Greek alphabet introduced into Italy. The ancient Roman name of the letter was *ix*, which is that given by Ælfric in his Grammar (*c* 1000).

Words having initial *x* (pronounced as *z*) in English are nearly all of Greek origin; a few, as *xebec*, *Xerez*, have *x* representing early Sp. *x* (now *j*). In OE. *x* was used medially and finally as a variant spelling of *cs* (whether original or standing for *sc*), e.g. *æx*, *eax* = *æcus*, *acus*, *æsc* AXE, *áxian* = *ácsian*, *áscian* to ASK, *fixas*, pl. of *fisc* FISH, *fixian* = *fiscian* to FISH, *waxan* = *wascan* to WASH. Other variants are *cx*, *hx*, *xs*, *cxs*, *hxs*, as *meohx*, *micxen* MIXEN, *axsan* ASHES. Similar spellings occur in the Cotton MS. of Cursor Mundi, e.g. *flexs*(*s* flesh, *wexs* wash, *fixses* fishes; the same MS. has the unexplained spellings *fux*(*o*)*l*, *foux*(*u*)*l*, etc. of FOWL *sb*. In East Anglian texts of the 14th to the 16th century *x* is frequently written for initial *sc*, *sch* in *xal* shall, *xuld* should; *xsal* also is found in the Paston Letters; instances of other words so written are only occasional, e.g. *xad* shed (pa. pple.), *xowyn* shove, *xuldrys* shoulders. Initial *x* stands for *sh* (or *s*) in early forms of some oriental words, as *xerif* SHEREEF (after early Sp. *xerife*), *xaraffe*, *-aff* SARAF, and *Xinto* SHINTO. Other temporary uses of *x*, but with its normal value (ks), are found in the once general *axes*, *axis* ACCESS, *hunx* HUNKS, and the less common *exelent* EXCELLENT, *exite* EXCITE; on the other hand *pox* = *pocks* has become permanent, and *sox* has been adopted, orig. in the hosiery trade, as a convenient shortening of *socks*.

The phonetic values of *x* in English are three, of which the commonest is (ks), as in *axis* (ˈæksɪs), *buxom* (ˈbʌksəm), *doxology* (dɒkˈsɒlədʒɪ), *excuse* (ɪkˈskjuːs), *expense* (ɪkˈspɛns), *oxen* (ˈɒks(ə)n), *proximity* (prɒkˈsɪmɪtɪ), *tax* (tæks). The pronunciation of the prefix *ex-* followed by a vowel or *h* varies according as it bears the stress or not, the general rule being that ˈ*ex*— = (ɛks) and *ex*—ˈ = (ɪgz), as *exile* (ˈɛksaɪl), *exact* (ɪgˈzækt), *exhort* (ɪgˈzɔːt); but there is considerable variety in individual words and individual usage: see EX- *prefix*[1] 1 note. The same general principle governs the pronunciation of *anxious* (ˈæŋkʃəs), *anxiety* (æŋˈzaɪɪtɪ), *luxury* (ˈlʌksjʊərɪ, ˈlʌkʃərɪ), *luxurious* (lʌgˈzjʊərɪəs, lʌgˈʒʊərɪəs) *Alexander* (ælɪgˈzɑːndə(r), -æ-), *Alexandrine* (ælɪgˈzɑːndrɪn, -æ-); but here also individual usage varies. The third value (z), arising from a reduction of (gz), is given in all cases to initial *x*, as *Xerxes* (ˈzɜːksiːz); this value is shown in many instances in the 17th and 18th centuries by the spelling with *z*, as *Zanthian*, *zebeck*, *Zerez*, and instances are not uncommon in the 19th century of *zantho-* and *zylo-* for *xantho-* and *xylo-*; early examples are *Zanctus* Xanthus (Lydg. *Troy Bk.* II. 731 rubric, 15th cent.), *zyphe* XIPH (1572). Cf. *Santippa* Xanthippe (Chaucer), *Cerses* Xerxes (Wyntoun *Chron.*, S.T.S., III. 54). A similar reduction of *x* took place in French:

x, if he be the fyrste letter of a worde, as *xenotróphe*, *xylobalsóme*, whiche they sounde but *s*, sayenge *senotrophe*, *sylobalsome*, for they can nat gyve *x*, whiche is also a greke letter, is true sownde. (**1530** PALSGR. *Esclarc.* I. xxv.)

I. 1. The letter or its sound. ***x-*** (rarely ***X-***)***height*** (Typogr.), the height of a printed lower-case *x*, esp. as representative of the size of the fount to which it belongs.

c **1000** ÆLFRIC *Gram.* (Z.) 6, *x* ana ongynð of þam stæfe *i* æfter uðwitena tæcinge. **1530** PALSGR. 38 Note that *x* shall never be sounded in frenche lyke as he is in latyn, or as we wolde do in our tonge, in no wyse, but lyke an *z*. *c* **1620** A. HUME *Brit. Tongue* (1865) 12 The top of the tongue stryking on the inward teeth formes d, l, n, r, s, t, and z. The midle tongue stryking on the rouf of the mouth formes the rest, c, g, k, j, q, and x. **1636** B. JONSON *Engl. Gram.* I. iv, X is rather an abbreviation, or way of writing with us, then a Letter;.. It begins no word with us, that I know, but ends many. **1735** MIDDLETON *Diss. Orig. Printing Eng.* 7, I take the Date in question to have been falsified originally by the Printer,.. and an x to have been dropt..in the Age of its Impression. *a* **1845** BARHAM *Ingol. Leg.* Ser. III. *Lord of Thoulouse* xxi, His cap, and his queer cloak all X's and Izzards. *a* **1849** POE *Tales*, *X-ing a Paragrab*, When the exigency does occur, it almost always happens that *x* is adopted as a substitute for the letter deficient. **1864** BOUTELL *Her. Hist. & Pop.* xxi. (ed. 3) 360 Az., on a cross arg. the letter X sa. **1878** W. J. CRIPPS *Old Engl. Plate* 110 Much of the old..plate of the sixteenth and seventeenth centuries that is still to be found in the counties of Devon and Cornwall bears the old Exeter mark, which was a large Roman capital letter X crowned. **1945** J. C. TARR *Printing To-day* 177 *x-height*, the height of lower-case letters (excluding descenders and ascenders), i.e. the height of a lower-case x. **1959** T. HARROD *Librar. Gloss.* (ed. 2), 99 *Descender*,..that part which extends below the 'X' height. **1964** P. A. D. MACCARTHY in D. Abercrombie et al. *Daniel Jones* 160 Any attempt to preserve traditional usage by having only x-height letters for vowels. **1978** J. LEWIS *Typography* ii. 79 Typefaces with a large x-height are more suitable for an age accustomed to reading sans serif signs... VIP Palatino is another large x-height typeface.

b. The letter considered with regard to its shape: chiefly *attrib.* and *Comb.* Hence identified with a cross. ***X's and O's***: the game of noughts and crosses. ***X chair***, a chair in which the underframe resembles the letter X in shape; so ***X-frame*** (usu. *attrib.*).

1545 ELYOT, *Decussis*..is also a fourme in any thynge representynge the letter X, whiche parted in the myddell maketh an other figure called *Quincunx*, V. **1769** in C. Welsh *Bookseller of Last Cent.* 354 Those [books] with an X. **1798** *Hull Advertiser* 28 July 2/1 Chairs in sets..with W tableau and X backs. **1837** HEBERT *Engin. & Mech. Encycl.* II. 876 The said pin traverses the X groove from side to side. **1839** *Penny Cycl.* XV. 176/1 Suppose a cross like an X or V to be cut out of brass-plate. **1861** HAGEN *Synopsis Neuroptera N. Amer.* 213 An *x*-shaped spot. **1866** BLACKMORE *Cradock Nowell* xii, The boy leaped the new X fence very cleverly. **1893** SELOUS *Trav. S.E. Africa* 402, I will write your name ..on the paper..and you must make an 'x' behind your name. **1894** CROCKETT *Raiders* 92 It wasna playing at x's and o's to be steering for that crossbones of a Dutchman. **1899** JESSE L. WILLIAMS *Stolen Story*, etc. 54 Billy, reaching the end of the page, made a double X mark to show that it was the end of the story. **1904** P. MACQUOID *Hist. Eng. Furnit.* iii. 52 It is a very common error to assign all these 'X' chairs to foreign importation. **1911** P. BRIDGES *Green Wave of Destiny* xiv. 211 There was just room between the humps for two narrow sacks placed X-wise. **1918** [see SAVONAROLA 2]. **1945** *Burlington Mag.* May 110/2 These X chairs throughout the sixteenth century, when made for the homes of the wealthy, were covered with rich cloths of gold, velvets, and silks. **1955** R. FASTNEDGE *Eng. Furnit. Styles* i. 33 (*caption*) Arm chair of X-frame construction... Early seventeenth century. **1961** L. G. G. RAMSEY *Connoisseur New Guide to Antique Eng. Furnit.* 20 Another form of chair, of different origin from the boxchair, was the X chair... Both chairs are assigned to about the same period—that is the middle of the sixteenth century. **1976** X-frame [see SADDLE SEAT 3 b].

c. Used like other letters of the alphabet to denote serial order, as in the signatures of the sheets of a book, the batteries of the Royal Horse Artillery, etc.

d. Used to mark a location on a map or the like; esp. in phr. ***X marks the spot*** and varr.

1813 M. EDGEWORTH *Let.* 16 May (1971) 59 The three crosses X mark the three places where we were let in. **1918** J. M. BARRIE *Echoes of War* 5 In the rough sketch drawn for to-morrow's press, 'Street in which the criminal resided'.. you will find Mrs. Dowey's home therein marked with a X. **1928** R. KNOX *Footsteps at Lock* iv. 36, I wish I could be there, to see you diving in the mud on the spot marked with an X. **1968** B. NORMAN *Hounds of Sparta* ix. 64 A message from our alcoholic friend. X seems to mark the spot where he lives.

II. Symbolic uses.

2. The Roman numeral symbol for ten (or †tenth); so xx = twenty (in early use also for 'score', as iij[xx] = 'three score', 60; also occas. xx[ti] = L. *viginti*), xxx, occas. xxx[ty] = thirty, etc.

c **1000** *O.E. Chron.* an. 409 (Parker MS.) þæt wæs embe .xi. hund wintra & x. wintra þes þe heo ȝetimbred was. *a* **1400** *Wyclif's Bible* Prol. (1850) I. 17 There weren not left ..no but v. hundrid horsmen, and x. charis, and x. thousind of footmen. **1426** AUDELAY *Poems* (Percy Soc.) 71 Ȝour x. comawndmentis ȝe most con. *c* **1450** *Mirour Saluacioun* (Roxb.) 146 The feest of kyng Aswere was ix[xx] dayes duryng. **1478** W. PASTON in *P. Lett.* III. 237 He seythe ye be xx[ti]s. in hys dette. **1481** *Howard Househ. Bks.* (Roxb.) 9 For j.m. j[c] iiij[xx] maryners. **1481–90** *Ibid.* 451 The nombir of the horse ys vij[xx] iij. **1488** *Henry's Wallace* v. 909 Xxx[ty] with him off nobill men at wage. **1489** MARG. PASTON in *P. Lett.* III. 350 Wretyn at London, the x. day of Februar. **1535** *Bury Wills* (Camden) 126 To my valentyn Agnes Illyon xs. **1537** CROMWELL in Merriman *Life & Lett.* (1902) II. 53 Frome London the xth daye of Apryll. **1638** FORD *Fancies* III. ii, If my watch keep faire decorum, Three quarters have neere past the figure X. **1686** BURNET *Trav.* 241 Pope Leo the Xs time.

†**b.** *x*[r]: abbreviation of *December*. *Obs.*

1624 SIR W. ASTON in Goodman *Court Jas. I* (1839) II. 369 Madrid, 24 of X[r] 1624.

c. ***x***: a ten-dollar note. ***XX***: a twenty-dollar note. *U.S. colloq.*

1837 *Knickerbocker Mag.* IX. 96 My wallet..distended with V's and X's to its utmost capacity. **1883** F. M. CRAWFORD *Dr. Claudius* xx, The Custom-House officials.. who know the green side of a XX.

3. In *Algebra* and *Higher Mathematics* used as the symbol for an unknown or variable quantity (or for the first of such quantities, the others being denoted by *y*, *z*, etc.); *spec.* in analytical geometry, the sign for an abscissa, or quantity measured along the principal axis of co-ordinates (hence called the †***axis of x***; now always ***x-axis***; also *transf.*). ***X-cut*** adj. (Electronics), of, pertaining to, or designating a quartz crystal cut in a plane normal to its X-axis; ***X-plate*** (Electronics), each of a pair of electrodes in an oscilloscope that control the horizontal movement of the spot across the screen. Hence allusively for something unknown or undetermined (also *attrib.* and in *Comb.*). See also X-RAY.

The introduction of *x*, *y*, *z* as symbols of unknown quantities is due to Descartes (*Géométrie*, 1637), who, in order to provide symbols of unknowns corresponding to the symbols *a*, *b*, *c* of knowns, took the last letter of the alphabet, *z*, for the first unknown and proceeded backwards to *y* and *x* for the second and third respectively. There is no evidence in support of the hypothesis that *x* is derived ultimately from the mediæval transliteration *xei* of شى *shei* 'thing', used by the Arabs to denote the unknown quantity, or from the compendium for L. *res* 'thing' or *radix* 'root' (resembling a loosely-written *x*), used by mediæval mathematicians.

1660 J. MOORE *Arith.* II. i. §19. 16 (*Algebra*) Note alwayes the given quantities or numbers with Consonants, and those which are sought with Vowels, or else the given quantities with the former letters in the Alphabet, and the sought with the last sort of letters, as *z y x*, &c. lest you make a confusion in your work. **1709** J. WARD *Yng. Math. Guide* IV. iii. (1713) 380 Let *y* = *As* the Abscissa, and *z* = *SP*, put *x* = *Aa* the Distance between the two Semi-ordinates; which we suppose to be infinitely near each other. **1726** E. STONE *New Math. Dict.* s.v. *Conoid*, If *a* be equal to the Transverse Axis of the Hyperbola, generating a Conoid, and *x* be the Heighth of the Conoid, or the Absciss of the Hyperbola. **1771** *Encycl. Brit.* II. 269 The equation of any curve, is an algebraic expression, which denotes the relation betwixt the ordinate and abscissa; the abscissa being equal to *x*, and the ordinate equal to *y*. **1839** *Penny Cycl.* XIII. 175/2 (*Kant*) What is that unknown principle (= X) on which the understanding relies, when of the subject A it finds a foreign predicate B, and believes itself justified in asserting their necessary connexion? **1885** J. CASEY *Treat. Analytical Geom.* ii. 22 If the equation of the line contains no *x*, it is parallel to the axis of *x*; and if it contains no *y*, it is parallel to the axis of *y*. **1886** W. B. SMITH *Elem. Co-Ordinate Geom.* I. i. 10 *OX*, *OY*, are called Co-ordinate Axes, or axes of *X* and *Y*, or *X*- and *Y*-axes. **1893** F. ADAMS *New Egypt* 29 The *x* of the Egyptian equation being pretty obviously the Egyptian people. **1898** W. T. STEAD in *Daily News* 8 Nov. 5/4 What manner of man is its author? He is the X in the equation. **1898** A. LANG *Making Relig.* ii. 15 Research in the X-region is not a new thing under the sun. **1903** GREENOUGH & KITTREDGE *Words* v. 53 To make fun of the x's and y's of the algebraist. **1906** *Daily Chron.* 12 May 4/3 There is 'a wholesome distrust,' says Professor Ewing, 'of what may be called *x*-chasing.' **1929** *Internat. Critical Tables* (U.S. Nat. Res. Council) VI. 211/1 The *z*-axis coincides with the crystallographic *c*-axis of 3-fold symmetry, the *y*-axis is ⊥ to a face of the hexagonal first order prism, and, in dextro crystals, the + direction of the *x*-axis is outward through one of the faces..of the trigonal pyramid. **1930** W. G. CADY in *Proc. IRE* XVIII. 2139 We consider first the manner of indicating the orientation of the more common 'cuts' [in quartz crystals]. .. In the first case, we have the cut variously referred to in the literature as 'Curie cut'..or 'normal cut'... However, a still more concise term would be the 'X-cut', denoting a plate the normal to whose face, and hence for which the applied electric field, is parallel to an X-axis. Similarly, the term 'Y-cut' would apply to the second type of quartz plate, which has hitherto been referred to as the '30-deg. cut' or 'parallel cut'. **1933** J. H. MORECROFT *Electron Tubes* xii. 337 The velocity of [compression] wave travel is different in the Y axis direction from that along the X axis. *Ibid.* 338 An X-cut plate has a negative temperature coefficient, i.e. the frequency of oscillation decreases as the temperature rises. .. The Y-cut plates have a positive coefficient. **1934** J. H. REYNER *Television* vii. 71 We then apply a suitable periodic voltage across the X plates which spreads the trace-out at right angles and produces a pattern on the screen. **1945** *Electronic Engin.* XVII. 723 These two equations define the components of the velocity of the spot along the X and Y axes. **1946** *Ibid.* XVIII. 23/1 A D.C. connexion must be made between the output of the time base and the X plates of the tube. **1969** *Funk & Wagnalls Dict. Electronics* 170/1 *X-axis*, in a quartz crystal, a reference axis chosen so as to connect two opposite vertices of its hexagonal cross section; one of the axes showing the greatest electrical activity. **1973** S. K. STEIN *Calculus & Analytic Geom.* ii. 26 Far to the right and to the left the graph gets closer and closer to the *x* axis without ever touching it. **1978** D. T. REES *Cathode Ray Oscilloscope* 9 A voltage applied to the X-plates will deflect the beam sideways. **1982** *IEEE Trans. Industr. Electronics* XXIX. 158/1 The rotated *X*-cut orientation has been found to be optimum from the viewpoint of its frequency versus temperature and pressure characteristics. **1983** V. M. Ristic *Princ. Acoustic Devices* vi. 180 The relationship between the natural axes *a*, *b*, *c* and the crystallographic axes *X*, *Y*, *Z* must be known in order to use the proper constants. These relationships, for each crystal system, have been adopted by convention. Various piezoelectric, elastic, and other constants of a particular crystal specimen are evaluated in terms of *X*, *Y*, *Z* axes.

b. Hence used *attrib.* as an indeterminate numeral adj. = 'an unknown number of..' Chiefly *humorous*.

1848 Thackeray *Van. Fair* xi, The black porker's killed —weighed *x* stone. **1904** *Brit. Med. Jrnl.* 15 Oct. 965 In the union of egg and sperm we witness the joining together of but two sets of characters and not that of 'x' sets derived from as many ancestors.

c. Put for a person's name when unknown or left undetermined. Also X. Y. (See also 5.)

1797 in *Corr. Pinckney, Marshall & Gerry* (1798) 36 We have promised Messrs. X. and Y. that their names shall in no event be made public. **1798** *Ibid.* 23 The names designated by the letters W. X. Y. Z. in the following copies of letters from the Envoys of the United States to the French Republic. **1810** Bentham *Packing* (1821) 125 As to Mr. *x*, I borrow, on this occasion for his use, one of the names employed by mathematicians for the designation of their unknown quantities. **1848** Thackeray *Ballads of Policeman X, Bow Street* ad fin., Pleaceman X 54. *Ibid.*, *Three Christmas Waits* 1 My name is Pleaceman X. **1853** Lytton *My Novel* xii. iv, The house-steward..was in fact the veritable XY of the *Times* [newspaper], for whom Dick Avenel had been mistaken. **1857** Dickens *Dorrit* ii. xii, The son of P. Q...whom we would call X. Y. **1873** H. Drummond *New Evangelism* etc. (1899) 199 X won't be preached to along with Y and Z and Q; that won't do X any good, for he thinks it is all meant for Y, Z, and Q. **1899** O. Seaman *In Cap & Bells* (1900) 47 For terror of the Law and him that waits Outside, the unknown X, to hale us hence. **1901** Elinor Glyn *Visits Elizabeth* (1906) 70 You feel obliged to ask the X's, the Y's, and the Z's from duty, and so you do... This is the kind of assortment that arrives: Papa X, Mamma X, and two girl X'es; Papa Y, Mamma Y, and Master and Miss Y; Papa Z, Mamma Z, Aunt Z, and Midlle. Z—such a party!

d. In wireless telegraphy (also in comb. ***x-stopper***): see quot.

1906 J. A. Fleming *Princ. Electric Wave Telegr.* ix. 611 The electric discharges due to atmospheric electricity create electromagnetic waves of an irregular type, which interfere with wireless telegraphy by causing irregular signals. These are technically termed X's... Means have been devised for sifting out the waves due to these irregular atmospheric disturbances... One of these devices, due to Mr. Marconi, has received the name of an X-stopper.

e. *Genetics.* (Now always as a capital.) [First used in German by H. Henking 1891, in *Zeitschr. f. wissensch. Zool.* LI. 706.] The symbol of the X chromosome. So **X-linked** (stress variable) *a.*, being or determined by a gene that is carried on the X chromosome.

1902 T. H. Montgomery in *Trans. Amer. Philos. Soc.* XX. 177 One of these three [chromosomes of *Protenor belfragei*], that designated *x* in Figs. 119–123, imposes by its relatively very large volume... We shall call this the 'chromosome *x*'. **1902** *Biol. Bull.* Dec. 29 (*caption*) All the chromosomes including the accessory (x), show indications of a longitudinal split. **1909** E. B. Wilson in *Science* 8 Jan. 57/1 In all the species half the spermatozoa are characterized by the presence of a special nuclear element which I shall call the 'X-element', while the other half fail to receive this element. **1910** [see heterogametic *a.*]. **1911** *Biol. Bull.* Jan. 118 The case of the aphids and phylloxerans has been the strongest argument for the hypothesis that two *X* chromosomes [in mosquitoes] give a female and..*XY* a male. **1949** Darlington & Mather *Elem. Genetics* ii. 49 The tortoiseshell cat is heterozygous for the X-linked gene, one allelomorph of which gives black, the other yellow, when homozygous. **1968** M. W. Strickberger *Genetics* xii. 216 In some instances, both compound X's and compound Y's may be found together in the same species. An extreme example of compound sex chromosomes occurs in the beetle *Blaps polychresta*, where the male has 12 X's and 6 Y's in addition to 18 autosomes. **1977** N. V. Rothwell *Human Genetics* iv. 83 One important point to note is that a male never passes an X-linked gene to his sons. **1983** *Oxf. Textbk. Med.* I. iv. 16/2 The triple X female with 47 chromosomes shows very little physical abnormality... It is possible that only one X is working in any cell at a given time. **1983** [see Y chromosome].

f. ***x-chaser***, etc.: a naval officer proficient in examinations or good at his work (see also quots. 1946, 1962). *slang*.

1904 'Vanderdecken' *Mod. Officer of Watch* vi. 64 To get on at sea it is not necessary to be an X hunter, a man may be a smart officer without ever having been near enough to an X to drop salt on its tail. **1912** 'Aurora' *Jock Scott, Midshipman* i. 4 He was what we called an *x* catcher; in fact, he passed out of the *Britannia* a midshipman and was wearing his patches the day he left. **1916** 'Taffrail' *Pincher Martin* v. 71 He was an *x*-chaser, in that he had done remarkably well in all his different examinations. **1946** J. Irving *Royal Navalese* 190 *X chaser*, a mathematically minded man; a theoretician. Also, a navigating officer who has qualified..as the navigator of a First Class ship. **1962** A. G. Course *Dict. Naut. Terms* 215 *X chaser*, a meticulous navigator in the Royal Navy.

g. In the analysis of games of Bridge x represents a card between 2 and 9, inclusive.

1920 A. G. L. Owen *Mod. Bridge* ii. 56 A similar position is this:—Z xxx A King xx BJ 10 xx YAQ. If A leads his King, Y makes Ace and Queen. **1933** C. Vandyck *Contract Contracted* i. 10 x = any small card... An easy way of remembering the Kx and Qx in different suits is to think of it as the *Grand Marriage*. **1959** Reese & Dormer *Bridge Player's Dict.* 14 East holds..Kxxxx. **1972** *Country Life* 4 May 1119/3 The trump finesse could not gain, even if East held Q xx.

h. ***x-question*** (Linguistics) (see quots.)

1924 Jespersen *Philos. Gram.* xxii. 303 In the other kind of questions we have an unknown 'quantity'... We may therefore use the well-known symbol x for the unknown and the term *x-question* for a question aiming at finding out what x stands for. **1957** S. Potter *Mod. Linguistics* iii. 71 Tune 1 falls after the turn. It is used in completed statements, in direct commands, and in special or x-questions which cannot be answered by 'yes' or 'no' and which are generally introduced by an interrogative pronoun or adverb. **1964** M. Chapallaz in D. Abercrombie et al. *Daniel Jones* 306 X-questions, that is, questions beginning with a specific interrogative word.

i. *Genetics.* (Now written as lower case.) A symbol representing the lowest number of chromosomes which make up a genome; freq. with preceding number, designating the number of sets of these in a cell, or in each cell of an organism.

1924 *Hereditas* V. 144 Summarizing our results on the chromosome set in *C[arex] pilulifera*, we may now state that this species has 9 chromosomes (X) of which there are 3 long, 4 medium and 2 short ones. *Ibid.* 161 In *Triticum* Sakamura..and Sax..found one species with 14 chromosomes (2X), four species with 28 and three with 42 chromosomes. **1932** C. D. Darlington *Recent Adv. Cytol.* iii. 61 Since a zygote usually receives two similar sets of chromosomes from its two parental gametes, their number is conventionally referred to as 2*n*; where the chromosomes pair regularly at meiosis they therefore form n pairs. Now in a particular individual these 2*n* chromosomes may consist of three sets or four sets of chromosomes relative to its own parents or ancestors. In the present work, therefore, the 'basic number' of this ancestral set is distinguished by the sign *x*. Thus in *Triticum vulgaer* $2n = 42$ and $x = 7$, the somatic chromosome number is therefore hexaploid (6*x*). **1979** A. F. Dyer *Investigating Chromosomes* ii. 47/2 *Rosa canina* ($2n = 5x = 35$ = AABCD). **1980** J. Schulz-Schaeffer *Cytogenetics* vii. 122 Very often, ploidy levels are erroneously reported for n-numbers. But the number reserved for ploidy levels is the x-number or basic genome number (x, 2x, 4x, 6x, etc.).

j. ***X factor*** (Mil. colloq.), the aspects of a serviceman's life that have no civilian equivalent; pay made in recognition of these.

1969 *Second Rep. Pay Armed Forces* (Nat. Board for Prices & Incomes) vi. 21 in *Parl. Papers* (Cmnd. 4079) 517 There are special conditions of employment..common to all servicemen and which.. make it more uncertain and on occasions more hazardous than the normal..employment in civilian life... The elements..constitute, what we have termed the X factor. **1979** *Navy News* May 48/3 The Ministry of Defence have proposed a substantial increase in the X factor across the board on the grounds that the elements that make up the justification for it have shifted to the disadvantage of the Services.

4. In designations of brands of ale, stout, or porter, XX or double X denotes a medium quality, XXX or treble X the strongest quality. Also in the marking of qualities of tin-plate.

1827 Hone *Every-day Bk.* II. 11 A lover of the best London porter and double XX. **1828** Miss Mitford *Village* Ser. iii. (1863) 47 His best double X. **1839** Barham *Ingol. Leg.* Ser. i. *St. Dunstan*, Keep clear of Broomsticks, Old Nick, and three XXX's. **1839** Ure *Dict. Arts*, etc. 1254 The following Table shows the several sizes of tin plates [and] the marks by which they are distinguished..Common, No. 1..c. 1... Two crosses, 1..xx. 1. Three crosses, 1..xxx. 1. Four crosses, 1..xxxx. 1. **1854** R. S. Surtees *Handley Cr.* ix. (1901) 75 'And you musicians', turning to the promenade band, who were hard at work with some XX, 'be getting your instruments ready.' **1856** Geo. Eliot *Ess.* (1884) 87 Barclay's treble X. **1886** A. G. Murdoch *Sc. Readings* Ser. i. 98 The XXX stout was brought in.

5. XYZ: used to denote some thing or person unknown or undetermined (cf. 3).

1808 Coleridge *Lett. to J. P. Estlin* (1884) 105, I use it rather as an X Y Z, an unknown quantity. **1813** Byron *Let.* 23 Nov., Wks. 1832 II. 269 Junius was X. Y. Z., Esq. *a* **1834** Coleridge *Ess. Faith* in *Lit. Rem.* (1839) IV. 426 [This] determines whether X Y Z be a thing or a person. **1885** J. K. Jerome *On the Stage* ii, Among the sham agents must be classed the 'Professors,' or 'X. Y. Z.'s.'

6. Used to represent a kiss, esp. in the subscription to a letter.

1763 G. White *Lett.* (1901) I. vii. 132, I am with many a xxxxxxx and many a Pater noster and Ave Maria, Gil. White. **1894** W. S. Churchill *Let.* 14 Mar. in R. S. Churchill *Winston S. Churchill* I. Compan. i. (1967) vii. 456 Please excuse bad writing as I am in an awful hurry. (Many kisses.) xxx WSC. **1951** S. Plath *Let.* 7 July (1975) i. 72 Some gal by the name of Sylvia Plath sure has something —but who is she anyhow?..x x Sivvy. **1953** Dylan Thomas *Under Milk Wood* (1954) 41 Yours for ever. Then twenty-one X's. **1982** C. Fremlin *Parasite Person* vi. 40 A row of 'X's', hurried kisses, all he had time to scribble.

7. ***X-band***: the range of microwave frequencies around 10,000 megahertz, used in radar transmission.

1946 *Radar: Summary Rep. & Harp Project* (U.S. Nat. Defense Res. Comm., Div. 14) 144/2 *X-band*, refers to wavelengths around 3 cm. **1952** [see *S-band* s.v. S. 12]. **1976** *Sci. Amer.* June 72/1 Most spacecraft now transmit to the earth a second radio signal at an X-band frequency (8·5 gigahertz).

8. *Cinemat.* X is used to denote films classified as suitable for adults only, or to which only those older than a certain age are to be admitted; so ***X-rated*** adj. (hence ***X-rate*** vb. trans.), ***X-rating*** vbl. sb. Also *fig.*

In Britain replaced by *15* and *18* in 1983.

1950 *Rep. Departm. Comm. on Children & Cinema* 64 in *Parl. Papers* (Cmd. 7945) VII. 238 We recommend that a new category of films be established (which might be called 'X') from which children under 16 should be entirely excluded. **1950** *Times* 14 July 8/4 The X certificates..will cover films other than those of a 'horrific' character, which are 'wholly adult in conception and treatment'. **1956** 'M. Innes' *Appleby plays Chicken* i. xvii. 139 'I'm going up.' 'You're doing nothing of the sort. It's X Certificate stuff, my boy, and not for general exhibition. There's a high-up copper who says so.' **1958** *Times* 9 July 6/3 Mr. Davie..has his 'X' certificate pictures..in which his obsessional imagery has taken on an existence, outside the vague allusiveness of the paint, which is too specific for comfort. **1970** *N.Y. Times Index* 1248/2 Panel of 3 Fed judges rules Penna's new law forbidding showing of previews of x-rated movies. **1972** *Daily Colonist* (Victoria, B.C.) 6 Feb. 2/3 There was only one explicit scene—the incest sequence—which caused the film to get an X (no one under 17 admitted). **1973** M. Amis *Rachel Papers* 136 Sebastian had gone into Oxford to see an X film ('any X film' he said) and to moon around looking for girls with his spotty mates. **1974** *Florida FL Reporter* XIII. 35/3 'Community standards' should determine whether X-rated movies should be allowed to be shown or not. **1974** *Newsweek* 20 May 23 His communicators..kept insisting that the transcripts actually clear the President of any crime more grievous than using X-rated language and thinking unsavory thoughts. **1976** *Publishers Weekly* 24 May 54/3 Most readers will surely X-rate the author's dicta; only the far-out minority will accept them. **1981** *TV Picture Life* Mar. 6/1 For it was daytime TV shows, or 'soaps' as they are affectionately called, that first explored the 'X'-rated areas of life. **1983** *Guardian* 15 Oct. 10/7 In America..X-rating is used only for out-and-out porn.

9. ***X-C*** (or ***XC***) ***skiing*** (N. Amer.) with pronunc. (krɒs), cross-country skiing.

1972 [see *ski-touring* s.v. ski *sb.* 2b]. **1976** *National Observer* (U.S.) 13 Mar. 11/1 Alpine and XC skiing. **1977** *N.Y. Rev. Books* 14 Apr. 42/4 (Advt.), Midwest Photographer, 33, likes bike rides, hikes, x-c skiing, concerts, theater,..seeks woman friend.

III. Abbreviations.

10. In writing the name Christ, esp. in abbreviated form, X or x represents the first letter (kaɪ) of Gr. ΧΡΙϹΤΟϹ *khristos*, and XP or xp the first two letters (kaɪrəʊ). Hence in early times Xp̄, in modern times Xt, X^t, and X, are used as abbreviations of the syllable *Christ*, alone or in derivatives; thus †***Xp̄en, Xp̄n*** = christen, †***Xp̄enned*** = christened; †***Xpian, Xtian(ity)*** = Christian(ity); Xmas (*Xstmas, Xtmas*) = Christmas.

†Xp̄c stands for ΧΡϹ contracted form of ΧΡΙϹΤΟϹ; cf. IHS.

a **1100** *O.E. Chron.* an. 1021 On Xp̄es mæsse uhtan. *c* **1380** Wyclif *Serm.* Sel. Wks. I. 337 In þis word Vix ben but þree lettris, V, and I, and X. And V bitokeneþ fyve; I bitokeneþ Jesus; and X bitokeneþ Crist. **1426** Lydg. *De Guil. Pilgr.* 19951 Xp̄c þi sone, þat in þis world alighte, Vp on þe cros to suffre his passioun. **1485** *Rolls of Parlt.* VI. 280/1 The most famous, blessed and Xpen Prince. *Ibid.* 336/1 Any Kyng or Prynce in England Xp̄enned. **1573** Baret *Alv.* s.v. *Y*, The long mistaking of this woorde Xp̄s, standing for Chrs by abbreuation which for lacke of knowledge in the greeke they tooke for x, p, and s, and so like-wise Xp̄ofer. **1598** Rowlands *Betraying of Christ* (Hunter. Cl.) 25 Xpian the outward, inward, not at all. **1634** *Documents, agst. Prynne* (Camden) 33 Such right..as your Xtianity, place, and function joyntly require. **1685–6** MS. in *Bk. Com. Pr. 1662* (Bodl.), My first child..Xstened on thursday the 28 of the same month. *a* **1697** Aubrey *Lives*, *Milton* (MS. Aubrey 8. lf. 63), He was so faire, that they called him the lady of X^{ts} coll. **1711** Hearne *Collect.* (O.H.S.) III. 155 This Note I took out of a Book of M^r. Urry of X^t. Church. **1811** Xtianity [see inerasable *a.*]. **1842** Francis *Dict. Arts*, etc. s.v., Xmas. for Christmas, Xpher. for Christopher, &c. **1845** M. Arnold *Let.* Mar. (1932) 55 When Tait had well observed that strict Calvinism devoted 1000s of mankind to be eternally,—and paused—I, with, I trust the true Xtian Simplicity suggested '—'. **1915** A. Huxley *Let.* Oct. (1969) 79 The ethics are identical with Xtian ethics. **1940** E. Pound *Cantos* lviii. 74 They drove the Xtians out of Japan. **1966** D. Jones *Let.* 8–16 June in R. Hague *Dai Greatcoat* (1980) iv. 223 All chaps should be awfully good..is..more or less what the present notion of Xtianity boils down to.

11. Put for the initial syllable *ex-* of a word, or as an abbreviation for a word beginning with *ex-*. ***x's*** (slang): expenses. Also, in Stock Exchange quotations, ***xd*** = ex dividend, etc.

1838 Manning *Let.* in Purcell *Life* (1896) I. xi. 230 All the 'Xs', I fear,..would go out. [*Note.* 'X's and Peculiars' were the nicknames given by the Tractarians to the Evangelicals ..who called themselves Christians *par excellence*.] *Ibid.*, He writes as tenderly as if he thought you a serious 'X'. *a* **1849** Poe *Tales*, *X-ing a Paragrab*, One gentleman thought the whole an X-ellent joke. **1885** *Daily News* 13 Mar. 2/1 New York Central Railway $92\frac{5}{8}$ $92\frac{7}{8}$ xd. **1894** Louise J. Miln *Strolling Players East* xv. 132, I think we might clear our X.'s... Perhaps I should explain that 'X.'s' means expenses. **1910** *Encycl. Brit.* V. 197/2 Canonists have continued to refer to the decretals of Gregory IX by the abbreviation X (*Extra*, i.e. *extra Decretum*).

b. In commercial and informal (esp. *U.S.*) use put for the final *-cks* (or *-cs*) of (esp. monosyllabic) words, as clox, pix[2], snax, sox.

12. *Chem.* = xenon.

x (ɛks), *v.* Pa. t. **x-ed, x'd.**

1. *trans.* To supply with x's in place of types that are wanting. $rare^{-1}$.

a **1849** Poe *Tales*, *X-ing a Paragrab*, 'I shell have to *x* this ere paragrab', said he to himself, as he read it over... So *x* it he did, unflinchingly, and to press it went *x-ed*.

2. *trans.* To obliterate (a typewritten character) by typing 'x' over it; to cross *out* in this way; = ex *v.* Also *fig.*

1942 W. Stevens *Let.* 28 Jan. (1967) 400, I felt that . . you had x-ed me out. *c***1945** U. Troubridge *Life & Death Radclyffe Hall* (1961) 71 As she dictated she continued to polish and the typist had always to be prepared to 'X' out at demand any word or sentence. **1958** C. Baker *Friend in Power* vi. 163 He set the capital key and X'd the sentence through. **1969** J. N. Chance *Abel Coincidence* iii. 54 You should x it off your card. **1977** J. Aiken *Last Movement* ii. 39 She crossed out that line, x-ing it vigorously to ensure its illegibility. **1978** H. Kemelman *Thursday the Rabbi walked Out* xxi. 89 You want me to make the correction on my typewriter? I can x it out.

Hence **x-ed** (*out*) *ppl. a.*, **'x-ing** (*out*) *vbl. sb.*

1966 *Punch* 31 Aug. 310/1 There shall be no 'X-ing out' of rival goods with black crosses. **1969** M. Land *Quicksand* 59 He knew the uneven lines of his portable and the X'd-out words would annoy Dave Winters. **1982** M. McMullen *Until Death do us Part* (1983) v. 29 A sheet of manila paper. . . A good deal of X-ing out to be seen.

xa, xabandar, obs. ff. SHAH, SHAHBANDAR.

xal, xall(e, obs. ff. SHALL.

Xanadu ('zænədu:). [Poetic ad. *Xandu*, i.e. Shang-tu, the Mongol city founded by Kublai Khan.] A place suggestive of the Xanadu portrayed in Coleridge's poem *Kubla Khan*, with its dream-like magnificence and luxury.

[**1625** *Purchas his Pilgrimes* III. I. iv. 80 Xandu, which the great Chan Cublay . . built; erecting . . a maruellous . . palace of marble. **1816** S. T. Coleridge *Kubla Khan* 55 In Xanadu did Kubla Khan A stately pleasure-dome decree.] **1948** 'J. Tey' *Franchise Affair* i. 7 To that douce country lawyer . . Scotland Yard was as exotic as Xanadu, Hollywood, or parachuting. **1958** M. Kennedy *Outlaws on Parnassus* xi. 165 Desirable readers . . do not expect Xanadu to put them in mind of Yarmouth. **1962** *Holiday* Aug. 70/1 It was only about half an hour's drive to the Xanadu of *le facteur* Cheval. **1969** *Guardian* 12 Nov. 5/7 Bob's double-tiered hideaway . . overlooking the fairy-lit battlements of his Xanadu in Mayfair. **1972** K. Bonfiglioli *Don't point that Thing at Me* viii. 76 The Ambassador was at some Xanadu-like golf-links far away. **1977** *Time* 25 July 2/1 We have lived in Southern California for twelve years and watched nearly everything encapsulate itself within a plastic bubble; not only giant 'pop Xanadus' like Sea World and Universal Studios, but also miniature golf courses, shopping centers and finally the American home.

Xanga, var. SHANG.

xanthæmatin to **xanthamide**: see XANTHO-.

xanthan ('zænθæn). *Chem.* Also **xantham**. [f. XANTH(O- + -AN; *-am* is unexplained.] A powdery polysaccharide composed of glucose, mannose, and glucuronic acid, produced by the bacterium *Xanthomonas campestris* and used in drilling muds and the food industry. Usu. as ***xanthan gum***.

1964 *Australasian Jrnl. Pharmacy* XLV. Suppl. No. 19. S80/1 The material is known variously as Polysaccharide B-1459, Xantham Gum, Corn Sugar Gum [etc.]. **1970** *Biotechnol. & Bioengin.* XII. 75 Previous publications from this Laboratory have reported batch fermentations to produce a biopolymer, xanthan, using *Xanthomonas campestris*. **1972** *Materials & Technol.* V. 44 Xanthan gum is used in oil well drilling muds, because of its heat stability and tolerance of salts. **1982** *S. Afr. Food Rev.* IX. 515/1 Since Xanthan gum solutions have a high viscosity at rest . . xanthan gum is widely used in food systems as a stabiliser for emulsions.

xanthane to **xantharsenite**: see XANTHO-.

xanthate ('zænθeɪt). *Chem.* [f. XANTHIC + -ATE[4].] **a.** A salt of xanthic (sulphocarbethylic) acid. Hence more widely, a salt or ester of any acid of the form RO·CS·SH, where R is an alkyl or similar radical. **b.** A compound of xanthic oxide (xanthine) with an alkali.

1831 [see XANTHIC 1 b]. **1868** Watts *Dict. Chem.* V. 498 Xanthate of sodium forms yellow needles. *Ibid.* 499 Xanthate of Antimony . . forms large, lemon-yellow, triclinic crystals. . . Xanthate of Bismuth . . crystallises in shining golden-yellow laminæ. **1887** A. M. Brown *Anim. Alkaloids* 79 [Xanthine] combines with the alkalies, . . forming xanthates. **1895** Cross & Bevan *Cellulose* III. 248 The precipitated xanthate may be treated with solutions of suitable salts of the heavy metals, and the cellulose xanthate of the metals prepared. **1945** *Jrnl. Chem. Soc.* 666 Debus . . showed that *O*-ethyl *S*-ethyl xanthate, EtO·CS·SEt, could be readily prepared by the interaction of potassium xanthate and ethyl iodide. **1951** C. R. Noller *Chem. Org. Compounds* xvi. 311 The sodium alkyl xanthates are used as collecting agents in the flotation process for the concentration of ores. **1974** *Encycl. Brit. Micropædia* X. 777/1 The most important group of xanthates are the sodium salts produced from cellulose.

xanthation (zæn'θeɪʃən). *Chem.* [f. XANTHATE + -TION.] A stage in the viscose process for making rayon, in which alkali-cellulose is treated with carbon disulphide to form cellulose xanthate.

1927 T. Woodhouse *Artificial Silk* iv. 30 The larger quantity of Viscose silk is made from wood-pulp. . . This process is termed Xanthation. **1962** J. T. Marsh *Self-Smoothing Fabrics* iv. 30 When xanthation is complete, the solid is dissolved in dilute caustic soda. **1978** *Nature* 12 Oct. 530/1 Mechanically pulped wood or papers are not generally useful, as the structure resists solution after xanthation.

So **'xanthate** *v. trans.*, to cause to undergo xanthation; also *absol.*; **xan'thated** *ppl. a.*, **xan'thating** *vbl. sb.*

1938 *Thorpe's Dict. Appl. Chem.* (ed. 4) II. 465/2 Surplus carbon disulphide is removed . . and the xanthated crumbs are then dispersed by churning with NaOH solution. **1952** *U.S. Patent* 2,592,355 1 In manufacturing viscose-rayon fiber, a low cellulose, high alkali and low viscosity is prepared . . by xanthating and dissolving same in usual way. *Ibid.* 4 Without subjecting to aging, it is xanthated in a xanthating apparatus. **1962** J. T. Marsh *Self-Smoothing Fabrics* iv. 30 The crumbs of alkali-cellulose are then xanthated by treatment with carbon disulphide in a rotating churn for about 3 to 4 hr. **1964** V. E. Yarsley et al. *Cellulosic Plastics* x. 149 The xanthated cellulose. *Ibid.*, The aged alkali-cellulose is charged to the xanthating churns, which rotate slowly. **1978** *Jrnl. Appl. Polymer Sci.* XXII. 897 Starch polyampholytes (xanthated starch amines) . . were prepared, characterized, and evaluated as wet- and dry-strength agents in paper handsheets. **1983** *Jrnl. Macromolecular Sci.: Chem.* A. XX. 218 Partially xanthated cellulose.

xanthein ('zænθi:ɪn). *Chem.* Also **-ine**. [ad. F. *xanthéine* (Frémy & Cloez, 1854), arbitrarily f. Gr. *ξανθός* yellow, to distinguish it from *xanthine* XANTHIN (1 b).] That part of the yellow colouring-matter of flowers which is soluble in water: cf. XANTHIN 1 b.

1857 Miller *Elem. Chem., Org.* 546 The yellow substance which is soluble in water is termed xantheine: it . . may be obtained from the yellow dahlia. **1864** Watts tr. *Gmelin's Hand-bk. Chem.* XVI. 513 Yellow of Flowers. . . the insoluble substance, called Xanthin by Frémy & Cloez, appears to correspond with Marquart's anthoxanthin; their Xantheïn, soluble in water, with Marquart's colourless extractive matter.

‖**xanthelasma** (zænθɪ'læzmə). *Path.* [mod.L., f. Gr. *ξανθός* yellow + *ἔλασμα* metal plate.] = XANTHOMA. Also *attrib.* Hence **xanthe'lasmic** *a.* = XANTHOMATOUS; ‖**xanthelasmoidea** [see -OID], a disease resembling xanthelasma, which leaves yellowish or brownish patches on the skin; also called *vitiligoidea*.

1867 W. J. E. Wilson *Diseases of Skin* (ed. 6) xxiv. 773 Epithelial hypertrophy . . to which from its colour and laminated appearance we have given the name of xanthelasma. **1900** J. Hutchinson in *Archives Surg.* XI. No. 41. 10 There is none of the characteristic xanthelasma leather. *Ibid.* 18 She . . had xanthelasma spots on the eyelids. *Ibid.* 2 The xanthelasmic [form of jaundice]. **1899** *Syd. Soc. Lex.*, Xanthelasmoidea. **1903** *Lancet* 30 May 1521/2 If further investigation should prove that in xanthelasmoidea the coagulability is high it will thus be more decisively separated from the urticarias.

xanthelene: see XANTHO-.

xanthene ('zænθi:n). *Chem.* Also **-en**. [f. XANTHO- + -ENE.] A tricyclic crystalline compound, $O(C_6H_4)_2CH_2$, derivatives of which are used as brilliant, often fluorescent, dyes. Usu. *attrib.*

1898 *Jrnl. Chem. Soc.* LXXIV. I. 643 Xanthen gives a *dichloro*-derivative, $C_{13}H_8Cl_2O$. **1902** *Chem. News* 17 Jan. 36/1 The mono-halogenated derivatives of the xanthene series possess basic properties. **1947** L. S. Pratt *Chem. & Physics Org. Pigments* viii. 189 The rhodamines are representative of the basic-type xanthene colors, and the fluoresceins, eosins, phloxins, erythrosins, and rose bengals are representative of the acid type. **1959** [see EUXANTHIC *a.*]. **1971** R. L. M. Allen *Colour Chem.* viii. 120 Xanthene dyes containing salicylic acid or other metallisable structures are manufactured as mordant dyes.

Xanthian ('zænθɪən), *a.* and *sb.* Also 7 **Zanthian**. [f. *Xanthus* (see def.) + -IAN.] Of or pertaining to (or an inhabitant of) Xanthus, an ancient town in Asia Minor; *spec.* of a collection of marbles discovered near it.

1685 Cotton *Montaigne* I. xl. (1711) I. 363 The Zanthians, who being besieg'd . . precipitated themselves . . into such a furious Appetite of dying, . . that Brutus had much ado to save but a very small number. **1697** Dryden *Æneid* I. 662 Ere yet the Food Of Troy they taste, or drink the Xanthian Flood. **1770** Langhorne *Plutarch* IV. 244 (*Alexander*) A spring in Lycia near the city of the Xanthians. **1842** Sir C. Fellows (*title*) The Xanthian Marbles, their acquisition and transmission to England.

xanthic ('zænθɪk), *a.* [ad. F. *xanthique*, f. Gr. *ξανθός* yellow: see -IC.]

1. *Chem.* Epithet of certain compounds which produce substances of a yellow colour, or of bodies connected with these. **a.** ***xanthic oxide***, the original name of XANTHINE; so ***xanthic calculus***, a urinary calculus containing xanthine.

1817 Marcet *Ess. Chem. Hist. Calculous Disorders* iv. 99 If the potash be added to the pure xanthic substance, . . no change of colour takes place. The residue of the solution of xanthic oxyd in water produces the yellow substance, when treated with nitric acid. *Ibid.* 101 Xanthic oxyd. *Ibid.* 102 In burning, it emitted an animal smell, which did not at all resemble that of the lithic, cystic, or xanthic calculus. **1857** Miller *Elem. Chem., Org.* 642 Xanthic or Uric Oxide ($C_{10}H_4N_4O_4$) was discovered by Dr. Marcet as the principal constituent of a very rare variety of urinary calculus. **1872** T. Bryant *Pract. Surg.* (1879) II. 84 Calculi of uric acid and the urates, with their modifications the oxalates, xanthic and cystic oxide.

b. ***xanthic acid***, a complex acid containing sulphur and carbon, also called sulpho-carbethylic or ethyldisulphocarbonic acid ($C_3H_6OS_2$), many of whose salts (*xanthates*) are yellow. Hence more widely, any acid of the general formula RO·CS·SH or RO·CS·SR′. So ***xanthic ether***, etc.

1831 T. Thomson *Syst. Chem.* (ed. 7) II. 176 Xanthic acid is characterized by precipitating the salts of copper yellow. *Ibid.*, During the distillation of xanthate of potash, a substance comes over which Zeise has distinguished by the name of xanthic oil. **1857** Miller *Elem. Chem., Org.* 146 Xanthic or Sulphocarbethylic Acid. **1868** Watts *Dict. Chem.* V. 498 Ethyldisulphocarbonic or Xanthic Acid . . is a colourless oil, heavier than water, . . its taste is acid, astringent, and bitter. *Ibid.* 500 Ethylic Disulphocarbonate or Xanthate, Xanthic Ether, $C^5H^{10}OS^2$ . . has a pale-yellow colour, a sweetish taste. **1945** *Jrnl. Chem. Soc.* 666 To interpret results obtained in other aspects of the chemistry of xanthic acid derivatives . ., we found it necessary . . to systematise current knowledge concerning the isomeric compounds RO·CS·SR′, R′O·CS·SR, RS·CO·SR′, the first two being esters of xanthic acids and the last an ester of *sym.* dithiocarbonic acid. **1956** Kirk & Othmer *Encycl. Chem. Technol.* XV. 150 The relatively unimportant xanthic acids are unstable, colorless or yellow oils, and have been known, on occasion, to decompose with explosive violence.

2. *Bot.* De Candolle's name for a series or class of colours in flowers, of which the type is yellow: opp. to *cyanic*.

1843 *Florist's Jrnl.* (1846) IV. 34 A most uncommon combination of colours—cyanic and xanthic tints in one and the same flower. **1885** Goodale *Physiol. Bot.* (1892) 454.

xanthide ('zænθaɪd). *Chem.* [f. Gr. *ξανθός* yellow + -IDE.] **a.** A compound of xanthogen (XANTHOGEN 1). **b.** A salt of xanthydric (persulphocyanic) acid.

1823 Henry *Elem. Chem.* (ed. 9) II. 667 The oxides of common metals (copper, lead, mercury, &c.) decompose it [*sc.* hydroxanthic acid] by giving up their oxygen to the hydrogen of the acid, and the xanthogene unites with the metal, forming xanthides. **1868** Watts *Dict. Chem.* V. 1050 *Xanthides*, syn. with *Persulphocyanates*.

xanthin ('zænθɪn). *Chem.* Also **xanthine, (zanthin)**. [ad. F. *xanthine* or G. *xanthin*, f. Gr. *ξανθός* yellow: see -IN[1].]

1. a. A yellow colouring-matter obtained from madder.

1838 T. Thomson *Chem. Org. Bodies* 387 Madder, according to Kuhlmann, contains two colouring matters, one, which is yellow, is soluble in cold water. Kuhlmann, who first obtained it, has given it the name of *xanthin*. **1839** Ure *Dict. Arts*, etc. 1329 *Xanthine*, is the name given by Kuhlmann to the yellow dyeing-matter contained in madder. *c***1865** J. Wylde in *Circ. Sc.* I. 421/1 Other principles may be extracted from madder, such as purpurine, alizarine, xanthine.

b. That part of the yellow colouring-matter of flowers which is insoluble in water: cf. XANTHEIN.

1857 Miller *Elem. Chem., Org.* 546. **1868** Watts *Dict. Chem.* V. 1050.

2. (See quot.)

1868 Watts *Dict. Chem.* V. 1050 *Xanthin*, . . applied . . 3. By Couerbe to a gaseous product of the decomposition of xanthates, to which he assigned the formula $C^2H^2S^2O^2$.

3. *attrib.* **xanthin-spar**, yellow lead-spar or WULFENITE.

1868 Watts *Dict. Chem.* V. 1052.

xanthine ('zænθaɪn). *Chem.* Also **-in**. [ad. F. *xanthine*, f. Gr. *ξανθός* yellow: see -INE[5].]

1. a. A substance ($C_5H_4N_4O_2$) allied to uric acid, found in various organs and secretions of the animal body; originally called *xanthic oxide* (see XANTHIC 1 a), from its forming a lemon-yellow compound with nitric acid.

1857 G. Bird *Urin. Deposits* (ed. 5) 46 This interesting body . . bears so close a resemblance to xanthine or uric oxide, that Scherer has named it hypoxanthine. **1862** H. Bence Jones in *Jrnl. Chem. Soc.* XV. 78 (*heading*) On a Deposit of Crystallized Xanthin in Human Urine. **1880** J. W. Legg *Bile* 582 The liver contained . . leucin, tyrosin, and xanthin. **1887** A. M. Brown *Anim. Alkaloids* 78 Xanthine may be extracted from muscular tissue in the same way as the sarkine.

attrib. and *Comb.* **1868** Watts *Dict. Chem.* V. 1050 *Xanthine* . . was discovered by Marcet in a urinary calculus weighing only 8 grains. Liebig and Wöhler afterwards found it in a larger calculus weighing between 18 and 20 grammes; these are the only known examples of xanthine calculi. **1873** Ralfe *Phys. Chem.* 93 Dr. Bence Jones has recorded an interesting case of xanthin gravel occurring in a lad aged nine and a half years. **1883** *Science* 23 Feb. 75/1 By heating xanthine-silver [= the silver-compound of xanthine] with methyl iodide, a methyl group was introduced. **1897** *Trans. Amer. Pediatric Soc.* IX. 123 Convulsive seizures, . . produced by the action of the poisonous xanthin bodies on the nerve centres. **1907** *Sat. Rev.* 16 Mar. 338/1 So called food reformers . . bandy about their catchwords—flesh-forming, . . xanthin-forming and the like.

b. Any of several substituted derivatives of xanthine.

1956 I. Finar *Org. Chem.* II. xvi. 613 Three important methylated xanthines that occur naturally are caffeine, theobromine and theophylline. **1974** M. C. Gerald *Pharmacol.* xv. 280 The xanthines . . have proved to be valuable drugs for the treatment of such respiratory diseases as asthma, bronchitis, and emphysema.

2. xanthine oxidase, an enzyme catalysing the oxidation of hypoxanthine to xanthine and of xanthine to uric acid.

1905 *Jrnl. Chem. Soc.* LXXXVIII. II. 271 The presence of oxygen is necessary to obtain in liver extract uric acid from the purine bases it contains, or that are added to it. The uric acid found comes almost exclusively from xanthine, and is due to a ferment, xanthine-oxydase. **1983** *Oxf. Textbk. Med.* I. IX. 79/1 Not all patients with xanthine stones have xanthine oxidase deficiency.

Hence **'xanthinine**, ‖**xanthi'nuria** (see quots.).

1868 WATTS *Dict. Chem.* V. 1051 *Xanthinine.* $C^4H^3N^3O^2$. .. A base produced .. by heating thionurate of ammonium to 200°... On boiling the resulting mass with water, the xanthinine remains as a yellow powder. **1890** BILLINGS *Nat. Med. Dict.*, *Xanthinuria*, passage of xanthin in the urine.

Xanthippe: see XANTIPPE.

xanthitane ('zænθɪteɪn). *Min.* [f. next + -ANE.] A mineral produced by alteration or decomposition of sphene or titanite: see quot.

1856 C. U. SHEPARD in *Amer. Jrnl. Sci.* Ser. II. XXII. 96 *Xanthitane.* In hollow crystals with the form of sphene, and pulverulent. Color pale yellowish white... It is found in a decomposing feldspar, .. and probably proceeds from the decomposition of sphene.

xanthite ('zænθaɪt). *Min.* [f. Gr. ξανθός yellow + -ITE[1].] A variety of vesuvianite or idocrase, occurring in yellowish crystals.

1828 THOMSON *Ann. Lyc. N. Hist. N.Y.* III. 44 (Dana). **1843** *Penny Cycl.* XXVII. 615/1 *Xanthite* consists of a congeries of small rounded grains, .. not larger than small grains of sand. **1851** MANTELL *Petrifactions* iv. §1. 364.

xantho- (zænθəʊ), before a vowel **xanth-**, repr. Gr. ξανθο-, combining form of ξανθός yellow; occurring as the first element in various compounds and derivatives, chiefly terms of chemistry, mineralogy, and pathology; the more important of these are given in their alphabetical places.

(Sometimes also erroneously *zantho-*: see X.)

1. *Chem.* In names of, or adjectives relating to, various compounds: (*a*) of a yellow colour, as ***xan'thæmatin***, ***'xanthaline***, ***,xantho'cobalt***, ***-co'baltic***, ***xantho'creatine*** (***-cre'atinine***), ***'xanthophane*** [Gr. φαν-, stem of φαίνειν to cause to appear], ***xantho'picrin*** (***-'picrite***) [Gr. πικρός bitter], ***xantho'protein***, ***xan'thopsin*** [Gr. ὄψις sight], ***xantho'puccine*** [PUCCOON], ***xantho-'purpurin***, ***xantho'rhamnin***; ***xantho'phenic***, ***xanthopro'teic***, ***xantho'tannic***, ***xan'thydric*** [Gr. ὕδωρ water] adjs.; (*b*) derived from or related to xanthic acid (XANTHIC 1 b), as ***'xanthamide***, ***'xantharin***, ***'xanthelene***; ***xan'theic***, ***,xanthome'thylic*** adjs.; (*c*) derived from or related to xanthydric acid, as ***'xanthane*** (***-an***): see quots.

1860 MAYNE *Expos. Lex.*, **Xanthæmatin* .. Term by Brett and Bird for a yellow, bitter substance found by dissolving hematin in weak nitric acid. **1893** *Pharmaceut. Jrnl.* 25 Mar. 793/2 *Xanthaline—A New Opium Alkaloid ($C_{37}H_{36}N_2O_9$). **1855** WATTS tr. *Gmelin's Chem.* IX. 276 *Xanthamide. $C^6NH^7S^2O^2$. *Ibid.* 277 Xanthamide exposed in a distillatory apparatus to a gradually increasing temperature is resolved into mercaptan and cyanuric acid. **1868** —— *Dict. Chem.* V. 1049 **Xanthan*, Berzelius's name for the group Cy^2S^3, regarded as the radicle of persulphocyanic or xanthydric acid. *Ibid.*, **Xantharin*, or *Xanthil*, an oily fetid compound, $C^4H^{10}O^3$, supposed by Couerbe .. to be produced by the dry distillation of xanthic ether. **1843** *Penny Cycl.* XXVII. 614/2 When xanthate of potash is subjected to distillation a limpid yellow coloured fluid comes over, which Zeise has called **xantheic oil.* **1868** WATTS *Dict. Chem.* V. 1049 **Xanthelene.* Zeise gave this name to an oil .. produced .. by precipitating potassic ethylsulphocarbonate with a cupric salt. **1856** GIBBS & GENTH *Res. Ammonia-cobalt Bases* in *Smithsonian Contrib. Knowl.* (1857) IX. v. 48 The salts of *Xanthocobalt. **1863** WATTS *Dict. Chem.* I. 1054 *Xanthocobaltic Salts. **1891** *Cent. Dict.*, **Xanthocreatine.* **1913** DORLAND *Med. Dict.* (ed. 7), *Xanthocreatin*, xanthocreatinin. **1887** A. M. BROWN *Anim. Alkaloids* 85 *Xanthocreatinine $C^5H^{10}N^4O$ .. closely resembles kreatinine... It shows in pellets of sulphur yellow, of slightly cadaveric odour. **1868** WATTS *Dict. Chem.* V. 1052 **Xanthoglobulin.* This name was given by Scherer .. to a substance which he obtained in yellow globules. **1880** J. W. LEGG *Bile* 515 Hypoxanthin and xanthoglobulin were also found. **1868** WATTS *Dict. Chem.* V. 501 Methyl-disulphocarbonic Acid $(CH^3)HCOS^2$. *Xanthomethylic Acid... Methylic Disulphocarbonate, $C^3H^6OS^2$... Xanthomethylic Ether. **1890** BILLINGS *Nat. Med. Dict.*, **Xanthophane*, an orange-yellow pigment obtained from the retina. **1868** WATTS *Dict. Chem.* V. 1052 **Xanthophenic acid.* A yellow colouring-matter, .. produced .. by heating phenol or cresol with arsenic acid... The *xanthophenates dye silk and wool red, of various shades. **1852** W. GREGORY *Handbk. Org. Chem.* 301 **Zanthopicrine* is a bitter crystalline substance from the bark of *Zanthoxylum Clava Herculis.* **1868** WATTS *Dict. Chem.* V. 1053 *Xanthopicrin*, *Xanthopicrite.* These names were given .. to a yellow colouring-matter from the bark of *Xanthoxylon caribœum*, since shown .. to be identical with berberine. **1838** T. THOMSON *Chem. Org. Bodies* 710 *Xanthopicrite .. was detected by Chevalier and Pelletan [1826], in the bark of the *Xanthoxylon carybœum*... It has .. a very bitter and astringent taste. **1847–9** *Todd's Cycl. Anat.* IV. 164/1 The alkaline *xanthoproteates. **1843** T. THOMSON *Chem. Anim. Bodies* 178 **Xantho-proteic Acid.* This name [*Xanthoproteinsäure*] has been given by Mulder [1838] to a yellow coloured acid, obtained first by Fourcroy, by treating fibrin, or albumen with nitric acid. **1873** RALFE *Phys. Chem.* 130 Heated with strong nitric acid pepsin does not give the xantho-proteic reaction; hence it would appear that pepsin is not an albuminoid substance. **1904** *Brit. Med. Jrnl.* 10 Sept. 601 The normal gland extract gave a positive result with the xanthoproteic test. **1883** OGILVIE (Annandale), **Xanthoprotein*, a yellow acid substance formed by the action of nitric acid upon fibrine. **1890** BILLINGS *Nat. Med. Dict.*, **Xanthopsin*, yellow pigment of the retina. **1901** DORLAND *Med. Dict.* (ed. 2), *Xanthopsin*, visual purple partially discolored or bleached by light; visual yellow. **1890** BILLINGS *Nat. Med. Dict.*, **Xanthopuccine*, name proposed by Lerchen (1878) for an alkaloid found in hydrastis. **1877** WATTS *Fownes' Chem.* II. 588 *Purpuroxanthin* (or **Xanthopurpurin*) .. is formed from purpurin by reduction with stannous chloride in alkaline solution. **1843** KANE in *Lond., Edinb., & Dubl. Philos. Mag.* July 3 The dark-coloured [Persian] berries .. give out to boiling water an olive-yellow material, to which .. I give the name of **xanthorhamnine.* **1862** WATTS tr. *Gmelin's Hand-bk. Chem.* XV. 533 *Xanthotannic Acid. Obtained from elm-leaves reddened in the autumn. **1868** WATTS *Dict. Chem.* V. 1054 **Xanthydric acid.* Syn. with *Persulphocyanic Acid* [obtained as 'a pale yellow crystalline powder', *ibid.* IV. 378].

2. In various compounds. **xan'tharsenite** *Min.*, a mineral allied to chondrarsenite, occurring in sulphur-yellow masses. **xantho'carpous** *a. Bot.* [Gr. καρπός fruit], having yellow fruit. **xantho'chromia** *Med.* [Gr. χρῶμα colour], (*a*) (see quot. 1894); = XANTHOCHROIA; (*b*) a yellowish discoloration of the cerebrospinal fluid as a result of haemorrhage in the spinal cord or brain; hence **xanthochro'matic**, **-'chromic** *adjs.* **xanthocomic** (-'kɒmɪk) *a.* (*nonce-wd.*) [Gr. κόμη hair], yellow-haired. **'xanthocone** (**-con**), **xan'thoconite** *Min.* [G. *xanthokon* (Breithaupt, 1840), f. Gr. κόνις dust], an arseniosulphide of silver, of a dull red or brown colour, yellow when pulverized. **xantho'cyanopsy**, **xanthocy'anopy** (**-kyan-**) *Path.* [Gr. κύανος blue + ὄψις, ὠπή sight], a form of colour-blindness in which yellow and blue are the only colours discerned. **'xanthoderm** (also **'Xantho-**) [Gr. δέρμ-α skin], a person of a yellow-skinned (mongoloid) race. ‖**xantho'derma**, **-'dermia** *Path.* [mod.L., f. Gr. δέρμα skin], yellowness of the skin. **'xanthodont**, **xantho'dontous** *adjs. Zool.* [Gr. ὀδούς, ὀδοντ- tooth], having yellow teeth, as certain rodents. **xan'thometer** [-METER], an instrument for determining the colour of sea or lake water by comparison with a scale of different-coloured solutions. ‖**xantho'pathia**, **xan'thopathy** *Path.* [Gr. -πάθεια -PATHY] = *xanthoderma.* **'xanthophore** *Zool.* [*a. G. xanthophor* (R. Keller 1895, in *Arch. f. Physiol.* LXI. 148): see -PHORE], a cell (as in an animal's skin) containing a yellow pigment. ‖**xan'thopsia**, **'xanthopsy** *Path.* [Gr. ὄφις appearance, sight], an affection of the eyes in which objects appear yellow; yellow vision. **xan'thopterin** *Chem.* [a. G. *xanthopterin* (Wieland & Schopf 1925, in *Ber. d. Deut. Chem. Ges.* LVIII. 2179): see PTERIN], a yellow pterin present in the wings of some butterflies and moths and in the urine of mammals and forming leucopterin upon oxidation; 2-amino-4,6-dihydroxypterine, $H_2NC_6HN_4(OH)_2$. **xan'thorthite** *Min.*, a yellow variety of orthite. **xantho'siderite** *Min.* [Gr. σίδηρος iron], a native hydrated oxide of iron, occurring in needle-shaped or fibrous crystals, or as an ochre, of a yellow, brown, or reddish colour. **xantho'spermous** *a. Bot.* [Gr. σπέρμα seed], having yellow seeds.

1892 DANA *Syst. Min.* 796 *Xantharsenite... Occurs with hausmannite, .. in crystalline limestone. **1862** MAYNE *Med. Vocab.* (ed. 2) 436/1 *Xanthocarpous. **1922** *Arch. Neurol. & Psychiatry* VIII. 24 Elsberg and Rochfort in a study of ninety-two cases of chronic diseases of the spinal cord found *xanthochromatic cerebrospinal fluid in fourteen instances. **1969** EDINGTON & GILLES *Path. in Tropics* ii. 79 [In congenital toxoplasmosis] the protein in the cerebrospinal fluid is increased and may be xanthochromatic. **1894** G. M. GOULD *Dict. Med.* 1622/2 **Xanthochromia*, a persistent condition of yellow skin, resembling but not identical with jaundice. **1905** —— *Dict. of New Med. Terms* 568/1 *Xanthochromia*, Tuffier and Miliau's [*read* Milian's] name (1902) for the yellow hemorrhagic discoloration of the cephalorachidian fluid, diagnostic of hemorrhage of the neuraxis. **1912** *Lancet* 7 Sept. 685/2 On the value of a quantitative albumin estimation of the cerebro-spinal fluid (with special reference to the syndrome of massive coagulation and xanthochromia). **1977** *Ibid.* 24–31 Dec. 1352/1 There were no cells in the C.S.F. and no xanthochromia. **1952** F. A. ELLIOTT et al. *Clin. Neurol.* ix. 184 *Xanthochromic fluid bleaches on exposure to daylight. **1979** *Jrnl. Neurosurg.* LI. 352/1 The presence of subarachnoid hemorrhage (SAH) is diagnostically confirmed by the detection of bloody and/or xanthochromic cerebrospinal fluid. **1861** WYNTER *Soc. Bees* 497 Europe is the chief seat of the *xantho-comic or light-haired races. **1846** WORCESTER, *Xanthocon (citing DANA). **1868** WATTS *Dict. Chem.* V. 1052 *Xanthocone*... A silver-ore from the Himmelfü rst mine, near Freiberg in Saxony. **1868** DANA *Min.* (ed. 5) 108 **Xanthoconite*... Color dull-red to clove-brown; crystals orange-yellow on the edges by transmitted light. **1891** *Cent. Dict.*, *Xanthocyanopsy. **1890** BILLINGS *Nat. Med. Dict.*, *Xanthokyanopy. **1924**, **1935** *Xanthoderm [see *melanoderm* sb. and adj. s.v. MELANO-]. **1935** [see *leucoderm* s.v. LEUCO-]. **1977** *Scripta Medica* L. 35 By and large, Melanoderms and Xanthoderms have either black or brown hair and there is not enough variation to be of practical interest. **1867** W. J. E. WILSON *Diseases of Skin* (ed. 6) 695 *Xanthoderma represents the yellow complexion of certain of the races of mankind. **1900** *Lancet* 11 Aug. 414/1 The mucous membranes were not coloured and the urine .. never showed a trace of bile pigment. This was in favour of the diagnosis of *xanthodermia. **1891** *Cent. Dict.*, *Xanthodont. **1862** MAYNE *Med. Vocab.* (ed. 2) 436 *Xanthodontous. **1902** *Westm. Gaz.* 8 April 8/3 When the Queen visited the Antarctic exploration ship *Discovery* she was particularly interested in Forel's *xanthometer. **1867** W. J. E. WILSON *Diseases of Skin* (ed. 6) 695 *Xanthopathia, or yellow discoloration of the skin, consists in the deposit in the cells of the rete mucosum of a yellow colouring principle. **1903** *Proc. Amer. Acad. Arts & Sci.* XXXIX. 261 The two remaining types of pigment bodies in the chameleon, erythrophores and *xanthophores, were not identified in Anolis. **1948** [see NEUROHUMOUR]. **1965** LEE & KNOWLES *Animal Hormones* x. 127 The hormone MSH [*sc.* melanocyte stimulating hormone] not only acts on the melanophores, but also on the xanthophores and erythrophores. **1974** D. & M. WEBSTER *Compar. Vertebr. Morphol.* viii. 173 Other chromatophores, called xanthophores, contain carotenoid and pteridine pigments and cause much of the yellow-to-red coloration. **1848** DUNGLISON *Med. Lex.* (ed. 7), **Xanthopsia*, yellow vision, —as sometimes occurs in jaundice. **1875** H. C. WOOD *Therap.* (1879) 603 A very curious symptom caused by zantonin .. is xanthopsia. **1926** *Chem. Abstr.* XX. 902 The residue was rubbed up 4 times with H_2O and centrifuged and the crude dirty yellow pasty pigment (*xanthopterin (I)) extd. with 20‰ HCl and pptd. wth NaOAc. **1974** *Encycl. Brit. Macropædia* IV. 922/2 Xanthopterin occurs in human urine. **1868** DANA *Min.* (ed. 5) 287 *Xanthorthite, of Hermann, .. is apparently an altered variety [of orthite]. **1868** WATTS *Dict. Chem.* V. 1054 **Xanthosiderite.* A hydrated ferric oxide. **1862** MAYNE *Med. Vocab.* (ed. 2) 436/2 *Xanthospermous.

‖**Xanthochroi** (zæn'θɒkrəʊaɪ, -'əʊkrɔɪ), *sb. pl. Anthropology.* [mod.L. (Huxley), app. meant as a transliteration of an assumed Gr. *ξάνθωχροι, f. ξανθός yellow + ὠχρός pale (the regular L. form of which would be **xanthōchrī*); by later writers and in Dicts. taken as *xanthŏchroī* (sing. *-chrous*), ad. Gr. ξανθόχροος, f. ξανθός yellow + χρόα skin: cf. MELANOCHROI.] In Huxley's classification of the varieties of mankind: A subdivision of the *Leiotrichi* or smooth-haired class, having yellow or light-coloured hair and pale complexion.

1866 [see XANTHOMELANOI]. **1875** TYLOR in *Encycl. Brit.* II. 113/2 The Xanthochroi, or fair whites .. are the prevalent inhabitants of Northern Europe.

Hence **xanthochroic** (-'krəʊɪk), **xanthochroid** (-'əʊkrɔɪd), **xanthochrooid** (-'ɒkrəʊɔɪd), **xanthochroous** (-'ɒkrəʊəs), **xanthochrous** (-'əʊkrəs) *adjs.*, of, pertaining to, or having the characters of the *Xanthochroi.* So ‖**xanthochroia** (-'krɔɪə) [mod.L. f. Gr. χροιά = χρόα skin], yellow discoloration of the skin from change in the pigment; **xanthochroism** (-'ɒkrəʊɪz(ə)m), *Ornith.*, abnormal replacement of another colour by yellow in the plumage of certain birds.

1867 W. J. E. WILSON *Diseases of Skin* (ed. 6) 695 Xanthopathia. Syn. Xanthoderma; *xanthochroia. **1870** HUXLEY in *Contemp. Rev.* July 515 The *Xanthochroic area. **1878** BARTLEY tr. *Topinard's Anthrop.* II. i. 202 The xanthochroic group: pale skin, blue eyes, and abundant fair hair. **1865** LUBBOCK *Preh. Times* xii. (1869) 378 [The] *Xanthochroid [group]. **1893** NEWTON *Dict. Birds* 421 There seems to be a certain correlation of colours in most cases of Heterochrosis: .. green feathers exhibit *xanthochroism. **1909** *Cent. Dict. Supp.*, **Xanthochroöid*, same as *Xanthochroic.* **1891** *Cent. Dict.*, *Xanthochroöus. **1865** *Xanthochrous [see MELANOCHROUS]. **1901** *Q. Rev.* July 230 Great stature and a xanthochrous complexion were .. the characteristics of the Celt or German.

xanthogen ('zænθədʒɛn). *Chem.* [f. XANTHO- + -GEN, after G. *xanthogensäure* (Zeise, 1822).]

1. The hypothetical radical of xanthic acid. Also *attrib.*

1823 HENRY *Elem. Chem.* (ed. 9) II. 665 This new acid contains sulphur, carbon, and hydrogen, the two first of which probably form a compound base, analogous to cyanogen... To the base, Mr. Zeise .. has given the name of *xanthogene* .. on account of the yellow colour of its compounds. **1868** WATTS *Dict. Chem.* V. 1052 *Xanthogen-oil.* Zeise's name for an oily product formed by the dry distillation of potassic xanthate.

2. A substance supposed to be contained in flowers: see quot.

1864 WATTS *Dict. Chem.* II. 668 According to Filhol, nearly all flowers contain a substance which forms colourless solutions with acids, and acquires a fine yellow colour when treated with alkalis: this substance was designated by Marquart as resin of flowers, and by Hope .. as xanthogen, which name is also retained by Filhol. He describes it as solid, of a light yellow colour, .. soluble in water, alcohol, and ether.

xantholiniform (zænθəʊ'lɪnɪfɔːm), *a. Entom.* [f. mod.L. *Xantholinus* (f. Gr. ξανθός yellow, with ending of *Staphylinus*, an allied genus) +

-(I)FORM.] Resembling in form the beetles of the genus *Xantholinus*.

1847 HARDY in *Proc. Berw. Nat. Club* II. No. 5. 250 *Ph[ilonthus] procerulus*.. Narrow, elongate, sub-parallel, xantholiniform.

‖**xanthoma** (zæn'θəʊmə). *Path.* Pl. **xanthomas, xanthomata.** [f. Gr. ξανθός yellow + -ωμα (cf. *sarcoma*).] An affection of the skin, characterized by the growth of yellowish patches or tubercles. Also, esp. in mod. use, such a patch or tubercle. Freq. with mod.L. adjs. Also *attrib.*

1869 *Jrnl. Cutaneous Med.* III. 241 (*heading*) On xanthoma, or vitiligoidea. *Ibid.* 317 After entry into hospital, patches of xanthoma developed in both eyelids. **1874** W. TAY tr. *Hebra & Kaposi's Dis. Skin* III. 345 There are two forms of the disease—1st, it occurs in the form of yellow patches—Xanthoma planum..; 2nd, in the form of tubercles—Xanthoma tuberosum. **1876** DUHRING *Dis. Skin* 410 Xanthoma is a connective-tissue new growth, characterized by the formation of yellowish, circumscribed, irregularly shaped,.. non-indurated patches or tubercles. **1896** N. WALKER tr. *Unna's Histopath. Dis. Skin* 945 The xanthoma of the eyelid may gradually develop protuberances, without giving up its own peculiar histological character. **1899** *Allbutt's Syst. Med.* VIII. 484 The chamois-leather-like patches may simulate xanthoma. *Ibid.* 896 The so-called 'xanthoma cell' is..a fragmented muscle fibre in a state of granulo-fatty degeneration. **1949** R. L. & R. L. SUTTON *Handbk. Dis. Skin* 385 Tuberous xanthomas are occasionally solitary. **1961** *Lancet* 12 Aug. 341/2 All her plasma-lipids tended to return to normal values..and her xanthomata completely disappeared. **1968** A. ROOK et al. *Textbk. Dermatol.* II. xxxviii. 1229/1 Xanthoma disseminatum is a rare histiocytic proliferative disorder characterized by widespread cutaneous xanthomata..but usually without evidence of systemic disturbance of lipid metabolism. **1974** S. L. ROBBINS *Pathologic Basis Dis.* xxx. 1410/1 These xanthomas may be widespread and occur in varied forms, such as xanthoma tuberosum.

Hence **xanthoma'tosis**, a metabolic disorder marked by the accumulation of excess lipid and by the presence of multiple and wide-spread xanthoma. **xanthomatous** (-'əʊmətəs) *a.*, pertaining to or of the nature of xanthoma.

1900 DORLAND *Med. Dict.* 764/1 Xanthomatosis. **1914** *Lancet* 13 June 1697/1 Xanthomatous nodules in the liver. **1923** *Brit. Jrnl. Dermatol.* XXXV. 90 Xanthomatosis is probably a process of infiltration dependent primarily upon hypercholesterolæmia. **1961** [see *hypercholesterolæmic* adj. s.v. HYPER- IV]. **1983** *Oxf. Textbk. Med.* I. IX. 113/1 The relationship between cerebrotendinous xanthomatosis and spinal cholesterosis..is uncertain.

‖**Xanthomelanoi** (zænθəʊ'mɛlənɔɪ), *sb. pl. Anthropology.* [mod.L. (Huxley), transliteration (instead of the regular L. form **xanthomelani*) of an assumed Gr. *ξανθομέλανοι, f. ξανθός yellow + μέλας, μελαν- black: cf. MELANOI and XANTHOCHROI. (On the analogy of the other terms, the word should have been *Melanoxanthoi*, the first element referring to the hair, the second to the skin.)] In Huxley's classification of the varieties of mankind: A subdivision of the *Leiotrichi* or smooth-haired class, having black hair and yellow, brown, or olive complexion. Hence **xantho'melanous** (-əs) *a.*, belonging to or having the characters of the *Xanthomelanoi*.

1865 HUXLEY *Crit. & Addr.* (1873) 153 The 'xanthomelanous,' with black hair and yellow, brown, or olive skins. **1866** —— *Laing's Preh. Rem. Caithn.* 132 The *Leiotrichi* may be best subdivided, according to their complexion, into *Xanthochroi, Melanochroi, Xanthomelanoi*, and *Melanoi*.

xanthone ('zænθəʊn). *Chem.* [f. Gr. ξανθός yellow + -ONE.] A compound which forms the basis of various natural colouring matters.

1894 MUIR & MORLEY *Watts' Dict. Chem.* IV. 867 *Xanthone* is Diphenylene ketone oxide.

xanthophyll ('zænθəʊfɪl). *Chem.* [ad. F. *xanthophylle* (Berzelius), f. Gr. ξανθός yellow + φύλλον leaf.] **a.** The yellow colouring-matter of leaves in autumn, a constituent or derivative of chlorophyll; also called *phylloxanthin*. (Now recognized as an oxygenated carotenoid identical with LUTEIN.)

1838 R. D. THOMSON in *Brit. Ann.* 334. **1868** WATTS *Dict. Chem.* V. 1052 *Xanthophyll*... Nothing certain is known respecting its composition, or of the manner in which it is formed from chlorophyll. **1891** *Science-Gossip* XXVII. 46/2 When the life of the leaf is destroyed by frost or drought, the chlorophyll is rapid changed to xanthophyll. **1934** *Science* 25 May 488/2 Xanthophyll (lutein) appears to be structurally related to α-carotene and zeaxanthin to β-carotene. **1945** *Biol. Rev.* XX. 115/1 Following a convention which is being more widely adopted the specific pigment which has been termed 'xanthophyll' is here called 'lutein'. **1964** E. J. H. CORNER *Life of Plants* i. 5 The orange-yellow carotin and the yellow xanthophyll..cause the yellow colour of those parts of variegated leaves unable through some deficiency to make chlorophyll.

b. [After R. Kuhn et al. 1931, in *Zeitschr. f. physiol. Chem.* CXCVII. 141.] Any of a group of yellow pigments (as lutein and violaxanthin) that are oxygenated carotenoids.

1931 *Chem. Abstr.* XXV. 3659 The term xanthophyll should be used to designate the entire group of OH-contg. carotenoids with 40 C atoms. The individuals thus far known are: lutein and zeaxanthin.., violaxanthin.., and fucoxanthin. **1952** *Chem. & Engin. News* 7 Jan. 104/2 Two of the rules on carotenoids adopted at the London Conference of 1947 were revised to give the following text: .. The name 'xanthophyll' is a group name..for carotene derivatives of natural origin which are soluble in alcohol and are not saponifiable. **1955** G. M. SMITH *Cryptogamic Bot.* (ed. 2) I. ii. 12 There are several xanthophylls [in the Chlorophyta] not found in other algae, and of these lutein is the most abundant. **1976** *Monitor* (McAllen, Texas) 27 Sept. 4A/2 Brown tannin pigments blend with xanthophylls to produce yellow-gold and gold-brown leaves.

Hence **xantho'phyllic** *a.*, of or containing xanthophyll.

1941 *Biol. Bull.* LXXX. 451 In the herbivores, the echinoids too contained some xanthophyllic pigments without exception. **1982** *Monitor* (McAllen, Texas) 2 Apr. 6-C/2 Miss Arden claims she now has a substance, extracted from a xanthophyllic-carotin mixture, which will drain the last vestige of visibility from succeeding generations of frogs but she feels it would serve no useful purpose.

xanthophyllite (zænθəʊ'fɪlaɪt). *Min.* [ad. G. *xanthophyllit* (G. Rose, 1840), f. Gr. ξανθός yellow + φύλλον leaf + -ITE[1] 2 b.] A micaceous mineral, a species of seybertite, occurring in yellowish crusts or implanted globules in talcose schist.

1844 DANA *Min.* (1862) 149.

‖**xanthorrhœa** (zænθəʊ'riːə). [mod.L., f. Gr. ξανθός yellow + ῥοία flowing, flow.]

1. *Bot.* A genus of Australian liliaceous plants, some species of which (called grass-trees or grass gum-trees) yield a yellow resin.

1868 WATTS *Dict. Chem.* V. 1054 Xanthorrhœa resin.

2. *Path.* A morbid affection resembling leucorrhœa (see quot.).

1891 *Lancet* 7 Nov. 1037/1 There is..more or less leucorrhœa, or xanthorrhœa, as it should rather be called, because the discharge is yellow, not white.

‖**xanthosis** (zæn'θəʊsɪs). *Path.* [mod.L., f. Gr. ξανθός yellow: see -OSIS.] (See quots.)

1857 DUNGLISON *Med. Lex.*, *Xanthosis*, a term applied to the yellow discolouration often observed in cancerous tumours. **1890** BILLINGS *Nat. Med. Dict.*, *Xanthosis*, formation of a yellow skin or pigment.

xanthous ('zænθəs), *a. Ethnology.* [f. Gr. ξανθός yellow + -OUS.] Applied to those races, or that type, of mankind characterized by yellow or yellowish hair and light complexion; fair, blond. Also said of the hair, complexion, etc. Opp. to MELANIC 1, MELANOUS.

1829 T. PRICE *Ess. Physiogn. & Physiol. Inhab. Brit.* 3 It is true that the Greek and Roman writers do describe the various barbarous tribes of Europe,..representing some to be of the fair, or, as it has been styled, Xanthous complexion; others of the dark, or Melanic. **1834** *Nat. Philos., Phys. Geog.* 64/1 (U.K.S.) Men of the xanthous variety of colour are known to spring up among the negroes in Africa. **1876** W. F. SKENE *Celtic Scot.* I. I. ii. 126 The Caledonii..were larger in body,..and less xanthous. **1896** *Allbutt's Syst. Med.* I. 35 The xanthous type with chestnut, red, or fair hair.

xanthoxenite (zænθəʊ'ziːnaɪt). *Min.* [ad. G. *xanthoxen* (Laubmann & Steinmetz 1920, in *Zeitschr. f. Krist.* LV. 580), f. Gr. ξανθο- XANTHO-, after G. *cacoxen* CACOXENITE: see -ITE[1].] A hydrated basic phosphate of calcium and ferric iron, $Ca_4Fe^{3+}{}_2(PO_4)_4(OH)_2.3H_2O$, occurring as yellow translucent triclinic crystals that are soft and have a waxy appearance.

1920 *Jrnl. Chem. Soc.* CXVIII. II. 698 Xanthoxenite, a new species from Rabenstein, occurring as small, wax-yellow, monoclinic crystals,..intimately associated with dufrenite and cacoxenite. **1949** *Amer. Mineralogist* XXXIV. 698 Xanthoxenite occurs abundantly although inconspicuously at the Palermo mine as one of the last formed of the hydrothermal reworked products of triphylite. **1978** *Mineral. Mag.* XLII. 309/1 Xanthoxenite of Laubmann and Steinmetz (1920) is probably stewartite (in part)... The xanthoxenite of Frondel (1949) is proposed as the species type. It is triclinic.

xanthoxin (zæn'θɒksɪn). *Biochem.* [f. VIOLA)XANTH(IN + OX- + -IN[1].] A photo-oxidation product, $C_{15}H_{22}O_3$, of violaxanthin that occurs in certain plant tissues as a growth inhibitor.

1970 TAYLOR & BURDEN in *Nature* 18 July 302/2 We have extracted a neutral growth inhibitor from the seedlings of dwarf bean..and wheat... The name xanthoxin is now proposed for the inhibitor, the activity of which in the *cis,trans* configuration is comparable with the known naturally occurring inhibitor abscisic acid (ABA). **1980** *Physiologia Plantarum* XLIX. 309/1 The inhibitory effect of both ABA and xanthoxin on total lateral root length was mainly due to their suppression of primordia emergence and their strong inhibition of elongation.

‖**xanthoxylon** (zæn'θɒksɪlɒn). *Bot.* Also 8 **zanthoxylon, -um.** [mod.L. *Xanthoxylon, -um* (by Linnæus spelt *Zanthoxylum*), f. Gr. ξανθός yellow + ξύλον wood.] A large and widely distributed genus of trees and shrubs of the N.O. *Rutaceæ* (type of the suborder *Xanthoxyleæ*, sometimes reckoned as an order *Xanthoxylaceæ*), yielding various products, esp. pungent and aromatic drugs and condiments; it includes the N. American Prickly Ash or Toothache-tree (*X. americanum* and *fraxineum*), the Chinese or Japanese Pepper (*X. piperitum*), the Prickly or W. Indian Yellow-wood (*X. Clava-Herculis*), etc. Hence **xan'thoxyl**, a plant of this genus, or of the order or suborder of which it is the type; **xanthoxylaceous** (-'eɪʃəs), **xanthoxyleous** (-'ɪlɪəs) *adjs.*, belonging to the *Xanthoxylaceæ* or *Xanthoxyleæ* (see above); **xan'thoxylene** (-iːn) *Chem.*, an aromatic volatile oil obtained from the fruit of *Xanthoxylon piperitum*; **xan'thoxylin** (-ɪn) *Chem.*, (*a*) a crystalline resin or camphor obtained from an oil distilled from the seeds of *X. piperitum*; (*b*) a crystallizable bitter principle contained in the bark of *X. Clava-Herculis* and other species; **xantho'xyloïn**, a neutral principle obtained from the bark of *X. americanum*.

1846 LINDLEY *Veg. Kingd.* 473 Several *Xanthoxyls have in their habit, and especially in their foliage, a marked resemblance to the Ash. **1876** HARLEY *Mat. Med.* (ed. 6) 679 The Xanthoxyl Family of the Rutal alliance. **1852** TH. ROSS tr. *Humboldt's Trav.* I. vi. 213 *note*, Among *xanthoxylaceous plants, the Cuspare of Angostura, known in America under the name of Orinoco bark. **1857** STENHOUSE in *Pharmaceut. Jrnl.* July 20 The pure hydrocarbon, to which I propose to give the name of *Xanthoxylene, is colourless, [etc.]. *Note*, The pleasant aromatic odour of Japanese pepper is due to Xanthoxylene. **1830** LINDLEY *Nat. Syst. Bot.* 131 Several *Xanthoxyleous plants have..a marked resemblance to the Ash. **1854** STENHOUSE in *Lond., Edin., & Dubl. Philos. Mag.* Jan. 28 The crystals of *xanthoxyline belong to the oblique system. **1765** J. BARTRAM *Jrnl.* 21 Dec. in Stork *Acc. E. Florida* (1766) 3 Some curious shrubs..we had never seen before,.. large *zanthoxylum, and purple-berried bay. **1799** *Med. Jrnl.* II. 32 A Negro woman, who had been affected for many years with several large phagædenic ulcers..was put under my care. I commenced the use of the Zanthoxylon, by bathing the sores with the decoction. **1868** WATTS *Dict. Chem.* V. 1054 *Xanthoxylon.* The bark of *X. caribæum*..or *X. Clava Herculis*..used in the Antilles as a febrifuge.

‖**Xantippe** (zæn'tɪpiː). Also 7 **Zentippe, Zantippe.** [Properly *Xanthippe*, Gr. Ξανθίππη.] The name of the wife of Socrates; hence *allusively*, an ill-tempered woman or wife, a shrew, a scold (with pl. *Xantippes*).

1596 SHAKS. *Tam. Shr.* I. ii. 71 As curst and shrow'd As Socrates Zentippe [*1st Fol., Qo.; 2nd-4th Fol.* Zantippe, *mod. edd.* Xanthippe]. **1691** WOOD *Ath. Oxon.* I. 262 Richard Hooker..married a clownish silly Woman and withal a meer Xantippe. **1749** FIELDING *Tom Jones* VIII. xi, An errant Vixen of a Wife... By this *Xantippe* he had two Sons. **1859** *Habits of Gd. Society* xiii. 339 For the time being the worst of Xantippes must turn into an angel of amiability if she gives a ball.

xaraf, -affe, -off, obs. ff. SARAF.

1628 in Foster *Eng. Factories India* (1909) III. 296 We lye at the mercy of the xaroffs or exchangers of monie. **1662** J. DAVIES tr. *Mandelslo's Trav.* 93 In the presence of the Xaraf, or Money-changers.

Xavante (ʃə'væntiː). Also **Chavante, Shavante.** [a. Port., of uncertain origin.] **a.** (A member of) any of several groups of semi-nomadic Indians of the interior savanna of central and east-central Brazil, esp. the Akwẽ-Xavante. **b.** The Ge language of the Akwẽ-Xavante, or the language of any group called Xavante. Also *attrib.* as *adj.*

1904 H. VON IHERING *Anthropol. State S. Paulo, Brazil* 10 Of all the Indians of S. Paulo, the Chavantes are the darkest, and the most backward. **1927** K. G. GRUBB *Lowland Indians Amazonia* vii. 121 The Chavante, irreconcilably hostile, occupy the River Manso or das Mortes. **1950** J. B. D'AVILA in J. H. Steward *Handbk. S. Amer. Indians* VI. 76 To the same [*sc.* Ge] group belong the Shavante, between the Araguaya and Tocantins Rivers;..the Sherente and Craho. **1950** J. A. MASON in *Ibid.* 299 Four groups of Southern Brazil of very different linguistic affinities are known to the Brazilian natives by the name *Chavanté*... Three of them.. form small independent (provisionally) families; the fourth is a *Ge* language. **1971** J. S. WEINER *Man's Natural Hist.* v. 221 'Micro-evolution' comparable to that found in the Xavante villages obtains in other South American aboriginal tribes. *Ibid.* 222 The extraordinary contrast between the high standard of physical fitness and stamina of the young Xavante and his later health and life expectation. **1978** *Sunday Times* (Colour Suppl.) 18 June 33 (*caption*) Xavante Indians in their village close to the River of the Dead..held the white off until recently. **1983** *Word* XXXIV. 61 A number of Brazilian Amazon languages (e.g., Apuriña, Urubú, Xavante, and Nadeb) also rely on both pragmatic and syntactic considerations in determining linear order.

Xaverian (zeɪ'vɪərɪən), *a.* and *sb.* [f. the name *Xav(i)er* + -IAN.] **A.** *adj.* **a.** Of, pertaining to, or designating a teaching order of Roman Catholic monks founded in 1839 and named in honour of St. Francis Xavier. **b.** Of or pertaining to St. Francis Xavier (1506–56), Spanish missionary. **B.** *sb.* A Brother of the Xaverian order.

1882 PABISCH & BYRNE tr. *Alzog's Man. Univ. Church Hist.* IV. 333 The Xaverian Brothers, founded at Bruges.. in 1839, and introduced into the United States..in 1854, have under their charge, Mt. St. Joseph's College,

Carrollton, Md. **1912** *Catholic Encycl.* XIII. 284/2 After holding the office of Superior General of the Xaverians for twenty-seven years. **1915** C. C. Martindale *In God's Army* I. 118 The whole Xaverian history had been one of deliberate ambition. **1931** M. Yeo *St. Francis Xavier* vi. 69 One sentence seems to have the true Xaverian ring. **1967** *New Catholic Encycl.* XIV. 1058/1 The Xaverian Brothers played an important role in the development of Catholic education. *Ibid.* 1058/2 In the U.S. the Xaverians staffed most of the parish schools of Louisville.

X chromosome. *Genetics.* Also †**x chromosome.** [X 3 e.] A chromosome with different morphology and properties from others in the complement, now recognized as a sex chromosome occurring in both sexes of a species, man and other mammals having one in the somatic cells of the male and two in those of the female.

[**1902**], **1911** [see X 3 e]. **1933** R. H. Wolcott *Animal Biol.* lxxiii. 537 In fowls and in moths females have either one *x*-chromosome or both an *x*-chromosome and a *y*-chromosome, while the males have the two *x*-chromosomes. **1961** P. Gray *Encycl. Biol. Sci.* 232/1 In most species of Spiders there are two different kinds of X-chromosomes but no Y, so that the males have X_1X_2 and the female $X_1X_1X_2X_2$. **1966** *Lancet* 24 Dec. 1397/1 The small size of the Y chromosome relative to the X chromosome has been attributed to the gradual loss of genetic material not concerned with sex determination. **1983** M. B. Zaleski et al. *Immunogenetics* ii. 36 The *X* chromosome carries a set of genes that determines a wide variety of traits that do not necessarily affect the sex of the organism.

X disease. [X 3.] **1.** *Path.* (chiefly *Austral.*) A disease now identified as Murray Valley encephalitis (see Murray Valley).

1918 *Med. Jrnl. Australia* 6 Apr. 278/2 On 25th August, 1917, I published in the *Journal* an account of an epidemic at Broken Hill of what is now called the 'X' disease. **1951** *Ibid.* 2 June 800/1 Our case differs from the classical picture of X disease .. in the lack of cellular infiltration in the brain. **1964** [see Q fever]. **1983** *Oxf. Textbk. Med.* I. v. 101/1 Murray Valley (formerly) Australia encephalitis. This disease was originally called Australian X disease.

2. *Vet. Sci.* = *blue comb* (*disease*) s.v. blue *a.* 13. (Now known to be caused by a mycotoxin.)

1950 [see *blue comb* (*disease*) s.v. blue *a.* 13]. **1961** *New Scientist* 17 Aug. 403/3 A consignment of groundnut meal from Brazil contained an agent toxic to young turkeys, which proved responsible for the death of some 100,000 birds from the hitherto mysterious X disease... The exact nature of the toxic principle has still not been found.

xebec ('ziːbɛk; also zɪ'bɛk). Also 8-9 **-eck, -eque, -ecque**; *β.* 8-9 **zebec(k,** 9 **zebecque.** See also chebec. [Altered form of chebec (F. *chebec*) after Sp. *xabeque*, now *jabeque*.] A small three-masted (originally two-masted) vessel, commonly lateen-rigged but with some square sails, used in the Mediterranean, formerly as a ship of war, now as a merchant-ship.

1756 *Gentl. Mag.* Aug. 409/2 Capt. Fortunatus Wright, of Liverpool, in the *King George* privateer off Leghorn, engaged a xebeck which had 280 men on board. **1760** *Ann. Reg., Chron.* 148/2 An Algerine xebeque of 20 guns .. was driven on shore near Penzance. **1762** More in *Phil. Trans.* LII. 450 There came a Spanish xebeck from the West, .. and .. was becalmed. **1769** Falconer *Dict. Marine* (1780) s.v., The sails of the xebec are in general similar to those of the polacre, but the hull is extremely different... The extremity of the stern .. projects further behind the counter and buttock than that of any European ship. **1794** *Rigging & Seamanship* I. 237 *Xebec.* A small vessel with three masts, navigated in the mediterranean. The fore and main-masts are called block-masts, being short... The mizen-mast is fitted with a topmast, &c., .. and .. has been lately added, to keep them better to the wind... The fore-mast rakes much forward. **1816** *Ann. Reg., Gen. Hist.* 133/2 A large Tunisian xebeck .. putting out two boats, gave a general chase. *a* **1829** I. Taylor *Ship* v. (1846) 118 The xebec very much resembles the galley in shape .., in its triangular sails and low masts. It is the corsair of the Algerines, .. and mounts from sixteen to twenty-four guns. **1851** Kipping *Sailmaking* (ed. 2) 158 The Spanish xebec has in general a lateen fore, with a square main-sail and mizen. **1884** Miss C. F. Woolson in *Harper's Mag.* Feb. 368/2 The coasting xebecs.

β. **1769** *Ann. Reg., Chron.* 164/1 A large Algerine zebeck, of 30 guns and 300 men. **1839** Marryat *Phant. Ship* xix, A three-masted zebecque. **1844** Hood *The Key* iv, The last Zebeck that came And moor'd within the Mole.

attrib. and *Comb.* **1780** Capt. Knowles in *Naval Chron.* II. 518 Two Spanish Xebec Ships, polacre rigged. **1801** Ld. Cochrane *ibid.* VI. 151 A Spanish xebeck frigate, of 32 guns. **1812** *Examiner* 4 May 280/2 A French xebeck-rigged privateer, of two guns.

xel, obs. form of shall *v.*

1429 in *Calr. Pat. Rolls 8 Hen. VI.* 30 A comon assemble which xel ben ordeyned be the mair.

xeme (ziːm). *Ornith.* [ad. mod.L. *Xema* (Leach, 1819), an arbitrarily formed word.] A bird of the genus *Xema*; a fork-tailed gull.

1836 Eyton *Rarer Brit. Birds* 64 Sabine's Xeme... was first observed by Captain Sabine in Greenland.

xenacanthine, xenarthral: see xeno-.

†**xenagogue** ('zɛnəgɒg). *Obs.* In 7 zen-. [ad. Gr. ξεναγωγός, f. ξένος stranger + -αγωγός leading.] One who conducts strangers; a guide. So †**xenagogy,** conduction of strangers: used as the title of a guide-book.

1570-6 Lambarde *Peramb. Kent* 386 The places, whereof I ment to make note in this my Xenagogie and perambulation of Kent. **1583** in Thynne *Animadv.* (1875) p. lxii, The Xenogogie of Bedfordshire. **1674** Josselyn *Voy. New Eng.* 136 They are generally excellent Zenagogues or guides through their Countrie.

xenelasy (zɛ'niːləsɪ). *Gr. Hist.* [ad. Gr. ξενηλασία, f. ξενηλατεῖν, f. ξένος foreigner + ἐλα- (ἐλαύνειν) to drive away.] A measure at Sparta for expulsion of foreigners.

1846 Grote *Greece* II. vi. II. 515 Nor were strangers permitted to stay at Sparta; they came thither it seems, by a sort of sufferance, but the uncourteous process called xenêlasy was always available to remove them.

‖**xenia** ('ziːnɪə). *Bot.* [mod.L., ad. Gr. ξενία state or relation of a guest, f. ξένος guest: see -ia[1].] A supposed direct action or influence of foreign pollen upon the seed or fruit which is pollinated.

1899 *Nat. Sci.* May 393 *Xenia* .., the direct action of the male element on the mother-plant, is an extremely hypothetical theory. **1901** *Nature* 12 Dec. 126/2 Xenia is the name given to the results of the crossing of the plant by a foreign pollen, exhibited in some peculiarity which appears in the seed itself.

xenia, pl. of xenium.

xenial ('ziːnɪəl), *a. Gr. Antiq.* [f. Gr. ξενία xenia + -al[1].] Of the nature of, or pertaining to, the relation between host and guest: applied to a friendly relation between two persons of different countries, or between a person and a foreign country. So '**xenian** *a.* (in quot. 1834 rendering Gr. ξένιος, a title of Zeus as protector of the rights of hospitality).

1834 *Fraser's Mag.* X. 533 The holy customs of the Xenian Jove. **1858** Gladstone *Homer* I. 220 The Taphians, .. from the xenial relation of their Lord Mentes to Ulysses, must in all likelihood have lived in the neighbourhood of Ithaca. **1869** —— *Juv. Mundi* iii. 87 Demetor Tasides .. is represented .. as being in xenial relations with Egypt.

‖**xenium** ('ziːnɪəm). Usually in pl. **xenia.** [L., ad. Gr. ξένιον, prop. neut. of ξένιος adj. pertaining to a guest, f. ξένος guest, stranger.] **a.** In *Gr.* and *Rom. Antiq.*, a present (esp. of table delicacies) given to a guest or stranger; *transf.*, in mediæval usage, an offering made (sometimes compulsorily) by subjects to their prince on the occasion of his passing through their estates; also extended to other kinds of offerings (see quots.).

1706 Phillips (ed. Kersey), *Xenia*, Presents bestowed by the Greeks to their Friends, Guests, or Strangers... In our old Records, it is taken for such Presents or Gifts as us'd to be made to Princes, or to the Governours of Provinces. **1772** [S. Denne] *Hist. Rochester* 106 That there be reserved to me .. out of the estates which I have assigned for the maintenance of the monks, such a xenium [orig. *exenium*] as is here specified. **1865** Stubbs *Chron. & Mem. Rich. I* (Rolls) II. Introd. p. xxx, The xenia, or Easter and Christmas offerings from [the monks'] manors, which were settled on the cellarer for the use of the sick and strangers.

b. (See quots.)

1791 Newton tr. *Vitruvius' Archit.* vi. x. 145 The pictures representing the sending of gifts to strangers are by the painters called *xenia*. **1854** Fairholt *Dict. Terms Art*, *Xenia*... Pictures of still-life, fruit, fish, &c., many of which have been found as decorations on the walls of houses in Pompeii.

xenization (zɛnaɪ'zeɪʃən). *rare*$^{-1}$. [f. Gr. ξενίζειν, trans. to entertain strangers, intr. to be a stranger, f. ξένος stranger: see -ize and -ation.] The fact of sojourning as a stranger.

1818 G. S. Faber *Horæ Mosaicæ* I. 231 The xenization of Abraham's seed in a foreign land.

xeno- (zɛnəʊ), before a vowel **xen-**, repr. Gr. ξενο-, ξεν-, combining form of ξένος a guest, stranger, foreigner, adj. foreign, strange; used in various scientific and other terms; for those not found here, see their alphabetical places. **xenacanthine** (-ə'kænθaɪn) *Zool.* [ad. mod.L. *Xenacanthini* pl., f. Gr. ἄκανθα spine], *a.* belonging to the extinct order *Xenacanthini* of selachian fishes, with long slender spines; *sb.* a fish of this order. **xe'narthral** *a. Zool.* [Gr. ἄρθρον joint], having peculiar accessory articulations in the vertebræ, as the American edentates. **xeno'antibody** *Immunol.*, an antibody produced in response to a xenoantigen. **xeno'antigen** *Immunol.*, a xenogeneic antigen; so ˌ**xenoanti'genic** *a.* **xeno-'antiserum** *Immunol.*, an antiserum rich in xenoantibodies. **xenobiosis** (-baɪ'əʊsɪs) *Zool.* [Gr. βίωσις manner of life], a form of symbiosis among ants in which two colonies of different species live together on friendly terms without rearing their broods in common. **xenobi'otic** *sb.* and *a.* [biotic *a.*], (designating) a substance foreign to the body. '**xenoblast** *Geol.* [a. G. *xenoblast* (F. Becke 1903, in *Compt. Rend. IX. Congr. Géol. Internat.* (1904) II. 564): see -blast] (see quot. 1920); hence **xeno'blastic** *a.* **xe'nocracy** [-cracy], a ruling body of foreigners. '**xenocryst** *Geol.*, a crystal not derived from the magma that gave rise to the igneous rock containing it; hence **xeno'crystal, -'crystic** *adjs.* '**xenoderm** *Zool.* [mod.L. *Xenoderma*, f. Gr. δέρμα skin], a snake of the genus *Xenoderma* or sub-family *Xenodermatinæ* (mod. Dicts.). ˌ**xenodiag'nosis** *Med.* [ad. F. *xénodiagnostic* (E. Brumpt 1914, in *Bull. de la Soc. de Path. Exotique* VII. 706)], a diagnostic procedure in which clean, laboratory-bred vectors of a disease are allowed to feed on the individual or material that may be infected and are then examined for the pathogen; hence ˌ**xenodiag'nostic** *a.* **xe'nogamy** *Bot.* [Gr. γάμος marriage], fertilization by pollen from another plant of the same species; cross-fertilization. **xenogenesis** (-'dʒɛnɪsɪs) *Biol.* [genesis], (supposed) production of offspring permanently unlike the parent (cf. heterogenesis 3); so **xenoge'netic, xeno'genic** *adjs.*, pertaining to or of the nature of xenogenesis; **xenogeny** (zɛ'nɒdʒɪnɪ), xenogenesis. **xe'nogenous** *a. Path.* (see quot.). **xeno'glossia,** '**xenoglossy** [Gr. γλῶσσα tongue], the practice or faculty of using intelligibly a language one has not learnt. '**xenograft** *Med.*, a graft of tissue between individuals of different species; = hetero-graft. **xeno'lalia** [Gr. -λαλία speaking, after glossolalia] = *xenoglossia* above. **xenolite** *Min.* [-lite], a silicate of aluminium, allied to fibrolite. '**xenolith** *Geol.* [-lith], a piece of rock in an igneous mass which differs from its surroundings and is considered to have been picked up by and incorporated into the mass when the latter was in the form of magma; hence **xeno'lithic** *a.*, containing xenoliths; also, occurring as a xenolith. **xenomania** (-'meɪnɪə), a mania or insane fancy for foreigners, or for something foreign; hence **xeno'maniac,** a person affected with 'xenomania'. **xeno-morphic** (-'mɔːfɪk) *a. Geol.* [Gr. μορφή form], applied to mineral constituents of a rock having a form different from the normal in consequence of the pressure of other constituents. **xeno'parasite, xeno'parasitism** *Biol.* (see quot.). '**xenophil(e** *a.* [-phil, -phile], fond of or attracted by foreign things or people; also as *sb.*, such a person; hence **xeno'philia,** the state of being xenophile; **xeno'philiac** *a.* [-ac] = *xenophil(e* adj. above; **xeno'philic, xe'nophilous** *adjs.* = *xenophil(e* adj.; **xenophilism** (-'ɒfɪlɪz(ə)m) *nonce-wd.* [Gr. φίλος loving, friendly], love of foreigners or of something foreign. **xenophoran** (-'ɒfərən) *a. Zool.* [f. mod.L. *Xenophora*, f. Gr. -φορος carrying], belonging or allied to the genus *Xenophora* (carrier-shells) of gastropod molluscs, distinguished by the habit of cementing stones and other foreign bodies to their shells. **xenopterygian** (-ptə'rɪdʒɪən), *Zool.* [Gr. πτέρυξ wing, fin], *a.* belonging to the suborder *Xenopterygii* of fishes, with spineless fins, scaleless skin, and a complex sucking-disk between the ventral fins; *sb.* a fish of this suborder. **xeno'thermal** *a. Petrol.*, applied to mineral deposits formed by hydrothermal action at high temperatures but at a shallow depth. **xeno'tropic** *a. Microbiology* [-tropic], (of a virus) present in a host species in an inactive form and only able to infect and replicate in organisms of other species; hence **xeno'tropism.** **xenurine** ('zɛnjʊraɪn), *Zool.* [f. mod.L. *Xenurus*, f. Gr. οὐρά tail], *a.* belonging to the genus *Xenurus* of armadillos, having the tail nearly naked; *sb.* an armadillo of this genus, a kabassou.

1974 *Brit. Jrnl. Cancer* XXX. 304/1 Gel filtration was used to show that the tumour specific *xenoantibody responsible for protection was not IgM but was in the IgG fraction. **1984** *Human Immunol.* X. 57 Xenoantibodies to idiotypes of the anti-HLA-A2, A28 MoAb CR11-351 were isolated from an antiserum raised in rabbit #81. **1975** *Nature* 24 Apr. 716/2 An important characteristic of the immune system is the ability to discriminate between antigens expressed on normal tissues within the individual and the many foreign antigens expressed on normal tissues of other species (*xenoantigens) and even on normal tissues of members of the same species (alloantigens). **1984** *Jrnl. Immunol.* CXXXII. 2522/1 An increase in specific antigenic activity for the *Rana*-specific xenoantigen. **1973** *Tissue Antigens* III. 5/1 Some of the eluted fractions possessed both alloantigenic and *xenoantigenic activity. *Ibid.* 18/2 Strain-discriminating effects of *xenoantisera were reported .. over thirty years ago. **1978** *Nature* 26 Oct. 711/1 Experiments with xenoantiserum to murine tissues provided the first, fortuitous indication that Thy-1 included an hitherto unrecognised specificity. **1885** *Stand. Nat. Hist.* (1888) V. 66 The geographical distribution of the Edentates. .. To America belong the *xenarthral or many-jointed forms. **1901** W. M. Wheeler in *Amer. Naturalist* July 535 *Xenobiosis... The best-known guest ant is the European *Formicoxenus nitidulus.* **1965** H. S. Mason et al. in

Federation Proc. XXIV. 1172 (*heading*) Microsomal mixed-function oxidations: the metabolism of *xenobiotics. *Ibid.*, We would like to call the components of this chemical environment which are foreign to the metabolic network of an organism 'xenobiotic' compounds. **1975** WILLIAMS & WILSON *Biologist's Guide to Princ. & Techniques Pract. Biochem.* i. 13 In order to study the metabolism of a xenobiotic, it is advantageous to administer it in an isotopically-labelled form. **1981** *Internat. Jrnl. Environ. Stud.* XVII. 11/2 Many xenobiotic substances reduce blood concentrations of one or more vitamins. **1920** A. HOLMES *Nomencl. Petrol.* 241 **xenoblast*, a term applied to crystals which have grown during metamorphism without the development of their characteristic faces. **1962** Xenoblast [see IDIOBLAST 3]. **1931** A. JOHANNSEN *Descr. Petrogr. Igneous Rocks* I. 232 **Xenoblastic*, a texture in metamorphic rocks corresponding to the xenomorphic in igneous rocks. The crystals lack proper crystal faces. **1980** *Mineral. Mag.* XLIII. 781/1 In thin-section all the felsic grains are seen to be xenoblastic. **1965** E. WEBER in Rogger & Weber *European Right* 507 Everywhere Eminescu looked.. he saw foreigners and cryptoforeigners; the intelligentsia, recruited from men who had inherited their character and ideas from Greek or Bulgarian fore-bears; the ruling Liberals, who drew their manners and policies from the Seine, the Spree, and the Bosphorus... Altogether one vast *xenocracy. **1975** H. LUKE in K. M. Setton *Hist. Crusades* III. xi. 394 While it is unlikely that the Cypriote peasantry under the Lusignan kingdom were politically worse off.. than the peasantry of other Near Eastern countries.., it is not surprising that by the end of the Venetian occupation they had come to conceive.. a profound hatred of the Latin xenocracy. **1894** W. J. SOLLAS in *Trans. R. Irish Acad.* XXX. 493 As a distinctive appelation appropriate to the crystals, both of pyroxene and of plagioclase felspar, which have found their way from the gabbro into the granophyre, the term '*xenocrysts' may be employed. Correspondingly included fragments of the whole rock may be called 'xenoliths'. **1964** G. A. JOPLIN *Petrogr. Austral. Igneous Rocks* ii. 26 Xenocrysts commonly show some resorption or corona indicating that they have reacted with the magma. **1983** *Jrnl. Geol.* XCI. 277 Xenocrysts and xenoliths from three Ithaca kimberlite localities are consistent with derivation from mantle depths of less than 150 km. **1963** *Amer. Mineralogist* XLVIII. 172 Classification of Kerguelen rocks is to a large extent dependent on the amount of *xenocrystal material present. **1981** *Jrnl. Geophysical Res.* LXXXVI. 10515 This particular granite cannot be a primary magma. .. It is a possible product of partial fusion of pelitic rocks between about 20 km and 40 km depth.. and xenocrystal muscovite or sillimanite from the source rocks. **1978** *Nature* 19 Oct. 640/1 The phlogopite is derived from the parental magma or its derivatives and is not a *xenocrystic phase. **1947** *Anales del Instituto de Medicina Regional* (Tucuman) II. 60 The authors describe.. artificial *xenodiagnosis for cases in which it is not possible to perform it directly upon patients. **1976** *Nature* 15 July 215/2 Using only male bugs of a susceptible stock for xenodiagnosis should enhance the sensitivity of this diagnostic test. **1955** *O Hospital* (Rio de Janeiro) XLVII/187 The authors make a comparison between the positivity of *xeno-diagnostic tests performed in two ways. **1974** R. ZELEDÓN in K. Elliott et al. *Trypanosomiasis & Leishmaniasis* 58 New xenodiagnostic tests in an endemic area of Chagas' disease in Costa Rica. **1877** DARWIN *Lett.* (1903) II. 413 Some such terms as autogamy, *xenogamy, etc. **1870** HUXLEY *Pres. Addr. Brit. Assoc., Rep.* p. lxxvii, The term Heterogenesis.. has.. been used in a different sense, and M. Milne-Edwards has therefore substituted for it **Xenogenesis*. *Ibid.* p. lxxxv, The analogy of pathological modification.. is in favour of the *xenogenetic origin of microzymes. **1901** DORLAND *Med. Dict.* (ed. 2), **Xenogenous*, caused by a foreign body, or originating outside the organism. **1913** *Ibid.* (ed. 7) *adds* 2. Formed or developed in the host: a term applied to toxins formed by the action of stimuli on the cells of the host. **1978** *Amer. Speech* LIII. 67 Samarin would call the event of persons speaking in a language unknown to them *xenoglossia, something different from glossolalia. **1981** *Times Lit. Suppl.* 3 July 765/3 The traditional view was that, while at Corinth glossolalia had occurred, meaning that there were lexically non-communicative utterances, at Pentecost what occurred was xenoglossia, utterance in an actual foreign language. **1914** A. TEIXEIRA DE MATTOS tr. *Maeterlinck's Unknown Guest* III. 101 *Xenoglossy is well known not to be unusual in automatic writing; sometimes even the 'automatist' speaks or writes languages of which he is completely ignorant. **1932** I. EMERSON tr. E. Bozzano (*title*) Polyglot mediumship (xenoglossy). **1980** *Brit. Med. Jrnl.* 9 Aug. 432/2 The investigators are reported to regard her xeno-glossy (ability to speak a foreign language without having learnt it) as a truly paranormal experience. **1961** *Nature* 25 Mar. 1024/2 Grafts between species.. of less general interest.. have been called *xenografts or heterografts. **1974** R. M. KIRK et al. *Surgery* ii. 35 A xenograft.. is poorly tolerated by the recipient. **1977** *Proc. R. Soc. Med.* LXX. 480/2 A xenograft in one patient was unsuccessful. **1984** *Times* 21 Aug. 4/1 Surgeons have a choice of artificial valves, or those made from human or animal tissue. The latter, xenografts, are silent and rendered rejection-proof. **1978** D. CHRISTIE-MURRAY *Voices from Gods* xii. 167 There appears to be no evidence of genuine, responsive *xenolalia (that is, intelligent conversation carried on in a recognized language completely unknown to the speaker) in any native culture studied by anthropologists. **1981** *Times* 8 Oct. 15/5 There is a distinction between glossolalia (paranormal speaking in tongues) and xenolalia (paranormal speaking in allegedly foreign languages). **1844** DANA *Min.* (1868) 374 *Xenolite.. resembles fibrolite.. excepting in the high specific gravity. **1894** *Xenolith [see *xenocryst* above]. **1942** [see METASOMATIZE *v.*]. **1956** 'H. MACDIARMID' *Stony Limits & Scots Unbound* 41 Ultra-basic xenoliths that make men look midges. **1975** *Nature* 10 Apr. 489/1 Xenoliths thought to represent material from the deeper parts of the upper mantle are brought to the surface in kimberlite magmas. **1900** *Q. Jrnl. Geol. Soc.* LVI. 665 The whole of the cliffs around Annestown Bay are composed of the widespread pink and greenish *xenolithic felsites. **1930** PEACH & HORNE *Geol. Scotl.* ii. 67 Grey igneous gneiss is interposed.. and is xenolithic. One of the pale xenoliths was found to consist of malacolite.. and green hornblende. **1980** *Sci. Amer.* May 97/1 With the exception of xenolithic.. fragments of mantle that are occasionally brought to the surface by kimberlite pipes and some basalt formations, direct sampling of the upper mantle is impossible. **1879** K. HILLEBRAND in *19th Cent.* Oct. 626 Germany received the first caresses of this strange *xenomania from the hands of youthful Carlyle and old Coleridge. **1887** SAINTSBURY *Hist. Elizab. Lit.* iv. 136 No writer of the period had such a command of pure English, unadulterated by xenomania and unweakened by purism, as Daniel. **1879** *Daily News* 30 Sept. 5/1 Are we all *Xenomaniacs? **1891** *Illustr. Lond. News* 7 Feb. 168/2 Sir Arthur Sullivan was never the least bit of a *xenomaniac*. **1888** HATCH in Teall *Brit. Petrography* Gloss. 423 *Allotriomorphic*, a term applied by Rosenbusch.. in contradistinction to idiomorphic. It is synonymous with *xenomorphic. **1905** E. S. SALMON in *Ann. Bot.* Jan. 127 To describe cases where a form of a Fungus which is specialized to certain host-plants.. proves able to infect injured parts of a strange host, I propose the terms *xenoparasite and *xenoparasitism. **1934** WEBSTER, *Xenophile, -phil *adjs.* **1945** W. PLOMER *Dorking Thigh* 10 And in fancy dress she lingers With a locket in her fingers Containing a curl from That xenophil Greek. **1948** *Penguin New Writing* XXXIV. 128 New York and Los Angeles seem to be replacing Paris as the goal of Colombian xenophiles. **1968** P. B. AUSTIN *On being Swedish* xx. 149 Almost in spite of herself, she becomes a xenophile. **1959** *Times* 3 Dec. 15/7 Among the subjects covered by books in our stock are X-rays, *xenophilia, [etc.]. **1964** *New Statesman* 1 May 694/1 The uniters are.. more prone to xenophilia. Literature being the least international of the arts, those who wish to infuse it with music and colour tend to be internationalists. **1982** *Times* 7 Aug. 8/5 When will Americans realise how *xenophiliac their short order cuisine is—hamburgers.. which Hamburg would not understand, French fries incomprehensible to the French. **1974** *Encycl. Brit. Macropædia* X. 309/2 Tension between the xenophobic (fear of strangers) and *xenophilic (love of strangers) in postexilic Judaism was finally resolved some two centuries later. **1912** W. SICKERT in *English Review* Apr. 147 Lest the writer be accused of *Xenophilism. **1984** *New Yorker* 16 Jan. 32/2 Even the most *xenophilous among us may feel a twinge of alarm. **1898** *Q. Jrnl. Microsc. Sci.* June 308 No Stromboid, Naticoid, or *Xenophoran molluscs have been found hitherto in any fresh water that is known. **1935** A. F. BUDDINGTON in *Econ. Geol.* XXX. 209 The writer therefore proposes the term **xenothermal* for these deposits,.. suggestive of the peculiar textures for the normal high-temperature mineral assemblages involved, of the abnormal association of high temperature with shallow depth, and of the 'telescoped' character of many of the deposits. **1976** *Nature* 10 June 482/2 The tin mineralisation of Missouri bears a resemblance to the subvolcanic (xenothermal) deposits of Japan. **1973** J. A. LEVY in *Science* 14 Dec. 1151/2 The results show that this NZB type virus is endogenous in other strains of mice and is *xenotropic; that is, it grows only in cells foreign to the host. **1978** *Nature* 30 Mar. 456/2 Defective type C RNA tumour viruses which are genetic recombinants between ecotropic and xenotropic viruses have been described and suggested to be the real transforming agents during the course of viral-induced lymphatic leukaemia. **1974** *Ibid.* 22 Mar. 279/3 Another example of *xenotropism is the endogenous feline virus which when activated replicates in human cells. **1982** *Jrnl. Virology* XLIII. 472 (*heading*) Monoclonal antibody to spleen focus-forming virus-encoded gp52 provides a probe for the amino-terminal region of retroviral envelope proteins that confers dual tropism and xenotropism. **1885** *Stand. Nat. Hist.* (1888) V. 50 The Kabassous, or *Xenurines, have the third as well as the fourth and fifth metacarpals abbreviated and broad.

† **xeno'dochial**, *a.* *Obs.* *rare*$^{-1}$. [f. Gr. *ξενοδοχία* (XENODOCHY^2) + -AL^1.] Given to receiving strangers; hospitable.

1716 M. DAVIES *Athen. Brit.* II. 402 The Insuperable Aversion, that those three Xenodochial Prelates seem'd always to exert against the French Nation. *Ibid.* 404.

‖**xenodochium** (zɛnəˈdɒkɪəm). Also -ion, -eum. Pl. -a. [Late L. *xenodochīum*, *-ēum*, ad. late Gr. *ξενοδοχεῖον*, f. *ξένος* stranger + *δέχεσθαι* to receive.] A house of reception for strangers and pilgrims; a hostel, guest-house, esp. in a monastery.

1612 CORYAT in Purchas *Pilgrims* (1625) II. 1829 In Constantinople, Peru, and Galata, there are.. Karabassaries or *Xenodochia* foure hundred and eighteen. **1736** DRAKE *Eboracum* I. vii. 246 [A] spital.. was an house of entertainment for poor travellers or pilgrims.. this [*sc.* spital of St. Catherine] was a *Xenodochium* of that kind. **1832** GELL *Pompeiana* II. xiii. 18 Many have supposed that the xenodochium, or hospitium, for the reception of strangers was placed in this division of the mansion. **1844** LINGARD *Anglo-Saxon Ch.* (1858) I. vi. 246 Within the precincts of the monastery stood an edifice, distinguished by the Greek name of *Xenodochium*, in which a certain number of paupers received their daily support, and which was gratuitously opened to every traveller who solicited relief. **1865** LECKY *Ration.* II. vi. 263 Long before the era of persecution had closed, the hospital and the Xenodochion, or refuge for strangers, was known among the Christians.

† **xenodochy**^{1}. *Obs.* *rare*$^{-1}$. [Anglicized form of prec.] = prec.

c **1540** tr. *Pol. Verg. Eng. Hist.* (Camden No. 29) 121 Ther was at York an auncyent and welthy xenodochye that ys to say, an hospytall.. wher powre and nedye people wer enterteynyd.

† **xenodochy**^{2}. *Obs.* *rare*$^{-1}$. In 7 xenodechie, zenodochie. [ad. Gr. *ξενοδοχία*: cf. XENODOCHIUM.] Entertainment of strangers; hospitality.

1623 COCKERAM, *Xenodechie*, hospitality. **1674** JOSSELYN *Voy. New Eng.* 181 Sincere and religious people.. descryed by their charity and humility.. by their Zenodochie or hospitality.

xenogeneic (zɛnəʊdʒɪˈniːɪk, -ˈeɪɪk), *a.* *Immunol.* [f. XENO- + Gr. *γενε-ά* race, stock + -IC.] Derived from an individual of a different species.

1961 P. A. GORER et al. in *Nature* 25 Mar. 1025/1 'Hetero-specific' has been used before and cannot be said to be illogical; but it is a Greco-Latin hybrid and we feel that 'xenogeneic' goes well with the other two terms we have suggested and is perhaps preferable. **1969** *Ibid.* 27 Sept. 1376/1 Until recently all procedures that were effective in prolonging the lives of allografts.. were usually ineffective for sustaining xenogeneic grafts. **1977** *Lancet* 21 May 1105/2 Patients with widespread metastatic melanoma were treated with.. xenogeneic anti-melanoma immunoglobulin. **1981** *Jrnl. Immunol.* CXXVI. 2397/1 Xenogeneic anti-Id antibodies.

xenon (ˈzɛnɒn). *Chem.* [ad. Gr. *ξένον*, neut. of *ξένος* strange.] A heavy inert gaseous element present in minute quantity in the atmosphere, discovered by Sir William Ramsay in 1898. Symbol Xe or X. Also *attrib.* and *Comb.*

1898 RAMSAY & TRAVERS in *Rep. Brit. Assoc. Bristol* 830 The last fractions of liquefied argon show the presence of three new gases. These are krypton.. metargon.. and a still heavier gas,.. which we propose to name 'xenon'. **1938** *Ann. Reg. 1937* 358 Laporte.. showed that white light could be obtained from a xenon tube through which brief but very intense currents were passed. **1957** T. L. J. BENTLEY *Man. Miniat. Camera* (ed. 5) v. 74 The practical uses of electronic flash sets are governed by the characteristics of the modern xenon-filled flash tube. **1959** *New Scientist* 1 Jan. 12/1 The main lighting was provided by a pulsed xenon compact source lamp, and its intensity was of the order of 50,000 foot candles. **1962** *Newnes Conc. Encycl. Nucl. Energy* 877/1 Xenon is of importance in nuclear technology because several radioactive isotopes of the element are found among the fission products. One of these, Xe^{135},.. gives rise to fission-product poisoning of the reactor. **1963** [see REACT *v.*^{1} 1 c]. **1971** Xenon arc [see SPECTRALLY *adv.* 2]. **1971** *Sci. Amer.* Oct. 92/3 The compounds they studied were two chlorides of xenon, $XeCl_2$ and $XeCl_4$, which they produced indirectly by synthesizing analogous compounds where radioactive iodine 129 took the place of xenon... It will be recalled that xenon used to be called an inert, or 'noble', gas because it was thought to be chemically completely unreactive. **1976** *Daily Times* (Lagos) 8 July 17/1 Most film theatres in this country operating in 35mm have such poor and antiquated projection equipment that a good 16mm heavy duty projector equipped with a xenon lamp will certainly achieve better picture and sound quality.

xenophobia (zɛnəˈfəʊbɪə). Also ˈ**xenophoby**, **zenophobia** (both *rare*). [f. XENO- + Gr. *φόβ-ος* fear + -IA^1, -Y^3.] A deep antipathy to foreigners.

1909 *Athenæum* 13 Mar. 325/3 Those whose sense of justice.. is not impaired by prejudice or 'xenophoby'. **1919** *Nation* 20 Dec. 800/1 We are often told in criticism of the Nationalist movements in Egypt, Turkey, Persia, and China that legitimate agitation for self-government and democratic institutions is marred by xenophobia. **1934** R. MACAULAY *Going Abroad* xxix. 249 Violent and inhospitable outbursts of xenophoby have.. characterised them [*sc.* the Basques] from their first appearance in history. **1936** E. WAUGH *Waugh in Abyssinia* i. 34 The zenophobia of the people was an insuperable barrier to all free co-operation. **1940** E. POUND *Cantos* lvi. 67 Showed no zenophobia. **1963** *Economist* 1 June 908/1 The mild xenophobia.. which informed such *Punch* lines as ''e's a stranger: 'eave 'arf a brick at 'im'. **1971** H. MACMILLAN *Riding Storm* ii. 49 This kind of isolationism or economic nationalism, amounting to xenophobia, seized all nations, great and small, from time to time. **1976** N. ROBERTS *Face of France* iv. 49 Eight per cent of France's total working population is immigrant... Here were all the conditions needed for the release of latent xenophobia.

Hence **xeno'phobic** *a.*, pertaining to or exhibiting xenophobia; **xeno'phobically** *adv.*; also ˈ**xenophobe**, a xenophobic person; also as *adj*.

1912 *Nation* 11 May 214/1 The popular attitude with regard to external politics is one of crude and xenophobic Imperialism. **1922** *Mail* 24 May 327/1 The Afghans are said to be suspicious of foreigners, even to be xenophobes. **1937** D. B. WYNDHAM-LEWIS in L. Russell *Press Gang!* 245 Grey, scrawny, xenophobe, oinophil NY chilled-steel tycoon. **1951** H. ARENDT *Burden of our Time* I. i. 3 The identification of antisemitism with rampant nationalism and its xenophobic outbursts. **1956** P. JENNINGS *Model Oddlies* 34 The kind of London pub which.. has a more closely-knit, xenophobe clientèle than the remotest village hostelry. **1977** T. HEALD *Just Desserts* vii. 146 It wasn't that he was.. a xenophobe.. but the foreignness was obtrusive. **1978** *Listener* 8 June 724/2 Xenophobically named after the old Roman province, the Dacia is, in fact, a licence-built French Renault. **1980** *Times Lit. Suppl.* 22 Aug. 937/5 At that moment [*sc.* the start of a major war], for discreditable xenophobic reasons, Haldane's reputation as a War Minister sank to its nadir, but from 1918 onwards it has always been high. **1983** P. LIVELY *Perfect Happiness* vi. 72 A stubborn and unfashionably xenophobic refusal to attempt foreign languages. **1983** N. FREELING *Back of North Wind* 77 'Another bloody foreigner! I hate a lot of foreigners,' said Castang xenophobically.

Xenophontean, -ian (zɛnəˈfɒntɪən), *a.* [f. Gr. *Ξενοφῶν, -ῶντος* Xenophon, name of an ancient Greek historian and biographer (*c* 444–354 B.C.) + -EAN, -IAN.] Pertaining to, characteristic of, described by, or resembling (that of) Xenophon.

1593 G. HARVEY *Pierce's Super.* Wks. (Grosart) II. 99 M. Thomas Blundeuil,.. whose painefull, and skillfull bookes of Horsemanship, deserue also to be registred in the Catalogue of Xenophontian woorkes. **1834** GEN. P. THOMPSON *Exerc.* (1842) III. 127 In all European services there is a class of officers who might not unaptly be termed Xenophontean; men.. zealous to know the most that is possible, for the sake of acting under its guidance. **1875** JOWETT *Plato* (ed. 2) I. 338 The Apology appears to combine the common characteristics both of the Xenophontean and Platonic Socrates.

So **Xeno'phontic** *a.*

1822 T. Mitchell *Aristoph.* II. 27 What..authority the poet had for engaging his Socrates in these ridiculous speculations, it is now impossible to ascertain; but..the Platonic, and even the Xenophontic, Socrates is sometimes almost as absurd. **1864** Sala in *Daily Tel.* 15 Aug., Colonel Fremantle, in one of the most Xenophontic little books that has seen the light within these latter days, tells us [etc.]. **1882** A. S. Walpole *Xenophon's Anab.* I. (1900) p. x, A Greek of Xenophontic age. **1904** *Times* 27 Aug. 10/1 A mere Xenophontic record of the length of stages in a journey.

Xenopus ('zɛnəpəs). [mod.L. (coined in Ger. by J. G. Wagler 1827, in *Isis von Oken* XX. 726/2), f. xeno- + Gr. πούς, πόδ- foot.] A toad of the African genus *Xenopus*, which has claws on its digits and which was formerly used in pregnancy testing, as it produces eggs when injected with the urine of a pregnant woman; a clawed toad.

1890 *Proc. Sci. Meetings Zool. Soc.* 70 *Xenopus* is a most admirable swimmer, and remarkable for the manner in which it remains poised for a long time immediately under the surface of the water. **1955** [see œstradiol]. **1974** *Encycl. Brit. Macropædia* XI. 803/2 In the toad *Xenopus*, each group of hair cells in a neuromast connects to its own nerve fibre.

xenotime ('zɛnəʊtaɪm). *Min.* [Named (in Fr.) by Beudant, 1832, as if f. Gr. ξένος strange + τιμή honour, but app. in error for **kenotime*, f. Gr. κενός empty, vain: see quot. below.] A native phosphate of yttrium.

1844 Dana *Min.* (1868) 528 Xenotime... Lustre resinous Color yellowish-brown, reddish-brown, hair-brown, flesh-red, grayish-white [etc.]... Beudant named the species *xenotime* (apparently from ξενός, stranger to, and τιμή, honor), but in the next line gives the derivation 'κενος, vain, et τιμή, honneur', as if the word were *kenotime*, and adds.. that this name is intended to recall the fact that the mineral was erroneously supposed by Berzelius..to contain a new metal. **1907** *Athenæum* 20 Apr. 479/1 M. Jean Becquerel.. has been engaged in magneto-optical researches... Most of his experiments have been made with crystals of xenotime (a magnetic phosphate of yttrium).

xeque, var. (Pg. spelling) of sheikh.

xerafeen, -in, var. seraphin *Obs.*

‖**xeranthemum** (zɪə'rænθɪməm). *Bot.* [mod.L. (Tournefort, 1700), f. Gr. ξηρός dry + ἄνθεμον blossom.] A plant of a genus of composites of the Mediterranean region, having flower-heads with dry chaffy bracts of a purplish or whitish colour; the genus itself; one kind of the plants commonly called *everlasting* or *immortelle*.

1741 *Compl. Fam.-Piece* II. iii. 385 Seeds of Jacea's,.. Xeranthemums,..and sweet Sultan. **1751** Hill *Hist. Plants* 574 The longleaved xeranthemum with paleaceous receptacles. It is a native of Germany and France; the flowers retain their beauty many years. **1786** Abercrombie *Gard. Assist.* 116 Virginia and English tobacco, Indian corn, xeranthemum, ten-week's stocks.

xerapheen, -phin, var. seraphin *Obs.*

xerarch ('zɛrɑːk), *a. Ecol.* [f. xer(o- + Gr. ἀρχ-ή beginning.] Of a plant succession: having its origin in a dry habitat.

1913, **1960** [see hydrarch *a.*]. **1973** P. A. Colinvaux *Introd. Ecol.* vi. 75 Later American work..sought to explain the existence of beech-maple forests on old sand dunes near the southern shore of Lake Michigan as resulting from a particularly dramatic xerarch succession.

‖**xerasia** (zɪə'reɪsɪə). *Path.* [mod.L., a. Gr. ξηρασία dryness, also in sense below (Galen).] A disease of the hair characterized by excessive dryness.

1706 Phillips (ed. Kersey), *Xerasia*, a fault in the Hairs when they appear like Down, as it were sprinkled with Dust. **1896** tr. *Balzac's César Birotteau* 152 To prevent xerasia and baldness.

Xeres ('zɛrɪs, 'zɪərɪz). Also 7 **Zerez**. Name of a town in Andalusia, famous for its wine; in full, ***Xeres sack, wine*** = sherris (*sack*), sherry *sb.*[1] 1.

a **1661** Fuller *Worthies, Bristol* (1662) III. 34 *Bristol Milk.* .. This Metaphorical Milk, whereby Xeres or Sherry-Sack is intended. **1662** Merret in Charleton *Myst. Vintners* (1675) 233 Most of the Canary is made with Malago and Zerez Sack. **1841** *Fraser's Mag.* XXIV. 26 The xeres and port Are of the right sort. **1869** Blackmore *Lorna D.* l, Do you like the wine of the Oporto, or the wine of Xeres? **1872** Ruskin *Fors Clav.* II. xvi. 13 So many skins of Xeres wine.

xeric ('zɪərɪk), *a. Ecol.* [f. xer(o- + -ic.] Having or characterized by a scanty amount of moisture.

1926, etc. [see hydric *a.*[2]]. **1932** Fuller & Conard tr. *Braun-Blanquet's Plant Sociol.* v. 115 In spite of this temporary excess of precipitation, the vegetation of the southern Cévennes has many xeric features. **1967** M. E. Hale *Biol. Lichens* vii. 94 Xeric savannas and mesic maple woods. **1979** *Jrnl. Arid Environments* II. 255 This soil represents an edaphically xeric condition.

xeriff, var. of sherifi.

xeriff, obs. form of shereef.

xero- ('zɪərəʊ), before a vowel **xer-**, repr. Gr. ξηρο-, ξηρ-, combining form of ξηρός dry, occurring in several scientific and technical terms. ‖**xero'derma, -'dermia**, *Path.* [mod.L., f. Gr. δέρμα skin], one of several diseases characterized by excessive dryness of the skin; hence **xeroder'matic, -'dermatous, -'dermic** *adjs.*, pertaining to or characteristic of xeroderma. **xeroderma pigmentosum** *Path.* [L. *pigmentōsus* pigmented], a rare, hereditary disorder in which skin exposed to the ultraviolet light of the sun becomes discoloured and swollen, chronic injury leading in childhood to cancer and often death. **'xeroform** *Med.* [after *chloroform*]: see quot. **'xeromorphy** *Bot.* [Gr. μορφή shape, form], the possession by a plant of features characteristic of a xerophilous plant; hence **xero'morphic** *a.*; also **'xeromorph**, a xeromorphic plant. **xero'philic** *a.* = *xerophilous* adj. **xerophilous** (-'ɒfɪləs) *a. Bot.* and *Zool.* [Gr. -φιλος -loving], adapted to a dry climate or habitat, or to conditions of scanty available moisture; so **xerophil(e** ('zɪərəʊfɪl), *sb.* [ad. F. *xérophile sb.* (J. Thurmann in *Essai de phytostatique* (1849) I. xiii. 268)], a xerophilous plant; also as *adj.*; **xe'rophily**, the condition or character of being xerophilous. **'xerophyte** (-faɪt), *Bot.* [Gr. φυτόν plant], a xerophilous plant (see above); so **xerophytic** (-'fɪtɪk) *a.*, pertaining to or having the character of a xerophyte, xerophilous; **xe'rophytism**, xerophytic character, xerophily. **'xerosere** *Ecol.* [sere *sb.*[2]], a plant succession having its origin in a dry habitat. ‖**xerostomia** (-'stəʊmɪə), *Path.* [mod.L., f. Gr. στόμα mouth], dryness of the mouth from insufficient secretion of saliva. **xero'thermic** *a.* [Gr. θερμός hot], dry and hot.

1848 Dunglison *Med. Lex.* (ed. 7), **Xeroderma*, diminution of secretion of the sebaceous glands. **1864** W. T. Fox *Skin Dis.* viii. 222 True xeroderma is in reality the early stage of ichthyosis, a true epithelial disease. **1899** *Allbutt's Syst. Med.* VIII. 786 [*Lichen pilaris*] is only a part of a general xeroderma. **1884** *Medico-Chir. Trans.* LXVII. 169 (*heading*) Three cases of *xeroderma pigmentosum, Kaposi or atrophoderma pigmentosum. **1952** C. P. Blacker *Eugenics* 248 Among these genes are those believed to determine retinitis pigmentosa, a severe disease of the eye leading to blindness; epidermolysis bullosa and xeroderma pigmentosum, both diseases of the skin. **1975** *Sci. Amer.* Nov. 68/2 An inherited defect in the enzymes that repair DNA damaged by ultraviolet light, called *xeroderma pigmentosum*, leads to multiple skin cancers. **1913** Dorland *Med. Dict.* (ed. 7), *Xerodermatic. **1899** *Allbutt's Syst. Med.* VIII. 851 The skin is dry and thin but not *xerodermatous. **1891** *Cent. Dict.*, **Xerodermia*, same as Xeroderma. **1899** [see xerosis]. **1890** *Retropsect Med.* CII. 92 Minute white, gray, or red scaly *xerodermic prominences, having a hair in the centre. **1901** Dorland *Med. Dict.* (ed. 2), **Xeroform*, a yellow neutral powder derived from tribromphenol and bismuth, $(C_6H_2Br_3O)_2$ BiOH + Bi_2O_3: useful in the treatment of wounds, abscesses, etc., and as an intestinal antiseptic. **1934** Webster, *Xeromorph. **1953** *Sci. News* XXVII. 10 The term 'xerophyte' is now limited to those plants able to endure conditions of drought, while salt-marsh plants are known as 'xeromorphs'. **1981** *Austral. Jrnl. Bot.* XXIX. 518 *G*[*revillea*] *annulifera* has the nutritional characteristics common to xeromorphs plus strategies to channel nutrients very efficiently to its seeds. **1909** E. Warming *Œcol. of Plants* xlvi. 194 There must be a causal connexion between the soil and the *xeromorphic structure which has been described. **1938** Weaver & Clements *Plant Ecol.* (ed. 2) xvi. 445 Xeromorphic structures such as thick cuticle, waxy covering, or abundant development of hairs have little value in directly reducing the rate of transpiration of xerophytes so long as the stomata are open. **1974** *Nature* 26 Apr. 807/2 The *Hybanthus* shrubs conspicuous by their apparent lack of xeromorphic adaptation to a climate which becomes increasingly arid towards the continental interior. **1909** E. Warming *Œcol. of Plants* xlvi. 194 This *xeromorphy of plants growing on wet moor-soil occurs all the world over. **1963** *Nature* 30 Nov. 909/2 It is well known that xeromorphy is of physiological importance to the aquatic plants which exhibit it and certain tissues become altered in relation to environment. **1980** *Bot. Jrnl. Linnean Soc.* LXXX. 319 Most of the variable characters are related to xeromorphy and are taxonomically useful within the framework of the present classification. **1878** *Xerophile [see hygrophilous *a.*]. **1884** *Trans. Victoria Inst.* 38 Xerophiles—plants such as pertain to very dry climates. **1921** H. Printz *Vegetation of Siberian-Mongolian Frontiers* 14 At a short distance from the river..the xerophile typical steppe vegetation predominates. **1936** *Hereditas* XXI. 290 *Viola crassa* is xerophile and alpine. **1985** *Times* 4 Jan. 12/2 The site was then abandoned, a conclusion that Dr Evans bases on the high diversity of snail species and the general paucity of xerophile species. **1961** Webster, *Xerophilic. **1965** B. E. Freeman tr. *Vandel's Biospeleology* xiii. 213 The Tenebrionidae are mainly xerophilic insects. **1972** *Science* 19 May 788/1 He is equally good when describing various kinds of vegetation, from the aquatic to the xerophilic. **1863** J. G. Baker *N. Yorksh.* xxii. 316 The *Xerophilous and Maritime species [of mosses] are very few in number. **1893** *Athenæum* 2 Dec. 774/3 A paper..by the Rev. G. Henslow 'On the Origin of Plant Structures by Self-adaptation to the Environment, exemplified by Desert and Xerophilous Plants.' **1968** *Jrnl. Zool.* CLV. 365 Many xerophilous species occupying desert or semi-arid areas have adapted their breeding physiology to take advantage of the unpredictable and sporadic rainfall that may occur at any time. **1904** *Science* 3 June 866/2 The causes of *xerophily in bog plants. **1897** Willis *Flower. Pl. & Ferns* I. 178 In countries with long dry seasons [etc.].., the plants..agree in having a lower rate of transpiration than plants living where there is plenty of available water. Plants of this kind are termed **xerophytes*. **1906** G. Henslow in *19th Cent.* Nov. 801 *E*[*uphoriba*] *Paralias* is a xerophyte with coriaceous leaves, because it has adapted itself to a maritime situation in England. **1897** Willis *Flower. Pl. & Ferns* I. 185 No plants..can be regular epiphytes unless they possess well-marked *xerophytic characters, including as a rule the capacity for water-storage. **1900** *Nature* 13 Dec. 150/1 Every one is aware how extremely intolerant of moisture are the cacti and some other xerophytic plants. *Ibid.* 15 Nov. 53/2 The stomatal grooves on the lower surface of the leaf [of *Lepidodendron*] suggest a xerophytic adaptation. Indications of *xerophytism are afforded by other anatomical characters in certain Palæozoic types. **1926** *Xerosere [see *hydrosere* s.v. hydro-]. **1952** P. W. Richards *Tropical Rain Forest* xii. 287 Opportunities for observing xeroseres in the tropics are ..not infrequent, particularly in regions of volcanic activity. **1890** Billings *Nat. Med. Dict.*, **Xerostomia*, dryness of the mouth. **1897** *Allbutt's Syst. Med.* III. 310 The salivary and buccal secretions may be totally arrested as in cases of xerostomia. **1904** *Bot. Gaz.* Apr. 312 (Cent. D. Suppl.) Jerosch holds that an interglacial *xerothermic or steppe period has been proved by the facts of plant geography, paleontology, and geology.

xerocopy ('zɪərəʊ-, 'zɛrəʊkɒpɪ). [f. next + copy *sb.* (*a.*).] A xerographic copy; a photocopy. Hence **'xerocopying** *vbl. sb.*

1963 *Fortune* Sept. 225/2 (Advt.), Which is the 5 c xerocopy? **1964** *Economist* 22 Aug. 695/1 (Advt.), Xerocopying is an essential part of modern business communication. **1966** *English Studies* XLVII. 152 Most of the items are also available as paperbound xerocopies. **1971** *Fremdsprachen* XV. 278 Dry permanent xerocopies at a ratio of 14·5 × are automatically reproduced on single cut sheets of ordinary unsensitised paper.

xerography (zɪə-, zə'rɒgrəfɪ). [f. xero- + -graphy, after *photography*.] A dry copying process in which an electrically charged surface retains both the charge and a pigmented powder on areas not illuminated by light from bright parts of the document, so that a permanent copy may be immediately obtained by placing paper on the surface and applying heat to fuse the powder to it; photocopying.

1948 *N.Y. Times* 23 Oct. 17/8 A revolutionary process of inkless printing..was announced yesterday... Invented by Chester F. Carlson, a New York lawyer, and known as 'Xerography', this basic addition to the graphic arts reproduces pictures and text at a speed of 1,200 a minute. **1957** *Technology* July 164/2 A new copying process, Xerography, attracted constant attention. **1962** *Daily Tel.* 30 Oct. 20 (Advt.), Xerography is capturing a growing share of a market in office copying. **1967** McLuhan & Fiore *Medium is Massage* 123 Xerography..heralds the times of instant publishing. **1970** A. Toffler *Future Shock* (1971) xii. 280 Advances in offset printing and xerography have radically lowered the costs of short-run publishing. **1976** *Globe & Mail* (Toronto) 1 Nov. 17/4 Asked whether xerography might become the next big movement in art, Bidner insisted on caution.

Hence **xero'graphic** *a.*, **xero'graphically** *adv.*

1948 *N.Y. Times* 23 Oct. 17/8 Even an unskilled person can make good Xerographic prints easily. **1958** *Times Lit. Suppl.* 5 Dec. 712/3 The enormous possibilities of applying the xerographic process to microfilms of books. **1968** *U.S. Patent 3,413,716* 1 A xerographically formed pattern of chemical resist is placed on the conductive material. **1976** *Nature* 22 Jan. 204/2 We sampled the air in an unventilated room..housing a xerographic machine. **1979** *Lore & Lang.* Jan. 14 This recitation has been printed many times and is common in the xerographically transmitted broadsheets. **1982** *Trans. Yorks. Dialect Soc.* LXXXII. 49 (Advt.), Available in microform and xerographic form.

‖**xeroma** (zɪə'rəʊmə). *Path.* [mod.L., f. Gr. ξηρός dry, after *sarcoma*, etc.] Abnormal dryness of some part from lack of fluid secretion; *spec.* = xerophthalmia. Hence **xe'romatous** *a.*, of the nature of or affected with xeroma.

1848 Dunglison *Med. Lex.* (ed. 7), *Xeroma*, xerophthalmia... *Xeroma, lachrymal*, suppression of the lachrymal secretion. **1860** Mayne *Expos. Lex.*, Xeromatous. **1875** H. Walton *Dis. Eye* (ed. 3) 876 The cornea passes into complete pannus or xeroma.

xerophagy (zɪə'rɒfədʒɪ). Also 7 **-fag-**. [ad. Gr. ξηροφαγία: see xero- and -phagy.] The eating of dry food, esp. as form of fasting practised in the early church.

1656 Blount *Glossogr.*, *Xerophagy*..the eating dry meats. **1671** F. S. tr. *Daille's Serm. Colossians* ii. 2 The stations, the xerofagies, and other disciplines of the Montanists. **1725** tr. *Dupin's Eccl. Hist. 17th C.* I. v. 157 In the Week which precedes the Feast of Easter, the Fast was more rigorous, and in some Places they eat nothing but dry'd things; which they call'd Xerophagy. **1884** *Catholic Dict.* (1897) 558/2 (*Lent*) Some kept the fast of extraordinary strictness known as xerophagy for one day. **1889** Farrar *Lives Fathers* I. v. 190 *note*, As for xerophagies, says Tertullian, they charge them with being a novel title for a pretended duty.

‖**xerophthalmia** (zɪərɒf'θælmɪə). *Path.* Also formerly anglicized as **xerophthalmy, -ie.** [L., ad. Gr. ξηροφθαλμία, f. ξηρός dry + ὀφθαλμία ophthalmia.] An ophthalmia without discharge; inflammation of the conjunctiva of the eye with abnormal dryness and corrugation.

1656 Blount *Glossogr.*, *Xerophthalmy*..soarness or bleäredness of the Eyes, when they neither swell, nor run. **1658** Phillips, Xerophthalmie. [**1684** tr. *Blancard's Phys. Dict.* (1693), *Xerophthalmia*, a dry Bleardness or Blood-shot of the Eyes.] **1875** H. Walton *Dis. Eye* (ed. 3) 885 (*heading*) Cuticular conjunctivitis or xerophthalmia.

xeroradiography (ˌzɪərəʊ-, ˌzɛrəʊreɪdɪˈɒgrəfi). [f. XEROGRAPHY + RADIOGRAPHY.] A xerographic process for obtaining an X-ray picture, the X-rays impinging on an electrically charged surface like light in conventional xerography. Hence **xeroˈradiograph**; **ˌxeroradioˈgraphic** *a.*

1950 *Non-Destructive Testing* IX. I. 11/1 Xeroradiography is a rapid, low-cost, all-electric method of obtaining permanent X-Ray images. *Ibid.*, The xeroradiographic plate.. may be made flexible, and placed in intimate contact with the curved surface of the test object. **1955** *Amer. Jrnl. Roentgenol.* LXXIII. 7/1 The xeroradiographic plate consists of a sheet of metal.. on which has been deposited.. a thin layer of selenium. *Ibid.* 8/1 (*caption*) Aluminum step-wedge xeroradiographs. **1960** *Aeroplane* XCIX. 722/2 The inspection of light-alloy castings, hidden structures and assemblies, is stated to be among the applications of xeroradiographic equipment. **1972** *Lancet* 2 Dec. 1186/1 A feature of the xeroradiograph is the remarkably sharp, clearcut 'edge effect' of the powder pattern. **1975** *Nature* 25 Sept. 276/2 The discharging of a selenium plate by X rays was embodied in the original Xerox patents but, despite some investigation in the 1950s, 'xeroradiography' has not been widely used.

‖**xerosis** (zɪəˈrəʊsɪs). *Path.* [mod.L., a. Gr. ξήρωσις, f. ξηρός dry: see -OSIS.] = XEROMA; spec. = *xeroderma* (see XERO-). Also *attrib.*

1890 BILLINGS *Nat. Med. Dict.*, *Xerosis*, a drying, dryness. **1899** *Allbutt's Syst. Med.* VIII. 661 To the milder forms [of ichthyosis] the names *xerodermia* and *xerosis* are frequently.. applied. **1900** *Brit. Med. Jrnl.* 17 Mar. 622/2 Xerosis bacilli were present.

So **xerotic** (zɪəˈrɒtɪk) *a.* [see -OTIC], affected with xerosis; **xerotine** (ˈzɪərətaɪn) *a.*, in ***xerotine siccative***, trade-name of a substance used for drying ships' bottoms.

1882 *Standard* 14 Jan. 5/8 We have had a terrible explosion of xerotine siccative on board here. **1890** BILLINGS *Nat. Med. Dict.*, *Xerotic*, dry. **1893** *Westm. Gaz.* 5 Oct. 3/1 The sad loss of H.M.S. *Dotterel*.., presumably from the effects of an explosion.. of Xerotine Siccative, supplied as patent driers. **1901** DORLAND *Med. Dict.* (ed. 2), *Xerotic*, characterized by xerosis, or dryness.

Xerox (ˈzɪərɒks, ˈzɛrɒks), *sb.* Also xerox. [Invented word f. XERO(GRAPHY.] A proprietary name for photocopiers (see quots. 1952, 1953); also used *loosely* (*attrib.* and *absol.*) to denote any photocopy.

1952 *Trade Marks Jrnl.* 19 Aug. 748/2 *Xerox*... Electro-photographic copying machines and apparatus for fusing powder images onto paper in connection with electro-photographic copying machines. The Haloid Company. **1953** *Official Gaz.* (U.S. Patent Office) 12 May 327/2 The Haloid Company, Rochester, N.Y... *Xerox* for electro-photographic copying machines, cameras, plates... Claims, use since June 22, 1949. **1966** *Economist* 15 Oct. 299/3 In most American offices executives instruct subordinates to 'make me a Xerox of this report' rather than 'make me a copy of it'. **1972** M. WILLIAMS *Inside Number 10* xi. 289 The Rank Organization in Brighton installed a xerox copying machine in the office and we also had an electric duplicating machine. **1975** D. LODGE *Changing Places* iii. 128, I enclose a Xerox of the anonymous letter. **1976** M. MACHLIN *Pipeline* xxvii. 317 It had appeared in Xerox form on bulletin boards in most of the administrative offices of Denali. **1977** M. FRENCH *Women's Room* (1978) iii. 272 They had a terrible fight one evening in the Xerox room of the library. **1979** *Author* XC. 157 Reprography..—xerox photocopying. **1980** *London Rev. Bks.* 15 May 8/3 How will the industry cope with new technologies, like tele-ordering, new EEC copyright complications and piracy both in the Middle East and (as we all guiltily know) in every xerox room in the British Isles? **1981** P. ROTH *Zuckerman Unbound* 52 Virtually all they had left in common was the rented Xerox machine.

fig. **1979** *Nature* 15 Mar. 209/3 The set is often referred to as 'the first generation of elementary particles'... Nature seems to have made xerox copies: a second generation (μ^- ν' and cs) and possibly a third.

xerox (ˈzɪərɒks, ˈzɛrɒks), *v.* Also **Xerox**. [f. prec.] *trans.* To reproduce by xerography; to photocopy.

1966 'E. V. CUNNINGHAM' *Helen* iv. 40 Anything you want copies of, why we'll Xerox it out. **1967** MCLUHAN & FIORE *Medium is Massage* 123 Custom-make your own book by simply Xeroxing a chapter from this one, a chapter from that one—instant steal! **1978** *Globe & Mail* (Toronto) *Weekend Mag.* 21 Oct. 14/3 He xeroxes the menu himself and stamps out to post it on the notice-board. **1979** N. MAILER *Executioner's Song* II. iv. 555 Tamera had gone to work at 5 A.M. and spent six hours Xeroxing Gary's letters. **1982** P. M. MARGOLIN *Last Innocent Man* II. iii. 115 He had Xeroxed the clippings for David.

Hence **ˈxeroxed** *ppl. a.*, **ˈxeroxing** *vbl. sb.* (both also with capital initial).

1965 *New Society* 14 Oct. 28/2 Inadequate library provision.. has forced university teachers to.. prepare.. roneoed or xeroxed material. **1973** *Jrnl. Social Psychol.* LX. 32 The Xeroxing, which made each sheet look less as though it had been individually prepared, was done to prevent distortion of the ratings. **1976** S. LLOYD *Mr Speaker, Sir* vii. 154 During July 1974, we frequently had to rely on Xeroxed copies of the order paper, amendments, and the Official Report. **1978** K. AMIS *Jake's Thing* xiv. 139 He.. reached for the xeroxed sheet on the bedside table. **1978** *Early Music* Oct. 605/3, I wonder how publishers who want to remain in business will react to Mr Rooley's complaint about xeroxing rules. **1980** E. BEHR *Getting Even* ii. 21 The xeroxing propensities of.. one of the top confidential secretaries. **1982** *Amer. Speech* LVII. 268 The dry duplicating process known as Xeroxing has gained great popularity. **1984** *Monitor* (McAllen, Texas) 15 Jan. 16A/6 Conference participants are also urged to bring xeroxed copies of their utility bills. **1985** A. S. BYATT *Still Life* 4 Schoolgirls were dutifully filling in xeroxed, hand-written, one-word-answerable questionnaires.

†**xesturgy**. *Obs. rare*⁻¹. [ad. Gr. ξεστουργία, f. ξεστός, vbl. adj. f. ξεῖν to polish: see -URGY.] The process of polishing.

1592 R. D. *Hypnerotomachia* 48 Diuers coulered stones.. so glistering and seuerly set of a diligent Xesturgie [orig. *xesturgia*].

Xhosa (ˈkəʊzə, ˈkɔːzə, -sə), *sb.* and *a.* Also 9 **Koossa**, etc.: 9– **Xosa**. [Their own name for themselves.] **A.** *sb.* **a.** A member of any of several related peoples in Cape Province, South Africa, that form part of the Nguni branch of the Bantu; such people collectively.

1801 J. BARROW *Trav. Interior S. Afr.* I. iii. 219 The Kaffers call themselves *Koussie*, which word is pronounced by the Hottentots with a strong palatal stroke of the tongue on the first syllable. **1812** A. PLUMPTRE tr. *Lichtenstein's Trav. Southern Afr.* I. xviii. 250 The tribe of which I mean more particularly to speak call themselves Koossas, or Kaussas. **1827** G. THOMPSON *Trav. Southern Afr.* App. No. I. 439 The national appellation of the Southern Caffers is *Amakosa*, the singular of which is *Kosa*. **1881** *Encycl. Brit.* XIII. 818/2 The Ama-Fengus are regarded both by the Ama-Zulus and Ama-Xosas as slaves or out-castes, without any right to the freedom and privilege of true-born Kaffres. **1948** B. G. M. SUNDKLER *Bantu Prophets in S. Afr.* iv. 96 The Zionist prophets, operating in Zululand, are in many cases not Zulus, but Sotho, Xhosa, or sometimes men from ..Nyasaland. **1981** A. PATON *Towards Mountain* xxii. 189 The suggestion was made at a white staff meeting that we should try allotting separate dormitories to Xhosas, Zulu, Basotho, and so on.

b. The Nguni language of the Xhosas, a tonal language of the Bantu family very similar to Zulu.

1872 W. J. DAVIS *Dict. Kaffir Lang.* p. vi, The author of this, the first Dictionary of Xosa Kaffir. **1928** *Africa* I. 479 Xosa is established as the literary language of Kaffraria and the Transkei. **1970** *Cape Times* 28 Oct. 2/6 Four hundred people of all races attended prayers for racial harmony, held at St. George's Cathedral, Cape Town last night. The service—conducted alternately in English, Afrikaans and Xhosa—formed part of 24 hours of continuous prayer. **1977** *N.Y. Rev. Bks.* 4 Aug. 41/2 After testifying for four days in his native Xhosa, he asked if he could address the court in English. **1983** M. KENYON *Free-Range Wife* i. 17 His English was so weird.. he might well, as compensation, have flawless French, German, Finnish, Xhosa too.

B. *adj.* Pertaining to or designating the Xhosas or their language.

1812 A. PLUMPTRE tr. *Lichtenstein's Trav. Southern Afr.* I. App. sig. a2ʳ In the Koossa dialect *u* is the vowel that occurs the most frequently. **1872** W. J. DAVIS *Dict. Kaffir Lang.* p. v, When a word is both Xosa and Zulu in form and signification, both these letters are prefixed to its meaning. **1935** *Critic* (Cape Town) Oct. 1 From the Xhosa verb *bonga* is derived the noun *isibongo*. **1948** B. G. SUNDKLER *Bantu Prophets S. Afr.* ii. 42 The Order of Ethiopia can hardly be said to have succeeded in attracting the broad masses of Ethiopians... It has remained exclusively Xhosa. **1963** *Times Lit. Suppl.* 17 May 354 A successful Xhosa cattle breeder. **1975** *Cricketer* May 15/2 A running commentary in the Xhosa language kept Bantu spectators in the picture.

xi (saɪ, zaɪ, ksaɪ, gzaɪ). *Particle Physics.* [Gr. ξεῖ, ξῖ, name of the fourteenth letter (Ξ, ξ) of the Greek alphabet.] Either of a pair of hyperons (and their antiparticles) having a mass of approximately 1320 MeV, spin of $\frac{1}{2}$, hypercharge -1, isospin $\frac{1}{2}$, and even parity, which on decaying usually produce a lambda particle and a pion. Freq. represented by Ξ. Usu. *attrib.*

1954 GELL-MANN & PAIS in *Proc. Glasgow Conf. Nucl. & Meson Physics* (1955) 344 It is interesting to consider the 'cascade particle', which we shall call Ξ^- and which has the decay scheme $\Xi^- \to \Lambda^0 + \pi^- + (\sim 65 \text{ MeV})$. **1964** *New Scientist* 20 Feb. 460/3 According to the conservation of baryons and hypercharge, the omega-minus should be produced in collisions between K-minus mesons and protons and should decay (weakly, with a change of hypercharge) to a xi-particle and pion, or to a lambda-particle and K-minus. **1974** *Nature* 13 Dec. 524/1 The elementary particles nearly obey a number of simple and elegant symmetry rules. Many useful approximate calculations can be made assuming that the symmetries are perfect—for instance.. by assuming that the proton and neutron have the same interactions as the lambda, sigma and xi hyperons. **1980** J. S. TREFIL *From Atoms to Quarks* vii. 109 There are two xi particles, one neutral and one with a negative charge.

xil-: see XYL-.

†**xilinous**, *a. Obs. rare*⁻⁰. [f. L. *xilinus*, *xylinus* (Pliny), a. Gr. ξύλινος, f. ξύλον cotton-tree: see -OUS.] Of cotton.

1656 BLOUNT *Glossogr.*, Xilinous.

Xinto, etc., obs. ff. SHINTO, etc.

1776 JUSTAMOND tr. *Raynal's Hist. Indies* I. 108 The sect of Xinto... The Xinto sect... The deity of the Xintoists [orig. *Sintos, Sintoistes*].

†**xiph**. *Obs. rare.* In 6 zyphe. [ad. L. *xiphias*: see next.] The swordfish, *Xiphias gladius*.

1572 BOSSEWELL *Armorie* II. 66 The fielde is of the Jacinthe, a pyle in pointe d'Ermyne, betwene two Zyphes hariante, Lunæ. This is a fishe whiche is named a sworde fishe.

xiphias (ˈzɪfiæs). Also 9 *erron.* **xy-**. [L., a. Gr. ξιφίας, f. ξίφος sword.]

1. A swordfish, esp. *X. gladius*; in mod. *Zool.*, the genus of fishes of which this is the common species, characterized by having the upper jaw prolonged into a sword-like weapon.

1667 *Phil. Trans.* II 492 Having.. dissected the head of a *Xiphias* or Sword-fish. **1763** C. SMART *Song to David* lxxv, Strong through the turbulent profound Shoots xiphias to his aim. **1860** WRAXALL *Life in Sea* v. 108 The heel of an East Indiaman was once bored by a twenty-foot Xyphias so violently, that the sword went in up to the root, and the fish was killed by the force of the blow.

2. *Astron.* A southern constellation, also called Dorado or the Sword-fish.

1728 CHAMBERS *Cycl.* s.v. *Constellation.* **1771** [see SWORDFISH 2].

Hence **xiphiad** (ˈzɪfiæd), a fish of the family *Xiphiidæ*.

1859–62 SIR J. RICHARDSON, etc. *Mus. Nat. Hist.* (1868) II. 137 Xiphiads or Sword-fishes.

xiphioid (ˈzɪfɪɔɪd), *a.* and *sb. Zool.* [f. prec. + -OID.] **a.** *adj.* Resembling or allied to the genus *Xiphias*; belonging to or having the characters of the family *Xiphiidæ*. **b.** *sb.* A xiphioid fish.

1851 MANTELL *Petrifactions* v. §1. 416 Cycloid Order... Xiphioids. **1891** *Cent. Dict.*, Xiphioid, *a.* and *n.*

‖**xiphiplastron** (zɪfɪˈplæstrən). *Anat.* and *Zool.* Pl. **-a**. Also (more correctly) **xipho-**. [mod.L., properly *xiphoplastron*, f. Gr. ξίφος sword + PLASTRON.] Each of the fourth or hindmost pair of lateral plates in the plastron of a turtle. Hence **xiphiˈplastral** *a.*, pertaining to or constituting a xiphiplastron; *sb.* a xiphiplastral plate, a xiphiplastron.

1871 HUXLEY *Anat. Vert.* v. 202 In the Turtle the plastron consists of nine pieces.. the fourth [lateral], xiphiplastron. **1889** NICHOLSON & LYDEKKER *Palæont.* liii. II. 1084 [The pubis and the ischium] may be anchylosed to the xiphiplastral. **1889** LYDEKKER in *Q. Jrnl. Geol. Soc.* 1 Aug. 511 The imperfect left xiphiplastral [of a Chelonian].

xiphisternal (zɪfɪˈstɜːnəl), *a.* and *sb. Anat.* and *Zool.* Also (more correctly) **xipho-**. [f. *xiphi-* for *xipho-*, Gr. ξίφος sword + STERNUM + -AL¹.]

a. *adj.* Belonging to or constituting the xiphisternum (see below). **b.** *sb.* A xiphisternal part or appendage. So ‖**xiphiˈsternum** (**xipho-**), the posterior division of the sternum, in some animals osseous and in others cartilaginous, in man constituting the xiphoid or ensiform cartilage; also sometimes applied to the XIPHIPLASTRON of a turtle.

1835–6 *Todd's Cycl. Anat.* I. 284/1 The posterior cartilaginous appendages [of the sternum in birds] he [*sc.* Geoffrey St. Hilaire] terms xiphi-sternals. **1839–47** *Ibid.* III. 838/1 The posterior [of the two pairs of elements of the 'sternum', i.e. plastron, of *Chelonia*] are fitly denominated the xiphosternal pieces. **1870** ROLLESTON *Anim. Life* 15 The posterior or xiphisternal end of the sternum. **1872** H. A. NICHOLSON *Palæont.* 399 The xiphisternum is the 'xiphoid cartilage' of human anatomy. **1888** ROLLESTON & JACKSON *Anim. Life* 362 The sternum [in *Mammalia*].. is divisible into three regions—a praesternum or manubrium sterni..; a mesosternum..; and a xiphisternum, sometimes cartilaginous, sometimes ossified. *Ibid.* 384 [The] bilateral origin [of the sternum in some *Lacertilia*] is evidenced.. by the prolongation backwards.. of two xiphisternal horns.

xiphocostal (zɪfəʊˈkɒstəl), *a. Anat.* [f. Gr. ξίφος sword + COSTAL.] Pertaining to or connected with the xiphoid cartilage and the ribs.

1899 in *Syd. Soc. Lex.*

xiphodyme (ˈzɪfəʊdaɪm). [ad. mod.L. *xiphodymus*, contr. f. *xiphodidymus*, f. Gr. ξίφος sword + δίδυμος twin.] = XIPHOPAGUS.

1861 *N. Syd. Soc. Year-bk. Med.* 404 A Monstrosity of the Genus Xiphodyme.

xiphoid (ˈzɪfɔɪd), *a.* (*sb.*) *Anat.* Also *erron.* 8–9 **xyphoid**, 9 **ziphoide**. [ad. mod.L. *xiphoidēs*, a. Gr. ξιφοειδής, f. ξίφος sword + εἶδος form: see -OID.] Sword-shaped, ensiform: a descriptive epithet of the cartilaginous or bony process at the lower or posterior end of the sternum in man and other animals (also called XIPHISTERNUM), and of a projecting bone at the back of the head in the cormorants and related birds (also called *occipital style*).

1746 GLASS *Dropsy* in *Phil. Trans.* XLIV. 338 We found the Circumference of her Abdomen to be just six Feet four Inches, and from the Xyphoid Cartilage to the Os Pubis it measur'd four Feet and half an Inch. **1782** A. MONRO *Anat.* 172 The outer surface of the xiphoid bone. **1802** HOME in *Phil. Trans.* XCII. 351 In the Hystrix, there is a xiphoid cartilage. **1847–9** *Todd's Cycl. Anat.* IV. 202/1 [The sternum] is connected.. with a xyphoid appendix. **1848** DUNGLISON *Med. Lex.* (ed. 7), *Xiphoid ligament*.. is a small, very thin, ligamentous fasciculus, which passes from the cartilage.. of the 7th rib to the anterior surface of the xiphoid cartilage. **1873** MIVART *Elem. Anat.* 35 The narrow lower end [of the sternum], which projects freely and remains cartilaginous till late in life, is called the xiphoid process. *Ibid.* 65 In Frogs and Toads we have a middle and xiphoid sternum.

So **xiˈphoidal**, **xiˈphoidan**, **xiˈphoidian** *adjs.*

1653 R. SANDERS *Physiogn.* 276 The brest..extended from the throat to the Diaphragma or Cartilagian Xiphoidan muscle or Midriff, which is round, lying overthwart the lower part of the brest, separating the heart and lights from the stomach. **1860** MAYNE *Expos. Lex.* 1345/2 Xiphoidian. **1904** *Amer. Nat.* Jan. 20 (Osteology of Pygopodes) A pair of flaring external xiphoidal processes, which curve outwards, then inwards.

xiphonite ('zɪfənaɪt). *Min.* [Named from *Xiphonia*, an ancient city in Sicily, where found: see -ITE[1].] A variety of amphibole, occurring in minute light yellow crystals in cavities of a volcanic rock.

1899 DANA *Syst. Min.* App. I. 3 Xiphonite is a name given by G. Platania..to a variety occurring in minute crystals with hematite in cavities of a slag-like rock.

‖**xiphopagus** (zɪ'fɒpəgəs). Pl. **-gi** (-dʒaɪ). [mod.L., f. Gr. ξίφος sword (here referring to the xiphoid cartilage) + πάγος something firmly fixed or set (:πηγνύναι to fix).] A twin monster united by a band extending downwards from the xiphoid cartilage, as in the case of the Siamese twins. Hence **xiphopagic** (zɪfəʊ'pædʒɪk), **xiphopagous** (zɪ'fɒpəgəs) *adjs.*, constituting a xiphopagus.

1848 DUNGLISON *Med. Lex.* (ed. 7), *Xiphopages* [sic]. **1890** BILLINGS *Nat. Med. Dict.*, Xiphorpagus. **1894** BATESON *Variation* 560 *note*, The relative position of xiphopagous twins may result simply from the way in which they happen to be laid by the mother or the midwife. **1901** *Brit. Med. Jrnl.* 6 Apr. 874/2 A new case of xiphopagous twins in two Chinese boys..who are united by a bridge running from the xiphoid cartilage to the umbilicus. **1901** *Lancet* 13 July 108/1 A Case of Xiphopagus or Double Monster. **190.** *Buck's Handbk. Med. Sci.* VII. 685 (Cent. D., Suppl.) Xiphopagic.

xiphosuran (zɪfəʊ'sjʊərən), *a.* and *sb.* *Zool.* [f. mod.L. *Xiphosūra* pl. (irreg. f. Gr. ξίφος sword + οὐρά tail, instead of the correct form *Xiphūra*) + -AN.] **a.** *adj.* Belonging to the order *Xiphosura* of *Arachnida*, including the king-crab (*Limulus*) with a long sharp telson, and the extinct genus *Belinurus*. **b.** *sb.* An arachnid of this order. So **'xiphosure** (= b); **xipho'surous, xi'phurous** *adjs.* (= a).

1837 *Penny Cycl.* IX. 460/1 Latreille..admitted into the class *Crustacea* 12 orders, viz., the Decapods,..the Xyphosures [*sic*], and the Siphonostomes. **1879** H. A. NICHOLSON *Palæont.* (ed. 2) I. xviii. 385 In the Devonian no certain traces of Xiphosurans have yet been detected, but several types occur in the Carboniferous. **1888** ROLLESTON & JACKSON *Anim. Life* 528 A Xiphosuran is found in the upper Silurian.

X-irradi'ation. [f. X (RAYS + IRRADIATION.] **a.** Irradiation with X-rays. **b.** X-rays, X-radiation.

1956 *Nature* 11 Feb. 287/1 A visible coloration is produced upon X-irradiation of the above silver-free base glass. **1962** O. HOCKWIN in A. Pirie *Lens Metabolism Rel. Cataract* 422 The application of a high dose of X-irradiation causes changes of lens metabolism immediately after the end of irradiation. **1964** G. H. HAGGIS et al. *Introd. Molecular Biol.* vii. 196 Chromosome breaks induced during leptotene by X-irradiation should..show up later as injuries to both daughter chromatids. **1976** *Internat. Jrnl. Radiation Biol.* XXIX. 367 X-irradiation..was delivered on four abdominal fields over 15 days.

Hence **X-i'rradiate** *v. trans.*, to irradiate with X-rays; **X-i'rradiated** *ppl. a.*

1958 *Jrnl. Compar. & Physiol. Psychol.* LI. 178 (*heading*) Maze learning in pre- and neonatally X-irradiated rats. **1971** *Nature* 9 Apr. 367/1 The solution was to X-irradiate the haploid sperms of one species. **1978** *Jrnl. Exper. Med.* CXLVIII. 15 Labeling studies in animals X-irradiated with hind-limb shielding gave a Kupffer cell labeling index of 5–10% of the normal values. **1980** *Photochem. & Photobiol.* XXXII. 183 With both treatment regimens, tumor susceptibility could be transferred to X-irradiated recipients with lymphoid cells.

Xmas, common abbreviation in writing of CHRISTMAS: see X 6. Also **Xmassing.**

1551 in E. Lodge *Illustr. Brit. Hist.* (1791) I. 145 From X'temmas next following. *c* **1755** in B. Ward *Hist. St. Edmund's Coll.* (1893) 303 In ye Xmas and Whitsuntide Vacations. **1799** COLERIDGE *Let. to Southey* 24 Dec., My Xstmas Carol is a quaint performance. **1801** —— *Let. to Southey* 31 Dec., On Xmas Day I breakfasted with Davy. **1875** S. G. THOMAS in R. W. Burnie *Mem. & Lett.* (1891) 55 We are not going to have any Xmas festivities or visitors of any kind. **1884** *Punch* 6 Dec. 268/1 He's beginning Xmassing already.

‖**xoanon** ('zəʊənɒn). Pl. **xoana** (-ə). *Gr. Antiq.* [Gr. ξόανον, related to ξύειν to scrape, carve.] A primitive rudely carved image or statue (originally wooden), esp. of a deity.

1706 PHILLIPS (ed. Kersey), *Xoana*, graven Images, Statues carv'd out of Wood or Stone. **1883** *Daily News* 10 May 5/2 This particular xoanon, if we may use that expression in lieu of 'idol'. **1893** W. M. RAMSAY *Church in Roman Empire* vii. 125 The primitive *xoana* of the nursing-mother (Artemis at Ephesus).

xography ('zɒgrəfɪ). [f. X (of unknown significance) + -OGRAPHY.] A photographic process producing images with a three-dimensional effect (see quots.). So **'xograph**, an image of this kind.

1965 R. R. KARCH *Graphic Arts Procedures* (ed. 3) xiii. 336 Xography provides three-dimensional printing which can be seen without benefit of special reading glasses. **1974** *Encycl. Brit. Macropædia* XIV. 1059/1 In the 1960s a three-dimensional print was developed, essentially an illustration bearing two views, superimposed, of the same image taken from slightly different angles, on a transparent mount striped with a multitude of imperceptible parallel strips (Xograph process). **1977** J. HEDGECOE *Photographer's Handbk.* 301 The basis of the xography process is a cylindrical 'lenticular' screen..which is built into the back of the camera just in front of the film plane.

xonotlite (zəʊ'nɒtlaɪt). *Min.* Also **xonaltite.** [First in erron. form *xonaltite*; named (in Ger., *xonaltit*, afterwards *xonotlit*) by Rammelsberg, 1866, 1875, from *Xonotla*, a village in Puebla, Mexico, where found: see -ITE[1].] A hard massive hydrated silicate of calcium.

1868 DANA *Min.* (ed. 5) 397 Xonaltite... Color white to bluish-gray... Occurs at Tetela de Xonalta, Mexico, in concentric layers, with apophyllite and bustamite. **1879** WATTS *Dict. Chem.* VI. 1128 *Xonaltite.* A hydrated calcium silicate, found at Tetela de Xonatla in Mexico. **1883** *Encycl. Brit.* XVI. 420/2 Xonotlite.

X organ. *Zool.* Also **x organ** and with hyphen. [After G. *organ X*, *X-organ* (B. Hanström 1931, in *Zeitschr. f. Morphol. u. Ökol. d. Tiere* XXIII. 200, 202), so called because indicated by the letter X in a diagram published by G. Bellonci 1882, in *Mem. dell' Accad. Sci. dell' Ist. di Bologna* III. 419 ff.] A group of neurosecretory cells in the eye-stalk of some crustaceans, one of the secretions of which inhibits the production of moulting hormone by the Y organ.

1938 [see *sinus gland* s.v. SINUS 6]. **1959** W. ANDREW *Textbk. Compar. Histol.* xiii. 513 There is a definite pathway ..by which the axons of the nerve cells of the x-organ travel to the sinus gland. **1975** *Sci. Amer.* Feb. 74/1 The eyes of crabs are mounted on movable stalks. The stalks also house a neuroendocrine unit called the X-organ sinus-gland complex, which secretes a hormone that causes the pigments to disperse within the chromatophores.

Xosa, var. XHOSA *sb.* and *a.*

xowyn, obs. form of SHOVE *v.*[1]

X-'radiograph. [After X-RAY.] A radiograph made using X-rays. So **X-radi'ography.**

1899 G. B. SHAW *Let.* 12 Apr. in *B. Shaw & Mrs. Campbell* (1952) 11, I have just had an Xradiograph [*sic*] taken; and lo! perfectly mended solid bone. **1948** *Endeavour* VII. 110/2 An X-radiograph [of the picture] made after cleaning revealed the density in the region near the proper right hand. **1961** M. LEVY *Studio Dict. Art Terms* 121 X-radiography. **1963** B. FOZARD *Instrumentation Nucl. Reactors* i. 7 The effect of radiation upon the crystals of silver bromide in a photographic emulsion is well known and the process is used in X- and gamma-radiography. **1975** *Nature* 26 June 697/1 Skeletal X radiography is a powerful tool for studying both modern and fossil corals. **1983** *National Gallery News* Oct. 4/1 This is a long and delicate process which involves..taking X-radiographs of the painting to ascertain its original state.

X-ray ('ɛks reɪ, ɛks 'reɪ). (Also without hyphen.) Also **x-ray.** [Orig. in pl., tr. Ger. *x-strahlen*, the name given by Röntgen to the rays in question, expressing the fact that their essential nature was unknown: cf. X 3.]

I. The pl. form *X-rays.* **1.** A form of radiation discovered by Prof. W. C. Röntgen of Würzburg in 1895, capable of passing in various degrees through many substances impervious to light, and of affecting a sensitized plate and thus producing shadow-photographs of objects inclosed within opaque receptacles or bodies, e.g. of the bones, or a bullet or other foreign body, within the flesh of a living person or animal; they also produce fluorescence, phosphorescence, and electrical effects, and have a curative operation in certain skin diseases; much used in modern surgical and medical practice. Now known to be a form of electromagnetic radiation of wavelength less than that of short-wave ultraviolet light (i.e. less than about 4 to 40 nm). Also called *Roentgen rays* (see ROENTGEN *sb.*[1] 1).

X-rays are often defined as being produced by deceleration of charged particles (esp. electrons) or by electron transitions in atoms, in contrast to the otherwise similar *gamma rays* which arise from radioactive decay of nuclei. Since gamma rays tend to be of shorter wavelength than most X-rays, they have been classified variously either as very short X-rays, or as constituting a separate class of very short wavelengths beyond X-rays. Cf. *gamma rays* s.v. GAMMA 1 c (ii).

1896 *Nature* 23 Jan. 274/1 (Röntgen in *Sitzungsberichte der Würzburger Phys.-Med. Gesellschaft* 1896, 133 tr. by A. Stanton) A piece of sheet aluminium, 15 mm. thick.. allowed the X-rays (as I will call the rays for the sake of brevity) to pass, but greatly reduced the fluorescence. **1897** *Allbutt's Syst. Med.* III. 362 Skiagraphs taken by means of the X Röntgen rays. **1899** *Ibid.* VI. 408 The application of the X rays to the diagnosis of internal aneurisms. *Ibid.* VIII. 717 The injury produced by the X rays of Röntgen. **1930** [see *gamma rays* s.v. GAMMA 1 c (ii)]. **1948** *Sci. News* VII. 35 Procedure for the generation of x-rays..is to accelerate a beam of electrons to the required energy, and then stop it by allowing the electrons to hit a metal target. **1958** CONDON & ODISHAW *Handbk. Physics* VII. viii. 118/2 Although there is no precise definition of the high-energy limit of the energy of quanta called X rays, this term is usually restricted to radiations of fewer than several million electron volts of energy, above which the radiation is referred to as γ radiation. **1971** D. W. SCIAMA *Mod. Cosmol.* ii. 31 The distinction between X- and γ-rays is a somewhat arbitrary one, but..we may take the dividing line to be an energy of 100 keV. **1983** *Oxf. Textbk. Med.* I. VI. 86/1 Gamma-rays. These are identical in properties to X-rays but are produced by the spontaneous disintegration of radioactive atoms.

II. The sing. form *X-ray.*

2. (An) examination of a person in which an X-ray picture is taken.

1933 V. BRITTAIN *Testament of Youth* viii. 409 Ten patients..were for immediate operation; a dozen more were for X-ray; several were likely to hæmorrhage at any moment. **1960** 'R. GORDON' *Doctor in Clover* vi. 47, I popped her in a taxi and drove her round to the casualty entrance at St Swithin's, where Miles organised X-rays. **1983** *Daily Tel.* 13 Oct. 18, I injured my back..and after a great deal of pain and misery I had an X-ray.

3. = X-RADIOGRAPH.

1934 in WEBSTER. **1942** M. DICKENS *One Pair of Feet* viii. 164 Siddons was subjected to all the indignities and discomforts of gastric investigation... X-ray after X-ray was taken and various different diets tried. **1957** 'R. GORDON' *Doctor in Love* xii. 107, I had a difficult x-ray which I thought she could help me interpret. **1969** *Ithaca Jrnl.* 27 Nov. 30 Some doctors try to head off possible litigation by ordering unnecessary and expensive x-rays. **1977** *Daily Tel.* 2 Mar. 19/5 It was not known when Miss Doris Hunt..swallowed the spoon, first seen on an X-ray last year.

4. (Without article.) An X-ray department in a hospital.

1955 'R. GORDON' *Doctor at Large* xiv. 143 Apart from the nurses, there were the buxom dieticians, the cheerful girls in X-ray, the neat secretaries, [etc.]. **1974** 'H. CARMICHAEL' *Motive* x. 116 Dr Egan had gone to X-ray but would be back soon. **1978** J. IRVING *World according to Garp* ii. 28 Her books..outgrew the shelf space and slid into the main infirmary..and into X-ray.

III. *attrib.* and *Comb.* (in sing. form '*X-ray*).

5. a. *gen.*

1896 *Boston Med. & Surg. Jrnl.* CXXXV. 610/2, I am.. nursing an X-ray finger. **1897** *Westm. Gaz.* 2 July 2/3 Radiations which have the X-ray-like property of passing through so-called opaque substances. **1899** *Allbutt's Syst. Med.* VI. 408 Aneurysms of the thoracic aorta can sometimes be detected earlier by X ray examination. **1907** *Westm. Gaz.* 21 Sept. 8/3 Another X-ray photograph..of a girl's wrist and hand, showing the thickening of the bone brought on by rheumatism. **1908** *Daily Chron.* 29 June 1/5 Dr. Hall Edwards, whose heroic fight against the inroads of X ray dermatitis has been compassionately followed by the King and public.

b. Applied to instruments and techniques using or producing X-rays, as ***X-ray analysis***, ***microscope***, ***microscopy***, ***spectrograph***, ***spectrometer***, ***spectroscopy*** (hence ***X-ray spectroscopic***), ***telescope***; **X-ray astronomy**, the branch of astronomy concerned with the X-ray emissions of heavenly bodies; so **X-ray astronomer.**

1924 *Econ. Geol.* XIX. 1 Physicists have developed X-ray analysis in recent years to such a point that the internal structure of any opaque crystalline substance can be determined. **1980** P. LUGER *Mod. X-Ray Analysis* vi. 288 The method which has been used from the earliest days of X-ray analysis is the drawing of contours obtained from the electron density map. **1969** *Times* 13 May 14/1 X-ray astronomers have to use rockets or balloons to carry their instruments above as much of the atmosphere as possible. **1982** *Jrnl. Brit. Interplanetary Soc.* XXXV. 291 Coded aperture techniques have been employed to great advantage by X-ray astronomers. **1963** *Daily Tel.* 6 June 21 The first news was given today by the United States at the International Space Research meeting in Warsaw of a new kind of astonomy, X-ray astronomy. **1964** *Space Res.* IV. 966 (*heading*) X-ray astronomy. **1970** *Sci. Jrnl.* May 17/4 It is some years since the accidental discovery of the X-ray source Sco X-1 ushered in the new field of X-ray astronomy. **1979** *Jrnl. R. Soc. Arts* CXXVII. 580/2 X-ray astronomy took its first real spurt forward in 1970 with the launch of NASA's small 'Uhuru' X-ray satellite. **1948** *Jrnl. Optical Soc. Amer.* XXXVIII. 774/1 It is clear that an x-ray microscope is now a definite possibility. *Ibid.* 766/1 A satisfactory x-ray microscopy would open up fields of investigation closed to the optical microscope because of its limited resolution. **1966** *McGraw-Hill Encycl. Sci. & Technol.* VIII. 368*b*/1 The x-ray microscopes used in microradiography utilize x-radiation to form images of resolution in the 0·2–2·0 micron..range. *Ibid.*, With this method, x-ray microscopy has not only become competitive with direct light microscopy in resolving power but has gained important advantages. **1981** *Rev. Sci. Instruments* LII. 211/2 The construction of a photoelectron x-ray microscope appears to be feasible and, moreover, this instrument should fairly fulfill the requirements demanded for the extension of x-ray microscopy. **1925** G. A. LINDSAY tr. *M. Siegbahn's Spectrosc. X-Rays* iv. 92 The evidence essential for a better answer to these questions was afforded by X-ray spectrographs and Röntgen tubes with hot cathodes. **1983** *IEEE Trans. Nucl. Sci.* XXX. 491 (*heading*) High throughput non-dispersive hard X-ray spectrograph. [*Note*] 'Spectrograph' and 'spectrometer' are used interchangeably in this paper. **1915** W. H. & W. L. BRAGG *X Rays & Crystal Structure* iii. 22 The X-ray spectrometer has already determined both the absolute wave lengths of various types of X-radiation and the arrangement of the atoms in several crystals. **1955** *Sci. News Let.* 23 July 1 The electronic assayer is known as an X-ray spectrometer, and the technique, which can be applied to most minerals, is called fluorescent X-ray analysis. **1977** A. HALLAM *Planet*

Earth 18/1 The X-ray spectrometer mapped aluminium:silicon ratios and delineated the extent of the aluminous highlands. **1925** G. A. LINDSAY tr. *M. Siegbahn's Spectrosc. X-Rays* iii. 33 In order to meet such demands of X-ray spectroscopic work, the firm of Emil Gundelach..has constructed tubes embodying a slight modification. *Ibid.* 52 This rotating crystal method was first employed in X-ray spectroscopy by de Broglie. **1966** J. G. BROWN *X-Rays & their Applic.* vii. 124 The methods of X-ray spectroscopy which depend on crystal diffraction are essentially methods of measuring the Bragg angle. **1983** *Jrnl. Physics B* XVI. L77 *(heading)* The determination of parameters of recombining laser-producing plasmas by means of x-ray spectroscopy. *Ibid.*, Among the various methods of plasma diagnostics the most preferable in this case are the x-ray spectroscopic methods. **1963** *Daily Tel.* 6 June 21/4 The X-ray telescope has to be raised above the earth's atmosphere and a technique found for focusing X-rays. **1978** PASACHOFF & KUTNER *University Astron.* xii. 333 It still looks as though Cygnus X-1 represents the first observational detection of a black hole. The new generation of x-ray telescopes should tell us more.

c. Applied to astronomical bodies that emit X-rays in detectable or significant quantities, as ***X-ray nova, pulsar, star***; **X-ray burster**, a cosmic source of intermittent, short-lived, powerful bursts of X-rays, typically lasting about a second.

1976 *Nature* 17 June 542/1 This object..is perhaps the most enigmatic 'X-ray burster' found to date. **1978** PASACHOFF & KUTNER *University Astron.* xxv. 632 *(caption)* Half a dozen of the strong x-ray sources in the galactic bulge region have been possibly identified with x-ray bursters. **1970** *Sci. Jrnl.* Apr. 64 The second example of an 'X-ray nova' was reported during the summer of 1969, based on observations from two US Vela satellites built to monitor man-made nuclear explosions in space. **1977** *Dædalus* Fall 53 One particular kind of variable X-ray stars are the *transient sources*, sometimes called X-ray novae. **1969** G. FRITZ et al. in *Science* 9 May 709/1 We wish to report the discovery of an x-ray pulsar in the general direction of the Crab Nebula. The data were obtained during an Aerobee rocket flight on 13 March 1969. **1978** PASACHOFF & KUTNER *University Astron.* xi. 315 *(caption)* The x-ray pulsar SMC X-1 in the Small Magellanic Cloud has a period of 0·716 sec. **1964** *Daily Tel.* 31 Mar. 17/1 Evidence of the existence of a previously unknown kind of star has been collected by American astronomers. Using an Aerobee rocket..they found two distinct 'X-ray stars'. **1977** *Sci. Amer.* Oct. 42/2 One can say with considerable certainty that X-ray stars are dense remnants of stars that have exhausted their supply of nuclear energy and have collapsed under the attractive force of their own gravity.

d. Used *attrib.* with reference to primitive pictures in which some representation is given of the insides of people and animals.

1940 L. ADAM *Primitive Art* xiv. 119 Characteristic of the northern territory are the so-called 'X-ray' drawings—a special variety of naturalistic art..whereby the artist, when drawing human beings and animals, represents the inner parts of the body. **1956** C. P. MOUNTFORD *Rec. Amer.-Austral. Scientific Exped. Arnhem Land* I. iii. 112 Nor do the subjects of the X-ray artists show any movement. It is essentially a static art. **1959** E. A. FISHER *Anglo-Saxon Archit. & Sculpture* 88 Still earlier in really primitive art, and among some primitive races today, the same idea of showing the inside, the backbone, ribs and internal organs.. is found, e.g. in the so-called X-ray drawings of some of the natives of the Melanesian area of the Pacific. **1977** G. CLARK *World Prehist.* (ed. 3) xi. 479 The X-ray figures of Arnhem Land..may well reflect exotic influences.

6. Special Combs.: **X-ray crystallography**, the study of crystals and their structure by means of X-ray diffraction techniques; hence **X-ray crystallographer**; **X-ray dermatitis**, dermatitis caused by X-rays; **X-ray diffraction**, the diffraction of X-rays by the regularly spaced atoms of a crystalline material, esp. as a technique of X-ray crystallography; **X-ray eyes**, the apparent ability to see beyond an outward form or through opaque material; very acute discernment; also, ***X-ray scrutiny***; **X-ray spectrum**, a graph of intensity against wavelength or frequency for the X-rays absorbed or emitted by a material; **X-ray tube**, an electron tube for generating X-rays by accelerating the electrons to high energies and causing them to strike a target that is also the anode, producing the X-rays.

1962 *Listener* 10 May 809/1 Botanists or X-ray crystallographers. **1971** J. W. JEFFERY *Methods X-Ray Crystallogr.* p. v, When one is generation 3..of X-ray crystallographers, one cannot expect to do much direct quarrying in that famous paper whose product, the Bernal chart, is known to every crystallographer. **1930** R. W. JAMES *X-Ray Crystallogr.* i. 2 X-ray crystallography is descended from, and constantly uses, the results of the older crystallography. **1968** M. PYKE *Food & Society* vii. 101 A few milligrams of vitamin B_{12} had been isolated and the nature of its complex molecule established by a combination of advanced organic chemistry and X-ray crystallography. **1977** R. S. DRAGO *Physical Methods in Chem.* xvii. 589 Using X-ray crystallography, one can generally determine the precise composition and atomic arrangement of almost any molecule. **1900** *Philadelphia Med. Jrnl.* V. 187 The believers in the electrical cause of x-ray dermatitis are found to be exclusively physicians. **1908** [sense 5 a]. **1959** *Med. Jrnl. Australia* I. 290/1 In November, 1897, Sylvanus Thompson described X-ray dermatitis, and in the following year the Röntgen Society set up a committee to investigate possible hazards. **1977** *Acta Dermato-Venereologica* LVII. 487/1 The fluid from spontaneous blisters in 15 patients with various bullous dermatoses, such as..X-ray dermatitis, all contained measurable amounts of activity. **1924** *Econ. Geol.* XIX. 15 A complete description of X-ray diffraction has been given by the Braggs. **1950** *Sci. News* XV. 139 The techniques of X-ray diffraction, which have contributed so much to the understanding of the inner structure of metals and alloys. **1969** *Times* 28 Jan. 6/6 X-ray diffraction techniques..show that the orientation of the graphite crystals in the fibre depends on the degree to which it is stretched during the heat treatment. **1982** R. M. SCHULTZ in T. M. Devlin *Textbk. Biochem.* ii. 73 The most important of the techniques for the study of a protein's secondary, tertiary, and quaternary structure is x-ray diffraction. **1939** M. ALLINGHAM *Mr. Campion & Others* ii. 36 The conviction that he had actually encountered a man with X-ray eyes at last. **1971** 'R. MACDONALD' *Underground Man* xxvi. 186 I've been feeling watched, tonight. Drawing the curtains doesn't really help. Whatever it is out there has X-ray eyes. Call it God, or call it the Devil, it hardly matters. **1976** J. WAINWRIGHT *Who goes Next?* 205 He didn't have X-ray eyes. He couldn't see through the sides of a parked van. **1982** M. MILLAR *Mermaid* vi. 68, I got X-ray eyes when it comes to people's weaknesses. **1899** G. ALLEN *Miss Cayley's Adventures* ii. 45 She looked me through and through again with her X-ray scrutiny. **1925** G. A. LINDSAY tr. *M. Siegbahn's Spectrosc. X-Rays* vi. 150 The X-ray spectrum is an atomic property... The frequencies involved in X-ray spectra are very great. **1983** *Jrnl. Physics B* XVI. L79 The large dimension of the spectrograph slit..allowed us to observe the x-ray spectra of H- and He-like F VIII and F IX ions. **1896** *Nature* 12 Nov. 31/2 Unexplained variations in the behaviour of the X-ray tubes. **1974** *Encycl. Brit. Macropædia* XIV. 345/1 Small gamma-ray sources are placed in areas inaccessible to X-ray tubes such as inside pipelines.

Hence **X-ray** ('ɛks,reɪ, older ɛks'reɪ) *v.*, *trans.* to examine or treat with X-rays; also *fig.*; hence **X-rayed** ('ɛks-) *ppl. a.*, **X-raying** ('ɛks-) *vbl. sb.* So **X-radi'ation**.

1896 *Strand* July 108/1 If a solid object is placed in the path of this stream..it may become the seat of the production of that which is..variously known as Röntgen radiation or X-radiation. **1899** *Bristol Med.-Chir. Jrnl.* XVII. 234 Cases that have to be X-rayed in their bedrooms. **1900** *Lancet* 17 Feb. 488/2 The patient's chest had been x-rayed, but the position of the bullet could not be localised. **1902** *Brit. Med. Jrnl.* 12 Apr. 894/2 The child was x rayed, and a large nail was seen. **1915** E. RUTHERFORD in *Nature* 9 Sept. 33/2 To examine the quantity and quality of the X-radiation scattered from crystals at different angles. **1920** *Glasgow Herald* 5 Oct. 7/2 Advantage is claimed for 'X-raying' over sterilization. **1941** *Cold Spring Harbor Symp. Quantitative Biol.* IX. 156/1 X-rayed Bar-M2 males (4000r) were crossed to females with the genes scute vermilion forked and carnation. **1973** *Sci. Amer.* Apr. 30/3 The only way to 'X ray' the earth for such fine structure is to use short-period seismic waves that interact with the boundary of the core. **1974** *Physics Bull.* Dec. 581/2 The developing use of synchrotrons as an intense source of x radiation. **1977** W. MARSHALL *Thin Air* i. 6 It took two hours for the poor old Japs to even clear body search... Let alone the X-raying of freight and luggage. **1977** *Time* 22 Aug. 30/3 The treaty will have to be X-rayed by the university. **1977** *New Yorker* 26 Sept. 43/3 She..could feel the plaster armoring his X-rayed ribs. **1980** J. O'FAOLAIN *No Country for Young Men* v. 102 The men were terrifying. She remembered their eyes X-raying her clothes.

X(s)tmas: see XMAS.

Xtal, xtal ('krɪstəl). [Cf. X 10.] Abbrev. of CRYSTAL *sb.* and *a.*

1957 *Practical Wireless* XXXIII. 454/1 Remove Xtal unit by cutting off all leads at the source. **1971** *Gramophone* July 257/2 The crystal pickup button is labelled 'xtal' which is engineer's shorthand.

xul, xuld(e, xwld: see SHALL *v.*

†**xylaloe(s, xyloaloe(s.** *Obs.* Forms: 6 xiloaloes, 6 (8) xyloaloe, 7 xylaloës, 7–8 (in Dicts.) xyloaloes. [a. late Gr. ξυλαλόη, f. ξύλον wood + ἀλόη ALOE. Cf. obs. F. *xilaloë* (Cotgr.).] = LIGN-ALOES, ALOE 1. Also *attrib.*

1545 RAYNOLD *Byrth Mankynde* 114 Wasshe them..with wyne, in the whiche is..soden myntes, roses, violettes, and xiloaloes. **1599** A. M. tr. *Gabelhouer's Bk. Physicke* 7/2 Take Xyloaloe woode j. G. *Ibid.* 11/2 Suger of Candy, xyloaloe, Cloves, Ginger. **1683** MORRISON tr. *Struys' Voy.* I. vi. 38 An Oyntment made of Xylaloës, or, wood of Aloës.

xylan ('zaɪlæn). *Chem.* [f. Gr. ξύλον wood + -AN.] A gelatinous compound contained in wood, also called *tree-gum, wood-gum.*

1894 MUIR & MORLEY *Watts' Dict. Chem.* IV. 868/1.

xylary ('zaɪlərɪ), *a. Bot.* [f. XYL(EM + -ARY[2].] Of, pertaining to, or constituting xylem.

1953 K. ESAU *Plant Anat.* xv. 367 The terms phloic procambium and xylary procambium..may be used to stress the early differentiation of the meristem into the two parts. **1973** *Nature* 13 Apr. 479/2 Between 2000 h and 2400 h the developing xylary tissues will rapidly withdraw water from the immediately adjacent developing phloem tissues.

xylate ('zaɪleɪt). *Chem.* [f. XYL-IC + -ATE[4].] A salt of xylic acid.

1873 WATTS *Fownes' Chem.* (ed. 11) 818. **1879** —— *Dict. Chem.* VI. 1130 Calcium salts, which may be separated by their different solubility in water, the xylate being more soluble than the paraxylate.

xylem ('zaɪlɛm). *Bot.* [mod. (Nägeli in Ger.) f. Gr. ξύλον wood: cf. PHLOEM.] Collective name for the cells, vessels, and fibres forming the harder portion of the fibrovascular tissue; the wood, as a tissue of the plant-body. Also *attrib.*

1875 BENNETT & DYER tr. *Sachs' Bot.* 94 The different forms of tissue of a differentiated fibro-vascular bundle may be classified into two groups, which Nägeli calls the *Phloëm*-(Bast) and *Xylem*- (Wood) portion of the bundle... The xylem-portion of the fibro-vascular bundle has mostly a strong tendency to thicken its cell-forms. *Ibid.* 95 These horizontal elements..may be..designated as rays; within the xylem they are called xylem-rays, within the phloëm, phloëm-rays. **1894** D. H. SCOTT *Struct. Bot.* I. *Flowering Pl.* 56 The woody character of the cell-walls of the xylem is due to the presence of a substance called lignine.

xylene ('zaɪliːn). *Chem.* [f. Gr. ξύλον wood + -ENE.] A mixture of three isomeric hydrocarbons having the formula C_8H_{10} = $C_6H_4(CH_3)_2$, obtained as a volatile colourless liquid from wood-spirit or coal-naphtha; any one of these three hydrocarbons: systematically named *dimethylbenzene*. Also *attrib.* (Also called XYLOL, q.v.)

1851 *Jrnl. Chem. Soc.* III. 184 Xylol or Xylene. **1859** WATTS tr. *Gmelin's Hand-bk. Chem.* XIII. 116 Xylene series... Primary Nucleus $C^{16}H^{10}$. Xylol $C^{16}H^{10}$. **1885** REMSEN *Org. Chem.* (1888) 241 Coal-tar xylene consists of three isomeric hydrocarbons..known as *ortho-xylene, meta-xylene,* and *para-xylene.*

Hence **xy'lenic** *a.*, **xylenol** ('zaɪlɪnɒl), **'xylenyl, xyle'nylamine**: see quots.

1868 WATTS *Dict. Chem.* V. 1059 *Xylenyl.* Syn. with *Xylyl. Ibid.*, *Xylenylamine.* Syn. with *Xylidine.* **1872** *Jrnl. Chem. Soc.* New Ser. X. 482 Liquid Xylenol is a colourless, highly refracting fluid, smelling strongly of phenol. **1873** WATTS *Fownes' Chem.* (ed. 11) 798 Xylenol is produced by fusing the potassium salt of xylyl sulphurous acid with potassium hydrate. **1879** —— *Dict. Chem.* VI. 1128 *Xylenol.* $C^8H^{10}O$ = $C^6H^3(CH^3)^2OH$. Dimethyl-phenol, Xenol, Xylylic phenol. *Ibid.* 1129 Solid xylenol dissolves abundantly in alcohol and ether... Liquid xylenol is colourless and strongly refractive. **1894** MUIR & MORLEY *Watts' Dict. Chem.* IV. 871/2 *Xylenic alcohol* is tolyl-carbinol.

xylic ('zaɪlɪk), *a. Chem.* [f. XYL-ENE + -IC.] *xylic acid*: dimethylbenzoic acid, $C_9H_{10}O_2$, also called XYLYLIC *acid* (see quots.).

1872 [see XYLIDIC]. **1873** WATTS *Fownes' Chem.* (ed. 11) 817 Xylic and Paraxylic..acid. **1879** —— *Dict. Chem.* VI. 1129 *Xylic* or *xylylic acid.* $C^9H^{10}O^2$ = $C^6H^3(CH^3)^2.CO^2H$. Two modifications of this acid, distinguished as *xylic* and *paraxylic*, are formed, together with xylidic acid..by oxidising pseudocumene..with dilute nitric acid..at the boiling heat.

xylidic (zaɪ'lɪdɪk), *a. Chem.* [f. XYL-IC + -ID[4] + -IC.] *xylidic acid*: either of two isomeric substances obtained by the oxidation of xylic and paraxylic acids: see quot. Hence **xylidate** ('zaɪlɪdeɪt) [-ATE[4]], a salt of xylidic acid.

1872 WATTS *Dict. Chem.* Suppl. 1130 *Xylidic acid.* $C^9H^8O^4$... This bibasic acid..is formed..by the oxidation of xylic or paraxylic acid. *Ibid.*, *Calcium xylidate*, $C^9H^6O^4Ca$, forms indistinct white scales, very soluble in water.

xylidine ('zaɪlɪdaɪn). *Chem.* [f. XYL-ENE or XYL-IC + -ID[4] + -INE[5].] **a.** An amine-derivative of xylene, homologous with aniline, occurring in several isomeric modifications having the formula $C_6H_3(CH_3)_2NH_2$; used in the preparation of artificial dyes. Called also **xy'lidamine. b.** = XYLOIDIN.

1850 *Jrnl. Chem. Soc.* III. 184 Mononitroxylol, when dissolved in alcohol, and treated with hydrosulphate of ammonia, yields a base analogous to toluidine; it may be called *Xylidine.* **1868** WATTS *Dict. Chem.* V. 1059 Xylidine is a colourless liquid, heavier than water.

xylite ('zaɪlaɪt). [ad. G. *xylit*, f. Gr. ξύλον wood: see -ITE[1].]

1. *Chem.* A volatile liquid obtained from wood-spirit, also called LIGNONE. Also *attrib.*

1843 *Penny Cycl.* XXVII. 634/2 With acids xylite..gives rise to xylitic acid, xylite naphtha, xylite resin, and xylite oil. **1855** WATTS tr. *Gmelin's Hand-bk. Chem.* IX. 48 Xylite-oil. $C^{12}H^9O$. Produced by the action of oil of vitriol, hydrate of potash, or potasium on lignone.

2. *Min.* An impure silicate of iron, occurring in brown fibrous masses resembling asbestos or 'mountain wood'.

1850 ANSTED *Elem. Geol., Min.* etc. §460 Hisingerite is another silicate of iron, and with it are associated.. Stilpnomelane, Chloropal,..Xylite. **1868** WATTS *Dict. Chem.* V. 1059 *Xylite.* This name is given by Hermann.. to a mineral..forming finely fibrous masses resembling mountain-wood.

Hence **xylitic** (zaɪ'lɪtɪk) *a. Chem.*, applied to compounds derived from xylite (sense 1): see quots.

1843 [see sense 1 above]. **1852** W. GREGORY *Handbk. Org. Chem.* 393 An excess of potash causes the formation of three products: xylitic naphtha, $C_{12}H_{12}O_3$; xylitic oil, $C_{12}H_9O$; and xylitic resin, C_8H_6O.

xylitol ('zaɪlɪtɒl). *Chem.* [ad. G. *xylit* (Fischer & Stahel 1891, in *Ber. d. Deut. Chem. Ges.* XXIV. 538), f. *xyl-ose* XYLOSE + *-it*, -ITE[1]: see -OL.] A sweet, crystalline, pentahydric alcohol, $CH_2OH(CHOH)_3CH_2OH$, derived from xylose and present in some plant tissues.

1891 *Jrnl. Chem. Soc.* LX. I. 668 Xylose yields a new compound, xylitol, which forms a non-crystallisable syrup. **1962** R. VAN HEYNINGEN in A. Pirie *Lens Metabolism Rel. Cataract* 402 The lens is the only mammalian tissue in which xylitol has been found. **1977** *Daily Colonist* (Victoria, B.C.) 1 Dec. 11/1 A storm of adverse publicity over the natural sweetener xylitol isn't going to deter major chewing gum manufacturers from marketing products containing the substance.

xylo ('zaɪləʊ). Colloq. abbrev. of XYLONITE.

1926 *Ironmonger* 16 Jan. (Suppl.) 50 (Advt.), This knife is made of stainless steel in four qualities with wood, xylo and ebonite handles. **1962** L. S. SASIENI *Optical Dispensing* ix. 218 Run the thumb-nail round between the xylo and the metal.

xylo- ('zaɪləʊ), before a vowel **xyl-**, repr. Gr. *ξυλο-, ξυλ-*, comb. form of *ξύλον* wood: the first element of various scientific and technical words, the more important of which see in their alphabetical places. **'xylochlore** (-klɔə(r)) *Min.* [ad. G. *xylochlor* (von Waltershausen, 1853), f. Gr. *χλωρός* green], an altered form of apophyllite, found in olive-green crystals in a fossil tree-stem in a volcanic rock in Iceland. **xylo'chloric** (-'chloeric) *a. Chem.* [ad. F. *xylochlorique*, *-chloérique*, f. Gr. *χλοερός* = *χλωρός* green], in *x. acid*: see quots. **'xylochrome** (-krəʊm) *Chem.* [Gr. *χρῶμα* colour], a colouring matter produced by chemical alteration of decayed wood. **xylocopid** (zaɪ'lɒkəpɪd), *a. Entom.* [mod.L. *Xylocopa*; Gr. *-κοπος* cutting, -ID[3]], belonging or related to the genus *Xylocopa*, comprising the carpenter-bees. **xylocryptite** (-'krɪptaɪt) *Min.* [Gr. *κρυπτός* hidden: see -ITE[1]]: see quots. **'xylolite**, *Min.* [-LITE]: see quot. **xylophilan** (-'ɒfɪlən) *Entom.* [Gr. *φίλος* loving: cf. -PHIL], *a.* belonging to the group *Xylophili* of beetles, which live in decayed wood; *sb.* a beetle of this group; so **xy'lophilous** *a.*, living or growing in or on wood, as an insect or a fungus. **xy'lopolist** *rare*$^{-0}$ [Gr. *ξυλοπώλης*], a timber-merchant. **xylopyrography** (-paɪ'rɒgrəfɪ) [Gr. *πῦρ* fire, -GRAPHY] = POKER-WORK. **xyloretin** (-'riːtɪn), **-retinite** (-'rɛtɪnaɪt) *Chem.* [G. *xyloretin* (Forchhammer, 1840), Gr. *ῥητίνη* resin], a white crystalline resin obtained from fossil pinewood. ‖**xylo'stroma** *Bot.* [mod.L., f. Gr. *στρῶμα* something spread out, a bed, coverlet], the mycelium of certain polyporoid fungi (originally supposed a distinct genus) which forms a dense leathery sheet on the surface of wood; hence **xylo'stromatoid** *a.* [-OID], resembling a xylostroma. **xylotherapy** (-'θɛrəpɪ) *Med.* [Gr. *θεραπεία* healing], the use of certain kinds of wood in the cure of disease (see quot.). **'xylotile** (-taɪl), **-til** (-tɪl) *Min.* [G. *xylotil*; Gr. *τίλος* down, fine hair], a mineral allied to (or a variety of) asbestos, also called *mountain-wood*. **xylotomous** (-'ɒtəməs) *a.* [Gr. *-τομος* cutting], that cuts or pierces wood, as an insect. **xylotypographic** (-taɪpəʊ'græfɪk) *a.* [TYPOGRAPHIC], printed from wooden blocks or types. **'xylulose** *Chem.* [-ULOSE[2]], a keto pentose that corresponds to the aldo pentose xylose and occurs in the urine of pentosurics.

1868 WATTS *Dict. Chem.* V. 1060 **Xylochlore*... Kenngott ..has shown that it is an altered form of apophyllite. **1862** —— tr. *Gmelin's Hand-bk. Chem.* XV. 534 *Xylochloric acid. $C^{30}H^{26}O^{34}$?.. A green colouring matter, which sometimes forms on decayed pieces of wood. **1868** —— *Dict. Chem.* V. 1060 *Xylochloeric acid*, a term applied by Fordos ..to the green colouring-matter of decayed wood, which may be extracted by chloroform. **1898** H. C. PORTER tr. *Strasburger's Text.-Bk. Bot.* 124 The tannins impart to the dead wood a distinct colour, often very characteristic, especially when it has been transformed into wood dyes, or so-called *xylochrome. **1904** *Athenæum* 24 Dec. 881/1 A photograph..showing the *Xylocopid model and its Asilid mimic. **1820** *Q. Jrnl. Sci. Lit. & Arts* VIII. 352 It may be named provisionally *Xylocryptite, expressive of its being hidden in fossil wood. **1868** WATTS *Dict. Chem.* V. 1060 *Xylocryptite*, a mineral apparently related to Scheererite, occurring in yellow waxy crystalline particles on lignite. (Becquerel.) *Ibid.* 1061 **Xylolite*. Syn. with mountain-wood, or ligniform asbestos. **1842** BRANDE *Dict. Sci.*, etc., **Xylophilans*,..the name of a tribe of beetles, consisting of those which live on decayed wood. **1862** MAYNE *Med. Vocab.* (ed. 2), *Xylophilus*..growing upon, or living in decayed wood; *xylophilous. **1656** BLOUNT *Glossogr.*, **Xylopolist*..a Woodmonger. **1850** OGILVIE, *Xylopyrography. **1901** *Daily Chron.* 27 May 6/1 [Baron Auer's] father was..an inventor in typography and xylopyrography. **1852** W. GREGORY *Handbk. Org. Chem.* 417 Tekoretine, Phylloretine, *Xyloretine, and Boloretine, are the names of four resinous compounds, found in the peat of Denmark, on the remains of pine-trees. **1868** DANA *Min.* (ed. 5) 743 *Xyloretinite was derived by Forchhammer through the action of alcohol on fossil pine-wood from the marshes of Holtegaard in Denmark. **1871** COOKE *Handbk. Brit. Fungi* I. 282 Polyporus vitreus... 'Glassy Polyporus.' .. Distinguished by its distinct *xylostromatoid substratum, which separates easily from the matrix. **1880** *Boston Jrnl. Chem.* Dec. 144 At a recent meeting of the Société de Thérapeutique M. Dujardin-Beaumetz read for M. Jourdanis a note on the æsthesiogenic properties of certain woods applied to the skin, which he calls *xylotherapy. M. Jourdanis has applied plates of wood to the insensible skin, and as with plates of metal, magnets,.. and blisters has obtained a return of sensibility. **1864** WEBSTER, *Xylotile. **1868** DANA *Min.* (ed. 5) 406 Xylotile.. is probably only an altered asbestus. It occurs delicately fibrous;..wood-brown, light or dark, and also green in color. **1872** W. SKEEN *Early Typogr.* 417 The *xylotypographic text. **1936** LEVENE & TIPSON in *Jrnl. Biol. Chem.* CXV. 731 For simplicity it would seem desirable to term the ketose '*d*-*xylulose', in conformity with the nomenclature accepted for other keto sugars. **1964**, **1968** [see PENTOSURIC *a.* and *sb.*]. **1974** B. S. HARTLEY in Carlile & Skehel *Evolution in Microbial World* 170 A mutant of this organism constitutive for ribitol dehydrogenase grows on xylitol by utilising a side specificity of this enzyme to produce xylulose.

‖**xylobalsamum** (zaɪləʊ'bælsəməm). Also 7 in anglicized form **xylobalsame**. [L. (Pliny), ad. Gr. *ξυλοβάλσαμον*: see XYLO- and BALSAM, BALM. Cf. F. *xylobalsame*, †*xilo-* (Cotgr.).] The fragrant wood of the tree *Balsamodendron gileadense*, which yields the resin called OPOBALSAMUM or Balm of Gilead.

[**1398** TREVISA *Barth. De P.R.* XVII. xviii. (Bodl. MS.) lf. 194 b/1 Balsamum is a tree..liche to a vyne..þe tre hatte Balsamum and þe stokke Xilobalsamum and the frute and þe sede Carpobalsamum and iuse Opobalsamum.] **1616** BULLOKAR *Eng. Expos.*, *Xylobalsamum*, a sweet wood out of which balme droppeth. **1728** CHAMBERS *Cycl.*, *Xylo-Balsamum*, a Name which Naturalists, &c. give to the Wood of the Tree which yields that precious Gum known to the Latins by the Name of *Opo-Balsamum*, and among us by the Name of *Balm of Gilead*... The *Xylo-balsamum* is reputed good to strengthen the Brain, and Stomach. **1868** WATTS *Dict. Chem.* V. 1060 *Xylobalsamum*, the commercial name of the odoriferous wood of *Amyris gileadensis*, which yields Mecca balsam.

xylocaine ('zaɪləʊkeɪn). *Pharm.* [f. XYLO- + *-caine*, after COCAINE.] = LIGNOCAINE.

1946 LÖFGREN & LUNDQVIST in *Svensk Kemisk. Tidskrift* LVIII. 208 The compound *ω*-diethylamino-2, 6-dimethylacetanilide is called xylocaine (LL 30) and is an ideal local anaesthetic, which seems to be superior to procaine in every respect. **1954** [see LIGNOCAINE]. **1961** *Times* 4 Feb. 12/2, I injected a total of 30 c.c. of xylocaine. **1978** *Jrnl. R. Soc. Med.* LXXI. 320/1 Shortening the duration of the convulsive activity in the brain by administering xylocaine before the inducing shock does reduce the therapeutic effects.

†**xylo'cassia**. *Obs.* Also 6 **xilo-**. [late L., ad. Gr. *ξυλοκασ(σ)ία* (Dioscorides): see XYLO- and CASSIA.] = CASSIA[1] 1 (cf. 1 b).

1555 EDEN *Decades* (Arb.) 284 Precious marchaundies were brought from the redde sea and India,..Cinamome. Longe pepper. Whyte pepper. Cloues... Cassia... Xilocassia... Xilocinamome, [etc.]. **1698** FRYER *Acc. E. India & P.* 178 In the Groves about Carwar grows *Cassia Lignum*, *Xylo-Cassia*, or Bastard Cinamon.

†**xylo'cinnamon**. *Obs.* In 6 **xilocinamome**. [ad. Gr. *ξυλοκιννάμωμον* (Dioscorides), L. *xylocinnamōmum* (Pliny): see XYLO- and CINNAMON.] Cinnamon-wood.

1555 Xilocinamome [see XYLOCASSIA]. **1706** PHILLIPS (ed. Kersey), *Xylocinnamon*, or *Xylocinnamomon*, the Wood of the Cinnamon-Tree.

xylograph ('zaɪləʊgrɑːf, -æ-), *sb.* Also **zylo-**. [The earliest words of the group are *xylography*, *xylographic*, *-ical*, ad. F. *xylographie* (18th cent.), *xylographique*: see XYLO- and -GRAPHY, -GRAPHIC.] A wood-engraving (i.e. either an engraving on wood, or an impression from one), esp. one of the early period. Hence **'xylograph** *v. trans.*, to execute from a wood-engraving. So **xylographer** (-'ɒgrəfə(r)), **xy'lographist**, a wood-engraver, esp. of the early period; **xylographic** (-'græfɪk), **-ical** *adjs.*, of, pertaining to, or executed by wood-engraving; **xylo'graphically** *adv.*, by the method of wood-engraving; **xylography** (-'ɒgrəfɪ), wood-engraving, esp. of the early period or of a primitive kind; also, more widely, printing from wood blocks as distinct from type.

1816 SINGER *Hist. Cards* Pref. p. xiii, The account which gives the honor of the invention of Xylography to the Cardmakers. *Ibid.* 176 The covers of books have of late been a fertile source of typographical and xylographical discoveries. *Ibid.* 205 Whether the xylographic art took its rise in Italy or Germany, cannot so clearly..be proved. **1824** DIBDIN *Libr. Comp.* 264 Many past and present 'Xylographers' (or wood-cutters) could do infinitely better. **1854** *Blackw. Mag.* LXXV. 60 Printing, or rather xylography, is said to have been invented about the beginning of the tenth century. **1855** tr. *Wedl's Rudim. Pathol. Histol.* (Sydenham Soc.) Auth. Pref. p. vi, The zylography was executed by A. Rosenzweig. **1859** J. P. BERJEAU *Biblia Pauperum* 15 Six editions of the Biblia pauperum due to the Netherlandish xylographers. **1863** *Sat. Rev.* 5 Dec. 738/1, The forthcoming edition of the New Testament, illustrated with all the powers of modern xylography. **1864** *Ibid.* 17 Dec. 758 The Brothers Dalziel are the xylographists, if there is such a word. **1864** WEBSTER, *Xylograph*, an engraving on wood, or the impression from such an engraving. **1878** *Print. Trades Jrnl.* XXIII. 6 Worked in red, blue and yellow, just as if they were the three colors of a xylograph. **1881** *Athenæum* 3 Sept. 310/2 The woodcuts, if..coarse from a xylographic point of view, are admirably characteristic. **1883** I. TAYLOR *Alphabet* viii. II. 221 The runes were essentially a xylographic script. **1887** HESSELS *Haarlem* xv. 53 Xylographic Donatuses. *Ibid.* xviii. 77 The *Doctrinales*..were not printed typographically but from wooden blocks (xylographically). **1892** *Nation* (N.Y.) 31 Mar. 249/2 We have received from Tokio, Japan, a copy of a handsome zylographed life-sized picture of Commodore Matthew C. Perry. *Ibid.*, The zylographic picture is a good specimen of popular art. **1905** E. CANDLER *Unveiling of Lhasa* iv. 67 Xylograph editions of the Lamaist scriptures and lives of the saints.

xylographica (zaɪləʊ'græfɪkə), *sb. pl.* [mod.L., f. XYLOGRAPHIC *a.* after TYPOGRAPHICA *sb. pl.*] Block-books, woodcuts, and the like; xylographic matter.

1931 M. B. STILLWELL *Incunabula & Americana* III. i. 177 Blockbooks, although produced during the same period [as incunabula], are those printed *a full page at a time*, each page being printed from a wooden block... Such books are sometimes called 'xylographic books', or 'xylographica', meaning that they are wood-engraved throughout. **1952** J. CARTER *ABC for Bk.-Collectors* 37 Block books, or xylographica, as produced in Europe are presumed..to have preceded the invention of printing from movable metal types. **1982** *Times Lit. Suppl.* 6 Aug. 866/1 Volume I will carry descriptions of block-books and other xylographica.

xyloidin (zaɪ'lɔɪdɪn, *formerly* zaɪ'ləʊɪdɪn). *Chem.* Also **-ine**. [ad. F. *xyloïdine* (Braconnot), f. Gr. *ξυλοειδής*, f. *ξύλον* wood: see -OID and -IN[1].] An explosive substance, $C_6H_9(NO_2)O_5$, allied to pyroxylin, obtained by treating starch or vegetable fibre with nitric acid.

1838 T. THOMSON *Chem. Org. Bodies* 664 *note*, M. Braconnot, by digesting saw-dust of wood, or potatoe starch, in concentrated nitric acid, obtained a mucilaginous solution... Water coagulated it, and separated a white caseous substance, to which he has given the name of *xyloidin*. **1850** *Fownes' Chem.* (ed. 3) 388 Both xyloidine and pyroxyline appear to be substitution-compounds, in which the elements of nitrous acid replace, to a certain extent, those of water in starch and lignine. **1868** WATTS *Dict. Chem.* V. 1060 Xyloïdin is a white, inodorous, and tasteless powder... Xyloïdin when struck decomposes with detonation, but not so violently as gun-cotton.

xylol ('zaɪlɒl). *Chem.* Also **-ole**. [f. Gr. *ξύλον* wood + -OL.] = XYLENE. Also *attrib.*

1851 [see XYLENE]. **1856** WARREN DE LA RUE & H. MILLER in *Proc. Roy. Soc.* VIII. 225 The Burmese naphtha products contain the corresponding hydrocarbons, namely,—Benzol ..$C_{12}H_6$. Toluol..$C_{14}H_8$ Xylol..$C_{16}H_{10}$. Cumol.. $C_{18}H_{12}$. **1894** *Brit. Jrnl. Photogr.* XLI. 5 Xylol is the best solvent of Canada balsam for such hermetical sealing. **1897** *Allbutt's Syst. Med.* II. 4 The section is to be dried with fine filter paper,..clarified with xylol, and mounted in xylol balsam.

xylonite ('zaɪlənaɪt). Also **zylo-** (see X). [Early form *xyloinite*, irreg. f. XYLOIDIN + -ITE[1], afterwards assimilated to Gr. *ξύλον* wood.] Another name for CELLULOID.

The invention originated with Alexander Sparkes, and was afterwards worked out by Daniel Spill (*Engl. Mechanic* XXIX. 93/1), who patented it 1867–75. An American company formed in 1881–2 adopted the form *zylonite*.

1869 The Xylonite Company Limited [incorporated 19 May]. **1870** *Provis. Specif. Patent* No. 787 In the production of those products which are similar to or such as are known as xyloinite or such compounds as contain xyloidine or soluble gun cotton. **1885** *Reader* 7 Mar. 455 Zylonite is the trade name of a substance that imitates amber, shell or ivory. **1888** *Pall Mall G.* 6 Dec. 3/2 The imitation ivory produced by the Xylonite Company, at their manufactory at Manningtree, in Suffolk. **1892** ELEANOR ROWE *Chip Carving* (1895) 52 Paper-knives, hairpin boxes, and various other small articles..made in Xylonite look remarkably well when carved.

xylophagous (zaɪ'lɒfəgəs), *a. Zool.* Also 9 *erron.* **zylo-**, **xilo-**. [f. mod.L. *xylophagus*, f. Gr. *ξύλον* wood + *-φαγος* eating: see -OUS. Cf. F. *xylophage*.] Feeding upon wood, as an insect larva, or boring into and destroying wood, as a mollusc or crustacean. So **xy'lophagan**, *a.* belonging to the *Xylophaga* or *Xylophagi*, names in different classifications for various groups of insects whose larvæ devour wood; *sb.* an insect belonging to one of these groups; **xylophage** ('zaɪləʊfeɪdʒ), a wood-eating insect.

1842 BRANDE *Dict. Sci.*, etc., **Xylophagans*, *Xylophaga*.. a tribe of Coleopterous insects,..also..a family of Dipterous insects. **1877** KURZ *Flora Brit. Burmah* I. 339 Wood..of a coarse fibre, soon attacked by *xylophages. **1739** *Phil. Trans.* XLI. 279 This *Xylophagous Worm. **1835–6** *Todd's Cycl. Anat.* I. 704/1 The..xilophagous Conchifera. **1836–9** *Ibid.* II. 862/1 The..Xylophagous insects of this tribe..are exceedingly destructive. **1864** OWEN *Power of God* 16 Tree-destroying Xylophagous larvæ.

xylophone ('zaɪləfəʊn). Also **zylo-** (see X). [f. Gr. *ξύλον* (see XYLO-) + *φωνή* voice, sound.] A musical instrument consisting of a graduated series of flat wooden bars, played by striking with a small hammer or by rubbing with rosined gloves.

1866 *Athenæum* 7 Apr. 470/3 A prodigy..who does wonderful things with little drumsticks on a machine of wooden keys, called the 'xylophone', almost five octaves in compass. **1890** HALLETT *1,000 Miles in Shan States* 322 A native zylophone made of eighteen sonorous strips of hard wood fastened side by side by strings and suspended over a boat-shaped sounding board. **1892** R. L. GARNER *Speech Monkeys* xiii. 135 Drawing a mallet rapidly across the keyboard of a xylophone.

Hence **xylophonic** (-'fɒnɪk) *a.*, of, pertaining to, or resembling a xylophone.

1899 MARY KINGSLEY *W. African Stud.* iii. 65 Many African instruments are..sweet..notably the xylophonic family. **1902** *Westm. Gaz.* 28 Aug. 10/2 Two swarthy bare-armed blacksmiths who extract zylophonic music from a couple of cart-wheels.

xylophonist (zaɪˈlɒfənɪst). [f. XYLOPHONE + -IST.] One who plays a xylophone.

1927 *Daily Tel.* 10 May 12/1 Teddy Brown the xylophonist. **1952** B. ULANOV *Hist. Jazz in Amer.* (1958) xvii. 207 He became a xylophonist. **1976** *Gramophone* Aug. 345/1 There is a really brilliant xylophonist in 'Fossils'.

xylophory (zaɪˈlɒfərɪ). *rare*⁻¹. [ad. Gr. ξυλοφορία wood-carrying, f. ξύλον wood + -φορος carrying (:φέρειν to carry).] Wood-carrying. ***festival of xylophory*** (Gr. ξυλοφόριος ἑορτή, Josephus), applied to the Feast of Tabernacles.

1737 WHISTON *Josephus, Jewish War* II. xvii. §6 The next day was the festival of Xylophory, upon which the custom was for every one to bring wood for the altar.

xylorimba (ˈzaɪlərɪmbə). [f. XYLO(PHONE + MA)RIMBA.] (See quots. 1938, 1980.)

1938 *Oxf. Compan. Mus.* 1026/2 *Xylorimba*, an American form of lightweight marimba. **1961** *Times* 10 Nov. 18/7 The icy, scientific precision of xylorimba. **1978** P. GRIFFITHS *Conc. Hist. Mod. Music* ix. 137 Xylorimba and percussion suggest the influence of black African music. **1980** *New Grove Dict. Music* XX. 564/2 *Xylorimba*... An instrument of the xylophone family with a compass sufficiently large to embrace the low-sounding bars of the Marimba and the highest-sounding bars of the xylophone.

xylose (ˈzaɪləʊs). *Chem.* [f. Gr. ξύλον wood + -OSE².] A colourless carbohydrate, $C_5H_{10}O_5$, obtained by the action of sulphuric acid on xylan; also called *wood-sugar*.

1894 MUIR & MORLEY *Watts' Dict. Chem.* IV. 538/2. **1899** CAGNEY tr. *von Jaksch's Clin. Diagn.* vii. (ed. 4) 334 [Pentose], in the form of arabinose, rhamnose and xylose, has been identified in the urine.

xylostein (zaɪˈlɒstɪɪn). *Chem.* [f. mod.L. *Xylosteum* (f. Gr. ξύλον wood + ὀστέον bone) + -IN¹.] A poisonous bitter substance found in the berries of the fly-honeysuckle, *Lonicera Xylosteum*.

1868 WATTS *Dict. Chem.* V. 1061. **1871** —— tr. *Gmelin's Hand-bk. Chem.* XVI. 102.

xylyl (ˈzaɪlɪl). *Chem.* [f. XYL-ENE + -YL.] The hypothetical radical (C_8H_9) of xylene and its derivatives. Hence **xylylamine**, **ˈxylylene**, †**xylylea** (= *xylylamine*), **xyˈlylic** *a.*, etc.: see quots.

1862 MILLER *Elem. Chem., Org.* vi. §2. (ed. 2) 453 Xylol, $C_{16}H_{10}$. Nitroxylol, $C_{16}H_9NO_4$. Xylylia, $C_{16}H_{11}N$. **1863** *Fownes' Chem.* (ed. 9) 694 The hydrate of oxide of xylyl.. has been observed by Mr. H. Müller. **1868** WATTS *Dict. Chem.* V. 1061 *Xylyl.* C^8H^9. A monatomic radicle, homologous with phenyl and tolyl, which may be supposed to exist in xylene.. and its derivatives. *Ibid., Xylylamine*.. a base..(not yet obtained), related to benzylamine.. as xylidine.. to toluidine. *Ibid., Xylylene.* C^8H^8. A diatomic radicle related to xylyl, C^8H^9, in the same way as ethylene to ethyl. *Ibid.* 1062 *Xylylic acid.* $C^9H^{10}O^2 = C^6H^3(CH^3)^2.CO^2H$... homologous with benzoic and toluic acids. *Ibid., Xylylic acetate, chloride*, &c. Syn. with *Toluylic Acetate, Chloride*, &c.

xyrid (ˈzaɪərɪd). *Bot.* [f. mod.L. *Xyrid-*, *Xyris*, ad. Gr. ξυρίς a species of iris, f. ξυρόν razor, so called from the sharp-edged leaves.] A plant belonging to the *Xyridaceæ*, an order of monocotyledons typified by the genus *Xyris*, comprising sedge-like herbs having flowers with three coloured petals like those of Spiderworts; chiefly tropical and North American. So **xyridal** (ˈzɪrɪdəl) *a.*, belonging to the alliance *Xyridales* in Lindley's classification, comprising the *Xyridaceæ* and allied orders; *sb.* a plant belonging to this alliance; **xyridaceous** (zɪrɪˈdeɪʃəs) *a.*, belonging to the *Xyridaceæ*.

1846 LINDLEY *Veg. Kingd.* 186 [The] nearest relationship [of *Philydraceæ*].. is plainly with Xyrids and Spiderworts. *Ibid.* 185 Alliance XIV. *Xyridales.*—The Xyridal Alliance .. Natural Orders of Xyridals. *Philydraceæ. Xyridaceæ. Commelynaceæ. Mayaceæ. Ibid.* 187 *Xyridaceæ.*—Xyrids.

xyst: see XYSTUS.

xystarch (ˈzɪstɑːk). *Gr. Antiq.* *rare*⁻⁰. [ad. Gr. ξυστάρχης, f. ξυστός XYSTUS + ἄρχειν to rule.] (See quot.)

1823 CRABB *Technol. Dict., Xystarch*.. an Athenian officer who presided over the gymnastic exercises of the Xystus.

‖**xyster** (ˈzɪstə(r)). *Surg.* [mod.L., a. Gr. ξυστήρ, f. ξύειν to scrape.] An instrument for scraping bones.

[**1684** tr. *Blancard's Phys. Dict.*] **1688** HOLME *Armoury* III. 429/1 Raspatorium, Rasping hookes;.. Scraping Instruments to shave and scrape filthy and scaly bones. Its called also Xyster.

‖**xyston** (ˈzɪstɒn). *Gr. Antiq.* [a. Gr. ξυστόν the polished shaft of a spear, hence a spear, neut. of ξυστός scraped, polished, f. ξύειν to scrape, polish.] (See quot., and cf. SARISSA.)

1856 GROTE *Greece* II. xcii. XII. 77 The regiments of cavalry called Sarissophori or Lancers.. carrying a long lance, and distinguished from the heavier cavalry.. who carried the xyston or short pike.

‖**xystus** (ˈzɪstəs). Pl. **xysti** (-aɪ). Also 7 **zystus**, pl. **xisti**; 8–9 **xystos**, 9 **zystos**; 8–9 **xystum**, pl. **xysta** (7 *erron.* **xystas**). Also in anglicized form **xyst**. [L. *xystus* masc., also *xystum* neut., ad. Gr. ξυστός, prop. sb. use of the masc. of ξυστός adj.: see prec.] Among the ancient Greeks, a long covered portico or court used for athletic exercises; among the ancient Romans, an open colonnade, or walk planted with trees, used for recreation and conversation; hence occas. allusively.

1664 EVELYN tr. *Freart's Archit.* 132 Those large Xystas, Porticos, Atrias and Vestibula of the Greeks and Romans. **1696** —— *Let. to Wotton* 28 Oct., Spacious plots of ground .. built about with porticos, xisti, & noble ranges of pillars. **1696** PHILLIPS (ed. 5), *Zystus*, was a Place where the Wrestlers exercis'd. **1706** *Ibid.* (ed. Kersey), *Xystos*, a large Portico or Gallery, where the Greek Wrestlers us'd to practise in Winter-time. *Ibid., Xystus* or *Xystum* (among the Romans) an open Walking-Place..; also a Knot-Garden. **1721** (*title*) The Architecture of A. Palladio.. containing A short Treatise of the Five Orders.. also The different Construction of Private and Publick Houses, High-ways, Bridges, Market-places, Xystes, and Temples... Revised.. By Giacomo Leoni. **1763** SMOLLETT *Trav.* xxx. (1766) II. 102 The *Xysta*, which were shady walks between two porticos. **1823** P. NICHOLSON *Pract. Builder* 596 Zystos; among the antients, a portico or aile of unusual length, commonly appropriated to gymnastic exercises. **1856** MACAULAY in Trevelyan *Life & Lett.* xiv. (1913) II. 405 [I] directed the workmen to set creepers in my xystus. **1871** FARRAR *Witn. Hist.* vi. 98 Philosophers who aired their elegant doubts in the shady xystus.

Y

Y (waɪ), pl. Y's, *Y*s (waɪz), the twenty-fifth letter of the modern and twenty-third of the ancient Roman alphabet, representing ultimately **Υ,** *Υ* (u psilon) of the Greek alphabet, a differentiated form of the primitive **V** which has given also U and V. It was adopted first in the Latin alphabet in the form **V** to express (u) and (w), and was later (after B.C. 100) readopted in the form **Y** to represent the *Υ* of borrowed Greek words.

The name of the letter in the Romanic languages, 'Greek i' (e.g. F. *i grec*, Sp. *i griega*), and the Ger. name *ipsilon*, It. *ipsilon*, *-onne* (†*yssilonne*), and Pg. *ypsilon*, preserve the fact of its Greek origin. The English name *wy* (waɪ) is of obscure origin.

The earliest available English evidence is in the MS. of the Ormulum, col. 109 (l. 4320), where pı is written, app. in the first hand (*c* 1200), over ẏ, the fifth letter of the name IESOẎS. Nothing certain is known about the historical relationship of the English name to the name VI or UI attributed to 'the Greek y' in the grammatical treatise (*a* 1150) contained in the Edda, or to the *ui* or *gui* of some OF. systems. Gawin Douglas rhymes Y with *sky* (see quot. 1513 in sense 2 below); other early references to the name are:—

1573 BARET *Alv.*, Y hath bene taken for a greeke vowel among our latin Grammarians a great while, which me thinke if we marke well we shall finde to be rather a diphthong: for it appeareth to be compounded of u and i, which both spelled togither soundeth as we write Wy. **1580** BULLOKAR *Amendm. Orthogr.* 8 The olde name of :y: (which is wy).

(1) The letter of which our *y* is the direct representative occurs from the earliest times in OE. script to express the *i*-mutation of *u*. It had various forms ranging from those resembling the Greek *u psilon*, in which the tops of the limbs turn outwards in opposite directions, to those in which both limbs turn in the same direction, whether to the right (forming an F-like character) or to the left. This last type with the right shank continued leftwards below the line was the form that prevailed in ME. script, and which, with the top closed (ƿ), became identical with the debased forms of þ: see (3) below. Most forms of the OE. *y* in the earliest manuscripts are written with a superposed dot, which is also a feature of the *y* in contemporary manuscripts of Latin texts. The dot fell out of use towards the end of the eighth century, but was revived towards the end of the tenth. The dotted *y* continued throughout the ME. period, and was carried into some of the early founts of type (e.g. in *The Book of St. Albans* of 1486 the dotted *y* is employed in the larger, but not in the smaller type).

In later (West-Saxon) OE., *y* was written alternatively for *i*, e.g. as representing older *ie*, as in *cyle*, *onʒytan*, *yld*, for *ciele*, *onʒietan*, *ield*; and, as its function of expressing rounded *i* (Y, y) was usurped by *u* in imitation of French usage, it became ultimately a possible substitute for vocalic *i* in any position. This use had become established by the middle of the 13th century, and, thenceforward, with the deterioration of script, *y* came to serve as a convenient means of breaking up an ambiguous series of minims produced by a succession of *i*, *u*, *n*, *m*, as *nym*, *myn*, *ynumen*, *unymete*, for *nim*, *min*, *inumen*, *unimete*. This free use of *y* was continued through the ME. period, and the tradition lasted for a long period after the introduction of printing; but *i* was gradually restored to its place, the resulting orthographic convention being that *y* is retained: (i) for final *i*-sounds, as in *fly*, *family*, *daily*, *destroy* (formerly spelt also *flie* and *flye*, *familie* and *familye*, etc.), only alien words being spelt with final *i*; (ii) in Greek words, representing *υ*, as in *hymn*; (iii) before *i*, in inflexional forms of verbs ending in *y* or *ie*, as *flying*, *lying*, *tying*, not *fliing*, etc.; (iv) in the plural of nouns ending in *y* preceded by another written vowel, as *boy boys*, *ray rays*, *alley alleys*, *money moneys* (but *monies* is still common, and *vallies*, *monkies*, etc. were equally so until recently). Particular usages, not falling under these categories, are the use of *y* to distinguish *dye* from *die*, and the fluctuation between *flyer* and *flier*, *tyre* and *tire*, *gipsy* and *gypsy*, *tiro* and *tyro*, *siphon* and *syphon*, *cipher* and *cypher*, *silva* and *sylva* (see each word for the special circumstances).

In some texts *y* is found substituted for *i* = French *j* (dʒ); e.g. in Shoreham's Poems *manyour* is written for *maniour* = manger, in Ayenbite *yyoyned* for *yioyned* joined, in the Camb. MS. of the 15th century version of Guy of Warwick occur *yoye*, *yolye*, *yelowse*, *harbenyoure*, *soyourned* = joy, jolly, jealous, harbinger, sojourned.

(2) About the middle of the 13th century *y* began to be used to represent the voiced palatal spirant (j), taking the place of the character ȝ (called YOGH, q.v.) in one of its values. ȝ is a loosely written form of OE. ᵹ, which had become appropriated in early ME. script to the guttural and palatal spirants, while the continental *g* was appropriated to the voiced guttural and palatal stops (though in some MSS. *g* stands for all these sounds: cf. G). The practice of contemporary scribes varied considerably, some restricting *y* to its vocalic use, others using it freely for both consonant and vowel. Northern scribes of the 14th and 15th centuries often write *yh* for *y* initially, as *yhit*, *yheyt*, yet, *yher* year, *yhoung* young.

In many late ME. scripts ȝ became identical in form with *z*, and it was retained by Scottish printers in this form; e.g. printed *zer*, *fenzeit*, *Dalziel*, represent *yer* year, *fenyeit* feigned, *Dalyiel*: see further s.v. Z.

(3) Another value of *y* arises from the assimilation of *y* and *þ*, the runic *thorn* (see TH), which had become indistinguishable from each other in some MSS. of the early 14th century (e.g. the Cotton MS. of Cursor Mundi). After 1400 *þ* fell more and more out of use, and in some scripts was represented only by the *y*-form in the compendia y^{e}, y^{t} or y^{at}, y^{ei}, y^{m}, y^{u} = the, that, they, them, thou, and the like, many of which continued to be extensively employed in manuscript in the 17th and 18th centuries. Two of these, y^{e} or $\overset{e}{y}$, y^{t} or $\overset{t}{y}$, were retained in printers' types during the 15th and 16th centuries, but often with a form of *y* somewhat different from that used in other positions. (In Sir John Cheke's translation of the New Testament, a dotted *y* stands for *th*.) In manuscript (e.g. in letter-writing) y^{e} lasted well into the 19th century. It is still often used pseudo-archaically, jocularly, or vulgarly (pronounced as *ye*), e.g. in Lewis Carroll's 'Ye Carpette Knyghte', and in shop-signs like 'Y^{e} Olde Booke Shoppe'.

c **1340** *Cursor M.* 17033–4 (MS. Cott. Vesp. A III, lf. 94 b) And es naman y^{t} es in skil yat agh sai her again. **14..** *Agincourt Song* (Pepys MS.), þat tounn he wan and mad a fray Yat fraunce xal rewe tyl domysday. *c* **1500** *Promp. Parv.* (Middle Hill MS.) 535 *note*[1], Yanne or thann, .. Yowtyng or thowtyng. *Ibid.* (MS. note in Brit. Mus. Copy of Pynson's ed.), All these Y. stande for Th. acordinge as the Saxon caracte was in this sorte þ. **1508** *Chapman & Myllar Prints* (S.T.S. 1918) 171 Thou ryall king all yis suld reull yi realme. **1551** SIR W. PICKERING *Let. to Sir W. Cecil* in *Nat. MSS.* II. l, At pares ye 27 of octobre. **1665** *Caldwell Papers* (Maitland Club) I. 62 Without any interuption yrupon. *Ibid.* 63 It may be clearlie answered yrto. **1680** P. HENRY *Diaries & Lett.* (1882) 292 Bo[reatton] where l^{d} Paget y^{en} was. **1705** J. ROGERS in *Mrs. E. Montagu's Corr.* (1906) I. 145, I had notice by my Mother yt you had ordered me £40. **1741** DK. PORTLAND *ibid.* 76, j am to inform you yt ye Duchess continues as well as can be, and ye Babe too. **1745** MRS. ROBINSON *ibid.* 225 [He] told y^{m} yt ye French was landing in the Marsh.

Pronunciation. The vocalic sounds now normally expressed by *y* are:—

1. (ɪ), as in h*y*mn (hɪm), s*y*non*y*m*y* (sɪ'nɒnɪmɪ), sill*y* ('sɪlɪ); in unstressed syllables there is more or less reduction or obscuration.

2. (aɪ), as in m*y* (maɪ), den*y* (dɪ'naɪ).

3. (aɪə), as in l*y*re (laɪə(r)).

4. (ɜː), as in m*y*rtle ('mɜːt(ə)l).

5. (ə), as in sat*y*r ('sætə(r)).

With *a*, *e*, *o*, *u*, it forms combinations having special values:—*ay* (final) = (eɪ), as in l*ay* (leɪ), ess*ay* ('ɛseɪ), = (aɪ) in *ay*e (aɪ); = (iː) in qu*ay* (kiː), = (ɛ) in s*ay*s (sɛz); *ey* = (eɪ), as in ob*ey* (əʊ'beɪ), conv*ey* (kən'veɪ), = (ɪ), as in all*ey* ('ælɪ), hon*ey* ('hʌnɪ), = (aɪ) in *ey*e (aɪ) and its derivatives, = (ɛə) in *ey*re (ɛə(r)); *oy* = (ɔɪ), as in b*oy* (bɔɪ), ann*oy* (ə'nɔɪ); *uy* (rare) = (aɪ) in b*uy* (baɪ).

The consonantal sound expressed by *y* is denoted in this Dictionary by (j), as *y*ew, *y*ou (juː).

II. 1. a. The letter or its sound.

c **1000** ÆLFRIC *Gram.* ii. (Z.) 5 To ðisum [*a*, *e*, *i*, *o*, *u*] is ᵹenumen se grecisca *y* for intingan greciscra namena, and se ylca *y* is on engliscum ᵹewritum swiðe ᵹewunelic. *c* **1440** *Promp. Parv.* 79/1 Quere plura vocabula similem sonum istis habencia in S literâ, ubi I vel Y sequitur hanc literam S immediate. [*c* **1465** *Pol. Rel. & L. Poems* (1903) 2 A. .3. for yorke.] **1521** BARCLAY *Introd. Fr.* B ij b, But specyally y: muste be wryten for I, in ye ende of englysshe wordes, and whan n: m, or u, is wryten before, or behynde it. **1530** PALSGR. 16 The writtynge of *i* and *y* in any frenche worde, eyther alone or as part of a diphthong, causeth no difference in sounde. **1599** in *Promp. Parv.* (Camden) 536 *note*, All these wordes of ȝ we pronounce with Y at this daye, and some of these ȝ here vsed haue that place of G in oure spekinge and writinge at this daye. **1636** B. JONSON *Eng. Gram.* I. iii, Y is also mere vowelish in our tongue, and hath only the power of an *i*, even where it obtains the seat of a consonant. **1693** DRYDEN *Disc. Satire* Ess. (1900) II. 67 [Satire] ought to be with *i*, and not with *y*, to distinguish its true derivation from *satura*, not from *satyrus*. **1755** JOHNSON *Dict.*, *Gram.* a 2 b, It may be observed of *y* as of *w*, that it follows a vowel without any hiatus, as *rosy youth*. **1785** PINKERTON *Lett. Lit.* xxxiv. 243 [Ending] in *y* we have no less than 4900 words, about an eighth of our language; our words amounting to about 35,000. **1848** MRS. GASKELL *Mary Barton* xxii, Tails of *ys* and *gs*. **1874** 'MAX ADELER' *Out of Hurly-burly* ix. (Rtldg.) 121 The Smith that spells without a y is not the Smith for me!

b. Used for the Greek letter *Υ* (*u psilon*), esp. as a Pythagorean symbol: see quots.

1430–40 LYDG. *Bochas* II. xv. (MS. Bodl. 263) lf. 117/2 Pithagorus .. Fond first out y a figur to discerne The liff heer short and liff that is eterne. **1587** GREENE *Tritam. Love* Wks. (Grosart) III. 96 Did not Pythagoras compare vertue to the letter Y, which is small at the foot but broad at the top: meaning that to obtaine vertue is verie painefull, but the possession thereof passing pleasant? **1616** HOLYDAY *Persius* III. 119 The Samian letter Y Whose spreading branches teach Philosophie, Hath marked out .. The high-rear'd right-hand path, wherein to walke. **1693** DRYDEN *Persius* iii. (1697) 443 Where the Samian Y directs thy Steps to run, To Virtue's narrow Steep, and Broad-way Vice to shun. **1771** *Encycl. Brit.* I. 272/1 The other two divaricate, like the branches of the greek Y.

2. The letter considered with regard to its shape; a figure or marking of this shape. Also Comb. ***y-shaped*** adj.

1513 DOUGLAS *Æneis* VII. Prol. 120 Palamedes byrdis crouping in the sky, Fleand on randoune schapin lik ane Y. **1591** SYLVESTER *Du Bartas* I. v. 871, I hear the Crane (if I mistake not) cry: Who in the Clouds forming the forkéd Y, .. Instructeth Souldiers in the Art of War. *a* **1817** T. DWIGHT *Trav. New Eng.*, etc. (1821) II. 265 The centre of the town is a pretty expansion, in the form of the Roman Y. **1849** ROCK *Ch. Fathers* I. v. 324 *note*, A rich orphrey .. dividing itself a little way below the neck, takes the shape of the letter Y, and passes, in that form, over the shoulders. **1861** HAGEN *Syn. Neuroptera N. Amer.* 214 Between the antennæ is a black Y. **1874** RAYMOND *Statist. Mines & Mining* 511 The bucket is then lowered into the Y-shaped rests. **1907** C. C. BROWN *China* xvi. 233 A Y-shaped divining rod.

3. a. A contrivance or piece of apparatus in the form of the letter Y; *esp.* a forked support for a telescope, theodolite, or piece of mechanism. Also *attrib.*, as ***Y axis***, ***bearing***, ***piece***; **Y branch**, a piece of piping with a branch at an acute angle to the main (cf. *T branch*, T 3 b); **Y cross**, (*a*) a cross in the form of the letter Y, often used as an ornamental device on ecclesiastical vestments; (*b*) a piece of piping consisting of three branches diverging at acute angles; hence **Y-crossed** *ppl. a.*; **Y-front**, a proprietary term for men's underwear, used esp. to denote close-fitting briefs with Y-shaped seaming at the front; freq. as *sb. pl.*, briefs of this kind; **Y gun** *U.S.*, an anti-submarine gun with two firing arms for discharging depth charges; **Y junction**, a junction at which a road forks into two branches, or one road joins another at an angle different from 90 degrees; **Y level**, the common spirit-level, used with a telescope or theodolite resting on Y's (also written *wye-level*, q.v.); **Y track**, a short track on a railway at right angles to the main track and connected with it by two switches in opposite directions, used for reversing an engine or car. Also in names of natural structures, as ***Y cartilage***, ***ligament***: see quot. 1890.

1793 WOLLASTON in *Phil. Trans.* LXXXIII. 137 The four pillars .. carry the Y*s* for the pivots of the transit. **1803** MUDGE *ibid.* XCIII. 407 The telescope was then quickly taken out of the Ys. **1864** WEBSTER, *Y*, .. 2. (Railways.) A portion of track consisting of two converging tracks connected by a cross-track. **1867** SMYTH *Sailor's Word-bk.*, *Journal*, .. the bearing part of a shaft, upon which it rests on its Y's or bearings. **1875** *Encycl. Brit.* III. 266/1 A wire, the axis of which coincides with the Y-axis. **1878** LOCKYER *Star-gazing* 314 The Y bearings of a theodolite. **1884** KNIGHT *Dict. Mech.* Suppl., *Y Branch*, a branch with a divergent stem. **1890** BILLINGS *Nat. Med. Dict.*, *Y cartilage*, the triradiate piece of true cartilage which, before puberty, unites the three portions of the hip-bone at the bottom of the acetabulum. **1881** G. G. SCOTT *Ess. Hist. Eng. Church Archit.* 114 St. Regnobert's chasuble at Bayeux, and St. Thomas's at Sens, are examples of the use of the Y cross in France. **1884** KNIGHT *Dict. Mech.* Suppl., *Y Cross*, a pipe with two divergent stems. **1881** G. G. SCOTT *Ess. Hist. Eng. Church Archit.* 114 The Y-crossed vestment of Ruben's picture. **1953** *Trade Marks Jrnl.* 17 June 526/1 *Y-front*... Pants and vests, all for men. Lyle and Scott Limited,.. Hawick, Scotland; manufacturers. **1959** H. HOBSON *Mission House Murder* xxix. 188 Here I was, in my athlete's vest and Y-front briefs. **1961** *Harper's Bazaar* May 103/1 The demand for a T-shirt and a Y-front in Act II. **1976** T. STOPPARD *Dirty Linen* 23 He produces.. a large pair of Y-front pants. **1978** M. PAGE *Pilate Plot* (1979) xii. 183 He stripped to his Y-fronts and plunged into the pool. **1918** *Ann. Rep. Secretary U.S. Navy Dept.* 56 A new gun known as the 'Y' gun has been designed and built especially for firing depth charges. **1937** *Jane's Fighting Ships* 471 Y-gun or Depth Charge Projector. **1961** *Guardian* 18 Sept. 3/4 Local Y junctions where drivers.. expect others prophetically to divine the route they are about to take. **1982** M. DUKE *Flashpoint* xxv. 182 When he came to a Y-junction he made a sharp turn right. **1838** P. BARLOW in *Encycl. Metrop.* (1845) XXV. 304 There are two constructions [of levels] that are commonly adopted, viz. the Y level and Troughton's level. **1890** BILLINGS *Nat. Med. Dict.*, *Y ligament*, ilio-femoral ligament. **1842** FRANCIS *Dict. Arts* s.v. *Beighton's Hand Gear*, The Y piece, as it is called, G, bearing the moveable weight F. **1886** CUMMING *Electricity* (1887) 40 A mounted telescope.. swinging on two Y pieces.

b. Collectors' name for various moths of the genus *Plusia*, having markings more or less resembling the letter Y.

1775 M. HARRIS *Engl. Lepid.* 59 Y moth.. Brown, having a mark in the middle of the wing like the letter Y. **1832** J. RENNIE *Butterfl. & Moths* 93 The Golden Y (*P. Iota*).. frequents woody places. *Ibid.*, The Yorkshire Y (*P. interrogationis*). *Ibid.* 94 The Essex Y (*P. circumflexa*). **1844** H. STEPHENS *Bk. Farm* III. 778 The Gamma or Y-moth, *Plusia gamma*. **1845** JAS. HAMILTON in W. Arnot *Life* vi. (1870) 289 The first capture was her favourite Golden Y-moth. **1903** *Blackw. Mag.* Apr. 490/1 Young missel-thrushes.. searching for the larvæ of the silver Y.

4. a. *Math.* Used to denote the second of a set of unknown or variable quantities (the first being denoted by *x*); *spec.* in Analytical Geometry, the symbol for an ordinate, or quantity measured in the direction of the second axis of co-ordinates (hence called † ***the axis of y***, now always ***y-axis***; also *transf.*); ***Y-cut*** adj. (Electronics), of, pertaining to, or designating a quartz crystal cut in a plane normal to its Y-axis; ***Y-plate*** (Electronics), each of a pair of electrodes in an oscilloscope that control the vertical movement of the spot on the screen.

1728 CHAMBERS *Cycl.* s.v. *Conic Sections*, If the *Latus Rectum* of any Diameter, as DK, be *y*; then, as the Diameter DK is to its conjugate *βγ*, or its equal *ων*; so that Conjugate *βγ*, or that Tangent *ων* is to *y*. **1885**, etc. [see X 3 a]. **1903** [see X 3]. **1930**, etc. Y-cut [see *X-cut adj.* s.v. X 3 a]. **1934** J. H. REYNER *Television* vii. 71 In the ordinary applications of the tube we apply the voltage to be examined across one pair of plates (usually termed the Y plates) which causes the spot to be elongated into a line. **1945** *Electronic Engin.* XVII. 723 These two equations define the components of the velocity of the spot along the X and Y axes. **1946** *Ibid.* XVIII. 23/2 The signal [may be] fed to one Y plate and a pulse derived from the anode of V_4 fed to the other Y plate. **1965** J. R. FREDERICK *Ultrasonic Engin.* iv. 65 If the second digit is 4, 5, or 6 this refers to a shear strain around the *x*, *y*, or *z* axes, respectively. **1969** MADDOX & DAVIES *Elem. Functions* i. 12 The graph is a straight line parallel to the *y*-axis and situated 2 units to the right of the *y*-axis. **1976** *Appl. Physics Lett.* XXIX. 76/1 Our measurements were made on a polished *Y*-cut single-crystal quartz substrate with a pair of aluminum thin-film interdigital transducers.. with orientation for wave propagation along the *X* axis. **1978** D. T. REES *Cathode Ray Oscilloscope* 9 A voltage applied to the Y-plates will move the beam and the spot in a vertical direction. **1979** FAUX & PRATT *Computational Geom.* i. 18 The most familiar equation of a straight line is $y = mx + c$, in which *m* is the slope, and *c* the intercept on the *y*-axis.

b. *Genetics.* (Now always as a capital.) [After X 3 e.] The symbol of the Y CHROMOSOME. So **Y-linked** (stress variable) *a.*, being or determined by a gene that is carried on the Y chromosome.

1909 E. B. WILSON in *Science* 8 Jan. 57/2 The X-element .. appears as a 'large idiochromosome' which has a synaptic mate... The latter chromosome, or its homologue, I shall designate as the 'Y-element'. **1910** *Amer. Naturalist* XLIV. 491 We should.. imagine that when a sperm bearing a Y enters an egg a male results. **1911**, etc. [see X 3 e]. **1917** *Amer. Naturalist* LI. 534 Y or W linked or plastid inheritance. **1949** DARLINGTON & MATHER *Elem. Genetics* ii. 51 In *Drosophila* and in man, there are completely Y-linked genes without any allelomorph in the X. **1981** *Heredity* XLVII. 238 A majority of male secondary sexual colour patterns are Y-linked [in the guppy]. **1983** M. B. ZALESKI et al. *Immunogenetics* ii. 36 For essentially all mammalian species discussed in this book, females are *X*/*X* and males are *X*/*Y*... Other types of sex determination are also known to exist in various species and are called *Protenor* (females are *X*/*X* and males are *X*/*O*), *Abraxas* (females are *X*/*Y* and males are *X*/*X*) and haploidy-diploidy (males are haploid and sterile, whereas females are diploid and fertile).

5. Used in abstract reasoning for the name of a person or thing (usually in connexion with X). Also ***Y.Z.***, used as the initials of a person remaining anonymous.

1765 *Museum Rust.* IV. 23, I am, Gentlemen, Yours, &c. Y.Z. **1867** SIR S. NORTHCOTE in A. Lang *Life, Lett.*, etc. (1890) I. ix. 293 The success of A. and B. will tempt Y. and Q. to enter upon the same field. **1873** [see X 3 c].

6. Used to denote position in a series, as of the batteries of the Royal Horse Artillery.

7. Abbreviations. (Abbreviations cited here with full stops are frequently used without them.) **y.** = year(s); **Y** = yttrium (*Chem.*); **Y** (*colloq.*, chiefly *U.S.*), short for *YMCA* or *YWCA*; **Y**, yuan; **YA** (*U.S.*), young adult; **YAG**: see YAG; **Y.C.** (see quot. 1883); **Y.E.**, Your Excellency; **Y.F.C.**, Young Farmers Club (formerly Clubs); **YHA**, Youth Hostels Association; **YIG**, yttrium iron garnet; **Y.M.** (*colloq.*), short for *YMCA*; also, a YMCA hostel; **YMCA**, Young Men's Christian Association; also, a hostel run by the YMCA; **YOP**, Youth Opportunities Programme; also, a young person taking part in this scheme; **Y.P.**, young prisoner; **yr**, year; **yr.**, **yr**, your; **yrs**, yours; **YTS**, Youth Training Scheme; **Y.W.** (*colloq.*), short for *YWCA*; also, a YWCA hostel; **YWCA**, Young Women's Christian Association; also, a hostel run by the YWCA.

1680 P. HENRY *Diaries & Lett.* (1882) 293 Hee is now 23. *y. old. **1915** *Dialect Notes* IV. 236 [College slang.] **Y*, abbreviation for the college Y.M.C.A. **1945** N. L. MCCLUNG *Stream runs Fast* xxvii. 259 Mary would have to have her bath at the 'Y'. **1956** H. KURNITZ *Invasion of Privacy* ii. 22 She's married to this English G.I. she met at the Y, where they have the service dances. **1977** *New Yorker* 27 June 35/3 Rose.. did not yet have a place to live; she was staying at the Y. **1962** in E. Snow *Other Side of River* (1963) lxv. 495 The State invested *Y. 37,000,000 in the livelihood needs and productive capital construction. **1973** *Times* 21 Mar. (China Trade Suppl.) p. iii/6 The basic unit of renminbi.. is the yuan, represented by the symbol Y. **1974** *Publishers Weekly* 7 Oct. 63/1 A powerful and tragic book, 'Betrayed' is as much for adults as *YAs. **1883** SIMMONDS *Dict. Trade* Suppl., **Y.C.*, an abbreviation for yellow candle tallow. **1870** *Weekly Standard* (Buenos Aires) 9 Mar. 14/2, I beg to communicate to *Y.E. the following despatch of Gen. Camara. **1945** G. CUNNINGHAM *Let.* 27 Nov. in N. Mitchell *Sir George Cunningham* (1968) v. 117, I feel terribly for Y.E. and for Claude A. in this. **1931** *Young Farmer* Mar. 77/1 The speakers.. had motored many miles to come to this .. third *Y.F.C. meeting. **1960** *Farmer & Stockbreeder* 8 Mar. 65/1 This competition.. is also of special interest to Y.F.C.s. **1982** *Financial Times* 30 Apr. 25/6 The YFC movement. **1931** *Ruc-Sac* July 18/1 The *Y.H.A. (the Youth Hostels Association of Great Britain) have sent us an advance copy of their handbook. **1982** R. HILL *Who guards Prince* IV. vi. 228 The best British equivalent [hotel] in terms of remoteness and height would be a YHA hut. **1959** *Physical Rev. Lett.* II. 499/1 (*caption*) The specific heat per unit volume of polycrystalline *YIG analyzed into its two components. **1975** D. G. FINK *Electronics Engineers' Handbk.* XIII. 113 In addition to mechanical tuning, both YIG and varactor tuning techniques are applicable. **1913** *Y.M. [see LOWBROW, LOW-BROW *a.*]. **1916** W. OWEN *Let.* 1 Feb. (1967) 377 We are refused admission to the Y.M. or Canteen. **1931** R. CAMPBELL *Georgiad* i. 25 Androgyno.. Well on the road... Half way to Georgiana's Y.M. hostel. **1881** *Y.M.C.A. Monthly Notes* Sept. 138/1 Pasteur Cook (Paris) said the *Y.M.C.As. were differently conducted in England to what they were in France. **1901** *Oxf. Times* 16 Mar. 12/1 A squad of eight Y.M.C.A. men.. gave a gymnastic display. **1920** S. LEWIS *Main St.* xxi. 257, I wish there were a Y.M.C.A. here, so I could take up regular exercise. **1931** R. CAMPBELL *Georgiad* i. 17 Like some Y.M. or W.C.A. It welcomes waifs whom love has cast away. **1956** R. MACAULAY *Towers of Trebizond* xiv. 157 There would be a Y.M.C.A. and a Y.W.C.A., where billiards and boxing would be played. **1978** *Times Higher Educ. Suppl.* 5 May 28/5 Young people.. eligible for the *YOP in Cardiff.. will be asked for their views. **1983** *Financial Times* 12 Apr. 19/3 One can employ a school leaver on the Youth Opportunities Scheme (YOP), the cost of whom is reimbursed by the MSC. All I had to do was take on a YOP as a personal assistant. **1952** *Chambers's Jrnl.* 1 June 356 They go all sentimental over the *Y.P.s. **1976** H. FERGUSON *Confessions of Long Distance Acid Head* 56 Ashford.. is also used as a place where young offenders who have done Borstal, and a Borstall [*sic*] re-call, serve their sentence. These are known as Y.P.'s (young prisoners). **1880** W. WHITMAN *Daybks. & Notebks.* (1978) I. 172 Robert Norris.. 28 *yrs old. **1942** W. FAULKNER *Go down, Moses* 264 Percavil Brownly 26 yr Old. cleark. **1968** E. KNIGHT in S. Henderson *Understanding New Black Poetry* (1973) III. 326 Last yr Like a salmon quitting The cold ocean.. I hitchhiked. **1772** J. KNYVETON *Jrnl.* 12 June in E. Gray *Man Midwife* (1946) I. 59 The two rooms and the closet will furnish *yr. obdt. with lecture rooms and office. **1811** SHELLEY *Let.* 3 Jan. (1964) I. 35 Not that I like yr. heroine. **1876** LD. BEACONSFIELD *Let.* 13 Sept. in R. S. Churchill *Winston S. Churchill* (1967) I. Compan. I. 54, I earnestly hope that these arrangements may be consistent with Yr Grace's decision to accept the high office of the Queen's Representative in Ireland. **1973** *Black World* Sept. 84 Ever get tired of people playing with yr life? **1811** SHELLEY *Let.* 11 Jan. (1964) I. 38 *Yr's with affection. PBS. **1922** JOYCE *Ulysses* 740 Yrs affly xxxxx. **1932** W. FAULKNER *Light in August* xviii. 412 Given it toe barer yrs truly. **1984** *Times* 17 Nov. 2/7 The *YTS is not available for many 17-year-olds. **1985** *Times Educ. Suppl.* 9 Aug. 4/1 Thus, all one's instincts and reflexes impel one to support YTS. **1937** PARTRIDGE *Dict. Slang* 968/1 **Y.W.*... The Young Women's Christian Association. **1979** M. SOAMES *Clementine Churchill* xxvi. 424 Clementine never severed her links with the 'Y.W.'. **1887** (*title*) *Y.W.C.A. Monthly Journal. **1931**, **1956** Y.W.C.A. [see Y.M.C.A. above]. **1961** *Times* 10 Oct. 16/1 A jolie-laide innocent looking for the Y.W.C.A.

8. In *Particle Physics*, *Y* denotes the hypercharge quantum number of sub-atomic particles.

1956 [see HYPERCHARGE]. **1974** S. GASIOROWICZ *Quantum Physics* xxvi. 443 The missing $I = 0$, $Y = 0$ pseudoscalar meson was found in the examination of $\pi^+ \pi^- \pi^0$ masses in bubble-chamber pictures.

y, obs. form of EYE, I *pron.*, IN *prep.*

y' (j). **a.** Abbrev. of YE *pers. pron.*, q.v., sense A. b.

b. Repr. a spoken abbrev. of YOU *pers. pron.* as subject, esp. in phrases of the type *you know*, *you see*.

1859 GEO. ELIOT *Adam Bede* I. I. i. 7 Ye might get religion, and that 'ud be the best day's earnings y'ever made. **1889** KIPLING *From Sea to Sea* (1899) I. 341 As a bell, y' know, it's rather a failure... They don't ring it properly. **1932** J. B. PRIESTLEY *Faraway* i. 49 Y'see, you know about the island. **1953** E. COXHEAD *Midlanders* vii. 168 Y'know.. I just wanted a spot of land to farm. **1981** J. WAINWRIGHT *All on Summer's Day* 14 But y'know... Sopworth money also meant Sopworth bobbying.

y- *prefix* (1 **ȝi-**, **ȝe-**, **ȝæ-**, **ȝie-**, **ȝy-**, 1–2 **ie-**, 2–3 **ȝe-**, 2–5 **i-**, **hi-**, 4–7 *dial.* **e-**, 3– now *dial.* **a-**, now *arch.* **y-**) represents OE. *ȝe-*, earlier (and Northumb.) *ȝi-*, = OFris. *gi-*, *ge-*, *ie-*, *e-*, *a-*, OS. *gi-*, *ge-*, *i-*, MLG., MDu. *ge-*, *ghe-*, locally *i-*, *y-*, *e-*, (LG., Du. *ge-*), OHG. *ga-*, *ka-*, *gi-*, *ki-*, *ge-*, (MHG., G. *ge-*, dial. *je-*, also *gi-*, *ga-*), Goth. *ga-*:—OTeut. **ga-*. The parallelism of formation and meaning exemplified by such forms as L. *commūnis* and Goth. *gamains*, OE. *ȝemǽne* common, I-MENE, L. *convenīre* and Goth. *gaqiman* to assemble, L. *conticēre* and Goth. *gaþahan* to be silent, L. *commemini* and Goth. *gamunan*, OE. *ȝemunan* to remember, L. *conferre* and Goth. *gabaíran* to compare, has suggested the probability of the etymological identity of Teut. *ga-* with L. *co-*, *com-*, and some scholars have accepted this on the assumption that Verner's law operated in some instances of initial consonants. (L. *com-* is normally represented by *ham-* in OFrank. *hamêdii*, synonymous with OHG. *geido*, MHG. *geeide* conspirator.)

The original form *ga-* is the only one found in Gothic (e.g. *galeiks* YLIKE); it was preserved also in OHG. (e.g. *galîh*), continued in MHG., and survives in a few words in some German dialects. The weakened (unstressed) form *gi-* was the prevailing one in OHG. and OS. and is the earliest form recorded in OFris. and OE., but it was early reduced to *ge-* in the whole of the Low German and High German area. In Scandinavian the prefix had disappeared entirely in prehistoric times as a living element, but relics of it remained in ON. *glíkr* YLIKE, *gnógr* ENOUGH, *greiðr* GRAITH *a.* (cf. READY).

The phonetic changes of OE. *ȝe-*, resulting in its complete disappearance in modern English as a living formative except in certain dialects, are in general paralleled in most of the LG. (as opposed to the HG.) dialects. While in HG. the vowel of the prefix not uncommonly underwent syncopation, which has become permanent (to the obscuration of the origin) in certain words, as G. *gleich* (OHG. *ga-*, *gi-*, *gelîk*) like (YLIKE), *gnade* (OHG. *ginâda*, OS. *ginâtha*, *nâtha*, Du. *genade*, ON. *náð*), in LG. dialects, on the other hand, there was a tendency for the consonant to fall, leaving *i-* or *e-*, in some dialects *a-*; e.g. OS. *unimetes* 'aliquid incommodum', MLG. *ilêtene*, pa. pple. of *lêten* to permit, *medeselle* (cf. G. *mitgesell*) companion, *enaugh* enough, *eschein* (cf. G. *geschehen*) happened, MDu. *idaen* done, *idragen* drawn, *yslagen* slain, Du. dial. *ivallig* weak, OFris. *idein* done, *islein* slain, *onebunden* unbound, *enôch*, *anôch* enough, *unaborn* unborn, *ofeslain*, *ofaslain* killed off, EFris. *unikaimed* unkempt, NFris. *-enogh* (in comp.) enough. Complete suppression of the prefix takes place in certain cases, as in MLG. *to lîke* (cf. G. *zugleich*) immediately, LG. *lîk* like, *naug* enough, *schein* happened, OFris. *bedda*, *sîth* companion, *fadera* godfather, *selscip* society, WFris. *nôch* adv. (beside *genôch* adj.-pron.), NFris. *nogh* enough; the suppression of the prefix is normal in pa. pples.; in words of other classes, it survives sporadically or has been revived through Du. or HG. influence.

The like developments of OE. *ȝe-* are traceable in the history of several words in which its identity and force have long ceased to be recognized, or from which all traces of the prefix have been obliterated: e.g. OE. *ȝeforðian*, ME. *iforð(i)e*, *aforth*, AFFORD *v.*, OE. *ȝewær*, ME.

iwar(e, *awar(e*, AWARE *a.*, OE. *ʒelíc(e*, ME. YLIKE, ALIKE, LIKE *a.* and *adv.*, OE. *ʒemang*, *onʒemang*, ME. YMONG, AMONG, MONG, OE. *ʒenoh*, ME. *inoȝ*, *anoȝ*, ENOUGH, *'nuff*, OE. *handʒeweorc* HANDIWORK (whence, by analogy, HANDICRAFT), OE. *ǽʒhwæðer* EITHER. For further examples of the complete disappearance of the prefix see below.

The general facts of the history and survival of OE. *ʒe-*, of which some details are given below, are:—In positions where it was still recognizable as a prefix, it had left few traces in northern English by 1200; its disappearance in the north was assisted by the absence of the prefix in ON. Substantival, adjectival, and verbal forms (other than pa. pples.) continued, not later than the end of the 14th century, only in southern and west-midland dialects. The pa. pple. was regularly formed with the prefix in southern ME. till about the middle of the 15th century, and its use in the form *a-* survives in south-western dialects to the present day. Pa. pples. so formed were a prominent feature of the archaistic language of Spenser and his imitators, and a few of them, the most notable of which is YCLEPT, persist as conventional archaisms of poetry.

In OE. and ME. the prefix was written either continuously with the body of the word of which it formed a part, or disjoined from it by a full or a half space; in the archaistic usage of the 16th and 17th centuries the general practice was to print the compound as one word, without hyphen. In this Dictionary established and well-known forms such as *yclad*, *yclept*, are printed without hyphen, but in other instances the convenience of the reader has been consulted, where occasion arises, in the avoidance of unhyphened forms where these would not suggest the nature of the word-formation.

Compounds of the prefix spelt with *y-* are entered in their alphabetical place, whether as full articles or as cross-references. Compounds which did not come down late enough for the spelling *y-* to have become established with them have been entered in their place in the letter I: see I-[1]. The choice of *y-* (and not *i-*) by Spenser and other archaists was determined by the prevalence of that form in the texts upon which he modelled his language. There are a few instances of the general survival of the *i-* form till a late date, e.g. I-THEE *v.*; the retention of *i-* in IWIS is due to the false etymologizing of it as *I wis*.

The original (physical) signification of the prefix, 'with', 'together', without admixture of transferred meaning, persists in some OE. words, such as *ʒedræʒ* lit. that which is drawn together, band, multitude (cf. Goth. *gadragan* to heap up or together), *ʒelaþian* to summon together, invite (cf. Goth. *galaþôn* συγκαλεῖν), *ʒerunnen* 'run together', coagulated (cf. Goth. *garinnan* to come together), *ʒeþéodan* 'conjungere', to join together, connect; but for the most part its meaning in OE. compounds falls under one or other of the following categories, which are arranged in the probable order of their development in primitive Germanic: the notion of physical accompaniment or conjunction passing into that of (1) association in life, occupation, etc., and hence, of suitability or appropriateness, and (2) collectivity, the final stage being (3) a perfective or intensive notion evolved in some measure from each of the others.

1. The associative meaning is exemplified by two classes of words in OE.:

a. Designations of persons associated or related by birth, family, or status, such as *ʒebedda* (I-BEDDE) 'one who shares a bed with another', bedfellow, consort, f. *bedd* bed, *ʒeféra* (YFERE, FERE *sb.*[1]) 'one who goes with another' (*faran* to go), companion, *ʒeháda* 'one of the same order as another', fellow-minister, f. *hád* condition, order, *ʒesíþ* (cf. Goth. *gasinþja*, OS. *gisīð*, OHG. *gisind*) 'one who shares a voyage with another', companion, f. *síþ* journey.

b. Adjectives and allied substantives denoting quality or condition, in which the purely associative sense readily passes into that of appropriateness, convenience, or similarity, such as *ʒecynd* (I-CUNDE *sb.*) nature, *ʒecynde* (I-CUNDE *a.*) natural, *ʒedéfe* (cf. Goth. *gadôbs*) becoming, fit, *ʒemæc* well-matched, *ʒemæcca* companion, mate, MATCH *sb.*[1], *ʒemaca* mate, MAKE *sb.*[1], *ʒelíc* lit. related in form to, of the same form as, LIKE *a.*, YLIKE, *ʒelíca* an equal, *ʒemet* sb., measure, proper measure, proportion, moderation, *ʒemet* adj., *ʒemǽte* lit. of suitable measure, fit, proper, MEET *a.*, *ʒerǽde* lit. suitably prepared (see I-REDE, I-REDY and READY *a.*), *ʒesibb* related, I-SIB(BE, *ʒeswéʒe* harmonious, *ʒetríewe* holding faith with, TRUE.

2. Compounds in which *mutual* relation is implied form a link between the associative and the collective uses, e.g. OE. *ʒefán*, *ʒefiend* (I-FEOND) enemies, *ʒefriend* (I-FREOND) friends, *ʒebróðor* (I-BROTHEREN) brothers, *ʒesweostor* sisters, *ʒemágas* kinsmen, *ʒescý* pair of shoes. The number of OE. words of purely collective meaning is not large; examples are *ʒebæcu* back parts, *ʒefylce* army, troop, *ʒemǽre*, pl. *ʒemǽru* limits, boundary, *ʒetimbru* pl. building, edifice, *ʒewǽde* clothing, I-WEDE, *ʒewider*, pl. *ʒewidru* weather (esp. as good or bad), storm cf. (G. *gewitter*).

b. What is probably to be regarded as a particular development of the collective sense appears in the OE. generalizing pronouns and corresponding adverbs, *ʒehwá* every or each one (cf. I-HWAT), *ʒehwilc* each or every one, ME. *i(l)ch*, ILK, *ʒehú* somehow or other, *ʒehwǽr* everywhere, YWHERE, *ʒehwider* in any or every direction. Some of them were reinforced by the prefixing of *á* ever, e.g. *ǽʒhwá* each or every one, *ǽʒhwæþer* each of two, both, EITHER, *ǽʒhwelc*, ME. *euch* (see EACH).

3. The perfective or intensive sense is found in the following classes of words:

a. Substantives denoting the result of an action, a stage in a process, or a particular state, as OE. *ʒemót* meeting, MOOT *sb.*[1], *ʒemynd* (cf. L. *commemini*) memory, remembrance, MIND *sb.*[1], *ʒesibb* relationship, *ʒesihþ* I-SIGHT, SIGHT, *ʒeswell* swelling, SWELL *sb.*, *ʒeweorc* working, what is done or built, fortification, WORK *sb.*, *ʒewitnes* testimony, I-WITNESS, WITNESS *sb.*, *ʒewrit* what is written, writing, I-WRIT, WRIT.

b. Adjectives denoting a state, as *ʒeclǽne* pure, *ʒehál* WHOLE, *ʒesund* uninjured, SOUND *a.*

c. Verbs which denote achievement of a result, the attainment of a stage in a process, or a special limitation of the general sense of the simple verb. The force of the prefix is clearly recognizable in examples like OE. *ʒeetan* to eat up, consume, 'comedere', *ʒestíʒan* to mount up, 'conscendere', and esp. in such pairs as *ærnan* to run, *ʒeærnan* to gain by running, *áscian*, *friʒnan* to ask, *ʒeáscian*, *ʒefriʒnan* to learn, *beran* to carry, *ʒeberan* to bring forth, *faran* to go, *ʒefaran* to depart this life, die, to get by going, occupy, *rǽcan* to stretch forth, offer, *ʒerǽcan* to reach, obtain, *rídan* to ride, *ʒerídan* to reach as by riding, get into one's power, *weorþan* to become, be, *ʒeweorþan* impers. to be agreed, *gán* to go, *ʒegán* to attain to, get, occupy, *winnan* to fight, strive, *ʒewinnan* to win. But in many instances no difference of meaning is discernible between the simplex and the compound, e.g. *beorʒan*, *ʒebeorʒan* to protect, *hátan*, *ʒehátan* to call, name, command, promise, *limpan*, *ʒelimpan* to happen, *secgan*, *ʒesecgan* to say, tell. There are also some causative compounds, as *ʒebétan* to make good, improve, BEET *v.*, *ʒeforðian* to further (see AFFORD), *ʒehefiʒian* to make heavy. Of such verbs many did not survive except in their pa. pples. into the ME. period; others survived only till about 1300, and that in southern areas; a certain number, such as *ʒehíeran* YHERE, *ʒeséon* YSEE, continued in use in present and past tenses till 1400 or later; very few lasted till 1500 or beyond. But from the middle of the 15th century onwards archaizing poets created (orig. after pa. ppl. forms) new formations in which the prefix was meaningless. Such are *ybete* (Kingis Quair), *ydrawe*, *yryve* (Lydgate), *yclepe* (after *yclept*), *yglaunst*, and *yshrilled* (Spenser), *ycharm'd*, *ysprout* (Robinson's *Mary Magdalene*), *ysteer* (Gosson), *ydrop* (Henry More), *ylipe*, *yminne*, *ypass*; there are also pres. pples. like Sackville's *ycausing* and Milton's *star-ypointing*.

4. The use of perfective or completive *ʒe-* had its most extensive development in the formation of pa. pples., a function common to the Low German and High German groups but not found in Gothic and Scandinavian. The prefix could be employed with any uncompounded verb, but the verbs corresp. to OE. *bringan* to bring, *cuman* to come, *findan* to find, *weorþan* to become, did not normally take it.

In OE. and in ME. (where the prefix continued in full use) it is often impossible to determine whether a particular pa. pple. with *ʒe-* (*i-*, *y-*) belongs to a simple verb or to its compound with *ʒe-*.

In OE. the prefix was employed in forms derived from Latin, as *ʒeplantod* = *plantatus*. Similarly in ME. it was freely employed with verbs of French origin, as *ybaptised*, *yblamed*, *ycircumcysed*, *iclosed*, *igranted*, *ikupled*, *ymartred*, *yoccupied*, *ipaied*, *ipassed*, *irobbet*, *isturbed*, *isued*, *isustened*, *iwarised*. Early loanwords from Scandinavian also took it, as *itaken* (12th cent.).

It came down into ME. as a peculiar characteristic of the language of the south and west-midland regions, and examples are consequently abundant in such texts as (in the 13th cent.) Layamon's Brut, the texts of 'the Katherine group', Owl and Nightingale, Robert of Gloucester, (in the 14th cent.) Ayenbite, Shoreham's poems, Piers Plowman, Trevisa's works, Sir Ferumbras, (in the 15th cent.) Yonge's translation (Anglo-Irish) of Secreta Secretorum and the anonymous Two Cookery Books (E.E.T.S.); its frequency in Lydgate is presumably due to metrical exigencies and to imitation of Chaucer, in whom it is fairly common, whereas it is almost entirely absent from the works of Gower. In the 16th century it was adopted as an archaistic feature from Chaucer and Lydgate by many poetical writers, among whom are Phaer, Sylvester, Arthur Hall, and, above all, Spenser. In the 17th cent. Henry More is a prominent user of these pa. pples., and in the 18th cent. Thomson and other Spenserians have many examples. Some of the most commonly occurring words are *ybent*, *ybound*, *ybrought*, *yclad*, *yclept*, *ydight*, *ydrad*, *ypent*, *ypight*, *ywrought*.

In modern dialects its use in the form *a* (ə) extends over a triangular area of which the angles lie in Worcestershire, Surrey, and Cornwall; it is found also in Pembrokeshire and Wexford. Modern examples of dialectal usage are:—

1568 HOWELL *Arbor of Amitie* 36 b, In husbandry, icham truely, ycounted to excell. **1605** *London Prodigal* IV. i. E 3 b, Such a lerripoope as thick ych was nere a sarued. *c* **1640** JOHN SMYTH *Descr. Hundr. Berkeley* (1885) 23 A native hundreder, beinge asked where hee was borne, answereth, where shu'd y bee y bore, but at Berkeley hurns, And there, begis, each was y bore. Or thus, Each was 'geboren at Berkeley hurns. **1746** *Exmoor Courtship* (E.D.S.) 326 Tha hast a creem'd ma Yearms, and a most a bost ma Neck. **1863** BARNES *Dorset Dial.* 27, I shall've a-meäde. *Ibid.* Gloss., *A-zet*, set, or planted. **1886** *W. Som. Word-bk.*, *Adood*, done.

5. In OE. *ʒe-* was used in the formation of adjs. from substantival stems to express the possession of, or being provided with, something, as *ʒefeax* having hair (of a certain colour), *ʒeheort* courageous, *ʒestence* odorous, *ʒewurms* purulent (f. *wurms* corruption; cf. Goth. *gascōhs* shod), but esp. with the ppl. ending *-od*, *-ed*, as *ʒefeaxod* (beside *ʒefeaxen*) having hair, *ʒehelmod*, *ʒehilmed* helmeted, *ʒehyrnd* horned, *ʒesperod* armed with a spear. The number of the latter was added to in ME., e.g. *ybonchyd* humped, (*wel*) *ycheryd* well-favoured, *ifeðered* (cf. OE. *ʒefeðerian*), *ileaded*, *ileðered*, *ypavylyound*, *iteiled*, (*old*) *i-yeerid*; in some instances the forms with the prefix are the more original forms of such adjs.: see e.g. FEATHERED, LEADED, LEATHERED, TAILED, YEARED. A few compounds of this class were coined by archaists of the 16th century; e.g. *ycrested* (A. Hall, 1581).

-y *suffix*[1] (Forms: 1 **-iʒ**, 2–5 **-i**, 4–6 **-ye**, 4–7 **-ie**, 4– **-y**, 6– now only in certain cases **-ey**), descending from the OE. adj. suffix *-iʒ*, which represents under a common form two OTeut. suffixes **-ĭʒa-*, *-aʒa-*, still distinguishable in OE. by the presence or absence respectively of mutation of the stem vowel of the sb. to which it is added, e.g. *módiʒ* MOODY:—**mōdaʒa-*, f. **mōda-* MOOD *sb.*[1], *mihtiʒ* MIGHTY:—**mahtĭʒa-*, f. **mahtiz* MIGHT, *stániʒ* STONY beside *stǽniʒ*, *þurstiʒ* beside *þyrstiʒ* THIRSTY.

OTeut. **-ĭʒa-*, *-aʒa-* are differentiated forms of Indo-eur. *-qo-* (Skr. *-ka-*, Gr. *-κο-*, L. *-cu-*) arising from application of the suffix to *i-* and *a-* stems respectively. In other Teut. languages the following forms are found: OFris. *-ig*, OS. *ig*, (MDu. *-ig*, *-ich*, Du. *-ig*), OHG. *-ĭg* (MHG. *-ig*, *-eg*, *-ec*, G. *-ig*), ON. *-igr*, Goth. *-eigs*, *-igs*; OS.

-ag, OHG. -ag, -ah, ON. -agr, Goth. -ags, -ahs; also OHG. -uh, ON. -ugr, Goth. -ugs.

When the suffix is appended to a sb. ending in *y*, the convention of modern spelling requires it to be spelt *-ey*, as in *clayey*, *skyey*, *wheyey*. When the sb. ends in *-e* preceded by a vowel, the *e* is retained, as *bluey*, *gluey*; in other cases there may be variation, as *homey*, *homy*, *liney*, *liny*, *nosey*, *nosy*.

1. The general sense of this suffix is 'having the qualities of' or 'full of' that which is denoted by the sb. to which it is added, as *icy* = (1) of the nature of, having the appearance, hardness, coldness, slipperiness, transparency, etc. of ice; (2) full of or covered with ice. In OE. there was a very large number of such adjs., many of which have a continuous history from the earliest times to the present day; in the case of some, however, e.g. *clayey*, *icy*, *rainy*, *wintry*, there is a significant gap in the evidence, which suggests that they may have dropped out of use and have been formed afresh later. There are some noteworthy instances of new formations in late OE., e.g. *dohtiᵹ* DOUGHTY replacing *dyhtiᵹ*, *dústiᵹ* DUSTY, *snáwiᵹ* SNOWY replacing *snáwlic*. To several OE. adjs. in *-iᵹ* there were parallel formations in *-iht*, as *ísiᵹ*, *ísiht* icy, *sandiᵹ*, *sandiht* sandy, *þorniᵹ*, *þorniht* and *þyrniht* thorny; the disappearance of this latter suffix left freer scope of development for the forms in *-iᵹ*.

In ME. the number of these derivatives does not seem to have been at first greatly increased; the following fresh coinages are exemplified first from texts before 1300, *dready*, *fiery*, *frighty*, *hairy* (cf. OE. *hæriht*), *happy*, *needy*, *sleepy* (but cf. OE. *unslǽpiᵹ*), *tidy* (*c* 1250 = in good condition); there are occasional parasynthetic compounds, as *sort-leui* short-lived. The addition of the suffix to non-native sbs. is at least as early as the 13th cent., e.g. *savoury* in the Ancren Riwle. The fourteenth cent., esp. the later half, was prolific in new formations; to this period belong *angry*, *bushy*, *earthy*, *fatty*, *flowery*, *heady*, *hearty*, *milky*, *miry*, *mouldy*, *mucky*, *naughty*, *smoky*, *sweaty*, and many more. The sixteenth cent. was also a prolific period; to it belong, e.g., *cottony*, *frothy*, *dirty*, *healthy*, *leafy* (but *leavy* is 15th cent.), *mealy*, *saucy*, *sugary*, *viny*, *woolly*, *yeasty*. Others, such as *bulky*, *measly*, *noisy* (Dryden), *peppery*, *racy*, *skyey* are recorded first from the 17th cent.

Later new derivatives tend in a large measure to be colloquial, undignified, or trivial, as *bumpy*, *dumpy*, *flighty*, *hammy*, *liney*, *loopy*, *lumpy*, *lungy*, *messy*, *oniony*, *treey*, *verminy*, *vipery*; some are from verbs, as *dangly*. Contextually, the application of the adj. may be narrowed in any direction, as *mousy* = (1) resembling a mouse, (2) quiet as a mouse, or (3) infested with mice. A sense 'addicted to' (cf. 3), as in *booky*, *doggy*, *horsy*, is of modern growth.

1850 THACKERAY *Contrib. to Punch* Wks. 1900 VI. 163 Grizzel had brought me an oniony knife to cut the bread. **1869** MRS. WHITNEY *We Girls* ii, Bedsteads and washstands and bureaus—the very things that made up-stairs look so very bedroomy. **1891** M. MURIEL DOWIE *Girl in Karp.* xi. 144 Fretwork brackets and crystal dangly things.

2. In the 15th cent., if not earlier, certain monosyllabic adjs. were extended by means of this suffix, app. with the design of giving them a more adjectival appearance, e.g. *hugy* f. *huge*, *leany* f. *lean*. The majority of such words arose in the 16th and 17th cent.; examples are: *bleaky*, *chilly*, *cooly*, *dusky*, *fainty*, *haughty*, *hoary*, *lanky*, *paly* adj.[1], *plumpy*, *slighty*, *slippery*, *stouty*, *swarty*, *thicky*, *vasty*. In this application the suffix has not infrequently come to express much the same notion as *-ish*; this is particularly so with colour-epithets, as *blacky*, *yellowy*, and esp. when these are used quasi-advb., as *greeny-blue*, *bluey-green*, *reddy-brown*.

3. As early as the 13th c. this suffix began to be used with verb-stems to express the meaning 'inclined or apt to' do something, or 'giving occasion to' a certain action; in the Ancren Riwle alone we have *slibbri*, *sliddri*, *sluggi*, *slummi*. Chaucer has *sleepy* = soporific. In the 16th cent. arose *choky*, *drowsy*, *slippy*, *sticky*; later we find *blowy*, *clingy*, *floaty*, *quavery*, *rollicky*. The immediate etymon of such adjs. cannot always be ascertained.

4. From the early years of the 19th cent. the suffix has been used still more freely in nonce-words designed to connote such characteristics of a person or thing as call for condemnation, ridicule, or contempt; hence such adjs. as *beery*, *catty*, *churchy*, *jumpy*, *newspapery*, *piggy*, *tinny*.

-y *suffix*[2] (1–3 **-ian, -iᵹan, -ia,** 2–4 **-ien, -ie,** 3 **-iȝen, -eȝen, -ye(n, -in,** 3–4 **-i,** 4–5 **-ey,** 8 **-ee,** 3– **-y**) represents OE. infin. ending *-ian* of the 2nd class of weak verbs (having pa. t. in *-ode* and pa. pple. in *-od*), corresp. to OFris. *-ia*, OS. *-ôian*, *-ôn*, (MLG., MDu. *-en*), OHG. *-ôn* (MHG., G. *-en*), Goth. *-ôn*:—OTeut. **-ōjan*. This class of verbs is denominative; e.g. *OE. sealfian* to anoint:—**salƀōjan*, f. **salƀō* ointment, salve, *hearpian* to harp, f. *hearp* harp, and contains many intrans. verbs derived from adjs., e.g. *cólian* to be cool (= OS. *côlôn*):—**kōlōjan*, f. **kōluz* cool, *nearwian* to be narrow, f. *nearu* narrow; it was swelled in prehistoric OE. by the passing over to it of many verbs that orig. belonged to the *-ǣjan* class, as *hatian* :—**hatōjan*, *-ǣjan* to hate (cf. OHG. *hazzôn* beside *hazzên*). Adoptions of foreign verbs were regularly taken into this class, e.g. OE. *fersian* to versify, (*ᵹe*)*temprian* to moderate, *offrian* to sacrifice.

By the 13th century this suffix had become restricted to the southern and western districts of England, and in the course of the century became generalized in those parts as the infin. ending of all verbs of whatever origin. The following are some examples of the extension of its use: in verbs orig. belonging to other conjugations, *brukien* (OE. *brúcan*) to enjoy, *nemni* (OE. *nemnan*) to name (Layamon); in new derivatives on native stems, *chapfari* to chaffer (Ayenbite), *grundien* to sink (Layamon), *kniȝti* to knight (King Horn); in verbs from Scandinavian, *lastin* (ON. *lasta*) to blame, *trosti* (Ayenbite); in verbs from French, not only those in *-ier*, *-ir*, *-ire* (the similarity of which to the ME. suffix would naturally suggest adoption into the *-ien* conjugation), *boili* (OF. *boillir*) to boil, *consenti* (OF. *consentir*), *herberȝi* (OF. *herbergier*) to harbour, *saisi* (OF. *saisir*) to seize, *trety* (OF. *traitier*) to treat—including those of the *-iss-* conjugation, *norisi*, *norischei* (OF. *noriss-*) to nourish, *perissy* (OF. *periss-*) to perish—but many also of other classes, *anuri* (OF. *anourer*) to worship, *fausie* (OF. *fauser*) to fail, *granti* (AF. *graunter*) to grant, *ioyni* (OF. *ioign-*) to join, *tempti* (OF. *tempter*) to tempt (these forms occur in various texts from Layamon to Ayenbite).

This suffix has been in continuous use in the south-west until the present day, when it is the regular infin. ending of verbs when used intrans. in the counties of Somerset, Devon, and Dorset. Examples and illustrations since 1400 are:—

c **1430** *Two Cookery-bks.* 7 Gadere alle þe kreme in þe clothe, an let hongy on an pyn. *Ibid.* 31 Take Porke or Beef, wheþer þe lykey. **1484** *Yatton Churchw. Acc.* (Som. Rec. Soc.) 115 To costs to rydy for the Chals that waste ystole xij[d]. **1746** *Exmoor Scolding* (E.D.S.) 143 Thee wut ruckee, and squattee, and doattee in the Chimley Coander lick an Axwaddle. **1825** JENNINGS *Observ. Dial. W. Eng.* 7 Another peculiarity is that of attaching to many of the common verbs in the infinitive mode, as well as to some other parts of different conjugations, the letter *y*. Thus it is very common to say *I can't sewy*, *I can't nursy*, *he can't reapy*, *he can't sawy*; as well as *to sewy*, *to nursy*, *to reapy*, *to sawy*, &c. but never, I think, without an auxiliary verb, or the sign of the infinitive *to*. **1863** BARNES *Dorset Dial.* 28 The truth is, that in the Dorset the verb takes *y* only when it is absolute, and never with an accusative case. We may say, 'Can ye zewy?' but never 'Wull ye zewy up theäse zēam?' 'Wull ye zew up theäse zēam?' would be good Dorset. Belonging to this use of the free infinitive *y*-ended verbs, is another kindred one, the showing of a repetition or habit of the action, as 'How the dog do jumpy,' i.e. keep jumping. 'The child do like to whippy,' amuse himself with whipping. 'Idle chap, He'll do nothèn but vishy, (spend his time in fishing,) if you do leäve en alwone.' 'He do markety,' He attends market.

-y *suffix*[3] (also 3–7 **-ie,** 4–6 **-ye**) represents ultimately, through F. *-ie*, Com. Romanic *-ía* = L. *-ĭa*, which comprised under one graphic form the Greek suffixes *-ία* and *-εια*, as in L. *mania* = Gr. *μανία*, whence F. *manie*, ME. MANIE, L. *sympathīa* = Gr. *συμπάθεια*, whence F. *sympathie*, Eng. SYMPATHY. Romanic *-ía* displaced L. ´*-ĭa* and became a living formative for abstract nouns of quality or condition; e.g. in OF. from *corteis* (COURTEOUS) was formed *corteisie* COURTESY, from *fol* (FOOL), *folie* FOLLY, from *gelos* (JEALOUS), *gelosie* JEALOUSY, and the like. When learned adoptions were made of L. nouns in ´*-ĭa*, this suffix was also represented by *-ie*, and so assimilated to *-ía*; e.g. F. *furie* FURY, ad. L. *furia* (whence also organic OF. *fuire*). In AF. preference was given to such forms as these over popular or semi-popular forms, e.g. AF. *accidie*, *glorie*, *estorie*, *victorie* = central F. *accide*, *gloire*, *estoire*, *victoire*, L. or med.L. *accīdia*, *glōria*, *historia* (Gr. *ἱστορία*), *victōria*; it is the AF. forms of such words that were adopted into English (see ACCIDIE, GLORY, STORY, VICTORY).

There were various new formations in late or med.L., in Romanic, or in individual Romance languages; examples are Romanic **libraría* LIBRARY, **poesía* (for *poesis*) POESY, OF. *navie* NAVY.

This suffix has never been in English a prolific formative, but from time to time new coinages have been made, e.g. in the 14th cent. *beggerie* BEGGARY and in the 16th COOPERY (= cooper's work or ware), f. *beggar* and *cooper*, both doubtless furthered by the prevalence of the suffix -ERY. Nonce-words like *orphany* and *tenanty* are of doubtful status, but the correspondence of adjs. in *-ic* and *-ous* to sbs. in *-y* has made possible in modern times the formation after Gr. types of such words as *brachycephaly*, *gymnospermy*, *synchrony*, *syntony* from *brachycephalic*, *gymnospermous*, *synchronous*, *syntonic*. The domain of the suffix is much enlarged by its constituting the final element of many compound suffixes, which receive separate treatment in this Dictionary in their alphabetical places; e.g. -ACY, -CY, -ERY, -GRAPHY, -LATRY, -LOGY, -MACHY, -PATHY, -PHAGY, -PHILY, -RY, -TOMY, -TONY.

Many important sbs. having this suffix appear as English adoptions of French words in the 13th century, as *barony*, *blasphemy*, *company*, *courtesy*, *felony*, *folly*, *jealousy*, *litany*, *story*, *villainy*; others, such as *comedy* and *tragedy*, *fury*, *glory*, *harmony*, *honesty*, *library*, *melancholy*, *memory*, *misery*, *navy*, *victory* date from the 14th century; in the 15th and 16th centuries another series of borrowings from French or from Latin appears, such as *family*, *industry*, *irony*, *liturgy*, *modesty*.

The majority denote a state, condition, or quality; others denote an activity or a result of it, as *blasphemy*, *felony*, *fury*, *harmony*, *history*, *liturgy*, *memory*, *phantasy*, *poesy*, *victory*. From either signification a definitely concrete meaning may be readily developed, which is found in *barony* (= baronial domain, body of barons), *company*, *family*, *library*, *navy*, *sacristy*, etc. The concrete application is abundantly illustrated also by names of countries, as †*Armony* (Armenia), *Italy*, †*Syrie* (Syria), *Brittany*; cf. -IA *suffix*[1].

-y *suffix*[4], representing, first through AF. forms in *-ie*, later by direct adaptation, L. *-ium*, which was added to verbal roots (primarily *i-* and *e-* stems) to denote an act, as in *beneficium* well-doing, good action, f. *beneficĕre* to do good, *colloquium* conference, conversation, f. *colloquī* to speak with, *gaudium* joy, f. *gaudēre* to rejoice, *suspīrium* sigh, f. *suspīrāre* to sigh. The earliest derivatives of this formation that were introduced into English are *remedy* (Ancren Riwle), through AF. *remedie*, from L. *remedium*, and †*sacrilegy* (early 14th c.), from AF. **sacrilegie* or L. *sacrilegium*. To both of these there are parallel forms, †*remede* and *sacrilege*, derived from continental Fr. forms *remede* and *sacrilege*; there are several similar pairs, of which the shorter form represents a continental Fr. form, the longer the corresponding AF. form or the orig. Latin, viz. †*augure*[1] and *augury*, *benefice* and †*beneficie* (rare), †*colloque* and *colloquy*, *empire* (F. *empire*) and †*empery* (AF. *emperie*, L. *imperium*), *homicide* sb.[2] and †*homicidie* (rare), †*perjure* sb.[2] (rare) and *perjury*, †*subside* (*c* 1450–1553) and *subsidy*; †*ingeny* 'mind', 'intellect' has its etymological doublet in *engine* 'native talent, genius, ingenuity, mechanical contrivance'. Most of these words, together with *obloquy*, came into the language before 1500. †*Relevy* sb.[1] (med.L. *relevium*) and *suspiry* (L. *suspīrium*) are rarities; *gaudy*, though partly from L. *gaudium*, is prob. of mixed origin; the derivation of *larceny* is somewhat obscure. *Horology*[1] (beside *horologe*) and *mystery*[1] are derived, through the medium of L. *-ium*, from Greek forms having the cognate termination *-ιον*.

This cannot be said to have been at any time a living suffix in Eng., but there appears to have been reminiscence of its function, combined with the false analogy of words in -RY, in the coining of a few nouns from verbs ending in an r-sound, viz. *enquery* (*c* 1440), *inquery, inquiry* (16th c.), f. *enquere, inquire, expiry* (from 1752) f. *expire*, and a rare *transpiry* f. *transpire*. *Entreaty* (16th c.) is f. *entreat* vb. on the analogy of *treat, treaty*.

-y *suffix*[5], representing AF., OF. *-e, -ee*, mod.F. *-é, -ée*:—L. *-ātu-, -āta-* (see -ATE[1], -ATE[2]).

a. In sbs. = -ATE[1], as in (i) COUNTY[1], OF. *counte*, F. *comté*, L. *comitātus*, f. *comit-*, *comes* count, DUCHY, F. *duché*, L. *ducātus*, f. *duc-*, *dux* duke, TREATY, F. *traité*, L. *tractātus*, f. *tractāre* to treat, (ii) ARMY, F. *armée*, Romanic **armāta* armed force, f. *armāre* to arm, DELIVERY, AF. *delivree*, ppl. sb. f. *delivrer* to deliver, ENTRY, F. *entrée*, Romanic **intrāta*, f. *intrāre* to enter.

This suffix is represented under other forms in certain words, e.g. *assignee, committee, refugee* (F. *assigné, comité, refugié*), *attorney* (OF. *atorné*), *alley, journey, valley* (F. *allée, journée, vallée*).

b. In adjs. = -ATE[2], as in *easy*, OF. *aisié* (F. *aisé*), f. *aisier* to ease. There are few general adjs. of this kind, but there is a considerable number of heraldic descriptive terms having this termination, the earliest example of which is *jerownde* (14th cent.), *gerundi* (1486), GYRONNY, a. OF. *geroné, gironné*, f. *giron* GYRON. Early adoptions of this class have the ending *-e*, later *-ee*, and (as early as the Book of St. Albans, 1486) often *-i*, later *-y*. With some, *-y* has become the regular form, as *barry, bendy, fretty, fusilly, gyronny, lozengy, nowy, paly* adj.[2], *sarcelly*; others are found commonly with either *-é, -ée, -ee*, or *-y*, as *botoné(e, -y, checky, chequee, nébulé, -y, tenné, -y, undé(e, undy*; others, of more modern introduction, usually retain the French spelling, as *coupé, dancetté(e* (cf. †*dancy*), *écartelé, renversé, semée*; some have been anglicized with the native ppl. suffix, either temporarily or permanently, as †*besantid* (= *bezanty*), *escarteled, paled* ppl. adj.[1], *resarcelled, sarcelled*. In *wavy* (after *undy*) we have a rare instance of an analogical use of the suffix with a sb. of native origin.

-y *suffix*[6], **-ie** (also 7–8 -ee, 7– -ey), used to form pet names and familiar diminutives. The forms *-y* and *-ie* are now almost equally common in proper names as such, but in a few instances one or other spelling is preferred, as *Annie, Betty, Sally* (rather than *Anny, Bettie, Sallie*); in the transferred applications of these, as *jemmy, tommy, dicky*, and the like, *-y* prevails; in general hypocoristic forms *-ie* is the favourite spelling after Scottish usage, as *dearie, mousie*. The use of *-ey* is subject to the same rules as for -Y *suffix*[1].

The use of this suffix in pet forms of proper names is found in Sc. as early as 1400; and in the 15th and 16th centuries instances become frequent; examples are *Cryste, Cristi* (f. *Cristin, Cristian*), *Pery* (f. *Pere* Peter), *Sandy* (f. *Sandre* for *Alisandre* Alexander), *Jamy* (f. *James*), *Michy* (f. *Michel*), *Richy* (f. *Richard*), *Roby* (f. *Robert*), *Edi* (f. *Ede, Ade* Adam), *Anny* (f. *Anne*), *Bessy* (f. *Elizabeth*). Such names were prob. modelled orig. upon forms like *Davy, Mathy* (= OF. *Davi, Mathé*), which have the appearance of being pet forms of *David, Mathou*. (Many have survived in Sc. surnames, as *Christie, Eadie, Pirrie, Ritchie, Christison, Mathieson, Robison*; *Davy* occurs as a surname in English use in the early 14th cent.)

The formation was greatly extended in Scottish and English use; whence *Annie*, BILLY, *Carrie* (f. *Caroline*), CHARLIE or CHARLEY, *Fanny* (f. *Frances*), JACKY, JENNY, JIMMY, JOHNNY, NANNY, *Nellie* (f. *Ellen*), PATTY, *Reggie* (f. *Reginald*), TOMMY, *Willie*. Many female names have corresponding forms in Du. names with the suffix *-je*, as in *huisje* little house, f. *huis* HOUSE *sb.*[1]; e.g. *Betty, Elsie, Hetty, Katy, Lottie, Matty, Sally* correspond to Du. *Betje, Elsje, Jetje, Kaatje, Lotje, Matje, Sellie*; but there is no evidence of historical contact.

Recently appended to surnames to form a familiar name. **1941** J. HILTON *Random Harvest* v. 352 She ran into his arms calling out: 'Oh, Smithy—Smithy—it may not be too late.' **1958** A. HACKNEY *Private Life* ix. 84 'Who's Old Kitey?' 'A Mr. Kite. He's our shop steward.' *Ibid.* xvii. 171 'Mr. Cox arranged it.'.. 'You've got to be careful with old Coxy.'

The earliest recorded instances of the use of such proper names as appellatives are Scottish and belong to the beginning of the 16th century: viz. *Lowrie* (f. *Lowrens* Laurence) used for 'fox'; *Katy* and *Kitty* (f. *Katherine*), with the meaning 'lass, wench', tending to a specifically depreciatory sense, 'wanton, loose woman', which senses belong also to the 18th century *Molly* and *Nanny* (as in *nanny-house* brothel); a few female names, viz. *Molly* and (dialectally) *Peggy*, have been used to designate an effeminate type of man.

The application of the female names to birds dates, according to our evidence, from the close of the 16th century; the wren is designated by *Kitty* and (more commonly) *Jenny*; in 1616 Ben Jonson calls a parrot *Polly*; in modern dialects *Peggy* is applied to various warblers and the pied wagtail, and *Betty* to the hedge-sparrow. Then, in the course of the 17th century, these names came to be applied to various mechanical contrivances, among which machines for spinning processes and the burglar's jemmy are prominent. This transference of application is illustrated by *Betty* (a burglar's jemmy, 1700), *Jenny* (in SPINNING-JENNY, 1783), *Jinny* (a stationary engine at a mine), *Peggy* (a washing-tub dolly, in various dialects).

Among male names the following are typical: *Johnny* is used for fellow, chap, *Jemmy* for the burglar's weapon, *Billy* for a roving machine; *Bobby, Charley, Dicky, Geordie, Jacky, Jockey, Tommy* exhibit a great variety of modes of application.

The first known instance of the application of the suffix to a common noun is LADDIE which appears in 1546 in the form *laddy*, used by John Bale; but there is no evidence until the 18th century of the generalization of *-y* for pet diminutives. Early instances are *dummie* (1595), *grannie* (1663), *dearie* (1681), *mousie* (1693, Sc.); *laddie, lassie*, and *sweetie* were used by Allan Ramsay, and these, with Burn's *birdie* and *mousie*, helped to popularize such formations in English generally; hence the appearance in the late 18th and early 19th century of *cooky, doggie, froggy, mannie, slavey*. In *blacky* and *darky* there remained something of the status of a proper name; cf. *Fatty* as a nickname. *Bookie* for *bookmaker* is a formation of a rare type; cf. *nighty* for *nightdress*.

There are two words that are generally held to contain this suffix, viz. *baby* (late 14th c.) and *puppy* (late 15th c.). With *baby* may perhaps be coupled *daddy* and *mammy*, although the evidence for these is not earlier than the 16th century; the pairs *babe* and *baby*, *dad* and *daddy*, *mam* and *mammy*, may have resulted from different phonetic reductions of original reduplicated forms **baba* (cf. BABAN), **dada*, **mama*. The source of *puppy* (spelt *popi* in the Bk. St. Albans) is doubtful; *pup* is a back-formation from it.

ya (jɑː, jə), repr. *U.S.* and *dial.* pronunc. of (*a*) YOU *pers. pron.*; (*b*) YOUR *poss. adj.*

(*a*) **1941** B. SCHULBERG *What makes Sammy Run?* xi. 193 Sunset Club... They've got a new dinge band there that'll kill ya. **1959** N. MAILER *Advts. for Myself* (1961) 46 Stay off the railroads, they bleed ya dry. **1973** E. BULLINS *Theme is Blackness* 64 Won't ya please move out of the way, honey? **1980** *Dirt Bike* Oct. 8/1 All of you mini riders can start drooling now, because as soon as we can get our gloves on one, we'll test it for ya.

(*b*) **1946** K. TENNANT *Lost Haven* (1947) iii. 50 What ya done with ya collar? **1970** K. PLATT *Pushbutton Butterfly* xi. 138 He waved the Luger. 'On ya feet.' I got up. **1973** *Black World* Oct. 56/2 Put ya hands on 'a table.

ya: see ONE, YAH, YE, YEA.

yaa-boo, var. YAH BOO *int.* (and *sb.*)

yaas (jæs, jɑːs), repr. a drawled pronunc. of YES *adv.*, esp. in U.S. speech.

1893 H. A. SHANDS *Some Peculiarities of Speech in Mississippi* 68 *Yaas*, the almost universal pronunciation of *yes*. **1895** A. W. PINERO *Second Mrs. Tanqueray* III. 104 *Paula*. Your wife? *Sir George*. Yaas—Birdie. **1913** KIPLING *Diversity of Creatures* (1917) 285 I've become an Episcopalian since I married. Ya-as. **1931** W. FAULKNER in *Harper's Mag.* Sept. 401/2 'Yaas,' the man in overalls said in a dry, drawling tone. 'Yaas. It got caught.'

ya bass (jæ bæs), repr. Sc. rendering of 'You bastard.'

1968 *Daily Tel.* (Colour Suppl.) 4 Oct. 21/2 We saw a film, *The Terror of the Tongs*... When we came out, we just started shouting: 'Tongs! Tongs, ya bass!' **1973** BOYD & PARKES *Dark Number* vii. 72 There was a crate of dead wine bottles... *Vino Fino* from Argentina, ya bass. **1974** *Punch* 6 Mar. p. v/1 That archetypal graffito, the Glaswegian *Ya bass*.

yabba ('jæbə). *Jamaica.* Also **yabah**. [Jamaican.] A large wooden or earthenware vessel used for cookery or storage.

1889 *Victoria Q.* (Kingston, Jamaica) May 50 The familiar 'Yabba' or earthen vessel. **1929** M. W. BECKWITH *Black Roadways* 27 Earthen bowls, hand turned and covered with a rude glaze, are always to be had in the Kingston market, but they are more rare in the hills where the old-time 'yabba' is being supplanted by tinware. **1953** *Caribbean Anthol. Short Stories* 103 She took a handful of cornmeal out of the wooden yabba. **1953** R. MAIS *Hills were Joyful Together* I. i. 11 Ras.. spat in an earthenware yabba set beside him for the purpose. **1959** A. SALKEY *Quality of Violence* iv. 56 He picked up an empty *yabah* which was resting on a Bible... He.. let it slip from his hands. It.. splintered in jagged pieces.

yabber ('jæbə(r)), *sb.* *Australia.* ['It is pronounced by the aborigines *yabba*, without a final *r*. *Ya* is an aboriginal stem, meaning to speak' (Morris *Austral Eng.*).] Speech, language, talk: applied to the speech of the Australian aborigines. So **yabber** *v.* (*intr.* and *trans.*), to talk, esp. in an aboriginal Australian language.

1855 R. CARBONI *Eureka Stockade* iv. 5 There was further a great waste of yabber-yabber about the diggers not being represented in the Legislative Council. **1874** BEVERIDGE *Lost Life* III. 37, I marked Much yabber that I did not know. **1885** MRS. C. PRAED *Austral. Life* 19 They yabbered unsuspiciously to each other. *Ibid.* 28 Longing to fire a volley of Black's yabber across a London dinner-table. **1887** FARRELL *How He Died* 126 He's yabbering some sort of stuff in his sleep. **1888** 'R. BOLDREWOOD' *Robbery under Arms* xxvii, They could speak a little Spanish and French, and got on with them. But Jim and I could only stare and stand open-mouthed.. while they'd yabber away quite comfortable.

yabble, Sc. var. GABBLE *sb.* and *v.*; hence **yabbler** = GABBLER. (Cf. *yab, yabber* = GAB, GABBER.)

1808 JAMIESON, To *yabble, v.n.*, to gabble, Fife. **1819** W. TENNANT *Papistry Storm'd* (1827) 204 And than sic skellochin' and shout,..Was never sic a yabble! **1871** W. ALEXANDER *Johnny Gibb* xi, There was a general.. clustering about him.. as Samie 'yabbled' out the particulars. **1901** LAWSON *Remin. Dollar Acad.* 48 An outpost of these cacklers and yablers sounded the alarm.

yabby ('jæbɪ), *sb.* *Austral.* Also **yabbie, yappy**. [Aboriginal.] **a.** A small, edible freshwater crayfish found in the eastern part of Australia, esp. one of the genus *Charax*. **b.** A burrowing, prawn-like, littoral crustacean of the order Thalassinidea.

1886 F. A. HAGENAUER in E. M. Curr *Austral. Race* III. 554/1 Crayfish—yappy. **1894** *Argus* (Melbourne) 6 Oct. 11/2 Small crayfish, called 'yabbies'.. may be found all over Australia, both in large and small lagoons. **1897** *Australasian* 30 Jan. 224/4 The bait used is 'yabby', a small crayfish found in the sand on the beach at low tide. **1930** V. PALMER *Men are Human* vi. 49 The yabbies they had cooked in a treacle-tin down by the lagoon. **1944** *Living off Land* iii. 49 Digging out these burrows will secure yabbies... The yabbie can be toasted. **1963** A. UPFIELD *Madman's Bend* xvi. 130 Been in the water days, by the look of him. Yabbies been at him too. No blood, but hole's here. **1966** *Courier-Mail* (Brisbane) 1 Oct. 2/6 This tasty fresh water crustacean is more frequently called the Yabby, which immediately brings about a confusion with the much-used marine Yabby. **1973** P. WHITE *Eye of Storm* x. 490 Used to come here after yabbies. I'd like to poke around a bit. **1977** *Caravan World* (Austral.) Jan. 105/1 A restaurant serving fresh, succulent yabbies has opened near the Murray Mouth.

'yabby, *v.* *Austral.* [f. prec. sb.] *intr.* To hunt for yabbies. So **'yabbying** *vbl. sb.*

1934 *Bulletin* (Sydney) 24 Oct. 21/2 Here's a sport for those who.. forget their bait when yabbying. **1941** K. TENNANT *Battlers* v. 53 He.. asked about the boys. 'They've gone yabbying.' **1964** *Sunday Mail* (Brisbane) 5 Apr., He participated personally in yabbying forays.

‖**yaboo** (jɑːˈbuː). Also 8 **yabou**, 9 **yabu**. [Hindustani = Persian *yābū*.] One of a breed of large ponies or small stout horses in Afghanistan, Persia, and adjacent countries.

1753 HANWAY *Trav.* (1762) II. XIV. vii. 367 *note*, There are in the highland country of Kandahar and Cabul a small kind of horses called yabous, which are very serviceable. **1831** *Lit. Souvenir* 153 What in England would have been termed a capital punch pony,—in Persia, a good stout yaboo. **1880** in Ld. Roberts *41 Years in India* lxi. (1897) II. 353 Yabus 1,592, mules and ponies 5,926.

ya boo, var. YAH BOO *int.* (and *sb.*)

‖**yacca** ('jækə). [Native name.] A West Indian evergreen tree, of either of two species of *Podocarpus* (*P. coriacea* and *P. Purdieana*, N. O. *Taxaceæ*), or its wood, used in cabinet-work, etc. Also *attrib.*

1843 HOLTZAPFFEL *Turning* I. 109 Yacca Wood, or Yacher, from Jamaica, is sent in short crooked pieces like roots. **1864** GRISEBACH *Flora W. Ind. Isl.* 789 Yacca tree, *Podocarpus coriacea*. **1890** H. THOMAS *Untrodden Jamaica* 10 A gate composed of closely set pales of Yacca.

yacca, var. YAKKA.

yacht (jɒt), *sb.* Forms: 6 **yeagh**, 7 **yoath, yolke** ?, **yaugh, yuaght, yought, y(e)aught**, (*Sc.* **z(e)aught**, with *z* for *ȝ*), **yaucht, jacht, yach, (yacth), yat, yott**, 7–9 **yatcht, yatch** (*pl.* 7–8 **yatchs**, 8 **yatches**), 7– **yacht**. [ad. early mod.Du. *jaght(e* (now *jacht*) = *jaghtschip* (lit. ship for chasing), light sailing vessels, fast piratical ship, f. *jag(h)t* hunting, chase (= G. *jagd*), f. *jagen* to hunt, chase (see -T *suffix*[3] a). Owing to the presence in the Du. word of the unfamiliar guttural spirant denoted by *g(h)*, the English spellings have been various and erratic; how far they represent varieties of pronunciation it is difficult to say. That a pronunciation (jɔtʃ) or (jatʃ), denoted by *yatch*, once existed seems to be indicated by the plural *yatches*; it may have been suggested by *catch*, *ketch*.

The word has been adopted in many European languages: F. *yacht* (jak), G. *jacht-*, *yacht(schiff)*, Da. *jagt*, MSw. *jackt* (15th c.), Icel., Sw. *jakt*, Sp. *yacte*, *yate*, *yac*, Pg. *hiate*, Russ. *yakta*.]

a. A light fast-sailing ship, in early use esp. for the conveyance of royal or other important persons; later, a vessel, usually light and comparatively small, propelled by motive power other than oars, and used for pleasure excursions, cruising, etc., and now esp. one built and rigged for racing.

1557 *Voy. Stephan Burrough* in Hakluyt *Voy.* (1598) I. 294 A barke which was of Dronton, and three or foure Norway yeaghes, belonging to Northberne. **1613** Phineas Pett *Autobiogr.* (Navy Rec. Soc. 1918) 109 [We anchored thwart of Sluis, where came on board us his] yoathes [the Prince of Orange]. **1616** R. Cocks *Diary* (Hakl. Soc.) I. 118, I esteemed he came to spie.. whether our shipp and the Duch yaught staid for to take the Amacon shipp. **1621** in Foster *Eng. Factories Ind.* (1906) 303 This smalle shippe or yolke is mostly ladne with pepper. **1630** *R. Johnson's Kingd. & Commw.* 40 The Emperour (who yet had never greater vessell than a Punt or Yaugh upon the Danuby). **1645** in *Sussex Archæol. Coll.* XLVIII. 129 Paid for tow and nails used aboute my Lords Yought at Pemsie. *Ibid.*, To unrig my Lord's Yaught. **1660** Sir W. Lower *Voy. Chas. II*, 12 Jachts or pinnaces. **1664** in *Maitl. Club Misc.* (1840) II. 518 To the sailors whair his Lordship breakfast in the Zeaught 001 10 00. To the sailleris of the Zaught at Owlage 003 12 00. **1666** in *10th Rep. Hist. MSS. Comm.* App. v. 10 Gunner of his Majestie's vessell the Mary yaucht. **1673** H. Stubbe *Further Justif. War Neth.* 5 They who had struck their Flags .. unto a Ketch of two Guns in the time of Cromwel, refuse to do it unto a Yacht of his Majesties. **1678** R. Ferrier *Jrnl.* 25 in *Camden Misc.* (1895) IX, A fair small River which yᵉ King has there cut to take his pleasure on, there being severall yotts. **1680** Alsop *Mischief Impos.* vi. 36 A.. Man of War as big as 2 or 3 Yatchs. **1688** in Boys *Sandwich* (1792) 759 About 20 small smacks and yats in the Downs. *a* **1700** Evelyn *Diary* 1 Oct. 1661, I sailed this morning with his Majesty in one of his Yatchts (or pleasure boats), vessels not known among us till the Dutch East India Company presented that curious piece to the King. **1710** J. Harris *Lex. Techn.* II, *Yatches*, are Vessels with one Deck carrying from 4 to 12 Guns, with from 20 to 40 Men; and are of Burden from 30 to 160 Tun. **1766** *Ann. Reg.*, *Chron.* 137/1 Admiral Keppel set out for Harwich, to take the command of the yatchs intended to carry over her R. Highness the Princess Carolina Matilda to Holland. **1769** Falconer *Dict. Marine* (1780) s.v., The royal yachts are commonly rigged as ketches, except the principal one reserved for the sovereign, which is equipped with three masts like a ship. **1790** H. Walpole *Let. to Miss Mary Berry* 10 July, The river was covered with little yatches and boats. **1811** *Self Instructor* 587 The Dutch yatchts are chiefly used on their rivers and canals. **1839** Darwin *Voy. Nat.* xxiii. 602 A yacht now with every luxury of life can circumnavigate the globe.

b. *attrib.* and *Comb.*, as ***yacht-berth***, ***-builder***, ***-building***, ***-club***, ***marina***, ***-race***, ***-racing***, ***-sailing***, ***-sailor***, ***-squadron***; **yacht basin**, a dock constructed for the mooring of yachts; a marina; **yacht broker**, a dealer in yachts; so **yacht brokerage**; **yacht-yard**, a yard where yachts are built or repaired.

1929 *Motorboat* 10 Mar. 20/1 For many years there has been much talk of public *yacht basins. **1952** P. Atkey *Juniper Rock* i. 2 An engine breakdown.. had compelled Roy to take the *Marsouin* limping into the yacht basin at Marseilles. **1981** L. Deighton *XPD* xii. 102 One of the parking places near the yacht basin. **1846** Mrs. Gore *Engl. Char.* (1852) 46 Insensible to the perils of any uneasy *yacht-berth. **1882** *Yachting Q.* July (Advt.), Cox and King, *Yacht brokers & Yachting auctioneers. **1982** N. J. Crisp *Brink* ix. 187 The yacht brokers were still in business... The pubs were still full of yachting types. **1974** J. Dimona *Last Man at Arlington* i. 51 In Nassau.. he had managed to set up a profitable *yacht brokerage. **1868** *Trollope's Brit. Sports* 195 The Swedes are skilful *yacht-builders. *Ibid.* 217 The progressive improvement in *yacht-building during the last twenty years. **1834** G. Crabbe Jr. in *Poet. Wks. G. Crabbe* I. 13 A party of amateur sailors was formed—the *yacht club of Aldborough. **1837** in *Yachting* (Badm. Libr.) II. 12 That the Commodore be requested to seek an.. audience with Her Majesty, with a view to the continuance of the Royal Cup to be presented to the Yacht Club at Cowes. **1981** L. Deighton *XPD* xii. 101 The Marina del Rey.. has the swanky yacht club as a centre-piece. **1973** 'A. York' *Captivator* ii. 32 The ah, sloop put into Cuxhaven... It entered the *yacht marina there, secured a berth. **1983** P. Ferris *Distant Country* ii. 15 The yacht marina.. would reopen with brand-new quays and pontoons. **1867** Dickens *Lett.* (1880) II. 271 The American *yacht race is the last sensation. **1868** *Trollope's Brit. Sports* 196 We do not mean to say that *yacht-racing has wholly escaped those sharp practices. **1833** W. H. Maxwell *Field Bk.* Introd., *Yacht-sailing has been slightly noticed. **1856** Marett *Yachts and Yacht Bldg.* Introd. p. ix, The designer [of a yacht] should .. be.. an experienced *yacht sailor. *Ibid.* 74 For many years after the establishment of the Royal *Yacht Squadron. **1933** 'L. Luard' *All Hands* 236 The proprietor of a *yacht-yard. **1980** P. Moyes *Angel Death* xx. 248 We have to get down there.. to the yacht yard. There's something wrong.

Hence (*nonce-wds.*) **'yachtdom**, **'yachtery**, yachts collectively; **'yachtian**, **'yachtist**, a yachtsman; **'yachtling**, a little yacht; **'yachty**, *a.*, pertaining to or characteristic of a yacht.

1901 *Pall Mall Gaz.* 12 Jan. 1/3 A yacht for her Majesty that would eclipse all examples in modern *yachtdom for luxurious comfort and sea-going qualities. **1861** J. G. Francis *Beach Rambles* 60 The flower of the *yachtery of England. **1842** *Blackw. Mag.* LI. 419 The assembled Thames *yachtians. **1895** *Nat. Observer* 21 Sept. 542 They went the way all *yachtists go. **1872** *Daily News* 21 Aug., The tiny *yachtlings (the largest of them measures but 10 tons, the smallest but four or five). **1892** *Field* 27 Feb. 279/2 The latest craft on the stocks—though of size that might be called '*yachty'—is.. thoroughly of the canoe family.

yacht (jɒt), *v.* [f. prec. sb., or back-formation from YACHTING *sb.*] *intr.* To make a trip in a yacht. (Chiefly in gerund or pres. pple.)

1836 Marryat *Midsh. Easy* xix, We must swear that it is a party of pleasure, and that we are gentlemen yachting. **1858** S. Wilberforce *Sp. Missions* (1874) 243 Sir James Brooke.. not content with yachting it about amidst orange flowering groves,.. conceived a great work amongst the Malay race. **1863** Speke *Jrnl.* 260 Sometimes the king spends a fortnight yachting. **1867** *Nation* (N.Y.) 3 Jan. 1/2 The only one of the owners who *yachted* as well as raced, by being on board his own craft.

yachter ('jɒtə(r)). [f. YACHT *sb.* or *v.* + -ER[1].] One who makes a trip in a yacht; a yachtsman.

1828 *Sporting Mag.* XXI. 341 Several East India ships.. with such saucy rigging that would have made the Yachters raving in envy. **1892** *Daily News* 22 Mar. 5/4 When in Bombay he was an enthusiastic yachter.

yachtie ('jɒtɪ), *sb. colloq.* (chiefly *Austral.* and *N.Z.*). Also **yachty**. [f. YACHT *sb.* + -IE.] A yachtsman.

1943 *Amer. Speech* XVIII. 88 [New Zealand English.] Yachty. **1965** G. McInnes *Road to Gundagai* x. 184 One should never.. leave them [*sc.* bottles] bobbing about the bay the way the careless 'yachties' did. **1972** *Sat. Rev.* 21 Oct. 62 Dunnie's a yachtie, he lives up on the cliff, and he's a rich guy. **1976–7** *Sea Spray* (N.Z.) Dec./Jan. 35/2 (Advt.), Laid polyester rope. The yachties' workhorse. **1977** *Herald* (Melbourne) 17 Jan. 19/2 They are really to cater for the spillover from Port Phillip Bay as more and more yachties realise that they can be much nearer to the blue water both inside and outside. **1977** *Pacific Islands Monthly* Feb. 25 (*heading*) Slugged yachtie.

yachting ('jɒtɪŋ), *vbl. sb.* [f. YACHT *sb.* or *v.* + -ING[1].] The action, practice, or amusement of cruising in a yacht; the art of navigating a yacht. Freq. *attrib.*, esp. applied to garments designed for use on yachts.

1836 Marryat *Three Cutters* i, Of all amusements, give me yachting. **1874** Burnand *My Time* xxix. 279 He.. never missed a season's yachting with them.

attrib. **1850** Ogilvie s.v., A yachting voyage. **1868** A. K. H. Boyd *Less. Mid. Age* 327 We had a pleasant yachting excursion. **1873** *Young Englishwoman* June 280/2, I always wear yachting shoes without heels, made of the white canvas, and with leather toes and straps, as now worn by boating and yachting gentlemen. **1884** *Harper's Mag.* Aug. 465/2 Invited to a yachting party. **1887** *Times* 27 Aug. 9 A sad yachting disaster occurred at Ilfracombe. **1894** *Country Gentlemen's Catal.* 155/1 Blue cloth yachting caps, from 8/6. **1931** E. F. Benson *Mapp & Lucia* vii. 200 Contempt for Georgie.. had been intensified by the sight of his yachting cap. **1976** 'A. Garve' *Home to Roost* iii. 37 He was wearing .. a battered old yachting cap. **1983** G. Thompson *Nobody cared for Kate* iv. 26 Maggie.. had dressed for the barge trip. .. She wore a yachting suit.

So **'yachting** *ppl. a.*, that sails in a yacht; addicted to yachting.

1848 Thackeray *Van. Fair* xxxix, Yachting men from Southampton. **1862** *Lond. Rev.* 16 Aug. 138 The yachting world is very variously composed.

yachtman ('jɒtmən). Now *rare*. Pl. **-men**. [f. YACHT *sb.* + MAN *sb.*[1]] = YACHTSMAN.

1820 *Examiner* No. 662. 807/1 The Royal Yachtman. **1856** 'Stonehenge' *Brit. Rur. Sports* 460/2 A variety of sails called flying-jibs, &c., which vary with every yachtman's fancy. **1868** *Trollope's Brit. Sports* 205 First-class yachtmen from Harwich.

yachtsman ('jɒtsmən). Pl. **-men**. [f. gen. of YACHT *sb.* + MAN *sb.*[1]] A man who owns, manages, or sails in a yacht; a man addicted to yachting.

1862 *Lond. Rev.* 16 Aug. 138 It.. requires a combination of those attributes which distinguish the modern Briton to make a great racing-man or a genuine yachtsman. **1868** *Trollope's Brit. Sports* 219 Nine out of ten yachtsmen build or buy their vessels in the dark.

Hence **'yachtsmanship**, the practice or skill of a yachtsman.

1862 Vanderdecken (*title*) The Yacht Sailor; a treatise on Practical Yachtsmanship. **1886** *St. James's Gaz.* 8 Sept. 4/2 The partisans of English yachtsmanship.

So **yachtswoman** ('jɒtswʊmən).

1888 *Athenæum* 1 Sept. 294/1 The Sea-Eagle.. is much exposed to the attacks of marauding yachtsmen and yachtswomen. **1906** *Daily Tel.* 29 Jan. 9/6 A well-known American yachtswoman.

yachty ('jɒtɪ), *a. colloq.* [f. YACHT *sb.* + -Y[1].] Of or pertaining to yachts.

1950 E. Allcard *Single-Handed Passage* 177 Don't use 'yachty' fittings. They are only good for the Solent. **1983** *Times* 19 Aug. 24/1 The yachts displace a lot of money which slops into the town to support.. galleries selling yachty prints.

yack (jæk), *sb.*

1. A syllable imitative of a snapping sound.

1861 Meredith *Evan Harrington* xli, Tom.. with a sound translated by 'yack', sent his leg out a long way.

2. *slang.* Also **yak**. Incessant talk of a trivial or boring nature. Freq. reduplicated and as *int.*

1958 J. Cannan *And be Villain* i. 5 That blasted Primrose will have arrived by now—yak yak yak, talking Eve into God knows what. **1965** W. King in *Black Short Story Anthol.* (1972) 306 Then, through the yak-yak, Mac began to tell us the 'unusual something' that he had just recently done. **1972** C. Weston *Poor, Poor Ophelia* (1973) xxxii. 205 A lot of yak in the news about the missing boot. **1983** N. Freeling *Back of North Wind* 99 The sudden head-down butt jabbed into someone's face, is a highly effective way of putting a stop to his yack.

b. An accent or tone of voice.

1957 M. Spark *Comforters* vi. 138 He fiddled with the tape machine... The voice came with an exaggerated soppy yak: 'Caroline, darling.' **1975** *Camping & Trailering Guide* Oct. 33/1 You will hear French Canadian patois mixed with Ontario English, down-Maine tones and New York yak.

yack (jæk), *v. slang.* Also **yak**. [Echoic, or f. YACK *sb.*] *intr.* **a.** *rare.* To make a snapping sound (cf. YACK *sb.* 1).

1873 W. Cory *Lett. & Jrnls.* (1897) 318 He opens his beak, and yacks like the young jackdaw.

b. To engage in trivial or unduly persistent conversation; to chatter.

1950 'P. Quentin' *Follower* v. 38 Yakked a lot. Know how she is. Talk your ear off... She yakked on about you being in South America. **1955** 'H. Robbins' *Stone for Danny Fisher* I. ix. 65, I was busy yakking with a broad. **1956** W. H. Whyte *Organization Man* (1957) xxvi. 359 Four or five of the girls and their kids will be yakking away. **1958** T. Roethke *Let.* 16 Aug. (1970) 220 I've spent nearly the whole of three sessions with my doctor yacking about you. **1958** L. Whishaw *As far as You'll take Me* iv. 47 Didn't have any breakfast, too busy yacking about women. **1977** J. Porter *Who the Heck is Sylvia?* vi. 57 She should have acted first and yacked about it afterwards. **1981** J. Trenhaile *Kyril* xix. 142 Those two will yak all day.

Hence **'yacking**, **yakking** *vbl. sb.* and *ppl. a.*

1959 'S. Ransome' *I'll die for You* ii. 29 She could sit at any bar.., with an ear out for all the yakking that goes on, and pick up any amount of gossip. **1971** *Time* 7 June 31/1 [The ability] to switch away from yakking actresses and the necessity of having yakking starlets for the ratings. **1976** N. Freeling *Lake Isle* xxvii. 192 Shop-keepers.. yelling in the street at yacking housewives. **1977** *N.Y. Rev. Bks.* 12 May 6/4 The sound which emerges from the pages is that of the yakking of debutantes.

yack, var. YERK, to beat; dial. f. OAK.

yacker ('jækə(r)), *sb. slang.* Also **yakker**.

1. [Echoic.] Talk, conversation, chatter. *Austral.*

1882 *Sydney Slang Dict.* 9/1 *Yacker*, talk. **1973** P. White *Eye of Storm* vii. 306 She wished it had been a hospital, when she could have produced a chart, handed over.., and swept off without further yakker. *Ibid.* ix. 441 Couldn't get on with me work—not with all the yakker that was goin' on in 'ere.

2. [f. YACK *v.* + -ER[1].] **a.** A chatterbox or gossip. **b.** = YACK *sb.* 2 b.

1959 G. Mitchell *Man who grew Tomatoes* vi. 87 Now that will be enough ammunition for the yakkers, if there are any present. **1960** 'R. Simons' *Frame for Murder* viii. 99 'What sort of a bloke?' 'Tall. Flashy dressed. Got a slight American yakker.' **1973** *Tel.* (Brisbane) 13 Sept. 30/1 Last, but hardly least, is the yakker, who talks continually to her passengers. **1984** *N.Y. Times* 28 Aug. B-2/5 She just brought the parrot along for the ride... He was quite a yakker.

yacker ('jækə(r)), *v. slang.* [f. YACK *v.* + -ER[5].] = YACK *v.*

1961 S. Price *Just for Record* x. 109 They're yackering away in the kitchen. **1982** *Financial Times* 20 Aug. 11/4 'Yellow Polka-Dot Bikini'—one of the scratchy 78s..—yackers melodiously while the characters gallivant through daytime Calcutta.

yacket ('jækɪt), *v. slang.* [f. YACKET(Y *int.*] *intr.* = YACK *v.* So **'yacketing** *ppl. a.*

[**1953**: see YACKETY-YACK(ET)ING *vbl. sb.* and *ppl. a.*] **1958** P. de Vries *Mackerel Plaza* 153 All this yacketing oratory. **1969** *New Yorker* 29 Nov. 51/3 We warn them, we yacket away night and day.. but they never learn.

yackety ('jækɪtɪ), *int. slang.* Also **yackity**, **yaketty**, **yakkety**, **yakkity**. [Echoic.] Expressing the sound of incessant chatter. Usu. reduplicated or with *ya(c)k*.

1953 Berrey & Van den Bark *Amer. Thes. Slang* (1954) §189/2 Idle talk; chatter... Yackety-yack,.. yackety-yackety. **1955** M. Millar *Beast in View* vi. 93 She.. parks herself in the phone booth, and there she sits, yackity, yackity, yackity. **1959** S. Gibbons *Pink Front Door* iii. 36 She went yaketty-yak to Katy. **1959** L. Smith *One Hour* (1960) xviii. 231 The TV going yakkety yak. **1959** 'J. Welcome' *Stop at Nothing* vii. 113 Mildred.. has been going yackety yack-yack about you to some purpose. **1976** *Billings* (Montana) *Gaz.* 26 June 5-B/5 I'm talking away, yakkity yak, and he started gasping for breath. **1982** D. Bagley *Windfall* xxix. 288 The Sergeant.. only talks when he has something to say. Everybody else goes yacketty-yack all the time.

Also **,yackety-'yack(ety** *sb.* = YACK *sb.* 2 a; *v. intr.* = YACK *v.*; **,yackety-'yack(et)ing** *vbl. sb.* and *ppl. a.*

1953 M. Dickens *No More Meadows* iv. 185 Our laundry's full of yackety-yacketing women this morning. **1958** *Observer* 15 June 15/7 A muddle-headed momma.. who knows no better than to drive away her husband.. by constant yackety-yack and pleas to stay at home. **1959** *Woman* 6 June 10/1 For once the place will be free of giggles and girlish yakitty-yak. **1960** *N.Y. Times Bk. Rev.* 3 July 1 (*heading*) How to dig the hips' yackety-yak. **1976** *Billings* (Montana) *Gaz.* 26 June B-14/8 A man working alone could never have enjoyed 'chewing the fat and the yakety yaking and drinking coffee'.

yad, obs. pa. t. of GO.
1424 in Picton *L'pool Munic. Rec.* (1883) I. 23 The Sheriffs..yadden up to the West Derby fen. *c* **1435** *Torr. Portugal* 1193 His squiers habite he had, Whan he to the deyse yad.

yad, var. YAUD *Sc.* and *north. dial.*, mare.

yadder, var. EDDER: see YEDDER *sb.* and *v.*

yae, Sc. dial. var. AE *a.*, one, only. Hence **yaefauldness,** 'onefoldness', simplicity.
a **1771** *Bonny Hind* viii. in Child *Ballads* (1884) I. 446/2 I'm Lord Randal's yae daughter, He has nae mair nor me. **1864** J. BROWN *Jeems* 8 His absolute downrightness and yaefauldness.

yaf, yafe, obs. pa. t. of GIVE *v.*

yaff (jæf), *v. Sc.* and *north. dial.* [Echoic: cf. YAFFLE *v.*[1] and WAFF.] *intr.* To bark, yelp; also, to prate, nag. Hence **'yaffing** *vbl. sb.* and *ppl. a.*; also **yaff** *sb.*, a bark or yelp.
1609 *Ravenscroft's Deuteromelia* 21 With all the hounds at her tail! With 'yeaffe a yaffe! yeaffe a yaffe!' **1808** JAMIESON, To *Yaff*,.. 1. To bark,..to yelp,..2. To prate, to talk pertly. **1815** SCOTT *Guy M.* i, Will ye no let me hear what the man wants, wi' your yaffing? **1844** G. J. PENNINGTON *Pronunc. Gk.* 22 A yaffing cur. **1910** G. J. LAURIE in *Poets of Ayrshire* 205 He'll row for fun amang the snaw And syne yaff at the moon.

yaffe, obs. pa. t. of GIVE.

yaffingale ('jæfɪŋgeɪl). *s.* and *s.w. dial.* Also 7 **yippingale,** 9 **yelpingal, yappingal(e.** [f. various echoic syllables with termination modelled on *nightingale*.] The green woodpecker; = YAFFLE *sb.*[1]
1609 C. BUTLER *Fem. Mon.* vii. § 5. H 5 b, The woodpecker or yippingale. **1802** [see YAFFLE *sb.*[1]]. **1865** *Cornh. Mag.* July 35 Mr. Matthew Arnold has very justly praised Maurice de Guérin for speaking of the woodpecker's laugh. But the West-country peasant ages ago called it the 'yaffingale', that is, the laugh-singer. **1866** BLACKMORE *Cradock Nowell* i, The tap of the yaffingale. **1871** TENNYSON *Last Tourn.* 696 The garnet-headed yaffingale. **1888** *Berksh. Gloss.*, *Yelpingal*, the woodpecker. **1906** G. A. B. DEWAR *Faery Year* 198 The statement of the gamekeeper that he had seen a 'black yappingal'.

yaffle ('jæf(ə)l), *sb.*[1] *dial.* Also -el, -il. [Echoic of the laughing cry of the bird: cf. YAFFLE *v.*[1] (See also HICKWALL.)] The green woodpecker.
1792 CHARLOTTE SMITH *Desmond* I. 173, I remember the cry of the wood-peckers, or yaffils, as we call them in that country [*sc.* Kent]. **1802** MONTAGU *Ornith. Dict.* (1831) 385 Green Woodpecker... Yappingale. Yaffle or Yaffler. **1856** KINGSLEY *South Wind* ii. Poems (1889) 292 O blessed yaffil, laughing loud! **1893** D. JORDAN & JEAN A. OWEN *Forest Tithes* 126 On their grey trunks the yaffle shins about, yells, laughs, and yikes to his heart's content.

yaffle, *sb.*[2] *dial.* [f. YAFFLE *v.*[1]]
1. A bark, a yelp.
1836 *Fraser's Mag.* XIII. 662 My faithful dog..sent up a loud 'yaffle'. **1856** AIRD *Winter Day* Poet. Wks. 192 The petulant yaffle of the cottage cur.
2. The call of the green woodpecker.
1955 D. A. BANNERMAN *Birds Brit. Isles* IV. 77 It [*sc.* the green woodpecker] is a bird which attracts attention by its loud cry or 'yaffle'. **1976** *Southern Even. Echo* (Southampton) 12 Nov. 18/4 The yaffle of a green woodpecker and needle-like sounds from the tits and goldcrests.

yaffle, *v.*[1] *dial.* [Echoic.] *intr.* **a.** To bark sharply, as a dog; to yelp. (Cf. YAFF *v.*) **b.** To talk indistinctly, to mumble. **c.** Of a woodpecker: To utter its characteristic cry. (Cf. YAFFLE *sb.*[1], YAFFLER.) Hence **'yaffling** *ppl. a.*
1847 HALLIWELL, *Yaffle*,..to bark. Same as *Yaff*. **1848** A. B. EVANS *Leicestersh. Words*, *Yaffle*, to yelp, or bark like a little dog... A yaffling little cur. **1875** *Anderida* xvi. II. 26 Then came three or four sounding taps from a woodpecker's beak, and a yaffling laugh as he flew away. **1887** *L'pool Daily Post* 12 Aug. 4/5 Yaffling little pet dogs.

yaffle ('jæf(ə)l, 'jɒf(ə)l), *v.*[2] *dial.* Also **yoffle.** [Echoic.] *intr.* To eat or drink, esp. noisily or greedily.
1788 GROSE *Dict. Vulgar T.*, *Yaffling*, eating. *a* **1821** J. W. MASTERS *Dick & Sal at Canterbury Fair* in Parish & Shaw *Dict. Kentish Dialect.* (1887) p. xx, Sa when we lickt de platters out, An yoffled down de beer. *a* **1935** T. E. LAWRENCE *Mint* (1955) viii. 30 You bloody swaddies can't half yaffle.

yaffler ('jæflə(r)). *dial.* [f. YAFFLE *v.*[1] + -ER[1].] The green woodpecker: = YAFFLE *sb.*[1]
1802 [see YAFFLE *sb.*[1]]. **1840** MACGILLIVRAY *Brit. Birds* III. 91 *Picus viridis.* The Green Woodpecker... Yaffler. Yappingale. **1863** J. C. ATKINSON *Stanton Grange* 70 Ta'n't a yaffler's [nest]; it's a black and white woodpecker's. **1906** *Sat. Rev.* 10 Feb. 169/1, I thought that would touch you, woodpecker! Ha, ha, ha—who's the yaffler now?

†**y-aforsayde** [Y- 4], aforesaid.
1422 YONGE tr. *Secr. Secr.* 147 And as y-aforsayde thes bene the foure cardynall vertues.

yag (jæg). Also **YAG.** [f. the initial letters of *y*ttrium *a*luminium *g*arnet.] A synthetic crystal of yttrium aluminium garnet, used in certain lasers and as a simulated diamond in jewellery.
1964 *Q. Rep. Bell Telephone Lab.* No. 2 (AD 439–628). 3 The splitting of the ^7F_J..manifolds of the trivalent Europium and Terbium ions..has been used to calculate crystal field parameters for Eu and Tb in YAG. **1964** *Appl. Physics Lett.* V. 201/2 Predictions of the laser behavior were tested on singly and doubly doped YAG crystals. **1971** *Daily Tel.* 22 Nov. 13 Have you got a yag yet? They are the latest form of simulated diamonds. Almost as hard as a sapphire, which is almost as hard as a diamond, they are 'grown' in America, brought over here to be faceted, set in 18-carat gold in Hatton Garden and sold as Diamonairs. **1977** *Jrnl. R. Soc. Arts* CXXV. 779/2 The YAG laser..is used routinely..for trimming resistors. **1979** [see SIMULANT *sb.*]. **1984** *National Geographic* Mar. 341/2 A flash lamp can excite atoms of neodymium, a rare earth, in a rod of YAG.

‖**yagé** ('jɑːʒeɪ, ja'xe). Also **yage, yajé.** [Amer. Sp.] **a.** A South American liana of the genus *Banisteriopsis* used by the Indians to make a hallucinogenic infusion. **b.** The drink made from this.
1924 C. W. DOMVILLE-FIFE *Among Wild Tribes of Amazons* xvi. 229 A curious potion is made from a plant called *yagé*. **1931** *Jrnl. Washington Acad. Sci.* XXI. 487 One of the most interesting plants found in the region of the upper courses of the Putumayo and Caquetá Rivers [in Colombia] is the *yagé*. The Indians make a beverage from either the wild or cultivated *yagé*, boiling it in a large earthenware vessel an entire day... They add to the *yagé* the leaves and the young shoots of the *oco yagé* or *chagro panga* ..and it is the addition of this plant which produces the 'bluish aureole' of their visions. **1945** F. R. FOSBERG in F. Verdoorn *Plants & Plant Sci. Lat. Amer.* 28/1 Two other plants..are used by the Amazonian Indians for their narcotic effect. *Maikoa* (*Brugmansia arborea*) and *yagé* or *caapi* (*Banisteriopsis caapi*) both produce hallucinations. **1953** W. BURROUGHS *Junkie* xv. 149 Maybe I will find in yage what I was looking for in junk and weed and coke. **1960** *Spectator* 29 July 176 Yage, a vine-bark stew..supposedly invests the user with telepathic powers. **1969** *Science* 17 Jan. 253/2 The Siona of today frequently mix *Datura* leaves with *Banisteriopsis* in preparing yajé. **1975** *High Times* Dec. 80/1 You trek 900 miles overland into the Amazon jungle to sample yagé in its natural habitat. **1977** LEWIS & ELVIN-LEWIS *Med. Bot.* xviii. 413/1 No more interesting or complex narcotic drink can be found than ayahuasca, caapi, or yaje.

yager ('jeɪgə(r)). Anglicized spelling of G. *jäger*, *jaeger*: see JÄGER 1, 2.
1804 *Ann. Reg.*, *Chron.* 424/2 The light companies and yagers were sent out and skirmished. **1809** BYRON *Bards & Rev.* xv, All hail, M.P...At whose command 'grim women' throng in crowds..With 'small gray men', 'wild yagers', and what not. **1809** CAMPBELL *Gert. Wyom.* III. xxi, And first the wild Moravian yagers pass. **1812** *Examiner* 7 Sept. 562/1 The 8th Uhlans, and the 10th regiments of foot Yagers; both Poles, are nearly cut up. **1876** BANCROFT *Hist. U.S.* V. lvii. 176 He [*sc.* the landgrave] bargained to supply four hundred Hessian yagers, armed with rifled guns.
b. An obsolete kind of rifle. Also *yager rifle*. *U.S.*
1817 E. P. FORDHAM *Narr. Trav.* (1906) 141 Sent the two P——s..for the yager rifle, and the Wallet. **1826** T. FLINT *Francis Berrian* I. 60 Their trade with the Americans supplied them with rifles and yagers. **1840** C. F. HOFFMAN *Greyslaer* I. i, He instantly brought his yager to his shoulder. **1848** H. W. HERBERT *Field Sports U.S.* II. 254 Throughout the South and South-West,..the *yager*, as it is called, or short-barrelled, large-bored piece, is universally preferred. *a* **1918** G. STUART *40 Yrs. on Frontier* (1925) I. 187 Nine Pipes..came to get a nipple to put on his Yager rifle.

yager, yagger, var. JAGGER[3].

yagger, var. JAGGER[2] *dial.*, pedlar.
1821 SCOTT *Pirate* v, I would take the lad for a yagger, but he has rather over good havings, and has no pack.

Yaghan, var. YAHGAN.

Yaghnobi (jɑːg'nəʊbɪ). Also **Yagnobi.** A modern Iranian language spoken by the Yaghnobs in parts of Tadzhikistan.
1932 W. L. GRAFF *Lang. & Languages* x. 372 Many..Iranian dialects..are spoken over large areas of Asia. The chief among them are the Caspian, the Kurdish,..the Yagnobi, and the Ossetic dialect. **1960** *Language* XLIV. 281 The alternative is to assume the more traditional view that Sogdian is a descendant of Avestan, and Yaghnobi of Sogdian. **1974** *Encycl. Brit. Macropædia* IX. 451/2 Yaghnobi is still spoken by a small number of people southeast of Samarkand. It has two main dialects.

Yagi ('jɑːgɪ). *Broadcasting.* The name of Hidetsugu *Yagi* (b. 1886), Japanese scholar and electrical engineer, used *attrib.* and *absol.* to designate a highly directional aerial that he invented (*Proc. IRE* (1928) XVI. 715) for receiving or transmitting VHF or UHF waves within a narrow frequency band, consisting of a number of short rods mounted transversely on an insulating support that points towards the signal source.
1943 *Gloss. Terms Telecomm.* (*B.S.I.*) 66 The term *Yagi aerial*, which relates to a particular form of end-fire array, should not be used as a generic term for all end-fire arrays. **1950** *Austral. Jrnl. Sci. Res.* A. III. 20 The array of nine Yagis in three groups of three, one wavelength apart, is fixed on an equatorial mounting. **1951** A. C. CLARKE *Sands of Mars* iv. 42 He produced a rough sketch of a simple Yagi aerial. **1960** *Practical Wireless* XXXVI. 362/2 (Advt.), 2 Metre beam 5 element W.S. Yagi. **1975** L. DEIGHTON *Yesterday's Spy* xi. 88 Did he think we needed the eight Yagi aerials for TV?

Yagnobi, var. YAGHNOBI.

yagona: see YANGGONA.

yaguarondi, -undi, var. JAGUARONDI.

yah (jɑː), *int.*[1] (and *sb.*) Also **ya, yar.** [Echoic.] An exclamation of disgust, aversion, or malicious defiance. Also used loosely as a vague or meaningless exclamation.
1812 H. & J. SMITH *Rej. Addr.*, *Rebuilding* v, While shout and scoff, Ya! ya! off! off! Like thunderbolt on Surya's ear-drum fell. **1840** DICKENS *Old C. Shop* lxii, 'A very excellent lodger, sir. I hope we may not lose him.' 'Yah!' cried the dwarf. 'Never thinking of anybody but yourself.' **1863** KINGSLEY *Water-Bab.* iv, He turned to bay..and bit the professor's finger till it bled. 'Oh! ah! yah!' cried he. *Ibid.* v, 'Yar!'..'you little meddlesome wretch.' **1863** READE *Hard Cash* xi, 'What him mean? what him mean? Yah! yah!' **1868** HOLME LEE *B. Godfrey* xxxvi, Gerrard, with a 'yah!' of repulsion, dropped the thing. **1890** HENTY *With Lee in Virg.* 299 'Yah!' the old man shouted. 'Do you suppose we are going to give in to five men?'
Hence **yah** *v. intr.*, to shout 'yah!' *nonce-wd.*
1904 *Sat. Rev.* 23 Jan. 101 Yahing at Russia and cheering the 'brave little Japs'.

yah, *int.*[2] Repeated, *yah! yah!*, denoting a perverted or affected pronunciation of 'hear! hear!'
1886 H. W. LUCY *Diary Gladstone Parlt.* 349 There are cheers of various kinds. There is Mr. Alderman Fowler's deep-chested 'Yah, yah, yah!' **1887** *Punch* 21 Mar. 132/1, I used to call out Yah! yah! as I do in House of Commons.

yah (jɑː, ja), *adv.* Dialectal for 'yea' or 'yes'; or in representations of Ger. or Du. speech. Cf. the earlier YAW *adv.*
1863 A. J. MUNBY *Diary* 20 Aug. in D. Hudson *Munby* (1972) 170 'Dus Jaan Brahn work here?' 'Yah!' said some of the maidens: 'Aye!' said others. **1889** RIDER HAGGARD *Allan's Wife* iv, 'Yah! yah! hold a light', put in one of the Boers. **1899** *Daily News* 5 Apr. 5/1 'Yah,' which the rustics of the Peak frequently use for 'Yes,' and which they employed exclusively thirty years ago. **1905** *Ibid.* 23 May 4/7 America..has two substitutes for 'yes.' One of them is 'yep' and the other is 'yah.'

yah boo (jɑː buː), *int.* (and *sb.*) *slang* (orig. *children's*). Also **ya(a) boo** and with hyphen. [f. YAH *int.*[1] + BOO *int.*] An exclamation of scorn or derision. Also *attrib.* and *transf.*
1921 H. WILLIAMSON *Beautiful Years* 83 Willie and Jack, scorning to reply to the yaa-boos of the retreating urchins, were licking their hurts. **1926** 'R. CROMPTON' *William the Conqueror* i. 16 'Yah—boo, softie!' he called over the wall. **1961** *Times* 7 Apr. 20/7 It [*sc.* a boo] is far from a pretty sound—rather moronic, in fact—and smacks too much of the 'yah boo' which used to be the height of brilliant preparatory school repartee. **1968** [see SUCK *sb.*[1] 11]. **1973** *Times* 28 Dec. 8/6 People..who are tired of the 'Yah-boo' school of debate. *a* **1976** A. CHRISTIE *Autobiogr.* (1977) II. ii. 76 Two small boys arrived..preparing as usual to say, 'Yah. Boo. Shan't go.' **1981** *London Rev. Bks.* 19 Nov.–2 Dec. 12/2 The impatient rejection of 'Ya! Boo!' politics.
Hence **yah boo sucks** [SUCK *sb.*[1] 11], used similarly.
1980 'A. SKINNER' *Mind's Eye* xiii. 181 Ya boo sucks to anyone who was interested. **1983** *Listener* 22 Dec. 62/2 This is neither a tranche of free advertising, nor a yah-boo-sucks to temperance advocates.

Yahgan ('jɑːgən). Also **Yaghan, -ane.** [App. a native name.] (A member of) one of the three indigenous peoples of Tierra del Fuego, found in the most southerly part of the islands. Also *attrib.* or as *adj.*
1884 *Proc. R. Geogr. Soc.* VI. 348 The natives, who inhabit Tierra del Fuego and this archipelago of Cape Horn, belong to three principal tribes:..(iii.) the Yaghanes, inhabiting both banks of the Beagle Passage and all the islands in the south of the archipelago. *Ibid.* 349 The Yaghane..passes his time squatting in his hut. **1961** G. CLARK *World Prehistory* ix. 238 (*heading*) Yahgan, Ona and Alacu peoples of Tierra del Fuego. *Ibid.*, The Yahgan and their neighbours the Ona and Alacu maintained down to modern times the most southerly settlements of mankind. **1972** *Bk. of Thousand Tongues* (rev. ed.) 459/1 The Yahgan language, which once comprised five mutually intelligible dialects, is related to no other known tongue. **1974** *Encycl. Brit. Macropædia* VIII. 1159/2 The Yahgan are canoe-using fishermen and shellfish gatherers. **1983** *Times* 9 July (Saturday Suppl.) 2/8 Of the poor, ill-clad and wretched Yahganes there is only one left.

yahoo (jɑː'huː), *sb.*
1. A name invented by Swift in *Gulliver's Travels* for an imaginary race of brutes having the form of men; hence *transf.* and *allusively*, a human being of a degraded or bestial type. (Cf. HOUYHNHNM.) Freq. in mod. use, a person lacking cultivation or sensibility, a philistine; a lout, a hooligan.
1726 SWIFT *Gulliver* IV. ii, The Fore-feet of the Yahoo differed from my Hands in nothing else, but the Length of the Nails, the Coarseness and Brownness of the Palms, and the Hairiness on the Backs. **1764** REID *Inquiry* i. § 5. 28 At the expence of disgracing reason and human nature, and making mankind yahoos. **1772** GRAVES *Spir. Quix.* IV. x, To see a noble creature start..at the passionate exclamation of a mere Yahoo of a stable-boy. **1829** MACAULAY *Mill on Govt.* Misc. Writ. (1868) 143/1 Because civilised men, pursuing their own happiness in a social state, are not Yahoos fighting for carrion. **1861** H. KINGSLEY *Ravenshoe* lv, 'And what sort of fellow is he?..a Yahoo, I suppose?' 'Not at all; he is..a perfect gentleman.' **1904** ASHBEE *Last Rec. Cotswold Community* p. xxiii, To have..the pleasant valleys of Saintbury and Weston tramped by armed bands of Birmingham yahoos. **1912** J. SANDILANDS *Western Canad. Dict. & Phrase-Bk.*, *Yahoo*, a lout from the back-country, an ignoramus, a know-nothing. **1914** 'I. HAY' *Lighter Side*

School Life iii. 83 You must not behave like a yahoo in my mathematical set. **1943** J. Lees-Milne *Ancestral Voices* (1975) 200, I took the young yahoo..to the station. **1968** *Courier-Mail* (Brisbane) 21 May 6/4 A Brisbane boat owner has complained that 'young yahoos' are stripping cars left at bayside boat ramps. **1977** *New Yorker* 20 June 56/2 Sarge Waller—who is, among other things, a professional riverman—later commented on Cook and Ulvi's journey and described them as 'yahoos'.

attrib. **1726** Swift *Gulliver* iv. iv, I told him, we had great Numbers [of Houyhnhnms]..[that] Yahoo-Servants were employed to rub their Skins smooth [etc.]. **1735** *Ibid., Let. to Sympson*, I must..confess, that..some Corruptions of my Yahoo Nature have revived in me. **1751** Warton *Newmarket* 192 That hated animal, a Yahoo-Squire. **1888** F. Harrison in *Fortn. Rev.* Nov. 681 Pessimist pictures of human destiny and Ya-hoo theories of human life.

2. = wild man 2.

c **1810–20** *Handbill*, During the Fair... Two surprising large Yohoes; or, Wild Men of the Woods, being the most Wonderful of the kind ever Exhibited. **1814** *Lincoln, Rutland & Stamford Mercury* 22 Apr. 3/5 Just arrived, and to be seen in a commodious booth, in the Crown and Anchor Yard, Lincoln... The Great Yahoo, or Wild Man of the Woods.

3. *Austral.* [Perh. a different word.] A probably mythical creature resembling a big hairy man, said to haunt eastern Australia. Cf. yowie[2].

1842 in G. C. Joyner *Hairy Man South Eastern Austral.* (1977) 5 A contested point has long existed among Australian naturalists whether or not such an animal as the Yahoo existed. **1844** L. A. Meredith *Notes & Sketches N.S.W.* x. 95 They have an *evil* spirit, which causes them great terror, whom they call 'Yahoo', or 'Devil-devil.' **1876** *Austral. Town & Country Jrnl.* 4 Nov. 729 For many years past it had been believed by the settlers of that wild part of the country, that the Walla Walla scrub was inhabited by a monster called 'the hairy man of the wood', or what all the blacks stand so much in dread of—the Yahoo. **1937** *Mankind* II. iv. 91 [J.N., a Kumtangerai, told me that big hairy men lived in the scrub at Nana Glen (North Coast, N.S.W.), and were called by the native Jarrā-wahu.] *Ibid.*, In the Mudgee district..a scrubby place was reputed to be the abode of a 'Yahu', and a resident in the Maitland district told me a 'Yahu' was reputed to live in thick scrub there. Each said he was a big hairy man.

Hence (*nonce-wds.*) **ya'hoo** *v. intr.*, to behave like a yahoo; **ya'hoodom**, the realm of yahoos, yahoos collectively; also, behaviour characteristic of a yahoo; **ya'hooish** *a.*, resembling or characteristic of a yahoo; **ya'hooism**, style or quality characteristic or suggestive of a yahoo.

1868 Yates *Rock Ahead* iii. v, A dam low-bred lot, *yahooin' all over the place. **1890** Kipling *Let.* in C. Carrington *Rudyard Kipling* (1955) vii. 162 The grotesque *Yahoodom of nipping pieces off a half-presented foetus and slamming it into the market. **1906** *Sun* (N.Y.) 17 Aug. 4/1 One dictum in a Judge's mouth can..unleash all Yahoodom. **1885** Masson *Carlyle* i. 37 The infrahuman, the *Yahooish, the diabolic. **1862** Rossetti in *Fraser's Mag.* July 70 Those '*yahooisms' are degrading in art. **1901** *Speaker* 5 Jan. 374/1 In the '*Scotsman*' we have Yahooism militant.

yahrzeit ('jɑːtsaɪt). Also **jahr-**; **yore-**, **yort-** ('jɔː-); and with capital initial. [Yiddish, f. MHG. *jârzît* anniversary, f. OHG. *jâr* year + *zît* time.] Among Jews, the anniversary of the death of someone, esp. a parent.

1852 *Asmonean* 10 Dec. 91/1 Men, who..when they have Yahrzeit, will go to congregational meetings, and oppose most violently every reform measure. **1876** Geo. Eliot *Dan. Deronda* II. iv. xxxiv. 359 'Your mother has been a widow a long while, perhaps.'..'Ay, ay, it's a good many *yore-zeit* since I had to manage for her and myself,' said Cohen. **1881** *Fraser's Mag.* Apr. 496 On the *Jahrzeit* Maier takes the boy to the synagogue. **1917** E. Ferber *Fanny Herself* 200 There would be no *Yahrzeit* light burning for twenty-four hours. **1964** W. Markfield *To an Early Grave* (1965) x. 177 They buried my brother-in-law... In two and a half weeks, God spare us, he'll have his *yahrzeit*. **1971** I. B. Singer *Isaac Bashevis Singer Reader* 300 Their 'questions' inevitably concerned the observance of a *yortzeit*.

Yahtzee ('jɑːtsiː). Chiefly *U.S.* [f. yacht *sb.*] The proprietary name of a game (orig. 'the yacht game') played with dice and a score sheet.

1957 *Official Gaz.* (U.S. Patent Office) 1 Jan. tm 12/2 E. S. Lowe Company, Inc., New York... *Yahtzee*. For poker dice games. **1970** *Trade Marks Jrnl.* 8 Apr. 563/1 *Yahtzee*. .. Boxed games; dice, boards, counters and cards (other than ordinary playing cards), all for games. E. S. Lowe Company, Inc... New York. **1973** M. Kaye *Toy is Born* 56 Initially popular as a men's game—probably because of the gambling mystique of dice—Yahtzee went on to fascinate women's clubs. **1974** *N.Y. Times* 10 Nov. ii. 37 We sat with a few friends and played Yahtzee all night long. **1977** *Monitor* (McAllen, Texas) 19 June 5c/1 Following the dinner, members met..and spent the evening listening to music and playing Yahtzee.

Yahudi (jəˈhuːdɪ). Also 9 **Yahooda**, **-ee**, **Yehoodi**; **Yehudi**. [Arab. *yahūdī*, Heb. *yehudi* Jew *sb.*] In Arabic-speaking or Muslim countries (in form *Yahudi*), and in some Jewish use, and hence in (chiefly *U.S.*) *slang* (in form *Yehudi*): **a.** A Jew; Jews. **b.** *attrib.* as *adj.* Jewish.

1823 C. M. Doughty *Trav. Arabia Deserta* II. 382 When I was trafficking in Irâk, I had dealings with a certain Yahûdi. **1858** *Asmonean* 19 Mar. 180/3 We are credibly informed that not less than eight hundred families of Yehoodim..are utterly destitute. **1862** J. A. Grant *Jrnl.* 14 Aug. in *Walk across Africa* (1864) xi. 264 Frij and all Seedees believe that the Jews, or Yahoodee, living in Calcutta, seize people, and tie them up by the heels till blood falls from them into a dish. **1900** G. Ade *More Fables* 117 The flip Yahooda, with the City Education and Thirty Centuries of Commercial Training.., saw that here was a Chance to work off some Old Stock. **1930** R. L. Strauss *Amer. Remnant* 117 Dot *mensch* certainly knew his bissness..and look at all the *Yehudim* here too! **1932** [see Hubshee *sb.* and *a.*]. **1959** I. Jefferies *Thirteen Days* i. 16 As far as the Yehudis were concerned I knew the dirt that was being done. *Ibid.* vi. 83 We ate well, and drank a good Yehudi wine. **1977** *Washington Post* 17 June c-5/3, I see the hate in your eyes, you Yahudi (Jewish) whore, and when we go to work on you, you'll be sorry.

Yahvism, -vist, etc.: see Jahvism.

Yahweh ('jɑːweɪ). Formerly also **Jahveh**, **Yahveh**, **Yahwe**. The usual form, among scholars, of the personal name of God in the Old Testament, representing the most likely vocalization of the 'sacred tetragrammaton' *YHWH* (see Jehovah).

1869 J. E. Carpenter tr. *Ewald's Hist. Israel* II. 130 Jahveh alone was the true defence. **1885** *Studia Biblica* I. 3 Delitzsch..propounds the following theory. The forms *Yahu, Yah*,..are of foreign origin. The form *Yahweh*, on the other hand, is distinctively Hebrew. **1892** Montefiore *Hibbert Lect.* 45 Yahveh, to the Israelite, was emphatically the God of Right. **1899** R. H. Charles *Eschatol., Heb., Jew. & Chr.* 8 As the natural God, Yahwè was the invisible Head of the nation. **1913** H. W. Robinson *Relig. Ideas of Old Test.* iii. 53 No certain evidence for the pre-Mosaic use of the form Yahweh..seems yet to have been brought forward. **1936** W. L. Wardle *Hist. & Relig. Israel* viii. 147 God reveals to Moses as something previously unknown that his name is Yahweh. **1958** S. Godman tr. *Noth's Hist. Israel* i. ii. 99 In Jos. xxiv, there is no mention at all of sacrifices, but rather of a profession of faith in Yahweh. **1973** D. J. Wiseman *Peoples Old Testament Times* p. xxi, The Sinai covenant was the seal of Yahweh's choice of the people. **1984** *Church Times* 23 Nov. 7/2 He is a New Testament scholar concerned to expound..the growth of the biblical idea of Yahweh as the God who cares for the poor.

yai, graphic variant of *þai*, obs. f. they: see th and Y.

yaid, ȝaid, var. yaud.

yaik, ȝaik, obs. Sc. ff. ache *v.*

yailing, variant of yiling.

†**yain**, *v. Obs.* Forms: 1 ȝiȝeȝnian, 3 aȝeine, ȝene, 4 ȝeyne, ȝayne. [OE. (Northumb.) *ȝiȝeȝnian*, **onȝeȝnian*, corresp. to OHG. *gaganan, gagenan*, ON. *gegna* (whence gain *v.*[1]), f. *ȝeȝn-, onȝeȝn* against (see again *adv.*).]

1. *trans.* To meet, encounter, oppose.

a **1000** *Rit. Dunelm.* (Surtees) 45/23 [*Justitia*] *obviabit illi quasi mater honorificata*, [soðfæstnis] ȝiȝeȝnað him svoelce moder arwyrðe. *c* **1205** Lay. 17854 He..aȝeineden þere uerde þe icumen wes to ærde. *a* **1250** *Owl & Night.* 845 Abid abid me shal þe ȝene [*v.r.* yene]. **13..** *Gaw. & Gr. Knt.* 1724 Loude he was ȝayned, with ȝarande speche.

2. *intr.* To avail: = gain *v.*[1] i.

c **1325** *Minor Poems fr. Vernon MS.* 661 For heer but ȝif we make vs euene, þer may no miht ne ȝiftes ȝeyne.

yair, yare (jɛə(r)), *sb. Sc.* and *north. dial.* Forms: 2–3 ihar, yhar, 3 yhare, (yere), 3–9 yare, 4 yar, 4–6 yaire, 5 ȝar, 6–9 yair, 9 yaar. [OE. *ȝear, ȝer*, recorded in comb. *mylenȝear, -ȝer* 'mill-yair'.]

a. An inclosure extending into a tide-way in a river or on the sea-shore, for catching fish; a fishgarth.

1178–1219 *Chartulary of Abbey of Lindores* (S.H.S.) 11 Omnes piscarias in they..preter vnam piscariam meam, scilicet, vnam iharam ad colcrike. *c* **1200** *Newminster Cartul.* (Surtees) 15 Piscarias meas de Benton in Tyna, &c. Hames yhare et Burnemuth yare. **1369** *Reg. Mag. Sig. Scot.* (1814) 66/1 Cum piscariis infra aquas de Northesk, et Suthesk, in crois, yaris, et Rethibus. **1408** *Durham Acc. Rolls* (Surtees) 53 In cccc sperlynges de nostro ȝar, ij s. **1511** *Exch. Rolls Scot.* XIII. 443 *note*, With all woddis, forestis, wateris, lowis, yairis and fischingis thaireof bath in fresch watir and in salt. **1580** *Burgh Rec. Edin.* (1882) IV. 553 The demolescheing and doun casting of the cruvis and yairis on the watter of Forth. *c* **1680** *Macfarlane's Geogr. Collect.* (S.H.S.) III. 211 Some of them [*sc.* herrings]..are taken in the Yairs. **1791** *Statist. Acc. Scot.* I. 282 There are a good number of salmon caught on the sea coast [Kiltearn]..by means of yaires, or small inclosures, built in a curve or semicircular form near the shore. At high water the salmon comes within these yaires, and at low water is easily taken. **1793** *Ibid.* VIII. 597 They erect what are called *yares*, a sort of scaffold projecting into the water; upon which they build little huts..; from these scaffolds they let down..their nets. **1883** *Standard* 10 May 3/6 He..destroyed a yare in which they often caught a number of herrings.

b. *attrib.* and *Comb.*: **yair-fishing**, fishing by means of yairs; **yair-net**, a long net fixed by poles and extending into a river so as to form a yair.

1796 *Statist. Acc. Scot.* XVII. 217 The Zair or Yair Fishings, so productive in this parish [*sc.* Cardross]. **1805** *State v. Leslie of Powis* 109 (Jam.) The yare-net is about thirty-six fathoms in length, and about two and one-half fathoms in depth. *Ibid.* 356 The..yare nets extend at least three fourths across the channel of the river.

yair (jɛə(r)), *adv.* Austral. var. of yeah *adv.*

1953 A. Upfield *Venom House* i. 3 'You manage all right without brakes?' 'Yair. Nothing wrong with the ruddy engine to ease her up.' **1959** S. H. Courtier *Death in Dream Time* xii. 164 'My coat still there?' 'Yair.' **1964** R. Braddon *Year Angry Rabbit* (1967) i. 8 'You can virtually rig the ballot in two of our most important rural divisions?' 'Yair,' said Alfill. **1977** C. McCullough *Thorn Birds* xv. 344 Yair, but in the glasshouse youse don't keep getting shot at. **1980** *Herald* (Melbourne) (City ed.) 14 Apr. 2/2 Yair, but it was only in Melbourne.

yair, graphic variant of *þair*, obs. f. their, there: so **yairfor**, **yairof**, etc., obs. Sc. ff. therefore, thereof, etc.

yait(t: see gate *sb.*[1]

yajé, var. yagé.

yak (jæk, jɑːk). [Tibetan *γyag* (Jäschke).]

a. A bovine animal (*Bos grunniens*), found wild and domesticated in Tibet and other high regions of central Asia, having the body and tail covered with long silky hair, which is made into various fabrics; the tails are used for decoration, and in India as fly-flappers (see chowry).

1795 *Asiatick Res.* IV. 351 The Yak of Tartary..is about the heighth of an English bull. **1799** S. Turner *Embassy Tibet* (1800) 186 The black chowry-tailed cattle..the Yak of Tartary. **1862** Torrens *Trav. Tartary* etc. 125 The oxen mostly used in Ladak are hybrids between the yâk and the common cow. **1893** Dunmore *Pamirs* I. 246, I remounted my yak. **1903** *Athenæum* 1 Aug. 163/1 Only in the valleys does scanty scrub give sustenance to the yaks, on whose services the travellers depended.

b. *attrib.* and *Comb.*, as **yak corps**, **-hair**, **-herd**, **-tail**; **yak butter**, butter made from the milk of the yak; **yak lace**, a heavy kind of lace made from the hair of the yak.

1962 L. Davidson *Rose of Tibet* v. 87 He had bought tea bricks..and a large cake of *yak butter. **1980** *Times* 12 Aug. 10/1 Crowds file through the little shrine rooms lit by flickering lamps of yak butter. **1904** *Times* 18 Jan. 5/6 The transport difficulties are still enormous, though the *Yak Corps is working well. **1905** E. Candler *Unveiling of Lhasa* xiv. 268 A heavy curtain of *yak-hair hangs above the entrance-gate. **1958** *Illustr. London News* 13 Dec. 1041/1 Greatest of all the village-festivals was the *Dumje*, celebrated in early July, before the villagers dispersed with their *yak-herds to the high pastures. **1872** *Young Englishwoman* Nov. 606/1 The trimming consists of a narrow passementrie border and black *yak lace. **1882** Caulfeild & Saward *Dict. Needlework* 525 *Yak Lace*..is a coarse Pillow Lace, made in Buckinghamshire and Northampton... The material used is from the fine wool of the Yak. **1902** *Q. Rev.* July 42 Strange gifts from the East..*yak-tails and peacock feathers.

yak, obs. Sc. f. ache *v.*; dial. f. oak.

yak, var. yack *sb.*, *v.*

‖**yakamik** ('jækəmɪk). Native name of a South American bird allied to the cranes, *Psophia crepitans*, also called Trumpeter, domesticated by the Indians.

In recent Dicts.

‖**yakdan** ('jakdaːn). Also 9 **yakhdan**. [Pers. *yakhdān* ice-house, (also) portmanteau, f. *yakh* ice + *dān*, (affix denoting) what holds or contains anything.] In Iran, a trunk or portmanteau.

1824 J. J. Morier *Adv. Hajji Baba* II. vii. 112, I was in want of a pair of *yakhdans*, or trunks. **1922** *Blackw. Mag.* June 761/1 The bachelor's rule should be never to possess anything which he cannot squeeze into a yakdan. **1954** J. Masters *Bhowani Junction* xxxvii. 320 Then he delved in a yakdan and brought out some food I'd had cooked. **1978** 'M. M. Kaye' *Far Pavilions* i. 13 Four locked *yakdans* containing botanical specimens.

yaketty, var. yackety *int.*

yakhdan, var. yakdan.

Yakima ('jækɪmə), *sb.* and *a.* Also 9 **Yacama**; **Iakima**. [Native name.] **A.** *sb.* **a.** (A member of) a group of American Indians who lived in the area of the Columbia and Yakima Rivers in south central Washington before their confinement, with other tribes, on the Yakima Reservation in 1858; since then, (a member of) the Indians of this reservation. **b.** The language of the Yakima, a member of the Sahaptin group. **B.** *adj.* Pertaining to or designating the Yakima.

1852 S. Eastman in H. R. Schoolcraft *Indian Tribes U.S.* (1853) III. *facing* p. 96 Yackimas. **1855** *N.Y. Herald* 15 Nov. 2/3 All the Yacama Indians are in the field, and the war has fairly begun. **1857** *Spirit of Times* 4 July 277/3, I have..become a sub in one of Uncle Sam's regular regiments engaged in the late campaigns against the Yakima. **1940** M. W. Smith *Puyallup-Nisqually* 20 The two Sahaptin dialects, Kittitas and Iakima. **1946** J. T. Adams *Album Amer. Hist.* III. 84 In 1855 the Yakimas attacked parties of prospectors. **1973** A. H. Whiteford *N. Amer. Indian Arts* 39 The..Yakima..make baskets with thick, hard coils of cedar root strips. **1976** *Billings* (Montana) *Gaz.* 1 July 3-b/2 Indians..led by Sid Mills, a Yakima Indian from Washington. **1978** [see rankle *v.* 5 b].

‖**yakitori** (jækɪ'tɔərɪ). Also **yaki-tori**. [Jap., f. *yaki* toasting, grilling + *tori* bird.] A Japanese dish consisting of pieces of chicken grilled on a skewer.

1962 M. Doi *Art of Jap. Cookery* 69 Yaki-tori... Chicken Meat.. cut into mouthfuls.. and soak ten minutes in *tare*... Place skewered chicken directly over fire and broil. **1970** J. Kirkup *Japan behind Fan* 4 *Yakitori* stands selling bamboo skewers of roasted bits of chicken and liver. **1983** *Daily Tel.* 10 Nov. 17/2 We have planned a modest meal.. making the main course one of two Japanese skewered specialities: one called Yakitori.

yakka ('jækə). *Austral. slang.* Also **yacca, yacka, yacker, yakker.** [Aboriginal.] Work, toil; esp. in phr. ***hard yakka.***

1888 *Boomerang* 14 Jan. 13 The Brisbane wharf labourers.. are so accustomed to hard yacker that they can't be happy for a single day without it. **1898** *Bulletin* (Sydney) 8 Oct. 31/2 Some [swagmen] ask for 'yacker', some's lookin' for 'graft', and some's 'after a job'. **1906** [see after *colloq. abbrev.*]. **1909** H. Thompson *Ballads about Business* 91 You'll be sure to get some yacker and more country you will see. **1939** X. Herbert in E. M. Fry *Tales by Australians* 133 It'd be a richer country if everyone.. did real hard honest yakker. **1944** *Coast to Coast 1943* 121 They'd been shoved in the background, told they weren't wanted, all the hard yacca put upon them in the home. **1946** K. Tennant *Lost Haven* (1947) 139, I vote we leave the Methodist part alone, and go and clear up where somebody's going to get some *benefit* out of our yacka. **1948** V. Palmer *Golconda* iv. 28 If there's a cove on this field making money at anything but hard yakker it isn't Macy Donovan. **1968** *Courier-Mail* (Brisbane) 13 Nov. 6/7 Australian scholarships have always been hard yakka. **1981** *National Times* (Austral.) 2 Aug. 29/1 He imposes some hard yakka on his readers.

yakker, var. yacker *sb.*, yakka.

yakkety, var. yackety *int.*

yakking, var. yacking *vbl. sb.*

yakkity, var. yackety *int.*

yakmak, erron. form of yashmak.

‖**yaksha** ('jakʃa). *Indian Mythol.* Also **yaksa**, and with capital initial. Fem. **yakshī, yak'shiṇī.** [Skr. *yakṣa*, fem. *yakṣī, yakṣiṇī.*]

a. Any of a class of demi-gods or nature spirits, often inoffensive tutelary guardians of a place; *esp.* one attendant upon Kubera, the god of wealth. **b.** A statue or carving representing one of these.

1785 C. Wilkins tr. *Bhăgvăt-Gēētā* xi. 92 The *Gāndhārvs* and the *Yăkshās*, with the holy tribes of *Soors*, all stand gazing on thee, and all alike amazed! **1810** E. Moor *Hindu Pantheon* 276 His servants and companions are the *Yakshas* and *Guhyakas*, into whose forms transmigrate the souls of those men who in this life are addicted to sordid and base passions, or absorbed in worldly prosperity. **1882** A. Barth *Religions of India* v. 164 Civa.. sits enthroned on Kailâsa, the fabulous mountain of the North.. surrounded and waited on by the Yakshas. **1928** A. K. Coomaraswamy *Yaksas* I. 17 The essential element of a Yakṣa holystead is a stone table or altar.. placed beneath the tree sacred to the Yakṣa. **1931** *Times Lit. Suppl.* 24 Dec. 1042/1 The important part played by *yakshas* in Buddhist religion and art is incontestable. **1963** *Times* 12 Feb. 12/4 The highest price of the afternoon was.. paid.. for a fifth century.. carving of a Yakshi or tree nymph, probably part of a pillar. **1971** *Illustr. Weekly India* 11 Apr. 9/1 (*caption*) Each Tirthankara is identified by the tree under which the vows of asceticism were taken and the attendant yakshas and yakshinis. **1977** *Jrnl. R. Soc. Arts* CXXV. 570/2 This seated *yakṣa*, perhaps Kubera, from Nagpur District.. has only recently come to light.

Yakut (jæ'kʊt), *sb.* and *a.* Also 8 **Yakouti, Yakuty,** 9 **Yakute.** [Russ.] **A.** *sb.* **a.** (A member of) a Mongoloid people of north-eastern Siberia which now constitutes the majority of the population of the Yakutsk Republic of the Soviet Union.

1763 J. Bell *Travels* I. 240 The Yakuty differ little from the Tongusians. **1797** *Encycl. Brit.* XVI. 570/2 Besides these, there are in the Russian dominions the Nagay Tartars;.. the Yakouti; and the white Kalmuks. **1890** J. G. Frazer *Golden Bough* I. i. 26 When the day is hot and a Yakut has a long way to go. **1974** T. P. Whitney tr. *Solzhenitsyn's Gulag Archipelago* I. I. ii. 51 The Yakuts were imprisoned after the revolt of 1928. **1981** M. C. Smith *Gorky Park* I. viii. 107 Some twenty-odd Russians and Yakuts surrounding a small group of Westerners and Japanese.

b. The language of the Yakuts, an Altaic one usually placed in the Turkic group.

1908 T. G. Tucker *Introd. Nat. Hist. of Lang.* viii. 134 The linguistic connection within this group is very close, the languages of the extremes, Turkish and Yakut, for instance, being at least as distinctly related as English and German. **1951** W. K. Matthews *Languages U.S.S.R.* ii. 8 Before the Revolution Yukagir was proscribed in favour of Yakut and Russian. **1976** 'S. Harvester' *Siberian Road* xiv. 165 The middle-aged woman translated what he said into a language he took to be Yakut.

B. *adj.* Pertaining to or designating the Yakuts.

1854 Max Müller in C. Bunsen *Outl. Philos. Universal Hist.* I. 279 The Yakute dialect became separated at a very early time from the still undivided Turko-Tataric speech. **1887** *Encycl. Brit.* XXII. 9/1 The Tunguses.. occupy as their hunting-grounds an immense region on the high plateau and its slopes to the Amur, but their limits are yearly becoming more and more circumscribed both by Russian gold-diggers and by Yakut settlers. **1963** V. Nabokov *Gift* iv. 267 Making clumsy paper boats for Yakut children. **1981** I. Boland tr. *Ginzburg's Within Whirlwind* II. iv. 218 He was a Yakut boy—or at least his mother was Yakut.

‖**yakuza** (jə'ku:zə). Also **yakusa.** [Jap., f. *ya* eight + *ku* nine + *za, sa* three (see below).] A Japanese gangster or racketeer; usu. in *pl.* sense, such people collectively.

8–9–3 is the worst set of cards in a player's hand at a gambling game: hence, the worst sort (K. Koike).

1964 *Newsweek* 14 Sept. 42/2 The youngsters had to listen to boss Sakamoto expound on the noble traditions of the *yakuza*, as gangsters are called in Japan. **1971** *Ibid.* 22 Mar. 42/1 The yakuza, or gangster, is an enduring feature of Japanese life. **1975** *New Yorker* 24 Mar. 98/2 The yakuza are the Japanese gangsters who in recent years have moved from gambling, drugs and prostitution into shakedown rackets. **1977** J. van de Wetering *Japanese Corpse* v. 53 Amsterdam is full of Japanese... Even their gangsters seem to be here, the yakusa. **1979** *Honolulu Advertiser* 8 Jan. A-6/1 Yakuza—the Japanese Mafia—are thriving in Hawaii as members of a crime syndicate.

yald, obs. f. old *a.*, yaud; var. yauld *a.*; Sc. pa. t. of yield *v.*

yaldran, -drin, var. yoldring.

yale[1] (jeɪl). Also 5 **gaill, gale,** 6 **jall,** 7 **yeale.** [ad. L. *eale* (Pliny *Nat. Hist.*).] A fabulous beast with horns and tusks, perhaps the two-horned rhinoceros; used *Her.* (see quot. 1910).

c **1425** Wyntoun *Cron.* I. ix. 754 In to þat lande [*sc.* India] þai say sulde be Ane oþer best, callyt Eale [*v.r.* Ane oþir beist is callit Gaill Into þat land foroutin faill], þat is lik al til a hors.. And has a gret tusk as a bare.. And in his hewide ar hornys twa. **1536** in *Archaeologia* (1910) LXII. 311 Paid to Ric. Rydge.. for lyke cuttyng carvyng.. and makyng of.. and jall and Iunecorne a dragon, a lyan a greyhonde [etc.] [**1601** Holland *Pliny* VIII. xxi. I. 206.] *a* **1660** *Contemp. Hist. Irel.* (Ir. Archæol. Soc.) I. 264 The Ethiopian yeale hath two hornes of a cubit longe. **1910** *Archaeologia* 313 The jall or yale.. is a rare and strange animal partaking of the nature of the heraldic antelope, that is to say, wearing horns and a large pair of projecting tusks:.. and he is silver bezanty, that is, white with yellow spots. He is one of the supporters of the Dukes of Somerset. *Ibid.* 314 *note*, The yale occurs as one of the supporters of the arms of the Lady Margaret Beaufort, mother of King Henry VII.

Yale[2] (jeɪl). [f. the name of the company founded by Yale (see def.).] A proprietary name for locks and keys, used esp. to denote a lock with a cylindrical barrel that can be turned only when a key with a specially serrated edge is inserted so as to displace a number of pins by the correct distances (invented by Linus Yale, Jr. (1821–68), U.S. locksmith).

1869 *Price List of Yale Lock Manfg. Co.* 3 The manufacturers of the Yale Locks desire to say a few words in relation to the recent changes in their organization, location and prices. **1875** *Iron Age* 1 July 10/1 (Advt.), Yale locks for all uses. **1885** *Trade Marks Jrnl.* 15 Apr. 346 *Yale.* The Yale and Towne Manufacturing Company (Incorporated), Stamford, Connecticut... Locks. Bronze hardware. **1895** *Montgomery Ward Catal.* Spring & Summer 375/2 Yale pattern night lock. *Ibid.* 382/1 Yale padlocks. **1907** *Official Gaz.* (U.S. Patent Office) 7 May 437/1 The Yale & Towne Mfg. Co., Stamford, Conn... *Yale*... Locks and keys. **1920** W. J. Locke *House of Baltazar* xxv. 306 The little brass Yale latchkey. **1930** W. de la Mare *On the Edge* 11 The Yale gear-key which usually lay in the little recess to the left of the dash-board was missing. **1949** M. Mead *Male & Female* v. 114 Each small family is so isolated from others that no one knows how peculiar or how usual are.. the behaviours that are shut behind each Yale lock. **1974** *Encycl. Brit. Macropædia* XI. 12/1 Magnetic forces can be used in locks working on the Yale principle. **1974** S. B. Hough *Fear Fortune, Father* vi. 45 It was a Yale key and the back door had a Yale lock. **1976** C. G. Smith *Let.* in *Daily Mail* 28 May 35/2 Yale is a registered trade-mark and in no way refers to one particular lock. Since 1949 we have specialised in marketing automatic, semi-automatic and double-locking night-latches, engineered to foil the glass-breaking and bolt-forcing intruder.

b. *ellipt.*

1918 G. Frankau *One of Them* xxx. 235 Where each man's latchkey fits his neighbours' Yales. **1954** R. Macaulay *Let.* 14 Mar. in *Last Lett. to Friend* (1962) 148, I have changed my lock, but they can pick 'Yales'. **1983** *Oxford Consumer* Autumn 11/2 Your cylinder-lock (what people are apt to call a 'Yale', whether it is actually made by the Yale Co. Ltd. or not).

yale, yall, obs. forms of ale, yawl.

‖**yali** (jə'li:). [ad. Turk. *yali* shore, waterside residence, f. Gk. αἰγιαλός sea-shore.] A house of a type found on the shore of the Bosporus.

1962 J. Fleming *When I grow Rich* i. 9 Most large wooden houses on the Bosphorus are called either *yalis* or palaces. **1976** *Times* 28 Feb. (Turkish Suppl.) p. i/3 Ahead.. flows the deep blue Bosporus. From its either shore rise green hills.. dotted with.. those lovely old wooden houses called *yalis.* **1978** S. Sheldon *Bloodline* i. 15 Not the tourist Istanbul.. but the out-of-the-way places.., the *yalis*, and the small markets beyond the *souks.*

Yalie ('jeɪlɪ). *U.S. colloq.* [f. *Yale* + -ie.] A student or graduate of Yale University.

1969 *Newsweek* 12 May 71/1 One new Yalie.. attended Harvard summer school and found time to visit New Haven to look Yale over. **1970** E. Segal *Love Story* xviii. 114 He's a Yalie, Ol... A total Yalie. College *and* Med School. **1972** *Nature* 4 Feb. 290/2 The availability of feminine companionship during the Monday-to-Friday period during which Yalies have traditionally gone without. **1983** *Washington Post* 21 Nov. B15/3 FDR, as editor of the Crimson, is said to have once gotten out a special post-victory edition, sticking it to the Yalies just as the fans were leaving the stadium.

y'all (jɔ:l). *U.S. dial.* Also **yall.** Abbrev. you-all *pers. pron.*

1909 *Dialect Notes* III. 390 Where are yall goin'? **1928** *Amer. Speech* IV. 103, I heard a young lady, in greeting a group of her friends, say, 'How're y'all this morning?' **1935** *Scribner's Mag.* Feb. 120/2 Ah ain' gwi' be wid yall long. **1944** C. Himes *Black on Black* (1973) 199 'Bout how much ken y'all pick, shawty? **1968** E. J. Gaines *Bloodline* 134 Unc' Toby won't feel right if y'all don't eat his lovely food. **1971** *Black World* Apr. 55 Yall woulda held a stop watch on God-all-mighty. **1982** J. S. Borthwick *Case of Hook-Billed Kites* xxxiv. 114 Yes, Doctor. You'll be in the breakfast room. Y'all have a nice day.

yaller, var. yellow *a.* and *sb.*

yalloch, yal(l)ow, yalp: see yelloch, yellow, yawp.

yalt, obs. pa. t. of yield *v.*

yam (jæm), *sb.*[1] Forms: [6 **nname, inany, ignane, iniamo,** 6–7 **inamia,** 6–8 **igname,** 7 **ignaman, ighname, iniamu,** 7–8 **inhame**], 7 **yeam(e, yawm, yaum, jamoo,** 7–8 **yame,** 8 **jamme, jamb, guam** (?), **yamm,** 7– **yam.** [a. Pg. *inhame* (Clusius 1567) or Sp. *igname* (Scaliger 1557), *ñame*, †*name*, whence F. *igname* (Thevet 1575); the ultimate origin is uncertain.

The foll. quots. contain unanglicized forms:—

1588 Hickock tr. *Frederick's Voy. E. Indies* 18 A fruite called Inany [It. *Ignami*]:.. lyke to our Turnops, but is verye sweete and good to eate. **1588** Parke tr. *Mendoza's Hist. China* Comm. xi. 342 These people [*sc.* of the Philippine Islands] do more esteeme yron than siluer or golde, and gaue for it fruites nnames [Sp. *ñames*] patatas, fish. **1588** in Hakluyt *Voy.* (1599) II. II. 129 Their bread is a kind of roots, they call it *Inamia*, and when it is well sodden I would leaue our bread to eat of it. **1598** W. Phillip tr. *Linschoten's Voy.* I. lv. 99/2 Iniamos were this yeare brought hether out of Guinea, as bigge as a mans legge. **1600** J. Pory tr. *Leo's Africa* Descr. Places 52 They haue good sustenance also by meanes of a root, called there Igname, but in the west Indies Batata. **1640** Parkinson *Theat. Bot.* xv. xxix. 1383 This manner of planting this Inhame savoureth something of that of the Manihot or Iucca, wherof the Cassavi is made. **1665** *Golden Coast* 65 The Battatas are.. in form almost like Iniamus. **1703** Petiver in *Phil. Trans.* XXIII. 1460 A sort of Inhame *vulgo* Yam or Potatoe. **1759** tr. *Adanson's Voy. Senegal* 165 The roots or manioc, igname [Fr.], and batatee multiply greatly in open places.]

1. The starchy tuberous root of various species of *Dioscorea*, largely cultivated for food in tropical and subtropical countries, where it takes the place of the potato; also, any plant of the genus *Dioscorea* (or, by extension, of the N.O. *Dioscoreaceæ*), comprising twining herbs or shrubs with spikes of small inconspicuous flowers.

With defining words, applied to various species of *Dioscorea*, and to plants of other genera in some way resembling these. **Chinese** or **Japanese yam**, *D. Batatas.* **coco** or **koko yam** = coco, koko[1]. **common yam**, *D. sativa.* **Granada** or **Guinea yam**, *D. bulbifera.* **Indian yam**, *D. trifida.* **long yam**, of Australia, *D. transversa.* **native yam**, a name for Australian species of *Ipomœa* (N.O. *Convolvulaceæ*) with edible tubers. **red, white, Negro Country,** or **winged yam**, *Dioscorea alata.* **round yam**, (*a*) a species of yam with a round tuber; (*b*) the Burdekin Vine of Australia, *Vitis* (*Cissus*) *opaca*, with an edible tuberous root. **wild yam**, *Dioscorea villosa* of N. America, the root of which is used medicinally, also called *colic-root*; also applied to two W. Indian climbing shrubs, *Rajania pleioneura* (N.O. *Dioscoreaceæ*) and *Cissus sicyoides* (N.O. *Vitaceæ*); also to an Australian parasitic orchid (*Gastrodia sesamoides*) with edible roots, called *native potato* in Tasmania.

1657 R. Ligon *Barbadoes* (1673) 94 Planting provisions of Corn, Yeams, Bonavista, Cassavie. **1659** in *Engl. Hist. Rev.* (1919) July 285 To procure.. planton rootes, cassada-sticks, large jamooes, potatoes and bonavist [in Cape Verde Is.]. **1661** Hickeringill *Jamaica* 16 Plentifull produce of Sugar-Canes, Tobacco, Cotten, Maiz.., Potato's, Yames [*printed* Yarnes]. **1697** Dampier *Voy.* (1699) 12 Yams, Potatoes and Plantains served us for Bread. **1699** Wafer *Voy.* 101 Yams, of which they have two sorts, a White and a Purple. **1705** tr. *Bosman's Guinea* i. 7 Jammes [orig. F. *jammes*]. *Ibid.* ii. 16 Jambs, Potatoes, and other Fruits. **1720** De Foe *Capt. Singleton* xiv. (1840) 236 Guams, potatoes. **1729** *Dampier's Voy.* III. 460 *Round Yam.* From the Root which is white raw, but when boyl'd red... *White Yam.* Its Root being of that Colour, the Leaves single and cordated. **1756** P. Browne *Jamaica* (1789) 360 The Wild Yam. This plant grows wild in the inland woods of Jamaica. *Ibid.* 359 The Negro Yam. **1830** Lindley *Nat. Syst. Bot.* 278 The yams, so important a food in all tropical countries, because of their large, fleshy, mucilaginous, sweetish tubers. **1858** Hogg *Veg. Kingd.* 718 The Chinese Yam (*D. Batatas*), recently introduced to this country as a substitute for the potatoe. **1864** Grisebach *Flora W. Ind. Isl.* 789 Yams, Indian, *Dioscorea trifida*... Yams, white, *Dioscorea alata.* Yams, wild, *Cissus sicyoides* and *Rajania pleioneura.* **1866** *Treas. Bot.* 411 Yams vary greatly in size and colour..; many attain a length of two or three feet, and weigh from 30 to 40 lbs.; some are white, others purplish throughout, while some have a purple skin with whitish flesh, and others are pink, or even black. **1887** Moloney *Forestry W. Afr.* 433 White Bockra or Winged Yam (*Dioscorea alata*, L.).—Square-stemmed climbing plant. The roots of this species afford a much more delicate.. food than those of *D. sativa.* **1889** Maiden *Useful Native Pl. Austral.* 67 *Vistis opaca*,.. Round Yam.

2. Applied to †(*a*) the mangrove, of which some species have an edible fruit; (*b*) varieties of the common potato (*Solanum tuberosum*), cultivated in Scotland; (*c*) *U.S.*, a variety of the sweet potato (*Batatas edulis*).

1753 *Chambers' Cycl. Suppl.* App., *Yams*, ..a name sometimes used for the *rhizophora* of Linnæus. *c* **1775** T. L. *Yankee Doodle* (song) ii. in *N. & Q.* 1st Ser. V. 87 Farewell all de yams, and farewell de salt fish. **1805** Forsyth *Beauties Scot.* II. 84 To give them [*sc.* horses]..a considerable quantity daily of potatoes, especially of the coarse sort, called yams. **1815** *Pennecuik's Wks.* 78 *note*, There is a demand for the large coarse varieties of potatoe, improperly called yams. **1844** H. Stephens *Bk. Farm* II. 30 The varieties raised exclusively for cattle are the common yam, red yam, and ox-noble. **1862** Whittier *At Port Royal, Song of the Negro Boatmen*, De yam will grow, de cotton blow, We'll hab de rice an' corn. **1892** *Kilmarnock Standard* 30 July 5/2 The Negro likes his yam.

3. *attrib.* and *Comb.*, as ***yam-hill***, ***-root***; **yam-bean**, either of two species of leguminous plants, *Pachyrrhizus* (*Dolichos*) *tuberosus* and *angulatus*, cultivated in the tropics for their pods and tubers, both of which are edible; **yam house**, a building in which to store yams; **yam potato** = sense 2 (*b*); **yam-stick**, a long stick sharpened at the end, used by Australian natives for digging and as a weapon; **yam-stock**, a nickname for an inhabitant of St. Helena; **yam-vine**, (*a*) a species of yam (*Dioscorea bulbifera*); (*b*) the 'vine' or climbing stem of the yam-plant.

1864 Grisebach *Flora W. Ind. Isl.* 789 *Yam-bean, *Dolichos tuberosus.* **1887** Moloney *Forestry W. Afr.* 321 Yam Bean (*Pachyrhizus angulatus*), its tubers are like turnips. **1867** Emerson *Lett. & Soc. Aims, Progr. Cult.* Wks. (Bohn) III. 228 Even the races that we still call savage ..vindicate their faculty by the skill with which they make their *yam-cloths. **1864–5** Wood *Homes without H.* iii. 85 A *Yam-hill—i.e. a bank of mould prepared for the purpose of growing yams. **1910** C. G. Seligmann *Melanesians Brit. New Guinea* xlix. 672 The number of *yam houses makes each hamlet look larger than it really is. **1949** M. Mead *Male & Female* ix. 190 Among the Trobriand Islanders, each man fills the yam-house of his sister, not that of his wife. **1801** *Farmer's Mag.* Aug. 324 The *yam potatoe. **1829** Loudon *Encycl. Plants* (1836) §2085 The juice of *yam-roots fresh is acrid. **1861** Bp. Mackenzie in H. Goodwin *Mem.* (1864) 349 Huge yam-roots, some weighing fifty pounds. **1863** M. K. Beveridge *Gatherings* 27 One leg's thin as Lierah's *yam-stick. **1833** T. Hook *Parson's Dau.* I. ii, The blonds of the Baltic, the brunettes of the Mediterranean,..and the fair *yam-stocks of St. Helena. **1792** Mar. Riddell *Voy. Madeira* 89 The *dioscorea bulbifera*, or *yam vine. **1894** B. Thomson *S. Sea Yarns* 186, I should soon..see the green yam-vines.

†**yam**, *sb.*² *Obs. rare.* [a. Russ. *yam* posting stage or house, Pers. *yām* post-horse.] A posting house.

1569 Turberv. *Trag. Tales*, etc. (1587) 147 b, If riding poast vpon a trotting Nagge. If homely yammes, in stead of Innes at night [etc.].

1800 *Asiat. Ann. Reg., Misc. Tracts* 236/2 Each night they reached a yam, and each week a city.

yam (jæm), *v. dial.* Also **nyam.** [Derived through W. Indian from W. African words such as Hausa *nama* flesh, meat, Swahili *nyama* meat, Fulah *nyama* to eat; ult. the same word as YAM *sb.*¹.] *trans.* To eat, esp. with relish.

1725 *New Canting Dict.*, *Yam*, to eat heartily, to stuff lustily. **1801** T. Dancer *Medical Assistant* 174 [Dirt-eaters] display as much curiosity and nicety in their choice of the earth they yam, as snuff-takers or smokers in the kind of tobacco they make use of. **1816** M. G. Lewis *Jrnl.* (1834) 256 There's rice in the pot, take it, and yam-yamme. **1841** Jamieson *Scottish Dict.*, *Nyam*, to chew. **1846** *Swell's Night Guide* 136/1 *Yam*, to eat hearty. **1862** W. G. Hamley *Captain Clutterbuck's Champagne* iv. 68 They purchased the congenial [sugar-cane] plant, and *nyaming* greedily its fibre, were entranced. **1864** Hotten *Slang Dict.* 273 *Yam*, to eat. This word is used by the lowest class all over the world; by the Wapping sailor, West India negro, or Chinese coolie. **1905** *Eng. Dialect Dict.* VI. 563/2 *Yam*, to eat greedily and with noise; to chew. **1970** C. Major *Dict. Afro-Amer. Slang* 125 *Yam*, to eat.

Also as *sb.*³, food.

1788 P. Marsden *Acct. Island Jamaica* 49 The negroes say, the black parroquets are good for *yam*, i.e. good to eat. **1828** *Marly; or Life of Planter in Jamaica* (ed. 2) 13 Eh! Mosquitoes hab grandy nyamn on dat new buckra! **1835** R. R. Madden *Twelvemonths Residence W. Indies* I. 188 Him want no nyam, no clothes, no sleep. **1903** Farmer & Henley *Slang* VII. 368/2 *Yam* (nautical), food. **1953** *Caribbean Q.* III. III. 176 That was a wicked Jamaican lizard 'mash up him common-law wife for mout'ful of nyam'.

yam(e, graphic var. *þam(e*, THEM: see Y 3.

‖**Yamato** (ja'mato). [Jap., = 'Japan'.]

1. The style or school of art in Japan which culminated in the 12th and 13th centuries and dealt with Japanese subjects in a distinctively Japanese (rather than Chinese) way. Usu. as **Yamato-e** († **-we**) [*e* picture]; also **-ryū** [*-ryū* style, orig. stream, school].

1879 *Trans. Asiatic Soc. Japan* VII. 345 Motomitsu is spoken of as the originator of the *Yamato-we. Ibid.* 346 Takanobu was a pupil of the Yamato riu. **1880** T. W. Cutler *Gram. Jap. Ornament* 5 In the thirteenth [century] was founded the Yamato, or Japanese school. **1911** *Encycl. Brit.* XV. 174/1 It did not take shape as a school until the beginning of the 11th century..; it then became known as *Yamato-ryū*, a title which two centuries later was changed to that of *Tosa*, on the occasion of one of its masters..assuming that appellation as a family name. **1935** K. Toda *Jap. Scroll Painting* ii. 19 Another important example of early *Yamato-e* is a series of wall paintings at Hōryūji. **1970** *Oxf. Compan. Art* 607/2 The demand for a more refined art from the aristocratic society of Kyoto, combined with the decline of the T'ang dynasty in China, encouraged the Japanese to incorporate more native elements in their art, especially in the picture scrolls..of the *yamato-e* style. **1980** R. Illing *Art Jap. Prints* vi. 87 In the 1720s Okumura Masanobu and Shigenaga produced prints of landscape views, rather in the style of the older *yamato-e* album paintings, showing the *Omi hakkei*.

2. ***Yamato-damashii***: the Japanese spirit.

1942 *R.A.F. Jrnl.* 13 June 6/2 He will be filled with what is called *yamato damashi* [sic] or the pure spirit of Japan. **1957** *Encycl. Brit.* XII. 954O/1 The Japanese..have been profoundly influenced by a specific type of ideology—sometimes known as *Yamato Damashii* (the soul of Japan), which was partly embodied in..the code of the warrior knight. **1974** in A. Murakami *Romanized Japanese* (1979) 23 And there was no doubt then that the warrior code ..*Bushido*..and the Japanese spirit..*Yamato-damashii*.. steeled the Japanese soldier.

yamboo, var. of (or error for) *jamboo*, JAMBO.

1777 G. Forster *Voy. round World* II. 302 The yamboos, (*eugenia*,) a cooling watery fruit, of the size of pears.

yamen, yamf: see YAMUN, YAMPH.

yammer ('jæmə(r)), *sb.* orig. *Sc.* and *dial.* Forms: 6 **ȝawmer, ȝamer**, 8 **yaumour, yaummer**, 8– **yammer**. [f. next. Cf. MDu., MLG. *jammer*.] An act, or the action, of 'yammering'; a cry of lamentation, a wail; a loud outcry, shout, yell; lamentation, complaint, querulous utterance.

In Standard English only in the general sense 'a loud noise, a din' (cf. YAMMER *v.* 2).

1500–20 Dunbar *Poems* xxxiii. 122 The air was dirkit with the fowlis, That come with ȝawmeris and with ȝowlis. **1552** Lyndesay *Monarche* 6002 Than sall those Creaturis forlorne Warie the hour that thay wer borne, With mony ȝamer, ȝewt, and ȝell. **1792** A. Wilson *Watty & Meg* xxxix, While the weans, wi' mornfu' yaummer, Round their sabbin mother flew. **1894** Crockett *Lilac Sunbonnet* ix, Gin ye dinna tak' tent to yersel'..wi' yer eternal yammer o' 'Peats, Jock Gordon', an' 'Water, Jock Gordon', ye'll maybes find yersel' whaur Jock Gordon 'll no be there to serve ye. **1932** 'L. G. Gibbon' *Sunset Song* 16 There the din of the gulls is a yammer night and day. **1978** *Poetry* Mar. 328 They huddle, and their tabled ground rejoices To the flat yammer of their American voices. **1984** *Washington Post* 11 June B4/3 Diamanda Gala's score, consisting of shrieks, yammers, gasps and vocal but incoherent hysterics.

yammer ('jæmə(r)), *v.* Forms: 5, 8 **yamer**, 6 **ȝammer, -ar, ȝalmer**, 7 **yalmer, -ur**, 8 **yommer**, 8–9 **yaumer**, 9 **yaummer, yawmer, yammar**, 6, 9 **yammer**. [Alteration of ME. *ȝomer*, YOMER, after MDu., MLG. *jammeren*.]

1. a. *intr.* To lament, mourn; to utter cries of lamentation or distress, to wail; to whine, whimper. *Obs.* exc. *Sc.* and *dial.*

[*c* **1400** *Anturs Arth.* ix, Hit ȝaulut, hit ȝamurt, lyke a woman.] **1481** Caxton *Reynard* xix. (Arb.) 47 He..fayned as he had wepte, right as he hadde yamerde in his herte. **1603** *Proph. of Waldhaue* (Bannatyne) 29 Thou shalt yalmur and yell: that al York shal it heare. **1818** Miss Ferrier *Marriage* xviii, It [*sc.* the child] does yammer constantly. **1820** Scott *Monast.* iv, The White Maiden of Avenel..is aye seen to yammer and wail before ony o' that family dies. **1861** Waugh *Birtle Carter's Tale* 27 To see poor wortchin folk's little bits o' childher yammerin' for a bite o' meight —when there's noan for 'em.

b. To murmur, complain, grumble; also *trans.* to say in a complaining or querulous tone.

1786 *Har'st Rig* cii, They ever and anon stand still, And yamour sair; 'We're sure we do our day fulfil, And meikle mair.' *c* **1826** Hogg in *J. Wilson's Noctes Ambr.* (1855) I. 224 There's some souls 'll yammer and cheep If a win'le-strae lie in their way. **1892** Kipling *Barrack-room Ballads, Tomlinson* 77 Then Tomlinson he gripped the bars and yammered, 'Let me in ——'. **1894** Crockett *Mad Sir Uchtred* ix, 'They chase us, Belus,' he yammered.

2. To make a loud unpleasant noise or outcry; to howl, yell; to roar, shout.

1513 Douglas *Æneis* VII. i. 38 Greit figuris of wolfis ..Ȝouland and ȝammerand grislie for to heyr. *c* **1550** *Clariodus* I. 738 (Maitland) 24 The cairfull echo ȝalmering to the sky. *a* **1585** Montgomerie *Flyting* 123 Hoy, hurson, to hell,..Where deuils in their den dois ȝammar and ȝell. **1603** *Proph. of Waldhaue* (Bannatyne) 27 He yelped, he yalmered, and youled loude. **1828** *Craven Gloss.* **1894** Crockett *Raiders* xx, Like fiends yammering and girning when Hell wins a soul. **1932** 'L. G. Gibbon' *Sunset Song* 38 Her five bairns were all yammering blue murder at the same minute. **1952** W. R. Burnett *Vanity Row* viii. 73 Joe Sert yammering and getting purple in the face. **1958** 'W. Henry' *Seven Men at Mimbres Springs* xi. 125 Somewhere off in the eastern hills a coyote yammered with the crazed wildness which never fails to startle the oldest listener. **1959** W. H. Canaway *Seal* i. 16 His guts clanked and yammered like air-locked water-pipes. **1970** C. Sandburg *Compl. Poems* 372 They banged their spoons and bowls on the table And went on yammering for more to eat. **1980** F. Weldon *Puffball* 202 In the kitchen..Mabs' children yammered and cowered and snivelled and were slapped and shouted at. **1984** *Times* 5 Nov. 13/6 Just when women are yammering to be the hand that holds the briefcase..here's this little upstart letting the side down.

3. To long, yearn, crave. *Obs.* exc. *Sc.* and *dial.*

1705 [see below]. *c* **1746** J. Collier (Tim Bobbin) *View Lanc. Dial.* Wks. (1775) 51 Boh I yammer t'hear heaw things turn's eawt. **1895** Crockett *Men of Moss-Hags* xxiii, When a' thae things are yammerin' to get haud o' ye.

Hence '**yammering** *vbl. sb.* and *ppl. a.*

1536 Bellenden *Cron. Scot.* (1821) I. 240 Terribil spraichis of yammering pepill in the deidthraw. **1705** J. Dunton *Life & Errors* 247 Mr. Ames..had always some Yammerings upon him after Learning and the Muses. **1722** Ramsay *Three Bonnets* IV. 191 A sucking weanie..to its yamering fa's again. **1807** Stagg *Poems* 21 Our wee yen's yammerin' noise. **1822** *Blackw. Mag.* XI. 486 Suppressed, discontented, yawmering..whiggism. **1870** Miss Broughton *Red as Rose* viii, The yammering of the baby. **1895** Crockett *Men of Moss-Hags* xxiii, 'Na, na', he cried, in the strange yammering speech of the creature. **1937** [see SKRIKING *vbl. sb.*]. **1940** L. MacNeice *Poems 1925–40* 249 The city's Yammering fire alarms. **1969** M. Braithwaite *Never sleep Three in Bed* ix. 105 There was always so much yammering from us kids that no adult had a chance to say anything. **1977** *Time* 31 Jan. 43/3 Visitors..shepherded round the Acropolis by yammering guides.

yampee. = YAM *sb.*

1796 Nemnich *Polygl.-Lex.*

yamph (jamf), *v. Sc.* and *north. dial.* Also **yamf.** [Echoic.] *intr.* To bark, as a dog, esp. a small dog; to yelp. Hence '**yamphing** *ppl. a.*

1718 Ramsay *Christ's Kirk Gr.* III. xix, The hale town tykes yamph loud. **1728** —— *Hackney Scribblers* xii, Nae mastive minds a yamphing cur. **1818** W. Muir *Poems* 33 Has wylie Reynard come thy way, Or peace-disturbing yamphing Tray. **1844** M. A. Richardson *Local Hist. Table-bk., Legend.* II. 136 The yamphin thing [*sc.* a dog] dee't the neist day.

Hence **yamph** *sb.*, a bark, a yelp.

1832–53 *Whistle-Binkie* (Scotch Songs) Ser. III. 69 She kend wha it was by the yamph o' his tyke.

‖**yamstchik** ('jæmstʃɪk). Also 8 **yamsheek**, 9 **yems(t)chick, -schik, yamshik.** [Russ. *yamshchik*, f. *yam* YAM *sb.*²] The driver of a post-horse.

1753 Hanway *Trav.* (1762) I. II. xii. 56 It was so worded as to signify either post-horses or *yamsheeks.* [**1833** R. Pinkerton *Russia* 21 The peasantry..furnish the horses, and each drives his own. They are called *yamstchiki.*] **1855** *Englishw. in Russia* 40 The yell of the yemstchick inciting his team to greater speed. **1896** 'H. S. Merriman' *Sowers* xxiv, Paul..driving with both hands and extended arms, after the manner of Russian yemschiks. **1911** *Encycl. Brit.* XXV. 15/1 Parties..of *yamshiks*—a special organization of Old Russia entrusted with the maintenance of horses for postal communication.

‖**yamun, yamen** ('jɑːmʌn). Also **-oun, -ên.** [Chinese *ya* tent or pavilion of a general, official residence, office + *mun* gate.] The office or official residence of a Chinese mandarin; hence, any department of the Chinese public service, as the *tsung li yamun* or Chinese 'foreign office', established in 1860.

1747 *Astley's New Gen. Coll. Voy.* IV. I. vi. 275 Each Magistrate, great or small, has his Tribunal, or *Ya-men.* **1827** H. E. Lloyd *Timkowski's Trav.* iii. I. 111 The tribunal (called the yamoun) is the supreme court of the country of the Kalkas: it has the civil and military jurisdiction, and administers justice: sentence is past according to the printed code of laws. **1858** *Merc. Marine Mag.* V. 45 He saw pagodas, and yamuns. **1883** *Sunday Mag.* 632 The yamun or official residence of the country magistrate. **1891** *Daily News* 28 July 5/1 He..made a run for the official yamen, but was overtaken..and murdered. **1907** *Times* 30 May 5/2 The intention is to attack every yamên and to exterminate all the officials.

yan, yance, north. dial. ff. ONE, ONCE.

Yana ('jɑːnə). [a. Central and Northern Yana (men's speech) *ya·na* person, people.]

a. The language of the Yana Indians (see below), a member of the Hokan group.

[**1888** *6th Ann. Rep. Bur. Amer. Ethnol.* p. xxxvii, Work was begun on the Nosa language (Yanan family) at Redding, Cal.] **1891** J. W. Powell in *7th Ann. Rep. Bureau Amer. Ethnol.* 135 Yanan Family. Derivation: Yana means 'people' in the Yanan language. **1903** *Amer. Anthropologist* V. 18 Yana shows so few similarities to other languages that it cannot be included in any group. **1913** [see HOKAN]. **1933** Bloomfield *Language* iii. 46 The differences between the two sets of Yana forms can be stated by means of a fairly complex set of rules. **1956** J. Lotz in Saporta & Bastian *Psycholinguistics* (1961) 12/1 In Yana, an Indian language of California, men and women use an entirely different vocabulary. **1971** *Language* XLVII. 831 Although most shifts move only one degree up the scale, Yana and Luiseño advance two degrees in shifting $l > n$ and $r > \eth$ respectively.

b. (A member of) an American Indian people formerly living in northern California. Also *attrib.*

1910 *Univ. Calif. Publ. Amer. Archeol. & Ethnol.* IX. 3 These boundaries are somewhat uncertain, it remaining doubtful whether the Yanas reached the Sacramento. **1933** Bloomfield *Language* iii. 46 The classical instance is that of the Carib Indians; a recently authenticated one is the language of the Yana Indians in northern California. **1962** *Guardian* 23 Feb. 7/3 In 1911..in California..a man..was identified as a survivor of a subtribe of Yana Indians thought to be extinct. **1974** *Encycl. Brit. Micropædia* X. 796/1 The last known Yahi survivor..died in 1916. Other Yana, if they survive, are intermixed with other northern Californian Indians.

yande, obs. form of YOND.

yandy ('jændɪ), *v. Austral.* [Aboriginal.] *trans.* To separate (grass seed) *from* refuse by shaking the mixture in a special way; to separate (ore) similarly or by winnowing. Hence '**yandying** *vbl. sb.*

1933 C. Fenner *Bunyips & Billabongs* vi. 158 When a gin has collected a coolamon..full of seed she has also a good deal of sand, dust, grass and leaves. But by shaking and twisting the coolamon in a particularly skilful way an almost perfect separation is made. This art of separation is called 'yandying'. **1937** E. HILL *Great Austral. Loneliness* vi. 50 The black woman...can yandy infinitesimal grass-seeds from their husks for the camp breakfast. **1944** M. J. O'REILLY *Bowyangs & Boomerangs* 48 Yandying, in blackfellow language, means shake-about. It is the natives' method of separating the grass seeds from the husks. **1962** D. STUART *Yaralie* i. 9 While her mother had sat resting from her work of yandying and specking..she had wandered about. **1975** *National Geographic* Feb. 166 [Native Australian] women often earn money by 'yandying'—winnowing by tossing panfuls of ore into the wind to separate dirt from tin or gold. **1978** O. WHITE *Silent Reach* xi. 113 The only tin that comes out of that country is what the gins yandi—dry blow by hand out of a coolamon.

yandy ('jændɪ), *sb. Austral.* [from prec.] (See quot. 1959.)

1959 D. STUART *Yandy* 158 *Yandy, tjardoo*: long shallow oval dish, of wood sometimes, but now almost always of sheet-iron, in which mineral is separated from the alluvial rubbish by means of a complicated racking action. **1962** —— *Yaralie* i. 12 Her mother and father had worked mightily, with the pick and shovel, and the yandy, and the loaming dish for days.

yane, north. dial. f. ONE; obs. f. YAWN.

‖**yang** (jæŋ). Also **Yang**. [Chinese *yáng* yang, sun, positive, male genitals.] In Chinese philosophy, the masculine or positive principle (characterized by light, warmth, dryness, activity, etc.) of the two opposing cosmic forces into which creative energy divides and whose fusion in physical matter brings the phenomenal world into being. Also *attrib.* or as *adj.* Cf. YIN.

1671 J. OGILBY tr. *Montanus' Atlas Chinensis* II. 549 The Chineses by these Strokes..declare..how much each Form or Sign receives from the two fore-mention'd Beginnings of Yn or Yang. **1736** R. BROOKES tr. *Du Halde's Gen. Hist. China* III. 357 The Chinese lay down two natural Principles of Life, vital Heat and radical Moisture..: They give the Name of Yang to the vital Heat, and that of Yn to the radical moisture. **1836** J. F. DAVIS *Chinese* II. xii. 65 The *Tae-keih* is said to have produced the *Yâng* and *Yin*, the active and passive, or male and female principle, and these last to have produced all things. **1845**, etc. [see T'AI CHI 1]. **1871** A. B. MITFORD *Tales of Old Japan* I. 150 The Chinese doctrine of the Yang and Yin, the male and female influences pervading all creation. **1934** R. FRY *Let.* 12 Apr. (1972) II. 690 Later on they discovered that the god of the furnace being male..to throw the wife in..alone sufficed to provide the Yang and the Yin. **1958** W. WILLETTS *Chinese Art* I. iv. 271 Light is the essence of *yang*. **1963** 'R. ERSKINE' *Passion Flowers in Italy* ix. 125 Giorgio looked even taller than usual..and (to all seeming) quite adequately Yang, whatever Consolata might say. **1969** *New Scientist* 10 July 53/1 For balance, the rational needs the irrational, the intellect must mesh with the emotions, the *yang* needs the *yin*. **1971** F. MANN *Acupuncture* (ed. 2) v. 63 In the treatment of disease, if Yang is hot and over-abundant, thus injuring the Yin fluid..the surplus Yang can be decreased by a method called 'cooling what is hot'. **1971** *Guardian* 18 Dec. 9/2 A macrobiotic diet..was the way Zen monks cooked... Foods were divided into Yin things and Yang things... Yang is meat for instance. **1980** *Holistic Health News* (Berkeley, Calif., Holistic Health Center) Sept./Oct. 1/3 In the past 300 years with the rise of empirical science, modern technology, property orientation, and the decline of the sacred, we have seen the creation of an extremely yang, overmasculine world-view.

b. Comb.: **yang-yin** = *yin-yang* s.v. YIN b.

1959 R. F. C. HULL tr. *Jung's Aion* in *Coll. Wks.* IX. II. v. 58 This vision..might easily be a description of a genuine yang-yin relationship. **1968** E. B. IRVING *Reading of Beowulf* iv. 179 The poem does seem to have something of a Yang-Yin structure to it..: as the kind of heroic achievement that Beowulf represents nears its end..self-destructiveness..—the negative side of the heroic ideal—comes into clearer and clearer focus. **1975** *New Yorker* 26 May 32/3 When I was a kid, the Technocrats used to drive these gray cars with the yang/yin symbol on the door.

‖**yangban** ('jæŋbæn). Also **yang-ban, yang ban; yangpan**; and with capital initial. [ad. Korean *'yăngpan*, f. *'yăng* both, a pair + *pan* social class.] **a.** The former ruling class in Korea. **b.** A member of this; an aristocrat or gentleman; (see also quot. 1972).

1898 I. L. BIRD *Korea & her Neighbours* I. iv. 60 The youths who swing and lounge on sunny afternoons along the broad streets, aping the gait of *yang-bans*, are aspirants for official position. **1904** W. E. GRIFFIS *Corea* (ed. 7) xlix. 443 In the Land of Morning Radiance there is a governing minority consisting of about one-tenth of the whole population. These, the Yangban..living on ancient privilege and prerogative and virtually paying no taxes or tolls, prey upon the common people. **1906** H. B. HULBERT *Passing of Korea* ii. 47 The common people constantly went down in the scale and the so-called *yangban* went up, until a condition of things was reached which formed the limit of the people's endurance. **1908** G. T. LADD *In Korea with Marquis Ito* xii. 292 As for the Yang-ban, on no account will he do manual work. **1952** C. OSGOOD *Koreans* viii. 147 The taking of concubines by rich husbands was a commonplace and, in the event that a son was not born to the legal wife..it became an almost inevitable procedure on the part of a Yangpan of distinguished family. **1972** P. M. BARTZ *South Korea* iv. 46/2 The civil service was known as *Tongban* (eastern class) and the military as *Soban* (western class), and the two together as *Yangban*, a word later used generally to refer to the nobility, and today used by women of the middle class in polite reference to their husbands or other men. **1977** *Korea Jrnl.* Dec. 21/2 All the citizens had to read the intentions of the ruling *yangban* class and Confucian scholars.

‖**yang ch'in** (jæŋ tʃɪn). Also **yang ching, jin, kin**, and as one word. [Chinese *yángqín*, f. *yáng* high-sounding or *yáng* foreign + *qín* musical instrument, zither.] A Chinese musical instrument similar to the dulcimer.

1876 STAINER & BARRETT *Dict. Mus. Terms* 455/1 *Yang Kin*, a Chinese instrument furnished with brass strings, which are struck with two small hammers, like a dulcimer. **1934** *Jrnl. R. Asiatic Soc.* Apr. 334 This would appear to have been similar to the dulcimer which is known to-day in China as the *yang-ch'in*. **1962** E. SNOW *Other Side of River* (1963) lxxiii. 566 They may specialize in piano, violin, cello, flute, or one of the standard Chinese strings: *p'i-p'a, yang-ch'in, yueh-ch'in*, and others. **1970** R. D. TARING *Daughter of Tibet* i. 2 His favourite instrument was the Chinese *yangjin*, which has strings like a harp and is beaten with two bamboo sticks. **1974** *Early Music* Oct. 250/2 One recent Chinese recording has the Yang Ching as an obbligato instrument backed by the classical orchestra. **1980** *New Grove Dict. Music* IV. 275/2 The *yan-ch'in* is used in many types of popular music, including various styles of regional opera, sung narratives and solos.

‖**Yang Dipertuan** (jæŋ diːpɜːˈtuːən). Also 9 **Iang de Pertuan; Yang di-Pertuan**, etc. [Malay, lit. 'he who is tuan': see TUAN.] In Malaysia, a king, an acknowledged ruler. Also with adjs., as **Yang Dipertuan Agung** [Malay *agung* principal], **Besar** [Malay *besar* important].

1834 P. J. BEGBIE *Malayan Peninsula* iv. 140 Rajah Alli..could not view the appointment of Rajah Laboo to the office of the Iang de Pertuan *Besar*, with any other feelings than those of great distrust. **1907** F. SWETTENHAM *Brit. Malaya* vi. 131 These places..were placed under the general control of a Raja from Mĕnangkâbau, in Sumatra, with the title Yang di Pertuan. **1947** R. WINSTEDT *Malays* 51 In Negri Sembilan, custom prescribed that only the Yang di-pertuan (or Ruler) could have four wives. **1972** *Straits Times* 23 Nov. 13/3 The hotel doormen should stop using the doormen's costume... The head-dress..is like the one worn by the Yang Dipertuan Agung.

‖**yanggona** (jæŋˈgəʊnə). Also (in Fiji) **yaqona** (with the same pronunc.). (Other spellings recorded below are 'South Sea solecisms' (G. B. Milner).) [Fijian.] The Fijian name for KAVA.

1858 T. WILLIAMS *Fiji* I. ii. 24 The leading men drink *yaqona* with the king elect. **1879** *Encycl. Brit.* IX. 156/2 The use of the kava root, here called yanggona.., was introduced, it is said, from Tonga. **1913** R. BROOKE *Let.* 15 Dec. (1968) 545 *Yagona* (pron. Yangona) is the drink: same as Samoan Kava. It is made by pounding up a root, and is non-intoxicant, though *slightly* narcotic. **1922** A. B. BREWSTER *Hill Tribes of Fiji* xviii. 179 Christening now takes the place of the old custom of sprinkling the children with water from the *yangona* bowls. **1953** G. K. ROTH *Fijian Way of Life* iii. 114 The vessel from which *yanggona* is regularly drunk nowadays is a cup made from the distal half of a coconut shell cut laterally. **1977** *Times* 17 Feb. 16/5 The Queen was..presented with..the potent locally-brewed drink called Yaqona. **1983** *Guardian Weekly* 25 Sept. 12/4 The great council of chiefs—the supreme body for Fijian affairs—met over a bowl of *yakona*.

yang jin, yang kin, varr. YANG CH'IN.

‖**yang-ko** (jæŋˈkəʊ, ‖ yaŋgə). Also **yangko** and as two words. [Chinese *yānggē*, f. *yāng* seedling, sprout + *gē* song.] A type of folk-dance popular in northern China.

1954 *Folk Arts of New China* 30 Well-known forms of folk art like the *yangko* dances of the Shansi peasants or the Yangtse River boatmen's songs. **1967** J. R. LEVENSON in A. Feuerwerker et al. *Approaches to Mod. Chinese Hist.* 278 Communists might trip the Shensi light fantastic, the *yang-ko*, partly to get themselves into Shensi—and partly to get Shensi into China. **1973** R. F. S. YANG in Yuan-li Wu *China* 750 Since its Yenan days, the Communist party has utilized the *yang ko* (songs in sprouting time), an improvised version of folksinging and folkdancing, as a very useful propaganda weapon. **1975** C. P. MACKERRAS *Chinese Theatre in Mod. Times* x. 165 The first [phase]..was characterized by an emphasis on the local peasant drama of the Communist base area in northern Shensi (in particular, the small-scale song-and-dance form called *yang-ko*).

yanglour, obs. form of JANGLER.

Yang-Mills (jæŋmɪlz). *Physics.* The names of C. N. *Yang* (b. 1922), Chinese-born physicist, and R. L. *Mills* (b. 1927), U.S. physicist, used *attrib.* with reference to a class of gauge theories with non-Abelian gauge invariance.

1961 *Bull. Amer. Physical Soc.* VI. 59/1 The Yang-Mills field has been quantized in the gauge $b_3 = 0$ (a similar analysis also holding in the gauges $b_1 = 0$ and $b_2 = 0$). **1977** *Nature* 21 July 207/2 There is wide agreement as to the ingredients in a prospective theory of hadrons: quarks, colour, gluons and the Yang-Mills interaction, to name the most obvious. **1979** *Sci. Amer.* Feb. 88/3 A Yang-Mills field is the essential element in a theory that seems to unify two of the four fundamental forces of nature, the weak force and the electromagnetic one. **1981** M. GELL-MANN in J. H. Mulvey *Nature of Matter* viii. 180 The theory of QCD and the theory of QFD..belong to the same class of theories. They are called Yang-Mills theories.

yangona: see YANGGONA.

yangpan, var. YANGBAN.

Yang-shao (jæŋ ʃaʊ). *Archæol.* Also **Yang Shao, Yang shao**. The name of a village in the Henan province of China, used *attrib.* and *absol.* to designate a Neolithic Chinese culture (*c* 5000–3000 B.C.), and its artefacts, evidence of which was first discovered there in 1921.

1923 J. G. ANDERSSON *Early Chinese Culture* 31, I propose that we coin a local term and name it from the type locality *The Yang Shao culture.* **1948** A. L. KROEBER *Anthropol.* (rev. ed.) xvii. 735 Various early polychrome wares of the West have been spoken of as 'similar' to Yang-shao. **1965** T. R. TREGEAR *Geogr. of China* ii. 47 Yang Shao pottery has several unique shapes. *Ibid.*, Yang Shao Man lived on the loess plateau at a time when the water-table must have been much higher than it is today. **1973** *Genius of China* 48/2 The pigment used in decorating Yang-shao bowls..was generally applied directly on the burnished clay surface. **1978** *Nagel's Encycl.-Guide: China* 106 Proof of cultivation of cereals..exists from the Yang shao period onwards.

yanizari: see JANIZARY.

yank (jæŋk), *sb.*[1] *colloq.* (orig. *dial.* and *U.S.*) [f. YANK *v.*] **a.** *Sc.* A sudden sharp blow or stroke. **b.** orig. *U.S.* A sudden vigorous pull, a jerk. Also *fig.*

1818 HOGG *Brownie of Bodsbeck* xiv. II. 18, I took up my neive an' gae him a yank on the haffat. **1888** GUNTER *Mr. Potter* viii. 100 Her brother giving her a masculine yank [from the gondola], and jumping her upon the steps. **1906** *N.Y. Globe* 20 Aug. 6 Here is a fantastic proposition from Germany, which takes one back with an unpleasant yank into the middle ages. **1913** M. ROBERTS *Salt of the Sea* xviii. 447 He gave the twine a yank.

Yank, *sb.*[2] (*a.*)

1. Colloq. abbreviation of YANKEE.

1778 *Conquerors* 14 Give me five hundred brave and chosen men, I'll drive the Yanks from north to south again. **1834** R. H. FROUDE in *Newman's Lett.* (1891) II. 77 The Yank edition of the 'Christian Year'. **1872** SCHELE DE VERE *Amer.* 23 During the war *the Yanks* became the universal designation of Federal soldiers in the Confederacy, even as they were called *Rebs*—not Rebels—by Northern men. **1886** *All Year Round* 14 Aug. 35 As clever at a trick as a Yank.

2. An American car.

1959 *Listener* 4 June 982/1 The young labourer..will invest his cash in buying a car 'on the 'ire'—not a modest second-hand British product but a 'big Yank'. **1977** *Hot Car* Oct. 11/3 It's not raunchy like a yank but it sure is clean and ripe for customising.

3. *Comb.* **'Yankland** *nonce-wd.*, the land of the Yankees, America.

1834 R. H. FROUDE in *Newman's Lett.* (1891) II. 37 When I shall go to Yankland I do not know.

yank (jæŋk), *v. colloq.* (orig. *dial.* and *U.S.*). [Origin unknown.]

1. a. *trans.* To pull with a sudden vigorous movement; to jerk or twitch vigorously.

1848 BARTLETT *Dict. Amer.*, To *Yank*, to twitch or jerk powerfully; a term used in New England. **1854** *Spirit of the Times* (N.Y.) (Thornton *Amer. Gloss.*), Afore you could say Sam Patch, them hogs were yanked aout of the lot, kilt and scraped. **1874** J. W. LONG *Amer. Wild-fowl* viii. 143 How angry it has made me to have a nervous know-nothing catch me by the arm and yank me down, for fear a duck that he happened to catch sight of half a mile off would see me and take alarm. **1902** *Sat. Rev.* 11 Jan. 39 Yanking up fence-posts that were wanted in a hurry. **1950** R. MACAULAY *World My Wilderness* xii. 102 His companion, a younger man with less of the Gael in his aspect and speech, jumped down into the copse,..and yanked her to her feet. **1964** F. CHICHESTER *Lonely Sea & Sky* xii. 129, I kept the seaplane on the surface, planing until I thought it was going as fast as it could, when I yanked the stick back hard, to pull her off suddenly. **1966** *Listener* 14 Apr. 534/1 Any incident, from three youths yanking a cigarette machine off a wall to the mods' and rockers' riots, qualifies as 'gang delinquency'. **1968** B. HINES *Kestrel for Knave* 57 Crossley grabbed a boy by the arm and began to yank him into the open. **1977** C. MCCULLOUGH *Thorn Birds* I. ii. 35 Fee's muscular arm yanked the brush ruthlessly through knots and tangles until Meggie's eyes watered. **1983** *Austral. Personal Computer* Aug. 62/1 If you want the disks back..you cannot just yank them out.

absol. **1867** *Visit to Nantucket* (Schele de Vere 649) He yanked and yanked, but the sapling wouldn't come, and that he was caught in his own trap. **1884** *Bath Herald* 11 Oct. 6/2 When a woman has a new pair of shoes sent home she..never shoves her toes into them, and yanks and hauls until she is red in the face.

b. *transf.*

1876 BESANT & RICE *Gold. Butterfly* xxvi, Yank them both to bed. **1896** G. B. SHAW *Let.* 7 Dec. in *Ellen Terry & Shaw* (1931) 139 Hearing that Janet..had no refuge but the Solferino, she promptly went to that haunt, yanked Janet..out of it,..and delivered her punctually..for the performance. **1901** F. HUME *Golden Wang-ho* xiii, I'd have yanked Jinfou to the police-station straight away. **1922** JOYCE *Ulysses* 421 Alexander J. Christ Dowie, that's yanked to glory most half this planet from 'Frisco Beach to Vladivostok. **1948** *Sunday Pictorial* 18 July 16/6 In the end attendants had to dive in and yank them out. **1977** J. I. M. STEWART *Madonna of Astrolabe* xiv. 197, I had to yank him out of Oxford—a shocking place, if Cambridge is anything to go by.

c. To withdraw (a theatrical show, an advertisement, etc.); to cancel. *U.S.*

1940 *Amer. Speech* XV. 205/1 *Yank*, to withdraw, usually because of poor attendance. **1976** *Time* 27 Sept. 65/1 The paper..ticked off 24 local real estate advertisers with a dispiriting account of development along a local lake; they have since yanked their ads. **1978** *Chicago* June 12/1 The *Tribune* flung up more flak for Greene in ads on TV and at the top of page one (it yanked an Arts & Fun ad that repeated the 'prostitute' column).

2. *intr.* To pull or jerk vigorously; *fig.* to be vigorously active. Usu. const. *at*.

1822 AINSLIE *Land of Burns* 1 They went not forth like gaugers, A yanking on their cloots. **1888** *Cassell's Encycl. Dict.* s.v., She yanked on at the work. **1906** 'O. HENRY' in

Munsey's Mag. Aug. 556/2 (1961) ix. 131 The drawer stuck, and he yanked at it savagely. **1912** MASEFIELD *Dauber* III. ii, The staysails flogged, the tackle yanked and shook. **1957** J. KEROUAC *On Road* I. ix. 55, I yanked at the window; it was nailed. **1977** C. MCCULLOUGH *Thorn Birds* i. 8 She.. began to comb Agnes's hair... She was yanking inexpertly at a large knot. **1981** *Sunday Express* (Colour Suppl.) 19 July/2 Suddenly Sally/Julie yanks at the neck-line of her dress.

Hence **yanking** *ppl. a.*, (*a*) active, 'pushing' (*Sc.*); (*b*) jerking, twitching.

1824 SCOTT *St. Ronan's* ii, I canna bide their yanking way of knapping English at every word. **1876** MRS. WHITNEY *Sights & Insights* xxix, Poor Emery Ann had had a yanking old horse, and a wretchedly uncomfortable saddle.

Yankee ('jæŋkɪ), *sb.* and *a.* Also 8-9 **Yankey, Yanky**, *pl.* **Yankies.** [Source unascertained.

The two earliest statements as to its origin were published in 1789: Thomas Anburey, a British officer who served under Burgoyne in the War of Independence, in his *Travels* II. 50 derives *Yankee* from Cherokee *eankke* slave, coward, which he says was applied to the inhabitants of New England by the Virginians for not assisiting them in a war with the Cherokees; William Gordon in *Hist. Amer. War* states that it was a favourite word with farmer Jonathan Hastings of Cambridge, Mass., *c* 1713, who used it in the sense of 'excellent'. Appearing next in order of date (1822) is the statement which has been most widely accepted, viz. that the word has been evolved from North American Indian corruptions of the word *English* through *Yengees* to *Yankees* (Heckewelder, *Indian Nations* iii. ed. 1876, p. 77); cf. YENGEES.

Perhaps the most plausible conjecture is that it comes from Du. *Janke*, dim. of *Jan* John, applied as a derisive nickname by either Dutch or English in the New England states (J. N. A. Thierry, 1838, in *Life of Ticknor*, 1876, II. vii. 124). The existence of *Yank(e)y, Yankee*, as a surname or nickname (often with Dutch associations) is vouched for by the following references:

1683 *Cal. St. Papers, Colon. Ser.* (1898) 457 They [*sc.* pirates] sailed from Bonaco..; chief commanders, Vanhorn, Laurens, and Yankey Duch. **1684** *Ibid.* 733 A sloop.. unlawfully seized by Captain Yankey. **1687** *Ibid.* (1899) 456 Captains John Williams (Yankey) and Jacob Everson (Jacob). **1687-8** *MSS. Earl of Dartmouth* in *11th Rep. Hist. MSS. Comm.* App. v. 136 The pirates Yanky and Jacobs. **1697** DAMPIER *Voy.* I. iii. 38. **1725** *Inventory of W. Marr of Carolina* in *N. & Q.* 5th Ser. X. 467 Item one negroe man named Yankee to be sold.

Cf. also 'Dutch yanky' s.v. YANKY.]

A. *sb.*

1. a. *U.S.* A nickname for a native or inhabitant of New England, or, more widely, of the northern States generally; during the War of Secession applied by the Confederates to the soldiers of the Federal army.

1765 *Oppression, a Poem by an American* (with notes by a North Briton) 17 From meanness first this Portsmouth Yankey rose. *Note*, 'Portsmouth Yankey', It seems, our hero being a New-Englander by birth, has a right to the epithet of Yankey; a name of derision, I have been informed, given by the Southern people on the Continent, to those of New-England: what meaning there is in the word, I never could learn. **1775** J. TRUMBULL *McFingal* I. 1 When Yankies, skill'd in martial rule, First put the British troops to school. *Editor's note*, Yankies—a term formerly of derision, but now merely of distinction, given to the people of the four eastern States. **1775** *Penna Gazette* 10 May in *N. & Q.* 1st Ser. VI. 57/1 They [*sc.* the British troops] were roughly handled by the Yankees, a term of reproach for the New Englanders, when applied by the regulars. **1778** *Muse's Mirrour* I. 220 O My Yankee, my Yankee, And O my Yankee, my sweet-ee, And was its nurse North asham'd Because such a bantling hath beat-ee? **1817** M. BIRKBECK *Notes Journ. Amer.* (1818) 19 The enterprising people [at Richmond, Virginia] are mostly strangers; Scotch, Irish, and especially New England men, or Yankees, as they are called. **1825** J. NEAL *Bro. Jonathan* i. I. 13 He was a Yankee, the very character of whom is, that he can 'turn his hand', as he says, 'to any thing'. **1891** DUNCAN *Amer. Girl in London* 23 The Yankees are the New Englanders,.. the name would once have been taken as an insult by a Southerner.

b. By English writers and speakers commonly applied to a native or inhabitant of the United States generally; an American.

Applied occas. to a ship (cf. *Frenchman*, etc.).

c **1784** NELSON *Let. to Locker* in A. Duncan *Life* (1806) 321, I.. am determined not to suffer the Yankies to come where the ship is. **1796** T. TWINING *Trav. Amer.* (1894) 68 Their wit was particularly directed against a 'Yankee' who was one of the company. We apply this designation as a term of ridicule or reproach to the inhabitants of all parts of the United States indiscriminately; but the Americans confine its application to their countrymen of the Northern or New England States. **1798** CHARLOTTE SMITH *Yng. Philos.* III. 11 If thou marriedst the heiress, thou must give up thy little American, thy fascinating yankey. **1836** HALIBURTON *Clockm.* Ser. I. ix, I'll be d——d, said he, if ever I saw a Yankee that didn't bolt his food whole like a Boa Constrictor. **1851** *Blackw. Mag.* LXIX. 409/2 When we next saw the Yankee [*sc.* a frigate], there we were coming right down upon him over the breast of the sea. **1887** 'EDNA LYALL' *Knight-Errant* xvii, I really am Italian, though Signor Sardoni will call me a little Yankee.

2. [ellipt. use of the adj.] The Yankee language, the dialect of New England; *loosely*, American English generally.

1824 J. GILCHRIST *Etymol. Interpr.* 8 The naked savages of Indiana already speak a corrupt English (or Yankee). **1836** HALIBURTON *Clockm.* Ser. I. i, You did not come form Halifax, I presume, sir, did you? in a dialect too rich to be mistaken as genuine Yankee. **1840** —— *Letter Bag* iii. 34 Coarse jokes in English, German, French, and Yankee.

3. Whisky sweetened with molasses. *local U.S. colloq.*

1804 FESSENDEN *Orig. Poems* 97 Call on me when you come this way, And take a dram of Yankee.

4. *pl. Stock Exchange slang.* American stocks or securities.

1887 *Pall Mall Gaz.* 6 Sept. 12/1 There was great excitement in the American market yesterday, and the bulls are cherishing the hope that there is to be a sustained boom in 'Yankees'. **1908** *Daily Chron.* 13 Mar. 1/7 Yankees finished higher on the lead from Wall Street.

5. A name for various special tools of American origin, or of ingenious design. (Cf. *Yankee notions* in C.)

1909 *Cent. Dict.* Supp.

6. = *Yankee jib* in sense C. b. below.

1912 HECKSTALL-SMITH & DU BOULAY *Compl. Yachtsman* vi. 152 The 'Yankee' is a strong pulling sail. **1953** *Yachting* June 48 We handed the yankee in favor of the working jib and forestops'l. **1967** J. ANDERSON *Vinland Voyage* 211 Peter decided to use the No. 2 yankee, leaving the big No. 1 to its proper job of pulling forward. **1974** *Islander* (Victoria, B.C.) 11 Aug. 11/1 We were lost without the mizzen. With motor and yankee we inched our way.. forward.

7. *Horse-racing.* A composite bet on four or more horses, composed of doubles, trebles, and one or more accumulators.

1967 C. COCKBURN *I, Claud* xxxiii. 404, I stepped into the betting-shop and placed the type of bet known as a 'Yankee' on four of the races... I was able to collect.. over £72 for the twenty-two shillings I had bet. **1970** *Guardian* 17 Apr. 12/3, I have.. won in 4-, 5- and 6-horse yankees sums of up to £200. **1981** B. HINES *Looks & Smiles* 184, I won it on the horses. Me and Phil had a Yankee up.

B. *adj.* **a.** That is a Yankee; pertaining to or characteristic of Yankees (often with the connotation of cleverness, cunning, or cold calculation); *loosely*, belonging to the United States, American.

1781 A. BELL in Southey *Life* (1844) I. 37 The whole coast infested with Yanky privateers. **1784** ABIGAIL ADAMS *Lett.* (1848) 161 We have curtains, it is true, and we only in part undress, about as much as the Yankee bundlers. **1822** COBBETT *Weekly Reg.* 9 Mar. 633, I was on board a little Yankee sloop in the Bay of Funday. **1828** (*title*) The Yankee and Boston Literary Gazette. **1829** MARRYAT *Frank Mildmay* xx, I will show you a Yankee trick. **1886** FROUDE *Oceana* 357 California with its gold and its cornfields,.. its 'heathen Chinese' and its Yankee millionaires, was a land of romance.

b. Used of or in reference to the language or dialect: cf. A. 2.

a **1854** WHITTIER *Charms & Fairy Faith* Pr. Wks. 1880 II. 239 A sort of Yankee-Irish dialect. **1866** LOWELL *Biglow P.* Introd., Wks. 1890 II. 170 Of Yankee preterites I find *risse* and *rize* for *rose* in Beaumont and Fletcher, Middleton and Dryden.

C. *Comb.*, etc. **a.** *gen.*, as *Yankee-like, -looking.*

1799 *Aurora* (Phila.) 30 Sept. (Thornton *Amer. Gloss.*) Faith, 'twill be Yankee like, and plagued funny. **1836** HALIBURTON *Clockm.* Ser. I. xvii, I heard him ax the groom who that are Yankee lookin feller was.

b. Special combinations and collocations. **Yankee bet** *Horse-racing* = sense A. 7 above; **Yankee gang**, name in Canada for a special arrangement of gang-saws (see quot.); **Yankee jib (topsail)**, a large jib topsail used in light winds, set on the topmast stay; **Yankee-land**, the land of Yankees, New England; *loosely*, the United States; **Yankee notions** [NOTION 9 b], small wares or useful articles made in New England or the northern States; **Yankee State**, a nickname for Ohio.

1964 A. WYKES *Gambling* viii. 194 (*caption*) The '*Yankee bet' (a permutation bet covering four horses) that can be made with off-course bookmakers in Britain. **1976** *Daily Record* (Glasgow) 29 Nov. 23/5 Yankee bet: Six doubles, four trebles and an accumulator—Pikey (12.0 Windsor), Escapologist (1.45 Wolverhampton), Corrieghoil (2.15 Wolverhampton), Heidelberg (3.0 Windsor). **1875** KNIGHT *Dict. Mech.*, * *Yankee Gang*, an arrangement in a saw-mill (Canada)... It consists of two sets of gang-saws, having parallel ways... One is the *slabbing-gang*, and reduces the log to a balk and slab-boards. The balk is then shifted to the *stock-gang*, which rips it into lumber. [**1904** B. HECKSTALL-SMITH *Dixon Kemp's Man. of Yacht & Boat Sailing* (ed. 10) v. 94 The sheeting of a modern large jackyard topsail requires a master hand's attention, especially when it is fitted 'Yankee fashion', having three sheets, as very many now are—namely, the main topsail sheet, the outer and inner sheets on the ends of the jackyard.] **1912** HECKSTALL-SMITH & DU BOULAY *Compl. Yachtsman* vi. 152 A useful sail is the *Yankee jib-topsail. This is the largest or balloon jib-topsail, and the modern and most efficient form of balloon jib-topsail is cut, like all modern head-sails should be, very high in the clew. **1928** *Daily Mail* 9 Aug. 19/6 There is a Yankee jib which, as one sail, covers more than the combined area of jib and foresail. **1939** U. FOX *Crest of Wave* 145 We had settled down with the large Yankee jib topsail set in the place of the double clewed jib. **1976** *Yachts & Yachting* 20 Aug. 339/3 At 30 knots across the deck she dropped her yankee jib and kept going under staysail and heavily reefed main. **1803** in *Spirit Publ. Jrnls.* VI. 350 More wit from *Yankee-land. **1837** HAWTHORNE *Amer. Note-bks.* 13 July (1883) 57 It sounds strangely to hear children bargaining in French on the borders of Yankee-land. **1819** *Mass. Spy* 8 Sept. (Thornton), I come here to retail My *Yankee notions,—cheese, wit, verse, codfishes, Cider, et cetera. **1825** J. NEAL *Bro. Jonathan* xxii. II. 298 The tallow, corn, cotton, hams, hides, and so forths, which we had got, in exchange for a load of Yankee notions. **1889** *Century Mag.* May 82/1, I saw the American tin-ware, lanterns, and 'Yankee notions'. **1884** *Harper's Mag.* June 125/1 Ohio was called 'the *Yankee State'.

Hence **Yankee** *v.* (*rare*$^{-1}$), *trans.* to deal cunningly with like a Yankee, to cheat; **'Yankeedom**, the realm or country of Yankees, the United States of America; Yankees as a body; **'Yankeyess**, a depreciatory term for an American woman; **'Yankeefied** (-faɪd) *ppl. a.*, made or become like a Yankee; characteristic of a Yankee; **'Yankeeish** *a.*, resembling a Yankee (whence **'Yankeeishly** *adv.*, like a Yankee); **'Yankeeism**, Yankee character or style; a Yankee characteristic or idiom; **'Yankeeize** *v.*, *trans.* to make Yankeeish, give a Yankee character to; **'Yankeeness**, Yankee character.

1837 *Fraser's Mag.* XVI. 683 [They] are considered capable of '*Yankeeing' the more simple-minded Canadians. **1851** *Blackw. Mag.* Apr. 417/1 He ought to take steamer direct for *Yankeedom;.. they'd make him President at once! **1890** MISS BROUGHTON *Alas* I. viii, Yankeedom and Cockneydom, rushing hand in hand through all earth's sacredness. **1852** *Q. Rev.* Mar. 297 The *Yankeyesses who urge the convenience of a manly garb. **1846** JAS. TAYLOR *Upper Canada* 47 Some of the Canadians indulge in the *Yankeefied habit of bolting down their victuals. **1897** *Voice* (N.Y.) 14 Jan. 8 Japan is getting Yankeefied in more ways than one. **1818** H. C. ROBINSON *Diary* 30 Apr. (1967) 58 Allston has a mild manner, a soft voice, and a sentimental air with him, not at all *Yankyish. **1830** *Collegian* (Cambridge, Mass.) Apr. 117 Comparisons are generally 'odorous', particularly Yankeeish, and decidedly condemned by Captain Basil Hall. **1855** DE QUINCEY in 'H. A. Page' *Life* (1877) II. xviii. 112 Waal, now, to speak *yankeeishly, I calculate your dander is rising. **1820** *Eclectic Rev.* Apr. 359 The term *unwell*, when first brought up, was ridiculed as a *Yankee-ism. **1836** *Fraser's Mag.* XIII. 653 Guilty of all those Yankeeisms which distinguish the lout from the gentleman. **1865** VISCT. MILTON & W. B. CHEADLE *N.-W. Pass. by Land* ii. (1867) 18 Irish or German Yankees;.. out-Heroding Herod in Yankeeism. **1864** *Guardian* 20 Apr. 386 We begin to fear that England is becoming *Yankeeised. **1877** SIR F. ELLIOT in Dowden *Corr. Sir H. Taylor* 377 The most certain of political tendencies in England is what.. I will call the Yankeeising tendency. **1882** H. E. SCUDDER *Noah Webster* viii. 289 Hawthorne, Yankeeizing the Greek myths, and finding all Rome but the background for his Puritan maiden, was asserting that new discovery of Europe by America. **1909** 'O. HENRY' *Roads of Destiny* xxi. 352 Any *Yankeeness I may have is geographical.

Yankee Doodle ('jæŋkɪ 'du:d(ə)l). [Origin uncertain.

The tune is said to have been composed in 1755 by Dr. Shuckburgh, a surgeon in Lord Amherst's army, in derision of the provincial troops (*Hist. & Misc. Coll. New Hampsh.* 1824, III. 217-18).]

1. The title of a popular air of the United States of America, considered to be characteristically national.

1768 *Jrnl. of the Times* (Boston) 29 Sept. in Lossing *Pict. Field-Bk. Revol.* (1851) I. 480 Those passing in boats observed great rejoicings, and that the Yankee Doodle Song was the capital piece in the band of music. **1775** *Pennsylvania Even. Post* 22 July 317/2 General Gage's troops are much dispirited;.. and.. disposed to leave off dancing any more to the tune of Yankey Doodle. *c* **1775** T. L. *Yankee Doodle; or the Negroe's farewell to America* (song) in *N. & Q.* 1st Ser. V. 87 Yankee doodle, yankee doodle dandy, I vow, Yankee doodle, yankee doodle, bow wow wow. **1836** HALIBURTON *Clockm.* Ser. I. xvii, He.. walked off, a whislin Yankee Doodle to himself.

2. A Yankee. Also *attrib.*

1787 J. F. BRYANT *Verses* 15 And we'll give the Yankee-doodles a dowse in the jaws. *a* **1807** J. SKINNER *Amusem. Leis. Hours* (1809) 78 Syne after him cam Yankie Doodle, Frae hyne ayont the muckle water. **1814** MOORE *Parody of Letter* 48, I might have withheld these political noodles From knocking their heads against hot Yankee Doodles. **1825** J. NEAL *Bro. Jonathan* xxiii. II. 319 One of your yankee doodle invitations, that,—happy to see you *another* time. **1830** SCOTT *Jrnl.* 5 Sept. (1890) II. 351 We have had.. Yankees male and female, and a Yankee-Doodle-Dandy into the bargain, a smart young Virginia man.

Hence **Yankeedoodle'dodom** *nonce-wd.* = YANKEEDOM; **yankee'doodledom, Yankee-'doodleism**, = YANKEEDOM, YANKEEISM (above).

1843 T. CARLYLE *Let.* 3 July in *Lett. Charles Dickens* (1974) III. 542/1 The last *Chuzzlewit* on *Yankeedoodledodom is capital. We read it with loud assent. **1845** P. HONE *Diary* 20 May (1889) II. 248 The ladies of this family (natives though they be of *Yankee-doodle-dom) seem to possess, in a high degree, the power of capturing the aristocracy of England. **1861** *Death of Lincoln Despotism* (Bartlett), And hold them Abe Lincoln, and all his Northern scum, Shall own our independence of Yankee Doodledom. **1836** *Fraser's Mag.* XIII. 468 The man's whole life.. was a long series of Frenchified *Yankeedoodleisms.

Yankeese (jæŋ'ki:z). *nonce-wd.* [f. YANKEE + -ESE.] American English.

1883 'OUIDA' *Frescoes, At Camaldoli* 119 They.. feel like two tame 'possums sitting on a gumtree. Now don't say I can't talk Yankeese!

yanker ('jæŋkə(r)). ? *Obs.* [f. YANK *v.* + -ER[1].]

1. *Sc.* = YANK *sb.*[1] a; *fig.* a big or 'thumping' lie.

1822 HOGG *Perils of Man* xii. I. 330 'Ay, billy, that is a yanker!' said Tam aside. 'When ane is gaun to tell a lie, there's naething like telling a plumper at aince.'

2. (See quot., but perh. an error for JANKER.)

1833 *Act 3 & 4 Will. IV*, c. 46 §89 If.. any person.. shall drive any four-wheeled cart, commonly called a wood yanker without a person in charge of each pair of wheels.

†**'yanky.** *Obs. rare.* [Of doubtful status, origin, and meaning. Perh. Du. *Janke*, applied orig. to

a particular ship, and so identical with YANKEE (q.v.). The following examples of *Yankee* in the proper names of ships may be compared:—

1776 M. CUTLER in *Life*, etc. (1888) I. 55 They were in the Yankee Hero. **1813** *Examiner* 11 Jan. 22/1 The Yankee, American schooner privateer.]

1760–1 SMOLLETT *Launcelot Greaves* iii, Proceed with thy story in a direct course, without yawing like a Dutch yanky. **1904** P. FOUNTAIN *Great North-West* xvii. 195 A yanki is a small kind of galiot, and the Dutch fur-traders used craft of this kind to ascend the rivers in search of their Indian customers.

yanolite (ˈjænəʊlaɪt). *Min.* [a. F. *yanolithe*, ? f. Gr. ἴανθος violet: see -LITE.] = AXINITE.

1850 ANSTED *Elem. Geol., Min.* etc. §438 *Axinite*, Thumite, Yanolite. In violet crystals, remarkable as one of the few representative forms of the unsymmetrical oblique prism. **1868** DANA *Min.* (ed. 5) 299.

Yanqui (ˈjæŋkɪ), *a.* and *sb.* [a. Sp. *Yanqui* YANKEE *sb.* and *a.*] = YANKEE *sb.* and *a.*: used esp. in Latin American contexts.

1929 [see PARROT-HOUSE]. **1937** [see PANAMAN *sb.* and *a.*]. **1952** *Caribbean Q.* II. IV. 9 Latin America replied with denunciations of what is called 'Yanqui Imperialism'. **1969** *Guardian* 6 Oct. 11/2 The Mexicans..naturally were loath to prosecute their own kind..on evidence collected by the Yanquis. **1975** *New Yorker* 30 June 23/3 Pelé, the King of Soccer, the Black Pearl, lured from Brazil by four million seventeen hundred thousand Yanqui dollars and his own sense of duty, was here to play his first game for Warner Communications' New York Cosmos. **1976** *Times Lit. Suppl.* 6 Aug. 989/4 Roosevelt's seizure of Panama led him to publish his archetypal anti-Yanqui diatribe. **1982** J. D. MACDONALD *Cinnamon Skin* xxiv. 257 It was a childish game with them, to effortlessly outdistance the heaving sweating Yanquis.

yantra (ˈjæntrə). [a. Skr. *yantra* device or mechanism for holding or fastening, f. *yam* to hold, support.] A geometrical diagram used as an aid to meditation in tantric worship; any object used similarly.

1877 M. WILLIAMS *Hinduism* ix. 129 As to the *Yantras* these are mystical diagrams—generally combinations of triangular figures. **1928** E. B. HAVELL *Indian Sculptures & Painting* (ed. 2) ii. 16 To this day *yantras*, or geometric symbols, are used in higher Brahmanical ritual in preference to images of the Hindu pantheon. **1946** H. ZIMMER in J. Campbell *Myths & Symbols in Indian Art* iv. 141 In Hindu devotional tradition, 'yantra' is the general term for instruments of worship, namely, idols, pictures, or geometrical diagrams. **1980** *Dædalus* Spring 123 The mouse child uses the image as a yantra to meditate on nothing and infinity. **1982** *N.Y. Times* 7 Nov. XXI. 35/2 An ecstatic state ..would be achieved..by contemplation of the mandalas and yantras, abstract diagrams of cosmic forces.

Yao (jaʊ), *a.*[1] and *sb.*[1] Also 9 Yaou. [Native name.] **A.** *adj.* Of, pertaining to, or designating a mountain-dwelling people of the Guangxi, Hunan, Yunnan, Guangdong, and Guizhou provinces of China and northern parts of Vietnam.

1834 C. GUTZLAFF *Sketch of Chinese Hist.* I. i. 30 In the mountains of Kwang-tung and Kwang-se live great numbers of the Meaou and Yaou tribes, who appear to be the aborigines of the country. **1897** *Fortn. Rev.* July 104, I will now close the subject by saying a few words touching the language of the Kakhyens. Like the Chinese, Annamese, Shan, Miao-tsze, Yao, and Burmese languages, it is monosyllabic and tonal. **1976** R. CONDON *Whisper of Axe* I. xv. 90 The KMT troops..took Shan or Yao or Lahu wives. **1977** YIN MING *United & Equal* 3 In the 1930s the reactionary warlords perpetrated massacres of the Hui people in Kansu and the Miao and Yao peoples in Kwangsi.

B. *sb.* **a.** The Yao people. **b.** The language of the Yao.

1883 *Encycl. Brit.* XVI. 224/1 The Yaou-jin, or Goblin clan, are said to have books, which though they are now unable to read, they still regard with reverent awe. **1901** E. H. PARKER *China* i. 7 In the southern portion of the eastern half there are still a few independent..tribes, known as Yao or Miao. **1939** [see MIAO *sb.* and *a.*]. **1948** R. A. D. FORREST *Chinese Lang.* v. 89 In Indo-China the Yao (akin to the Miao) are also known as Man. *Ibid.* 91 Miao and Yao were assigned by..Schmidt, along with Khamti, Shan, and Ahom, to the northern group of T'ai languages. **1982** B. HOOK *Cambridge Encycl. China* 102/1 Because of culture-contact they were..familiar with the notion of writing, and consequently came to employ a neighbouring language, using its script as their own written language. This happened with the Yao, who wrote their poems and hymns in a..modified form of Han Chinese.

Yao (jaʊ), *sb.*[2] and *a.*[2] [Native name.]

A. *sb.* **a.** (A member of) a Bantu people found east and south of Lake Nyasa in East Africa. **b.** The language of the Yao.

1894 *Rep. Admin. Brit. Central Africa* 23 in *Parl. Papers* (C. 7504) LVII. 771 As the coast people and Arabs began to penetrate East Central Africa they came in contact with the Yao, who, from his predatory nature, took to the idea of slave-raiding with real appreciation. **1916** *Blackw. Mag.* Apr. 551/1 The Africans were Yaos, little men, affectionately termed 'Golliwogs' by their British officers. **1924** [see NYANJA *sb.* and *a.*]. **1957** LD. HAILEY *African Survey 1956* iii. 97 Nyanja is the lingua franca throughout Nyasaland..though Tumbuka has also been recently recognized as the medium in the Northern Province, and Yao in the Yao-speaking areas. **1974** *Encycl. Brit. Micropædia* X. 799/3 Through Arab contact most Yao are Muslims.

B. *adj.* Pertaining to or designating a Yao or the Yao.

1910 *Encycl. Brit.* III. 360/1 The extensive *Yao* genus of languages stretches from just behind the coast of the Lindi settlements..to the north-east shores of Lake Nyasa. **1955** M. GLUCKMAN *Custom & Conflict in Afr.* iv. 96 When a Yao headman in Nyasaland is installed his taste for human meat is tested in the installation ceremony: because Yao witches eat the corpses of those they kill. **1974** *Encycl. Brit. Micropædia* X. 799/3 Yao social life features annual initiation ceremonies involving circumcisions for boys.

yaoor, var. GIAOUR.

‖**yaourt** (ˈjaʊrt). Also yao(o)rt, you(a)rt. [Turkish *yoǧhurt* (with quiescent *gh*) YOGURT.] A fermented liquor made by the Turks from milk.

1819 T. HOPE *Anastasius* (1820) I. vii. 137 Once on a fast-day eating some nice Yaoort. **1844** KINGLAKE *Eothen* xvii. 250 The 'youart', or curds and whey, which is the principal delicacy to be found amongst the wandering tribes. **1858** SIMMONDS *Dict. Trade*, *Yaourt*, a fermented liquor or milk-beer, similar to koumis. **1887** T. STEVENS *Around World on Bicycle* xviii. 427 The *yaort* bowl contains one solitary wooden spoon.

yap (jæp), *sb.*[1] [Echoic. Cf. YAWP.]

1. a. A dog that yaps; a yelping cur. Now *dial.*

1603 SIR C. HEYDON *Jud. Astrol.* i. 4 Those bawling yappes, that barke rather of fashion, then fiercenes. **1692** R. L'ESTRANGE *Fables* cclxxxiv. 248 'Tis a Common Thing upon the Passing of a Strange Dog through a Town, to have a Hundred Curs Bawling at his Breech, and Every Yap gets a Snap at him. *a* **1825** FORBY *Voc. E. Anglia.*

b. A fool, someone easily taken in; also, an uncultured or unsophisticated person. *dial.* and *U.S. slang.*

c **1894** C. H. HOYT *Texas Steer* (1899) III. 6 Instead of his being the only 'yap', as he calls it, in Congress there were about two hundred other members. **1895** W. STEVENS *Let.* 4 Aug. (1967) 6 Paul and Several other Yaps are up with them. **1898** B. KIRKBY *Lakeland Words* 157 *Yap*, a chap 'at's a bit ov o gomeril. **1901** 'FLYNT' & 'WALTON' *Powers that Prey* I. iii. 21 This yap from the country. *Ibid.* III. i. 60 I've seen those yaps come to town an' throw up their hands at sights that a Bowery kid wouldn't drop a cigarette snipe to see. **1915** W. CHURCHILL *Far Country* xxiv. 452 The yaps that listen to him don't understand him, but somehow he gets under their skins. **1926** J. BLACK *You can't Win* iv. 36 You are just the kind of a yap that gets up in the middle of the night and hides his money so carefully that he has to have a policeman find it for him in the morning. **1977** *New Musical Express* 12 Feb. 12/2 Then this yap starts yowling about anarchy,..and eventually the record seems to end in the middle.

2. a. A sound expressible by the syllable 'yap'; a short sharp bark or cry.

1826 LAMB *Ess., Pop. Fallacies* xiii, But *yap, yap, yap!*—what is the confounded cur? **1864** *Daily Tel.* 8 Oct., A small dog,..giving a quick series of sharp low barks, or yaps. **1879** JEFFERIES *Wild Life in S. Co.* 258 A weasel rushes past... He utters a strange startled 'yap'. **1901** *Pall Mall Mag.* July 328 The sub. gave a little yap of joy.

b. The mouth. *U.S. slang.*

1900 *Dialect Notes* II. 70 *Yap*, the mouth. **1937** J. WEIDMAN *I can get it for you Wholesale* i. 8 Every time you open your yap to say something. **1959** N. MAILER *Advts. for Myself* (1961) 43 There was a guy screaming his yap off next to him,..holding his face. **1977** H. FAST *Immigrants* IV. 243 They know that if they open their yaps, we'll close them down.

c. Idle or loquacious talk; chatter; = YAWP, YAUP *sb.* b. *slang.*

1907 *Dialect Notes* III. 204 *Yap*, offensive or superfluous talk. 'Shut up your yap.' **1926** KIPLING *Debits & Credits* 314 He'd preserved it in his head through all those weeks..o' Bert's yap. **1928** A. P. HERBERT *Trials of Topsy* 133 All this *pragmatical* yap about *tea* being a necessity and *beer* being a vice. **1945** *Coast to Coast 1944* 1 It wasn't much fun listening to all that yap when it really didn't mean a thing. **1968** K. WEATHERLY *Roo Shooter* 21 Never mind that yap. Where's the tucker?

d. A chat. *slang.*

1930 SAYERS & 'EUSTACE' *Documents in Case* 145 I'd like to have a yap with somebody who talks my language. **1957** R. LAWLER *Summer of Seventeenth Doll* II. i. 66 Real ear-basher he is, always on for a yap.

Yap (jæp), *sb.*[2] (See quots.)

1984 *Chicago Sun-Times* 25 Mar. (Views) 7/1 Yumpies, young upwardly mobile professionals, a.k.a. Yaps (young aspiring professionals). **1984** *Sunday Times* (Colour Suppl.) 28 Oct. 12/3 Phillips' Yaps believe in vigorous self-advancement, jogging and BMWs. **1985** *Times* 9 Feb. 11/1 (*heading*) Yaps, or Young Aspiring Professionals are brash, bright and bound for the top.

yap, yaup (jap, jɑp), *a.* Chiefly *Sc.* and *north.* Forms: 4–6 ʒape, 5 ʒop(e, 5–6 ʒaip(e, 6 yaip, 8–9 yap, 9 yaup. [Northern ME. *ʒape*, with rare southern var. *ʒop*, representing *ȝeáp*, alteration of OE. *ȝéap* YEPE by conversion of the falling into a rising diphthong.]

1. Clever, cunning; shrewd, astute; nimble, active: = YEPE I.

13.. *Northern Passion* (H.) 1944 ʒe haue ʒape men him forto ʒeme. *c* **1375** *Cursor M.* 9019 (Fairf.) Haue he bene before neuer sa ʒape [*Cotton* yepe] Fra þen I telle him for a nape. *c* **1375** *Sc. Leg. Saints* v. (*Johannes*) 318 Of þar ydolis þe bischope, Aristodemus, þat wes ʒape, Raisit a gret sedicione In þe puple of þat towne. *c* **1400** *Destr. Troy* 6642 A ʒop knyght & a ʒonge. *a* **1450** MYRC *Par. Pr.* 1651 Bvt, confessour, be wys and ʒop, And sende forth þese to þe byschop. *c* **1475** *Rauf Coilʒear* 628 The ʒaip ʒeman to the ʒet is gane. *a* **1508** DUNBAR *Tua Mariit Wemen* 79 Ane grume, ..ʒaip, and ʒing. **15..** *Christ's Kirk* 100 (Bann. MS.) A yaip yung man,..Lowsd of a schot. **1825** BROCKETT *N.C. Gloss.*, *Yap*, apt, quick. **1891** 'H. HALIBURTON' *Ochil Idylls* 40 I'm juist as yap an' yauld As e'er was youth.

†**2.** Eager or ready, esp. *to do* something. *Obs.*

c **1450** HOLLAND *Howlat* 602 ʒaipe, thocht he ʒong was, to faynd his offens. *c* **1500** *Rowll's Cursing* 205 (Bann. MS.) With gaipand mowth richt yaip to swelly. **1513** DOUGLAS *Æneis* XII. ii. 88 The byssy knaipis and verlettis of his stabill About thame stud, full ʒaip and seruyabill. **1728** RAMSAY *Daft Bargain* 11 [He] seem'd right yap His mealtith quickly up to gawp.

3. Eager or ready to eat, hungry.

1768 ROSS *Helenore* I. 20 Right yape she yoked to the pleasing feast. *a* **1774** FERGUSSON *Rising of Session* Poems (1845) 29 The farmers' sons, as yap as sparrows. **1832** CARRICK in *Whistle-Binkie* (Scotch Songs) Ser. I. (1839) 74 Like leeches when yaup. **1871** W. ALEXANDER *Johnny Gibb* ii, Gi'e the bairns a bit piece,..the like o' them's aye yap.

yap, *v.* Also **yap-yap**. [Echoic. Cf. YAWP.]

1. *intr.* To bark sharply, as a small dog; to yelp.

1668 [see *yapping* vbl. sb.]. *a* **1825** FORBY *Voc. E. Anglia.* **1854** R. S. SURTEES *Handley Cr.* i, Up come the hounds.. yelping, yapping, puffing, and blowing. **1865** ANNE MANNING *Belforest* II. 100 A little dog that..yap-yapped at every visitor. **1901** MEREDITH *Poems, Forest Hist.* xvii, Where long forlorn the lone dog whines and yaps.

2. *transf.* To speak snappishly.

1864 'ANNIE THOMAS' *D. Donne* III. 204 Dora was not one of the women who yap and scream in wrath or excitement. **1893** KIPLING *Many Invent.* 130 Ortheris yapped indignantly.

b. To talk idly or loquaciously; to chatter. Also *trans.*, with quoted words as obj. *slang* (orig. *dial.*).

1886 F. T. ELWORTHY *W. Somerset Word-Bk.* 844 *Yappy*, ..to chatter. The use of the word is distinctly depreciatory. Mind yer work, and neet bide there yappin. **1893** DARTNELL & GODDARD *Gloss. Words Wilts.* 185 *Yap*, *Yop*, to talk noisily. 'What be a yopping there for?' **1898** R. BLAKEBOROUGH *Wit, Character, Folklore, & Customs N. Riding Yorks.* 473 *Yap*, to talk foolishly. **1899** S. CRANE *Monster* xviii. 76, I told him to keep his trap shut. But then you know how he'll go all over town yapping about the thing. **1922** S. LEWIS *Babbitt* x. 141 He hands me the cold-boiled stare and yaps, 'I dunno, friend, I'll see.' **1937** J. WEIDMAN *I can get it for you Wholesale* iii. 28 You've been yapping away. **1946** K. TENNANT *Lost Haven* (1947) xix. 315 Len wished Alec wouldn't yap so much. **1963** *Australasian Post* 14 Mar. 51/2 If you want to yap on like a drongo in the DTs..go ahead: be a gig! **1975** *Daily Tel.* 30 June 13/7 A lot of women who are happy to yap away normally, became tongue-tied when they had to talk and drive. **1985** A. T. ELLIS *Unexplained Laughter* 49 They end up writing books about it and yapping away on the television.

Hence **ˈyapping** *vbl. sb.* and *ppl. a.*; **ˈyappingly** *adv.*; also **ˈyapper**, a dog or person that yaps.

1823 *New Monthly Mag.* VIII. 499 Some dozen *yappers and yellers of all shapes and breeds. **1901** *Longm. Mag.* May 46 His enemies said 'Job wer' a proper yapper'. **1668** R. L'ESTRANGE *Vis. Quev.* (1708) 243 A Voice not unlike the *yapping of a foysting Cur. **1891** CONAN DOYLE *White Company* ix, The shrill yapping of the hounds. **1894** *Sat. Rev.* 3 Mar. 214 There was some rather feeble yap yapping at the Peers. **1865** ANNE MANNING *Belforest* I. 265 Every little *yap-yapping dog. **1868** MISS BRADDON *Dead-sea Fruit* xxv, Half a dozen little yapping dogs..assailed me. **1924** *Chambers's Jrnl.* Feb. 128/1 Bob danced *yappingly around him.

ˈyaply, *adv.* Chiefly *Sc.* and *north.* Forms: 4–5 ʒap(e)ly, 5 yappely, ʒopely, 8–9 yaply. [f. YAP *a.* + -LY[2].] Actively, nimbly; readily, eagerly; in mod.Sc. hungrily. So **ˈyapness**, hunger.

a **1400** *Pistill of Susan* 228 To the ʒate ʒaply þei ʒeoden wel ʒare. *c* **1400** *Rule St. Benet* (verse) 1674 A souerayn aw forto be-hald ʒapli vnto ʒong & ald. *a* **1400–50** *Wars Alex.* 1393 (Dubl. MS.), And þai ʒopely ayayn ʒeldyn þaim swythe. *c* **1440** *York Myst.* xxx. 231 We muste yappely wende in at þis yate. **1768** ROSS *Helenore* II. 68 Unto their supper they right yaply fa'. **1828** MOIR *Mansie Wauch* iv, My yapness and stiff appetite.

yapock (ˈjæpɒk). Also **yapok, yapach.** [f. *Oyapok*, name of a river between French Guyana and Brazil, spelt earlier *Wiapoco* (Harcourt *Voy. Guyana*, 1613).] The South American water-opossum, *Chironectes variegatus*, having webbed toes.

1827 GRIFFITH tr. *Cuvier's Anim. Kingd.* III. 35 There are ..Yapocks of a smaller size... Found on the banks of the Yapoch river of Guyana. **1840** *Cuvier's Anim. Kingd.* 103 The Yapach..frequents the rivers of Guiana. **1892** J. A. THOMSON *Outl. Zool.* 569 The aquatic Yapock (*Chironectes*) ..feeds on fish and smaller water animals.

yapon, yaupon (ˈjɔːpɒn). Also 8 yaupan, yopon, yappon, 9 yupon. [North Carolina.] An evergreen shrub or small tree (*Ilex Cassine* or *vomitoria*), allied to the holly, growing in Texas and Southern U.S.; a decoction of the leaves (*yapon tea*) is used as an emetic and purgative. Also called *Appalachian* or *Carolina tea.*

a **1712** LAWSON *Hist. Carolina* (1714) 91 *Yaupon*, call'd by the South Carolina Indians *cassena*, is a bush that grows chiefly on the sand banks and islands. **1723** J. BRICKELL *Nat. Hist. Carolina* (1737) 319 They drink great quantities of yaupan tea. **1775** ADAIR *Amer. Ind.* 361 The Yopon, or Cusseena. **1786** ABERCROMBIE *Arr.* in *Gard. Assist.* 42 Yappon tree. **1884** G. P. LATHROP *True* ii. 13 That kind of holly known in the region [N. Carolina coast] as yaupon. **1895** *Advance* (Chicago) 19 Dec. 909/1 That horrid yupon and sassafras tea.

yapp (jæp). [Name of a London bookseller to whose order this style of binding was first made, about 1860 (*N. & Q.* 9th Ser., 1890, IV. 256).] Name for a style of bookbinding in limp leather with overlapping edges or flaps. Hence **yapped** (jæpt) *a.*, made in this style.

1882 *Publishers' Circular* 15 Feb. 163 Bagster's Bibles. In Sheep Yapped, with Elastic Band. **1883** *N. & Q.* 6th Ser. VII. 313 *Yapp*, as applied to binding, is the name of the binder [*sic*] who originally employed the style now so known. **1889** *Rep. Artisans Paris Univ. Exhib.* 31 Bagster & Co. have a good variety of work in the Bible line, especially their india-rubber kid-lined Yapps. **1894** *Guardian* 31 Oct. 1712 An ingenious method of appending markers to Bibles with yapped or overlapping bindings. **1910** *Athenæum* 26 Feb. 239/1 In velvet persian, yapp edges, boxed.

yappet ('jæpɪt), *v.* [frequent. f. YAP *v.*: see -ET[1].] *intr.* = YAP *v.* 1. Hence '**yappeting** *ppl. a.*

1681 T. FLATMAN *Heraclitus Ridens* No. 39 (1713) I. 255 It is a little Tutty-nos'd yappeting Sprite; the Good Old Cause's Lap-Dog. **1868** HELPS *Realmah* xix. I. 290 The likeness he was pleased to discover between my poor self and a yappeting suburban poodle.

yappy ('jæpɪ), *a.* [f. YAP *sb.* or *v.* + -Y[1].]

a. Given to yapping. **b.** Suggestive of a dog's yap.

1909 in *Cent. Dict.* Suppl. **1937** H. T. MILLER *Let me die Tuesday* i. 12 You're a yappy kid with no bringing up whatever. **1977** P. CARTER *Under Goliath* vi. 31 He had a wee tight face like one of those little dogs that snap at your heels, and he had a voice like one, thin and yappy. **1977** R. PERRY *Dead End* ii. 21 One yappy white poodle.

Hence '**yappiness**.

1928 *Daily Express* 28 Aug. 4/4 Pekingese..are not addicted to 'yappiness', and thus differ from many toys.

yaqona, var. YANGGONA.

Yaqui ('jækɪ), *sb.* and *a.* [a. Sp., earlier *Hiaquis* pl., ad. Yaqui *hiaki*.]

A. *sb.* **a.** (A member of) an Indian people of north-western Mexico.

1861 *Hist. Mag.* V. 164/2 The Indian population is large, and, properly regulated, would be exceedingly useful... The most numerous tribe is that of the Yaquis. **1875** H. H. BANCROFT *Native Races of Pacific States* I. v. 575 The Chinipas, Yaquis, Ópatas and Conchos build..more substantial dwellings of timber and adobes. **1946** *Nature* 13 July 69/2 The Cáhita Indians of western Mexico consist of two surviving groups, the Yaqui and the Mayo. **1953** E. HAUGEN *Norwegian Lang. in Amer.* II. xiv. 367 An interesting description is available of conditions among the Yaqui, a tribe in Arizona, whose villages were hispanicized by missionaries and political functionaries by the end of the 17th century. **1977** C. SCHAEFFER tr. *Simenon's Bottom of Bottle* vi. 95 He was a Yaqui, bigger and stronger than I am.

b. The Uto-Aztecan language of the Yaqui.

1911 *Bull. U.S. Bureau Amer. Ethnol.* No. 44. 12 Three dialects—Yaqui, Mayo, and Tehueco—are usually mentioned. **1943** *Amer. Anthropologist* XLV. 428 Yaqui and Mayo stand in the relation of mutually intelligible dialects. **1957** *Publ. Amer. Dial. Soc. 1956* XXVI. 55 In Yaqui the Spanish word *díos* 'God' appears both as *díos* and *líos*.

B. *adj.* Of, pertaining to, or designating the Yaqui.

1861 *Hist. Mag.* V. 165/1 From that day [*sc.* 1609] to this, the Yaqui Indians have retained their pueblos, or towns, along their river, governed by chiefs of their own tribe, appointed by the Spanish and Mexican governments. **1884** H. H. BANCROFT *Hist. N. Amer. States* ix. 216 A party of Tehuecos were..sent with two converted Yaqui women. **1943** *Amer. Anthropologist* XLV. 428 A fuller consideration ..of Yaqui history. **1964** F. O'ROURKE *Mule for Marquesa* (1967) ii. 24 From Nogales he peddled arms and ammunition.., his most valued customers the Yaqui Indians. **1978** *Tucson Mag.* Dec. 104/3 They perform a Yaqui Deer Dance in addition to Aztec dances and a variety of regional folk dances.

yar(r, *v. Obs.* exc. *dial.* Also 4 **ȝar(r)en**, 7 **yarre**. [Imitative. Cf. ARR *v.*[2], GARRE *v.*, YIRR.] *intr.* To snarl or growl, as or like a dog. Hence '**yarrer**; '**yarring** *vbl. sb.* and *ppl. a.*

13.. *Gaw. & Gr. Knt.* 1595, & he ȝarrande hym ȝelde. *Ibid.* 1724 Loude he was ȝayned, with ȝarande speche. **1611** COTGR., *S'entregratter*, to whurre, yarre, grumble, one at another. *Ibid.*, *Gronderie*,..whurling, yarring. *Ibid.*, *Grondeur*,..a whurrer, or yarrer. **1653** URQUHART *Rabelais* II. xxii. 153 When he saw that all the dogs were flocking about her, yarring at the retardment of their accesse to her. **1768** BEATTIE *To Mr. A. Ross* in *Helenore* (1812) 132 In kittle times, when faes are yarring. **1866** J. E. BROGDEN *Provincial Words & Expressions Lincs.* 227 *Yar*, to snarl. **1953** G. M. DURRELL *Overloaded Ark* x. 181 A young and foolish bitch ..had yapped and yarred herself into a fit of hysterical bravery.

yar, obs. or dial. f. EARTH, ERE, THEIR, YAIR *sb.*, YOUR; var. YAH *int.*[1]

† '**yarage.** *Naut. Obs.* [? f. YARE *a.* or *v.* + -AGE.] The power of moving or being managed at sea.

1579–80 NORTH *Plutarch* (1595) 997 They were light of yarage: armed and furnished with water-men as many as they needed. *Ibid.* 999 The gallies of the enemies, the which were heauie of yarage, both for their bignes, as also for lacke of watermen to row them.

yarak ('jæræk). *Falconry.* [? Pers. *yārakī* power, strength, ability.] ***in yarak***: (of a hawk) in proper condition for hunting.

1855 SALVIN & BRODRICK *Falc. Brit. Isles* 105 The Goshawk..will not work at all unless in good temper and proper flying order, termed in the East '*yarak*'. *Ibid.* 108 It requires about ten days to get this Hawk into '*yarak*'. **1900** MICHELL *Hawking* xii. 162 Unless the hawk was in first-rate condition,—in what is called 'screaming yarak'. **1901** KIPLING *Kim* x, He's in yarak Plumed to the very point.

yarb, dial. form of HERB.

1845 S. JUDD *Margaret* v. (1871) 23 Stultiloquent yarbmonger. **1847** THOREAU *Let.* in *Atlantic Monthly* (1892) June 736, I hope he got 'yarbs' enough to satisfy him. **1855** KINGSLEY *Westw. Ho!* iv, Some skill in 'yarbs', as she called her simples.

yarborough ('jɑːbərə). *Cards.* [Said to be so called because a certain Earl of Yarborough used to bet 1,000 to 1 against the occurrence of such a hand.] In whist and bridge, a hand which contains no card above a nine.

1900 J. DOE *Bridge Man.* 35 If he has a Yarborough, you will lose the game. **1910** *Blackw. Mag.* Dec. 809/2, I have held yarboroughs and been doubled and roughed all the evening.

yard (jɑːd), *sb.*[1] Forms: 1 **ᵹeard**, 4–5 **ȝerd(e**, 4–6 **ȝard(e**, **yerde**, 4–8 **yerd**, 4–9 **yaird**, (4 **ȝherd**, 5 **ȝeard**, **ȝord**, **yorde**, 6 **ȝharde**, 7 **yearde**, 8 *Sc.* **yeard**), 5–6 **ȝaird**, 6–7 **yarde**, 3– **yard**. [OE. *ᵹeard* str. masc. fence, dwelling, house, region = OS. *gard* enclosure, field, dwelling, MDu., Du. *gaard* garden, OHG. *gart* circle, ring, ON. *garðr* GARTH, (Sw. *gård* yard, Da. *gard* yard, farm), Goth. *gards* house, with corresp. wk. forms OFris. *garda* garden, OS. *gardo*, OHG. *garto* (MHG. *garte*, G. *garten*) garden, Goth. *garda* enclosure, stall. (OE. *ᵹeard* is the second element of *middanᵹeard* MIDDENERD, *ortᵹeard* ORCHARD, *wínᵹeard* WINYARD.)

The ulterior relations of these words are uncertain. Close affinity of sense is exhibited by the words derived from the Teut. root *gerd-*: *gard-*: *gurd-*, represented by GIRD *v.*[1] (OE. *gyrdan*, OHG. *gurten*, ON. *gyrða*) and GIRTH *sb.*[1] (ON. *gjǫrð*, Goth. *gairda*), and those derived from an Indo-European root *ghort-*, viz. Gr. *χόρτος* farm-yard, feeding-place, food, fodder, L. *hortus* garden, *co-hors* enclosure, yard, pen for cattle and poultry, COHORT, COURT, OIr. *gort* cornfield; but there are phonological difficulties in the way of equating both groups of words. (OSl. *gradŭ* enclosure, town, Russ. *grad*, *gorod* town, as in *Petrograd*, *Novgorod*, Lith. *gàrdas* hurdle, fold, are prob. borrowed from Teutonic.)

The general signification of the word is 'enclosure', the particular character of which is usually to be inferred from the context; the simple word is thus often felt to be short for a specific compound of it (see references in the various senses).]

1. a. A comparatively small uncultivated area attached to a house or other building or enclosed by it; *esp.* such an area surrounded by walls or buildings within the precincts of a house, castle, inn, etc. Cf. *back-yard*, *castle yard*, *chapel yard*, COURTYARD, *inn-yard*, *palace yard*, *stable-yard*.

In OE. used in sing. and pl. = dwelling, house, home, the 'courts of heaven'; also, region, tract (cf. *middanᵹeard* MIDDENERD).

Beowulf 2459 Nis þær hearpan sweᵹ, ᵹomen in ᵹeardum. *a* **1000** *Cædmon's Gen.* 740 (Gr.) Wit..forleton on heofonrice heahᵹetimbro, godlice ᵹeardas. *a* **1000** *Guthlac* 763 (Gr.) Swa soðfæstra sawla motun in ecne ᵹeard up ᵹestiᵹan rodera rice. *c* **1375** *Sc. Leg. Saints* xviii. (*Egipciane*) 571 To þe tempil men cane draw; & of It til in þe ȝarde I wes cummyne, I ne spard. *c* **1400** *St. Alexius* (Laud 108) 302 Alex..Is dweld in his fader ȝerd As a pore man. **1524** *Test. Ebor.* (Surtees) VI. 10 A litile howse with a yerde. **1562** J. HEYWOOD *Prov. & Epigr.* (1867) 100, I kepe doggis..in my yarde. **1565** in Hay Fleming *Reform. Scotl.* (1910) 613 Part of ane yard within the abbay place of Sanctandrois. *a* **1657** SIR J. BALFOUR *Ann. Scot.* Hist. Wks. 1825 II. 71 He was brought vpone a scaffold in the parliament yaird. **1711** ADDISON *Spect.* No. 121 ¶1 As I was walking..in the great Yard that belongs to my Friend's Country-House. *a* **1720** SEWEL *Hist. Quakers* (1795) I. II. 96 The steeple-house yard. **1818** SCOTT *Rob Roy* xxv, I wandered from one quadrangle of old-fashioned buildings to another, and from thence to the College-yards, or walking ground. **1838** LYTTON *Alice* v. iv, Four horses, that had been only fourteen miles, had just re-entered the yard. **1842** DICKENS *Amer. Notes* v, An old cathedral yard. *Ibid.* viii, A long row of small houses fronting on the street, and opening at the back upon a common yard. **1908** [MISS FOWLER] *Betw. Trent & Ancholme* 20 The small yard between the stables.

b. *spec.* † (*a*) The 'ground' of a playhouse, orig. an inn-yard; (*b*) *Sc. pl.* a school playground; (*c*) = COURT *sb.*[1] 3 (esp. in proper names, as *Carter's Yard*, *Thompson's Yard* in Oxford).

1609 DEKKER *Gull's Horn-bk.* vi. 29 Neither are you to be hunted from thence though the Scar-crowes in the yard, hoot at you. **1808** SCOTT *Autobiogr.* in *Lockhart* (1839) I. 41, I made a brighter figure in the yards than in the class. **1815** —— *Guy M.* ii, Half the youthful mob of 'the yards' used to assemble..to see Dominie Sampson..descend the stairs from the Greek class. **1851** in Mayhew *Lond. Labour* (1861) II. 211/1 Every Street, Lane, Square, Yard, Court, Alley, Passage, and Place..are to be thus cleansed.

c. Contextually = CHURCHYARD, GRAVE-YARD.

[**1617** MORYSON *Itin.* I. 145 Not farre thence is a yard vsed for common buriall, called the holy field, vulgarly *Campo Santo*.] **1791** BURNS *There'll never be peace* ii, And now I greet round their green beds in the yerd. **1836** [HOOTON] *Bilberry Thurland* I. xi. 217 The road he had taken brought him at length to the church, through the yard of which it led. **1856** MISS YONGE *Daisy Chain* I. xxii, The little..church, its yard shaded with trees.

d. An inclosure attached to a prison, in which the prisoners take exercise. ***liberty of the yard*** (U.S.): see quot. 1828–32.

1777 HOWARD *Prisons Eng.* iii. 74 Why were not the walls of the yards repaired in time, that prisoners might with safety be allowed the proper use of them? **1828–32** WEBSTER s.v. *Yard*, *Liberty of the yard*, is a liberty granted to persons imprisoned for debt, of walking in the yard, or within any other limits prescribed by law. **1851** MAYHEW *Lond. Labour* (1861) III. 438/1 This person..took me into the yard and stripped me.

e. ***the Yard***, short for 'Scotland Yard', the chief London police office.

1888 GUNTER *Mr. Potter* xviii. 221 They're tired of paying your old master's salary up at the Yard. **1904** SWEENEY *At Scotland Yard* ii, W. E. Monro..was one of the greatest public servants who ever worked at the Yard.

f. *U.S.* A college campus or the area enclosed by its main buildings; *spec.* at Harvard: ***the Yard***, the quadrangle formed by the original college buildings.

1637–9 *Harvard Coll. Rec.* in *Publ. Colonial Soc. Mass.* (1925) I. 172 Mr Nathaniel Eatons Account... The frame in the Colledge Yard & digging the cellar. **1841** *Harvard Faculty Orders & Regul.* 6 Collecting in groups round the doors of the College buildings or in the yard [shall be considered a violation of decorum]. **1871** L. H. BAGG *Four Years at Yale* 27 Besides the fourteen buildings already described, the only others within the yard..were the two wooden dwelling-houses. **1902** *Boston Even. Record* 18 Mar. 8/4 (*heading*) Out of the 'Yard'—how the Harvard students have gone to the 'Gold Coast'. **1942** BERREY & VAN DEN BARK *Amer. Thes. Slang* §829.12 *Campus*, camp, orchard,.. yard. **1947** *Harvard Alumni Bull.* 12 Apr. 586/2 Few people have likely ever thought of the Yard as a bird sanctuary... What of the Yard? There must be bird records. **1970** 'E. QUEEN' *Last Women in his Life* III. 163, I found out the truth about myself in my freshman year at Harvard... There was an episode in a bar, well away from the Yard. **1981** 'D. JORDAN' *Double Red* xv. 71 Stumbling across the Yard.. after too much Harvard Provision Co. gin.

2. An inclosure forming a pen for cattle or poultry, a storing place for hay, or the like, belonging to a farm-house or surrounded by farm-buildings, or one in which a barn or similar building stands. (Cf. *barn-yard*, FARM-YARD, *poultry-yard*.)

c **1300** *Havelok* 702 Þe hennes of þe yerd. *c* **1386** CHAUCER *Nun's Pr. T.* 27 A yeerd she hadde enclosed al aboute With stikkes and a drye dych with-oute In which she hadde a Cok. *Ibid.* 177 Oon of hem was logged in a stalle Fer in a yeerd with Oxen of the plough. **1481** CAXTON *Reynard* v. (Arb.) 10, I [*sc.* chantecleer] had viij fayr sones and seuen fayr doughters whiche..wente in a yerde whiche was walled round a boute. **1551** *N. Country Wills* (Surtees 1908) 218 To Jhon Collin,..one lode of heye in my yarde. **1573–80** TUSSER *Husb.* (1878) 58 All maner of strawe that is scattered in yard. **1646** SIR T. BROWNE *Pseud. Ep.* III. xxv. 175 One of the Lyons leaped downe into a neighbours yard, where nothing regarding the crowing or noise of the Cocks, hee eat them up. **1697** DRYDEN *Virg. Georg.* II. 766 His wanton Kids..Fight harmless Battels in his homely Yard. **1749** FIELDING *Tom Jones* IV. viii, A vast herd of cows in a rich farmer's yard. **1840** DICKENS *Old C. Shop* xv, A thriving farm with sleepy cows lying about the yard.

3. A piece of inclosed ground of moderate size, often adjoining a house and covered with grass or planted with trees; a garden. Now chiefly *N. Amer.* and *dial.*, a kitchen or cottage-garden (cf. DOOR-YARD, KAIL-YARD).

See also *grass-yard*, GREEN-YARD.

a **1300** *Cursor M.* 1027 Paradis..es a yard cald o delites Wit all maner of suet spices. *Ibid.* 12522 He sent him to þe yerd..For to gedir þam sum cale. **1390** GOWER *Conf.* II. 30 And after Phillis Philliberd This tre was cleped in the yerd. *c* **1400** *Sc. Trojan War* (Horstm.) I. 255 Ȝardes for herbys ande for virgerys. *c* **1440** *Gesta Rom.* xxvii. 111 (Add. MS.), He had a faire yerde [*Harl. MS.* gardin], that he mekell loved. *c* **1440** *Promp. Parv.* 537/2 Ȝerd, or ȝorde.., *ortus*. **1477** in *Exch. Rolls Scot.* IX. 101 *note*, Oure landis of Auld Lindoris with the brewlandis cotagiis and yairdis therof. **1536** BELLENDEN *Cron. Scot.* (1821) I. p. lvi, Aqua vite.. maid..of sic naturall herbis as grew in thair awin yardis. **1589** R. BRUCE *Serm.* v. (1590) T 2 b, Quhat Christ suffered for thame in the zarde [*sc.* Gethsemane], and on the crosse. **1718** in *Nairne Peerage Evid.* (1874) 33 Houses biggings yairds orchyairds. **1792** BURNS *Auld Rob Morris* iii, My daddie has nought but a cot-house and yard. **1818** SCOTT *Hrt. Midl.* ix, Any of her apple-trees or cabbages which she had left rooted in the 'yard' at Woodend. *a* **1825** FORBY *Voc. E. Anglia*, *Yard*, the garden belonging to a cottage or ordinary messuage. **1835** J. H. INGRAHAM *South-West* II. 88 Striped grass, cultivated in yards at the north. **1877** H. G. MURRAY *Tom Kittle's Wake* 21 My daughter, Molly tief pass, maam, den go da him yard. **1889** MARY E. WILKINS *Far Away Melody* etc. (1891) 11 Four..old apple-trees, which stood promiscuously about the yard back of the Cottage. **1907** W. JEKYLL *Jamaican Song & Story* 163 The immediate surroundings of the house are called the yard. They seldom speak of going to a friend's house. They say they are going to his yard. **1932** 'L. G. GIBBON' *Sunset Song* 97 The berries hung ripe in the yard of the gardener Galt. **1947** J. A. LOMAX *Adventures Ballad Hunter* vii. 185 She says, 'Can you cut yards?' an' I says, 'Yes ma'am.' She says, 'Go roun,..to de back.., you'll find a lawn-mower there, and then begin cuttin'.' **1956** G. E. EVANS *Ask Fellows who cut Hay* iv. 55 The village was almost entirely self-supporting, most families living on what they grew or reared on their *yards* or allotments. **1980** W. MAXWELL *So Long, see you Tomorrow* (1981) ii. 22 The rented house had no yard to speak of.

4. a. An inclosure set apart for the growing, rearing, breeding, or storing of something or the carrying on of some work or business. Cf. *brickyard*, DOCKYARD, *dung-yard*, *hemp-yard*, ORCHARD (OE. *ortᵹeard*), SHIPYARD, *tan-yard*, VINEYARD, † *winyard* (OE. *wínᵹeard*).

1378 [see *hemp-yard*, HEMP *sb.* 6 b]. **1520** *Perth Hammermen Bk.* (1889) 15 Ressavit fra John Kynloch of this yeres excrestes of the yairds. **1523** LD. BERNERS *Froiss.* I. xvi. 7/2 Great leuers..the whiche they founde in a carpenters yarde. **1555** *Act 2 & 3 Phil. & Mary* c. 16 §7 Before the said Boate..bee lanched out of the Yarde or Grounde wherin the same Boate..shall fortune to bee made. *a* **1610** HEALEY *Theophrastus* (1636) 23 He hath a little yard, gravelled fit for wrestling. **1696** *Cal. St. Pap., Dom.* 282 The porter, master-caulker and 'teamer' of Deptford Yard. **1748** *Anson's Voy.* II. vi. 200 A ship-carpenter in the yard at Portsmouth. **1803** PERING in *Naval Chron.* XV. 61 The yard is paid quarterly. **1835** DICKENS *Sk. Boz, River*, What can be more amusing than Searle's yard on a fine Sunday morning? **1837** —— *Pickw.* ii, 'What's Mr. Smithie?' inquired Mr. Tracy Tupman. 'Something in the yard [= the Dockyard]', replied the stranger. **1855** *Poultry Chron.* III. 191 Eggs from the Yards of Mr. Punchard. **1873** G. S. BADEN-POWELL *New Homes* 194 The 'yards'..are usually situated near the head station. **1891** W. K. BROOKS *Oyster* 131 Around each claire is built a levee or dirt wall called a yard... This yard retains the water filling the basin.

b. The piece of ground adjacent to a railway station or terminus, used for making up trains, storing rolling-stock, etc.; also an inclosure in which cabs, trams, etc. are kept when not in use.

1827 [see *wagon-yard*, WAGON *sb.* 13]. **1837** DICKENS *Pickw.* ii, A..young man,.. emerging suddenly from the coach yard. **1894** *Daily News* 18 May 5/4 Yesterday his cabs were still in the yard. **1903** *Westm. Gaz.* 8 Jan. 7/3 The yard foreman knows the capacity of each of the engines he sends out from his yard.

c. ***the Yards***, the stockyards where cattle are collected for slaughter, esp. in Chicago. *U.S.*

1865 *Atlantic Monthly* Jan. 83/2 The average weekly expenditure by butchers at the New York yards during the year 1863 was $328,865. **1906** U. SINCLAIR *Jungle* xv. 170 Already the yards were full of activity. **1935** A. G. MACDONELL *Visit to America* vii. 114 As in Chicago, the pride of Omaha is the Stock-yards... I was looking straight down into the Yards. **1974** 'M. ALLEN' *Super Tour* ii. 57 I've been called all kinds of things ever since I was a kid back of the Yards.

5. *U.S.* and *Canada.* An area in which moose and deer congregate, esp. during the winter months.

1829 HALIBURTON *Nova-Scotia* II. ix. 392 In winter they [*sc.* moose] form herds, and when the snow is deep, they describe a circle, and press the snow with their feet, until it becomes hard, which is called by hunters a yard, or pen. **1864-5** WOOD *Homes without H.* 614 So confident is the Elk in the security of the 'yard', that it can scarcely ever be induced to leave its snowy fortification. **1884** *Science* 28 Mar. 394/1 Immense yards, containing hundreds of deer, existed along the various tributaries [of the Ottawa]. **1903** *Longman's Mag.* July 248 [They] never failed to destroy a 'yard' to the last fawn.

6. *attrib.* and *Comb.* (*a*) in sense 1, as ***yard-broom, door, gate, wall***; **yard-dog**, a watchdog kept in the yard of a house or dwelling; (*b*) in sense 2, as ***yard-bar, -dung, -liquor, -pond, -room***; †(*c*) in sense 3, (*Sc.* and *U.S.*), as ***yard door, end, house, tack***; **yard-boy**, a general labourer; a gardener or gardener's boy (*obs.* exc. *Caribbean*); †**yard-dike**, a garden wall; **yard-grass**, a low annual grass, *Eleusine indica*, common in 'yards' about houses in parts of U.S.A.; also *Cynodon Dactylon*; **yard sale** *U.S.*, a sale of miscellaneous second-hand items held in the garden of a private house; (*d*) in sense 4, 4 b, esp. relating to dockyards, ship-yards, cab yards, or railway yards, as ***yard clerk, craft, -keeper, -lighter, -master***; **yard-money**, fees payable by hirers of cabs from cab-owners to stablemen, etc. on returning them to the yard.

(*a*) **1580** in *Archaeologia* LXIV. 358 To mak and hang a yard dor at the nether end of the turrit at the bridg. **1795** HAIGHTON in *Phil. Trans.* LXXXV. 197, I kept this animal nineteen months, during the greatest part of which he performed the office of a yard dog. **1823** SCOTT *Quentin D.* Introd. (*init.*), Trusty, the yard-dog. **1857** KINGSLEY *Two Yrs. Ago* iii, Lofty garden and yard walls of grey stone. **1865** —— *Herew.* xix, Let me and my serving-man go free out of thy yard gate. **1905** A. C. BENSON *Thread of Gold* ii, A big black yard-dog. **1908** [MISS FOWLER] *Betw. Trent & Ancholme* 29 Near the yard doors. **1921** *Blackw. Mag.* Feb. 195/1 Dip an old yard-broom in a bucket of water. **1982** J. SCOTT *Local Lads* iii. 32 Billy took up an aged, patchily moulted yardbroom.

(*b*) **1573-80** TUSSER *Husb.* (1878) 119 Some barnroome haue little, and yardroome as much. **1744** W. ELLIS *Mod. Husb.* Jan. xi. 73 He may now carry out his Stable or Yard Dung. **1764** *Museum Rusticum* II. I. 3 When I make use of yard dung, I take care it is very rotten. **1778** [W. MARSHALL] *Minutes Agric., Digest* 23 It is better management to prevent, than either to waste or cart-out a superfluity of Yard-liquor. **1827** CLARE *Sheph. Cal.* 20 While ducks and geese..Plunge in the yard-pond brimming o'er. **1869** MRS. WHITNEY *Hitherto* xi, The lowing of cattle at their yard-bars.

(*c*) **1473** *Rental Bk. Cupar-Angus* (1879) I. 189 He sal put bath husband tak and ȝard tak til al possibil polyci. **1505** *Ibid.* 260 Biggind of gud ȝerd hous, sufficiand chawmeris and stabulis to resaue and herbry..xij or xvj hors. **1532** *Abst. Protocols Town Clerks Glasgow* (1897) IV. 57 The rademyng and lowsing of twa riggis of land, lyand at his yard end. **1595** *Reg. Mag. Sig. Scot.* 132/2 Up the saidis Alesteris eist yaird-dyk to the mairch of Galdwalmoir. **1691** *Jedburgh Counc. Rec.* 19 Mar. (MS.), For his wrongous..awaytakeing of certaine stones out of the minister's yeard dyke at his awn hand. **1788** J. WOODFORDE *Diary* 7 Jan. (1927) III. 2 To my Yard Boy, Charles Crossley, for 3 Quarters of a Years Wages pd 0. 15. 9. **1809** A. HENRY *Trav.* 79 Behind the yard-door of my own house,..there was a low fence. **1822** J. WOODS *Two Yrs.' Resid. Illinois* 199 Yard-grass comes on land that has been much trodden; it is something like cock's-foot-grass, except the seed. **1831** C. FARQUHARSON *Jrnl.* 2 Dec. in *Relic of Slavery* (1957) 47 Employed all hands weeding.. along with the yard boys. **1848** SCHOMBURGK *Hist. Barbados* 586 *Cynodon dactylon.* Devil's Grass. Bahama, or Yard Grass. **1907** A. LANG *Hist. Scot.* IV. xvi. 392 A minister's yard dyke, or garden wall, was overthrown. **1958** S. SELVON *Turn again Tiger* viii. 185, I take the worst job that was going —as a kind of yard-boy by the white people house. **1975** *New Rev.* May 10/2 In and around Port of Spain cooks, ironers and yardboys in attendance. **1976** *Flint* (Michigan) *Jrnl.* 12 July C-5 *Yard sale*—1508 Webber canning jars, screen tent, patterns, books, [etc.]. **1982** M. MCMULLEN *Until Death do us Part* (1983) vii. 46 There was a yard sale down our street.

(*d*) *a* **1647** PETTE in *Archaeologia* (1796) XII. 266 Those businesses, which were put out by the great to divers yard-keepers. **1737** *J. Chamberlayne's St. Gt. Brit.* (ed. 33) II. 87 Yard-keeper and Fire-maker. **1804** *Naval Chron.* XII. 504 Six Gun-vessels and Yard-lighters. **1861** (16 Apr.) in *Orders of Council Naval Service* (1904) II. 29 Pensions..granted to the Riggers employed in Your Majesty's Dock-yards, and the Seamen belonging to the Yard Craft. **1864** *Rep. Children's Employment Comm.* 139/1 in *Parl. Papers* XXII. 487/1 Mr Thomas Wheat, yard-master... My duty is to give orders..and manage the work. **1883** SIMMONDS *Dict. Trade* Suppl., *Yard Clerk*, one who has the overlooking of the yard of a brewery, builder, etc. **1884** *Bath Jrnl.* 26 July 7/3 On returning to the yard at night he has to stump up ten shillings more, plus a mysterious fee of two shillings called 'yard money'. **1889** *Boston* (Mass.) *Jrnl.* 9 Apr. 3/4 [A] yardmaster at Brattleboro' had one leg cut off by a switching train. **1891** C. ROBERTS *Adrift Amer.* 93 The brakesman was standing by to couple the cars that the yard engine was backing down on to the rest of the train. **1898** *Engineering Mag.* XVI. 67 The ordinary yard-handling of, say, an army corps.

yard (jɑːd), *sb.*[2] Forms: 1 **ᵹyrd, ᵹerd,** (**ierd**), 1–2 **ᵹird,** 3–6 **ȝerd(e, yerd(e,** 4–5 **ȝarde,** 4–7 **yarde,** (3 **ȝerrde, ȝeord, yeorde, yherde,** 4 **ȝierd(e, ȝeird, yeird, ȝeerde, ȝurde,** 5 **ȝearde, ȝherde, yeerde, yerede,** 6 **yerdde**), 5–7 **yeard(e,** (9 *Sc.* **yaird**), 5– **yard.** [OE. **ᵹierd, ᵹyrd, ᵹird*, Angl. *ᵹerd* = OFris. *ierde* (EFris. *jœd*), OS. *-gerda* (in *segalgerda* SAILYARD), MLG. *gerde*, MDu. *gherde, garde*, Du. *garde, gard*, OHG. **gartja, gardea, gerta*, MHG., G. *gerte*, generally taken to represent OTeut. **gazdjō*, deriv. of **gazdaz* (whence OE. *ᵹeard*?, MLG. *gaert*, OHG. *gart*, ON. *gaddr* GAD *sb.*[1], Goth. *gazds* prickle), prob. related to L. *hasta* (:—**ghazdhā*) spear, OIr. *gat* rod.

Some, however, regard the *r* in this word as original and connect it with OSl. *žrŭdĭ*, Russ. *zherd'* thin pole.]

†**1. a.** A straight slender shoot or branch of a tree; a twig, stick. *Obs.*

c **950** *Lindisf. Gosp.* Matt. xi. 7 ðerd..from uinde styrende [*arundinem uento agitatum*]. *c* **1000** ÆLFRIC *Hom.* II. 8 Seo driᵹe ᵹyrd, þe næs on eorðan aplantod,..and swa-ðeah greow. **1297** R. GLOUC. (Rolls) 510 A gret ok he wolde braide adoun as it a smal ȝerd were. *c* **1374** CHAUCER *Boeth.* III. met. ii. (1868) 68 þe ȝerde of a tree þat is haled adoun by myȝty strengþe bowiþ redely þe croppe adoun. *a* **1425** *Cursor M.* 5614 (Trin.) A cofur of ȝerdes dud she be wrouȝt. *c* **1425** *Engl. Conq. Irel.* 30 Thay arered a dyche, & a feble castel vpon, of yardes and turues. *c* **1450** *Mirk's Festial* 221 A branche of palme of paradyse of þe wheche þe ȝearde was grene as gresse.

†**b.** *fig.* in reference to Isaiah xi. 1: cf. ROD *sb.*[1] 1 b. *Obs.*

c **1200** *Trin. Coll. Hom.* 217 An ȝerd sal spruten of iesse more. *a* **1400** *Minor Poems fr. Vernon MS.* 57/169 Heil þou ȝerde of Iesse. *a* **1400** *Leg. Rood* (1871) 212 Þou seydest a ȝerd schulde sprynge Oute of þe rote of Ientill Iesse. **1450-1530** *Myrr. our Ladye* II. 172.

†**c.** In reference to taking or surrendering land, esp. in phr. ***by the yard*** (law-Fr. *per le virge*): see quots. and cf. ROD *sb.*[1] 1 c. *Obs.*

1523 FITZHERB. *Surv.* 13 b, There be other tenantes by copy of court role, and is called tenauntes per le virge .s. by the yerde. And they be called so bycause whan they wolde surrendre their tenementes in to the lordes handes to the vse of another, they shall haue a lytell yerde in his hande by custome of the courte, and that he shall delyuer vnto the stewarde. **1559** *Bk. Presidentes* 48 b, How the copy should be made of landes holden by the yarde.

†**d.** Used typically of a thing of no value.

c **1400** *Laud Troy Bk.* 9660 He ȝeues of hem not a ȝerd.

†**2. a.** A staff or stick carried in the hand as a walking stick, or by a shepherd or herdsman. *Obs.*

c **1000** *Ags. Gosp.* Matt. x. 10 Næbbe ᵹe gold..ne codd on weᵹe ne twa tunecan ne ᵹe-scy ne ᵹyrde [*Lindisf.* ᵹerd; *Rushw.* ierde]. *c* **1000** ÆLFRIC *Num.* xvii. 10 Ber Aarones ᵹirde in to þam ᵹetelde. *c* **1250** *Gen. & Exod.* 2987 He smot wið ðat ȝerde on ðe lond. *a* **1300** *Cursor M.* 5894 Þan tok aaron þis ilk yeird, And on þe flore he kest it don. *a* **1400** *Leg. Rood* (1871) 141 Þe heerdes ȝerde. *a* **1450** *Knt. de la Tour* lxxv, The yerde wherewith Moyses departed the see. **1538** BALE *Thre Lawes* (facs.) B v, For horse take Moyses yearde, There is no better charme.

†**b.** (Also ***golden yard***; cf. *yard-band* in sense 13, and *ell-wand*.) The Belt of Orion. *Obs.*

1551 [see GOLDEN *a.* 10]. **1651** *Loves of Hero & Leander* (1653) 23 The Yard, Orion, and Charles Wain.

†**3. a.** A stick or rod used as an instrument for administering strokes by way of punishment or otherwise. *Obs.*

c **1000** *Sax. Leechd.* II. 290 ðenim ane ᵹirde, sleah on þæt bæc þonne biþ þæt hors hal. *a* **1175** *Cott. Hom.* 243 Þu ahst to habben..Stede and twei sporen and ane smearte ȝerd. *c* **1205** LAY. 20318 Ofte me hine smæt mid smærte ȝerden [*c* **1275** ȝerdes]. *a* **1250** *Prov. Ælfred* 451 in *O.E. Misc.* 130 Þe mon þe spareþ yeorde and yonge childe. *a* **1250** *Owl & Night.* 777 Hit [*sc.* a horse]..þoleþ boþe ȝerd & spure. *c* **1374** CHAUCER *Troylus* II. 1427 Tristith wele that I Wole be her champioun with spore and yerd. *a* **1400** *Minor Poems fr. Vernon MS.* 537 Ȝif þi child be not a-fert, Ȝif him i-nouh of þe ȝerd. **1430-40** LYDG. *Bochas* (1554) Prol. xxviii, His yard of castigacion. *c* **1450** *Mirk's Festial* 40 He made hys confessour bete hym wyth a ȝarde apon þe backe al bare, as a chyld ys beten yn scole. *c* **1450** *Mirour Saluacioun* (1888) 5 The payens bett him with scourgis & with scharp ȝerds eke.

†**b.** *fig.* A means or instrument of punishment; hence, punishment, chastisement. *Obs.*

a **1225** *Ancr. R.* 184 Þench ȝet þet hwose euer hermeð þe, ..þench þet he is Godes ȝerd, & tet God bet þe mide him. *Ibid.* 324 Ase ofte ase þe hund of helle keccheð ei god from þe, smit him anonriht mid te ȝerde of tunge schrifte. **1389** in *Eng. Gilds* (1870) 95 Qwo-so make any noyse..and þe den comaunde him to ben stille, and he ne wil nouth, scal taken him þe ȝerde. *c* **1400** *Pilgr. Sowle* I. xxii. (1859) 24 Tretyng with yerd of loue, and discipline. *c* **1449** PECOCK *Repr.* IV. ii. 424 He thretened hem that he wolde come to hem in ȝerde, that is to seie, in peyne. *c* **1530** *Crt. Love* 363, I shall.. meekly take her chastisement and yerd.

†**4.** A wand, rod, or staff carried as a symbol of office, authority, etc.; hence in fig. phr. ***under the yard***, under (the) rule or discipline (of). *Obs.*

c **1205** LAY. 22480 He bar on his honde ænne mucle ȝeord of golde. *c* **1275** *Passion our Lord* 382 in *O.E. Misc.* 48 Seþþe hi nomen a red cloþ and duden him a-bute And one yerd on his hond. **13..** *Seuyn Sag.* (W.) 142 Dioclician the maistres herde, He strok his berd, and schok his yerde. *c* **1386** CHAUCER *Clerk's Prol.* 22 Hoost quod he I am vnder youre yerde Ye han of vs as now the gouernance. *a* **1400-50** *Wars Alex.* 813 Þen was him geuyn vp þe ȝerde & ȝolden þe rewme. *c* **1440** *Promp. Parv.* 537/2 Ȝerde, borne a-forne a worthyman. *c* **1470** HARDING *Chron.* CCXXII. iv, Compleyntes..Refourmed were well vnder his yerd egall.

5. *Naut.* A wooden (or steel) spar, comparatively long and slender, slung at its centre from, and forward of, a mast and serving to support and extend a square sail which is bent to it.

(See also JACKYARD, MIZEN-YARD, SAILYARD, TOPGALLANT-*yard*.)

c **725**-*c* **1440** [see SAILYARD 1]. **1336-7** [see YARD-ROPE]. **1465** *Mann. & Househ. Exp.* (Roxb.) 199 My mastyr paid for the yerde [of the said ship]. **1591** HARINGTON *Orl. Fur.* XLI. xvii, At last with striuing, yard and all was torne, And part therof into the sea was borne. **1624** CAPT. J. SMITH *Virginia* III. xii. 90 Some [ships] lost their Masts, some their Sayles blowne from their Yards. **1633** T. JAMES *Voy.* 19 We put abroad all the sayle that was at yards. **1745** P. THOMAS *Jrnl. Anson's Voy.* 21 The Sails were almost always splitting and blowing from the Yards. **1814** SCOTT *Ld. of Isles* III. xii, Fain to strike the galley's yard, And take them to the oar. **1853** DICKENS *Bleak Ho.* i, Fog lying out on the yards, and hovering in the rigging of great ships. **1868** MORRIS *Earthly Par.* Prol. (1870) I. 26 We saw the yards swing creaking round the mast.

†**6.** A straight rod or bar used in various connexions (see quots.). *Obs.*

a **1490** BOTONER *Itin.* (1778) 260 The yerdys called sparres of the halle ryalle. **1538** ELYOT, *Radius*,..a rodde or yerde, that Geometricians haue to describe lynes. **1594** BLUNDEVIL *Exerc., Navig.* xii. (1597) 322 b, In vsing M. Hoods staffe they shall..need..onely to marke vpon what degree of the yarde the shadow of the Vane streeketh.

†**7.** A measuring-rod; *spec.* a measuring-rod or -stick of the length of three feet; a yard-measure.

See also CLOTH-YARD, *ell-yard* (ELL[1] 5), METEYARD (OE. *meteᵹyrd*), *tailor's yard* (TAILOR *sb.* 6 b).

c **1000-1050** *Instit. Pol.* xii. [vii.] (Liebermann 478) And riht is, þæt ne beo æniᵹ meteᵹyrd [*Quadripartitus* mensuralis uirga] lengre þonne oðer. *c* **1430** Met yerde [see METEYARD]. *c* **1440** *Promp. Parv.* 537/2 Ȝerde, metwande, *ulna.* **1557** NORTH *Gueuara's Diall Princes* Gen. Prol. A ij, By the yarde the marchaunte measureth al his war. **1656** EARL MONM. tr. *Boccalini's Advts. fr. Parnass.* I. x. (1674) 13 He had a very just yard at home. *a* **1658** CLEVELAND *London Lady* 81 The Heroes of the Yard have shut Their Shops. **1712** ARBUTHNOT *John Bull* III. v, If they offered to come into the warehouse, then strait went the yard slap over their noddle. **1751** JOHNSON *Rambler* No. 116 ¶7, I was..bound to a haberdasher... I learned in a few weeks to handle a yard with great dexterity.

8. A unit of linear measure equal to $16\frac{1}{2}$ feet or $5\frac{1}{2}$ yards (but varying locally); a rod, pole, or perch. Now *local.*

Sometimes spec. distinguished as *land-yard*.

900 in Earle *Land-Charters* (1888) 351, xvi. ᵹyrda gauoltininga. **901-9** in Thorpe *Dipl. Angl. Ævi Sax.* (1865) 156 Ðæs landes be suðan ðære cirican..xxiiii. ᵹerda on lange & on bræde ðar hit bradest is fif ᵹeurda, & ðær hit unbradost is anne ᵹeurde. **11..** *Textus Roffensis* in Birch *Cart. Sax.* III. 659 To wercene þa land peran & þreo ᵹyrda to þillianæ [L. *tres virgatas plancas ponere*]. *c* **1330** *Arth. & Merl.* 1449 Her vnder is a ȝerde depe A water. **1828** [see *land-yard*, LAND *sb.*[1] 12]. **1858** SIMMONDS *Dict. Trade* s.v., As a linear measure, the yard varies considerably in different parts of the kingdom; at Hertford the land-yard is 3 feet; at Saltash, $16\frac{1}{2}$ feet; at Falmouth and Bridgend 18 feet; and at Dowspatrick, 21 feet. **1886** ELWORTHY *W. Som. Word-bk.*, *Yard*, a measure of five and a half yards ($16\frac{1}{2}$ feet) both long and square, *i.e.* the same as a rod, pole, or perch.

9. a. A measure of length (traditionally the standard unit of English long measure) equal to three feet or thirty-six inches. (See quot. 1867.) Also the corresponding measure of area (***square yard*** = 9 square feet) or of solidity (***cubic yard*** = 27 cubic feet).

The earlier standard was the ell = 45 inches (*ulna* in Stat. de Pistoribus, 13th cent.); this was succeeded by the *verge* (1353) Act 27 Edw. III, stat. 2, c. 10), of which *yard* is the English equivalent.

1377 LANGL. *P. Pl.* B. v. 214 Thanne drowe I me amonges draperes my donet to lerne,..Amonge þe riche rayes I rendred a lessoun, To broche hem with a pak-nedle..And put hem in a presse and pynned hem þerinne, Tyl ten ȝerdes or twelue hadde tolled out threttene. **1426-7** *Rec. St. Mary at Hill* 64 For v ȝerdis and a half of grene bokeram iij s. iij d.

1496–7 *Ibid.* 32 An Awlter cloth.. conteynyng in lengthe iij yardes di. **1518** *Star Chamber Cases* (Selden Soc.) II. 152 A gowne of vi brode yardes at vj^{s} the yard xxxvj^{s}. **1598** SHAKS. *Merry W.* I. iii. 46, I am in the waste two yards about. **1617** J. TAYLOR (Water P.) *Three Weekes Observ.* E 4 b, I bought .. a yard and halfe of pudding for fiue pence. **1663** GERBIER *Counsel* 78 One hundred of Lathes will cover six yards of seeling, and lathing is worth six pence the yard. **1762–71** H. WALPOLE *Vertue's Anecd. Painting* (1786) IV. 43 Sir James could obtain but 40*s.* a yard square for the cupola of St. Paul's. **1825** SCOTT *Betrothed* vii, Sir Cook, let me have half a yard or so of broiled beef. **1835** DICKENS *Sk. Boz, Seven-Dials*, When penny magazines shall have superseded penny yards of song. **1848** —— *Dombey* xxxv, Mrs. Perch.. has made the tour of the establishment, and priced the silks and damasks by the yard. **1867** THOMSON & TAIT *Nat. Phil.* I. I. §407 The British standard of length is the Imperial Yard, defined as the distance between two marks on a certain metallic bar, preserved in the Tower of London, when the whole has a temperature of 60° Fahrenheit. **1896** *Law Times Rep.* LXXIII. 615/1 The railway line.. was perfectly straight for a distance of over 700 yards.

fig. **1583** GOLDING *Calvin on Deut.* iv. 27–31 We imagine God to be lyke our selues, & we measure him by our owne yard. *a* **1626** BACON (J.), A peer, a counsellor, and a judge are not to be measured by the common yard.

b. Vaguely, hyperbolically, or fig.; phr. ***by the yard***, at great length, without end; also, of books or paintings: bought by quantity or size rather than for quality.

c **1386** CHAUCER *Knt.'s T.* 192 Hir yelow heer was broyded in a tresse Bihynde hir bak a yerde long. **1842** TENNYSON *Godiva* 19 His beard a foot before him, and his hair A yard behind. *a* **1843** SOUTHEY *Comm.-pl. Bk.* Ser. II. (1849) 209 Latinisms,—yard-and-half-long words. **1845** J. W. TURNER *Razor Strop Man* 3 He was spinning poetical rhyme by the yard; Had Shakespear been living 'twould astonish'd the bard. **1853** 'C. BEDE' *Verdant Green*, I. viii, Spit us out a yard or two more, Gig-lamps. **1869** 'WAT BRADWOOD' *The O.V.H.* v, He.. could talk by the yard of what little he did know. **1881** H. JAMES Jun. *Portrait of Lady* xlii, He had a face a yard long; I wondered what ailed him. **1900** ELINOR GLYN *Visits Elizabeth* (1906) 117, I danced it with some idiot who almost at once let yards and yards of my gauze frills get torn. **1933** J. BETJEMAN *Ghastly Good Taste* i. 12 The old books.. can be sold.. by the yard to America as wall decoration. **1976** 'O. BLEECK' *No Questions Asked* ii. 29 He bought fine paintings by the yard and rare books by the case.

c. Phr. ***yard of ale***, etc., a deep slender glass for liquor, or the amount of liquor contained in it. ***yard of clay*** (***clay yard***), a long clay tobacco-pipe. ***yard of satin*** (slang), a glass of gin (see SATIN *sb.* 4). ***yard of tin***, a coachman's horn.

[**1828** W. T. MONCRIEFF *Tom & Jerry* III. vi, *Log.* The haberdasher is.. the spirit-merchant,.. and tape the commodity he deals in.. white is Max, and red is Cognac. *Jerry.* Then give me a yard and a half of red.] **1842** *Punch* II. 23 His Highness condescendingly indulged in a pot of half-and-half and a yard of clay. **1866** *Lond. Misc.* 19 May 235/2 The stolidity of a mynheer smoking his clay yard. **1872** *N. & Q.* 4th Ser. X. 49 At the annual Vinis, or feast, of the mock corporation of Hanley (Staffordshire), the initiation of each member, in 1783, consisted in his swearing fealty to the body, and drinking a yard of wine—i.e., a pint of port or sherry out of a glass one yard in length. **1899** *Ibid.* 9th Ser. III. 97/1 The (disused and probably illegal) 'yard' of ale. This is a measure a yard long, holding, I should fancy, more than a pint. **1902** *Tatler* 8 Jan. 52 A 'Yard of Ale' Glass. It is 38 in. high and contains two pints of ale. **1903** C. G. HARPER *Stage-Coach & Mail* I. xii. 279 That instrument [*sc.* the key-bugle] came over from Germany in 1818, and for a time pretty thoroughly displaced the old 'yard of tin' the earlier guards had blown so lustily.

d. In Building: ***yard of lime, mortar, stone***, etc.: see quots.

1851 LAXTON *Builder's Price Bk.* 9, 27 cubic feet, or 1 cubic yard, contains 21 striked bushels, which is considered a single load. *Ibid.* 12 A rod of brickwork requires $1\frac{1}{2}$ cubic yard of chalk lime, and 3 single loads or yards of drift. **1881** *Dict. Archit.* VI. 84/2 A standard perch being taken as 21 ft. (or $16\frac{1}{2}$ ft.) long, 18 ins. high, and 12 ins. thick. This is about 'a yard of stone', or a ton, or a horse-load. **1892** *Ibid.* VIII, *Yard of Lime*; or load. In 1750 it was equal to 30 or 32 bushels.

10. a. In full ***yard of land*** (OE. *ȝyrd landes* = L. *virgata terræ*): An area of land of varying extent according to the locality, but most freq. 30 acres: commonly taken as = a fourth of a hide. See also YARDLAND.

688–95 *Laws Ine* cxi. (Liebermann), Ᵹif mon ȝeþingað ȝyrde landes [*Quadripartitus* uirgata terre] oþþe mare to rædeȝafole & ȝeereð, ȝif se hlaford him wile þæt land aræran to weorce & to ȝafole, ne þearf he him onfon, ȝif he him nan botl ne selð, & þolie þara æcra. **937** in Earle *LandCharters* (1888) 322 Þis synd þære anre ȝyrde landȝemæro æt æschyrste þe ȝebyrað into þære hyde æt toppeshamme. **978–992** *Charter of Oswald* in Kemble *Cod. Dipl.* III. 263 Landes sumne dæl ðæt syndon .iii. hida æt Bradingcotan and an ȝyrd æt Genenofre. *a* **1122** *O.E. Chron.* an. 1085 (Laud MS.) Swa swyðe nearwelice he hit lett ut aspyrian, þæt næs an ælpiȝ hide ne an ȝyrde landes.. þæt næs ȝesæt on his ȝewrite. **14..** *Tretyce* in *W. of Henley's Husb.* (1890) 44, iiij acres makithe a yerde of londe and v yerdis makithe a hyde off lande. *c* **1450** *Godstow Reg.* 559 A Charter.. confermyng to ser Iohn Trillawe.. and to Edmond Mabaunke, v. mesis, viij. yerdis of lond. **1534** *Star Chamber Cases* (Selden Soc.) II. 307 Seased.. of and in a messe half a yard of land a closse called Grymes closse.. in thyngden. **1567** in F. J. Baigent *Rec. Crondal* (1891) 163 One yarde of customary lande,.. graunted to and with the said messuage or messuages. **1618** *Crt.-roll Gt. Waltham Manor*, Ad tres rodas prati, parcellam de Alizaunder's yardland,.. et ad unam croftam terre.. parcell. unius virgate terre vocat. Alisaunder's yarde.

b. An area of land of the extent of a quarter of an acre, being, theoretically, a strip of land bounded by a 'yard' (sense 8) and a furlong, i.e. $5\frac{1}{2} \times 220$ yards; a rood.

c **1450** *Godstow Reg.* 290, v acris and a yerd of his arable lond. **1613** *MS. Acc. St. John's Hosp., Canterb.*, One acer of land and iij yeardes & viij pearches. **1726** in W. Wing *Ann. Steeple Aston* (1875) 54 Fourth part of an acre of meadow ground, called a yerd. **1893** MRS. B. STAPLETON *Three Oxf. Parishes* 309 A yard is a fourth part of a lot.. An acre is a lot.

†**11. a.** The virile member, penis; also = PHALLUS 1. (So L. *virga.*) *Obs.*

1379 *Glouc. Cath. MS.* 19 No. I, lib. 1, ca. 3, fo. 5 [The urine] passith out by the ȝerde. **1382** WYCLIF *Gen.* xvii. 11 Ȝe shulen circumside the flehs of the ferthermore parti of ȝoure ȝeerde. *a* **1425** tr. *Arderne's Treat. Fistula*, etc. 92, I haue oft tyme sene puluis grecus for to availe in þe cancre of a mannez ȝerde. **1588** SHAKS. *L.L.L.* v. ii. 676. **1607** MARKHAM *Caval.* I. (1617) 23 You must haue care that your Stallyons yarde be all of one colour. **1613** PURCHAS *Pilgrimage* VI. iv. 479 This yard, which they called *Phallus*, was vsually made of Figge-tree. **1693** WOOD *Life* (O.H.S.) III. 420 A monstrous child.. It hath three yards and he makes use of them all at once. **1748** tr. *Vegetius Renatus' Distemp. Horses* 87 His Yard drops Matter. **1884** J. PAYNE *Tales fr. Arabic* I. 30 Aboulhusn.. abode naked, with his yard and his arse exposed.

transf. **1683** SNAPE *Anat. Horse* III. v. (1686) 114 It [*sc.* the pineal gland] is also called the Yard or Prick of the Brain.. because it resembleth a Man's Yard.

†**b.** = *pintle-fish* (see PINTLE 3). *Obs.*

1655 MOUFET & BENNET *Health's Improv.* xviii. 174 *Colybdænæ*, Yards or shamefishes.. Gesner.. saith that the French men call this fish the Asses-prick, and Dr Wotton termeth it grosly the Pintle fish. **1661** LOVELL *Hist. Anim.* 232.

12. *U.S. slang.* One hundred dollars; one thousand dollars; a bill for this amount.

1926 *Amer. Mercury* Dec. 465/2 One hundred dollars is a *century* or a *yard.* **1929** C. F. COE *Hooch* vi. 130 He slips him $300 an' promises him $700 more if they'll spring him... Baldy.. promises to come right to me for the seven yards that make the grand. **1932** *Amer. Speech* VII. 118 *Yard*,.. a thousand-dollar bill. **1942** BERRREY & VAN DEN BARK *Amer. Thes. Slang* §18.5 (*One*) *G, -gee* or *grand, thou*, (*one*) *yard*, one thousand. *Ibid.* §467.2 *One C, yard*, a hundred dollars. **1979** V. PATRICK *Pope of Greenwich Village* vii. 70 You throw a hundred to the guy who makes the loan... He writes the loan for thirteen hundred, you take twelve, and a yard goes south to him.

13. *attrib.* and *Comb.* as (sense 5) ***yard-mast, -tackle***; (sense 9) ***yard-band, -glass, -length, -rule***; ***yard-broad, -deep, -long, -square, -thick, -wide*** adjs.; (sense 11) ***yard-ball, -mattering, -syringe***; ***yard-fallen*** adj.; **yard-coal, yard-seam**, a seam of coal a yard thick; †**yard-fell**, the foreskin; **yard goods**, fabric sold by the yard; **yard-stick**, a rigid yard-measure; also *fig.*, a standard of comparison; **yard-work** = YARDAGE^{2} 1. Also YARDARM, -MEASURE, -ROPE, -WAND.

1650 BULWER *Anthropomet.* Descr. *j, *Yard-bals or Bels hung 'twixt the flesh and skin. **1828** *Craven Gloss.*, **Yerd-band*, a rod of a yard in length. 'The Ladies yerd-band', the belt of Orion. **1711** *Act 10 Anne* c. 18 §104 All such Callicoes .. which shall be within One Eighth Part of a Yard of *Yard broad.. shall pay as Yard broad. **1855** J. PHILLIPS *Man. Geol.* 188 *Yard coal. 3 feet. **1753** *Chambers' Cycl.* Suppl. s.v., **Yard-fallen*, a term.. to express a malady to which horses are sometimes subject, which is the hanging down of the penis from its sheath.., the creature not being able to draw it up again. **1382** WYCLIF *Jer.* iv. 4 *Ȝerde felles. **1882** *N. & Q.* 6th Ser. V. 456/1 The expense of 7*s.* 6*d.* was not his main reason for the non-replacement of the absent *yard-glass. **1941** L. I. WILDER *Little Town on Prairie* v. 33 He'll get most of the trade in *yard goods, with somebody there in the store making them up into shirts. **1964** M. LAURENCE *Stone Angel* iv. 113 At the back was the section where yard-goods were sold, and ladies' and children's ready-to-wear garments hanging dejectedly on racks. **1982** S. T. HAYMON *Ritual Murder* xix. 134 Patter of the travelling men who sold crockery and yard goods. **1843** J. WARD *Borough Stoke-upon-Trent* 367 The drinking off a *yard-length-glass of ale at a single draught. *a* **1711** KEN *Edmund* Poet. Wks. II. 52 In Ewen Bows they *Yard long Arrows shot. **1798** in *Spirit Publ. Jrnls.* (1799) II. 276 A rope of yard-long words. **1822** SCOTT *Nigel* i, A nod of his yard-long visage. **1890** 'R. BOLDREWOOD' *Col. Reformer* (1891) 171 A yard-long dog-fish was dropped into.. the boat. **1579–80** NORTH *Plutarch* (1595) 1000 They sawe the threescore shippes of Cleopatra busie about their *yard-masts, and hoysing saile to flie. **1708** KERSEY, **Yard-mattering*, a Distemper in Horses. **1862** *Times* 21 Jan., Strong active relays of pitmen and miners can soon clear the shaft from the *yard-seam. **1799** in *Spirit Publ. Jrnls.* III. 388 Their *yard-square towels. **1822** in W. R. Alger *Life Edwin Forrest* (1877) I. 100 Furnish me with every particular, especially how our Tid is, and whether she reads with the *yard-stick. **1828–32** WEBSTER, Yard-stick. **1844** EMERSON *Lect., Yng. American* Wks. (Bohn) II. 293 It has great value as a sort of yard-stick, and surveyor's line. **1878** *N. Amer. Rev.* CXXVI. 507 Senator Huerman was content to measure the Bland Bill with the yard-stick of the constitutional lawyer. **1883** GRESLEY *Gloss. Coal-mining*, *Yard-stick*, an ash walking-stick, 3 feet in length.. which a manager or underviewer carries with him in the pit, with which he roughly measures any lengths or work done.. and with which he chastises unruly lads. **1929** *Morning Post* 4 June 15/6 This is considered more effective than a rough comparison by means of tonnage or range... It is hoped that this new American 'yardstick' will be ready for General Dawes when he leaves for London. **1949** *Here & Now* (N.Z.) Oct. 33/2 What yardstick should we use in assessing success or failure in farming? **1960** A. S. NEILL *Summerhill* (1962) VI. 334 We all have our standards of values and we measure others by our personal yardstick. **1984** A. SMITH *Mind* IV. xiv. 262 Whatever yardstick is used, it is probable that at least a million people on this planet kill themselves each year. **1694** SALMON *Bate's Dispens.* (1715) 455/1 Make an Injection into the Yard, with a proper *Yard-Syringe. **1867** SMYTH *Sailor's Word-bk.*, **Yard-tackles*, tackles attached to the fore and main yards.. whereby.. the boats.. are hoisted in and out. **1901** K. STEWART *By Allan Water* i. 1 *Yard-thick walls bear testimony to its own great age. **1766** W. GORDON *Gen. Counting-ho.* 427, 1 piece *yard-wide quilt. **1832** BABBAGE *Econ. Manuf.* xv. (ed. 3) 139 The practice, in retail linen-drapers' shops, of calling certain articles *yard-wide*, when the real width is, perhaps, only seven-eigths or three-quarters. **1865** BRIERLEY *Irkdale* I. 9 Newspapers in his 'yardwide days', as he would term the period of his earliest acquaintance with manhood. **1893** *Lady* 17 Aug. 173/2 The yard-wide tweed usually sold for trousers. **1883** GRESLEY *Gloss. Coal-mining*, **Yard Work*,.. synonymous with yardage.

yard, *v.*^{1} Chiefly *N. Amer.* [f. YARD *sb.*^{1}]

1. a. *trans.* To inclose (cattle, etc.) in a yard. Also with *up*.

1758 in *Essex Inst. Hist. Coll.* (1874) XII. 140 The Dutch here have a nasty practice of yarding their cows in ye Street before their doors. **1826** J. ATKINSON *Agric. & Grazing N.S.W.* 66 When they seem pretty well reconciled to the place, they are *bedded* out one night, and *yarded* the next. **1828–32** WEBSTER, *Yard, v.t.*, to confine cattle to the yard; as, to *yard* cows. (A farmer's word.) **1840** BUEL *Farmer's Comp.* 68 The cattle should be kept constantly yarded in winter. **1855** *Poultry Chron.* III. 201 An old Creeper hen that had been yarded with the Chittagong rooster. **1859** H. KINGSLEY *G. Hamlyn* xxxi, Well, lad, suppose we yard these rams? **1865** [see ROUND *v.*^{1} 5 f]. **1885** FINCH-HATTON *Advance Australia!* 83 Seven or eight men were yarding up a mob of cattle.

b. To store up (wood) in a yard.

1878 *Lumberman's Gaz.* Jan. 12 The logs which have been yarded or piled up in the woods. **1903** *Windsor Mag.* Sept. 405/2 They [*sc.* beavers] commence to build their houses and yard-up wood for the winter in September.

c. To shoot deer in their yards.

a **1891** *Tribune Bk. Sports* 432 (Cent. D.) 'Pot-hunters' have other methods of shooting the Adirondack deer, such as yarding and establishing salt licks.

2. *intr.* Of moose, etc.: To resort to winter quarters (see YARD *sb.*^{1} 5). Also with *up*.

1852 H. W. HERBERT *Field Sports* (ed. 4) II. 199 Here it [*sc.* the moose] still breeds, and yards in winter. **1874** W. STAMER *Gentl. Emigrant* I. 293 The caribou do not yard. They winter it out on the bogs. **1894** *Century Mag.* Jan. 354 They do not.. yard up until the deep snow comes.

yard, *v.*^{2} [f. YARD *sb.*^{2} In sense 1 used to render Manx *slattys*, f. *slat* rod, wand of authority.]

1. *trans.* In the Isle of Man, to summon for hiring: used of the hiring of servants by the coroner of a sheading on behalf of those entitled to a prior claim for their services at a low wage.

1662 in M. A. Mills *Stat. Laws I. of Man* (1821) 116 That the Coroners of this Isle, who.. by Statute have had the Benefit of yarding of three Servants within their Sheading, .. shall for the future have but the Benefit of one yarded Servant. **1667** *Ibid.* 138 The Wages mentioned in the said Statute was only intended for such Servants as were made by Jurys and Yarding. **1726–31** WALDRON *Descr. Isle of Man* (1865) 39 If any man or maid-servant be esteemed extraordinary in their way, either he [*sc.* the lord's steward], the Governour, or the two Deempsters have the power to oblige such a servant to live with them for the space of a year, and receive no more than six shillings for their service during the said time. This they call yarding. *Ibid.*, All servants who have any apprehensions of being yarded. **1892** *Denham Tracts* I. 199 The old privilege of yarding, given by ancient customary law to the Lords, Deemsters, and Chief Officers in the island.

2. To furnish with sailyards.

1676 T. MILLER *Modellist* Index, In the second Page is shewed a Rule for Masting and Yarding. **1705** *Lond. Gaz.* No. 4117/4 Easy Directions to Build, Rigg, Yard, and Mast any Ship.

yardage^{1} (ˈjɑːdɪdʒ). [f. YARD *sb.*^{1} + -AGE.] The use of or charge for a yard in which commodities are stored, cattle inclosed, or the like.

1867 *Trans. Illinois Agric. Soc.* VI. 322 Net cash receipt for yardage, and profit on feed. **1889** *Baltimore Sun* in *Public Opinion* 16 Feb., The object of the company.. is to regulate the price of pig-iron by holding it in stock in yards leased by the company at the furnaces... Each furnace is to turn over all its product to the company,.. the furnace-master paying the company yardage at the rate of 25 cents per ton.

ˈ**yardage**^{2}. [f. YARD *sb.*^{2} + -AGE.]

1. The cutting of coal at a fixed rate per yard.

1877 RAYMOND *Statist. Mines & Mining* 8 The amount for yardage.. includes powder, fuse, and candles furnished by contractors and paid for as labor. **1887** *Manch. Exam.* 8 Dec. 5/2 The men employed at the.. Colliery.. have struck for an advance of wages of 10 per cent. They also demand an extra 25 per cent. on yardage.

2. The aggregate number of yards; amount estimated in yards.

1900 *Referee* 23 Sept. 1 (Cass. Suppl.) That the courses as measured from end were as represented in yardage. **1906** *Daily News* 3 Feb. 8 The yardage of linen goods exported in 1905 was the largest in any year during the last twenty.

yardang (ˈjɑːdæŋ). *Physical Geogr.* Also **jardang.** [a. Turk., abl. of *yar* steep bank, precipice.] A sharp, irregular ridge of sand or the like, lying in the direction of the prevailing wind in exposed desert regions and formed by erosion by the wind of adjacent less resistant material.

1904 S. HEDIN *Sci. Results Journey in Central Asia* I. xxvii. 439 At intervals furrows or trenches in the clay sub-soil, called *jardangs*, traced between long elevations or ridges, crop up amongst the dunes. **1934** *Bull. Geol. Soc. Amer.* XLV. (*caption facing* p. 160) Looking down one of the narrower wind-scoured troughs, with a sharp yardang (seven feet high) on the left and a higher one on the right. **1970** R. J. SMALL *Study of Landforms* ix. 301 Probably the only landforms of deserts that can be confidently ascribed to wind abrasion alone are the comparatively unimportant 'yardangs' and allied 'ridge-and-furrow' features. **1979** *Nature* 5 Apr. 535/1 In other regions [of Mars], the surface has been stripped, yardangs have formed, and in general the topography seems to have been largely configured by aeolian activity.

'yard-arm, *sb. Naut.* Also 6 yardes-, 7 yards-, 7–8 yard's-. [f. YARD *sb.*[2] 5 + ARM *sb.*[1] 8 a.]

a. Either of the two ends of a yard; *esp.* that part of either end which is outside the sheave-hole. Often used for the yard as a whole.

1553, etc. [see b]. **1665** PEPYS *Diary* 18 Sept., It being a place just wide enough, and not so much hardly, for ships to go through to it, the yard-armes sticking in the very rocks. **1756** *Gentl. Mag.* Nov. 506/2 So near as to be almost on board each other, our yard-arms very near touching hers. **1833** M. SCOTT *Tom Cringle* vi, Aloft there! lie out, you Perkins, and reeve a whip on the starboard yard-arm. **1855** MACAULAY *Hist. Eng.* xv. III. 609 The vast wood of masts and yardarms below London Bridge.

b. in reference to hanging or ducking a person from the extremity of a yard as a punishment.

1553 in Hakluyt *Voy.* (1589) 266 For pickerie ducked at the yardes arme, and so discharged. **1585** T. WASHINGTON tr. *Nicholay's Voy.* II. x. 44 b, [He had] three stroppados at the yardes arme of the gally. **1627** J. TAYLOR (Water P.) *Armado* B 7, They are duck'd from the yeard arme of State, into the deep sea of disgrace. **1746** *Brit. Mag.* 48, I..shall go near to complement you with the Ceremony of the Yard-arm. **1755** SMOLLETT *Quix.* IV. xi. (1803) IV. 235 He ordered the two Turks..to be hanged at the yard's arm. **1870** THORNBURY *Tour rd. Eng.* I. ix. 188 It was the time of hard fighting,..and frequent stringing up at the yard-arm. **1887** *Times* 11 Aug. 13/2 The improbability of seeing them ..in their proper place at the yard-arm of one of Her Majesty's ships.

c. advb. phr. ***yard-arm and*** (or ***to***) ***yard-arm***, said of two ships so near to one another that their yard-arms touch or cross. Also ***yard-arm to*** or ***with*** (another ship).

1666 *Lond. Gaz.* No. 60/1 The Saphire and Success.. bore in among them, laying yard-arm to yard-arm with the Admiral and Vice-Admiral. **1697** *Ibid.* 3288/2 They lay Yards-Arm and Yards-Arm for 5 Glasses. **1759** *Ann. Reg., Chron.* 62/1 The second lieutenant then came upon deck, and fought the ship bravely, yard-arm and yard-arm. **1781** *Log of Albemarle* 30 Oct. in Nicolas *Disp. Nelson* (1846) VII. p. iii, Finding the Albemarle yard-arm with them they submitted. **1867** H. KINGSLEY *Silcote of S.* xlvii, The old English (and French) method of laying himself yardarm to the enemy, and boarding him suddenly. **1887** BESANT *The World went* etc. vi, An engagement, yard-arm to yard-arm, with a Frenchman.

transf. **1862** THORNBURY *Turner* I. xvi. 299 To leave it [*sc.* a picture by Turner] to the nation on condition of its being hung yard-arm and yard-arm with Claude.

d. *attrib.*

c **1860** H. STUART *Seaman's Catech.* 18 The goose neck or yard arm iron. **1867** SMYTH *Sailor's Word-bk.*, *Yard-arm cleats*, wooden wedges fixed on the yards at those points where they support the lifts and braces. *Ibid.*, *Yard-arm piece*, an octagonal piece of timber supplied to replace a yard-arm if shot away. **1883** *Man. Seamanship for Boys* 68 The yard-arm men get hold of the head-earrings.

e. Phr. ***when the sun is over the yard-arm*** and varr., the time of day when it is permissible to begin drinking. Cf. SUN *sb.* 1 e (*i*).

1899 KIPLING *From Sea to Sea* I. xxiv. 454 The American does not drink at meals as a sensible man should... Also he has no decent notions about the sun being over the yard-arm or below the horizon. **1945** J. C. COLCORD *Sea Lang. comes Ashore* 211 An officers' quip..is 'When the sun is over the yardarm..it's time to take a drink'. **1964** *Amer. N. & Q.* III. 23/2 Frequent reference is made to the undesirability of drinking before 'the sun has crossed the yardarm'. **1968** 'J. LE CARRÉ' *Small Town in Germany* ii. 20 Just one hour till the sun was over the yardarm... He'd have a beer first. **1979** A. MORICE *Murder in Outline* iii. 26, I had promised to take a jugful of dry martini with him and Vera..as soon as the sun went over the yardarm.

Hence **yard-arm** *v. nonce-wd.* (*a*) ***yard-arm and yard-arm*** (*intr.*), to be yard-arm and yard-arm; also ***to yard-arm it***: *transf.* of persons, to fight at close quarters; (*b*) *trans.* to hang (a person) from the yard-arm.

1829 P. EGAN *Boxiana* 2nd Ser. II. 358 'Long bowls,' said Curtis to Savage, 'will not answer: you must *yard-arm* it with your adversary.' **1840** THACKERAY *George Cruikshank* Wks. 1900 XIII. 312 They are yard-arm and yard-arming, athwart-hawsing, marlinspiking,..as honest seamen invariably do, in novels. **1902** *Munsey's Mag.* (U.S.) XXVI. 499/2, I wish to God you'd been yard armed ten years back!

'yardbird. *U.S. slang.* Also yard bird. [f. YARD *sb.*[1] + BIRD *sb.* (see sense 1 e), perh. after *jail-bird*.] **a.** *Mil.* A recruit, a newly-enlisted serviceman; also, a serviceman under discipline for a misdemeanour; one assigned to menial tasks. Also *transf.*

1941 *Amer. Speech* XVI. 169/2 *Yard bird*, a raw recruit. **1942** [see RED-LINE *v.*]. **1943** J. GOODELL *They sent me to Iceland* 102 With this wealth of jargon we were able to produce a quiz on army slang..for the benefit of the newly arrived men—better known as 'yardbirds'. **1943** *American Mercury* Nov. 552/1 If he's in the Army he's referred to as a *yardbird*..an old Army term for camp-confined newcomers. **1947** *Amer. Speech* XXII. 111 A soldier, sailor, or marine who frequently receives punishments for offenses against the regulations is designated as a *Y.B.* or 'yard bird'. **1965** C. BROWN *Manchild in Promised Land* iii. 80 For the next two weeks, K. B. was Claiborne's yardbird. He had to go everywhere Claiborne went from morning till night. He even had to ask Claiborne when he wanted to go to the bathroom.

b. A convict.

1956 S. LONGSTREET *Real Jazz, Old & New* 148 A yard-bird is a low mug. **1980** A. PEARL *Dict. Popular Slang* 189/1 *Yardbird*, a convict..an ex-convict.

c. A worker in a yard (YARD *sb.*[1] 4) (see quots.).

1963 T. PYNCHON *V.* xvi. 427 'Yardbirds are the same all over,' Pappy said... The dock workers fled by, jostling them. **1968** *Amer. Speech* XLIII. 290 *Yard bird*, a disabled engineer, fireman, or switchman who may work only within the yard limits. **1971** M. TAK *Truck Talk* 190 *Yard bird*, a driver who spots trailers and moves vehicles around a terminal yard.

'yarded, *ppl. a.* [f. YARD *sb.*[2] or *v.*[2] + -ED.]

1. Furnished with a yard or yards.

1654 T. W[EAVER] *Songs & Poems of Love & Drollery* 42 How you are yarded both in flesh and Land Is all on which they stand.

2. (See YARD *v.*[2] 1.)

† **'yardel.** *Obs. rare.* A yard-measure.

1804 W. TAYLOR in Robberds *Mem.* (1843) I. 493, I am glad you..disdain measuring lines like linen by a yardel.

yarder ('jɑːdə(r)). *N. Amer.* [f. YARD *v.*[1] + -ER.] A kind of donkey-engine used in logging.

1911 *Pacific Monthly* Apr. 376/2 The hook-tender gives the signal to the engineer of the 'yarder' as the donkey-engine is termed. **1919** *Camp Worker* 2 June 3/3 [There were] two Ledgerwood skidders, one yarder, one swing and one roader. **1942** BERREY & VAN DEN BARK *Amer. Thes. Slang* §512.10 *Yarder*, a donkey engine which hauls logs from where they are felled to the landing or skid road. **1955** *Bush News* (Port Arthur, Ont.) Feb. 7/1 About 1,100 men are involved on the haul plus 450 horses, 125 trucks,..and 4 yarders. **1979** *Beautiful Brit. Columbia* Fall 37 In some logging areas, mechanical grapple yarders, machines that resemble construction cranes, settle into the forest floor.

'yardful. [f. YARD *sb.*[1] + -FUL 2.] As much or as many as a yard will hold. Also *fig.*

1860 in WEBSTER. **1960** *Farmer & Stockbreeder* 15 Mar. 95 A yardful of well-finished Hereford-cross beef. **1978** J. L. HENSLEY *Killing in Gold* xii. 165 I'm surprised you haven't a yardful of law around here.

† **yardhove.** *Obs.* In 5 yerdhoue. [f. YARD *sb.*[1] + HOVE *sb.*[1] Cf. TUNHOOF.] prob. Ground Ivy (*Nepeta Glechoma*).

c **1430** *M.E. Med. Bk.* (Heinrich) 221 *Herbe pro balneis.* Tak yerdhoue [etc.]. *c* **1460** J. RUSSELL *Bk. Nurture* 991 The makyng of a bathe medicinable. Holy hokke & yardehok [? *error for* yardehof].

'yarding, *vbl. sb.*[1] [f. YARD *v.*[1] + -ING[1].]

1. *concr.* (See quot.) *U.S.*

1840 BUEL *Farmer's Comp.* 315 *Summer yarding*, stuff carted into the yard, and trodden by the cattle, for manure.

2. Storage in a yard.

1865 GRANDY *Timber Importer's Guide* 129 Market value of bricks,..allowing for..expenses of yarding, &c. **1886** *Law Times* LXXX. 149/2 The freight and yarding charges.

3. (See YARD *v.*[1] 1.)

1898 'R. BOLDREWOOD' *Rom. Canvas Town* 97 The same process of yarding-up, catching, and cropping proceeds.

yarding, *vbl. sb.*[2]: see YARD *v.*[2]

yardland ('jɑːdlənd). Forms: see YARD *sb.*[2] and LAND *sb.*[1]; also 5 *Sc.* **yertland.** [= *yard of land*, OE. *ʒyrd landes*: see YARD *sb.*[2] 10 a.]

1. = YARD *sb.*[2] 10 a.

c **1450** *Godstow Reg.* 205 [She] ȝaf & confermyd þe same ȝerdelonde þat reynolde of halso ȝaf to mynchons of Godestow. **14..** *Voc.* in Wr.-Wülcker 619 *Virgata*, a yerdlond. **1464** *Rolls of Parlt.* V. 516/2 A Mese, a Yerdland, 111 Acres of Medowe. **1496** *Reg. Mag. Sig. Scot.* 492/1 Aliam peciam terre prope australem partem dicti tenementi inter le yertland ejusdem et terram quond. dicti Nich. **1517** *Lincoln Dioc. Doc.* (1914) 265, I bequeth to Robert my sone fforethers hous with the yarde londe. **1527** in Leadam *Sel. Cases Star Chamber* (Selden Soc.) II. 17 John Selby..was seased of a Mese a close and di. yeerd land with thappourtenaunces. **1551** in Phillipps *Wills* (*c* 1830) 199 A hous with on yeardland, lyging in Bloklley. **1581** *Stanford Churchw. Acc.* in *Antiquary* Apr. (1888) 172 Rec. of parisheoners by the yard lands towards the bell. **1592–3** *Act 35 Eliz.* c. 7 §8 Everie person havinge One Yarde Lande or more in his Possession lying w[th]in the sayde Fyve Miles [of Oxford]. **1607** NORDEN *Surv. Dial.* III. 97 How are the tenants stinted, whether by the yard-land, plow-land, oxe-gang, acres or rent. **1684** E. CHAMBERLAYNE *Pres. St. Eng.* (ed. 15) I. 17, 30 acres ordinarily make a yard-land. **1716** *Lond. Gaz.* No. 5487/4 A Messuage, Close, and half a Yard Land. **1720** KENNETT *Monitions & Advices* II. 55 The same worthy Benefactor gave another half yard Land unto the poor People of the Parish of Blaxley. **1740** in *N. & Q.* 7th Ser. I. 244/2 The said Mr. Cooper hath lett to the said John Weston..part of an Estate in Hugglescote, in the name of one Yard Land with Common for the said Yard Land. **1794** T. DAVIS *Agric. Wilts* 14 The tenantry yard-lands (or customary tenements) which are still subject to rights of common. *Ibid.* 15 There are many instances where a yard-land of about £20 per annum, contains about two acres of meadow land, eighteen acres of arable.., and a right on the common fields..for perhaps forty sheep. **1883** SEEBOHM *Engl. Vill. Comm.* v. 164 The yard-land was the normal holding of the *gebur* or *villanus*.

2. Incorrectly used for YARD *sb.*[2] 10 b.

1542 RECORDE *Gr. Artes* K vij, A rodde of lande, whiche some call a roode, some a yarde londe. **1674** JEAKE *Arith.* (1696) 67 A Rood is somtime called..a Yardland, but..very corruptly, for a Yardland containeth much more than an Acre.

3. *Comb.*, as ***yardland-holder***.

1890 E. W. WATSON *Ashmore* 31 The two plough-oxen, the universal outfit of the English yardland-holder.

Hence **'yardlander**, a yardland-holder.

1891 *Athenæum* 16 May 632/3 The notes he gives as to the families of the yardlanders are most interesting. **1906** N. J. HONE *Manor* I. i. 11 In 1279 a yard-lander at Newington, Oxon, was bound to plough an acre of winter tillage. **1964** H. P. R. FINBERG *Lucerna* ii. 32 It would obviously make for convenience to group the strips of each yardlander.

yardman[1] ('jɑːdmən). [YARD *sb.*[1]] A man who has charge of, or is employed in, a yard, e.g. a farm-yard, builder's yard, stable-yard, railway-yard, etc.

a **1825** FORBY *Voc. E. Anglia*, *Yard-man*, the hind who has the particular care of the farm-yard, and of the cattle fed there. **1858** SIMMONDS *Dict. Trade*, *Yard-man*, a manager or overlooker in a builder's yard. **1864** *Social Sci. Rev.* 406 The payment of washers, ostlers, and harness cleaners who are all classed together as yard-men is ordinarily divided between the cab-owners and the drivers. **1876** *Belfast Newsletter* 22 Nov. 3/3 Yardman wanted..in the neighbourhood of Belfast; would be required to clean boots, &c., and make himself generally useful. **1903** *Hull & East Yorksh. Times* 28 Feb. 1/1 Yardman Wanted,..must be good milker.

'yardman[2]. *Naut.* [YARD *sb.*[2]] In ***royal yardman***, ***upper yardman***, etc., a sailor occupied on the royal yards, the upper yards, etc.

1886 ALBERT VICTOR & GEORGE *Cruise H.M.S. Bacchante* I. 551 He was a smart royal yardman. **1903** *Sat. Rev.* 27 June 815/1 An unfortunate upper yardman made some blunder aloft.

'yard-'measure. [f. YARD *sb.*[2] + MEASURE *sb.*] A rod, bar, or tape for measuring by the yard (but not necessarily restricted to that length).

1831–4 R. S. SURTEES *Jorrocks's Jaunts* (1838) 192 A silk yard-measure in a walnut-shell. **1850** DICKENS *Dav. Copp.* ii, I..looked..at the little bit of wax-candle she kept for her thread—..at the little house with a thatched roof, where the yard-measure lived; at her work-box with a sliding lid.

'yard-rope. *Naut.* [f. YARD *sb.*[2] + ROPE *sb.*[1]]

†**a.** (*pl.*) The permanent rigging of a yard.

1336–7 *Acc. Exch. K.R.* 19/31 m. 4 (P.R.O.) In viij. petris cord' de canabo..pro duobus yerderopes inde faciendis. **1356** in *Pipe Roll 32 Edw. III*, m. 34/2, xlvij. trusseropes, xxv. ȝerderopes, xiiij. Wyndyngropes, ij. Cranelynes. **1420** in *For. Acc. 3 Hen. VI*, I, De..ij Trippetropes ij. Trusses pro ȝerdrope. **1487** *Naval Accts. Hen. VII* (1896) 68 Yerd ropes for the top.

b. (See quot. 1867.)

1850 J. S. CARDEN *Curtail'd Mem.* iii. (1912) 89 The intended Victim was on the Forecastle, the Yard Rope from the Fore Yard rove round his neck, The Yard Rope Man'd. **1867** SMYTH *Sailor's Word-bk.*, *Yard-rope*,..that by which a yard is hoisted for crossing, or sent down. Also, rove for execution.

yardsman ('jɑːdzmən). [f. gen. of YARD *sb.*[1] + MAN *sb.*[1]] = YARDMAN[1].

1872 *Daily News* 1 Aug., The Guardians of Mile-End Old Town require, for their industrial schools,..a..man..as Yardsman. **1885** *Law Times* LXXX. 79/2 The servant was *bonâ fide* employed by the defendant as yardsman and labourer. **1888** *Daily News* 12 Dec. 5/4 A yardsman who saw the approaching train shouted to the guard.

So **'yardswoman.**

1817 in A. J. C. Hare *The Gurneys of Earlham* (1895) I. 282, I was conducted by..the newly appointed yards-woman, to the door of a ward. **1905** *Daily Chron.* 1 Sept. 1/6 Holborn Union... The Guardians of the above Union require a Girls' Yardswoman at the Schools, Mitcham, Surrey.

'yard-wand. [f. YARD *sb.*[2] + WAND *sb.*] A three-foot rod for measuring. Also *fig.*

14.. *Customs of Malton* in *Surtees Misc.* (1890) 61, j ȝerde wande, and weghttes. **1586** *Durham Depos.* (Surtees) 321 The yerdwand was not a lawfull yerdwand. **1614** CORNWALLIS in Gutch *Coll. Cur.* I. 165 Whom [*sc.* his daughter] had he measured by the yard-wand of the world he might perhaps have bestowed upon one of the greatest Monarchs in Christendom. **1651** CLEVELAND *Poems* 26 And were 't not pity But both should serve the yardwand of the city? **1774** *Westm. Mag.* II. 453 He is sure to be..a mere yard-wand of Nature, and marked with as much brass as the implement he uses to measure frippery with. **1850** DENISON *Clock & Watch-m.* 7 If all our yard-wands and other measures were burnt. **1855** TENNYSON *Maud* I. I. xiii, That the smooth-faced snubnosed rogue would leap from his counter and till, And strike, if he could, were it but with his cheating yardwand, home.

yare (jɛə(r)), *a. arch.* and *dial.* Forms: 1 **ʒearo, ʒearu, ʒearw-, -ow-, -uw-,** 2–3 **ȝaru,** 3 **ȝareou, -ew, -ue, -ow, ȝeærwe, ȝæru, -ew, ȝeruh,** *pl.* **ȝarre,** 3–4 **ȝar,** 3–5 **ȝare,** 4 **yarwe, ȝeare,** *Sc.* **ȝair, yhar,** (4–5 **yore, ȝere, yere),** 5 **yar, youre,** 6 *Sc.* **ȝor(e, ȝoir, yoir,** 3– **yare.** [OE. *ʒearu, -o*, = OS. *garu*, MDu. **gare* (Du. *gaar* done, dressed), OHG. *garo, garaw-* ready, prepared, complete (MHG. *gara, gar, gar(e)w-*), ON. *gǫrr* ready made, prompt, skilled (see GARE *a.*); prob. a compound of OTeut. **ga-* Y- *prefix* and **arw-*, represented by OE. *earu* ready (? in Exodus 339 for MS. *ʒearu*), OS. *aru* (MS. pl. *aroa*) ready (for reaping), ON. *ǫrr* ready, liberal-handed, in neut. *ǫrt* advb. quite, OE. *earwunga*, (late

Northumb.) *arwunge* gratis, freely, and perhaps Goth. *arwjô*, OHG. *arawûn* in vain.]

1. Ready, prepared. **a.** of persons: const. *to* with sb. or inf.

Beowulf 211 (Gr.) Beornas ʒearwe on stefn stiʒon. *c* **888** ÆLFRED *Boeth.* xxxvi. §6 Ic hæbbe nu onʒiten þæt ðu eart ʒearo to onʒitanne mina lara. *a* **1000** *Andreas* 234 (Gr.) He wæs..ʒearo ʒuðe. *c* **1205** LAY. 9457 Weoren alle þa cnihtes ȝærewe [*c* **1275** ȝar] to þon fihte. *Ibid.* 22278 We beoð alle ȝarewe [*c* **1275** ȝarue] To ganne & to ride. *a* **1225** *Leg. Kath.* 2334 Ich am ȝarow to al þe wa þet tu const me ȝarkin. *a* **1240** *Ureisun* 132 in *O.E. Hom.* I. 197 ȝif he is to bote ȝeruh and bit þe uorȝiuenesse. **13..** *Coer de L.* 343 Stylle he hovyd and bode yore; To them he thought to ryde more. **1375** BARBOUR *Bruce* II. 346 On athir syd thus war thai yhar, And till assemble all redy war. *c* **1440** *York Myst.* vii. 30 To offyr loke þat ye be yore [*rime* nomore]. *c* **1460** *Towneley Myst.* xiii. 704, I am redy and yare, go we in fere To that bright. **1603** HARSNET *Pop. Impost.* 143 And so the second may be yare and ready, to take his cue and turne of the former. **1603** SHAKS. *Meas. for M.* IV. ii. 61, I hope, if you haue occasion to vse me for your owne turne, you shall finde me yare.

b. of things; in later use, (of implements) ready for use.

a **900** CYNEWULF *Crist* 1270 þæt hy him yrmþa to fela grim hellefyr ʒearo to wite and weard seoð. **971** *Blickl. Hom.* 39 Seðoþ þæt eow sy mete ʒearo on minum huse. *c* **1205** LAY. 7783 þe tur wes al ȝaru. *a* **1225** *Ancr. R.* 394 His merci is hire euer ȝeruh. *a* **1250** *Owl & Night.* 378 ȝif hundes urneþ to him ward He..hokeþ paþes sviþe narewe & haueþ mid him his blenches ȝarewe. *c* **1350** *Will. Palerne* 895 Mi dere gode damisele my deþ is al ȝare. *Ibid.* 2729 þe werwolf waited wiȝtly which schip was ȝarest, to fare forþ at þat flod. *c* **1400** *Gamelyn* 90 Afterward came his brother..And seide to gamelyn is oure mete ȝare? *c* **1595** CAPT. WYATT *R. Dudley's Voy. W. Ind.* (Hakl. Soc.) 59 To see that..everie souldier [should have] his furniture as yare and fine as might be. **1627** CAPT. J. SMITH *Sea Gram.* viii. 35 The Corporall is to..see ..the souldiers..keepe their armes cleane, neat, and yare. **1631** MARKHAM *Country Contentm.* (ed. 4) I. xi. 78 You shall obserue that all your Tooles, Lines, or Implements be (as the Sea-man sayth) yare, fit, and ready. **1799** SCOTT *Covenanter's Fate* xxxiii, At each pommel there, for battle yare, A Jedwood axe was slung. **1808** —— *Marmion* I. ix, The gunner held his linstock yare.

c. *to make yare*: to make ready, get ready, prepare (also *refl.*).

c **1290** *Beket* 821 in *S. Eng. Leg.* 130 þare-fore make þe ȝare i-nov þine a-countes to ȝelde. **13..** *Coer de L.* 1185 The knyght it takes withouten let, Dyghtes hym, and made hym yare. *c* **1385** CHAUCER *L.G.W.* 2270 *Philomela*, This Therius let make hise shepis ȝare And In-to grece hymself is forth I-fare. *c* **1460** *Towneley Myst.* iv. 121, I shall found to make me yare. **1865** TOM TAYLOR *Ball. of Brittany, Bran* II, To-night make me a good ship yare.

2. Alert, nimble, active, brisk, quick.

13.. *Coer de L.* 6751 The Sarezynes fledde..; In there herte they were soo yarwe, Alle here yates they thought too narwe. *c* **1425** *Engl. Conq. Irel.* 114 Thys legat was youre aboute, pees to make betwene the kynge & Iohn. *c* **1425** *Cast. Persev.* 18 in *Macro Plays* 77 God hym ȝeuyth to aungelis Ful ȝep & ful ȝare. **1606** SHAKS. *Ant. & Cl.* III. xiii. 131 A halter'd necke, which do's the Hangman thanke, For being yare about him. **1626** CAPT. J. SMITH *Accid. Yng. Seamen* 18 Be yare at the helme. **1698** VANBRUGH *Short Vind* 27, I believe, had the Obscenity he has routed up here, been buried as deep in his Church-yard, the Yarest Boar in his Parish wou'd hardly have tost up his Snout at it. **1706** E. WARD *Wooden World Diss.* (1708) 11 It's the Trick of a Hound to be yare at Hares only. **1831** CARLYLE *Misc.* (1857) II. 253 Like a right yare steersman. **1869** *Athenæum* 28 Aug. 284/2 *Yare*, which is still current in Norfolk, and is pronounced yar, = brisk, active, lively.

b. Of a ship: Moving lightly and easily; answering readily to the helm; easily manageable.

1390 GOWER *Conf.* II. 237 The wynd was good, the Schip was yare. **1579–80** NORTH *Plutarch* (1595) 131 The Persian gallies, being high cargged, heauy, and not yare of steredge. **1606** SHAKS. *Ant. & Cl.* III. vii. 39 Their shippes are yare, yours heauy. **1610** —— *Temp.* V. i. 224 Our Ship..Is tyte, and yare. *a* **1642** SIR W. MONSON *Naval Tracts* III. (1704) 357/1 She is Roomsom for her Men, and yare to run too and again in. *a* **1656** USSHER *Ann.* VI. (1658) 749 Caesars ships being more yare, and ready for any needs of service. **1658** EARL MONM. tr. *Paruta's Wars Cyprus* 177 Vluzzali..commanded 25 of his yarer gallies..to assault our right Wing.

3. *Comb.*, as *yare-handed*; †**yare-witel**, quick-witted.

[*c* **900** tr. *Bæda's Hist.* V. ii, Se ʒeonga wæs ʒeworden hale lichaman..& ʒearowyrde on ʒespræce.] *c* **1205** LAY. 3028 Heo was alre ȝungest Of soðe ȝær witelest. *Ibid.* 5639 þa cnihtes weoren wise & ful ȝere witele. **1728** W. BETAGH *Voy. rd. World* 26 Don Pedro..took care however to be very officious or yare handed (as we say) with his present.

yare, *adv. Obs.* or *arch.* Forms: 1 **ʒeara**, **ʒeare**, **ʒearo**, **ʒere**, 2–4 **ȝeare**, 3 **ȝære**, 3–5 **ȝare**, 4 **ȝaire**, **ȝhare**, **ȝar**, **yaar(e**, **yarre**, 4–5 **yhare**, (4–6 **ȝore**, 5 **yore**, **yere**), 5–6 *Sc.* **ȝair**, (6 **ȝoir**, **ȝor**), 4–7 (9 *arch.*) **yare**. [OE. *ʒeara*, *-o*, *-e*, also *ʒear(e)we*, *-uwe*, corresp. to OS. *garo* (Du. *gaar*), OHG. *garo*, also *garawo* (MHG. *gare*, *gar*, also *garwe*, G. *gar*) completely, quite, ON. *g(j)ǫrva*, *gerva* quite, clearly, plainly; adv. of *ʒearu*, etc.: see YARE *a.*]

†**1.** Quickly, without delay, promptly, immediately, soon. (Often used vaguely, esp. in *full yare*, as a riming tag.) *Obs.*

Beowulf 2748 (Gr.) þæt ic..ʒearo sceawiʒe sweʒle searoʒimmas. *c* **1250** *Gen. & Ex.* 2866 Ðat, bi ði leue, hise folc vt-fare, Ðre daiȝes gon and ðor ȝare, In ðe deserd. *a* **1300** *K. Horn* 497 (Cambr. MS.) Aþelbrus..tolde him ful ȝare Hu he hadde ifare. *a* **1300** *Cursor M.* 2837 'Haste', he said, 'þan þeder yaar, For i do noght til þou come þar'. *Ibid.* 5225 þan was iacob busked yare, Wit al þe gynge þat wit him ware. **1375** BARBOUR *Bruce* III. 696 And by the mole thai passyt ȝar, And entryt sone in-to the rase. *c* **1435** *Torr. Portugale* 1320 The emperoure of Rome was there, The kynges of Pervens and of Calabere yare, And other two or thre. *a* **1450** *Le Morte Arth.* 3536 The ermyte Answeryd swythe yare. **14..** *Guy Warw.* (C.) 5944 And wyth hys fyste he smote me sore: Sythen he flewe awey full ȝore. **1513** DOUGLAS *Æneis* I. v. 37 Ane duelling place for Troianis biggit hes he,..and full ȝor, The armes of Troy has set wp in memor. *Ibid.* II. xi. 21 Send ws thi help als ȝoir, And conferme all thir takinnis sene befoir.

†**b.** Nimbly, briskly. *Obs. rare.*

1622 J. TAYLOR (Water P.) *Merrie Wherrie-Ferry-Voy.* Wks. 1630 II. 8/1 Though it [*sc.* a tongue] continuall toyl'd, And went as yare, as if it had bin Oyl'd.

c. As exclamation: = Quick! esp. in nautical use. *arch.*

1606 SHAKS. *Ant. & Cl.* V. ii. 286 Yare, yare, good Iras; quicke: Me thinkes I heare Anthony call. **1610** —— *Temp.* I. i. 7 Cheerely, cheerely my harts: yare, yare: Take in the toppe-sale. **1822** HOGG *Perils of Man* III. vii. 204 Yare, yare! Lord sauff us! Here they come! What's to be our fate? Keep close for a wee while. **1867** MORRIS *Jason* IX. 241 Yare!—for the ebb runs strongly towards the sea.

†**2.** Well, thoroughly; (often with *know*, etc.) certainly, plainly, without doubt. (Often used vaguely as in 1.) *Obs.*

Beowulf 2656 (Gr.) Ic wat ʒeare þæt næron ealdʒewyrht þæt [etc.]. *a* **900** CYNEWULF *Crist* 109 God of gode ʒearo acenned sunu soþan fæder. *a* **1000** *Boeth. Metr.* ix. 9 He het him to gamene ʒeara forbærnan Romana buriʒ. *c* **1000** *Ags. Gosp.* Luke xx. 6 Hi wiston ʒere þæt iohannes wæs witeʒa. *c* **1205** LAY. 18816 Ah ful ȝare ich hit wiste. **13..** *E.E. Allit. P.* A. 834 þe þryde tyme is þer-to ful mete In apokalypez wryten ful ȝare. *a* **1425** *Cursor M.* 4866 (Trin.) Gode men, he seide, ȝe shal fare, But of oure kyng I warn ȝou ȝare. *c* **1475** *Rauf Coilȝear* 641 Se that thow leis thame not, bot ȝeme thame full ȝair. **1513** DOUGLAS *Æneis* V. iv. 97 Now quha was blyth bot Menestheus, full ȝore?

†**yare**, *v. Obs.* Forms: 1 **ʒearwian**, 3 **ȝ(e)arwen**, **ȝ(e)ærwen**, **ȝarewen**, 3–5 **ȝare**, 4 **ȝhare**, **yare**. [OE. *ʒearwian*, f. *ʒearu* YARE *a.*

Cf. OE. *ʒierwan*, OS. *garuwian*, *gerwean*, MDu. *gherwen*, *garwen*, *gerwen*, OHG. *garawen* (MHG., G. *gerben*, *gärben*), ON. *gǫr(v)a*, *gjǫr(v)a*, *gera* (see GAR *v.*).]

trans. To make or get ready, to prepare.

c **888** ÆLFRED *Boeth.* xxxix. §13 Se hata sumor dryʒð & ʒearwað sæd & bleda. *c* **1000** *Ags. Gosp.* Luke i. 76 þu gæst beforan drihtnes ansyne his weʒas ʒearwian. *c* **1205** LAY. 220 He makede ane heȝe burh..þa burh wes wel iȝarwed [*c* 1275 iȝarket]. *Ibid.* 29834 Bruchinal..ȝarewede his ferde. *a* **1300** *St. Gregory* 1178 in Herrig's *Archiv* LVII. 71 Whan þe nyȝt was al a gone a bote þe fisschere he gan ȝare. **1338** R. BRUNNE *Chron.* (1810) 58 þe kyng ȝared his folk, on haste alle þat he myght.

refl. *c* **975** *Rushw. Gosp.* Matt. vi. 25 Hu ʒe eowic ʒearwiʒe. *c* **1205** LAY. 7473 ȝarewieð eow to fihte. **1338** R. BRUNNE *Chron.* (1810) 90 He ȝared him to bataile. *a* **1400–50** *Alexander* 4866 þan ȝaris he him ȝapely & a-ȝayne turnes.

yare, var. YAIR *sb.*; obs. f. YORE.

yare, y'are, abbreviation of *ye are*.

1607 HEYWOOD *Fayre Mayde Exch.* I 3 b, Welcome M. Golding yare very welcome sir.

yarely (ˈjɛəlɪ), *adv. arch.* Forms: 5 **ȝarely**, **ȝarle**, **-ly**, 6 **yeerlie**, 7–9 **yarely**. [OE. *ʒearolíce*: see YARE *a.* and -LY[2], and cf. OS. *garolîko*, OHG. *garalîhho* (MHG. *garlîche*).] Quickly, promptly; nimbly, briskly; †diligently; = YARE *adv.* in various senses.

a **900** CYNEWULF *Elene* 288 Ic þæt ʒearolice onʒiten hæbbe. *a* **1400–50** *Wars Alex.* 1035 Outhire macches ȝow maynly þerto..Or ȝefes ȝarely vp þe ȝerde & ȝeld me þe cite. **1573–80** TUSSER *Husb.* (1878) 144 Actes lawles to doo without feare, how yeerlie togither they band. **1606** SHAKS. *Ant. & Cl.* II. ii. 216 The Silken Tackle, Swell with the touches of those Flower-soft hands, That yarely frame the office. **1610** —— *Temp.* I. i. 4 Fall too 't, yarely, or we run our selues a ground. **1627** J. SMITH in J. Taylor (Water P.) *Armado* A 8, This new Fleete runnes ouer Seas and Lands, And's now so victua'ld, rigd and yarely plyes. **1668** DRYDEN *Even. Love* V. i. (1671) 77 Come yarely my mates, every man to his share of the burthen. *a* **1681** T. RAYMOND *Autobiog.* (Camden 1917) 29 In London great out-cryes about this tyme [*c* 1631] against shom [*sic*] whoe they called Armynians as if shom of that opinion intended yarely to introduce Poperie. **1812** W. TENNANT *Anster F.* IV. ix, Till..The younker Curtius..Down headlong yarely gallop'd, horse and all. **1827** CARLYLE *Germ. Rom.* I. 186 The Count..kept plunging, yarely, through the ranks. [**1897** LD. TENNYSON *Tennyson* II. 133 *note*, He revived many fine old words which had fallen into disuse: and I heard him regret that he had never employed the word 'yarely'.]

‖**yari-yari** (ˈjɑːriːˈjɑːriː). [Native name.] Name in Guyana for the wood of *Duguetia quitarensis*, also called *lance-wood*.

1858 HOGG *Veg. Kingd.* 27. **1862** *List* in Veness *El Dorado* (1866) App. 144 A piece of tough wood from the Yari-yari tree.

†**yark**, *v. Obs.* Forms: 1 **ʒearcian**, 2 **ȝearceon**, **ȝeirke**, 2–5 **ȝarke**, 3 **ȝarrkenn** (*Orm.*), **ȝearkien**, **ȝarki**, **-i(e)n**, **ȝærek-**, **ȝarekien**, **ȝerke**, 4 **yark**. [OE. *ʒearcian*, f. *ʒearu* YARE *a.* with factitive suffix as in *ieldcian* to delay, f. *eald* old.] *trans.* (and *refl.*) To make ready, prepare.

c **1000** ÆLFRIC *Gen.* xix. 3 He þa ʒearcode him ʒereord and hiʒ æton. *a* **1122** *O.E. Chron.* an. 1091 (Laud MS.) þa ʒearcode he his fare & to Englelande com. *c* **1175** *Lamb. Hom.* 19 He haueð us iȝarket þa ecche blisse ȝif we wulleð hit iernien in heuene riche. *c* **1200** ORMIN 9151 Forr þatt he wollde ȝarrkenn hemm Onnȝæness Cristess come. *c* **1205** LAY. 23275 ȝarkieð bi þan flode Mine scipen gode. *a* **1225** [see YARE *a.* 1]. *a* **1300** *Cursor M.* 8856 Was neuer man born þat cuth wirc Ne yark suilk a-noþer kirc. **1377** LANGL. *P. Pl.* B. VII. 80 He þat ȝiueth, ȝeldeth and ȝarketh hym to reste. *c* **1400** *Destr. Troy* 882 He forȝet not, but ȝepely ȝarkit hym þerfore. *c* **1400** *Laud Troy Bk.* 6070 His men he ȝarked Euerychon vnto that fyght. **1708** KERSEY, To *Yark*, (N[orth] C[ountry]) to prepare.

b. To put in a position; to set, place. ***yark to***, to shut; ***yark up***, to open. Also *fig.*, *pass.* and *intr.*, to pass *into* a state.

13.. *Gaw. & Gr. Knt.* 820 þay ȝolden hym þe brode ȝate, ȝarked vp wyde. *c* **1400** *Destr. Troy* 414 Yong men yepely yarke into Elde. *Ibid.* 5595 Now is ȝepely a yere yarket to end. *Ibid.* 6081 For to ȝarpe [*sic*] vp the ȝate he ȝepely comaund. *Ibid.* 10738 þai ȝarkit to þe yatis ȝepely onon. *Ibid.* 11265 þai kepyn the cloyse of this clene burgh, With ȝep men at þe yatis ȝarkit full þik.

c. To ordain, decree, appoint; to grant, bestow.

a **1300** *Cursor M.* 8982 Hard it es, þe wird o sin þat yarked was til adam kin! **13..** *E.E. Allit. P.* B. 758 ȝif þou ȝernez hit, ȝet ȝark I hem grace. *a* **1400** *Emare* 329 Such sorow was here ȝarked ȝore.

Hence †ˈ**yarking** *vbl. sb.*, preparation.

c **1000** *Ags. Ps.* (Spelman) second ix. 20 [x. 17] Ðearcunge heortan [Vulg. *præparationem cordis*]. *c* **1200** ORMIN 10800 Itt [*sc.* John's baptism] wass ȝarrkinng ȝæn fulluhht þatt Crist sellf shollde settenn.

yark, var. YERK, YORK *sb.*[2]

Yarkand (ˈjɑːkænd, jɑːˈkænd). [The name of a river, district, and city in Sinkiang Uighur (formerly Chinese Turkestan), an autonomous region of western China.] **1.** A language or dialect of the central Turkic or Turco-Tatar group of Altaic languages, spoken in the district of Yarkand. Also *attrib.*

1875 [see KASHGAR 1]. **1954** M. A. PEI *Dict. Linguistics* 236 *Yarkand*, an Asiatic language, member of the Central Turkish group of the Altaic sub-family of the Ural-Altaic family of languages.

2. Used *attrib.* and *absol.* to designate a type of Turkoman carpet.

1880 G. C. M. BIRDWOOD *Industrial Arts of India* II. 168 The tree of life represented on modern Yarkand rugs is always a pomegranate tree. **1913** W. A. HAWLEY *Oriental Rugs* xii. 251 In Plate L..are two of the most typical and interesting stripes of Samarkands and Yarkands... A stripe with simple archaic pattern peculiar to Yarkands is seen in Plate L. **1931** [see KASHGAR 2]. **1967** U. SCHÜRMANN *Oriental Carpets* 72 The eastern Turkestan rugs commonly known..as 'Samarkand' come..from the three oasis-cities of Kashgar, Yarkand and Khotan... A small number of silk Yarkands also exist. **1970** J. FRANSES *European & Oriental Rugs* 146 (*caption*) Eastern Turkestan Yarkand runner in the form of a saph. *Circa* 1800.

3. *Zool.* Used *attrib.* to designate a heavily built kind of red deer with short antlers that is found in Sinkiang Uighur.

1892 *Proc. Zool. Soc.* 116 Mr. W. T. Blanford exhibited two heads..and a skin of the Yarkand Stag. *Ibid.* 117 The name *C[ervus] yarkandensis* may be applied to the Yarkand and Tarim Deer. **1918** R. LYDEKKER *Wild Life of World* II. 231 Very distinct from the wapiti type is the Yarkand deer ..of the forests of the Tarim Valley. **1982** G. K. WHITEHEAD *Hunting & stalking Deer* iv. 111 Among the most endangered are the Yarkand deer..of Chinese Turkestan.

Yarkandi (jɑːˈkændɪ), *sb.* and *a.* Also 9– **Yarkundi.** [f. prec.] **A.** *sb.* A native or inhabitant of the city or district of Yarkand.

1841 H. H. WILSON *Trav. Moorcroft & Trebeck* I. II. iii. 351 A Yarkandi asserted that an infusion of poppy-heads was employed to render the leaves of the tea adhesive. **1875** in T. D. Forsyth *Report Mission to Yarkund* iii. (*facing page*) 118 (*caption*) Yarkundis. **1901** P. W. CHURCH *Chinese Turkestan* iii. 33 The guileless Yarkandis. **1926** C. P. SKRINE *Chinese Central Asia* viii. 106 A charming..and well educated Yarkandi called Murad Qari..partook of tea. **1981** A. ALI in *Himalayan Jrnl.* XXXVII. 115 The Yarkandis used this route [*sc.* Saser La in the Karakorams] for trade and for going on haj to Mecca.

B. *adj.* Of or pertaining to Yarkand or its people.

1854 A. CUNNINGHAM *Ladák* iii. 49 My informants, who were also Yarkandi merchants, stated exactly the reverse. **1893** H. LANSDELL *Chinese Central Asia* II. xxxiv. 108 Turdi Akhoon, a Yarkandi merchant..had arrived from India. **1928** 'GANPAT' *Magic Ladakh* xiv. 255 It is a hard life on the Central Asian trade route if you happen to be a hired ponyman travelling with a callous Yarkandi merchant. **1973** M. BENCE-JONES *Palaces of Raj* viii. 144 A portly General endeavoured to stop his Yarkundi pony from jumping over the railings.

‖**yarke, -kee** (ˈjɑːkiː). [Native name.] A South American monkey of the genus *Pithecia*, esp. the white-headed saki, *P. leucocephala*.

1834 MCMURTRIE *Cuvier's Anim. Kingd.* 48 *Simia pithecia*, L. (The Yarke.) Blackish; circumference of the face whitish. **1855** DALTON *Brit. Guiana* II. 449 The yarkee is the name given by some to the white-faced Saki.

†ˈ**yarken**, *v. Obs.* [f. YARK *v.* + -EN[5].] *trans.* To prepare.

c **1205** LAY. 7384 Leteð ȝarkni [*c* **1275** ȝarki] mine scipen. *c* **1250** *Gen. & Ex.* 3240 Hold up ðin ȝerde to ðe se And del it so on sundri del, Ðat ȝu ben ȝarknede weiȝes wel. **14..** *Chaucer's Rom. Rose* (MS.) 716 Layes of loue ful wel sownyng They songen in their yarkonyng [*ed. Thynne* 1532 iargoning; Fr. *en lor serventois*, v.r. *en son patois*].

yarl: see JARL.

yarling (ˈjɑːlɪŋ), *ppl. a. Midl.* (and *north.*) *dial.* [f. dial. *yarl* vb. to utter a loud discordant sound: see *Eng. Dial. Dict.*] Howling, wailing.

1911 D. H. LAWRENCE *White Peacock* I. vii. 119, I heard more plainly..the peevish, wailing, yarling cry of some beast in the wood. **1972** LD. ROBENS *Ten Year Stint* ii. 32 They were a 'yarling mob'—crude, vulgar and unfit to lead the decent men I know in the pits.

yarly, obs. Sc. form of EARLY *adv.*

yarm (jɑːm), *sb.* Now *dial.* [Goes with next.] A discordant outcry; a scream, yell.

13.. *E.E. Allit. P.* B. 971 Such a ȝomerly ȝarm of ȝellyng þer rysed. **1898** *Shetl. News* 26 Mar. (E.D.D.) Da yarms an' spittin' o' da cat.

yarm (jɑːm), *v.* Now *dial.* Also 4 **ȝerme**, 9 **yerm, yirm.** [OE. **ȝierman, ȝyrman.*] *intr.* To utter a discordant or mournful cry; to scream, yell, howl; to wail.

c **1000** *Lambeth Ps.* xxxvii. 9 Ic ȝyrmde for ȝeomrunge heortan minre. **13..** *S. Cristofer* 119 in Horstm. *Altengl. Leg.* (1881) 456 þe fende bygane to crye & ȝarme. ? *a* **1400** *Morte Arth.* 3911 Than cho ȝermys and ȝee[s] at Ʒorke in hir chambire. *a* **1400–50** *Alexander* 4745 Vmquile he noys as a nowte as a nox quen he lawes, Ʒarmand & ȝerand.

1615 BRATHWAIT *Strappado* (1878) 178 In hels abisse: Where they may yaule and yarme til that they burst. **1680** HICKERINGILL *Curse ye Meroz* 26 A Holder-forth may Yawle and Yarne [*sic*]..'till his Lungs..ake. **1808** JAMIESON, *To yirm*, to whine, to complain; also, to ask in a querulous tone; implying the idea of continuation. *a* **1825** FORBY *Voc. E. Anglia*, *Yarm*, *Yawm*, to shriek or yell. *a* **1835** HOGG *Miser's Warning* xxii, They yermit and flaitte a summer's day.

† **y-armed**, *pa. pple.* [Y- 4, ARM *v.*] Armed.

1297 R. GLOUC. (Rolls) 4522 Eiȝte hundred ssipes.. Vol of saracens yarmed. **1340** *Ayenb.* 83 Godes knyȝtes, þet þe holy gost heþ y-dobbed and y-armed. *c* **1400** *Laud Troy Bk.* 6976 He nas yarmed nother lym ne lyth. **1426** LYDG. *De Guil. Pilgr.* 7810 Hys handys wern yarmyd wel.

Yarmouth (ˈjɑːməθ). Name of a fishing town on the coast of Norfolk: used *attrib.* in ***Yarmouth bloater*** (also *transf.* a native of Yarmouth), †***capon***, †***coach*** (see quots.), ***herring***. Hence **Yarmouthian** (jɑːˈmaʊθɪən), *a.* belonging to Yarmouth; *sb.* an inhabitant of Yarmouth.

1614 T. GENTLEMAN *England's Way* 15 The Hollanders be very welcome guests vnto the Yermothian Herring-buyers. *Ibid.* 26 These Hollanders be Hosted with the Layestof men, as they be with the Yermothians. *a* **1661** FULLER *Worthies*, *Norfolk* (1662) II. 248 A Yarmouth Capon. That is a red-herring. *a* **1700** B. E. *Dict. Cant. Crew*, *Yarmouth-Coach*, a sorry low Cart to ride on, drawn by one Horse. *Yarmouth Pie*, made of Herrings, highly Spic'd, and Presented by the City of Norwich (upon the forfeiture of their Charter) annually to the King. **1732** *MSS. Dk. Portland* (Hist. MSS. Comm.) VI. 153 These machines, which now in merriment are called Yarmouth coaches... They are something of the nature of a sledge, as at Bristol, with one horse. **1832** Yarmouth bloaters [see BLOATER]. **1850** DICKENS *Dav. Copp.* iii, Peggotty said..that..she was proud to call herself a Yarmouth Bloater. **1867** SMYTH *Sailor's Word-bk.*, *Yarmouth herring-boat*, a clincher-built vessel with lug-sails, similar to the drift or mackerel boats.

yarmulke (ˈjɑːməlkə). Also **yarmulka**; (more rarely) **jarmulka, yarmolka**, etc. [ad. Yiddish *yarmolke*, ad. Polish *jarmulka* cap.] A skull-cap worn by male Orthodox Jews at all times, and by other male Jews on religious occasions: = KOPPEL.

1903 *Jewish Encycl.* IV. 301/2 The so-called Jewish garb of Poland, including even the 'jarmulka' (under-cap), is simply the old Polish costume which the Jews retained. **1929** *Menorah Jrnl.* XVI. 37 Jacob..saw and did not revere the squat figure clumsy in its..*yarmelke*. **1930** M. GOLD *Jews without Money* 95 My father took me to the tailor and had made a handsome velvet *yamalka*. **1941** B. SCHULBERG *What makes Sammy Run?* ix. 232 There in the synagogue,.. with his impressive shawl, his *yarmolka* and his great beard, there life was rich. **1957** L. STERN *Midas Touch* I. v. 45 He wore his *yamulka* (skull cap) when it was ritually required. **1962** 'E. MCBAIN' *Empty Hours* 111, I was collecting the prayers shawls and the *yarmelkas*. **1963** T. PYNCHON *V.* iv. 97 He went out of his way to cultivate the Tagliacozzi look: ..wearing a bushy mustache, pointed beard, sometimes even a skull-cap, his old schoolboy yarmulke. **1966** L. DAVIDSON *Long Way to Shiloh* xv. 221 You have the yarmulkah? Remember to put it on. **1966** H. KEMELMAN *Saturday Rabbi went Hungry* (1969) i. 14 He wondered if the cantor had put on his robes and tall white yarmulka. **1971** B. MALAMUD *Tenants* 90 Sam Clemence, a Mephistophelean type in yarmulke and yellow dashiki. **1975** *Church Times* 7 Nov. 5/1 A lively man in a business suit and embroidered *yarmulka*—the little skull-cap worn by orthodox Jews. **1979** 'A. HAILEY' *Overload* III. xi. 244 Hardly any of us took a yarmulke. I didn't. Had to borrow one when I went to the Wall in Jerusalem. **1984** *Times* 24 Sept. 4/6 The captain, who wore Israeli army uniform with a red yarmulka fringed with gold on his head.

yarn (jɑːn), *sb.* Forms: 1 **ȝearn**, 4 **ȝern, iern, yaarn**, 4–6 **yern(e**, 5 **ȝarn(e, ȝieren, yeern**, 5–7 **yarne**, 6 **yaren, yarone, yeryn, yorne**, 6–7 **yearne**, 7 **yearn**, 5– **yarn**. [OE. *ȝearn* str. n. = WFris. *jern*, NFris. *jaarn*, *juarn*, MDu. *gaern*, *gar(e)n* (Du. *garen*), OHG., MHG., G. *garn* yarn, †net, ON. (Sw., Da.) *garn* (whence GARN *sb.*); app. f. the root represented also by **garnô* in ON. *gǫrn*, pl. *garnar* guts, and **garnjo-* in OE. *micgern*, OS. *midgarni*, OHG. *mittigarni* MIDGERN (= entrail-fat, suet), and related (outside Teutonic) to Lith. *žárna* intestine, L. *hariolus* soothsayer, *haruspex* one who divined the future from an inspection of the entrails of victims, Gr. *χορδή* intestine (CHORD). (Cf., moreover, Skr. *hirā́* vein, L. *hīra* empty gut, *hillæ*:—**hirl-* smaller intestines.)]

1. a. Originally, spun fibre, as of cotton, silk, wool, flax; now, usually, fibre spun and prepared for use in weaving, knitting, the manufacture of sewing-thread, etc.

Also with qualification, as *cotton*, *linen*, *woollen yarn*.

c **1000** *Voc.* in Wr.-Wülcker 238/27 *Filatum*, ȝearn. *c* **1050** *Suppl. Ælfric's Gloss.* ibid. 187/30 *Glomus*, unwunden ȝearn. *c* **1325** *Gloss. W. de Bibbesw.* in Wright *Voc.* 157 A klewe of yarn. *Ibid.*, Do my yaarn on the reel. **1376** *Rolls of Parlt.* II. 353/1 Tout maner de ȝern. **1391** in W. Hudson *Leet Jurisd. Norwich* (1892) 75, x hespys de Irlondyern pretii iiij. d. **1420** *E.E. Wills* (1882) 46 Item dimidium þe ȝieren and wolle that is in this house. **1511–12** *Act 3 Hen. VIII.* c. 6 §1 The carder and Spynner to delyver agayn to the same Clothier yerne of the same Woll. *a* **1552** LELAND *Itin.* (1769) VII. 47 Good Marchandis at Lyrpole, and moch Yrisch Yarn that Manchester Men do by ther. **1552–3** *Inv. Ch. Goods, Stafford* in *Ann. Lichfield* (1863) IV. 6 On cope of whitte & blewe yorne. **1607** SHAKS. *Cor.* I. iii. 93 You would be another Penelope: yet they say, all the yearne she spun in Vlisses absence, did but fill Athica full of Mothes. **1748** in *Jrnl. Friends Hist. Soc.* (1918) 28 We had about eighty Score of Yarn stole out of garth. **1784** COWPER *Task* I. 53 Well-tann'd hides,.. With here and there a tuft of crimson yarn.. in the cushion fixt. **1846** MCCULLOCH *Acc. Brit. Empire* (1854) I. 707 The manufacturers obtain the finer sorts of yarn chiefly from Yorkshire and Ireland. **1852** MRS. STOWE *Uncle Tom's C.* xiii, A long stocking of mixed blue and white yarn.

fig. **1601** SHAKS. *All's Well* IV. iii. 84 The webbe of our life, is of a mingled yarne, good and ill together. **1832–4** DE QUINCEY *Cæsars* Wks. 1862 IX. 32 In the mingled yarn of human life.

transf. **1862** JOHNS *Brit. Birds* 56 Eggs, from which emerge..bodies enveloped in a soft plush of grey yarn.

b. *collect. sing.* put for fishermen's nets. *dial.*

1535 COVERDALE *Ezek.* xvii. 20, I wil cast my net aboute him, and catch him in my yarne. —— *Hab.* i. 15 They take vp all with their angle, they catch it in their net, & gather it in their yarne [Luther *Garn*]. **1880** *Antrim & Down Gloss.*, *Yarn*, 'Take the yarn', said of herrings when they strike the net.

c. In *Rope-making*, one of the threads of which a strand of rope is composed (= ROPE-YARN 1), or these threads collectively.

1627 [see SPUN-YARN 2]. **1794** *Rigging & Seamanship* I. 59 *Yarn*, called twenty-five, twenty, and eighteen thread yarn, differs only in the fineness; the twenty-five being finer than the twenty. **1831–3** P. BARLOW in *Encycl. Metrop.* (1845) VIII. 753 The first part of the process of rope-making is that of spinning the yarn or threads. *c* **1860** H. STUART *Seaman's Catech.* 28, 18-yarn spunyarn. *Ibid.* 51 If it is for boltrope 3 inches in circumference, each strand will have 30 yarns.

2. a. ***to spin a yarn*** (*fig.*, orig. *Naut. slang*), to tell a story (usually a long one); also, 'to pitch a tale'. Hence *yarn* = a (long) story or tale: sometimes implying one of a marvellous or incredible kind; also, a mere tale. *colloq.*

1812 J. H. VAUX *Flash Dict.* s.v., *Yarning* or *spinning a yarn*, signifying to relate their various adventures, exploits, and escapes to each other. **1835** MARRYAT *Jacob Faithful* ix, Come, spin us a good yarn, father. **1835** —— *Pacha of Many T.* xvii, 'You must tell lies, and you will have gold.' 'Tell lies! that is, spin a yarn; well, I can do that.' **1837–42** HAWTHORNE *Twice-told T.* (1851) II. vi. 97 Like uncle Parker,.. I am a spinner of long yarns. **1888** *Poor Nellie* 162 Catch them spinning any of their yarns to me. **1897** HALL CAINE in *Humanitarian* XI. 234 What I mean is that without motive a story in not a novel, but only a yarn. **1903** *Dublin Rev.* July 131 All further developments of these traditions were mere 'yarns'.

b. A chat, a talk. *colloq.* (chiefly *Austral.* and *N.Z.*).

1857 H. W. HARPER *Lett. from N.Z.* (1914) iii. 49 This has been a long yarn. **1883** STEVENSON *Treasure I.* x. 80 'Come away, Hawkins,' he would say; 'come and have a yarn with John.' **1888** 'R. BOLDREWOOD' *Robbery under Arms* I. xii. 156 After tea father and I and Jim had a long yarn. **1929** K. S. PRICHARD *Coonardoo* xv. 147 Meenie and Bandogera had taken advantage of her absence to have a smoke and a yarn together at the wood-heap. **1937** D. COWIE *N.Z. from Within* vii. 109 The word is used in its oldest sense. The New Zealander's 'yarn' is the Scotsman's 'news'. **1966** G. W. TURNER *Eng. Lang. Austral. & N.Z.* vi. 124 Other counts have been based on written material and the Australian one on spoken. This accounts for the inclusion of *kid* ('child').., *yarn* ('talk').., [etc.]. **1979** B. MOORE *Mangan Inheritance* II. 295 We can take it easy for a while and have a real yarn together. **1984** *Times* 11 Sept. 32/8, I still see some of the Roman Catholics in the street..and we have a yarn.

3. *attrib.* and *Comb.*, as (sense 1) ***yarn ball***, ***-carrier***, ***hose***, ***-man***, ***rope***, ***scales***, ***spindle***, ***stockings***, ***thread***, ***twine***; ***yarn-buyer***, ***-factoring***, ***-jobber***, ***manufacture***, ***-manufacturer***, ***-seller***; (sense 2) ***yarn-slinger***, ***-teller***; **yarn-clue**, a ball of yarn; **yarn count** = COUNT *sb.*[1] 2 b; **yarn-croft** *Obs.* exc. *dial.*, a rope-yard; **yarn-dyed** *a.*, dyed while in the state of yarn or thread; **yarn-frame, -guide** (see quots.); **yarn-house**, a building in which yarns are stored; **yarn-reel** (see quot.); **yarn-roll** = YARN-BEAM.

For other names of apparatus used in yarn manufacture see Knight's *Dict. Mech.*

1585 HIGINS *Junius' Nomencl.* 295/2 *Pila paganica*,.. a bal stuft with soft wooll or haire, and vsed to be tossed from hand to hand: a tossing ball: a *yarne ball. **1763** *Museum Rust.* I. 11 The eagle-sighted *yarn-buyer. **1927** T. WOODHOUSE *Artificial Silk* 100 The yarns now pass to their respective *yarn carriers, the function of which is to place the yarn in the path of the single set of sinkers. **1957** *Textile Terms & Definitions* (Textile Inst.) (ed. 3) 109 *Yarn carrier*, ..the final element which guides the yarn to the knitting instruments. **1820** SCOTT *Monast.* xxxiii. (*Old Play*), Like to the *yarn-clew of the drowsy knitter, Dragg'd by the frolic kitten through the cabin. **1923** *Yarn count [see NUMBER *sb.* 6 g]. **1963** JERRARD & MCNEILL *Dict. Sci. Units* 154 In the textile industry the yarn count or yarn number gives either the mass per unit length or the length per unit mass of a yarn fibre. **1634–5** BRERETON *Trav.* (Chetham Soc.) 11 A dainty quay here is, and many *yarne-crofts here about. **1885** HUMMEL *Dyeing Textile Fabrics* 289 If in any dyed woollen fabric..the dyeing took place while it was in the state of thread or yarn, it is said to be *yarn-dyed. **1841** LEVER *O'Malley* xxviii, A race of linen-weaving, Presbyterian-*yarn factoring fellows. **1831–3** P. BARLOW in *Encycl. Metrop.* (1845) VIII. 755/1 The yarn reels were placed individually in a stationary frame at the head of the rope-ground; and it appears that the register was to be conveyed onwards towards the *yarn frame, as the strand was twisted by the hook of a sledge, at the end where the process commenced, until the whole strand was made. *Ibid.* 756/2 The *yarn guide, or perforated plate, through which the rope yarns pass individually to concentre at the press block. **1578** in Nichols *Progr. Q. Eliz.* (1823) II. 144 Eyght small women chyldren spinnyng worsted yarne, and..as many knittyng of worsted *yarne hose. **1794** *Rigging & Seamanship* I. 60 After yarn is tarred, it is laid in the *yarn-house..to harden. **1720** *Lond. Gaz.* No. 5878/8 William Hill,..*Yarne-jobber. **1637** *Bury Wills* (Camden) 168 Goodman Howes, of Bury, *yarneman. **1882** *Encycl. Brit.* XIV. 664/2 The whole operations in *yarn manufacture comprise (1) heckling, (2) preparing, and (3) spinning. **1783** *Specif. Patent* No. 1365. 1 Thomas Baker, of Derby..*Yarn Manufacturer. **1794** *Rigging & Seamanship* I. 88 A *Yarn-reel is a circular board, nailed in the middle to a piece of oak, ..16 inches long, and is used to wind spun-yarn on. **1831** G. R. PORTER *Silk Manuf.* III. iii. 215 A weight..suspended over the *yarn-roll to produce..the requisite tension of the threads of the warp. **1534** in F. W. Weaver *Wells Wills* (1890) 49 A *yerynrope. **1818** SCOTT *Rob Roy* xxxi, The *yarn scales in the weigh-house. **1705** *Lond. Gaz.* No. 4188/4 Richard Corbett, of Spittle-fields, *Yarn-seller. **1897** BARRÈRE & LELAND *Dict. Slang*, **Yarn-slinger*, one who writes tales in newspapers. **1820** W. TOOKE tr. *Lucian* I. 736 She draws the *yarn-spindle from her bosom. **1704** *Lond. Gaz.* No. 4056/8 Blue *Yarn Stockings. **1863** HAWTHORNE *Our Old Home* II. 219 Knitting coarse yarn stockings. **1891** *Tablet* 7 Nov. 742 The most confirmed American *yarn-teller. **1833** J. RENNIE *Alph. Angling* Pref. p. xiii, My '*yarn thread' was strong enough to twitch out the trout to the green bank where I stood. *c* **1600** J. KEYMER *Dutch Fishing* (1664) 7 To make Cables and Cordage, likewise *Yarn Twine, and Thred for the makeing of Nets and Lines.

yarn (jɑːn), *v. colloq.* [f. prec. (sense 2).]

a. *intr.* To 'spin a yarn', tell a story; also, to chat or talk. Hence ˈ**yarning** *vbl. sb.* and *ppl. a.*

1812 [see YARN *sb.* 2 a]. **1849** CUPPLES *Green Hand* i, Somehow or another I was al'ays a yarning sort of a customer. **1857** *St Leonard's Station Diary* 14 May, in L. R. C. MacFarlane *Amuri* (1946) III. 125 Hanging round the station, yarning and sleeping. **1859** H. KINGSLEY *G. Hamlyn* xxxi, The head man of that there gang is..a-sitting yarning with your boss. **1880** *19th Cent.* No. 38. 655 So we talked and yarned till I grew sleepy and dozed off. **1888** W. CLARK RUSSELL *Death Ship* vii, We speedily fell to yarning. **1901** M. FRANKLIN *My Brilliant Career* (1966) iii. 3 Too friendly to pay a short call, they came and sat for hours yarning about nothing in particular. **1939** A. POWELL *What's become of Waring* vii. 206 If I..start yarning with him..we shall be late for dinner. **1941** I. L. IDRIESS *Great Boomerang* xvii. 122 In the whitewashed Birdsville Hotel, low-roofed but with dim, cool rooms, the blokes yarn the time away. **1944** *R.A.F. Jrnl.* Aug. 256 There is practically nothing to do but ..yarn with your friends. **1958** L. DURRELL *Balthazar* ii. 37 We were sitting at a café yarning. *a* **1966** 'M. NA GOPALEEN' *Best of Myles* (1977) 55 He does be yarnin with the brother above in the digs of a Sunday. **1972** M. SHADBOLT *Strangers & Journeys* xi. 195 In the town, where men gathered to yarn on street corners. **1977** C. MCCULLOUGH *Thorn Birds* vi. 120 Their parents yarned over cups of tea, swapped tall stories and books.

† **b.** *trans.* To recount or narrate. *Obs. rare.*

1840 A. RUSSELL *Tour Austral. Colonies* 40 One who can yarn the dangers of the deep so well.

yarn: see EARN *v.*[1], YEARN *v.*, YERN.

ˈ**yarn-beam.** *Weaving.* [Cf. G. *garnbaum.*] The roller on which the yarn is wound.

1598 FLORIO, *Subbio*,..the roule whereon the weauer rouleth vp his web or worke, called a yarne-beame. **1797** *Encycl. Brit.* (ed. 3) XVIII. 835/2 The cane-roll or yarn-beam, on which the warp is rolled when put into the loom. **1844** G. DODD *Textile Manuf.* i. 40 The yarn-beam is capable of revolving on its axis.

Hence **yarn-beaming** *a.*

1875 KNIGHT *Dict. Mech.*, *Yarn-beaming Machine*, a machine for winding the warp-yarn on to the beam.

† **yarn-chopper.** *Obs.* [f. YARN *sb.* + CHOPPER[2].] A dealer in yarn.

Also in various corrupt forms in Law Dicts., etc.: see JOURN-CHOPPER.

1429 *Act 8 Hen. VI*, c. 5 Les regratours du file appelles Yernchoppers.

†**yarndle.** *dial. Obs.* Shortened form of YARNWINDLE.

1682 MARTINDALE *Countrey-Surv.-Bk.* x. 69 Those things which here in Cheshire we call Yarndles, being used by Country Housewives in winding of their Yarn.

yarned (jɑːnd), *a.* [f. YARN *sb.* + -ED[2].] Furnished with yarn.

1653 URQUHART *Rabelais* I. ii. 16 Five spindles yarnd.

†**yarnen,** *a. Obs.* [f. YARN *sb.* + -EN[4].] Made of yarn.

1568 TURBERV. *Trag. T., Epit.* etc. (1587) 190 b, A paire of yornen [*v.r.* yarnen] stockes to keepe the cold away.

'yarnets, -its. *Sc.* [Of obscure formation.] = YARNWINDLE.

1808 JAMIESON, *Yarnets*, an instrument for winding yarn. **1842** *Whistle-Binkie* Ser. IV. 94 The aefauld yarn was ta'en awa', To the yarnits niest, to lay an' twist.

'yarn-spinner. [f. YARN *sb.* + SPINNER.]

1. A workman who spins yarn.

1813 *Examiner* 1 Mar. 137/2 T. Kemp, Knaresborough, yarn-spinner. **1895** *Daily News* 10 May 9/3 Yarn spinners are.. very busy on old orders.

2. One who 'spins a yarn'; a story-teller. *colloq.*

1865 MRS. WHITNEY *Gayworthys* xxvi, 'Captain Vorse, we want a yarn—a real sailor's yarn!'..'Oh, I'm no yarn-spinner', said the young captain, evasively. **1883** *Harper's Mag.* Jan. 323/2 The story was 'improved' by the marine yarn-spinners of that port.

So **'yarn-spinning.**

1867 SMYTH *Sailor's Word-bk.*, *Yarn-spinning*, a figurative expression for telling a story. **1888** *Encycl. Brit.* XXIV. 731/1 These inventions are at the foundation of all modern systems of yarn-spinning.

yar-nut, north. dial. var. *ernut*, EARTH-NUT. (Cf. GERNUT, JURNUT.)

1828 *Craven Gloss.*, *Yar-nut*, earth nut, or pig-nut. **1908** [MISS FOWLER] *Betw. Trent & Ancholme* 230 The earth-nut, or 'Yar-nut'.

'yarnwind. *Obs.* exc. *dial.* Also 9 **yarewind.** [OE. *ȝearnwinde* (= WFris. *jernwine*, NFris. *juarnwinj*, Flem. *garenwinde*, MHG., G. *garnwinde*, Icel. *garnvinda* skein of yarn), f. *ȝearn* YARN *sb.* + **winde* = OHG. *winta* (G. *winde*) winder. Cf. GARNWIN.] = YARNWINDLE.

c **725** *Corpus Gloss.* (Hessels) R 168 *Reponile*, ȝearnuuinde. *c* **1000** *Gloss.* in Wr.-Wülcker 213/11 *Conductum*, ȝearnwinde. **1879** MISS JACKSON *Shropsh. Word-bk.*, *Yarewinds* (yaa·r'winz).. a machine for holding yarn intended to be made into skeins or wound into balls... The yarewinds consisted of a reel and stand. **1903** *Eng. Dial. Dict.*, *Yarnwinds* [Shetland, Caithness].

yarn-winder. Also 5 yernwynder. [In ME. an alteration of OE. *ȝearnwinde* or of YARNWINDLE by association with *winder* (cf. Du. *garenwinder*); in mod.E. f. YARN *sb.* + WINDER.] An apparatus for winding yarn, as a yarn-reel or a yarn-spooler.

14.. *Voc.* in Wr.-Wülcker 564/31 *Appendium*,.. a yern-wynder, or a reel. **1875** KNIGHT *Dict. Mech.*, Yarn-winder.

yarnwindle ('jɑːn,wɪnd(ə)l). *Obs.* exc. *dial.* Forms: 4 **yar-, ȝarewyndel,** 5 **ȝarn(e wyndel, ȝarwyndyl(l, yerwyndylle,** 6 **yarne wyndell,** 9 **yarn-windle,** *Sc.* **yarn-winle.** Also YARNDLE, YARRINGLE. [f. YARN *sb.* + *-windle*, instrumental formation on WIND *v.*[1] (see -LE 1); cf. YARNWIND.] An appliance for winding a skein of yarn into a ball: = GARNWINDLE.

c **1325** *Gloss. W. de Bibbesw.* in Wright *Voc.* 157 A yarwyndel. *c* **1340** *Nominale* (Skeat) 547 *Serence lussel et voydere*, hechele clewen ȝarewyndul. *c* **1440** *Promp. Parv.* 536/2 ȝarne wyndel, or ga(r)wyndel (*S.* or ȝarwyndyl), *girgillus*. *c* **1475** *Pict. Voc.* in Wr.-Wülcker 794/33 *Hic virgillus*, a yerwyndylleblad. **1530** PALSGR. 291/1 Yarne wyndell, *tornette*. **1611** COTGR., *Desvidoir*, a paire of blades, or yarnwindles. **1818** SCOTT *Rob Roy* xxxii, Nae man willingly wad cut short his thread of life before the end o' his pirn was fairly measured off on the yarn-winles. **1821** —— *Pirate* v, Speak her fair and canny, or we will have a ravelled hasp on the yarn-windles!

yarooh (ja'ruː), *int.* Also **yaroo.** A humorous stylized representation of a cry of pain. (One of Billy Bunter's characteristic exclamations: see quots.)

1909 *Magnet* 20 Nov. 4/2 'Oh!' roared Bunter, as Bulstrode's heavy boot biffed on him. 'Ow! Yah! Yarooh!' **1918** *Ibid.* 8 June 12/2 'Don't keep me waiting, or I shall help you on—like that!' 'Yarooh!' **1940** 'G. ORWELL' in *Horizon* Mar. 178 'Oooogh!', 'Grooo!' and 'Yaroo!' (stylized cries of pain). **1953** *Manch. Guardian Weekly* 23 July 11/2 With a 'Yarooh!' on nearly every page William G. Bunter is on the war-path again. **1972** *Guardian* 21 Jan. 1/5 'Yarooh!' they yelled... 'Get out, you cad!' **1977** M. AMIS in A. Thwaite *My Oxford* 205 A sign reading 'Yaroo—College Squit!' suspended from my neck.

yarpha ('jafa). *Sc. dial.* Also **yarff** (see *Eng. Dial. Dict.*). [ON. *jǫrfi* (*jǫrva-*) gravel.] A peat-bog; peat combined with clay or sand.

1805 G. BARRY *Orkney* I. i. 10 *Yarpha*, or bog soil, whose characteristic is a black colour connected with the power of retaining moisture. *Ibid.*, In those places that are most elevated, the *yarpha* soil is most frequent. **1808** JAMIESON, *Yarpha*, I. Peat full of fibres and roots, *Orkney*. **1821** SCOTT *Pirate* xxxv, The poor *yarpha*, as the benighted creatures here call their peat-bogs.

yarr (jar), *sb. Sc.* and *north. dial.* [Cf. NFris. (Föhr) *jïr* spurrey.] The corn-spurrey, *Spergula arvensis*.

1775 *Essays Agric.* 435 Farmers in Scotland will take notice that this [*sc.* yarrow] is not the plant known among them by the name of *Yarr*, spurrey, *Spergula*. **1812** SOUTER *Agric. Banff* App. 46 Those lesser weeds that go under the common appellation of skellach, gule, yarr, &c. **1829** LOUDON *Encycl. Plants* 390 S[pergula] arvensis is a common weed in sandy soils, in Scotland called yarr.

yarr, *v.*: see YAR.

†**yarraman** ('jærəmən). *Obs.* Pl. **yarramen, -mans.** An Australian Aboriginal word for a horse.

1848 H. W. HAYGARTH *Bush Life in Austral.* x. 108 A stockman.. meets some of the blacks, to whom his first question is 'You make a light yarraman belonging to me' (*i.e.* Have you seen my horses?). **1882** A. J. BOYD *Old Colonials* 69 There's seventeen yarramen—call 'em thirty pounds a head. **1905–6** 'T. COLLINS' *Rigby's Romance* (1971) v. 21 He needn't be frightened o' these yarramans. I got them like lambs. **1930** A. W. GROOM *Merry Christmas* xx. 156 'We tie yarraman here,' he suggested. They fastened their horses to low snags on the dead tree. **1959** BAKER *Drum* 158 *Yarraman*, an outlaw horse or wildly behaved station hack. **1964** W. S. RAMSON in *Southerly* I. 58 Other aboriginal words, *bora*, *coolamon*, *goondie*, *humpy*, and *yarraman*, came from tribes in the Sydney and Moreton Bay districts.

‖**yarran** ('jærən). *Australia.* [Native name.] Name for several Australian species of *Acacia*.

1888 'R. BOLDREWOOD' *Robbery under Arms* xlvi, We stopped inside a yarran scrub.

†**yarringle.** *Obs.* Also 7 **yarwingle.** Corrupt form of *yarwindle*, YARNWINDLE.

Cf. *garwyngyll* in ed. 1499 of *Promp. Parv.* (Camd. 188/1).

1611 COTGR., *Tournette*, a Rice, or Yarwingle to wind yarne on. **1687** *Mother Shipton* 7 A pair of Yarwingles, made in the form of a Cross. **1688** HOLME *Armoury* III. 287/2 A Pair of Yarringles with its Pins, set upon its Stock... This Instrument is also of great use with Housewives, by the help whereof Yarn Slippings or Hanks is wound... Some term these a Pair of Yarringles or Yarringle Blades. *Ibid.* 288/1 The Yarringle foot. **1879** MISS JACKSON *Shropsh. Word-bk.*, *Yarringles*, same as *Yarnacles* [= *Yarewinds*].

yarrow ('jærəʊ), *sb.* Forms: 1 **ȝear(e)we,** 5 **ȝarwe, ȝarow(e,** 5–6 **yarow,** 6 **yarowe, yarrowe,** 6– **yarrow.** [OE. *ȝearwe* = Du. *gerw* (:—**garwe*), OHG. *gar(a)wa* (G. *garbe*), of uncertain etym.] The common name of the herb *Achillea Millefolium* (N.O. *Compositæ*), also called MILFOIL and NOSE-BLEED, frequent on roadsides, dry meadows, and waste ground, with tough greyish stem, finely-divided bipinnate leaves, and close flat clusters of flower-heads of a somewhat dull white, often varying to pink or crimson; sometimes used medicinally as a tonic. Also extended to other species of *Achillea*. **b.** Applied with defining words to plants of other genera. **soldier's yarrow,** *Stratiotes aloides*. **water yarrow,** a name for various water plants with finely divided leaves, as *Ranunculus aquatilis*, *Hottonia palustris*, and the genus *Myriophyllum*. (Cf. MILFOIL 2.)

c **725** *Corpus Gloss.* (Hessels) M 204 *Mirifillo*, ȝearwe. *c* **1000** *Sax. Leechd.* II. 354 Wyl on meolcum þa readan ȝearwan. *c* **1050** *Ags. Voc.* in Wr.-Wülcker 297/31 *Millefolium*, ȝearewe. *a* **1400–50** *Stockholm Med. MS.* 202 Millefoly or neseblod or ȝarwe. **14..** *Nom.* in Wr.-Wülcker 711/26 *Hoc millefolium*, ȝarow. *c* **1440** *Promp. Parv.* 536/2 ȝarowe, myllefoyle, herbe for nese blederys. **1503** DUNBAR *Thistle & Rose* 83 Full craftely conjurit scho the Yarrow. **1546** LANGLEY tr. *Pol. Verg. De Invent.* I. xvii. 32 b, Mercurie founde the vse of Moly, Achilles Yarowe, Esculapius, Panace. **1578** LYTE *Dodoens* I. ci. 142 Water Milfoyle or Yearrow. *Ibid.* 143 Knights Milfoyle: souldiers Yerrow. **1597** GERARDE *Herbal* II. cclxxxvi. 678 Water Milfoile, or water Yarrow, hath long and large leaues. **1612** DRAYTON *Poly-olb.* xiii. 203 The Yarrow, where-with-all he stops the wound-made gore. **1614** MARKHAM *Cheap Husb.* Table Hard Wds., *Yarrow*, is an hearbe called the water-Violet, and growes in Lakes, or marrish grounds. **1784** J. TWAMLEY *Dairying Exempl.* 91, I take yarrow to be an ill favoured Plant for Cheese where it prevails much in Land. **1789** J. PILKINGTON *View Derbysh.* I. viii. 348 *Hottonia palustris*. Water Violet. Water Yarrow. **1866** MRS. RIDDELL *Race for Wealth* xxiii, A lawn in which I have gathered yarrow.

†**'yarrow,** *a. dial. Obs.* [dial. var. ARGH (OE. *earȝ*); cf. Sussex *yar* (W. D. Cooper *Sussex Gloss.* 1853).] (See quot.)

1616 BULLOKAR *Eng. Expos.*, *Yarrow*, fearefull, faint-hearted.

yarrum ('jærəm). *Thieves' Cant.* Also 6 **yaram,** 6–7 **yarum.** [?] Milk.

1567 HARMAN *Caveat* (1869) 83 Yaram [*v.r.* yarum], mylke. **1608** DEKKER *Lanth. & Candle Lt.* i, If we mawnd Pannam, lap, or Ruff-peck, Or poplars of yarum. **1641** BROME *Joviall Crew* II. (1652) F 3, Here's Pannum and Lap, and good Poplars of Yarrum. *a* **1700** B. E. *Dict. Cant. Crew.*

yarth(e, obs. or dial. ff. EARTH.

a **1500** *Cov. Corp. Christi Pl.* 36/79 Apon the yarthe. **1688** HOLME *Armoury* III. xvii. (Roxb.) 120/1 The yarthing Hooke, or forke is an Instrument of Husbandry as well as warre. **1825** JENNINGS *Obs. Dial. W. Eng.*, *Yarth*, earth.

'yarwhelp. *local.* Also 6 **yerwhelp,** 7 **yarewhelp, yarwell,** 7–9 **yarwip,** 8 **yarwhelph,** 8–9 **yarwhip.** [? Imitative of the goat-like cry of the godwit; cf. YAR *v.*] The bar-tailed godwit (*Limosa lapponica* or *rufa*) and the black-tailed godwit (*L. ægocephala* or *melanura*).

1577 in *Archaeologia* (1821) XIX. 289 Yerwhelps ij.. ijs. **1579** J. JONES *Preserv. Bodie & Soule* I. xiv. 26 The flesh of .. Towin, Yarwhelpe, Plover, Wodcocke. **1634** in Simpkinson *Washingtons* (1860) App. p. xiii, Yarwell 1 dozen and 11 02 14 02. **1668** SIR T. BROWNE *Let. to Dr. Merrett* 29 Dec., A Yarwhelp, Barker, or Latrator a marsh bird about the bignesse of a Godwitt. **1678** RAY *Willughby's Ornith.* 292 The Godwit, called in some places the Yarwhelp, or Yarwip. **1744** *Ant. & Pres. St. Co. Down* xviii. 227 The Yarwhelp or Yarwip, is something like a Wood-cock.

yarwingle, yarwyndel: see YARRINGLE, YARNWINDLE.

yary ('jɛərɪ), *a. dial.* (chiefly *Newfoundland*). Also **yarry.** [var. of YARE *a.*] Quick, sharp; alert, energetic; wary, wide awake; rising early.

1855 *Trans. Philol. Soc.* 38 [Norfolk] *Yary*, brisk. **1863** J. MORETON *Life & Work in Newfoundland* iii. 35 *Yary*, wary. **1868** in *Dict. Newfoundland Eng.* (1982) 622/2 Here we saw a great number of wild geese in the lagoon.. but it was impossible to get within shooting distance of them, these birds are so wild and extremely yarry. **1881** *Even. Telegram* (St. John's, Newfoundland) 20 Sept. 1 We don't find the cruising war-ships of our yarry neighbours the French and the Americans, lying in port for weeks at a time. **1906** N. DUNCAN *Adventures Billy Topsail* 256 'Hi, b'y! Get yarry (wide awake)!' cried the captain in the morning. **1925** *Dialect Notes* V. 346 *Yary*,.. 1. energetic; smart. 2. early. 3. wary. **1966** A. R. SCAMMELL *My Newfoundland* 90 That would be Skipper John Elliott, yary as ever, hi-tailing it for Jacob's ground before the Eastern Tickle crowd got the choice berths for the day.

yas (jæs), repr. colloq. and U.S. Blacks' pronunc. of *yes adv.* See YASSUH *int.*

1887 H. BAUMANN *Londinismen* 238 *Yas*,.. yes. **1909** L. M. MONTGOMERY *Anne of Avonlea* xxiv. 279 'Was Ginger hurt?'.. 'Yas'm. He was hurt pretty bad. He was killed.' **1927** *N.Y. Times Mag.* 24 Apr. 4/2 Yas, sir. Dat right, sir. **1936** M. MITCHELL *Gone with Wind* xxxii. 546 'I suppose you heard Jonas Wilkerson and that Emmie—'Yas'm,' said Mammy. **1966** *Keystone Folklore Q.* XI. 85 Caddy always taught the children not to say 'Yas suh, No suh and Yas 'um' .. to white folks.

‖**yashiki** ('jaʃiki). Also 9 **yaski.** Pl. **yashiki,** (anglicized) **-s.** [Jap., f. *ya* house + *shiki* a space, site.] The residence of a Japanese feudal nobleman, including the palace or mansion and grounds, and the quarters for his retainers.

1727 J. G. SCHEUCHZER tr. *Kæmpfer's Hist. Japan* II. ix. 486 *Sokkokf Dai Mio Jassiki*, that is, Palaces and houses of the princes and Lords of the Empire.] **1863** R. ALCOCK *Capital of Tycoon* II. xiii. 280 The Daimios' *Yaskis* are merely a low line of barracks of the same construction, rather higher in the roofs. **1871** A. B. MITFORD *Tales of Old Japan* II. 206 The principal yashikis (palaces) of the nobles are for the most part immediately round the Shogun's castle. **1906** R. A. CRAM *Impressions Jap. Archit.* iii. 57 The arrangement of these 'yashiki' varied but little: a hollow square.. was formed by the barracks for the daimyo's retainers; these barracks were usually two stories in height. **1959** R. KIRKBRIDE *Tamiko* ix. 65 It was at once obvious to him that it was part of the ruins of a magnificent yashiki, destroyed by fire during the war. **1970** J. W. HALL *Japan* x. 170 All daimyo were obliged to build residences (*yashiki*) in Edo where they kept their wives and children.

‖**yashmak** ('jæʃmæk). Also **-mack, -mac, yasmak, yashmac** (*erron.* **yakmak, yaknack**). [Arab. *yashmaq*.] The double veil concealing the part of the face below the eyes, worn by Muslim women in public.

1844 KINGLAKE *Eothen* iii. 47 *note*, The yashmak.. is not a mere, semi-transparent veil, but rather a good substantial petticoat applied to the face. **1848** THACKERAY *Van. Fair* xviii, We let their bodies go abroad liberally enough, with smiles and ringlets and pink bonnets to disguise them instead of veils and yakmaks. **1885** *Times* 25 May 10 A Turkish lady is shocked if a strange man sees her without a yashmak. **1895** P. HEMINGWAY *Out of Egypt* II. 167, I gave her [*sc.* an old Arab woman] a cigarette, and she consented to accept a light from me, raising her yashmak for a moment.

Hence **'yashmaked** *a.*, wearing a yashmak.

1904 OXENHAM *Weaver of Webs* xiii, The simple pleasure of exciting the envious admiration of their yashmaked and unemancipated sisters.

yask *sb.* and *v.*, local variant of *yesk*, YEX.

1580 HOLLYBAND *Treas. Fr. Tong*, *Baailler*, to gape, yaske, to yawne. **1879** MISS JACKSON *Shropsh. Word-bk.*, *Yask*, a term used to express the sound made by a violent effort to get quit of something in the throat.

†**yasked** [Y- 4], asked.

1377 LANGL. *P. Pl.* B. XVIII. 294, I haue.. hym.. yasked Where he were god. **1426** LYDG. *De Guil. Pilgr.* 7048 Thow sholdest.. Fyrst yaxyd A Bordoun.

yaspen, yaspin: see YEPSEN.

yassuh ('jæsʌ), *int.* Chiefly *U.S.* Repr. Black colloq. pronunc. of 'yes, sir' (often somewhat obsequious). Cf. YAS + SUH.

1936 M. MITCHELL *Gone with Wind* xxiii. 391 'She's not dead? Is she breathing?' 'Yassuh, she breathin'.' **1944** C. HIMES *Black on Black* (1973) 199 'Take good care of me, Chops,' I said... 'Yassuh.' **1963** PRANGE & VITOLS in A.

Dundes *Mother Wit* (1973) 631/2 Yassuh, I sees all dat. **1973** J. Pattinson *Search Warrant* ii. 33 'You live alone here?' 'Yassuh. Jus' me an' my mem'ries.'

†**yasured** [Y- 4], azured.
c **1483** Caxton *Dialogues* 14/36 *Bleu asuret*, Blyew y-asured.

yat: see GATE *sb.*[1], THAT, YACHT.

yataghan ('jætəgæn). Also **yatagan**; ATAGHAN. [Turkish *yātāghan.*] A sword of Muslim countries, having a handle without a guard and often a double-curved blade.
1819 T. Hope *Anastasius* (1820) I. iii. 52, I began hacking and hewing with my yatagan. **1837** *Gambler's Dream* I. 144 With our flowing garments, our turbans, and our yataghans, we conquered Asia under the standard of the Prophet. **1881** *Blackw. Mag.* May 566/1 The curved Arab yataghans with an outside edge. **1894** D. C. Murray *Making of Novelist* 125 A Circassian..flourishing..a formidable looking yataghan.

yatch, yatcht, obs. ff. YACHT.

yate (jeɪt), *sb.* Also **yeit**. [Native name.] Either of two species of gum-tree, *Eucalyptus cornuta* and *E. occidentalis* (flat-topped yate), of south-western Australia, yielding a tough wood; also the wood itself.
1880 Von Mueller *Select Extra-trop. Plants* 110. **1884** Miller *Plant-n.*, Yate-tree, or Yeit-tree, *Eucalyptus cornuta*. **1907** *Westm. Gaz.* 20 Nov. 12/1 The extraordinary properties of yate, believed to be the strongest of all known woods.

†**yate**, *v. Obs.* Forms: 2 **ȝeatan, ȝætan, ȝetan, ietan**, (*Orm.*) **ȝatenn**, 3–4 **ȝette, ȝet**, 4 **ȝete, yete**, *north.* **ȝiate**, 4–5 *north.* **ȝate, yate**, 5 **ȝote**. *Pa. t.* 2 **ȝeatte, ȝætte, ȝeotte, iætte, iette**, 2–3 **ȝatte**, 3 **ȝet(te**, 4 **yatt(e, ȝat(e, yeitt**; 3 **ȝet(t)ed(e**. *Pa. pple.* 2 (*Orm.*) **ȝatedd**, 3 **iȝetted**. [late OE. *ȝéatan* (Peterborough Chron.), f. *ȝéa* YEA, app. after ON. *játa*, also *játta* to assent, acknowledge, confess, promise, grant (cf. OHG. *gijâzan*, MHG. *jâzen* to assent); for the formation cf. ON. *neita* NAIT *v.*[2] to refuse.
The northern form *ȝate* is directly from or influenced by ON. The west-midland present *ȝette* is prob. due to the pa. t. *ȝette*.]

1. *trans.* To grant, bestow, concede. Also *absol.*
a **1122** *O.E. Chron.* (Laud MS.) an. 656 Ic Uitalianus papa ȝeate þe Wulfhere cyning & Deusdedit ærcebiscop & Saxulf abbod ealle þe þing þe ȝe ȝearnon. *Ibid.* 675 Ic ȝæte þæs ilce curs..Ic Adrianus legat hit iete. *Ibid.* 1066 Se æðeling hit him ȝeatte þa bliþolice. *c* **1200** Ormin 154 Godd Allwældennd hafeþþ herrd & ȝatedd tine beness. *c* **1205** Lay. 10994, & al ich þe ȝette Swa þu hit ȝirnest. *Ibid.* 14267 Þe king him ȝette swa Hengest hit wolde. *a* **1225** *Ancr. R.* 230 ȝif þu driuest us heonene, do us iðeos swin her, & he ȝettede ham. *a* **1225** *Leg. Kath.* 2402 He ȝettede hire & ȝef bliðeliche leaue. *a* **1300** *Cursor M.* 8414 And curtaisli, wit-vten hone, He yatte hir freli al hir bone. *Ibid.* 22413 Fourti dais he sal tham yate þat fallen ar ute of þair state..þat þai mai þam wit penance bete. **13..** *Gaw. & Gr. Knt.* 776 'Now bone hostel', coþe þe burne, 'I be-seche yow ȝette!' *c* **1440** *Promp. Parv.* 201 God ȝate (*K.* Godȝote, *H.* Goodȝoth, *P.* Godwolde), *utinam*.

2. To acknowledge, confess.
c **1200** Ormin 9819 Ne wolldenn þeȝȝ nohht cnawenn Ne ȝatenn þatt teȝȝ wærenn ohht Sinnfulle onn aniȝ wise. *a* **1300** *Cursor M.* 26946 þou he yeitt [*Fairf.* ȝeted] his wickedhede It moght him to no merci lede. *Ibid.* 27428 A man him cums al for to scriue..And yetes..þat he es fallen in miskenyng.

3. To provide, give, offer.
13.. *E.E. Allit. P.* A. 558 Frende no wrang I wyl þe ȝete. *a* **1420** *Cursor M.* 29047 (Cotton Galba) Als oure lord crist at þe last Gat vs ensaumple forto fast.
1788 *Voc. Forth & Bargie* in *Trans. R. Irish Acad.* II. 34 *Yate*, give.

Hence †**yating** (ȝettung) *vbl. sb.*, granting, consent.
a **1225** *Ancr. R.* 204 On is ful wil uorte don þet fulðe, mid skilles ȝettunge.

yate: see GATE *sb.*[1], YET.

Yates (jeɪts). *Statistics.* [The name of Frank *Yates* (b. 1902), English statistician, who published the correction in 1934 (*Suppl. Jrnl. R. Statistical Soc.* I. 217).] ***Yates'(s) correction***: a correction for the discreteness of the data that is made in the chi-square test when the number of cases in any class is small and there is one degree of freedom, consisting in the subtraction of ½ from each difference when evaluating chi square.
1934 R. A. Fisher *Statistical Methods for Research Workers* (ed. 5) iv. 96 (*heading*) Yates' correction for continuity. **1968** P. A. P. Moran *Introd. Probability Theory* ii. 76 The use of the correction ½ results in a closer numerical approximation and is known as Yates's correction. **1972** *Jrnl. Social Psychol.* LXXXVII. 53 As the expected frequency in some cells was less than 10, Yate's [*sic*] correction for continuity was applied. **1977** R. Holland *Self & Social Context* vi. 211 Cooper..shows with the help of chi-squared and Yates' correction the effectiveness of conjoint family and milieu therapy.

yatte, obs. form of GATE *sb.*[1]

yatter ('jætə(r)), *v. colloq.* (orig. *Sc. dial.*). [Imitative, perh. after YAMMER *v.* + CHATTER *v.*; cf. also NATTER *v.*] *intr.* To talk idly and incessantly; to chatter, or gossip; to gabble; to complain peevishly. Freq. const. (*on*) (*about* something or *at* someone). Occas. *trans.*
1825 Jamieson (Suppl.) II. 703/2 She's ay yatter-yatterin, and never devaulds. **1831** *Gasometer* 457 She yattered about an ugly man that cam' in a fiddle case. **1896** P. A. Graham *Red Scaur* viii. 121 Grace likes to yatter about the days when she bondaged for him. **1919** J. Buchan *Mr. Standfast* i. vi. 122 No company but a wheen ignorant Hielanders that yatter Gawlic. **1942** N. Streatfeild *I ordered Table for Six* 203, I don't like to yatter about flying much. **1950** 'P. Woodruff' *Island of Chamba* 124 As long as the British yatter on about going and don't go, things are bound to get worse in India. **1963** J. N. Harris *Weird World of Wes Beattie* (1964) v. 62 This dear old Betty was yattering at me on Sunday morning when I was hung over to the eyeballs. **1977** J. I. M. Stewart *Madonna of Astrolabe* ii. 48 The confounded thing might tumble around our ears while we yattered.

Hence '**yattering** *vbl. sb.* and *ppl. a.*
1859 J. Watson *Living Bards of Border* 193, I winna get up, sae yer yatterin's vain. **1878** R. Ford *Hamespun Days* 105 A thrawart, yatterin', blatterin' mither. **1935** D. Rorie *Lum Hat* 58 Ta'en in By a yatterin' lump o' original sin. **1972** *Hawick News* 7 Jan. 7/4 Their yatterin', like the stream, goes on for ever.

'**yatter**, *sb. colloq.* (orig. *Sc. dial.*). [See prec.] Idle talk; incessant chatter or gossip.
1827 J. Watt *Poems* 72 Gin ane hae walth to keep him lievin', Nae cravin' body's yater deevin'. **1898** J. Buchan *John Burnet of Barns* ii. ix. 188 The shrill yatter of the fishwives. **1935** F. Niven *Flying Years* i. 10 Any yatter of human follies and failings. **1955** E. Pound *Section: Rock-Drill* xciv. 95 To the Odes to escape abstract yatter. **1978** *Sunday Mail* (Brisbane) 28 May 3/4 No one in the Brisbane Valley any longer believes the tourist yatter given out by Government..circles.

yaucht, obs. form of YACHT.

yaud (jɔːd, jɑːd). *Sc.* and *north. dial.* Forms: 4–6 **ȝald**, 6 **ȝad, ȝaid**, 6–7 **yawde**, 6–9 **yawd**, 8 **yade**, 8–9 **yad, yode**, 8- **yaud**. [a. ON. *jalda* (Sw. dial. *jälda*), poet. word for 'mare'.]

1. A mare: usually applied to an old mare; also *loosely* to an old or worn-out horse (associated with JADE).
1500–20 Dunbar *Petit. of Gray Horse* Poems lxi. *refrain*, Schir, lett it nevir in toun be tald, That I sould be ane ȝuillis ȝald! **1641** Brome *Joviall Crew* iv. i. (1652) Kjb, Your Yawdes may take cold, and never be good after it. **1709** *Queen Anne; or, the Auld Grey Mare* iv. in *Jacobite Songs & Ball.* (1887) 57 And they hae seized the yaud And tied her head and heel. **1719** D'Urfey *Pills* V. 326 She's have a Yode to ride out; She's neither drive the Swine, nor the Plough. **1724** Ramsay *Tea-t. Misc.* (1733) I. 8, I have three owsen in a plough Twa good ga'en yads and gear enough. **1816** Scott *Bl. Dwarf* i, Landlord, get us our breakfast, and see an' get the yauds fed. **1866** Mrs. Lynn Linton *Lizzie Lorton* II. 294 [They] sneered at her as the 'grey yaud wha'd be better rode wi' martingal nor snaffle'.

b. *Comb.*, as ***yaud-stealer***; †**yaud-swiver**, one who commits buggery with a mare.
1508 Dunbar *Flyting* 246 Muttoun dryver, girnall ryver, ȝadswyvar, fowll fell the. *c* **1560** *Durham Depos.* (Surtees) 60 And yett Ednam shuld still be his father yawd steiller.

c. *attrib.* or *adj.* Of a horse: Worn out.
1500–20 Dunbar *Petit. of Gray Horse* 25 Poems lxi, Suppois I war ane ald ȝaid aver, Schott furth our clewch to pull the clever.

†**2.** A strumpet, whore. *Comb.* **ȝaldson**, the 'son of a whore'; a term of abuse (cf. *whoreson*).
a **1400** *Morte Arth.* 3809 ȝondire to ȝone ȝaldsones he þat ȝeldes hyme ever,..Be he neuer mo sauede. **1545** *Burgh Rec. Stirling* (1887) 41 You leid that said Annapill Graheme wes ane freris get and freris yawde.

yaue, obs. pa. t. of GIVE *v.*

yauger, variant of JAGGER[3].
1808 Forsyth *Beauties Scot.* V. 390 The fishing fleet was often attended by certain vessels, called *yaugers*, that carried salt, casks, and victuals, to barter with the busses for their herrings.

yaugh, yaught, obs. ff. YACHT.

yaul: see YAULD, YAWL.

yauld, yald (jɔːld), *a. Sc.* and *north. dial.* Also 8 **yawl**, 9 **yaul**. [Origin unknown.] Active, sprightly, nimble; strong, vigorous.
1786 *Har'st Rig* viii, A bang O' Highlanders, a fendy rout, Baith yawl and strang. **1787** Burns *Let. to W. Nicol* 1 June, She's a yauld, poutherie Girran. **1816** Scott *Antiq.* xliv, There's mony yauld chiels amang thae volunteers. **1873** D. Maclagan *Heather* iii. in *Mod. Scott. Poets* Ser. iii. (1881) 177 Though somethin' auld An' no sae yauld.

yauld, yaulew, yaulpe, yaumer, -our: see YIELD, YELLOW, YAWP, YAMMER.

yaup: see YAP *a.*, YAWP.

'**yaupish**, '**yawpish**, *a. Sc.* [f. *yaup*, YAP *a.* + -ISH[1].] Hungry.
1789 Davidson *Seasons, Spring* 31 Take thou thy way To where the lusty tenant o' the floods Has, yaupish, ta'en his stan' in quest of food. **1835** D. Webster *Paisley Fair* in *Harp of Renfrewshire* Ser. ii. (1873) 153 I'm e'en growing yawpish, We maun hae some buns and some ale.

yaupon, var. YAPON.

yautia (jaʊ'tiːə). [Amer. Sp.] In the West Indies, any of various herbaceous perennials of the genus *Xanthosoma*, esp. *X. sagittifolia*, which belong to the arum family and are widely cultivated for their edible tubers; = TANIA, TANIER, TANNIER.
1899 W. Dinwiddie *Puerto Rico* xii. 141 The other root, ..known commonly as 'yautia', is much cultivated by the peasantry and held in high esteem, being always on sale in the markets. *Ibid.*, From the 'yautia' roots considerable starch is made..and is sold principally for laundry purposes. **1917** L. H. Bailey *Stand. Cycl. Hort.* VI. 3523/1 The corms and cormels (offsets) of some taros, and the cormels of some varieties of yautia, are free from acridity even in the raw state as cultivated in southern United States. **1975** E. L. Ortiz *Best of Caribbean Cooking* 135 Add the yautia, yams, pumpkin, cassava, plantains, salt and Tabasco to taste. **1981** P. Theroux *Mosquito Coast* xvii. 223 Seeing me with some yautia plants..I told them they were yautias and that their roots were as tasty as carrots.

‖**yava** ('jɑːvə). Variant of KAVA; cf. AVA.
1774 W. Wales *Jrnl.* 26 June in J. Cook *Jrnls.* (1961) II. 846 They [*sc.* the Tongans] brought off with them the Yauva, or pepper-Root. **1804** *Ann. Rev.* II. 196/1 The eyes of the great yavva drinkers are much blood-shot. **1822–7** Good *Study Med.* (1829) II. 641 It [*sc. Bucnemia tropica*] is also indigenous to the Polynesian isles, where it takes the name of yava-skin, as being supposed to originate from drinking the heating beverage called yava.

yave, obs. pa. t. of GIVE *v.*

yaw (jɔː), *sb.*[1] *Naut.*, *Aeronaut.*, and *Astronaut.* Also 7 **yawe, yogh**. [Related to YAW *v.*[1]]

a. An act of yawing; a movement of deviation from the direct course, as from bad steering; angular motion or displacement about a yawing axis.
1546 Gardiner *Declar. Joye* 91 Lyke a shyppe without anker holde or rother, ye wander as the variable wynde tosseth you, and so make yawes in and oute, without any right course. ?**1565** Sir J. Hawkins *2nd Voy. W. Ind.* (Hakl. Soc.) 9 To make three yawes, and to strike the Myson three times. **1667** (Nov. 5) *Admiralty Crt. Exam.* 77, Made a yogh. **1697** *Lond. Gaz.* No. 3315/1, I crouded Sail to Leeward to him,..making a little Yaw sometimes to shew my French Ensign. **1725** H. de Saumarez in *Phil. Trans.* XXXIII. 425 It cannot be expected but that a Ship before the Wind will deviate from her true Course, sometimes one Way, sometimes another, in her Yaws and Sheers. **1793** Smeaton *Edystone L.* §254 *note*, The boat took a sudden yaw or sheer, which canted me overboard. **1840** R. H. Dana *Bef. Mast* xxxiii, Another wide yaw and a come-to snapped the guys. **1875** Bedford *Sailor's Pocket Bk.* iii. (ed. 2) 59 If under steam, a slight yaw with the helm will serve to show the direction you intend to take. **1916** G. C. Loening *Military Aeroplanes* xii. 166 Struts of large fineness ratio..present considerable side surface and affect the directional center, at different angles of yaw. **1935** [see PITCH *sb.*[2] 2b]. **1950** *Engineering* 3 Mar. 255/2 The Desynn type of transmitter and indicator..is used to transmit to the recording apparatus such variables as control forces, angle of yaw, pressures, etc. [in a prototype aircraft]. **1974** *Physics Bull.* Jan. 11/1 The six component wind tunnel balance..will be able to measure three forces (lift, drag and side force) and three moments (pitch, yaw and roll) on any aircraft model it supports. **1977** *Offshore Engineer* May 44/3 During these tests, the data acquisition system recorded..pitch, roll, heave, surge, sway and yaw of the lay barge, pull and length of mooring cables, and anchor positions. **1978** R. Jansson *News Caper* 7 The Captain manoeuvred the big jet back to stability, damping out yaw and roll.

b. *transf.* and *fig.*: cf. YAW *v.*[1] 2.
1597 J. Payne *Royal Exch.* 34 Now and then we make yawes agaynste our wills. **1634** Massinger *Very Woman* iii. v, 'Tis strong, strong Wine: O the yaws that she'll make! **1870** Reade *Put yourself in his Place* III. 163 Putting her left hand to his breast, she gave a great yaw, and then a forward rush with her mighty loins. **1885** Stevenson *Prince Otto* i. iv, He gave a beery yaw in the saddle.

c. *Comb.* **yaw axis** = *yawing axis* s.v. YAWING *vbl. sb.*; **yaw-sighted** *a.* (*Naut. slang*), cross-eyed, squinting.
1751 Smollett *Per. Pickle* (1779) I. vi. 45 A yaw-sighted bitch. **1867** Smyth *Sailor's Word-bk.* **1959** F. D. Adams *Aeronaut. Dict.* 184/1 Yaw axis. **1962** F. I. Ordway et al. *Basic Astronaut.* ix. 368 Any vehicle motion will take place about three axes... These axes are the yaw axis, the pitch axis, and the roll axis. **1978** *Sci. Amer.* Nov. 137/1 For the first time the machine included a pair of fixed vertical surfaces behind the wings to stabilize motion about the yaw axis.

yaw, *sb.*[2] [Back-formation from YAWS apprehended as a plural.] Each of the excrescences or spots of eruption in yaws.
1744 *Med. Essays Soc. Edinb.* V. ii. 793 Sometimes after all the other Yaws are fallen off..there remains one large Yaw, high knobbed, red and moist; this is commonly called the Master-yaw. **1888** *Encycl. Brit.* XXIV. 732/2 Hairs at the seat of a yaw turn white. **1898** P. Manson *Trop. Diseases* xxvii. 427 The crust which caps and encloses an uninjured yaw is yellowish.

b. Used as attrib. form of YAWS, as ***yaw matter***, ***taint***, ***tubercle***; **yaw-house**, a hospital for persons affected with yaws; **yaw-weed**, a shrubby plant, *Morinda Royoc* (N.O. *Cinchonaceæ*), used in the West Indies as a remedy for yaws.
1679 Trapham *Disc. Health Jamaica* 122 The..long Guinny Worms, arising from the Yaw teint found..in the Children..of the Blacks. **1822–7** Good *Study Med.* (1829) III. 171 The revolting scene of a yaw-house. **1834** *Good's Study Med.* (ed. 4) II. 433 *note*, The time that elapses between the inoculation with yaw matter and the first

appearance of a yaw tubercle. **1864** GRISEBACH *Flora W. Ind. Isl.* 789 Yaw-weed, *Morinda Royoc.*

yaw, *v.*[1] [Of obscure origin. ON. *jaga* to move to and fro as a door on its hinges, has been compared.]

1. *intr.* **a.** *Naut.* Of a vessel: To deviate temporarily from the straight course, as through faulty or unsteady steering; to turn to one side or from side to side in her course.

1586 [see YAWING *vbl. sb.*]. **1612** DEKKER *If it be not Good* Wks. 1873 III. 293, I spie two Shippes yonder, that yaw too and agen. **1769** FALCONER *Dict. Marine* (1780) E ee 2, She had yawed to leeward. **1769** *St. James's Chron.* 5–8 Aug. 4/2, I..see the Ship yaw as if there was not a Seaman aboard. **1830** MARRYAT *King's Own* xiii, The frigate yawed-to with all her sails set. **1885** RUNCIMAN *Skippers & Shellbacks* 54 The barque yawed as far as the hawser would allow.

b. *Aeronaut.* and *Astronaut.* Of an aircraft or spacecraft: to rotate about a vertical axis, to undergo yawing.

1912 *Q. Rev.* July 243 This disposition tends to offer an ever-increasing amount of surface sideways to the air when a turn is begun, thus accentuating the turn initiated by the rudder and causing the craft to yaw. **1935** C. G. BURGE *Compl. Bk. Aviation* 108 The forces on the two wing tips are neither steady nor equal, so that the aeroplane tends to roll and yaw. **1964** [see PITCH *v.*[1] 19 f]. **1979** *Daily Tel.* 7 Apr. 3/2 It then yawed to the right, did a barrel roll like a light aircraft starting at an aerial show, and went into a nose-dive.

2. *transf.* and *fig.* To deviate, go out of course, go or move unsteadily. (Often with direct allusion to sense 1.)

1584 R. SCOT *Discov. Witchcr.* XII. vii. (1886) 183 The daie delaied by length of night which made both daie and night to yawe. **1604** SHAKS. *Ham.* v. ii. 120 (Qo. 2) To deuide him inuentorially, would dosie th' arithmaticke of memory, and yet but yaw neither in respect of his quick saile. **1834** MARRYAT *P. Simple* xvi, I shot ahead, and yawed a little—caught a peep at her through her veil. **1896** *Pall Mall Mag.* May 80 The rider yawed in his saddle as a boat..yaws on a cross-sea swell.

3. *trans.* To cause to yaw (*lit.* and *fig.*); to move (something) unsteadily from side to side.

1746 W. HORSLEY *Fool* (1748) I. 201 The Ship of State was, as the Seamen phrase it, yawed to and fro. **1807** E. S. BARRETT *Rising Sun* xxxvii. III. 48 Owing to the unskilfulness of her pilots, she was so *yawed* about, that it was quite uncertain when she would be moored in a safe port. **1827** HOOD *Sailor's Apol. for Bow-legs* 41 [She] yaw'd her head about all sorts of ways. **1845** GOSSE *Ocean* iv. (1849) 168 The man at the wheel,..neglecting his helm, 'yaws' the ship about sadly. **1920** *Engineering* 8 Oct. 462/2 It was found that the control was not reversed at large angles of incidence up to 20 deg. unless the model was yawed. **1960** WELCH & DENES *Go Gliding* i. 20 Moving the left foot forward yaws the glider's nose to the left. **1975** L. J. CLANCY *Aerodynamics* xvi. 525 The aircraft is yawed to starboard.

yaw, *v.*[2] *dial.* (see Eng. Dial. Dict.) [Of obscure origin.] *intr.* To be wide open; to yawn.

1596 LODGE *Wits' Miseries* 71 His browes bent, his hand shaking, his nostrils yawning. *Ibid.* 103 A fellow stretching himselfe at his window, yawing, and starting.

yaw, *adv.* [Used in representations of Ger. and Du. speech: cf. YAH *adv.*] Yes.

1667 DAVENANT & DRYDEN *Tempest* I. i, *Steph.* Boy! *Boy.* Yaw, yaw, here Master. **1697** VANBRUGH *2nd Pt. Æsop* II. iii, *Æsop.* Have you then a mind to a Wife, Sir? *Beau.* Yaw myn Heer. **1815** SCOTT *Guy M.* xxxiv, [Dirk Hatteraick loq.] Wetter and donner! yaw—What do you take me for?

yaw, *int.* An affected exclamation. Also as vb. (cf. YAW-HAW, YAW-YAW).

1797 MRS. A. M. BENNETT *Beggar Girl* (1813) III. 277 He will yaw a parcel of nonsense about jukes and lords. **1826** F. REYNOLDS *Life & Times* II. 94 Yawning and muttering, 'Reynolds is an humorist, not a wit—yaw! yaw! I am a wit!'

yaw, local form of HEW *v.*

a **1529** SKELTON *Col. Cloute* 1206 Ye prechers shall be yawde; And some shall be sawde. **1847** HALLIWELL, *Yaw*,..to hew. *West.*

yawd(e, var. YAUD, mare.

yawe, obs. f. *gave*, pa. t. of GIVE *v.*

yawer, var. YURE, *dial.*, udder.

yawey, var. YAWY.

yawger, var. JAGGER[3].

yaw-haw (ˈjɔːˈhɔː), *v.* [Echoic.] *intr.* To laugh rudely or noisily. Hence **yaw-haw** *sb.*, a loud or rude laugh; **yaw-hawing** *ppl. a.*

1836 HALIBURTON *Clockm.* Ser. I. xix, I had to pucker up my mouth..to keep from yawhawin in her face. **1912** H. MACFALL in *English Rev.* Jan. 334 A booth at a fair, a place set up but to tickle the country-bumpkins into yaw-haws.

yaw-haw. Intended to represent an affected pronunciation characterized by loose articulation in which open vowel sounds predominate. Hence attrib., as sb. (= affected person) and vb. (cf. YAW *int.* and *v.*, YAW-YAW *v.*).

1867 E. B. RAMSAY *Art of Reading* 9 All reading where sounding the vowels predominates is indistinct. At Cambridge, in my time, it used to be called a 'yaw-haw' reading. **1876** J. GRANT *One of the '600'* vii, That yaw-hawing donkey, Berkeley.

yawing (ˈjɔːɪŋ), *vbl. sb.* [f. YAW *v.*[1] + -ING[1].] The action of the verb YAW; temporary deviation of a vessel from her course; unsteady movement from side to side; also *fig.* and *attrib.*

1586 J. MELVILL *Diary* (Wodrow Soc.) 253 Be hir tumbling and yeawing, the mast schouk sa louse, that Mr. Robert.. haid mikle ado to fasten the sam. **1627** CAPT. J. SMITH *Sea Gram.* ix. 38 He that keepes the Ship most from yawing doth commonly vse the lest motion with the Helme. **1793** NELSON 22 Oct. in Nicolas *Disp.* (1845) I. 335 The Chase..by yawing, which her superiority in sailing enabled her to do, gave us many broadsides. **1858** R. S. SURTEES *Ask Mamma* lii, There is a great yawing of mouths and.. renewed inquiries for fords. **1870** LOWELL *Among my Bks.* Ser. I. (1873) 293 The language has such a fatal genius for going stern-foremost, for yawing. **1915** A. FAGE *Aeroplane* vi. 86 An indifference [on the part of pilots] to yawing, and possibly to rolling, is regarded favourably in many aeronautical circles. **1935** C. G. BURGE *Compl. Bk. Aviation* 238/1 This causes a 'yawing' effect in the opposite direction to the turning effect of the rudder [of the plane]. **1975** L. J. CLANCY *Aerodynamics* xvi. 525 If the aircraft has a yawing velocity, *r*, this affects the fin incidence in the same way that pitching velocity affects the tail incidence.

b. Special Comb.: **yawing axis**, a vertical axis through a ship or aircraft; an axis through a spacecraft normal to both the longitudinal and lateral axes.

1953 [see *rolling axis* s.v. ROLLING *vbl. sb.*[2] 9 a]. **1978** *Jrnl. Fluid Mech.* LXXXVII. 533 These passive yawing motions are studied to find their amplitude, the yawing axis and any associated energy dissipation.

So ˈ**yawing** *ppl. a.*, that yaws (*lit.* and *fig.*).

1835 WHATELY in *Life* (1866) I. 292 Another [evil] will be a sort of unsteady yawing course of the state-ship. **1850** 'H. HIEOVER' *Pract. Horsemanship* v. 92 A more yawing, pully-hauly brute I had scarcely ever ridden.

yawl (jɔːl), *sb.*[1] Forms: 7 **yaule, yale,** 7–8 **yall, yaul,** 8 **yawle, (youghall),** 8–9 **yole, yoal, yoll,** 7– **yawl.** [app. ad. MLG. *jolle* (LG. *jolle, jölle, jelle*), or Du. *jol* (17th c.) explained by Sewel, 1708, as 'a Jutland boat', whence dim. *jolleken* (1660, Hexham), cf. Sw. *julle*, Da. *jolle*; of unknown origin. F. *yole*, †*iol(e*, It. *jolo*, Russ. *yal* are from Germanic.]

1. A ship's boat resembling a pinnace, but somewhat smaller, usually with four or six oars.

1670 COVEL in *Early Voy. Levant* (Hakl. Soc.) 131 Next morning our Captain and I..went on shore in the yale betimes. **1685** *Lond. Gaz.* No. 2054/3 The *Larks* Boat being Commanded by Captain Leightons Brother, the *Bonadventures* Pinnace by Mr. Harrises accompanied with Mr. Littleton, and the Yaule by Mr. Brisbane. **1687** W. HEDGES *Diary* (Hakl. Soc.) I. 240 Capt. Milborne, perceiving yͤ Hazard, came off in his Yall to our assistance. **1742** WOODROOFE in Hanway *Trav.* (1762) I. II. xvii. 76 We had..a long-boat of five tuns, and a yaul, each with six oars. **1775** DALRYMPLE in *Phil. Trans.* LXVIII. 397 Hove the ship to, and sent jolly boat and yawl in search of him. **1776** *Pennsylvania Even. Post* 4 June 280/2 A small Youghall belonging to some vessel. **1834** MARRYAT *P. Simple* xxxiii, The launch, yawl, first and second cutters, were the boats appointed for the expedition. **1875** KNIGHT *Dict. Mech.*, *Yawl*..In the British navy it is the fifth boat in point of size; the others being the launch, long-boat, barge, and pinnace.

2. A small sailing-boat of the cutter class, with a jigger.

1684 *Lond. Gaz.* No. 1898/4 Some Deal men have tried to go off to her in one of our Yaules. **1692** *Ibid.* No. 2808/4 A Deale built Yawl with 6 Oars. **1713** *Order in Council* 13 Sept. in *Lond. Gaz.* No. 5155/1 There came on Board the said Bark Seven Men in a Deal-Yawl. **1798** CRUTTWELL *Gazetteer* (1808) III. s.v. *Orkney*, The inhabitants..sail from island to island in small boats, called yoals. **1873** *Daily News* 22 Aug., The Pantomime takes the schooners' prize, the Oimara that for cutters, and the Florinda for yawls.

3. A small kind of fishing-boat.

1670 J. SMITH *Eng. Improv. Reviv'd* 254 The Commodities of Shotland which the Inhabitants do for the most part Trade withal is Ling and Cod, which they take with Hooks and Lines in small Boats, called Yalls, about the bigness of Gravesend Oars. **1854** H. MILLER *Sch. & Schm.* iii. (1858) 42 All sorts of barques and carvels, from the fishing yawl to the frigate. **1865** *Leeds Mercury* 22 Feb., Three more of the fishing yawls being missing.

4. *attrib.* and *Comb.*

1865 *Guardian* 17 May 478 A yawl-boat was landed bottom up from the hurricane-deck upon the heads of those below. **1881** MISS BRADDON *Asphodel* xvi, His little yawl-rigged yacht. **1894** HALL CAINE *Manxman* VI. i, Pete began to think of buying a Dandie, which being smaller than a Nickey, and of yawl rig, he could sail of himself.

yawl (jɔːl), *sb.*[2] [f. YAWL *v.*[1]] An act of 'yawling'; a shout, yell.

1728 FIELDING *Love in several Masques* IV. ii, To me, the Turkish Yawl at an On-set, the Irish Howl at a Funeral, or the Indian Exclamation at an Eclipse, are all soft Musick to that single Noise.

yawl (jɔːl), *v.*[1] Now *dial.* Forms: 4–5 **ȝaule,** 4, 7–8 **yall,** 6 **yalle,** 6–7 **yaule, yawle,** 7–8 **yaul,** 8–9 **yole,** 7– **yawl.** [Parallel to YOWL, with alternation of vowel designed to express a variety of the sound echoed. Cf. LG. *jaueln* (of cats).]

1. *intr.* **a.** To cry out loudly from pain, grief, or distress: also said of the howling of dogs, the 'wauling' of cats, the screaming of peacocks.

13.. *Gaw. & Gr. Knt.* 1453 He hurtez of þe houndez, & þay Ful ȝomerly ȝaule & ȝelle. *c* **1395** *Plowman's Tale* 386 To catche catell as covytous As hound, that for hunger woll yall [*rime* fall]. *c* **1400** *Anturs Arth.* ix, Hit ȝaulut, hit ȝamurt, lyke a woman. *Ibid.* vii. (Douce MS.) Ther come a lede of þe lawe..ȝauland and ȝomerand, with many loude ȝelles. **1615** BRATHWAIT *Strappado* (1878) 178 In hels abisse: Where they may yaule and yarme til that they burst. **1621** J. TAYLOR (Water P.) *Begger* B iv, I (like many other froward boyes) Would yaule, and baule, and make a wawling noyse. **1681** HICKERINGILL *Sin Man-Catching* I. 16 The little Peacocks shreame out and yawle amain, pluming themselves. *a* **1825** FORBY *Voc. E. Anglia* s.v., The cry of a peacock is an excellent instance of yawling. **1833** TENNYSON *Goose* ix, Then yelp'd the cur, and yawl'd the cat. **1870** E. PEACOCK *Ralf Skirl.* II. 193 Give a look to that bairn, it yawls sorely.

b. To call aloud, shout, bawl, scream, vociferate.

1542 UDALL *Erasm. Apoph.* 288 Cato right eagrely yallyng at Pompeius. **1620** QUARLES *Feast for Wormes* iii. D ij b, The haplesse Pylot..mainly calls; Calls *Ionah, Ionah*; and yet lowder yawles. **1719** DE FOE *Crusoe* II. (Globe) 405 They all ran skreaming and yawling away. **1808** JAMIESON, *To Yaul*, to yell.

transf. **1575** *Gammer Gurton* II. i, My gutts they yawle crawle and all my belly rumbleth.

2. *trans.* **a.** (with *simple obj.* or *obj. cl.*) To shout out, utter with shouting.

1542 UDALL *Erasm. Apoph.* 172 b, Thei..whiche yalle and rore, that learnyng..is vtterly nothyng auailable to the gouernaunce..of a commenweale. **1613** WITHER *Abuses Stript* II. iii. Q vj b, Such as haue yauld Ergo in the schooles. *Ibid.*, *Scourge* V ij b, The nimble Tapster..Still yalling, *here, anon sir, by and by.* **1679** *Pol. Ball.* (1860) I. 220 They baul and they yaul aloud thro' the whole town The rights to succession and claims to the Crown. **1859** *Habits of Gd. Society* v. (new ed.) 217 A man..should never yawl out the namby-pamby ballads beloved of young ladies.

b. (with *compl.*) To bring into a specified state by 'yawling'.

a **1627** MIDDLETON *Widow* II. i, Ile make 'em yaul one an other deaf, but ile have thee.

Hence ˈ**yawling** *vbl. sb.* and *ppl. a.*

1568 *Hist. Jacob & Esau* I. i. A ij, The deuill stoppe that same yallyng throte..Somwhiles. **1598** SYLVESTER *Du Bartas* II. ii. II. *Babylon* 228 Nigh breathlesse all, with their confused yawling. **1619** *Pasquil's Palin.* (1877) 146 Young Beagles..Whose yawling throats will never let him sleepe. **1715** *C'tess D'Aunoy's Wks.* 454 The hideous Outcries that he made, and his continual Yauling. **1719** D'URFEY *Pills* III. 31 A Wife, That makes him weary of his Life With Scolding, yoleing in the House.

yawl, *v.*[2] *nonce-wd.* [f. YAWL *sb.*[1]] *trans.* To convey in a yawl.

1884 'MARK TWAIN' *Huck. Finn* xxiv, When we got to the village, they yawled us ashore.

yawl (jɔːl, jɑːl), repr. (Southern) U.S. pronunc. of Y'ALL *pers. pron.*

1919 *Dialect Notes* V. 40 *Yawl*,..you-all. **1938** C. HIMES in *Black on Black* (1973) 167 Why doesn't yuh git happy an' praise de Lawd? Doesn' yawl know who Ah is? **1978** J. R. GASKIN in *Sewanee Rev.* LXXXVI. 426 Dillard accounts for *y'awl*, or *you all*, not as the simple concatenation of two English forms.

yawl, var. YAULD *a.*

yawler[1] (ˈjɔːlə(r)). *rare*[−0]. [f. YAWL *v.*[1] + -ER[1] 2.] One who 'yawls' or howls.

1611 COTGR., *Glatisseur*, a barker; bawler, yawler.

yawler[2] (ˈjɔːlə(r)). Also **yoler.** [f. YAWL *sb.*[1] + -ER[1] 1.] A sailor who rows or sails in a yawl; one of the crew of a yawl.

1833 M. SCOTT *Tom Cringle* xviii, Pipe away the yawlers, boatswain's mate. **1867** *Engineer* 27 Sept. 283/3 'Yolers'.

ˈ**yawling.** *local.* Also 8 **yaulin.** A young herring.

1758 *Descr. Thames* 227 A young Herring is by some termed a Yaulin. **1879** T. SATCHELL *Index Gloss. Fish Names* (E.D.S.) 8 *Clupea Harengus*,..Yarmouth-capon, Yawlings, Whitebait, White-Herring.

yawlsman (ˈjɔːlzmən). *rare*[−1]. [f. *yawl's*, gen. of YAWL *sb.*[1] + MAN *sb.*[1]] = YAWLER[2].

1885 *Chamb. Jrnl.* 15 Aug. 513/2 The bluff yawlsman riding to his nets far out at sea.

yawmer, var. YAMMER *v.*

yawmeter (ˈjɔːmiːtə(r)). [f. YAW *sb.*[1] + -METER.] An instrument used to detect changes in the direction of flow round an aircraft or other body.

1921 *Flight* 28 July 511/1 A new direction and velocity meter (yawmeter) has recently been constructed. **1947** *Jrnl. R. Aeronaut. Soc.* LI. 15/2 We imagine aerofoil and observer to be stationary and the aerofoil to be immersed in a stream of air of speed *V* normal to the span..the direction of the stream being made known to the observer by, for example, a yawmeter. **1969** *Jrnl. Physics E* II. 989/1 Calibration of the instrument as a yawmeter. Most of the tests on the instrument have been made near the outlet end of an open water channel. **1983** *Ibid.* XVI. 231/1 (*heading*) A yawmeter for steady and low-frequency unsteady flows.

yawn (jɔːn), *sb.* [f. YAWN *v.*]

1. Something that yawns; a gaping opening or entrance; *esp.* a chasm, abyss.

1602 MARSTON *Antonio's Rev.* III. iii. Wks. 1856 I. 111 Now gapes the graves, and through their yawnes let loose Imprison'd spirits to revisit earth. **1755** AMORY *Mem.* (1766) II. 56 The billows that were all in wild uproar, and then came down into the dreadful yawn. **1820** L. HUNT *Indicator* No. 22 (1822) I. 170 Trust not the tempting yawn of stable-yard or gateway. *a* **1821** KEATS *Hyperion* I. 120 Spaces of fire, and all the yawn of hell. **1894** *Idler* Sept. 134 The stubborn, wonderful old piece of timber-frame was picked out of the yawn of the hatch in splinters.

2. The or an act of yawning: **a.** Gaping or opening wide.

1697 CONGREVE *Mourn. Bride* II. v, Sure, 'tis the Friendly Yawn of Death for me. **1705** ADDISON *Italy* 248 And sometimes with a mighty Yawn, 'tis said, Opens a dismal Passage to the Dead.

b. Involuntary opening of the mouth, as from drowsiness.

1706 E. WARD *Wooden World Diss.* (1708) 96 After..a few hearty Yawns, he crawls up upon Deck. **1712** STEELE *Spect.* No. 320 ¶5 Our Salutation at Entrance is a Yawn and a Stretch. **1742** POPE *Dunc.* IV. 343 She..heard thy everlasting yawn confess The Pains and Penalties of Idleness. **1875** TENNYSON *Q. Mary* I. iii, A life of nods and yawns.

c. *transf.* and in *transf.* contexts, denoting something that induces boredom; a tedious activity. *colloq.*

1889 E. C. DOWSON *Let.* 3 Feb. (1967) 32 My dear Moore. Here goes for my accustomed Sunday yawn to you! Thanks for your note. **1974** D. GRAY *Dead Give Away* ii. 24 To you it may be one big yawn, or the laugh of a life-time... But to me it's important. **1978** G. A. SHEEHAN *Running & Being* viii. 102 For them the Super Bowl is three hours of yawns. **1979** *Broadcast* 4 June 8/3, 7 June will be a major event for psephologists..if..a yawn a minute for British voters. **1984** *Times* 3 Oct. 13/1 So much proscription may sound like a recipe for a great gastronomic yawn.

Hence (*nonce-wds.*) **'yawnful** *a.*, **'yawnfully** *adv.*, **'yawnish** *a.*, **'yawnless** *a.*, **'yawnsome** *a.*, **'yawnsomely** *adv.*

1855 ANNE MANNING *Old Chelsea Bun-Ho.* ix. 156, I awoke..chilly and yawnish. **1878** J. THOMSON *Plenip. Key* 26 His mouth and arms stretched yawnful. **1881** J. M. BROWN *Student Life* 4 A yawnless languor. **1898** *Blackw. Mag.* Apr. 498/1 Fifty dull, stiff-jointed, yawnful years. **1900** *Yorksh. Post* 28 July 6/6 A jaded and yawnsome and even jaundiced assemblage. **1908** *Standard* 18 Feb. 7 A..yawnsomely dull debate. **1914** W. DE MORGAN *When Ghost meets Ghost* I. xviii. 691 'On my way to Poynders,' said the Countess yawnfully.

yawn (jɔːn), *v.* Forms: α. 1 **ȝinian, ȝyn-, ȝionian, ȝeon-, ieon-, ȝenian,** 3 **ȝeon(i)e, ȝonie,** 3–4 **ȝone, yone,** 3–5 **ȝeone, ȝene, yene,** 4 **ȝyne,** 6 **yeane.** β. 4–5 **ȝane,** 4–6 **yane.** γ. 6–7 **yawne,** 6–8 **yaun,** 6– **yawn.** [OE. *ȝinian, ȝeonian* = OHG. *ginôn, -ên* (MHG. *ginen*), MDu. *gênen* to gape, yawn, related to the synonymous OE. *gánian* GANE *v.* (q.v.), OHG. *geinôn*, and OE. *ȝinan*, ON. *gína.* The vocalism of the present form of this word is difficult to account for. The normal representatives of the OE. and early ME. forms (*ȝene, ȝone*) would be **yeen* and **yoan.* Later ME. *yane* prob. arose through regional contact with GANE *v.* The 16th cent. *yaun, yawn*, may have been the result of special local development of *yane* or *yone.*]

†**1.** *intr.* To open the mouth wide voluntarily, esp. in order to swallow or devour something; in early use often, to have the mouth wide open; to gape. Said also of the mouth. *Obs.*

α. *c* **725** *Corpus Gloss.* (Hessels) B 24 *Battat*, ȝeonath. *Ibid.* G 4 *Garrit*, ȝionat. *c* **1000** *Sax. Leechd.* II. 50 Bewyl twy dæl on wætre ȝeot on bollan & ȝeona ymb. *c* **1000** *Ags. Ps.* (Th.) xxi. 11 [xxii. 13] Hi todydon heora muð onȝean me, swa swa leo, þonne he ȝeonað. *a* **1100** *Aldhelm Gloss.* I. 2409 (Napier 65) *Hiulco, i. aperto*, ieoniendum. *rostro, i. ore*, bile. *a* **1225** *Ancr. R.* 242 3if þu iseie..ȝeonien wide uppon þe, þene deouel of helle. *a* **1250** *Owl & Night.* 292 þat me ne chide wit þe gidie Ne wit þan ofne me ȝonie. *a* **1290** *S. Eustace* 156 in Horstm. *Altengl. Leg.* (1881) 214 A wilde lioun..kipt his ȝonge sone anon, On him he ȝenede wide. **13..** *Sir Beues* (A.) 2763 ȝenande & gapande on him so, Ase he wolde him swolwe þo. **13..** *K. Alis.* 485 (Linc. Inn MS.) Him þouȝte a goshauk wiþ gret flyȝt Setliþ on his herberyng And ȝeniþ [*Laud MS.* ȝyneþ] and sprad abrod his wyngyn. *c* **1400** *Arth. & Merl.* 1583 (Linc. Inn MS.) His mouþ and þrote ȝonede wide. **14..** *Ibid.* 1117 (Douce MS.) And wiþ his mouþ he ȝenede wyde. *c* **1450** *Mirk's Festial* 200 Then anon come..a gret horryble dragon and ȝeonet [*v.r.* ȝanyng] on her.

β. **13..** *Coer de L.* 276 Upon hys crest a raven stode, That yaned as he wer wode. **1382** WYCLIF *2 Macc.* vi. 18 Eleasarus..ȝanynge [*v.r.* ȝonyng] with open mouth, was compellid for to ete swynys flesh. **1398** TREVISA *Barth. De P.R.* XII. x. (Tollem. MS.), The rauen biholdeþ þe mouþe of hire briddes, whan þey ȝaneþ. *Ibid.* XVI. vi, [Auripigmentum] helpeþ tisik..if þey ȝaneþ þeron and takeþ þe smoke þerof. **1555** EDEN *Decades* (Arb.) 151 Multitudes of Crocodiles lyinge in the sande, and yanyng to take the heate of the soonne.

γ. **1568** HACKET tr. *Thevet's New found World* xx. 32 This fish is named Marsouin,..he hath..on the heade a certayne cundite or opening, by the which he yawneth or pupeth, euen as the Whale [orig. Fr. *par lequel il respire ainsi que la balene*]. **1603** HOLLAND *Plutarch's Mor.* 970 The crocodiles ..yawne and offer there teeth unto them to be picked and clensed with there hands.

2. To lie, stand, or be wide open, as a chasm, abyss, or the like; to have or form a wide opening, gap, or chasm.

α. *c* **890** WÆRFERTH tr. *Gregory's Dial.* 52 Beneoðan swiðe deop niwolnys ȝinode [*v.r.* ȝeonode]. *a* **1225** *Ancr. R.* 304 Bineoðen us, ȝeoniinde wide þe wide þreote of helle. *c* **1450** *Mirk's Festial* 4 Vndyr hym helle ȝeonyng, and galpyng, and spyttyng fyre.

γ. **1599** SHAKS. *Hen. V*, IV. vi. 14 The gashes That bloodily did yawne vpon his face. **1742** YOUNG *Nt. Th.* VI. 730 Wide yawns the gap; connexion is no more. **1795** COWPER *Needless Alarm* 14 And where the land slopes to its wat'ry bourn, Wide yawns a gulph beside a ragged thorn. **1810** SCOTT *Lady of L.* II. xxxi, As sudden ruin yawned around. **1829** —— *Anne of G.* xxxiii, A private staircase which yawned in the floor to admit their descent. **1865** GOSSE *Land & Sea* (1874) 241 The beach yawning some thirty feet below. **1877** MISS A. B. EDWARDS *Up Nile* xxi. 648 Here yawns a great pit half full of débris. **1890** W. CLARK RUSSELL *Ocean Trag.* ii, It was the Isle of Wight, and the shore on either hand went yawning to it till it looked a day's sail away.

fig. **1580** SPENSER *Let. to Harvey* H.'s Wks. (Grosart) I. 35 The onely, or chiefest hardnesse,..is in the Accente: whyche sometime gapeth, and as it were yawneth ilfauouredly.

†**3.** *to yawn after* or *for*, to be eager to obtain, to long for. *Obs.*

a **1250** *Owl & Night.* 1403 þe gost..ȝeoneþ after more & more An lutel rehþ of milce & ore. **1576** FLEMING *Panopl. Epist.* 283 After he hath caught that within his clawes, after which he was euer yawning. **1594** HOOKER *Eccl. Pol.* Pref. iv. §3 The chiefest thing which lay reformers yawne for is, that the Cleargie may..be Apostolicall.

4. To make involuntarily a prolonged inspiration with the mouth wide open and the lower jaw much depressed, as from drowsiness or fatigue.

α. **1450–80** tr. *Secr. Secr.* xxxiv. 23 Suche a man yeneth often, and hath sumtime disese in his eyen. **1547** BOORDE *Brev. Health* cxlvii. 54 The pacient wyll be colde and oft yeane or gape, yf this feuer be putryfied. **1598** BP. HALL *Sat.* VI. ii. 101 Had he heard the Female Fathers grone, Yeaning in mids of her procession.

β. *c* **1430** *How Good Wife taught Dau.* 56 in *Babees Bk.* (1868) 38 Lauȝe þou not to loude, ne ȝane þou not to wide. *a* **1529** SKELTON *E. Rummyng* 331 She began to yane and gaspy. **1548** UDALL *Erasm. Par. Luke* viii. 78 [He] wil stande gapyng & yanyng whan he should geue eare as though he wer more then half in slepe. **1557** EDGEWORTH *Serm.* 261 He yaned seuen tymes, and opened his eyes, reuiued, and liued. **1570** LEVINS *Manip.* 19/7 To Gane, yane, *oscitare.*

γ. **1549** COVERDALE, etc. *Erasm. Par. Thess.* 7 Those that yawne and slumbre in naughtinesse, are occupied in darknesse of the soule. **1622** GATAKER *Spirituall Watch* (ed. 2) 67 The very sight of those that yawne is wont to set others also on yawning. **1721** BOLINGBROKE in *Swift's Lett.* (1766) II. 41 You shall be forced to read it out, though you yawn from the first to the last page. **1836** J. H. BARROW *Mirr. Parl.* I. 818/1 Mr. O'Connell here yawned so loudly as to interrupt the Honourable Member. **1852** THACKERAY *Esmond* III. iii, It must be owned that the audience yawned through the play; and that it perished on the third night. **1880** 'OUIDA' *Moths* ii, I thought I should have yawned till I broke my neck.

b. To open the mouth wide from surprise or the like; to gape. *Obs.* or *dial.*

1604 SHAKS. *Oth.* v. ii. 101 Me thinkes, it should be now a huge Eclipse Of Sunne, and Moone; and that th'affrighted Globe Did yawne at Alteration. **1607** —— *Cor.* III. ii. 11 To shew bare heads In Congregations, to yawne, be still, and wonder [etc.]. **1887** F. T. HAVERGAL *Heref. Gloss.*, *Yarning*, = staring. 'Stand *yarning* there'. E.

c. *trans.* To say or utter with a yawn or with wide-open mouth. Also with cognate object.

1718 ROWE tr. *Lucan* I. 394 Scorning the wound he [*sc.* the lion] yawns a dreadful roar. **1828** MACAULAY *Poems, Political Georgics* 30 Let all in bulky majesty appear, Roll the dull eye, and yawn th'unmeaning cheer. **1854** DICKENS *Hard T.* III. ii, 'It wouldn't be bad', he yawned at one time, 'to give the waiter five shillings, and throw him.' **1897** MARY KINGSLEY *W. Africa* 243 One immense fellow..yawns a yawn a yard wide.

d. To bring into some position or condition by, or to the accompaniment of, yawning; also *occas.*, to pass through in a lethargic manner.

1742 YOUNG *Nt. Th.* III. 336 For what live ever here?.. To surfeit on the same, And yawn our joys? *Ibid.* VIII. 614 No man e'er found a happy life by chance; Or yawn'd it into being, with a wish. **1817** LADY MORGAN *France* II. (1818) I. 247 The *Dalai lamas* of *haut ton*, who yawn away their existence in the assemblies of London. **1880** *Daily News* 29 Oct. 6/2 He literally yawned us out of the room. *a* **1903** 'H. S. MERRIMAN' *Last Hope* i, He..politely yawned that reminiscent fish-curer into silence.

5. *intr.* To open wide as a mouth; to form a chasm; to gape, part asunder.

1599 SHAKS. *Much Ado* v. iii. 19 Graues yawne and yeelde your dead. **1667** MILTON *P.L.* VI. 875 Hell at last Yawning receavd them whole, and on them clos'd. *a* **1700** EVELYN *Diary* 7 Feb. 1645, The sea retiring neere 200 paces, and yawning on the sudaine, it continued to vomit forth flames and fiery stones. **1713** YOUNG *Last Day* I. 87 The valleys [shall] yawn, the troubled ocean roar. **1820** SCOTT *Monast.* xii, If the earth yawned and gave up a demon. **1848** DICKENS *Dombey* lvi, When the silent tomb shall yawn, Captain Gills, I shall be ready for burial; not before. **1852** TENNYSON *Ode Wellington* 269 The black earth yawns: the mortal disappears; Ashes to ashes, dust to dust.

6. *trans.* To cause to open wide.

1382 WYCLIF *Ps.* xxxiv. [xxxv.] 21 Thei ȝeneden [*v.r.* maden large, *Vulg.* dilataverunt] their mouth upon me. *a* **1653** G. DANIEL *Idyll.* II. 31 The monstrous Whale (w[ch] Roles The Ocean, wth his Breath, and Yawnes the Brine As its Recesse). **1798** SOUTHEY *Grandmother's Tale* 85 She stood beside the murderer's bed, and yawn'd Her ghastly wound.

7. To make, produce, or afford by opening wide.

1605 SYLVESTER *Du Bartas* II. iii. III. *Law* 1220 The groaning Earth..Tearing her rocks, untill she Yawn a way To let it out, and to let-in the Day. **1818** BYRON *Ch. Har.* IV. lxiii, None felt stern Nature..yawning forth a grave for those who lay Upon their bucklers for a winding-sheet. **1821** —— *Sardanap.* II. i. 422 The realm itself, in all its wide extension, Yawns dungeons at each step for thee and me. **1907** *Smart Set* Mar. 41/2 The prison doors were yawning a welcome for the runaways.

8. *Comb.* **yawn-mouthed** *a.*, yawning, gaping.

1861 CHR. ROSSETTI *Prince's Progr.* xxix, Out it [*sc.* a light] flashed from a yawn-mouthed cave, Like a red-hot eye from a grave.

yawner ('jɔːnə(r)). [f. YAWN *v.* + -ER[1].]

1. a. One who yawns, as from drowsiness.

1687 MIÈGE *Gt. Fr. Dict.* I, *C'est un Baailleur perpetual*, he is an everlasting Yawner. **1818** BENTHAM *Ch. Engl.* 130 To procure upon an average half a dozen voluntary yawners, in addition to the compulsory ones. **1897** *Voice* (N.Y.) 9 Sept. 5/5 The yawner..is not being intentionally rude, but is exercising muscles which have been for a long time inactive.

b. *transf.* Something dreary or boring. *colloq.* (orig. *U.S.*).

1942 BERREY & VAN DEN BARK *Amer. Thes. Slang* §276/2 *Something uninteresting*,..washout, yawner. **1969** A. GLYN *Dragon Variation* ii. 42 The game between him and Wheaton, still to be played, should be a real yawner. **1980** *Globe & Mail* (Toronto) 5 Nov. 17 (*heading*) The Awakening is a real yawner. **1983** *Chicago Sun-Times* 6 Aug. 76 (*heading*) Opener likely to be yawner.

2. Something that yawns; a wide ditch.

1832 *Egan's Bk. Sports* 220/2 Sir Francis Burdett, sitting erect upon Sampson, and putting his head straight at a yawner. **1852** R. S. SURTEES *Sponge's Sp. Tour* vii. **1862** *Sporting Mag.* June 511 In clearing a yawner The King of the Valley covered the extraordinary space of 31 feet.

yawning ('jɔːnɪŋ), *vbl. sb.* [f. YAWN *v.* + -ING[1].] The action of the verb YAWN.

1. The action of opening the mouth wide, esp. involuntarily from drowsiness.

c **725** *Corpus Gloss.* (Hessels) B 23 *Barritus*, ȝenung. *c* **1050** *Voc.* in Wr.-Wülcker 412/5 *Garrulitas*, ȝeonung. *c* **1440** *Promp. Parv.* 536/1 ȝanynge, or gapynge wythe the mowthe .., *hiatus.* **1552** HULOET, Yauninge, *oscedo.* **1581** MULCASTER *Positions* xv. 69 Those..that be cumbred with much gaping & yawning. **1605** WILLET *Hexapla Gen.* 353 Yawning in trauaile to women is mortall. **1707** PRIOR *Sat. Poets* 200 Your Yawning prompts me to give o'er. **1755** STRYPE *Stow's Surv.* II. 774/1 Near to this, is a large handsome Monument, erected to the Memory of James Cooper of this Parish, Gent. remarkable for his loud Yawning during the Time of Divine Service. **1838** W. C. HARRIS *Narr. Exped. S. Africa* 15 [They] were very slow in taking the hint conveyed by his violent yawnings, that he was anxious to retire to rest. **1899** *Allbutt's Syst. Med.* VIII. 98 Abnormal visceral or reflex movements such as paroxysmal hurry of the heart, or of respiration—sneezings, yawnings, or hiccoughings.

†**2.** Longing *after* (something). *Obs.*

1634 RAINBOW *Labour* (1635) 33 Ambitious yawning after outward dignitie and honour.

3. The action of opening wide.

1820 W. IRVING *Sketch Bk.* (1859) 7 The yawning of a seam [in a boat].

yawning ('jɔːnɪŋ), *ppl. a.* [f. YAWN *v.* + -ING[2].] That yawns.

1. That opens the mouth wide, esp. in order to swallow or devour something; chiefly *transf.* of the mouth, wide open.

c **890** WÆRFERTH tr. *Gregory's Dial.* 156 He ȝemette on þam weȝe standan sumne dracan onȝæn hine mid ȝeniendum [*v.r.* ȝiniendum] muþe. *a* **1225** *Ancr. R.* 80 Ne blowe ȝe hire nout ut mid maðelinde muðe, ne mid ȝeoniinde tuteles. **13..** *Guy Warw.* (A.) 4117 A lyoun þai seye cominde þo,..Wiþ ȝenende [**14..** *Caius MS.* yanyng] mouþe, & weri he was. *c* **1475** *Partenay* 5852 An horrible serpent..With a yanyng throte gain hym gan Auaunce. **1555** EDEN *Decades* (Arb.) 187 As thoughe they wolde with yanynge mouthes haue torne in sunder the bealy of the mannes Image. **1593** SHAKS. *2 Hen. VI*, IV. i. 73 Now will I dam vp this thy yawning mouth, For swallowing the Treasure of the Realme. **1617** J. TAYLOR (Water P.) *Three Weekes Observ.* B iv b, His eies well dried, would make good Tennis-balls,..his yawning mouth would serue for a Conniborrow. **1693** CONGREVE in *Dryden's Juvenal* xi. (1697) 289 Large yawning Panthers.

2. Opening, or open wide, as the earth, a chasm, abyss, etc.

c **893** ÆLFRED *Oros.* Contents III. iii, Hu Marcus Curtius besceat on þa ȝeniȝendan [*v.r.* ȝyniendan] eorþan. *c* **900** tr. *Bæda's Hist.* IV. xxi. [xix.] (1890) 322 For openre wunde & ȝeoniendre. **1590** SPENSER *F.Q.* I. xi. 35 He..Vpon his crested scalpe so sore did smite, That to the scull a yawning wound it made. **1667** MILTON *P.L.* x. 635 Both Sin, and Death, and yawning Grave. **1780** COWPER *Progr. Err.* 172 Cards, with what rapture, and the polish'd die, The yawning chasm of indolence supply! **1830** LYELL *Princ. Geol.* xxiv. I. 420 Many houses were swallowed up by the yawning earth, which closed immediately over them. **1860** TYNDALL *Glac.* II. xxv. 363 Strains which, having once rent the ice, tend subsequently to..produce yawning crevasses. **1884** GILMOUR *Mongols* 87 A lofty pass..surrounded with yawning precipices.

3. That yawns from weariness; *transf.* characterized by or producing yawning, drowsy, sleepy.

1575 GASCOIGNE *Flowers* Wks. 1907 I. 58 The stretching armes, y[e] yauning breath, which I to bedward use. **1599** SHAKS. *Hen. V*, I. ii. 204 The sad-ey'd Iustice..Deliuering ore to Executors pale The lazie yawning Drone. **1605** —— *Macb.* III. ii. 43 The shard-borne Beetle, with his drowsie hums, Hath rung Nights yawning Peale. **1617** HIERON *Wks.* II. 108 Many formall, idle, and (as I may call them) yawning requests for mercy. **1649** JER. TAYLOR *Gt. Exemp.* II. Disc. ix. 122 It is impossible to prevent them..any more than we can..refuse to yawn when I see a yawning sleepy person. **1740** RICHARDSON *Pamela* (1824) I. 204 Everyone sees that the yawning husband, and the vapourish wife, are truly insupportable to one another. **1764** WILKES *Corr.* (1805) II. 96 The account of the character of Mr. Legge is the most yawning pamphlet I ever read. **1826** SCOTT *Woodst.* xv, Here am I..ready to fight, if this yawning fit will give me leave. **1848** DICKENS *Dombey* xxx, The yawning, shaking, peevish figure of the mother.

Hence **'yawningly** *adv.*

1629 BP. HALL *Hypocrite* Wks. 1634 II. 361 Leaning upon your idle elbow yawningly. **1840** *Fraser's Mag.* XXII. 17 The caliph received..yawningly the countless homages.

1876 Miss Broughton *Joan* I. x, She looks out yawningly towards her friend, the sea.

yawny ('jɔːnɪ), *a.* Also **yawney**. [f. yawn *sb.* or *v.* + -y¹.] Characterized by yawns or (much) yawning; inclined to, or provocative of, yawning.

1805 [implied in *yawniness*]. **1813** *Examiner* 1 Feb. 74/2 His laugh relaxed into a yawny simper. **1830** *Ibid.* 410/2 His Discourses are.. what our departed friend Nollekens would have described as 'yawney'—that is, somewhat heavy. **1888** Meredith *Let. to Miss Meredith* 5 Jan., Bruny and Koby in Lapinland last night, very yawny to-day.

Hence **'yawniness.**

1805 Southey in Robberds *Mem. W. Taylor* (1843) II. 115 The old yawniness comes on at times. **1898** Shiel *Yellow Danger* 176 The day has that very-early-morning grayness for which one can find no adjective to express its utter yawniness.

yawp, yaup (jɔːp), *sb.* Also **yop**. [f. next.]

a. A harsh, hoarse, or querulous cry, esp. of a bird.

1824 Mactaggart *Gallovid. Encycl.*, *Yawp*, the cry of a sickly bird; or one in distress. **1879** Black *Macleod of D.* ix, The eagle raised its great wings, and.. flapped them.. while it uttered a succession of shrill yawps. **1905** *Sat. Rev.* 12 Aug. 207/2 He can only tell us how bad he is by hideous grimaces and inarticulate yawps.

b. *fig.* Applied in contempt to speech or utterance likened to this. Chiefly *U.S.*, sometimes in allusion to Whitman's use.

1835 J. H. Ingraham *South-West* I. 29 'Hold your yaup, you youngster you,' roared the old man in reply. **1844** 'Jonathan Slick' *High Life N. York* I. 114 He looked round as if he wanted to say something..; but I told him to go ahead and hold his yop. **1855** W. Whitman *Leaves of Grass* 55, I sound my barbaric yawp over the roofs of the world. **1870** 'Mark Twain' in *Galaxy* Oct. 571/1 He.. ordered me to 'hold my yop'. **1882** Stevenson *Fam. Stud.* 93 When Mr. Spencer found his Synthetic Philosophy reverberated from the other shores of the Atlantic in the 'barbaric yawp' of Whitman. **1904** *Buffalo* (N.Y.) *Commercial* 25 Aug. 6 When this contest is ended, the insincere and ridiculous yawp about the fierce belligerency of Theodore Roosevelt will be laid away with the other feeble fakes. **1973** *Publishers' Weekly* 26 Mar. 61/3 American readers may miss the experimentation and 'barbaric yawp' of avant-garde American poetry.

yawp, yaup (jɔːp), *v.* Chiefly *dial.* Also 4 **ȝolp**, 6 **yaulpe, yolp(e**, 6–7 **yalp**, 7, 9 **yope**. [Echoic. Cf. yap *v.* and yelp *v.*]

1. a. *intr.* To shout or exclaim hoarsely; to yelp, as a dog; to cry harshly or querulously, as a bird.

13.. *E.E. Allit. P.* B. 846 What! þay ȝeȝed & ȝolped of ȝestande sorȝe. *a* **1560** Phaer *Æneid* ix. (1562) Eeijb, Thereupon men shout, yᵗ hye heauen yalping yells. **1573** Baret *Alv.* Y 3 To Yaulpe and barke like a dogge, and a foxe, *gannio.* **1580** Fulke *Retentive* 51 They like impudent dogges yolpe & barke against vs. **1599** Sandys *Europæ Spec.* (1632) 114 To stop their adversaries mouthes, alwayes yolping and crying with hatefull sounds. **1623** Jobson *Golden Trade* 145 The Lyon.. remaines feeding.. whilest his small seruant [*sc.* the Jackal] stands barking, and yalping by. **1654–1787** [implied in *yawper* (*yoper*), *yawping*: see below]. **1802** Sibbald *Chron. Scot. Poetry* IV. Gloss., *Yaup*, ..more commonly denotes the incessant crying of birds. **1880** *Spec. Westmoreland Dial.* II. 52 (E.D.D.) We yoped an' shoot't ta egg folk on. **1885** *Letts's Househ. Mag.* 620/2 'That's it!' yawped Mr. Spoopendyke. 'You've been thinking again!' **1915** *Daily Mail* 12 Mar. 4/5 The Press of the Fatherland yelped and yawped at America's heels.

b. To speak foolishly or noisily. *U.S. colloq.*

1872 S. Hale *Let.* 28 Oct. (1919) 90 Perhaps it is just as well, however, not to yawp much about our going *alone*, as it may be considered loose in America. **1926** T. Beer *Mauve Decade* vi. 233 Where the boys who badgered Richard Harding Davis for autographs in 1890 will be yawping over 'Billy Baxter's Letters' in 1900.

2. *trans.* To utter with a strident or harsh voice.

1567 Painter *Pal. Pleas.* II. 161 b, To pacify this immoderate rage which in vaine yᵘ yalpest forth against this troupe. **1596** Nashe *Saffron Walden* Wks. (Grosart) III. 198 What more haue I in my Proclamation to yalp out?

3. *intr.* To gape. *dial.* (Cf. gawp *v.*)

1836 Haliburton *Clockm.* Ser. I. xxxi, They stand starin and yawpin, all eyes and mouth. **1895** *Pall Mall Mag.* Jan. 7 'Sue! Wot yer yawpin' at thar?'

Hence **'yawping, yauping** *vbl. sb.* and *ppl. a.*; also **'yawper, yauper (yoper)**, one that yawps.

1576 Fleming tr. *Caius' Dogs* (1880) 31 The older dogges ..cease from yolping. **1599** Nashe *Lenten Stuffe* Wks. (Grosart) V. 214 The apostacie of the sands from the yalping world was so great, that they ioynd themselues to the maine land of Eastflege. **1654** Gataker *Disc. Apol.* 97 The yalping of maungie Whelps. **1678** E. Howard *Man of Newmarket* iv. i. 43 Thou art so earnest still to follow Yopers, that make so much haste to devour a simple Hare. **1787** Grose *Provinc. Gloss.* (1790), *Yaaping*, crying in despair, lamenting. Applied to chickens lamenting the absence of their parent hen. **1825** Jamieson, *Yauping, part. adj.*, ill-natured, peevish. **1846** Worcester, *Yauper*, one that yaups. *A. Everett.* **1896** Crockett *Grey Man* xxxvii, The.. yawping and crying of the seabirds. **1899** Jesse L. Williams *Stolen Story* etc. 206 When the time came,.. a goodly number of these same yawping lads went to the front to get shot at.

yaws (jɔːz). [Origin uncertain; identity with pian *sb.* has been suggested (*N. & Q.* Ser. x. I. 5).] A contagious disease of tropical countries, characterized by raspberry-like excrescences or tubercles on the skin; also called *frambœsia*. Also *attrib.* See also yaw *sb.*²

1679 Trapham *Disc. Health Jamaica* ix. 113 Both which quarters of the world [*sc.* American and African deserts] bring forth the monstrous Yaws as a proper Stock to engraft a new cion of Disease. **1739** Huxham in *Phil. Trans.* XLI. 667 He had frequent impure Conversation with some of the Negro Hussies (who probably laboured under the worst Species of Pox, called the Yaws). **1766** Hillary *Air of Barbadoes* 346 Whether it be the *Yaws* or a sort of itch which the Negroes call in their language *Crowcrow*. **1804** Southey in C. C. Southey *Life* (1849) II. 257 The yellow fever will not take root in a negro, nor the yaws in a white man. **1897** *Allbutt's Syst. Med.* II. 502 Paulet, who inoculated healthy negroes with yaws-fluid. *Ibid.* 506 Syphilis never itches, yaws nearly always does. **1898** P. Manson *Trop. Diseases* xxvii. 430 Yaws virus applied to a pre-existing ulcer may.. cause it to fungate like an ordinary yaw.

yawy ('jɔːɪ), *a.* Also **yawey**. [f. yaw(s, yaw *sb.*² + -y¹.] Affected with or characteristic of yaws.

1679 Trapham *Disc. Health Jamaica* ix. 119 The Yawy Patients. **1744** *Med. Essays Soc. Edinb.* V. II. 794 The Yawy Matter. **1888** *Encycl. Brit.* XXIV. 732/2 If the yawey matter finds access to a pre-existing sore or ulcer.

yaw-yaw ('jɔː'jɔː), *v.* [Cf. yaw *int.*] *intr.*

a. To say 'yaw! yaw!'; to talk affectedly. **b.** To utter inarticulate cries resembling the syllables 'yaw, yaw'. Hence **yawyawdom** (*nonce-wd.*), an affected expression.

1854 Dickens *Hard T.* II. ii, They liked fine gentlemen... They became exhausted in imitation of them; and they yaw-yawed in their speech like them. **1862** —— in R. C. Lehmann *C. D. as Editor* (1912) 319 The word 'shindy', or any similar yaw-yawdom. **1885** Hornaday *2 Yrs. in Jungle* vi. 63 The jackals.. broke out into a perfect concert of agonized yelping and yaw-yawing.

yawyn, obs. 3 pl. pa. t. of give *v.*

yax(e, dial. ff. axe.

1504 in *Archaeologia* (1846) XXXI. 208, ij. yaxronges weyeng iiij li. et di. **1808** Jamieson, *Yaxe*, an axe, Buchan.

yaxyd: see yasked.

yay (jeɪ), *adv. U.S. slang.* Also **yea**. [Prob. f. yea *adv.*] In phrases ***yay big*** (or ***high***), 'this big', 'this high': freq. accompanied by a gesture indicating the size intended.

1960 Wentworth & Flexner *Dict. Amer. Slang* 591 *Yea big, yea high*, 1. This big, or this high, accompanied with the spreading of the hands to indicate the size; very large, or high, overwhelmingly large or tall. 2. Not very big or high. **1972** T. Kochman *Rappin' & Stylin' Out* 242 Jeff fired on him. He came back and all this was swelled up bout yay big, you know. **1978** P. Theroux *Picture Palace* 259 Why does a daughter of mine, whom I've loved and respected ever since she was yay high, go out of her way to make a jackass of me?

yay, obs. graphic variant of *þay*, they.

‖**yayla** ('jeɪlə). Also 9 **yaila**; **yaylak**. [Turk.] A summer camping-ground in the mountains of Turkestan used by Kurdish and other semi-nomadic peoples; the encampment pitched there.

1864 A. Vambery *Trav. Central Asia* xvi. 308 A Yaylak (summer abode), near to the hill on the sea-shore. **1896** D. G. Hogarth *Wandering Scholar in Levant* iii. 53 Others come and go, and the place of the summer *yaila* is fixed hard by the village itself. **1953** O. Caroe *Soviet Empire* xi. 181 In the same country in winter the *yaylaks* will be deep under snow. **1975** J. Rathbone *Kill Cure* III. ii. 85 At last they had come to the yayla or summer pasture.

Yayoi ('jɑːjɔɪ). The name of a quarter in Tokyo, used *attrib.* and *absol.* to designate a type of early Japanese (wheel-thrown) pottery first discovered at this site in 1884, and hence applied to the mainly neolithic culture characterized by this ware. Cf. Jomon.

1906 N. G. Munro in *Trans. Asiatic Soc. Japan* XXXIV. 24 The pottery.. is called *Yayoishiki*, 'Yayoi sort', because it was first encountered in breaking ground at Yoyoi [*sic*] Street in Tokyo. **1931** G. B. Sansom *Japan* I. i. 3 This latter type is known as the Yayoi type, because of certain characteristic earthenware first found in a neolithic site at a place of that name. **1955** *Far Eastern Q.* XIV. 329 It is not entirely clear why so few workers paid any serious attention until extremely recent years to the archaeology of the Yayoi period. **1960** B. Leach *Potter in Japan* vi. 136 Jomon pottery 3,000 B.C. on to Yayoi from A.D.o. **1968** *Encycl. Brit.* XVIII. 523/3 The prehistoric period in Japan is characterized by two principal cultures known as Jōmon and Yayoi... Yayoi pottery seems to have its beginnings in the 3rd century B.C. and is mostly wheel-thrown. **1970** J. W. Hall *Japan* iii. 19 The Yayoi people brought with them the horse and the cow, though not in abundance.

†**ybake(n** [y- 4], baked.

1340 *Ayenb.* 112 Bread tuies ybake. **1377** Langl. *P. Pl.* B. vi. 184 Benes and bren ybaken togideres. *c* **1430** *Two Cookery-bks.* 54 Tyl it be y-baken y-now. **1513** Douglas *Æneis* xi. xi. 47 The schaft was sad and sound, and weill ybaik [orig. *solidum nodis et robore cocto*].

ybanysshed, banished.

c **1385** [see banish *v.* 2 c]. *c* **1400** tr. *Higden* (Rolls) VII. App. 510 Somme of hem were slayn.. and somme y-banysched.

ybaptized.

1297 [see baptize *v.* 1].

ybarnd: see ybrent.

ybarred, barred.

1377 Langl. *P. Pl.* B. xix. 162 In an hous al bishette & her dore ybarred. **1470–85** Malory *Arthur* xix. v. 780 That wyndowe was y barryd with yron.

ybathed.

c **1300** [see bathe *v.* 3]. *c* **1374** Chaucer *Troylus* iv. 815 With here salte terys Here brest here face y-baþed was ful wete.

ybatrid.

c **1380** [see batter *v.*¹ 1 b].

ybe, yben(e, yby, earlier *ȝebeon, ib(e)on, ibi*, etc. (see be *v.* A. 8).

1297 R. Glouc. (Rolls) 5729 Sein swithin.. þat longe adde vnder erþe ybe. *c* **1320** *Sir Tristr.* 1203 Sche.. sleiȝest had y bene. **1340** *Ayenb.* 239 Ane cite huer he hedde y-by at ane bredale. *a* **1500** *Flower and Leaf* 375 The grete affray That they in greene without had in ybe. **1513** Douglas *Æneis* xi. i. 73 The quhilk Acetes had tofor ybe Squyer to kyng Evander.

ybedded [y- 5], provided with beds.

1377 Langl. *P. Pl.* B. xv. 498 Yuel yclothed [þei] ȝeden, Badly ybedded.

ybede [y- 4, bid *v.*], asked for.

1340 *Ayenb.* 117 Huanne god heþ y-yeue to man þet he him heþ ybede.

ybegunne, begun.

1432–50 tr. *Higden* (Rolls) III. 147 The batelle ybegunne, men of Persides.. fledde.

ybeld: see ybuld.

ybenched [y- 5], furnished with benches.

c **1394** *P. Pl. Crede* 205 An halle.. Wiþ brode bordes aboute y-benched wel clene.

ybent, bent.

c **1330** [see bent *ppl. a.* 2]. **1399** Langl. *Rich. Redeles* III. 214 Grette browis y-bente. **1508** Dunbar *Gold. Targe* 110 Cupide the king, wyth bow in hand ybent. **1579** Hake *Newes out of Powles* (1872) G iij b, That Broking trade might practizd be by men so well ybent. **1595** *Locrine* I. Prol. 9 A dreadfull Archer with his bow ybent.

yber, pa. t. of i-bere *v.*¹

yberyit, obs. Sc. pa. pple. of bury *v.*: see yburied.

ybet(te [beet *v.*], amended; improved; kindled.

c **1000** [see beet *v.* 1]. **1377** Langl. *P. Pl.* B. iv. 93 Bettere is þat bote bale adoun brynge, þan bale be ybette & bote neuere þe bettere. *a* **1400** *Octouian* 235 Anoon a fyer ther was y-beet [*rime* y-set]. **1501** Douglas *Pal. Hon.* Prol. 14 Vapours hote, richt fresche, and weill ybet. **1581** A. Hall *Iliad* II. 19 And to his side a sworde he girt, with golden nayles ybet.

ybete *v.* [y- 3 c], to beat.

1423 Jas. I *Kingis Q.* cxvi, My teris.. That ȝe se on the ground so fast ybete.

ybete(n [beat *v.*¹], beaten.

13.. *K. Alis.* 1518 An ymage.. Y-beten al with gold fyne. **1340** *Ayenb.* 236 Behoueþ þet he by ybeate and y-wesse. *c* **1385** Chaucer *L.G.W.* 1122 *Dido*, Ne coupe of gold with floreynys newe I-bete [*v.rr.* ybet, ybete, ybette]. ? *a* **1400** *Arthur* 609 And Arthour [was] y-bete wyþ wounde. *c* **1520** Skelton *Magnyf.* 2017 Nowe must ye be storm ybeten with showres and raynes.

ybite, bitten.

c **1460** *Stans Puer ad Mensam* in *Rel. Ant.* I. 157 Off brede y-bite no soppis that thu make.

yblamed, blamed.

1377 Langl. *P. Pl.* B. III. 281 Who-so seyth hem sothes is sonnest yblamed.

yblaunchyd, blanched.

c **1430** *Two Cookery-bks.* 31 Draw vppe a þrifti Mylke of Almaundys y-blaunchyd.

ybleft, var. ybleued.

†**y'blent**, *pa. pple.*¹ *Obs.* Also 4 **yblend**. [y- 4, blend *v.*¹] Blinded; dazed; 'clouded'.

a **1225–1450** iblend, iblent [see blend *v.*¹]. **1340** *Ayenb.* 201 Huo þet is beueld mid þo lac he is riȝtuolliche yblent. **1387** Trevisa *Higden* (Rolls) VII. 457 þat was i-blend wiþ [*MS.* γ yblend be] þe chaungynge of hap of mankynde [orig. *hoc obnubilavit sortis humanae varietas*]. *c* **1407** Lydg. *Reson & Sens.* 3659 Shippes.. With her songe so fonned bee, So supprysed, and y-blent. **1423** Jas. I *Kingis Q.* lxxiv, All my body so It hath ouerwent, That of my sicht the vertew hale Iblent. **1590** Spenser *F.Q.* I. ii. 5 The eye of reason was with rage yblent. **1590** Greene *Neuer too late* (1600) 60 Beeing all with cares yblent, When he thought on yeeres mispent.

y'blent, *pa. pple.*² *Obs.* or *arch.* [y- 4, blend *v.*²] Blended, mingled; confused, blurred.

1426 Lydg. *De Guil. Pilgr.* 10978 Thys Rud entendement Ys wyth Rudnesse so yblent, That dyamaunt,.. ys noon.. So indurat.. As he. **1591** Sylvester *Du Bartas* I. iv. 108 When I observe their Light and Heat yblent. **1642** H. More *Song of Soul* I. II. lvi, He was bent To keep the credit which he then had got, As he conceiv'd: for it had been yblent. **1748** Thomson *Cast. Indol.* I. iv, All these sounds yblent inclined all to sleep.

†**yblessed, yblest**, *pa. pple. Obs.* Also 1 **ȝebletsod**, 2 **iblecced, -sced** (see bless *v.*), 4 **ybli(s)ced**, etc. [y- 4.] Blessed, blest.

1297 R. Glouc. (Rolls) 6285 Yblessed be þe moder wombe þat him to monne bere. **13..** *Cursor M.* 23081

(Edinb.) Ybliced folk. **1377** LANGL. *P. Pl.* B. VII. 13 Bisshopes yblessed, ȝif þey ben as þei shulden. **1422** YONGE tr. *Secr. Secr.* xxi. 148 Than was the worlde y-blessyd whan wyse men regnyd. **1591** GREENE *Maiden's Dr.* xxxiv, Bausis and Philemon were iblest For feasting Iupiter in strangers stead.

†**ybleued**, pa. pple. of BELEAVE, to remain.
1340 *Ayenb.* 225 Þe ilke þet is ybleued ine lyue he ssel him loki chastliche.

yblowe, yblown, blown.
1377, *c* **1384** [see BLOW *v.*[1] 13, 17 c]. **14..** *Pol. Poems* (Rolls) II. 245 Ther is a bitter blast yblowe. **1642** H. MORE *Song of Soul* II. I. II. ix, Lest we..be yblown about with wanton wind.

yblynd(ed, blinded, blindfolded.
1387 TREVISA *Higden* (Rolls) VII. 497 Yblynd wiþ þe blasynge of þe snowe. **1426** LYDG. *De Guil. Pilgr.* 3681 Entendement Ys with Ire yblynded so. *c* **1489** CAXTON *Blanchardyn* xxx. 113 The handes ybounde & the eyen yblynded.

yblyndfalled: see BLINDFOLD *v.*
c **1380** *Sir Ferumb.* 3011 Gy of Borgoyngne þar afond y-blyndfalled, and by-bounde.

ybode(n, proclaimed, bidden, prayed.
a **935** *Laws of Æthelstan* II. c. 20 ðif..hit beo seofon nihtum ær ȝeboden ær ðæt ȝemot sy. *c* **1175** *Lamb. Hom.* 69 Þurh festing and þurh wacunge and ec þurh ibodenes biddunge. *c* **1330** *Arth. & Merl.* 498 Of mani noble he nam ȝeme, Þat he hadde y-boden flem. **1387** TREVISA *Higden* (Rolls) VII. 111 Þre dayes fastynge y-bode for þat.

yboffeted, buffeted.
1387 TREVISA *Higden* (Rolls) IV. 261 Þe myȝt in whiche Crist was..i-buffeted [*v.r.* yboffeted].

ybonchyd, = BUNCHED, humped.
1426 LYDG. *De Guil. Pilgr.* 18299 The bo[n]ch..with whiche this folke relygious bene ybonchyd.

ybontyd [BUNT *v.*[3]], sifted.
c **1430** *Two Cookery-bks.* 38 Take Almaunde mylke, & y-bontyd flour.

ybord *v. pseudo-arch.* [see Y- 3 and ABORD *v.* 2], to accost.
1768 DOWNMAN *Land of Muses* xx, Them Alma gracefully y-bording.

yborȝe [Y- 4, BERGH], saved; hence **yborȝing**, *vbl. sb.*, salvation.
1340 *Ayenb.* 121 Vor tuo þinges is þe man yborȝe, be þe be-uliynge of kueade and do þet guode. *Ibid.* 201 Þet his holy zaule..miȝte ysy and knawe god, and al þet him is niede and guod to his yborȝinge.

†**y'born**, *pa. pple. Obs.* (from 16th c. *arch.*) Forms: 1 **ȝeboren**, 2–3 **iboren**, 4–5 **yboren**, **iborne**, 4–6 **yborne**, **ybore**, (6 **ybor**), 4–8 **y-born**. [OE. *ȝeboren*, pa. pple. of OE. *ȝeberan* I-BERE *v.*[1], *beran* BEAR *v.*[1]]

1. Born.
Beowulf 1703 Þæt ðes eorl wære ȝeboren betera. **900–930** *O.E. Chron.* an. 855 (Parker MS.) Itermon Hraþraing, se wæs ȝeboren in þære earce. *c* **1175** *Lamb. Hom.* 55 Weo beon swa his sunes iborene. **13..** *K. Alis.* 5024 Alsone as that childe y-borne is. *a* **1310** in Wright *Lyric P.* xxxix. 110 He is the sloweste mon that ever wes y-boren. *c* **1330** *Arth. & Merl.* 7780 Ywain bastard ybore. *c* **1400** MAUNDEV. (1839) 286 Wommen maken gret Sorwe, whan hire Children ben y born. **1513** DOUGLAS *Æneis* x. Prol. 58 Ne so the Son of hys kynd is ybor, That he a part hes tharof, and na mor. **1634** SIR T. HERBERT *Trav.* 220 Woe be to that Priest yborne That will not cleanly weed his corne. **1642** H. MORE *Song of Soul* I. III. xxxiii, Or was he to continuall pain of God yborn? **1748** THOMSON *Cast. Indol.* II. lxi, Heirs of eternity! yborn to rise Through endless states of being. **1755** MENDEZ *Sqr. Dames* II. xxix. in Dodsley *Coll. Poems* IV. 150 A young swain on Shannon's banks yborn.

2. Borne.
c **725** *Corpus Gloss.* (Hessels) E 390 *Exposito*, ȝeborone. **11..** *O.E. Chron.* an. 3 (MS. F) Þæt cild Crist wearð ȝeboren aȝean of Egiptan. **1297** R. GLOUC. (Rolls) 3442 After þat he was in þe hors bere ybore. *c* **1325** in *Pol. Songs* (Camden) 70 He hath robbed Engelond, the mores, ant the fenne, The gold, ant the selver, ant y-boren henne. *c* **1380** *Sir Ferumb.* 1810 Þe oþre relyqes..þat þou hast away y-born. **1387** TREVISA *Higden* (Rolls) VII. 319 Whanne þei haveþ y-bore doun here enemyes. **1642** H. MORE *Song of Soul* II. III. I. xxv, Fair clustred buildings..with high spires to heaven yborn.

†**yborned**, **ybornsched**: see YBRENT, YBURNUSCHT.

yborwed [Y- 4, BORROW *v.*[1]].
1377 LANGL. *P. Pl.* B. xv. 307 Fonde þei þat Freres wolde forsake her almesses, And bidden hem bere it þere it was yborwed.

ybosted, boasted.
1377 LANGL. *P. Pl.* B. XVII. 59 Hope cam hippyng after þat hadde so ybosted.

ybought, pa. t. of I-BYE, to buy.
1446 ? LYDG. *Nightingale Poems* i. 396 This blessid lord þat..Vpon a crosse oure soules dere y-bought.

ybought, -oht, -oȝt, pa. pple. of BUY *v.* or I-BYE *v.*
c **1300** *Harrow. Hell* (L.) 182 For my deþ wes monkune yboht.

†**ybound**, *pa. pple. Obs.* (from 16th c. *arch.*) Forms: 1 **ȝebunden**, 4–6 **ybounde(n**, 6 **ibund**, 4–8 **ybound**. [pa. pple. of OE. *ȝebindan* I-BINDE, *bindan* BIND.] Bound.
Beowulf 871 Cyninges þeȝn..word oþer fand soðe ȝebunden. *Ibid.* 1531 Wundenmæl wrættum ȝebunden. *c* **1330** *Arth. & Merl.* 5863 Ȝond men ledeþ Leodegan Ybounden toward king Rion. **1426** LYDG. *De Guil. Pilgr.* 2861, I to-forn hadde nat seyn Som other folk ybounde so. **1513** DOUGLAS *Æneis* IV. Prol. 40 The God abufe, from his hie maieste, With the ibund, law in a maid did lycht. **1563** [see BIND *v.* 1 c]. **1647** H. MORE *Song of Soul* II. *Democr. Plat.* viii, The low Cusp's a figure circular, Whose compasse is ybound, but centre's every where. **1714** GAY *Sheph. Week* Prol. 84 Thy joyous Madrigals twice three, With Preface meet, and Notes profound, Imprinted fair, and well y-bound.

†**ybowed** [Y- 4, BOW *v.*[1]], influenced.
1387 TREVISA *Higden* (Rolls) VII. 451 [He] was ybowed vor favour [*orig. inflexus favoribus*].

ybowne, *pseudo-arch.* [Y-, *bowne*, BOUND *ppl. a.*[1]], about to go or start.
c **1572** GASCOIGNE *Posies, Fruites Warre* cxl, A daye before he was from thence ybowne.

yboylid, boiled.
c **1430** *Two Cookery-bks.* 48 Hony y-boylid hote.

ybrad [BREDE *v.*[1], to roast], tortured as with fire.
a **1310** in Wright *Lyric P.* xi. 39 The care that icham yn y-brad, y wyte a wyf.

ybraid [BRAY *v.*[2]], pounded.
c **1430** *Two Cookery-bks.* 48 A pece of Milwelle..y-braid with-al.

†**y'brent**, *pa. pple. Obs.* (from 16th c. *arch.*) Forms: 3–4 **ibrend(e**, 4–5 **ybrend**, **-te**, 6 **ybrint**, 4– **ybrent**; 3–4 **ybarn(e)d**, 4 **ybernde**, 5 **yborned**. [See Y- 4 and BURN *v.*[1]] Burnt; *occas.* burnished.
1297 R. GLOUC. (Rolls) 2890 Þe king vortiger was ybarnd to doust wiþinne. *c* **1300** *Prov. Hending* xliii. in *Anglia* IV. 199 So þe child þat draweþ is hond..fro þe brond þat is enes ibrend. *c* **1305** *St. Katherine* 148 in *E.E.P.* (1862) 94 In þe fur me hem caste þo hi hadde longe ibrend. **1340** *Ayenb.* 116 Þe ybernde uer dret. *c* **1384** CHAUCER *H. Fame* II. 432 Y-brent wyth hete. *c* **1450** LYDG. *Life Our Lady* xlix. (1484) g viij, With golde of fayth fayr bright y borned. **1513** DOUGLAS *Æneis* III. i. 7 Ybrint in smoke of flambis. **1590** SPENSER *F.Q.* III. ix. 53 And heauenly lampes were halfendeale ybrent. **1647** H. MORE *Song of Soul* I. I. xvii, The proud Phaeton, Who clomb the fiery car and was ybrent. **1767** MICKLE *Concub.* I. xxviii, With feverish Thirste ybrent. *Ibid.* II. liii, The ragged Walls with Lightning seemd ybrent.

†**ybroached**: see BROACH *v.*[1] I.

ybroke: see BREAK *v.* and I-BROKE.
1297 R. GLOUC. (Rolls) 4985 Þe fourme of þes was vaste ymad..þat ne miȝte noȝt wel be ybroke. **1422** YONGE tr. *Secr. Secr.* 143 Throgh a feyth y-broke.

ybrought, brought.
1297 R. GLOUC. (Rolls) 2505 Rowen..among hom ybroȝt was. *c* **1325** *Poem temp. Edw. II* (Percy) viii, Holy cherche Is mych ibrowt adoun. **1340–70** *Alex. & Dind.* 586 Ȝe were..y-brouht forþ & bred of þat modur. *c* **1489** CAXTON *Blanchardyn* xxix. 107 The kynge of polonye, that sawe..his standarde ybrought to the grounde. **1647** H. MORE *Song of Soul* II. *Democr. Plat.* ii, As men ybrought Into some spacious room.

ybroylid, broiled.
c **1430** *Two Cookery-bks.* 47 Porke y-broylid.

ybuld, -beld, etc. [Y- 4, BUILD *v.*], built.
c **1380** *Sir Ferumb.* 1331 Ne sawe þay neuere by-fore þat a place so faire ybuld. *c* **1394** *P. Pl. Crede* 172 A woon wonderlie well ybeld. *c* **1400** in *26 Pol. Poems* xxvi. 195 Withyn y-bylde halles and bowres. **1422** YONGE tr. *Secr. Secr.* 201 The tempill y-bylid. [For form cf. *bylled*, quot. *c* 1400 s.v. BUILD *v.* I.]

ybulled [BULL *v.*[2]], issued a bull against.
c **1400** *Langland's P. Pl.* A. v. 77 (MS. H) [Ichaue] y-bulled hem to þe lord to make hem lese siluer.

yburied, -bir-, -ber- [Y- 4, BURY *v.*], buried.
c **1250** [see BURY *v.* I]. **1297** [see FALL *v.* 33 b]. **1387** TREVISA *Higden* (Rolls) V. 45 He..was i-slawe and y-buried þere. **1513** DOUGLAS *Æneis* II. v. 28 With wyne and sleip yberyit and at rest.

yburnuscht, ybornsched, burnished.
c **1330** R. BRUNNE *Chron. Wace* (Rolls) 3622 Wel y-burnuscht fair & bryght. **1380** *Sir Ferumb.* 3587 Sherpe swerdes y-bornsched briȝte.

yburþananseca: see BYRTHYNSAK.

†**ycalled**[1], **-yd, ycalde** [Y- 4], called.
1377 LANGL. *P. Pl.* B. xv. 32 Þanne am I conscience ycalde. **14..** *R. Gloucester's Chron.* (Rolls) 212 A woman þat heleine was icluped [*MS. β* ycallyde, *γ* ycallyd]. **1426** LYDG. *De Guil. Pilgr.* 2904 To-forn or he had makyd man,..He was ycallyd but God only.

ycalled[2] [Y- 5, CAUL *sb.*[1]], wearing a 'caul'.
1377 LANGL. *P. Pl.* B. xv. 223 In riche robes rathest he walketh, Ycalled and ycrimiled.

ycapred, capered.
c **1634** CARTWRIGHT *Ordinary* III. i, Huh, huh, huh, so; ycapred very wele.

ycarked, ykarked, loaded, burdened.
1340 [see CARK *v.* I].

ycarped, talked.
1377 LANGL. *P. Pl.* B. xv. 296 If þei couth han ycarped by cryst.

ycast.
1297 R. GLOUC. (Rolls) 5122 Þe englisse þo & saxons..castles bigonne bulde..þat hii adde er ycast adoun. **1340** *Ayenb.* 108 Huanne..he heþ alle his uelþes ykest out. *c* **1489** CAXTON *Blanchardyn* xxx. 111 They were..y-caste from the realme of Tourmaday.

ycaught, yca(u)ȝt.
1297 R. GLOUC. (Rolls) 4372 Hii wende wel hor owe sleuþe on ȝou abbe ycaȝt. *c* **1570** icaught [see CATCH *v.* 32].

ycausing *pr. pple.* [Y- 3 c], causing.
1563 SACKVILLE *Mirr. Mag., Compl. Henry Dk. Buckhm.* xlix, The Tyrant kyng..Saunce earthly gylt ycausing both be slayne.

ycch(e, yce, obs. forms of ITCH, ICE.

ycclipped, obs. form of YCLEPT.

†**ycesed** [Y- 4, CEASE], appeased, quieted.
1387 TREVISA *Higden* III. 155 Whanne þe Babilons were i-sesed [*MS. γ* ycesed].

ych(e, obs. ff. EACH, I *pron.*, ITCH *v.*[1]

†**ychaf(f)ed**, warmed.
1422 YONGE tr. *Secr. Secr.* 242 That syde is moste colde and moste nedyth to be ychafit. *c* **1460** J. RUSSELL *Bk. Nurture* 893 His stomachere welle y-chaffed to kepe hym fro harme.

ychained.
c **1393** [see CHAIN *v.* 2 b]. **1629** MILTON *Hymn Nativ.* xvi, Those ychain'd in sleep.

ychanged.
1297 R. GLOUC. (Rolls) 3325 Þis art was al clene ydo þat ychanged hii were. **1340** *Ayenb.* 242 Hi wes ychonged in-to an ymage of zalt. **1422** YONGE tr. *Secr. Secr.* 172 The herte y-changed fro ayse to mysayse. **1647** H. MORE *Song of Soul* III. App. xxv, The bare bones..First into liquour melt to air ychanged been.

ycharged, charged, laden.
a **1225** icharged [see CHARGE *v.* 4]. **1297** R. GLOUC. (Rolls) 2504 Ycharged mid gode kniȝtes ssipes eiȝtetene. **1340** *Ayenb.* 260 Þet youre herten ne by..y-charged of glotounie. **1399** LANGL. *Rich. Redeles* III. 230 Ich man y-charchid to schoppe at his croune. *c* **1425** *Engl. Conq. Irel.* 12 O shippe ..y-charget with whet. *a* **1542** WYATT in *Tottel's Misc.* (Arb.) 224 And though with Indian stones..Ycharged were thy backe.

ycharm *v.* (pseudo-*arch.*) [Y- 3], to charm.
c **1620** T. ROBINSON *Mary Magd.* 1438 Seu'n sprights, with thunder hee ycharm'd from out my brest.

ychased, -ced.
1387 TREVISA *Higden* (Rolls) VI. 323 Þere Lotharius fliȝ and was i-chasede [*MS. β* ychaced]. *c* **1460** [see CHASE *v.*[1] 2 c].

yche, var. ECHE *v. Obs.* to augment, increase.
1398 TREVISA *Barth. De P.R.* IV. vii. (Tollem. MS.), [Blood] is..more scharpe for þe ychynge of hete.

†**ycheckt**, checked.
1642 H. MORE *Song of Soul* III. III. xxviii, It would project Dark powerfull beams, that solar life ycheckt.., all things would die.

ychele, var. ICKLE *sb.*, icicle.

ycheon, obs. f. *each one*: see EACH B. I c.

†**ycheryd** [Y- 5], (well) favoured.
c **1407** LYDG. *Reson & Sens.* 5373 Wel y-cheryd of lokyng.

ychesyled.
1509 [see CHISEL *v.*[1] I].

ycheued [CHEVE *v.* 5], done homage.
c **1330** R. BRUNNE *Chron. Wace* (Rolls) 15062 Ȝit y ne may Leten oure forfadres lay, þat we longe on haue y-leued, & til oure Godes þer-inne y-cheued.

ychid, chidden.
1387 TREVISA *Higden* (Rolls) VII. 35 Þere Dunston was strongliche despised and i-ched [*v.rr.* y-chidde, y-chyd].

ychon(e, obs. ff. *each one*: see EACH B. I c.

†**ychoppid** [Y- 4], chopped.
c **1430** *Two Cookery-bks.* 46 A litel soþe Porke or vele y-choppid.

ychose(n [Y- 4, CHOOSE, I-CHEOSE], chosen. (Cf. YCORE.)
1297 R. GLOUC. (Rolls) 2419 Ychose we beþ þer to. **1340** *Ayenb.* 68 Þe holi gost..makeþ his ychosene zinge..þe zuete zonges of heuene. *c* **1400** tr. *Higden* (Rolls) VII. App. 529 He was lawfullich y-chose pope.

Y chromosome. *Genetics.* Also †**y chromosome.** [Y 4 b.] A sex chromosome which occurs in only one of the sexes (in man and other mammals, the male) or in some species is absent altogether, its presence or absence in the zygote determining in man and many other species the sex of the organism.
1911 *Biol. Bull.* Jan. 119 We have associated the *X* and *Y* chromosomes of the male with sex-determination, but possibly they have some other meaning. **1933**, etc. [see X CHROMOSOME]. **1965** R. P. MOREHEAD *Human Path.* vi. 170/1 Proved cases of mutation involving the Y chromosome are

extremely rare... As Y chromosomes occur only in males, the characteristic pedigree of such mutations should contain only affected males, never affected females, and all affected males should transmit the defect to all their sons. **1974** P. Cave *Dirtiest Picture Postcard* x. 57 You've buttonholed me to give me long and boring lectures upon Germaine Greer, the faulty Y chromosome and the drudgeries of housework and child-bearing. **1982** *Nature* 2 Dec. 404/2 When a Y chromosome is present the foetal gonad, which has the potential to become either ovary or testis, differentiates into a testis and, when absent, into an ovary... Recent genetic analysis shows that this first step is not as simple as first thought and appears to be controlled by an interaction between autosomal genes and a gene(s) on the Y chromosome, for normal male differentiation. **1983** J. R. S. Fincham *Genetics* ii. 72 In grasshoppers and other insects of the order Orthoptera.. there is usually no Y-chromosome. The females are XX and the males just X.

ycicle, ycie, obs. ff. ICICLE, ICY.

yclad (ɪ'klæd), *pa. pple. arch.* (since 16th c.). Also 4–5 **ycladde, ycledde,** (also 7) **iclad,** 6 **ycladd.** [See Y- 4 and CLAD.] Clothed (*lit.* and *fig.*).
c **1320** *Sir Tristr.* 2843 Mark y clad in palle. ? *a* **1366** Chaucer *Rom. Rose* 472 Al to selde.. Is ony pouere man wel fedde Or wel araied or [y]cledde. *c* **1386** —— *Miller's T.* 134 Yclad [*v.rr.* iclad, y-cladde] he was.. Al in a kirtel of a lyght waget. **1460** Capgrave *Chron.* (Rolls) 363 Iff a man se an other naked he shalle have mo sekernes of hym thanne iff he se hym yclad. *c* **1474** Caxton *Recuyell* (1894) 615 A place voyde, where the maysters.. putte the body of hector.. y cladde in his beste garementes and robes. **1568** T. Howell *Arb. Amitie* (1879) 97 My carefull corps yclad with heauinesse. **1583** Melbancke *Philotimus* Ff ij, All yclad in grene.. he paced forward to the parke. **1590** Spenser *F.Q.* I. i. 29 An aged Sire, in long blacke weedes yclad. **1593** Shaks. *2 Hen. VI*, I. i. 33 Her words yclad with wisedomes Maiesty. **1603** Holland *Plutarch's Mor.* 30 In pure white clothes iclad. **1616** R. C. *Times' Whistle* ii. (1871) 30 Ignorance in his scarlet robe yclad. **1676** Hobbes *Iliad* XIX. 371 Yclad in Armour shining like the Sun. **1748** Thomson *Cast. Indol.* II. x, Yclad in steel, and bright with burnish'd mail. **1751** R. Lloyd *Progr. Envy* xv, In flowing sable stole she was yclad. **1812** Byron *Ch. Har.* II. liv, Spring yclad in grassy dye.

†**yclansed, yclensed**, pa. pple. of CLEANSE, YCLENSE.
c **1175** *Lamb. Hom.* 59 In þe font.. we iclensed weren. **1297** R. Glouc. (Rolls) 1012 Þoru graces of þe londe Idronke hii beþ iclansed sone. **1340** *Ayenb.* 74 Þe fornayse huerinne berneþ þe zaules al-huet hi byeþ yclenzed. **1387** Trevisa *Higden* (Rolls) I. 337 Whete cornes beeþ þere ful smal, vnneþe i-clansed wiþ manis hond.

ycleap'd, obs. form of YCLEPT.

†**yclense**, *v.* [Y- 3 c, CLEANSE.] To cleanse.
971 *Blickl. Hom.* 21 We sceolan.. ure heortan ʒeclænsian from oþrum ʒeþohtum. *c* **1394** *P. Pl. Crede* 760 Her kynde were more to y-clense diches.

†**yclepe** (ɪ'kliːp), *v. Obs.* Also 6 **ycleepe.** [OE. *ʒeclipian, ʒecleopian* to call (in various senses): see Y- 3 c and CLEPE *v.* Spenser's *ycleepe* is a new back-formation on YCLEPT. In quot. 1901 'ycleping' is an error for 'clipping' (CLIP *v.*[1]).] *trans.* To call by name, name.
c **950**, *c* **1100** [see YCLEPT]. **1595** Spenser *Col. Clout* 65 Himselfe he did ycleepe, The shepheard of the Ocean by name. **1901** *Westm. Gaz.* 23 Oct. 8/2 The old Saxon custom of 'ycleping', or naming, the Church has just been revived at Painswick, in the Cotswolds.

yclept (ɪ'klɛpt), **ycleped** (ɪ'kliːpt, *poet.* ɪ'kliːpɪd), *pa. pple. arch.* Forms: 1 **ʒeclypod,** *Northumb.* **ʒicliop(p)ad,** 2 **ȝecleped, iclipet,** 2–3 **iclepet, i-, ycluped,** 4 **yclepud,** 4–5 **icleped, yclepid,** 5 **iclepyd,** 6 **iclipped, iclipt, ycliped, ycclipped, ycleapt, -ed,** *Sc.* **yclepit,** 6–7 **yclipt,** 7 **i-, ycleeped, ycleep'd, ycleap'd, yclipped, ecleaped, eclip't,** 8 **yclyped,** 4– **ycleped** (7–9 **yclep'd**), 8– **yclept.** [OE. *ʒeclypod*, pa. pple. of *(ʒe)clypian*, *(ʒe)clipian* CLEPE, YCLEPE: see Y- 4. Adopted by Gawin Douglas from his ME. models, and much affected as a literary archaism by Elizabethan and subsequent poets; in less dignified writing often used for the sake of quaintness or with serio-comic intention.] Called (so-and-so), named, styled.
c **950** *Durham Ritual* (Surtees) 60 *Dignus vocari apostolus*, wyrðe þætte ic se ʒicliopad erendwraca. *c* **1100** *O.E. Chron.* an. 1057 (MS. D.) [Eadmund] Irensid wæs ʒeclypod for his snellscipe. *c* **1175** *Lamb. Hom.* 9 Heo weren iclipet synagoge al swa is nu iclepet al cristen folc. *c* **1200** *Vices & Virtues* 7 Ðurh ane oðre senne þe is ȝecleped inobediencia. *c* **1230** *Hali Meid.* 5 Syon was sum hwile iclepet þe hehe tur of Jerusalem. **1297** R. Glouc. (Rolls) 110 Al þis was ȝwile icluped [*v.rr.* ycleped, icleped, clepud, callyde, callyd] þe march of walis. *c* **1330** *Arth. & Merl.* 5560 Her ost was ycleped Blaire. **1340** *Ayenb.* 18 A vice þet is y-cleped ine clergie ingratitude. *c* **1350** *Will. Palerne* 121 & braunde was þat bold quene of burnes y-clepud. *c* **1430** *Two Cookery-bks.* 43 Make round-lyke Fretourys.. þat ben y-clepid Ragons. *c* **1440** *Stac. Rome* 674 in *Pol. Rel. & L. Poems* (1903) 166 A lytylle chapelle yeet there is, I-clepyd 'titulus pastoris'. **1509** Hawes *Past. Pleas.* iii. (1555) C j b, They pyped a daunce Iclipped, amour de la hault plesaunce. **1513** Douglas *Æneis* III. ii. 23 The king thairof yclepit Anyus. **1581** Howell *Deuises* (1879) 244 By name yclipt Endimion. **1588** Shaks. *L.L.L.* I. i. 242 Now for the ground Which? which I meane I walkt vpon, it is ycliped, Thy Parke. **1592** *Soliman & Pers.* v. iii. 74 That fraudfull squire of Ithaca, iclipt Vlisses. **1598** Tofte *Alba* III. G v, Loves Labor Lost, I once did see a Play, Ycleped so. **1611** Cotgr., *Nommé*.. named, called, cleaped, ecleaped. **1616** R. C. *Times' Whistle* ii. (1871) 22 The dredfull beast, yclepèd crocodile. **1632** Milton *L'Allegro* 12 But com thou Goddes fair and free, In Heav'n ycleap'd Euphrosyne. **1638** Heywood *Wise Wom.* II. i, *Seuc.* Is thy name Taber? *Tab.* I am so eclip't Sir. **1663** Butler *Hud.* I. i. 904 A valiant Mamaluke, In Foreign Land yclep'd (Sir Samuel Luke). **1664** *Ibid.* II. i. 46 A tall long-sided dame (But wondrous light) ycleped Fame. **1717** Lady M. W. Montagu *Let. to C'tess of Bristol* 1 Apr., Attending damsels yclep'd maids of honour. *a* **1764** Lloyd *Poetry Prof.* Wks. 1774 I. 31 Tho' not one wit bestrides the back Of useful drudge, ycleped hack. **1822** Lamb *Elia* Ser. I. *Praise of Chimney-Sweepers*, The sweet wood yclept sassafras. **1849** C. Brontë *Shirley* xi, The old and tenantless dwelling yclept Fieldhead. **1877** Gladstone *Glean.* (1879) I. 169 It is yclept 'redistribution of seats'. **1900** *Westm. Gaz.* 23 Feb. 9/1 The Associated South London Extended Gold Mines Corporation, Limited, yclept in the market Suds.

¶ irreg. predicated of the name. **1653** J. Taylor (Water P.) *Cert. Trav. Uncert. Journ.* 17 The name of *Wheat ears*, on them is ycleap'd, Because they come when wheat is yeerly reap'd.

†**yclepte, ycliȝt** [Y- 4], pa. pples. of CLIP *v.*[1], CLITCH *v.*

ycleyed, stopped with clay.
c **1440** *Pallad. on Husb.* IV. 438 Another list ycleyed hem to se.

yclinge *v.* (*pseudo-arch.*) [Y- 3 c], to cling.
c **1620** T. Robinson *Mary Magd.* 339 Yet to ye banckes his tender rootes yclinge.

y-clive[1], obs. pa. pple. of *clive*, CLEAVE *v.*[2]
a **1325** *Maudelain* 323 in Horstm. *Altengl. Leg.* (1878) 166 So michel pain is in hir ycliue, ȝete ich wene wele þat sche liue.

yclive[2], pa. pple. of CLIVE *v.*, to climb.

yclomben, climbed.
c **1412** Hoccleve *De Reg. Princ.* 904 Þou þat yclomben art in hy honoures.

yclosed, closed.
1377, *c* **1420** [see CLOSE *v.* 1 b, 3]. *c* **1430** *Two Cookery-bks.* 48 And so noȝt y-closyd, serue forth. **1647** H. More *Song of Soul* III. App. xviii, The ghosts Of men deceas'd.. in sleep yclos'd.

yclothed, clothed.
1297 R. Glouc. (Rolls) 3949 Noble men ycloþed in ermine. *a* **1400** *Adam Davy* 140 Þe kyng stood, ycloþed al in rede. *c* **1450** *Mirk's Festial* 4 To haue fed me.. and ȝeue me dryngke, ycloþet me.

yclouted, patched.
1377 Langl. *P. Pl.* B. VI. 61, I shal.. cast on me my clothes yclouted and hole.

yclove, obs. pa. pple. of CLEAVE *v.*[1] (3 β).

yclyketed, latched.
1393 Langl. *P. Pl.* C. VIII. 266 Þe dore.. Y-keyed and yclyketed.

yclyped, obs. form of YCLEPT.

†**yclypyd** [Y- 4], obs. pa. pple. of CLIP *v.*[2]
1426 Lydg. *De Guil. Pilgr.* 2012 Yclypyd & yshaue Vp-on your hedys.

y-colded, made cold, cooled.
a **1425** tr. *Arderne's Treat. Fistula* etc. 80 And þe potte y-colded, be it opned.

ycoled, obs. pa. pple of CULL *v.*[1]
13.. *K. Alis.* 2686 Foure thousand knyghtis,.. Y-coled alle for the nones.

y-colo(u)rid, coloured.
1422 Yonge tr. *Secr. Secr.* 230 Eyen y-colorid like rede wyne.

ycome(n, come.
1297 R. Glouc. (Rolls) 4249 Þo king arþures men ycome were echon. **1340** *Ayenb.* 262 Þis boc is ycome to þe ende. **1426** Lydg. *De Guil. Pilgr.* 3617 Now ye ben ykome ageyn.

ycompaced.
1297 [see COMPASS *v.*[1] 2].

ycomparisoned.
1340 [see COMPARISON *v.* 1].

yconceyued.
1340 [see CONCEIVE *v.* 7].

yconfirmed.
1297 R. Glouc. (Rolls) 4882 Þoru hard oþ & god ostage yconfermed was al þis. **1340** *Ayenb.* 106 Þi beleaue by y-confermed ine ous.

yconfortid, comforted.
1422 Yonge tr. *Secr. Secr.* 247 The kyndly hette shal be y-confortid.

yconfounded.
1297 R. Glouc. (Rolls) 8419 Al clene þe ssrewen were confounded [*MS. α* yconfounded].

ycongeyed, pa. pple. of CONGEE *v.*, to permit.
1387 Trevisa *Higden* (Rolls) VI. 259 Whan eny man is i-congyed [*MS. γ* ycongeyed] þere to commence in eny faculte [etc.].

yconomie, yconomus (-imus), obs. ff. ECONOMY, ŒCONOMUS.

†**yconquest** [see Y- 4 and CONQUEST *pa. pple.*], acquired.
1513 Douglas *Æneis* XII. ii. 50 Rewardis.. Yconquest in this batall Laurentane.

yconsayled, counselled.
1387 Trevisa *Higden* (Rolls) VII. App. 509 *note*, As Edricus hadde yconsayled while a was alyve.

ycontined, -contyened, contained.
1340 *Ayenb.* 39 Zome byeþ y-contined ope þan þet byeþ yzed. *Ibid.* 118 [see CONTAIN *v.* 2].

yconyd, pa. pple. of COIN *v.*[1]

y-coped [Y- 5] *a.*, early form of COPED *a.*, wearing a cope.
1377 Langl. *P. Pl.* B. XX. 342, I knewe such one.. Come in þus ycoped at a courte.

†**y'core**, *pa. pple.* and *ppl. a. Obs.* Forms: 1 **ʒecoren,** 2–3 **icoren,** 3–4 **icore,** 4 **i-, ycorn,** 3–5 **ycore.** [OE. *ʒecoren*, pa. pple. of *céosan* to CHOOSE, *ʒecéosan* I-CHEOSE.] Chosen; often predicative and as adj., elect; 'choice', fair, comely (cf. the uses of *corn* s.v. CHOOSE *v.* A. 6 a); hence in ME. used as a meaningless tag often riming with *before*; *absol.* elect one, the elect.
Beowulf 206 He hæfde cempan ʒecorone. *a* **900** Cynewulf *Juliana* 299 Wiþ þa ʒecorenan Cristes þeʒnas. *c* **900** tr. *Bæda's Hist.* II. xviii, Honorius.. to bisceope ʒecoren wæs. *a* **1000** *Cædmon's Gen.* 1818 Abraham.. drihtne ʒecoren. *c* **1000** *Ags. Ps.* (Th.) cxxxi. 18 [cxxxii. 17] Ic.. fæʒre ʒearuwe byrnende blac-ern bere for minum criste ʒecorenum [orig. *christo meo*]. *c* **1175** *Lamb. Hom.* 45 Nu ic þe bidde for þine kinedome.. and for alle þine haleȝen and ec þine icorene. *a* **1200** *Moral Ode* 104 Hwi boð fole iclepede and swa lut icorene. *c* **1200** *Trin. Coll. Hom.* 167 Hwat is þis þe astihȝð alse dai rieme, fair alse mone, icoren [orig. *electa*, Song of Songs vi. 10] alse sunne? *c* **1300** *Harrow. Hell* (L.) 244 Let vs neuer be forloren for no sunne, crist ycoren. *c* **1330** *Amis & Amil.* 579 Of wel heighe kin y-corn. *c* **1330** *King of Tars* 544 [The child] as a roonde of flesche icore In chaumbre lay hire bifore, Withouten blod or bon. **13..** *Coer de L.* 146 With a coron off gold i-corn. **1340–70** *Alex. & Dind.* 978 Þe kiddeste y-core þat corone weldus! *c* **1380** *Sir Ferumb.* 766 Charlis kyng þe beste knyȝt y-core þat is owar now lyuyng. *c* **1420** *Chron. Vilod.* 789 Edgar.. To þe kyndam of Englonde was y-core.

†**ycoroned**: see YCROWNED.

ycorumped [Y- 4], pa. pple. of CORRUMP *v.*, to corrupt.

ycorve(n, carved.
1297 R. Glouc. (Rolls) 4240 He vel adoun as a gret ok þat bineþe ykorue wer. *c* **1394** *P. Pl. Crede* 173 A woon wonderlie well y-beld, Wiþ arches on eueriche half & belliche y-corven. *c* **1430** *Two Cookery-bks.* 23 Rasonys y-corven.

ycoryd, cored.
c **1430** *Two Cookery-bks.* 46 Take perys y-coryd.

ycounted.
1568 [see Y- 4].

ycouped, pa. pple. of COUP *v.*[2], to cut.

ycoupled.
1387 Trevisa *Higden* (Rolls) VII. 445 Ȝif a ȝong sheep.. schal be y-coupled and y-ȝoked to a wylde bole.

ycovered (see also *ykeuered*), covered.
1742 Shenstone *Schoolmistr.* xxxiii, Apples with cabbage-net y-cover'd o'er.

ycraul *v.* [Y- 3 c], to crawl.
1594 Carew *Tasso* (1881) 75 Vile man from vilest durt on earth ycrauld.

ycrested *a.* [Y- 5], crested.
1581 A. Hall *Iliad* v. 97 A heauie helmet.. with crests ycrested three.

ycrimiled, pa. pple. of CREMIL *v.*

ycristened, christened.
1387 Trevisa *Higden* (Rolls) V. 37 Sche was y-cristened and i-cleped Eugenius, and i-made monk. **1393** Langl. *P. Pl.* C. XVIII. 165 Men fyndeþ þat makamede was a man ycrystned.

ycrost, crossed.
1603 J. Davies *Microcosmos* 243 For, Crownes are richly blest, with Peace y-crost.

ycrowned, -coro(u)ned, -cronet, crowned.
1297 R. Glouc. (Rolls) 3934 In þe oþer half þe quene was of erchebissops al so Ylad & ycrouned ek as riȝt was uor to do. **1340** *Ayenb.* 267 Ich y-zeȝ.. þe innumerable uelaȝrede of þe holy martires mid blisse and worþssipe y-corouned. **1387** Trevisa *Higden* (Rolls) V. 71 Þou schalt be y-crowned bisshop at Rome. **1422** Yonge tr. *Secr. Secr.* 199 Than he hym bethoght of the grete noble that he demenyd in Ierusalem, ther as he was kynge y-cronet. **1642** H. More *Song of Soul* II. III. III. xiii, With fair flowers from unknown root ycrownd.

ycullid, obs. pa. pple. of KILL *v.*
1393 Langl. *P. Pl.* C. I. 199 Thauh we hadde ycullid þe catte ȝut sholde þer come anoþer.

ycus(s)ed, obs. pa. pple. of KISS *v.*

ycustumet, pa. pple. of CUSTOM *v.* (sense 1).
1422 Yonge tr. *Secr. Secr.* 247 Aftyr the tyme of the yere and the houre of the day y-custumet or vset.

ycutte (see also *ykyt*, etc.), cut.
c **1430** *Two Cookery-bks.* 51 Datys y-cutte in .ij. or .iij.

ycy, yd, obs. forms of ICY, IT.
c **1400** *Rule St. Benet* (verse) 78 To fulfyll yd in word and dede.

†**ydad,** a minced oath: cf. EDAD.
c **1680** HICKERINGILL *Hist. Whiggism* I. Wks. 1716 I. 42 Ydad, I think I am just of that Opinion myself.

†**ydamned, -dampned,** obs. pa. pple. of DAMN *v.*
1340 *Ayenb.* 78 Vor manye filozofes oþer of greate clierkes and of kynges and of emperours.. byeþ ydampned ine helle. *c* **1395** *Plowman's Tale* 1243 Thou shalt be..clene y-dampned into hell. *c* **1400** *R. Gloucester's Chron.* (Rolls) 8679 He was þere idemd [*MS. C* ydampned] to þe pine of helle stronge.

ydan(t, obs. ff. EIDENT, IDENT *Sc.*, diligent.

†**ydarted** [Y- 4], pierced as with a dart.
c **1374** [see DART *v.* 1]. *c* **1407** LYDG. *Reson & Sens.* 6878 With wo they be throgh-out y-darted.

ydaunted, overcome.
1581 A. HALL *Iliad* v. 80 Chromius eke fel deade in fielde y-daunted by his might.

ydder, obs. form of UDDER.

†**ydead, ydede** [Y- 4], dead.
1387 TREVISA *Higden* (Rolls) VII. 169 þis ȝere Levyngus þe bisshop of Worcestre y-dede. **1642** H. MORE *Song of Soul* III. I. v, Old Adam.. Under some senselesse sod with sleep ydead.

ydee, ydene [OE. *ȝedén, ȝedœ́n*, pa. pple. of DO *v.*, I-DO *v.*], done.
a **900** CYNEWULF *Crist* 1266 Synne..ær ȝedenra. *c* **1420** *Chron. Vilod.* 290 When þe masse was alle y-dee. *c* **1425** *Engl. Conq. Irel.* 28 That thou ne hast y-dene troght some grete lette, hastyly be about to do.

ydel, obs. form of IDLE, IDOL.

†**ydel(e)d** [Y- 4, DEAL *v.*], divided.
1297 R. GLOUC. (Rolls) 542 þis lond was þo ideled [*MS. α* ydeld; *β, γ* ydelde] a þre. **1387** TREVISA *Higden* (Rolls) II. 107 þese tweie kyngdoms were..y-deled bytwene tweye kynges.

†**ydem(e)d** [Y- 4, DEEM *v.*], judged, condemned.
c **1200** *Trin. Coll. Hom.* 75 He is idemd to eche wowe on helle. **1297** R. GLOUC. (Rolls) 6381 þin owe mouþ þe aþ ydemd. **1340–70** *Alex. & Dind.* 909 We faiþful folk.. Ben y-demed to do dedus of rihte. **1399** LANGL. *Rich. Redeles* III. 229 His dwellinge [was] ydemed a bowe-drawte ffrom hem.

†**ydemptifically,** *adv. Obs. rare*$^{-1}$. [app. ad. med.L. **identificē*, adv. of **identificus* IDENTIFIC.] With actual identity.
1432–50 tr. *Higden, Harl. Contin.* (Rolls) VIII. 461 Criste is not in that sacramente ydemptifically, veryly and really in his propre presence corporealle.

ydenly, obs. form of IDENTLY *adv. Sc.*

ydeot(e, obs. form of IDIOT.

†**ydept** [Y- 4], dipped.
1340 *Ayenb.* 106 Y-dept ine blod.

y-det [Y- 4, DIT *v.*], stopped, closed.
a **1340** in *Rel. Ant.* I. 30 Hwan Banockesbourne is y-det myd mannis bonis.

y-dicyd [Y- 4], cut into dice.
c **1430** *Two Cookery-bks.* 22 Hard Wastel y-dicyd.

†**y'dight,** *pa. pple. Obs.* (after 1500 *arch.*) [Y- 4, DIGHT *v.*] Prepared, furnished, dressed.
1297 R. GLOUC. (Rolls) 5581 þe welisse ver in engelond vorte he it adde ydiȝt. *c* **1394** *P. Pl. Crede* 211 Her dortour y-diȝte wiþ dores ful stronge. *c* **1510** *Lytell Geste R. Hode* VII, Full hastly was theyr dyner I dyght. **1522** *World & Child* A j b, Stretes and strondes full strongely ydyght. **1579** FULKE *Refut. Rastell* 722 The Aultars bright, that were rounde ydight.

ydil(l, -illy, ydiome, ydiot(e, obs. ff. IDLE *a.*, IDLY *adv.*, IDIOM, IDIOT.

†**ydo(n** [Y- 4, DO *v.*, I-DO *v.*], done, put. ***wel idon*** (cf. MHG. *wol getân*): excellent.
1123, etc. [see DO *v.* A. 8]. *c* **1205** LAY. 910 Membricius, þet wes a riche mon, þe wes swiðe wel idon [Wace *saives hom*]. **1297** R. GLOUC. (Rolls) 9535 Wircestere was þus ibarnd and oþer harm ido. *c* **1320** *Cast. Love* 312 A þral.. To strong prison was i-don. **1387** TREVISA *Higden* (Rolls) VI. 71 What hast y-doo, sire bisshop? **1392** *E.E. Wills* (1882) 3 þat þe hows be ysold, and þe Almes yi-do in þe worst ȝere. **1426** LYDG. *De Guil. Pilgr.* 17310 Thys mescheff.. Ys ydon and wrouht by me.

ydobbed: see YDUBBED.

ydodded, shorn.
a **1400** *N.T.* (Paues) 1 Cor. xi. 6 ȝif it be foul for a womman to ben y-dodded oþer balled.

ydolve [DELVE *v.*], undermined; buried.
1340 *Ayenb.* 263 Vor huych hord þet ilke zelue hous ne by y-dolue heȝlyche he wakeþ. **1430–40** LYDG. *Bochas* IV. ii. (1554) 102 She was ydolue lowe.

ydoubled, -dobbled, doubled.
1340 *Ayenb.* 230 Yef þou me beuelst aye mi wyl, my chasthede hit ssel by me ydobbled. **1399** LANGL. *Rich. Redeles* III. 275 With deyntes y-doublid and daunsinge to pipis.

ydought [DOW *v.*[1]], grown strong.
13.. *K. Alis.* 5906 Tho the kyng was hool, and wel y-doughth.

ydous, obs. form of HIDEOUS.

†**ydout** *v.* [Y- 3 c], to fear.
1297 R. GLOUC. (Rolls) 6328 Ech prince & ech lond ydouted hom tuo.

ydouted [Y- 4], feared.
1399 LANGL. *Rich. Redeles* I. 42 With diamauntis derne y-doutid of all.

ydrad(de: see DREAD *v.*, YDRED.
1642 H. MORE *Song of Soul* I. li, O happy man that full perswasion had Of this! if right at home, nought of him were ydrad.

ydrawe *v.* [Y- 3 c], to draw.
1426 LYDG. *De Guil. Pilgr.* 3037 A cause evydent That thow mayst wel.. The swerd ydrawe.

ydrawe, ydraȝe, *pa. pple.* [Y- 4], drawn.
1297 R. GLOUC. (Rolls) 5905 þou art mid vnriȝt her to ydrawe. **1340** *Ayenb.* 133 He wes villiche y-draȝe ase a þyef. **1393** LANGL. *P. Pl.* C. XIX. 218 Eue was of adam and out of hym ydrawe. *c* **1430** *Two Cookery-bks.* 26 Take gode mylke of Almaundys y-drawe with wyne.

ydre: see HYDRE.

†**ydred** (also *ydreddyd, ydrad, ydraded*), pa. pple. of DREAD *v.*
1340 *Ayenb.* 104 He ys ald and yknawe and ydred and yworþssiped and yloued. **1422** YONGE tr. *Secr. Secr.* 137 Wyrchippyd, ylowid, and ydreddyd. **1513** DOUGLAS *Æneis* XII. iv. 55 Abuf the hevin ydred and starrit sky. **1590** SPENSER *F.Q.* I. I. 2 Yet nothing did he dread, but euer was ydrad. **1610** G. FLETCHER *Christ's Vict. Heaven* I. xl, Euery one shakes his ydraded speare. **1642** H. MORE *Song of Soul* II. I. II. xix, Mans awfull majesty of every beast ydred.

ydremed, dreamt.
1387 TREVISA *Higden* (Rolls) VIII. 49 Wheþer I have i-mette [CAXTON hath ydremed] þis tale or nouȝt.

ydrenched, drenched.
1610 HOLLAND *Camden's Brit.* 285 And how the fields ydrenched were with bloud.

ydressid, ydrest, prepared, equipped, adorned.
c **1386** i-dressed [see DRESS *v.* 3]. **1422** YONGE tr. *Secr. Secr.* 165 Anoone aftyr the Iue Saw that he was wel ydressid. *c* **1430** *Two Cookery-bks.* 11 Make a dragge of powder Gyngere,.. an caste þer-on When it is y-dressid. **1642** H. MORE *Song of Soul* I. III. lvi, Their face with love and vigour was ydrest.

ydreyght, obs. pa. pple. of DRAW *v.*

ydreynt [DRENCH *v.*], drowned.
1426 LYDG. *De Guil. Pilgr.* 14464 Swych wynsyng.. Made hym that he was atteynt And myddes off the see ydreynt.

ydrife, ydrive, driven.
1297 R. GLOUC. (Rolls) 4803 þe brutons were ydriue [*v.r.* ydrife] al in to west walis. **1387** TREVISA *Higden* (Rolls) III. 109 He hadde wiþ his prayers y-dryue away addres and cokedrilles from þe Egypcians.

ydromancy, ydromel, obs. ff. HYDROMANCY, HYDROMEL.

†**ydronke(n, -drunke,** drunk.
a **1275** *Prov. Ælfred* 476 in *O.E. Misc.* (1872) 131 Werse þe swo on euen yuele haued y-dronken. **1340** *Ayenb.* 51 Ich ne ssel by an eyse al-huet ich habbe ydronke. **1377** LANGL. *P. Pl.* B. VI. 281 Til I haue dyned bi þis day and ydronke bothe. **1432–50** tr. *Higden* (Rolls) III. 75 Mida.. was sleyne þro the bloode of a bulle ydrunke.

ydrop *v.* [Y- 3 c], to drop.
a **1718** PARNELL *Fairy Tale* 171 And down ydrops the knight.

ydropesey, -ie, etc., **ydropike, ydrosacre,** obs. ff. HYDROPSY, HYDROPIC, HYDROSACRE.

†**ydrownd** [Y- 4], drowned.
1603 J. DAVIES *Microcosmos* Pref. 23 In Teares ydrownd.

ydubbed, dubbed.
1340 *Ayenb.* 83 Godes knyȝtes þet þe holy gost heþ y-dobbed. **1399** LANGL. *Rich. Redeles* III. 363 Tyll degon and dobyn.. were y-dubbid of a duke ffor her while domes.

ydul, ydy, obs. ff. IDLE *a.*, EDDY.

†**ydyned** [Y- 4], dined.
1393 LANGL. *P. Pl.* C. IX. 303 Er ich haue y-dyned by þys day and y-dronke boþe!

ydyt [DIT *v.*], closed, shut up.
1303 R. BRUNNE *Handl. Synne* 3186 Wyþ hys hede [he haþ] my mouþ y-dyt. *c* **1400** *Solomon's Bk. Wisdom* 242 A pytte, þere seuen hungri lyouns weren þereinne all ydytte.

ye (jiː, jɪ), *pers. pron. 2nd pers. nom.* (*obj.*), *pl.* (*sing.*). Forms: see below. [OE. *ȝe*, stressed *ȝē, ȝie*, corresp. to OFris. *jī*, OS. *gi, ge*, (MLG., MDu. *ghi, -i*, LG., Du. *gij*), OHG., MHG. *ir* (G. *ihr*), ON. *ér* (:— **jēr*), Sw., Da. *i*: analogically modified forms (after the 1st pers. pl. pron., e.g. OE. *ȝe* after *we*, ON. *ér* after *vér*, HG. *ir* after *wir*) of OTeut. **jūs*, unaccented **juz*, represented by Goth. *jus*, f. root *yu-* with pl. ending *-s* (cf. Zend *yūš*, Lith. *jūs*, and Skr. *yū-yám*).
For the declension of the 2nd pers. pron. in OE. and ME. see THOU.
In the earliest periods of English *ye* was restricted to the nom. pl. In the 13th c. it came to be used as a nom. sing. = 'thou', first as a respectful form addressed to a superior. This use survives in modern dialects, esp. (in the form *ee*) in interrog. and imperative formulæ (e.g. *Dee* = 'do ye'), but also in objective uses = 'thee' (e.g. *Oi tell ee*). When *you* had usurped the place of *ye* as a nom., *ye* came to be used (in the 15th c.), vice versa, as an objective sing. and pl. (= 'thee' and 'you').]
Now (in all uses) only *dial.*, *arch.*, or *poet.*; in ordinary use replaced by YOU.

A. Illustration of Forms:
1 **ȝe, ȝie, ȝee,** 2–3 **ȝie,** (**gie, ge**), 2–5 (6–8 *Sc.* printed **ze**) **ȝe,** 4–5 **ȝee,** *north.* **yhe,** 4–6 *north.* **ȝhe,** 4–7 **yee** (3 **jȝe, hye,** 4 **iȝe, iye,** (**i**)**he,** 7, 9 *dial.* **yea**), 3– **ye.**
c **950** *Lindisf. Gosp.* Matt. v. 13 Ȝee sint salt eorðes. *Ibid.* Luke xvi. 15 ðie sindon ða ðe ȝie soðfæstigeð iuih foræ monnum. *a* **1175** *Cott. Hom.* 217 þenche ȝie aelc word of him swete. *c* **1175** *Lamb. Hom.* 127 Ȝe ne beoð ne alesde of deofles anwalde mid golde ne mid seolure. *c* **1200** *Trin. Coll. Hom.* 143 Nu ȝie habbeð iherd þes wimmanes name. *c* **1200** ORMIN 1118 Hu ȝe muȝhenn lakenn Godd. *c* **1250** *Kent. Serm.* in *O.E. Misc.* 28 Hye habbet to gode i-offred of yure selure. *c* **1275** *Sinners Beware* 320 ibid. 82 To day ye schulle myd blysse To heueryche wende. **1297** R. GLOUC. (Rolls) 9360 Louerdinges jȝe wute wel þat [etc.]. *a* **1300** *Cursor M.* 411 (Cott.) Als yee herd me neuen. *Ibid.* 19094 (Edin.) His sone.. Gie.. demid als ge seluin wate. **13..** *Gosp. Nicod.* 1105 Wende we to þaime, if yhe [*v.r.* ȝhe] rede. **13..** *Northern Passion* 157 He seid wol iye yeue me mede? **1340** HAMPOLE *Pr. Consc.* 68 Als yhe sal here aftirward sone. **1382** WYCLIF *Matt.* xxii. 29 Ȝee erren, nether knowynge the scripturis. **14..** *Northern Passion* II. 172/306 Me þenkeþ he saide ihe habbet wrong. **1508** DUNBAR *Poems* v. 38 Drink with my Guddame, as ȝe ga by. **1510** *Reg. Privy Seal Scotl.* I. 314/1 Wit zhe us to have made.. oure lovit Alexander Andersoun.. settar and sear of all skynnys. **1611** *Bible* Gen. iii. 5 Yee shall bee as Gods. **1639** MURE *Ps.* cxlviii. 9 Yea mountaines and yea hills. **1683** *Col. Rec. Pennsylv.* I. 72 All yee that are willing yt the last proposition should stand so as it is. **1878** *Cumbld. Gloss.*, *Yea's*, you shall.

b. In combination, proclitically or enclitically, with other words, as: †***ȝet*** = ye it, ***yare*** = ye are, ***y'have***; ***d'ee, dee*** = do ye, ***hark'ee, harkee***. Now *dial.*
c **1200** ORMIN 9006 Loc ȝiff ȝet wilenn follȝhenn. **1611, 1625, 1632** [see DEE]. **1631** KNEVET *Rhodon & Iris* v. vi. I 3, An ample restitution, Of what y'have tane from her. **1632** BROME *Northern Lass* I. ii, If I interrupt you, hang me. Dee hear? **1634** FORD *Perk. Warbeck* II. i, Madam, yare passionate. **1708**, etc. harkee, hark'ee [see HARK *v.* 2 c]. **1746** *Exmoor Courtship* (E.D.S.) 485 No, es thankee, Cozen Magery. **1775** SHERIDAN *St. Patr. Day* I. i, There's a discipline, look'ee in all things. *Ibid.*, Hark'ee, lads, I must have no grumbling.
Cf. the rimes in the following:—*a* **1721** PRIOR *Cupid Mistaken* 14 Indeed, Mamma, I did not know Ye:.. I took You for your Likeness, Cloe. **1774** GOLDSM. *Retaliation* 136 Then what was his failing? come tell it, and burn ye. He was —could he help it?—a special attorney.

B. Uses.
1. The pronoun used (as the plural of THOU) in addressing a number of persons (or, rhetorically, of things), in the nominative (or vocative).
Beowulf 237 Hwæt syndon ȝe searohæbbendra? *c* **1000** *Ags. Gosp.* Matt. vi. 5 þonne ȝe eow ȝebiddon, ne beo ȝe swylce liceteras. *c* **1175** *Lamb. Hom.* 15 Ȝe herde wilche laȝe weren er crist wes iboren. *c* **1200** *Vices & Virtues* 19 Ȝie ðe berð iwant fram me. *a* **1250** *Prov. Ælfred* 27 in *O.E. Misc.* 104 Wolde ye, mi leode, lusten eure louerde, he ou wolde wyssye wisliche þinges. *c* **1300** *Harrow. Hell* (E.) 142 Helle ȝates, y com ȝou to, Now ich wil þat ȝe vndo. **1390** GOWER *Conf.* III. 37 Thus be yee parted nou atuo. *c* **1450** *Mirk's Festial* 1 Good men and woymen, þys day, as ȝe knowen well, ys cleped Sonenday yn þe Aduent. **1470–80** MALORY *Arthur* x. lxxx. 555 My fayre felawes wete ye wel that I will torne vnto kynge Arthurs party. *a* **1529** SKELTON *Agst. Garnesche* ii. 32 Cum Garnyche, cum Godfrey, with as many as ȝe may. **1610** SHAKS. *Temp.* v. i. 34 Ye, that on the sands with printlesse foote Doe chase the ebbing-Neptune.. and you, whose pastime Is to make midnight-Mushrumps. **1662** *Bk. Com. Pr., Comm., Conf.*, Ye [*1st Pr. Bk.* 1549 You] that do truly and earnestly repent you of your sins. **1781** SIR J. BANKS in *Phil. Trans.* LXXI. 7 Shew the World that ye still are as ye always have been, worthy the Patronage of your King! **1798** WORDSW. *We are Seven* vii, Yet ye are seven! —I pray you tell, Sweet Maid, how this may be. **1833** TENNYSON *Death of Old Year* i, Toll ye the church-bell sad and slow. **1841** LANE *Arab. Nts.* I. ii. 95 The King answered, Ye know not the reason wherefore I would kill the sage. **1902** BRIDGES *Matres Dolorosæ*, They rode to war as if to the hunt, But ye at home, ye bore the brunt.

†**b.** In apposition with *self* (*ye self, selven* = yourselves): see SELF A. 2. *Obs.*
a **1300** *Cursor M.* 6786 (Cott.) To cumlinges do yee right na suike, For quilum war yee seluen slike. *Ibid.* 14691 Bot.. if yee self willi be blind. **1388** WYCLIF *1 Pet.* ii. 5 And ȝe silf as quyk stoonys be ȝe aboue bildid in to spiritual housis.

c. In apposition with and preceding a sb. (or adj. used *absol.*) in the vocative.
1362 LANGL. *P. Pl.* A. VIII. 62 Ȝe Legistres and lawyers ȝe witen wher I lyȝe. *c* **1374** CHAUCER *Troylus* III. 1809 Ye sustren nyne. **1377** LANGL. *P. Pl.* B. XV. 333 Ȝe riche, ȝe robeth and fedeth Hem þat han as ȝe han. **1549** LATIMER *3rd*

Serm. bef. Edw. VI (Arb.) 84 Ye brainsycke fooles, Ye hoddy peckes, Ye doddye poulles, ye huddes. **1593** SHAKS. *Rich. II*, III. ii. 88 Looke not to the ground, Ye Fauorites of a King. **1681** BAXTER *Hymn*, Ye holy Angels bright, Which stand before God's Throne. **1697** DRYDEN *Æneid* VIII. 634 That Blood, those Murthers, O ye Gods replace On his own Head. **1730** THOMSON *A Hymn* 76 Ye woodlands all, awake. **1803–6** WORDSW. *Ode Intim. Immort.* iv, Ye blessed creatures, I have heard the call Ye to each other make.

2. Used instead of *thou* in addressing a single person (originally as a mark of respect or deference, later generally: cf. THOU, YOU).

1297 R. GLOUC. (Rolls) 1341 Sire emperour quaþ þe erl þo, ne be ȝe no so bolde. *a* **1300** *Cursor M.* 8721 'Lauerd', sco said, 'god it witschild þat þou britten sua mi child. Yee giue him all til hir allan, Me es it leuer þan he be slan'. **1390** GOWER *Conf.* I. 47 Ma dame, if ye wolde have rowthe. **1411** *Rolls of Parlt.* III. 650/2 My Lord.. I knowe wele that ye be of such birth estate and myghte that [etc.]. *c* **1450** *Merlin* i. 15 Moder,.. be not dismayed, for ye shull neuer be Iuged to deth for my cause. *c* **1460** *Promp. Parv.* 549 (Winch.) ȝetyng, with worshyp seyng ȝe not þu, *vosacio.* **1481** CAXTON *Reynard* xxi. (Arb.) 51 Saye that ye your self haue made the lettre. *c* **1489** —— *Sonnes of Aymon* xiv. 336 Good lord, ye created & made our fader Adam. **1516** in *Acts Parlt. Scot.* (1875) XII. 36/2 We with oure lauthfull service thankis ȝoure grace of the grete Regarde ȝe Beir to the weill.. of our kingis gracis person. **1590** SPENSER *F.Q.* I. viii. 26 The royall Virgin.. him thus bespake.. How shall I quite the paines, ye suffer for my sake? **1591** SHAKS. *Two Gent.* I. ii. 49 *Iul*[*ia*]. Will ye be gon? *Lu*[*cetta*]. That you may ruminate. *c* **1730** RAMSAY *Eagle & Robin* 45 Ze sing sae dull and ruch, Ze haif deivt our lugs. **1786** BURNS *To a Louse* 19 Now haud you there, ye're out o' sight. **1866** MRS. LYNN LINTON *Lizzie Lorton* III. 159 Ye've dune summut ye're sorry for. **1872** TENNYSON *Gareth & Lynette* 1142 'Damsel', he said, 'ye be not all to blame'. **1873** *Oxfordshire Gloss.*, *Ee*.. is a more refined word than *thee*.. 'Who did ee see up strit?'.. *Ee* is used to a superior, and not *thee*. **1878** HARDY *Ret. Native* I. iii, Be ye a-cold, Christian?

b. In apposition with and preceding a sb. in the vocative.

a **1596** *Sir T. More* I. i. 11 Compell me, ye dogges face! **1599** CHAPMAN *Hum. dayes Myrth* Plays 1873 I. 69 O ye impudent gossip. **1886** STEVENSON *Kidnapped* xxix, Ye donnered auld runt.

3. Used as objective (accusative or dative) instead of *you* (in plural or singular sense).

c **1449** PECOCK *Repr.* I. xvi. 86 Y preie ȝe seie ȝe to me [etc.]. **1538** BALE *Thre Lawes* 163 We leaue ye here behynde. **1594** MARLOWE & NASHE *Dido* IV. iv, For this will Dido tye ye full of knots,.. Ye shall no more offend the Carthage Queene. *a* **1596** *Sir T. More* I. i. 110 He is in a good forwardnesse, I tell ye, if all hit right. **1613** SHAKS. *Hen. VIII*, v. iii. 181 As I haue made ye one Lords, one remaine: So I grow stronger, you more Honour gaine. **1624** BEDELL *Lett.* iv. 73 This no Protestant will grant yee. *c* **1650** MILTON *Sonn.*, *On new Forcers Consc.*, To.. ride us with a classic Hierarchy Taught ye by meer A.S. and Rotherford. **1667** —— *P.L.* II. 840, I.. shall.. bring ye to the place. **1721** RAMSAY *Richy & Sandy* 18 I'll bear ye Company for Year and Day. **1815** SCOTT *Guy M.* xxii, There's saxpence t' ye to buy half a mutchkin. **1820** BYRON *Mar. Fal.* v. i. 198 Was not the place of Doge sufficient for ye? **1827** KEBLE *Chr. Y.*, *2nd Sunday Advent* vi, Ye, who your Lord's commission bear, His way of mercy to prepare: Angels He calls ye. **1840** DICKENS *Old C. Shop* lxxii, 'Go thy ways with him, sir,' cried the sexton, 'and Heaven be with ye both!' **1847** HALLIWELL *Dict.* (1889) I. p. xiv/1 I'd soon yarn sum munney, I warrant ye. **1866** LYTTON *Lost Tales Miletus* 127 The morrow's sun shall light ye homeward both.

†**b.** Used redundantly ('ethical dative'). *Obs.*

1668 R. L'ESTRANGE *Vis. Quev.* (1708) 6 He comes ye laden forsooth, with Letters of Recommendations. **1768** TUCKER *Lt. Nat.* (1834) I. 471 He cannot make a handsome bow, nor run ye off an elegant period.

Hence †**ye** *v.*, to use 'ye' instead of 'thou' in addressing a single person: cf. THOU *v.*, YEET *v.*

1483 *Cath. Angl.* 426/1 To ȝe, *vosare jn plurali numero vos vestrum vel tibi.* **1510** *Promp. Parv.* 537/2 (W. de W.) Yeyn or sey ye, *voso.*

†**ye**, *conj.* and *adv.* *Obs.* Forms: 1 ᵹe, 2–3 ȝe, 3 *Orm.* ȝa. [OE. ᵹe, corresp. in use to OS. *ge, gi*(*e*, *gia*, and *ja*, OHG. *ja* and *jauh, joh, jouh* (MHG. *ja, joch, jouch*), Goth. *jah.*] And; also, too. **ȝe** ... **ȝe** (or **and**): both... and; as well... as.

Beowulf 1864 ðe wið feond ᵹe wið freond. *a* **900** CYNEWULF *Crist* 847 þonne herᵹa fruma æþelinga ord eallum demeð leofum ᵹe laðum lean æfter ryhte. **900–30** *O.E. Chron.* (Parker MS.) an. 835 [He] þær ᵹefliemde ᵹe þa Walas ᵹe þa Deniscan. *c* **1000** *Sax. Leechd.* II. 204 Her sint tacn aheardodre lifre ᵹe on þam læppum & healocum & filmenum. *c* **1175** *Lamb. Hom.* 103 Ðeos sunne fordeð eiðer ȝe saule ȝe lichoma. *c* **1200** ORMIN 846 He turrnde mikell follc till Godd ȝa læwedd follc, ȝa læredd.

ye, obs. dial. form of GIVE *v.*

1788 *Voc. Forth & Bargie* in *Trans. R. Irish Acad.* II. 34 *Y'oure*, give over, cease.

ye: see EYE, YEA; graphic var. THE, THEE, cf. Y (3).

yea (jeɪ), *adv.* (*sb.*) Now *dial.* and *arch.* Forms: α. 1 ᵹæ, ᵹee, ᵹe, 2–5 (6 *Sc.*) ȝe, 4–5 ȝhe, 4–6 ȝee, ye, 4–7 yee, 5 yhe, 6 je. β. 1 ᵹea, 1–2 ia, 3–5 ȝea, (also 6 *Sc.*) ȝa, 4 yaa, iaa, ȝia, ȝai, 4–5 ȝaa, ȝha, ya, yai, 5 yha, yae, 5– yea; 4 ȝo, ioo, ȝoo, 5 yoe, 5–7 yoo. γ. 3 ȝei, 4–5 ȝey, 5 yei, ȝeyȝe. δ. 1 ᵹiee, ᵹi, 4 yie, 5 (6 *Sc.*) ȝie, 8 *dial.* yoy, 9 *dial.* yi, yigh. ε. 3 ȝeoi, ȝui, 5 ȝoye. [An affirmative particle having forms corresponding more or less exactly in all the other Teutonic languages: OFris. *gê, jê*, OS. *jâ*, (M)LG. *ja*, (M)Du., OHG., MHG. *ja, jâ*, (G. *ja*), ON. *já*, Goth. *ja, jai*, all derivable ultimately from a primitive Teut. **ja, je*, which has undergone modification in different directions as the result of sentence stress or emotional emphasis.

OE. (WS.) *ᵹéa* combined with the corresp. Anglian *ᵹé* to produce the ME. type *ȝe*(*e*, *ye*(*e*; the Northumb. development of the Anglian form, *ᵹie*, *ᵹí* (cf. Northumb. **scíep*, *scip* = WS. *scéap* SHEEP), gave a ME. type *ȝie*, continued in mod. north. dial. in *yi, yigh, yoi.* In later WS. the falling diphthong of *ᵹéa* became a rising one, *ᵹeá, iá*, whence arose southern *ȝo* and northern *ȝa* (but cf. ON. *já*). In other respects the phonology of the English forms is obscure. The modern standard spelling *yea* and pronunciation (jeɪ) show arrested development of the vowel, but the pronunciation (jiː) is current locally. ME. *ȝei, ȝey, ȝeyȝe* seem to point back to a doubled form **ȝeȝe.* The ε-forms *ȝui, ȝoi* constitute a distinct southern type, with possibly a modern representative in Hampshire *yigh.*]

A. *adv.* A word used to express affirmation or assent: now ordinarily replaced by YES.

1. a. As simple affirmative, in answer to a question not involving a negative: = YES 1.

For the distinction formerly observed between *yea* and *yes*, see NAY *adv.*[1] 1 and YES 2.

In ME. *ȝe* is sometimes accompanied by a pronoun repeating the pronominal subj. of the question (see quots. from *Ancren Riwle*, *a* 1225, and cf. the first quot. from the same text in 1 c).

731 BÆDA *Hist. Eccl.* v. ii, 'Dicito,' inquiens, 'aliquod verbum, dicito Gæ [*OE. transl.* (*c* 900) cweð nu ᵹee],' quod est, lingua Anglorum, verbum adfirmandi et consentiendi, id est, etiam. *c* **1000** *Ags. Gosp.* John xxi. 15 þa cwæð se hælend.. Simon iohannis lufast ðu me swiðor þænne ðas; He cwæð to him, ᵹea [*Lind. & Rushw.* ᵹee] drihten þu wast þæt ic þe lufiᵹe. *c* **1000** ÆLFRIC *Gen.* xxvii. 24 Eart þu Esau min sunu? And he cwæð: Ia leof, ic hit eom. *c* **1175** *Lamb. Hom.* 47 Is hit god for to hiheren godes weordes and heom athalden? ȝe fuliwis. *c* **1200** ORMIN 4452 Maȝȝ aniȝ mann slan oþerr mann & cwellenn himm wiþþ herrte? ȝa full wel seȝȝþ þatt Latin boc. *a* **1225** *St. Marher.* 4 Hwet godd heiestu ant hersumest? Ich heie qð ha godd feder... ȝe [see sense 4] qð he lude, leuestu ant luuest him þe reowðfulliche deide.. on rode? Yai quoð heo. *a* **1225** *Ancr. R.* 52 Is hit nu so ouer vuel uor te toten utward? ȝe hit. *Ibid.* 408 Mei ich preouen ou þis? ȝe ich sikerliche. *a* **1300** *Cursor M.* 772 'And wenis þou þat it be sua Sum he has said yow?' 'certes, ya!' *c* **1330** *Florice & Bl.* (1857) 598 ȝhe ne answerede nai ne ȝo. *c* **1350** *Will. Palerne* 268 'What? sone', seide þe couherde 'seidestow i was here?' 'ȝa, sire, sertes', seid þe child. *c* **1380** *Sir Ferumb.* 1575 'Wolleþ ȝe ȝou defende ouþer ȝe wolleþ flen?' 'ȝea, so god me mende.' *c* **1420** *Avow. Arth.* xxiv, Gauan asshes, 'Is hit soe?' To tother knyȝt grauntus, ȝoe. *c* **1440** *Generydes* 294 His moder.. Askyd medeyn if she hadde done wele And she seid yae. *a* **1450** MYRC *Par. Pr.* 69 Belevest thowe fully alle the pryncipalle articles of the Feithe..? The Sike persone answerethe, Yee. *a* **1466** GREGORY *Chron.* in *Hist. Coll. Cit. Lond.* (Camden) 165 'Yf ye holde you welle plesyd.. say you nowe, ye!'.. And thenne alle the pepylle cryde with oo voyce, 'Ye! ye!' *c* **1470** HENRY *Wallace* IV. 364 At him he speryt, all Scottis gyff thai be. Wallace said 'ȝa'. *c* **1500** *Lancelot* 2843 'Madem, if ȝhe remembir, so it was The red knycht.. That wencust al'... 'ȝha,' quod the qwen, 'rycht well remembir I'. **1500–20** DUNBAR *Poems* xlii. 15, I said, 'Is this ȝour guirnance, To tak men for thair luking heir?' Bewty sayis, 'ȝa, schir'. **1526** TINDALE *Matt.* xiii. 51 Jesus sayde vnto them; have ye vnderstonde all these thynges: they sayde, ye syr. *a* **1553** UDALL *Royster D.* III. iii. (Arb.) 46 *R. Royster.* Trowest thou so? *M. Mery.* Ye plain. **1593** SHAKS. *Rich. II*, III. ii. 2 *Rich.* Barkloughly Castle call you this at hand? *Au.* Yea, my Lord. **1602** *Contention betw. Liberalitie & Prodigalitie* II. iii. (Malone Soc.) 345 *Van*... What, still so hastily? *Ten.* Yoo by gisse, sir, tis high time. **1611** W. ADAMS *Let.* in Rundall *Mem. Japon* (Hakl. Soc.) 39 He asked whether our countrey had warres? I answered him yea. **1796** PEGGE *Derbicisms* (E.D.S.) 86 *Yoy*, yes, from *yea* or *ay* rather than *yes.* **1859** TENNYSON *Marr. Geraint* 688 'Look on it, child, and tell me if ye know it.' And Enid.. answer'd, 'Yea, I know it'. **1865** 'ARTEMUS WARD' *His Bk., Shakers*, When we broke up, sez I, 'my pretty dears, ear I go you hav no objections, hav you, to a innersent kiss at partin?' 'Yay,' thay sed. **1909** K. D. WIGGIN *Susanna & Sue* i. 13 [Shaker Eldress loq.] 'Yee, yee! I remember well!' [*footnote* Yea is always thus pronounced among the Shakers.]

b. Expressing assent to a statement, command, etc.: = YES 3. (See also 4.)

a **1000** *Colloq. Ælfric* in Wr.-Wülcker 96 *M.* And maniᵹe fedaþ þa ᵹetemodon ofer sumor þæt eft hiᵹ habban ᵹearuwe. *A.* ðea swa hiᵹ doþ. *a* **1300** *Cursor M.* 1246 'Sun,' he said, 'þou most now ga To paradis þat i com fra.'.. 'Yai, sir, wist i wyderward þat tat vncuth contre ware.' *a* **1330** *Otuel* 303 'Euele mote he þriue & þe, þat ferst faillep of me & te.' 'ȝe leue ȝa,' quaþ otuwel þo. *a* **1375** *Joseph Arim.* 170, 'I trouwe þat beo þi sone' bi Iosaphe he seide. 'ȝe, sire, so he is. *c* **1412** HOCCLEVE *De Reg. Princ.* 2979 'Ye shul vnto me swere þe lawes kepe til I agayn come,'.. to which þei gan answere, 'ȝee, ȝee, man, ȝee!' **1535** COVERDALE *Josh.* xxiv. 22 Ye are witnesses ouer youre selues, that ye haue chosen you the Lorde, to serue him. And they sayde: Yee. **1599** SHAKS. *Much Ado* II. ii. 3 *Ioh.* It is so, the Count Claudio shal marry the daughter of Leonato. *Bora.* Yea my Lord, but I can crosse it. **1859** TENNYSON *Geraint & Enid* 757 'Then, Enid, shall you ride Behind me.' 'Yea,' said Enid, 'let us go.'

c. Rarely in answer to a negative question (*obs.*: = YES 2 a), or in contradiction of a negative statement (now *dial.*: = YES 2 b).

a **1000** *Colloq. Ælfric* in Wr.-Wülcker 92 *M.* Ne canst þu huntian buton mid nettum? *V.* ðea butan nettum huntian ic mæᵹ. *a* **1225** *Ancr. R.* 334 Nis nout, cweð he, God so grim ase ȝe him uore makieð. No, he seið, Dauid, ȝuihe [*MS. T.* ȝeoi he, *MS. C.* ȝeihe], and seið þenne hwareuore. *Ibid.* 392 Ne muhte he mid lesse geref habben ared us? ȝe siker [*v.rr.* ȝuse I wis, ȝes I wis], ful lihtliche. **1382** WYCLIF *Matt.* xvii. 23 Thei.. seiden to hym, ȝoure maister payeth nat tribute? And he seith, ȝhe [1388 ȝhis]. **1423** JAS. I *Kingis Q.* lxviii, Quhare[un]to lyve I langer? Wofullest wicht, and subiect vnto peyne; Of peyne? no: god wote, ȝa. **1876** WAUGH *Chimney Corner* (1879) 149 'This is th' house isn't it, Matty?' 'Yigh. We're just i' time.' **1886** CUNLIFFE *Gloss. Rochdale-w.-Rossendale Wds. & Phr.*, *Yi*.. is.. a negative [answer] to a statement, as, 'You have not been at home to-day,' to which 'yi' means that the statement made is untrue.

d. *to say yea*: to answer in the affirmative; hence, to give assent.

c **1100** *O.E. Chron.* (MS. D.) an. 1067 Se kyng befealh ᵹeorne hire breðer oð þæt he cwæð ia wið. *c* **1300** *Beket* 36 This Gilbert seide ȝe. **1390** GOWER *Conf.* I. 288 And to the kniht sche seide: 'Yee.' *c* **1400** *Apol. Loll.* 29 To a ferme.. oiþer ȝie or nay. *c* **1440** *Generydes* 3164 They praed them to say In all this mater playnly ye or nay. **1513** DOUGLAS *Æneis* I. Prol. 93 Nocht fullie grantand, nor anis sayand ȝe. **1568** GRAFTON *Chron.* II. 128 A folkemot was an assembly of people to say yea or nay to that which should be declared vnto them. **1683** *Col. Rec. Pennsylv.* I. 72 All yee that are willing y[t] the last proposition should stand so as it is, see yee.

†**e.** Standing for an affirmative dependent clause after a verb of saying or believing: = YES 5. *Obs.*

c **1375** *Cursor M.* 772 (Fairf.) And wenis þou þat hit is squa? Certis, ho sayde I traw ya [*v.rr.* ȝa, ȝe]. **1397** *Rolls of Parlt.* III. 379/1, I trowe rather ȝe than nay. *c* **1489** CAXTON *Sonnes of Aymon* xxiv. 511 Alas, doo they not remembre me, I byleve better ye than nay. *c* **1500** *Melusine* 263 Yf they swere ye they are your enemyes and to the contrary, yf they swere that noo.

†**f.** *yea or no*, after *whether*, in an alternative dependent question = 'whether.. or not'. So in an alternative dependent clause, as ***would I yea or no*** = 'whether I would or not'. *Obs.*

1515 in Leadam *Sel. Cases Star Chamber* (Selden Soc.) II. 93 To the Interrogatory Whethir thei had this by the Comen assent ye or noo [etc.]. *c* **1540** *B.N.C.* (Oxf.) *Munim.* 27. 112 (MS.) Whether J. S. was cosyn and heire of [A. B.], ye or naye, he knoweth not. **1577** BRETON *Floorish upon Fancie* Wks. (Grosart) I. 7/1 Would I ye or no, I learnd some of his raging rules. **1670** in *Extr. St. Papers rel. Friends* Ser. IV. (1913) 313 In that time I shall tell thee whether I shall make them yea or no. **1727** DE FOE *Hist. Appar.* iv. (1840) 30 Whether they really do converse familiarly with us, yea or no?

†**2.** Used as an ordinary adverb directly qualifying a clause or word: Even; truly, verily. *Obs.*

In the Lindisfarne and Rushworth glosses on the Gospels it freq. renders L. *etiam*, *jam* = *sóðlice, witodlice.*

c **950** *Lindisf. Gosp.* Mark xiii. 22 *Ad seducendos si potest fieri etiam electos*, to ᵹesuicanne ᵹif mæᵹe wosa ᵹee ða ᵹecoreno. *Ibid.* John xvi. 32 *Ecce uenit hora et iam uenit*, heono cuom ðio tid ᵹee cuom [*marg.* ᵹi nu cummen; *Rushw.* & ᵹe comon]. *c* **1250** *Hymn* in *Trin. Coll. Hom.* App. 258 Iherd ȝe beo þin holi nome in heouene & in eorþe. *a* **1300** *Cursor M.* 13050 þou luues hir yaa again þi liue. **1387** TREVISA *Higden* (Rolls) VII. 129 þe kyng.. forbeed þat any schulde selle hym woode ȝe [L. *etiam*] forto seþe his mete and vitailles wiþ. **1388** WYCLIF *Prov.* xiv. 20 A pore man schal be hateful, ȝhe [Vulg. *etiam*], to his neiȝbore. *c* **1460** *Wisdom* 895 in *Macro Plays* 64 Schulde we lyve þis lyue, ya whowe, We may a-mende wen we be sage. **1581** A. HALL *Iliad* III. 58 Helene.. did him earnestly behold, and swelling yea with wrath [etc.].

3. Used to introduce a statement, phrase, or word, stronger or more emphatic than that immediately preceding: = 'indeed'; 'and more': = YES 4.

Often practically coinciding with NAY *adv.*[1] 5, which however properly expresses the contrast in degree between the statements, etc., whereas *yea* expresses their identity in substance.

a **1240** *Ureisun* in *O.E. Hom.* I. 185 He openeþ swa þe moder hire earmes hire leoue child for to cluppen, ȝe soþes. **1297** R. GLOUC. (Rolls) 4797 Seint patric was þere monek & suþþe abbot þer ȝe ar seint austin come mo þen an hundred ȝer. **13..** *Cursor M.* 19752 (Edin.) He fande a man unfere In parlesie gia aȝte ȝier. **13..** in *Pol. Rel. & L. Poems* (1903) 261 þou þeng wel on þese þinges yie, wat tou art, & wat tou were. *c* **1375** *Sc. Leg. Saints* xxvii. (*Machor*) 153 þai.. Ioy mad, ȝey, mare þan ma nemmyt be. *c* **1380** WYCLIF *Wks.* (1880) 10 þei seyn þat an heþene philosofre.. is wittiere and trewere þan almyȝti god, ȝe þat god is fals and a fole. *a* **1533** LD. BERNERS *Huon* clxix. 565, I had rather haue lost .iiii. of my best cityes, ye and all my countre.. destroyed. **1533** GAU *Richt Vay* 38 Giff we be the barnis of God thane ar we alsua heritours, ȝei heritours of God. **1579** LYLY *Euphues* (Arb.) 106 How wantonly, yea, and how willingly haue we abused our golden time. **1605** CAMDEN *Rem.* 3 As that the true Christian Religion was planted heere most auntiently by Ioseph of Arimathia,.. yea by saint Peter, and saint Paul. *c* **1620** A. HUME *Brit. Tongue* (1865) 14 We see, not onelie in our idiom, but in the latin alsoe, one symbol to have sundrie soundes, ye, and that in one word; as lego, legis. **1671** MILTON *P.R.* I. 117 Regents and Potentates, and Kings, yea gods, Of many a pleasant Realm. **1690** W. WALKER *Idiomat. Anglo-Lat.* Pref. 3, I did not always particularly quote the place of my author..; yea sometimes I did not so much as set down my author at all. **1786** WESLEY *Jrnl.* 3 May, Some of them use improper, yea, indecent, expressions in prayer. **1813** SHELLEY *Q. Mab* II. 130 Those Pyramids shall fall! Yea! not a stone shall stand to tell The spot whereon they stood! **1859** TENNYSON *Marr. Geraint* 704, I.. kept it for a sweet surprise at morn. Yea, truly is it not a sweet surprise?

4. a. Introducing a question or remark in reply to a statement, etc., expressing either vague assent or (more commonly) opposition or objection: = 'Indeed?'; 'Well', 'well then'.

a **1225** [see sense 1]. *c* **1230** *Hali Meid.* 25 Nu þu art iwedded, & of se heh se lahe iliht... ȝei nu, hwat frut, & for hwuch þing meast hit is? **1377** LANGL. *P. Pl.* B. xi. 33 'ȝee, recche þe neuere,' quod recchelesnes. *c* **1420** *Chron. Vilod.* 3357 'þis childe rose vp, and alyue he ys'... 'ȝe', quod þe kyng, 'he nasnot dede þo, y-wys.' 'ȝeysse, for god', quod þe knyȝt, 'dede he was & his body golde.' 'ȝoye, sire', quod þe archebisshop.., 'Mony grette meracle þis mayden has do.' 'ȝe, syre archebysshop, holde þou þy clappe! For y ȝeue no by-leue þerto.' *c* **1475** *Rauf Coilȝear* 376 'Hald ȝow fra the Court, for ocht that may be; ȝone man that thow outrayd Is not sa simpill as he said..' 'ȝea, Dame, haue nane dreid of my lyfe to day.' *c* **1520** SKELTON *Magnyf.* 942 *Fan...* They fell a chydynge With Crafty Conuayaunce. *Con. Ab.* Ye, dyd they so? **1535** COVERDALE *Gen.* iii. 1 The serpent.. sayde vnto the woman: Yee, hath God sayde in dede: Ye shall not eate of all maner trees in the garden? **1590** SHAKS. *Mids. N.* III. ii. 411 *Rob.* Come, recreant... *Dem.* Yea, art thou there? **1605** —— *Lear* I. iv. 326 (Qo.) Yea, is it come to this? **1859** TENNYSON *Geraint & Enid* 128 'Yonder comes a knight.'.. 'Yea, but one? Wait here, and when he passes fall upon him.'

†**b.** As a mere introductory interjection, emphasizing the statement following. *Obs.*

a **1450** *Le Morte Arth.* 1626 Kynge Arthur than loude spake A-monge hys knyghtis to the quene: 'ȝa, yonder is launcelot du lake, Yiff I hym euyr with syght haue sene.'

B. as *sb.*

1. a. An utterance of the word 'yea'; an affirmative reply or statement; an expression of assent. (Usually opposed to *nay* or *no*: see also 3.)

1228 *Mem. Ripon* (Surtees) I. 53 Credendi.. per suum na vel suum ya. *a* **1400** *Cristene-mon & Jew* 125 in *Minor Poems fr. Vernon MS.* 488 Oþer a nay, or A ȝa? Soone tel þou me swa. *c* **1480** HENRYSON *Orpheus & Eurydice* 574 (Bann. MS.) Thingis.. Till ȝe or na quhilk ar indefferent. **1500–20** DUNBAR *Poems* xv. 36 Sum micht haif ȝe, with littill cure, That hes oft nay, with grit labour. **1534** TINDALE *James* v. 12 Sweare not... Let youre ye be ye, and youre naye naye. **1578** H. WOTTON *Courtlie Controv.* 230 Take pitie of him which attendeth life or death of your yea or nay. **1588** SHAKS. *L.L.L.* v. ii. 413 My woing minde shall be exprest In russet yeas, and honest kersie noes. **1611** in *10th Rep. Hist. MSS. Comm.* App. I. 538 Their No should be as welcome unto him as their Yea. **1714** tr. *Joutel's Jrnl. Voy. Mexico* (1719) 34 We observ'd that their Yea consisted in a Cry, fetch'd from the Bottom of the Throat. **1812** JEFFERSON *Writ.* (1830) IV. 178 Their nay is the yea of truth, and its best test. **1846** TRENCH *Mirac.* xxxiii. (1862) 473 Not seldom He gives even in the very act of seeming to deny; his Nay proving indeed a veiled Yea.

b. More vaguely: Affirmation, assurance, certainty, absolute truth; a positive statement or principle.

1382 WYCLIF *2 Cor.* i. 18 For oure word the which was at ȝou, ther is not in it is [*v.rr.* ȝea, ȝhe] and nay [Vulg. *est et non*], but in it is is, that is, treuthe. **1526** TINDALE *2 Cor.* i. 19–20 Goddis sonne Jesus Christ.. was not ye and naye: but in hym it was ye. For all the promises of God, in hym are ye [**1881** *R.V.* in him is yea. For how many soever be the promises of God, in him is the yea]: and are in hym Amen. **1831** CARLYLE *Sart. Res.* II. ix, Love God. This is the Everlasting Yea, wherein all contradiction is solved.

2. An affirmative vote; a person who votes in the affirmative: usually *pl.*, opposed to *nays* (or *noes*).

Still in use in the U.S. Congress. Cf. AYE.

1657 *Burton's Diary* (1828) II. 58 After a short debate.. the House was divided. The yeas went forth. **1706** HEARNE *Collect.* (O.H.S.) 203 'Twas carried in yᵉ Affirmative Yeas 141, Noes 71. **1781** HATSELL *Prec. Proc. Ho. Comm.* (1796) II. 106 *note*, If this question for adjournment takes place before four o'clock in the afternoon, and there is a division upon it, the Yeas go forth; if after four o'clock, the Noes. **1789** *Massachusetts Spy* 29 Jan. 3/2, 197 Members present —Yeas 101. **1838** *Congr. Globe* 24 Dec. 33/1 Mr. Tillinghast asked for the yeas and nays, which were ordered. **1888** BRYCE *Amer. Commw.* xiii. I. 176 If one fifth of a quorum demand a call of yeas and nays, this is taken.

3. a. *yea and nay* (or *no*): positive and negative statement (or command); affirmation and denial (or injunction and prohibition); sometimes, alternate affirmation and denial, vacillating statement, shilly-shallying. Also *attrib.* (see C. below).

1382 WYCLIF *2 Cor.* i. 17 Is and not, or ȝhe and nay. **1387** TREVISA *Higden* (Rolls) VII. 297 He folwede þe kynges wille and his ȝee [*v.r.* ȝhe] and nay in al manere wise. **1526** TINDALE *2 Cor.* i. 18 Oure preachynge vnto you, was not ye and naye. **1540** PALSGR. *Acolastus* Declar. Names b 4, To flatter hym, and holde hym vp with ye and nay. **1598** SHAKS. *Merry W.* I. iv. 99 The very yea, & the no is, yᵉ French Doctor my Master [etc.]. **1720** PRIOR *Conversation* 34 These two went on, With yea and nay, and pro and con. **1886** RUSKIN *Præterita* II. i. 27 There had been a good deal of dealers' yea and nay about it. **1913** H. BROWN *Our Renaissance* ii. (1918) 56 Beyond yea or nay he inspired the greatest of all philosophers.

b. *by yea and nay* (or *no*): a formula of asseveration in the form of, and substituted for, an oath (cf. Matt. v. 34–37). ? *Obs.*

1588 SHAKS. *L.L.L.* I. i. 54 *Longa.* You swore to that Berowne, and to the rest. *Berow.* By yea and nay sir, than I swore in iest. **1598** —— *Merry W.* I. i. 88. [**1641** BROME *Joviall Crew* I. (1652) C 3, By yea-cock and naycock The Fields will afford us a Hedge or a Hay-cock.] **1661** W. N. etc. *Merry Drollery* I. 2 b, He swore by yea and nay He would have no denial. **1682** MRS. BEHN *False Count* Prol. A ij b, By Yea and Nay, shee'll throw her self on you. **1828** *Craven Gloss.* s.v., 'By fair yea and nay,' by a solemn affirmation. *a* **1839** PRAED *Charades & Enigmas* xvii, But still the Lady shook her head, and swore by yea and nay.

C. *Comb.* **yea-and-nay** *a.* [attrib. use of phrase: see B. 3], (*a*) whose 'communication' is 'yea, yea, nay, nay'; spec. †***yea-and-nay man***, a quaker; ***Richard Yea-and-Nay***, a nickname for King Richard I; (*b*) of indefinite or indeterminate character, 'neither one thing nor another', ambiguous; (*c*) disposed to assent or deny indifferently or according to expediency; hesitating, vacillating, undecided; also *sb.* a Quaker; hence ***yea-and-nayish*** adj. (*nonce-wd.*) in sense (*b*); **yea-forsooth** *a.*, addicted to saying 'yea forsooth' in the way of superficial assent; **yea-nay** *a.* = *yea-and-nay*; **yea-say** *v.* [after NAY-SAY *v.*], *intr.* to say 'yea', to assent; *trans.* to assent to; hence **yea-saying** *vbl. sb.* and *ppl. a.*; **yea-sayer**, one who says 'yea' or who agrees; a person inclined by nature to assent, or to act in a positive manner; **yea-word**, a word of assent.

1656 FLECKNOE *Diarium* 35 Above all of your *yea and nay Man, take especial heed I pray. **1678** (*title*) A Yea and Nay Almanack for the people call'd Quakers. *a* **1700** B. E. *Dict. Cant. Crew*, *Yea and Nay-Men*, Quakers. **1775** MME. D'ARBLAY *Early Diary* Jan. (1889) II. 9 He was a *yea and nay* man not worth remembering. **1781** C. JOHNSTON *Hist. J. Juniper* I. 81 One of your water-gruel, yea-and-nay good boys. **1807** *Antid. Miseries Hum. Life* 4 They were Yeas and Nays. 'What's that?' said I... 'O quack, quack I suppose', said the squire. **1828** L. HUNT *Ld. Byron* etc. I. 309 Shelley ..had only to become a yea and nay man in the House of Commons, to be one of the richest men in Sussex. **1865** ANNE MANNING *Belforest* I. 200, I hate yea-and-nay persons that don't care, and leave it to you. **1900** M. HEWLETT (*title*) The Life and Death of Richard Yea-and-Nay. **1911** FLETCHER & KIPLING *School Hist. Eng.* 70 'Richard Yea and Nay', so called because he spoke the truth. **1957** A. DUGGAN *Devil's Brood* xii. 165 Because he [*sc.* Bertrand de Born] could not persuade Richard to make war at his bidding he gave him the opprobrious nickname Yea-and-Nay. **1777** MME. D'ARBLAY *Early Diary* July (1889) II. 202 Our journey proved very *yea and *nayish*. **1597** SHAKS. *2 Hen. IV*, I. ii. 41 A Rascally-*yea-forsooth-knaue, to beare a Gentleman in hand, and then stand vpon Security. **1847** MRS. GORE *Castles in Air* iii, The executor was an infirm *yea-nay old gentleman. **1856** R. A. VAUGHAN *Mystics* VIII. ii. (1860) II. 279 *note*¹, It was indeed no time for compliment —for hesitant, yea-nay utterance upon the question. **1875** MORRIS *Æneids* VII. 615 Whom all men follow straight, The while their brazen *yea-saying the griding trumpets blare. *Ibid.* XII. 841 And yea-saying she bowed. **1887** —— *Odyss.* XIII. 47 So he spake; and all yea-said him and bade the thing to be. **1934** WEBSTER, Yea-sayer. **1940** 'G. ORWELL' *Inside Whale* 176 There are the 'progressives', the yea-sayers, the Shaw-Wells type, always leaping forward to embrace the ego-projections which they mistake for the future. **1972** A. FRIEDMAN in Cox & Dyson *20th-Cent. Mind* I. xii. 434 The Wilcoxes..are businessmen, robust, conservative, organized, practical yea-sayers who lead lives of 'telegrams and anger'. **1960** *Partisan Rev.* Fall 609 In literary criticism ..artless enthusiasm..has modulated into..more restrained yea-saying. **1960** *Times* 14 Oct. 18/3 Matthew Smith's art, so much..in tune with the traditional, yea-saying materialism of French painting. **1972** *Jrnl. Social Psychol.* LXXXVI. 220 Subjects who obtained scores of 0, 1, and 11, 12 were dropped from the analysis as representing extremes of yeasaying or naysaying. *a* **1861** SIR F. PALGRAVE *Norm. & Eng.* (1864) III. 82 Nor did any bashfulness real or conventional, delay his *yea-word.

yea, *v.* [f. prec.] *intr.* (or with *it*): To say 'yea'; to reply affirmatively: opp. to NAY *v.* 2 b.

1598 BP. HALL *Sat.* VI. i. 82 No more smell-feast Vitellio ..loues him in his maw, loaths in his heart, Yet soothes, and yeas, and Nayes on eyther part. **1657** J. GOODWIN *Triers Tried* 6 Such as will swallow their camels, and yea it, and nay it, with them from the one end of their faith unto the other. **1679** *Establ. Test* 23 A..Jesuit..can thou and thee, and yea and nay, as well as the best of them [*sc.* Quakers].

yead, obs. form of EYED.

1598 Q. ELIZ. *Plutarch* 134 Thre yead men.

yead, dial. form of HEAD *sb.*¹

1746 *Exmoor Scolding* (E.D.S.) 97 Chell make thy Yead addle. **1864** TENNYSON *North. Farmer* v, A bummin' awaäy loike a buzzard-clock ower my yeäd.

yead(e, obs. pa. t. of GO: see YODE.

yeaf, obs. pa. t. of GIVE.

yeaghe, obs. f. YACHT.

yeah (jɛə), *adv. colloq.* (orig. *U.S.*). Repr. a casual pronunc. of YES *adv.* Cf. OH YEAH.

1905 *Dialect Notes* III. 67 *Yeah, yep*,..variants of *yes*. **1925** F. S. FITZGERALD *Great Gatsby* iv. 87 'That's a very interesting idea.' 'Yeah.' He flipped his sleeves up under his coat. **1936** M. KENNEDY *Together & Apart* IV. 293 'You were in Sweden with him last year, weren't you?' 'Yeah.' **1940** *Music Makers* May 37/3 *Yeah, man*, exclamation of assent. **1949** E. BIRNEY *Turvey* 153 'Yeah, yeah, Hayes was pretty hot but the ref——'. **1950** 'D. DIVINE' *King of Fassarai* xx. 166 'I take it the natives are friendly?'.. 'Yeah. .. We had us a party last night.' **1961** J. HELLER *Catch-22* (1962) xix. 194 'Will that be all, sir?' asked the chaplain. 'Yeah,' said Colonel Cathcart. 'Unless you've got something else to suggest.' **1977** B. LANGLEY *Death Stalk* ix. 104 'The shooting. That was Tony.' 'Tony?' 'Yeah, he done that.'

yeal, dial. form of ALE.

yeald: see GUILD, OLD, YELD, YIELD.

yealdon, var. ELDING¹, fuel.

1818 SCOTT *Hrt. Midl.* xlv, Take awa yealdon, take awa low.

yeale, obs. form of EEL *sb.*

a **1625** in *Engl. Hist. Rev.* Jan. (1915) 25 Some of the yeales being worth 2*s.* a peece.

yeale, obs. form of YALE¹.

'yealing. *Sc.* Also 8 eeldin, 9 yeildin, yeelin', eelin. [? For *even eilding*, one of *even eild* (ELD *sb.*) or equal age with another. Cf. *evineld, evin eild* = contemporary in Douglas *Æn.* III. xii. 42.] A contemporary in age. Also *attrib.*

1728 RAMSAY *Phœnix and Owl* vi, You, a Species by your sell, Near Eeldins with the Sun your God. **1787** BURNS *Brigs of Ayr* 150 My dear-remember'd, ancient yealings. **1804** COUPER *Macguldrochiana* I. xvi, His bonny, various, yeelin' frien's. **1808** JAMIESON, *Yeildins, Yealings.*

yealk, obs. form of YOLK.

yeallow, yealow, obs. ff. YELLOW.

yealte, obs. var. YELT.

†**yean**, *sb. Obs.* Also 5 ȝeeene, ȝe(e)ne, yene, e(e)ne, yn. [app. f. next.] A young lamb, yeanling.

1408 *Wycl. Bible* Ps. cxliii. 13 (MS. Fairf. 2) þe sheep of hem ben wþ ȝeeene [*v.rr.* ȝene, ȝeene, ene, eene, yn]. *Ibid.* Isa. xl. 11 He shal bere sheep wiþ eene eþer wþ lombe [*v.rr.* yene, ene].

a **1650** in J. E. T. Rogers *Hist. Agriculture & Prices* (1887) V. 341 [Besides the general names of sheep, ewes, rams, wethers or muttons, and lambs, I find tups, tegs, yeans,.. crones and hoggs].

yean (ji:n), *v.* Now *arch.* and *dial.* Forms: 4 ȝene, 6 yene, 6–7 yeane, 6– yean. [? OE. *ȝeéanian, related to ȝeéan 'feta', pregnant: see Y- and EAN *v.*]

1. *trans.* Of a ewe: To bring forth (a lamb); also said of goats and occas. other beasts.

1387 TREVISA *Higden* (Rolls) II. 303 Alle þe splekked lamberne and kedes þat schulden be i-ȝened. *a* **1513** FABYAN *Chron.* VII. (1811) 368 A lambe was yenyd, hauynge .ii. perfyte bodyes. **1523** FITZHERB. *Husb.* §37 An ewe goth with lambe .xx. wekes, and shall yeane her lambe in the .xxi. weke. **1605** WILLET *Hexapla Gen.* 319 There is a riuer in Assyria..which causeth the sheepe that drinke thereof to yeane blacke lambes. **1644** QUARLES *Sheph. Orac.* vii, They'l conspire To yeane their jolly lambs within thy cot. **1759** R. BROWN *Compl. Farmer* 32 The ewes yean the polled lamb with the least danger. **1800** WORDSW. *Pet Lamb* 39 The dam that did thee yean Upon the mountain-tops. **1806** SOUTHEY in *Ann. Rev.* IV. 51 To record the day and hour when a sheep died, a lamb was yeaned, or one of the flock stolen. **1862** TRENCH *Poems, Vis. Tusculum* 15 Watching the white goats..their young Tending, new yeaned. **1871** R. ELLIS tr. *Catullus* lxiv. 154 What grim lioness yeaned thee, aneath what rock's desolation?

b. *fig.* To produce, give birth to.

1598 MARSTON *Sco. of Villanie* VI. 39 Yon's one hath yean'd a fearefull prodigie. **1847** EMERSON *Poems, Wood Notes* 11, Trenchant time behoves to hurry All to yean and all to bury.

2. *intr.* To bring forth young, as a sheep.

1548 ELYOT, *Adasia*, an olde yewe, whiche hath lately yeaned or had a lambe. **1565** STAPLETON *Fortr. Faith* 99 Like an ewe when she is yeaning and wringeth for deliueraunce. **1573–80** TUSSER *Husb.* (1878) 73 Eawes readie to yeane craues ground rid cleane. **1615** SYLVESTER *Job Triumph.* IV. 478 The time when mountain Goats and Hinds Do yean and calve. *a* **1661** HOLYDAY *Juvenal* (1673) 22 To see a woman calve, or a cow yean. **1794** T. DAVIS *Agric. Wilts* 17 By the time all the ewes have yeaned. **1835** THIRLWALL *Greece* vi. I. 212 The ewes yean twice a year. **1854** *Jrnl. R. Agric. Soc.* XV. I. 232 The ewes yean in a yard or standing pen. **1879** BUTCHER & LANG *Odyssey* 51 The ewes yean thrice within the full circle of a year.

Hence **yeaned** *ppl. a.*, **'yeaning** *vbl. sb.* (also *attrib.*) and *ppl. a.*

1567–1849 [see NEW-YEANED *ppl. a.*]. **1574** HELLOWES *Gueuara's Fam. Ep.* (1577) 253 His eawes to haue good yeaning. **1577** B. GOOGE *Heresbach's Husb.* III. (1586) 139 The shepeheard must be as careful as a midwife in the yeaning time. **1686** PLOT *Staffordsh.* 258 Within thirteen months she brought 7 Lambs at three yeanings. **1697** DRYDEN *Virg. Georg.* II. 751 The yeaning Ewes prevent the springing Year. **1775** ADAIR *Amer. Ind.* 309 The she bear takes an old large hollow tree for her yeaning winter-house. **1776** *Complete Grazier* (ed. 4) xxvi. 144 It is necessary she [*sc.* a ewe] should at her yeaning have the benefit of springing grass. **1866** COPLEY *Agric.* IX. xvi. 487 Late yeaned lambs..are generally delicate.

yean(e, obs. forms of YAWN.

yeane-sherre, obs. form of JANIZARY.

1704 J. PITTS *Acc. Mohammetans* vii. 73 They are all *Yeane-Sherres*, or *Janizaries*, i.e. Soldiers.

yeanling ('ji:nlɪŋ). *arch.* [f. YEAN *v.* + -LING. Cf. EANLING.] A young lamb or kid. Also *fig.*

1637 B. JONSON *Sad Shepherd* I. ii, When in their store They add the poor man's yeanling. **1644** QUARLES *Sheph. Orac.* i, One of my weaker yeanlings hapt to stray. **1791** COWPER *Odyss.* IX. 283 As he milked his ewes.. All in their turns, her yeanling [he] gave to each. **1862** MRS. NORTON *Lady of La Garaye* IV. 411 Still to the schools the ancient chiming clock Calls the poor yeanlings of a simple flock. **1869** SWINBURNE *Ess. & Stud.* (1875) 207 Take the young ones to the teat, Left in yeanlings' penfolds pent.

b. appositive or as *adj.* That is a yeanling; young or new-born: esp. of a lamb. Also *fig.*

1658 *Topsell's Four-f. Beasts* 495 The common Epithets expressing the nature of this Beast [*sc.* the lamb] are these, rough, yeanling [*ed.* 1607 yearling], weak, unripe, sucking, tender. **1667** MILTON *P.L.* III. 434 The flesh of Lambs or yeanling Kids. **1760–72** H. BROOKE *Fool of Qual.* (1809) I. p. xiv, The yeanling kids and cooing turtles. **1812** W. TAYLOR in *Monthly Mag.* XXXIII. 239 To surround himself with ushers, proportioned to the number of boys, and more advanced in acquirement than these yeanling monitors. *a* **1873** R. BUCHANAN *Man and Shadow* I. Poet. Wks. 1874 III. 61 By the yeanling Lambkin's side.

yeant, obs. f. GIANT: see Y (I) *note.*

a **1440** *Sir Eglam.* 233 Ther dwellyth a yeant in a foreste. *Ibid.* 301 He come where the yeant was.

year[1] (jɪə(r)). Forms: 1 ȝear, ȝer, (ear, ȝar), 2–5 ȝear, 2–5 (6 *Sc.*) ȝer, (3 ȝeor, ȝeær, ȝær, hier, 3–4 ȝier, 4 ȝiere), 3–6 yer, (4 yerr, yeier, yeire, ȝher, *Sc.* ȝheir), 4–5 ȝeer, (yher, yhere), 4–5 (6 *Sc.*) ȝere, yeir, 4–7 yere, yeer, 5 ȝeere, (ȝeyre, heire, heyre, here, ȝhere, eer, *Sc.* yheir, ȝhir, 5–6 yeyr), 5–7 yeere, 5–6 *Sc.* ȝeir (6–8 zeir), 6–7 yeare, (*Sc.* zeare, 7 *Sc.* zear), 6– year. [OE. (WS.) *ȝéar* str. n., also masc., (Anglian) *ȝér*, = OFris. *jâr, jêr* (NFris. *jûar, jôr*, EFris. *jir, îr*, WFris. *jier*), OS. *jâr, gêr*, MLG. *jâr*, MDu. *jaer* (LG., Du. *jaar*), OHG., MHG. *jâr* (G. *jahr*), ON. *ár* (Sw. *år*, Da. *aar*), Goth. *jēr*:—**jǣrom*, cognate with Zend *yāre* year, Gr. ὧρος year, ὥρα time of year, season, year, time of day, OSl. *jarŭ* spring (Russ., Pol., etc. *jar* spring, Serb. summer); cf. also L. *hornus* of this year (:—**ho-jōrinus*). The normal OE. (flexionless) pl. *ȝéar* is represented still in dialectal usage; for illustration of the history see 1 *β*.]

1. a. The time occupied by the sun in its apparent passage through the signs of the zodiac, *i.e.* (according to modern astronomy) the period of the earth's revolution round the sun, forming a natural unit of time (nearly = 365¼ days); hence, a space of time approximately equal to this in any conventional practical reckoning (considered with respect to its length, without reference to its limits: cf. 3).

c **960** ÆTHELWOLD *Rule St. Benet* liii. (Schröer 1885) 85 To ȝeares fæce tweȝen ȝebroðra into cumena cicenan gan. *c* **1000** *Sax. Leechd.* I. 204 Hyt bynnan healfon ȝeare ealne þone wætan ut atyhþ. *c* **1200** *Trin. Coll. Hom.* 53 Nu aȝe we ..leten alse fele daȝes, alse hie diden ȝeres... þat we ne singeð þo blisfulle songes. *c* **1205** LAY. 217 Asscanius heold þis drihliche lond Daiȝes & ȝeres. *c* **1290** *S. Eng. Leg.* 2/33 Twelf Monþe it was þare-afterward and half ȝer and more. *a* **1300** *Cursor M.* 4705 Be þe thrid yeir was gan, Vnnethes was þer beist left an. **1362** LANGL. *P. Pl.* A. VII. 43 þou schalt ȝelden hit a-ȝeyn at one ȝeeres ende. *c* **1400** *St. Alexius* (Laud 463) 58 More he lerned in on ȝer þan any of his oþer fere dide in ȝeres tene. **1428** *E.E. Wills* (1882) 80 Competent saleri for an hole here. **1456–70** *Acts Parlt. Scot.* (1875) XII. 27/2 Landis..quhilkis our predecessoris hes iosyt..ii hundreth ȝeirys befor thir days. **1500–20** DUNBAR *Poems* xxx. 32 Gif evir my fortoun wes to be a freir, The dait thairof is past full mony a ȝeir. **1598** SHAKS. *Merry W.* I. i. 13, I that I doe, and haue done any time these three hundred yeeres. **1637** *Decree Star Chamb.* x. in *Milton's Areop.* (Arb.) 14 No Haberdasher of small wares,..not hauing beene seuen yeeres apprentice to the trade. **1718–19** SWIFT *Stella's Birthday* Wks. 1841 I. 682/2 Stella this day is thirty-four (We shan't dispute a year or more). **1819** SCOTT *Leg. Montrose* vi, A family of four hundred years' standing. **1842** DICKENS *Amer. Notes* xviii, A gentleman..within a year or two on either side of thirty. **1884** GOLDWIN SMITH in *Contemp. Rev.* Apr. 533 The idea that the United States are disposed to aggress upon Canada cannot survive a year's intercourse with their people.

β. **900–30** *O.E. Chron.* (Parker MS.) Pref. 4 þa feng Æþelbryht his broþur to, & heold .v. ȝear. *c* **1000** *Ags. Gosp.* Matt. ix. 20 An wif þe þolode blod-ryne twelf ȝear. *c* **1200** *Vices & Virtues* 143 þrie hier and six moneþes. *c* **1205** LAY. 3789 Ale þe twa ȝere. *a* **1225** *Ancr. R.* 218 Efter ueole ȝer. **1340** HAMPOLE *Pr. Consc.* 741 An hundreth and twenti yhere. *c* **1386** CHAUCER *Knt.'s T.* 588 And thre yeer in this wise his lif he ladde. *c* **1449** PECOCK *Repr.* I. xi. 56 Poul was slain bifore the tyme of this exile bi almost xxx[ti]. ȝeer. **1526** *Pilgr. Perf.* (W. de W. 1531) 118b, A thynge done perauenture a dosyn yere before. **1535** STEWART *Cron. Scot.* (Rolls) II. 121 Mony ȝeir. **1553** BECON *Reliques of Rome* (1563) 200 He had burned in Purgatorye a greate number of yeare. **1602** SHAKS. *Ham.* V. i. 183 He will last you some eight yeare, or nine yeare. **1699** BENTLEY *Phal.* Pref. p. lxxxv, Sir Henry Spelman..used it lxxx Year since. **1701** in *Cath. Rec. Soc. Publ.* VII. 101 The Curé is now stone blinde, & has been this 4 year. **1815** SCOTT *Guy M.* xxxix, At last they didna 'gree at a' for twa or three year.

b. Following and qualifying a date: = a year before or after...; †*was a year*, a year ago. More commonly expressed by *twelvemonth* (TWELVEMONTH 1 b).

1533 CROMWELL in Merriman *Life & Lett.* (1902) I. 362 That..your pleasure maye be to suffer it to bere date from Mydsomer Was a yere. **1606** G. W[OODCOCKE] *Lives Emp.* in *Hist. Ivstine* L I 5, The Emperor..tooke him prisoner vppon the same day twentye yeares, after that his father was taken prisoner by Charles the fift. *a* **1873** WILBERFORCE *Ch. & Emp.* (1874) 8 On the day year on which he had received our Lord's servants into his house. **1880** DISRAELI *Endym.* xxxv, I should not be surprised..if he were to change his name again before this time year.

c. In reference to the duration of some (usually painful) experience, as the sufferings of purgatory (always in reference to ***years of pardon***), a term of imprisonment, etc. (Usually *pl.* with numeral.)

c **1200** *Trin. Coll. Hom.* 61 Vuele god us briseð,..oðer þurh orf qualm oðer þurh smerte ȝier [cf. G. *schmerzenjahr*]. **1357** *Lay Folks Catech.* (L.) 221 And so myȝt pardoun be gotun to sey yche day a lady sawter ȝhe ten þowsand ȝer in on ȝere. *c* **1400** *Apol. Loll.* 8 þewenti þowzand ȝer of pardoun. *c* **1489** CAXTON *Sonnes of Aymon* x. 271 'Goodys curse have he for it', sayd Charlemagne, 'and an evyll yere.' **1533** GAU *Richt Vay* 5 Sa mony thousand ȝeris of pardone pouers and remissione of sine and payne. **1874** W. S. GILBERT *Charity* II, *Mr. S...* There is nothing to connect me with that matter... *Ruth.* Nothing?.. I've writin' of yours which is fourteen year [*i.e.* penal servitude], if it's a day. **1901** *Scotsman* 27 Feb. 11/1 The woman also told him that..if he was not careful she could get him fifteen years.

d. *pl.* with numeral, expressing a person's age. (Cf. 5.)

More usually either followed by *of age* or *old*, or omitted by ellipsis; e.g. 'a man fifty years of age', or 'fifty years old', or 'a man of fifty'. For obs. variants of expression see quots.

a **1300** *Cursor M.* 11315 O gode haliman..O sex scor yeire, hight symeon. **13..**, etc. [see OLD *a.* 4b]. *c* **1380** WYCLIF *Serm.* Sel. Wks. I. 83 Whan [Crist] was twelfe ȝeer olde. **1382** —— *Matt.* ii. 16 Alle the children,..fro two ȝeer age and with ynne. *c* **1386** CHAUCER *Merch. T.* 177, I wol no womman thritty yeer of age. **1390** GOWER *Conf.* I. 148 The yongest of hem hadde of age Fourtiene yer. *a* **1425** *Cursor M.* 12386 (Trin.) Ihesu was þat tyme þore Of eiȝte yeer olde & more. *c* **1450** *Merlin* i. 15 It semed ij yere age or more. *c* **1480** *Childe of Bristowe* 37 in Hazl. *E.P.P.* I. 112 When the child was xij yere and more. **1523** FITZHERB. *Husb.* §67 Put theym bothe in one pasture, tyll they be foure or fyue yere olde. **1570** *Satir. Poems Reform.* x. 14 Ane woundit man, of aucht and threttie ȝeiris. **1600** SHAKS. *A.Y.L.* II. iii. 73 At seauenteene yeeres, many their fortunes seeke But at fourescore, it is too late a weeke. **1609** SKENE *Reg. Maj.*, *Table* 62b, The heire of ane Soccoman is of perfite age, quhen he is passed fivetene zeares. **1675** HOBBES *Odyssey* (1677) 32 Wine, that aged was eleven year. **1695** SIBBALD *Autobiog.* (1834) 127 Four children..who died all before they were full four year old. **1847** TENNYSON *Princess* v. 544 A nurse of ninety years.

e. In special or idiomatic genitive or attrib. uses, qualified by *a* or a numeral.

c **1000** ÆLFRIC *Gram.* xlix. (Z.) 287 *Anniculus*, anes ȝeares cild oððe lamb. **1451**, **1552** [see DAY *sb.* 11]. **1475** *Bk. Noblesse* (Roxb.) 8 The dyvysyon..dured in Fraunce continuelly by .xj. yeerday. **1559** *Mirr. Mag.* (1563) C iv, My enmy straunged but for a ten yeares daye. **1609** C. BUTLER *Fem. Mon.* (1623) D iij, The Bee is but a yeares Bird, with some advantage. **1635** in Foster *Crt. Min. E. Ind. Comp.* (1907) 67 [At 4l. per hundred at] a yeares day of payment. **1654** CROMWELL *Sp.* 12 Sept., A people that have been unhinged this twelve-years day, and are unhinged still. **1860** *Merc. Marine Mag.* VII. 181 She..is classed in Lloyd's Register as an eight years' ship.

2. a. With qualifying words, denoting periods differing in length according to the manner in which they are computed in some scientific or conventional reckoning.

anomalistic, astronomical, canicular, civil, embolismic, equinoctial, Gregorian, Julian, lunar, lunisolar, natural, sidereal, solar, Sothic, tropical, vague (etc.) ***year***: see the adjs.

c **1055** *Byrhtferth's Handboc* in *Anglia* VIII. 316 þæs ȝeares daȝas þe ȝetelwise witan nemniað on lyden solaris annus, & on englisc þære sunnan ȝear. **1579–80** NORTH *Plutarch* (1595) 79 For the Romaines at the beginning had but 10. moneths in the yere: as some of the barbarous people make but three moneths for their yere. **1592** [see JULIAN]. **1594** BLUNDEVIL *Exerc.* II. I. xlii. (1597) 171b, The Egyptian yeare containeth the iust number of 365. dayes. **1728** CHAMBERS *Cycl.* s.v. *Period*, *Victorian Period*, an Interval of 532 Julian Years. **1757** J. FERGUSON *Astron.* (ed. 2) xxi. §408 The Solar or Tropical Year, which contains 365 days, 5 hours, 48 minutes, 57 seconds; and is the only proper or natural year, because it always keeps the same seasons to the same months. **1841** WILKINSON *Mann. & Cust. Anc. Egypt.* xi. Ser. II. I. 17 The sacred was the same as the solar or vague year. **1860** R. S. POOLE in W. Smith *Dict. Bible* I. 505/1 There appear to have been at least three years in use with the Egyptians before the Roman domination, the Vague Year, the Tropical Year, and the Sothic Year.

b. *transf.* Applied to a very long period or cycle (in chronology or mythology, or vaguely in poetic use).

cynic year: see CYNIC *a.* 3. ***great year*** (Gr. μέγας ἐνιαυτός), the period (variously reckoned) after which all the heavenly bodies were supposed to return to their original positions, also called ***Platonic year*** (see PLATONIC *a.* 3b); also occas. used of certain cycles in modern chronology.

1398 TREVISA *Barth. De P.R.* VIII. xxi. (Bodl. MS.) lf. 86/1 Chaunging of roundenes and cercles of sterres..þe chaungeing of hem falleþ in euerich xxxvj. M. ȝeere. And þis þe greete ȝere þat is the laste of alle þinges. **1585** T. WASHINGTON tr. *Nicholay's Voy.* IV. xi. 123b, With the life of this bird [*sc.* the phœnix], the reuolution of the great yere is made, which diuers..say to consist, not in 540. yeres, but in 12950. yeres. **1587** GOLDING *De Mornay* xxvi. (1592) 402 If they had liued lesse than Sixe hundred yeares, their obseruations had bene in vaine, because the great yeare continueth so long. **1594** BLUNDEVIL *Exerc.* II. I. xxxvii. (1597) 170 It is called of some the yeare of the worlde, and of some the great yeare of Plato, which contayneth according to Alphonsus, 49000. yeares..yet some affirme that the perfect yeare of the worlde contayneth but 36000 yeares. **1666** S. PARKER *Free & Impart. Censure* (1667) 91, I will engage you shall never be one of their Disciples, though you should study them [*sc.* Platonists] to the revolution of their Great Year. **1667** MILTON *P.L.* v. 583 On such day As Heav'ns great Year brings forth. **1737** WHISTON *Josephus, Antiq.* I. iii. §9 Unless they had lived six hundred years: for the Great Year is compleated in that interval. **1830** LYELL *Princ. Geol.* I. 116 The 'great year,' or geological cycle. **1871** ALABASTER *Wheel of Law* 89 Five thousand angelic years, which are five hundred and eighty-six millions of the years of men. **1893** HUXLEY *Romanes Lect.* 36 The suggestion that the power and the intelligence of man can ever arrest the procession of the great year.

c. The period of revolution of any planet round the sun (***planetary year***).

1728 CHAMBERS *Cycl.* s.v., The Times wherein Jupiter, Saturn, the Sun, Moon, &c. finish their Revolutions..are respectively call'd the Years of Jupiter, and Saturn, [etc.]. **1870** E. F. BURR *Ecce Coelum* iv. 104 According to the Neptunian calendar, it is only thirty-six years since the creation of Adam.

3. A space of time, of the length stated in sense 1, with fixed limits. **a.** *esp.* Such a space of time as reckoned in a calendar and denoted by a number in a particular era: commonly divided into twelve calendar months, in the ordinary (Roman) calendar beginning with January and ending with December, and consisting of 365 (or 366) days: see CALENDAR 1. (Distinctively called the ***civil year***.)

year of Christ, † ***of God*** (Sc.), ***of our Lord*** (LORD *sb.* 7b), ***of grace*** (GRACE *sb.* 12), †***of salvation*** (SALVATION 1c), a particular year of the Christian era (denoted by a number following).

Also with cardinal number following, denoting a period of a political regime as a means of calendar reckoning. Formerly also in *pl.* with numeral, denoting a particular year of an era.

c **1000** *Ags. Gosp.* Luke ii. 41 His maȝas ferdon ælce ȝere to hierusalem. *c* **1132** *O.E. Chron.* (Laud MS.) an. 1132 Ðis ȝear com Henri king to þis land. *c* **1205** LAY. 7220 He makede þane kalend þe dihteð þane moneð & þeȝer. *a* **1250** *Owl & Night.* 101 þat oþer ȝer a faukun bredde. *c* **1250** *Gen. & Ex.* 150 Two geuelengðhes timen her, And two solstices in ðe ȝer. **1357** *Lay Folks Mass Bk.* (1879) 118 The sacrement of the auter..whilk ilk man and woman..aught forto resceyve anes in the yhere. **1396** in *Scott. Antiq.* (1900) XIV. 217 The secvnde day of May the yher of our lorde MCCC neynty and sex. *a* **1500** *Bernard. de cura rei fam.*, etc. (E.E.T.S.) 32 Be the yheris of cryst comyn and gone, Fully nynty ande nyne. **1556** LAUDER *Tractate of Kyngis* 19 The ȝeir of God Ane M.V.C.LVI. **1584** in *Cath. Rec. Soc. Publ.* V. 64 The lettre from Richard Hutton written in September withowt yere. **1607** TOPSELL *Four-f. Beasts* 297 Stalions are to be seperated from Mares al the yeare long, except at the time of procreation. *a* **1646** J. GREGORY *Learned Tracts* (1649) 164 The Christians did not use to reckon by the years of Christ, until the 532 of the Incarnation. *Ibid.* 165 That the first year Dionysian of Christ ought to bee reckoned the third. **1657** *North's Plutarch, Add. Lives* 4 In the yeer of the Salvation of all mankinde, three hundred thirty and nine. *a* **1700** in *Cath. Rec. Soc. Publ.* IX. 335 [They] were al by holy obedience sent to Paris in the yeare 1652. **1788** COWPER *Stanzas Bill of Mortality* 2 Could I..as sure presage To whom the rising year shall prove the last. **1818** SCOTT *Rob Roy* xxvi, The Hielands hae been keepit quiet since the year aughty-nine—that was Killiecrankie year. **1861** M. PATTISON *Ess.* (1889) I. 36 Dr. Pauli..more than once gives the day and the month, without remembering to add the year of an event. **1933** E. WAUGH *Scoop* II. iv. 226 New Calendar. Year One of the Soviet State of Ishmaelia. **1971** *Times Lit. Suppl.* 27 Aug. 1015/2 When he refers to 'the language of the Year III', he means that of the Year II [of the 1870 Commune]. **1972** R. COBB *Reactions to French Revolution* i. 38 The *coup d'état* of Fructidor year V (Sept. 1797). **1980** P. VAN GREENAWAY *Dissident* vii. 147 The Seventeen Revolution is Year One to our country.

c **1440** *Alphabet of Tales* 265 Abowte þe yeris of our Lord cccc vj. **1474** *Acc. Ld. High Treas. Scot.* I. 1 The ferd day of the moneth of August, the ȝere of God etc. lxxiij ȝeris.

b. Such a space of time, with limits not necessarily coinciding with those of the civil year, forming a division of a period (or the whole period) of office, study, or other occupation, or of a person's lifetime (in these cases commonly with ordinal numeral, often with possessive noun or pronoun), or taken between definite dates for some special purpose, e.g. taxation, payment of dividends, agricultural operations, etc.

c **1000** *Lambeth Ps.* xxx. 11 Lif min and ȝearas mine. *c* **1200** ORMIN 9503, & ta wass Kayfasess ȝer þe fifte ȝer bigunnenn. *a* **1225** *Leg. Kath.* 43 þe fif & þrittuðe ȝer of his [*sc.* Maxence's] rixlinge. **1338** R. BRUNNE *Chron.* (1725) I. 10 In his elleuent ȝere com folk, þat misleued. *c* **1425** *Cursor M.* 3893 (Trin.) His ȝeres passed & seuen dayes Rachel he weddide þe story sayes. *c* **1450** *Godstow Reg.* 138 þe v. yer of þe reine of kinge Edwarde. **1518** *Star Chamber Cases* (Selden Soc.) II. 162 Suche greate charges as they [*sc.* sheriffs]..must bere by Reason of the same Office after their yer Ended. **1611** B. JONSON *Catiline* III. i, Which I'll perform..not for my year, But for my life. **1616** in *Cath. Rec. Soc. Publ.* III. 34 There in your English Colledge,..he liued and heard his course of philosophie and almost two yeares of school diuinitie. **1631** MILTON *Sonn.* vii. 2 How soon hath Time..Stoln on his wing my three and twentith yeer! **1635** A. STAFFORD *Fem. Glory* (1869) 61 His living in obscurity from His twelfth to His thirtieth yeere. **1848** E. S. CREASY *Eton Coll.* 42 The relative positions which the boys of each year had occupied in the school. **1871** SMILES *Charac.* iii. (1876) 68 At the following Christmas examination he was the first of his year.

(*a*) Freq. with qualifying word, as ***financial, fiscal, sabbatical, school, tax year***: see under the first elements; ***academic year***: in a school, college, etc., in the Northern hemisphere usu. reckoned from the beginning of the autumn term until the end of the summer term.

1932 *Handbk. Univ. Oxford* 103 An overseas application made..a few weeks before the beginning of the academic year has little or no prospect of success. **1957** *Encycl. Brit.* XXII. 876/2 The master's degree is usually obtained for one academic year of graduate work. **1971** *Morning Star* 28 Dec. 4 Every September boys and girls..return to school..to begin a new academic year. **1983** *Oxf. Univ. Gaz.* 10 Nov. 218/2 The college proposes to elect a distinguished visitor to a Visiting Senior Research Fellowship during the academic year 1984–5.

(*b*) Used *attrib.* or *absol.* with preceding ordinal numeral to denote a student at a particular stage of education. Also *collect.*

1851 B. H. HALL *Coll. College Words & Customs* 266 In the University of Cambridge, Eng., the title of *Second-Year Men*..is given to students during the second year of their residence at the University. **1894** A. MORRISON *Tales of Mean Streets* iii. 50 A fourth-year London Hospital student. **1913** J. VAIZEY *College Girl* II. xix. 268 One word in your ear! Don't ask a third-year girl to dance with you. **1927** R. LEHMANN *Dusty Answer* III. i. 124 I've done six hours every day this vac... Sibyl Jones has done ten hours every day... Third years ought to be more sensible. **1935** D. L. SAYERS *Gaudy Night* vii. 139 There are some oddities in the First Year... I expect the Third Year said the same about us ..but..I should call the whole of our year pretty sound. **1966** E. H. JONES *Margery Fry* v. 44 Margery..was the obvious choice from the First Year when a committee was formed to arrange a garden-party in May 1895. **1979** D. BRIERLEY *Cold War* iii. 26 Sociology second years from Nanterre. **1982** D. CLARK *Doone Walk* viii. 179 He's a Bristol University third-year bloke.

c. Such a space of time as arranged for religious observance in the Christian Church, with special seasons and holy days, beginning with Advent (but, formerly or locally, with other periods).

a **1400** *Wyclif's Bible* (1850) IV. 683 The lessouns, pistlis, and gospels, that ben rad in the chirche al the ȝeer. **1657** SPARROW *Bk. Com. Prayer* 106 We begin..our Ecclesiastical year (as to some accounts, though not as to the order of our service) with the glorious Annunciation of his Birth by angelical message. **1827** KEBLE (*title*) The Christian Year; Thoughts in Verse for the Sundays and Holydays throughout the year. **1875** *W. Smith's Dict. Chr. Antiq.* I. 33/1 The first Sunday in Advent was not always the beginning of the liturgical year... The *Antiphonarius* of St. Gregory begins 1 Advent, and the *Liber Responsalis* with its Vigil. But the earlier practice was to begin the ecclesiastical year with the month of March, as being that in which our Lord was crucified (March 25).

d. Such a period officially designated for special celebration or to focus public attention on a particular object of concern; esp. ***Holy Year***, a year so designated by the Pope, now usu. once every 25 years, during which special Indulgences are granted and ceremonies held.

1699 J. JACKSON *Let.* 25 Dec. in *Lett. & Second Diary of Samuel Pepys* (1932) 291 Wee made our entry here on Tuesday last, about 23 a clock, and were soon after deafned with the jangling of all the bells of the town, which for severall days, morning and evening, had proclaimed the approach of the Holy Year. **1776** PIUS VI (*title*) Instructions & Directions for Gaining the Grand Jubilee of the Holy Year, celebrated at Rome anno 1775, and extended to the universal Church anno 1776, by his Holiness Pius VI. **1858** H. E. WISEMAN *Recoll. Last Four Popes* II. iv. 270 The practice has been, that on Ascension Day of the preceding year, the Pope promulgates the Holy Year, or Jubilee. **1900** H. THURSTON *Holy Year of Jubilee* ix. 358 During the Holy Year, and also during the time of the extension of the Jubilee to the rest of Christendom, the Holy Father grants extraordinary powers to confessors. **1957** J. S. HUXLEY *Relig. without Revelation* (rev. ed.) ix. 205 Mass celebrations, like those of the Holy Year or the rallies and parades of Nazism and Communism. **1960** *Stamp Mag.* May 454/1 Commemorative. For World Refugee Year (Overprint on the rest of the 1958 World Exhibition stamps, with surcharge in aid of World Refugee Year 1960). **1965** *Ibid.* Apr. 244/1 The Australian Post Office will issue a stamp this year to commemorate International Co-operation Year. **1971** M. LEE *Dying for Fun* xliv. 212 He..decided to organize and launch Compassion Year. **1974** *Times* 7 Feb. 15/8 In the year 2073..many of the trees planted in Tree Planting Year 1973 will still be with us. **1983** *Out of Town* Dec. 52/4 Those of us who go to church already know that 1984 is Christian Heritage Year.

4. a. As the period of the seasons, and of the growth of crops and vegetation in general; *spec.* with reference to the vintage of wine. Hence *poet.* connoting the phenomena of growth and decay.

c **1386** CHAUCER *Merch. T.* 222 Myn herte and alle my lymes been as grene As laurer thurgh the yeer is for to sene. *c* **1430** *Two Cookery-bks.* 29 Take Strawberys, & waysshe hem in tyme of ȝere in gode red wyne. **1573–80** TUSSER *Husb.* (1878) 59 Make hillocks of molehils, in field thorough out, and so to remaine, till the yeere go about. **1637** MILTON *Lycidas* 5 Shatter your leaves before the mellowing year. **1728–46** THOMSON *Spring* 18 As yet the trembling year is unconfirmed, And Winter oft at eve resumes the breeze. **1781** COWPER *Heroism* 24 Vines, olives, herbage, forests disappear, And all the charms of a Sicilian year. **1842** TENNYSON *Day Dream, Sleeping Palace* i, The varying year with blade and sheaf Clothes and reclothes the happy plains. **1864** 'J. WARD' *Diary* 22 May in J. Burnett *Useful Toil* (1974) I. 85 Everything looks well in fields and gardens, with every prospect of a good fruit year. **1941** B. SCHULBERG *What makes Sammy Run?* xi. 206 Laurette..told the waiter to send it back. 'If you haven't *1927*, don't bother. That's the only good year left.' **1967** 'L. BLACK' *Two Ladies in Verona* x. 161 A bottle of Mumm Cordon Rouge. I leave the year to you, but it'd better be good. **1984** *Sunday Tel.* 20 May 12/8, I bought the wine. 1964 was quite a good year.

b. *transf.* A year's produce. (A literalism.)

1382 WYCLIF *Joel* ii. 25, Y shal ȝeelde to you the ȝeris whom the locust eete.

c. Each of the annual rings in the wood of a tree. *rare.*

1708 *Phil. Trans.* XXVI. 163 The Circles, or (as they are commonly call'd) Years, are closer.

5. a. *pl.* Age (of a person).

years of discretion: see DISCRETION 6 b.

a **1000** *Cædmon's Gen.* 2381 Ðearum frod. *c* **1200** ORMIN 10885 Himm birrþ beon fullwaxenn mann, & shadd fra childless ȝæress. *a* **1225** *Juliana* 5 Ȝunge mon of ȝeres. *c* **1400** *Destr. Troy* 12759 He was yong & yepe, of yeris but iyte. *c* **1500** *Lancelot* 1431 Euery gilt..Done frome he passith the ȝeris of Innocens. *a* **1529** SKELTON *Death K. Edw. IV* 37, I se wyll, they leve that doble my ȝeris. **1577** HANMER *Anc. Eccl. Hist.* (1619) 231, I my selfe learned it of one of no small credite, of great yeares. **1598** R. BERNARD tr. *Terence, Hecyra* V. i, I am of that yeares now that it were no reason to remit mine offence. *c* **1610** *Women Saints* (1886) 39 When she was of yeares fitt for marriage. **16..** MIDDLETON, etc. *Old Law* II. ii, Ere they be thought at years to welcome misery! **1624** QUARLES *Job Militant* Medit. xvi, Dayes, produced to decrepit yeeres, Fild with experience, and grizly haires. *c* **1652** MILTON *Sonn. to Sir H. Vane* 1 Vane, young in yeares, but in sage counsell old. **1700** S. L. tr. *Fryke's Voy. E. Ind.* 1 Ever since I came to years, that I could tell my own inclinations. **1749** FIELDING *Tom Jones* XII. xiii, You may change your Opinion, if you live to my Years. **1794** MRS. RADCLIFFE *Myst. Udolpho* xiii, That Madame Cheron, at her years, should elect a second husband, was ridiculous. **1867** FREEMAN *Norm. Conq.* I. vi. 594 William, still a boy in years but a man in conduct and counsel.

b. Full or mature age (esp. in phr. ***into*** or ***to years***, ***of years***); old age (esp. in phr. ***in years*** = old, aged). Now *arch.* or *poet.*

stricken, struck, strucken in years: see the pa. pples.

1579 E. K. in *Spenser's Sheph. Cal.* Feb., Emblem, Men of yeares haue no feare of god at al. **1581** PETTIE tr. *Guazzo's Civ. Conv.* III. (1586) 130 It is better for a man to chuse a young wife, then one in yeares. **1593** SHAKS. *Rich. II*, II. iii. 66 Till my infant-fortune comes to yeeres. **1605** *First Pt. Jeronimo* I. iii, Had not your reuerend yeares beene present heere, I should haue ponyarded the Villaynes bowels. **1607** TOPSELL *Four-f. Beasts* 392 If the horse be of yeeres. **1623** COCKERAM II, *Vnder Yeeres*, Minoritie, Nonage. **1633** LAUD in *Strafford's Lett.* (1739) I. 111, I am in Years, and have had a troublesome Life. **1724** A. COLLINS *Gr. Chr. Relig.* 85 As they grew into Years. **1773** BURNEY *Pres. St. Mus. Germany* (1775) I. 329 Wagenseil is rather in years. **1813** SCOTT *Trierm.* I. viii, The Man of Years mused long and deep. **1868** BROWNING *Ring & Bk.* III. 284 He was slipping into years apace, And years make men restless.

6. a. *pl.* (more or less vaguely): Age, period, times; with *poss. pron.* time or period of life.

a **1225** *Ancr. R.* 218 Iðe uorme ȝeres [of monastic life] nis hit bute bal-pleouwe. **1340–70** *Alex. & Dind.* 215 Fram þe ȝouþe of my ȝer ȝerned ich haue Of wide werkus to wite. **1382** WYCLIF *Isa.* xxxviii. 15, I shal eft thenke to thee alle my ȝeres, in the bitternesse of my soule. **1430–40** LYDG. *Bochas* VIII. xii. (MS. Bodl. 263) 379/1 The lord of lordis, lord of longest yeeris. *a* **1542** WYATT *Penit. Ps.* CII. xxiii, Take me not Lord away In myddes off my yeres. **1659** H. PLUMPTRE in *12th Rep. Hist. MSS. Comm.* App. v. 6 Wishing that all your yeares yet to come may passe over with mirth and jollityes. **1719** WATTS *Ps.* xc, Our God, our help in ages past, Our hope for years to come. **1762–71** H. WALPOLE *Vertue's Anecd. Paint.* (1786) IV. 28 Those who know any thing of the state of painting in this country of late years. **1874** GREEN *Short Hist.* vii. §8. 430 The last years of Elizabeth's reign were years of splendour and triumph abroad.

b. In emphatic or hyperbolical use, chiefly in *pl.*: A very long time. (Cf. AGE *sb.* 10 b.)

1692 DRYDEN *Cleomenes* I. i, Where hast thou been this long long year of hours? *c* **1759** J. GOFF in *Jrnl. Friends Hist. Soc.* (1918) 69 Dr Betty, I think every Day Absent from thee, Years. **1852** THACKERAY *Esmond* II. i, At certain periods of life we live years of emotion in a few weeks. **1853** M. ARNOLD *Scholar Gipsy* v, Once, years after, in the country lanes, Two scholars whom at college erst he knew Met him.

7. a. Phrases. (See also senses 2, 3, 5.) **a year**, formerly also ***aȝere***, ***ayeer***, ***a-year*** [A *adj.*[2] 4, *prep.*[1] 8 b]: every year, yearly, *per annum.* †**by (the) year** [BY *prep.* 24 c]: in the same sense; rarely †***by years***; also ***by the year***, from year to year (as a tenancy, etc.). **of the year**: denoting things or persons considered to be outstanding examples of their kind in a particular year. **the year dot**: see DOT *sb.*[1] 4 c. **the year one**: see ONE *numeral* 4. **year after year** [AFTER *prep.* 6], **year by year** [BY *prep.* 25 c], **from year to year** [FROM *prep.* 3 b]: through a succession of years, either continuously or at some particular time in each year; every year successively; (hence ***year-to-year*** adj. phr., occurring or done from year to year); also †***for year and year***, †***from*** x ***year to*** x ***year***, x ***year and*** x ***year***: every *x* years; †***year, year, and year***: on a stated occasion every year in succession. **year in (and) year out** [IN *adv.* 2]: as each year begins and until it ends; continually throughout the year (and through successive years). **year-on-year** *adj. phr.*: in *Economics*, used with reference to a comparison of figures with corresponding ones for a date twelve months earlier.

a **1250** *Owl & Night.* 1133 Þar treon schulleþ a yer blowe. **1398** TREVISA *Barth. De P.R.* XVII. lxi. (Tollem. MS.), The fige tre..bereþ frute þries or fowre siþes aȝere. **1435** in Heath *Grocers' Comp.* (1869) 417 Paid..the mairalte dew ffor the ground in the Groceres' Hall,..ipurchased ayeer.. xl lb. **1573–80** TUSSER *Husb.* (1878) 28 Christmas comes but once a yeere. *a* **1791** WESLEY *Wks.* (1872) VIII. 327 Every worn-out Preacher shall receive..at least ten pounds a-year. **1849** MACAULAY *Hist. Eng.* iii. I. 291 Every man who had fifty pounds a year derived from land. **1861** BROUGHAM *Brit. Const.* vi. (1862) 84 He pays £10 a-year to the owner.

a **1300** *Cursor M.* 10212 Þai halud alle þe festes dere þe Iues war wonto halu bi yere. **14..** *Customs of Malton* in *Surtees Misc.* (1890) 59, ij suttes by þe ȝer' to þe sayd cowrtt. **1430–40** LYDG. *Bochas* I. v. (MS. Bodl. 263) 22/2 She.. tauhte ther laboreris To sowe ther greyn & multeplie bi yeris. *a* **1450** *Knt. de la Tour* xvii. 23 A ladi..that might spende more thanne fyue hundred pounde bi yeere. **1544** tr. *Littleton's Tenures* III. viii. 108 b, If such lande be worth xl. s. by yere. **1640** HABINGTON *Edw. IV* 95 The reward of a hundred pound by the yeare during life. **1797** [see BY *prep.* 24 c].

1883 H. JAMES in *Atlantic Monthly* Sept. 316/1 Wherever the traveler goes, in France, he is reminded of this very honorable practice—the purchase by the government of a certain number of 'pictures of the year'. **1936** L. P. SMITH *S.P.E. Tract* XLVI. 220 The market-place where the books of the year are sold in large editions. **1968** 'E. LATHEN' *Stitch in Time* vi. 46, I hope they haven't confused Wendell Martin with the GP of the year. **1983** *Daily Tel.* 18 Aug. 8/4 A 35-year-old mother..beat 523 competitors to win the London Chamber of Commerce and Industry's award as top secretary of the year.

1611 *Bible* 2 Sam. xxi. 1 There was a famine..three yeeres, yeere after yeere. **1830** TENNYSON *Day Dream, Sleeping Beauty* i, Year after year unto her feet..The maiden's jet-black hair has grown.

c **1380** *Antecrist* in Todd *Three Treat. Wyclif* (1851) 131 Þe almes of þise bischoppes of so old synne is gedren for a certeyn rente ȝer bi ȝer in lecherie to lige. *c* **1400** *Pilgr. Sowle* (Caxton 1483) IV. xxxiv. 82 In euery countre ben certeyne officers yere by yere chaunged for the more sykernes. **1539** *Bible* (Great) 1 Kings x. 25 [They] brought hym euery man his present, vesselles of syluer [etc.] yere by yere. **1585** HIGINS *Junius' Nomencl.* 5/2 *Annales*,..Chronicles: records of matters done yeare by yeare. **1793** COWPER *A Tale* 77 Be it your fortune, year by year, The same resource to prove. **1885** SIR H. COTTON in *Law Rep. 30 Chanc. Div.* 12 The accounts were delivered year by year to Mr. Norton.

c **1380** WYCLIF *Wks.* (1880) 62 Fro ȝer to ȝer, fro seuene ȝer to seuene ȝer. **1436** *Pol. Poems* (Rolls) II. 175 Now wolle ye here how they in Cotteswolde Were wonte to borowe, or they schulde be solde, Here wolle gode, as for yere and yere [*v.r.* fro yere to yere]. *Ibid.* 176 Ffor yere and yere they schulde make paymente, And some tyme als too yere and too yere. *c* **1485** *E.E. Misc.* (Warton Club) 20 There as thou hast deyllyd from heyre to ȝere. **1539** *Bible* (Great) 1 Sam. ii. 19 Hys mother made hym a lytle coate, and brought it to him from yere to yere. **1594** R. ASHLEY tr. *Loys le Roy* 68 From three yeares to three. *c* **1630** MILTON *Sonn.* i. 11 As thou from yeer to yeer hast sung too late For my relief. **1635** in Foster *Crt. Min. E. India Comp.* (1907) 29 At yeare, yeare, and yeare from the first of March next. *Ibid.* 93 Yeare, yeare and yeare, upon rebate. **1838** H. H. WHITE *Watkins' Princ. Conveyancing* ii. (ed. 8) 28 *note*, A tenancy from year to year. **1845** A. POLSON in *Encycl. Metrop.* II. 829/1 An estate from year to year may arise not only from express stipulation, but even from that general letting heretofore held to constitute an estate at will. **1855** I. TAYLOR *Restor. Belief* (1856) 218 A year-to-year reading of the Gospels. **1870** HUXLEY *Lay Serm.* etc. (1877) 251 That the energy radiated from year to year was supplied from year to year. **1962** *Lebende Sprachen* VII. 113/3 Year-to-year growth ratio. **1977** J. L. HARPER *Population Biol. Plants* 203 The relative constancy of mean seed weight over a density range in this experiment is particularly interesting because the year to year variation in seed weight is quite large.

1830 *Massachusetts Spy* 28 July 4/1 I've been to..school *year in and year out*. **1868** LOUISA M. ALCOTT *Little Women* xv, You see other girls having splendid times, while you grind, grind, year in and year out. **1881** MRS. RIDDELL *Senior Partner* III. 135 At Mr. McCullagh's the same faces greeted customers year in year out.

1976 *Daily Tel.* 20 July 1/5 It is hoped this will show a year on year rise in average earnings of between 14 and 15 per cent. **1982** *Listener* 16 Dec. 27/3 Over a ten-week period from September to November, the year-on-year decline recorded is equivalent to 12 per cent of individuals, or 7 per cent of households.

b. *Law.* (*a*) ***year and day***, a period constituting a term for certain purposes, in order to ensure the completion of a full year. ***year, day, and waste***, a prerogative whereby the sovereign was entitled to the profits for a year and a day of a tenement held by a person attainted of petty treason or felony, with the right of wasting the tenement: finally abolished in 1870.

Cf. MDu. *jaer en dagh*, a year and six months (and, locally, three days).

c **1450** *Merlin* xxxiii. 682, I shall seche hym a yere and a day, but with-ynne that space I may knowe trewe tidinges. **1454** *Rolls of Parlt.* V. 274/2 In case the Maire, Constables, and Felawship aforesaid, commence not their accion.. within the yer and day next after thoffence. **1514** *Extr. Aberd. Reg.* (1844) I. 90 Vnder the pane of banyssing of the toune for ȝer and day. **1548** STAUNFORD *Kinges Prerog.* xvi. (1567) 49 b, If the husband be atteinted of felonie the kinge shall haue the yeare, daye and wast of the lands of the wife. **1659** HICKS tr. *Plowden's Abridgm. Comm.* 212 So by the custom of many Mannors, one shall lose Copyhold if he claims it not within a year and a day after the death of his ancestor. *a* **1768** ERSKINE *Inst. Law Scot.* I. vi. §42. **1820** SCOTT *Monast.* xxv, When we are handfasted,..we are man and wife for a year and day; that space gone by, each may choose another mate. **1913** *Act 3 & 4 Geo. V.* c. 20 §103 When the sequestration is dated within year and day of any effectual adjudication.

(*b*) ***years and terms***, in full ***books of years and terms***, the year-books.

1528 MORE *Dyaloge* III. Wks. 239/1 In the yeres and termes called Hunnes case. **1883** *Wharton's Law Lex.*, Year-books, or Books of years and terms.

c. ***to see the New*** (***Old***) ***Year in*** (***out***) and varr.: to stay up until after midnight on 31 December, to celebrate the start of a new year.

1840 DICKENS *Let.* ? 18 Dec. (1969) II. 169 Will you dine with us on the last day of the old year—just to see it jollily out. **1875** L. TROUBRIDGE *Life Amongst Troubridges* (1966) 134 It's eleven o'clock now, and shall I tell you what we three are doing? Watching the Old Year out and the New Year in. **1916** M. DIVER *Desmond's Daughter* III. x. 227 Accepting an invitation to..'see the New Year in' with Thea. **1921** W. DE LA MARE *Mem. of Midget* xv. 99, I had written..an invitation to herself and Fanny to sit with me and 'see in' the New Year. **1939** H. NICOLSON *Diary* 31 Dec.

(1967) II. 52, I do not stay to watch the New Year in or the Old Year out. I write this diary at 11.45 and shall not wait.

See also GOODYEAR, NEW-YEAR, TO-YEAR.

8. *Comb.*, as ***year-end, -spinner; year-born, -counted, -hedged, -marked*** adjs.; **year-bird**, a name for *Rhyticeros plicatus*, a bird of the Malay archipelago, having a very large beak with a wrinkled growth on the top, which was believed to develop a fresh wrinkle every year; **year class**, the individuals of a particular kind of animal (usu. a fish) that were born in any one year; **year-count**, among the N. American Indians, a series of figures each symbolizing the chief event of a year, usually painted on hide, and forming a record or chronicle (also called *winter-count*); **year-ring**, each of the rings formed by successive years' growth in the wood of a tree; † **year-tack**, a lease for a year. See also YEAR-BOOK, etc.

1873 *Cassell's Bk. Birds* III. 137 The plumage of the *Year Bird is principally black. *a* **1882** ROSSETTI *Soothsay* i, Let no man ask thee of anything Not *yearborn between Spring and Spring. **1910** J. HJORT in *Publications de Circonstance* No. 53. 18 Very characteristic in this respect are the analyses of samples of the typical Norse spring-herring, where the *year-class which formed its first winter-ring in 1904 preponderates largely over all the other year-classes. **1958** *Jrnl. Marine Res.* XVII. 505 The population [of sea-urchins] probably consists of four year-classes. **1967** [see RECRUIT *v.* 3 e]. **1981** *Trans. Amer. Fisheries Soc.* CX. 185/1 By optimizing the yield from dominant year classes, greater yields from the fishery can be realized for all groups involved. *a* **1896** D. G. BRINTON in Keane *Ethnol.* (1896) 218 There is absolutely no similarity between the Tibetan calendar and the primitive form of the American, which was not intended as a *year-count, but as a ritual and formulary. **1876** GEO. ELIOT *Dan. Der.* xliii, My own small *year-counted existence. **1872** HARTLEY *Yorksh. Ditties* Ser. II. 106 A nice little bit to fall back on i' th' Savings bank at th' *year end. **1899** *Westm. Gaz.* 4 Jan. 6/3 The year-end stocktaking results. **1936** DYLAN THOMAS *25 Poems* 41 The *year-hedged row is lame with flint, Blunt scythe and water blade. **1873** MRS. WHITNEY *Other Girls* xxiii, Old and *year-marked faces. **1854** RONALDS & RICHARDSON *Chem. Technol.* (ed. 2) I. 58 The original form and structure of wood..are retained by the charcoal left by each, so that *year-rings and cells may be distinguished in wood-charcoal. **1598** SYLVESTER *Du Bartas* II. ii. II. *Babylon* 512 One [language], ..becomming old, Is cradle-toomb'd: another warreth bold With the *yeer-spinners. **1532** *Abst. Protocols Town Clerks Glasgow* (1879) IV. 57 James Grahame sall haef ane *yeyrtak for the yeyr that he has gewin our to hyme.

year[2] (jɪə(r), jɜː(r)). Repr. dial. (chiefly U.S.) pronunc. of EAR *sb.*[1]

1863 *Southern Confederacy* (Atlanta, Georgia) 9 May 1/2 You should git the strait of it from one who seed it with his eyes, and hearn it with his years. **1886** *West Somerset Word-Bk.* 845 *Year*.., the ear. **1891** *Dial. Hartland, Devonshire* 122 *Year* (yur), the ear. **1929** W. FAULKNER *Sound & Fury* 72, I wish I was young like I use to be, I'd tear them years right off your head. **1935** Z. N. HURSTON *Mules & Men* (1970) I. viii. 173 He took and galloped out in de middle of de road right in front of John's horse and laid his years back.

year, obs. f. ERE; ***year whayle*** = EREWHILE.

a **1592** GREENE *Jas. IV*, I. Induct., What were those Puppits that hopt and skipt about me year whayle?

year-book ('jɪəbʊk). [Cf. MLG. *jârbôk*, MDu. *jaerboeck* (Du. *jaarboek*), OHG. *jârpuoh* (G. *jahrbuch*), etc.]

1. *pl.* The books of reports of cases in the English law-courts published annually during several periods from the reign of Edward II to that of Henry VIII.

1588 FRAUNCE *Lawiers Logike* I. xvii. 61 b, Uncoherent cases in yeare-bookes. **1639** SANDERSON *Serm.* (1657) II. ix. 189 The Reports and year-books of our Common Law. **1688** SIR E. HERBERT *Acc. Auth. Hales's Case* 12 Plowden, who.. is as little like to be mistaken in the sense of the Year-books as any Reporter we have. **1796** SEWARD *Anecd.* IV. 501 [Ld. Mansfield] said, that, when he was young, few persons would confess they had not read a considerable part, at least, of the Year Books. **1824** J. JOHNSON *Typographia* I. 431 It has been supposed that Pynson printed above forty year-books.

2. **a.** A book published annually and containing information for the year, e.g. in connexion with a society or religious denomination; an annual.

1710 STEELE *Tatler* No. 261 ¶4 The following Fragment out of much more which is written in my Year-Book. **1839** TIMBS (*title*) The Year-book of Facts in Science and Art: exhibiting the most important discoveries and improvements of the past year. **1847** (*title*) The Congregational Year Book, for 1846. **1858** SIMMONDS *Dict. Trade*, *Year-book*, an annual; a book of law cases; a turf register. **1883** (*title*) The official Year-book of the Church of England.

b. *U.S.* An album published annually by the graduating class of a high school or college.

1926 B. MANBERT (*title*) Inter-Scholastic Year Book Manual. **1928** A. H. ANDERSON *School-Built Annual* 21 Don't think you can get out an annual in a week. A yearbook is a year's job. **1939** D. E. MITCHELL *Journalism & Life* xxx. 413 The yearbook is a more formal and permanent production than a newspaper. **1972** M. MEAD *Blackberry Winter* vii. 83, I did not see Luther again, but he sent me his yearbook... Luther was four years older than I and a senior in college. **1978** S. BRILL *Teamsters* vi. 233 The mob looks at high-school yearbooks and picks a hundred guys who look smart and clean.

3. A book of information about the various days and seasons of the year, as Hone's Year-Book (1829). Now freq. as one word.

yeard, ȝeard, Sc. forms of EARTH.

1596 DALRYMPLE tr. *Leslie's Hist. Scot.* (S.T.S.) I. 35 Out of the ȝeard we cutt peates and turfes. *a* **1783** *Burd Ellen* xi. in Child *Ballads* III. 88/1 A yeard-fast stane.

yeard, obs. form of YARD.

'year-day. Forms: see YEAR[1] and DAY; also **year's day** (*yeeres dai*, etc.). [In OE. *ȝéares dæȝ* = OFris. *ierisdei*, MDu. *jaersdagh*, OHG. *jâr(s)tac* (MHG. *jarstag*, G. *jahrstag*).]

† **1.** (*year's day.*) The first day of the year, New Year's Day. *Obs.* (Cf. F. *jour de l'an.*)

a **1122** *O.E. Chron.* (Laud MS.) an. 1096 To ȝeares dæȝe. **1387** TREVISA *Higden* (Rolls) IV. 275 [Christ] hadde of þe firste ȝere of his burþe but sevene dayes from þe nativite to ȝeresday.

2. A day observed every year in commemoration of a person or event, an anniversary; *esp.* a day on which requiem services were held every year in commemoration of a deceased person: cf. OBIT 2 b and YEAR'S MIND. *Obs.* exc. *Hist.*

1390 GOWER *Conf.* II. 171 To every godd.. Thei made a temple forth withal, And ech of hem his yeeres dai Attitled hadde. *c* **1440** *Promp. Parv.* 537/2 3erday, *anniversarius.* **1448** in *Eng. Gilds* (1870) 281 We haue ordeyned..for to kepe the ȝereday of Jon lyster of Cambryge ȝerely. *c* **1450** in Aungier *Syon* (1840) 275 How be it the fyrst dirige may be differred,..ȝet the xxx[ti] day and ȝeres day schal neuer be differed. **1526** *Lincoln Wills* (1914) I. 179 That the sayd feoffers..yerely kepe up the aforsayd tyme my yereday for my soule. **1579–80** NORTH *Plutarch* (1595) 584 The very daies on the which the women celebrated the feast and yeareday of Adonis death.

3. *pl.* Days of the year.

1897–8 *Ann. Rep. Bur. Amer. Ethnol.* p. xliii. (Cent. Dict. Suppl.) A simple observation on the setting sun behind a distant sierra, which would in itself permit a count of year-days, if not the recognition of the bissextile.

yeard-hunger: see YERD-HUNGER.

yeare, obs. form of EAR, YEAR[1].

yeared (jɪəd, *poet.* 'jɪərɪd), *a.* or *pa. pple.* Also 5 **i-yeerid.** [f. YEAR[1] + -ED.]

1. † That has lived or lasted a given number of years; so many years of age, or of so many years' standing: as ***old i-yeerid*** = of old standing; ***twice yeared*** = that has lasted two years; ***yeared to thirty*** = thirty years of age (*obs.*). Also without qualification, That has lasted many years (*poet.*).

c **1412** HOCCLEVE *De Reg. Princ.* 1858 þou of þe pryue seel art old I-yeerid. **1583** BURGHLEY in Nicolas *Mem. Sir C. Hatton* (1847) 323 His [*sc.* Oxford's] fall in her Court, which is now twice yeared. **1603** B. JONSON *Sejanus* I. i, Year'd but to thirty. **1848** BAILEY *Festus* (1852) 282 White with all yearéd snows and radiant rime.

2. Phr. ***yeared and dayed***, said of property left unclaimed for a year and a day, after which time the original owner's claim lapsed: see YEAR[1] 7 b (*a*).

1523 FITZHERB. *Surv.* xv. 28 b, They maye..cease theym as streyes and put them in sauegarde to the lordes vse tyll they be yered and deyed. **1579** *Admiralty Crt. Exemplifications* 19 Nov. 105 There was driven..upon my libertie of Alverstoke..a certaine shipp..wheare she being yeered and daied according to the law of Oleron hath ever since remayned.

yearethlye, obs. form of EARTHLY.

1553 *Respublica* II. i. 1 What yearethlye thinge is permanent or stable?

yearful ('jɪəfʊl), *sb. nonce-wd.* [f. YEAR[1] + -FUL 2.] As much as fills a year.

1889 H. M. STANLEY in *Daily News* 25 Nov. 5/4 Over a yearful of stirring events.

† **yearing**, *sb.* and *a. Obs.* Forms: see YEAR[1]; also 6 **yeoryng.** [f. YEAR[1] + -ING[3].]

A. *sb.* = YEARLING A. 1; also with numeral, as ***three yearing***, an animal three years old.

1460 CAPGRAVE *Chron.* (Rolls) 8 Jabel departed the flokkis of scheep fro the flokkis of goot..aftir here age ȝeringis be hem selve, and elder be hem selve. **1586** *Wills & Inv. N.C.* (Surtees) II. 131, ij coulte foles, not yearingers [*sic*]. **1607** TOPSELL *Four-f. Beasts* 122 The french haue no proper name for this beast that I can learn vntil he be a three yearing, and then they call him (*ein Gabler*). **1611** COTGR., *Borret*, a yearing. **1641** BEST *Farm. Bks.* (Surtees) 120 The yearinges weare large, and the two yeares little.

B. *adj.* = YEARLING B. 1.

1451 *Lincoln Dioc. Doc.* (1914) 51 A ȝeryng calf. **1516** in *5th Rep. Hist. MSS. Comm.* (1876) App. 596/2 A yeoryng boloke. **1558** *Test. Ebor.* (Surtees) VI. 81, ij yeringe foolles.

yeark, obs. form of YERK.

yearlily, error in mod. Dicts. for *yearely*, YEARLY *adv.*

yearling ('jɪəlɪŋ), *sb.* and *a.* Forms: see YEAR[1]; also 6 **erlynge.** [f. YEAR[1] + -LING[1]. Cf. early mod.Du. *jaerlingh*, G. *jährling.*]

A. *sb.* **1. a.** An animal a year old, or in its second year (esp. a sheep, calf, or foal; also applied to certain birds and fishes; rarely to a child).

1465 *Mann. & Househ. Exp.* (Roxb.) 554, .x. yerlynges. **1531** *Lincoln Dioc. Doc.* (1914) 247, I bequeth to Jane Hay a yereling, that is to say, a cowe heifer. **1541** in Leadam *Sel. Cases Crt. Requests* (Selden Soc.) 53 One heyffer oone Erlynge & xj Shepe. **1577** B. GOOGE *Heresbach's Husb.* I. (1586) 43 b, In the next [pasture] are my young breede, Yeerelinges, and Twoyeerelinges. **1607** MARKHAM *Cavel.* I. (1617) 66 To seperate your horse-colts from your Mare Colts,..and your yearelings from your two yeares olde. **1847** STODDART *Angler's Comp.* 208 The parr of Tweed.. descend to the sea in the shape of smolts, as yearlings. **1847** *Bewick's Brit. Birds* I. 11 *note*, The female yearling is termed a red Falcon, the male a red Tiercel. **1877** J. A. ALLEN *Amer. Bison* 463 The cows, on the other hand, as well as the yearlings and two-year-olds, are generally fattest in June. **1902** WISTER *Virginian* xi, Alfred..is a little more than a yearlin', and of course he'll snuffle.

b. *transf.* The fleece of a yearling sheep.

1888 R. BEAUMONT *Woollen Manuf.* i. 7 The second clip, which is somewhat thicker in fibre [than 'lambs'], and both longer and stronger in staple, is styled 'yearlings'.

2. A plant a year old; *spec.* applied to hops of the previous year's growth.

1849 *Florist* 247 Matthew's Juno, large and full, lavender, purple-edge, noticed by us as a yearling last season. **1887** *Pall Mall Gaz.* 6 Oct. 12/1 Messrs. Woolloton and Son state that 'brewers hold exceptionally large stocks of yearlings'. **1902** *Times* 19 Sept. 2/5 Yearlings are in good request at 70*s.* to 100*s.*

3. *U.S. colloq.* A student in his first year or beginning his second year at college.

1900 *Dialect Notes* II. 70 *Yearling*, a second year man. **1940** BERREY & VAN DEN BARK *Amer. Thes. Slang* §825/6 *Freshman*...yearling. **1944** *Collier's* 23 Sept. 69/1 His femme fell for a [West Point] yearling.

4. *Econ.* A yearling bond (see sense 3 of the adj. below).

1966 *This is Bill-Broking* (Allen, Harvey & Ross Ltd.) 38/1 *Yearlings*, stocks issued by local authorities for a period of a year and quoted either on the stock exchange or in the discount market. **1970** *Daily Tel.* 29 Sept. 17/5 (*heading*) Local authority yearlings at 8p.c. **1977** *Guardian* 19 Apr. 17/2 At the moment the yearlings give a return of 10 per cent which may be lower than what is available on the ordinary bonds, but are flexible. **1981** *Observer* 18 Oct. 20/1 An interesting alternative [to Government stocks] is the local authority negotiable bond—or the 'yearling', so-called because of its one-year term.

B. *adj.* **1. a.** Of an animal (rarely of a child): A year old; in its second year.

1528 PAYNELL *Salerne's Regim.* Fj, The fleshe of.. yerelynge wethers..is conuenient inoughe to eate. **1605** SYLVESTER *Du Bartas* II. iii. III. *Law* 585 Yearly, the Jews a Yearling Lamb must slay. *a* **1682** SIR T. BROWNE *Tracts* i. (1683) 80 So many thousand male unblemished yearling lambs. **1719** DE FOE *Crusoe* I. (Globe) 246, I order'd Friday to take a yearling Goat. **1729** SWIFT *Modest Proposal* 13 A well grown, fat Yearling Child. **1814** SOUTHEY *Roderick* I. 244 Even like a yearling child, a fosterer's care. **1859** *Sporting Mag.* Oct. 240 The yearling filly by him [*sc.* Rataplan], out of Musjid's dam. **1900** *Jrnl. Sch. Geog.* (U.S.) Apr. 148 Kips—the skins of small or yearling cattle, exceeding the size of the calf skins.

b. Of plants or seeds, esp. of hops: Of the previous year's growth.

1846 J. BAXTER *Libr. Pract. Agric.* (ed. 4) I. 246 Cuttings, or yearling plants, for hedge-planting. **1888** *Daily News* 13 Oct. 2/6 Yearling and old hops are at present quite neglected. **1892** *Ibid.* 11 Oct. 6/4 Yearling red cloverseed.

2. Of a year's standing; that has been such for a year.

1854 THACKERAY *Newcomes* i, As yearling brides provide lace caps, and work rich clothes, for the expected darling.

3. *Econ.* Applied to bonds issued by a local authority usu. for one year.

1964 *Times* 2 Apr. 18/1 Under present conditions a quotation for a yearling bond would mean additional expense. **1969** *Daily Tel.* 12 Apr. 5/7 Most yearling bonds mature in..a year, sometimes two to five years. **1975** *Economist* 19 July 95 The explosion in the yearling bond market. **1977** *Guardian* 19 Apr. 17/2 Yearling bonds.. which come in units of £1,000, are much more flexible—and like the local authority bonds disgorge interest twice a year. They last for 12 months only and then investors have to start again.

'year-long, *a.* [f. YEAR[1] + LONG *a.* Cf. OE. *ȝéarlanges* adv. for a year, MHG. *jârlanc*, (G. *jahrelang*), ON. *árlangt* (as adv.)] Of the length of a year; lasting for a year, or throughout the year; often, lasting for years in succession, (sometimes) age-long.

1813 COLERIDGE *Lett., to T. Poole* (1895) 612 The year-long difference [*viz.* Feb. 1812–13] between me and Wordsworth. **1847** TENNYSON *Princess* VII. 319 Thee.. From year-long poring on thy pictured eyes, Ere seen I loved. **1868** MORRIS *Earthly Par.* (1870) I. I. 16 No Greenland winter waits us there, No year-long night. **1886** A. WEIR *Hist. Basis Mod. Europe* (1889) 44 Her legislative assembly..did good service to her fame at the time, but the year-long farce soon lost its plausibility. **1886** W. WALLACE in *Encycl. Brit.* XXI. 453/1 The yearlong alliance between philosophy and theology.

b. *hyperbolically.* Seeming as long as a year.

1871 PALGRAVE *Lyr. Poems* 92 Through year-long hours of hope and woe She sits and waits.

So **'years-long** *a.* (*rare*[−1]), lasting for several or many years.

1887 HARDY *Woodlanders* I. xiii. 235 The years-long regard that she had had for him.

yearly ('jɪəlɪ), *a.* (*sb.*) [OE. *ȝéarlic* = OFris. *ier(a)lik*, MLG. *jârlik*, *jaerlije*, OHG. *jârlich*

(MHG. *jaerlich*, G. *jährlich*), ON. *árligr*: see YEAR[1] and -LY[1].]

† **1.** Of the year; belonging or relating to a year. *Obs. rare.*

c **1000** *Hexameron of St. Basil* (1849) 12 Næron nane tida on ðam ȝearlican ȝetæle ær ðam ðe se ælmihtiȝa scyppend ȝesceop ða tunglan to ȝearlicum tidum. **1557** *Order of Hospitalls* F v b, Yow shall kepe an Yerely-Booke for Collections, Legacies and Benevolences. **1613** PURCHAS *Pilgrimage* To Rdr., The naturall Philosophers may obserue ..the varietie of heauenly influence, of the yearely seasons. *c* **1811** in *Rep. Comm. Publ. Rec. Irel.* (1815) 104 The Recognizances..are regularly arranged in yearly bundles according to their Receipts.

2. Done, made, observed, happening, coming, produced, etc. every year or once a year; annual.

c **725** *Corpus Gloss.* (Hessels) A 618 *Annua*, ȝerlice. **925-36** *Laws of Æthelstan* Prol., ðe ðæs libbendes yrfes, ȝe ðæs ȝearlices westmes. *c* **1449** PECOCK *Repr.* II. xi. 216 The seid solempne ȝeerli goyng bi ij. tymes in ech ȝeer. **1531** *Test. Ebor.* (Surtees) VI. 24, I will that ther be a yerlie obit done. **1561** WINȜET *Bk. Questions* §63 Wks. (S.T.S.) I. 115 The ȝierly celebratioun of the Pasche day. **1595** SHAKS. *John* III. i. 81 The yearely course that brings this day about. **1697** DRYDEN *Æneis* v. 77 And yearly Games may spread the Gods renown. *a* **1721** PRIOR *New-Year's Gift to Phyllis* i, The circling months begin this day, To run their yearly ring. **1857** H. MILLER *Test. Rocks* xii. 470 In some of the fossil-trees these yearly rings are of great breadth. **1868** FREEMAN *Norm. Conq.* II. vii. 85 An officer, who provided them with daily food and with a yearly change of raiment.

b. esp. of payments, charges, revenue.

a **1400-50** *Wars Alex.* 2406 Þai..ȝerely tribute him to geue ȝapely him hetis. **1452** *Lincoln Dioc. Doc.* (1914) 61 To whome I haue granted any fees, annuetes, yerely rentis, or fermes. **1524** *Act 14 & 15 Hen. VIII*, c. 3 §8 Landes and tenementes to the yerely value of xx. s. **1599** SHAKS. *Hen. V*, IV. i. 315 Fiue hundred poore I haue in yeerely pay. **1610** HOLLAND *Camden's Brit.* (1637) 318 Having received an yearely pension of Lewis the eleaventh. **1712** HUGHES *Spect.* No. 316 ¶6 The yearly Rent which gives the Value to the Estate. **1855** KINGSLEY *Heroes, Theseus* II. 237 O people and King of Athens, where is your yearly tribute?

c. Engaged or hired by the year.

[*1611 Bible* Lev. xxv. 53 As a yeerely hired seruant shall he be with him.] **1891** *Daily News* 28 Mar. 2/6 Wages had gone up 5*l*. a year for yearly men.

d. ***Yearly Meeting***, in the Society of Friends (Quakers), a national assembly held annually to deal with legislation and questions of policy (see *esp.* quot. 1869). Cf. *quarterly-meeting* (*a*) s.v. QUARTERLY *a.* 3.

1688 *Testimony for the Lord, & His Truth* (Women Friends, York) 1 Given forth by the Women Friends at their Yearly Meeting at York, being a Tender Salutation of Love to their Friends and Sisters in their several Monthly Meetings. **1714** in *Jrnl. Friends Hist. Soc.* (1918) 28 Thence into Maryland to friends yearly-meeting at Tradaven-Creek ..wherein Truth was plentifully afforded to ye bowing of many souls here. **1831** in S. B. Weeks *Southern Quakers & Slavery* (1896) xi. 300 There is not a school in the limits of the [North Carolina] Yearly Meeting that is under the care of a committee of either monthly or preparative meeting. **1869** BECK & BALL *London Friends' Meetings* v. 53 The Yearly Meeting was from its commencement..first and chiefly, a gathering of public Friends (i.e. ministers), to confer together on matters of faith and doctrine... The ministers alone formed the Annual Assembly in London; but in 1677 the invitation for deputies from the Quarterly Meetings was renewed... The representative element has been formally recognised, and thereby the Yearly Meeting has come to its position of legislative importance in the Church. **1923** E. B. EMMOTT *Short Hist. Quakerism* xi. 171 The proposal for a General Meeting for the whole country (which we now call the Yearly Meeting) came in the first instance from Durham Friends..in 1659. **1949** *Friend* 17 June 497/1 When the Clerk, in Yearly Meeting, announces the Report of the Committee on Accounts, it is quite astonishing to note how many Friends..get up and walk out. **1974** G. HUBBARD *Quaker by Convincement* I. iii. 41 Through the queries answered in writing four times a year by Monthly Meetings, the Yearly Meeting kept a watchful eye on departures from the norm.

yearly (ˈjɪəlɪ), *adv.* [OE. *ȝéarlíce* = MLG. *jârlik*, OHG. *jârlich*, ON. *árliga*, etc.: see YEAR[1] and -LY[2].] Every year, once a year, year by year, annually.

c **1050** *Voc.* in Wr.-Wülcker 347/9 *Annuatim*, ȝearlice. *c* **1375** *Sc. Leg. Saints* xl. (*Ninian*) 1079 Þat man syne ȝerly can hym seke..Ilke ȝere..fra quhare he duelt in Ingland. *a* **1400** *Relig. Pieces fr. Thornton MS.* (1914) 58 Þe gernare þat kepis ȝerely þe whete þat es rede with-owte and white with-in. *c* **1450** *Godstow Reg.* 47 A feld yerly tyllyd, or ellys euyry othyr yere. *c* **1460** FORTESCUE *Abs. & Lim. Mon.* v. (1885) 119 Such as wolde haue ben feyner of a c. li in hand, than of xl. li worth lande yerely. **1500** *Reg. Privy Seal Scot.* I. 68/1 To haf merkatis and fairis in the said burgh ȝerle, with a merkat cors. **1583** STUBBES *Anat. Abus.* II. (1882) 31, I thought one might haue had a farme or a lease for a reasonable rent yeerely. **1687** A. LOVELL tr. *Thevenot's Trav.* I. 177 There is a Caravan that yearly in Lent goes from Caire to Jerusalem. *a* **1715** BURNET *Own Time* (1766) I. 536 He gave yearly great sums in charity. **1830** A. CUNNINGHAM *Brit. Painters* II. 176 The demand for his works lessened yearly. **1849** MACAULAY *Hist. Eng.* vi. II. 65 It was agreed that Sunderland should receive this sum yearly.

yearly, dial. form of EARLY.

1797 MRS. A. M. BENNETT *Beggar Girl* (1813) IV. 209 A monstrous pretty garden, Miss;..I am up yearly and late at it myself.

†**yearman.** *Obs.* In 5 yerman. [f. YEAR[1] + MAN *sb.*[1]] A man hired by the year. (Cf. YEARSMAN.)

1481-90 *Howard Househ. Bks.* (Roxb.) 210 My Lord toke the stward to pay the yermen for wages as folew.

year-mind: see YEAR'S MIND.

yearn (jɜːn), *sb.* [f. next.] A yearning.

a **1797** MRS. M. W. GODWIN *Wks.* (1798) III. xliv. 134, I feel my fate united to yours by..the yearns of..a true, unsophisticated heart. **1853** KINGSLEY *Misc., Shelley & Byron* (1859) I. 307 In one mighty yearn after that beauty from which he is debarred, [Keats] breaks his young heart, and dies. **1862** 'ARTEMUS WARD' *His Bk.* (1865) 35 'Hast thou not yearned for me?' she yelled... 'Not a yearn!' I bellered. **1890** W. CLARK RUSSELL *Ocean Trag.* I. v. 106 The rounds of her canvas whitened into marble hardness with the yearn and lean of the distended cloths.

yearn (jɜːn), *v.*[1] Forms: 1 **ȝiorna, ȝeornan, ȝiernan, ȝirnan, ȝyrnan,** 2-4 **ȝierne, ierne,** 2-5 **ȝerne,** 3 **ȝirn(e,** (*Orm.*) **ȝeorrnenn,** 3-4 **ȝorn(e** 3-6 **ȝern,** 4 **ȝiern, yhern(e, ȝharn(e, ȝaren,** 4-5 **ȝyrn(e,** 4-6 **ȝarn(e, yarne,** 4-7 **yerne,** 4-8 **yern,** 5 **yurn, herne,** 6 **yo(u)rn,** *Sc.* **ȝairne, yairne,** 6-7 **yearne,** 6- **yearn.** [OE., Northumb. *ȝiorna*, Mercian *ȝeornan*, WS. *ȝiernan*, corresp. to OS. *girnean, gernean*, ON. *girna* (see GREEN *v.*[2]), Goth. *gairnjan*, related to OE. *ȝeorn*, Goth. *-gaírns*: see YERN *a.* and YERE *v.*]

I. † **1.** *trans.* To desire earnestly; to experience a strong desire or longing for. **a.** with simple obj.

c **888** ÆLFRED *Boeth.* xv, Ne diorwyrðra hræȝla hi ne ȝirndon. *c* **1000** *Ags. Gosp.* Luke xxii. 71 Hwi ȝyrne we ȝyt ȝewitnesse? *c* **1100** *O.E. Chron.* (MS. D) an. 1067 Ða begann se cyngc Malcholom ȝyrnan his sweostor him to wife. *c* **1200** *Vices & Virtues* 43 Ðare ðinge ðe on ðesse worlde waren he ne ȝernde. *c* **1205** LAY. 17795 Cnihtes feollen a-dun & ȝirnden heore dæðes. *a* **1225** *Ancr. R.* 192 Muche word is of ou hu..ȝe beoð vor godleic & for ureoleic iȝerned of monie. *a* **1300** *Cursor M.* 23458 Fair Iuels..men yerns oft. *c* **1374** CHAUCER *Troylus* III. 152 Þis man wole no þyng yerne But youre honour. *c* **1400** *Rule St. Benet* (Verse) 485 Mor we suld ȝern hele of saule þan of bodi. *c* **1412** HOCCLEVE *De Reg. Princ.* 1407 For þat þou art brent With couetyse now,..þou ȝernest soules cure. *a* **1450** *Ratis Raving* 3790 At E nocht seis, hart nocht ȝarnis. **1500-20** DUNBAR *Poems* lxxi. 19 We ȝarne thy presens, bot oft thow hes refusit Till cum ws till. **1568** LAUDER *Godlie Tractate* 627 That death ȝe ȝairne, it sall fast frome ȝow fle.

† **b.** with obj. clause. *Obs.*

c **897** ÆLFRED *Gregory's Past. C.* xliv. 331 Hwile ðe he ȝiernð ðæt he his weolan iece. *c* **1000** *Ags. Gosp.* Matt. xxiii. 8 Ne ȝyrne ȝe þæt eow man lareowas nemne. *a* **1310** in Wright *Lyric P.* vi. 28 Lest eny reve me my make, ychabbe y-ȝyrned ȝore. **13..** *Cursor M.* 1801 (Gött.) Þai ȝernid þan, þa caitifes madd, þat þai had ben wid noe stadd. *c* **1375** *Sc. Leg. Saints* iii. (*Andrew*) 423, I ȝarne þe Of corse to here þe priwete. *c* **1425** WYNTOUN *Cron.* v. ii. 260 Octoviane ȝarnyt hym to be His ayr.

2. *intr.* To have a strong desire or longing; to long. **a.** Const. inf. with († or without) *to*.

971 *Blickl. Hom.* 53 Þa halȝan..naht ne..ȝyrndon to hæbbenne. *c* **1000** *Poenitentiale Ecgberti* I. §10 in Thorpe *Laws* II. 176 Ȝif se man..ȝyrneð Cristes lichaman to underfonne. *c* **1200** ORMIN 3578 Crist wass æfre swillc to sen ..þatt gode ȝeorrndenn himm to sen. *a* **1300** *Cursor M.* 1 Man yhernes rimes for to here. *Ibid.* 6479 Þi neghbur wijf ȝerne noght at haue. **1340** HAMPOLE *Pr. Consc.* 6705 For hungre þai sal yherne it ete. **1375** BARBOUR *Bruce* I. 158 The kynryk ȝharn I nocht to have. *a* **1395** HYLTON *Scala Perf.* (W. de W. 1494) I. xvi, Ȝit shalt thou ȝerne..for to come as nere as þou mayst to þat state. *a* **1568** *Wowing of Jok and Jynny* 9 in *Bannatyne MS.* (Hunter. Club) 387, I yern full fane To..sit down by yow. *a* **1616** BEAUM. & FL. *Bonduca* II. iv, I must do that my heart-strings yern to do. **1711** STEELE *Spect.* No. 142 ¶3 My gushing Heart, that..yearns to tell you all its Achings. **1805** SOUTHEY *Madoc* II. xiii, A female tenderness which yearn'd, As with maternal love, to cherish him. **1840** DICKENS *Old C. Shop* lv, The child yearned to be out of doors. **1879** DIXON *Windsor* II. iv. 38 He had a daughter whom he yearned to hail as queen.

b. Const. *after, for,* †*to, towards.* Also *absol.*

c **893** ÆLFRED *Oros.* VI. xxviii, He ofsloȝ Proculus & Bonorum, þa ȝierndon eac æfter þæm onwalde. *c* **1200** *Trin. Coll. Hom.* 27 Þe godfrihte..ne ȝierneð to none þinge bute after godes wille. *Ibid.* 183 Ðus wareð þe sowle þe licame, for þat hit haueð þarafter ierned. *a* **1225** *Juliana* 8 He biȝet et te keiser þat he him ȝettede reue to beonne as þat he iȝirnd hefde. **1340** *Ayenb.* 55 Þe þridde boȝ of þise zenne is to uerliche yerne to þe mete ase deþ þe hond. **1357** *Lay Folks Catech.* (T.) 560 Tham that ledis thair lifs als thaire flesch yhernes. *c* **1400** *Destr. Troy* 2937 Yonge men & yeuerus.. yurnes to gaumes. **1573** *Satir. Poems Reform.* xlii. 750 Thay pepill..That..ȝarnis for fude with sa greit zeill. *c* **1645** HOWELL *Lett.* (1688) IV. 503 His Maw began to yern again after some of the Figs. **1820** W. IRVING *Sketch Bk.* II. 367 His heart yearned after the damsel who was to inherit these domains. **1868** TENNYSON *Lucretius* 266 Yearn'd after by the wisest of the wise. **1870** DICKENS *Lett.* (1880) II. 440, I yearn for the country again.

transf. **1635** PAGITT *Christianogr.* 213 Sacriledge is one of the most detestable sinnes, after which Gods curse yearneth, til he be revenged.

† **3.** *trans.* To express a wish or desire for (an object); to ask for, request. Also *absol.* or *intr.*

c **950** *Lindisf. Gosp.* Mark x. 46 *Mendicans*, ȝiornade [*Rushw.* ȝiornde]. *c* **1000** *Ags. Gosp.* Mark xi. 24 Swa hwæt swa ȝe ȝyrnende biddað ȝelyfað þæt ȝe hit onfoð. *a* **1122** *O.E. Chron.* (Laud MS.) an. 656 Þa ȝeornde seo abbe þet he scolde him tyþian þet he æt him ȝeornde. *Ibid.* 777 He ȝeornde at se kyning þet he scolde for his luuen freon his ane mynstre Wooingas het. *Ibid.* 1011 Se cyng & his witan ..ȝeorndon friðes. *c* **1205** LAY. 929 Ȝirne we to þane kinge Ȝeuen suiðe gode. *Ibid.* 8250 King Androgeus ȝeorneð þi grið. *a* **1225** *Leg. Kath.* 2420 Lauerd,..ȝette me þet ich ȝirne. **1340** *Ayenb.* 39 Þe uerþe boȝ of auarice is acsynge, þet is, to yerne ope oþre mid wrong. **1340-70** *Alex. & Dind.* 67 Ȝernes now of my ȝift þat ȝou leue were, & what it be þat ȝe bidde ȝour bonus i graunte.

† **4.** *intr.* Of hounds: To cry out eagerly, give tongue. Also *trans.* to give tongue after. *Obs.*

1523 SKELTON *Garl. Laurel* 1409 The howndes began to yerne and to quest. *a* **1530** HEYWOOD *Weather* (Brandl) 276 That after our houndes yournynge so meryly,..In herynge we may folow. **1576** TURBERV. *Venerie* lxv. 181 You muste holde your yong Terryers euery one of them at a sundrie hole of some angle or mouth of the earth, that they may herken and heare theyr fellowes yearne. *Ibid.* lxvi. 185 When they percieue the Terryers beginne to yearne them. **1674** N. COX *Gentl. Recr.* I. (1677) 18 When Beagles bark and cry at their Prey, we say, they Yearn.

† **b.** *transf. Obs.*

1582 STANYHURST *Æneis* IV. (Arb.) 100 Nymphs in mountayns high typ doe squeak, hullelo, yearning. **1639** G. DANIEL *Ecclus.* xxii. 4 He shall be soiled in the vnsavory Slime From Dunghills gather'd; all Men yerne at him. **1680** HICKERINGILL *Curse ye Meroz* 26 A Holder-forth may yawl and yerne, snivle and whine, thump and bawl.

5. a. *intr.* To give a sound suggestive of strong desire; to express yearning or strong desire; also *trans.* to utter in emotional voice.

1816 L. HUNT *Rimini* I. 40 Yearns the deep talk, the ready laugh ascends. **1820** KEATS *Eve St. Agnes* vii, The music, yearning like a God in pain. **1856** DICKENS *Househ. Words* 3 May 368/2 While the organ was yearning its last, and the great throng was pushing to the doors. **1894** LE GALLIENNE *Prose Fancies* 22 The kind of voice..in which Socialist actresses yearn out passages from 'The Cenci'.

b. To have an appearance as of longing.

1870 ROSSETTI *Burden of Nineveh* ix, The faces of thy ministers Yearned pale with bitter ecstasy. **1871** SWINBURNE *Songs bef. Sunrise, Tenebrae* 92 The blossom of man from his tomb Yearns open. **1890** W. CLARK RUSSELL *Ocean Trag.* I. v. 95 The jibs yearning from their sheets taut as fiddle-strings.

II. 6. *intr.* To be deeply moved; to be moved with compassion; to have tender feelings; †to mourn, grieve. In first quot. app. *trans.* to have compassion upon.

1500-20 DUNBAR *Poems* lxxxv. 11 Ȝerne ws, guberne, wirgin matern. *a* **1533** FRITH *Another Bk. agst. Rastell* ii. B iv, The..slender reasons that those ii. wytted men, syr Thomas More and my lorde of Rochestre had brought to confyrme purgatory made my harte to yerne. **1539** *Bible* (Great) 1 Kings iii. 26 Her bowelles yerned vpon her sonne. **1562** COOPER *Answ. Priv. Masse* (1850) 56 Any christian heart may rather yearn and lament to remember so ungodly profanation of the holy sacrament. **1577** HARRISON *England* II. x. (1877) I. 217 To raise pitifull and odious sores, and mooue the goers by such places where they lie, to yerne at their miserie. **1602** DAVISON *Rhapsody* (1611) 30 They in their bleating voice did seeme to yearne. **1649** G. DANIEL *Trinarch., Hen. IV*, ci, The horror of Imaginary Death Strikes deep wth flesh; and all Mortalitye Yernes at a Change. **1665** BRATHWAIT *Comm. Two Tales* (1901) 21 It would make any ones heart yern within him, that has any man's blood in him. **1711** ADDISON *Spect.* No. 123 ¶5, I have left your Mother in the next Room. Her Heart yearns towards you. **1848** DICKENS *Dombey* xliii, With her gentle nature yearning to them both, feeling the misery of both. **1866** G. MACDONALD *Ann. Q. Neighb.* xxii. (1878) 406 My heart was yearning over her.

† **b.** To be reluctant *to do* something. *Obs. rare.*

1597 BEARD *Theatre God's Judgem.* (1612) 53 [He] committed such excesse of crueltie, that the most barbarous heathen in the world would haue yearned to doe.

† **7.** *trans.* To cause to mourn; to move to compassion. *Obs.*

1593 SHAKS. *Rich. II*, v. v. 76 O how it yern'd my heart, when I beheld..That horse. **1598** —— *Merry W.* III. v. 45 She laments Sir for it, that it would yern your heart to see it. **1641** J. SHUTE *Sarah & Hagar* (1649) 94 Who..torture them, in that manner, that it yerns a mans bowels to observe!

Hence **yearned** *ppl. a.*; also **'yearner**, one who yearns.

c **1375** *Sc. Leg. Saints* xl. (*Ninian*) 724 Lofare of vertu & dyspysare Of þe warld, of hewine ȝ arnar. **1616** B. JONSON *Epigr.* xlii, That his long yearn'd life Were quite out-spun. **1838** S. BELLAMY *Betrayal* 82 What if that vow Thy Father's yearn'd heart, all impatiently, Hath quench'd in its embrace. **1896** *Westm. Gaz.* 30 Oct. 10/1 The yearned-for visitor. **1915** A. BENNETT *Over There* 186 The yearners after Calais did themselves no good by exterminating fine architecture and breaking up innocent homes, but they did experience the relief of smashing something.

yearn (jɜːn), *v.*[2] Chiefly *north. dial.* and *Sc.* Forms: 4 **yern,** 6 *Sc.* **yyrne,** 8- **yirn,** 7- **yearn.** [Probably dial. variant of EARN *v.*[2], with initial *y*-glide; cf. YEARTH, etc. Continuity with OE. *ȝeyrnan* (pa. pple. *ȝeurnen*) is improbable.]

a. *intr.* To coagulate, curdle. **b.** *trans.* To curdle (milk), esp. for making into cheese; to make (cheese) of curdled milk. Hence **yearned** *ppl. a.*

1371-3 [implied in YEARNING *vbl. sb.*[2]]. *a* **1568** *Wyfe of Auchtermuchty* xi. (Bann. MS.) He het the milk our hett, And sorrow spark of it wald yyrne. **1635** D. DICKSON *Pract. Wks.* (1845) I. 33 The making of cheese of yearned milk. ? **17**.. *Gaberlunyie Man* vi. in *Songs of Scotl.* (1862) 177 The kirn's to kirn, and milk to yirne. **1818** SCOTT *Hrt. Midl.* xxxix, His honour the Duke will accept ane of our Dunlop cheeses, and it sall be my faut if a better was ever yearned in Lowden. **1866** 'SARAH TYTLER' *Days of Yore* II. 219 Mrs. Hoy was salting Elspa's butter, and 'yearning' her cheese. **1868** R. L. STEVENSON in *Scribner's Mag.* (1899) XXV. 36/2 Curds called 'yearned milk' hereaway.

yearn, (yarn(e, yern(e), *v.*[3], obs. or dial. f. EARN *v.*[1]

a **1175** *Cott. Hom.* 221 Þat he eorðlic man sceolde ȝeðeon, and ȝearnian mid admodnisse þet wuniunge on hefen rice. *c* **1530** *Crt. Love* 367 Thy-self art never like to yern..her mercy. **1557** TUSSER *100 Points Husb.* xxxvi, Beware they threshe clene, though the lesser they yarne. **1596** SPENSER *F.Q.* VI. i. 40 Put away proud looke, and vsage sterne, The which shal nought to you but foule dishonor yearne. ?*c* **1600** *Distr. Emperor* II. i. in Bullen *Old Pl.* (1884) III. 189 Those worthye deeds Whereby y'ave yearn'd all wellcome. **1626** *Essex Archdeaconries, Depos. Bk.* 27 June lf. 77 (MS.) He sayd that he was ever yearning of money. **1851** MAYHEW *Lond. Labour* I. 359/2 She..told me, I must look out and *yearn* my own living.

yearn, obs. Sc. f. ERNE, eagle.
1790 BURNS *Elegy on Capt. M—— H——* iii, Ye cliffs, the haunts of sailing yearns.

yearn(e, obs. ff. YARN.

†**yearnandlike,** *a. Obs. rare.* In quots. yorn-, yhern-. [f. YEARNING *ppl. a.* + -LIKE, rendering L. *desiderabilis.*] Desirable.
a **1300** *E.E. Psalter* xviii. 11 [xix. 10] Yornand-like over þe golde. *Ibid.* cv. 23 [cvi. 24] And for noghte þai had þe land þat yhernandlike was in þar hand.

yearnful ('jɜːnfʊl), *a.* [In sense 1 OE. *ȝeornfull*, f. *ȝeorn* YERN *a.*; in senses 2 and 3 f. YEARN *v.*[1]: see -FUL 1.]
†**1.** Eagerly desirous, anxious, solicitous. *Obs.*
c **888** ÆLFRED *Boeth.* xxii. §2 Ðu ær sædest þæt þu swiðe ȝeornfull wære hit to ȝehyranne. *c* **1000** *Ags. Gosp.* Luke x. 41 Martha martha ȝeornfull þu eart & embe fela þinga ȝedrefed. *c* **1200** ORMIN 1631 Beo ȝeorrnfull Crist to cwemenn. *c* **1275** *Duty of Christians* 100 in *O.E. Misc.* 144 We schulde abute cristes lay Beon yeornfulle & clybbe. *c* **1375** *Sc. Leg. Saints* xvi. (*Magdalen*) 780, & scho sa ȝarnful wes þar-til, þat scho til wildirnes has socht, & fand a derne sted, was wrocht In til a crage of angil wark.
2. Mournful, sorrowful.
a **1566** R. EDWARDS *Damon & Pithias* (1571) Dj, Oh Musicke,..lend me thy yernfull tunes, to vtter my sorow. **1583** MELBANCKE *Philotimus* Tj, So out of thy stonye hearte maye yet flowe such water, as may wash and purge my yearnfull woundes. **1591** GREENE *Maidens Dr.* Wks. (Grosart) XIV. 303 She wet his visage with a yearnfull streame. **1613** PURCHAS *Pilgrimage* VI. xi. 522 *Ala, Ala,* was their yernfull note. **1889** J. K. JEROME *Three Men in a Boat* xix, The wild yearnful melody.
†**3.** Full of compassion. *Obs.*
1633 P. FLETCHER *Purple Isl.* IX. xlvi, His yearnfull heart pitying that wretched sight.
Hence **'yearnfully** *adv.*; †**'yearnfulness,** eagerness, diligence.
c **888** ÆLFRED *Boeth.* xxiv. §3 Sume tiliað mid micelre ȝeornfulnesse wifa. *c* **960** ÆTHELWOLD *Rule St. Benet* iv. (Schröer 1885) 17 þæs ecean lifes he sceal mid ealre ȝeornfulnesse ȝirnan. *c* **1200** ORMIN 11181 Swa þatt himm birrþ fra þeþennforþ Wiþþ mikell ȝeorrnfullnesse... To follȝhenn Godess laȝheboc. *a* **1884** WALT WHITMAN *After the Sea-Ship* 9 Larger and smaller waves in the spread of the ocean yearnfully flowing.

yearning ('jɜːnɪŋ), *vbl. sb.*[1] [f. YEARN *v.*[1] + -ING[1].]
1. The action of YEARN *v.*[1]; intense longing or desire *after, for,* †*of, to,* or *to do* something; an instance of this.
c **897** ÆLFRED *Gregory's Past. C.* v. 45 Mid ðære ȝierninge [*v.r.* ȝirninge] ðara smeaunga Godes wisdomes anes. *a* **1050** *Liber Scintill.* xi. (1889) 59 Se na wiðsæcð middanearde þam eorðlicre æhte ȝegladað ȝyrnincg [L. *ambitio*]. *a* **1225** *Ancr. R.* 114 His þurst nis nout buten ȝirnunge of ure soule hele. *Ibid.* 130 þuruh ȝirnunge of heorte to heouenliche þinges. **13..** *Cursor M.* 10513 (Gött.) þi ȝerning gode and þi prayere, Es comyn now to goddes ere. **1340** HAMPOLE *Pr. Consc.* 1127-8 Outher yhernyng of þe flesshe of man, Or yhernyng of eghe,.. Or pride of lyfe. **1357** *Lay Folks Catech.* (T.) 507 A urangwise wilnyng Or yernyng to hafe any kyns gode that us augh noght. **1375** BARBOUR *Bruce* III. 742 Thai, to fullfill hys ȝarnyng, Become his men euirilkane. *a* **1395** HYLTON *Scala Perf.* (W. de W. 1494) II. xxi, The yernyng of thyn herte to Jhesu. *c* **1440** *Promp. Parv.* 536/2 ȝarnynge, or ȝernynge, or desyrynge, *desiderium, optacio, exoptacio.* *a* **1450** *Ratis Raving* 975 It makis the knawleginge, And ledis the at thi ȝarnynge Fra place to place, quhar þow wald be. **1821** BYRON *Cain* III. i, Such melancholy yearnings o'er the past. **1836** KINGSLEY in *Life & Lett.* (1878) I. 33 Her restless yearnings after future things. **1840** BARHAM *Ingol. Leg.* Ser. I. *Mr. Peter's Story,* A strong disposition to doze, And a yearning to seek 'horizontal repose'. **1848** DICKENS *Dombey* xliii, Her doubts and fears between the two; the yearning of her innocent breast to both. **1850** TENNYSON *In Mem.* cxvi, Less yearning for the friendship fled. **1872** LIDDON *Elem. Relig.* i. 24 That Being to Whom the highest yearnings of his inmost self constantly point.
b. *transf.* (contextually) An object of intense desire.
c **1430** *Hymns Virgin* (1867) 23 Take to þee al myn entente þat þou be to me myn ȝerninge. **1869** MOZLEY *Univ. Serm.* ii. (1876) 40 The great yearning of prophecy was the total destruction of idolatry.
†**2.** The baying of hounds. Also *transf. Obs.*
1531 ELYOT *Gov.* I. xviii, If they wold use but a fewe nombre of houndes, onely to harborowe, or rouse, the game, and by their yorning to gyue knowlege whiche way it fleeth. **1576** TURBERV. *Venerie* lxv. 181 When they beginne to baye, (whiche in the earth is called Yearnyng). **1582** STANYHURST *Æneis* II. (Arb.) 53 Thee skrich rings mounting, increast is the horror of armoure, From sleepe I broad waked,.. And to the shril yerning with tentiue greedines harckned.
3. The state of being moved with compassion.
1603 FLORIO *Montaigne* II. xi. 247 Amongst all other vices, there is none I hate moore, than crueltie... But it is with such an yearning [F. *mollesse*] and faint-hartednes, that if I see but a chickins necke pulld off,.. I cannot choose but grieve. *c* **1625** BP. HALL *St. Paul's Combat* I. Wks. 1634 II. 441 Of pitty and yearning of bowels. **1647** S. M[OORE] (*title*) The Yernings of Christs bowels towards his languishing Friends. **1690** NORRIS *Beatitudes* (1694) 134 All that inward Feeling and Yerning of the Heart and Soul at a pitiful Object.
4. *attrib.* †**yearning-meat,** the meat for which one yearns.
a **1300** *Cursor M.* 3684 'Fader', he said, 'sitt vp and ete, I ha broght þi ȝerning mete.'

yearning ('jɜːnɪŋ), *vbl. sb.*[2] *Sc.* and *n. dial.* [f. YEARN *v.*[2] + -ING[1].] Rennet. Also *attrib.*
1371-3 *Durham Acc. Rolls* (Surtees) 577 Pro yernyng et Cheseclotes emp. pro vaccaria. **1581-2** *Inv.* in Best *Farm. Bks.* (Surtees) 172 Yerens [? yernens], oitemeell, and onions 13*s.* 4*d.* **1753** *Chambers' Cycl.* Suppl. App., *Earning,* or *Yearning,* a name used in several parts of the kingdom for rennet. **1788** W. MARSHALL *E. Yorksh.* Gloss. (E.D.S.), *Cheslip-skin,* the calf's bag, used in making yerning. *c* **1820** [see EARNING *vbl. sb.*[2] 2]. **1825** BROCKETT *N.C. Gloss.* s.v., A plant used in North Tindale to curdle milk for cheese is called yerning grass. **1825** JAMIESON s.v., The yirnin is the maw or stomach of the calf.

yearning, obs. var. EARNING *vbl. sb.*[1] (1 b).
1581 B. RICH *Farew.* Ej, With her yearnynges to helpe to releue hym.

yearning ('jɜːnɪŋ), *ppl. a.* [f. YEARN *v.*[1] + -ING[2].]
1. a. That yearns; characterized by longing desire or compassion.
1627 DRAYTON *Agincourt* cccx, These yearning cryes, that from the Caridge came. **1652** BENLOWES *Theoph.* IV. lxxiii, This Devota breaths out yerning Cries. *a* **1704** T. BROWN *Two Oxf. Schol.* Wks. 1730 I. 10 Some tenderhearted virgin ..who with yearning bowels will offer me her best assistance. **1819** KEATS *Fall of Hyperion* I. 39 Appetite More yearning than on Earth I ever felt. **1859** GEO. ELIOT *Adam Bede* xlv, The two pale faces..: one with a wild hard despair in it, the other full of sad, yearning love. **1873** E. E. HALE *In His Name* viii, As if the Holy Spirit had sent the immediate answer to his yearning prayer. **1891** W. CLARK RUSSELL *Marriage at Sea* iv, A full-rigged ship..with yearning canvas and ocean-worn sides.
transf. **1865** SWINBURNE *Poems & Ball., Anactoria* 228 By the yearning in my veins I know The yearning sound of waters.
†**b.** *yearning mood*: optative mood. *Obs.*
1522 VAUS *Rudim. Gram.* Bb ij (Jam.), *Optatiuo modo,* yarnand mode.
†**2.** Of hounds: see YEARN *v.*[1] 4. *Obs.*
1706 J. PHILIPS *Cerealia* 190 As the tall stag..quits his lair, And flies the yearning pack which close pursue.
Hence **'yearningly** *adv.*; (*nonce-wd.*) **'yearningness.**
1840 *New Monthly Mag.* LIX. 402 She felt yearningly enough for both. **1861** H. MACMILLAN *Footn. Page Nat.* 197 The geranium growing in the cottage window yearningly stretches out its tender leaves..to the smiling sunshine. **1894** HALL CAINE *Manxman* V. iii, He looked at it lovingly, fondly, yearningly. *a* **1916** H. JAMES *Sense of Past* (1917) 304 The ideal thing for dramatic interest..would be that there is just one matter in which..he betrays himself, gives himself away..it should..affect her..with but a finer yearningness of interest.

yearnling ('jɜːnlɪŋ). *nonce-wd.* [f. YEARN *v.*[1] + -LING.] A young child over which one yearns.
1829 LAMB *Let. to Procter* 29 June, She visited..a poor man's cottage that had a pretty baby (O the yearnling!).

'year-old, *a.* and *sb.*
A. *adj.* A year old; of the age of one year.
1767 ABERCROMBIE *Ev. Man his own Gardener* (1803) 85 Young shoots rising in the spring from the year-old plants. **1818** SCOTT *Rob Roy* iv, Was it not Wat the Devil who drove all the year-old hogs off the braes of Lanthorn-side? **1883** GUSTAFSON in *Harper's Mag.* Nov. 894/2 The little year-old Edgar..was very sick.
B. *sb.* A beast a year old, a yearling.
1539 *Wills & Inv. N.C.* (Surtees) I. 114, xj ky & iiij quyes iiij yer olds iiij ij yere olds. **1583** *Durham Wills* (Surtees) II. 82 Eight younge cattell, yeare-olds, and tuantays. **1774** GOLDSM. *Nat. Hist.* (1824) I. xlv. 381 None but the year olds remain together. **1816** SCOTT *Bl. Dwarf* i, To see if him and me can gree about the luckpenny I am to gie him for his year-aulds. *c* **1830** *Glouc. Farm Rep.* 17 in *Libr. Usef. Knowl., Husb.* III, The year-olds are kept in the field all winter.

year-round, *a.* and *adv.* [f. the phr. *all the year round* s.v. ROUND *adv.* 1 e.] **A.** *adj.* That exists, occurs, is used, etc., all the year round. Also of persons: residing in a place for the whole year.
1939 *Florida* (Federal Writers' Project) II. 177 The western district..contains..many homes of year-round residents. **1939** R. CAMPBELL *Flowering Rifle* II. 38 And thaws numbed strikers from their year-round frost. **1945** NELSON & WRIGHT *Tomorrow's House* x. 111/1 One advantage of the inside bathroom..is that it has year-round ventilation. **1960** *House & Garden* Aug. 40/1 A skilfully-planned year-round family house. **1961** *Guardian* 8 May 8/6 A moment, known increasingly to year-round Londoners. **1976** *Sci. Amer.* July 118/1 Where the diversion of local streams would not provide a year-round supply of water it was necessary to build a reservoir. **1980** P. MOYES *Angel Death* i 7 Year-round sunshine.
B. *adv.* = *all the year round.*
1968 *Globe & Mail* (Toronto) 17 Feb. 47/8 Enjoy swimming year-round in the outdoor and indoor pools. **1979** *Wall Street Jrnl.* 20 Dec. 18/1 The yuletide bulge chiefly reflects the greater number of people in the stores at that time. However, the crime is rising year-round. **1981** C. MILLER *Childhood in Scotland* 58 Rabbits..were shot year-round.

year's day: see YEAR-DAY.

yearsman ('jɪəzmən). *local.* [f. *year's,* gen. of YEAR[1] + MAN *sb.*[1]] A labourer hired by the year.
1891 *Daily News* 12 Sept. 3/6 Our labourers are divided into two classes: the day labourer and the yearsman.

year's mind, 'year-mind. [OE. *ȝéarȝemynd*: see YEAR *sb.* and MIND *sb.*[1] 5 b.] The commemoration of a deceased person by the celebration of requiem services a year after, or every year on the anniversary of, his death or funeral; a yearly obit. Cf. *twelvemonth's,* MONTH'S MIND.
a. a **1100** in Napier *Contrib. OE. Lexicogr.* (1906) 28 Ðis is seo caritas þe Baldwine abbod hæfð ȝeunnon his ȝebroðrum for Eadwardes sawle, þæs godan kynges, þæt is healf pund æt his ȝearȝemynde to fisce. **1489** *Will of R. Partrich of Sudbury, Suff.* 5 Dec. (P.C.C., 1 dogett), vs. yerely to the keping of a yer minde for my soule. **1579-80** NORTH *Plutarch* (1595) 1104 For keeping of a yeare minde and for making feastfull dayes In honour of that worthy wight. **1587** GOLDING *De Mornay* xv. (1592) 229 Hee commaunded an Anniuersarie or Yeere-minde to be kept in remembrance of him. **1606** HOLLAND *Sueton.* 19 b, Augustus had in mirth giuen him the name of *Founder,* he was so reputed, and his yeares-mind after his death solemnized accordingly.
β. **1408** *E.E. Wills* (1882) 15 That..hys Executours.. haue..rewlyng of my obytis, that ys for to sayn, my ȝerys mynde, xx wynter Af[t]er my deses. *c* **1420** *Prymer* 56 Graunte þou to þe soule of þi seruaunt, whos ȝeris mynde we maken to dai, a seete of refreschinge blisse. **1520** SIR R. ELYOT *Will* in T. Elyot *Gov.* (1883) App. A, The prest executing the service at myn enteryng, moneth mynde, and yeres mynde. **1558** PHAER *Æneid* Gen. Somme a iij, For his fathers honoure he deuised games of actiuitie, and set-foorthe his Obite or yeres mynde, with greate solempnitie. **1561** VERON *Hunt. Purgat.* 25 The moneth myndes and yeares minds other wyse called Anniversaries. **1849** ROCK *Ch. Fathers* I. vii. II. 350 No others' names were read out but of those whose anniversary or year's mind fell upon that very Sunday or festival. **1902** *Westm. Gaz.* 4 Feb. 7/3 The 'Year's Mind' of her late Majesty Queen Victoria was celebrated at St. Matthew's, Westminster, this morning.

yearth, etc., obs. or dial. ff. EARTH *sb.*[1], etc.
1542 UDALL *Erasm. Apoph.* 49 An yearthen potte. **1561** *Plowman's T.* in *Chaucer's Wks.* 95 b/2 That taketh maistrie in his name Ghostly, and for yearthly good. *c* **1581** LODGE *Repl. Gosson's Sch. Abuse* (Shaks. Soc.) 6 To make a yearthly creature to beare the person of the Creator. **1582** HESTER *Secr. Phiorav.* III. i. 2 Drie the Vitrioll in a yearthen pan. **1688** HOLME *Armoury* III. 261/2 *Yearthing,* put Earth about [the kiln]. **1828** *Craven Gloss., Yearthen,* earthen.

yeast (jiːst), *sb.* Forms: 1 **ȝist, ȝyst,** 5 **ȝest(e, ȝeest, yeest,** 6-9 **yest,** 7 **eyst** (?), 8-9 *dial.* **east,** 9 *dial.* **yist,** 7- **yeast.** [OE. (late WS.) *ȝist,* Anglian **ȝest,* corresp. to MLG. *gest* dregs, dirt, MDu. *ghist,* Du. *gist, gest* yeast, MHG. *jest, gest, gist* (G. *gischt, gäscht*) yeast, froth, ON. *jastr* yeast, related to OHG. *jeasan, gesan* (MHG. *jesen, gesen, gern,* G. *gähren* to ferment), the causative OHG. *jerian, gerian* to cause to ferment, and ON. *gerð* yeast. The underlying base *jes-* is found also in Skr. *yás(y)ati* to seethe, boil, *práyastas* bubbling over, Zend *yah-* to boil (intr.), Alb. *ğeš buken* I knead bread, Gr. ζέω I boil, ζεστός boiled, W. *iās* seething.]
1. a. A yellowish substance produced as a froth or as a sediment during the alcoholic fermentation of malt worts and other saccharine fluids, and used in the manufacture of beer and to leaven bread.
Modern science distinguishes two kinds of yeast, ***surface*** or ***top yeast*** (G. *oberhefe*) and ***under, sediment,*** or ***bottom yeast*** (G. *unterhefe*), the former propagated by buds, the latter by spores, of the fungus *Saccharomyces cerevisiæ*. The yeast of beer is used medicinally as an antiseptic and stimulant in low fevers, and as an application to ulcers.
c **1000** *Sax. Leechd.* II. 266 Læt þonne hwon ȝestandan, do of þa ȝaȝellan, do þonne niwne ȝist. **1530** PALSGR. 291/1 Yest or barme for ale, *leueton.* **1591** A. W. *Bk. Cookrye* 8 Put into your broth a spoonfull of yest. **1600** SURFLET *Country Farm* V. xxiii. 725 They renewe the force and strength of the yeast or leuen euerie hower with beere already made, so long as till the said leuen or yeast become strong inough of it selfe. **1612** *Househ. Bks. Howard of Naworth* (Surtees) 41 To Harry Baker to bestow in eyst v[s]. **1664** BUTLER *Hud.* II. iii. 119 When Yeast, and outward means do fail, And have no pow'r to work on Ale. **1666** G. HARVEY *Morb. Angl.* viii. (1672) 19 Those sharp scorbutick dregs imitating the nature of yist. **1743** *Lond. & Country Brewer* III. (ed. 2) 214 Yeast.. consists of a great Quantity of subtile and spirituous Particles, wrapped up in such as are viscid. **1804** *Med. Jrnl.* XII. 192 An instance of a young gentleman in the last stage of typhus fever, being cured by the use of yeast. **1843** R. J. GRAVES *Syst. Clin. Med.* Introd. Lect. 34 Sugar by presence of yeast [is made to resolve itself] into alcohol and carbonic acid. **1858** LEWES *Sea-side Studies* 314 There are two kinds of yeast, or rather two forms of the same plant. The one is called 'surface' yeast, the other 'sediment' yeast. The former requires a temperature of 70° to 80° Fahrenheit; the latter 32° to 45°. **1877** HUXLEY *Physiogr.* 193 The porous texture of bread is due to the presence of bubbles of gas evolved by the fermentation of the yeast.
b. With qualifying word, as ***beer-yeast***; applied esp. to common yeast drained, pressed dry, and made into a cake in order to be kept for a time: see quots. and cf. *yeast-cake, -powder* (4).
[**1781** T. HENRY *Acc. Method Pres. Water,* etc. 26 The Process for making artificial Yeast. Boil flour and water together to the consistence of treacle... In about two days, such a degree of fermentation will have taken place, as to give the mixture the appearance of yeast.] **1845** E. ACTON

Mod. Cookery xxviii. 650 German yeast, imported in a solid state, is now much sold in London. **1858** SIMMONDS *Dict. Trade* s.v., German yeast is now imported to a considerable extent in a dried form from the Continent. **1878** *Chambers's Encycl.* s.v. *Yeast*, Patent Yeast is exactly similar [to German Yeast], but is raised from a wort made purposely from malt and hops. Artificial Yeast is a dough of wheat or other flour, mixed with a small quantity of common yeast, and made into small cakes, which are dried. **1879** WEBSTER Suppl., *Press-yeast*, the yeasty froth from the surface of a fermenting fluid, washed and pressed into cakes for bakers' use. **1889** *Pall Mall Gaz.* 1 July 3/3 Patent yeast is either made by the baker himself or is bought from the yeast merchant. It..leaves an unpleasant smell and taste in the bread.

c. *fig.* = LEAVEN *sb.* 2 a.

1760–72 H. BROOKE *Fool of Qual.* (1809) III. 35 Though liberty has no relation to party.., there is yet a kind of yest observable in its nature, which may be necessary to the fermentation and working up of virtue. **1818** KEATS *Let.* Wks. 1889 III. 105 The best of men have but a portion of good in them—a kind of spiritual yeast in their frames, which creates the ferment of existence. **1873** DIXON *Two Queens* VI. iv. I. 324 The Plantagenet yeast being strong within his sons.

d. A fungus that exists predominantly as single cells rather than a mycelium and in which vegetative reproduction takes place by budding or fission.

Now not usu. regarded as constituting any particular taxon.

1899 *Allbutt's Syst. Med.* VIII. 760 The common saccharomyces or yeast of the scalp. **1906** G. MASSEE *Text-bk. Fungi* III. 275 Symbiotic relationship between yeasts and bacteria is not uncommon. **1922** H. GWYNNE-VAUGHAN *Fungi* i. 7 Yeasts and filamentous fungi are abundant in woodland soils. **1930** H. M. FITZPATRICK *Lower Fungi* i. 16 In the lower Ascomycetes the asci are formed without order throughout a mould-like mycelium, or exist as isolated cells as in the yeasts. **1977** R. C. COOKE *Fungi, Man & his Environment* i. 14 Yeasts appear in the Ascomycetes, Basidiomycetes, and Fungi Imperfecti. This is because the term 'yeast' refers to a special mode of growth and does not describe a particular, special assemblage of fungi. **1983** *Oxf. Textbk. Med.* I. v. 372/2 *Candida albicans*... It is a saprophytic yeast often found as a commensal in the mouth and gastrointestinal tract and commonly present in the vagina.

†**2.** The froth or 'head' of new or fermenting beer. *Obs.*

c **1430** *Two Cookery-bks.* 10 Þen take ȝest of New ale an caste þer-to. *c* **1440** *Promp. Parv.* 537/2 Ȝeest, berme, *spuma.* **1683** SALMON *Doron Med.* I. 241 Let not the Head, or Yest work over at the bungs. **1716** GAY *Trivia* II. 290 When drays bound high, they never cross behind, When bubbling yest is blown by gusts of wind.

3. *transf.* Foam or froth, as of troubled water.

1611 SHAKS. *Wint. T.* III. iii. 94 The Shippe boaring the Moone with her maine Mast, and anon swallowed with yest and froth. **1818** BYRON *Ch. Har.* IV. clxxxi, They melt into thy yeast of waves. **1864** *Q. Rev.* Apr. 311 The dim headlands of new empires which are already looming darkly up out of the yeast of stormy waves.

4. *attrib.* and *Comb.*, as ***yeast-ash, -cell, -culture, dumpling, -fungus, -germ, -poultice, -scum; yeast-like*** adj. and adv.; **yeast-beer**, new beer with which a small quantity of fermenting wort has been mixed to make it 'work'; **yeast-bitten** *a.* (see quot.); **yeast bread**, bread made with yeast (i.e. ordinary bread); **yeast-budding**, a direct budding or germination of spores from other spores as occurring in *Saccharomyces* and other fungi; **yeast-cake**, (*a*) (see 1 b); (*b*) a cake made light with yeast; †**yeast-fat**, a fermenting-vat; **yeast-plant**, any plant of the genus *Saccharomyces*, esp. *S. cerevisiæ*, which produces fermentation in saccharine fluids; **yeast-powder**, the powder of dried yeast (cf. 1 b), also (*U.S.*) baking-powder.

1875 HUXLEY & MARTIN *Elem. Biol.* (1877) 6 Pasteur himself used actual *yeast ash. **1829** *Art of Brewing* (ed. 2) 54/2 (L.U.K.) The gas being too weak to buoy up the now close head of the tun, the yeast might partially or wholly subside, and the ale would become **yeast-bitten*; it would receive that disagreeable taste which the head had acquired by too long exposure to the atmospheric air. **1853** *Southern Ladies Bk.* (New Orleans) I. 130 The chicks in the free states live on *yeast bread. **1945** *ABC of Cookery* (Ministry of Food) xviii. 67 Nowadays yeast bread is seldom made in the home. **1898** PORTER tr. *Strasburger's Bot.* 350 Such a method of multiplication of conidia by budding is termed *yeast budding, and the conidia are termed yeast conidia. **1795** SIR J. DALRYMPLE *Let. to Admiralty* 4, I put in the Wort-cake and *Yeast-cake at his sight. **1855** E. ACTON *Mod. Cookery* (rev. ed.) xxxi. 604 To test bread that has been cut (or yeast-cakes), press down the crumb..with the thumb. **1897** R. M. STUART *Simpkinsville* 136 Here, too, had passed pantalet patterns, bits of yeast-cake and preserving-kettles. **1908** *McClure's Mag.* Feb. 421/2 We are to be the yeast-cake for democracy's dough. **1973** *Listener* 20 Sept. 377/2 Tea was served by Auntie Golda..thick slices of cinnamon-veined yeast-cake. **1847–9** *Todd's Cycl. Anat.* IV. I. 101/2 The importance of *yeast-cells in the phenomena of fermentation. **1899** CAGNEY tr. *von Jaksch's Clin. Diagn.* v. (ed. 4) 200 Yeast-cells (Saccharomycetes) are the commonest form of parasite in the intestinal discharges. **1898** *Allbutt's Syst. Med.* V. 420 Protein or dead cultures of bacteria, filtered *yeast-cultures. **1747** MRS. GLASSE *Cookery* ix. 112 *East Dumplings. First make a light Dough ..with Flour, Water, Salt, and Yeast. **1367** *Priory of Finchale* (Surtees) p. lxxviii, j. *yestefatt. **1876** tr. *Wagner's Gen. Pathol.* 86 The several fermentation or *yeast-fungi. **1867** *Edin. Rev.* Apr. 395 The fermentation occurs only in presence of the *yeast germs. **1868** *Rep. U.S. Comm. Agric.* (1869) 277 The..*yeast-like appearance of the decomposing brood. **1857** HENFREY *Bot.* §813 What is called the '*Yeast-plant' consists of a particular form of the vegetative structure (*mycelium*) of a Fungus. **1871** TYNDALL *Fragm. Sci.* (1879) II. xii. 257 The brewer deliberately sows the yeast-plant. **1860** MAYNE *Expos. Lex., Cataplasma Fermenti*, ..the *yeast poultice, for sloughing and mortification; flour mixed with yeast and heated till it rise. **1795** SIR J. DALRYMPLE *Let. to Admiralty* 2 Wort-cake and *Yeast-powder made at the King's breweries. **1857** W. CHANDLESS *Visit Salt Lake* I. vi. 95 Three boxes of yeast-powder (at thirty cents each) to improve our bread. **1876** *Amer. Cycl.* XVI. 777 Yeast powders, or baking powders, substitutes for yeast, used in making bread. **1888** *Encycl. Brit.* XXIV. 602/1 After ten to fourteen days the *yeast-scum on the surface disappears.

yeast (jiːst), *v. rare.* [f. prec.] *intr.* (also *refl.*) To ferment; to be covered with froth, as agitated water. Also *fig.* and with *up.* **'yeasting** *vbl. sb.* and *ppl. a.*

1819 KEATS *Otho* III. ii, To thee only I appeal, Not to thy noble son, whose yeasting youth Will clear itself, and crystal turn again. **1880** BLACKMORE *Mary Anerley* I. ix. 113 (Like dough before the fire) every well belaboured [bed] tick was left to yeast itself awhile. **1891** C. DAWSON *Avonmore* II. 35 Racing seas, with their yeasting waves. **1902** *Brit. Med. Jrnl.* 14 June 1463 The presence of purin bodies in beers is probably due to the yeasting and processes of manufacture. **1921** A. HUXLEY *Crome Yellow* ix. 88 It must inevitably take a long time for Armageddon to ripen, to yeast itself up.

yeast, obs. form of EAST.

yeasty ('jiːstɪ), *a.* Also 7–9 **yesty**. [f. YEAST *sb.* + -Y[1].]

1. Of, pertaining to, full of, covered with, like or resembling yeast.

1599 PORTER *Angry Wom. Abington* D j, His beard, Thats glewed together with his slauering droppes, Of yesty ale. **1600** MARSTON, etc. *Jack Drums Entert.* I. (1601) A iij, Each ..yeastie bowzing bench. **1602** MARSTON *Ant. & Mel.* Ind., Wks. 1856 I. 5 As slovenly as the yeasty breast of an ale-knight. **1676** COTTON *Walton's Angler* II. viii. 75 We have then [*sc.* in June] another Dunne, call'd the Barm-flie, from it's yesty colour. **1683** TRYON *Way to Health* 25 That Yeasty quality that most Ale in Cities, especially in London, is subject unto. **1743** *Lond. & Country Brewer* II. (ed. 2) 84 He fell into Drinking such Quantities of their yeasty Ale, as made him distracted. **1836** [see *yeastiness* below]. **1849** CUPPLES *Green Hand* ii. (1856) 15 From foaming whiteness it melted into yesty green.

transf. **1668** CULPEPPER & COLE *Barthol. Anat.* I. xvi. 39 The Arterial, fermentative, or leavening, and yeasty Blood.

2. *fig.* with various connotations: 'Swelling', 'working'; light and superficial, 'frothy'.

1598 E. GUILPIN *Skial.* (1878) 36 Like a Swartrutters hose his puffe thoughts swell With yeastie ambition. **1602** SHAKS. *Ham.* v. ii. 199 He..only got the tune of the time, and outward habite of encounter, a kinde of yesty collection, which carries them through & through the most fond and winnowed opinions. **1627** DRAYTON *Moon-calf* in *Agincourt* etc. 161 Knowledge with him is idle, if it straine Aboue the compasse of his yestie braine. **1826** DISRAELI *Viv. Grey* IV. i, Byron's mind was like his own ocean, sublime in its yesty madness. **1904** *Athenæum* 2 Apr. 425/2 Burying his thought in a yeasty mass of adjectives.

3. *transf.* Foamy, frothy, like troubled water.

1605 SHAKS. *Macb.* IV. i. 53 Though the yesty Waues Confound and swallow Nauigation vp. **1798** *Poetry of Anti-Jacobin* No. 36. 236 And Whitbread wallowing in the yeasty main. **1802** PALEY *Nat. Theol.* xxi. (1819) 331 The yesty waves which confound the heaven and the sea. **1819** CRABBE *T. of Hall* IV. 472 Far up the beach, the yesty sea-foam roll'd. **1820** BYRON *Juan* III. lviii, The ocean when its yeasty war is waging Is awful. **1899** F. T. BULLEN *Log Sea-waif* 254 We were over the bar and in smooth water, only the yeasty flakes of the spent breakers following us.

Hence **'yeastily** *adv.*, **'yeastiness**.

1778 H. BROOKE *Antony & Cl.* IV. iv, I know not why of late This yestiness of temper comes upon me. **1836** *Penny Cycl.* V. 405/1 It [*sc.* creamy scum] however rises again, becomes yesty, the bladders enlarge in size, the yestiness increases, and, when ready for cleansing, it has a vigorous, rich, yesty brown and bladdery head. **1890** W. CLARK RUSSELL *Ocean Trag.* I. viii. 162 The pale blue brine that melted yeastily from her metalled forefoot.

yeat, obs. Anglo-Irish f. GET *v.*

1554 in *10th Rep. Hist. MSS. Comm.* App. v. 415 If the creditore can not yeat the owner nor his attorney.

yeat(e: see GATE *sb.*[1], YET.

yeather, var. EDDER: see YEDDER *sb.* and *v.*

Yeatsian ('jeɪtsɪən), *a.* (*sb.*) Also **Yeatsean**. [f. the name of the Irish poet and playwright William Butler *Yeats* (1865–1939) + -IAN.] Of, pertaining to, or characteristic of Yeats or his writing. Also as *sb.*, an admirer of Yeats.

1928 S. O'CASEY *Let.* 5 June (1975) I. 261 Since Mr. Yeats has..shouted a lot of things in at O'Casey's window, he shouldn't be surprised,..when he finds O'Casey hammering at the Yeatsian door. **1941** *Scrutiny* IX. 381 Mr. MacNeice does attempt to define the essence of the Yeatsian idiom. **1954** *N. & Q.* CXCIX. 535/2 Yeatsians are doubtless all familiar with Dr. Jeffares' story of the composition of 'The Wheel' at Euston on 17 September 1921. **1959** *Encounter* Nov. 78/2 The misguided Neo-Platonism of some Yeatsians. **1969** *Listener* 13 Mar. 361/2 Though Reisz can give us a Yeatsian despair ('Ah dancer, ah, sweet dancer'), he fails to evoke a Yeatsian gaiety. **1978** *Studies in Eng. Lit.: Eng. Number* (Tokyo) 157 Through his long poetic career, he changed from his early Yeatsean stance to his later self-assurance. **1982** J. GROSS in A. Thwaite *Larkin at Sixty* 86 Larkinesque irony..and high Yeatsian romance.

yeaught, obs. form of YACHT.

yeauman, obs. form of YEOMAN.

yeaunt, obs. form of GIANT: see YEANT.

yeave, obs. form of EWE *sb.*[1]

yeaven, obs. pa. pple. of GIVE *v.*

1592 *B.N.C.* (Oxf.) *Muniments* 18. 73 (MS.).

yeax, yeck, obs. ff. YEX, ITCH *v.*[1]

yech (jɛk, jɛx), *int. U.S. slang.* Also **yecch, yeck**; (*rare*) **yee(c)ch**. [Imitative. Cf. YUCK *int.*, *sb.*[2], and *a.*] = YUCK *int.*

1969 C. BURKE *God is Beautiful, Man* (1970) 76 Well, Jesus did the craziest thing you ever heard. He took some clay from the road and he spit on it...yeck! **1972** *Even. Telegram* (St. John's, Newfoundland) 23 June 3/1 Yeecchhhh! How messy. A St. John's pigeon just passed his opinion of a Bayman. **1973** *Daily Tel.* (Sydney) 17 May 36/1 She (yecch) pins a plastic gardenia into her hair. **1975** *Hi-Fi Answers* Feb. 41/1 Colouration introduced by the cartridge will be carried right through the system and emerge at the other end added to the inevitable individual speaker character, result...yeech! **1979** 'A. HAILEY' *Overload* IV. xviii. 389 As for the food there—yech! **1984** *N.Y. Times* 30 Mar. A. 6/2 We come up with new information and we tell them and they go 'Yecch—what a mess.'

yechy ('jɛkɪ), *a. U.S. slang.* Also **yecchy**. [f. prec. + -Y[1]. Cf. YUCKY *a.*] = YUCKY *a.*

1969 *Current Slang* (Univ. S. Dakota) Summer 17 *Yecchy*, adj. Extremely unpalatable (of food or drink). **1975** *New Yorker* 16 June 25/1 They thought the green peppers and onions were 'yechy'. **1983** *Washington Post* 23 Dec. 15/1 She goes on and on about him in yecchy voice-overs: He was like 'a licorice billygoat sniffing the wind for sexual sweat'.

yed (jɛd), *sb.* Now *Sc.* Forms: 1 **ȝied(d, ȝed(d, ȝid(d, ȝyd(d**, 3 **ȝed**, 8– **yed**. [OE. *ȝiedd*: see next.]

†**1.** A song, poem, speech, tale, riddle. *Obs.*

Beowulf 1160 Leoð wæs asungen, gleomannes ȝyd. *Ibid.* 1723 Ic þis ȝid be þe awræc. *c* **1205** LAY. 25853 Heo..hire ȝeddes [*later version* wordes] sæide ȝeomere stefne.

b. A fib, an exaggerated tale (Jam.). *Sc.*

2. Contention, wrangling; strife.

1719 RAMSAY *3rd Answ. to Hamilton* ii, [The soldier] Wha now to youngsters leaves the yed, To 'tend his fauld. **1808**, etc. [see *Eng. Dial. Dict.*].

yed (jɛd), *v.* Now *Sc.* Forms: 1 **ȝieddian, ȝeddian, ȝiddian, ȝyddian**, 3–7 **ȝedde**, 3–5 **ȝede**, 6 **yedde**, 8– **yed**. [OE. *ȝieddian*, f. *ȝiedd* (see prec.), ? f. root *gad-* to put together, as in GATHER, TOGETHER. For the development of sense 2 cf. OE. *ȝieddum wrixlan* to dispute, and the use of the vb. in Daniel 728.]

1. *intr.* To sing, recite, talk, discourse.

c **888** ÆLFRED *Boeth.* xii. 26 Þa ongan se Wisdom gliowian & ȝeoddode þus. *Ibid.* xxxi. 71 Þa ongan he eft ȝiddian & þus singende cwæð. *c* **1205** LAY. 21429 Arður..þus ȝeddien agon [*later version* þes word saide] Mid gomenfulle worden. **1362** LANGL. *P. Pl.* A. I. 138 Prechet in þin harpe þer þou art Murie at þi mete whon me biddeþ þe ȝedde. *c* **1425** *Seven Sages* (P.) 215 Thay nolden no langer with hym ȝede, Ne suffry langer lygge in bede.

b. To fib, exaggerate a tale (Jam.). *Sc.*

2. To contend, wrangle.

1570 LEVINS *Manip.* 48/35 To Yedde, chide, *iurgare.* **1721** RAMSAY *Poems* I. 398 Gloss., *Yed*, to contend, wrangle. Contention, Wrangling.

yed, yedd(e, obs. pa. t. of GO: see YODE.

yedda ('jɛdə). Also **yeddo**. [Origin unknown.] A type of grass used for making straw hats (see quot. 1925). Freq. *attrib.* as ***yedda braid, plait, straw***.

1918 C. R. AIKEN *Millinery Dept.* 28 Yedda braid was first produced in Italy, but the Japanese have made an imitation. ... Yedda is a tall grass grown in Italy, Japan, and the Philippines. **1922** F. ANSLOW *Pract. Millinery* viii. 93 The Yedda plaits, made of Japanese and Chinese grass, are soft and pliable, and can be dyed in most beautiful shades, of which, perhaps, the mole, grey and blue are the most attractive. **1923** *Sketch* 9 May 300 Dove-grey yedda straw makes this attractive shady hat. **1925** N. KNEELAND *Millinery* ii. 17 Yeddo is a tall grass grown in Italy, Japan, and the Philippines. The hats made from this fiber are loosely woven, light, and delicate. **1927** *Daily News* 20 June 2/4 A smart little hat of varnished black yedda straw. **1929** *Millinery Trade Rev.* May 46 A diversity of summer fabrics is being featured..as well as the ever popular straw items, Bakou, balibuntal, yedda, [etc.]. **1957** E. R. E. LANGRIDGE *Textbk. Mod. Millinery* vi. 62 Yeddo is a knotted straw made entirely by hand and worked up by the Swiss peasants in their houses.

yedder ('jɛdə(r)), *sb. north. dial.* Forms: 5 **ȝedd-, yeddyr**, 6 **ȝedder**, 7–9 **yeather**, 8–9 **yether**, 9 **yadder**, 6– **yedder**. [Variant of EDDER *sb.*]

1. An osier, or rod of pliant wood, used for binding a hedge. Also *attrib.*

1512–13 *Durham Acc. Rolls* (Surtees) 106 Pro cariag. xij plaustrat. lez thornes, ȝedders, et rysez ad prædict. sepes. **17**.. [see STRUT *sb.*[2] 1 b]. **1691** RAY *N.C. Words* 152 A yeather, *vimen.* **1764** *Museum Rust.* III. iv. 10 Yethers (as binders of hassel or willow are here [*sc.* Yorks.] called). **1779** CHARLTON *Hist. Whitby* 96 A certain stake and yether hedge. **1829** J. HODGSON in J. Raine *Mem.* (1858) II. 156 Great abundance of fine osiers will be thus produced, but a few of the strongest shoots should be left on each stake, for other stakes and poles and yeathers. **1852** *Jrnl. R. Agric. Soc.* XIII. II. 281 Farmers find posts and rails cheaper.. than the old system of 'stake and vice'. *Footnote.* Called..in some parts..'stower and yedder'. **1876** *Whitby Gloss.*, *Yethers*, oziers and similar flexibilities.

2. The mark of a blow or stripe, or that made by tight binding; a weal. Also, a smart blow.

c **1440** *Alphabet of Tales* 286 He..grapyd his bakk, & it was passand sare & full of yeddyrs & wowndis as he had bene betyn. **1483** *Cath. Angl.* 426/1 A ȝeddyr, *liuor*, *vibex*. **1535** COVERDALE *Ecclus.* xxviii. 17 The stroke of yᵉ rod maketh yedders. **1802** SIBBALD *Chron. S.P.* IV. Gloss., *Yether*, the mark left by tight binding, as with a small cord. **1825** JAMIESON, *Yether*,..a severe blow, Upp. Clydes. **1877** *Holderness Gloss.*, *Yether*, a discolouration of the skin caused by a blow.

Hence **yedder** *v.* (see quots.).

[**1523** edderinges: see EDDER. **1691** RAY *N.C. Words* 152 Eathering of hedges being binding the tops of them with small sticks as it were wooven on the stakes.] **1818** HOGG *Brownie of Bodsbeck* etc. II. 131, I hae heard o' some o' them that fought the deil,..yethered him and yerked him till he coudna mou' another curse. **1825** JAMIESON, To *Yether*,..to bind firmly, Roxb. **1825** in Hone *Every-day Bk.* I. 1381 Yadder them with your yadders, and..stake them on each side, with street stowers. **1855** ROBINSON *Whitby Gloss.*, To *Yedder* or *Yether*, to interweave or connect with pliable twigs or osiers a row of upright sticks or stobs in hedge work. **1876** *Ibid.*, *Yether*, v. to interweave with twigs, as in basket-making. **1877** *Holderness Gloss.*, *Yether*, v. to lash with a whip.

† **yedding**, *vbl. sb.* [OE. *ʒiedding*, f. *ʒieddian*, YED *v.* + -ING¹.] A song; a speech, discourse; *spec.* a 'gest' or romance in verse.

c **950** *Lindisf. Gosp.* Luke xv. 3 *Et ait ad illos parabolam istam*, & cuoeð to ðæm ʒeddung ðics. *a* **1350** in *Thornton Rom.* (Camden) 261 Ȝeddyngis, japis, and folies. *c* **1386** CHAUCER *Cant. T.* Prol. 237 Wel koude he synge and pleyen on a rote Of yeddynges he baar outrely the pris. *a* **1440** *Sir Degrev.* 1421 And evere Myldore sche sete Harpyng notus ful swet..Songe ȝeddyngus above. *c* **1440** *Promp. Parv.* 537/1 Ȝeddynge, or geest, *idem quod* geest (or rowmamnce).

Yeddo (ˈjɛdəʊ). The former name of Tokyo, used *attrib.* to designate materials, etc., originating there (before 1868, in which year the name was changed), as † *Yeddo crepe*, *poplin*; **Yeddo spruce**, the Japanese spruce, *Picea jezoensis*.

1866 in A. Adburgham *Shops & Shopping* (1964) xii. 126 Costumes at reduced prices in Yeddo Poplin. [**1906** ELWES & HENRY *Trees Gr. Brit. & Ireland* 87 Mayr informed me last year that the Yezo spruce was not introduced into Europe until 1891.] **1932** W. DALLIMORE in F. J. Chittenden *Conifers in Cultivation* 26 Picea...jezoensis Carr... Yeddo Spruce—N.E. Asia to N. Japan. **1952** A. G. L. HELLYER *Sanders' Encycl. Gardening* (ed. 22) 378 *Picea..jezoensis*, 'Yeddo Spruce', not so hardy as var. *hondoensis*, 80 to 100 ft., Japan. **1960** C. W. CUNNINGTON et al. *Dict. Eng. Costume* 280/2 *Yeddo crepe*, 1880, a cotton fabric thick as linen but soft... *Yeddo poplin*, 1865, of pure llama wool, resembling French merino. **1981** F. B. HORA in *Oxf. Encycl. Trees of World* 70/2 *P. jezoensis* Yeddo Spruce. NE Asia, Japan.

yeddo, var. YEDDA.

† **yede**, *v. Obs.* Also 6 yead, 6–7 yeed(e, 7 yed. [A pseudo-archaism of 16th cent. poets and their imitators; *yede*, pa. t. of GO (see YODE) used erron. as an infin.] *intr.* To go, proceed.

1563 SACKVILLE *Induct. Mirr. Mag.* xxx, Yeding forth, anone An horrible lothly lake we might discerne. *a* **1578** DRANT (Webster) Years yead away, and faces fair deflower. **1579** SPENSER *Sheph. Cal.* Sept. 145 They wander at wil, and stray at pleasure, And to theyr foldes yead at their owne leasure. **1590** —— *F.Q.* I. xi. 5 Then bad the knight his Lady yede aloofe. **1602** CAREW *Cornwall* 116 Downeuet ..(perhaps so called) of downe yeeding, as hauing a steep hill. **1614** GORGES *Lucan* v. 174 Yet she, poore soule, was sore adread Into the horrid cell to yed. **1633** FISHER *Fuimus Troes* III. ix, Vnneath thilke borrells May well ne yede, ne stand. **1768** DOWNMAN *Land of Muses* xii, Early the morn we will forth yede yfere.

yede, ȝede, obs. pa. t. of GO: see YODE.

† **ˈyeder**, *a. Obs.* In 4 ȝeder, 5 ȝedire. [Origin unknown.] Quick; frequent. Hence † **ˈyederly** *adv.*, quickly.

13.. *E.E. Allit. P.* B. 463 He..sone ȝederly for-ȝete ȝister-day steuen. **13..** *Gaw. & Gr. Knt.* 1215, I ȝelde me ȝederly, & ȝeȝe after grace. *a* **1400–50** *Wars Alex.* 5042 So did his princes..for pete of him-selfe, With ȝedire ȝoskingis & ȝerre ȝett out to grete.

yee, obs. f. EYE, YE, YEA.

yeed(e, ȝeed(e, obs. pa. t. of GO: see YODE.

yee-ho: see YO *int.*

yeel(e, obs. form of EEL *sb.*

yeelaman, variant of HIELAMAN, shield of Australian aborigines.

1862 KENDALL *Poems* 19 Yeelamans splinter and boomerangs clash.

yeeld, etc., obs. form of GUILD, YIELD, etc.

yeelde, obs. pa. t. of AIL *v.*

c **1489** CAXTON *Sonnes of Aymon* ii. 66 The duke knewe wel what she yeelde.

yeen, obs. pl. of EYE *sb.*¹

ˈyeender. *north. dial.* Forms: 7 earnder, eender, 7–9 yeender, 7, 9 yender; also 8–9 yeandurth. [Representing OE. *ǽr undern* 'mane' (Ælfric *Lev.* vi. 20) = OFris. *êr unden* in the forenoon, NFris. (Sylt) *îrönner*, *îrner* forenoon, MDu. *eeronderen* (*broot*) 12 o'clock meal (cf. early Flem. *eronderen* 'meridiari', Kilian): see ERE *prep.* and UNDERN.] The forenoon.

12.. *Ancrene Wisse* in J. Hall *Early M.E.* (1920) 74 Cumeð to ham to þe þurl earunder & ouerunder eanes oðer twien. *c* **1663** KYNDER *Hist. Darby*, §7 But these and yᵉ Moorelanders add three more [meales], yᵉ bitt in the morning, yᵉ Anders-meate, and yenders meate, and soe make up seaven. **1674** RAY *N.C. Words* 55 The *Yeender* or *Eender*, the Forenoon, *Derbysh.* **1684** G. M[ERITON] *Yorkshire Dial.* 195 (E.D.S.) It comes ith Earnder, Wife, or else by Neaun. **1703** THORESBY *Let. to Ray* (E.D.S.), *The Yeender* or *Earnder*, the forenoon. Hallifax, in Yorkshire. *c* **1746** J. COLLIER (Tim Bobbin) *View Lanc. Dial.* (1770) 25 Sed I, I'r there last Oandurth, on he'd leet o oneth' Yeandurth ofore. **1855** J. DAVIES *Races Lanc.* in *Trans. Philol. Soc.* 236 The equivalent of the Lanc. 'oandurth' [afternoon] and 'yeandurth', forenoon.

yeep (jiːp), *v. rare.* [Imitative.] *intr.* To cheep. Hence ˈ**yeeping** *ppl. a.* and *vbl. sb.*

1834 T. KEIGHTLEY *Tales & Popular Fictions* i. 11 His feathered charge, who go along *yeeping* and leisurely picking their steps. **1945** B. MACDONALD *Egg & I* (1946) iii. 44 Seven hundred and fifty yeeping chicks. *Ibid.* vii. 91 The yelping of a puppy and the stronger, louder yeeping of the chicks.

yeep (ȝeep), var. YEPE *a.*

yeepsen: see YEPSEN.

yeer, yeere, obs. ff. ERE, YEAR¹.

yeerde, obs. f. YARD *sb.*²

yees: see YEZ.

yees(y, ȝees(y, obs. ff. EASE, EASY.

† **yeet**, *v. Obs.* In 5 ȝeetyn, ȝet-, ȝyt-. [f. YE *pron.* + *-t*, as in THOWT. Cf. MHG. *ir(e)zen*, med.L. *vosare*, *vobissare*, *vositare*, *vobissitare*, and YE *v.*] To use the pronoun *ye* in addressing a person. Hence † **yeeting** *vbl. sb.*

c **1440** *Promp. Parv.* 537/2 Ȝeetyn, or sey ȝee (*P.* ȝetyn or sey ȝe with worship), *voso*. *Ibid.* 538/1 Ȝytynge, wythe wurchyp seyynge ȝe, and not thow (*K.* ȝetynge), *vosacio*.

yeet, ȝeet: see YET *v.*, to melt, cast.

yeewk, obs. form of YUKE *sb.*, itch.

yef(e: see GIVE, IF.

yeff(e: see GIFT, GIVE, IF.

yeffell, obs. f. EVIL *adv.*

yeffor, obs. form of EVER *adv.*

yef(f)t(e, obs. ff. GIFT.

yegg (jɛg). *U.S.* [Said to be the surname of a certain American burglar and safe-breaker.] A burglar or safe-breaker. So ˈ**yeggman**.

1903 *N.Y. Even. Post* 23 June (Cent. D. Supp.), The prompt breaking up of the organized gangs of professional beggars and yeggs. **1905** *N.Y. Times* 2 Jan. (ibid.), Detective Sergeants..captured on the Bowery three men who, they say, are among the most successful 'yeggmen', or safe-crackers, in the business. **1906** A. STRINGER *Wire Tappers* 100 'Now, nitro-glycerine I object to, it's so abominably crude.'.. 'And so odiously criminal!' she interpolated. 'Precisely. We're not exactly yeggmen yet.'

† **yegged** [Y- 5], edged.

1297 R. GLOUC. (Rolls) 5542 Þat suerd..Yegged it is in þe on half & in þe oþer noȝt.

yeh (jɛə), *colloq.* or *dial.* var. of YES or YEA. Cf. YEAH *adv.*

1920 GALSWORTHY *Skin Game* I. 13 *Hillcrist.* Did you meet the Jackmans? *Dawker.* Yeh. **1934** J. FRANKLYN *This Gutter Life* xx. 160 'I hope your son will be happy'. 'Yeh! —I 'opes so lidy.' **1955** W. GADDIS *Recognitions* I. vi. 206 Yeh, I could write a book. **1962** G. E. EVANS *Ask Fellows who cut Hay* (ed. 2) xxv. 235 The affirmative in the East Anglian dialect is 'yeh', which is undoubtedly not a corruption of yes, but a true survival of the early 'ye' ('Let youre ye be ye, and youre naye naye' of Tindal's Bible). **1963** LENNON & MCCARTNEY in *Golden Beatles Bk.* (1966) 37 She loves you yeh yeh yeh. **1973** *Black World* Nov. 91 Can you imagine the R&B band funky as they want to be, using a bass figure that kind of remind you of sweetback, yeh sweetback.

ye-ho: see YOHO *int.*

Yehudi, var. YAHUDI.

† **yei**, *sb. Obs.* [f. YEIE *v.*] A cry, wail.

a **1225** *Ancr. R.* 306 Mid tisse schulen þe uorlorene worpen a swuch ȝeor [*MS. T.* ȝur, *MS. C.* ȝei] þet heouene & eorðe muwen beoðe grisliche agrisen.

yei, obs. form of EYE *sb.*¹

1553 *Respublica* II. ii, I praie god she bee blynde: I am haulf afraide leste she have an yei behynde.

yei, obs. graphic variant of THEY.

yeid(e, ȝeid(e, obs. pa. t. of GO: see YODE.

† **yeie**, *v. Obs.* Forms: 2–3 ȝeiȝe, 3–4 ȝeie, yeie. 4 ȝeye, ȝyȝe, yeye. [OE. *ʒieʒan, *ʒéʒan = WFris. *geije* to cry out, ON. *geyja* to bark, to blaspheme:—**gaujan*, f. **gau* (cf. ON. *-gá* barking, blasphemy, as in *guðgá*).

Prob. related forms with *-t-* suffix are Du. *guiten* to bark, scold, G. dial. *gauzen*, *gäuzen* to yelp, scold, ON. *gaunta* to boast, prate.]

1. *intr.* To cry out, shout.

c **1175** *Lamb. Hom.* 43 Summe þer wepeð..and swiðe reowliche ilome ȝeiȝeð. *c* **1205** LAY. 27750 Þa ȝeiden lude Alle Rom-leode. *Ibid.* 29563 Heo..seoððe ȝeiden him on Mid ȝeomerliche stanen. *a* **1225** *Leg. Kath.* 162 Ifont ter swiðe feole ȝeinde & ȝurinde. *a* **1225** *Juliana* 44 Þeo ilke þat beoð stalewurðe..ȝeornliche ȝeieð [*v.r.* ȝeiȝeð] efter godes grace to helpe. *a* **1310** in Wright *Lyric P.* xxxix. 111 Thah ich ȝeȝe upon heth. *c* **1320** *Cast. Love* (Halliw.) 1541 The loude cry and ȝeiyng That heo wolleth with loude stevyn Ȝevyn. **13..** *Northern Passion* (G_1) 139 Men ne sschulle noth yeye þos longe. **13..** [see YEDERLY].

2. *trans.* To utter in a loud voice; to call out; to announce for sale in a loud voice, to 'cry'.

a **1225** *Ancr. R.* 66 Þe wreche peoddare more noise he makeð to ȝeien his sope, þen a riche mercer al his deorewurðe ware. *Ibid.* 126 For þi we ȝeieð to him iðe Paternostere, 'Et dimitte nobis debita nostra'. *a* **1225** *Leg. Kath.* 1265 Þes keiser..wodeliche ȝeide: Hwet nu, unwreste men.

3. To ask for, as with a loud voice.

c **1320** *Cast. Love* (Halliw.) 358 How Mercy here sistur heore herte ȝyȝth. **13..** *Gaw. & Gr. Knt.* 67 Syþen riche forth runnen to reche honde-selle, Ȝeȝed ȝeres ȝiftes on hiȝ.

yeild, ȝeild, obs. forms of YELD, YIELD.

yeild (ȝeild), obs. Sc. f. ELD *sb.*², age.

1513 *Sc. Acts Jas. IV* (1814) II. 278/2 Dispensand wᵗ his aige quhat ȝeild þat euir he be of.

yeinder, obs. f. YONDER.

yeir(e, obs. ff. YEAR¹.

yeird (ȝeird), obs. Sc. and north. dial. f. EARTH.

1533 GAU *Richt Vay* 41 He sufert onder poncio pilat to be crucifeit to de and to be zeirdit. *c* **1575** *Balfour's Practicks* (1754) 482 Thair to tak sasine thairof..be deliverance of zeird and stane.

yeirne, obs. form of IRON.

yeisk (ȝeisk), Sc. f. *yesk*: see YEX.

yeistrein, obs. f. YESTREEN.

yeit, obs. Sc. f. YET.

yek, dial. form of OAK.

† **yeke**, *sb. Obs.* Forms: 1 ʒeac, ʒaec, ʒec, iac, iec, 4–5 ȝeke, yeke. [OE. *ʒéac* cuckoo = MLG. *gôk* simpleton, MDu. *gooc*, OHG., MHG. *gouh*, *gouch* cuckoo, bastard, fool, (G. *gauch* provincial name of cuckoo, etc., simpleton, gawk), ON. *gaukr* cuckoo (whence Sc. GOWK); perhaps f. *gau-* as in **gaujan* (see YEIE *v.*).] The cuckoo. Also in comb. (with gen.) † **yekesterse** [TARSE¹] = CUCKOO-PINT.

With OE. *ʒéaces súre* 'cuckoo's sorrel' cf. ME. *goukesures* glossing *Alleluia* in MS. Rawl. C. 607 lf. 1 b.

c **725** *Corpus Gloss.* (Hessels) A 131 *Accitulium*, ʒeces sure [*Epinal* ʒeacaes; *Erfurt* ʒ ecaes]. *Ibid.* C 121 *Calciculium*, ieces surae [*Erfurt* iaces sura]. *Ibid.* G 87 *Geumatrix*, ʒeac. *a* **1000** *Guthlac* 716 Ȝeacas ʒear budon. *a* **1387** *Sinon. Barthol.* (Anecd. Oxon.) 24 *Iarus*, *barba aaron*, *pes vituli*,.. i. ȝekesterse. **14..** *MS. Porkington* lf. 59 (Halliw.) Whene the ȝeke gynnys to synge, Thenne the schrewe begynnys to sprynge. **14..** *MS. Rawl. C.* 506, lf. 249 b, *Iarus aaron*, ȝeksters, gauk pyntill.

yeke (ȝeke), obs. f. EKE *v.*, *adv.*, ITCH *sb.*, *v.*¹

† **yekth.** *Obs.* Forms: 1 ʒiecða, ʒicða, ʒihða, ʒyhða, 3 ȝecðe, ȝeohðe, 5 ȝykthe, yeketh, ȝeght, ȝight. [OE. *ʒiecða* = OHG. *jukido* (MHG. *jukede*):—OTeut. **jukiþon-*, f. *juk-*: see ITCH *v.*¹ (The suffix occurs in other names of physical disorders, as *clęweþa* itch, *spéowþa* vomit.)] Itching, itch.

c **897** ÆLFRED *Gregory's Past. C.* xi. 70 Se ʒicða [*Hatt.* ʒiecða] bið swiðe unsar, & se cleweða bið swiðe row. *c* **1000** *Sax. Leechd.* II. 252 Þes læcedom deah ʒe wiþ hriefðo & ʒicþan. *c* **1000** ÆLFRIC *Hom.* I. 86 Unaberendlic ʒyhða ofereode ealne ðone lichaman. *c* **1230** *Hali Meid.* 9 Þat bearninde ȝecðe [*v.r.* ȝeohðe] of þat licomliche lust. *c* **1440** *Promp. Parv.* 538/2 Ȝykynge, or ȝykth'e [**1499** *P.* ȝekyn or yeketh], *pruritus*. **14..** *Medulla Gram.* (Rawl. MS.), *Prurigo*, a scabbe a ȝeght. **14..** *Medulla* (Cant. Cath. MS.), *Pruritus*, ȝight.

yelamber, -bre: see YELLOW-HAMMER.

yeld (jɛld), *a.* (*sb.*) *Sc.* and *north. dial.* Forms: 1 ʒelde, 5– yeld, 6 ȝeld, ȝeild, ȝeald, 6–9 yeild, yeeld, 7 yeell, 8–9 yeald, 9 yield, yeal, yeel, yill. See also EILD. [late OE. *ʒielde, *ʒelde* (in glosses), corresp. to MLG. *galt*, OHG., MHG. *galt* (MG. *gelde*, *gelle*, G. *gelt*), ON. *geldr* (MSw. *galder*, etc.): cf. GELD *a.* and *v.*¹]

1. Of an animal: Barren; that has missed having her young, or is not old enough to bear.

a **1100** *Ags. Voc.* in Wr.-Wülcker 226/22 *Effeta*, ʒelde. *Ibid.* 394/26. **1411** *Priory of Finchale* (Surtees) 158, ix yeldbestis videlicet iiij vaccæ j stot ij quioks, ij stirketts. **1513** DOUGLAS *Æneis* VI. iv. 32 Enee hym self..to the, Proserpyne, A ȝeld kow all to trynschit. **1538** *Reg. Privy Seal Scot.* II. 386/2, xl ȝeild scheip. *a* **1598** D. FERGUSSON

Scot. Prov. (1641) No. 47 A yeeld sow was never good to gryces. **1726** *Fleming's Fulfilling Script.* (ed. 5) Table Scots Phr., *Yeald*, barren or dry. **1808** JAMIESON, *Yeld*, .. 3. Applied to cattle or sheep that are too young to bear, Dumfr. **1831** *Sutherland Farm Rep.* 79 in *Libr. Usef. Knowl., Husb.* III, Yill gimmers. *Ibid.* 81 The yell ewes being all sorted off the herding a few days before the lambing begins. **1844** H. STEPHENS *Bk. Farm* II. 38 If she has never been put to the ram she gets the name of *yeld-gimmer*. **1886** *Athenæum* 30 Oct. 560/2 To shoot the yeld hinds on the 15th of October. **1897** *Badminton Mag.* Apr. 474 We have got altogether four bucks and a good yeld doe.

b. Of birds: In a single state, unmated. *Sc.*

1535 STEWART *Cron. Scot.* III. 388 Birdis clekkit as tha war wont till do, .. No nestis maid bot all that tyme war ȝeild. **1809** EDMONSTON *Zetl. Isl.* II. 280 [They], not paring, are called yield kittiwakes.

2. Of cattle: Not yielding milk, from being in calf or from age; 'dry'. Also of a nurse.

1670 *Contract* in *Proc. Soc. Ant. Scot.* (1896) XXX. 20 Too tydie kay & four yeell kay. **1785** BURNS *Addr. to Deil* x, An' dawtet, twal-pint Hawkie's gane As yell's the Bill. **1793** *Statist. Acc. Scot.* IX. 317 The yell cattle vary in numbers according to the seasons of the year. **1808** JAMIESON, *Yeld, Yeald, Yell, Eild*.. A cow, although with calf, is said to *gang yeld*, when her milk dries up. A yeld nurse signifies a dry nurse. **1818** SCOTT *Hrt. Midl.* xxxix, A wild farm in Northumberland, well stocked with milk-cows, yeald beasts, and sheep. **1864** A. LEIGHTON *Myst. Leg. Edin.* (1886) 8 'And wha will pay for the wet nurse?' said I, 'for ye ken I am as dry as a yeld crummie.'

3. Applied to inanimate objects that are sterile, unproductive, etc. (see quots.).

1721 KELLY *Scot. Prov.* 42 Any thing is better than the Yell Kail. An Apology for having little, or bad, Fleshmeat. *Ibid. foot-n.*, Yell is properly what gives no Milk, here it signifies boil'd without Meat, or having no Butter. **1824** MACTAGGART *Gallovid. Encycl.* s.v. *Yell*, A rock is said to be yell when it will not quarry but with gunpowder; a field is said to be yell when nothing will grow on it. **1825** JAMIESON, *Yeld*.. 8. Bleak, cold; applied to the weather, as denoting that it has no tendency to fruitfulness, or that it threatens sterility.

B. *sb.* A barren cow or ewe; a hind that is not pregnant.

1856 MORTON *Cycl. Agric.* II. 727. **1886** *W. Somerset Word-bk.*, *Yeld*.. a female deer not pregnant.

Hence **yeld (yell)** *v. trans.*, to make 'yell', keep from breeding.

1831 *Sutherland Farm Rep.* 81 in *Libr. Usef. Knowl., Husb.* III, That.. those least fit for breeding be yelled off for sale. *Ibid.*, The contrivance of yelling or breeching a certain number of ewes in each herding.

yeld, obs. form of ELD *sb.*[2], age.

a **1529** SKELTON *Death Edw. IV*, 86 Of no great yeld.

yeld(e, (ȝeld(e), var. *ilde*, obs. form of AISLE.

1527 *Dunmow Churchw. MS.* lf. 6 b, For mendynge of lede over the new chapell and over the ȝelde on the same syde. **1535** in Weaver *Wells Wills* (1890) 82 In makyn and byldyn of the new yeld in the ch[urch] of B[romfelde]. xl[s].

yeld(e, obs. form of GUILD, YIELD.

yelden, variant of YOLDEN.

yelderin, -drin(g, var. YOLDRING.

yele, var. AIL *sb.*[2], awn.

1510 STANBRIDGE *Vocabula* C iv, *Arista*, the yele.

yele, obs. form of AISLE.

1498 *Churchw. Acc., Pilton* (Som. Rec. Soc.) 66 For takyng downe off the nort wyndow yn our lady yele. *c* **1600** *Inscr. Northam Church, Devon* in *N. & Q.* 8th Ser. I. 463/1 This Yele was made Anno 1593.

yele (ȝele): see EEL *sb.*, HEAL *sb.*

y-eled [Y- 4, ELE *v.*[1]], anointed.

1297 R. GLOUC. (Rolls) 5331 He was king of engelond .. þat verst þus yeled was of þe pope of rome. **1387** TREVISA *Higden* (Rolls) VI. 225 He was i-led [*MS. γ* yeeled] and anoynt and i-housled.

yeled, obs. form of EYELID.

14.. in Wr.-Wülcker 600/2 *Palpebra*, an yeled.

yeleinge, var. YILING.

yelek ('jɛlɛk). Also JELICK. [Turk. *yelek*.] A long outer garment worn by Turkish women.

1836 LANE *Mod. Egypt.* I. i. 49 Over the shirt and shintiyan is worn a long vest (called *yelek*), .. the yelek is cut in such a manner as to leave half of the bosom uncovered, except by the shirt; but many ladies have it made more ample at that part; and, according to the most approved fashion, it should be of a sufficient length to reach to the ground. **1865** W. HEPWORTH *Holy Land* II. 49 The yelek, a vest, is worn by these ladies open at the front.

yeles, obs. form of EYELESS.

1593 Q. ELIZ. *Boeth.* IV. met. vii. 100 Poleφemus .. with his yeles hed.

yelf, obs. variant of YELVE.

yelfat, obs. f. *ale-fat, -vat* (ALE II).

yeliche, obs. form of YLIKE.

yelk: see YOLK.

yell (jɛl), *sb.* Forms: 4–6 ȝell, 5 ȝelle, yelle, 6–7 yel, 6– yell. [Earlier *iȝel* (LAY. 17799); f. YELL *v.*]

a. An act of yelling; a sharp loud outcry, such as is described s.v. YELL *v.* 1.

c **1375** *Sc. Leg. Saints* vi. (*Thomas*) 659 þan al þe prestis gef a ȝell, As þai had bene fendis of hell. *c* **1400** *Anturs Arth.* vii, Ȝauland ful ȝamerly, with mony loude ȝelles. **1509** BARCLAY *Shyp of Folys* (1570) 122 One woman chiding maketh greater yell Than should an hundred pyes in one cage. **1572** *Satir. Poems Reform.* xxxii. 79 Than cryit my bairnis with mony ȝout and ȝell. **1604** SHAKS. *Oth.* I. i. 75 *Rodo*... Ile call aloud. *Iago*. Doe, with like timerous accent, and dire yell, As when (by Night and Negligence) the Fire Is spied in populus Citties. **1758** JOHNSON *Idler* No. 25 ¶7 The yell of inarticulate distress. **1784** COWPER *Task* VI. 420 The patient ox, with stripes and yells Driv'n to the slaughter. **1816** BYRON *Siege of Corinth* xxviii, Fearfully the yell arose Of his followers, and his foes; These in joy, in fury those. **1827** SCOTT *Chron. Canongate* v, Janet gave three skips on the floor, and uttered as many short shrill yells of joy. **1841** J. F. COOPER *Deerslayer* xix, Once or twice the Indian yell was given. **1850** PRESCOTT *Peru* II. 212 Closely followed by the victorious enemy, who celebrated their success with songs or rather yells of triumph. **1855** TENNYSON *Maud* I. I. x, The vitriol madness flushes up in the ruffian's head, Till the filthy by-lane rings to the yell of the trampled wife.

b. Of animals.

1579 SPENSER *Sheph. Cal.* Aug. 178 As my cryes .. You heare all night, .. so let your yrksome yells augment. **1592** SHAKS. *Ven. & Ad.* 688 Sometime he [*sc.* a hare] runnes .. where earth-deluing Conies keepe, To stop the loud pursuers [*sc.* hounds] in their yell. **1697** DRYDEN *Æneis* III. 550 The loud yell of watry Wolves to hear. **1860** TYNDALL *Glac.* I. iii. 26 Marmots .. with yells of terror scattered themselves among the rocks. **1862** BURTON *Bk. Hunter* (1863) 45 The terrific yells of that cursed biped [*sc.* a peacock].

c. An outcry in writing, e.g. in a newspaper.

1853 BP. WILBERFORCE in R. G. Wilberforce *Life* (1881) II. v. 210 Once let such a course be begun, and though the yell of 'The Record' will be with you, it will be impossible to halt there. **1887** *Spectator* 4 June 758/1 This, from the 'United Irishman', is of course a mere yell, not to be taken seriously.

d. A cry consisting of a set of words or syllables shouted on certain occasions, as by American college students.

18.. *St. Nicholas* XVII. 837 (Cent. Dict.) The young men .. are giving the mountain calls or yells—cries adopted according to the well-known college custom. **1913** *Spectator* 8 Mar. 386/1 The undergraduates of Princeton and Virginia University .. acclaimed their academic head .. with their characteristic college yells.

e. *slang.* Something or someone extremely amusing; a joke, a 'scream'.

1926 E. HEMINGWAY *Sun also Rises* xvi. 179 'Bill's a yell of laughter,' Mike said. **1938** N. MARSH *Artists in Crime* xv. 238 'Well, of course!' exclaimed Miss O'Dawne, greatly diverted. 'Aren't you a yell!' **1949** E. COXHEAD *Wind in West* ii. 32 All these doctors and their ecologists—what a yell. **1970** [see LOOK *v.* 10 a].

yell (jɛl), *v.* Forms: 1 ᵹellan, ᵹiellan, ᵹillan, ᵹyllan, 3 ȝeolle, 3–5 ȝelle, 4 ȝel, ȝele, yhelle, ȝolle, ȝulle, 4–6 yel, yelle, 5 ȝhelle, 6 *Sc.* ȝell, 5– yell. *Pa. t. str.* 1 ᵹeal, *pl.* gullon, 3 yal, *pl.* gullen, ȝulle(n, ȝollen, 3–5 ȝal; *wk.* 4–5 ȝelled, 5 ȝellede, yellid, -yd, 6 yeald, *Sc.* ȝeld, 6– yelled. [OE. (Anglian) *ᵹellan*, (WS.) *ᵹiellan, ᵹyllan, ᵹillan* str. vb., pa. t. *ᵹeal*, pl. *ᵹullon* = MLG. *gellen, gillen* wk., MDu. *gellen* str. (Du. *gillen*), OHG. *gellan* str. (MHG., G. wk. *gellen*), ON. *gjalla*, pa. t. *gall* (Sw. *gälla*, Norw. *giella*); f. *gell-*, extended form of *gel-*: *gal-*, whence OE. *galan* to sing, GALE *v.*[1], *-gale* in *nihtegale* NIGHT(IN)GALE, ON. *-gal* in *hanagal* cockcrow, OS., (M)Du., OHG. *galm* outcry.]

1. *intr.* To utter a loud strident cry, esp. from some strong and sudden emotion, as rage, horror, or agony.

a **1225** *Leg. Kath.* 2040 þer me mahte iheren þe heaðene hundes ȝellen & ȝeien & ȝuren. *c* **1290** *S. Eng. Leg.* 3/87 þo cam þe deouel ȝeollinde forth. *c* **1290** *St. Brandan* 583 *ibid.* 235 Huy weopen ant ȝollen [*Harl. MS.* ȝulle] faste. **1297** R. GLOUC. (Rolls) 4239 So grisliche ȝal [*v.rr.* ȝolled, ȝelled] þat ssrewe þo. *c* **1305** *St. Katherine* 241 in *E.E.P.* (1862) 96 þo gan þemperour for wraþþe loude ȝulle and rore. *c* **1386** CHAUCER *Nun's Pr. T.* 569 They yelleden as fendes doon in helle. *c* **1450** *Brut* II. 422 Thei cryed alle 'nowelle' as high as thei myght yelle. **1553** T. WILSON *Rhet.* (1580) 176 Women are saied to chatter, churles to grunt, boies to whine, & yongmen to yel. **1575** LANEHAM *Let.* G iv b, Knights stampt, Squiers startld az steeds in a stoour Yeemen & Pagez yeald oout in the hall. **1671** MILTON *P.R.* IV. 423 Infernal Ghosts, and Hellish Furies, round Environ'd thee, some howl'd, some yell'd, some shriek'd. **1821** SCOTT *Kenilw.* v, She yelled out on seeing him as if an adder had stung her. **1835** W. IRVING *Tour Prairies* xii. 93 They whooped and yelled in the Indian style. **1877** TENNYSON *Harold* v. i. 229 When all was lost, he yell'd, And bit his shield, and dash'd it on the ground.

fig. **1602** MARSTON *Antonio's Rev.* v. v. Wks. 1856 I. 141 Murder for murder, blood for blood, doth yell!

b. Of certain birds and beasts: To emit a loud cry, either as their natural utterance or when hurt or from rage.

a **1000** *Finnsburg* 6 Fuᵹelas singað, ᵹylleð græᵹhama. *a* **1000** *Riddles* xxv. 3 Ic eom wunderlicu wiht, .. hwilum græde swa gos, hwilum ᵹielle swa hafoc. *a* **1250** *Owl & Night* 112 þe faucun was wroþ wit his bridde & lude ȝal & sterne chidde. **13..** *Gaw. & Gr. Knt.* 1453 He hurtez of þe houndez, & þay Ful ȝomerly ȝaule & ȝelle. *c* **1425** WYNTOUN *Cron.* IV. xxiv. 2116 Alkyn best .. ȝhellande ran as þai war wode Til woddis and til wildirnes. *a* **1529** SKELTON *E. Rummyng* 500 She yelled lyke a calfe. **1560** *Bible* (Genev.) Jer. ii. 15 The lyons roared vpon him & yelled. **1588** SHAKS. *L.L.L.* IV. ii. 60 The Dogges did yell. **1590** SPENSER *F.Q.* I. xi. 37 The cruell wound enraged him so sore, That loud he [*sc.* the dragon] yelled for exceeding paine. **1810** SCOTT *Lady of L.* I. iii, Yell'd on the view the opening pack; .. A hundred dogs bay'd deep and strong. **1863** W. C. BALDWIN *Afr. Hunting* ix. 408 Innumerable hyenas, .. fighting, running, and yelling like demons.

†**c.** Applied to loud singing or chanting.

1387 TREVISA *Higden* (Rolls) IV. 395 Nero .. gan to ȝelle [*v.r.* ȝolle] and songe þe gestes of Troye. **1395** PURVEY *Remonstr.* (1851) 18 What wisdom is this to hiren hem so dere to yellen in chirchis and abbeies.

†**d.** *trans.* To protrude (the tongue) in uttering a yell. *Obs.*

1480 *Robt. Devyll* 229 in Hazl. *E.P.P.* 1864 I. 228 Behynde them woulde he steale, And geve them a sowce .. To cause some to yell out theyr tongues longe.

e. To urge *on* by yelling.

1868 G. MEREDITH *Poems, Orchard & Heath* ix, They raced; their brothers yelled them on.

†**2.** *intr.* Of an inanimate thing: To make a strident or crashing noise. *Obs.*

a **1000** *Riddles* xxxiii. 4 Ic seah searo hweorfan, grindan wið greote, ᵹiellende faran. *a* **1000** *Andreas* 127 Guðsearo gullon, garas hrysedon. *c* **1205** LAY. 9797 Helmes þer gullen [*c* **1275** ȝollen]. *c* **1330** *Florice & Bl.* (1857) 302 The water wille ȝelle als hit ware wode And bicome on hire so red so blod. **1470–85** MALORY *Arthur* XIV. x. 654 Soo she wente with the wynde rorynge and yellynge that it semed alle the water brent after her. **1560** B. GOOGE tr. *Palingenius' Zodiac* v. (1561) M iij b, Black storms he sends with thondres rore he makes the skies to yel. **1606** *Wily Beguiled* F 2, Let .. sounding musicke yell Through hils, through dales.

3. *trans.* To utter with a yell. Also *transf.*

[*a* **1000** *Seafarer* 24 Ful oft þæt earn biᵹeal uriᵹfeþra.] **13..** *Gosp. Nicodemus* (A.) 1796 Howe þai lay in droupand drede And non so ȝhepe a worde to ȝelle. **1370–80** *Visions of St. Paul* 275 in *O.E. Misc.* 230 þei ȝelleden wiþ lodly cry, 'Poul, Michael, on vs ha merci.' *a* **1450** *Mirk's Festial* 5 þay styntyn neuer to cry and ȝelle: 'Woo ys hym þat þedyr schall goo.' **1577** WHETSTONE *Gascoigne* xxvi, The Nightingale, .. When she might mourn, her sweetest layes doth yel. **1605** SHAKS. *Macb.* IV. iii. 7 It [*sc.* heaven] resounds As if it felt with Scotland, and yell'd out Like Syllable of Dolour. **1663** BUTLER *Hud.* I. iii. 540 He tumbled down, and as he fell, Did Murther, murther, murther yell. **1700** T. BROWN tr. *Fresny's Amusem.* 21 Another Son of a Whore yells louder than Homer's Stentor, Two a Groat. **1810** SCOTT *Lady of L.* III. i, Clamorous war-pipes yell'd the gathering sound. **1812** BYRON *Ch. Har.* II. lxxi, Yelling their uncouth dirge, long daunced the kirtled clan. **1852** MISS YONGE *Cameos* I. xxviii. 230 Otho .. fled .. , hunted by the students, all yelling abuse.

Hence **yelled** (jɛld) *ppl. a.*; **'yeller**, one who yells.

1823 *New Monthly Mag.* VIII. 499 Some dozen yappers and yellers of all shapes and breeds. **1895** S. CRANE *Red Badge* xxiii, At the yelled words of command the soldiers sprang forward. **1900** *Lancet* 3 Mar. 637/2 To prosecute a newspaper yeller for obtaining money under false pretences.

yell, obs. form of AISLE.

1503–4 *Rec. St. Mary at Hill* (1904) 252 þe gret vynddow vythe þe Trenyte in the sovthe yell. **1540** *Lincoln Dioc. Doc.* (1914) 230 Within ye churche of saynte peter .. in ye myddell yell.

yell, local variant of HEALD.

1883 SIMMONDS *Dict. Trade* Suppl., *Yells*, in weaving, guides for the warp-threads.

yell, obs. or dial. f. ALE, EVIL, HALE *a.*, YELD.

yelld, var. *ilde*, obs. form of ISLE.

1612 *MS. Acc. St. John's Hosp., Canterb.*, St. Larances in the yelld of Teneth.

yelling ('jɛlɪŋ), *vbl. sb.* [f. YELL *v.* + -ING[1].] The action of the verb YELL; *esp.* the uttering of a sharp loud cry of rage, agony, etc.

a **1250** *Owl & Night.* 1643 An mid ȝulinge [*Jesus MS.* yollinge] & mid igrede. *c* **1290** *St. Brandan* 493 in *S. Eng. Leg.* 233 Ȝeot heo i-heorden heore ȝeollinge [*Harl. MS.* ȝullinge]. **13..** *E.E. Allit. P.* B. 971 Such a ȝomerly ȝarm of ȝellyng þer rysed. **1395** PURVEY *Remonstr.* (1851) 112 Hou abhominable is the feynid preiere othir hidous yellinge of siche prelatis. *a* **1450** *Mirk's Festial* 240 þes fendes madyn a ȝellyng and a cryyng, þat any myght be agast forto here hit. **1556** LAUDER *Tractate of Kyngis* 92 With gretyng, raryng, and with ȝellyng. **1577** tr. *Bullinger's Decades* v. v. 936/1 Often times the Singers striue among themselues for the excellencie of voyces, whereby it commeth to passe that the whole Churche ringeth with an hoarse kinde of yellinge. **1612** DRAYTON *Poly-olb.* xiii. 124 When after goes the cry with yellings lowd and deepe That all the forrest rings. **1653** H. COGAN tr. *Pinto's Trav.* lxix. (1663) 281 The dreadful yelling of six thousand Elephants. **1666** SPURSTOWE *Spir. Chym.* 151 Cries .. that are like the yellings of the damned. **1740** RICHARDSON *Pamela* I. xxvi. 78 The cursed Yellings of you both made me not myself. **1816** SCOTT *Antiq.* xxvii, The yelling and screaming of the children. **1818** —— *Br. Lamm.* ix, The impatient yelling of the hounds. **1871** R. ELLIS tr. *Catullus* xlii. 18 Swell your voices in higher harsher yellings.

'yelling, *ppl. a.* [f. YELL *v.* + -ING[2].] That yells; that utters a loud strident cry or noise.

c **1000** *Widsið* 128 (Gr.) Ful oft of þam heape hwinende fleaᵹ ᵹiellende ᵹar on grome þeode. *c* **1000** *Sax. Leechd.* III. 52 Hy ᵹyllende garas sændan. **1590** SPENSER *F.Q.* I. ii. 31 A piteous yelling voyce. **1667** MILTON *P.L.* II. 795 These yelling Monsters that with ceasless cry Surround me. **1727–46** THOMSON *Summer* 1681 The lonely tower .. whose mournful chambers hold .. the yelling ghost. **1823** SCOTT *Quentin D.* vi, The disordered and yelling group. **1879** *Daily News* 1 Mar. leading art., To force their horses through the ring of yelling savages. **1899** SOMERVILLE & ROSS *Irish R.M.* 179 The tall old house quivered, and the yelling wind drove against it.

b. Characterized by or filled with yells.

a **1000** *Cædmon's Exod.* 489 He maneᵹum ᵹ esceod ᵹyllende gryre. **1549** COVERDALE, etc. *Erasm. Par. Eph.* v. 12 Not with vncomly yellyng noyses, as madde droncken men are vsed to dooe. **1595** *Locrine* I. Prol. 4 A Mightie Lion, ruler of the woods,.. With yelling clamors shaking all the earth. 1697 DRYDEN *Æneis* III. 887 His brother Cyclops hear the yelling Roar. 1825 SCOTT *Talism.* v, A loud yelling laugh. 1906 'MARJORIE BOWEN' *Viper of Milan* xxxiv, The garden was one wild, yelling confusion.

yelling, variant of YILING *Obs.*

yellm, obs. form of YELM *v.*

yelloch ('jɛləx), *sb. Sc.* Forms: 6 **ȝelloch, ȝalloch,** 7 **yellough,** 9 **yill-, yelloch.** [app. f. YELL with symbolic ending: cf. *belloch, skelloch.*] A yell.

1513 DOUGLAS *Æneis* XII. xiv. 100 With a ȝelloch [*v.r.* ȝalloch] and cairfull womentyng. 1697 CLELAND *Poems* 17 His brains with shouts and yelloughs tumbled. 1824 SCOTT *Redgauntlet* Let. xi, Sir Robert gied a yelloch that garr'd the castle rock. 1880 *Antrim & Down Gloss.*

yelloch ('jɛləx), *v. Sc.* Also 8 **yellowch,** 9 **yello.** [f. prec.] *intr.* To yell; *trans.* to utter with a yell. Hence '**yelloching** *vbl. sb.*

1773 FERGUSSON *Hallowfair* viii, Than there's sic yellowchin and din, Wi' wives and wee-anes gablin. 1821 SCOTT *Pirate* xxx, An auld useless carline, called Tronda Drons-daughter,.. yelloched and skirled.

yellow ('jɛləʊ), *a.* and *sb.* Forms: *α.* 1 **ᵹelu, -o, ᵹeolu, ᵹeolo, ᵹiolu, ᵹeolw-, -uw-, -ew-,** 2 **ȝeoluw, ȝeolew, ȝeluw,** 3 **ȝeolu(h, ȝeleu,** 4 **ȝelew(e, ȝelugh(e, ȝelogh, ȝelowȝ, ȝelȝ, ȝelw, (ȝealwe),** 4–5 **ȝelwe, yelwe, ȝelou, ȝelow(e,** 5 **yelu, (ȝelwh(e, ȝelhew(e),** 5–6 **ȝellow, yelow(e, (**6 **ȝello, yelloo, yealow(e),** 6–7 **yellowe, (yeallow),** 6– **yellow** (9 *dial.* and *vulgar* **yeller).** *β.* 2 **ȝolewe,** 4 **ȝolȝe, yolwe, ȝolow,** 5 **yolgh, yolow,** 5–6 **yolowe,** 6 **yollow(e, yolo,** 9 *dial.* **yollo(w.** *γ.* (chiefly *Sc.* and *north. dial.*) 4–5 **ȝalou,** 4–6 **ȝalow, yalow,** 5 **ȝalowe, yalowe, ȝalwe, (ȝalo, yhalou),** 5–7 **ȝallow,** 6 **ȝallou, yallowe, (ȝallo, yalley),** 7–9 *dial.* and *vulgar* **yallow,** (9 esp. *U.S.*, **yaller, yallah).** *δ.* 4 **yaulew,** 6 **yewlow, ewlow, yeolow, youlowe, jowllo.** [OE. *ᵹeolu, -o* = OS. *gelo*, (M)LG. *gel*, MDu. *gel(e)u, geluw, geel* (Du. *geel*, Flem. *geluw, geelw, gilw*), OHG. *gelo*, (MHG. *gel, gelw-*, G. *gelb*):—OTeut. **gelwa-*:—Indo-eur. **ghelwo-* (cf. L. *helvus* greyish yellow, Lith. *želvas* greenish).

For other derivatives of the Indo-eur. *ghol-*: *ghel-*: *ghl-*, see GALL *sb.*[1], GOLD[1], and cf. also L. *holus* vegetable, OIr. *gel* white, OSl. *zelije* cabbage, *zelenŭ* green, Skr. *hári-*, Zend *zaranya-* Pers. *zer* gold, ON. *gulr* yellow.]

A. *adj.*

1. a. Of the colour of gold, butter, the yolk of an egg, various flowers, and other objects; constituting one (the most luminous) of the primary colours, occurring in the spectrum between green and orange.

α. *Beowulf* 2610 Hond rond ᵹefeng, ᵹeolwe linde. *c*700 *Epinal Gloss.* 242 *Crocus*, ᵹelu. *c*725 *Corpus Gloss.* (Hessels) C 876 *Crucus*, ᵹelo. *Ibid.* F 219 *Flabum*, ᵹeolu. *a*900 *Leiden Riddle* 10 Uyrmas mec ni auefun uyrdi cræftum, ða ði ᵹoelu godueb ᵹeatum fraetuath. *c*1175 *Lamb. Hom.* 51 Blake tadden.. ȝeluwe froggen and crabben. *Ibid.* 53 Alswa doð monie of þas wimmen heo.. claþeð heom mid ȝeoluwe claþe. *c*1290 *St. Eustace* 182 in *S. Eng. Leg.* 398 With red heued, ȝeolu and crips. 1303 R. BRUNNE *Handl. Synne* 3978 Þe ye þat ys ful of Iawnes, Alle þenkeþ hym ȝelogh yn hys auys. *c*1380 *Sir Ferumb.* 5881 Wyþ eȝene graye, and browes bent, And ȝealwe traces. *c*1386 CHAUCER *Prol.* 675 This Pardoner hadde heer as yelow as wex [*v.rr.* ȝelw, ȝelowe, ȝalowe]. 1431 *Rec. St. Mary at Hill* (1904) 27 Also j ȝelew cope of selk. *c*1440 *Promp. Parv.* 537/1 Ȝelhwe of colure (*K.*, *H.* ȝelwe, *S.* ȝelhewe, *P.* ȝelowe colowre). 1523–34 FITZHERB. *Husb.* §14 Red otes are the beste otes, and whan they be thresshed, they be yelowe in the busshell. 1601 SHAKS. *Twel. N.* II. v. 166 Remember who commended thy yellow stockings, and wish'd to see thee euer crosse garter'd. 1610 —— *Temp.* I. ii. 376 Come vnto these yellow sands. 1630 MILTON *On May Morning* 4 The yellow Cowslip, and the pale Primrose. 1784 COWPER *Task* VI. 302 King-cups in the yellow mead. 1855 HT. MARTINEAU *Autobiog.* (1877) I. 383 Yellow as a guinea. 1860 FITZ-ROY in *Merc. Marine Mag.* VII. 342 A bright yellow sky at sunset presages wind.

β. *c*1175 *Lamb. Hom.* 53 Þe ȝolewe frogge. 1382 WYCLIF *Gen.* xxx. 32 Seuer alle thi speckid sheep, and with speckyd flese, and what euere ȝolow. *a*1400 *Pistill of Susan* 192 Hir hed was ȝolow as wyre Of gold fyned wiþ fyre. *c*1440 *Pallad. on Husb.* I. 579 Ek best are hennis blake, & werst ar white And good ar yolgh. 1540 *Test. Ebor.* (Surtees) VI. 107 The sparver of buckeram yolowe and rede. 1571 in Feuillerat *Revels Q. Eliz.* (1908) 146 One maske was yolowe. 1828 *Craven Gloss.* 296 As yollo as a daffodowndilly. 1888 *Sheffield Gloss.*, *Yollow*, yellow.

γ. *c*1375 *Sc. Leg. Saints* xxix. (*Placidas*) 23 Quhen for elde ..his tetht waxis ȝalou with-al. 1397 *Priory of Finchale* (Surtees) 117, j coopertorium cum rosys ȝalow. *c*1400 MAUNDEV. (1839) vii. 48 His Nekke is ȝalowe. 1483 *Cath. Angl.* 425/1 Ȝalowe, *aureus.* 1500 *Ortus Vocab.*, *Glaucus*, ȝalo or yrne graye. 1535 COVERDALE *Jer.* x. 9 Clothed with yalow sylck and scarlet. 1546 *Test. Ebor.* (Surtees) VI. 239 Too yalley coverlettes. 16.. SIR W. MURE *Sonn. to Margareit* ix. 10 Yallow curls of gold. 1863 *Macm. Mag.* Dec. 101 'Do you remember the lilies at Stanlake?' .. 'Acres on 'em,.. Yallah ones as well.'

δ. 13.. *Seuyn Sag.* (W.) 477 Here yaulew here Out of the tresses sche hit tere. 1513 *Inv.* in *Archaeologia* LXVI. 343 A pece of youlowe lawne. 1541 *Lanc. Wills* (Chetham Soc.) I. 80, iij old ewlow quishens. 1550 *Ibid.* II. 103 A yewlow coverlet. 1591 SPENSER *Ruins of Time* 10 Rending her yeolow locks.

b. Of the complexion in age or disease; also as the colour of faded leaves, ripe corn, old discoloured paper, etc.; hence *allusively*.

The phrase in quot. 1605 has been freq. echoed.

*c*1000 *Sax. Leechd.* II. 106 Wiþ þære ᵹeolwan adle hune bisceop wyrt.. menge þa togædere. *Ibid.* 348 Ȝif him biþ ælfsoᵹoþa him beoþ þa eaᵹan ᵹeolwe þær hi reade beon sceoldon. ?*a*1366 CHAUCER *Rom. Rose* 310 Sorowe, thought, and greet distresse,.. Made hir ful yelwe [*MS.* yolare]. 13.. *Gaw. & Gr. Knt.* 951 Bot vn-lyke on to loke þo ladyes were, For if þe ȝonge was ȝep, ȝolȝe was þat oþer. 1422 YONGE tr. *Secr. Secr.* 222 Yolow coloure in the face meddelite with palnesse. 1590 GREENE *Never too late* Wks. (Grosart) VIII. 225 The riping corne growes yeolow in the stalke. 1597 SHAKS. *2 Hen. IV*, I. ii. 204 Haue you not a moist eye? a dry hand? a yellow cheeke? a white beard? *c*1600 —— *Sonn.* civ. 5 Three Winters colde, Haue from the forrests shooke three summers pride, Three beautious springs to yellow Autumne turn'd. 1605 —— *Macb.* V. iii. 23 My way of life Is falne into the Seare, the yellow Leafe. 1667 MILTON *P.L.* XI. 435 The green Eare, and the yellow Sheaf. 1730–46 THOMSON *Autumn* 1322 When Autumn's yellow lustre gilds the world. 1817 BYRON *Beppo* xcii, No, I never Saw a man grown so yellow! How's your liver? 1824 —— *''Tis time this heart'* ii, My days are in the yellow leaf. 1836 DICKENS *Sk. Boz, Sentiment*, 'The Misses Crumpton' were ..very upright, and very yellow. 1847 EMERSON *Repr. Men, Shakespeare* Wks. (Bohn) I. 358 They [*sc.* the Shakespeare Society] have left.. no file of old yellow accounts to decompose.. to discover whether the boy Shakespeare poached. 1849 JAMES *Woodman* vii, The yellow autumn time of the year.

†**c.** With allusion to the use of yellow starch (coloured with saffron). *Obs.*

1614 TOMKIS *Albumazar* II. i. (1615) D j, Trincalo, what price beare's wheate, and Saffron, that your band's so stiffe and yellow? 1616 B. JONSON *Devil is an Ass* I. i, Car-men Are got into the yellow starch. 1619 RICH *Irish Hubbub* 4 Yellow bands are become so common, to euery young giddy-headed Gallant, and light-heel'd Mistresse, that me thinks a man should not hardly be hanged without a yellow band, a fashion so much in vse with the vaine fantasticke fooles of this age. *a*1626 MIDDLETON *Widow* V. i, That Suit.. will disgrace my Masters fashion for ever, and make it as hatefull as yellow bands. *c*1645 [see STARCH *sb.* 1].

d. Having a naturally yellowish skin or complexion: applied chiefly (often somewhat depreciatorily) to persons of Asiatic, esp. Oriental, origin, but also in the *U.S.* to persons of mixed white and Black origin and (freq. as *yaller*) to light-skinned Blacks.

In modern use also *transf.* in ***yellow peril*** and similar phrases, denoting a supposed danger that the Asiatic peoples will overwhelm the white, or overrun the world.

1787 *Asiatick Researches* (1790) II. 2 That the Turks have any just reason for holding the coast of Yemen to be a part of India, and called its inhabitants Yellow Indians. 1834 [see MONGOLIAN *a.* 2]. 1834 *Sun* (N.Y.) 20 Mar. 2/2 A huge looking 'yaller gall' was hammering away at the eyes of a small white man.., because he called her a *snow* ball. 186. *Amer. Song*, *'Cheer up Sam'* i, I lov'd a dark-eyed yellow girl, And thought that she lov'd me. 1888 L. A. SMITH *Music of Waters* 37 Oh, sigh her up, my yaller gals. 1892 E. REEVES *Homeward Bound* 5 The 'yellow agony', as the Chinese, the best market gardeners in the world, are called. 1900 *Daily News* 21 July 3/5 The 'yellow peril' in its most serious form. 1910 *Encycl. Brit.* IX. 851/1 Mongolic or Yellow Man prevails over the vast area lying east of a line drawn from Lapland to Siam. 1913 *Punch* 19 Feb. 138/3 Believers in the Yellow Peril who wish everyone else to realise the importance of that menace are proposing to bring it home by means of All Yellow Suppers. 1927 [see *monkey-man* s.v. MONKEY *sb.* 18 a]. 1937 C. HIMES *Black on Black* (1973) 141 The nervous profile of the driver bent low over the wheel. A yellow nigger. 1942 Z. N. HURSTON in A. Dundes *Mother Wit* (1973) 28/2, I done slept with yaller women. 1956 J. BARTH *Floating Opera* xxviii. 268 Ah fails to unnerstan' How a wuthless, shif'less dahkie such as you, sah, Kin conglomerate de money fo' a Caddylac sedan, Jest to keep yo' yaller gal fren' sweet and true, sah. 1966 *Listener* 17 Mar. 401/1 The setting is.. England now, with a cold war and a yellow peril. 1977 C. MCCULLOUGH *Thorn Birds* xv. 348 But Japan was Asia, part of the Yellow Peril poised like a descending pendulum above Australia's rich, empty, underpopulated pit.

e. Applied to naval captains retired as rear admirals in H.M. Fleet without being attached to a particular squadron (red, white, or blue). (Cf. YELLOW *v.*[1] 2 c.)

1788 *Parl. Hist.* XXVII. 22 An establishment planned in 1747, for the maintenance and support of such officers as were passed by in a promotion of captains to flags, and this was the first (as it was commonly called) of Yellow admls. 1854 DE QUINCEY *War* Wks. 1862 IV. 264 That's a sort of plagiarism from Themistocles... I have as good a right to the words.. as that most classical of yellow admirals. 1867 SMYTH *Sailor's Word-bk.*, *Yellow-admiral*, a retired post-captain, who, not having served his time in that rank, is not entitled to his promotion to the active flag. 1898 *Westm. Gaz.* 11 July 1/2 For the remainder of those in the senior rank there is.. a prospect of their attaining the rank of flag officer with the 'yellow' attachment.

f. *transf.* Dressed in yellow.

1848 THACKERAY *Van. Fair* lxvi, The yellow postillion was cracking his whip gently.

2. *fig.* †**a.** Affected with jealousy, jealous. (Cf. JAUNDICED 3.) Also in allusive phrases, as ***to wear yellow hose*** = to be jealous. *Obs.*

1602 MIDDLETON *Blurt, Master Constable* V. ii, Ha, ha, ha; by my ventoy (yellow Lady) you take your marke improper. 1607 DEKKER & WEBSTER *Northw. Hoe* I. Wks. 1873 III. 14 Iealous men are eyther Knaues or Coxcombes, bee you neither: you weare yellow hose without cause. 1623 MASSINGER *Dk. Milan* IV. ii, If I were The Duke.. I should weare yellow breeches. 1632 MASSINGER & FIELD *Fatal Dowry* III. i, If my Lord Bee now growne yellow. 1665 BRATHWAIT *Comm. Two Tales* (1900) 47 Your yellow humour interprets this to be too much familiarity. *c*1680 *Roxb. Ball.* (1874) II. 61 Why, therefore, Shouldst thou deplore, Or weare stockings that are yellow? *c*1680 *Man's Felicity* xiii, My Wife will wear no yellow hose. 1812 J. H. VAUX *Flash Dict.*, *Yellow*, jealous; a jealous husband is called a *yellow gloak*. 1858 AIDÉ *Rita* xvi, Well, the filly's cut you out, Rita: won in a canter, you see! You've got to wear the yellow shoes, and all your own fault.

b. Craven, cowardly. *colloq.* (orig. *U.S.*).

1856 in P. T. Barnum *Struggles & Triumphs* (1869) 400 We never thought your heart was yellow. 1918 J. M. GRIDER *War Birds* (1927) 264 One of our noblest he-men, a regular fire-eater to hear him tell it, has turned yellow at the front. 1932 E. WALLACE *When Gangs came to London* xv. 121 The yellow jury.. acquitted 'em on a murder charge. 1950 J. AGEE in *Botteghe Oscure* VI. 392 Then something happened that made me know I was scared of them and I admitted to myself: I'm yellow. 1974 *Guardian* 30 Jan. 24/3 It frightens me when moderate voices are taken to be from weak and yellow men. 1977 'O. JACKS' *Autumn Heroes* xiv. 203 You're yellow scum. You'll fight when the odds are with you.

c. Of or pertaining to an organization, a policy, or to persons opposed to militant action by a trade union or trade unions. See also *yellow union*, sense C. 1 e below.

1913 J. A. ESTEY *Revolutionary Syndicalism* ii. 47 The so-called *syndicats jaunes*, or yellow syndicats, formed in the interest of employers for the purpose of strike-breaking. 1920 *Glasgow Herald* 12 Sept. 7 The railwaymen.. will be content to follow the lead of the General Confederation of labour and stick to the Amsterdam International, which the dictators of Russia have labelled 'yellow'—that is to say 'blackleg'. *Ibid.* 24 Nov. 8/3 The Russian Soviet Republic has insolently rejected it as 'a Congress of yellow leaders who continually betray the fundamental interests of the Labour movement'. 1922 B. G. DE MONTGOMERY *Brit. & Continental Labour Policy* vi. 58 The bus-traffic and road-transport were organized by the members of the 'yellow' or anti-strike syndicates, and by the *bourgeois* class. 1939 A. PHILIP in H. A. Marquand *Organized Labour in Four Continents* 51 The Confederation of Professional Unions, a 'yellow' organization benefiting from employer support. 1972 G. L. MOSSE in *Jrnl. Contemp. Hist.* VII. 206 France was regarded as the classical land of yellow trade unionism.

3. (orig. *U.S.*) Applied to newspapers (or writers of newspaper articles) of a recklessly or unscrupulously sensational character.

A use derived from the appearance in 1895 of a number of the *New York World* in which a child in a yellow dress ('The Yellow Kid') was the central figure of the cartoon, this being an experiment in colour-printing designed to attract purchasers.

1898 *Daily News* 2 Mar. 7/2 The yellow Press is for a war with Spain, at all costs. 1898 ELIZ. L. BANKS in *19th Cent.* Aug. 328 All American journalism is not 'yellow', though all strictly 'up-to-date' yellow journalism is American! *Ibid.* 332 Its [sc. *New York Journal*] Sunday editions, with its 'yellow kids' and 'blackberry blossoms' and various other 'special features'. 1902 —— *Newspaper Girl* xviii, The very first thing I was asked to do in the line of 'yellow' work was to walk along Broadway at midnight and 'allow' myself to be arrested. 1906 *Times* (weekly ed.) 9 Nov. 714 The President of the United States sent his Secretary of State to New York to throw the whole weight of Mr. Roosevelt's.. authority and influence against the 'yellow' candidate [*sc.* Hearst].

4. Of or pertaining to a political party whose colour is yellow. Cf. sense 4 of the *sb.*

1834 F. WITTS *Diary* 12 Aug. (1978) 97 The respective parties mustered when the poll was over at their head-quarters, the Bell Hotel being the Blue house and the King's Head the yellow. 1874 TROLLOPE *Phineas Redux* I. ii. 14 He remained there for three or four days.. staying at the 'Yellow' inn.

B. *sb.*

1. a. The colour described in YELLOW *a.* 1, or a shade, pigment, fabric, or stuff of this colour.

1303 R. BRUNNE *Handl. Synne* 3446 Ȝelugh vnder ȝelugh þey hyde. *c*1386 CHAUCER *Nun's Pr. T.* 82 His colour was bitwixe yelow [*v.r.* ȝelw] and reed. 1396–7 *Durham Acc. Rolls* (Surtees) 214 [Hangings] cum avibus de yalow. *c*1400 *Destr. Troy* 5462 All hor colouris to ken were of clene yalow. *c*1450 in *Maitl. Club Misc.* III. 199 Courtenes of singill worsat palyt of red and grein and yhalou. *c*1532 in E. Law *Hampton Crt. Palace* (1885) 363 For 4000 flemyshe pavyng tyll of grene and jowllo. 1541 *Test. Ebor.* (Surtees) VI. 135 A crose of yolowe opone his brest. *a*1548 HALL *Chron., Hen. VIII*, 227 Quene Anne ware yelowe for the mournyng. 1577 B. GOOGE *Heresbach's Husb.* III. (1586) 133 b, The sicknesse of the Gall.. is also discerned by the browne yellowes vnder the vpper lippe. 1600 NASHE *Summer's Last Will* B 3 b, Wks. (Grosart) VI. 94 To weare the blacke and yellow [*rime* followe]. 1609 B. JONSON *Silent Wom.* I. iv, Wee doe beare for our Coat Yellow, or Or, checker'd Azure, and Gules. 1613 SHAKS. *Hen. VIII* Prol. 16 A long Motley Coate, garded with Yellow. 1633 BP. HALL *Occas. Medit.* (ed. 3) §54, I doe not like these reds, and blewes, and yellowes, amongst these plaine stalkes and eares. *c*1665 in *Verney Mem.* (1907) II. 275 Ribband knots for her head of sky collor, or yallow. 1715 ADDISON *Freeholder* No. 10. 60 When he appear'd in Yellow, his Great Men hid themselves in Corners. 1824 MISS MITFORD *Village* Ser. I. (1863) 58 The narrow lane bordered with elms, whose fallen leaves have made the road one yellow. 1859 GULLICK & TIMBS *Painting* 224 The ochres are the most permanent yellows. 1889 J. K. JEROME *Three Men in Boat* vii, His complexion is too dark for yellows. Yellows don't suit him.

b. With qualifying words, denoting different shade of the colour, as ***brass-, bronze-, canary-, gold-, Isabella-, lemon-, primrose-, rust-, straw-, sulphur-*** (etc.) ***yellow***, or various pigments and dyes, as ***aniline y., Chinese y., cobalt y., imperial y., Indian y., King's y., Mars y., Naples y., strontian y.***, etc., for which see the first element.

1532 *Acc. Ld. High Treas. Scot.* VI. 23 Tway elnis franche ʒallow to lyne the said cote. **1794** KIRWAN *Elem. Min.* (ed. 2) I. 89 Isabella yellow. **1805–17** R. JAMESON *Char. Min.* (ed. 3) 69 Brass-yellow, gold-yellow, and bronze-yellow. **1831–3** BARLOW in *Encycl. Metrop.* (1845) VIII. 539/1 A yellow termed rust yellow is made with acetate of iron thickened with gum for light yellows. **1899** *Daily News* 29 Dec. 5/1 Martius's yellow. This substance has many an alias, some alluring, some otherwise, golden yellow, Manchester yellow, saffron yellow, nap[h]thalene yellow.

†**c.** *allusively*, as the colour attributed to jealousy: cf. A. 2. *Obs.*

1611 SHAKS. *Wint. T.* II. iii. 107 If thou hast The ordering of the Mind too, mongst all Colours No Yellow in't.

d. Cowardice. Cf. sense 2 b of the adj. above.

1896 G. ADE *Artie* vi. 57 This is how I found that streak of yellow in him. **1914** B. M. BOWER *Flying U Ranch* 146, I was just b'ginnin' to think this bunch was gitting all streaked up with yeller.

2. a. Denoting various objects of a yellow colour, as the yolk of an egg, the stigmas of the saffron crocus (quot. 1587), a yellow carriage (quot. 1833), or any yellow substance, as sulphur (quot. 1649), gold (*U.S.*), old faded paper; also *ellipt.* for a yellow variety of any flower, fruit, root, etc.

c **700** *Epinal Gloss.* 429 *Fitilium* [Erfurt *vitellus*], æʒerʒelu. *c* **1000** *Sax. Leechd.* II. 22 Ðenim æʒes þæt ʒeoluwe & meng lythwon wið huniʒ. *Ibid.* 130 Banwyrt do on sure fletan & on huniʒ æʒes ʒeola, meng tosomne, smire mid. **1587** HARRISON *England* III. viii. 232/2 in *Holinshed*, In euerie floure [of saffron] we finde commonlie three chiues, and three yellowes. **1649** *Woodstock Scuffle* xxiv, The men were frighted, and did smell O' th' yellow. **1738** DEERING *Cat. Stirp.* 149 *Napus sylvestris*..the Country People here call them the *Yellows*. **1833** T. HOOK *Parson's Dau.* II. vii, The arrival..of Lady Frances Sheringham herself and her maid, in a 'yellow and two'. **1844** H. STEPHENS *Bk. Farm* II. 14 The yellows [*sc.* turnips] then follow, and last for about 2 months. *a* **1845** SYD. SMITH in Lady Holland *Mem.* (1855) I. 373 To make this condiment, your poet begs The pounded yellow of two hard-boil'd eggs. **1849** CUPPLES *Green Hand* xvi, As he [*sc.* the aged Negro] sat..leering out of the yellows of his eyes. **1858** *Pike's Peak Guide Bk.* 329 We commenced sending prospecting parties into the mountains, but they returned every night with 'nary yellow'. **1886** C. SCOTT *Sheep-farming* 43 Yellows or swedes. **1901** M. E. RYAN *That Girl Montana* xviii. 227 She would watch some strange miner dig and wash the soil in his search for the precious yellow.

b. A particular yellow species or variety of bird, butterfly (= SULPHUR 5 a), or moth.

1816 STEPHENS in Shaw *Gen. Zool.* IX. II. 464 [American Gold-finches] are called York Yellows. **1855** *Poultry Chron.* II. 515 Tumblers, Blues, Blacks, Silver, Yellows. **1880** A. H. SWINTON *Insect Variety* 51 Our English Clouded Yellows. **1896** W. F. KIRBY *Handbk. Order Lepidopt.* II. 214 Both our Clouded Yellows are very rare in Scandinavia.

c. A yellow ball used in the game of snooker.

1910 *Encycl. Brit.* III. 938/2 If it is pocketed, the player scores one and is at liberty to play on any of the coloured balls; though in some clubs he is compelled to play on the yellow. **1950** L. H. DAWSON *Hoyle's Games Modernized* III. 346 At the beginning of the game [of snooker] Yellow is placed on the right-hand corner of the D. **1977** *Cleethorpes News* 6 May 29/4 After potting the yellow he more or less forced Barnes to take green, brown and blue.

d. A golden Labrador.

1945 C. L. B. HUBBARD *Observer's Bk. Dogs* 97 As long as we have bred Labradors we have had yellows. **1973** *Country Life* 8 Feb. (Suppl.) 325/1 Some of the yellows were a light creamy colour.

3. A person with a naturally yellowish skin or complexion (see A. 1 d). Only *pl.* (Cf. *black*, *white*.) See also *high yellow* s.v. HIGH *a.* 21. (Somewhat *depreciatory*.)

1808 C. SCHULTZ Jr. *Trav.* (1810) II. 198 In attending to the amusements of the whites, the yellows, and the blacks, I had almost forgotten to mention the reds. **1886** *Cornh. Mag.* July 50 The 'whites' have made a complete surrender to the 'yellows'. **1901** *19th Cent.* May 837 If they [*sc.* Japanese] are to colonise at all they must colonise among the yellows and the blacks.

4. As the colour of a party badge; hence *transf.* an adherent of a party whose colour is yellow.

1755 *Gentl. Mag.* Aug. 339/2 The blues being in the old interest, and the yellows in the new. **1868** HOLME LEE *B. Godfrey* li, He would not vote yellow. **1881** [see BLUE *sb.* 8].

5. A 'yellow' journal or writer: see A. 3.

1898 *Daily News* 27 July 5/7 This deliberate attempt to stir up animosities..is worthy of 'the yellows' at their worst. **1901** *Scribner's Mag.* Apr. 408/2 The killing at the Vulcan Shops made the yellows froth head-lines.

6. *ellipt.* for *yellow alert*, sense C. 1 e below.

1940 *Mass-Observation Archive* 1 Aug. in Calder & Sheridan *Speak for Yourself* (1984) iii. 78 Soon after eleven we were remarking that it was time we got the yellow, when the telephone went. **1943** [see RED *sb.*[1] 8]. **1949** [see ALERT *sb.* 1 b]. **1978** 'G. VAUGHAN' *Belgrade Drop* xiii. 84 President Turner had been in touch with the other Nato head of state and their forces had gone on yellow.

⁂ For specialized uses of the plural in singular sense, see YELLOWS.

C. Collocations and Combinations.

1. Special collocations. **a.** In names of species or varieties of animals distinguished by their yellow colour or colouring: as ***yellow ant***, ***baboon***, ***bass***, ***bittern***, ***boa***, ***chatterer***, ***fly***, ***fly-catcher***, ***grosbeak***, ***Labrador***, ***perch***, ***redpoll***, ***tanager***, ***underwing***, ***wagtail***, ***warbler***, ***weasel***, ***woodpecker***, ***yite***, for which see the sbs.; also **yellow-bob**, a shrike-robin, *Eopsaltria australis*, found in forested areas of south-eastern Australia; **Yellow Sally**, name for a species of stone-fly used as a bait by anglers; **yellow snake**, one of several yellowish snakes, esp. a boa, *Epicrates subflavus*, found in the West Indies; **yellow warbler**, one of several North American warblers of the genus *Dendroica*; see also YELLOW-BIRD, YELLOW-FISH, YELLOW-HAMMER. **b.** In names of plants distinguished by having flowers (or sometimes fruit, wood, etc.) of a yellow colour: as ***yellow archangel***, ***balsam***, ***bedstraw***, ***bugle***, ***camomile***, ***centaury***, ***cress***, ***crocus***, ***daffodil***, ***dead-nettle***, ***fir***, ***flag***, ***gentian***, ***gilliflower***, ***gold*** (GOLD[2]), ***gowan***, ***jasmine***, ***loosestrife***, ***medick***, ***ox-eye***, ***pearmain***, ***pimpernel***, ***pine***, ***poppy***, ***rattle***, ***rocket***, ***rose***, ***sedge***, ***succory***, ***sultan***, ***thistle***, ***vetch***, ***vetchling***, ***water-cress***, ***water-lily***, for which see the sbs.; also **yellow bean**, the yellow seeds of one of several varieties of soya bean; **yellow birch**, a North American tree, *Betula lutea*, which has yellow or grey bark; **yellow box**, an Australian gum-tree, *Eucalyptus melliodora*, which has yellowish inner bark; **yellow cedar** = *Nootka cypress* s.v. NOOTKA *a.* 2; **yellow poplar**, one of several North American softwood trees or their wood, esp. the tulip-tree, *Liriodendron tulipifera*; **yellow-weed**, (*a*) *dial.* dyer's-weed, *Reseda Luteola*; (*b*) common ragwort, *Senecio Jacobæa*; (*c*) in *U.S.* a name for some species of golden-rod (*Solidago*); **yellow-wort**, a gentianaceous plant, *Chlora perfoliata*, having bright yellow flowers and yielding a yellow dye; yellow centaury; **yellow yam**, one of several species of *Dioscorea* producing yellow-fleshed tubers; also, the tubers themselves. **c.** In names of minerals, and of chemical or other products, of a yellow colour: as ***yellow arsenic***, ***copper***, ***copperas***, ***corallin***, ***jasper***, ***lake*** (LAKE *sb.*[6] 3), ***ochre***, ***orpiment***, ***quartz***, ***sandalwood***, ***sanders***, ***ultramarine***, ***wash***, ***wax***, for which see the sbs.; also **yellow bark**, any variety of Peruvian bark of a yellow colour, as Calisaya bark; **yellow berries**, the fruit of *Rhamnus infectorius* and other species, yielding a yellow dye; also called *Persian berries*; **yellow deal**, the wood of the Scotch fir, *Pinus sylvestris*; **yellow earth**, †(*a*) a generic term for minerals or 'earths' of a yellow colour; (*b*) a yellowish clay, coloured by iron, used as a pigment; a variety of bole; **yellow ground**, kimberlite that is exposed at the surface and has become yellow as a result of atmospheric oxidation; **yellow jack** = *yellow jacket* (*b*), sense C. 2 c; **yellow metal**, an alloy of two parts of copper and one of zinc, used for sheathing vessels; **yellow ore**, yellow copper ore, copper pyrites (see COPPER *sb.*[1] 12); **yellow phosphorus** = *white phosphorus* s.v. WHITE *a.* 11 c; **yellow share**, ? *sb.* or *a.* (? *obs.*) [cf. REDSHIRE, -SHARE], a name or epithet for a brittle or friable iron ore (see quot.); **yellow soap**, a common soap made of tallow, rosin, and soda; hence **yellow-soap** *v. trans.* (*nonce-wd.*), to wash or rub with yellow soap; **yellow ware**, yellow earthenware or stoneware; **yellow wove** (see quot.). **d.** In names of diseases characterized by yellowness of the skin, or of some tissue, secretion, etc.: as ***yellow jaundice*** (see JAUNDICE), ***softening***, ***typhus***; **(acute) yellow atrophy**, 'atrophy and yellow discoloration of the liver with jaundice' (Dorland s.v. *Atrophy*); †**yellow evil**, jaundice, or (app.) some epidemic disease of which jaundice was a symptom; **yellow gum**, jaundice in infants, characterized by yellowness of the gums; **yellow Jack**, **yellow jack**, a slang name for yellow fever; **yellow plague** = *yellow evil*; **yellow sickness**, (*a*) = prec.; (*b*) a disease of hyacinth-plants (see quot. 1887); †**yellow sought** [SOUGHT *sb.*], jaundice: see also YELLOW FEVER. **e.** Miscellaneous: **yellow admiral** (see A. 1 e); **yellow alert**, an instruction to be prepared for or an initial state of readiness to cope with an emergency (cf. *red alert* s.v. RED *a.* 19 a); **yellow badge**, a badge of identification that Jews have sometimes been required to wear, esp. by the Nazis in Germany (cf. *yellow star* below); **yellow band**, a mark on a lamp-post to indicate that motor vehicles are not permitted to wait in the vicinity; freq. *attrib.*; also = *yellow line* below; **yellow belt**, the belt worn by one who has attained a certain standard of proficiency in judo (see quots.); **yellow book**, (*a*) an official report of government affairs in various European countries; (*b*) a report issued by the Liberal Party in 1928 on the industrial future of Britain; **yellow card**, in Association Football, a card shown by the referee to a player when he is cautioned; **yellow cartilage** *Anat.*, cartilage containing *yellow fibres*, elastic cartilage; **yellow cell** *Biol.*, one of the small yellow bodies found in many radiolarians, now held to be symbiotic algæ; **yellow dirt**, a contemptuous appellation for gold; **yellow fibre** *Anat.*, one of the elastic fibres of a yellow colour occurring in certain tissues (so **yellow fibrous tissue** = *yellow tissue*); **yellow flag**, a flag of a yellow colour displayed on board ship, formerly as a signal of capital punishment, now as a signal of infectious disease or of quarantine, and hoisted in war time on hospitals, etc.; **Yellow George** (see GEORGE 4 b); †**yellow jacket**, a military decoration in imperial China (*obs.* exc. *Hist.*); **yellow jersey** [tr. F. *maillot jaune*], a jersey awarded to the winner of (a stage of) a cycle race, *esp.* the *Tour de France*; **yellow leaf**, used (in allusion to quot. 1605) to refer to the process of ageing; **yellow light** *U.S.* a yellow-coloured cautionary light in traffic signals (cf. AMBER *a.* b); also *fig.*; **yellow line**, a yellow road-marking, usu. parallel to the kerb, indicating that parking of motor vehicles is restricted (though local regulations vary); also **double yellow line** indicating that parking is forbidden; **yellow-man**, †(*a*) a yellow silk handkerchief (*slang*); (*b*) a person with naturally yellowish skin or complexion (see A. 1 d); **yellow pages** *sb. pl.* orig. *U.S.*, an index printed on yellow paper; *spec.* the classified section of or supplement to a telephone directory, listing firms, products, and services; **yellow peril** (see A. 1 d); **yellow press** (see A. 3); **Yellow Pressman**, a journalist or reporter working for the yellow press (cf. sense 3 of the adj.); **yellow rain** = *sulphur rain* (see SULPHUR *sb.* 8); a yellow powder reported as falling through the air in S.E. Asia and causing severe blistering and sometimes death; **yellow rust**, a disease of wheat caused by the fungus *Puccinia glumarium*; **yellow spot** *Anat.*, a yellowish circular depression in the middle of the retina, being the region of most distinct vision; = *macula lutea* s.v. MACULA 2; **yellow star**, a piece of yellow cloth bearing the Magen David, which the Nazis required Jews to wear; **yellow stick** (see quots.); **yellow streak**, a trait of cowardice; **yellow tissue** *Anat.*, tissue containing *yellow fibres*, elastic tissue; **yellow union** [tr. F. *syndicat jaune*: cf. sense 2 c of the *adj.* above] a union of workers favouring free enterprise and usually opposed to strike action; **yellow warning** = *yellow alert* above. See also YELLOW-BOY.

1968 *Punch* 28 Aug. 279/1 NATO forces had quickly been placed on 'Yellow *Alert'. **1969** *Times* 17 Sept. 1/8 A yellow alert..on hospital beds..means that all cases not in need of immediate attention will not be admitted to hospitals. **1978** 'G. VAUGHAN' *Belgrade Drop* iii. 23 The United States president.. put his missile submarines throughout the world on yellow alert. **1815** KIRBY & SP. *Entomol.* x. (1818) I. 310 Piso speaks of yellow *ants called *Cupiá* inhabiting Brazil. **1864–5** WOOD *Homes without H.* vii. (1868) 129 The common Yellow Ant (*Formica flava*) so abundant in marshes and gardens. **1845** BUDD *Dis. Liver* 204 The yellow *atrophy is distinguished by a deep yellow colour; imbibition of the whole tissue of the organ with bile [etc.]. **1876** GEO. ELIOT *Daniel Deronda* III. v. xxxvii. 127 To Deronda just now the name Cohen was equivalent to the ugliest of yellow *badges. **1892** I. ZANGWILL *Childr. Ghetto* I. 2 People who have been living in a ghetto for a couple of centuries are not able..to efface the brands on their souls by putting off the yellow badges. **1942** I. COHEN *Jews in War* iii. 31 *The Yellow Badge* The crowning device for humiliating the Jews was the revival of a mediæval practice. In October 1941, a decree was issued requiring them to wear a yellow armlet marked with the 'Shield of David', which the Jews of Poland had been wearing for the past two years. **1962** BRIDGER & WOLK *New Jewish Encycl.* 38/1 (*caption*) The yellow badge the Nazis required Jews to wear in Germany and Nazi-occupied countries. **1948** *Times* 13 May 2/3 When the no-waiting order was first introduced in the West End it was announced that permanent signs would be erected as soon as the materials were available, the yellow *bands being temporary. **1959** *Times* 8 Dec. 5/6 Vast numbers of cars..are left at the kerbside all day in all parts of central London except the yellow-band streets. **1962** R. JEFFRIES *Exhibit No. Thirteen* iv. 36 Parked my car in a yellow-band area. **1967** R. RENDELL *Wolf to Slaughter* ii. 17 The car drew up... 'Not on the yellow band, Drayton,' Burden said sharply. **1796** NEMNICH *Polygl.-Lex.* 960 Yellow *bark. **1837**, **1875** [see CALISAYA]. **1838** THOMSON *Chem. Org. Bodies* 802 The yellow bark is the most employed, and most highly esteemed in this country. It is the bark of the *cinchona cordifolia* of Mutis. **1888** GOODE *Amer. Fishes* 33 Another species which closely resembles the Striped Bass is the *Morone interrupta*, generally known as the Yellow *Bass. **1965** H. BURKE *Chinese Cooking for Pleasure* 150 In small cans are bamboo shoots,..red bean curd, black bean, yellow soy *bean, [etc.]. **1972** CLAIBORNE & LEE *Chinese Cookbk.* (1973) xi. 422 *Bean Sauce*... Also called 'Whole Bean Sauce' or 'Yellow Bean Sauce', this thick sauce is made from yellow beans, flour, and water and is sold in..tins. **1983** *Observer* 16 Jan. (Colour Suppl.: Living Extra) 7/4 Black beans..and yellow beans..are both products of the versatile soya bean. **1941** M. Feldenkrais *Judo* 166 A white belt is worn by beginners, corresponding to the sixth Kyu. The next grade, the fifth, is indicated by a yellow *belt. **1979** *Observer Mag.* 17 June 39/1 For several years he went to judo classes, reached yellow-belt standard (three below black belt). **1712** tr. *Pomet's Hist. Drugs* I. 13 The Yellow *Berry is the Fruit of a Shrub which Authors call Licium. **1812** J. Smyth *Pract. Customs* (1821) 46 Yellow Berries are the fruit of a species of Lycium, growing plentifully in different parts of France... It is much used by the Dyers and Painters. **1787** W. Sargent in *Mem. Amer. Acad.* IX. 158 Black and Yellow *Birch... The bark of the latter is used by the Indians for making canoes. **1851** J. S. Springer *Forest Life* 23 The general outlines of the Yellow Birch often resemble the Elm. **1943** R. Peattie *Great Smokies* 156 A yellow birch on Whitetop Mountain was found to be seven feet three inches thick. **1974** M. Braithwaite *Ontario* xi. 169 Hemlock, oak, maple, and yellow birch, they were all there, just waiting to be cut down and sawed up into lumber. **1909** A. E. Mack *Bush Calendar* 68 Then a yellow-*bob came to visit us. **1965** *Austral. Encycl.* VII. 470/1 Another common and familiar bird is the yellow robin ('yellowbob') of eastern Australia, a species with a breast of bright yellow. **1883** *Pall Mall Gaz.* 5 Dec. 8/1 Paris, Dec. 5.—The first volume of the new Yellow-*book on Tonkin affairs. **1897** *Times* 23 Nov. 5/1 The *Berliner Neueste Nachrichten* reminds the French Republic that..in former Yellow-books there is plenty of evidence to show how generous was the help afforded by Germany to France. **1929** D. Lloyd George *We can conquer Unemployment* 3 In the 'Yellow Book', published a year ago, the Liberal Industrial Enquiry presented exhaustive proposals for dealing with the grave unemployment situation with which Britain was, and is still, faced. **1949** *Time* (Atlantic ed.) 14 Feb. 18/1 The Communists issued a 'Yellow Book' containing what they called Mindszenty's written confession. **1983** *Daily Tel.* 24 Nov. 18/4 Had the Liberal Yellow Book been published in 1920 our history might have been different. **1877** F. von Mueller *Introd. to Bot. Teaching at Schools of Victoria* 15 This tree passes by the very unapt vernacular name Yellow *Box-tree. **1934** *Bulletin* (Sydney) 31 Jan. 21/2 We lop mainly yellow box. **1977** *Meanjin* (Austral.) XXXVI. I. 71 I'll..split off kindling wood From the yellow-box log. **1776** Pennant *Brit. Zool.* I. 276 Yellow *Bunting..; the crown of the head is of a pleasant pale yellow. **1548** Turner *Names Herbes* (E.D.S.) 14 The secund [kind of Camomile] is called in greke chrysanthemon..it maye be called in englishe yealowe *camomyle. **1882** *Garden* 29 July 85/2 The Yellow Camomile..seems to be almost unknown. **1976** *Times* 11 Nov. 12/4 Two Villa men were shown the yellow *card for fairly innocuous offences. **1884** *N.Y. Times* 5 Oct. 5/2 Red and yellow *cedar..are the other trees most frequently met with. **1910** [see Alaska]. **1957** *Handbk. of Softwoods* (Forest Prod. Res. Lab.) 61 'Yellow cedar'..is confined to the Pacific Coast area from Alaska south to southern Oregon. **1879** tr. *Semper's Anim. Life* 74 Most of the Radiolaria.. bear in their body certain..particles known as the yellow *cells. **1796** Kirwan *Elem. Min.* (ed. 2) II. 140 Yellow *Copper Ore. Copper Pyrites. **1876** Voyle & Stevenson *Milit. Dict.* 488/1 Yellow copper is more brittle, stiffer, and less malleable [than the red]. **1548** Turner *Names Herbes* (E.D.S.) 55 Plenie maketh mention of a kynde called Narcissus herbaceus, whiche is after my iudgement our yealowe *daffodyl. **1766** *Complete Farmer* s.v. *Trellis*, Trellises..being generally made of regularly cut yellow-*deal, or oak. **1753** A. Murphy *Gray's Inn Jrnl.* No. 42 Convenience stamped an imaginary Value upon yellow *Dirt. **1794** Charlotte Smith *Wand. Warwick* 152 While you hesitate about receiving from me a little yellow dirt, for which I have no use. **1552** Huloet, Yellow *earth founde in the mynes of golde or syluer, *sandaraca*. **1688** Holme *Armoury* II. 38/2 Yellow earth, as Durry, Yellow Occar, Sand. **1794** Kirwan *Elem. Min.* (ed. 2) I. 194 This yellow earth differs from ochres only in containing a greater proportion of argill. **1883** *Encycl. Brit.* XVI. 425/1 Bole.. Stolpenite, Rock Soap, Plinthite, Yellow Earth or Felinite, Fetbol, and Ochran are varieties. **1387** Trevisa *Higden* (Rolls) II. 113 Afterward fel a pestilence in to al Wales of þe ȝelowe *yuel þat is i-cleped þe iaundys. **1494** [see jaundice 1 β]. **1667** Primatt *City & C. Builder* 61 Yellow *Fir, called Dram,..is the best sort of Fir for flooring. **1882** *Garden* 30 Sept. 301/3 The principal tree in these forests is the yellow Fir. **1783** *Ann. Reg., Chron.* 213/2 The other three were hanged..a yellow *flag was flying from each ship during the execution. **1805** *Act 45 Geo. III*, c. 10 §14 If the said ship.. have a clean bill of health, a large yellow flag of six breadths of bunting at the main-topmast head. **1836** Mrs. C. P. Traill *Backwoods of Canada* 19 [Our ship bears] the melancholy symbol of disease, the yellow flag. **1863** *Ann. Reg., For. Hist.* 326 The yellow flag, ordinarily held so sacred in modern war, has..been but the mark for the hottest and most deadly fire. **1867** Smyth *Sailor's Word-bk.*, *Yellow-flag*, the signal of quarantine. **1750** G. Edwards *Nat. Hist. Birds* III. Index 243 The great Yellow *Fly with black Spots. **1902** *Westm. Gaz.* 31 May 2/1 A banded yellow-fly. *c* **1386** Yelewe *gooldes [see gold² 1]. **1625** B. Jonson *Pan's Anniv.* Wks. (1641) I. 119 Gladdest myrtle for these postes to weare..star'd with yellow-golds, and Meadowes Queene. **1783** Latham *Gen. Synopsis Birds* III. 139 Yellow *Grosbeak...head, neck, breast, belly, and vent, yellow..Inhabits Asia. **1886** Yellow *ground [see *blue ground* s.v. blue *a.* 13]. **1947** *E. African Ann.* 1946–7 122/1 The portion of a pipe at the surface which has been altered or weathered and is usually of a yellowish colour is known as 'yellow ground', in contrast to the blue-green colour of the unaltered kimberlite or blue ground. **1978** *Sci. Amer.* Apr. 120/3 Most kimberlite exposed at the surface, called 'yellow ground' by miners and prospectors, is severely weathered. **1799** Underwood *Dis. Childhood* (ed. 4) I. 26 Nurses have usually accounted the yellowness that appears about the third day after birth, if unusually deep (termed by some the yellow *gum) as the true jaundice. **1836** E. Howard *R. Reefer* xxxiii, Misgivings about Yellow *Jack. **1857** Kingsley *Two Y. Ago* iv, Have seen three choleras, two army fevers, and yellow-jack without end. **1897** Mary Kingsley *W. Africa* 1, I knew a good deal..of South East America, and remembered that Yellow Jack was endemic. **1927** M. M. Bennett *Christison of Lammermoor* iv. 49 These trees called yellowjacks are soft wood, so white ants enclose them with earth walls and eat the wood out. **1943** A. Marshall in *Coast to Coast 1942* 14, I tied the horse to a yellowjack and crept towards the river. **1864** *North-China Herald* 18 June 99/2 [They] being each and all pre-eminent for bravery, contempt for death, and a generous emulation, are invested with the yellow *jacket as a reqard for their merits. **1878** H. A. Giles *Gloss. Ref. Far East* 84 A yellow *ma-kwa* is a distinction conferred by the Emperor on high officials; sometimes called the *Yellow Jacket*. **1918** H. B. Morse *International Relations Chinese Empire* II. v. 104 On Li Hung-chung was conferred the military distinction of the Yellow Jacket and the civil distinction of Junior Guardian to the heir apparent. **1964** *Guardian* 16 June 6/6 Metcalfe (England) won his seventh yellow *jersey with another aggressively defensive ride. **1983** *Times* 1 July 12/5 It's hard enough even to get a ride in the Tour [de France]... To be the raceleader, to wear the yellow jersey, that's almost worth dying for. **1948** C. L. B. Hubbard *Dogs in Britain* xix. 232 The Yellow *Labrador sometimes called the Golden Labrador..differs in several respects from the black Labrador. **1974** *Times* 4 May 23/8 (Advt.), Country home urgently wanted for two purebred Yellow Labrador bitches. [**1605**: see sere, sear *a.*¹ 1 b]. **1913** L. Strachey in *Edin. Rev.* Jan. 68 The radiant creatures of Sceaux had fallen into the yellow *leaf. **1935** C. Isherwood *Mr. Norris changes Trains* vii. 107 Yes, I shall be fifty-three... I find it difficult to become accustomed to the thought that the yellow leaf is upon me. **1974** A. A. Thompson *Swiss Legacy* xvi. 157 He guided the Mercedes through the traffic..taking chances... He ran a yellow *light and then a red one. **1977** *N.Y. Rev. Bks.* 27 Oct. 16/4 They only ask a 'yellow' light—the right to proceed with caution. **1965** *Autocar* 24 Sept. 609/1 The leaflet recently published by RoSPA in conjunction with the Ministry of Transport..states that a yellow *line by the kerb means no waiting *except* for loading and unloading. **1968** J. Fleming *Kill or Cure* iv. 56 The local police..allow me to park on the double yellow line with impunity, when absolutely necesesary. **1975** J. Symons *Three Pipe Problem* xviii. 180 Traffic wardens can start booking cars on yellow lines after eight o'clock. **1983** *Church Times* 23 Dec. 11/1 Christmas shoppers who had taken the risk of parking on the single yellow line. **1821** *Sporting Mag.* (N.S.) IX. 27 A prime yellow-*man round his squeeze. **1823** 'Jon Bee' *Dict. Turf* s.v., John Gully introduced the yellowman. **1898** *Westm. Gaz.* 5 Jan. 1/2 Convinced free-traders from the Colonies..draw the line at the free invasion of the Yellow-man. **1647** in W. M. Williams *Ann. Founders' Co.* (1867) 103 Wayghtes of Brass..shall not..be..made of any worse Brass than Yellow *Mettell. **1860** *Merc. Marine Mag.* VII. 284 A ship fastened with yellow metal ought not to be put under the head of 'copper fastened'. **1878** Ure *Dict. Arts* IV, Yellow-metal sheathing. **1481–90** Yelu *okyr [see ochre *sb.* 1]. **1599** in *Archaeologia* LXIV. 384 For too pounde of yellow Oker for the said seeling iiij d. **1799** G. Smith *Laboratory* I. 185 Take yellow ochre, neal it well, and it will turn to a brown red. **1899** Cagney tr. *von Jaksch's Clin. Diagn.* (ed. 4) 143 The expectoration, which was of a yellow-ochre tint. **1843** R. J. Graves *Syst. Clin. Med.* xxix. 391 The ulcer was dressed with yellow *ointment. **1881** Raymond *Mining Gloss.*, *Yellow-*ore*..Chalcopyrite. **1908** *Sears, Roebuck Catal.* (*verso rear cover*), See the yellow *pages in back of this book. **1956** R. A. Heinlein in *Mag. of Fantasy & Sci. Fiction* Oct. 51/2 Get me the yellow-pages phone book... I want to check the exact phrasing of a firm name. **1966** D. G. Hays in *Automatic Transl. of Lang.* (NATO Summer School, Venice, 1962) 152 In a telephone book..in the..'Yellow Pages', the major variable is name of product or service. **1969** *Times* 5 May 26/2 Yellow Pages are the classified guide that will be part of everyone's GPO telephone directory soon. **1982** S. Brett *Murder Unprompted* i. 10 The random selection method of sticking a pin in the 'Theatrical and Variety Agents' section of the Yellow Pages. **1985** *Punch* 23 Jan. 24/2 I started by ringing a few cowboys through the *Yellow Pages*, just to check on prices. **1866** H. E. Roscoe *Less. Elem. Chem.* xv. 133 The weight of red substance produced is exactly equal to that of yellow *phosphorus used. **1944** J. A. Timm *Gen. Chem.* xli. 443 Yellow phosphorus is formed when the liquid solidifies. **1819** Lingard *Hist. Eng.* I. ii. 108 A pestilence of the most fatal description (it was called the yellow *plague) depopulated the island. **1887** [see plague *sb.* 3 b]. **1774** J. R. Peyton *Let.* 21 July in J. L. Peyton *Adv. My Grandfather* (1867) 127 The forest of Kentucky consists of yellow and white *poplar, walnut, red bud. **1876** W. Whitman *Specimen Days* (1882–3) 89 Here is one of my favorites now before me, a fine yellow poplar, quite straight, perhaps 90 feet high. **1955** *Sci. News Let.* 7 May 302/2 The tulip tree is also variously known as tulip poplar, yellow poplar, whitewood and fiddle-tree. **1909** G. K. Chesterton *Tremendous Trifles* 131 The Yellow *Pressman seems to have no power of catching the first fresh fact about a man. **1918** S. Sassoon *Counter-Attack* 29 The boys came back... And Yellow-Pressmen thronged the sunlit street To cheer the soldiers who'd refrained from dying. **1891** *Cent. Dict.* s.v. *Rain, Sulphur-rain* or *yellow *rain* is a similar precipitation of the pollen of fir-trees, etc. **1903** *Daily Chron.* 5 Mar. 5/2 The phenomenon of 'yellow rain' was observed at some of the southern..stations. **1979** W. Safire in *N.Y. Times* 13 Dec. A31/5 The Laotians call it 'the yellow rain'. **1981** *N.Y. Times* 24 Nov. C-1/5 The United States has been trying since 1976 to verify reports that chemical weapons, known popularly as 'the yellow rain', are being used against remote villages in Laos, Cambodia and, more recently, Afghanistan. **1982** *Sci. News* 20 Feb. 122/1 Blood samples were drawn from nine individuals supposedly exposed to a 'yellow rain' gas attack in the fall of 1981... Mirocha 'was able to tentatively identify'..a metabolite of the trichothecene mycotoxin T_2, in samples from only two. **1907** *Jrnl. Agri. Sci.* II. 129 He [*sc.* Mr. Biffen] has discovered and grown several wheats which show to a greater or lesser degree immunity to the attacks of *Puccinia glumarum*, Yellow *Rust. **1973** *Scotsman* 7 Aug. 4/6 Mr Blakebell was speaking of yellow rust in wheats. **1855** Kingsley *Glaucus* (1859) 195 The delicate lemon-coloured 'Yellow *Sally' (Chrysoperla viridis). **1867** F. Francis *Bk. Angling* vi. (1880) 231 The Yellow Sally..has..a high character with some anglers. **1686** Plot *Staffordsh.* 160 The first and meanest whereof [*sc.* Iron Ore], they call yellow *share an ill sort that runs all to dirt and is good for nothing ..this sort some others are please'd to call Redshare. **1747** Carte *Hist. Eng.* I. 214 *note*, The yellow *sickness, a pestilential distemper which is mentioned by abundance of ancient writers, as laying Wales almost desolate. **1807** *Ess. Highl. Soc.* III. 437 *note*, Yellows,..Yellow sickness, or Jaundice. **1887** Garnsey & Balfour tr. *De Bary's Fungi* 482 A disease in the hyacinth known in Holland as the yellow sickness, the characteristic symptom of which is the presence of yellow slimy masses of Bacteria in the vessels. **1725** H. Sloane *Voy. Jamaica* II. 325 Serpens major subflavus..The yellow *Snake. **1851** P. H. Gosse *Naturalist's Sojourn in Jamaica* 314 A serpent of the Boa kind..is distinguished by the appellation of Yellow Snake. **1860** Mayne Reid *Odd People* 22 The 'Yellow Snake', or South African Cobra. **1868** J. G. Wood *Homes without Hands* iii. 85 A Yellow Snake..is very plentiful in Jamaica and is perfectly harmless to man. **1813** *Gentl. Mag.* Jan. 95/1 *Soap, Yellow, 104*s.* Mottled 114*s.* **1837** Dickens *Pickw.* xxv, Applying plenty of yellow soap to the towel, and rubbing away till his face shone again. **1835** —— *Sk. Boz, Parish* vi, The children were yellow-*soaped and flannelled, and towelled, till their faces shone again. **1845** Yellow *softening [see softening *vbl. sb.* 1 b]. **1873** T. H. Green *Introd. Pathol.* (ed. 2) 42 Yellow Softening.., in which, from the fine state of division and close aggregation of the fatty particles, a dead yellowish-white colour is imparted to the softened tissue. **14..** Ȝalow *souȝt [see sought *sb.*]. **1578** Lyte *Dodoens* I. ii. 6 The infusion..cureth the Iaundise or Yealowsought. **1819** *Phil. Trans. R. Soc.* CIX. 302 The yellow *spot of Soemmerring..is never seen to advantage until this membrane be removed. **1869** Huxley *Physiol.* ix. (ed. 3) 241 Exactly opposite the middle of the posterior wall, it [*sc.* the retina] presents a slight circular depression of a yellowish hue, the *macula lutea*, or yellow spot. **1899** *Allbutt's Syst. Med.* VII. 730 Ophthalmoscopic examination reveals a peculiar..appearance in the region of each yellow spot. **1967** *Guardian* 21 Oct. 8/3 'Private Eye' recently labelled me 'D. A. N. Jew'. Now it happens that I haven't the right to claim the yellow *star. **1981** *Times Lit. Suppl.* 6 Nov. 1296/5 Germans like Captain Ernst Janger..who declared himself 'ashamed'..when he saw Jews in Paris wearing their yellow stars. **1861** Macleod *Devot. to B.V.M. in N. Amer.* 342 *note*, Hebridean Protestants..are..called Protestants of the Yellow *Stick. **1880** W. G. Blaikie *Life Livingstone* i. 3 A tradition that the people of the island [Ulva] were converted from being Roman Catholics 'by the laird coming round with a man having a yellow staff,..the new religion went long afterwards..by the name of the religion of the yellow stick'. **1911** H. S. Harrison *Queed* v. 55 'A yellow *streak in him, and we didn't know it!' bellowed the Major. **1977** 'D. MacNeil' *Wolf in Fold* xi. 116 I'm not showing a yellow streak! But we're going to have casualties. **1876** Quain *Anat.* (ed. 8) II. 67 Yellow or Elastic *Tissue. **1822–34** *Good's Study Med.* (ed. 4) I. 585 *Typhus icterodes* or yellow *typhus. **1947** H. W. Ehrmann *French Labor* vii. 126 The CGT could not properly identify the Catholic trade unions with the various movements, in French usage commonly referred to as 'yellow' *unions, which were organized under the auspices of the employers. **1957** M. P. Fogarty *Christian Democracy* xv. 192 Widespread support was given to the yellow unions, notably by the clergy. **1970** R. A. H. Robinson *Origins of Franco's Spain* 331 Socialists were also determined that no 'yellow' unions should flourish, eg a strike-threat by the UGT procured the dismissal of 20 members of the *Federación Española de Trabajadores*. **1783** J. Latham *Gen. Synopsis Birds* II. 482 Spotted Yellow *Warbler. **1845** S. Judd *Margaret* I. 160 The leafless Butternut, whereon..the yellow warbler made its nest, sprawls its naked arms. **1938** M. Thompson *High Trails* 153 The yellow warbler..and many other birds fill the air with their songs. **1971** *Islander* (Victoria, B.C.) 13 June 13/2 Overhead a pair of yellow warblers trilled out their song. **1785** J. Woodforde *Diary* 7 Nov. (1926) II. 213 To Nancy for 2 new yellow *Ware Chamber Pots 1. 0. **1827** Lytton *Pelham* lxiii, A comfortless sort of dressing-room,..where I found a yellow-ware jug and basin. **1887** *Harper's Mag.* Dec. 31/1 Sometimes a cherry would fall upon her dark braids, and drop thence in among the verdant contents of the yellow-ware bowl. **1967** *Canadian Antiques Collector* Apr. 9/2 During the next ten years the Bells extended their pottery production to include Rockingham and yellow wares. **1963** *Times* 22 Jan. 10/3 The service have issued a 'yellow *warning'. This is intended to warn hospitals to cut down on routine admissions so as to make room for emergencies. **1973** *Times* 13 Nov. 1/2 In electricity supply terms a national 'yellow warning'..means possible voltage reductions. **1760** J. Lee *Introd. Bot.* App. 332 Yellow *weed, *Reseda*. **1853** G. Johnston *Bot. E. Borders* 111 *S[enecio] Jacobæa*. Ragwort: Yellow-weed. **1884** Miller *Plant-n.*, *Reseda Luteola*..Dyer's-Rocket, Dyer's-weed, Dyer's Yellow-weed,..Yellow-weed. **1789** Pilkington *View Derbysh.* I. 384 *Chlora perfoliata*, perforated [*sic*] Yellow-*Wort. **1859** *Stationers' Handbk.* 12 In woven papers may be mentioned *Blue Wove*—that is, a paper of woven texture, but blue in colour; then comes another, which, although in point of fact white, or an extremely pale cast of blue, is termed *Yellow *Wove*. **1913** W. Harris *Notes Fruit & Veg. Jamaica* 42 Yellow *yam and its varieties belong to *Dioscorea cayennensis*. **1971** [see *negro yam* s.v. Negro 7]. **1973** N. Farki *Countryman Karl Black* iv. 38 Rice and two pieces of yellow yam in one plate.

2. Combinations. **a.** Qualifying other adjs. (or sbs.) of colour (= yellowish, inclining to or tinged with yellow): as ***yellow-black, -blue, -brown, -dun, -golden, -green, -grey, -olive, -red, -white***; also occas. other adjs., as ***yellow-fluffy, -gleamy, -pale, -ripe***.

In OE. expressed by *ȝeolu* in comb. or by the adv. *ȝeolwe*, as *ȝeoluréad, ȝeolwe réad*.

1841 Clough *Poems, Song of Autumn* 5 My gay green leaves are *yellow-black, Upon the dank autumnal floor. **1940** W. Faulkner *Hamlet* IV. ii. 328 There were three buzzards soaring against the high *yellow-blue. **1796** Withering *Brit. Plants* (ed. 3) IV. 177 Pileus *yellow brown. **1859** Geo. Eliot in Cross *Life* (1885) II. 109 The rich yellow-brown of the oaks. **1639** T. de Grey *Compl. Horsem.* 59 The horse which is milke white, *yellow-dunne, sanded or pie-bald. **1832** Lytton *Eugene Aram* I. ix, He.. drew up his line, and replaced the contemned beauty of the violet-fly with the novel attractions of the yellow-dun. **1837** Kirkbride *Northern Angler* 32 The Yellow Dun..makes its appearance on the northern rivers some time in May. **1916** D. H. Lawrence *Amores* 50 Flutter for a moment, oh the beast is quick and keen,—Extinct one *yellow-fluffy spark. *a* **1930** —— *Phoenix* (1936) I. 3 In the *yellow-gleamy sunset, wild birds began to whistle faintly. **1946** S. Spender *European Witness* i. 15 In the foreground *yellow-golden fields, with above a flat wall of greyish sky. *a* **1963** L.

MacNeice *Astrol.* (1964) iii. 96 Leo the yellow-golden fire of organized mentality. **1768** G. White *Selborne, To Pennant* 17 Aug., The *yellow-green of the whole upper part of the body is more vivid. **1816** Stephens in Shaw *Gen. Zool.* IX. II. 404 Upper part of the back and scapulars yellow-green. *a* **1887** Jefferies *Field & Hedgerow* (1889) 269 The broad descending surfaces of yellow-green oak. **1811** Shaw *Gen. Zool.* VIII. 466 *Yellow-olive Parrakeet. *a* **1930** D. H. Lawrence *Last Poems* (1932) 315 Black lamps.. Giving off darkness, blue darkness, upon Demeter's *yellow-pale day. *c* **1050** *Voc.* in Wr.-Wülcker 437/20 *Lutea*, þæt *ȝioluréade. **1398** Trevisa *Barth. De P.R.* v. xiv. (Tollem. MS.), Yf þey ben browne in coloure, oþer citryn ȝolwer[e]de. **1819** Stephens in Shaw *Gen. Zool.* XI. II. 324 The breast is yellow-red. **1886** R. F. Burton *Arab. Nts.* (abr. ed.) III. 3 All manner trees bearing *yellow-ripe fruits. **1614** Sylvester *Parl. Vertues Royall* 1288 Her *yellow-sallow skin. *c* **1000** Ælfric *Gloss.* in Wr.-Wülcker 163/21 *Giluus*, *ȝeoluhwit. **1591** Sylvester *Du Bartas* I. i. 337 A Hen that fain would hatch a Brood.. Sits close thereon, and with her lively heat, Of yellow-white bals, doth live birds beget. **1891** Farrar *Darkn. & Dawn* xli. That yellow-white plant, which grows on an old oak in the wood. **1898** *Eliz. & her German Garden* 55 Coral-pink petals, paling.. to a yellow-white.

b. Parasynthetic and instrumental combs. (many of which are used in the names of species or varieties of animals or plants): as ***yellow-backed, -banded, -barked, -barred, -belled, -billed, -blossomed, -bodied, -breasted, -browed, -cheeked, -chinned, -coloured, -covered, -crested, -crowned, -eyed, -faced, -fanged, -finned, -flagged, -flecked, -fleshed, -flowered, -flowering, -footed, -fringed, -fronted, -girted, -gloved, -haired, -headed, -hilted, -horned, -jerkined, -leaved, legged, -lit, -livered, -locked, -lustred, -maned, -marked, -mottled, -necked, -painted, pinioned, -ringed, -ringleted, -robed, -rumped, -sealed, -shafted, -shanked, -shouldered, -skinned, -skirted, -slashed, -slobbered, -spotted, -sprinkled, -stained, -tailed, -throated, -tinged, -tinging, -toed, -tressed, -vented, -wamed*** (Sc. = -bellied), ***-washed, -winged***, etc., adjs. Also YELLOW-HAIRED.

1783 Latham *Gen. Synopsis Birds* IV. 440 *Yellow-backed Warbler. **1874** *Baily's Mag.* Jan. 346 One or two yellow-backed railway novels. **1833** Tennyson *Eleänore* 22 The *yellow-banded bees. **1611** Cotgr., *Saulx vitelline*, ..*yellow-barked Willow. **1824** Loudon *Green-house Comp.* I. 68 Yellow-barked shoots and leaves. **1832** J. Rennie *Butterfl. & Moths* 174 The *Yellow-barred Iron.. occurs in woods. **1752** Hill *Hist. Anim.* 328 The *yellow-beaked, American Owl. **1966** E. Palmer *Plains of Camdeboo* xvi. 262 By far the showiest is the yellow-beaked Stapelia, *Stapelia flavirostris*, with dark flowers marked with yellow and ornamented with silver hairs. **1881** O. Wilde *Poems* 122 On this side and on that a rocky cave, Hung with the *yellow-belled laburnum stands. **1822** Latham *Gen. Hist. Birds* II. 331 *Yellow-billed Horn-bill. **1859** Geo. Eliot *Adam Bede* I. vi, Turning even the muddy water..into a mirror for the yellow-billed ducks. **1764** Goldsm. *Trav.* 292 The *yellow-blossom'd vale. **1852** Mundy *Antipodes* (1857) 31 The delicate yellow-blossomed acacia. **1752** Hill *Hist. Anim.* 30 The black and *yellow-bodied Œstrus. **1864–5** Wood *Homes without H.* vi. 139 To see the yellow-bodied Wasp..dart into the dark mass. **1730** Mortimer in *Phil. Trans.* XXXVI. 432 The *Yellow-breasted Chat. **1776** Brown *Illustr. Zool.* 80 The yellow-breasted Flycatcher. **1849** Macaulay *Hist. Eng.* iii. I. 313 The yellow-breasted martin was still pursued in Cranbourne Chase for his fur. **1783** Latham *Gen. Synopsis Birds* IV. 459 *Yellow-browed Warbler. **1913** H. K. Swann *Dict. Names Brit. Birds* 264 Yellow-browed Warbler... A Siberian species of Willow Warbler. **1971** *Country Life* 25 Mar. 705/3 Almost any rarity can turn up, such as..yellow-browed warbler. **1872** *Routledge's Ev. Boy's Ann.* 419/1 White petaled, *yellow-centred flowers. **1765** Layard in *Phil. Trans.* LVI. 13 A rusty *yellow-colored crust covering the stalactites. **1849** *Merchants' Mag.* XX. 118 The *yellow-covered literature of the day—translations from the French. **1915** H. Young *Hard Knocks* 23 The little yellow covered novels were the cause of it. **1776** Brown *Illustr. Zool.* 24 The *Yellow-crested Woodpecker. **1894** A. Robertson *Nuggets* 127 A flock of yellow-crested cockatoos. **1776** Brown *Illustr. Zool.* 50 *Yellow crowned Thrush. **1817** Stephens in Shaw *Gen. Zool.* X. 623 Yellow-crowned Warbler. **1925** J. Ferguson in *Oxf. Poetry* 18 Like stately flowers, yellow-crowned. **1950** *Caribbean Q.* II. III. 41 Nor were the larger and stronger Yellow crowned Night Herons, to be outdone. **1752** Hill *Hist. Anim.* 322 The *yellow-eyed Owl. **1845–50** Mrs. Lincoln *Lect. Bot.* App. 187 *Xyris..caroliniana* (yellow-eyed grass). **1881** O. Wilde *Poems* 180 The hot jungle where the yellow-eyed huge lions sleep. **1957** T. Hughes *Hawk in Rain* 39 A square-pupilled yellow-eyed look. **1592** Nashe *P. Penilesse* Wks. (Grosart) II. 27 In praise of Lady Swinsnout, his *yeolow-fac'd Mistres. **1758** G. Edwards *Glean. Nat. Hist.* I. 49 The Yellow-faced Parrakeet. **1811** Shaw *Gen. Zool.* VIII. 445 Yellow-faced Parrakeet. **1954** J. R. R. Tolkien *Two Towers* III. iii. 50 It was the *yellow-fanged guard. **1804** Shaw *Gen. Zool.* V. 176 *Yellow-finned Herring. **1908** C. F. Holder *Big Game at Sea* xxiii. 342 The boatmen..called it the 'yellow-finned tuna'... This was in 1904, and ever since the new tuna, with its vivid lemon finlets, has appeared every August or September. **1936** *Zoologica* XXI. 190 The various nominal forms of the yellow-finned tuna belong to the same species. **1868** J. E. Ollivant tr. *P. Kollonitz's Crt. Mexico* 16 The *yellow-flagged boat of the quarantine. **1920** D. H. Lawrence *Lost Girl* iv. 55 The seam of *yellow-flecked coal. **1885–94** R. Bridges *Eros & Psyche* Dec. 12 The *yellow-fleecèd flocks. **1859** Darwin *Orig. Spec.* iv. (1860) 85 Another disease attacks *yellow-fleshed peaches far more than those with other coloured flesh. **1721** Mortimer *Husb.* II. 239 The Toad Flax of Valentia is *yellow-Flowered. **1845** *Florist's Jrnl.* (1846) VI. 270 A yellow-flowered Sea-Lavender is a rarity. **1888** J. & E. R. Pennell *Sent. Journ.* 11 Across the yellow flowered sand-dunes. **1832** *Veg. Subst. Food of Man* 213 The *yellow flowering pea. **1894** Lydekker *Marsupialia* 172 *Yellow-footed Pouched Mouse, *Phascologale flavipes*. **1832** J. Rennie *Butterfl. & Moths* 221 The *Yellow-fringed White [Moth] (*Y*[*psolophus*] *flaviciliatus*). **1781** Pennant *Gen. Birds* 62 *Yellow-fronted Honey-Sucker. **1783** Latham *Gen. Synopsis Birds* IV. 461 Yellow-fronted Warbler. The forehead and crown are of a bright yellow. **1901** *Nature* 19 Sept. 523/2 A Yellow-fronted Amazon (*Chrysotis ochrocephala*) from Guiana. **1880** *Daily News* 16 Aug. 6/5 The..*yellow-funnelled White Star liner steams slowly in. **1818** Keats *Endym.* I. 253 *Yellow girted bees. **1771** Smollett *Humphrey Cl.* II. 10 June, let. i, It was the singularity in S——'s conduct that reconciled him to the *yellow-gloved philosopher. **1743** G. Edwards *Nat. Hist. Birds* 44 The *Yellow-headed Linnet. This Bird being of kin to Linnets or Canary-Birds, I choose to call it by this Name. **1783** Latham *Gen. Synopsis Birds* IV. 401 Yellow-headed Wagtail. **1846** *Ex. Doc. 30th U.S. Congress I Sess. House* No. 41. 436 [We saw] large flocks of the yellow headed black bird. **1972** R. & R. Wright *Cariboo Mileposts* 50 Stands of tules or reeds will hold the woven nests of red-wing and yellow-headed blackbirds. **1787** Hawkins *Life of Johnson* 233 A long *yellow-hilted sword. **1832** J. Rennie *Butterfl. & Moths* 83 The *Yellow-horned [Moth] (*C*[*eropacha*] *flavicornis*)..antennæ yellow. **1860** Motley *Netherl.* ii. I. 35 Battling..breast to breast with the *yellow-jerkined pikemen of Spain and Italy. **1766** *Complete Farmer* s.v. *Purslane*, The red or *yellow leaved, commonly called golden purslane. **1824** Longf. *Autumn* 20 Maple yellow-leaved. **1752** Hill *Hist. Anim.* 340 The *yellow-legged Falco. **1865** Dickens *Mut. Fr.* III. viii, A..bystander, *yellow-legginged and purple-faced. **1877** Black *Green Past.* vi, Asleep in the hushed *yellow-lit room. **1935** S. Lewis *It can't happen Here* 156 The meanest, lowest, cowardliest gang of *yellow-livered, back-slapping, hypocritical gun-toters. **1979** *PN Rev.* No. 9. 27/1 O green, green eating out my eyes, A yellow-livered green in a wet light. **1697** Dryden *Æneis* x. 786 Camers the *yellow Lock'd. **1878** Longf. *Kéramos* 182 A ground of deepest blue With *yellow-lustred stars o'erlaid. **1863** W. C. Baldwin *Afr. Hunting* ix. 416 He was only a *yellow-maned one [*sc.* lion]. **1916** Blunden *Harbingers* 64 Toadstools.. Yellow, and *yellow-mottled red, and black. **1783** Latham *Gen. Synopsis Birds* III. 337 *Yellow-necked Flycatcher. **1889** *Cent. Dict.* 7016/3 The yellow-necked caterpillar..feeds in communities on the foliage of apple, hickory, and walnut in the United States. **1908** E. J. Banfield *Confessions of Beachcomber* I. iii. 98 Yellow-necked Mangrove Bittern. **1921** G. E. H. Barrett-Hamilton *Hist. Brit. Mammals* II. 547 The Yellow-necked Field Mouse is distinguished from *A. sylvaticus* by its larger size. **1979** *Essex Countryside* XXVII. 72/2 The hoarding habits of yellow-necked mice are well known. **1861** W. F. Collier *Hist. Eng. Lit.* 104 Those *yellow-painted wooden caravans. **1735** Somerville *Chase* I. 243 His glossy Skin, or *Yellow-py'd, or blue. **1624** Heriot in *Mem.* (1822) App. III. 98 My *yellow-pointed diamond-ring. **1880** A. H. Swinton *Insect Variety* 94 The groups of *Yellow-ringed Gnats. **1864** Tennyson *Boadicea* 55 Thither at their will they haled the *yellow-ringleted Britoness. **1819** *Methodist Mag.* Oct. 723 We took leave of our *yellow-robed acquaintances. **1889** S. Langdon *Appeal to Serpent* iii. 50 A long procession of yellow-robed.. monks. **1758** G. Edwards *Glean. Nat. Hist.* I. 97 The *Yellow-rumped Fly-catcher. **1808–13** A. Wilson *Amer. Ornith.* (1832) I. 280 Yellow-rumped Warbler.—Sylvia Coronata. **1841** *Yellow-sealed [see *yellow-seal* in c]. **1848** Thackeray *Van. Fair* xi, My yellow-sealed wine, which costs me ten shillings a bottle. **1822** Latham *Gen. Hist. Birds* III. 410 *Yellow-shafted Woodpecker;..tail dusky yellow, with black spots, and yellow shafts. **1844** H. Stephens *Bk. Farm* II. 248 A *yellow-skinned chicken makes the most delicate roast. **1629** Milton *Hymn Nativ.* xxvi, The *yellow-skirted Fayes. **1928** V. Woolf *Orlando* v. 225 The *yellow-slashed sky of dawn. **1922** Joyce *Ulysses* 222 Two barefoot urchins, sucking long liquorice laces, halted near him, gaping..with their *yellowslobbered mouths. **1869** 'Mark Twain' *Innoc. Abr.* vii. 43 The tall *yellow-splotched hills. **1828** Latham *Index Gen. Hist. Birds* III, Woodpecker, *yellow spotted. **1853** Mrs. Gaskell *Cranford* xiii, The yellow-spotted lilac gown. **1619** Rich *Irish Hubbub* 4 A *yellow-starcht band about his necke. **1758** G. Edwards *Glean. Nat. Hist.* I. 101 The *Yellow-tailed Fly-catcher. **1823** Latham *Gen. Hist. Birds* VI. 232 Yellow-tailed Warbler. *a* **1749** M. Catesby *Nat. Hist. Carolina* (1754) I. 62 The *yellow-throated creeper. **1859** Tennyson *Elaine* 12 Yellow-throated nestling in the nest. **1826** J. Wilson *Noct. Ambr.* Wks. 1855 I. 174 In their *yellow-tinged-lookin blankets. **1728–46** Thomson *Spring* 1082 The *yellow-tinging Plague Internal Vision taints. *a* **1593** Marlowe *Ovid's Elegies* II. iv, Amber trest [*v.r.* *Yellow trest] is she. **1838** *Wilson's Tales of Borders* IV. 176 He can..lurk in the green moss like the *yellow-wamed ask. **1859** Hawthorne *Marble Faun* xxxvi, Those immense seven-storied, *yellow-washed hovels. **1764** G. Edwards *Glean. Nat. Hist.* III. 239 The *Yellow-winged Pye. **1808–13** A. Wilson *Amer. Ornith.* (1831) II. 259 Yellow-Winged Sparrow..inhabits the lower parts of New York and Pennsylvania. **1844** Kinglake *Eothen* xviii, The yellow-winged Angel [of Death].

c. Forming sbs. (or adjs.), the names (or descriptive epithets) of animals and other objects, in which *yellow* qualifies the name of some part or distinctive feature: **yellow-back**, (*a*) some kind of fish (see quot. 1796); (*b*) a cheap yellow-backed (esp. French) novel; more widely, any cheaply issued or reprinted novel; (*c*) a U.S. currency note having the back coloured yellow; **yellow-beak** = BEJAN; **yellow-bill**, name for various birds with a yellow bill or yellow coloration on the bill, as the American scoter, *Œdemia americana*; **yellow-cup**, a buttercup; **yellow-fin**, name for various fishes with yellow fins or yellow coloration on the fins (see quots.); esp. **yellow-fin tuna**, one of several species of *Thunnus*, esp. *T. albacares*, a large fish found in warmer parts of both the Atlantic and Pacific oceans; **yellow-foot** *a.* (Sc. -fit), yellow-footed; **Yellow Hat**, *colloq.*, used *attrib.* or *absol.* in *pl.* to denote a Tibetan Buddhist sect (Gelugpa) founded in the fourteenth century by Tsong-kha-pa; **yellow-head**, (*a*) an African plant of the genus *Helichrysum* having brilliant yellow flowers; (*b*) a species of moth (see quot. 1832); (*c*) the American yellow-headed blackbird, *Xanthocephalus icterocephalus*; (*d*) a warbler, *Mohoua ochrocephala*, found in the South Island of New Zealand; **yellow jacket**, (*a*) *U.S. colloq.*, name for a wasp or hornet; (*b*) name for various species of *Eucalyptus* with yellowish bark (Morris *Austral Eng.*); (*c*) *slang* (orig. *U.S.*), a pentobarbitone capsule; **yellow-leg, -legs**, (*a*) a bird with yellow legs, esp. either of two N. American sandpipers, *Totanus flavipes* and *T. melanoleucus*; (*b*) *N. Amer. colloq.* [from the yellow stripe down the side of the breeches], a U.S. cavalryman or a member of the Royal Canadian Mounted Police; **yellow-line**, collectors' name for species of moths of the genus *Orthosia* (see quots.); **yellow-neb** = *yellow-beak*, BEJAN; **yellow-pate**, the yellow-hammer; **yellow-poll (warbler)**, the summer warbler of N. America, *Dendrœca æstiva*; **yellow-rump (warbler)**, *Dendrœca coronata*, also called *yellow-crowned warbler* or *myrtle-bird*; also *D. maculosa*; **yellow-seal** (*nonce-use*), wine in bottles bearing a yellow seal; **yellowseed**, a name for *Lepidium campestre*, also called *mithridate mustard* or *m. pepperwort*; **yellow-shank, -shanks** = *yellow-leg*(*s*; **yellow-shell**, collectors' name for a species of moth (see quot.); **yellow-skin**, one of an ethnic type having a yellow skin or complexion (see A. 1 d); **yellow-spot**, collectors' name for a species of skipper (butterfly), *Polites peckius*, having a yellow spot on each hind wing; also (***yellow-spot unicorn hawk***) for a species of hawk-moth, *Sphinx quinque-maculatus*; **yellow-throat**, any species of warbler of the N. American genus *Geothlypis*, esp. *G. trichas*, the Maryland yellow-throat; **yellow-top**, (*a*) a N. American species of reed-grass, *Calamagrostis hyperborea Americana*, valued for hay; (*b*) the early golden-rod, *Solidago juncea*, common in eastern N. America; (*c*) a variety of turnip, having the top of the root of a yellow colour; **yellow underwing**, one of several noctuid moths. See also YELLOW-BELLY, YELLOW-ROOT, YELLOW-TAIL, YELLOW-WOOD.

1796 Stedman *Surinam* II. xxix. 368 The fisher-men having caught a quantity of large fish, I discovered one among them..the *yellow-back...thus called from its colour, which almost resembles that of a lemon. **1877** *Living Age* 14 Apr. 128/1 Four days ago Ley and I started down the river on an exploring expedition, and he took it into his head to rope ('lasso', as the yellow-backs have it) a buffalo. **1890** *Q. Rev.* Oct. 443 A well-thumbed 'Yellow-back'. **1902** H. L. Wilson *Spenders* xiv. 150 She was dead in love with the nice long yellow-backs that I've piled up. **1928** M. Sadleir *Trollope: a Bibliogr.* 68 In 1868 *The Belton Estate* was issued at two shillings as a 'yellow back'. **1943** *Copper Camp* (Writers' Program, Montana) 37 They occasionally found yellowbacks tucked in their shoes. **1976** T. Eagleton *Crit. & Ideology* ii. 47 The 'yellowback' railway novel is available to a mass public. **1865** G. Macdonald *Alec Forbes* xxxiv, The speaker kindled with wrath at the presumption of the *yellow-beaks. **1868** [see BEJAN]. **1865** Gosse *Land & Sea* (1874) 321 Yonder floats by a flock of Parrots with a most abominable combination of harsh screams. It is the *Yellow-bill. **1824** W. Irving *T. Trav.* I. 251 A bed of daisies and *yellow-cups. **1818** Hogg *Brownie of Bodsbeck*, etc. II. 167 At length a *yellowfin rose... 'I wish your honour had hookit that ane.' **1825** Jamieson, *Yellowfin*, a species of trout, so named from the colour of its fins..; apparently the same with the *Finnoc* or *Finner*. **1845** Gosse *Ocean* iv. (1849) 206 The Yellow-fin (*Sparus synagris*, Linn.), which has its body marked with longitudinal bands of delicate pink and yellow alternately. **1888** Goode *Amer. Fishes* 111 About Cape Cod they [*sc.* squeteague] are called 'Drummers'; about Buzzard's Bay and in the vicinity the largest are known as 'Yellow-fins'. **1922** *Pacific Fisherman* Feb. 12/1 Each of these new species—bluefin tuna, yellowfin tuna and striped tuna—proved itself well adapted to the same canning method as the albacore. **1975** *Islander* (Victoria, B.C.) 7 Sept. 4/2 They [*sc.* whales] travel in schools in the eastern Pacific, followed by yellow-fin tuna which feed on their leavings. **1796** Nemnich *Polygl.-Lex.* 944 *Yellow fingers, *Strombus lambis*. *c* **1780** *Johnstone Hey & Yng. Caldwell* xxiv. in Child *Ballads* IV. 293 'Nut-brown was his hawk', they said, 'And *yellow-fit was his hound'. **1747** *Astley's New Gen. Coll. Voy.* IV. II. iv. 450/2 They being of the *yellow Hat, or Chinese party. **1931** C. Bell *Relig. Tibet* viii. 129 With the enthronement of the fifth Dalai Lama as sovereign over the whole country, the power of the Yellow Hats was greatly increased. **1962** H. E. Richardson *Tibet & its Hist.* ii. 40 The Dalai Lamas.. owed their appearance to the great religious teacher known as Tsong Khapa (1357–1417), the founder of a new sect, the Gelugpa, popularly called the Yellow Hats. **1978** C. Humphreys *Both Sides Circle* xx. 212 The famous monastery at Ghoom..belongs to the Gelug-pa or Yellow Hat sect of Tibetan Buddhism. **1712** Petiver in *Phil. Trans.* XXVII. 419 Narrow-leaved Cape *yellow Heads [*Elichrysum Africanum*, Ray]. **1832** J. Rennie *Butterfl. & Moths* 210 The Yellow Head ([*Porrectaria*] *flavi-frontella*).. the head tawny. **1873** *Trans. N.Z. Inst.* VI. 144 Yellowhead. Average weight of specimens, 1½ ounce. **1897** *Yearbk. U.S. Dept. Agric.* 351 In complaints made against the redwing the yellowhead is frequently included as equally guilty. **1966** *Encycl. N.Z.* I. 206/2 Still widely distributed in the deeper forests are..whitehead..and yellowhead. **1868** *Amer. Naturalist* May 123 [Bears] also dig up '*yellow-jackets', wasp's-nests, for the larvæ. **1897** HOWELLS *Landlord at Lion's Head* 381 He remembered stumbling.. into a nest of yellow-jackets. **1953, 1969** Yellow jacket [see NEMBIE]. **1974** M. C. GERALD *Pharmacol.* xi. 205 Short-acting barbiturates such as pentobarbital ('yellow jackets'). **1772** FORSTER in *Phil. Trans.* LXII. 410 This bird is called a *yellow leg at Albany fort. **1854** *Poultry Chron.* II. 129 A pen of Brahmas—one pea-comb, two single-combs, one white-legs, two yellow-legs. **1894** J. A. FRYE *Fables of Field & Staff* 109 The 'Yellow-Legs' are always great on dismounted duty. **1895** *Outing* (U.S.) XXVI. 70/2 The winter yellowlegs were less numerous. **1943** W. CHASE *Sourdough Pot* xix. 120 Numbers of these prisoners were marched down the main street in charge of a Mountie, or 'Yellow-leg', as they were called on account of the yellow strip running down the outside of their trouser leg. **1957** G. SHIRREFFS *Rio Bravo* (1972) i. 6 He glanced back at the rough country through which they had come, almost as though looking for the beefy figure of Francis Xavier Feeley, one of the best yellowlegs who had ever forked a McClellan. **1974** W. HUNT *North of 53* xix. 139 The 'yellow legs'—the Mounties—were not permissive in law enforcement. **1832** J. RENNIE *Butterfl. & Moths* 59 The *Yellow Line (*Orthosia flavilinea*)..Wings..brownish; first pair with a slanting, but very straight yellowish streak. **1869** E. NEWMAN *Brit. Moths* 365/2 The Yellow-Line Quaker (*Orthosia macilenta*). **1899** H. G. GRAHAM *Soc. Life Scot. 18th Cent.* xii. II. 196 These first year's students were popularly called '*yellow-nebs'. **1612** DRAYTON *Poly-olb.* xiii. 75 The *Yellow-pate, which though she hurt the blooming tree Yet scarce had any bird a finer pype than shee. **1783** LATHAM *Gen. Synopsis Birds* IV. 515 *Yellow-Poll. Rather less than the Pettichaps:.. This species is found in America,..but its chief residence is in Guiana. **1785** PENNANT *Arct. Zool.* II. 402 Yellow-poll Warbler... Inhabits Canada. **1730** MORTIMER in *Phil. Trans.* XXXVI. 433 *Parus uropygeo luteo*, the *yellow Rump. **1785** PENNANT *Arct. Zool.* II. 400 Yellow-rump Warbler. **1841** THACKERAY *Gt. Hoggarty Diam.* vii, 'Get some of that yellow-sealed wine, Tiggins,' says the captain. .. I must say I liked the *yellow-seal much better than aunt Hoggarty's Rosolio. **1846–50** A. WOOD *Class-bk. Bot.* 161 *L[epidium] campestre*..*Yellow Seed. **1785** PENNANT *Arct. Zool.* II. 468 *Yellow-shanks Snipe. With a slender black bill. **1835** AUDUBON *Ornith. Biog.* III. 573 The Yellowshank is much more abundant..to the westward of the Alleghany Mountains than along our Atlantic coast. **1832** J. RENNIE *Butterfl. & Moths* 128 The *Yellow Shell (*C[amptogramma] bilineata*). **1851** MAYNE REID *Rifle Rangers* xiii. (1853) 89, I was in hopes we'd have a brush with the *yellow-skins. **1904** *Contemp. Rev.* Aug. 289 Russia has ever regarded herself as the dear friend of the nations who are now contemptuously nick-named 'yellowskins'. **1832** J. RENNIE *Butterfl. & Moths* 24 The *Yellow-spot Unicorn Hawk (*Sphinx quinque Maculatus*). **1702** PETIVER *Gazophyl.* i. 6 *Avis Mary-Landica gutture luteo.* The Mary-Land *Yellow-Throat. **1865** *Atlantic Monthly* XV. 521, I miss in the woods..the Yellow Throat. **1949** V. S. REID *New Day* I. xxviii. 143 A.. yellowthroat warbler whistles back. **1977** *Blair & Ketchum's Country Jrnl.* May 43/1 The yellow-throats will reemerge on other days. **1846** WORCESTER, **Yellow-Top*, a species of grass, called also white-top. *Farm. Ency.* **1749**, etc. *Yellow underwing [see UNDERWING 2]. *a* **1941** V. WOOLF *Death of Moth* (1942) 9 The commonest yellow-underwing asleep in the shadow of the curtain. **1968** *Oxf. Bk. Insects* 72/1 Like the other Yellow Underwings..this species baffles its enemies by the way it shows its colours.

ˈyellow, *v.*[1] [f. YELLOW *a.*]

1. *intr.* To become yellow, turn yellow.

a **1050** *Liber Scintill.* xxviii. (1889) 105 Na beheald þu win þænne hit ȝeoluwað [L. *flauescit*]. **1821** CLARE *Vill. Minstr.* II. 157 Ash or maple 'neath thy colour yellows. **1851** MAYNE REID *Scalp Hunters* xxxviii, The peak [of the temple] is yellowing downward [in the sunlight]. **1868** *Jrnl. R. Agric. Soc.* Ser. II. IV. II. 425 In one part of the field the oats 'yellow off'. **1888** RIDER HAGGARD *Col. Quaritch* xxi, Their foliage yellowing to its fall, rose the giant oaks. **1902** CUTCLIFFE HYNE *Thompson's Progr.* vii. 184 When the wick yellowed out into flame.

2. *trans.* To make or render yellow; to impart a yellow colour to.

1598 SYLVESTER *Du Bartas* II. i. III. *Furies* 457 Her fiery poyson, yellowing all without. *c* **1600** SHAKS. *Sonn.* xvii, My papers (yellowed with their age). **1743** FRANCIS tr. *Hor., Odes* I. xxxi. 6 The swelling Grain, That yellows o'er Sardinia's Plain. **1805** WORDSW. *Prelude* v. 560 While the morning light Was yellowing the hill tops. **1863** GEO. ELIOT *Romola* v, The vellum is yellowed in these thirteen years. **1885** MEREDITH *Diana* iv, On that fine spring morning, when..cowslips yellowed the meadow-flats. **1907** J. A. HODGES *Elem. Photogr.* (ed. 6) 25 Some modern lenses.. become..yellowed by exposure to strong light.

b. *spec.* in pin-manufacture: see quot.

1839 URE *Dict. Arts* etc. 956 *Yellowing or cleaning the pins*, is effected by boiling them for half an hour in sour beer, wine lees, or solution of tartar.

c. *Naut. colloq.* To make a 'yellow admiral' of (see YELLOW *a.* 1 e). Also *transf.* to retire (a person).

1747 in Mahan *Types Naval Off.* (1902) 85 'I will not have Hawke "yellowed"' [was the royal fiat]. **1820** LADY GRANVILLE *Lett.* (1894) I. 171 He..gave a droll description of himself as old and fairly yellowed out of the service. **1867** [see YELLOWING *vbl. sb.*[1]].

†**yellow**, *v.*[2] *Obs. rare.* [app. extension of YELL *v.* on the analogy of BELL *v.*[4], BELLOW *v.* Cf. YELLOCH.] *intr.* To yelp; to bellow. Hence **yellowing** *vbl. sb.*[2] and *ppl. a.*[2]

1600 SHAKS. *Tit. A.* II. iii. 20 (Qo.) Whilst the babling Ecchoe mocks the hounds,..Let us sit downe and marke theyr yellowing [*Folios* yelping] noyse. **1629** MABBE tr. *Fonseca's Dev. Contemp.* 244 Roaring and yellowing like so many mad Bulls. **1652** LOVEDAY tr. *Calprenede's Cassandra* II. 124 Running about the Camp with horrible yellowings.

yellow-ammer: see YELLOW-HAMMER.

ˈyellow-ˌbellied, *a.* **1.** Applied to birds or animals having yellow underparts. Also in extended use (in quot. 1909 of an airship).

1709 T. ROBINSON *Nat. Hist. Westmld.* x. 60 The Male is grey, the Female yellow-bellied. **1783** LATHAM *Gen. Synopsis Birds* III. 42 Yellow-bellied Thrush..the under parts of the body of a pale rusty yellow. **1827** J. L. WILLIAMS *View W. Florida* 30 Black-head fly catcher... Yellow-bellied do. **1869** [see SCRUNCHING *vbl. sb.*]. **1908** E. J. BANFIELD *Confessions of Beachcomber* I. iii. 95 Yellow-bellied Fig-bird. **1909** KIPLING *Actions & Reactions* 140 Yellow-bellied ore-flats..punted down leisurely out of the north. **1936** *Discovery* Oct. 307/2 There are many varieties of flying phalanger, the yellow-bellied 25 inches in length with a bushy tail an inch longer than the body. **1942** R. PEATTIE *Friendly Mts.* 210 A sweet or black birch tree..had been tapped by a yellow-bellied sapsucker. **1971** *Islander* (Victoria, B.C.) 25 July 16/2 Most members of his species (the yellow-bellied marmot) weigh about 13 pounds at maturity.

2. *fig.* Cowardly, craven. Cf. YELLOW *a.* 2 b, YELLOW-BELLY 5. *slang* (orig. *U.S.*).

1924 P. MARKS *Plastic Age* ix. 75 Yellow-bellied quiters. **1930** [see *potato-mouthed a.* s.v. POTATO *sb.* 7]. **1943** J. MITCHELL *McSorley's Wonderful Saloon* (1946) I. 24 You yellow-bellied jerk. **1965** J. PORTER *Dover Two* xiv. 185 Anything to save his own skin, the yellow-bellied rat! **1971** [see MALT *sb.*[2]]. **1979** 'M. HEBDEN' *Pel & Faceless Corpse* vi. 58 I'm..a yellow-bellied, lily-livered coward.

ˈyellow-ˌbelly.

1. a. A name for a frog.

1825 *Houlston Tracts* I. No. 28. 4 The Frenchman's soupe-maigre and fricasseed yellow-bellies. **18..** *Nursery Rime*, Yellow-belly, yellow-belly, come and have a swim.

b. A native of the fens (in humorous allusion to a frog).

1787 GROSE *Provincial Gloss.* s.v. *Lincolnshire*, Yellow bellies. This is an appellation given to persons born in the Fens, who, it is jocularly said, have yellow bellies, like their eels. **1796** *Grose's Dict. Vulgar T.* (ed. 3), *Yellow Belly*, a native of the Fens of Lincolnshire: an allusion to the eels caught there. **1846** J. KEEGAN *Leg. & Poems* (1907) 362, I would rather dig my daughter's grave..than see her tied to Lanty Wolfe. or any other yellow belly of the County Wexford. **1847** HALLIWELL, *Yellow-belly*, a person born in the fens of Lincolnshire. *Linc.* **1982** *Times* 5 Oct. 4/5 The Lincolnshire 'yellowbellies' of south Humberside..for generations have entertained a healthy disregard for Yorkshire 'tykes' on the north bank of the Humber.

2. A kind of tortoise, or the tortoiseshell obtained from it.

1843 HOLTZAPFFEL *Turning* I. 127 *note*, The Yellow Belly, which plates are very thin and yellow. **1905** *Times* 15 Sept. 11/5 Tortoiseshell,..yellowbelly about 5*s.* dearer.

3. (See quots.) *derog.*

1842 *New Orleans Crescent* 16 Mar. (Extra) 1 God send that they bayonet every 'yellow belly' in the Mexican army. **1845** [see COPPERHEAD 3]. **1850** MAYNE REID *Rifle Rangers* I. ii. 12 I've a mighty puncheon, as the Frenchmen say, to hev a crack at them yeller-bellies. *Footn.* Yellow bellies—a name given by Western hunters and soldiers of the U.S.A. to the Mexicans. **1867** SMYTH *Sailor's Word-bk.*, *Yellow-belly*, a name given..occasionally to half-castes, &c. **1934** 'G. ORWELL' *Burmese Days* x. 155 They're Eurasians—sons of white fathers and native mothers. Yellow-bellies is our friendly nickname for them. **1966** [see *slant-eye(s)* s.v. SLANT *a.* 3].

4. Name for various fishes having the under parts yellow (see quots.).

1890 *Science* 28 Feb. 141/2 A sole (*Peltorhamphus novæ-zealandiæ*) and a sole-like flounder (*Rhombosolea leporina*), commonly known as 'yellow-belly', are also frequently caught. **1896** JORDAN & EVERMANN *Fishes N. Amer.* 1001 *Lepomis Auritus*... Yellow Belly; Redbreast Bream. **1898** MORRIS *Austral Eng.*, *Yellow-belly*. In New South Wales, the name is given to a fresh-water fish, *Ctenolates auratus*; called also Golden-Perch... In Dunedin especially, and New Zealand generally, it is a large flounder, also called Lemon-Sole [*Ammotretis guntheri*]. **1899** *Cumbld. Gloss.*, *Yalla belly*, a young salmon-trout returning from the sea.

5. A coward. Cf. YELLOW *a.* 2 b, YELLOW-BELLIED *a.* 2. *slang* (orig. *U.S.*).

1930 J. LAIT *Put on Spot* 215 Yellow-belly. Coward. **1942** BERREY & VAN DEN BARK *Amer. Thes. Slang* §404/3 *Coward* ..yellow-back, -belly or guts. **1952** H. INNES *Campbell's Kingdom* III. ii. 271 What are you?.. A bunch of yellow-bellies to be fooled into hiding away. **1952** J. STEINBECK *East of Eden* 517 I'm a cowardly yellow-belly. **1965** *Austral. Women's Weekly* 20 Jan. 50/5 'Yellowbelly baby... Spoiled-cat crybaby,' Steve yelled at him. **1969** K. M. WELLS *Owl Pen Reader* II. 209 Grandad's knees shook, and he wasn't no yellow-belly either. **1972** 'H. HOWARD' *Nice Day for Funeral* ix. 128 She'd call me every kind of yellow belly if I suggested throwing in my hand.

yellow-bird (ˈjɛləʊbɜːd). Name for several birds having yellow plumage; now *esp.* the North American goldfinch or thistle-bird, *Chrysomitris* (*Spinus, Carduelis*) *tristis*, and the North American summer warbler (distinctively called ***summer yellowbird***), *Dendrœca æstiva*.

a **1705** RAY *Syn. Avium* (1713) 80 *Regulus non cristatus Aldrov[andi]*... The small Yellow-Bird. **1738** ALBIN *Nat. Hist. Birds* III. 19 The yellow Bird, from Bengall... This Bird was about the bigness of a Fieldfare. **1792** W. BARTRAM *Trav. N. & S. Carolina* 290 *P[arus] luteus*; the summer yellow bird. **1860** S. F. BAIRD, etc. *Birds N. Amer.* 421 *Chrysomitris Tristis.* Yellow Bird; Thistle Bird. **1884** E. P. ROE in *Harper's Mag.* Mar. 617/2 The American gold-finch, or yellow-bird. **1896** NEWTON *Dict. Birds* 1056 Yellowbird is the North-American Siskin..and perhaps more than one of the *Mniotiltidæ*. **1898** *Atlantic Monthly* LXXXII. 495/2 The summer yellow-bird, which pushes its hardy spring flight beyond the Arctic circle.

ˈyellow-ˌbottle.

1. [cf. BLUEBOTTLE 1, BOTTLE *sb.*[4]] The marigold (*obs.*); also the corn-marigold (*dial.*).

c **1450** *Alphita* (Anecd. Oxon.) 112 *Menelaca*, gall. gounde, anglice yellebotel [*v.r.* yelebothel]. **1847** HALLIWELL, *Yellow-bottle*, corn marigold. *Kent.*

2. *nonce-use* [after BLUEBOTTLE 3]. (See quot.)

1898 MORRIS *Austral Eng.*, *Korrumburra*, aboriginal name for the common blow-fly, which in Australia is a yellow-bottle, not a blue-bottle.

ˈyellow-boy. *slang. Obs.* exc. *Hist.* (Also as two words.) A gold coin; a guinea or sovereign.

1662 J. WILSON *Cheats* I. i, Do they cry Chink in thy Pocket?—How many yellow Boyes (Rogue) How many yellow Boyes? **1663** DRYDEN *Wild Gallant* III. i, If one could see the yellow boyes peeping underneath the brims now. **1700** T. BROWN tr. *Fresny's Amusem.* 129, I have..in my Pocket brave Yellow-Boys, to pay for a Coat of Arms. **1712** ARBUTHNOT *John Bull* I. vi, Yellow-boys to fee counsel, hire witnesses, and bribe juries. **1838** JAS. GRANT *Sk. Lond.* 182 If you don't fork out the yellow boys (sovereigns) presently, I'll send a ball through your carcass. **1840** DICKENS *Old C. Shop* xlii, The delight of picking up the money—the bright, shining yellow-boys. **1883** 'MARK TWAIN' *Life on Miss.* xxxvi. 389 A round ten thousand dollars in yellow-boys. **1898** A. M. BINSTEAD *Pink 'Un & Pelican* x. 219 Gazing contemptuously at the yellow-boy, and then at its donor, she cried: 'An' since when has a "new hat" ceased to be a guinea?' **1957** A. BRYANT in J. B. Booth *Palmy Days* p. xi, He reconstructs a vanished world: the last age of horses and 'yellow boys'.

ˈyellowcake. Also **yellow cake.** [f. YELLOW *a.* + CAKE *sb.*] An oxide of uranium (and other elements) obtained as a yellow precipitate in the processing of uranium ores.

1950 *Mining Congr. Jrnl.* Oct. 30/2 Through pH adjustment by regulated additions of sulphuric acid virtually all of the uranium is precipitated as 'yellowcake', an artificial carnotite. **1955** KIRK & OTHMER *Encycl. Chem. Technol.* XIV. 439 If the uranium and vanadium are present in the carbonate leach liquors in the proper stoichiometric ratio, then neutralization by acid leads to the very complete precipitation of sodium uranyl vanadate, the 'yellow cake' of Colorado Plateau extractive metallurgy. **1971** *Daily Colonist* (Victoria, B.C.) 11 June 7/7 A West German..group has undertaken to find a market for 4 million pounds of uranium oxide (yellow cake) annually. **1977** *Telegraph* (Brisbane) 5 Sept. 5/1 Police and 200 anti-uranium demonstrators traded kicks and punches, when a fresh consignment of yellowcake reached the White Bay container terminal today. **1981** T. BARLING *Bikini Red North* i. 34 Will anything positive be done to stop the French selling yellowcake or hardware on the open market?

yellow dog. *U.S.* **1.** A mongrel dog of a yellowish colour.

c **1770** T. FAIRFAX *Compl. Sportsman* 97 Yellow dogs, are those which have red hairs, inclining to brown. **1840** *Daily Pennant* (St. Louis) Apr. 20 (Thornton *Amer. Gloss.*) One of those interesting animals, a yellow dog, with a bullet-hole through his breast. **1860** O. W. HOLMES *Elsie V.* iii, A 'yallah dog' is a large canine brute, of a dingy old-flannel colour, of no particular breed except his own. **1873** M. HOLLEY *My Opinions* 237 If I was a yeller dog, she couldn't seem to look down on me any more, and treat me any worse. **1895** BRET HARTE *Clarence* III. iii, In Illinois we wouldn't hang a yellow dog on that evidence.

2. *fig.* **a.** A person or thing of no account or of a low type.

1881 E. W. NYE *Bill Nye & Boomerang* 166 The presiding officer had lost control, and a surging crowd of yellow dogs had the floor. **1903** *Everybody's Mag.* Oct. 562 In a cut-rate combination you are lucky if you get what you pay for. If there are five magazines in the combination, two of them are good. The rest are 'yellow-dogs'. **1924** A. J. SMALL *Frozen Gold* i. 44 Understand, I won't allow no yellow dog of a Siwash to step over me. **1975** *New Yorker* 8 Dec. 126/2 Calling someone a yellow dog would not imply that the person so called was actually yellow and wagged his tail. It is just the sort of cultural misunderstanding that student-exchange programs were once expected to clear up.

b. *attrib.*; applied *spec.* to organizations, etc., opposed to trade unionism.

1894 KIPLING *Day's Work* (1898) 71 America's paved with the kind er horse you are—jist plain yaller-dog horse —waitin' ter be whipped inter shape. **1902** —— *Just So Stories* 92 Old Man Kangaroo is being rude to Yellow-Dog Dingo. Yellow-Dog Dingo has been trying to catch Kangaroo all across Australia. **1902** *Mine Workers' Jrnl.* July 1 A yellow dog lease. **1903** *Outlook* 15 Aug. 931/2 In preference to a Tammany 'yellow dog' ticket his organization would support the Fusion candidate. **1920** *Motorman & Conductor* Oct. 34 A yellow dog contract. **1930** *Sun* (Baltimore) 6 May 12/2 The 'yellow dog' contract, requiring men to barter away their right to organize as the price of a job. **1956** *Mag. of Fantasy & Sci. Fiction* Oct. 32/2 It was the latest form of the yellow-dog clause, one in which the employee agrees to refrain from engaging in a competing occupation for five years by letting his former employers pay him cash to option his services on a first-refusal basis. **1976** *Amer. N. & Q.* XIV. 136/1 The committee scrutinized the records and books of the four major New York companies uncovering the existence of the so-called 'yellow dog funds'.

yellowed (ˈjɛləʊd), *ppl. a.* [f. YELLOW *a.* or *v.*[1] + -ED.] Made yellow.

a **1100** *Aldhelm Gloss.* I. 108 (Napier 4/2) *Crocata*, þa ȝeȝeolewedan. **1824** *Examiner* 307/1 A sun-yellowed river softly flows. **1851** ROBERTSON in S. A. Brooke *Life & Lett.* (1865) II. 73 The peculiar watery shine cast on the yellowed leaves. **1906** R. C. BAYLEY *Compl. Photogr.* 114 A yellowed lens.

yellow fever.

1. A dangerous infectious febrile disease of hot climates, characterized by vomiting, constipation, fatty degeneration of the liver, jaundice, etc.

1748 J. Lining in *Ess. Phys. & Lit.* (1756) II. 370 That fever, which continues two or three days, and terminates without any critical discharge,..and which is soon succeeded with an icteritious colour in the white of the eyes and the skin, vomiting, hæmorrhages, &c...is called in America, the yellow fever. **1758** *Let. to Mayor of* —— 47 Seamen seized by the Yellow Fever in the West Indies. **1825** Southey *Let. to John May* 16 Mar. in *Life* (1849) I. 156 He had had the yellow fever three times, and...still bore strong vestiges of it in his complexion. **1877** F. T. Roberts *Handbk. Med.* (ed. 3) I. 204 Most authorities hold that true yellow-fever is of the continued type. **1898** P. Manson *Trop. Diseases* vii. 138 Inoculations by the bites of mosquitoes previously fed on yellow fever patients. **1898** *Jrnl. Sch. Geog.* (U.S.) Oct. 300 When a sufficient altitude is reached, the yellow fever zone is left behind.

2. In various allusive uses, chiefly humorous.

1854 *Poultry Chron.* I. 582 After this we got the yellow fever, and the clear buff and silver cinnamon fever. We did not care for a thing except speckless colour. *c* **1856** *Denham Tracts* (1892) I. 336 When the 'Runch' is in bloom the appearance is called 'the Yellow Fever'. **1867** Smyth *Sailor's Word-bk.*, *Yellow fever*, a cant term for drunkenness at Greenwich Hospital; the sailors when punished wearing a parti-coloured coat, in which yellow predominates. **1884** *Illustr. Sydney News* 26 Aug. 5/3 He said I had the yellow fever [*i.e.* for gold], and was to go to the diggings to get cured.

ˈyellow-fish. a. Name for several fishes with yellow coloration; now *esp.* a species of rock-trout, *Pleurogrammus* (*Hexagrammus*) *monopterygius*, of the coast of Alaska, olive on the back and yellowish below.

1734 Mortimer in *Phil. Trans.* XXXVIII. 317 *Turdus cauda convexa.* The Yellow-Fish. *a* **1749** Catesby *Nat. Hist. Carolina*, etc. (1754) II. 10 The Yellow Fish. Some of these Fish were a foot in length: this had small thin scales of a reddish yellow colour. **1796** Nemnich *Polygl.-Lex.* 944 Yellow fish, *Labrus fulvus.* **1888** Goode *Amer. Fishes* 272 The 'Yellow-fish', 'Striped Fish', or 'Atka Mackerel', *Pleurogrammus monopterygius.*

b. In South Africa, one of several freshwater fishes of the genus *Barbus.*

1834 A. Smith *Diary* 9 Dec. (1939) I. 168 Fish in the pools of this river of two kinds, the flat head and the bearded yellow fish. **1896** H. A. Bryden *Tales S. Afr.* i. 18 The pouch contained..a 'yellow fish', a barbel-like fish of a pound and a half. **1912** J. Stevenson-Hamilton *Animal Life Afr.* xix. 334 The yellow fish..is the commonest fish of South Africa. **1952** [see kurper]. **1975** *Stand. Encycl. S. Afr.* XI. 563/1 The yellow-fishes..are popular angling fishes, ranging from one kg to over 14 kg in weight.

yellow-haired (-hɛəd: stress variable), *a.* Having yellow (flaxen, auburn, or golden) hair. Also *fig.*

1580 Hollyband *Treas. Fr. Tong*, *Blond*, yellow haired. **1690** *Lond. Gaz.* No. 2569/4 Edmond Barber, aged about 30, Yellow Hair'd. **1721** Ramsay *Content* 208 A tall yellow-hair'd young pensive swain. **1812** Byron *Ch. Har.* II. lxxii, Let the yellow-hair'd Giaours view his horsetail with dread. **1842** Prichard *Nat. Hist. Man* 196 The Britons are taller than the Gauls, and less yellow-haired. **1887** Hall Caine *Son of Hagar* I. ii, The yellow-haired elderly gentleman with the perpetual smile. **1917** D. H. Lawrence *Look! We have come Through!* 155 Scyllas and yellow-haired hellebore, jonquils, dim anemones.

yellow-ham. *Obs.* exc. *dial.* (yellow an-). = next, q.v.

1544 Turner *Avium Præcip.* F4, Χλώρευς, luteus siue lutea, Anglicè a yelow ham, a yowlryng. Germanicè *eyn geelgorst.* **1657** C. Beck *Univ. Char.* M4b, The yellow-ham bird. **1905** *Eng. Dial. Dict.*, *Yellow an-bird*, the yellow-ammer [Kent].

ˈyellow-ˌhammer, -ˈammer. Forms: 6 **yelambre**, 7 **yelamber, yellow-hamer**, 7, 9 *dial.* **-amber**, 9 **-ammer**, *dial.* **-ommer, -omber, -homber**, 6– **yellow-hammer.** [In the earliest recorded form, *yelambre*, app. representing OE. **ȝeolo-amore* = *ȝeolo* yellow + *amore* 'scorellus' (unidentified), corresp. to OHG. *amero* (MHG. *amer*, G. *ammer*), of which there are various cognate or derivative forms, viz. OE. *omer*, *emer*, *emaer*, 'scorellus', OHG. *amerinc*, MHG. *gold(en)emer*, G. *emmerling*, †*emmering*, *emmeritze*, †*embritze* (whence mod.L. *emberiza*), LG. *geelemerken* (dim., with *geel* 'yellow' prefixed). Besides these forms there is a type represented by OE. *clodhamer* (coupled with *feldeware*) 'scorellus', of doubtful formation (? corruption of **goldhamer*) and MHG. *hamere*, *golthamere* 'amarellus'. The origin and identity of *hamer*, *-ere* are uncertain; but connexion with or assimilation to OE. *-hama*, OHG. *-hamo* covering, skin, feathers (see hame¹) seems probable, and the form yellow-ham, which may go back to an OE. type **ȝeolo-hama* the yellow-feathered bird, gives support to the hypothesis.

Both forms *-hammer* and *-ammer* are historically justifiable; Yarrell's proposed rejection of *-hammer* (see *British Birds*, 1843, I. 446) is based on insufficient evidence.

The bird has many local names into which the word *yellow* or *gold* enters, viz. yowlring (yorling), yoldring, yowley, *yellow bunting*, *yellow yite*, *gold spink*, *gold finch.* Cf. (in addition to the names given above) MLG. *gelegorsse*, *-gersse*, Du. *geelgors*, LG. *gelgans*, *-gôs*, G. *gelbling*, *gelbammer*, *goldfink*, MHG. *gollhans*, *gol(l)ammer*, G. dial. *golmer*, Sw. *gulsparf*, dial. *golspink*, Norw. dial. *gulspikke*, *gulsporv*, *gulskur*, Du. *guulspurv.*]

1. A species of bunting, *Emberiza citrinella*, common in Britain and Europe generally, having the head, throat, and under parts of a bright yellow.

1556 Withals *Dict.* (1562) 5/2 A yelambre, *luteus*, *vel lutea.* **1587** Harrison *England* III. ii. 223/2 in *Holinshed*, Washtailes, cheriecrackers, yellowhamers, felfares. **1598** Florio, *Spaiarda*, a birde called a yellow hammer, or yowlring. **1656** W. Du Gard tr. *Comenius' Gate Lat. Unl.* 43 The songsters, living on seeds; the Yelamber of Poppie; the Linnet, of flax. **1674** Ray *Coll. Words*, *Engl. Birds* 88 The Yellow-hammer, or amber, *Emberiza flava*, Gesn. **1763** *Ann. Reg.*, *Chron.* 59 Contents of a pye lately made at Lowther-hall, in Westmoreland,..forty-six yellow-hammers. **1789** Mrs. Piozzi *Journ. France* II. 377 Flights of yellow-hammers..enliven the fields. **1855** Kingsley *Westw. Ho!* xxx, These same beggarly croakers, that be only fit to be turned into yellow-hammers...and sit on a tor all day, and cry 'Very little bit of bread, and no chee-e-ese!' **1898** F. C. Gould in *Westm. Gaz.* 13 Apr. 2/1 Chaffinches and yellow-ammers give flashes of colour as they pass the glades.

b. *U.S.* The golden-winged woodpecker, *Colaptes auratus.*

Also locally in England, the skylark, the yellow wagtail, and the chaffinch.

1857 Thoreau *Maine W.* (1894) 31 A 'yellow-hammer', as they called the pigeon-woodpecker. **1874** Baird, Brewer, & Ridgway *N. Amer. Birds* II. 581 This bird [sc. *Colaptes Mexicanus*], in some parts of California, is known as the Yellow-Hammer, a name given in some parts of New England to the *Colaptes auratus.*

†**2.** *fig.* Applied in contempt to a person, esp. a jealous husband (cf. yellow *a.* 2). *Obs.*

1602 Middleton *Blurt, Master-Constable* III. i. D3b, Heere's a Yellow-hammer flew to me with thy water, and I cast it, and finde, that his Mistris being giuen to this newe falling-sicknesse, will cure thee. **1605** *Tryall Chev.* II. i, Bowyer a Captayne? a Capon,..a red beard Sprat, a Yellow-hammer, a bow case. **1620** Middleton & Rowley *Courtly Masque* D2, Much of the complexion Of high Shroue-Tuesday Batter, yallow-hammer. **1634** ?Rowley *Noble Soldier* II. i, You yellow hammer.

†**3.** A gold coin. *Obs. slang.*

1626 Middleton *Mayor Quinb.* II. i, *Sym...* Now by this light a nest of Yellow Hammers!.. Ile undertake, Sir, you shall have All the skins in our Parish at this price. **1633** Shirley *Bird in a Cage* II. i, Is that he that has gold enough? would I had some of his yellow hammers.

4. A nickname for a charity boy in yellow breeches.

1861 *City Press* May, In Worrall's school, founded in 1689, for poor boys born in Cripplegate, the coat is still red; the orange breeches, shoes, and hose of orange, which secured the boys the *sobriquet* of 'yellow hammers' have been discontinued.

ˈyellowing, *vbl. sb.*¹ [f. yellow *v.*¹ + -ing¹.] The action of imparting a yellow colour.

1611 Cotgr., *Iaulnissure*,..a yellowing, or making yellow. **1622** T. Stoughton *Chr. Sacrif.* xii. 166 Thrift..is pleaded for this yellowing of linnen as the which being so yellowed needeth not so much washing. **1858** Simmonds *Dict. Trade*, *Yellowing*, a manufacturing term for cleaning pins. **1859** A. Smith in *Macm. Mag.* I. 125 The slow yellowing of wheaten plains. **1867** Smyth *Sailor's Word-bk.*, *Yellowing*, the passing over of captains at a flag promotion. **1894** *Brit. Jrnl. Photog.* XLI. 25 There would be no yellowing if the paper was good.

So **ˈyellowing** *ppl. a.*, turning yellow, becoming yellow. Also *fig.*

1757 Dyer *Fleece* IV. 576 The op'ning vallies, and the yellowing plains. **1840** Browning *Sordello* I. 452 The noisy flock of thievish birds at work Among the yellowing vineyards. **1842** Tennyson *Launcelot & Guinev.* ii, In curves the yellowing river ran. **1859** Gullick & Timbs *Painting* 208 The yellowing tendency of oils on blue. **1908** S. E. White *Riverman* viii, The old piano with the yellowing keys. **1961** E. Williams *George* xxi. 339 Divvers—..a routine side-exam based on the yellowing idea that an Oxford graduate must have a solid religious training. **1977** *Guardian Weekly* 10 July 17/4 All that is left is a batch of yellowing declarations of good intentions.

yellowing *vbl. sb.*²: see yellow *v.*²

yellowish (ˈjɛləʊɪʃ), *a.* Forms: see yellow *a.* [f. yellow *a.* + -ish¹.] Somewhat yellow; of a colour inclining or approaching to yellow; having a tinge of yellow.

1379 *Glouc. Cath. MS.* 19 No. I. i. iv. lf. 11 It ys evirmare whitytssh or ȝolowyssh. **1398** Trevisa *Barth. De P.R.* XIII. xxi. (Bodl. MS.), Nowe he [*sc.* the sea] is whitissche and ȝelowissche now white & clere. **1576** Turberv. *Venerie* 184 The Badgerdwhelpes haue theyr nose, their throte and their eares yellowyshe. **1622** Peacham *Compl. Gentl.* xii. 111 Linseede oyle will turne yeallowish. **1781** Pennant *Hist. Quadrup.* I. 188 Yellowish monkey with a black face. **1823** Scott *Quentin D.* Introd., His clean silk stockings, washed till their tint had become yellowish. **1884** A. Lang in *Century Mag.* Jan. 323/1 The London houses of dirty, yellowish brick.

b. Qualifying adjs. or sbs. of colour.

1615 G. Sandys *Trav.* 68 They paint their nailes with a yellowish red. **1688** *Lond. Gaz.* No. 2411/4 A yellowish bay Stone-horse. **1752** Hill *Hist. Anim.* 499 The yellowish-grey Fringilla. **1816** Stephens in Shaw *Gen. Zool.* IX. II. 310 Yellowish-green Grosbeak. **1843** Portlock *Geol.* 214 Miemite of a rich yellowish-green. **1882** *Garden* 12 Aug. 145/3 Lovely yellow or yellowish scarlet tints.

c. *Comb.*

1693 Moxon *Mech. Exerc.* (1703) 238 A yellowish coloured fat Earth. **1725** *Bradley's Fam. Dict.* s.v. *Goose*, A goose..if yellowish footed and bill'd, [is] young. **1840** G. V. Ellis *Anat.* 41 A thin, yellowish-looking band.

Hence †**ˈyellowish** *v.*, to turn yellowish; **ˈyellowishness**, yellowish colour or tinge.

1590 Barrough *Meth. Phisick* III. xxvi. (1639) 146 His tongue is *yellowished. **1547** Boorde *Brev. Health* lxxiii, An uryne that is yelow lyke the *yelowyshenes of an horne of a lanterne that is bryght. **1657** W. Rand tr. *Gassendi's Life Peiresc* I. 196 A certain dark and obscure yellowishness [in a picture]. **1663** Boyle *Exp. Hist. Colours* III. xxviii, Bruis'd Madder..being drench'd with the like Alcalizate Solution, exchang'd..its Yellowishness for a Redness. **1941** E. R. Eddison *Fish Dinner* xi. 184 The cloud-bank was indigo against that yellowishness of the sky.

yellowly (ˈjɛləʊlɪ), *adv.* [f. as yellowish *a.* + -ly².] With a yellow colour or light.

1611 Cotgr., *Iaulnement*, yellowly. **1796** W. Taylor in *Monthly Mag.* I. 404 Whether thy fair locks Yellowly curl in the clouds of the morning, or red in the West wave Quivering dip. **1833** Tennyson *Hesperides* iv, When the fullfaced sunset yellowly Stays on the flowering arch of the bough. **1886** Hardy *Mayor Casterbr.* xiii, The evening sun seemed to shine more yellowly. **1932** W. Faulkner *Light in August* xiv. 314 He saw before daylight a lamp come yellowly alive in the kitchen. **1958** I. Fleming *Dr. No* vi. 78 The centipede was whipping from side to side in its agony. .. Bond hit it again. It burst open, yellowly. **1968** P. Dickinson *Skin Deep* ix. 165 The home-made candles burnt yellowly. **1978** H. Wouk *War & Remembrance* x. 100 The lights flickered yellowly on.

yellowness (ˈjɛləʊnɪs). Forms: see yellow *a.* [f. as prec. + -ness.]

1. The quality or state of being yellow; yellow colour.

1398 Trevisa *Barth. De P.R.* v. vi. (Bodl. MS.), Aristotel seith ȝelownes of yȝen is meuynge of feblenes. *a* **1400** Chaucer *Purse* 11 That I..may..see your colour lyke the sonne bryght That of yelownesse hadde neuere pere. *c* **1460** *Promp Parv.* 548 Ȝelhewnesse, *glavcedo.* *c* **1475** *Partenay* 3887 Adieu, my lady, with heres yowlownesse! *a* **1586** Sidney *Arcadia* IV. Wks. 1724 II. 739 A dark yellowness dying his Skin. **1663** Dryden *Rival Ladies* III. i, Like the Sun (ev'n while Eclips'd) she casts A Yellowness upon all other Faces. **1765** Delaval in *Phil. Trans.* LV. 17 *note m*, The Hyacinth is a stone..which is red with a certain yellowness. **1844** Kinglake *Eothen* viii, Doctors will tell you that the drinking of milk gives yellowness to the complexion. **1889** *Chamb. Jrnl.* 30 Nov. 760/1 There is a solidity and yellowness about Jupiter's light.

†**2.** *fig.* Jealousy: see yellow *a.* 2. *Obs.*

1598 Shaks. *Merry W.* I. iii. 111, I will incense Ford to deale with poyson: I will possesse him with yallownesse. **1621** Burton *Anat. Mel.* III. iii. I. ii. (1651) 606 The undiscreet carriage of some..gallant..may..if he be inclined to yellowness, colour him quite.

ˈyellowplush. Plush of a yellow colour, as worn by footmen; hence *transf.* as a humorous appellation for a footman.

[**1837** Thackeray (*title*) The Yellowplush Correspondence.] **1841** —— *Gt. Hoggarty Diam.* ii, A great powdered fellow in yellowplush breeches. **1842** *Punch* III. 133 He fetched the dishes, drew the corks and performed all the duties of His Majesty's yellowplush.

yellow-rattle: see rattle *sb.*¹ 3 a.

ˈyellow-root. (Also as two words.) Name for two N. American ranunculaceous plants, the one a herb, *Hydrastis canadensis*, of Canada and Northern U.S. (***Canadian yellow-root***, *goldenseal*, or *yellow puccoon*), the other a sub-shrub, *Xanthorrhiza apiifolia*, of Southern U.S. (***shrub yellow-root***), or for their roots, which yield yellow dyes, and are used in medicine as tonics.

1796 Nemnich *Polygl.-Lex.* 944 Yellow root, *Hydrastis canadensis.* **1814** Pursh *Plants N. Amer.* Ind. 712 Yellow Root, *Zantorrhiza.* **1856** A. Gray *Man. Bot.* 13 *Zanthorhiza.* Shrub Yellow-root. **1866** *Treas. Bot.* 605 Yellow Puccoon, Orange root, or Canadian Yellow root. **1876** Harley *Mat. Med.* (ed. 6) 781 Yellow Root is an article of the United States Pharmacopœia.

yellows (ˈjɛləʊz). [Plural of yellow *sb.*, used in specific senses.]

I. 1. Jaundice, chiefly in horses and cattle.

1561 *Norwich Depos.* (1905) 65 The horse had a disease running through him which was called the yellows. **1585** Higins *Junius' Nomencl.* 454/1 *Arquatus*,..that hath the yellowes, or the iaunders. **1596** Shaks. *Tam. Shr.* III. ii. 54 His horse..raied with the Yellowes. **1607** *Merry Devil Edmonton* v. ii. 16 If I doe not indite him at the next assises for Burglary, let me die of the yellowes. **1616** Surfl. & Markh. *Country Farm* 147 For a Horse that is troubled with the Yellowes, you shall first let him bloud. **1733** W. Ellis *Chiltern & Vale Farm.* 220 This is apt to gripe them, and bring on the Yellows. **1799** A. Young *Agric. Linc.* 377 They lose many lambs of the yellows, from August to the middle of September. **1805** R. W. Dickson *Pract. Agric.* II. 1133 The Yellows, which is a disease to which cows are very subject. **1871** Napheys *Prev. & Cure Dis.* III. ix. 995 Jaundice is also known under the name of the yellows.

†**2.** *fig.* Jealousy: see yellow *a.* 2. *Obs.*

1601 B. Jonson *Ev. Man in Hum.* (Qo.) V. i, You haue a spice of the yealous yet both of you, (in your hose I meane). **1638** Ford *Fancies* II. ii, *Troy.* Yet is this Batchelor miracle not free From the epidemical head-ach. *Liv.* The Yellowes. *Troy.* Huge jealous fits. **1638** Brathwait *Barnabees Jrnl.* Fij, Alwayes frolick, free from yellows.

3. a. A disease of wheat: see quots. 1771, 1815.

b. A disease of peach-trees, in which many

sterile shoots are produced and the leaves turn yellow (= *peach-yellows*: see PEACH *sb.*[1] 6).

1771 GULLET in *Phil. Trans.* LXII. 350 What the farmers call the yellows in wheat,.. occasioned by a small yellow fly with blue wings, about the size of a gnat. **1808** [see *peach yellows* s.v. PEACH *sb.*[1] 6]. **1815** *Farmer's Mag.* 385 The yellows in wheat is a small grub that eats the corn out of the ear before it is ripe. **1848** LOWELL *Biglow P.* I. 111 'Fore they think on 't they will sprout (Like a peach thet's got the yellers), With the meanness bustin' out. **1897** L. H. BAILEY *Fruit-growing* 45 In New York the failure [of peach-growing] is often attributed to yellows.

c. A similar virus or deficiency disease in other plants.

1822 S. DEANE *New-England Farmer* (ed. 3) 318/2 Peach trees are subject to a disease called the 'Yellows', of which we have seen no particular description. **1926** *Amer. Jrnl. Bot.* XIII. 647 Asters affected with yellows never show mottling. **1933** *Times Lit. Suppl.* 16 Mar. 187/2 A disease of the tea-bush known as 'yellows' is due to a deficiency of sulphur in the soil. **1957** *New Scientist* 8 Aug. 31/3 At least 2,800 tons of beet were lost from yellows infection.. in the Shotley peninsula.

II. 4. Name for certain plants yielding a yellow dye, as *Genista tinctoria* and *Reseda Luteola*; also *dial.* for certain plants with yellow flowers, as the wild mustard, *Sinapis arvensis*, and the wild cabbage, *Brassica campestris*.

1601 HOLLAND *Pliny* XXXIII. v. II. 471 An hearb called likewise Lutea. *marg.*, Some take it to be weld or yellows. **1638** FORD *Fancies* V. ii, Burnish my forehead with the juyce of yellowes. **1790** W. MARSHALL *Rural Econ. Midl. Co.* (1796) II. Gloss. (E.D.S.), Yellows, dyers' broom.

5. A miner's term for yellow copper ore occurring in tin mines.

1859 R. HUNT *Guide Mus. Pract. Geol.* (ed. 2) 122 Several tin mines were abandoned when the miners came to the 'yellows'; this was the yellow copper ore, and their saying was that the 'yellows cut out the tin'.

yellowtail ('jɛləʊteɪl), *sb.* (*a.*) A name (or epithet = *yellow-tailed*) for various animals with yellow tails or yellow coloration on the tail.

†**1.** A kind of earthworm: cf. GILT-TAIL. *Obs.*

1608 TOPSELL *Serpents* 307 Othersome againe are yellow onely about the tayle: Whereuppon they haue purchased the name of Yellow-tayles. **1688** HOLME *Armoury* II. 210/2 The Ascarides, or lesser Earth-worm,.. Some are yellow, called Yellow-Tails, or Golden Tails.

2. Name for various fishes, chiefly of N. America, Australia, and New Zealand, as various species of *Seriola*, *Caranx*, and *Latris*, and many others.

1709 *Dampier's Voy.* III. II. 143 The Sea and Rivers [New Guinea] have plenty of Fish;.. we catch'd but few, and these were Cavallies, Yellow-tails and Whip-rays. **1796** NEMNICH *Polygl.-Lex.* 944 Yellow tail, (*a*) *Perca punctata*. (*b*) *Scomber*. **1838** *Encycl. Metrop.* (1845) XXIV. 370/2 *S*[*ciæna*] *Xanthurus*;.. Yellow-tailed Smooth-mouth... Found on the Carolina coast, where it is called the Yellow-tail. **1847** J. C. ROSS *Voy. Antarctic Reg.* II. 117 A kind of mackarel, called yellow tail, and sometimes cavallo. **1867** SMYTH *Sailor's Word-bk.*, *Yellow-tail*, a well-known tropical fish often in company with whip-rays; it is about 4 feet long, with a great head, large eyes, and many fins. *Leiostomas*. **1875** MELLISS *St. Helena* 106 *Seriola lalandii*,.. The Yellow Tail of St. Helena is obtained also in the Atlantic, at Japan and Australia. **1888** *Rep. U.S. Comm. Fish* (1892) XVI. 45 The yellow-tail rockfish (*S*[*ebastichthys*] *flavidus*). **1888** GOODE *Amer. Fishes* 99 The 'Sailor's Choice' [*Lagodon rhomboides*].. bears several other names,.. being known.. in the Indian River region as the.. 'Scup', and 'Yellow-tail'. *Ibid.* 131 The Yellow Tail, *Bairdiella chrysura*, known as 'Silver Perch' on the coast of New Jersey. *Ibid.* 386 In North Carolina.. the names 'Yellow-tail' and 'Yellow-tail Shad' [for the Menhaden] are occasionally heard. **1897** BEATRICE HARRADEN in *Blackw. Mag.* Feb. 179 The yellow-tail is rather like a solid beefsteak of coarse fibre. **1898** MORRIS *Austral Eng.*

3. (Also *yellow-tail warbler*.) The female or young male of the American Redstart.

1775 DALRYMPLE in *Phil. Trans.* (1779) LXVIII. 410 Many yellow tails. **1785** PENNANT *Arct. Zool.* II. 406 Yellow-tail Warbler. With an ash-colored crown:.. Taken.. off Hispaniola, at sea.

4. Collectors' name for a species of moth, also called *gold-tail* (see GOLD[1] 10).

1749 B. WILKES *Eng. Moths*, etc. 28 The Yellow-tail Moth.. may be found sticking against the Barks of the Trees in Parks. **1815** KIRBY & SP. *Entomol.* ii. (1818) I. 30 The yellow-tail moth (*Bombyx chrysorhœa*, F.).

yellow-wood ('jɛləʊwʊd). Name for various trees and shrubs having yellow wood, or for the wood of any of these. Also *attrib.*

Some furnish yellow dyes, as *Maclura tinctoria* (FUSTIC) of the W. Indies and S. America, and the N. American *M. aurantiaca* (Osage ORANGE), *Cladrastis tinctoria* (**American** or **Kentucky y.**), and *Xanthorrhiza apiifolia* (shrub YELLOW-ROOT); others are used for ornamental purposes, as species of *Flindersia* (white TEAK) of Queensland and *Rhus rhodanthema* of New South Wales (both called **light y.**), *Podocarpus Thunbergii* (**Cape y.**) of S. Africa, and *Chloroxylon Swietenia* (SATIN-WOOD) of the E. Indies; others as timber or for other purposes, as *Schæfferia frutescens* of Florida, *Podocarpus elongata* (**Natal y.**) and *P. pruinosa* (**bastard y.**) of S. Africa, *P. latifolia* of the E. Indies, and *Xanthoxylon Clava-Herculis* and other species (**prickly y.**) of the W. Indies.

1666 J. DAVIES *Hist. Caribbee Isles* 43 The Island of S. Croix is the most famous of all the Islands for its abundance in rare and precious Trees. There is one very much esteem'd for its usefulness in Dying: It is called the Yellow-wood from its colour. **1716** *Petiveriana* I. 243 Prickley Yellow wood. **1752** *Rec. Elgin* (New Spald. Club 1903) I. 465 Ilk cwt. brown Brisiell wood, sweet wood, yellow wood or fustic 8d. **1767** in *Country Life* (1973) 7 June 1607/1 A mahogany Commode, with yellow wood ornaments, and Drawers for medals. **1790**, **1801** [see GEELHOUT]. **1812** BRACKENRIDGE *Views Louisiana* (1814) 59 One very beautiful [forest tree], *bois jaune*, or yellow wood: by some called the mock orange. **1830** LINDLEY *Nat. Syst. Bot.* 122 Oxleya xanthoxyla, a large tree, is the Yellow-wood of New South Wales. **1834** PRINGLE *Afr. Sk.* vi. 219 A tree greatly resembling the cedar in its external aspect,.. termed.. geelhout, or yellow-wood (*taxus elongata*). **1868** *Rep. U.S. Comm. Agric.* (1869) 199 Yellow wood (*Cladrastis tinctoria*) is a western tree. **1871** H. H. DUGMORE *Reminisc. Albany Settler* 27 Plain dinners and hearty suppers,.. served up in tin dishes on yellow wood benches. **1875** *Ure's Dict. Arts* II. 527 *Fustic*, or *Yellow Wood.* The old fustic of the English dyer. It is the wood of the *Morus tinctoria*. **1888** E. E. MONEY *Dutch Maiden* 238 The tree, a huge yellow-wood, stood at the edge of the bush. **1915** RIDER HAGGARD *Holy Flower* iv. 63 It.. rolled under a great yellow-wood chest. **1952** G. M. MILLS *First Ladies of Cape* 42 Cupboards.. were usually framed by stinkwood and yellow-wood doors. **1981** *N. & Q.* June 193/2 The most important furnishings of the *groote kamer* were a yellow-wood cupboard and a stink-wood four-poster bed. **1985** *New Yorker* 18 Mar. 65/2 Old yellowwood and stinkwood chests.

yellowy ('jɛləʊɪ), *a.* [f. YELLOW *a.* + -Y[1] 2.] Having a yellow tinge; yellowish.

1667 E. KING in *Phil. Trans.* II. 426 The head, with two little yellowy specks where the Eyes are design'd. **1876** MISS BROUGHTON *Joan* II. ii, A little kerchief of cobweb muslin and ancient yellowy lace. **1883** J. PARKER *Tyne Chylde* 107 They took their tumblers and looked at each other across the yellowy foam.

yelm (jɛlm), *sb.* Now *dial.* [OE. *ȝielm*, *ȝelm*, *ȝilm*, *ȝylm*.] In OE., a handful, bundle, sheaf, as of reaped corn; in mod. *dial.* use, a bundle of straw laid straight for thatching (see YELM *v.*): = HELM *sb.*[3] 1.

c **1000** ÆLFRIC *Gen.* xxxvii. 7 Eowre ȝilmas stodon ymbutan and abuȝon to minum sceafe. *c* **1000** *Sax. Leechd.* II. 120 Ðenim grene mintan ænne ȝelm. *a* **1100** *Aldhelm Gloss.* I. 5252 (Napier 133/1) *Manipulorum*, ȝylma, wræda. *c* **1390** *B.N.C.* (Oxf.) *Docts.* C.[2] 56 We will make 200 yelmes. **1649** BLITHE *Eng. Improv. Impr.* (1652) Kkj, You must reap it.. and lay it upon little yelmes, or two or three handfuls together till it be dry. *a* **1825** FORBY *Voc. E. Anglia*, *Yelm*, *s.* a portion of straw laid for that purpose [*viz.* thatching]; or as much as can be conveniently carried under the arm for any purpose. **1879** JEFFERIES *Wild Life in S. Co.* 124 [The thatcher] is attended by a man to carry up the 'yelms'.

yelm (jɛlm), *v. dial.* Also 6 **yellm**, 8 **yealm**, 9 **yalm**, **yolm**. [f. prec.] *trans.* and *intr.* To separate and select straw and lay it in order for thatching: = HELM *v.*[3] Hence **'yelming** *vbl. sb.*, the action of the verb; also *concr.* = prec.

1581 *Stanford Churchw. Acc.* in *Antiquary* (1888) Apr. 172 For a yellmyng of straw xij[d]. **1589** in H. Hall *Soc. Eliz. Age* (1886) 203 A woman 'yelming' 14 days, 1[s], 9[d]. **1601** in Glasscock *Rec. St. Michael's*, *Bp.'s Stortford* (1882) 67 Pd for strawe, vs. Pd for yelmyng, xd. Pd to the thatcher and fixer, iiijs. ijd. **1629** *Ibid.* 71 Pd to Gryces wife for yelming strawe for her house, xviijd. **1765** *Museum Rust.* IV. xviii. 79 Thatching per square, yelming and serving included, 2s. 6d. **1850** *Jrnl. R. Agric. Soc.* XI. II. 400 Cornes's new chaff cutter dispenses with the women yelming. **1879** JEFFERIES *Wild Life in S. Co.* 124 Two or three women are busy yelming, *i.e.* separating the straw, selecting the largest, and laying it level and parallel, damping it with water, and preparing it for the yokes. **1890** *Glouc. Gloss.*, *Yolm* or *Yalm*.. (Stow-on-Wold).

Hence **'yelmer**, one who lays out yelms.

1808 BATCHELOR *Agric. Bedford* 109 These [two men], together with the four yelmers and servers, cost about 20s. per day.

yelow, **ȝelow**, etc., obs. ff. YELLOW.

yelowse, obs. form of JEALOUS.

14.. *Guy Warw.* (Camb. MS.) 801 Thou woldest be so yelowse And of me so amerowse.

yelp (jɛlp), *sb.* Forms: 1 **ȝielp**, **ȝelp**, **ȝilp**, **ȝylp**, 2–6 **ȝelp(e**, (3 **ȝealp**, **ȝælp**, **ȝeolp**, *Orm.* **ȝellp**), 5– **yelp.** [OE. *ȝielp*, etc. vainglory, pride = OS. *gelp* defiant or arrogant speech, OHG., MHG. *gelph*, *gelf* loud crying, outcry, cheerfulness, exuberance, ON. *gjalp* ? boasting, noise of the sea: see next.]

I. †**1.** Boasting, vainglorious speaking. *idle yelp*, vain boasting. *Obs.*

Beowulf 2521 Ðif ic wiste hu wið ðam aȝlæcean elles meahte ȝylpe wiðgripan. *c* **888** ÆLFRED *Boeth.* xix. § 1 Hwæt forstent eow þonne se ȝilp? *c* **900** tr. *Bæda's Hist.* III. xvii. (1890) 206 Næfde he on him naðer ne yrre ne oferhyd ne ȝytsunge, ne idel ȝylp him on ne ricsade. *c* **1000** ÆLFRIC *Hom.* II. 220 Se seofoða heafod-leahter is ȝehaten idelwuldor, þæt is ȝylp. *c* **1175** *Lamb. Hom.* 103 [He] deð for ȝelpe mare þenne for godes luue ȝif he awiht delan wule. *c* **1200** ORMIN 4902 Þiss mahhte.. cwennkeþþ i þin herrte All rosinng & all idell ȝellp. *a* **1225** *Leg. Kath.* 865 Ha beoð ful of idel ȝelp. *c* **1330** R. BRUNNE *Chron. Wace* (Rolls) 9836 Of gret los mighte he make his ȝelpe. *a* **1400**–*c* **1460** *Towneley Myst.* iii. 321 Without any yelp, At my myght shall I help. *c* **1400** *Laud Troy Bk.* 15602 Off her goddis myȝt made thei ȝelp.

†**b.** An object of boasting. *Obs.*

c **1320** *Cast. Love* 1364 Þis is vre child and vre help, Vre strengþe and vre ȝelp.

II. 2. A cry characteristic of dogs and some other animals, resembling a bark but distinguished from it by being sharp and shrill.

1500–20 DUNBAR *Poems* xxxii. 10 He [*sc.* a tod] braisit hir [*sc.* a lamb's] bony body sweit,.. Syne schuk his taill, with quhinge and ȝelp. **1501** DOUGLAS *Pal. Hon.* I. iii, This laithlie flude.. In quhome the fisch ȝelland as eluis schoutit, Thair ȝelpis wilde my heiring all fordeifit. *a* **1627** MIDDLETON *Witch* III. iii, No howles of woolves, no yelpes of hounds. **1681** CROWNE *Hen. VI*, I. II. 14, I.. hear the Howles of Wolves, and Yelpes of Foxes. **1682** FLAVEL *Fear* 1 Some are as timorous as hares and start at every sound or yelp of a dog. **1801** SOUTHEY *Thalaba* IX. xviii, The dogs, with eager yelp, Are struggling to be free. **1840** THACKERAY *Barber Cox* Mar., After hearing a yelp here, and a howl there, tow, row, yow, yow, yow! bursts out. **1848** 'F. FORESTER' *Field Sports* II. 325 A sort of pipe or call by which the cry or yelp, as it is termed, of the female [*sc.* the wild turkey-hen] may be simulated. **1868** TENNYSON *Lucretius* 45 The dog With inward yelp and restless forefoot plies His function of the woodland. **1886** J. K. JEROME *Idle Thoughts* 129 The watch-dog.. wakes with a yelp of gladness to greet a caressing hand.

b. *transf.* and *fig.*

1775 JOHNSON *Tax. no Tyr.* 89 If slavery be thus fatally contagious, how is it that we hear the loudest yelps for liberty among the drivers of negroes? **1825** CROKER *Fairy Leg. Irel.* I. 48 The whinge, and the yelp, and the screech, and the yowl, was never out of his mouth. **1866** BALLANTYNE *Shifting Winds* xxiv, The [engine] driver vented his impatience.. by causing the whistle to give three sharp yelps. **1885** RUNCIMAN *Skippers & Shellbacks* 241 The yelp of a Norwegian seaman who was hauling on a rope.

c. The syllable *yelp* used imitatively.

1831–4 R. S. SURTEES *Jorrocks's Jaunts* i. (1838) 10 'Yelp, yelp, yelp,' howl the hounds. **1835** W. IRVING *Tour Prairies* 299 Yelp! yelp! yelp! passed from mouth to mouth. There was a sudden dispersal.

yelp (jɛlp), *v.* Forms: 1 **ȝielpan**, **ȝelpan**, **ȝilpan**, **ȝylpan**, 2–5 **ȝelpe**, 4–7 **yelpe**, (3 **ȝælpe**, **ȝeolp**, **ȝeilp**, **ȝulp**, *Orm.* **ȝellpenn**, 4 **ȝilpe**, 5 **yilp**, 7 **yealp**), 3– **yelp.** *Pa. t.* 1 **ȝealp**, *pl.* **ȝulpon**, 3 **ȝ(e)alp**, **yelp**, *pl.* **ȝulpe**, 4 **yalp**; 4 **ȝolped**, 6 **yalpid**, *Sc.* **ȝelpit**, 4– **yelped.** *Pa. pple.* 1 **ȝolpen**, 4 **y-yolpe**; 4– **yelped.** [OE. *ȝielpan*, etc., = MHG. *gelfen*:—**galpjan*, f. root represented by OS. *galpôn* to cry aloud, boast, LG. *galpen* to croak, MG. *galpen* to bark, yelp, MHG. *galf*, MG. *galp* loud cry, barking, Sw. dial. *galpa* to cry (of certain birds). Cf. GALP, GAWP, *yalp*, YAWP.]

I. †**1.** *intr.* To boast, speak vaingloriously. Const. *of* (= OE. gen.). *Obs.*

Beowulf 2583 Hreðsiȝora ne ȝealp goldwine ȝeata. *c* **888** ÆLFRED *Boeth.* xiv. § 1 Ðif þu ȝilpan wille, ȝilp Godes. *a* **1000** *Daniel* 714 Ða wearð bliðemod burȝa aldor, ȝealp gramlice gode on andan. *c* **1200** ORMIN 2042 Þuss mihhte ȝho full modiȝliȝ Off hire sinne ȝellpenn. *a* **1225** *Ancr. R.* 128 [Heo] ȝelstreð, ase þe uox deð, & ȝelpeð of hore god. *a* **1250** *Owl & Night.* 1299 Þu ȝeolpest of seolliche wisdome, þu nustest wanene he þe come. **1340** *Ayenb.* 208 Þe fariseu þet yalp ine his benes and onworþede þane pubblycan. *c* **1380** *Sir Ferumb.* 694 Ne schaltou by þat tyme noþyng ȝilpe of þy doynge here. *c* **1386** CHAUCER *Knt.'s T.* 1380, I kepe noght of armes for to yelpe, Ne I ne axe nat to-morwe to have victorie. *c* **1425** *Cast. Persev.* 2865 in *Macro Plays* 162 Sum bote of bale þou me brewe, Þat I may of þee ȝelpe.

†**b.** *refl.* in same sense. *Obs.*

1340 *Ayenb.* 79 Huanne hi ham yelpeþ oþer hi ham prodeþ. **1390** GOWER *Conf.* I. 97 He hath trewly supposed That he him may of nothing yelpe, Bot if [etc.].

†**c.** Const. clause. *Obs.*

c **888** ÆLFRED *Boeth.* xiv. § 1 Hwæðer þu dyrre ȝilpan þæt hiora fæȝernes þin sie? *a* **1023** WULFSTAN *Hom.* xvi. (1883) 99 Þa wende he þæt hit godes aȝen wære; and se deofles man ȝealp þæt he eac swa wære. *c* **1205** LAY. 26835 þu ȝulpe biforen þan kaisere þat þu me woldest a-quellen. *a* **1250** *Owl & Night.* 971 Ac ȝet þu ȝelpst of þine songe þat þu canst ȝ olle wroþe & stronge. *c* **1275** *Passion of our Lord* 330 in *O.E. Misc.* 46 He yelp to-vore vs alle þat he is vre king. *c* **1400** *Death of Robin Lyth* 82 in Ritson *Anc. Songs* (1877) 74 Now xalt thu never yelpe, Wrennok, At ale ne at wyn, That thu hast slawe goode Robyn. *c* **1420** *Chron. Vilod*, 53 Bot how þay deden after, y nylt not ȝelpe.

II. †**2.** To lift up one's voice; to cry aloud; to sing loud or on a high note. *Obs.*

Cf. the OE. sense (with gen.) 'to applaud, praise'.

c **1450** *St. Cuthbert* (Surtees) 4697 Gude fadir,.. To þe we crye and ȝelpe. *c* **1460** *Towneley Myst.* xii. 422 Brek outt youre voce, let se as ye yelp. **1549** *Compl. Scot.* vi. 39 The lyntquhit sang cuntirpoint quhen the osȝil ȝelpit.

†**b.** *trans.* To call out, utter. *Obs.*

c **1400** *Laud Troy Bk.* 13520 And he myȝt not him selff helpe; His sorwe coude he to no man ȝelpe.

3. *intr.* To utter a yelp or yelps: said of dogs and related animals, and certain birds (see quots.).

1553 M. WOOD tr. *Gardiner's True Obed.* To Rdr. A v, A rash bethlem brained hound,.. rushing he careth not which wai, so he be yelpyng. **1593** PEELE *Hon. Garter* C 3 b, Enuy will bite, or snarle and barke at least, As dogs against the Moone that yelpe in vayne. **1596** W. SMITH *Chloris* xiii, A lust-led Satyre hauing hir in chace Which after hir, about the fields did yelpe. **1688** HOLME *Armoury* II. 134/2 A Dog Barketh, & Baugheth, being smitten Yelpeth. **1706** E. WARD *Wooden World Diss.* (1708) 32 Oft does he make the poor Tars yelp and run about, like Dogs in a Church, under the Correction of a Sexton. **1708** DERHAM in *Phil. Trans.* XXVI. 124 April 1, the Jynx first yelped here. **1751** JOHNSON *Rambler* No. 119 ¶5 Compassion once obliged me to.. chide off a dog that yelped at his heels. **1845** DARWIN *Voy. Nat.* vii. (1879) 135 The jaguar, when wandering about at night, is much tormented by the foxes yelping as they follow him. **1847** TENNYSON *Princess* VII. 196 Let the wild Lean-headed Eagles yelp alone. **1848** in 'F. Forester' *Field Sports* II. 326 The gobblers continued yelping in answer to the female, which all this time remained on the fence. **1865** DICKENS *Mut. Fr.* III. xi, A scholastic huntsman clad for the field, with his fresh pack yelping and barking around him. **1879** J. BURROUGHS *Locusts & Wild H.* (1884) 56 [The fledgling] left the nest and clung to the.. tree, and yelped and piped for an hour.

fig. **1577** GRANGE *Golden Aphrod.* G iv b, To Veronas well he hies whose wante of bloud doth yelpe. **1885** TENNYSON *Balin & Balan* 314 That chain'd rage, which ever yelpt within.

4. *fig.* To complain, whine.

1706 HEARNE *Collect.* 16 Sept. (O.H.S.) I. 288 'Twill make ye Whig Pamphlettiers yelp. **1792** ALEX. WILSON *Watty & Meg* x, Night and day she's ever yelpin, Wi' the weans she ne'er can gree. **1801** JEFFERSON *Writ.* (1830) III. 469 The nominations have accordingly furnished something to yelp on. **1881** BESANT & RICE *Chapl. Fleet* II. xx. 167, I might, if I pleased, yelp and cry for my lord and his precious friend, Sir Miles Lackington.

5. *trans.* **a.** To utter with a loud cry; to express by yelping or in a yelping tone.

a **1654** W. PRICE in C. Wase *Gratius' Cyneget.* Illustr. 70 There lurks the pride o' th' woods, the Lyon fell, At whose decease our troops [of hounds] shall yelpe a knell. *a* **1704** T. BROWN tr. *Fresny's Amusem.* iii. (1709) 17 Another Son of a Whore yelps [*ed.* 1700 yells] louder than Homer's Stentor, Two a groat, and Four for Six-pence Mackerel. **1828** *Examiner* 98/1 Lord Ellenborough 'gave tongue' on Monday, and yelped an explanation most melodiously. **1865** PARKMAN *Champlain* x. (1875) 311 On their arrival, they.. yelped consternation at the sharp explosion of the arquebuse.

b. To bring into some condition by yelping.

1711 BUDGELL *Spect.* No. 116 ¶6 A raw Dog.. might have yelped his Heart out, without being taken notice of.

yelper ('jɛlpə(r)). [f. YELP *v.* + -ER¹.]

†**1.** A boaster. *Obs.*

1340 *Ayenb.* 22 Þe yelpere is þe cockou þet ne kan naȝt zinge bote of him-zelue.

2. An animal that yelps or gives a sharp shrill cry; also, a person who 'yelps', etc.

a. A dog that yelps, a whelp. b. The avocet. *local.* c. A young partridge. d. A redshank. e. A 'call' used by sportsmen to imitate the 'yelp' of the wild turkey-hen. f. *slang.* A town-crier. g. *slang.* A wild beast.

a. **1673**, **1825** [implied in 3]. **1847** HALLIWELL, *Yelper*, a young dog; a whelp. **1850** DOBELL *Roman* vi. Poet. Wks. (1875) 90 But let one miscreant yelper howl, and mark How all the pack gives tongue. **1886** H. F. LESTER *Under Two Fig Trees* ii, I was strolling.. through the establishment [*sc.* a dog's home], looking into one cage of yelpers after another.

b. **1770** PENNANT *Brit. Zool.* IV. 69 [Avosettas] are found in considerable numbers during the breeding season, near Fossdyke Wash, in Lincolnshire, called there Yelpers. *c* **1818** *Britton's Lincolnshire* 725.

c. **1802** W. B. DANIEL *Rur. Sports* II. 518 Vos teneri *Yelpers*, vos grandævique parentes.

d. **1892** D. JORDAN *Within an Hour of London T.* ix, The 'cussed' redshank or pool-snipe was dubbed the red-legged yelper. *Ibid.* xiii, If wild-fowl possess the virtue of gratitude, they must quack, bark, whistle, shriek, and grunt untold blessings on the redshank's head, for the yelper is their feathered sentinel. **18..** ROOSEVELT *Florida & Game Water-Birds* 196 The yelper has a strong, rapid, and often irregular flight and a loud cry.

e. **1884** *Sport with Gun and Rod* II. 762 We now take our yelper, and give a few sharp yelps; he [*sc.* a wild turkey] hears the call.

f. **1725** *New Cant. Dict.*, *Yelper*, a Town-Cryer; also, one subject to complain. **1823** 'JON BEE' *Dict. Turf* 197 *Yelper*, a town-crier. Also, a discontented cove, who is forward to complain of his woes, and the imaginary evils of life.

g. **1823** *Grose's Dict. Vulgar T.*, *Yelpers*, wild beasts.

3. Applied contemptuously to a speaker or writer, whose utterance is compared to a dog's yelp.

1673 S. PARKER *Reproof Reh. Transp.* 268 He will never take any notice of such a despicable yelper as you, unless with a Dog-whip. **1703** T. BAKER *Tunbridge Walks* III. 31 Now shall I be ask'd, a thousand more Whimsical Cross Questions, than a Bashful Witness, by an Impudent Yelper at the Old-Bayley. **1821** *Blackw. Mag.* IX. 61 When they reflect on thy strength, and think of their own petty yelpers. **1825** *Blackw. Mag.* XVII. 467 A pretty pack of yelpers they are, to be sure, that the Whigs *hound* at the Chancellor. **1827** SCOTT *Diary* 10 Aug. in *Lockhart*, In the house of commons he [*sc.* Canning] was the terror of that species of orators called the Yelpers. **1873** J. GREENWOOD *In Strange Company* 281 The other merciless howlers and yelpers.

yelping ('jɛlpɪŋ), *vbl. sb.* [f. YELP *v.* + -ING¹.]

†**1.** Boasting, proud or pompous talk. *Obs.*

a **1050** *Liber Scintill.* xliii. (1889) 144 *Pro sola inani gloria*, for sylfre idelre ʒylpincge. *c* **1175** *Lamb. Hom.* 11 Ne haue þu þines drihtenes nome in nane aða ne.. in nane idel ȝelpunge. *a* **1225** *Ancr. R.* 330 A derne ȝelpunge & huntunge efter hereword of more holinesse. **1297** R. GLOUC. (Rolls) 4266 Quintylian.. ansuerede.. þat bote ȝelpinge [*v.r.* ȝulpynge] & bost mid brutons noþing nas. **13..** *Gaw. & Gr. Knt.* 492 He ȝerned ȝelpyng to here. **1340** *Ayenb.* 59 In þise boȝe byeþ vif leaues, þet byeþ vif manere of yelpinges. *c* **1400** T. CHESTRE *Launfal* 762 Why madest thou swyche yelpyng? That thy lemmannes lodlokest mayde Was fayrer than my wyf, thou seyde. *c* **1440** *Promp. Parv.* 537/1 Ȝelpynge, or boostynge, *jactancia.*

2. The utterance of a sharp shrill cry. **a.** Of dogs or birds.

1592 SHAKS. *Ven. & Ad.* 881 The timerous yelping of the hounds. **1782** MISS BURNEY *Cecilia* VII. ix, The poor little animal, forgotten by its mistress,.. was now discovered by its yelping. **1809–10** COLERIDGE *Friend* (1837) II. 24 Like children we ran away from the yelping of a cur. **1847** *Bewick's Brit. Birds* I. 7 [Eagles] often soar out of the reach of human sight: and notwithstanding the immense distance, their cry is still heard, and then resembles the yelping of a dog. **1863** BATES *Nat. Amazons* ii. (1864) 33 We often heard the shrill yelping of the toucans.

b. Of persons. Also *fig.*

1632 LITHGOW *Trav.* IX. 395 A ceremonious mourning.. with such yelping, howling, shouting, and clapping of hands [etc.]. **1854** MACAULAY in Trevelyan *Life* (1880) II. 376 The yelping against Prince Albert is a mere way of filling up the time. **1894** *Forum* (N.Y.) Aug. 643 The incessant snarling and yelping of demagogues at capitalists.

yelping ('jɛlpɪŋ), *ppl. a.* [f. YELP *v.* + -ING².] That yelps; given to or characterized by yelping.

1591 SHAKS. *1 Hen. VI*, IV. ii. 47 A litle Heard of Englands timorous Deere, Maz'd with a yelping kennell of French Curres. **1623** —— *Tit. A.* II. iii. 20 Let vs sit downe, and marke their [*sc.* the hounds'] yelping [*Qq.* yellowing] noyse. **1664** in *Verney Mem.* (1907) II. 212 A little yealping Dogg. **1712** ARBUTHNOT *John Bull* IV. i, The Tradesmen.. began to surround Lewis like so many yelping curs about a great boar. **1820** W. IRVING *Sketch Bk.*, *Rip van Winkle* 55 At the least flourish of a broomstick or ladle, he would fly to the door with yelping precipitation. **1840** DICKENS *Old C. Shop* li, Kit is.. a crouching cur to those that feed and coax him, and a barking yelping dog to all besides. **1848** in 'F. Forester' *Field Sports* II. 326, I heard the yelping notes of some gobblers. **1906** ALICE WERNER *Natives Brit. Central Africa* viii. 188 The miserable, yelping mongrels which infest the villages.

transf. and *fig.* **1607** BEAUM. & FL. *Woman Hater* I. ii, The very comfort of whose presence shuts The monster hunger from your yelping guts. **1607** LEVER *Crucifixe* xx, And like the hunted deere, Of our loud yelping sinnes, we stand in feere. **1787** HAWKINS *Life of Johnson* 100 The deep-mouthed rancour of Pulteney, and the yelping pertinacity of Pitt. **1871** B'NESS BUNSEN in Hare *Life* (1879) II. vii. 416 The yelping, barking crowds in Trafalgar Square.

yelpingal: see YAFFINGALE.

yelt (jɛlt). *dial.* Forms: 1 **ʒilte**, 5 **yelte**, 7 **yealte**, (8 **ilt**, 8–9 **elt**, 9 **hilt**), 6– **yelt**. [late OE. *ʒilte*, **ʒielte* = MLG. *gelte* spayed sow:—**galtjōn-*: see GALT, GILT *sb.*²] A young sow.

c **1000** ÆLFRIC *Gloss.* in Wr.-Wülcker 119/25 *Suilla, uel sucula*, ʒilte. **14..** *Voc.* ibid. 614/30 *Suillus, i. parva sus*, a yelte. **1562** WITHALS *Dict.* 17 b/1 A yelt or yonge sow, *sucula.* **1607** TOPSELL *Four-f. Beasts* 661 We call a young swine a Pigge, A weaning Pigge, a sheate, a Yealke [*read* Yealte], and so foorth. **1746** *Exmoor Courtship* (E.D.S.) 409 Es must ha' wone that es can trest.. to zar tha Ilt and tha Barra. **1790** GROSE *Prov. Gloss.* s.v. *Elt*, Elt, or ilt, is also a spayed sow. Exm. **1903** *E. Angl. Daily Times* 24 Aug. 3/7 Some grand young Boars and Yelts for sale at moderate prices.

yelt(e, ȝelt(e: see YIELD *v.*

yelting ('jɛltɪŋ). A name for fishes of the genus *Lutianus*.

1873 T. GILL *Catal. Fishes E. Coast N. Amer.* 28 *Lutjanus caxis*... Yelting, glass-eyed snapper. **1876** GOODE *Fishes of Bermudas* 55.

yelu, etc., obs. ff. YELLOW.

yelve (jɛlv), *sb. dial.* Also 7 **yelf**, 9 **yilve**. [Metathetic f. ME. *ȝevel*:—OE. *ʒeafel* fork, more directly represented by dial. *yeevil*, EVIL *sb.*³, in use along the Celtic border from Cheshire to Cornwall.] A dung- or garden-fork. Hence **yelve** *v.*, to use a yelve.

[*c* **1000** ÆLFRIC *Hom.* I. 430 Hi.. hine ufan mid isenum ʒeaflum ðydon. *a* **1100** *Voc.* in Wr.-Wülcker 241/36 *Forcelle*, ʒæfle, *dictae quod frumenta celluntur, i. commouentur.* *a* **1100** *Gerefa* in *Anglia* IX. 263 He sceal fela tola.. habban.. bærwan, besman, race, ʒeafle. **1398** TREVISA *Barth. De P.R.* XVII. lxx[ii]. (Tollem. MS.), Hey.. is houe, turnid and wende with pikes, ȝeuels [*ed.* 1495 forkees] and rakes.] **1688** HOLME *Armoury* II. 173/2 Yelf or Yelve, an Iron with three fork ends, by which Dung is taken from the Beast, and the house made clean. *Ibid.* III. 337/1 A Yelve Iron with two Ends. *Ibid.*, With the same Forke or Yelve, (or Evill, as some call it). **1817** WILBRAHAM *Gloss. Cheshire* (1818) 32 *Yelve*, to dig chiefly with the yelve. **1841** HARTSHORNE *Salopia Antiqua* 622 *Yilve*, a dung fork, an *evil*, as we more commonly call it. **1879** MISS JACKSON *Shropsh. Word-bk.*, *Yelve*.. a garden-fork. **1886** *Cheshire Gloss.*, *Yelve*, a potato fork... *Yelve*, *v.* to dig, chiefly with the yelve.

yelvean, early variant of ELVAN.

a **1728** LOWER in Woodward *Fossils* (1729) I. I. 201 A sort of Yelvean Stone, and Earth, mixed together, down to the Load. [Cf. *Ibid.* 202 A dun Stone which the Miners call Elvean Stone.]

yelver, obs. form of ELVER.

1655 WALTON *Angler* xiii. (1661) 189 In Severn, (where they [*sc.* young eels] are call'd Yelvers).

yelwe, ȝelwe, etc., obs. ff. YELLOW.

yelyng, variant of YILING *Obs.*

yem: see EME, YEME.

yeman, obs. form of YEOMAN.

†**yeme**, *sb. Obs.* Forms: 1 **ʒieme**, **ʒyme**, 2–5 **ȝeme**, 3–5 **yeme**, 4 **yem**, **ȝeeme**, 5 **yeeme**, **eme**. [OE. *ʒieme* fem. (also *ʒiemen*), f. OTeut. *gaum-*: see next. Cf. OS. *gôma* fem., attention, entertaining, feast, banquet, OHG. *gouma* (MHG. *goume*) fem., observation, feasting, opulence, ON. *gaumr* masc., *gaum* fem., care (see GOME²).] Care, heed, attention. ***in yeme***, in one's care, in charge.

c **893** ÆLFRED *Oros.* III. xix. 134 Hie þæs wealles nane ʒieman ne dydon. *c* **897** —— *Gregory's Past. C.* v. 44 Ðif we ðonne habbað swæ micle sorʒe & swæ micle ʒ ieman urra nihstena swæ swæ ure selfra. *c* **1175** *Lamb. Hom.* 117 He is iset to þon þet he scal ouerscawian mid his ȝeme þa lewedan. *a* **1225** *Ancr. R.* 344 Wiðuten ȝeme of heorte. *a* **1300** *Cursor M.* 7015 (Cott.) Tene yeir had he þe folk in yeme [*other MSS.* to ȝeme].

b. In ME. almost always in phr. ***to nim*** or ***take yeme***: to take note, notice, observe; to give heed, attend; to heed, care; to take heed, take care, be careful (corresponding to various senses of YEME *v.*).

c **1175** *Lamb. Hom.* 19 Nimað ȝeme nu.. hwilche ȝife he us ȝefeð. *Ibid.* 75 Numeð nu ȝeme þerto, and ic ou wile seggen word efter word. *c* **1200** *Trin. Coll. Hom.* 77 Þe heuenliche leche seinte poul nimeð ȝeme of ure saule sicnesse. *a* **1225** *Ancr. R.* 78 Nimeð ȝeme hu wel he seið. *a* **1250** *Owl & Night.* 649 We nimeþ ȝeme of manne bure An after þan we makeþ ure. *c* **1290** *Beket* 1942 in *S. Eng. Leg.* 162 Holi church.. þat geth al-mest nouþe to grounde bote god nime ȝeme þar-to. *a* **1300** *Cursor M.* 17536 For goddes luue tas yeme Quat yee sai. **13..** *K. Alis.* 7415 (Linc. Inn MS.) Pors gan abak renne And nom þiderward ȝeme And loked toward heore crye. **1340** *Ayenb.* 54 Nim yeme of þe guodes þet þou dest oþer miȝt do. **1362** LANGL. *P. Pl.* A. VII. 14 Þe Neodi and þe Nakede nym ȝeeme hou þei liggen. **1421** HOCCLEVE *Lerne to Dye* 521 They.. list take no yeeme Vn-to the ende which mighte hem profyte. **1426** AUDELAY *Poems* 12 He that sayth he lovys his Lord, on hym take good eme. *c* **1430** *Syr Gener.* (Roxb.) 7085 Had she kept furth hir way, He wold of hir haue take no yeme. *c* **1450** *St. Cuthbert* (Surtees) 582 Ȝit biddes he to þaim take ȝeme.

†**yeme**, *v. Obs.* Forms: 1 **ʒieman**, **ʒiman**, **ʒyman**, **ʒeman**, 2–6 **ȝeme**, 3 **ȝeome**, 3–4 **ȝiem(e**, 3–6 **ȝime**, 4 **ȝheme**, **ȝheyme**, **yeeme**, **yem**, 4–5 **yheme**, 4–6 **yeme**, 5 **ȝem**, **ȝyme**, 6 **ȝym**. [OE. *ʒieman* = OS. *gômean* to care for, guard, entertain (guests), OHG. *goumjan*, *goumôn* (MHG. *goumen*) to give heed to, observe, feast, ON. *geyma* to heed, watch (Sw. *gömma* to keep, hide, Da. *gjemme* to keep, guard, save), Goth. *gaumjan* to perceive, observe f. OTeut. *gaum-*, whence also the forms s.v. prec.; the ultimate origin is disputed. In OE. constructed with a genitive of the object, which was succeeded in ME. by *of*, and ultimately by a simple object.]

1. To care for, take notice of, consider.

c **888** ÆLFRED *Boeth.* xv. §1 Ne ʒemdon hie nanes fyrenlustes. **971** *Blickl. Hom.* 99 Hie.. nystan ne ne ʒemdon hwonne hie þæt eall anforlætan sceoldan. *c* **1000** ÆLFRIC *De Vet. Test.* Pref. (Gr.) 3/16 He ætes ne ʒimde. *c* **1205** LAY. 9168 Bruttes her of ȝemden & noht hit ne forȝeten.

b. To give heed or attention to, attend to, look after; to take heed, take care (*to do* something).

c **897** ÆLFRED *Gregory's Past. C.* xxi. 160 Swiðe ʒeornlice ʒiemað ðæt hie ða eorðlican heortan ʒelæren. *c* **1205** LAY. 12581 For þa arewen ne mihte þa Bruttes ȝemen nanes fihtes. *a* **1225** *Ancr. R.* 98 Heo went in hire þuhte ofte swuche wordes, hwon heo schulde oðerhwat ȝeorneliche ȝemen. *c* **1440** *York Myst.* xxvii. 66 Euer for to ȝeme in ȝouþe and elde, To be buxsome in boure and hall. *c* **1450** *St. Cuthbert* (Surtees) 2819 All othir thinges he ȝemed þat to a bischope degre semed.

c. *intr.* To attend; to look attentively *upon*.

a **1225** *Ancr. R.* 44 (MS. C.) Of ower kneolunge, hwense ȝe maȝen iȝemen, ear mete & efter [etc.]. **13..** *Cursor M.* 17297 (Gött.) Al þai hidd þaim-self to ȝeme. *c* **1394** *P. Pl. Crede* 159 Y ȝemede vpon þat house & ȝerne þeron loked.

2. To take care of, keep; to have charge of, have in keeping; to guard, protect, preserve from injury.

a **900** CYNEWULF *Crist* 1546 Se deopa seað.. ʒiemeð gæsta. *c* **1000** ÆLFRIC *Num.* iii. 38 Moises and Aaron and hira bearn ʒimdon þæs temples on middan Israhela folce. *c* **1175** *Lamb. Hom.* 23 Þa men þe beoð in þe castel and hin ȝemeð. *Ibid.* 115 He scal wicche creft aleggan and wiȝelunge ne ȝeman. *c* **1200** ORMIN 5595 Himm reoweþþ þatt he nohht ne maȝȝ Himm ȝemenn all fra sinne. *c* **1205** LAY. 369 Children & hinen þa ure nete sculen ȝemen. *c* **1320** *Cast. Love* 448 Nis þer nout in world bi-leued þat nis destrued.. But eiȝte soulen þᵗ weren i-ȝemed In þe schup. *c* **1330** *Arth. & Merl.* 968 In a tour þai han hir do, þat noman miȝt hir com to, Bot an eld midwiif, þat schuld ȝemen hir liif. **13..** *Gosp. Nicod.* (G.) 468 His lare be þine algate, And his pese might þe ȝeme. **1357** *Lay Folks Catech.* (T.) 443 The seuent vertu.. is methe.. That.. yhemes us fro yernynges of worldely godes. **1375** BARBOUR *Bruce* XIII. 230 Ȝhemen, swanys, and poveraill, That in the parc to ȝheyme vittale War left. *a* **1400** *Leges Burgorum* c. 57 in *Acts Parl. Scot.* (1844) I. 344/2 He sal be lede to þe house of þe kyngis seriand.. and þar he sal be yhemyt fra his challangeouris. *c* **1400** *Destr. Troy* 8254 He hurlet thurgh the helme, þat the hed yemed. *Ibid.* 10791 The yates to yeme he yepely comaundit. *c* **1450** HOLLAND *Howlat* 132 The said secretar. that the sele ȝemyt. **1500–20** DUNBAR *Poems* xxxviii. 39 Dispulit of the tresur that he ȝemit. **1513** DOUGLAS *Æneis* III. ix. 97 Poliphemus, ȝymmand his beistis rowch. *Ibid.* VII. x. 23 [He] heyrdis wyde, As storoure to the king, did kep and ȝime. *a* **1568** W. BROWN *Lett. Gold* in *Bannatyne MS.* (Hunter Cl.) 141 Ye men of kirk, that cure hes tane Of sawlis for to wetsche [*v.r.* yeme] and keip.

absol. *a* **1300** *Sarmun* xviii. in *E.E.P.* (1862) 3 Hi nul noȝt spene bot ȝime in store. *a* **1400** *Sir Perc.* 1136 He lefte mene many ane... Be the ȝates ȝemande.

3. To have the command or oversight of; to rule, govern, manage, control.

c **1000** ÆLFRIC *Gen.* i. 18 Þæt hiʒ.. ʒimdon þæs dæʒes and þære nihte. *a* **1300** *Cursor M.* 9541 On na manere Moght he in pes his kingrik yeme. **1399** LANGL. *Rich. Redeles* I. 89 The cheuyteyns.. Weren all to yonge of ȝeris to yeme swyche a rewme. *c* **1400** *Ywaine & Gaw.* 1185 My landes forto lede and yeme. *c* **1400** *Rule St. Benet* (verse) 1052 Vs aw to ȝem our tong And spek not bot we be requerde. *c* **1400** *Destr. Troy* 5338 The septur & the soile sithyn haue I ȝemyt.

4. To keep, observe (a command, festival, etc.).

c **1000** ÆLFRIC *Lev.* xxvi. 42 Ic ʒyme min wedd. *c* **1175** *Lamb. Hom.* 11 Þe pridde godes heste.. Wite ȝe þet ȝe ȝemen þenne halie sunnedei. *a* **1300** *Ten Commandm.* in *O.E. Misc.* 200 Þe halidayes þu shalt ȝieme [*pr.* þieme; *rime* queme].

a **1300** *Cursor M.* 2690 Ful wel þis lagh sal he yeme. **13..** *Ibid.* 9980 (Gött.) Euer scho lyues in maydenhede, þat scho hir ches þe first day, Scho ȝemed it in mekenes ay. **1389** in Sir W. Fraser *Wemyss of Wemyss* (1888) II. 24 Til there thyngys al and syndry lelily and fermly to befulfyllyt and yhemmyt bath the partys. *c* **1400** MAUNDEV. (Roxb.) xiv. 61 In þe whilk er many gude Cristen men, ȝemaund þe same rytes..þat we vsen. *c* **1400** *Destr. Troy* 869, I am ferd lest þou..for ȝeuernes for-ȝete þat þe ȝeme shuld. *c* **1450** *Bk. Curtasye* 304 in *Babees Bk.*, With freres on pilgrimage yf þat þou go, þat þei wille ȝyme, wilne þou also.

†**yemeles**, *a.* *Obs.* Forms: 1 **ᵹieme-**, **ᵹime-**, **ᵹymeleas**, 2–3 **ȝemeles**, 3 **ȝemeleas**. [OE. *ᵹiemeléas*, f. *ᵹieme* YEME *sb.* + *-léas* -LESS.] Careless, heedless, negligent. Hence †**yemelesliche** *adv.* [OE. *ᵹiemeléaslíce*: see -LY²], carelessly, heedlessly; †**yemeleaschipe** [-SHIP], †**yemelest** [OE. *ᵹiemeléast*: see -T³], heedlessness, negligence.

c **897** ÆLFRED *Gregory's Past. C.* xxi. 164 Ond swæ hwelc swæ mid ðæm Godes andan bið onæled, ne bið he for ᵹiemeliste [*Hatton MS.* ᵹiemeleste] ᵹehiened. *Ibid.* xlii. 305 Ðæm unbealdum is to cyðanne hu ᵹiemelease hie bioð ðonne hie hie selfe to suiðe forsioð. *c* **1000** *Sax. Leechd.* II. 84 Þara stowa sum raþe rotaþ ᵹif hire mon ᵹimeleaslice tilað. *c* **1175** *Lamb. Hom.* 109 ȝif þe king bið unrihtwis and ȝif þe biscop bið ȝemeles. *c* **1200** ORMIN 2913 Þatt teȝȝ ne falle nohht i gillt þurrh ȝure ȝemelæste. *a* **1225** *Ancr. R.* 92 Hwo se ȝemelesliche witeð hire uttre eien. *Ibid.* 172 ȝif heo wit ham vuele, & let ham þuruh ȝemeleaste etfleon hire seruise. *Ibid.* 202 ȝemeleaschipe, oðer to siggen, oðer to don,..oðer miswiten ei þing þet heo haueð to witene. *a* **1240** *Lofsong* in *O.E. Hom.* I. 205 ȝemeleas and unlusti.

†**yemelich**, *a.* *Obs.* *rare*⁻¹. [f. YEME *sb.* + *-lich*, -LY¹.] Full of care, anxious.

c **1205** LAY. 3356 Þai ȝedede þe king Mid ȝemeliche worden.

Yemeni (ˈjɛmənɪ); *sb.* and *a.* [ad. Arab. *yamanī*, f. *Yemen* name of two States in the south-west of the Arabian peninsula.] **A.** *sb.* A native or inhabitant of North Yemen or South Yemen. **B.** *adj.* Of or pertaining to North Yemen, South Yemen, or the inhabitants of either.

[**1888** C. M. DOUGHTY *Trav. Arabia Deserta* II. 688 *Yémeny*, a man of el-Yémen.] **1916** *Handbk. Arabia* I. vi. 151 The Yemeni is not regarded as particularly fanatical. **1955** *Times* 1 July 11/6 Britain was obliged to deliver a strong Note protesting about border raiding. This pointed out..that in June there had been a serious attack on Mukeiras by a mixed force of Yemeni troops and tribesmen. **1959** W. THESIGER *Arabian Sands* xiii. 247, I had ridden..with two Arab companions and three..Yemeni pilgrims. *Ibid.*, One of the Yemenis fetched us food from the market. **1959** *Listener* 27 Aug. 308/2 The southern Yemeni provinces. **1968** *Ibid.* 4 Jan. 7/1 A guerrilla attack on the outskirts of Sanaa for a few Yemini riyals. **1973** 'D. JORDAN' *Nile Green* xxv. 105 Mara was wearing..a silver medallion. .. I decided it must be Yemini. **1982** P. WAY *Belshazzar's Feast* xix. 208 Would these people have been Arabs, Yemeni Arabs? *Ibid.* xx. 223 The Soviets..have used their East German puppets, the Yemenis, to create trouble. **1982** M. A. ZABARAH *Yemen* 53 Through the Yemeni emigrant and the Yemeni commercial entrepreneur, modern ideas were reaching not only city dwellers but also the tribes.

Yemenite (ˈjɛmənaɪt), *sb.* and *a.* [Sense a (see below); senses b, c f. prec. + -ITE¹.]

A. *sb.* †**a.** [f. an earlier form of the personal name.] A member of a family belonging to the tribe of Benjamin. *Obs.* **b.** = YEMENI *sb.* **c.** A Jew who was, or whose ancestors were, formerly resident in the Yemen.

1566 BIBLE *1 Sam.* ix. 21 Am not I the sonne of a Jaminite of the smallest tribe of Israel: and my kyured is the leest of all the kyuredes of the trybe of Ben Jamin. **1568** *Ibid.*, Am not I the sonne of a Jeminite. **1864** J. T. THOMSON *Some Glimpses Life Far East* xlii. 323 By race he was a Yemenite. **1902** *Encycl. Brit.* XXV. 518/2 The Yemenites rashly invited Turkish intervention. **1926** tr. *Granovsky's Land Prob. Palestine* I. 18 The history of Jewish colonization in Palestine shows many attempts to create a class of Jewish farm laborers..by establishing small settlements for Yemenites (Jewish immigrants from Southern Arabia). **1935** A. REVUSKY *Jews in Palestine* xii. 206 The Sephardim and Yemenites, the two main groups of Oriental Jews. **1965** M. SPARK *Mandelbaum Gate* iv. 91 Those Arab girls, those Yemenites, Syrians, those Israelites, Samaritans. **1976** C. BERMANT *Coming Home* II. iii. 154 One of those private schools..basically..for the sons of Arab oil sheiks, but it also housed..tall, lean Persians, tiny, dusky Yemenites, a few bombastic Greeks.

B. *adj.* Of, pertaining to, or designating a Yemeni Arab or a Yemeni Jew.

1876 R. D. OSBORN *Islam under Arabs* III. i. 296 The Yemenite Arabs of Syria were known as the Kelbites. **1902** *Encycl. Brit.* XXXI. 329/2 The present Sultan, a descendant of those Yemenite Imams who consolidated Arab power in Zanzibar. **1926** *Sunday at Home* July 636/1 Another industry which has been revived in Jerusalem is the silver filigree work of the Yemenite Jews. **1949** [see *gun moll* s.v. GUN *sb.* 17]. **1955** S. N. EISENSTADT in *Public Opinion Q.* XIX. 156 (*heading*) Communication in a traditional Yemenite community. **1978** *Church Times* 16 June 11/2 In the Flea Market [of Tel Aviv]..the Guide did not want us to miss the sight of Arabs buying from Yemenite salesmen. **1982** D. WILTSE *Wedding Guest* ix. 113 He was an Arab, but he could have been anything from Moroccan to Yemenite.

†**yemer.** *Obs.* [f. YEME *v.* + -ER¹. Cf. ON. *geymari* keeper.] A keeper, guardian; a ruler.

c **1320** *Sir Tristr.* 831 ȝif tristrem be now sleyn, Yuel ȝemers er we. **1375** BARBOUR *Bruce* II. 123 Thow sall tak Ferrand my palfray..And gyff his ȝhemar oucht gruchys, Luk that thow tak him magre his. *c* **1400** *Rule St. Benet* (verse) 2244 So þat in godes hows may be A gude ȝemer of godes menȝe. **14..** *Tundale's Vis.* (Turnbull) 239, Y was thi yemer evon and moron Seython thou was of thi moder boron. **1482** *Cely Papers* (Camden) 94 My emer & I be greed that I schold have xl li.

yemer, ȝemer, variant of YOMER.

†**yeming**, *vbl. sb.* *Obs.* [f. YEME *v.* + -ING¹.] The action of the verb YEME; care, keeping, protection, charge.

c **1250** *Gen. & Ex.* 2783 Hic am god ðe in min ȝeming nam Iacob, ysaac, and abraham. *a* **1300** *Cursor M.* 16894 For-þi es skil þir dais thre Yeming on him yee lai. *c* **1330** *Arth. & Merl.* 2034 He..proferd him al his þing To ben vnder his ȝemeing. *c* **1400** *Rule St. Benet* (prose) lviii. 38 Suilk yeming sal sho haue, þat te saule be turnid to god alle-mihtye. *c* **1440** *York Myst.* xliii. 46 Mankynde was thyne whome þu be-kende And toke me to þi ȝemyng right.

y-emptid, ME. pa. pple. of EMPTY *v.*

c **1412** HOCCLEVE *De Reg. Princ.* 4435 Whan þat þe peple ..Hir purs y-emptid haue.

yemschi(c)k, yemstchick, variants of YAMSTCHIK.

†**yemsel.** Chiefly *Sc.* *Obs.* Forms: 3 **ȝemsle**, 4 **ȝemsel**, **-sele**, **-sale**, **-seill**, **-schele**, **ȝeymseill**, **ȝeemsell**, **ȝhemsall**, **-sell**, **yhemsale**, 4–5 **ȝemsall**, 5 **ȝhemsayl**, **yhemselle**. [ad. ON. *geymsla* (f. *geyma* YEME *v.* + *-sla* = OE. *-els*), with assimilation to the native *ȝeme* YEME *v.*] Keeping, care, charge, custody.

c **1200** ORMIN 5095 Ne segge icc þe nohht tatt te birrþ.. All all se mikell ȝemsle, þwerrt ut onn iwhillc oþerr mann Alls o þe sellfenn leggenn. *c* **1375** *Sc. Leg. Saints* I. (*Petrus*) 601 þe quhilk gaff þame ine ȝemsale Of twa knychttis, þat war fell. *Ibid.* xii. (*Mathias*) 245 Cryste gef it hyme ay in ȝemsele, þo he wes thefe & ay wald steyle. **1375** BARBOUR *Bruce* XI. 329, I trow he sall..Do his dewour, and virk so weill, That hym sall neyd no mair ȝeymseill [*MS. E.* ȝemseill]. *a* **1400** *Leges Burgorum* c. 3 in *Acts Parl. Scot.* (1844) I. 333/2 Bot gif..he [*sc.* ane uplandis man] war in þe kyngis oste or in yhemsale of þe kyngis castell. *c* **1425** WYNTOUN *Cron.* VIII. xxvi. 4352 Keparis, þat it [*sc.* a castle] in ȝhemsayl [*v.r.* ȝemsall] hade.

‖**yen**¹ (jɛn). [Japanese, ad. Chinese *yüan* round, round thing, circle, dollar.] A Japanese coin, of gold or silver, representing the monetary unit of Japan since 1871, formerly of about the value of the United States dollar. Also *collect.* as *pl.*

1875 JEVONS *Money* xii. 147 Even Japan has imitated European nations, and introduced a gold coinage of twenty, ten, five, two, and one-yen pieces, the yen being only three per mille less in value than the American gold dollar. **1875** BEDFORD *Sailor's Pocket Bk.* ix. 316 The Yen is divided into 100 Sen, and the Sen into 10 Rin. **1883** SIMMONDS *Dict. Trade* Suppl., *Yen*, a name for the dollar in Japan, in former years worth 3*s.* 9*d.*, but now only about 3*s.* 2*d.* **1904** *Times* 16 Jan. 11/3 Japan has..specie to the unprecedented amount of 113 million yen, or £11,300,000.

yen² (jɛn). *slang* (orig. *U.S.*). Also **yin**, **ying**. [Prob. of Chinese origin. The most likely etymon is Chinese (Cantonese) *yǎn* craving; the forms *yin* and *ying* may reflect the Mandarin pronunciation *yǐn* of the same character. Reinforcement from YEN³ is possible. See also YEN-YEN.

See E. C. Knowlton in *Amer. Speech* (1961) XXXVI. 175–80 for further discussion and documentation of this word, YEN³, and YEN-YEN.]

1. The craving of a drug-addict for his drug (orig. for opium). (See also quots. 1929, 1937, 1974.)

1876 H. A. GILES *Chinese Sketches* 115 Chinamen ask if an opium-smoker has the *yin* or not; meaning thereby, has he gradually increased his doses of opium until he has established a craving for the drug. **1891** A. W. DOUTHWAITE *Opium Habit* 5 The frequent and regular repetition of this process of stimulation and depression induces the '*ying*', or carving, which is simply a demand by the nervous system for its accustomed stimulant, without which it is unable to properly perform its functions. **1912** D. LOWRIE *My Life in Prison* vii. 79, I even saw two or three guys eat chloride o' lime to stop their yen. **1922** E. MURPHY *Black Candle* II. i. 113 When 'the black candle' is ready for lighting and the smoker has the *ying* upon him—that is to say the mad longing for indulgence—the procedure is like this [etc.]. **1929** LIGHT & TORRANCE in *Arch. Internal Med.* XLIII. 210 If he falls asleep, which is often the case, he falls into a deep slumber well known as the 'yen'. **1933** [see MUGGLE³]. **1937** A. R. LINDESMITH *Nature of Opiate Addiction* iv. 107 The drug user does not ordinarily find that his efforts to explain what he means by 'yen' (which signifies both withdrawal symptoms and desire for opiates) are very successful. *Ibid.*, The drug user says, 'he wakes up some morning with a yen.' **1948** F. BROWN *Murder can be Fun* v. 78 He hadn't thought Wilkins would know a biological urge from an opium yen. **1974** M. C. GERALD *Pharmacol.* xiii. 251 Symptoms begin within 8 to 12 hours after the last dose... The addict experiences tearing, a running nose, sweating, yawning, and difficulty in sleeping. This restless sleep is commonly referred to as the 'yen'.

2. *gen.* A craving, a yearning or longing.

1906 H. GREEN *Actors' Boarding House* 248 He had a yen to gamble and bet high. **1928** J. O'CONNOR *Broadway Racketeers* ix. 107 The kid..had a burning yen for champagne and poker. **1932** S. GIBBONS *Cold Comfort Farm* xx. 267 Ezra, who had a secret yen for horticulture. **1952** *Here & Now* (N.Z.) Jan. 19 This yen for a dog that will do everything has had a lot to do with the waning of pointers, setters and retrievers. **1961** *Time* 6 Jan. 4/2 The yen of Christian churchmen for achieving church unity is more pathetic than peculiar to behold. **1967** A. CHRISTIE *Endless Night* ii. 21 He'd got such a yen for a picture that he managed to get the money together. **1983** *Listener* 7 July 17/3 You write your music because you have a real yen to write it.

Hence **yen** *v. intr.*, to crave for a drug; to yearn, desire strongly; ˈ**yenny** *a.*, affected by a craving for drugs.

1919 MENCKEN *Amer. Lang.* iii. 93 A great many of them [*sc.* Chinese words] have remained California localisms, among them such verbs as *to yen* (to desire strongly, as a Chinaman desires opium). **1935** N. ERSINE *Underworld & Prison Slang* 80 He's yenning for morph. **1936** F. M. FORD *Let.* 6 Sept. (1965) 261 Not that I particularly yen to mention the Deity, but that I believe that publishers should be as sadistically punished as possible. **1936** E. POUND *Let.* Sept. (1971) 282 Am afraid I got 'em stuck with some bad grub, but it was the only place I cd. count on being open... The violin player yenned toward another place, where I thought they wd. git stuck a price. **1953** W. BURROUGHS *Junkie* (1972) vi. 63 Nick is followed all the time now. You know yourself when a guy is yenning, he doesn't look behind him. He's running. **1975** H. WHITE *Raincoast Chron.* (1976) 147/1 'We brought a bit of shit in with us to taper off on... Too bad she's all gone.' 'Yeah,' said Pat longingly, 'I sure get yenny sometimes.' **1977** *Times* 11 Feb. 12/2 The need for new educational certainties..cannot be met by yenning for the relative simplicities of the old 'elementary' education.

yen³ (jɛn). *U.S. slang* and *techn.* [Prob. a. Chinese (Cantonese) *yīn* opium, or (Mandarin) *yān* opium: cf. YEN² and YEN-YEN.]

1. Opium.

1926 J. COLTON *Shanghai Gesture* III. 188 [Servant enters with..opium...] Here's the yen! **1935** A. J. POLLOCK *Underworld Speaks* 135/1 *Yen in the cheek*, gum opium or yen shee placed and sucked in back of lower teeth which produces comfort to the addict (this is frequently used when traveling in public conveyances). **1942** BERREY & VAN DEN BARK *Amer. Thes. Slang* §509/2 Opium..yen.

2. *attrib.* and *Comb.*, as (sense 1, with varying degrees of naturalization) **yen hock, hok**, and varr., a needle used in the preparation of opium in the form of pills; **yen hop**, an opium pipe; **yen pock, pox**, and varr. (see quots. 1935 and 1959); **yen she(e)** and varr., the deposit of opium ashes formed in the bowl of an opium pipe; also *loosely*, opium; **yen siang, tsiang**, an opium pipe.

1882 H. H. KANE *Opium-Smoking in Amer. & China* iii. 35 The other articles..for a smoker's outfit are..a needle (*yen hauck*) on the end of which the opium is taken up, 'cooked', and placed over the small opening in the upper surface of the bowl. **1886** T. BYRNES *Professional Criminals Amer.* 385 Among the frequenters of his place could be seen ..such noted characters as..'Yen Hock' Harry, who earned his title by stabbling a man with a 'yen hock'. **1909** I. L. NASCHER *Wretches of Povertyville* II. v. 176 The needle or yen hok is merely a short knitting needle, sometimes with a handle. **1926** *Variety* 29 Dec. 7/4 The dopes and hop heads, with their 'stem', 'yen hok', [etc.]. **1955** *U.S. Senate Hearings* (1956) VIII. 4162 *Yen hock*, a long needle-shaped instrument, flat on one end and used to roll the 'pill' and hold same for cooking. **1968–70** *Current Slang* (Univ. S. Dakota) III–IV. 140 *Yen hok, n.*, a slender needle used in preparing opium for smoking. (Drug users' jargon). **1901** C. R. WOOLDRIDGE *Hands Up!* 215 It consists of the 'yen hop', or pipe, usually made of a section and a half of heavy bamboo. **1918** F. HUNT *Blown in by Draft* iii. 60 In the rare old fiction days 'corking a pill' had to do with yen hop, today it tells of naught but rolling a cigarette. **1934** *Detective Fiction Weekly* 21 Apr. 114/1 Yen pok, pill of opium after being prepared for smoking. **1935** A. J. POLLOCK *Underworld Speaks* 135/1 *Yen pock*, a cooked opium pill often eaten by addicts to produce normalcy and temporary relief. **1946** MEZZROW & WOLFE *Really Blues* xiv. 249 We'd ..pack along some yen pox (opium pills that you eat). **1955** [see MUD *sb.*¹ 2 d]. **1959** W. BURROUGHS *Naked Lunch* 12 Yen pox is the ash of smoked opium. **1882** H. H. KANE *Opium-Smoking in Amer. & China* iii. 35 A straight and curved knife for cleaning the bowl of the ash (*yen tshi*) that rapidly collects and renders the pipe foul. **1892** H. CAMPBELL *Darkness & Daylight* xxviii. 565 And a little box of tin held the *yen she* or bits of refuse opium. **1901** C. R. WOOLDRIDGE *Hands Up!* 215 The 'yen she gow', or small chisel, for cleaning out the bowl of the pipe. **1912** A. H. LEWIS *Apaches of New York* xi. 229 Number-one hop is $87.50 a can, an' yee-chee..not less'n $32. **1918** *Policeman's Monthly* Oct. 16/3 In answer to this, it was learned that fifty-eight began by smoking opium..eight ate morphine, three ate 'yen shee', the ashes of opium, and the remaining cases started by using cocaine and laudanum, or eating opium. **1947** A. MEYERS in J. H. Jackson *San Francisco Murders* 291 Liu uttered..a pathetic plea that he be allowed his daily pipe of 'yen-shee' or opium. **1952** J. STEINBECK *East of Eden* xix. 219 Odors from Chinatown, roasting pork and punk and black tobacco and yen shi. **1882** H. H. KANE *Opium-Smoking in Amer. & China* iii. 35 The whole pipe is called the *Yen Tsiang*, or opium pistol. **1909** J. S. THOMPSON *Chinese* viii. 336 At last its consistency suits. He places the gummy head on the large flute-like pipe, or *yen siang* (smoking pistol).

yen, obs. pl. of EYE *sb.*; Sc. and north. dial. f. ONE; dial. f. YON; graphic var. *þen* THAN, THEN.

Yenan (jɛˈnæn). [Chinese (Pinyin) *Yan'an*.] The name of a town in northern Shaanxi province, China, which was the headquarters of the Chinese Communist Party in the years 1936–49, used *attrib.* to designate this period in the history of the Party, or to describe the principles and policies evolved by it at that time.

1949 F. C. JONES *Manchuria since 1931* xii. 231 The Yenan régime had no hold upon the country in general before August 1945. **1957** P. S. H. TANG *Communist China Today: Domestic & Foreign Policies* v. 197 Thoroughness of rural regimentation characterized..administration of the Shensi-Kansu-Ninghsia border region during the Yenan period. **1966** F. SCHURMANN *Ideology & Organization in Communist China* i. 59 The scattered guerrilla forces of the Yenan period had to report back to headquarters in systematic ways. **1970** E. SNOW *Red China Today* (1971) xxxii. 257 After 1966 foreign ballets were seen no more in China; traditional Chinese opera was also overhauled to make it conform to Yenan principles. Mao Tse-tung's dicta, *Talks at the Yenan Forum on Art and Literature*, became the guide-lines for stage and screen performances. **1975** I. C. Y. Hsü *Rise of Mod. China* (ed. 2) xxiv. 714 The heart of the Yenan Way was the perfection of the mass line and the sharpening of revolutionary nationalism in the countryside, which became the twin pillars of Maoism. **1979** *Encounter* Feb. 74/1 The 'Great Leap Forward' led to a re-evaluation of the significance of the Yenan period of the late 1930s and early 1940s.

yence, Sc. and north. dial. f. ONCE.

yench, obs. form of INCH *sb.*[1]

1493 [see THICK *a.* 2].

†**yend**, *v.* *Obs.* Forms: 1 **ȝeendian**, 2–3 (**ȝ**)**ienden**, 5 **ȝynde**. [OE. *ȝeendian*: see Y- 3 c and END *v.* For the form in quot. *c* 1430 cf. END *sb.* etym. note.] *trans.* To end.

c **1000** *Ags. Gosp.* Matt. xxviii. 20 Ic beo mid eow ealle daȝas oð worulde ȝe-endunge. *Ibid.* Luke xiv. 30 Hwæt þes man agan timbrian & ne mihte hit ȝe-endian. *c* **1175** *Lamb. Hom.* 129 Iwilch mon bið iboren mid muchele sara and mid muchele sorȝe his lif iendað. *a* **1240** *Lofsong* in *O.E. Hom.* I. 217 He is ænde buton ælcere ȝiendunge. *c* **1430** *Freemasonry* (1840) 12 The multytude that was comynge Of here chyldryn after here ȝyndynge.

yend, obs. or dial. var. YOND.

yend(e, ȝend(e, obs. ff. END *sb.* and *v.*

Yende, obs. f. IND.

yended, obs. pa. pple. of END *v.*

yender: see YEENDER, YONDER.

yene, obs. pl. of EYE *sb.*; obs. f. YAWN *v.*

yenesherre, obs. form of JANIZARY.

yeng, ȝeng, obs. ff. YOUNG.

Yengees ('jɛŋgiːz). Also **-eese**, *pl.*, whence **Yengee** ('jɛŋgiː) *sing.* Stated to be a N. American Indian corruption of *English*, applied to the people of New England. (Cf. YANKEE.)

1819 HECKEWELDER *Ind. Nations* iii. (1876) 77 When the Yengeese arrived at Machtitschwanne, they looked about everywhere for good spots of land. *Ibid.* xiii. 143 *Yengees.* This name they [*sc.* the Chippeways and some other nations] now exclusively applied to the people of New England... They say they know the *Yengees*, and can distinguish them by their dress and personal appearance... The proper English they call *Saggenash.* **1826** J. F. COOPER *Last of Mohicans* xxix, 'What art thou?' 'A woman; one of a hated race, if thou wilt—a Yengee.' *Ibid.*, It is a redskin in the pay of the Yengeese. **1834** WHITTIER *Mogg Megone* 40 A scalp or twain from the Yengees torn.

Yenisei ('jɛnɪseɪ, jɛnɪ'seɪ). [a. the name of the river *Yenisei* in Siberia.] One of a group of Palæo-Siberian languages belonging to the Finno-Ugric group. Usu. in *Comb.*, esp. as **Yenisei-Ostiak**, the designation of this linguistic group.

1888 *Encycl. Brit.* XXIV. 1/1 *Samoyedic. Yurak* and *Yenisei*, White-Sea to the Yenisei. **1908** T. G. TUCKER *Introd. Nat. Hist. Lang.* viii. 149 The Hyberborean speeches of Asia, some of which may or may not form a family, include..Yenissei-Ostiak (a tongue to be distinguished from the Ural-Altaic Ostiak, with which it agrees neither in its roots nor in the principle of vowel-harmony). **1932** W. L. GRAFF *Lang. & Languages* 406 The Yenisei-Ostiak variety is believed to be related to Tibeto-Chinese. **1939** L. H. GRAY *Foundations of Lang.* 369 The languages of the Uralic family are as follows:..Samoyede group: Yurak, Yenisei-Samoyede, [etc.]. **1948** R. A. D. FORREST *Chinese Lang.* 22 A remarkable outlier of the Sinitic family, and more specifically of the Tibeto-Burman group, is..a group of dialects known as Yenisei-Ostiak and Kottish. They are now spoken by a few villagers far in the north of Siberia, on the river Yenisei, northwards of Yeniseisk. **1951** W. K. MATTHEWS *Languages U.S.S.R.* iii. 17 Yurak (Nenets)..is spoken from the Kanin peninsula to the estuary of the Yenisei river, Yenisei (Enets) along its lower course. **1958** A. S. C. ROSS *Etymology* i. 27 In the language called Yenisei-Ostyak..a variation of a kind very similar to M[oder]n E[nglish]..is found. **1967** [see NENETS].

yenite ('jiːnaɪt). *Min.* [ad. F. *yénite* (Lelièvre, *Jrnl. des Mines*, 1807), f. *Jena* + -ITE[1]: see quot. 1868.] A former synonym of ILVAITE.

1816 P. CLEAVELAND *Min.* (1822) I. 394 Before the blow-pipe the Yenite is easily fusible into a dull, opaque, black globule. **1868** DANA *Min.* 297 Named *Ilvaite* from the Latin name of the island (Elba) on which it was found; *Lievrite* after its discoverer [Lelièvre]; *Yenite* (should have been Jenite) in commemoration of the battle of Jena, in 1806. The Germans, and later the French, have rightly rejected the name *yenite*, on the ground that commemorations of political hostility or triumph are opposed to the spirit of science.

yenne, obs. form of EVEN *sb.*[1]

1478–9 *Stonor Lett.* (Roy. Hist. Soc.) II. 72 Payd for a cope for the caponys on candelmas yenne, vi. d.

yenny, *a.*: see YEN[2].

yenough, obs. form of ENOUGH.

1577 B. GOOGE *Heresbach's Husb.* I. (1586) 9 b, And suche as I found sounde, I thought yenough for me to keepe the reparations.

yenta ('jɛntə). *U.S.* Also **yente**, (*rare*) **yenteh**. [Yiddish, orig. a personal name.] A gossip or busybody; a noisy, vulgar person; a scolding woman or shrew.

1923 A. YEZIERSKA *Salome of Tenements* 12 The slattern *yentehs* lounging on the stoops..were transfigured. **1931** B. HECHT *Jew in Love* 122 Jesus God, you talk like a typical *yenta.* **1948** *Commentary* V. 500/1 *Yente* has become synonymous with noisiness and vulgarity, plus implications of rough good-heartedness. **1968** *Encounter* Sept. 27/1 *Yenta*, I am told, was a perfectly acceptably name for a lady, derived from the Italian *gentile*—until some ungracious *yenta* gave it a bad name. **1970** S. ELLIN *Bind* xxiii. 114 A couple of *yentas* got nothing better to do, they'll take a sunbath right by my window. **1975** *New Yorker* 24 Nov. 167/3 It is to the director's credit that she manages to hold down Doris Roberts' performance as the *yente.* **1978** I. B. SINGER *Shosha* ii. 38 You were always ready to trade me for the first available yenta.

yent (**ȝent**), var. *yend*, YOND *Obs.*

yentred, ME. pa. pple. of ENTER *v.*

1377 LANGL. *P. Pl.* B. x. 375 þat I man made was and my name yentred In þe legende of lyf longe er I were.

yentyll, obs. form of GENTLE *a.*

a **1533** LD. BERNERS *Huon* viii. 20 It neuer commyth of a yentyll courage of any knyght to assayle any person without armure.

yentz (jɛnts), *v.* *U.S. slang.* [Yiddish, f. *yentzen* to copulate.] *trans.* To cheat, to swindle (see also quot. 1939). Also *fig.* Cf. SCREW *v.* 6 d, 13.

1930 *Amer. Mercury* Dec. 458/2 *Yentz*, to cheat. 'They try to yentz me out of me end.' **1939** *Amer. Speech* XIV. 240/2 *To yentz*, to cheat; to fornicate. **1969** S. J. PERELMAN in *Holiday* Mar. 104/4 The faintness one characteristically experiences on discovering that he has been yentzed. **1978** J. KRANTZ *Scruples* x. 276 'I don't *yentz* them,' Maggie explained, Coca-Cola-colored eyes all innocence, 'they just yentz themselves and I try not to run out of tape.'

yen-yen ('jɛnjɛn). *U.S. slang.* Also †**inyun**. [Prob. ad. Chinese (Cantonese) *yīnyǎn* craving for opium, f. *yīn* opium + *yǎn* craving: cf. YEN[2] and YEN[3].] A craving for opium, the 'opium-habit'.

1886 T. BYRNES *Professional Criminals Amer.* 385 A fiend suffering with the *inyun* is a man to be avoided. *Ibid.* 384, I was a victim to the opium habit, or, as the Chinese have it, *inyun fun.* **1892** H. CAMPBELL *Darkness & Daylight* xxviii. 569 'I've got the *yen-yen* (opium habit) the worst way', said one woman, 'and must have my pipe every night.' **1904** H. HAPGOOD *Autobiogr. of Thief* x. 207 Perhaps it was the sight or smell of the hop, but anyway I got the yen-yen and shook as in the ague. **1926** J. BLACK *You can't Win* xvii. 238 He [*sc.* the old Chinaman] was shaking with the 'yen yen', the hop habit. **1961** *Amer. Speech* XXXVI. 178 If Cantonese *yen yen* be regarded as the probable source of English *yen-yen* we may assume that the syllables represent the individual etymons for *yen* 'opium' and *yen* 'craving'.

yeo, *sb.*[1] *local* (south-west). [repr. OE. **eá*, **iá* for *éa* stream, river: see Æ *sb.*[1], EA, and cf. AA[1].] A stream or drain (in mining).

[In the following 16th cent. quots. the forms *yew*, *yo* are of doubtful identity; the river-name *Yeo* (OE. *Eowan* in oblique cases) may be intended:

1521 *Yatton Churchw. Acc.* (Som. Rec. Soc.) 139 In expenses for dyking yᵉ new yew..xxiijs. iiijd. **1543** *Ibid.* 157 Payd for mowyng the yew..iijs. iiijd. **1558** *Ibid.* 170 Fo Dychinge..the parishe woorke in yᵉ Yo..xvjᵈ and xijᵈ.]

1725 PEARCE *Laws Stannaries* Introd. p. xiii, Every Work may lawfully bring their Water from the River, which the Tinners [in Cornwall and Devon] commonly call the *Yeo*, without Denial or Contention. *Ibid.*, Then they go [to] the *Yeo*, or River, and fetch home the Water which serves this Work. **1873** *Q. Rev.* CXXXV. 157 'Girts' or 'gulphs' are names given by the moormen [of Dartmoor] to the long, and sometimes deep, excavations seaming the hill-sides, down which the miners led their stream, generally known as the 'yeo'. **1873** WILLIAMS & JONES *Gloss. Som.*, *Yeo*, main drain of a level.

yeo (jəʊ), *sb.*[2] Colloq. abbrev. of YEOMAN; commonly in *pl.* = YEOMANRY 3.

[**1710** J. CHAMBERLAYNE *St. Gt. Brit.* II. III. (ed. 23) 534 M. Alford *Yeo.*] **1831** LOVER *Leg. Irel.*, *Paddy the Piper* 150 If the Husshians or the Yeo's ketches you. **1898** K. TYNAN in *Westm. Gaz.* 12 Oct. 2/1 The yeos at Rathdrum had information that a house..was to be robbed.

yeo, *sb.*[3] Dial. form of EWE; also in comb. *yeo-necked* = EWE-NECKED.

1746 *Exmoor Scolding* (E.D.S.) 210 Tha cortst tha natted Yeo now-reert,..laping o'er the Yoanna Lock. **1878** G. MURRAY *Russians of To-day* 15 Mounted upon yeo-necked galloways.

yeofaile, obs. form of JEOFAIL.

yeo-(heave-)ho: see YO-HEAVE-HO, YOHO.

ye olde (jiː əʊld, 'əʊldiː), *a.* [f. *ye* graphic var. of THE *dem. adj.* (see Y 3) + OLDE *a.*] Employed esp. commercially to suggest (spurious) antiquity in collocations the other words of which are often also archaistically spelt. Also *absol.* as *sb.*, a building characterized by (spurious) antique furnishings.

1896 W. WROTH *London Pleasure Gardens* I. 56 A modern public-house. 'Ye olde Bagnigge Wells.' **1900** *Confectioners' Union Hand-bk.* 167 Ye olde English toffee. **1919** WODEHOUSE *Damsel in Distress* xxvi. 298 In London, when a gentlewoman becomes distressed..she collects about her two or three other distressed gentlewomen..and starts a tea-shop in the West-End, which she calls Ye Oak Leaf, Ye Olde Willow-Pattern, Ye Linden-Tree, or Ye Snug Harbour, according to personal taste. **1933** [see OLDE *a.*]. **1951** 'M. INNES' *Operation Pax* V. ii. 197 Not a tourist centre. Nothing ye olde. **1972** P. CLEIFE *Slick & Dead* iv. 36 The Inn was the complete trendy-contemporary Ye Olde —all ship's lanterns, copper pans, chintz and candelabra. **1977** *New Yorker* 16 May 107/1 Quincy Market..basically a suburban shopping mall done up in the instant charm of ye olde exposed brick.

yeolke, yeolow, obs. ff. YOLK, YELLOW.

yeoman ('jəʊmən). Pl. **yeomen** ('jəʊmɛn). Forms: α. 4–5 **ȝoman, ȝhoman**, (4 **ȝhuman, ȝouman**), 4–7 **yoman**, 5 **ȝoman(n)e, ȝomon, yomon**, (**yhoman**), **ȝuman**, 6–7 **yoeman**. β. 4–6 **ȝeman**, (4 **ȝheman**), 5–7 **yeman**, (5 **ȝemman, yemon**, 6 **ȝeaman**, *Sc.* **ȝieman**, 8 **ye'man**). γ. 4–5 **ȝiman, ȝyman**, (4 **ȝymman**, 5 **ȝimman, ȝymanne**). δ. 5– **yeoman**, (7–8 *Sc.* **zeoman**). [ME. (14th cent.) *ȝoman, ȝuman, ȝeman, ȝiman*, prob. reduced forms of *ȝong-, ȝung-, ȝeng-, ȝingman*: see YOUNGMAN, which is itself used as a designation of an attendant or servant (cf. sense 1 below), while a 12th cent. *yongerman* is given in Pseudo-Cnut de Foresta §2 as a synonym of *læsspeȝenes* 'mediocres homines' (cf. sense 4), who were intermediate between the *þeȝenes* 'liberales homines' and the *tunmen* 'villani' (cf. also OE. *ȝingra* vassal, follower of a prince, etc.).

The *mm* found in some forms (*ȝemman, ȝimman*) may be a survival of the *ngm* of *yongman.* Cf. MSw., Da. *jomfru*, Icel. *jumfrú* (after LG. *jumfer*), and Du. *juffrouw* beside *jonkvrouw* young lady.

The pronunciation ('jiːmən) is evidenced as late as the time of Swift (see quot. 1706 in 4 β and cf. 1687 in 4 δ).

If this word is ultimately identical with *youngman*, the derivation has possibly a remarkable parallel in s.w. dial. *yeomath, yeemath, yemmath, youmath, yummath* = aftermath, which is app. for **young math* = late mowing.]

I. 1. a. A servant or attendant in a royal or noble household, usually of a superior grade, ranking between a sergeant (SERGEANT *sb.* 7) and a groom (GROOM *sb.*[1] 4) or between a squire and a page.

α. **13..** *K. Alis.* 835 (Laud MS.), To ȝoman page & joglers. **1377** LANGL. *P. Pl.* B. III. 213 (MS. R.) Emperoures ..han ȝoumen [C. IV. 271 ȝemen, *v.rr.* ȝomen, ȝimmen, ȝemmen, ȝonge men] to ȝernen and to ride. ? *a* **1400** *Morte Arth.* 2628 He [*sc.* Arthur] made me ȝomane at Ȝole, and gafe me gret gyftes, And c. pounde, and a horse, and harnayse fulle ryche. **14..** in *Monum. Francisc.* (Rolls) 583 Commaunde ȝe that ȝoure gentilmen yomen and other dayly bere and were there robis in ȝoure presence. *c* **1420** *Chron. Vilod.* 4558 Knyȝt, squiere, ȝomon & page. **1449** *Rolls of Parlt.* V. 157/2 Yomen of the moste honourable Houshold of the Kyng. *c* **1489** CAXTON *Sonnes of Aymon* iv. 123 Came there a yoman that sayd to the duchesse..the meete is redy. *c* **1520** SKELTON *Magnyf.* 2542 To day hote, to morowe outragyous colde; To day a yoman, to morowe made of page. **1593** *Lanc. Wills* (Chetham Soc.) 155, I gyve unto everye one of my yomen suche as are my howseholde servants over and besyds theire waigs xxˢ a peece.

β. **1345–8** in *Househ. Ord.* (1790) 9 The Kinges archers, vinteners, yemen of offices in the Kinges howse. **1375** BARBOUR *Bruce* v. 235 Quhill I liff, and may haf mycht To lede a ȝheman or a swane. *c* **1470** HENRY *Wallace* II. 388 A bauld squier, with him gud ȝemen twa. **1470–85** MALORY *Arthur* XXI. iii. 845 The kyng callyd vpon hys knyghtes squyers and yemen. **1584** WHETSTONE *Mirr. Mag., Cities* 15 b, Were this a lawe in England, I feare mee..we shuld haue more Gentlemen bondmen, then Yemen trustie seruantes.

δ. *a* **1483** *Liber Niger* in *Househ. Ord.* (1790) 19 Our sovereyn lordes household is now discharged..of the Court of Marshalsy, and all his clerkes and yeomen. **1561** *Old Cheque-Bk. Chapel Royal* (Camden) 1 Mr. Paternoster was sworne gent' the 24th of Marche, and Jones, Gospeller, and Thos. Rawlins, Yeoman. **1571** GOLDING *Calvin on Ps.* vii. 14 Saule..had many yeomen at hand, that wold gladly have employed their labour too destroye David. **1607** DEKKER & WEBSTER *Westw. Hoe* III. D 4, Come Sergeant Ambush, come yeoman Clutch, yons the Tauerne, the Gentleman will come out presently. **1713** SWIFT *On Himself* 35 The waiters stand in ranks; the yeomen cry, Make room; as if a duke were passing by. **1814** SCOTT *Ld. of Isles* I. xxix, Where squire and yeoman, page and groom, Plied their loud revelry. **1864** TENNYSON *Aylmer's F.* 497 The folly..became in other fields A mockery to the yeomen over ale, And laughter to their lords.

b. An attendant or assistant to an official, etc.

13.. *E.E. Allit. P.* A. 535 Gos to my vyne, ȝemen ȝonge, & wyrkes & dos þat at ȝe moun. **1363** *Rolls of Parlt.* II. 278/2 Gentz de Mestere, d'Artifice & d'Office, appellez Yomen. *c* **1386** CHAUCER *Prol.* 101 A Yeman [*v.rr.* ȝeman, ȝ oman] hadde he, and seruantz namo. **1552** in Feuillerat *Revels Edw. VI* (1914) 124 Lyuery for his yemen and other baser officers. **1568** GRAFTON *Chron.* II. 84 Robyn Hood had at his rule and commaundement an hundreth tall yomen. **1597** SHAKS. *2 Hen. IV*, II. i. 4 *Hostesse.* Mr. Fang, haue you entred the Action? *Fang.* It is enter'd. *Hostesse.* Wher's your

Yeoman? Is it a lusty yeoman? 1627 J. Taylor (Water P.) *Armado* C 8, Nimble tongu'd Pettifoggers, greedy Serieants, hungry Yeomen, deuoureing Catchpoles. 1766 Entick *London* IV. 47 Eighteen serjeants at mace, and every serjeant hath his yeoman. 1861 *Times* 26 July, The senior Sheriff's yeoman read Her Majesty's writ, authorizing the Sheriffs to proceed to the election of 'a fit and discreet citizen' to serve in Parliament. 1897 J. D. Walker in *Rec. Lincoln's Inn* I. Pref. 7 A Bencher in 1442 was entitled as of right to have a yeoman (*valettus*) boarded in the Inn at a charge of 14d. per week.

c. ***yeoman's service*** (also ***yeoman service***): good, efficient, or useful service, such as is rendered by a faithful servant of good standing.

[*a* 1500 *Gest of Robyn Hode* lxxx, It were greate shame sayd Robyn A knyght a lone to ryde, Without squyer yeman or page,.. I shall the lene lytyll Johan my man,.. In a yemans stede he may the stande, Yf thou grete nede haue.] 1602 Shaks. *Ham.* v. ii. 36, I once did hold it.. A basenesse to write faire;.. but Sir now, It did me Yeomans seruice. 1613 Hoby *Counter-snarle* 75 You may doe the Pope yeoman seruice indeede. 1807 Scott 11 Aug. in *Fam. Lett.* (1894) I. iii. 77 This [law] has done me yeoman's service in the hour of necessity. 1857 Hughes *Tom Brown* i, These stalwart sons of the Browns have done yeomen's work. 1858 De Quincey *Language* Wks. 1890 X. 247 The word *ignore*.. has now assumed [a general meaning], with little offence to good taste, and with yeoman service to the intellect. 1884 *Illustr. Lond. News* 29 Nov. 84 The.. Society has done yeoman's service during the ten years of its existence.

2. a. With *of* (or *for*) followed by a word indicating the particular department or function, in the titles of various officials, esp. of a royal or noble household, as ***yeoman of the bottles, of the buttery, of the cellar, of the chamber, of the crown, of the ewery, of the horse(s, for the household, of the larder, for the mouth*** (mouth *sb.* 2 d), ***of the revels, of the robes, of the stable, of the stirrup, of the tents, of the wardrobe***; so ***yeoman of the channel*** (an official of the Corporation of London: see channel *sb.*[1] 3 a). Hence in humorous allusion, as ***yeoman of the collar***, a prisoner with an iron band round his neck (collar *sb.* 5); ***yeoman of the cord, of the halter***, a hangman, or hangman's assistant.

1455 in *Househ. Ord.* (1790) 18 Richard Clerk, Yoman of the *Armurie. *Ibid.*, Henri Est, Yoman of the *Beddes. *Ibid.* 19 William Wytnall, Yoman for the *botilles. 1591 *Murther John Ld. Bourgh* A 4 b, One Iohn Powell yeoman of the bottels. 1531 in Butt *Ford's Archery* (1887) 141 Yoeman of the Kinges *bowes. 1473 *Rolls of Parlt.* VI. 97/2 Richard Forster, Yoman of the *Botry of oure Houshold. 1513 *Bk. Keruynge* in *Babees Bk.* 270 Yoman of the *seller and ewery. 1345–8 in *Househ. Ord.* (1790) 4 Yeomen of the Kinges *chamber. 1390 Gower *Conf.* III. 62 Thre yomen of his chambre. 1438 *E.E. Wills* (1882) 110 The yomen of my lordys chambre. 1708 J. Chamberlayne *St. Gt. Brit.* ii. iii. xliii. (ed. 22) 688 Yeoman of the *Channel. 1647 Haward *Crown Rev.* 33 Yeoman of the Stirrup... Yeoman of the Male... Yeoman of the *close Carte. 1530 *Hickscorner* (Manly) 239 *Frewyll.* Syr, laye you beneth, or on hye on the soller? *Imag.* Nay, ywys, amonge the thyckest of yemen of the *coller. *c* 1640 J. Day *Peregr. Schol.* xvii. (1881) 72 A kinsman of myne that is grome of the ladder and yeoman of the *corde. 1450 *Rolls of Parlt.* V. 192/2 Yoman of the *Coroune, and Ussher of oure Chambre. 1498 in Leadam *Sel. Cases Crt. Requests* (Selden Soc.) 5 William Frost oon of your Yomons of the Crowne. 1450 *Rolls of Parlt.* V. 194/1 Watkyn Bedell, Yoman of oure *Ewre. 1455 in *Househ. Ord.* (1790) 20 John Canne, Yomen for the *halle. 1802 J. T. Smith *Bk. for Rainy Day* (1861) 169 A most diabolical-looking little wretch, denominated 'the Yeoman of the *Halter', Jack Ketch's head man. 1455 in *Househ. Ord.* (1790) 23, 1 Yoman of *Horse. 1530 Palsgr. 291/1 Yeman of the horse, *palfrenier*. 1586 T. B. *La Primaud. Fr. Acad.* i. 320 The yomen of his horses. 1585 Higins *Junius' Nomencl.* 510/2 *Promus*,.. a butler: a yeoman of the *larder. 1455 in *Househ. Ord.* (1790) 20 William Pratte, Yoman for the King's *mouth. 1531 Elyot *Gov.* iii. v, Yoman for the mouthe with the kynge. *a* 1700 B. E. *Dict. Cant. Crew*, *Yeoman of the Mouth*, an Officer belonging to his Majestie's Pantry. 1345–8 in *Househ. Ord.* (1790) 4 Yeomen of the *offices. 1552–3 in Feuillerat *Revels Edw. VI* (1914) 111 Iohn howlte yeman of the *Revelles. 1455 in *Househ. Ord.* (1790) 17 John Slytherst, Yoman of the *Robes. 1552 Huloet, Yoman or master of the robes, *vestiarius*. 1728 Chambers *Cycl.* s.v. *Acatery*, A Yeoman of the *Salt-Stores. 1650 in *Archaeologia* V. 435 The Saucery House, conteyning foure little roomes used by the yeoman of the *sauces. 1455 in *Househ. Ord.* (1790) 21 Roger Sutton, Yoman for the *sething place. *Ibid.* 23, 11 Yeoman and Gromes of the *Stable. 1473 *Acc. Ld. High Treas. Scot.* I. 55 The Hensmen and ȝomen of the stablis for the King and the Quene. *a* 1578 Lindesay (Pitscottie) *Chron. Scot.* (S.T.S.) I. 325 The king callit on ane ȝemen of the stabill and desyrit ane of his abullȝementis. 1526, 1538, 1647, 1692 Yeoman of the *stirrup [see stirrup *sb.* 1 d]. 1455 in *Househ. Ord.* (1790) 18 Yoman of the *Stoole. 1552–3 in Feuillerat *Revels Edw. VI* (1914) 111 Yeman of the *Tentes. 1679–88 *Moneys Secr. Serv. Chas. II & Jas. II* (Camden) 135 To Thomas Howard, yeoman of the tents and toyles, for his charge in removing the toyles and waggons. 1523–34 Fitzherb. *Husb.* §151 The yomen of the *wardropes of noble men. 1601 Shaks. *Twel. N.* ii. v. 45 The Lady of the Strachy, married the yeoman of the wardrob.

b. ***Yeoman of the Guard***: a member of the body-guard of the sovereign of England (first appointed at the accession of Henry VII, and originally archers). Also ***Extraordinary Yeoman***: see beefeater 2.

1485 in Hennell *Hist. Yeom. Gd.* (1904) 23 Oure humble and feithful subgiet William Browne yoman of oure garde. 1509–10 *Act 1 Hen. VIII*, c. 14 A Yoman of the Crowne or of the Kynges garde. 1519–20 *Rec. St. Mary at Hill* (1904) 307 Ress' for the Buryall of a yoman of the Gard þat dyed at þe Swan.. ij s. 1552 in Hennell *Hist. Yeom. Gd.* (1904) 292 The Garde, 1552... Ordinarie Yeomen in number cc... Extraordinarie Yeomen in number cc & vii. 1573 *Ibid.* 293 Raulf Colborne an extraordinarye yeoman. 1613 J. Taylor (Water P.) *Watermen's Suit* Wks. 1630 i. 175 Gentlemen of the priuy Chamber, or Yeomen of the Gard at least. 1647 Haward *Crown Rev.* 19 Captaine of the Guard.. Ordinary Yeomen of the Guard, 200..50 Extraordinary. 1675 in *Verney Mem.* (1907) II. 305 A L[d] Chamberlain was never before turned out for striking a yeoman of the guard. 1711 Steele *Spect.* No. 109 ¶2 The vast jetting Coat and small Bonnet, which was the Habit in Harry the Seventh's Time, is kept on in the Yeomen of the Guard. 1745 Mrs. E. Montagu *Corr.* (1906) I. 202, I can eat more buttered roll in a morning than a great girl at a boarding school, and more beef at dinner than a yeoman of the Guards. 1904 Hennell *Hist. Yeom. Gd.* 62 In the Yeomen of the Guard the yeomen are all non-commissioned officers, sergeants or sergeant-majors.

c. In the British and U.S. navies, an inferior officer who has charge of the stores in a particular department: with *of* or possessive, as ***yeoman of the powder-room, of the sheets*** (now abolished), ***y. of (the) signals, of the store-room, boatswain's y., engineer's y., paymaster's y., ship's y.*** Also *ellipt.*

[*c* 1400 *Beryn* 2997 Why goon the ȝemen to bote, Ankirs to hale?] 1669 Sturmy *Mariner's Mag.* v. xii. 46 A Gunner.. must be careful in making Choice of a sober honest Man, for the Yeoman of the Powder. 1698 in *MSS. Ho. Lords* (N.S.) III. (1905) 346 The gunner and the yeoman ordered him to assist him. 1702 in *Lond. Gaz.* No. 3815/2 Yeomen of the Sheets,.. Yeomen of the Powder Room. 1816 in *Ord. Council Naval Service* (1866) I. 300 We further submit to your Royal Highness to be pleased to sanction the abolition of the following obsolete or unnecessary ratings:—Yeoman of the Powder Room. —— of the Sheets. 1833 *Ibid.* 511 Yeoman of the Store Rooms. 1850 H. Melville *White Jacket* I. xxx. 194 The ship's yeoman's store-room. 1891 C. Roberts *Adrift Amer.* 234 The boatswain's yeoman. 1898 Kipling *Fleet in Being* 82 The Yeoman of Signals came to the captain's cabin at the regulation pace... 'Signal from the flagship, sir.' 1899 F. T. Bullen *Way Navy* 28 The chief petty officer, who is entitled chief yeoman of the signals. 1918 T. S. Eliot *Let.* 13 Nov. in *Waste Land Drafts* (1971) p. xv, I was *sent for* by the Navy Intelligence, who said.. that ..they would make me a Chief Yeoman and raise me to a commission in a few months. 1978 H. Wouk *War & Remembrance* i 6 My chief yeoman's got the logs and other records all lined up.

3. Used appositively in the titles of various attendants and officials, as ***yeoman bedel***, †***brever, cook, farrier*** (†***ferrer***), †***fewterer***, †***furner***, †***garneter, gunner***, †***herbergeour*** (harbinger), ***porter, pricker*** (pricker 3), ***purveyor, usher, waiter, warder***, etc.: see also these words.

1641 *Yeoman-bedels [see beadle 3 a]. 1853 'C. Bede' *Verdant Green* i. vii, The Vice-Chancellor, with his Esquire and Yeoman-bedels. 1553 in *Archaeologia* XII. 359 The celler. Servauntes.. John Thorowgood and Jeffrey Perrens, *yeomen brevers. 1450 *Rolls of Parlt.* V. 195/1 To Thomas Cateby, *Yoman Cooke for oure mouth. 1454 *Acts Privy Council* (1837) VI. 213 Robert Pilchard *yoman ferrour. 1455 [see ferrer 3]. 1647 [see farrier *sb.* 3]. 1599 *Yeoman pheuterer [see fewterer]. 1629 Massinger *Picture* v. i, If you will bee An honest yeoman pheuterer, feed vs first, And walke vs after. 1650 B. *Discolliminium* 52 The rest of the Subjects [shall be] Yeomen-futerers and Gold-finders. 1553 in *Archaeologia* XII. 357 The Countinge howse. Servants.. Rauffe Englishe, *yeoman furnator.. Robert Style, yeoman garnator. 1455 in *Househ. Ord.* (1790) 19 William Peye, *Yoman Fourner. 1454 *Acts Privy Council* (1837) VI. 213 Thomas Wente, *yoman garnetter. 1553 in *Archaeologia* XII. 357 Robarte Style, yeoman garnator. 1647 Haward *Crown Rev.* 33 Three Yeomen granators: Fee a peice per diem 9 d. 1450 *Rolls of Parlt.* V. 198/1 The office of *Yoman Gonner of oure Citee and Castell of Westchestre. *Ibid.* 195/1 Oure servaunt John Ripon, one of oure *Yomen Herbergeours. 1642 *Docq. Lett. Pat. at Oxf.* (1837) 341 His Ma[te] gent' & yeomen Harbingers. 1455 in *Househ. Ord.* (1790) 21, 1 *Yoman Herde. *Ibid.* 19 John Swyllyngton, *Yoman Messenger. *Ibid.*, William Brynklowe, *Yoman Paymenbaker. 1470–85 Malory *Arthur* vi. ix. 196 He fond a *yoman porter kepyng ther many keyes. 1560 in J. Scott *Berwick-upon-Tweed* (1888) 449 The yeoman porters at any of the gates of this towne. 1708 J. Chamberlayne *St. Gt. Brit.* ii. iii. (ed. 22) 628 Yeoman Porter for Oil and Candle for the Gate. 1766 Entick *London* IV. 347 The yeoman porter goes to the governor's house for the keys. 1455, 1601 *Yeoman powder-beater [see powder *sb.*[1] 5 b]. 1586, 1760, 1891 *Yeoman pricker [see pricker 3]. *c* 1767 G. White *Selborne, To Pennant* vi, I saw myself one of the yeomen-prickers single out a stag from the herd. 1820 Scott *Monast.* xvii, Were you to put in for it, I would warrant you were made one of the Abbot's yeomen-prickers. 1454 *Acts Privy Council* (1837) VI. 213 Richard Walgrave and John Glover *yomen purveours. 1647 Haward *Crown Rev.* 33 Foure Yeomen Purveiours: Fee a peice per diem 9 d. 1455 in *Househ. Ord.* (1790) 18 Stephen Coote, *Yoman Skynner. *Ibid.*, John Marchall, *Yoman Surgeon. *a* 1400–50 *Bk. Curtasye* 519 in *Babees Bk.* 316 *Ȝomon vssher be-fore þe dore, In vttur chambur lies on þe flore. 1614 *Nottingham Rec.* IV. 319 To the Yeoman Vsher's grooms and pages.. xl s. 1649 Milton *Eikon.* xxiv. 192 The Yeomen Ushers of Devotion. 1708 J. Chamberlayne *St. Gt. Brit.* ii. iii. (ed. 22) 555 Mr. Ric. Pearson, Yeoman Usher. 1523–34 Fitzherb. *Husb.* §152 There was.. as many good housholdes kept, and as many *yomenne wayters therin as be nowe. 1526 *Househ. Ord.* (1790) 152 The yeoman ushers and yeoman wayters for that day. 1573 in Hennell *Hist. Yeom. Gd.* (1904) 293 The *yeomen warders of our Tower of London. 1947 *Tower of London* (Min. of Works) 13/2 The interior is shown to the public.. on application to the Yeoman-Warder on duty. 1979 J. Gardner *Nostradamus Traitor* i. 2 'You are a Beefeater, yes?' 'Yeoman Warder, Ma'am. Beefeater's a kind of nickname.'

II. 4. a. A man holding a small landed estate; a freeholder under the rank of a gentleman; hence *vaguely*, a commoner or countryman of respectable standing, *esp.* one who cultivates his own land.

α. 1411 *Rolls of Parlt.* III. 650/2 All the Knyghtes and Esquiers and Yomen that had ledynge of men. *c* 1425 Wyntoun *Cron.* viii. xi. 1825 Ȝhomen and gentil men alsua. *c* 1449 Pecock *Repr.* iii. xiv. 371 Whether he be knyȝt, squyer, gentilman, ȝoman, or louȝer. *c* 1460 Fortescue *Abs. & Lim. Mon.* xvii. (1885) 151 A c.s. off ffee or rente, wich is a feyre lyuynge ffor a yoman. 1473 Warkw. *Chron.* (Camden) 1 And othere of gentylmen and yomenne he made knyghtes and squyres, as thei hade desserved. 1549 Latimer *1st Serm. bef. Edw. VI* (Arb.) 40 My father was a Yoman, and had no landes of his owne, onlye he had a farme of iii. or iiii. pound by yere at the vttermost... He had walke for a hundred shepe, and my mother mylked xxx. kyne. 1642 in Rushw. *Hist. Coll.* (1692) iii. I. 680 Though many of the Chief Gentry of those Counties were for paying Obedience to his Majestie's Commission of Array, yet the Free-holders and Yoemen being generally of the other side, ..they were crush'd. 1648 *Hunting of Fox* 39 The sufferings of the Yoemen, Farmers, and other poor Countrymen.

β. 1455 *Cal. Anc. Rec. Dublin* (1889) 288 Arlaton Hussher, merchant.. and Harry White, yeman. 1486 *Bk. St. Albans* d iv, Ther is a Goshawke, and that hauke is for a yeman. 1500–20 Dunbar *Poems* xxxix. 25 Honest ȝemen in every toun War wont to weir baith reid and broun. 1542–3 *Act 34 & 35 Hen. VIII*, c. 26 §26 [70] Twoo substanciall Gentlemen or Yeomen to be chief Constables of the Hundred wherin they inhabyte. 1567 Harman *Caveat* (1869) 22 The honorable wyl abhore them, The worshipfull wyll reiecte them, The yemen wyll sharpely tawnte them, The Husband men vtterly defye them, The laboryng men bluntly chyde them. *a* 1578 Lindesay (Pitscottie) *Chron. Scot.* (S.T.S.) I. 283 Money wther gentillmen and ȝemenis. 1596 Dalrymple tr. *Leslie's Hist. Scot.* (S.T.S.) I. 36 Ȝiemen and housbandmen thair sal ȝe sie gang weil arrayed. 1706 Swift *Baucis & Phil.* 19 A good old honest ye'man, Call'd in the neighbourhood Philemon.

γ. 1387 Trevisa *Higden* (Rolls) II. 171 Þerfore hit is þat a ȝeman [*v.r.* ȝymman; L. *vernaculus*] arraieþ hym as a squyer, a squyer as a knyȝt, a kniȝt as a duke and a duke as a kyng.

δ. *a* 1577 Sir T. Smith *Commw. Eng.* i. xxiii. (1584) 30, I call him a yeoman whom our Lawes doe call *Legalem hominem*,.. which is a freeman borne English, and may dispend of his owne free lande in yerely reuenue to the summe of xl. s. sterling. *Ibid.* 32 Yeoman: which worde now signifieth among vs, a man well at ease and hauing honestlie to liue, and yet not a gentleman. 1591 Shaks. *1 Hen. VI*, ii. iv. 86 His Grandfather was Lyonel Duke of Clarence,.. Spring Crestlesse Yeomen from so deepe a Root? 1640–1 *Kirkcudbr. War-Comm. Min. Bk.* (1855) 4 To be peyit be the tennants and yeomanes. 1647 Clarendon *Hist. Reb.* vi. §4 The other party.. persuading the substantial yeomen and freeholders that at least two parts of their estates would.. be taken from them. 1687 in *Third Coll. Poems* (1689) 21 The Admiral may now turn common Seaman, Or Fer——s like; from Court to Country Yeoman. 1716 Gay *Trivia* iii. 285, I knew a yeoman, who.. To the great city drove, from Devon's plain His num'rous lowing herd. 1812 Shelley *Devil's Walk* xix, The wealthy yeoman, as he wanders His fertile fields among, And on his thriving cattle ponders. 1815 Scott *Guy M.* Note B, An old and sturdy yeoman belonging to the Scottish side,.. well known by his soubriquet of Fighting Charlie of Liddesdale. 1861 Geo. Eliot *Silas M.* i. iii, The fall of prices had not yet come to carry the race of small squires and yeomen down that road to ruin.

transf. and *fig.* *a* 1586 Sidney *Arcadia* ii. iv. (1912) 167 The first might seeme the Lords, the second the Gentlemen, and the last the Yeomen of dogges. 1863 Longf. *Wayside Inn, K. Olaf* xx. iii, Turning to a Lapland yeoman. 1865 *Spectator* 14 Jan. 32 Never.. since yeoman Cain killed nomad Abel. 1879 Froude *Cæsar* ii. 14 The grandsons of the yeomen who had held at bay Pyrrhus and Hannibal sold their farms and went away.

†**b.** Used as a term of disparagement. *rare*$^{-1}$.

c 1440 *Gesta Rom.* lxix. 318 Thenne þe Emperour turnyd to his brothir, and saide, 'Þou ȝoman, what soory wrecchidnesse is in þe?'

†**c.** Applied to the pawns at chess. *Obs. rare.*

1523–34 Fitzherb. *Husb.* Prol., That boke [*sc.* of chess] is deuyded in vi. degrees,.. the kynge, the quene, the byshops, the knightes, the iudges, and the yomenne.

5. a. A man of the standing or rank described in 4 serving as a (foot) soldier. Now *Hist.* or *arch.* exc. as in b.

1375 Barbour *Bruce* xvi. 101 Schir Richard of Clare.. Send wicht ȝhomen that veill couth schut To bikkir the reirward apon fut. *a* 1400 *Sqr. lowe Degre* 232 Thus in your warres shall you ryde, With syxe good yemen by your syde. *a* 1577 Sir T. Smith *Commw. Eng.* i. xxiii. (1589) 41 The gentlemen of Fraunce and the yeomen of England are renowned, because in battle of horsemen Fraunce was many times too good for vs, as we againe away for them on foote. And Gentlemen for the most part be men at armes and horsemen, and yeomen commonly on foote. 1599 Shaks. *Hen. V*, iii. i. 25 And you good Yeomen, Whose Lyms were made in England; shew vs here The mettell of your Pasture. 1612 Drayton *Poly-olb.* xi. 29 Our Armies in those times.. Of our tall Yeomen were, and foot-men for the most. 1814 Scott *Ld. of Isles* v. xxix, Two hundred yeomen on that morn The castle left, and none return.

b. *spec.* A member of the (Imperial) Yeomanry: see yeomanry 3.

1798 in *Ld. Auckland's Corr.* (1862) III. 429 Two of the yeomen of Lord Ely's corps.. were hanged.., being condemned by a Courtmartial. 1812 *Ann. Reg., Chron.* 93 It being reported that a poor old woman had been killed by the carelessness of the yeomen, the crowd began to follow the cavalry. 1828 Scott *Jrnl.* 18 Mar. (1891) 558, I am one of the oldest, if not the very oldest Yeoman in Scotland, and have seen the rise, progress, and now the fall of this very constitutional part of the national force. 1912 L. Tracy *Mirabel's Isl.* iv. (1915) 65 'Were you in a Highland regiment?' 'No. I was a mere worm, an Imperial Yeoman.'

III. 6. *attrib.* and *Comb.* **a.** *attrib.*, as ***yeoman class, rank, throng***; appositive (see also 3), as ***yeoman farmer, gentleman, man, proprietor, servant, soldier,*** † ***sprat, volunteer***; † **yeoman ale,** † **yeoman bread** (also *yeoman's bread*), names for second qualities of ale or bread; **yeoman service** (see 1 c).

1532 *Cartular. Abb. de Rievalle* (Surtees) 355 Of *yoman aile of the great fatt, v gallons. **1430** *Charters Selby Abbey, York* (B.M. Add. Ch. 45849), 8 panes secundarios vocatos *yhomanbreed. **1552** Huloet, Bread called Yomens bread, *domesticus panis.* **1620** Venner *Via Recta* i. 18 *Secundarium* is that part of the meale, whereof yeoman-bread is made, which some call second bread. **1876** Miss Braddon *J. Haggard's Dau.* i, The new-comer's costume was that of the *yeoman class. **1878** Stubbs *Const. Hist.* §803 After the economical changes which marked the early years of the fifteenth century, the yeoman class was strengthened by the addition of the body of the tenant farmers. **1821** Cobbett *Rur. Rides* (1885) I. 17 Those only who rent..are, properly speaking, farmers. Those who till their own land are yeomen; and, when I was a boy, it was the common practice to call the former farmers and the latter *yeomen-farmers. **1375** Barbour *Bruce* xiii. 225 *heading*, How the *ȝhemen men and the pouer men maid of schetis the maner of baneris. **1481** *Acts Parl. Scot., Jas. III* (1814) II. 139/2 For the slaying..of ony tratour..cummyn of gentill blude, thare salbe payit xx li And for a ȝeman man x li. *a* **1578** Lindesay (Pitscottie) *Chron. Scot.* (S.T.S.) I. 98 Witht sindrie wther gentillmen and money ȝeamen men of commons. **1593** *Sc. Acts Jas. VI* (1816) IV. 18/2 The panis and vnlawes of lawborrous..salbe of euery erll or lord Tua thowsand pund ..and for euerie ȝeman man Ane hundreth markis. **1873** Hamerton *Intell. Life* iii. iii. 83 A small *yeoman proprietor cultivates his own land. **1862** Thornbury *Turner* I. 5 A family like Turner's that produced a small tradesman, a bank-clerk, and a solicitor, must have at least been of as good *yeoman rank as Shakspeare's. **1498** in *Somerset Med. Wills* (1901) 375 To every of my servants y callid *yemen servants, 6*s.* 8*d.* **1880** Hardy *Trumpet-Major* v, No impossible contingency with the *yeoman-soldier. **1622** Massinger & Dekker *Virg. Mart.* ii. i, She tooke vs, tis true, from the gallowes, yet I hope she will not barre *yeomen sprats to haue their swinge. **1808** Scott *Marm.* iii. xxvi, And on the tale the *yeoman-throng Had made a comment sage and long. **1808** in C. W. Thompson *Rec. Dorset Yeomanry* (1894) 87 Report of the Dorset *Yeomen Volunteers.

b. *Comb.*, as ***yeoman-like*** adj., ***yeoman-wise*** adv.

1674 N. Fairfax *Bulk & Selv.* 90 They could neither speak with nor make one another, (if I may word it so much Yeoman-wise). **1682** H. More in *Glanvill's Sadducismus, Contin. Coll.* 38 A proper Yeomen-like Man. **1828** tr. *Manzoni's Betrothed Lovers* Pref. p. viii, His bold, and honest, and yeoman-like bearing.

Hence **yeomaness** = yeowoman; **yeomanhood,** the position or station of a yeoman.

1623 Wodroephe *Marrowe Fr. Tongue* 211/2 *Yeamanesse, good wife, haue you no fresh egges? *Ibid.* 283/2 Valiant like the yeamenesses [orig. *Paysantes*] of Lombardie. **1889** Saintsbury *Ess. Engl. Lit.* (1890) 6 They had apparently lost even the dignity of *yeomanhood.

yeomanly (ˈjəʊmənlɪ), *a.* [f. yeoman + -ly[1].]

1. Having the rank, or the character, of a yeoman.

1576 A. Hall *Acc. Quarrel w. Mallerie* etc., Misc. Antiq. Angl. (1816) I. 97 A yeomanly man. *c* **1590** Greene *Fr. Bacon* xv. (1594) H6b, I warrant you hees as yeomanly a man, as you shall see, marke you maisters, heeres a plaine honest man, without welt or garde. **1621** Donne *Serm., 1 Cor.* xv. 26 (1640) 148 Who will undertake to sift those dusts again, and to pronounce, This is the Patrician, this is the noble flowre, and this the yeomanly, this the Plebeian bran? **1680** Aubrey in *Lett. Emin. Persons* (1813) III. 530 His father was an yeomanly man. **1853** Raine in *Richmond Wills* (Surtees) 36 *note*, The Fells were and are still a clan of yeomanly gentry in the neighbourhood of Ulverston.

2. Pertaining to, characteristic of, or befitting a yeoman; (*a*) sturdy; (*b*) homely.

c **1626** Donne *Serm., Ps.* xxxviii. 4 (1649) 181 Hee will come to think it..a sordid, a yeomanly thing, still to be plowing, and weeding, and worming a conscience. **1641** Milton *Reform.* i. 28 A homely and Yeomanly Religion. **1673** S. Parker *Reproof Reh. Transp.* 30 It is but a blunt and Yeomanly Jest. **1827** *Blackw. Mag.* XXII. 596 Merry Shrovetide, with its rustic feast, and yeomanly feats. **1830** Miss Mitford *Village* Ser. iv. *Going to Races*, One of a fine yeomanly spirit, not ashamed of his station,..sowing his own corn, driving his own team, and occasionally ploughing his own land. **1897** Howells *Landlord at Lion's Head* 132 There was something in Jeff's figure..of a yeomanly vigour.

ˈyeomanly, *adv.* [f. as prec. + -ly[2].] In the manner of or befitting a yeoman; like a yeoman; doughtily, handsomely.

c **1386** Chaucer *Prol.* 106 Wel koude he dresse his takel yemanly [*v.rr.* ȝemanly, ȝimanly, ȝemonlie]. **1819** Scott *Ivanhoe* xxix, 'Do the false yeomen give way?' 'No!'..'they bear themselves right yeomanly.' **1843** James *Forest Days* ix, 'Right yeomanly done', cried Robin Hood.

yeomanry (ˈjəʊmənrɪ). Forms: see yeoman; also 5 **yemandry, yomandrye,** 6–7 **yeomandrie, -dry,** (7–8 **-try**). [f. yeoman + -ry.]

I. 1. The body of yeomen or small landed proprietors, yeomen collectively; †a company of yeomen.

1375 Barbour *Bruce* iv. 386 Schir Iohne the Hastyngis,.. With knychtis of full mekill pryde, With squyaris and gude ȝhemanry. **1477** Earl Rivers (Caxton) *Dictes* Fiij, The nombre of his knyghtes were comonli of his retenew..were ccc .xiij. thousand wythout yomanrye and other men necessary to his warres. **1538** Starkey *England* (1878) 79 Yf the yeomanry of Englond were not, in tyme of warre we schold be in schrode case. **1549** Latimer *1st Serm. bef. Edw. VI* (Arb.) 40 Suche procedynges..do intend plainly, to make the yeomanry slauery and the Cleargye shauery. **1607** Markham *Cavel.* Ded. (1617) Aj, The three great Columbes of this Empire: the Nobilitie, the Gentrie, and Yeomanrie of Great Brittaine. **1692** R. Meeke *Diary* 2 Sept. 54 My father was born in a very mean house: my mother in a comely hall... I am a branch of Yeomanry by the father, of gentility by my mother. **1693** *Humours Town* 103 The Yeomandry trudge on honestly in their several Vocations. **1704** Swift *T. Tub* x. 184 The Clergy, and Gentry, and Yeomantry of this Land. **1837** Ht. Martineau *Soc. Amer.* III. 67 The free yeomanry, and the youth of the towns, have an eye for the right, and a heart for the true. **1868** Rogers *Pol. Econ.* xiii. (1876) 171 A hardy and prosperous yeomanry, who either purchased the land in parcels, or bargained to work it with their own capital.

b. The general body of freemen of a livery company. *Obs. exc. Hist.*

1497 in J. Nicholl *Comp. Ironm.* (1866) 50 The yemenry of this yo[r] worshipfull feliship of this craffte of Iermongers. **1532** *Ibid.* 54 The..wardens of the yemanry of Iremongeres. **1578** in *East Anglian* June (1910) 275 [Provision is made for two] banketts [to friends and to the] companye of yeomanrye. **1637** *Decree Star Chamb. conc. Printing* §19 Euery Master-printer of the Yeomanry of the Company may haue one Apprentice.

†**2. a.** A company of yeomen or attendants. **b.** The yeomen of the guard. *Obs. rare.*

16.. *Robin Hood & Beggar* xxxi. in Child *Ballads* (1888) III. 157/2 And Robin took these brethren good To be of his yeomandrie. **1673** Marvell in *Coll. Poems* 254 [It is] Dishonourable to the Nation He should have any other Guards but the Yeomanry.

3. A volunteer cavalry force in the British army, originally formed at the time of the French revolution, and consisting chiefly of men of the yeomanry class or status; first embodied in 1794 (Act 34 Geo. III, c. 31). The force has now been amalgamated with the Volunteers to form the Territorial Army (q.v.), which has five Yeomanry units.

The full designation was ***The Yeomanry Cavalry***, but was subsequently (1908) ***The Yeomanry***. In 1899 the formation of a new corps was provided for, entitled ***The Imperial Yeomanry***, recruited for service in the South African War (1899–1902) from the yeomanry, the volunteers, and civilians; this title was subsequently extended to the original yeomanry, and was retained until 1908.

1794, 1798 [see sense 6]. *c* **1800** A. Young in *Autobiog.* (1898) 206, I sat at dinner by a gentleman of great property, captain of a troop of yeomanry. **1802** *Act 42 Geo. III*, c. 66 (*title*) An Act to enable his Majesty to avail himself of the Offers of certain Yeomanry and Volunteer Corps to continue their Services. **1828** Scott *Jrnl.* 18 Mar. (1891) 558, I dined at the Club of the Selkirkshire yeomanry, now disbanded. **1846** McCulloch *Acc. Brit. Empire* (1854) II. 139 The management of the militia, yeomanry, and other domestic forces, is regulated by various statutes. **1866** Geo. Eliot *F. Holt* Introd. 10 Their notion of Reform was a confused combination of rick-burners, trades-unions, Nottingham riots, and in general whatever required the calling-out of the yeomanry. **1899** *Daily News* 30 Dec. 8/5 No mounted corps from this country will be accepted for service in South Africa except as part of the Imperial Yeomanry.

II. †**4.** The condition of a yeoman; yeomanhood. *Obs.*

c **1386** Chaucer *Reeve's T.* 29 For Symkyn wolde no wyf, as he sayde, But if she were wel ynorissed and a mayde, To sauen his estaat of yomanrye [*v.r.* yemanrye]. **1611** Cotgr., *Roture*, yeomanrie; the estate, condition, or calling of such as are not of gentle bloud. **1612** Drayton *Poly-olb.* xi. 25 They, of all England, most to ancient customes cleaue, Their Yeomanry and still endeuoured to vphold.

†**5.** Something pertaining to or characteristic of a yeoman. **a.** Speech befitting a (good) yeoman, homely or honest speech. **b.** Yeoman's dress. *Obs.*

c **1500** *Robin Hood & Potter* xxiii. in Child *Ballads* (1888) III. 110/2 'Be mey trowet, thou seys soyt', seyde Roben, 'Thow seys god yemenrey.' **1592** *Arden of Feversham* iv. ii. 38 *Fran.* And, sirra, as we go, let vs haue som more of your bolde yeomandry. *Fer.* Nay, by my troth, sir, but flat knauery. **1597** Bp. Hall *Sat.* iii. i, Husbanding it in workday yeomanrie.

III. 6. *attrib.*, as ***yeomanry cavalry*** (= 3), ***corps, cut, dress, family, horse, man, officer.***

1794 in Q. L. *Yeom. Cav. Worc.* (1914) 5 The proposed Corps of *Yeomanry Cavalry for the County of Worcester. **1798** *Act 38 Geo. III*, c. 51 (*title*), An Act for authorizing the billetting such Troops of Yeomanry Cavalry as may be desirous of assembling for the Purpose of being trained together. **1825** M'Watt (*title*) Letters to Officers and Privates of the Berwickshire Yeomanry Cavalry. **1886** H. Graham (*title*) Annals of the Yeomanry Cavalry of Wiltshire, a History of the Prince of Wales' Own Royal Regiment. *c* **1800** A. Young in *Autobiog.* (1898) 206 The undisputed origin of all the *yeomanry corps in the kingdom. **1816** Scott *Bl. Dwarf* i, With a saddle of the *yeomanry cut, and a double-bitted military bridle. **1877** Mrs. Forrester *Mignon* xviii, How handsome he looks in his *yeomanry dress. **1868** *Chamb. Encycl.* X. 315/2 The horses employed on *yeomanry duty. **1885** J. Gillow *Lit. & Biog. Hist. Eng. Cath.* II. 47 The Dennetts, a Lancashire *yeomanry family. **1833** Gen. P. Thompson *Exerc.* (1842) II. 426 The landlords..have martial law in their view before they will give up the Corn Laws; they fat their *yeomanry horses for that very chase. **1884** Jefferies *Life of Fields* 132 There are *yeomanry-men still living who remember how they rode about at night after the rioters. **1902** Violet Jacob *Sheep-Stealers* ix, The *yeomanry officer who had been present at the riot.

yeopardie, obs. f. jeopardy: see Y (1) *note*.

1535 in *Lett. Suppr. Monast.* (Camden) 81 Withowt great yeopardie of my liffe.

yeorling, var. yorling *dial.*, yellow-hammer.

yeorned, ME. pa. pple. of run *v.*

yeoven, obs. pa. pple. to give *v.*

1551–2 in Aungier *Syon Mon.* (1840) 94 Yeoven under our signet at our pallaice of Westminster. **1581** Lambarde *Eiren.* i. xvi. 107 Yeouen at Ightham aforesaid vnder my seale. **1780** *B.N.C.* (Oxf.) *Munim.* 40. 35 (MS.) Yeoven.

yeowe, obs. f. ewe.

1547–8 in E. Green *Somerset Chantries* (1888) 32 Six yeowe shepe.

yeowoman (ˈjəʊwʊmən). Pl. **yeowomen** (-wɪmən). [After yeoman.] A woman having the rank or position of a yeoman.

1852 W. Cory *Lett. & Jrnls.* (1897) 58 With a young yeowoman called Miss Brook he sang 'All's Well'. **1892** Tennyson *Foresters* iii, *Robin.* Nay, no Earl am I. I am English yeoman. *Marian.* Then I am yeo-woman. O the clumsy word!

yeox(e, var. yex *Obs.*

yep, *int.* (7 **yeap.**) A call to urge on a horse.

1690 Dryden *Don Sebastian* i. i. (1692) 15 To your paces villain, amble, trot, and gallop!—Quick about there.—Yeap. **1869** *Lonsdale Gloss., Yep!* a word of command to horses.

yep, repr. a dial. (esp. U.S.) or vulgar pronunc. of yes; cf. nope.

1891 *Harper's Mag.* Nov. 970 He gently and peacefully murmured, 'Yep'. **1897** Kipling *Capt. Cour.* x. 222 'Like Lorry Tuck?' Harvey put in. 'Yep.' **1905** [see yah *adv.*]. **1907** J. W. Schultz *My Life as an Indian* xxv. 284 'You must cut your hair.' 'Yep.'..'An' quit gamblin.' 'Yep.' **1926** J. Galsworthy in *Scribner's Mag.* Dec. 581/1 Their 'Yeahs!' and their 'Yeps!' Americans no longer said 'Yes' it seemed! **1962** E. Birney *Sel. Poems* (1966) iv. 99 Yep ain't nothin we kin do. **1967** *Listener* 19 Jan. 96/3 'Would you like a cigarette?' I got a typically aggressive 'Yep'. **1977** *Time* 16 May 39/2 Yep, I let the American people down. **1979** R. Jaffe *Class Reunion* (1980) i. vi. 74 'Oh? You got a new car?' ..'Yep... Look out the window.'

†**yepe,** *a.* (*sb.*) *Obs.* Forms: 1 **ȝeap,** (**ȝep**), 3 **ȝeap, ȝæp, ȝiap, ȝiep,** 3–5 **ȝep,** (4 **ȝhepe, ȝeep, yeepe,** 6 **epe**), 4–5 **ȝepe, yepe.** See also yap *a.* [OE. *ȝéap* open, wide, spacious, curved, crooked, vaulted, crafty, astute; repr. OTeut. root *gaup-*, and prob. related to ON. *gaupn* hollow made by both hands held together, hollow of the foot, two-hands-ful, etc. (cf. *geypna* to encompass): see gowpen and yepsen.]

1. Cunning, crafty, sly, wily.

c **1000** Ælfric *Gen.* iii. 1 Seo næddre wæs ȝeappre þonne ealle þa oðre nytenu. *c* **1000** *Life St. Neot* in Cockayne *Shrine* (1864) 14 An fox þe is ȝeapest ealra deora. *a* **1225** *Ancr. R.* 280 þe ȝeape wrastlare nimeð ȝeme hwat turn his fere ne cunne nout, þet he mid wrastleð. *Ibid.* 362 þeos ȝeape children þet habbeð riche uederes,..tetereð hore cloðes forto habben neowe.

2. Prudent, wise, sagacious, shrewd, astute.

c **1000** *Sax. Leechd.* III. 184 Cild acenned wis, milde, ȝeap, ȝesæliȝ. *c* **1200** *Trin. Coll. Hom.* 193 Beð ȝiepe, and warre, and wakieð. *c* **1205** Lay. 7581 Julius Cesar He wes ȝep and swuðe i-wær. *a* **1300** *Cursor M.* 5370 A wis man es þi lord iuseph, In al egypti es nan sa yepe [*MS. Gött.* ȝep]. *c* **1400** *Land Troy Bk.* 3812 That we sende oure Messager, Wise and ȝepe. *c* **1485** *Digby Myst.* iv. 724 Iohn, your cosyn, most virtuus & ȝepe.

3. Active, nimble, brisk, alert; bold, daring.

c **1205** Lay. 21503 Cheorles ful ȝepe Mid clubben swiðe græte. **13..** *Guy Warw.* (A.) 3983 Gij to aseylen þai wer ȝep. **13..** *Sir Beues* (A.) 88 Maseger, be ȝep and snel. **13..** *Gosp. Nicod.* (A.) 1796 þai lay in droupand drede And non so ȝhepe a worde to ȝelle. **1377** Langl. *P. Pl.* B. xi. 17 þow art ȝonge and ȝepe and hast ȝeres ynowe, Forto lyue longe. *c* **1400** *Destr. Troy* 11265 þai kepyn the cloyse of this clene burgh, With ȝep men at þe yatis ȝarkit full þik. *c* **1515** *Scottish Field* 491 (Chetham Misc. II.) And of Yorkshire a yong knight, that epe was of deedes.

B. *absol.* as *sb.*

a **1225** *Ancr. R.* 66 Kumeð þe coue [*MS. T.* cumes te ȝeape] anonriht & reueð hire hire eiren. **13..** *E.E. Allit. P.* B. 796 For aungels hit wern, & þat þe ȝep vnder-ȝede þat in þe ȝate syttez. *c* **1400** *Destr. Troy* 13231 With-in a yere..þat yepe was with child.

Hence †**yephede** [-head], †**yepleȝȝc** [-laik], †**yepship** [-ship], cunning; astuteness, sagacity.

c **1000** Ælfric *Josh.* ix. 16 Eall heora ȝeapscipe wearð ameldod Israhela bearnum. *c* **1200** Ormin 2523 ȝho wass, wiss to fulle soþ, All full..Off soþ clænleȝȝc, off god ȝæpleȝȝc. *c* **1200** *Trin. Coll. Hom.* 193 þe apostel..muneȝeð us to þrie þinges, On is ȝiepshipe, þat oðer is wakienge, þe þridde is bede. *Ibid.* 195 He notede þe naddre ȝiapshipe. *c* **1205** Lay. 2760 Heo færden mid ȝeapscipe & mid wisdome. *a* **1250** *Owl & Night.* 683 (Jesus MS.) þanne erest cumeþ his yephede Hwenne hit is alremest on drede.

†**yeply,** *adv. Obs.* [OE. *ȝéaplíce*: see yepe *a.* and -ly[2].]

1. Cunningly, craftily; shrewdly, sagaciously.

a **900** *Kent. Gl.* xxi, *Procaciter*, ȝeaplice. *c* **1000** Ælfric *Hom.* I. 80 þa betealde he [*sc.* Herod] hine swiðe ȝeaplice, swa swa he wæs snotorwyrde. *c* **1055** *Byrhtferth's Handboc* in *Anglia* VIII. 313 Hiȝ eac toscead ð þæt stæfgefeȝ on þrym wisan ȝeaplice swyðe.

2. Quickly, briskly; promptly, without delay.

13.. *Gaw. & Gr. Knt.* 1981 Fele þryuande þonkkez he þrat hom to haue, & þay ȝelden hym aȝayn ȝeply þat ilk. *c* **1350** *Will. Palerne* 3346 [He] ȝerne opened þe ȝates & ȝepli out rides. **1393** Langl. *P. Pl.* C. xvii. 328 Then he ȝerneþ in-to þouht and ȝepliche he secheþ Pruyde. *c* **1400** *Destr. Troy* 6081 For to ȝarke vp the ȝate, he ȝepely comaund. *c* **1430** *Pistill of Susan* 118 (Cott. MS.) Thus þe ȝonge ȝepply ȝede in here ȝerde.

yepsen ('jɛps(ə)n). *dial.* ? *Obs.* Forms: 4 **ȝyspun, -on, yepsene, yespen,** 5 **ȝespyn, yespon, ȝespe,** (? **ȝelspe, ȝelpe**), 7 **yeaspen, yaspen, yaspin, yeapsond,** 7–9 **yeepsen,** 8 **yepsond, eapns, espin,** 8–9 **yepsintle,** 9 **ipson.** [ME. *ȝespon, ȝyspon, yepsen,* prob.:—unrecorded OE. **ȝiepsen,* **ȝiespen,* corresp. to MLG. *gespe, gepse,* (*göpse*), LG. *gepse, geps, göpse, göps* (G. *gäspe*).

Various other formations are found in LG. dialects, e.g. *göppsche,. göpske, göppelsche, -ske*; also early Flem. *gaspe, gaps,* Du. dial. *gap(e,* LG. *gåpske, gäppelsche, -ske.*

Affinity of sense suggests derivation from the Teut. stem *gaup-* appearing in OHG. **goufana* (in dat. pl. *coufanôm*), MHG. *goufen,* later and dial. *gauf,* ON. *gaupn* (whence GOWPEN). In the present state of the evidence it is impossible to determine the relationship of these forms and of Lith. *žiùpsnis* = as much as can be seized with two or three fingers, a small handful or armful.]

The two hands placed together so as to form a bowl-shaped cavity; as much as can be held in this; = GOWPEN 1.

c **1325** *Gloss. W. de Bibbesw.* in Wright *Voc.* 147 Deus meyns ensemble, vodes ou pleyns, Sount apelés les galeyns [*gloss* yepsene; *v.rr.* yespone, ȝespyns, ȝyspun, goupynes].. Cent galeynes [*gloss* yespen; *v.r.* ȝyspones]. *c* **1440** *Pallad. on Husb.* XII. 561 A yespon al to grounde Of cyner. *c* **1440** *Promp. Parv.* 537/2 ȝelspe, handfulle (*K., H.* ȝespe, *S.* ȝelpe, *P.* ȝespyn), *vola.* **1611** COTGR., *Iointée,*.. in some countries of England it is called a yeaspen, in others a goppenful of. **1662** ATWELL *Faithf. Surveyor* 109 Out of every hors-footing,.. I could take up whole yeapsonds [of wild oats] that were never the worse for the fire. **1664** GOULDMAN *Dict.* I. (1669), A yaspin or handful, *vola.* **1674** RAY *S. & E.C. Words* 80 A *Yaspen* or *Yeepsen*: in Essex signifies as much as can be taken up in both hands joyn'd together. **1703** THORESBY *Let. to Ray* (E.D.S.) *Eapns, sb.* 'an eapns', hands full. *c* **1746** J. COLLIER (Tim Bobbin) *View Lanc. Dial.* Wks. (1775) 59 There wou'd not I ha com'n for a Yepsintle a Ginneys. **1796** PEGGE *Derbicisms* (E.D.S.) *Espin, sb.* a handful of anything. **1892** C. T. MARTIN *Rec. Interpr.* 256 'A little ipson', in Somerset, is a double handful.

yer[1] (jɜː(r)), repr. a dial. or vulgar pronunc. of YOU.

1848 A. B. EVANS *Leicestersh. Wds.* 109 You're a bigger fool, nur oi took yer to be. **1856** *Punch* 2 Feb. 41/1 (*caption*) That's how it was, yer see. **1867** [see YERE]. **1880** A. E. HOUSMAN *Let.* 10 May (1971) 20 Yah! yer aint got no votes! **1916** G. B. SHAW *Pygmalion* I. 106 Theres manners f' yer! Te-oo banches o voylets trod into the mad. **1946** K. TENNANT *Lost Haven* (1947) iii. 50 Hey! Wait a minute... I want to see yer. **1978** *Hot Car* June 93/1 Brian *would* like to get in a plug for Micky Mees who helped with the heavy stuff. Good on yer, Mick.

yer[2] (jɜː(r)), repr. a dial. or vulgar pronunc. of YOUR.

1814 SCOTT *Wav.* xxx, D'ye hear wha's coming to cow yer cracks? **1894** *Jrnl. Amer. Folk-Lore* VII. 148 She is gwine ter keep de house straight and yer britches mended. **1922** JOYCE *Ulysses* 419 Aweel, ye maun e'en gang yer gates. **1954** W. FAULKNER *Fable* 85 'Use yer boot,' the sergeant muttered. **1973** J. SPEIGHT *Thoughts of Chairman Alf* 26 Yer Queen should have a veto to.. overrule Parliament... 'Cos she's born to rule. Not like yer Labour rubbish. **1980** *Herald* (Melbourne) 3 Apr. (City ed.) 2 Wouldn't it rot yer footy socks! Someone's about to contest Cazaly's musical mark.

yer, obs. f. ERE, IRE, YEAR[1]; obs. graphic var. THEIR, THERE.

-yer, *suffix,* old variant of -IER, now used after *w* or a vowel, as *bowyer, great oneyer, lawyer, sawyer, stuccoyer* (s.v. STUCCOER).

yerabyll, var. EARABLE *a. Obs.,* ploughable.

1517 *Domesday Inclos.* (1897) I. 220, viij acars of yerabyll lond in Wygbarow.

yerb, obs. or dial. f. HERB.

‖**yerba** ('jɜːbə). Also **yerva.** [Sp. *yerba* herb (+ *mate* MATÉ).] In full **yerba-maté** ('jɜːbə 'mæteɪ): = MATÉ 2 a, b.

1818 *Amer. State Papers, For. Relat.* (1834) IV. 279 The yerba is used in decoction, like the tea of China. **1839** [see PARAGUAY 1]. **1843** *Chem. Gaz.* 1 Mar. 233 Yerba Maté, or Paraguay Tea. **1855** J. F. W. JOHNSTON *Chem. Common Life* vii. I. 184 A kind of arch.. upon which the Yerba branches are placed. **1858** SIMMONDS *Dict. Trade,* Yerva-mate. **1902** H. HESKETH PRICHARD *Thro' Heart of Patagonia* xii. 177 He seemed to have no provisions, only a bag of *yerba.*

Hence **yerbal** (jɜː'bɑːl) [Sp. *yerbál*], a grove or plantation of yerba.

1858 SIMMONDS *Dict. Trade, Yerbal,* a forest or wild grove of the *Ilex Paraguayensis,* the holly from the leaves of which the Paraguay tea is obtained. **1883** [see MATÉ 2 c].

yerba buena ('jɜːbə bʊ'eɪnə). [Sp., lit. 'good herb': cf. YERBA.] A trailing perennial herb, *Satureja douglasii* (formerly *Micromeria chamissonis*) of the family Labiatæ, native to western North America and bearing aromatic leaves and white or purplish flowers.

1847 *Calif. Star* (San Francisco) 30 Jan. 2/3 The town [*sc.* San Francisco] takes its name from an herb to be found all around it which is said to make good tea; and possessing medicinal qualities; it is called good herb or Yerba Buena. **1882** B. HARTE *Flip, & Found at Blazing Star* 15 He seized a few of the young tender green leaves of the yerba buena vine.. and ate them. **1915** ARMSTRONG & THORNBER *Western Wild Flowers* 436 Yerba Buena, Tea-vine.. was used medicinally by California Indians, so it was called 'good herb' by the Mission Fathers, and it still used as a tea. **1935** J. STEINBECK *Tortilla Flat* xv. 261 Tea made from yerba buena will be good. **1975** *Islander* (Victoria, B.C.) 3 Aug. 3/3 Beside the pond speedwell.. yerba buena [etc.].

yerbua, obs. form of JERBOA.

‖**yercum** ('jɜːkəm). [Tamil.] An East Indian shrub, *Calotropis gigantea* (N.O. *Asclepiadaceæ*), or the fibre obtained from its bark; also the allied species *C. procera*; both used medicinally.

1826 [see MUDAR]. **1838** LINDLEY *Flora Med.* §1144. 540 Under the names of Mador, Mudar, Akum, and Yercund, the root and bark.. are used as.. purgatives.

†**yerd,** *v. Obs. rare*[−1]. [f. *yerd,* YARD *sb.*[2]; cf. OHG. *gerten, kertin* to drive with a stick.] *trans.* To beat with a rod.

a **1225** *St. Marher.* (1862) 6 Hwil me yerdede hire.

yerd, ȝerd, etc.: see YARD, YIRD.

yerde, var. ERDE *v.,* to dwell.

c **1515** *Scottish Field* 648 (Chetham Misc. II.) His ancetors of long tyme, have yerded there long.

yerd-hunger. *Sc.* 'Earth-hunger': (*a*) voracious desire for land (cf. *eard-hunger* in Scott *Nigel* ix); (*b*) see quot. 1825. So **yerd-hungry** *a.* See also YIRD.

1823 SCOTT *Let.* in *Lockhart* (1839) VII. 155 About the land, I have no doubt your Lordship is quite right, but I have something of what is called the *yeard hunger.* **1825** JAMIESON, *Yerd-hunger*.. 1. That keen desire of food, which is sometimes manifested by persons before death... 2. Voraciousness; the term being used in a general sense. *Ibid., Yerd-hungry,*.. voraciously hungry.

†**yere,** *v. Obs.* Forms: 3–4 **ȝere,** 4 **ȝeore;** 3 *pa. t.* **ȝerde, ȝirde, ȝurde.** [ME. *ȝere,* representing an OE. **ȝerian* = OFris. *geria, ieria,* OS. *gerôn* (MLG. *geren*), OHG. *gerôn, -ên, -ân* (MHG. *geren, gern, be-gern,* G. *begehren*) to desire, related to OHG., MHG. *ger,* ON. *gerr* greedy (cf. OHG. *girî,* G. *gier* desire, OHG. *girîg,* G. *gierig* desirous, covetous, etc.); f. Teut. *ger-,* whence also YERN *a.,* YEARN *v.*

With Teut. *ger-*:—Indo-eur. *gher-* (*:ghor-*: *ghr-*) to long, desire, have pleasure, are prob. allied Skr. *háryati* finds pleasure, *háršatē* rejoices, Zend *zara-* striving, goal, *χαίρειν, χαρῆναι* to rejoice, *χάρις* favour, grace, L. *horiri, hortārī, hortārī* to cheer, exhort.]

trans. To desire, long or yearn for; to express a desire for, request.

c **1205** LAY. 4790 Belin king him ȝette þæt forward þat he ȝerde [*c* 1275 ȝornde]. *Ibid.* 5515 Heo forȝeten here ȝisles & þat griþ þat heo ȝurden [*c* 1275 ȝeornden]. *Ibid.* 11514 Al swa þe king ȝirde Mauric hit him ȝette. *a* **1300** *Cursor M.* 28982 þat es to be here ai ȝerand þat ilk liue is ai lastand. **1362** LANGL. *P. Pl.* A. I. 33 Mesure is Medicine þauh þou muche ȝeore.

Hence †**yering** *vbl. sb.,* desire, longing; request.

13.. *Ball. on Scottish Wars* xx. (Ritson), Al my yering he me tald, And yatid me, als we went bi waye. *c* **1400** *Cursor M.* 27930 (Cott. Galba) Fole couaitise and fole ȝering.

yere, repr. a dial. (esp. U.S.) or vulgar pronunc. of HERE.

1867 *Harper's Mag.* Feb. 274/2 This yere is Colonel N—— who wants ter know yer. **1907** J. W. SCHULTZ *My Life as an Indian* xxv. 284 You must.. help me run this yere boardin' house. **1929** W. FAULKNER *Sartoris* IV. i. 270 Yere day is, Cunnel. **1956** [see JONG[1]]. **1973** J. PATTINSON *Search Warrant* ii. 34 Like young folks is these yere days—long hair, beards.

yere, obs. f. EAR, ERE, HEAR, HEIR, YEAR[1]; Sc. and dial. f. YOUR.

†**yeresgift, -ȝift.** *Obs.* = next.

14.. [see next]. *c* **1425** *Orolog. Sapient.* vii. in *Anglia* X. 386/24 In þis daye begynneþ þe ȝeere, and.. þey þat ben knytte to-gedir by love specyalle vsen to ȝeve eche oþere ȝeerys-ȝiftis. **1545** in *Shropsh. Par. Doc.* (1903) 79 For or. ladys yeres gyft.

†**yeresyeve.** *Obs.* Forms: 2 **ȝieresȝieve,** 3 **jherscheve, jaresive,** 3–4 **ȝeres-, yeresȝyve, -ȝiue, -ȝeue, -yeve,** 5 **ȝereseffe.** [f. *yeres,* gen. of YEAR *sb.* + *ȝive, ȝeue* GIVE *sb.*[1]] A gift customarily given or exacted at the New Year, or at the beginning of a year of office.

1194 *Charter Rich. I* in Rymer *Fœdera* (1816) I. 52/2 Concessimus, quod sint quieti de bridtol, & de childwite, & de ȝieresȝieve. **1201** *Charter Cambr.* in *Rot. Chart.* (1837) 83/2 Quod omnes burgenses de Cantebruge sint quieti de jherscheve et de scothale. **1231** in *Cal. Charter Rolls* (1903) I. 130 [20 s. which were paid yearly to the constable of Bristoll from the land of Mangodesfeld by way of] jaresive. **1362** LANGL. *P. Pl.* A. XI. 34 Wolde neuer kyng ne kniht ne Canoun of Seynt poules ȝeuen hem to heore ȝeres-ȝiue þe value of a grote! **1377** *Ibid.* B. III. 99 Hem þat desireth ȝiftes or ȝeresȝyues [*MS. R.* (14..) ȝereȝiftes] bi-cause of here offices. *Ibid.* VIII. 52 He ȝaf þe to ȝeresȝyue to ȝeme wel þiselue. *c* **1460** *Promp. Parv.* 548 (Winch.), ȝereseffe, *encennium.* [**1723** BOHUN *Priv. Lond.* (ed. 3) 35 *Jeresgive,* is a Toll or Fine, taken by the King's Officers, on a Person's entring into an Office; or rather, a.. Bribe, given to them to connive at Extortion, or other Offence in him that gives it.]

yerfull, obs. form of IREFUL.

yeri ('jɛrɪ). [Russ.] The name of the Russian vowel *ÿ,* the twenty-eighth letter of the Russian alphabet.

1921 E. SAPIR *Language* ix. 212 Both nasalized vowels and the Slavic 'yeri' are demonstrably of secondary origin in Indo-European. **1977** *Word 1972* XXVIII. 249 The /i/ is a back unrounded vowel, similar to the Russian yeri.

yerk (jɜːk), **yark** (jɑːk), *sb.* Now *Sc.* and *dial.* Forms: see the vb. [f. YERK *v.*: see also YORK *sb.*[2]]

1. a. A smart blow or stroke, as of a whip or rod, or of a heavy body falling; a lash; also, the sound of such a blow; the crack of a whip; a thud.

1509 HAWES *Past. Pleas.* IV. (Percy Soc.) 18 And in her hande a strong knotted whippe; At every yarke she made hym for to skyppe. **1565** COOPER *Thesaurus, Crepitus plagarum*.. a yerke, or girke. **1583** GOLDING *Calvin on Deut.* xxiv. 143/2 As soone as the wicked feele but one yirke of the rod with Gods hand. **1593** CHURCHYARD *Challenge, Murton's Trag.* xcix, No wisdomes lore, nor men of noble fame, Can scape thy scourge, it giues so sore a yarke. **1622** MABBE tr. *Aleman's Guzman d'Alf.* I. 35 They gaue mee the yarke with the spurre. **1682** FLATMAN *Heraclitus Ridens* No. 56 (1713) II. 99 Our Province is to lash a rout of wanton and disloyal People; and if any will be outer-most, and so get a Yerk that makes 'em smart, let them hereafter learn to hide themselves in the Crowd. *a* **1807** J. SKINNER *Amusem. Leis. Hours* (1809) 47 Wi' a yawfu' yark,.. He derfly dang the bark Frae's shins that day. **1826** T. WILSON *Pitman's Pay* etc. 80 The blacksmith's hammer, yark for yark, We hear ne langer bangin'. **1860** RAMSAY *Remin.* (ed. 7) Pref. p. xxiii, Clinching every decision with the 'yerk' of a spadeful of earth on the grave's brink. **1871** J. MILNE *Sel. Poems & Songs* 89 It flew oure the houses like a lark An doun on the fouk's taes fell wi' a yark.

fig. **1682** FLATMAN *Heraclitus Ridens* No. 82 (1713) II. 249 More out of dread of a Yerk from Heraclitus, than of all the Penalties in the Statue-Book. **1689** *Answ. Desertion Disc.* in *11th Coll. Papers rel. Pres. Juncture of Affairs* 5 To call the Breach of the Original Contract pretended, and a Popular Flourish, is a yerk of Malitious Reflection.

†**b.** *fig.* An impulse, eager desire. *Obs. rare*[−1].

1577 HELLOWES *Gueuara's Chron.* 308 Ciucius did much delight to goe on hunting, & had a fine yearke to kill the Bore & other uenerie in the mountaines.

2. a. The act of lashing out with the heels, as a horse; a kick; a sudden or abrupt movement, a jerk, twitch.

1581 A. HALL *Iliad* VI. 120 The horse, That.. With many frisks and yerks behinde, his head doth cast aloft. **1618** M. BARET *Hippon.* I. 9 There is no foale.. but will both leap,.. turne loftily, fetch such yarks behind, that it is very delightfull to behold. **1623** MARKHAM *Cheap Husb.* (ed. 3) I. ii. 26 With your rod giue him a good ierke vnder the belly.. when you please to giue the ierke, he will then giue the yerke. **1679** SHADWELL *True Widow* IV. 56 Let's fight here; I would have my Mistress see how I put in my Pass, and what a yerk I give it. **1726** SWIFT *Gulliver* IV. xii. 191 Twenty thousand of them.. battering the Warriors Faces into Mummy, by terrible Yerks from their hinder Hoofs. **1822** HOGG *Perils of Man* III. 357 He.. attacked the couple with his heels, prostrate as they were, yerk for yerk, indiscriminately.

b. A jerking or twitching sensation. ? *Obs.*

1806 J. BERESFORD *Miseries Hum. Life* ix. (ed. 3) 195 The yerk, or throe, in the throat, that follows your last bumper of port. **1831** *Examiner* 290/1 The yerk of the third bottle of hot nastiness [*sc.* port].

yerk (jɜːk), **yark** (jɑːk), *v.* Now *Sc.* and *dial.* Forms: 5–7 **yarke,** 5–9 **yerk,** 6–7 **yerke, yeark(e,** 6–9 **yark, yirk,** 9 (*U.S.*) **yawk.** [ME. *yerk* (15th cent.), appearing first as a technical term of bootmaking. Of obscure origin, but prob. in part phonetically symbolic; cf. the largely synonymous *jerk, firk.*]

1. To draw stitches tight, to twitch, as a shoemaker in sewing (*trans.* with the leather, etc. as obj., or *intr.*); also, to bind tightly with cords.

c **1430** *York Mem. Bk.* (Surtees) I. 194 Pro sutura xij parium sotularium yerkyd ad manum, iiij d. **1600** DEKKER *Shoomakers Hol.* (1610) D 3. *Eyre.* Yarke and seame, yark and seame. *Firke.* For yarking & seaming let me alone & I come toot. **1630** *Tincker of Turvey* 27 His Wife sitting by him when hee was yerking of his shooes. **1805** SCOTT *Last Minstr.* (1894) Note xlviii, 'Sutor Watt, ye cannot sew your boots; the heels *risp,* and the seams *rive.*'—'If I cannot sew,' retorted Tinlinn, discharging a shaft, which nailed the captain's thigh to his saddle,—'If I cannot sew, I can yerk.' **1813** HOGG *Queen's Wake* I. III. lxiv, And they yerkit his limbis with twine. **1818** SCOTT *Hrt. Midl.* lii, His hands and feet are yerked as tight as cords can be drawn. **1822** HOGG *Perils of Man* II. vii. 269 Eight horses,.. every one with its head yerked to the tail of the one before him. **1825** [see *yerking* below].

2. *trans.* To strike smartly, esp. with a rod or whip; to beat, flog, lash; to drive with a whip.

c **1520** SKELTON *Magnyf.* 484 A carter.. That with his whyp his mares was wonte to yarke. **1550** COVERDALE *Spir. Perle* vi. 54 Like as the carter or foore man yerketh his horsse with the whyp. **1595** SPENSER *F.Q.* VI. vii. 44 That same foole.. Was Scorne, who hauing in his hand a whip, Her therewith yirks. **1604** SHAKS. *Oth.* I. ii. 5 Nine, or ten times I had thought t'haue yerk'd him here vnder the Ribbes. **1631** J. DONE *Polydoron* (1650) 211 When I observe a cruell Carter yerke and slash but a poore over-toyld Iade. **1703** MRS. CENTLIVRE *Love's Contriv.* IV. i. 45 I'll yerk the sullen Devil out of you. *a* **1774** FERGUSSON *Leith Races* Poems (1845) 34 Their skins are gaily yarkit And peel'd thir days. **1825** BROCKETT *N.C. Gloss.* s.v., Aw'l yark yah, yah dirty bastard yah. **1833** *Blackw. Mag.* XXXIV. 550 We should yerk the yokel of a Yankee with the knout.

b. To smack or crack (a whip); also *intr.* of the whip, to crack.

a **1566** R. EDWARDS *Damon & Pithias* (1571) F ij b, When ich was a lusty fellow, and could yarke a whip trimly. **1603** FLORIO *Montaigne* I. xxii. (1632) 48 He would..make a whip to yarke and lash, as cunningly as any Carter in France. **1606** G. W[OODCOCKE] *Hist. Ivstine* II. 9 Euery man drew forth his whip, and began to yerke the same.

c. *intr.* To strike, deal blows.

1815 G. BEATTIE *John O'Arnha* (1826) 30 He swat and yarkit wi' his hammer.

3. *fig.* To beat, lash, flagellate (as with sharp words or treatment); hence, to stir up, excite.

1593 G. HARVEY *Pierce's Super.* 10 Arrius will shake the Church: Macchiauell will yerke the Commonwealth. **1607** MIDDLETON *Fam. Love* III. (1608) E 2, If it hit, and that I yearke my familist out of the Spirit. **1639** J. TAYLOR (Water P.) *Part Summers Trav.* C 5, I with my Pen doe meane to yerke and ferke ye. **1786** BURNS *To J. S——* iv, My fancy yerket up sublime Wi' hasty summon. **1797** T. POOLE in Mrs. H. Sandford *T. P. & Friends* (1888) I. 221 The weight of government, which our ministry has cause[d] to touch and yark every individual where he never felt it before. **1819** KEATS *Otho* III. ii, Aye, Satan! does that yerk ye? **1825** JAMIESON, *To Yerk, Yark*, figuratively applied to the rays of the sun, when they beat powerfully on any object. **1874** OUTRAM *Annuity* vi, In vain he yerked his souple head, To find an ambiguity.

b. *intr.* To gird or carp *at.*

1621 BP. MOUNTAGU *Diatribæ* 392 Almost in euery Paragraph, either he yerketh at his neighbours credit, or commendeth his owne chickens. **1826** J. WILSON *Noctes Ambr.* Wks. 1855 I. 114 Onything's mair preferable than yerk yerkin at every thing said by a wiser man than yoursel.

4. *trans.* To pull, push, or throw with a sudden movement; to jerk.

1568 J. FEN tr. *Osorius' Confut. Haddon* I. 7 b, When you are pricked and yearked foorth with the goades of your owne madnes. **1575** GASCOIGNE *Flowers* Wks. 1907 I. 65 He that yerks old angells out apace. **1604** T. M. *Black Bk.* D 3 b, But when I yerkt them [*sc.* dice] forth, away they ranne like Irish Lackeys. **1644** MANWAYRING *Sea-mans Dict.* 83 When a great sea comes to yerk up the ship. **1780** HUTTON *Tour to Caves* (ed. 2) Gloss., *Yark*, to push or strike. **1825** J. NEAL *Bro. Jonathan* III. 236 A gray beaver..yerked a little on one side. **1836** [HOOTON] *Bilberry Thurland* I. xiv. 258 He..seized the parson by the chin and ears and yerked him upwards several times. **1840** HALIBURTON *Clockm.* Ser. III. xiii, I'd larn him how..to yawk the reins with both hands. **1861** *Stamford Merc.* 27 Sept., He saw him knocking and yarking the horse about and swearing at it. **1882** *Jamieson's Sc. Dict.* s.v., He yerkit to the yett wi' a bang. **1904** *Dundee Adv.* 2 Dec. 7 If any person went and asked a civil question he might get a besom 'yarked' at his head.

b. To utter spasmodically, 'jerk *out*' (words); to start, strike up (a song, etc.).

1604 MIDDLETON *Fr. Hubburd's T.* C 3, He began to speake to the richest of our number, euer and anon, yerking out the word Fines. **1719** RAMSAY *To Arbuckle* 14 Yerking those words out which lye nearest. **1815** G. BEATTIE *John O'Arnha* (1826) 57 A' the devils in a ring Yarkit up the Highland fling. **1892** LUMSDEN *Sheep-head & Trotters* 287 Yerk us aff a sang belyve.

†**c.** To 'get *up*' or compose rapidly or hastily, to 'dash off'. *Obs.*

1592 NASHE *Strange Newes* E 4 b, In a night & a day would he haue yarkt vp a Pamphlet as well as in seauen yeare. **1621** BP. MOUNTAGU *Diatribæ* 88 You are able to shape your aduersary an answere, and yerke vp a booke in a night.

5. To move (some part of the body) with a jerk or twitch; *esp.* to lash out with (the legs), as a horse.

1599 SHAKS. *Hen. V*, IV. vii. 83 [Wounded steeds] with wilde rage Yerke out their armed heeles at their dead masters. **1607** MARKHAM *Cavel.* II. (1617) 171 You shall obserue that when he yarketh, he yark out his hinder feete euen and close together. **1623** —— *Cheap Husb.* (ed. 3) I. ii. 17 When a horse yerketh out his nose. **1651** *Loves of Hero & Leander* (1653) 16 Leander now turns on his back, He yerks out legs and lets arme slack. **1726** *Dict. Rusticum* (ed. 3) s.v. *Capriole*, The Goat-leap, when a horse at the full height of his Leap, yerks or strikes out his hind legs. **1825** SCOTT *Betrothed* xiii, Mahound yerked out his hoofs. **1828** *Craven Gloss.* s.v., T'horse yarkd out baath his hinder fit.

b. *intr.* To lash or strike *out* with the heels, to kick.

1565 [see *yerking* below]. **1573–80** TUSSER *Husb.* (1878) 150 The sooner that poore beast is strucke the sooner doth he yerke. **1579–80** NORTH *Plutarch* (1595) 719 The horse.. would let no man get vp on his backe,..but would yerke out at them. **1581** J. BELL *Haddon's Answ. Osor.* 158 b, He [*sc.* the horse] chaufeth & champeth vpon the bridle, commeth a loft, yorketh out with his heeles behinde. **1611** COTGR. s.v. *s' Agrouper*, He would yearke out behind. **1694** MOTTEUX *Rabelais* v. viii. 36 He fell a Trotting, and Winsing, and Yerking.

transf. **1622** FLETCHER *Sea-Voy.* I. i, How she [*sc.* a ship] kicks and yerks.

6. *intr.* To spring or rise suddenly: esp. of animals.

1612 DRAYTON *Poly-olb.* vi. 54 So doth the Salmon vaut; And if at first he faile, his second summersaut Hee instantlie assaies, and from his nimble ring Still yarking [etc.]. **1828** *Craven Gloss.*, *Yark*, to rise hastily. 'He yarks up i' th' snert of a cat [= instantly]. **1892** *Mem. Dean Hole* xvi. (1893) 193 It [*sc.* a snipe] yarked up, and screeted, and I nipped round, and blazed. **1893** STEVENSON *Catriona* xv, We saw the wee flag yirk up to the maist-heid.

b. *fig.* To engage eagerly in some proceeding, to 'pitch *into*'.

1737 RAMSAY *Sc. Prov.* (1750) 103 Thoughts are free, tho' I mayna sae mickle I can yerk at the thinking. **1807** J. STAGG *Poems* 52 Some teymes i' th winter neeghts, when dark We'd into th' Ladies Di'rys yark. **1892** LUMSDEN *Sheep-head & Trotters* 181 We hae a lang tramp to yerk till in the morning. *Ibid.* 257 Now Dominie, yerk in.

Hence **yerking, yarking** *vbl. sb.* and *ppl. a.* (in various senses: see above and quots.).

1565 COOPER *Thesaurus*, *Excussores equi*, flingyng and yerkyng horses. **1587** FLEMING in Holinshed *Chron.* III. 819 The fox..not able to beare the yerking of his [*sc.* the lion's] taile, or a pelt of his paw. **1589** —— *Virg. Georg.* III. 348 Seest thou not that neither bit and bridle..Nor cruell yerkings,..do stop or stay Horsses from mares. **1593** G. HARVEY *Pierce's Super.* 11 And what comparable to this spowte of yarking eloquence? **1598** MARSTON *Sco. Villanie* Proem., Quake guzzell dogs,..Skud from the lashes of my yerking rime. **1605** *Play Stucley* in Simpson *Sch. Shaks.* (1878) I. 254 We'll spur your Iennet..Until with yarking she do break her girths. **1624** GEE *Foot out of Snare* App. 114 A song of the same smart-yerking tune. **1639** T. DE GREY *Compl. Horsem.* 2 The horse..never gave over flinging, yarking, plunging, and bownding. **1689** T. PLUNKET *Char. Gd. Comm.* 47 Are all the yerking Muses fallen asleep? **1787** W. TAYLOR *Sc. Poems* 177 Mornin clocks an' yarkin hammers Reviv'd us by their tunefu' yammers. **1825** JAMIESON, *Yerkin*, the seam by which the hinder part of the upper leather of a shoe is joined to the forepart, Berwicks., Dumfr. **1892** LUMSDEN *Sheep-head & Trotters* 286 Hootsman..proposed that Rob Clarty..should..give us some of his reels..for the yerking off of which Rob..is..a famous hand.

yerk, obs. form of IRK.

'yerker. [f. YERK *v.* + -ER[1].] **a.** One who yerks; a kicker; a flogger. **b.** A sudden and very severe blow' (Jam. 1825).

1664 GOULDMAN *Dict.* I. (1669), A yerker out, *sternax*. **1678** LITTLETON *Eng.-Lat. Dict.*, A yerker or whipster, *plagosus Orbilius*.

Yerkish ('jɜːkɪʃ), *sb.* (and *a.*). [f. the name of R. M. *Yerkes* (1876–1956), U.S. primatologist + -ISH[1].] A sign language for chimpanzees based on geometric symbols, chiefly devised by E. C. von Glasersfeld for experimental purposes and first published in 1973. Also *attrib.* or as *adj.*

1973 D. M. RUMBAUGH et al. in *Behavior Research Methods & Instrumentation* Sept. 385/2 The study program ..included the design of the language system (Yerkish). *Ibid.* 387/2 Each correlator links two items that are expressed in the Yerkish phrase or sentence. **1973** *Science* 16 Nov. 731 Each Yerkish word, or 'lexigram', is a distinctive geometric white symbol on a colored background. **1974** E. C. VON GLASERSFELD in *Amer. Jrnl. Computational Linguistics* (microfiche 12), The Yerkish language for nonhuman primates. **1974** *N.Y. Times* 29 May 52/3 Lana's [*sc.* a chimpanzee's] computerized language, called *Yerkish* in honor of the primate center's founder, Dr. Robert M. Yerkes. **1977** E. C. VON GLASERSFELD in D. M. Rumbaugh *Language Learning by Chimpanzee* v. 114 The grammar of Yerkish had to be kept as simple as possible for several reasons. **1980** *Times* 3 July 16/3 'Yerkish', an artificial language especially developed by Professor D. M. Rumbaugh at the Yerkes Primate Research Centre, Emory University, near Atlanta, United States, for a chimpanzee called Lana.

yerl, yerle, obs. or Sc. ff. EARL.

yerle, -ly, obs. ff. EARLY, YEARLY.

yerm, variant of YARM *v.*

†**yern**, *a. Obs.* Forms: 1 **ȝeorn**, 3 **ȝeorn**, 3–5 **ȝern**, (4 **ȝarn, yerin**), 4–5 **ȝerne, yerne**, 5 **yarne, yherne**, 6 **yorne, yearne**, (9 *dial.* **jern**). [OE. *ȝeorn* = OS. *gern*, OHG. *gern, kern* (MHG. *gern*, G. *-gern*), ON. *gjarn*, Goth. *-gaírns* (in *seinagaírns* selfish, *faíhugaírns* covetous), also OS. *-gerni* (MLG. *gerne*), OHG. **gerni, kerni* (MHG. *-gerne*); f. Teut. *ger-*: see YERE *v.* and cf. YEARN *v.*]

1. Eager, earnestly or keenly desirous; also, greedy, covetous.

c **893** ÆLFRED *Oros.* III. viii. 122 For þæm þe æȝþer þara folca wæs þæs ȝefeohtes ȝeorn. **971** *Blickl. Hom.* 43 Ne sceal he eac beon to ȝeorn deadra manna feos. *a* **1000** *Guthlac* 1051 Ic eom siþes fus..edleanan ȝeorn. *a* **1200** *Moral Ode* 256 in *O.E. Hom.* I. 175 Þa þe weren swa lese þet me hom ne mihte ileuen Med-ierne domes men & wrong-wise reuen. **13..** *Cursor M.* 14638 (Gött.) Þat ȝe war sauf ȝarn haue i bene. *c* **1425** WYNTOUN *Cron.* VI. x. 852 To fecht wiþ him þai wer full ȝarne [*v.r.* yherne]. [**1905** *Engl. Dial. Dict.* s.v. *Yearn*, In phr. *to be jern on a thing*, to be bent on it. Shr., Mtg. I'm jern on this or that.]

b. Earnestly occupied or engaged, busy (*about* something).

a **1300** *Cursor M.* 8205 (Cott.) O þaa wandes grett lose þai made, þe king abute þam was ful gern [*v.rr.* ȝern(e)]. *c* **1450** *Mirk's Festial* 147 Þer was a tonne of bras..into þe wheche tonne he was put and closyd þeryn, and fure made vndyr hote, and so þei weren ȝerne about for þat Seynt Ion schuld haue ben brent þeryn.

2. Swift, rapid; brisk, lively; nimble, active.

13.. *Cursor M.* 23588 (Edinb.) Sun and mon, and water and stern, þat rinnes now wit ras sa yerin. *c* **1386** CHAUCER *Miller's T.* 71 But of hir song, it was as loude and yerne As any swalwe sittynge on a berne. *c* **1515** *Scottish Field* 571 (Chetham Misc. II.) Yorkshippe [*sic*] like yorne [*v.r.* (Percy MS.) yearne] men, egerly they foughten!

†**yern**, *v. Obs.* Forms: 1 **ȝeiernan, ȝeyrnan**, *Nth.* **ȝeiorna**, 3–4 **ȝurne, ȝirne**, 4–5 **ȝerne, yerne.** *Pa. t. a.* (*str.*) 1 **ȝearn**, (**ȝarn, ȝeharn**), **ȝiarn**, *pl.* **ȝeurnon, ȝe-uurnun, ȝiurnun**, 3–4 **ȝorn**, 4 **yorn, ȝorne, yorne, yourne, ȝarn, yarn**, 5 **yarne, yurne**; *β.* (*wk.*) 1 *pl.* **ȝeærndon**, 4 **yerned.** *Pa. pple.* 1 **ȝeurnen** (see YEARN *v.*[2] etym.); 4 **yȝarned.** [OE. *ȝeiernan, ȝeærnan*: see Y- *prefix* 3 c and RUN *v.* For the specific sense 'to curdle' see YEARN *v.*[2]]

1. *intr.* = RUN *v.* 1, 4, 5.

c **900** tr. *Bæda's Hist.* v. vi. (1890) 400 Þa ȝeærndon hio sume ðraȝe, & eft hwurfon. *c* **900** WÆRFERTH tr. *Gregory's Dial.* xii. (1900) 88, & þa him gangendum in þam weȝe him onȝen ȝeurnon [*v.r.* urnon] þer ærendracan. *c* **1300** *K. Horn* 749 (Laud 108), To boure he gan ȝerne. **13..** *K. Alis.* 565 (Laud MS.), Of wilde beestes com a grete pray, Ȝerned þorouȝout þe contray. *Ibid.* 2699 Forthe [he] is wiþ þat yȝarned [*rime* forbarnd; *v.r.* yroune, *rime* brenne]. **13..** *E.E. Allit. P.* B. 881 Bot þat þe ȝonge men, so ȝepe, ȝornen þer-oute. **1377** LANGL. *P. Pl.* B. III. 213 (MS. R.) Emperoures ..þurȝ ȝiftes han ȝoumen to ȝernen [*v.r.* renne] and to ride. *a* **1400** *Octouian* 561 The maryners..yorne awey, with good wylle, Well hastyly. *Ibid.* 965 Vpon a stede he gan yerne With sper and scheld. *c* **1400** *St. Jer.* 15 *Tokens* 45 Þe deuelen willen come ȝernend & speten fire & blast. *c* **1425** *Engl. Conq. Irel.* 74 He saw a mych flote of wylde swyne yernynge vp-on hugh & moryce. *Ibid.* 82 He yarne to snellych for to socur hym.

b. = RUN *v.* 9.

c **1055** *Byrhtferth's Handboc* in *Anglia* VIII. 298 Þes circul ys todæled ontwelf, & seo sunne ȝeyrnð þas twelf fætu binnan .XII. monðum. *Ibid.* 320 Saturnus ys se ytemesta he ȝeyrnð his ryne binnan þrittiȝum wintrum. **1340** *Ayenb.* 84 Stedeuest and lestinde ase þe zonne, þet alneway yernþ and ne is neure wery. *Ibid.* 141 [see *yerning* below].

2. = RUN *v.* 20.

1340 *Ayenb.* 27 Vor hit behoueþ þet zuich wyn yerne by þe teppe, ase þer is ine þe tonne. **1377** LANGL. *P. Pl.* B. XIX. 376 (MS. B) Water..Egerlich ȝernynge out of mennes eyen. **1387** TREVISA *Higden* (Rolls) I. 105 Þe streem of Egipte þat ȝerneþ westward in to þe grete see. *a* **1400** *R. Gloucester's Chron.* (Rolls) 8671 (MS. C) Þe blod ȝorn to grounde.

3. *fig.* = RUN *v.* 27, 29, 31.

c **900** tr. *Bæda's Hist.* IV. xxviii[i]. (1890) 366 Þa ȝeorn ðær sona upp ȝenihtsumlic yrð & wæstm. *c* **900** WÆRFERTH tr. *Gregory's Dial.* xxi. (1900) 147 Swa hwæt swa þe on mod ȝeurne [orig. *quidquid animo occurrit*]. **13..** *Gaw. & Gr. Knt.* 529 Þenne al rypez & rotez þat ros vpon fyrst, & þus ȝirnez þe ȝere in ȝisterdayez mony. **1377** LANGL. *P. Pl.* B. XI. 59, I forȝat ȝouthe and ȝarn [*v.rr.* yarne, ȝerne; **1393** ȝorn(e, ȝarn] in-to elde. **1393** *Ibid.* C. XIX. 165 Enuye and vuel will ȝorn in þe Iewes.

Hence †**yerning** *vbl. sb.*, running, course; *ppl. a.*, running; also †**yerner**, a runner.

1340 *Ayenb.* 141 Þe sterre þet hatte staturne,..þet asemoche yernþ in onelepi daye mid þe firmament..ase he deþ ine þritti yer ine his oȝene sercle and ine his oȝene yerninge. *Ibid.* 255 Þe melle wyþoute scluse þet alne-way went be þe yernynge of þe wetere. **1387** TREVISA *Higden* (Rolls) VI. 13 Þanne þe province was swiþe destourbed by rennynge of [*MS.* γ ȝurnyng and] reses of straungers. *a* **1400** *Praier & Compl. Ploughman* (1531) F ij, Thou ne madest none suche shepherdes ne kepers of thy schepe, that weren yerners aboute countreys. *a* **1400** *R. Gloucester's Chron.* (Rolls) 8288 (MS. C) Þe ȝurnende water was of hor blod al red. *c* **1425** *Engl. Conq. Irel.* 94 Bytwene twe perylle:—on on halue, þe wode-yernynge watyr so grysly; on other halue, hys fomen.

yern(e, obs. ff. EARN *v.*[1], IRON, YARN, YEARN.

yern-bliter, var. EARN-BLEATER, snipe.

1755 R. FORBES *Jrnl. from London* in *Ajax his Sp.* 35 Afore the levrick or yern-bliter began to sing.

†**yerne**, *adv. Obs.* Forms: 1 **ȝeorne, ȝyrne**, 2–4 **ȝeorne**, 2–5 **ȝorne**, 2–6 **ȝerne**, 3 (*Orm.*) **ȝerrne**, 4 **ȝern, ȝiern(e**, 4–5 **yerne, ȝurne, ȝarne**, 4–6 **yern, ȝarn**, 5 **ȝyrne, yorne, yurne, yarn**, 6 **yarne.** [OE. *ȝeorne* = OFris. *gerne, jerne* (Fris. *jearn*), OS. *gerno* (MDu. *gherne, geerne*, Du. *gaarne*), OHG. *gerno* (MHG. *gerne*, G. *gern*), ON. *gjarna* (Sw. *gerna, gärna*, Da. *gerne*); adv. of OE. *ȝeorn*, etc.: see YERN *a.*]

1. Eagerly, earnestly, diligently, zealously, heartily.

Beowulf 2294 Hordweard sohte ȝeorne æfter grunde. *a* **1122** *O.E. Chron.* (Laud MS.) an. 1083 Þa wreccan munecas..ȝyrne cleopedon to Gode his miltse biddende. *c* **1175** *Lamb. Hom.* 11 Muchel is us þenne neod..ȝerne bidden ure milciende drihten þet [etc.]. *a* **1200** *Moral Ode* 49 Þider ȝe sculen ȝorne draȝen. *c* **1200** *Trin. Coll. Hom.* 3 Men ..wisten ȝerne after ure lauerd ihesu cristes tocume. *a* **1250** *Prov. Ælfred* 101 in *O.E. Misc.* (1872) 108 Þe mon þe on his youhþe yeorne lernet wit and wisdom. *c* **1290** *St. Brandan* 94 in *S. Eng. Leg.* 222, & bede ȝurne oure louerdes grace þulke veyage to do. *a* **1300** *Cursor M.* 2789 (Cott.) Ȝern [*Fairf.* ȝ orne] on þaim he cried merci! **1375** BARBOUR *Bruce* III. 547 The king then at thaim speryt ȝarne, How thai..had farne. *c* **1400** *St. Alexius* (Laud 463) 35 Boþe be day, & be nyght, Ȝerne þei þonked our dright, & Seinte Marie. *c* **1400** *Rom. Rose* 6719 Thanne may he go abegging yerne Til he somme maner crafte kan lerne. *c* **1420** *Chron. Vilod.* 727 Seynt Dunstone heyȝede hym fulle faste And ȝyrne to god for hym he bedde. *c* **1425** *Engl. Conq. Irel.* 92 He..besoght ful yorne þat he most allyaunce haue to har kynrede. *c* **1440** *Pallad. on Husb.* I. 447 Mynge hit yurne Tyl euery part vntyl on body turne. **1513** DOUGLAS *Æneis* IV. vii. 83 The blak swarm our the feildis walkis ȝarn, Tursand throw the gers thar pray to hiddillis dern. *Ibid.* VI. vii. 44 The hiddillis held thai and the roddis darn, A myrtre wod about thaim lowkit ȝarn.

b. Willingly, gladly, 'fain'; *occas.* wilfully.

c **888** ÆLFRED *Boeth.* vii. § 2 Þonne scealt þu ȝeorne ȝeðolian ȝehwæt þæs þe to heora þenungum..belimpet. *c* **1200** *Trin. Coll. Hom.* 9 Ȝif þu ȝierne waxest on godnesse, ..after þing þe ðe beð biheue. **13..** *Gaw. & Gr. Knt.* 1526 Ȝe, þat ar so cortays & coynt of your hetes, Oghe to a ȝonke þynk ȝern to schewe, & teche sum tokenez of trweluf craftes. **1414** BRAMPTON *Penit. Ps.* (Percy Soc.) 12 And I trespase aȝens the ȝerne. *a* **1508** DUNBAR *Tua Mariit Wemen* 129 He trowis that ȝoung folk I ȝerne ȝeild.

c. Thoroughly, well.

c **1000** ÆLFRIC *Gen.* xxxix. 3 He wiste ful ȝeorne þæt god hine lufode. **12..** *Moral Ode* 346 (Egerton MS.) þat buð ða þe heom sculdeð ȝeorne, wid elche un-ðeawe. *a* **1225** *Leg. Kath.* 1588 Hire lust swiðe ȝeorne speoken mit te meiden. *a* **1240** *Ureisun* in *O.E. Hom.* I. 199 þu hit wost ful ȝeorne þet þe deouel hateð me.

2. a. Quickly, swiftly, rapidly, fast, briskly, at a great rate.

a **1023** WULFSTAN *Hom.* ii. (1883) 18 Hit to ðam dome nu ȝeorne nealæcð. **13..** *Gaw. & Gr. Knt.* 498 A ȝere ȝernes ful ȝerne, & ȝeldez neuer lyke. *c* **1386** CHAUCER *Pard. T.* 70 Myne handes and my tonge goon so yerne That it is ioye to se my bisynesse. **1393** LANGL. *P. Pl.* C. XXIII. 159 Sleuthe wax wonder ȝerne and sone was of age. *c* **1430** *Freemasonry* 174 The mayster may his prentes so enforme, That hys hure may crese ful ȝurne. *c* **1440** *Promp. Parv.* 536/2 Ȝarne, hastyly (*P.* ȝarne or fast), *festinanter.* **1443-9** *Paston Lett.* Suppl. (1901) 12 There he lyted and knokkyd on the gate, and we folwyd as yarn as we myth. **1493** *Dives & Pauper* (W. de W. 1496) IX. viii. 358/1 Bere he his sayle neuer soo hyghe, & go he neuer soo yerne. *c* **1530** *Crt. of Love* 1299 There nis no swallow swift..ne half so yern can fly.

b. Quickly, without delay, immediately, directly, soon. Also *as yerne* (see AS A. 5 c).

c **1320** *Sir Tristr.* 3065 Hennes ȝern þou fle Out of siȝt mine. *c* **1350** *Will. Palerne* 1252 Ȝeld þe to me ȝeply or ȝerne þou schalt deie. *c* **1374** CHAUCER *Troylus* III. 376 Achilles with his spere Myn herte cleue,..yf I late or yerne Wolde it by-wreye. *c* **1384** —— *H. Fame* II. 402 Wyth that he spack to me so yerne And seyde. *c* **1440** *Jacob's Well* 12 Ȝif ȝe by gylty, be sory in herte,..and ȝerne, wyth full sorwe of herte, beeth schreuyn. *c* **1470** HARDING *Chron.* CIX. vi, And then the kyng made hym byshop as yerne Of Winchester.

†**yernly**, *adv. Obs.* Forms: 1 **ȝeornlice**, 2-3 **ȝeornliche**, 3 **ȝeorneliche**, **ȝernliche**, **ȝierneliche**, **ȝornliche**, 4 **ȝernely**; *comp.* 3 **ȝerenluker**, **ȝeorneluker**, 4 **ȝernloker**; *sup.* 2 **ȝeornlucost**. [OE. *ȝeornlíce* = OHG. *gernlîhho* = ON. *giarnliga*: see YERN *a.* and -LY[2].] = prec. 1.

c **725** *Corpus Gloss.* (Hessels) O 38 *Obuixe*, ȝeornlice. *c* **900** tr. *Bæda's Hist.* IV. iii. (1890) 268 He..ȝeornlice in his ȝebede hleoðrade. *c* **1000** *Ags. Gosp.* Matt. ii. 8 Farað & axiað ȝeornlice be þam cilde. *c* **1175** *Lamb. Hom.* 109 þe feorðe unþeu is þet þe riche mon..bihude his feh, and ȝeornliche halde hit. *c* **1200** *Trin. Coll. Hom.* 121 Men bien swo wiðerfulle þat, swo he ȝerenluker clepeð hem to him, swo hie wiðere turneð froward him. *a* **1225** *Ancr. R.* 100 Hercneð nu ȝeorneliche, mine leoue sustren. *c* **1275** LAY. 15593 Hii ..ȝornliche luste Of þes vncouþe tale. *a* **1375** *Joseph Arim.* 593 Nas þer ȝong mon ne old þat ȝernloker wrouȝte. *a* **1400** *Relig. Pieces fr. Thornton MS.* (1914) 55 Damsele Discrecyone..sall..ȝernely luke þat all go wele.

†**yerr**, *sb. Obs.* In 3 **ȝeor**, **ȝur**, 4-5 **ȝerre**. [f. next.] A loud or harsh cry, yell, howl.

a **1225** *Ancr. R.* 306 Mid tisse schulen þe uorlorene worpen a swuch ȝeor [*MS. T.* ȝur, *MS. C.* ȝei] þet heouene & eorðe muwen beoðe grisliche agrisen. *a* **1225** *Juliana* (Bodl. MS.) 51 [He] bigon swa te ȝuren þat monie weren awundret hwet tet ȝur were. *a* **1400-50** *Wars Alex.* 5042 So did his princes..With ȝedire ȝoskingis & ȝerre ȝett out to grete.

†**yerr**, *v. Obs.* Forms: 1 **ȝyrran**, 3 **yeorre**, **ȝure** (*pa. t. pl.* **ȝurren**), 4-5 **ȝere**. [OE. **ȝierran*, *ȝyrran* str. vb., f. echoic stem *gar-*: cf. GARRE, YAR(R, etc.] *intr.* To make a harsh noise, creak, roar, rattle; to cry out loudly, yell, howl.

a **1000** *Andreas* 374 Strengas ȝurron. *a* **1100** in Napier *O.E. Glosses* (1900) 194/13 *Garrio*, ic [*sc.* a file] ȝyrre. *c* **1205** LAY. 28358 Ȝurren þa stanes Mid þan blod-stremes. *a* **1225** *Leg. Kath.* 2041 þer me mahte iheren þe heaðene hundes ȝellen & ȝeien & ȝuren. *a* **1225** *Juliana* (Royal MS.) 50 Monie weren awundret hwet te ȝuring mahte beon. *c* **1275** *Sinners Beware* 325 in *O.E. Misc.* 83 He yeorreþ & heo gredeþ, þe feondes heom forþ ledeþ. *a* **1400-50** *Wars Alex.* 4745 Vmquile he noys as a nowte as a nox quen he lawes, Ȝarmand & ȝerand a ȝoten him semed.

yerra ('jɛrə), *int. Anglo-Ir.* Also **yerrah**. [Ir.] An asseverative oath or exclamation.

1892 E. LAWLESS *Grania* II. iii. 32 Yerra! give him his bit and his sup and his bed,..and 'tis all he wants. **1898** M. MACDONAGH *Irish Life & Character* ix. 156 'What's the matter with the old gentleman?' he was asked. 'What's the matter with him! Yerrah, look at the walk of him... Begor, he only touches the ground in an odd place.' **1914** JOYCE *Dubliners* 155 Yerra, sure the little hop-o'-my-thumb has forgotten all about it. **1939** —— *Finnegans Wake* 95 Yerra, why would he heed that old gasometer. **1958** B. BEHAN *Borstal Boy* III. 218 'Yerra, 'tis nothing,' said I, jovial and Irish, but making every move to work on a bit more. **1965** *N. Munster Antiquarian Jrnl.* IX. IV. 186 Yerra there's no good in talking to you. **1977** J. HODGINS *Invention of World* iii. 83 This is no ordinary boy... Yerra, this is a boy apart.

yerse (jɜːs), repr. a non-Standard pronunc. of YES. Also **yers**.

1937 PARTRIDGE *Dict. Slang* 970/2 *Yers; yerse*, yes: sol.: C. 19-20. **1965** J. PORTER *Dover Two* vi. 69 Yerse, we was. Only they nabbed us first. **1969** J. GARDNER *Founder Member* ii. 16 'All three of us going to New York..' parried Boysie. 'Yerse,' said Griffin. **1980** P. G. WINSLOW *Counsellor Heart* v. 80 'A plant?'..'Yerse.' She described the plant. **1985** M. GILBERT *Long Journey Home* xii. 125 'Was it as obvious as that?' 'Yers. Well, you can always tell.'

yersel, Sc. form of YOURSELF.

yersinia (jɜː'sɪnɪə). *Bacteriol.* Also **Yersinia**. Pl. **-ae**. [mod.L. (J. J. Van Loghem 1944, in *Antonie van Leeuwenhoek* X. 15), f. the name of A. E. J. *Yersin* (1863-1943), Swiss-born French bacteriologist + -IA[1].] A bacterium of the genus *Yersinia* (formerly included in *Pasteurella*), which includes Gram-negative rods that are facultative anærobes present in many animals causing plague and yersiniosis in man.

1967 *Acta Path. & Microbiol. Scand.* LXXI. 384 Morphologically, they were fairly easy to distinguish from Yersinia. **1982** E. A. GORZYNSKI in Milgrom & Flanagan *Med. Microbiol.* xxi. 316/1 Yersiniae are facultative intracellular parasites. **1983** *McGraw-Hill Yearbk. Sci. & Technol.* 482/1 Once isolation of a suspect yersinia has been accomplished, the biochemical identification ensues more logically.

Hence **yersini'osis** [-OSIS], infection with or a disease caused by yersiniæ (other than *Y. pestis*, the cause of plague), which in man is self-limiting and usu. marked by lymphadenitis of the mesentery and ileitis or by enteritis and occurs chiefly in children and young adults.

1971 *Country Life* 2 Dec. 1530/1 In older leverets, parasitism may be the main problem, and in adults yersiniosis, formerly called pseudotuberculosis, a bacterial disease occurring in either the acute or chronic form, appears to be a common cause of death. **1983** *Brit. Med. Jrnl.* 27 Aug. 593/1 A large outbreak of yersiniosis in 1980 in a boys' school in Dorset was attributed to contact with a pig kept on the school farm.

yerst, yerstendai, obs. ff. ERST, YESTERDAY.

†**yert.** *Obs. rare.* [Of obscure origin; combines the symbolic elements, initially of *yerk*, finally of *blurt*, *flirt*, *spirt*, *squirt*.] = YERK *sb.* 1. **yert-point**, name of some game (cf. *blow-point* s.v. BLOW- 3).

1509 HAWES *Past. Pleas.* XXXI. (1555) T ij, At euery yerte she made godfrey to skyppe. **1659** *Lady Alimony* II. v, All his games..Are yert-point, ninepins, job-nut, or span-counter.

yerth, obs. form of EARTH.

yerva: see HERBA, YERBA.

yes, *sb.*[1] *dial.* Also 8 **yesse**, 9 **yis**, **yesh**. [Variant of EASSE, prob. the same word as EES, OE. *ǽs* food, bait.] The earthworm.

1787 GROSE *Prov. Gloss.*, *Yesse*, an earth-worm, particularly those called dew-worms. W. *c* **1820** *Quekett's Sayings* (1888) 33 Yeshes..are large worms which they make use of as baits..to catch eels. **1825** JENNINGS *Obs. Dial. W. Eng.*, *Yes.* **1863** BARNES *Dorset Gloss.*, *Yis.*

yes (jɛs), *adv.* (*sb.*[2]) Forms: α. 1 **ȝese**, 3-4 **ȝes**, 4-5 **ȝeis**, (5 **yhes**, **ȝeysse**, **yesse**, 9 *dial.* **ees**), 5- **yes**. β. 1 **ȝise**, 2-4 **ȝise**, (4 **yijs**), 4-5 **ȝhis**, **ȝys**, 4-6 **ȝis**, 4-6 (9 *dial.*) **yis**, (5 **yhis**, **yys**, **ȝisse**, 6 **yisse**, 6-7 **is**, 9 *dial.* **iss**). γ. 1 **ȝyse**, 3 **ȝuse**, 4 **ȝhus**, **yus**, 4-5 **ȝus**, (5 **ȝeus**). [An affirmative word confined to English: OE. *ȝése*, *ȝíse*, *ȝýse*, the forms of which point to early WS. **ȝíese*:—**ȝéasī*, prob. f. *ȝéa* YEA + *sí* 3 sing. pres. subj. of *bēon* to be; a similar formation is seen in *nese* (Northumb. *næse*, *næsi*), prob. f. *ne* NE *adv.* + *sī* (as above).

The acceptance of this derivation necessitates the assumption that *ȝése* was orig. applicable as an answer to a particular class of question, which is intrinsically not improbable. The suggested derivation from **ȝéa swā* 'yea, so' is phonologically inadequate.

The pronunciation (jɪs), still widespread in dialects, was formerly current in polite speech and is recorded as such in Walker's *Pronouncing Dict.*]

A. *adv.* A word used to express an affirmative reply to a question, statement, command, etc.

1. a. In answer to a question not involving a negative; standing for the affirmative sentence corresponding to the interrogative one constituting the question: = 'It is so.' Phr. *to say yes*: to assent, comply; *spec.* to accept a proposal of marriage.

Formerly usually more emphatic than *yea* or *ay*; in later use taking the place of these as the ordinary affirmative particle: cf. 2 below.

c **1000** ÆLFRIC *Hom.* I. 14 Hwi! wolde God swa lytles þinges him forwyrnan..? Ȝyse; hu mihte Adam tocnawan [etc.]. *c* **1200** *Vices & Virtues* 31 Hwat seist þu, Dauið? Hafst þu aniȝe sikernesse herof?.. 'Ȝise,' [he] seið, 'we bieð all siker of godes behate.' **1375** BARBOUR *Bruce* IV. 470 (MS. E.) The kyng..sperit..Giff ony man couth tell tithand Of any strange man in that land. 'Ȝhis [*v.r.* ȝai]', said a voman, 'schir, perfay, Of strange men I can ȝow say'. **1387** TREVISA *Higden* (Rolls) VI. 341 þanne þe kyng com, and þe pope axede of hym ȝif he hadde i-holde his oth... þe kyng..seide 'Ȝis al at þe fulle'. *Ibid.* VIII. 313 Of þis erle..is ofte greet stryf.., wheþer he schulde be acounted for [*v.r.* among] seyntes oþer none. Some seyn ȝis... Oþer seien þe contrarie. *c* **1440** *Promp. Parv.* 539/1 Ȝys, *ita*, *eciam*. **1509** HAWES *Past. Pleas.* XXXIV. ix, Haue you hym sene in any time before? Yes yes quod she. **1583** HOLLYBAND *Campo di Fior* 227 Hast thou found thy Tusculans questions? Is, so evill favoured that I knew them not. **1603** SHAKS. *Meas. for M.* II. iii. 25 *Duk.* Loue you the man that wrong'd you? *Iul.* Yes, as I loue the woman that wrong'd him. **1634** MILTON *Comus* 584, *2. Bro*... Is this the confidence You gave me Brother? *Eld. Bro.* Yes and keep it still. **1747** H. WALPOLE *Let. to Mann* 28 July, Bergen-op-zoom still holds out, and is the first place that has not said yes, the moment the French asked it the question. **1808** SCOTT *Marm.* I. Introd. 45 Will spring return,..And blossoms clothe the hawthorn spray? Yes, prattlers, yes; the daisy's flower Again shall paint your summer bower. **1866** MRS. LYNN LINTON *Lizzie Lorton* xvi, 'Is it a nice clean place?' asked Aunt Harriet... 'Yis! yis! clean eneugh!' said Isaac. **1883** D. C. MURRAY *Hearts* xiv. (1885) 111 She'd never say 'Yes' to a man she didn't care for. **1917** G. W. E. RUSSELL *Pol. & Pers.* IV. x. 364 It is wise to be prepared for this evil? Until the dream of a universal.. disarmament is realized, surely yes.

b. *Yes and No*: a round game (see quots.).

1843 DICKENS *Chr. Carol* iii, It was a Game called Yes and No, where Scrooge's nephew had to think of something, and the rest must find out what; he only answering to their questions yes or no, as the case was. **1854** *Round Games* (ed. 2) 111 Yes and No. This game..was formerly called *Animal, Vegetable, and Mineral.* A player was sent out of the room, and a word (or rather thing) thought of. The player was called in, and proceeded to ask certain members of the company to which of the three kingdoms—*animal*, *vegetable*, or *mineral*—the object in question belonged... He then proceeded to ask other questions, to which the players were only compelled to answer 'Yes' or 'No'.

c. *yes and no*, in answer to a question to which it is difficult to reply: partly, perhaps, to a certain degree.

1873 C. M. YONGE *Pillars of House* I. vii. 154 'Do you come from his father?' 'Well—yes and no. His father is still in Oregon; but he and I have always been one.' **1896** 'M. RUTHERFORD' *Clara Hopgood* xxii. 212, I said 'yes and no' and there is another side. **1933** W. S. MAUGHAM *Sheppey* III. 75 *Bessie*:..Expecting somebody? *Florrie*: Yes and no. **1964** R. PETRIE *Murder by Precedent* v. 78 'That's why you gave him a home?' he asked. 'Well yes and no.' **1981** B. MURPHY *Enigma Variations* xiii. 137 'Do you believe that if you continue seeing me you'll be damned?' 'Yes and no.'

d. *yes or no*: used *attrib.* (freq. hyphenated) to denote a question, etc., answerable by, or definable in terms of, *yes* or *no*; *spec.* in *Linguistics*. Also *ellipt.* as **yes-no**.

1924 [see PRONOMINAL *a.* 2]. **1935** [see OKEY-DOKE *a.*]. **1952** *Mind* LXI. 52 The yes-or-no question is the one we like to ask. **1957** D. L. BOLINGER in *Publ. Amer. Dialect Soc.* XXVIII. 24 Yes-no Qs are essentially true-false Qs. **1961** F. W. HOUSEHOLDER in Saporta & Bastian *Psycholinguistics* 17/1 Beside this graded kind of 'grammaticalness'..there is also an absolute yes-or-no type. **1963**, **1964** [see MORE C. *adv.* 2]. **1966** A. BATTERSBY *Math. in Management* vii. 180 This type of work [*sc.* simulation] lends itself very readily to electronic computation, because it comprises a number of repetitive 'loops' of instructions, controlled by simple 'yes-no' decisions. **1976** H. KEMELMAN *Wednesday Rabbi got Wet* xlvi. 257 The law is not a yes-or-no thing. **1977** *Times* 8 Feb. 17/1 The Government is proposing to put a single yes-no question to the voters of Scotland and Wales. **1979** *Economist* 16 June 98/2 Whitehall's traditional passion for compromise only makes for trouble in a crisis which needs yes-or-no decisions, fast. **1984** *Word* XXXV. 188 Sentences other than declaratives are broken up into a speech act operator (a wh-question operator, a yes-no question operator, a command operator, etc.) and a propositional kernel.

2. a. In answer to a question involving a negative.

Formerly regularly used thus (and as in b) in distinction from *yea* (see YEA 1); the distinction became obsolete soon after 1600, and since then *yes* has been the ordinary affirmative particle in reply to any question positive or negative, and *yea* has become archaic. The distinction was still observed in the Bible of 1611, in which *yes* occurs four times (all in N.T.), always after a negative question or statement; the Revisers of 1881, apparently in ignorance of the usage, altered it in all these instances to *yea*.

c **888** ÆLFRED *Boeth.* xvi. §4 Wenst ðu þæt se godcunda anweald ne mihte afyrran þone anweald þam unrihtwisan kasere,..ȝif he wolde? þise, la, ȝese; ic wat þæt he mihte, ȝif he wolde. *Ibid.* xxxiv. § 6 Ða cwæð he: Ne sæde ic þe ær þæt sio ȝesælð good wære? Ȝyse, cwæð ic, ȝe þu þæt sædest þæt hio þæt hehste good wære. *c* **1000** *Ags. Gosp.* Matt. xvii. 25 Eower lareow, ne ȝylt he gafol? þa cwæð he: Ȝyse, he deð. *a* **1225** *Ancr. R.* 392 Ne muhte he mid lesse gref habben ared us? Ȝe siker [*MS. T.* ȝuse I wis, *MS. C.* ȝes I wis]. *a* **1300** *Cursor M.* 5208 (Cott.) 'How sua, es þar na noþer king?' 'Yus [*Gött.* Ȝes], bot he dus nakins thing.' *c* **1315** SHOREHAM *Poems* VII. 499 Nys þys god laȝe? Ȝes, y-wys, god laȝe hys. **13..** *Cursor M.* 2761 (Gött.) 'Ne sal þai all þar-fore liue?' 'Yis,' said vr lauerd. **1375** BARBOUR *Bruce* IX. 84 Trow ȝe nocht than that thai Sall vencust in thair hertis be? Ȝhus, sall thai. *c* **1400** *Pilgr. Sowle* (Caxton 1483) IV. xx. 66 Myn hertes greef, mote I not wepe? O yis. *c* **1450** *Merlin* iii. 54 'Haue ye no mynde of the sarazins..?' And thei seide, 'Yesse, full wele.' *c* **1450** *Cov. Myst.* xxx. (Shaks. Soc.) 296 Thynk ȝe not he is worthy to dey? *Et clamabant omnes.* 'ȝys! ȝys! ȝys! alle we seye his is worthy to dey, ȝa! ȝa! ȝa!' **1533** MORE *Debell. Salem* Wks. 997/1 Wold not the iudges trow you geue them y[e] hearing; yes yes I dout not. **1545** JOYE *Exp. Dan.* iii. 38 b, Did we not cast thre men bownde into the fyer? which answerd, yisse trwly oh kynge. **1591** SHAKS. *Two Gent.* II. i. 128 *Val.* What meanes your Ladiship? Doe you not like it? *Sil.* Yes, yes. **1632** LITHGOW *Trav.* VI. 255 Was not the hand of the Almighty..able also, to drowne their..plaines with water? Yes and doubtlesse yes. **1646** VAUGHAN *Juv. Sat. x.* 485 But thy spruce boy must touch no other face Then a Patrician? Is of any race So they be rich. **1779** JOHNSON in *Boswell* (1904) II. 308 *B.* 'Is not the Giant's Causeway worth seeing?'—*J.* 'Worth seeing, yes; but not worth going to see.' **1865** DICKENS *Mut. Fr.* III. xvi, 'You never can have walked, my dear?' 'Yes, I have.' **1880** 'MARK TWAIN' *Tramp Abr.* xxvii, 'I like to be always making acquaintances, don't you?' 'Lord, yes!'

b. In contradiction of or opposition to a negative statement expressed or implied, or a negative command or request.

Now usually accompanied by a short asseverative phrase echoing the preceding statement; e.g. in quot. 1611, mod. colloq. usage would require *Yes, it was.*

c **1205** LAY. 17208 þa andswarede þe king: Mærlin þu sæist sællic þing þe nauere nan iboren mon Ne maie heom bringgen þenne... Hu mihte ich heom þenne Heom bringen þeonne? þa andswerede Mærlin þan kinge..Ȝuse, ȝuse lauerd king. **13..** *Cursor M.* 1249 (Gött.) 'Sun,' he said, 'þe bus ga To paradis þat I cam fra...' 'Ȝa, sir, wist i queþirward.'.. 'Ȝeis,' he said, 'i sal þe tell and say, Hugat þu sal ta þi right way.' *c* **1350** *Will. Palerne* 1567 'Ȝe, wist y þat,' seide william 'witterly to speke, Of alle harmes were ich hol.' .. 'Ȝis, be marie,' seide meliors 'misdrede ȝow neuer.' *c* **1375** *Cursor M.* 5066 (Fairf.) We ar noȝt of a kithe saide he, Ȝus þat salle I shew to þe. *c* **1400** *Rom. Rose* 4659 Knowest hym ought? *Lamaunt.* Yhe, dame, parde. *Raisoun.* Nay, nay. *Lamaunt.* Yhis, I. *c* **1420** [see YEA 4]. *c* **1450** *Mirk's Festial* 252 Then..þe Iewe..sayde hit was not soo. 'Ȝeus' quod þe cristyn man. **1470-85** MALORY *Arthur* I. xx. 66 How sholdest thou knowe it, for thow arte not so old of yeres to knowe my fader, yes sayd Merlyn I knowe it better than ye or ony man lyuynge. **1552** LYNDESAY *Monarche* 5952 We neuer saw thyne excellence Subdewit to sic Indigence. Ȝis, sall he [*sc.* Christ] say,..Quhen euer ȝe did ressaue the pure. **1603** SHAKS. *Meas. for M.* II. ii. 49 *Isab.* Must he needs die? *Ang.* Maiden, no remedie. *Isab.* Yes: I doe thinke that you might pardon him. **1611** —— *Cymb.* I. iv. 52 *Post...* My Quarrell was not altogether slight. *French.* Faith yes, to be put to the arbiterment of Swords. **1779** JOHNSON in *Boswell* (1904) II. 304 *Boswell.* 'You did now know what you were undertaking.' *Johnson.* 'Yes, Sir, I knew very well what I was undertaking.' **1865** DICKENS *Mut. Fr.* II. xv, 'But it's not in the way, Charley.' 'Yes, it is,' said the boy, petulantly. **1880** 'MARK TWAIN' *Tramp Abr.* xxvii, 'I do not know he ever preached there.' 'Oh, yes, he did.'

3. a. Expressing assent to a command, request, proposal, or summons.

a **1300** *Cursor M.* 4341 'Lauedi', he said, 'com to þi mete.' 'Yus', sco said. *Ibid.* 7363 'Þat childs nam yee will me scau.' 'Yijs', he said, 'i sal þe ken To knau him a-mang oþer men.' *c* **1320** *Sir Tristr.* 436 He bede hem pens mo..Ȝif þai wald wiþ him go... 'Ȝis' þai sworen þo. *c* **1369** CHAUCER *Dethe Blaunche* 753, I telle hyt the vp a condicion That thou shalt hooly..Doo thyn entent to herkene hitte. Yis syr. *c* **1425** *Cast. Persev.* 440 in *Macro Plays* 90 Now go we forth..& bere þee manly euere a-mong..*Humanum genus.* Ȝys, & ellys haue þou my necke. **1470-85** MALORY *Arthur* II. xv. 93 Hast thow slayn my broder, thow shalt dye therfor or thou departe, wel said balen do it your self, yis sayde kyng pellam, ther shall no man haue ado with the, but my self. **1728** DE FOE *Street Robb. Consid.* 15 Prithee call him, Child, said he, to me,..Yes, Sir, said I. **1837** DICKENS *Pickw.* iv, 'Joe!' 'Yes, sir.' **1859** RUSKIN *Two Paths* iii. §82 Nay, but you will take Christian ornament—purest mediæval Christian—thirteenth century! Yes: and do you suppose you will find the Christian less human? **1898** G. B. SHAW *Mrs. Warren's Prof.* I, *The Clergyman* [calling]. Frank! *Frank...* Yes, gov'nor.

b. Expressing assent to a statement or implication.

a **1400-50** *Wars Alex.* 2079 'Be his kniȝtis as kene as me þis cornes shewis, All þe werd war to waike his wrothe to with-stand.'.. 'Ȝ is, he ledis bot a lite, lord, with ȝoure lefe..Bot mare fersere in feld fell neuire of modire.' **1633** MARMION *Fine Comp.* IV. vi, *Spr.* I heare she is runne mad. *Aur.* Is. **1723** C. WALKER *Mem. Sally Salisb.* 26 She would bring out a Word something like Abdication, in this manner, Yes, yes, Abdillication was of great use to you, &c. **1732** POPE *Ep. Cobham* 1 Yes, you despise the man to books confin'd, Who from his study rails at human kind. **1818** SHELLEY *Rosal. & Helen* 77 *Henry.* This is not the way, Mamma; it leads behind those trees that grow Close to the little river. *Helen.* Yes: I know: I was bewildered. **1837** DICKENS *Pickw.* xiv, 'They must have been very nice men, both of 'em.'.. 'Yes, they were,..very nice men indeed!' **1898** 'MERRIMAN' *Roden's Corner* vii. 74 The exquisite sense of humour had also slightly evaporated. People said, 'Oh yes, very funny,' than which nothing is more fatal to humour. *Ibid.* viii. 82 'But we were talking of Mr. Cornish.' 'Yes', answered Dorothy... 'Yes; but I must not talk any longer or I shall be late.'

c. Expressing concessive assent (sometimes sarcastically), and introducing an objection: often repeated in sign of impatience.

1596 SHAKS. *Merch. V.* I. iii. 34 *Iew...* May I speake with Anthonio? *Bass.* If it please you to dine with vs. *Iew.* Yes, to smell porke. **1852** MRS. STOWE *Uncle Tom's C.* xxii, 'Miss Ophelia has taught Topsy to read', continued Eva. 'Yes, and you see how much good it does.' **1865** 'L. CARROLL' *Alice's Adv. in Wonderland* vii, 'It was the *best* butter.'.. 'Yes, but some crumbs must have got in as well.' **1880** 'MARK TWAIN' *Tramp Abr.* xxv, One morning I said:—'There is an American party.' Harris said,—'Yes, but name the State.'

d. (Usually interrogative.) Expressing provisional assent, with desire for further information or statement; hence as an inquiry addressed to a person waiting in silence (= 'what is it?' 'what do you want?'); also as a mere expression of interest (= 'indeed?' 'is it so?').

1842 DICKENS *Amer. Notes* iv, If you are an Englishman, he expects that that railroad is pretty much like an English railroad. If you say 'No', he says 'Yes?' (interrogatively) and asks in what respect they differ. You enumerate the heads of difference one by one, and he says 'yes?' (still interrogatively) to each. **1858** O. W. HOLMES *Aut. Breakf.-t.* i, My landlady's daughter... Tender-eyed blonde. Long ringlets... Says 'Yes?' when you tell her anything. *Ibid.*, 'I was only giving some hints on the fine arts.' 'Yes?' **1898** *Punch* 16 Apr. 173/1 After a few moments I was joined by a gentleman... 'Yes?' he said, in a tone of interrogation.

4. Used to emphasize or strengthen the speaker's own preceding statement: = YEA 3.

In first quot. perh. used as an ordinary intensive adverb: = YEA 2.

1598 SHAKS. *Merry W.* II. ii. 108 Surely I thinke you haue charmes, la: yes in truth. **1613** —— *Hen. VIII*, I. ii. 176, I say, take heed; Yes, heartily beseech you. **1766** GOLDSM. *Vicar W.* xxii, 'Ah, Madam', cried her mother, 'this is but a poor place you are come to after so much finery... Yes, Miss Livy, your poor father and I have suffered very much of late.' **1810** CRABBE *Borough* xxii. 12 His father's love he scorn'd,..But being drunk, wept sorely when he died. Yes! then he wept. **1827** SCOTT *Highl. Widow* iv, 'The race of Dermid, whose children murdered—yes', she added, with a wild shriek, 'murdered your mother's fathers.' **1866** MEREDITH *Vittoria* iv, 'He rendered payment for it', said Agostino. 'He perished; yes! as we shake dust to the winds.' **1888** 'J. S. WINTER' *Bootle's Childr.* ii, He was living a month ago, and drunk enough to knock me down. Yes, *me* ..*me* with a babe of a month old.

†5. In construction after a verb of thinking, etc., standing for a clause expressing affirmation or assent: = YEA 1 e. *Obs.*

a **1533** LD. BERNERS *Huon* ix. 24 Then Huon..demandyd yf he myght ryde or not, 'brother' quod Gerarde 'I thynke yes.' **1634** CAINE *Necess. Separ.* v. 218 His wordes import positively *no*, but we are sure *yes*. **1843** CARLYLE *Past & Pr.* III. xv, Thou shalt not disobey them. It were better for thee not. Better a hundred deaths than yes.

¶ *O yes* (formula introducing a crier's announcement): see OYEZ.

B. as *sb.* (Pl. **yes's, yeses.**) An utterance of the word 'yes'; an affirmative reply, or expression of assent: often opposed to *no*.

[*c* **897** ÆLFRED *Gregory's Past. C.* xlii. 308 Wene ȝe ðæt æȝðer sie mid me ȝe ȝise ȝe nese?] **1712** STEELE *Spect.* No. 266 ¶4 Her innocent forsooths, yes's, and't please you's.. moved the good old Lady to..hire her for her own Maid. **1775** SHERIDAN in *Sheridaniana* (1826) 62 No pearly teeth rejoice my view, Unless a 'yes' displays their hue. **1805** SOUTHEY *Madoc* I. xvii. 29 Madoc smiling on the Maid,.. lightly gave the yes. **1818** KEATS *Endym.* IV. 898 Striving their ghastly malady to cheer, By thinking it a thing of yes and no, That housewives talk of. **1840** THACKERAY *Shabby Genteel Story* v, Dear yeses and noes, how beautiful you are when gently whispered by pretty lips! **1855** TENNYSON *Maud* I. XVII. 9 Roses are her cheeks, And a rose her mouth When the happy Yes Falters from her lips. **1866** MEREDITH *Vittoria* ii, 'Said yes!' he remarked. 'He might say no, for a diversion. He has yeses enough in his pay to earn a Cardinal's hat.' **1879** 'L. HOFFMANN' *Drawing-r. Amusem.* ii. 41 The 'Twenty questions'... He is limited to twenty questions, which, with one exception, must be of such a character as to be answered by a simple 'Yes' or 'No'.

yes, *v.* [f. the adv.]

1. *intr.* To say 'yes'; to assent: opp. to NO *v.* (see after NO *adv.*[3] and *sb.*).

1820 *Blackw. Mag.* VIII. 271 Thy hat low dangling from thy better hand, *Yes*-ing and *No*-ing to the great man's will. **1891** J. K. STEPHEN *Quo Musa Tendis?* 56, I don't know what we talked about; I smiled; the same old smile: I 'yes'd' and 'no'd' and 'really'd', till I thought he must discover That I was listening to the band.

2. *trans.* To say 'yes' to or agree with (someone); to flatter by habitual assent. *U.S.*

1921 R. W. LARDNER in Mencken *Amer. Lang.* (rev. ed.) 393 He..crossed me up. I ast him for a hook and he yessed me and then throwed a fast one. **1928** J. P. MCEVOY *Show Girl* ix. 134 They yes you to death. **1933** *Times Lit. Suppl.* 23 Nov. 844/2 For Mr. Leonard..there is no fun in life as lived in the United States. Too much work..yessing the boss and dud liquor. **1935** [see RAVE *sb.*[2] 2 b]. **1945** S. LEWIS *Cass Timberlane* xvi. 89 A lot of bums are always yessing you ..but me and Boone are good-enough friends to tell you the truth. **1983** *N.Y. Times* 23 Oct. 19/6 Mr. Reagan..is unable to get his proposal off the ground..; his aids yes him to death with plans.

yes, obs. pl. of EYE; obs. f. ICE.

ye'se = *ye shall*: see SHALL A. 5.

yeshiva (jə'ʃiːvə). Also **yeshiba(h, yeshivah,** and with capital initial. Pl. **yeshivoth, yeshiva(h)s;** also **yeshibot.** [a. Heb. *yĕšīḇāh*, f. *yashav* to sit.] An Orthodox Jewish college or seminary; a Talmudic academy.

1851 *Living Age* XXIX. 154/2 The hope of seeing him one day decorated with the dignity of rabbi..will impel them cheerfully to make all the sacrifices which his outfit and partial support at the yeshibah (*academy*) entail. **1881** *Encycl. Brit.* XIII. 681/2 The rabbis received their education at the Yeshiboth ('sessions' of academies devoted to the Talmud, the *Shulchan Aruch*, and their commentators). **1904** *Sat. Rev.* 24 Sept. 404/1 The Jewish orphan..is brought up..at a yeshiva, or seminary, where the Talmud is almost the sole object of study. **1916** H. SACHER *Zionism & Jewish Future* 38 They had passed by so swift and drastic a revolution from the *Cheder* and the *Yeshiba* to the Gymnasium and the University, that the only culture they were interested in was German culture. **1926** S. ASH *Kiddush Ha-Shem* x. 88 Famed far and wide were the yeshivahs of Poland. **1949** KOESTLER *Promise & Fulfulment* III. i. 295 Israel's first Prime Minister..and many of the other political leaders, started their education in the *Yeshivot*, the religious schools of Russian Jewry. **1957** *Encycl. Brit.* XIII. 63D/1 Orthodox Judaism created the Rabbi Isaac Elchanan Theological seminary in New York (1896), which developed into the Yeshiva university, a liberal arts college. **1960** L. P. GARTNER *Jewish Immigrant in England, 1870–1914* ii. 39 Yekuthiel Sussmann Schlosser.. arrived in 1852 as an itinerant solicitor for a projected yeshibah in Kalish. **1965** J. A. MICHENER *Source* 461 Sometimes the yeshiva students contrived ingenious answers. *Ibid.* 705 He..tries always to attend one of the yeshivot. **1976** C. BERMANT *Coming Home* I. i. 17 Yeghivah students..had been equipped for a life of prayer, contemplation and study. **1981** *Amer. Speech* LVI. 3 Orthodox Jews are typically strict Sabbath observers who maintain their own religious day schools and yeshivas. **1985** *Listener* 3 Jan. 27/3 He overcomes this obstacle by making a donation to a yeshiva, or religious seminar.

yesk: see YEX.

'yes-man. *colloq.* (orig. *U.S.*). Also **yes man.** [f. YES *adv.* + MAN *sb.*[1]] A man who agrees from self-interest or fear with everything put to him by a superior; an obsequious subordinate.

1912 *Century Mag.* July 339/2 We're both yes-men, Edward. We've got to take orders now. **1924** H. C. WITWER in *Cosmopolitan* Apr. 69/2, I thoroughly enjoy..the yes-men who hang about the executives and hold their jobs by simply being constantly affirmative. **1928** *Sunday Express* 15 July 3/6 Heeney is paying the strictest attention to his instructors, and in this respect is very different from Tunney, who directs his own training, and whose camp associates are all 'Yes' men. **1933** C. DAY LEWIS *Magnetic Mountain* 51 What do they believe in, these yellow yes-men. **1949** [see *closed shop* s.v. CLOSED *ppl. a.* 3]. **1954** D. UNWIN *Governor's Wife* v. 119 Your administration..favours the boot-lickers, the sycophants, the yes-men who do as they're told and don't make trouble. **1959** [see BAND-WAGON]. **1973** *Times* 31 Jan. 14/3 This is not a demand for 'yes men' but for common standards. **1979** J. WAINWRIGHT *Duty Elsewhere* i. 8 The heavies and the molls—the pimps and the yes-men.

Hence **'yes-girl, -woman,** an obsequiously subordinate woman.

1930 K. BRUSH *Young Man of Manhattan* v. 56 Her attitude.., so respectful, so impressed, hardened his heart. 'Just a yes-girl!' he thought bitterly. **1933** S. LEWIS *Ann Vickers* xxxviii. 454 They want to boss a gang of meek yes-women or they want to be received socially, like princesses. **1937** H. G. WELLS *Star Begotten* vii. 128 All his most trusted henchmen, tools, stooges, subordinates, intimates, Watsons, yes-girls. **1942** E. WAUGH *Put out More Flags* i. 17 'That's right,' said the yes-woman. **1950** D. CUSACK *Morning Sacrifice* in *3 Austral. Three-Act Plays* I. 188 It..Prepares them to accept all, question nothing, and grow into nice well-behaved yes-girls. **1979** M. SOAMES *Clementine Churchill* xvi. 235 Devoted and fiercely loyal, she never became a 'yes-woman'.

yesse, obs. f. YES *sb.* and *adv.*

yessir ('jɛsə(r), jɛs'sɜː(r)). *colloq.* [Repr. an informal pronunc. of *yes, sir*: see SIR *sb.* 8 c.]

a. = *yes, sir* s.v. SIR *sb.* 8 c. **b.** A formula of assent to a superior. Occas. as *sb.*, a quick utterance of 'yes, sir'. Cf. NOSSIR.

There is much variation in the placing of the main stress in both the ordinary use and in the verbal forms.

1913 R. BROOKE *Let.* 17 Sept. (1968) 511 That note-book. .. I lost it in British Columbia—yessir, isn't it *too* bloody. **1930** [see NOSSIR]. **1931** M. ALLINGHAM *Look to Lady* xxi. 215 The girl vanished with a startled 'yessir'. **1933** D. L. SAYERS *Murder must Advertise* vi. 102 'Yessir.' Ginger grinned confidentially. **1936** WODEHOUSE *Laughing Gas* xxiv. 262 'And,' said George, 'it's yessir sure enough the picture of the dead wife he loved.' **1962** L. DEIGHTON *Ipcress File* xviii. 118 A couple of 'yessirs' when you know that 'not on your life' is the thing to say. **1968** *Globe & Mail* (Toronto) (Mag.) 17 Feb. 1 A perfect specimen, yessir, the Canadian Hercules. **1973** A. BROINOWSKI *Take One Ambassador* ix. 125 The commanding officer went past, giving you marks for..the crispness of your Yessir. **1982** M. NABB *Death of Dutchman* vii. 143 'Do you understand me?' 'Yessir!'

Hence **yes(-)'sir, yes'sir** *v.*, (*a*) *trans.*, to defer to (someone) as a superior; (*b*) *intr.*, to say 'yes, sir', esp. obsequiously; **yes-'sirring** *vbl. sb.*

1966 *Punch* 21 Sept. 454/2 Yessiring in the office is insufficient, he offers his clammy devotion to the whole family as well. **1968** L. DEIGHTON *Only when I Larf* i. 16 Imagine..yes sirring the boss until superannuation... Not me, man. I'm for the open road. **1977** 'J. D. WHITE' *Salzburg Affair* xii. 104 He came in bowing and yes-sirring, although no one..was there to overhear. **1980** H. R. F. KEATING *Murder of Maharajah* xv. 182 You're used to people yessirring you left and right.

yes siree (jɛs sɜː'riː). *U.S. colloq.* Also **yes sir-ee, yes sirree.** [f. YES *adv.* + SIRREE.] Yes indeed; certainly. Cf. NO SIREE.

1846 *Dollar Newspaper* (Philadelphia) 1 July 3/4 'Will you take this man to be your lawful husband?' said the Justice; to which she responded with breathless haste, '*Yes, sir-ee*'. **1898** J. C. HARRIS *Tales of Home Folks* 225 Cassy Tatum! Yes, siree! The very gal! **1900** R. H. SAVAGE *Brought to Bay* I. ii, 'So, the title is secure!' cried the overjoyed Hawtrey. 'Yes, Sir-ee!' frankly answered Texas Dave. **1924** H. J. LASKI *Let.* 29 July (1953) I. 638 For local colour he added that when you emphatically approve of an opinion you write 'yes, sirree' on it. **1927** J. N. MCILWRAITH *Kinsmen at War* xxvii. 277 Yes, siree, our army's been going ashore plundering and destroying helpless villages all along the sea-coast of the United States. **1956** B. HOLIDAY *Lady sings Blues* (1973) xxiv. 203 Yes siree bob, life is just a bowl of cherries.

‖**yesso.** *Obs.* [Sp. *yeso* GYPSUM.] = GESSO.

a **1533** LD. BERNERS *Gold. Bk. M. Aurel.* let. xiv. (1535) 149 Ye made my figure with fete of straw, my legges of ambre,..the heed of yesso. **1619** *Pasquil's Palin.* lxix, With Yesso they him purge, with Lime they choake him.

b. Applied to a kind of plaster which is trodden with grapes in the making of wine in Spain.

1875 *Jrnl. Chem. Soc.* 952.

yessum ('jɛs(ə)m). *U.S. dial.* contraction of *yes, ma'am* [cf. MA'AM], a polite form of assent addressed to a woman.

1913 *Dialect Notes* IV. 1 *Yessum*, adv., yes, ma'am. **1929** W. FAULKNER *Sound & Fury* 6 'Take his overcoat and overshoes off.'.. 'Yessum.' Versh said. **1938** M. K. RAWLINGS *Yearling* x. 88 'You feel all right?' she asked. 'Yessum. Sort o' weakified.' **1942** W. FAULKNER *Go down, Moses* 11 Miss Sophonsiba said..neighbors just a half day's ride apart ought not to go so long as Uncle Buck, and Uncle Buck said Yessum.

yest, slang or epistolary abbreviation of YESTERDAY.

1725 *New Cant. Dict.*, *Yest*, a Diminutive of *Yesterday*. **1894** DUCHESS OF MARLBOROUGH *Let.* 21 May in R. S. Churchill *Winston S. Churchill* (1967) I. Compan. I. vii. 486 Your father returned yest morn and went to Harrow.

yest, etc., obs. f. YEAST, etc.

yeste, obs. graphic variant of *ieste*, GEST *sb.*[1]

13.. *Octavian* 279 (MS. Ff. ii. 38, lf. 84) In yeste as we rede. **13..** *Sir Beues* 3693 (ibid. lf. 121 b) Now begynnyth a yeste ageyn Of King Quore & Armyn.

yesteneuen, var. YESTERNEVEN *Obs.*

yester ('jɛstə(r)), *a.*, *adv.*, *sb.* [The first element of *yesterday*, *yestereve*, etc., used as a separate word. Cf. next.]

A. *adj.* Of or belonging to yesterday. *poet.*

1577 HOLINSHED *Chron.*, *Descr. Scot.* ix. 12/1 We haue such plenty of fishe, . . that although Millions . . of them be taken on the one day, yet on the next their losse wil so be supplied with new store, that nothing shal be missing by reason of the yesterfang. **1690** DRYDEN *Don Sebastian* II. i. (1692) D 1 b, To love an Enemy, . . whom yester Sun beheld, Must'ring her Charms. **1725** POPE *Odyss.* IV. 881 When the glimm'ring ray Of yester dawn disclos'd the tender day. **1737** GLOVER *Leonidas* VII. 31 Opposition more tremendous still And ruinous, than yester sun beheld. **1848** LYTTON *K. Arthur* XI. cxliv, Thro' paths his yester steps had fail'd to find. **1889** *Universal Rev.* Nov. 427 There all day long my yester journey was.

†B. *adv.* Yesterday. *Obs.*

1647 in *Essex Rev.* (1908) XVII. 134 Sir thomas farfax yester dined at the Tower. **1653** *Nicholas Papers* (Camden) II. 6 The other took his advertisement so ill that they were like to have fallen by the ears yester. **1790** GROSE *Prov. Gloss.* (ed. 2) Suppl., All the day yester.

†C. *sb.* Yesterday. Also *transf.* *Obs.*

a **1701** SEDLEY *Virg. Past.* vi. Wks. 1778 I. 307 With fumes of yester's wine the god was doz'd. **1837** WHITTOCK, etc. *Bk. Trades* (1842) 390 (*Printer*), Ornamental printing—the last thing of yester's date.

yester-, in comb. or as prefix = immediately preceding the present, last, in YESTEREVE, etc., after YESTERDAY, YESTERNIGHT; e.g. ***yester-afternoon***, ***-age***, ***-noon***, ***-tempest***, ***-week***. See also YESTER-YEAR.

1806 COLERIDGE *Let. to D. Stuart* 18 Aug., I . . have found myself so unusually better ever since I leaped on land *yester-afternoon. **1870** SWINBURNE *Ess. & Stud.* (1875) 97 A poet of the first order . . puts the life-blood of an equal interest into Hebrew forms or Greek, mediæval or modern, yesterday or *yesterage. **1855** HYDE CLARKE *Dict.*, *Yesternoon. **1872** M. COLLINS in Frances Collins *M.C.*, *Lett.* etc., (1877) I. 106, I saw some swallows yesternoon at the parsonage. **1888** G. M. HOPKINS *Poems* (1967) 105 Delightfully the bright wind boisterous ropes, wrestles, beats earth bare Of *yestertempest's creases. **1839** MRS. BROWNING *Rom. Page* xii, The lady Abbess dead before it, And the chanting nuns whom *yester-week Her voice did charge and bless.

yesterday ('jɛstədeɪ, -dɪ), *adv.*, *sb.*, and *a.* Forms: *α.* 1 **ȝeostran-**, **ȝystran-**, **ȝioster-**, **ȝestor dæȝ**, 3–6 **ȝister-** (3 **yhistre-**, 4 **ȝester-**, **ȝistir(e-**, **ȝystir-**, **ȝystyre-**, **ȝhister-**, **yhister-**, **ȝhystir-**, **ȝuster-**, 5 **ȝistur-**, **ȝystyr-**, **ȝyster-**, **ȝustir-**, 6 **ȝeister-**, **yister-**, **-ir-**, 9 *dial.* **yisser-**), 4– **yesterday**. *β.* 1 **ȝyrstan-**, **ȝierstandæȝ**, 3 **ȝersten-**, **ȝurster-**, **ȝursten-**, **ȝorsten-**, **ȝorstnen-**, 4 **ȝursday**, 5 **ȝurston-**, **yerstenday**; 4 **ȝistai**, **-av**, 8 **ye(r)stei**. (Also 1–6 occas. as two words.) [OE. *ȝeostran*, *ȝystran dæȝ*, Lindisf. Gosp. *ȝioster doeȝ*, Rushw. Gosp. *ȝestor dæȝe*, also with metathesis (WS.) *ȝierstan*, *ȝyrstan dæȝ*. The only known parallel to this collocation is Goth. *gistradagis* αὔριον, tomorrow; in OE., the simple *ȝiestron* is found only once, but in the other languages the simple word is regularly used alone in the sense of 'yesterday': OFris. **iester*, **iers(t)ne* (NFris., WFris. *jister*, EFris. *jursen*, *jersten*), MLG. *gisteren*, *-ern(e*, (LG. *gistern*, *güster(n)*, MDu. *ghisteren*, *ghister* (Du. *gisteren*, also *dag van gister*), OHG. *gestaron*, *gest(e)ren* (MHG. *gestern*, *gester*, G. *gestern*). The word has the form (with and without inflexional *-n*) of a comparative **ghistr-*, *ghjestr-* (cf. L. *hester-nus* of yesterday) of an Indo-eur. **ghjes* represented outside Teutonic by Skr. *hyás*, Gr. χθές, Alb. *dje*, L. *heri* yesterday (ON. *í gǽr* yesterday, tomorrow, shows a variant with long vowel).

The twofold meaning exhibited in the above forms and in OHG. *ēgestern* day before yesterday, day after tomorrow, indicates that the original application of the word was to a day preceding or following the present. The following apparent example of the English word with the meaning 'tomorrow' is isolated:—

1533 MORE *Apol.* 201, I geue them all playn peremptory warnynge now, that they dreue yt of no lenger. For yf they tarye tyll yesterday . . I purpose to purchace suche a proteccyon for them [etc.].]

A. *adv.* **1.** On the day immediately preceding the present day. Also, in reported speech, on the day last past, the day before.

†***ere yesterday***: the day before yesterday.

α. *c* **950** *Lindisf. Gosp.* John iv. 52 *Heri*, ȝioster doeȝ [*Rushw.* ȝestor dæȝe, *Ags. Gosp.* ȝyrstan dæȝ, *Hatton* ȝystendaiȝ]. *c* **1250** *Gen. & Ex.* 2732 We witen wel quat is bi-tid, Quuow ȝister-dai was slaȝen and hid. *a* **1375** *Joseph Arim.* 330 Þou toldest me ȝusterday. **1375** BARBOUR *Bruce* I. 124 Wnfayr thingis may fall, perfay, Alss weill to-morn as ȝhisterday. *c* **1380** *Sir Ferumb.* 1632 Ȝester day, . . as we ryde forþ ryȝtes, Wiþ seuen glotouns mette we. *c* **1450** *Northern Passion* 160/404 Ȝistirday were þay redis thre, Now are thay closed in to a tre. *c* **1450** tr. *De Imitatione* III. lv. 131 As it was ȝisterday and þe oþir day. **1535** COVERDALE *Gen.* xxxi. 2 Iacob behelde Labans countenaunce, & beholde, it was not towarde him as yesterdaye and yer-yesterdaye. *a* **1578** LINDESAY (Pitscottie) *Chron. Scot.* (S.T.S.) II. 76 Mr George ansuerit and said, . . wald they send to him the honest and godlie man that maid the sermone ȝeisterday, he wald oppin his mynd into him. **1585** WHITNEY *Choice Emblems* (1586) Ep. Ded. 1 For hereby, this present time behouldeth the accidentes of former times, as if they had bin done but yesterdaie. **1601** SHAKS. *Jul. C.* III. ii. 123 But yesterday, the word of Cæsar might Haue stood against the World: Now lies he there, And none so poore to do him reuerence. **1675** LD. CONWAY in *Essex Papers* (Camden 1013) 11 The Debate there was yesterday and to day in the House of Commons. **1814** JANE AUSTEN *Mansf. Park* xl, He was well, had left them all well at Mapsfield, and was to dine, as yesterday, with the Frasers. **1842** TENNYSON *Gard. Dau.* 81 As tho' 'twere yesterday, as tho' it were The hour just flown. **1849** M. ARNOLD *Forsaken Merman* 30 Children dear, was it yesterday We heard the sweet bells over the bay? **1860** TYNDALL *Glac.* I. xxvii. 212 All evidence of the deep track which they had formed yesterday having been swept away.

β. *c* **1000** ÆLFRIC *Gen.* xxxi. 5 Ic ȝeseo on eowres fæder þeawum, þæt he nys swa wel wið me ȝeworht, swa he wæs ȝyrstan dæȝ and þis æran dæȝ. *c* **1000** —— *Saints' Lives* xxiii. 468 And biȝe us swa ðeah rumlicor to-dæȝ be hlafe þonne ðu ȝebohtest ȝyrstan dæȝ. *c* **1050** *Voc.* in Wr.-Wülcker 418/9 *Horno* [sic], ȝierstandæȝe. *c* **1205** LAY. 17063 Ȝurstendæi [*c* **1275** ȝorstendai] ær none Ich wuste þat ȝe comen. *c* **1290** *St. Dominic* 198 in *S. Eng. Leg.* 283 Þes frere cam ȝursterday to toune. **1455** *Paston Lett.* (1897) I. 326 Yerstenday we wrote our lettres of our entent to . . the Archebysshop of Caunterburye. **1788** *Voc. Forth & Bargie* in *Trans. R. Irish Acad.* II. 34 *Yerstei*, yesterday; *ear yestei*, the day before yesterday.

2. *transf.* A short time ago; only lately; the other day; now esp. in prov. phr. ***I was not born yesterday***, etc.

1387 TREVISA *Higden* (Rolls) IV. 15 Anoþer seide, 'Ȝister-day [*MS.* γ ȝurstonday] he hadde þe peple at his hestes, and now þe peple haþ hym at here heste.' *a* **1400–50** *Wars Alex.* 3304 (Ashm. MS.), I, þat was ȝustirday so ȝape & ȝemed all þe werld, To day am dreuyn all to dust. **1509** BARCLAY *Shyp of Folys* 153 b, From the kechyn to the quere and so to a state One yester day a courter is nowe a prest become. **1718** PRIOR *Solomon* III. 116 Naked from the Womb We yesterday came forth; that in the Tomb Naked again We must Tomorrow lye. **1757** R. DEMERE *Let.* 10 Aug. in W. L. McDowell *Docs. relating to Indian Affairs* (1970) II. 398, I was not born Yesterday. **1837** MARRYAT *Snarleyyow* xii. 62, I was not born yesterday, as the saying is. **1856** *N. Brit. Rev.* XXVI. 264 Edinburgh . . outstripped in population daily by towns that yesterday were hamlets. **1860** WHYTE-MELVILLE *Mkt. Harb.* xii, It is needless for me to observe that Mr. Sawyer was one of those individuals who are described in common parlance as not having been 'born yesterday'. **1895** SNAITH *Mistr. Dor. Marvin* xlviii, 'I wasn't born yesterday', he returned sweetly; 'methinks I am rather old in the tooth.'

3. *fig.* Used to suggest extreme urgency or impatience, esp. in phr. ***to want*** (or ***need***) ***something yesterday***. *colloq.*

1974 *Times* 7 Feb. 14/7 Attacks by Miss Brigid Brophy and her group, whose case was, roughly, that they wanted everything, and wanted it yesterday. **1978** D. A. STANWOOD *Memory of Eva Ryker* xxi. 196, I need the information yesterday. **1980** T. BARLING *Goodbye Piccadilly* xv. 309 Don't ask me. . . Just get us down there yesterday.

B. *sb.* **1.** The day next before the present; also *pl.* past days (often in echoes of quot. 1605).

c **1000** *Ags. Ps.* (Th.) lxxxix. [xc.] 4 Þusend wintra bið þon anlicast, swa ȝeostran dæȝ ȝegan wære [*a* **1300** *E.E. Ps.* Als yhistre-dai þat forth-yhed here]. **13..** *E.E. Allit. P.* B. 463 He . . sone ȝederly for-ȝete ȝister-day steuen. **1387** TREVISA *Higden* (Rolls) III. 145 Who þat foloweþ þe Medes, he schal haue þe trauaille of ȝister day [*MS.* γ ȝursday]. **1542** UDALL *Erasm. Apoph.* II. 252 My yesterdayes araye was to please my housbande. **1562** J. HEYWOOD *Prov. & Epigr.* (1867) 74 Well well (quoth she) what euer ye now saie, It is to late to call again yesterdaie. **1605** SHAKS. *Macb.* V. v. 22 And all our yesterdayes, haue lighted Fooles The way to dusty death. **1627** DONNE *Serm.*, *John xiv. 26* (1640) 285 Not for your yester-dayes, not for your yester-nights sins. **1779** FARR in *Earl Malmesbury's Lett.* (1870) I. 425 The wind blowing very hard at east all that day, and still more so in the night and on yesterday. **1809** BYRON in Dallas *Corr. of B.* (1825) I. 39 Did you receive my yesterday's note? **1814** SCOTT *Ld. of Isles* III. xxiii, More of the youth I cannot say, Our captive but since yesterday. **1827** SOUTHEY *Hist. Penins. War* xviii. II. 144 The Junta, he said, had commenced their sittings on the yesterday. **1841** DICKENS *Barn. Rudge* lxxv, The same . . gentleman he had seen yesterday, and many yesterdays before. **1899** FAIRBAIRN *Catholicism* I. §5. 34 They tried to enrich the church of to-day with the wealth of all her yesterdays.

2. *transf.* Time not long past.

1382 WYCLIF *Job* viii. 9 (MS. Douce 369), Wee ben as ȝistai born, and wee han vnkunnyng. —— *Isa.* xxx. 33 Greiþid is forsoþe fro ȝistai tofeth. **1399** LANGL. *Rich. Redeles* III. 261 It ffallith as well to ffodis of xxiiij ȝeris, Or yonge men of yistirday to ȝeue good redis, As be cometh a kow to hoppe in a cage! **1555** PHILPOT in Foxe *A. & M.* (1570) 2012/2 We are but yesterdayes children, . . & our dayes are lyke a shadow. **1570** *Ibid.* (ed. 2) 125/1 Thy crucified Christe is but an yesterdayes God, the gods of ye Gentiles are of most antiquitie. **1653** ASHWELL *Fides Apost.* 85 Praxeas a fellow of yesterday. **1790** BURKE *Fr. Rev.* 187 By a revolution in the state, the fawning sycophant of yesterday, is converted into the austere critic of the present hour. **1865** KINGSLEY *Herew.* xli, Their skin-deep yesterday's civilisation. **1876** J. PARKER *Paracl.* II. xviii. 311 As compared with Christian Theology, science as it is now urged upon us is but of yesterday. **1897** KIPLING *Recessional* 15 Lo, all our pomp of yesterday Is one with Nineveh and Tyre!

3. a. *attrib.* with times of the day: ***yesterday afternoon***, ***evening***, ***morning***, ***night***, ***noon***. The combination is used both as *sb.* and as *adv.* Cf. YESTER-.

1654–5 *Clarke Papers* (Camden) III. 26 Yesterday night came letters from Collonell Hacker. **1711** *Lond. Gaz.* No. 4892/2 The Bridge was finished Yesterday-Morning. **1782** MISS BURNEY *Cecilia* I. vi, She enquired how long he had left Suffolk? 'But yesterday noon, ma'am', he answered. **1837** DICKENS *Pickw.* xi, Yesterday morning, when a letter was received from Mr. Wardle.

b. In the possessive, as ***yesterday's man***, a man, esp. a politician, whose career is finished or past its peak.

1966 'G. BLACK' *You want to die, Johnny?* ii. 27 John saw himself as one of yesterday's men, a survivor. **1972** *Guardian* 14 Jan. 13/8 Support for Nkrumuh still remains limited to his fellow tribesmen in the remote South-west and to those who fell off the high-living Fascist bandwagon when he was overthrown. These people are 'yesterday's men' in the eyes of most Ghanaians. **1979** *Jrnl. R. Soc. Arts* CXXVII. 349/2 The politicians . . do not know if they will walk out as ministers . . or as yesterday's men.

C. as *adj.* Belonging to yesterday or the immediate past; very recent. Now *rare* or *Obs.*

1553 BECON *Reliques of Rome* (1563) 78 b, A late and an yesterday byrde, hatched and brought forthe of many Popes. **1646** R. BAILLIE *Anabaptism* (1647) 163 An yesterday conceit of the English Anabaptists. **1657** J. WATTS *Scribe, Pharisee*, etc. III. 51 You may ere long, lay down your Novelties, and the yesterday fashions of your new Brotherhood. **1665** J. WEBB *Stone-Heng* (1725) 41 His Judgment dictated, that Yesterday Writers are most proper for Matters of Antiquity. **1690** C. NESSE *O. & N. Test.* I. 189 The covenant of reconciliation . . was but a yesterday covenant . . in comparison of this covenant of redemption . . which was from eternity.

Hence '**yesterdayness** (*nonce-wd.*), the distinctive quality of being yesterday or of belonging to the recent past.

1897 *Bookman* Nov. 235 Yesterday, as such and in its essential yesterdayness, has no objective existence. **1909** *Times Lit. Suppl.* 3 June 202/2 That disquieting sense of 'yesterdayness' that attaches to most collections of essays . . that have already severally seen the light.

yestereve (jɛstə'riːv), *adv.* (*sb.*) Chiefly *poet.* [f. YESTER- + EVE *sb.*[1]] = YESTER-EVENING.

1603 B. JONSON *Entertainm. at Althrope* Wks. (1616) 873 In hope that you would come here Yester-eue the lady Summer, Shee inuited to a banquet. **1794** MRS. RADCLIFFE *Myst. Udolpho* i, Who . . jealous is of me, That yester-eve I lighted them, along the dewy green. *a* **1850** ROSSETTI *Dante & Circle* II. (1874) 271, I marked thee here all yestereve Lurking about my home. **1850** HAWTHORNE *Scarlet Let.* xiv. (1883) 204 No longer ago than yester-eve. **1859** TENNYSON *Marr. Geraint* 702 And yester-eve I would not tell you of it, But kept it for a sweet surprise at morn. **1864** W. C. BRYANT *Italy* 39 Slaves but yester-eve were they—Freeman with the dawning day.

yester-even (jɛstə'riːv(ə)n), **yestere'en**, *adv.* and *sb.* *arch.* and *dial.* Forms: 5 **ȝistir-**, **ȝister-**, **ȝistur-**, **yster-**, 5– **yester-**: see EVEN *sb.* [f. YESTER- + EVEN *sb.* Cf. YESTREEN.]

A. *adv.* = YESTER-EVENING *adv.*

c **1420** *Avow. Arth.* xlii, Ȝistur euyn I the king hiȝte, To cumme to my mete. *c* **1440** *Partonope* 10025 (Univ. Coll. MS.) These twyn that yster even full late Caught the last stroke. *c* **1450** *Merlin* 172 Yester even ye sente for vs, and I am now come. ? **1452** *Paston Lett.* (1897) I. 247 My doughter your wyf told me yester even the man that suyth him will not stonde to your awarde.

1822 BYRON *Werner* III. iv, The myrmidons . . who were Dogging him yester-even. **1840** TALFOURD *Glencoe* II. i, He has not return'd Since, yestere'en, he left us. **1857** MRS. CARLYLE *Lett.* II. 313, I had yester-even a presentiment I should die before I got back. **1863** READE *Hard Cash* x, 'When was your last spasm?' 'No longer agone than yestereen, ma'am.' **1880** EMMA MARSHALL *Troub. Times* 295, I did stop yestereven when, in a rage, I was going to strike Lily, for breaking the toy gun James Ellis bought for me.

B. *sb.* = YESTER-EVENING *sb.*

1820 SCOTT *Abbot* xxxi, To endure the cruel disappointment of yester even. **1888** STEVENSON *Black Arrow* IV. iv, Thy swinishness of yestereven.

attrib. **1578** H. WOTTON *Courtlie Controv.* 203 Let vs returne then vnto our yester euen lecture.

yester-evening (jɛstə'riːvnɪŋ), *adv.* and *sb.* *arch.* [f. YESTER- + EVENING *sb.*[1]]

A. *adv.* Yesterday evening.

1715 ROWE *Lady Jane Gray* III. i, This Morn a trusty Spy, Has brought me Word that yester Evening late, . . Your Friends were marry'd. *a* **1774** TUCKER *Lt. Nat.* (1777) III. IV. xxvi. 46 If he be asked why he . . played at cards yester-evening, to answer, For the glory of God would be untrue, or if true would be a profanation of his name. **1826** SCOTT *Woodst.* xvii, I had taken my post yester evening in the half-furnished apartment. **1889** CONAN DOYLE *Micah Clarke* vii, Yester-evening I left Monmouth's camp.

B. *sb.* The evening of yesterday.

1796 COLERIDGE *Dest. Nations* 235 Late on the yester-evening. **1808** —— *Let. to F. Jeffrey* 20 July, The Review was sent, addressed to you, by the post of yester-evening. **1822** BYRON *Werner* II. ii, Me! whom he ne'er saw Till yester' evening. **1853** G. J. CAYLEY *Las Alforjas* II. 209 Yester-evening's sunset.

yesterfang (FANG *sb.* 2): see YESTER *a.*

yestermorn (jɛstə'mɔːn), *adv.* and *sb.* Chiefly *poet.* [f. YESTER- + MORN *sb.*] Yesterday morning.

1702 ROWE *Tamerl.* II. i, From yester Morn till Even. *a* **1769** FALCONER *Shipwr.* III. 813 Ah! how unlike what yester-morn enjoy'd! *c* **1815** JANE AUSTEN *Persuasion* xiii, Each lady dated her intelligence [of the accident] from the same hour of yestermorn. **1846** TENNYSON *Golden Year* 21 But if you care indeed to listen, hear These measured words, my work of yestermorn. **1895** *Chamb. Jrnl.* XII. 828/1 The lover wrote yestermorn, making light of the story. **1896** KIPLING *Seven Seas*, *Song of Banjo* 90 To the tune of yestermorn I set the truth.

yester-'morning, *adv.* and *sb.* *arch.* and *dial.* [f. YESTER- + MORNING *sb.*] = prec.

1654-5 *Clarke Papers* (Camden) III. 26, 300.. Cavalieres tooke yestermorning.. Judge Rolls out of his bed. **1764** H. WALPOLE *Otranto* v, My Lady Matilda told me but yester-morning that her Highness Hippolita knows something. **1775** MRS. THRALE *Let. to Johnson* 24 June, So yestermorning, a flag flying from some conspicuous steeple in Westminster gave notice of the approaching festival. **1821** SCOTT *Kenilw.* xl, Those expressions, which were yester-morning accounted but a light offence. **1848** MRS. GASKELL *Mary Barton* ix, He dropped down dead in Oxford Road yester morning. **1889** CONAN DOYLE *Micah Clarke* vi, There was the Squire o' Milton over here yester morning. **1893** STEVENSON *Catriona* I. i, Even so late as yester-morning, I was like a beggarman by the wayside.

yestern ('jɛstən), *a.* and *adv.* *dial.* or *arch.* [? f. YESTER after adjs. in *-ern*, as *eastern.*] **a.** *adj.* Of yesterday. **b.** *adv.* Yesterday.

[*a* **1000** *Riddles* xli. 44 Ic ʒiestron wæs ʒeong acenned.] **1860** WORCESTER cites *Wright*. **1877** *Holderness Gloss.*, *Yesthern*, W., yesterday. **1891** LD. HOUGHTON *Stray Verses* 85, I linger on the oaken bridge Fine-filigreed with yestern snow.

†**yesterneve(n**, *adv.* *Obs.* Forms: 1 **ʒyrstanæfen**, 4 **yesteneuen**, **ȝister-neue**. [OE.: f. *ʒyrstan* (see YESTERDAY) + *ǽfen* EVEN *sb.*] Yesterday evening.

c **900** WÆRFERTH tr. *Gregory's Dial.* 22 Ʒyrstanæfen [*v.r.* ʒyrstanæfenne] me ʒelamp, þæt ic unʒewealdes ætsporn æt anum fotscamele. *c* **1000** ÆLFRIC *Saints' Lives* xxiii. 469 Forþon þe þa halfas wæron swiðe eaðelice þe us ʒyrstan æfen comon. **1340** *Ayenb.* 51 We hedde guod wyn yesterneuen and guode metes. *c* **1350** *Will. Palerne* 2160, I sai a selkouþe siȝt mi-self ȝister-neue.

yesternight (jɛstə'naɪt), *adv.* and *sb.* Chiefly *dial.* or *arch.* Forms: 1 **ʒystran-**, 3–7 **yister-**, 4 **ȝistir-**, **ȝuster-**, **ȝerstene-**, 4– 6 **ȝester-**, **ȝister-**, 5 **ȝistyr-**, **yistre-**, **ȝustir-**, 6 **yeaster-**, 5– **yester-**. [OE.: f. *ʒystran* (see YESTERDAY) + *niht* NIGHT *sb.*] **A.** *adv.* On the night of yesterday, last night.

In early use not necessarily restricted to the night.

Beowulf 1334 Heo þa fæhðe wræc, þe þu ʒystran niht Grendel cwealdest. *a* **1300** *Cursor M.* 15988 Ne sal he neuer vp-rise eft,.. Ar sal þis cok vp-rise Was skald yisternight [*other texts* ȝister-, ȝuster-]. **13..** *Sir Beues* (A.) 3088 Wel þe grete þat ilche kniȝt, Þat sopede wiþ þe ȝerstene niȝt. *c* **1374** CHAUCER *Troylus* v. 221 (MS. Gg. 4. 27) Where ben hire armys & hire eyen clere Þat ȝistyr nyȝt þis tyme with me were? *c* **1380** *Sir Ferumb.* 148 Ȝester neite wan we had fiȝt ȝonder out on þ[e] playne. *a* **1450** *Paston Lett.* (1897) I. 97 And now yistre nyght my Lord Welles come to Boston with iiij[xx] horses. **1500-20** DUNBAR *Poems* lxxviii. 1 My heid did ȝak ȝesternicht. **1546** J. HEYWOOD *Prov.* (1867) 32 Toward night yesternight.. we came thyther. **1566** GASCOIGNE *Supposes* II. i, Yesternight in the evening I walked out, and founde Pasiphilo. **1612** SAVILE in *Buccleuch MSS.* (Hist. MSS. Comm.) I. 123 Sir Th. Bodley.. died yesternight between 5 and 6 of the clock after noon. **1775** JOHNSON *Let. to Mrs. Thrale* 1 Aug., I forgot that the post went out yesternight, I therefore put this by the by-post. **1808** SOUTHEY *Let. to J. N. White* 9 Jan., I have received two letters, both from persons whom I have never seen, one yesternight, and the other this evening. **1814** CARY *Dante, Inf.* xx. 125 Yesternight The moon was round. **1828** SCOTT *F. M. Perth* xviii, His beautiful daughter was a bride yesternight—this morning the Fair Maid of Perth is a widow before she has been a wife! **1888** FENN *Dick o' the Fens* xii, After our bad time with him yesternight, I mean to have some sleep.

B. *sb.* The night last past.

1513 DOUGLAS *Æneis* X. iii. 54 Mnestheus.. Quham the renowne of this ȝistir nycht,.. Full prowd maid in hys curage our the laif. **1591** SAVILE *Tacitus, Hist.* I. xviii. 46 Excessiue affection it was towarde mee,.. which bred.. yeasternights trouble. *a* **1631** DONNE *Lett.* (1651) 83 To know.. whether you suffered anie thing, or no, by the ill accident of yester-night. **1700** PENN in *Pa. Hist. Soc. Mem.* IX. 5 Thow wilt by this time have mine of yesternight. **1797** COLERIDGE *Christabel* I. iv, She had dreams all yesternight Of her own betrothed knight. **1812** —— *Let. to W. Wordsworth* 7 Dec., They reminded me of my words the very yester-night. **1830** TENNYSON *Ode to Memory* 9 Flinging the gloom of yesternight On the white day. **1865** SWINBURNE *Chastelard* II. i, I have slept so well and sweet since yesternight.

yester-year. [Coined by D. G. Rossetti to render F. *antan* (:—L. *ante annum*) in François Villon's *Grand Testament, Ball.* I.] Last year.

1870 ROSSETTI *Three Transl. fr. Villon* I, But where are the snows of yester-year? **1871** R. BUCHANAN in *St. Paul's Mag.* Apr. 88 No crime of yesterday or yesteryear. **1888** MRS. H. WARD *Robt. Elsmere* xxxi, Where had the crude pretty child of yester-year departed to? **1893** *Daily Chron.* 13 Sept. 3/1 The vogue of 'Ernest Maltravers' has gone with the snows of yesteryear.

yestewarde, obs. f. EASTWARD.

1482 *Monk of Evesham* (Arb.) 36 Thenne went we yestewarde.

yestreen (jɛ'striːn), *adv.* and *sb.* Chiefly *Sc.* and *poet.* Forms: *α.* 4 **ȝhistrewyn**, **ȝystrewine**, 5 **yistrevyn**, **ȝistreuen**. *β.* 6 **ȝestrene**, **ȝistrene**, **yestrene**, **yeistrein**, 8– **yestreen**. *γ. corruptly.* 6 **the strene**, 8 **the straine**, 9 **the streen**, **thestreen**. [MSc. *ȝystrewin* = *ȝystir* (see YESTERDAY) + *ewin* EVEN *sb.*, in the 16th c. contracted to *ȝistrene*, later *yestreen* (18th cent.), in which form it was taken up by English writers.]

A. *adv.* On the evening of yesterday; yesterday evening.

α. *c* **1375** *Sc. Leg. Saints* xxiii. (*vii Sleepers*) 229 Ȝystrewine wele lat. *a* **1400** *Northern Passion* 1489 Ȝhistrewyn when þe day was gane. *c* **1440** *Alphabet of Tales* 245 Yone gude liberall monke, your hostley, servid me yistrevyn at my supper wurthelie. *c* **1450** *St. Cuthbert* (Surtees) 7426 Ȝistreuen he was in his awen steed.

β. **1513** DOUGLAS *Æneis* V. xi. 72 In my sleip ȝestrene. **1583** in *3rd Rep. Hist. MSS. Comm.* 422/2 Twa missives, the ane .. quhilk he ressauit yeistrein. *a* **1600** MONTGOMERIE *Sonn.* xli. 1 So suete a kis ȝistrene fra thee I reft. **1721** RAMSAY *Bessy Bell & Mary Gray* i, Bessy Bell I loo'd yestreen. **1785** BURNS *Halloween* xv, I mind't as weel's yestreen. **1821** SCOTT *Pirate* vii, I did feel a rheumatize in my back-spauld yestreen. **1837** LOWELL *Let. to G. B. Loring* 23 Aug., An' 'twas but late yestreen I met her And—ah! those een! **1894** CROCKETT *Raiders* iii, He was tired yestreen, and he's the better o' a rest this morning.

γ. **1587** W. FOWLER *Wks.* (S.T.S.) I. 129/88 That which long tyme past before or present is in sight, which was the strene, or yit tomorrow. **1711** *Sir Eger, Sir Grahame, & Sir Gray-Steel* 1753 The streen to chamber I him led. **1790** MORISON *Poems* 134 The merligoes are yet before your e'en And paint to you the sight ye've seen the streen. ? *a* **1800** *Fair Ellen* xxiv. in Child *Ballads* (1894) V. 221/2, I dreamed a dream san the strain. **1873** [P. BUCHAN] *Leg. North* 29 Quo he, 'Guidwife! I had a thocht thestreen'.

B. *sb.* The evening of yesterday.

1816 SCOTT *Antiq.* xi, When the sea was working like barm wi' yestreen's wind. **1861** J. R. GREEN *Lett.* (1901) II. 75, I spent yestreen at the Crystal Palace.

yet, *v.* *Obs.* exc. *dial.* Forms: 1 **ʒeotan**, 2–4 **ȝeote(n**, 3 **yeote**, (*Orm.*) **ȝetenn**, 3–5 **yhet**, 3–6 **ȝet**, 4 **yete**, **ȝhet**, **ȝit**, 4–5 **ȝete**, **ȝeete**, **ȝute**, 5 **ȝett(e**, **ȝut**, 5–7 **yet**, 6 **yette**, 7 **yeat**, 9 **yett**, **yat**. *Pa. t.* *α.* 1 **ʒeat**, **ʒet**, *pl.* **ʒ uton**, 3 **ȝeat**, **yhet**, *pl.* **ȝeoten**, 3–4 **ȝette**, 4 **ȝete**, **yeett**, **yeyt**, 4–6 **ȝet**, 5 **yette**, 6 **yet**. *β.* 3 **yhotte**, 4 **yot**, **ȝot**, 5 **ȝote**. *γ.* 2 **ȝettede**, 4 **ȝetede**, **-id(e**, **ȝeetide**, 4–5 **ȝettid(e**. *Pa. pple.* *α.* 1 **ʒoten**, 3 **yhoten**, **-in** (*Orm.* **ȝotenn**), **ȝhutten**, **yotten**, **iȝoten**, **iȝotten**, 3–4 **iȝote**, 4 **ȝoten**, **ȝooten**, **ȝote**, **yȝote**, 4–6 **yoten**, 5 **yȝutte**, **ȝut**, **yat**, 6 **iȝotun**. *β.* 4–5 **yeten**, **ȝette**, (4 **ȝitte**), 5 **ȝeten**, 5–6 **ȝett**, 6 *Sc.* **ȝet**, **ȝit**, **ȝyt**. *γ.* 5 **ȝetted**, **-yd**. [Com. Teut. str. vb. = to pour, to melt metal, pour out, flow: OE. *ʒéotan*, pa. t. *ʒéat*, *guton*, pa. pple. *goten*, = OFris. *giata*, *iata*, (NFris. *jit*, WFris. *jiette*, EFris. *jôte*), (M)LG. *geten*, (M)Du. *gieten*, OHG. *giozan* (MHG. *giozen*, G. *giessen*), ON. *gjóta* only in senses, to drop one's young, twinkle with the eyes, Goth. *giutan*; f. Teut. *geut-* (:*gaut-*: *gut-*):—*gheud-* (:*ghoud-*: *ghud-*), whence L. *fŭd-* in *fundĕre*, pa. t. *fūdī* to pour. For other derivatives and cognates, see GOTE *sb.*, GUSH *v.*, GUT *sb.* The simpler form of the root (*gheu-*) is found in Gr. χέϝω I pour, χεῦμα pouring, Skr. *hu*, *juhóti* to pour in sacrifice. (Compounds are BIGETEN, INYET, OUTYET.)]

1. *trans.* To pour. Also *absol.*

c **1000** ÆLFRIC *Lev.* viii. 24 He ʒet þæt blod uppan þæt weofod. *c* **1000** *Sax. Leechd.* II. 98 Ʒeot on fæt, þonne hio ʒenoh þicce sie. *Ibid.* III. 246 Aquarius, þæt is.. se þe wæter ʒyt. *c* **1205** LAY. 19771 Six amppullen fulle Heo ȝeoten i þan welle. *Ibid.* 29255 Þer biforen he gon ȝeoten Draf and chaf and aten. *a* **1300** *Cursor M.* 3805 And oyel he yeett apon þat stan And made to godd a voo onan. *c* **1375** *Sc. Leg. Saints* xii. (*Mathias*) 251 [She] brocht a preciuse vnyment, Til ennownte hymne in entent, & apone cristis hed it ȝete. *a* **1425** tr. *Arderne's Treat. Fistula* etc. 35 Be þer ȝette in of a ȝolk of an ey. *c* **1450** *St. Cuthbert* (Surtees) 2789 With þis haly water he yode To þe seke man for his gode. In his mouthe he ȝettid thryse. **1483** *Cath. Angl.* 426/2 To ȝett be twene, *jnterfundere*. *a* **1500** BOLLARD in Arnolde *Chron.* (1502) 64/1 Than thou most moyst them twyes or thries in the day not yeting [*v.r.* ȝitteng] but dewyng or springling. **1513** DOUGLAS *Æneis* VI. iv. 37 The fat olie did he ȝet and peir Apoun the entraillis, to mak thaim birn cleir. **1666** *Despaut. Gram.* F ij, (Jam.) *Fundo*, to yet, or power forth. *Ibid.* G j, *Fundo*.., to yeat forth. **1866** EDMONDSTON *Gloss. Shetland & Orkney*, *Yat*, to pour in large quantity, S.

b. To shed (tears or blood; also light).

a **900** CYNEWULF *Crist* 173 Ic tearas sceal ʒeotan ʒeomormod. *c* **900** tr. *Bæda's Hist.* II. vi. (1890) 114 Ond þa ærest longe nihtes in halʒum ʒebedum [he] wæs, & his tearas ʒeat. *c* **1175** *Lamb. Hom.* 39 Þu scalt.. ȝeoten þine teres swiðe sariliche. *c* **1200** ORMIN 1773 Þatt blod tacnede Cristess blod Þatt ȝotenn wass o rode. *c* **1275** LAY. 19142 Þar was mochel blod iȝote. *a* **1300** *E.E. Psalter* lxxviii[i]. 3 Þai yhotten blode, als watre strem, In vmgange of Ierusalem. *c* **1374** CHAUCER *Boeth.* I. met. vii. (1868) 29 Þe sterres couered wiþ blak cloudes ne mowen geten a doun no lyȝt. **1501** DOUGLAS *Pal. Hon.* Prol. 47 Phebus furth ȝet depured bemis cleir. **1513** —— *Æneis* III. v. 121 And with lang sobbis furth ȝettand teris in vane.

Const. *inf.* *a* **1400-50** *Wars Alex.* 5042 So did his princes .. With ȝedire ȝoskingis & ȝerre ȝett out to grete.

c. To pour forth or cause to flow in a flood. *Sc.*

1513 DOUGLAS *Æneis* V. xii. 36 Thar wes na strenth of valeant men to waill, Nor large fludis on ȝet that mycht avail. **1533** BELLENDEN *Livy* I. ii. (S.T.S.) I. 17 This Ryver be divyne purviance was ȝett furth with large flude abone þe brayis. **1536** —— *Cron. Scot.* (1821) I. p. xlviii, The see, be contrarius stremes, makis collision; sum times yettand out the tid, and sum times swelleand and soukand it in agane.

d. *fig.* To pour, shed, infuse. Often rendering L. *fundere* and its compounds in mere literalisms.

c **897** ÆLFRED *Gregory's Past. C.* xxxix. 282 Sio slæwð ʒiett slæp on ðone monnan. *a* **1000** *Guthlac* 1206 Þy læs þæt wundredan weras & idesa & on ʒeað ʒutan. *a* **1240** *Lofsong* in *O.E. Hom.* I. 209 Þe holi goste þet þu.. sendest þine deorewurðe deciples and ȝettedest to þeo þet rith luuieð þe. *a* **1300** *E.E. Psalter* xliv. 3 [xlv. 2] Yhotin es hap in þi lippes twai [Vulg. *diffusa est gratia in labiis tuis*]. **1393** LANGL. *P. Pl.* C. II. 151 Heuene holde hit [*sc.* love] ne myȝte so heuy hit semede, Til hit hadde on erthe ȝoten [*v.r.* I-ȝotun, ȝeten] hym-selue. *c* **1450** *Mirour Saluacioun* (Roxb.) 20 For in hir moders wombe whils this virgine was shette On hire the haly Gast his speciell blissing yette. **1502** ATKYNSON tr. *De Imitatione* III. xxx. (1893) 221 For all carnall loue yet into my soule the loue of thyne holy name. **1509** BARCLAY *Shyp of Folys* 219 Some with a fals herte,.. Into his lordes erys yetyth secretly Lyes venomous. **1563** WINȜET tr. *Vincent. Lirin.* v. Wks. (S.T.S.) II. 21 A certane mist wes ȝet vpon the myndis of al the Bischopes of the Latin toung.

e. *transf.* To pour fluid into (a cavity).

1560 ROLLAND *Seven Sages* (Bann. Cl.) 157 Thay ȝet his mouth full of het meltit gold.

2. *intr.* To gush forth or flow in a stream, as water, tears, blood.

a **900** CYNEWULF *Elene* 1132 Hat heafodwylm ofer hleor ʒoten. *a* **1000** *Guthlac* 1029 He hate let torn þoliende tearas ʒeotan. *a* **1225** *Juliana* 17 Me nom hire & dude swa þat hit [*sc.* blood] ȝeat adun of þe ȝerden. *c* **1250** *Gen. & Ex.* 582 Reyn ȝette dun on euerilk stede. *c* **1400** *Laud Troy Bk.* 12941 For so faste doun the water ȝet, That thei were alle thorow wet. *c* **1450** *St. Cuthbert* (Surtees) 7811 Teris oute of þaire eyen ȝote. **1533** BELLENDEN *Livy* V. iii. (S.T.S.) II. 152 The teris for blyithnes.. ȝet fra þe ene of faderis.

3. *trans.* To form (an object) by running molten metal into a mould; to found; = CAST *v.* 51.

c **1000** *Ags. Ps.* (Th.) cxxxiv. [cxxxv.] 15 Gold and seolfur, þe her ʒeotað menn, and mid heora folmum fæʒere wyrceað. *c* **1000** ÆLFRIC *Deut.* ix. 12 Hiʒ ʒuton him hæðenne god. *c* **1200** ORMIN 17418 Drihhtinn.. badd he shollde melltenn brass & ȝetenn himm a neddre. *a* **1225** *Juliana* 38 Ich makede nabugodonosor.. makien þe mawmez igoten of golde. *c* **1300** in *T. North's Engl. Bells* (1888) 8 [Inscription on bell] IOH:ME:YEYT. **1382** WYCLIF *Isa.* xliv. 10 Who foormede God, and a grauen thing ȝetede, to no thing profitable? **1387** TREVISA *Higden* (Rolls) VI. 185 Þis picher het ȝit [*v.r.* ȝute] Dunstan. *c* **1449** PECOCK *Repr.* II. v. 163 Ymagis graued, coruun, or ȝut. *c* **1450** *St. Cuthbert* (Surtees) 6021 He made it [*sc.* a bell] to be ȝett. **1533** *Acc. Ld. High Treas. Scot.* VI. 104 To Peris and the laif of the werkmen ȝettand the gunnis in the castell.

b. To form (metal) into a shape, by pouring it when melted into a mould; = CAST *v.* 50.

1387 TREVISA *Higden* (Rolls) I. 235 And wonderliche by craft of ȝetynge þat bas is i-ȝote. *c* **1425** WYNTOUN *Cron.* I. v. 252 (Edin. MS.) To wirk metall, Yrne and steill, leid and tyn, To ȝet [*v.r.* ȝett] or bet or graif þar in. *c* **1475** *Promp. Parv.* 538/1 (MS. K.) Ȝetyn metall. **1513** DOUGLAS *Æneis* VIII. Prol. 94 Sum goukis quhill the glas pyg grow full of gold ȝit. **1531** ELYOT *Gov.* I. viii. (1883) I. 48 A commune painter or keruer,.. stained or embrued with sondry colours,.. or perfumed with tedious sauours of the metalles by him yoten. **1552** HULOET, Yet, or caste mettall, *fundo*.

4. To melt down (metal). Also *fig.*

1382 WYCLIF *Jer.* ix. 7 Lo! I shall ȝ eete and preue them. **1387** TREVISA *Higden* (Rolls) VIII. 129 Vessel, croyses, and chalys were y-take, and golde i-schave of seyntes schrynes and i-ȝote. **1570** LEVINS *Manip.* 86/16 To Yette metal, *fundere, liquefacere*.

5. To set or fasten (as iron in stone) by means of molten lead. Hence, to fix firmly.

1387 TREVISA *Higden* (Rolls) IV. 185 Þe stakes were grete, i-schape as a manis þigh, and i-ȝote aboute wiþ leed. **1554-5** *Burgh Rec. Edin.* (1871) II. 302 Item for vj greit cruks fra Johne Alhanny,.. Item for ane stane of leid to yet thame with,.. viij[s]. **1808** JAMIESON, To *yett*, *v. a.*, to fasten in the firmest manner, to rivet, Loth.

Hence **yet**, **'yetted** *ppl. a.*, poured; molten, cast; **'yetting** *vbl. sb.*, casting, founding.

1387 Ȝetynge [see 3 b]. *c* **1450** *Mirour Sauacioun* (Roxb.) 5 The mawmetiers vnto y[e] ȝette [*printed* ȝerte] calf of gold prefigured thes thinges. **1483** *Cath. Angl.* 426/2 Ȝettyd, *fusilis*. **1504-5** *Acc. Ld. High Treas. Scot.* II. 294 Item, for lede to ȝet the pulleis and the pais, and for ȝetting of thaim, .. ij s. viij d. **1513** DOUGLAS *Æneis* IX. xi. 12 Als violent as euyr the ȝet doun rane Furth of the west dois smyte apon the wald.

yet (jɛt), *adv.* (*adj.*) and *conj.* Forms: *α.* 1 **ʒiet**, **ʒit**, **ʒieta**, 2–4 **ȝiete**, 2–5 (6–7 *Sc.*) **ȝit**, 3–4 **ȝiet**, **ȝite**, 3–5 **ȝyt**, **ȝitte**, 3–6 **yitte**, 4 **yiet**, (**ytt**, **ȝhyt**, **yhitte**, 4–5 **ȝhit**, **yhit**), 4–6 **ȝitt**, (**ȝhitt**), 4–7 **yitt**, (5 **ihit**, **yt**), 5–6 **ȝytt**, 4–6, 7–8 *Sc.*, 9– *dial.* **yit**. *β.* 1 **ʒet**, **ʒeta**, 2 **ȝeat**, **ȝæt**, **iett**, 2–5 **ȝet**, **ȝette**, (2 **ȝeiet**, 3 **ȝæte**, **ȝeht**, **hyet**), 3–4 **yete**, 3–5 **ȝete**, 4 **ȝeitt**, **yeitt**, **ȝeite**, (**ȝate**, **ihet**, *Sc.* **ȝeyt**, **yhet(e**, **yheit**, **yheyt(e)**, 4, 5–6 *Sc.* **ȝeit**, 4–6 **yeit**, 4–7 **yett**, 5 **ȝeet**, **ȝett**, 5–6 **yette**, 6 **yeat**, (**yate**, 9 *dial.* **yeet**), 3– **yet**. *γ.* 1 *Northumb.* **ʒeot**, 3 **ȝeot**, **ȝot**. *δ.* 1–2 **ʒyt**, 2–5 **ȝut**, 3 **ȝuet**, **ȝuyt**, (**ȝuȝt**), 3–4 **ȝ uit**, **ȝute**, 4 **yute**, **ȝutte**, 5 **ȝutt**, **ȝuite**, **yut**. [OE. *ʒíet* and *ʒíeta*, corresp. to OFris. *ieta*, *eta*, *ita* (WFris. *yette*, NFris. *jit*); of obscure origin. (The synonymous OE. (Anglian) *ʒén*, *ʒéna* show the same parallelism of formation.)

The meanings of *yet* are generally expressed in the Teut. langs. outside the Anglo-Frisian group by **noh* (OS., OHG. *noh*; but in Goth. *naūh* is an interrog. particle):—Indo-eur. **nu-qe* and now.]

I. 1. a. In addition, or in continuation; besides, also; further, furthermore, moreover; with a numeral or the like = 'more', as ***yet a***, ***yet one*** = 'another', 'one more' (= F. *encore un*, G. *noch ein*). *Obs.* or *arch.* (now chiefly with *again* or *once more*: cf. d below).

For the use with words denoting time see 5 c.

Beowulf 47 þa ȝyt hie him asetton seȝen gyldenne. c900 Wærferth tr. *Gregory's Dial.* iv. (1900) 42 þa þing, þe ic her to ȝita ȝeþeode [L. *ea quae subjungo*]. c1000 *Ags. Gosp.* Matt. xviii. 16 Ðyf he þe ne ȝehyrð, nim þonne ȝyt ænne oððe tweȝen to þe. c1175 *Lamb. Hom.* 13 ȝet cweð ure lauerd to moyses. ȝif ȝe cherrat from me ower heortan [etc.]. *Ibid.* 41 ȝette he him sceawede ane welle of fure. a1225 *Leg. Kath.* 70 A meiden.. feier & freolich o wlite & o westum ah ȝet, þet is mare wurð, steðelfest wiðinnen. a1225 *Ancr. R.* 312 Auh wostu hwat me deð ȝet [*MS. T.* ȝeddes; *MS. C.* ȝeddeð]? a1250 *Owl & Night.* 309 ȝet þu me seist of oþer þinge. 1297 R. Glouc. (Rolls) 287 Man þou art iwis To winne ȝvt [*v.r.* ȝuyt] a kinedom wel betere þan min is. c1350 *Will. Palerne* 186 þe herde & his hende wif þat bold barn wiþ his bowe.. fedde, & ȝit hadde fele felawes in þe forest. 1375 in Horstmann *Altengl. Leg.* (1878) 130/2 ȝut after he gat þretty sones mo, And þretty douȝtres and two. 1456 Sir G. Haye *Law Arms* (S.T.S.) 87 Alssua ane othir ȝit resoun is [etc.]. c1460 *Towneley Myst.* ii. 30 Yit, shrew, yit, pull on a thraw! 1497 *Naval Acc. Hen. VII* (1896) 219 Wages of maryners.. ix^{li} vij^{s}. Vitayle.. vij^{li} xx^{d}. Yet Wages of maryners.. iiij^{li} x^{s} x^{d}. 1534 More *Answ. Poys. Bk.* i. xiii. 54b, They that call it brede declare yet that in dede it is not brede but the body of Chryste. 1599 B. Jonson *Cynthia's Rev.* i. iii, Stay let me obserue this portent yet. 1637 Milton *Lycidas* 1 Yet once more, O ye Laurels.. I com to pluck your Berries. c1643 Ld. Herbert *Autobiog.* (1824) 7 Notwithstanding yet these expences at home, he brought up his children well. 1660 Marvell *Corr.* Wks. (Grosart) II. 17 There is yet brought in an Act in which of all others your corporation is the least concerned. 1705 Addison *Italy* Ded., I had a very early Ambition to recommend my self to Your Lordship's Patronage, which yet encreas'd in me as I Travell'd through the Countries. 1831 Wordsw. *On Dep. Sir W. Scott* 7 While Tweed, best pleased in chanting a blithe strain, Saddens his voice again, and yet again. 1875 Jowett *Plato* (ed. 2) I. 273 Yet once more, fair friend. 1895 Petrie *Egypt. Tales* Ser. i. 73 The Sekhti came yet, and yet again, even unto the ninth time.

b. Used to strengthen a comparative: now more commonly expressed by even (*adv.* 9 e) or still (*adv.* 5 a). †Also formerly with a superlative (= very *adv.* 3 a) or an ordinal numeral.

c888 Ælfred *Boeth.* v. §3 Ac wit sculon þeah ȝiet dioplicor ymb ðæt bion. a1000 *Judith* 182 þe us monna mæst morðra ȝefremede,.. & þæt swyðor ȝyt ycan wolde. a1122 *O.E. Chron.* (Laud MS.) an. 1087 He.. dyde ȝit eallra wærst. c1175 *Lamb. Hom.* 123 Luuian we ure drihten, for þon þe he luuede us er we hine.. ȝit we sculen mare, we sculan luuian ure nehstan. c1200 Ormin Ded. 6 Broþerr min i Godess hus, ȝet o þe þride wise. *Ibid.* 780, & Godess enngell seȝȝde þær Off Sannt Johan ȝet mare. c1275 Lay. 28538 Sixti þousend manne And mo þousendes ȝite. a1352 Minot *Poems* (ed. Hall) i. 49 Ma manasinges ȝit haue þai maked. 1390 Gower *Conf.* III. 132 Alpheta.. is the twelfthe sterre yit. c1400 *Rule St. Benet* (verse) 299 þe fortt degre ȝit es þair als Of sum þat er in order fals. c1425 Wyntoun *Cron.* iii. ix. 1044 þis kynge mony sonnys hade, Off ane of þa ȝhit mast he made. 1567 *Satir. Poems Reform.* vi. 112 Thairfoir ye fand thame prickis vnto your ene, And, ȝif ye spair thame, yit sall find thame moir. 1626 Gouge *Dign. Chiv.* §5, I purpose to dive yet more deeply into the depth of my Text. 1665 Hooke *Microgr.* 2 Being able to include as great a variety of parts.. in the yet smallest Discernable Point, as in those vaster bodies such as the Earth, Sun, or Planets. 1724 Ramsay *Vision* x, That's yit worse. 1782 Miss Burney *Cecilia* viii. v, Which can only awaken painful recollections, or give rise to yet more painful new anxieties. 1819 Scott *Ivanhoe* xxiv, The thought.. gave a yet deeper colour of carnation to her complexion. 1847 H. Melville *Omoo* lxvii, My sandals were worse yet. 1889 'J. S. Winter' *Mrs. Bob* x. (1891) 121 'And you're quite sure.. that you really like me.' 'Yes, I'm quite sure,' said he, holding her yet more closely to him.

c. Used for emphasis after *nor* (†*na, ne, neither*): ***nor yet*** = and also not. †Also formerly after *or*: ***or yet*** = or else, or even (cf. e below).

a1300 *Cursor M.* 12811 Neþer am i crist ne yeitt heli. c1375 *Sc. Leg. Saints* iii. (*Andreas*) 3 In word, in thocht, or yhet in dede. c1386 Chaucer *Knt.'s T.* 1084 Nat was foryeten, the porter ydelnesse Ne Narcisus.. Ne yet the folie of kyng Salomon. 1513 Douglas *Æneis* i. vi. 98 All thai quhilk haitis the cruel tirrantis dedis, Or ȝit his felloun violence sair dredis. 1526 Tindale *Luke* xxiii. 15, I.. founde noo faute in this man.. No nor yett Herode. 1581 Mulcaster *Positions* xxxvii. (1888) 152 Neither he, ne yet his parentes, can forsake their prince. 1588 A. King tr. *Canisius' Catech.* g vij, Quhatsoeuer do proceid ather from the hail body thairof, ather yeit ony particular membre of the same. 1625 Hart *Anat. Ur.* ii. iv. 68 Such an excretion of bloud, which cometh thus to passe by reason of the loosenesse.. of the mouthes of the small veines, or yet of the thinnesse of bloud. 1637–50 Row *Hist. Kirk* (Wodrow Soc.) 121 Yit the samine can noth be conceiled.. Neither ȝit can the men of God.. dissemble the samine. c1639 in *10th Rep. Hist. MSS. Comm.* App. i. 35 He does not rekon the samen nether yett his owne charges. 1884 W. C. Smith *Kildrostan* 88, I never handled rope, Nor held a tiller, nor yet mean to do.

†**d.** Denoting repetition of an act: Again. *Obs.*

a1300 *Cursor M.* 1197 Bad him [*sc.* Adam] thoru an angel steuen, þat he suld wit his wijf yete mete. c1385 Chaucer *L.G.W.* 2687 *Hypermnestra*, She rist ȝit vp, & stakerith her & ther. a1400–50 *Wars Alex.* 3163 First warte I to ȝour worthines, ȝit write I þe same. 1431 *Test. Ebor.* (Surtees) II. 15 Unum flatt pece cum scriptura in cooperculo Drynk and fyll ȝytt. 1564–5 *Reg. Privy Council Scot.* I. 316 To charge the said Gilbert.. yit as of befoir, to bring the saidis Urchid Makdowell and Patrik Makdowell.

†**e.** Emphasizing an extreme case: = even *adv.* 9. *Obs. rare.*

a1300 *Cursor M.* 11575 Ar he self wald.. To ded it moght naman him bring, And not yeitt þan þat he ne suld rise, Al at his aun deuise. 1382 Wyclif *Luke* xiv. 26 If ony.. hatith not his.. britheren, and douȝtris, ȝit forsoth and his lyf [*2nd vers.* and ȝit his owne lijf]. a1450 *Le Morte Arth.* 2248 All landys northe and southe Off thys werre the word spronge, And yit at Rome it was full couthe.

f. Used as an ironic intensive at the end of a sentence, clause, etc. (imitating the use of Yiddish *noch*). *colloq.* (orig. *U.S.*).

1936 *Sat. Even. Post* 19 Dec. 11/3 'The only kinda men I want are ones who wouldn't be afraid to try out for Whiteman.' 'Whiteman yet!' scoffed one. 1943 M. Shulman *Barefoot Boy with Cheek* vii. 68 'Not just a little story, but a big story, and on the front page and with pictures.' There were admiring whistles and cries of 'Pictures, yet!' from the audience. 1957 *N.Y. Times Book Rev.* 17 Mar. 8 The counter-claim was dismissed (with costs yet). 1962 T. Meehan in *Sunday Times* 5 Aug. 20/3 And that spooky organ music they got piped in all over the place—E. Power Biggs instead of Muzak, yet. 1972 D. S. Viscott *Making of a Psychiatrist* ii. 32 You can bet your Phi Beta Kappa pin, junior year yet, that D. J. Marley knows exactly what to put down. 1975 *Times Lit. Suppl.* 7 Mar. 250/2 If you own a Beaumont and Fletcher folio, don't lend it. At least not to someone who will return it with extensive annotations (in ink yet!). 1980 *Oxford Times* 22 Aug. 13/3 The tracks include.. 'To Know Him is to Love Him' (with David Bowie on saxophone, yet!).

II. Senses relating to time.

2. a. (*a*) Implying continuance from a previous time up to and at the present (or some stated) time: Now as until now (or then as until then): = still *adv.* 4 a. Often also implying contrast to a future or subsequent state more emphatically expressed by *as yet* (7 a): cf. c below, and still *adv.* 4 b. *arch.* or *dial.* exc. in negative context: see esp. (*b*).

c897 Ælfred *Gregory's Past. C.* Pref. 5 Her mon mæȝ ȝiet ȝesion hiora swæð. 971 *Blickl. Hom.* 231 Nu ȝit þry daȝas to lafe syndon. a1000 *Harrow. Hell* 73 (Gr.) A ic þæt heold nu ȝiet. a1122 *O.E. Chron.* (Laud. MS.) an. 449 þæt cyn on West Sexum þe man ȝit hæt Iutna cyn. c1160 *Hatton Gosp.* Matt. xv. 16 And synd ȝe ȝeot buton andȝytte? c1200 *Trin. Coll. Hom.* 83 Al to fele swiche men bien ȝet þe ne wilen noht here sinnes forleten. c1205 Lay. 28636 Bruttes ileueð ȝete þat he bon on liue. 1297 R. Glouc. (Rolls) 1574 Seint Iones de lateran.. þat stont ȝute & heued churche of al cristendom is. a1300 *Cursor M.* 796 For of þat ilk appel bitt þair suns tethe ar eggeid yitt. a1375 *Joseph Arim.* 334 þat I tolde þe þo I telle þe ȝitte. c1400 *Destr. Troy* 1628 Somur qwenes, and qwaintans, & oþer qwaint gaumes, Ther foundyn was first, & yet ben forthe haunted. c1450 *St. Cuthbert* (Surtees) 306 þat he had sene before in spirit, he held it all pryue ȝyt. 1534 *Star Chamber Cases* (Selden Soc.) II. 309 Robert hunte baylyf.. did take and kepe and yeat kepeth a cowe of your said oratours. a1548 Hall *Chron., Edw. V* 11 It wer as great commoditee to theim bothe, as for yet a while too bee in the custody of their mother. 1588 A. King tr. *Canisius' Catech.* N v b, Euerie moneth was reconed to begin on ye day of ye change, as is obserued ȝeit in ye Hebrew kallendar. 1611 *Bible* Jer. xv. 9 Her sunne is gone down while it was yet day. 1700 *Stanley's Hist. Philos., Life* a j, While he continued yet in the University. 1711 Addison *Spect.* No. 164. ¶3 While her Beauty was yet in all its Height and Bloom. 1756 Mrs. Calderwood in *Coltness Collect.* (Maitland Club) 187 This man was from Nidsdale, and had been out of the country since he was ten years old, but he spoke the language pretty well yet. 1802 Wordsw. *To the Cuckoo* iv, Even yet thou art to me No bird, but an invisible thing. 1839 Bywater *Sheff. Dial.* ii. 22 Dusta work at flat backs yit, as thahs been used to do? 1848 Mrs. Gaskell *Mary Barton* vii, Earnest as the father was in watching the yet-living, he had eyes and ears for all that concerned the dead. 1872 Tennyson *Gareth & Lynette* 79 A yet-warm corpse, and yet unburiable. 1874 Mahaffy *Soc. Life Greece* iv. 81 No students of history can fail to observe that even yet very few nations in the world are fit for diffused political privileges. 1888 'J. S. Winter' *Bootle's Childr.* v, You know you look ill yet, very ill.

(*b*) With negative pples. and adjs.: cf. *not yet* (4).

1535 Coverdale *Ps.* lxxvii[i]. 6 The children which were yet vnborne. 1697 Dryden *Virg. Georg.* iv. 782 Four fair Heifars yet in Yoke untry'd. 1705 Stanhope *Paraphr.* I. 282 The ravishing Discovery of that which is yet unattainable. 1706 Pope *Let. to Wycherley* 10 Apr., Till you have finish'd these that are yet unprinted. 1725 —— *Odyss.* v. 382 Then shook the Heroe,.. And question'd thus his yet-unconquer'd mind. 1839 Kemble *Resid. Georgia* (1863) 19 The swampy patches of yet unreclaimed forest. 1859 Tennyson *Elaine* 378 The yet-unblazon'd shield. 1860 Pusey *Min. Proph.* 544 The children in their yet undeveloped strength, the very old in their yet sustained weakness.

†**b.** Qualified by a negative, implying discontinuance before the present time: ***not yet*** = no longer. *Obs. rare.*

a1000 *Cædmon's Gen.* 1038 Ne þearft ðu þe ondrædan.. nu ȝiet. 1530 Palsgr. 506/2, I darrayne (Lydgat).. This worde is nat yet admytted in our comen spetche. *Ibid.* 598/2, I kydde (Lydgate), I knowe.. This terme is nat yet in use.

c. Followed by an infinitive referring to the future, and thus implying incompleteness (e.g. *yet to be done*, implying 'not hitherto done'; *I have yet to learn*, implying 'I have not hitherto learnt'). Cf. also 5.

1659 Plumptre in *12th Rep. Hist. MSS. Comm.* App. v. 6 Wishing that all your yeares yet to come may passe over with mirth and jollityes. 1756 Mrs. Calderwood in *Coltness Collect.* (Maitland Club) 188 He has three years of study yet to come. 1848 Lushington in *Notes of Cases* VI. 11, I have yet to learn that.. those on board the steam-tug had a right to.. overrule the order of the pilot. 1849 Macaulay *Hist. Eng.* v. I. 564 The earl.. had prepared himself for what was yet to be endured. 1885 Sir J. Bacon in *Law Times Rep.* (N.S.) LII. 569/2 None of them had been completely finished, the painting and papering being yet to be done.

3. a. Referring to the period preceding the present or some stated time, without necessarily implying continuance: Up to this (or that) time, till now (or till then), hitherto, thus far; with a superlative, or *only*, etc. = at any time up to the present. Usually implying expectation of possible change, more fully expressed (as in 2) by *as yet* (7 a).

a1000 *Colloq. Ælfric* in Wr.-Wülcker 101 ðyt [*adhuc*] þeah-hwæþere deoplicor mid us þu smeaȝst þonne yld ure onfon mæȝe. c1175 *Lamb. Hom.* 139 þis dei is.. þe formeste dei þet eauer ȝiete was iseȝen buuen eorðe. a1300 *Cursor M.* 9321 'Ful littel se we ȝeitt', coth þai, 'Of al þat euer we her þai sai.' c1375 *Ibid.* 10078 (Laud) Now blessid be that byrd of grace The worthiest that euyr yet was. c1475 *Rauf Coilȝear* 80 Na, thank me not ouir airlie, for dreid that we threip, For I haue seruit the ȝit of lytill thing to ruse. 1539 Cranmer *Let. to Cromwell* in *Misc. Writ.* (Parker Soc.) 388 The state of things standing as they do at this present, so far as yet I do know. 1596 Spenser *F.Q.* vi. ii. 5 A slender slip, that scarse did see Yet seuenteene yeares. 1690 Locke *Hum. Und.* ii. xxvi. §4 When we say a Man is Young, we mean, that his Age is yet but a small part of that which usually Men attain to. 1761 Warburton in *W. & Hurd's Lett.* (1809) 335, I have yet printed off but 72 pages. 1815 Scott *Guy M.* xlviii, This is the queerest thing yet! 1857 Buckle *Civiliz.* I. viii. 471 The most important event that had yet occurred in the history of French civilization. 1870 L'Estrange *Life of Miss Mitford* I. x. 147 'Blanch' is to consist of five thousand lines, and only eleven hundred are yet written.

b. By this (or that) time, so soon as this: chiefly in questions, direct or indirect, to which the negative answer would be *not yet* (4): nearly = 'already', but not expressing surprise as that word would in a question.

a1250 *Owl & Night.* 541 Hu þincþ þe, artu ȝut inume, Artu mid riȝte ouercume? c1375 *Cursor M.* 1876 (Fairf.) How sal we of þes waters wete, Queþer þai be fully fallyn ȝete? c1440 *York Myst.* ix. 186 It waxes clere aboute.. Loke þar owte, Yf þat þe water wane ought ȝitt. 1596 Shaks. *1 Hen. IV*, iii. iii. 61 Haue you enquir'd yet who pick'd my Pocket? 1634 Massinger *Very Woman* iii. v, I am glad you have found your tongue yet. 1823 Scott *Quentin D.* xxxiii, 'Have you yet done?' said the Duke to the herald. 'One word more,' answered Rouge Sanglier. 1916 D. Hankey *Student in Arms* (1917) 51 *Potentate*... Has a counter-attack been launched yet? *General.* Not yet, Sire.

c. With *ere, before*, etc. indicating the ultimate occurrence of something after an interval of time: before *ere*, etc., nearly = 'already'; after *ere*, etc., nearly = 'at length' (cf. 5 a). Now only in *ere yet* (arch.).

13.. *Gaw. & Gr. Knt.* 1122 To bed ȝet er þay ȝede, Recorded couenauntez ofte. c1450 Holland *Howlat* 196 ȝit or ewyn enterit come that bur office, Obeyand thir bischoppis, and bydand tham by. 1592 *Arden of Feversham* i. i. 92 Meanewhile prepare our breakfast,.. For yet ere noone wele take horse and away. c1643 Ld. Herbert *Autobiog.* (1824) 80 Before I departed yet I left her with child of a son. 1795 Southey *Joan of Arc* viii. 70 Ere yet from Orleans to the war we went. 1828 Scott *Death Laird's Jock* ¶13 Ere yet the fight began, the old men gazed on their chief. 1866 Spurgeon *Hymn, 'Sweetly the holy hymn'* ii, Ere yet the sun the day renews, O Lord, Thy spirit send.

†**d.** At some time in the past; 'once'; previously, before, already. *Obs.*

Beowulf 956 Alwalda þec gode forȝylde, swa he nu ȝyt dyde! a1300 *Cursor M.* 367 þe werld i call wit min entens þe mater of þe four elements, þat yeit was tan o forme mischapen. *Ibid.* 1198 Ur lord had aghteld yete A child to rais of his oxspring. c1460 J. Russell *Bk. Nurture* 389 þan take youre loof of light payne as y haue said ȝett.

4. With a negative, in sense 2 or 3 (*yet* qualifying the whole sentence or clause including the negative): ***not yet***, †***yet not***, still not, thus far not, not hitherto, not by this (or that) time, not till now (or then) and not now (or then): implying expectation or recognized possibility of subsequent change (cf. 7 a).

a. With negative preceding. (The more usual, now the only regular, construction.)

Beowulf 583 Breca næfre ȝit æt heaðolace.. swa deorlice dæd ȝefremede faȝum sweordum. c1000 *Ags. Gosp.* Matt. xxiv. 6 Ðas þing sceolon ȝewurþan, ac nys þonne ȝyt se ende. *Ibid.* John vii. 8 Min tid nis ȝyt ȝefylled. c1200 *Vices & Virtues* 17 Ðar næure ȝiete liht ne cam. c1200 Ormin 14371 Abid, abid, wifman, abid, Ne comm nohht ȝet min time. c1205 Lay. 109 Nas ȝet Rome bi-wonnen. c1275 *Passion of our Lord* 583 in *O.E. Misc.* 53 Ich ne astey nouht yete vp to myne vadere. c1386 Chaucer *Prol.* 293 (Harl. 7334), He hadde nouȝt geten hym ȝit a benefice. 1470–85 Malory *Arthur* viii. vi. 282 Neuer yet was I preued with good knyghte. 1539 *Bible* (Great) Mark xi. 13 The tyme of fygges was not yet. a1548 Hall *Chron., Edw. IV* 207b, Because Quene Margaret and her sonne were not fully yet furnished for suche a iorney. 1605 Shaks. *Macb.* ii. iii. 50 *Macd.* Is the King stirring, worthy Thane? *Macb.* Not yet. 1654 Gataker *Disc. Apol.* 24 Such a manner of Prelacie, I say, I never durst, nor yet dare condemn. 1708 Addison *Pres. St. War* 3 This Kingdom was never yet engag'd in a War of so great consequence. 1776 Gibbon *Let. to Holroyd* 18 Jan., Quebec is not yet taken. 1849 Macaulay *Hist. Eng.* ii. I. 175 A body of representatives was returned, such as England had never yet seen. *Ibid.* iv. 447 As to Halifax, Ormond, and Guildford, he determined not yet to dismiss them. 1861 M. Pattison *Ess.* (1889) I. 46 In the reign of James I,.. when the world of fashion had not yet migrated wholly to the west-end. 1880 [see shoot *v.* 23 g]. 1908 Kipling *Lett. of Travel* (1920) 146 There's them that can't see *yit*. 1977 *Transatlantic Rev.* lx. 147 'Naw', he says. 'Least, no yit.'

b. With negative following. (Cf. G. *noch nicht.*) *Obs.* or *arch.* exc. when preceded by *even*, or *as* (7 a).

c1000 *Ags. Gosp.* John vii. 6 Ðyt ne com min tid. c1205 Lay. 20571 Ah he heo þa ȝæte [c1275 ȝet] Nefde noht bi-wunnen. c1250 *Gen. & Ex.* 3558 'Louerd, merci!' quad moyses, 'ȝet ne let hem noȝt helpe-les.' a1300 *Cursor M.* 5904 þe king hert wex herd as bras, 'þe folk', he said, 'yeitt sal noght pas.' 1377 Langl. *P. Pl.* B. viii. 108 Ac ȝete sauoureth me nouȝt þi seggyng. 1460 Capgrave *Chron.*

(Rolls) 302 And ȝet was not the erl of Arundel and his retenew com hom. **1567** *Satir. Poems Reform.* iii. 37 ȝit neuer did sho se his maik in France. **1613** SHAKS. *Hen. VIII*, II. iv. 204 My Conscience, which I then did feele full sicke, and yet not well. **1642** D. ROGERS *Naaman* 423 Such confession was yet never extorted from some of you. **1827** SCOTT *Highl. Widow* iv, I leave you to comfort and certainty, which you have yet never known. **1830** MOORE *Mem.* (1854) VI. 127 Even yet not quite finished.

5. In reference to future time (see also 2 c, 3 c). **a.** At some time in the future (usually implying 'though not hitherto'); hereafter; at length, ultimately, before all is over; often with mixture of sense 9 ('after all').

c **897** ÆLFRED *Gregory's Past. C.* xxxv. 245 ðiet [*v.r.* ȝit] cymð se micla.. Godes dæȝ. **971** *Blickl. Hom.* iv. 47 On ealra eorþlicra ȝebedrædenne þe Cristene wæron, oþþe ȝyt syn. *a* **1300** *Leg. Rood* (1871) 32 Vor þer scholde ȝut a mon deie on þulke tre. *c* **1400** *Brut* i. 90 þe Britons supposen þat he [*sc.* Arthur] Leueþ in a-noþere lande, and þat he shal come ȝit and conquere al Britaigne. *c* **1440** *York Myst.* i. 87 Abowne ȝhit sall I be beeldand, On heghte in þe hyeste of heuwen. **1535** COVERDALE *Ps.* xlii. 7 [5] Put thy trust in God, for I wil yet geue him thankes for yᵉ helpe of his countenaunce. *a* **1586** SIDNEY *Ps.* XVII. iv, [I] pray that still you guide my way, Least yet I slipp, or goe astray. **1760–2** GOLDSM. *Cit. W.* xliv, He sees that he may yet be happy, and wishes the hour was come. **1841** BROWNING *Pippa Passes* III. ad fin. (Song), You'll love me yet!—and I can tarry Your love's protracted growing. **1849** MACAULAY *Hist. Eng.* v. I. 524 Their chief employment is to talk of what they once were, and of what they may yet be. **1902** VIOLET JACOB *Sheep-stealers* viii, 'You couldn't be safer, not if you was in Hereford jail itself.'.. 'That's where I may be yet,' he said.

b. With reference to the immediate future: (*a*) Even now (though not till now): often with mixture of sense 9 ('after all'); sometimes implying 'while there is still time' (cf. sense 2).

a **1000** *Cædmon's Gen.* 618 ðif ȝiet.. læst mina lara, þonne ȝife ic him þæs leohtes ȝenoȝ. *c* **1375** *Sc. Leg. Saints* v. (*Johannes*) 251 And of paynis hard and fell, He tald þam, þat he schaw in hell, And sad: 'wrechis, mend ȝow ȝeit!' *Ibid.* l. (*Katerine*) 921 Lewe þine errour,..& ask forgiffnes of þi syne, Yheit mycht þu sauchtyng with hym wine. *c* **1430** *Hymns Virgin* (1867) 128 To hevyns blys yhit may he ryse, Thurghe helpe of Marie. *c* **1450** *St. Cuthbert* (Surtees) 3367 ȝon gose I bad ȝow is noȝy etyn... I bid ȝow þat ȝe take it ȝit. *a* **1529** SKELTON *Woffully araid* 43 Wks. 1843 I. 142 Cum ȝytt, and thou schalt fynde Myne endlys mercy and grace. **1689** *Act. Parlt. Scot.* (1875) XII. 77/1 þat if he will yett delyver up the Bass & prisoners þerin he should have his bygone arears to himself & garrisone. **1867** MORRIS *Jason* II. 850 Bethink ye yet of death, And misery, And dull despair, before ye arm to go. **1879** WEBBER *Pigskin & Willow* xiv. 197 Time enough yet? No, there isn't time enough yet.

† (*b*) Not later than (a specified time). (Cf. 3 b, c.) *Obs.*

c **1250** *Gen. & Ex.* 313 For ȝef he don ð ad god for-bead, Ðat sal hem bringen to ðo dead, And sal ȝet ðis ilke dai. *a* **1300** *Cursor M.* 15567 þou sal þam se yeitt to night Do me ful gret spite. *a* **1352** MINOT *Poems* (ed. Hall) vii. 129 Inglis men sall ȝit to ȝere Knok þi palet or þou pas.

c. From this (or some stated or implied) time onwards; henceforth (or thenceforth). Chiefly, now only, contextually with words denoting time, the sense being then strictly 1 ('further, more'); with a negative, nearly coinciding with 4; often replaceable by 'to come'.

c **1000** ÆLFRIC *Gen.* viii. 10 He abad þa ȝit oðre seofon daȝas and asende ut eft culfran. *a* **1300** *Cursor M.* 12920 Bot ar he wild him fulli scau, For yeitt a quille he wild abide. **1382** WYCLIF *Luke* i. 15 He schal be fulfillid of the Hooly Gost ȝit of his modir wombe. —— *John* vii. 33 ȝit a litel tyme I am with ȝou, and I go to the fadir, that sente me. *c* **1420** *Chron. Vilod.* 3367 He leyȝe in þe vrthe ȝet þrettene ȝere & more. **1535** COVERDALE *Jonah* iii. 4 There are yet xl. dayes, and then shal Niniue be ouerthrowen. **1628** DIGBY *Voy. Mediterr.* (Camden) 56 It was so hott that all men said in a moneth yet meate could not take salt. **1849** M. ARNOLD *Sick King in Bokhara* 5 O merchants, tarry yet a day Here in Bokhara.

†**6.** ME. *þe ȝet* [OE. *þá ȝíet* then yet, when yet: see THO *adv.* 1, 2]: **a.** Still (= 2); also, while still, when as yet. *Obs.*

a **930** *O.E. Chron.* (Parker MS.) an. 921 þa æfter þam þa ȝiet þæs ilcan hærfestes ȝegadorode micel here hine of East Englum. *c* **1000** *Ags. Gosp.* Luke xv. 20 þa ȝyt [*Lindisf.* ȝet] þa he wæs feorr, his fæder he hyne ȝeseah. *a* **1122** *O.E. Chron.* (Laud MS.) an. 1106 Feawa oðre of þam heafodmannan þe mid þam eorle of Normandiȝe þe ȝyt heoldan. *c* **1175** *Lamb. Hom.* 99 þa ȝet wuniende on þissere weorlde, þe helende ableu his gast on his apostlas. *c* **1205** LAY. 7079 þe ȝeht þe [*c* **1275** þe ȝet þat] Lud king ahte þis lond hehte Lundene Trinouant. *c* **1290** *St. Dunstan* 2 in *S. Eng. Leg.* 19 Miracle ore louerd dude for him þe ȝuyt he was un-bore.

†**b.** with negative: = 4. *Obs.*

a **1000** *Cædmon's Gen.* 103 Ne wæ s her þa ȝiet nymþe heolsterseeado wiht ȝeworden. *a* **1100** *Aldhelm Gloss.* I. 1296 (Napier 35/2) *Nondum*, na þa ȝyt næs. *c* **1290** *Beket* 1433 in *S. Eng. Leg.* 147 Ake he ne scholde nouȝt þe ȝeot to engelonde wende. *c* **1380** *Sir Ferumb.* 750 Of herte was he hol & pleynede him þe ȝute no þyng.

7. *as yet* [AS B. 34 a]: **a.** Hitherto, up to this time, = 3; with a negative = 4; implying expectation or recognized possibility of coming change.

c **1384** CHAUCER *H. Fame* II. 91 Thow demest of thy selfe amys, For Ioues ys not ther aboute.. To make of the as yet a sterre. *c* **1386** —— *Frankl. T.* 849, I failled neuere of my trouthe as yit, For sikerly my dette shal be quyt. **1484** *Cely Papers* (Camden) 153 Here ys noo goode wyne to gett for noo mony as yett, but I understond ther schall come from Bruges som. **1592** Q. ELIZ. in *Archaeologia* XIX. 12 If your long expected and never had as yet answer had not lingard. **1665** BOYLE *Occas. Refl.* IV. i. 1 The Sun had as yet but approach'd the East, and my Body as yet lay moveless in the Bed. **1682** BUNYAN *Holy War* 68 Thou hast heard what the Captains have said, but as yet thou shuttest thy Gates. **1708** ADDISON *Pres. St. War* 19 That War continued Nine Years, and this hath as yet lasted but Six. **1823** SCOTT *Quentin D.* xxix, 'No,' answered the Astrologer, 'the End is not as yet.' **1848** THACKERAY *Van. Fair* lxiii, She had never..met a professional ladies' man as yet. **1849** MACAULAY *Hist. Eng.* ii. I. 171 As yet the Duke professed himself a member of the Anglican Church. **1850** TENNYSON *In Mem.* cxiv, Half-grown as yet, a child, and vain. **1874** MAHAFFY *Soc. Life Greece* vii. 226 But there were.. extensions of this practice as yet but little noticed.

†**b.** Without implied expectation of change: Still, even now or then, to this day, = 2. *Obs.*

1483 CAXTON *G. de la Tour* f iv b, As yet they kepe and hold that custome. **1530** PALSGR. 509/2 As for *polu*, defyled, thoughe he be used of Johan le Mayre, there is no verbe used in this sence in the frenche tonge as yet. **1577** HANMER *Anc. Eccl. Hist.* III. vi. 38 The meate as yet rawe, was snatched from the coales. **1585** T. WASHINGTON tr. *Nicholay's Voy.* II. iii. 33 The foundations.. are there as yet apparant. **1611** *Bible* Exod. ix. 17 As yet exaltest thou thy selfe against my people, that thou wilt not let them goe? **1632** LITHGOW *Trav.* VII. 321 Ægypt was made a Prouince of the Turkish Empire, and so continueth as yet. **1651** [see AS B. 34 a].

8. as *adj.* in sense 2 or 3: That is still or as yet such; still continuing or subsisting. (Cf. NOW 16, STILL *adv.* 4 a ¶, THEN 9 b.)

1606 SYLVESTER *Du Bartas* II. iv. II. *Magnificence* 356 Let, with her staffe, my yet-Youth govern well.. the Flock of Israel. **1629** W. SCLATER *Exp. 2 Thess.* 83 That the yet aliens in euery quarter of the World may bee wonne by the example of dispersed Saints. *c* **1634** STAFFORD in Browning *Life* (1892) 117 The certainty of your lordship's yet abode at West-Chester. **1653** *Cloria & Narcissus* 181 Her yet safety. **1817** KEATINGE *Trav.* II. 269 He was one of the numerous party of yet walkers in the world. **1874** KEY *Lang.* i. 7 In the yet non-existence of language.

III. 9. a. as *conj. adv.* or *conj.* (developed from 1), introducing an additional fact or circumstance which is adverse to, or the contrary of what would naturally be expected from, that just mentioned: In spite of that, for all that, nevertheless, notwithstanding. Sometimes strengthened by *nevertheless*, etc. Often correlative to *though*, etc.

More emphatically adversative than BUT *conj.* 24, and freer in construction; formerly sometimes placed after, and still sometimes in the midst of, its clause; *and* or *but* may precede *yet*. Nearly equivalent to STILL *adv.* 6 b; but *still* indicates mainly that the fact or condition remains unaltered by the adverse one; *yet* usually expresses some degree of surprise at it as something unexpected.

[*c* **1205** LAY. 28112 ȝif hit weore ilimpe.. þat Modred.. hafde þine quene inume... þe ȝet þu mihtest þe awreken Wurðliche mid wepnen.] *a* **1250** *Owl & Night.* 995 So bo hit euer in unker siþe þat þu bo sori & ich bliþe; ȝut þu aisheist wi ich ne fare Into oþer londe & singe þare. **1297** R. GLOUC. (Rolls) 3344 þe castel was ynome & þat folc to sprad þere. ȝute þo hii adde al ydo hii ne founde noȝt þe king þere. *Ibid.* 8804 In prison was roberd al is lif & ȝut ich vnder-stonde, Him adde betere abbe ibe king of þe holi londe. **13..** *Cursor M.* 786 (Gött.) þis heting was.. ful mekil, Bot ȝeit it was bath fals and fikil. **1377** LANGL. *P. Pl.* B. Prol. 185 Thouȝ we culled þe catte, ȝut sholde þe come another To cracchy vs. **1390** GOWER *Conf.* II. 140 He hath ynowh and yit him nedeth. *c* **1420** *Liber Cocorum* (1862) 5 And make þo flesshe to seme, iwys, As hit were raw, and ȝyt hit nys. *c* **1450** *Lay Folks Mass Bk.* (MS. F.) 149, I haw done.. Synnes diuers, .. And ȝut art thu redi.. To graunt me ay forȝefnesse. *c* **1470** *Gol. & Gaw.* 95 Suppose thi birny be bright, as bachiler suld ben, Yhit ar thi latis vnlufsum. **1470–85** MALORY *Arthur* XX. vii. 809 Oftymes we doo many thynges that we wene it be for the best & yet peradaunture hit torneth to the werst. *c* **1475** *Partenay* 21 Al-be-hit I.. can noght peynt my boke as other be, Vnder youre supporte yut aunter wyl me. **1545** RAYNALDE *Byrth Mankynde* I. iii. (1552) 5 Plenty of flesh.. knitting to geather the muskles: not so yet, but that neuerthelesse they haue theyr free motion. **1596** SPENSER *Prothalamion* 117 As he would speake, but that he lackt a tong Yeat did by signes his glad affection show. **1644** MILTON *Areop.* 26 Though his belief be true, yet the very truth he holds, becomes his heresie. **1697** DRYDEN *Æneis* XI. 188 Auspicious Prince, in Arms a mighty Name, But yet whose Actions far transcend your Fame. **1764** GOLDSM. *Trav.* 28 Some fleeting good, that.. Allures from far, yet, as I follow, flies. **1814** SCOTT *Wav.* iv, The splendid yet useless imagery. **1831** —— *Ct. Rob.* xxiv, Although they did not all agree on the precise cause of danger, it was yet generally allowed that something of a dreadful kind was impending. **1845** M. PATTISON *Ess.* (1889) I. 13 The style of Bede, if not elegant Latin, is yet correct, sufficiently classical. **1857** H. S. RIDDELL *Book of Psalms in Lowland Scotch* lxviii. 61 Thouch ye hae læyne amang the pats, yit sall ye be as the wings o' ane dow. **1939** JOYCE *Finnegans Wake* 138 An yit he wanna git all his flesch nuemaid.

†**b.** *yet (that)*, notwithstanding that, although.

c **1320** *Cast. Love* 1422 In whonhope and doute heo weoren vchon, ȝit heo seȝen him alyue a lyues-mon. *c* **1425** *Cursor M.* 12119 (Trin.) And ȝit þou wenest makeles to be þat noon in lore shulde teche þe, I con þe teche þat þou not can. **1556** *Aurelio & Isab.* (1608) M ij, Contente you than, for yette that me strenghste be litell, the desiere is grete.

yet(e, ȝet(e, obs. ff. GATE *sb.*¹

†**yete(n**, *pa. pple. Obs.* Forms: 1 **ȝeeten**, 3 **iȝeten**, (iheote), 3–4 **iȝet(t)e**, **yȝete**, **iete(n**, 4 **y-yete**, **i-eete**, 4–5 **yete(n**, 5 **yheete**. [OE. *ȝeeten*, pa. pple. of *etan* and *ȝeetan* to EAT.] Eaten.

c **1000** ÆLFRIC *Gen.* xxxi. 54 þa hiȝ ȝeeten hæfdon, hiȝ wunedon þær. *c* **1205** LAY. 6691 þeær heo hæfden wel iȝeten [*c* **1275** iheote] and seoððen idrunken. *Ibid.* 31773 Ær þe uisc i-eten weore. *c* **1290** *St. Brandan* 309 in *S. Eng. Leg.* 228 Heo a-risen op and wenden to churche þo heo hadden yȝete. *c* **1330** *Arth. & Merl.* 3127 þo þai hadde yeten alle, Heiȝe & lowe in þe halle. **1340** *Ayenb.* 13 Efter his arizinge, huanne he hedde y-yete mid his deciples. **1387** TREVISA *Higden* (Rolls) VII. 511 Thei.. hadde nouȝt y-ete ne dronke nother y-slepe. **1398** —— *Barth. De P.R.* IX. xxxi. (1495) z iv b/2 A lambe was offryd rosted and yeten. **1426** LYDG. *De Guil. Pilgr.* 6849 Whan they be fumous, ful off heete, And han yheete & dronke at large.

†**yeter, yetter.** *Obs.* Forms: 1 **ȝeotere**, 3–4 **ȝeter**, 4 **ȝeoter**, **ȝeetere**, 5 **ȝetare**, 6 **ȝettare**, **yetter**. See also YOTER. [f. YET *v.* + -ER¹. Cf. MSw. *giutare* 'fictor'.] A caster of metal; a founder. Also in comb. *bellyeter*.

c **893** ÆLFRED *Oros.* I. xii. 54 þa þæt þa onhæt wæs, & eall ȝedon swa se ȝeotere þæm æðelinge ær behet. **1298** in Stow *Surv.* (1908) II. 290 Belȝeterslane. **13..** *K. Alis.* 6735 (Laud MS.) A queynt man, & metal ȝeters [*v.r.* ȝeoter]. **1382** WYCLIF *Jer.* li. 17 Confoundid is eche ȝeetere [1388 wellere] in grauen thing; for fals is his ȝeting. *c* **1440** Bellȝetare [see BELL *sb.*¹ 12]. **1512** *Reg. Privy Seal Scot.* I. 360/2 Robert Borthuik, ȝettare of the kingis gunnys. **1552** HULOET, Karuer or yetter of Images, *statuarius.*

yether, var. EDDER; see YEDDER *sb.* and *v.*

yeti ('jɛtɪ). Also **Yeti.** [ad. Tibetan *yeh-teh* little manlike animal.] Native (Sherpa) name for a hypothetical ape-like animal whose tracks have supposedly been found in snow on the Himalayan mountains; = *Abominable Snowman* s.v. ABOMINABLE *a.* 1 c.

1937 *Times* 13 Nov. 13/5 The Sherpas had no hesitation in pronouncing them [*sc.* tracks] to be those of a Snowman or 'Yeti'. **1951** *Times* 6 Dec. 5/7 Sen Tensing immediately pronounced them to be tracks of yetis or Abominable Snowmen... He describes it as half man half beast, about five feet six inches tall, covered with reddish-brown hair but with a hairless face. **1955** [see *Abominable Snowman* s.v. ABOMINABLE *a.* 1 c]. **1956** C. EVANS *On Climbing* xiii. 185, I had heard that there was a *yeti* scalp there, and I wanted to see it. **1972** J. NAPIER (*title*) Bigfoot: the yeti and sasquatch in myth and reality. **1975** E. HILLARY *Nothing venture Nothing Win* xv. 238 Even in the Thyangboche Monastery —traditionally the source of much Yeti lore and Yeti sightings—we were unable to find anyone who had seen a Yeti.

†**yeting**, *vbl. sb. Obs.* [f. YET *v.* + -ING¹. Cf. YOTING.]

1. Casting of metal or a metal object.

1382 [see YETER]. *c* **1440** *Promp. Parv.* 538/1 ȝytynge [*Winch. MS.* ȝetyng] of metelle, as bellys, pannys, potys, and other lyke, *fusio.* *c* **1449** PECOCK *Repr.* II. ii. 138 Forwhi in kinde of ymagis no difference the grauyng makith fro the ȝutting, or the ȝutting fro the grauyng. **1453–4** *Durham Acc. Rolls* (Surtees) 191 Pro uno novo axiltre cum ȝattynges et factura, xxij s. iij d. **1473–4** *Acc. Ld. High Treas. Scot.* I. 65 For the mending and theking of a hous in thare place that wes revin at the ȝetting of the gwn, viij li.

2. Pouring down, forth, etc.; shedding.

c **1400** *Destr. Troy* 8175 Now is.. yomeryng for-yeton, & yettyng of teres. *a* **1425** tr. *Arderne's Treat. Fistula* etc. 36 Aftir þe ȝettyng in of tapsimel wiþ þe forseid poudre. **1483** *Cath. Angl.* 426/2 A ȝettynge jn, *jnfusio.* A ȝettynge oute, *effusio.*

3. *attrib.* and *Comb.*, as *yeting-place, -vessel.*

1382 WYCLIF *Prov.* xxvii. 21 What maner wise siluer is preued in the ȝeting vessel. **1483** *Cath. Angl.* 426/2 A ȝettynge place, *fusorium.*

yetling ('jɛtlɪŋ), *sb.* and *a. Sc.* and *north.* Also 4–5 **ȝet(t)lyng**, 5 **ȝettlyne**, **yetteling**, 5–6 **yetlyn(g**, **-line**, 6 **ȝet-**, **yaitling**, 8 **yetlen**, (**atelin**), 8–9 **yet(t)lin**, **yetland**, 9 **yetlan**, **yettling**. [f. YET *v.* + -LING¹.]

A. *sb.* **1.** A pot or boiler, usually of cast iron; esp. one with a bow-handle and three feet.

1378–9 *Durham Acc. Rolls* (Surtees) 588 In factura unius yetling. **1472** *Ibid.* 246, ij ȝetlynges enee. **1559** *Wills & Inv. N.C.* (Surtees 1835) 183 One yaitling of brasse. **1564** *Ibid.* 223 First a pan wᵗʰ eares vˢ—ij yetlinges iiijˢ. **1702** in *Northumbld. Gloss.* (1892) 19 Itm. an atelin in the Abbey great kitchen. **1787** GROSE *Prov. Gloss.*, *Yetling*, a small iron boiler. N. **1865** CORVAN, etc. *Tyneside Songs* 9 A kyel pot an a yetlin fell a-top iv his head. **1892** RAINE *Handbk. York Mus.* 173 A fine.. camp-kettle or yetling, 16½ in. high by 12 in. diameter, with three tall legs ending in claws.

2. Applied to various articles made of cast iron; † (*a*) a small cannon; (*b*) a 'girdle' on which cakes are baked; (*c*) a ball used in bowls.

1566 *Acc. Ld. High Treas. Scot.* XI. 518 Twa culvering moyanis of found and ane grit ȝetling of irne. **1576** *Burgh Rec. Edin.* (1882) IV. 51 The tovnis yetlingis lyand vpon the kirk of feild steipill, with thair fourniture. **1866** EDMONDSTON *Shetland & Orkney Gloss.* 147 *Yetlin*, a girdle on which cakes are baked. **1868** GORRIE *Summ. & Wint. in Orkneys* ix. 354 Flat stones which served the purpose of yettlins, or girdles for firing cakes and scones. **1895** *Fife News* 19 Jan. 7 The 'yettling' measures some seven inches in circumference, and its regulation weight is from twenty two to twenty four ounces.

3. Cast iron.

1777 W. NIMMO *Stirlingsh.* xiii. 309 It [*sc.* the pint jug] is made of a sort of yetlin, and appears to be very old. **1845** *New Statist. Acc. Scot.* VIII. II. 413 The Stirling Jug.. is made of a kind of brass or yettlin. **1883** J. MARTIN *Remin. Old Haddington* 384 The land was as hard as 'yetlan' and would soon kill them and their horses.

B. *adj.* Made of cast iron; (of iron) cast.

1495–6 *Priory of Finchale* (Surtees) 394, j yetlyng pan et iiij laddels de auricalco. **1572** *Wills & Inv. N.C.* (Surtees 1835) 381 Two yetling pans viijˢ. **1578** in *Inv. Royal Wardr.* (1815) 253 Ane demy culvering of yetline yron. **1703** *Househ. Bk. Lady G. Baillie* (1911) 170 A little yetlin kettle. **1792** *Statist. Acc. Scot.* IV. 167 The ploughs.. have a cast yetland mould-board. **1836** M. MACKINTOSH *Cottager's*

Dau. 190 My heart..As hard as ony yetlin floor Or whunstane rock.

yett, ȝett, Sc. ff. GATE *sb.*[1]

yette (ȝette), var. YATE *v. Obs.*

yetter: see YETER.

yeue, obs. form of EWE *sb.*[1]
c **1340** *Nominale* (Skeat) 404 Ram blismyth a yeue.

yeugh, yeuk, yeule: see YEW, YUKE, YULE.

yeve, ȝeve, etc.: see GIVE, etc.

yeve, obs. f. EVE *sb.*[1], IF.

yevel (ȝevel), yevill, etc., obs. ff. EVIL, etc.

yeven (ȝeven), -yn, obs. ff. EVEN *sb.*

ˈ**yever,** *a. Obs.* exc. *Sc.* Forms: 1 **ʒifre, ʒyfre, ʒifer-,** 2 **ȝifer,** (*Orm.*) **ȝiferr,** 2–4 **ȝiuer,** 3 **ȝifre, ȝiure, ȝefere, yuer,** 5 **ȝeuer, yeuer, ȝyuer, youre,** 9 *Sc.* **aiver.** [OE. *ʒífre*, corresp. to ON. *gifr* (found only in pl. witches, fiends), whence *gífrliga* savagely, in mod.Icel. exorbitantly, *gífrligr* in mod.Icel. immoderate, exorbitant. The Icel. form is represented by north. Engl. *givour* 'greedy', *giverous* (see YEVEROUS).]

1. Greedy, covetous.
Beowulf 1277 And his modor þa ʒyt ʒifre and galʒmod ʒegan wolde sorhfulne sið. *c* **888** ÆLFRED *Boeth.* xxxv. §7 Tantulus se cyning ðe on ðisse worulde unʒemetlice ʒifre wæs. *c* **1205** LAY. 7337 þu sulf ært swiðe gripel þine gumen sunden ȝefere [*c* **1275** ȝifre]. *a* **1225** *Ancr. R.* 214 þe ȝiure glutun is þes feondes manciple.

2. Eager, quick, prompt.
c **1400** *Destr. Troy* 3955 Polidamas þe pert..was..Full ȝeuer and ȝepe, and a yong knight. *c* **1425** *Engl. Conq. Irel.* 114 Thys legat was youre [*v.r.* besy] aboute, pees to make betwene the kynge & Iohn. **1847** J. HALLIDAY *Rustic Bard* 94 Forbye the body's clean an' aiver, Wi' little blust, he's doonright clever.

Hence ˈ**yeverly** *adv.*, greedily; quickly; ˈ**yeverness,** greediness, gluttony; eagerness, impetuosity.
c **888** ÆLFRED *Boeth.* xxxv. §7 Him ðær ðæt ilce yfel filʒde ðære ʒifernesse. *c* **900** tr. *Bæda's Hist.* III. ix. (1890) 178 Ongon ʒiferlice þæt gærs etan. **971** *Blickl. Hom.* 25 þurh heora ʒifernesse & oferhyʒde. *a* **1100** *Aldhelm Gloss.* I. 766 (Napier 22/1) *Pertinaciter, i. insuperabiliter,* ʒyferlice. *c* **1175** *Lamb. Hom.* 33 Hordomes and ȝifernesse and druncnesse. *a* **1225** *Ancr. R.* 240 Ne beo hit neuer so bitter, ne iueleð heo hit neuer: auh gulcheð in ȝiuerliche, & ne nimeð neuer ȝeme. *Ibid.* 286 Golnesse cumeð of ȝiuernesse & of flesches eise. *c* **1250** *Lutel Soth Serm.* 11 in *O.E. Misc.* 186 To ȝiuernesse and prude none neode he nedde. *c* **1400** *Destr. Troy* 543, I haue pittye of your person & your pert face, And ȝeuernes of ȝowthe. *Ibid.* 869, I am ferd lest þou..for ȝeuernes for-ȝete þat þe ȝeme shuld. *Ibid.* 13231 With-in a yere, full yeuerly, þat yepe was with child.

†ˈ**yeverous,** *a. Obs.* Forms: 5 **ȝyueris, -us, ȝeuerus, ȝeferous.** [f. YEVER + -OUS. The north. form *giverous* (see YEVER etym.) is found from 17th c. = 'greedy, avaricous' (1677 Nicolson in Ray *Coll. Words* (1691) 141).] Eager, impetuous.
c **1400** *Destr. Troy* 357 So ȝonge and so yepe, ȝyuerus of wille. *Ibid.* 1242 Ȝyueris of hert. **1483** *Cath. Angl.* 426/1 Ȝeferous, *ambroninus.*

yevery (ˈjɛvərɪ), *a. Sc.* and *north. dial.* Forms: 6, 9 **yevery,** 8 **aevery,** 9 **yeovery, e(e)very, aiverie.** [f. YEVER *a.* + -Y[1].] Greedy, voracious.
1536 BELLENDEN *Cron. Scot.* (1821) II. 272 Utheris, quhilkis war mair yevery and tume. **17..** *Dick o the Cow* xxv. in Child *Ballads* (1889) III. 465 The lads, that hungry and aevery was. **1825** JAMIESON, *Aiverie*, adj., very hungry, Roxb.; a term nearly obsolete. **1847** HALLIWELL, *Yeovery*, hungry. *Northumb.*

Hence ˈ**yevrisome** *a.*, ravenously greedy.
1825 JAMIESON, *Yevrisome*, having an appetite habitually craving, Dumfr.

yew (juː), *sb.* Forms: 1 **iuu, iw, eow, eoh,** 4–7 **ewe,** 4–8 **ew,** (4 **w, hw, hue,** 5 **hew, uu, uv, new**), 5–6 **u,** 5–7 **eu,** 6 **yeue, yue, yow(e, iewe, eughe, u(g)he,** 6–7 **ewgh,** 6–8 **ugh, yeugh, eugh,** 7 **yugh, yewgh, eue,** 6– **yew.** Also 6 **veiwe,** 6–7 **vewe,** 7– **view,** etc.: see VEW. [OE. *íw, éow*, late *éoh*, str. masc., corresp., with consonant-alternation and variation of gender, to OS. *îh*, pl. *îchas*, MLG., MDu. *îwe, iewe, uwe*, OHG. *îuu, îuui* str. masc., *îuua* wk. fem., *îga* str. fem. (MHG. *îwe, îbe*, G. *eibe*, Swiss dial. *îche, îge*), ON. *ýr* (chiefly, bow):—OTeut. **îhwaz*, **îʒwaz*, **îhwō*, **îʒwō*. (F. *if*, Sp. *iva*, med.L. *ivus*, are from Germanic; (M)Du. *ijf* is ad. F. *if*.)

Related obscurely to the Germanic forms are: OIr. *eo*, W. *ywen*, Cornish *hivin*, Breton *iven*, going back to OCeltic **ivos*; Lith. *jëvà*, Lett. *ëwa* black alder (OPruss. *iuwis*, Lett. *iwe* yew, are from MLG.); OSl. (Russ., Serb.) *iva* willow.]

1. a. A tree of the genus *Taxus* (N.O. *Coniferæ*) widely distributed in the North Temperate Zone, esp. *T. baccata*, the common yew of Europe and Asia, having heavy elastic wood and dense dark-green foliage; often planted in churchyards, and regarded as symbolic of sadness.
c **725** *Corpus Gloss.* (Hessels) T 15 *Taxus*, iuu. **985** *Charter of Æðelred* in Kemble *Cod. Dipl.* III. 218 Of wænhyrste on ðone eald iw; ðonone of ðon iwe to Lullan setle. *a* **1000** *Riddles* lvi. 9 þær wæs hlin & ac & se hearda iw & se fealwa holen. *c* **1000** ÆLFRIC *Gloss.* in Wr.-Wülcker 139/14 *Ornus*, eow. *c* **1325** *Gloss. W. de Bibbesw.* in *Rel. Ant.* II. 82/2 *Eye*, w [*Arundel MS.*, *if*, ew]. *c* **1340** *Nominale* (Skeat) 667 Hw, rosetre and hawetre. *c* **1386** CHAUCER *Knt.'s T.* 2065 Mapul, thorn, bech, hasel, Ew, whippeltre. *a* **1400** *Gloss.* in *Rel. Ant.* I. 7 *Taxus*, ewe. **1535** in E. Law *Hampton Crt. Pal.* (1885) 372 Treys of Yow, Sypers, Genaper, and Bayes. **1562** TURNER *Herbal* II. 150 The berries of the Italian Ughe. **1587** MASCALL *Govt. Cattle, Oxen* (1596) 36 Yeugh is euill for cattell to eate. **1588** SHAKS. *Tit. A.* II. iii. 107 They told me they would binde me heere, Vnto the body of a dismall yew. **1612** WEBSTER *White Devil* I. ii. 262 Under that Eu, As I sat sadly leaning on a grave. **1625** BACON *Ess., Gardens* (Arb.) 555 Iuniper; Cipresse Trees; Eugh. **1663** COWLEY *Verses on Sev. Occas., Complaint* 4 Beneath a Bow'r for sorrow made, ..Of the black Yew's unlucky green. **1699** GARTH *Dispens.* II. 11 Beneath the gloomy Covert of an Eugh. **1706** HEARNE *Coll.* (O.H.S.) I. 223 Robinson..pull'd up some of ye Ews. **1715** *Ibid.* V. 39 Some say that tis to be planted with Ugh, dwarf Ughs. **1750** JOHNSON *Rambler* No. 44, I threw myself beneath a blasted yeugh. **1799** J. ROBERTSON *Agric. Perth* 478 Ews 6 [feet in circumference]. **1872** OLIVER *Elem. Bot.* II. 247 The wood of the Yew is said never to be attacked by insects.

b. The wood of this tree, esp. as the material of bows.
a **1400** *King & Hermit* 199 Wyth a bow of hue full strong And arowys knyte in a thong. **1524** *Test. Ebor.* (Surtees) V. 177 A bowe of u. **1530** PALSGR. 234/1 Iewe wode to make bowes, *hyf. Ibid.* 291/2 Yowe to make bowes of, *hyf.* **1545** ASCHAM *Toxoph.* (Arb.) 113 Ewe of all other thynges, is that, wherof perfite shootyng woulde haue a bowe made. **1590** SPENSER *F.Q.* I. i. 9 The Eugh obedient to the benders will. **1593** SHAKS. *Rich. II*, III. ii. 117 Their Bowes Of double fatall Eugh. **1619** DRAYTON *Odes* xvii. 73 With Spanish Ewgh so strong, Arrowes a Clothyard long. *a* **1700** EVELYN *Diary* 18 Apr. 1680, One roome parquetted with yew, which I lik'd well. **1805** SCOTT *Last Minstr.* III. xx, My bow of yew to a hazel wand. **1899** E. J. CHAPMAN *Drama of Two Lives, Snake-Witch* 32 The chevron bands that edg'd the floor All shapely set in oak and yew.

c. Branches or sprigs of the tree, esp. as symbols of sadness.
c **1450** in Aungier *Syon* (1840) 349 Two bysoms made of boxe and ewe. *c* **1450** *Mirk's Festial* (MS. Claud. A. II. lf. 52), We have non olyfe þat beruth grene leves, we takon in stede of hit hew and palmes wyth, and beruth abowte on procession. **1547** *Ludlow Churchw. Acc.* (Camden) 29 Yeve and candelles at Ester to hange in the churche. **1601** SHAKS. *Twel. N.* II. iv. 56 My shrowd of white, stuck all with Ew. **1697** DRYDEN *Æneis* IV. 731 Sad Cypress, Vervain, Eugh, compose the Wreath. **1820** SHELLEY *Prometh. Unb.* IV. 16 Strew, oh, strew Hair, not yew! Wet the dusty pall with tears, not dew!

¶ **d.** Applied to some flowering plants.
1653 R. SANDERS *Physiogn.* Pref. b 2, The flowers of plants having the resemblance of Butterflies..; as our English Gandergoose, the flower of Beans, Woodbine, Ew, and Ragwort. **1674** tr. *Scheffer's Lapland* 141 The thin leaved heath, that bears a Berry, which some call ground Ewe.

2. A bow made of the wood of the yew.
1598 SYLVESTER *Du Bartas* II. i. IV. *Handicrafts* 490 Through a Forrest Tubal (with his Yew And ready quiver) did a Boar pursue. **1697** DRYDEN *Æneis* IX. 854 At the full stretch of both his Hands, he drew, And almost join'd the Horns of the tough Eugh. *a* **1718** PRIOR *Henry & Emma* 345 To send the Arrow from the twanging Yew. **1728** RAMSAY *Archers diverting themselves* 13 To see them draw the bended yew. **1817** SCOTT *Harold* II. iii, When from Wulfstane's bended yew Sprung forth the grey-goose shaft.

3. *attrib.* and *Comb.*, as ***yew-berry, -bough, -flat, -frond, -hedge, -leaf, -stock, -wood;*** made of yew-wood, as ***yew-bow, -panel; yew-besprinkled, -crested, -hedged, -leaved, -roofed*** adjs. See also YEW-TREE.
c **1000** *Sax. Leechd.* II. 350 Do him þis læcedome ..*eowberʒe..ofʒeot mid ealaþ. **1768** G. WHITE *Selborne, To Pennant* 8 Oct., The ousel..fed on yew-berries. **1820** KEATS *Melancholy* i, Make not your rosary of yew-berries. **1851** G. MEREDITH *Love in the Valley* vii, Threading it with colour, like yewberries the yew. **1868** MORRIS *Earthly Par.*, *Man born to be King* 1479 The feet Of the long *yew-besprinkled hill. **1867** —— *Jason* VII. 137 She..to a *yew-bough made the boat's head fast. **1558** *Nottingham Rec.* IV. 123 A dosyn of *ewe bowes. [**1622** *Inv.* (Nottingham) in *N. & Q.* 1st Ser. VI. 10/1 Foure Spanishe viewe bowes.] **1727** SOMERVILLE *Yeoman of Kent* 9 Bow-men..Whose good yew-bows, and sinews strong, Drew arrows of a cloth-yard long. **1860** LONGF. *Wayside Inn, K. Olaf* xx. i, From his yew-bow, tipped with silver, Flew the arrows fast. **1814** SCOTT *Flora Macivor's Song* xi, The *yew-crested bonnet o'er tresses of grey! **1922** JOYCE *Ulysses* 491 The walls are tapestried with a paper of *yewfronds. *a* **1763** SHENSTONE *Ess. Men & Mann.* Wks. 1777 II. 116 Lord D——'s high shorn *yew-edges. **1777** MRS. THRALE *Let. to Johnson* 18 Sept., A spirit of innovation has however reached even these at last... A yew hedge, or an eugh hedge if you will. **1832** MISS MITFORD *Village* Ser. v. *Christmas Amusem.* 105 From the yew-hedge to the fountain. **1830** SCOTT *Doom of Devorgoil* I. i, The *yew-hedged garden. **1688** HOLME *Armoury* II. 80/1 He beareth Argent, a *Yew leaf slipped. **1731** MILLER *Gard. Dict.* s.v. *Abies*, The Silver, or *Yew-leav'd Firr Tree. **1776** WITHERING *Bot. Arrangem.* I. 680 Yew-leaved Feathermoss. *a* **1691** AUBREY *Wilts* (Royal Soc. MS.) 263 (Halliw.) With box and *ewgh pannells of about six inches square. **1897** A. DE VERE in Ld. Tennyson *Tennyson* I. xiii. 293 The *yew-roofed cloister of Muckross. **1483** *Cath. Angl.* 118 An *Ev stok, *taxum.* **1613** *Holmesfield Crt. Rolls* in *Sheffield Gloss.* (1888) Addenda s.v. *Ewe forth*, *Ewe Wood. **1830** TENNYSON *Oriana* 19 In the yew-wood black as night.

†**yew,** *v. local. Obs.* Also **yaw.** (See quots.)
1748 W. BROWNRIGG *Art of Making Common Salt* II. iv. 131 At the Lemington works.. They boil the brine violently till a thin skin of salt appears on its surface. [*Note*] They say then that the brine begins to yew. **1828-32** WEBSTER, *Yaw*, To rise in blisters, breaking in white froth, as cane juice in the sugar works... West Indies. *Ibid.*, *Yew*, to rise, as scum on the brine in boiling at the salt works.

yew, repr. a vulgar pronunc. of YOU. Also **yewall** = YOU-ALL *pers. pron.*
1890 KIPLING *Abaft Funnel* (1909) 272 'Do *yew* know,' as the Private Secretary said at Simla,..'it's remarkably hard for an Anglo-Indian to get along in England.' **1921** H. WILLIAMSON *Beautiful Years* 204 'Yew wait... Common as dirt, are we?..Yew wait, young cocky-boy.' 'Yes, yew wait, yew slug-face, bag o' bones.' **1968** A. DIMENT *Great Spy Race* i. 8 How can I help yew? **1977** *Custom Car* Nov. 14/1 Thank yewall. **1981** P. MACDONALD *One Way Street* xix. 189 Yew just scoot, yew an' young John.

yew(e: see EWE *sb.*[1], GIVE, YEO *sb.*[1], YOU, YULE.

yewar, -er, obs. forms of EWER[2].
1538 ELYOT, *Gutturnium*, a lauer, or yewer [**1552** HULOET, yewar]. **1582** N. LICHEFIELD tr. *Castanheda's Conq. E. Ind.* xvii. 44 A certein yewer ye which had a high foot.

yewel, obs. form of JEWEL.

yewen (ˈjuːən), *a.* Now *rare* or *arch.* Also 6 **ewghen, eughen,** 6–8 **ewen,** 7 **yeughen.** [f. YEW *sb.* + -EN[4]. Cf. MHG. *îwîn*, G. *eiben*.] Made of the wood of the yew; consisting of yew-trees.
1563 *Norwich Depos.* (1905) 77 A ewen bow. **1590** SPENSER *F.Q.* I. xi. 19 So farre as Ewghen bow a shaft may send. **1591** —— *M. Hubberd* 747 His stiffe armes to stretch with Eughen bowe. **1654** C. WASE *Gratius' Cyneget.* Pref. b 3 b, A round hoop of yeughen wood made of boughs. *a* **1700** KEN *Edmund* Poet. Wks. 1721 II. 262 As warlike Archers bend long ewen Bows. **1861** READE *Cloister & H.* xxiv, In spite of their laws and their proclamations to keep up the yewen bow. **1884** E. V. BOYLE *Days & Hours in Garden* vi. 89 The square-topped Yewen hedge.

yewer: see YURE.

yewisse, yewl, yewlow, yewre, yewrie: see IWIS, YULE, YELLOW, EWER[1], EWERY[1].

yew-tree (ˈjuːtriː). = YEW *sb.* 1.
1398 TREVISA *Barth. De P.R.* XVII. clxi. (1495) Vj/1 An Ewe tree..is a tree with venim & poyson. *c* **1425** *Voc.* in Wr.-Wülcker 646/13 *Hec taxus*, hawtre [*sic*], newtre. *c* **1440** *Promp. Parv.* 507/2 V tree (*K.* uv tre), *taxus.* **1538** TURNER *Libellus, Taxus*, an Vhe tre. **1593** in *N. & Q.* 1st Ser. (1852) VI. 64/1 Itm. for leadinge of earthe to ye benche about the yewe tree,..ij^s. iiij^d. **1607** TOPSELL *Four-f. Beasts* 554 The rotten part of Eue-tree. **1612** WEBSTER *White Devil* I. ii. 261 Into a church-yard, where a goodly Eu tree Spred her large roote in ground. *a* **1697** AUBREY *Surrey* (1718) III. 46 In this Church-Yard is an Ew-Tree, ten Yards in Compass. **1750** GRAY *Elegy* iv, Beneath those rugged elms, that yew-tree's shade, Where heaves the turf in many a mould'ring heap. **1814** SCOTT *Ld. of Isles* v. xix, The yew-tree lent its shadow dark. **1864** TENNYSON *En. Ard.* 732 An ancient evergreen, A yewtree.

attrib. and *Comb.* **1688** HOLME *Armoury* II. 52/1 He beareth Argent, a Yew Tree Branch Fructed. **1845** R. S. SURTEES *Hillingdon Hall* x. 145 A massive yew-tree-lined walk. **1866** GEO. ELIOT *F. Holt* Introd. 4 Its untidy kitchen-garden and cone-shaped yew-tree arbour. **1889** *Science-Gossip* XXV. 118/2 The poisonous nature of yew-tree leaves.

Hence **yew-tree'd** *a.*, planted with yew-trees.
1872 MRS. A. GATTY *Bk. Sun-dials* Introd. p. xxii, The quaint yew-tree'd garden.

yewys, obs. form of IWIS.

yex (jɛks), **yesk** (jɛsk), *sb.* Now *dial.* Forms: 1 **ʒesca, iesca, ʒescea, ʒeocsa, ʒeoxa, ʒeohsa, ʒihsa,** 4–6 **yoxe,** 5–7 **yexe,** 6 **yeax, yeske,** 6–7 **yeox(e,** 7 **yex, yox,** 7, 9 *Sc.* **yesk,** 9 **yisk, yucks, yeux, yokes.** [OE. *ʒesca, ʒeocsa*, **ʒicsa* (*ʒihsa*), related to next.] An act of yexing; †a sob (*obs.*); a hiccup or the hiccups.
a **700** *Epinal Gloss.* 958 *Singultus*, iesca. *c* **725** *Corpus Gloss.* (Hessels) T 71 *Tentigo*, ʒesca. *a* **1000** *Boeth. Metr.* ii. 5 Me þios siccetung hafað agæled, ðes ʒeocsa. *c* **1000** *Sax. Leechd.* II. 60 þam monnum þe for fylle ʒihsa sliђð. **1398** TREVISA *Barth. De P.R.* XVII. ix. (Tollem. MS.), To abate þe ȝoxe [*ed.* **1495** yexe] þat comeþ of fulnesse. **1530** PALSGR. 291/1 Yeske that cometh of the stomake, *sanglout.* **1547** BOORDE *Brev. Health* cccxxv, It is named the yexe or the hicket, and of some the dronken mans cough. **1548** PATTEN *Exped. Scot.* Pref. c vj b *marg.*, [They] w^t a yoxe, do soon dye. **1565** HARDING *Answ. Jewel* ii. 138 The yeax and vomite followed. **1578** LYTE *Dodoens* II. lxxiv. 246 Two or three branches of Myntes..do swage and appease the Hicquet or yeoxe. **1601** HOLLAND *Pliny* XXVIII. xx. II. 342 They shall find a remedie for the yox. **1609** —— *Amm. Marcell.* XXX. ix. 392 The yex that often shooke his flankes and small guts. **1621** J. TAYLOR (Water P.) *Goose* Wks. (1630) I. 110/2 One staggering there hath got the drunken yox. **1808** JAMIESON, *Yeisk, Yesk, s.*, a single affection of hiccup, S. as, He gae a great yesk, S. B. *eesk*, id. **1818** TODD, *Yux*..: sometimes pronounced *yex*, and *yox*, or *yokes*.., the hiccough. **1824** MACTAGGART *Gallovid. Encycl.* 266 Drink..Which cures the yisk and waterbrash. **1876** *Whitby Gloss.*, *Yeux*, a hiccup. **1886** ELWORTHY *W. Somerset Word-bk.* s.v. *Yucks*, Why Tommy, you've a-got the yucks—drink some cold water.

yex, yesk, *v.* Now *Sc.* and *dial.* Forms: α.[1] 1 **ʒeocsian, ʒeoxian,** 3–4 **ȝoxe,** 4–6 **yoxe,** 4–7 **yexe,** 5 **ȝexe,** 6 **yeax, youx, yowx,** 6– **yex,** 9 *dial.* **yox, yocks, yaux;** α.[2] 5–6 **yeske,** 6 **yeask,** 6– **yesk;** α.[3]

4–5 ȝoske, 5 yoske. β.[1] 1 ȝiscian, 5 yiske, ȝyske, 5–6 ȝisk, ȝeisk, 9 yisk; β.[2] 5 ȝyxe. [OE. *ȝeocsian*, *ȝiscian*, corresp. to OHG. *geskôn*, *gesgizôn* 'oscitare': of imitative origin.]

†**1.** *intr.* To sob. *Obs.*

c888 ÆLFRED *Boeth.* ii. §1 Ac ic nu wepende & ȝisciende ofgeradra worda misfo. c1290 [see YEXING]. c1290 *Beket* 1536 in *S. Eng. Leg.* 150 And sore wepinde he wende forth, he ȝoxede and siȝte wel ofte. 13.. *S. Erkenwolde* 312 in Horstm. *Altengl. Leg.* (1881) 312 Þe bysshop..hade no space to speke, so spakly he ȝoskyd. 1388 WYCLIF *2 Kings* iv. 35 The child ȝoxide [1382 brethed] seuene sithis. c1440 *Alphabet of Tales* 29 And agayn he suld dy, he began at yiske. 1510 STANBRIDGE *Vocabula* (W. de W.) A iv, *Singultio*, to yeske or to sob. 1601 HOLLAND *Pliny* XVIII. xxxv. I. 614 Ravens crying one to another as if they sobbed or yexed therewith. 1629 GAULE *Holy Madn.* 283 What thinkst thou of the Body, that yelpes and yexes, at any small push?

2. To hiccup.

a1400 *Arund. MS. 42* lf. 28 b in *Promp. Parv.* 539 *note*, Anet..the sed coct, and al hot put to þe nostrelle, soffreth noȝt to galpyn, ne to rospyn, ne to ȝexyn. 1432–50, etc. [see YEXING]. c1460 J. RUSSELL *Bk. Nurture* 298 Be yoxinge, ne bolkynge, ne gronynge. 1530 PALSGR. 786/2 Whan he yesketh next, tell hym some straunge newes, and he shall leave it. 1544 PHAER *Regim. Lyfe* (1545) X vij, It chaunceth oftentymes that a chylde yeaxeth out of measure. Wherfore it is expedyent to make the stomake eygre afore it be fed. 1653 URQUHART *Rabelais* I. xxi. 90 He..yawned, spitted, coughed, yexed. 1656 BLOUNT *Glossogr.*, To *Yex*, is that we do, when we have the Hicket or Hick up. 1711 RAMSAY *On Maggy Johnstoun* vi, We did baith glow'r and gaunt..yesk, and maunt. 1804 COUPER *Poetry* II. 220 Weel like ye, yeeskin', to be there, Though morn's a head-ach.

3. *trans.* To belch forth. Also *intr.* to belch; to hawk; to expectorate.

c1386 CHAUCER *Reeve's T.* 231 (Ellesm.) He yexeth [*v.rr.* ȝeskeþ, ȝoxeth] and he speketh thurgh the nose As he were on the quakke or on the pose. 1513 DOUGLAS *Æneis* III. ix. 82 His nek fourth of the cave He straucht, fordrunkin,.. Bokkis furth and ȝiskis of ȝoustir mony streme. *Ibid.* VIII. iv. 36 At his mouth..His faderis reky flamb furth ȝiskit he. *Ibid.* 154 A laithly smok he ȝiskis blak as hell. a1555 LYNDESAY in *Bannatyne MS.* (Hunter. Club) 521/1441 Scho puft and yiskit with sic riftis, That verry dirt come furth with driftis. 1560 PHAER *Æneid.* IX. (1562) D iv, He their maisters head wt sword ofchopt, & left his tronke furth yexing belching blood. 1567 GOLDING *Ovid's Met.* V. 58 He ..Beheld him yesking forth his ghost. 1819 W. TENNANT *Papistry Storm'd* (1827) 154 It garr'd him yesk his drammach. 1882 *W. Worc. Gloss.*, *Yox*, *v.* to cough, or spit up. 1893 *S.E. Worc. Gloss.*, *Yaux*, *v.* to cough, or expectorate. 'I don't want no bacca smokers in my kitchen, yauxin' an' spettin' about.'

Hence **'yexer**, one who yexes.

1611 COTGR., *Sengloteur*, one that hath the hickocke; a yexer.

†**'yexen**, *v. Obs.* In 5 ȝyksen, ȝosken. [f. YEX *v.* + -EN[5].] = YEX *v.*

14.. *Chaucer's Reeve's T.* 231 (Camb. MS.) He ȝyksneth & spekyth þourw þe nose. c1430 *Chev. Assigne* 108 They chyuered for colde as cheuerynge chyldren, They ȝoskened, & cryde out & þat a man herde.

†**yexiled** [Y- 4], exiled.

1340 *Ayenb.* 30 Men and wyfmen and children deserited and y-exiled.

yexing, yesking, *vbl. sb.* Now *Sc.* and *dial.* Forms: see YEX, YESK *v.* [OE. *ȝeocsung*, *ȝeoxung* = OHG. *gesgizunga*: see YEX, YESK *v.* and -ING[1].] The action of the vb. YEX; †sobbing (*obs.*); (most freq.) hiccuping.

c1050 *Voc.* in Wr.-Wülcker 423/12 *In singultum*, in sicettunge and ȝeoxunge. c1050 *Suppl. Ælfic's Gloss.* ibid. 179/4 *Singultus*, ȝoecsung. 1297 R. GLOUC. (Rolls) 801 Mid ȝoxinge & gret wop þus he bigan is mone. 1382 WYCLIF *Lam.* iii. 56 Ne turne thou awei thin ere fro my sobbing [*v.r.* ȝoxyng] and cries. 1387–8 T. USK *Test. Love* I. i. (Skeat) l. 6 Any maner disese outward, is sobbing maner, sheweth sorowful yexinge from within. 1398 TREVISA *Barth. De P.R.* VII. xlvi. (1495) q vj b, Yoxynge is the sowne in the nose of vyolent meuynge of ye stomak. a1400–50 *Wars Alex.* 5042 So did his princes..With ȝedire ȝoskingis & ȝerre ȝett out to grete. 1432–50 tr. *Higden* (Rolls) V. 389 Pereschenge moche peple in yoskenge or nesynge. c1440 *Promp. Parv.* 539/1 Ȝyxynge, *singultus.* a1470 TIPTOFT *Orat. G. Flamineus* (Caxton 1481) f iv, He in his drunkenesse with his stombling yoxing & prating. 1483 *Cath. Angl.* 426/2 A ȝiskynge, *singultus.* 1510 STANBRIDGE *Vocabula* (W. de W.) A v, *Oscedo*, yeskynge. 1530 PALSGR. 291/1 Yexing, *hocquet.* 1543 TRAHERON tr. *Vigo's Chirurg.* III. ix. 96 b/1 Great apostemations..whyche cause rigours, fieuers, spasmes, youxinge. 1544 PHAER *Regim. Lyfe* (1545) F j, Hycket or yeaskyng, is an euyll mouyng of the vertue expulsiue of the stomake. 1562 TURNER *Bathes* 9 b, It healeth also the hitchcock or yiskinge. 1569 R. ANDROSE tr. *Alexis' Secr.* IV. I. 35 To remedie the yexings of the stomacke and vomitings. 1600 DARRELL *True Narr.* 6 A bygg blacke catt..threwe her backward taking from her the vse both of her eyes and handes, which with yesking were euer losed. 1613 BP. ANDREWES *96 Serm., Eph.* iv. 30 (1629) 652 The upbraiding or yexing of the heart (as Abigail excellently termeth it). 1684 ROBT. JOHNSON *Enchir. Med.* III. iv. 152 [The Hicket] is called in English a sobbing or yexing. 1887 F. T. HAVERGAL *Heref. Wds.* 38 He suffers so from yocksing. 1887 *Jamieson's Dict., Suppl.* s.v. *Yeterie*, A yetrie yisking.

yé-yé (jeje), *a.* (*sb.*) Also Ye-Ye. [a. Fr., tr. of *yeah-yeah*, redupl. of YEAH *adv.*; the form *yeah-yeah* freq. occurred in Eng. popular songs of the 1960s.] Designating or pertaining to the modern style of music, dress, etc., associated with France in the 1960s. Also applied to persons. Occas. as *sb.*

1960 *Daily Tel.* 24 Oct. 9/3, I found one dramatically *yé-yé* shop in old Lyons..which sells only British goods of a somewhat bizarre kind. 1966 *Guardian* 1 Apr. 10/7 In Paris, clothes are still a lot more class-divisive with Ye-Ye girls and debutantes thoroughly opposed. *Ibid.* 7 Apr. 8 Paris once had twenty music halls; now it has two—the Olympia, which caters more for *yé-yé* singers, and Bobino. *Ibid.*, The Bobino..is no place for *yé-yés.* 1967 *Sat. Rev.* 4 Mar. 49 Amplified like yé-yé music. 1968 *N.Y. Times* 3 July 30 The orchestra Chez Régine will play anything 'from yé-yé to regular music'. *Ibid.* 23 July 42 The name of a high-priced haute couture boutique here, run by Arlette Nastat, a forever yé-yé designer. 1972 M. GOLDBERG *Karamanov Equations* xvii. 161 He sipped a coffee and a Cinzano..watching the mini-skirted yé-yé girls and their hairy escorts parading by. 1979 J. WYLLIE *To catch Viper* viii. 49 Coca-Cola signs and bars, fashionable young women in miniskirts and teen-age *yé-yé* boys.

yeyed, ? = *yeþed*, pa. pple. of EATHE *v.*, to ease.

c1425 *Abraham's Sacr.* 334 in *Non-Cycle Myst. Plays* (1909) 49 A! Lord, I thanke The of Thy gret grace, Now am I yeyed on dyuers wysse.

yeyn-, ȝeyn-: see GAIN-.

yeyr, obs. Sc. form of YEAR[1].

yeyrd, yeyre, obs. Sc. form of EARTH, AIR *sb.*[1]

1533 *Abstr. Protocols Town Clerks of Glasgow* (1879) IV. 60 Jhon Muir..gaef staet, be yeyrd and stane, of ane bak tenement. a1500 *Coventry Corpus Chr. Pl.* 37/126 When the sun and the stare In the yeyre togeythur warre.

yez, *pers. pron. dial.* (esp. *Anglo-Ir.*). Also **yees, yeez, yiz.** [f. YE with plural inflexion *s.*] You (said to more than one).

1804 MARIA EDGEWORTH *Ennui* vi, Mind the big hole in the middle of the bridge, God bless *yees!* 1828 T. C. CROKER *Fairy Leg. S. Irel.* II. 110 'Boys', says she, 'I hope yez have made a good dinner.' 1842 S. LOVER *Handy Andy* xxxiv. 280 Who are yiz at all, gintlemin? 1884 D. BOUCICAULT *Shaughraun* I. iv. 10/2 Away with yeez—hide! 1901 M. FRANKLIN *My Brilliant Career* xvii. 147, I have the table laid out for both of yez. 1908 J. JOYCE *Let.* 8 Dec. (1966) II. 226, I will send him very gladly if that will make yiz all happy and loving. 1939 —— *Finnegans Wake* 8 Now yiz are in the Willingdone Museyroom. 1962 D. PHILLIPS *Lichty Nichts* 30 Yez ur gitn a rare day. 1966 [see JACK *sb.*[1] 1 d]. 1969 in Halpert & Story *Christmas Mumming in Newfoundland* 211 Some people will say, 'How many of yez?' and the janneys will shout back, 'Two or three.' 1977 *Transatlantic Rev.* LX. 147 'Aye, OK,' I says. 'How but? Did yiz arrange that afore?' 1977 *Sounds* 9 July 8/5 It's not going to be on general release and yez can't buy it at general outlets.

Yezidi, -dee ('jɛzɪdiː). Also Yeze(e)dee, Izedi, Zezidee. [Of disputed origin.] One of a religious sect found in Kurdistan, Armenia, and the Caucasus, which, while believing in a Supreme God, regards the Devil with reverential fear.

1818 KINNEIR *Journ. Asia Minor* 414 The Zezidees live in enmity with the Christians. 1819 T. HOPE *Anastasius* (1820) III. 114 The strangers were Yezidees. 1842 J. B. FRASER *Mesop. & Assyria* xiv. 328 The Yezidee religion appears to be a compound of many others strangely jumbled together. 1848 LAYARD (*title*) Nineveh and its Remains: with an Account of..the Yezidis, or Devil-Worshippers. 1852 BADGER *Nestor.* I. x. 112, I think it cannot be doubted that the term 'Yezeedee' is derived from Yezd, one of the titles applied by the ancient Persians to the Supreme Being. 1871 TYLOR *Prim. Cult.* II. xvii. 299 The Izedis or Yezidis, the so-called Devil-worshippers.

yezzy, dial. form of EASY.

1896 AUG. J. C. HARE *Story of my Life* I. iii. 178 The old Cheshire proverb—'Bout's bare but it's yezzy.'

yf, obs. form of GIVE *v.*, IF.

†**yfaȝe**, *adv. Obs.* Also 4 ifaie. [repr. OE. *ȝefæȝen* adj.: see Y- and FAIN *a.* (southern ME. *faȝe*).] Fain, gladly.

a1300 *Vox & Wolf* 199 in *Rel. Ant.* II. 276 'Woltou', quod the vox, 'srift ounderfonge, Tel thine sunnen on and on, That ther bileve never on.' 'Sone', quad the wolf, 'wel i-faie.' c1315 SHOREHAM I. 1862 Ne forþe þe moder þet hyt beer, Ne woldest þou nase y-faȝe.

†**yfailed, yfayl(l)ed** [Y- 4], failed.

c1315 SHOREHAM I. 56 Yf þou nelt nauȝt climme þos, Of heuene þou hest yfayled. 13.. *Pol. Songs* (Camden) 202 Trewth is i-faillid with fremid and sibbe. 1340 *Ayenb.* 71 Alle guodes byeþ ous yfayled. c1394 i-failed [see FAIL *v.* 12 b].

yfaired, yuayred [FAIR *v.*], made clean or pure.

1340 *Ayenb.* 107 Þane gost of wysdom, be huam bi we zuo yclensed ase gold and yuayred of alle uelþe. *Ibid.* 200.

y'faith, in faith: see FAITH *sb.* 12 b.

15.. *Chevy Chase* II. 124 'Such A-nothar captayn skotland within', he sayd, 'ye-feth shuld neuer be.' a1596 *Sir T. More* I. ii. 152 Yfaith, yfaith, they are too short for me. 1607 Y'faith [see FAITH *sb.* 12 b]. 1619 DRAYTON *Heroic. Ep.* xiii. 108 Yfaith her Queeneship little Rest should take.

†**y-falle**, *v. Obs.* Also 4 yualle. [OE. *ȝefeallan* = OHG. *gifallan*: see Y- 3 c and FALL *v.*] *intr.* To fall; to befall.

971 *Blickl. Hom.* 93 Þonne ȝefeallaþ ealle deofolȝyld. 1340 *Ayenb.* 36 Huet cas yualle. *Ibid.* 48 Hit yualþ oþerhuyl desertesoun of eyr and ualse mariages.

†**yfalle(n**, *pa. pple. Obs.* Forms: 1 ȝefeallen, 6 ivalle(n, ifalle(n, 4 yvalle, yfall, 4–5 yfalle(n, 3 yfalne. [OE. *ȝefeallen*, pa. pple. of *feallan* to FALL, *ȝefallan* (see prec.).] Fallen; also *fig.*

971 *Blickl. Hom.* 93 Seo heofon biþ ȝefeallen æt þæm feower endum middanȝeardes. c1000 *Ags. Ps.* (Th.) cxlviii. 8 Fyr, forst, hægel, and ȝefeallen snaw. a1225 *Ancr. R.* 58 Heo schulen ȝelden þet best þet is þer inne ivallen. a1250 *Owl & Night.* 514 Vor hwanne he haueþ ido his dede Ifalle is al his boldhede. 1297 R. GLOUC. (Rolls) 1537 Þe king..let bulde vp grete tounes þat were ney adoun ivalle [*MS δ* yfalle]. 1340 *Ayenb.* 176 Hou ofte he heþ yualle into zenne. 1393 LANGL. *P. Pl.* C. x. 179 Men yfalle in myschef. 1589 PUTTENHAM *Engl. Poesie* III. iv. (Arb.) 160 Many a word yfalne shall eft arise.

yfalt, ME. pa. pple. of FOLD *v.*[1]

yfare, var. I-FARE *v. Obs.*

1593 *Jack Straw* II. C iv, So did they all yfare like franticke men.

†**yfare(n** [Y- 4, FARE *v.*[1]: cf. I-FARE *v.*], gone; travelled; dealt *with.*

900–30 *O.E. Chron.* (Parker MS.) an. 894 Þa he þær to ȝefaren wæs, þa eodon hie to hiora scipum. c1205 LAY. 4690 Nes hit buten feower wiken þat þas kinge ifaren [*c* 1275 i-vare] weoren, cam Brennes riden. *Ibid.* 26425 Þa þis wes al iuare, þa wes Brennes kæisere. a1250 *Owl & Night.* 400 Ho ..wes aferd þat hire answare Ne wrþe nouht ariht ivare [*v.r.* ifare]. c1374 CHAUCER *Troylus* III. 577 Whan þat he seyde so, That Troylus was out of town y-fare. 1387 TREVISA *Higden* (Rolls) VII. 385 He was piled and i-robbed, and fare [*MS. γ* yvare] wiþ as it were a þeef. 1432–50 tr. *Higden*, *Harl. Contin.* (Rolls) VII. 515 The cuntray was foule yfare with.

yfarsyd [FARCE *v.*], stuffed.

c1430 *Two Cookery-bks.* 40 Pygge y-farsyd.

yfast, yvast [FAST *v.*[2]], fasted.

971 *Blickl. Hom.* 205 Ðære nihte þe hie þæt fæsten ȝefæst hæfdon. c1275 yuast [see FAST *v.*[2] 3]. 13.. *K. Alis.* 2419 (Laud MS.) As a wolf, þat fele dawes had yfast. c1380 *Sir Ferumb.* 2822 Gyoun þanne was teynt & paal so longe he hadde yuaste.

yfastened, set fast, fixed, fastened.

c1000 *Ags. Ps.* (Th.) lvii[i]. 7 Swa weax melteð, ȝif hit byð wearmum neah fyre ȝefæstnad. 1340 *Ayenb.* 107 Zuo yuestned ine þe loue and adrayngt in þe zuetnesse of god. c1430 *Two Cookery-bks.* 50 Þan take a dysshe y-fastenyd on þe pelys ende.

yfebled, enfeebled.

1387 TREVISA *Higden* (Rolls) VI. 363 Englisshe men.. were moche i-feble [*MSS. β and γ* yfebled].

†**yfed**, *pa. pple. Obs.* [OE. *ȝeféd*, pa. pple. of *fédan* FEED *v.*] Fed.

a1100 *Aldhelm Gloss.* I. 3753 (Napier 100/1) *Holusculis uesceretur*,..ofætum wære ȝefed. c1205 LAY. 13573 He us haueð wel iued. a1310 in Wright *Lyric P.* xxxix. 110 Wher he were ythe mone boren ant y-fed. 1387 TREVISA *Higden* (Rolls) VI. 251 Realliche i-cloþed and likyngliche i-fedde [*MS. γ* yved]. c1450 *Crt. of Love* 975 In wofull hour I got was, welaway! In wofull hour fostred and y-fed. 1647 H. MORE *Song of Soul* II. *Infin. Worlds* c, Where all take life,.. And then renew'd with pleasure be yfed. 1728 POPE *Dunc.* III. 188 On parchment scraps y-fed.

yfel(l, obs. ff. EVIL.

†**yfele**, *v. Obs.* Forms: 1 ȝefelan, 2–4 ifele, 3 ivele, 3–4 yvele, 4 yfele, 7 yfeele. [OE. *ȝefélan*: see Y- 3 c and FEEL *v.*] To feel.

c893 [see FEEL *v.* 1]. a1240 *Ureisun* in *O.E. Hom.* I. 201 Hwi ne iuele ich þe imine breoste so swete ase þu ert? c1305 *Judas Isc.* 18 in *E.E.P.* (1862) 107 Swiþe heo gan iwite And yfele þat he was mid childe. 1387 TREVISA *Higden* (Rolls) VI. 13 Þe same merk and tokene þat he hadde i-felt [*MS. γ* yveld] in his soule he bare alwey after i-sene. c1634 CARTWRIGHT *Ordinary* III. i. (1651) 36, I no where hoart yfeele, but on mine head.

†**yfell**, *v. Obs.* Also 3–4 yvelle. [OE. *ȝefyllan*, *-fiellan*: see Y- 3 c and FELL *v.*] *trans.* To strike down, fell. Also **yfelled** *pa. pple.*

c893 ÆLFRED *Oros.* IV. vi. §7 Þa hio [*sc.* seo nædre] ȝefylled wæs. 971 *Blickl. Hom.* 221 Ða wolde he Sanctus Martinus..ðæt gyld abrecan & ȝefyllan. c1205 LAY. 14838 We heom habbeoð ifelled..& mid wepnen ifelled. a1300 *K. Horn* 58 Hy smyten vnder schelde Þat sume hit yfelde. 13.. *K. Alis.* 3363 (Laud MS.) Wiþ dynt of spere þou were yfeld. a1400 *Octouian* 1525 Syx baners were y-feld.

†**yfere**, *sb. Obs.* Forms: 1 ȝefera, 2–3 ifere, ivere, 3 iuære, iuare, ifære, ifeire, yfere. *Pl.* 1 ȝeferan, 2 ȝeferen, 2–3 iferen, 2–4 ifere, iuere, 3–4 yfere, yuere, 3 iveres. [OE. *ȝeféra*, f. *ȝe-* Y- 1 a + *fœr-*, mutated f. *fōr-*: *faran* to go.] A companion, mate, fellow, associate.

c870 *Codex Aureus Inscr.*, Ic Aelfred aldormon & Werburg min ȝefera. c1000 ÆLFRIC *Gen.* iii. 12 Þæt wif, þæt þu me forȝeafe to ȝeferan. a1200 *Moral Ode* 229 In helle his hunger and þurst, twa uuele iuere. c1205 LAY. 26012 Arður hine teh Bi-siden his iferen [*c* 1275 iveres]. a1225 *Juliana* 48 Englene ifere ant arcanglene freond. 1297 R. GLOUC. (Rolls) 5994 Vor suan..adde euere is yuere, Þre velawes þat next him were. a1300 *K. Horn* 235 Hom rod Aylmer þe kyng, Ant horn wiþ him..Ant alle his yfere. 13.. *K. Alis.* 6906 (Laud MS.) Þoo wepe þe kyng & hise yfere.

†**yfere**, *adv. Obs.* (from 6 to 8 *arch.*) Forms: 3–4 ifere, yvere, 4–8 yfere, 5 yfeere, yffere, 6 yfeere, yfeare, *Sc.* yfeir. β. 4 yferes, 6 *Sc.* yferis. [Origin uncertain. The available evidence favours on

the whole the supposition that the adverb arose out of the predicative use of *ifere*, pl. of YFERE *sb.* 'companions, associates', hence 'associated' (see introductory quots. below); if this were so, the form *in fere* (from *c* 1330) arose from analysing *ifere* as *i*, IN *prep.* + FERE *sb.*² With the *β*-form cf. TOGETHERS, and see -S *suffix*.] In company; together. (Extensively used in ME. poetry as a riming tag; rare in prose.)

[*a* **1200** [see YFERE *sb.*]. *c* **1205** LAY. 27435 Twein kinges þere æuere weoren ifere. *c* **1275** *Ibid.* 24750 Euere tweine and tweyne wenden i-vere [*earlier text* Æuer tweie and tweie tuhte to-somne ælc mid his honde heold his iuere]. *a* **1300** *S. Michael* in *Pop. Treat. Sci.* (1841) 136 Ther is turment strong Of wynd, of water, and of fure, and thaye threo were i-fere.]

a **1300** *XV Signa* 117 in *E.E.P.* (1862) 11 Al þe see sal draw ifere as a walle to stand up ri3t. *c* **1330** *Assump. Virg.* (B.M. MS.) 859 Cryst of heuene.. Amonge þe apostles sone he ly3t, And gret hem alle yfere. *c* **1350** *Will. Palerne* 2267 In caue þei lyen, & slepen samen y-fere. **13..** *Gosp. Nicod.* (A.) 751 And þai for skorne sayd alle yfere. *c* **1374** CHAUCER *Troylus* II. 1116 With þat þey wente arm in arm y fere [*v. rr.* in fere, yfere] In to þe gardeyn from þe chaumbre doun. *c* **1380** *Sir Ferumb.* 1269 We buþ kny3tes alle y-vere y-born in douce fraunce. *c* **1400** *26 Pol. Poems* xvii. 192 What soule is syk, lay þat herbe aboue, Hit makeþ hool al y-fere. **1426** LYDG. *De Guil. Pilgr.* 2295 And whan I herde al thys yfere, I wex abaysshed in my chere. *c* **1430** *Two Cookery-bks.* 18 Þan take Pepyr, an Safroun, an Brede, y-grounde y-fere. **1508** DUNBAR *Goldyn Targe* 147 Syne folowit all hir dameselis yfere. **1566** DRANT *Horace Sat.* I. i. A ij b, They feede and feele the fruit of that, which once they gott yfeare. **1583** MELBANCKE *Philotimus* S ij, As litle ioy I feare, should we feele yfere, as did the two vnsensible pictures. **1590** SPENSER *F.Q.* I. ix. 1 O goodly golden chaine, wherewith yfere The vertues linked are in louely wize. **1600** *England's Helicon* F j b, Harpalus and eke Corin were Heard-men both yfere. **1642** H. MORE *Song of Soul* I. II. lxxv, Then let's all go yfere. **1748** THOMSON *Cast. Indol.* II. xxxv, And much they moraliz'd as thus yfere they yode. **1768** DOWNMAN *Land of Muses* lv, There passed by the sister Graces bright, .. Benevolence and Gratitude y-fere.

β. ? *c* **1390** *Form of Cury* I. xxii. (1780) 20 Take brede and þᵉ self broth and drawe it up yferes. **1513** DOUGLAS *Æneis* VI. v. 25 Baith matrouns, and thair husbandis, all yferis.

yfern: see FERN *a.* and *adv. Obs.*

yferre, pseudo-arch. f. AFAR *adv.*

c **1634** CARTWRIGHT *Ordinary* v. iv. (1651) 84, I do not reche One bean for all. This Buss is a blive guerdon. Hence Carlishnesse yferre.

†**yfet**, *pa. pple. Obs.* Also 1 **3efett**, 2–4 **ifet**, 3 **ifat**, 3–4 **yuet**, 4 **y-feet**. [OE. *3efett*, pa. pple. of (*3e*)*fetian*: see Y- 4 and FET *v.*] Brought, carried, fetched; acquired.

c **893** ÆLFRED *Oros.* IV. vi. §8 Amilcor, se wæs of Sicilium him to fultume 3efett. *c* **1175** *Lamb. Hom.* 147 And wunie ine þet clenesse þet he haueð et his fulluhte ifet. *a* **1225** *Leg. Kath.* 1296 Fif siðe tene, icudde & icorene & of feorrene ifat. **1297** R. GLOUC. (Rolls) 5721 Þe monekes out of abendone verst were þuder yuet. *c* **1330** R. BRUNNE *Chron. Wace* (Rolls) 1624 Þe castel was mad & set, & þer godes þerto yfet. *a* **1400** *Octouian* 237 Floraunce was dyder y-feet. **1555** PHAER *Æneid.* I. (1558) C j b, Giftes with him he had to bring from Troy destroyed yfet.

†**yfetered** [Y- 4], fettered.

a **1000** *Riddles* liii. 4 Þa wæron 3enumne nearwum bendum, 3efeterade fæste togædre. *a* **1225** *Ancr. R.* 32 Heo liggeð mid iren heuie iveotered. **13..** *Pol. Songs* (Camden) 218 Yfetered were ys legges under his horse wombe. *c* **1420** [see FETTER *v.*¹ 1].

yfethered, yfeyned, ME. pa. pples. of FEATHER, FEIGN.

yff, obs. form of IF.

yff, yffen, obs. ff. *give, given*: see GIVE *v.*

c **1435** *Torr. Portugale* 2009 God, that died vppon the Rode, Yff grace, that she mete with good! **1484** *Cov. Leet Bk.* 519 Of which somme x li. was yffen to theym a3eyn.

†**y'filled**, *pa. pple. Obs.* [OE. *3efylled*, pa. pple. of (*3e*)*fyllan*: see Y- 4 and FILL *v.*] Filled; fulfilled.

c **900** tr. *Bæda's Hist.* IV. iii. (1890) 266 Þæt wæs swa soðlice mid dæd 3efylled, swa him to cweden wæs. *c* **1175** *Lamb. Hom.* 5 Þa hit wes ifullet þet ysaias þe prophete iwite3ede. *c* **1205** LAY. 6942 Þis lond wes on griðe and ifulled mid gode. **1297** R. GLOUC. (Rolls) 1072 Wonder it is.. of þi noble gentrise þat is so noble anerþe iwolt wiþ so vil coueitise. **1387** TREVISA *Higden* (Rolls) VII. 337 Lanfranc hadde y-fylled [*MS. γ* y-vulled] his witt wiþ al vertues. **1422** YONGE tr. *Secr. Secr.* 241 Whan a man sittyth atte mette he sholde wythdrawe his honde afor that he be y-fillit. **1642** H. MORE *Song of Soul* II. III. IV. xxiv, So all things he yfild with their wish'd good.

†**y'find**, *v. Obs.* [OE. *3efindan*: see Y- 3 c and FIND *v.*] To find.

c **950** *Lindisf. Gosp.* Matt. xviii. 28 *Inuenit unum de conseruis suis*,.. 3efand enne of efne-ðegnum. *c* **1200** *Moral Ode* 243 (Trin. Coll. MS.) Hie secheð reste þar non nis ac hie hies ne mu3en ifinden. **1297** R. GLOUC. (Rolls) 5779 Vor he sende þe kinge word þat he ne mi3te namo vinde. **1340** *Ayenb.* 130 Þou gest in-to helle huer þou sselt yuinde ver and bernston. **1387** TREVISA *Higden* (Rolls) VI. 405 Ethelwoldus .. destroyede al þat he my3te fynde [*MS. γ* yvynde] anon to Crekanforde. **1412–20** LYDG. *Chron. Troy* I. 537 Famous Argus, þat.. first þat art y-founde.

†**yfixed** [Y- 4], fixed.

1742 SHENSTONE *Schoolmistr.* xviii, This Hand in Mouth y-fix'd, that rends his Hair.

yflawe, ivla3en [FLAY *v.*], flayed.

c **1205** LAY. 27377 Heo sculleð beon isla3ene, and summe quic iula3ene. **13..** *K. Alis.* 894 (Laud MS.) Þou shalt ben .. quyk of þine hyde y-flawe.

yfled [FLEE *v.*], fled.

c **1374** CHAUCER *Troylus* IV. 661 The swyfte fame.. was þorugh-out Troye y-fled with preste wynges.

yflemed, yvlemd [FLEME *v.*], put to flight; exiled.

c **893** ÆLFRED *Oros.* VI. xxxiv. §4 He 3efeaht wiþ Gotan, & 3efliemed wearð. *c* **1205** LAY. 7658 Hu he wæs mid his færde i-flæmde of þissen earde. **1297** R. GLOUC. (Rolls) 5609 Vor a traytour of is lond lof was is name Yflemd was out of engelond. **1340** *Ayenb.* 39 Þe oþre byeþ, þe ualse yulemde, þet vlyeþ.

yflesshide [Y- 5]: see FLESHED 1.

yflet [FLEET *v.*], removed.

c **1430** *Hymns Virg.* (1867) 92 Þanne foond y me ful fer y-flet Al from god in maieste.

yfloured [Y- 5], having flowers.

1340 *Ayenb.* 136 He is ase þe smale ule3e þet make3 þet hony.. and zekþ þe ueldes yfloured.

yflowe(n¹, **iflo3e, yvlowe**, etc. [FLEE *v.*], fled.

c **1205** LAY. 5953 Alle þe flæmen þe iflowe buð of Rome. *Ibid.* 21463 Nu is Childric iulo3en. **13..** *K. Alis.* 4486 (Linc. Inn MS.) Darie þe kyng is yflowe. **1387** TREVISA *Higden* (Rolls) IV. 225 Marcus Antonius was i-flowe [*v. rr.* yflowe, fledde].

yflowe(n², **yflone** [FLY *v.*¹], flown.

c **1000** ÆLFRIC *Hom.* II. 140 Se earn on ðam ofre 3esæt, mid fisce 3eflo3en, þone he ðærrihte 3efeng. **1297** R. GLOUC. (Rolls) 672 He let him makie wengen.. & þo he was iflowe [*v.r.* yflowe] an hei [etc.]. **1642** H. MORE *Song of Soul* II. III. IV. xxxvii, They'll all be gone In a short time, like Bats and Owls yflone At dayes approch.

y'flown [FLOW *v.*], over-flowed.

1576 FLEMING *Panopl. Epist.* 379 The land of Tyre with seas yflown.

yfo3te, yfou3te(n [FIGHT *v.*], fought.

688–95 *Laws Ine* vi. (Liebermann), Þeah hit sie on middum felda 3efohten. *c* **1205** LAY. 25693 We habbeð wið him iuohten. *c* **1330** *Arth. & Merl.* 9923 On hors keuered Cleodalis, þat al so wele yfou3ten, cert. **1387** TREVISA *Higden* (Rolls) VII. 229 Þe tweie breþeren eorles.. hadde stalworthliche i-fou3te [*MS. γ* yvo3te].

yfoiled, ME. pa. pple. of FOIL *v.*¹

yfold, -e(n [FOLD *v.*¹], folded; closed.

c **1000** *Ags. Gosp.* John xx. 7 & þæt swat-lin.. onsundron 3efealden on anre stowe. *c* **1330** *Arth. & Merl.* 1454 Vnder þo stones beþ depe in mold To dragouns fast yfold. *c* **1380** *Sir Ferumb.* 5796 Þe Ameral.. gurde hym with ys fuste y-volde. **1432–50** tr. *Higden* (Rolls) III. 253 The Roman.. helde his honde y-folden to geder.

yfolewed, yfolled: see YFULLED.

yfol3ed, yfol(o)wed, followed.

a **1175** *Cott. Hom.* 237 Se gode man þe godes lufe hað 3efol3ed. **1340** *Ayenb.* 99 Þis uerste word.. yef hit is wel onderstonde and yuol3ed. **1377** LANGL. *P. Pl.* B. III. 39 Falsenesse haued yfolwed þe al þis fyfty wyntre.

yfonded [FAND, FOND *v.*], attempted, tried, tested, tempted.

Beowulf 2301 Ðæt hæfde 3umena sum goldes 3efandod. *c* **1175** *Lamb. Hom.* 27 A þet he hine haueð al ifonded to his wille þurhut. *a* **1225** *Ancr. R.* 94 Holi men wuteð wel þet habbeð hit iuonded. **1297** R. GLOUC. (Rolls) 2245 My broþer þat god kni3t is.. & wel yfonded in armes. **1340** *Ayenb.* 117 We wylleþ wel þet we by yuonded.

yfong [FANG *v.*¹], taken, seized, received.

c **1000** ÆLFRIC *Gen.* xliv. 4 Aris and far æfter þisum mannum, and þonne þu hi3 3efangen hæbbe [etc.]. *c* **1275** *Passion of our Lord* 460 in *O.E. Misc.* 50 We after vre gultes mede habbeþ yuonge. **1297** R. GLOUC. (Rolls) 6620 At rome he was vaire auonge [*MS. δ* yfonge] & asoiled al so. **1387** TREVISA *Higden* (Rolls) V. 357 He.. deide þe 3ere after he hadde i-fonge [*MS. γ* yvonge] þe fey of holy chirche oon and twenty.

yforged, forged.

c **1386** [see FORGED *ppl. a.* 2]. **1426** LYDG. *De Guil. Pilgr.* 7671 Whan they.. Ben yforgyd off malys.

yfost(e)red, fostered.

a **1225** *Leg. Kath.* 95 Þeo.. þet hire forðfederes hefden ifostret. *c* **1325** *Lai le Freine* 389 In a covent y-fostered to be. *c* **1386** CHAUCER *Reeve's T.* 26 She was yfostred in a Nonnerye. *c* **1407** LYDG. *Reson & Sens.* 1633 That wisdam and philosophie Yfostred ben with rychesse.

†**yfound**, *pa. pple. Obs.* [Y- 4.] Found.

c **900** tr. *Bæda's Hist.* III. xi. (Schipper) 235/1 Þa his ban 3efunden & 3emeted wæron & to þære cyricean 3elædde. *c* **1175** *Lamb. Hom.* 35 Oðer he heo wat ðurh þet he heo dude him seolf, oðer he heo hafð i-escad, oðer hafð ifunden on boke. *a* **1250** *Owl & Night.* 705 Þe Nihtegale.. hedde onswere god ifunde. **1387** TREVISA *Higden* (Rolls) V. 333 Aftirward his body and þe body of his wif Gwenvere were i-founde [*MS. γ* yvounde]. **1422** YONGE tr. *Secr. Secr.* 160, I haue y-founde a man aftyr myn herte. **1470–85** MALORY *Arthur* XVII. vii. 699 Ye be wel y fonde said sir Bors. **1522** *World & Child* A v b, So fell a fyghter in a felde was there neuer yfounde.

†**yfounded** [Y- 4, FOUND *v.*²], founded.

c **1290**, etc. i-founded [see FOUND *v.*²]. **1399** LANGL. *Rich. Redeles* III. 265 It is not vnknowen.. That rewlers of rewmes .. Were not yffoundid.. To leue al at likynge. *c* **1430** *Freemasonry* 394 He schal thenne be chasted after the lawe That was y-fownded by olde dawe.

yfo(u)rmed, formed, informed.

1297 R. GLOUC. (Rolls) 3179 Yfourmed [*v.r.* yformed] as a dragon as red ase fur. *c* **1374** CHAUCER *Troylus* IV. 451 Make no comparyson To creature y-formed here by kynde. **1402** *Pol. Poems* (Rolls) II. 43 Jak, thi formur is a fole, that thus thee hath yfourmed. *c* **1420** [see FORM *v.*¹ 3].

yfracled, yfreklet: see FRECKLED *ppl. a.* 2.

yfra(u)ght, fraught.

c **1412** HOCCLEVE *De Reg. Princ.* 858 My schip is wel ney with dispeir y-fraght. **1576** GASCOIGNE *Steele Glas* 363 Such as have their stables ful yfraught, With pampred Jades. **1598** SYLVESTER *Du Bartas* II. i. IV. *Handicrafts* 108 The Trees with thousand fruits yfraught. **1647** H. MORE *Song of Soul* II. *Infin. Worlds* xlv, As if this empty space with bodies were yfraught.

yfrayght [cf. FREIGHT *pa. pple.*], freighted.

1561 B. GOOGE *Palingenius' Zodiac Life* Bk. to Rdr., Momus there doth ryde at flote, with scornefull tonges yfrayght.

yfrede *v.* [Y- 3 c], to feel, perceive, experience.

c **888**, etc. [see FREDE *v.*]. *c* **1275** *Sinners Beware* 316 in *O.E. Misc.* 82 To day ye schuleþ y-frede And vnder-fo luþre mede. *c* **1315** SHOREHAM I. 170 Þa3 we ne mowe hyt nau3t ise, Ne forþe ine bodie iurede.

yfree *v.* [Y- 3 c], to free.

688–95 *Laws Ine* lxxiv. (Liebermann), Þonne mot hine se hlaford 3efreo3ean. *a* **1000** *Paternoster* ii. 31 Wið yfele 3efreo us. *c* **1205** LAY. 475 Heo biddeð þe mid freonscipe, þat þu heom ifreoie. **1340** *Ayenb.* 86 Þe guodemen in þise wordle, þet god heþ yvryd be grace.. uram þe þreldome of þe dyeule. *c* **1425** [see FREE *v.* 2].

yfrendg'de [Y- 4], fringed.

1594 CAREW *Tasso* I. xiv, He puts on siluer wings, yfrendg'de with gold.

yfret(ed¹ [FRET *v.*¹], eaten, worn away or into holes.

c **950** *Lindisf. Gosp.* Matt. vi. 19 *Ubi aerugo et tinea demolitur*, huer rust & mohða 3freten bið. *c* **1275**, *a* **1577** [see FRET *v.*¹ 2, 3]. **13..** *Pol. Songs* (Camden) 201 That his fleis be al i-frette. *a* **1425** tr. *Arderne's Treat. Fistula*, etc. 58 Þe substance of þe veyne yfreted may no3t be souded with-out disese. **1426** LYDG. *De Guil. Pilgr.* 17468 Conswmyd, and yffret a-way. **1568** T. HOWELL *Arb. Amitie* 2 b, Thy prisonere, Whose chaines hath through his hart yfreat.

yfret(ed² [FRET *v.*⁶], furnished, studded.

1426 LYDG. *De Guil. Pilgr.* 588, I sawh ther cordys rovnd & long, Al yffret with knottys strong. *c* **1440** *Pallad. on Husb.* IV. 725 His necke in many a ruge Yfretted grete.

yfretized, pa. pple. of FRETISH, FRETIZE *v.*² *Obs.*

yfrore [FREEZE *v.*], frozen.

c **1275** *XI Pains of Hell* 181 in *O.E. Misc.* 152 Summe beoþ fur-brend, and summe ifrore. **1297** R. GLOUC. (Rolls) 5354 More vor þe harde vorst þat þut water yurore is. **1387** TREVISA *Higden* (Rolls) VII. 497 Þe emperesse.. scapede awey over Temse, þat was i-frore [*MS. β* yfrore] and heled wiþ snowe. *c* **1403** LYDG. *Temple of Glas* 20 A craggy roche, Like ise Ifrore.

yfrote, ME. pa. pple. of FROT *v.*

yfrounct [FROUNCE *v.*], wrinkled.

c **1634** CARTWRIGHT *Ordinary* v. iv. (1651) 84 His Visage foul, yfrounct with glowing eyn.

yfruited, yfry(e)d, ME. pa. pples. of FRUIT *v.*, FRY *v.*¹

yft(e, obs. forms of GIFT.

1422 YONGE tr. *Secr. Secr.* xxxi. 173 A wyse and a worthy man þat lowid not yftis to rescewe. *c* **1450** *Godstow Reg.* 177 Þᵉ yfte þat Raf þᵉ sone of wayfere & hys heyrys made. **1486** *Churchw. Acc., Croscombe* (Somerset Rec. Soc.) 15 John a Dene owth for the yfte of hys syster iij selver sponys.. xxs.

†**yfuled, yvyled** [Y- 4, FILE *v.*²], rendered foul.

a **1100** *Aldhelm Gloss.* I. 653 (Napier 19/1) *Foedatos*, 3efylede. *a* **1240** *Lofsong* in *O.E. Hom.* I. 205 Ich habbe.. mid flesches fulðe ifuled me. **13..** *R. Gloucester's Chron.* (Rolls) 8971 Wanne he þi mouþ cusste þat so villiche isoiled [*MS. B* yuyled] is.

yfulled, yfolled [FULL *v.*¹], baptized.

c **897** ÆLFRED *Gregory's Past. C.* lviii. 443 Doð ærest hreowsunga, & weorðað siððan 3 efullwade. *c* **1175–1297** ifulsed, ifulhet, yuolled [see FULL *v.*¹]. **1387** TREVISA *Higden* (Rolls) VI. 157 Þere he was i-cristned [*v.rr.* yfulled, yvolled] of pope Sergius. *a* **1400** *New Test.* (Paues) 47/16 To byleuen in Crist, & ben y-folewed.

yfurred, furred.

13.. *K. Alis.* 5502 (Laud MS.) Twoo þik mantels, yfurred wiþ grys. **13..** *Coer de L.* 6526 A robe i-furryd with blaun and nere. *c* **1450** *Mirk's Festial* 40 A cloþe.. þat was of fyne scarlad, well yfurred wyth grys.

yfurthered, furthered.

c **1402** LYDG. *Compl. Bl. Knt.* xlvii, The trewe man Was put abakke, wher-as the falshede Y-furthered was.

yfycched [FICCHE *v.*], fixed.
c **1412** HOCCLEVE *De Reg. Princ.* 856 That after-clap, in my mynde so deepe Y-fycched is.

yfyned [FINE *v.*[3]], refined.
14.. LYDG. *Beware Doubleness* 99 O ye women, which been enclyned.. To been as pure as gold y-fyned.

yfyred, ME. pa. pple. of FIRE *v.*[1]

†**ygad(e)red, ygedred** [Y- 4], gathered.
c **891**–c **1275** [see GATHER *v.*]. **1297** R. GLOUC. (Rolls) 4527 In is ost þo hii were ygadered in þis cas. c **1394** *P. Pl. Crede* 189 Þouȝ þe tax of ten ȝer were trewly y-gadered. c **1489** CAXTON *Blanchardyn* xxxix. 144 So grete a tresoure was ther wyth-in the paleys, ygadred by the kyng.

ygalled = GALLED *ppl. a.*[2] 1.
1742 SHENSTONE *Schoolmistr.* xviii, See! to their Seats all hie with merry Glee,.. All, but the Wight of Bum y-galled.

ygan, ME. pa. pple. of GO *v.*

ygathering, *pr. pple.* [Y- 3 c; cf. *ycausing*], gathering.
1866 J. B. ROSE *Ovid's Met.* 163 Rustics there, ygathering osiers.

ygazed, arch. pa. pple. of GAZE *v.*
1812 BYRON *Ch. Har.* II. lxxi, He that unawares had there ygazed.

ygazing, *pr. pple.* [Y- 3 c], gazing.
1742 SHENSTONE *Schoolmistr.* xiii, Thilk Wight that has y-gazing been.

ygelt, ygerdonyd, ME. pa. pples. of GILD *v.*[1], GUERDON *v.*

ygerd, ygert: see YGURD.

ygete, got.
1297 R. GLOUC. (Rolls) 225 Ʒwat man þe child ssolde be þat he adde bi ȝete [*MS. B* y gete]. **1387** TREVISA *Higden* (Rolls) V. 61 Whan he hadde y-gete his axynge.

ygeve: see GIVE *v.*

‖**Yggdrasil** (ˈɪgdrəsɪl). *Myth.* Forms: 8 Ydrasil, 9 Ig-, Y(g)gdrasil. [ON. *yg(g)drasill*, also *askr yg(g)drasils* lit. ash-tree of *Yggdrasil* (? f. *Yggr* name of Odin + *drasill* horse; but the formation is obscure).] In Scandinavian mythology, the great tree whose branches and roots extend through the universe. Also *allusively*.
1770 tr. *Mallet's Northern Antiq.* II. Fab. viii. 49 Gangler demanded: Which is the capital of the Gods, or the sacred city: Har answers, It is under the Ash Ydrasil; where the Gods assemble every day, and administer justice. **1840** CARLYLE *Heroes* iii. 165 The Tree Igdrasil, that has its roots down in the Kingdoms of Hela and Death, and whose boughs overspread the highest Heaven! **1865** W. H. GILLESPIE *Argt. Mor. Attrib. God* 51 It [*sc.* Love] is, in fact, the mundane Yggdrasil. **1865** LOWELL *Thoreau* Wks. 1890 I. 361 The nameless eagle of the tree Ygdrasil. **1878** EMERSON in *N. Amer. Rev.* CXXVI. 413 You say: 'Cut away; my tree is Ygdrasil—the tree of life.'

yghe, yȝe, obs. forms of EYE *sb.*[1]

†**yȝeld(e, yȝened**, ME. pa. pples. of YIELD *v.*, YEAN *v.*

yȝete, yyete: see I-YETEN, Y-ETE(N.

†**ygiled, ygyled** [Y- 4, GUILE *v.*], beguiled.
1340 *Ayenb.* 124 Lokeþ þane man þet he ne by be none sleȝþe of þe kueade y-gyled. *Ibid.* 256 Hi byeþ ofte y-giled.

ygilt[1] [GUILT *v.*], sinned, offended.
1387 TREVISA *Higden* (Rolls) IV. 219 Noþer for noblete of þe persone þat hadde agult [*MS. β* ygilt].

ygilt[2] = GILT *ppl. a.*
1434 [see GILT *ppl. a.* 1 b]. **1589** NASHE *Martin's Months Minde* Wks. (Grosart) I. 196 My hope once was my old shooes should be sticht, My thumbes ygilt, thai were before bepitcht.

ygladed [GLAD *v.*], made glad.
c **950** [see GLAD *v.* 1]. c **1205** LAY. 19587 Þa wes Vðer bliðe & igladed swuðe. c **1350** *Will. Palerne* 850 Þanne was þat menskful meliors muchel y-gladed.

yglased, ME. pa. pple. of GLAZE *v.*[1]

yglent [GLENT *v.*], made radiant.
c **1530** *Songs, Carols*, etc. (E.E.T.S.) 65 Gaude Maria, yglent with grace!

yglewed, yglosed, etc., ME. pa. pples. of GLUE, GLOZE *v.*[1], etc.

ygloved [Y- 5, GLOVE *sb.*], gloved.
c **1400** *Laud Troy Bk.* 6542 Agamenon on syde houed, With gode Armes and wel y-gloued.

†**y'go**, *adv. Obs.* Also 6 ygone, 6, 8 ygoe. [Spenserian pseudo-arch. form of AGO *adv.*] Ago; formerly. *late ygo*: recently.
[**1426** LYDG. *De Guil. Pilgr.* 6276 Yt ys not yet ygon ful yore.. When thow doutest the off thys bred.] **1579** SPENSER *Sheph. Cal.* Oct. 62 And great Augustus long ygoe is dead. **1590** —— *F.Q.* II. i. 2 Whom his victorious hands did earst restore To natiue crowne and kingdome late ygoe. **1596** *Ibid.* IV. xi. 39 And following Dee, which Britons long ygone Did call diuine, that doth by Chester tend. **1767** MICKLE *Concub.* I. xliii, And what ygoe the Place of Herbs had bene, Is now a Turnip Fielde. **1768** DOWNMAN *Land of Muses* lx, Her heart had long y-go transmewed bin to stone.

†**ygo(e**, ME. pa. pple. of GO *v.*

ygolped, ME. pa. pple. of GULP *v.*

ygon(e, ygoon, yguo, ME. pa. pples. of GO *v.*
1340 *Ayenb.* 142 He is y-guo into þe hole of þo roche ase þe colure ine his coluerhous. c **1440** *Pallad. on Husb.* I. 788 Another with a diche aboute ygoon is. **1642** H. MORE *Song of Soul* I. III. xliii, But when from Aptery we were ygone.

ygot(en [Y- 4, GET *v.*], got.
c **1430** *Pilgr. Lyf Manhode* I. cxlv. (1869) 74 Litel is woorth thing ygoten if after the getinge it ne be kept.

ygovernet, governed.
1422 YONGE tr. *Secr. Secr.* 207 By Iustice Is al the worlde y-gouernet.

ygraced, ME. pa. pple. of GRACE *v.*

ygrad, ygred, ME. pa. pples. of GREDE *v. Obs.*

ygraithed, ygreithed [GRAITH *v.*], prepared, equipped.
a **1225** *Leg. Kath.* 1993 Þis pinfule gin wes.. se grisliche igreiðet. **13..** *K. Alis.* 7536 (Laud MS.) Ygreiþed ben his foure þousynde. c **1460** J. RUSSELL *Bk. Nurture* 225 When he is so y-graithed.. þen shalle ye open hym thus.

ygratyd, grated.
c **1430** *Two Cookery-bks.* 15 Brede y-gratyd.

ygra(u)nted, ygrawnt, granted.
1340 *Ayenb.* 264 Huyche y-graunted þus he begynþ. **1387** TREVISA *Higden* (Rolls) VIII. 227 Whanne þe legacye of þe cros was commytted to hym he took no procuracies þat hym were y-graunted. **1456** *Cal. Anc. Rec. Dublin* (1889) 292 Had and ygrawnt by the fellyst of the sayd comynes.

†**ygrave(n, ygraved**, *pa. pple. Obs.* [See Y- 4 and GRAVE *v.*] Buried; graven, engraved.
c **1205** LAY. 21153 Ænne sceld deore.. þer wes innen igrauen [c **1275** igraued] mid rede golde stauen. c **1369** CHAUCER *Dethe Blaunche* 164 By a caue That was vnder a rocke ygraue. **1387** TREVISA *Higden* (Rolls) V. 379 A cros i-grave in þe pavement of marbilston. c **1500** *Lancelot* 1798 But be als dep in to the erd y-grave. **1559** *Mirr. Mag.* (1563) T j, And in the hart it is so diepe ygrave. **1594** CAREW *Tasso* III. lxxiii, Where after was ygrau'd: Here lyes Dudon.

†**ygret**, ME. pa. pple. of GREET *v.*[1]

ygreved, ygrewid, grieved.
13.. *K. Alis.* 841 (Linc. Inn MS.) A kyng þer was.. þat had ygreued muchul his kynne. **1422** YONGE tr. *Secr. Secr.* 241 Sone he shal be seke and his body y-grewid.

ygromony, obs. form of AGRIMONY.
c **1475** *Pict. Voc.* in Wr.-Wülcker 786/12 *Hec igromonia*, a ygromony.

†**ygronde, ygrounde(n** [Y- 4, GRIND *v.*[1]], ground.
c **1000** ÆLFRIC *Gloss.* in Wr.-Wülcker 131/2 *Commolitus*, ȝegrunde. **1362** LANGL. *P. Pl.* A. VII. 171 To Abate þe Barli bred and þe Benes I-grounde. c **1386** CHAUCER *Knt.'s T.* 1691 A sharpe ygrounde spere. c **1430** *Two Cookery-bks.* 13 Temper vp þine Almaundys þat þou hast y-grounde.

ygrope, ME. pa. pple. of GROPE *v.*

ygrounded [GROUND *v.*], grounded.
c **1369** CHAUCER *Dethe Blaunche* 921 So frendly and so wel ygrounded, Vpon al reason so wel yfounded. **1426** LYDG. *De Guil. Pilgr.* 3942 Knowyng that.. hyr compleynte.. Was ygroundyd on folye. **1556** LAUDER *Tractate of Kyngis* 191 Without kyngs Y-groundit be In Goddis wourd of verytie [etc.].

ygrowe(n [GROW *v.*], grown.
c **900** WÆRFERTH tr. *Gregory's Dial.* III. xiii. (1900) 198 Swa fæste his heafod wæs ȝegrowen to ðam lichaman, swylce hit næfre of acorfen nære. **13..** *K. Alis.* 6491 (Laud MS.) Þer hij founde Wymmen growen out of þe grounde... Somme weren to þe nauel ygrowe;.. And summe weren ygrowe al out. c **1386** CHAUCER *Reeve's T.* 53 This wenche thikke and wel ygrowen was.

yguana, obs. form of IGUANA.

†**yguld, -t, ygyld, -t**, ME. pa. pples. of GILD *v.*[1]

ygulpid, ME. pa. pple. of GULP *v.*

ygurd, -t [GIRD *v.*[1]], girt.
1340 *Ayenb.* 236 Y-gert aboue mid huite linene gerdles. **1387** TREVISA *Higden* (Rolls) VII. 403 Þey slepeþ i-cloþed and i-gerd [*MS. β* y-gurde]. **14..** *Voc.* in Wr.-Wülcker 604/30 *Precinctus*, ygurd.

ygyved, fettered.
c **1290** i-gwiued [see GYVE *v.*]. **1387** TREVISA *Higden* (Rolls) III. 145 Sabar þat fliȝe out of prisoun [*added in MS. γ* ygyued].

yha, ȝha, obs. forms of YEA.

†**yhabited** [Y- 5, HABIT *sb.*], clothed.
1377 LANGL. *P. Pl.* B. XIII. 285 Y-habited as an hermyte an ordre by hymselue.

yhacked [Y- 4], hacked.
a **1225** *Ancr. R.* 298 His heaued is ihacked of. **1387** TREVISA *Higden* (Rolls) V. 9 His herte was i-hakked [*MS. γ* y-hakket] to smal gobettes. c **1430** *Two Cookery-bks.* 55 Porke y-soþe, & smale y-hackyd.

yhad(de, ME. pa. pple. of HAVE *v.*

yhaded, yhoded [HADE, HODE *v.*[1]], consecrated, ordained.
900–930 *O.E. Chron.* (Parker MS.) an. 625 Her Paulinus fram Iusto þam ercebiscep wæs ȝehadod Norþhymbrum to biscepe. c **1175** *Lamb. Hom.* 131 Ihadede men he muneges wel to lerene ilewede men. a **1250** *Owl & Night.* 1177 Hwat queþ heo ertu ihoded? **1340** *Ayenb.* 49 Clerkes y-hoded. c **1425** I-hode [see HODE].

yhaht, ME. pa. pple. of HATCH *v.*[1]

yhald, obs. pa. t. of YIELD *v.*

†**yhalde(n**, ME. pa. pple. of HOLD *v.*

yhalewed, yhalȝed, yhal(o)wed [Y- 4, HALLOW *v.*[1]], hallowed.
c **900**, etc. [see HALLOW *v.*[1], HALLOWED]. c **1205** LAY. 29443 Na chirche þer nes ihaleȝed. **1340** *Ayenb.* 40 Þe y-halȝede stedes þet byeþ apropred to guodes seruise. **1387** TREVISA *Higden* (Rolls) III. 13 Þe temple was i-halowed [*MS. γ* yhalwed]. c **1450** LYDG. *Life Our Lady* xlix. (1484) g viij, In al the erthe y halowed and y holde.

yhalou, obs. form of YELLOW.

†**yhamled**, ME. pa. pple. of HAMBLE *v.*

yhandled [Y- 4, HANDLE *v.*[1], I-HANDLE], handled.
a **1225** *Juliana* 51 Neauer adet tis dei nes ich þus ihondlet. **1387–8** T. USK *Test. Love* II. xi. (Skeat) l. 101 Is vertue the hye way to this knot that long we have y-handled?

yhanted [HAUNT *v.*], practised.
1340–70 *Alex. & Dind.* 988 Ne we sitte in no sete þere sinne is y-hanteþ.

yhar(e, obs. ff. YAIR *sb.*, YARE, fishgarth.

†**yharded** [Y- 4, HARD *v.*], hardened.
1297 R. GLOUC. (1724) 352 Þe folkes herte ys So yharded [*v.r.* iharded]. c **1374** CHAUCER *Boeth.* IV. met. v. (1868) 133 Þe weyȝte of þe snowe yhardid by þe colde. c **1430** *Two Cookery-bks.* 52 Whan he is a lytel y-hardid in þe ouen.

yharmed[1], var. Y-ARMED, armed.
1297 R. GLOUC. (Rolls) 2633 Þre hondred þousend men mid him yharmed he nom.

yharmed[2], harmed.
1340 *Ayenb.* 238 Vor yef hi byeþ queade hi ssolle by þe more y-harmed þanne þe oþre.

yharneysed, yhasped, yhat, ME. pa. pples. of HARNESS *v.*, HASP *v.*, HEAT *v.*

†**yhate(n**: see YHOTE.

yhated, hated.
1297 R. GLOUC. (Rolls) 2254 Wiþ gret poer.. Of scottes & of picars.. þat euere abbeþ þis lond yhated. **1377** LANGL. *P. Pl.* B. IX. 99 Is moste yhated vp erthe of hem þat beth in heuene.

yhatered, ME. pa. pple. of HATER *v.*, to clothe.

yhat (ȝhat), yhate, obs. ff. GATE *sb.*[1]

yhaved, had.
c **1315** SHOREHAM VII. 434 We nedde y-haued ryȝt no profyȝt Ine heuene a-boue.

yhe, obs. f. EYE, YE, YEA.

yhed(de, var. of YHID.

yhed (ȝhed(e), obs. pa. t. of GO: see YODE.

yheedid, -yd: see HEADED.

yhefyr, obs. form of HEIFER.
1446 *Churchw. Acc., Yatton* (Somerset Rec. Soc.) 85 It. of J. Meke vor a yhefyr.. iij s.

yheid (ȝheid(e), obs. pa. t. of GO: see YODE.

yheir, yheit, obs. ff. YEAR[1], YET, GATE *sb.*[1]

yheld(e, obs. ff. YIELD *v.*

†**yheled**[1] [Y- 4] *pa. pple.*, healed.
c **900** tr. *Bæda's Hist.* IV. iii. (Schipper) 366 & þa on morȝenne ȝehælede ȝewitte aras & ut eode. c **1175**, c **1200** [see HEAL *v.*[1] 1, 3 b]. **1377** LANGL. *P. Pl.* B. XIV. 96 A wounde yheled.

yheled[2] [HELE *v.*[2]], covered, concealed.
c **1000** ÆLFRIC *Gen.* xxix. 2 Se pitt wæs ȝeheled mid anum stane. **1297** R. GLOUC. (1724) 305 Myd blod þe erþe was yheled. **13..** *K. Alis.* 278 Þeo lady lyȝt on hire bedde Yheoled [*MS. Laud* yhiled] wel wiþ selkyn webbe. **1399** LANGL. *Rich. Redeles* III. 212 An herne at þe halle ende, Well homelich yhelid. c **1430** *Two Cookery-bks.* 40 Straw on pouder Canelle y-now, þat þe stekys be al y-helid þer-wyth.

yheled[3], var. Y-ELED, anointed.
c **1275** iheled [see ELE *v.*[1]]. **1297** R. GLOUC. (Rolls) 7243 King alfred þe kunde more þat uerst was yeled [*MS. B.* yheled] at rome.

yhelle, obs. form of YELL *v.*

yheme, etc., var. YEME, etc.

yhen, obs. pl. of EYE *sb.*[1]

†**yhende**, *a.* and *adv.* [OE. *ȝehende*: see Y- 1 b and HEND(E], near, at hand.
c **893**, c **1000** [see HEND *a.* 1, 2 and *adv.* 1]. a **1250** *Owl & Night.* 1263 Þer hi wel vnderstonde scholde þat sum vnsel

heom is ihende. **1340** *Ayenb.* 212 þer bieþ oþre þet gredeþ hare benes zuo lhoude þet þo þet byeþ y-hende byeþ desstorbed.

yhent [Y- 4, HENT *v.*], caught.
1297 [see HENT *v.* 1]. **14..** *St. Jeremie's 15 Tokens* 96 Miȝth þai hym haue yhent fast by þe crovne.

yheped, heaped.
c **1440** *Pallad. on Husb.* XII. 334 Yf they mende not, yheped se Askis or flood grauel aboute her roote.

yher(e, obs. forms of YEAR[1].

†**yherber(e)ȝed, yherborwed** [Y- 4], harboured.
c **1200** *Trin. Coll. Hom.* 143 Seuen awergede gostes ware on hire ȝeherbereȝede. **1340** *Ayenb.* 130 Ine zuo poure house yherberȝed. **1393** LANGL. *P. Pl.* C. VII. 235 Ich was yherborwed with an hep of chapmen.

yherde, early var. of YIRD *Sc.*, earth.

†**yherdling.** *Obs.* The holder of a yardland.
11.. *Cartulary of Battle* in Vinogradoff *Villainage in Eng.* (1892) 148 *note*, Yherdlinges..customarii [cf. *Ibid.*, Majores Erdlinges scil. virgarii Halferdlinges (majores cottarii) Minores cottarii].

†**yhere**, *a. Obs. rare.* [repr. OE. *ȝehíere, f. ȝehíeran: see next. Cf. MHG. *gehære*.] Obedient.
c **1315** SHOREHAM I. 732 Þeȝ he ne be nauȝt yhere, Ac wykke.

†**yhere**, *v. Obs.* Forms: see Y- and HEAR *v.* [OE. *ȝehíeran*, etc. = OS. *gihôrian*, MLG., MDu. *gehoren*, OHG. *gahôrjan* (MHG. *gehœren*, G. *gehören* with special sense-development, to belong), Goth. *gahausjan*: see Y- 3 c and HEAR *v.* (The instances of the pa. pple. may belong to the simplex or the compound.)] To hear.
c **825** *Vesp. Psalter* ix. 38 [x. 17] Lustas heortan heara ȝeherde eare ðin. *Ibid.* liv. 2 [lv. 1] Ðeher god ȝebed min & ne forseh ðu boene mine. *c* **1000** *Ags. Gosp.* Matt. xviii. 15 Ðyf he þe ȝehyrð, þu ȝestaþelast þinne broðor. *c* **1000** ÆLFRIC *Saints' Lives* xxxiii. 201 Ðehyredum þysum wordum hi ongunnon ealle weopan. *c* **1175** *Lamb. Hom.* 5 Ȝe iherden er on þe godspel hu [etc.]. *c* **1200** *Trin. Coll. Hom.* 143 Nu ȝie habbeð iherd þes wimmanes name. **1297** R. GLOUC. (Rolls) 3440 Ac suþþe hii wonne al clene out as ȝe ssulle after yhure. *c* **1330** *Assump. Virg.* (B.M. MS.) 9 Þar auenture ȝe haue noȝt iherde How oure ladi went out of þis werde. **1340** *Ayenb.* 265 Nou broþren and zostren y-hyreþ my red. **1387** TREVISA *Higden* (Rolls) III. 355 Þe iuge swoor þat he hadde i-herde [*MS.* γ yhurd] suche tales of Zenocrates his mouth. **1393** LANGL. *P. Pl.* C. v. 157 Loue..cryed vp-on conscience, þe kynge hit myghte yhure. **1422** YONGE tr. *Secr. Secr.* 235 Who-so hath a smale neke, he sholde haue a swete voyce and wel y-harde.

yhere (ȝhere), obs. form of EAR *sb.*[1]

†**yher(i)ed, yher(y)ed** [Y- 4, HERY *v.*], praised.
c **1175** *Lamb. Hom.* 107 Þet ure drihten beo eure ihered on ure godan weorcan. *a* **1310** in Wright *Lyric P.* xvi. 52 A betere burde never nes y-heryed with the heste. *c* **1450** *Crt. of Love* 592 Venus,..Goddes eterne, thy name y-heried is!

yhern(e: see YEARN *v.*[1], YERN *a.*

†**yhert** [Y- 4, HARD *v.*], hardened.
1340 *Ayenb.* 29 Huanne man is y-hert ine his kueadnesse þet me ne may him wende.

yheryd [EAR *v.*[1]], ploughed.
1426 LYDG. *De Guil. Pilgr.* 5398 That erthe..Wher as sowe was thys greyn, Was nat..yheryd neueradel.

yheryȝed [HARRY *v.*], ravaged.
a **1440** *Sir Degrev.* 140 Hys husbondus that yaf rent Was y-heryȝed dounryght.

yhes, obs. form of YES.

yhet: see GATE *sb.*[1], HAVE, YET.

†**yhevid** [Y- 4, HEAVY *v.*; cf. I-HEVEȜED], grieved.
c **1440** *Gesta Rom.* 51 Sith my two doughters haue thus yhevid me, sothely I shal preve the thrid.

yhewe(d, hewn.
c **950** *Lindisf. Gosp.* Mark xv. 46 *Excisum de petra*, ..ȝeheawen of carre *vel* stane. **11..** *Voc.* in Wr.-Wülcker 545/36 *Lignum*, iheawen treow. **1387** TREVISA *Higden* (Rolls) VIII. 283 Þat tyme the woodes in Wales were i-hewe [*MS.* γ yheuwe] adoun. **1430–40** LYDG. *Bochas* VIII. xi. (1558) 6 b, Vnto the death was wounded and yhewe.

yheyt(e, obs. forms of YET *adv.*

†**yhid(de, yhud(de, yhyd(de**, etc. [Y- 4, HIDE *v.*[1], I-HEDE], hidden.
c **888** ÆLFRED *Boeth.* xxxv. § 1 Þon fint he þær þa ryhtwisnesse ȝehydde mid þæs lichoman hæfiȝnesse. *a* **1225** *Ancr. R.* 146 Hester, on Ebrewish, þet is ihud, an English. **1297** R. GLOUC. (Rolls) 5099 Wanne þe relikes of halwen yfounde were & ykud þat vor drede of saxons er wide were yhud. *a* **1300** *Sarmun* xi. in *E.E.P.* (1862) 2 Þer nis no þing a-boute þe bone to ȝeme þat was ihuddid here. **1340** *Ayenb.* 109 Godes riche is ase on tresor in þe uelde yhed. *c* **1369** CHAUCER *Dethe Blaunche* 175 Some..slepte vpright her heed yhed. *c* **1374** [see HIDE *v.*[1] 4]. **1387** TREVISA *Higden* (Rolls) IV. 431 Iosephus was i-founde y-hid among useles. *c* **1440** *Pallad. on Husb.* IV. 487 By nyght, and vndir cloude yhid the mone.

yhifte, obs. form of GIFT *sb.*
a **1500** *Bernard. de cura rei fam.*, etc. (E.E.T.S.) 36 Of all yhiftes þat gode yevith to man.

†**yhight**, ME. pa. pple. of HIGHT *v.*[1]

yhillid [Y- 4, HILD *v.*], flayed.
1387 TREVISA *Higden* (Rolls) VIII. 167 [He] made hym be i-hylde [*MSS.* β, γ y-huld] al quyk. **1422** YONGE tr. *Secr. Secr.* 167 Wherfor this kynge comandid that he were y-hillid.

yhis, etc., obs. ff. YES, etc.

yhit(te, obs. ff. YET *adv.*

yhode, obs. pa. t. of GO: see YODE.

yhoded: see YHADED.

yholde(n, obs. pa. pples. of HOLD *v.*, YIELD *v.*

yhole, pa. pple. of HELE *v.*[1], to conceal.

†**yhole**, *a. Obs.* Forms: 1 ȝehal, 3 ihal, 3–4 ihol, 4 yhol, 4–5 yhole. [OE. *ȝehál*: see Y- 3 b and WHOLE *a.*] Whole, sound.
c **1000** ÆLFRIC *Hom.* II. 154 Ða ȝemette he þæt fæt..swa ȝehal þæt ðær nan cinu on næs ȝesewen. *c* **1000** *Sax. Leechd.* I. 354 Wyrc swa hit man ȝehal forswelȝan mæȝe. *c* **1205** LAY. 821 Al ihal & al isund. *a* **1225** *Ancr. R.* 80 Hope halt þe heorte i hol. **1340** *Ayenb.* 228 Huo þet is yhol of bodie and uoul ine herte is ase þe berieles yhuited. *c* **1430** *Two Cookery-bks.* 22 Þen take figys, an kerue hem a-to, or Roysonys y-hole.

Hence †**yholliche**, wholly; †**yholnesse**, †**yholschipe**, wholeness.
a **1240** *Ureisun* in *O.E. Hom.* I. 203 Moder of swich sune wið iholschipe of meiden. *c* **1315** SHOREHAM III. 223 Þarefore do þe al y-holliche þat day [*sc.* mass-day] to holy þynge. **1340** *Ayenb.* 127 Þe loue of þe herte huerby he him yefþ y-holliche and wyþoute corrupcion to þet ha loueþ. *Ibid.* 230 Yholnesse and clennesse of bodye þet is to zigge þet þet body by y-hol wyþoute uelþe of lecherie. *a* **1400** in *Eng. Gilds* (1870) 362 Ȝif þ[t] þe axkere bryngeþ skore oþer wryt, and aske þe berynge y-holecheche [*sic*].

yholk, obs. form of YOLK.

†**yholpe(n** [Y- 4, HELP *v.*], helped.
a **1240** *Ureisun* in *O.E. Hom.* I. 191 Þu me hauest iholpen aueole kunne wise. **1297** R. GLOUC. (Rolls) 8358 Ich hom abbe quaþ vr louerd iholpe [*v. rr.* yholpe, yholpen] er ywis. **1377** LANGL. *P. Pl.* B. XVII. 60 How he with Moyses maundement hadde many men y-holpe. *c* **1400** *Rom. Rose* 5505 Socoured ofte And most I hope [*Thynne's ed.* yholpe] in all her neede.

yhon(e, yhong, obs. ff. YON, YOUNG.

†**yhonge, -ed** [Y- 4, HANG *v.*], hung, hanged.
a **1000** *Phœnix* 38 Wintres & sumeres wudu bið ȝelice bledum ȝehongen. *a* **1250** *Owl & Night.* 1136 If þu art þar ouer ihonge þi lif is euer luþer and qued. **13..** *Seuyn Sag.* (W.) 2612 The thre theues were knightes, That were i-honged. **1340** *Ayenb.* 241 Al alsuo ase þe wordle him hild uor uyl and uor wlatuol, ase me deþ enne y-honged. *a* **1425** tr. *Arderne's Treat. Fistula*, etc. 34 Þe legges y-raised vp and wiþ a towel y-hungen.

†**yhorsed**, *a. Obs.* [OE. *ȝehorsed*: see Y- 5.] Horsed; on horseback.
c **893** ÆLFRED *Oros.* III. ix. § 1 On his feðehere wæron xxxii M. & þæs ȝehorsedan fifte healf M. *a* **1122** *O.E. Chron.* (Laud MS.) an. 1010 Þa Dæniscan..þær wurdon ȝehorsode. *c* **1350** *Will. Palerne* 1950 Alle on stalworþ stedes stoutliche i-horsed. *c* **1380** *Sir Ferumb.* 801 Y-horced & y-armed. *c* **1489** CAXTON *Blanchardyn* xxvii. 102 Yf wele yhorsed I had not ben I shulde neuer haue escaped.

yhote(n [HIGHT *v.*[1]], called; commanded; promised; bidden, etc.
c **1000** ÆLFRIC *Gen.* ii. 11 Þæt land, þe ys ȝehaten Euilað. **1154**, etc. [see HIGHT *v.*[1] A. 3, B. 1]. *c* **1175** *Lamb. Hom.* 159 Þe fuwer wateres þa þe beoð ihaten us on to weschen. *c* **1200** ORMIN 3360, I Daviþþ kingess chesstre, Þatt iss ȝehatenn Beþþleæm. *c* **1250** *Gen. & Ex.* 2416 Siðen ðor was mad on scite, Ðe was y-oten Ramesé. **1340** *Ayenb.* 119 Þise graces byeþ yhote yefþes uor þri skeles. *c* **1400** TREVISA *Higden* (Rolls) VII. App. 521 The emperour had y-hote his servauntes that thei schuld go after hym privylich. **14..** *K. Sol. Bk. Wisd.* 156 Þe widewe son died, he was yhote Ionas.

yhoten, var. ETEN *Obs.*, giant.

yhou, yhour(e, yhouth(e, obs. ff. YOU, YOUR, YOUTH.

†**yho(u)sled** [Y- 4], houselled, communicated.
a **1000** in *Anglia* XIII. 425/860 Þænne hi beoþ ȝehuslude, *dum communicantur*. **1387** TREVISA *Higden* (Rolls) V. 73 He ..was i-houseled [*MS.* γ y-housled] to fore al þe peple in an Esterday.

†**yhove** [Y- 4, HEAVE *v.*], heaved.
1387 TREVISA *Higden* (Rolls) VII. 455 Y-meoved and y-hove fer out of oon place into anoþer.

yhow, yhownge, yhowthe, obs. ff. YOU, YOUNG, YOUTH.

yhowted, ME. pa. pple. of HOOT *v.*

yhte, rare var. of ME. *ehte*: see AUGHT *sb.*[1]
1390 GOWER *Conf.* II. 378 This Priamus hadde in his yhte A wif, and Hecuba sche hyhte.

yhu, ȝhu, obs. forms of YOU.

yhude, ME. variant of YODE.

†**yhugged** [Y- 4], hugged.
1614 J. DAVIES *Eclogue* 188, I ne wot, on mould what feater skill Can bee yhugg'd in Lordings pectorall.

yhuited [WHITE *v.*], whitened.
1340 *Ayenb.* 178 Line cloþ þet is y-huyted be ofte wessinge. *Ibid.* 228 Þe berieles yhuited þet is uayr wyþ-oute and wyþ-inne uol of stench.

yhuld: see YHILLED.

yhule, yhung, obs. ff. YULE, YOUNG.

†**yhungen**: see YHONGE.

yhuntid [Y- 4], hunted.
1399 LANGL. *Rich. Redeles* III. 228 He was halowid and y-huntid and y-hote trusse.

yhurt(e, ME. pa. pple. of HURT *v.*

yhu(y)red, yhyred, hired.
c **1000** ÆLFRIC *Gloss.* in Wr.-Wülcker 115/21 *Locatio*, behyring, *uel* ȝehyred feoh. **1387** TREVISA *Higden* (Rolls) IV. 51 An oost þat was i-hered [*MS.* γ yhuyred] out of Grecia. **1393** LANGL. *P. Pl.* C. IX. 336 Bote he be heyliche yhyred elles wol he chide.

yhy(e)alde, ME. (Kentish) pa. pple. of HOLD *v.*
1340 *Ayenb.* 8 Zuich wreþe longe yhyealde and byuealde ine herte.

yhyȝed [Y- 4, HIE *v.*[1]], hastened,
a **1400** *New Test.* (Paues) 1 Thess. ii. 17 We..hafeþ muche y-hyȝed to sen ȝoure vysage.

yhyled [HILL *v.*[1]], covered.
c **1394** *P. Pl. Crede* 193 Þat cloister..All y-hyled wiþ leed lowe to þe stones.

Yi (iː). [Chinese.] The name of a minority nationality in China, distributed over Yunnan, Sichuan, and Guizhou; = LOLO. Also, the language of this people. Also *attrib.* or as *adj.*
1960 CHANG-TU HU et al. *China* v. 66 The Yi (Lolo) are located principally in the Liang Shan area on the borders of Szechwan and Yunnan. **1962** E. SNOW *Other Side of River* (1963) lxxviii. 596 Some of the Yi people in Yunnan planted grain as the American Indians did. **1968** [see LOLO]. **1974** *Encycl. Brit. Micropæ dia* X. 818/3 The traditional Yi culture includes a primitive hoe-using agriculture, livestock herding, and hunting. **1978** *Nagel's Encycl.-Guide: China* 65 The Tibeto-Burmese group includes Tibetan, Yi (or Lolo), Hani and Tujia. **1979** *China Now* Mar./Apr. 16/1 The Yi people, like many peasant societies, still want lots of children. **1984** *National Geographic* Mar. 290/2 These people number about 750,000 and belong to the larger group of five million Yi scattered over a wider area.

yi, graphic var. *þi*, THY; dial. f. YEA.

‖**yichus** (ˈjɪkəs, ˈjɪxəs). Also **yiches**. [Yiddish f. Heb. *yiḥūs* pedigree.] Honour, prestige, status.
1907 tr. *Frank's Simon Eichelkatz* 431/2 *Yichus*, aristocracy; good family connection. **1927** *Amer. Mercury* X. 172/2 There was a steady demand from wealthy prospective fathers-in-law for professional men whose titles would add *yiches* (prestige) to their wealth. **1946** *Commentary* May 63/1 On the other hand our butcher's daughters..had even less *yichus*. **1964** S. BELLOW *Herzog* 86, I know you Herzogs and your *Yiches*. Don't give me that hoity-toity. *Ibid.* 141 All branches of the family had the caste madness of *yichus*. No life so barren..that it didn't have imaginary dignities, honors to come. **1976** C. BERMANT *Coming Home* I. vii. 99 If I could become a doctor he might recover something of his former grace. A doctor meant *yichus*, social status, prestige.

yicker, var. YIKKER *v.*

Yid (jɪd). *slang.* Also †**Yit(t**. [Back-formation f. next.] A (usu. offensive) name for a Jew.
1874 HOTTEN *Slang Dict.* 344 *Yid*, or *Yit*, a Jew. *Yidden*, the Jewish people. The Jews use these terms very frequently. *a* **1890** *Sporting Times* (Leland), I might, if I had poached upon the province of the Pitcher, Have devoted just a verse or two to love among the Yids. **1898** [see SCHLEMIEL]. **1912** G. FRANKAU *One of Us* vi. 53 As the Yid Knows well the slump-signs ere the slump convulses. **1935** [see CRAP *sb.*[1] 7 b]. **1940** E. POUND *Cantos* lii. 11 Sin drawing vengeance, poor yitts paying for——. **1946** KOESTLER *Thieves in Night* 279, I became a socialist because I hated the poor; and I became a Hebrew because I hated the Yid. **1963** V. NABOKOV *Gift* iii. 180 Then she went and married a yid. **1971** B. MALAMUD *Tenants* 203 Then they go to a synagogue late at night,..and make Yid noises, praying.

Yiddish (ˈjɪdɪʃ), *sb.* (*a.*) [Anglicization of G. *jüdisch* (ˈjyːdɪʃ) Jewish; the full German name is *jüdisch deutsch* 'Jewish-German'. The English word has been adopted in German as *jiddisch*.] The language used by Jews in Europe and America, consisting mainly of German (orig. from the Middle Rhine area) with admixture (according to local or individual usage) of Balto-Slavic or Hebrew words, and printed in Hebrew characters.
1875 *New Era* 5 May 285 In fact, this corrupt German is known as Yiddish or Jewish German. **1886** BESANT *Childr. Gibeon* II. vii, [German immigrants] tell me their wants in their own language, which is generally Yiddish. **1892** *Chamb. Encycl.* IX. 496/2 There were at one time two newspapers in London alone published in Yiddish. **1894** DU MAURIER *Trilby* VII. (1912) 368 Several of the band stood round gesticulating, and talking German or Polish or Yiddish. **1900** C. RUSSELL *Jew in London* ii. 18 The Yiddish-speaking community. **1917** *Edin. Rev.* Apr. 310 In 1903.. Yiddish was solemnly proclaimed the Jewish national

language. **1938** *Better English* Feb. 50 As a rule, Yiddish-speaking people do not move in higher society. **1939** [see Judæo-, Judeo-]. **1970** *Language* XLVI. 939 Standard Yiddish is the only variety taught in the schools. **1979** *Guardian* 28 May 11/8 The Jewish community of eastern Europe, the Yiddish-speaking, Ashkenazi quasi-state. **1981** G. Clare *Last Waltz in Vienna* (1982) I. 11 He must also have spoken Yiddish, the language of the ghetto.

adj. **1886** Besant *Childr. Gibeon* II. xxviii, A large importation of Polish Jews who were making a little Yiddish Poland for themselves up a court. **1892** *Chamb. Encycl.* IX. 496/1 Martin Luther compiled a dictionary of *Rotwälsch*.. used by the thieves of his time, in which half the words are Hebrew, derived from the receivers of stolen goods and their Yiddish dialect. **1977** *Rolling Stone* 16 June 43/2 'Never point your gun at someone,' Prince clucked in a Yiddish accent.

'Yiddisher, *sb.* and *a.* Also **yiddisher,** † **Yidisher.** [ad. G. *Jüdischer* Jew.] **A.** *sb.* A Jew. Also *transf.* (cf. Jew *sb.* 2).

1859 Matsell *Vocabulum* 97 *Yidisher*, a Jew. **1890** Barrère & Leland *Dict. Slang.* **1896** E. Turner *Little Larrikin* xxiv. 292 But why.. that agent.. refused to take the premium.. beats me.. for he's more than a bit of a yiddisher. **1931** R. Campbell *Georgiad* iii. 62 Doctors much to praise in it can see And with the ancient Yiddishers agree. **1933** L. Golding *Magnolia Street* I. iii. 59 Can't he mind his own business, now.. he's got hold of a stinking Yiddisher? **1976** *Publishers Weekly* 19 Apr. 81/3 With yiddishers, reasonableness and gentle satire, Vorspan.. sets out to convince you that a bit of suffering is good for you.

B. *adj.* Also **Yiddische,** etc. [ad. G. *jüdische* (inflectional form of *jüdisch*).]

1892 I. Zangwill *Childr. of Ghetto* I. iii. 94 At least, she would have starved in a Yiddishë country, not in a land of heathens. **1898** A. M. Binstead *Pink 'Un & Pelican* xii. 276 One very enquiring Yiddisher youth stood munching a shoot of celery. **1925** J. Yellen (*song-title*) My Yiddishe Momma. **1961** P. De Vries *Through Fields of Clover* i. 27 Jokes about hot pastrami... To say nothing of Yiddisher Mamas. **1965** D. S. Davis *Pale Betrayer* iv. 52 I'm a real *Yiddishe* mama. **1971** C. Fick *Danziger Transcript* 177, I laughed like a Yiddische baby. **1973** *Jewish Chron.* 18 May 15/3 A Clever Yiddisher boy working next door, heard strange noises. **1976** R. Sanders in D. Villiers *Next Year in Jerusalem* 198 The young Irving Berlin composed both Italian and Yiddisha pastiche. **1979** *Guardian* 22 Mar. 9/1 In Israel.. plangent Yiddischer mammas are passé.

'Yiddishism. orig. *U.S.* [f. Yiddish *sb.* (*a.*) + -ism.] **a.** A linguistic feature influenced by or derived from Yiddish. **b.** Advocacy of Yiddish culture and language.

1926 *Amer. Mercury* VII. 207/1 Most Yidgin writers qualify their Yiddishisms with parenthetical English explanations. **1933** in A. A. Roback *Curiosities of Jewish Lit.* viii. 124 Doeblin sees his model in something on the lines of Yiddishism on a world scale. **1938** *Better Eng.* Feb. 50 No one has yet made an attempt to collect all these Yiddishisms into a single collection. **1962** *Amer. Speech* XXXVII. 202 The use of *better* with *should* here is another Yiddishism.. repeated in the announcer's next sentence: 'Better we should stop the clock.' **1966** *New Society* 12 May 9/2 The idiom of the New Yorker—Gentile or Jew—is.. full of translated Yiddishisms ('I should live so long', 'Who needs it?' 'You should pardon the expression' and 'Now he tells me'.) **1978** *Soviet Jewish Affairs* VIII. 73 Since Tsinberg's claim, there has been debate as to whether the sixteenth, seventeenth and eighteenth century 'Yiddishists' can properly be viewed as forerunners of modern Yiddishism. **1981** *Amer. Speech* LVI. 17 The noun *glitsh* is a Yiddishism .. from the verb *glitshn* 'to slide'.

'Yiddishist, *sb.* (*a.*) [f. Yiddish *sb.* (*a.*) + -ist.] An adherent or supporter of Yiddishism (sense a); *spec.*, an advocate of the exclusive use of Yiddish by Jews. Also, a student of Yiddish language or literature. Also *attrib.* or as *adj.*

1917 *Edin. Rev.* Apr. 310 Russian Jewry rang for a time with the bitter controversy of the so-called Hebraists and Yiddishists. The Yiddishists.. won... In 1903.. Yiddish was solemnly proclaimed the Jewish national language. **1933** *B'nai B'rith Mag.* XLVIII. 32/3 What will the Yiddishists.. say to this? **1964** S. Bellow *Herzog* 108 Her father had been.. a member of the Arbeiter-Ring, a Yiddishist. **1970** *Language* XLVI. 938 The title of this book [sc. *The Field of Yiddish*] suggests that it is primarily of interest to Yiddishists. **1971** *Encycl. Judaica* X. 62/2 The Yiddish movement which came at the beginning of the 20th century, laid the accent on Yiddish as the spoken and living language of the vast majority of world Jewry. **1972** H. Kemelman *Monday Rabbi took Off* xlvii. 276 'My husband was a Yiddishist,' said Gittel stiffly, 'He did not speak the language out of principle.' **1976** I. B. Singer in D. Villiers *Next Year in Jerusalem* 62 The leftist Yiddishists tried to identify Yiddish with the social revolution... Russia had promised its Jews a Yiddishist cultural autonomy. **1982** *Lang. Problems & Lang. Planning* VI. II. 208 Yiddishists apply the term [Yiddish] retroactively to all earlier stages of the language, until its very beginnings about a thousand years ago.

‖ **Yiddishkeit** ('jɪdɪʃkaɪt). Also **yiddishkeit.** [ad. Yiddish *yidishkeyt.*] = Jewishness, Judaism 1; Yiddishness.

1892 I. Zangwill *Childr. of Ghetto* I. iii. 87 All they teach them in the school is English nonsense... The good Yiddishkeit goes to the wall. **1901** M. Wolfenstein *Idylls of Gass* 25 They do say she reads German books with not a word of *Yiddishkeit* (Judaism) in them. **1956** 'H. MacDiarmid' *Stony Limits & Scots Unbound* 28 A *Yiddishkeit* crutch. **1966** *New Statesman* 6 May 648/2 The most sophisticated Israelis are those who are often most attached to *yiddishkeit* and many accept the rabbinical regime as part of Jewish culture without which Israel would have no identity. **1976** B. Williams *Making of Manchester Jewry* xi. 271 A.. strictly observant Jewish society based upon the exclusive *Yiddishkeit* of the Eastern European ghetto. **1984** *Listener* 20 Sept. 14/2 With them the immigrants brought their richest possessions: Yiddish and Yiddishkeit—their language and their way of life.

yie, obs. form of eye, yea.

yieft, ȝiefte, obs. ff. gift *sb.*

yield (ji:ld), *sb.* Forms: 1 **ᵹeld, ᵹield, ᵹild, ᵹyld, ᵹeold,** 2 **ȝæild,** 2–3 **ȝield,** 2–5 **ȝeld,** 4 **eild, yilde,** 4–5 **ȝeild, yeild,** 4–6 **yeld,** 5 **ȝelde, yelde,** 6 **yalde,** 6–7 **yeeld(e,** 6– **yield.** [In senses 1–3 OE. *ᵹield*, etc., str. neut. (cf. guild etym.) = OFris. *geld*, *ield* (Fris. *jild*, *jil*), OS. *geld* (senses as in OE.), MLG., MDu. *gelt* payment, money (Du. *geld* money), OHG., MHG. *gelt* (senses as in OE.), (G. *geld* money), ON. *gjald* (Sw. *gäld*, Da. *gjeld*), Goth. *gild* tax: f. stem of **gelðan* (see next). In senses 4–6 directly f. yield *v.*]

†**1. a.** Payment; a sum of money paid or exacted, as a tribute, tax, etc.: *spec.* = geld *sb.* *Obs.*

c **950** *Lindisf. Gosp.* Mark Introd. 4 *De reddendo caesaris tributo*, of ᵹyld æs cæseres ᵹeselenne. *a* **1122** *O.E. Chron.* (Laud MS.) an. 1013 Bead þa Sweᵹen full ᵹild & metsunga to his here þone winter. *Ibid.* 1087 Ælc unriht ᵹeold he forbead. *a* **1154** *Ibid.* 1137 Hi læiden ᵹæildes on þe tunes. *c* **1200** Ormin 10170 Þeȝȝ haffdenn wikenn off þe king To sammnenn hise ȝeldess. *c* **1205** Lay. 7194 Romleode.. þe.. ne dursten hider liðen Axien king of þissen londe þat he ȝefue ȝeld in to Rome. *a* **1300** *Cursor M.* 27831 Strenth, þat lauerding agh to meild, þat o þair men tas wrangwis yeild. **13**.. *K. Alis.* 2959 (Linc. Inn MS.) Ȝef þow wold aske suche a ȝeld Com and haue hit in þe feild. **1424** *Sc. Acts Jas. I* (1814) II. 4 It is accordit þt a ȝelde be raisit þt is to say xijd of ilk pvnde. *c* **1450** *Godstow Reg.* 652 That the lady.. shold hold and haue.. all yelde and all quarels and exaccions fre and quyte. **1494** *Burgh Rec. Edin.* (1869) I. 67 And this ȝeild to be gadderit yeirly anes in the yeir. **1531** in *Eng. Gilds* (1870) 329 Euery mannys wief, after the deth of hur husbond, beyng a taillor, shall kepe as many servaunts as they wille,.. so she bere scotte and lotte, yeve and yeld, wt the occupacion. **1582** *Shuttleworths' Acc.* (Chetham Soc.) 6 The constablye of Sharpelles for a yalde vijd.

†**b.** Payment for loss or injury, compensation.

601–4 *Laws of Ethelbert* xxviii, Ᵹif man inne feoh ᵹenimeþ, se man III ᵹelde ᵹebete. *a* **1225** *Ancr. R.* 58 Strong ȝeld is her mid alle & Godes dom is, & his heste, þet heo hit ȝelde allegate. *c* **1500** *Priests of Peblis* in Pinkerton *Scot. Poems* (1792) I. 29 Upon the day of Dome, For mans body thair to give ane yeild.

†**2.** The offering of sacrifice to a deity; worship.

a **900** Cynewulf *Juliana* 146 Þu goda ussa ᵹield forhogdest. *a* **1225** *Leg. Kath.* 212 Þis ilke ȝeld, þet tu dest to deouelen.

†**3.** Reward, recompense; retribution. *Obs.*

a **1200** *Moral Ode* 45 (Trin. Coll. MS.) He deð his aihte an siker stede þe hit sent to heueriche, þar ne þarf he habben care of here ne of ȝielde. *a* **1225** *Ancr. R.* 376 Þe þolemode þolie bitter one hwule uor he schal sone.. habben ȝeld of blisse.

4. a. The action of yielding crops or other products, production; that which is produced, produce; *esp.* amount of produce.

c **1440** *Pallad. on Husb.* I. 216 Eek hillis yeld is Wel gretter grayn and fewer, then in feeld is. *a* **1483** *Liber Niger* in *Househ. Ord.* (1790) 69 Beyng in some yeres, or in sundrye countreys, thynne wheete, or thycke husked, or bettyr and heavyer of yelde, some tyme whiter flower or browner. **1543** Grafton *Contn. Harding* 157 After haruest for so muche as wheat.. was of so smal yelde, it was solde for .xii.s. and .xiii.s. iiii.d. a quarter. **1563** Hyll *Art Garden.* (1593) 126 The yong plants ought daily to be plucked vp from the old, for feare of hindring the yeeld of the old. **1577** Googe *Heresbach's Husb.* 17b, To knowe the nature of euery grounde, Iscomachus in Xenophon, dooth wyll you to marke wel the plantes and the yeeld of the Countrey. **1611** R. Fenton *Usurie* II. xiii. 91 That increase which God gaue by the yeeld of the earth and liuing creatures. **1773** Burke *Lett., to Marq. Rockingham* (1844) I. 445 The wheat was large in show upon the ground, but the yield in flour is not extraordinary. **1799** A. Young *Agric. Linc.* 213 His yield 12 guineas an acre. **1854** Ronalds & Richardson *Chem. Technol.* (ed. 2) I. 131 The coking lasts about twenty-four hours, and the yield of coke in the ovens averages 67 per cent. **1863** Fawcett *Pol. Econ.* III. xv. 489 Since the year 1850, the average of the yield of gold in Australia has been 10,000,000*l.* **1868** Dasent *Jest & Earnest* (1873) II. 381 He had a farm just outside the town on the yield of which he lived. **1893** Traill *Soc. Eng.* Introd. p. xlviii, Their earliest trade.. is.. in the surface products of the earth—in corn or wine, in the yields of the olive-grove or the orchard.

b. The amount obtained from some financial transaction, impost, etc. (e.g. of interest from an investment, of revenue from a tax).

1877 R. Giffen *Stock Exch. Securities* 152 The higher the yield of a security. **1884** *Manch. Exam.* 12 Sept. 5/1 A tax.. which, moreover, is considerably reduced in its yield by the cost of collection. **1912** *Times* 19 Dec. 15/4 The present value of the three Central London stocks.. affords a yield of over 5 per cent.

†**5.** The action of yielding or giving in; surrender, submission. *Obs. rare.*

1600 W. Watson *Decacordon* (1602) 193 Their consent, yeeld and concurrence. *Ibid.* 351 No such yeelde, as the Iesuiticall faction report we haue made.

6. The action of yielding or giving way, as under pressure or tension, and esp. under a stress greater than the yield stress; also, the stage in the progressive stressing and deformation of a body when the yield stress is reached.

1889 *Telegr. Jrnl. & Electr. Rev.* 20 Dec. 707/1 It was concluded that the increase of [elastic resistance] during 'yield' is the same for all the specimens. **1913** *Proc. R. Soc.* A. LXXXVIII. 464 Yield occurred.. while there was still a large margin of elasticity left in the side bars. **1925** J. Case *Strength of Materials* xxxiv. 538 The drop of stress which occurs at yield with materials like wrought-iron and mild steel. **1967** J. G. Ramsay *Folding & Fracturing of Rocks* vi. 314 The stress conditions which initiate plastic yield. **1981** C. Hall *Polymer Materials* iii. 73 The search for improved impact performance has more recently stimulated a similar systematic study of yield and fracture processes in polymers.

7. Special Comb.: **yield table** *Forestry*, a table giving (usu. with other information) the average value or volume of a species of timber that can be expected from unit area of woodland each successive year.

1888 W. Weise (*title*) Yield tables for the Scotch pine. **1953** H. L. Edlin *Forester's Handbk.* xiv. 222 Yield tables.. show the likely rate of growth and timber yield of tree crops of a certain kind of tree, grown in a certain country. **1980** *Forestry* LIII. 23 These regressions were solved for the appropriate values of volume or volume increment from published yield tables for this species.

yield (ji:ld), *v.* Forms: see below. [Com. Teut. str. vb.: OE. (WS.) *ᵹieldan*, (Angl. & Kent.) *ᵹeldan*, pa. t. *ᵹeald*, *ᵹuldon*, pa. pple. *ᵹolden* = OFris. *gelda*, *ielda* (WFris. *jilde*, EFris. *jêlde*, NFris. *jill*), OS. *geldan*, MDu. *g*(*h*)*elden* (Du. *gelden*), OHG. *geltan*, (MHG., G. *gelten*), ON. *gjalda*, Goth. *-gildan* (in compounds *fragildan*, *usgildan* to compensate):—OTeut. **gelðan*, of which the ultimate relations are uncertain.

This verb has had a remarkable sense-development in English owing to its having been used as an equivalent of L. *reddere* and F. *rendre*, or their compounds. In some of the related languages the word has shown tendencies to develop in the same directions, but the only generally surviving senses on the Continent are 'to be worth, to be valid, to concern, apply to', which are not represented at all in the English word.]

A. Illustration of Forms.

1. a. *Infinitive and Present Stem.* α. 1 **ᵹieldan, ᵹeldan,** 2–5 **ȝelde(n,** 3–7 **yeld,** 4 **ȝielde, ȝeilde, yeilde, yhelde,** (also 8 *Sc.*) **ȝield,** 4–5 **ȝhelde,** (also 7 *Sc.*) **ȝeeld(e,** 4–6 **ȝeld, yelde,** 4–7 **ȝeild,** 4–7 **yeild,** 5 **ȝheylde, eylde, elde,** 5–7 **yeeld(e,** 6 **ealde,** 6–7 **yeald,** 7 **yielde, eyld,** 4, 6– **yield.**

c **825**–*a* **900** [see B. 1–7]. *c* **1200** Ormin 19903 Whanne & hu He wollde hiss dere kemmpe Hiss mede ȝeldenn. *c* **1250** yeld [see B. 6]. **1297** R. Glouc. (Rolls) 6369 Icholle wel þin mede ȝelde. **13**.. *Cursor M.* 110 (Cott.) Scho sal þam ȝeld a hundreth fald. *Ibid.* 260 Traistli acuntes sal we yeild. *Ibid.* 28738 Resun to yield well better is O merci þan of cruelnes. **13**.. *Ibid.* 19472 (Edinb.) To þe ihesu Ȝield I mi gaste. **1340** Hampole *Pr. Consc.* 5503 Acount to yhelde of þair kepyng. **1375** Barbour *Bruce* XI. 33 To ȝeld or reskew Strewilling. **1382** Wyclif *Isa.* xlii. 22 And ther is not that seie, Ȝeeld. *c* **1430** *Syr Gener.* (Roxb.) 9792 Darel fast he behelde, And seid, 'Sir, crist you yelde Of this comyng.' *c* **1440** *Promp. Parv.* 537/1 Ȝeelde þe goost, or deyyn. *a* **1483** Elde [see B. 10a]. ? *a* **1500** *Chester Pl.* (Shaks. Soc.) 169 The high father of heaven I praie To eylde your good deed to daie. **1535** Coverdale *Ecclus.* li. 1, I wil yelde prayse vnto thy name. *a* **1548** Hall *Chron., Hen. VI*, 126b, Twoo so inuincible nacions, which neuer would yeild or bowe. **1572** Yeald [see B. 17b]. **1598** Sir T. Norreys in *Lismore Papers* Ser. II. (1887) I. 16 His purpose is not to ealde the posesion. **1605** Shaks. *Macb.* I. vi. 13 How you shall bid God-eyld vs for your paines. **1611** Mure *Misc. Poems* i. 25 Ȝeeld to his powar. **1647** H. More *Song of Soul* III. App. xix, That light Orb of air.. must yielden evermore To phansies beck. **1659** Hammond *On Ps.* Pref. ¶ 18 To yeeld him an intire Body of necessary Theology. *c* **1730** Ramsay *Some of the Contents* ii, He to best poets skairslie zields in ocht.

β. 1 **ᵹildan, ᵹyldan,** 3–5 **ȝulde(n,** 4–5 **ȝild(e, ȝyld(e,** 4–6 **yild(e,** 6 **ild, ylde** (in *God dild*, etc.).

c **1000** Ælfric *Exod.* xxii. 4 Ᵹif man cucu finde, þæt he stæl.. ᵹilde be twifealdon. *a* **1122** [see B. 1]. *c* **1205** ȝulden [see B. 1]. *a* **1300** *Cursor M.* 28833 Þe pouer man es like þe fild, þat corn plente is wont to yild. *c* **1305** in *E.E.P.* (1862) 58 An heȝere Justise þat þe schal þe trecherie ȝulde. **1389** ȝyld [see B. 2]. *a* **1400–50** *Wars Alex.* 80 Ȝild vp þi rewme. **1493** *Cov. Leet Bk.* 550 Due therfor paying, gyffyng, or ȝilding. **1575** God dylde [see B. 7]. **1590** Spenser *F.Q.* I. vi. 3 That stubborne fort to yilde. **1608** Sylvester *Du Bartas* II. iv. *Decay* 138 God dild you.

γ. *Sc.* 5 **ȝauld,** 5–6 **ȝald, yald.**

c **1450** *Sc. Leg. Saints* iv. (*Jacobus*) 142 Þat criste.. can vs kene Gud fore ewil to ȝald almene. **1489** *Barbour's Bruce* x. 824 He suld the castell ȝeld [*MS. E.* ȝauld] quytly. *c* **1500** *Lancelot* 553 He bidis yow your londe Ye yald hyme our. **1513** Douglas *Æneis* x. x. 136 He weltis our, and ȝaldis vp the breith.

δ. 5 **yolde.**

c **1400** *Sowdone Bab.* 403 Yolde youe here to me. **1432–50** tr. *Higden* (Rolls) IV. 55 Cownsaylenge theyme to yolde vp the cite. *c* **1482** J. Kay tr. *Caoursin's Siege of Rhodes* ¶ 1 (1870), So that they wold knowlege hym as theyre souuerayn: and yerely yold hym a lytyll trybute.

b. *Pres. Ind.* (contracted forms) *2nd sing.* 1 **ᵹieltst, ᵹiltst, ᵹilst, ᵹyltst,** 3–4 **ȝelst, yelst.** *3rd sing.* 1 **ᵹielt, ᵹilt, ᵹylt,** 2 **ȝeelt,** 3 **ȝilt, ȝeldþ,** 3–5 **ȝelt,** 4–5 **yelt,** 5 **yalte.**

c **888** Ælfred *Boeth.* xl. §7 Ælmihtiᵹ God.. ᵹilt ælcum æfter his ᵹewyrhtum. *a* **1175** *Cott. Hom.* 231 Elc ȝeelt efter his ȝearnunge. *c* **1205** Lay. 21071 Nu he me ȝilt [*c* **1275** ȝelt] mede For mire god dede. *a* **1225** *Ancr. R.* 232 Hwoso is siker of sukurs.. & ȝelt tauh up his kastel to his wiðerwines. **1297** R. Glouc. (Rolls) 100 Ac ssropssire ȝeldþ haluendel to þulke bissopriche iwis. *Ibid.* 729 þou ȝelst nou my loue wroþe. **1340** *Ayenb.* 18 He . . þet . . yelt him kuead uor guod. *Ibid.* 38 Vor yef þe vinst and naȝt ne yelst, þou hit stelst. *c* **1400** *Rom. Rose* 4904 He chaungith purpos and entente And yalte into somme couente.

2. a. *Pa. t.* α. 1 **ᵹeald,** 3 **ȝeald,** 3–4 **ȝiald, ȝeld,** 3–5 **ȝelde,** 4 **eild, ȝilde,** (also 6 *Sc.*) **ȝeild,** 4–5 **yeld,** 4–6 **yelde,** 5 **ȝylde, ȝeelde,** 6 *Sc.* **yeild,** 7 *Sc.* **yeeld.**

971 [see B. 5]. *c* **1200** *Trin. Coll. Hom.* 45 Ich ȝeald þat ich noht ne nam. *a* **1225** *Leg. Kath.* 128 Ah se sone ha ȝeald ham swucche ȝeincleppes. **1297** R. Glouc. (Rolls) 9216 He . . ȝeld him is godnesse þat he dude him. **13 . .** *Cursor M.* 9484 (Cott.) Sathanas . . To wais seruis straitt he him eild. **13 . .** *Ibid.* 6398 (Gött.) þai ȝeild him ay ful littel thanc. **1387** Trevisa *Higden* (Rolls) III. 95 þe kyng Ieconias . . ȝilde hym . . to Nabugodonosor. **14 . .** *Sir Beues* 4306 (Pynson) And both in armes yeld vp the gaste. *a* **1585** Montgomerie *Cherrie & Slae* 1024 Ȝit Hope and Curage wan the field, Thocht Dreid and Danger nevir ȝeild. **1632** Lithgow *Trav.* IX. 418, I yeeld to the Noble mans counsell, and giuing him all dutifull thankes, he sent a guide with mee.

b. *2nd sing.* 1 **ᵹulde,** 3 **ȝulde;** *3rd sing.* 4 **ȝuld(e.** *pl.* 1 **ᵹuldon, -an,** 3–4 **ȝulde(n,** 4 **ȝuld.**

a **1000** *Cædmon's Gen.* 2419 Duᵹuðum wlance drihtne ᵹuldon god mid gnyrne. *c* **1000** *Ags. Ps.* (Th.) cv. 26 [cvi. 36] Sceuccgyldum swyþe ᵹuldan. *a* **1225** *Ancr. R.* 406 þu ȝulde þet tu ouhtest. *c* **1380** *Sir Ferumb.* 953 Al þe feldes þo wern y-fuld of dede . . Saue an vewe þat leye & ȝulde & abide hure deþes stounde. **1387** Trevisa *Higden* (Rolls) III. 77 He ȝelde [*MS.* γ a ȝuld] vp þe goost. *Ibid.* 95 (MS. γ) þeos þat ȝuld [*v.r.* ȝilde] ham wylfolych [orig. *isti qui sponte se dederunt*]. *Ibid.* 269 Whan þe men of þe citee sigh þat þey ȝelde hem self [*MS.* γ hy ȝulde ham sylf].

β. 3–5 **ȝold, ȝolde, yolde,** 4 **youlde,** 4–5 **ȝoulde,** 4–6 **yold.**

In the earliest quots. a variant of *ȝulde*: see α b.

c **1275** *Passion our Lord* 61 in *O.E. Misc.* 39 Vor alle þe gode þat he heom dude, hi yolde him luþre mede. *c* **1290** *Beket* 819 in *S. Eng. Leg.* 130 And þov ne ȝolde me þar-of none a-countes. **1297** R. Glouc. (Rolls) 3847 & to þe king arthure hom ȝolde ech man þat was wys. *Ibid.* 11800 þe castel of penneseie heo ȝolde vp þe kinge. *c* **1320** *Sir Tristr.* 307 For hauke siluer he ȝold. **1340–70** *Alisaunder* 304 Hur ȝates ȝeede þei too & youlden hem soone. *c* **1420** *Chron. Vilod.* 562 þe kyng of Denmarke ȝolde hym anone þo. **1460** Capgrave *Chron.* (Rolls) 187 But aftirward alle went bak, and ȝold hem to the Kyng. *c* **1482** J. Kay tr. *Caoursin's Siege of Rhodes* ¶10 (1870), There he kneled downe and yold thankynges . . unto God. **1590** Spenser *F.Q.* III. xi. 25 To her yold the flames.

γ. Chiefly *north.* 4–5 (6 *Sc.*) **ȝald, ȝalde,** (also 6, 9 *Sc.*) **yald,** (4 **ȝialde, yalld, yhald**); 4–5 **yauld,** 5 **ȝauld, ȝaulde.**

13 . . *Cursor M.* 1208 (Cott.) Lelli yald he him his teind. **13 . .** *Ibid.* 19794 (Edinb.) He hir raisid . . And ȝialde hir quic up for þaim alle. *c* **1320** *Sir Tristr.* 390 To crist his bodi he ȝald. *c* **1350** *Will. Palerne* 3661 þe kinges sone of spayne . . to hire ȝalde. **1375** Barbour *Bruce* IX. 320 Syne ȝald the castell to the king. *c* **1375** *Sc. Leg. Saints* xxii. (*Laurentius*) 496 He . . ȝauld þe spryt. *c* **1400** *Destr. Troy* 6499 He gird to þe ground, & þe gost yalde. *a* **1450** *Knt. de la Tour* lxxx, Whanne it plesed vnto God, he yalde ayen the sight vnto this good man. **1513** Douglas *Æneis* II. ix. 46 The gaist he ȝald with habundance of blude. **1552** Ȝald [see B. 14 c]. **1819** W. Tennant *Papistry Storm'd* (1827) 168 The kirk-yard's coffins yald and broke.

δ. 4 **ȝalt, ȝalte, yalt;** 4 **ȝelt(e,** 5 **yelte, yilt.**

c **1300** *Seynt Mergrete* in *Leg. Cath.* (1840) 100 He . . ȝelt hem her seruise With wel michel wouȝ. **13 . .** *Guy Warw.* (A.) 927 & wele he ȝalt him his while. *c* **1320** *Sir Tristr.* 261 Durst non oȝain him kiþe, Bot ȝalt him tour & toun. **1377** Langl. *P. Pl.* B. XII. 214 Why þat one thef on þe crosse creaunt hym ȝelt. *Ibid.* XVIII. 100 Ȝowre champioun chiualer . . Ȝelt [*v.rr.* ȝelte, yelde, yilt] hym recreaunt. *c* **1430** *Pilgr. Lyf Manhode* III. xxv. (1869) 150 Whan j sigh that he hadde don euele, he yelte ayen the pens.

ε. 4 **ȝeldid, yhelded, ȝeilded,** 4–5 **ȝeldede, yeldid,** 5 **ȝeldide, yeldyd, yeildyd, yyldyd,** 5–6 **yelded,** 6 **yealded,** *Sc.* **ȝeildit, yeldit,** 6–7 **yeelded,** 7–8 **yeilded,** 7– **yielded.**

a **1340** Hampole *Psalter* vii. 4 If i ȝeldid ill til ȝeldand til me ill for goed. **1340** —— *Pr. Consc.* 2272 He yhelded þe gast to God and dyghed. **13 . .** *Cursor M.* 696 (Gött.) Alkines thing in diuers wise ȝeilded to Adam þair seruise. *c* **1440** *York Myst.* xli. 356 Whose wombe that yeildyd fresh and fayr. **1474** Caxton *Chesse* II. v. (1883) 60 They opend the yates and yelded them vnto hym. *a* **1578** Lindesay (Pitscottie) *Chron. Scot.* (S.T.S.) I. 408 He . . held wpe his handis to god and ȝeildit the spreit. **1610** Holland *Camden's Brit.* I. 297 He yeelded unto nature, and ended his life. **1617** Moryson *Itin.* I. 241 The Mountaine . . of it selfe . . yeelded many wilde but pleasant fruits. *a* **1647** Clarendon *Hist. Reb.* I. §30 The King Yeilded. **1874** [see B. 10 b].

ζ. 5 **yoldede.**

1432–50 tr. *Higden* (Rolls) III. 269 The citesynnes . . yoldede the cite.

3. *Pa. pple.* α. 1 **ᵹolden,** 4 **yȝolden, ȝoldine, -un, yoldon, -un,** 4–5 **ȝolden, -yn,** (**yholden**), 4–6 **yolden, -in, -yn,** 5 **y-yolden,** (**ȝoldyne, ȝholden**), 5 (6 *Sc.*) **ȝoldin;** 5 **ȝoulden,** 6 **youlden,** *Sc.* **ȝowdin, yowdin,** 9 *Sc.* **yowden.**

a **900** *Kent. Glosses* in Wr.-Wülcker 67/9 *Et . . retribuetur*, and bið ᵹolden. *a* **1000** [see B. 6]. **13 . .** *Cursor M.* 23192 (Edinb.) þar sal be yoldin him his hire. **13 . .** *Guy Warw.* (A.) 1572 Ful iuel ichaue y-ȝolden it þe. *a* **1340** Hampole *Psalter* lxiv. 1 Body and saule, sall be ȝolden till þe in ierusalem. **1375** Barbour *Bruce* x. 804 He set ane sege thar-to stoutly, And lay thair quhill it ȝoldyn was. *c* **1400** *Rom. Rose* 4556 Curtesie certeyn dide he me So mych that may not yolden be. *c* **1450** *Brut* II. 492 þe town of Melun was yholden to þe Kynge. **1483** Caxton *Gold. Leg.* 67 b/1 Our lord hath yolden the malyce of Nabal on his owen heed. **1513** Douglas *Æneis* I. iii. 9 Quhy mycht I nocht on fieldis of Troy haue deid, And by thi richt hand ȝowdin furth my spreit? **15 . .** *Christ's Kirk* 151 in *Bannatyne MS.* (Hunter. Cl.) 287 For hir saik he wes nocht yoldin. **1553** Brende *Q. Curtius* III. 25 b, All the Cities . . that had bene youlden vnto hym. **1836** youden [see yolden 2].

β. 3–5 **iȝolde, yȝolde, yolde,** 4 **iȝoulde, hyȝolde, iȝulde, yȝulde,** 4–5 **y-yolde, ȝulde,** 4–6 **ȝolde,** 5 **i-yolde;** 5 **ȝold,** 5–6 **yold.**

1297 R. Glouc. (Rolls) 9223 Ar þe castel him were iȝolde. *a* **1300** *Floriz & Bl.* 809 To hire he haþ iȝolde Twenti pond of ride golde. **13 . .** *Bonaventura's Medit.* 346 Wheþer nat euyl be ȝulde for gode. **1340** *Ayenb.* 73 Hou uirtues and guode dedes byeþ heȝliche yolde. *Ibid.* 163 þ is dette ne may by uolliche y-yolde. **1412–20** Lydg. *Chron. Troy* I. 2220 With-out assaut þe castel were y-ȝolde. *a* **1450** *Knt. de la Tour* lxxxviii, Whanne they shalle be yolde ayenne an hundred folde more. *c* **1500** *Lancelot* 380 She aȝeine to hyme haith ansuer ȝolde. **1596** Spenser *F.Q.* VII. vii. 30 To reape the ripened fruits the which the earth had yold.

γ. 5 **ȝ(h)eldyn,** 5–6 **yelden(e,** 6 **-yn, yeelden.**

c **1425** Wyntoun *Cron.* III. ii. 276 þat he Sulde bundyn and syne ȝeldyn [*v.r.* ȝoldin] be. **1471** yelden [see B. 8]. **1556** *Chron. Grey Friars* (Camden) 14 This yere . . was the towne of Rome yeldene to the emperor. **1568** Grafton *Chron.* II. 80 Thinke . . what thou hast yelden to him againe. *a* **1586** Sidney *Arcadia* (1622) 95 Klaius . . who lately yeelden was To beare the bonds which time nor wit could breake.

δ. 4 **iyelt, iȝilde,** 5 **yȝeld, yelde,** 5, 7 **yeld,** 6 **yeeld.**

13 . . *Seuyn Sages* (W.) 1698 Oure gode dede schal ben iuel i-yelt. **1387** Trevisa *Higden* (Rolls) VII. 485 Forto he hadde i-ȝilde hym þe castel of Newerk. **1401** in Ellis *Orig. Lett.* Ser. II. I. 14 [He] hadd yȝeld op the Castell of Kermerdyn. *c* **1440** *Generydes* 4781 Townys and Castelys are yelde to his hand. **1578** Whetstone *Promos & Cass.* I. v. iii, Who (wonne by loue) hast yeeld the spoyle of thy virginity. *a* **1660** *Contemp. Hist. Irel.* (Ir. Archæol. Soc.) II. 24 Mariborough was . . treacherously yeld to Castlhauen the 9th of May.

ε. 5 **iȝelded, ȝeldid, yeldyde,** 5–6 **yelded,** 6–7 **yeelded,** 7– **yielded.**

c **1460** *Oseney Reg.* 128, j.d. ȝerely to be i-ȝelded to me and to my heyres. *c* **1489** Caxton *Sonnes of Aymon* xii. 304, I have yelded you agen that ye lended me right now. **1540** yelded [see B. 9]. **1561** Norton & Sackv. *Gorboduc* V. ii, Who fearing to be yelded fled before. **1651** Hobbes *Leviath.* III. xxxvi. 230 Before hee yeeld them obedience; unlesse he have yeelded it them already. **1875** Jowett *Plato* (ed. 2) I. 365, I should never have yielded to injustice from any fear of death.

ζ. 5 **yolded, -yd.**

1449 *Paston Lett.* I. 85 And ther they were yolded all the hundret schyppys to go with me in what port that me lust. *a* **1466** Gregory *Chron.* in *Hist. Coll. Cit. Lond.* (Camden) 115 The towne whythe grete sawte was yoldyd and wonne.

B. Signification.

I. To pay, repay, requite.

†**1.** *trans.* To give in payment, render as due, pay (money, a debt, tribute, tax, etc.). *Obs.*

c **893** Ælfred *Oros.* I. x. §1 þæt him leofre wære wið hiene to feohtanne þonne gafol to ᵹieldanne. *c* **950** *Lindisf. Gosp.* Matt. xviii. 30 *Donec redderet debitum*, wið he ᵹulde þæt scyld. *a* **1122** *O.E. Chron.* (Laud MS.) an. 1014 Se cyning het ᵹyldan þam here þe on Grenewic læᵹ .xxi. þusend punda. *c* **1205** Lay. 7372 þu ahtest me to ȝulden [*c* **1275** ȝelde] ȝauel of þine londe. *a* **1225** *Ancr. R.* 404 Iðen euentid, hwon me ȝelt werc-men hore deies hure. *a* **1300** *Cursor M.* 1985 And ȝeildes til your creatur þe tend part o your labour. *c* **1330** *Arth. & Merl.* 5219 Today ich ȝeld ȝour rentes Wiþ hard woundes & deþ dentes. *c* **1400** Maundev. (Roxb.) xxii. 104 þis citee ȝeldez ȝerely to þe Grete Caan . . l. thousand comacyes of florenes of gold. *c* **1450** *Godstow Reg.* 318 Symon Holle held j. Cotage, vj. acris of bond-lond, and shold yelde by the yere iij. shillings at two termes of the yere in even porcions. **1491** *Act 7 Hen. VII.* c. 19 §1 By the service of a redde rose . . to the same late Kyng and his heires for all maner services to be yolden. **1553** T. Wilson *Rhet.* 15 To performe their bargaines, to stand to their promises, & yelde their debtes. **1598** Manwood *Lawes Forest* iv. §1. 21 b, The killing of them [*sc.* foxes] is a breach of the kings Royal free Chase, and for that the offender shall yeelde a recompence. **1652** Needham tr. *Selden's Mare Cl.* II. xi. 272 Glocester yielded [orig. *reddebat*] xxxvi Dicres of Iron and c. iron rods fitted to make nails for the Kings ships.

2. a. To give as due or of right, or as demanded or required; to render (service, obedience, account, reward, thanks, etc.). Now somewhat *arch.*

c **1000** *Ags. Ps.* (Th.) cxviii[i]. 17 Ᵹild þinum esne gode dæde. *c* **1200** Ormin 5214 Lef faderr, ȝeld me nu Forr all min swinnc rihht mede. *a* **1225** *Ancr. R.* 186 þencheð anon þet he is ower uederes ȝerde, & þet he wule ȝelden him ȝerde seruise. *a* **1225** *Leg. Kath.* 2248 Ich am her, . . mid alle mine hirdmen, to ȝelden reisun for ham. **13 . .** *K. Alis.* 7420 (Laud MS.), Ȝeldeþ me homage alle. **13 . .** *Cursor M.* 461 (Gött.) Qui suld i him seruise ȝeilde? All sal be at mine aun weilde. **1362** Langl. *P. Pl.* A. VIII. 175 þer dede schullen a-rysen, . . and a-Countes ȝelden How þou laddest þi lyf. **1389** in *Eng. Gilds* (1870) 3 Which wardeins schul gadere þe qwarterage . . and trewelich ȝyld here acompt þerof. *c* **1400** tr. *Secr. Secr., Gov. Lordsh.* 49 With ioye y wente hoome ȝeldand to oure creatour gret þankynges. **1470–85** Malory *Arthur* XVII. xix. 717 They yelded hym honour and good aduenture. **1560** Daus tr. *Sleidane's Comm.* 49 They shal yeld an accompt for it one day. **1588** J. Udall *Diotrephes* (Arb.) 33 And so we her subiects should yeeld continual thanks vnto her highnesse. *c* **1610** *Women Saints* (1886) 170 Seeing we haue beene reserued to yield these funerall speeches to our brother and sister. **1663** Patrick *Parab. Pilgr.* xxxviii, That he might be moved to let go his right to punish us, and we not moved to be careless in yielding him the rest of his right which he hath to our . . obedience. **1823** Scott *Quentin D.* xv, What token canst thou give me, that we should yield credence to thee? **1831** James *Phil. Augustus* II. ii, Yield him obedience in lawful things. **1850** Tennyson *In Mem.* xxxvi, We yield all blessing to the name Of Him that made them current coin.

†**b.** To perform (a promise), pay (a vow). *Obs.*

c **825** *Vesp. Psalter* xlix. [l.] 14 Ᵹeld ðæm hestan ᵹehat ð in. **13 . .** *E.E. Allit. P.* B. 665, I schal . . ȝelde þat I hyȝt. **1382** Wyclif *Isa.* xix. 21 Thei shul vouwe vouwes to the Lord, and ȝeelde. *c* **1400** Maundev. ix. [xiii.], þei ȝolden vp here avowes. *c* **1400** tr. *Secr. Secr., Gov. Lordsh.* 110 Ȝelde þy hetynges.

†**c.** To give thanks to. *Obs. rare.*

c **1440** *York Myst.* x. 53 Nowe awe I gretely god to yeelde, That so walde telle me his entente.

†**3.** To pay for loss of or injury to (something); to make compensation for (loss or injury); to make up for, make good. (Also *absol.*) *Obs.*

a **900** *Laws of Ælfred* Introd. xxii, Ᵹif hwa adelfe wæterpyt . . & hine eft ne betyne, ᵹelde swelc neat swelc ðær on befealle. *c* **1000** Ælfric *Exod.* xxii. 6 Ᵹif fyr bærne muᵹan oððe standende æceras, ᵹylde þone byrst þe þæt fyr ontende. *c* **1175** *Lamb. Hom.* 31 þah ic hefde al þet ic efre biȝet, ne mahtic ȝelden swa muchel swa ic habbe idon to herme. *a* **1225** *Ancr. R.* 58 Heo schulen ȝelden þat best þat is þer inne ivallen. *Ibid.*, Heo is gulti of þe bestes deaðe . . & schal . . ȝelden þe bestes lure. **1340** *Ayenb.* 31 Uor hi ne moȝe amendi ne yelde þe harmes þet hi habbeþ ydo, and hit behoueþ yelde oþer hongy.

†**4.** To pay back, repay; to give back, restore. (In later use mostly with *again.*) *Obs.*

c **897** Ælfred *Gregory's Past. C.* liv. 425 Wenstu . . hwæðer he hine mid ðy ᵹehealdan mæᵹe ðæt he him nauht mare on ne nime, ne ðæt ne ᵹielde ðæt he ær nam? *c* **1175** *Lamb. Hom.* 79 Ȝif þu mare spenest of þine, hwan ic aȝen cherre, al ic þe ȝelde. *a* **1225** *Ancr. R.* 302 Schrift ȝelt eft al þet god þet we hefden uorloren. **13 . .** *E.E. Allit. P.* B. 1708 So ȝeply was ȝarked & ȝolden his state. **1362** Langl. *P. Pl.* A. v. 236 And ȝit I-chulle ȝelden aȝeyn ȝif I so muche haue. *c* **1400** *Cursor M.* 27867 (Cott. Galba) Till wrang tane thing be ȝolden ogayne. *a* **1450** *Knt. de la Tour* lxxx, And whanne it plesed vnto God, he yalde ayen the sight vnto this good man. **1450–1530** *Myrr. our Ladye* III. 295 So peace that was loste by Adams synne, he restored & yelded ageyne. **1489** Caxton *Faytes of A.* II. xxi. 219 He ought to be yolden ageyn to his frendes. **1552** Huloet, Yeld eftesones a thinge receiued, or taken, . . money borowed or suche like.

†**5. a.** To give (something) in return for something received; to render, return (a benefit or injury, etc.); const. *for.* *Obs.*

971 *Blickl. Hom.* 223 Ne he næniᵹne man unrihtlice fordemde, ne næniᵹum yfel wiþ yfele ᵹeald. *c* **1175** *Lamb. Hom.* 15 Ne scalt þu ȝelden vuel onȝein uuel nuða. *a* **1225** *Ancr. R.* 186 Ase þe apostle lereð, ne ȝelde neuer vuel uor god. *a* **1300** *Cursor M.* 4424 For þi leute and þi truthhede Ful iuel es yolden þe þi mede! **1387–8** T. Usk *Test. Love* I. iii. (Skeat) l. 107 Yvels for my goodnesse arn manyfolde to me yolden. **1390** Gower *Conf.* II. 292 It with kinde nevere stod A man to yelden evil for good. **1484** Caxton *Fables of Æsop* I. x, Euyll folk . . for the good done to them, they yeld ageyne euyll. *a* **1586** Sidney *Ps.* VII. iv, If I wrought not for his freedom's sake, Who causlesse now yeeldes me a hatefull hart: Then let my foe chase me.

b. To return (an answer, a greeting, or the like). Now only (with admixture of 10 b or 14), to vouchsafe (an assent) *to.*

a **1225** *Ancr. R.* 64 He . . þe sit & spekeð touward him, & ȝelt him word aȝein word. *a* **1300** *Cursor M.* 8166 And þair hailsing þai til him tald, Ful hendeli to þam he yald. *c* **1320** *Sir Tristr.* 1987 Brengwain answere ȝolde. *c* **1350** *Will. Palerne* 234 In hast þemperour hendely his gretyng him ȝeldes. *c* **1475** *Rauf Coilȝear* 224 And euer to his asking ane answer he ȝ ald. **1501** Douglas *Pal. Hon.* II. xix, Venus again ȝald thame thair salusing. **1526** *Pilgr. Perf.* (W. de W. 1531) 142 Than yf we be touched with a sharpe worde, we shal yelde a benigne & gentyll answere. **1603** Shaks. *Meas. for M.* IV. ii. 6 Leaue me your snatches, and yeeld mee a direct answere. **1840** Dickens *Old C. Shop* xvi, As he yielded to this suggestion a ready and rapturous assent, they all rose. **1875** Jowett *Plato* (ed. 2) I. 111 To this Protagoras yields a reluctant assent.

†**6.** To give something in return for, make return for, pay for, repay; to reward, recompense, requite (an action, etc., in good or bad sense; often with dative of person). Often in phr. ***God yield it you***: cf. 7 a. *Obs.*

a **1000** *Cædmon's Gen.* 413 þonne he me na on leofran tid leanum ne meahte Mine ᵹife ᵹyldan. *Ibid.* 1102 Min sceal swiðor mid grimme gryre ᵹolden wurðan fyll & feorhcwealm, þonne ic forð scio. *c* **1200** *Trin. Coll. Hom.* 5 For þanne he wile ðere ȝelden elch man his hwile mid swilch mede swo he ernede here. *c* **1200** Ormin 6239 þatt heore daȝȝwhammlike swinnc Beo daȝȝwhammlike hemm ȝoldenn. *c* **1250** *Kent. Serm.* in *O.E. Misc.* 33 Clepe þo werkmen and yeld hem here trauail. *a* **1300** *Cursor M.* 4996 'Sir', þai said, 'godd yeild [*v.rr.* ȝilde, ȝeild, ȝelde] it yow'. *a* **1300** *Assump. Virg.* (Camb. MS.) 249 Thu hast made me ofte glad; Thu has done as my sone bad, My sone shal it yelde to the. **13 . .** *K. Alis.* 132 (Laud MS.) He . . þinkeþ ȝelde his iniquite. *c* **1330** *Arth. & Merl.* 9241 He hadde iuel ȝolden þe kisseinge þat Gvenour him ȝaf at his arminge. *c* **1350** *Will. Palerne* 319 þat god for his grete miȝt al here god hem ȝeld. ? **1370** *Robt. Cisyle* 128 in Hazl. *E.P.P.* I. 274 The portar ȝalde hym hys travayle, He smote hym agayne withowten fayle. *c* **1400** *Destr. Troy* 7941 The dethe of þat doughty shalbe dere yolden With the blode of þi body. *c* **1400** *Gamelyn* 368 If . . thou thenke as thou seyst, god yelde it thee. *a* **1450** *Knt. de la Tour* lxxxviii, Suche good dedes, it is noble thinge to be do, and to vse, whanne they shall be yolde ayenne an hundred folde more. **1530** Palsgr. 786/1 Where I can nat, God yelde it you.

absol. **1382** Wyclif *Ps.* cxxxvii[i]. 8 The Lord shal ȝelde for me.

7. With personal object (orig. dative; sometimes with *to*). To reward, remunerate, recompense, repay. **a.** in good or neutral sense: esp. (in later use only) in phr. ***God yield*** (***you*** etc.), also corruptly ***God eyld . .***, ***God dild . .***, etc. (see god 8), from *c* 1400 to *c* 1600 a common expression of gratitude or goodwill. *Obs.* or *rare arch.*

Beowulf 1184 Wene ic þæt he mid gode ᵹyldan wille uncran eaferan. **971** *Blickl. Hom.* 123 Se ilca Drihten . . us þonne wile . . æᵹhwylcum anum men ᵹyldan & leaniᵹean æfter his sylfes weorcum. *a* **1175** *Cott. Hom.* 231 He . . elc ȝeelt efter his ȝearnunge. *c* **1250** *Gen. & Ex.* 2581 God it ȝeald ðese wifes wel, On hom, on haȝte, eddi sel! *c* **1300** *Havelok* 803 God yelde him þer i ne may, þat haueth me fed to þis day! *c* **1350** *Will. Palerne* 1547 But loueliche lemman oure lord mot þe ȝeld þat þi worþi wille was to come to me nouþe. *c* **1400** *Beryn* 1680 A Ml in this town Wold do hym worshipp.. God hem ȝeld! so have þey offt or nowe. *c* **1430** *Pilgr. Lyf Manhode* I. cxlvii. (1869) 75 Whan þei weren trussed, grace dieu, god yilde hire wel, goodliche spak to me. **1454** *Paston Lett.* (1904) II. 331 Suster, God ȝelde ȝow for ȝowre labore fore me, for gaderyng of my mony. *c* **1489** Caxton *Sonnes of Aymon* xxiii. 495 'Gramercy, sir', sayd the duke rycharde, 'and god yelde you!' **1575** *Gammer Gurton* v. ii, *Baily*. God blesse you gammer Gurton. *Gamer*. God dylde you master mine. **1602** Shaks. *Ham.* IV. v. 41 How do ye, pretty Lady? *Ophelia*. Well, God dil'd you. **1606** —— *Ant. & Cl.* IV. ii. 33 Tend me to night two houres, I aske no more, And the Gods yeeld you for't. **1608** Chapman *Byron's Conspir.* v. *ad fin.*, Marry God dild him. **1872** Tennyson *Gareth & Lynette* 18 Heaven yield her for it.

†**b.** in bad sense: To take vengeance on, 'pay out'. *Obs.*

13.. *Sir Beues* (A.) 318 Al þat haþ me fader islawe,.. Ich schel hem ȝilden [14.. *MS. M.* I shall be vengid]. *c* **1380** Wyclif *Sel. Wks.* III. 43 Myn is þe veniaunce, and I schal ȝelde hem in tyme. **1382** —— *Ps.* xl. 11 [xli. 10] Thou.. Lord.. aȝeen rere me, and I shal ȝelde to them.

II. To give or put forth, produce, furnish, exhibit.

8. a. To give forth from its own substance by a natural process, or in return for cultivation or labour; to produce, bear, generate (fruit, seed, vegetation, minerals, etc.); to put forth (a bud, shoot, etc.); †to bring forth, give birth to, bear (offspring). Now chiefly *arch.* or *poet.*

In first quot. with partitive object.

a **1300** *Cursor M.* 4720 þof men ouer all has saun feilds, O corn es þar noght as þat yeilds. **1471** Caxton *Recuyell* (Sommer) 31 She this day hath rendred & yelden þe fruyt of her wombe a sone and a doughter. **1573–80** Tusser *Husb.* (1878) 31 For want of seede, land yeeldeth weede. **1577** Googe tr. *Heresbach's Husb.* 39 b, The Female [hemp].. dooth yeelde a white flowre. **1577** Harrison *England* II. xv. 90 b/2 in *Holinshed*, Till they.. spread or yeld their rootes down right into the soyle about them. **1591** Shaks. *Two Gent.* I. ii. 107 Iniurious Waspes, to feede on such sweet hony, And kill the Bees that yeelde it, with your stings. **1608** —— *Per.* v. iii. 48 Thy burden at the Sea, and call'd Marina, for she was yeelded there. **1611** *Bible* Gen. i. 29 Euery tree, in the which is the fruit of a tree yeelding seed. **1613** Purchas *Pilgrimage* VII. xi. 595 The soile yeeldeth Cloues, Ginger, and Siluer. **1651** Bp. Hall *Soliloquies* xvi, If I look into my orchard I see the well grafted scions yield, first a tender bud. **1672** Grew *Idea Philos. Hist. Pl.* §43 Turpentine, which, in Distillation, yieldeth Oyl and Water, both limpid. **1697** Dryden *Virg. Georg.* III. 482 The salacious Goat encreases more; And twice as largely yields her milky Store. **1744** Berkeley *Siris* §25 Trees growing in low and shady places do not yield so good tar. **1857** Miller *Elem. Chem., Org.* (1862) iii. §3. 194 They all combine with the elements of water and yield one of the acids homologous with formic acid. **1859** E. FitzGerald *Omar* v, But still the Vine her ancient Ruby yields.

fig. **1587** Golding *De Mornay* xvi. (1592) 262 This minde of ours doth also yeeldfoorth words. *Ibid.* 267 When did euer purenesse yeeldfoorth corruption?

b. To furnish (a produce of so much). Also with *up*.

a **1300** *Cursor M.* 12329 þan quen it [*sc.* wheat] scorn was, weil it yalld A hundret o þair mettes tald. **1577** Harrison *England* I. xiii. 38/1 in *Holinshed*, Eche acre of Whete.. will yeeld commonly twentie bushelles. **1577** Googe tr. *Heresbach's Husb.* 30 b, The other kinde [of oats] is lyghter.. and yeeldeth but little flowre. **1667** Primatt *City & C. Builder* 4 Inclosed Lands in many places doth yeild half as much, or as much more, as Lands in common fields. **1833** Ht. Martineau *Briery Creek* iii. 63 The farmer makes his land yield double by good tillage. **1888** P. Strutt in *Homilist* Sept. 391, I have seen a barrowful of crushed quartz-rock yield up at last.. a little spoonful of gold.

c. To produce as a result; to give as a mathematical product. Now *rare* or *Obs.*

1542 Recorde *Gr. Arts* L vij, I multiply the first numbre 3 into yᵉ second 40000, and it yeldeth 120000. **1593** Fale *Horologiogr.* 31 The quotient Sine shall yeeld an arke, whose Complement shall be named the Complement repeated. **1876** R. H. Hutton *Ess.* (ed. 2) I. Pref. 26 Wherever two or more independent and equally worthy sources of information appear to yield up inconsistent results.

d. *absol.* To bear produce; to be productive or fertile. †Hence, to turn out (in a certain way).

1297 R. Glouc. (Rolls) 5696 þe erþe ȝeld betere & þet weder was murgore bi is daye.. þan me er ysaye. *c* **1300** *Prov. Hendyng* in *Sal. & Sat.* (1848) 277 Lyþt chep luþere ȝeldes, quoþ Hendyng. **13..** *Gaw. & Gr. Knt.* 498 A ȝere ȝernes ful ȝerne, & ȝeldez neuer lyke. *c* **1386** [see yielding *vbl. sb.* 4]. *c* **1425** Wyntoun *Cron.* II. v. 316 He couythe weil bathe ken and se Qwhat lande sulde ȝhelde or fertile be. *c* **1440** *York Myst.* x. 30 Sara was vncertan thanne That euere oure seede shulde sagates ȝelde. **1523–34** Fitzherb. *Husb.* §10 If the grounde be good, putte the more beanes to the pease, and the better shall they yelde. **1639** J. Taylor (Water P.) *Part Summers Trav.* 14 A good Myne that doth hold out, and yield plentifully. **1760** R. Brown *Compl. Farmer* II. 38 It makes corn to yield well. **1856** Morton *Cycl. Agric.* II. 1132/1 Spalding's Prolific Red Wheat.. yields remarkably well, and weighs well in the bushel.

†**9.** (with compl.) To render, make, cause to be; also occas. to make, cause (*to do* something).

c **1430** *Pilgr. Lyf Manhode* I. cli. (1869) 76, I haue a stoon þat to þe folk, whan j wole, yelt inuisible. *c* **1450** *Mankind* 733 in *Macro Plays* 27 My inwarde afflixcyon ȝeldyth me tedyouse wn-to yowur presens. **1540** Palsgr. *Acolastus* I. i. D iv, What? is not he yelded quiete (with these wordes)? **1581** A. Hall *Iliad* v. 83 For doubt that this our forwardnesse may yeelde vs both to die. *Ibid.* VIII. 135 This threat and surly speech doth yeelde the Gods amazde and dum. **1609** *J. Rainolds's Def. Judgm.* Pref. A ij b, That.. holy man, whose learning.. and pietie.. may perhaps yeeld him more admirable to posteretie. **1674** *T. Campion's Art Descant* II. 35 Example will yield it more plain.

10. To give, in various senses. †**a.** To deliver, hand over, present, offer. Also with *up*. *Obs.* or merged in other senses.

a **1300** *Cursor M.* 8743 (Cott.) Me think.. þe child be nawight don to ded, Bot he be yoldon to yond wijf. **13..** *Ibid.* 10220 (Gött.) Ilkan to þe temple broght Sere giftes.. All þair giftes þai ȝeld vp þar. **13..** *Gaw. & Gr. Knt.* 67 Syþen riche forth runnen to reche honde-selle, Ȝeȝed ȝeres ȝiftes on hiȝ, ȝelde hem bi hond. **1382** Wyclif *Prov.* xxvii. 24 A croune shal be ȝolde [*late vers.* ȝouun] to thee. *a* **1483** in *Engl. Gilds* (1870) 316 þᵗ euery prentes.. shall elde a brekefast to the forsayde M. and Wardons. **1603** Shaks. *Meas. for M.* v. i. 7 Our soule Cannot but yeeld you forth to publique thankes. **1613** Purchas *Pilgrimage* II. i. 90 Where the holy Trinitie did first yeeld it selfe in sensible apparition to the world. **1807** J. Barlow *Columb.* III. 212 No furious God bestorms our soil and skies, Nor yield our hands the bloody sacrifice.

b. To give as a favour, or as an act of grace; to grant, accord, allow, let (one) have, bestow.

a **1225** *Juliana* 72 Schendeð hire nuðen ant ȝeldeð hire ȝarew borh. *a* **1300** *K. Horn* 1066 (Cambr. MS.) King þe wise, Ȝeld me mi seruise. Rymenhild help me winne. *a* **1450** *Knt. de la Tour* lxx, Afterwarde God yelde her that she had deseruid. **1575** Gascoigne *Glasse Govt.* Wks. 1910 II. 48 God is.. bountifull, yelding unto every man that is industrious the open way to knowledge. **1582** Stanyhurst *Æneis* I. (Arb.) 35 Yeeld pytye, graunt mercy. *c* **1586** C'tess Pembroke *Ps.* CXL. iv, Yeeld, O Lord, that ev'n the head of those That me enclose, Of this their hott pursute May tast the frute. **1590** Spenser *F.Q.* III. xi. 17 To yield him loue she doth deny. **1624** Sir J. Davies *Ps.* iii. 4 Wks. (Grosart) I. 365 His God to him not safety yeilds nor aid. **1825** Scott *Betrothed* xxxi, 'I know but one [jugglers' feat]', said Vidal, 'and I will shew it, if you will yield me some room.' **1833** Tennyson *Miller's Dau.* xviii, And slowly was my mother brought To yield consent to my desire. **1874** Green *Short Hist.* ii. §6. 89 The King yielded the citizens the right of justice. **1885–94** R. Bridges *Eros & Psyche* May xxiv, His name she never learn'd, Nor was his image yielded to her sight.

†**c.** To exercise, exert (a function, force, etc.); to deliver, deal (blows), to give (battle); to execute, inflict (a sentence, vengeance). *Obs.*

a **1300** *Cursor M.* 5872 And taron sett he men at ask Of ilk dai to yeild þair task. *c* **1315** Shoreham VII. 893 God þe fader hys leue sone Engendrede out of alle wone,.. Ac man haþ certayn tyme of elde Wanne he may engendrure ȝelde. **13..** *Seuyn Sag.* (W.) 1932 Thries misdede this womman bald, And thre vengaunces he hire yald. *c* **1350** *Will. Palerne* 2708 þe selcouþ a-sautes þat þei samen ȝolde. *a* **1400–50** *Wars Alex.* 3126 He.. Bid buske him eft to þe bent vs bataill to ȝeld. *c* **1400** *Destr. Troy* 1177 Iche buerne on his best wise batell to yelde. *c* **1435** *Torr. Portugal* 2572 Smert boffettes there they yeld. **1561** Googe tr. *Palingenius' Zodiac* v. O v, Of custome long is nature bred and yeldes her force alway To vse that long time hath bene kept. **1581** A. Hall *Iliad* I. 3 The rancor ceaseth not, til they do yeeld their vengeance due. **1581** J. Bell *Haddon's Answ. Osor.* 118 b, Christ.. doth encourage them.. which do yeld their endeuour.. to performe yᵉ rule of the Gospell.

11. To give forth, emit, discharge; to utter. Also *absol.* *Obs.* exc. as represented by weakened uses of other senses, as 8, 14.

c **1450** Lovelich *Grail* lvi. 481 And the tombe owt blood gan ȝelde. **1535** Lyndesay *Satyre* 4354 Scho riftit, routit, and maid sic stends, Scho ȝeild, and gaid at baith the ends. **1548–77** Vicary *Anat.* v. (1888) 44 It causeth the stomacke to yeld from him that is within him. **1552** Huloet, Yeld forth licoure, or moystnes, *exsudo*. **1581** A. Hall *Iliad* IV. 72 They cries and clamors yeeld. **1591–5** Spenser *Colin Clout* 822 Ne is there shepheard.. That dare.. Blaspheme his powre, or termes vnworthie yield. **1626** Bacon *Sylva* §22 So we finde that Violets.. yeeld a pleasing Sent. **1853** M. Arnold *Scholar Gipsy* iii, Air-swept lindens yield Their scent. **1872** Tennyson *Gareth & Lynette* 1344 The huge pavilion slowly yielded up.. that which housed therein.

†**12. a.** To give, render, state, declare, deliver, communicate (speech, or something expressible in speech, as a reason, etc.). *Obs.*

a **1350** *St. Sextus* 109 in Horstm. *Altengl. Leg.* (1881) 107 Decius Cesar.. Demed þam al thre to ded. And when þe dome was ȝolden swa, þan answerd þe dekins twa [etc.]. **1382** Wyclif *1 Tim.* vi. 13 Crist Jhesu, that ȝelde a witnessing vndir Pilat of Pounce. *a* **1400–50** *Wars Alex.* 5192 Lat þi semblance be sadd quen þou þi saȝe ȝildis. **1575–85** Sandys *Serm.* i. §24 We haue no other reason to yeeld of our dooing, but onely this. *a* **1577** Sir T. Smith *Commw. Eng.* (1633) 230 The order of proceeding to judgment is by assent of voyces and open yeelding their mind in court. **1581** J. Bell *Haddon's Answ. Osor.* 104 b, Yeldyng the same in the Latine toung almost, which Basile before him dyd expresse most manifestly in the Greeke toung. **1601** Shaks. *All's Well* III. i. 10 The reasons of our state I cannot yeelde. **1602** Marston *Ant. & Mel.* I. I. B 3, Hast thou yeelded vp our fixt decree Vnto the Genoan Embassadour? *Ibid.* IV. G 4, She were no woman, if shee could not yeelde strange language. **1607** Rowlands *Diogines Lanthorne* E 3 b, Morrow (quoth he) Philosopher, I yeild thee time of day. **1645** Ussher *Body Div.* 43 What reason can you yeeld for this?

†**b.** To report as being so-and-so: = deliver *v.*[1] II c. *Obs.* *rare*$^{-1}$.

1606 Shaks. *Ant. & Cl.* II. v. 28 Anthony's dead. If thou say so Villaine, thou kil'st thy Mistris. But well and free, if thou so yeild him, there is Gold.

13. a. To give so as to supply a need or serve a purpose; to give or provide for use, furnish, afford.

a **1548** Hall *Chron., Edw. IV*, 226 b, They could none otherwise do, but.. yelde & geue hym a reasonable reward. **1560** Daus tr. *Sleidane's Comm.* 282 b, He made a goodly librarie, whiche yelded certen notable bookes afterwardes. **1585** Higins *Junius' Nomencl.* 392/2 *Castellum*,.. a conduit built with cocks and spowts to yeeld water. *a* **1586** Sidney *Ps.* XVIII. iv, The cherubins their backs, the winds did yeild their wings To beare his sacred flight. **1605** Camden *Rem.* 1 Navigable rivers, which yeelde safe havens and roads. **1607** Topsell *Four-f. Beasts* 594 That there is such a beast in the world, both Pliny.. and others, doe yeald erefrigable testimony. **1661** J. Childrey *Brit. Baconica* 103 This County also yeilds good store of Honey. **1674** Playford *Skill Mus.* (ed. 7) II. 102 Making each several string yield a clear sound. **1781** Cowper *Retirem.* 326 Man is an harp whose chords elude the sight, Each yielding harmony, dispos'd aright. **1836** W. Irving *Astoria* II. 128 The narrow valley.. being watered by a running stream, yielded fresh pasturage. **1862** Spencer *First Princ.* II. v. §57 (1875) 185 A ball fastened to the end of an india-rubber string yields a clear idea of the correlation between perceptible activity and latent activity. **1894** H. Drummond *Ascent of Man* 251 Two flints struck together yielded fire.

b. To give rise to, cause, occasion (a state or feeling). Now *rare*.

1576 Gascoigne *Steele Glas* 709 But if it.. might empaire, offende, or yeld anoy Unto the state. **1581** A. Hall *Iliad* I. 15 Yeelding the Greekes a thorough feare, the Troyans courage hie. **1618** J. Taylor (Water P.) *Penniless Pilgr.* B 3, We made a field-bed in the field, Which sleepe, and rest, and much content did yeeld. **1632** Lithgow *Trav.* x. 448 The English Fleete.. comming, yeelded no small feare to the affrighted Towne. **1746** Francis tr. *Hor. Epist.* II. ii. 120 [He] Yields Diversion to the gaping Throng. **1855** Bain *Senses & Int.* II. i. §49. 400 Curved forms and winding movements yield of themselves a certain satisfaction through the muscular sensibility of the eye.

c. To furnish or produce as profit, bring in.

1573–80 Tusser *Husb.* (1878) 74 Good cow & good ground Yeelds yeerely a pound. **1599** B. Jonson *Cynthia's Rev.* v. iv, I frotted a jerkin, for a new-reuenu'd gentleman, yeelded me threescore crownes, but this morning. **1603** G. Owen *Pembrokeshire* (1892) 114 Rockes yeldinge small proffitte. **1700** S. L. tr. *Fryke's Voy. E. Ind.* 96, I.. please my self with the thoughts of what it would yeild me among the Chineeses, and the English. **1840** Dickens *Old C. Shop* xii, I have sold the things. They have not yielded quite as much as they might have done. **1895** *Manch. Guardian* 14 Oct. 5/5 It has cost altogether Rx. 875,000, and will yield a revenue to the Government of Rx. 50,000.

†**d.** To present to view, exhibit. *Obs.*

1622 Peacham *Compl. Gentl.* xvi. 206 The valley yeelding so goodly a prospect, as I neuer beheld a better. *a* **1700** Evelyn *Diary* 20 July 1654, The stables are well order'd and yeild a gracefull front. **1726** Shelvocke *Voy. round World* 69 We had a clear view of Staten land, which yields a most uncomfortable landskip.

III. To surrender, give way, submit.

14. a. To hand over, give up, relinquish possession of, surrender, resign. *arch.* or *poet.*

(*a*) in material sense, esp. of surrendering a military position or forces to an enemy.

1297 R. Glouc. (Rolls) 3366 þat hii ssolde him þe castel ȝelde ar he wiþ strengþe him nome. *a* **1300** *Cursor M.* 7164 þe Iuus was þan þair vnder-lute, Sampson bunden þai yald for dute. *c* **1300** *Havelok* 2717 Do nu wel with-uten fiht, Yeld hire þe lond. *c* **1386** Chaucer *Wife's T.* 56 And suretee wol I han er þat thou pace Thy body for to yelden in this place. **1460** Capgrave *Chron.* (Rolls) 161 Had he not come, the cyte had be ȝoldyn. *c* **1470** *Gol. & Gaw.* 1032 Gif thou luffis thi life,.. Yeld me thi bright brand, burnist sa bene. **1508** Kennedie *Flyting w. Dunbar* 545 Deulbere, thy spere of were, but feir, thou yelde. **1582** N. Lichefield tr. *Castanheda's Conq. E. Ind.* I. lxxviii. 158 The shippe beeing yeelded, our men did enter the same. **1617** Moryson *Itin.* II. 233 The besieged did yeeld the place to the Queene. **1698** Fryer *Acc. E. India & P.* 151 We soon made him yield his Prize to engage with us. **1850** Tennyson *In Mem.* xc, The hard heir strides about their lands, And will not yield them for a day.

(*b*) in immaterial sense.

a **1300** *Cursor M.* 10602 þai yald hir [*sc.* the child Mary] to þe temple þan. **1486** in *Surtees Misc.* (1890) 54 Yelding his title and his crowne unto the king. **1570** Foxe *A. & M.* (ed. 2) 2296/2 [Queen Mary] who beyng long sicke before, vpon the sayd xvii. day of Nouember,.. yelded her life to nature. **1586** A. Day *Engl. Secretorie* II. (1595) 28, I was content to yeeld my interest for eleuen hundred and three score poundes. **1611** *Bible* Rom. vi. 13 Neither yeeld yee your members as instruments of vnrighteousnes vnto sinne. **1623** J. Taylor (water P.) *New Discov.* Bj, We.. Were glad to yeeld the honour of the day Vnto our foes. **1656** Bramhall *Replic.* App. 34 He is well contented to pass by them all in silence, which is as much as yeeld the Cause. **1748** Gray *Alliance* 53 The prostrate South to the Destroyer yields Her boasted Titles. **1802** Maria Edgeworth *Moral T., Forester* xvii, It will be imagined that I yield my opinions from meanness of spirit. **1833** Newman *Arians* IV. i. 312 The timid Constantius, yielding to fear what he denied to justice. **1838** James *Robber* vii, You have yielded your heart and your happiness to one of whose.. family you know nothing.

†(*c*) To give up, resign (mentally). *Obs. rare.*

1697 Dampier *Voy.* (1699) 17 Those two men that we left the day before did not come to us till we were in the North Seas, so we yielded them also for lost.

(*d*) To relinquish, surrender (a position of advantage or point of superiority).

1590 Spenser *F.Q.* I. ii. 15 Each to other yeeldeth land. **1647** Cowley *Mistr., Bathing in River* iii, And still old Lovers yield the place to new. *a* **1700** Evelyn *Diary* 3 June 1666, [This] put new courage into our Fleete, now in a manner yielding ground. **1797** Godwin *Enquirer* I. viii. 69 Grief does not easily yield its place to joy. **1851** Mrs. Browning *Casa Guidi Wind.* I. 1074 Living heroes who will scorn to yield A hair's-breadth even. **1864** *Congressional Globe* 5 Mar. 934/2 *Mr. Schenck*. I ask the gentleman from Vermont to yield to me for about five minutes. *Mr. Morrill*. I will yield the gentleman ten minutes of my time. **1869** Swinburne *Ess. & Stud.* (1875) 268 The finest of Coleridge's Odes is beyond all doubt the 'Ode to France'... It were profitless now to discuss whether it should take or yield precedence when weighed with the 'Ode to Liberty'.

b. with *up*; rarely with *over*.

a **1225** *Ancr. R.* 266 þreateð þet ȝe wulleð ȝelden up þene castel bute ȝif he sende ou þe sonre help. *c* **1290** *St. Lucy* 83 in *S. Eng. Leg.* 103 Ich ȝelde him op al mi bodi. *c* **1350** *Will. Palerne* 1256 He ȝald vp his swerd to saue þanne his liue. *a* **1400–50** *Wars Alex.* 1140 Or he ȝode þai ȝolde hym vp þe realm. *a* **1548** Hall *Chron., Hen. VIII*, 258 He tolde them ..that onlesse thei woulde yelde vp the toune..he would put them to the sword. **1600** *Old Cheque-Bk. Chapel Royal* (Camden) 5 Edward Pearce yealded up his place for the Mastership of the children of Poules. **1611** *Bible* 1 Macc. x. 32, I yeeld vp my authoritie ouer it. **1814** Scott *Ld. of Isles* iv. xxix, The ring which bound the faith he swore, By Edith freely yielded o'er. **1842** Dickens *Amer. Notes* ix, He had kindly yielded up to us his wife's own little parlour. **1852** —— *Bleak Ho.* xvi, Sir Leicester yields up his family legs to the family disorder [*sc.* gout].

c. *to yield* (*up*) *the ghost* (*soul, breath, life, spirit*): to 'give up the ghost', die, expire. *arch.*

c **1290** *S. Eng. Leg.* 211 He was neiȝ ope þe pointe þene gost op to ȝelde. *a* **1300** *Cursor M.* 209 How our leuedi endid and yald Hir sely saul. *c* **1330** R. Brunne *Chron. Wace* (Rolls) 13262 þey fond hym sone, ȝeldyng þe gast. *c* **1386** Chaucer *Knt.'s T.* 2194 Whan with honour vp yolden is his breeth. *c* **1430** *Chev. Assigne* 335 He bowethe hym down & ȝeldethe vp þe lyfe. *c* **1500** *Lancelot* 1088 The batell was richt crewell to behold, Of knychtis wich that haith there lyvis ȝolde. **1552** Lyndesay *Monarche* 4000 Thay,..For extreme hunger, ȝald the spreit. **1610** Holland *Camden's Brit.* i. 303 Canutus the Hardie..who there amid his cups yeelded up his vitall breath. **1611** *Bible* Gen. xlix. 33 He..yeelded vp the ghost, and was gathered vnto his people. **1627** J. Taylor (Water P.) *Armado* C 4, The Horse proued himselfe a mortall beast, yeelding his breath into the ayre. **1844** Mrs. Browning *Romaunt of Page* xviii, Out upon the traitor's corse Was yielded the true spirit. *a* **1845** Hood *Fall of Deer* 35 Nor like a Craven yeeld his Breath.

d. *refl.* and †*pass.* To be dedicated or devoted *to*; to give oneself up or be addicted *to*.

? *a* **1366** Chaucer *Rom. Rose* 429 As she were, for the love of God, Yolden to religioun. **1390** Gower *Conf.* III. 317 In blake clothes thei hem clothe,..And yolde hem to religion. *c* **1500** *Lancelot* 951 Y ware ȝolde euermore to be your knyght. **1621** T. Williamson tr. *Goulart's Wise Vieillard* 124 Eleazar..was gone and yeelded to prophane ceremonies. **1825** Scott *Talism.* iv, All the extravagances which strong affection suggests and vindicates to those who yield themselves up to it. **1852** Dickens *Bleak Ho.* xiii, I.. yielded myself for a little while to the interest of the scene.

15. *refl.* To give oneself up, surrender, submit, as to a conqueror (now *rare*; superseded by 16). Also with *up*.

1297 R. Glouc. (Rolls) 5447 þe maystres of þe lond ȝolde hom to hom echon [*v.rr.* ȝulde, ȝoulde, ȝeldede, ȝelden]. *a* **1300** *Cursor M.* 23769 Hardili es he cuward,..þat yeildes him ar he be soght. **13..** *Gaw. & Gr. Knt.* 1215, I ȝelde me ȝederly, & ȝeȝe after grace. *c* **1400** *Brut* cxcvii. 219 Anone he & his company comen to the Gentil Knyght..& saiden 'ȝelde þe, traitour! ȝelde þe!' **1470–85** Malory *Arthur* viii. xxii. 306 Rather shalle he slee me than I shal yelde me as recreaunt. **1567** *Gude & Godlie B.* (S.T.S.) 237 Quhen deith cummis thair is na vther grace, Bot ȝeild the than, for doutles thow mon die. **1596** Shaks. *1 Hen. IV*, v. iii. 10 Vnlesse thou yeeld thee as a Prisoner. **1611** Speed *Hist. Gt. Brit.* ix. xix. 724/1 The sight of vs their annointed Soueraign shall..cause them..submissiuely to yeeld themselues to our mercy. **1642** J. Taylor (Water P.) *Life Henry Walker* A 3 b, Others would have him come on Land and yeeld himselfe. *a* **1648** Ld. Herbert *Hen. VIII* (1683) 243 Genoua also was constrained to yield it self, and shake off the French yoke. **1847** Tennyson *Princess* vii. 343 Indeed I love thee: come, Yield thyself up.

with *compl.* **1377** Langl. *P. Pl.* B. xii. 193 He ȝelte [*v.rr.* yald, ȝelde, yelde, ȝalte, ȝald] hym creaunt to cryst on þe crosse & knewleched hym gulty. *c* **1500** *Melusine* 335 My intencion is thither to goo and to yeld my self there hermyte. **1560** Daus tr. *Sleidane's Comm.* 284 b, I yelde my self prisoner to you saith he. *c* **1645** Howell *Lett.* I. iii. xxxi. (1655) 157 My Don will..yeeld himself his prisoner. **1651** Hobbes *Leviath.* i. xii. 54 To those that have yeelded themselves subjects. **1802** Maria Edgeworth *Moral T., Prussian Vase*, He..yielded himself up a prisoner. **1813** Scott *Rokeby* iv. xvi, He..yielded him an easy prey To those who led the Knight away.

const. *inf.* **1590** Sir J. Smythe *Disc. Weapons* Ded. 1 b, [They] will (with humility) yeeld themselues to heare and learne by their experiences.

16. a. *intr.* To give oneself up, surrender, submit (as overcome in fight). Also with *up* (*obs. rare*).

c **1330** *Arth. & Merl.* 3451 Seuen kniȝtes..to hem ward gun priken..& bad hem ȝeld. *c* **1450** *Merlin* 461 Sir knyght, thow art take: yelde thow to me. **1509** Hawes *Past. Pleas.* xvi. lxx, It [*sc.* a castle] must yelde vp, or els be wonne at length. **1599** Shaks. *Hen. V*, iv. ii. 37 England shall couch downe in feare, and yeeld. **1605** Camden *Rem.* 28 The rebells therewith weere so terrified, that they forthwith yeelded. **1672** Marvell *Corr.* Wks. (Grosart) II. 400 The whole Province of Utrecht is yielding up. **1719** De Foe *Crusoe* i. (Globe) 270 There needed very few Arguments to perswade a single Man to yield, when he saw five Men upon him, and his Comrade knock'd down. **1791** Cowper *Iliad* xvii. 16 Yield. Leave the body and these gory spoils.

†with *compl.* *a* **1547** Surrey *Æneis* ii. 77 [They] brought ..A yongman, bound his handes behinde his back Whoe willingly had yelden prisoner.

b. In wider sense: To give way, be subjected, submit (cf. 17); *occas.* to break down, succumb.

1576 Gascoigne *Steele Glas* Ep. Ded., Shall I yelde to mysery as a just plague apointed for my portion? **1577** tr. *Bullinger's Decades* iv. ii. 566 The worldly griefe is the sorrowe of such men..as yeeld vnder the burthen of sorrowe. **1593** Shaks. *3 Hen. VI*, v. ii. 11 Thus yeelds the Cedar to the Axes edge. **1640** G. Sandys *Christ's Passion* i. 184 Not yeelding to the charmes of Sleep. *a* **1721** Prior *Turtle & Sparrow* 86 Sorrow shou'd to Prudence yield. **1750** Gray *Elegy* 25 Oft did the harvest to their sickle yield. **1813** Scott *Rokeby* vi. xxiii, The night has yielded to the morn. **1840** Dickens *Old C. Shop* xliv, The child..soon yielded to the drowsiness that came upon her. *a* **1862** Buckle *Civiliz.* (1873) III. v. 355 Theory should yield to fact, and not fact to theory. **1896** *Pall Mall Mag.* May 17 The night was yielding, and the dawn came up in a thin white mist.

†**c.** *pa. pple.* in *refl.* or *intr.* sense = that has surrendered. Hence in *pass.* sense = forced to surrender, subdued. *Obs.* Cf. yielded, -en, yolden.

In first quot. with mixed constr.

a **1330** *Otuel* 862 Hit where sschame..To sslen a man þat ȝolden him is. *c* **1374** Chaucer *Troylus* iii. 1211 Now yeldeth yow, for oþer bote is noon. To þat Criseyde answered þus a-noon, Ne hadde I er now, my swete herte dere, Ben yolden, y-wys I were now not here. **1387–8** T. Usk *Test. Love* i. vii. (Skeat) l. 30 Although the party be yolden, he may with wordes saye his quarel is trewe. *a* **1400–50** *Wars Alex.* 1899 þe erthe at to myne enpire enterely bees ȝolden. **1470–85** Malory *Arthur* vii. xi. 228 Whan ye see me beten or yolden as recreaunt. **1533** Bellenden *Livy* iv. xii. (S.T.S.) II. 91 þe Inemyis kest away þare wappynnys and war ȝoldin presoneris. *a* **1547** Surrey *Æneis* ii. 827 Like as the elm..doth bend his top, Till yold with strokes..with ruin it doth fall. *a* **1600** Montgomerie *Sonn.* xxxvi. 7, I ȝoldin am, and ȝit am stryving still. *a* **1600** —— *Misc. Poems* xxi. 11 To prove on me thy pith,..That ȝoldin am in will.

†**d.** To give place, give way *to*. *Obs.*

1604 E. G[rimstone] *D'Acosta's Hist. Indies* iii. xxvii. 201 In some partes one element ends and another beginnes, yeelding by degrees one vnto another. **1611** Mure *Misc. Poems* ii. 42, I yeild to the, more worthie thame nor I.

e. To be inferior *to*. Now *rare*.

[**1604** E. G[rimstone] *D'Acosta's Hist. Indies* iv. xxvi. 281 But as touching almonds and other fruites, all trees must yeelde to the almonds of Chachapoyas.] **1617** Moryson *Itin.* i. 18 The City [of Nuremberg]..may perhaps yield to Augsburg in treasure and riches. **1726** Swift *Gulliver* i. vi, Their mutton yields to ours, but their beef is excellent. **1826** Syd. Smith *Wks.* (1859) II. 74 Demerara yields to no country in the world in her birds. **1832** R. & J. Lander *Exped. Niger* I. iv. 187 The vast plain on which it stands, although exceedingly fine, yields in..fertility and..beauty ..to the delightful country surrounding the..city of Bohoo.

17. a. To give way *to* persuasion, entreaty, or the like; to cease to oppose or object; to submit, comply, consent. Also with *up* (*obs. rare*).

? *a* **1500** *Chester Pl.* (E.E.T.S.) vii. 647 Turne to thie fellowes and kis! I yeald, for in my youth we haue bene fellowes, I wis. **1531** Elyot *Gov.* iii. xviii. (1883) II. 315 Ther lacked litle that the yonge man was nat vainquisshed; and that the flesshe yelded nat to the seruice of Venus. **1561** T. Hoby tr. *Castiglione's Courtyer* ii. Q iv b, He woulde neuer yelde at the perswasion of many Scholars. **1583** in *Cath. Rec. Soc. Publ.* V. 43 Yealdinge to the froward importunities of the Donatists. **1589** Hakluyt *Voy.* To Rdr. ¶8, I haue yeelded vnto those my freindes which pressed me in the matter. **1596** Shaks. *Merch. V.* iv. i. 425 You presse mee farre, and therefore I will yeeld. **1630** Prynne *Anti-Armin.* 2 We will forthwith yeeld up to them without any more dispute. **1671** Milton *P.R.* ii. 409 Thy temperance..For no allurement yields to appetite. **1749** Fielding *Tom Jones* x. iii, He..yielded to the dissuasions of his friend from searching any farther after her that night. **1866** G. Macdonald *Ann. Q. Neighb.* xxvi, As soon as they had yielded to my arguments. **1874** Green *Short Hist.* viii. §5. 516 The danger at last forced the King to yield to the Scotch demands.

†**b.** with *inf.* or *clause*, or with *to* and sb.: To submit, consent, agree (*to do* something, *that* something should be done, or *to* something proposed).

1572 in *13th Rep. Hist. MSS. Comm.* App. iv. 13 If such reasons shall not move him for to yeald to departe. **1597** Hooker *Eccl. Pol.* v. lxxi. §7 To..graunt that what their fancie will not yeelde to like, their iudgement cannot with reason condemne. **1598** Grenewey *Tacitus, Ann.* i. xvi. 31 The Reatins..no way yeelding that the mouth of the lake Velinus should be dammed vp. **1604** E. G[rimstone] *D'Acosta's Hist. Indies* vii. xii. 529 As this was preparing, and every one yeelded to this treatie of peace [etc.]. **1626** in Ellis *Orig. Lett.* Ser. i. III. 245 Which news so soon as the French heard, their courage came downe, and they yielded to be gone the next tyde. **1667** Milton *P.L.* ix. 248 To short absence I could yeild, For solitude somtimes is best societie. *Ibid.* 902 How hast thou yeelded to transgress The strict forbiddance? *a* **1763** Shenstone *Elegies* vii. 55 Should some patron yield my stores to bless. **1799** Jane West *Tale of Times* xxxiii, Nor can I yield to sully my integrity by basely framing a forged accusation. **1814** —— *Alicia de Lacy* IV. 265 He yielded to ask for mercy, but he yielded without hope of success.

18. *trans.* †**a.** With compl. adj. or adj. phr.: To acknowledge or admit that a person or thing is so-and-so. *Obs.*

a **1300** *Cursor M.* 28077 Til our lauerd crist and þe, M. gastli fader, yeild i me Plighti for my syn o pride. **1377** Langl. *P. Pl.* B. v. 374, I, glotoun,..gylti me ȝelde, þat I haue trespassed with my tonge. *c* **1400** Maundev. (1839) x. 120 Ȝeldynge him self gylty, and cryenge him mercy. **1450–1530** *Myrr. our Ladye* ii. 87 Yeldyng vs gylty not for the thanke of man but *Coram domino*. **1591** Shaks. *1 Hen. VI*, ii. iv. 42 Till you conclude, that he vpon whose side The fewest Roses are cropt from the Tree, Shall yeeld the other in the right opinion. **1630** W. Freake *Doctr. Jesuits* 17 Which thing, if I shall yeeld unto you as lawfully done [etc.]. **1667** Milton *P.L.* xi. 526, I yeild it just, said Adam, and submit. **1673** *Lady's Call.* i. iv. ¶19, I shall be thought to have out-run my subject... Yet I cannot yield it wholly impertinent. **1676** Dryden *Aurengz.* i. i, He yields his Arms unjust if he withdraws. **1744** Eliza Haywood *Female Spect.* viii. (1748) II. 65, I knocked under, in token of yielding myself in the wrong.

†**b.** With clause or acc. and inf.: To concede or admit that a thing is so. *Obs.*

1590 Spenser *F.Q.* ii. ix. 38 Pensiue I yeeld I am, and sad in mind. **1605** Chapman *All Fooles* ii. i, I must yeeld,..I did..Make such a frivall promise. **1628** T. Spencer *Logick* 242 The Apostle Paul 2 Cor. ii. 6 is content to yeeld his accusers, that, he was 'rude in speech'. **1633** Bp. Hall *Hard Texts* 1 Cor. vii. 40, I thinke that I also shall be yeelded to have the Spirit of God. **1692** Locke *3rd Let. Toleration* iv. 114, I will yield my self to have mistaken you. *a* **1697** Aubrey *Lives, Suckling* (1898) II. 241 Sir John Digby.. yielded to be the best swordsman of his time. **1703** Rowe *Fair Penit.* v. i, 'Tis hard for Souls like mine..to yield they have done amiss.

c. With simple obj., with or without dative of the person: To grant, allow, concede the fact, validity, or cogency of. Now *rare* (and associated with 14).

1571 Campion *Hist. Irel.* vii. (1633) 20 The honourable Historian Titus Livius, yeeldeth certaine priviledge to antiquitie. **1611** Shaks. *Wint. T.* iv. iv. 421, I yeeld all this. *c* **1620** A. Hume *Brit. Tongue* (1865) 22 This idle e;..in wordes ending in c..as peace, face..these I yeld because I ken noe other waye to help this necessitie. **1652** Brome *Queenes Exch.* i. i, Tis true, the King Osriick..may be thought fit To be endow'd with all you seem to yeild him. **1713** Swift *Cadenus & Vanessa* 265 And Pallas, if she broke the laws, Must yield her foe the stronger cause. **1713** Steele *Englishman* No. 55. 354 All which wise Men mean was yielded on both sides by our Lawyers. **1907** *Verney Mem.* I. 63 The point appears to have been yielded.

†**19.** *refl.* To betake oneself (cf. F. *se rendre*); hence ***yield-you*** as a nonce-rendering of *rendez-vous*.

c **1330** R. Brunne *Chron. Wace* (Rolls) 14225 [Guenevere] ȝald hure til þat nonnerye. *c* **1400** *Rom. Rose* 4904 He..yalte [him] into somme couente. **1470–85** Malory *Arthur* xvii. xxiii. 724 Sire Percyual yelded hym to an hermytage oute of the cyte. **1578** H. Wotton *Courtlie Controv.* 295 He tooke his leaue of hir, and went out..into a narrowe by lane, where from thenceforth euer after the (yeeld you) was giuen him.

20. a. *intr.* To give way under some natural or mechanical force, so as to collapse, stretch, bend, crack, etc.; *spec.* To deform inelastically; to undergo a large increase in strain without a corresponding increase in stress. Const. *to* (the force, pressure, etc.).

1552 Huloet, Yeld againe as dankysh, *contabesco*. **1577** [see yielding *ppl. a.* 4]. *c* **1580** Lodge *Reply Gosson's Sch. Abuse* (Hunter. Cl.) 26 Looke for wonders where musike worketh,..the bowels of the earth yeld where the instrument soundeth. **1590** Greene *Neuer too late* (1600) E j, As there is a Topace that will yeeld to euery stamp, so there is an Emerald that will yeeld to no impression. **1603** G. Owen *Pembrokeshire* (1892) 2 [The sea] doth not..seeme to yeld to the lande in anye parte. *c* **1610** *Women Saints* (1886) 64 The same stone moste miraculouslie being pulled, would yield like a bowe. **1735** Johnson *Lobo's Abyssinia, Descr.* x. 98 After Rains,..the Ground yields and sinks so much, that [etc.]. **1830** R. Knox *Béclard's Anat.* 196 If they [*sc.* the arteries] be distended in the longitudinal direction, they yield and elongate. **1860** Tyndall *Glac.* i. xiv. 96 The snow yielded, he fell, and slid swiftly downwards. **1883** Gresley *Gloss. Coal M.* s.v., Pillars of coal are said to yield when they commence to give way or crush. **1900** *Phil. Mag.* L. 77 The assumption..that the material yields when one of the principal stresses reaches a certain amount. **1927** F. V. Warnock *Strength of Materials* iii. 46 At the point *C* the material has yielded a large amount, and the corresponding stress is known as the 'Yield Stress'. **1968** A. H. Cottrell *Introd. Metallurgy* xxi. 395 Suppose that the central grain.. has in fact so yielded (e.g. because of the stress-concentrating effect of a foreign inclusion in it), but its neighbours are still elastic.

b. To submit *to* some physical action or agent (e.g. pressure, friction, heat, etc.) so as to be affected by it.

1794 Kirwan *Elem. Min.* (ed. 2) I. 37 He distinguishes those that yield to the file, as the white copper ore, hæmatites, etc. **1827–35** N. P. Willis *Idleness* 49 When the frost has yielded to the sun. **1838** Dickens *O. Twist.* xxi, The door yielded to the pressure. **1847** W. C. L. Martin *Ox* 158/1 Ophthalmia arising..from blows, generally yields to bleeding. **1867** H. Macmillan *Bible Teach.* Pref. (1870) p. vii, The mountain must yield to the action of cold and heat. **1908** H. Wales *Old Alleg.* xvii. 292, I was surprised that you didn't yield to brandy.

†**21.** To decline, turn aside, be deflected *from* a path or course: *lit.* and *fig.* *Obs.*

1576 Fleming tr. *Caius' Dogs* 15 [Setters] attend diligently vpon theyr Master,..inclining to the right hand, or yealding toward the left. **1631** Markham *Cheap Husb.* (ed. 6) i. ii. 22 Ease your hand, and draw it up againe, letting it come and goe till hee yeeld and goe backeward. **1806** *Simple Narrative* I. 21 Without yielding, in the smallest degree, from the resolution she had formed.

IV. 22. *Comb.*: **yield-capacity**, capacity of yielding or producing; **yield gap**, the excess rate of return of long-dated or undated Government stocks over that of ordinary shares; **yield-point**, (the stress corresponding to) the point on a stress–strain diagram at which the strain begins to increase substantially without a corresponding increase in stress: in some metals differentiated as ***upper yield point***, a point at which the stress ceases to increase as the strain increases, prior to a fall to the *lower yield point*, from which the strain increases while the stress remains almost constant at the lower value; also, esp. in *Geol.*, the elastic limit or the yield strength; **yield sign** *U.S.* = give-way sign; **yield strength**, in materials that do not exhibit a well-defined yield point, the stress at which (in addition to the elastic deformation) a definite amount of plastic deformation is produced (usu.

taken as 0·2 per cent of the unstressed length); **yield stress**, the value of stress at a yield point or at the yield strength.

1889 *Nature* 12 Dec. 122 To assess the yield-capacity of any locality stocked with Scotch pine. **1959** *Economist* 25 Apr. 353/1 Investors today keep a careful eye on the 'yield gap'—the margin between dividend yields on ordinary shares and long term rates of interest set by the yield on irredeemable Consols. **1981** *Observer* 4 Oct. 19/2 It would also draw attention to the widening yield gap between gilts and shares. [**1870** G. Berkeley in *Exper. Mech. & Other Properties Steel* 4 Within the 'yielding point' of Steel the amount of lengthening from tension, or shortening from compression, produced by equal forces per unit of area is nearly the same.] **1886** K. Pearson in I. Todhunter *Hist. Theory Elasticity & Strength of Materials* I. 887 When a bar is subjected to increasing traction, a certain stretch is reached after which there is a sudden and rapid increase of stretch... The point at which this change takes place is very marked, and various names have been suggested for it, as the limit of fatigue, the limit of stability, and the break-down point. The latter name brings out the character of the phenomenon, but at the same time suggests a point related to absolute strength or cohesion; I have therefore spoken of this point in the present work as the yield-point. **1889** *Telegr. Jrnl. & Electr. Rev.* 20 Dec. 707/1 The question of discontinuity of the curves about the 'yield point' was next discussed. **1919** Fuller & Johnston *Appl. Mech.* II. x. 378 If the material is very ductile a yield point in torsion will appear at a torque somewhat higher than the elastic limit, similar to the yield point in tension. **1967** J. G. Ramsay *Folding & Fracturing of Rocks* vi. 258 The specimen has.. been permanently strained because the elastic limit has been exceeded. The point where this limit is first exceeded is known as the yield point. **1968** A. H. Cottrell *Introd. Metallurgy* xxi. 390 In some materials.. general yielding can begin in a very striking manner with a yield drop in which the applied stress falls, during yielding, from an upper yield point to a lower yield point. **1971** B. Scharf *Engin. & its Lang.* iv. 23 Many metals such as aluminium, copper and brass have high ductility but no definite yield point (yield stress). **1981** *Pop. Hot Rodding* Feb. 66/1 To delve into this whole subject more deeply, we discussed it with SPS engineer Jack Schmidt, who spoke to us of tensile strength, yield points, and clamping loads. **1951** C. E. Riggs in *Amer. City* June 133/1 On one street of each open intersection the sign reading *slow yield right of way* is erected... The new 'yield' signs are.. of distinctive shape. **1977** J. Cheever *Falconer* 48 Putting up traffic signs, speeding signs, yield signs, stop signs. **1935** *Proc. Amer. Soc. Testing Materials* XXXVIII. 1315 *Yield strength*, the stress at which a material exhibits a specified limiting permanent set. **1967** *Times Rev. Industry* Feb. 45/2 Some British orders went overseas because of the inability.. to cope with the more difficult combinations of pipe diameter, wall thickness and yield strength. **1982** *Materials Sci. & Engin.* LVI. 10/1 The yield strength of tempered lath martensitic 0·4% C steels is generally independent of packet size. **1913** *Proc. R. Soc.* A. LXXXVIII. 465 The observed stress at yield might.. be below the true yield stress. **1954** C. W. MacGregor in W. R. Osgood *Residual Stresses in Metals* 110 Local yielding occurred with an applied uniform tensile stress considerably less than the yield stress. **1971** [see *yield-point* above]. **1973** C. R. Barrett et al. *Princ. Engin. Materials* vi. 208 The applied tensile stress required to induce plastic behavior is known as the elastic limit or yield stress. **1973** J. G. Tweeddale *Materials Technol.* I. iv. 81 The yield stress is slightly above the elastic limit since it clearly represents the incidence of gross plastic strain.

yieldable ('jiːldəb(ə)l), *a. rare.* [f. yield *v.* + -able.] †**a.** Having the quality of yielding, productive *of.* †**b.** Disposed to yield, submissive. **c.** That can be yielded. *rare*⁻⁰ (mod. Dicts.). Hence **'yieldableness** (in quot., †submissiveness).

1577 Harrison *England* I. viii. 17 b, in *Holinshed*, If.. the soyle [were] yeeldable of woode. **1603** H. Crosse *Vertue's Commw.* (1878) 19 She is euer readie to dwel where she findeth the heart yeeldable to honestie. **1645** Bp. Hall *Three Tract., Peace-maker* §13 The fourth disposition for Peace, a yeeldablenesse upon sight of clearer Truths.

†**'yieldance.** *Obs.* [f. yield *v.* + -ance. (A favourite word with Bp. Joseph Hall.)] The action of yielding, in various senses.

1. Surrender, submission, compliance.

1610 Bp. Hall *Apol. Brownists* 2 The spirits of these men are two-well knowne, to admit any expectation of yeeldance. **1633** —— *Hard Texts* Rom. vii. 8 Had not the law strictly restrained us from the yeildance unto sinne. **1657** Trapp *Comm. Job* ix. 14, 87 Seeking to disarm his indignation by an humble yeildance. *a* **1716** South *Serm., Gal.* ii. 5 (1727) V. 490 For if the things under Debate be given up to the Adversary, it must be upon one of these two Accounts; either, 1. That the Persons who thus yield them up, judge them unfit to be retained. Or, 2. That they find themselves unable to retain them; one or both of these must of necessity be implied in such a Yieldance.

b. Granting, allowance.

a **1656** Bp. Hall *Specialities Life* Rem. Wks. (1660) 23 If .. I might draw him to a willing yieldance of that parcell of my due maintenance, which was kept back from my not over-deserving predecessor.

2. Production, yield.

a **1656** Bp. Hall *Serm., Ps. cvii.* 34 Wks. 1662 III. 197 How should the corn, wine, oyl, be had without the yieldance of the earth? **1668** Steele *Husbandman's Calling* vii. 183 When it [*sc.* harvest] comes, sometimes the poor yieldance of it utterly disappoints him.

yielded ('jiːldɪd), *ppl. a.* [f. yield *v.* + -ed¹.] Surrendered, given up, granted, etc.: see the verb.

1591 Savile *Tacitus, Hist.* iv. lxxx. 231 A dishonoured captiue, and yeelded person. **1595** Shaks. *John* v. ii. 107 Haue I not heere the best Cards for the game..? And shall I now giue ore the yeelded Set? **1697** Dryden *Æneis* xii. 1359 Against a yielded Man, 'tis mean ignoble Strife. **1801** Southey *Thalaba* iii. xix, The rushing flow, the flowing roar, Filling his yielded faculties. **1810** Scott *Lady of L.* i. xxxiv, He sought her yielded hand to clasp. **1868** Morris *Earthly Par., Watching of Falcon* (1870) I. 582 And yielded towns were set aflame. **1895** W. Watson *Odes* etc. 53 O yielded lips, O captive breast!

†**yielden**, *ppl. a. Obs.* [pa. pple. of yield *v.* (A. 3 γ). Cf. yolden.] = prec.

a **1542** Wyatt in *Tottel's Misc.* (1557) H ij b, The fierce lyon will hurt no yelden thinges. *a* **1547** Surrey *Æneis* ii. 196 Ye sacred bandes I wore as yelden hoste. **1561** Norton & Sackv. *Gorboduc* ii. ii, Shall I abide,.. And holde my yelden throate to traitours knife?

yielder ('jiːldə(r)). Forms: see yield *v.* [f. yield *v.* + -er¹.] One who or that which yields.

†**1.** One who has to pay, i.e. owes, something; a debtor. *Obs.*

1340 *Ayenb.* 163 He ne is naȝt riȝtuol, þet ne yziȝþ naȝt ine his herte,.. and onderstant, þet he is yeldere, and a-yens god of treuþe, toppe alle þing. *Ibid.* 262 [see yielding *vbl. sb.* 1].

†**2.** A rewarder. *Obs.*

1382 Wyclif *Judith* Prol., Ȝeldere of hir chastite. **1388** —— *Ecclus.* xxxv. 13 For whi the Lord is a ȝeldere [1382 ȝeldende], and he schal ȝelde seuene fold so myche to thee.

3. One who gives something up, or gives in; a surrenderer (also with *up*); one who concedes.

1590 Shaks. *Mids. N.* iii. ii. 30 For briars and thornes at their apparell snatch, Some sleeues, some hats, from yeelders all things catch. **1597** —— *2 Hen. IV*, iv. ii. 123 The Block of Death, Treasons true Bed, and yeelder vp of breath. **1598** —— *1 Hen. IV*, v. iii. 11 (Qo. 1), I was not borne a yeelder thou proud Scot. **1893** *Daily News* 25 May 5/6 In the hope that they might get concessions from this universal yielder.

4. Something that produces or furnishes, a producer; now esp. with qualifying word referring to the amount or quality of the produce.

1733 W. Ellis *Chiltern & Vale Farm.* 198 A sort [of wheat].. that.. is a great Yielder to the Barn. **1861** W. Barnes in *Macm. Mag.* June 132 Nature's yielders of good. **1906** *Westm. Gaz.* 6 Dec. 2/3 The quality of the good milker's milk is better than that produced by the small yielder.

yieldiness: see yieldy.

yielding ('jiːldɪŋ), *vbl. sb.* [f. yield *v.* + -ing¹.] The action of the verb yield.

†**1.** Payment; *transf.* obligation to pay, debt.

1340 *Ayenb.* 115 Ich am mochel ine dette ayen þe.. and.. ich ne habbe huer-of maki þe yeldinge. *Ibid.* 262 Uorlet ous oure yeldinges, ase and we uorleteþ oure yelderes. *c* **1380** Wyclif *Wks.* (1880) 423 þis is.. but ȝilding of dette bi mannus lawe.

2. The giving of something as due, or as a favour; rendering; bestowal.

1340 Hampole *Pr. Consc.* 7846 Yheldyng of mede for ilk gud dede. **1382** Wyclif *Ps.* cii[i]. 2 And wile thou not forȝete alle the ȝeldingus of hym.

†**3.** Repayment, reward, recompense, retribution.

a **1340** Hampole *Psalter* xciii[i]. 2 Ȝelde ȝeldynge til proude. **1382** Wyclif *Isa.* lxvi. 6 Vois of the Lord ȝeldende ȝelding to his enemys. **1382** —— *Luke* iv. 19 He sente me.. to preche the ȝeer of the Lord plesaunt, and the day of ȝeldynge. **1388** —— *Ps.* cxxx. 3 [cxxxi. 2] As a child wenyde on his modir, so ȝelding be in my soule. *c* **1440** *Promp. Parv.* 537/1 Ȝeldynge, *reddicio.* **1530** Palsgr. 291/1 Yeldeng, *retribution.*

4. Production of crops or the like; produce.

c **1386** Chaucer *Prol.* 598 Wel wiste he by the droghte and by the reyn The yeldynge of his seed and of his greyn. **1547–8** in E. Green *Somerset Chantries* (1888) 32 A tenement in Pytmyster.. the yelding wherof John Forde.. solde unto William Voysey.. for xij. li. sterling. **1903** *Smart Set* IX. 127/2 Speculating as to the profit of this year's yielding. **1922** W. Schlich *Man. Forestry* (ed. 4) I. 97 Timber fit for sawing would begin to be cut about 10 to 15 years later, and by the eightieth year the forests should be in full yielding.

5. a. Giving *up*, giving in, surrender, submission.

c **1425** Wyntoun *Cron.* viii. xxv. 3833 Syn of þe ȝeldyn [*v.r.* ȝelding] tretyt þai, þat gif þai be a certane day War noucht reskewit.. þai sulde gif vp þe towne. *c* **1475** *Rauf Coilȝear* 837 'Ȝarne efter ȝ eilding,' on ilk syde thay call. **1544** in Leadam *Sel. Cases Crt. Requests* (Selden Soc.) 112 To make an yeldynge yf she lyst.. by the delieueryng of a mote to any of the seyd tenauntes to the vse of them whom shall please her. **1568** Grafton *Chron.* I. 427 Eche part with an hundred Knightes and Esquiers,.. to fight and combate to the yeldyng. **1583** Melbancke *Philotimus* R iv, But this, nor anye thinge coulde enforce him to relinquish his suite, sauing the yelding of her battered brest. **1606** Shaks. *Tr. & Cr.* ii. ii. 25 What merit's in that reason which denies The yeelding of her vp? **1631** Weever *Anc. Funeral Mon.* 769 At the battaile, and yeelding vp of Mont de dier. **1711** Shaftesb. *Charac.* II. 214 A Sacrifice and mutual yielding of Natures one to another. **1818** Keats *Endym.* i. 411 She.. breath'd a sister's sorrow to persuade A yielding up. **1885** *Athenæum* 17 Oct. 499/2 More or less cowardly yieldings to panic and sedition.

b. Giving way, as to persuasion or the like; compliance, concession, consent.

1588 Shaks. *L.L.L.* i. i. 118 How well this yeelding rescues thee from shame. **1592** —— *Rom. & Jul.* ii. ii. 105 Therefore pardon me, And not impute this yeelding to light Loue. **1611** *Bible* Eccl. x. 4 Yeelding pacifieth great offences. **1634** Canne *Necess. Separ.* (1849) 108 Their bare presence argues their approbation and yielding in show to ceremonies. *a* **1647** Clarendon *Hist. Reb.* i. §22 (1702) I. 12 His Yeilding to the violent passion. **1749** Fielding *Tom Jones* iv. vi, He.. imputed her yielding, to the ungovernable force of her love towards him. **1844** Kinglake *Eothen* xv, I can see no limit to the yielding, and bending of his mind when it is worked upon by the idea of power. **1856** Froude *Hist. Eng.* II. vii. 130 Nothing was to be gained by yielding in minor points.

6. Giving way, as to pressure or other physical force. Cf. yield *v.* 20.

1665 Hooke *Microgr.* 41 It is.. shrunk,.. which is caused by the yielding a little of the hardened Skin to a Contraction. **1683** Moxon *Mech. Exerc., Printing* xxiv. ¶7 The softness or yielding of the Paper, Tympan, and Blankets. **1688** Boyle *Final Causes* iv. 176 The Yielding of the Flexible Branch or Twigs whereto the Nest is fastened. **1860** Tyndall *Glac.* i. ii. 10 There will be a gradual yielding of its mass under the pressure. **1899** J. A. Ewing *Strength of Materials* iii. 31 There is.. a well-marked yield point.. at which extension goes on for a time through a considerable distance without increase of load. After this the extension becomes less rapid until the final yielding occurs just before rupture. **1961** Lubahn & Felgar *Plasticity & Creep in Metals* v. 104 When a piece of metal is loaded in such a way that the elastic stress is non-uniform,.. yielding begins at the most highly stressed point. **1973** C. R. Barrett et al. *Princ. Engin. Materials* viii. 257 The yielding usually starts at a small notch or irregularity in the sample and subsequently propagates throughout the sample.

'yielding, *ppl. a.* [f. as prec. + -ing².] That yields, in various senses.

†**1.** Owing, indebted: cf. yielder 1, yielding *vbl. sb.* 1. *Obs. rare.*

1340 *Ayenb.* 169 Asemoche ase he is worþ betere þanne ich, zuo moche ich am yeldinde be riȝte riȝtuolnesse.

2. Bearing produce, productive, fertile. ? *Obs.*

1553 Grimalde *Cicero's Offices* i. (1556) 59 b, Nothing is better than groundtilth and trimmyng, nothing yeeldinger, nothing sweeter, nothing meeter for a freeborne man. **1598** Yong *Diana* 441 The fertilitie of the yeelding soyle. **1777** [W. Marshall] *Minutes Agric., Digest* 45 *note*, In a yielding Year, a Jag of equal size to those alluded to will afford from two Quarters to twenty Bushels of Wheat. **1849** C. Lanman *Lett. Alleghany Mts.* xx. 159 The yielding wells are somewhat over two hundred feet deep.

3. Giving in, surrendering, submitting; disposed to submit, submissive, compliant, unresisting.

1578 H. Wotton *Courtlie Controv.* 44 As the Hunter who pleasureth not to take the yeilding pray, thou shunnest me. **1599** B. Jonson *Ev. Man out of Hum.* iv. v, I am eas'ly yeelding to any good Impressions. **1698** [Ferguson] *View Ecclesiastick* 5 To become Guilty of the Little and mean Vanity of Attacking a yielding as well as a Routed Enemy. **1741–2** Gray *Agrippina* 197 With fond reluctance, yielding modesty. **1749** Fielding *Tom Jones* xi. iii, Sophia, who was yielding to an excess,.. at last gave way. **1801** Scott *Glenfinlas* xvii, Fair woman's yielding kiss. **1811** W. R. Spencer *Poems* 75 You may press her yielding hand. **1848** Dickens *Dombey* xxxv, There are yielding moments in the lives of the sternest and harshest men.

4. Giving way to pressure or other physical force; not stiff or rigid; taking impression, bending, collapsing, etc.

1577 T. Kendall *Flowers Epigr.* 42 Can Flint or Marble harde be made, as yeldyng Butter softe? **1590** Spenser *F.Q.* iii. xi. 25 A thunder bolt Perceth the yielding ayre. **1613** Purchas *Pilgrimage* viii. iii. 618 Neither can the hard-hearted Rockes breake these yeelding Vessells. **1639** T. de Grey *Compl. Horsem.* 313 By some fall upon yeelding or slippery ground. **1697** Dryden *Æneis* ii. 66 His forceful Spear.. Pierc'd through the yielding Planks of jointed Wood. *a* **1732** T. Boston *Crook in Lot* (1805) 132 The cannon ball breaks down a stone wall, while the yielding packs of wool take away its force. **1827** Keble *Chr. Y., Prayers at Sea*, Beneath the shadowy clouds The yielding waters darken in the breeze. **1890** *Retrospect Med.* CII. 258 The shafts of all the long bones being so soft and yielding that the mere weight of the limbs is sufficient to produce their distortion.

Hence **'yieldingly** *adv.*, **'yieldingness** (see senses 3 and 4 above).

1560 A. L. tr. *Calvin's Four Serm. Song Ezech.* (1574) Ep., You see him sometyme *yeldingly stretch out, sometyme struglingly throw his weakend legges. **1592** Warner *Alb. Eng.* viii. xlii. 28 As Mayds that know themselues belou'd and yeeldingly resist. **1823** Moore *Loves of Angels* Introd. 53 A Spirit of light mould, that took The prints of earth most yieldingly. **1862** Lytton *Str. Story* lxxxvi, Like the clouds that are yieldingly pierced by the light of the evening star. **1607** Hieron *Wks.* I. 282 This readinesse and *yeeldingnesse of the inward man. **1766** Fordyce *Serm. Yng. Women* (1767) II. xiii. 222 A degree of complacence, yieldingness, and sweetness, beyond what we look for in men. **1802** Paley *Nat. Theol.* viii. 124 The yieldingness of the cartilaginous substance. **1838** Lytton *Alice* viii. vi, Evelyn was gentle, even to yieldingness. **1880** J. E. Burton *Handbk. Midwives* 227 The thinness and yieldingness of the bones.

'yieldless, *a. poet. rare.* [f. yield *v.* + -less.] Unyielding; not surrendering; not productive.

1651 Davenant *Gondibert* iii. ii. civ, A Fort so yeildless, that it fears to treat. **1703** Rowe *Ulysses* iii. i, Undaunted, yieldless, firm. **1974** R. Adams *Shardik* xxxiv. 285 There was.. something sinister about this place, unhusbanded and yieldless in the midst of the abundant land all about.

yieldy ('jiːldɪ), *a. rare.* [f. yield *sb.* or *v.* + -y¹.] **a.** Productive, fertile. **b.** Having the quality of yielding or giving way physically. Hence **'yieldiness.**

1598 Chapman *Iliad* v. [ix.] 92 Of the most fat and yeeldie soile. **1757** tr. *Henckel's Pyritologia* 42 Themselves containing nothing of the noble metals, yet mixed with other ores.. prove yieldy. **1857** Mayne Reid *War-Trail* xiii, A.. serpentine yieldiness of movement. **1933** *Amer. Speech*

VIII. I. 53/2 That 'ar west bottom never was much yieldy, nohow.

yien, yiet, yif(f, yift, yigh: see EYE *sb.*[1], YET, GIVE, IF, GIFT, YEA.

‖**Yigdal** ('jɪgdəl). *Judaism.* Also 9 Yigdol. [Heb., = 'may he be magnified', the opening word of the hymn.] A Hebrew hymn, thought to have been composed by Daniel ben Judah (fl. *c* 1300), embodying the thirteen articles of the Jewish faith, and recited at morning prayer and on Sabbath and festival eves.

1845 *Jewish Chron.* 19 Sept. 244/1 The children sang in a beautiful manner the hymn Yigdol (Sabbath Hymn). **1892** I. ZANGWILL *Childr. Ghetto* I. xii. 269 You confound the air of the Passover *Yigdal* with the New Year ditto. **1907** J. JULIAN *Dict. Hymnol.* (ed. 2) II. 1149/2 The hymn [sc. *The God of Abraham Praise*] is a free rendering, with, as Olivers puts it, as decided 'a Christian character' as he could give to it, of the Hebrew *Yigdal* or Doxology, which rehearses in metrical form the thirteen articles of the Hebrew Creed.

yight, obs. form of OUGHT *v.* (q.v., 6 b γ.)

c **1386** CHAUCER *Pars. T.* ¶ 321 (Egerton MS.) He þat.. hath despite to doon þat hym yight to do.

Yi Hsing (iː ʃɪŋ). Also **I-hsing, Yi-hsing.** [f. the name *Yi Xing* of a town in Jiangsu prov., China.] In full ***Yi Hsing yao, Yi Hsing ware.*** A type of unglazed stoneware (esp. for teapots) first produced at Yi Xing in the Song dynasty and reaching its height in the later part of the Ming dynasty.

1904 E. DILLON *Porcelain* x. 165 The Yi-hsing yao, made at a place of that name.. includes the red unglazed ware. **1910** *Encycl. Brit.* V. 744/2 The manufacture of red teapots, mugs, bowls, cups, &c., in imitation of the Yi-Hsing-Yao was widespread during the late 17th and early 18th centuries under the name of red porcelain. **1915** R. L. HOBSON *Chinese Pott. & Porc.* xv. 178 The Yi-hsing wares in the celebrated Chinese ceramic collection formed by Augustus the Strong at Dresden supplied designs for the fine red stoneware made in the first years of the eighteenth century by Böttger. **1945** [see BOCCARO]. **1970** *Ashmolean Mus.: Rep. Visitors 1969* 47 Tea-pot, I-hsing brown stoneware, Chinese, 18th century. **1971** L. A. BOGER *Dict. World Pott. & Porc.* 378/2 Yi Hsing Yao.. an unglazed stoneware produced at Yi-hsing-hsien in Kiang-su province... Its greatest productive period was during the latter part of the Ming dynasty and during the Ch'ing period.

yijs, obs. form of YES.

yike (jaɪk), *sb.*[1] An imitation of the cry of the woodpecker. So **yike** *v.*

1889 D. JORDAN & JEAN A. OWEN *Woodland, Moor,* etc. 38 The yikeing laugh of the green woodpecker. **1891** —— *Within an Hour London T.* xi, [The green woodpecker] making the woods ring with his maniacal yikes! **1892** —— *Forest Tithes* (1893) 126 The yaffle shins about, yells, laughs, and yikes to his heart's content.

yike (jaɪk), *sb.*[2] *Austral. slang.* [Origin unknown.] An argument, a dispute; a fight, a brawl. Occas. as *v. intr.*

1940 *Mod. Standard Eng. Dict.* (rev. ed.) 697/2 *Yike,* v. to fight. **1945** R. RENE *Mo's Memoirs* 186 There's that tram connie having a yike with a drunk. **1951** D. STIVENS *Jimmy Brockett* 86 It was a pretty good yike while it lasted. **1952** T. A. G. HUNGERFORD *Ridge & River* 213 Don't let's yike about it. **1964** G. JOHNSTON *My Brother Jack* 244 Sorry your party ended up in a yike. **1976** *Sunday Sun* (Brisbane) 11 Apr. 6/2 ALP circles have scoffed at suggestions of a political 'yike' between State Opposition Leader Tom Burns and TLC chief Egerton. **1984** *Business Rev. Weekly* (Australia) 7–13 Jan. 18/1 We have had a couple of small yikes, mainly on things like contract prices.

yikes (jaɪks), *int. colloq.* [Origin unknown, but cf. YOICKS *int.*] An exclamation of astonishment.

1971 *TV Comic* 5 June 8 Yikes! He's blown out the candles all right.. blown them out of the cake! **1973** G. SIMS *Hunters Point* xiii. 115 Holding her nose.. and exclaiming: 'Yikes! It seems that a cat has been shut up there.' **1978** *Detroit Free Press* 5 Mar. B 5/1 Yikes! Even Paul Newman loses the woman in this new breed of movies.

yikker ('jɪkə(r)), *v.* Also **yicker.** [Echoic, f. *yik* + -ER[5].] *intr.* Of a bird or other animal: to make repeated short, sharp cries.

1951 *Chambers's Jrnl.* Sept. 528/2 As we pushed through the bilberry bushes, rowan, and stunted Scots fir, a lemming yikkered angrily at the disturbance. **1959** W. K. RICHMOND *Brit. Birds of Prey* ix. 113 Sometimes he yikkers to himself as he goes,.. a low, emphatic chatter. **1960** 'L. LAMPLUGH' *Sixpenny Runner* xiii. 137 Good track dogs wait.. yickering eagerly and ready to fly out. **1964** T. H. WHITE *Goshawk* III. 154 A pair of young badgers.. greedily fought for warm milk and sugar out of a champagne bottle, and nipped my ankles yikkering when they were not nipping the rubber teat.

yild(e, ȝild(e, obs. ff. GUILD, YIELD.

†**yile,** obs. var. GYLE. **ȝeeltonne** for *yile-tun = *gyle-tun,* GYLE-FAT.

c **1425** *Stonor Papers* (Camden) I. 43 Item ij ȝeeltonnys, ij mashfattes.. pro cerevisia.

yile, obs. Sc. form of ISLE.

a **1578** LINDESAY (Pitscottie) *Chron. Scot.* (S.T.S.) I. 389 The Yile of Rosa.

†**yiling,** *vbl. sb. Obs.* Forms: 5 **yelyng,** 5–6 **yilyng(e,** 6 **yailinge, yeleinge,** 7 **yelling.** Variant of GYLING *vbl. sb.*

c **1440** *Inv.* in *Camden Misc.* (1895) IX. p. xviii, Unum yilyngfatte. **1488–9** *Rep. MSS. Ld. Middleton* (Hist. MSS. Comm. 1911) 471, iiij. yelyng tubbys. **1556** *Lanc. Wills* (Chetham Soc. 1884) 14 On yilynge toobe and on saltynge toobe. **1573** *Ibid.* 64 One brewinge keare and a troghe for y[e] same, ij[s]. A yailinge keare, xij[d]. **1588** *Ibid.* (1861) III. 137 One yeleinge combe v[s]. **1688** HOLME *Armoury* III. 319/2 The Yelling Comb or Tub is that Vessel into which the Wort is put to Work with the Yeast, or Bearm.

yill (jɪl), *sb.* Scotch variant of ALE.

1785 BURNS *Death & Dr. Hornbook* iii, The Clachan yill had made me canty. ? *a* **1800** *Bonnie Earl o' Murry* in Child *Ballads* (1889) III. 449/2 Her bread it's to bake, Her yill is to brew. **1818** SCOTT *Br. Lamm.* xii, If they offer ye a drink o' yill, or a cup o' wine. **1885** RUNCIMAN *Skippers & Shellbacks* 98 The guests in the sanded kitchen were content with twopenny bottles of 'yill'.

b. *attrib.* and *Comb.,* as ***yill-caup*** [CAP *sb.*[3]], ***-house, -maker, -making, -seller, -selling, -shop, -wife*** (see also Eng. Dial. Dict.).

1786 BURNS *Holy Fair* xviii, The Change-house fills, Wi' yill-caup Commentators. **1789** D. DAVIDSON *Seasons* 13 Chiels wi' sooty skins, an' yill-caup een. **1790** JAS. FISHER *Poems* 59 Ye're welcome neighbour yill wives here.

Hence **yill** *v. trans.,* to entertain with ale.

1808 JAMIESON, To *Yill, v.a.,* to entertain with ale, a term commonly used by the vulgar.. to denote one special mode in which a lover entertains his Dulcinea at a fair or market. **1890** SERVICE *Notandums* ii. 11 He forgot.. to bid Maggie.. to the yuillin'.

yill, yilt, yin, yinder, ying (ȝing): see YELD *a.,* YIELD *v.,* ONE, YON, YONDER, YOUNG.

‖**yimkin** ('jɪmkɪn), *adv. slang.* Also **yimpkin.** [a. Iraqi Arabic *yimkin.*] Perhaps (see also quot. 1966).

1925 FRASER & GIBBONS *Soldier & Sailor Words* 311 *Yimkin,* perhaps. An Arabic word used colloquially among troops on the Eastern Fronts. **1966** 'L. LANE' *ABZ of Scouse* 120 *Yimkin,* nonsense; I don't believe it. **1967** *Sunday Times* (Colour Suppl.) 10 Sept. 46/4 Yimpkin, perhaps. Expressive of extreme scepticism. 'When Tunis falls we're all going home, yimpkin!' (Ar.)

‖**yin** (jɪn). Also **Yin, Yn.** [Chinese *yīn* shade, feminine; the moon.] **a.** In Chinese philosophy, the feminine or negative principle (characterized by dark, wetness, cold, passivity, disintegration, etc.) of the two opposing cosmic forces into which creative energy divides and whose fusion in physical matter brings the phenomenal world into being. Also *attrib.* or as *adj.,* and *transf.* Cf. YANG.

1671, etc. [see YANG]. **1845,** etc. [see T'AI CHI 1]. **1850** [see QI]. **1911** *Encycl. Brit.* XXIII. 68/1 The altar to the Earth is dark and square, on the north side of the city, the region of *yin,* the principle of cold and gloom. **1931** A. U. DILLEY *Oriental Rugs & Carpets* ix. 210 Other primitive motives are .. male and female forms called Yin and Yang. **1963** 'R. ERSKINE' *Passion Flowers in Italy* xi. 144 The things that woman was doing to us.. More truly Yin than you could believe. **1976** H. FERGUSON *Confessions of Long Distance Acid Head* 17 Lucy was so yin, receptive and feminine, that the passions, slumbering in my bosom, were consciously aroused.

b. *Comb.,* as **yin-yang,** the combination or fusion of the two cosmic forces; freq. *attrib.,* esp. as ***yin-yang symbol,*** a circle divided by an S-shaped line into a dark and a light segment, representing respectively *yin* and *yang,* each containing a 'seed' of the other.

1850 *Chinese Repository* XIX. 375 The Great Extreme.. is not exterior to or separate from the Yin-yáng. **1934** A. D. WALEY *Way & its Power* App. II. 112 The aim of the *yin-yang* philosophers was not the triumph of Light, but the attainment in human life of perfect balance between the two principles. **1958** W. WILLETTS *Chinese Art* I. iv. 273 The observed behaviour of this stellar couple accorded perfectly with the *yin yang* theory. **1972** MANAKA & URQUHART *Layman's Guide Acupuncture* (1977) I. 32 Their relativity and inseparability are symbolized by the inclusion, in the Chinese yin-yang symbol, of a small portion of each within the other. **1976** C. SOO *Chinese Art of T'ai Chi Ch'uan* iii. 19 When these [outlines] are put together, the Yin-Yang symbol is obtained. **1977** MILLER & SWIFT *Words & Women* iv. 69 The ancient belief that contrasting male and female forces are at work in everything—the yin-yang of dark and light.. too easily becomes an adversary concept.

yin, ying, varr. YEN[2].

‖**ying ch'ing** (jɪŋ tʃɪŋ). Also **Ying Ch'ing, Ying ch'ing,** etc. [Chinese, lit. 'shadowy blue'.] A type of glazed porcelain produced in Jiangxi and other provinces, chiefly during the Song dynasty. Freq. *attrib.*

1922 A. L. HETHERINGTON *Early Ceramic Wares China* xix. 139 The ware.. with a very translucent, white sugary body and a bluish-white glaze tending to a more pronounced blue.. is known as *ying ch'ing yao*..: *ying ching*.. may be translated 'shadowy blue'. **1934** *Burlington Mag.* May 214/1 The *ying ch'ing* species of white porcelain. **1936** *Ibid.* Jan. 10/1 With pale bluish glaze currently known as Ying Ch'ing (misty blue). **1943** [see SUNG *sb.* b]. **1949** [see JU]. **1954** H. GARNER *Oriental Blue & White* ii. 9 *Ying ch'ing* (shadow blue) is a thin translucent white porcelain covered with a clear glaze of bluish tint. The term is a modern one, invented by Chinese dealers, which has unfortunately become established in the West. **1977** O. IMPEY *Chinoiserie* II. vii. 89/2 The famous 'Fonthill vase', a Yüan dynasty *ying ch'ing* bottle fitted with a gothic silver-gilt and enamel mount.

Yinglish ('jɪŋglɪʃ), *sb.* (*a.*) orig. *U.S.* [f. Y1(DDISH *sb.* (*a.*) + E)NGLISH *sb.*] A jocular name for a blend of English and Yiddish spoken in the United States; a form of English containing many Yiddishisms. Also *attrib.* or as *adj.*

1951 W. & S. SCHACK in *Commentary* Dec. 586/2 A Jewish American theater in which.. the material is of mixed nature, and the language neither the King's English nor the *rebbetzin's* Yiddish but a crossbreed that we might call 'Yinglish'. **1953** H. J. GANS in *Amer. Q.* V. 213 (*title*) The 'Yinglish' music of Mickey Katz. *Ibid.* 215 Katz's life is as Yinglish as the concept of a Bar Mitzvah ranch. **1967** *N.Y. Times* 6 Apr. 44 This show.. is a mixture of Yinglish (English with Yiddish) and Yidlish (Yiddish with English). **1968** [see O.K. *adj.* a]. **1970** L. M. FEINSILVER *Taste of Yiddish* iii. 372 *Yinglish.* This coined term describes English that contains Yiddish idiom, pronunciation and/or intonation. **1974** *Observer* 31 Mar. 39/4 The text, written in Yinglish and American, abounds in euphemisms. **1983** *Listener* 7 July 20/3 One of the joys of the *Oxford American Dictionary* is searching out the progress of Yinglish.

yio, var. HEO *Obs.,* she.

13.. *Northern Passion* 104 In holy wrytte of here men rede þat sche [*v.r.* yio] hade donen synfulle dede.

yioyned, ME. pa. pple. of JOIN *v.*[1]

yip (jɪp), *v.* In 5 **ȝyppe, ȝippe, yepe.** [Echoic.] **1.** *intr.* To cheep, as a young bird. *Obs.* or *dial.*

c **1440** *Promp. Parv.* 401/2 Pypyn, or ȝyppe, as henn byrdys (*K., H.* ȝippyn, as bryddys, *P.* yepyn). *a* **1825** FORBY *Voc. E. Anglia, Yip, v.* to chirp like a newly hatched chicken, or other very young bird.

2. *intr.* To utter a sharp cry or yelp (with a dog or human being as subj.); to shout; to complain. orig. *U.S.*

1907 K. D. WIGGIN *New Chron. Rebecca* vii. 177 He would walk right up close and cuff 'em if they dared to yip. **1922** S. LEWIS *Babbitt* vii. 99 There's a swell bunch of Lizzie boys and lemon-suckers.. that love to fire off their filthy mouths and yip that Mike Monday is vulgar and full of mush. **1927** P. MARKS *Lord of Himself* 15, I love to hear you yip at him. **1945** B. MACDONALD *Egg & I* ii. 176 Sport and the puppy.. yapping and yipping at each other. **1963** *New Statesman* 11 Jan. 38/3 Yet how does the victim react? He yips with delight. **1978** S. RADLEY *Death & Maiden* i. 6 [The] Jack Russell terrier had yipped itself to the edge of hysteria.

3. *trans.* To cry or exclaim (with the words spoken as direct obj.). *U.S.*

1927 *Sat. Even. Post* 24 Dec. 84/2 'Hey!' Jim yipped, ..'Get away from there!' **1974** WODEHOUSE *Aunts aren't Gentlemen* x. 81 'Has he brought it yet?' she yipped.

Hence '**yipping** *vbl. sb.* and *ppl. a.*; also **yip-yipping.**

1910 *N.Y. Even. Post* 14 Oct. 4 The applause was really deafening..; not yip-yipping.. but steady volume of vocal uproar. **1951** J. MASTERS *Nightrunners of Bengal* xv. 195 Women's voices rang clear.. on the verandah, and a child's excited yipping. **1956** H. GOLD *Man who was not with It* (1965) xi. 85 The inner yipping of a man who had assaulted the Pittsburgh of his babyhood may have given them obscure desires to kick me. **1960** I. CROSS *Backward Sex* ii. 60, I could not help making a slight yipping noise as I tried to clear my throat. **1977** *New Yorker* 26 Sept. 42/1, I have spoken to those people about that yipping dog. **1980** A. DESAI *Clear Light of Day* i. 3 He [*sc.* a dog] has such a beautiful voice, it's a pleasure to hear him. Not like the yipping and yapping of other people's little lap dogs.

yip (jɪp), *sb.* orig. *U.S.* [Echoic: see prec.] A short high-pitched cry, as from a dog; a shout, an exclamation; a complaint, an expostulation.

1911 H. QUICK *Yellowstone Nights* xii. 303 They chase 'em, with wild whoops an' yips over the undulatin' reservation. **1928** WODEHOUSE *Money for Nothing* ix. 208 If I'd been a life-insurance company I'd have paid up on him without a yip. **1945** B. MACDONALD *Egg & I* xii. 179 The dog began to bark and, guided by his excited yips, I was able to follow the progress of the hunt around the ranch. **1946** E. HODGINS *Mr. Blandings* iii. 48 This is the first faint yip of pain he's drawn. **1962** J. STEINBECK *Travels with Charley* 221 He [*sc.* a dog] ran.. and laughed and gave little yips of pure joy. **1971** *Shankar's Weekly* (Delhi) 4 Apr. 5/1 In the old days, there would have been a spate of.. discussions... But today? Not a yip.

yip (jɪp), colloq. pronunc. of YES. Cf. YEP.

1934 'R. CROMPTON' *William—the Gangster* iii. 49 'Is that a fair down there?' 'Yip,' answered William. **1954** —— *William & Moon Rocket* i. 13 'That's fixed it,' said the youth. 'Yip,' said the man.

yippee (jɪpiː, stress variable), *sb.* and *int.* orig. *U.S.* Also **yip-ee.** [Perh. connected with HIP *int.* (*sb.*[4]).] An exclamation of delight or excitement.

1920 S. LEWIS *Main St.* 86 She galloped down a block, and as she jumped from a curb across a welter of slush, she gave a student 'Yippee!' **1939** R. CHANDLER *Big Sleep* xii. 80, I was being brought into camp. I was going to yell 'Yippee!' **1947** N. MARSH *Final Curtain* xvi. 246 She said 'Yip-ee' like a cow-girl. **1951** J. FLEMING *Man who looked Back* xvi. 212 He permitted himself a loud 'Yippee!' **1961** *Guardian* 19 Apr. 5/1 Yippee. I've been blooded. It's lovely. **1976** BOTHAM & DONNELLY *Valentino* vii. 51 Rodolpho let rip a great cowboy yippee. **1980** A. CORNELISEN *Strangers & Pilgrims* viii. 162 It's a boy! *A boy!* Yippee!

Hence as *v. intr.,* to make this exclamation; **yi'ppeeing** *vbl. sb.*

1938 M. K. RAWLINGS *Yearling* xxvi. 351 They capered together and shouted and yipped until their throats were hoarse. **1963** A. LUBBOCK *Austral. Roundabout* 182 There was bush ballads, and a whistling and yippeeing! **1977** 'E. CRISPIN' *Glimpses of Moon* v. 69 Clarence Tully hilloed. His sons yippeed.

yippie, Yippie ('jɪpɪ). orig. *U.S.* Also **yippy**. [f. the initials of *Y*outh *I*nternational *P*arty + -IE, influenced by HIPPIE, HIPPY *sb.* and *a.*] A member of a group of politically active hippies, orig. in the United States.

1968 *Time* 5 Apr. 55/1 The Yippies—1968's version of the hippies... The term Yippie comes from Youth International Party. **1968** *Listener* 3 Oct. 428/2 One student outlines his own theories to me. 'This whole scene began with Dylan, the Beatles, and of course pot.' Another complains that the militants need a sense of humour and hopes the Yippies move in with their 'politics of ecstasy'. **1968** *Time* 11 Oct. 28 Pierson had infiltrated a yippie group known as the Headhunters, and soon rose to the dizzying position of personal bodyguard to the yippie leader. **1971** *Bulletin* (Sydney) 19 June 15/3 The news that Sydney's Yippies ('Yippie is a fun Revolution') were preparing to play an energetic part in the strenuously humorless Vietnam Moratorium came as a surprise. **1976** *Times* 18 Aug. 4/7 If we're going to save democracy, we've got to put an end to all this yippy filth, these abortions, [etc.]. **1981** J. DUNNING *Deadline* (1982) xiv. 138 Bill Neal was one of those yippie types... One of those bearded nonconformists.

yips (jɪps), *sb. pl. colloq.* [Origin obscure.] In *Golf*, a state of nervousness which causes a player to miss an easy putt in a competition. Usu. with the def. article.

1963 *Times* 10 June 4/2 His left-below-right putting stroke designed to prevent the 'yips', is most effective once it begins to flow. **1972** *Tel.* (Brisbane) 1 Jan. 5/7 Nevertheless, Jones got a dose of what golfers call 'the yips'. **1984** *Times* 21 Sept. 9/4 Golfers suffer from the 'yips', which means that their muscles seize up and freeze when they are faced with a short putt and they cannot play the stroke.

yir, graphic var. *þir* THIR, these.

1572 *Satir. Poems Reform.* xxxi. 199 Thairfor, yir plaigs wald yai eschew.

yirb, Sc. and n. dial. f. HERB.

yird (also 4 **ȝerd(e**, 4, 8–9 **yerd**, 5 **yherde**, 6 **ȝird**). Sc. and north. f. EARTH *sb.*, and *v.* (to bury).

c **1375** *Sc. Leg. Saints* i. (*Petrus*) 681 Ihesu,.. þat in þis ȝerd com fra hewine. **1433** *Deeds rel. Orkney* vi, Aisiamentis .. as weill under yherde as boufe yherde. **1550** *Rental Bk. Cupar-Angus* (1880) II. 74 All.. pertenens quhatsumeuir.. als weill vnder the ȝird as abouf. **1562** *Acc. Ld. High Treas. Scot.* XI. 214 To David Ellis for ȝerding of Johnne Gordoune.. xx s. *a* **1670** SPALDING *Troub. Chas. I* (Bannatyne Club) II. 221 They fand yirdit in the yaird of Drum ane trunk full of silver plait. **1785** BURNS *Jolly Beggars* Recit. i, When lyart leaves bestrew the yird. **1824** MACTAGGART *Gallovid. Encycl.* s.v. *Yird-fasts*, The cauld yird, the grave. **1825** JAMIESON s.v., '*Fairly yirdit*', dead and buried. **1851** *Cumbld. Gloss.*, *Yerd*, a fox-earth. **1882** *Proc. Berw. Nat. Club* IX. No. 3. 511 The 'Yirding of a live Cock' to cure epilepsy. **1894** CROCKETT *Raiders* xxiv, To afford yirds and secret caves for our Solway smugglers.

b. *Comb.*: esp. in **yirdfast** = EARTHFAST (cf. ON. *jarðfastr*). See also YERD-HUNGER.

1545 *Aberd. Reg.* XIX. (Jam.) Tuelf pennis Scottis of yerd-siluer. **1785** *Poems in Buchan Dial.* 6 Whare now thy groans in dowy dens The yerd-fast stanes do thirle. **1808** JAMIESON, *Yirdin*, thunder [see EARTH-DIN]. **1820** *Blackw. Mag.* VI. 568 A penetrating and even suffocating yird-drift. **1824** MACTAGGART *Gallovid. Encycl.*, *Yird-fasts*, large stones sticking in the yird, or earth, that the plough cannot move. **1825** JAMIESON, *Yird-drift*, snow, not in the act of falling, but lifted up from the ground, and driven by the wind, after it has lain for some time.

yire, yirk, yirm, yirn: see IRE, YERK, YARM, IRON.

yirr (jɪr), *v. Sc.* [Possibly repr. OE. *ȝyrran*, **ȝirran* (see YERR), but probably an independent echoic formation.] *intr.* To snarl, growl. So **yirr** *sb.*, a snarl, growl.

1786 BURNS *Ep. to Maj. Logan* ii, When idly goavan whyles we saunter; Yirr! fancy barks. **1815** G. BEATTIE *John o' Arnha'* (1826) 63 The watch-dogs yirr'd and yowf'd wi' fright. **1825** JAMIESON, *Yirr*, the growl of a dog. **1890** SERVICE *Notandums* xix. 125 If ony whillywha o' an Englisher should yirr and mak a kilfudyoch aboot the words he doesna ken.

yirth, Sc. form of EARTH.

yis, obs. pl. of EYE *sb.*[1]

c **1425** *Found. St. Bartholomew's* (E.E.T.S.) 11 Beholdyng .. thynges to cumme.. with the yis of his soule.

yis: see THIS, YES.

yisce, variant of YISSE.

yise, obs. f. ICE, YES.

† **yisel**. *Obs.* Forms 1 **ȝisel**, 2 **ȝysel**, 3 **ȝisel**, **ȝæsel**. [OE. *ȝísel* = OHG. *gîsal* (MHG. *gîsel*, G. *geisel*), ON. *gísl* (Sw. *gislan*, Da. *gidsel*, *gissel*) GISEL; cf. OIr. *giall*.] A hostage.

c **893** ÆLFRED *Oros.* III. vii. §2 Philippus þa he cniht wæs, wæs Thebanum to ȝisle ȝeseald. *c* **1205** LAY. 21103 Bringeð her þa ȝæsles Biforen ure cnihtes. *Ibid.* 22790 He wes iȝefen Arður To halden to ȝisle.

Yishuv (jɪ'ʃuːv, 'jɪʃʊv). Also **Yishub**. [ad. Heb. *yiššūḇ* settlement.] The Jewish community or settlement in Palestine during the nineteenth century and until the formation of the State of Israel in 1948.

1918 *Round Table* VIII. 321 The Jewish *Yishub*, or settlement in Palestine. **1922** *Encycl. Brit.* XXXII. 1130/1 This new Palestinian *Yishub* (settlement), strengthened in the early years of the present century by a number of young men and women who went to Palestine with the ideal of working as labourers on its soil, became the basis of the political success which Zionism achieved during the World War. **1940** *Contemp. Jewish Rec.* III. 599 The Yishub has made available over £P200,000 for emergency purposes. **1940** A. ULITZUR *Two Decades of Keren Hayesod* ii. 40 From the beginning of the Third *Aliyah* until the end of September, 1940.. the Yishuv grew by about 432,000 persons. **1949** KOESTLER *Promise & Fulfilment* I. xii. 130 Let the Yishuv, the Diaspora and the whole world know what Bevin, Attlee and their henchmen are preparing for us. **1962** *Observer* 20 May 25/5 The British Zionists with whom I worked—infected, no doubt, by the free life of the Yishuv in Palestine—did not give me an inkling of what goes on in the mind of an orthodox Jew. **1970** I. SIEFF *Memoirs* vi. 107 These Jews of the old *Yishuv* (meaning settlement) were usually advanced in years before they left their country of origin. **1980** *Times Lit. Suppl.* 14 Nov. 1288/5 The extent and scale of the massacres tended to be underestimated for a while by Jews in the West.., by the *Yishuv* in Palestine, and even by Jews in Europe themselves.

yisk, Sc. f. *yesk*, YEX.

† **yisse**, *v. Obs.* Forms: 1 **ȝitsian**, **ȝietsian**, **ȝidsian**, 2–3 **ȝitsen**, 2–4 **ȝissen**, (2 **ȝitcen**, 3 **ȝiscen**, **ȝyscen**, **ȝescen**, **ȝietcen**, **ȝetsen**, 4 **yisse**; in vbl. sb. 3 **ȝittsunng**, **yssyng**, 4 **icinge**). [OE. *ȝítsian*, *ȝídsian* = OHG. **gîtisôn* (MHG. *gîzen*, *gîtsen*, G. *geizen*), f. Teut. *gīd-*, whence also OHG. *kît* (MHG. *gît*, G. *geiz*) covetousness, OHG. *kîtac* (MHG. *gîtec*, G. *geizig*) covetous; ultimately related to Lith. *geidžu* to covet, Lettish *gaida* desire, OSl. *židati* to expect.] *trans.* (in OE. const. gen. or dat.) and *intr.* To covet. Hence **yisser**, a covetous person; **yissing** *vbl. sb.*, coveting, covetousness.

Beowulf 1749 [He] ȝytsað gromhydiȝ. *c* **700** *Epinal Gloss.* 82 *Appetitus*, ȝitsung [*Corpus Gloss.* ȝidsung]. *c* **888** ÆLFRED *Boeth.* xiii. §1 Sio ȝitsung ȝedeð heore ȝitseras laðe. *Ibid.* xxvi. §2 Ælc bit þæs reaflaces þe him on ȝenumen bið, oððe eft oðres ȝitsað. *c* **897** —— *Gregory's Past. C.* xli. 298 (Cotton MS.) Hu ȝewitende ða ðing sint þe hie ȝidsiað [*v.r.* ȝietsiað]. *a* **1175** *Cott. Hom.* 233 He wat wel þat maniȝe men bieð sa ful of ȝescung. *c* **1200** *Moral Ode* 271 (Trin. Coll. MS.) Þo þe waren ȝietceres of þis wereldes aihte. *c* **1200** ORMIN 4560 Ȝæn ȝittsunng & grediȝleȝȝc. *c* **1205** LAY. 5332 Þe kinges beoð ȝunge Of æhte ȝissinge. *a* **1225** *Ancr. R.* 202 Al so ȝisceð a ȝissare [*v.r.* ȝiscere] þet moni þusunt muhten biflutten. *c* **1250** *Gen. & Ex.* 3515 Ne ȝisce ðu noȝt ðin nestes ðing, Hus, ne aȝte, ne wif, in ðin ȝiscing. *c* **1275** *Passion our Lord* 35 in *O.E. Misc.* 38 Mid yuernesse and prude and yssyng wes þat on. *c* **1315** SHOREHAM IV. 357 Þorȝ ȝeskynge efter gode. **1340** *Ayenb.* 16 Icinge, in cle[r]gie auarice oþer couaytise. *a* **1400** in *Pol. Rel. & L. Poems* (1903) 251 Ȝissinge and glosinge and felsship beon riue. *Ibid.* 269 Worldes yissyng Me haueth schent.

yisse, ȝ-, obs. ff. YES.

yist, dial. f. YEAST *sb.*

yistai, -ay, (ȝistai, -ay), contr. ff. YESTERDAY.

yister-, ȝister-, etc., obs. or dial. ff. YESTER-.

† **yit**, *pron. Obs.* Forms: 1 **ȝit**, **ȝyt**, 2–3 **ȝit**, 3 **ȝet**, (*Orm.*) **ȝitt**. [OE. *ȝit* = OFris. **jit* (NFris. *jat*, *jæt*, Sylt *at*), OS. *git*, ON. (MSw.) *it*; f. unstressed form of YE with an obscure dental element.] Ye two, both of you.

Beowulf 508 Ðær ȝit for wlence wada cunnedon. **971** *Blickl. Hom.* 187 Ȝyt ȝit þurhwuniað on incre anwilnesse. *c* **1000** *Ags. Gosp.* Matt. xx. 22 Ȝyt nyton hwæt ȝyt biddaþ. *c* **1175** *Lamb. Hom.* 93 Hwi iwearð hinc swa þet ȝit dursten fondian godes? *c* **1200** ORMIN 4498 Butt iff ȝitt muȝhenn betenn itt Onn aniȝ kinne wise. *c* **1205** LAY. 5020 Ne beon ȝit [*c* 1275 ȝe] bute tweien, mine sunen ȝit [*c* 1275 ȝeo] beoð beien.

yit(e, ȝit(e, obs. ff. YET.

yite (jaɪt). *dial.* Also **yeite**, **yoit**. [Obscure.] The yellow-hammer, *Emberiza citrinella*.

1812 P. FORBES *Poems* 104 (E.D.D.) Herryin' linties, yites an' kays. **1830** J. WILSON *Noctes Ambr.* Wks. 1856 III. 4 Lark, lintie, yellow-yite,.. shilfa, and goldfinch. **1888** BARRIE *Auld Licht Idylls* ii. 54, I have known a black-fishing expedition stopped because a 'yellow yite', or yellowhammer, hovered round the gang when they were setting out.

Yit(t), varr. YID.

† **yiug(g)ed** [Y- 4], judged.

1297 R. GLOUC. (Rolls) 7082 Þo was it ilugged þat he ssolde be.. Hardi kniȝt. *c* **1315** SHOREHAM V. 101 Y-iuged by þe lawe To by stend wyþ stone. **1387** TREVISA *Higden* (Rolls) V. 45 Geta was i-iuged [*MS.* γ y-juget] for a comoun enemy.

yive, ȝive, obs. ff. GIVE, IF.

yiz, var. YEZ.

Yizkor ('jɪzkə(r)). Also **Yiskor**, **Yizcor**. [Heb., lit. 'may he [*sc.* God] remember'.] A memorial service, formally known as *Hazkarat Neshamot*, held by Jews on certain holy days for deceased relatives, martyrs, etc.

1934 *Encycl. Jewish Knowl.* 644/1 *Yizkor*, popular name for Memorial Service, the full title being Hazcarath Neshoma. **1946** *Commentary* Aug. 173/1 They may still be on time to say *Yizcor*. **1956** S. BELLOW *Seize Day* v. 86 He asked him whether he had reserved his seat in the synagogue for Yom Kippur... 'Well, you better hurry up if you expect to say Yiskor for your parents.' **1966** H. KEMELMAN *Saturday Rabbi went Hungry* viii. 46 The Memorial Service for the Dead.. the Yizkor service. **1976** C. BERMANT *Coming Home* II. v. 189 Four times a year special remembrance prayers, known as *yizkor*, are read in synagogue... The word means memorial.

yk, obs. form of I *pers. pron.*

ykeld, ykend, ykened, ME. pa. pples. of KILL, KEN *v.*[2], KENE.

† **ykep(t** [Y- 4, KEEP, I-KEPE *vbs.*], kept.

13.. *Seuyn Sag.* 460 To the ich have i-kept mi maidenhod. *c* **1380** *Sir Ferumb.* 2125 Þis ys þat tresour.. Which þat my fader.. haueþ y-kept hit in-to þis day. **1399** *Pol. Poems* (Rolls) I. 365 Roton corne, So long ykep, hit is forlorne. **1422** YONGE tr. *Secr. Secr.* lxix. 246 Als longe as the natural hette duryth.. the helth of man shal be y-keppit. **1593** [see KEEP *v.* 14].

ykest: see CAST *v.*, YCAST.

† **ykeuered** [Y- 4, COVER *v.*[1]], covered.

1393 LANGL. *P. Pl.* C. x. 138 Vnder godes secre seel here synnes ben ykeuered. **1420** *E.E. Wills* (1882) 45, I ȝewe to Iohn Forster my godsonne a becure of selur y-keueryd.

† **ykid**, *pa. pple.* and *ppl. a. Obs.* Forms: 1 **ȝecyd**, 2 **ȝekyd**, 3 **ikud(d**, 3–4 **icud(de**, 3–5 **ykud**, 4–5 **ykid(de**, **ykyd**, 5 **ykyde**, (4 **ykudde**, **ycud**, **ikid**, **yked**, **ikedde**). [OE. *ȝecýd*, contracted pa. pple. of *cýþan*, *ȝecýþan*: see KID *ppl. a.* and KITHE *v.*] Made known; hence, well known, renowned: sometimes (like YCORE) a vague epithet of commendation.

a **1100** in *Leg. Rood* (1871) 3 Þa wearð hit sona þam mæran constantine þam kasere ȝecyd. *a* **1122** *O.E. Chron.* (Laud MS.) an. 1093 Se cyng.. wæs ofer eall dead ȝekyd. *c* **1205** LAY. 24671 Þat nan lauerd taken nolde.. Næuer nænne cniht,.. Bute he icostned weoren þrie inne compe, & his oht-scipen icudde. *a* **1225** *Leg. Kath.* 1295 Italde bi tale, fif siðe tene, icudde & icorene. *Ibid.* 1933 O icudd keiser! *c* **1315** SHOREHAM I. 633 Bote wanne þer hys o þyng yked, An oþer to onderstonde þerinne. **13..** *K. Alis.* 3359 (Linc. Inn MS.) Y say Darie.. þat he was god knyȝt y kud. **1340–70** *Alex. & Dind.* 64 Þe king cortais i-kid cofliche saide. **1362** LANGL. *P. Pl.* A. IV. 140 Bote he beo A Coke-wold I-kore [*MS. H.* ykyd] cut of boþe myn Eres! *c* **1380** *Sir Ferumb.* 4344 Y schal.. haue wyþ me of ȝour knyȝtes .V. hundred gode y-kudde. **1393** LANGL. *P. Pl.* C. XIII. 196 A confessour ykud [*MSS. M.*, *T.* i-kid] that couteþ nat a ruysshe Fere, ne famyne, ne false menne tonges. **14..** *K. Sol. Bk. Wisd.* 78 Wisdom yheled, litel is worþ oiþer treuþ ihyd; Bot boþe þai wexen swiþe ȝif þai ben y-kyd.

† **ykitt, ykut, ykutted, ykyt** [Y- 4], cut.

c **1300**, *c* **1330** [see CUT *v.* I, 7]. **1387** TREVISA *Higden* (Rolls) V. 391 He made alle þe hedes and lymes of mawmettes i-kut [*MS.* γ ykitt] of. *a* **1425** tr. *Arderne's Treat. Fistula*, etc. 69 Smal y-kutted. *c* **1430** *Two Cookery-bks.* 55 Taylid Datys y-kyt a-long.

yknet(t, yknit, yknyt, knit.

13.. *Leg. Greg.* 481 Þe ropes wer fast yknett. *c* **1374** CHAUCER *Boeth.* IV. pr. vi. (1868) 134 While þat I weue.. to þe resouns yknyt by ordre. **1426** LYDG. *De Guil. Pilgr.* 4924 Whan thys lettrys [*sc.* P, A, X] ben yknet,.. Parfyt pes they sygnyfye. *c* **1440** *Promp. Parv.* 154/1 Felowys, y-knytte togedyr in wykydnesse, *complices*.

† **yknow**, *v. Obs.* Forms: 1 **ȝecnawan**, 2 **ȝecnowen**, **ikna(u)wen**, 2–3 **icnawe(n**, 3 **icnowe(n**, 3–4 **iknowe(n**, 3–5 **yknowe(n**, 4 **yknawe(n**, **yknaue(n**, 5 **iknow**. *Pa. t.* 1 **ȝecneow**, 2–3 **icnew**, 2 **ȝecnew**, **ȝicneow(e**, 3–4 **iknewe**, **ikneu**. *Pa. pple.* 1 **ȝecnawen**, 2–3 **icnawe(n**, 2 **ȝecnowe**, 3 **icnowe(n**, **iknowe**, 4 **yknawe**, **yknowe(n**, **ycnowen**, 5 **yknow**. [OE. *ȝecnáwan*: see Y- 3 c and KNOW *v.*] To know (in various senses); to acknowledge.

971 *Blickl. Hom.* 71 He wæs.. of cilda muþe ȝecnawen & weorþad. *a* **1000**, etc. [see KNOW *v.* I, II, etc.]. *c* **1175** *Lamb. Hom.* 49 Betre hit is þet mon ne iknawe noht þe wei to godalmihtin þe he hine icnawe and seodðe hine for-hoȝie. *c* **1200** *Trin. Coll. Hom.* 143 Ða biðohte heo on hire liflode and ȝe-cnew þat hie was lað gode. *c* **1205** LAY. 24805 Ȝif þu wult icnawen þat he is king ouer þe. *a* **1240** *Lofsong* in *O.E. Hom.* I. 205 Ich icnowe me gulti and creie þe leafdi merci. **1297** R. GLOUC. (Rolls) App. H. 122 Ich ne dar þat þe folc yhure þat ich yknowe þe. *c* **1320** *Cast. Love* 36 For him þat con not i-knowen Nouþer French ne Latyn. *c* **1330** *Arth. & Merl.* 9049 Herui Riuel þis iknewe. **1340** *Ayenb.* 104 He is þe eldeste and þe meste yknawe and þe meste beloued. *Ibid.* 201 Zuo þet he ne may y-knawe his sseppere. **1377** LANGL. *P. Pl.* B. XI. 225 In her lyknesse owre lorde ofte hath ben y-knowe. **1387** TREVISA *Higden* (Rolls) VII. 205 A lewed goost, þat kouþe not y-knowe þe cause.. of verray martirdom. *c* **1394** *P. Pl. Crede* 252 We ben clerkes y-cnowen cunnynge in scole. **1422** YONGE tr. *Secr. Secr.* 123 Whath awaylyth Sotilte of vndyrstondynge and connynge, and how thay byth y-know. *c* **1430** *Syr Gener.* (Roxb.) 6737 If ye can me tech Hou I may I-know him.

b. To make known; = KNOW *v.* 13.

a **1400** *New Test.* (Paues) Col. i. 27 To whom God wolde y-knowe þe richesse of þe blisse of þis sacrement.

† **ykorve(n**: see YCORVE(N.

ykoweryn, ME. pa. pple. of COVER *v.*[1]
?**1466** *Stonor Papers* (Camden) I. 77 To send hym worde wher to [= whether the] Mylle of Ermyngton schall be y-koweryn with stone or strawe.

ykoyned [Y- 4, COIN *v.*[1]], coined.
1423 *Rolls of Parlt.* IV. 256/2 Silver is..no better.. thenne xxxii *s.* the seid pound of troie ykoyned.

ykremyd [CRIM *v.*], crumbled.
c **1430** *Two Cookery-bks.* 40 A fewe ȝolkys of hard Eyroun y-kremyd þer-on.

ykuenct: see YQUENCT.

ykynde [Y- 5, KIN *sb.*[1]], of (high) kin or lineage.
1420 *Proc. Privy Council* (1834) II. 273 The whiche partyes bothe beth weel ykynde and of gret allyaunce.

ykyt: see YKITT.

yl, obs. form of ILL, ISLE.

-yl (ɪl, aɪl), formerly occas. **-ule**, a terminal element of chemical terms, ad. G. *-yl*, f. Gr. ὕλη wood, matter, substance (see HYLE), used for 'chemical principle, radical'. It was introduced by Wöhler and Liebig (*Ann. der Pharm.* (1832) III. 262), and first used by them in the term *benzoyl*; other early names were *éthyle* (*éthule*), *élayle* (Berzelius), *dadyle*, *peucyle*, *citronyle*, *citryle* (Blanchet and Sell). Some fifteen in anglicized form, including *acetyl*, *amyl*, *cinnamyl*, *glyceryl*, *salicyl*, appear in the *Elements of Chemistry* by T. Graham, 1842, who also invented the general term *basyle* for a body which unites with oxygen to form a base. *Methyl* is peculiar in being a back-formation from *methylene*.

-yl is used in forming the names of radicals compounded of two or three elements in various atomic proportions, which behave in combination like simple elements and are the constant bases of series of compounds (though they may not be themselves obtainable in a free state). Thus *carbonyl* CO, *hydroxyl* HO, *sulphuryl* SO_2, are compounds of carbon, hydrogen, and sulphur respectively. The greater number are compounds of carbon and hydrogen, either alone, as *amyl*, *ethyl*, *deutyl*, *trityl*, or with oxygen, as *acetyl*, *lactyl*.

b. Now also in more formal use in *Organic Chem.*
1952 *Jrnl. Chem. Soc.* 5075 Rule 58.5. Radicals derived from amino-acids which have trivial names in *ine* by removal of OH from all $-CH(NH_2){\cdot}CO_2H$ and related groups will be named by replacing the ending *ine* with *yl*. **1965** *Recommended Names for Chemicals used in Industry* (*B.S.I.*) 11 Univalent radicals derived from cycloalkanes with no side chain are named by replacing the ending '-ane' of the hydrocarbon name by '-yl'. **1966** [see FURYL]. **1971** *Nomencl. Org. Chem.* (I.U.P.A.C.) (ed. 3) A. 5 Univalent radicals derived from saturated unbranched acyclic hydrocarbons by removal of hydrogen from a terminal carbon atom are named by replacing the ending '-ane' of the name of the hydrocarbon by '-yl'. *Ibid.* B. 70 Univalent heterocyclic radicals whose names end in '-yl'. *Ibid.* C. 128 Radicals derived from unsubstituted ring assemblies are named by adding '-yl',..*etc.*, to the name of the assembly.

ylacay, obs. Sc. var. LACKEY.
1512 *Acc. Ld. High Treas. Scot.* IV. 342 Item, to ane Franche ylacay,..xiiij s.

†**ylacet** [Y- 4, LACE *v.*], laced.
c **1425** *Engl. Conq. Irel.* 52 þay..turneden toward weysford by Odroon, wyth baners y-lacet.

ylad(d [LEAD *v.*[1]], led, conveyed, carried.
1297 R. GLOUC. (Rolls) 2424 Mercurius us aþ ylad in to þin londe. **1387** TREVISA *Higden* (Rolls) V. 99 Numerianus was y-lad in a liter. *c* **1400** MAUNDEV. (1839) ii. 13 Oure Lord Jesu, in that Nyghte that he was taken, he was y lad in to a Gardyn. **14..** *K. Sol. Bk. Wisd.* 211 þo Ely in þis fair cart to heuen was ylad, Elisee his felawe was sory. **1426** LYDG. *De Guil. Pilgr.* 9772 The maryner..Ledeth the shyp,..And ys hym sylff ylad also.

ylaft(e: see YLEFT.

ylaht [LATCH *v.*[1], I-LECCHE], seized, caught.
c **1306** *Pol. Songs* (Camden) 214 The Bisshop of Glascou ychot he was y-laht.

ylaid, ylayd, yleid, yleyd, ME. pa. pples. of LAY *v.*[1]
12.. *Moral Ode* vi. in *E.E.P.* (1862) 22 Al to muchel ic habbe i-spend, to litel y-leid an horde. *c* **1330** *Assump. Virg.* (B.M. MS.) 842 It was in þe tumbe ylaide. *c* **1380** *Sir Ferumb.* 2427 þe cloþes þat wern on hure bed ilaid. **1426** LYDG. *De Guil. Pilgr.* 5415 Ther was no chaff ysene, And the strawh yleyd a-syde.

ylakked [LACK *v.*[1]], blamed.
1377 LANGL. *P. Pl.* B. II. 21 That is Mede þe Mayde.. hath noyed me ful oft, And ylakked my lemman.

yland(e, obs. forms of ISLAND.

ylang-ylang ('iːlæŋ'iːlæŋ). Also **yhlang-, i(h)lang-**. [Tagalog *álang-ílang*.] An anonaceous tree (*Canangium odoratum*) of Malaysia, the Philippines, etc., with fragrant greenish-yellow flowers from which a perfume is distilled; hence, the perfume itself.
1876 *Jrnl. Chem. Soc.* I. 243 Oxidation of Essential Oils. .. *Citronella* and *yhlang yhlang* developed no hydrogen peroxide. **1881** *Ibid.* XL. 916 Cananga Oil... This oil, also known as Hang-lang or Alanguilan oil. **1882** *Englishman* (Calcutta) 2 Dec. 4/5 Atkinson's Perfumery. Ess. Ylang Ylang, Frangipanne. **1884** MILLER *Plant-n.*, *Cananga odorata*, Ilang-Ilang-tree.

Hence **y'langol** *Chem.* (See quot.)
1895 *Jrnl. Chem. Soc.* LXVIII. I. 243 *Ylangol*, $C_{10}H_{18}O$, the isomeride of geraniol.

†**y'last**, *v.* *Obs.* Forms: 1–5 **ȝelæstan**, etc. as in LAST *v.*[1]; also 3–4 **ylaste, yleste**. *Pa. t.* 1 **ȝelæste**, 2 **ȝelest**, 3–4 **ilast(e, ilest(e**, 3–5 **ylast(e**. *Pa. pple.* 1 **ȝelæst, ȝelæsted**, 2 **ȝelest**, 3 **ilæst, ilast**, 4 **ylast(ed**. [OE. *ȝelǽstan*: see Y- 3 c and LAST *v.*[1]]

1. *trans.* To carry out, perform: = LAST *v.*[1] 1 b.
Beowulf 524 Beot eal wið þe sunu Beanstanes soðe ȝelæste. *c* **888** ÆLFRED *Boeth.* xxxvi. §4 Ic eac nauht ne tweoȝe ðæt ðu hit mæȝ e ȝelæstan. *a* **1000** *Cædmon's Gen.* 2762 He..hæfde wordbeot leofum ȝelæsted. *a* **1122** *O.E. Chron.* (Laud MS.) an. 1012 Ða þet gafol ȝelest wæs. *a* **1200** *Moral Ode* 242 þa þe gode biheten heste and nolden hit ileste. *c* **1205** LAY. 31109 ȝif þu miht under criste þis forward me ileste.

2. *intr.* To last, continue, endure; = LAST *v.*[1] 2.
a **1000** *Boeth. Metr.* vii. 19 Ne mæȝ hæleþa ȝehwæm hus on munte lange ȝelæstan. *c* **1175** *Lamb. Hom.* 157 Wa is mine saule þet mi lif þus longe ilest. *c* **1200** *Trin. Coll. Hom.* 151 Letitia sempiterna, þat is ilestende liht. *a* **1250** *Prov. Ælfred* 387 in *O.E. Misc.* 126 Alle world-ayhte schulle bi-cumen to nouhte... And vre owe lif lutel hwile ileste. **1297** R. GLOUC. (Rolls) 208 þe bataile of troye þat ilast vale ȝer. **1377** LANGL. *P. Pl.* B. III. 191 [þow] wendest þat wyntre wolde han y-lasted euere. *c* **1400** *St. Jer.* 15 *Tokens* 32 Leuere had his owen moder in helle pyne to be, Al þe while þe dom ylast, þan her sones face to see.

b. To stretch, extend; = LAST *v.*[1] 4.
a **1175** *Cott. Hom.* 231 His land ȝelest wide and side.

†**ylat**: see YLET.

ylauenyt, ME. pa. pple. of LEAVEN *v.*
1422 [see LEAVEN *v.* 1].

ylauȝte, ylauȝthe, ME. pa. pples. of LATCH *v.*[1], I-LECCHE.

ylay(e, yleie, yleighe, yleiȝe, yleine, yleye(n, yly, ME. pa. pples. of LIE *v.*[1]
1297 R. GLOUC. (Rolls) 5729 He sein swithin..þat longe adde vnder erþe ybe [*v.r.* yleye] verst broȝte in to ssryne. **13..** *K. Alis.* 508 (Linc. Inn MS.) A god..þat haþ ylaye by þe quene. **1377** LANGL. *P. Pl.* B. v. 82 As a leke hadde yleye longe in þe sonne. *c* **1400** MAUNDEV. xiii. [ix.], ȝif here fader had not ben dronken he hadde not yleye with hem.

ylde, obs. by-form of ISLE.

yle: see AIL *sb.*[2], AISLE, HYLE, ILL, ISLE.

†**yleave**. *Obs.* [OE. *ȝeléaf*: see Y- 3 a, LEAVE *sb.*[1]] Permission; leave.
a **1050** *Liber Scintill.* l. (1889) 165 *Iniquorum potestas super te ex dei datur licentia*, unrihtwisra miht ofer þe of godes ys ȝeseald ȝeleaf. *a* **1122** *O.E. Chron.* (Laud MS.) an. 1043 Be þes cynges ȝelæfan. *c* **1315** SHOREHAM I. 1269 ȝef eny oþer hyt doþ, Nys hyt ordre, ac ileaue. **1340** *Ayenb.* 50 God yaf yleaue þe dyeulen to guo in to þe zuyn. *Ibid.* 112 At his yleaue nymynge.

ylechyd, ME. pa. pple. of LEACH *v.*[1]

†**y'left, y'laft**, *pa. pple.* *Obs.* Forms: 1 **ȝelæfed**, 3 **ileaued, ileued**, 4 **yleued, -yd**, 4–5 **yleft(e, ylafte**, 7 **ylaft**. [OE. *ȝelǽfed*, pa. pple. of *(ȝe)lǽfan*: see Y- 4 and LEAVE *v.*[1]] Left.
c **950** *Lindisf. Gosp.* Matt. xv. 37 *Et quod superfuit de fragmentis*, & þ ȝelæfed wæs of screadungum. *a* **1225** *Ancr. R.* 168 Oure large relef þet we habbeð ileaued. *c* **1275** LAY. 28583 þo nas þar na more ileued in þan fihte..bote Arthur þe king. **1297** R. GLOUC. (Rolls) 6722 He was al one of þe tem bileued [*v.r.* yleft] there. *c* **1380** *Sir Ferumb.* 3349 þe Assege þanne þay y-lafte. *Ibid.* 5121 Tho was þe assaut y-leuyd clene. **1405** in *Royal & Hist. Lett. Hen. IV* (Rolls) 158, I have nought ylafte with me over two men. **1422** YONGE tr. *Secr. Secr.* lxiv. 240 Yf anythynge be y-lefte in the stomake. *c* **1634** W. CARTWRIGHT *Ordinary* II. ii. (1651) 25 None pleasaunce is me ylaft.

†**yleid, yleie, yleighe, yleine**, etc.: see YLAID, YLAY(E.

ylem ('iːlɛm). *Astr.* [f. med.L. *hȳlem*, acc. of *hȳlē* HYLE.] In the big-bang theory, the primordial matter of the universe, orig. conceived as composed of neutrons at high temperature and density.
[**1390**: see HYLE.] **1948** R. A. ALPHER in *Physical Rev.* LXXIV. 1581/1 Very shortly after the beginning of the universal expansion, the ylem was a gas of neutrons only. [*Note*] According to Webster's New International Dictionary..the word 'ylem' is an obsolete noun meaning 'The primordial substance from which the elements were formed.' It seems highly desirable that a word of so appropriate a meaning be resurrected. **1954** *Sci. Amer.* Mar. 61/2 As the Universe went on expanding and the temperature of ylem dropped, protons and neutrons began to stick together, forming deuterons..and heavier elements. **1959** J. BLISH *Clash of Cymbals* vii. 171 The ylem was the primordial flux of neutrons out of which all else emerged. **1974** FRAUENFELDER & HENLEY *Subatomic Physics* xviii. 475 It is interpreted as the radiation that is left over from the primordial fireball and thus provides some information about the conditions in the ylem.

ylend, ylent, pa. pples. of LEND *v.*[1] and *v.*[2]
a **1310** [see LEND *v.*[1] 2]. **13..** *Leg. Greg.* 259 þat day was hem no grace ylent. **1340** *Ayenb.* 19 þe greate guodes þet god ham heþ ylend. **1647** H. MORE *Song of Soul* II. II. II. iv, The hearing never knew the verdant peint Of springs gay mantle, nor heavens light ylent That must discover all that goodly pride. *Ibid.* IV. xxii, Their life ylent And subtill being quite away are flone.

ylengd, pa. pple. of LENG *v.*

†**y'leof**, *a.* (*sb.*) *Obs.* Forms: 1 **ȝeleof**, 3 *pl.* **yleoue, iloue**. [OE. *ȝeléof* = MHG. *geliep* (also as sb. pl.): see *ȝe-* Y- 1 b, 2 and *léof* LIEF.] Mutually loving or beloved; *sb. pl.* a pair of lovers.
a **1000** *Confess. Ecgberti* xxviii. in Thorpe *Laws* (1840) II. 152 On þære fiftan cneorysse ȝeleofe men hiȝ moton ȝesamniȝan. *c* **1000** *Ags. Gloss.* in Haupt's *Zeitschr.* (1853) IX. 461 *Contubernali sodalitate*,..mid ȝeleofre ferrædene. *a* **1250** *Owl & Night.* 1047 þar two yleoue [*Cott.* ilove] in one bedde Liggeþ iclupt & wel bihedde.

†**ylepe, ylope** [Y- 4, LEAP *v.*], leapt.
c **1380** *Sir Ferumb.* 4626 Many wer ouer y-lepe. *Ibid.* 5059 þe tour þay hauede y-take þo Nadde duk Naymes y-lope hem to.

†**y'lere**, *v.* *Obs.* [OE. *ȝelǽran*: see Y- 3 c and LERE *v.*] To teach; to learn.
Beowulf 3079 Ne meahton we ȝelæran leofne þeoden.. ræd æniȝne. *c* **1290** *Beket* 216 in *S. Eng. Leg.* 112 Seli child is sone i-lered. *c* **1300** *Havelok* 12 þat ye mowen nou y-here, And þe tale ye mowen y-lere. **1393** LANGL. *P. Pl.* C. XII. 128 Thus þorw my lore beþ men ylered.

†**ylered**, *ppl. a.* *Obs.* [OE. *ȝelǽred*, pa. pple. of *(ȝe)lǽran*: see prec.] = LERED, learned.
c **897** ÆLFRED *Gregory's Past. C.* 8 Uncuð hu longe þær swæ ȝelærede biscopas sien. **11..** *Fragm. Ælfric's Gram.* (1838) 6 Ilærede men. *c* **1205** LAY. 21858 þreo biscopes wise, a boke wel ilæred. *a* **1225** *Ancr. R.* 64 Sum is so wel ilered, oðer se wis iworded. **1377** LANGL. *P. Pl.* B. XIII. 213 My deuore to shewen, And conformen fauntekynes and other folke ylered. *c* **1440** *Partonope* 1994 And eke in armes full wele ylered.

†**ylerned** [Y- 4], learnt.
1340 *Ayenb.* 70 Non wel libbe ne ssel conne þet to sterue ylyerned ne heþ. **1362** LANGL. *P. Pl.* A. IX. 10 Ich heilede hem hendeli as Ich hedde I-leorned [*C-text* hadde ylerned]. **1387** TREVISA *Higden* (Rolls) VII. 219 þat þey hadde i-lerned [*MS. γ* ylurned] of here sovereynes to meyntene fredom.

yleslipe, ylespile, var. *ilespil*: see under IL, ILE.

ylessed, ME. pa. pple. of LESS *v.*

ylet, obs. form of EYELET.
14.. *Voc.* in Wr.-Wülcker 598/39 *Ocellulus*, an ylet.

†**ylet**[1], **ylat**, earlier *ȝelǽten*, *ileten*, *ilate(n* [Y- 4, LET *v.*[1]], let, allowed, left, etc.
13.. *K. Alis.* 2414 (Linc. Inn MS.) þer was..mony a veyne ylat blode. **1340** *Ayenb.* 115 þe guodes þet ich habbe uoryete and ylete to done. **1387** TREVISA *Higden* (Rolls) V. 109 He was i-closed wiþ ynne þe citee, and y-let out by a roop over þe wal.

ylet[2], **ylettyd**, earlier *ȝelet(t*, *ilet* [LET *v.*[2]], hindered.
13.. *K. Alis.* 1776 (Linc. Inn MS.) Ac he was y-lat by þe way. *Ibid.* 3221 þer þey weoren fouly ylet, þe gates weoren ageyns him scheot. **1422** YONGE tr. *Secr. Secr.* xxxi. 174 He was moche y-lettyd by an hugy ryuer.

ylettert, ylettred, early varr. of LETTERED.
1303 y-lettrede [see LETTERED *ppl. a.*]. **1387** TREVISA *Higden* (Rolls) VI. 141 Well i-lettred [*MS. γ* ylettert].

†**yleve**, *sb.* *Obs.* Forms: 1 **ȝeleafa**, 2 **ȝel(e)afe, ileafe, ileave**, 2–3 **ileve**, 3 **ȝielefe, ilæfe**. [OE. *ȝeléafa*: see LEVE *sb.*] Belief, faith.
c **888** ÆLFRED *Boeth.* v. §3 Nu þu ðone ȝeleafan hæfst. *c* **1175** *Lamb. Hom.* 5 þet we sulen..habben godne ileafe to ure drihten. *Ibid.* 73 þet an is rihte ileue, þet oðer fulluht. *c* **1200** *Trin. Coll. Hom.* 143 þurh rihte ȝielefe, and clene liflade. *c* **1205** LAY. 2974 Swa helpe me Apollin, for min ilæfe is al on him.

†**yleve**, *v.* *Obs.* Forms: 1 **ȝeliefan, ȝelyfan, ȝelefan**, 2 **ȝelifen, ȝelyfen, ileafen**, 2–5 **ileve(n**, 3 **ilæiven, ilæfen, iluven**, 3–4 **ilefe(n, ylefe(n, ileove(n**, 4 **ileave, ileeve, ilyve, yleve, ylif**. [OE. *ȝelíefan* = OS. *gilôbjan* (MDu. *ghelooven*, Du. *gelooven*), OHG. *gilouben* (MHG. *gelouben*, *glouben*, *glöuben*, early mod.G. *gleuben*, G. *glauben*), Goth. *galaubjan*: f. Teut. *ga-* Y- + *laub-* dear (related to *leub-* LIEF and *lub-* LOVE).] To believe.
c **888** ÆLFRED *Boeth.* v. §3 ðelefst ðu þet sio wyrd wealde þisse worulde? *a* **1000** *Boeth. Metr.* xxvi. 99 Ða dyseȝan men þe ðysum drycræftum long ȝelyfdon. *c* **1175** *Lamb. Hom.* 65 Wenne ic ileue and wel iso þet no gult me forȝeuen bo. *c* **1205** LAY. 29022 Karic ileouede to soðe Sexisce monne lare. *a* **1250** *Prov. Ælfred* 352 in *O.E. Misc.* 124 Ne ilef þu neuer þane mon þat is of feole speche. *c* **1380** *Sir Ferumb.* 4097 þou ne dost noȝt ase þe wys If þow ylyuest sir Alorys. **1387** TREVISA *Higden* (Rolls) VIII. 177 Men of þe contray aboute longe tyme þerafter myȝte unneþe i-leve þat þat citee was i-take. *c* **1400** *Lanfranc's Cirurg.* 267 I-leue þe wordis þat I seie.

yleve: see YLIVE, to live.

yleved, yleyd, yleye, yliac: see YLEFT, YLAID, YLAY, ILIAC.

ylid ('ɪlɪd). *Chem.* Also **ylide** (-aɪd). [a. G. *ylid* (Wittig & Felletschin 1944, in *Ann. d. Chem.* DLV. 133): see -YL, -ID[4].] Any neutral compound containing a negatively charged carbon atom directly bonded to a positively charged atom of another element (commonly sulphur, phosphorus, or nitrogen). Hence **y'lidic** *a.*

1951 *Chem. Abstr.* XLV. 6166 The reaction of PhLi upon suitable quaternary ammonium salts results in compds. with a semipolar bond between N and adjacent C. These compds. are called ylides. **1970** *Nature* 25 July 335/2 Silylated ylides of phosphorus, arsenic and sulphur, in which the silyl group is both a stabilizing and an efficient leaving group, transferring the ylidic moiety in very mild conditions. **1972** S. J. WEININGER *Contemporary Org. Chem.* xviii. 491 Ylids are extremely useful reactive intermediates for syntheses and are the subject of a good deal of research effort at the present time. **1979** *Nature* 15 Nov. 231/3 The zwitterionic ylides were obtained from the reaction of phenyl-lithium with quaternary ammonium halides. **1982** *Heterocycles* XIX. 1849 Cycloimmonium ylides.. possessing two electron-withdrawing groups covalently bonded to the ylidic carbon..can be isolated.

-ylidene (-'ɪl-, -'aɪlɪdiːn), *suffix. Chem.* [f. as -IDENE.] Used in place of -IDINE when the name of the parent compound does not end in *-yl*.

1971 *Nomencl. Org. Chem.* (I.U.P.A.C.) (ed. 3) A. 17 Names of bivalent radicals derived from saturated or unsaturated monocyclic hydrocarbons by removal of two atoms of hydrogen from the same carbon atom of the ring are obtained by replacing the endings '-ane', '-ene', '-yne', by '-ylidene', '-enylidene' and '-ynylidene', respectively.

†**ylight(ed** [Y- 4, LIGHT *v.*[2]], lighted.

1422 YONGE tr. *Secr. Secr.* lxi. 237 The mecche of a candill whych is ylyghtid. *c* **1450** *Brut* II. 313 With candels ylight.

†**ylike**, *a.* and *sb. Obs.* Forms: *a.* 1 **ȝelic**, 2 **ȝelic(h)**, 2–5 **ilich(e**, **ylych(e**, 3–5 **ylich(e**, 4 **ileche**, 4–5 **yleche**, **ilyche**. *β.* 2–5 **ilik(e**, 3–5 **ilyke**, 4 **ylik**, **ilek**, 4–5 **ylyk(e**, **illike**, **ylike**. [OE. *ȝelíc*: see Y- 1 b and LIKE *a.* Represented now by ALIKE, q.v.; see also INLIKE.]

A. *adj.* **1.** Like, similar (const. dat. or *to*).

a **900** CYNEWULF *Juliana* 549 Ic ær ne sið ænig ne mette in woruldrice wiþ þe ȝelic. *c* **900** tr. *Bæda's Hist.* IV. xix. (1890) 322 [Se lichoma] wæs slæpendum men ȝelicra þonne deadum. *c* **1175** *Lamb. Hom.* 109 Þe alde mon þe bið butan treowscipe bið iliche þan treo þe bereð lef and blosman and nane westmas ne bereð. *c* **1200** *Vices & Virtues* 9 Ic scal bien ȝelich ðan heisten [orig. *ero similis altissimo*]. *a* **1225** *Ancr. R.* 200 Hwose haueð eni unðeau of þeo þet ich er nemde, oðer ham iliche. **1340–70** *Alex. & Dind.* 792 Ȝe ben to þe hellehond holliche i-like. *c* **1380** *Sir Ferumb.* 2336 A semede þe diuel ileche. **1422** YONGE tr. *Secr. Secr.* xxii. 149 None afore the hath be y-lyke the, ne, aftyre the shall come. *c* **1474** CAXTON *Recuyell* (1894) 321 A geant named Cerberus ynowh ylyke vnto pluto of condicions.

2. Of a number of things: Like one another; alike; equal. ***ever ylike***: always the same.

Beowulf 2164 Feower mearas..ȝelice. *c* **890–***c* **1060** *Laws of Æthelred* VI. lii. (Liebermann) 258 Se maȝa & se unmaȝa ne beoð na ȝelice, ne ne maȝon na ȝelice byrþene ahebban. *a* **1240** *Ureisun* in *O.E. Hom.* I. 203 Þet naueþ nouðer ende ne biginnunge þet is euer iliche wiðute sturiunge. **1387** TREVISA *Higden* (Rolls) IV. 355 Þinges þat beeth i-liche [*MS. γ* buþ ylyche] acordeþ to gidres. *c* **1391** CHAUCER *Astrol.* I. §17 Than ben the daies & the nyhtes illike of lenghthe in al the world. *c* **1420** *Chron. Vilod.* 399 Thre waxe-candels he let make þen, Euery candelle y-leyche of weyȝt. **1422** YONGE tr. *Secr. Secr.* xxiii. 151 Yestyrday he hadd frendys Speciall, but to-day he haue ham all y-lyke. **1430–40** LYDG. *Bochas* IV. xi. (1558) 103 Fortunes gyftes be nat aye ylyche.

3. Fitting, suitable. (Cf. LIKE *a.* 6 a.)

c **1205** LAY. 15117 Nusten heo an world-riche ræd þat heom weore ilike.

B. *sb.* **1.** (One's) like, equal, counterpart.

a **1000** *Boeth. Metr.* xx. 37 Nan þing nis þin ȝelica. *c* **1175** *Lamb. Hom.* 151 Iob wes..swa godmon þet ure drihten..seide þet under houene ne nan his ilike. *c* **1205** LAY. 25378 Nes þer na king his ilike. *c* **1305** *Judas* 66 in *E.E.P.* (1862) 109 Ech þing loueþ his iliche.

2. Outward appearance, likeness, semblance; *concr.* an image, 'likeness'.

a **1225** *Leg. Kath.* 1843 Crist..þurh his ahne engel i culurene iliche, fedde hire. *a* **1225** *Ancr. R.* 136 Loke þet tu habbe his iliche, þet is þet crucifix. *a* **1300** *K. Horn* 305 In hornes ilike þu schalt hure biswike. *c* **1315** SHOREHAM VII. 883 Ase mannes ylyche ymad of tre May nauȝt be al ase man may be..Ne godes ylyche, man, y-wys Ne may nauȝt be al ase god ys.

†**y'like**, *adv. Obs.* Forms: 1 **ȝelíce**, 2 **ȝelic(h)e**, 3–5 **iliche**, **yliche**, 4–5 **ilike**, 4–7 **ylike**, etc. (cf. prec.); also 4 **eliche**, **elike**, **elyke**, 5 **yeliche**. [OE. *ȝelíce* = OS. *gilîco* (MDu. *gelike*, Du. *gelijk*), OHG. *galîhho*, *g(i)lîcho* (MHG. *g(e)lîche*, *g(e)lîch*, G. *gleich*), Goth. *galeikô*; f. prec.]

1. Similarly; likewise; alike; equally. ***ever ylike***: unceasingly, continuously.

971 *Blickl. Hom.* 119 Ne wæron þas ealle ȝelice lange. *c* **1000** *Ags. Gosp.* Matt. xx. 5 Eft he ut-eode embe þa sixtan & niȝoþan tide & dyde þam swa ȝelice. *c* **1200** *Moral Ode* 66 (Trin. Coll. MS.) Africh man mid þat he haueð mai bugge heueriche þe þe more haueð and þe þe lasse boðe iliche. **1297** R. GLOUC. (Rolls) 152 Þat water of baþe is þat on þat euere is iliche hot. **1377** LANGL. *P. Pl.* B. XIX. 436 Al tymes ylyke. *c* **1386** CHAUCER *Knt.'s T.* 1668 Til that the Thebane knyghtes bothe yliche Honured, were in to the paleys fet. *c* **1391** —— *Astrol.* II. §39 The longitude of a clymat ys a lyne ymagined fro Est to west, illike distant by-twene them alle. *a* **1395** HYLTON *Scala Perf.* (W. de W. 1494) I. xxxiv, Who soo is euer ylyke wyse in knowyng of god & ghostly thynges. *c* **1400** LYDG. *Chorle & Bird* 48 (MS. Harl. 116) Of lengthe and brede yeliche square and longe. *c* **1403** CLANVOWE *Cuckow & Night.* 64 The floures and the gras y-lyke hye. **1423** JAS. I *Kingis Q.* lxx, Tantalus..That euer ylike hailith at the well Water to draw with buket botemles. *c* **1460** *Towneley Myst.* viii. 106 A bush I se burnand full bryght, and euer elyke the leyfes are greyn. **1486** *Bk. St. Albans* c vj b, Take Fenell Maryall and Kersis ilich moch.

2. Const. dative: In the same manner (as), like, as. Also with *as* (OE. *swá*), as conj. or conj. adv.

c **893** ÆLFRED *Oros.* V. vii. §2 Þe elpendes hyd wile drincan wætan, ȝelice & spynge deð. **971** *Blickl. Hom.* 17 He him ȝehet his æriste,..ȝelice swa he ær þa þrowunge dyde. **1393** LANGL. *P. Pl.* C. XX. 330 Wusshen and wylnen Alle manere of men mercy and forȝeuenesse, And louye hem yliche hymsylf. **1579** SPENSER *Sheph. Cal.* May 4 How falles it then, we no merrier bene, Ylike as others, girt in gawdy greene? *c* **1634** W. CARTWRIGHT *Ordinary* II. ii. (1651) 25 If I kissen, These thick stark bristles of mine beard will pricken Ylike the skin of Hownd-fish.

†**y'like**, *v. Obs.* [OE. *ȝelícian* (cf. MDu. *ghelîken*, MHG. *gelîchen*, Goth. *galeikan*): see Y- 3 c and LIKE *v.*[1]] *trans.* To please.

c **893** ÆLFRED *Oros.* V. i, Ascian þonne Italie hiera aȝne londleode, hu him þa tida ȝelicoden. **1340** *Ayenb.* 109 Leue uader ylyky þe þet þe holy gost ous wille alyȝte þe hert.

†**ylik(e)ned** [Y- 4], likened.

1340 *Ayenb.* 234 No þing ne is worþi to be ylykned to þe chaste herte. **1393** LANGL. *P. Pl.* C. XVII. 265 Ypocrisie is..ylikned to latyn to a lothliche dounghep. **1422** YONGE tr. *Secr. Secr.* lviii. 228 They bene folis y-lykenyd to assis.

y'likewise, *adv.* = ALIKEWISE: cf. YLIKE *a.*

1460 *Cal. Anc. Rec. Dublin* (1889) 305 And of fysherys ylykewis for the fysch.

ylin(c)ked [Y- 4], linked.

a **1565** SIR T. CHALLONER in Q. Eliz. *Boeth.* etc. 156/56 What ere thow be that thinges ylynked hast In league so olde. **1590** [see LINKED *ppl. a.*].

yliþe *v.* [Y- 3 c, LITHE *v.*[3]], to hearken, listen.

a **1300** *K. Horn* (Harl. MS.) 2 Alle heo ben blyþe þat to my song ylyþe.

†**ylive**, *v. Obs.* Forms: 1 **ȝelifian**, 4 **yleue**; *pa. pple.* 1 **ȝelifd**, 3–4 **ilyued**, **yliued**, **ylyued**, 4 **yleued**. [OE. *ȝelibban*, *ȝelifian* (cf. OHG. *gileben*): see Y- 3 c and LIVE *v.*[1]] To live.

c **950** *Lindisf. Gosp.* Luke x. 28 *Hoc fac et uiues*, ðis do þætte ðu ȝelifiȝe. *c* **1000** in *Narrat. Angl.* (1861) 30 Fulne ende þines lifes þu hæfst ȝelifd. **1297**, etc. Yliued, etc. [see LIVE *v.*[1]]. **1340** *Ayenb.* 93 Þet is guod lyf and yblyssed þet cristene ssolle yleue. *Ibid.* 130 Huanne þe man þengþ..ine huet trauail he heþ yleued. **1393** LANGL. *P. Pl.* C. XII. 255 A goode fryday..a felon was ysaued That vnlawefulliche hadde ylyued.

ylk(e, **ylkan**, **yll**, obs. ff. ILK, ILKA, ILL.

ylle, obs. form of AISLE, ILL, ISLE.

yllischman, **yllisman**, obs. ff. ISLESMAN.

a **1578** LINDESAY (Pitscottie) *Chron. Scot.* (S.T.S.) I. 29 Of grett oppressioun maid be the yllismen [*cf. infra* men of the yllis]. **1610** *Reg. Privy Council Scot.* VIII. 615 What cours salbe takin with these Yllischmen.

yllond, obs. form of ISLAND.

ylls, obs. form of ELSE.

1461 in *Jarrow & Wearmouth* (Surtees) 245 Y[t] he..apper be for ye said holy fader ye pope, or ylls ye wirschipfull doctour Bernardus Romia.

†**ylog(g)ed** [Y- 4], lodged.

13.. *K. Alis.* 3132 (Laud MS.) Forto he com to þat plas, Þer Alisaunder ylogged was. *c* **1380** *Sir Ferumb.* 4001 Wel y-loged ther on pauyllouns.

yloȝe, **ylow(e**, ME. pa. pple. of LIE *v.*[2]

yloȝed, **ylowed** [LOW *v.*[1]], subjected, humbled.

1340 *Ayenb.* 144 Hi ham byeþ zuo moche yloȝed. **1422** YONGE tr. *Secr. Secr.* xxx. 172 He ne holdyth hym not y-lowet ne vndyrfote of the dyssayses whyche he hathe escapid.

yloke, **ylokked**, ME. pa. pples. of LOCK *v.*[1]

13.. *K. Alis.* 2769 (Laud MS.) Ar þe ȝates weren yloke. **1399** LANGL. *Rich. Redeles* I. 44 With lewte and loue yloke to þi peeris. *c* **1400** *Trevisa's Higden* (Rolls) VII. App. 525 That the dores be fast y-loke and barred. *c* **1400** y lokked [see LOCK *v.*[1] 3].

yloked [LOOK *v.*], looked, observed, etc.

1340 *Ayenb.* 7 Þe sabat, þet wes straytliche y-loked ine þe yalde laȝe.

†**ylome**, *adv. Obs.* Forms: 1 **ȝelome**, 2–5 **ilome**, 3 **ȝelome**, 3–5 **ylome**. [OE. *ȝelóme*, f. *ȝe-* Y-, with an element of obscure origin: see LOOM *sb.*[1]] Frequently, often; phr. ***oft and ylome***.

a **1000** *Cædmon's Gen.* 1539 Ðe on wolcnum þæs oft ȝelome andȝiettacen maȝon sceawiȝan. *c* **1175** *Lamb. Hom.* 13 Westmes þorð uuele wederas oft and ilome scal for-wurðan. *c* **1200** *Trin. Coll. Hom.* 31 Heald þin cunde, and þine licames lust kel ilome. *a* **1250** *Owl & Night.* 595 Þar me mai þe ilomest finde, þar men worpeþ hore bihinde. **1340–70** *Alisaunder* 521 A Lioun in a launde may lightlych driue Of hertes an holle herde, as happes ilome. *c* **1400** *St. Alexius* (Laud 622) 69 Men speken of hym ylome In alle þinges wiþouten strijf.

ylond, obs. form of ISLAND.

†**ylong**, obs. var. ALONG *a.*[1] (in sense 'depending *on*').

1297 R. GLOUC. (Rolls) 2711 Þe king esste at enchantors war on it were ylong. *a* **1310** in Wright *Lyric P.* xxi. 61 My joie ant eke my blisse on him is al y-long. *c* **1400** *Pilgr. Sowle* (Caxton 1483) IV. xxx. 78 Yf it soo be that in his hede be founde ony defaute, hit wylle seme..that hit is y long vppon his counceyl.

ylope: see YLEPE.

ylore(n, **ylorn(e**, ME. pa. pple. of LEESE *v.*[1] to lose.

1297 R. GLOUC. (Rolls) 5133 Hii ssolleþ ȝut keuery moche lond þat hii abbeþ y lore. *a* **1310** in Wright *Lyric P.* xxxix. 110 Al is dayes werk ther were y-loren. **1393** LANGL. *P. Pl.* C. XIII. 182 Oþer sedes..That ben leide on louh erthe ylore as hit were. *c* **1430** *Hymns Virg.* (1867) 79 At euery hour a poynt is y-loore.

ylosed, **ylost(e**, ME. pa. pple. of LOSE *v.*[1]

13.. *K. Alis.* 4282 (Linc. Inn MS.) Darie haþ ylost his pray. **1387** TREVISA *Higden* (Rolls) IV. 461 Allas! my freendes, þis day I have y-lost. **1407** SCOGAN *Mor. Balade* 36 Tyme y-lost in youthe folily Greveth a wight goostly and bodily.

ylosed[1], loosed, loosened.

1387 TREVISA *Higden* (Rolls) VII. 151 Þe skyn y-loused [orig. *soluta cute*].

ylosed[2], freed from lice.

1387 TREVISA *Higden* (Rolls) III. 353 Þey hadde i-lowsed [*MS. γ* ylosed] her cloþes.

yloved, **ylowid**, ME. pa. pple. of LOVE *v.*[1]

13.. *Coer de L.* 1744 Friends, with the best That might be in any lond Y-loved. **1422** YONGE tr. *Secr. Secr.* vii. 137 Wyrchippyd, ylowid, and ydreddyd.

ylow(e, **ylowed**: see YLOȜE, YLOȜED.

yluggyd, lugged, pulled.

1399 LANGL. *Rich. Redeles* III. 336 He was lyghtliche y-lauȝte and y-luggyd of many.

ylurned, **ylyerned**: see YLERNED.

yly: see YLAY(E.

ylych(e, **ylyk(e**, varr. YLIKE.

ylyft(e, lifted.

1387 TREVISA *Higden* (Rolls) VI. 9 Þanne he was ileft [*MS. γ* ylyft] an hiȝe.

ymaad, **ymad(e**, obs. pa. pples. of MAKE *v.*[1]

ymaced, ME. pa. pple. of MASS *v.*[2]

ymadge, **ymag(e**, etc., obs. ff. IMAGE, etc.

†**ymake**, **ymaked**, ME. pa. pples. of MAKE *v.*[1]

ymanered, **ymanerit(e** [Y- 5, MANNER *sb.*[1]], mannered.

1393 LANGL. *P. Pl.* C. XI. 260 A mayde wel ymanered of good men yspronge. **1422** YONGE tr. *Secr. Secr.* lviii. 226 Tho that haue the flesshe of the brestis lytill and dry bene ille-ymanerite.

ymanned, **-yd** [Y- 4], manned.

c **1450** *Brut* II. 434 The toune of Orliaunce was..well ymannyd and vitailid.

ymaried, married.

1377 LANGL. *P. Pl.* B. II. 39 Now worth þis Mede ymaried al to a mansed schrewe.

ymariss(ch)ed, pa. pple. of MARISSE *v.*

ymarked, **-yd**, ME. pa. pple. of MARK *v.*

13.. *Sir Orfeo* 546 (Zielke) A way!..þat him was so hard Grace yȝarked, And so vile deþ ymarked! **1422** YONGE tr. *Secr. Secr.* xl. 199 Euery manes lyfe is y-markyd by kynde, how longe he shal mow doure.

ymart(i)red, **ymartyred**, ME. pa. pple. of MARTYR *v.*

1297 R. GLOUC. (Rolls) 1819 Ymartred [*v.rr.* y martired, y martred] uor vre louerdes loue. **1387** TREVISA *Higden* (Rolls) V. 19 Þat ȝere Eustas..was y-martired.

ymasked, **ymaymed**, ME. pa. pples. of MASK, MAIM.

ymbar, obs. form of EMBER[2].

1550 *Acts Privy Council* (1891) III. 68 Holiedaies or fastinge daies as Lent, Ymbar daies, or any such lyke.

ymbarge, obs. form of EMBARGE *v.*

1585 *MS. Tanner 78*, 52 They shall ymbarge or arrest the Duke of Florrences Gallion.

ymbassator, **-bassutt**, obs. var. AMBASSADOR, AMBASSADE.

1484 *Cely Papers* (Camden) 149 To goo as ymbassutt for the stappell to Dewke Phyllypp. **1543** in Lodge *Illustr. Brit. Hist.* (1791) I. 45 The Frenche Ymbassator has not proponyt that matt[r] as yet.

ymber, **ymbre**, obs. forms of EMBER[1].

c **1450** *Mirk's Festial* 254 Our old faders wolden ete þes dayes kakes bakyn yn þe ymbres. **1588** KYD *Househ. Phil.* Wks. (1901) 273 She gins the ymbers vp to rake.

ymbir-, ymbre(n, etc., obs. ff. EMBER².

ymbolden, obs. f. EMBOLDEN, IMBOLDEN.
1611 W. ADAMS *Let.* in Rundall *Mem. Japon* (Hakl. Soc.) 31, I haue ymboldened my selfe to write these few lines.

ymbrasour, obs. form of EMBRACER².

ymbroder, obs. form of EMBROIDER.
1562-3 *N. Country Wills* (Surtees 1912) 37 A suyte of blewe velvet ymbrodered. **1638** *Abridgm. Specif. Patents, Furniture* (1869) 1 Ymbrodering or hufling of guilded leather.

†**ymed(e)led** [Y- 4, MEDDLE *v.*], mixed.
c **1374** CHAUCER *Troylus* III. 815 So worldly selynesse.. y-medled is with many a bitternesse. *c* **1394** *P. Pl. Crede* 177 Wyde wyndowes..Schynen wiþ schapen scheldes..Wiþ merkes of marchauntes y-medled bytwene.

ymedicable, ymedyat, obs. ff. IMMEDICABLE, IMMEDIATE.

†**ymeint,** pa. pple. (ME. and 7 *arch.*) of MENG *v.*, to mix.

ymel(le: see IMELLE.

ymelked [Y- 4], milked.
13.. *St. Kenelm* 234 in *E.E.P.* (1862) 54 As ful heo wolde a morwe beo, þeȝ heo were vmelked an eue.

†**ymelled, -yd** [MELL *v.*²], mixed.
1387 TREVISA *Higden* (Rolls) III. 469 Þe elementes i-medled [*MS. γ* ymelled] to gidres. *c* **1430** *Two Cookery-bks.* 28 Pouder Gyngere y-mellyd with Sugre.

ymelt(ed, ME. pa. pple. of MELT *v.*¹
1387 TREVISA *Higden* (Rolls) III. 13 A streem of gold of nayles i-melt [*MS. γ* ymelt]. **1432-50** tr. *Higden* (Rolls) IV. 187 Golde y-meltede.

ymende [Y- 3 c, *mende* MIND *v.*], to remember.
1340 [see MIND *v.* 2 c].

ymene: see I-MENE.

ymeneȝed, pa. pple. of MING *v.*

ymeng, ymeng(e)d, -id, -yd, ME. pa. pples. of MENG *v.*, to mingle.
1297 R. GLOUC. (Rolls) 2541 Þo were among cristinemen þis paiens þus imenged [*v.r.* y menged]. *Ibid.* 3437 Þus were in worre & in wo ymeng þe saxons..myd þe brutons. **1340** *Ayenb.* 196 Loke þet ydele blisse..ne by naȝt y-mengd. *c* **1430** *Two Cookery-bks.* 38 Ȝolkys of Eyroun y-mengyd with þe Ius of haselle leuys.

yment, ME. pa. pple. of MEAN *v.*¹

ymered, pa. pple. of MERE *v.*¹, to purify.

ymesurid, ME. f. MEASURED; *well y-mesurid*, well-proportioned.
1422 YONGE tr. *Secr. Secr.* lxix. 236 The hede well y-mesurid.

ymet¹, ME. pa. pple. of METE *v.*², to dream.
c **1380** *Sir Ferumb.* 335 Þou hast y met of venysoun; þou mostest drynke a torn. *c* **1430** [see METE *v.*² 2].

ymet², pa. pple. (ME. and 6-7 *arch.*) of MEET *v.*
1522 *World & Child* (facs.) C v b, Well ymet syr, well ymet. **1642** H. MORE *Song of Soul* I. III. ii, Last time we were together here ymet.

†**ymete,** *v. Obs.* [OE. *ȝemétan*: see Y- 3 c and MEET *v.*] To meet, meet with, encounter.
c **893** ÆLFRED *Oros.* VI. xxxi. 286 Mid þæm þæt hiene ȝemette an mon, þa he for from Actesiphonte þære byriȝ. *c* **1175** *Lamb. Hom.* 109 Iselie beoð efre þa mildheortan for þi heo imetað þa mildheortnesse. *c* **1275** *Wom. Samaria* 67 in *O.E. Misc.* 86 To alle þat heo myhte iseon oþer y-mete. **1297** R. GLOUC. (Rolls) 1437 Him þouȝte imete mid is ost ar he at hom were. *c* **1300** *Names of Hare* 1 in *Rel. Ant.* I. 133 The mon that the hare i-met, Ne shal him nevere be the bet. *c* **1305** *St. Christopher* 37 in *E.E.P.* (1862) 60 Þe maistre þat was firs ynouȝ com & ymette him anon.

†**ymete(n,** ME. pa. pple. of METE *v.*¹, to measure.
c **1380** *Sir Ferumb.* 2092 Fuliche ne is he noȝt now fram þe vj fet ymete in brede.

ymeved, ymeoved, ymoved, ME. pa. pple. of MOVE *v.*
1387 TREVISA *Higden* (Rolls) III. 301 Þe Frensche men.. were i-meved [MS. *γ* ymeoued] by likynge of þat wyn. **1422** YONGE tr. *Secr. Secr.* xxxiv. 189 Yf he thyn answere in dispite haue, neuer for that be thow ymeuet. **1432-50** tr. *Higden* (Rolls) V. 143 To decide the maters y-movede.

ymeynd, ymeynt = YMEINT.

ymgrame, error (in T. Wilson's *Rhet.* p. 37, edd. 1580, etc.) for *yngrame*, INGRAM.

ymidde, ymydde, var. IMID *Obs.*
c **1400** *26 Pol. Poems* xi. 66 God may say, fern ȝere, folk were fayn To resceyue me ymydde here brest. *c* **1450** *St. Cuthbert* (Surtees) 7794 He..went forth his enmys y midde.

†**yminne** *v.* [Y- 3 c, MIN *v.*²], to mention.
a **1325** *Maudelain* 579 in Horstm. *Altengl. Leg.* (1878) 169 Herdestow euer in spelle yminne Of a woman þat was in sinne?

yminted, pseudo-arch. pa. pple. of MINT *v.*²
1835 CLARE *Rural Muse* 10 Like gold yminted new.

ymixt, mixed.
a **1600** MONTGOMERIE *Misc. Poems* xxxv. 38 Hir comelie cheeks of vive colour, Of rid and vhyt ymixt.

ymnake, error for *ynmake*, INMAKE, inmate.
1536 *Act 28 Hen. VIII.* c. 24 in Bolton *Stat. Irel.* (1621) 175 Euery person and persons..which in the haruest season, receiue..in his or their houses..any person or persons called ymnakes.

ymne, etc., obs. forms of HYMN, etc.

†**ymolt(en** = YMELT(ED.
1387 TREVISA *Higden* (Rolls) VIII. 129 Golde i-schave of seyntes schrynes and i-ȝote [*MS. β* y-molt]. *a* **1425** tr. *Arderne's Treat. Fistula*, etc. 31 Whiche y-molten and þe forseid þingis beyng hote. **1590** [see MELT *v.*¹ 8]. **1748** [see MELT *v.*¹ 11].

†**y'mone,** *sb. Obs.* [OE. *ȝemána*: see MONE *sb.*¹, MENE, MEAN *a.*¹]
1. Companionship, fellowship.
c **888** ÆLFRED *Boeth.* v. § 1 Þonne wære he mid his aȝnum cynne..þonne he wæs on ðara ryhtwisena ȝemanan. *a* **1175** *Cott. Hom.* 245 For ðan þe se helende underfeng þa sinfullan, and ham mid imone hafede. *c* **1205** LAY. 21308 Þeh þe wulf beon ane buten ælc imane [*c* **1275** one..imone]. *c* **1260** *K. Horn* (Camb. MS.) 834 Sire, ischal al one Wiþute more ymone..Bringe hem þre to deþe.
2. Sexual intercourse.
c **950** *Lindisf. Gosp.* Mark xii. 25 *rubric*, Ne ceorl hæfis wifes ȝemana. *c* **1275** *Wom. Samaria* 32 in *O.E. Misc.* 85 Nabbe ich of wepmonne nones kunnes y-mone. *c* **1275** *Annunc. Virg.* 10 ibid. 100 Hw myhte hit iwurþe þat ich were myd childe, Monnes imone on me ne may nomon fynde. *c* **1275** LAY. 25916 Ne mihte þat maide his imone [*c* 1205 mone] þolie. *c* **1315** SHOREHAM v. 28 Hy wyþ-oute mannes ymone In body,..to manne hyne broute.
3. A companion. (? A scribal error.)
a **1300** *K. Horn* (Harl. MS.) 530 He nolde gon is one, Athulf wes hys ymone [*Camb. MS.* mone].

†**ymone,** *a.* and *adv. Obs.* [Alteration of IMENE *a.* and *adv.* after YMONE *sb.*]
A. *adj.* Common, shared by two or more.
1205 LAY. 978 Ȝif we sceoteð to heora mæðe, þat bið ure imone deað. **1297** R. GLOUC. (Rolls) 6359 He..sede, hail þou be King one. Se nis it noȝt, quaþ þe King, uor mi Kinedom is ymone.
B. *adv.* Together.
c **1300** *St. Brandan* 380 Anon so hi seȝe the monekes come, hi gonne to singe ymone. *c* **1380** *Sir Ferumb.* 99 If þat on of hem ne dar him self wiþ me fiȝte al one Send hem boþe on þyn helf to fiȝte wiþ me ymone.

†**ymong,** *sb. Obs.* [OE. *ȝemang*, f. *ȝe-* Y- 3 a + root *mang-* to mix, found in MENG *v.* Cf. next.] Mixture (OE. only); company, assembly.
a **1000** *Judith* 193 Berað..Scire helmas in sceaðena ȝemong. *c* **1205** LAY. 10868, & sloh þene king..Imong þissen imonge [*c* 1275 motinge].

†**y'mong,** *prep.* and *conj. Obs.* Forms: 1 **ȝemang, ȝemong,** 2-3 **imong,** 3-7 **ymong,** 4 **imang(e,** 4-5 **ymang(e,** 4-6 **ymonge;** also 5 *Sc.* **ymangis** (after *amonges*, AMONGST). [OE. *ȝemang, ȝemong*, used beside *onȝemang* AMONG *prep.*, which is f. *on* ON *prep.* + *ȝemang* company, YMONG *sb.*] **A.** *prep.* Among, in the midst of.
c **893** ÆLFRED *Oros.* IV. iv, & þeah ȝemong þære heringe þyllica bismra on hie selfe asædon. *c* **1000** *Ags. Gosp.* Matt. x. 16 Nu ic eow sende swa sceap ȝemang [*Lindisf.* inmong, *Hatton* onmang] wulfas. *Ibid.* John xxi. 23 Ðeos spræc com ut ȝemang broþrum þæt se leorning-cniht ne swylt. *c* **1175** *Lamb. Hom.* 27 Hu derst þu mon þer on-ȝein underfon drihtenes fleis and his blod in þine licome imong þan unwreste sunne and ec imong þan deofle þe wuneð in him? *c* **1205** LAY. 13116 Þe þer sæt..imong alle þan cnihten. *c* **1250** *Gen. & Ex.* 3419 If ymong .x. wurð oȝt mis-don. *c* **1325** *Metr. Hom.* 48 Imang you wonand he isse. *c* **1330** R. BRUNNE *Chron. Wace* (Rolls) 369 Y-monge þe pres. *a* **1400** *Isumbras* 368 In his mantille of skarlet rede Ymange his golde he did his brede. *c* **1450** *St. Cuthbert* (Surtees) 5646 Be takyns he aspyed þe thefe ymang ilkane. **1474** *Acc. Ld. High Treas. Scot.* I. 53 Item to the batis that carijt our the King, the Quene, and the Courte, ymangis thaim,..xl. s. *c* **1500** *Lancelot* 820 He goith ymong them in his hie curage. **1536** in J. Nicolson & R. Burn *Westmld. & Cumbld.* (1777) 613 *note*, Every on of the other iiii prysts to have vi d, and to have to drynke ymonge theym viii d. **1642** H. MORE *Song of Soul, Paraphr. Interpr. Answ. Apollo* 15, I Phœbus with my lovely locks ymong The midst of you shall sit.
b. *her* (*þer*)..*ymong*: among or with them; herewith, therewith.
c **1205** LAY. 22702 Her wes fiðelinge and song, her wes harpinge imong. *Ibid.* 24194 Þer wes harepinge and song, þer weoren blissen imong. *a* **1225** *Leg. Kath.* 1580 Heo wes hire seolf þer imong, as hire þuhte.
B. *conj. ymong þat*: while.
Cf. OE. *ȝemang þæm*, meanwhile.
c **893** ÆLFRED *Oros.* IV. i. § 9 Ȝemong þæm þe Pirrus wið Romane winnende wæs. *c* **1205** LAY. 18174 Imong þat he king wæs..Merlin him æt-wende.

†**ymorþred,** ME. pa. pple. of MURDER *v.*
1297 [see MURDER *v.* 1 a]. **1393** LANGL. *P. Pl.* C. XIII. 242 And so is meny man ymorþred for hus money and goodes.

ymortified, ME. pa. pple. of MORTIFY.
a **1425** tr. *Arderne's Treat. Fistula* etc. 45 A gret quantite y-mortified.

ymoselyd, ME. pa. pple. of MUZZLE *v.*¹

Y-moth: see Y 3 b.

ymounted, pseudo-arch. pa. pple. of MOUNT *v.*
1590 MARLOWE *2nd Pt. Tamburl.* IV. iii, Like to an almond tree ymounted high.

ymovede: see YMEVED.

ympes(c)he, obs. forms of IMPEACH.

ympliȝeþly, obs. form of IMPLIEDLY.

ympn(e, obs. forms of HYMN.

ympreif, var. IMPREVE *v. Obs.*

ymree, obs. form of EMERY.

ymston, var. ME. *ȝymston*: see GEMSTONE.
a **1272** *Luue Ron* 175 in *O.E. Misc.* 98 Among alle oþre ymstone þes beoþ deorre in vyche place. *Ibid.* 178 Mayde al so ich þe tolde þe ymston of þi bur.

ymulis, obs. Sc. form of EMULOUS.

†**ymummyd,** ME. pa. pple. of MUM *v.*

ymund, -munt: see YMINT.

ymunde: see MIND *sb.*¹, *a.*

ymundified, ME. pa. pple. of MUNDIFY *v.*
a **1425** tr. *Arderne's Treat. Fistula* etc. 27 Þe wounde ymundified if it be wele tretable.

†**ymur.** *Obs.* [? a. dial. var. of OF. *umor* HUMOUR *sb.* (cf. Picard *himeur*, Walloon *imeure*).] ? Atmospheric moisture.
c **1400** *Destr. Troy* 897 All cold it became & the course helde, Bothe of ymur & aire after I-wise. *Ibid.* 1575 The Stretis were streght & of a stronge brede, For ymur & aire opon in þe myddis.

†**ymurdred,** arch. pa. pple. of MURDER *v.*
1581 A. HALL *Iliad* v. 95 Here dy thou shalt ymurdred by my hand.

ymuwed, ME. pa. pple. of MEW *v.*¹

ymyd(de, ymyddes, -is, -ys, ymydward, obs. varr. AMID (cf. YMIDDE), AMIDST, AMIDWARD.
c **1400** *Destr. Troy* 8769 The body..Was..set in a seate vnder, Ymydward the mayne towmbe.

†**ymylded,** ME. pa. pple. of MILD *v.*

ymynced, ymynsyd, ME. pa. pple. of MINCE *v.*
c **1430** *Two Cookery-bks.* 6 Oynons y-mynced. *Ibid.* 13 Oynonys y-mynsyd.

ymyned, ME. pa. pple. of MINE *v.*

ymynt(e: see YMINT.
1297 R. GLOUC. (Rolls) 4920 + 31 Þe nyȝt þet he adde imund [*MS. δ* ymynte] vort abbe ywend a-morwe. *c* **1380** *Sir Ferumb.* 576 Hadd y þat stronge strok y-take þou haddest to me ymynt.

ymynused, pa. pple. of MINISH *v.*
a **1400** *New Test.* (Paues) Col. i. 21 Whan ȝe weren sumtyme y-alyened & y-mynused in wyt in efel werkes.

yn, obs. f. IN *prep.* and *adv.*, INN *sb.*

Yn: see YIN.

ynail(l)ed, ynamyd, ME. pa. pples. of NAIL *v.*, NAME *v.*¹

Ynca, obs. f. INCA.

ynce, obs. Sc. form of HENCE *adv.*

ynch(e, obs. ff. INCH.

yncke, ync(k)le, ynclynge, yncorne, obs. ff. INK, INKLE, INKLING, INK-HORN.

ynd(e: see END *sb.*, HIND *sb.*¹, IND, INDE.

Yndeen, -ien, Yndewes, obs. ff. INDIAN, INDIES.

yndling, var. INDLING, EYNDLING *sb. Obs.*, jealous.

yndoys, var. *Yndes* (see IND 2).

yndrest, var. INNEREST *Obs.*, innermost.

yne, obs. pl. of EYE *sb.*¹, obs. f. IN *prep.*

-yne (-aɪn), orig. var. -INE⁵, now used in its own right to denote a triple bond between carbon atoms, as in BUTYNE, PROPYNE.
1931 *Jrnl. Chem. Soc.* 1610 Definitive Report of the Committee [of the International Union of Chemistry] for the Reform of Nomenclature in Organic Chemistry... The name of hydrocarbons containing the triple linkage will end in *yne, diyne*, etc.

†**ynem(p)ned,** pa. pple. of NEMN *v.*, to name.
1297 R. GLOUC. (Rolls) App. H. 10 After þe quene y nempned heo was. **1340** *Ayenb.* 66 Alle þise zennes þet we habbeþ hyer ynemned. **1417** *E.E. Wills* (1882) 27 All my pourest tenauntes..excepte ham þat I haue ynemned in þis bok.

†**ynence, -ens, -entes,** *prep. Obs.* [var. ff. *enence, anentes* ANENT.] Towards; in relation to.
a **1340** HAMPOLE *Psalter* ix. 2 Ynence my selfe i. sall be glad in þe. *Ibid.* x. 8 Euennes is sen in his knawynge, ynentes bath þe partis of goed and ill. *c* **1340** —— *Prose Treat.* 8 Many are þat neuer haue halde þe ordyre of lufe ynesche [*read* ynence] þaire frendys sybbe or ffremede. *a* **1400** *Relig. Pieces fr. Thornton MS.* (1914) 26 Thurghe þis commandement es man ordaynede ynence God þe Fadire. *c* **1400** MAUNDEV. (Roxb.) x. 40 Ynentes þe kirk of þe Sepulchre es þe citee maste wayke. *c* **1400** tr. *Secr. Secr., Gov. Lordsh.* 106 Conferme my louynge in þe, ynens þis Iew.

yneuch(t, ynew(cht: see ENOUGH, ENOW.

ynewe, obs. var. ANEW *adv.*
c **1380** *Sir Ferumb.* 626, & þo by-gan ynewe fiȝt be-twene þis knyȝtes tweye.

†**ynewed** [Y- 4, NEW *v.*], renewed.
1340 *Ayenb.* 107 Ynewed and eft ycristned ine þe bloode of Iesu crist.

yngde, obs. f. IND.

ynge, obs. f. HINGE, ING, YOUNG.

ynȝoin, ynion, obs. ff. ONION.

Yngles, -is(se, etc., obs. ff. ENGLISH, INGLIS.

yngynore, obs. form of ENGINEER.

ynke, ynkell, obs. forms of INK, INKLE.

ynkirly, -urly, var. ENKERLY *adv. Obs.*

ynkleth: see INKLETH.

ynmast, -most, obs. forms of INMOST.

ynn(e, ynner: see IN, INN, INNE, INNER.

ynnion, obs. form of ONION.
c **1580** in *Engl. Hist. Rev.* (1914) July 519 Greate ynnions that be xij or xiiij ynches abowte.

ynogh(e, ynoh(e, etc.: see ENOUGH, ENOW.

†**ynombred,** ME. pa. pple. of NUMBER *v.*
1470–85 MALORY *Arthur* v. x. 178 His armye..with the garneson of godard and sarasyns of Southland ynombred lx M of good men of armes.

ynome(n, ynume, ME. pa. pple. of NIM *v.*, to take.
c **1275** in *O.E. Misc.* 43/206 So me doþ to þeoue þat schal beon ynume. **1297** R. GLOUC. (Rolls) 2421 Vor to be maistres of þis folc we beþ ychose & ynome. **13..** *K. Alis.* 4668 (Laud MS.), Þe boweles weren ynomen oute. *c* **1380** *Sir Ferumb.* 1105 Erld Olyuer & his felawes þat Sarazyns habbeþ ynome. *c* **1470** HENRY *Wallace* IX. 53 Leyt salys fall, and has thar cours ynom.

ynon, obs. form of ONION.

†**ynorisched, -issed, ynorsched,** ME. pa. pples. of NOURISH, NORSH.
1297 R. GLOUC. (Rolls) 1450 He spac engliss vor he was at rome inorssed [*MS. B.* ynorisched] biuore. **1340** *Ayenb.* 205 þe children þet weren y-norissed mid greate metes. **1387** TREVISA *Higden* (Rolls) VIII. 35 While he was a child y-norsched in þe kynges court of Fraunce. *c* **1450** *Mirk's Festial* 9, I..haue ben cheresly ynorysched.

ynot = *y not*, I do not know: see NOT *v.*[2]
1297 R. GLOUC. (Rolls) 5628 þere he liþ ȝut to þis day ac ynot to wuche dome þe toun suþþe of pokel chirche fram glastingbury come. **13..** in Ritson *Anc. Songs* (1877) 57 Ynot non so freoh flour, Ase ledies that beth bryght in bour.

ynou(gh, ynow(gh, etc.: see ENOUGH, ENOW.

ynoumbred, ME. pa. pple. of NUMBER *v.*

ynpossybull, ynpugne, obs. ff. IMPOSSIBLE, IMPUGN.

yn sted, stude, styd, obs. ff. INSTEAD.

ynsyte, obs. form of INCITE.

†**ynued** [Y- 4, NOY *v.*], harmed.
1422 YONGE tr. *Secr. Secr.* xxx. 170 By this vertu Is the herte of a man I-Stabelid, in so myche that for no chaunce hit is not y-nued.

ynug(h, ynume(n: see ENOUGH, YNOME(N.

ynuste = *y nuste*, I knew not: see NIST.

yo (jəʊ), *int.* (*sb.*[1]) Forms: 5 ȝo, io, ȝaw, 9 yo, yeo(h. An exclamation of incitement, warning, etc. (also repeated). In nautical use = YOHO. Occas. as sb. and in vbl. sb. *yo-yoing*.
c **1420** *Avow. Arth.* vii. [*To hounds*], ȝaw thar suche him no mare. *c* **1450** *Mankind* 450 in *Macro Plays* 17 *Myscheff.* How, New-gyse, Now-a-days! herke or I goo! When owur hedis wer to-gethere, I spake of 'si dedero'. *New-gyse.* ȝo! go þi wey! we xall gaþer mony on-to. *c* **1460** *Towneley Myst.* ii. 25 Io furth, greyn-horne! and war oute, gryme! **1772** *Monthly Rev.* XLII. 191/1 The scene was quite chang'd, 'twas no more yo, yo-ho. **1806** PINCKARD *Tour W. Indies* III. 343 A string of negroes singing out in the sailors' cry —yeoh-yeoh, yeoh-yeoh, and hauling at a long rope. **1837** DICKENS *Pickw.* ix, He was roused by a loud shouting of the post-boy on the leader. 'Yo—yo—yo—yo—yoe,' went the first boy. 'Yo—yo—yo—yoe!' went the second... And amidst the yo-yoing..the chaise stopped. **1839** HOOD *Storm at Hastings* xiii, Sundry boatmen, that with quick yeo's, Lest it should *blow*,—were pulling up the *Rose.* **1859** DICKENS *T. Two Cities* I. ii, Yo there! Stand! I shall fire!

yo (jəʊ), *sb.*[2] Also yoe. Repr. dial. (esp. U.S.) pronunc. of EWE *sb.*[1] Cf. YOW(E.
1891 *Dialect Notes* I. 71 *Yo*, ewe. **1899** B. W. GREEN *Word-bk. Virginia Folk-Speech* 434 *Yoe, n.*: yow, yeo; eow; yowe; a female sheep. 'Breeding yoes & a Ramm.' **1922** BLUNDEN *Shepherd* 12 While each one came from the poor frightened yoes. **1946** *Amer. Speech* XXI. 98 [S. Illinois] *Yo*, ewe.

yo, [historically an obs. form of YOU]: in mod. use, repr. dial. pronunc. of *you, your*, esp. in Black English.
1848 MRS. GASKELL *Mary Barton* I. vi. 90 Yo stop here, and I'll be back in half-an-hour. **1897** [see SHOOT *v.* 2 d]. **1931** W. FAULKNER *Sanctuary* xxiv. 271 Minnie tapped at the door. 'Here yo dinner.' **1937** C. HIMES *Black on Black* (1973) 139 Niggah, ef'n yo is talkin' tuh me, Ah ain' liss'nin'. **1969** R. FAIR in A. Chapman *New Black Voices* (1972) 114 Oh, shut yo mouf up man. **1973** *Black World* June 61 Saturday nite take yo shoes off at the door.

yoak(e: see OAK, YOKE, YOLK.

yoaks, yoax (jəʊks), *int. Obs.* exc. *dial.* (yocks). A hunting cry; also as vb. (Cf. YOICKS.)
1778 GARRICK in *Monthly Rev.* (1779) LX. 59 'Squire Western, reeling, with October mellow, Tall, yo!—Boys! —Yoax—Criticks! hunt the fellow! **1828** *Sporting Mag.* (N.S.) XXII. 129 He yoaksed in a whisper, he cheered in a whisper. **1905** *Eng. Dial. Dict.*, *Yocks*, a call of encouragement to a dog hunting rabbits, &c. n. Yks.

yoalk, obs. form of YOLK.

yob (jɒb). *slang.* [Backslang for BOY *sb.*[1]] Orig. simply, a boy, a youth; in mod. use, a lout, a hooligan; (see also quot. 1918).
1859 HOTTEN *Dict. Slang* 131 *Yob*, a boy. **1886–96** in Farmer & Henley *Slang* (1903) VII. 375/1 And you bet that each gal, not to mention each yob, Didn't care how much ooftish it cost 'em per nob. **1908** A. N. LYONS *Arthur's* II. i. 108 It'd take more'n a yob in a squash 'at to call *me* a blighted sooper. **1918** FARROW *Dict. Milit. Terms* 673 *Yob*, a slang term used by soldiers meaning an officer or one who is easily fooled. **1927** J. C. GOODWIN *Crook Pie* iii. 71 A yob shouted: 'Now for yer belts, boys!' and my friend was thrashed. **1930** P. MACDONALD *Link* 130 Well, sir, I sez to meself, what does A do? Then I thinks, keep the mob off. So I jest backs into the door of the public, and doesn't let any of the yobs get out. **1957** J. OSBORNE *Look Back in Anger* I. 15 'Let's go to the pictures.'.. 'And have my enjoyment ruined by the Sunday night yobs in the front row?' **1962** J. WAIN *Strike Father Dead* 303 If you're expecting a description of what those yobs did to us, please forget it. **1977** *Western Morning News* 30 Aug. 1/3 One police officer sheltering from a bombardment of missiles behind a plastic shield said: 'It's just a bunch of yobs.' **1984** *Times* 16 Feb. 3/1, I would not want anybody looking at me to think this man is a thick, stupid, illiterate yob.
Hence **'yobbery**, hooliganism; **'yobbish** *a.* characteristic of a yob; **'yobby** *a.*, loutish.
1955 E. BLISHEN *Roaring Boys* iv. 210 Though I don't hold with Grimes' yobby way of dressing, I think the Edwardian style's a good thing in itself. **1972** *Guardian* 16 Feb. 12/1 The 16-year-old boy..was..adopting a yobbish air which drove his mother into nerve-twanging tantrums. **1974** *Times Lit. Suppl.* 1 Mar. 215/2 A comparative study of urban adolescent vandalism and upper-class yobbery. **1980** *Observer* 9 Nov. 12/4 It is one thing to deplore the collective yobbery of Mr. Benn's supporters. **1982** E. NORTH *Ancient Enemies* ii. 19 The boys, although none of them as individuals are that dim or yobby, jeered. **1984** *Listener* 27 Sept. 22/1 A club with one of the worst records for drunken yobbery, Tottenham Hotspur,..brazenly makes a deal with the makers of Holstein lager. **1984** *Sunday Tel.* 2 Dec. 20/6 The loony Left should not be confused with that other Left which has been described as the Left of the yobbish tendency.

yobbo ('jɒbəʊ). *slang.* Also yobo. Pl. yobbos, occas. yobboes. [An extended form of prec.] A lout, a hooligan.
1922 *Contemp. Rev.* CXXII. 368 To him the boys are always the 'yobos'. **1938** *Evening News* 7 Mar. 11/5 A few inverted words have found common acceptance; slop (policeman), yob or yobbo (street rough, an inverted form of boy). **1940** R. POSTGATE *Verdict of Twelve* I. v. 74 Hardly any one about except a few yobos who had got nothing to do, and hung around in irritated idleness, spitting manfully in the gutter and telling dirty stories. **1955** E. BLISHEN *Roaring Boys* III. 147 'Yoboes!' said my colleague. 'My God, I wouldn't teach again in a senior school... Their insolence and rowdiness.' **1959** J. BRAINE *Vodi* xii. 165 Some yobbos in 1916 broke Nisbauer's shop window. **1960** *News Chron.* 9 Feb. 6/6 The local Teddies and yobbos swing their dubious weight behind the strike. **1964** in Hamblett & Deverson *Generation X* 56 Ever since that Profumo lark I've come to the conclusion that we working class yobos, as they like to call us, have less to be ashamed of than those establishment geezers. **1972** T. STOPPARD *Jumpers* II. 80 That astronaut yobbo is good for twenty years hard. **1978** [see *street-corner* s.v. STREET *sb.* 4 b]. **1982** *Age* (Melbourne) 4 Feb. 9/4 We get the odd guarded comment from the yobbo on the street about our dress.

yoberte, obs. form of JEOPARDY.
1539 *St. Pap. Hen. VIII* III. 161 Yn gret yoberte of lyff.

yobliged, ME. pa. pple. of OBLIGE *v.*

yochomdale, yockynggale, var. YOKINDALE.

yock (jɒk), *sb.* (and *v.*) *Theatr. slang* (chiefly *U.S.*). Also yok. [Cf. Eng. dial. *yocha* to laugh.] A laugh. Also as *v. intr.* (and quasi-*trans.*).
1938 H. M. ALEXANDER *Strip Tease* 83 'Listen to 'em yock out there,' says the comic... 'Yock' is a belly laugh. **1949** *N.Y. Times* 4 Sept. 7/6 It makes me furious when I have a corny line and it gets a yock. **1951** *New Yorker* 12 May 32/3 There'd be Don, yockin' it up like crazy,..he's so hysterical with loyalty laughter. **1957** S. J. PERELMAN *Road to Miltown* 73 Brother, I've heard some dillies in my day, but that's the payoff... What a yock this'll give the mob at Sardi's! **1957** WODEHOUSE *Over Seventy* xiii. 134 A few gay observations on the weather and he is ready for the big yoks. **1961** *Daily Mail* 4 Mar. 8 'I'm right in saying that you wouldn't do this to me, madam?' asked the colonel... The producer said, 'You'd have got a helpful yok from the audience there, colonel.' **1965** *New Yorker* 31 July 56/3 A chuckle or even a short, muted yock is acceptable from time to time. **1973** *Publishers Weekly* 26 Feb. 50/1 (Advt.), An hilarious collection of jokes, rhymes, riddles, tongue twisters, teasers and other assorted high-flying nonsense. The riddles and illustrations sprinkled throughout this page give just a brief taste of this yok-filled book. **1975** *New Yorker* 2 June 36/3 'Maybe you were a king in Babylon and I was a Christian slave,' I chaffed him. 'But enough with the yocks.'

yock, yocke, obs. forms of YOKE.

yod (jɒd, jəʊd). Also yodh. [See JOD.]
1. Name of the tenth (the smallest) letter of the Hebrew alphabet.
1735 LYONS *Scholars Instr.* (1757) 25 Those Verbs which have Vau Consonant, or Yod Consonant for the second Radical. **1769** PARKHURST *Grk. Eng. Lexicon N.T.* (1794) 385/2 An Iota, Jod, or Yod. **1861** *Grammatography* 10 Yodh. **1879** FARRAR *St. Paul* I. II. viii. 143 They remembered.. what He had said about the permanence of every yod and horn of a letter in the Law. **1958** D. DIRINGER *Story of Aleph Beth* I. iii. 36 Several letters in the Aḥiram sarcophagus (*aleph, waw,..yodh,..*and *resh*) indicate a cursive rather a monumental development. **1982** *Canad. Jrnl. Linguistics* XXVII. 76 Part II also has several appendices, dealing with Middle High German and Old Yiddish transcription, with the source of double waw and double yodh.
2. *Phonetics.* Also jod. The semi-vowel (j).
1934 M. K. POPE *From Lat. to Mod. Fr.* II. i. 55 The voiced fricative sound *j* (*jod*), heard in *bien* bjẽ. **1954** PEI *Dict. Linguistics* 237 *Yodization*, the changing of a pure-vowel (usually *e* or *i*) in hiatus into the semivowel which in English orthography is usually written *y*, and called *yod* after a letter of the Hebrew alphabet. **1971** *Canad. Jrnl. Linguistics* XVII. 19 Discussion is limited to two aspects of palatization in French: velars followed by front vowels, and clusters of single consonant plus yod. **1982** J. C. WELLS *Accents of English* I. ii. 163 The *cure* vowel is frequently preceded by a yod, /j/... GenAm reflects more widespread Yod Dropping than RP and most other British accents. *Ibid.* II. v. 435 Yod Coalescence in stressed syllables is common in Dublin..; *dew* = *due* = *Jew.* **1984** *Word* XXXV. 70 The consequence of this for yod assibilation in Irish English is that it is not found in instances where it might be expected.

†**yode, yede,** *v.*[1] *Obs.* Past tense of GO *v.* (= went, went away, proceeded, took his course). [12th cent. ME. (north-east midland) *ȝode, ȝede* (*iede*), prob. altered form of OE., ME. *eode* (*ede, ode*), pa. t. of GO *v.*, by prothesis of *ȝ*-glide induced by the hiatus in such collocations as *he eode, we eoden.* Later, when the form *ȝode*, arising from the development of *eo* as a rising diphthong, became established, it would help to extend the currency of the form *ȝede* by analogical influence upon *ede*, the normal representative of *éode* with a falling diphthong. A parallel development is furnished by ME. *York, Yerk*:—OE. *Eoforwic* (see YORK). Moreover, the OE. compound form *ᵹeéode*, pa. t. of *ᵹegán* IGO *v.*, examples of which are here given with the meaning of the simple *éode*, may have survived in localities where the prefix *ȝe-* = Y- persisted in ME., and so have furthered the spread of *ȝede* and *ȝode*.
Beowulf 1967 Hi sið druᵹon, elne ᵹeeodon. *Ibid.* 2676 Ac se maᵹa ᵹeonga under his mæᵹes scyld elne ᵹeeode. *c* **725** *Corpus Gloss.* (Hessels) A 217 *Adgrediuntur*, ᵹeeodun [*Epinal* 76 ᵹihiodun]. *c* **950** *Lindisf. Gosp.* Matt. xx. 5 *Exiit*, ᵹe-eode. *Ibid.* John x. 23 *Ambulabat*, ᵹe-eade.]
Illustration of Forms.
α. 2–4 **ȝeode** (4 **ȝiode**).
a **1122** *O.E. Chron.* (Laud MS.) an. 1070 Hi..ᵹeodon into þe mynstre. *c* **1260** *K. Horn* (Camb. MS.) 401 He ȝeode in wel riȝte To Rymenhild þe briȝte. *c* **1275** LAY. 25331–2 Ofte hii ȝeode [*c* 1205 eoden] to reade, ofte hii ȝeode to roune. *c* **1305** *Judas* 31 in *E.E.P.* (1862) 108 þe quene ȝeode adai and pleide bi þe stronde. **13..** *Cursor M.* 19920 (Edin.) Quen þai of Petir undirstode, His coming, sone gain him þai ȝiode. **1387** TREVISA *Higden* (Rolls) IV. 397 A lampe..in þat hevene..þat ȝede [*MS.* γ ȝeode] adoun westward as it were þe sonne. *a* **1400** *Pistill of Susan* 228 To the ȝate ȝaply þei ȝeoden [*v.rr.* ȝedyn, ȝede] wel ȝare. *c* **1400** *R. Gloucester's Chron.* (Rolls) 8409 (MS. α) þoru wham þe heþene men ȝeoden al to schonde.
β. 2. **ᵹæde**, **iede**, **iæde**, 2–5 **ȝede**, 3–4 **ȝiede**, 4 **ȝide**, **ȝed**, **yhed**, *Sc.* **ȝheid**, 4–5 **ȝeide**, **ȝhede**, **ȝeede**, 4–6 **yeede**, (also 9 *Sc.*) **yede**, 5 **ȝeyde**, **ȝhed**, *Sc.* **ȝheide**, 5–6 *Sc.* **ȝeid**, **yeid**, 5–6 (8 *Sc.*) **yeed**, 6 **yheid**, **yead(e**, 8 **yee'd**.
a **1122** *O.E. Chron.* (Laud MS.) an. 1070 Syððon ᵹeden heom to scipe, ferden heom to Eliᵹ. **1154** *Ibid.* an. 1137 Sume ieden on ælmes þe waren sum wile rice men. *Ibid.*, Me dide cnotted strenges abuton here hæued & uurythen to ðet it ᵹæde to þe hærnes. *Ibid.* 1140 Scæ fleh & iæde on fote to Walingford. *c* **1200** *Vices & Virtues* 69 Ðies ȝunge mann ȝiede awei sari. **1297** R. GLOUC. (Rolls) 1766 Ac basian & al is folc ȝede anon to gronde. *a* **1300** *Cursor M.* 1086 Quen caym had don þat dreri dide, Til his fader hamward he ȝeide. *Ibid.* 21093 He prechid þare wiþ fote he ȝide. *c* **1330** R. BRUNNE *Chron. Wace* (Rolls) 14308 þyse were þe lordes of renoun þat on Moddredes side ȝed doun. **1340** HAMPOLE *Pr.*

Consc. 4851 þat day, þat Loth yhed out of Sodome. **1340–70** *Alisaunder* 304 Hur ȝates ȝeede þei too & youlden hem soone. **1375** BARBOUR *Bruce* I. 90 Bot othir wayis all ȝheid the gle. *Ibid.* 333 And till swylk thowlesnes he ȝeid, As the courss askis off ȝowtheid. **1423** *Acts Privy Council* III. 97 He yeed in ambassiate to..ye Kyng of Polayn. *c* **1470** *Gol. & Gaw.* 228 The day yeid doun. **1487** *Cely Papers* (Camden) 158, I had xx[li] more wheyr of ȝeyde xij[li] and mor for carryayge of wholl. **1508** DUNBAR *Kynd Kittok* 33 Becaus the wif ȝeid wrang. **1566** DRANT *Horace, Sat.* v. C vij, When you..yeade to Louaine there to heare the Latine Romishe worde. **1575** *Gammer Gurton* IV. ii, My Gammer then she yeede, see now hir neele again to bring. **1583** *Leg. Bp. St. Androis* 327 With this the word yead through the toun. *a* **1600** MONTGOMERIE *Devot. Poems* iii. 29 That leddir.. Quhairby the angels come and ȝeid From hevin to earth. **1768** ROSS *Helenore* I. 7 They Yeed hand in hand together. **1808** JAMIESON, *Yede* is still used in Ang[us] although almost obsolete.

β^2. 3–4 **ȝet.**

c **1275** LAY. 2647 þis wes þe ereste king þet ȝet vt to reuing. *c* **1375** *Sc. Leg. Saints* xxix. (*Placidas*) 297 þane wes þe feynd wondir wa, þat placydas lewit hym sa & ȝet on crist.

γ. ? 1 **ᵹode,** 3–5 **ȝod,** 4–5 **yhode,** (also 6 *Sc.*) **ȝode,** (also 7–8 *dial.*) **yod,** (4 **ȝood, ȝodd, yoede,** 5 **ȝ-, yoode,** 6 **yood,** *Sc.* **ȝoid,** 7 **youd**), 4–6 (6–9 *arch.*) **yode.**

c **1030** *Rule of S. Benet* xxvii. (ed. Logeman) 58 *Abiit*, se ðe ᵹode [How this spelling is to be interpreted in this instance is doubtful]. *c* **1250** *Gen. & Ex.* 2030 Sone ȝhe mai hire louerd sen, Ȝhe ȝod him bitterlike a-ȝen. *a* **1300** *Cursor M.* 1806 He wist noght wyder-ward he ȝodd. *Ibid.* 6264 þe see on aiþer side þam stod Als walles tua, quils þai for yod. **13..** *Ibid.* 24360 (Gött.) þe nailes þat him fest on rode Thoru in hend and fete þai ȝode. **13..** *Gaw. & Gr. Knt.* 1146 A hundreth of hunteres..To trystors vewters ȝod. *c* **1400** *Melayne* 449 The fire ȝode owtt þat come þer nee. *c* **1400** [see GO *v.* B. 21 b]. *c* **1440** *York Myst.* ix. 151 My frendis þat I fra yoode Are ouere flowen with floode. *c* **1450** *St. Cuthbert* (Surtees) 643 Him thoght oute of þe shipp he yhode. **1513** DOUGLAS *Æneis* II. xii. 21 Throw howsis and the citie quhar I ȝoid. **1524** in Ellis *Orig. Lett.* Ser. I. I. 244 Saing if he yode awaye she must neds do for her self. *a* **1533** LD. BERNERS *Huon* clxiii. 636 He issued out of the gate and yode towardes the tentes of his enemyes. **1590** SPENSER *F.Q.* I. x. 53 Such one, as that same mighty man of God, That bloud-red billowes..disparted with his rod, Till that his army dry-foot through them yod. **1596** *Ibid.* IV. viii. 34 So forth they yode, and forward softly paced. **1600** FAIRFAX *Tasso* XX. xcii, An armed stead fast by the Soldan yood. **1615** BRATHWAIT *Strappado* (1878) 130 A lang youd I. *a* **1650** *Glasgerion* 46 in Furniv. & Hales *Percy Folio* I. 250 He did not kisse that Lady gay when he came nor when he youd. **1748** THOMSON *Cast. Indol.* II. xxxv, And much they moraliz'd as thus yfere they yode. **1808** SCOTT *Marm.* III. xxxi, In other pace than forth he yode, Returned Lord Marmion.

γ^2. 4 **ȝot, yot.**

13.. *E.E. Allit. P.* A. 10, I leste hyr in on erbere, þurȝ gresse to grounde hit fro me yot. *c* **1380** *Sir Ferumb.* 3690 A rideþ to Richard wyþ a spere,..& on þe scheld hym smot; þorȝ-out ys scheld..& iakke & ioupoun, þorȝ-out al it ȝot.

δ. 4 **ȝud,** 4–5 **yude,** (**yhude, ȝhude,** 5 **ȝhuyde**), 4–6 **ȝude,** 7 *dial.* **yud,** 7–8 *dial.* **yewd.**

1375 BARBOUR *Bruce* XII. 560 Quhill throu the byrneis brist the blud, That till the erd doune stremand ȝud [*MS. Edin.* ȝhude]. **1387** TREVISA *Higden* (Rolls) V. 423 þe kyng meked hym, and ȝeede [*MS.* γ ȝude] barfoot. *c* **1425** WYNTOUN *Cron.* II. v. 330 His breþir..Slew a kyde and in þe blude Wet þe gowne þat he in ȝhuyde. ? *a* **1550** *Freiris of Berwik* 563 in *Dunbar's Poems* 303 And throw the myre full smertly than he ȝude. **1674** RAY *N.C. Words* 55 *Yewd* or *Yod*: Went, *Yewing*: Going.

ϵ. 5 **yad.**

1424 in Picton *L'pool Munic. Rec.* (1883) I. 23 The Sheriffs..yadden up to the West Derby fen. *c* **1435** *Torr. Portugal* 1192 His squiers habite he had, Whan he to the deyse yad.

† **yode,** *v.*[2] *Obs. rare.* [Pseudo-archaic use of prec. as infin. or pres.; cf. YEDE *v.*] *intr.* To go.

1587 M. GROVE *Pelops & Hippod.* (1878) 42 Then foorth one yodeth fast And sayes [etc.].

yode, var. YAUD, mare.

yodel ('jəʊdəl), *sb.* Also **jodel, yodle,** *erron.* **jödel.** [f. next.] A melody or musical phrase inarticulately sung with interchange of the ordinary and falsetto voice, as by Swiss and Tyrolese mountaineers. Also *transf.* any cry resembling this.

1849 THACKERAY *Pendennis* lxv, Fanny's little sisters were taught a particular cry or *jödel*, which they innocently whooped in the court. **1864** *Cornh. Mag.* Aug. 230, I heard singing and wild jodels about this dissipated city of Innsbrück. **1883** *Harper's Mag.* July 907/2 As he joined his own vibrant baritone to the Tyrolese song-music, his yodel drowned all other sounds. **1894** DU MAURIER *Trilby* I. 22 The British milkman's yodel, 'Milk below!'

Comb. **1874** MISS R. H. BUSK *Vall. Tirol* Pref. p. vi, Just as the shriek of the whistle overpowers the Jödel-call.

yodel ('jəʊdəl), *v.* Also **youdle, yoddle, yodle, jodel,** *erron.* **jödel.** [ad. G. *jodeln* (Bavarian dial. *jodln, jolen*), properly, to utter the syllable *jo.*]

a. *intr.* To sing or warble with interchange of the ordinary and falsetto voice, in the manner of Swiss and Tyrolese mountaineers. Also *transf.*

1838 LADY GRANVILLE *Lett.* (1894) II. 266 Listening to three little peasant girls, all youdling to perfection in parts. **1841** in J. F. Campbell *Frost & Fire* (1865) I. 156 We went yoddling and shouting to rouse the echoes. **1850** *The Initials* v, A loud gay voice was heard in the distance jodling. **1876** BESANT & RICE *Gold. Butterfly* xxv, The shepherds jodel in the valleys. **1878** H. S. WILSON *Alpine Ascents* i. 21 Our guides shout and jödel. **1890** LOWELL *Let. to Miss E. G. Norton* 7 Sept., The screech-owl..every night yodels mournfully about the house like a banshee.

b. *trans.* with the melody as object.

1839 LONGF. *Hyperion* III. iii, A single voice..was heard yodling forth a ballad. **1879** BARING-GOULD *Germany* xi. II. 52 From far away comes the refrain jödeled back to her.

Hence **yodel(l)ing (yoddling, jodel(l)ing)** *vbl. sb.*; also **yodel(l)er (yodler, jodler), yodelist,** one who yodels.

1827 M. WILMOT *Jrnl.* 18 Aug. in *More Lett.* (1935) 288 The wild yodling of two young girls, who suddenly begun [*sic*] to sing their mountain melody. **1830** SCOTT *Jrnl.* 4 June, Anne wants me to go to hear the Tyrolese Minstrels, but..I cannot but think their yodeling..is a variation.. upon the tones of a jackass. **1841** in J. F. Campbell *Frost & Fire* (1865) I. 155 We stepped out for our stone house, from which came yoddling and screaming and all sorts of noises. **1880** 'MARK TWAIN' *Tramp Abroad* xxviii. 289 Now the jodeler appeared..and..we gave him a franc to jodel some more. **1885** MRS. C. PRAED *Head Stat.* xxviii, Clephane and Wyatt executed..an effective jodelling chorus. **1885** *Detroit Free Press* 7 Nov. (Cassell), The yodelist began to play once more. **1910** *Blackw. Mag.* Oct. 469/2 A Swiss yodeler.

yodization (jɒdaɪ'zeɪʃən). *Phonetics.* [f. YOD 2 + -IZATION.] = YOTIZATION.

1954 [see YOD 2]. **1966** [see PROSODY 3]. **1982** *Times Lit. Suppl.* 3 Sept. 953/5 Such phonological phenomena as yodization and consonantal dissimilation.

yoe, obs. form of JOY.

yoe: see YO, repr. EWE *sb.*[1]

yoede: see YODE.

yoelle, obs. form of JEWEL.

1536 in Archbold *Somerset. Relig. Houses* (1892) 62 The crosses, chalysshes and other yoelles of the churches.

yoeman, obs. form of YEOMAN.

yoen, yoene, obs. forms of YON.

yof, graphic var. *þof*, obs. f. THOUGH: see Y 3.

yof, variant of YOUF.

yoff, intended to imitate the grunt of a pig.

c **1630** *Song* ii. in De Foe *Mem. Cavalier* (1840) Notes 323 Yoffing, crying, youlling, yelling, Lyk ane citie swyne summonds out with an horne.

† **y-offred** (earlier *ioffred*, OE. *ᵹeoffrod*), offered, sacrificed.

1340–70 *Alex. & Dind.* 738 Of swiche bestus þat ben of burnus yofreed. **1387** TREVISA *Higden* (Rolls) IV. 427 þe bisshop acountede þis nombre by þe nombre of oystes þat were y-offred. **1432–50** tr. *Higden* (Rolls) V. 169 The bowelles of a beste y-offrede.

yoga ('jəʊgə). [Hind., Skr. *yoga* lit. union: see YOKE *sb.*[1]] In Hindu religious philosophy, Union with the Supreme Spirit; a system of ascetic practice, abstract meditation, and mental concentration, used as a method of attaining this; now a widespread cult in many countries outside India. Also *attrib.*

1820 W. WARD *View Hindoos* (ed. 3) IV. 125 Clear knowledge of spirit arises from yogŭ, or abstraction of mind. **1832** H. H. WILSON in *Asiatic Researches* XVII. 184 The Yoga, or Pátanjala school of philosophy. **1843** *Penny Cycl.* XXVII. 657/2 *Yoga*..chiefly consists in a continual meditation on the sacred monosyllable *Om*.., profound contemplation of the divine excellence, and various acts of self-denial... The *Yoga* is often practised for the purpose of obtaining the eight magical properties of power... In the Purân'as and other works, Yoga very often means magic. **1881** *Contemp. Rev.* Oct. 583 The *yoga* faculty, or the power of spiritual communion and absorption, is specially claimed for the Hindu race. **1886** 'F. ANSTEY' *Fallen Idol* viii, A yogi performing his *japa* in the yoga posture. **1934** A. HUXLEY *Let.* 22 July (1969) 382 Some modification of this yoga technique may provide what's needed..since it is as.. independent of religion..as Freudism—many Indian yogis being in fact atheists. **1937** 'G. ORWELL' *Road to Wigan Pier* xiii. 254 If only..every..creeping Jesus [could be] sent home..to do his yoga exercises quietly! **1967** *Daily Tel.* 1 Feb. 13/1 All kinds of yoga (*the word means 'union' or 'joining'*) are practised, including yoga of action, wisdom, knowledge, devotion, sounds and higher faculties, but far the most common in Britain is hatha yoga, the philosophy of physical well-being. **1977** 'M. YORKE' *Cost of Silence* iv. 31 She had managed..to enrol..in a weekly yoga class. **1977** J. A. KOTARBA in Douglas & Johnson *Existential Sociol.* ix. 266 Osteopaths, naturopaths, yoga instructors, acupuncturists, and anyone else who offers hope. **1979** R. JAFFE *Class Reunion* (1980) III. i. 308 She took all sorts of lessons: gourmet cooking,..macramé, origami, yoga. **1982** 'A. J. QUINNELL' *Snap Shot* i. 27 She had immersed herself in the expatriate social routine... Ikebana classes on Tuesdays and Yoga on Thursdays. **1984** *Times* 17 Mar. 15/3 Yoga postures..are demonstrated by a small group.

Yogacara (jəʊgə'tʃɑːrə). [ad. Skr. *yogāćāra* (also used), f. *yoga* YOGA + *ā-cāra* conduct, practice.]

a. A school of Mahayana Buddhism which teaches that only consciousness is real.

1889 M. MONIER-WILLIAMS *Buddhism* x. 225 Our present concern is..with the growth and development of mystical Buddhism in India.., through its connexion with the system of philosophy called Yoga and Yogāćāra. **1932** M. HIRIYANNA *Outl. Indian Philos.* ix. 219 Objects according to the Yogācāra are not..encountered by the mind, but are created by it. **1951** E. CONZE *Buddhism* vii. 165 The tradition of Yogacara logic is still active in Tibet. *Ibid.*, Together with Buddhism, the Yogacara school disappeared from India about 1,100 A.D. **1960** J. HEWITT *Teach Yourself Yoga* 11 Buddhist meditation utilizes Yoga, especially the Yogacara school which lays emphasis on the trance. **1978** *Pacific Affairs* LI. 513 The author's equation of Yogacara philosophy with 'mind-only doctrine'..is, on the basis of Tibetan writings, open to doubt.

b. An adherent of the Yogacara school.

1915 R. W. FRAZER *Indian Thought* ix. 181 This sect was known as Yogācāras; the only thing they would admit the reality of was a series of thoughts or consciousnesses... As Yogācāras, teachers of Yoga, they adhered to a Yoga system of philosophy. **1922** S. DASGUPTA *Hist. Indian Philos.* I. x. 411 The Yogācāras or idealistic Buddhists..say that since we can come into touch with knowledge and knowledge alone, what is the use of admitting an external world of objects as the data of sensation determining our knowledge? **1933** E. J. THOMAS *Hist. Buddhist Thought* xvii. 246 It was among the Yogāchāras that Tantrism developed.

Hence **Yoga'carin** = sense b above.

1951 E. CONZE *Buddhism* vii. 161 It was the function and purpose of the Yogacarins to give due emphasis to the outlook on the world revealed by withdrawal into trance. **1974** *Encycl. Brit. Micropædia* X. 822/3 Yogācārins were not unique among Buddhists in practicing meditation.

yogee: see YOGI.

yogh (jɒg, -x). Also **ȝok, ȝoch,** etc. (see quots.). [See *Mod. Lang. Review* VI. (1911) 441 seqq., VII. (1912) 520–1.] The name of the ME. letter ȝ: see G, Y.

The use of L. *jugum* 'joke' to designate this letter (see quot. *a* 1440) points to the prevalence of the English form *ȝok.*

c **1300** *MS. McClean 123*, lf. 114 b in *Mod. Lang. Rev.* (1911) VI. 442 · Yoȝ · ȝ · [*examples*] ȝef · ȝus · ȝer · ȝender · draȝ · sclaȝ · arȝ · marȝ. *a* **1400** *Maundeville's Travels* (Fr. text, MS. Brit. Mus. Harl. 4383, lf. 31) ibid. 444 Nous auons en nostre parleure en Engleterre deux lettres pluis qils nount en lour a b c, cest assauoir þ et ȝ, qi sont appelez thorn et yogh [*v.rr.* ȝogh, iogh, ȝok]. **1410–20** *Ibid.* (Eng. text, MS. Cott. Tit. C. xvi, lf. 60 b) ibid. 445 þ & ȝ, the whiche ben clept þorn and ȝogh [*v.rr.* ȝoch, ȝoche, ȝoghe, ȝouh, yowh, yough, ȝouȝ, ȝowȝe, ȝow, ȝoux, youx]. **14..** *MS. Reg. 17, B. 1*, lf. 14 b, ibid. 442 þe carect yogh, þat is to seie ·ȝ· is figurid lijk a ȝed. [*a* **1440** THOMAS ELMHAM *Liber Metr. de Hen. V* ii. in *Mem. Henry V* (Rolls) 195 Praeposita litera Anglica, scilicet ȝ quae jugum sonat. *c* **1465**: see Y 1].

yogh, obs. form of YAW *sb.*[1]

yoghourt, yoghurd, yoghurt, varr. YOGURT.

‖ **yogi** ('jəʊgiː). Forms: 7 **ioggue, iogue,** 9 **jogee, jogi,** 7, 9 **jogue,** 8 **jougie, joguey,** 9 **yoguee, yogue, yogee, yogi; yogin.** [Hind. *yogī* (Skr. *yogi-n*), f. *yoga*: see YOGA.]

1. An Indian devotee or ascetic who practises the system of YOGA, q.v.

1619 PURCHAS *Microcosmus* lvii. 543 The Indian Gymnosophists..offering violence to Nature in nakednesse, and strict absurd Niceties, wherein they are followed to this day by the Bramenes, Ioggues, and others. **1625** —— *Pilgrims* I. II. 31 An Indian Iogue, a begging Frier of that Bramene Religion. **1727** A. HAMILTON *New Acc. E. Ind.* I. 152 There is another Sort called *Jougies*, who..go naked, except a Bit of Cloth about their Loyns. **1734** *Cerem. & Relig. Customs Nat.* III. 480 The *Joguis*, who affect to devote themselves to the most dreadful Torments, from a Principle of Pride and Fanaticism. **1810** SOUTHEY *Kehama* XIII. xvi, A band Of Yoguees, as they roam'd the land Seeking a spouse for Jaga-Naut their God. **1813** J. FORBES *Oriental Mem.* III. 14 A Yogee, who lives under the tree on the skin of a tiger or leopard, which they are very fond of. **1824** HEBER *Narr. Journ.* (1828) I. 133 A 'Yogi' (a religious mendicant). **1854** MILMAN *Lat. Christ.* VIII. iv. III. 335 He attained a height of abstraction from earthly things which might have been envied by an Indian Yogue. **1864** J. A. GRANT *Walk across Afr.* 317 Like mad 'jogees' or devotees. **1871** TYLOR *Prim. Cult.* II. xviii. 375 No wonder that..the Hindu yogi should bring on by fasting a state in which he can with bodily eyes behold the gods. **1899** *Folk-Lore* X. 394 The struggle for local supremacy between a Musalman saint and his rival and counterpart, a Hindu *jogi*. **1922** *Chambers's Jrnl.* 29 Apr. 343/2 Other *jogis* there are, with heavy iron rings in their ears.

(*b*) **1841** *Penny Cycl.* XX. 402/1 Hence has arisen the saying, that the 'yogin' is exalted above the Vedas. **1959** *Times Lit. Suppl.* 27 Mar. 181/5 It is not to divide Time and Eternity that the yogin undertakes his arduous task of re-creation, but to restore to them their true relation. **1962** A. HUXLEY *Island* v. 39 The Yogin and the Stoic—two righteous egos who achieve their very considerable results by pretending, systematically, to be somebody else. **1965** P. WYLIE *They both were Naked* I. iii. 131 Sitting opposite me on my divan cross-legged as a yogin etc. **1973** J. BLOFELD *Secret & Sublime* i. 19 To yogins steeped in the arts of rejuvenation, prolonging life and achieving one of several kinds of immortality, it meant both of these. **1979** R. CASSILIS *Arrow of God* IV. vii. 121 A little rent in the seamless garment of self-mastery. On, yogin, heal thyself!

2. = YOGA.

1925 A. HUXLEY *Let.* 25 Feb. (1969) 242 His little book.. is a sort of explanation of the ethics of Christianity... Lose one's life in order to gain it... It is the same idea as lies at the bottom of the Yogi system. **1943** D. POWELL *Time to be Born* i. 22 He had no pot at all due to his Yogi exercises. **1952** 'R. GORDON' *Doctor in House* iv. 43 There was another medical student there, a man from St. Mary's who kept tropical fish in a tank in his bedroom and practised Yogi. **1960** R. CROFT-COOKE *Thief* i. 9 One day he was in a shop with her when she put her bag down on a chair while she looked at something. I don't know how he got out with it, but then..I'm not a thief. It seemed like Yogi to me, or at least conjuring.

So '**yogified** *a. nonce-wd.*, treated in a yogic manner; **yogi-man** *poet.*, a devotee of yoga; '**yogism,** '**yogeeism,** the system of yoga or of the yogis; '**yogist,** a yogi.

1881 SINNETT *Occ. World* 27 The ethereal yogeeism which is called *Ragi yog.* **1881** *N. & Q.* 6th Ser. III. 291 The Indian yogist (or fakeer) Haridas. **1893** A. LANG in *Daily News* 20 Apr. 5/1 He reckons about 90,000 believers in Yogism. **1938** L. MACNEICE *Mod. Poetry* v. 78 In T. S. Eliot Hyde is the yogi-man. **1938** —— *Earth Compels* 58 It's no go the Yogi-Man, it's no go Blavatsky. *a* **1960** E. M. FORSTER *Maurice* (1971) 235 Carpenter's yogified mysticism.

Yogi Bear ('jəʊgɪ bɛə(r)). The name of a popular U.S. cartoon character, used *attrib.* of toys, garments, etc., featuring the bear.

1960 *Newsweek* 18 July 84/2 Yogi Bear, who lives with a small bear-buddy, Boo-Boo, in a national preserve called Jellystone Park, spends a good deal of his time trying to cadge food. **1962** *Punch* 19 Dec. p. xviii, Marshall & Snelgrove's Toy Shop features.. Yogi bear hobby sticks. **1963** *Sunday Express* 3 Mar. 15/4 Another baby bit a chunk out of a yogi bear hat. **1974** P. DICKINSON *Poison Oracle* 188 The Shaikhah had easily found jeans and a Yogi-Bear tee-shirt to fit her.

yogi'bogeybox. *nonce-wd.* [f. YOGI + BOGY, BOGEY + BOX *sb.*[2]] The paraphernalia of a spiritualist.

1922 JOYCE *Ulysses* 189 Yogibogeybox in Dawson Chambers. *Isis Unveiled.* Their Pali-book we tried to pawn... He thrones an Aztec logos, functioning on astral levels, their oversoul mahamahatma. **1965** *Spectator* 15 Jan. 73/1 Yeats, like AE.. stood for the whirlpool, Madame Blavatsky and the yogibogeybox.

yogic ('jəʊgɪk), *a.* Also Yogic. [f. YOG(A + -IC.] Of or pertaining to yoga.

1921 STREETER & APPASAMY *Sadhu* v. 136 The object of the Yogic trance is not the heart but the head. **1946** A. HUXLEY *Let.* 26 Oct. (1969) 551 In yogic practices there is a form of intense concentration which induces 'false samadhi', or self-hypnosis. **1960** J. HEWITT *Teach Yourself Yoga* 17 The Yogic internal cleansing method of swallowing a long strip of cloth, retaining it for a while in the stomach to absorb bile, etc. **1960** R. P. JHABVALA *Householder* i. 58 Yogic exercises, you know. He's getting quite good at them. **1967** *Listener* 7 Sept. 298/1 A few serious young people squatting in Yogic postures, spines straight, hands receptively cupped. **1980** *Dædalus* Spring 103 Repressed Hindus rejoice in myths of extreme forms of ascetic yogic mortification.

yogini (jəʊgɪ'niː). [a. Skr. *yoginī* (also used), fem. of *yogī*, f. *yoga* YOGA.] **a.** In India, a female demon or sorceress, esp. one of a group attendant on Durga or Siva. **b.** A female yogi.

1883 M. WILLIAMS *Relig. Thought & Life in India* vii. 188 Another class of manifestation is that of the Yoginīs. These are sometimes represented as eight fairies or sorceresses.. sometimes as mere forms of that goddess [*sc.* Durgā], sixty or sixty-five in number. **1910** *Encycl. Brit.* XIII. 512/1 The different classes of sorceresses and ogresses, called *Yoginis, Dakinis* and *Sakinis.* **1928** A. K. COOMARASWAMY *Yakṣas* I. 9 The Seven Mothers.., the Sixty-four Joginīs,.. and some forms of Devī.. must have been Yakṣinīs. **1969** 'R. FARRE' *Beckoning Land* xvi. 196 She wore an unbleached off-white sari and her black hair hung loose denoting that she had freed herself from worldly ties and that she was a yogini (a female yogi). **1972** B. N. SHARMA *Social & Cultural Hist. N. India* iv. 76 There was a *Yoginī Saṁpradāya* among the *Sāktas* and many persons received the highest knowledge from the female ascetics. **1979** *Telegraph* (Brisbane) 15 Aug. 7/4 Meditation can cure many illnesses caused by mental and physical tension, according to a yogini (female yogi) visiting Brisbane.

yogurt ('jɒgət, older 'jəʊguət). Forms: 7 **yoghurd, yogourt,** 9 **yahourt, yaghourt, yogurd, yoghourt, yooghort, yughard, -urt, yohourth,** 9– **yogurt,** 20 **yoghurt.** See also YAOURT. [Turkish *yōghurt.*] Properly, a sour fermented liquor made from milk, used in Turkey and other countries of the Levant; now common in many English-speaking countries as a commercial semi-solid, often flavoured, foodstuff.

1625 PURCHAS *Pilgrims* II. IX. xv. §9. 1601 Neither doe they [*sc.* the Turks] eate much Milke, except it bee made sower, which they call *Yoghurd.* **1687** A. LOVELL tr. *Thevenot's Trav.* II. 25 A kind of Butter-milk by them [*sc.* Turks] called *Yogourt*, which they drink. **1837** PARDOE *City of Sultan* (1838) III. vi. 83 The *yahourt*-merchant, with his .. trays covered with little brown clay basins, showing forth the creamy whiteness of his merchandize. **1883** E. O'DONOVAN *Merv* xviii. 216 We halted to.. refresh ourselves with a draught of *yaghourt.* **1912** *Dundee Adv.* 2 Nov. 7 Servian yoghourt is well known. **1925** C. H. BROWNING *Bacteriol.* vii. 154 'Yoghurt', which contains very little alcohol, is prepared by the Bulgarians, Greeks and Turks from cow's milk. **1934** E. WAUGH *Handful of Dust* i. 13 Mrs. Beaver stood with her back to the fire, eating her morning yoghourt. She held the carton close under her chin and gobbled with a spoon. **1955** G. FREEMAN *Liberty Man* I. ii. 32 Miss Parrot, who ate only yoghourt for lunch, would dip a teaspoon into the bottle. **1970** R. LOWELL *Notebook* 185 Open books, yogurt cups in the unmade bed. **1980** *Sunday Times* (Colour Suppl.) 14 Sept. 85/4 Stokowski.. was concerned with retaining his youth—and Garbo, always a food faddist, was into the 'yoga and yoghourt' experience.

Hence **'yog(h)urty** *a.* (and varr.), fed on or smeared with yoghurt; containing or being yoghurt.

1981 *Times* 20 June 12/3 The dull and dispirited expressions that lie on their yoghurty faces. **1983** *N.Y. Mag.* 18 July 15 Not everything yogurty, performs magically—certainly, frozen yogurt hasn't in the last few years.

yo-hah, yohay, *int.* (*sb.*) An exclamation of pleasure among N. American Indians.

1751 J. BARTRAM *Observ. Trav. Pennsylv.* 22 They gave us the Yohay, a particular Indian expression of approbation. **1791** J. LONG *Voy. Ind. Interpr.* 56 These [gifts] were received with a full yo-hah.

yo-heave-ho ('jəʊ'hiːv'həʊ), *int.* (*sb.*) Also **-oh, -o; yeo-heave-o', -yeo.** [See YO *int.* and HEAVE HO.] An exclamation of sailors when hauling at a rope or a capstan, heaving an anchor up, etc. Hence **yo-heave-hoing** *vbl. sb.*

1803 DIBDIN *Songs* II. 254 To the windlass let us go, With yo heave ho! **1840** R. H. DANA *Bef. Mast* xv, Yo, heave ho! Heave and pawl! Heave hearty ho! **1867** SMYTH *Sailor's Word-bk.*, *Yeo-heave-yeoing*, the chant or noise made at the windlass and purchase-falls in a merchantman, to cheer and lighten labour, but not permitted in a man-of-war. **1872** LOWELL *Milton* Wks. 1890 IV. 102 He offers a striking contrast with Wordsworth, who has to go through with a great deal of *yo-heave-ohing* before he gets under way. **1883** S. FERGUSON *Forging of Anchor* v, Our Anchor soon must change the lay of merry craftsmen here, For the Yeo-heave-o', and the Heave-away, and the sighing seaman's cheer.

yo'himbenine, yo'himbine. *Chem.* Also **-in.** [See def. and -INE[5].] Names of two colourless alkaloids obtained from the bark and leaves of the *yohimbé*, a West African rubiaceous tree. Also **yo'himbic** *acid.*

1898 *Jrnl. Chem. Soc.* LXXIV. I. 679 An extract of the acid of the rind of the yohimbehe has been recommended as an aphrodisiac. Two substances named yohimbine and yohimbenine have been separated from it. *Ibid.*, Yohimbic acid, $C_{20}H_{24}O_6N_2$, is soluble. **1977** E. J. TRIMMER et al. *Visual Dict. Sex* (1978) vi. 65 Yohimbine is incorporated in a preparation that many doctors prescribe for patients with loss of sexual desire and ability. **1979** *Nature* 29 Feb. 600/1 (*caption*) Inhibition by yohimbine and indoramin of the response of human platelets to adrenaline. **1983** *Guardian* 11 Aug. 18/4 Curare blocks acetylcholine receptors, another alkaloid, yohimbine, does the same for noradrenaline. **1984** *Observer* 9 Dec. 14/4 The detailed promotional material claims that the drug—containing.. yohimbine and strychnone—will improve both erections and sperm.

yoho (jə'həʊ), *int.* Also as two words, or with hyphen; also 8 **yoa hoa, yoe-hoe,** 9 **yeo-ho, -hoy, ye(e) ho.** [See YO *int.*, HO *int.*[1] and [3].] An exclamation used to call attention: orig. in nautical use, hence generally; also sometimes used like YO-HEAVE-HO, q.v.

1769 FALCONER *Dict. Marine* (1780) 11, *Hola-ho*, a cry which answers to yoe-hoe. *Ibid.* s.v. *O! d'en haut*, Yoa-hoe, aloft there! **1803** DIBDIN *Songs* III. 47 He can pull away, Cast off, belay, Aloft, alow, Avast, yo ho! **1825** L. HUNT *Redi's Bacchus in Tuscany* 153 The yeo-hoys on board a ship. **1833** M. SCOTT *Tom Cringle* ii, Yo ho, my young un! whence and whither bound, my hearty? **1844** DICKENS *Mart. Chuz.* xxxvi, Yoho, past hedges... Yoho, past donkey-chaises... Yoho, down the pebbly dip... Yoho! Yoho! **1849** LEVER *Con Cregan* xiii, The very voices that ye-hoed.. made delicious music to my ear. *Ibid.* xviii, The pleasant ye-ho! of the sailors. *a* **1880** WEATHERLY *Song, Nancy Lee*, The sailor's wife the sailor's star shall be, Yeo ho! we go across the sea. **1883** STEVENSON *Treas. Isl.* i, Fifteen men on the Dead Man's Chest—Yo-ho-ho, and a bottle of rum!

attrib. **1887** *Academy* 7 May 317/3 The despised bow-wow theory [BOW-WOW 2 b] would, after all, have something in it. On the analogy of that famous nickname, one may, perhaps, venture to suggest the yo-ho theory as a convenient appellation for Noiré's view; yo-ho being.. the *clamor concomitans* of sailors engaged in working a capstan. **1888** MAX MÜLLER *Nat. Relig.* xiv. (1889) 373 The *Pooh-pooh* theory, the *Bow-wow* theory, and the *Yo-heho* theory, completely fail to explain.. how conceptual words arose.

Hence **yo'ho** *v.*, *intr.* to shout 'yoho!' (whence **yo'hoing** *vbl. sb.*); **yo'hoic** *a.*, *nonce-wd.* after *echoic* (cf. quot. 1887 above).

1772 *Gentl. Mag.* Apr. 191/1 The passengers bawling, the sailors yo-ho-ing. **1840** R. H. DANA *Bef. Mast* xv, After two or three hours of constant labour at the windlass, heaving and 'Yo-ho!'-ing with all our might, we brought up an anchor. **1843** THACKERAY *Irish Sk.-bk.* vii, Seamen are singing and yeehoing on board. **1888** HENLEY *Bk. Verses* 128 Hark! the echoes are yeo-hoing Valiantly from vale and hill! **1888** MAX MÜLLER *Nat. Relig.* viii. (1889) 211 The Yo-heoic theory [of language]. **1901** BESANT *Lady of Lynn* viii, The bargemen brought their.. craft alongside with many loud-sounding oaths and the yohoing without which they can do nothing.

yoi, *int.* ? *Obs.* Also **yooi.** A huntsman's cry to encourage the hounds: cf. YOICKS.

1826 *Sporting Mag.* (N.S.) XVII. 270 The word was given 'Yoi—hark on, hark'. **1831–4** R. S. SURTEES *Jorrocks's Jaunts* i. (1838) 10 'Yooi in there!' shouts Tom Hill, who has long hunted this crack pack. **1832** *Egan's Bk. Sports* 221/2 'Yooi, over he goes!' holloas the Squire. **1869** WHYTE-MELVILLE *Songs & Verses* 90 Yoi! wind him! and rouse him! By Jove, he's away.

yoi, obs. form of JOY.

yoicks (jɔɪks), *int.* Also 8–9 **yoics,** 9 **yoix, yooicks.** [Cf. YOAKS, YOI, and HOICKS, earlier *hoik* (1607), *hoic*, which is used similarly to, and appears to be a variant of, *hike, hyke*, as in *hike hallow, hyke a Bewmont* (see Turbervile *Hunting* 31, 112, 175).] A call used in fox-hunting to urge on the hounds; also occas. *gen.* as an exclamation of excitement or exultation.

1774 *Westm. Mag.* II. 657 The bold Fox-hunter, just come up to town, From 'Yoicks, hark forward', loves to seem a clown. **1777** T. SWIFT *Gamblers* 54 'Hark forward! Yoics!' with rough delight he hears. *c* **1800** *Armiger's Sportsman's Vocal Cabinet* (1830) 112 Old Juno, young Scentwell, bold Jowler, and Tray, Yoix! yoix! have compelled him to yield. **1831–4** R. S. SURTEES *Jorrocks's Jaunts* i. (1838) 11 The wood begins to resound with shouts of 'Yoicks True-bo-y, yoicks True-bo-y, yoicks push him up, yoicks wind him!' **1858** in *Morn. Chron.* 5 Nov. 7/1 The energetic 'view-holloa', and the hearty cheerful 'yoicks-tally ho'. **1875** F. T. BUCKLAND *Log-Bk.* 3 Yoicks! tear him, my beauties! **1884** *Blackw. Mag.* May 642/1 With renewed spirits he jumped into a hansom, and gave the direction—— ..'Yoicks!' cried he to himself, 'I'm going it!'

Hence **yoicks** (also **yoick**) *v.*, *intr.* to cry 'yoicks!'; *trans.* to urge on by crying 'yoicks!'

1847 R. S. SURTEES *Hawbuck Gr.* xiv, The swell huntsman yoicked his hounds into cover. **1854** —— *Handley Cr.* xlvii. (1901) II. 63 The hounds dashed into cover, and master and man proceeded to 'yoicks' and crack their whips.

yoike, obs. form of YOKE.

‖**yojan** ('jəʊdʒən), **yojana** ('jəʊdʒənə). *E. Indian.* Also **-en, -unu.** [Hindi *yójan*, Skr. *yójana*, yoking, measure of distance (lit. that travelled at one time without unyoking), f. *yóga*: see YOKE *sb.*[1]] A measure of distance, varying locally from about four to ten miles.

1784 W. CHAMBERS in *Asiatick Researches* (1788) I. 155 South of the Ganges two hundred Yojen. **1784** W. HASTINGS *ibid.* 259 That ancient city [*sc.* Audh] extended.. over a line of ten Yojans, or about forty miles. **1820** W. WARD *View Hindoos* (ed. 3) IV. 315 The circumference of the earth is 5,059 yojŭnŭs. **1834** *Nat. Philos.* III. *Hist. Astron.* App. 122 (U.K.S.) The Brahmins suppose the Earth to be spherical: they suppose the diameter divided into 1600 equal parts called yojanas. **1883** E. ARNOLD *Ind. Idylls* 171 Who else Could in one day drive fivescore yojanas?

yok (jɒk). *slang.* [Yiddish, GOY reversed with unvoicing of final consonant.] A pejorative Jewish term for a non-Jew, a Gentile.

1923 A. YEZIERSKA *Children of Loneliness* 75 She stands there like a *yok* with her eyes in the air! **1960** *Times* 17 May 17/4 Mr. Faulks.. said that on February 10, 1958, Mr. Daniels had said to Mr. Lincoln: 'Unless you join me and Mr. Jackson against that bloody Yok I will crush you, smash you and drag you into the gutter.' His Lordship asked the meaning of 'Yok' and was told that it was a Yiddish word meaning a Gentile, a rude way of saying a 'Goy'. A woman member of the jury.—It is not rude. **1969** R. ESSER *Hot Potato* 34 My God, this could all be a Nasser plot. And you let this yok into our Intelligence camp! **1970** *Guardian* 21 July 8 Jews.. in the arts area *are* pretty smashing but then some of the yoks are fabulous. **1981** R. SAMUEL *East End Underworld* vii. 76 There were five Jewish boys in the gang —I was the only 'Yok'.

yok, var. YOCK *sb.* (and *v.*).

yoke (jəʊk), *sb.*[1] Forms: 1 **ȝeoc, ȝioc, ioc, iuc,** 2–3 **ȝoc,** 3 **ȝeoc, ȝiok,** (*Orm.*) **ȝocc,** 3–5 (6 *Sc.*) **ȝok,** 4 **ȝook,** 4–5 (6 *Sc.*) **ȝokke, ȝoke,** (6–7 *Sc.*) **ȝock,** 4–6 (8–9 *dial.*) **yok,** 4–7 (8–9 *dial.*) **yock,** 5 **ȝokk, youk(k)e,** 5–7 **yocke,** 6 **youck, yowcke, yowg, yoike,** (*pl.* **yoixe?**), *Sc.* **ȝoik,** (**ȝoilk**), 6–7 **yoake,** (7 **yolke, oak**), 6–8 **yoak,** (8 **yolk**), 4– **yoke.** [Com. Teut. str. neuter: OE. *ȝeoc* = OS. *juc* (MLG. *juk*, MDu. *juc, joc*, LG., Du. *juk, jok*), OHG. *juh, joch*, (MHG., G. *joch*), ON. *ok* (Sw. *åka*, Da. *aag*), Goth. *juk*, corresp. to L. *jugum*, Gr. *ζυγόν*, W. *iau*, OSl. *igo*, Skr. *yugá-m*:—Indo-eur. **jugóm.*

The Indo-eur. series *jeug-: joug-: jug-* is represented also by OHG., MHG. *giuh, jiuch* yoke, 'yoke' of land (whence late OHG. *jûhhart*, MHG. *jûchert*, dial. G. *jauchert, juchert*), L. *jūgerum* measure of land, Gr. *ζεῦγος* yoke of beasts, couple; ON. *eykr* (:—Teut- **jaukiz*), Skr. *yógya* beast of draught; Skr. *yuj*, Gr. *ζευγνύναι*, L. *jungere*, Lith. *jungiù* to yoke, couple, join, Skr. *yóga* union.

On the analogy of LOCK *sb.*[1] from OE. *loc*, the modern standard form would be *yock*, which survives in certain (chiefly north-midland) districts. Orthographic evidence for the lengthening of the stem vowel (which began first in the inflected forms) appears in the latter part of the 14th century.]

I. 1. a. A contrivance, used from ancient times, by which two animals, esp. oxen, are coupled together for drawing a plough or vehicle; usually consisting of a somewhat curved or hollowed piece of wood fitted with 'bows' or hoops at the ends which are passed round the animals' necks, and having a ring or hook attached to the middle to which is fastened a chain or trace extending backward by which the plough or vehicle is drawn.

in the yoke: with the oxen yoked up.

c **1050** *Ags. Voc.* in Wr.-Wülcker 267/34 *Iugum*, iuc. *Ibid.* 313/37 *Jugum*, ȝeoc. *a* **1300** *Cursor M.* 21288 þe carter self is iesus crist, His bodi es yock [*v.rr.* ȝok, ȝock] he has stablist. *c* **1325** *Gloss. W. de Bibbesw.* in Wright *Voc.* 169 *Les juges*, the yokkes. *a* **1340** HAMPOLE *Psalter* cxxxii. 3 A wylde beste in þe ȝoke. **1390** GOWER *Conf.* II. 131 Hou that an Oxe his yock hath bore For thing that scholde him noght availe. *c* **1425** WYNTOUN *Cron.* I. xvi. 1615 He gert bestis vndyr ȝok [*v.r.* ȝoke] Thoil broddis sare and mony knok. **1523–34** FITZHERB. *Husb.* §5 To lerne to make his yokes, oxe-bowes, stooles, and all maner of plough-geare. **1526** TINDALE *Matt.* xxi. 5 The foole off an asse vsed to the yooke. **1534** in Weaver *Wells Wills* (1890) 6 Ye plow and all belongyn therto, cheyns, yowgs and such other. **1535** COVERDALE *Job* xxxix. 10 Canst thou bynde yᵉ yock aboute him in thy forowes? **1563** *Richmond Wills* (Surtees) 169 Four yokes for oxen. **1593** *Lanc. Wills* (Chetham Soc. 1884) 121 Plowe harrowes

Cheynes and Yockes to yt belonginge. **1599** Shaks. *Much Ado* I. i. 263 In time the sauage Bull doth beare the yoake. **1642** in *Verney Mem.* (1907) I. 232 Beasts that have bine used to the yooke. **1697** Dryden *Virg. Georg.* III. 227 Let 'em..never know The taming Yoak, or draw the crooked Plough. **1728–46** Thomson *Spring* 38 There, unrefusing, to the harness'd yoke They lend their shoulder and begin their toil. **1834** *Brit. Husb.* I. 194 In England the custom is to attach the yoke round the neck by a hoop of alder, or of elm, fixed under it, which, passing through the yoke, is then fastened to the upper part with buttons, or pegs, upon the ends of the hoop, which is called a bow. **1846** J. Baxter *Libr. Pract. Agric.* (ed. 4) II. 107 It is a question, whether it is most advantageous to work oxen by the collar or harness single, or in double yoke. **1850** R. G. Cumming *Hunter's Life S. Afr.* xii, We were in the yoke soon after daybreak. **1860** Tennyson *Tithonus* 40 The wild team Which love thee, yearning for thy yoke. **1876** Voyle & Stevenson *Milit. Dict.* s.v., Yokes are required for bullock draught, and are used either for pole or trace.

b. A similar appliance anciently placed on the neck of a captive or conquered enemy; among the ancient Romans and others, a symbol of this consisting of two spears fixed upright in the ground with another on the top of them, under which vanquished enemies were compelled to pass.

a **1000** *Ags. Voc.* in Wr.-Wülcker 195/7 *Boia, arcus, uel* ʒeoc. *c* **1050** *Ibid.* 336/38 *Bogia*, iuc oððe swurcops. **1549** *Compl. Scot.* xii. 101 Ve sal put ȝour cragis in ane ȝoik to be ane perpetual takyn that ȝe ar vencust be vs. **1600** Holland *Livy* III. xxviii. 107 His..pleasure was, they should passe al under the yoke or gallowes. **1649** *Alcoran* 151 They shall have Oaks [*ed.* 1734 collars] upon their necks. **1720** Ozell tr. *Vertot's Rom. Rep.* II. IX. 93 Jugurtha grants the Romans Life and Liberty but upon Condition that they should pass under the Yoke. **1875** Merivale *Gen. Hist. Rome* xxx. 209 His army was routed, and passed under the yoke.

c. A figure or representation of a yoke.

stone yoke, an ancient Mexican carving representing a yoke, supposed to have been placed on the necks of victims when sacrificed.

a **1548** Hall *Chron., Hen. VIII*, 8b, Garmentes.. travessed with cloth of gold, cut in Pomegranettes and yokes, strynged after the facion of Spaygne. **1688** Holme *Armoury* III. 335/2 He beareth Vert, a Yoke. **1899** *Smithsonian Rep.* 41 A beautiful example of the stone yoke, or ceremonial collar.

2. A wooden frame or collar fitted on the neck of a hog or other animal, to prevent it from breaking through or leaping over a hedge, fence, etc.

1573–80 Tusser *Husb.* (1878) 38 Strong yoke for a hog. **1669** Worlidge *Syst. Agric.* 278 A *Yoak*, ..an Instrument ..to put on Swine or other unruly Creatures, to keep them from running through Hedges. **1886** *Cheshire Gloss.* s.v., I have never seen a pig yoked, but yokes are still in common use for cattle and sheep; and I have, on one occasion at least, seen a number of hens all wearing yokes.

3. a. A frame fitted to the neck and shoulders of a person for carrying a pair of pails, baskets, etc.

c **1618** Moryson *Itin.* IV. iii. (1903) 383, I haue seene men ..carry the milke in two payles fastned to a wooden yoke before them. *c* **1700** Kennett *MS. Lansd. 1033*, A yoak of milk, two pailes. **1821** Clare *Vill. Minstr.* I. 155 Whenever to rest she her buckets set down, She jinkled her yokes to and fro. **1876** Hardy *Ethelberta* i, The speaker, who had been carrying a pair of pails on a yoke, deposited them upon the edge of the pavement.

b. A part of a garment, made to fit the shoulders (or the hips), and supporting the depending parts, often of double thickness, of special material, or particularly ornamented.

1880 *Girl's Own Paper* 20 Mar. 191/3 Make a new yoke and sleeves, and add a scarf to tie round the neck. **1882** Caulfeild & Saward *Dict. Needlework* 527 *Yokes.*—These are headings, or shaped bands, into which plaitings or gatherings of garments are sewn, and which are so cut as to fit either the shoulders or the hips, and from which the rest of the bodice, nightdress, dressing gown, or the skirt is to depend. **1891** *Truth* 10 Dec. 1240/2 The front [of a teagown] was all white satin,..with a yoke of gold and white embroidery. **1903** *Daily Chron.* 24 Jan. 8/4 The hip-yoke is a plain piece, sometimes, however, covered with embroidery, that is moulded to the figure below the waist.

4. a. Applied to various objects resembling the yoke of a plough.

e.g. †a ridge of hill connecting two peaks (after L. *jugum*), an arched convex frame, timber, bar, etc. (see quots.).

1382 Wyclif *Isa.* xxxvii. 24, I steȝede vp the heiȝtus of mounteynes, ȝokes [*later vers.* ȝockis] of Liban. **1489** Caxton *Faytes of A.* II. xxviii. 139 Leuers of yron youkes for brygges to make with. **1577** Googe *Heresbach's Husb.* II. 84 The Uine keeper must often goe about his Uines, and set vp his proppes, and make euen his yokes. **1864** Webster, *Yoke.* .. A frame or convex piece by which a bell is hung for ringing it. **1875** Knight *Dict. Mech.*, *Yoke*... A branching coupling-section, connecting two pipes with a single one, as the hot and cold water pipes with a single pipe for a shower-bath. **1883** Gresley *Gloss. Coal M.*, *Yokes*, short sawn timbers placed across biats for steadying pump trees. **1888** *Encycl. Brit.* XXIV. 242/1 The fidicula or lyre consisted of a resonant box, having a yoke (*jugum* or *transtillum*) instead of a neck. **1902** *Ibid.* (ed. 10) XXVII. 584/1 The yoke, which joins the [magnet] limbs together and conducts the flux between them.

b. *Naut.* A board or bar fixed transversely to the head of the rudder, and having two cords or ropes (*yoke-lines*) attached for steering: see also quots. 1627, 1769.

a **1625** *Nomencl. Navalis* (Harl. MS. 2301). **1627** Capt. J. Smith *Sea. Gram.* ix. 41 A yoke is when the Sea is so rough as that men cannot gouern the Helme with their hands, and then they sease a block to the Helme on each side at the end, and reeuing two fals thorow them like Gunners Tackles brings them to the ships side, and so some being at the one side of the Tackle, some at the other, they steare her with much more ease than they can with a single rope with a double Turne about the Helme. **1769** Falconer *Dict. Marine* (1780), *Yoke*, a name formerly given to the tiller, when communicating with two blocks or sheaves affixed to the inner end of the tiller. It is now applied to a small board or bar which crosses the upper end of a boat's rudder at right angles. **1792** *Jrnl. Ho. Comm.* XLVII. 364/1 Those Ships that have no Roundhouse, their Rudders should run up, and steer with a Yoke abaft the Rudder Head. **1840** R. H. Dana *Bef. Mast* xxiii, The bowman had charge of the boat-hook and painter, and the coxswain of the rudder, yoke, and stern-sheets.

c. *Electr. Engin.* The part of a magnet or electromagnet that joins the poles or pole-pieces.

1884 S. P. Thompson *Dynamo-Electric Machinery* vii. 145 One such iron mass..is attached solidly to each pole-piece, and the two are united at the top by a still heavier yoke of iron. **1924** A. L. Cook *Elements Electr. Engin.* xi. 88 On the ring-shaped portion or yoke are inwardly projecting cores, which carry the exciting windings and have pole pieces, curved to fit the armature. **1951** R. B. Dome *Television Princ.* ix. 230 Another problem, that of high-voltage surges across the yoke and tube during flyback, must be taken into account in designing the components. **1975** D. G. Fink *Electronics Engineers' Handbk.* XI. 42 For PPI deflection one common arrangement is to have the single-axis yoke rotated physically by an external motor..driven by the radar antenna.

d. *Aeronaut.* = *control column* s.v. CONTROL *sb.* 5.

1934 in Webster. **1956** W. A. Heflin *U.S. Air Force Dict.* 576/2 *Yoke*,..a control column, esp. a dual control column. **1971** R. Dentry *Encounter at Kharmel* ix. 151 Ed eased back on the yoke and made a slow, climbing turn. **1984** *Miami Herald* 27 Mar. 2D/5 A co-pilot immediately pulled back on the yoke.

II. 5. a. *transf.* A pair of animals, esp. oxen, that are or may be coupled by a yoke.

In this sense the plural after a numeral is often *yoke*.

688–95 *Laws of Ine* lx. (Liebermann) 116 Se ceorl se ðe hæfð oðres ʒeoht [*v.r.* ʒeoc] ahyrod..aʒife ealle. *c* **1200** *Trin. Coll. Hom.* 195 Half hundre ȝiokes of ocsen. **13..** *E.E. Allit. P.* B. 66, I haf ȝerned & ȝat ȝokkez of oxen. *c* **1375** *Sc. Leg. Saints* xliv. (*Lucy*) 252 Fyfty ȝok of oxine. **1535** Coverdale *Job* xlii. 12 A M. yock oxen [**1539** *Gt. Bible* a M. youck of oxen]. **1551** in Phillipps *Wills* (*c* 1830) 201, I wyll that Ihon my sun, and William my sun, shall have every of them..a yowcke of Oxyn. **1606** *Shuttleworths' Acc.* (Chetham Soc.) 173 One yocke of draft oxen, viij^{li} xiij^{s} iiij^{d}. **1660** F. Brooke tr. *Le Blanc's Trav.* 18 A deep well whence they draw water, with a wheel turned round by a yoke of Bulls. **1778** *Eng. Gazetteer* (ed. 2) s.v. *Wergins*, One of them required 9 yoke of oxen to draw it. **1879** Bartlett *Egypt to Pal.* xix. 408 We ..saw men plowing, sometimes with a camel, and oftener with a yoke of cattle.

†**b.** *gen.* A pair, couple. *Obs.*

c **1380** Wyclif *Sel. Wks.* II. 224 þe þridde ȝok þat Poul forfendiþ, is chiding and envie. *c* **1380** —— *Wks.* (1880) 354 þis first ȝock bigynniþ wiþ paciens. **1598** Shaks. *Merry W.* II. i. 181 These that accuse him in his intent towards our wiues, are a yoake of his discarded men.

6. One-fourth of a SULING, about 50 or 60 acres (cf. *oxgang* as $\frac{1}{8}$ of a plough-land); hence, later, applied vaguely to small manors. (Cf. YOKLET.) *Kent.*

837 *Kent. Charters* 42 in Sweet *O.E. Texts* 450, xvi ʒioc ærðelondes. *c* **1050** *Ags. Voc.* in Wr.-Wülcker 424/2 *Iuger*, iuc. **1653** in Hasted *Hist. Kent* (1782) II. 525 [In the survey of Milton manor, taken anno 1653, there is mention made, as held of that manor, of the] yoke of Hamons atte Deane. [*Note*, Upon these hills, the smaller manors are frequently called *yokes*.] **1772** Shrubsole & Denne *Hist. Roch.* 44 The originals..mention certain persons by name, with the number of yokes and acres belonging to them. **1886** *Archæol. Cant.* XVI. 167 The yoke of Henwood or Hewitt.. at the east end of the town [of Ashford] extended into Willesboro'.

7. A spell of work at the plough (cf. YOKING *vbl. sb.* 4). *local* (*Kent*).

1796 Boys *Agric. Kent* 157 An acre a day is the common yoke for eight or ten oxen in wet, heavy, land, where four horses would plough an acre and a quarter. **1805** *Ibid.* (ed. 2) 183 When two yokes are made in a day, which is the usual practice of East Kent, the time of going to work is at six o'clock in the morning, returning home at ten; and then going out again at one, and returning at six.

III. 8. *fig.* or in fig. phr. **a.** Denoting servitude, subjection, restraint, humiliation, oppression, etc.

c **888** Ælfred *Boeth.* xix. §1 Æala, ofermodan, hwi ʒe wilniʒen þæt ʒe underlutan mid eowrum swiran þæt deaðlice ʒeoc. *c* **897** —— *Gregory's Past. C.* xxix. 200 Ælc ðara þe sie under ðæm ʒeoke hlafordsciepes. *c* **1000** *Ags. Gosp.* Matt. xi. 29 Nimaþ min ʒeoc ofer eow. *c* **1200** *Vices & Virtues* 71 Se ðe..Cristes ȝoc wile beren, and forlat al ðe woreld. *c* **1200** Ormin 4045 þatt tanne shollde itt lesedd ben Fra dæþess ȝocc. *c* **1380** Wyclif *Wks.* (1880) 228 What kynne seruauntis ben vnder ȝook of seruage deme þei here lordis worþ i alle manere honour or worschipe. **1387** Trevisa *Higden* (Rolls) V. 357 He brouȝte alle þe kynges þat were nyh hym under his ȝok. *c* **1449** Pecock *Repr.* IV. i. 420 What euer seruauntis ben vndir ȝok, deeme thei her lordis worthi al honour. *c* **1450** Capgrave *Life St. Gilbert* 90 þe ȝok of all þis birden was leid in his nek. **1549** *Compl. Scot.* iv. 31 Tyl al them that hes resauit the ȝoilk ande the confessione of crist. **1573** *Satir. Poems Reform.* xli. 68 This day thy heid is in the ȝock. **1588** Shaks. *Tit. A.* I. i. 69 He circumscribed with his Sword, And brought to yoke the Enemies of Rome. **1596** Spenser *State Irel.* Wks. (Globe) 610/2 Having quite shaken of theyr yoke, and broken the bandes of theyre obedience. **1610** Holland *Camden's Brit.* I. 719 It [*sc.* a castle] became a most grievous yoke unto the neighbour Inhabitants. **1648** J. Beaumont *Psyche* XI. xxxiv, Impudent Boldness! which can..make the Bond of Sweetness their pretence, To break all other yoaks. **1709** Steele *Tatler* No. 36 ¶1 Termagant Wives who make Wedlock a Yoke. **1756** Burke *Subl. & Beaut.* Introd., In tying us down to the disagreeable yoke of our reason. **1837** Howitt *Rur. Life* I. iv. (1862) 36 The weary yoke of business. **1849** Macaulay *Hist. Eng.* iii. I. 400 The Restoration emancipated thousands of minds from a yoke which had become insupportable. **1879** Dixon *Windsor* I. ii. 11 His province..had never yet submitted to the Norman yoke.

b. With various other implications, as of connexion, co-operation, labour, etc.; in reference to marriage, combining the ideas of union or co-operation and subjection or restraint.

1382 Wyclif *2 Cor.* vi. 14 Nyle ȝe lede ȝok [Vulg. *jugum ducere*] with vnfeithful men. *a* **1400–50** *Wars Alex.* 818* (Dubl. MS.), He..fair enformed þam of fight & fetez of armez For ȝapest in hys awne yoke ȝarly to drawe. *c* **1403** Clanvowe *Cuckow & Night.* 140 Myn entent is neither for to dye, Ne, whyl I live, in loves yok to draw. *c* **1412** Hoccleve *De Reg. Princ.* 3992 Ȝok of mariage. **1475** *Stonor Papers* (Camden) I. 158 Tyll..þat youkke of wedlokke ly in my nekke as hyt dose now in yours. **1555** Eden *Decades* (Arb.) 128 We haue byn ioyned togyther with the yoke of holy matrimonie. **1596** Shaks. *Merch. V.* III. iv. 13 Companions..Whose soules doe beare an equal yoke of loue. **1645** Fuller *Good Th. in Bad T.* 228 It is therefore some comfort that I draw in the same Yoak with my Neighbours. **1697** Dryden *Æneis* IV. 22 Were I not resolv'd against the Yoke Of hapless Marriage. **1847** Tennyson *Princess* VI. 188 If thou needs must bear the yoke, I wish it Gentle as freedom. **1885** Haggard *K. Sol. Mines* i, Well I had better come to the yoke [*i.e.* begin my task].

IV. 9. *Comb.*, as (sense 1) ***yoke-bar***, ***-bow***, ***-gear***, ***-peg***, ***-pin***, ***-ring***, ***-work***; ***yoke-weary*** adj.; (sense 3) ***yoke-shouldering*** adj.; (sense 3 b) ***yoke-back***, ***-bodice***, ***-collar***, ***front***, ***piece***; **yoke-arbor** (see quot.); **yoke-band** (= Gr. ζυγόδεσμον), a band for fastening the yoke to the pole; †**yoke-bone**, the jugal or malar bone of the cheek, forming part of the zygomatic arch; †**yoke-devils** *sb. pl.* (*nonce-wd.*), companion devils; **yoke-elm**, a name for the hornbeam, from the wood being used for yokes, and the leaves resembling those of the elm; **yoke-horse** (= Gr. ζύγιος ἵππος), a horse yoked to another; **yoke-line** *Naut.*, each of the two cords or ropes attached to a yoke (sense 4 b) for steering; **yoke-skey** *S. Africa*, = SKEY *sb.*^{2}; see also JUKSKEI; **yoke-steed** = *yoke-horse*; **yoke-stick**, (*a*) = sense 1; (*b*) = sense 3; (*c*) a stick, or one of two crossed sticks, attached to an animal's neck (cf. sense 2); **yoke-strap**, **-thong** = *yoke-band*; **yoke-toed** *a.*, having the toes joined together in pairs, as scansorial birds; zygodactylous; **yoke-tree**, †(*a*) = *yoke-elm*; (*b*) the body or main part of a yoke.

1875 Knight *Dict. Mech.*, **Yoke-arbor*, a form of double journal-box for pulley-spindles, in which a curved branch extending from one bearing to the other on each side of the pulley serves to protect the belt from being chafed or otherwise injured. **1895** *Montgomery Ward Catal.* Spring & Summer 278/3 Men's Overshirts..Gathered *yoke back. **1981** *Country Life* 22 Jan. 226/2 Mr. Tommy Nutter wears ..a jacket of honey-toned Donegal tweed, yoke back, single-breasted. **1585** Higins *Junius' Nomencl.* 270/2 *Subiugium lorum*,..the yoke thong, or *yoke band. **1848** Buckley *Iliad* 452 Then they brought out the yoke-band, nine cubits in length, along with the yoke. **1844** H. Stephens *Bk. Farm* II. 320 The *yoke-bars..are made of hard-wood. **1888** *Bow-Bells Weekly* 4 May 286/3 A serviceable navy serge *yoke bodice, with belt. **1615** Crooke *Body of Man* 755 The first paire of the vpper Lip..ariseth from the vtter seame of the Iugall or *yoke-bone. **1634** T. Johnson tr. *Parey's Chirurg.* v. xi. (1678) 117 There is a cleft under the yoke-bone ascending into the orb of the eye. *c* **725** *Corpus Gloss.* (Hessels) Int. 185 *Iungula*, *ʒeocboʒa. **1587** Mascall *Govt. Cattle, Oxen* (1596) 73 If ye tie them as plow oxen be, with a sole and a with, which is made like a yoke bowe. **1891** Meredith *Horses of Achilles* 15 Poet. Wks. (1912) 560 All their lustrous manes..Right side and left of the yoke-ring tossed, to the breadth of the yoke-bow. **1906** *Daily Chron.* 5 Apr. 8/5 A *yoke collar of fine Irish lace. **1599** Shaks. *Hen. V*, II. ii. 106 Treason, and murther, euer kept together, As two *yoake diuels sworne to eythers purpose. **1687** Miège *Gt. Fr. Dict.* 11, *Yoke-elm, *un Charme, sorte d'Arbre de bois dur.* **1706** London & Wise *Retir'd Gard'ner* I. 261 The Gard'ner who has a fence of Yoke-Elms. **1768** T. Nugent *Trav. Germany* II. 89 A beech or elder, a yok-elm, an aspin and a crab. **1901** Levett-Yeats *Traitor's Way* x, We had reined up under a huge yoke-elm. **1888** *Bow-Bells Weekly* 4 May 286/3 Six chemises, made with pointed *yoke fronts. **1844** H. Stephens *Bk. Farm* III. 1181 The *yoke-geer of this cart. **1837** B. D. Walsh *Aristoph., Clouds* I. i, Neither you, sir, nor your *yoke-horse,..shall eat my goods. **1849** Cupples *Green Hand* xvi, The fat midshipman..watching me critically as I handled the *yokelines. **1585** Higins *Junius' Nomencl.* 269/1 *Radius*,..the yoke sticke: the yoke pin or *yoke peg. **1885** *Letts's Househ. Mag.* 93/2 A *yoke piece of velveteen. **1819** Rees *Cycl.* XXXIX. s.v. *Yoking*, The *yoke-ring and ox-chain. **1891** [see *yoke-bow*]. **1895** K. Grahame *Golden Age* 42 The *yoke-shouldering village folk were wont to come to fill their clinking buckets. **1817** G. Barker *Diary* 29 May (MS.), Made *yoke schegen. **1835** A. Smith *Diary* 31 Mar. (1939) I. 338 The woman looked at her for a moment and then took up a yokeskey. **1850** R. G. Cumming *Hunter's Life S. Afr.* ii, Passing through each end of the yoke, at distances of 18 inches from one another, are two parallel bars of tough wood about 18 inches in length; these are called yoke-skeys. In inspanning, the yoke is placed on the back of the neck of the ox, with one of these skeys on either side. **1934** B. Buchanan *Pioneer Days in Natal* 31 The straight yoke was placed across their necks and secured by the throat strap attached to the wooden yokeskeys. **1948** W. S. Chadwick *Mother Africa hits Back*

i. 21 When transport riding in Barotseland I had two good but rather cheeky Zulu drivers. One night after an argument they threatened me with yoke-skeys and I got in the first blow. **1880** L. Wallace *Ben-Hur* 208 They termed the two next the pole *yoke-steeds. *c* **725** *Corpus Gloss.* (Hessels) O 108 *Obicula*, *ᵹeocstecca. **1483** *Cath. Angl.* 427/1 A ȝoke styke, *fisticulus.* **1614** R. Tailor *Hog hath lost Pearl* Prol., Ovr long time rumor'd Hogge..is at length got loose, Leauing his seruile yoake-sticke to the goose. **1684** [Meriton] *Yorksh. Dial.* 100 (E.D.S. No. 76), Yoakes and Bowes and Gad and Yoak-sticks. **1855** Robinson *Whitby Gloss.*, *Yoke-stick*, the wooden shoulder-bar for carrying the milk pails by suspension... 'As crooked as a yoke-stick,' deformed. Also the wooden horseshoe-shaped collar with which oxen are yoked. **1837** B. D. Walsh *Aristoph.*, *Knights* II. iii, May I die,..And be cut into *yoke-straps and traces. **1585** *Yoke-thong [see *yoke-band*]. **1835** *Yoke-toed [see zygodactylic]. **1872** Coues *N. Amer. Birds* 199 The parrots..are yoke-toed. **1585** Higins *Junius' Nomencl.* 149 *Carpinus*,..a kind of tree, called in olde time the *yoke tree, the wood whereof was easie to be cleft. **1844** H. Stephens *Bk. Farm* II. 322 The draught-chains, hooked to the lever, and passed under the pulleys of the yoke-trees. **1910** Kipling *Rewards & Fairies* 219 And a wet *yoke-weary bullock Pushed in through the open door. **1890** Crawfurd *Round Cal. in Portugal* 32 One may see oxen and even cows—for they too do their share of *yoke-work—harnessed to the net.

yoke (jəʊk), *sb.*^{2} *Anglo-Irish.* [Origin unknown.] A thing; a thingummy.

1910 P. W. Joyce *English as we speak it in Ireland* xiii. 352 Yoke; any article, contrivance, or apparatus, for use in some work. 'That's a *quare* yoke Bill,' says a countryman when he first saw a motor car. **1958** N. Fitzgerald *Student Body* v. 69 Don stooped to pick up the gun... 'Where's the safety-catch on these yokes?' **1979** K. Dowling *Interface: Ireland* I. iii. 26 This fecking yoke is maggots up to here!

yoke (jəʊk), *v.* Forms: see yoke *sb.*^{1}; also 1 *pa. pple.* **ᵹeiukod**, 3 *pa. t.* **ȝeokede, ȝogede**, 4 **oak**, *pa. pple.* **y-ȝoket, y-yokyd**, *Sc.* **ȝakkit**, 5 *pa. pple.* **ȝeokyn**, 6 *Sc.* **ȝolk**, *pa. pple.* **iooked**. [OE. *ᵹeocian*, f. *ᵹeoc* yoke *sb.*^{1}]

1. *trans.* To put a yoke on (a pair of draught-animals, etc.); to couple with a yoke. Also with *up* (? *Colonial*).

a **1000** *Colloq. Ælfric* in Wr.-Wülcker 90 *Iunctis bobus*, ᵹeiukodan oxan. *c* **1000** Ælfric *Gram.* (Z.) 174 *Iungo*, ic iuciᵹe [*v.r.* ᵹeociᵹe]. **1399** Langl. *Rich. Redeles* III. 251 Steeris well y-yokyd. *c* **1400** Maundev. (1839) xxvi. 269 For o Griffoun there wil bere, fleynge to his Nest, a gret Hors or 2 Oxen ȝoked to gidere, as thei gon at the Plowghe. *c* **1400** *Destr. Troy* 902 Ȝyuerly the ȝepe knight ȝokit hom belyue, Pight hom into ploghe. *c* **1440** *Promp. Parv.* 539/1 Ȝokke beestys (*S.* ȝok, *P.* ȝockyn, *W.* yoken). **1530** Palsgr. 786/2 Yoke the oxen, for I wyll go to the plough this mornyng. **1641** J. Jackson *True Evang. T.* III. 166 It was cautioned in the Law not to yoake an Oxe, and an Asse together. **1724** Swift *Drapier's Lett.* Wks. 1755 V. II. 100, I shall..learn to consider my driver, the road I am in, and with whom I am yoked. **1775** *Ann. Reg., Chron.* 98/2 The prisoners were all secured and yoked. **1859** H. Kingsley *G. Hamlyn* xviii, A bullock-driver yoking-up his beast. **1880** 'Mark Twain' *Tramp Abr.* xi, A peasant's cart,..drawn by a small cow and a smaller donkey yoked together.

2. a. To attach (a draught-animal) *to* a plough or vehicle (orig. with a yoke); to 'put in', 'put to'.

c **1375** *Sc. Leg. Saints* iv. (*Jacobus*) 329, 332 Scho had bulis wilde and tate, þat scho nocht trewit mycht ȝakkit be In carte,..And, gyf It hapnyt þat þai Var ȝokit, suld ryne away. **1398** Trevisa *Barth. De P.R.* XVIII. lxiii[i]. (Bodl. MS.), A ȝonge cowe þat is able to be ȝoked [*ed.* **1495** yockid] to drawe at plowȝ. *c* **1420** *Prose Life Alex.* 78 We tille na lande,..ne ȝokes noþer ox ne horse in plughe ne in carte. *c* **1450** *Mirk's Festial* 211 Þe bulles mekely stodyn styll, tyll þay had ȝeokyn ham yn þe wayne. **1535** Coverdale *1 Sam.* vi. 7 Take two mylke kyne,..and yocke them to ye cart. **1650** J. Nicoll *Diary* (Bann. Club) 12 The hangman rydand on ane hors befoir him yockit in that cairt. **1697** Dryden *Virg. Georg.* I. 69 Produce the Plough, and yoke the sturdy Steer. **1774** Goldsm. *Nat. Hist.* (1776) III. 199 Lions have been yoked to the chariots of conquerors. **1856** Kane *Arctic Expl.* I. xvii. 210 They yoked in their dogs in less than two minutes. **1871** C. Gibbon *For Lack of Gold* xvii, Four fresh horses which had been 'yoked' at Abbotskirk. **1882** 'Ouida' *Maremma* ii, Twice a year regularly she yoked her mule to her cart and drove into Grosseto.

b. with the plough or vehicle as object.

a **1568** *Wyfe of Auchtermuchty* i. (Bann. MS.) He yokkit his plwch vpoun the plane. **1635** *Reg. Privy Council Scot.* Ser. II. VI. 37 He yocked the cairt wherein Cokstouns chartour kist wes caried away. **1638** A. Henderson *Serm.*, *Ps. cxxix. 3* (1867) 276 Without his license the pleugh cannot be yoked. **1697** Dryden *Æneis* XII. 433 These on their Horses vault, those yoke the Car. *a* **1774** Fergusson *Hame Content* 62 The chaise is yokit in a trice. **1869** Gibbon *Robin Gray* xxii, He said he would 'yoke the cart'. **1871** Ellis *Catullus* lv. 18 Rhesus' chariot yok'd to snowy coursers.

c. *gen.* To attach, put on or in (as a yoke).

c **1848** Keegan *Leg. & Poems* (1907) 470 The Scotchman ..'yoked on' his war-pipes, and the..rafters..rang..with the martial strains of the Highland Pibroch. **1853** Kane *Grinnell Exp.* xxiv. (1856) 196 By the time I had yoked my neck in its serape.

3. To fasten a yoke round the neck of (a hog or other animal): see yoke *sb.*^{1} 2.

1530 Palsgr. 786/2 You muste yoke your hogge, for he ronneth thorowe every hedge. **1607** in *Eng. Gilds* (1870) 442 That all thinhabitants of this lordship yoke or ring their swine sufficiently. **1657** J. Watts *Scribe, Pharisee*, etc. Ep. Rdr. c j b, So yoking and ringling the wild Boars amongst them..that they may not break through the hedges, or down the walls of the vineyard of the Lord. **1708** in *Hist. Anc. Chapel Stretford* (Chetham Soc.) II. 84 Wm. Moss for not yoaking and ringing his swine, 2*s.* **1840** Colquitt in *Congr. Globe* Jan., App. 145/2 If they think it..a duty..to yoke the geese to keep them from going in washing in violation of the Sabbath. **1886** [see yoke *sb.*^{1} 2].

4. To suspend (a bell) on a yoke (see yoke *sb.*^{1} 4, quot. 1864).

1701 in W. S. Banks *Walks Yorksh., Wakefield* etc. (1871) 44 John Hinchliff for yoaking ye bell 2 18 6.

5. *Mining.* To mark out (a claim) with 'yokings' (see yoking *vbl. sb.* 6).

? **1556** in Pettus *Fodinæ Reg.* (1670) 96 All Grounds, as Crosses and Holes that be not stowed nor yoked lawfully. **1664** [see stowce].

6. *trans.* To bring into or hold in subjection or servitude; to subjugate, oppress. Now *rare* or *Obs.*

c **1325** *Old Age* iii. in *E.E.P.* (1862) 149 Y-ȝoket ic am of ȝore wiþ last an luþer lore. *a* **1529** Skelton *Col. Cloute* 325 The pore people they yoke With sommons and citacyons. **1542** Udall *Erasm. Apoph.* 300 b, Vntill thei wer yoked by the thirtie tyrannes, and afterwarde conquered and subdued by Philippus. **1567** *Gude & Godlie B.* (S.T.S.) 185 With traditiounis of men we haif thame ȝockit. **1592** Kyd *Sol. & Pers.* IV. i, All Rhodes is yoakt, and stoopes to Soliman. **1605** Camden *Rem.* (1637) 29 The Normans, who..would have yoaked the English under their tongue, as they did under their command. **1647** N. Bacon *Disc. Govt. Eng.* I. lvii. (1739) 106 He was fain to yoke his lawless will under the grand Charter. **1667** Milton *P.L.* x. 307 Xerxes, the Libertie of Greece to yoke. **1671** —— *Samson* 410 But foul effeminacy held me yok't Her Bond-slave. **1781** Cowper *Table T.* 258 As well be yok'd by despotism's hand, As dwell at large in Britain's charter'd land.

7. *fig.* **a.** To join, link, couple, connect, associate; †*occas.* to embrace.

c **1205** Lay. 1872 Heo ȝeokeden [*c* **1275** ȝogede] heora earmes & ȝarweden heom seoluan. *a* **1400** *Prymer* (1891) 111 Oak nouȝt me to gydere with synneres. **1490** Caxton *Eneydos* xxiv. 89 Whiles that the sterres ben in theyr courses well yocked. *a* **1508** Dunbar *Tua Mariit Wemen* 220 [He] with a ȝoldin ȝerd, dois ȝolk me in armys. **1561** Winȝet *Bk. Questions* §53 Wks. (S.T.S.) I. 110 The matrimonie to be dissoluit, and the twa harlotis to be ȝokit vp in a prætendit band of matrimonie. *a* **1578** Lindesay (Pitscottie) *Chron. Scot.* (S.T.S.) I. 319 The Earle of Angus and the Earle of Glencairneis was ȝokit togither. **1611** Shaks. *Wint. T.* I. ii. 419 Oh then,..my Name Be yoak'd with his, that did betray the Best. **1612** T. Taylor *Comm. Titus* i. 16 Let euery of vs be carefull to approoue our sinceritie to God..by yoking answerable practise to our profession. **1614** Raleigh *Hist. World* I. viii. 171 The two Riuers (as it were) yoked together goe along it. **1638** Farley *Moral Embl.* x, Foure Elements in this my body are All yockt in one. **1818** Scott *Rob Roy* xiv, Sae mony royal boroughs yoked on end to end, like ropes of ingans. **1865** J. G. Holland *Plain Talks* ii. 67 Ambition, when yoked with genius. **1867** Dk. Argyll *Reign of Law* ii. 103 It often happens that some common law is yoked to extraordinary conditions. **1879** Froude *Cæsar* xxiv. 420 Cato was one of those better natured men whom revolution yokes so often with base companionship.

b. With reference to marriage: only in *pa. pple.*

1604 Shaks. *Oth.* IV. i. 67 Thinke euery bearded fellow that's but yoak'd May draw with you. **1632** Sanderson *Serm.* 364 He that is yoaked with a wife must not put her away. **1712** Steele *Spect.* No. 455 ¶3, I have the Honour to be yok'd to a young Lady. **1847** Tennyson *Princess* VII. 340 My bride, My wife, my life. O we will walk this world, Yoked in all exercise of noble end.

c. To join or couple the ridges in ploughing.

1812 Souter *Agric. Banff* App. 82 We are directed to yoke awal and bear-root, that is to plow the ridges by pairs. *Ibid.*, We must take care not to yoke twice one way, other-wise it will impoverish the one half, and thicken the other too much. **1844** H. Stephens *Bk. Farm* I. 471 Another mode of ploughing land from the flat surface is *casting* or *yoking* or *coupling* the ridges.

8. a. *intr.* (for *refl.*) To join, associate oneself, be or become connected or linked. Now *rare.*

1500–20 Dunbar *Poems* lv. 33 Keip ȝou fra harlattis nycht and day; Thay sall repent quha with thame ȝockis. *a* **1592** Greene *Jas. IV*, v. ii, That galling grief and I may yoke in one. **1607** Shaks. *Cor.* III. i. 57 You must enquire your way, ..with a gentler spirit, Or neuer be so Noble as a Consull, Nor yoake with him for Tribune. **1851** Tennyson *To the Queen* 10 The care That yokes with empire.

b. with reference to the married state.

1593 Shaks. *3 Hen. VI*, IV. i. 23 God forbid, that I should wish them seuer'd, Whom God hath ioyn'd together: I, and 'twere pittie, to sunder them, That yoake so well together. **1624** Fletcher *Rule a Wife*, I. iv, *Alt.* Shee would faine marry. I. *Lady*... Who would she yoke with? **1765** Boswell *Let.* 11 May in *Corr. Boswell & Johnson* (1966) 167 At any trade I shall be in no hurry to *yoke* as my Father calls it. **1920** R. Macaulay *Potterism* II. i. 61 She is yoking together with an unbeliever.

9. *intr.* To join battle, engage (*with* an enemy); to engage in a contest or dispute; rarely *trans.* to engage in dispute with, attack. *Sc.*

1535 Stewart *Cron. Scot.* (Rolls) III. 333 Syne he and tha hes ȝokkit sone togidder In plane battell. **1581** A. Hall *Iliad* v. 92 We sooner see goe to the hacke, the dull and fearful foke, Than hardie souldiors in the field, who wishe with foes to yoke. **1587** Montgomerie *Sonn.* xix. 12 Ȝok when we will, I hope to gar him ȝeild. **1646** R. Baillie *Lett. & Jrnls.* (1841) II. 398 The orthodoxe and heterodoxe partie will yoke about it with all their strength. **1822** Chalmers in Hanna *Mem.* (1850) II. 360, I..yoked upon him, and posed him well with questions. **1901** N. Munro *Doom Castle* xv, She yoked himsel' on his jyling the lassie.

10. *trans.* To set (a person or thing) to work or service (usually consciously *fig.* from 2); *dial.* to urge to attack, set (a dog) *upon* a person.

1606 Shaks. *Tr. & Cr.* II. i. 116 There's Vlysses, and old Nestor,..yoke you like draft-Oxen, and make you plough vp the warre. **1637** Rutherford *Lett.* (1862) I. cxiv. 285 He hath yoked me to work, to wrestle with Christ's love. **1681** Colvil *Whigs Supplic.* (1751) 98 Bishops either will cause stone him, Or else yoak butcher dogs upon him. **1805** MacIndoe in Chambers *Pop. Hum. Scot. Poems* (1862) 152 To count, his man and Tam were yoket, Ten hunder thousand tatties. **1807** Coleridge *Let. to H. Coleridge* 3 Apr., Mere natural qualities..must not be deemed virtues until they are broken in and yoked to the plough of Reason. **1867** Dk. Argyll *Reign of Law* iii. 128 It is by wisdom and knowledge that the Forces of Nature..are yoked to service. **1910** W. R. Nicoll *Round of Clock* xv. 230 He yoked his great imagination to constant labour.

11. *intr.* To engage vigorously in some occupation; to set to work, set to; to put one's hands *to*; to set *on* a person. *Sc.*

1554 in Tytler *Hist. Scot.* (1864) III. 29 ['Oh!' said Angus, 'that I had here my white goss-hawk: we should then all] yoke [at once']. **1637** Rutherford *Lett.* (1862) I. xciv. 243 O, if I could yoke in amongst the thick of angels and seraphims and now-glorified saints! **1685** Peden *Let. to Prisoners* July, He is the easiest merchant ever the people of God yoked with. **1768** Ross *Helenore* 20 Right yape she yoked to the pleasing feast. **1816** Chalmers in Hanna *Mem.* (1850) II. 83, I yoked to the review of 'Jones'. **1818** *Ibid.* 444 In homely phrase..she *yoked* to the reading of the Bible upon that principle. **1823** Mrs. E. Logan *St. Johnstoun* ix, Wi' that they a' yoked to me, and hoisted me ower into the cobble. **1886** J. Barrowman *Sc. Mining Terms* 74 To *Yoke*, to resume work. **1895** Marchbank *Coven. Annandale* xi, They yoked on the man as he was riding alang in his carriage.

yoke: see yolk, yuke.

'**yok(e)able**, *a. rare.* [f. yoke *v.* + -able.] Capable of being or adapted to be yoked. Hence '**yokeableness** (in quot., readiness to be held in subjection, submissiveness).

1483 *Cath. Angl.* 427/1 Ȝokabylle, *iugalis.* **1611** Cotgr., *Accouplable*, yoakeable. *a* **1638** Mede *Wks.* (1672) 161 Yokeableness, or a pliableness and tractableness to be ordered.

yokeage ('jəʊkɪdʒ). *U.S.* = rokeage, q.v.

yoked (jəʊkt, *poet.* 'jəʊkɪd), *ppl. a.* [f. yoke *sb.*^{1} + -ed.]

1. Coupled by a yoke, as a pair of draught-animals; also, attached to a vehicle or plough, as a draught-animal.

c **1480** Henryson *Test. Cress.* 209 This goldin Cart..Four ȝokkit steidis..throw the Spheiris drew. *c* **1485** *Digby Myst.* II. 119 He was nother horse ne mare, nor yet yokyd sow. *c* **1550** Cheke *Matt.* xxi. 5 A foole of an iooked as. **1568** Howell *Arb. Amitie* 24 The yoked Oxe doth smell his strawie stall. **1607** Topsell *Four-f. Beasts* 42 The Septentrions call them *Triones*, that is yoked Oxen. **1716** in Cramond *Ann. Banff* (1893) II. 86 John Gregor cited for going with his yoked horse through the country on the Sabbath day. **1819** Chalmers *Serm.*, *Job ix. 30–33*, 124 The yoked and the tortured negro is compelled to yield to the whip of the overseer. **1902** Fairbairn *Philos. Chr. Relig.* II. iv. 384 The yoked oxen plough the fields.

2. Connected, coupled, linked; in *Bot.* said of a leaf consisting of one or more pairs of opposite leaflets; now called conjugate (*a.* 4 a), jugate (*a.* 1).

1551 T. Wilson *Logic* K v, Yoked wordes whiche beyng deriued of one, are chaunged in the speakyng. **1807** J. E. Smith *Phys. Bot.* (1814) 137 *Conjugatum*, conjugate, or yoked [leaf], consists of only a pair of *pinnæ* or leaflets, and is much the same as *binatum*. **1829** T. Castle *Introd. Bot.* 70 It is said to be simply yoked, when one pair only of opposite leaflets, is supported on the common foot-stalk... Double-yoked—when there are two pairs, and so on.

3. Carried on a yoke, as a pail; furnished with a yoke, as a garment: see yoke *sb.*^{1} 3, 3 b.

1866 Geo. Eliot *F. Holt* Introd. 6 At the well, clean and comely women carrying yoked buckets. **1913** *Play Pictorial* No. 133. 78/3 With an original trimming of diamanté on the yoked back and down the fronts.

yoke-fellow ('jəʊkˌfɛləʊ). [f. yoke *sb.*^{1} + fellow *sb.*, transl. Gr. *σύζυγος*.]

1. A person 'yoked' or associated with another, esp. in some work or occupation; a fellow-worker; an associate or partner, esp. in a task.

1526 Tindale *Phil.* iv. 3 Yee and I beseche the faythfull yockfelowe, helpe the wemen which labored with me in the gospell. **1559** *Mirr. Mag., Dk. Clarence* xli, He tolde me to, my youkefelow should dye. **1599** Shaks. *Hen. V*, II. iii. 56 Yoke-fellowes in Armes, let vs to France. *a* **1659** Bp. Brownrig *Serm.* (1674) I. iv. 61 We must not..be Yoke-fellows with them in their Religion. **1664** Butler *Hud.* II. i. 672, I know you cannot think me fit, To be th' Yoke-fellow of your Wit. **1815** Scott *Guy M.* lvi, 'Mr. Corsand,' said Glossin to the other yoke-fellow of justice [after Shaks. *Lear* III. vi. 39], 'your most humble servant.' **1850** Merivale *Rom. Emp.* iv. I. 193 This was the second time that these reluctant yoke-fellows had been joined together in public office. **1908** *Ch. Times* 5 June 762/1 An able, Catholic-minded and devout Prince having for his yokefellow a resolute and saintly Primate.

b. Applied to things.

1579 Tomson *Calvin's Serm. Tim.* 411/1 Doctrine & an honest & godly life, are two yokfelows y^t cannot be sundred. **1670** Maynwaring *Vita Sana* xv. 140 Unwilling is the Soul to move her yoak-fellow, farther then the enforcing Law of Nature..commands. **1675** T. Brooks *Gold. Key* 183 Those two sinful Yoke-fellows, the soul and the body. **1852** H. Rogers *Essays* (1874) I. vii. 378 Unhappy mind!..so strictly is it united to that mad yokefellow, Matter..that it can find a tongue only by its aid. **1871** Freeman *Norm. Conq.* IV. xviii. 211 The castle..still crowns the height as no unworthy yokefellow of its ecclesiastical neighbour.

2. *spec.* A person joined in marriage to another; a husband or wife, spouse.

? **1545** Brinklow *Compl.* xxiv. (1874) 68 This fast..is good to be vsed..of such as be absent from their yockfelows, & prycked to fylthynes. **1629** Winthrop *Let. to Wife* in *New*

Eng. (1825) I. 366 It grieveth me much, that I want time and freedom of mind to discourse with thee (my faithful yokefellow). **1693** CONGREVE *Old Bach.* IV. xxii, I have been a tender Husband, a tender Yoke-fellow. **1712** ADDISON *Spect.* No. 530 ¶1 Those who have most distinguished themselves by railing at the sex in general, very often make an honourable amends, by choosing one of the most worthless persons of it for a companion and yoke-fellow. **1838** DICKENS *O. Twist* xxxviii, Mrs. Bumble..did not want for spirit, as her yokefellow could abundantly testify. **1871** MEREDITH *H. Richmond* lv, Was it possible I had ever refused to be her yokefellow?

Hence **yoke-fellowship**, association, partnership.

1816 *Sporting Mag.* XLVIII. 57 We never heard that Godwin..slighted..the yoke-fellowship. **1856** *N. Brit. Rev.* XXVI. 113 The forced yoke-fellowship of slaves. **1879** FARRAR *St. Paul* II. 108 They would..separate themselves from their incongruous yoke-fellowship with unbelief.

yokel (ˈjəʊk(ə)l). Also **youkell**. [Of uncertain origin. Perh. a fig. application of dial. *yokel* (1) green woodpecker, (2) yellow-hammer.] A contemptuous term for a (stupid or ignorant) countryman or rustic; a country bumpkin. Also quasi-*adv.*, as ***yokel-stubborn***.

1812 J. H. VAUX *Flash Dict.*, *Youkell*, a countryman or clown. **1820** *Sporting Mag.* (N.S.) VI. 193 It was thought Redgreaves was a Yokel; but upon further scrutiny, it turned out that he was a Clerkenweller. **1823** 'JON BEE' (*title*) A Dictionary of the Turf,..useful..for Novices, Flats, and Yokels. **1828** P. CUNNINGHAM *N.S. Wales* (ed. 3) II. 222 A raw yokel [*note*, Countryman] was once complained of to me by a messmate of his, for robbing him of a dollar. **1861** THACKERAY *Four Georges* iv, Black legs.. inveigle silly yokels with greasy packs of cards in railroad cars. **1883** D. C. MURRAY *Hearts* xxv, The yokel, being a yokel, was not good at the reading of facial expression. **1935** L. MACNEICE *Poems* 15 The moon's glare, Goggling yokel-stubborn.

attrib. **1829** P. EGAN *Boxiana* 2nd Ser. II. 665 If he stood still, in his *yokel* attitude, he was laughed at by the spectators. **1844** DICKENS *Mart. Chuz.* xxxvi, None of your steady-going, yokel coaches, but a swaggering, rakish,.. London coach. **1891** C. T. C. JAMES *Rom. Rigmarole* ix, Maidservants..looked eagerly for their yokel sweethearts.

Hence ˈ**yokeldom**, yokels collectively; ˈ**yokelish** *a.*, characteristic of a yokel.

1886 *Manch. Exam.* 16 Feb. 5/3 The chosen home of rural stupidity and yokeldom. **1886** *Jrnl. Anthrop. Inst.* Nov. 236 A very good rural population, with somewhat yokelish notions.

yokel, obs. var. of ICKLE *sb.*, icicle.

yokeless (ˈjəʊklɪs), *a. rare.* [f. YOKE *sb.*^{1} + -LESS. Used as a rendering of L. *absque jugo* 'without yoke', the interpretation given by Jerome of Heb. *b'li-yaʕal* BELIAL, as *b'li* without + *ʕōl* yoke.] Without a yoke; *fig.* not under subjection or restraint, unrestrained, dissolute.

1596 LODGE *Divel Coniured* (Hunter. Cl.) 21 He is likewise called Sathan, because an aduersary:..and Belial, because yoakles. **1641** TRAPPE *Theol. Theol.* iv. 180 These Yokelesse Belialists snuffe at it as over-strict. **1675** BROOKS *Gold. Key* Wks. 1867 V. 464 Brainless fellows, light and empty, yokeless and masterless persons. **1680** C. NESSE *Church Hist.* 104 Those men of Belial or, as the word signifies, yokeless ones.

yokeless (jəʊk(ə)ˈlɛs), *sb. nonce-wd.* [f. YOKEL + -ESS.] A female yokel.

1925 D. H. LAWRENCE *Refl. on Death of Porcupine* 182 As for the yokel, his little stream may have flowed out of commonplace little hills, and been ready to mingle with the streams of any easy, puddly little yokeless.

ˈ**yoke-mate.** [f. YOKE *sb.*^{1} + MATE *sb.*^{2}] = YOKE-FELLOW. Chiefly *fig.* So **yoke-mated** *a.* (*rare*).

c **1555** HARPSFIELD *Divorce Hen. VIII* (Camden) 276 [She] all to beat her yokemate with a washbutte. **1581** MARBECK *Bk. Notes* 1015 [1013] He had to his yoke mate one Helen. **1581** HANMER *Jesuites Banner* G 4 b, Neyther may they bee ioyned as yokemates, to drawe in the vineyarde of the Church. **1684** J. S. *Profit & Pleas. United* 10 Some were wont to yoke them together,..putting one of them yokemate with an Ox. **1704** SWIFT *T. Tub* Ep. Ded., He is a worthy yokemate to his forementioned friend. **1776** G. CAMPBELL *Philos. Rhet.* II. 296 *note*, Such yokemates as these, *immortal mark*, *great captain*, *illustrious place*. **1848** THACKERAY *Van. Fair* xxv, Rebecca..trying to soothe her angry yoke-mate. **1857** GLADSTONE *Glean.* (1879) VI. 58 Inasmuch as St. Paul has declared that a Christian husband or wife married to an unbeliever is to suffer the unbelieving yoke-mate to depart. **1882** G. M. HOPKINS *Let.* 1 Jan. (1956) 162 One of our Fathers, who was..my yokemate on that laborious mission, died there yesterday night. **1911** FLETCHER & KIPLING *School Hist. England* 223 The very marrow of Youth's dream, and still, Yoke-mate of wisest Age that worked her will! **1914** *Nineteenth Cent.* July 111 In water, Oxygen is still further subjugated by its yoke-mate, Hydrogen. **1917** *Q. Rev.* Apr. 276 The Austrians..to the disgust of their German allies, did nothing to endear themselves to their unequal yoke-mates, the Italians. **1929** R. BRIDGES *Test. Beauty* IV. 145 Where lay the harness'd bones of the yoke-mated oxen. **1973** L. RUSSELL *Colonial Canada* iv. 46 If one ox of a pair were lost or killed, the other was usually unfit to work, because it would not function in unison with a new yoke-mate.

So ˈ**yoke-mating**, marriage.

1891 MEREDITH *One of our Conq.* xiv, On some future day of a perchance miserable yokemating.

yoker (ˈjəʊkə(r)). *rare.* [f. YOKE *v.* + -ER^1.] One who yokes.

1483 *Cath. Angl.* 427/1 A ȝoker, *iugator*. **1731** A. HILL *Advice to Poets* Ep. p. v, How little is it suspected, by Thousands,..that a Poet is no Yoker of Sounds, or idle Assayer of Syllables. **1913** R. HARRIS *Boanerges* xxxvii. 341 Since Jason is alone, another pair of twin yokers will come to his assistance.

yokewise (ˈjəʊkwaɪz), *adv. rare*$^{-1}$. [f. YOKE *sb.*^{1} + -WISE.] In the manner or form of a yoke.

1577 GOOGE *Heresbach's Husb.* III. 128 In the stable, you must haue certayne stalles, or boordes, yokewyse set vp. [**1684** J. S. *Profit & Pleas. United* 9.]

† **yokindale.** *Obs.* Also **yochomdale, youkyndall, yockynggale; youghendale;** *Sc.* **yopeindail, ȝ(e)op-, ȝewp-, yopindaill, -dale, -dall, yowpindail.** [ad. early LG. *jochimdailer*, var. of *joachimsdaler* (whence also early Da. *iochim-*, *iocumdaller*, *iochimsdaler*, *-dale*, and 16th c. F. *jocondal(l)e*) = G. *joachimstaler*, 'the coin of Joachimstal' (in Bohemia), the orig. name of the THALER: see DOLLAR. (The Sc. forms *yop-*, *yowp-* are prob. due to contamination with GOWPEN 'double-handful'.)] A silver coin of the 16th century varying in value from 15 to 20 shillings Scots.

1536 in *Diplom. Island.* (1910) IX. 758 Declaring iiij^{xx} ml. yochomdales to be ready at Breame to be conveyed to Copmanhaven. **1541** *Aberd. Reg.* XVII. (Jam.), To deliuer Johnn Auchtquholly ane yopindaill, or than xv sh. Scottis thairfor. **1557** *Richmond Wills* (Surtees) 103 To John Teysdayll a yokindale of syluer. **1557** *Will of R. Pickworth* (Somerset Ho.), I geve to..my suster a youkyndall of silver. **1558–9** in *N. & Q.* (1901) 9th Ser. VII. 288 Halfe a yockynggale of silver. **1572** *Will of James Innes of Drennie* (Jam.), Be Thomas Innes of Pethnik auchtene yowpindailes, pryce of the pece xxs. **1580** R. HITCHCOCK *Pol. Plat* d iv Paiyng their custome (a Youghendale vppon euery Laste) to the king of Denmarke.

yoking (ˈjəʊkɪŋ), *vbl. sb.* [f. YOKE *v.* + -ING^1.]

I. The action of YOKE *v.* in various senses.

1. The action of coupling draught-animals together with a yoke, or of attaching a draught-animal to a vehicle, etc.; also with *up*. Also *attrib.*, as ***yoking-gear***.

1580 HOLLYBAND *Treas. Fr. Tong*, *Accouplement de bœufs*, a yoking of oxen. **1844** H. STEPHENS *Bk. Farm* III. 1176 The yoking-geer of the shafts. **1881** A. C. GRANT *Bush Life in Queensland* I. iv. 39 They passed camp after camp of bullock-drags, the drivers and assistants all busy in yoking-up for the day.

b. *concr.* Harness. *U.S.*

1873 *Routledge's Ev. Boy's Ann.* 579 'Do your horses bear yokings?' asked Trick... 'We have often used them for driving, but we have no harness,' was the answer.

†**2.** Subduing, subjugation. *Obs. rare.*

1604 HIERON *Wks.* (1634) I. 548 The yoking and hampering, and restraining of mans naturall disposition.

3. The action of engaging in a contest; attack, onset; contest; a spell, turn, or bout of any occupation. *Sc.*

1596 DALRYMPLE tr. *Leslie's Hist. Scot.* (S.T.S.) I. 177 Seuerus at the first ȝoking [*orig.* congressu] slewe of Albion xx thousand. **1637** RUTHERFORD *Lett.* (1862) I. cxvii. 294 Three yokings laid him by. **1785** BURNS *Ep. to J. L——k* ii, At length we had a hearty yokin, At sang about. **1816** SCOTT *Old Mort.* viii, Sitting amang the wat moss-hags for four hours at a yoking. **1882** CUPPLES *Mem. Mrs. Valentine* vi. 88 'A double yoking', as was the phrase for a service when two successive sermons were preached without any mid-day interval. **1883** J. MARTIN *Remin. Old Haddington* 203 One 'yoking' [of Sunday School attendance] might have been sufficient for young folk.

4. A spell of work at the plough, or with a cart, etc., done at a stretch, between the times of yoking and unyoking the beasts; *locally*, a day's ploughing, carting, etc.

1765 A. DICKSON *Treat. Agric.* (ed. 2) 127 An acre was plowed at one yoking. **1787** BURNS *Answ. to Gudewife* i, When I..first could thresh the barn; Or haud a yokin at the pleugh. **1811** KEITH *Agric. Aberd.* 500 A pair of horses can plough an English acre in three journies, or yokings, of four hours each. **1812** SIR J. SINCLAIR *Syst. Husb. Scot.* II. 124 The work-horses also go two journeys or yokings in the day. **1832** *Scoreby Farm Rep.* 4 in *Lib. Usef. Knowl.*, *Husb.* III, It is very general to average full two acres per day,..with a pair of light horses in two yokings of five hours each. **1844** H. STEPHENS *Bk. Farm* II. 691 Colts..will soon submit to work, and become harmless in the course of a few short yokings.

II. †**5.** A measure of land (see quot. 1888). *Obs.*

1587 *Lanc. Wills* (Chetham Soc. 1893) 147 In plowyng of syx and twentye yockynge of land. **1888** *Sheffield Gloss.* s.v., Broad 'lands' in a ploughed field sixteen yards in width are called *yockings*. They are only made in dry flat fields. The word yoking is also applied to two 'lands' or 'roods' lying side by side in a ploughed field, the united breadth of the two 'lands' being from sixteen to seventeen yards.

6. *Mining.* (*pl.*) Pieces of wood joined together in a 'grove' or pit to prevent the earth from falling; also used in conjunction with 'stows' or 'stowces' for marking out a claim.

1653 MANLOVE *Lead-Mines* 14 If that the Stowes be pinned and well wrought With yokings, sole-trees. **1664** [see STOWCE]. **1747** HOOSON *Miner's Dict.* T j b, In Sinking with Square Wood or Yokings. **1802** MAWE *Min. Derbysh.* Gloss., *Yokings*, pieces of wood ascertaining possession.

ˈ**yoking**, *ppl. a.* [f. as prec. + -ING^2.] That yokes, in various senses: see the verb.

1592 SHAKS. *Ven. & Ad.* 592 And on his neck her yoaking armes she throwes. **1643** MILTON *Divorce* I. xiii. 21 An improper and ill-yoking couple. **1645** —— *Tetrach.* Matt. v. 31 What can be more..disparaging to the cov'nant of love.. then to bee made the yoaking pedagogue of new severities?

yokle, obs. var. of ICKLE *sb.*, icicle.

† **yoklet.** *Obs.* Also **joclet.** [OE. *ȝeocled*, *iocled*, *-let*, *-leta*, f. *ȝeoc* YOKE *sb.*^{1} with obscure second element.] In Kent, A small manor. (Cf. YOKE *sb.*^{1} 6.)

805 in Sweet *O.E. Texts* 455 *Mediam partem unius mansiunculae, id est* an ȝeocled. **811, 812** in Birch *Cartul. Sax.* I. 462, 476 Iocled, ioclet. **1704** *Dict. Rusticum*, *Joclet*, is a little Farm, or Mannor, called in some parts of Kent a Yoklet, as requiring but a small Yoke of Oxen to Till it.

Yokohama (jəʊkəʊˈhɑːmə). The name of a city in Japan, used as a specific epithet (see quots.); also as *sb.* (*ellipt.*).

1882 CAULFEILD & SAWARD *Dict. Needlework*, *Yokohama Crape*, this is a very fine, close make of Crape, otherwise known as Canton Crape... The Yokohama is the costliest of all descriptions of Crape, and the most durable in wear. **1885** *Encycl. Brit.* XIX. 646/1 Long-tailed fowls, under the ..names of Yokohama or Phœnix fowls, or Shinotawaro fowls, are..varieties recently introduced from Japan. **1910** *Ibid.* (ed. 10) X. 227/1 A domesticated breed of jungle-fowl known as the 'Japanese long-tailed fowls' or as 'Yokohamas'.

‖**yokozuna** (jəʊkəˈzuːnə). [Jap., f. *yoko* across + *zuna*, f. *tsuna* rope, festoon, orig. a sacred straw festoon presented to a champion wrestler.] A grand champion sumo wrestler.

1966 *Manch. Guardian Weekly* 9 June 7 The last six bouts were the most important with two yokozuna (grand champions) and several ozeki (champions) fighting. **1972** *Times* 19 July 6/7 The only *Yokozuna* or grand champion at present active, Kitanofuji, was unable to take part in the Nagoya tournament because of injury. **1974** *Daily Tel.* (Colour Suppl.) 22 Feb. 40/3 The *yokozuna* is the embodiment of all the highest virtues of Sumo and no slightly less than brilliant *sumotori* will ever be allowed to degrade the status of the Grand Champion.

yökul, variant of JOKUL.

1818 E. HENDERSON *Iceland* I. p. viii, The most extensive of all the Icelandic Yökuls is that called Klofa Yökul.

Yokuts (ˈjəʊkʌts), *sb.* and *a.* [Yawelmani Yokuts *yok^{h}oč* person, people.]

A. *sb.* **a.** (A member of) any of about 40 closely related Indian peoples of central California; these peoples collectively.

1877 *Contrib. N. Amer. Ethnol.* III. 370 At the time of the American advent..the Yokuts occupied the south bank of the Fresno. **1929** A. H. GAYTON *Yokuts & Western Mono Pottery-Making* 249 These sherds are related stylistically to southern California ware rather than to that of the Yokuts. **1973** A. H. WHITEFORD *N. Amer. Indian Arts* 39 In southern California the baskets of the Yokuts and Mono have thin grass coils.

b. The language family of the Yokuts, or the language of any Yokuts group.

1912 [see PENUTIAN *sb.* and *a.*]. **1921** E. SAPIR *Lang.* iv. 77 In another Indian language, Yokuts, vocalic modifications affect both noun and verb forms. **1965** *Canad. Jrnl. Linguistics* X. 139 Yokuts is a language family that is centered in the San Joaquin Valley and is flanked by languages of the Uto-Aztecan family.

B. *adj.* Of, pertaining to, or designating the Yokuts.

1877 *Contrib. N. Amer. Ethnol.* III. 370 In the Yokuts nation there appears to be more political solidarity..than is common in the State. **1944** S. S. NEWMAN (*title*) Yokuts language of California. **1974** *Encycl. Brit. Micropædia* X. 824/2 Yokuts ceremonies included puberty rite for boys, involving use of the hallucinogen *tolguache*, made from jimsonweed.

yoky (ˈjəʊkɪ), *a. rare.* Also 7 -ie. [f. YOKE *sb.*^{1} + -Y^1.] **a.** Having, or coupled by, a yoke; yoked. **b.** Consisting of or constituting a yoke.

c **1590** MARLOWE *Faustus* vi. Chorus, A chariot..Drawn by the strength of yoky dragons' necks. *c* **1611** CHAPMAN *Iliad* XVII. 382 Their manes..fell through the yokie sphere, Ruth-fully rufl'd and defilde. *a* **1660** *Contemp. Hist. Irel.* (Ir. Archæol. Soc.) I. 61 Hoisinge theire thundringe instruments upon the unconstant wheeles of yokie beasts.

yol, ȝol, obs. forms of YULE.

yold(e, ȝold(e: see YIELD *v.*, YULE.

yolden, yold, *ppl. a. Obs.* exc. *Sc.* Forms: see YIELD *v.* A. 3. [pa. pple. of YIELD *v.*]

†**1.** Surrendered (as a prisoner); that has surrendered or submitted; hence, submissive. *Obs.*

c **1374** CHAUCER *Troylus* III. 96 With lok doun cast & vmbele & ȝoldyn chere. *c* **1440** *Promp. Parv.* 539/2 Ȝolde manne, yn werre, *daticius*. **1470–85** MALORY *Arthur* XIX. ix. 787, I wylle neuer aryse vntyll ye take me as yolden & recreaunt. *a* **1547** SURREY *Eccles.* iv. 107 The yolden goost His marcy doth requyre. **1553** BRENDE *Q. Curtius* v. 86 His promis keaping towards ye yelden, his clemencie towardes prisoners.

2. Wearied, exhausted. *Sc.*

a **1508** DUNBAR *Tua Mariit Wemen* 220 [He] with a ȝoldin ȝerd, dois ȝolk me in armys. **15..** *Christ's Kirk* 151 in *Bannatyne MS.* (Hunter. Cl.) 287 For hir saik he wes nocht yoldin. **1836** M. MACKINTOSH *Cottager's Dau.* 62 O deed quo' William I am youden now.

ˈ**yoldring,** ˈ**yeldring.** *Sc.* and *north. dial.* Also **youldring, yowdring, yoldrin, yaldrin, -an,**

yeld(e)rin, yieldrin. [Variant of YOWLRING.] (Also *yellow y.*) A yellow-hammer.

1790 GROSE *Prov. Gloss.* (ed. 2), *Yold-ring*, a yellow-hammer. North. *a* **1810** TANNAHILL *Midges dance aboon the burn* ii, While weary yeldrins seem to wail Their little nestlings torn. **1815** G. BEATTIE *John o' Arnha'* (1826) 37 Three yaldrin's eggs. **1820** SCOTT *Abbot* xvii, You heed me no more than a goss-hawk minds a yellow yoldring. **1865** ALEX. SMITH *A. Hagart's Househ.* v, The yellow yelderin builds in dry banks.

yole, early var. of YAWL *v.*[1]

? *a* **1500** *Chester Plays* (Shaks. Soc.) xiii. 229 See, ffellowe, for cokes soule! This freeke begines to reme and yole.

yole: see YAWL *sb.*[1], YULE.

yolgh, ʒolʒe, obs. ff. YELLOW.

yolk (jəʊk), **yelk** (jɛlk), *sb.*[1] Forms: α. 1 **ʒeolca, ʒeoloca, ʒioleca,** 3 **ʒeolke,** 4 **yholk(e,** 4–5 **ʒolke,** 5 **ʒolk,** 7 **yeolke, yoke, yowlk, yoalk(e,** 8– *Sc.* **yowk,** (9 **yoke**), 7– **yolk.** β. 4–5 **ʒelke,** 4–7 **yelke,** 5 **ʒelk,** 7 **yealk,** 6– **yelk.** [OE. *ʒeolca, ʒeoleca, -oca,* f. *ʒeolu* yellow.

The spelling *yelk* appears to have ceased to be frequent since the third quarter of the 19th century, but it is found in later scientific and technical works. The pronunciation (jɛlk) survives locally; it is not clear during what period or to what extent it has been current in standard English.]

1. a. The yellow internal part of an egg, surrounded by the 'white' or albumen, and serving as nourishment for the young before it is hatched.

α. *a* **1000** *Boeth. Metr.* xx. 170 þæm anlicost þe on æʒe bið ʒioleca onmiddan. *c* **1000** *Sax. Leechd.* II. 38 Hænne æʒes ʒeolocan. *c* **1000** ÆLFRIC *Hom.* I. 40 Sceawa nu on anum æʒe, hu þæt hwite ne bið ʒemenged to ðam ʒeolcan. *c* **1290** *St. Michael* 635 in *S. Eng. Leg.* 317 Ase þe ʒwyte of þe Eye goth a-boute þe ʒeolke. **1340** HAMPOLE *Pr. Consc.* 6446 An egge yholke. **1398** TREVISA *Barth. De P.R.* XII. xix (Bodl. MS.), þe chiken is ibred of þe white and ynorissched wiþ þe ʒolke. *c* **1420** *Liber Cocorum* (1862) 18 Take ʒolkes of eyren þat harde bene. **1486** *Bk. St. Albans* b vj b, Tempere it with clere wyne and with the yolke of an egge. **1604** MARSTON *Malcontent* II. iv. D 1 b, Seauen and thirty yowlks of Barbarie hennes eggs. **1605** TIMME *Quersit.* I. xiv. 67 The yeolke of the egge..is the true sulphur. **1666** *Third Adv. to Painter* 18 An Addle-egg with double Yoalk. *a* **1756** MRS. HAYWOOD *New Present* (1771) 158 Beat up the yolks of three eggs. **1842** TENNYSON *Audley Court* 24 A pasty costly-made, Where quail and pigeon, lark and leveret lay,..with golden yolks Imbedded and injellied.

β. *c* **1325** *Gloss. W. de Bibbesw.* in Wright *Voc.* 150 *Le moiel*, a yelke. *c* **1400** *Lanfranc's Cirurg.* I. iii. 53 Wiþinne þe wounde leie þe ʒelke of an ey. **1560** WHITEHORNE *Ord. Souldiours* (1588) 46 b, Oile of the yelkes of egges. **1600** SURFLET *Country Farm* VII. lxv. 895 Putting thereto the yelkes of two egs and a little saffron. *a* **1625** FLETCHER *Wife for Month* II. i, Like to poch'd eggs That had the yelks suckt out. **1650** SIR T. BROWNE *Pseud. Ep.* III. xxviii. (ed. 2) 150 That a Chicken is formed out of the yelk of the egge,..the people still opinion. *a* **1700** EVELYN *Diary* 29 Sept. 1645, He abounded in things petrified, wallnuts, eggs in which ye yealk rattl'd. **1756** C. LUCAS *Ess. Waters* I. 73 [These] divided and inviscated by the yelk of an egg become miscible in..water. **1864** *Reader* 5 Nov. 572/2 The embryos of man [etc.] are nourished..by the mother's blood,..and those of birds by the yelk of the egg. **1884** *Health Exhib. Catal.* 39 The leather is..soaked in liquor made of the yelks of eggs.

b. in *Biol.* extended to the corresponding part in any animal ovum, which serves for the nutrition of the embryo (***nutritive*** or ***food-yolk***), and to the protoplasmic substance from which the embryo is developed (***formative*** or ***germ-yolk***): = VITELLUS 1.

1835–6 [see 5]. **1851** WOODWARD *Mollusca* 51 After impregnation, the germinal vesicle, which then subsides into the centre of the yolk, divides spontaneously into two. **1879** *Haeckel's Evol. Man* I. ii. 28 Cephalopods, the embryo of which has a bag of yelk protruding from the mouth. **1889** GEDDES & THOMSON *Evol. Sex* viii. 101 The yolk..is more or less readily distinguished from what is often called the formative protoplasm. *c* **1909** E. RAY LANKESTER *Science fr. Easy Chair* xxii. 209 The 'yelk' of the bird's egg.. corresponds to the black sphere of the frog's egg—the actual germ.

†**c.** *Bot.* = VITELLUS 2. *Obs. rare.*

1807 J. E. SMITH *Phys. Bot.* xix. (1814) 222 *Vitellus*, the Yolk, first named and fully illustrated by Gaertner.

†**2.** *fig.* Centre; innermost part, 'core'; also, best part.

1387–8 T. USK *Test. Love* III. iv. (Skeat) I. 198 Of loue (quod she) wol I nowe ensample make, sithen I knowe the heed knotte in that yelke.

1614 T. GENTLEMAN *England's Way* 12 Then being the very heart of Summer, and the very yoalke of all the yeare. **1637** RUTHERFORD *Let. to Parishioners* 13 July, Christ hath the yolke and heart of my love. **1637** —— *Let. to J. Kennedy* Lett. (1664) 187 Then Christ would..conquer to himself a lodging in the inmost yolk of our heart. **1695** J. SAGE *Fund. Charter Presbyt.* Pref., Wks. 1844 I. 32 The true yolk of the mystery. *c* **1730** RAMSAY *To Duncan Forbes* iv, Chance gi'es them of gear the yowk, And better chiels the shell.

3. (Also *y. of egg.*) Name for a gastropod mollusc of the genus *Nerita*, from the appearance of its shell.

1796 NEMNICH *Polygl.-Lex.* 945 *Yolk nerita*, nerita vitellus and albumen. **1815** S. BROOKES *Introd. Conchol.* 157 Yolk of Egg, *Nerita Vitellus*.

4. a. A rounded opaque or semi-opaque part occurring in window-glass; also, a pane of rough or thick glass. **b.** A hard or otherwise differentiated nodule in stone, rock, etc. *local.*

1808 JAMIESON s.v., Those round, opaque and radiated crystallizations, which are found in window-glass, in consequence of being too slowly cooled, are generally termed yolks in S[cotland]. **1811** *Acc. Game Curling* 3 Those whinstone nodules..called yolks, on account of their toughness. **1883** SIMMONDS *Dict. Trade* Suppl., *Yolk*, a local name in the Forest of Dean for masses of rotten stone intervening in the grey stone. **1886** J. BARROWMAN *Sc. Mining Terms* 74 *Yolk coal*, or *Yolks*, free or soft coal. **1901** W. LAIDLAW *Poetry & Prose* 34 They [*sc.* windows] were of yolks of darkish green, Sae dim they didna need a screen.

5. *attrib.* and *Comb.* in sense 1 b.

The most important are: ***yolk-bag, -sac***, the sac or vesicle inclosing the yolk, esp. when attached to the umbilicus as an organ of nutrition; it is connected with the intestine of the embryo by the ***yolk-duct*** or ***yolk-stalk***; ***yolk-cleavage, -division, -segmentation***, the division of the (formative) yolk as the initial process in the development of the embryo; ***yolk-membrane, -skin***, the delicate membrane surrounding the yolk of some ova; ***yolk plug***, a mass of yolk cells partly filling the blastopore in the development of certain fish, amphibians, and insects. Also ***yolk-coloured*** adj.

1835–6 *Todd's Cycl. Anat.* I. 560/2 The point of attachment of the yolk-bag [in the Cephalopod], which is suspended from the head of the embryo. **1849–52** *Ibid.* IV. 1223/2 The central yolk-mass of the body. **1857** GOSSE *Omphalos* xi. 330 The yelk-globe, fastened by its twisted *chalazæ*, is suspended in a glairy fluid (albumen). **1859** *Todd's Cycl. Anat.* V. 46/1 The process of yolk-segmentation. *Ibid.* 51/2 The ovum of the frog..consists of the yolk-ball,..surrounded by a..layer of..albuminous matter. *Ibid.* [124/1] The germ-forming and yolk-forming portions. **1861** J. R. GREENE *Man. Anim. Kingd., Cœlent.* 15 Many ova are provided with an outer envelope, known as the yolk-sac or 'vitelline membrane'. *Ibid.*, After fecundation, the ovum exhibits a series of changes inaugurated by the process of 'segmentation' or yolk-division. *Ibid.* 181 After yolk-cleavage the embryo appears rudely cylindrical in form. **1869** G. M. HOPKINS *Jrnls. & Papers* (1959) 189 The other evening..there was a slash of glowing yolk-coloured sunset. **1878** BELL tr. *Gegenbaur's Comp. Anat.* 18 Special particles—yolk-granules—may appear in its protoplasm. *Ibid.* 53 Special glands, Yolk glands, are formed from the ovary. **1879** *Haeckel's Evol. Man* I. x. 284 Connected with the central portion of the intestinal tube by a thin stalk, the yelk-duct. [**1881** F. M. BALFOUR *Treat. Compar. Embryol.* II. vii. 102 Shortly after the stage represented in fig. 71 B, the plug of yolk, which fills up the opening of the blastopore, disappears, and the mesenteron communicates freely with the exterior by a small circular blastopore.] **1888** GOODE *Amer. Fishes* 190 The comparatively large yelk-sac. **1889** ROLLESTON & JACKSON *Anim. Life* Introd. p. xxvii, The Gastrula is derived either by invagination or by differentiation of the yolk-cells. **1892** E. L. MARK tr. *O. Hertwig's Text-bk. Embryol. of Man & Mammals* vi. 117 The inner lamella [of the *Triton* embryo]..is connected with the mass of yolk-cells.., which lies like a wall in front of the blastopore and even projects into it as the Rusconian yolk-plug. **1898** P. MANSON *Trop. Diseases* xxxvi. 532 The points to be attended to in the diagnosis of ova are size, shape, colour..the presence or otherwise of yolk spheres. **1900** *Q. Jrnl. Microsc. Sci.* Feb. 7 The thin..yolk-stalk carrying the vitelline artery. **1928** [see INDUCTION 9 b]. **1959** SOUTHWOOD & LESTON *Land & Water Bugs* 299 Fertile eggs [of the bug *Capsus ater*] commence to develop at once and the grey band of the yolk plug forms just below the operculum about 2 weeks after laying. **1980** *Jrnl. Exper. Zool.* CCXIV. 323 YSL [*sc.* yolk syncytial layer] cytoplasm which reaches the yolk plug during epiboly is not a part of the syncytium when gastrulation begins.

yolk (jəʊk), *sb.*[2] Also **yoak, yoke, yok, yelk.** [OE. **eowoca* (whence *eowociʒ* YOLKY *a.*[2]), corresp. to Flem. *ieke* (*iecke* in Kilian; in comb. *ie(c)kwoll* yolky wool), whence Sc. EIK. The spelling of the Eng. word has been influenced by association with YOLK *sb.*[1]] The greasy substance secreted by the sebaceous glands in the skin of a sheep, which serves to moisten and soften the wool. Also called *suint, wool-oil*, and (as a chemical substance) *lanolin*.

in the yolk: said of wool in its natural state, containing the yolk.

1607 TOPSELL *Four-f. Beasts* 686 The panch of a sucking pig being taken out and mingled with the yolke which sticketh to the inner parts of the skin. **1798** *Young's Ann. Agric.* XXX. 73 The wool on the moor [*sc.* Dartmoor] 5 lb. on an average, in the yoak, that is unwashed. **1805** LUCCOCK *Nat. Wool* 81 The power of producing a copious supply of healthy and nutritious yolk is one of the most important qualities of wool-bearing animals. **1858** SIMMONDS *Dict. Trade, Yolk, Yelk*, a natural oily secretion or greasy substance in wool. **1884** JEFFERIES *Red Deer* viii. 165 The water is fouled by the grease, called the 'yok'. **1901** *Dundee Adv.* 17 May 5 [Wool] in 'the yoke'..was only fetching about 4½d. a lb.

attrib. **1808** VANCOUVER *Agric. Devon* 343 Eight pounds of yoak wool to the fleece.

yolk, *sb.*[3] *local.* Also **yoak, yoke.** [f. next.] Hiccup.

c **1700** KENNETT *MS. Lansd.* 1033 lf. 481 *Yoaks*, hiccup. **1825** JENNINGS *Obs. Dial. W. Eng.*, *Yokes*.

yolk, yelk, *v. dial.* Also 7 **yoke, yeke,** 8– **yock, yeck,** etc. [app. alteration of *yox*, YEX (q.v.) with subsequent assimilation to *bolk, belk* to belch. In mod. dials. *yolk, yoak, yock* are south-western and *yeck* is Sc.] *intr.* To hiccup; also, to utter a short cough, as a sheep. Hence **yolking, yelking** *vbl. sb.* and *ppl. a.*

α. **1585** *MS. Ashmole 208* lf. 237 b Whose vgly locks and yolkinge voice Did make all men a feard. **1598** SYLVESTER *Du Bartas* II. i. III. *Furies* 414 Thirst, Yawning, Yolking, Casting, Shivering, Shaking. *c* **1700** KENNETT *MS. Lansd. 1033* (E.D.D.) Applied to the short cough of a sheep, as the sheep yekes or yokes, or has a yeking or yoking.

β. **1527** ANDREW *Brunswyke's Distyll. Waters* H ij b, The same dronke in the maner aforesayd is good for the yelkyng, named Singultus. *c* **1532** DU WES *Introd. Fr.* in *Palsgr.* 954 To yelke, *sangloutir*. **1590** BARROUGH *Meth. Phisick* III. xi. (1596) 117 The meate being..so corrupted, causeth some to yelke. *Ibid.*, When yelking is caused of fulnesse, vomiting is the best remedie. **1653** R. SANDERS *Physiogn.* 191 A yelking which followeth vomiting.

yolk, yolke, obs. forms of YOKE.

yolked (jəʊkt), *a.* [f. YOLK *sb.*[1] + -ED[2].] Having or containing a yolk or yolks: chiefly in comb. as ***double-, large-, two-yolked***.

1585 HIGINS *Junius' Nomencl.* 54/1 *Ouum geminum*,..a two yolked egge. **1599** T. M[OUFET] *Silkwormes* 66 Whited alike, and yellow yolked all. **1859** *Todd's Cycl. Anat.* V. 51/2 Animals..with the large-yolked ova. **1889** *Science Gossip* 118/1, I know that 'double-yolked' eggs are not uncommon. **1900** *Q. Jrnl. Microsc. Sci.* Feb. 75 Small-yolked, holoblastic eggs.

yolkiness ('jəʊkɪnɪs). [f. YOLKY *a.*[1] + -NESS.] Yolky quality or condition.

1528 PAYNELL *Salerne's Regim.* (1541) 98 b, Coler prassine, lyke the colour of the herbe Prassion..is engendred of the yolkynes whan hit is burned: for burnyng causeth a yolky blackenes in the coler.

yolkless ('jəʊklɪs), *a.* [f. YOLK *sb.*[1] + -LESS.] Destitute of yolk; containing no yolk.

1897 *Brit. Birds, their Nests & Eggs* II. 163 Three full-sized eggs and one small yolkless one.

yolky ('jəʊkɪ), *a.*[1] Also 6 **yelky,** 9 **yoky.** [f. YOLK *sb.*[1] + -Y[1].] **a.** Resembling or consisting of (egg) yolk; of or pertaining to yolk; full of or abounding in yolk.

1528 [see YOLKINESS]. **1533** ELYOT *Cast. Helthe* (1541) 9 Yelky choler, like to the yelkes of egges. **1576** NEWTON *Lemnie's Complex.* 147 The seconde [melancholy]..is compact and made of yealowe or yolkie Choler aduste. **1841** J. T. HEWLETT *Parish Clerk* I. 80 Vield's eggs was more yokier than their's was. **1889** *Q. Jrnl. Microsc. Sci.* May 11 Small round, highly refractive yolky particles were present in the egg protoplasm. **1918** W. J. LOCKE *Rough Road* ix. 104 With a hazardous plunge of his spoon he had made a yellow yelky horror of the egg-shell.

b. in reference to stone or other mineral: cf. YOLK *sb.*[1] 4 b. ***yolky-stone***, a local name for a kind of conglomerate.

1805 MUSHET in *Phil. Trans.* XCV. 167 The fracture [of the bars] was gray, tore out a little in breaking, but was otherwise yolky and excessively dense. **1813** HEADRICK *Agric. Angus* 34 Beds of coarse pudding-stone, or gravel, or yolky-stone, as it is here called.

yolky ('jəʊkɪ), *a.*[2] Also **yoky.** [OE. *eow(o)ciʒ*, f. **eowoca* YOLK *sb.*[2]: see -Y[1] 1.] Containing 'yolk'; greasy with yolk, as unwashed wool.

c **1000** *Sax. Leechd.* II. 42 Genim ele, do on mid eowociʒ re wulle. *Ibid.* 74 Mid eowciʒre wulle. **1847** HALLIWELL, *Yoky-wool*, unwashed wool as it comes from the sheep's back. *Devon.* **1854** MISS BAKER *Northampt. Gloss.*, *Yolk*, the grease of wool. Wool that is oily is said to be *yolky*. **1886** C. SCOTT *Sheep-farming* 130 The fleece falls to pieces in a vexatious fashion on the table, especially if the sheep has been fed for the shambles, or is naturally very yolky.

†**yoll,** *v. Obs.* Forms: 3–5 **ʒolle,** 4 **ʒol,** 4–5 **yolle.** [Imitative. Cf. NFris. *jolli*, and for similar forms with vowel-variation YAWL *v.*[1], YOWL *v.*] *intr.* To cry aloud, howl; = YAWL *v.*[1] 1 a. Hence †**yolling** *vbl. sb.*

a **1250** *Owl & Night.* 223 þu schirchest & ʒollest to þine fere. *Ibid.* 1643 Myd yollinge [*v.r.* ʒulinge] & myd igrede. *a* **1300** *Leg. Rood* (1871) 44 þo com þe deuel ʒollynge uorþ. *c* **1325** *Gloss. W. de Bibbesw.* in Wright *Voc.* 152 *note, Oule*, [glossed] yolles. *c* **1386** CHAUCER *Knt.'s T.* 1814 The heraudes, that ful loude yolle and crie. *c* **1400** *Anturs Arth.* 86 (Thornton MS.) ʒollande ʒamyrly, withe many lowde ʒelle. **1483** CAXTON *Gold. Leg.* 81 b/1 Whan they had made thys pyetous cryeng and yollyng.

yolle, yol(l)ow, obs. ff. OIL *sb.*[1], YELLOW.

yolp, *v. Obs.* or *dial.* Also **yollop.** = GULP *v.*

1579 HAKE *Newes out of Powles* (1872) D vij b, The pitchie burning pit..Shall yolpe them vp. **1881** *Leic. Gloss.*, *Yollop*, or *Yolp*, *v.a.*, var. pron. of 'gulp' and 'gulf'.

yolp. The cry of hounds. Cf. YAWP *v.*, YOUP.

1602 *Narcissus* (1893) 17 Then woe bee vnto little Watt, Yolp, yolp, yolp, yolp!

†**yolster.** *Obs.* [perh. of Scand. origin (cf. Sw. *(h)jolster, (h)jelster, (h)ilster*, Norw. *ister*, ON. **jǫlstr, ilstri*, pointing to orig. **elustr-* and **elustrj-*); but possibly from an unrecorded OE. **eolstr.*] Some kind of willow or osier.

1387 *Demise of site in Scagglethorpe, Yorks.* (MS.), Omnes yolstres crescen[tes] super ripam de Ouse infra dominium de Scahylthorp. **1396** *Ibid.*, Yholsters. [See *Yorks. Deeds* (Yorks. Archæol. Soc.) II. 161.]

yoly, obs. form of JOLLY *a.*

yoman, ʒoman(n)e, obs. forms of YEOMAN.

† **'yomer, 'ȝomer,** *a. Obs.* Forms: 1 **ȝeomor,** 3 **ȝeo(u)mer, ȝimer,** 3–4 **ȝomer,** *Kentish* **ȝemer, yemer.** [OE. *ȝeómor* = OS., OHG. *jâmar.* A neut. sb. is represented by OFris. *iâmer,* OHG. *jâmar,* also *âmar,* MHG. *jâmer* (G. *jammer*) sorrowful desire. (ME. *yēmer* may partly reflect OE. *ȝéamrung, ȝémrung* of Vesp. Psalter.)] Sorrowful, wretched; grievous, doleful.

Beowulf 49 Him wæs ȝeomor sefa. *a* **1000** *Husband's Message* 22 (Gr.) Siððan ðu ȝehyrde on hliþes oran galan ȝeomorne ȝeac on bearwe. *c* **1200** *Trin. Coll. Hom.* 169 Þe he þolede þe ȝimere pine he makede ane reuliche meninge. *c* **1205** LAY. 16566 Þer wes þa Hengest cnihten alre ȝeomerest. *a* **1225** *Leg. Kath.* 1831 Twa hundret cnihtes, ..þat ȝeuen anan up hare ȝeomere bileaue. *c* **1250** *Kent. Serm.* in *O.E. Misc.* 30 Þo..þet þurch yemere werkes oþer þurch yemer i-wil liesed þo blisce of heuene. **1340** *Ayenb.* 215 Þer me ssel..do al out alle seculere niedes, yemere þoȝtes, and þenche an his sseppere.

Hence † **'yomerness** *Obs.,* wretchedness, misery.

c **1250** *Kent. Serm.* in *O.E. Misc.* 28 Þo gode werkes þet is biter to þo yemernesse of ure flesce.

† **'yomer, 'ȝomer,** *v. Obs.* Forms: 1 **ȝeom(e)rian,** 2–3 **ȝeomer,** 3 **ȝeoumer,** 5 **ȝomer, yomer.** [OE. *ȝeómrian,* f. *ȝeómor*: see prec. Cf. OHG. *jâmarôn,* MHG. *jâmern,* and YAMMER *v.*] *intr.* To murmur, complain; to lament, mourn. Hence † **yomering** *vbl. sb.*

Beowulf 1118 Earme on eaxle ides gnornode, ȝeomrode ȝiddum. **971** *Blickl. Hom.* 113 For þære ȝeomrunga þæs oþres deaþes. *c* **1000** in *Lat. Hymns A.-S. Ch.* (Surtees No. 23) 21 Bena ȝeomriȝende we asendaþ. *c* **1205** LAY. 23492 Gullen þa helmes ȝeoumereden eorles. *c* **1230** *Hali Meid.* 35 Þat unrotes uuel, þat pine upo pine, þat wondrende ȝeomerunge. *c* **1400** *Destr. Troy* 1722 The Grekes..vs to grefe broght,..And to yow & also yours ȝomeryng for euer. *c* **1400** [see YAWL *v.*[1] 1 a].

† **'yomere, 'ȝomere,** *adv. Obs.* [f. YOMER *a.*] Sorrowfully, dolefully.

a **1250** *Owl & Night.* 415 A wintere þu singest wroþe and ȝomere [*Jesus MS.* yomere], And eure þu art dumb a sumere.

† **'yomerly, 'ȝomerly,** *a. Obs.* Forms: see YOMER *a.* [OE. *ȝeómorlic,* f. *ȝeómor* YOMER *a.* + *-lic* -LY[1]. Cf. OHG. *jâmarlîh,* ON. *ámorlegr.*] = YOMER *a.*

Beowulf 2444 Bið ȝeomorlic gomelum ceorle to ȝebidanne, þæt his byre ride ȝiong on galȝan. *c* **1205** LAY. 29564 Heo.. seoððe ȝeiden him on mid ȝeomerliche stanen. **13..** *E.E. Allit. P.* B. 971 Such a ȝomerly ȝarm of ȝellyng þer rysed.

† **'yomerly, 'ȝomerly,** *adv. Obs.* Forms: see YOMER *a.*; also 5 **ȝamyrly, ȝamerly** (but cf. YAMMER *v.*). [OE. *ȝeómorlíce,* f. *ȝeómor* YOMER *a.* + *-líce* -LY[2]. Cf. OHG. *jâmarlîcho.*]

Sorrowfully, dolefully.

a **1000** *Sal. & Sat.* 267 Se fugol..ȝilleð ȝeomorlice. *c* **1200** *Trin. Coll. Hom.* 35 His ofspring al þrowude on synne..and ȝemerliche pineden. **13..** *Gaw. & Gr. Knt.* 1453 He hurtez of þe houndez, & þay Ful ȝomerly ȝaule & ȝelle. *c* **1400** *Anturs Arth.* vii, Ȝauland ful ȝamerly, with many loude ȝelles.

Yom Kippur (jɒm 'kɪpə(r), kɪ'pʊə(r)). Also 9 **Jaumkipur.** [a. Heb. *Yōm Kippūr,* f. *yōm* day + *kippūr* atonement.] The Day of Atonement, the annual Jewish fast day of repentance and expiation that ends the Ten Days of Penitence.

1854 *Asmonean* 6 Oct. 198/3, I will tell thee now why the Jews in Gneson do not wear the *kittel* at *Jaumkipur.* **1878** *Harper's* Oct. 768/2 This..is a *Shophar,* such as is blown in the synagogues on the Jewish New Year..and the Day of Atonement (*Yom Kippur*). **1907** I. ZANGWILL *Ghetto Comedies* 20 With a woman *Yom Kippur* is a wonder-working day. **1922** JOYCE *Ulysses* 149 Their butteries and larders. I'd like to see them do the black fast Yom Kippur. **1941** *Contemp. Jewish Record* IV. 429/2 Last Yom Kippur.. Nazi elite guards..evicted Jews from a synagogue in Szczucin. **1974** *Ann. Reg. 1973* 200 Yom Kippur (the Day of Atonement), when there is no public transport [in Israel] or private or public business and even non-observant Jews stay at home, fell on 6 October. **1981** C. MACLEOD *Palace Guard* xii. 89 'Have you ever in your life seen anybody eat the way he does?' 'Yes, my Uncle Hymie on the night after Yom Kippur.'

b. *Comb.* **Yom Kippur War,** an Arab-Israeli war that began on Yom Kippur on 6 October 1973 and ended in the same month.

1973 *Guardian* 29 Oct. 3/5 The Yom Kippur war had given them [*sc.* the superpowers] a greater hold over their respective clients. **1980** 'E. ANTHONY' *Defector* v. 101 We [Russians] made very good use of the opportunities given to us by the Yom Kippur war.

yommer, obs. f. YAMMER *v.*

yomon, ȝomon, obs. forms of YEOMAN.

yomp (jɒmp), *v.* orig. *Mil.* [Origin unknown. The word came into prominence when used by the Royal Marines during the Falklands conflict of 1982. It was subsequently identified with YUMP *v.* by correspondents familiar with the terminology of rally driving, but whether correctly or not has not been confirmed.]

a. *intr.* To march with heavy equipment over difficult terrain. Also *fig.* **b.** *trans.* To cover (a certain distance) in this way.

1982 *Daily Tel.* 3 June 36/6 And always in the cold light of the Falklands dawn, the..Marines..have been ready to 'yomp on' for the next stage of the journey. **1982** *Observer* 20 June 3/2 Yomping round the sodden and trackless wastes of the constituency, I found the voters in less martial mood. **1983** *Listener* 20 Jan. 31/2 Mrs. Thatcher may begin yomping..around the hustings considerably sooner. **1983** *Guardian* 15 Apr. 10/1 Our boys..who yomped all those miles in the Falklands. **1984** *Sunday Times* 14 Oct. 9/3 So the sweaty soldier yomping to battle ends up with blisters and a pool of water inside the boot.

So **'yomping** *vbl. sb.* and *ppl. a.*; also **'yomper.**

1982 *Daily Tel.* 3 June 1/1 (*heading*) Yompers surprise the enemy. *Ibid.*, Yomping they call it in the Royal Marine Commandos. It means marching, humping up to 120 lb. of equipment and all the arms needed for attack at the far end of the trek. **1982** *Standard* 6 Aug. 8/1 (Advt.), Yompers wanted..in teams of 3 for 40 mile mountain express 24-hour walk. **1983** *Financial Times* 28 Jan. 16/6 Will robots replace the 'yomping' soldier in the army of the future?

yom tov ('jɒm tɒv). Also **yomtov,** 9 **yontef,** and with capital initial(s). [Yiddish, f. Heb. *yōm* day + *ṭōḇ* good.] A Jewish holiday or holy day.

1854 *Asmonean* 7 July 96/2 Now, Shlome's grand-father was a kind of careless man who preferred making 'yontef' throughout the year. **1892** I. ZANGWILL *Childr. Ghetto* II. 166 He had been so proud of having earned enough money to make a good *Yomtov.* **1933** A. VAN SON tr. C. van Bruggen in J. Leftwich *Ysräel* 1012 A Jewish woman cannot be too ill to hear the Seder... That's right, it's Yomtov now. **1962** B. ABRAHAMS tr. *Life Glückel of Hameln* iii. 51 Before we eat I must first take my child..some food. It is *Yom Tov.* **1976** M. HOROVITZ in D. Villiers *Next Year in Jerusalem* 113 Quite often, in the midst of supra-national poetry events, I find myself involuntarily imagining *yom tov.*

Yomud ('jəʊmʌd, jɒ'mu:d). Also 9 **Yimoot; Yomut.** [Native name.] **a.** (A member of) an ethnic group of Turkmen people (once a nomadic tribe) inhabiting the Turkmen Soviet Socialist Republic of the U.S.S.R. Also *attrib.*

1834 A. CONOLLY *Journey India Overland* I. iv. 35 The large tribe of Yimoot occupy the banks of the Goorgaun river. **1864** A. VÁMBÉRY *Trav. Central Asia* xvi. 307 The Yomuts inhabit the East shore of the Caspian Sea and some of its islands. **1889** G. N. CURZON *Russia in Central Asia* viii. 275 The Turkomans under Khivan rule are Yomuds, Chadars, Emrali, Ata and Alili. **1938** E. O. LORIMER tr. *Krist's Alone through Forbidden Land* ii. 38 We had reached Qala-Qaya, the standing camp or village of the Yomut. **1963** L. KRADER *Peoples Central Asia* iii. 58 Yomud had an alternative division, based on subsistence type rather than genealogy. **1974** *Even. Stand.* 12 Feb. 48/5 (Advt.), Superb oriental carpets & rugs. Including:..A special collection of unique Persian Nomadic rugs from the Yomut..and Quashgai tribes.

b. *attrib.* Designating rugs made by this people, often distinguished by a diamond-shaped motif.

1900 J. K. MUMFORD *Oriental Rugs* xii. 234 One might reasonably say, looking at some of the Yomud rugs, that they had come from the Shirvan or Dagestan looms. **1940** A. B. THACHER *Turkoman Rugs* 24 This type of juval is the aristocrat of Yomud rugs in respect to density of knotting. **1974** *Encycl. Brit. Micropædia* X. 825/2 The large Yomud carpets are entirely of wool or of goat hair.

yon (jɒn), *dem. a.* and *pron.* Now *arch.* and *dial.* Forms: α. 1 **ȝeon,** 4 **ȝion, yoene, ȝhone, yhon(e,** 4–5 **yone,** 4–6 **ȝone,** (6, 8 *Sc.*) **ȝon,** 5 **yhonne,** 6 **yoen,** (7–8 **yon'**), 4– **yon.** β. 5 **ȝene,** (6 **ien**), 6, 9 *dial.* **yen,** 9 *dial.* **yin.** [OE. *ȝeon* adj. (rare), corresp., with variation of vowel, to OFris. *iêna, gêna* (*ienn-, inn-*), WFris. *jinge,* OHG. *jenêr,* MHG., G. *jener,* also OHG., MHG. *enêr,* G. dial. *ene(r,* ON. *enn, inn, hinn,* def. art. (Sw., Da. *hin*), Goth. *jains* that. The Teut. bases underlying these forms, or other variants of them, are represented also in OHG. *ennân,* MHG. *enne(n* from there, hither, OHG. *en(n)ônt,* MHG. *en(n)ent* yonder, G. dial. *jenntak, jennabend* yesterday, Goth. *jainar* there; Du. and LG. show forms with initial guttural, viz. MDu. *ghene, gone, göne* (Du. *gene*) that, LG. *gunnen* that, there, *gunsiet* yonder. Related forms outside Teut. are recognized in Skr. *ēna-* 3rd pers. pron., *anēna, anayā* (instr.), that (one), OSlav. *onŭ* he, Lith. *añs* he. See also YOND, YONDER.

In OE. the only members of this family of words for which evidence is forthcoming are *ȝeon* adj. and *ȝeond, ȝeondan* YOND prep. (? orig. adv. like Goth. *jaind*), together with *biȝeonan* (*-ȝinan, -ȝenan*) 'trans', *beȝeondan* (Northumb. *biȝeanda, biȝienda*) BEYOND *adv.* and *prep.* From these the various parallel uses of *yon, yond,* and *yonder* have arisen through the extension to other members of applications originally appropriated to one of them.

The 17–18th cent. spelling of the word with an apostrophe (*yon'*) indicates that it was regarded as short for *yond.*]

A. *adj.*

1. A demonstrative word used in concord with a sb. to indicate a thing or person as (literally, or sometimes mentally) pointed out: cf. THAT *dem. adj.* 1. Formerly often, as still in some dialects, simply equivalent to *that* (*those*); but chiefly, and in later literary use almost always, referring to a visible object at a distance but within view: = 'that (those)...over there'.

α. *c* **897** ÆLFRED *Gregory's Past. C.* lviii. 443 Aris, & gong to ȝeonre byrȝ. *a* **1300** *Cursor M.* 654 Bot yhon tre cum þou nawight to, Þat standes in midward paradis. *Ibid.* 3027 Sco sceud abraham, 'yon bastard Do him a-wai.' **1393** LANGL. *P. Pl.* C. XXI. 149 Patriarkes and prophetes þat in peyne liggen, Leyf hit neuere þat ȝon [*v.rr.* ȝeon, ȝone, ȝonde, ȝynen, ȝeond] lyght hem a-lofte brynge. *a* **1400** *Northern Passion* 9/70, I wyll weynd to ȝhone cyte. *c* **1400** *Cursor M.* 27684 (Cott. Galba) Ȝone man ledes His life in praiers and almus dedes. *a* **1400–50** *Wars Alex.* 498 Ȝone selfe dragon forsothe I saȝe with myne eȝen. *c* **1450** *St. Cuthbert* (Surtees) 7398 Knawes þou noȝt ȝone ȝonge man? **15..** *Sonnge Sir Andraye Barton* xxii. in *Surtees Misc.* (1890) 70 'Fetch me yoen English dogs,' he saide. **1621** G. SANDYS *Ovid's Met.* VIII. (1626) 168 And to yon' hill Follow our steps. *c* **1630** MILTON *Sonn.* i, O Nightingale, that on yon bloomy Spray Warbl'st at eeve. *c* **1645** HOWELL *Lett.* (1890) I. i. 62 When we have gain'd yon Maiden City. **1652** URQUHART *Jewel* 189 Because of his being of this or this, or that, or yon, or of that other Religion. **1712** POPE *Vertumnus* 100 The fair fruit that on yon' branches glows. **1766** GOLDSM. *Hermit* i, To where yon taper cheers the vale With hospitable ray. **1818** SCOTT *Hrt. Midl.* xxx, I mind aye the drink o' milk ye gae me yon day. **1833** HT. MARTINEAU *Tale of Tyne* i. 16, I must go somewhere away from yon great town. **1890** W. A. WALLACE *Only a Sister?* xxix, There's a man in yon brake listening to what we're a-saying.

β. *c* **1425** *Cast. Persev.* 1765 in *Macro Plays* 129 All ȝene maydnys on ȝone playn. *c* **1550** CHEKE *Matt.* xxvii. 64 We remember y[t] ien deceiver said, whil he was iet alijv. J wil rijs again after iij dais. **1583** MELBANCKE *Philot.* Dd iij b, Seest thou not yen milke white pathe that crosse the welkin wendes? *a* **1825** FORBY *Voc. E. Anglia, Yin,* adj., yon.

2. *the yon*: the farther, the more distant: = YOND *a.*[1] 1, YONDER *a.* 1. *local.*

1700 *B.N.C.* (Oxf.) *Munim.* 33. 15 (MS.) The yon acre in Bindffield. **1897** *Outing* (U.S.) XXX. 384/1 We were told that Bill Ryder lived on the yon side of the mountain.

B. *pron.* (*sing.* or *pl.*) The adj. used *absol.,* usually denoting a visible object (or objects) pointed out, at a distance but within view: = 'that (*or* those) over there'; but sometimes simply = 'that' (or 'those'): cf. A. 1. Now only *Sc.* and *dial.*

a **1300** *Cursor M.* 3358 (Cott.) Yon es mi lauerd ysaac, Yon es þi keiser sal be þin. **13..** *Ibid.* 15919 (Gött.) 'Yoene,' he said, 'es ane of his þat wid vs es in band.' *Ibid.* 19700 (Edinb.) Na es noȝt ȝion He þat we saȝ þis ender dai Gain name of ihesu sua werrai? **1375** BARBOUR *Bruce* XIV. 280 Ȝone ar gadering of the cuntre. *c* **1470** HENRY *Wallace* III. 123 Yhonne is Wallace, that chapit our presoune. *c* **1480** HENRYSON *Test. Cress.* 533 Quhat Lord is ȝone (quod scho)? **1533** BELLENDEN *Livy* IV. ix. (S.T.S.) II. 79 Ȝone Is he þat has violate þe law of pepil. **1616** *Marlowe's Faustus* xi, What strange beast is yon, that thrusts his head out at window? **1621** G. SANDYS *Ovid's Met.* VIII. (1626) 165 What place Is yon', and of what name, that stands alone? *a* **1704** T. BROWN *Misc., Campaign* iii. Wks. 1711 IV. 143 Now, now we are there; yon's the General's Tent. **1822** SCOTT *Peveril* xl, Was yon the messenger? **1829** MARRYAT *Frank Mildmay* xix, 'D—— n the dog that says yon of Jock Thompson,' replied the Caledonian. **1895** 'IAN MACLAREN' *Brier Bush, Highl. Mystic* i. 60 Yon were verra suitable words at the second table [i.e. at the Communion]. **1896** KIPLING *Seven Seas, M'Andrews' Hymn* 108 Yon's strain, hard strain, o' head an' hand.

yon, *dem. adv.* Forms: 5–6 **ȝone,** 7 **yonn,** 7– **yon.** [See prec.] **a.** = YOND *adv.*, YONDER *adv. Obs.* exc. *dial.* and as in b.

c **1475** *Rauf Coilȝear* 706 In clais of clene gold, kythand ȝone cleir. *c* **1500** *Lancelot* 2826 Who is he ȝone? **1608** MIDDLETON *Five Gallants* II. iii, *Fulk.* Where sir? *Gold.* Peepe yon sir vnder. **1622** WITHER *Philarete* B j b, Here, you might (through the water) see the land, Appeare,..Yonn, deeper was it. **1628** —— *Brit. Rememb.* 116 b, Yonn lay a heape of skulls. **1632** MILTON *Penseroso* 52 But..with thee bring, Him that yon soars on golden wing. **1896** A. E. HOUSMAN *Shropsh. Lad* ix, And yon the gallows used to clank Fast by the four cross ways.

b. *hither and yon*: hither and thither, this way and that. orig. *dial.* Cf. YONDER *adv.* 1 c.

1787 GROSE *Prov. Gloss., Hither and yon,* here and there, backwards and forwards. *North.* **1836** GALT in *Tait's Mag.* III. 33 She swayed hither and yon, and was so coggly that I had fears of a catastrophe on the floor. **1883** *Century Mag.* July 379/2 The bass dashed hither and yon at the end of his tether, but all the time working up-stream and toward the rod. **1903** H. JAMES *Ambassadors* II. v. 53 What carried him hither and yon was an admirable theory that nothing he could do would not be in some manner related to what he fundamentally had on hand. **1939** W. S. MAUGHAM *Christmas Holiday* iv. 94 The wan characters of Chekov's stories drifted hither and yon at the breath of circumstance like dead leaves before the wind. **1963** BIRD & HUTTON-STOTT *Veteran Motor-Car* 52 Untidy chain or belt drives running hither and yon. **1978** *Nature* 27 Apr. 768/2 It is inaccurate, full of fanciful and unilluminating analogies, infuriatingly unsystematic, and skims hither and yon over the surface of the subject.

† **yon,** *prep. Obs.* In 3 **ȝeon, ȝen.** [See YON *a.*] = YOND *prep.* 1.

c **1205** LAY. 4401 To færen ȝeon þan eærde. *Ibid.* 6087 Þat me mihte hine bi-halden wide ȝeon þeon londe. *Ibid.* 6109 He seonde his sonde wide ȝen his londe.

† **yon,** *v. Obs. rare.* [ad. early Du. *gonnen,* now *gunnen,* to favour, vouchsafe.] *trans.* To wish.

1481 CAXTON *Reynard* xxvii. (Arb.) 66 He sawe there many of his kynne standyng which yonned hym but lytyl good.

yoncker, obs. form of YOUNKER.

yond (jɒnd), *a.*[1] and *pron. Obs.* exc. *dial.* Forms: α. 3 **yeonde,** *Orm.* **ȝonnd,** 3–4 (6 *Sc.*) **ȝond,** 4 **ȝonde, ȝund, yend,** 5–6 **yonde,** (6 **ȝound,** 7 **yon'd,**

yond', yound'), 4– **yond.** [adj. use of YOND *adv.*, after YON *a.* Cf. EFris. *juntî*, MLG. *gint*, Du. *gindsch.*

The 17th cent. spelling of the word with an apostrophe (*yond'*) indicates that it was regarded as short for *yonder.*]

A. *adj.*

†**1.** Qualifying *half, side*, or the like (with or without *the* preceding): The farther, the more distant, 'the other'. *Obs.*

c **1200** ORMIN 10588 Þatt an wass o ȝonnd hallf þe flumm & o þiss hallf þatt oþerr. **1340** *Ayenb.* 256 Þis waye ne ssel hongi of þis half ne of yend half, ariȝthalf ne alefthalf. **13..** *Ball. on Scottish Wars* 91 (Ritson) On yonde-alf Humbre. **1375** BARBOUR *Bruce* XVII. 191 Nane that wes that tyme wonand On ȝond half Tweid durst weill apeir. **1495** *Trevisa's Barth. De P.R.* XV. lxxxii. (W. de W.) H iij, The next party therof beerith corne... The yonde [*Bodl. MS.* ȝendre] party toward Mundia is ocupied wᵗ beestis. **1553** *Douglas' Æneis* VI. v. 166 Vncallit on the ȝound bray wald thou be? **1561** *Reg. Privy Council Scot.* I. 194 Beneficit men on the yond syde of the Month [*sc.* Grampians]. **1596** DALRYMPLE tr. *Leslie's Hist. Scot.* (S.T.S.) II. 122 To this end Andro Bartayne saylet with a multitud of marineris to the ȝond syd. **1623** WEBSTER *Duchess Malfi* V. iii, To yond side o' th' riuer lies a wall.

2. = YON *a.* 1.

Rarely preceded by *the*, as in quot. *c* 1380 (cf. YONDER *a.* 1 b).

a **1300** *Cursor M.* 8743 Me think sua, if yee rede, þe child be nawight don to ded, Bot he be yoldon to yond wijf. *c* **1330** *Arth. & Merl.* 5862 Ȝond men ledeþ Leodegan Ybounden toward king Rion. *c* **1380** *Sir Ferumb.* 5367 Fro þe ȝond pauyllons prykeþ a knyȝt. *c* **1400** *Destr. Troy* 3160 And prise of þis prouynse are in yond proude yle. *c* **1500** *Melusine* 70 Lepe on horsbak and ryde on your way to mete yonde straungers. **1583** GOLDING *Calvin on Deut.* iv. 5 In a Countrie where there is a Prince, euerie man may well say, yondsame is the king, yondsame is the Prince. **1602** SHAKS. *Ham.* I. i. 36 When yond same Starre that's Westward from the Pole Had made his course. *a* **1616** BEAUM. & FL. *Bonduca* III. iii, The Roman is advanc'd from yound' his bow. **1641** BROME *Joviall Crew* II, But do you see yon'd Fellow? **1672** DRYDEN *Assignation* II. ii, There's the Wall: Behind yond' Pane of it we'll set up the Ladder. **1708** *Brit. Apollo* No. 67. 3/2 Yond Azure Roof. **1886** BRIERLEY *Cast upon World* xiv, I'd rayther live at yond farmhouse than here.

B. *pron.* (the adj. used *absol.*) = YON *pron.*

In early use preceded by *the.*

a **1250** *Owl & Night.* 119 Iwis hit was ure oȝe broþer þe ȝond [*Jesus MS.* þat yeonde] þat haved þat grete heued. *c* **1350** *Will. Palerne* 3052 Þe ȝond is þat semly and his selue make. *c* **1520** SKELTON *Magnyf.* 780 Who is yonde that for the dothe call? **1601** SHAKS. *All's Well* III. v. 85 Yonds that same knaue That leades him to these places. **1623** WEBSTER *Duchess Malfi* V. iii, Yond's the Cardinall's window. **1886** BRIERLEY *Cast upon World* ii, Come, Tummy, let's goo,.. I conno abide t' yer yond.

†**yond**, *a.*² *Obs. pseudo-arch.* Spenserian word, with the sense 'furious, savage', due to misunderstanding of a passage containing YOND *a.*¹ or *adv.*, prob. the following:—

Beth egre as is a Tygre yond in Ynde (Chaucer *Clerk's T.* 1143).

1590 SPENSER *F.Q.* II. viii. 40 Like a Lion, which hath long time saught His robbed whelpes, and at the last them fond .., then wexeth wood and yond. *Ibid.* III. vii. 26 As Florimell fled from that Monster yond. **1600** FAIRFAX *Tasso* I. lv, Those three brethren, Lombards fierce and yond [orig. *i tre fratei lombardi al chiaro mondo Involi*].

yond, *prep.* and *adv. Obs.* exc. *dial.* Forms: 1 **ȝeond, ȝiond, ȝeondan, iand,** 2–3 **ȝeond,** 3 **ȝeont, þuond,** 3–4 **ȝeonde, ȝund, ȝont,** 3–5 (6 *Sc.*) **ȝond,** 4–5 **ȝonde, yonde,** (5 **yande,** 6 *Sc.* **ȝound**), 6, 8–9 *Sc.* **yont,** (prep. only 8 *Sc.* **'yont,** 8–9 **'yond**), 4– **yond.** *β.* 3–4 **ȝend,** 4 **ȝende, ȝent, yent,** (**ȝendis**). [OE. *ȝeond* prep., also *ȝeondan* (cf. BEYOND), corresp. to MLG. *gint, genten, jint* there, LG. *gunt, gunten*, early Flem. *ghins*, Du. *ginds*, Goth. *jaind*: see YON *a.*] **A.** *prep.*

†**1.** Through, throughout, over, across. *Obs.*

c **888** ÆLFRED *Boeth.* xviii. §2 Þæt ȝe woldon eowerne naman tobrædan ȝeond ealle eorþan. *a* **1000** *Gloria* 2 (Gr.) Sy þe wuldor & lof wide ȝeopenod ȝeond ealle þeoda. *c* **1000** *Ags. Gosp.* Matt. xii. 43 He gæð ȝeond driȝe stowa secende reste. *a* **1122** *O.E. Chron.* (Laud MS.) an. 1048 & com þa Eustatius fram ȝeondan sæ sona æfter þam biscop. *c* **1205** LAY. 28 Laȝamon gon liðen wide ȝond þas leode. *Ibid.* 423 Wide ȝend [*c* **1275** ȝeont] þane londe. **13..** *K. Horn* (Harl. MS.) 1078 He sende þo by sonde, ȝend al is londe, after knyhtes to fyhte. *c* **1320** *Cast. Love* 1448 He .. sette tweyne and tweyne to gon Ȝond al þe world to prechen vchon. *c* **1325** *Chron. Eng.* 809 in Ritson *Metr. Rom.* II. 304 He wes.. Cleped yent this lond wide Edmound Irneneside.

2. On (or to) the farther side of, beyond. In later use *poet.*, or *Sc.* (chiefly in form *yont*); often written with apostrophe as if aphetic f. *beyond* or *ayont.*

1388 WYCLIF *Ezra* iv. 16 Thou schalt not haue possessioun biȝende [*v.r.* ȝendis] the flood [Vulg. *trans fluvium*]. **1567** DRANT *Horace, Ep.* I. xi. E ij, If those chaunge weather, not their wit, which yont the sea do run. **1579** HAKE *Newes out of Powles* (1872) E iij b, Thou God of grace,.. yond whome we can not roaue Or raunge aright. **1720** RAMSAY *Rise & Fall of Stocks* 169 'Yond Seas I saw the Upstarts drifting. **1725** —— *Gentle Sheph.* III. ii, A' that's done In ilka place beneath, or yont the moon. *c* **1730** —— *Eclipse* iv, Imprudent men.. Rax yont their reach. **1789** D. DAVIDSON *Seasons* 58 The silent night.. sinks 'yond the western main. **1866** 'SARAH TYTLER' *Days of Yore* IV. iv, She would have a hoard to fill Elspa's drawer 'yont the coast'. *a* **1870** RIDDELL *Poet. Wks.* (1871) II. 317 Desperate deeds 'Yond ocean [they] had been doomed to dare.

B. *adv.* **1.** = YONDER *adv.* 1.

c **1300** *St. Brandan* 1 Seint Brendan the holi man was ȝund of Irlande. *a* **1327** in *Rel. Ant.* I. 123 Ȝent ryd Maximon. *c* **1386** CHAUCER *Knt.'s T.* 241 The fairnesse of that lady þat I see Yond in the gardyn romen to and fro. **1393** LANGL. *P. Pl.* C. XXI. 263 Ihesus as a gyaunt with a gyn comeþ ȝonde [*v.rr.* ȝont, ȝeonde, ȝende, ȝender]. *c* **1475** *Partenay* 5827 Behold yande that hiduous montain. *a* **1553** UDALL *Royster D.* I. ii. (Arb.) 10 Who commeth forth yond from my swete hearte Custance? *a* **1592** GREENE *Jas. IV*, II. ii, Yond comes the messenger of weale or woe. **1610** SHAKS. *Temp.* I. ii. 409 Say what thou see'st yond. **1639** COKAINE *Masque* Poems (1669) 124 Sweet youth! yon'd is your Father, kiss his hand. **1815** SCOTT *Guy M.* iii, Sit down yont there at the door. **1898** HARDY *Wessex Poems* 204 Young Tim away yond.. Through brimble and underwood tears.

b. = YONDER *adv.* 1 b.

c **975** *Rushw. Gosp.* Matt. xxvi. 36 Sittaþ her oþ þæt ic gange ȝeond [*Lindisf.* ðider; *Ags. Gosp. & Hatton* hiderȝeond]. *c* **1350** *Will. Palerne* 263 Goþ yond to a gret lord þat gayly is tyred. *c* **1375** *Cursor M.* 3065 (Fairf.) Lede him ȝonde.

c. †*here and yond*, here and there (*obs.*); *hither and yond* (now *Sc.*), hither and thither. Cf. YON *adv.* b, YONDER *adv.* 1 c.

c **900** tr. *Bæda's Hist.* v. xiii. [xii.] (1890) 428 Ða ahof ic mine eaȝan upp & locade hider & ȝeond. *c* **1250** *Gen. & Ex.* 3851 Her and ȝund ðor he biried lin. **1831** CAMPBELL *Lines on View from St. Leonards* 83 Moored as they cast the shadows of their masts In long array, or hither flit and yond Mysteriously.

2. At or to a distance; (far or farther) away. *far yond*, in an extremely bad state, 'far gone'. In later use *Sc.*

13.. *K. Horn* (Harl. MS.) 1261 Ich eode mony a myle, wel fer ȝent by weste [*Camb. MS.* Wel feor bi ȝonde weste]. **1513** DOUGLAS *Æneis* XII. Prol. 9 Nor frawart Saturn.. Durst langar.. appeir, Bot stall abak ȝond in his regioun far Behynd the circulat warld of Jupiter. *a* **1665** W. GUTHRIE *Serm.* (1709) 24 (Jam.) When he that reproves in the gate makes himself a prey, then they are far yond, when they refuse to return. **1721** RAMSAY *Prosp. Plenty* 19 Sweet prolifick Plains.. Stand yont; for Amphitrite claims our Sang. **1893** STEVENSON *Catriona* xxx, I'll be getting a wee yont amang the bents, so that I can see what way James goes.

yonder ('jɒndə(r)), *adv.* and *a.* (*pron., sb.*) Now only *literary* and somewhat *arch.*, or *dial.* Forms: *α.* 4–5 (6 *Sc.*) **ȝonder, -ir,** (4 **ȝionder, ȝundir, yunder,** 5 **ȝondur, -yr, yondur**), 5–6 **yondre,** (6 **ȝondar,** *Sc.* **ȝounder,** 7 **younder**), 4– **yonder;** 4 **yonþer,** 6–7 **yonther;** 6, 9 *dial.* **yander.** *β.* 4 **ȝender,** 5 **-ir, -yr, yendre, yeinder,** 5–6 **yender,** 7 *dial.* **yeander,** 9 *dial.* **yinder.** [ME. *ȝonder, ȝender*, corresp. to OS. *gendra* adj. on this side, MLG. *ginder, gender*, LG. *gunter*, Du., WFris. *ginder*, Goth. *jaindrê* (cf. *hidrê* HITHER): see YON *a.*]

A. *adv.* **1. a.** At or in that place; there; usually implying that the object spoken of is at some distance but within sight: Over there, away there.

α. a **1300** *Cursor M.* 2717 Þan asked þai quare was sarra. Abraham said, 'yonder wit-in'. *Ibid.* 3148 'Yonder vp,' he said, 'on yon fell Sal þou bren þi sun for me'. **13..** *Ibid.* 19899 (Edinb.) Lo! ȝionder þre Men.. er sende to seke þe. **13..** *Ibid.* 14976 (Gött.) Þe stede es yonþer, lo! *c* **1380** WYCLIF *Sel. Wks.* II. 402 Sum men seien þat he is ȝundir at Rome. *c* **1386** CHAUCER *Man of Law's T.* 920 Whos is that faire child that stondeth yonder? **1523** LD. BERNERS *Froiss.* I. lxxxii. 43/1, I wyll nat departe hens tyll I se what company is yonder within the castell. **1598** SHAKS. *Merry W.* II. i. 163 Looke who comes yonder. **1641** BROME *Joviall Crew* I. (1652) C 2 b, I left the merry Griggs.. in such a Hoigh younder! **1667** DAVENANT & DRYDEN *Tempest* IV. iii. (1670) 63 Mark her behaviour too, she's tippling yonder with the serving-men. **1766** GOLDSM. *Vicar W.* xii, But, as I live, yonder comes Moses. **1818** SCOTT *Rob Roy* xxvi, 'The limes', he assured us, 'were from his own little farm yonder-awa' (indicating the West Indies with a knowing shrug of his shoulders). **1863** READE *Hard Cash* x, You sits yander fit to bust: but.. ye never offers me none on't. **1876** MISS BRADDON *J. Haggard's Dau.* x, To the white cottage yonder on the lower ground across the meadows.

β. **13..** *E.E. Allit. P.* B. 1617 Þaȝ þe mater be merk þat merked is ȝender. *c* **1380** WYCLIF *Sel. Wks.* II. 138 Þis man is Jesus þat stondiþ ȝendre on þe banke. *c* **1450** LYDG. *Life Our Lady* lii. (MS. Ashm. 39), Loke vp yender & se the sercle of golde. *c* **1485** *Digby Myst.* III. 1438 Yender is þe lond of satyllye. **1674** RAY *N.C. Words* 55 *Yeander*, Yonder, *Var. Dial.* *a* **1825** FORBY *Voc. E. Anglia, Yinder, adv.* yonder.

b. To that place; thither.

c **1300** *Havelok* 922 Go þu yunder, and sit þore. **13..** *Cursor M.* 3065 (Gött.) Lede him ȝender [*Cott.* yonder]. *c* **1489** CAXTON *Sonnes of Aymon* iv. 127 Lady, I goo yonder wythout. **1535** COVERDALE *Gen.* xxii. 5 As for me and the childe, we wyl go yonder.

c. in phr. *here and yonder, hither and yonder*: cf. YON *adv.* b, YOND *adv.* 1 c.

1412–20 LYDG. *Chron. Troy* I. 4291 As he rod among hem here & ȝonder. *c* **1485** *Digby Myst.* III. 1346 Now have þe dysypylles take þer passage to dyvers contreys her and ȝondyr. **1883** *Century Mag.* XXVI. 221/2 Gangs of street paviors were seen and heard here, there, and yonder.

†**2.** Farther. *Obs. rare.*

1387 TREVISA *Higden* (Rolls) II. 33 Som men wolde mene þat Loegria endeþ at Homber, and streccheþ no ȝonder [*Caxton* ferther] northward.

B. *adj.* **1.** With *the.* **a.** Farther, more distant, 'other': = YON *a.* 2, YOND *a.*¹ 1.

13.. *Gaw. & Gr. Knt.* 2440 Syn ȝe be lorde of þe ȝonder londe. **1387** TREVISA *Higden* (Rolls) I. 173 Þere is anoþer Pannonia be ȝonde þe wateres Meotides in þe ȝonder Scythia. *Ibid.* 299 Þe hyder bygynneþ from þe pleynes and valeys of Pireneies... Þe ȝonder Spayne conteyneþ þe west partye anoon to þe see Gaditanus. *c* **1450** in Aungier *Syon* (1840) 345 The seyd brother schal se that ther be a lectron set in the ȝendyr corner of the ambytus for redyng of the gosbel towarde the este. **1513** DOUGLAS *Æneis* VI. v. 166 Vncallit, on the ȝondir bray wald thow be. **1609** *Reg. Mag. Sig. Scot.* 51/2 Terras de Bruntskeath,.. Over et Nethir Lagane,.. Hither and Yonther Barscheuallis. **1899** MRS. HUGH FRASER *Dipl. Wife in Japan* xxxv. II. 313 His dead name, the one by which his shadowy companions call him in the yonder world. **1909** MEREDITH '*The Years had worn their seasons' belt*' ix, O she was fair as a beech in May With the sun on the yonder side. **1910** *Dublin Rev.* Jan. 64 Something on the yonder side of imagery.

b. = 2.

c **1374** CHAUCER *Troylus* II. 1188 Nece who hath arayed þus The yonder hous þat stant a-forn yeyn vs? *c* **1380** *Sir Ferumb.* 930 Olyuer my felaw ys take! y-seeþ þat ȝonder company how þay him ledeþ away. *c* **1400** *Rom. Rose* 4018 The yonder man to shenden vs alle. *a* **1425** *Cursor M.* 1251 (Trin.) Towarde þe eest ende of þe ȝondur [*Cott., Fairf.* þis, *Gött.* þe] vale. *c* **1430** *Syr Gener.* (Roxb.) 4727 Toward the ost of the yendre kinges Ne made I neuer louely lookinges. *c* **1480** HENRYSON *Paddock & Mouse* 77 That thow wald gyde me to ȝone ȝonder land [*Bann.* How thow wald gyd me to þe ȝondir land].

2. That is yonder; usually, and in later literary use always, implying that the thing spoken of is at some distance but within sight: cf. YON *a.* 1.

α. c **1400** *Destr. Troy* 8837 We hade hertely no hope.. Yonder toun for to take. *a* **1413** *Anturs of Arthur* (Ireland MS.) xlix, Ȝondur byrnes [*Thornton MS.* ȝone beryns] in batelle, that bidus on the bent. *c* **1450** *Mirk's Festial* 39 Hit wer almes forto ȝeue ȝondyr pore man warmer cloþes þen he haþe. **1523** LD. BERNERS *Froiss.* I. lxxxvii. h iij, It shuld be great honour for vs if we might delyuer out of daunger yonther two knyghtes. *a* **1533** —— *Huon* xxiv. 70 Yonder company are fooles. **1590** SHAKS. *Mids. N.* III. ii. 61 Yet you, the murtherer, looke as bright, as cleare, As yonder Venus, in her glimmering spheare. **1615** JACKSON *Creed* IV. vi. §7 This is profitable, That is pleasant, we shall not then say, but yonder other truly good and honest. **1671** MILTON *Samson* 3 Yonder bank hath choice of sun or shade. **1770** GOLDSM. *Des. Vill.* 219 Near yonder thorn, that lifts its head on high. **1842** TENNYSON *E. Gray* i, Sweet Emma Moreland of yonder town Met me walking on yonder way. **1850** —— *In Mem.* xv, To-night the winds begin to rise And roar from yonder dropping day.

β. c **1440** *Generydes* 2777 On yender towre on highe. *? a* **1500** *Chester Pl.* (Shaks. Soc.) iii. 52 Mother, my father after thee sende, And byddes thee into yeinder shippe wende. **1563** GOOGE *Eglogs* i. (Arb.) 32 The Hylles.. that ioyne to yender towne. **1755** *Gammer Gurton* I. v, Chaue tost and tumbled yender heap ouer and ouer againe.

†**3.** (with *this* or *that*) Qualifying *day, night*: Lately past, 'other'. (Cf. ENDER *a.*, HINDER *a.* 2, and YONDERS.) *Obs.*

a **1425** *Cursor M.* 4561 (Trin.) Me pouȝte þat þis ȝonder [*v.r.* ender] nyȝt I coom in a medewe briȝt. *Ibid.* 13559 Art þou not he þat ȝondir day miȝtes not se? *a* **1450** *Le Morte Arth.* 1105, I gabbyd on hym thys ȝendyr day.

C. *pron.* (*sing.* or *pl.*: †also with *the*: absol. use of B. 1 b, 2): = YON *pron.* Now *dial.*

c **1375** *Cursor M.* 4891 (Fairf.) Ȝonder ar theues we lelmen wende. *c* **1430** *Chev. Assigne* 232 And þe ȝondur is my qwene betryce she hette. **1855** BROWNING *Grammarian's Funeral* 7 Look out if yonder be not day again Rimming the rock-row! **1880** *Sat. Rev.* 2 Oct. 423/2 A closely-shaven curate, who was walking down a street clad in his cassock, was once horrified by hearing shouted across the road an inquiry whether 'yonder was a lad or a lass'.

D. as *sb.* **1.** (*nonce-use.*) Something beyond.

1888 MEREDITH *Hymn to Colour* vii, His touch is infinite and lends A yonder to all ends.

2. [After quot. 1939.] The far and trackless distance; usu. with preceding adj.

1939 R. CRAWFORD *Army Air Corps* (song), Off we go in to the wild blue yonder, Climbing high into the sun. **1948** *N.Y. World Telegram* 30 Dec. 11/6 A pilot.. took wing into that wonderful yonder on a training flight. **1967** C. COCKBURN *I, Claud* xxxiii. 410 The ex-editor of *The Week* had suddenly appeared out of the deep green yonder of Ireland. **1974** *Times* 26 Feb. 12/3 Mr. Wilson's.. policy for controlling inflation, which consists of holding down prices by law while letting wages go up, up, up into the wide blue yonder. **1979** 'D. KYLE' *Green River High* viii. 103 My father had vanished into the great green yonder of a million square miles of jungle. **1985** W. GOLDING *Egyptian Journal* iv. 57 Minya is a centre for scarpering, for fading away, for disappearing into the blue yonder.

Hence '**yonderly** *a., dial.*, 'distant', reserved, sullen; depressed, gloomy, melancholy; †**yondermair** *adv. Sc.*, farther; †**yondermest** *a. Sc.*, farthest, most distant (cf. YONDMOST); †**yonderward** *adv.* [cf. Du. *ginderwaerts*], in yonder or the other direction, thither; farther off; †**yonderway**, by that way, in that manner.

1828 *Craven Gloss.*, **Yonderly*, grave, sullen, distant. I have not often heard this word. **1863** WAUGH *Lanc. Songs* 28 Thae's looked very yonderly mony a day. **1513** DOUGLAS *Æneis* VIII. xi. 48 Syne *ȝonder mayr was schapin in the feild The dansand prestis, clepit Salii. **1808** JAMIESON s.v. *Yound, Sit yontermert*,.. sit farther off. **1513** DOUGLAS *Æneis* VIII. xii. 31 The *ȝondermaist [*v.r.* The ȝoundermest] pepill, clepit Baktranis. *Ibid.* X. vi. 148 Nou presis this syde, and now *ȝonderwart. **1535** COVERDALE *1 Sam.* xx. 37 The arowe lyeth yonderwarde before the. **1570** LEVINS *Manip.* 197/7 *Yonderway, *illac, illo modo.*

†**yonders**, *a. Obs. rare*⁻¹. **a.** = YONDER *a.* 3. (Cf. *enders*, ENDER *a.*) **b.** Next following.

c **1510** *Songs* (MS. Royal, App. 58) in *Anglia* XII. 265 This yonders nyght I herd a wyght most heuyly complayne.

a **1650** *Sir Lambewell* 232 in Furniv. & Hales *Percy Folio* (1867) I. 153, I shall die this yenders night.

'yondmost, *a. Sc. ? Obs.* Also 7 **yonmest**. [f. YOND *a.* + -MOST.] Farthest, most distant; farthest advanced, extreme, utmost; also *absol.* (*the yondmost*) = the uttermost.

1608 *Burgh Rec. Glasgow* (1876) 286 It is maist necesser that ane bulwork or butradge be bigit befoir the yonmest piller of the said brig except ane. **1640** R. BAILLIE *Canterb. Self-convict.* 3 They..at last have wrought their yondmost myne to that perfection, that it is now readie to spring under our wals. **1650** MONTROSE in M. Napier *M. & Covenanters* (1838) II. 539 That then you should have..entered into a League and Covenant with them against the King, was the thing I judged my duty to oppose to the yondmost. a **1653** BINNING *Serm.* (1845) 468 A Christian assaulted with many temptations should unite his strength and try the yondmost. a **1658** DURHAM *Comm. Rev.* VI. vi. (1660) 360 Death and the Grave came as the yondmost step of temporall affliction. **1716** WISHART *Theologia* 393 Here the Mercy of God is gone to the Yondmost.

yondsame: see YOND *a.*[1] 2.

†**yondward**, *adv. Obs.* In 3 **ȝeondward**, 5 **yondewarde**. [f. YOND + -WARD. Cf. (M)Du. *ginswaert(s*, Goth. *jaindwairþs*. Cf. YONWARD.] In a direction away from the speaker; thither.

c **1205** LAY. 30781 Þe an hine putte hiderward and þe oðer hine putte ȝeondward. **1485** CAXTON *Trevisa's Higden* II. ii. (1527) 59 b, Antypodes..theyr fete towarde oures and theyr hede yondewarde [**1387** TREVISA ȝonward].

yone, obs. form of YON.

yo-necked, corrupt or dial. f. EWE-NECKED.

1836 HALIBURTON *Clockm.* Ser. I. ix, The nasty yo necked, cat hammed,..good for nothin brutes.

†**y-oned** [OE. *ȝeáned*: Y- 4, ONE *v.*], united.

1387 TREVISA *Higden* (Rolls) VI. 341 Ȝe moste commune wiþ us þat ȝe be i-oned [*MS. β* yooned; *γ* y-oned] to Crist his lymes. *Ibid.* VII. App. 534 He helde..these bischopriches so ooned [*MS. γ* y-oned] with thre cuntrayes that longed therto.

†**yong**, *sb. Obs.* Forms: 1 *Northumb.* (hin)iong, **ȝeong**, 3 **ȝeong(e**, (**ȝoing**?, **ȝeonc-**), 3-4 **ȝong(e**. [OE. (Northumb.) *ȝeong*, and in comp. *hiniong* departure, *inȝeong* entrance, *útȝeong* exit, *ymbȝeong* 'decursus, ambitus': of obscure origin; cf. next.] Going; gait; travelling, journey; course.

ȝongdawes, Rogation Days; cf. GANG-DAYS.

c **950** *Lindisf. Gosp.* Mark i. 3 *Rectas facite semitas eius*, rehta doeð *vel* wyrcas stiȝ *vel* ȝeongas his. *Ibid.* Luke ii. 44 *Uenerunt iter diei*, cuomon ȝeong dæȝes. *c* **1205** LAY. 1298 Þeonene he ferden forð wel feole dawen ȝong. a **1225** *Leg. Kath.* 500 Earen buten herunge, honden buten felunge, fet buten ȝonge. *Ibid.* 569 Ich..wule..wið kinewurðe ȝeoues ȝelden ow hehliche ower ȝong hider. a **1225** *Ancr. R.* 412 Uridawes and umbridawes and ȝoing dawes [*v.rr.* ȝong dahes, ȝeoncdaȝes]. a **1300** *Sayings of Bernard* 184 (MS. Laud 108) in Herrig's *Archiv* LII. 33 Ȝis ridingue and þis proute ȝong. a **1327** in *Rel. Ant.* I. 124 Nou nabbe y nout that ȝong, That speche, ne that song.

** Illustration of compounds (see etym. above).

a **900** *Bede's Death-song* in *O.E. Texts* 149 Aer his hiniongæ. *c* **950** *Lindisf. Gosp.* Mark Introd. 4 Of uneaðalice wlonga innȝeonges in ric godes. *Ibid.* Matt. xxii. 9 Ðeongas forðon to utȝeong ðære weȝana [*Rushw.* utgengum]. *c* **1205** LAY. 28370 Þa burhweren..warnden him inȝeong. a **1225** *Ancr. R.* 62 Þurh eie þurles deað haueð hire inȝong into þe soule. *Ibid.* 206 To openen þet inȝong & leten in sunne. a **1240** *Sawles Ward* in *O.E. Hom.* I. 247 Forte sechen in ȝong abute þe wahes. *c* **1320** *Cast. Love* 878 Þorw þe faste ȝat he con in teo, And at þe out-ȝong he lette faste beo.

†**yong**, *v. Obs.* Forms: 1 *Northumb.* **ȝeonga**, 3 **ȝunge**, **ȝeonge**, **-ȝenge**, **-yenge** [see MISYENGE, to go astray], 3-4 **ȝonge**, 4-5 **yonge**, 5 **ȝynge**; *pa. pple.* 3 **-ȝeong**, **-e(n**, **-ed**. [OE. (Northumb.) *ȝeonga*, and in comp. *foreȝeonga* to go forward, *inȝeonga* to enter, *útȝeonga* to go out, **ymbȝeonga* to surround (pa. t. *ymbéade*): cf. prec.] *intr.* To go.

c **950** *Lindisf. Gosp.* Mark xiv. 42 *Surgite eamus*, arisað gæ we *vel* wutun ȝeonga. *c* **1205** LAY. 8436 Euelin i-seh enne gume ȝungen him bi-halfues. *c* **1275** *Ibid.* 9061 Nas hit noht longe þat he ne com ȝonge. **13..** *Pol. Songs* (Camden) 216 Now Kyng Hobbe in the mures ȝongeth. a **1375** *Joseph Arim.* 313 Þenne þei wenden heore wei and to þe court ȝongen. *c* **1440** *Pallad. on Husb.* IV. 641 And wrie hem fest, lest wynd therynto yonge. a **1450** MYRC *Par. Pr.* 1851 Make þy clerk before þe ȝynge, To bere lyȝt, and belle rynge.

** Illustration of compounds (see etym. above; also ME. pa. pples. *aȝeong(en)* passed, *biȝeonge* surrounded).

c **950** *Lindisf. Gosp.* Matt. xix. 23 Wlonc uneaðe innȝeongas in ric heofna. *c* **1205** LAY. 9364 Þe sæ wes iȝeonged [*MS.* -eð], þe scipen stoden a londe. *Ibid.* 23557 Þa feouwer wiken weoren aȝonged [*c* **1275** agon]. *Ibid.* 23702 In þan æitlonde þe mid watere is biȝeonge. *Ibid.* 28893 þe alde king deȝede, his daȝes weoren aȝeongen. *Ibid.* 30552 Þa niȝen dæȝes weoren aȝeong. *c* **1440** *Pallad. on Husb.* II. 214 Vp they goth vche as her seed is, And letuce in their leues vmbiyonge. *Ibid.* IV. 437 With seefroth other haue hem vmbiyonge.

yong(e, **ȝong(e**, etc., obs. ff. YOUNG, etc.

†**yongate**, *adv. Sc. Obs.* In 4 **ȝongat**. [f. YON *a.* + GATE *sb.*[2] 9 b.] In that way.

1375 BARBOUR *Bruce* III. 171 It semys it likis the perfay, That he slayis ȝongat our mengȝe.

yongfrow: see YUFFROUW.

yongker, obs. form of YOUNKER.

‖**yoni** ('jəʊnɪ). [Skr.] A figure or symbol of the female organ of generation as an object of veneration among the Hindus and others. Hence **'yonic** *a.*

1799 *Asiatick Researches* III. 363 The navel of Vishnu, by which they mean the *os tincæ*, is worshipped as one and the same with the sacred *yóni*. **1879** M. MACFIE *Relig. Parall.* 27 The *yonic* or moon-worshippers of Chaldea... The yonic symbolism professed by their remote ancestors in Turkestan, who were originally worshippers of the female principle. **1906** WHATHAM in *Amer. Jrnl. Relig. & Psychol.* II. 44 In nature-worship, all natural orifices were reverenced as representing the yoni of the mother-earth goddess.

yonike, obs. form of IONIC *a.*[1]

1598 FLORIO, *Cartoccio*,..a kinde of yonike worke in building.

yonk, yonker: see JUNK *sb.*[3], YOUNKER.

yonks (jɒŋks). *slang.* [Origin unknown.] A long time, 'ages'; chiefly in phr. ***for yonks***.

1968 *Daily Mirror* 27 Aug. 7/1, I rang singer Julie Driscoll... She said: 'I haven't heard from you for yonks.' **1977** 'J. GASH' *Judas Pair* iv. 54 Any man that says he can remain celibate for yonks on end is not quite telling the truth. **1980** *Oxford Times* 20 June 18 Even though Gabriel left Genesis yonks ago, his music and particularly his vocals remind one of Genesis. **1984** *Listener* 10 May 32/2 The English have been writing poetry for yonks, and have become damned good at it too. **1985** A. BLOND *Book Book* ix. 142 Nicholas Bagnall and David Holloway have run the *Telegraph's* book pages for yonks.

yonnie ('jɒnɪ). *Austral. slang.* [Origin unknown.] A small stone; a pebble.

1941 BAKER *Dict. Austral. Slang* 84 *Yonnie*, a small stone, a pebble. **1979** *Sun-Herald* (Sydney) 18 Mar. 79 There were two lamp posts..each equipped with one electric bulb... Young couples courting would smash each of them with a well-aimed 'yonnie' on pay night.

yons (**ȝons**), obs. form of ONCE *adv.*

c **1400** tr. *Secr. Secr., Gov. Lordsh.* 100 And he ȝons put him to folk of disceplyne.

†**yonsame** (in rustic speech), = *yon same*: see YON *a.* 1.

1565 GOLDING *Ovid's Met.* II. (1567) 26 Vnder yonsame hill they were, and vnder yonsame hill Cham zure they are.

yonside ('jɒnsaɪd), *sb.*, *adv.*, and *prep.* [The phrase *yon side* (YON *a.*, SIDE *sb.*[1]) taken as one word: cf. INSIDE, OUTSIDE. Cf. LG. *gunsiet*, *-syts*, G. *jenseits*.] **A.** *sb.* The farther side; the other side.

1535 COVERDALE *Hos.* v. 8 Crie out at Bethauen vpon the yonside of Ben Iamin. **1856** MEREDITH *Shav. Shagpat, Well of Paravid* 156 The sun..sank on the yonside of the mountain. **1912** *Sat. Rev.* 1 June 690/2 Visions of the things of the 'yonside' as his Lincolnshire flock love to term the hereafter.

B. *adv.* On the farther side (*of*).

1681 W. ROBERTSON *Phraseol. Gen.* 1361 Yonside, *ab illa regione*. **1878–9** LANIER *Street-Cries, How Love looked for Hell* 23 As I rode down, and the River was black, And yonside, lo! an endless wrack. **1901** H. TRENCH *Deirdre Wed* II. 12 Yonside of Assaroe the swineherd found her.

C. *prep.* On the farther side of; beyond.

1856 MEREDITH *Shav. Shagpat, Genie Karaz* 147 A phial full of the waters of Paravid from the wells in the mountain yonside the desert.

†**yonste**. *Obs. rare.* [ad. early Du. *gonst*, now *gunst* favour; cf. YON *v.*] Favour.

1481 CAXTON *Reynard* viii. (Arb.) 14 Ye shal wel vnderstande the very yonste and good wyl that I bere to you ward.

yont, var. YOND.

yont(e, **yonture**, obs. ff. JOINT *sb.*, JOINTURE.

1422 YONGE tr. *Secr. Secr.* 225 That haue..moore flesshe fro the Ioyntures vpwarde, than fro the yontures downwarde. **1597** *Pilgr. Parnass.* I. 62 Whose yonts youe see are dryde, benumd and coulde.

yonthe (**ȝonþe**), var. YOUNGTH *Obs.*, youth.

yonther, obs. form of YONDER.

†**yonward**, *adv. Obs. rare*[−1]. [f. YON + -WARD.] = YONDWARD.

1387 TREVISA *Higden* (Rolls) II. 205 [Antipodes] here feet toward oure, and hire heed ȝonward.

yoo, yooff, yook, yool(e: see EWE *sb.*[1], YEA, YOUF *v.*, YUKE, YULE.

yoo-hoo ('juːhuː), *int.* (*sb.*) [Cf. YOHO *int.*] A call made to attract attention, esp. to one's arrival or presence; also as *sb.*

1924 *Dialect Notes* V. 280 *Yoo-hoo* (call). **1926** *New Yorker* 2 Jan. 18/3 Yoo-hoo! When did your school let out? **1937** M. ALLINGHAM *Case of Late Pig* vii. 49 He opened the breakfast-room door. 'Yoo-hoo!' said someone inside. **1946** A. MARSHALL in Murdoch & Drake-Brockman *Austral. Short Stories* (1951) 316 There was a faint 'yoo-hoo!' from behind us. We all turned. **1959** L. LEE *Cider with Rosie* 150 I'm coming—yoo-hoo! Just mislaid my gloves. **1959** A. WESKER *Roots* I. 16 Girl's Voice (off): Yoo-hoo! Any one home? **1970** J. UPDIKE *Bech* 182 Mildred..waved an alabaster, muscular arm: 'Yoo-hoo, Henry, over here.' **1973** E. BULLINS *Theme is Blackness* 62 Yoo Hoo up there! Someone will be up to give you a hand with the rest of those things. **1983** 'J. GASH' *Sleepers of Erin* viii. 61 Patrick.. trilled a roguish yoo-hoo.

Hence **'yoohoo**, **'yoo-hoo** *v. intr.* and *trans.*, to call 'yoo-hoo!' (to); **'yoohooing** *vbl. sb.*

1948 D. BALLANTYNE *Cunninghams* 14 He..yoohooed for a chair. **1954** *Partisan Rev.* Nov.–Dec. 599 Life, despite their frantic yoohooing, had passed them by. **1957** J. KEROUAC *On Road* I. xiii. 88 Then they yoohooed us. **1969** 'E. LATHEN' *When in Greece* xxii. 231 Leaving the ladies to their yoohooing, the three men followed the officer's directions. **1978** 'J. GASH' *Gold from Gemini* iii. 24 Patrick yoo-hooed me over to his place. **1982** —— *Firefly Gadroon* xiii. 122 Margaret blew a kiss... Patrick yoohooed.

yoolughan, var. ULLAGONE.

yoong, **yoonker**, obs. ff. YOUNG, YOUNKER.

yoop (juːp), *sb.* and *int.* Also **youp**. A word expressing the sound made by convulsive sobbing; also as an exclamation.

1848 THACKERAY *Van. Fair* i, The hysterical yoops of Miss Swartz. **1854** —— *Rose & Ring* xix, Mrs. Jenkins, giving a dreadful youp, fell down in a fit. **1865** DICKENS *Mut. Fr.* III. vii, 'Yoop!' cried Wegg. 'You're there, are you?'

yoore, **yoow**, obs. forms of YORE, YOU.

yop, var. YAWP, YAUP *sb.*

yop(e)indail(l, etc.: see YOKINDALE.

†**y-opened** [Y- 4], opened.

1297, etc. [see OPEN *v.*] *c* **1450** *Two Cookery-bks.* 114 Yopened & ywasshe clene.

yopon, **yor** (**ȝor**), **Yordan**, obs. ff. YAPON, YOUR, JORDAN.

†**y-ordayned**, **-deined**, ME. pa. pple. of ORDAIN *v.*

yore (jɔə(r)), *adv.* (*a.*) *arch.* Forms: 1 **ȝeara**, **ȝara**, **iara**, **ȝeare**, **ȝearo**, 3 **ȝar**, **ȝeare**, **ȝaure**, 3-5 **ȝare**, 3-6 **yare**, **ȝore**, 4 **yar**, 5 **yoore**, 6 **ȝoir**, **youre**, 4- **yore**. [OE. *ȝeára*, also *ȝeáre*, *ȝeáro*, advb. formations of obscure origin.]

†**1.** A long time ago; of old; freq. strengthened by *full*; also in collocation with *ago*, *agone*. Phr. ***it is*** (***gone***) ***yore*** (***that***...): long ago. *Obs.*

Beowulf 2664 Swa ðu on ȝeoȝuðfeore ȝeara ȝecwæde. *c* **900** tr. *Bæda's Hist.* II. xiii, Ðeare ic þæt onȝeat þæt ðæt nowiht wæs þæt we beeodan. *Ibid.* III. xxii, Is se [*sc.* tun] be ðam wealle þe ȝearo Romane Breotone ealonde begyrdon twelf milum fram eastsæ. *c* **975** *Rushw. Gosp.* Matt. xi. 21 *Olim*, Iara. a **1000** *Boeth. Metr.* i. 1 Hit wæs ȝeara iu ðætte Gotan eastan of Sciððia sceldas læddon. *c* **1050** *Voc.* in Wr.-Wülcker 427/6 *Iam*, ȝeara, oþþe ȝeoȝara. *c* **1205** LAY. 4650 Þe king him ȝef Delcan þe ȝare wes mi leouemon. a **1225** *Ancr. R.* 88 Ȝare hit is þet ich wuste herof. a **1300** *Floriz & Bl.* 653 Nis noȝt ȝore þat i ne com And fond hire wiþ hordom. *c* **1386** CHAUCER *Sir Thopas* Prol. 19 (Harl. 7334) Other tale certes can I noon But of a rym I lerned ȝore agoon. *c* **1400** *Gamelyn* 257 Sithen I wrastelet first it is gone ȝore. *c* **1400** *Destr. Troy* 13968 Til a ȝer was full yore yarkit to end, And a halfe, er þat end happit to fare. a **1400–50** *Wars Alex.* 1008 All þe ȝeris of oure ȝouthe es ȝare syne passid. a **1425** *Cursor M.* 5672 (Trin.) Woltou me sle herfore As þou didest þe egipcian not ȝore? **1426** LYDG. *De Guil. Pilgr.* 5696 And for that skyle gon ful yore,..I callede the my paramour. ? a **1500** *Chester Pl.* (E.E.T.S.) xx. 27 He dyed on Rood, gone is not yore. **1513** DOUGLAS *Æneis* XIII. Pref. 3 Ȝoir ago, in myne ondantit ȝowth. *c* **1532** DU WES *Introd. Fr.* in *Palsgr.* 927 Yare so, *aincois ainsy*. a **1542** WYATT *Poems*, '*Ryght true it is*', Ryght true it is, and said full yore agoo. a **1550** in *Dunbar's Poems* (S.T.S.) 320 The Gret Forlore Of Babylon, that I full yore Espousit. **1613** CAWDREY *Table Alph.*, *Yore*, long agoe, before.

†**2.** In time past; formerly, before. *Obs.*

a **1250** *Owl & Night.* 1180 Ich not ȝef þu were ȝaure prest. *c* **1350** *Will. Palerne* 1503 God..graunt ȝou ioye, For þe worchipe þat ȝe han wruȝt to me ȝore. *c* **1375** *Sc. Leg. Saints* xxiii. (*vii Sleperis*) 258 [He] lukyt vpe, & saw þare þe sammyne takine he saw yare. *c* **1400** *Rom. Rose* 7597 Thus seide I now, and haue seid yore. *c* **1450** *Cursor M.* 2651 (Laud) Abraham hast þou yore by cald, That name no lengger shalt þou hald. ? a **1500** *Chester Pl.* (E.E.T.S.) xxiv. 513 Doe as thou hast yore behight. **1570** LEVINS *Manip.* 174/34 Yore, before, *ante*, *prius*. **1574** *Mirr. Mag.*, *Kimarus* xii, A iust rewarde, for so vniust a life, No worse a death, then I deserued yore.

†**3.** For a long time (past, or *rarely* to come).

c **1275** *XI Pains of Hell* 23 in *O.E. Misc.* 147 In helle ich habbe yare ibeo. a **1300** *Vox & Wolf* 169 in Hazl. *E.P.P.* I. 63 The wolf haueth hounger swithe gret, For he nedde ȝare i-ete. *c* **1386** CHAUCER *Clerk's T.* 12 Thus in delit he lyueth and hath doon yoore. *c* **1430** LYDG. *Chichevache & Bycorne* in Dodsley *O. Pl.* (1827) XII. 304 And thus ye stonde and have don yore. **1522** *World & Child* C j, In englonde haue I dwelled yore.

4. ***of yore***: **a.** in *advb.* use: Of old, in time long past, anciently, formerly. Also † ***of yore ago(ne***, † ***long yore***: long ago.

a **1375** *Joseph Arim.* 317 Werdes of Ebreu weren I-writen of ȝore. *c* **1385** CHAUCER *L.G.W.* Prol. 13 For that he say it nat of ȝore a-go. **1430–40** LYDG. *Bochas* IX. xiv. (1554) 202 b/2 She was the same that of yore agon, Unworthelye sate in Peters place. **1579** SPENSER *Sheph. Cal.* July 116 The sayncts Which han be dead of yore [*Gloss* long agoe]. *c* **1600** SHAKS. *Sonn.* lxviii, To shew faulse Art what beauty was of yore. **1632** MILTON *Penseroso* 23 Thee bright-hair'd Vesta long of yore, To solitary Saturn bore. **1784** COWPER *Task* II.

591 A form, not now gymnastic as of yore. **1819** SCOTT *Ivanhoe* i, Here haunted of yore the fabulous Dragon of Wantley. **1862** KINGSLEY in *Life & Lett.* (1877) I. 477, I have defended the right of combination among the work-men, in hope that they would become wiser than of yore. **1867** 'OUIDA' *Cecil Castlemaine's Gage* 19 Proud Cecil Castlemaine was yet prouder than of yore.

b. in *adj.* use: Belonging to time long past, ancient, former.

1598 *Mucedorus* IV. iii. 72 In time of yore. **1612** DRAYTON *Poly-olb.* v. 338 His Bishoprick of yore. *c* **1705** POPE *Jan. & May* 514 Well sung sweet Ovid, in the days of yore. **1809–10** COLERIDGE *Friend* I. v. (1865) 134 This is altogether different from the village politics of yore. **1814** WORDSW. *Excurs.* II. 1 In days of yore how fortunately fared The Minstrel! **1820** W. IRVING *Sketch Bk.* I. 80 (*Rip van Winkle*) The quiet little Dutch inn of yore. **1883** WHITELAW *Sophocles, Philoct.* 1151 For now I hold not in my hands The mighty shafts of yore.

c. With other preps.: e.g. †*for yore* (obs.); *in yore* (pseudo-arch.). *rare.*

13.. *E.E. Allit. P.* A. 586 ȝet oþer þer werne..þat swange & swat for long ȝore. *c* **1350** *Will. Palerne* 4174 Hire mi sone is founde þat sche for ȝore saide was sonk in þe see. **1876** MORRIS *Æneids* v. 865 In yore agone.

5. as *adj.* Of old time; ancient, former. *arch.* and *dial.* †*yore while* (advb. phr.), some time ago. *Yore-flood* (nonce-use), the biblical Flood.

yore-day is an echo of OE. *on ȝeárdaȝum*, ON. *í árdaga* in days of yore.

13.. *E.E. Allit. P.* A. 322 Oure ȝore fader hit con mysseȝeme. *Ibid.* B. 842 þete vus out þose ȝong men þat ȝore-whyle here entred. *c* **1400** *Destr. Troy* 9959 So hatnet hir hert in his hegh loue, And all ȝomeryng for-yeton of hir yore dedes. **1866** G. STEPHENS *Runic Mon.* I. p. v, Thousands of books and yore-day things. **1876** G. M. HOPKINS *Wreck of Deutschland* xxxii, in *Poems* (1967) 62, I admire thee, master of the tides, Of the Yore-flood.

yore, ȝore: see EWER², ORE¹, YARE, YOUR.

yores, dial. or obs. form of YOURS.

yorezeit, var. YAHRZEIT.

‖**yorgan** (jɔːˈgʌn). Also **yorghan**. [Turk.] A quilt.

1914 *Blackw. Mag.* Dec. 759/2 He..brought a heavy quilted *yorghan*, a warm covering for the coldest night. **1962** *Times* 6 June 16/7 Blankets and silk *yorgans*—Turkish eiderdowns.

Y organ. *Zool.* Also **y organ** and with hyphen. [tr. F. *organe Y* (M. Gabe 1953, in *Compt. Rend.* CCXXXVII. 111), after X ORGAN.] An endocrine gland in certain crustaceans which secretes a hormone that causes moulting.

1959 E. SCHARRER in E. Gorbman *Compar. Endocrinol.* 239 The final common path for the resulting decision to molt is represented by the neurosecretory cell which presumably activates the Y-organ. **1965** LEE & KNOWLES *Animal Hormones* xi. 137 The Y organ is located in the antennary segment of those species which have a maxillary excretory organ, and in the second maxillary segment of those which have an antennary excretory organ. **1973** *Nature* 9 Mar. 133/2 An insect does not enter premoult if its thoracic glands have been removed, nor a crustacean if its y-organs have been removed.

York (jɔːk), *sb.*¹ [OE. *Eoforwíc*, later *Efer-*, *Euerwíc*, ME. *Everwik*, also *Yerk* (Havelok), surviving in Lincolnshire dial. *Yerksheer*, and *York* (cf. ON. *c* 960 *Jorvik*, later *Jork*), ad. L. *Eboracum*, with addition of *wíc* dwelling.]

1. a. The name of a city in N. Yorkshire (the capital of the former county of Yorkshire); used attrib. in names of things originating from or peculiar to York or Yorkshire, as *York ham*, †*York robe*, *York tan*. **York-Antwerp rules** [adopted at *York* in 1864 and modified at *Antwerp* in 1877], an international set of rules governing the application of general average in marine insurance. **York-paving**, paving with Yorkshire stone. **York pitch** (of a plane): see quot. 1875 and PITCH *sb.*² 24 g; hence **York-pitched** *a.* **York use** *Eccl.*: see USE *sb.*¹

1794 WALDRON *Heigho for Husb.* III. i. 27 There's not a week goes over her head, but she [*sc.* the mistress] says to me ..Maria, my dear, you may take that polonese, or York-robe, or pierrot, or whatever dress it happens to be. **1815** JANE AUSTEN *Emma* xxiv, While the sleek, well tied parcels of 'Men's Beavers' and 'York Tan' were..displaying on the counter. **1826** MISS MITFORD *Village* Ser. II. *My Godfather's Manœuvring*, [He] actually drew my York-tan gloves from my astonished hands, and substituted a pair of his own best white kid. **1853** WHYTE-MELVILLE *Digby Grand* x, The Major's York-tan gaiters. **1861** *Skyring's Builders' Prices* 87 York paving, per foot super..os. 8d. **1875** *Carpentry & Join.* 144 Knotted or crosse-grained wood can [only] be planed..with a special tool, of which the iron is placed at a more obtuse angle... For deal and soft wood this is 45 degs., or common pitch; for mahogany and hard wood 50 degs., or York pitch. **1877** HELLYER *Plumber* vii. 54 The other compartment should be sealed over..with a piece of York stone. [**1877** TWISS & JENCKEN in H. D. Jencken *York & Antwerp Rules* 20 The Rules which your committee now bring before you as the basis for a uniform system of General Average for all maritime countries, and to which the title might be given of the 'York and Antwerp Rules', are appended.] **1881** R. LOWNDES *Pract. Treat. Law Marine Insurance* vii. 203 The York-Antwerp Rules constitute a sort of international code of general average, not as yet obligatory. **1897** *Westm. Gaz.* 7 Apr. 2/3 A ham is a 'York' ham if composed of English meat and prepared in Yorkshire or 'in contiguous counties or places'. **1913** *Engl. Rev.* Apr. 110 The wood, being cut, is planed up and finished with a 'York-pitched' plane. **1970** York ham [see *Cambridge sausage* s.v. CAMBRIDGE]. **1974** E. R. H. IVAMY *Marine Insurance* (ed. 2) xiv. 191 The policy almost invariably provides that either a foreign law or the York-Antwerp Rules 1974 shall apply. **1983** *Harrods Mag.* Xmas. 44/1 At Christmas the whole York ham, costing £35. **1984** J. GRIGSON *Brit. Cookery* 122 Today, York ham has become a generalised term, meaning no more than a mild cured ham.

b. as predicative adj. connoting the character of a Yorkshireman: cf. YORKSHIRE 2.

1856 LEVER *Martins of Cro' M.* xxxix, Don't lose your time trying to humbug me, I'm 'York' too.

c. Short for *Yorkshire cabbage.*

1823 COBBETT *Rur. Rides* 26 July (1885) I. 210 They appear to be early Yorks, and look very well. **1841** J. T. HEWLETT *Parish Clerk* I. 102 Large patches of early yorks.

2. Pertaining to the royal house of York; *spec.* = YORKIST 1 b.

York pence, copper coins of the reign of Henry VI. *York and Lancaster rose* (see quots.); hence allusive use of *York and Lancaster* in quot. 1653.

14.. *Norwich Corporation Records* (Halliw.) Pens of topens fabricatis de ære vocatis brasenpens, secundum formam et similitudinem denar. vocat. Yorkpens. **1653** CLEVELAND *Upon Phillis walking* 26 Poems 22 And he that for their colour seeks, May find it vaulting in her cheeks, Where Roses mix: no civill war Between her York and Lancaster. **1688** HOLME *Armoury* II. 62/2 The York and Landcaster Rose, is half white, half red in the leaves: but in Herauldry it is a white Rose, in a red Rose. **1759** HUME *Hist. Eng.* I. i. 4 Henry himself..had imbibed a violent antipathy to the York party. *Ibid.* 8 The retainers of the York family. **1837** RIVERS *Rose Amateur's G.* 12 The true York and Lancaster Rose is a Damask Rose.

3. One of the heralds of the College of Arms.

1630 B. JONSON *New Inn* II. vi, She's a wild-Irish borne! Sir, and a Hybride, That..studies Vincent against Yorke. **1766** [see HERALD *sb.* 1 c].

4. = New York; in *York shilling*, (*a*) in U.S.A. 12½ cents, (*b*) in Canada sixpence.

1824 *Microscope* (Albany) 27 Mar. (Thornton *Dict. Amer.*), The bill amounted to the enormous sum of one York shilling for each gentleman. **1883** SIMMONDS *Dict. Trade* Suppl., *York shilling*, a name in Western Canada for the English sixpence.

5. The name of *York Factory*, a trading settlement in northeastern Manitoba, used *attrib.* in **York boat**, a type of inland cargo boat used in Canada between *c* 1790 and 1930.

1864 *Nor' Wester* (Red River Settlement) 26 Apr. 2/5 Gentlemen of practical experience gave their opinion that the present York boats (bateaux) could be used for the transportation of goods from Lake of the Woods to Lake Superior with as little difficulty as is encountered between this place and York Factory. **1909** G. BRYCE *Romantic Settlement Lord Selkirk's Colonists* 71 The birch-bark canoe is a mere trifle on the portage, but the heavy York boat capable of carrying three or four tons is a clumsy lugger. **1971** R. RUSSELL *Carlton Trail* 10 The company hired Scotsmen, Metis, and Indians to man brigades of York Boats.

york (jɔːk), *sb.*² *dial.* Also **yark**, **yerk**. [Perh. the same word as YERK, YARK *sb.*] Something used to tie a trouser leg beneath the knee. Usu. *pl.*

1905 *Eng. Dialect Dict.* V, *Yark*, a strap or piece of string to fasten the trousers to keep them free from mud. [*Cites a quot. with 'yerks'.*] **1958** K. ETHERIDGE *Welsh Costume* 66 When kneeling at the coal-face, dirt and small coal are apt to get inside the trouser-leg... Tying of the trouser leg just below the knee prevents this. A piece of string, or a leather strap..may be used for this. The strap..is called a 'york'. **1967** *Listener* 19 Oct. 504/3 The 'tyings' or straps worn below the knees..are, or were, used by the South Wales colliers, whose term for them is 'yorks'. **1977** SCOLLINS & TITFORD *Ey up, mi Duck!* III. 12 Mr. Flint, who played the Fool, wore moleskin trousers tied with 'yorks'. **1984** *Guardian Weekly* 22 Jan. 4/2 They wore corduroy trousers fastened below the knee with leather straps ('yarks' is the technical name).

york (jɔːk), *v.*¹ *Cricket.* [Back-formation f. YORKER².] *trans.* To bowl (a batsman) out or strike (the wicket) with a yorker.

1882 *Australians in Engl.* 42 Butler was 'yorked' the second ball he received. **1888** A. G. STEEL *Cricket* (Badm. Libr.) iii. 169 [W. G. Grace loq.] I'm never frightened of him; he is always trying to 'york' you, and bowls any amount of half-volleys. **1904** *Daily Chron.* 19 July 7/3 The ball that bowled Tunnicliffe started its flight a foot outside the off stump, at the finish it 'yorked' the middle stump.

york (jɔːk), *v.*² [f. YORK *sb.*² Cf. YERK, YARK *v.*] *trans.* To keep *up* trouser legs by tying them with 'yorks'.

1960 R. WILLIAMS *Border Country* 258 The thongs which yorked the trouser legs just below the knees. **1969** M. HARRIS *Kind of Magic* 178 He always wore thick brown cord trousers yorked up below the knee with leather straps, and his face was the colour of a bit of old leather.

Yorker¹ (ˈjɔːkə(r)). [f. YORK *sb.*¹ + -ER¹.]

1. An inhabitant of York or Yorkshire; applied allusively (cf. YORKSHIRE 2).

1599 BUTTES *Diets Dry Dinner* Ep. Ded. A a j b, As for the Middle-sex or Londoner, I smell his Diet.. Here is a Pipe of right Trinidado for him. The Yorkers they will bee content with bald Tabacodocko. What should I say? here is good Veale for the Essex-man. **1673** KIRKMAN *Unlucky Citizen* 158 She was a right Yorker, being of that Countrey breed, and as full of dissimulation and hipocrisy as most of that Countrey. **1847** H. MILLER *First Impr.* xiii. 232 The Yorkers contend that their organ is not only the greater, but also the finer organ of the two; whereas the Birminghamers assert, on the contrary, that theirs..plays vastly better. **1849** H. W. HERBERT *Frank Forester* I. 75 Here's Archer, and another Yorker with him—leastwise an Englisher I should say.

2. An inhabitant or a soldier of New York.

1776 ABIGAIL ADAMS in *Fam. Lett.* (1876) 229 We are told for truth that a regiment of Yorkers refused to quit the city. **1876** BANCROFT *Hist. U.S.* V. xxii. 587 Sir John Johnson and some part of his royal Yorkers. **1883** *Harper's Mag.* Nov. 821/1 The settlers..hated..the 'Yorkers'.

yorker² (ˈjɔːkə(r)). *Cricket.* [? Same word as prec.] (See quot. 1888.)

1861 *Bell's Life* 25 Aug. (Suppl.) 2/1 Buchanan stopped sometime, and bothered the bowlers much, as he would not hit even a 'Yorker'. **1870** *Sporting Mag.* Oct. 99 A fast Yorker is as disagreeable a first ball as an incoming batsman could receive. **1888** A. G. STEEL *Cricket* (Badm. Libr.) iii. 133 The ordinary definition of a 'yorker' is a ball that pitches inside the crease, and this, no doubt, is correct so far as it goes, but it does not go far enough. It really should be, any ball that pitches directly underneath the bat. It is quite possible for a man to be bowled out with a 'yorker' when he is two or three yards out of his ground, if he misjudges the ball, and allows it to pitch directly beneath his bat, although the ball pitches as far from the crease as he is standing. The most deadly sort of 'yorker', however, is the one that pitches about three or four inches inside the crease.

yorker³ (ˈjɔːkə(r)). [f. YORK *sb.*² + -ER¹.] = YORK *sb.*²

1940 H. SPRING *Fame is Spur* xiii. 362 Checked mufflers ..were at the throats of most [miners], and their trousers were hitched up with yorkers below the knee. **1972** [see NICKY TAM].

York gum. [Named after *York*, a town in Western Australia east of Perth.] A gum-tree, *Eucalyptus loxophleba*, of Western Australia, or its timber.

1846 [see GUM *sb.*² 5]. **1889** J. H. MAIDEN *Useful Native Plants Austral.* ix. 449 Samples of this timber were sent to the Colonial and Indian Exhibition under the name 'York gum' (*E. loxophleba*). **1934** T. WOOD *Cobbers* viii. 101 In addition to seeds for me—yates gum and york gum and mallee wattle—a cold turkey sat in the back seat. **1944** *Coast to Coast 1943* 60 The slope..rose towards his own home, a thin tracery of york-gums screening the house. **1965** *Austral. Encycl.* III. 407/1 York gum..and wandoo..are pale-coloured Western Australian timbers.

Yorkie (ˈjɔːkɪ). Also 9 **Yorky**. [f. YORK(SHIRE + -IE, -Y⁶.]

1. A Yorkshireman; †a nickname for a Yorkshireman. *colloq.*

1818 P. EGAN *Boxiana* (ed. 2) II. 301 Yorky did not appear wholly without judgment. **1938** 'J. CURTIS' *They drive by Night* xiii. 144 You're in Yorkshire now... Them Yorkies never was any good. **1950** W. BIRD *This is Nova Scotia* 14 The gallant young Yorkie hushed up her every attempt to talk. **1980** 'J. GASH' *Spend Game* x. 107 Joseph Bramah was a Yorkie, and a genius... His legendary lock patent is dated 1784.

2. A Yorkshire terrier. *colloq.*

1950 A. C. SMITH *Dogs since 1900* xiii. 321 A bigger Yorkie ..is as satisfactory a companion as could be desired. **1967** 'A. GILBERT' *Visitor* vi. 95 'Mrs. Warren is telling me poodles are out!'.. 'And Yorkies are in?' I suggested. **1977** *S. Wales Echo* 18 Jan. 12/3 (Advt.), Wanted, Toy Poodles.. and Yorkies. **1984** *Hampstead & Highgate Express* 14 Dec. 27/5 Yorkie and Westie pups, inoculated, guaranteed.

Yorkish (ˈjɔːkɪʃ), *a. rare.* [f. YORK *sb.*¹ + -ISH¹.] = YORKIST 1 b.

a **1548** HALL *Chron., Hen. VI*, 171 b, As the Iewes disdayned the company of the Samaritans, so the Lancastrians abhorred the familiaritie of Yorkysh lynage. **1634** FORD *Perkin Warbeck* I. i, Idolls of Yorkish malice. **1829** SCOTT *Anne of G.* xxiv, Does Burgundy prepare to.. make common cause with this Yorkish host against King Louis of France? **1884** *Leisure Hour* Feb. 102/2 All colours being admissible except the Yorkish white.

Yorkist (ˈjɔːkɪst), *sb.* (*a.*) [f. YORK *sb.*¹ (see below) + -IST.]

1. An adherent of the house of York, the English royal family which based its title on its descent from Lionel, Duke of Clarence, and Edmund, Duke of York (died 1402), the third and the fifth sons of Edw. III; or one of the party (whose emblem was the White Rose) which supported this family in the Wars of the Roses.

1601 WEEVER *Mirr. Mart.* C v, Then high-resolued Hotspur,..Join'd with the Yorkists, made a mutinie. **1643** BAKER *Chron., Hen. VI* (1653) 280 From whence Richard Beauchampe Bishop of Salisbury, is sent to offer the Yorkists a full and generall pardon. **1726–31** TINDAL *Rapin's Hist. Eng.* (1743) I. XII. 583/1 The King having advanced with design to give Battle, the Yorkists sent him a very submissive Letter. **1829** SCOTT *Anne of G.* xxiv, Offering with large sums of money to purchase England to the Yorkists. **1856** MISS MULOCK *John Halifax* v, The Vineyards had been a battle-field; and under the long wavy grass..slept many a Yorkist and Lancastrian.

b. *attrib.* or as *adj.*

1823 S. TURNER *Hist. Eng.* III. II. 321 The Christmas of 1469, seemed to have ended all hostilities between these two Yorkist parties. **1861** *Sat. Rev.* 7 Dec. 586 The Yorkist poems are numerous. There is one on the reconciliation of Henry and Duke Richard. **1864** BOUTELL *Her. Hist. & Pop.* xx. (ed. 3) 339 The Yorkist Collar is formed of suns and roses.

2. A supporter of James, Duke of York (*c* 1680), in his claim to succeed to the crown on the death of his brother, Charles II.

1681 LUTTRELL *Brief Rel.* (1857) I. 124 The former [party] are called by the latter, tories, tantivies, Yorkists, high-flown church men, &c. *a* **1734** NORTH *Examen* II. v. §9

(1740) 321 It is easy to imagine how rampant these Procurators of Power, the Exclusioners, were..: Every where insulting and menacing the Loyallists... This Trade ..naturally led to a common Use of slighting and opprobrious Words; such as Yorkist. [**1858** KNIGHT *Pop. Hist. Eng.* IV. xxi. 350 The anti-exclusionists were first called Yorkists.]

3. An inhabitant of York: = YORKER[1] 1. *rare.*

1796 *Sporting Mag.* VII. 55 Once a Cockney and Yorkist maintain'd a dispute, Whether London or York was of oldest repute.

Yorkshire (ˈjɔːkʃə(r)). [f. YORK *sb.*[1] + SHIRE 5.] Formerly, the name of the largest of the northern counties of England (comprising three ridings or administrative divisions). As a result of local-government re-organization in 1974, this region was divided into the three counties of North, West, and South Yorkshire (and some territory originally included in Yorkshire became part of Humberside). The name is still used loosely to designate the region covered by the former county or, more accurately, to that formed by the present three counties.

1. *attrib.* **a.** Pertaining to or characteristic of Yorkshire.

1683 G. M[ERITON] (*title*) A York-shire Dialogue, in its pure Natural Dialect. **1685** DRYDEN *Sylvæ* Pref. a6, Like a fair Shepherdess in her Country Russet, talking in a Yorkshire Tone. **1826** *Zool. Jrnl.* II. 555 An undescribed Fossil Animal from the Yorkshire Coal-field. **1859** *Househ. Words* 15 Jan. 148/2 His sullen, self-willed, local Yorkshire nature. **1886** KINGTON OLIPHANT *New Engl.* I. 31 Hampole's..'Pricke of Conscience'..is in the Yorkshire dialect.

b. Applied to things originating in or cultivated especially in Yorkshire, as ***Yorkshire ale, cabbage, cord, drab, fog***, (FOG *sb.*[1]), ***fustian, gray, grit*** (GRIT *sb.*[1] 2), ***kidney*** (potato), ***pie, sanicle*** (SANICLE 2), ***shoe, stone, tyke*** (TYKE 3), ***white(s***; **Yorkshire bond, cement, light, maiden, mile** (see quots.); **Yorkshire chair**, a type of 17th-century upright chair, usu. distinguished by an open backrest and arched cross-rails; **Yorkshire fog**, a perennial greyish-green grass, *Holcus lanatus*, bearing pale green or purplish panicles; **Yorkshire pudding**, a batter-pudding orig. baked under meat, now usu. cooked and served as a separate item to accompany roast beef; hence **Yorkshire pud** *colloq.*; **Yorkshire Relish**, the proprietary name of a kind of savoury sauce; **Yorkshire teacake**, a kind of baked yeast teacake occas. made with currants or sultanas; **Yorkshire terrier**, a small, long-coated, tan and blue-grey terrier belonging to a breed developed in the West Riding of Yorkshire about 1870.

1683 G. MERITON (*title*) The Praise of *York-shire Ale. **1892** *Dict. Archit.*, **Yorkshire bond*, or flying, or garden wall, bond, is chiefly used in building garden walls, one brick thick; the face shows three or four stretchers to one header; or five courses of stretchers to one of headers. **1786** ABERCROMBIE *Gard. Assist.* 228 Cabbage seed..some early dwarf sorts, early *Yorkshire. **1892** *Dict. Archit.*, **Yorkshire cement*, the same as Mulgrave, Whitby, or Atkinson's cement. [**1900** E. SINGLETON *Furnit. of Our Forefathers* I. i. 46 There were not so many kinds of single chairs in the seventeenth century... There were two very favourite patterns, the Derbyshire and the Yorkshire... The Yorkshire model..is rather more ornamental.] **1906** W. E. MALLETT *Introd. Old Eng. Furnit.* 20 A solid oak chair of the Stuart period. These are often called *Yorkshire chairs. **1976** *Southern Even. Echo* (Southampton) 12 Nov. (Advt. Suppl.) 19/3, 4 Yorkshire chairs and 1 carver, £300. **1849** H. W. HERBERT *Frank Forester* I. 3 A pair of most voluminous unmentionables, of thick *Yorkshire cord. **1810** *Sporting Mag.* XXXVI. 240 A driving coat of *Yorkshire drab. **1874** C. C. BABINGTON *Man. Brit. Bot.* (ed. 7) 419 *H. lanatus*... Meadows and pastures... *Yorkshire Fog. **1954** C. E. HUBBARD *Grasses* 237 'Yorkshire Fog' is generally regarded as a weed, but when young it has some value for grazing. **1977** *New Yorker* 8 Aug. 58/3 The fairways were edged by the wispiest kind of rough—a thin, random collection of fescue, buttercups, plantain shoreweed, Yorkshire fog, dandelions, and assorted other weeds, grasses and wild flowers. **1612** in *Halyburton's Ledger* (1867) 308 *Yorkshyre or Northern fusteanes. **1679** *Trials of T. White & Other Jesuits* 83 In Gray Cloaths, a Gray Coat like a Shepherds Coat, a *Yorkshire-Gray. **1892** *Dict. Archit.* s.v., *Yorkshire stone or Grit, is a name sometimes given to Bramley Fall stone; it is one of the most general of the sandstones sent to London, and is used for paving, copings, and other rough work. **1849** H. W. HERBERT *Frank Forester* III. 144 There was a *Yorkshire ham, which had not suffered so deeply by the last night's onslaught. **1842** LOUDON *Suburban Hort.* 639 The red-nosed kidney and the white *Yorkshire kidney. **1892** *Dict. Archit.*, **Yorkshire light*, a term used in Lancashire, for a sliding sash. **1752** *Gentl. Mag.* Jan. 32/2 A Machine for washing of Linnen, called a *Yorkshire Maiden. **1711** E. WARD *Quix.* I. 44 Not caring to perform much more Than one good *Yorkshire Mile an Hour. **1889** *N.W. Linc. Gloss., Yerksheer mile*, a long distance. **1838** DICKENS *Nich. Nick.* vii, A young servant girl brought in a *Yorkshire pie. **1894** *Garrett's Encycl. Pract. Cookery* II. 803/1 *Yorkshire Pie.* A pie under this name sold at Italian warehouses is nothing more than a galantine packed in terrines of different sizes. **1794** WEDGE *Agric. Chester* 23 The Rotherham or *Yorkshire plough. **1747** MRS. GLASSE *Cookery* 69 A *Yorkshire Pudding. Take a Quart of Milk, four Eggs,..make it up into a thick Batter with Flour, like a Pancake Batter. **1832** MACAULAY in Trevelyan *Life* (1876) I. v. 272 They feed me on roast-beef and Yorkshire pudding. **1836** [HOOTON] *Bilberry Thurland* I. vii. 140 At the bottom of all..lay about half an acre of sad and heavy Yorkshire pudding, like a leaden pancake. **1975** *New Society* 21 Aug. 411/2 The roast beef and *Yorkshire pud dinners provided on Sundays. **1976** C. BERMANT *Coming Home* II. iv. 169, I was given roast beef and Yorkshire pud. **1877** *Trade Marks Jrnl.* 13 Jan. 78 **Yorkshire Relish*... William Powell, of..the firm of Goodall Backhouse and Co., Leeds..; drysalters and general merchants. **1881** *Cassell's Family Mag.* Dec. 46/1 And two table-spoonfuls of Yorkshire Relish. **1926** *Daily Colonist* (Victoria, B.C.) 17 Jan. 7/7 (Advt.), Genuine Yorkshire Relish. **1770** BRIDGES *Burlesque Transl. Homer* (1797) II. 30 One Tychius, who dwelt in Hyle, Where *Yorkshire shoes are made most vilely. **1569** in *Black Bks. Linc. Inn* (1897) I. 449 For vj fote of *Yorkeshere stone for bassys of dorys. **1877** *Cassell's Dict. Cookery* 1157/2 **Yorkshire tea-cakes*... Two pounds of good flour;..an ounce of German yeast..two well-beaten eggs and six ounces of butter... Leave it in a warm place to rise... Divide it into ten portions. **1945** 'R. CROMPTON' *William & Brains Trust* v. 84 One of his happiest memories was the Yorkshire tea cakes that his mother used to make. **1977** E. DAVID *Eng. Bread & Yeast Cookery* 488 The following nineteenth-century recipe for plain Yorkshire tea cakes comes from..Marcus Woodward. [**1871** R. PEARSON in *Field* 13 May 386/2 Some friends of mine in Yorkshire wish me to put a matter right in connection with dog shows, namely, the classification of a breed of dogs they claim as of Yorkshire origin—those beautiful blue and tan long-haired terriers, now sometimes entered in the Scotch and broken-haired, also rough-haired terrier classes. They with myself think it would much simplify the matter by calling them the 'Yorkshire blue and tan long-haired terrier'.] **1872** 'STONEHENGE' *Dogs of Brit. Islands* (ed. 2) v. 108 The silver-grey *Yorkshire terrier is not a distinct breed, being merely a paler variety of the blue-tan. **1922** D. MATHESON *Terriers* i. 188 Yorkshire Terriers are hardy, game little dogs. **1959** *Observer* 1 Feb. 12 Yorkshire Terrier. Coat should hang straight and evenly down each side. **1971** *Country Life* 6 May 1098/3 Mrs. Huxham makes it clear..how much pleasure and entertainment she gets from her gay little Yorkshire terriers.

c. The name of a breed of white pig, now widely bred for bacon.

1770 BRIDGES *Burlesque Transl. Homer* (1797) II. 319 A pastry-cook, That made good pigeon-pie of rook, Cut venison from Yorkshire hogs. **1845** *Encycl. Metrop.* XXV. 310/1 The Old Yorkshire Pig is by some considered as the very worst of the large varieties, very long legged, weak loined, not of strong constitution, nor good stye pigs, but yet quicker feeders. **1856** J. C. MORTON *Cycl. Agric.* II. 942/1 The Old Lincolnshire, or Yorkshire Pig, was one of largest breeds in the kingdom, and probably the worst... The large breed, or *improved* wold pig, has probably undergone as great a change as any, and has become..the most profitable kind we have. **1914** 'SAKI' *Beasts & Super-beasts* 24 Tarquin, the huge white Yorkshire boar-pig, had exchanged the narrow limits of his stye for the wider range of the grass paddock. **1974** *Encycl. Brit. Macropædia* X. 1281/2 The Yorkshire pig, which originated early in the 19th century in England, where it was considered a bacon type, is long, lean, and trim with white hair and skin. Found in most countries, this breed is probably the most widely-distributed in the world.

2. Used allusively, esp. in reference to the †boorishness, cunning, sharpness, or trickery attributed to Yorkshire people. ***to come*** (or ***put***) ***Yorkshire on one***, to cheat, dupe, overreach him. ***Yorkshire bite***, a sharp overreaching action or person. †Also in prov. phr. ***a pair of Yorkshire sleeves in a goldsmith's shop***, said of anything worthless.

1620 *Westward for Smelts* (Percy Soc.) 36 If she lived now, she would shew as vild as a paire of Yorkeshire sleeves in a goldsmiths shop. **1624** A. HOLLAND *Contin. Inquis. Paper-Persec.* 85 England is all turn'd Yorkeshire, and the Age Extremely sottish, or too nicely sage. **1650** *Brief Disc. betw. Yorkshirem. & Scottish-man* 1 *Yorks.* I am a Yorkshireman born and bred, I care not who knowes it: I hope true Yorkshire never denies his county. *Scot.* I thought you looked like a subtle blade. **1700** *Step to the Bath* 10, I ask'd what Countrey-Man my Landlord was? Answer was made full North; and Faith 'twas very Evident, for he had put the Yorkshire most Damnably upon us. **1706** E. WARD *Wooden World Diss.* (1708) 53 He's more confident of his Way, than a Yorkshire Carrier. *c* **1747** J. COLLIER (Tim Bobbin) *View Lanc. Dial.* (1770) Gloss., *Yorshar*, Yorkshire; to put Yorkshire of a Man, is to trick, cheat, or deceive him. **1795** *Gentl. Mag.* Aug. 629/1, I flatter myself that this will turn out to be a Yorkshire bite, and that the biter will be bit. **1796** HOLMAN *Abroad & at Home* I. i, I dare say, his Yorkshire simplicity will qualify him admirably for the profession! **1801** *Sporting Mag.* XIX. 114, I will not denominate your coursing correspondent a Yorkshire bite, for he only snaps. **1877** *N.W. Linc. Gloss., Yerksheer*, Yorkshire. When anything is done very sharp or clever, we say 'that's real Yerksheer'. **1887** *S. Cheshire Gloss., Yorkshire*, cajolery, blarney, attempt to hoodwink or deceive. 'Let's ha' none o' yur Yorkshire.'

3. *ellipt.* as the designation of a thick coarse cloth made in Yorkshire, a breed of canary, (*pl.*) soldiers of a Yorkshire regiment; also short for *Yorkshire dialect*; *Yorkshire pudding*; a *Yorkshire pig*; a *Yorkshire terrier*.

1717 M. W. MONTAGU *Let.* 1 Apr. (1965) I. 333 'Tis as ridiculous to make use of the expressions commonly us'd, in speaking to a Great Man or a Lady, as it would be to talk broad Yorkshire or Somersetshire in the drawing room. **1726** *Lond. Gaz.* No. 6444/5 Speaks Yorkshire. **1753** HANWAY *Trav.* (1762) I. VI. lxxxv. 390 Soldiers cloths, yorkshires, and flannels. **1849** PATON *Highl. Adriatic* II. xvii. 215 The Hausknecht and Stallknecht..speaking the broad dialect of the south-eastern provinces, a kind of Yorkshire to the classic language of the Schillers and Herders. **1898** *Westm. Gaz.* 31 Jan. 7/1 Fifteen of the Yorkshire Light Infantry killed; two Sikhs and thirty-one Yorkshires wounded. **1898** *Daily News* 28 Nov. 3/3 Slim and sprightly Yorkshires..contrast strongly with the equally esteemed Lancashires of pale yellow plumage. **1898** J. D. BRAYSHAW *Slum Silhouettes* 235 Now's yer time, gents, fer a nice 'ot dinner, cut off the jint.., an' two wedgetables; plum-tart or Yorkshire—a shilling. **1902** *Encycl. Brit.* XXV. 194/2 The latter [*sc.* recognized breeds] include the Large White, Middle White, and Small White, which were all formerly embraced under the general term of Yorkshires, and are still so called in other countries. **1908** *Daily Chron.* 7 Feb. 3/5 [Women] much prefer the graceful, stylish Yorkshire to the more rotund Norwich. **1922** D. MATHESON *Terriers* i. 181 Originally designed as a sporting dog, the Yorkshire has gradually passed into a lap-dog. **1956** A. WILSON *Anglo-Saxon Attitudes* I. ii. 41 Theo..said, 'Shame!' in his broadest Yorkshire. **1967** M. KENYON *Whole Hog* viii. 93 They're Large Whites. You [*sc.* Americans] call them Yorkshire. **1971** R. J. WHITE *Second-Hand Tomb* ix. 95 Rammel. That's Yorkshire for rubbish. **1977** J. WAMBAUGH *Black Marble* (1978) viii. 105 The handler two stations down had a Yorkshire with a touch-up. **1977** *S. Wales Guardian* 27 Oct. 5/3 Oh the joy of digging into tender roast beef and Yorkshire!

†**4.** = YORKIST b. *Obs.*

1643 BAKER *Chron., Hen. VI* (1653) 278 All the enemies of the Yorkshire Faction are assembled by the Queen at Greenwich. **1792** E. SPELMAN & LEMON *Hist. Civ. Wars* 125 The earl of Warwick..came over to England, in order to put himself at the head of the Yorkshire insurgents.

Hence **ˈYorkshiredom**, the character of a Yorkshireman; **ˈYorkshir(e)ism**, an action or expression characteristic of a Yorkshireman.

1849 *Athenæum* 7 Apr. 356/2 Tim Matlock..who keeps his 'canny Yorkshire-dom' intact even on Jonathan's hunting-ground. **1849** C. BRONTE *Shirley* xviii, Mr. Hall's sincere friendly homily, with all its racy Yorkshireisms. **1962** P. BENTLEY '*O Dreams, O Destinations*' iv. 56 Her voice was pleasant, quite devoid of Yorkshirisms. **1971** J. WAINWRIGHT *Dig Grave & let him Lie* 128 'Aye.' The open-vowelled Yorkshirism was heavy with self-disgust.

Yorkshireman (ˈjɔːkʃəmən). A man of Yorkshire.

1549 THOMAS *Hist. Italie* 3 b, Betwene the Florentine and Uenetian is great diuersitee in speeche, as with vs betwene a Londoner and a Yorkeshyreman. **1650** [see YORKSHIRE 2]. **1752** HUME *Ess., Bal. Trade* (1777) I. 332 A melancholy Yorkshireman. **1808** SCOTT *Marmion* v. xvii, Yorkshiremen are stern of mood. **1820** —— *Abbot* xvi, He was a bluff Yorkshireman. **1856** [H. H. HALL] *Post & Paddock* i, The Yorkshiremen generally direct their attention to quick returns.

ˈyorlin(g. *Sc.* and *north. dial.* Also 7 yourling, 9 **yorline, yeorling, yarlin, yerlin.** [Variant of YOWLRING; cf. YOLDRING.] A yellow-hammer.

1679 LOVELL *Indic. Univ.* 31 A Yellow-hammer or Yourling. **1789** D. DAVIDSON *Seasons* 151 Should at his feet a scared yorlin bir. **1813** HOGG *Queen's Wake, Kilmeny* i, It was only to heire the yorline syng. **1861** ATKINSON *Brit. Birds' Eggs* 50, I used to hear in Berwickshire, that 'The Brock, the Toad, and the Yellow Yeörling, Get a drap o' the Deil's bluid ilka May morning.'

yorn(e, ȝorn(e: see YARN, YERN, YERNE.

yornyman, obs. form of JOURNEYMAN.

1553 *Cov. Leet Bk.* 806 For a yornyman or a Suffycyent servaunte not aboue vj d. a daye.

yort(e, obs. or dial. (Lancs.) f. YARD *sb.*[1]

c **1515** *Exam. towcheynge Cokeye More* 9 (Chetham Misc. II.) & so vnto Ryngley yorte.

yort, yorth, ȝorth, yoske, ȝoske: see YOURT, EARTH, YEX.

yortzeit, var. YAHRZEIT.

Yoruba (ˈjɒrʊbə), *sb.* and *a.* Also 9 **Yarriba.** [Native name.] **A.** *sb.* **a.** The language of the Yorubas, a tonal language of the Kwa group.

1841 *Outl. Vocab. Lang Western & Central Africa* 2 (*heading*) Ako, Eyo, Yabú, or Yarriba. **1843** S. CROWTHER (*title*) Vocabulary of the Yoruba language. Part I.—English and Yoruba, Part II.—Yoruba and English. **1888** *Encycl. Brit.* XXIV. 755/1 The Bible and several religious treatises have been translated into Yoruba. **1927** E. S. PANKHURST *Delphos* v. 51 Yoruba, one of the African languages, conjugates its verbs as in English, though its vocabulary is entirely different. **1964** *New Statesman* 1 May 681/1 In Accra recently a Nigerian company, under the direction of the brilliant young artist Demas Nwoko, presented a dramatised version, in Yoruba, of Amos Tutuola's *The Palm-Wine Drinkard.* **1972** B. EMECHETA *In Ditch* i. 6 The landlady started scolding her husband in Yoruba.

b. (A member of) a Black people of western Nigeria and neighbouring parts.

1843 S. CROWTHER *Vocab. Yoruba Lang.* p. iii, The Yorubas, like other nations, have always considered themselves the first people in the world. **1897** M. H. KINGSLEY *Trav. W. Afr.* xiii. 526, I had a set of porters composed of four Bassa boys, two Wei Weis, one Dualla, and two Yorubas. **1937** *Discovery* July 225/1 The Yoruba have only the vaguest tradition of their own past. **1960** *Guardian* 15 July 14/3 The Yorubas live in the largest urban agglomerations to be found in traditional Africa. **1970** P. OLIVER *Savannah Syncopators* 32 Between the lands of the Ibo and those of the Ashanti (Akan) of the old Gold Coast (Ghana) lie the domains of the Yoruba of Nigeria and Dahomey.

B. *adj.* Of, pertaining to, or characteristic of this people.

1843 [see sense A. b above]. **1883** *Encycl. Brit.* XVI. 517/1 In the Yoruba lands the Church Missionary Society has 11 stations. **1938** J. CARY *Castle Corner* 357 Four big Yoruba soldiers. **1957** M. BANTON *W. Afr. City* viii. 153 A Yoruba secret society called *Engugun.* **1978** *Jrnl. R. Soc. Arts* CXXVI. 366/2 In Nigeria, Yoruba woodcarvers have adapted their techniques to work in concrete.

Hence **ˈYoruban** *sb.* and *a.*

1853 S. TUCKER *Abbeokuta* (ed. 2) ii. 15 There were few or no Yorubans brought to Sierra Leone till the year 1822. *Ibid.* viii. 100 It afforded Mr. Townsend the opportunity of becoming in some degree acquainted with the Yoruban language. **1879** J. A. FARRER *Primitive Manners* iii. 89 Captain Burton justly calls attention to the possibility of many Yoruban proverbs being relics of the Moslems. **1936** V. A. DEMANT *Christian Polity* xi. 193 The thunder-god of the Yorubans is decidedly an earthly king who became a god. **1957** M. STEARNS *Story of Jazz* iii. 27 The musical instruments for such occasions consist of Yoruban drums, shaped like hour glasses, and the drumming and singing are in the Yoruban style.

Yoshiwara (jɒʃɪˈwɑːrə). Also **yoshiwara**. In Japan, an area (esp. one in Tokyo) where brothels were officially recognized. Freq. *attrib.*

Official recognition was withdrawn in May 1958.

1870 *Fortn. Rev.* Aug. 154 At Yokohama, indeed, and at the other open ports, the women of the Yoshiwara are loud in their invitations to visitors. **1877** A. C. MACLAY *Let.* 25 Nov. in *Budget of Lett. from Japan* (1886) xix. 342 That strange institution of the feudal Government of Japan known as the *Yoshiwara* system..This was a system of legalized prostitution..under government patronage. **1896** KIPLING *Seven Seas* 70 And tell the Yoshiwara girls to burn a stick for him. **1911** *Daily Colonist* (Victoria, B.C.) 27 Apr. 3/4 The fire..destroyed the new yoshiwara at Tokyo, sweeping away 6555 houses. **1944** H. G. WELLS *'42 to '44* 102 The child may be apprenticed to Fagin's academy, it may be sold into the Yoshiwara. **1966** *New Statesman* 2 Dec. 840/1 A short look at *A Harlot's Progress*, and then—if not at a yoshiwara house by a Japanese master of the Floating World—at Botticelli's *Venus*. **1978** *Country Life* 24 Aug. 500/2 The brothels in the red light district of Edo, the Yoshiwara.

yosted: see HOST *v.*[1]

yostregere, obs. form of OSTREGER.

1563 in *N. & Q.* (1889) 7th Ser. VIII. 106 Here vnder lyeth Xp'ofor Walasto' who somtyme was..on of ye yostregere unto ye late kynges & quenes of famous memorye.

yot(e, ȝot(e: see YET.

†yote, *sb.* [f. next.] Casting (of a metal object).

1474–5 in Swayne *Churchw. Acc. Sarum* (1896) 19 Brasse that remayned of the yote of the grete bell.

yote, *v. dial.* Also 4 **ȝ(e)ote,** *pa. pple.* **ȝotted,** 6 **yout,** *vbl. sb.* **yotting,** 6–7 **yowt, yeot,** 7 **yoat.** [Local (chiefly west and south-west) development of OE. *ȝéotan* YET *v.*]

1. *trans.* To pour.

a **1400** *New Test.* (Paues) Acts ii. 18 Vpon my honde-maydens I schal ȝote oute of my spiritte in þoo dais. *Ibid.* 33 He has ȝotted downe þis, þat ȝhe see ande here. *Ibid.* x. 45 For in nacyons þo grace was ȝotted oute of þo Holygoste. **1878** [see 2].

2. To pour liquid upon; to soak.

1615 CHAPMAN *Odyss.* XIX. 760 My Fowles,..I..found feeding at their Trough, Their yoted wheate. **1787** GROSE *Prov. Gloss.* s.v., The brewer's grains must be well yoted, or whesed for the pigs. **1878** *N. & Q.* 5th Ser. IX. 328 Workmen are said to 'yote in' metal to fix iron clamps or railings. The word 'yote' also signifies to water, to pour water on.

3. a. To cast in metal.

1387 TREVISA *Higden* (Rolls) VII. 77 Þis Gerebertus.. dede ȝote [*MS. β* ȝeote] an hede þat spak nouȝt but whanne me axede of hym.

b. To fasten in (a metal bar, a stone block, etc.) with lead; to 'lead in'.

1535 *MS. Rawl. D.* 777, lf. 85 Youtyng the hookes of the Kechyn Dores in to the stone Walles. **1572** in Swayne *Churchw. Acc. Sarum* (1896) 287 White for his labore for the yoting of them 6d. **1692** WOOD *Ath. Oxon.* II. 111 [Selden's] grave was nine foot deep at least, the bottom pav'd with bricks and walled about two foot high, with grey marble coarsly polished, each piece being yoated (that is fastned with lead molted in) with iron champs. **1850** *N. & Q.* 1st Ser. II. 89/2 *Yote* or *Yeot*, a term used in Gloucestershire and Somersetshire for 'leading in' iron work to stone.

Hence ˈ**yoting** *vbl. sb.* (*attrib.*); also †ˈ**yoter,** a caster of metal.

1479–80 in Swayne *Churchw. Acc. Sarum* (1896) 367 Castyng 3 C lede to y^e^ *yoters 2s. **1543** *Will of Ric. Elyot* (Somerset Ho.) *Yowtyng faate. **1534** in Weaver *Wells Wills* (1890) 176 Iohn labur a *ȝottingston. **1597** in Phillipps *Wills* (*c* 1830) 40, I give and bequeath to my son..one yeoting stone. **1602** *Will of Albyn* (Somerset Ho.) Yowting stone. **1652** *Will of M. Reeve* (Somerset Ho.) The yeoting stone, the mowstadells. **1592–3** *Will of B. Saunders* (Somerset Ho.) One broache and my plumpe and *yottinge vate and garnett. **1602** *Inv.* in *Collect. Archæol.* (1863) II. 111 In the well yarde. One yotinge vate and frame xxs. *c* **1530** in Weaver *Wells Wills* (1890) 176 *margin*, One *yotinge vault in the house at Tolland. **1511** in *Somerset Med. Wills* (1903) 151 A *yoting wessaile of lede.

†ˈyoten, *ppl. a. Obs.* Forms: 4 **ȝoten, -un, ȝetun,** 4–6 **yoten.** [pa. pple. of YET *v.*] Cast.

13.. *Coer de L.* 371 Hys mase..That was made of yoten bras. **1382** WYCLIF *Prol. Bible* iii. 4 Thei forsoken the feith ..of God, and onoureden ȝoten calues. —— *Exod.* xxxiv. 17 Ȝotun goddis thow shalt not make to thee. **1555** WATREMAN *Fardle Facions* II. viii. M iv b, Some worship the sonne, some ye moone. Other, ymages of yoten metalle.

yotization (jəʊtaɪˈzeɪʃən). *Phonetics.* [f. *yot-*, repr. IOTA + -IZATION.] The prefixing of the semivowel (j) to another sound or syllable; the change of a sound into (j). So ˈ**yotized** *ppl. a.*

1936 *Bull. School Oriental Stud.* VIII. 525 Peanius.. presents various types of syllable such as those 'quibus copulatur *ja*, seu *jota*', which we may describe as 'yotized'. *Ibid.* 532 Basic type of articulation..yotization..labio-velarization..nasalization. **1951** [see PROSODY 3].

yott, obs. form of YACHT.

you (juː, jə), *pers. pron.*, *2nd pers. obj.* (*nom.*), *pl.* (*sing.*). Forms: 1–3 **eow,** (1 **ieow, iow,** 2 **ȝeau, heou, heow, how, ȝehw,**) 2–3 **eou, ȝeu, ȝew,** 2–4 **ou, hou, ȝu,** 3 **iou, æu, ew, heu, eo, oeu, howe, ȝeow, ȝuw, ov,** 3–4 **ow, owe, ȝiu,** 3–5 **eu, yu,** (6 *Sc.*) **ȝou,** 4 **iow, ȝue, ȝuu, ȝouȝ, yuu, youu, yhow,** 4–5 **ȝowe, ȝhow, ȝo,** (6–7 *Sc.*) **ȝow,** 4–7 **yow,** 5 **ȝoue, ȝewe, ȝhu, yowe, yoow, yw, yo, yewe,** *Sc.* **yhu, yhw,** 5–6 **youe,** 6 **iow,** 7 **yew,** 4– **you,** (9 *dial.* & *vulgar* **yah, yer,** also YEZ). [OE. *éow* acc. and dat. (also *éowic*, Northumb. *íuih*, etc.) = OFris. *iuwe*, *iwe*, OS. *iu*, MDu., Du. *u*, OHG., MHG. *iu*, *eu*; deriving from earlier **īuw*:—OTeut. **iwwiz*. A parallel formation is represented by ON. *yðr* (MSw. *iþer*) for **iðwir*, ? **iRwiR*, Goth. *izwis*.

Originally the accusative and dative plural of the second personal pronoun: see THOU for the declension of the 2nd pers. pron. in OE. and ME. Between 1300 and 1400 it began to be used also for the nominative YE, which it had replaced in general use by about 1600. During the 14th century it also appears as a substitute for the singular obj. THEE and nom. THOU, being originally used in token of respect in addressing a superior, but later also to an equal, and ultimately generally: cf. THOU 1. Thus *you* is now the general pronoun of the second person, nominative or objective, singular or plural.]

I. As plural, used in addressing a number of persons (or, rhetorically, of things).

1. *Objective.* **a.** as direct object of a verb.

a **900** CYNEWULF *Elene* 551 Eow þeos cwen laþaþ, secgas, to salore. **1155** in *Anglia* VII. 1. 220 God ȝeau ȝehealde. *a* **1175** *Cott. Hom.* 233 Unwraste man wat lacede ȝeu? *c* **1175** *Lamb. Hom.* 13 Swa þet heo eow tintraȝed and heow i-swenchet. *c* **1205** LAY. 4556 Æuere mare ich æu leouie. *Ibid.* 5455 Leou wer here ic eow [*c* **1275** ȝou] abide. *c* **1250** *Kent. Serm.* in *O.E. Misc.* 32 Wat dret yw, folk of litle beliaue? **1389** in *Eng. Gilds* (1870) 53 To certefyen ȝ^u^ of godes and chateux. *a* **1400** *Pol. Rel. & L. Poems* (1903) 254, I come to leden ou swiþe. *c* **1420** *Sir Amadace* (Camden) lviii, Butte, alle my men, I ȝo cummawunde, To serue him wele to fote and honde. **14..** *Northern Passion* II. 173 In heuene ich wole ȝo cloþy & fede. **1450** in *Exch. Rolls Scot.* V. 425 *note*, Oure will is and we charge yhw that [etc.]. **1482** *Cov. Leet Bk.* 504 Ryght trusty & wele-belouеd, we grete yewe wele. **1567** *Gude & Godlie B.* (S.T.S.) 15 To him I ȝow commit baith small and greit. **1607** TOMKIS *Lingua* IV. i, I will be Iudicium, the moderator betwixt you, and make you both friends. **1766** GOLDSM. *Elegy Death Mad Dog* i, Good people all, of every sort, Give ear unto my song; And if you find it wondrous short,—It cannot hold you long. **1848** THACKERAY *Van. Fair* lxii, Fair scenes of peace and sunshine..who has ever seen you, that has not a grateful memory of those scenes of friendly repose and beauty? **1859** GEO. ELIOT *Adam Bede* ii, The lost!..Sinners!..Ah! dear friends, does that mean you and me?

b. as indirect object.

c **897** ÆLFRED *Gregory's Past. C.* xxvi. 181 (Hatton MS.) Waa ieow weleȝum. *c* **1160** *Hatton Gosp.* Matt. xxv. 45 Soð ic ȝu segge [etc.]. *c* **1175** *Lamb. Hom.* 49 Nu we sculen heow sceawen hwilc hit is heom for to heren. *c* **1200** *Trin. Coll. Hom.* 117 Ich wile ȝiu senden þe heuenliche frefringe. *c* **1205** LAY. 26515 Hit is eo muchel sceome þat ȝe wulleð at-sceken. *a* **1250** *Prov. Ælfred* 29 in *O.E. Misc.* 104 He ou wolde wyssye wisliche þinges. *a* **1250** *Owl & Night.* 115 Hit wes idon eu [*Cotton MS.* ov] a loþe custe. **1297** R. GLOUC. (Rolls) 10997 Ȝuf we doþ ou wrong wo ssal ou do riȝt? *a* **1300** *Cursor M.* 139 Sythen sal i tell yow [*v.rr.* ȝaw, ȝou] Of iacob and of esau. *c* **1320** *Cast. Love* 567 Ȝe habbeþ i-herd, as Ich ow tolde, For-whi God þe world maken wolde. **1340** HAMPOLE *Pr. Consc.* 3560 Here haf I shewed yhow, on Inglys, Som syns þat Saynt Austyn specifys. *c* **1400** *Pilgr. Sowle* (Caxton 1483) IV. v. 61, I graunte you leue, seyth what yow semyth eueryche in his parte. **1481** CAXTON *Godfrey* vi. 25, I shal shew yow one exampel. **1567** *Gude & Godlie B.* (S.T.S.) 29, I will ȝow giue Eternall lyfe. **1638** BROME *Antipodes* IV. vi, Ile give you halfe a dozen At the next Ale-house, to set all right. **1722** DE FOE *Plague* (1840) 129, I tell you, that we have not made use of the barn. **1859** KINGSLEY *Good News of God* xiii, I preach to you a Spirit..who has given you all the life you have.

c. As object of a preposition.

c **975** *Rushw. Gosp.* Matt. xii. 28 Cuðlice becymeþ in eow godes rice. *a* **1175** *Cott. Hom.* 225 Betwuxe me and eow. *c* **1175** *Lamb. Hom.* 149 Þene fule onkume..þa þe douel haueð in ow ibroht of sunne. *c* **1275** *Sinners Beware* 272 in *O.E. Misc.* 81 Loke seyde god nuþe Hwat ich for ou ouþe. *c* **1290** *St. Patrick* 612 in *S. Eng. Leg.* 218 Ȝif ich fram eov wende. *c* **1300** *Harrow. Hell* (E.) 141 Helle ȝates, y com ȝou to, Now ich wil þat ȝe vndo. **1382** WYCLIF *John* xviii. 39 It is a custom to ȝou, that I delyuer oon to ȝou in pask. *c* **1400** *Apol. Loll.* 1, I witnes bifor God Almiȝty, and alle trewe cristunmen and wommen, and ȝowe. *c* **1460** *Towneley Myst.* xx. 464 And I in you, and ye in me. **1536** WRIOTHESLEY *Chron.* (Camden) I. 42 Longe to reigne over yow. **1567** *Gude & Godlie B.* (S.T.S.) 31 Mark weill..How Christis croce, is for ȝow meit. **1609** B. JONSON *Epicœne* v. iii, That it be not strange to you, I will tell you. **1722** DE FOE *Plague* (1840) 130 The danger is as great from you to us, as from us to you. **1821** SCOTT *Kenilw.* i, Here's an unbelieving Pagan for you, gentlemen! **1896** MRS. FORRESTER *Harlow's Ideal* etc. 46 You have killed me between you.

d. As *reflexive pron.* (*acc.* or *dat.*) Yourselves. *arch.* See also *youself* s.v. SELF A. 2–4.

c **897** ÆLFRED *Gregory's Past. C.* xv. 93 (Hatton MS.) Habbað ȝe sealt on ieow, & sibbe habbað betweoh iow [*Cott. MS.* eow]. *c* **1175** *Lamb. Hom.* 73 Wascheð ou and wonieð clene. *c* **1200** ORMIN 5273 Þatt iss min bodeword, tatt ȝe ȝuw lufenn swa bitwenenn Rihht alls icc hafe lufedd ȝuw. *c* **1205** LAY. 7473 Ȝarewieð eow [*c* **1275** Greiþeh ow] to fihte. *Ibid.* 26447 Cnihtes fareð eou aȝæin. *a* **1225** *Leg. Kath.* 1403 Ne drede ȝe ow nawiht. *c* **1350** *Will. Palerne* 106 Haldes ow stille. **1375** BARBOUR *Bruce* I. 92 Haid ȝe wmbethocht ȝow enkrely, Quhat perell to ȝow mycht apper. *c* **1450** *St. Cuthbert* (Surtees) 3689 Demys ȝow na better in ȝour doyng þan othir of þe same leuyng. *c* **1560** A. SCOTT *Poems* (S.T.S.) iv. 103, I will nocht brek my brane, Suppois ȝe sowld mischeif ȝow. **1601** SHAKS. *Jul. C.* I. i. 1 Hence: home you idle Creatures, get you home. **1611** *Bible* Isa. i. 16 Wash yee [*mod. edd.* you], make you cleane. **1881** W. S. GILBERT *Patience* I, Now tell us, we pray you, Why thus you array you.

2. a. *Nominative*, replacing YE (sense 1).

In early use sometimes app. for emphasis, as opposed to *ye* unemphatic; but often beside *ye* as a mere alternative.

13.. *Cursor M.* 23160 (Gött.) Vnto mi blis haf ȝue na right. *c* **1400** *Destr. Troy* 7600 And, as yo [*sc.* Æneas and Hector] counsell in the cas, I comaund be done. **1526** *Pilgr. Perf.* (W. de W. 1531) 8 b, What ye rede, se you practise it in lyfe and dede. **1582** *N.T.* (Rhem.) Matt. v. 47 And if you salute your brethren only, what do you more? **1605** SHAKS. *Macb.* I. iii. 47 *Mac.* Speake if you can: what are you? **1611** *Bible* Ruth i. 11 Turne againe, my daughters; Why will you goe with mee? **1637** *Sc. Bk. Com. Prayer, Publ. Bapt.* Exhort., Friends, you heare in this Gospel the words of our Saviour Christ. **1652** BENLOWES *Theoph.* VI. lxxiii, Pure, scientifick and illustrious Spirits You'are. **1722** DE FOE *Plague* (1840) 129 And do you assure us that you are all sound men? **1868** HELPS *Realmah* xiii, I declare you are all very unkind to me.

b. As *vocative*, chiefly in apposition with a sb. following.

1569 PRESTON *Cambyses* (*c* 1584) F 3, Farwell you Ladies of the Court. **1594** SHAKS. *Rich. III*, I. iii. 158 Heare me, you wrangling Pyrates, that fall out, In sharing that which you haue pill'd from me. **1658** COKAINE *Trappolin* v. v, You Lords of Florence, wise Machavil, and You Lord Barbarino, will you never come Out of this frenzie? **1799** SHERIDAN *Pizarro* II. ii, And you, my daughters,..away to the appointed place of safety. **1875** JOWETT *Plato* (ed. 2) I. 37 You sirs, I said, what are you conspiring about? **1885** TENNYSON *The Fleet* i, You, you, if you shall fail to understand, What England is,..On you will come the curse of all the land.

3. In apposition with a sb., a numeral, *all*, *both*, in nominative or objective case.

c **1205** LAY. 5453, & ȝif ȝe þis nulleð, alle ich ȝeow [*c* **1275** ȝou] aquelle. *c* **1320** *Sir Tristr.* 2184 Loke now on aday And blod lat ȝou þre. **1340–70** *Alex. & Dind.* 65, I haue founde ȝou folk faiþful of speche. **1470–85** MALORY *Arthur* x. lv. 506 Is þ^t^ the rule of yow arraunt knyghtes for to make a knyght to Iuste wil he or nyll. **1549** COVERDALE *Erasm. Par. Phil.* i. 8, I longe after you all, from the very hart rote in Iesus Christ. *a* **1596** *Sir T. More* I. i. 120 If you men durst not vndertake it, before God, we women would. **1610** SHAKS. *Temp.* III. iii. 69 You three From Milan did supplant good Prospero. *c* **1720** DE FOE *Mem. Cavalier* iv. (1840) 61 You English gentlemen..are too forward in the wars. **1837** DICKENS *Pickw.* xlvi, If you law-gentlemen do these things on speculation. **1884** 'EDNA LYALL' *We Two* xxi, You don't know how I love you all.

II. As singular, used in addressing one person (or thing); orig. as a mark of respect, later *gen.*

4. *Objective*, replacing the earlier THEE.

a. as direct object of a verb.

13.. *Bonaventura's Medit.* 314 My wurschypful fadyr,.. Here my bone..For sorowe my soule haþ ȝow soȝt. *c* **1350** *Will. Palerne* 634 Madame,..nis it no sekenes bote þat so sore ȝouȝ eiles, I schal þurth craft þat ich kan keuer ȝou i hope. *c* **1440** *York Myst.* xxx. 58, I beseke you my soueraynе, assente to my sawes. *c* **1470** *Gol. & Gaw.* 147 To mak you lord of your avne, me think it grete skill. **1585** JAS. I *Ess. Poesie* Pref. (Arb.) 55, I will also wish ȝow (docile Reidar) that or ȝe cummer ȝow with reiding thir reulis [etc.]. **1587** in *Cath. Rec. Soc. Publ.* V. 138, I committ youe to the tuition of Jesu. **1650** in *Verney Mem.* (1907) I. 465 If yew love your selfe, and those that love yew. **1749** FIELDING *Tom Jones* XII. iv, Your religion..serves you only for an excuse for your faults. **1837** DICKENS *Pickw.* ii, It will afford me the greatest pleasure to know you, sir. **1857** *Chamb. Jrnl.* 8 Aug. 83/1 When I say mammon, I don't mean idle dukes or greedy merchant-princes; my small adulterating shopkeeper I mean you!

b. as indirect object. (See also 7.)

a **1352** MINOT *Poems* (ed. Hall) vi. 23 No bowes now thar ȝow bende; Of blis ȝe er all bare. *c* **1375** *Sc. Leg. Saints* v. (*Johannes*) 643 Myn lord,..þis ringe, þat I yu present now, Me gafe a pilgram to gyf ȝow,..And bad I suld gyf it ȝov til, & thange ȝou of ȝore gud vyl. **1471** MARG. PASTON in *P. Lett.* III. 24, I can yw thanke for ywyr lettyr that ye sente me. *c* **1520** SKELTON *Magnyf.* 2355 Nowe must I make you a lectuary softe. **1567** *Satir. Poems Reform.* iii. 64 My Lord, ane taikin I ȝow plycht. **1646** *Hamilton Papers* (Camden) 114 The drawing of that whereof the copy is sent yow. **1749** FIELDING *Tom Jones* VII. viii, Let me tell you that. **1826** SCOTT *Woodst.* xviii, 'Hold, woman, hold!' said Alice Lee; 'the dog will not do you harm.'

c. as object of a preposition.

a **1352** MINOT *Poems* (ed. Hall) vi. 28 Oure men sall with ȝow mote. *c* **1375** *Sc. Leg. Saints* xl. (*Ninian*) 1123 Lord,.. of þat land ȝet brocht haf I a man to ȝou as presonere. *c* **1420** *Chron. Vilod.* 2417 Me thouȝt þat assemely lady come me to ..& badde þat y chulde heyȝe & to ȝow go. *a* **1455** MARG. ANJOU *Let. to Abbot of St. Osy* (Camden) 124 Unto you that bene a member of chirche. **1482** in *Engl. Hist. Rev.* XXV. 122 This owre ordinance made for yowe Thomas Raile nowe keper of þ^e^ said Brethernes locutorie. **15..** *Adam Bel* 47 in Ritson *Anc. Pop. Poetry* 7 Thys place hath ben besette for you, Thys half yere and more. **1596** DALRYMPLE tr. *Leslie's Hist. Scot.* (S.T.S.) I. 296 This goldne aple..I preparit and decoret vnto ȝow my Souerane. **1607** TOMKIS *Lingua* IV. i, Mendatio you offer mee great wrong to hold me, in good-faith I shall fall out with you. **1780** *Mirror* No. 97 'Quantity of syllables,' exclaimed the Captain, 'there is a modern education for you!' **1852** MRS. STOWE *Uncle Tom's C.* xx, I bought her, and I'll give her to you.

d. As *refl. pron.* (*acc.* or *dat.*). Yourself. *arch.*

c**1400** *Anturs Arth.* 100 Thus he comforthede þe qwene . . 'At this gaste,' quod Sir Gaweayne, 'greue ȝowe no more.' c**1420** *Chron. Vilod.* 3470 Seynt Ede . . sayde: syre kyng, drede ȝow nomore! c**1500** *Three Kings' Sons* 29 Y thought that ye wolde kepe you here aboute hym. ?a**1550** *Freiris Berwik* 512 in *Dunbar's Poems* (1893) 302 And neir the dur ȝe hyd ȝow prevely. **1585** [see a]. **1610** Shaks. *Temp.* iii. i. 18 Pray set it downe, and rest you . . Pray now rest your selfe. **1712** [see get *v.* 28 c]. **1884** W. S. Gilbert *Princ. Ida* iii, Coward! get you hence.

5. a. *Nominative*, replacing thou.

Always const. with pl. verb, exc. in the collocation *you was*, prevalent in 17th and 18th c., for which see be *v.* 6 ¶. For phr. such as *you bet, you know, you see*, see the verbs.

14.. *Guy W.* (Cambr. MS.) 4192 'Syr Gye,' he seyde, . . 'To morowe schall yow weddyd bee.' **1489** *Barbour's Bruce* vi. 657 (Edin. MS.) Bot the gret part ȝe tuk ȝe, That slew iiij off the fyve ȝow ane. **1555** Eden *Decades* (Arb.) 380 Ouer the sayde byght, yow shall se a greate gappe in the mountayne. **1588** Shaks. *L.L.L.* i. i. 53 You swore to that Berowne, and to the rest. a**1596** *Sir T. More* i. ii. 194 Well, Maister Moore, you are a merie man. **1648** *Hamilton Papers* (Camden) 236 Yow shall, if yow finde it necessary, goe from Holland to France, and deliver to the Queen's Majtie this our letter. **1740** Richardson *Pamela* I. 163 Well, Jacob, what do you stare at? Pray mind what you're upon. **1821** Clare *Vill. Minstrel* I. 34 If yah set any store by one yah will! **1833** Tennyson *Death of Old Year* ii, Old year, you must not go; . . Old year, you shall not go.

b. As *vocative*, chiefly in apposition with a sb. following; in reproach or contempt often repeated after the sb. (cf. thou 1 b).

c**1500** *Melusine* 182 My lord and you my lady, yf ye vouchsaf it were tyme that we went thrugh the world at our auenture. **1590** Shaks. *Mids. N.* iii. ii. 288 Fie, fie, you counterfeit, you puppet, you. **1606** Chapman *Gentl. Usher* iii. i, You asse you, d'ee call my Lord horse? **1667** Dryden & Dk. Newcastle *Sir M. Mar-all* v. iii, You old Sot you, to be caught so sillily! **1768** Goldsm. *Goodn. Man* ii, And you have but too well succeeded, you little hussy, you! **1840** Thackeray *Catherine* ix, You young hangdog, you! **1849** H. W. Herbert *Frank Forester* II. 179 Walk a few yards ahead of me, and look out you for all that cross you! **1852** E. Burne-Jones *Let.* 24 Jan. in *Mem.* (1904) I. 63 You scamp not to write before. **1919** Capes *Skel. Key* xxi. 273 'I love you for trying, you dear,' he said.

c. Phr. *you and your* ——: a contemptuous, impatient, or good-natured dismissal of the thing or person mentioned. *colloq.*

1607 Shakes. *Coriolanus* iv. vi. 97 You haue made good worke, You and your Apron men. **1837** H. Martineau *Society in America* III. iii. i. 80 An old acquintance of Noah's . . said . . , 'Go, get along, you and your old ark! I don't believe we are going to have much of a shower.' **1899** Kipling *Stalky & Co.* 177 'I was born there . . . It was called after my uncle.' 'Shut up—you and your uncle!' **1943** J. B. Priestley *Daylight on Saturday* xxii. 172 I've told 'im . . . 'You an' your Teds!' I told 'im. **1955** E. Blishen *Roaring Boys* i. 27 'Progressing!' He relished it. 'You and your long words!' **1980** P. G. Winslow *Counsellor Heart* xiv. 171 Ah, you and your Colonel. Worms' meat, he is now.

d. *you and who else?*: see who *pron.* 4 a; *you and yours*: see yours *poss. pron.* 2 b.

III. Special uses.

6. Denoting any hearer or reader; hence as an indef. pers. pron.: One, any one.

1577 Googe *Heresbach's Husb.* ii. (1586) 87 You shall sometime have one branch more gallant than his fellowes. **1614** Tomkis *Albumazar* i. iii, With this [perspicill] Ile read a leafe of that small Iliade . . as plainly Twelue long miles off, as you see Pauls from Highgate. **1625** Bacon *Ess., Atheism* (Arb.) 333 Nay more, you shall haue Atheists striue to get Disciples, as it fareth with other Sects. **1707** *Lond. Gaz.* No. 4351/3 One Red Buoy to the Eastward of you, as you pass this Chanel. **1726** Swift *Gulliver* ii. i, A child . . began a squall that you might have heard from London Bridge to Chelsea. **1865** Ruskin *Sesame* i. §30 You can talk a mob into anything. **1870** *Good Words* 133/2 The slope [is] so rapid that you can scarcely find footing when once off the beaten road.

7. Used with no definite meaning as indirect object ('ethical dative'). Cf. me 2 c. *arch.*

1590 Shaks. *Mids. N.* i. ii. 84, I will roare you as gently as any Sucking Doue; I will roare and 'twere any Nightingale. **1602** —— *Ham.* v. i. 183 If he be not rotten before he die . . , he will last you some eight yeare, or nine yeare. A Tanner will last you nine yeare. **1624** Bedell *Lett.* xii. 162 Vnto him . . I doe . . commend you: and rest you, Your very louing brother. **1874** Geo. Eliot *Coll. Breakf.-P.* 388 Anti-social force that sweeps you down The world in one cascade of molecules.

†**8.** As *possessive* = your. *Obs.* or *dial. rare.*

1642 D. Rogers *Naaman* 272 You rather will quarrel with God for not fulfilling you wills. *Ibid.* 290 You make benefit thereof for you owne behoofe and content. **1888** Elworthy *W. Somerset Word-bk.*

9. Qualified by a preceding adj.

c**1600** Shaks. *Sonn.* lxxxvi. 2 Bound for the prize of (all to precious) you. **1895** Mrs. Forrester *Too Late Repented* viii, 'Oh', muttered Ethel . . 'poor you, poor you!' **1904** F. Whishaw *Tiger of Muscovy* xi. 95 How should poor little you deal with a maiden who dares to call the Tsar a bear?

10. As *sb.* **a.** The word as used in addressing a person or persons.

c**1645** Howell *Lett.* iv. xix. (1890) 596 The Courtiers began to magnify him, and treat him in the plural number by *You*, and by degrees to deify him by transcending Titles. **1669** Penn (*title*) No Cross, No Crown: or Several Sober Reasons against Hat-Honour, Titular Respects, You to a Single Person, . . with Testimonies of the most famous Persons in defence of the poor despised Quakers.

b. The person (or such a person as the one) addressed; the personality of the one addressed.

1700 Dryden *Fables* Poet. Ded. 138 Or Heav'n . . So lik'd the Frame, he would not work anew, To save the Charges of another You. **1724-5** Swift *Receipt to restore Stella's Youth* 38 If your flesh and blood be new, You'll be no more the former you. **1729** Law *Serious C.* xix. 361, I don't mean that you have not bodies . . , but that all that deserves to be called *you*, is nothing else but spirit. **1911** Marett *Anthropol.* viii. 231 Though the language may seem to imply a 'you', he would mean, I believe, to impute to the flint just as much, or as little, of personality as we should mean to do when using similar language. **1964** 'E. Lathen' *Accounting for Murder* xv. 142 We run tests. . . Then, once we had really found the real you, we . . would try to find a place that provided a challenge to your best creative talents. **1974** *Spartanburg* (S. Carolina) *Herald* 25 Apr. a-5 (Advt.), Vicaltein can be your ticket to a newer, slimmer you. **1978** J. Grenfell *Stately as Galleon* 38 Learn . . to dance the natural nature way. Let the music through, find the inner you. **1981** *Sci. Amer.* July 14/3 For every quantum-mechanical branch point in your life . . you have split into two or more you's riding along parallel but disconnected branches of one gigantic universal wave function.

11. As *adj.*: expressive of or suited to your taste, personality, etc.

1918 R. Fry *Let.* 12 Mar. (1972) II. 425 I've read your *Lucretius*. . . I feel sure it's both immensely him and also very much you. **1936** U. Orange *Begin Again* xi. 247 'I think it's lovely,' said Jane unkindly, 'So *you*, somehow.' **1960** N. Marsh *False Scent* viii. 232 The boudoir . . had been created by Bertie. . . 'Almost indecently *you*, darling!' Bertie had told Miss Bellamy. **1981** M. Spark *Loitering with Intent* ii. 44, I thought your piece was very much you.

12. Phrasal combinations: **you-be-damned** *a.*, addicted to saying 'you be damned!'; contemptuously overbearing; hence *you-be-damnedness*; **you-know-what**, †**you-wot-what** *sb.*, used instead of the name of something which it is needless or undesirable to specify; also as *vb.*; **you-know-who, -whom**, a deliberately unnamed person whose identity is apparent to the hearer.

1545 Ascham *Toxoph.* ii. (Arb.) 145 As though they were doyng you wotte what. **1605** Camden *Rem.* (1623) 29 *Κακάω*, to you know what. **1766** O. Goldsmith *Vicar of Wakefield* II. ix. 143, I danced last night with Lady G——, and could I forget you know whom, I might be perhaps successful. **1796** M. Edgeworth *Parent's Assistant* (ed. 2) i. 174 Do nothing in this till we have consulted *you know who* about whether it's right or wrong. a**1845** Hood *Tale of Trumpet* xxvi, And down you go, in you know what. **1857** *Commerc. Trav. Mag.* II. 240 First give me, Marguerite, just a little drop of you know what. I'm quite husky. **1885** *Society in London* ix. 204 What I principally like about your Lord Hartington is his you-be-damnedness. **1891** Kipling *Light that Failed* vi, He is such an aggressive, cocksure, you-be-damned fellow. **1912** C. Mackenzie *Carnival* xiii. 167, I don't think I'm jealous of you know who. **1936** O. Nash *Primrose Path* 198 Be my gazelle, my wishing well . . But never my you-know-what. **1937** M. Allingham *Dancers in Mourning* xiii. 179 Not a word to Mrs. You Know Who. **1956** L. McIntosh *Oxford Folly* 37 She's madly gay, but hard as nails when it comes to you know what. **1975** *Verbatim* Dec. 1/2 John O'Donnell expressed his delight that 'we're going to arm German panzer divisions for you-know-what'. **1976** *New Yorker* 26 Apr. 99/1 She gives me a pain in my you-know-what. **1978** J. Irving *World according to Garp* xviii. 390 Old You-Know-Who—the Under Toad, that's who, Helen thought. **1981** Q. Crisp *How to become Virgin* vi. 81 Since neither I nor Mr. Hurt . . flashed you-know-what before the cameras . . we might both by modern standards be considered old-fashioned.

Hence **you** *v. trans.*, to address (a person) by the pronoun *you* (instead of *thou*); *intr.* with *it*, to use the pronoun *you* repeatedly. (Cf. thou *v.*)

1564 Bulleyn *Dial. agst. Pest.* (1573) 1 He [*sc.* a beggar] thowes not God, but you[s] hym. **1675** H. More in R. Ward *Life* (1710) 341 No Man will *You* God, but use the Pronoun *Thou* to him. **1676** Bunyan *Strait Gate* 55 *I say unto you.* Had not the Lord Jesus designed by these words, to shew what an overthrow will one day be made among professors, he needed not to have *you'ed* it at this rate. **1848** A. B. Evans *Leicestersh. Wds.* 109 Says I, 'Do yeaow mane to bully me? . . Yeaow come here to bully me? So I yeaowed him out o' the field.

you, obs. f. ewe *sb.*[1]

1523-4 *Churchw. Acc., Croscombe* (Som. Rec. Soc.) 37 The whych you scheppes beth delyvered unto Hew Morganne.

you, graphic variant of þou, thou.

you-all ('juːɔːl, juː'ɔːl), *pers. pron. U.S. dial.* Also **you all**. [f. you *pers. pron.* + all *a.*] Used in place of you *pers. pron.*

Used, with no clear pattern, both as *sing.* and as *pl.*

1824 'A. Singleton' *Lett. South & West* 82 Children learn from the slaves some odd phrases; . . as . . will you *all* do this? for, will *one* of you do this? **1871** R. M. Johnston *Dukesborough Tales* vii. 95 You all little fellows was . . skeered. **1875** [see we-all *pron.*]. **1901** A. H. Rice *Mrs. Wiggs of Cabbage Patch* vi. 81 Some of you all shake down the stove an' pull the door to fer me. **1919** R. Frost *Let.* 24 Mar. (1972) 56 The second thing is to ask you what you-all are thinking of to want me to judge in a lyric contest. **1924** W. M. Raine *Troubled Water* xix. 201 You-all are losing a better man than Missie ever had. **1926** E. Ferber *Show Boat* 299 You-all one of them Suhveys? **1926** *Amer. Speech* II. 476/1, I was born in South Carolina . . and have worked on a New Orleans paper for two years, and I have not once in my life heard the expression 'you-all' used except in plural address. **1927** *Ibid.* III. 5 *You-all* certainly is used as singular in the Ozarks—I have heard it daily for weeks at a time. *You-uns*, however, . . is nearly always plural in the Ozark country. **1928** *Ibid.* IV. 54 Here in Missouri . . I have again and again heard 'you all' used in speaking to one person. **1942** M. K. Rawlings *Cross Creek* xxii. 344, I ain't never been as far as you-all aim to go. **1944** *Amer. Speech* XIX. 147/2 In almost a score of years of residence in North Carolina I have never heard anyone say 'you all', unless the plural was definitely and distinctly intended. **1954** G. Durrell *Three Singles to Adventure* 15 Is youall to catch the Parika train? **1981** *TV Picture Life* Mar. 46/3 Then I walked into this audition, put my feet up on the desk, finished my beer, and drawled, 'What kind of character you-all looking for?'

So **you-all's** and varr., your.

1869 *Overland Monthly* Aug. 131 During the war we all heard enough of 'we-uns' and 'you-uns', but 'you-alls' was to me something fresh. **1887** *Scribner's Mag.* Oct. 478/1 How are you all's little trick? **1929** W. Faulkner *Sound & Fury* 347, I try to obey his wishes for you alls' sakes. **1934** C. Carmer *Stars fell on Alabama* 190 We are honored to have you-all's company.

youden-drift, variant of ewden-drift.

'**youdith.** *Sc.* [f. *youd*, obs. Sc. var. youth + *-ith*, after *poortith*.] Youth.

1728 Ramsay *Fair Assembly* xiv, Her Cheek, where Roses free from Stain, In Glows of Youdith beek. **1810** in Cromek's *Sel. Scot. Songs* II. 54 Sae lang's ye hae youdith.

youdle, var. yodel *v.*

youf (jaʊf), *v. Sc.* Forms: 7 **youph, yooff**, 8-9 **youf, yuff**, 9 **youff(e, yowf(f.** [Echoic. Cf. yaff.] *intr.* To bark, esp. in a suppressed manner.

1682 Law *Mem.* (1818) 224 His dogs . . howling, yelling, and youphing. *Ibid.*, Howling and yooffing. a**1774** Fergusson *Poems* (1789) II. 6 My colley, Ringie, youf'd an yowl'd a' night. **1789** D. Davidson *Seasons* 41 And, Cerberus, though but just whelped, Did stan' an' yuff. **1826** J. Wilson *Noctes Ambr.* Wks. 1855 I. 173 A' the collies began yelpin and youffin. **1842** *Whistle-Binkie* Ser. iii. *Last Laird o' the Auld Mint* viii, A kind yowffin bark.

So **youf** *int.* (also reduplicated) and *sb.*

1842 J. Wilson *Chr. North* I. 18 Youf—youf—youf—go the terriers. **1866** Gregor *Banffsh. Gloss.*, *Youff*, the bark of a dog. *Youff* conveys the notion of a softer sound than *youp*.

youf(f, youft, variants of yowf, yuft.

youghendale, youkyndall, var. yokindale.

yough fro, obs. form of yuffrouw.

yought, youghten, youghthe, yougth: see yacht, youth, yuft.

youhoge, obs. form of ewe-hog.

1531 in Weaver *Wells Wills* (1890) 29 My sister-in-law Marg. Pinare a youhoge.

youk, youk(e, obs. ff. yoke, yuke.

youl(e, youll, youlan: see oil *sb.*[1], yowl, yulan.

youlde, -en, obs. pa. t. and pple. of yield *v.*

youle, obs. spelling of *you'll*, = *you will*.

1607 Tomkis *Lingua* iii. vi, Leaue iesting, youle put the fresh Actor out of countenance.

youlowe, obs. form of yellow.

youl(w)ring: see yowlring.

yound (ȝ-), -er, obs. ff. yond, yonder.

young (jʌŋ), *a.* (*sb.*[1]). Forms: α. 1 **ȝeong, ȝiong, ȝung, iung**, 2 **jung**, 2-5 (6 *Sc.*) **ȝung**, 3 **ȝeung**, 3-5 **ȝeong(e, ȝonge, ȝunge, yung**, (6 *Sc.*) **ȝong**, 3-7 **yong**, (4 **ȝonke, ȝhoung, yhung**), 4-5 **yunge**, 4-6 **yonge, ȝoung(e**, (5 **yhonge, ȝoyng**, 6 **yownge, yongue**), 6-7 **yoong, younge**, 6- **young**. β. 1 **ȝing**, 3 **ȝuing**, 3-5 **ȝinge**, 4-5 **ȝyng(e**, 4-6 **ȝing, ying**, (4 **yyng**, 5 **yinge, yynge, ynge, yhyng**). γ. 3 **ȝenge**, 3-5 **ȝeng**, (4 **ȝeing**), 4-5 **yeng**. See also younger, youngest. [OE. *ȝeong, ȝung, iung*, (Northumbrian) *ȝing*, = OFris., OS. *jung*, MDu. *jonc* (Du. *jong*), MLG. *junk* (LG. *jung*), OHG., MHG. *junc* (G. *jung*), ON. *ungr* (Sw., Da. *ung*), Goth. *juggs*:—OTeut. **jūŋgaz*, contraction of **juwuŋgaz*:—Indo-Eur. **juwn̥kós* (whence Skr. *juvaçás* youthful, youngling, L. *juvencus* young bull, W. *ieuanc*, OIr. *óac, óc* young), f. **juwen-* (*jūn-, jun-*), which is represented also by Skr. *yúvan-, yūn-*, L. *juvenis*, comp. *jūnior*, Lith. *jáunas*, OSl. *junŭ* young, L. *juventūs, juventa*, OIr. *óitiu*, youth.]

A. *adj.*

1. That has lived a relatively short time; that is in the early stage of life or growth; youthful: opp. to old *a.* 1. **a.** of persons.

not so young as** (one) **was (or ***used to be***): getting old, advanced in years (*colloq.*, often *jocular*).

α. *Beowulf* 13 Ðæm eafera wæs æfter cenned ȝeong in ȝeardum. a**1000** *Andreas* 392 Nu synt ȝeƿreade þeȝnas mine, ȝeonge guðrincas. a**1100** *Aldhelm Gloss.* i. 2591 (Napier 70/2) *Lactantes, .i. infantes*, iung cildra. c**1200** Ormin 1212 Ȝiff þu . . hafesst ȝet, tohh þu be ȝung, Elldernemanness late. a**1225** *Leg. Kath.* 66 A meiden swiðe ȝung of ȝeres. c**1290** *S. Eng. Leg.* 7/209 On ouewarde he i-saiȝ a luyte ȝong child. a**1300** *Cursor M.* 12460 Quen iesus com in-to þat scole, Þof he was yong was he na fole. **1362** Langl. *P. Pl.* A. x. 181 Hit is an vn-Comely Couple be Cryst, as me þinkeþ, To ȝeuen a ȝong wenche to an old feble Mon. **1375** Barbour *Bruce* xii. 322 His air . . his land sall weild, All be he neuir so ȝhoung of eild. c**1450** Capgrave *Life St. Aug.* iii, Wher ȝong damesellis be with chateryng tongis. c**1460** *Emare* 707 Up he toke that fayre ladye, And the yonge chylde her by. **1551** Robinson tr. *More's Utopia* ii. (1895) 162 The nourceis sitte seuerall alone with their yonge suckelinges. **1617** MORYSON *Itin.* III. 185 Philip.. died young before his Father. **1682** DRYDEN *Mac. Fl.* 3 Who, like Augustus, young Was call'd to Empire and had govern'd long. **1751** SMOLLETT *Per. Pickle* xvi, He.. instructed the young boys in the games of hustle-cap, leap-frog, and chuck-farthing. **1821** SCOTT *Kenilw.* xli, Young in years but old in grief. **1852** MISS MULOCK *Agatha's Husb.* vii, Judging such things by what they were when I was young. *Ibid.*, He is not so young as he used to be. **1859** H. KINGSLEY *G. Hamlyn* xxxvii, George Hawker, it's many years since we met, and I'm not so young as I was. **1888** 'J. S. WINTER' *Bootle's Childr.* vi, Somehow the laugh had made her look young and pretty again.

β. *a* **900** CYNEWULF *Elene* 353 Ic up ahof eaforan ᵹinge. *Ibid.* 464 Onᵹit, guma ᵹinga, godes heahmæᵹen, nerᵹendes naman. *c* **1250** [see YOUNG WOMAN 1]. *a* **1300** *Cursor M.* 3224 A sargiant.. þat had ben als of his fostring, Ai siþen he was a barn ying. **13..** *Coer de L.* 924 Forleyn was his doughter yyng. **1447** BOKENHAM *Seyntys* (Roxb.) 195 That ageynys oo maydyn tendyr & ying Fyfty greth clerkys þou doost furth bryng. *c* **1450** *Merlin* 198 As soone as thei hem saugh, thei ne douted nothinge so small a peple that were so ynge. **1522** *World & Child* A ij b, I wyll the fynde whyle thou art yinge, So thou wylte be obedyent to my byddynge. **1570** *Satir. Poems Reform.* xvii. 188 In him I hope releif, Of ȝeiris thocht he be ȝing. *a* **1600** MONTGOMERIE *Misc. Poems* xxxiv. 2 Sueit thing, bening and ȝing.

γ. *c* **1205** LAY. 3123 He wes a ȝenge king. **13..** *Cursor M.* 24030 (Gött.), þat wreche womman ȝeng [*rime* steng]. *c* **1400** [see YOUNG MAN 1]. *c* **1430** *Syr Gener.* (Roxb.) 3305 Among the lordes old and yeng For gladnes of thes new tithing. *c* **1450** *Cursor M.* 10618 (Laud) There was no maide of none osprynd So holy of lyf old nor yeng. *c* **1450** *St. Cuthbert* (Surtees) 591 He had sex childre ȝeng A lang tyme in his kepyng.

b. (*a*) In collocations of specific meaning, as ***young creature***, ***young folk***(*s*, ***young fry***, ***young master***, ***young people***, ***young person***, ***young thing***: see the sbs. CREATURE 3, FOLK 3, 4, FRY[1] 4 b, MASTER *sb.*[1] 23, PEOPLE 6 b, PERSON 2 e, THING[1] 10, and quots. below. ***young one***: †a young person; (usually with poss.) offspring, pl. ***young ones***, offspring, progeny; = B. 2; also in colloq. form ***young 'un***, ***youngun*** = YOUNGSTER. See also YOUNG LADY, YOUNG MAN, YOUNG WOMAN, and C. below.

Certain collocations, e.g. *young man*, *gentleman*, *woman*, *lady*, are colloq. used vocatively in addressing reproof or warning to persons of almost any age. See YOUNG MAN 1, quot. 1865, YOUNG WOMAN 1, quot. 1864.

1297 R. GLOUC. (Rolls) 6446 Awey seli ȝonge þinges. **13..** *Gaw. & Gr. Knt.* 1526 Ȝe.. Oghe to a ȝonke þynk ȝern to schewe, & teche sum tokenez of trweluf craftes. **1382** WYCLIF *Mark* xvi. 5 Thei goynge yn into the sepulcre syȝen a ȝong oon, hilid with a whit stoole. *c* **1412** HOCCLEVE *De Reg. Princ.* 147 Ful seelde is, þat ȝong folk wyse been. *c* **1450** *Brut* II. 349 A yong creature of ix yere of age, Dame Isabell. **1474** CAXTON *Chesse* II. iv. (1883) 55 That the yonge peple shold not haue but on gowne or garment in the yere. **1533** GAU *Richt Vay* 3 Mony guyd men and vemen and specialie ȝung persons. **1535** COVERDALE *Isa.* xi. 7 The cowe and the Bere shal fede together, and their yongones shal lye together. **1542** [see THING *sb.*[1] 10]. **1601** SHAKS. *All's Well* v. iii. 303 Dead though she be, she feeles her yong one kicke. **1605** —— *Macb.* IV. ii. 11 The poore Wren.. will fight, Her yong ones in her Nest, against the Owle. **1653** W. HARVEY *Anat. Exerc.* xi. 53 The superficies of this Island (in the moneths of May and June) is almost covered quite over with Nests, Egges, and Young-Ones. **1693** *Humours Town* 118 If you want a Foil, as indeed 'tis generally the Care of you young Ones, now-a-days, to get one that's Ugly or Old. **1709** MRS. MANLEY *Secret Mem.* (1720) IV. 190 My Eyes, like most young Peoples, were perpetually at the Windows. **1753** SMOLLETT *Count Fathom* viii, Certain dangerous books, calculated to debauch the minds of young people. *c* **1810** W. HICKEY *Mem.* (1960) iv. 64 So the young'un there wanted to be off, but I said as how I knew a trick worth two of that. **1814** SCOTT *Wav.* lxxi, The Baron, while he assumed the lower end of the table, insisted that Lady Emily should do the honours of the head, that they might, he said, set a meet example to the *young folk*. **1833** [see FOLK 3 b]. **1838** EGAN *Pilgr. Thames* x. 200 'Where's the kids?' 'Kids!' reiterated Mrs. Brindle, interrogatively. 'Yes, the young 'uns!' said Mrs. Bodger. 'Oh, the children!' **1852** MRS. STOWE *Uncle Tom's C.* xviii, Dinah would.. tell all marauding 'young uns'.. to keep out of the kitchen. **1852** MISS MULOCK *Agatha's Husb.* x, The young couple were excellent listeners. **1855** LEIFCHILD *Cornwall* 281 'Young persons' have been defined to be males and females from thirteen to eighteen years of age. **1860** GEO. ELIOT *Mill on Fl.* III. iii, Well, young sir, we've been talking as we should want your pen and ink. **1876** MISS BRADDON *J. Haggard's Dau.* i, You beware o' that young 'un. He's bound to be your foe. **1886** BESANT *Childr. Gibeon* I. ix, She could be properly described as a Young Girl, which is the general name for the workwoman in youth, but no one would think of calling her a young lady. **1918** *Act 8 & 9 Geo. V*, c. 39. §48 The expression 'young person' means a person under eighteen years of age who is no longer a child. **1922** JOYCE *Ulysses* 418 Collar the leather, Youngun. **1940** C. MCCULLERS *Heart is Lonely Hunter* I. iv. 56 A youngun was sitting on the banisters... He had seen her somewhere before. **1981** J. D. MACDONALD *Free Fall in Crimson* xix. 219 Here and there are little groups of younguns who know what an original idea tastes like.

(*b*) Such collocations may be used attrib. or as adj., may be converted into verbs, or may take a suffix; e.g. ***young-girl*** adj. (pertaining to a young girl), hence ***young-girlish*** adj., ***-girlishly*** adv.; ***young-master*** vb. (to address or treat as a young master); ***young-gentlemanly*** adj. (pertaining to or characteristic of a young gentleman).

1613 *Sidney's Arcadia* II. xxix. (ed. 4) 210 Looking to haue bin yong-mastred among those great estates, as he was among his abusing vnderlings. **1854** THACKERAY *Leech's Pict.* Wks. 1900 XIII. 488 What fine young-gentlemanly wags they are. **1868** SILL *Hermitage* i, A well-bred, fair, young-gentlemanly life. **1880** 'MARK TWAIN' *Tramp Abr.* ix, She was absorbed in.. her own young-girl dreams. **1928** A. HUXLEY *Point Counter Point* xi. 174 She flushed with a young-girlishly timid pleasure. **1975** *New Yorker* 28 Apr. 66/3 Her young-girlish way of lowering her eyes with an air of anguish when I asked her what had happened to her affair with the man she said she had loved.

c. Used to distinguish the younger of two persons of the same name or title in a family (esp. a son from his father); equivalent to *junior*.

1340 *Ayenb.* 48 þe holy mayde sare þet zeþþe wes yonge thobyes wyf. **1375** BARBOUR *Bruce* III. 216 Scipio the ying. ? *a* **1461** *Stonor Papers* (Camden) I. 55 Yn Abraham tyme, and in Balky tyme the yongge. **1533** BELLENDEN *Livy* I. xviii. (S.T.S.) I. 101 Ȝoung [*v.r.* ȝing] terquyne and þis feirs tullia war maryit togiddir. **1563–1693** [see MASTER *sb.*[1] 23]. **1572** in *Buccleuch MSS.* (Hist. MSS. Comm. 1899) I. 23 For maring of zoung Quein Marie with Prince Edward. **1647** CLARENDON *Hist. Reb.* III. §147 The chief leaders, Nathaniel Fynes and young Sir H. Vane. **1753** SMOLLETT *Count Fathom* xliii, Young Melvil.. implicitly believed the story and protestations of Fathom. **1817** MARIA EDGEWORTH *Ormond* i, Young Ormond was the son of the friend of Sir Ulick O'Shane's youthful and warm-hearted days. **1885** 'MRS. ALEXANDER' *At Bay* xi, Lady Frances keeps her dower, and young Deering the estates for his life.

d. of animals (or their flesh as food).

young fry: see FRY *sb.*[1] 4.

c **950** *Lindisf. Gosp.* Luke xv. 23 *Uitulum saginatum*, ᵹing oxo fætt. *c* **1200** *Trin. Coll. Hom.* 201 Đe neddre bileued hire hude baften hire, and cumeð newe fel and hie wurð jung. **1390** in W. Hudson *Leet Jurisd. Norwich* (1892) 73 Capere yongfry in Regia Ripa et vendere hominibus de Crowmeer.. pro bayte. *c* **1430** *Two Cookery-bks.* 54 Take kydes Fleyssche & ȝong porke. *c* **1440** *York Myst.* ix. 139 Of beestis and foules ȝynge,.. a peyre. **1573–80** TUSSER *Husb.* (1878) 82 Thy colts for thy saddle geld yoong to be light. **1599** PORTER *Angry Wom. Abingt.* (Percy Soc.) 43 As soone goes the yong sheep to the pot as the olde. **1653** W. HARVEY *Anat. Exerc.* v. 20 Pullets or young Hens. *c* **1730** RAMSAY *Eagle & Robin* 23 A tunefull Robin trig and ȝung. **1803–6** WORDSW. *Ode Intim. Immort.* iii, While the young lambs bound As to the tabor's sound. **1828** G. F. LYON *Jrnl. Mexico* I. 109 A steak which I cooked tasted so like well-fed young pork.

e. of plants, or their parts or products.

a **800** *Blickl. Glosses* in *O.E. Texts* 122 þa ᵹingan eletriow. *a* **1100** *Aldhelm Gloss.* I. 3750 (Napier 99/2) Iungum wyrtuna ofætum. *a* **1250** *Owl & Night.* 1134 þar tron shulle a ȝere blowe An ȝunge sedes springe & growe. *a* **1300** *Cursor M.* 1418 þar ras o þam thre wandes yong. *c* **1420** *Liber Cocorum* (1862) 11 Do þer to sage and persely ȝoyng. **1508** DUNBAR *Gold. Targe* 22 The rosis yong.. War powderit brycht with hevinly beriall droppis. **1600** SHAKS. *A.Y.L.* III. ii. 378 There is a man haunts the Forrest, that abuses our yong plants with caruing Rosalinde on their barkes. **1678** MOXON *Mech. Exerc.* vi. 108 If it [*sc.* cross-grain] grew up young with the Trunk, then instead of a Knot you will find a Curling in the Stuff when it is wrought. **1716** 'H. S. PHILOKEPOS' *Yng. Gard. Director* 108 Young Onions. **1824** MISS MITFORD *Village* Ser. I. 15 The sunny colouring of the young leaves. **1828** G. F. LYON *Jrnl. Mexico* II. 249 The cattle.. make sad incursions amongst the young crops. **1842** LOUDON *Suburban Hort.* 29 The heart wood is.. of a darker colour than the soft or young wood.

2. *transf.* Belonging or pertaining to a young person or persons, or to youth. **a.** with *age*, *days*, *years*, etc.: the age or time when one is young; youth. *Obs.* exc. in ***young days***.

c **1000** *Rule St. Benet* (1888) 99 Ᵹif he þæt sylfe cild on iunre ylde is. *a* **1100** *Aldhelm Gloss.* I. 2275 (Napier 61/2) Iunges cildhades. *Ibid.* 2843 (77/1) *Teneritudine*, iungan iuᵹeþe. **13..** *Gaw. & Gr. Knt.* 492 This hanselle has Arthur of auenturus on fyrst, In ȝonge ȝer. **1389** in *Eng. Gilds* (1870) 53 Children in ȝonge age. **1460** CAPGRAVE *Chron.* (Rolls) 131 Whan his ȝong dayes were go, he went to Rome. *a* **1548** HALL *Chron.*, *Hen. V*, 79 At these yong yeres of age. *c* **1570** *Satir. Poems Reform.* xiv. 27 Than vp thow rasit to reule my Ring, In to my tender yeiris ȝing. *c* **1610** *Women Saints* (1886) 77 Cuthburge.. from her yong yeares soughte to please Christ. **1852** MISS MULOCK *Agatha's Husb.* xv, A remnant of my young days.

b. of bodily members, faculties, acts, etc.

a **1250** *Owl & Night.* 1434 His ȝunge blod hit draȝeþ amis. *c* **1400** *Brut* I. 251 He was wonder sory, and ful hertly wepte wiþ his ȝonge eyne. **1535** STEWART *Cron. Scot.* (Rolls) II. 308 Ane ȝoung stomack.. of groiss meittis.. ma tak skayth and harme. *a* **1548** HALL *Chron.*, *Edw. IV*, 204 Hauyng a yonge and a lusty courage,.. he set on hys enemyes. **1591** SHAKS. *Two Gent.* I. i. 47 By Loue, the yong, and tender wit Is turn'd to folly. **1852** THACKERAY *Esmond* I. xi, She.. made eyes at him, and directed her young smiles at him. **1876** MISS BRADDON *J. Haggard's Dau.* i, A homily, in which he held up to his son the picture of his young infirmities. **1883** D. C. MURRAY *Hearts* ix. (1885) 66 A young eye beneath a grey eyebrow is a prettier thing than a grey head on young shoulders.

3. Having the characteristics of young persons, or of youth; youthful in bodily condition or mental disposition (with various connotations); *esp.* having the freshness or vigour of youth.

1513 BRADSHAW *St. Werburge* I. 1400 To se the a quene wyll make vs yonge agayne. **1600** SHAKS. *A.Y.L.* I. i. 57 *Oli.* What Boy. *Orl.* Come, come elder brother, you are too yong in this. **1678** WANLEY *Wond. Lit. World* I. xxxii. 52 An old Abbatess, being decrepit, suddenly became young, her monthly courses return'd [etc.]. **1712** LADY M. W. MONTAGU *Let. to W. Montagu* 9 Dec., 'Tis a maxim with me to be young as long as one can. **1815** J. C. HOBHOUSE *Substance Lett.* (1816) I. 454 Napoleon's mother.., a very handsome, regular featured, princely personage, young of her age. **1824** MISS MITFORD *Village* Ser. I. *Lucy*, The affectation of age and wisdom, which contrast so oddly with his young unmeaning face. **1858** TROLLOPE *Dr. Thorne* iii, Mr. Gresham was young for his age, and the doctor old. **1894** MAX PEMBERTON *Sea-Wolves* i, Why, man, she must be a hundred and four, and young at that.

4. a. That has newly or not long since entered upon some course of action, or having the character of such a one; newly or recently initiated; inexperienced, or having little experience; unpractised; 'raw'.

Also in Australian use, Newly arrived; that is a new-comer.

a **1100** *Aldhelm Gloss.* I. 1673 (Napier 45/1) Iungum, *neutericis*, i. *nouellis* (*catholicæ fidei sectatoribus*). *a* **1200** *Moral Ode* 4 þah ich bo a wintre ald, to ȝung ich em on rede. **1340** *Ayenb.* 162 Nou yziȝ ane yongne boryeis and ane newene kniȝt. **1423** JAS. I *Kingis Q.* vii, Quhich to declare my scole is ouer ȝong. **1496–7** *Act 12 Hen. VII*, c. 6 The seid felishippe and Marchauntes of London take of every English man or yonge merchaunte beyng there att his first commyng xx li. sterling. **1561** WINȜET *Bk. Questions* Wks. (S.T.S.) I. 101 Men in this vocatioun.. suld nocht be ȝoung of leirning. **1605** SHAKS. *Macb.* III. iv. 144 We are yet but yong indeed. **1650** HUBBERT *Pill Formality* 161 Its not with thee as with a yong Christian. **1722** DE FOE *Col. Jack* iv. (1840) 67, I was but young at the work. **1768** STERNE *Sent. Journey*, *Montriul*, The landlord supposing I was young in French. **1796** H. HUNTER tr. *St. Pierre's Study Nat.* (1799) II. 77 We are still so young in the study of Nature. **1859** H. KINGSLEY *G. Hamlyn* xxxi, 'Matey, what station are you on?' 'Maraganoa', says he. 'So', says I, 'you're rather young there, ain't you?' **1867** SMYTH *Sailor's Word-bk.*, *Young gentlemen*, a general designation for midshipmen, whatever their age.

†**b.** *transf.* Characteristic of a young person, or of a beginner; showing inexperience; juvenile; immature; *occas.* childish, infantile. *Obs.*

c **1200** *Moral Ode* 10 (Trin. Coll. MS.), Fele idel word ich habbe ispeken seðen ich speken cuðe, And fele ȝeunge [*v.r.* ȝuinge] dade idon þe me ofðinkeð nuðe. **1623** COCKERAM II, *Young*, childish. **1663** GERBIER *Counsel* 9 To excuse his young Experience. **1718** J. HUGHES in *J. Duncombe's Lett.* (1773) I. 205 He has.. inserted some trifles of mine which were very young performances.

5. a. Of a thing (concrete or abstract): That is in its early stage; lately begun, formed, introduced, or brought into use; not far advanced; recent, new.

In quot. 1402 applied to something resulting or 'springing' from something else, as compared to offspring (cf. 1 d).

1402 *Pol. Poems* (Rolls) II. 103 And alle siche ȝonge impossibilitees folowen therof. **1538** ELYOT, *Mustus*.., newe, yonge, late made. **1553** *Respublica* III. iii. 731 It ys but yong daies yet. **1569** UNDERDOWNE *Heliodorus* VII. 93 b, A little yonge yellowe bearde. **1577** HARRISON *England* II. ii. (1877) I. 50 Oxford hath Oxfordshire onelie, a verie yoong iurisdiction, erected by king Henrie the eight. **1592** SHAKS. *Rom. & Jul.* I. i. 166 *Rom.* Is the day so young? *Ben.* But new strooke nine. **1631** MARKHAM *Country Contentm.* (ed. 4) I. xiii. 89 Take the Kidney-Tallow of a Sheep, and as much young Cheese. **1697** DRYDEN *Virg. Georg.* I. 64 While yet the Spring is young. *Ibid.* III. 752 Such are the Symptoms of the young Disease. **1743** *Lond. & Country Brewer* II. (ed. 2) 113 To tun or put up their Drink young, as the Brewers call it, that is before it hath, fermented too much. **1859** H. KINGSLEY *G. Hamlyn* xxxviii, It's a young country, but there's been muckle wickedness done in it. **1869** BLACKMORE *Lorna D.* xvi, The water.. spread with that young blue which never lives beyond the April. **1880** O. CRAWFURD *Portugal* 253 New port wine—the trade speak of it as *young* wine. **1884** BESANT *Dorothy Forster* xi, They.. left the table when the night was yet young, and the bottle just beginning. **1886** CUMMING *Electr. treated Experim.* (1887) 63 It is.. necessary, while the ship is young, to make a new correction for magnetism after each voyage. **1893** STEVENSON *Catriona* iii, A.. gabled house set by the walk-side among some brave young woods. **1913** *Times* 13 Sept. 15/6 [This] was a severe tax on a young concern not earning profits.

b. Applied to the moon in the early part of the lunar month, soon after 'new moon', when it appears as a crescent.

In quot. *c* 1386 applied to the sun at the season just after the vernal equinox.

c **1386** CHAUCER *Prol.* 8 The yonge sonne Hath in the Ram his halfe cours yronne. **1813** [see *May moon*, MAY *sb.*[3] 5]. **1821** SHELLEY *Hellas* 168 When the young moon is westering as now. **1849** H. W. HERBERT *Frank Forester* III. 95 The dark azure vault, up which the thread-like crescent of the young moon was climbing.

c. *spec.* in nautical uses (see quots.).

1596 SIR W. SLINGSBY *Voy. Cadiz* (Navy Rec. Soc. XX.) 71 At six hours' end,.. upon the opportunity of the young flood, the San Felipe, the San Matias, the San Andrés, and the San Tomaso.. were abandoned by the Spaniards. **1774** C. J. PHIPPS *Voy. N. Pole* 60 The pools of water in the middle of the pieces were frozen over with young ice. **1833** M. SCOTT *Tom Cringle* i, We.. ran up the river with the young flood for about an hour. **1853** KANE *Grinnell Exp.* xv. (1856) 109 The 'young', or as it is called by the whalers, the 'bay ice'. **1867** SMYTH *Sailor's Word-bk.* s.v. *Flood*, When the water begins to rise, it is called a young flood. *Ibid.*, *Young wind*, the commencement of the land or sea breeze.

†**d.** ***young with child***: newly pregnant, in the early stage of pregnancy; also loosely used for 'pregnant' (app. by confusion of *with child* and *with young*). *Obs.*

1613–18 DANIEL *Coll. Hist. Eng.* (1626) 187 Charles [King of France] dying leaues his Wife young with childe. **1652** FRENCH *Yorksh. Spaw* viii. 78 When they have been very young with child. **1758** MRS. LENNOX *Henrietta* I. x, My mother, being young with child when my father died, miscarried. *a* **1800** T. BELLAMY *Beggar Boy* (1801) III. 51 When my father was commanded on board, he left my mother young with child of me.

6. a. *fig.* Small, diminutive, miniature, not fullsized. Now *colloq.* and *jocular*.

1550 J. COKE *Eng. & Fr. Heralds* §8 (1877) 60 We have in England great corne countres, groves, yongsprynges, great ryvers and swete brockes. **1577** GOOGE *Heresbach's Husb.* IV.

(1586) 173 It is best to bring from the Sea, little Rockes with the weedes and all vppon them, and to place them in the middest of your Ponds, and to make a young Sea of them. **1851** *Amer. Mag.* Nov. 92 I'll turn all the drawers inside out, wus than a young earthquake. **1854** GRACE GREENWOOD *Haps & Mishaps* 10, I left Liverpool on an afternoon of unusual brightness, but plunged immediately into a young night, in the shape of the longest tunnel I ever passed through. **1885** HORNADAY *Two Yrs. in Jungle* xvii. 192 Such a weapon is really a young cannon.

†**b.** Technically applied to a lens of low magnifying power. *Obs.*

1667 PEPYS *Diary* 4 Nov., To Turlington, the great spectacle-maker,..who dissuades me from using old spectacles, but rather young ones. **1718** J. CHAMBERLAYNE *Relig. Philos.* (1730) I. xii. §22 To speak in the Language of the Glass-Grinders, of younger or older Spectacles.

B. *absol.* or as *sb.*

1. a. *absol.* in pl. sense (with def. art., or without art. in conjunction with *old*): Young people.

c **825** *Vesp. Psalter* lxxvii[i]. 63 *Juvenes eorum comedit ignis*, ȝunge heara et fyr. *c* **1000** *Rule of Chrodegang* ii, Ælfre þa ȝeongan wurðian þa ealdan, & þa ealdan lufien þa ȝingran. *c* **1205** LAY. 28444 þa ȝeonge and þa alde alle he aqualde. *a* **1300** *Cursor M.* 20495 ȝong and ald and euerilkan All þar fell to slepe onan. **1390** GOWER *Conf.* I. 112 And how that love among the yonge Began the hertes thanne awake. *c* **1460** *Towneley Myst.* ix. 217 Therfor thou byd both old and ying, That ich man know me for his kyng. **1567** *Gude & Godlie B.* (S.T.S.) 29 Cum ȝung and auld, baith man and wyfe, I will ȝow giue Eternall lyfe. **1598** SHAKS. *Merry W.* II. i. 118 He wooes both high and low, both rich and poor, both yong and old. **1611** *Bible* 2 Macc. v. 13 Thus there was killing of yong and old. **1632** [see OLD *a.* 1]. **1710** STEELE *Tatler* No. 207 ¶1 Old Age, which is a Decay from that Vigour which the Young possess. **1770** [see OLD *a.* 1]. **1817** MARIA EDGEWORTH *Ormond* i, She saw herself surrounded by the young, the fair, and the gay. **1841–4** [see OLD *a.* 1]. **1885** 'MRS. ALEXANDER' *Valerie's Fate* v, I have always lived with people older than myself,..so I do not feel it, though it is very nice to be with the young.

†**b.** *absol.* or as *sb. sing.* A young person, *esp.* a young woman or girl. *Obs.*

c **897** ÆLFRED *Gregory's Past. C.* xlix. 385 Ðu ȝionga, bio ðe uniðe to clipianne & to læranne. *c* **1000** *Ags. Gosp.* Matt. xix. 20 þa cwæð se ȝeonga, eall þiss ic ȝeheold. *a* **1300** *K. Horn* 137 (Cambr. MS.) 'Feren', quaþ he, 'ȝonge [*v.r.* ȝynge], Ihc telle ȝou tiþinge.' **13..** *Gaw. & Gr. Knt.* 951 Vn-lyke on to loke þo ladyes were, For if þe ȝonge was ȝep, ȝolȝe was þat oþer. ? **1402** in *Yorksh. Archæol. Jrnl.* (1909) XX. 43 Vlixes..Brak hir his trowth, & toke another yhyng, Circes, to loue. *c* **1430** [see YEPLY 2]. **14..** *Pol. Rel. & L. Poems* (1903) 77 This goodly yong and fresche of face.

c. as *sb.* in *pl.* Young or newly initiated persons, new-comers, novices. *nonce-use.*

1890 *Pall Mall Gaz.* 30 Aug. 2/2 Although the 'Olds' have been the pioneers..of the movement, the 'Youngs' show an impatience with them at every meeting.

2. † **a.** A young one; esp. with *a* and *pl.* (chiefly in imitation of foreign idiom). *Obs. rare.*

a **1300** *Cursor M.* 10977 Til þat he be born, þat yung, þan sal he do þe haue þe tung. *c* **1520** ANDREW *Noble Lyfe* xxxviii. in *Babees Bk.* (1868) 234 Halata is a beste that dothe on-naturall dedys, for whan she feleth her yonges quycke, or stere in her body, than she draweth them out & loketh vpon them. **1527** —— *Brunswyke's Distyll. Waters* Fiјb, A Scorpyon, whyche kylleth the yonges of the lyon with his venymous stynges. **1759** B. STILLINGFLEET tr. *Riberg's Econ. Nat.* in *Misc. Tracts* (1762) 90 The elephant scarcely produces one young in two years. **1797** *Encycl. Brit.* (ed. 3) XIV. 612/1 It [*sc.* the great seal] breeds about the month of March, and brings forth a single young on the ice.

b. Young animals collectively in relation to the parent; young ones, offspring.

1484 CAXTON *Fables of Æsop* I. xiii, The tree where vpon the egle and his yonge were in theyr nest. **1535** COVERDALE *Ps.* lxxxiii[i]. 3 The sparow hath founde hir an house, & the swalowe a nest, where she maye laye hir yonge. —— *Jer.* xvii. 11 The disceatfull maketh a nest, but bringeth forth no yonge. **1593** SHAKS. *Lucr.* 863 So then he hath it when he cannot vse it, And leaues it to be maistred by his yong. **1596** DALRYMPLE tr. *Leslie's Hist. Scot.* (S.T.S.) I. 123 Gif a Sou eit his ȝoung, stane him. **1697** DRYDEN *Virg. Georg.* III. 382 'Tis with this rage, the Mother Lion stung, Scours o're the Plain; regardless of her young. **1820** SHELLEY *Witch Atl.* vii, The brinded lioness led forth her young. **1849** *Sk. Nat. Hist., Mammalia* IV. 63 The field mouse breeds twice in the year, producing from six to ten young at a time.

c. Phr. ***with young*** (also ***in young***), of a female animal: Pregnant.

1535 COVERDALE *Ps.* lxxvii[i]. 71 The yowes greate with yonge. **1593** SHAKS. *3 Hen. VI*, II. v. 35 So many Dayes, my Ewes haue bene with yong. **1607** TOPSELL *Four-f. Beasts* 241 Goats grow fat when they are with young. **1774** GOLDSM. *Nat. Hist.* III. vii. 203 The cat goes with young fifty-six days. **1846** J. BAXTER *Libr. Pract. Agric.* (ed. 4) II. 309 The breeding sow, when in young, and near farrowing, should be kept in good condition.

†**3.** (? *ellipt.* for *young age*: see the adj. 2 a.) The time of life when one is young; youth. *rare.*

c **1450** *Cov. Myst.* (Shaks. Soc.) v. 50 In thi ȝonge lerne God to plese. **1639** G. DANIEL *Ecclus.* End 60 In the strong Estate of Man, and the sweet Time of younge.

C. Special collocations and Combinations. (See also A. 1 b.)

1. a. With the names of countries or their inhabitants, in the designations of political parties chiefly composed of young men: as **young** (or **Young**) **America,** (*a*) a slogan used in connection with an expansionist movement within the Democratic Party in the 1840s and 1850s (*obs.* exc. *Hist.*); (*b*) American youth collectively; **Young England,** name assumed by a group of Tory politicians in the early part of the reign of Queen Victoria (hence ***Young-Englander***, a member of this group; ***Young-Englandism***, the principles of 'Young England'); **Young Europe,** a group of associations of republican agitators of various nations which arose after the July revolution (1830) in France, known severally as ***Young France***, ***Young Germany***, ***Young Italy***, ***Young Poland***; **Young Ireland,** a group of Irish agitators about 1840–50 (hence ***Young-Irelander***, ***Young-Irelandism***); **Young Turk,** a member of a party of Turkish agitators which brought about the revolution of 1908 (hence ***Young Turkish*** adj.); see also TURK[1] 2 e. (Such phrases may also be used in a general sense, as ***Young England*** = the typical young Englishman, or the rising generation of Englishmen.) Also with names of political parties and movements, denoting a young member or (*pl.*) a section organized by and for young members, as ***Young Communist***, ***Conservative***, ***Farmers***, etc.

1844 *St. Louis Reveille* 30 Nov. 2/2 No mammoth bank.. can form any part of the creed of the **Young America!* **1852** *U.S. Mag. & Democratic Rev.* Feb. 185/2 We are not for all the young men before the country, but only for the bold, active honor and talent of Young America. **1880** 'MARK TWAIN' *Tramp Abr.* xxxviii. 444 He and the innocent chatterbox whom I met on the Swiss lake are the most unique and interesting specimens of Young America I came across during my foreign tramping. **1924** *Outlook* 10 Sept. 45/1 Young America could with profit leave such affairs alone. **1962** E. WILSON *Patriotic Gore* p. xxii, Douglas..had been the leader of the 'Young America' movement in the Democratic Party, which had favored..the annexation of Mexico, Cuba and..Central America. **1936** J. BELL *Let.* 4 Jan. in *Ess., Poems & Lett.* (1938) II. 294 While I have been writing these last pages, I have been acutely aware of 'the adversary'. He takes the form of an enthusiastic member of the *Young Communist League and he bellows incessantly. **1966** 'H. MACDIARMID' *Company I've Kept* viii. 188 Some of the Edinburgh University students, members of the Young Communist League,..came to the rescue. **1982** *Manch. Guardian Weekly* 21 Nov. 10/3 He had a good secondary education and joined the Young Communists in 1923 while he was at a metallurgical school. **1924** *Times* 17 Mar. 13/5 (*heading*) The '*Young Conservatives Union'. *Ibid.*, This union has been formed by Young Conservatives who desire to prove by attaching themselves to constituencies for social service that their Conservative ideal is one which they are prepared to maintain by action. **1938** B. R. BRAINE in *Torchbearer* Apr. 41/3 The prefix 'Junior' we dislike, and the word 'Imps' infers an extreme and irresponsible youthfulness that is certainly not in accordance with reality..I suggest..that we take steps to become the 'Young Conservative League'. **1944** *Times* 11 July 2/2 The Conservative Party has decided to establish a new Young Conservative movement which will take the place of the Junior Imperial League. **1959** E. H. CLEMENTS *High Tension* x. 165 Fiona isn't a Young Conservative! She's a Communist. **1977** J. WAINWRIGHT *Do Nothin' till You hear from Me* iv. 52 It is a Young Conservative hop, in a neighbouring town. **1838** R. MONCKTON MILNES *Let. to C. J. MacCarthy* 13 Mar., I go on with small '*Young Englands' on Sunday evenings, which unfortunately excludes the more severe members—Acland, Gladstone, &c. **1843** *Times* 17 Aug. 5/2 It is not to defend 'Young England'..that we make these remarks. **1848** KINGSLEY *Yeast* vi, Young England or Peelite, this is all right and noble. **1859** *New Sporting Mag.* (N.S.) LVIII. 425 Now Master Young England I am afraid I have been rather angry with you. **1886** KEBBEL *Hist. Toryism* v. 273 That distrust of Sir Robert Peel which alone made the Young England Party possible. **1837** in T. W. Reid *R. M. Milnes* (1890) I. 205 We may both rejoice that our two *young Englanders [*sc.* Milnes and Acland] have come out so well. **1848** KINGSLEY *Yeast* iii, She would have started as from a snake, from the issue.. that Lancelot would fall in love, not with *Young Englandism, but with Argemone Lavington. **1840** T. GORDON tr. *W. Menzel's Ger. Lit.* IV. 309 The coterie took the name of Young Germany (*das junge Deutschland*) only, however, as an emanation from *Young Europe. **1968** P. JENNINGS *Living Village* 71 The flourishing *Young Farmers Club movement. **1981** J. WAINWRIGHT *Urge for Justice* I. v. 35 The lads from the local Young Farmers branch put on a New Year's Ball. **1835** *Ann. Reg., Hist. Eur.* 478/1 Germany had found in her political reformers a new school of literature and morals, as well as of civil rights... Under the appellation of '*young Germany', or 'young literature', aping the French..disregard of all authority,.. they preached up their extravagant doctrines in corrupting publications. **1845** R. MONCKTON MILNES *Let. to C. J. MacCarthy* 26 Mar., *Young Ireland would separate from Rome to-morrow if they dared. **1884** *Dict. Eng. Hist.* 610/1 The 'Young Ireland' party..made a foolish attempt at rebellion in 1848. **1855** MORIARTY in W. Ward *Life Newman* (1912) I. 361, I do not at all share..in Dr. Cullen's distrust of those he calls *Young Irelanders. **1851** *Edin. Rev.* Jan. 224 Rise and Progress of *Young-Irelandism. **1844** R. MONCKTON MILNES *Let. to C. J. MacCarthy* 1 July, Mazzini,..who has been organising a '*Young Italian' descent on Italy from Malta. **1983** *Economist* 21 May 37/1 As usual, the *Young Liberals attacked it from a neo-Trotskyite stand. **1980** *Christian Science Monitor* 28 Jan. 12/3, 80,000 pounds—none of which, say the editors, came from abroad. Much of it probably came through the Labour youth movement, *Young Socialists, where the tendency reportedly has strong support. **1901** *Scotsman* 4 Sept. 7/6 As regards the *Young Turks, the Sultan hopes that Munir Bey will be able to keep them under surveillance. **1909** *Westm. Gaz.* 17 Aug. 9/1 Salonika, the head-quarters of the Young Turk Party. **1911** *Encycl. Brit.* XXVII. 463/2 The *Young Turkish party had long been preparing for the overthrow of the old régime.

b. In other special collocations, as *young* FUSTIC, *young* HYSON, *Young* PRETENDER, for which see the sbs.; **young grammarians** *sb. pl. Philol.* [tr. Ger.] = JUNGGRAMMATIKER *sb. pl.*; cf. NEO-GRAMMARIAN; so **young-grammarian** *a.*; **young lion,** a young and vigorous man.

1922 Young-grammarian [see JUNGGRAMMATIKER *sb. pl.*]. **1947** *Essays & Studies* XXXII. 89 This was bound to shake the young-grammarian theory of the inviolability of the sound laws. **1856** C. M. YONGE *Daisy Chain* ix. 92 Take care of my arm!..I was..a little in dread of such a young lion! **1917** H. JAMES *Middle Years* iii. 36 Frederic Harrison..one of his [*sc.* Matthew Arnold's] too confidently roaring 'young lions' of the periodical press. **1937** K. BLIXEN *Out of Africa* v. v. 407 It was curious to hear the young Kikuyu lions speak with reverence and awe of..the old dancers. **1977** *Listener* 17 Feb. 216/2 An orchestra comprising most of the 'young lions' from the home front.

2. *Comb.* **a.** Adverbial and predicative, as ***young-born*** (cf. 'new-born': also *absol.*), ***-fed***, ***-looking***, ***-old*** (old in years but young in condition or disposition), ***-seeming***, ***-sprung*** adjs. **b.** Parasynthetic, etc. as ***young-bladed***, ***-conscienced***, ***-headed***, ***-hearted***, ***-minded***, ***-winged***, †***-yeared*** adjs.; **young-blood,** a 'young-blooded' person, a young hothead; recently revived in *U.S.* as a hyphenated or one-word form of *young blood* (see BLOOD *sb.* 15); †**young-head,** a headstrong young man. Also YOUNG-EYED, YOUNG-LIKE.

1551 ROBINSON tr. *More's Utopia* Ep. (1895) 5 This *yong bladed and newe shotte vp corne. **1630** BRATHWAIT *Eng. Gentleman* 12 These *Young-blouds use rather, Catiline-like, to speake much, and doe little. **1946** MEZZROW & WOLFE *Really the Blues* viii. 106 He was a tall blond good-looking *youngblood. **1979** *N.Y. Times Mag.* 30 Sept. 28/4 The fault always lay with..veterans rather than the youngbloods that Willis himself had drafted. **1874** *Edin. Rev.* July 80 The first-fruits of the *young-born eruptive power. **1915** D. H. LAWRENCE *Rainbow* i. 2 Every year throws forward the seed to begetting, and..leaves the young-born on the earth. **1651** DAVENANT *Gondibert* II. VII. xxx, She.., like *Young Conscienc'd Casuists, thinks that sin, Which will by talk and practise lawfull seeme. **1608** SYLVESTER *Du Bartas* II. iv. *Schisme* 1 Rejecting Old, *Young-Counsail'd rash Roboam Loseth Ten Tribes, which fall to Jeroboam. **1598** *Mucedorus* IV. i. 29 What ..*young-fed humour moist within the braine? **1630** BRATHWAIT *Eng. Gentleman* 12 It is intolerable for these *Young-heads to be opposed: they are deafe to reason. **1588** FRAUNCE in *Brit. Bibliogr.* (1812) II. 280 Owld dotinge graye beardes talke muche of Baralipton, whiles *young headed boyes beare awaye logike. **1868** LYNCH *Rivulet* CL. vi, *Young-hearted, gay Summer shall fling Thy doubts away. **1824** MISS MITFORD *Village* Ser. I. *Mod. Ant.*, A man of seventy,..but wonderfully *young-looking and well-preserved. **1930** *Daily Express* 23 May 10/4 The Italians and the Russians are *young-minded. **1558** R. RAMSEY *Boy Bp.'s Serm.* 14 in *Camden Misc.* (1875) VII, All you that are no childer, but men, women, and *yonggolds, of years and discretion. **1650** FULLER *Pisgah* II. xiii. 274 Caleb was that young-old man, whose strength contradicted his years. **1903** *Westm. Gaz.* 21 Feb. 2/1 A tall, ascetic-looking, young-old man. **1951** S. SPENDER *World within World* 113 An old man. .. With *young-seeming nervous fingers he touched the rim of his glass. **1614** R. TAILOR *Hog hath lost Pearl* IV. i, All thy *young sprung griefes shall seeme but sparkes To the great fire of my calamities. **1706** WATTS *Horæ Lyr.* II. xxxiii. 149 A generous Pair Of *young-wing'd Eaglets. **1596** R. LINCHE *Diella* Fjb, This *young-year'd Hermit. **1599** —— *Fount. Anc. Fiction* Hij, A carelesse crue of young-year'd Nimphs.

Young (jʌŋ), *sb.*[2] *Physics* and *Mech.* [The name of Thomas *Young* (1773–1829), English physician and physicist.] ***Young's modulus***: = *modulus of elasticity* s.v. MODULUS 3.

1865 *Proc. R. Soc.* XIV. 293 Young's 'modulus', which has generally been called simply *the* modulus of elasticity of a solid, is the longitudinal traction of a stretched rod or wire of the substance, divided by the extension produced by it. *Ibid.*, Several accurate determinations of Young's modulus have been made upon wires of different substances hung in the College Tower of the University of Glasgow. **1930** *Engineering* 11 Apr. 465/1 The modern theory of the elasticity of isotropic materials makes use of a number of physical constants, all of which are definitely related to Young's Modulus E. **1967** M. CHANDLER *Ceramics in Mod. World* iv. 118 The harder it is to stretch a material, the higher is its Young's modulus. **1978** *Jrnl. R. Soc. Arts* CXXVI. 683/1 The stresses built up in a structure due to these temperature differences are proportional to E (Young's Modulus), α (the linear coefficient of expansion) and ΔT (the temperature difference).

young (jʌŋ), *v. Geol.* [f. YOUNG *a.*] *intr.* Of a structure or formation: to present the apparently younger side (in a specified direction). Hence **'younging** *vbl. sb.*

1934 E. B. BAILEY in *Q. Jrnl. Geol. Soc.* XC. 469, I have ..been forced to coin the barbaric verb 'to young', in the sense 'to present the younger aspect'. **1969** BENNISON & WRIGHT *Geol. Hist. Brit. Isles* viii. 164 It seems probable that beds 'young' both southwards and northwards from the St. Austell Granite. **1972** *Nature* 28 Apr. 431/2 The eastward younging of plutons was taken to indicate an eastward migration of the downwelling plate margin. **1975** TINDALL & THORNHILL *Blandford Rock & Mineral Guide* I. 30 The direction of younging in a single layer of rock can sometimes be established if there is clear evidence of erosion. **1982** COLLINSON & THOMPSON *Sedimentary Structures* ii. 9/2 A sequence [of beds] could therefore be reported as 'younging to the east' for example.

youngberry ('jʌŋbərɪ). Also Young-. [f. the name of B. M. *Young* (fl. 1905), U.S.

horticulturist, who first produced it + BERRY *sb.*[1]] A dewberry derived from a cross made in Louisiana in 1905 between a blackberry and a dewberry; also, a fruit of this plant, similar to a loganberry.

1927 *Calif. Cultivator* 30 July 104 (*heading*) The Youngberry. *Ibid.* 20 Aug. 178/4 As to the Youngberry plant it does not produce a dewberry fruit and if the name dewberry cheapens a most excellent fruit and is misleading as well we can see no reason why, in California, dewberry should not be dropped and Youngberry..adopted. **1935** *Ann. Rep. Oregon State Hort. Soc.* XXVII. 74 Our oldest Youngberries were set in the spring of 1931. **1971** *Post* (Cape ed.) 9 May (Suppl.) 10/4 Ingredients:..Apple Jelly, ..2 cups boiling water, 2 cups milk, 1 tin youngberries or loganberries. **1980** *Times* 9 June 6/4 A few untended youngberry bushes are all that remain of the thriving farming community that once lived here [in Zimbabwe].

younger (ˈjʌŋgə(r)), *a.* (*sb.*) Forms: 1 **ʒingra, ʒyngra, ʒeongra,** 3 **ȝeong(e)re, ȝengere, ȝ(e)unger, ȝungre** (*Orm.* **ȝunngre**), **yungre, ȝongor(e,** 3–4 **ȝongere,** 3–5 **ȝungar,** (6 *Sc.*) **ȝonger,** 4 **yunger,** 4–6 **yongar,** *Sc.* **ȝongar(e,** 4–7 **yonger,** 5 **ȝongir(e, ȝungir, yungur,** 5–6 **yongir,** 6 *Sc.* **ȝoungar, youngar, yonngar(e,** 7 *Sc.* **ȝonnegar,** 6– **younger.** [f. YOUNG *a.* + -ER[3]. (The normal mutated OE. comp. *ʒingra, ʒyngra* did not survive.)] **A.** *adj.* The comparative degree of YOUNG *a.*; opposed to ELDER *a.*, OLDER.

1. a. In senses 1 and 3 of YOUNG: Of less age; that has lived a shorter time; more youthful (in years, or *fig.* in disposition, etc.).

c **930–40** *Laws Æthelstan* VI. xii. §1 Cwæð þa þæt him þuhte..þæt man nænne ʒingran mann ne sloʒe þonne xv wintre man. *c* **1000** *Ags. Ps.* (Spelman) xxxvi. 26 [xxxvii. 25] ðyngra [*v.rr.* ʒeongra, ʒongre] ic wæs, witendlice ic ealdode. **1297** R. GLOUC. (Rolls) 8753 Hit ne likede noþing wel Roberd courtehese þoru is ȝongore broþer so engelond to lese. *a* **1300** *Cursor M.* 3493 Iacob hight þe yonger broþer. **1390** GOWER *Conf.* II. 308 Fedra hire yonger Soster. *a* **1400–50** *Wars Alex.* 1474 Athils of all age eldire & ȝongire. **1523–34** FITZHERB. *Husb.* §23 The yonger and the grener that the grasse is, the softer and the sweter it wyll be. *c* **1600** G. HARVEY *Marginalia* (1913) App. ii. 232 The younger sort takes much delight in Shakespeares Venus, & Adonis. *c* **1626** *Dicke of Devon.* IV. i. in Bullen *Old Pl.* (1883) II. 62 All younger brothers Must sitt beneath the salt & take what dishes The elder shoves downe to them. **1678** WANLEY *Wond. Lit. World* I. xxxii. 52 They are proverbially said to have eaten a snake, who look younger than accustomed. **1718** POPE *Let. to Lady M. W. Montagu* 1 Sept., I shall look upon you as so many years younger than you was, so much nearer innocence. **1838** LYTTON *Alice* IX. ii, Evelyn was younger than her years! **1844** R. MONCKTON MILNES *Let. to C. F. MacCarthy* 1 July, Sir F. Doyle is going to marry the younger Miss Wynn. **1897** MARY KINGSLEY *W. Africa* 484 The younger brother may not marry the elder brother's widows.

(*b*) ***younger generation***, the next or rising generation, seen in contrast to the current one or one's own.

1896 G. B. SHAW *Our Theatres in Nineties* (1932) II. 289 A fine young woman in rational dress who..treads the boards with no little authority and assurance as one of the younger generation knocking vigorously at the door. **1914** L. WOOLF *Wise Virgins* iv. 93 'Most lakes..are repulsive,' ejaculated Harry. 'Ah,' said Mr. Macausland tolerantly, 'there spoke the younger generation.' **1931** R. CAMPBELL *Georgiad* i. 25 Writers of the younger generation. **1939** T. S. ELIOT *Family Reunion* I. i. 14 The younger generation Are undoubtedly decadent. **1976** 'J. FRASER' *Who steals my Name?* ii. 22 Mr. Cedric was a member of the younger generation.

b. Used after a person's name for distinction from an older person of the same name; = JUNIOR 1. Chiefly *Sc.*

esp. in the titles of Scottish heirs.

c **1375** *Sc. Leg. Saints* ii. (*Paulus*) 1138 Iustine yungre. *c* **1460** *Oseney Reg.* 84 Aleyne Romely þe yongur. **1529** *Reg. Privy Seal Scot.* 62/2 Umquhill Johnne Culquhone, eldar, and Johnne Culquhone, ȝounger. **1567** in R. Pitcairn *Criminal Trials in Scotland* (1833) I. II. 496 (*heading*) Deposition by John Hay, ȝounger of Tallo. **1627** HAKEWILL *Apol.* (1630) 163 Tobias the Elder lived to one hundred fifty and eight, the yonger to one hundred twenty seven. **1684** *Procl.* in Wodrow *Hist. Suff. Ch. Scot.* (1722) II. App. 109 John Baxters elder and younger, Tenants to Robert Campbel. **1734** *Parish Reg. Forres* 23 Feb. (MS.), Witnesses Alexander Dunbar younger and Elder of Boath. **1815** SCOTT *Guy M.* xli, Charles Hazlewood, younger of Hazlewood. **1982** *Who's Who* 1425/2 Hugh Magnus Macleod, younger of Macleod.

†**c.** ***youngerman***: see quot. and YEOMAN etym.

Cf. MLG. *jungerman*, newly elected judge or counsellor, newly admitted member of a guild.

?*c* **1185** *Pseudo-Cnut De Foresta* ii. (Liebermann) 620 Sintque sub quolibet horum [primariorum] quatuor ex mediocribus hominibus, quos Angli læsþegenes nuncupant, Dani uero yongermen uocant.

2. *transf.* in sense 2 of YOUNG: Belonging to the earlier part of life; earlier. Now only in ***younger days***.

1578 *Reg. Privy Council Scot.* Ser. I. II. 707 Gude will schawin unto him in his youngar aige. **1605** SHAKS. *Lear* I. i. 41 (Qo. 1) To shake all cares and busines of our state, Confirming them on yonger yeares. **1676** GLANVILL *Ess. Philos. & Relig.* III. 52 They [*sc.* the Peripatetick Disputers] imployed their Younger Studies upon the Philosophy of Disputation. **1741** WATTS *Improv*,. *Mind* I. xvii. §8 Whether in their chamber, parlour or study, in the younger or elder years of life. **1827** LYTTON *Pelham* lxi, He had been an old votary of the turf in his younger days.

3. a. In senses 4 and 5 of YOUNG: More lately initiated, begun, introduced, etc.; having less experience or practice; that is in an earlier stage; less advanced; later, more recent.

1593 G. HARVEY *Pierce's Super.* 122 Thou art young in yeares, I suppose: but younger in enterprise, I am assured. **1609** BP. HALL *Disswas. Poperie* Wks. (1625) 614 If there be any point of our Religion yonger than the Patriarchs, and Prophets. **1662** STILLINGFL. *Orig. Sacræ* I. iii. §10 We have made it evident, that these two great historians are younger even then the translation of the Bible into Greek. **1706** PHILLIPS (ed. Kersey), *Younger Regiment* or *Officer*, in Military Affairs, that Regiment is counted Youngest, which was last rais'd, and that Officer youngest, whose Commission is of the latest Date. **1794** J. BOYS *Agric. Kent* 58 The second year after planting [hops], full size poles..are placed to the hills instead of the seconds, which are removed to younger grounds. **1849** MACAULAY *Hist. Eng.* iii. I. 340 Younger towns, towns which are rarely or never mentioned in our early history and which sent no representatives to our early parliaments. **1854** MURCHISON *Siluria* i. 13 The Silurian rocks of the Ural chain are succeeded by younger palæozoic deposits. **1874** SAYCE *Compar. Philol.* ii. 60 The younger the science, the smaller will be the amount of known facts. **1915** *Daily Tel.* 5 May 2/3 The directors decided not to commence tapping on the younger [rubber] fields.

b. ***younger hand*** (in Card-playing): the second player in a two-handed game (opp. to *elder hand*, ELDER *a.* 4).

1744 HOYLE *Piquet* iii. 28 If the younger-hand has one Ace dealt him, what are the Odds of his taking in one or two of the three remaining Aces?

B. *absol.* or as *sb.*

1. *absol.* (usually, now always, with def. art.) in *sing.* or *pl.* sense; One who is, or those who are, younger. (Most commonly contrasted with *elder*.)

OE. *ʒingra* (fem. *ʒingre*) spec. = follower, disciple, vassal.

c **900** tr. *Bæda's Hist.* III. v. (1890) 160 Se bisceop, betwih oþre lare mannum to lyfiʒeanne, þa fæʒerestan bysene his ʒingrum forlet. *a* **1000** *Cædmon's Gen.* 291 Ne wille ic leng his ʒeongra wurþan. *c* **1200** *Moral Ode* 326 (Trin. Coll. MS.) Ne muȝe we werien naðer ne wið þurst ne wið hunger..þe elder ne þe ȝeunger. *c* **1205** LAY. 3927 þe king hauede tweie sunen..þe ȝengere [*c* **1275** þe ȝeongre] hehte Poreus. *Ibid.* 9189 Wiðer wes þa ældere Aruiragun þe ȝungere [*c* **1275** ȝeongere]. *a* **1225** *Ancr. R.* 424 Nenne mon ne leten heo in ne þe ȝungre ne speke mid none monne bute leaue. *a* **1300** *Cursor M.* 2934 þe elder to þe yonger spak. *c* **1380** WYCLIF *Wks.* (1880) 383 He þat is gratter of ȝow, loke þat he be made as ȝongar in sympilnes. *c* **1400** *Apol. Loll.* 2 Wan þe synne of þe heldar man drawiþ not be his ensaumple þe hertis of þe ȝungar in to deþ. **1526** TINDALE *Rom.* ix. 12 The elder shall serve the yonger. **1612** WOODALL *Surg. Mate* Pref., Wks. (1653) 16 It is fit that the yonger obey the elder.

2. (In early use *absol.* without change in pl.; later as *sb.* with pl. in *-s*.) With preceding possessive: (A person's) inferior in age: = JUNIOR B. b. Now *rare*.

c **1200** ORMIN 13279 þatt uss birrþ follȝhenn bliþeliȝ þatt ure ȝunngre uss læreþþ, ȝiff þatt iss þatt hiss lare iss god. **1493** [H. PARKER] *Dives & Pauper* (W. de W. 1496) I. xxxvi. 78/1 Than begyn they moost to dote and to teche theyr yonger many folyes. **1523** [COVERDALE] *Old God* (1534) Rj, Suche thinges do theyr yongers here. *a* **1540** in T. West *Antiq. Furness* (1807) 157 They shall diligently instruct their juniors and yongers. **1595** SOUTHWELL *Image of Death* 33 My youngers daily drop away, And can I think to 'scape alone? **1639** LD. DIGBY *Lett. conc. Relig.* (1651) 90 No false doctrine whatsoever can be admitted into the Church in any age, unless they of that age do unanimously conspire to deceive their children and yongers. **1742** YOUNG *Nt. Th.* IV. 22, I scarce can meet a monument, but holds My younger. **1836** *Going to Service* viii. 87 [Lady's maid loq.] It is very mortifying to be obliged to one's youngers. **1872** TENNYSON *Gareth & Lynette* 1380 Answer'd Sir Gareth graciously to one Not many a moon his younger.

3. (As *sb.* with pl. in *-s*.) A younger person: = JUNIOR B. (Chiefly, in later use only, in *pl.*; commonly contrasted with *elder*.)

c **1449** PECOCK *Repr.* III. iv. 302 He muste nedis meene that he allowith oon to be grettist among hem, and that he in sum other maner louȝe him as a ȝonger. **1551** ROBINSON tr. *More's Utopia* II. (1895) 164 To the intent that the sage grauitie..of the elders should kepe the yongers from wanton licence. **1596** SHAKS. *Merch. V.* II. vi. 14 How like a yonger or a prodigall The skarfed barke puts from her natiue bay. **1658** OSBORN *Queen Eliz.* Ep. A3b, So have I a little wondred at Age, to finde it so tetchy, when Younger in years lay any claim to Knowledge. *a* **1734** NORTH *Lives* (1826) III. 175 The two youngers [of the family] were also well placed. **1885** MOZLEY *Remin.* I. xxiv. 138 In 1823 all we youngers were at a small farmhouse between Filey and Scarborough. **1894** 'EDNA LYALL' *To Right the Wrong* v, He himself was one of the despised youngers of the family.

C. *Comb.*, as ***younger-born***; **younger-brotherish, -sisterish** *adjs.* (*nonce-wds.*), having the character of a younger brother or sister.

1530 PALSGR. 291/2 Yongar borne, *maisne*. **1856** LEVER *Martins of Cro' M.* lxv, His preference for the younger-born. **1864** MISS YONGE *Trial* v, She is painfully meek and younger-sisterish. **1885** WINGFIELD *Barb. Philpot* xii, To sell smiles to such a beggarly younger-brotherish runagate!

Hence **ˈyoungerly** *a.* (*U.S. colloq.*), somewhat young (opp. to *elderly*); **ˈyoungership** (*rare*), the condition of one who is younger, juniority.

1868 *Church Union* 11 Jan. (Cent. Dict.), The life-blood of Christendom flows in the veins of her *youngerly men. **1611** COTGR., *Iuveignerie*, *youngership. **1898–9** *Ann. Rep. Bur. Amer. Ethnol.* p. cxiii, The captive is thus doomed to perpetual youngership, if the term may be permitted—that is, to perpetual servitude.

youngest (ˈjʌŋgɪst), *a.* Forms: 1 **ʒingest, ʒingæst, ʒingst,** 3 **ȝeongeste, ȝengestte, ȝongest(e, -ist, -ost(e,** 3–6 **ȝungest(e,** 4 **ȝingest, yongeist,** *Sc.* **ȝongast, ȝungaste,** 4–6 **ȝongest, yongest,** 5 **ȝongust,** 6 **yoongest,** 6– **youngest.** [f. YOUNG *a.* + -EST. (The normal mutated OE. form *ʒingest* did not survive.)] The superlative degree of YOUNG *a.*; opposed to ELDEST, OLDEST.

1. In sense 1 of YOUNG: Of least age. Also *absol.*

c **893** ÆLFRED *Oros.* I. iv. §1 Ioseph, se þe ʒingst wæs hys ʒebroðra. *c* **1205** LAY. 3460 Mi ȝengestte [*c* **1275** ȝeongeste] dohter. *Ibid.* 6955 þe ȝungeste of þan breðeren. **13..** *Cursor M.* 7391 (Gött.) Quer es þin alder ȝingest son? **1390** GOWER *Conf.* I. 148 The yongest of hem hadde of age Fourtiene yer. **1464** *Paston Lett.* II. 153 Your sone and lowly servant, John Paston, the yongest. **1568** GRAFTON *Chron.* II. 391 When suche questions be asked, the yongest both of the spiritualitie and temporalitie say their opinions first. **1611** COTGR., *Quloculi*,..the last, or youngest child one hath. **1826** MISS MITFORD *Village* Ser. II. *Walk through Vill.*, They are a fine family from the eldest to the youngest. **1852** MISS MULOCK *Agatha's Husb.* xii, She and the youngest Miss Harper eyed one another uncomfortably. **1860** TYNDALL *Glac.* I. xxii. 156 My guide,..with his strong right arm round the youngest of the party.

2. In senses 2 and 3 of YOUNG: Belonging to the earliest part of life, earliest; most youthful in character or aspect, freshest. *rare*.

c **1586** C'TESS PEMBROKE *Ps.* LXXXVIII. xi, Thou dost me fill, And hast from yongest yeares, With terrifying feares. **1818** KEATS *Endym.* I. 42 While the early budders are just new, And run in mazes of the youngest hue About old forests.

3. In senses 4 and 5 of YOUNG: Most newly initiated, begun, introduced, etc.; latest, most recent.

Beowulf 2817 þæt wæs þam gomelan ðingæste word breostʒehyʒdum, ær he bæl cure, hate heaðowylmas. *c* **897** ÆLFRED *Gregory's Past. C.* xli. 300 Ure Aliesend..he hiene ʒemedemade to bionne betweox ðæm læstum & ðæm ʒingestum monnum. *c* **1586** C'TESS PEMBROKE *Ps.* CXXXIX. ii, Not yongest thought in me doth grow,..But yet unutt'red thou dost know. **1596** *Edw. III*, II. ii. 117 Since Letherne Adam till this youngest howre. **1797** NELSON 5 Apr. in Nicolas *Disp.* (1845) II. 27 To go youngest into the Britannia.

b. ***youngest hand*** (in Card-playing): the last player, or the last except the dealer (opp. to *eldest hand*, ELDEST 5).

1680 COTTON *Compl. Gamester* 66 If the eldest and second hand pass the Ruff the youngest hath power to double it, and then it is to be plaid for the next deal. *Ibid.* 89 This being done, the eldest must show how many Chalks he hath in his hand to set up, and after him the youngest. **1720** R. SEYMOUR *Compl. Gamester* (1734) 74 If the youngest Hand names his Trump without asking Leave.

4. *Comb.*, as ***youngest-born***.

1596 MARKHAM *Poem of Poems* II. xi, Now with their [*sc.* the vines'] smallest grapes, times yongest borne Clustred in bunches like a countlesse broode. **1833** GEN. P. THOMPSON *Exerc.* (1842) II. 414 Music, the youngest-born heaven's benevolence. **1838** LYTTON *Alice* VIII. iii, Our youngest-born affection is our darling and our idol.

young-eyed (ˈjʌŋaɪd), *a.* Having the bright or lively eyes of a young person; also *fig.*; *occas.* having a youthful vision. (In later use an echo of Shaks.)

1596 SHAKS. *Merch. V.* V. i. 62 There's not the smallest orbe..But in his motion like an Angell sings, Still quiring to the young eyed Cherubins. **1777** POTTER *Æschylus, Agamemnon* 749 To Troy the shining mischief came, Before her young-ey'd pleasures play. **1796** COLERIDGE *Death of Chatterton* xiv, And we..would round thee throng,..And greet with smiles the young-eyed Poesy All deftly mask'd as hoar Antiquity. **1812** BYRON *Ch. Har.* I. xlvi, Young-eyed Lewdness walks her midnight rounds. **1820** HAZLITT *Lect. Dram. Lit.* 14 The grace of Fletcher and his young-eyed wit. **1902** *Q. Rev.* Oct. 575 The fantastic visions of a young-eyed people.

young fogey. Also **young fogy** and with capital initials. [f. YOUNG *a.* + FOGY, FOGEY 2.] A young person of noticeably conservative tastes or outlook. Cf. *old fogey* s.v. FOGY, FOGEY 2.

Though occasionally used at an earlier date in contrast with *old fogey*, the expression did not become common until the 1980s.

c **1909** C. S. PEIRCE *Coll. Papers* (1935) VI. I. xii. 218, I expect the day will come when another generation of old and young fogies will be equally indisposed to admit that there is any corner of the whole field that I have not turned up. **1929** 'D. YATES' *Maiden Stakes* 11 Fashions, outlook, the spirit and manners of the age—I found the lot beyond me... I was a young fogey. **1980** *Business Week* 6 Oct. 95 Noting a split in the profession between 'old Turks and young fogies', Aaron says: 'The older generation of economists was stimulated by external problems.' **1981** *N.Y. Times* 18 Mar. A27/1 At their worst, conservatives were old fogeys. There were some young conservatives, of course, but they were unbrilliant young fogeys. **1983** *Listener* 27 Jan. 21/3 He implies that this is a consequence of the decline in educational standards of the past decades. Mr. Wilson, though he has many admirable qualities, is a bit of a professional young fogey. **1985** *Times* 16 July 30 Mr. Gorbachov is something of a young fogy, though with an inquiring mind. **1985** S. LOWRY *Young Fogey Handbk.* i. 8 The present resurgence of the Young Fogey ties up neatly with the reinvention of the class system that has been going on at least in the South of England ever since Tina Brown revamped *Tatler*.

youngfrow (**ȝoung-**): see YUFFROUW.

†**younghede.** *Obs.* [f. YOUNG *a.* + *-hede*, -HEAD.] Youth (*abstr.* and *concr.*).

c **1275** *Moral Ode* 369 in *O.E. Misc.* 71 þer is yonghede buten ealde. **1297** R. GLOUC. (Rolls) 2195 Alle vre kniȝtes & swaines & alle vre ȝonghede. *c* **1305** *St. Lucy* 21 in *E.E.P.*

(1862) 102 To an heþene man Lucie was iwedded in ȝunghede. ?*a***1366** CHAUCER *Rom. Rose* 351 Elde..That shorter was a foot, ywis, Than she was wont in her yonghede.

Young-Helmholtz (jʌŋ ˈhɛlmhɒlts). The names of Thomas YOUNG and von HELMHOLTZ used *attrib.* to designate the theory that in the eye there are receptors sensitive to one or other of three colours (red, green, violet) and every colour sensation is due to the stimulation of these in different proportions.

1889 in *Cent. Dict.* **1896** [see TRICHROMATIC *a.*]. **1935** *Discovery* July 187/2 In 1801, Dr. Thomas Young (1773–1829),..propounded the theory which now, as the result of the latter work of Helmholtz, commonly bears the name of the Young-Helmholtz theory of colour vision. **1974** *Encycl. Brit. Macropædia* VII. 108/2 All the evidence points to the correctness of the Young-Helmholtz hypothesis with respect to the three colour basis.

youngish (ˈjʌŋɪʃ), *a.* [f. YOUNG *a.* + -ISH¹.] Somewhat young.

1667 PEPYS *Diary* 10 Apr., It is strange..that Mr. Weaver,..who was..a youngish man, should be dead. **1712** STEELE *Spect.* No. 282 ¶2 Our Father is a youngish Man. **1860** O. W. HOLMES *Elsie V.* vii. (1891) 102 Judge Thornton,..as good at sixty as he was at forty, with a youngish second wife. **1903** *Times* 18 Mar. 10/5 These senile parts generally appeal to young or youngish actors.

youngker, obs. form of YOUNKER.

ˈyoung ˈlady.

1. A lady who is young; a young woman, usually unmarried, or a girl, orig. one of superior social position; formerly often used to connote the artificiality, primness, sentimentality, etc., attributed to young ladies.

'This expression is now avoided in polite use, except among some old-fashioned speakers and jocularly. Various particular applications formerly existed; thus, from the 17th to the early 19th cent. a young woman or a girl waited upon by a maid-servant was called "her young lady"; until late in the 19th cent. girls at boarding schools were spoken of and addressed as young ladies. At the present day, the term is freq. applied, with the intention of avoiding the supposed derogatory implication of *young woman*, to female shop assistants or clerks of good appearance and manners.' *N.E.D.*

For the vocative use, see YOUNG *a.* 1 b.

?**1402** QUIXLEY *Ball.* 160 in *Yorksh. Archæol. Jrnl.* (1908) XX. 44 The yhonge lady then praysed of beautee. *c***1450** *Mirk's Festial* 291, I rede þat þer was an olde knythe and weddud a ȝung ladi. **1669** COKAINE *Choice Poems* 35 Ask but a Chamber-maid..what her young Lady Doth. **1749** SMOLLETT *Gil Blas* IV. vii. (1816) 128 It is a long time since I left her, and went to serve a young lady of fashion. *a***1800** *The Governess* in Miss Yonge *Storehouse of Stories* (1870) 188 Two young ladies, Lady Caroline and Lady Fanny Delun... Lady Caroline was fourteen years of age,..Lady Fanny, who was one year younger than her sister, was rather little of her age. **1824** MISS MITFORD *Village* Ser. I. *Ellen*, A life, and freedom, and buoyancy, quite unusual in that artificial personage, a young lady. **1837** ELIZA FARRAR *Yng. Lady's Friend* i. 1 When they cease to attend school, and begin their career as young ladies. **1837** DICKENS *Pickw.* xvi, The premises of Westgate House Establishment for Young Ladies. *Ibid.* xl, 'Good morning, my dear,' said the principal, addressing the young lady at the bar. **1842** MOTLEY *Corr.* (1889) I. iv. 95, I have been young lady enough to keep a journal. **1848** DICKENS *Dombey* xxiii, 'Fetch him home', said Miss Ripper with authority, 'and say that my young lady's here.' **1856** LEVER *Martins of Cro' M.* xii, 'A young lady, did you say, Collins?' 'Yes, my Lady.' 'Then you were very wrong, Collins. You meant to say a young person.' 'Yes, my Lady—a young person, like a lady.' **1856** *Amy Carlton* 42 Miss Colman..pronounced the oracular words, 'Your lessons, young ladies, immediately'. **1886** [see YOUNG *a.* 1 b]. **1920** *Oxford Times* 24 Dec. 1/2 Young Lady Wanted, with good experience, as Book-keeper.

attrib. **1784** BAGE *Barham Downs* I. 43 Amongst young-lady-correspondents especially, it is a sort of petty treason, to send blank paper to a friend. **1857** *Chamb. Jrnl.* 2 May 274/2 My young-lady friends, of from seventeen upwards. **1865** LE FANU *Guy Dev.* iii. I. 42 Beatrix was in a young-lady reverie.

2. A female sweetheart; a fiancée. *vulgar.*

1896 G. B. SHAW *You Never Can Tell* IV, My wife was like your young lady: she was of a commanding..disposition.

Hence (chiefly *nonce-wds.*) **young-ˈladydom**, young ladies collectively; **young-ˈladyfied** (-faɪd) *a.*, having acquired, or having, the style of a young lady; **young-ˈladyhood**, the condition or status of a young lady; also *concr.* young ladies collectively; **young-ˈladyish, young-ˈladylike** *adjs.*, resembling or characteristic of a young lady; **young-ˈladyism**, the style, or a phrase, characteristic of young ladies; **young-ˈladyship**, the personality of a young lady.

1866 *Sat. Rev.* 14 Apr. 439 The virtuous young man.. monopolized the sympathies of *young-ladydom. **1882** *Pall Mall Gaz.* 31 Oct. 4/2 A general air of 'young-ladydom' prevails, each second name in the catalogue is a Lily or a Jessie or a Letitia. **1863** MISS BRADDON *Aur. Floyd* vi, No stiff, embroidered, *young-ladyfied garment. **1853** MISS YONGE *Heir of Redclyffe* iv, They had not arrived at perceiving that they were on the equal terms of *youngladyhood. **1858** TROLLOPE *Dr. Thorne* xxxi, No bevy of Greshamsbury young ladies had fairly represented the Greshamsbury young-ladyhood if Mary Thorne was not there. **1860** *Sat. Rev.* 7 Jan. 12/1 It is not to be wondered at ..that there should be something eminently *young ladyish in the clergyman's way of doing parochial business. **1884** HOWELLS *Silas Lapham* I. iv, The Colonel, in fond enjoyment of their *young ladyishness. **1853** MISS YONGE *Heir of Redclyffe* x, I am not fallen so low as the essence of *young-ladyism. **1832** E. FITZGERALD *Lett.* (1889) I. 12, I am sorry to say that I have a very *young-lady-like partiality to writing to those that I love. **1852** MISS MULOCK *Agatha's Husb.* iv, To judge whether, young-lady-like, she had told his secret to all her female friends. **1871** *Young-ladyship [see GROWN-UP-DOM]. **1891** BARRIE *Little Min.* iv, 'Hae you ever looked on a lord?' 'No.' 'Or on an auld lord's young leddyship? I have.'

younglet (ˈjʌŋlɪt). *rare.* [f. YOUNG + -LET.] = YOUNGLING 1 b.

1852 BAILEY *Festus* (ed. 5) 240 E'en as an eagle drops a hare Brought for her callow younglets' fare. **1890** 'R. BOLDREWOOD' *Col. Reformer* xxiii, The angular cows [grow] into..matrons..with younglets.

ˈyoung-like, *a.* [f. YOUNG + -LIKE. Cf. YOUNGLY *a.*] Resembling, or having the nature of, one that is young; youthful in condition or character.

1530 PALSGR. 330/2 Yonglyke,..*juuenil.* **1562** TURNER *Bathes* 11 b, They kepe a man yonge like and lustye. **1756** MRS. CALDERWOOD in *Coltness Collect.* (Maitland Club) 268 The old countess was too young-like for the other to be her daughter. **1878** BRET HARTE *Hoodlum Band* i, We used to call him little Weevils, he was so young-like.

youngling (ˈjʌŋlɪŋ). *arch.* Forms: see YOUNG. [OE. *ȝeongling* = OS. *iungling* (MLG., Du. *jongelinc*, Du. *jongeling*), OHG., MHG. *jungeling* (G. *jüngling*), whence Icel. *unglingr*: see YOUNG and -LING.]

1. One who is young; a young person, young man or woman, youth or child, youngster.

*c***900** WÆRFERTH *Gregory's Dial.* (1900) 89/2 Us utgangendum com ongean sum iungling. *c***1160** *Hatton Gosp.* Matt. xviii. 2 þa clypede se hælend enne ȝeongling & sette on heora midlen. *c***1205** LAY. 28681 Siȝen toward hirede ȝeonglinges snelle. *a***1300** *Floriz & Bl.* 705 Floriz was so fair ȝongling, And blauncheflur so suete þing. **1387** TREVISA *Higden* (Rolls) I. 165 Dido..went oute of Phenicia wiþ a grete companye of ȝonglynges i-chose. *c***1450** in *Cov. Myst.* (Shaks. Soc.) 414 This pore yongling For whom we do singe By, by, lully, lullay. **1481** *Churchw. Acc., Croscombe* (Somerset Rec. Soc.) 9 Comes yonglens and presents in Rich. Costrell's hands..vjs. *xd.* **1513** DOUGLAS *Æneis* x. xiii. 155 O douchty ȝingling [Virg. *puer*]. **1522** SKELTON *Why not to Court* 345 He is but an yonglyng, A stalworthy stryplyng. **1578** H. WOTTON *Courtlie Controv.* 95 This vertuous youngling..made hir hearing deafe vnto his sugred talke. **1620** QUARLES *Feast for Wormes* G 3, Like as a yongling that to schoole is set, (Scarce weaned from his dandling mothers tet). **1779** JOHNSON *Let. to Mrs. Thrale* 16 Oct., You say nothing of the younglings; I hope they are not spoiled with the pleasures of Brighthelmston, a dangerous place, we were told, for children. **1837** HOOD in *Mem.* (1860) I. 280 Little Tom is a capital traveller,..our trouble was less than might have been expected with such a youngling. **1876** MORRIS *Sigurd* I. 65 The smooth-lipped youngling's kiss.

fig. **1812** J. JEBB *Corr.* (1834) II. 116 He recommended me to publish. England I have looked to as the proper sphere in which to bring my youngling out. **1880** W. WATSON *Prince's Quest* IX, A grassy vale..Where..a pure stream ran, as yet A youngling.

b. A young animal; the young or offspring of an animal.

*c***1220** *Bestiary* 667 Ðanne remen he alle a rem,..For here mikle reming rennande cumeð a ȝungling. **1576** BAKER *Gesner's Jewell of Health* 51 b, This druncke in lyke quantitie ..expelleth the youngling dead. **1596** *Edw. III*, III. i. 119 Be like the fielde of Beares, When they defend their younglings in their Caues! **1646** SIR T. BROWNE *Pseud. Ep.* III. vi. 116 The parturition or very birth it selfe: wherein not only the Dam, but the younglings play their parts. **1772** MACKENZIE *Man of World* I. iii. (1773) 39 The linnet..was bringing out her younglings to their first imperfect flight. **1807** WORDSW. *White Doe* VII. 256 A spotless Youngling white as foam. **1883** *Century Mag.* XXVI. 487/1 If rain should come on,.. the mother calls her younglings under her wings.

c. A young plant, sapling; a young shoot or blossom of a plant.

1559 MORWYNG *Evonymus* 382 The yonglinges or shoutes of bremble. **1818** KEATS *Endym.* I. 138 Each having a white wicker over brimm'd with April's tender younglings. *a***1822** SHELLEY *Coliseum* Ess. (1840) I. 174 The shattered masses of precipitous ruin, overgrown with the younglings of the forest.

†**2.** A young scholar or student, a disciple; a beginner, novice, tiro; one who is unpractised or inexperienced (usually with implication of actual youth). *Obs.*

*a***1175** *Cott. Hom.* 237 þa apostles and hare iunglenges. **1387** TREVISA *Higden* (Rolls) I. 387 He seiþ þat Chadde was a ȝongelyng, and lerned the rule of monkes in Hibernia. **1548** UDALL *Erasm. Par. N.T.* To Rdr. B vj b, Younglynges in the feith. **1590** SIR J. SMYTHE *Disc. Weapons* 34 b, Whose weapons of fire..doo..terrifie..yonglings and nouices of warre. **1649** AMBROSE *Media* x. (1652) 277 Let our Lord Iesus his tender-heartedness in Spirituall younglings, teach us mercy. **1682** T. FLATMAN *Heraclitus Ridens* No. 78 (1713) II. 226 From the Seminary there, a small Detachment was made of Yonglings that were got as far as *Asserit A, negat E.*

3. *attrib.* **a.** That is a 'youngling'; young, youthful; †inexperienced (*obs.*).

1382 WYCLIF *Judges* xviii. 3 Knowynge the voys of the ȝonglynge Leuyte. **1595** MARKHAM *Trag. Sir R. Grinuile* Ep. Ded. A 2, Fier to my hart, & wings to my youngling Muse. **1664** POWER *Exp. Philos.* I. 15 The youngling Spiders (that were either hatching, or newly hatch'd). **1785** BURNS *Cotter's Sat. Nt.* xviii, The youngling Cottagers retire to rest. **1800** WORDSW. *Idle Sheph.-Boys* 6 The mountain raven's youngling brood. **1880** L. MORRIS *Ode of Life* 45 Since Artemia first trod the youngling earth.

b. Pertaining to or characteristic of a 'youngling'; juvenile, immature; in quot. *a* 1616, belonging to the production or rearing of young.

1582 T. WATSON *Cent. Love* To Rdr. A 4, Idle toyes proceedinge from a youngling frenzie. **1615** BRATHWAIT *Strappado* (1878) 77 To thee (young youth) these youngling lines I write. *a***1616** BEAUM. & FL. *Wit at Sev. Weapons* II. i, You have built a Nest That will stand all storms,..and one day it may be The youngling season too, then I hope You'll ne'er fly out of sight.

†**youngly**, *a. Obs.* [OE. *ȝeonglic* = MDu. *jongelîk*, OHG., MHG. *junglich*, ON. *ungligr*: see YOUNG *a.* and -LY¹.] Young, youthful, juvenile (in years, in appearance or condition).

*c***1000** ÆLFRIC *Gram.* ix. (Z.) 54 *Iuuenilis*, iunglic. *c***1000** —— *Hom.* II. 118 On ȝeonglicum ȝearum. *a***1225** *Leg. Kath.* 544 A meiden ȝunglich of ȝeres. *c***1290** *St. Brendan* 704 in *S. Eng. Leg.* 239 þo cam to heom a ȝonglich man. *a***1300** *E.E. Psalter* cxviii[i]. 141 Yongelike am I, and hated for-þi. **1390** GOWER *Conf.* II. 369 Beerdles with a yongly face. **1478** EARL RIVERS *Crystyne's Mor. Prov.* (1859) 2 b, A yongly man of chastisyng content Is signe of grace & of a good entent. **1542** BOORDE *Dyetary* xxxix. (1870) 300 A mery herte and mynde ..causeth a man to lyue longe, and to loke yongly. *a***1577** SIR T. SMITH in Strype *Life* (1698) App. 42 Look what Ladies and Gentlewomen be most fruitful, and have most Children, if they look not for their Age most youngly, best coloured, and be clearest from Diseases. **1634** [see INFANTRY 2].

youngly (ˈjʌŋlɪ), *adv.* Now *rare.* [f. YOUNG *a.* + -LY².]

1. In youth; when one is young; early in life.

1559 *Mirr. Mag.* (1563) P j, Euen in thy Swathebands out commission goeth To loose thy breath, that yet but yongly bloweth. *c***1600** SHAKS. *Sonn.* xi, That fresh blood which yongly thou bestow'st. **1607** —— *Cor.* II. iii. 244 How youngly he began to serue his Countrey. **1888** MEREDITH *Reading of Earth* i, Flowers of the clematis drip in beard, Slack from the fir-tree youngly climbed.

2. In the manner of a young person; youthfully, immaturely.

*c***1530** MORE *Answ. Frith* Wks. 841/2 This point is as ye see well of thys young man very younglye handeled. *a***1596** *Sir T. More* IV. ii. 29 As tis the custome in this place The youngest should speake first, so, if I chaunce In this case to speake youngly, pardon me. **1607** MARKHAM *Cavel.* Ded., About foureteene yeres agone (when myne experience was but youngly fortified). **1922** JOYCE *Ulysses* 192 Yes, Mr. Best said youngly, I feel Hamlet quite young.

young man. Also **youngman.** [Cf. NFris. *ongman* lad, fellow, Du. *jongmensch* young man, *jonkman* bachelor, G. *jungmann* deckhand, ordinary seaman, ON. *ungmenni* youths.]

1. A man who is young; one in early manhood.

For the vocative use, see YOUNG *a.* 1 b.

*a***1122** *O.E. Chron.* (Laud MS.) an. 1052 Rodberd..& Vlf ..ofslogon & elles amyrdon maniȝe iunge men. *c***1200** *Vices & Virtues* 69 Ðies ȝunge mann ȝiede a-wei sari. *c***1205** LAY. 376 A ȝung mon of þriti ȝeren. *a***1375** *Joseph Arim.* 437 þou weore a ȝong mon in þi grete strengþe. **1607–12** BACON *Ess.*, *Youth & Age* (Arb.) 258 Yonge men in the Conduct..of accions embrace more then they can hold. **1687** A. LOVELL tr. *Thevenot's Trav.* I. 278 When Young-men find themselves all of a sudden advanc'd to so great power. **1840** DICKENS *Old C. Shop* xiv, Abel has not been brought up like the run of young men. **1865** —— *Mut. Fr.* III. vii, You had better provide yourself with another situation, young man.

b. Written as one word. (Not now in standard use.)

*a***1250** *Prov. Ælfred* 134 in *O.E. Misc.* (1872) 110 Ne scolde neuer yongmon howyen to swiþe þeih him his wyse wel ne lykie. *a***1300** *Cursor M.* 18984 Yur suns and yur doghteres fre, And yur yongmen sightes se. *c***1400** *Apol. Loll.* 59 Ȝengmen. **1486** in *Surtees Misc.* (1890) 47 If this slaunderous report come to the eers of some yongmen of the blode that he is of. **1591** SPENSER *Virg. Gnat* 431 A rulesse rout of yongmen..lie wallowed in their blood. **1961** *Evergreen Rev.* July–Aug. 15 There was a youngman I had seen often around Times Square. Like me, he was.. hustling. **1963** J. RECHY *City of Night* I. 43 Part of Pete's technique as a hustler was to tell the men he'd been with that he knew other youngmen like himself. **1967** R. MCGOUGH in A. Henri et al. *Mersey Sound* 91 Let me die a youngman's death not a clean & inbetween the sheets holywater death. **1977** *Sunday Times* (Lagos) 6 Feb. 3/3 A police dog also bit a youngman who was rushed to the hospital for treatment.

Comb. **1551** T. WILSON *Logic* T j b, He went in freshe apparell, yong man like.

2. With special application or connotation.

a. Various uses: see quots.

Quots. 1577 and *c* 1643 relate to Galway; cf. the following:—'In 1611, the "young men" obtained a charter from the corporation, instituting them a body politic of themselves... Their "captain" was privileged to sit next the sheriffs... They were also exempt from paying taxes; in consideration of which, they were bound to keep watch and ward' (Hardiman, *Hist. Galway* (1820) 212 *note*).

963–84 in Birch *Cartul. Sax.* III. 366 Þonne is æt Farresheafde .xvi. weorc wurðe men, & .viii. iunge men. **1577** in *10th Rep. Hist. MSS. Comm.* App. v. 447 This indenture, made..betwixt William Halloran, yongman, and ..Edmond Ffrench. **1589** PUTTENHAM *Engl. Poesie* I. xxvi. (Arb.) 66 The skreeking and outcry of the young damosell [on the marriage night] feeling the first forces of her stiffe and rigorous young man. *c***1643** in *10th Rep. Hist. MSS. Comm.* App. v. 493 The Captaine of the Youngmen. **1799** NELSON in Nicolas *Disp.* (1845) IV. 82 The first act of my command was to name Sidney Smith's First Lieutenant to the death-vacancy of Captain Miller. I have placed two of his young men in Gun-boats. **1858** *Phytologist* Jan. 320 The Windsor-street Young Men's Society. **1862** C. C. ROBINSON *Dial. Leeds* 199 A Young Men's Mutual Improvement, and all the rest of it, Society. **1863** B. A. HEYWOOD *Vac. Tour Antipodes* 153 A Young Men's Christian Association Room.

†**b.** A man in the service of, or in attendance upon, a person of high rank or an official: = YEOMAN 1, 1 b. *Obs.*

Cf. also *youngerman* s.v. YOUNGER *a.* 1 c.

1362 LANGL. *P. Pl.* A. III. 207 Emperours..þorw ȝiftes han ȝonge men to renne and to ride. [Cf. quot. 1377 s.v. YEOMAN 1.] **1382** WYCLIF *Acts* v. 10 The ȝonge men entrynge founden hir deed, and thei baren out, and birieden to hir hosebonde. *c* **1400** *Gamelyn* 793 He..seide to his ȝong men, dighteþ ȝow ȝare. **1530** PALSGR. 291/1 Yongman a servaunt, *ualeton.* **1541–2** *Act 33 Hen. VIII*, c. 10 §6 Any servantes comonly called yongemen [*orig.* Yeomen] or gromes.

c. A youth employed by a tradesman, etc.

1751 JOHNSON *Rambler* No. 116 ¶11 The term of *Young Man*, with which I was sometimes honoured, as I carried a parcel to the door of a coach, tortured my imagination. **1836** DICKENS *Sk. Boz, Scenes* i, She discovers..that Mr. Todd's young man over the way is..taking down his master's shutters. **1887** G. R. SIMS *Mary Jane's Mem.* vi, While the grocer's young man was waiting inside for orders.

3. A lover, a male sweetheart; a fiancé. *vulgar.*

1851 MAYHEW *Lond. Labour* I. 207/2 Treated to an ice by her young man—they seemed as if they were keeping company. **1887** G. R. SIMS *Mary Jane's Mem.* iv, And cook she shouted 'Murder!' too, and asked us..to spare his life, as it was only her young man.

Hence **young-'manhood**, †(*a*) the valour befitting a young man (*obs.*); (*b*) the condition of being a young man, early manhood; **young-'mannish** *a.*, resembling, pertaining to, or characteristic of a young man (chiefly in a derogatory sense); hence **young-'mannishness**.

1422 YONGE tr. *Secr. Secr.* v. 134 Ther-as thay hath.. stowtly demenet ham-Selfe in grete *yonge-man-hode. **1784** BAGE *Barham Downs* I. 19 Eight of the first years of my young-man-hood. **1875** SWINBURNE *Let. to E. C. Stedman* 21 Feb., One must..jump from little-boyhood into young-manhood. **1854** C. M. YONGE *Heartsease* I. II. xii. 310 He looked more *young-mannish and sentimental than he does now. **1887** MISS BRADDON *Like & Unlike* iii, Father has talked so much of your girlish days and his young mannish days. **1873** FURNIVALL in *Biogr.* (1911) p. liii, The boyish romanticism or the sharp *youngmanishness of his [*sc.* Shakspere's] early plays.

youngness ('jʌŋnɪs). [f. YOUNG *a.* + -NESS.] The state or quality of being young; youthfulness: = YOUTH 1, 3 (but usually expressing the character or appearance of one who is young, rather than the mere fact of being young).

1528 PAYNELL *Salerne's Regim.* F j, Their drines is abated with the humidite of theyr yongnes. *a* **1600** MONTGOMERIE *Misc. Poems* xxiii. 38 Will he my ȝongnes ȝit With mercy once remit, I trou to faill no more. **1678** CUDWORTH *Intell. Syst.* I. iv. §18. 312 The Youngness and Newness of its Duration. *a* **1735** EARL HADDINGTON *Forest-Trees* (1756) 27 The youngness of the plants made them take root sooner than if they had been older. **1835** LYTTON *Rienzi* I. vii, How flushed and mighty as with the youngness of a god. **1901** *Munsey's Mag.* XXV. 694/1 The first cabin passengers.. exclaimed over his youngness and his good looks. **1919** C'TESS VON ARNIM *Chris. & Col.* xxx. 394 Those cunning little bits of youngness, the Twinkler sisters.

†**b.** The time when one is young; the early period of life or existence: = YOUTH 2. *Obs.*

1510–20 *Compl. of them that ben to late maryed* (1862) 12 We twayne sholde have all our yongenesse..Passed in joye. **1579** KNEWSTUB *Confut.* 35 They let passe the childhood, or the yongnes of the holy vnderstanding, & grew vp..vnto the manly agednes of Christ.

youngster ('jʌŋstə(r)). Now chiefly *colloq.* Forms: see YOUNG; also 6–7 **younckster, ounster.** [f. YOUNG *a.* + -STER, suggested by YOUNKER.]

1. A young person, *esp.* a young man, and, formerly, a lively or vigorous young fellow; †a novice. Now only as extension of sense 3 with connotation of inexperience or immaturity.

1589 GREENE *Menaphon* (Arb.) 23 Menaphon,..a man.. loued of the Nymphes, as the paragon of all their countrey youngsters. **1594** NASHE *Unfort. Trav.* Wks. (Grosart) V. 158, I am halfe in a iealozie hee is some fantasticall amorous yonckster, who to dishonor me hath hyr'd you to this stratagem. **1642** H. MORE *Song of Soul* I. II. xxxviii, A youngster gent, With bever cockt. **1670** EACHARD *Cont. Clergy* 18, I cannot foresee any other Remedy, but that most of those University Youngsters must fall to the Parish. **1706** PHILLIPS (ed. Kersey), *Youngster*, an airy, brisk young Man; a raw or unexperienced Youth, a Novice. **1798** *Lit. Mem. Living Authors* I. 116 This..is adapted to youngsters rather than the higher classes of readers. **1824** MISS MITFORD *Village* Ser. I. *Hannah*, John Wilson has no rival,..for the Robert Ellis, whom certain youngsters would fain exalt to a co-partnery of fame, is simply nobody. **1825** BROCKETT *N.C. Gloss.*, *Youngster*, a novitiate in any thing. **1866** OXENDEN *Our Church* ii. 15 If, for instance, we wanted a Counsellor, we should not consult a mere youngster.

attrib. **1623** LISLE *Ælfric on O. & N. Test.* 36 They called straight vnto him their yongster captain.

2. Familiarly applied to a boy or junior seaman on board ship (cf. YOUNKER 2 b); also to a junior officer in the army or navy.

1608 *Relat. Trav. W. Bush* B 4 b, At length a nimble younckster gets him to the very top of the foremast. **1802** C. JAMES *Milit. Dict.*, *Youngsters*, a familiar term to signify the junior officers of a troop or company. The word youngster is like-used in the navy. **1850** HANNAY *Sing. Font.* v. v, The shrill, squeaking voices of 'youngsters' in the tops. **1857** *Chamb. Jrnl.* 9 May 290/2 Nowhere was the excitement more intense than in the midshipmen's berth, and on no one had the intelligence a more surprising effect than on Bobstay, our junior youngster.

3. A young person who is not of age; a child, *esp.* a boy. *colloq.*

1732 BERKELEY *Alciphr.* VII. §20 Appetite..which is elder Brother to Reason,..is sure..to take the advantage of drawing all to his own side: And Will..is but at best a Football or Top between those Youngsters who prove very unfortunately matched. **1788** COWPER *Pity for Poor Afr.* 21 A youngster at school, more sedate than the rest. **1852** MRS. STOWE *Uncle Tom's C.* iv, 'Now for the cake,' said Mas'r George..; and with that the youngster flourished a large knife over the article in question. **1886** SPURGEON *Treas. Dav.* Ps. cxxviii. 3 The wife is busy all over the house, but the youngsters are busiest at meal-times.

4. A young animal.

1849 W. S. MAYO *Kaloolah* xxxvii. (1851) 341 A youngster of a crocodile who had come out of the water. **1854** *Poultry Chron.* I. 598 All the chickens hatched prior to the 22nd of May, dwindled away one by one, and scarcely left a single youngster from many clutches. **1873** *Baily's Mag.* Nov. 193 The rest of the youngsters [*sc.* young racehorses]..had gone away for change of air to Newmarket.

youngstock ('jʌŋstɒk). [f. YOUNG *a.* + STOCK *sb.*[1]] Young (domestic) animals.

[**1888** W. DAY *Horse* xviii. 250 To put them [*sc.* yearlings] into small paddocks totally unfitted for rearing young stock in is a sad blunder.] **1963** *Times*, 9 May 17/6 Some excellent hunter youngstock classes came before Major Stoddart at the Oxfordshire Show today. **1971** *Pony* Oct. 6/3 There were 325 entries in the classes for pony youngstock. **1979** *Proc. 11th Ann. Convention Amer. Assoc. Bovine Practitioners* 72/2 Cold housing is generally preferred for youngstock. **1982** *Proc. Internat. Conf. Goat Production & Disease* III. 499/1 Perinatal and youngstock mortality data of a 5 year period..of 8 goat breeding farms.

†**youngth.** *Obs.* Forms: α. 4 **ȝungþe, ȝonkþe, yongþe, -the,** 4–5 **ȝongþe, -the, yongthe,** 4–6 **yongth,** 5 **ȝungth(e, yongith, ȝonþ,** 6–7 **youngth.** β. 4 **ȝingþe, ȝyngheth, ȝinkthe.** [f. YOUNG *a.* + -TH[1].]

1. The state of being young, or period of life when one is young: = YOUTH 1, 2.

1303 R. BRUNNE *Handl. Synne* 2807 Yn ȝungþe or elde. *c* **1330** *Arth. & Merl.* 6269 Þe leuedis..hadde wonder of his ȝingþe [*rime* strengþe]. *c* **1440** *Gesta Rom.* xiv. 47 (Harl. MS.) [He] servid god in all the tyme of his yongith. **1531** ELYOT *Gov.* III. xxii. (1883) II. 343, I haue knowen men of worshippe..whiche duryng their yongth haue dronken for the more parte water. **1590** SPENSER *Muiop.* 34 The fresh yong flie, in whom the kindly fire Of lustfull youngth began to kindle fast. **1602** DAVISON *Rhapsody* C 12, Ah Thenot, be not all thy teeth on edge, To see youngths folke to sport in pastimes gay? [After Spenser *Sheph. Cal.* May 9 Yougthes folke: see YOUTH 4.]

2. Young people collectively: = YOUTH 5.

1483 CAXTON *G. de la Tour* cxxi, The goddesse Venus, whiche hath grete power vpon yongthe. **1542** UDALL *Erasm. Apoph.* Pref. **vij, The vnbroken youngth not yet full rype for the serious precepies of philosophie.

Hence †**youngthed** *pa. pple.*, made young; †**youngthly** *a.*, pertaining to youth, youthful.

c **1440** CAPGRAVE *Life St. Kath.* III. 126 Hys body is *ȝonthyd [*v.r.* yongthed], he þinketh hym-self ful lygth. **1602** DAVISON *Rhapsody* C 11 b, All for he feeles the heate of *youngthly dayes.

young woman.

1. A woman who is young; one in early womanhood.

For the vocative use, see YOUNG *a.* 1 b.

a **1100** *Voc.* in Wr.-Wülcker 310/9 *Puella*, mæden, oððe geong wifman. *c* **1205** LAY. 261 Þeos ȝunge wiman [*c* **1275** ȝonge] Iwerð hire mid childe. *c* **1250** *Gen. & Ex.* 4049 Ðe ȝinge wimmen of ðin lond, Faiȝer on siȝte and softe on hond. *c* **1449** PECOCK *Repr.* II. xiii. 226 A ȝong womman, which gate myche money to her maistris. **1589** PUTTENHAM *Engl. Poesie* I. xxvi. (Arb.) 67 Such as had tasted the frutes of loue before, (we call them well experienced young women). **1775** SHERIDAN *Rivals* I. ii, You thought, miss! I don't know any business you have to think at all—thought does not become a young woman. **1864** MISS YONGE *Trial* vi, Let me tell you, young woman, it is hard on a man who has been at work all day to come home and find a dark house and nobody to speak to. **1887** *Blackw. Mag.* Dec. 774/2 Hannah More was still a young woman, and also remarkably young for her years.

2. A female sweetheart; a fiancée. *vulgar.*

1858 *Househ. Words* 27 Mar. 338/1 It was assumed that I had fallen in love, had made my offer, and had been accepted by my young woman and her family.

Hence **young'womanhood**, the condition of being a young woman; young women as a class; **young'womanly** *a.*, like a young woman.

1885 R. BUCHANAN *Matt.* iii, [Her change of costume] made her look several years older—in fact, quite young-womanly. **1892** *Athenæum* 20 Feb. 240/3 The Girton girl [is] treated as a distinct species of young-womanhood.

younker ('jʌŋkə(r)). Forms: 6 **yonckher, yongker, yonkar, yooncker, yoonker, yunker,** *Sc.* **ȝungker, ȝoungker, ȝounker, ȝonkier,** 6–7 **yoncker,** *Sc.* **ȝonker,** 7 **youngker,** 6, 9 **yunker,** 8 **youkier,** 6– **yonker, younker.** [ad. MDu. *jonckher, jonghheer, jonchere* (mod.Du. *jonker, jonkheer*) = *jonc* YOUNG + *hêre* lord, master (HER, HERE *sb.*). Cf. OFris. *ionker*, MHG. *junchêrre* (G. *junker*: see JUNKER[1]).]

†**1.** A young nobleman or gentleman, a youth of high rank (orig. Dutch or German, hence generally). Cf. JUNKER[1]. *Obs.*

1505 in *Lett. Rich. III & Hen. VII* (Rolls) I. 253 Also go to yonker [*sic*] Flovrens, and sae I recommand me to hem. *Ibid.* II. 383 The king made knightes of the Toyson at Myddelburgh..amonges whiche were my Lord Nassou, Don John Emanuel,..Yonker Florens and Monsieur de la Layn. **1513** DOUGLAS *Æneis* I. viii. 8 The quene Dido..To temple cummis with ane fair menȝie Of lustie ȝonkeris walking hir about. **1533** BELLENDEN *Livy* III. xii. (S.T.S.) I. 296 With þe patricians & nobil ȝounkeris of þe ciete. **1547** BOORDE *Introd. Knowl.* xiv. (1870) 160 The people of Hygh Almayne..yf some of them can get a fox tale or two.. standyng vp ryght vpon theyr cappe,..or that he maye haue ..any long feder on his cap, than he is called a 'yonker'. ? **1560** COVERDALE *Treat. Death* III. iii, Some say (and speciallye great yonkers) mi mourning..is, because my kinred..perysheth. **1617** J. TAYLOR (Water P.) *Three Wks. Observ.* F 2, A man is in almost as high promotion to bee a knaue in England, as a Knight in Germany, for there a Gentleman is called a Youngcurr, and a Knight is but a Youngcurs man. *c* **1645** HOWELL *Lett.* (1890) 301 There was a Parliament then at Rhensburgh, where all the Younkers met.

2. A young man generally, in early use *esp.* a gay or fashionable young man: = YOUNGSTER 1.

1513 DOUGLAS *Æneis* I. vi. 29 How, say me, ȝonkeris, saw ȝe walkand heir, By aventure ony of my sisteres deir? ? **1560** COVERDALE *Treat. Death* I. xii, Then were we forced to receiue & loue the gospel, which els here to fore might not come to such stout and ioly yonkers. **1578** LYTE *Dodoens* VI. i. 656 Venus loued the younker Adonis better then the warrier Mars. **1596** H. CLAPHAM *Briefe Bible* II. 152 The yonker Saul, consented to the death of Steuen. **1611** CHAPMAN *May Day* IV. 60 How now? whom doe I see? my daughter and a yonker together? **1748** RICHARDSON *Clarissa* III. 59 When put to the university, the same course of initial studies will qualify the yonker for the one line or for the other. **1880** DISRAELI *Endym.* xlvii, He always encouraged one. A younker likes that. **1885** C. F. HOLDER *Marvels Anim. Life* 227 He was as wild a yonker as they make 'em.

†**b.** *spec.* A boy or junior seaman on board ship: cf. YOUNGSTER 2. *Obs.*

c **1595** CAPT. WYATT *R. Dudley's Voy. W. Ind.* (Hakl. Soc.) 36 Two proper younkers sailers, and two painfull and able Dutchmen. **1622** R. HAWKINS *Voy. S. Sea* (1847) 44 To have younkers in the top continually, is most convenient. **1626** CAPT. J. SMITH *Accid. Yng. Seamen* 6 The Younkers are the yong men called Fore-mast men, to take in the Topsayles, or Top and yeard; Furle, and Sling the maine Saile; Bousing or Trysing; and take their turne at Helme. **1786** NELSON in Nicolas *Disp.* (1845) I. 160 To Lord Ducie say compliments; why has he never sent the younker? *a* **1818** MISS ROSE in *G. Rose's Diaries* (1860) I. 9 He..served..as a younker and midshipman.

3. A child: = YOUNGSTER 3.

1601 DENT *Pathw. Heaven* 131 Two beares came out of the forrest, and tare in peeces two and fortie yonkers, which mocked Elisha. **1648** HERRICK *Hesper.*, *Upon Pagget*, Pagget, a School-boy, got a Sword..Who wo'd not think this Yonker fierce to fight? **1742** BLAIR *Grave* 461 Yet ne'er Yonker on the Green laughs louder. **1815** SCOTT *Guy M.* xxxiv, Do you think the younker knows much of his own origin now? **1838** DICKENS *O. Twist* xxii, Sit down by the fire, younker, and rest yourself. **1842** TENNYSON *Walking to the Mail* 25 And there he caught the younker tickling trout. **1866** R. CHAMBERS *Ess.* Ser. I. 157 A merry group of human younkers.

b. Of animals.

1868 GORRIE *Summ. & Wint. in Orkneys* vii. 260 [276] Some old fellows thumping the yunkers with their finny paws while they tumbled headlong out of harm's way.

Hence (only with spelling *yonk-*) †**'younkerkin** [-KIN], a little younker; †**'younkerly** *a.* [-LY[1]], befitting or characteristic of a younker, juvenile; †**'younkery (-erie)** [-Y[3]], younkers collectively.

a **1529** SKELTON *Replyc.* Wks. 1843 I. 209 These demy diuines, and Stoicall studiantes, and friscaioly *yonkerkyns. **1579** G. HARVEY *Let. to Spenser* Wks. (Grosart) I. 24 Youre Latine Farewell is a goodly braue *yonkerly peece of work. **1593** —— *Pierce's Super.* 121 That yonkerly & presumptuous enterprise. **1594** O. B. *Quest. Profit. Concern.* 13 We haue spent our selues thus vpon our *yonkerie, euen to that which would haue proued honest portions for them to haue liued all their life thorough.

youp, yowp, *int.*, *sb.*, and *v.* Variant of YAWP.

1808 JAMIESON, *Youp*, a scream. **1855** ROBINSON *Whitby Gloss.*, To *Yowp* or *Yope*, to yelp. **1856** OLMSTED *Slave States* 63 They [*sc.* hounds] contented themselves with dolefully *youping* as long as we continued in sight. **1881** JEFFERIES *Wood Magic* I. ii. 22 'Yowp, yow; wow-wow!' The yelling of Pan woke Bevis.

youp, variant of YOOP.

youph, obs. form of YOUF.

your (jʊə(r), *usually unemphatic* jɔː(r)), *poss. pron.* and *a.* Forms: 1 **iower,** *Northumb.* **iuer, iwer,** 1–3 **eower,** 2 **euwer, ȝuer, ower,** 3 **eouwer, eou(e)r, æ(o)uwer, eur, ouwer, owur, our, or, ȝiuer, ȝiwer, ȝiuwer,** 3–4 **oure, ȝ(i)ur,** 3–5 **ȝure, yure,** (6 *Sc.*) **ȝoure,** (6–8 *Sc.*) **ȝour,** 4 **hour, ȝiuor, ȝouure, yur, yor,** 4–5 **ȝor, ȝore, ȝowr(e, youre, ȝhour(e, yhour(e,** 5 **yowr(e, yowyr, -ur, ywyr, yooure, iho(i)re,** 5–6 **yower,** 6 **iour,** 9 *Sc.* **yere,** *dial.* **yore,** and *vulgar* 4– **your.** See also YER[2]. (For inflexional adj. forms see 2 a β.) [I. OE. *éower*, usually in partitive sense, the genitive of *ȝé* YE *pron.*, corresponding to OFris. *iuwer*, OS. *iuwar, iwar*, OHG. *iuwêr* (MHG. *iuwer*, G. *euer*); cf. ON. *yðr*, Goth. *izvara*. II. OE. *éower, éowru, éower*, poss. adj., corresponding to OHG. *iuwar, iwar* (MHG. *iuwer, iwer*, G. *euer*); cf. ON. *yð(v)arr*, Goth. *izvar*. The other langs. had a distinct formation for the adj.: OFris. *iuwe*, OS. *i(u)wa* (MDu. *u*, inflected *uwe*, Du. *uw*).

On the pronunciation John Walker in his *Pronouncing Dict.* 1791, says: 'When the emphasis is upon this word, it is always pronounced full and open like the noun *Ewer*; as, "The moment I had read *Your* letter I sat down to write *Mine*"; but when it is not emphatical it generally sinks into *yur*, exactly like the last syllable of *Law-yer*; as, "I had just answered *yur* first letter as *yur* last arrived." Here if we were to say, "I had just answered *your* first letter as *your* last arrived," with *your* sounded full and open like *Ewer*, as in the former sentence, every delicate ear would be offended.'

Since this was written, there has been a reaction in favour of less obscuration of the vowel.]

1. As genitive case of the 2nd personal pronoun. †**a.** (*pl.*) in partitive sense: Of you. ***your aller***: see ALL D. 4. *Obs.*

Beowulf 248 Eower sum. *c* **950** *Lindisf. Gosp.* Matt. vi. 27 *Quis..uestrum*, huælc..iurre [*Rushw.* hwilc eower]. *c* **1175** *Lamb. Hom.* 15 Swa muchel þa wreðða bid þe mare bitwenen eow and eour eyþer sunezað. *c* **1250** *Gen. & Ex.* 3471 Ilc ȝure. **13..** *K. Horn* 821 (Harl. MS.) Ȝef oure þre sleh ure on. *c* **1330** *Amis & Amil.* 852 Your noither it may forsake. **1338** R. BRUNNE *Chron.* (1725) 162 Þat I be ȝour aller broþer. *c* **1380** *Sir Ferumb.* 4146 Bote it be amended,..ȝour summe it schal abye. **1423** JAS. I *Kingis Q.* cxiii, I will that gude hope seruand to the be, Ȝoure alleris frend. [**1556** CARELESS in Coverdale *Lett. Martyrs* (1564) 610, I woulde haue stryken iij. strokes the more for your two sakes.]

b. (*pl.* or *sing.*) in certain absolute constructions, as †*your* ALONE, Sc. *your lane* (LONE *a.* 6b), †*your* UNWITTING: see these words.

2. As possessive pronoun and adjective of the 2nd person: Of or belonging to you, that you have.

This includes three uses: the possessive proper, as *your books, your hands, your friends*; the subjective, as *your attention, your promise*; and the objective with an agent-noun, or in any way involving the possessive idea, as *your persecutors, your benefit*. (For other objective uses see 4.) Cf. note s.v. HIS *poss. pron.* 2a.

a. as possessive plural, referring to a number of persons addressed.

c **825** *Vesp. Psalter* xxx. 25 *Cor vestrum*, heorte eower. *a* **1000** *Cædmon's Exod.* 563 Bið eower blæd micel. *c* **1175** *Lamb. Hom.* 13 Ȝe beoð iseald eower feonde to prisune. *Ibid.* 29 For godes luue beteð ower sunnen. *c* **1200** *Vices & Virtues* 7 For ȝuer lieue saule. *a* **1250** *Owl & Night.* 1699 Ich eu wolde alle rede..þat eur [*Cott.* ower] fihtlak leteþ beo. **1297** R. GLOUC. (Rolls) 10285 Inot nout, quaþ þe king, wat ower demande be. Commune riȝt, quaþ pandulf, we esseþ & nammore. *a* **1300** *Cursor M.* 4844 Tells me Quat-kin man yur fader be. **1303** R. BRUNNE *Handl. Synne* 976 Blessede mote ȝe alle be For ȝoure preyers haþ saued me. **1370–80** *Visions of St. Paul* 313 in *O.E. Misc.* 231 Ȝe weore lyȝers al ȝor lyf. *c* **1386** CHAUCER *Knt.'s T.* 701 Allas thou felle Mars, allas Iuno, Thus hath youre Ire oure kynrede al fordo. *c* **1450** CAPGRAVE *Life St. Aug.* 6 Ȝour tables matrimonial þat wer mad be-twix ȝou and ȝour husbandis at ȝour weddyng. **1508** DUNBAR *Gold. Targe* 265 Your angel mouthis most mellifluate Our rude langage has clere illumynate. **1591** SHAKS. *1 Hen. VI*, II. iv. 26 In dumbe significants proclayme your thoughts. **1616** SIR W. MURE *Misc. Poems* xi. 1 Gaise, eyes, on nocht quhich can content ȝoʳ sight. **1780** COWPER *Progr. Err.* 185 Let him your rubric and your feasts prescribe. **1790** BURKE *Fr. Rev.* 66 The power..of the house of commons..is as a drop of water in the ocean, compared to that residing in a settled majority of your National Assembly. **1872** 'MARK TWAIN' *Sp.* (1910) 97 The names rise up in your own memories at the mere suggestion.

β. OE. and ME. inflexional adj. forms: 1 **eowre, -u** (etc.), 2 **(ȝ)iure**, 2–3 **eo(u)were, eowre**, 3 **ȝ(o)ure, (e)ore, æ(o)ure, oure, owre, woure.**

Beowulf 2889 Syððan æðelingas Feorran ȝefricgean fleam eowerne. *c* **897** ÆLFRED *Gregory's Past. C.* xvi. 98 Eft sona cirrað to eowrum ryhthæmde. *Ibid.* xxxii. 211 For eowerre fortruwodnesse. *Ibid.* lix. 451 Ðios eowru leaf. **971** *Blickl. Hom.* 171 Godes Gast eowres Fæder. *a* **1122** *O.E. Chron.* (Laud MS.) an. 656 Þet ȝeo hit write mid iure fingre. *a* **1175** *Cott. Hom.* 217 Al swa an huni tiar felle upe ȝiure hierte. *c* **1200** *Trin. Coll. Hom.* 5 Beð wakiende and forleteð ȝure synne. *a* **1250** *Prov. Ælfred* 33 in *O.E. Misc.* 104 Hw ye myhte worldes wrþsipes welde, and ek eure saule somnen to criste. *c* **1250** *Doomsday* 68 in *O.E. Misc.* 166 Comeþ her mine freond oure [*c* **1275** eure] sunnes for to lete. *c* **1290** *St. Eustace* 28 in *S. Eng. Leg.* 393 Nim hire and evwere twei sones. *c* **1300** *Havelok* 171 Mi douther þat shal be Yure leuedi after me.

b. as possessive singular, referring to one person addressed (originally as a mark of respect, later generally: cf. YOU II.): replacing THY.

1297 R. GLOUC. (Rolls) 10310 Ȝe mowe þretni ynou, Ower dede ne may be no wors þan ower word is. **13..** *Bonaventura's Medit.* 469 To þe fadyr of heuene she [*sc.* Our Lady] made þys mone:..He [*sc.* Christ] ys so buxum to do ȝoure wyl, þat he nat chargeþ hym self to spyl. **1377** LANGL. *P. Pl.* B. I. 43 'Madame, mercy,' quod I 'me liketh wel ȝowre wordes.' *c* **1400** *Rule St. Benet* (Prose) xxx. 23 Lauerd, for yure pite ye gete vs fra sinne. *c* **1470** *Gol. & Gaw.* 114 Lord, wendis on your way. **1613** SHAKS. *Hen. VIII*, v. i. 167 Sir, your Queen Desires your Visitation. **1668** DRYDEN *Even. Love* IV. iii, Take back your oathes and protestations..take 'em..for the use of your next Mistress. **1726** GAY in *Swift's Lett.* (1766) II. 68, I gave your service to lady Harvey. **1802** MARIA EDGEWORTH *Moral T., Prussian Vase*, Take your time to speak. We are in no hurry. **1884** 'EDNA LYALL' *We Two* i, You must be content with your own people.

c. In titles of honour substituted for *you* in addressing a person (or persons) of high rank, as ***your Excellency, your Grace, your Highness, your Honour, your Lordship, your Majesty***: see the sbs.

c **1368** CHAUCER *Compl. Pite* 59 Sheweth vn-to youre rialle excellence Youre servaunt, yf I durst me so calle, Hys mortal harme. **1423** *Rolls of Parlt.* IV. 249 Please it your full wyse discretions, to consider the matier. **1433** in *Hist. Sudbury* (1896) 125 To youre ryght Reverent lordshepe and faderhod in God. *c* **1590** GREENE *Fr. Bacon* xvi, In Royallizing Henries Albion With presence of your princely mightinesse. **1601** B. JONSON *Poetaster* III. i, Sir, your silkenesse Cleerely mistakes Mecænas, and his house. **1656** HARRINGTON *Oceana* (1658) 198 These are to certifie unto your Fatherhoods, that the said Votes of the People were as followeth. **1709** MRS. MANLEY *Secret Mem.* 19 Your Mightiness has indeed guess'd at my Thoughts. *a* **1814** *Gonzanga* II. ii. in *New Brit. Theatre* III. 119 My son wasn't grand enough for your Royal Highness-ship! **1851** *Househ. Words* III. 64/1 Never was there one of the cloth who addressed a fare otherwise than as 'Your Grace'.

d. Qualifying a sb. denoting the speaker or writer himself, esp. in the subscription of a letter: see also SERVANT *sb.* 4d.

1418 ABP. CHICHELE in Ellis *Orig. Lett.* Ser. I. I. 5 Wryten at Lamhyth xvj day of Febr. ȝour preest and bedeman H. C. **1477** *Paston Lett.* III. 186 By your John Pympe. *c* **1514** in Ellis *Orig. Lett.* Ser. I. I. 119 Yowr on whyl I lefe Mary. *c* **1560** A. SCOTT *Poems* (S.T.S.) ix. 13 This woundit hairt, sweit hairt, ressaif, Quhilk is..Ȝour fayᵗfull hairt wᵗ trew intent. **1611** SHAKS. *Cymb.* III. ii. 47 So he wishes you all happinesse, that remaines loyall to his Vow, and your encreasing in Loue, Leonatus Posthumus. **1629** SIR F. HUBERT *Hist. Edw. II.* Ep. Ded., And so..I rest, not your Servant according to the new and fine, but false Phrase of the Time, but in honest old English, your loving Brother, and true Friend for euer. **1647** CHAS. I. in *Antiquary* (1880) I. 97/1 Yoʳ loving Father Charles R. **1654** WHITLOCK *Zootomia* 352 Some counts it as pleasant to converse with Historians,..though now rotten, as with the finest perfumed Your-humble-Servant-Madam alive. **1721** RAMSAY *Patie & Roger* 36 Yet may I please you, while I'm your Devoted Allan. **1746** FRANCIS tr. *Hor., Epist.* I. vii. 3 Yet August roll'd away, And left your Loiterer here. **1837** HOOD in *Mem.* (1860) I. 217 Your old Unitarian in love, T. H. **1848** KINGSLEY *Let.* in *Life* (1879) I. 146 Your own Daddy, Charles Kingsley.

†**3.** *absol.* or as *pron.* (predicatively, or standing for *your* + sb.) = YOURS. *Obs.*

971 *Blickl. Hom.* xi. 117 Nis þæt eower..þæt ȝe witan þa þraȝe & þa tide þa þe Fæder ȝesette on his mihte. *a* **1250** *Prov. Ælfred* 213 in *O.E. Misc.* 114 Lvsteþ ye me, leode; ower is þe neode, And ich eu wille lere wit and wisdom. **1297** R. GLOUC. (Rolls) 8174 Ne se ȝe þat ȝare hors beþ sulftore þan ȝoure be? **13..** *K. Alis.* 2138 (Linc. Inn MS.) Y kepe nouȝt bote honour, Al þe bygate schal beo ȝour. *c* **1386** CHAUCER *Can. Yeom. Prol. & T.* 695, I wol be youre in al that euere I may. *a* **1400** *Sqr. lowe Degre* 546 For ye are myne and i am your. ? *a* **1400** *Arthur* 286 Hys worthynesse, sur Emperour, Passeþ Muche alle ȝowre. **1540** J. HEYWOOD *Four P.P.* (Manly) 838 Helpe me to speke with my lorde and your. **1556** —— *Spider & F.* lxxiv, I had woordes of thanke from the mouth of your. *a* **1625** FLETCHER *Fair Maid* II. i, This affront of your.

4. As objective genitive, qualifying a noun of action or the like: Of you. Now *rare* or *Obs.* exc. in certain phrases, as ***in your despite***.

c **1175** *Pater Noster* 221 in *Lamb. Hom.* 67 Ower hating forȝefe ȝe; þin sunful efenling luue him for godes þing. **1481** CAXTON *Reynard the Fox* xxxiv. (Arb.) 100 One..whiche..was your better and wyser. **1562** WINȜET *Cert. Tractates* Wks. (S.T.S.) I. 4 Quhidder sal we begin ȝour commendation and louing at ȝour haly lyfes, or at ȝoure helthful doctrine, we ar doutsum. **1659** FULLER *Appeal, Let. to Dr. C. Burges*, Abler Men are undertaking your Confutation. **1661** FELTHAM *Lusoria* etc. 79 While I stay, you cannot want an Agent that will glory in your imployment. **1690** DRYDEN *Don Sebastian* v. (1692) 102, I can hold my breath in your despight. **1751** CHESTERF. *Lett.* (1892) I. cliii. 386, I have not yet heard from Lady Hervey upon your subject. **1760–72** H. BROOKE *Fool of Qual.* (1809) IV. 136 [He] would be nearly distracted with joy at your sight. **1822** MRS. ELIZA NATHAN *Langreath* III. 253, I hope our union will be the means of renewing your intimacy.

5. a. Used more or less vaguely of something which the person or persons addressed may be expected to possess, or have to do with in some way: cf. HIS *poss. pron.* 2b.

c **1200** *Trin. Coll. Hom.* 17 Alle cunne ower crede..þeih ȝe alle nuten hwat hit biqueðe. **1585** JAS. I *Ess. Poesie* (Arb.) 55 To knaw the quantitie of zour lang or short fete in they lynes. **1682** DRYDEN & LEE *Dk. Guise* II. ii, Your Air, your Mien,..Will kill at least your thousand in a Day. **1773** MRS. CHAPONE *Improv. Mind* x. (1774) II. 183 The most ancient of all histories, you will read in your Bible. **1808** SYD. SMITH *Lett. on Cath.* i, You (if you had lived in those times) would certainly have roasted your Catholic. **1865** RUSKIN *Sesame* i. §23 Take up your Latin and Greek dictionaries, and find out the meaning of 'Spirit'.

b. Used with no definite meaning, or vaguely implying 'that you know of', corresponding to the 'ethical dative' *you* (YOU 7): often expressing contempt.

a **1568** ASCHAM *Scholem.* I. (Arb.) 32 Euen the wisest of your great beaters, do as oft punishe nature, as they do correcte faultes. **1590** SHAKS. *Mids. N.* III. i. 33 There is not a more fearefull wilde foule then your Lyon liuing. **1602** —— *Ham.* v. i. 188 Your water is a sore Decayer of your horson dead body. **1610** B. JONSON *Alch.* IV. iv, Your Spanish Pauin is the best daunce. **1653** H. MORE *Antid. Ath.* II. ix. §3 That grave Awfulness, as in your best breed of Mastiffs. **1703** ROWE *Ulysses* Epil. 18 Your Sal, and Hartshorn Drops, they deal not in. **1759** R. BROWN *Compl. Farmer* 19 A good hardy sort [of cows] are your Angleseys and Welsh. **1791** 'G. GAMBADO' *Ann. Horsem.* xv. (1809) 122 Your Gentleman now-a-days, must have to his bridle two head stalls, and two reins. **1851** E. FITZGERALD *Euphranor* 76 They *valse* very well, which is enough for me, —I hate your accomplished women. **1884** W. C. SMITH *Kildrostan* 92, I hate Your meek and milky girls that dare not kiss A burning passion, clinging to your lips.

6. As possessive of the indefinite pronoun (YOU 6): One's, any one's.

1598 SHAKS. *Merry W.* II. i. 233 In these times you stand on distance: your Passes, Stoccado's, and I know not what. **1708** *Caldwell Papers* (Maitland Club) I. 213 Here [*sc.* Hanover] there is no living without them [*sc.* curtains], one whole side of your house being glass. **1709** MRS. MANLEY *Secret Mem.* 115 They may be well term'd discharging ones Duty with a good Grace, wearing your Fetters with no Inclination to Freedom. **1870** LOWELL *Study Wind., Thoreau*, He wishes..to trump your suit and to *ruff* when you least expect it.

youraballi, var. JURIBALLI.

yourn (jʊən), *poss. pron. dial.* Also 4 **ȝouren**, 9 **your'n.** [f. YOUR + *-n* as in HERN, HISN, OURN, q.v.] = YOURS.

1382 WYCLIF *Gen.* xxxiv. 16 Thanne we shulen ȝyue and take togidere our dowȝtris and ȝouren. **1825** JENNINGS *Obs. Dial. W. Eng.*, *Yourn*, yours. **1837** DICKENS *Pickw.* xxiii, Sam..replied that his master was extremely well. 'Oh, I am so glad,' replied Mr. Trotter, 'is he here?' 'Is your'n?' asked Sam. **1858** *Househ. Words* 14 Sept. 298/1 Famous top-coat that o' your'n, sir.

yours (jʊəz, jɔːz), *poss. pron.* Forms: 4 **ȝures, -is, ȝurs, yurs**, 4–6 **ȝouris**, 4–7 **youres**, 5 **ȝoures, -ys, ȝowres, ȝowers, yowres, yowers, yourez, -is, yor(e)s, -ys, yowrs**, 6 *Sc.* **yowris**, 8–9 **your's**, 5– **yours.** [f. YOUR + *-s* as in HERS, OURS, q.v.] The absolute form of YOUR, used when no sb. follows (originally, like *you* and *your*, referring to a number of persons, later also to a single person): That or those belonging to you.

1. a. Predicatively.

1375 BARBOUR *Bruce* I. 497 All hale my land sall ȝouris be. *c* **1440** *Generydes* 2869 The felisheppe is yourez that yender ye see. **1535** COVERDALE *Gen.* xlv. 20 The goodes of all the lande of Egipte shalbe yours. **1603** SHAKS. *Meas. for M.* v. i. 543 If you'll a willing eare incline; What's mine is yours, and what is yours is mine. **1625** B. JONSON *Staple of N.* II. i, All this Nether-world Is yours, you command it, and doe sway it. **1709** MRS. MANLEY *Secret Mem.* 31 Take all that an over-indulgent Monarch has enrich'd me with! these Jewels! these Bills must be yours! **1825** MARIA EDGEWORTH *Harry & Lucy* (1858) 174 You should not meddle with them; they are not yours. **1845** LADY DUFFERIN *Irish Emigrant* 33 Yours was the good brave heart, Mary, That still kept hoping on.

†**b.** With *both, two*, etc. following. *Obs.*

a **1300** *Cursor M.* 2068 Drightin graunt þat it be sua, þat al þis werld be yurs tua. **1671** H. M. tr. *Erasm. Colloq.* 162 Moreover remember that boy which is yours both.

c. In the subscription of a letter (cf. YOUR 2d): often qualified by an advb. phr., or an adv., as *faithfully, sincerely, truly* (see also these words). Hence ***yours truly***, etc. humorously for 'I' or 'me', 'myself'.

? **1430** W. PASTON in *P. Lett.* I. 30 Yowres, Will. Paston. **1438–9** *Priory of Coldingham* (Surtees) 109 Be ȝoʳs in all thyng, David Home of Wederburn. **1516** LD. DACRE in Ellis *Orig. Lett.* Ser. I. I. 133 At Kirkoswald the xxiij. daye of Auguste Yowrs with hyes serves Thomas Dacre. **1582** in Allen *Martyrdom Campion* (1908) 77 Yours to death, and after death, Luke Kirbie. *c* **1680** *Let.* in Hickes *Sp. Popery* (1680) 75 Yours in the Lord, Subscribed, J. B. **1682** J. W. *Let. fr. New-Eng.* 9 end, Sir, I shall trouble you no more at present, onely that I am Yours, J. W. **1718** *Illustr. Modern* 19, I depend on your mighty Talent,..and on that Score, remain, Most Lovingly Yours. **1798** FERRIAR *Illustr. Sterne* Ded., I am, most truly and faithfully your's, The Author. **1833** DICKENS *Let.* Oct. (1965) I. 31 Pray give my love to Letitia; 'accept the same from yours truly' as school-boys say. **1860** SALA *Baddington P.* xxvii, The verdict will be 'Guilty, my Lord,' against yours truly. *Ibid.*, It's ill..with yours obediently. **1890** 'R. BOLDREWOOD' *Col. Reformer* xx, And they were his faithfully, etc. 'Hang their "yours faithfully"', banged out Ernest.

d. = Your business or affair.

1841 MIALL in *Nonconf.* I. 409 Be it your's to help him.

2. a. Standing (esp. in collocation with another possessive) for *your* + a sb. to be supplied from the context.

a **1300** *Cursor M.* 5061 Knauing of yours haue i nan. *c* **1300** *Havelok* 2798 Leuedi, kristes ore, And youres! *c* **1450** *Merlin* iv. 68 The kynge that is my lorde and yowres. **1596** SHAKS. *Merch. V.* IV. i. 96 Let their beds Be made as soft as yours. *a* **1707** PRIOR *To the Lady Dursley* 13 With Virtue strong as Your's had Eve been arm'd. **1777** BOSWELL *Let. to Johnson* 29 Nov., I was, indeed, doubly uneasy;—on my own account and yours. **1827** DISRAELI *Viv. Grey* v. vii, Such a father as yours. **1837** DICKENS *Pickw.* xliv, 'Will you take a glass of wine?' 'You're very good, sir,' replied Mr. Roker, accepting the proffered glass. 'Yours, sir.' 'Thank you,' said Mr. Pickwick. **1840** —— *Old C. Shop* li, 'It shall [be done], sir,' said Sampson. 'Then give me your hand,' retorted Quilp. 'Sally, girl, yours.'

b. Those who belong to you; your family, kindred, or friends: chiefly in phr. ***you and yours.***

a **1300** *Cursor M.* 17340 It sal i wene On yow and yours bath be sene. *c* **1400** *Destr. Troy* 1722 Bothe to me & to myne mykull vnright, And to yow & also yours ȝomeryng for euer. *c* **1465** *Stonor Papers* (Camden) I. 70 Allmyty God have you in ys kepyng, and all yowrys. *a* **1533** LD. BERNERS *Huon* lxi. 212 You & al yours shal be ryche for euer. **1605** SHAKS. *Macb.* III. i. 91 Whose heauie hand Hath bow'd you to the Graue, and begger'd Yours for euer. **1645** CHAS. I in *12th Rep. Hist. MSS. Comm.* App. IX. 14 Some considerations hinder me from doing all I would towards you and yours. **1772** MACKENZIE *Man of World* I. ii. (1773) 32, I had looked forward to some happy days, amidst a race of my Harriet's and yours. **1838** HOOD in *Mem.* (1860) I. 313 And now, God bless you and yours. **1847** TENNYSON *Princess* VI. 282 Yourself and yours shall have Free adit.

c. That which belongs to you, your property.

1526 TINDALE *2 Cor.* xii. 14, I seke not youres but you.

d. In epistolary (now chiefly commercial) correspondence: Your letter, the letter from you.

1536 in Ellis *Orig. Lett.* Ser. II. II. 77, I have yours of the last of April. *c* **1645** HOWELL *Lett.* (1892) 515, I had yours of the last week. **1755** CHATHAM *Let. to Nephew* 15 Apr., Pardon an observation on style: 'I received yours' is vulgar and mercantile; 'your letter' is the way of writing. **1775** CHALLONER in E. H. Burton *Life* (1909) II. xxviii. 116 Yours with the enclosed draught for 50-ll. came safe to hand. **1821** BYRON *Let. to Moore* 3 May, Though I wrote to you on the 28th ultimo, I must acknowledge yours of this day.

e. Phr. ***what's yours?*** (colloq.): what would you like to drink?

1930 AUDEN *Poems* 12 There's time for a quick one before changing. What's yours? **1982** P. LOVESEY *False Inspector Dead* v. 177 What's yours, Inspector?

3. Used instead of *your* before another possessive, etc. qualifying the same sb. Now *rare* or *Obs.*

1534 CRANMER *Let. to Warden of All Souls' Coll.* Misc. Writ. (Parker Soc.) 279 So that by yours and their agreement I may obtain the next lease. **1610** SHAKS. *Temp.* II. i. 254 Yours and my discharge. *a* **1634** CHAPMAN *Rev. for Honour* III. i, Despight of yours and your Maids weak resistance. **1710** ADDISON *Let. to Swift* 11 Apr., I suppose you know, that I obeyed your's, and the Bishop of Clogher's commands. **1791** BURKE *Let. to Member of Nat. Ass.* 66 This adaptation of contending parts, as it has not been in our's, so it can never be in your's, or in any country, the effect [etc.].

4. ***of yours***: see OF 44.

a **1300** *Cursor M.* 15409 If yee me oght of yurs giue. *c* **1470** *Gol. & Gaw.* 164 Ane knyght of youris. **1471** *Paston Lett.* Suppl. (1901) 140 ȝe schuld borow of my brother Sir John, or of sum other frend of ȝowers. **1539** *Bible* (Great) 1 Cor. viii. 9 Lest..thys libertye of yours be an occasyon of falling. **1601** SHAKS. *All's Well* v. iii. 209 She hath that Ring of yours. **1709** MRS. MANLEY *Secret Mem.* Ded. p. iv, So near a Resemblance of Yours to the Young Prince. **1851** *Amer. Mag.* Dec. 116/2 This charming new sister of your's. **1894** W. E. NORRIS *St. Ann's* xxiv, That dictatorial Colonel of yours.

yourself (jʊə'sɛlf, jɔː'sɛlf), *pron.* Forms: see YOUR and SELF. [ME. *ȝour self(e, ȝour selven*, superseding earlier nom. *ȝe selfe*, and acc.-dat. *eow selve(n, ȝou self*: see SELF A. 2–4. The development of the sing. use through the honorific pl. use followed the precedent of YE, YOU, YOUR.] The emphatic and reflexive pronoun corresponding to *you*.

I. In plural sense: now replaced by *yourselves*.

†**1.** *emphatic*, = YOURSELVES 1, 2. *Obs.*

c **1325** in *E.E.P.* (1862) 134 þe soþeȝe may ȝor self ise. **1340–70** *Alex. & Dind.* 1095 Al þe nede & þe noy þat ȝe now suffren By a-sent of ȝour-silf, ȝe sain þat ȝe dryen. *c* **1380** WYCLIF *Wks.* (1880) 179 þat.. her-by schulde be.. worschipe to god & endeles good to ȝouwre self. *c* **1400** *Destr. Troy* 5036 All the wise how it was ȝe wetyn your selfe. **1567** *Gude & Godlie B.* (S.T.S.) 195 Preistis, thole to preiche, Sen ȝe ȝour self can preiche na thing.

β. **13..** *Cursor M.* 780 (Gött.) Als goddes suld ȝur seluen be. *c* **1420** *Sir Amadace* (Camden) xxx, ȝe most noue take ȝour leue, For ȝoure seluun knauyn the cace.

†**2.** *refl.* = YOURSELVES 4. *Obs.*

13.. *Cursor M.* 16653 (Gött.) Ne wepe ȝe noght for me, Bot on ȝur childer and ȝurself [*Cott.* ȝowself]. *c* **1400** *Apol. Loll.* 4 Wil ȝe not sei wiþin ȝor self we haue þe fadir Abraham. **1426** AUDELAY *Poems* 9 Do fore ȝoure self ore ȝe gone, Or mede of God get ȝe none. **1509** BARCLAY *Shyp of Folys* (1570) 9 Ye proude galants that thus your selfe disguise. **1572** ABP. PARKER *Corr.* (Parker Soc.) 391 Think you, that this way you among yourself shall escape?

β. *c* **1400** *Destr. Troy* 12843 But the noble Duke Nestor onon to hom said:..'Sendis fro youre-seluyn to your syde londis.' **1426** LYDG. *De Guil. Pilgr.* 2730 Ye sholde alway your syluen shewe Wyth cherysshyng ffyr of plesaunce.

II. In singular sense (originally as a honorific plural: cf. YOU II, YOUR 2 b): replacing THYSELF.

* Emphatic. **3. a.** In apposition with *ye* or *you* (usually as subj., less commonly as pred. or obj.), or after a verb in the imperative.

13.. *Gaw. & Gr. Knt.* 350 þaȝ ȝe ȝour-self be talenttyf to take hit to your-seluen. *c* **1400** *Destr. Troy* 3309 And ye sothely, your selfe,.. Shal be worshipped worthely. *a* **1553** UDALL *Royster D.* III. v. (Arb.) 58 *R. Royster.* If it were an other but thou, it were a knaue. *M. Mery.* Ye are an other your selfe, sir. **1591** SHAKS. *Two Gent.* I. i. 154 Henceforth, carry your letters youre selfe. *c* **1600** —— *Sonn.* xiii, You are No longer yours, then you your selfe here liue. **1707** FREIND *Peterborow's Cond. Sp.* 211 You will hardly believe your self, what this Letter informs you of. **1749** FIELDING *Tom Jones* VI. ii, Suppose she should have fixed on the very Person whom you yourself would wish. **1859** H. KINGSLEY *G. Hamlyn* xxvii, I hope I may see you happily married yourself some of these days. **1861** MISS YONGE *Stokesley Secret* vi, 'Johnnie!—get sticks, I say.'..Johnnie uttered a gruff 'Get 'em yourself.' **1890** BURNAND *Very Much Abr.* 103 You certainly gave me to understand you had been there yourself.

b. Added as a retort after repeating something just said to oneself. *colloq.*

1897 H. G. WELLS *Plattner Story, & Others* 214 William came up beside her and said, 'Hello!' 'Hello yourself!' she said. **1944** S. BELLOW *Dangling Man* 39 'Minna,' I said, 'Minna yourself!' *a* **1945** C. WILLIAMS *Seed of Adam* (1948) 77 *Hell* (*to Grace*) Stop that noise! *Grace* Noise yourself!

4. a. Used as simple subject, with the verb either in the pl. (as with *you*), or in the 3rd pers. sing. (*self* being taken as a sb.).

c **1400** *Destr. Troy* 2489 Your seluyn sothely asayet haue before. **1509** HAWES *Past. Pleas.* XVIII. (Percy Soc.) 81 Your selfe hath caught it in so sure a net. **1586** A. DAY *Engl. Secretorie* II. (1625) 22 Your owne selfe doe know, that both he and the rest were to me knowne before time. **1594** SHAKS. *Rich. III*, II. i. 18 Madam, your selfe is not exempt from this. **1621** BP. MOUNTAGU *Diatribæ* 47 Your selfe deny this elsewhere. **1641** 'SMECTYMNUUS' *Vind. Answ.* §13. 122 But your selfe grants..that Timothy was not yet Bishop. *a* **1745** SWIFT *Verses, To a Lady* 126 Conversation is but carving; Carve for all, yourself is starving. **1799** WASHINGTON *Lett.* Writ. 1893 XIV. 150 Does the Presidt. and yourself wear them? *Mod.* (*vulgar*) How's yourself?

b. as predicate, or after *as* or *than*. Now esp. in Anglo-Irish.

c **1400** *Destr. Troy* 1849 Sho might haue bene mariede to more þen your selfe. **1601** SHAKS. *All's Well* III. v. 46 Is it your selfe? **1709** MRS. MANLEY *Secret Mem.* 31, I know nothing so valuable as your self. **1805** G. COLMAN *John Bull* IV. i. 65 Och! and is it yourself I see, at last? **1847** R. S. SURTEES *Hawbuck Gr.* xii, 'Why, what a mess you're in, Beaney!'..'Am I?.. I can't be much worse than yourself; look at your breeches!' **1896** MARY BEAUMONT *Joan Seaton* x, It's yourself, Sweetheart, it's yourself I think most of now. **1896** C. M. YONGE *Release* II. ix. 160 And is it yourself, Miss Caroline, as would honour me by sailing under my flag. **1907** J. M. SYNGE *Tinker's Wedding* II. 32 And it's yourself is wedding her, Michael Byrne? **1970** N. MARSH *When in Rome* iv. 92 The monk..spoke with a superb brogue... 'Ah, it's yourself again,' he said.

c. as direct or indirect object, or after a preposition (or *like* adj. and adv.).

13.. *Gaw. & Gr. Knt.* 1548, I..euer-more wylle Be seruaunt to your-seluen. *c* **1400** *Destr. Troy* 2327 Yff it like your Aliegiaunce, þat I, your lefe son, Be sent from your seluon. **1634** PRYNNE in *Documents agst. P.* (Camden) 34 This odious scandall..which I wish may not truly reflect upon your self. **1725** RAMSAY *Gentle Sheph.* II. i, Spoke like ye'rsell, auld birky. **1766** *Gentl. Mag.* May 234/1 Good fortune befall Yourself, and the B-n-r-d family all. **1807** ANNA SEWARD *Lett.* (1811) VI. 331 On a balance of their beauty and deformity, not one of them equals yourself or Southey. **1852** MISS MULOCK *Agatha's Husb.* iv, What a strong friendship used to exist between Uncle Brian, yourself, and Anne Valery.

5. In pregnant sense: Your being or personality; also, your true self, you as you are in your natural or normal condition: cf. SELF D. 1, 2.

1590 SPENSER *F.Q.* I. viii. 42 What euill starre On you hath frownd,..That of your selfe ye thus berobbed arre. *c* **1600** SHAKS. *Sonn.* xiii, O that you were your selfe. **1740** RICHARDSON *Pamela* (1741) I. ii. 5 For fear you should be brought to any thing..wicked, by being set so above yourself. **1749** FIELDING *Tom Jones* VI. v, 'Dear aunt, you frighten me out of my senses.' 'O, my dear,..you will soon come to youself again.' **1889** 'J. S. WINTER' *Mrs. Bob* viii, 'Now you look like yourself', she said fondly.

** **6.** Reflexive, as direct or indirect object, or after a preposition: taking the place of YOU 4 d.

13.. to your-seluen [see 3]. **1426** LYDG. *De Guil. Pilgr.* 3759 To occupye your sylff alway. **1568** GRAFTON *Chron.* II. 102 Least that by the doyng the contrary, you bring your selfe into such a pecke of troubles. **1598** B. JONSON *Ev. Man in Hum.* I. i, Nor would I, you should melt away your selfe In flashing brav'rie. **1606** SHAKS. *Ant. & Cl.* II. v. 75 Good Madam keepe your selfe within your selfe. **1680** R. L'ESTRANGE *Erasm. Colloq.* 127 'Twas well you bethought your self before you were in for good and all. **1717** LADY M. W. MONTAGU *Let. to Mrs. S. C——* 1 Apr., I am going to tell you a thing that will make you wish yourself here. **1865** 'L. CARROLL' *Alice's Adv. in Wonderland* ix, Pray don't trouble yourself. **1882** 'EDNA LYALL' *Donovan* xix, You'll do for yourself one of these days.

*** **7.** As indefinite pronoun (emphatic or reflexive): = ONESELF: cf. YOU 6, YOUR 6.

1669 STURMY *Mariner's Mag.* II. iii. 56 Here is a Table of Latitudes..and the way to calculate it your self. **1881** *Baily's Mag.* Apr. 97 Our friend learned that one of the secrets of their success was picking the line of country quickly yourself. **1918** *Times Lit. Suppl.* 2 May 207/2 The monkey..has a rule that everything which cannot be eaten must be used to scratch yourself with.

yourselves (jʊə'sɛlvz, jɔː'-), *pron. pl.* Forms: see YOUR and SELF. [f. prec., in the 16th cent., with pl. inflexion, like *ourselves*, *theirselves*, *themselves*, in order to provide an unambiguous form for the pl. use.] The emphatic and reflexive pronoun corresponding to *you* in plural sense: replacing the earlier *yourself* (see prec. 1, 2).

I. Emphatic.

1. In apposition with *ye* or *you* (as subj., pred., or obj.), expressed or implied.

1526 TINDALE *Matt.* xxiii. 13 Ye youre selves goo nott in, nother [**1611** yee neither goe in your selues, neither] suffre ye them that come to enter in. *c* **1550** LYNDESAY *Monarche, Trag. Dauid* 312 It is ȝour craft,..ȝour selfis, in ȝour Templis, for to teche. **1611** *Bible* Luke xiii. 28 When yee shall see..all the Prophets in the kingdome of God, and you your selues thrust out [**1526** TINDALE, and youre selves thrust oute a dores]. **1881** 'MARK TWAIN' *Sp.* (1910) 24, I think I honor and appreciate your Pilgrim stock as much as you do yourselves, perhaps.

2. As simple subject (now *arch.* or *poet.*), predicate, or object.

1526 [see quot. 1611 in 1]. *a* **1578** LINDESAY (Pitscottie) *Chron. Scot.* (S.T.S.) II. 58 To manefest ȝourselfis quhat men ȝe ar. **1582** *N.T.* (Rhem.) 1 Thess. ii. 1 For your selues know, brethren, our entrance vnto you, that it was not vaine. **1608** SHAKS. *Lear* II. iv. 194 (Qo. 1) If you doe loue old men, ..if your selues are old. **1709** MRS. MANLEY *Secret Mem.* 110, I intend to carry you where your selves shall be Judges of his Conversation. **1728** POPE *Dunc.* I. 3 Say great Patricians! (since yourselves inspire These wond'rous works). **1881** 'MARK TWAIN' *Sp.* (1910) 20, I ask you to put yourselves in his place.

3. In pregnant sense: cf. prec. 5.

1718 POPE *Iliad* XIV. 428 Be still your selves, and we shall need no more.

II. 4. Reflexive, as direct or indirect object, or after a preposition: taking the place of YOU 1 d.

1523 LD. BERNERS *Froiss.* I. cxlvi. 71 b/2 It is his wyll that ye all shulde put your selfes into his pure wyll. **1526** TINDALE *Luke* xvii. 3 Take hede to youre selves. **1539** *Bible* (Great) Matt. vi. 19 Laye not vp for your selues treasure vpon earth. **1632** BROME *Novella* I. i, Not to wanton out your holy vowes Dancing your selfes to th' Devill. **1790** BURKE *Fr. Rev.* 52 Respecting your forefathers, you would have been taught to respect yourselves. **1837** DICKENS *Pickw.* xxxii, 'You ought to be ashamed of yourselves,' said the voice of Mr. Raddle. **1847** R. S. SURTEES *Hawbuck Gr.* xvi, It is all very well for you to give yourselves airs among other girls.

yourt, var. YAOURT.

yous (juːz). Also **youse**. Dial. varr. YOU *pers. pron.* (with pl. inflection, though used in sing. sense also). Cf. YEZ.

1893 S. CRANE *Maggie* i. 8 Youse kids makes me tired. *Ibid.* ii. 13 Ah, Jimmie, youse bin fightin' agin. **1901** M. FRANKLIN *My Brilliant Career* xxx. 256 Ye and Lizer can have a little fly round. It'll do yous good. **1907** J. M. SYNGE *Playboy of Western World* III. 63 Is it mad yous are? **1929** WODEHOUSE *Gentleman of Leisure* xiv. 110 Say, youse won't want me any more, boss. **1930** J. DOS PASSOS *42nd Parallel* I. 102 Say, yous guys, this is fellowworker McCreary. **1939** X. HERBERT *Capricornia* xiii. 183, I want yous two back here at Black Adder. **1968** S. L. ELLIOTT in E. Hanger *Three Austral. Plays* II. i. 74 Good luck to youse. **1975** [see STORE *sb.* 12 a]. **1981** S. RENA *Painless Death* xx. 132 We've a telephone installed in the lounge since yesterday and none of yous even noticed it!

yous, yoush, dial. contractions of *you shall*: see SHALL A. 5.

1575 *Gammer Gurton* I. v. Bj, Yoush beare the blame.

youst, obs. form of JOUST *v.*[1]

youster, *sb. north. dial.* Forms: 1 **ȝelostr, ȝeolster, -or**, 6 *Sc.* **ȝoustir**, 7 **yowster**, 9 **youster**. [OE. *ȝeolster* (late also *ȝillister*) suppuration, pus, related to LG. *galster* mouldy spot in cheese, bacon, etc., whence Du. *galsterig* rank, rancid (cf. OE. *ȝeolstriȝ* purulent, poisonous).] Fetid discharge from a wound; pus, sanies. Hence **youster** *v.*, to fester; **youstered** *pa. pple.* (see quot. 1894).

c **725** *Corpus Gloss.* (Hessels) S 709 *Supuratio*, ȝelostr. *a* **1100** *Aldhelm Gloss.* I. 3585 (Napier 95/2) *Tabo, .i. sanie*, wyrmse, ȝeolstre. **1513** DOUGLAS *Æneis* III. ix. 72 The ȝoustir tharfra chirtand and blak blud. **1691** RAY *N.C. Words, Yowster* [*printed* Yowfter], to fester. **1894** *Northumbld. Gloss., Youstered*, puffed or swollen in the cellular membranes of the skin.

yout, variant of YOWT.

youth (juːθ). Forms: 1 **ȝeoȝuþ, ȝioȝuþ, iuȝuð, -oð**, 1–2 **ȝeoȝoþ, iuȝeþ**, 2–3 **ȝeoȝeð, ȝuheð**, 3–5 **ȝouþ(e**, 4–5 **ȝowthe, youghthe, yhouth(e**, 4–6 **youthe**, 4–5 (6–7 *Sc.*) **ȝouth**, (7 *Sc.*) **yowthe**, 5–6 **ȝouthe, ȝowth, yought(e, yougth(e**, (3 **ȝuweð, -wuð, -ȝeð, ȝueþ, ȝoeþ, ȝieuð, youhþ, ȝuð**, 4 **ȝoweþ, ȝougheþ, ȝuth**, 5 **ȝowith, yowith, yowuthe, ȝougeþe, ȝougthe, youþe, yuþ e, ȝouhetȝ**, *Sc.* **ȝowutht**, 5–6 **vthe**, 6 **yowght**, *Sc.* **ȝow**[t], 7 **yewth**), 5– **youth**. [OE. *ȝeoȝuþ* = OS. *juguð* (MLG., MDu. *jôghet*, Du. *jeugd*), OHG. *jugund* (MHG. *jugent*, G. *jugend*):—Com. W. Ger. **jugunþi-*, app. an alteration on the analogy of **dugunþ-* DOUTH of **juwunþi-*:—pre-Teut. **juwənti-* (cf. the parallel formation in L. *juventa*, Goth. *junda*). See YOUNG and -TH[1].]

1. a. The fact or state of being young; youngness. (Often blending with sense 2.)

a **1100** *Aldhelm Gloss.* I. 2843 (Napier 77/1) *Teneritudine*, iungan iuȝeþe. *c* **1100** *O.E. Chron.* (MS. D) an. 975 On his daȝum for his iuȝoðe, Godes wiþærsacan Godes laȝe bræcon. *a* **1225** *Leg. Kath.* 1462 Nim ȝeme of þi ȝuheðe. *c* **1380** WYCLIF *Sel. Wks.* I. 84 Seynge þe ȝouþe of þe childe. *c* **1425** *Engl. Conq. Irel.* (1896) 68 Other tweyn of hys bretheren, (that throgh yought & foolrede hym folwed). *a* **1500** *Cov. Corpus Chr. Pl.* ii. 751 Thogh thatt my vthe frome me be worne. *a* **1533** LD. BERNERS *Huon* xxii. 65 They knewe well by the reason of his yought hunger opressyd hym more then it dyde to them of gretter age. *a* **1572** KNOX *Hist. Ref.* Wks. 1846 I. 195 By your authoritie, the people may be moved the rather to beleve the trewth, whareof many dowbtes be reassone of our yowght. **1601** SHAKS. *Jul. C.* II. i. 148 Our youths, and wildenesse, shall no whit appeare, But all be buried in his Grauity. **1697** DRYDEN *Virg. Georg.* III. 664 A Snake..renew'd in all the speckl'd Pride Of pompous Youth. **1709** MRS. MANLEY *Secret Mem.* 122 Their free-behaviour are generally attributed to Youth and Gaiety. **1796** BURKE *Let. to Hussey* Dec., Corr. 1844 IV. 401 If I had youth and strength, I would go myself over to Ireland to work on that plan. **1803** BEDDOES in *Med. Jrnl.* X. 572 He has youth on his side, and it is odds but he gets over it [*sc.* a disease].

b. *fig.* Newness, novelty, recentness.

1596 SHAKS. *Merch. V.* III. ii. 224 If that the youth of my new interest here Have power to bid you welcome. *a* **1600** HOOKER *Eccl. Pol.* VI. iv. §13 These opinions have youth in their countenance.

2. a. The time when one is young; the early part or period of life; more specifically, the period from puberty till the attainment of full growth, between childhood and adult age.

c **897** Ælfred *Gregory's Past. C.* xxxi. 206 Ðære scame & ðære scande þe ðu on iuguðe worhtes ic ȝedo ðæt ðu forȝitst. *c* **1000** *Ags. Gosp.* Luke xviii. 21 Eall þis ic heold of minre ȝeoȝuþe. *c* **1200** *Trin. Coll. Hom.* 127 On his ȝuweðe he fleh fro folke to weste. *a* **1250** *Prov. Ælfred* 100 in *O.E. Misc.* (1872) 108 þe mon þe on his youhþe yeorne leorneþ wit and wisdom. *c* **1330** R. Brunne *Chron. Wace* (Rolls) 10436 Alle þe ȝongest bachelers þat..were of ȝouþe. *c* **1400** *Rule St. Benet* (verse) 14 Women..þat leris no latyn in þar ȝouth. **1508** Dunbar *Poems* vii. 63 Most fortunable chiftane, bothe in yhouth and eild. **1535** Coverdale *Gen.* viii. 21 The ymaginacion of mans hert is euell, euen from the very youth of him [**1611** from his youth]. **1749** Smollett *Gil Blas* IV. vii. (1816) 126/2 One of those old boys who had been great rakes in their youth. **1839** Fr. A. Kemble *Resid. Georgia* (1863) 11 As soon as they begin to grow up and pass from infancy to youth. **1879** Harlan *Eyesight* vii. 103 In the case of any kind of optical defect, it is a great advantage to begin the use of glasses in youth.

b. *transf.* and *fig.* Early stage or period of existence.

1602 Shaks. *Ham.* I. iii. 7 A Violet in the youth of Primy Nature. **1678** Moxon *Mech. Exerc.* vi. 108 As the Bough grew in the youth of the Tree. **1733** W. Ellis *Chiltern & Vale Farm.* 14 One very bad [quality]..that often ruins part of its Crop, while in their youth. **1883** *Ch. Times* 9 Nov. 813/2 Lutheranism..covers a smaller area to-day than it did in its early youth.

3. A quality or condition characteristic of the young; e.g. youthful freshness or vigour; youthful wantonness, folly, or rashness; youthful appearance or aspect.

971 *Blickl. Hom.* 65 þær is ȝeoȝoþ buton ylde. *c* **1175** *Lamb. Hom.* 145 þer scal beon..Ivȝeðe [*v.rr.* ȝeoȝeðe, ȝieuð] wið-uten elde. *a* **1300** *E.E. Psalter* cii[i]. 5 Als erne þi yhouthe be newed sal. **1390** Gower *Conf.* II. 263 Sche..preide hem alle..To grante Eson his ferste youthe. **1475** *Stonor Papers* (Camden) I. 158 Tyll..þat youkke of wedlokke ly in my nekke..youth shall rene in me as hyt has done in you afore tyme. *c* **1489** Caxton *Sonnes of Aymon* ix. 244 Now is loste our beaulte and our yougthe thorughe grete synne. **1525** Ld. Berners *Froiss.* II. cxxv. 140b/2 Though ..that youthe of wytte haue made hym to defye the kynge. *a* **1653** Binning *Serm., John i.* 5 Wks. (1725) 410/2 [The sun] puts a Youth upon the World. **1709** Mrs. Manley *Secret Mem.* 16 The Enervating of their Youth and Vigour. **1817** Maria Edgeworth *Ormond* i, After she had purchased all of youth which age can purchase for money. **1844** Mrs. Browning *Rhaps. Life's Progr.* viii, Oh, the soul keeps its youth! But the body faints sore.

4. Personified, or vaguely denoting any young person or persons (without article).

Here perhaps belongs *yougthes folke* (Spenser *Sheph. Cal.* May 9), which was imitated by Davison (see youngth 1, quot. 1602).

1390 Gower *Conf.* III. 358, I sih wher lusty Youthe tho ..Stod with his route wel begon. **1399** Langl. *Rich. Redeles* Prol. 69 They shall fynde ffele ffawtis ffoure score and odde, That youghthe weneth alwey þat it be witte euere. *c* **1400** *Beryn* 1052 Ȝowith is recheles. *c* **1430** *Hymns Virg.* (1867) 93 Ful of corage is ȝouȝeþe in herte. **1513** More *Rich. III* Wks. 39/1 Slipper youth [must be] vnderpropped with elder counsayle. **1579** Lyly *Euphues* (Arb.) 124 We haue an olde prouerbe youth wil haue his course. **1675** Brooks *Gold. Key* 27 Youth enclines to Wantonness and Prodigality. **1757** Gray *Bard* 74 Youth on the prow, and Pleasure at the helm. **1844** Disraeli *Coningsby* III. i, Almost everything that is great has been done by youth.

5. Young people (or creatures) collectively; the young. (With or without *the*; now always construed as plural.)

Beowulf 66 Oð þæt seo ȝeoȝoð ȝeweox. *c* **897** Ælfred *Gregory's Past. C.* Pref. 7 Eall sio ȝioȝuð ðe nu is on Angelcynne friora monna. *c* **1205** Lay. 15372, & inne Æstsaxe heore aðeleste ȝuȝeðe. *Ibid.* 19837 Bezst alre ȝeoȝeðe þa..a þan dæȝen weore Ærður ihaten. **1538** Starkey *England* (1878) 152 The yl and idul bryngyng vp of youth here in our cuntrey. *Ibid.* 156 To ouerse the educatyon of vthe. **1581** Mulcaster *Positions* xxxiii. (1888) 119 Youth from seuen till one and twenty, will abyde much exercising. **1599** Shaks. *Hen. V.* II. Chorus 1 Now all the Youth of England are on fire. **1656** Harrington *Oceana* (1658) 204 The Elders could remember that they had been Youth. **1742** Gray *Spring* 25 The insect youth are on the wing. **1818** Byron *Juan* I. cxxv, The unexpected death of some old lady Or gentleman..Who've made 'us youth' wait too—too long already For an estate. **1874** Stubbs *Const. Hist.* I. ii. 25 When there was peace at home, the youth sought opportunities of distinguishing..themselves in distant warfare. **1883** *Century Mag.* XXVI. 292/1 There was a native innocence in the New York youth of both sexes that was pleasing to our pride.

6. a. A young person; *esp.* a young man between boyhood and mature age; sometimes, esp. in earlier use, more widely (see quots.).

Formerly sometimes (and still in dialect or vulgar speech) pleonastically qualified by *young*.

c **1250** *Gen. & Ex.* 2665 Bi ðat time ðat he was ȝuð, Wið faiȝered and strengthe kuð. *a* **1400** *Pistill of Susan* 230 He lift vp þe lach and leop ouer þe lake, þat ȝouthe. ? **1580** W. Hergest (*title*) The Right Rule of Christian Chastitie; profitable to bee read of all godly and vertuous Youthes of both sexe. **1583** Stocker *Civ. Warres Lowe C.* I. 32b, Accompanied with a multitude of women, young youthes and children. **1599** Shaks. *Much Ado* II. i. 40 He that hath a beard, is more then a youth: and he that hath no beard, is lesse then a man. **1605** Treswell *Journ. Earl Nott.* 32 A youth of ten yeares of age. **1611** *Bible* Susanna 45 The Lord raised vp the holy spirit of a young youth, whose name was Daniel. **1632** Milton *L'Allegro* 95 The jocond rebecks sound To many a youth, and many a maid. **1687** [? W. Penn] *Reason. Toleration* 16 He ended his days a young Youth, in the 24th Year of his Age. **1711** Hearne *Collect.* (O.H.S.) III. 263 Wch was in the eleventh Year of his Age, and yt he was then a very hopefull Youth. **1774** tr. *Chesterfield's Lett.* Kal. May 1741, To-morrow..you will attain your ninth year; so that, for the future, I shall treat you as a youth. **1805** *Ann. Reg., Chron.* 396/2 Two youths, one 14 and the other 8 years of age, sons of a poor man. **1837** Dickens *Pickw.* xxxii, The pot-boy, the muffin youth, and the baked-potato man. **1881** *19th Cent.* May 780 Before she was twenty she wrote verses like other youths.

b. (esp. ***college youth***.) Applied technically to societies of bellringers. *Obs.* exc. *Hist.*

1668 [Stedman] *Tintinnalogia* (1671) Ded., To the Noble Society of Colledge-Youths. **1816** Shipway *Campanal.* p. xix, The Society of College Youths, in the summer of 1657, on a visit to Cambridge, were presented by Mr. Stedman with his peculiar production on five bells. **1855** T. Bailey *Ann. Notts.* IV. 29 The bells at St. Peter's church re-cast this year;..The following are the inscriptions upon them: First, or Treble.—'I was given by the Society of Northern Youths, in 1672, and recast by the Sherwood Youths, in 1771.'

7. *attrib.* and *Comb.*, as ***youth cult***, ***culture***, ***-day***, ***-group***, ***movement***, ***organization***, ***-slip***, ***-state***, ***-tide***, ***-time***; ***youth-bold***, ***-consuming*** adjs.; ***youth-bereft***, ***-charmed***, ***-oriented*** ppl. adjs; **Youth Aliyah** [Heb. *ăliyah* ascent], a movement begun in 1933 for the emigration of young Jews to Palestine; **youth and old age** = zinnia; **youth camp**, one of the camps of various kinds that were established for young people in Germany under the Nazis; **youth centre**, a building providing social and recreational facilities for young people; **youth club**, a social club provided for the spare-time activities of young people; the premises of such a club; **Youth Employment Service**, an advisory service for school leavers set up in 1948 and superseded by the Careers Advisory Service; also *ellipt.*; so ***Youth Employment office***, ***officer***; †**youthgrass**, †**youthwort**, names for sundew; **youth hostel** [tr. G. *jugendherberge*], a hostel providing cheap overnight accommodation for young travellers and holiday-makers; hence **youth-hostel** *v. intr.*, **-hostelling** *vbl. sb.*; **youth hosteller**; **youth leader**, a person having charge of young people in a youth club or other youth organization; †**youthlike** *a.*, resembling or having the character of youth, juvenile (cf. youthly *a.*); *adv.*, like a youth, or in the manner of youth; hence †*youthlikeness*; †**youth-master**, a master who teaches young people; **Youth Opportunities Programme**, a Government-sponsored service introduced in 1978 to provide temporary work experience for unemployed young people and replaced in 1983 by the *Youth Training Scheme* (see below); **youth orchestra**, an orchestra open only to young musicians; **youth-potion**, a potion supposed to restore youth; **youth service**, a service, esp. of local government, providing social and recreational facilities for young people; **Youth Training Scheme**, a Government-sponsored scheme introduced in 1983 to replace the *Youth Opportunities Programme* (see above) and offering job experience and training for unemployed school leavers; **youth work**, social work among young people; hence **youth worker**.

1936 H. Szold *Let.* 4 Sept. in M. Lowenthal *Henrietta Szold: Life & Lett.* (1942) xvi. 312 We build homes, we work our heads off over *Youth Aliyah and social service. **1968** P. Durst *Badge of Infamy* i. 3 A Youth Aliyah village in a kibbutz south of Tel Aviv. **1975** E. Avriel *Open the Gates!* vi. 62 We had a number of special immigration certificates for youngsters from the separately functioning body of Youth Aliyah. **1889** G. Nicholson *Illustr. Dict. Gardening* IV. 241/2 Zinnia... *Youth and Old Age. **1971** *Farmer & Stockbreeder* 16 Feb. 80/1 Zinnias—common name 'youth-and-old-age'—have normally bloomed in late summer. **1911** M. Beerbohm *Zuleika Dobson* xix. 292 As on the towing-path, so on the *youth-bereft rafts of the barges, yonder, stood many stupefied elders, staring at the river. *a* **1618** Sylvester *Sonn. Mirac. Peace* xii, My *youth-bold thoughts. [**1936** *Liverpool Echo* 5 Sept. 4/1 (*heading*) A visit to a Hitler youth camp.] **1942** E. Waugh *Put out More Flags* iii. 217 Those absurd instructors who harangued the *youth camps. **1975** H. W. Koch *Hitler Youth* ix. 196 Officials of the party and the Hitler Youth participated. Final selection of candidates was made early each year in what was described as 'Youth Camp'. **1942** H. C. Warner *Christian Youth Leadership* ii. 26 We have seen the sudden outcrop of *Youth Centres, Youth Service Corps, Juvenile Civil Defence Units, etc. **1958** I. Murdoch *Bell* xx. 251 The opening of a new youth centre. **1976** 'W. Trevor' *Children of Dynmouth* i. 21 The Youth Centre curtains are apparently unavailable for the Easter Fête, dear. **1943** C. Day Lewis *Word over All* 16 Oh *youth-charmed hours. **1940** *Times* 19 Sept. 7/3 *Youth clubs may be found in all districts of the city. **1955** E. Blishen *Roaring Boys* IV. 249 Some of the blocks..had community centres and youth clubs. **1957** J. Osborne *Entertainer* 28, I was teaching Art to a bunch of Youth Club kids. **1980** P. Lively *Judgement Day* i. 7 He was no good at Youth Clubs and disturbed black teenagers. **1610** Fletcher *Faithf. Sheph.* I. i, That heavy *youth-consuming Miserie. **1968** *Harper's* Oct. 8/3 That temptation to jump on the *youthcult bandwagon is hard to resist. **1976** B. Bova *Multiple Man* vii. 73 Aspen was once a center of the youth cult... Kids from all over the country flocked there. **1980** J. O'Faolain *No Country for Young Men* x. 209 Typical Ireland! They got the youth cult ten years late. **1958** *Listener* 28 Aug. 308/2 We know little or nothing about the motivation of the new *youth culture, whose emergence is one of the key phenomena of the 'fifties. **1977** M. Dickstein *Gates of Eden* 289 The best ongoing rock criticism, some of it quite sharp, appeared in periodicals associated with the youth culture of the sixties, such as *Rolling Stone*, *Creem*, *Crawdaddy* and the *Village Voice*. **1985** *Isis* 3 May 4/2 Youth culture implies the new, the non-conformist, the intractable, yet these still form themselves into cults with rules to keep you right. **1953** C. Day Lewis *Italian Visit* v. 55 I too gave tongue in my piping *youth-days. **1948** *Youth Employment Service* (Min. Labour) 1 Local Education Authorities in England and Wales..may be authorised by means of a scheme approved by the Minister of Labour and National Service to operate a *Youth Employment Service. **1966** P. Willmott *Adolescent Boys* vi. 105 In theory, the youth employment service is available to help school leavers find suitable work. In fact, although more of the boys in the sample had got their first job through the Youth Employment Officer than any other single source, they were not a majority. **1976** L. Thomas *Dangerous Davies* iv. 30 She had gone to the youth employment office..to inquire about ..becoming a nurse. **1584** Cogan *Haven Health* ccxxiv. 228 In Lankashire..the common people do call it *youth grasse, and they think that it rotteth sheepe. **1946** Koestler *Thieves in Night* 155 The *youth-group for a while looked on critically at us rapturous elders. **1929** *Liverpool Post & Mercury* 13 Dec. 7/5 (*heading*) *Youth hostels. *Ibid.*, A meeting..held last evening in Liverpool, passed a resolution in favour of proceeding with the formation of a local Youth Hostel Association for the purpose of providing hostels in North Wales for holiday sojourns on the lines of those already existing on the Continent, in Scotland, and Northumberland. **1948** 'N. Shute' *No Highway* ix. 185 'Are you fond of hiking?' 'We used to do a lot,' he said. 'Staying in Youth Hostels?' she inquired. **1972** D. Devine *Three Green Bottles* I. iv. 39, I was youth-hostelling on a hired bicycle. **1977** *Daily Colonist* (Victoria, B.C.) 5 June 24/4 When the original—and still operating—youth hostel opened its doors in the West German town of Altena 68 years ago, its purpose was to provide inexpensive accommodations for young students on walking trips. **1977** C. McCullough *Thorn Birds* xvii. 441 The typical fate of Australians in England, youth-hosteling on a shoestring, working for a pittance. **1933** *Y.H.A. Rucksack* Summer 42/1 This is written as a challenge to *Youth Hostellers everywhere to send us word whether they want such a hostel. **1977** M. Drabble *Ice Age* II. 152 Whenever he went to any of the three pubs..he had to spend his time listening to complaints about the behaviour of delinquent youth hostellers. **1947** (*title*) *Youth hostelling abroad. **1959** *Woman* 2 May 3/4 Youth Hostelling *is* great fun, for those who enjoy an outdoor holiday, with a sufficiency of male escorts. **1936** *Liverpool Echo* 5 Sept. 4/1 In the streets [of Germany] we met policemen, storm-troopers, *youth-leaders, soldiers,..all in their various uniforms. **1958** *Listener* 21 Aug. 256/1 Youth leaders trained in Spain by Franco's Falange. **1973** 'B. Mather' *Snowline* i. 10 A youth leader at a church club in London. **1582** Stanyhurst *Æneis* II. 518 When shee saw Priamus *youthlik surcharged in armour. *a* **1586** Sidney *Arcadia* III. iv. (1912) 371 All such, whom either youthfull age, or youth-like mindes did fill with unlimited desires. **1549** Chaloner *Erasm. on Folly* C iij b, Women with their smoth chekes, small voyces, and fine skinnes, doo euer shewe a certayne *youthlikeness. **1550** Harington tr. *Cicero's Bk. Friendship* (1562) 48b, For so shall nursses and *youthmaisters chalenge muche frendshyp. **1921** *Survey* 31 Dec. 487 (*heading*) *Youth movement of Germany. **1941** 'G. Orwell' *Lion & Unicorn* I. 16 No party rallies, no *Youth Movements. **1982** *Listener* 11 Feb. 3/1 The youth movements and their clashes with the police in the 1960s. **1977** *Dept. of Employment Press Notice* 29 June 1 Up to 230,000 unemployed youngsters each year will have a chance of work experience or training under a new £160 million *Youth Opportunities Programme announced today by Mr. Albert Booth, Secretary of State for Employment. **1983** *Sunday Tel.* 16 Oct. 11/4 A Midlands businessman who has successfully employed Jamaican youngsters under the Youth Opportunities Programme. **1948** *Times* 22 Apr. 7/4 The Bath Assembly.. opened this afternoon in the Pavilion with a concert given by the National *Youth Orchestra. **1972** *Daily Tel.* 18 Jan. 9/5 Leicestershire Schools Symphony Orchestra, a 100-strong unit which has a considerable reputation as a youth orchestra. **1959** *Listener* 2 July 17/2 Local institutions: for example, water boards, *youth organizations and universities. **1977** *Gay News* 7–20 Apr. 8/3 It's always been known as a *youth-oriented action spot. **1982** S. Brett *Murder Unprompted* v. 51 The new youth-oriented culture. **1876** Geo. Eliot *Dan. Der.* liii, A sorceress..to mix *youth-potions for others. **1943** *Ann. Reg. 1942* 68 The Council.. advocated..adequate *youth services. **1962** *Guardian* 25 Sept. 6/4 A great impact would be felt if this country had a fully developed..youth service staffed by trained social workers and youth leaders. **1975** *Times* 2 Jan. 3/1 Libraries and the youth services will be among the main victims of cuts..in 1975. **1605** Sylvester *Du Bartas* II. iii. IV. *Captains* 1220 'Tis better bear the *Youth-slips of a King..Then to fill all with Bloud-flouds of Debate. **1553** Grimalde *Cicero's Offices* II. xiii. (1556) 81 Publius Rutilius *youth-state [orig. *adolescentiam*]. **1873** Brennan *Witch of Nemi*, etc. 291 The seeds that in *youth-tide we sow. **1845** S. Austin *Ranke's Hist. Ref.* I. 307 Their works, produced in the *youth-time of the human race. **1895** *Educat. Rev.* Sept. 190 Miss Cobbe regrets the banished grace of her mother's youthtime. **1981** *Hansard Commons* 15 Dec. 153 We are able to ask the Manpower Services Commission to ensure that this new *youth training scheme is in full operation by the autumn of 1983. **1983** *Times* 18 Jan. 1/4 The Government is putting a £100-a-head value on the work and training opportunities created by new jobs 'brokers' under the £1000m Youth Training Scheme, which starts in Sept. **1944** *Ann. Reg. 1943* 306 Trust funds..for the development of *youth work. **1964** 'J. H. Roberts' '*Q' Document* (1965) iv. 84 She..had pangs of conscience and decided to go into youth work. **1976** *Equals* Dec. 6/1 A *youth worker is to be appointed to escort young people to interviews,..and generally support those making an uncertain start in work or training. **1597** Gerarde *Herbal* III. clv. 1366 Called in English Sunne deaw, *Ros Solis*, *Youth woort. **1598** R. Chester *Poems* (1914) 18 Youthwort faire Affections lover.

Hence **youthen** (ˈjuːθ(ə)n) *v.* [-EN⁵], *trans.* to make youthful, impart a youthful appearance to; *intr.* to become youthful, acquire youthful qualities; **ˈyouthless** *a.*, having no youth, lacking the ordinary characteristics of youth (whence **ˈyouthlessness**); †**ˈyouthness**, youth; **ˈyouthship**, with poss. adj., used as a title (cf. *worship*); †**ˈyouthsome** *a.*, youthful in disposition, juvenile.

1882 *Even. Star* (Philad.) 28 Apr., No dress *youthens a girl so much as white. **1916** C. H. Sorley *Lett.* (1919) 140 You will always be forty to strangers perhaps: and youthen as you get to know them. **1906** Mansfield *Girl & Gods* xiii, A *youthless, over-developed girl of fifteen. **1909** *Times Lit. Suppl.* 17 June 225/2 It is his own letters..his cold *youthlessness..that are his enemy. *c* **1475** *Partenay* 5221 Þat he had don in his *youthnesse soo. **1906** A. & E. Castle '*If Youth but knew*' ii, Heaven knows..what sweet hostess may not greet your *youthship tonight. **1661** Pepys *Diary* 31 Oct., I found him drinking and very jolly and *youthsome.

youthful (ˈjuːθfʊl), *a.* [f. YOUTH + -FUL.]

1. Having or characterized by youth; that is still young.

1590 Spenser *F.Q.* I. i. 14 The youthfull knight could not for ought be staide. **1590** Shaks. *Com. Err.* v. i. 52 In vnlawfull loue, A sinne preuailing much in youthfull men. **1610** Holland *Camden's Brit.* I. 77 This Prince being youthfull, cast behinde him all care of the Empire. **1703** Rowe *Fair Penit.* III. 32 Is she not more than Painting can express, Or youthful Poets fancy, when they love? **1832** W. Irving *Alhambra* xxiii. II. 37 A youthful princess, in the very sweetness and bloom of her years. **1875** Jowett *Plato* (ed. 2) IV. 129 Here we have..an unmistakable attack made by the youthful Socrates.

2. *transf.* Of, pertaining to, characteristic of, or suitable for, youth or the young; juvenile.

1561 T. Hoby tr. *Castiglione's Courtyer* II. Xiij, Alonso Carillo..hauynge committed certein youthfull partes that were of no great importance, was..caried to prison. **1579** Lyly *Euphues* (Arb.) 111 Idlenesse is..ye sole maintenaunce of youthful [*later edd.* youthly] affection. **1600** Shaks. *A.Y.L.* II. vii. 160 The leane and slipper'd Pantaloone,..His youthfull hose well sau'd, a world too wide, For his shrunke shanke. **1632** Milton *L'Allegro* 26 Jest and youthful Jollity. **1723** C. Walker *Mem. Sally Salisb.* 10 Dress and Dancing were the sole Youthful Delights of our Sally. **1799** Han. More *Fem. Educ.* (ed. 4) I. 173 That profusion of little..sentimental books with which the youthful library overflows. **1848** Dickens *Dombey* xxxv, Mrs. Skewton..appropriately attired for that purpose in a very youthful costume. **1901** Jacobs *Light Freights* 228 An ancient eye watched with almost youthful impatience the slow warming of a mug of beer on the hob.

3. *fig.* That is in its early stage, early, new; also, having the freshness or vigour of youth.

1588 Shaks. *Tit. A.* III. i. 18 O earth! I will befriend thee more with raine That shall distill from these two ancient ruines, Then youthfull Aprill shall with all his showres In summers drought. **1613** Purchas *Pilgrimage* I. vii. 34 The larger stature..of men in those youthfull times and age of the world. **1692** Bentley *Boyle Lect.* i. 24 Perfect Felicity, such as after millions and millions of Ages is still youthfull and flourishing. **1777** Potter *Æschylus, Agamemnon* 256 The youthfull bloom of rosy love. **1830** Lyell *Princ. Geol.* I. 147 There may be a connexion between an extraordinary profusion of monocotyledonous plants and a youthful condition of the world. **1877** *Pall Mall Gaz.* 17 Oct. 11/1 A youthful and astringent Tinta, an aromatic Malmsey of fabulous value.

4. Comb. *youthful-looking* adj.

1846 Poe in *Godey's Mag.* July 15/1 The likeness conveys a good general idea of the man, but it is far too stout and youthful-looking for his appearance at present. **1954** W. Faulkner *Fable* 8 A man not so young actually, but rather simply youthful-looking. **1977** *New Yorker* 19 Sept. 66/3 Mrs. McCabe is a youthful-looking woman.

Hence **youthfullity** (*nonce-wd.*), youthfulness; *pl.* youthful acts or follies.

1763 H. Walpole *Let. to G. Montagu* 15 Aug., You see my impetuosity does not abate much: no, nor my youthfullity. **1764** —— *Let. to C. Churchill* 27 Mar., You do not suspect me, I hope, of any youthfullities.

youthfully (ˈjuːθfʊlɪ), *adv.* [f. prec. + -LY².] In a youthful manner; with the freshness, vigour, or other characteristic of youth; like a young person; in a juvenile style.

1581 Mulcaster *Positions* xxxix. (1888) 209 Let them..defende that stoutly, which they haue begone youthfully. **1582** Hester *Secr. Phiorav.* III. ii. 6 The face beyng washed therwith, it maketh it very faire, and preserueth it youthfully. **1638** Junius *Paint. Ancients* 195 If anything seemeth to be painted somewhat youthfully, it is esteemed to proceed out of a promising forwardnesse of our naturall inclinations. **1665** Manley *Grotius' Low C. Wars* 87 Youthfully impatient of all delay. **1808** Han. More *Cœlebs* ix, Rather youthfully drest. **1875** Browning *Aristoph. Apol.* 5289 Now that the cloud has broken, sky laughs blue, Earth blossoms youthfully!

youthfulness (ˈjuːθfʊlnɪs). [f. as prec. + -NESS.] The fact or quality of being youthful; youthful condition or character.

1587 Golding *De Mornay* viii. 117 Should we rather graunt an euerlasting ignorance in man, than a kynd of youthfulnesse which hath learned things according to the growths thereof in ages? **1622** Mabbe tr. *Aleman's Guzman d'Alf.* II. 139 He might either doe it out of youthfulnesse..or out of want. **1717** Addison tr. *Ovid's Met.* III. Wks. 1726 I. 213 With all the purple youthfulness of face, That gently blushes in the wat'ry glass. **1840** Dickens *Old C. Shop* i, Her very small and delicate frame imparted a peculiar youthfulness to her appearance. **1898** 'H. S. Merriman' *Roden's Corner* xii. 124 A complexion almost dazzling in its youthfulness and brilliancy.

youthhead (ˈjuːθhɛd). Chiefly *Sc.* Forms: 3 **ȝuðhede**, 4 **ȝouþehede**, **-heed**, **ȝouthhede**, **yhouthede**, **ȝuthed**, 4–5 **ȝowthed(e**, **-eid**, **youthed(e**, 4–6 **ȝouthed(e**, **-eid**, 5 **yowthid**, **ȝowthehede**, **youtheed**, **(yuȝhed)**, 5–6 **ȝowthheid**, **youtheid**, **yowthed**, 6 **ȝouthhed**, **ȝhouthhed**, **yowth(h)eid**, **ȝeutheid**, **yutheid**, **ȝowcht-heid**, **youitheid**, 6, 8 **ȝouthheid**, *arch.* 8 **youthhede**, 9 **-hed**, 9 **youth-head**, **youthhead** (*Sc.* -heid). [f. YOUTH + -HEAD.]

1. The state of youth, youngness: = YOUTH 1.

c **1220** *Bestiary* 55 Wu he neweð his ȝuðhede, hu he cumeð ut of elde. *c* **1375** *Sc. Leg. Saints* ii. (*Paulus*) 862 Quhare hele beis ay but seknes, ȝouthed but eld or wrechitnes. **1456** Sir G. Haye *Law Arms* (S.T.S.) 3 Till enforme ȝour ȝouthede of mony syndry knaulagis. **1535** Stewart *Cron. Scot.* (Rolls) I. 67 ȝouthheid is without ressoun or ryme. *c* **1560** A. Scott *Poems* (S.T.S.) xvi. 50 Quha wald the rege of ȝowᵗheid dant. *c* **1730** Ramsay *Some of the Contents* vi, Quhen eild and spyte takis place of ȝouthheids flame. **1819** Scott *Let. to Cornet W. Scott* 3 Dec. in *Lockhart*, Mamma and the girls are quite well, and so is Master Charles, who is of course more magnificent, as being the only specimen of youthhead at home.

2. The time of youth, adolescence: = YOUTH 2.

a **1300** *Cursor M.* 3592 Quen þai it [*sc.* eld] haue þai are vnfayn, And wald ha youthed þan again. *c* **1375** *Sc. Leg. Saints* xiv. (*Lucas*) 3 In his ȝouthede leyrit he In antyoche leche to be. *c* **1440** *Gesta Rom.* lxix. 317 (Harl. MS.) My lord god, þat hast y-kept me fro my ȝowthede, kepe me now in þis hour. **1526** *Extr. Burgh Rec. Stirling* (1887) 29 He was within youitheid and of mynor aige. **1588** A. King tr. *Canisius' Catech.* k iv, All the iust men, florising in thair ȝouthheid. **1798** H. Macneill *Scot. Muse* xiv, Year after year in youtheid's prime, Wander he will, frae clime to clime. **1814** Southey *Roderick* XVII. 17 The children, free In youthhead's happy season from all cares. **1826** J. Wilson *Noctes Ambr.* Wks. 1856 I. 170 That never was Mr. North's character, even in lusty youth-head.

3. Youths collectively: = YOUTH 5.

1562 Winȝet *Cert. Tractates* Wks. (S.T.S.) I. 23, I iugeit the teching of the ȝouthed in vertew and science, nixt efter the auctoritie with the ministeris of iustice vnder it. **1567** *Reg. Privy Council Scot.* I. 535 Privatlie or publictlie to instruct the youtheid. **1848** *Tait's Mag.* XV. 123 They are ..guilty of having committed the education of 'the youth-head' of the country to men whom they consider disqualified.

youthhood (ˈjuːθhʊd). Now *rare* or *arch.* Forms: 1 **ȝeoȝoþhad**, **ȝeoȝuþhad**, 3 **ȝuweðehode**; 7–9 **youthood**, **youth-hood**, **youthhood**. [OE. *ȝeoȝuþhád*, f. *ȝeoȝuþ* YOUTH + *-hád* -HOOD; cf. OS. *juguðhêd*, MHG. *jugentheit*. In mod.E. a new formation.]

1. = YOUTH 1, 2, 3.

971 *Blickl. Hom.* 59 Swa þonne ȝelice bið þære menniscan ȝecynde þæs lichoman, þonne se ȝeoȝoþ-hád ærest bloweþ & fæȝerost bið. *a* **1050** *Liber Scintill.* lxii. (1889) 189 Se þe estelice fram ȝeoȝuðhade [L. *pueritia*] fet þeow his þær-æfter hyne onȝyt ofermodiȝne. *a* **1225** *Ancr. R.* 342 Of al þin elde, of childhode, of ȝuweðehode.

1623 tr. *Favine's Theat. Hon.* I. vi. 49 In this age of youth-hood, (commonly called Adolescency). **1637** Gillespie *Engl. Pop. Cerem.* II. iii. 17 From his youthood he was most observant of Ecclesiasticall Ceremonies. **1680** in Sprat *Relat. Wicked Contriv.* II. (1693) 64 It was a folly of Youth-hood. **1724** Warburton *Tracts* (1789) 36 My Governess Philosophy, under whose Roof I spent my Youth-hood. *a* **1807** J. Skinner *Amusem. Leis. Hours* (1809) 49 A gawsie gurk, wi' phiz o' yellow, In youthood's sappy bud. **1837** Carlyle *Fr. Rev.* I. VII. x, With the down of youthhood still on his chin. **1887** Smiles *Life & Lab.* 143 All new ideas are young, and originate for the most part in youth-hood.

b. *fig.* Early stage or period: = YOUTH 2 b.

1828 D'Israeli *Chas. I*, II. xii. 343 The native of a land where, in the youthhood of the Republic, a nation's independence had broke forth. **1880** W. Watson *Prince's Quest* 101 And night and day its crystal heart doth yearn To wed its youthhood with the sea's old age.

2. *concr.* Young people collectively: = YOUTH 5.

1690 J. Mackenzie *Siege London-Derry* 48 The Youth-hood by a strange impulse ran in one Body and shut the Gates. **1834** H. Miller *Scenes & Leg.* xxviii. (1857) 412 The urchin who, in behalf of the outraged youthhood of the place, wore the white sheet on this interesting occasion.

youthify (ˈjuːθifaɪ), *v.* [f. YOUTH + -IFY.] *trans.* To make (a person) appear more youthful. Hence **ˈyouthifying** *ppl. a.*

1945 H. L. Mencken *Amer. Lang.* Suppl. I. 573 *Beauty-parlor*..was displaced by *beauty-shop*... The girls have produced a considerable vocabulary of elegant terms to designate their operations, *e.g. to youthify*. **1960** *Housewife* May 24/3 She..has both to 'youthify' and age actors. **1976** U. Holden *String Horses* iii. 41 He wasn't such a bad looker .., his summer tan was youthifying.

youthily, youthiness: see after YOUTHY.

youthless: see after YOUTH.

youthly (ˈjuːθlɪ), *a.* Now *rare.* [f. YOUTH + -LY¹. In OE. *ȝeoȝuþlic*; cf. OHG. *jugundlîh*.]

1. Pertaining to or characteristic of youth: = YOUTHFUL 2.

c **900** tr. *Bæda's Hist.* v. vi. (1890) 398 Ic ne wæs min mod fulfremedlice bewerȝende þæm ȝeoȝuðlicum unalefednessum. **1922** E. R. Eddison *Worm Ouroboros* xxvi. 323 Yet is Corinius..a valiant and puissant soldier,..and this one in his youthly age. **1923** H. J. Laski *Let.* 23 Oct. in *Holmes-Laski Lett.* (1953) I. 553, I have read a new *Early Life of Burke* which is full of good things, especially in its recovery of some youthly essays of his which have not appeared before.

a **1536** Wyatt *Love's Arraignm.* v, Alwayes whetting my youthely desyer On the cruell whetstone tempered with fier. **1577** Hanmer *Anc. Eccl. Hist.* VIII. xii. 152 Two doughters, ..which passed all other in..youthly comlines. **1590** Spenser *Muiop.* 431 And all his yougthly forces idly spent. **1685** Burnet *Trav.* iii. (1687) 97 Pope Nicolas the IV. who had..a youthly and womanish face. **1817** Shelley *To Wm. Shelley* 14 To a blighting faith and a cause of crime They have bound them slaves in youthly prime.

2. Having youth or the characteristics of youth: = YOUTHFUL 1.

1566 Painter *Pal. Pleas.* I. Pref. 8 Faulting fooles and youthly heades. **1596** Spenser *F.Q.* IV. ii. 40 All that youthly rout. *a* **1629** Hinde *J. Bruen* xxxvii. (1641) 116 This Master Done being young and youthly. **1767** Mickle *Concub.* I. xxxiii, While thus the Knight persewd the Shadow Joy As youthly Spirits thoughtlesse led the Way. **1856** *Chamb. Jrnl.* 8 Nov. 301 Although still something too youthly in figure, [he] had a frame well knit. **1925** T. Dreiser *Amer. Tragedy* (1926) II. II. xxviii. 347 All seeking a glimpse of the astonishingly youthly slayer.

So †**ˈyouthly** *adv.* *Obs.* = YOUTHFULLY.

1541 Paynell *Conspir. Catil.* I b, With men of sadnesse he lyued soberly,..with youth youthely. **1581** A. Hall *Iliad* VII. 131 Paris..youthly thus doth answere him. **1582** Stanyhurst *Æneis* I. 590 His heunly moother amended His bush with trimming, his sight was yoouthlye bepurpled.

youthness to **youthsome**: see after YOUTH.

youthquake (ˈjuːθkweɪk). *colloq.* [f. YOUTH after EARTHQUAKE.] The series of radical political and cultural upheavals occurring among students and young people in the 1960s.

1967 *Punch* 8 Nov. 708/2 Mary Quant opened her first Bazaar shop..simultaneously with the first tremors of the youthquake. **1970** R. Neville *Play Power* 18 A unique feature of today's Youthquake—as *Vogue* once dubbed it —is its intense, spontaneous internationalism. **1976** *Sunday Mail* (Brisbane) 5 Sept. 19/3 He's built an empire based on the youthquake.

ˈyouthy, *sb. Sc.* [f. YOUTH + -Y⁶.] A youthful person.

1795 Macneill *Scotl. Scaith* I. xviii, The mair they crack'd, the mair ilk youthy Pray'd for drink to wash news down.

youthy (ˈjuːθɪ), *a.* Now *rare* or *Obs.* [f. YOUTH + -Y¹. 'A bad word' (J.).] Having or affecting the character of youth: usually connoting a youthful appearance or behaviour inconsistent with the person's years.

1712 Steele *Spect.* No. 296 ¶5 Affecting a youthier Turn than is consistent with my Time of Day. **1819** Scott *Let. to J. Richardson* 18 Jan. in *Lockhart*, A withered beauty who persists in looking youthy. **1841** Caroline Fox *Mem. Old Friends* (1882) I. 231 When at college, Sterling had venerated and defended Shelley as a moralist as well as a poet, 'being rather youthy'.

Hence **ˈyouthily** *adv.*, with the appearance of youth; **ˈyouthiness**, youthfulness, juvenility.

1821 *Blackw. Mag.* VIII. 517 Bringing back with me..a sort of youthiness that lasted sometimes more than a fortnight. **1839** Galt *Demon of Dest.* 6 His bright eyes shone youthily.

you-uns (ˈjuːʌnz), *pron. U.S. dial.* Also 9 **youns**; 20– **you uns**. [f. YOU *pers. pron.* + *uns*, dial. var. *ones* (ONE *pron.*).] Used in place of YOU *pers. pron.*

1810 M. V. H. Dwight *Jrnl.* 10 Nov. in *Journey to Ohio* (1912) 37 Youns is a word I have heard used several times, but what it means I don't know. **1869** [see *you-all's* s.v. YOU-ALL *pers. pron.*]. **1885** 'C. E. Craddock' *Prophet Great Smokey Mountains* 7, I hev no call ter spen' words 'bout sech ez that, with a free-spoken man like you-uns. **1927** *Amer. Speech* II. 345 The paterfamilias questioned solicitously: Did you uns sleep good last night? **1934** W. Faulkner *Dr. Martino* 341 Why did you uns have to stop here? **1941** *Amer. Mercury* June 660/2 'Proud to know ye!' Sam will beam. 'Why, you-uns be a-comin' in ter th' fire an' set a spell.'

youward(s, in phr. *to youward(s*: see -WARD(S.

yove, yoven, -yn, ȝove, etc., occas. **yoved**, obs. pa. t. and pple. of GIVE.

c **1300** *Harrow. Hell* (E.) 189 Y haue ȝouen my liif for þe. **13..** *Northern Passion* 130/1255 Ageyn oure law he haþ ȝoue red. **1390** Gower *Conf.* II. 192 Unto thidoles yove and granted. **1426** Lydg. *De Guil. Pilgr.* 24360 Whan Iuges, for offence Han yoved hir sentence. *c* **1460** *Wisdom* 945 in *Macro Plays* 66 My wyll was full yowe to syne. **1532** Cromwell in Merriman *Life & Lett.* (1902) I. 344 According to your high commawndment to me youyn yesterdaye. **1552** Huloet, Yoven or enclined to couetousenes or crueltye.

yow (jaʊ), *int.* [Imitative.]

a. An exclamation of vague meaning.

c **1440** *York Myst.* xxx. 295 Yowe! þat schalke shuld not shamely be shente.

(*b*) In mod.Austral. and N.Z. use = WOW *int.* 2.

a **1943** L. Esson in *Penguin Bk. Austral. Ballads* (1964) 232 Not er shutter lifted Since they jugged 'im. Yow! **1978** P. Grace *Mutuwhenua* vi. 35, I know. Matter of fact, some of those girls you went round with. Yow! **1983** 'F. Parrish' *Bait on Hook* viii. 111 The rain came... 'Yow,' said Cedric, and shot back into the pub.

b. An imitation of the yelp or bark of a dog, or the miaow of a cat; also as *sb.* and *v.* (reduplicated *yow-yow*).

1820 *Edin. Mag.* May 452 *To yow*, to caterwaul. **1837** Barham *Ingol. Leg.* Ser. I. *Spectre Tapp.*, Yow!—yeough!

—yeough!—yow!—yow! yelled a hapless sufferer from beneath the table. **1839** *Ibid., Cynotaph*, Cupid, of 'Yow-Yow'-ing memory. **1866** SIR T. SEATON *From Cadet to Col.* I. iv. 103 A mob of pretty dogs, yow-yowing musically after a poor little beast.

yow (jaʊ), *sb. Austral. slang.* [Origin unknown.] In phr. ***to keep yow***, to keep a look-out, esp. in order to protect some criminal activity.

1942 E. LANGLEY *Pea Pickers* xix. 283 You keep yow,.. and whistle..if anyone comes along. **1965** G. MCINNES *Road to Gundagai* xii. 206 Molly kept a look out ('kept yow', as we used to say).

yow(e: see YOVE; obs. f. YEW, YOU.

yow(e, obs. (exc. *dial.*) ff. EWE *sb.*[1]; also *attrib.*

1459–60 *Durham Acc. Rolls* (Surtees) 320 Pro emend. unius muri juxta le yowecote. **1521–2** *Churchw. Acc., Croscombe* (Somerset Rec. Soc.) 36 Ed. Wynsor geve unto the chorch ij. yows the prisse iij^s. iiij^d. **1566** in *Reg. Mag. Sig. Scot.* 1584, 208/2 Pastura *lie yow-flokkis* sive aliarum ovium quarumcunque de Pawinshill. **1903** 'T. COLLINS' *Such is Life* (1937) v. 249 He went out back, Cooper's creek way, with three thousand gunbar yowes. **1925** 'H. MCDIARMID' *Sangschaw* 2 Ae weet forenicht i' the yow-trummle I saw yon antrin thing. **1978** *Jnl. Lakeland Dial. Soc.* XL. 14 I' a field wid sum yows in ther was a crab apple tree. **1979** L. DERWENT *Border Bairn* i. 15 Her brother, the shepherd..accepted me more or less as one of his flock. A yowe or a glimmer, a stirk or a stot.

yowcke, yowg, obs. forms of YOKE.

yowden-drift, variant of EWDEN-DRIFT, snow driven by the wind.

1815 G. BEATTIE *John O' Arnha'* (1826) 58 Choakin' thick as yowden drift.

yowdin, ȝowdin, obs. Sc. pa. pple. of YIELD *v.*: see YOLDEN.

yowele, yower, yowese, obs. ff. JEWEL, EWER[2], YOUR, YURE, USE.

yowf (jaʊf), *sb. Sc.* Also yowff, youf(f. [Echoic.] A smart swingeing blow. Hence **yowf** *v. trans.*, to strike with such a blow.

1711 RAMSAY *On Maggy Johnstoun* vii, Death wi' his rung rax'd her a yowff. *c* **1738** J. SKINNER *Christmas Ba'ing* ii, They yowff'd the ba' frae dyke to dyke. **1808** JAMIESON, *Youff, Yowff*, a swinging blow, Loth.

yowght, obs. Sc. form of YOUTH.

yowie[1]. *Sc.* [f. *yow*, EWE *sb.*[1] + *-ie*, -Y[6].] A little ewe.

1783 BURNS *Death & Dying Wds. Poor Mailie* ix, An' niest my yowie, silly thing, Gude keep thee frae a tether string!

yowie[2] (ˈjaʊɪ). *Austral.* [Origin unknown.] A large, hairy, man-like creature supposedly inhabiting south-eastern Australia.

1976 *Australasian Express* 17 Sept. 10/4 Since 1795 there have been over 3,000 reported sightings of the Snowy Mountains version of the abominable Snowman nick-named the Yowie. **1980** *Courier-Mail* (Brisbane) 4 Jan. 1/8 The 'yowie', a large hairy animal similar to the Himalayan yeti and American Big Foot, has existed in Aboriginal folklore for thousands of years. **1984** *Truckin' Life* (Austral.) Feb. 80/1 'In search of a Yowie.' That was how Theiss Toyota promoted its media function for the release of its new HiLux [*sc.* type of van]..last year.

yowith, obs. form of YOUTH.

yowl (jaʊl), *sb.* Also 5–6 ȝowle, 7 youle, 9 youl. [f. next.] An act of yowling; a prolonged loud cry, now esp. of a dog or cat.

c **1450** HOLLAND *Howlat* 53 He grat grysly grym, and gaif a gret ȝowle. **1500–20** DUNBAR *Poems* xxi. 69 Pitt obscure, Quhair ȝoulis ar hard with horreble stevin. **1622** MABBE tr. *Aleman's Guzman d' Alf.* I. 36 He brake forth into such a Youle of laughing, that he was ready to burst. **1820** HOGG *Tales & Sk., Sheph. Cal.* i, A dog..gae two or three melancholy yowls. *a* **1877** JAS. BALLANTINE in *Mod. Scott. Poets* Ser. III. (1881) 31 At your feet wi' kindly yowl, Whurrs your wee catty. **1917** P. MACGILL *Gt. Push* i, The cats raise their primordial, instinctive yowl.

yowl (jaʊl), *v.* Forms: 3 ȝoȝele, ȝuhele, ȝule, 4–5 (6 *Sc.*) ȝoule, ȝowle, 5–6 yowle, 5–7 youle, 5, 7, 9 youll, 7, 9 youl, 9 yowll, 8– yowl. [ME. *ȝoȝele*, *ȝoule*, *ȝuhele*, *ȝule*. Cf. ME. *ȝaule*, YAWL *v.*[1] and GOWL (ON. *gaula*).]

1. a. *intr.* To cry out loudly from pain, grief, or distress; also said of the howling of dogs and various wild animals, the 'wauling' of cats, and (formerly) of the hooting of owls, the cooing of doves.

a **1225**, *a* **1250** [see YOWLING *vbl. sb.*]. *c* **1375** *Sc. Leg. Saints* iv. (*Jacobus*) 102 Þe fendis furth can fare..ȝouland and cryand in þe ayre. *c* **1380** WYCLIF *Sel. Wks.* I. 200 Whanne þei [*sc.* wolves] bigynen to ȝoule, þei turnen her snowte to hevene ward. *c* **1410** *Master of Game* (MS. Digby 182) 66/60 A bolde hounde shulde neuer pleyne nor yowle, but if he were oute of þe reghtes. **1483** *Cath. Angl.* 427/2 To ȝowle, *vlulare.* **1513** DOUGLAS *Æneis* IV. viii. 112 The nycht oule..was hard ȝoule With langsum voce. **1535** COVERDALE *Ps.* lviii. [lix.] 14 Let them go to & fro, & runne aboute the cite, youlinge like dogges. **1549** *Compl. Scot.* vi. 39 The turtil began for to greit, quhen the cuschet ȝoulit. **1674** RAY *N.C. Words* 22 To Greet and Yowl, *Cumberland*, to weep and cry. **1728** RAMSAY *Robt., Richy, & Sandy* 24 His dog its lane sat yowling on a brae. **1820** *Marmaiden of Clyde* vii. in *Edin. Mag.* VI. 422 An' the wilcat yowl't through its dowie vowts. **1848** THACKERAY *Dr. Birch* (1849) 18 She is always croaking, scolding, bullying—yowling at the housemaids, snarling at Miss Raby [etc.]. **1862** SALA *Seven Sons* I. vii. 161 The Blenheim spaniel..yowled fractiously. **1896** BARING-GOULD *Broom-Squire* i, [The child] yowlin' enough to tear a fellow's nerves to pieces.

transf. **1513** DOUGLAS *Æneis* II. viii. 84 The whole howsis ȝowlit and resoundit For womenting of ladyis and wemen.

†**b.** Applied to loud singing or shouting. *Obs.*

1509 BARCLAY *Shyp of Folys* (1874) I. 297 Yowlynge with theyr folysshe songe and cry. *c* **1630** *Song* ii. in De Foe *Mem. Cavalier* (1840) Notes 323 Yoffing, crying, youlling, yelling, Lyk ane citie swyne summonds out with an horne.

2. *trans.* To express by yowling; to utter with a yowl.

1842 J. WILSON *Chr. North* I. i. 13 The chained mastiff in the yard yowls his admiration. **1889** RUSKIN *Præterita* III. iv. 175 However fast the clergyman may gabble, or the choir-boys yowl, their psalms.

Hence **ˈyowler**, one who or that which yowls (in quot. 1935 applied to a crooner).

1935 WODEHOUSE *Blandings Castle* v. 120 He's a yowler, and girls always fall for yowlers. They have a glamour. **1966** 'L. LANE' *ABZ of Scouse* 120 *Yowler*, a cat. **1979** *Tucson* (Arizona) *Citizen* 20 Sept. 10A/3 In every airport I stand, sip, sleep, weep, wail and yowl in, I find an equal number of other standers, sippers, sleepers, weepers, wailers and yowlers.

yowle, obs. form of YULE.

ˈyowley. *north. dial.* [? f. YOWLRING + *-ey*, -Y[6].] A yellow-hammer.

1797 BEWICK *Brit. Birds* I. 143 Yellow Bunting. Yellow Hammer, or Yellow Yowley. **1862** *Tyneside Songs* (1863) 56 They've a bunch ov hair upon their jaws Just like a yowley's nest.

yowling (ˈjaʊlɪŋ), *vbl. sb.* [f. YOWL *v.* + -ING[1].] The action of the verb YOWL; *esp.* the uttering of a prolonged wailing cry.

a **1225** *Juliana* 57 Ȝe, quoð eleusius, haldest tu ȝetten up o þi ȝuhelunge? *a* **1250** *Owl & Night.* 40 Me luste bet speten þane singe Of þine fule ȝoȝelinge [*Jesus MS.* howelynge]. *Ibid.* 1643 Mid ȝulinge & mid igrede. **1382** WYCLIF *Gen.* xxvii. 38 With a greet ȝowlyng [**1388** ȝellyng; Vulg. *ejulatu*] he wepte. *c* **1440** *Alphabet of Tales* 179 He vanysshid away with grete cryand & yowlyng. **1528** LYNDESAY *Dreme* 165 Ȝowtyng and ȝowlyng we hard, with mony ȝell. **1632** LITHGOW *Trav.* x. 466 The water..strangled and swallowed vp my breath from youling and groaning. **1710** *Acc. Last Distemper of Tom Whigg* I. 19 He..set all the Dogs in the Town a yowling. **1844** THACKERAY *White Squall* vi, Then the wind set up a howling, And the poodle dog a yowling. **1894** W. CLARK RUSSELL *Good Ship 'Mohock'* vii, The hoarse yowling of pulling and dragging sailors.

So **ˈyowling** *ppl. a.*, that yowls.

c **1590** W. FOWLER *Wks.* (S.T.S.) I. 193/11 All thir cold nights..I wishe for day,..disturb'd with youling hounds. **1790** ALEX. WILSON *Callamphitres Elegy* Poet. Wks. (1846) 104 Wi' yowling clinch auld Jennock ran. **1843** THACKERAY *Men's Wives, Mr. & Mrs. Berry* ii, Her little yowling black-muzzled darling of a Fido. **1899** BARING-GOULD *Furze Bloom* iii. 33 Think what it 'ud be wi' two yowlin' females under one roof!

yowlk, obs. form of YOLK.

yowlring. *dial.* Also 6 yowlo-, youlw-, 6–7 yowle-, 9 youlring, yo(u)rin, yowring. See also YOLDRING, YORLIN(G. [f. *yowlo(w)*, YELLOW *a.* + RING *sb.*] A yellow-hammer.

1544 [see YELLOW-HAM]. **1591** *Shuttleworths' Acc.* (Chetham Soc.) 70 Larkes and yowloringes. **1595** *Ibid.* 104 Sixtine sparrowes and youlwringes. **1828** *Craven Gloss.*, *Yellow-yowring*, a yellow hammer.

yowndrift, var. EWDEN-DRIFT, snow driven by the wind.

1834 H. MILLER *Scenes & Leg.* xviii. (1850) 265 I'll be lost, I'm feared, in the yowndrift.

yownge, yowp, yowr(e, obs. forms of YOUNG, YOUP, YOUR, YURE.

yowpindail: see YOKINDALE.

yowt (jaʊt), *sb.* Chiefly *Sc.* Forms: 6 ȝewt, ȝout(t, 9 yout(t, yowte, 8– yowt. [f. next.] A yell, yelp.

1552 LYNDESAY *Monarche* 6002 With mony ȝamer, ȝewt, and ȝell. **1567** *Satir. Poems Reform.* iii. 189 Cerberus..Sall gar hir cry, with mony ȝout and ȝell. *c* **1590** BURREL *Pass. Pilgr.* I. xxxvii. in Jas. Watson *Coll. Scots Poems* (1709) II. 33 And vther sum with zouts and zells, Maist cairfully did cry. **1806** R. JAMIESON *Pop. Ballads* I. 233 The sichts to see, the yowts to hear That stound upon mine ear.

yowt (jaʊt), *v.* Chiefly *Sc.* Forms: 5 ȝowt, 6, 9 yout, 9 yowt. [Cf. Flem. *juyten* 'iubilare & vociferari & ouare' (Kilian). Verbs of similar meaning and differing in form by the initial consonant are *howt* (HOOT), ROUT *vbs.*[2] and [3], SHOUT.] *intr.* To yell, yelp, howl, bellow.

c **1450** HOLLAND *Howlat* 102 To ȝowt and to ȝowle, As ane horrible Owle. **1528** [see YOWLING *vbl. sb.*]. **1808** JAMIESON s.v., A cow is said to yout, when she makes a noise. **1819** W. TENNANT *Papistry Storm'd* (1827) 38 Yelpin' and youtin' in his face. **1848** A. B. EVANS *Leicestersh. Wds.* s.v. *Yowt*, I yeard the dogs yowting.

yowthe, yowuthe, obs. ff. YOUTH.

yowx, yox(e (ȝoxe), obs. or dial. ff. YEX.

yoy(e, ȝoye: see JOY, YEA.

yoyle, yoylle, yoyn, yoyntor, yoyste, obs. ff. OIL *sb.*[1], YULE, JOIN, JOINTURE, JOIST *sb.*[1]

1557 in *Archaeologia* I. 13 For wast of the paschall, and for holye yoyle 5s. 10d. **1585** *Knaresb. Wills* (Surtees) I. 149 In full recompence of her thirdes or yoyntor. **1536** *MS. Rawl. D. 780* lf. 68 The flore with plates yoystes and other nedfull for the same.

yo-yo (ˈjəʊjəʊ), *sb.* [Origin uncertain, but prob. from one of the Philippines languages.]

1. Also **Yo-Yo.** A proprietary name for a toy in the form of two conjoined cones or discs with a deep groove between them in which a string is attached and wound, its free end being held so that the toy can be made to fall under its own weight and rise again by its momentum.

1915 *Philippine Craftsman* Dec. 363 Sumpit (blowgun), pana (arrow), and yo-yo, however, are names very generally used throughout the islands. *Ibid.* 364 There is evidently some commercial possibility in Filipino toys, for a patent was recently secured upon the yo-yo by a firm in the United States. **1932** *Trade Marks Jrnl.* 2 Mar. 279/2 *Yo Yo*... All good included in Class 49 [*i.e.* toys and games equipment]. Henry Clement Conlin,..Vancouver, British Columbia, Canada; merchant. **1932** *Evening Standard* 1 June 17/4 He asked me to hold his hand until he became proficient, and I experienced a queer thrill as I brought his hand slowly up and down to make the Yo-Yo respond to the twitch of the string. **1932** AUDEN in *Rev. Eng. Stud.* (1978) Aug. 281 In the year of my youth when yoyos came in The carriage was sunny and the Clyde was bright. **1933** D. L. SAYERS *Murder must Advertise* vi. 99 Ginger brought a Yo-Yo to the office with him and broke the window in the boys' room practising 'Round the World' in his lunch-hour. **1958** *Observer* 12 Oct. 15/7 The yo-yo craze of the thirties. **1972** *Daily Tel.* 20 Dec. 14 Overall trading was at a low ebb and bored dealers spent a very quiet afternoon in yo-yo competitions and other pre-Christmas pastimes. **1984** *New Yorker* 23 July 76/2 They've got the right string but the wrong yo-yo.

b. The pastime of playing with a yo-yo.

1932 *Daily Express* 2 July 3/3 Some boys playing yo-yo attracted the Queen's attention. **1932** *Morning Post* 15 July 10/5 Games similar to Yo-Yo have been played in almost every age.

2. *fig.* or in fig. context. **a.** Something or someone going continually up and down, or to and fro; also, such a motion or fluctuation. Freq. used in comparative phrases referring to emotions or spirits rising and falling like a yo-yo.

1958 *Listener* 16 Oct. 623/2 What is it like to be a human yo-yo, driving all day on a ten-minute bus route. **1963** L. DEIGHTON *Horse under Water* xi. 47 Singleton was jumping in and out of the water like a yo-yo. **1973** C. BONINGTON *Next Horizon* xii. 168 With a bit of luck the constant yo-yo between Scheidegg and the snow cave would be over. **1975** *Times Lit. Suppl.* 12 Dec. 1496/4 Confronted by these dramatic developments, transport policy ceased to be the political yo-yo it had previously been. **1976** J. GRENFELL *Joyce Grenfell requests Pleasure* xvi. 230 Our spirits went up and down like yo-yos. **1980** *Times* 13 Sept. 10/5 Alarming yo-yos in the quality of food and service. **1981** *Daily Tel.* 19 Oct. 25/4 (*heading*) Interest rates all a big yo-yo. **1984** S. TOWNSEND *Growing Pains A. Mole* 23 Your emotions are up and down like a yo-yo.

b. A stupid person, a fool. *U.S. slang.*

1970 *New Yorker* 28 Nov. 40 He would leer, and categorize them in a loud, mocking voice. ('Weirdo' was one of his favourite appellations; also 'Freak', 'Yo-Yo', and creep.) **1975** *Ibid.* 20 Jan. 29/1 Some yo-yo of a technician there pulls the control rods out of the core to polish them with Rally wax. **1978** V. BUGLIOSI *Till Death us do Part* xi. 325 I've got enough problems without some punk yo-yo threatening me.

3. *attrib.* Marked by a continual up-and-down or to-and-fro motion; continually passing from and into a condition. Also *fig.*

1932 *Amer. Speech* VII. 272 *Yo-yo driller*, a cable-tool driller. **1960** *Spectator* 30 Sept. 501 It isn't the industry's fault that we have a yo-yo economy. **1963** T. PYNCHON *V.* i. 29 Though they only thought about one another at random, though her yo-yo hand was usually busy at other things, now and then would come the invisible, umbilical tug. **1977** *Lancet* 15 Oct. 792/1 There was no improvement in patients with severe on-off disabilities with freezing and rapid oscillations ('yo-yo' effect). **1979** *Globe & Mail* (Toronto) 22 Jan. 4/3, I want this job because all the jobs I've had have been yo-yo jobs, I've been laid off my job four times in the last six years.

ˈyo-yo, *v.* [f. prec. sb.] **1.** *intr.* To play with a yo-yo.

1932 *Daily Express* 30 June 12/6 (*heading*) Do you yo-yo? **1973** *N.Y. Times* 14 Apr. 18/2 The idea is to go where the kids are and to teach them how to yo-yo.

2. *fig.* To move up and down, or between one point and another; to fluctuate.

1967 *Punch* 12 Apr. 514 The hard facts underlying our economic health—as opposed to the headlines and Treasury press releases—just don't yo-yo about like this. **1973** C. BONINGTON *Next Horizon* xi. 166 In those early stages of the climb we yo-yo'd back and forth between Kleine Scheidegg and the Rock Band. **1976** *Time* 20 Dec. 23/2 He has yo-yoed between 210 and 296 lbs., now carries a bulky 263. **1978** *Sunday Times* 21 May 53/1 City rates of interest have yo-yoed.

Hence **ˈyo-yoing** *vbl. sb.* and *ppl. a.*; also **ˈyo-yoer, ˈyo-yoist**, one who plays or performs with yo-yos.

1933 *Spectator* 6 Jan. 23/2 Surely the unkind girl of figure fifty-eight is the precursor of the modern yoyoist. **1947** *Sat. Even. Post* 10 May 12 His Casper Milquetoast model for timid yo-yoists was lighter, and, he added, prettier. **1963** T. PYNCHON *V.* i 30 As it turned out, the New Year's party was to end all yo-yoing. **1967** F. CONROY *Stop-Time* viii. 114

The greatest pleasure in yo-yoing was an abstract pleasure—watching the dramatization of simple physical laws. **1973** *N.Y. Times* 14 Apr. 18/2 When you're a professional yo-yoer, how can you take anything very seriously? **1976** *Alyn & Deeside Observer* 10 Dec. 34/5 It is more volatile than the yo-yoing pound. **1980** *Illustr. London News* Mar. 56/1 The uncomfortable and costly yo-yoing of temperature experienced in light-weight buildings with large areas of window.

†**ypaid, ypay(e)d** [Y- 4, PAY *v.*[1]], paid, pleased.
1297 R. GLOUC. (Rolls) 1842 þat folc was þo of þis lond ypaid wel ynou. **1393** LANGL. *P. Pl.* C. IV. 393 Be þe pecunie y-payed þauh parties chide.

ypaised, yparroked, ME. pa. pples. of PEASE *v.*, PARROCK *v.*

ypass *v.* [Y- 3 c], to pass.
13.. *K. Alis.* 5606 (Laud MS.) A northhalf ne mowen ȝee nouȝth ypasse For deserte & wildernesse.

ypas(s)ed, ypast, ME. pa. pple. of PASS *v.*
13.. *K. Alis.* 5460 (Laud MS.) Nov it is ypassed hy ne don þerof. **1422** YONGE tr. *Secr. Secr.* 157 Who-so nothynge thynkyth of thyngis y-passet. **1432-50** tr. *Higden* (Rolls) III. 195, vij. year ypaste. *Ibid.* 335 A litelle season y-passede.

ypaved, -yd, paved.
c **1394** *P. Pl. Crede* 194 Y-paued wiþ peynt til. **1426** LYDG. *De Guil. Pilgr.* 331 For al the weyes & paament Wer ypavyd all off gold.

ypavylounded, ME. pa. pple. of PAVILION *v.*

†**ypaynt(ed, ypeint, ypeynt(ed**, ME. pa. pples. of PAINT *v.*[1]
c **1290** ypeint, **13..** y-paynted [see PAINT *v.*[1] 1]. *c* **1440** *Gesta Rom.* 8 þis ymage that is thus y-paynt.

y-pekyd: see YPIKED.

ypend, obs. pa. pple. of PEN *v.*[1]
1591 SYLVESTER *Du Bartas* I. i. 429 Though yet he seem in feeble flesh ypend.

†**ypent**, *pa. pple. Obs.* [Y- 4.] = PENT *pa. pple.* and *ppl. a.*
c **1395** *Plowman's T.* 22 He nas nat alway in cloystre y-pent. *Ibid.* 939 Proude pendaunts at hir ars y-pent. **1579, 1728** [see PENT *pa. pple.* 1]. **1642** H. MORE *Song of Soul* III. I. xxv, Those powers be all or more or lesse ypent In this grosse life. **1839** KINGSLEY *Poems, In Illum. Missal* 7 My love.. Have I within this seely book y-pent.

†**yperced, -sed** [Y- 4], ME. pa. pple. of PIERCE.

yperisched, yperis(s)ed, etc., ME. pa. pple. of PERISH *v.*
1297 [see PERISH *v.* 2]. **1377** LANGL. *P. Pl.* B. XVII. 189 Were þe myddel of myn honde ymaymed or yperisshed.

yperite ('iːpəraɪt). [ad. F. *ypérite*, f. *Ypres*, name of the town in Belgium where the gas was first used, in 1917: see -ITE[1].] = *mustard gas* s.v. MUSTARD *sb.* 4 c.
1919 *Chem. Abstracts* XIII. 3063 (*heading*) Yperite and poisonous gases. **1940** *Times* 17 Aug. 4/4 Dr. Gerard C. Savoy, of Lausanne, has produced a preparation which is the most efficient known antidote to yperite (mustard gas). *Ibid.*, Fifty per cent. of the yperite present in the wound is destroyed after one hour. **1979** *Microbiology* XLVIII. 246 Nitrous yperite and other alkylating substances with a radiomimetic effect can inhibit cell division in *Escherichia coli* B.

ypeyred [PAIR *v.*[2]], impaired.
1387 TREVISA *Higden* (Rolls) III. 225 What is amended and apeyred [*MS.* γ ypeyred].

ypicking, *pr. pple.* [Y- 3 c], picking.
1656 *Choyce Drollery* 74 And as she romed here, and there, Y-picking of the bloomed brier.

ypiȝt(e, ypight, ypyȝt, ypyght, *pa. pple.*, pitched.
c **1435, 1489, 1590** [see PITCH *v.*[1] A. 3 *a*]. **1768** DOWNMAN *Land of Muses* xxii, A wond'rous tow'r, Which hence thou seest high in the air y-pight.

ypiked [PICK *v.*[1]], picked.
c **1407** LYDG. *Reson & Sens.* 5422 Hys firste bowe.. Is wroght.. of yvory, Y-piked out ful craftyly. *c* **1430** *Two Cookery-bks.* 41 Pigis fete clene y-pekyd.

ypined [PINE *v.*], put to suffering or torment.
12.. in *Rel. Ant.* I. 282 Jhesu Crist.. y-boren of þen mayden Marie, y-pined under Ponce Pilate. **1340** *Ayenb.* 213 Hi ssolle by more y-pined.. ine þe oþre wordle.

†**ypir.** *Obs.* [Flem. *Yper.*] app. Cloth of Ypres.
1517 *Caldwell Papers* (Maitland Club) I. 57 Tua capis, ane of scarlet and ane uther of ypir.

†**ypitched**, obs. pa. pple. of PITCH *v.*
1581 A. HALL *Iliad* IV. 71 His campe ypitched By Asope floud.

ypitte, ME. pa. pple. of PUT *v.*[1]

yplaied, played.
13.. *K. Alis.* 7734 (Linc. Inn MS.) So longe þey hadde þus yplaied.

ypleite, yplight [PLIGHT *v.*[2]], pleated.
1421 HOCCLEVE *Min. Poems* xxii. 928 And from hire heed shee hath hir veil y-plight. *c* **1430** *Pol. Rel. & L. Poems* (1903) 209 þi gowne y-pleite.

yplet [PLEAT *v.*], plaited.
1513 DOUGLAS *Æneis* XII. ii. 126 Hys.. hayr,.. Yplet ilk nycht on the warm broch of steill.

ypleynted, ME. pa. pple. of PLAINT *v.*

ypliȝt, -ight, -yȝt, -yght, ME. pa. pple. of PLIGHT *v.*[1]

yplonged, plunged.
c **1407** [see PLUNGE *v.* 2]. *a* **1565** SIR T. CHALLONER *Boeth.* I. ii. in *Q. Eliz. Engl.* (1899) 151 The mynde yplonged in worldlye thoughte.

ypocrafet, ypocras, ypocr(e)it, -cryte, -cricy, -crisy: see APOCRYPHATE, HIPPOCRAS, HYPOCRITE, HYPOCRISY.

ypodeakon, var. *hypodeacon* (see HYPO- II).

ypointing, in *star-ypointing*: see STAR *sb.*[1] 20 and Y- 3 c.

ypoquistid, -is, var. HYPOCISTIS.
a **1425** tr. *Arderne's Treat. Fistula*, etc. 63 Medicynez restrictyuez bene þise;.. ypoquistid, gallez cupule.

†**yporchaced, ypurchasede** [Y- 4], purchased.
1340 *Ayenb.* 35 þet hire uaderes.. habbeþ yporchaced be gauelinge. *c* **1425** y-purchasede [see PURCHASE *v.* 4 b].

yportreyd, ME. pa. pple. of PORTRAY *v.*

yporveide, -veyid, purveyed.
13.. *R. Gloucester's Chron.* (Rolls) 7473 þe normans were þo wel porueid [*MS. C.* wel yporueide].

yposarca, obs. form of HYPOSARCA.

ypotam(e, -tamos, etc., obs. ff. HIPPOPOTAMUS.

†**ypothecar, -gar.** ? obs. Sc. ff. APOTHECARY.
1509 *Burgh Rec. Edin.* (1869) I. 125 Our familiar and daily seruitour Maister Stephane, ypothegar. **1574** *Reg. Privy Council Scot.* Ser. I. II. 377 [Thomas Davidson] ypothecar [and burgess of Edinburgh].

†**ypoudred, -ide, ypouthered** [Y- 4, POWDER *v.*[1]], powdered, sprinkled.
c **1380** *Sir Ferumb.* 1327 þe wyndowes wern y-mad of iaspre.. Ypoudred wyþ perree of polastre. **1395** *E.E. Wills* (1882) 4 A bed of tapicers werk.. ypouthered with chapes and scochons. *c* **1403** CLANVOWE *Cuckow & Night.* 63 The ground was grene, y-poudred with daisye.

ypowred, poured.
a **1565** SIR T. CHALLONER *Boeth.* II. ii. in *Q. Eliz. Engl.* (1899) 160 Of Goodes somoche ypowred owte, With never stayed hande.

ypoynet, ME. pa. pple. of POIN *v.*

†**ypoynt**, = *in point*: see POINT *sb.*[1] D. 4 f.
a **1340** HAMPOLE *Psalter* ix. 1 When he was in þe se ypoynt to perisch.

†**ypoynt** [Y- 4], ME. pa. pple. of POINT *v.*[1]

ypraised, ypraysed, ypreised, praised.
c **1330** y-praised [see PRAISE *v.* 2]. **1422** YONGE tr. *Secr. Secr.* 172 He haue no cure that he be y-praysid ne that otheris be blamyd.

yprast, ypreost, ypressede, ME. pa. pples. of PRESS *v.*[1]
13.. *K. Alis.* 2342 (Linc. Inn MS.) His hors he gaf to orest, þat was to grounde ypreost.

ypreked, ypricked, yprykked, pricked.
1377 LANGL. *P. Pl.* B. XX. 85 Frenesyes, & foule yueles.. Hadde yprykked and prayed polles of peple. **1387** TREVISA *Higden* (Rolls) V. 371 He were priked [*MS.* γ ypreked] wiþ spores. **1748** THOMSON *Cast. Indol.* I. lxvii, In soul ypricked deep.

ypre(o)ved, yproved, yprowed, etc., proved.
1297 R. GLOUC. (Rolls) 3958 Bote he were in armes wel yproued [*v.rr.* yprowed, ypreuede, ypreuyd]. **1422** YONGE tr. *Secr. Secr.* 134 They hathe vertue and Streynth of consaill y-prowide. **1522** *World & Child* A v, I am a prynce, peryllous yprovyde.

Ypresian (iː'prɛsɪən), *a. Geol.* [ad. F. *ypresien* (A. H. Dumont 1850, in *Bull. de l'Acad. des Sci.*, etc., *de Bruxelles* XVI. II. 368), f. as YPERITE: see -IAN.] Of, pertaining to, or designating the lowest stage of the Eocene in western Europe, lying above the Landenian. Also *absol.*
[**1852** *Q. Jrnl. Geol. Soc.* VIII. 323 The group of tertiary strata which we meet with next in the descending order in Belgium (comprising the 'Systèmes Laekenien, Bruxellien et Ypresien' of M. Dumont) corresponds most nearly.. in age with the Barton, Bagshot, and Bracklesham beds.] **1880** J. D. DANA *Man. Geol.* (ed. 3) III. 512 London Clay; Lower Ypresian of Belgium. **1969** BENNISON & WRIGHT *Geol. Hist. Brit. Isles* xv. 339 The Ypresian cycle commenced with the basement bed of the London clay. **1977** A. HALLAM *Planet Earth* 227 The most commonly accepted stages [of the Eocene] include (from oldest to youngest) the Ypresian, Lutetian and Bartonian.

†**yprimisined, yprimsened** [Y- 4], pa. pple. of PRIME-SIGN.

yprisoned, prisoned.
a **1450** *Knt. de la Tour* lxxxviii, Any pore prisonere that was yprisoned for ani necessite of wronge.

yprived, ypryved, ME. pa. pple. of PRIVE *v.*

yprocred, yprokered, procured.
1387 TREVISA *Higden* (Rolls) V. 215 þe emperesse Eudoxia had i-procured [*MS.* β y-prokered] þe out puttynge of Iohn.

yprofred [PROFFER *v.*], offered.
1340-70 *Alex. & Dind.* 187 As sone as his king say þat sonde him yprofred.

ypsiliform (ɪp'sɪlɪfɔːm), *a.* [f. YPSILON + -(*i*) FORM.] Shaped like the Greek letter upsilon; Y-shaped. Cf. HYPSILOID.
1886 *Encycl. Brit.* XX. 417/1 The T-shaped gradually passes into the 'ypsiliform' figure.

ypsilon. *rare.* [So med.L., OF., etc.] = UPSILON.
1567 SALESBURY in Ellis *E.E. Pronunc.* 763 *marg.*, The englishe Scolers tongues be marueilously tormented in soundyng of the Greke *ypsilon* and yet atain not to the right sound.

†**ypullished** [Y- 4], polished.
c **1460** J. RUSSELL *Bk. Nurture* 63 Bryght y-pullished youre table knyve.

ypult [Y- 4, PILT, PULT *v.*], thrust.
1297 [see PILT *v.* 1 *a*]. **1393** LANGL. *P. Pl.* C. XII. 208 Ypult out of grace.

ypunched, ypunsed, ypunyss(h)ed, punished.
1340 [see PUNISH *v.* B. 1 b]. **1340-70** *Alex. & Dind.* 395 Where-fore we miht aftur Ben y-punched in paine. **1426** LYDG. *De Guil. Pilgr.* 2404 They.. wer.. ypunysshed by that swerd.

yput(te, ME. pa. pple. of PUT *v.*[1]
1377 [see PUT *v.*[1] B. 27]. ? **1466** *Stonor Papers* (Camden) I. 77 Y haue.. y-putte yn iij seuryteys.

ypuysned, poisoned.
1387 TREVISA *Higden* (Rolls) VI. 287 I-poysoned [*MS.* γ ypuysned] by þe venym of his wyf.

ypyȝt, ypynned: see YPIȜT(E, PINNED *a.*

†**yquartred** [Y- 4], quartered.
1387 TREVISA *Higden* (Rolls) VIII. 317 His bowels i-brent and y-quartred.

yquaysched, ME. pa. pple. of QUASH *v.*

Yquem (iː'kɛm). The name of Château d'*Yquem*, a vineyard in the Gironde, France, used *absol.* and (*rarely*) *attrib.* to denote a variety of fine, rich Sauternes wine produced and bottled there.
1869 A. TROLLOPE *Phineas Finn.* I. viii. 29 They give you a capital little dinner at Moroni's, and they've the best Chateau Yquem in London. **1902** BELLOC *Path to Rome* 396 He had.. Yquem with his fish, the best Chambertin during the dinner. **1927** C. CONNOLLY *Let.* 11 Feb. in *Romantic Friendship* (1975) 252, I drank.. Yquem at 300 francs the bottle. **1959** *Sunday Times* 1 Nov. 32/5, I find Yquem too sweet. **1982** D. PEPPERCORN *Bordeaux* xi. 315 A good vintage of Yquem is the quintessence of Sauternes.

yqueme, var. IQUEME *v.*

yquenct, yqueynte, ME. pa. pple. of QUENCH *v.*
1340 *Ayenb.* 205 Zenne of lecherie þet is yquenct mid uorberinge of mete. *c* **1440** *Pallad. on Husb.* IX. 111 A light.. Yf hit be founde yqueynte, ther is a veyne Of water nygh.

yquit, yquyt(te, ME. pa. pple. of QUIT *v.*

yr, obs. f. HER, *poss. pron., 3rd sing. fem.*, IRE; graphic var. *þr*, THEIR.

†**yrad** [Y- 4, REDE *v.*[1]], counselled.
1297 [see REDE *v.*[1] 6 g]. *c* **1380** *Sir Ferumb.* 4083 Gweneloun.. haþ y-rad the at oure deuys, As it wil best auayle.

yrad(e, yredde [READ *v.*], read.
c **1380** *Sir Ferumb.* 5789 þe bysschop.. þat had.. ouer y-rad Alle ys orysouns.

yraft, ME. pa. pple. of REAVE *v.*[1]
c **1380** *Sir Ferumb.* 1934 þe other relyqes ryche wyche þov him hast y-raft.

†**yraȝte, yrapt**, obs. pa. pples. of REACH *v.*[1], WRAP *v.*

yrare [cf. Y- 3 b], pseudo-arch. f. RARE *a.*[1]
1742 SHENSTONE *Schoolmistr.* xvii, With sugar'd Cates she doth them greet, And Gingerbread y-rare.

yrast ('ɪræst), *a. Nucl. Physics.* [See quot. 1967.] Pertaining to or designating any nuclear energy level that is the lowest for some value of the spin; *yrast line*, a line on a graph of spin against nuclear rotational energy (or some function of each of these), connecting points representing the various yrast states of a nuclide.
1967 J. B. GROVER in *Physical Rev.* CLVII. 832 It has been proposed that the lowest-energy excited state at a given

angular momentum be called 'yrast' level for that angular momentum. *Ibid.* 832/1 The yrast levels play a crucial role in deciding the course and outcome of many nuclear reactions. [*Note*] By 'yrast' level of a given nucleus, at a given angular momentum, is meant the level with least energy at that angular momentum. The English language seems not to have a graceful superlative form for adjectives expressing rotation. Professor F. Ruplin (of the Germanic Languages Department of the State University of New York, Stony Brook) suggested the use of the Swedish adjective *yr* for designating these special levels. This word derives from the same Old Norse verb *hvirfla* (to whirl) as the English verb *whirl*, and forms the natural superlative, *yrast*. It can thus be understood to mean 'whirlingest', although literally translated from Swedish it means 'dizziest' or 'most bewildered'. **1971** *Physics Lett.* XXXIVB. 575 Non-axially symmetric deformation of a nucleus is introduced to account for the admixture of the collective rotational bands and the distribution of the yrast levels. **1974** FRAUENFELDER & HENLEY *Subatomic Physics* xvi. 435 The yrast line of a nucleus gives *E* as a function of *J*. **1983** *Nucl. Physics* A. CDIII. 421 Precession of the yrast 2^+_1, and 4^+_1, and the second 2^+_2 states in ^{24}Mg have been measured.

†**yrauissed, -isshid, yravesed** [Y- 4], ravished, carried away.
1340 *Ayenb.* 231 Hi wes y-rauissed of þe princes zone of þe cite. **1362** [see RAVISH *v.* 1 b]. **1387** TREVISA *Higden* (Rolls) VI. 9 He.. i-was i-ravished [*MS. γ* yravesed] out of his body anon to þe holy siȝt of aungles.

yraunceouned, -soned, ransomed.

†**yravish** [Y- 3 c], pseudo-arch. f. RAVISH.
1608 SHAKS. *Per.* III. Prol. 35 The sum of this, Brought hither to Pentapolis, Y-ravished [*so Malone*; Q1 Iranyshed] the regions round.

†**yraylle** [Y- 3 c], variant of RAIL *v.*[1], to arrange, and RAIL *v.*[3], to flow.
1426 LYDG. *De Guil. Pilgr.* 246 In ordre dresse hyt, & yraylle. *Ibid.* 4740 And doun therby hys blood yraylled.

†**yrayn(e.** *Obs.* Also i-, yreyn(e, -eine. [a. OF. *iraine*, var. *araine* ARAIN. Cf. IRANE.] A spider.
1382 WYCLIF *Hosea* viii. 6 The calf of Samarie shal be into webbis of yreinus [**1388** ireyns]. *c* **1430** *Pilgr. Lyf Manhode* III. xvi. (1869) 143, I do as the yrayne doth; for as longe as any blood.. is in the flye, al she souketh it. *c* **1450** *St. Cuthbert* (Surtees) 2646 All oure ȝeris.. Sall be thoght as an yrayn [Psalm xc. 9].

yrchen, -on, -oun, var. IRCHIN.

yre, var. (perh. erron.) of EYRE, in phr. (***wiþ***) ***gret yre*** = OF. *de grant erre* with great speed.
13.. *R. Gloucester's Chron.* (Rolls) 1183 As þe ssipes wiþ gret eir [*v.rr.* heir, yre, Ire] come toward londe. *Ibid.* 3824 Wiþ hard dunt & gret eir [*v.r.* yre] to gadere sone hii come.

yre, obs. form of IRE, IRON *sb.*[1]

†**yre(a)ued** [Y- 4], ME. pa. pple. of REAVE *v.*[1]

yrebuked, ill-used.
1377 LANGL. *P. Pl.* B. XIV. 162 A-fyrst sore and afyngred and foule yrebuked.

yredliche, yredy, var. I-RADLICHE, I-REDY.

yregned, reigned.
1387 TREVISA *Higden* (Rolls) VIII. 73 Hyderto þou hast y-regned gloriousliche.

Yreis, obs. form of IRISH.
1297 R. GLOUC. (Rolls) 5551 þer were of deneys & of scottes aslawe & al so of yreis.

†**yreke(n** [Y- 4], obs. pa. pple. of REKE *v.*[3], to cover up.
c **1386** yreke [see REKE *v.*[3]]. *c* **1634** W. CARTWRIGHT *Ordinary* II. ii, My fire yreken is in Ashen cold.

yremuwed, ME. pa. pple. of REMUE, to remove.

yren(e, yrenen, obs. ff. IRON *sb.*[1], *a.*, IRNEN.

†**yrent** [Y- 4, REND *v.*[1]], rent.
c **1395** *Plowman's T.* 256 These wollen.. Christes membres all to-tere On rode as he wer newe y-rent.

yrented: see RENTED *ppl. a.*[1]

yreos, variant of IREOS *Obs.*

†**yrerd** [Y- 4, REAR *v.*[1]], raised.
1297 R. GLOUC. (Rolls) 5740 Ar vre king þat we abbeþ nou adde yrerd so vale.

Yres(she, obs. forms of IRISH.
c **1450** *St. Cuthbert* (Surtees) 64 Of auncetry In yres kynges mast worthy. **1509** BARCLAY *Shyp of Folys* (1874) I. 21 Thoughe one know but the yresshe game.

†**yrest** [Y- 4], ME. pa. pple. of REST *v.*[1]
1297 R. GLOUC. (Rolls) 3763 Him þoȝte he adde yrest ynou, no leng he nolde abyde. *c* **1350** *Libeaus Desc.* (Kaluza) 1192 Al day þey hadde y-rest.

yreued, ME. pa. pple. of REAVE *v.*[1]

yreuerenced, reverenced.
1393 LANGL. *P. Pl.* C. XVII. 49 The ryche is yreuerenced by reson of his richesse.

yreuested [REVEST *v.*[1]], robed.
c **1290** [see REVEST *v.*[1] 1]. **1387** TREVISA *Higden* (Rolls) VII. 453 [He] sigh þe bisshop of Salisbury y-revested to doo þe solempnite of þat weddynge.

yreuled, ME. pa. pple. of RULE *v.*

yride, yrifled, ME. pa. pples. of RIDE *v.*, RIFLE *v.*[1]

yrin, yringe, yrios, Yrisch(e, -iss(h, etc., **yrk**: see IRON, ERYNGE, IREOS, IRISH, IRK.

†**yrle.** *Sc. Obs.* [Cf. north. dial. *urling*, *yurlin*, and *wurlin*, WIRLING.] A dwarfish person.
1508 KENNEDIE *Flyting w. Dunbar* 38 Wan-fukkit funling, that natour maid ane yrle.

yrmonger, obs. form of IRONMONGER.
1297-8 *MS. Pipe Roll*, De Randulfo le yrmonger.

yrn(e, yrnen, obs. ff. IRON, IRNEN.

yrof, graphic var. *þrof*, THEREOF.
1517 *Knaresb. Wills* (Surtees) I. 6 According to a dede yrof.

†**yroked** [Y- 4], rocked.
c **1425** *Engl. Conq. Irel.* 42 Old men that fore eld yroked weren yn her cradelys.

yrold, yrollyd [ROLL *v.*[2]], rolled.
c **1430** *Two Cookery-bks.* 48 Y-rollyd with þin hond. **1642** H. MORE *Song of Soul* I. I. xviii, Things 'fore our feet yrold.

yron(e, obs. forms of IRON.

yron, yronge, yronne(n, yrosted, yroted, ME. pa. pples. of RUN *v.*, RING *v.*[2], ROAST *v.*, ROOT *v.*[1]

yrous, -ows, etc., var. IROUS, etc.

yrþe, obs. form of EARTH *sb.*[1]
?*c* **1400** *Emare* 285 He felle down in sowenynge, To þe yrþe was he dyght.

yrubde, yruled, ME. pa. pples. of RUB *v.*[1], RULE *v.*

yrun, yryn, obs. forms of IRON.

†**yruyfled** [Y- 4, RIFLE *v.*[1]], plundered.
1393 LANGL. *P. Pl.* C. XX. 90 For wente neuere man þis way þat he ne was here rifled [*MS. I* y-ruyfled].

yrymed [RIME *v.*[1]], rimed.
1340 *Ayenb.* 99 Uor he ne heþ none hede of longe ryote of tales y-slyked ne y-rymed.

yrynged: see RINGED *ppl. a.* 2.

Yrysch, Yryssh(e, obs. forms of IRISH.

†**yryve** [Y- 3 c], variant of RIVE *v.*[1]
1426 LYDG. *De Guil. Pilgr.* 4814 Wych shal thorgh hyr herte blyve Sharper than any swerd y-Ryve.

ys, obs. f. HIS, ICE, *is* (see BE *v.*).

ys, var. ES *pers. pron.*, them.
14.. *Stockholm Med. MS.* I. 79 in *Anglia* XVIII. 297 Take rwe [&] heysele & meng ys with hony.

†**ysackte** [Y- 4], obs. pa. pple. of SACK *v.*[2]
1581 A. HALL *Iliad* v. 90 Their.. Citie spoild, ysackte, and pilled bare.

ysacred(e, -yd, ME. pa. pple. of SACRE *v.*
1387 TREVISA *Higden* (Rolls) VII. 445 Anselyn fonge þe investiture, and was y-sacrede. *c* **1407** [see SACRED *a.* 2].

ysade, ME. pa. pple. of SAY *v.*[1]

ysaluwed [SALUE *v.*], saluted.
1387 TREVISA *Higden* (Rolls) V. 101 þey emperoures þat were to fore hym were i-salwed [*MS. γ* y-saluwed] as iuges.

ysamed, pa. pple. of SAM *v.*[1]

ysam(m)e, var. I-SAME *adv.*, together.
c **1330** y-same [see I-SAME]. **1362** LANGL. *P. Pl.* A. x. 193 Bote Maydens and Maydens maccheþ ou ysamme. **1596** SPENSER *F.Q.* VII. vii. 32 And in a bag all sorts of seeds ysame.

ysatled, ME. pa. pple. of SETTLE *v.*

ysaued(e, -id, etc., saved.
1297 R. GLOUC. (Rolls) 5835 þat hente him by a bem and ysaued was. **1387** TREVISA *Higden* (Rolls) VI. 461 Who þat comeþ in þat helle schal nevere after be saved [*MS. γ* ysaved].

ysawed, ME. pa. pple. of SHOW *v.*

ysay, pa. t. of YSEE.

ysayd(e, yscalded, yscend, ME. pa. pples. of SAY *v.*[1], SCALD *v.*, SHEND *v.*[1]

yscha, obs. Sc. form of ISSUE *sb.*
1531 *Abstr. Protocols Town Clerks of Glasgow* (1897) IV. 43 G. B... hes tane in prenteischip P.D... for the space of fyff yeiris, and to be fre at the yscha of the saydis fyff yeiris.

†**yschad, yschape(d, -en, -schappit, yschatred** [Y- 4], obs. pa. pples. of SHED *v.*[1], SHAPE *v.*, SCATTER.
1340-70 *Alex. & Dind.* 647 Al so many as a man haþ membrys y-schape. **1501** DOUGLAS *Pal. Hon.* Prol. 41 The vmbrate treis.. War portrait, and on the eirth yschappit Be goldin bemis viuificatiue.

ysche, var. ISH *sb.*, *v.*[1], to issue.

ysched(de, ME. pa. pple. of SHED *v.*[1]

yscheill, var. ESCHELE *Obs.*, squadron.
1375 BARBOUR *Bruce* XII. 214 Ilk man in-till his awne yscheill.

†**yschend(e, -ent, ysche(o)t** [Y- 4], ME. pa. pples. of SHEND *v.*[1], SHUT *v.*

yschete, ME. pa. pple. of SHIT *v.*
1387 TREVISA *Higden* (Rolls) IV. 441 Oon of þe Assiries aspied þat doynge by oon þat hadde yschete golde.

yschew(e, yschey, obs. Sc. ff. ISSUE *sb.*
1498 *Acta Dom. Conc.* II. 137 To begin on Friday.. and sa furth quhil the yschey of aire.

†**yschewede, -owed, yschod, yschoded, yschore, yschorn(e, yschote(n, yschott(e** [Y- 4], ME. pa. pples. of SHOW *v.*, SHOE *v.*, SHED *v.*[1], SHEAR *v.*, SHOOT *v.*

yschred(yd, ME. pa. pples. of SHRED *v.*
c **1430** *Two Cookery-bks.* 29 Almaundys y-schredyd. *Ibid.* 49 þan take Almaundys & Dates y-schred þer-to.

yschrined, shrined.
1297 R. GLOUC. (Rolls) 5730 Yssryned [*v.rr.* yschrined, yshryned] he was nyn hondred & on & seuentiþe ȝere.

yschrowd [SHROUD *v.*[1]], clothed.
1513 DOUGLAS *Æneis* XI. xv. 36 This precyus spulȝe.. Quharwith, as said is, was this preist yschrowd.

yschryve(n, ME. pa. pple. of SHRIVE *v.*
c **1412** HOCCLEVE *De Reg. Princ.* 1802, I am yschryue So ny, þat oþer way ne se I noon.

yschue, obs. form of ISSUE *sb.*
1393 LANGL. *P. Pl.* C. XI. 243 God seide ensample of suche manere isshue [*v.r.* yschue] That kynde folweþ kynde.

†**yschutte** [Y- 4], shut.
1432-50 tr. *Higden* (Rolls) III. 163 Fyndenge the ȝates yschutte.

ysclayn, ME. pa. pple. of SLAY *v.*[1]

yscore [SHEAR *v.*], shorn.
1387 TREVISA *Higden* (Rolls) VI. 173 Etheldredus.. was i-schore [*MS. γ* yscore] monk at Bardeneye.

yscote, shot.
1387 TREVISA *Higden* (Rolls) VII. 411 He was i-schote [*MS. γ* yscote] of oon Walter Tirel.

yscredde [SHRED *v.*], shredded.
c **1430** *Two Cookery-bks.* 40 Oynonys smal y-scredde.

yscryve, shriven.
1387 TREVISA *Higden* (Rolls) VII. 345 He.. was i-schryve [*MS. γ* yscryve] and i-houseled.

yse, obs. form of ICE *sb.*, IRON *sb.*[1]

yse, variant of ISH, ISS *v.*[1]
c **1430** *Pilgr. Lyf Manhode* I. vi. (1869) 4 þanne j ysede me out of myn hous.

ysed, obs. pa. pple. of SAY *v.*[1]

†**ysee**, *v. Obs.* [OE. *ȝeséon*: see Y- 3 c and SEE *v.*] *trans.* To see, behold.
[For early quots. see SEE *v.* and I-SEE].
1297 R. GLOUC. (Rolls) 3329 þe porter ysei is louerd come. *Ibid.* 5615 þe king bi huld aboute & þe traytour ysay. **1340** *Ayenb.* 27 þet he ne may oþre manne guod yzy. *Ibid.* 130 He yziþ þane greate heap of his zennes. *Ibid.* 264 Me him acseþ huo he ys, huannes he comþ, huet he heþ ysoȝe. *c* **1460** J. RUSSELL *Bk. Nurture* 1222 Now dar y do seruice diligent to dyuers of dignyte, where for scantnes of connynge y durst no man y-se.

†**ysegede** [Y- 4, SIEGE *v.*], besieged.
1432-50 tr. *Higden* (Rolls) III. 377 For to socoure that cite y-segede.

yseid(e, ME. pa. pple. of SAY *v.*[1]
1387 TREVISA *Higden* (Rolls) VII. 445 [He] put of al þat was good y-seide to hym wiþ swellynge wreþþe. *c* **1412** HOCCLEVE *De Reg. Princ.* 1991 What I haue y-seid þe, naght forgete.

ysekele, obs. form of ICICLE.

ysel, obs. form of ISEL, ashes, etc.

ysell, variant of EISELL *Obs.*, vinegar.
1552 HULOET, Ysell, *acetum*.

†**yselþe**, variant of I-SELTH, success.
12.. *Moral Ode* 8 in *E.E.P.* (1862) 22 Ic myhte habbe bet i-don hadde ic þer y-selþe.

†**ysemblid** [Y- 4, SEMBLE *v.*[2]], likened.
1393 LANGL. *P. Pl.* C. XV. 188 To lowe-lyuynge men þe larke is resembled [*MS. S* y-semblid].

ysen, obs. f. IRON *sb.*[1]; pa. pple. of SEE, YSEE.

†**ysend(e, ysent** [Y- 4], ME. pa. pple. of SEND *v.*[1]
1297 R. GLOUC. (Rolls) 4332 Ac þo com þe duc of peyto as god adde þe grace ysend [*MS. ε* ysent]. *a* **1440** *Sir Degrev.* 121 Hys steward hadd a lettre y-sent.

yserched, yserued, ME. pa. pples. of SEARCH *v.*, SERVE *v.*[1], [2].
1297 R. GLOUC. (Rolls) 6365 þer nis non aliue nou þat þe abbe yserued so. **1340** *Ayenb.* 115 þine greate guodnesses.. huyche ich habbe kueadliche yvzed and þe kueadliche yserued.

yse-schokkill, -s(c)hokle, obs. ff. ICICLE.

†**ysesid, yseysed** [Y- 4], seized.

ysessed, ceased.
1387 TREVISA *Higden* (Rolls) VI. 389 þe monkes of Turon hadde al þe offrynge for to þe werre was i-sesede [*MS. γ* ysessed].

yset, ysett(e, yseuered, -et, ME. pa. pples. of SET *v.*, SEVER.

ysewed, ME. pa. pple. of SEW *v.*^{1}
c 1394 *P. Pl. Crede* 229 His kyrtel of clene whijt clenlyche y-sewed.

yse-yckel, obs. form of ICICLE.

†**yseyd(e** [Y- 4], ME. pa. pple. of SAY *v.*^{1}
c 1380 WYCLIF *Sel. Wks.* III. 102 On þe þrydde manere is holy Churche yseyd to be disposed. 1426 LYDG. *De Guil. Pilgr.* 150 My wrytyng..ys al yseyd vnder correcion.

yseye, yseyne, ME. pa. pple. of SEE *v.*

yshad(e, ME. pa. pple. of SHED *v.*^{1}
c 1400 *Pety Job* 172 in *26 Pol. Poems* 126 Ryght as the hardnesse of chese yshade.

yshadewed, shadowed, darkened.
c 1400 *St. Alexius* (Laud 622) 1082 Yshadewed is al my myroure.

yshape, ME. pa. pple. of SHAPE *v.*
1393 LANGL. *P. Pl.* C. XVI. 301 To wroþer-hele was he wrouȝt þat neuere was ioye yshape.

yshave, ME. pa. pple. of SHAVE *v.*
c 1386 Y-shaue [see SHAVE *v.* 3]. 1426 LYDG. *De Guil. Pilgr.* 2012 Thogh ye now..Ben yclypyd & yshaue Vp-on your hedys euerychon. 1480 CAXTON *Trevisa's Higden* (Rolls) VIII. 129 Gold of seventene shrynes y-shave and molten.

yshend *v.* [Y- 3 c], pseudo-arch. f. SHEND *v.*^{1}
1579 SPENSER *Sheph. Cal.* Aug. 139 Should it not yshend Your roundels fresh, to heare a doolefull verse Of Rosalend.

yshent(e, yshet [Y- 4], ME. pa. pples. of SHEND *v.*^{1}, SHUT *v.*

ysheued, yshewed, -yd, ME. pa. pple. of SHOW *v.*
1362 LANGL. *P. Pl.* A. XII. 34 When scripture þe skolde hadde þus wyt y-sheued. 1426 LYDG. *De Guil. Pilgr.* 5795 Yiff the valu off thys bred Were yshewyd.

yshildred: see SHOULDERED *ppl. a.* I.

yshogged, ME. pa. pple. of SHOG *v.*

yshoned, shunned.
1387–8 T. USK *Test. Love* II. xi. (Skeat) l. 10 These olde philosophers..wenden that of pure nature..me might have y-shoned th'other livinges.

yshood, ME. pa. pple. of SHOE *v.*

yshore, yshorne, obs. pa. pples. of SHEAR *v.*

yshorted, shortened.
c 1400 *26 Pol. Poems* xxiv. 252 My dayes shulle yshorted be.

yshote, ME. pa. pple. of SHOOT *v.*

yshrad, ME. pa. pple. of SHRED *v.*

yshred, -id, ME. pa. pple. of SHRIDE *v.*^{1}

yshriuen, yshryue(n, ME. pa. pple. of SHRIVE *v.*
1377 LANGL. *P. Pl.* B. v. 91, I wolde ben yshryue,..and I for shame durst.

yshryned, shrined.

yshuldred: see SHOULDERED *ppl. a.* I.

ysibbe, variant of I-SIB.
c 1315 SHOREHAM I. 1931 ȝef hy ysibbe ine degres Ryȝt wyþ-inne þe ferþe.

ysicle, obs. form of ICICLE.

†**ysinwed** [Y- 4], sinned.
a 1400 *Leg. Rood* (1871) 176 þat pine be my socour there That y haue y-sinwed with myn here.

ysiwed, ME. pa. pple. of SUE *v.*

yskaldyd, scalded.
c 1430 *Two Cookery-bks.* 22 Brede y-Skaldyd.

yslaȝe, ysla(i)ne, yslawe(n, yslayn(e, obs. pa. pples. of SLAY *v.*^{1}
13.. *Coer de L.* 1788 That six and thirty they had y-slowe. 1387 TREVISA *Higden* (Rolls) V. 71 Gordianus..was y-slawe of oon Phelip. 1616 R. C. *Times' Whistle*, etc. (1871) 122 The dead body was a calfe yslaine.

yslaked, obs. pa. pple. of SLAKE *v.*^{1}

yslape, yslepe, ME. pa. pple. of SLEEP *v.*

ysle, yslelonde, obs. ff. ISLE, ISLAND.

†**yslente** [Y- 4], pa. pple. of SLENT *v.*^{2}

ysleyn(e, ME. pa. pple. of SLAY *v.*^{1}
1432–50 tr. *Higden* (Rolls) III. 133 Balthasar ysleyne, Darius did translate the realme of men of Babilon..in to Persia.

ysliked, yslyked, ysmacked, ysmer(e)d, ME. pa. pples. of SLICK, SMACK, SMEAR *vbs.*

ysmete, ysmite, ysmyte(n, ME. pa. pple. of SMITE *v.*
1297, etc. [see SMITE *v.*]. *c* 1400 *Parce Mihi* 117 in *26 Pol. Poems* 146 Nowe hathe age y-smyte [*v.r.* y-smete] me fro My secund feder. *c* 1430 *Two Cookery-bks.* 55 Nym raw ȝolkys of Eyroun, & melle hem a-mong chikonys y-smete.

ysmoþed, -smothed, ME. pa. pple. of SMOOTH *v.*

ysmytted [SMIT *v.*], infected.
1387 TREVISA *Higden* (Rolls) VII. 477 He was i-smeten [*MSS. β* & *γ* ysmytted] wiþ þe vice of pride.

ysnes, obs. pl. of IRON *sb.*^{1}

†**ysnyt** [Y- 4], ME. pa. pple. of SNITE *v.*

yso(c)ht [SEEK *v.*], sought.
c 1306 *Ball. agst. Scots* 79 (Ritson), He bith y-soht out. 1568 *Hoccleve's Let. Cupid* 128 in *Bannatyne MS.* (Hunter. Club) 787 Every woman..is licht to get..gife scho be weill ysocht [*v.r.* I-soght].

ysocoured, ysocyed, ysode(n, ysoȝe, ysoiled, ME. pa. pples. of SUCCOUR, SOCIE, SEETHE, SEE and YSEE, SOIL *vbs.*

ysojourned, sojourned.
1576 GASCOIGNE *Steele Glas* 91 Where when she had some yeeres ysojorned,..A deepe Desire hir loving hart enflamde.

ysome: see I-SOM.

†**ysomned** [Y- 4, SOMNE *v.*^{2}], summoned.
1387 TREVISA *Higden* (Rolls) VIII. 151 He com at þe tyme as he was sommed [*MS. γ* ysomned].

ysondred, sundered.
c 1380 *Sir Ferumb.* 1737 Of grete hertes..y asky of ȝow an hundred, & clene maydens faire smal al-so manye y-sondred.

ysondur: see SUNDER *a.* and *adv.* B.

†**ysonge** [Y- 4, SING *v.*^{1}], sung.
1387 TREVISA *Higden* (Rolls) VII. 467 þe same day after þat he hadde i-songen [*MS. β* ysonge] masse.

ysoop, ysop(e, obs. forms of HYSSOP.

†**yso(o)the(n** [Y- 4, SEETHE *v.*], boiled.
1377 LANGL. *P. Pl.* B. xv. 425 Ysothe [*v.rr.* ysoden, y-sothen, ysoothe] or ybake. *a* 1425 tr. *Arderne's Treat. Fistula* etc. 31 Not wele y-soþen. *c* 1430 *Two Cookery-bks.* 23 Take a tenche whan he is y-sothe.

ysophage, -gus, var. ŒSOPHAGE, -GUS.
c 1400 *Lanfranc's Cirurg.* 153 þouȝ þat trache arterie be peersid or ellis ysophage.

†**ysoþt, ysouȝt, ysou(g)ht** [Y- 4, SEEK *v.*], sought.
1377 LANGL. *P. Pl.* B. Prol. 50, I seigh somme that seiden þei had ysouȝt seyntes. 1470–85 MALORY *Arthur* XVIII. xvi. 754, I haue the same y sought.

ysound, var. ISOUND.
1297 R. GLOUC. (Rolls) App. H. 52 Morbidus huld þis lond..Freliche wel on griþ and his men y sounde.

ysoupid [Y- 4, SUP *v.*^{1}], supped.
1399 LANGL. *Rich. Redeles* IV. 55 Some had ysoupid with Symond ouere euen.

ysow(e, ysowȝ, ysown(e: see SWOW, SWOWN *pa. pple. Obs.*

ysowe(n [Y- 4], ME. pa. pple. of SOW *v.*^{1}

ysowndir, asunder: see SUNDER *a.* and *adv.* B.
1513 DOUGLAS *Æneis* I. iii. 59 Eneas navy skatterit fer ysowndir.

ysowpit [Y- 4], obs. pa. pple. of SOWP *v.*^{2}

†**ysped(d(e, yspeke,** ME. pa. pples. of SPEED *v.*, SPEAK *v.*

yspend(ed, -dyth, yspent [SPEND *v.*^{1}], spent.
13.. *R. Gloucester's Chron.* (1724) 404 Hii þo adde yspend þat wyþynne was. 1340 *Ayenb.* 171 He hise heþ folliche y-spended. 1408 *E.E. Wills* (1882) 15 That ther be yspendyth ..of my good,..Cs'. 1581 A. HALL *Iliad* II. 22 Our saile yards rotten, our masts yspent. 1647 H. MORE *Song of Soul* III. App. lxxxvi, Grosse sperm yspent in Nuptiall bed.

ysperde, ysper(r)ed(e, ysperyd [SPEAR *v.*^{1}], bolted, shut.
1377 LANGL. *P. Pl.* B. XIX. 162 In an hous al bishette & her dore ybarred [*v.rr.* ysperrede, yspered].

yspewed, yspild, -lt, etc., **yspited, yspoke(n, -yn, ysponne,** ME. pa. pples. of SPEW, SPILL, SPIT, SPEAK, SPIN *vbs.*

yspouse(d [SPOUSE *v.*], espoused.
13.. *R. Gloucester's Chron.* (1724) 13 þis mayde y spoused was of so riche blode.

ysprad(de, yspre(a)d, ME. pa. pple. of SPREAD *v.*
1297, etc. ysprad, yspred [see SPREAD *v.*]. 1616 R. C. *Times' Whistle* v. (1871) 64 Who..Knewe..on which side of his bread The sweetnesse of the butter was yspread.

ypraind, ysprengd(e, yspreynd, etc., **yspratelid,** ME. pa. pples. of SPRENGE *v.*, SPRATTLE *v.*^{1}

ysprinkled, pseudo-arch. f. *sprinkled*, pa. pple. of SPRINKLE *v.*^{1}
1867 JEAN INGELOW *Song Nt. Christ's Resurr.* iv, Her star y-sprinkled gown.

ysprong(e, -en, ysprung(e, obs. pa. pple. of SPRING *v.*^{1}
a 1300, etc. [see SPRING *v.*^{1}]. 1586 MARLOWE *1st Pt. Tamburl.* III. iii, The brats ysprong from Typhons loins. 1748 THOMSON *Cast. Indol.* II. xxvi, From heaven this life ysprung, from hell thy glories vild!

ysprout [Y- 3 c], pseudo-arch. f. SPROUT *v.*^{1}
c 1620 T. ROBINSON *Mary Magd.* 349 And farther in, ye laden vines ysprout.

yspunne, arch. pa. pple. of SPIN *v.*
1616 R. C. *Times' Whistle* ii. (1871) 27 His stockings of the coursest woole yspunne.

yspuwed, ME. pa. pple. of SPEW *v.*

ysquaryd, squared.
1426 LYDG. *De Guil. Pilgr.* 7672 Yforgyd off malys, And ysquaryd by fals devys.

ysrive, ME. pa. pple. of SHRIVE *v.*

yss, ysse-ikkle: see ICE, ISH, ISS *v.*^{1}, ICICLE.

yssant, var. ISSANT = ISSUANT I.
1482 *Paston Lett.* III. 298 To be yssant or chargeabill oute or upon the seid tenement.

†**yssape** [Y- 4], ME. pa. pple. of SHAPE *v.*
1340 *Ayenb.* 87 þe zoþe uorbisne huer-by we byeþ yssape to his ymage.

ysse, obs. f. *is* (see BE *v.*); var. ISH, ISS *v.*^{1}

†**ysse(a)wed, yssed** [Y- 4], ME. pa. pples. of SHOW *v.*, SHED *v.*^{1}

yssend, yssent, ysset, yssette, ME. pa. pples. of SHEND *v.*^{1}, SHUT *v.*, SET *v.*
1422 YONGE tr. *Secr. Secr.* 237 Yf the mecche be ouer depe y-sette in the oyle.

yssew(e, ysshue, yssu(e, obs. ff. ISSUE.

yssh(e, var. ISH, ISS *v.*^{1}

†**yssored, yssot(t)e, yssred, yssriue, yssryned** [Y- 4], ME. pa. pples. of SHORE *v.*^{1}, SHOOT *v.*, SHRIDE *v.*^{1}, SHRIVE *v.*, SHRINE *v.*
13.. *R. Gloucester's Chron.* (1724) 353 Wyllam, þe rede kyng, yssote was by cas. 1340 *Ayenb.* 188 Martin..me heþ yssred mid þise cloþe. *Ibid.* 70 Nou ssel..þe ilke..yzy diligentliche to by yssriue.

ysstreynned: see YSTRAINYD.

yst = IS'T, *is it.*
1553 *Respublica* I. iv, Youe that sholde have wytte, yst youre Descretion Bluntlye to goe forth, and be called Oppression?

†**ystabelid, ystabled, -yd** [Y- 4], ME. pa. pples. of STABLE *v.*^{1}, ^{2}.
13.. *K. Alis.* 4690 (Linc. Inn MS.) Whan he hadde ystabled þat lay, þus he saide. 1422 YONGE tr. *Secr. Secr.* 135 The lawes y-stabelid in the Pepill.

ystade [STEAD *v.*], beset (with difficulties).
a 1440 *Sir Degrev.* 1631 He was never so hard y-stade.

ystal(l)ed, ME. pa. pple. of STALL *v.*^{1}

ystamped, pounded.
c 1410 *Master of Game* (MS. Digby 182) xii, Take of blac pycche and of rosyn as myche of one as of an oþer wele ystamped.

ystatut, obs. pa. pple. of STATUTE *v.*^{1}

ysteare [Y- 3 c], pseudo-arch. f. STEER *v.*^{1}

ysteke, -yd [Y- 4], ME. pa. pples. of STEEK *v.*^{1}, ^{2}.

ystept [STEP *v.*], advanced.
c 1634 W. CARTWRIGHT *Ordinary* II. ii, A Norice Some dele ystept in age!

ysteynud, ME. f. STAINED.

ystik(k)ed, ystyked, -yd, ME. pa. pple. of STICK *v.*^{1}

ystocked [STOCK *v.*^{1}], imprisoned.
1387–8 T. USK *Test. Love* I. i. (Skeat) l. 41 Depe in this pyninge pitte with wo I ligge y-stocked.

ystoffed, ystoke(n, ystol(n)e, ystond(e, ystonge(n, ystonnge, ystope, ystored, -id,

obs. pa. pples. of STUFF *v.*[2], STEEK *v.*[1], STEAL *v.*[1], STAND *v.*, STING *v.*[1], STEP *v.*, STORE *v.*

ystowe [STY *v.*[1]], ascended.
1387 TREVISA *Higden* (Rolls) VI. 227 Oo Kyng of bliss, ..þat..art þis day i-steie [*MS. γ* ystowe] up above alle hevenes.

ystrainyd, ystraynid [STRAIN *v.*[1]], fastened; strained.
c **1325** *Gloss. W. de Bibbesw.* in Wright *Voc.* 169 Sunt les boufs si fort artes, *gloss* ysstreynned [*v.r.* streingned]. *c* **1430** *Two Cookery-bks.* 17 Take Eyroun, þe ȝolke an þe Whyte y-strainyd a lyte.

ystrawed, ystreiȝt, -streight, -streith, ME. pa. pples. of STRAW *v.*[1], STRETCH *v.*

ystrengþed [STRENGTH *v.*], strengthened.
1340 *Ayenb.* 201 Y-strengþed be þe yefþe of onderstonndinge.

ystrewed, ME. pa. pple. of STREW *v.*

ystrick(en, ystrike, ystruck, obs. pa. pples. of STRIKE *v.*
1583 MELBANCKE *Philotimus* Z ij, To rescue Phedimus and Tantalus ystrick with pearcing shaft yfere. **1642** H. MORE *Song of Soul* III. I. i, Ystruck with mighty rage.

ystrived, ME. pa. pple. of STRIVE *v.*

ystuded [STUDY *v.*], endeavoured.
1387 TREVISA *Higden* (Rolls) VIII. 83, I have studied [*MS. γ* y-studed] to take þe floures of Stevenes book.

ystured, ystwyde, -yed, ME. pa. pples. of STIR *v.*, STEW *v.*[2]

ystyffled [Y- 5, STIFLE *sb.*[1]], having (weak) stifle-bones.
c **1410** *Master of Game* (MS. Digby 182) xii, Somtyme an hounde is euyl astyfled [*v.r.* y styffled], so þat he shall somtyme abydenn halfe a yere or more, or he be wele ferme.

ysucrod, obs. pa. pple. of SUCCOUR *v.*
1387 TREVISA *Higden* (Rolls) V. 157 þere he was i-socoured [*MS. γ* ysucrod] awhile wiþ oon Maximus.

ysue, obs. form of ISSUE.

†**ysuffred** [Y- 4], suffered.
c **1374** CHAUCER *Troylus* v. 415 This knowen folk þat han y-suffred peyne.

ysuled [SULE *v.*], sullied.
c **1394** *P. Pl. Crede* 752 A soutere y-suled in grees.

ysunged, etc., sinned.
13.. *Marina* 119 in Bödddeker *Altengl. Dicht.* (1878) 260 Ich habbe ysunged, merci y crie. **1362** LANGL. *P. Pl.* A. VIII. 165 Soules þat han sunget [*MS. T* ysynned] seuen siþes dedlich. **1393** *Ibid.* C. XI. 213 After þat adam and eue hadden ysynged. **1387** TREVISA *Higden* (Rolls) VI. 47 We haveþ i-synned [*MS. γ* ysynwed] grevously.

ysuore, ME. pa. pple. of SWEAR *v.*

ysustained, -teyned, sustained.
1340–70 *Alex. & Dind.* 877 ȝe han..ben y-sustained so wiþ sorwe in þis worde.

ysuwed [SEW *v.*[1]], sewn.
c **1400** TREVISA *Higden* (Rolls) VII. App. 535 On caas ȝe mowe kepe my body ȝif hit is sewide [*MS. γ* ysuwed] in hertes lether.

ysuyled [SOIL *v.*[1]], soiled.
1377 LANGL. *P. Pl.* B. XIII. 458 Thus haukyn þe actyf man hadde ysoiled [*MS. O* ysuyled] his cote.

yswathid, swathed.
c **1325** *Gloss. W. de Bibbesw.* in Wright *Voc.* 143 Lors deyt estre maylolez, *gloss* yswathid.

yswengyd, ME. pa. pple. of SWENGE *v. Obs.*

yswepe, yswepped, ME. pa. pples. of SWEEP *v.*

yswered, ME. pa. pple. of SWEAR *v.*

yswerred [Y- 5, SWIRE], necked.
13.. *K. Alis.* 6264 (Linc. Inn MS.) Schorte y-swerred.

yswoȝe [Y- 4]: see SWOW, SWOWN *pa. pple. Obs.*

yswolle, yswolwet, ME. pa. pples. of SWELL *v.*, SWALLOW *v.*

yswone, yswounyng: see SWOW(N, SWOON *v.*
1297 R. GLOUC. (Rolls) 305 Heo criede & wep mid sorwe inou & ofte iswowe [*MS. B* yswone] lay. *Ibid.* 829 þe quene þo ȝo ihurde þis nei iswowe [*MS. B* yswounyng] was.

yswonge(n, yswonnge, ME. pa. pples. of SWING *v.*[1]

yswope(n, -ed, yswore, ysworn, ME. pa. pples. of SWOPE *v.*[1], SWEAR *v.*

yswowe: see SWOW, SWOWN *pa. pple.*
13.. *K. Alis.* 2262 (Linc. Inn MS.) þat heo to grounde yswowe sletten. **1387** TREVISA *Higden* (Rolls) VI. 477 þe kyng..fil doun to þe grounde as þeyȝ he were i-sowe [*MS. γ* y-swowe].

yswyke, variant of I-SWIKE *v. Obs.*
1297 R. GLOUC. (Rolls) 3261 Nou hii beþ al onywar hii wolleþ yswyke by daye.

ysy, ysyb, ysyle: see YSEE, I-SIB, ISEL.

†**ysynged, -synned, -synwed** [Y- 4]: see YSUNGED.

ysywed [SUE *v.*], followed.
1297 R. GLOUC. (Rolls) 2743 þo he adde ysywed me longe in þisse fare.

ysz, obs. form of ICE.

yt, obs. f. IT; (also *yt*) contr. graphic var. THAT.

†**ytachid** [Y- 4, TACHE *v.*[2]], attached.
1393 LANGL. *P. Pl.* C. XIX. 279 Hit is a preciouse present, ..ac þe pouke hit haþ attached [*v.r.* y-tachid].

Ytaile, var. ITAILE *Obs.*, Italian.

†**ytailed** [Y- 5], var. TAILED *a.* and *ppl. a.*[1]

ytailled, ytayled [Y- 4], ME. pa. pple. of TAIL *v.*[2]

ytak(e, -en, -yn, ytan, ME. pa. pples. of TAKE *v.*

ytald, ME. pa. pple. of TELL *v.*
1340 *Ayenb.* 70 Nou we habbeþ ytald ten manere zennes of þe tonge.

Ytalian, etc., obs. ff. ITALIAN, etc.

†**ytamet** [Y- 4, TAME *v.*[2]], broken into.
c **1450** *Mirk's Festial* 276 þer was no clothe of hors, ny heere of hor hede ytamet wyth þe fyre.

ytaried, ME. pa. pple. of TARRY *v.*

yta(u)ȝt, ytaught, ytawȝt(te, obs. pa. pple. of TEACH *v.*
1297 R. GLOUC. (Rolls) 2197 ȝe beþ men bet iteiȝt [*v.rr.* ytaȝt, ytauȝt] to ssofle & to spade. **13..** *K. Alis.* 3141 (Linc. Inn MS.) Bote he beo wel ytauȝt, Wiþoute skorn passiþ he nouȝt. **1642** H. MORE *Song of Soul* II. III. IV. viii, Thinking how all doth flee What-ever we have painfully ytaught.

ytch(e, obs. ff. ITCH.

yte, obs. pa. t. of EAT *v.*

†**yteld** [Y- 4], ME. pa. pple. of TELL *v.*
13.. *Coer de L.* 1972 His foe, That had his good knights queld, And eke on him despite y-teld. **13..** *K. Alis.* 7870 (Laud MS.) What helpeþ it lenger yteld?

yteld(e, ytelt, ME. pa. pple. of TELD *v. Obs.*

ytelle, var. I-TELLE *v. Obs.*
1387 TREVISA *Higden* (Rolls) VIII. 49 But þou doo as I ytelle and amende þy lyf.

ytemperit, -yd, ytempred, -id, -yd, ytempted, ME. pa. pples. of TEMPER *v.*, TEMPT *v.*
1340 *Ayenb.* 257 And zuo ssolde he by wel ytempred and amesured. **1422** YONGE tr. *Secr. Secr.* 186 In ettynge and drynkynge be thou y-temperit. **14..** *Voc.* in Wr.-Wülcker 615/36 *Temporatus*, ytempored.

ytend, ytent, yteyned, ME. pa. pple. of TIND *v.*
1387 TREVISA *Higden* (Rolls) III. 395 þe taperes þat were i-tend [*MS. γ* ytent]. *a* **1400** *New Test.* (Paues) James iii. 6 Heo is y-tend of þe fuyr of helle.

ytent, ytented, ME. pa. pple. of TENT *v.*[3]

ytenþed [TENTH *v.*], tithed.
a **1400** *N.T.* (Paues) Heb. vii. 9 And ȝef it mowe be seyd so, by Abraham Leui, þat vnderfong tenþinges, was y-tenþed.

ytermenyd, -myned, ME. pa. pple. of TERMINE *v.*
1377 LANGL. *P. Pl.* B. I. 97 Til treuthe had ytermyned her trespas to þe ende.

ytesed, teased.
a **1425** tr. *Arderne's Treat. Fistula*, etc. 68 Streche þam on wolle y-tesed or subtile stupez of line.

yteyd, yteynd(e, ME. pa. pples. of TIE *v.*, TINE *v.*[1]

yth = *in the*: see I'TH'.

ythan(d, -en, etc., var. ITHAND, etc.

†**ythe.** *Obs.* Forms: 1–2 **yþ**, 2 **uþe**, 3 **uðe**, 4–5 **yþe**, 5 **ythe, ithe.** [OE. *ýþ* str. fem., also *ýþe* wk. fem. = OS. *ūðia*, OHG. *undea, unda* (MHG. *unde, ünde*), ON. *unnr, uðr*.] A wave of the sea.
Beowulf 1918 þy læs hym yða ðrym wudu wynsuman forwrecan meahte. *a* **1000** *Andreas* 466 Mere sweoðerade, yða onȝin eft oncyrde. *c* **1175** *Lamb. Hom.* 43 Innan þan sea weren .vii. bittere uþe. *c* **1205** LAY. 4578 þe wind com on weðere and þa sæ he wraðede; vðen þer urnen. **13..** *E.E. Allit. P.* C. 147 Hit reled on round vpon þe roȝe yþes. *a* **1400–50** *Wars Alex.* 63 Carrygis comand he knew keruand þe ithis. *c* **1400** *Destr. Troy* 1992 So wode were the waghes & þe wilde ythes. **14..** *Siege Jerus.* (E.E.T.S.) 3/50 Myd þe grym yþes.

†**ythewed** [Y- 5], var. THEWED *ppl. a.*, mannered.
13.. *K. Alis.* 3209 (Linc. Inn MS.) Mony baroun ful wel y-þewed.

ythe (yþe), obs. f. EATH *a.*, easy; var. I-THEE *v.*

ythied, obs. var. THIGHED.

yþirled, yþurled [Y- 4, THIRL *v.*[1]], pierced.
1387 TREVISA *Higden* (Rolls) IV. 397 I-bored and i-þrulled [*v.rr.* yþirled, yþurled] wiþ meny smale holes.

yþoȝt, yþoght, yþou(ȝ)t, ME. pa. pple. of THINK *v.*[2]
c **1315** SHOREHAM IV. 413 Wanne hy y-þouȝt beþ oþer y-speke, Oþer y-don in stat. **1422** YONGE tr. *Secr. Secr.* 157 Whan thou haste all y-thoght, mowrnynge and wrothi thow shalte reme.

ytholed [THOLE *v.*], suffered.
13.. *K. Alis.* 7138 (Linc. Inn MS.) Al his damage þat he hadde yþoled in þat vyage.

yþonked, yþorsse, ythrysshe, yþraw, ythrest, ythreve, ME. pa. pples. of THANK *v.*, THRASH *v.*, THROW *v.*[1], THREST *v.*, THRIVE *v.*

ythrotelede, throttled.
1432–50 tr. *Higden* (Rolls) III. 161 A nakede man ythrotelede to the dedde.

yþrowe, ME. pa. pple. of THROW *v.*[1]

ythrungin [THRING *v.*], hurled.
1423 JAS. I *Kingis Q.* clxv, Be quhirlyng of the quhele, vnto the ground, Full sudaynly sche hath thaim vp ythrungin.

ythrust, ythryste, thrust.
1422 YONGE tr. *Secr. Secr.* 220 Ouer-oppyn eyen, lyke as they were y-thryste owte.

ytielde, ytilde, ytiȝt, ME. pa. pples. of TELD, TILD *v.*, TIGHT *v.*[2]

ytilied, -lled [TILL *v.*[1]], obtained.
1377 LANGL. *P. Pl.* B. XV. 105 Tythes of vntrewe þinge ytilied or chaffared.

ytint, ME. pa. pple. of TINE *v.*[2]

ytoȝte, ytought [TEACH *v.*], taught.
1340 *Ayenb.* 254 þe wyse and þe wel ytoȝte tempreþ..his wordes. **1656** *Choyce Drollery* 73 Full well she was y-tought the leire Of mickle courtesie.

ytokenyd, ME. pa. pple. of TOKEN *v.*

ytold, ytolte, ME. pa. pple. of TELL *v.*

ytore, ytorn [TEAR *v.*[1]], torn.
1647 H. MORE *Song of Soul* I. II. cxxix, The tallest trees up by the root ytorn. *Ibid.* III. App. xvii, Sith unwillingly they were ytore From their dear carkasses their fate they rue.

ytormentet, tormented.
c **1400** TREVISA *Higden* (Rolls) VII. App. 505 Grevouslich tormented [*MS. γ* ytormentet].

ytornd, ytourned, -yd, ytost, ytoted, ytouchide, ytowchid, ytouked, obs. pa. pples. of TURN *v.*, TOSS *v.*, TOOT *v.*[1], TOUCH *v.*, TUCK *v.*[1]

ytranslatid, translated.
1422 YONGE tr. *Secr. Secr.* 236, I..haue y-translatid to youre excellence by this boke afor, the techynges [etc.].

ytraualid, -aillit, -ayled [TRAVAIL *v.*], troubled, harassed.
1387 TREVISA *Higden* (Rolls) V. 85 Decius and Valerius were i-travailled [*MS. γ* y-travayled] wiþ a fend. **1422** YONGE tr. *Secr. Secr.* 162 He was ytraualid with the Deuyl.

ytreated, treated.
1480 [see HANDLE *v.*[1] 6.].

ytredde, ytrodde, ME. pa. pples. of TREAD *v.*
c **1410** *Master of Game* (MS. Digby 182) xxiv, If ye se it gret and brode and wele ytredde [*MS. Reg.* ytrodde].

ytrent, ME. pa. pple. of TREND *v.*

ytressed, var. TRESSED *ppl. a.*
c **1374** CHAUCER *Troylus* v. 810 To gon y-tressed with hire heerys clere Doun by hire coler.

ytried, ytryed, -id, ME. pa. pple. of TRY *v.*

ytrowbelid, troubled.
1422 YONGE tr. *Secr. Secr.* 173 His Spirite is not by rancoure y-trowbelid.

ytrowe, ME. pa. pple. of THROW *v.*[1]

ytt, obs. form of IT, YET *adv.*

ytter (ˈɪtə(r)). *Min.* The first element of *Ytterby* (see next) used attrib. = combined with yttria, yttriferous, yttrious, in imitation of Sw. or Ger., as in Sw. *ytterjord*, G. *yttererde* (ytter earth).
1805 R. JAMESON *Syst. Min.* II. 585 Yttertantalite... According to Eckeberg, it is composed of tantalium, the new earth called yttria, and iron. **1877** *E. B. Dana's Text-bk. Min.* 281 Yttriferous, or Ytter-garnet. **1897** *Ann. Rep. Smithsonian Inst.* 239 As early as 1794 Gadolin had separated from the gadolinite of Ytterby an earth which he called ytter earth.

ytterbite (ˈɪtəbaɪt). *Min.* [Named by Gadolin 1794, from *Ytterby* in Sweden, where found: see -ITE[1].] A synonym of GADOLINITE. So **ytterbia** (ɪˈtɜːbɪə) *Chem.*, the oxide of ytterbium; **ytterbic**

(ɪ'tɜːbɪk) *a.*, containing ytterbium; **ytterbium** (ɪ'tɜːbɪəm) [mod.L. (Marignac)], a rare metallic element occurring in gadolinite, etc.

1839 URE *Dict. Arts* 541 Gadolinite; called also Yttrite and Ytterbite. **1879** *Jrnl. Chem. Soc.* XXXVI. 118 Ytterbium, a new Metal from Gadolinite... Solutions of ytterbia give no absorption-spectrum... Ytterbium sulphate resembles.. the sulphates of yttrium and erbium.

ytterite ('ɪtəraɪt). *Min.* [f. *Ytter(by* (see YTTERBITE) + -ITE[1].] A synonym of GADOLINITE.

1849 WATTS tr. *Gmelin's Handbk. Chem.* III. 409 Silicate of Yttria.—Gadolinite, or Ytterite.

yttria ('ɪtrɪə). *Chem.* Also **ittria**. [mod.L. (Ekeberg, 1797), f. the name of *Ytterby*: see YTTERBITE.] An earth obtained as a white powder from gadolinite and other rare minerals, consisting of sesquioxide of yttrium (Y_2O_3).

1800 HENRY *Epit. Chem.* (1808) 105 Yttria, or Ittria.—This earth was discovered in 1794.. in a stone from Ytterby in Sweden. **1873** *Fownes' Chem.* (ed. 11) 382 To obtain the earths, yttria and erbia, in the separate state, gadolinite is digested with hydrochloric acid.

yttrium ('ɪtrɪəm). *Chem.* [mod.L., f. YTTRIA, after names of other metals in *-ium*.] A rare metal of the cerium group, the base of the earth YTTRIA. Symbol Y.

1822 *Imison's Sci. & Art* II. 93 The base of yttria has been supposed to be a metallic substance, which would receive the name of yttrium. **1866** ROSCOE *Elem. Chem.* 8 The metals yttrium, erbium, indium, &c. have only as yet been met with in most minute quantities.

Hence (or from prec.) **yttrialite** ('ɪtrɪəlaɪt) *Min.*, a silicate of thorium and the yttrium metals; **yttric** ('ɪtrɪk) *a. Chem.*, related to or containing yttrium; **y'ttriferous** *a.*, containing or yielding yttrium; **yttrious** ('ɪtrɪəs) *a.*, pertaining to or containing yttria; **yttrite** ('ɪtraɪt) *Min.*, a synonym of GADOLINITE.

1889 *Amer. Jrnl. Sci.* XXXVIII. 477 *Yttrialite. **1860** MAYNE *Expos. Lex.*, *Yttricus*..*yttric. **1877** *yttriferous [see YTTER]. **1828–32** WEBSTER, **Yttrious*, pertaining to yttria; containing yttria; as, the yttrious oxyd of columbium. *Cleaveland*. **1839** URE *Dict. Arts* 541 Gadolinite; called also *Yttrite and Ytterbite.

yttro- (ˌɪtrəʊ), *Min.*, used as combining form of YTTRIUM in names of minerals containing yttrium, the second element usually indicating the other metallic constituent, sometimes an allied mineral: as **yttrocerite** (-'sɪəraɪt) [CERIUM], **yttroco'lumbite** [COLUMBIUM], **yttro'gummite** [GUMMITE], **yttro'tantalite** [TANTALUM], **yttro'titanite** [TITANIUM]: see quots. **yttro'tungstite**, a basic oxide of yttrium and tungsten, $YW_2O_6(OH)_3$, occurring as yellow monoclinic crystals.

1817 T. THOMSON *Syst. Chem.* (ed. 5) III. 495 *Yttrocerite.. occurs at Finbo in Sweden... It is found in amorphous masses,.. disseminated through quartz. **1868** WATTS *Dict. Chem.* V. 1065 *Yttrocerite*, a mineral consisting of fluoride of yttrium mixed with the fluorides of cerium and calcium. **1819** W. PHILLIPS *Elem. Introd. Min.* (ed. 2) 202 *Yttro-columbite... It consists, according to Vauquelin, of 45 oxide of columbium, 55 of yttria and oxide of iron. **1879** *Jrnl. Chem. Soc.* XXXVI. 365 *Yttrogummite.. is the final product of the decomposition of clevite. **1850** WATTS tr. *Gmelin's Handbk. Chem.* IV. 19 *Samarskite*.—This mineral, first named Urano-tantalite or Columbite, and afterwards called *Yttro-ilmenite by Hermann. **1809** WOLLASTON in *Phil. Trans.* XCIX. 246 The two Swedish minerals, tantalite and *yttro-tantalite, from which I could obtain tantalum. **1868** DANA *Min.* (ed. 5) 519 Yttrotantalite.. Color black, brown, brownish-yellow, straw-yellow... Tantalate of yttria and lime, or yttria, lime, and iron, with some protoxyd of uranium. **1828** WHEWELL *Ess. Min. Classif. & Nomencl.* 52 *Yttro-Tantalum Oxide. **1854** DANA *Syst. Min.* (ed. 4) II. 341 Keilhauite,..*Yttrotitanite. **1868** WATTS *Dict. Chem.* V. 1065 *Yttrotitanite. Keilhauite*. A silicotitanate containing lime, yttria, ferric oxide, and alumina, with small quantities of other bases. **1950** E. H. BEARD in *Colonial Geol. & Mineral Resources* I. 51 The results show conclusively that the term 'thorotungstite' is inapplicable as a true description of the mineral... It is suggested that the mineral in future be called yttrotungstite. **1971** *Mineral. Mag.* XXXVIII. 262 All the specimens studied consisted mainly of a fine-grained aggregate of pale-yellow earthy yttrotungstite, with rare druses lined by yttrotungstite crystals.

†**ytuckde, ytukked** [Y- 4], obs. pa. pple. of TUCK *v.*[1]

ytueþed, ME. pa. pple. of TITHE *v.*[2]

c **1400** TREVISA *Higden* (Rolls) VII. App. 504 Cristes flok was tethed [*MS.* γ ytueþed], the nyne were slayn and the tenthe was kept.

ytund, ME. pa. pple. of TINE *v.*[1]

yturnde, -ed, ME. pa. pple. of TURN *v.*

1387 TREVISA *Higden* (Rolls) IV. 443 þe wombe and þe bowels were i-slitte and y-turned to seche gold wiþ ynne.

†**ytwyn** = *itwin, in twin*, apart: see TWIN *sb.* 4.

1375 BARBOUR *Bruce* VIII. 175 Thai War in-twyn [*v.r.* ytwyn] a bow-draucht & mar. **1513** DOUGLAS *Æneis* IX. i. 3 In diuers placis set full fer ytwyn.

†**ytwynned** [Y- 4, TWIN *v.*[1]], separated.

c **1374** CHAUCER *Troylus* IV. 788 (Corpus MS.) Though in erthe ytwynned be we tweyne.

ytyed, tied.

1402 HOCCLEVE *Let. Cupid* 226 Ful mony of hem wer in my cheyne y-tyed.

ytynt, ME. pa. pple. of TINE *v.*[2]

yu (juː). *Archæol.* [Chinese.] An ancient Chinese wine vessel in the form of a small metal pail with a swing handle and a decorative cover, popular in the Shang and Early Zhou periods.

1904 S. W. BUSHELL *Chinese Art* I. iv. 90 The sacrificial wine vessels illustrated.. have been selected as the most ancient pieces in the collection... The first is an ovoid jar (*yu*), of the shape used by the old kings for presents of wine to deserving subjects, with a cover surmounted by a knob, and a loop handle ending in dragons' heads. **1945** P. ACKERMAN *Ritual Bronzes of Anc. China* iv. 99/1 *Yu* range from six to nine inches high... They often come in pairs. **1973** W. WATSON in *Genius of China* (R. Acad.) II. 74/2 The *yu* with its high handle is an invention of late Shang.

yu, obs. form of YOU.

Yuan[1] (jʊ'ɑːn, ‖yu'ɛn). Also 7 Ivena, 8 Ywen, 8–9 Yuen; Yüan. [a. Chinese *yuán*, lit. 'first'.] **a.** The name of the Mongol dynasty established as rulers of all China by Kublai Khan in 1279 and in power until 1368.

Kublai Khan named his kingdom Yuan in 1271, and the Yuan dynasty is often described as beginning in that year.

1673 [see SUNG *sb.* a]. **1738** tr. *J. B. Du Halde's Descr. of Empire of China & Chinese Tartary* I. 214 (*heading*) The twentieth dynasty, call'd Ywen, which contains nine emperors in the space of eighty nine years. **1788** GIBBON *Decl. & Fall* VI. lxiv. 298 The annals of the Moguls or Yuen. **1836** J. F. DAVIS *Chinese* I. v. 182 On the accession of Koblai Khan, the first of the *Yuen* dynasty,.. an order was promulgated to burn all the books of the Taou sect. **1948** D. DIRINGER *Alphabet* 355 This character.. was only sparsely used but it lingered on at the imperial Chancery under the Yüan dynasty. **1966** F. SCHURMANN *Ideology & Organization in Communist China* i. 53 The Yüan Mongols relied heavily on a traditional bureaucratic elite to rule the country. Many of these bureaucrats remained loyal to the Yüan after 1368. **1977** *N.Y. Rev. Bks.* 26 May 22/1 The wreckers had found, during their work, the foundations of a gate of the Yuan era.

b. Used *attrib.* and *absol.* of the art and porcelain of the Yuan period.

1888 F. HIRTH *Ancient Porc.* 50 Pieces of a surface which bears no resemblance to any of the classical Sung or Yüan monochrome vessels.. are very common. **1933** [see SUNG *sb.* b]. **1969** R. QUEST *Cerberus Murders* iv. 30 Whistler and his circle went in for blue-and-white.. but it was all late stuff... This is all Hsüan-tê or Yüan. **1978** *Nagel's Encycl.-Guide: China* 199 In old Yuan opera, one actor alone, the hero of the play, had the privilege of singing certain parts of his role.

yuan[2] (jʊ'ɑːn). Also yüan. Pl. yuan. [a. Chinese *yuán* round.] **1.** A Chinese unit of currency introduced in 1914, equal to 10 *jiao*; a coin of this value.

1921 J. V. A. MACMURRAY *Treaties & Agreements with China 1894–1919* I. 853 The Law for the National Currency.—January 1914... Article 2.—The unit of the national coins shall be called *yuan*, and the *yuan* shall contain.. 23·97795048 grammes of pure silver. **1927** *Glasgow Herald* 14 Jan. 8 The surtax imposition will yield.. an advantage of 12,000,000 yuan of revenue. **1949**, etc. [see JIAO]. **1962** E. SNOW *Other Side of River* (1963) ii. 23 At the Hsin Ch'iao a small suite consisting of a sitting room, bedroom and bath cost me 24 yuan.. a day. **1976** W. H. CANAWAY *Willow-Pattern War* xvii. 173 Yang Ma-wei gave me a fistful of yüan and told me to.. find Thupten at the tea-house, and pay him. **1982** C. THOMAS *Jade Tiger* ii. 51 He offered the stallkeeper one of his own grubby ten yuan notes.

2. *Chinese Archæol.* A flat ring or perforated disc made of jade, widely circulated from the Shang period to the Hang dynasty.

1912 *Field Museum Nat. Hist.* X. v. 154 There are three kinds of annular jade objects, called *pi*.. *yüan*.. and *huan*... The former is a disk with a round perforation in the centre, the two latter are rings. **1958** W. WILLETTS *Chinese Art* I. ii. 89 The *yüan* has a perforation twice the width of the body substance, so that its diameter is half that of the whole ring. **1963** K. CHANG *Archaeol. Anc. China* ix. 276 A ceremonial pit was uncovered which contained over twenty stone discs of various sizes and a number of jade and stone ceremonial objects (circular *yüan*, square *tsung* tubes, *wuan-kui*, etc.).

yuan[3] (jʊ'ɑːn). Also Yuan. Pl. yuan. [a. Chinese *yuàn* courtyard, yard.] Each of several government institutions (e.g. *guo wu yuan* the State Council, *waiyuxueyuan* a foreign languages institute) in China.

1928 *China Year Bk.* xxvi. 1234 Administrative Court (*P'ing Cheng Yuan*)... The principal officials of the Administrative Court are the President (Yuan Chang).. and 15 judges. **1938** E. TEICHMAN *Affairs of China* xiv. 205 On the governmental side the Central Executive Committee of the Kuomintang gives birth to the National Government of the Republic of China, composed of a President.. and five *Yuan*, or governing committees: the Legislative *Yuan*, charged with the making of laws; the Judicial *Yuan*, charged with the administration of justice.. the Examination *Yuan* charged with selection of officials of the public service; the Control *Yuan*, charged with the supervision of the national administration.. and the Executive *Yuan*, charged with the actual administration of the government. **1947** *Sun* (Baltimore) 22 Aug. 6/3 They.. will be asked to participate in the selection of the National Assembly and the legislative Yuan. **1967** *Sunday Times* 14 May 6/1 Chiang's executive Yuan (Cabinet) has discussed measures. **1979** *China Yearbk.* ix. 98/2 In the event of a dispute among the various Yuan, the President may call a meeting of the Presidents of the Yuan concerned for consultation on a solution.

‖**yuan hsiao** (jyɑn çiau). Also yüan hsiao and with hyphen. [Chinese *yuánxiāo* (in Wade-Giles *yüanhsiao*), f. *yuán* first + *xiāo* night.] A sweet rice-flour dumpling made for the Chinese Lantern Festival (15 January in the lunar calendar).

1956 B. Y. CHAO *How to cook & eat in Chinese* II. xvii. 210 Orange soup with *yüan-hsiao*... Knead the glutinous rice flour with ½ cup hot.. water. Then make into globules of about ⅜ inch in diameter. These are the *yüan-hsiao*. **1972** K. LO *Chinese Food* I. 56 *Yuan hsiao* is a form of Chinese festival sweet, served in a rather bland rice soup. *Ibid.* 57 We Chinese love these *yuan hsiaos*, partly, I think, because of happy childhood memories of being allowed to do the rolling.

†**yuarȝed, yuarwed**, ME. pa. pple. of FARROW *v.*

yuast(e: see YFAST.

Yucatec ('juːkətɛk). Also Yuca'teco and with lower-case initial. [ad. Sp. *yucateco*, f. *Yucatán*, earlier *Yocotán*, adapted from a Maya name for the language of the Mayan Chontal Indians.]

a. An American Indian of the Yucatán Peninsula in eastern Mexico; such Indians collectively. **b.** *colloq.* Any present-day inhabitant of the Peninsula or of the Mexican state of Yucatán in its northern part.

1843 J. L. STEPHENS *Incidents of Travel in Yucatan* I. vi. 139 No native ever calls himself a Yucateco, but always a Macegual or native of the land of Maya. **1845** *Trans. Amer. Ethnol. Soc.* I. 107 The Yucatecs differed materially from the Mexicans with regard to the time of the solar year. **1875** H. H. BANCROFT *Native Races Pacific States* II. xxi. 675 So great was the horror in which the Yucatecs held this crime that they did not always wait for conviction,.. but sometimes punished a suspected person. **1912** *Contemp. Rev.* Feb. 257 The better Yucatecos do not lean to this profession [of clergyman], which is unendowed. **1966** T. PYNCHON *Crying of Lot 49* v. 119 He was part-owner here with a yucateco who still believed in the Revolution. **1974** *Encycl. Brit. Micropædia* X. 841 The Yucatec were the Classical Maya who were conquered by the Spanish and whose calendar, architecture, and hieroglyphic writing marked them as a highly civilized people. **1983** *Word Ways* Aug. 152 Originate in Yucatan and you are a Yucatec.

c. The language of the Yucatán Indians, a Mayan language.

1940 F. JOHNSON in *Maya & their Neighbors* vi. 107 The divisions of the Yucatec-speaking Maya are relatively indistinct. **1954** J. E. S. THOMPSON *Rise & Fall Maya Civilization* i. 28 Yucatec is spoken by many whites and mestizos of Yucatán as a second language and is said to be easy to learn. **1977** *Language* LIII. 296 Tall people can be reclassified by one of the long classifiers in Bantu.., Japanese, and Yucatec.

d. *attrib.* or as *adj.*

1875 H. H. BANCROFT *Native Races of Pacific States* II. xxi. 665 A Yucatec noble who wedded a woman of inferior degree, descended to her social level. **1934** A. TOYNBEE *Study of Hist.* I. 123 The Yucatec Society was apparently incorporated into the Mexic Society by conquest at about the turn of the twelfth and thirteenth centuries of the Christian Era. **1956** *Publ. Amer. Dial. Soc.* XXVI. 25 It is their speech which Vasquez.. describes as 'yucateco Spanish', characterized by Mayan phonemes and Mayan phrases. **1975** *Sci. Amer.* Oct. 74/3 They spoke a dialect unlike the Yucatec Maya dialect heard generally throughout Yucatán; it was Chontal Maya, one of the dialects of the Cholan Maya group. **1983** *Washington Post* 13 July E-3/1 You can be sure that Yucatec farmers don't waste maize on their cows. **1983** *Times Lit. Suppl.* 7 Oct. 1090/5 The Yucatec city of Chichen Itza.

Hence **Yuca'tecan** *a.* and *sb.*

1869 *Proc. Amer. Philos. Soc.* XI. 5 The most important dialects of the Maya are the Yucatecan, the Quiche, the Cakcquichel, [etc.]. **1886** *U.S. Cons. Rep.* LXVII. 495 A fair sample of Yucatecan agriculture. **1909** *Athenæum* 4 Dec. 688/1 Of the Yucatecans themselves the authors have nothing good to say. **1931** E. H. MORRIS *Temple of Warriors* xix. 228 Gold and copper were the only metals known to pre-Columbian Yucatecans. **1950** *Caribbean Q.* II. II. 30 Actual settlement was limited at first to the Belize district, and even that was made precarious by the attack of the Spaniards and Yucatecan Indians.

yucca ('jʌkə), **yuca** ('juːkə). Forms: 6–7 iucca, 6–9 yuca, 7–8 jucca, 7– yucca. [In sense 1, found in the forms *juca* (Amerigo Vespucci, 1497), *yuca* (Clusius, 1567); of Carib origin.]

1. The common name in Western South America and Central America for the CASSAVA. (Now usually in form *yuca*, for distinction from sense 2.)

1555 EDEN *Decades* (Arb.) 67 They haue also an other kynde of rootes, whiche they call *Iucca*, wherof they make breade in lyke maner. **1597** GERARDE *Herbal* III. cxlix. 1359 Of Yuca or Iucca... The roote wherof the bread Casaua, or Cazaua is made. **1631** R. H. *Arraignm. Whole Creature* ix. 67 Figs and Lemmans from Spaine, Jucca from Cuba, Mayze from Peru. **1726** J. STEVENS tr. *A. de Herrera Tordesillas' Hist. Amer.* IV. 135 A Roll of Yuca, being a clammy Root, like a Patata. **1851** MAYNE REID *Scalp Hunters* xx, There were 'lairs' among the underwood thatched with the palmated leaves of the yuca. **1894** C. D. TYLER in *Georg. Jrnl.* III. 481 The *masato*.. is.. the masticated and fermented root of the yuca.

2. Any plant of the liliaceous genus *Yucca*, native of the warmer parts of N. America, and extensively cultivated for ornament, characterized by a woody stem with a crown of usually rigid narrow pointed leaves and an upright cluster of white bell-shaped flowers; popularly known as *Adam's needle*, particular species being also called *Spanish bayonet* and *Spanish dagger*. (Almost always in form *yucca*.)

1664 EVELYN *Kal. Hort.* 83 [Plants] not perishing but in excessive Colds,..Opuntia, or the smaller Indian Fig, Jucca, Seseli Æthiop. **1731** MILLER *Gard. Dict.* s.v., The Narrow-leav'd Carolina Yucca. **1841** MANTELL in *Phil. Trans.* CXXXI. 140 The..trunks of the *Clathrariæ*,.. *Yuccæ*, and arborescent ferns. **1851** MAYNE REID *Rifle Rangers* i. (1853) 18 The thickets of yucca and acacia-trees. **1872** C. KING *Mountain. Sierra Nev.* i. 20 Tall stems of yucca bore up their magnificent bunches of bluish flowers.

3. *attrib.* and *Comb.*, as *yucca-flower*, *-plant*, *-root*; **yucca-borer**, (*a*) a N. American moth, *Megathymus yuccæ*, whose larva bores into the roots of yucca-plants; (*b*) a Californian weevil, *Yuccaborus frontalis*; **yucca-moth**, a tineid moth of the genus *Pronuba*, esp. *P. yuccasella*, which lays its eggs in the ovary of the yucca-plant, and deposits a ball of pollen on the stigma, thus fertilizing the seeds on which the larvæ feed; **yucca-palm**, **yucca-tree**, any arborescent species of *Yucca*.

1895 COMSTOCK *St. Insects* 367 A much better known species is the *Yucca-borer, *Megathymus yuccæ*. **1753** *Chambers' Cycl. Suppl.*, *Yucca-Bread, or Cassada-Bread. **1892** *Rep. Missouri Bot. Gard.* 99 The *Yucca moth and Yucca Pollination. **1851** MAYNE REID *Scalp Hunters* xviii. 124 She was standing near one of the *yuca palm trees that grew up from the azotéa. **1828–31** TENNYSON in Ld. Tennyson *Mem.* (1897) I. 57 She gave them the *yuccaroot ..Of sweet Xaraguay. **1828** G. F. LYON *Jrnl. Mexico* I. 142 Most uninteresting country, bearing here and there a stunted bush or a *Yucca-tree.

Yuchi (ˈjuːtʃɪ). Also 8–9 **Euchee**, **Euchi(e**, **Uchee**. [a. Creek, of uncertain origin.]

a. (A member of) an Indian people formerly inhabiting the region of the Savannah river in Georgia and South Carolina, and now incorporated into the Creek nation in Oklahoma.

1738 W. STEPHENS *Jrnl.* in *Colonial Rec. Georgia* (1906) IV. 75 He understood they were a Party of the Euchies. **1741** in *South Carolina Hist. Soc. Coll.* (1887) IV. 40 Thomas Jones..was Employed..as a Linguist to the Creeks and Euchees. **1744** in *Georgia Hist. Soc. Coll.* (1840) I. 145 Their cattle..had strayed away and eat the Uckee's corn. **1818** *Lynchburg* (Va.) *Press* 25 Dec. 3/1 The captain..reports to have taken three warriors, a Creek, a Choctaw, and a Uchee. **1893** *Amer. Anthropologist* VI. 280 The Yuchi believe themselves to be the offspring of the sun. **1965** [see CREEK *sb.*[3]]. **1975** W. L. BALLARD in J. M. Crawford *Stud. Southeastern Indian Lang.* 163, I spent approximately six weeks in Sapulpa, Oklahoma, interviewing Yuchis.

b. The language of this people.

1836 *Trans. & Coll. Amer. Antiq. Soc.* II. 96 These five languages, the Muskhogee and the Hitchittee, the Uchee, the Natches, and the Alibamon or Coosada are, it is believed, the only ones spoken by the different tribes of the Creek confederacy. **1909** F. S. SPECK *Ethnol. Yuchi Indians* 15 It is quite certain now that Yuchi is spoken in only one dialect. **1975** W. L. BALLARD in J. M. Crawford *Stud. Southeastern Indian Lang.* 163 A number of tapes of conversations in Yuchi were made.

yuck (jʌk), *sb.*[1] *slang* (orig. *U.S.*). Also **yuk**. [Origin unknown.] A fool; a boor; anyone disliked or despised.

1943 H. A. SMITH *Life in Putty Knife Factory* xiv. 239 *Yuck* is a word introduced into the language by Fred Allen. A yuck is a dope who makes a practice of going around appearing on quiz programs. That was its original definition; it now means a dope of any description. **1948** R. CHANDLER *Let.* 27 Jan. (1981) 105 The public's capacity and adaptability to a quality of entertainment which the yucks seem to be afraid to give them. **1957** M. SHULMAN *Rally round Flag, Boys!* (1958) vi. 67 The yucks who look at television don't know the difference between Ernest Hemingway and Huntz Hall. **1972** P. ROWLANDS *Fugitive Mind* xi. 132 'Is your brother a yuk?' Clare asked Sally. 'Oh yes! He's a *terrible* yuk! He shouts a lot, he breaks my toys, he pushes me over.' **1979** J. WAINWRIGHT *Duty Elsewhere* xx. 56 Three no-good yucks had felt like playing footsie with the law.

yuck (jʌk), *int.*, *sb.*[2], and *a. slang.* Also **yuk**. [Imitative. Cf. YECH *int.*, YUCK *v.*[1]] **A.** *int.* An expression of strong distaste or disgust.

1966 R. H. RIMMER *Harrad Experiment* (1967) 25 Across the table; Dorothy Stapleton and Valerie Something-or-other belong (yucks, is that the right word?) to Herber Snyder and Peter Longini. **1970** *It* 12–25 Feb. 16/4 The whole tenor of the epistle is that of one elite talking to another without reference to..those who have paid... Yuk. **1976** G. MOFFAT *Short Time to Live* vii. 58 'Fish pie perhaps, and parsley sauce.' 'Yuk,' said Arabella. **1981** P. DICKINSON *Seventh Raven* x. 130 You took a harmless animal and chopped it up..to please your God—yuck, they thought. **1983** D. SIMPSON *Puppet for Corpse* xx. 172 It was the way he talked about her... 'You know what older women are, wink, wink.'.. Yuk!

B. *sb.*[2] Messy, unpleasant, or distasteful material. *lit.* and *fig.*

1966 *New Statesman* 19 Aug. 258/1 Rotting wodges of chilly yuck which once were apples and pears. **1971** P. PURSER *Holy Father's Navy* xxxviii. 187 There was a lot of yuk which I didn't investigate too closely, and a bit of ear definitely in the wrong place. **1977** *Times* 17 Oct. 12/6, I asked Nancy Grimes, a freelance who arranges plants for people... 'The offices now are so ugly and so standard, such standardized urban yuk... They want to see something that can actually survive and grow here. It gives them reassurance.' **1981** M. E. ATKINS *Palimpsest* xii. 118 One of those syndicated advice columns... All noble sentiments and romantic yuk.

C. *adj.* **1.** = YUCKY *a.* a.

1971 *TV Times* (Austral.) 24 Feb. 39/2 Business was a bit yuk and I was bugged by this lack of confidence. **1973** P. DICKINSON *Green Gene* ii. 28 She's got a really yuck family, even worse than mine.

2. Comb. **yuck-making** *ppl. a.* = *sick-making* ppl. adj. s.v. SICK *a.* 11.

1972 *Courier-Mail* (Brisbane) 30 Mar. 1/10 The BBC yesterday described a song about the former Australian Prime Minister..as the biggest 'yuk-making' piece of propaganda in politics. **1975** *Listener* 7 Aug. 168/3 Nasty, yuk-making remarks.

yuck (jʌk), *v.*[1] *Canad. dial.* [Imitative.] *intr.* To vomit.

1963 *Amer. Speech* XXXVIII. 301 [Newfoundland.] *Yuck*, to vomit. **1981** *Publ. Amer. Dial. Soc.* LXVIII. 54 [Newfoundland.] *To vomit*, yuck.

yuck (jʌk), *v.*[2] *slang.* (chiefly *N. Amer.*). Also **yuk**. [Origin unknown. Cf. YOCK *sb.* (and *v.*).] *intr.* **a.** To fool around; to act so as to cause laughter. **b.** To laugh. Also *to yuck it up*.

1964 S. BELLOW *Herzog* 119 And Gersbach, boisterous, yucking it up, poured whisky, wine, pounded the table. **1967** *Boston Sunday Herald* 2 Apr. (T.V. Mag.) 9/2 Russ Tamblyn and Sidney Poitier yuk it up as the lightly clad barbarians; Rosanna Schiaffino and Beba Loncar play it cool as the lightly clad camp followers. **1969** *Listener* 23 Jan. 98/3 An American watches British television..for visions of America. Stray ones move us: Wally Schirra yukking it up in space. **1974** *Publishers Weekly* 12 Aug. 55/3 Laurel and Hardy fans..should enjoy this semi-biography... Old-timers who yukked when they saw the movies way-back-when should swell the market. **1975** *Time Out* 11 Apr. 36/4 Pryor has them yukking at whitey one moment and at themselves the next.

Hence **yuck** *sb.*[3], a laugh.

1971 *Daily Colonist* (Victoria, B.C.) 10 Feb. 5/2 The biggest yuks, as might be expected, are to be found right here in Canada. **1976** *National Observer* (U.S.) 16 Oct. 10/3 The biggest yuck of the night was when Mr. T. called Mrs. Llewelyn 'Mrs. Rreweryn'. **1977** *Canadian* 2 Apr. 20/1 Humor is his forte. Looking for yuks? Phone Sammy. **1984** *Sun-Times* (Chicago) 17 Feb. 49/2 The movie gets its yuks with slapstick scenes where one guy goes out the window when the other guy comes in the door.

yuck, variant of YUKE.

yuckle (ˈjʌk(ə)l). *dial.* Also **yuckel**, **yuccle**, **yukkel**, **yockel**. [var. of *hickle*, HICKWALL, influenced by YAFFLE.] The green woodpecker.

1847–78 HALLIWELL, *Yuckel*, a woodpecker. *Wilts.* **1861** HUGHES *Tom Brown at Oxf.* xli, I feels sum how as peert as a yukkel.

yucky (ˈjʌkɪ), *a. slang.* Also **yukky**. [f. YUCK *a.*] **a.** Nasty, unpleasant; sickly sentimental.

1970 D. UHNAK *Ledger* v. 79 She wanted to go to a lousy, yukky secretarial college. **1977** *Oxford Times* 1 July 15 The sweetness is fused with enough real feeling to avoid being sugary, except for the rather yucky spoken introduction to 'Meadows of Springtime'. **1980** *Sunday Times* 13 Jan. 61/1 To develop an improved instrument for doctors dealing with emergency cases of perforated lungs, the research boys set to work with butchers' skewers and a lot of belly of pork. It may sound yukky to the squeamish. **1981** M. GORDON *Company of Women* III. 240 It's only bats, I say... 'They're weird,' says Linda. 'Yucky.'

b. Messy, 'gooey'.

1975 *Times Lit. Suppl.* 13 June 661/3 Peanut butter, that yucky staple standby of the American snack-eater. **1977** J. WILSON *Making Hate* v. 62 Let's get these yucky things off and get you washed.

Hence **ˈyuckiness**.

1982 E. NORTH *Ancient Enemies* ix. 120 The ringing in my ears and general lassitude and yuckiness. **1984** *Info World* 14 May 18/1 So you go for 100 shares... Let's say that by November it soars back up to 68 5/8, where it peaked before all this market yuckiness began.

yud (jʊd), dial. var. HEAD *sb.*[1] *rare.*

1874 [see INNARDS *sb. pl.*]. **1882** E. L. CHAMBERLAIN *Gloss. W. Worcestershire Words* 35 Yud,..head. **1974** W. FOLEY *Child in Forest* I. 100 I'll 'old her yud still, and..you get a good dose down 'er gullet.

yud(e, **ȝud(e**, obs. pa. t. of GO: see YODE.

yue, obs. form of GIVE *v.*

1340 *Ayenb.* 265 Nou broþren and zostren y-hyreþ my red and yueþ youre. *Ibid.* 271 Yue.

†**yued**, ME. pa. pple. of FEED *v.*

1340 *Ayenb.* 141 þo hedde ypreched and yued þet uolk.

Yüeh[1] (ˈjyə). Also **Yueh**. [f. the name *Yüeh* Chou of a town (now called Shaoxing) in Zhejiang Province, China.] A type of stoneware distinguished by a celadon glaze, first produced in the Six Dynasties period and perfected during the Tang dynasty. Freq. *attrib.*, esp. as *Yüeh ware*.

[**1887** *Jrnl. R. Asiatic Soc. N. China Branch* XXII. 134 The author of the *T'ao-Shuo* begins his treatise on ancient porcelains with the Yüeh-chou potteries of the T'ang dynasty.] **1910** S. W. BUSHELL *Descr. Chinese Pott. & Porc.* II. ii. 35 The Hsing-chou porcelain resembles silver, while the Yueh-chou porcelain resembles jade... Hsing is inferior to Yueh. **1915** R. L. HOBSON *Chinese Pott. & Porc.* v. 59 Surely this cannot be far removed from the 'secret colour' of the Yueh ware. **1933** *Burlington Mag.* Sept. 122/2 When Yüeh Chou was capital of a principality, Yüeh ware was made exclusively for the princely court and was known as *pi sê yao* or ware of forbidden colour. **1958** W. WILLETTS *Chinese Art* II. vi. 439 In 1930 a Yüeh Kiln was found by Yonayama at Tê-ch'ing near Hangchow. *Ibid.* vi. 442 A number of whole bowls in the shape of lotus flowers are illustrated, all reputedly being Yüeh *yao*. **1972** *Trans. Oriental Ceramic Soc.* XXXVIII. 23 The fully evolved ware which T'ang poets praised is generally termed *Yüeh ware*.. the earlier product being called *Old Yüeh* by the Japanese.

Yüeh[2] (ˈjyə). Also **Yueh**. [Chinese.] (A member of) a group of peoples originally living in the coastal provinces of southern China, who expanded into south-east Asia during the third century B.C.

1901 E. A. PARKER *China* ii. 23 The..Yüeh tribes..seem to have very soon lost their separate identity, and to have either permanently retired into Annam proper or to have been merged into the Chinese. **1934** K. S. LATOURETTE *Chinese* I. ii. 51 Both Wu and Yüeh seem to have depended in part upon boats for their victories, navigating these craft on the sea and on the rivers and lakes in which their possessions abounded. **1966** W. G. GODDARD *Formosa* i. 16 The Yueh in coastal China. **1972** M. SHEPPARD *Taman Indera* 5 At the beginning of the Christian era well-established trade links existed between South China, India and the Red Sea. Many different traders and sailors joined in operating this route,..leaving the Yuehs to control the final sector. **1974** *Encycl. Brit. Macropædia* XIX. 120/1 A long-held notion that identified the Vietnamese with one tribe of the Viets of southern China (Yüeh in Chinese) has been abandoned.

Yüeh[3] (ˈjyə). Also **Yue**. [ad. Chinese *Yuè*, a former name for Guangdong province.] A Chinese dialect spoken in parts of the provinces of Guangdong and Guangxi. Freq. *attrib.*

1954 M. A. PEI *Dict. Ling.* 34 *Cantonese*..spoken in Kwang-tung... The indigenous name of this vernacular is *Yüeh*. **1961** CHANG-TU HU et al. *China* v. 101 Yüeh or Cantonese is spoken by some forty million people in China and abroad. **1974** *Encycl. Brit. Macropædia* XVI. 801/2 The most important representative of the Yüeh languages is Standard Cantonese of Canton, Hong Kong, and Macao. **1978** *Nagel's Encycl.-Guide: China* 70 *Yue* dialect: most of Guang dong and south eastern Guang xi. **1982** C. THOMAS *Jade Tiger* ii. 43 The man spoke in northern Min dialect as opposed to his own expatriate Yue dialect.

‖**yüeh**[4] (ˈjyə). *Archæol.* Also **yueh**. [Chinese *yuè*.] A bronze battle-axe or halberd, esp. one of the Shang period.

1956 W. C. WHITE *Bronze Culture Ancient China* 4 *Axes* (Yüeh), the most common type of axe is found in a variety of shapes. *Ibid.* 58 (*caption*) Axe-head (Yüeh), with socket for hafting. **1960** CHENG TE-K'UN *Archaeol. in China* II. iv. 69 Larger, and consequently richer, tombs would be provided with bronze vessels as well as weapons, such as *ko* dagger axes..*yueh* broad-axes. **1964** M. MEDLEY *Handbk. Chinese Art* 14/2 Axes, called *yüeh*, *ch'i* or *fu*, are either tanged or socketed. **1978** *New Archaeol. Finds in China* II. 29 Also found was a bronze weapon *yueh*.

‖**yüeh ch'in** (ˈjyə tʃɪn, kɪn). Also **yueh-ch'in**, **yu-kin**, **yukin**, 9 **yuĕ kin**. [Chinese (Pinyin *yuè qín*), lit. 'moon guitar'.] A Chinese lute with four strings and a flat, circular body.

1839 *Chinese Repository* VIII. 44 The *pepa* and *yuĕ kin* are of easy purchase. **1909** *Cent. Dict.* Suppl. *Yu-kin*,..a Chinese lute or guitar with a large circular body, a short neck, and four strings. **1954** *Grove's Dict. Mus.* (ed. 5) II. 239/2 *Yüeh ch'in*.., flat lute of four strings. Used..to accompany ballads. Now rare. **1962** E. SNOW *Other Side of River* (1963) lxxiii. 566 They may specialize in piano, violin, cello, flute, or one of the standard Chinese strings: *p'i-p'a*, *yang-ch'in*, *yueh-ch'in*, and others. **1971** J. R. BERNASCONI *Collectors' Gloss.* 396 *Yukin*, a Chinese instrument with four strings played by plucking. **1975** [see SAN HSIEN].

yuel(l, **-lle**, obs. ff. EVIL.

yuer, var. YURE, udder.

yuer, **yuery(e**, **yuerene**, obs. ff. IVORY, IVORINE.

yuerred, ME. pa. pple. of FAR *v.*

yuert, variant of YOURT.

yuff, variant of YOUF.

‖**yuffrouw** (ˈjʊfraʊ). Forms: 5–6 **ȝong-**, 6 **ȝoung frow**, **yong frow**, 7 **yough Fro**, 9 **yuffro(u)w**, **yungfrau**, **euvrou**, **uvrou**, **-ow**: see also EUPHROE. [ad. early mod.Du. *jongvrouw(e* (cf. FROW *sb.*), now *juffrouw* young lady, miss, and (in shortened form) *juffer* young lady, beam in shipbuilding, rammer (see JUFFER, UFER). See also EUPHROE.]

1. A young lady, girl.

1589 GREENE *Menaphon* (Arb.) 45 To see the fashion of these countrey yong frowes. **1673** DRYDEN *Amboyna* IV. i, And it may be then in stead of kissing, desir'd yough Fro to hold his head. **1810** W. IRVING *Let. to Mrs. Hoffman* 26 Feb., I have..formed acquaintance with some of the good people, and several of the little Y[u]ffrouws.

2. *Naut.* **a.** ? A dead-eye. *Obs.* **b.** (See quots. 1810, 1867.)

1494 *Acc. Ld. High Treas. Scot.* I. 254 ȝong frowis and collaris, seme and rufe to the bote. **1505** *Ibid.* III. 86 Blokkis and brassin schiffis, paralingis, and ȝong frowes. **1810** J. DESSIOU *Moore's Pract. Navigator* 291 *Uvrou*, the piece of wood by which the legs of the crow-foot are extended. **1815–** [see EUPHROE]. **1867** SMYTH *Sailor's Word-bk.*, *Crow-foot*, a number of small lines spreading out from an uvrow or long block, used to spread awnings by.

‖**yuft** (jʌft). Also 9 **youghten, jucten, juff, juft, youft.** [a. Russ. *yuft'*, *yukht'*, whence also G. *juften, juchten.*] Russia leather (see RUSSIA 1).
1799 W. TOOKE *View Russ. Emp.* III. 514 The chief products of the tanneries of this country..are the yufts. **1802–3** tr. *Pallas's Trav.* (1812) I. 45 Russian leather, or Youghten. **1853** URE *Dict. Arts* (ed. 4) II. 60 The Russians have long been possessed of a method of making a peculiar leather, called by them *jucten*, dyed red with the aromatic saunders wood. **1858** SIMMONDS *Dict. Trade*, *Juff*, *Youft*.

‖**yug** (jʊg), **yuga** ('jʊgə). Also yoog, yoogu. [Hindi *yug*, Skr. *yugá-* YOKE, an age of the world.] In Hindu cosmology, any of the four ages in the duration of the world, the four ages comprising 4,320,000 years and constituting a great yuga (*Mahāyuga*).
1784 W. HASTINGS in *Asiatick Researches* (1788) I. 237 The duration of the Historical ages must needs be very unequal..; while that of the Indian Yugs is disposed so regularly and artifically, that it cannot be admitted as natural or probable. **1820** W. WARD *View Hindoos* (ed. 3) IV. 315 The amount of these four yoogŭs form a mŭhu or great yoogŭ, viz. 4,320,000 years. **1883** *Encycl. Brit.* XVI. 207/2 The Hindu doctrine of the four ages or yuga.

yugawaralite (jʊ'gæwərəlaɪt). *Min.* [f. *Yugawara*, name of a town in Japan near where it was first found + *-l-* + -ITE¹.] A hydrated aluminosilicate of calcium, $CaAl_2Si_6O_{16}.4H_2O$, that is a member of the zeolite group and occurs as colourless or white monoclinic crystals having a vitreous lustre.
1952 SAKURAI & HAYASHI in *Sci. Rep. Yokohama Nat. Univ.* Section II. I. 77 We can not identify this mineral with the other zeolites, and we may consider this to be a new zeolite. We wish to [call] it 'Yugawaralite' after its locality. **1969** *Acta Cryst.* B. XXV. 1190/1 It is difficult to place yugawaralite in any of the seven recognized groups of zeolites, although it shows certain similarities to both mordenite and heulandite. **1978** *Mineral. Rec.* IX. 296/1 Yugawaralite, a relatively rare calcium zeolite,..has been found in specimens mined from the Khandivali quarry near Bombay, India.

yugement, obs. form of JUDGEMENT.

‖**yugen** ('juːgən). Also yūgen and with capital initial. [Jap., f. *yū* dark + *gen* the unfathomable.] In traditional Japanese Court culture, esp. poetry and, later, the No play, a hidden quality of graceful beauty or mystery; profound aestheticism.
1921 A. WALEY *Nō Plays of Japan* 21 The difficult term yūgen which occurs constantly..is derived from Zen literature. It means 'what lies beneath the surface'; the subtle, as opposed to the obvious; the hint as opposed to the statement. **1932** *Times Lit. Suppl.* 6 Oct. 715/1 Such a couplet..can hardly be said to capture the spirit of *yugen*. **1959** *Ibid.* 15 May 291/2 This brief basking in the Shōgun's favour led Zeami to stress the importance in performance of Yūgen, or elegant beauty and gentleness. **1970** *Daily Tel.* 16 May 9/4 His smooth curving movements of a fan, together with circling movements across the stage..gave a poetic suggestion of flight, illustrating the *Yugen*—indirection, allusiveness, mystery—which lies at the heart of No.

Yugo ('juːgəʊ), colloq. abbrev. of YUGOSLAVIAN *a.* and *sb.*
1941 *Daily News* (N.Y.) 20 Mar. 19/1 (*heading*) Yugos and Axis in compromise. *Ibid.* 24 Mar. 3/3 (*heading*) Yugo disorders, Greek warning stay Axis pact. **1963** I. FLEMING *On H.M. Secret Service* xi. 117 'Which one was it, anyway?' 'One of the Yugos. Bertil.' **1982** 'I. I. MAGDALEN' *Search for Anderson* I. x. 47 There was someing wrong about that Yugo shoot-out. It stank.

Yugoslav ('juːgəʊslɑːv, juːgəʊ'slɑːv), *sb.* and *a.* Also Jugo-; 9 **Iugo-Slav, Yougo-Slave, Yugo-Slave.** [ad. G. *Jugoslawe* (F. *Yougoslave*), f. Serbo-Croat *jugo-*, comb. form of *jug* south + G. *Slawe* SLAV *sb.*] **A.** *sb.* **a.** (A member of) various groups of southern Slavs, comprising the Serbs, Croats, and Slovenes; also, since 30 Oct. 1918, a native or inhabitant of the State of Yugoslavia. **b.** *rare.* The Slavonic language dominant in Yugoslavia; = *Serbo-Croat* s.v. SERBO-.
1853 L. H. KERR tr. *Robert's Slave Prov. Turkey* in *Ranke's Hist. Servia* (ed. 2) 382 Toasts were drunk to..the New Servian Kingdom, which will reunite all the Yugo-Slaves under the eternal patronage of the house of Romanoff. **1867** MACKENZIE & IRBY *Trav. Slavonic Provinces of Turkey-in-Europe* xxv. 369 The situation was reversed when the Russians had shaken off the Tartar, and the Iugo-Slav fell under the Turk. **1881** MRS. A. O. BRODIE tr. *Tissot's Unknown Hungary* I. 111 The Yougo-Slaves, or Slaves of the south of Austria. **1917** F. S. COPELAND tr. *Vosnjak's Bulwark against Germany* xv. 250 The unification of the Jugoslavs. **1922** *Encycl. Brit.* XXX. 372/1 The Yugoslavs..are the most numerous people in the [Balkan] peninsula. **1943** J. B. PRIESTLEY *Daylight on Saturday* xxv. 194 If you've got the morale—and even if you've got hardly anything else, like the Jugo-Slavs—you stand up and fight. **1948** R. A. D. FORREST *Chinese Lang.* i. 28 The feature [*sc.* distinctive tone]..survives to this day in one Lithuanian dialect, with traces in Scandinavian and in a variety of Yugoslav. **1973** *Times* 29 Oct. 12/7 The new Electra is Danica Mastilovic, a Yugoslav, making her debut in the house.

B. *adj.* Of, pertaining to, or designating the people or state of Yugoslavia.
1853 L. H. KERR tr. *Robert's Slave Prov. Turkey* in *Ranke's Hist. Servia* (ed. 2) 378 Gaï's 'Illyrian Journal', the organ of the Serb and Yugo-Slave interests. **1916** B. VOSNJAK *Jugoslav Nationalism* 11 There have been..three Jugoslav state creations. **1920** *Edin. Rev.* July 42 Whatever else may be said of the Yugoslav movement..it is at any rate a national movement having its origins within..the peoples whose destiny it affects. **1967** *Listener* 29 June 843/3 Italian, Yugoslav, or Spanish workers have migrated to West Germany..or Switzerland. **1981** L. DEIGHTON *XPD* xxviii. 226 The duty officers could be sure of a bottle of Yugoslav riesling.

Yugoslavian (juːgəʊ'slɑːvɪən), *a.* and *sb.* Also Jugo-. [f. prec. + -IAN.]
A. *adj.* = YUGOSLAV *a.* **B.** *sb.* **a.** A native or inhabitant of Yugoslavia. **b.** *rare.* The Serbo-Croat language.
1923 W. J. LOCKE *Moordius & Co.* xiii. 180, I must be back to give dinner to the Jugo-Slavian minister. **1924** *Contemp. Rev.* Apr. 448 They cannot effectively crush the revolutionaries on Yugoslavian soil. **1949** E. POUND *Pisan Cantos* lxxx. 96 White boy says: do you speak Jugoslavian? **1953** A. SMITH *Blind White Fish in Persia* x. 204 Firstly, our Yugoslavian visas had not come through. **1962** A. LURIE *Love & Friendship* ii. 31 They didn't have them [*sc.* Boy Scouts] in Yugoslavia. Anyway, only for Yugoslavians. **1977** *New Yorker* 19 Sept. 49/2 There was a Yugoslavian boy who had brought along a portable silent keyboard with a weight attached to each key, to regulate the action. **1983** *Times* 3 Oct. 1/4 The Greek and the Yugoslavian were accustomed to the heat.

yuh (jʌ), repr. a colloq. (esp. Black English) pronunc. of YOU.
1906 [see OUTA]. **1922** [see *tough nut* s.v. TOUGH *a.* 10a]. **1933** *Publ. Texas Folklore Soc.* XI. 101 She tol' me to ax yuh. **1952** [see MACOUMÈRE]. **1967** E. BRATHWAITE in Ramchand & Gray *West Indian Poetry* (1972) 25 Yuh does get up, walk 'bout. **1969** [see SECKO]. **1977** *Rolling Stone* 30 June 80/3 So get back to me as soon as you can, will yuh.

yuill, obs. Sc. form of YULE.

yuk, var. YUCK *int.*, *sb.*², and *a.*

Yukaghir ('juːkəgɪə(r), juːkə'gɪə(r)), *sb.* (*a.*) Also **Yukaghire, Yukagir(e).** **a.** (A member of) a Mongoloid people of Arctic Siberia. **b.** The Palæo-Siberian language (of unknown affiliation) of this people. Also *attrib.* or as *adj.*
1842 C. H. COTTRELL *Recoll. Siberia* iv. 104 The Yukaghires, settled on the banks of the river Anuiy, maintain themselves the whole year on the reindeer they kill in spring and autumn. **1879** C. H. EDEN *Frozen Asia* ix. 208 The head-quarters of the Yukagires is on the River Anyui. **1898** [see KORYAK]. **1906** *Daily Chron.* 4 Apr. 7/5 The sole survivors of a group of ten Yukagirs, are charged with having eaten the man's nephew... After that the Yukagir, although he had caught a swan, continued to eat human flesh. **1908** T. G. TUCKER *Introd. Natural Hist. Lang.* 149 The Hyperborean speeches of Asia, some of which may or may not form a family, include..*Yukaghir.* **1932** [see CHUKCHEE, CHUKCHI *sb.* and *a.*]. **1948** D. DIRINGER *Alphabet* 35 Sad love-story of a Yukaghir girl. **1951** W. K. MATTHEWS *Languages U.S.S.R.* ii. 3 Yukagir (Odul), the mother-tongue of fewer than 500 persons in Northern Yakutia. **1964** tr. *Levin & Potapov's Peoples of Siberia* 789 The name 'Yukagir' was borrowed by the Russians from the Yakuts, but its origin is probably Tungusic. **1972** W. B. LOCKWOOD *Panorama Indo-Europ. Lang.* 154 There are isolated languages spoken by diminutive populations. These are Gilyak..and, with a thousand speakers..or less ..Yukagir (Yukagir National Area). **1981** M. C. SMITH *Gorky Park* I. xiv. 213 He was more Siberian than any of us. .. The Borodins..lived with the Yukagir, the reindeer herders. **1983** *Word* XXXIV. 217 The focus system of Yukagir, and case and negation in Uralic are treated in syntax sections.

‖**yukata** (ju'kata). Also **Yukata, yukatta;** 9 **ukata.** [Jap., f. *yu* hot water, bath + *kata* short for *katabira* a light kimono.] A light cotton kimono, freq. with stencil designs, orig. intended to be worn after a bath, but now also used as a housecoat.
1822 F. SHOBERL tr. *Titsingh's Illustr. Japan* II. 254 The *ukata.*, a robe of fine linen; it is put on in coming out of the bath to dry the body. **1881** SATOW & HAWES *Handbk. Japan* p. xvi, Japanese loose cotton gowns (*yukata*). **1886** J. LA FARGE *Let.* 3 Sept. in *Artist's Lett. from Japan* 229 A——.. rode along with only a partial covering of *yukatta*, and attracted no attention. **1936** K. NOHARA *True Face of Japan* v. 130 Dons the *yukata*, the light, informal, Japanese house-jacket of coloured cotton. **1960** B. LEACH *Potter in Japan* vi. 133 My Yukata (provided cotton kimono) reached to my knees. *Ibid.* ix. 195 Visitors were strolling the streets in 'yukatta' (cotton kimono provided by hotels). **1970** *Guardian* 12 Dec. 6/6 The donning of the cool cotton *yukata* robe and slippers is the first sloughing of Western identity. **1981** J. MELVILLE *Sort of Samurai* ix. 75 All four of them were now wearing cotton *yukatas.*

Yukawa (jʊ'kɑːwə). *Nucl. Physics.* The name of H. *Yukawa* (b. 1907), Japanese physicist, used *attrib.* with reference to the theory of the strong interaction between nucleons put forward by him, in which it is mediated by the exchange of particles (***Yukawa particles***) subsequently identified with pions; **Yukawa potential**, a potential function of the form $V = V_0(r/r_0)^{-1} \exp(-r/r_0)$, occurring in Yukawa's theory of the nuclear force.
1938 *Nature* 1 Oct. 592/2 The discovery of a new particle, the Yukawa particle or 'heavy electron', has given a new orientation to many of our ideas. **1948** *Proc. Cambr. Philos. Soc.* XLIV. 90 As an illustration of the treatment developed above the nuclear field as described by the Yukawa potential $U(r) = -b\lambda r^{-1}e^{-\lambda r}$ will be treated. **1964** *Listener* 29 Oct. 661/1 Immediately after the war, many physicists..became deeply involved in these problems, especially the nature of protons, neutrons, and the Yukawa mesons. **1968** C. G. KUPER *Introd. Theory Superconductivity* xv. 258 The Yukawa force between nucleons has a pairing part, and the methods of the BCS theory are applicable. **1973** R. J. BLIN-STOYLE *Fund. Interactions & Nucleus* i. 3 The earlier Lagrangian formulation of strong interactions based on Yukawa type interactions has continued to play an important role. **1974** FRAUENFELDER & HENLEY *Subatomic Physics* viii. 187 If virtual pions are exchanged between nucleons, the basic Yukawa reaction $N \rightarrow N' + \pi$ should conserve isospin. **1977** P. D. B. COLLINS *Introd. Regge Theory & High Energy Physics* i. 42 The simplest form of potential which has the short-range character appropriate to strong interactions is the Yukawa potential $U(r) = g^2e^{-\mu r}/r$, where g^2 is the coupling strength and μ^{-1} is the range.

yuke (juːk), *sb. Sc.* and *north. dial.* Forms: see the vb. [f. next.] Itching, itch.
1551 TURNER *Herbal* I. A v b, Wormwood..helyth also the yche or yuke. *Ibid.* P iv, The broth of hem is good..for itche or yeewk that goeth ouer the hole body. **1572** BUCHANAN *Detectioun* in Jas. Anderson *Coll.* (1727) II. 16 Certane blak Pimples..brak out ouer all his haill Body, with sa greit Zuik,..that he lingerit out his Lyfe with verray small Hope of Eschaip. **1715** RAMSAY *Christ's Kirk Gr.* II. ix, When their hands he shook, Ga'e them what he got frae his dad, Videlicet, the yuke. **1722** in *C'tess Suffolk's Lett.* (1824) I. 93 All the best families in the parish are laid up with what they call the yoke—which in England is the itch. **1824** W. OLIVER *Songs* 7 For fear that..Scotch Donald chance to myek owr free, An' gie wor king the yuick. [**1901** *Let. to Editor*, Among stablemen, coachmen, &c., the itch goes by the name of the 'dukes' (or dooks), and horses suffering from the complaint are referred to as 'dukey (or dooky) horses'.]

yuke (juːk), *v. Sc.* and *north. dial.* Forms: 5 **ȝhuyk, ȝoke, ȝouk,** 5–6 **ȝuke,** 6 **ȝoik, yuik, iuke, yeewk,** 7 **yeauk,** 6– **yeuk, yuke,** 7– **yuck,** 8–9 **yook,** (**youk, yoke,** 9 **yuk, yuc, yewk, yeuck, yuick, ewk, euk(e, uke).** [app. alteration of north. ME. *ȝeke, ȝike* (see ITCH *v.*¹), prob. under the influence of MDu. *jeuken.*] *intr.* To itch.
c **1425** WYNTOUN *Cron.* II. vii. 574 Senyphes..And alkyn kynde of cleggis als þat gert ȝhuyk [*v.r.* ȝuke] bathe heid and hals. *a* **1508** DUNBAR *Tua Mariit Wemen* 130 Bot I may ȝuke all this ȝer, or his ȝerd help. *a* **1600** MONTGOMERIE *Sonn.* xxvi. 3 Quhais craig ȝoiks fastest, let tham sey thame sell. **1674** RAY *N.C. Words* 56 *Yuck*; Linc. **1790** BURNS '*Kind Sir, I've read*,' etc. 26 How Daddie Burke the plea was cookin', If Warren Hastings' neck was yeukin'. **1796** —— *Poem on Life* vi, Ah Nick!.. Thy auld, damned elbow yeuks wi' joy, And hellish pleasure. **1804** R. ANDERSON *Cumbld. Ball.* (*c* 1850) 99 She'll scart my back whene'er it yuks. **1816** SCOTT *Antiq.* xxi, It wad hae been a fashious job that; by my certie, some o' our necks wad hae been ewking. **1882** JAS. WALKER *Jaunt to Auld Reekie* etc. 42 For poachin' aye his heart it yeukit.
Hence **yuking** *vbl. sb.* and *ppl. a.*
a **1449** W. BOWER in *Fordun's Scotichron.* (1759) II. 376 Wyth prik ȝoukand eeris, as the awsk gleg [tr. L. *auribus indisciplinata, ut aspis*]. **1562** TURNER *Bathes* I b, Good..for the sciatica, and for all kindes of itche or iukinge. **1600** J. HAMILTON *Facile Traictise* 40 Sik as flatters thair zeuking earis. **1886** *S.W. Linc. Gloss.* s.v. *Yuck*, Such a nasty yucking pain comes on in the legs. **1894** CROCKETT *Raiders* xxiv, When I get that dry yeukin' in my thrapple.

Yuki ('juːkɪ), *sb.* (*a.*) Also 9 **Yuka, Yukeh,** etc. [a. Wintu *yu-keh*, lit. 'stranger, enemy'.]
a. (A member of) a group of linguistically related American Indian peoples, comprising the Yuki, Huchnom, and Wappo tribes, inhabiting the coast of north-western California. **b.** The language spoken by this people. Also *attrib.* or as *adj.*
1858 S. P. STORMS *Let.* 14 Aug. in *Ann. Rep. Commissioner of Indian Affairs for 1858* CIX. 307 About three thousand Nome Cults or Yukas make this valley [*sc.* Round Valley in northern California] their headquarters. **1863** *Hist. Mag.* VII. 123/1 The Yukeh, or as the name is variously spelt, Yuka, Yuques, and Uca, are the original inhabitants of the ..Round Valley in Tehama County, California. **1875** H. H. BANCROFT *Native Races Pacific States* III. II. iii. 648 In Round Valley, northern California, there is the..Yuka language. *Ibid.* 643 At Humboldt Bay a language called Patawat is mentioned, and in Round Valley the Yuka. **1877** S. POWERS *Tribes Calif.* xiv. 129 If a Yuki stumbles and falls on the march..it is a bad omen. *Ibid.*, He has seen Yuki dead left on the field. **1900** J. FRAZER *Golden Bough* (ed. 2) I. i. 34 When the men of the Yuki tribe of Indians in California were away fighting, the women at home..danced ..in a circle, chanting and waving leafy wands. **1923** A. L. KROEBER *Anthropol.* iii. 90 In the native Californian language known as Yuki, *ko* means *go.* **1939** H. M. WORMINGTON *Ancient Man in North Amer.* vi. 256 Among living Indians in North America the Cahuilla tribes of inland southern California and the Pomo and Yuki of northern coastal California, are thought to show the greatest number of Amurian traits. **1965** *Canad. Jrnl. Linguistics* X. 99 Hokan-Siouan in Sapir's arrangement includes six major constituent units..Hokan-Coahuiltecan, Yuki, [etc.]. **1974** *Encycl. Brit. Micropædia* X. 844/1 Warfare was apparently frequent—between certain communities, between the different Yuki groups, and with other Californian Indians. *Ibid.* 844/2 The Yuki..were organized into communities composed of several scattered settlements. **1981** A. B.

KEHOE *North Amer. Indians* vii. 376/2 Yuki and its sister language Wappo, both spoken north of San Francisco Bay.

yukky, var. YUCKY *a.*

Yukon ('ju:kɒn). [The name of the *Yukon* Territory in north-west Canada.] ***Yukon stove***, a lightweight portable stove consisting of a small metal box divided into firebox and oven.

1898 W. B. HASKELL *Two Years in Klondyke* 75 The 'Yukon stove'..is a small sheet iron box with an oven at the back and a telescope pipe. **1943** W. CHASE *Sourdough Pot* xvi. 97 The stove, a sheet-iron affair, known as a Yukon stove, had a limited capacity. **1974** W. HUNT *North of 53* iv. 15 A wood-fired 'Yukon' stove, either square or round bottomed, and containing a small oven at the back end, provided cooking facilities and kept the cabin warm in the winter.

Also **'Yukoner**, an inhabitant of the Yukon Territory; **'Yukonesque** *a.*

c **1898** Yukoner [see HOOCHINOO 2]. **1924** M. H. MASON *Arctic Forests* 84 These things have made the Yukoners the finest, most generous, and most virile population to be found on the whole continent of America. **1934** A. HUXLEY *Beyond Mexique Bay* 128 Our Yukonesque stampedes into any business that seems, at any given moment, to be doing well. **1977** Yukoner [see OUTSIDER 1].

yuky ('ju:kɪ), *a. Sc.* and *north. dial.* [f. YUKE + -Y[1].] Itchy; itching with curiosity.

1719 RAMSAY *3rd Answ. to Hamilton* xv, We, like nags whase necks are yucky, Ha'e us'd our teeth. **1722** —— *Three Bonnets* III. 46 While haste his youky mind expresses. *c* **1750** J. COLLIER (Tim Bobbin) *Fratres in Malo*, Scratching his Yuky arm. **1789** D. DAVIDSON *Seasons* 46 Unto thy smooth'ning tongue they fainly turn Their yeuky rumps. **1867** RAMSAY *Remin.* (ed. 15) 86 I'm unco yuckie to hear a blaud o' your gab.

Hence **'yukiness**.

1853 G. JOHNSTON *Nat. Hist. E. Bord.* I. 74 If the hairs get into the neck, a youkiness (itch) is the..consequence.

‖**yulan** ('ju:lən). Also **youlan**. [Chinese, f. *yu* a gem + *lan* plant.] A Chinese species of magnolia, *M. conspicua* (*M. Yulan*).

1822 *Hortus Anglicus* II. 55 Lily flowered Magnolia, or Youlan. **1882** *Garden* 6 May 311/1 The Yulan..forms a conspicuous object amongst spring flowering trees.

yule (ju:l), *sb.* Forms: 1 **ȝeol, ȝeochol, ȝeoh(h)ol, -el, ȝeh(h)ol, ȝehhel, ȝeola, iula,** 2 **iol,** 2–4 **ȝol** (**yol**), 3 **ȝeol,** 4 **ȝool,** 4–5 **ȝole,** 5 **ȝoil(l, yoyll(e, ȝowle, yowle, youle, yole, yoole, ȝwle, (yold(e),** 5–7 **ȝule,** 6 **ȝoile, ȝuill, ȝull, ȝowill, -ell, ȝoull, ȝeoll, (ewle),** 6–7 **yeul, yewl, yool, yuill, ȝuil, (ule,** 9 **yuhl),** 6– **yule.** Also *dial.* (in comb.) 7 **yew,** 7–8 **yu, u.** [The modern form descends from OE. *ȝeól*, earlier *ȝeoh(h)ol, ȝeh(h)ol*, also *ȝeóla* sometimes pl.) Christmas day or Christmastide, and in phr. *se ærra ȝeóla* December, *se æftera ȝeóla* January; corresp. to ON. *jól* pl. a heathen feast lasting twelve days, (later) Christmas. An Old Anglian *ȝiuli*, recorded by Bede (see quot. 726 in sense 1) as the name of December and January, corresponds to ON. *ýlir* month beginning on the second day of the week falling within Nov. 10–17, and Goth. *jiuleis* in *fruma jiuleis* November. The ultimate origin of the Teut. types **jeul-* (*jeȝul-*) and **jeχul-*:—pre-Teut. **jeqᵘl-* is obscure.]

†**1.** December or January. *Obs.*

726 BÆDA *De Temp. Rat.* xv, De Mensibus Anglorum.. Primusque eorum mensis, quem Latini Januarium vocant, dicitur Giuli... December Giuli, eodem quo Januarius nomine, vocatur... Menses Giuli a conversione solis in auctum diei, quia unus eorum præcedit, alius subsequitur, nomina accipiunt. *a* **900** *O.E. Martyrol.* 1 Jan. 12 Ianuarius, þæt is on ure ȝeþeode se æftera ȝeola. *Ibid.* 10 Dec. 216 Se monað ys nemned on leden Decembris ond on ure ȝeþeode se ærra ȝeola. *c* **1200** ORMIN 1910–15 Crist wass borenn i þiss lif Wiþinnen ȝoless moneþþ,..þatt wass o þe fiffte daȝȝ Att twenntiȝ daȝhess ende Off ȝol.

2. Christmas and the festivities connected therewith. (Still the name in *Sc.* and *north. dial.*; since *c* 1850 also a literary archaism in Eng.)

a **900** *O.E. Martyrol.* 6 May 76 Feowertiȝ daȝa ær Criste acennisse, þæt is ær ȝeolum [*v.r.* ȝyhhelum]. *c* **900** tr. *Bæda's Hist.* IV. xix. (1890) 318 Þy twelftan deȝe ofer ȝeochol [*v.rr.* ȝeohol, ȝeohhel]. *a* **901** *Laws of Ælfred* §43, xii daȝas on ȝehhol [*v.rr.* ȝehol, ȝehhel, ȝeol]. ? **12..** *Charter of Eadweard* an. 1067 in Kemble *Cod. Dipl.* IV. 209 Ealle ða gyltes ða belimpeð to mine kinehelme inne Iol and inne Easterne. **13..** *Gaw. & Gr. Knt.* 284, I craue..a crystemas gomen, For hit is ȝol & nwe ȝer. **1338** R. BRUNNE *Chron.* (1725) 49 Þe kyng one on þe morn went to London, His ȝole forto hold was his encheson. *c* **1425** *Engl. Conq. Irel.* (1896) 42 Seynt Tomas-ys day, Apostle, ys þe fyft day afor yold. *c* **1440** *Bone Flor.* 1897 Of seynt Hyllary the churche ys, The twenty day of yowle y wys. *c* **1450** *Merlin* vi. 96 The kynge is now deed sithe Martin-masse, and fro hens to yoole is but litill space. **1533** *Extr. Aberd. Reg.* (1844) I. 149 At the natiuite of our Lord, callit ȝowill. **1536** BELLENDEN *Cron. Scot.* XIII. xiv. (1821) II. 340 Quhen he wes sittand with his modir, on the Epiphany Day, at his yuill. *a* **1580** SIR R. MAITLAND *Sat. Age* 45 Thai..yat held grit ȝulis. **1589** WARNER *Alb. Eng.* v. xxiv. 108 At Ewle we wonten, gambole, daunce, to carrole, and to sing. **1637** *Bk. Com. Prayer Scotland* Table Proper Ps., Yule, or Christmas day. **1644** in Row *Hist. Kirk* (Wodrow Soc.) p. xxix, Knowing that the superstitious dayis of Yool was approching. **1753** *Stewart's Trial* App. 61 About Yule last. **1794** BURNS *Bonie Peggy Ramsay* i, And dawin' it is dreary, When birks are bare at Yule. **1816** SCOTT *Antiq.* xxiii, Ye ken a green Yule makes a fat kirk-yard. **1850** TENNYSON *In Mem.* xxviii, They bring me sorrow touch'd with joy, The merry merry bells of Yule. **1878** SUSAN PHILLIPS *On Sea-board* 74 And many a Yule since..You chose a spray all brightly berried over.

¶ ***Yule of August, Lammas Yule***: the festival of Lammas, the first of August. *Obs.*

This use has arisen from confusion of this word with GULE *sb.*[2] (Lammas Day).

1643 HAMMOND *Let. Resol. Six Quæres* vi. §65. 465 *Gula Augusti*, or the Yule of August. *a* **1661** FULLER *Worthies, Northumbld.* (1662) II. 304 It [*sc.* Yule] is a name general for festivals, as Lammas Yule, &c.

†**3.** Used as an exclamation of joy or revelry at the Christmas festivities. *Obs.*

1546 J. HEYWOOD *Prov.* (1867) 28 It is easy to cry vle at other mens coste. *a* **1568** in *Bannatyne MS.* (Hunter. Club) 380 It is eith [*pr.* dith] to cry yule [*Maitl. Fo. MS.* hailȝule] On ane vder manis coist. **1661** BLOUNT *Glossogr.* s.v. *Ule*, In Yorkshire and our other Northern parts, they have an old Custom, after Sermon or Service on Christmas day, the people will, even in the Churches cry *Vle, Vle,*..and the common people run about the streets singing Ule, Ule, Ule, Three Puddings in a Pule, Crack nuts and cry Ule. **1737** RAMSAY *Sc. Prov.* (1750) 58 It is eith crying yool on anither man's stool. **1853** W. SANDYS *Christmastide* 143 In some places it seems to have been the custom to dance in the country churches, after prayers, crying out, 'Yole, yole, yole!' &c.

4. *attrib.* and *Comb.*, as ***yule banquet, batch, common*** (COMMON *sb.*[1] 8), ***fare, feast, hearth, night*** [cf. ON. *jólanótt*], ***time***; locally applied to articles of food made specially for Christmas as ***yule-bread, -cake, -dough, -loaf*** (see quots.); also **yule-block** = *yule-log*; **yule-candle** = *Christmas candle* (CHRISTMAS 4); **yule-clog** = *yule-log*; **yule-game**, a Christmas game or sport; †a frolic, gambol; †**yule-girth** [see GRITH *sb.* 6; cf. ON. *jólagrið*], the peace of Christmas; **yule-log**, a large log of wood burnt on the hearth at Christmas; **yule-song** *dial.*, a Christmas carol; †**yule-stock**, (*a*) [? STOCK *sb.*[1] 20, 47], ? contribution to Christmas festivities; (*b*) = *yule-log*; **yule-tide** [cf. ON. *jólatíð*], the season of Yule, Christmas-tide; †**yule-waiting** (*yolwayting*) [app. ON. *veiting*, WAITING *vbl. sb.*[2]], app. a due paid by bondmen at Christmas; †**yule-waitstand** (*yolwayte-*), ? the place where the waits (WAIT *sb.* 8 a) stood at Christmas; †**yule-work** (Sc. *ȝeoll vark*), ? preparations for Christmas festivities.

1629 *Orkney Witch Trial* in *N.B. Advertiser* Oct. (1894), If ever the guidman of the hous sould mak ane other *yull bankett. **1674** RAY *N.C. Words*, *Yu-batch. **1796** PEGGE *Derbicisms* (E.D.S.), *U-back, U-block*. See *Yu-batch*.. *Yu-bach*. *a* **1661** FULLER *Worthies, Northumberland* (1662) II. 304 The Northern parts call Christmas Yule, (hence the *Yule-block, *Yule-cakes [*pr.* oakes], Yule-songs, &c.). **1820** *Sporting Mag.* (N.S.) VI. 283 Yule Cake, a kind of spiced cake, often supplies the place of gingerbread. **1884** BESANT *Dor. Forster* xiii, The tables were covered with Yule-cakes (which are, in the north, shaped like a baby, and Christmas pies in form of a cradle. **1808** JAMIESON s.v., The candle, that is lighted on Yule, must be so large as to burn from the time of its being lighted till the day be done... Hence large candles are by the vulgar called *Yule-candles. **1820** *Sporting Mag.* (N.S.) VI. 283 The yule candle, a tall mould candle, is lighted and set on the table. **1725** BOURNE *Antiq. Vulg.* xiii. in Brand *Pop. Antiq.* xiii. (1777) 155 Our Fore-Fathers..were wont..to lay a Log of Wood upon the Fire, whlch they termed a *Yule-Clog, or Christmas-Block. **1836** R. FURNESS *Astrol.* III. Wks. (1858) 163 When ample yule-clogs lent their heat and light, And all-spiced possets warm'd the Christmas night. **1850** TENNYSON *In Mem.* lxxviii, The yule-clog sparkled keen with frost. *a* **1614** J. MELVILL *Autob. & Diary* (Wodrow Soc.) 274 That *Yuill comoun they thought to repey weill now at Pasch. **1777** BRAND *Pop. Antiq.* 163 The *Yule-Dough,..a Kind of Baby or little Image of Paste, which our Bakers used formerly to bake at this Season, and present to their Customers. **1888** JESSIE M. E. SAXBY *Lads of Lunda* 210 Such bounty, in the form of *Yule-fare, as the folks are pleased to bestow. *a* **1661** FULLER *Worthies, Northumbld.* (1662) II. 304 A *Yule feast may be quat at Pasche. That is Christmas-cheer may be digested, and the party hungry again at Easter. *a* **1774** FERGUSSON *Geordie & Davie* 14 Poems (1789) II. 6 For the Yule-feast a sautit mart's prepar'd. **1611** COTGR., *Gambade*, a gamboll, *yew-game, tumbling tricke. **1632** SHERWOOD, A yew-game, or yeule-game, *gambade*. **1615** R. COCKS *Diary* (Hakl. Soc.) I. 93 The shipps company..plaied Christmas ule games in good sort. **1621** BURTON *Anat. Mel.* II. ii. IV. 346 Masks, singing, dancing, vlegames. **1674** RAY *N.C. Words*, Yu-game. **1569–70** *Rec. Inverness* (New Spalding Club) I. 182 For breking of *Yule gerthe and trubling of the towne. ? **16..** in F. Drake *Eboracum* I. vi. (1736) 197 The fower serjeants shall go and ride..and so go forth to the fower barrs of the citty and blow the youle-girthe. *Ibid.*, To make proclamation at the pillory of the Yoole-girthol. **1656** MENNIS & J. SMITH *Mus. Delic.* (ed. 2) 23 Thrice had all New-yeares Guests their *yewl guts fill'd With embalm'd Veal, buried in Christmas Past. **1848** LYTTON *Harold* IV. vi, We strip not the green leaves for our *yule-hearths. **1729** WALKDEN *Diary* (1866) 85 A *yule loaf, 3d. **1725** BOURNE *Antiq. Vulg.* xiii. in Brand *Pop. Antiq.* (1777) 157, I am apt to believe, the Log has had the Name of the *Yule-Log, from its being burnt as an Emblem of the returning Sun. **1848** LONGF. *K. Witlaf's Drinking-horn* viii, The Yule-log cracked in the chimney. **1303** R. BRUNNE *Handl. Synne* 4648 Howe God was born yn *ȝole nyght. *c* **1325** *Metr. Hom.* 101 On feld thar thai woc on yol niht. *c* **1475** *Rauf Coilȝear* 342 Betuix none of the day and ȝule nicht. **1792** BURNS *Duncan Gray* i, On blythe yule night when we were fu'. *a* **1661** *Yule-songs [see *yule-block*]. **1876** ROBINSON *Whitby Gloss.*, *Yule-sangs*, s. pl. Christmas carols. **1282** *Yorksh. Inquis.* (Yorks. Rec. Soc. 1892) I. 244 [The same pays 12d. at Christmas, which is called] *Yolstoch. *c* **1480** HENRYSON *Sum Practysis Med.* 77 (Bann. MS.) With thre crawis of the cok, The schadow of ane ȝule stok, Is gud for þe host. *c* **1475** *Rauf Coilȝear* 4 Quhair Empreouris and Erlis, and vther mony ane, Turnit fra Sanct Thomas befoir the *ȝule tyde. **1860** LONGF. *Way-side Inn* I. *Musician's T.* XII. ii, Three days his Yule-tide feasts He held. **1787** W. TAYLOR *Poems* 44 About *Yule-time an' Hogmenai. **1864** PRIOR in *Athenæum* 2 Jan. 10/2 [Mistletoe] ripened its snow-white fruit just at Yule-time. **1183** *Boldon Bk.* (Surtees) 20 Dant cum villanis partem suam de scat et de metride et de *yolwayting. *c* **1380** *Bp. Hatfield's Surv.* (Surtees) 22 Iidem tenentes red. p. a. pro yol-wayting, ad festum Nativitatis Domini, 5s. **1413–14** *Boldon Bk.* (Surtees) Gloss. p. lxxii, De quadam placea vocata *Yolewaytestand. **1540** *Rec. Elgin* (New Spald. Cl. 1903) I. 47 Dauid Hardy..sall pay ane stane wax to the nixt *Ȝeoll vark.

Hence **yule** *v.*, *intr.* to keep Christmas. *Sc.* and *north. dial.*

a **1670** SPALDING *Troub. Chas. I* (Bannatyne Club) I. 39 The lords refuised to lett the lady marchioness go to the castle with her husband, except she would waird also, and with great intreatie had the favour, to Yule with him, but to stay no longer. **1828** *Craven Gloss.*, *Yuling*, Christmas feasting.

yule-day. Chiefly *Sc.* Forms: see YULE *sb.* and DAY *sb.* [OE. *ȝeohheldæȝ*; cf. ON. *jóladagr*.] Christmas Day.

a **900** *O.E. Martyrol.* 1 Nov. 198 Se ærysta dæȝ in *natale domini*, þæt is ærysta ȝeohheldæȝ. *c* **1200** ORMIN 11063 Itt iss þe þrittennde daȝȝ Fra ȝoldaȝȝ, nohht te twellfte. *c* **1205** LAY. 22737 Hit wes in ane ȝeol-dæie þat Arður in Lundene lai. *c* **1330** R. BRUNNE *Chron. Wace* (Rolls) 10371 On þe ȝol day he made his feste. *c* **1425** WYNTOUN *Cron.* v. vii. 1381 On ȝoil [*v.r.* ȝule] day He bad thre messis be said ay. **1488** *Acc. Ld. High Treas. Scot.* I. 100 To the Kingis offerande on ȝwle da, ij demyss. **1596** DALRYMPLE tr. *Leslie's Hist. Scot.* (S.T.S.) II. 462 Euin ȝuil day, Christes awne day. **1600** J. HAMILTON *Facile Traictise* 174 Thay cause thair wyfis and seruants spin in oppin sicht of the people vpon zeul day. *a* **1670** SPALDING *Troub. Chas. I* (Bannatyne Club) I. 85 Doctor Scrogie gave the communion, upon Yeull day, in Old Aberdein. *a* **1774** FERGUSSON *Daft Days* v, Whan merry Yule-day comes, I trow, You'll scantlins fin' a hungry mou.

yule-even. *Sc.* Forms: see YULE *sb.* and EVEN *sb.* [Cf. ON. *jólaaptann*.] Christmas Eve.

1375 BARBOUR *Bruce* IX. 204 Befor ȝoill-evyn ane nycht bot mair. **1473–4** *Acc. Ld. High Treas. Scot.* I. 67 Gevin to Rob Purvas,..on ȝule evin,..xxiiij s. **1567** *Gude & Godlie B.* (S.T.S.) 72 Ane Carrell of the Epistill on ȝule Euin. **1570–1** *Rec. Inverness* (New Spalding Club) I. 198 Vpon the xxiiij day of December last being Yule Ewin. *a* **1653** BINNING *Serm., Isa. lxiv. 6* Wks. (1735) 618/1 Sin rising up to Iniquities..hath accomplished the Judgment, put Fire up among us, made us as the Birk in Yule-even. *a* **1670** SPALDING *Troub. Chas. I* (Bannatyne Club) I. 85 The marquess of Hamilton..upon Yeull evin, takes journey towards London. **1808** JAMIESON s.v., Some farmers..are so extremely superstitious, as to go into their stables and cow-houses on Yule-e'en, and read a chapter of the Bible behind their horses and cattle, to preserve them from harm.

yulo ('ju:ləʊ). Also **yuloh, yulow,** etc. [Prob. ad. Chinese (Cantonese) *iū-lǒ* to scull a boat, f. *iū* to shake + *lǒ* oar.] A Chinese sculling oar (see quot. 1899). So also as *v. intr.* to scull a boat with such an oar. Hence **'yulohing** *vbl. sb.*

1878 H. A. GILES *Gloss. Reference* 170 *Yuloh, to*, to scull a boat with an oar at the stern. From the Shanghai pronunciation of..*yao* to work..*lu* an oar. **1888** A. J. LITTLE *Through Yang-tse Gorges* 320 In addition to these, two lateral yuloes (sculls worked by a screw motion),..were attached to the sides. **1899** I. L. BISHOP *Yangtze Valley & Beyond* xiii. 145 Others are toiling at *yu-lows*, big broad-bladed sculls, worked over the stern or parallel to the junk's side. **1905** *N. & Q.* 22 Apr. 305/1 The *yuloh* is the single oar used over the stern for the propulsion of sampans and barges, after the manner sometimes called sculling in England. To *yuloh* is to row a boat in that fashion. The meaning is literally 'push and pull wood'. **1911** J. D. BALL *Chinese at Home* xvi. 203 Ferryboats slowly cross the river. .. The loads of the coolies are put in the bows of the boat, where also occasionally is to be seen a leper, who is not allowed amongst the other passengers. The ferryman *yeeoo-loes* at the stern. **1921** *Outward Bound* June 36/1 The junk is propelled when possible by great oars, called by the Chinese 'yulos', projecting out from either side. **1927** *Chambers's Jrnl.* Mar. 163/1 We pass a fishing boat; a woman with a willowy figure bending to the yulow at one end. **1941** J. HOMER *Dawn Watch in China* iv. 93 Junks bound downstream were manned on the foredeck with six or eight or a dozen oarsmen, who stood, each to his oar poling forward into the fast water and singing in unison the minor wordless river chant of the sacred Yangtze. Now and then, the helmsman would *yuloh* in a high-pitched scream were he called forth the wind. **1966** G. R. G. WORCESTER *Sail & Sweep in China* ii. 11 In rowing, as in so many other arts, the Chinese show their great independence of thought; and in the yuloh or sculling oar, they demonstrate a perfect example of applied mechanics which can, confidently, be dated back to the Later Han Dynasty AD25–220. *Ibid.* 12 When operated by a Chinese, even by a child, yulohing appears to be supremely simple. **1981** *Jrnl. R. Naval Med. Service* LXVII. 46/2 Navigable by one man using a large yulo at the stern.

yum (jʌm), *int.* [Echoic.] An exclamation of pleasurable anticipation, with implication of sensual or gustatory satisfaction; freq. reduplicated as ***yum-yum***, etc.

Some of the reduplicated examples are not clearly distinguishable from those given s.v. YUM-YUM *sb.* and *a.* below.

1878 *Burlington Hawkeye* in *Irish Monthly* VI. 688 How we would like to get hold of the man... Alone. In the woods, with a revolver in our hip-pocket. Revenge is sweet; yum, yum, yum. **1899** KIPLING *Stalky & Co.* 239 Pretty lips.. Seem to say—Come away. Kissy! come, come!.. Yummy-yum-yum! **1922** JOYCE *Ulysses* 173 Kissed her mouth. Yum. **1942** O. NASH *Good Intentions* 143 And fish are only something about which some people say, 'Yum yum, right out of the water and fried to a delicate golden brown.' **1959** 'J. CHRISTOPHER' *Scent of White Poppies* iii. 40 When she had gone, Bella said: 'Yum-yum. Really luscious.' **1962** A. LURIE *Love & Friendship* iii. 45 Miranda cut a piece of warm coffee cake, handed it to Emmy... 'Oh, yum. Thank you.' **1982** S. PARETSKY *Indemnity Only* xii. 155 'Lotty talked her into..making homemade enchiladas, yum-yum.' 'Yum-yum,' the two little girls chorused.

Hence **'yummy** *a. colloq.*, delicious, delectable; also as *int.*

1899 [see YUM *int.*]. **1934** WEBSTER, Yummy *adj.* **1950** 'S. RANSOME' *Deadly Miss Ashley* xii. 147 Lora's attractive face or Dorothea's yummy figure. **1955** J. P. DONLEAVY *Ginger Man* xix. 213 Sitting, facing one another across the white table. Bacon and eggs, tea, bread and butter. Yummy. **1955** H. KURNITZ *Invasion of Privacy* (1956) vi 47, I adore movie stars. Gregory Peck! Yummy! **1970** P. ZELVER *Honey Bunch* xx. 96 Thanks a lot for the lemonade. It was yummy. **1979** *Evening Standard* 18 Sept. 23/2 Mr. Zamoyski is a handsome devil himself—such a yummy photograph on the back of the jacket.

Yuma ('ju:mə), *sb.*[1] and *a.* Also 9 **Umea**. [a. Sp., ad. Pima-Papago *'yumĭ*.] **A.** *sb.* **a.** (A member of) an Indian people inhabiting south-west Arizona and the adjoining areas of Mexico and California, now officially referred to as the Quechan. **b.** The language of this people. **B.** *adj.* Of, pertaining to, or designating this people or their language.

1831 J. O. PATTIE in R. G. Thwaite *Early Western Trav.* (1905) XVIII. 188 Here we found the tribe of Umeas. **1849** A. W. WHIPPLE *Jrnl.* 1 Dec. in H. R. Schodcraft *Hist. & Stat. Information Indian Tribes* (1852) II. IV. 118 To this day among the Yumas I have never seen anger expressed. *Ibid.*, I will add a vocabulary of the Yuma (or rather Cuchan) language. **1877** H. S. GATSCHET *Indian Lang. Pacific States* 156 The term *opa*, composing several of these tribal names, is taken from the Yuma, and means man. **1891** D. G. BRINTON *Amer. Race* II. ii. 109 It has also been called..the Apache, that being the Yuma word for 'fighting men'. **1892** *Amer. Anthropologist* Oct. 326 This pamphlet..is the fourth of the author's Yuma series. **1907** [see G STRING 2 a]. **1942** *Amer. Anthropologist* July-Sept. 425 Certain structural features of the Yuma language should be outlined... Yuma has three 'parts of speech'. **1965** *Language* XLI. 305 Yuma has /a/. **1973** A. H. WHITEFORD *North Amer. Indian Arts* 13 Modeling and paddling is a technique..still used by the Papago and Yuma of Arizona. **1979** *Tucson Mag.* Apr. 27/3 In 1780 Teodoro de Croix..ordered that two new settlements of Spaniards be established among the Yuma Indians on the Lower Colorado River.

Yuma ('ju:mə), *sb.*[2] The name of *Yuma* county in north-eastern Colorado, used chiefly *attrib.* to designate the remains of a prehistoric culture discovered there, and applied esp. to a type of projectile point. Cf. FOLSOM.

1932 E. B. RENAUD in *Proc. Colorado Museum Nat. Hist.* 19 Nov. 5 Yuma and Folsom artifacts. *Ibid.*, The number and variety of artifacts of this splendid collection from the Yuma district contributed greatly to our better knowledge of the points which, in recognition, we named 'Yuma points' to distinguish them from the true Folsom type. **1948** A. L. KROEBER *Anthropol.* (rev. ed.) xvi. 684 Points called Yumas have now and then been found in Folsom association, as at Clovis. **1949** *Time* 12 Sept. 69/1 Not much is known about Yuma Man, for no Yuma skeleton has yet been found. **1960** C. WINICK *Dict. Anthropol.* 277/2 Yuma implements are unfluted.

Yuman ('ju:mən), *a.* and *sb.* [YUMA *sb.*[1]: cf. -AN.]

A. *adj.* Of, pertaining to, or designating various related Indian peoples of Arizona, Mexico and California, or the languages spoken by them. **B.** *sb.* **a.** A member of this group of peoples. **b.** A language family of Hokan stock to which the languages of these peoples belong.

1891 J. W. POWELL in *7th Ann. Rep. Bureau Amer. Ethnol.* 13 With the exception of certain small areas possessed by Shoshonean tribes, Indians of the Yuman stock occupied the Colorado River from its mouth as far up as Cataract Creek. **1901** G. W. JAMES *Indian Basketry* x. 161 The carrying frame and net of the Mohave Indians, of the Yuman stock, dwelling about the mouth of the Colorado River. **1920** *Univ. Calif. Publ. Amer. Archaeol. & Ethnol.* XVI. 478 The Yuma, who call themselves Kwichyana..are known to other Yumans by dialect variants of the same name. **1933** L. SPIER *Yuman Tribes of Gila River* 151 The Maricopa have transposed the normal Yuman word from south to west. **1950** *Nat. Hist.* Feb. 76/3 They speak essentially the same language—a dialect of the Yuman tongue. **1952** *Amer. Anthropologist* Jan.-Mar. 80 The cultivated plants and the agricultural methods of the Yumans. **1963** [see SHASTAN *a.* and *sb.*]. **1965** [see MOHAVE]. **1970** *Language* XLVI. 533 The Yuman languages..were early recognized as constituting a linguistic family. **1974** *Encycl. Brit. Micropædia* X. 845/3 The total number of Yuman peoples remaining in the 1970s..was uncertain. **1978** *Language* LIV. 219 It crops up again in Southern California, in one subgroup of the Yuman family. *Ibid.* 505 The present collection indicates that such a tradition has now also been established for Yuman, a Hokan family of Arizona, California.

yump (jʌmp), *v. slang.* [Alteration of JUMP *v.*, repr. the supposed pronunciation of it by Swedish speakers or the Norw. *jump* jump (sb.), *jumpe* jump (vb.).] *intr.* Of a rally car or its driver: to leave the ground while taking a crest at speed. So **'yumping** *vbl. sb.*

1962 *Motoring News* 22 Nov. 7 (*caption*) 'Yumping', a pastime dear to Scandinavian rallyists, was seen practised to the full for the first time in this country during the R.A.C. Rally. **1968** [see ROLL *v.*[2] 19 a]. **1968** *Sun* 12 Nov. 8/5 Yumping happens..when cars literally jump into the air. They take off when taking crests at speed.

Also as *sb.*, an instance of 'yumping' (see also quot. 1980).

1975 *Country Life* 4 Dec. 1529/2 Clark had an enormous 'yump' (Swedish rally parlance for a car leaving the ground and hurtling for some distance before landing heavily). **1980** *Sunday Express* 24 Aug. 23 (Advt.), Yump: Rally jargon for a sharp crest in the road, which causes a car to take off at speed.

yumpie ('jʌmpɪ). *colloq.* (orig. *U.S.*). Also **yump, Yumpie.** [f. the initial letters of *y*oung *u*pwardly *m*obile *p*eople: see -IE.] = YUPPIE.

1984 *Economist* 17 Mar. 40 Mr. Hart seems to have drawn much of his support from young upwardly mobile people and young urban professionals—yumps and yuppies, as they are called. **1984** *Times* 21 Mar. 14/2 Sometimes 'Yuppies' are referred to as 'Yumpies', meaning Young, upwardly-mobile people. **1984** *N.Y. Times Mag.* 25 Mar. 20 The yumpies climbing the ladder of success with great agility can be described as upscaling. **1984** *Chicago Sun-Times* 25 Mar. 7 The ultimate Yumpie status symbol is to have a child suffering flash-card burn-out.

yum-yum: see YUM *int.*

yum-yum (ˌjʌm'jʌm), *sb. slang.* [Redupl. of YUM *int.*] **a.** An action providing a pleasurable or delicious sensation; love-making; also (*Naval slang*), love-letters. Also ***yum-yum girl*** (euphem.), prostitute.

1885 *Punch* 3 Jan. 4/1 You and me's got our notions of yum-yum, as isn't fur wide o' the mark. **1939** A. HUXLEY *After Many a Summer* I. iv. 45 Enjoying what she called 'a bit of yum-yum'. **1943** HUNT & PRINGLE *Service Slang* 71 *Yum yum*, love letters. **1960** 'S. HARVESTER' *Chinese Hammer* xxv. 202 Yum-yum tarts from Hong Kong or ex-temple dancers from Java. **1962** A. BUCHWALD *How Much is that in Dollars?* 124 One of the chiefs said, 'Don't let her kid you. All her girls are really yum-yum girls from the dance halls'. **1962** *Times* 12 July 13/5 Would the sin bosun (chaplain) frown, one wonders, at hearing a love-letter described as a 'yum-yum'? **1967** S. BECKETT *Texts for Nothing* III. 86 Come, ducky, it's time for yum-yum.

b. *spec.* Tasty food (of various kinds).

1889 '*Aunt Babette's*' *Cook Book* 330 *Yum-Yums.* Grate one cocoanut, reserving the milk; one pound and a half of pulverized sugar, whites of three eggs. **1932** O. O. MCINTYRE *Another 'Odd' Book* 5 Whenever I mention a longing for such old-fashioned yum-yums as gingersnaps.. the response is immediate. **1941** J. SMILEY *Hash House Lingo* 58 *Yum-yum*, sugar.

yum-yum, *a. slang.* [f. as prec.] Excellent, first-class; delectable.

1890 BARRÈRE & LELAND *Dict. Slang* II. 428/2 *Yum-yum* (London), first-rate, elegant. **1922** JOYCE *Ulysses* 372 Howth settled for slumber tired of long days, of yumyum rhododendrons. **1962** R. PRAWER JHABVALA *Get Ready for Battle* iii. 135, I wish my cook could learn..how to make cheese pakoras like these, they are absolutely yum-yum.

Yunani (ju:'nɑ:nɪ), *a.* Also **Unani.** [a. Arab. *yūnānī*, lit. 'Greek'.] Designating a Western system of medicine (opp. AYURVEDIC *a.*). Occas. also applied to other disciplines (see quot. 1958).

1922 [see AYURVEDIC *a.*]. **1958** O. CAROE *Pathans* iii. 45 The Yunani or Greek lore which so largely influenced Islamic *literae humaniores*. **1977** *Times Lit. Suppl.* 3 June 684/2 The traditional Hindu (Ayurvedic), Muslim (Unani) and Chinese medicine... Unani is Arabic for 'Ionian' and thus declares its descent from Greek medical thought. **1979** *Social Sci. & Med.* XIII.B. 339 Yūnāni medicine which lasted for a few centuries in the court of medieval Baghdad. **1979** V. MEHTA *Mamaji* iii. 39 The Unani system, which is based on ancient Greek medicine and relies on metallic compounds.

Yunca ('jʊŋkə). Also **Yunga, Yunka.** [Amer. Sp., a. Quechua *yunca* plain, valley.]

a. The Chipayan language formerly spoken by a group of Indian peoples inhabiting the coast of Peru; = MOCHICA *sb.* **b.** **b.** A member of such a people. Also *attrib.* or as *adj.*

1853 F. L. HAWKS tr. *Von Tschudi's Peruv. Antiquities* v. 117 The Quichua language has various dialects strongly marked..the *Yunca*, in the bishopric of Truxillo. **1871**, etc. [see MOCHICA *a.* and *sb.*]. **1908** *Athenæum* 11 Apr. 447/1 Customary with the Natchez, Muizcas, Pokomames, Yuncas, and Incas of the American continent. **1950** J. A. MASON in J. H. Steward *Handbk. S. Amer. Indians* VI. 194 The *Yunca*, *Mochica*, or *Chimu* language..is practically extinct. **1954** *Internat. Jrnl. Amer. Ling.* Jan. 24 (*heading*) Yunka, language of the Peruvian coastal culture. *Ibid.*, A comparison of the Yunka language with Quechua has been made.

yuncte, obs. form of JOINT *sb.*

yund(ʒ-), yunder(ʒ-), obs. ff. YOND, YONDER.

yung, yunker, obs. ff. YOUNG, YOUNKER.

Yung Chêng (jʊŋ tʃɛŋ). Also **Yung Cheng, Yung-ching,** etc. The name of the reign of the third Chinese Emperor of the Ching dynasty (1723–35), used *attrib.* and *absol.* to denote a kind of porcelain produced during his reign, characterized by its delicate colouring.

1902 W. G. GULLAND *Chinese Porcelain* II. 384 It [is].. impossible to tell whether many of these rose pieces were made during this reign or early in the following, but they are all spoken of as Yung-ching pieces. **1906** R. L. HOBSON *Porcelain* iv. 34 The Yung-chêng porcelain has a character of its own and includes many innovations worthy of separate notice. **1908** J. F. BLACKER *Chats on Oriental China* ix. 115 The contrast between the delicacy of the detail is striking when compared with the broad treatment of the Kang-he period. On the one hand there is fine stipple work. This is Yung-ching. On the other hand there is a broad wash of colour. **1925** R. L. HOBSON *Later Ceramic Wares of China* vii. 62 (*heading*) Yung Chêng Porcelain (1723–35). **1949** G. SAVAGE *Ceramics for Collector* ii. 83 Celadons take on a bluish tinge, and obviously have some cobalt mixed with the glaze colour. Colour is applied in washes and fine, detailed drawing usually indicates Yung Chêng. **1971** R. QUEST *Death of Sinner* v. 42 'You mean it's not K'ang Hsi?' 'It's later—Yung Cheng.' **1976** SCOTT & KOSKI *Walk-In* x. 55 A wealthy importer of usually genuine Chinese *objets d'art*, mostly Yung-chêng porcelain.

yungth(e (ʒungth(e), var. YOUNGTH *Obs.*

Yunnanese (jʊnə'ni:z), *sb.* and *a.* Also 9 **Yun-Nese.** [f. *Yunnan* (see below: Chinese *Yúnnán*) + -ESE.]

A. *sb.* **a.** A native or inhabitant of Yunnan, a province in S.W. China; also *collect.*, the people of Yunnan. **b.** The dialect of Yunnan. **B.** *adj.* Of or pertaining to Yunnan.

1849 *Ann. Propagation Faith* Mar. 109 A young physician from the province of Yun-nan evinced more generosity... This young Yun-Nese had led so strange a life. **1909** *N. China Herald* 18 Sept. 671/3 With their catch crops the Yunnanese in the eastern part of the province seemed as satisfied as they were at the time before wheat took the place of the now-departed opium. **1927** *Blackw. Mag.* Mar. 308/1 He had a full knowledge of Yunnanese, but these men were Lolos from Szechuan, and understood not a word. **1933** N. WALN *House of Exile* III. ii. 200 These Yunnanese soldiers were hired henchmen that Sun Yat-sen had brought to Canton to police the city. **1948** G. H. JOHNSTON *Death takes Small Bites* iv. 85 'It's usually thronged with people,' Coates continued boredly. 'Kachins and Shans, Yunnanese, Lisus, Burmese, Miaos.' **1959** C. OGBURN *Maurauders* (1960) iii. 92 Cantonese and Yunnanese..slammed their vehicles from one gear to another with a grinding scream. **1959** *Times* 19 Mar. 14/7 It was found expedient not to have Yunnanese mules in Lucifer's section. **1964** M. A. K. HALLIDAY et al. in J. A. Fishman *Readings Sociol. of Lang.* (1968) 145 In China, you speak Cantonese if you come from Canton, Pekinese if you come from Peking and Yunnanese if you come from Yunnan. **1981** P. BARR *Chinese Alice* iv. 94 Golden Persimmon sang..and the Yunnanese watched her.

‖**yunx** (jʌŋks). Aberrant mod.L. a. Gr. ἴυγξ *iynx*, JYNX; adopted by Linnæus.

1694 RAY in *Lett. Lit. Men* (Camden) 200 The Yunx, a genuine Woodpecker, hath a tail as long [as the Cuckow] in proportion to his body, and marked with crosse-bars too.

†**yuo,** pl. yuon [OE. *ȝefá(n*: see Y- 2 and FOE], an enemy.

1340 *Ayenb.* 171 þe castel of his herte..he heþ yolde to his yuo dyadlich.

yuoȝte [Y- 4, FIGHT *v.*], fought.

1340 *Ayenb.* 176 Efterward me ssel zigge yef he ne heþ naȝt yuoȝte aye þe uondinge.

yuori(e, -ory(e, obs. forms of IVORY.

1589 LODGE *Scillaes Metam.* B 2, An yuorie shadowed front. **1593** Q. ELIZ. *Boeth.* I. pr. v. 20 Nor doo I desyre my shops walles adornid with yuory or glasse.

†**yuorþed** [Y- 4, FORTH *v.*], supplied, kept going.

1340 *Ayenb.* 186 Vor be oyle is y-uorþed þet uer ine þe lompe.

yup (jʌp), colloq. (orig. U.S.) var. of YES. Cf. YEP, dial. pron. of YES.

1906 *Cent. Mag.* Jan. 410/2 'Will you go—if I swear?' 'Yup,' said Pinchas, airing his American. **1919** G. MURRAY *Aristophanes & War Party* 36 *Demos.* You see those rows and rows of people? *Offal-monger.* Yup. **1923** E. F. WYATT *Invisible Gods* II. iv. 78 'Paul as mean as ever?' 'Yup,' replied Hancock..'and a little meaner.' **1947** [see *supercolossal* adj. s.v. SUPER- 9 a]. **1959** E. H. CLEMENTS *High Tension* iv. 63 'You're staying here, then?' 'Yup.' **1968** S. CHALLIS *Death on Quiet Beach* v. 75 'Will you pay the fine?'..'Yup.' **1978** J. IRVING *World according to Garp* xii. 232 'Is that you, Roger?' 'Yup.'

Yupik ('ju:pɪk), *a.* and *sb.* [See quot. 1951[1].]

A. *adj.* Of, pertaining to, or designating an Eskimo-Aleut language spoken in Siberia and Alaska, or the speakers of it. **B.** *sb.* This language.

1951 M. SWADESH *Internat. Jrnl. Amer. Ling.* Apr. 69/1 The phonologic material shows an unmistakable cleavage between two groups of dialects which may be conveniently called the Yupic and Inupik divisions by reference to their treatment of the root for *human being* (juk versus inuk; these are the words for *real person* in Kuskokwim and Barrow respectively). *Ibid.* 70/2 The dichotomy between Yupik and Inupik is clear and geographically abrupt. *Ibid.*, We find nothing in the [Wales] dialect which minimizes the depth of its separation from Yupik Eskimo. **1967** W. H. OSWALT *Alaskan Eskimos* p. xiv, In Alaska two languages, Inupik and Yupik are spoken. *Ibid.* iv. 115 The Yupik speakers..would be expected to have had a greater long-term stability than the Inuit. **1974** *Encycl. Brit. Macropædia* VI. 963/2 In 1961 a program was started..with the active participation of Yupik Eskimos, for working out a systematic Eskimo orthography in the Roman alphabet. *Ibid.*, Greenlandic *ûvoq*..is related to the Asian Yupik form *ugu-*. **1977** *New Yorker* 20 June 55/2 The big river delivers the wood to the Yupik Esimos of the western coast. **1980** M. E. Krauss *Alaska Native Languages* App. ii. 91 There is..the well known sharp division between Yupik and what we in Alaska usually call Inupiaq. *Ibid.* 103 With a dense and increasing population, almost entirely Yupik, the Yupik language remained..strong.

yupon, variant of YAPON.

yuppie (ˈjʌpɪ). *colloq.* (orig. *U.S.*). Also **Yuppie, yuppy.** [Orig. f. the initial letters of *y*oung *u*rban *p*rofessional; now also freq. interpreted as *y*oung *up*wardly mobile *p*rofessional (or *p*erson, *p*eople): see YUMPIE and -IE.] A jocular term for a member of a socio-economic group comprising young professional people working in cities. Also *attrib.* Cf. YUMPIE.

1984 Piesman & Hartley *(title)* The yuppie handbook. **1984** [see YUMPIE]. **1984** *Times* 21 Mar. 14/2 A new term has been introduced into the American political lexicon... It is 'Yuppie', which stands for Young, urban professional people. **1984** *Observer* 8 Apr. 12/1 We have got to break this yuppie image. **1984** *Guardian* 22 Oct. 6/6 The yuppies themselves, in the 25–34 age group, supported Senator Gary Hart in the primaries. **1984** *Washington Post* 29 Mar. VA1/5 The two yuppy, upwardly mobile professional capitals of Virginia. **1985** *Investors Chron.* 8–14 Nov. 8/1 It also announced that it will change its name to Next—the yuppy clothes-chain responsible for its meteoric rise.

Hence **ˈyuppi(e)ness; ˈyuppyish** *a.*

1984 *N.Y. Times* 28 May 22/6 Yuppiness depends on the prestige of gaining; happiness on the satisfaction of giving. **1986** *Courier-Mail* (Brisbane) 8 Jan. 5/4 There is a serious side to yuppieness, as advertisers are discovering. **1986** *Financial Times* 22 Apr. 25/1 There is nothing yuppyish about the Folkes Group. **1987** *Athletics Today* Apr. 33/1 The area, fast becoming the hot-bed of 'Yuppiness', was first vacated several years ago when the ships left London's docks. **1988** *Fortune* 15 Feb. 124/3 This declaration points to upscale yuppyish types plainly able to afford $100 a week.

ˈyuppiedom. *colloq.* (orig. *U.S.*). Also **yuppydom.** [f. YUPPIE + -DOM.] The condition or fact of being a yuppie; the domain of yuppies; yuppies as a class.

1984 *MacNeil-Lehrer NewsHour* 4 June, What a curve, that from hippiedom to Yuppiedom. Is it really possible that these Yuppies are the same people who were the counterculture? **1984** *Washington Post* 20 June A21/5 Yuppiedom does not conduce to a realistic view of the human condition or of American society. **1985** *Sunday Tel.* 26 May 11/6 Occasionally they [*sc.* Yuppies] are overcome by the instinct to perpetuate Yuppiedom with their little Yuppies. **1987** *New Musical Express* 14 Feb. 42/4 Real yuppiedom is an absence more than a presence—an absence of social conscience, of tolerance and of depth. **1988** *Guardian* 13 Apr. 20/2 'There was a great rush into the City in the early to mid-Eighties,' reflects Mark, 'a great boom in yuppiedom.'

ˈyuppieism. *colloq.* (orig. *U.S.*). Also **yuppie-ism, yuppyism.** [f. YUPPIE + -ISM.] The state of being a yuppie; behaviour characteristic of yuppies. Also, a yuppyish phrase, expression, etc.

1984 *New Republic* 6 Aug. 11/2 Neoliberalism, generational politics, faith in the 'future', yuppie-ism. **1984** *Washington Post* 21 Oct. C3/4 Baez says she's sick to death of the '60s. Eldridge Cleaver is a Republican and Jerry Rubin has traded in Yippieism for Yuppieism. **1985** *Christian Science Monitor* 17 Jan. 8/2 All who sit here silent,..betray the oppressed... It is institutionalized yuppyism. **1987** *N.Y. Times Mag.* 5 July 8/5, I played second base for Our Lady of the Assumption... I don't deal in yuppie-isms.

yuppifiˈcation. *colloq.* (orig. *U.S.*). Also **yuppiefication.** [f. YUPPIE + -FICATION; cf. GENTRIFICATION.] The action or process by which an area, building, clothing, etc., becomes or is rendered characteristic of or suitable for yuppies. (Usu. *disparaging.*)

1984 *Time* 9 Jan. 66 Some signs of imminent Yupification [*sic*]: forced relocation of candy stores and laundromats, the proliferation of gourmet-food stores, [etc.]. **1985** *Los Angeles Times* 10 Mar. 76/5 The association with three Japanese masters brings conflicting thoughts. There are still places for the loner artist to escape 'yuppification'. **1987** *Independent* 17 Sep. 18/2 What Dickens is describing, I suddenly realised, is yuppification. The trendies were moving in. **1987** *Daily Tel.* 26 Sept. 9/3 At a pre-conference meeting of Labour's National Executive, Left-wing critics such as Dennis Skinner scornfully dismissed what they describe as the 'Yuppiefication' of the party. **1988** *Christian Science Monitor* 4 Feb. 23/1 In some ways the change reflects a trend—'yuppification' or 'gentrification' which is transforming many inner cities in the West.

Also **ˈyuppify** *v. trans.*, to subject to yuppification; **ˈyuppified** *ppl. a.*

1984 *Listener* 8 Mar. 27/1 They get into a district before anyone else and really yuppify it. **1984** *Adweek* 17 Dec. 42/2 The marketer's never-never land between the 12-to-18-year-old MTV set and the yuppified Rolling Stone audience. **1985** *Washington Post* 13 Feb. B4/1 A yuppified suit that converts to something sexier for after-hours wear. **1986** *Daily News* (N.Y.) 23 May 41/1 Betty gets (shudder) yuppified. **1987** *Observer* 16 Aug. 3/4 Their 'bashers' (shacks) will be forcibly removed by police to make way for developers who want to 'yuppify' the Charing Cross area. **1987** *Listener* 24 Sept. 38/2 The dramatist sketches a new breed of yuppified 'social managers', obsessed with image-building and politicking to the exclusion of..justice.

yur, yure, obs. forms of YOUR.

Yurak (ˈjʊəræk). [Native name.] = NENETS (see quot. 1972). Also *Comb.*, as ***Yurak-Samoyed(e)***.

1882 H. Lansdell *Through Siberia* I. viii. 103 Reclus.. speaks of the Yurak-Samoyedes as still practising their bloody rites. **1911** *Daily News* 3 Nov. 1 Great praise is due to the Russian Red Cross Society for the noble way in which the women of this corps work among the revolting and diseased Yuraks. **1939** L. H. Gray *Foundations of Lang.* 369 The languages of the Uralic family are as follows ..*Samoyede* group: Yurak, Yenisei-Samoyede, [etc.]. **1952** *Trans. Philol. Soc.* 118 Yurak-Samoyede *paju, pal'* 'close, thick'. **1954**, etc. [see NENETS]. **1964** tr. *Levin & Potapov's Peoples of Siberia* 547 Before the Revolution the Russians called the Nentsy Samoyeds or Yuraks. **1972** *Language* XLVIII. 208 Calling the language and people 'Yurak' is an anachronism. Since 1917 a native self-designation has come into use in the Soviet Union, which I render as 'Nenets'. 'Yurak' arose from a term applied to the eastern Nenets by their Enets and Nganasan neighbours. **1975** G. F. Cushing tr. *Hajdu's Finno-Ugrian Languages & Peoples* iii. 216 The Nenets are generally termed Yurak-Samoyeds.

yure (jʊə(r)). *Sc.* and *north. dial.* Forms: 5 **ȝowre,** 7– **yower, ure, ewr,** 8–9 **yewer, ewer,** 9 **yure (yuer, yoo(e)r, yowr,** etc.). [Obscurely connected with ON. *júgr* (Norw. *juver*, MSw. *juver, juger*, Sw. *jufver*, Da. *yver*), f. unexplained variant of the Teut. stem represented by OE. *úder* UDDER.] An udder.

1483 *Cath. Angl.* 427/2 A ȝowre, *vber.* **1641** Best *Farm. Bks.* (Surtees) 8 It is goode to admonish the shepheard to pluck the wolle away from the yower of the ewe, thereby to make more way for weake lambes to finde the pappe. *Ibid.* 80 If an ewe bee kittle on her yower, or unkinde to her lambe. **1691** Ray *N.C. Words* (ed. 2), *Ure*, udder. **1787** Grose *Prov. Gloss.*, *Ewer*, an udder. **1825** Jamieson, *Ure*, the dug or udder of an animal, particularly of a sheep or cow. *Ibid.*, *Ure-lock*, the name given to the locks of wool growing round the udder of a sheep, which are pulled off when it is near lambing-time. **1828** *Craven Gloss.*, *Yower-joint*, the joint near the udder or thigh of the horse, opposite the hock or hough.

yurn, yurne, yurt: see YEARN *v.*[1], YERN *v.*, YERNE *adv.*, YOURT.

Yurok (ˈjʊərɒk), *sb.* and *a.* Also 9 **Euroc, Youruk.** [a. Karok *yúruk* (a considerable distance) downriver; cf. *yurúk'varara* Yurok Indian, lit. 'downriver person'.]

A. *sb.* **a.** (A member of) an Indian people of northern California. **b.** The language of this people, distantly related to Algonquian and Wiyot. **B.** *adj.* Of, pertaining to, or designating this people or their language.

1851 [see KAROK]. **1872** *Overland Monthly* Apr. 326/2, I have seen a half-dozen tatterdemalion Eurocs..come rushing down through the *chaparral*. **1875** H. H. Bancroft *Native Races Pacific States* III. 641 On the lower Klamath, the Euroc language prevails. **1904** *Univ. Calif. Publ. Amer. Anthrop. & Ethnol.* II. iii. 95 The belief in a previous world ..is not uncommon. The Torint of the Eskimo..the Waghe of the Yurok. **1913** *Amer. Anthropologist* XV. 621 Our knowledge of Wiyot and Yurok is still very incomplete. **1921** [see CULTURALLY *adv.*]. **1946** L. Bloomfield in H. Hoijer et al. *Ling. Structures Native America* 85 Two languages of California, Wiyot and Yurok, have been suspected of kinship with Algonquian. **1954** E. A. Hoebel *Law of Primitive Man* ii. 25 An aggrieved Yoruk who felt he had a legitimate claim engaged the legal services of two nonrelatives from a community other than his own. **1962** [see KAROK]. **1973** A. H. Whiteford *N. Amer. Indian Arts* 47 Half-twist overlay was used by the Yurok..for fine flexible mats. **1977** R. Holland *Self & Social Context* ii. 40 Witness the astonishingly beautiful analogy between the oral anxiety of the Yurok people and the uncertainty of the salmon run on which they depend as a culture. **1981** A. B. Kehoe *N. Amer. Indians* vii. 376/2 Macro-Algonkian is represented by two language isolates, Yurok..and Wiyot.

Yurrup (ˈjʌrəp). Repr. a supposed U.S. pronunc. of *Europe*.

1883 *National Police Gaz.* 17 Mar. 3/1 The entire court of shyster lawyers, wives and contractors' daughters who have been to Yurrup. **1960** N. Mitford *Don't tell Alfred* iii. 34 There are the [American] business men trying to make a better position for themselves at home as experts on Yurrup. **1980** R. McCrum *In Secret State* xiii. 123 American students enthusing about Yurrup.

‖**yurt** (jʊət). Forms: 8–9 **jourt,** 9 **jurt, y(o)urte, yurta, yuert, yort,** 9–**yurt, yurta,** 8– **yourt.** [ad. Russ. *yurta*, through F. *yourte* or G. *jurte*.] A semi-subterranean dwelling or hut of the natives of northern and central Asia, usually formed of timber covered with earth or turf. Also, a circular skin- or felt-covered tent, with collapsible frame, used by the nomadic peoples of Siberia and Central Asia. Also *transf.* and *attrib.*

1784 King *Cook's Voy. Pacific* III. 9 May 1779, Natcheekin is a very inconsiderable *ostrog*, having only one log-house, the residence of the *Toion*; five *balagans*, and one *jourt*. **1780** Coxe *Russ. Discov.* 259 Six or seven of these huts or yourts make a village. **1858** Anne Bowman *Yng. Exiles* xii. 154 They made no scruple to enter the warm, though uninviting *yurte*. **1865** Tylor *Early Hist. Man.* viii. 207 Stone knives..have been found in the high northeast of Siberia, on the site of deserted yourts of modern date. **1883** S. W. Williams *Middle Kingdom* (rev. ed.) I. iv. 206 A first-class *yurt* is by no means an uncomfortable dwelling, with its furniture, lining, shrine, and hot kettle in the centre. **1899** Baring-Gould *Furze Bloom* iii. 29 A Khan's yourte on the steppes of Central Asia. **1904** H. G. C. Swayne *Through Highlands Siberia* vi. 98 Occasional groups of true Kalmak huts, extinguisher-shaped,..felt 'yurtas', which are used by the richer Kalmuks, though I believe they are properly the Kirghiz type of dwelling. **1911** P. T. Etherton *Across Roof of World* iv. 60 The habitations of the Kirghiz are the 'yurts', or 'khirgas', constructed of felt on a wooden framework, with an opening at the top to let out smoke from the fire lighted in the centre. **1924** *Blackw. Mag.* Aug. 255/2 We had seen little camps of their Yurtas, large black tents. **1940** *Antiquity* XIV. 410 Dwelling of the semi-dugout type. This was probably a conical structure similar to a yurt. **1953** J. Masters *Lotus & Wind* xx. 247 Groups of the round black felt tents called yurts dotted the grass. **1974** *Publishers Weekly* 4 Mar. 5/2 (Advt.), Build a yurt. The round house you can make... It's a portable dwelling for people and pets. .. Inspired by the ancient Mongolian felt-and-hide structures, the yurt is the newest thing in housing. **1978** A. Grey *Chinese Assassin* ii. 38 The yurt camps..were now quickly dispersing..across the steppes. **1979** J. Halifax *Shamanic Voices* (1980) ii. 49 Kyzlasov lived a distance from his village..in an isolated and impoverished yurta constructed of logs and surrounded by birch trees. **1981** *Nordic Skiing* Jan. 51/2 Skiing the system of five yurts set five miles apart in the Sawtooth Mountains is what Leonard Expeditions is all about.

Yuruk (ˈjʊərʊk), *sb.* (*a.*). [a. Turk. *yürük* (also used) = nomad.] (A member of) a nomadic people inhabiting Anatolia. Also *attrib.* or as *adj.*

1869 H. F. Tozer *Researches Highlands of Turkey* I. i. 13 In one of these glades we found a tribe of Yuruk with their flocks. **1896** D. G. Hogarth *Wandering Scholar in Levant* iii. 53 The 'Turk', most rightly so called, is the despised *Yuruk*, the 'wanderer', a name applied to the half-settled population, roaming in summer.., collected in the winter into villages. **1907** G. Bell *Let.* 1 May (1927) I. xi. 233 So we rode back along the beautiful grassy shores of the lake, where the Yuruks were watching their flocks and herds. **1959** *Listener* 6 Aug. 221/1 Three weeks among the Yuruks. **1963** *Times* 9 May 14/6 The Yürüks are a tribe of nomads who spend their winter in the equable south of Anatolia and move up to the plateaux and highlands for the summer. **1974** *Encycl. Brit. Micropædia* X. 848/2 *Yü rük rugs*, handwoven by nomadic people in various parts of Anatolia. .. Rugs from Eastern Anatolia, many of them Kurdish rugs ..but classed as Yürük, show a wide range of rich and unusual colour shades. **1983** J. Thompson *Carpet Magic* 19/2 *(caption)* One member of a Turkish nomad, or Yuruk, family on migration.

yus, *adv.* Also **yhus** (*once*), **yuss.** Repr. *dial.* and non-Standard form of YES.

1828 W. Carr *Dial. Craven* (ed. 2) II. 279 *Yus*, Yes. **1888** S. O. Addy *Gloss. Words Sheffield* 292 *Yus, adv.*, yes. **1890** Kipling *Many Inventions* (1893) 284 Ho yuss! 'Taint much though, is it? **1898** J. D. Brayshaw *Slum Silhouettes* 15 'Yus!' responded his wife. **1934** J. Franklyn *This Gutter Life* xx. 159 Yhus, movin' aht, are yer? Norra bad flet. **1968** C. M. Vines *Little Nut-Brown Man* i. 32 'Please, may I ask you something?' 'Yus!' said he [*sc.* Lord Beaverbrook], employing, in good humour, this cheerful Canadianism.

yus, ȝus, obs. forms of YES.

yused, ME. pa. pple. of USE *v.*

yusho (ˈjuːʃəʊ). *Path.* [Jap., f. *yu* oil + *sho* disease.] A disease characterized by the development of brown staining of the skin and severe acne, caused by the ingestion of polychlorinated biphenyls.

1969 Goto & Higuchi in *Fukuoka Acta Med.* LX. 409 *(heading)* The symptomatology of yusho (chlorobiphenyls poisoning) in dermatology. *Ibid.*, We thought its cause might be rice oil... The case has been called Yusho. **1973** G. L. Waldbott *Health Effects of Environmental Pollutants* xviii. 226/1 In 1968 about 1000 persons in southern Japan developed darkened skin..and severe acne... The illness was named 'Yusho', or rice oil disease, because the patients had eaten food cooked with contaminated rice oil. **1977** *Lancet* 22 Jan. 176/1 Chisato Hirayama provides a chapter on the clinical aspects of *yusho* (oil disease), the important skin symptoms being reviewed separately.

yust, obs. f. JOUST *v.*[1]

Yusufzai (ˈjuːsʊfzaɪ), *sb.* and *a.* Also **Yusafzai;** 9 **Eusofzye, Eusafzai,** etc. [a. Pers., f. *yūsuf* Joseph + *-zāī* bringing forth.] **A.** *sb.* (A member of) a Pathan tribal group inhabiting the North-West Frontier Province of Pakistan. **B.** *adj.* Of, pertaining to, or designating this people.

1815 M. Elphinstone *Caubul* iii. i. 328 The Eusofzyes are a very numerous tribe. **1838** in *Parl. Papers 1839* XL. 29 Shah Shooja-ool-Moolk disclaims all title..to..Peshaur, with the Eusefzye territory. **1857** S. Cotton *Nine Years on North-West Frontier* (1868) ix. 220 The column placed under his orders on the Euzofzaie Border. **1886** [see -OLOGY, OLOGY 2]. **1887** Kipling *Plain Tales from Hills* (1888) 24 A Eusufzai horse-thief. **1899** *Dict. Pathan Tribes* 234/1 *Yusufzai* (73,000), a great group of Pathan tribes which includes those of the Black Mountain, the Bunerwals, the Swatis, the people of Dir and the Panjkora valley, and the inhabitants of the Yusufzai plain in British territory. **1900** R. Warburton *Eighteen Years in Khyber* v. 52 Mukarrub Khan of Panjtar..was another pleasing character connected with Yusufzai politics. **1940** P. Sykes *Hist. Afghanistan* I. xix. 290 In the autumn of that same year Babur..decided on an expedition against the Yusufzais. **1953** O. Caroe *Soviet Empire* v. 86 Another Yusufzai *maira*. **1958** —— *Pathans* i. 14 A Yusufzai or a Khalil..if he is asked who he is, will always reply, 'I am an Afghan.' **1978** 'M. M. Kaye' *Far Pavilions* xi. 170 The men of his own troop were drawn largely from the Border tribes: Yusafzai, Orakzai and

Khattak. **1983** J. C. GRIFFITHS *Queen of Spades* ii. 26 Hussein Rahman, a Yusufzai Pathan.

yut(e, ȝut(e, obs. ff. YET.

yuþe, obs. f. YOUTH.

yuu, obs. f. YOU.

Yuvaraja (jʊvə'rɑːdʒə). Also **Jubaraj, Yuvaraj, Yuveraj, Yuvraj.** [a. Hindi, f. Skr. *yuva-* young + *rājā*: see RAJA, RAJAH.] The male heir to an Indian state or principality; the crown prince.

1893 R. LETHBRIDGE *Golden Bk. India* p. xv, In some of the Orissa Tributary Mahâls..the heir-apparent is styled *Jubaraj* or *Yuvaraj*. **1916** N. SINGH *King's Indian Allies* I. xii. 150 To distinguish the heir-apparent from the other sons, it is customary to call the former by some distinctive title, *Yuvaraja* in the case of Hindus. **1931** *Times of India* 6 Nov. 5/4 On May 28, 1930, he was received, with the Yuvraj, at Court at Buckingham Palace. **1937** W. H. SAUMAREZ SMITH *Let.* 3 Jan. in *Young Man's Country* (1977) ii. 50 On the 30th, I saw Prince Jaya's father, the Yuvaraja. **1953** E. M. FORSTER *Hill of Devi* 161 Vikky, henceforward to be referred to as the Yuvraj (Crown Prince), had now developed into a charming and intelligent youth. **1978** 'M. M. KAYE' *Far Pavilions* iii. 54 The young crown-prince, Lalji, Yuveraj of Gulkote. **1982** K. SINGH *Heir Apparent* i. 1 The birth of a Yuvaraj (heir apparent) was always a matter for rejoicing.

yuy(e, yve, obs. ff. IVY.

yuzbashi (juːz'bɑːʃɪ). Also **Yuzbachi, Yuz-bashi, Yuzbashi.** [Turk. *yüzbaşı*, lit. 'one who is head of a hundred', f. *yüz* hundred + *baş* head.] A captain in the Turkish army; in the Turkish navy, a first lieutenant. Cf. BIMBASHI.

1876 [see BIMBASHI]. **1907** *Blackw. Mag.* June 806/2 Our procession was headed by a Yuz-bashi. **1908** M. PICKTHALL *Children of Nile* xxxiii. 268 Word of his coolness during the bombardment having reached the ear of power, he found himself raised to the rank of yuzbashi and honoured with a small command. **1920** *Glasgow Herald* 21 Jan. 4 The author ..is an umquile Yuzbashi of the Imperial Ottoman Naval College. **1969** R. MILLAR *Kut* v. 87 The Turkish *yuzbashi* (equivalent to a captain, literally means the commander of 100 troops) was ushered into the office still blindfolded.

‖**yūzen** ('juːzɛn). Also **yuzen** and with capital initial. The name of Miyazaki *Yūzen*-sai (fl. mid-18th cent.), Japanese inventor of a technique of dyeing silk fabric in which rice-paste is applied to areas which are not to be dyed, used *attrib.* and *absol.* with reference to this process and the designs produced. Also **yūzen-zome** (see quot. 1983).

1902 [see HABUTAI]. **1911** *Encycl. Brit.* XV. 183 The difference between the results of the ordinary and the yūzen process of dyeing is, in fact, the difference between a stencilled sketch and a finished picture. **1958** K. NOMACHI *Jap. Textiles* 21 Yuzen pattern is the design printed by the Yuzen process, with beautiful and graceful flowers and birds ..as the motifs. The Yuzen process is of three kinds: Yuzen proper, hand painting, and stencil printing. **1964** NEWMAN & RYERSON *Jap. Art* x. 77 *Yūzen zome*, a method of producing elaborate multi-colour designs by starch dyeing. Came into vogue in the Edo period. **1968** G. T. WEBB tr. *Seiroku's Arts Japan* II. 214/2 The design of this *furisode*.. a garment traditionally worn only by young girls, is executed in a variety of techniques, including *yūzen* and *shibori* dyeing and gold appliqué. In *yūzen-zome*, a hand-painted dyeing method, the patterns are first outlined with a color-resist of rice paste applied with a paper funnel or a chopstick-like wooden implement, and later filled in with dyes of any color desired. **1980** *Textile Designs Japan* (rev. ed.) I. 21 The invention of a new starch-resist dyeing technique, known as *yūzen*, during this period..led to undreamed of achievements in the dyeing of free-style graphic designs. **1983** Y. TAZAWA *Biogr. Dict. Jap. Art* 652 During and after the Genroku era..stencil dyeing was developed and became popular, for a large number of *yūzen* designs are mentioned. ..From amongst these dyes, the term *yūzen-zome* came to be used thereafter to refer to *all* such pattern dyeing and it is still used thus to the present day.

yvel, -ll(e, yven, obs. ff. EVIL, IVY.

yvenkessyd, -kised, -quyst, ME. pa. pple. of VANQUISH.

yver(e, -ery(e, obs. ff. IVORY.

†**yveresce.** *Obs.* [a. OF. (F.) *ivresse*, f. *ivre*:—pop. L. **ēbriu-s*, for *ēbriu-s* drunk: see -ESS.] Drunkenness.

c **1430** *Pilgr. Lyf Manhode* III. xliii. (1869) 159 Twey wombes..Of whiche yueresce [*gloss* drunkeshipe] is that oon seid. And that oother the gulf that to ete is euere redy.

†**yverysshe,** *a. Obs.* [f. *yvery*, IVORY + -ISH.] Of or like ivory.

1530 PALSGR. 330/2 Yverysshe,..*eburnyn*.

†**yves.** *Obs.* Also 8 **ives.** = VIVES.

1578 H. WOTTON *Courtlie Controv.* 301 To the ende the horse by his continuall trembling mighte seeme to haue the Yues. **1753** BARTLET *Gentl. Farriery* 104 The vives or ives differs from the strangles only in this [etc.].

†**yvewdid,** ME. pa. pple. of VOID *v.*

yvi(e, yvle, yvoire, yvor(e, -ie, etc., obs. ff. IVY, EVIL, IVORY.

†**yvitaillid** [VICTUAL *v.*], supplied with victuals.

1422 YONGE tr. *Secr. Secr.* 215 That thou be..well y-vitaillid.

†**yvolvuld** [Y- 4, FULFIL *v.*], fulfilled.

c **1330** *Hymn* in *Rel. Ant.* I. 87 Y-volvuld ys Davidthes sawe.

Yvorne (iː'vɔːn). The name of a village in the Vaud canton of S.W. Switzerland, used *absol.* to designate a white wine produced in the region.

1871 J. MURRAY *Handbk. for Travellers in Switzerland* (ed. 14) p. xxxii, *Yvorne* is considered the best Swiss white wine. **1888** [see CORTAILLOD]. **1935** A. L. SIMON *Wines & Liqueurs* 61 *Yvorne*, one of the best Swiss white wines from Aigle, in the Upper Rhône Valley. **1962** *Economist* 29 Dec. 1283/1 The best whites are perhaps Yvorne and Dézaley. **1980** G. GREENE *Doctor Fischer of Geneva* ix. 54 Beside every plate was a bottle of good Yvorne.

y-vowted, ME. pa. pple. of VAULT *v.*[1]

yvsed, yvzed, ME. pa. pple. of USE *v.*

1340 *Ayenb.* 115 Þine greate guodnesses þet ich habbe eche daye onderuonge, huyche ich habbe kueadliche yvzed. *c* **1394** *P. Pl. Crede* 510 And also Domynikes dedes weren deruelich y-vsed.

yvy, yvyl, obs. forms of IVY, EVIL.

yvyned, obs. form of VINNIED, mouldy.

14.. *Voc.* in Wr.-Wülcker 597/2 *Mucidus*, yvyned.

yw, obs. form of YOU.

†**ywaged** [Y- 4, WAGE *v.*], hired.

1393 LANGL. *P. Pl.* C. XXIII. 261 Bote hij beon nempned in þe numbre of hem þat ben ywaged.

ywalked, ME. pa. pple. of WALK *v.*[2]

ywalled, obs. f. WALLED *ppl. a.*

ywalwed, pa. pple. of WALLOW *v.*[1]

ywar, obs. form of AWARE.

ywarded, ywareschid, ywarnist, ywarred, ywasche, ywasshe(n, ywasted, ywatert, -eryd, ywedded, ME. pa. pples. of WARD *v.*[1], WARISH *v.*, WARNISH, WAR *v.*[1], WASH, WASTE, WATER, WED *vbs.*

ywel(l, obs. forms of EVIL.

†**ywelde,** variant of I-WELDE *v. Obs.*, to carry into effect.

1387 TREVISA *Higden* (Rolls) VII. 491 He..assaieþ dedes þat he may nouȝt y-welde.

ywemmed, ME. pa. pple. of WEM *v.*

ywend(e, ywent(e, ywenkused, ywept, ME. pa. pples. of WEND *v.*, VANQUISH *v.*, WEEP *v.*

ywende, var. I-WENDE *v. Obs.*, to go, progress.

13.. *R. Gloucester's Chron.* (Rolls) 4063 Ȝif we in þisse manere wendeþ [*MS. a* ywendeþ] we ne fayleþ on none wyse þat we ne wolleþ abbe þe maistrie. **1393** LANGL. *P. Pl.* C. IX. 62 Ich..wol y-wende To pylgrimages, as palmers don pardon to wynne.

ywer, ME. var. of AWARE *a.*, wary.

1340 *Ayenb.* 100 By wys and y-wer.

†**ywerche** [Y- 3 c], var. I-WURCHE *v. Obs.*

ywerred, ywess(h)e, ywet(te [Y- 4], ME. pa. pples. of WAR *v.*[1], WASH *v.*, WET *v.*

ywete, var. I-WITE *v.*[1] *Obs.*, to know; to preserve, keep.

1387 TREVISA *Higden* (Rolls) VII. 59 Ȝif any good counsaile..were i-ȝeve, anon enemyes schulde wite [*MS. a* ywete] for al. *a* **1400** in *Eng. Gilds* (1870) 360 þ[t] þe seal by-fore y-seyd shal be y-weted vnder þre heuedes.

ywetered, yweved, ywexed, ME. pa. pples. of WATER *v.*, WEVE *v.*, WAX *v.*

†**y'whelped,** *pa. pple.* and *ppl. a. Obs.* [pa. pple. of WHELP *v.* or f. WHELP *sb.*[1]: see Y- 4 and 5.]

a. Brought forth as whelps.

1398 TREVISA *Barth. De P.R.* XVIII. xxiv. (Bodl. MS.), Þe sonner þei haue here sight whan þey beþ ywhelpid.

b. In kindle with whelps.

a **1400** *Octouian* 433 A grysly best, A greet y-whelpyd lyonesse.

†**ywhere,** *adv. Obs.* Forms: 1 **ᵹehwær,** 2 **ȝewer, uwer,** 3 **ihwar(e, ihwær, ihwer, iwar(e, iwære, iwere.** [OE. *ᵹehwǽr*: see Y- 2 b and WHERE.] Everywhere.

Beowulf 526 Ðeah þu heaðoræsa ᵹehwær dohte. *c* **1000** ÆLFRIC *Hom.* I. 2 His ᵹebyrd and goodnys sind ᵹehwær cuþe. *a* **1175** *Cott. Hom.* 231 His under-þeoden ȝewer on his cyne rice wuneden. *a* **1200** *Moral Ode* 88 Þe þe deð godes wille uwer he mei him finden. *c* **1205** LAY. 260 Hit iwerð þere swa hit deð wel iwere [*c* **1275** iware]. *a* **1240** *Ureisun* in *O.E. Hom.* I. 189 Þet he wule þet al þine wil ihwer beo iforþed. *a* **1250** *Owl & Night.* 216 Þe Nihtegale were al ware heo hedde ileorned wel ihware [*Cott. MS.* aiware].

ywhet(t, ME. pa. pple. of WHET *v.*

†**ywhether** [Y- 2 b], obs. var. WHETHER.

c **1400** *26 Pol. Poems* 113 Ywhether þou art alone, withoute mene?

ywhyngged [Y- 4], ME. var. WINGED.

ywil(le, var. I-WILL *Obs.*, will, desire.

12.. *Moral Ode* 14 in *E.E.P.* (1862) 22 Þe muchel folȝeþ his y-wil him sulfne he bi-swikeð. *a* **1275** *Prov. Ælfred* 423 in *O.E. Misc.* (1872) 129 Ich telle him for a dote, þat sait al is y-wille, þanne he sulde ben stille.

ywilned, ME. pa. pple. of WILN *v.*

ywis, ywiss(e: see IWIS.

†**ywist,** pa. pple. of I-WITE, YWITE *v.*[1] *Obs.*

1340–70 *Alex. & Dind.* 582 Of richesse & of renoun romme be ȝe kidde, & ben baldere y-wist þan any burn elles.

ywite, var. I-WITE *v.*[1] *Obs.*

ywitted, ME. form of WITTED.

1393 LANGL. *P. Pl.* C. XII. 235 Ryght wel ywittede men.

ywive, var. I-WIVE *v. Obs.*, to marry.

ywon(e, ywonne(n, ywonde(d, ywonden, ywon(e)d, -et, ywonte, -wonyd, yworewid, ME. pa. pples. of WIN *v.* (cf. I-WIN(NE *v.*), WOUND *v.*, WIND *v.*, WON *v.* (see WONT *a.*), WORRY *v.*

ywori, obs. form of IVORY.

†**yworred, yworschiped, -wor(þ)sshipid,** etc., ME. pa. pples. of WAR *v.*[1], WORSHIP *v.*

yworþ(e, -worth(e, -wourthe, var. I-WORTH *v. Obs.*

1422 YONGE tr. *Secr. Secr.* 217 The chylde wox,..but for no-thynge he hit myght lerne;..And ther-for they lettyn hym y-wourthe.

ywounded, ywounden, obs. pa. pples. of WOUND, WIND *vbs.*

ywoven, obs. pa. pple. of WEAVE *v.*

1610 HOLLAND *Camden's Brit.* I. 285 Faire Reading towne,..where Cloth's ywoven be.

ywowed, ywoxe, obs. pa. pples. of WOO, WAX *vbs.*

ywrapped, ywrapt, obs. pa. pple. of WRAP *v.*

c **1400** MAUNDEV. ix. (E.E.T.S.) 39 In þat same cloth so ywrapped the aungeles beren hire body to the mount Synay. *a* **1425** *Cursor M.* 23324 (Trin.) Iwrapped alle in gome & gle. **1572** GASCOIGNE *Voy. Holland* Wks. 1907 I. 358 A wretch ywrapt in wroth. **1583** MELBANCKE *Philotimus* I iv b, Pills ywrapt in sugar. **1642** H. MORE *Song of Soul* I. I. i, Nor Ladies loves, nor Knights brave Martiall deeds, Ywrapt in rolls of hid Antiquity.

ywraþþed, ywreȝe, ywreke, obs. pa. pples. of WRATH, WRY, WREAK *vbs.*

†**ywrit,** *pa. pple. Obs.* Forms: 1 **ᵹewriten,** 2–4 **iwrite(n,** 3–4 **ywrite, ywryte,** 4 **iwritten,** (**i-, ywrete,** 5 **iwreten**), 5–7 **ywrit.** [OE. *ᵹewriten*, pa. pple. of (*ᵹe*)*wrītan* to WRITE.] Written.

c **1000** *Ags. Gosp.* Luke x. 26 Hwæt is ᵹewriten on þære æ? *c* **1175** *Lamb. Hom.* 11 Þe þridde godes heste was iwriten inne þa table. *c* **1200** *Moral Ode* 118 (Trin. Coll. MS.) Swo he hit iseie aboc iwrite. **1297** R. GLOUC. (Rolls) 1901 An aungel he sey þat huld an croiz & þer on ywrite was lo þis. *c* **1315** SHOREHAM v. 320 Þer-bye we mowe wel y-wyte, þaȝ þer be nauȝt of y-wryte, þat cryst hym self was þere. **1377** LANGL. *P. Pl.* B. XI. 220 Sum wordes I fynde ywryten were of faithes techynge. **1387** TREVISA *Higden* (Rolls) V. 15 Whanne bookes of oure byleve were y-wrete. *Ibid.* VIII. 41 Foure famous men discreved his lyf and his dedes as it is i-written in his lyf. **1422** YONGE tr. *Secr. Secr.* 149 In the thyrde boke of kynges we fyndyth y-writ that [etc.]. *c* **1450** *Merlin* 279 Whan it was I-wreten. **1642** H. MORE *Song of Soul* I. III. xxvi, On which in golden letters be ywrit These words.

ywroȝt, ywroht: see YWROUGHT.

ywroken (ɪ'rəʊk(ə)n), *pa. pple. arch.* Forms: 1 **ᵹewrecen,** 3 **iwreken,** 4 **iwrokin,** 5 **ywrekyd, ywroke,** 4– **ywroken.** [OE. *ᵹewrecen*, pa. pple. of (*ᵹe*)*wrecan*: see Y- 4 and WREAK *v.*] Avenged; taken vengeance upon, punished.

c **893** ÆLFRED *Oros.* I. xiv, Ær hie þæt ᵹewrecen hæfden. *c* **1250** *Gen. & Ex.* 1856 Symeon and leui..hauen here sister ðor i-wreken. **13..** *Cursor M.* 4416 (Gött.) As þu art man for þe Loke on him i-wrokin be. **1377** LANGL. *P. Pl.* B. XX. 203 Ȝif þow wilt ben ywroken wende in-to vnite. **14..** *Tundale's Vis.* (Turnbull) 1304 But they schall soo y-wrekyd bee That non of hem schall see the. *c* **1430** LYDG. *Misc. Poems* (Percy Soc.) 41 Ther was no speke y-broke, Nor wrestelyng wherby he was y-wroke. **1595** SPENSER *Col. Clout* 921 Through iudgement of the Gods to been ywroken. **1825** SCOTT *Betrothed* Concl., Vanda's wrong has been y-wroken. *a* **1835** MOTHERWELL *Clerke Richard & Maid Margaret* xi, And now that hatred was ywroken, A wondrous joy in them had sprung.

ywronge, ME. pa. pple. of WRING *v.*

ywrought (ɪ'rɔːt), *pa. pple. arch.* Forms: 1 **ᵹeworht,** 3–4 **iworht, iwroht,** 3–4 **ywro(u)ȝt,** 4–5 **ywroght,** (3 **iwraht, ywort,** 4 **ywroht,** 5 **ywrouht, ywrowte**), 5– **ywrought.** [OE. *ᵹeworht*, pa. pple. of *ᵹewyrcan* IWURCHE, *wyrcan* to WORK.] Worked, wrought, made.

971 *Blickl. Hom.* 127 Ehta eaᵹþyrelu swiþe mycele of glæse ᵹeworht. *c* **1230** *Hali Meid.* 25 Þe þat art i wit iwraht to godes ilicnesse. **1297** R. Glouc. (Rolls) 3613 Aboute is ssoldren & þeron ypeint was & ybroȝt [? ywroȝt; *v.rr.* ywrouȝt, ywort] þe ymage of vre leuedy. *a* **1310** in Wright *Lyric P.* ix. 36 Hit is wonder wele y-wroht. **14..** *Pol. Poems* (Rolls) II. 284 When suche clothe ys alle ywrowte, To the maker it waylyth lytylle or nowȝtte. **1426** Lydg. *De Guil. Pilgr.* 3593 Ye han ywrouht ageynys kynde. *a* **1500** *Flower & Leaf* 49 A plesaunt herber, wel y-wrought. **1610** Holland *Camden's Brit.* i. 196 This by-word.. (Hengston downe well ywrought Is worth London deere ybought). **1642** H. More *Song of Soul* iii. ii. xx, What's gnawing conscience from impietie By highest parts of humane soul ywrought?

ywrye, ywryed, ywryȝe, obs. pa. pples. of wry *v.*

†**ywryȝeliche,** *adv. Obs.* [repr. OE. type **ȝewriȝenlíce*, f. *ȝewriȝen*, pa. pple. of *wréon* to cover, conceal + *-líce* -ly².] Secretly.
1340 *Ayenb.* 37 Þe þyef y-wreȝe is þet steleþ ine halkes and ywryȝeliche greate þinges oþer little.

†**ywrythe, ywurnd, ywuste,** ME. pa. pples. of writhe, warn, wit *vbs.* (cf. i-wite *v.*).

ywus, obs. form of iwis.

ywyl, var. i-will *Obs.*

ywylned, pa. pple. of wiln *v.*

ywympillit [obs. Sc. var. wimpled], wrapped.
1513 Douglas *Æneis* xi. xi. 48 Ywympillit [orig. *clausam*] in this bark tho did he take Hys ȝong douchtyr.

ywynne, var. i-win(ne *v. Obs.*, to win.

ywyryed, ME. pa. pple. of worry *v.*

ywys(se, ywysed, ywyte, ywyve: see iwis, iwisse *v.*, i-wite *v.*¹, i-wive *v.*

yye, obs. form of eye.
c **1485** *Digby Myst.* iii. 1124 Þer xall þey se me.. with here carnall yye. *a* **1539** in *Archaeologia* XLVII. 53 That ther vayle come as lowe as ther yye ledes.

yyeve, yȝeve, yȝive, ME. pa. pple. of give *v.*

yyf(e, ȝyf(e, yyff: see give *v.*, if.

†**yyȝt,** ME. pa. pple. of hight *v.*³, to augment, enhance.
1387 Trevisa *Higden* (Rolls) VII. 455 By his studie and travaille þis storie is greetliche i-hiȝt [*MS.* γ y-yȝt].

yyldyd, obs. f. *yielded*, pa. t. of yield *v.*

yym(m)an(e, ȝym(m)an(e, obs. ff. yeoman.

yynge, obs. f. young.

yyoked, yyolde (-ȝ-), yȝulde, yyolpe, yyoyned, ME. pa. pples. of yoke, yield, yelp, join *vbs.*

yyrne, obs. f. yearn *v.*²

yys, obs. pl. of eye *sb.*¹; obs. f. yes.
c **1485** *Digby Myst.* iii. 640 Her xal Mary wasche þe fett of þe prophet with þe terres of hur yys.

yzard, obs. form of izzard.
1669 [see zad].

yzawe, yzed, ME. pa. pples. of sow *v.*¹, say *v.*¹

yzen, obs. var. iron *sb.*¹

†**yzendred:** see sendre.

yzen(e)ȝed, yzet, ME. pa. pples. of sin *v.*, set *v.*¹
1340 *Ayenb.* 21 Þou sselt ysi þet þou hest more ziþe y-zeneȝd.. þet þou ne kanst naȝt telle. *Ibid.* 7 Zonday and þe oþre heȝe festes þet byeþ y-zet to loky ine holy cherche.

yziȝþ, yzy: see ysee *v.*

Z

Z (zɛd, *U.S.* ziː), the twenty-sixth and last letter of the English and other modern alphabets, derives its form, through the medium of the Latin and Greek alphabets, from the Phœnician and ancient Hebrew ⌶ ⌶ ⌶ (Hebrew ז *zayin*); in the Phœnician, Greek, and earlier Roman alphabets it was the seventh letter, in the later Roman alphabet the twenty-third. Greek *Ζ ζ* seems to have had originally the phonetic value (zd) or (dz), but later simple (z). Instances of *z* are found in early Latin, but Greek ζ was more commonly represented initially by *s*, e.g. *sōna* (Plautus) = ζώνη, and medially by *ss*, e.g. *cōmissor* = κωμάζω, *massa* = μᾶζα MASS *sb.*[2], but after B.C. 100 *z* came into regular use to render the ζ of Greek loan-words. In consequence of the phonetic change of (dz) to (dj) exemplified by the spelling *baptidiare* for *baptizare*, Gr. βαπτίζειν to baptize, *z* in popular Latin came to denote (dj) and probably (j), as in *zaconus* for *diaconus* deacon, *zeta* for *dieta* (see ZETA[1]), *zunior* for *junior* (cf. the spellings *Zopen*, *Zope* in Cursor Mundi for *Joppa*). For the use of *z* for initial *x* see X.

Z was used in OE. in the spelling of alien words, and (with or without *t* or *d*) in certain loan-words, as *bæ(d)zere* (L. *baptista* + *-ere* -ER[1]) baptist, *mertze* (L. *mercem*, *merx*), with the value (ts); this use was continued in ME., e.g. *mildze*, *milz(c)e*, MILCE *sb.*, and was reinforced by French usage, as shown in forms like *caliz* chalice, *croiz* cross, *voiz* voice, *vestimenz*, pl. of *vestiment*. This phonetic value is preserved in, and indicated by the spelling of, mod.E. *assets* (AF. *asetz*, OF. *asez* enough, pop.L. *ad-satis*) and the patronymic prefix *Fitz-* (AF. *fiz* = *fius*, *fils*, L. *filius*).

In French, the reduction of (ts) to (s) brought about a change of spelling from *z* to *s* (often alternating with *x*, e.g. *vois*, *voix*), and this helped to set free *z* to denote the voiced s appropriate to such 'learned' adoptions as *zone* (which appears as early as the 12th c., Ph. de Thaun). In English, by the end of the 13th c., *z* is found with the later OF. value (z) in 'learned' words, e.g. *zizanny* tares (Cursor Mundi 1138); it is conspicuous in the Ayenbite of Inwyt (*c* 1340) as the symbol for the voiced s characteristic of southern dialects (e.g. Kentish *zenne*, OE. *synn* sin); by the end of the 14th c. the character had become general, e.g. *gaze*, *mazed*, *canonize*.

In MSS. of 1300 onwards the tailed *z* and *ȝ* came to be indistinguishable in form (cf. first quot. s.v. ZED); hence in modern editions are found many instances of spellings such as *ȝelot* zealot, *Sarȝine* Saracen. This identity of the two symbols was perpetuated in the typography of early Scottish printers, who represented the sounds (j) and (z) by the same characters, as in such words as *ze* ye, *zeir* year, *forzet* forget, *fenzeit* feigned, and *azure*, *zele* zeal. This confusion has led to the general mispronunciation by Englishmen of *capercailzie* (-ˈkeːlji, corruptly -ˈkeɪlzɪ), and proper names such as *Cadzow*, *Dalziel*, *Mackenzie*, *Menzies* (ˈmiŋɪs).

a **1814** J. RAMSAY *Scot. & Scotsm. 18th Cent.* (1888) I. 212 *note*, He [*sc.* Lord Kames] used to say that pronouncing the letter *z* in the names Mackenzie and Menzies in the English was enough to turn his stomach.

The name given to the letter in England (presumably since the Norman Conquest) has been ZED, q.v., or one of its variants, †ZAD, †ZARD, IZZARD, EZOD, UZZARD. With the disyllabic forms, which survive dialectally, cf. F. *edez*, ? for *ezed* (Coyfurelly, 14th cent.), *ézed* (Claude de Saint-Lien, 1580), Prov. *izedo*, Cat. *idzeta*, app. from pop.L. **idzēta*, a. Gr. ζῆτα (ˈdzɛːta). The names *ez* (Gil, Logonomia Anglica, 1619) and *ze* (C. Butler, Eng. Gram., 1633) do not seem to represent actual usage, but are (like *ya* and *yi* as names of *y*) systematic inventions of these phonetic writers. The name ZEE, now standard in the United States of America, appears to have had some early currency in England.

Initially and medially *z* occurs largely in words of Greek or Oriental origin, e.g. *zeal*, *azimuth*, *Amazon*, *zenith*; and in this Dictionary the spelling of the suffix derived ultimately from Greek -ίζειν has been normalized throughout as -IZE, q.v. In other classes of words the use of *z* has been determined by various circumstances, e.g. the immediate source of the word, as in *bronze*, or the desirability of an unambiguous or distinctive spelling, as in *ooze* (cf. *loose*), *prize* (cf. *price*). It is found in a number of monosyllabic words (and their derivatives), as *craze*, *daze*, *laze*, *maze*, *doze*, *gloze*, *gauze*, *furze*, *blowze*, *size*, *assize*, *seize*, *freeze*, *wheeze*.

One fact which has told against an extensive use of it instead of *s* to represent the sound (z) is the difficulty of writing the character rapidly and intelligibly; this is referred to by Mulcaster, 1st Part of Elementarie, 1582, p. 123:—

Z, is a consonant much heard amongst vs, and seldom sene. I think by reason it is not so redie to the pen as s, is, which is become lieutenant generall to z, as gàse, amàse, ràsur, where z, is heard, but, s, sene.

It is remarkable that in the three words cited by him the ultimate decision has been in favour of the spelling with *z*. In certain words usage fluctuated even in modern times until *s* or *z* prevailed, as in *tease* and †*teaze*, *pose* and †*poze*, *surprise* and †*surprize*; *rase* and *raze* are specifically differentiated.

Z is normally employed to denote (z), the blade-open-voice consonant, the voiced analogue of (s). In the combination *-zure* in *azure* it denotes (ʒ), a sound commonly denoted by other means, as in *pleasure*, *decision*, *lesion*, *transition*.

I. 1. The letter, or its sound.

c **1000** ÆLFRIC *Gram.* ii. (Z.) 6 *Z*, eac, se grecisca stæf, ȝeendaδ on *a*. Se stæf is ȝenumen of Grecum to ledenspræce for greciscum wordum. **1528** in Ellis *E.E. Pron.* III. 816 S betwene two vowelles, pronounceth [*sic*] by .z. **1530** PALSGR. 38 The *x* by this rule shalbe sounded lyke an *z* [*i.e.* ezod]. *c* **1532** DU WES *Introd. Fr.* in *Palsgr.* 901 If ye do adde a *z*, at the latter ende of them, than are they plurell nombres. **1611** COTGR. *Fr. Dict.* Brief Direct. Nnnn j b, The tongue in the former [*guerre*] giuing onely a touch to the palate, and sounding the later [*poison*] as if it were a *Z*. **1668** WILKINS *Real Char.* III. xii. 369 (*Z*) is by some stiled (*S*) *molle*... (*Zh*) the sonorous Consonant, and (*Sh*) its correspondent mute. **1669** HOLDER *Elem. Speech* 43 The vowel I, partaking also of the nature of a Consonant, added to Z, comes very near to the sound of *Zh*, as *Zya*. **1792** W. ROBERTS *Looker-on* No. 32 ¶8 The Z's, an ancient sign at grocers shops, look very enigmatical; but I am told they allude to the word zinziber, or ginger, and intimated the sale of that article. **1838** DICKENS *O. Twist* ii, I have got names ready made to the end of the alphabet, and all the way through it again, when we come to Z.

2. The letter considered with respect to its shape; a figure or object of this shape. Also *attrib.*, as **Z-bar**, a metal bar having a cross-section of a form resembling a Z; so ***Z-iron***; **Z-bend**, a series of bends in a road forming a shape like a letter Z; **Z-crank**, a crank of zigzag form, used in marine engines; **Z-fold** *a.* (of print-out paper) in a continuous strip that comes folded in alternate directions in a stacked pile; **Z-plan** *Archit.*, the ground-plan of a type of Scottish castle having a central block with a tower placed at each of two diagonally opposite corners; **Z-plastic** *a. Surg.*, involving the use of Z-shaped incisions; also as *sb.*, Z-plastic surgery; so **Z-plasty**, a technique in which one or more Z-shaped incisions is made (the diagonals forming one straight line) and the two triangular flaps of skin so formed are rotated and drawn across the diagonal before being stitched, so as to give a less obvious Z-shaped scar and minimize the effect of contraction; an operation in which this technique is used; also *Comb.*, as **Z-shaped** *a.*, in the shape of a Z; *spec.* in *Archæol.*, designating a rod motif found on Pictish stones.

1680 MOXON *Mech. Exerc.* xiii. 223 Bent backwards and forwards..somewhat like an ʒ [i.e. ezod or izzard]. **1688** HOLME *Armoury* III. 408/2 A Roman Z. **1711** STEELE *Spect.* No. 17. ¶2 The Irregularity of his Shape, which he describes as very much resembling the Letter Z. **1820** *Death of Minuet* 24 in *Edin. Mag.* VI. 453 No more the well taught feet shall tread The figure of the mazy Z. **1852** *Househ. Words* IV. 423/1 The road winds up the side of the cone like a strung series of Zs. **1858** SIMMONDS *Dict. Trade*, *Z-crank*, the peculiarly-shaped crank of a cylinder, in a newly-invented engine for marine propulsion. **1877** W. H. WHITE *Naval Archit.* ix. 360 Provided the thin iron plating..be stiffened by angle-bars, T bars, or Z bars riveted to its surface. *Ibid.* x. 386 Z-iron..is used for frames behind armour in ironclads. **1880** JOS. ANDERSON *Scotl. in Early Chr. T.* Ser. II. (1881) 114 The Z and kindred varieties of this ornament. **1887** MACGIBBON & ROSS *Castellated & Domestic Architect. Scotl.* II. 6 As one form of plan is designated the L plan, it has occurred to us that the form we are now considering might..be called the Z plan. We have accordingly adopted this nomenclature. **1889** WELCH *Text Bk. Naval Archit.* vi. 89 Instead of these Z bars, earlier vessels have the frames at their ends made up of two angle bars riveted back to back. **1893** MADAN *Bks. in MS.* 53 The Z-patterns (fine lines arranged diagonally, like natural and reversed Zeds combined). **1901** *Proc. Soc. Antiquaries Scotl.* XI. 91 The double-disc and crescent symbols of the Pictish stones may be connected with the worship of the Blessed Virgin, the Z and V-shaped rods being her floriated sceptre. **1908** F. R. FRAPRIE *Castles & Keeps of Scotl.* i. 22 A new and entirely Scotch plan is very common. This has been called the zigzag or Z plan. **1913** S. L. MCCURDY in *Surg., Gynecol. & Obstetr.* XVI. 209 (*heading*) Z-plastic surgery. *Ibid.* 212/2 (*caption*) Z-plastic operation of the neck for burn scar. **1927** *Sc. N & Q.* 3rd Ser. V. 2/1 Two plates of silver engraved with the double disc and Z-shaped rod symbol. **1934** *Surg., Gynecol. & Obstetr.* LVIII. 178/1 Davis has been interested in tracing the history of the use of Z plastic. **1940** *Ibid.* LXX. 942/1, 2 patients returned for further work after a Z plasty with skin graft. **1958** *New Statesman* 1 Nov. 590/2 The shops were grouped round the angles of a Z-bend in the road. **1964** R. BATTLE *Plastic Surg.* xii. 316 A Z-plasty should be done only on one aspect of the finger at a time, thereby avoiding complete disruption of the circulation. **1967** *Electronics* 6 Mar. 282/2 The smudge is gone from Z-fold paper. **1967** I. HENDERSON *Picts* v. 104 A selection of the commoner symbols is illustrated here, the most common of all being the crescent with an applied V-shaped rod, the double disc with an applied Z-shaped rod. **1973** J. LEASOR *Host of Extras* v. 69 About twelve miles of diabolical Z-bends. **1977** *Proc. R. Soc. Med.* LXX. 256/2 The Achilles tendon is lengthened by Z-plasty and then the posterior capsules of the ankle and subtalar joints are incised transversely. **1977** *Clinics in Plastic Surg.* IV. 207/1 Z-shaped techniques other than Z-plasties, which are referred to as 'Z-plastics', differ in the movement or lack of movement of the flaps formed by the zigzag incision. **1978** A. & G. RITCHIE *Anc. Monuments Orkney* 79 Began 1560, it is an excellent example of a Z-plan castle, comprising towers at diagonally opposite corners of a main block. **1982** *Computerworld* (U.S.) 15 Mar. 66 It [*sc.* a digital plotter] also uses Z-fold paper and disposable fiber-tip pens.

3. As the last letter of the alphabet; hence allusively for 'end', esp. in phr. ***from A to Z*** = from beginning to end, all through, in every particular. (Cf. It. *dall' A alla Zeta*.)

1819 KEATS *Otho* v. v, We must obey The prince from A to Z. **1876** BROWNING *Fears & Scruples* v, Ask the experts! How they shake the head O'er these characters,..Call them forgery from A to Z! **1877** JAS. WELLS *Bible Echoes* 297 Christ is the A, and the Z of the Bible. **1912** L. TRACY *Mirabel's Isl.* v. (1915) 77, I know Ealing from A to Z, but have never visited Regent Street.

4. Used (usually repeated) to represent a buzzing sound; also conventionally representing the sound of snoring. Hence ***Z-ing*** vbl. sb., and as *v. intr.* to make such a noise or noises.

1852 THOREAU *Summer* 15 June, The dry z-ing of the locust is heard. **1884** R. W. BUCHANAN *New Abelard* i, The bats were seen flitting with thin z-like cry high up over the waterside. **1893** KIPLING *Many Invent.* 103 The oars rip out and go z-zzp all along the line. **1902** S. E. WHITE *Blazed Trail* ii, The rhythmical *z-z-z! z-z-z!* [of the saw]. **1909** H. G. WELLS *Tono-Bungay* I. ii. 67 He had a way of drawing air in at times through his teeth that gave a whispering zest to his speech. It's a sound I can only represent as a soft Zzzz. *Ibid.* III. ii. 326 He meditated for a time and Zzzzed softly. **1924** *Dialect Notes* V. 259 *Z-z-z* (buzzing, or snoring). **1951** *Blue Book Magazine* Jan. 25/1 A spark danced between two terminals, a filament snake spat an irate, 'Zzzt!' **1966** L. COHEN *Beautiful Losers* I. 16 Hiccup, jerk, zzzzzz, snort. **1967** V. C. WELBURN *Johnny so Long* II. i. 46 Lola: (*makes buzzing noise*) Zzzzzzz. **1975** *New Yorker* 21 Apr. 36/3 David sits in the chair, puts his arms on the armrests, presses his neck against the back of the chair, and moves his feet together. 'Zzzz,' he says, and his head falls forward. **1976** *Cambridge Independent Press* 16 Dec. II. 3/2 The zzzzz-noise of the electric hare gliding past the opening traps grabs everyone's attention. **1983** *Private Eye* 4 Nov. 6/2 Once you have hit on a commercial product you just go on producing more of the same, over and..zzzz..over and..zzzz..over and..zzzzzzzzzzzzzzzzzzzzzzzzzzzzzzzzzzzzzzzzz. **1984** *Wall Street Jrnl.* 9 Oct. 28/2 We suspect public interest.. more nearly resembles a cartoonist's depiction of a man sawing wood—ZZZZZZZZZ. **1984** *Oxford Star* 29/30 Nov. 19/3 Zzzzing off for forty winks on a regular basis may not sound much like Action Man stuff, but for Alex Gardner it's the most exciting part of the day.

b. In *colloq.* phr. ***to catch some z's*** and varr., to get some sleep (where z represents the sound of snoring). *U.S.*

Pronounced (ziːz) in the U.S.

1963 *Amer. Speech* XXXVIII. 174 An onomatopoetic construction reported four times is *get some Z's*... Variants occurring once were: *bagging Z's*, *copping some Z's*, *cutting Z's*, and *knocking out Z's*. **1973** A. DUNDES *Mother Wit* 238 Got to go..cop me some z's. **1977** C. MCFADDEN *Serial*

(1978) xxxii. 71/1 All Harvey wanted..was to pop his Sominex and catch a few z's.

II. Symbolic uses.

5. *Math.* Used as the symbol for the third of a set of unknown or variable quantities (the first and second being denoted by *x* and *y*); *spec.* in Analytical Geometry of three dimensions, for a quantity measured in the direction of the third axis of coordinates (hence called the † ***axis of z***, now always ***z-axis***; also *transf.*).

For the history see X 3 *note*.

1660, 1709 [see X 3]. **1929**, etc. [see X 3 a]. **1967** *Electronics* 6 Mar. 2 (Advt.), Plug-in markers offer not only variable band-width, but also Z-axis or pulse-type marking.

6. Used abstractly for the name of a person or thing: cf. X 3, 3 c, Y 5.

1798, 1873, 1901 [see X 3 c]. **1833** Newman *Let. to Froude* 13 Nov., Palmer musters the Z.'s [*sc.* Establishment men] in great force against the tracts, and some Evangelicals. **1848** Hannay *Biscuits & Grog* 109 Lord X, the Marquis of Y, and Baron Z. **1880** 'Mark Twain' *Tramp Abr.* xiii, Mr. X. pranced in in his long night garment with a candle, young Z. after him with another candle.

7. Used, like the other letters of the alphabet, to denote position in a series.

1842 Dickens *Amer. Notes* viii, We dismounted with as much ease and comfort as though we had been escorted by the whole Metropolitan Force from A to Z inclusive. **1860** Sala *Baddington P.* xxiv, A very Rabelais of the Z division. *Ibid.*, Z. 92 saw the striped bracelet of a sergeantcy in perspective. **1862** Thackeray *Philip* xxxviii, 'Tell that to his worship,' says the incredulous Z. **1867** 'Ouida' *Cecil Castlemaine's Gage* etc. 381 He exchanged into the Z Battery going out to India.

8. *Genetics.* *Z* is used to designate the male-determining sex chromosome in species in which the female rather than the male is the heterogametic sex.

1917 T. H. Morgan in *Amer. Naturalist* LI. 534 Since the female here [*sc.* in pigeons] is the heterozygotic sex (ZW) the results are such as would follow a direct influence on the sex chromosomes when the polar body is eliminated. **1925** *Ibid.* LIX. 133 The locus of the male tendency gene (M) is in the 'Z-chromosome' of which two are present in the male and one in the female. **1966** *Lancet* 24 Dec. 1397/2 The phenotypic expression of plumage factors on the Z chromosome of birds seems to be a function, principally, of gene dosage. **1971** [see heterogametic *a.*]. **1976** *Nature* 17 June 598/2 In avian species, the heterogametic (Z W) female sex possesses W-linked histocompatibility antigen.

9. *Physics.* *Z* is the symbol for the atomic number of an element.

1931 *Proc. R. Soc.* A. CXXXIII. 234 We have taken Z = 8 (oxygen). **1962** F. I. Ordway et al. *Basic Astronautics* xii. 502 Electrons such as those in the outer Van Allen radiation belt are easily stopped by a few millimeters of a low-*Z* material such as aluminum or magnesium. **1978** P. W. Atkins *Physical Chem.* xiv. 438 The next atom to build is lithium, $Z = 3$.

10. *Z* is used to denote one of the two directions of twist in spinning (see quot. 1935); hence ***z-spun*** adj.

1935 [see S II. 8]. **1964** H. Hodges *Artifacts* ix. 128 In thigh spinning, for example, a right-handed person will almost always produce Z-spun yarn. **1980** A. Fritz *Fibre of Clothing* iii. 40 There are two types of twist possible in a yarn. One is an S twist, the other a Z twist.

11. *Particle Physics.* *Z* is the symbol of a heavy, uncharged vector boson that forms a triplet with the two Ws.

1967 S. Weinberg in *Physical Rev. Lett.* XIX. 1265/2 The only unequivocal new predictions made by this model have to do with the couplings of the neutral intermediate meson Z_μ. *Ibid.* 1266/1 Our Z_μ and W_μ mesons get their mass from the spontaneous breaking of the symmetry. **1971** —— in *Ibid.* XXVII. 1688 This procedure..resulted in a model involving electrons, electron-type neutrinos, charged intermediate bosons (W_μ), neutral intermediate bosons (Z_μ), [etc.]. **1977** *Dædalus* Fall 32 The family of intermediate vector bosons, of which the photon is a member, is believed to contain one heavy charged particle and its anti-particle, called the W^+ and W^-, and one even heavier neutral particle, called the Z^0. **1982** [see W 4 b]. **1983** *New Scientist* 12 May 355 (*heading*) CERN physicists find the Z particle. **1983** *Nature* 25 Aug. 686/2 This resulted in a total of six examples of the Z particle (four decaying into e^+e^- and two into $\mu^+\mu^-$) and 52 W± particles.

III. Abbreviations.

12. a. ZANU, Zanu, Zimbabwe African National Union; **ZAPU, Zapu,** Zimbabwe African People's Union; **ZBB** (*U.S.*), zero-base(d) budgeting; **Z-DNA** (*Biochem.*), DNA in which the double helix has a left-handed rather than the usual right-handed twist and the sugar phosphate backbone follows a zigzagged course; **ZPG**, zero population growth. See also *Z band* (s.v. Z line), Z line.

1963 *Times* 10 Aug. 5/2 The split in the Southern Rhodesian African nationalist movement has come to a head. A breakaway group..has formed..the Zimbabwe African National Union. The president is the Rev. Ndabaninge Sithole, formerly one of Mr. Nkomo's staunchest lieutenants, as are all the members of the new *Zanu executive. **1964** *Ann. Reg. 1963* ii. v. 105 On 8 August a new organization, the Zimbabwe African National Union (Z.A.N.U.), was formed with the Rev. Sithole as leader. **1977** *Times* 17 Sept. 15/3 Nobody wants to clear an arena for a final fight between Zapu and Zanu armies for supremacy. **1961** *Guardian* 18 Dec. 1/3 A new African political party, to be known as the Zimbabwe African People's Union, has been launched in Southern Rhodesia.. by Mr. J. M. Nkomo... Mr. Nkomo said..*ZAPU would press for immediate negotiations for a fresh constitutional arrangement. **1972** J. Biggs-Davison *Africa —Hope Deferred* xi. 100 The rival parties Z.A.P.U. and Z.A.N.U. **1977** *Daily Times* (Lagos) 27 Jan. 3/2 Mr. Moyo ..was with Nkomo in ZAPU before the revolt which Nkomo faced prior to 1963. **1976** *N.Y. Times* 27 Aug. d 1 *Z.B.B., as it is widely known, calls for the justification of all spending in relation to priorities. **1978** *National Civic Review* LXVII. 132 ZBB was formally delineated and put into practice for the first time by Texas Instruments, Inc., 15 years ago. **1979** A. H.-J. Wang et al. in *Nature* 13 Dec. 681/2 In looking at this left-handed helix..it is apparent that the ribose-phosphate backbone follows a zig-zag course resulting from alternating residue conformations. Accordingly, we propose to call this *Z-DNA. **1983** *Sci. Amer.* Dec. 92/1 In Z DNA..the repeating unit of the helix is not a single base pair, as it is in *A* and *B* DNA, but rather two successive base pairs: *G–C* followed by *C–G*. **1970** *N.Y. Times* 3 June 61/6 Of all the cries that have arisen, perhaps none is quite so superficially appealing, or so profound in its long-range social and economic implications, as zero population growth—'*ZPG' in the slogans of the day. **1978** *Nature* 6 Apr. 491/3 This may have reduced the maximum possible number of children per female to around five, and it does not then require harsh assumptions about mortality rates to end up with ZPG.

b. In combinations containing the abbreviation Z followed by a word, as **Z-car**, a police patrol car (after the title of a popular U.K. television series, from the radio call-sign 'zulu' allotted therein to a group of such cars); also used allusively; **Z-day** *Mil.* = *zero day* s.v. zero *sb.* 7 a.

1961 *Radio Times* 28 Dec. 29/2 The call-sign is ZULU —they call them Z-cars. There are two young constables in each, ready to deal with trouble. **1963** *Daily Mail* 23 Apr. 1/6 (*heading*) Z-car crashes. **1965** *Sunday Mail* (Brisbane) 19 Dec. 32/5 Two black Z-cars—powerful Humbers—keep driving around the half-mile circle every five minutes watching for strangers. **1976** 'D. Craig' *Faith Hope & Death* xviii. 127 It's not like Barlow and Z Cars, all that shouting stuff and strong jaws. These boys, they was slimy. **1925** Fraser & Gibbons *Soldier & Sailor Words & Phrases* 312 The opening of the main attack of the battle of the Somme was fixed for June 29th, and notified beforehand as 'Z Day'. **1930** S. Sassoon *Mem. Infantry Officer* iv. 61 Operation Orders..notified us that Thursday was 'Z' (or zero) day. **1938** Blunden *On Several Occasions* In the sour concrete hole the corporal shows his muddy map, his Z Day zone of fire.

'Z, phonetic spelling of 'S as a euphemistic shortening of *God's* in certain oaths: see 'Zbloud, 'Zdeath, 'Zfoot, 'Zlife, &c.

za (zɑː). Also **'za**. U.S. slang abbrev. of pizza.

1968–70 *Current Slang* (Univ. S. Dakota) III–IV. 140 *Za* .., pizza. **1980** L. Birnbach et al. *Official Preppy Handbk.* 44/2 You can go for 'za, burgers, and ice cream without signing out. **1983** *Verbatim* IX. iv. 1/1 One of the boys called up and asked the parlor to *bag the za* (meaning 'cancel the pizza'). **1984** *Amer. Speech* LIX. 89 In surveying my classes for campus slang I learned that pizza is referred to as *za* and to get or eat a pizza is to *do a za*.

Zaara(h, Zaarra, variants of Sahara.

Zabæan, variant of Sabian.

zabaglione (zɑːbɑːˈljəʊneɪ). Also **sambaglione, zabaione,** etc. [a. It., perh. ult. ad. late Lat. *sabaia* an Illyrian drink.] A dessert consisting of egg yolks, sugar, and (usu. Marsala) wine, whipped to a frothy texture over a gentle heat and served either hot or cold. Cf. sabayon.

1899 M. Ninet *Dainty Meals for Small Households* xiv. xiv. 223 *Sambaglione.*—Put into a saucepan about six new-laid eggs, and two sherry-glassfuls of Madeira. **1901** W. G. Waters *Cook's Decameron* 175/1 Zabajone is a kind of syllabub. *Ibid.* 175/2 (*heading*) Iced zabajone. **1914** C. E. Edwards *Bohemian in San Francisco* 104 This was followed by a glass of zabaione for dessert. **1917** *Blackw. Mag.* Jan. 111/1 We dined off onion pilaff, and sponge-cake of maize flour with zabayone. **1924** M. Kennedy *Constant Nymph* xvi. 222 She had instructed Roberto to beat up some eggs.. that she might make zabaglione. **1932** *Times Lit. Suppl.* 10 Nov. 836/4 At a single opening of the book we find.. zambaglione (the reviewer would prefer to omit the lemon-juice but to add a pinch of yeast). **1958** *Times* 2 Oct. 11/4 A nation that is content at midday with shepherd's pie..must dine out off kebabs and zabagliones. **1960** *House & Garden* May 94/3 A copper zabaglione pan. **1974** *Country Life* 25 Apr. 1006/1 The best-known Italian sweet, *zabaglione.* **1981** R. Airth *Once a Spy* ix. 100 Zac ordered blackberry, peach, pineapple [ices] and *zabaione.* **1984** *Listener* 1 Nov. 42/2 Whatever food is mentioned, from aubergines to zabaglione, they are ready to garnish it with some unsavoury gobbet of introductory junk music.

Zabaism (Zabiism), variant of Sabaism. So **zabaist**, one who practises Sabaism.

1662 Stillingfl. *Orig. Sacræ* ii. vii. §9 The rites and customs of these Zabaists. **1669** Gale *Crt. Gentiles* i. ii. i. 3 Zabaisme,..gave a Deitie..to the Sun, Moon, and Stars. **1748** T. Blackwell *Lett. conc. Mythol.* 364 That Religion which is still known under the Name of Zabiism among the Eastern Writers. **1775** J. Bryant *Mythol.* II. 443 Addicted to Zabaism, and other species of idolatry.

†**zabernism** (ˈzæbənɪz(ə)m). *Obs.* [f. *Zabern*, German name of the village of Saverne in Alsace + -ism.] The misuse of military power or authority; bullying, aggression (see quot. 1921). Also **'zabernize** *v. intr.*

1914 *Daily News & Leader* 6 Apr. 1/7 A quaint illustration of an attempt to 'zabernise' in business life..is published.. to-night. **1916** [see rounding *vbl. sb.*[1] 1 a]. **1918** *Nineteenth Cent.* Dec. 992 The acquisitive commercialists and financiers of Germany—the Zabernism of industry and *l.s.d.* —were up to the eyes in it [*sc.* the war]. **1918** H. G. Wells *In Fourth Year* iii. 36 Both countries have been slaves to Kruppism and Zabernism. **1920** *Glasgow Herald* 7 Apr. 8 The advance of the Government troops into the Ruhr district, coupled with a marked exhibition of 'Zabernism', has stiffened the Spartacist resistance. **1921** E. Weekley *Etym. Dict. Mod. Eng.* 1658/2 *Zabernism* (*hist.*), military jackbootery. From an incident at *Saverne* (Ger. *Zabern*) in Alsace (1912), when an excited Ger. subaltern cut down a lame cobbler who smiled at him.

Zabian, Zabianism, var. Sabian, Sabianism.

zable, var. sable *sb.*[3] *Obs.*, sabre.

‖**zabra** (ˈθabra, ˈzɑːbrə). Also 6 **zabre, azabra,** 9 **zumbra.** [Sp.] A small vessel used off the coasts of Spain and Portugal.

1523 Wolsey in *St. Papers Hen. VIII*, VI. 118 That the Emperour..do sende also 2 zabres of the portage of 30 or 40 ton a pece. **1588** Archdeacon tr. *True Disc. Army K. Spain* 19 The Zabra Augusta, of 166 tunnes. **1589** Greene *Span. Masq.* Wks. (Grosart) V. 274 Of Gallions, Hulkes, Pataches, Zabres, Galeasses, and Gallies 130. **1607** Dekker *Whore Bab.* H 4, Our Galeons, Galeasses, Zabraes, Gallies. **1860** Motley *Netherl.* xix. II. 507 Of the tenders and zabras, seventeen were lost. **1867** Smyth *Sailor's Word-bk.*, *Zumbra*, a Spanish skiff or yawl.

zabra, obs. form of zebra.

‖**zabuton** (zaˈbuton). [Jap., f. *za* sitting, a seat + *buton* f. *futon* cushion, padded mattress.] A flat floor cushion on which one sits or kneels.

1889 M. B. Huish *Japan & its Art* vii. 85 The Japanese.. is only comfortable when resting on his knees and heels on a cushion (*zabuton*). **1928** J. I. Bryan *Jap. All* vi. 76 In a Japanese house the guest does not sit, but kneels down and rests on the heels with toes out behind. A cushion, called *zabuton*, is given to rest the knees on. **1960** *Sunset* Mar. 137/1 The word *zabuton* applies to a Japanese floor cushion designed for sitting. It comes from the Japanese words *za* meaning to sit, and *futon* meaning bedding. **1973** A. Broinowski *Take One Ambassador* v. 57 There were *shoji* screens and *zabuton* cushions on the *tatami* round the table. *Ibid.* xii. 193 She brought a *zabuton* and sat on the floor on that.

zac (zæk). *Austral. slang.* Also **zack, zak.** [Origin unknown.] A sixpence.

1898 *Bulletin* (Sydney) 1 Oct. 14 6d., a 'zack'. **1924** *Truth* (Sydney) 27 Apr. 6 *Zack*, sixpence. **1941** *Coast to Coast 1941* 213 'Only one, then,' I said. 'We'll only have one more, so we'll make it a sixpence in.' 'Don't worry about the zac,' said Tom. **1952** M. Tripp *Faith is Windsock* ii. 29 Arthur spent the break losing bobs and tanners while the tall Australian reckoned his profits in dieners and zaks. **1962** *John o' London's* 8 Mar. 229/2 And all you get for it is a zack. **1966** *Tel.* (Brisbane) 13 Oct. 13/2 The zack, now the 5c piece, is in such demand that very often its scarcity makes one wonder if it is gradually going out of circulation. **1966** P. Mathers *Trap* ii. 31 Two taps with an improvised hammer and anvil, a two bob and a zac. **1977** *Sunday Sun* (Brisbane) 1 May 16 When it comes to unique competitions the people of outback Winton reckon they're the full quid—and you can bet your last zac or traybit on it.

zacate: see sacate, zacate.

zacaton: see sacaton, zacaton.

'zackly, 'zactly (ˈzæklɪ, ˈzæktlɪ). Repr. a dial. or colloq. pronunc. of exactly *adv.*

1886 Baumann *Londinismen* 239/1 *'Zactly..*, exactly. **1893** H. A. Shands *Some Peculiarities of Speech in Mississippi* 69 *Zackly..*, negro for *exactly*. **1929** W. Faulkner *Sartoris* iii. vi. 232 'Yessuh,' Simon agreed readily. 'Hit struck me jes' 'zackly dat way.' **1929** H. Williamson *Beautiful Years* (rev. ed.) vi. 63 'Isn't the sunshine lovely, Mr. Lewis?' 'Eh, ooh? 'Zactly!' **1973** *Amer. Speech* 1970 XLV. 77 Her dress was 'zactly like mine. **1983** R. Sutcliff *Blue Remembered Hills* xii. 91 Some people believed that Mr. Snow was, in West Country parlance 'not quite zackly'... I think he was just simple in the true sense of the word.

zad. *Obs.* exc. *dial.* Variant of zed, name of the letter Z; hence (*slang*) applied to a thing or person of crooked form. (Cf. zard.)

1669 Holder *Elem. Speech* 140 We may imagine it to have been anciently pronounced, as it is now by the Italians, Ds or Ts; and so to be called *Zad* from the Hebrew *Tsadi*: but yet..we..do as often call it *Yzard.* **1725** *New Cant. Dict.* s.v., *A meer Zad*, used of any bandy-legg'd, crouch-back'd ..Person. **1728** De Foe *Street Robb. Consid.* 35 *Zad*, crooked. **1778** Halhed *Gram. Bengal Lang.* 6 W is defined from its form only, not from its use; and Z *zad*, or *izard* is an appellation equally useless. **1810** Crabbe *Borough* xviii. 30 And how she soothed me, when, with study sad, I labour'd on to reach the final Zad. **1877** *Reports Provinc.* (E.D.D.) Labouring man said at a night school, 'I can't made a zad.'

zaddik, zadik, varr. tsaddik.

Zadokite (ˈzeɪdəkaɪt), *sb.* and *a.* [f. the name of *Zadok*, a high priest of Israel in the time of King David + -ite[1].] **A.** *sb.* A member of a Jewish sect which seceded from orthodox Judaism in the second century b.c., and traced its authority back to Zadok.

1910 S. Schechter *Fragments of Zadokite Work* p. xxi, It is the Zadokites from which the Sect derived its spiritual pedigree. **1920** *Encycl. Relig. & Ethics* XI. 43/2 The Sadducees were thus not a religious party at all, but simply a body of people bound together by a common interest to maintain the existing *régime*. The name is explained as meaning 'Zadokites', and was given to them by their opponents, the Pharisees, who borrowed it from an earlier age..when the descendants of Zadok, who then filled the high-priestly office, identified themselves with Hellenism in its most dangerous forms. **1960** tr. *Noth's Hist. Israel* III. ii. 316 It may also be that..some deported Zadokites returned to Jerusalem. **1974** *Encycl. Brit. Macropædia* XIV. 190/1 The Zadokites may have constituted the survival of an ancient Jebusite (Canaanite) royal priesthood.

B. *adj.* Of, pertaining to, or designating the members of this sect; *spec.* applied to fragments of sectarian texts discovered in Cairo in 1896–7 and later traced back to the Dead Sea Scrolls.

1910 S. Schechter (*title*) Fragments of a Zadokite work. **1912** R. H. Charles *Fragments of Zadokite Work* p. vii, There is no question as to the genuineness of the orders of the Zadokite Priests and Levites. *Ibid.* p. x, The Zadokite Party represents an attempt at reform beginning within the ranks of the priesthood and extending outwards so as to embrace a strong lay element. **1921** J. Moffatt *Approach to New Testament* i. 60 In the so called Zadokite document of Jewish piety, just before the days of Jesus, the idea of a new covenant, a covenant of repentance, began to be linked to the expectation of a messiah. **1954** [see Qumran]. **1974** *Encycl. Brit. Macropædia* II. 938/2 Another sectarian book of ordinances is the Damascus Document (the Zadokite Fragments). The work was already known from two medieval copies before the discovery of the Dead Sea Scrolls, but fragments of it also were found in Qumrān.

‖**zadruga** (za'druga). Pl. **zadrugas, zadruge.** Also with capital initial. [Serbo-Croat, = patriarchal commune, association.] A type of patriarchal social unit traditional to (agricultural) Serbians and other southern Slavic peoples, orig. comprising an extended family group which worked the land and lived communally round the main house; the customs and rules associated with this type of unit.

1887 *Encycl. Brit.* XXII. 146/2 The Slavs know nothing of private property,—the land being held in common under the care of the *vladika* or *stareshina*, as in the Servian *xadrugas* at the present day. **1900** 'Odysseus' *Turkey in Europe* viii. 375 The old system of Zadruga, or communal village based upon the family. **1911** Prince Lazarovich-Hrebelianovich *Servian People* i. 39 The basis of the Serb organisation is the family, either in its narrowest sense of blood-relationship, in communistic organisation, or other individuals grouped together for common work and with common possessions. These forms are called 'Zadruga'. **1934** *N.Y. Times* 24 June iv. 3/4 Zadruga in Serbia means a big family where brothers and sisters..lead a community life, under the leadership usually of the eldest member of the family. **1943** L. Adamic *My Native Land* 214 From their Russian homeland the Slavs brought a democratic institution called *zadruga*, a clan or family cooperative, which some of the tribes tried to extend and adjust to the wider forms of government necessary in their new homelands. *Ibid.* 216 They lived in their primitive villages and held onto their Old-Slavic *zadrugé* and 'heart culture'—decency, friendliness, hospitality. **1963** *Times Lit. Suppl.* 25 Jan. 49/3 The *dvor* or peasant household..is the same elastic unit which was familiar in medieval Europe, and survives today in the *zadruge* of the Balkans. **1979** *Internat. Jrnl. Sociol. of Law* VII. 270 The old customary Slavonic 'family' law, the zadruga. **1980** A. Toffler *Third Wave* ii. 44 People tended to live in large, multi-generational households,..from the 'joint family' in India to the 'zadruga' in the Balkans.

zaffre, zaffer ('zæfə(r)). Also (7 **zaphara, saffera**), 9 **saffre, saffer,** (**zaffira, suphara**). [ad. It. *zaffera* (Neri) or F. *zafre, saffre* (12–13th c.); cf. Sp. *zafre, safre*, G. *zaffer, zaffra*: of uncertain origin.] An impure oxide of cobalt, obtained by roasting cobalt-ore, and used in the preparation of smalt and as a blue colouring-matter (cobalt blue) for pottery, glass, etc.

1662 Merrett tr. *Neri's Art of Glass* xii, Take Zaffer in gross pieces. **1686** *Phil. Trans.* XVI. 26 Smalt is made of Zaffer and Pot-ashes. **1693** tr. *Blancard's Phys. Dict.* (ed. 2), *Zaphara* or *Saffera*. **1745** Watson in *Phil. Trans.* XLIII. 497 Zaffer, which is used by the Glass-makers and Enamellers, is made of Cobalt..calcined after the subliming the Flowers. **1804** tr. *Tingry's Paint. & Varn. Guide* 301 Smalt, or vitreous oxide of cobalt, is saffer reduced to blue glass by the action of a violent fire. **1843** Poe *Tales, Gold-Bug*, Zaffre, digested in *aqua regia*, and diluted with four times its weight of water, is sometimes employed; a green tint results. **1912** *Contemp. Rev.* Dec. 860 The Egyptian porcelain..manufacturer, who used for the zaffre the Cyprus blue-stone.

‖**zaftig** ('zæftɪg), *a.* *U.S. colloq.* Also **zoftig, zofti(c)k.** [Yiddish, a. G. *saftig* juicy.] Of a woman: plump, curvaceous, 'sexy'.

1937 M. Levin *Old Bunch* ii. 394 He could see himself on the road, whizzing by a flaming poster—a beautiful..girl, snappy, modern, *zaftig*. **1950** *Commentary* IX. 460/2 The owner of the local barber shop..installed a *zoftig* blond manicurist. **1960** 'E. McBain' *Heckler* x. 91 A *zaftig* redhead..in her early thirties. **1967** P. Welles *Babyhip* (1969) xxiv. 139 'And see how *zoftik* she is.' Mrs. Green felt pleased she had spotted someone over-weight. **1970** S. J. Perelman *Baby, it's Cold Inside* 188 This demure but *zoftick* freshman, with a brain rivalling Spinoza's encased in the body of a Lollobrigida. **1973** R. Hayes *Hungarian Game* xxx. 179 That *zoftig* colonel wasn't a colonel at all. I checked her out in Budapest. **1981** *Gossip* (Holiday Special) 11/2 Zaftig Dolly Parton..once described herself as looking like a 'hooker with a heart of gold'.

zag (zæg). The second syllable of *zigzag* used as a separate word (*adv.*, *vb.*, or *sb.*) to express a movement or direction inclined at an angle to that indicated by *zig*.

1793 Burns *Let. to R. Ainslie* 26 Apr., I have written many a letter in return for letters received, but, then, they were original matter. Spurt away! zig here, zag there. **1840** Arnold in A. P. Stanley *Life & Corr.* (1844) II. 403 We go down by zig and zag towards the level of the Tiber. **1900** H. Sutcliffe *Shameless Wayne* xii, His steel zags down like lightning before a man's eye can teach his hand to parry. **1906** *Spectator* 1 Dec. 879/2 One of the chief difficulties of walking up snipe is that when you shoot zig he goes zag, and when you shoot zag he goes zig.

†**za'gaie, za'gaye.** *Obs.* Also 6 **zagaia,** 7 **sagay.** [a. F. *zagaie*, reduced form of *azagaye*: see assagai *sb.*] = assagai *sb.*

1590 Sir J. Smythe *Disc. Weapons* L 4, Some numbers of *Zagaias* (which are double headed Lances). **1687** A. Lovell tr. *Thevenot's Trav.* i. 35 They are very dextrous at the *Zagaye*. *a* **1693** *Urquhart's Rabelais* iii. Prol., Long Hooks, Lances, Zagayes [Rabelais *azzesgayes*]. **1698** Froger *Voy.* 12 The Sagay, which is a very light Half-Pike. [**1702** W. J. tr. *Bruyn's Voy. Levant* xxii. 95 They..excell [in] the managing of the Zagaie; which is a sort of Stick about four Foot long, about an Inch Thick, round before and flat behind. **1869** Boutell *Arms & Armour* vii. 102 The 'Estradiots,'..armed with a *zagaie*, or javelin, pointed at both ends.]

Zaghlulist (zæ'glu:lɪst), *sb.* and *a.* Also **Zaghloulist.** [f. the name of the Egyptian politician *Zaghlūl Sa'd* (1857–1927) + -ist.]

A. *sb.* An adherent or supporter of the nationalist and separatist principles and policies of Zaghlūl Sa'd. **B.** *adj.* Of, pertaining to, or designating members of this political group.

1921 *Times* 29 Dec. 9/3 The Zaghlulists have raised the familiar Indian cry of non-cooperation. **1924** *Times* 14 Jan. 11/5 The comparative nonentity who was his Zaghlulist opponent. **1924** [see omdah, omdeh]. **1927** *Daily Express* 9 Sept. 1/1 A congress of Zaghlulist parliamentarians to decide on a policy consequent on the death of their leader will open on September 15 or immediately after, when the Wafdists (champions of Home Rule)..arrive. **1943** Ld. Wavell *Allenby in Egypt* vii. 102 The completeness of the Zaghlulist victory surprised every one..even Zaghlulists themselves. **1955** H. W. Jarvis *Pharaoh to Farouk* xxxii. 267 The Zaghloulists, however, were determined that a 'Tantah' incident *should* be repeated in some part of Egypt. **1971** P. Mansfield *British in Egypt* xxii. 252 Allenby..departed to genuine expressions of regret from the Egyptian public including the Zaghlulists.

‖**zaguan** (za'gwan, sa-). Also 9 **saguan.** [Sp., = vestibule, hallway.] The passage running from the front door to the central patio in houses in South and Central America and in the south-western U.S.

1851 *Harper's Mag.* Sept. 465/2 Don Pedro was heard within, moving toward the 'Saguan'. **1863** *Rio Abajo Press* 28 Apr. 1/2 She had just seen Juanito's ghost in the saguan door. **1880** G. W. Cable *Grandissimes* 131 It was a long, narrowing perspective of arcades, lattices, balconies, *zaguans*, dormer windows, and blue sky. **1921** *Chambers's Jrnl.* Mar. 258/1 There is the *zaguan* or vestibule at the outside, then the *cancel* or grating, and next the *patio* within. *Ibid.* Nov. 821/1 A couple of Moors—in the vestibule or *zaguan*—conduct a peculiar performance. **1927** D. H. Lawrence *Mornings in Mexico* 12 Some stranger comes into the *zaguan*.

Zahal (‖tsa'hal). [Heb., f. *Ṣĕḇā' Hăgānāh Lĕ-Yiśrā'ēl* Israel Defence Force.] The name applied by the Israelis to their defence forces, formed originally in 1948 by the fusion of pre-independence military organizations.

1959 A. M. Heller *Israel's Odyssey* 61 The Haganah disbanded, the Irgunist and the Sternist forces and their members were fused into the Zahal, made up of the initial Hebrew letters of Zva Haganah L'Israel—Israel's National Army. **1969** A. Perlmutter *Mil. & Politics in Israel* v. 55 Zahal's chief of staff was delegated the operational function of maintaining and training the army. **1971** *Scope* (S. Afr.) 19 Mar. 17/3 Very few top-ranking Israeli officers gave their Zahal (Defence Force) more than one chance in three of pulling it off. **1975** C. A. Haddad *Moroccan* i. 7 The twins did not have to lose two years to the Zahal, as the [Israeli] army does not draft religious girls. **1982** Murray & Viotti *Defense Policies of Nations* ix. 378 The leadership opted for a unified command for *Zahal* in which there would be one general headquarters and a chief of staff.

Zahara, variant of Sahara.

‖**zaibatsu** (zaɪ'bætsu:). Also **Zaibatsu.** [Jap., f. *zai* wealth + *batzu* clique.] In Japan, a large capitalist organization, usu. based on a single family having controlling interests in a variety of companies, of a type that existed before the war of 1939–45; since 1947, a cartel or conglomerate. Also, the members of such an enterprise.

1937 *Econ. Jrnl.* June 272 These concerns are popularly known in Japan as the *Zaibatsu* or money-cliques. **1947** R. Benedict *Chrysanthemum & Sword* iv. 93 A chosen financial oligarchy, the famous Zaibatsu. **1957** *Pacific Affairs* XXX. 219 The *zaibatsu* and the landlords. **1959** R. Kirkbride *Tamiko* (1960) vi. 41 By getting the right people to sit for you. The zaibatsu. The Royal Family. **1964** *Asia Mag.* 26 July 15/2 While the companies being merged presently are old Zaibatsu connected firms, and the groups are sponsoring the moves, the economics of the mergers themselves have little to do with such connections. **1965** *Economist* 11 Dec. 1219/2 The *Zaibatsu* are becoming concerned about the problems of seniority and management. **1970** [see conglomerate *sb.* 3]. **1974** P. Gore-Booth *With Great Truth & Respect* 45 When a community, historically prone to become the victim of unreason, finds itself in a position of success amid failure, its only recourse is probably to go to ground. The Japanese *Zaibatsu* understood this; a really successful Japanese business man was and is rarely obtrusive. **1982** K. Ohmae *Mind of Strategist* (1983) ix. 109 Japan's prewar *zaibatsu* holding companies.

‖**zaikai** ('zaikai). [Jap., f. *zai* wealth + *kai* community.] In Japan: financial circles; the business world or power élite who control it.

1968 C. Yanaga *Big Business in Jap. Politics* ii. 32 A new postwar term, zaikai,..practically supersedes zaibatsu... It is frequently interpreted..as a synonym for 'business circles', 'financial circles', and even 'business community'. More inclusive than zaibatu, it is nevertheless restricted to big business... Zaikai also denotes the place where the craving for political power is openly expressed and gratified. **1970** *Times* 19 Aug. 5/2 A Japanese economic magazine recently conducted a survey of opinion among leading representatives of the *zaikai*, the world of business and high finance. **1975** G. L. Curtis in E. F. Vogel *Mod. Jap. Organization & Decision-Making* 38 The men who make up this elite in Japan spend an extraordinary amount of time in so-called *zaikai* activities..that are not directly related to their own companies, but which seek to represent the interests of the business community as a whole. **1981** J. B. Kidd in P. G. O'Neill *Tradition & Mod. Japan* 50 The process of *nemawashi* operating in the senior levels of the *zaikai* world enable the companies to secure long-term goals.

zaire (zaɪ'ɪə(r)). [f. *Zaïre*, local name of the Congo River in Central Africa.] The basic monetary unit of the Republic of Zaïre; a coin of this value, equal to 100 makuta (see likuta).

1967 *Times* 9 Nov. 6 They tried to recruit former Katangese gendarmes... They offered seven zaires (£5) to every man who enlisted. **1971, 1972** [see likuta]. **1976** L. Sanders *Hamlet Warning* (1977) xvi. 133 A bribe... Five thousand zaire—ten thousand dollars.

Zairean (zaɪ'ɪərɪən), *sb.* and *a.* Also **Zairian.** [f. the name of the Republic of *Zaïre* (cf. prec.) + -an, -ian.] **A.** *sb.* A native or inhabitant of the Republic of Zaïre, formerly the Democratic Republic of the Congo. **B.** *adj.* Of or pertaining to Zaïre.

1972 *Observer* 19 Nov. 2/1 Dead victims..have been found dumped close to the frontier with Zaire... They were taken there by contract drivers, many of them Zaireans. **1973** *Black World* May 80 The dollar value of this manpower is considerable and most of it is defrayed by the Zairian Government. **1973** *Daily Tel.* 1 Oct. 19 Two British geologists yesterday described their fortnight's ordeal under armed Zairean Gendarme guards. **1973** *Times* 11 Dec. (Zaire Suppl.) p. vii/2 None of the young Zairians danced. **1977** *Times* 12 Apr. 13/1 Both the Moroccans and Zaireans are using their own planes to transport the troops. **1977** *Daily Tel.* 14 Apr. 1/8 The spokesman said that on Saturday two Zairean jets violated Zambian airspace. **1982** S. Johnson *Marburg Virus* x. 121 The logistic support of the Zairian army.

Zairese (zaɪ,ɪə'ri:z), *a.* and *sb.* [f. as prec. + -ese.] = Zairean *sb.* and *a.* Cf. next.

1974 *N.Y. Times* 10 Feb. 11/1 A 700-page, 30,000 word Swahili dictionary..is the work of a Zairese priest. **1975** *Business Week* (Industrial ed.) 27 Oct. 94H On the other side of the lake, the Zairese would like to build a new recovery unit. **1977** *Bangladesh Times* 19 Jan. 11/6 A lack of co-ordination between Belgian and Zairese security officials at Brussels airport, where the Belgian monarch was greeting President Mobutu. **1978** *Washington Post* 18 June A18/4 In the name of 'authenticity', he declared that in French revolution fashion Zairese should call each other 'citizen'.

Zairois (zaɪ,ɪər'wɑ:), *sb.* and *a.* Also **Zaïrois.** [a. Fr.] = Zairean *sb.* and *a.*

1973 J. J. MacKelvey *Man against Tsetse* iv. 228 The state of war against tsetse as the Zairois assess it will dictate the role that this institution may play in further research. **1974** *Observer* 22 Sept. 20/3 The Zairois people are warm, helpful and charming. **1975** R. Barclay *Ernest Bevin & Foreign Office* viii. 159 It is in any case an offence for a Zaïrois to wear such an 'un-authentic' item of dress as a tie. **1977** *New Day* Summer 10 (*caption*) A Zairois student learns how to take a skin smear. **1982** *Financial Times* 26 Jan. 22/1 The Government intends the industry to employ an eventual 700 Zairois.

‖**zakat** (za'kɑt). Also **zakah, zakkat,** †**zecchat.** [Pers. *zakāt*, Turk. *zekât*, etc., ad. Arab. *zakāh*.] An obligatory tax payable annually under Islamic law on certain kinds of property in order to raise money for charitable and religious objects.

1802 J. Pinkerton *Mod. Geogr.* I. 452 [Turkey.] This revenue is partly derived from..the *zecchat*. **1875** Bellew & Chapman in T. D. Forsyth *Rep. Mission to Yarkund* ii. 103 The *zakât* is a Mahommedan tax... It is one part in forty of all live-stock, and of merchandise entering the country. **1957** Ld. Hailey *African Survey 1956* x. 671 In Mauretania those who are not liable to *zakkat* pay the personal tax and in addition a capitation fee on every animal. **1960** C. Geertz *Religion of Java* x. 123 The fifth pillar [of Islam] is the *zakah*, the religious tax. **1979** *Observer* 4 Mar. 12/3 Their principal objection was to 'zakat', a partly-compulsory Islamic welfare tax which General Zia proposes to introduce in July. According to Shi-ism zakat has to be an individual act of conscience and can never be levied compulsorily by the State, he said.

‖**zakuska** (za'kuska). Also **zakouska**. Pl. **zakuskas, zakuski.** [a. Russ. *zakúska* (usu. as pl. *zakúski*).] An hors d'œuvre. Freq. pl.

The sing. form is occas. erron. const. as pl.

1885 A. J. C. HARE *Stud. in Russia* v. 203 The refreshment-room is enormous,..with a great buffet at one end, whither the Russians resort before dinner for the customary *zakuska* of pickles, sardines, vodki, &c. **1919** H. WALPOLE *Secret City* I. xii. 79 The 'Zakuska' were on a side-table near the door—herrings and ham and smoked fish and radishes and mushrooms and tongue and caviare. **1920** E. & P. SYKES *Through Deserts & Oases Central Asia* iv. 73 It began with many *zakuskas*, consisting principally of dubious-looking tinned fish. **1922** W. S. MAUGHAM *On Chinese Screen* vi. 27 The emotion..was diverted by the appearance of two Chinese servants in long silk robes and four-sided hats with cocktails and zakouski. **1933** H. NICOLSON *Let.* 7 Nov. (1966) 156 There were also little snippets of lobster in tomato cocktails, which were among the least successful of *zakouska* that I have ever known. **1951** V. NABOKOV *Speak, Memory* xiv. 213, I detest crowds, harried waiters, Bohemians, vermouth concoctions, coffee, *zakuski*, floor shows and so forth. **1981** T. KEENE *Skyshroud* i. 18 The *Zakouski*, the *borshch* and the *blini* of his homeland.

zalambdodont (zə'læmdədɒnt), *a. Zool.* [f. Gr. ζα-, intensive prefix + λάμβδα the letter lambda, Λ + ὀδούς, ὀδοντ- tooth.] Belonging to the division *Zalambdodonta* of insectivorous mammals, characterized by short molar teeth with a single Λ- or **V**-shaped ridge: opp. to DILAMBDODONT.

1885 *Riverside Nat. Hist.* (1888) V. 136 The zalambdodont dentition.

zalandyne, obs. form of CELANDINE.

1530 PALSGR. 291/2 Zalandyne an herbe, *esclaire.*

‖**zamacueca** (zama'kweka, sa-) Also 9 **-cuca.** [Amer. Sp.] A South American, esp. Chilean, dance in which a couple move around one another, accompanied by chords on the guitar and rhythmical handclapping. Shortened as CUECA.

1855 E. R. SMITH *Araucanians* vi. 65 The fashionable dances soon gave way to the more national *Zamacúca*. The Zamacúca has been very much reviled by foreigners, who have seen it only in sea-port towns. **1895** L. GROVE et al. *Dancing* xii. 375 The 'Zamacueca' is an inimitable dance, in which the handkerchief plays a prominent part. **1917** [see CUECA]. **1974** *Encycl. Brit. Macropædia* I. 669/1 The Creole people of the coast and plains [of South America] have been replacing the indigenous music of the mountains with their own music, especially with the ubiquitous *cueca*, or *zamacueca*.

‖**zamang** ('zæmæŋ). Also **zaman, saman.** [Native name.] A large ornamental leguminous tree (*Pithecolobium Saman*, suborder *Mimoseæ*) of tropical S. America, having a spreading head of branches of immense extent.

1819 HEL. M. WILLIAMS tr. *A. von Humboldt's Pers. Narr.* IV. 116 The famous *zamang del Guayre*, known throughout the province for the enormous extent of it's branches, which form a hemispheric head five hundred and seventy-six feet in circumference. The zamang is a fine species of mimosa, ..The branches extend like an immense umbrella, and bend toward the ground, from which they remain at a uniform distance of twelve or fifteen feet. **1852** E. SULLIVAN *Rambles N. & S. Amer.* 400 The zamang is a species of mimosa,..the leaves of this giant of nature are as small and delicate as those of the silver-willow.

‖**zamarra** (θa'marra). Also 9 **semara.** [Sp.] A sheepskin jacket worn by Spaniards.

1839 E. E. NAPIER *Jrnl.* 4 May in *Excursions along Shores of Mediterranean* (1842) II. vi. 81, I observed a tall, gentlemanly-looking man, dressed in a semara. **1841** G. BORROW *Zincali* I. II. i. 231 Another Gypsy..dressed in a zamarra of sheep-skin. **1842** BORROW *Bible in Sp.* ix. 53 The gipsy Antonio..dressed in his zamarra and high-peaked Andalusian hat. **1894** MAX PEMBERTON *Sea Wolves* xxii, Swarthy Galicians, in the black zamarra.

Zamazim, -zin, obs. corrupt ff. AMAZON.

a **1300** *Cursor M.* 7043 Zamazims [*c* **1425** *Trin. MS.* zamazinis] þat sith be-gan, þe wimmen land wit-outen man.

Zambian ('zæmbɪən), *sb.* and *a.* [f. *Zambia* (see def.) + -AN.] **A.** *sb.* A native, citizen, or inhabitant of Zambia (formerly Northern Rhodesia), a country in south central Africa.

1964 *Economist* 15 Feb. 607/2 With only 180 'Zambians' (Northern Rhodesia's name when independent) taking school certificate this year. **1976** *Drum* (E. Afr. ed.) Aug. 8/1 Another reason for the shortage here is that the township council has turned down licence applications from non-black Zambians and foreigners. **1977** 'O. JACKS' *Autumn Heroes* xiv. 207 *Everyone* had learned to freeze into silence the moment the Zambian made pronouncements.

B. *adj.* Of, pertaining to, or characteristic of Zambia or its people.

1964 *Times* 13 Nov. 11/3 A European in Zambia whose father was born in Britain might decide after a year to acquire Zambian citizenship. **1966** *Listener* 15 Dec. 879/2 The whole Rhodesian situation has driven Zambian politicians into a kind of neurosis. **1970** *Cape Times* 28 Oct. 2/5, I was furious when we found ourselves on the Zambian side of the lake. **1977** *Whitaker's Almanack 1978* 588/1 The Zambian Minister of Home Affairs signed deportation orders for 55 aliens who it was said had entered the country illegally.

Hence **'Zambianize** *v. trans.*, to make Zambian in character, by replacing foreign personnel by native Zambians; **Zambiani'zation.**

1968 *Times* 18 Nov. (Zambia Suppl.) p. v/2 The Zambian government wants to see the whole industry Zambianized, with no whites and indeed no foreign Africans in any jobs. **1968** *Economist* 14 Dec. 26/2 ANC claims simply that it could have done better, picking out the soaring cost of living, wasteful public expenditure and falling standards in the police force—the last two linked with too-rapid Zambianisation. **1969** *Listener* 14 Aug. 221/3 That may have led to the proposal to 'Zambianise' the judiciary. **1976** G. C. BOND *Politics of Change in Zambian Community* x. 166 Its policy of rapid Zambianization siphoned off the more educated and progressive elements. **1984** *Mining Jrnl.* 26 Oct. 287/2 Zambianization of the mining industry was a natural consequence of independence.

zambo ('zæmbəʊ). [Sp.: see SAMBO.]

1. = SAMBO 1.

1819 HEL. M. WILLIAMS tr. *A. von Humboldt's Pers. Narr.* IV. 430 He was..of a dark brown complexion like a Zambo. **1851** MAYNE REID *Rifle Rangers* xi. (1853) 72 In the sparse settlements of the country [*sc.* Mexico] you meet with a strange race—the cross of the negro with the ancient inhabitants of the country—the 'zamboes'. **1896** W. E. CURTIS *Venezuela* xii. 159 The zambos, the offspring of the imported negro and the native Indian stock.

2. A species of American monkey.

1851 MAYNE REID *Rifle Rangers* i. (1853) 11 The ferocious zambo fills the woods with its hideous half-human voice. *Ibid.* 350 The 'zambo' monkey is one of the largest and fiercest of the family of *quadrumana*.

Zamboni (zæm'bəʊnɪ). Chiefly *N. Amer.* Also **zamboni.** [See quot. 1965.] A proprietary name for a machine used to resurface ice rinks.

1965 *Official Gaz.* (U.S. Patent Office) 16 Feb. TM 93 Frank J. Zamboni & Co., Paramount, Calif... *Zamboni* for ice resurfacing machines and dump attachments therefor. First use July 1962. **1968** *Trade Marks Jrnl.* 3 Apr. 517/2 *Zamboni*... Machines for resurfacing ice rinks and parts and fittings therefor. **1974** *Kingston* (Ontario) *Whig-Standard* 11 July 14/2 With 12 scrapers, I could do that ice in nine minutes. With the Zamboni, it took a little longer..but I will have to admit it does do a better job. **1978** *Winnipeg Free Press* 25 Sept. 53/4 A crack in the boards near the door used by the zamboni helped Guindon open the scoring. **1984** *N.Y. Times* 11 Feb. I. 22/6 Then the ice was glazed by a smooth-nosed French cousin of the Zamboni before another Soviet skater..glided to gold medals.

zamboorak, zambourouk: see ZUMBOORUK.

‖**zambra** ('θambra, 'zæmbrə). [Sp.] A Spanish or Moorish dance.

1670 DRYDEN *Conq. Granada* I. i, Fair Almahide.. Prepares a Zambra to be danc'd this Night. **1832** W. IRVING *Alhambra* II. 46 In wanton Seville, where black-eyed damsels dance the zambra under every orange grove. **1906** *19th Cent.* June 942 The knights..often joined them in the graceful dance of the zambra.

zambuck, variant of SAMBUK.

zambuk ('zæmbʌk). *Austral.* and *N.Z. colloq.* Also **zambuc, -buck,** and with capital initial. [A proprietary name of a type of antiseptic ointment.] A first-aider, a St. John's ambulance man or woman, esp. at a sporting occasion. Also *attrib.* and *transf.*

[**1904** *Trade Marks Jrnl.* 23 Nov. 1406 *Zam-buk*... Chemical substances prepared for use in medicine and pharmacy, but not including gelatine capsules... The Bile Bean Manufacturing Company,..Leeds; vendors of proprietary medicines.] **1918** [see GUTSER]. **1943** *Amer. Speech* XVIII. 95 A few trade names have caught the public fancy, and become generalised. Thus *Zambuk*, a brand of ointment, is regularly used for a 'first-aid man' (usually a member of the St. John's Ambulance Corps), or even as an appeal for first aid. **1950** B. SUTTON-SMITH *Our Street* iv. 50 Everybody would shout, 'Zambuk! Zambuk!' until the first-aid man came to the rescue. **1965** *N.Z. Listener* 5 Nov. 4/5 Perhaps he might have concussion... A zambuck came with sal volatile. **1968** *Wanganui Photo News* 31 Aug. 13 (*caption*) No injuries to attend to so these 'Zambuk' ladies get on with their knitting at the basketball recently. **1969** *N.Z. Listener* 23 May 12/3 The driver was dead... There was a girl in a bad way mixed up with him. 'Better leave it for the zambucs,' Payne said. **1972** P. MATHERS *Wort Papers* 95 They even supplied the zambuck, a priest with brown attaché case containing oils and waters for extreme unction.

‖**Zamia** ('zeɪmɪə). *Bot.* [mod.L. (Linnæus, 1767), taken from *zamiæ*, misreading for *azaniæ* pine-nuts which open on the tree, in Pliny *N.H.* XVI. xxvi. 44.] A genus of cycadaceous plants, natives of the tropical and sub-tropical parts of N. America, the W. Indies, and S. Africa, resembling dwarf palms, with fern-like leaves and oblong cones; a plant of this genus.

1819 LINDLEY tr. *Richard's Obs. Fruits & Seeds* 74 The embryo of *Zamia* is reversed with regard to the pericarp, and occupies an axile cavity in a large endosperm. **1827** *Gard. Mag.* II. 425 The Zamia is a palm with a large scaly protuberance above the surface. **1841** G. GREY *Jrnl. Two Exped. Discov.* II. iii. 61 The native had..gone away to look for Zamia nuts. **1847** ANSTED *Anc. World* ix. 219 Zamias, cycadeæ, and such plants.

Hence **zamioid** ('zeɪmɪɔɪd) *a.*, belonging to the genus *Zamia* or tribe *Zamieæ*.

1860 J. PHILLIPS *Life on Earth* 145 Stems and fronds of Zamioid and Cycadeoid plants.

zamindar, variant of ZEMINDAR.

zamindari, -y, varr. ZEMINDARY.

‖**zamorin** ('zæmərɪn). *East Indies.* Forms: 6 **samoryn,** 7 **samorine, -orein, -aryn, -arine, zamori, -ourin,** (**-erhin**), 7–8 **samori,** 7, 9 **samorin,** 8–9 **zamorim,** 9 **zamorine,** 7– **zamorin.** [a. Pg. *samorim*, *çamorim* (It. *samory*, 16th c.), ad. Malayalam *sāmūri*, of disputed origin.] 'The title for many centuries of the Hindu Sovereign of Calicut and the country round' (Yule).

1582 N. LICHEFIELD tr. *Castanheda's Conq. E. Ind.* I. xiv. 33 b, They called him Samoryn, which in theyr tongue is Emperour. **1601** R. JOHNSON *Kingd. & Commw.* (1603) 204 All souerayne authority shuld rest in the king of Calecute, with the title of Samori. **1662** J. DAVIES tr. *Mandelslo's Trav.* 111 Since the establishment of the Portuguez in those parts, the power of Zamourin is grown so low,..the King of Cochim is more powerful then he. **1776** MICKLE tr. *Camoens' Lusiad* Introd. p. xlvii, Gama sent two of his officers with Monzaida to wait upon the Zamorim at his palace of Pandarene. **1862** BEVERIDGE *Hist. India* I. I. vii. 156 Calicut,..was then the capital of a Hindoo sovereign, who, under the title of *samiry* or *zamorin*, ruled a considerable extent of country. **1883** F. DAY *Indian Fish* (Fish. Exhib. Publ.) 17 The Samorin, in 1513, sent a deputation to Portugal.

zampatan, variant of SUMPITAN.

‖**zampogna** (tsam'poɲɲa, z-). *Mus.* [It.:—LL. **sumpōnia*, *symphōnia* (see SYMPHONY). Cf. Sp. *zampoña*, Pg. *sanfon(h)a*.] A traditional wind-blown bagpipe of southern Italy having two chanters and two drones; also, any wood-wind instrument.

1740 GRASSINEAU *Mus. Dict.* 343 *Zampogna*, sometimes written *Sampogna*..is..any instrument that sounds like a Flute and particularly a Bag-pipe, being an assemblage of divers pipes of different sizes. **1801** T. BUSBY *Dict. Mus.*, *Zampogna*, or *Sampogna*, the flute-à-bec, or common flute. **1826** M. KELLY *Reminisc* (1975) ii. 30 The peasantry and shepherds from Abruzzo, Calabria, and Apulia,..come from the mountains in their sheepskin dresses, playing on their various instruments, some on the Zampogna, (a kind of bagpipe), others on the Colascione. **1876** STAINER & BARRETT *Dict. Mus. Terms* 455/1 A rough-toned reed instrument without a bag is also called Zampogna or Zampugna. **1954** *Grove's Dict. Mus.* (ed. 5) I. 351/1 Italian pipers..make a practice of coming into the towns at the Christmas season to serenade the images of the Infant Christ, which are set up at the roadside. They also formerly visited Britain as strolling musicians, but they appear to have abandoned this habit many years ago; they were all players of the *zampogna*. **1977** *Early Mus.* Oct. 555/2 It was ..good to see no less than two sets of zampognas, from the early 19th century. **1983** *N.Y. Times* 26 June XI. (Westchester Weekly) 13/1 Vocalists will be accompanied on such classic Old World instruments as the zampogna.

‖**Zamzummim.** Also 6 **Zamzumym, Samsumim,** 7 **Zanzummin(e, -im.** [Heb. pl. *zamzummîm*.] A name of 'a people great, and many, and tall, as the Anakims' (Deut. ii. 21); used *allusively* or *fig.*

1530 TINDALE *Deut.* ii. 20 That also was taken for a londe of geauntes and geauntes dwelt therin in olde tyme, and the Ammonites called them Zamzumyms. **1530** —— *Answ. Sir T. More's Dial.* Pref., Wks. (1573) 249/1 Haue they not compelled the Emperours of the earth..to be their tormentours, and the Samsumims them selues do but imagine mischief and inspire them. **1628** BURTON *Anat. Mel.* II. iii. II. (ed. 3) 290 Aiax, Caligula, and the rest of those great Zanzummins, or giganticall Anakims. **1642** DRUMM. OF HAWTH. *Skiamachia* Wks. (1711) 201 Such numbers of arm'd enemies, so many Nimrods, Zanzummims, adversaries to our opinions. **1660** *England's Mon. Asserted* 9 Those two great Zanzummines of Church and State, the Arch-bishop of Canterbury, and the Earl of Strafford.

zanana(h: see ZENANA.

zanbuc(o, var. SAMBUK.

Zand: see ZEND.

Zande ('zændiː). Also 9 **Zandey;** 9– **Zandeh.** Pl. **Zandes, Azande** (†**A-Zande**). [Native name.] **a.** (A member of) a people of mixed ethnic origin inhabiting central Africa. **b.** The language of this people. Also *attrib.* as *adj.*

1873 E. E. FREWER tr. *Schweinfurth's Heart of Afr.* II. xiii. 6 As marks of nationality, all the 'Zandey' score themselves with three or four tattooed squares. **1884** *Encycl. Brit.* XVII. 474/1 The A-Zandey are to be regarded as rather of mixed Negroid than of pure Negro stock. *Ibid.* The Zandey language..appears to be everywhere spoken with considerable uniformity. **1891** A. H. KEANE tr. *W. Junker's Trav. in Africa* II. iv. 102 The hair, arranged Zandeh-fashion, though somewhat carelessly, in tresses, projected under a tarbush round the occiput. **1902** *Encycl. Brit.* XXXI. 230/1 The Zandehs proper..are now found to stretch, with interruptions, from the White Nile above the Sobat confluence to the Shari affluent of Lake Chad. **1918** R. G. C. BROCK in *Sudan Notes & Records* Oct. 249 The Zande tribe. *Ibid.*, The true Azande live in the Belgian Congo. *Ibid.* 253 The Azande are divided into different clans and most of these believe that they return to the earth in the form of some animal. *Ibid.* 257 The ordinary Zande dance is a very dull affair. **1938** E. M. NORTH *Bk. of*

Thousand Tongues 353/2 Zande... Spoken by perhaps 300,000 people in northeastern Belgian Congo, eastern French Equatorial Africa and southern Anglo-Egyptian Sudan. **1955** M. Gluckman *Custom & Conflict in Afr.* iv. 85 If a Zande murdered a fellow-tribesman with his spear he was tried in court by his chief. *Ibid.* 90, I find it difficult to see exactly how the Azande witchcraft charges work. **1978** J. Skorupski in Hookway & Pettit *Action & Interpretation* 85 Winch's account of the meaning of Zande magic is ultimately not at all unlike that which some symbolist writers might give.

zander (ˈzændə(r)). Also **sandre, sander.** [G. *zander*; in mod.L. *sandra* (Cuvier).] A common European species of pike-perch, *Stizostedion lucioperca* (*Lucioperca sandra*), valued as a food-fish.

1854 Badham *Halieut.* 114 The German *sandre*, pike-perch, one of the best-flavoured of the family. **1888** Goode *Amer. Fishes* 14 In the Old World,..there are two well marked species, the Zander, or Schill, *S*[*tizostedion*] *lucioperca*, and the Berschick, or Sekret, *S. volgensis*.

zanella (zəˈnɛlə). Also 9 **zenilla**. [? f. name of Antonio *Zanelli* (author of *Le lane italiane*, 1878).] (See quot. 1882.)

1876 F. Kilvert *Diary* 28 Apr. (1940) III. 272, I found she had taken my umbrella and left me a much better one, a fine silk umbrella in place of my zenilla. **1880** *Gt. Industr. Gt. Brit.* III. 213 Since 1848 a material called zanella cloth, which has a cotton warp, has been largely made. **1882** Beck *Draper's Dict.*, *Zanella*, a mixed twilled fabric introduced of late years, and used for covering umbrellas.

zaniacci, -o, zanjack, obs. ff. SANJAK.

1663 Davenant *Siege of Rhodes* II. III. i, A *Zanjack* from the Camp attends Behind the out-let of the Peer.

Zante (ˈzænti:). Also 7 **Zant.** A name of one of the Ionian islands, anciently *Zacynthus*: used attrib. in the names of certain products (see quots.); also short for *Zante wine, wood*, etc.

1615 E. S. *Brit. Buss* in Arber *Eng. Garner* III. 634 Physic and Surgery helps... Zante Oil. **1825** W. Weldon *Chem.* 560 Claret. Zante. Malmsey Madeira. **1835** *R. D. Thomson's Rec. Gen. Sci.* I. 387 A black juicy berry resembling the Zante grape. **1843** Holtzapffel *Turning* I. 110 Zante, or Young Fustic, from the Mediterranean, is a species of sumach, (*Rhus Cotinus*). **1858** Simmonds *Dict. Trade*, *Zante-wood*, a name for the *Rhus Cotinus* and for the *Chloroxylon Swietenia*.

zantho-, misspelling of XANTHO-.

zany (ˈzeɪnɪ), *sb.* (*a.*) Also 6–7 **zani, zanie,** 7 **zane, zanee, zanni,** (*pl.* **zaneese**), 8 **zaney.** [a. F. *zani*, or its source It. *zani, zanni* name of servants who act as clowns in the 'Commedia dell' arte'.

Properly, the Venetian and Lombardic form of *Gianni* = *Giovanni* John (cf. *Zanipolo* the title of the church of St. John and St. Paul in Venice) used as an appellative for a porter (or the like) from the mountain country of Bergamo who had taken service in a seaside town.

In the following the French word is app. intended:—*a* **1566** R. Edwards *Damon and Pithias* (1571) F ij, *Iacke.* Iebit avow mon companion. *Grimme.* Ihar vow pleadge pety Zawne. *Iacke.* Can you speake Frenche, here is a trimme colier by this day.]

1. A comic performer attending on a clown, acrobat, or mountebank, who imitates his master's acts in a ludicrously awkward way; a clown's or mountebank's assistant, a merry-andrew, jack-pudding; sometimes used vaguely for a professional jester or buffoon in general. Now *Hist.* or *arch.*

1588 Shaks. *L.L.L.* v. ii. 463 Some carry-tale, some please-man, some slight Zanie,..That..knowes the trick To make my Lady laugh. **1596** Lodge *Wits Mis.* M iv b, Here marcheth forth Scurilitie,..the first time he lookt out of Italy into England, it was in the habite of a Zani. **1599** B. Jonson *Ev. Man out of Hum.* IV. i, Hee's like a *Zani* to a Tumbler, That tries trickes after him to make men laugh. **1601** Shaks. *Twel. N.* I. v. 96, I protest I take these Wisemen ..no better then the fooles Zanies. **1648** Winyard *Mids.-Moon* 2 Cheynell among the visitors, is a mountebanke extraordinary with 4 zanyes. **1652** Urquhart *Jewel* 104 They go..in the disguise of a *Zanni* or *Pantaloon* to ventilate their fopperies. **1682** *New News fr. Tory-Land* 7 He may serve for some Zany to a Mountebank, to jest off Medicines for the Tooth-ach to the Rabble in Southwark. **1760** C. Johnston *Chrysal* lxix, A mountebank-doctor, and his zany. **1810** Crabbe *Borough* vii. 66 There was a time, when we beheld the quack, On public stage, the licensed trade attack; He made his labour'd speech with poor parade; And then a laughing zany lent him aid. **1848** L. Hunt *Jar of Honey* vi. 75 Those who had flattered him most when a king, were the loudest in their contempt, now that he was the court-zany. **1883** Miss M. Betham-Edwards *Disarmed* viii, Everybody is good to the Court-fool, the zany!

2. Hence in transf. and allusive uses, with various shades of meaning: **a.** An attendant, follower, companion, assistant: almost always contemptuous (sometimes, hanger-on, parasite), and with direct reference to sense 1. Now *rare* or *arch.*

1601 B. Jonson *Ev. Man in Hum.* II. iii. (Qo.), I pray thee be acquainted with my two Zanies [1616 *Fol.* hang-by's] heere. **1602** Middleton *Blurt* III. i. E 2, Lady Imperia (the Curtezan's Zani). **1616** R. C. *Times' Whistle* (1871) 136 Ye Aristippian zanies,..Leave off at last your poysning honnied speach. **1631** Chapman *Cæsar & Pompey* IV. i, Protean fortune, and her zany, warre. **1673** Hickeringill *Greg. Fr.-Greyb.* 50 The Directory, and the geud Covenant, (its *zanee*). **1746** Francis tr. *Hor., Ep.* I. xv. 37 A vagrant Zany, of no certain Manger, Who knew not, ere he din'd, or Friend or Stranger. **1746–7** Smollett *Advice* 181 To shine confess'd her zany and her tool, And fall by what I rose, low ridicule. **1760** H. Walpole *Let. to G. Montagu* 24 Nov., On the Address, Pitt and his zany Beckford quarrelled. **1817** [see MOUNTEBANK *sb.* 2]. **1880** *Q. Rev.* Jan. 14 St. John was not content to be a mere zany, he aspired to rival his master as a wit, and to outstrip him as a libertine. **1911** *Athenæum* 25 Mar. 343/3 To figure as a zany of a peer.

†**b.** An imitator, mimic; *esp.* a poor, bad, feeble, or ludicrous imitator. *Obs.*

1606 Dekker *Seven Sins* v. 31 An Ape is Zani to a man, doing ouer those trickes..which hee sees done before him. **1627** Drayton *Ep. to H. Reynolds* 93 As th' English Apes and very Zanies be Of euery thing that they doe heare and see. **1678** Dryden *All for Love* Pref. b 3 b, They are for persecuting Horace and Virgil, in the persons of their Successors... Some of their little Zanies yet go farther; for they are Persecutors even of Horace himself. **1730** *Flying Post* 22 Dec., Their little Zanies about the Country have learnt their Cant.

c. One who resembles, or acts like, a merry-andrew or buffoon; one who plays the fool for the amusement, or so as to be the laughing-stock, of others. Now *rare*.

1606 *Sir G. Goosecappe* III. i. in Bullen *Old Pl.* (1884) III. 42 Goe too, you French Zanies you. **1630** Bp. Hall *Serm., 2 Tim. iii.* 5 Wks. 1808 V. 393 What is a Hypocrite but a Player; the Zany of religion? **1728** Pope *Dunc.* III. 206 Oh great Restorer of the good old Stage, Preacher at once, and Zany of thy age! **1790** Wolcot (P. Pindar) *Adv. to Fut. Laureat* xv, I'll not be Zany to a King, not I. **1846** *Eclectic Rev.* June 662 Sydney Smith..was a West-end chapel preacher,..a lecturer in Albemarle-street, and Zany to Holland-house. **1925** *Sunday at Home* Nov. 91/2 He went capering about all his tasks with a zany-like glee. **1929** C. Day Lewis *Transitional Poem* I. 11 A burly wind playing the zany In fields of barleycorn. **1976** G. Langford (*title*) Death of the early morning hero. Episodes of a zany in love.

d. A fool, simpleton, 'idiot'. Still *dial.*

a **1784** Johnson in R. Cumberland *Mem.* (1806) I. 263 The lady asked me for no other purpose than to make a Zany of me. **1847** Tennyson in Ld. Tennyson *Mem.* (1897) I. 241 The printers are awful zanies, they print erasures and corrections too, and other sins they commit of the utmost inhumanity. **1862** Thackeray *Philip* iii, Whether Andrew was a genius, or whether he was a zany, was always a moot question. **1897** Watts-Dunton *Aylwin* III. i, A heaven for zanies and tom-fools!

B. *attrib.* passing into *adj.* **a.** *attrib.* That is a zany, or characteristic of a zany; †imitative; clownish; foolish, idiotic. **b.** *adj.* Comically idiotic, crazily ridiculous.

The adjectival use of the word (as if an adj. formed with -Y[1]) is now the dominant one. In quot. 1938, 'simple-minded' (cf. sense 2 d).

1616 Anton *Philos. Sat.* C 2, Like a gorgeous robe, Purl'd ore with natures Ape, and Zany-art. **1618** J. Taylor (Water P.) *Pennyles Pilgr.* E 2, Nor Britaines Odcomb (Zanye braue Vlissis) In all his ambling saw the like as this is. **1869** Blackmore *Lorna D.* xv, He will make some of your zany squires shake in their shoes. **1890** Hall Caine *Bondman* II. ii, Your zany doings have shut every other door against you. **1918** G. B. Shaw in *Nation* 22 June 308/2 Before Shakespear touched Hamlet there was a zany Hamlet who mopped and mowed. **1938** L. MacNeice *I crossed Minch* viii. 117 The gardener who was apparently zany, used to level his stick at an obelisk. **1957** Manvell & Huntley *Technique Film Music* v. 204 *Sloppy Jalopy* (UPA), a zany cartoon. **1959** *House & Garden* June 76 Luncheon-mats of the subtlest as well as the zaniest designs. **1978** J. Krantz *Scruples* xii. 349 Television shows that lean heavily on the brand of humor known as 'zany', consisting largely of sight gags and the sight of appealing people making cheerful fools of themselves. **1983** D. Cecil *Portrait of Lamb* II. ii. 143 A sympathetic spirit able to appreciate his more characteristic and zany vein of humour.

Hence **ˈzanily** *adv.*; **ˈzaniness**.

1958 S. Ellin *Eighth Circle* (1959) I. i. 11 In Central Park sea lions barked zanily at the sky. **1960** *Sat. Rev.* 6 Feb. 13/2 Ginsberg, for all his carefully cultivated (and natural) zaniness, is a writer far above Kerouac. **1966** M. Laurence *Jest of God* ix. 170 I've..emptied the crucial and precious capsules out of my window, zanily. **1976** *Times Lit. Suppl.* 21 May 602/2 His wider appeal owes much more to his modern zaniness and irreverence. **1980** L. Birnbach et al. *Official Preppy Handbk.* 111/1 Many of these forays into zaniness actually wind up involving mayhem or destruction of property. **1984** *Financial Times* 25 July 13/6 The play is a staple of the repertory and amateur theatre diet, and while it may not inspire to the zanily surreal heights of *See How They Run* or *Madame Louise*, Dighton is certainly a name worth conjuring with. **1985** *Listener* 21 Mar. 28/3 How could anything with Jerry Lewis not fall into a comic range somewhere between surrealistic zaniness and childish destructiveness?

ˈzany, *v. Obs.* or *rare arch.* [f. prec.] *trans.* To play the zany to; to imitate poorly or awkwardly like a zany; hence *gen.* to imitate, mimic.

1602 Marston *Antonio's Rev.* IV. i, Who..Laughes them to scorne, as man doth busie apes When they will zanie men. *a* **1619** Fletcher, etc. *Q. Cor.* I. ii, [He] takes his oath..that all excellence In other Madams doe but zany hers. **1691** Langbaine *Acc. Dram. Poets* 351 Francisco's zanying the Person and Humour of Albano, is an incident in several Plays. **1894** H. Pease *Mark o' Deil* Pref. 7 If the delicious original be beyond capture, why essay to zany it?

zanyism (ˈzeɪnɪɪz(ə)m). [f. as prec. + -ISM.] The character or style of a zany; action or language like that of a zany; fantastic folly; buffoonery.

1818 Coleridge *Lit. Rem.* (1836) I. 138 The caricature of his [*sc.* Rabelais'] filth and zanyism. **1823** *Blackw. Mag.* XIII. 662 Such zanyisms as these.

So **ˈzanyship**, the condition or character of a zany.

1766 J. Adams *Diary* 7 Jan., Wks. 1850 II. 175 Y. Z. and H. had attacked him about idleness, and familiar spirits, and zanyship.

zanza, zanze, varr. SANSA.

zanzack, -ziac, Zanzummim, -in(e, zaphire, zapota, -ote, zapotilla, obs. ff. SANJAK, ZAMZUMMIM, SAPPHIRE, SAPOTA, SAPODILLA.

Zanzibari (ˌzænzɪˈbɑːrɪ), *sb.* and *a.* [f. *Zanzibar*, name of an island off the east coast of Africa, now part of Tanzania + -I.] **A.** *sb.* A native or inhabitant of Zanzibar. **B.** *adj.* Of, pertaining to, or characteristic of Zanzibar or its people.

1888 G. W. Brooke *Let.* 18 July in M. E. Herbert *Afr. Slave Trade* (1890) 12 The Zanzibaris express horror and disgust at the bare idea of associating with them. *Ibid.* 13 The women and children are hurried off to the Zanzibari camps. **1890** W. Booth *In Darkest Eng.* I. i. 12 Mr. Stanley's Zanzibaris lost faith. **1917** G. B. Shaw in *Daily Express* 28 Nov. 3/2 When the Sultan of Zanzibar ordered the admiral of his second-hand penny steamboat to go out and sink the British fleet, and the poor devil actually went, we laughed... No doubt Ireland, north and south, teems with Zanzibari courage. **1959** *Daily Tel.* 1 Dec. 8/6 It is uphill work to persuade the Zanzibaris to make a partial switch to other products, which they could fairly easily do in their fertile island. **1966** D. Wilson *Quarter of Mankind* xvi. 205, I have sat on a train in Manchuria and heard Zanzibari visitors ask their guides why colonialism had not yet been expelled from Hong-kong. **1975** *Nat. Geographic* Apr. 501/1 Towering above all a tree bearing tiny reddish buds—the famous cloves, basis of the Zanzibari economy. **1985** *Daily Tel.* 20 Aug. 4/7 Zanzibaris with foreign exchange were allowed to import essential goods.

zaouia, var. ZAWIYA.

zap (zæp), *int. slang* (orig. *U.S.*). [Echoic.]

1. Used to represent the sound of a ray gun, laser, bullet, etc.; also *fig.*, expressing any sudden or dramatic event.

1929 P. F. Nowlan in *Washington Post* 7 May 16/3 Ahead of me was one of those golden dragon Mongols, with a deadly disintegrator ray... Br-r-rr-r-z-zzz-zap. **1962** *Amer. Speech* XXXVII. 288 The jokester, pretending to be a creature from outer space, pointed his cosmic ray gun (finger) at his friend's genitals and exclaimed, 'Zap! You're sterile.' **1967** L. Deighton *Only when I Larf* (1968) xii. 160 Shouting idiotic things and going, 'Whoop,' 'Zap,' and 'Yap,' all the time. **1968** *Maclean's Mag.* Mar. 77 Bang! Zap! Pow! With laser beams and cracking doomsday machines, the deadly-serious super-heroes. **1970** *Daily Tel.* (Colour Suppl.) 15 May 34/4 I'm against the war in Vietnam. But I'm not among the people who say let's stop Vietnam, zap. **1971** *Frendz* 21 May 17/1 Getting down to a blow job, she suddenly produces a razor and zap—the man bleeding and gushing blood, is screaming on the floor. **1974** *Globe & Mail* (Toronto) 12 Sept. 7/2 We have been told..we needn't worry, the sections are not being enforced. Then zap, another homosexual is denied entry for being honest. **1978** *Fortune* 18 Dec. 101 (Advt.), The solution receives a positive charge, the truck a negative charge. Zap! The primer and the GMC are joined with a magnetic-like bond. **1985** *Parade Mag.* 31 Mar. 9 A staff meeting will be Wick just shooting out those things one after another—zap, zap, zap.

2. zap gun, a ray gun or the like.

1969 K. Vonnegut *Slaughterhouse-Five* iv. 65 Billy's will was paralyzed by a zap gun aimed at him from one of the portholes. **1976** *Publishers' Weekly* 15 Mar. 59/1 Plot is subordinated to character exploration, but there's more adventure in that than in many a zap-gun epic. **1977** *Sunday Sun* (Brisbane) 30 Jan. 7/1 New York police have confiscated two space-age 'zap' guns from blind singer Stevie Wonder... The guns look like flashlights and fire two darts attached to 20 ft. thin copper wires.

zap (zæp), *v. slang* (orig. *U.S.*). Also (*rare*) **zapp.** [Echoic.] **I.** *trans.* **1. a.** To kill, esp. with a gun; to deal a sudden blow to.

1942 Berry & Van den Bark *Amer. Thes. Slang* §118/3 *Kill; murder*,..wipe out, work off, zap. **1965** *Time* 10 Dec. 34 *Zap*..means to clobber. **1966** *Current Slang* (Univ. S. Dakota) Fall 6 *Zap*, v., to slap... I got *zapped* when I tried that. **1969** I. Brown *Rhapsody of Words* 143 In Vietnam a man knocked out was said to be zapped. **1970** *Courier-Mail* (Brisbane) 14 Dec. 3/3 A council workman on-duty during the week zapped any rat foolish enough to wiggle a whisker within a hundred yards of the place. **1971** *Sunday Times* 28 Mar. 9/1 He wants to prove a Hanoi man can zapp a Saigon man. **1971** *Radio Times* 18 Nov. 15/4 This year the system has zapped the counter-culture member in the sneakiest way of all, by robbing him of a decent way of making a living after graduation. **1977** *Time* 6 June 55/2 Proto..fires a beam of electrons at the pellet, zapping it with a jolt equal to 8 trillion watts. **1979** *Mod. Photogr.* Oct. 64 You can't run a darkroom without plug-in power, so you'd better make it electrically safe or you might get zapped! **1981** *Observer* 2 Aug. 10 God is not going to zap women for coming forth. **1982** N. Freeling *Wolfnight* 161 Unbureaucratically, any bugger who shoots, you zap. **1984** *Weekly World News* (U.S.) 25 Dec. 29/1 Teenager Vickie Parker was zapped to death by 640 volts of electricity when she wandered onto the tracks of an elevated train and accidentally touched the 'live' third rail. **1985** *N.Y. Rev. Bks.* 9 May 23/3 (Advt.), In a New York restaurant, a young man celebrating with friends was zapped in the face by a man with an aerosol spray can.

b. To put an end to, do away with.

1976 *Courier-Mail* (Brisbane) 22 Apr. 21/4 We can zap a headache almost immediately. **1982** *Sunday Sun-Times* (Chicago) 17 Oct. 62 (*heading*) Atari seeks to zap X-rated video games.

2. To fail (someone) in a test, course, etc.; to punish (see also quot. 1969).

1961 *Amer. Speech* XXXVI. 149 The cadet who is *zapped* is the recipient of a large number of demerits or other cadet punishments. The term was probably taken from a favorite cadet newspaper comic strip, 'B.C.', where *zapp* is used as the sound of any blow. **1969** *Current Slang* (Univ. S. Dakota) Winter 12 *Zap*, v., to 'put down'; to put someone in his place. **1976** *National Observer* (U.S.) 17 Jan. 8/5 A graduate student whose 'scholarly potential' is not overwhelmingly lauded 'is going to get zapped'.

3. To overwhelm emotionally.

1967 *Punch* 26 July 123/1 I'll be zapped with love, blow the mind of straight people. **1970** *New Yorker* 22 July 4/3 If the music doesn't zap you..you can contemplate..movies on the wall. **1971** *Daily Colonist* (Victoria, B.C.) 30 May 47/1 Our politicians turn to the architects, presuming them to be the theatrical stage managers of the city to zap the masses with compelling masques and follies. **1974** A. LURIE *War between Tates* (1977) vi. 134 If The Book is published in time, and the right people in Washington read it, it's going to really zap them. **1977** *It* May 31/3 (Advt.), Bring you own sounds!!, and get zapped. **1983** *Theology* Jan. 15 A well-known evangelist invited the undergraduates of Oxford to allow themselves to be 'zapped by the Holy Spirit'.

4. To send, put, or hit in a forceful way.

1967 *Time* 22 Dec. 56 For quick acceleration..the nickel-cadmium batteries would cut in briefly, could zap the car from a standstill to 50 m.p.h. in 20 seconds. **1972** D. DELMAN *Week to Kill* 139, I nosed the car out of town and on to 118, where I zapped it into high. **1974** *Farm & Country* 9 Apr. 11 (*heading*) Computers zap farmers through space-age door. **1976** *National Observer* (U.S.) 29 May 12/4 Won't they be surprised when Ms. Klutz limberly zaps the ball over the net.

5. To demonstrate against or at.

1972 *Sat. Rev.* 12 Feb. 24/1 Homosexuals..'zap' (confront) politicians until they express themselves..on equal housing..for homosexuals. **1980** *Observer* 3 Aug. 8/5 Columbia and Warner Bros. were 'zapped' last week; this Tuesday it's the turn of 20th Century Fox. An itinerant army of 1,000 striking actors..will parade at the old studio's grimy portals.

6. *Computers.* To erase or change (an item in a program).

1982 *Times* 14 Jan. (Information Technol. Suppl.) p. v/5 When the program is erased, the PROM is said to be 'zapped'. **1983** *80 Microcomputing* Jan. 29/3 On DRS 304, RB 2C you will find the byte to be 20H. Zap this to 18H. **1983** *Your Computer* Sept. 86/1 Since I keep a hard copy listing of the assembly of MODEM7, the easiest thing to do was to zap the offending byte.

II. *intr.* **7.** To move quickly and with vigour.

1968 *Maclean's* Sept. 55 Nothing is quite as sad as watching Lynn watching Lightfoot zap off out of a parking lot. **1972** *Observer* 27 Feb. 33/5 The well-known routine of zapping from studio to studio. **1977** *Mod. Boating* (Austral.) Jan. 30/3 We're zapping over Kogarah Bay with 45 miles an hour on the clock. **1981** *Times* 22 July 12/4 When those self-satisfied pop singers and dizzy girls from Hollywood zap in and out they are not drinking themselves silly at our expense. **1985** *Times* 6 Apr. 11/1 Several smaller craft zap past.

8. To use a fast-forward facility on a video recorder to go quickly *through* the advertisements in a recorded television programme; to switch *through* other channels for the duration of the advertisements when watching programmes off-air.

1983 [implied in ZAPPING *vbl. sb.*]. **1984** *Broadcast* 7 Dec. 27/2 People are beginning to record the best commercial programmes on their VCRs so they can zap through the commercials. **1985** *Marxism Today* May 34/1 People with the technology use it to avoid commercial breaks, either by zapping through other channels or by fast-forwarding material recorded off-air.

Hence **zapped** *ppl. a.* and *pa. pple.*

1962 *Amer. Speech* XXXVII. 71 'Zapped.'.. I first heard it in 1952 while I was an undergraduate at Brown University. The term was in vogue..to designate precisely the process by which a student..had his 'come-uppance' in class or on an examination. **1966** *Punch* 21 Dec. 911/3 Maybe truce negotiations won't be possible until the Viet Cong are zapped to the point of accepting the impossibility of military victory. **1976** *National Observer* (U.S.) 22 May 12/4 Despite his allure, could she really endure him? But the chap's got her zapped. **1980** R. ADAMS *Girl in Swing* xix. 254 She was pale and sweating; clearly what Mr. Steinberg would call 'zapped'.

zap (zæp), *sb. slang* (orig. *U.S.*). [f. ZAP *v.*, *int.*]

1. Liveliness, energy, power, drive; also, a strong emotional effect.

1968 *N.Y. Times* 2 Aug. 3 When the heat's too much and the gin's lost its zap.., tranquilize your jangled nerves with the Swinging Wonder. **1972** *Publishers' Weekly* 6 Mar. 62/2 As for those lyrics—probably only the over-30s will dig them. Anyone older or younger won't grasp the 'organic' zap of rock's years of innocence. **1975** *Harpers & Queen* May 128/3 The zap of his language drawn from every dialect of the underground. **1979** *Chatelaine* (Canada) Jan. 50 She loves sports, especially skiing, but found she had lost some of her old zap. **1979** *Mod. Photogr.* Oct. 68 Electricity arrives at your neighborhood at a level of 2400 [*read* 240] volts... If the transformers were perfect you would get precisely the 110 volts you wanted and could care less about the big zap lurking outside. **1984** *New Yorker* 16 Apr. 141/1 He gives the film a manic zap.

2. A demonstration (by a group against something).

1972 *Sat. Rev.* 12 Feb. 26 Despite six zaps, New York's Mayor Lindsay has consistently refused to meet with any homosexual delegation. **1974** *Times* 7 Oct. 12/3 A demonstration, alternatively described as a community action or a zap, had been planned..in Brixton's Tesco supermarket.

3. *Computers.* A change in a program.

1983 *80 Microcomputing* Jan. 29/1, I would like to provide the following zaps to TRSDOS 1·3 for the Model III. To provide a 30ms track stepping rate you must change the nine bytes listed below.

4. A short, varying sound of the kind expressed by 'zap!'

1984 *Verbatim* X. III. 17/2 The whir of the flippers—pinball machines—the zaps of the video games.

Zapata (zəˈpɑːtə). The name of Emilio *Zapata* (1879–1919), Mexican revolutionary, used *attrib.* to designate a type of moustache in which the two ends extend downwards to the chin.

Zapata was portrayed with a moustache of this kind by Marlon Brando in the film *Viva Zapata!* in 1952.

1968 *Punch* 25 Dec. 903/1 He stood now, in the centre of the enormous white vault of the school's auditorium, a willowy figure in a green velveteen frock-coat, Zapata moustache and a Donovan cap. **1972** A. ROSS *London Assignment* 84 One of the younger men, wearing nothing now but his Zapata moustache.., came up for a fresh joint. **1977** *N.Y. Rev. Bks.* 4 Aug. 11/1 He is a heavy, buccaneering figure with a Zapata mustache. **1983** *Manch. Guardian Weekly* 22 May 20/1, I was delighted to see a few shots of Karajan as stage actor—hiding behind a Zapata moustache as a bit-part cardsharper in the Carmen film he made in 1967.

‖**zapateado** (θapateˈaðo). Also **Zapateado.** [Sp., f. *zapato* shoe.] **a.** A flamenco dance which involves complex rhythmic syncopated stamping of the heels and toes in imitation of castanets.

1845 R. FORD *Handbk. Spain* I. 190 The chief dances are the *Jota* of Arragon..the *Zapateado* and *Seguidilla* of La Mancha..and the *Zortico* of Biscay. **1902** *Encycl. Brit.* XXVII. 374/2 Other provincial dances now in existence are the *Jaleo de Jerez*,..the *Zapateado*, the *Zorongo*..and the *Tripola Trapola.* **1952** *Ballet Ann.* VI. 30 Antonio is in certain details of the Spanish dance the greatest exponent I have seen... Both his Bolero and his Zapateado must be seen to be believed. **1958** *Times* 23 Sept. 3/4 There is a good selection of flamenco dances, including solo and *à deux* Zapateados. **1973** *Daily Tel.* 19 Nov. 12/1 They danced without music and—like flamenco dancers performing a Zapateado—they used a very wide variety of sounds produced with their heels and toes so that music was superfluous. **1985** *Listener* 28 Feb. 18/3 Soon the girls are dancing with sensuous frenzy and a young man leaps on a table to execute a fine *zapateado.*

b. Dancing or footwork of this kind.

1959 *Sunday Times* 17 May 20/8 José's imprisonment, his rage expressed in zapateado, and the drama of Carmen's death, are adroitly planned. **1980** 'M. FONTEYN' *Magic of Dance* 56 Antonio, an electrifying dancer of flamenco and particularly of the language of foot and heel beats called zapateado. **1981** *Daily Tel.* 26 Aug. 9/8 Maya..has a superb grasp of subtle and varied zapateado.

zapote (zəˈpəʊteɪ). [Sp.: see SAPOTA.] = SAPOTE.

1842 S. MAVERICK *Jrnl.* 16 Dec. (1953) ix. 185 Fruit—oranges, Zapotes, etc. **1909** *Chambers's Jrnl.* Aug. 557/2 The Zapote..should secure the appreciation of the English fruitarian. **1926** D. H. LAWRENCE *Plumed Serpent* xiv. 229 A big basket piled with mangoes, papayas, zapotes—all the tropical fruits one did not want, in hot weather. **1948** G. M. FOSTER *Empire's Children* 27/2 Fruit trees include the fig,.. white and black *zapotes.*

Zapotec (ˈzæpəʊtɛk), *sb.* and *a.* Also 8– Zapoteca, -o, 9 **Zapoteque.** [ad. Sp. *zapoteco*, *zapoteca*, ad. Nahuatl *tzapoteca*, pl. of *tzapotecatl*, lit. 'person of the place of the sapodilla'.]

A. *sb.* A member of an American Indian people of southern Mexico.

1797 *Encycl. Brit.* XI. 668/1 To the south-east..were the great provinces of the Mixtecas, the Zapotecas, and the Chiapanecas. **1875** *Ibid.* I. 694/2 In Chiapa were the Zapotecs, in Yucatan the Mayas. **1877** L. H. MORGAN *Anc. Soc.* II. vii. 195 The confederacy was confronted by hostile ..tribes..: the tribes of Chiapas, and the Zapotecs. **1953** S. BEDFORD *Sudden View* III. v. 231 The ancient Zapotecs.. who may have come from Asia across the Behring Straits, and who are believed to have built..these temples at Mitla and Monte Albàn. **1979** P. THEROUX *Old Patagonian Express* v. 75 These Indians—the Zapotecs—were a matrilineal people.

b. Any of several dialects or languages of the Zapotecs.

1881 *Encycl. Brit.* XII. 828/1 The other chief stock or at least not yet classified Mexican tongues are the Miztec and Zapotec of Oajaca, [etc.]. **1936** E. C. PARSONS *Mitla* i. 16 These ladies understand Zapoteco..but they do not speak it. **1965** *Language* XLI. 73 In Trique, Isthmus Zapotec, and certain other languages of Mexico, certain clause types have the preferred ordering predicate, subject, object. **1973** *Times* 24 Mar. 11/8 The student of architecture we met in the square of Oaxaca was talking Zapotec to his girl-friend.

B. *adj.* Of or pertaining to the Zapotecs.

1861 [see EXPECTANT *ppl. a.* 1 b]. **1927** D. H. LAWRENCE *Mornings in Mexico* 45 Four words in the *idioma*, the Zapotec language..'You understand them?' **1934** A. HUXLEY *Beyond Mexique Bay* 46 A bas-relief of an ithyphallic man—the work..of the pre-Zapotec occupants of the site. **1972** *Bk. Thousand Tongues* (rev. ed.) 464/2 The Zapoteco language is spoken in a number of regional dialects. **1980** *Sci. Amer.* Feb. 46/3 Its hieroglyphs, mostly carved from 500 B.C. to A.D. 700, record the rise and decline of the Zapotec state.

Hence **Zapoˈtecan** *a.* and *sb.*

1922 K. AL-SHIMAS *Mexican Southland* vii. 122 The Zapotecan tongue is spoken by at least 500,000 souls. *Ibid.* 126 Those accosted made answer in Zapotecan. **1962** E. BIRNEY *Ice Cod Bell or Stone* 54 Rhythmic and Zapotecan-proud the classic women dance. **1978** *Language* 506/2 In the Zapotecan family of Oaxaca, 'Choapan Zapotec phonology', by Larry and Rosemary Lyman..employs 'a hierarchically oriented framework' of five levels, from phoneme to 'phonological sentence'.

zappe (cf. It. *zappare*), obs. f. SAP *sb.*[3] and *v.*[1]

1600 DYMMOK *Ireland* (1843) 38 When that rampart which is, shall either be beaten or zapped.

zapper (ˈzæpə(r)). [f. ZAP *v.* + -ER[1].]

a. A person, technique, etc., that kills or does away with something. **b.** *spec.* Any of various devices for destroying or warding off pests; also (properly with capital initial), a proprietary name in the U.S. for an agricultural machine of this kind.

1969 *Guardian* 27 May 8/5 The United States colonel who formerly commanded them.. is now busy evolving a 'zapper' technique for scything down nippa palm groves where Vietcong are reported to be hiding with direct fire artillery. **1970** *Courier-Mail* (Brisbane) 14 Dec. 3/3 The rat zapper does not work on Saturdays or Sundays, but there were still no rats to be seen there yesterday. **1973** *Sci. Amer.* Sept. 74/2 One particularly promising application, making use of small portable zappers, is for greenhouses and other horticultural enterprises where the cost of soil preparation per acre is not an important consideration. For row crops.. the self-propelled Zapper is presently economic only when chemical weed-control costs are higher than $15 per acre. **1975** *Official Gaz.* (U.S. Patent Office) 25 Mar. TM 271/2 *Zapper.* For agricultural machine which employs microwaves to control vegetation and vegetation damaging pests. **1976** *Nature* 12 Feb. 441/1 The general message is that although various alternatives are promising, there is no magic 'insect zapper', as Kennedy put it, to replace chemical poisons in the near future. **1977** *Globe & Mail* (Toronto) 30 July 4/1 How many bugs do zappers zap? **1983** *Monitor* (McAllen, Texas) 23 June 10C (Advt.), 1 acre bug zapper. $59·97. 35 watt ultraviolet fluorescent bulb has an effective range up to 1 acre for outdoor comfort.

zapping (ˈzæpɪŋ), *vbl. sb. slang.* [f. ZAP *v.* + -ING[1].] The action of ZAP *v.*; *spec.* the practice of skipping advertisements when watching television programmes.

1972 *Daily Colonist* (Victoria, B.C.) 8 Jan. 17/7, I wouldn't take the zapping he has taken, to use the contemporary word, for a million dollars. **1983** *Times* 27 Oct. 8/3 The practice is known in the US as 'zapping'. Apparently people who have remote control devices are substantially more likely..to switch over to another channel when ads come on. **1983** *Austral. Personal Computer* Nov. 32/2 You could add suitable sound-effects to an applications program—zapping noises as a word processor deletes characters, maybe? **1984** *Listener* 9 Feb. 14/2 For the ITV companies there is the additional problem of 'zapping' to contend with—the habitual use of the fast-forward button to bypass the commercial breaks in recorded material.

zappy (ˈzæpɪ), *a. slang.* [f. ZAP *sb.* + -Y[1].] Lively, amusing, energetic; striking.

1969 *Guardian* 1 Mar. 5/2 The Minister wore in his lapel ..a zappy coloured badge of the 'Cocoa makes you sterile' type. **1971** 'J. MAYO' *Asking for It* xxiv. 155 They were both giving each other big zappy grins. **1972** *Observer* 16 July 30/2 We badly need some zappy young editor who will start making his more garrulous authors prune their books. **1983** *Times Lit. Suppl.* 30 Dec. 1448/3 The best of contemporary American prose sometimes has a zappy elegance. **1984** *Listener* 3 May 30/4 The company felt the need for a zappier profile.

‖**zaptieh** (ˈzæptɪeɪ). Also **-ié.** [Turkish *ḍabtiyeh*, f. Arab. *ḍabt* administration, regulation.] A Turkish policeman.

1869 TOZER *Highl. Turkey* II. 100 A young Turkish Zaptié, or policeman. **1878** tr. *F. von Löher's Cyprus* xxi. 177 A wretched coffee-house, which was full of zaptiehs, who were quartered here.

zarab, early var. *sharab*, SHRAB, wine, etc.

1477 EARL RIVERS (Caxton) *Dictes* 27 b, He that seketh the delices of this worlde is like vnto him that seketh to drink zarab wenyng it were water.

zarape, U.S. var. of SERAPE.

Zarathustrian (zærəˈθʊstrɪən), *a.* and *sb.* [f. *Zarathustra*, the Old Iranian form of the name of the founder of the ancient Persian religion.] = ZOROASTRIAN. So **Zaraˈthustrianism, Zaraˈthustric** *a.*, **Zaraˈthustrism.**

1871 TYLOR *Prim. Cult.* I. ii. 49 Brahmanism, Zarathustrism, and Buddhism. *Ibid.* II. xv. 219 The Wicked Serpent of the Zarathustrians. **1886** *Encycl. Brit.* XX. 361/1 The Vedic and Zarathustric religions. *Ibid.* 370/1 Mazdaism (Zarathustrianism), with its sects. **1891** CHEYNE *Orig. Psalter* viii. 401 The Bundahis is thoroughly Zarathustrian in spirit when it states [etc.].

zaratite (ˈzærətaɪt). *Min.* [a. Sp. *zaratita* (Casares, 1851), f. the name of Señor *Zarate*: see -ITE[1].] A hydrous carbonate of nickel, of a green colour, found as an incrustation and in stalactites.

1858 SIMMONDS *Dict. Trade* [erron. as *Zamtite*]. **1861** BRISTOW *Gloss. Min.* [erron. as *Zavalite*]. **1868** DANA *Min.* (ed. 5) 710 Zaratite.

‖**zarcole.** Also 6 saracoll, 6–7 zarcola, 7 -cull, zercola. [Turkish.] A high cylindrical head-dress such as was worn by janizaries.

1585 T. WASHINGTON tr. *Nicholay's Voy.* I. vi. 4 b, Slaues bearyng on theyr heads a Saracoll of Crymson veluet. *Ibid.* III. iii. 73 b, A hood of fine white felt, whiche they call Zarcola. *Ibid.* x. 91 b, A white Zarcole. **1603** KNOLLES *Hist. Turks* (1621) 831 His slaues with their red zarcull on their heads. **1696** tr. *Du Mont's Voy. Levant* 176 A Thousand Janisaries.. with Zercola's on their Head.

†**zard.** *Obs.* Variant of IZZARD; cf. ZAD.

1608 J. DAY *Humour out of Breath* III. i, *Asp.* Marry, buz. *Flo.* Double the zard and take the whole meaning for your labour.

zareba, zareeba: see ZARIBA.

‖**zarf** (zɑːf), **zurf** (zɜːf). [Arab. *ẓarf* vessel.] A cup-shaped holder for a hot coffee-cup, used in the Levant, usually of metal and of ornamental design.

1836 LANE *Mod. Egypt.* I. 168 Zurf. **1854** R. CURZON *Armenia* 80 One brought coffee on a tray.. and then came a man bringing to each of us a cup, well frothed up, and in a zarf, or outer cup. **1978** *Times* 2 May 13/3 (*caption*) A diamond and emerald zarf, mounted in gold and silver, 19th century, 6·5 cm high.

‖**zariba, zareba** (zəˈriːbə), *sb.* Also **seriba, sariba, zerybeh, zareeba, zer(r)iba, zereba.** [Arab. *zarībaʰ* pen or enclosure for cattle (*zarb* sheep-fold).] **a.** In the Sudan and adjacent parts of Africa, A fence or inclosure, usually constructed of thorn-bushes, for defence against the attacks of enemies or wild beasts; a fenced or fortified camp.

1849 O'REILLY tr. *Werne's Exped. Sources White Nile* II. 112 A shining seriba of reeds, the stalks of which.. perhaps only afford resistance to tame animals. **1852** *Eliza Cook's Jrnl.* 27 Mar. 337 The Sultan has planted a zerybeh, or circular inclosure, with two issues. **1867** BAKER *Nile Trib.* xii. 315 We employed ourselves.. in cutting thorn branches, and constructing a zareeba. **1884** *Times* 11 Mar. 5 The Black Watch (Royal Highlanders) advanced this morning to Baker Pasha's zariba.

b. Applied to a formation of troops for defence against attack.

1887 *Times* 9 Apr. 5/5 Forming a zariba, or square, to resist cavalry.

c. *transf.* and *fig.* In these uses usu. as **zareba.**

1885 *Glasgow Her.* 19 Mar. 4/5 It is when he advances from these elementary zarebas that he loses himself in the wilderness, and, apparently from an inherent inability to state any fact correctly. **1898** A. WHITE in *Nat. Rev.* Aug. 804 The.. Tsar.. is.. surrounded by a zereba of detail and enticed from affairs of State by organized diversions. **1916** 'TAFFRAIL' *Pincher Martin* iii. 42 The orchestra.. took their places behind a zareba of bunting-covered biscuit-boxes and hired palms erected in front of the stage. **1940** G. GREENE *Power & Glory* II. ii. 128 The shadows of the palms pointed at him like a zareba of sabres. **1961** WODEHOUSE *Ice in Bedroom* vii. 52 Owing to his *obiter dicta* having to be filtered through a zareba of white hair, it was not always easy to catch exactly what Mr. Cornelius said. **1965** G. MAXWELL *House of Elrig* x. 139 The final approach to any birds' nest was an affair of struggle and achievement. My hand reaches through the twigged zareba of basket and basket handle, touches the soft lining, touches the firm intimacy of the eggs. **1974** *Author* Spring 33 A novelist.. has direct access to his readers, with no thorny zariba of a cast of actors to battle through. **1984** *Listener* 3 May 24/2 The two previous ones faced the reader in their opening chapters with an almost impenetrable zareba of thickset descriptions of the committee structure.

d. *attrib.*

1895 A. H. KEANE *Africa* I. v. 245 The expression 'zeriba country' applied by some geographers to the northern slope of the Nile-Congo divide. **1901** H. VIVIAN *Abyss.* vii. 184 A succession of enclosures, each with a zareba wall.

Hence **za'riba** *v. trans.*, to surround or inclose with a zariba; *intr.* to construct or form a zariba.

1885 *19th Cent.* July 89 Orders were given to zereba ourselves... The Brigadier ordered the force to zereba on the best position that was near. **1886** *Contemp. Rev.* June 850 A large garden, zerebaed in with aloes and henna.

zarish, obs. form of TSARISH.

1814 tr. *Klaproth's Trav. Cauc.* 181 The ambassadors of his Zarish Majesty.

‖**zarnich** (ˈzɑːnɪk). Also 7 **zernich,** 9 **zarnac, -ec, -eg, -ek.** [Arab. *zarnīkh*, f. Pers. *zernī* orpiment, f. *zer* gold.] A name for the yellow and red sulphides of arsenic, usually called respectively *orpiment* and *realgar*.

1610 B. JONSON *Alch.* II. iii, Your lato, azoch, zernich, chibrit, heautarit. **1748** J. HILL *Hist. Fossils* 406 Bright red Zarnich, the Sandarach of Authors. **1867** BRANDE & COX *Dict. Sci.* s.v. *Yellow Orpiment*, In its native state it [*sc.* yellow arsenic] is used under the name of Zarnic or Zarnich.

Zarp (zɑːp). *S. Africa.* Now *Hist.* [From the initials of Du. *Zuid Afrikaansch Republikeinsch Politie* South African Republican Police.] An appellation for a member of the Boer police force in the pre-1902 South African Republic; a Boer constable. Hence **Zarpine** *a.*, of or belonging to the 'Zarps'.

1895 *Standard & Diggers News* (Johannesburg) 23 Nov. 21 The Zarp produces his latest capture. Jan, an Ethiop, is a vagrant who resisted Zarpine authority, and even attempted to test the Zarpine probity by the bribe of a sixpence.

zarza parilla: see SARSAPARILLA.

‖**zarzuela** (θarˈθwela). [Sp.] A traditional form of popular musical comedy in Spain.

In its theatrical sense the word is said to be derived from the name *Real Sitio de la Zarzuela* in Madrid, where these works were first performed in the early 17th century.

1888 *Lippincott's Mag.* July 51 It had all transpired in a flash, like some of the absurd things he had seen in pantomimes by the *zarzuela* companies at the theatres. **1922** J. HERGESHEIMER *Bright Shawl* (1923) 54 The zarzuelas, the operettas of one act, largely improvised with local allusions. **1947** A. EINSTEIN *Music in Romantic Era* xvii. 328 The way was being prepared for the Italianization of Spanish music as early as Calderón's period, which brought forth the old *zarzuela*, a mixture of song and dance with spoken dramatic dialogue. **1973** *Oxford Times* 30 Mar. 14/5 The modern zarzuelas are really operettas or lyric dramas, which are a kind of Spanish equivalent of Gilbert and Sullivan and the Viennese operetta, full of tunes which have become part of Spain's popular culture. **1973** R. A. CRAMPSEY *Puerto Rico* viii. 130 Less common are the old *zarzuelas*, the traditional musical dramas. **1983** *Listener* 21 Apr. 31/2 A Catalan born in 1871,.. he [*sc.* Amadeo Vives] was evidently best known as a *zarzuela* composer.

zastruga, var. SASTRUGA.

zat (zæt), repr. a colloq. pronunc. of the cricket appeal 'How's that?' (see HOW *adv.* 2 b).

1934 *Humorist* 27 Jan. 38/3 Not a bad record.. for a game that consists chiefly of standing about.. and shouting 'Zat?' at intervals. **1966** M. WOODHOUSE *Tree Frog* xxiii. 167 Outside the window a sharp yelp of 'Zat?' sounded.

zatch (zætʃ). *vulg.* [Perh. corruption of SATCHEL in similar slang sense.] The buttocks; the female genitals; an act of copulation.

1950 E. B. WHITE *Let.* 6 June (1976) 321 You are just sticking out your zatch, and many a tosspan and strutfart will run you through. **1971** R. DENTRY *Encounter at Kharmel* v. 88 Scotsmen playing the bagpipes give me a pain in the prick... Pathan tribesmen playing them is enough to make the harlot of Jerusalem snatch her zatch! **1980** J. KRANTZ *Princess Daisy* xii. 191 You're going to take her home and give her a zatch.

zaught, zaunders, zauns, zavana: see YACHT, SANDERS[1], ZOUNDS, SAVANNAH.

‖**zawiya** (ˈzɑːwɪə). Also **zawia, zawiyah, zawya; zaouia.** [Arab. *zāwiya* (hence F. *zaouia*) corner, prayer room.] In North Africa, a Muslim religious community or its mosque, usually containing the shrine of a holy person.

1836 E. W. LANE *Acct. Manners & Customs Mod. Egyptians* II. xi. 190 These lights were not hung merely in honour of the Prophet: they were near a *zawiyeh* (or small mosque) in which is buried the sheykh Durweesh El-Ashmawee; and this night was his Moolid. **1874** R. L. PLAYFAIR *Handbk. Trav. Algeria* II. 70/2 The *Djamâa*, or rather *Zaouia* of *Abd-er-Rahman eth-Thalebi*.. contains the tomb of that saint, who died in 1471. **1911** *Encycl. Brit.* XXVII. 289/1 Kufra.. is a centre of the Senūssite brotherhood, whose *zawya* (convent) at Jof, in Kebabo, ranks in importance with that of Jarabub. **1911** D. S. MARGOLIOUTH *Mohammedanism* v. 184 A *zawiyah*, or 'hermitage' was offered him by the Pasha. **1924** W. M. SLOANE *Greater France in Afr.* viii. 166 The sacred colleges of the Moslem fraternities, zaouias, are the scenes of wild, maniacal, religious orgies. **1958** N. EPTON *Saints & Sorcerers* ii. 28 The sheikh (this word signifies either the head of a *zaouia* or of a tribe..) lives close to the *zaouia* with his family and the devotees. **1968** T. BLUNSUM *Libya* x. 105 The *zawias*, or houses of learning and worship, were documentation centres where copies of the Koran were prepared for distribution. **1977** *Times* 30 Apr. 11/3 Nefta.. a village.. whose roof lines are broken by the cupolas of mosques and zaouias. **1978** J. UPDIKE *Coup* (1979) iii. 122 Who was it used to tell reporters I was a *zawiya* Berber too pious to be seen?

zax, dial. form of SAX *sb.*[1], tool for cutting slates.

zay, dial. form of SAY *v.*[1]

‖**zayat** (ˈzɑːjət). [Burmese.] A public hall or shed for worship, meetings, or shelter.

1823 MRS. A. JUDSON *Amer. Bapt. Miss. Burman Emp.* 145 The Zayat, the Burman name for a place for public worship, was erected. **1852** PIERSON *Miss. Mem.* 89 In April 1819 the first zayat was opened for Christian worship. **1906** *Blackw. Mag.* Aug. 230/2 They went straight to the *zayat*, the strangers' rest-house.

‖**zazen** (zɑːˈzɛn). Also 8 **Sasen; Zazen.** [Jap., f. *za* sitting, a seat + *zen* ZEN.] Zen meditation.

1727 J. G. SCHEUCHZER tr. *Kæmpfer's Hist. Japan* I. III. i. 242 A posture, which is thought to engage one's mind in so profound a meditation, and to wrap it up so entirely within itself, that the body lies for a while as it were sens less... This profound Enthusiasm is by them call'd *Safen* [sic: read *Sasen*]. **1897** *Princ., Pract. & Enlightenment Soto Sect* 22 How can you think of not-thinking? That is thinking of nothing. This is the most important art of Zazen. **1907** *Jrnl. Pali Text Soc. 1906–7* 36 Zazen is not meant to induce a trance or a state of self-hypnotization. **1960** KOESTLER *Lotus & Robot* II. xi. 257 Zazen meditation, unlike Yoga, holds no promise of supernatural rewards. **1973** A. BROINOWSKI *Take One Ambassador* viii. 108 Three hours of daily *zazen* meditation. **1983** M. FURLONG *Cousins* xxi. 167 He had taken to practising what he hoped was *zazen* in the yard.

Z band: see Z LINE (as a main entry).

Zbloud, 'Zbud, Z'death, obs. ff. 'SBLOOD, 'SBUD, 'SDEATH.

1620 I. C. *Two Merry Milk-maids* IV. iii. M 2, Zbloud I heard otherwise. **1676** ETHEREDGE *Man of Mode* I. i, 'Zbud, I think you men of quality will grow As unreasonable as the Women. **1689** N. LEE *Princ. Cleve* II. ii, Z'Death and Fury, if they shou'd try.

ze, obs. form or graphic var. of THE, YE.

‖**zea** (ˈziːə). [late and mod.L. *zēa*, a. Gr. ζειά.] †**1.** A Latin name for the grain called spelt. *Obs.*

1577 GOOGE tr. *Heresbach's Husb.* 29 Next to Wheate and Barley, foloweth Zea. **1611** COTGR., *Bled leger*, Spelt or Zea; a corne which makes light and sauorie.. bread.

2. *Bot.* Adopted by Linnæus as the name of a genus of graminaceous plants, comprising the one species *Z. Mays* (sometimes anglicized as *zea maize*), Maize or Indian corn.

1787 tr. *Linnæus' Fam. Plants* II. 633 *Zéa*... Indian, or Turkey Wheat. **1808** BARTRAM in A. Wilson *Amer. Ornith.* (1832) I. 8, I fed him with corn, (zea, maize). **1820** *Amer. Jrnl. Sci.* II. 46 The smut upon an ear of Zea-Mays. **1851** MAYNE REID *Rifle Rangers* i. (1853) 16 The lance-like blades of the zea maize.

zeagonite (zɪˈægənaɪt). *Min.* [Named in 1816 by Gismondi, f. Gr. ζεῖν to boil + ἄγονος barren: see -ITE[1].] = GISMONDINE.

c **1840** *Encycl. Metrop.* (1845) VI. 519/2.

zeal (ziːl), *sb.* Forms: 4–7 **zele,** 5 **zel,** 5–6 **zeel(e,** 5–7 **zeale,** 6 **zealle,** *Sc.* **zeil(e, zeill, (syil),** 4– **zeal.** [Late ME. *zele*, ad. L. *zēlus*, a. Gr. ζῆλος. Cf. OF. *zel* (F. *zèle*), It., Pg. *zelo*, Sp. *celo*.]

1. In biblical language, rendering L. *zelus* (or *æmulatio*), Gr. ζῆλος, denoting ardent feeling or fervour (taking the form of love, wrath, 'jealousy', or righteous indignation), with contextual tendency to unfavourable implications (emulation, rivalry, partisanship).

1382 WYCLIF *2 Kings* xix. 31 The zeel [1388 feruent loue, COVERDALE gelousy] of the Lord of hoostis schal done that. —— *Ezek.* viii. 3 The north, where the idol of zele [*gloss* or enuye], was set. **1526** TINDALE *Gal.* v. 20 The dedes of the fleesshe.. hatred, lawynge, zele [1611 emulations, 1881 (*R.V.*) jealousies]. **1535** COVERDALE *Ecclus.* xlviii. 2 He brought an honger vpon them and in his zele he made them few in nombre. **1575** tr. *Luther's Comm. Gal.* iii. 88 These kindes of anger are good, and are called in the scripture ielousies or zeales. **1604** T. WRIGHT *Passions* II. iii. 63 Zeale (that is, envie, emulation or indignation) and anger shorten thy dayes. **1611** *Bible* Ezek. v. 13 They shal know that I the Lord haue spoken it in my zeale, when I haue accomplished my fury in them.

†**2.** In a specialized sense: Ardent love or affection; fervent devotion or attachment (to a person or thing). *Obs.* or merged in sense 4.

c **1400** *Rule St. Benet* (prose) lxxii. 139 As there is an euyll zele, loue, or affeccyon the whiche departyth one from god .. soo there is a zele or affeccion.. the whiche departyth one from synne. **1412–20** LYDG. *Chron. Troy* II. 3168 With zel of feith I brenne as doth þe glede, Of alle harmys to bidden ȝow be war. *c* **1449** PECOCK *Repr.* I. xiii. 71 Bi cause noon of hem .. wole so allegge aȝens me for eny zele or credence which he him silf hath to what he schal so allegge. *c* **1450** tr. *De Imitatione* II. iii. 43 Haue þerfore first zeel to þiself, & þan maist þou haue zeel to þi neiȝbore [*Habe primo zelum super te ipsum, et tunc juste zelare poteris etiam proximum tuum*]. **1485** *Cov. Leet Bk.* 524 The loue and zele that ye owe.. to the wele.. of our said Citie. **1513** MORE *Rich. III* (1883) 36 Hath the protectour so tender zele to him that he fereth nothing but lest he should escape hym? **1559** *Mirr. Mag., Salisbury* xxviii, For though no cause be found, so nature frames, Men haue a zeale to such as beare their names. *a* **1562** G. CAVENDISH *Wolsey* (1893) 51 The Cardynall espieng the great zeale that the kyng had conceyved in this gentilwoman. **1606** G. W[OODCOCKE] *Hist. Ivstine* xxxv. 113 Demetryus.. spared his life not for any zeale hee had toward him. **1685** in *Verney Mem.* (1907) II. 403, I thought I had ground for those hopes, which.. the zeal of my soul formed into wishes for her recovery.

†**3.** Ardent, earnest, or eager desire; longing. Also const. inf. or clause. *Obs.* or merged in 4.

c **1450** CAPGRAVE *Life St. Gilbert* 65 Gilberd.. had.. so grete zel to lede soules to heuene. *c* **1450** *Brut* II. 522 Wherfore he might nat performe his zele & desire þat he had conceyved Agenst þe Turke. **1474** CAXTON *Chesse* II. iv. (1883) 54 Thus shold the knightes haue grete zele that the lawe be kept. **1547** in Strype *Eccl. Mem.* (1721) II. App. K. 39 Upon the confydence of whych your accomplyschment to my expectation, zele, and request. **1581** A. HALL *Iliad* II. 21 Yᵉ rout with zeale of news now goes. **1597** SHAKS. *2 Hen. IV*, v. v. 14 This doth inferre the zeale I had to see him. **1658** SLINGSBY *Father's Leg.* in *Diary* (1836) 211 My tender zeal .. of your future welfare. **1697** DRYDEN *Virg. Georg.* IV. 300 Such Rage of Honey in their Bosom beats And such a Zeal they have for flow'ry Sweets.

4. (*a*) Intense ardour in the pursuit of some end; passionate eagerness in favour of a person or cause; enthusiasm as displayed in action. Const. *for*; †formerly *to*, occas. *of*.

[*c* **1520** NISBET *N.T.* Eph. iv. 26 *marg.*, This angre and wraith was bot a weray zeill vnto the law of God. **1535** COVERDALE *Ps.* lxviii[i]. 9 The zele of thine house hath euen eaten me.] ? **1545** BRINKLOW *Compl.* xxv. (1874) 74 Let all thinges be done of zeale only for Gods truthes sake. **1555** EDEN *Decades* (Arb.) 50 By whose.. godly zeale this myghtie portion of the worlde hath byn added to the flocke of Chrystes congregation. **1593** G. HARVEY *Pierce's Super.* Wks. (Grosart) II. 175 Inordinate Zeale is a pernitious Reformer. **1610** B. JONSON *Alch.* III. i, In pure zeale, I doe not like the man: He is a heathen. **1611** *Bible* Transl. Pref. ¶1 Zeale to promote the common good. **1641** J. JACKSON *True Evang. T.* III. 197 They deride our worship, and zeale, as Michall did Davids. **1681** TATE *Lear* Ep. Ded., My Zeal for all the Remains of Shakespear. *a* **1700** EVELYN *Diary* 19 Aug. 1641, Popular reformers, whose zeale had foolishly transported them in other places rather to act like mad-men than religious. **1727–46** THOMSON *Summer* 1615 That first paternal virtue, Public Zeal. **1816** BYRON *Siege Cor.* iv, With all the zeal Which young and fiery converts feel. **1835** THIRLWALL *Greece* vi. I. 209 A mean between this irreverent criticism, and the excessive zeal of those who regarded Homer as a master of all arts and sciences. **1860** E. B. RAMSAY *Remin.* v. (ed. 6) 183 He joined with his drinking propensities a great zeal for the Episcopal Church. **1874**

GREEN *Short Hist.* vii. §6. 400 The decay of Catholicism appealed strongly to the new spirit of Catholic zeal.

†(*b*) In obsolete constructions.

1526 *Pilgr. Perf.* (W. de W. 1531) 122 b, Many hath a good zele to perfeccyon, whiche for lacke of this lyght.. knoweth not what is to be done. **1535** STEWART *Cron. Scot.* (Rolls) II. 535 His gude Lyfe and Maneris, and Zeill of Justice. **1561** WINȝET *Bk. Questions* To Rdr., Wks. (S.T.S.) I. 53 Blindit be feruent zele towart the Mosaical law. **1597** SHAKS. *2 Hen. IV*, IV. ii. 27 Vnder the counterfeited Zeale of Heauen. **1723** *Pres. St. Russia* II. 86 A Zeal of converting the neighboring Nations.

†(*c*) In plural. *Obs.*

c **1533** LATIMER in Foxe *A. & M.* (1563) 1309/2 Such ar zeles without knowlege, and iudgement. **1625** BACON *Ess., Viciss. Things* (Arb.) 570, I doe not finde, that those Zeales, doe any great Effects. **1654** Z. COKE *Logick* Pref., Whereof (my Lords).. we.. by your unwearied Zeals may.. obtain the full.. Fruition.

†**5.** In weakened sense, with qualifying adj.: Intent, purpose, will, disposition (chiefly *good zeal*). *Obs.* (chiefly *Sc.*).

1513 DOUGLAS *Æneis* III. Prol. 29 Gentill curtas redaris of guide zeill. *a* **1533** FRITH *Answ. More* (1548) A 3 b, Master More which of late hath busyed him selfe to medle in al such matters (of what zele I will not defyne). **1536** BELLENDEN *Cron. Scot.* VI. v. (1821) I. 207 Thus grew he, ilk day, more terribill and odius to his pepill, and governit the realme with na better zeil than he gat it. **1537** *St. Papers Hen. VIII*, VII. 707 The many discomoditeis,.. the wiche be like were unknowen to hym or them that have preffarrid the same, who myght of a good syil doo it. *a* **1578** LINDESAY (Pitscottie) *Chron. Scot.* (S.T.S.) I. 14 Men of guid zeall and conscience.

†**6.** *transf.* (from 4). A zealous person, zealot.

1614 B. JONSON *Barth. Fair* I. iii, As errant a Zeale as he. **1643** SIR T. BROWNE *Relig. Med.* I. §3 There are.. both in Greek, Roman, and African Churches, solemnities,.. whereof the wiser zeales doe make a Christian use. **1647** JER. TAYLOR *Lib. Proph.* Ep. Ded. 9 Although some Zeales are so hot, and their eyes so inflamed with their ardors.

7. *attrib.* and *Comb.*

a **1613** OVERBURY *A Wife*, etc. (1638) 140 The hooke and crooke of his *Zeale-blind Shepheard. **1628** LEIGHTON *App. Parlt.* ix. 202 The fyrie *zeal-consuming love of Gods howse. **1648** J. BEAUMONT *Psyche* XII. ccii, The Stranger's *zeal-inflamed Eye. **1736** THOMSON *Liberty* IV. 919 The worst the zeal-inflam'd Barbarian drew. **1774** J. ADAMS in *Fam. Lett.* (1876) 23 This zeal will prove fatal to the fortune and felicity of my family... Colonel Otis's phrase is, 'The *zeal-pot boils over'. **1671** FOULIS *Hist. Romish Treasons* (1681) 110 *Zeal-pretending gravity. **1727** P. WALKER in *Biogr. Presbyt.* (1827) I. 304 The Christ-dethroning, Church-ruining,.. *Zeal-quenching Indulgence. **1598** SYLVESTER *Du Bartas* II. i. II. *Imposture* 35 The profane *zeal-scoffing Atheist. *a* **1644** QUARLES *Sol. Recant.* solil. v. 37 O but my *zeal-transported soul, take heed. **1797** BENTHAM in Betham-Edwards *Autob. A. Young* (1898) 309 Knowing.. your zeal for all *zeal-worthy objects.

Hence **'zealful** *a.*, full of zeal, zealous; †**'zealist**, a zealot; **'zealless** *a.*, wanting in zeal (whence **'zeallessness**).

1602 FULBECKE *2nd Pt. Parall.* Ded. 1 My dutifull thankfull and *zealefull affection toward your graces person. **1605** SYLVESTER *Tri. Faith* iv, Meek Moses with a zeal-full ire. **1614** C. BROOKE *Ghost Rich. III*, lxxiv. Poems (1872) 107 Proue not a *Zelist in fond purity, Nor paint a heauen, nor counterfeit a hell. **1638** SIR T. HERBERT *Trav.* (ed. 2) 27 The Meccan zealists have here a few poore built Mosques. **1613** SPELMAN *De non Temer. Eccl.* (1646) 30 O thou *zeleless mortality. **1643** HAMMOND *Serm., John xviii. 40* Wks. 1684 IV. 514 That heartless zealless behaviour in this very house of God. **1868** PUSEY *Our Pharis.* 15 A zealless, loveless, lifeless worship of God. **1667** WATERHOUSE *Narr. Fire Lond.* 65 Levity and *Zealesness for Reformed Religion.

†**zeal**, *v. Obs.* Also zele. [ad. late L. *zēlāre*, ad. Gr. ζηλοῦν, f. ζῆλος ZEAL *sb.*]

1. *trans.* To be zealous for; to pursue with zeal or passionate ardour.

1542 UDALL *Erasm. Apoph.* I. 69 A notable exaumple of sapience with whole herte & mynde, feruently desired and zeled. **1609** *Bible* (Douay) Wisd. i. 12 Zeale not death in the errour of your life. **1623** NAUNTON in *Fortescue Papers* (Camden) 193 Blesse and prosper it to both yourselves and to all that truely zeale your truest prosperities.

2. To inspire with zeal.

1549 CHEKE *Hurt Sedit.* (1569) L iij b, Men zealed towarde God, but not fit to iudge. **1642** FEATLY *Vertumnus* 85 They will.. stirre up an earnestnesse in them in religion, as zealing their owne being opposed by falshood.

3. *intr.* To act with zeal, show zeal, be zealous.

1459 [see *zealing* below]. *a* **1626** BACON *Disc. conc. Ch. Aff.* (1641) 19 Stiffe fellowes, and such as zeale marvellously for those whom they have chosen to be their masters.

Hence †**zealed** *ppl. a.*, full of zeal, zealous (see also OVER-ZEALED); †**'zealing** *ppl. a.*

1459 *Rolls of Parlt.* V. 348/2 Subtily coloured, and feyned zelyng Justice. **1600** W. WATSON *Decacordon* (1602) 68 A faire seeming.. fountaine of zealing christall streames. ? **1635** FLETCHER, etc. *Love's Pilgr.* IV. i, You might have done, but for that zeald religion You women bear to swownings.

Zealander ('zi:ləndə(r)). Forms: 6 Zelender, 7 Zelander, 7– Zealander. [f. *Zealand* = Du. *Zeeland* + -ER[1].] **a.** A native or inhabitant of Zealand, a province of the Netherlands.

1573 BEDINGFIELD tr. *Cardanus' Comf.* II. (1576) 21 Gulielmus a Zelender. **1656** EARL MONM. tr. *Boccalini's Pol. Touchstone* (1674) 254 She doth.. make more.. War upon the Spaniards, than do the Hollanders and Zealanders. **1766** *Compl. Farmer* 5 H b/1 The Zealanders let their's [*sc.* madder] grow larger. **1855** MACAULAY *Hist. Eng.* xx. IV. 485 Every merchant ship that cleared out from the Thames or the Severn would be manned by Zealanders and Hollanders and Frieslanders.

b. A native or inhabitant of New Zealand; orig. and esp. a Maori.

1773 W. BAYLY *Jrnl.* 12 Apr. in R. McNab *Hist. Rec. N.Z.* (1914) II. 207 The Zeelanders never eat greens of any kind. **1821** M. EDGEWORTH *Let.* 7 Dec. (1971) 288 Captain Thompson.. went some years ago to New Zealand and when he was taking leave of the Zealanders one of their chiefs consented to accompany him to England. **1949** E. POUND *Pisan Cantos* lxxx. 92 And persuaded an Aussie or Zealander or S. African To kneel with him in prayer.

⁂ See also NEW ZEALANDER.

zeale, obs. form of SEAL *sb.*[1]

1666 *Chirk Castle Acc.* (1908) 129 Paid Sir Thomas Myddelton.. what he gave the men that came to shew the zeale fish.

zealot ('zɛlət). Forms: [4], 6–7 zelote, 4–8 zelot, 7 zelott, 6– zealot. [ad. eccl. L. *zēlōtes*, a. Gr. ζηλωτής, f. ζηλοῦν to be zealous (see ZEAL *v.*).]

1. A member of a Jewish sect which aimed at a Jewish theocracy over the earth and fiercely resisted the Romans till the fall of Jerusalem in A.D. 70.

[*a* **1300** *Cursor M.* 21165 Symon zelote.] **1537** [COVERDALE] *Orig. & Sprynge of Sectes* 55 Zelotes or Gelous secte. These were suttyll and sedicious rascals amonge the Iewes of Ierusalem. **1644** HAMMOND (*title*) Of Resisting the Lawfull Magistrate under colour of Religion... Also, Of the Zelots among the Jewes. **1671** STILLINGFL. *Serm., Matt. xxi. 43* Wks. 1710 I. 107 That desperate Faction of the Zealots, who.. soon put the whole Nation into Flames. **1831** E. BURTON *Eccl. Hist.* i. 11 The persons who were called *Zealots*, from their zeal for the national religion and independence. **1882** FARRAR *Early Chr.* II. 111 *note*, The Zealots formed the 'extreme left' division of the Pharisees politically, as the Essenes did religiously.

2. One who is zealous or full of zeal; one who pursues his object with passionate ardour; usually in disparaging sense, one who is carried away by excess of zeal; an immoderate partisan, a fanatical enthusiast. Const. *for*, †*of*, †*to*.

a **1638** MEDE *Diatribæ* lii. Wks. I. (1672) 300 The true Zealot whom God approveth, namely, He whose Spirit is in Fervency and not in Shew. **1651** HOWELL *Venice* 5 Though they continue still such great Zelotts to their own Country.. they are not so to the Church. *c* **1665** MRS. HUTCHINSON *Mem. Col. Hutchinson* (1838) 25/1 The more religious zealots, who afterward were branded with the name of Puritan. **1706** PHILLIPS (ed. Kersey), *Zelot*.. is often taken in an ill Sense, for a Separatist or Schismatick, a Fanatick. **1712** ADDISON *Spect.* No. 445 ⁋6 The insignificant Party Zealots on both sides. **1758** JOHNSON *Idler* No. 11 ⁋3 Slavery is now no where more patiently endured than in countries once inhabited by the zealots of liberty. **1779** BURKE *Let. to J. Erskine* Apr., I do not aspire to the glory of being a zealot for any particular national Church. **1827** HALLAM *Const. Hist.* I. iii. 168 The queen [*sc.* Elizabeth] was as a mark for the pistol or dagger of every zealot. **1851** *Househ. Words* III. 386/2 A horde of Methodists, Baptists, Campbellites, and other burning zealots. **1892** MEREDITH *Lett.* (1912) II. 448 They are both zealots of the rod [*i.e.* keen anglers].

3. *attrib.* or as *adj.* That is a zealot; characteristic of a zealot.

1670 PERWICH *Desp.* (1903) 73 The old zelot Card[lls] have made a great noyse, being much offended. **1711** SHAFTESB. *Charac.* (1737) III. 322 Our gentleman by these expressions had already given considerable offence to his zealot-auditors. **1713** *Guardian* No. 93 ⁋10, I would not willingly lie at a zealot papist's mercy. **1879** FARRAR *St. Paul* II. 262 It was not likely that at Rome there should be any of that zealot fanaticism which held it unlawful for a Jew to recognise any other earthly ruler besides God.

zealoter, zealotic, -ical, -ism: see ZELATOR, ZELOTIC, etc.

zealotry ('zɛlətrɪ). Also 7 zel-. [f. ZEALOT + -RY: cf. *bigotry*.] Action or feeling characteristic of a zealot; an instance of this.

1656 *Artif. Handsom.* 63 Some mens and womens more plebeian Zelotry. **1661** GAUDEN *Consid. Liturgy* 29 The late inordinate zealotries, and desperate frolicks of Religion. **1797** W. TAYLOR in *Monthly Rev.* XXIII. 573 The ecstasy of eulogy and the zealotry of panegyric. **1839** DE QUINCEY *Wordsw.* Wks. 1854 II. 287 A more apostolic fervour of holy zealotry in this great cause. **1898** BODLEY *France* II. III. vi. 316 A bigot whose zealotry could not be pierced with sentiments of patriotism.

zealous ('zɛləs), *a.* Also 6–7 zelous. [ad. med.L. *zēlōsus* (cf. It., Pg. *zeloso*, Sp. *celoso*), f. *zēlus* ZEAL *sb.*: see -OUS.]

1. Full of or incited by zeal; characterized by zeal or passionate ardour; fervently devoted to the promotion of some person or cause; intensely earnest; actively enthusiastic.

a. of persons. Const. *for*.

In the 17th cent. sometimes connoting puritanical zeal.

1535 COVERDALE *1 Kings* xix. 10, I haue bene zelous for the Lorde God Zebaoth. **1585** WHITNEY *Choice Embl.* (1586) Ep. Ded. *3, A zelous fauorer of the Gospell, and of the godlie Preachers thereof. *a* **1591** H. SMITH *Serm., Acts xxvi. 27–9* (1592) 921 As some giddy spirites thinke now, that they which are zelouser than themselues know not what they say nor doe. **1617** MORYSON *Itin.* III. 32 Let them stay at home who are so zealous, as they will pull the *Hostia* or Sacrament out of the Priests hand. **1653** MILTON *Hirelings* Wks. 1851 V. 368 Out of the ablest and zealousest among them to create Elders. **1673** J. W[ADE] *Vin. & Must.* (1873) 15 Are they not reverend botchers,.. or some weavers, Some zealous cobblers, hatmakers and glovers? **1733** in *Swift's Lett.* (1768) IV. 47 Be assured that none is more truly zealous for your welfare, than your F. A. Kelly. **1849** MACAULAY *Hist. Eng.* ii. I. 175 The House of Commons.. more zealous for royalty than the king, more zealous for episcopacy than the bishops. **1874** GREEN *Short Hist.* viii. §5. 508 Episcopacy had become identified among the more zealous Scotchmen with the old Catholicism.

(*b*) Const. inf., occas. clause (the sense passing into: Eagerly desirous).

1605 BACON *Adv. Learn.* II. vii. §2. 24, I am.. zealous and affectionate to recede as little from Antiquitie.. as may stand with truth. **1667** MILTON *P.L.* IV. 565 A Spirit, zealous, as he seem'd, to know More of th' Almighties works. *a* **1700** EVELYN *Diary* 1 Apr. 1688, Multitudes zealous to hear the second sermon. **1847** TENNYSON *Princess* IV. 403 Not a scorner of your sex But venerator, zealous it should be All that it might be. **1852** MRS. STOWE *Uncle Tom's C.* viii, I's so zealous to be cotchin' Lizy, that I couldn't hold in.

†(*c*) In obs. const. with preps.

1526 TINDALE *Acts* xxi. 20 They are all zelous over the lawe [*Geneva* zelous of the Lawe]. **1611** *Bible* Acts xxii. 3, I.. was zealous towards God. *Ibid.* Titus ii. 14 A peculiar people, zealous of good workes. **1644** MILTON *Judgm. Bucer* xxii. Wks. 1851 IV. 313 Jerom.. though zealous of single life more then enough,.. defended Fabiola.

b. Of passions, actions, etc.

1563 *Mirr. Mag., Hastings* xiv, The many meanes, wherby I dyd bewraye My zelous wyll, to earne my prynces grace. **1594** SHAKS. *Rich. III*, III. vii. 94 When.. Religious men Are at their Beades, 'tis much to draw them thence, So sweet is zealous Contemplation. **1595** —— *John* II. i. 19 This zelous kisse. **1649** BP. HALL *Cases Consc.* II. iii. 130 Then w[ch] [sc. *Bulla Cruciatæ*] there was never a more zealous piece, published to the world. **1808** W. WILSON *Hist. Diss. Ch.* I. 391 To those doctrines he expressed a zealous attachment. **1851** GLADSTONE *Glean.* VI. lxiv. 42 Zealous and intelligent co-operation.

†**2.** = JEALOUS 4, 4 c. *Obs. rare.*

1563 *Homilies* II. *Agst. Idol.* III. Tt ij b, To spoyle the zelous God of his honour. **1630** HAKEWILL *Apol.* (ed. 2) IV. x. §4. 433 That this people should be so wonderfully zealous of the renowne of their nation.

zealously ('zɛləslɪ), *adv.* Also 6–7 zel-, (7 selusslie). [f. prec. + -LY[2].] In a zealous manner; with zeal or passionate ardour; with enthusiastic eagerness.

1575 tr. *Luther's Comm. Gal.* 24 b, At the first when the light of the gospel.. began to appeare, many were zelously bent to godlines. **1611** *Bible* Transl. Pref. ⁋3 To professe it [*sc.* Religion] zealously. *Ibid.* Gal. iv. 17 They zelously affect you, but not well [TINDALE They are gelous over you amysse]. *c* **1630** MILTON *Sonn.* ix, Thy care is fixt and zealously attends To fill thy odorous Lamp with deeds of light. **1661** *Lauderdale Papers* (Camden 1884) I. 92 The chanslir is selusslie your frind. **1769** *Junius Lett.* iii, You zealously undertook the cause of that gallant army. **1879** LUBBOCK *Sci. Lect.* ii. 36 We know how fond ants are of honey, and how zealously and unremittingly they search for food. **1886** BESANT *Childr. Gibeon* II. v, A place.. where there was no prospect of improvement, however zealously one worked.

†**b.** In the way of religious zeal or devotion.

1644 MILTON *Divorce* I. viii. Wks. 1851 IV. 40 It will easily be true that a father or brother may be hated zealously, and lov'd civilly or naturally.

zealousness ('zɛləsnɪs). Now *rare*. [f. ZEALOUS + -NESS.] The quality of being zealous; zeal.

c **1555** in Strype *Eccl. Mem.* (1721) III. App. xliii. 122 Mark.. Christ's Words, which he spake with Zealousnes and Power. **1579** W. WILKINSON *Confut. Fam. Love* A iv, The old Fathers grew out of a zealousnes of the mynde towardes God.. to institute certaine Ceremonies. *c* **1662** BOYLE *Motives Love of God* (1708) 169 The Zealousness of our Endeavours. **1803** *Ann. Reg., Chron.* 608/1, I will not betray his confidence nor that zealousness in his cause which he has a right to expect. **1903** M[c]LEAN *Stud. Apost.* xiii. 194 It is difficult to draw the line between zealousness and zealotry.

†**zealousy.** *Obs.* Forms: 6 zelousie, -ye, zelosie, -zie. [f. ZEALOUS + -Y[3].]

1. Jealousy.

1542 UDALL *Erasm. Apoph.* II. 177 b, Whiche grudges;.. the zelousie, and the eagre feersenes of Olympias did augmente. **1598** Q. ELIZ. *Plutarch* 126/25 Or Zelozie of wife, or Sons suspect, or dout of frind.

2. Zealousness, zeal.

1597 MIDDLETON *Wisd. Solomon* v. G 2 b, His armour zealousie, his breast-plate heauen.

zearalenone (zi:ə'rælənəʊn). *Biochem.* [f. ZEA + *-ralenone*, f. *r*esorcylic *a*cid *l*actone + -ENE, repr. a double bond + -ONE.] A white crystalline bicyclic latone, $C_{18}H_{22}O_5$, that is a metabolic product of certain cereal fungi and causes disorders of the reproductive system in pigs.

1966 W. H. URRY et al. in *Tetrahedron Lett.* XXVII. 3109 Study of the substance of striking physiological activity isolated from the mycelia of the fungus Gibberella zeae.. has shown that it is one of the enantiomorphs of 6-(10-hydroxy-6-oxo-*trans*-1-undecenyl)-β-resorcylic acid lactone I... Zearalenone I.. gives reactions that indicate it has one olefinic and one ketonic group, and two phenolic hydroxyls and an ester group in a β-resorcylate structure. **1977** *Lancet* 26 Mar. 671/2 Analytical tests failed to show the presence of aflatoxin,.. although zearalenone was found in maize samples. **1978** [see TRICHOTHECENE]. **1981** M. L. CLARKE et al. *Veterinary Toxicol.* (ed. 2) VIII. 277/1 The phenolic macrolide zearalenone (F-2 toxin) produced by *Fusarium graminearum*.. and other *Fusarium* species growing on maize, barley and wheat destined for incorporation into animal feeds, is probably one of the most widespread and economically important mycotoxins.

zearat, var. ZIARAT.

zeatin ('ziːətɪn). *Biochem.* [f. ZEA + *-t-* + -IN[1].] A purine derivative occurring as a cytokinin in maize kernels and other plants; 6-(4-hydroxy-3-methylbut-2-enyl)-aminopurine, $C_{10}H_{13}N_5O$.
1963 D. S. LETHAM in *Life Sciences* No. 8. 572 For this factor the name zeatin is proposed since it was first isolated in crystalline form from *Zea mays.* **1973** D. W. KROGMANN *Biochem. Green Plants* xi. 196 Coconut milk..contains a high concentration of zeatin. **1980** *Physiologia Plantarum* XLIX. 304/1 All the cytokinins, at $10^{-6}M$ and above, inhibited both the initiation and the emergence of lateral roots, zeatin being the most powerful inhibitor.

zeaught, obs. Sc. form of YACHT.

zeaxanthin (ziːə'zænθɪn). *Biochem.* [a. G. *zeaxanthin* (P. Karrer et al. 1929, in *Helvetica Chim. Acta* XII. 791): see ZEA and XANTHIN.] A xanthophyll, $C_{40}H_{56}O_4$, originally isolated from Indian corn, *Zea mays*.
1929 *Chem. Abstr.* XXIII. 4480 (*heading*) Zeaxanthin, a new carotinoid pigment in maize. **1934** [see XANTHOPHYLL a]. **1978** [see VIOLAXANTHIN].

zeayde, obs. Kent. ind. past of SAY *v.*[1]

zebec(k, variant of XEBEC.

† **'Zebedist.** *Obs. nonce-wd.* [f. the name *Zebedee* + -IST.] One who acts like the sons of Zebedee (see Matt. xx. 20–22).
1574 tr. *Josselin's Life* 70 *Abp.* To Rdr. E iij, Like a pore blinde zebediste to aske he knoweth not what.

zebelin, -elline, -iline, obs. ff. ZIBELINE.

zebra ('ziːbrə, 'zɛbrə), *sb.* Also 7 **zabra, zeuera, sebra, zebre, zevre, (zembra)**, 7–8 **zeura**; 7 *pl.* **zebrae.** [Congolese. Cf. F. *zèbre*, It. (Florio, 1598), Pg. *zebra*, Sp. *cebra*.]
1. A South African equine quadruped (*Equus* or *Hippotigris zebra*), of a whitish ground-colour striped all over with regular bars of black; inhabiting mountainous regions, and noted for its wildness and swiftness.
With qualifying words, applied to other species, as Burchell's Zebra, *E.* or *H. Burchelli* (also called DAUW); Grévy's Zebra, *E.* or *H. Grevyi.* Sometimes applied generically to the whole subgenus *Hippotigris*, comprising all the striped species of African wild horses, including the Quagga.
1600 J. PORY tr. *Leo's Africa* Introd. 39 The Zebra or Zabra of this countrey [*sc.* Congo] being about the bignes of a mule, is a beast of incomparable swiftnes. **1625** PURCHAS *Pilgrims* VII. iii. §3. 977 Holding in each hand a *Zeueras*, or wilde horses tayle. **1638** SIR T. HERBERT *Trav.* (ed. 2) 14 Apes, Baboons,..Zebrae, Wolves, Foxes. **1653** H. COGAN tr. *Pinto's Trav.* lv. 216 Some applied themselves..to the pursuing of Tygers, Rhinocerots, Ounces, Zevres. **1683** *Weekly Mem.* 15 A Beast called *Zecora* or *Zembra.* **1735** JOHNSON *Lobo's Abyssinia, Voy.* i. 5 A *Zeura* or Wild-Ass, a Creature of large Size, and admirable Beauty. **1776** GIBBON *Decl. & F.* xii. I. 350 Twenty zebras displayed their elegant forms and variegated beauty to the eyes of the Roman people. **1857** LIVINGSTONE *Trav.* iii. 56 The presence of the ..zebra..is always a certain indication of water being within a distance of seven or eight miles. **1886** BESANT *Childr. Gibeon* II. vi, You might as well put a zebra in harness as Melenda into any kind of service.
2. *transf.* Applied to things having stripes resembling or suggesting those of a zebra:
a. natural objects (see quots.).
1811 PINKERTON *Petral.* II. 101 There is also a rare kind [of agate] called the zebra, from its regular black bands upon a white ground. **1815** BURROW *Elem. Conchol.* 200 *Bulla Achatina*, Broad-striped Zebra, or Pink-mouthed Chersina. **1901** *Field* 23 Nov. 812/2 Howietoun still supplies..two-year-old 'zebras', a name given to a very beautiful hybrid between our English trout and the American char.
b. *Comm.* Name for a striped shawl, scarf, or the like.
1851 *Illustr. Exhibitor* 7/1 Coloured goods, such as handkerchiefs, ginghams, checks,..scarfs, and zebras. **1858** SIMMONDS *Dict. Trade, Zebras*, a name given to Paisley shawls, which are very generally worn in Turkey, as sashes or other parts of dress.
c. Humorous name for a convict in striped prison dress. Also, a striped prison uniform.
1882 SALA *Amer. Revis.* (1885) 218 A 'Zebra' is the humorous nickname for a convict. **1895** *Harper's Weekly* 10 Aug. 753/3 At present I understand that he is in limbo, wearing the famous 'zebra'—the penitentiary dress. **1935** A. J. POLLOCK *Underworld Speaks* 136/1 *Zebra*, striped prison clothing.
d. A zebra crossing. *colloq.*
1951 O. LANCASTER in *Daily Express* 15 Dec. 1/5 If we can only find a Zebra, we can sit down and relax. **1959** *Woman* 24 Jan. 4/3, I often wait ten minutes or more, even at a zebra, while super new cars speed past. **1968** *Listener* 15 Aug. 201/3 Outside, on the road, trucks wait for me to cross a zebra. **1976** *S. Wales Echo* 27 Nov. 9/2 [He] pleaded guilty to stopping a car in a zebra-controlled area.
3. *attrib.* and *Comb.*, as ***zebra mark, marking, meat, skin, stripe***; ***zebra-like, -marked, -striped*** adjs.; esp. in names of genera, species, or varieties of animals having stripes like those of a zebra, as ***zebra caterpillar, finch, frog, mackerel, mussel, parakeet, rush, shark, sole, woodpecker*** (see quots.); also **zebra crossing**, a pedestrian crossing marked by broad black and white stripes on the road and Belisha beacons on the kerb; **zebra danio** ('deɪnɪəʊ), a small Indian freshwater fish with horizontal dark and light stripes, *Brachydanio rerio* (family Cyprinidæ), which is popular as an aquarium fish; **zebra fish**, an Australian fish (*Neotephrœops zebra*) of the perch kind; also, any of several striped tropical fishes, esp. the zebra danio; **zebra-opossum** = *zebra-wolf*; **zebra-plant**, a tropical American plant, *Maranta* (*Calathea*) *zebrina*, having large ornamental leaves marked with dark stripes (*Treas. Bot.* 1866); **zebra-poison**, a South African tree, *Euphorbia arborea*, with highly poisonous milky juice (see quot.); **zebra spider**, any of several striped spiders of the family Salticidæ; **zebra-wolf**, the striped Tasmanian 'wolf' = THYLACINE; **zebra-wood**, name for several kinds of ornamentally striped wood used by cabinet-makers, furnished by various trees and shrubs, as *Omphalobium Lambertii* of S. America, *Eugenia fragrans* of the W. Indies, and *Guettarda speciosa* of various tropical regions; also for the plants themselves.
1895 J. H. & A. B. COMSTOCK *Study of Insects* 305 The *Zebra Caterpillar, *Mamestra picta.* [**1949** *Surveyor* 8 July 407/1 Investigations by the Road Research Laboratory.. have led to the full-scale trials of the striped (zebra) markings for pedestrian crossings. **1950** *Times* 18 Feb. 2/5 Experiments are now being carried out..to test the efficacy of the zebra striped pedestrian crossing when illuminated at night.] **1950** *Surveyor* 23 June 365/2 The initial values of the percentage of drivers giving way are higher on the '*zebra' crossings than on the plain. **1977** B. PYM *Quartet in Autumn* ii. 23 He..called out angrily after a car which had failed to stop at a zebra crossing. **1917** W. T. INNES *Goldfish Varieties & Tropical Aquarium Fishes* (ed. 2) vii. 86 *Danio rerio*, *Zebra Danio. **1962** D. W. TUCKER tr. *Sterba's Freshw. Fishes of World* 265 Some species, such as the Zebra Danio, will spawn over gravelly bottoms even when there are no plants present. **1980** *Sci. Amer.* Feb. 127/2 McCutchen has employed his rig to study the motion of a small fish, a zebra danio (*Brachydanio rerio*), which is about three centimeters long. **1889** *Science-Gossip* XXV. 215 *Zebra finches. **1771** LORT in *Phil. Trans.* LXI. 247 It is called by the Commodore the *Zebra fish. **1895** *Aquarium* Apr. 172/1 (*heading*) Brazilian Zebra Fish (*Heros facetus*). **1925** *Aquatic Life* June 18/1 Danio rerio, those swift, graceful, blue and white and sometimes golden striped zebra fish, have many admirers. **1934** C. W. COATES *Tropical Fishes as Pets* v. 49 The Zebra Fish (*Pterois volitans*), a marine beast from the Indian Ocean, erects all his fins, faces his future meal, and appears to drift toward it. **1962** *Listener* 22 Nov. 852/2 The three black-and-white-striped zebra fish were speed-merchants [in the tank]. **1979** H. F. AXELROD et al. *Exotic Marine Fishes* 121 The scorpion fishes..often called butterfly cod or zebra fishes..are mostly hardy, attractive predators. **1802** SHAW *Gen. Zool.* III. 123 *Zebra Frog... This appears to be..the largest of all the..slender-bodied Frogs, and is, according to Seba, a native of Carolina and Virginia. Its colour is an elegant pale rufous brown, beautifully marked..with transverse chesnut-coloured bands. **1815** BURROW *Elem. Conchol.* 201 *Buccinum Rugosum*, *Zebra Helmet. **1872** *Daily Tel.* 11 Jan., Certain most brilliant fish, covered with *zebra-like stripes of green and pink. **1802** SHAW *Gen. Zool.* IV. 587 *Zebra Mackrel. *Scomber Zebra*..bands of the body continued nearly through the dorsal and anal fin. **1869** J. PAGET in *Mem. & Lett.* (1901) 408 A note from Lord Fitzwilliam about his horse with *zebra-marks. **1924** J. A. THOMSON *Science Old & New* v. 30 Butterflies like the unpalatable *zebra-marked Heliconius, which insectivorous birds leave unmolested. **1949** *Zebra marking [see *zebra crossing* above]. **1907** J. H. PATTERSON *Man-Eaters of Tsavo* xxiii. 262 He was afraid that they would seize all the *zebra-meat that the lions had not already eaten. **1883** *Goole Weekly Times* 7 Sept. 8/4 Down among the side stones are *zebra-mussels (*Dreissena polymorpha*). **1899** *Speaker* 18 Feb. 204/1 The zebra mussel is a native of the rivers of Southern Russia. **1855** *Engl. Cycl., Nat. Hist.* III. 697 *T*[*hylacinus*] *cynocephalus*,..the Tasmanian Wolf, *Zebra Opossum, and Zebra Wolf. **1865** H. KINGSLEY *Hillyars & Burtons* l, Others..now so popular in London as *Zebra parakeets. **1882** J. SMITH *Dict. Pop. Names Plants* 449 *Zebra Poison... Its milky juice is highly poisonous, whole herds of zebras having been killed by branches of it being placed in the water which they drink. **1796** NEMNICH *Polygl.-Lex.* 946 *Zebra rhomb, *Voluta paupercula.* **1882** *Garden* 2 Sept. 203/1 The Eulalia although very beautiful..is still surpassed by the *Zebra Rush. **1804** SHAW *Gen. Zool.* V. 352 *Zebra Shark... *Squalus tigrinus*... Of a dark brown colour,..barred with..milk-white,.. somewhat undulating stripes. **1973** G. BEARE *Snake on Grave* xiii. 68 Walls, floor, and ceiling were all done in a *zebra-skin motif. Everything..was covered in zebra skin. **1978** S. NAIPAUL *North of South* II. vi. 230 Copies of *Playboy* were scattered on a zebra-skin rug. **1803** SHAW, *Gen. Zool.* IV. 305 *Zebra Sole... Marked from head to tail by numerous..deep brown..bands. **1866** *Hours at Home* III. 331/1 Next to the garden-spider, the hunting or *zebra spider is the most common. **1966** C. SWEENEY *Scurrying Bush* vi. 87 The commonest of these [jumping spiders] was banded black and white like a zebra... Zebra spiders are able to leap..in an eighteen-inch arc. **1890** BURNAND *Very Much Abr.* 332 The Merry Swiss Boy, in canary-coloured uniform with *zebra stripes over it. **1852** *Zebra-striped [see *dove orchis* s.v. DOVE *sb.* 5 b]. **1950** [see *zebra crossing* above]. **1976** *National Observer* (U.S.) 21 Aug. 1/3 There was Clarabell in his green-and-white zebra-striped clown suit. **1895** J. H. & A. B. COMSTOCK *Study of Insects* 379 The *Zebra Swallow-tail, *Iphiclides ajax.* **1853** *Househ. Wds.* VII. 210/2 The skin of the *Zebra-Wolf is smooth and glossy, somewhat resembling in its colour that of the Bengal tiger... Zebra-Wolves are now extremely scarce. **1783** *Trans. Soc. Arts* I. 22 For importing Earth Nuts, Myrtle Wax, Sturgeon, and *Zebra Wood. £175. **1852** R. S. SURTEES *Sponge's Sp. Tour* xlii, A beautiful Devonport of zebra-wood, with a plate-glass back. **1934** [see ZINGANA 2].

Hence **zebraed** ('ziːbrəd) *pa. pple.* or *ppl. a.* (cf. F. *zébré*), striped like a zebra; **ze'braic** [irreg. after *Hebraic*], **zebrine** ('ziːbraɪn) [-INE[1]] *adjs.*, related to, or characteristic of, the zebra.
1839 *New Monthly Mag.* LVI. 311 The whole garment *zebraed with tarnished lace. **1855** *Engl. Cycl., Nat. Hist.* III. 697 Barred or zebraed on the lower part of the back and rump with about 16 jet-black transverse stripes. **1890** *Sat. Rev.* 6 Sept. 287/2 Its multi-coloured zebraed form. **1895** W. WRIGHT *Palmyra & Zenobia* xxiv. 277 Hermon itself, streaked and zebraed with snow. **1898** A. LANG in *Longm. Mag.* Oct. 559 The horse is supposed to have been developed out of the zebra, or a *zebraic animal. **1868** DARWIN *Anim. & Pl.* II. 373 The *zebrine stripes on dun-coloured horses.

zebrano (zə-, zɪ'brɑːnəʊ). [Irreg. f. ZEBRA *sb.*] Striped wood furnished by various species of African trees, esp. those of the genus *Microberlinia*.
1928 *Sunday Express* 29 July 15/4 We take the most handsome pieces of..sapele mahogany, or of lesser known woods like macassar, ebony, zebrano, amboyna. **1934** *Archit. Rev.* LXXV. 144 (*caption*) The furniture is in Indian rosewood and Japanese chestnut and the panelling in zebrano. **1965** *Wireless World* Sept. 37 (Advt.), Finish zebrano, mahogany, walnut or teak veneers. **1980** E. SCOTT *Illustr. Encycl. Working in Wood* 248 *Microberlinia brazzavillensis* Zebrano. Normally coarse texture; interlocked grain.

zebrina (zə'braɪnə). *Bot.* Also **Zebrina.** [mod.L. (A. Schnitzlein 1849, in *Bot. Zeitung* VII. 870/2), f. ZEBR(A, in allusion to the striped leaves of some species + -INA[2].] A creeping recumbent herb of the genus of this name (family Commelinaceæ) that is native to central America, bears ovate, often striped, leaves and clusters of small flowers, and is grown as a greenhouse and indoor plant.
1946 M. FREE *All about House Plants* iii. 15 English Ivy, Tradescantia, and Zebrina (to trail over edge [of a window-box]). **1960** *Times* 30 Jan. 11/2 The green or white and green striped zebrinas. **1963** [see PERICLINAL *a.* (*sb.*) 2 b]. **1978** *Homes & Gardens* Oct. 42/2 Among these summer sun-lovers are beloperone..and zebrina.

zebroid ('ziː-, 'zɛbrɔɪd), *a.* and *sb.* [f. ZEBR(A + -OID.] **A.** *adj.* Resembling or characteristic of a zebra.
1899 *Nat. Science* Mar. 209 The reproductive organs, which were of a zebroid type. **1974** *Nature* 22 Mar. 296/2 G. Nobis's study of the horse teeth recognised three groups: two larger species with primitive 'zebroid' features.
B. *sb.* The offspring of a horse and a zebra.
1899 *Tablet* 25 Nov. 848/2 The zebroid, or hybrid between the horse and the zebra, 'will be the mule of the 20th century'. **1926** *Daily Colonist* (Victoria, B.C.) 18 July 24/1 The first man to have any practical success in crossbreeding the zebra and the horse is Dr. W. E. Hastings of Mt. Vernon, Ind. The result is a new mule, the zebroid. **1973** *Daily Tel.* (Colour Suppl.) 5 Oct. 31/4 Another Kenya 'character'..crossed ponies with zebras, and used the resulting 'zebroids' as pack animals for safaris. **1983** *Listener* 20 Jan. 25/1 Christina Dodwell, in *Travels with Fortune*, paddled a dug-out canoe, and rode a camel and a zebroid, in her journey through Africa.

zebrule ('ziː-, 'zɛbruːl). [f. ZEBR(A + M)ULE[1].] = ZEDONK.
1903 in P. Fleming *Bayonets to Lhasa* (1961) viii. 102 In my Section are two Zebrules, half zebra and half donkey. **1978** J. MORRIS *Farewell the Trumpets* vii. 132 By December 13, 1903 every last yak and zebrule had crossed the frontier of Tibet.

zebu ('ziːbjuː). [ad. F. *zébu* (Buffon, who states that it was shown under this name at a fair in Paris in 1752).] A humped species of ox, *Bos indicus*, domesticated from the most ancient times in India, China, Japan, and parts of Africa.
1774 GOLDSM. *Nat. Hist.* (1776) III. 23 Others among them [*sc.* bisons], such as the zebu, or Barbary cow, are very small. **1844** CARPENTER *Zool.* §269 The Zebu or Brahmin Ox. **1894** *Chambers's Jrnl.* 2 July 488/1 Zebus (the pigmy cattle of Ceylon).
attrib. **1847** W. C. L. MARTIN *Ox* 19/1 The zebu race is not confined to India, China, and the Indian islands, but is found on the eastern coast of Africa, and in..Madagascar. **1903** *Times* 9 Jan. 5/2 He bred a female hybrid from a zebu bull and a gayal cow.

zecchin ('zɛkɪn). Forms: 6–7 **zechine**, 7 **-yne**, 8–9 **zechin**, (8 **zeckin, zequeen**), 7– **zecchin, -ine.** [ad. It. *zecchino*, f. *zecca* the mint at Venice = Sp. *seca*, a. Arab. *sekkah* coin.] A former gold coin of Venice and Turkey: = CHEQUEEN, SEQUIN 1.
1575 GASCOIGNE *Flowers* Wks. 1907 I. 77 Zechines of glistering golde, two thousand was his price. **1615** G. SANDYS *Trav.* 3 They pay tribute to the Turke, 14000 Zecchins yearely. **1617** MORYSON *Itin.* I. 88 The gold coyne of the Venetians is called Zecchino. *Ibid.* 276 In Turkey the gold zechines of Venice are most currant. **1702** W. J. tr. *Bruyn's Voy. Levant* xl. 160 A Subsidy of 600000 Zechins; worth about seven Franks and a half a piece. **1727** A. HAMILTON *New Acc. E. Ind.* I. 304, I presented the Officer ..with five Zequeens. **1789** MRS. PIOZZI *Journ. France* I. 195 A zecchine will bend between your fingers. **1819** SCOTT *Ivanhoe* xxxvi, They would swear the mother that bore them a sorceress for a zecchin. **1857** RUSKIN *Pol. Econ. Art* ii. (1868) 124 If you don't choose to submit to be cheated by

them out of a ducat here and a zecchin there, you will be cheated by them out of your picture.

Zechian, var. CZECHIAN, a Czech.
1847 MRS. A. KERR tr. *Ranke's Hist. Servia* i. 5 The Western races—the Moravians, Zechians, Carantaneans, and to some extent, even the Poles.

‖**Zechstein** ('zɛkstaɪn). *Geol.* [Ger., lit. minestone.] A limestone stratum of the Permian system as developed in parts of Germany, corresponding to the Magnesian Limestone of the N.E. of England; also extended to the series of rocks containing this, forming the upper division of the Permian.
1823 *Amer. Jrnl. Sci.* VI. 189 On the Rhine.., the Zechstein or 1st floetz limestone is imbedded in the coal-field. **1885** GEIKIE *Text-bk. Geol.* (ed. 2) VI. ii. v. §2. 754 Zechstein, an argillaceous thin-bedded compact limestone.

zed. Also 5-6 **zedde**. [a. F. *zède* (= It. *zeta*, †*zette*, Sp. *zeta*, *zeda*), ad. L. *zēta*, a. Gr. ζῆτα.]
1. Name of the letter Z.
In quot. 1605 applied contemptuously to a person.
14.. *MS. Reg. 17, B. 1, f. 146* in *Mod. Lang. Rev.* (1911) VI. 442 For as miche as þe carect yogh, þat is to seie ·ȝ· is figurid lijk a zed, þerfore alle þe wordis of þis table þat biginnen wiþ þat carect, ben set in zed, which is þe laste lettre of þe a·b·c. **14..** MAUNDEV. (MS. Laud 699 f. 37) Too lettres.. þat is to sey ·y· [*i.e.* þ] & ·z· which is called thorn and zedde. **1582** MULCASTER *1st Pt. Elem.* xxiii. 161 Hence cummeth it that so manie zeds in our tung are herd, and so few sene, for dexteritie and spede in the currantnesse of writing. **1605** SHAKS. *Lear* II. ii. 69 Thou whoreson Zed, thou vnnecessary letter. **1755** JOHNSON *Dict., Gram.*, Z ..[Name] *zed*, more commonly *izzard* or *uzzard*, that is, *shard*. **1817** *Err. Pron. Lond.* 38 Children.. often call this letter *Izard*... They should be taught to pronounce it Zed. **1882** E. A. FREEMAN in *Longman's Mag.* I. 94 The name.. given to the last letter of the alphabet.. in New England is always *zee*; in the South it is *zed*. **1893** [see Z 2].
2. *zed-bar*, also simply *zed* = Z-bar: see Z 2.
a **1891** *Engineer* LXXI. Advts. p. xxxviii. (Cent. Dict.), Angles, Zeds, Channels, Beams, Bars. **1892** *Daily News* 9 Sept. 6/1 The improved sections of steel known as channel and zed bars.

zed(e: see SAD *a.*, SAY *v.*[1], SEED.

zedewal, -wal(l)e, -ward, obs. ff. SETWALL (= ZEDOARY).
1310 *Acc. Exors. T. Bp. of Exeter* (Camden) 9 De xd. de j libra de zedewand [*sic*] vendita.

zedge, obs. dial. form of SAY *v.*[1]

zedoary ('zɛdəʊərɪ). Forms: 5-6 **zeduarye, -ie,** 6 **zedwary,** 6-7 **zedoarie,** 6- **zedoary.** [ad. med.L. *zedoārium*, *-ia* (also *zedu-*), ad. Arab. *zedwār*: cf. OF. *zedouar*, *zedoar*, mod.F. *zédoaire*, Prov. *zeduari*, Sp., It. *zedoaria*, Pg. *zeduaria*, It. *zettovario*, OHG., MHG. *zitwar* (G. *zitwer*). See also SETWALL.] The aromatic tuberous root of one or more species of *Curcuma* (N.O. *Zingiberaceæ*), of the East Indies and neighbouring countries, sold in two forms, ***long zedoary*** and ***round zedoary***, and used as a drug, having properties resembling those of ginger; also the plant itself. ***yellow zedoary*** = CASSUMUNAR.
c **1475** *Nominale* in Wr.-Wülcker 714/11 *Hoc zeduarium*, zeduarye. *c* **1550** LLOYD *Treas. Health* I vj, Zedwary, chawed.. and swallowed.. taketh awaye the grefe of the bely. **1684** tr. *Bonet's Merc. Compit.* III. 103 Zedoary is most powerfull against vitreous Phlegm. **1760** J. LEE *Introd. Bot.* App. 332 Zedoary, round, *Kæmpferia*. Zedoary, long, *Amomum*. **1773** W. LEWIS *C. Neumann's Chem. Wks.* (ed. 2) II. 201 Zedoary is the root of a plant said to be of the Ginger kind, growing in different parts of the East Indies, and brought to us chiefly from Bengal. **1858** HOGG *Veg. Kingd.* 784 From the roots of *Zingiber casumunar*, the article known in commerce as Casumunar, or Yellow Zedoary, is obtained. .. Long Zedoary is the root of *Curcuma zerumbet*, a native of the East Indies... Round Zedoary is furnished by *C. zedoaria*. **1880** C. R. MARKHAM *Peruv. Bark* 347 The undergrowth.. consists of cardamom, wild ginger, zedoary, rattan, a small bamboo,.. and a few ferns.
attrib. **1741** *Compl. Fam.-Piece* I. i. 40 Take.. Zedoary Root 10 Grains. **1866** *Treas. Bot.* s.v. *Curcuma*, *C. aromatica* and *C. Zedoaria* furnish Zedoary tubers,.. used by the natives of India as aromatic tonics, and as a perfume.

zedonk ('zi:dɒŋk, 'zɛdɒŋk). Also **zeedonk.** [f. ZE(BRA + DONK(EY.] The offspring of a male zebra and a female donkey. Cf. ZONKEY.
1971 *Daily Tel.* 17 Apr. 8/5 The staff at Colchester Zoo have described their newcomer as a 'Zedonk'. **1976** *Observer* (Colour Suppl.) 5 Sept. 42/3 Donkeys crossed with zebras, sometimes called zeedonks, have been used like mules.. as pack animals. **1978** *Panorama* (Austral.) Aug. 13/2 Zareeba the zedonk (half zebra, half donkey) is one of only five of his kind known in the world.

zeduale, obs. form of SETWALL (= ZEDOARY).

zee (zi:). A name, esp. now in U.S., of the letter Z.
1677 T. LYE *New Spelling Bk.* II. 5 Zz zee Z-eal, thou shalt be my charret, whilst I ride, Elijah-like, with Word and Spirit, my Guide. **1797** *Gazette of U.S.* No. 1429. 3/3 Younker yield the yawning yea—Zounds, I'm safe at zig-zag zee. **1828** WEBSTER, *Z*... It is pronounced *zee*. **1882** [see ZED 1].

zeel(e, obs. forms of ZEAL.

zeelde, variant of SELD *adv. Obs.*
c **1374** CHAUCER *Boeth.* II. met. iii. 26 (Camb. MS.) ȝif the forme of this worlde is so zeelde stable.

Zeeman ('zeɪmən). *Physics.* The name of P. *Zeeman* (1865-1943), Dutch physicist, used *attrib.* with reference to the splitting of a spectral line into three or more closely spaced components when the light source is in a magnetic field not strong enough to produce the Paschen-Back effect.
Observed by Zeeman in 1897.
[**1897** *Phil. Mag.* XLIV. 503 A theoretical analysis.. can be developed in connexion with Zeeman's phenomenon, which may help to throw light on the nature of the electric vibrations in the molecule.] **1899** *Rep. Brit. Assoc. Adv. Sci. 1898* 789 An effect converse to the Zeeman effect occurs in those cases where the body is absorbing instead of emitting light. **1904** [see MAGNETOGYRIC *a.* 1]. **1926** [see LARMOR]. **1962** W. B. THOMPSON *Introd. Plasma Physics* i. 3 There are several ways of inferring the existence of magnetic fields, of which the most direct is from a measurement of the Zeeman splitting of spectral lines. **1971** *New Scientist* 18 Feb. 381/1 When a nucleus is placed in a high magnetic field, each energy level splits into several sublevels known as magnetic sublevels or Zeeman levels. **1978** PASACHOFF & KUTNER *University Astron.* viii. 219 (*caption*) From studies of the splitting of lines that are sensitive to the Zeeman effect, the magnetic field on the sun can be mapped.

zeep (zi:p), *v. rare*⁻¹. [? var. ZIP *v.*] *trans.* To elicit a zipping sound from.
1935 S. BECKETT *Echo's Bones*, Tires bleeding voiding zeep the highway.

zeferus: see ZEPHYRUS.

†**zegedine.** *Obs.* Also **zega(r)dine.** [? f. *Szegedin* in Hungary.] A drinking cup of silver (?).
1643 *Ball. Coll. Oxf. List of Plate* (MS.), Given to the King in the year 1642—silver plate—5 great two-ear'd pots: called Zegardines. **1650** *Balliol Coll. Reg.* (MS.), Mr. Robt. Pudsey a Zegadine 15 [oz.] 02 [dwt.]. **1651** BARKSDALE *Nympha Lib.* IV. xlv. 91 Oft have we discours'd 'ore a Zegedine Of Double, and now and then a pot of wine. **1688** *Ball. Coll. Oxf. List of Plate* (MS.), Mag. Price, a Bedmaker in the Colledge gave the 5th zegadine of 5 *li.* price.

zeil(e, zeill, obs. Sc. forms of ZEAL.

zeilanite ('zaɪlənaɪt). *Min.* Also **zey-**. [ad. G. *zeilanit*, f. *Zeilan* CEYLON.] A variety of spinel, found in Sri Lanka (Ceylon); = CANDITE, CEYLONITE.
1851 WATTS tr. *Gmelin's Handbk. Chem.* V. 275 Aluminate of Ferrous Oxide.—Zeilanite.

zein ('zi:ɪn). *Chem.* Also **-ine.** [f. ZEA + -IN[1].] A protein found in maize, analogous to gluten.
1822 *Q. Jrnl. Sci.* XIII. 402 The zëine of John Gorham, is obtained from Indian corn, by infusing it in water. **1877** WATTS *Dict. Chem.* V. 1066.

zeinte, obs. form of SAINT.

zeir, Sc. graphic var. *ȝeir*, YEAR[1].

Zeiss (zaɪs). The name of Carl *Zeiss* (1816-88), German optical instrument maker, used *attrib.* to designate binoculars manufactured by the firm he founded.
1905 W. JAMES *Let.* 3 Apr. (1920) II. 224 Now I will stop, and use my Zeiss glass on the land, which is getting nearer. **1912** A. CONAN DOYLE *Lost World* vii. 126 He had his Zeiss glasses in his hand. **1938** S. BECKETT *Murphy* iv. 60, I have worshipped her from afar... All last June, through Zeiss glasses. **1971** R. DENTRY *Encounter at Kharmel* vii. 127 There were.. Zeiss binoculars.. at the back of the glove compartment. **1983** T. POCOCK *1945* vii. 217 The luckiest found Leica cameras and Zeiss binoculars.

‖**zeitgeber** ('tsaɪtge:bər). *Physiol.* Pl. same or (anglicized) **zeitgebers.** [Ger. (J. Aschoff 1954, in *Naturwissenschaften* XLI. 49), f. *zeit* time + *geber* giver.] A rhythmically occurring event, esp. in the environment, which acts as a cue in the regulation of certain biological rhythms in an organism.
1964 E. BÜNNING *Physiological Clock* ii. 9 The change of light and dark or alternations of high and low temperatures have a synchronizing effect on the endodiurnal rhythm; they function as 'Zeitgeber' (cues, synchronizers). **1969** *New Scientist* 21 Aug. 369/2 Light is known to be the *zeitgeber* for the ant-lion's solar-day rhythm. **1975** D. VINCE-PRUE *Photoperiodism in Plants* v. 169 The signals responsible for entrainment have been called *zeitgebers*. **1975** *Nature* 27 Nov. 291/2 The various rhythms respond to changes in the phase or the period of the entraining cycle (the Zeitgeber). **1983** *Brit. Med. Jrnl.* 6 Aug. 426/2 Melatonin is secreted by the pineal gland during the night... In rats it will act as a 'zeitgeber' or synchroniser of the rest-activity cycle under conditions of zero environmental input.

‖**Zeitgeist** ('tsaɪtgaɪst). Also **Zeit Geist, Zeit-Geist** (both *rare*), and with lower-case initial. [G., f. *zeit* time + *geist* spirit.] The spirit or genius which marks the thought or feeling of a period or age.
1848 M. ARNOLD *Let.* Nov. (1932) 95, I.. took up Obermann, and refuged myself with him.. against your Zeit Geist. **1873** M. ARNOLD *Lit. & Dogma* v. 129 It is what we call the *Time-Spirit* that is sapping the proof from miracles,—it is the 'Zeit-Geist' itself. **1876** *Mind* I. 369 There is a *Zeitgeist*, he says. **1884** *Macmillan's Mag.* Aug. 254 For realism in one form or another is the zeitgeist which will master us all. **1889** G. B. SHAW *Let.* Aug. (1965) I. 222 My business is to incarnate the Zeitgeist. **1893** *Nation* (N.Y.) 5 Jan. 15/2 Rome has undergone radical changes, for the year 1870 has intervened, and the *Zeitgeist* has occupied and is rebuilding the city. **1933** A. HUXLEY *Let.* 9 Oct. (1969) 374 The Zeitgeist is a most dismal animal and I wish to heaven one cd escape from its clutches. **1946** AUDEN *Litany & Anthem for S. Matthew's Day*, May we worship neither the flux of chance, nor the wheel of fortune, nor the spiral of the zeit-geist. **1972** *Science* 2 June 991/3 A clear mark of the Zeitgeist of the late 1960's and the 1970's is the increased demand for participation in decision-making by those affected by it. **1982** D. PIPER *Image of Poet* i. 13 Shakespeare becomes in a sense an ever-changing embodiment of the *Zeitgeist*.

zek (zɛk). [Russ., prob. repr. pronunc. of *z/k*, abbrev. of *zaklyuchënnyĭ* prisoner.] In the U.S.S.R., a person confined in a prison or forced labour camp.
1968 T. P. WHITNEY tr. *Solzhenitsyn's First Circle* p. x, All the zeks at the Mavrino sharashka belonged, though they were not at the time in hard-labor camps, to the realm of GULAG. **1977** *Guardian Weekly* 26 June 22/2 And didn't his author work gratefully too in the same *sharashka*, or Island of Paradise, as the zeks called these 'soft' research camps? **1982** T. BINYON *Swan Song* viii. 58 They got him for parasitism and a few other offences. Now he was presumably.. east of the Urals and taking the zeks for their bread ration.

zekill, obs. form of SICKLE *sb.*

zel. Also **zell.** [Turkish *zil* (Redhouse).] A kind of cymbal.
1817 MOORE *Lalla Rookh, Fire-Worshippers* I. 8 Where, some hours since, was heard the swell Of trumpet and the clash of zel. **1838** LYTTON *Leila* IV. i, The clash of the zell, the boom of the African drum, and the wild and barbarous blast of the Moorish clarion.

zel, obs. form of SELL *v.*, ZEAL.

Zelander, obs. form of ZEALANDER.

†'**zelant.** *Obs. rare.* [ad. late L. *zēlant-*, *zēlans*, pr. pple. of *zēlāre*: see ZEAL *v.* Cf. It. *zelante* zealous.] A zealot.
1625 BACON *Ess., Unity in Relig.* (Arb.) 427 To certaine Zelants all Speech of Pacification is odious. [**1885** E. A. ABBOTT *Bacon* 426 An *Advertisement touching an Holy War* .., in which the interlocutors represent a Moderate Divine, a Protestant Zelant, a Romish Catholic Zelant.]

zelator ('zɛlətə(r)). Also 5-6 **zelatour,** 6 **zelat(e)ur, -oure, zealatour,** 9 **zealator, zealoter.** [a. OF. *zelateur* (= It. *zelatore*, Sp. *celador*, Pg. *zelador*) or its source eccl. L. *zēlātor*, f. *zēlāre*: see ZEAL *v.* The spellings with *zeal-* are due to assimilation to *zeal*, *zealot*.]
1. A zealous defender or supporter; one who zealously furthers the cause *of*. *rare.*
1460 CAPGRAVE *Chron.* (Rolls) 195 That the qween and the prince schuld be receyved as good zelatores of the rem. **1531** ELYOT *Gov.* III. xxvii. (1883) II. 426 Many zelatours or fauourers of the publyke weale. **1549** *Compl. Scot.* ix. 76, I praye ȝou to be zelaturs of the lau of gode. **1600** HAMILTON *Facile Traictise* Ded., Al zelateurs of the trew seruice of God. **1865** W. G. PALGRAVE *Journ. Arabia* I. 408 'Meddey' yeeyah', 'men of zeal', or 'Zelators'. *Ibid.* II. 3 He had figured conspicuously in the first band of Zelators at the epoch of their foundation in 1855. **1891** *Catholic News* 25 July 8/6 The Salford Diocesan Branch of the Zelators of St. Joseph's Foreign Missionary Society.
2. = ZEALOT 1, 2. *rare.*
1644 H. LESLIE *Blessing of Judah* 41, I can best compare them.. with that Rebellious rout of the Iewes, who called themselves Zelators. **1867** PALGRAVE in *Macm. Mag.* XVI. 143 Even stoutest parliamentary 'zealoters' must yield to utter weariness of body.
3. A sister in a religious community whose duty is to keep a check upon the conduct of the mother superior or of the younger religious and novices.
[**1671** WOODHEAD *St. Teresa* II. xvi. 113 Nor was there any accusation against her in the Chapter concerning the least defect; although the smallest, and most minute matters are by the *Zelatore* observed, and mentioned there.] **1851** ULLATHORNE *Plea Rights Relig. Women* 11 The rule commonly requires also that there should be two prudent sisters who are called *Zealators*, and whose duty it is to admonish the superioress, should she exceed or fail in her duties.

zelatrice ('zɛlətrɪs), **zelatrix** (-ɪks). [ad. F. *zélatrice* and its source eccl. L. *zēlātrix*, fem. of *zēlātor*: see prec.] A female zelator.
1890 *Tablet* 17 May 794 The Superioress of a Convent, a most fervent zelatrix. **1902** M. J. F. MCCARTHY *Priests & People in Irel.* 200 A zelatrice is a curiosity of religion in Ireland. *Ibid.* 201 A zelatrice for the Œuvre Expiatoire.

zelde, zele, Zelender, zelie, zell, Zelonian, zelot, -(t)e: see SELD *adv.*, ZEAL, ZEALANDER, SEELY, SELL, ZEYLONIAN, ZEALOT.

Zeldovich ('zɛldəvɪtʃ). *Chem.* The name of Y. B. *Zeldovich* (b. 1914), U.S.S.R. physicist, used *attrib.* to designate a mechanism proposed by him for the oxidation of nitrogen to nitric oxide in flames via a two-stage free-radical reaction.

1973 S. J. WILLIAMSON *Fund. Air Pollution* x. 298 The formation of NO occurs primarily through two simultaneous reactions known as the Zeldovich mechanism: $N + O_2 = NO + O; O + N_2 = NO + N$. **1982** *Sci. Amer.* Feb. 94/1 At temperatures low enough to suppress the Zeldovich reactions other reactions still generate nitric oxide.

zelkova (zɛl'kəʊvə). Also **Zelkova**. [mod.L. (E. Spach 1841, in *Ann. des Sci. Nat.*: *Bot.* 2nd Ser. XV. 352), f. *zelkoua*, *tselkwa*, cited by Spach as local names for *Z. carpinifolia* in the Caucasus: cf. mod.Russ. *dzel'kova grabolistnaya*.] A deciduous tree of the genus of this name (family Ulmaceæ), which is native to China, Japan, and the Caucasus, and bears toothed leaves and small green flowers. Also ***zelkova tree***.

1893 A. D. WEBSTER *Hardy Ornamental Flowering Trees & Shrubs* 134 Zelkova Tree..is a handsome, large growing tree, with oblong deeply-crenated leaves, and small inconspicuous flowers. **1957** M. HADFIELD *Brit. Trees* 226 The zelkova..deserves more extensive planting. **1976** *Daily Tel.* 5 July 8/6 Three thousand Zelkova trees imported from Germany are being planted in Peterborough to replace elms killed by Dutch Elm disease. **1978** *Vole* Dec. 27/1 Zelkovas are a rather special group of trees. They belong to the Elm family and have delicate, toothed leaves.

zelotic, zealotic (ziː'lɒtɪk), *a.* [f. ZEALOT + -IC; now often assimilated to Gr. ζηλωτικός, f. ζηλωτής zealot.] Of the nature of, or characteristic of, a zealot.

1657 GAUDEN *F. Watts' Scribe, Pharisee*, etc. To Rdr., He ..is void as of all superstitious novelties, so, of all zealotick transports. **1743** J. MORRIS *Serm.* iv. 90 In such a legal and zelotic, such a passionate and fierce..spirit. **1889** J. B. BURY *Later Roman Empire* I. i. 3 We have the zelotic dogmatism of Epiphanes. **1899** STALKER *Christol. Jesus* iv. 152 Such zealotic enthusiasm. **1916** P. T. FORSYTH in *Contemp. Rev.* June 762 The Pharisees were doing that passionately. It was their whole zealotic programme about which they had no misgivings.

So † **ze'lotical** *a.*

1630 in *Crt. & Times Chas. I* (1848) II. 80 One Leviston, a zealotical Scotsman. *a* **1638** MEDE *Par. Peter* Wks. III. (1672) 611 The zelotical Anti-chiliasts. **1694** STRYPE *Cranmer* III. xix. 373 Dr. Marshal Dean of Christ's-Church, a most furious and zelotical Man.

zelotism, zealotism ('zɛlətɪz(ə)m). [f. ZEALOT + -ISM; for the spelling cf. prec. So F. *zélotisme*.] Action, thought, or feeling characteristic of a zealot; zealotry.

1716 M. DAVIES *Athen. Brit.* III. *Suppl. Diss. Drama* 2 His Embassador's indefatigable Zelotism. **1751** GRAY *Let. to Walpole* 8 Oct., Wks. 1825 II. 165 The folly and cruelty of stiffness and zealotism in religion. **1885** J. F. SMITH tr. *Ewald's Hist. Israel* VII. 615 Zealotism itself did not..cease to ferment in the hearts..of many..adherents of the party. **1888** DOUGHTY *Arabia Deserta* I. 548, I could not altogether escape..the Mohammedan zelotism.

So † **zelotist** *Obs.*, a zealot.

1593 G. HARVEY *Pierce's Super.* Wks. (Grosart) II. 173 Their feruent, and illuminate Zelotistes. **1608** H. CLAPHAM *Errour Left Hand* 8, I haue sinned much in following blind Zelo[t]ists, setting al on fire with Samsons foxes. **1640** [see SCIOLOUS].

‖**zelo'typia**. *Obs. rare.* [late L., a. Gr. ζηλοτυπία, f. ζηλότυπος, f. ζῆλος ZEAL *sb.* + τυπ-, stem of τύπτειν to strike.] Jealousy. So † **zelotypie** [cf. F. *zélotypie*, Cotgr.]. Hence † **zelotyping** *a.*, jealous; † **zelotypist** (-tɪp-), a person characterized by excessive zeal, a zealot.

1601 T. WRIGHT *Passions* I. vi. (1604) 26 Every diversity or change we finde in passions,..as, Mercy, Shamefastnesse,..Zelotypia, Exanimation. **1623** COCKERAM, *Zelotypie*, iealousie. **1631** R. H. *Arraignm. Whole Creat.* xvii. 302 In all the hot Countries, where hotspurre Zelotipists have resided. *a* **1660** *Contemp. Hist. Irel.* (Ir. Archæol. Soc.) II. 159 Castlhauen..apointinge there his temptinge and zelopytinge [*sic*] spirits, deserted the towne.

zely, obs. form of SEELY *a.*

1496 *Bk. St. Albans, Fishing* h j b, Who soo woll ryse erly shall be holy helthy & zely. **1555** PENDLETON in *Bonner's Hom.* 38 b, The impudente procedars haue taught the zely people that euerye man..maye be a iudge of controuersyes.

'Zembl(i)an, *a.* and *sb. rare.* [f. (*Nova*) *Zembla* = Russ. *Novaya Zemlya* 'new land'.]

a. *adj.* Belonging to Nova Zembla, a group of islands in the Arctic Ocean north of Archangel in Russia; hence, arctic. **b.** *sb.* A native or inhabitant of Nova Zembla.

1674 tr. *La Martinière's New Voy.* 34 Samoiedes, Siberians, Zemblians. *Ibid.* 122 We descryed..a Zemblane in a Canoe. **1749** CAWTHORN *Poems* (1771) 179 Thy unwearied soul..gave to Britain half the zemblian sky. **1806** SHEE *Rhymes Art* (ed. 3) 10 Lybian sands, or Zemblan snows.

† **'zembletee**. *Obs. rare.* (illiterate.) [f. SEMBLE *a.* + *-tee*, -TY.] ***by zembletee***, in appearance: = *by semblant* (see SEMBLANT *sb.* 2 b).

a **1553** UDALL *Royster D.* I. iv, A sore man by zembletee.

zembra, obs. var. ZEBRA.

zeme, zemi ('ziːmɪ). [Carib *cemi*.] An idol, or a tutelary spirit represented thereby, worshipped by the aborigines of the West Indian islands. Hence **'zemeism** (see quot. 1902); **zeme'istic** *a.*

1613 PURCHAS *Pilgrimage* IX. xiv. 743 These Images they made of Gossampine cotton hard stopped, sitting, like the pictures of the Deuill, which they called *Zemes*. *Ibid.*, Euery King hath his particular *Zemes*, which he honoureth. **1663** J. OWEN *Vind. Animadv. Fiat Lux* xxi. 487 In the Indies, the Catholick Spaniards took away the *Zemes* or Images of their Idols. **1902** FEWKES in *Science* 18 July 104 The whole social and religious organization was knit together by a form of totemism or tutelary clan ancients worship which I shall call *Zemeism*. **1903–4** *Ann. Rep. Bur. Amer. Ethnol.* 54 Zemiism. *Ibid.* 59 Her body was painted with figures and..flowers, evidently zemeistic or totemistic.

zeme, obs. form of SEAM *sb.*[2]

zemindar (zə'miːndɑː(r)). *E. Ind.* Forms: 7 **gemidar**, 7–8 **jem(m)idar**, 8 **jemitdar**, **jemendar**, **zemidar**, **zemendar**, **zimeendar**, 8–9 **zamindar**, 9 **zem-**, **zumeendar**, 8– **zemindar**. [Hind., a. Pers. *zamīndār* (also *zamīdar*), f. *zamīn*, *zamī* earth + *dār* holder.

The pronunciation shown by the earliest forms *gemi-*, *jemidar*, is that of the North-West Provinces of India today, where 'the rustic pronunciation of the word *zamīndār* is hardly distinguishable from the Anglo-Indian pronunciation of *Jama'dār*' (Yule).]

Formerly, a collector of the revenue from land held by a number of cultivators; subsequently, an Indian who held land for which he paid revenue direct to the British government.

1683 W. HEDGES *Diary* (Hakl. Soc.) I. 77 We lay at Bogatchera,..y[e] Gemidar invited us ashore, and showed us Store of Deer, Peacocks, &c. **1698** *Ext. Consultations at Chuttanutte* 31 Oct. (Yule) Paying the said Rent to the King as the Jemidars have successively done. **1713** *MS. Records* in Yule & Burnell *Anglo-Ind. Gloss.* s.v., Mr. Edwd. Page... Jemendar. **1753** HANWAY *Trav.* (1762) II. XIV. iv. 357 *note*, *Rajahs*, who are the chiefs of those people who are distinguished by the name of *zemidars*, which signifies possessors of lands. **1764** *Ann. Reg.*, *St. Papers* 188/1 To all governors, officers..and zemindars..in the provinces of Bengal. **1776** JAS. RENNELL *MS. Let.* 5 Aug. (Yule), The Countrey Jemitdars remote from Calcutta, treat us frequently with great Insolence. **1781** *Ann. Reg.*, *Hist. Eur.* 177/1 The Zemindars, who are the present great landholders of India, are likewise a sort of hereditary princes of the country. **1844** H. H. WILSON *Brit. India* I. I. vii. 401 The Zemindars had been formerly charged with the management of the police, and were held accountable for all acts of robbery or violence committed within their Zemindaris. **1890** *Times* 8 Mar. 4/1 The zemindar of Devarakota.

Hence **'zemindarship**, zemindary.

1698 *Ext. Consultations at Chuttanutte* 31 Oct. (1788) (Yule), The Prince having given us..the Jemmidarship of the said towns. **1860** [C. GRANT] *Rur. Life Bengal* 64 For the honour and glory of Zumeendarship he cares not a fig. **1878** JAS. GRANT *Hist. India* I. ii. 9 For a good round sum he sold to the East India Company the zemindarships of Govindpore, Chutanutty, and Calcutta.

zemindary (zə'miːndərɪ). *E. Ind.* Forms: 8 **zemidary**, 8–9 **zemindarry**, **-aree**, 9 **zeme(e)ndary**, **zam-**, **zemindari**, **zam-**, **zumeen-**, **zemindary**. [Hind., a. Pers. *zamīndārī*, f. *zamīndār*: see prec.]

1. The system of holding lands and farming revenue by means of zemindars; the office or jurisdiction of a zemindar.

1757 in Scrafton *Indostan* (1770) 81 All the land lying south of Calcutta, as far as Culpee, shall be under the Zemindary of the English Company. **1758** in *Jrnl. Ho. Comm.* XXXIII. 850/1 Sunnud from the Dewan of the Subah of Bengal, for the Zemindarry of the Lands granted to the Company. **1783** *Ann. Reg.*, *Hist. Eur.* 5/2 The zemidary was secured to the family..of Bulwant Sing. **1890** *Times* 8 Mar. 4/1 The appellant, who was the eldest son of the late zemindar..contended that the zemindary was impartible. **1917** *Chambers's Jrnl.* Dec. 781/1 There is no such man within my zamindary as can catch the living snake.

attrib. **1790** J. GRANT (*title*) An Inquiry into the nature of Zemindary Tenures in the landed property of Bengal. **1885** G. S. FORBES *Wild Life in Canara* 171 They now..cultivate the lands of some eight or ten zemindari estates. **1914** W. G. LAWRENCE *Let.* 30 July in *Home Lett. T. E. Lawrence* (1954) 563 We all ate together of food one could stick one's teeth in, thick Zamindari bread. **1932** *Ann. Reg. 1931* I. 155 Movements against the payment of rents and land revenue, particularly in the United Provinces, where the *zamindari* (landlord) system is prevalent. **1968** *Times* 6 Apr. (Pakistan Suppl.) p. v/4 After independence, many Hindu zamindars fled, the zamindary system was abolished and the land divided into tiny portions and sold to the Muslims. **1976** M. S. HOQUE *Hunger* II. vi. 41 Parents now think that their son is a Zamindari estate on auction sale.

2. The territory administered by a zemindar.

1764 *Ann. Reg.*, *St. Papers* 191/2 If the French come into the country, I will not allow them to..hold lands, zemindaries, &c. **1858** J. B. NORTON *Topics* 165 The ancient zemindarry of Golugondah, which yields about 10,000 rupees of clear surplus annually. **1878** *Macm. Mag.* Jan. 250/2 The actual extent of land cultivated in the Madras Presidency (excluding Zemindary), amounted to 14,236,072 acres of dry and 3,510,615 acres of wet.

‖**zemirah** (zə'mɪərə). *Judaism.* Pl. **zemirot(h** (zə'miːrəʊt, s-). [Heb.] A religious song sung in Hebrew at Sabbath meals.

1831 [see MITZVAH]. **1892** I. ZANGWILL *Childr. Ghetto* II. xviii. 82 When supper was over grace was chanted, and then the *Zemiroth* were sung—songs summing up, in light and jingling metre, the very essence of holy joyousness. **1973** *Jewish Chron.* 9 Feb. 21/5 The service was followed by supper and zemirot in the communal hall.

‖**zemni** ('zɛmnɪ). Also 8 **ziemni**, 9 **zemmi**. [Short for Russ. dial. *schenók zemnói* 'puppy of earth' (*zemnói* adj. f. *zemlya* earth).] The blind mole-rat, *Spalax typhlus*. Also ***zemni-rat***.

1785 SMELLIE tr. *Buffon's Nat. Hist.* (1791) VIII. 232 In Poland and Russia there is another animal called *ziemni* or *zemni*, which is of the same genus with the zisel. **1836–9** *Todd's Cycl. Anat.* II. 571/2 Some..are devoid of the auricle, as the mole, the zemni-rat, the mole-rat.

‖**zemstvo** ('zɛmstvo). Also **zem(p)stwo**. Pl. **zemstvos**, ‖**zemstva**. [Russ., f. *zemlya* land.] An elective district or provincial council in Russia for purposes of local government, created by Alexander II in 1864.

1865 *Saunder's Newsletter* 8 Feb., He..sneered at the upstart ambition of the *Zempstwo* class, by which is meant the mere owners of certain acreable amount of the soil. **1877** D. M. WALLACE *Russia* xiv. (ed. 2) I. 326 The Zemstvo is a kind of local administration. **1896** *Jewish Chron.* 17 Jan. 8/1 The Zemstwo of Odessa. **1958** *Times Lit. Suppl.* 10 Jan. 14/3 The history of the pressure for political freedom was closely interwoven with the development of the organs of local self-government, the *Zemstva*. **1967** *Listener* 2 Nov. 559/1 At any time in those final decades of the last century even a central assembly of representatives of the *zemstvos* would have constituted an important safety-valve. **1980** *Times. Lit. Suppl.* 14 Nov. 1306/3 Linked closely to the work of the *zemstva*, new local units of administration, medicine became the first true profession in Russia. **1983** P. USTINOV *My Russia* xi. 122 Members of local *zemstvos* might soon enjoy a voice in the internal government of the country.

Hence **'zemstvoist**, a member of zemstvo.

1905 *Times* 8 May 5/3 The Zemstvoists have split over the question of universal suffrage.

Zen (zɛn). Also 8 **Sen**. [a. Jap. *zen*, ad. Chin. *chán* quietude, ad. Skr. *dhyāna* meditation.] A school of Mahayana Buddhism that emphasizes meditation and personal awareness and became influential in Japanese life from the 13th century after being introduced from China.

1727 J. G. SCHEUCHZER tr. *Kæmpfer's Hist. Jap.* I. II. v. 199 In the 1850 streets of this city, there were 1050 [families] of the *Ten Dai's* Religion,..11 016 of *Sen*. **1834** [see SHINGON]. **1911** *Encycl. Relig. & Ethics* IV. 704/1 Meditation came to have more weight than the other two factors, until in China and Japan there arose a sect, the Zen ..in which it is the most essential part of the entire teaching. **1921** *Eastern Buddhist* (Japan) I. 13 Zen in its essence is the art of seeing into the nature of one's own being. **1960** *Spectator* 15 July 101 *What* do they know about Zen—the programme-writer, the film-makers, the beatniks, the lot? **1967** D. & E. T. RIESMAN *Conversations in Japan* 123 Another boy, who..was their top judo athlete, said that he got his values from Zen. **1976** A. DAVIS *Television* 122 By the late sixties, religious programmes were beginning to reflect the interest of young people in Eastern religions such as Buddhism, Hinduism, Zen and the cult of the Maharishi. **1977** J. F. FIXX *Compl. Bk. Running* ii. 14 Our society puts considerable emphasis on personal development and the maximizing of one's potential. Zen, transcendental meditation, assertiveness training..and similar movements are all directed at making us fulfilled human beings.

2. *attrib.* and *Comb.*, esp. in ***Zen Buddhism***, ***Buddhist***.

1881 *Trans. Asiatic Soc. Japan* IX. 179 (*heading*) Zen sect. **1894**, etc. [see SOTO]. **1902** *Encycl. Brit.* XXIX. 681/1 The Zen doctrines of Buddhism, which contributed so much to the development of the heroic and the sentimental,..were therefore favourable to the stability of military feudalism. **1921** *Eastern Buddhist* (Japan) I. 13 (*heading*) Zen Buddhism as purifier and liberator of life. *Ibid.* 26 Whether an enlightened Zen master or an ignoramus of the first degree, neigher can escape the so-called laws of nature. **1923** *Ibid.* II. 341 It remained for the Chinese Zen Buddhists to invent their own methods according to their own needs and insight. **1947** *Archit. Rev.* CII. 32/2 Taoism and nature mysticism, transmitted through the vehicle of Zen Buddhism. **1950** A. HUXLEY *Themes & Variations* 98 As the Zen Masters like paradoxically to put it, 'Buddha never taught the saving truth.' **1960** KOESTLER *Lotus & Robot* II. x. 234 The monk's rudeness..was in the right tradition of Zen-teasing. **1965** W. SWAAN *Jap. Lantern* v. 58 The canons of Japanese aesthetic appreciations were formulated to a very large degree under the influence of Zen Buddhist philosophy. **1971** 'G. BLACK' *Time for Pirates* iii. 45 Mr. Akamoro.. contrived..to leak the thought..that it is time for Japanese initiative to take over with Zen Buddhism for the moral trimmings. **1979** B. MALAMUD *Dubin's Lives* viii. 280 She said she had been talking to a Zen Master in South San Francisco... 'I'm thinking of entering a Zen commune... I expect to become a Zen disciple.'

zenana (zə'nɑːnə). Also 8–9 **zananah**, **zenanah**, **zunana**, (8 **jenana**), 9 **zennanah**, **zanana**. [Hind. *zenāna*, a. Pers. *zanāna*, f. *zan* woman (related to Gr. γυνή woman: see QUEAN *sb.*).]

1. In India and Persia, that part of a dwelling-house in which the women of a family are secluded; an East Indian harem.

1761 COOTE in Vansittart *Narr. Trans. Bengal* (1766) I. 245, I asked him where the Nabob was? Who replied, he was asleep in his Zenana. **1776** *Trial of Nundocomar* 66/2 Sujah Dowlah..plundered all the goods..of Cossim Ally; he even infringed the rights of his Zenana. **1790** in Yule & Burnell *Anglo-Ind. Gloss.* s.v., The Jenanas or Women's apartments of principal Natives. **1889** G. HOOPER *Wellington* ii. 45 He was disgusted with an order to search the zenana for treasure.

2. (Also ***zenana-cloth***.) A light thin fabric used for women's dresses.

1900 *Westm. Gaz.* 6 Dec. 2/2 A bolero of pale blue zenana. **1903** *Daily Chron.* 17 Jan. 8/4 Such combinations of wool and silk as Zenana cloth.

3. *attrib.*, esp. of missionary work carried on by Christian women among native women in India.

1810 T. WILLIAMSON *E. Ind. Vade Mecum* I. 244 The *zenanah* apparel is given to him [*sc.* the doby] to wash, and to iron. **1872** E. BRADDON *Life in India* iii. 57 The influence of zenana society told upon his character. **1882** CUPPLES *Mem. Mrs. Valentine* ix. 146 For the purpose of assisting her to pursue Zenana-work when she returned to India. **1886** YULE & BURNELL *Anglo-Ind. Gloss.* s.v., The growth of the admirable Zenana missions has of late years made this word more familiar in England.

Zend (zɛnd). Also **Zand, Zund.** [a. F. *zend* (used as the name of the language by Anquetil du Perron, 1771): see ZEND-AVESTA.]

I. = ZEND-AVESTA.

In T. Hyde *Hist. Relig. Vet. Pers.*, 1700, it is usually designated *liber Zend*, but it is also referred to as *Zendavestâ, Vestâvazend, Avesta, Vesta, Avestak*, etc.

1715 PRIDEAUX *O. & N. Test.* I. (1718) 176 This book is called *Zendavesta*, and by contraction *Zend*, the vulgar pronounce it *Zundavestow*, and *Zund*. *Ibid.*, In their language they call a righteous action *Zend-aver*, i.e. what the book Zend allows. **1789** SIR W. JONES *Disc. Persians* Wks. 1799 I. 79 Besides the Pársi and Pahlavi, a very ancient and abstruse tongue was known to the priests and philosophers, called the language of the Zend. **1790** FRANCKLIN *Obs. Tour Bengal to Persia* 29 Their sacred book, the Zend, which is said to have been written by their celebrated prophet Zerdusht.

2. The language of the Avesta (see ZEND-AVESTA): also called *Old Bactrian*, forming with Old Persian the Iranian group of the Indo-European languages. Also *attrib.*

In early use, attrib. use of sense 1, = pertaining to or used in the Zend-Avesta.

1700 T. HYDE *Hist. Relig. Vet. Pers.* xxvi. 338 Literæ.. quæ..apud incolas vulgò audiunt *Literæ Zundicæ*, seu *Character Zundicus*, vel si Anglicè loquimur, the *Zund Character*. **1788** *Asiatick Researches* I. 45 *note*, The Zend Letters. **1789** SIR W. JONES *Disc. Persians* Wks. 1799 I. 83 M. Anquetil..has exhibited in his work, entitled *Zendávestà*, two vocabularies in Zend and Pahlavi. **1815** ELPHINSTONE *Acc. Caubul* (1842) I. 251 Some of this very class [of words] belong to the Zend and Pehlevee. **1842** (*title*) The Vandidad Sádí of the Pársis in the Zand Language. **1878** G. SMITH *Life John Wilson* vii. 213 He was the first English scholar to master the original Zand texts.

Hence **'Zendic** *a.* [cf. mod.L. *Zundicus*, T. Hyde, 1700], belonging to Zend; so **'Zendish** *a.* (also as *sb.* = Zend); **'Zendist**, one versed in Zend.

1813 *Q. Rev.* Oct. 266 In ancient Media, Zendish was the language of the northern, and Pehlvi, or Parthian, of the southern parts. **1842** W. C. TAYLOR *Anc. Hist.* App. II. (ed. 3) 581 The Zendic and Pehlvi dialects of Persia. **1893** *Nation* (N.Y.) 22 June 457/2 That persons professing to be specialists in Zend should be able to read the Pahlavi language..in MS.—an accomplishment which..very few professed Zendists possess.

†**zendalet.** *Obs.* Also **zendaletto.** [It. *zendaletto*, dim. of *zendale* SENDAL.]

1. In Venice, a large square woollen shawl, usually black, folded triangularly and worn either over the head (in the 18th cent. upon a wire frame) or over the shoulders.

1789 MRS. PIOZZI *Journ. France* I. 184 A Venetian lady's mode of appearance in her zendalet, without which nobody stirs out of their house in a morning. It consists of a full black silk petticoat..flounced with gauze... A skeleton wire upon the head,..over it a large piece of black mode or persian, so as to shade the face like a curtain. [**1910** tr. *P. Monnier's Venice 18th Cent.* iv. 57 Over their heads they fasten that *zendaletto* of white lace, which inwreathes the waist, the shoulders, and the smile.]

2. A long piece of cloth falling from the back of the hood of a gondola into the water; hence, the gondola itself.

1794 MRS. RADCLIFFE *Myst. Udolpho* xvii, The count led Emily to his *zendaletto*. *a* **1814** *Gondolier* II. i. in *New Brit. Theatre* III. 183 When moonlight cheers the scenes we love, ..And zendalettos seem to move Upon a sea of liquid light.

Zend-Avesta (zɛndə'vɛstə). Also 7–8 **Zundavastaw.** [Alteration (cf. Pers. *zand(a)-wastā, zandastā*) of *Avestá-va-Zend* (Pehlevi *Avistāk va Zend*), i.e. the Avesta with the interpretation. The word *Zend* was taken as an attrib. element denoting the language of the books, and was hence used independently as its name: see ZEND.] The sacred writings of the Parsees, usually attributed to Zoroaster.

1630 LORD *Relig. Persees* Proeme, A booke writ in the Persian Character, containing their Scripture, and in their owne language, called their Zvndavastaw. **1760–2** GOLDSM. *Cit. W.* xv, 'Kabul', says the Zendavesta, 'was born on the rushy banks of the river Mawra.' **1854** [see VATICAN 1 b]. **1878** *N. Amer. Rev.* CXXVII. 323 The Zendavesta of the Persians.

Hence **Zend-Ave'staic** *a.*

1816 G. S. FABER *Orig. Pagan Idol.* I. p. xxxii, The materials of the Zend-Avestaic history seem to be genuine.

zende, obs. form of SEND *v.*[1]

Zendik ('zɛndɪk). [a. Arab. *zindīq* atheist, fire-worshipper, disbeliever in a future state, etc., Pers. *zandīq* fire-worshipper; cf. late Avestic *zandā-* a kind of heretic (Bartholomae).] A name given in the East to a disbeliever in revealed religion or a practiser of heretical magic. Also **Zen'dician.** Hence **'Zendicism,** the belief of a zendik; **'Zendikite (Zin-),** a believer in zendicism.

1697 PRIDEAUX *Mahomet* (1708) 13 Zendicism, an Error among the Arabs near of kin to the Sadducism of the Jews, ..denying Providence, the Resurrection, and a Future State. **1842** BRANDE *Dict. Sci.*, etc. s.v., The sect of Zendiks opposed the progress of Mohammedanism in Arabia with great obstinacy. **1845** *Encycl. Metrop.* XI. 558/2 The Zendicians... Their belief seems to have been a medley formed from the doctrines of the Magians and Paulicians. **1877** *Smith & Wace's Dict. Chr. Biog.* I. 477/2 The Persians exulted in crimes and Zendicism abounded. *Ibid.* 478/1 Hareth, son of Amr,..who is said by Hamza to have been a Zendikite, was of Kendite race.

zendo ('zɛndəʊ). [a. Jap. *zendō*, f. *zen* ZEN + *dō* hall.] A place for Zen Buddhist meditation and study.

1959 *Encounter* XII. I. 20 The *Zendo* or meditation-hall. **1968** *Time* 18 Oct. 62/3 Students must report to the *zendo* (meditation hall) by 5. **1974** *Country Life* 14 Feb. 326/1, I was taken to the Zendo, the special hall for contemplation, by a young monk. **1981** 'E. V. CUNNINGHAM' *Case of Sliding Pool* vii. 77, I thought I would drive down to the Zendo... I feel a need to talk to the Roshi.

zeneȝi, zeng, obs. ff. SIN *v.*, SINGE *v.*

Zener ('zi:nə(r)). Also **zener.**

1. The name of K. E. *Zener* (1903–61), U.S. psychologist, used *attrib.* to designate a pack of 25 cards that he designed for use in parapsychology experiments, containing five each of five different cards, each showing a simple symbol.

1934 J. B. RHINE *Extra-Sensory Perception* iv. 50 We have once since substituted a 'heart' for the 'waves' figure but later returned to the latter. I shall hereinafter call these cards the 'Zener cards'. **1940** *Proc. Soc. Psychical Res.* XLVI. 153 The guesser at Zener cards all unwittingly was guessing correctly..a card which was one or two places earlier or later in the sequence. **1949** *Mind* LVIII. 390 Extra-sensory perception (ESP) is investigated by means of the card-guessing technique. Zener cards are generally used. **1969** *Listener* 6 Mar. 301/2 Rhine devised a new kind of test for ESP. He made packs of 25 cards called Zenercards, with geometrical designs: cross, square, circle, waves and star. **1978** D. BLOODWORTH *Crosstalk* xiv. 119 There are a dozen ways of beating the odds with the Zener packs they use for card-guessing tests.

2. *Electronics.* The name of C. M. *Zener* (b. 1905), U.S. physicist. **a.** Used *attrib.* to denote various concepts, etc., connected with or arising from his researches, as **Zener breakdown** = *Zener effect* below; **Zener diode,** a junction diode in which the forward characteristic is like that of an ordinary diode but there is a sudden large increase in reverse current at a certain constant reverse voltage owing to the Zener effect or the avalanche effect, making it useful as a voltage regulator and in switching circuits; **Zener effect,** the increase in reverse current of a Zener diode when attributed to the tunnelling of current-carriers through the transition region rather than to the avalanche effect; **Zener voltage,** the voltage at which Zener breakdown occurs; the reverse breakdown voltage of a Zener diode.

1956 L. P. HUNTER *Handbk. Semiconductor Electronics* III. 17 The two mechanisms which have been observed for semiconductor contacts in the absence of thermal breakdown are Zener breakdown..and avalanche breakdown. **1962** [see *Zener effect* below]. **1981** NASHELSKY & BOYLESTAD *Devices: Discrete & Integrated* ii. 29 As V_z [*sc.* the Zener voltage] decreases to very low levels, such as −5V, another mechanism, called Zener breakdown, will contribute to the sharp change in the characteristic. **1957** R. F. SHEA *Transistor Circuit Engineering* iii. 62 One of the simplest methods of obtaining such a [stable collector-voltage] supply is with the aid of a diode biased into breakdown in the reverse direction (so-called Zener diode). **1975** *Gramophone* Aug. 384/3 Stabilisation of the feedback input stages is achieved with a zener diode. **1981** J. C. SPROTT *Introd. Mod. Electronics* vi. 136 In the forward direction a Zener diode behaves like any other diode. **1957** W. C. DUNLAP *Introd. Semiconductors* viii. 168 Internal field emission, often called Zener effect because of the early theoretical contributions made to the subject by C. Zener,.. is analogous to field emission from metals. **1962** SIMPSON & RICHARDS *Physical Princ. Junction Transistors* iv. 69 Lower voltage units usually have negative temperature coefficients indicating the existence of Zener effect. In such devices the transition region is apparently too thin to allow appreciable carrier multiplication to take place and Zener breakdown occurs before the critical avalanche condition has been reached. **1952** *Proc. IRE* XL. 1349/2 The Zener voltage for this junction was 21·5 volts. **1969** J. J. SPARKES *Transistor Switching* i. 13 At Zener voltages of about 6V the slope resistance of the diode characteristic is minimal. **1980** C. F. G. DELANEY *Electronics for Physicist* ix. 215 The Zener voltage..is a function of the resistivity (that is, of the doping) of the materials from which the diode is constructed.

b. *ellipt.* A Zener diode.

1965 *Wireless World* July 14 (Advt.), Ask for details of zeners from 400 mW to 50W, and 3·6V to 200V. **1976** *Pract. Electronics* Oct. 791/1 To provide any given voltage, it is only necessary to select a Zener having a voltage exceeding the required voltage by 0·7 volts.

Zengakuren (zɛŋgə'ku:rən). [Jap., acronym f. *Zen* Nihon *Gaku*sei Jichikai So*ren*go, = All-Japan Federation of Student Self-Government Associations (formed in 1948).] In Japan, an extreme left-wing student movement, noted for its violent interventions in national politics. Also *attrib.* or as *adj.*

1952 E. S. COLBERT *Left Wing in Japanese Politics* v. 299 The Communist-dominated student organization, the *Zengakuren*. *Ibid.* 300 On May 23, [1950] at a *Zengakuren* convention. **1960** *Times* 21 Sept. 16/6 He is rather naturally unloved by the members of Zengakuren, the radical student movement. **1967** D. & E. T. RIESMAN *Conversations in Japan* 121 The large Zengakuren ideas and practical accomplishments. **1970** *Guardian* 1 Apr. 11/1 The students, armed with quarter-staves,..with the colours and battle-cry of the Zengakuren sect to which they belonged. **1975** *New Yorker* 18 Aug. 50/2 Five student groups, including two main ones called Kakumaruha (the Revolutionary Marxists) and Chukakuha (the Middle Core), both composed of self-styled Trotskyites, are offshoots of the original Zengakuren, a radical association that led demonstrations against the security treaty and instigated campus riots that succeeded in closing down a number of universities over a period of months in 1969.

zenick ('zi:nɪk). Also **zenik.** [a. F. *zénik* (Sonnerat *Voy. aux Indes Orientales*, 1806).] The African suricate, *Suricata suricatta.* = MEERKAT 2 b, SURICATE.

1801 J. BARROW *Acct. Trav. S. Afr.* I. iii. 231 Others of this genus [*sc.* Viverra] are the muskiliatte cat, or zenik,.. the tigrina [etc.]. **1843** *Penny Cycl.* XXVII. 764. **1875** BUCKLAND *Log-Bk.* 96.

zenilla, obs. var. ZANELLA.

zenith ('zɛnɪθ, 'zi:nɪθ). Forms: 4–5 **cinit, cenith, -yth, senith, -yth,** 5 **cenit, senit,** 6 **zenit, -ithe, -yth, ceneth,** 6– **zenith.** [a. OF. *cenit(h* (F. *zénith*) or med.L. *cenit* (cf. It. *zenit*, Sp. *cenit*, Pg. *zenith*, G. *zenith*, etc.), obscurely ad. Arab. *samt*, in *samt ar-rās* lit. way or path over the head (*samt* way, *al* the, *rās* head); cf. AZIMUTH (*al* the, *sumūt* pl. of *samt*).]

1. The point of the sky directly overhead; the highest point of the celestial sphere as viewed from any particular place; the upper pole of the horizon (opp. to NADIR).

†Sometimes, as in quots. 1555, 1638, used like a predicative adj. = in the zenith, 'vertical': cf. also quot. 1604.

1387 TREVISA *Higden* (Rolls) II. 177 Cinit, þat is þe point þat is in þe welken euen aȝenst hem in þe oþer side of þe erþe. *c* **1391** CHAUCER *Astrol.* I. §18 The centre þat standith a-Middes the narwest cercle is cleped the senyth...this forseide cenyth is ymagened to ben the verrey point ouer the crowne of thyn heued, & also this senyth is the verrey pool of the orisonte in euery regioun. *Ibid.* II. §22 As fer is the heued of aries..from owre orisonte as is the cenyth fro the pole artik. *c* **1495** *The Epitaffe*, etc. in *Skelton's Wks.* (1843) II. 393 Creatures more maddyr In erthe none wandreth atwene senit and naddyr. **1549** *Compl. Scot.* vi. 50 The point that is rycht abufe our hede is callit zenyth,..ande as oft as ve change fra place to place, as oft ve sal hef ane vthir zenytht. **1555** EDEN *Decades* (Arb.) 251 The sonne beinge there Zenith (that is the poynt of heauen directly ouer theyr heades) they felte greater heate..then when they were vnder the Equinoctiall line. **1604** E. G[RIMSTONE] *D'Acosta's Hist. Indies* II. ix. 101 When I passed, which was when the sun was there for Zenith, being entered into Aries. **1638** SIR T. HERBERT *Trav.* (ed. 2) 6 Shadowlesse, when Sol is Zenith. **1667** MILTON *P.L.* I. 745 From Morn To Noon he fell, from Noon to dewy Eve..; and with the setting Sun Dropt from the Zenith like a falling Star. **1733** BERKELEY *Th. Vision* §60 As an object gradually ascends from the horizon towards the zenith. **1849** H. W. HERBERT *Frank Forester* I. 144 There was not a speck of cloud from east to west, from zenith to horizon. **1860** TYNDALL *Glac.* I. xi. 72 The stars..near the zenith shine with a steady light. **1885–94** R. BRIDGES *Eros & Psyche* Mar. xxiv, She saw the evening light In shifting colour to the zenith tower.

†**b.** The point of the horizon at which a heavenly body rises; the point of intersection of an azimuth-circle with the horizon; hence by extension = AZIMUTH 2. *Obs.*

c **1391** CHAUCER *Astrol.* I. §19 Thise Azimutz seruen..for to knowe the cenyth of the sonne & of euery sterre. *Ibid.* II. §33 To knowe the senyth of the Altitude of the sonne, &c... Any tyme of the day tak the altitude of the sonne, & by the Azymut in which he stondith, Maistou sen in which partie of the firmament he is.

†**c.** *transf.* Course towards the zenith. *Obs.*

1667 MILTON *P.L.* X. 329 Satan..Betwixt the Centaure and the Scorpion stearing His Zenith, while the Sun in Aries rose.

d. *magnetic zenith*: the point of the sky directly above the magnetic pole of the earth.

1885 S. TROMHOLT *Aur. Bor.* x. I. 221 The Auroral Corona..is produced by the streamers shooting from every part of the sky towards a common point, viz., the magnetic zenith.

2. *loosely.* The expanse of sky overhead, the upper region of the sky; the highest or culminating point of a heavenly body.

[**1592** SIR J. DAVIES *Nosce Teipsum* L 2 b, If we beleeue, that men do liue Vnder the Zenith of both frozen Poles.] **1631** MASSINGER *Believe as you List* I. ii, Two-and-twentye yeares of miserie..that longe time spent in Vnder distant zeniths. **1704** SWIFT *Batt. Bks.* T. Tub, etc. 271 The conscious Moon, now in her Zenith. **1791** E. DARWIN *Bot. Gard.* I. 118 As Night's pale Queen..climbs the zenith. **1827–35** N. P. WILLIS *Starlight* 11 Above To the far-stretching zenith. **1864** TENNYSON *En. Arden* 587 Huge trees that branch'd And blossom'd in the zenith. **1898** E. V. LUCAS *Willow & Leather* 106 Jack would..brandish the bat,

And away the balls would go,..sometimes bang into the zenith.

3. *fig.* Highest point or state, culmination, climax, acme.

1610 SHAKS. *Temp.* I. ii. 181, I finde my Zenith doth depend vpon A most auspitious starre, whose influence If now I court not,..my fortunes Will euer after droope. **1627** DONNE *Serm., Acts vii. 60* (1661) 214 Gods suffering for man was the Nadir the lowest point of Gods humiliation, mans suffering for God is the Zenith, the highest point of mans exaltation. **1643** SIR T. BROWNE *Relig. Med.* I. §17 The hand of God, whereby all Estates arise to their Zenith and verticall points. **1728** MORGAN *Algiers* I. iv. 149 In S. Augustine's Time, the Christian affairs seem to have been in their Zenith of Prosperity. **1820** BYRON *Mar. Fal.* IV. i, I left the festival before It reach'd its zenith. **1837** MACAULAY *Ess., Bacon* (1851) I. 377 Bacon had reached the zenith of his fortunes. **1884** F. HARRISON *Choice of Bks.* (1886) 251 Built ..in the zenith of the pointed style, [Westminster Abbey] is one of the most exquisite examples of its class.

†**b.** *Med.* (See quot.) *Obs.*

1753 *Chambers' Cycl.* Suppl., *Zenith*,..a word used by some medical writers to express the first appearance of the menses in young women.

4. *attrib.* and *Comb.* **a.** *attrib.* (quasi-*adj.*: cf. quots. 1555, 1638 in 1): Belonging to or situated in the zenith, directly overhead, as ***zenith sky, star, sun***; also *fig.* (cf. 3) highest, supreme, culminating, as ***zenith happiness, hour***. **b.** *Astron.*, etc. In names of instruments used for determining the *zenith distance* (see c) of a heavenly body, as **zenith sector, telescope, tube** (see quots.). **c.** Other special combs.: **zenith-borne** *a.*, borne to or towards the zenith; **zenith distance**, the angular distance of a heavenly body from the zenith (the complement of its *altitude* or angular distance from the horizon); †**zenith line**, used for a vertical line or arc extending from the zenith to the horizon (= AZIMUTH 1); so †**zenith point**, the point at which such a line meets the horizon (cf. sense 1 b); **zenith sweep** (SWEEP *sb.* 7), a series of observations of a region of the sky passing through the zenith.

1886 M. F. TUPPER *My Life as an Author* 365 Liberty!.. Rise to thy height upon *zenith-borne wings! **1704** J. HARRIS *Lex. Techn.*, **Zenith Distance*, is the Complement of the Sun, or Stars Meridian Altitude, or what the Meridian Altitude wants of 90 Degrees. **1854** TOMLINSON *Arago's Astron.* 41 Zenith-distances and azimuths form..a system of angles, by means of which it is easy to fix the positions of the stars with extreme precision. **1869** DUNKIN *Midn. Sky* 156 The zenith-distance of Gamma Draconis is daily observed at Greenwich. **1875** W. CORY *Lett. & Jrnls.* (1897) 405 Scott's year of *zenith happiness. **1853** WHITTIER *Rantoul* iii, Dead! in..That triumph of life's *zenith hour! **1596** BLAGRAVE *Astrol. Uran.* i. Bj b, The 90. lower ends of the 90. *zenith lines, which before I called the 90. *zenith points. **1776** MASKELYNE *Astron. Observ.* I. Pref. p. ix, The *zenith sector,..constructed by that excellent artist Mr. Graham,..was fixed up at Wanstead in the year 1727, for the use of that great astronomer Dr. Bradley; who, from his first year's observations with it, discovered the apparent motion of the fixed stars, which he called the aberration of light. **1802** A. ELLICOTT *Jrnl.* (1803) 185 The pack-horse-men likewise brought on my small zenith sector. **1829** W. PEARSON *Pract. Astron.* II. 531 The zenith sector..can be used only on the meridian; and its measures are referred to the zenith point of the place of observation. Its principal uses are to determine the latitude of the place of observation by a star of known zenith distance; to measure the zenith distance of a star..; and to ascertain the zenith point... The first zenith sector was..constructed by the ingenious Dr. Hooke [*c* 1700], with an intention of determining whether or not a fixed star has a measurable annual parallax. **1862** F. T. PALGRAVE *Hymn, 'Lord God of morning and of night'* iii, The sun may stand in *zenith skies. **1817** SHELLEY *Rev. Islam* VII. xx, When *zenith-stars were trembling on the wave. **1903** HARDY *Dynasts* I. v. v, This Trafalgar Will..Pitt exalt As zenith-star of England's firmament. **1826** CARRINGTON *Dartmoor* 3 Deep-hued flowers that light Their tints at *zenith suns. **1789** HERSCHEL in *Phil. Trans.* LXXX. 10 My twenty-feet speculum was so much tarnished by *zenith sweeps, in which it had been..exposed to falling dews. **1834** POND *ibid.* CXXIV. 209 The erection of a *zenith telescope of twenty-five feet focal length.., for the purpose of measuring the zenith distance of γ Draconis. **1836** G. B. AIRY *Autobiog.* (1896) 123 The North Terrace was the official passage to the North-west Dome, where there was a miserable Equatoreal, and to the 25-foot *Zenith Tube. **1847** *Ibid.* 184 On Nov. 13th I circulated an Address, proposing to discontinue the use of the Zenith Tube, because it had been found..that the Zenith Tube was not more accurate than the Mural Circle. **1869** DUNKIN *Midn. Sky* 15 The reflex zenith-tube.

Hence †**zenithfer**, a part of an astrolabe used for measuring zenith distances; **'zenithward(s)** *adv.*, towards the zenith.

1596 BLAGRAVE *Astrol. Uran.* i. B 1, This Astrolabe hath three generall partes, that is to say, the Celestiall, the *Zenitfer with his Cursor, and the Almicantifer with his Pointer. *Ibid.* B 1 b, As farre as the Zenithfer will giue leaue. **1868** CARLYLE *Jrnl.* 8 June in J. A. Froude *T. Carlyle* (1884) II. xxxi. 371 It was as a ray of everlasting light and insight this, that had shot itself **zenithward* from the soul of a man. **1871** A. STEWART *Nether Lochaber* xxii. (1883) 128 The meridian sun..is..climbing zenithwards. **1881** TRAILL in *Nature* 10 Feb. 351/1 The streamers..still ascending zenithward.

'zenithal, *a.* [f. ZENITH + -AL[1].]

Pertaining or relating to, situated or occurring at, the zenith; also *fig.* supreme, 'culminating'. ***zenithal projection***, any of a class of map projections in which a portion of the globe is projected on to a plane tangential to a point on that portion, usu. made the centre of the map.

1860 TYNDALL *Glac.* I. v. 39 The deep zenithal blue. **1869** DUNKIN *Midn. Sky* 57 Beta and Gamma Draconis..were the two zenithal stars in June. **1882** T. CRAIG *Treat. on Projections* v. 89 The name zenithal projections is..derived from the fact that they can always be considered as the representation of the hemisphere situated above the horizon of the given point, and having the zenith for pole. **1891** HARDY *Tess* xxv, A zenithal paradise, a nadiral hell. **1903** *Blackw. Mag.* Nov. 651/1 They have known the zenithal instant of piscatorial life. **1910**, etc. [see PROJECTION *sb.* 7 b]. **1961** L. F. BROSNAHAN *Sounds of Language* iii. 74 A continuous distribution of the O blood-group gene frequencies in Europe was..redrawn on a map of zenithal equal-area projection. **1974** *Encycl. Brit. Micropædia* IV. 587/3 *Gnomic map*, type of zenithal projection in which the Earth's grid is projected by radials from a point at the centre of the sphere into a tangent plane so that all great circles are represented by straight lines.

Zenker ('zɛŋkə(r)). **1.** The name of F. A. *Zenker* (1825–98), German pathologist, used in the possessive and occas. *attrib.* to designate (*a*) a hyaline degeneration of striated muscle occurring chiefly in cases of acute infectious disease, esp. typhoid and cholera (described by Zenker in 1864); (*b*) a pathological diverticulum at the junction of the pharynx and œsophagus (described by Zenker & von Ziemssen in *Cycl. Practice of Med.* (1878) VIII. 1–214).

1890 BILLINGS *Med. Dict.* II. 789/2 *Zenker's degeneration*, waxy degeneration as seen in muscles after acute attacks of fever. **1898** W. S. LAZARUS-BARLOW *Man. Gen. Path.* xii. 521 In Zenker's degeneration the muscular fibres themselves look dull and semi-opaque, and microscopically are found to have lost their striation. **1910** *Lippincott's New Med. Dict.* 1103/2 Zenker's pulsion diverticulum. **1932** *Jrnl. Amer. Med. Assoc.* XCVIII. 965/2 The symptoms of a Zenker pulsion diverticulum depend on the size of the pouch. **1970** PASSMORE & ROBSON *Compan. Med. Stud.* II. xxiv. 25/1 In typhoid fever, patches of necrosis develop in striated muscles. Here, the fibres lose all structure and become glassy and eosinophilic (Zenker's hyaline degeneration). **1975** *Year Bk. Ear, Nose & Throat* 279 A variety of neuro-muscular disorders, with or without Zenker's diverticulum.

2. *Histology.* [The name of Konrad *Zenker*, German histologist, who described the fluid in 1894 (*Arch. f. path. Anat. und Physiol.* CXXXV. 147).] ***Zenker's fluid***: a fixative (see quot. 1902).

1902 E. A. SCHÄFER *Essentials of Histol.* (ed. 6) 397 General methods of preserving and hardening tissues and organs.—The fluids which are more commonly used are.. Müller's fluid (bichromate of potash 2½ parts, sulphate of soda 1 part, water 100 parts); Zenker's fluid (which is Müller's fluid containing 5 parts per cent. of mercuric chloride, to which 5 c.c. of acetic acid is added at the time of use); [etc.]. **1941** [see FIXER 2]. **1976** *Path. Ann.* XI. 130 Tumors that have been fixed in Zenker's fluid almost invariably show affinity for chrome salts, so that brown granules are easily discerned.

zeno- (ziːnəʊ), f. Gr. Ζηνο-, comb. form of Ζεύς, used as a word-forming element with the sense 'the planet Jupiter', as **zeno'centric** *a.*, measured or expressed with reference to the centre of Jupiter; **zeno'graphic** *a.*, measured or expressed with reference to the surface of Jupiter.

1968 *Dissertation Abstr.* B. XXIX. 858/1 For each year the study has reconfirmed that there are two zenocentric intervals of Io's position in which we observe this influence. **1978** *Nature* 14 Sept. 111/1 The ±3·3° variation of the zenocentric declination of the Earth is sufficient to lead to a 15° variation of the..sub-Io longitude of the emission. **1971** *Icarus* XIV. 343 A bright spot at zenographic latitude 23°.8 N displayed the shortest rotation period ever recorded on Jupiter. **1979** *Nature* 5 July 42/2 Values..synthesised on a 10° by 10° zenographic θ (co-latitude) and λ (longitude) grid.

zenober, obs. var. of SINOPER.

1535 COVERDALE *Jer.* xxii. 14 The sylinges and geastes maketh he off Cedre, and paynteth them with Zenober.

†**zeno'cratically**, *adv. Obs. nonce-wd.* [f. Gr. Ζηνο-, combining form of Ζεύς + κράτος power, rule + -ICALLY; cf. *autocratically*.] With the power or authority of Zeus or Jove.

1588 J. HARVEY *Disc. Probl.* 35 They will seeme..to haue borrowed euen from the mouth of mightie Ioue, or the oracle of wise Apollo himselfe, or Zenocratically, and Pythagorically to haue remained..*Instar Sybillæ cuiusdam vaticinantis, furentisque.*

zenography (ziː'nɒgrəfɪ). *rare*[−0]. [f. Gr. Ζηνο- (see prec.) + -GRAPHY: cf. AREOGRAPHY.] The description or study of the planet Jupiter. So **zenographical** (ziːnəʊ'græfɪkəl) *a.*, pertaining to zenography.

1889 A. S. WILLIAMS (*title*) Zenographical Fragments, Part I, The Motions and Changes of the Markings of Jupiter in..1886–87.

Zenonian (ziː'nəʊnɪən), *a.* and *sb.* [f. L. *Zēno*, *Zēnōn*, Gr. Ζήνων + -IAN.] **a.** *adj.* (*a*) Of or pertaining to Zeno of Elea, a philosopher of the 5th century B.C., famed for his paradoxical arguments about motion. (*b*) Of or pertaining to Zeno of Citium (*c* 300 B.C.), the founder of the Stoic school of philosophy. **b.** *sb.* A follower of Zeno, esp. of Zeno of Citium; a Stoic. So **Zenonic** (ziː'nɒnɪk) *a.* = a.; **Zenonism** ('ziːnənɪz(ə)m), the philosophy of Zeno, Stoicism.

1843 *Penny Cycl.* XXVII. 769/1 They [*sc.* Stoics] were at first called Zenonians from the name of their master. **1850** GROTE *Greece* II. lxviii. VIII. 565 Generalising dialectics and Zenonian negation. **1866** CHARNOCK *Verba Nom.* 343 Zenonism. **1888** *Encycl. Brit.* XXIV. 779/1 Gorgias's sceptical development of the Zenonian logic. *Ibid.* 779/2 The Zenonian difficulty continued to demand and to receive Plato's best attention. **1888** *Academy* 21 Apr. 278/1 Heraclitus's system was the polar antithesis to this Zenonic position.

zenophobia: see XENOPHOBIA.

zenvy, dial. form of SENVY *Obs.*, mustard.

1519 HORMAN *Vulg.* 172 b, Zenvy sede ones sowed wyll neuer almoste oute of the grounde. **1825** JENNINGS *Obs. Dial. W. Eng.*, *Zenvy*, wild mustard.

†**'zenzic,** *a.* and *sb. Math. Obs.* [ad. mod.L. *zenzicus*, *zens-*, f. *zensus*, Germanized f. *census* (1202 in Leonardo of Pisa), transl. Arab. *māl* possessions, property, as used spec. in mathematics. Cf. It. *censo* (13th c.).]

a. *adj.* Of a number or root: = SQUARE *a.* 2, 2 b. **b.** *sb.* A square number: = SQUARE *sb.* 8.

So various compounds denoting higher powers or roots, as **'zenzicube** (the square of the cube, the sixth power), **zenzi'cubic** *a.*, **zenzi'cubicube, zenzi'zenzic** *a.* and *sb.*, **zenzi'zenzicube, -'cubic** *a.*, **zenzizenzi'zenzic**, etc. (Cf. 13th c. It. *censo di censo*, *censo di cubi*, *censo cubo*, etc.)

1557 RECORDE *Whetst.* Hij b, Squares of Squares..of some men..are named *Zenzizenzikes*, as square nombers are called *Zenzikes*. *Ibid.* Hiij, 81 whiche is a *Zenzizenzike* number. *Ibid.* Hiij b, If I name it [*sc.* 64] to bee a Square of Cubes, or *zenzicube*: then is..2. his roote. *Ibid.* Hiv b, *Zenzizenzizenzikes*, that is squares of squared squares. *Ibid.* Kj, *Zenzicubike*, or Squared Cube. *Ibid.* Qiv, When Squares and Cubes be compounde together: as *Zenzicubes*, *Zenzizenzicubes*, *Zenzicubicubes*.... 3. is the Zenzizenzicubike roote of .531441. **1571** DIGGES *Pantom.* Ddj b, Extracte the Zenzike rootes of these numbers. **1674** JEAKE *Arith.* (1696) 177 A Zenzicube, or a Squared Cube Number made by multiplying the Sursolide into the Root.

zenzyber, -yr, obs. forms of GINGER.

c **1485** *Digby Myst.* III. 343 Zenzybyr and synamom.

zeolite ('ziːəlaɪt). *Min.* Also 8–9 *erron.* **-yte**. [ad. Sw., G., etc. *zeolit*, f. Gr. ζεῖν to boil, seethe + λίθος stone, -LITE; so named from its boiling and swelling under the blowpipe: see quot. 1777.] Generic name for a large and varied group of minerals, consisting of hydrous silicates in which the bases are alumina and the alkalies and alkaline earths; generally characterized by swelling up and fusing to a glass or enamel before the blowpipe, and often by gelatinizing with acids; commonly found in the cavities of igneous rocks.

Examples are ANALCITE, BREWSTERITE, CHABAZITE, HARMOTOME, NATROLITE, PHILLIPSITE, STILBITE, THOMSONITE, etc.

1777 *Dict. Chem.* III. X 8, *Zeolites.* This name is given by Mr. Cronstedt to a stone described by him in the Transactions of the Academy of Sciences at Stockholm for the year 1756, the peculiar properties of which have induced that mineralogist to consider it as forming a distinct order of earths, called *zeolites*. **1777** PRIESTLEY *Exper. Air* III. 39 The sparry zeolyte from the Ferro Isles. **1803** *Edin. Rev.* Jan. 510 This Zeolite, found in the rocks of Edinburgh Castle. **1804** *Ibid.* Jan. 311 Zeolytes [see CHABAZITE]. **1842** T. GRAHAM *Elem. Chem.* 145 Chabasie and other minerals of the zeolite family. **1880** HAUGHTON *Phys. Geog.* v. 214 *note*, Tabular trap, which..contains abundant zeolites.

Hence **zeolitic** (-'ɪtɪk), † **-ical** *adjs.*, pertaining to, consisting of, or of the nature of zeolite; **zeo'litically** *adv.*, as in a zeolite; **zeolitiform** (-'ɪtɪfɔːm) *a.* 'having the form of zeolite' (Webster, 1828); **,zeoliti'zation**, transformation into a zeolite; so **'zeolitize** *v.* (in mod. Dicts.).

1828–32 WEBSTER, *Zeolitic. **1848** DAUBENY *Volcanoes* (ed. 2) 18 An intimate mixture of augite and magnetic iron with a mineral of the zeolitic family. **1857** *G. Bird's Urin. Deposits* (ed. 5) 231 Four-sided prisms, which exhibited, like the zeolitic crystals, beautiful coloured bands, when examined with polarized light. **1807** HEADRICK *Arran* 86 *Zeolitical concretions. **1951** C. PALACHE et al. *Dana's Syst. Min.* (ed. 7) II. 993 The water content can vary *zeolitically over a range from $8H_2O$ to $5H_2O$. **1969** H. T. EVANS tr. *G. Hägg's Gen. & Inorg. Chem.* xxi. 510 Water in a solid phase may..be zeolitically bound.., so that the proportion of water can vary without breaking down the crystal structure. **1980** *Nuclear Technol.* LI. 143/2 This study shows that similar enrichment of ^{234}U occurs in zeolitically altered volcanic ash and tuff. **1891** *Cent. Dict.*, **Zeolitization*, the process by which a mineral is converted into a zeolite by alteration—for example, nepheline into thomsonite.

Zep (zɛp), *sb.* and *v.* Also Zepp and with lower-case initial. Colloq. abbrev. of ZEPPELIN *sb.*, *v.* Also *attrib.*

1915 JESSIE POPE *Simple Rhymes, Mariana*, The night those Zeps bombarded town. **1915** A. HUXLEY *Let.* Oct. (1969) 79 The dear old Boches and their Zepps, which always get back bomb for bomb. **1915** W. OWEN *Let.* 12 June (1967) 338 The spot where a Zep. Bomb fell in a cross-roads. **1916** *Morning Post* 15 Mar. 1 (Advt.), Anti-Zep blinds. **1916** *Times Lit. Suppl.* 27 Jan. 40/3 A hostile raiding 'Zepp.' **1919** C. ORR *Glorious Thing* ii. 20 We're exceedingly preoccupied with the war—Zepp. raids and things. **1920** W.

J. LOCKE *House of Baltazar* vii. 83 'So you've been Zepped, I hear,' she said. **1931** *Flight* 28 Aug. 855/1 The most interesting feature of our trip was a personally escorted tour of the entire Zep whilst crossing over France. *a* **1935** T. E. LAWRENCE *Mint* (1955) II. xxii. 159 There were Zepps in a cloud (sausages and mashed) and Adam and Eve on a raft (Hoxtonian for fried eggs on toast). **1974** *Listener* 7 Feb. 177/3 This aeroplane..flew towards the zepp, and he started firing.

zep, obs. form of SAP *sb.*[1]

Zephiran ('zɛfirən). *Pharm.* A proprietary name for an antiseptic preparation of benzalkonium chloride.

1935 *Trade Marks Jrnl.* 17 July 887/1 *Zephiran*... Chemical substances prepared for use in medicine and pharmacy. Bayer Products Limited,..London, E.C.2; merchants and manufacturers. **1936** *Official Gaz.* (U.S. Patent Office) 28 Jan. 687/2 I. G. Farbenindustrie Aktiengesellschaft, Frankfort-on-the-Main... *Zephiran* for antiseptic and disinfectant. **1951** A. GROLLMAN *Pharmacol. & Therapeutics* xxv. 503 Benzalkonium chloride (Zephiran ®) is of comparatively low toxicity. **1974** M. C. GERALD *Pharmacology* xxvi. 448 Iodine tincture.., Zephiran, and hexachlorophene are representative examples of local anti-infective agents.

Zéphirine Drouhin ('zeɪfiriːn 'druːæ̃). A thornless shrub or climbing Bourbon rose of the variety of this name, which bears fragrant pink flowers and was first introduced in France in 1868.

1931 H. H. THOMAS *Rose Bk.* viii. 72 The old thornless Rose (Zéphirine Drouhin) makes an excellent bush, and its lovely, fragrant blooms of soft rose-colour..are freely produced for weeks together. **1940** A. CHRISTIE *Sad Cypress* II. xii. 193 Do you know the name of this rose? It is Zephyrine Droughin [*sic*]. **1983** *Woman's Jrnl.* Jan. 85/2 Zephirine Drouhin is a fragrant climber with cerise-pink semi-double flowers and is thornless.

zephyr ('zɛfə(r)), *sb.* Forms: α. (in Latin form) 1 **zefferus**, 4 **zeferus**, 4–7 **zephirus**, 5 **zeforus**, 5–6 **zepherus**, 6– **zephyrus**; β. 7 **zephir(e**, **-yre**, 7– **zephyr**. [a. or ad. L. *zephyrus*, a. Gr. ζέφυρος: cf. F. *zéphire*, It. *zefiro*, *zeffiro*, Sp. *cefiro*, Pg. *zephyro*, G. *zephyr*, etc.]

1. The west wind, esp. as personified, or the god of the west wind.

α. *a* **1000** *Riddles* xl[i]. 68 Nis zefferus se swifta wind þæt swa fromlice mæȝ feran æȝhwær. **13..** *E.E. Allit. P.* C. 470 & sayez vnte Zeferus þat he syfle warme. *c* **1386** CHAUCER *Prol.* 5 Zephirus..with his swete breeth. *c* **1520** SKELTON *Garl. Laurel* 677 There blew in that gardynge a soft piplyng colde, Enbrethyng of Zepherus with his pleasant wynde. **1594** *Selimus* ad fin., Zephyrus sweete smelling blast. **1616** R. C. *Times' Whistle* (1871) 116 Art thou perhaps that purest breathing aire, Sweet Zephirus? **1667** MILTON *P.L.* v. 16 With voice Milde, as when Zephyrus on Flora breathes. **1898** MEREDITH *Lett.* (1912) II. 498 Like a gossamer puffed by summer Zephyrus.

β. **1598** CHAPMAN *Iliad* VII. [XI.] 120 When the hollow floode of ayre in Zephyres cheeks doth swel. **1605** DRAYTON *Idea* liii, Sweet mirrh-breathing Zephire. **1632** MILTON *L'Allegro* 19 Zephir with Aurora playing, As he met her once a Maying. **1750** JOHNSON *Rambler* No. 80 ¶3 Regions in which no wind is heard but the gentle Zephyr. **1823** B. W. PROCTER *Flood of Thess.* I. 89 Words more soft than Zephyr.

2. A soft mild gentle wind or breeze.

1611 SHAKS. *Cymb.* IV. ii. 172 They are as gentle As Zephires blowing below the Violet, Not wagging his sweet head. **1683** TRYON *Way to Health* 47 The pure thin sweet Vapours of the Air (which are the Refreshing *Zephiri* of Nature). **1718** PRIOR *Henry & Emma* 389 While gentle Zephyrs play in prosp'rous Gales. **1764** GOLDSM. *Trav.* 173 No zephyr fondly sues the mountain's breast. **1807** W. IRVING *Salmag.* (1824) 187 The flowers, the zephyrs, and the warblers of spring, returning after their tedious absence. **1883** MISS M. BETHAM-EDWARDS *Disarmed* x, The zephyrs breathed softly from the south.

3. a. Applied to various very light articles of clothing; e.g. a light shawl; a light dust-coat; *esp.* a light shirt worn by athletes.

1774 *Westm. Mag.* II. 259 Negligees of pale lutestring,..with tassels and zephyrs in fancy, or of muslin. **1830** *Lady's Mag.* 31 May 284/2 Some wear little square shawls of soft crape, called zephyrs. **1879** F. W. ROBINSON *Coward Consc.* I. ii, The gentleman's light overcoat had once done duty as a 'zephyr' at the races. **1887** SHEARMAN *Athletics* 68 When the athlete has got a pair of the best shoes, a zephyr, and a pair of silk or merino drawers,..he has got all the stock-in-trade required to win half-a-dozen championships. **1891** R. F. MURRAY *Scarlet Gown* 6 He sat upon the sofa, where my hat, My wanton Zephyr, rested on its rim.

b. [after Ger.] A fine light cotton cloth of the gingham type used for women's dresses, having the colours woven into the fabric.

1849, etc. [see 6 b]. **1863** B. TAYLOR *Han. Thurston* I. 128 [To] measure a yard of calico..or choose a shade of zephyr. **1866** in *Abridgm. Specif. Patents, Spinning* II. (1868) 490 Equal in appearance to the finest German zephyr. **1905** WELLS *Kipps* I. vi. §1 I'm sorting up zephyrs to-morrow, Sir.

c. *Cookery.* (See quot.)

1894 *Garrett's Encycl. Cookery, Zephyrs.* These might almost be described under the heading of *Soufflés*.

4. A butterfly of the genus *Zephyrus*.

5. [after Fr.] A soldier of the Algerian light infantry.

1854 *Househ. Words* VIII. 145/1 Zephyrs is a nickname given in Algeria to a corps which is recruited from..the French army. **1911** *Blackw. Mag.* May 595/2 Service with the 'Zephyrs', the malefactors of the French army.

6. *attrib.* and *Comb.*, as (sense 2) ***zephyr-bough***, ***-breath***, ***-sigh***, ***-whispering***; ***zephyr-fanned***, ***-haunted***, ***-kissed*** adjs.; **zephyr-flower** = ZEPHYRANTH (Miller *Plant-n.* 1884).

1818 KEATS *Endym.* II. 318 Within my breast there lives a choking flame—O let me cool't the *zephyr-boughs among! **1854** BREWSTER *More Worlds* ii. 17 The *zephyr breath among the distant foliage. **1880** A. H. SWINTON *Insect Var.* 96 The *zephyr-fanned summits of the oak wood. ? **1793** COLERIDGE *Lines to a beautiful Spring* 5 Ere from thy *zephyr-haunted brink I turn. *c* **1840** ELIZA COOK *Spring* v, The *zephyr-kissed grass. **1818** KEATS *Endym.* I. 376 Where every *zephyr-sigh pouts, and endows Her lips with music for the welcoming. **1842** DICKENS *Amer. Notes* x, Nor was the atmosphere quite free from *zephyr whisperings of the thirty beds which had just been cleared away.

b. Applied to certain light yarns and fabrics (see quots.); also = made of zephyr (sense 3 b).

1849 *Jrnl. Design* Aug. 143 Zephyr Silk Barège... This is one of those light and elegant fabrics which have done so much to reduce the demand for the higher class of light printed goods. **1852** *Househ. Words* IV. 398/2 We have Paletôts,..Zephyr wrappers,..and a host of other garments. **1858** SIMMONDS *Dict. Trade, Zephyr-cloth*, a kind of kerseymere made in Belgium; a waterproof fabric. *Ibid.*, *Zephyr-shawl*, a kind of thin light worsted and cotton embroidered shawl. **1864** WEBSTER, *Zephyr yarn*, or *worsted*, a fine kind of yarn or worsted, called also *Berlin wool*. **1882** CAULFEILD & SAWARD *Dict. Needlework, Zephyr Ginghams* or *Prings*. These are pretty delicate textiles, resembling a cotton batiste. *Zephyr Merino Yarn*, the term employed by the wool staplers of Germany to signify what is usually called German or Berlin. *Zephyr Shirting*..a kind of gauze flannel, having a silk warp. **1883** *Truth* 31 May 768/2 Two sisters in blue zephyr gowns. **1888** MAUDE BRADSHAW *Ind. Outfits* 31 Two pairs of zephyr stays,..besides a few pairs of ordinary stays.

Hence **zephy'rean**, **ze'phyrian**, **'zephyrous**, **'zephyry** *adjs.*, of, pertaining to, or of the nature of a zephyr; full of or having zephyrs; **'zephyret**, a gentle zephyr; **'zephyrine**, the name of a light thin material or a garment made of this; also *attrib.*; **'zephyrless** *a.*, destitute of zephyrs.

1837 *Blackw. Mag.* XLI. 146 The voice of Reason, like the *zephyrean breath of summer. **1848** tr. *J. P. F. Richter's Levana* III. iii. §54 To..send the *zephyrets of pleasure through artistic bellows and air-pumps, to the little flowers. **1734** *Poor Robin* Mar. A7, And from the West with a *Zephyrian Breath, Plants seeming dead he re-revives from Death. **1873** MRS. WHITNEY *Other Girls* iii, A span new tea-coloured *zephyrine polonaise. *Ibid.*, Her zephyrine, with its silky shine. **1819** KEATS *Lines to Fanny* 37 Whose winds, all *zephyrless, hold scourging rods. **1847** *Tait's Mag.* XIV. 267 This soft *zephyrous breeze. **1791** LEARMONT *Poems* 188 The *Zephiry Summer breeze. **1880** A. H. SWINTON *Insect Var.* 169 In zephyry hay-fields.

zephyr ('zɛfə(r)), *v.* [f. the sb.] *intr.* To blow like a zephyr. Hence **'zephyring** *ppl. a.*

1922 HARDY *Late Lyrics & Earlier* 111 An aura zephyring round, That care infected not. **1939** JOYCE *Finnegans Wake* 418 Since longsephyring sighs sought heartseast for their orience? **1973** J. JONES *Touch of Danger* xxiii. 131 A light little breeze zephyred in..from the open water.

zephyranth ('zɛfɪrænθ). [ad. mod.L. *Zephyranthes*, f. Gr. ζέφυρος ZEPHYR *sb.* + ἄνθος flower: with allusion to the waving flower-stalks.] A plant of the genus *Zephyranthes*.

1845 *Florist's Jrnl.* (1846) VI. 248 In habit the one-flowered Habranths are the same as the Zephyranths.

Zepp: see ZEP.

Zeppelin ('zɛpəlɪn), *sb.* [The name of the German Count Ferdinand von *Zeppelin*.] In full ***Zeppelin airship***: a dirigible airship; properly, one of a type constructed by Count Zeppelin of Germany in 1900.

Sometimes colloquially abbreviated ZEP(P.

1900 *Whitaker's Alm.* 665/2 The Zeppelin Air-ship, now [1899] in construction on an island of the Boden See, is a cylindrical frame of aluminium in partitions, each holding a gas-bag. **1914** F. T. JANE in *Land & Water* 12 Sept. 15*/1 A Zeppelin has dropped bombs on Antwerp. *Ibid.* 19 Sept. 19*/1 Alarming rumours of a German Zeppelin invasion of England *viâ* Calais. *Ibid.* 26 Sept. 16*/2 It takes something like a year to build a Zeppelin shed.

Hence **'Zeppelin** *v. trans.*, to drop bombs on from a Zeppelin (see also ZEP *v.*); **'Zeppelinite**, one who advocates the use of Zeppelins as an engine of war, esp. against non-combatants; **'Zeppelinist**, a member of the crew of a Zeppelin; **Zeppeli'nistic** *a.*, resembling a Zeppelin in shape; (both *rare*[−1]).

1916 WELLS *Mr. Britling* I. v. §12 They will Zeppelin the fleet and walk through our army. **1916** *Daily Express* 29 Mar. 4/7 The battle royal between the Zeppelinites and the anti-Zeppelinites [in Germany] continues. **1930** KIPLING *Limits & Renewals* (1932) 328 He called Saint Jukamus a militarist and an impostor—this defaitist of a Zeppelinistic belly! **1937** F. MORISON *War on Great Cities* iv. 127 The demons who drove and dealt death cared as little for us as the earlier Zeppelinists cared.

zeppole ('zɛpɒleɪ). *U.S.* Pl. zeppoli. [It.] A kind of doughnut.

1976 *Monitor* (McAllen, Texas) 14 Oct. c 2/6 The mingled smells of salsiccia, bracciola, zeppole and calzone wafted from the stalls of food vendors around Father Zemo Square. **1979** *New Yorker* 8 Oct. 32/1 There aren't a lot of food venders. We wanted to differentiate this from other street fairs. Also, I didn't want people dropping zeppoli all over our books.

zequi, zequin(e, obs. forms of SEQUIN.

1613 PURCHAS *Pilgrimage* VII. iv. (1614) 675 Euery Zequi being sixteene ryals, and with vs eight shillings. *a* **1701** [see SEQUIN *sb.* 1]. **1765** SMOLLETT *Trav.* xxx. (1766) II. 107 Two scudi make a zequine; and a French loui'dore is worth about two zequines.

zeraphim, var. SERAPHIN.

zerbaffe, zerbaft, variants of SHERBAFF *Obs.*

1686 tr. *Chardin's Coronat. Solyman* 81 Seventy Pieces of Zer-baffè, which is a very rich sort of Persian Tissue. **1687** A. LOVELL *tr. Thevenot's Trav.* II. 92 Zerbaft, which is the Bocart of Persia.

zerbet, obs. form of SHERBET.

zerda ('zɜːdə). *Zool.* [So called by the 'Moors' (*Kongliga Svenska Vetenskaps Handlingar*, 1777, XXXVIII. 265).] The fennec, *Canis zerda*.

1781 PENNANT *Hist. Quadrup.* I. 248.

zereba, zeriba: see ZARIBA.

zereglia, Zerez, obs. ff. SERAGLIO, XERES.

zeriff, var. SHERIFI.

zernich, obs. form of ZARNICH.

zero ('zɪərəʊ), *sb.* Pl. zeroes (-əʊz). [ad. F. *zéro* (1515 in Hatz.-Darm.) or its source It. *zero*, for *zefiro*, ad. Arab. *çifr* CIPHER *sb.*]

1. a. The arithmetical figure 0 which denotes 'nought': = CIPHER *sb.* 1.

1604 E. G[RIMSTONE] *D'Acosta's Hist. Indies* VI. ii. 435 They accompted their weekes by thirteene dayes, marking the dayes with a Zero or cipher. **1706** PHILLIPS (ed. Kersey), *Zero*, a Word sometimes us'd especially among the French, for a Cipher or Nought (0). **1799** *Tilloch's Philos. Mag.* II. 413 Every letter..marked with a figure followed by a zero. **1854** *Orr's Circ. Sci., Math. Sci.* 16 Sometimes the divisor ends with zeros or noughts. **1857** *Househ. Words* 8 Aug. 143/2 A five, with a zero to the right, and a three to the left. **1878** GURNEY *Crystallogr.* 15 If we have two zeros in the symbol. **1940** E. T. BELL *Devel. Math.* iii. 48 The introduction of zero as a symbol denoting the absence of units or of certain powers of ten..has been rated as one of the greatest practical inventions of all time. **1959** KOESTLER *Sleepwalkers* II. iii. 105 The Indian system of numerals based on the symbol zero. **1969** P. B. JORDAIN *Condensed Computer Encycl.* 572 Users can be confused and misled by leading zeros: they may hide the true size of the numeral and make it harder to grasp at a glance.

b. The compartment numbered 0 on a roulette table.

1859 LEVER *Dav. Dunn* xlvi, I have been sketching out a little plan of a martingale for the roulette-table. There's only one zero at Homburg, and we can try it there as we go up. **1889** J.-S. BOND *Roulette* 29 If for 150 years Roulette has held its own against all comers, it is zero that has done it. **1911** tr. *Silberer's Roulette* 50 When the zéro comes out, the Bank takes the half of all stakes on the *chances simples* and the whole of all stakes upon the *chances multiples* (excepting, of course, stakes laid upon zéro, or on a combination including zéro, which alone it pays).

2. The point or line marked 0 on a graduated scale, from which the reckoning begins: esp. in a thermometer or other measuring instrument.

1795 *Phil. Trans.* LXXXV. 446 When the instrument is adjusted, and the index belonging to the micrometer-screw stands at the zero on its circle. **1826** *Art of Brewing* (Libr. Usef. Knowl. 1829) 19/2 If the saccharometer be made so as to sink to a certain point marked zero (a cypher) in distilled water. **1826** HENRY *Elem. Chem.* II. 639 The Centigrade thermometer places the zero at the freezing point. **1840** LARDNER *Geom.* 208 The French adopt as their zero of longitude the meridian which passes through the Observatory at Paris. **1890** W. F. STANLEY *Surv. & Lev. Instr.* 439 These rollers are fixed in such a manner as to turn in a circumference concentric with the zero of the alidade.

3. The temperature corresponding to the zero of a thermometer; that degree of heat (or cold) which is reckoned as 0°: i.e. in the Centigrade and Réaumur's scales, the freezing-point of water; in Fahrenheit's scale (traditionally the usual one in Eng. use), 32° below this, or 'thirty-two degrees of frost'.

absolute zero, the lowest temperature possible in the nature of things, at which the molecular motion which constitutes heat would cease; the zero of absolute temperature, reckoned as −273° C.

1800 tr. *Lagrange's Chem.* I. 78 That the melting of ice produces cold, is proved by the custom which confectioners have of melting certain salts with ice to produce a cold below zero. **1809** *Med. Jrnl.* XXI. 525 On the 23d of January, at sunrise, the thermometer was 10 deg., on the 26th 13 deg. below Zero; the coldest weather ever recorded in this town. **1823** BYRON *Juan* x. xxxiii, Thermometers sunk down to..zero. **1848** WATTS tr. *Gmelin's Handbk. Chem.* I. 303 Clement and Desormes place the absolute zero at −266·6° C. (−447·9° Fah.). **1905** *Times* 24 Jan. 4/6 In a terrible surf, with the glass near zero, they finally brought the remnant of the crew off safely.

4. a. In abstract sense: Nought or nothing reckoned as a number denoted by the figure 0, and constituting the starting-point of the series of natural numbers; the total absence of quantity considered as a quantity (in *Alg.* and *Higher Math.* as intermediate between positive and negative quantities); hence as expressing the amount of something = 'none at all'.

1823 BYRON *Juan* IX. ii, Though your years as man tend fast to zero. **1831** *Phil. Trans.* CXXI. 113 This sum is equal to zero in all positions of the line *d s* round the point (*x*, *y*, *z*). **1831** CARLYLE *Sart. Res.* II. ix, Unless my Algebra deceive me, Unity itself divided by Zero will give Infinity. **1872** LOWELL *Dante* Pr. Wks. 1890 IV. 155 Dante's direct acquaintance with Plato may be reckoned at zero. **1899** *Allbutt's Syst. Med.* VII. 248 In a certain patient, I have observed the intercranial tension to be slightly below zero while he was standing upright.

b. In the theory of functions, A value of a variable for which a function vanishes.

1893 A. R. FORSYTH *Functions* 62 The number of distinct zeros in the limited area is finite. **1902** E. T. WHITTAKER *Mod. Anal.* 94 A polynomial of degree *n* has *n* zeros.

c. *Linguistics.* In grammar, the absence of an overt mark, written or spoken, as against its presence in corresponding positions elsewhere (e.g. *cut* pa. t. as against *putted*).

1891 S. C. VASU *Ashṭádhyáyí of Pánini* 56 In Sanskrit Grammar, this 'lopa' is considered as a substitute or âdeṣa, and as such this grammatical *zero* has all the rights and liabilities of the thing it replaces. **1914** BLOOMFIELD *Introd. Study Lang.* v. 154 If..we take into view..*amo* 'I love', *amāvit* 'he loved', *amētur* 'he may be loved', it is possible to call them all related by affixation, the kernel being *am-*... In this instance the group does not contain a word that equals the kernel, or, as we might say, has 'affix zero'. **1933** —— *Language* xiii. 209 In *sheep* : *sheep* the plural-suffix is replaced by zero. **1946** *Jrnl. Amer. Oriental Soc.* LXVI. 98/1 Zero counts as an ending if it has the same function as an overt ending in another paradigm. **1957** *Eng. Lang. Teaching* (British Council) Oct.-Dec. 11 If the pronoun is object, zero should be used if the subject is a personal pronoun. **1972** R. QUIRK et al. *Gram. Contemporary Eng.* xiii. 866 With time adjuncts, omission of the preposition is usual whether the pronoun is *that* or zero..: That is the time (that) he arrives (at). **1979** *Amer. Speech* LIV. 31 Fifteen items take zero as the plural suffix.

5. *fig.* (from 4). Something that counts as or amounts to nothing; a worthless thing or person, one of no account; a 'cipher', 'nonentity'; a 'nothing' or 'nobody'.

1813 MARIA EDGEWORTH *Patronage* xxiv, The other gentlemen are zeros. **1858** CARLYLE *Fredk. Gt.* VI. ix. II. 126 Whatever the answer now be from England, I will have nothing to do with it..to me it shall be zero. **1861** *Macm. Mag.* III. 322 A man who *will* not work..is as complete a zero in the labour supply as if he were dead. **1870** H. MACMILLAN *True Vine* iii. (1872) 82 He is not surrounded with a vast zero, an all-absorbing negation.

6. *fig.* (from 2 and 3). **a.** The lowest point or degree; vanishing-point; nothingness, nullity. Also, an absence or lack of anything; nothing. (Sometimes coinciding with b.)

1820 BYRON *Juan* III. cx, Sure my invention must be down at zero. **1837** HOOD *Desert-Born* 64 Merely to look at such a sight my courage sinks to zero. **1867** 'MARK TWAIN' *Jumping Frog, Curing a Cold*, I got to coughing incessantly, and my voice fell below zero. **1883** *Proc. Inst. Mech. Engineers* Jan. 74 We have again a zero of current. **1894** DRUMMOND *Ascent of Man* 176 Man began the Ascent of Civilization at zero. **1915** J. HUNEKER *Ivory, Apes & Peacocks* iii. 35 We should soon reach a zero if we only registered the absence of 'necessary' traits in our poet. **1967** *Boston Globe* 21 May (Confidential Chat) 8/3 True, there is a certain amount of 'freedom' in their use but the wearing of them adds up to absolutely zero! **1977** C. MCCARRY *Secret Lovers* xii. 159 'What about the airlines, the hotel, car rentals.' 'Zero, I'd have used phony paper, wouldn't you?'

b. The initial point of a process or reckoning; the starting-point, the absolute beginning; *spec. Mil.*, the time or the day when an attack or operation is due to begin.

† ***hour of zero***, *Mil. Obs.* = *zero hour* (see 7 a).

1849 H. MILLER *Footpr. Creator* x. 193 The vegetation of the Silurian system, from its upper beds down till where we reach the zero of life. **1866** J. MARTINEAU *Ess.* I. 7 He.. makes 1788 his zero of human history. **1916** P. GIBBS *Battles of Somme* xxviii. 248 When the hour of 'zero' came for the attack. **1916** *King's R. Rifle Corps Chron. 1915* 104 Zero, the time the gas and smoke was to start, was 5.50 a.m. **1918** E. A. MACKINTOSH *War, the Liberator* IV. 124 We've got to be at Battalion Headquarters at 5, although I don't suppose zero'll be for a good time after that. **1924** KIPLING *Debits & Credits* (1926) 314 The men's teeth chatterin' behind their masks between rum-issue an' zero. **1942** W. S. CHURCHILL in *Second World War* (1950) IV. I. xiii. 225 It should be assumed..that zero [for an attack on Madagascar] should be about April 30. **1954** W. FAULKNER *Fable* 10 At zero, nobody left the trench except the officers and a few N.C.O.'s. **1983** L. MACDONALD *Somme* v. 41 The main body was ordered to Thiepval..timing their arrival for Zero plus two hours..to stride on to consolidate the third objective.

7. *attrib.* **a.** in sense 2 (or 6 b), as ***zero-line***, ***-mark***, ***-plane***, ***-point***; **zero-base**, **-based** *adjs.*, applied to a budget and to budgeting in which each item is costed anew, rather than in relation to its size or status in the previous budget; cf. *ZBB* s.v. Z 12 a; **zero creep**, spontaneous slow displacement of the zero-point on a graduated scale; **zero-crossing**, the crossing of the horizontal axis by a function as it passes through zero and changes sign; a point where this occurs; also *attrib.* with reference to the analysis of complex wave-forms through the study of such points; **zero day** *Mil.*, the day on which an attack or operation is scheduled to begin; also *transf.*; **zero hour**, (*a*) *Mil.*, the hour at which an attack or operation is timed to begin; also *transf.*; (*b*) the hour when something is at its lowest ebb (*nonce-use*); (*c*) the hour from which the time of day is measured; **zero magnet**, a magnet for adjusting the zero, e.g. of a galvanometer; **zero mark**, **post**, a mark or post from which distances along roads are measured; **zero-point** (POINT *sb.*[1] A. 22), *spec.* in *Physics*, used *attrib.* with reference to properties and phenomena in quantized systems at absolute zero; esp. ***zero-point energy*** (see quot. 1935).

1970 P. A. PYHRR in *Harvard Business Rev.* Nov.-Dec. 111 In this speech [Arthur F.] Burns identified the basic need for what we at Texas Instruments have come to call *zero-base budgeting... Burns was advocating that government agencies start from ground zero, as it were, with each year's budget and present their requests for appropriations in such a fashion that all funds can be allocated on the basis of cost/benefit or some similar kind of evaluative analysis. **1977** *Wisconsin State Jrnl.* 1 Feb. 1 Zero-base budgeting was used by President Carter when he was governor of Georgia. He asked state agencies to justify their existence and the programs they administer from zero up, rather than merely bringing in requests for more programs, money and staff. **1976** *National Observer* (U.S.) 27 Mar. 3/3 To curb inflation, he advocates a '*zero based' Federal budget, in which each program must be justified every year. **1983** *Financial Times* 10 Nov. 9/1 Sir Douglas Wass..proposed two specific changes... The first would be to introduce 'zero-based budgetting' to make spending departments consider their action if the money available to them were drastically cut. **1906** *Athenæum* 19 May 612/2 A very ingenious bifilar galvanometer..warranted free from the tendency to *zero creep. **1950** *Jrnl. Acoustical Soc. Amer.* XXII. 821/2 Vowel sounds were the first to become intelligible, presumably because for them the density of *zero crossings in the input to the time quantizer is lower than it is for consonants. **1969** *New Scientist* 1 May 225/1 Equipment capable of analysing and recognizing speech.. has achieved considerable success using the so-called zero crossing technique. **1982** *Electronics Today Internat.* Oct. 78/2 Switching the zero-crossing point of the mains cycle eliminates the need for RFI suppression. **1929** *Papers Mich. Acad. Sci., Arts & Lett.* X. 335/2 **Zero day*, the day for an attack. **1938** *Brit. Jrnl. Psychol.* XXVIII. 325 On zero-day (the day preceding the beginning of training with the aid of the electric shock) each rat was immersed six times in the tank. **1947** L. HASTINGS *Dragons are Extra* iv. 80, I..fixed a zero-day three months ahead. **1978** R. V. JONES *Most Secret War* xxxix. 350, 20th October had been fixed as Zero Day for rocket attacks on London to begin. **1917** W. BEACH THOMAS *With British on Somme* II. v, The coming of the *zero hour of 3.30 in the morning. **1930** *Daily Express* 23 May 1/6 Psychologists have fixed 11 a.m. as the zero hour of the worker. **1939** WODEHOUSE *Uncle Fred in Springtime* xviii. 269 Your duties will not begin till after dinner. Zero hour is at nine-thirty sharp. **1939** JOYCE *Finnegans Wake* 403 Methought..I heard at zero hour as 'twere the peal of vixen's laughter among midnight's chimes. **1946** K. TENNANT *Lost Haven* (1947) vii. 98 Desperate over the nearness of zero hour for the punt service, he seized her by the hand and snatched her along. **1953** A. HUXLEY *Let.* 2 Feb. (1969) 664 Incidentally, zero hour for tax-payments is approaching. **1978** A. PRICE *'44 Vintage* viii. 86 He had.. the..impression..that they had been travelling at breakneck speed,..as though the Americans were determined to deliver them on time for some impossible pre-arranged zero hour. **1915** A. KEITH *Antiq. Man* xxi. 341 The horizontal or *zero line, which crosses the hinder and lower angles of the right and left parietal bones. **1862** TYNDALL *Heat* i. (1863) 3 At the present moment the needle ..points to the *zero mark on the graduated disc. **1908** *Times* 2 Jan. 8/6 The iron tablet marking the position of Tyburn-gate..is virtually a milestone, marking, as it does, a spot from which the miles on the two great roads that join at Marble Arch are measured. It is perhaps the sole survivor of the zero marks of London. **1880** HAUGHTON *Phys. Geog.* ii. 51 The *zero plane is the surface of the ellipsoid similar to the sea surface. **1810** T. THOMSON *Syst. Chem.* (ed. 4) I. 565 A thermometer, the *zero point of which indicates absolute cold. **1826** *Mem. Astron. Soc.* II. 469 Every star observed in the course of the sweep which can be identified with a star in any catalogue, and whose place is determined with certainty, is taken as a zero point. **1895** *Physical Rev.* II. 326 The balls were placed horizontally in their neutral position, and the reading of the zero-point of the scale taken. **1935** J. DOUGALL tr. *Born's Atomic Physics* 339 According to the classical theory, the state of least energy of an oscillator is that of zero energy. According to wave mechanics, however, the ground state has a finite energy $E = \frac{1}{2}h\nu_0$... This zero-point energy can be explained by Heisenberg's uncertainty principle. **1938** R. W. LAWSON tr. *Hevesy & Paneth's Man. Radioactivity* (ed. 2) xx. 194 If account be taken of zero-point energy, it is found that at low temperatures the lighter isotope must have the higher vapour pressure, whereas if there is no zero-point energy it will have the lesser vapour pressure. **1955** H. B. G. CASIMIR in W. Pauli *Niels Bohr* 130 The interaction with the zero point vibrations of the crystal lattice leads to an interaction between electrons. **1969** P. ANDERSON in Cockburn & Blackburn *Student Power* 263 When neither society nor man are anywhere put in question, culture stops. In England, it has gradually slowed towards zero point. **1970** G. K. WOODGATE *Elem. Atomic Struct.* iv. 67 A quantized radiation field has a zero-point energy equivalent to a mean-square electric field so that even in a vacuum there are fluctuations in this zero-point radiation field. *Ibid.*, Zero-point fluctuations. **1973** *Sci. Amer.* Jan. 91/1 In quantum physics the ground state is not a state of absolute rest or motionlessness but only a singular 'zero point' form of motion in which there are no quasiparticles. **1908** *Daily Chron.* 9 Jan. 3/3 The *zero posts which formerly stood on the present site of the Marble Arch, and at Hyde-park-corner.

b. in sense 3, as ***zero night***, ***temperature***, ***weather***.

1854 HAWTHORNE *Engl. Note-bks.* (1870) I. 162 In the zero atmosphere of America. **1855** BROWNING *Old Pict. in Flor.* xxxiv, Feel truth at blood-heat and falsehood at zero rate. **1884** E. P. ROE in *Harper's Mag.* Jan. 288/2, I can keep my..hens warm even in zero weather. **1899** *Edin. Rev.* Apr. 323 Molecular rest—the theoretical condition of zero-temperature. **1902** *Encycl. Brit.* XXXIII. 299/2 The zero reading and the steam reading would both generally correspond to a falling meniscus.

c. in sense 4: That is of the amount expressed by zero, i.e. none at all; in *Math.* also *transf.* applied to a value of a function corresponding to the value 0 of the variable or variables. Hence (*colloq.*) more widely as adj. in the sense 'no, not any'.

1879 CAYLEY *Math. Papers* X. 499 The letter *c* is used in connexion with the zero values $u = 0$, $v = 0$... $\vartheta_0, \vartheta_1, \vartheta_2$,.. are even functions, and the corresponding zero-functions are denoted by c_0, c_1, c_2,... When (u, v) are indefinitely small each of these functions is of course equal to its zero-value *plus* a quadric term in (u, v). **1882** MINCHIN *Unipl. Kinemat.* 25 The surface of still water is agitated by wave disturbances proceeding from three fixed points..: find the points of zero disturbance. **1920** *Conquest* Apr. 257/2 Years of tedious work out of which there was always the chance of a zero result. **1938** *Brit. Jrnl. Psychol.* XXVIII. 329 If each such contact [*sc.* a mild electric shock received by rats] had been counted as an error, the number of cases of zero-error would have been considerably reduced. **1960** [see *social distance* s.v. SOCIAL *a.* 12]. **1962** *Times* 30 Oct. 4/6 Good design points include 'zero torque'. **1972** *Listener* 22 June 820/3 Why is the notion of zero economic growth so seductive for those who embrace environmental causes? **1976** *New Yorker* 24 May 28/1 Because he had zero toads, Howard had to content himself with the tub of thin green gruel. **1978** *Peace News* 6 Oct. 2/1 We can't call together the group at zero notice. **1981** *TV Picture Life* Mar. 39/3 Jackie claims they now have 'zero communication'.

d. In sense 4 c: denoting an absence of a feature (as an inflection, or a phonetic or syntactic element) that is present in other cases, and is often indicated by the following word; **zero-derivation** *Linguistics*, derivation in which the parent word is not altered; the use of a word with a different grammatical function or in a different (though related) sense; hence **zero-derivative** *a.* and *sb.*, **-derived** *a.*; **zero grade** *Philol.*, the absence or extreme reduction of an ablaut vowel from a syllable.

1905 *Amer. Jrnl. Philol.* XXVI. 179 The intrusion of the *é* grade on the zero grade..is..attested for the nasal verbs of the Indo-Iranian group. **1926** BLOOMFIELD in *Language* II. 160 *Alternation*... Absence of sound may be a phonetic or formal alternant... Such an alternant is a zero element. The postulation of zero elements is necessary for Sanskrit..for Primitive Indo-European..and probably economical for English (singular *book* with affix zero, as opposed to *book-s*, cf *f-oo-t*; *f-ee-t*). **1933** —— *Language* xiii. 215 Another extreme case is that of zero-alternants.., in which a constituent is entirely lacking, as in the plurals *sheep*, *deer*, *moose*, *fish*. *Ibid.* xiv. 236 In English, the nouns *longlegs*, *bright-eyes*, *butterfingers* are exocentric, because they occur both as singulars, and, with a zero-affix, as plurals (*that longlegs*, *those longlegs*). *Ibid.* xv. 252 We have zero-anaphora for participles after forms of *be* and *have*, as in *You were running faster than I was.* **1942** *Language* XVIII. 170 In *He cut it* there is a zero morpheme meaning 'past time' after *cut*. **1947** *Ibid.* XXIII. 340 We may set up the tentative portmanteau..as an alternant of that constituent morpheme which it resembles phonemically, and set up a zero morph as an alternant of the other constituent morpheme. **1954** M. PEI *Dict. Linguistics* 238 *Zero ending*, in morphology, the bare stem of a word when used as such in discourse is said to have zero ending. **1959** *Brno Studies in English* I. 43 The indefinite article and its zero plural variant. **1960** H. MARCHAND *Categories & Types of Present-Day English Word-Formation* v. 295 (*heading*) Zero-derivation as a 'specifically English' process. *Ibid.* 297 There are quite a few vbs with French roots for which no French verbs are recorded and which may accordingly be treated as zero derivatives: *feeble* vb.., *master* vb, [etc.]. **1963** F. T. VISSER *Hist. Syntax Eng. Lang.* I. iv. 538 The Authorized Version of the Bible clearly fights shy of it: in those places where the Hebrew has a zero-clause, it uses a relative pronoun printed in italics (e.g. Ps. 7, 5, 'he is fallen into the ditch *which* he made'). **1964** *English Studies* XLV. (Suppl.) 63 The *be going + infinitive* group has had a partially independent development. Its opposite in this case is the *will + zero infinitive* group. **1965** *Language* XLI. 519 The unfortunate myth that there is some essential connection between aorist aspect and stems consisting of zero-grade root plus accented thematic vowel in Indo-European. **1971** *Canad. Jrnl. Linguistics* Fall 31 The use of zero morphs would have greatly facilitated the description..of several problems in Japanese. **1976** *Archivum Linguisticum* VII. 129 Zero-derivation..must be regarded an extremely productive word-formative process both in English and German, but also in other languages. *Ibid.* 132 The Direct Object-type based on (17b) has two different surface realizations in English: payMENT and also the zero-derived noun *payØ*. *Ibid.* 133, I believe..that *act* (noun) must be regarded as zero-derivative (*actØ*) from the corresponding verb. **1979** *Dictionaries* I. 19 The last point concerns zero-derivatives or homographs. **1981** *Amer. Speech* LVI. 229 Other details on which there have been ethnic speculations are the zero genitive of nouns..and the zero subject of a relative clause.

e. Special Combs. (see also sense 7 a, d): **zero-balance** *a.*, applied to a bank account operated with no continuing balance, funds being transferred into it when necessary to just the extent required to meet drawings made on it; **zero beat**, a condition existing between two equal frequencies, in which no beats are produced; *spec.* in *Radio*, applied *attrib.* to a method of reception in which the incoming signal is mixed with a receiver-generated oscillation of the same frequency as the carrier wave (see *homodyne* s.v. HOMO-); **zero-coupon** *a.*, applied to a bond carrying no interest but issued below its redemption price; **zero-energy** *a.* (Nucl. Physics), applied to a small reactor, usu. built for research purposes, that develops so little power that no cooling and little shielding are required; **zero g** or **G** = *zero gravity* below; **zero gravity**, the state or condition in which there is no apparent force of gravity acting on a body, either because the force is locally weak, or because both the body and its surroundings are freely and equally accelerating under the force; = WEIGHTLESSNESS; **zero grazing** *vbl. sb.* (Agric.) = SOILING *vbl. sb.*[4] 1; so **zero-graze** *v. trans.* = SOIL *v.*[4] 1; **zero-grazed** *ppl. a.* = SOILED *ppl. a.*[2]; **zero growth**, an absence of increase (in population, production, etc.); **zero-length** *a.* (of a rocket launcher) no longer than the rocket it supports; **zero norm**, in a period of pay restraint, a recommended value of zero for the percentage increase in pay; **zero option**, a disarmament proposal that if the Soviet Union would withdraw its SS-20 missiles from Europe the U.S.A. would abandon its plan to deploy Pershing and cruise missiles there; **zero population growth**, an absence of any increase (or decrease) in a population over a period of time; abbrev. *ZPG* s.v. Z 12 a; **zero-power** *a.* (Nucl. Physics) = *zero-energy* adj. above; **zero rating**, a rating of zero for the purposes of value added tax; also as *vbl. sb.*, the practice of assessing the VAT at zero for a particular item; so **zero-rate** *v. trans.*, to assess at a VAT rate of zero; **zero-rated** *a.*; **zero sound**: see SOUND *sb.*[3] 1 d; **zero-sum** *a.*, in the theory of games, applied to a game in which the sum of the winnings of all the players is always zero; also *transf.*, denoting any situation in which advantage to one participant necessarily leads to disadvantage to one or more of the others; **zero tillage** (Agric.) = *sod planting* s.v. SOD *sb.*[1] 5 b; **zero-zero** (Aeronaut.), (*a*) a situation in which both the (horizontal) visibility and the cloud ceiling are technically zero; (*b*) used *attrib.* to designate an ejection seat that works even at rest and at zero altitude.

1974 *U.S. Investor/Eastern Banker* 26 Aug. 42/2 With a Zero Balance account, a customer will pay a small charge for actual activity. **1983** *Fortune* 18 Apr. 76/2 A controlled disbursement account is a type that bankers call a 'zero balance account'—it contains no cash at the end of the day after all checks have been paid. There are no funds left idle. **1927** *Mod. Wireless* Mar. 334/2 The results of fading on an ordinary set using high-frequency amplification were large compared with these effects in zero-beat reception. **1957** *Practical Wireless* XXXIII. 370/1 Tune a signal to zero-beat at the high-wavelength end of the scale. **1982** *Amer. Jrnl. Physics* L. 137/1 With this arrangement, one can explore the zero-beat situation (when frequencies are matched) as well as a variety of non-zero-beat situations. **1979** *Jrnl. Finance* XXXIV. 189 The relationship between yield curves for zero coupon bonds and coupon-bearing bonds is important. **1983** *Chicago Sun-Times* 29 May 5 Following the birth of their first child, the couple purchased $7,000 worth of zero coupon bonds in their daughter's name. **1951** *Canad. Chem. & Process Industries* Jan. 42 (*heading*) Zero Energy Experimental Pile. **1954** R. STEPHENSON *Introd. Nucl. Engin.* iii. 82 The smaller one is known as ZEEP (zero energy experimental pile) and is very similar . . except that its power level is limited to a few watts. **1981** *Nucl. Energy* XX. 467 Fast neutron fluence measurements in the core of a zero-energy research reactor. **1952** A. C. CLARKE *Islands in Sky* v. 80 She was escorted by an elderly woman who seemed to be quite at home under zero 'g' and gave Linda a helpful push when she showed signs of being stuck. **1962** F. I. ORDWAY et al. *Basic Astronautics* xii. 477 Walking will be impossible in zero G. **1970** N. ARMSTRONG et al. *First on Moon* vi. 127 Deke Slayton ate the same food we did... In our zero-G situation we were always full. **1978** *Radio Times* 28 Jan. 59/2 *Horizon* explores all these aspects, with footage from Skylab and reminiscences from ex-inhabitants—the astronauts who call this world zero gravity—zero G for short. **1951** A. C. CLARKE *Sands of Mars* i. 5 I'll take you into the zero-gravity section and see how you manage there. **1968** *New Scientist* 12 Sept. 545/1 Astronauts of the future will probably have to build vehicles in space. This will entail joining different metals together under zero-gravity conditions. **1978** [see *zero g* above]. **1979** *United States 1980/81* (Penguin Travel Guides) 553 You'll be offered the opportunity to . . experience weightlessness in a zero-gravity machine. **1984** *News* (Mexico City) 12 Mar. 22/4 Two of the first drugs that will be produced in zero gravity in mass quantities are beta cells . . and interferon. **1956** *Britannica Bk. of Year* 316/1 Studies indicated that green-chopping, sometimes called zero-grazing or soiling (bringing the pasture to the livestock), resulted in forage yields about double those from grazing. **1958** *Agriculture* LXV. 129 Zero grazed animals also put on greater weight during the summer months than those out grazing. *Ibid.* 131 The cattle have been zero grazed since May 1956. **1970** R. JEFFRIES *Dead Man's Bluff* vi. 56 Cows were zero-grazed and never stepped off concrete. **1978** *Exper. Husbandry* No. 33, 18 (*heading*) Beef from spring-born zero-grazed Friesians—comparison of bulls, steers and late castrates. **1984** 'D. ARCHER' *Ambridge Yrs.* 19 There are other herds that never go out into pasture... They have their grass cut and carted to them, a method called 'zero-grazing'. **1973** *Science* 15 June 1143 The possibility of zero growth in the population of the United States. **1976** *Atlantic Monthly* Jan. 4 Can economies have simultaneously zero growth, rapid inflation, substantial unemployment, and a balance of payments deficit? **1976** *N.Y. Times Mag.* 4 July 73 Power to stop new construction is wielded through the . . water board . . , a majority of which is dedicated to zero growth. **1954** K. W. GATLAND *Developm. Guided Missile* (ed. 2) iii. 79 (*caption*) A later G.A.P.A. rocket being adjusted on a 'zero-length' launcher. **1966** *Economist* 17 Dec. 1214/1 There is no bogy-man so dismal to those who run Britain's economy as the dreaded Zero Norm, the spectre who is supposed to rule over pay negotiations in the six-month period of 'severe restraint' that replaces the total pay freeze from New Year's Day. **1976** F. ZWEIG *New Acquisitive Society* II. i. 80 A zero norm which equalizes everybody is easier to endure. **1981** *Washington Post* 5 July A20/1 By reviving controversy about a moratorium and the 'zero option', Brandt's trip appears to have realized some of the fears of those in the West German government and opposition party. **1983** *Financial Times* 10 Feb. 11/6 Mr. George Bush, the U.S. Vice-President, last night confirmed Washington's willingness to consider alternatives to its zero option proposals for banning intermediate range nuclear missiles from Europe. **1967** *Science* 10 Nov. 732/2 Most discussions of the population crisis lead logically to zero population growth as the ultimate goal. **1974** *Environmental Conservation* I. 15/1 It is my estimate that zero population growth will be reached . . some time during the next decade. **1950** *Nucleonics* Sept. 104/2 *Zero-power reactor*, an experimental nuclear reactor operated at low neutron flux and at a power level so low that not only is no forced cooling required but also fission-product activity in the fuel is sufficiently low to allow the fuel to be handled after use without serious hazard. **1983** *Trans. Amer. Nucl. Soc.* XLIV. 528/2 Plate versus pin geometry continues to be an issue for Zero-Power Plutonium Reactor (ZPPR) analysis. **1972** *Daily Tel.* 22 Mar. 19/3 Zero-rating a transaction, rather than exempting it, is advantageous, because a trader is allowed credit for any VAT paid on his inputs. **1975** *Times* 11 Feb. 6/4 The first thing the Government could do would be to zero-rate the theatre for VAT. **1972** *Daily Tel.* 22 Mar. 17/4 A firm which supplies zero-rated goods or services gets complete relief from Value Added Tax both on its purchases and on its sales. **1976** *Horse & Hound* 3 Dec. 28 (Advt.), Rubber riding boots. Best quality, shiny leather-look finish. Price £3·45 (zero rated). **1971** *Nature* 3 Dec. 310/3 The recently reported claim of the salvage industries to be given zero rating for value-added tax . . can also be extended. **1972** *Daily Tel.* 22 Mar. 17 Mr Barber explained the difference between exemption from VAT and 'zero rating'. **1984** *Bookseller* 3 Nov. 1857/1 Books are the essential tools of society and zero-rating is a very efficient way of encouraging their wide availability. **1944** VON NEUMANN & MORGENSTERN *Theory of Games* ii. 47 An important viewpoint in classifying games is this: Is the sum of all payments received by all players (at the end of the game) always zero; or is this not the case? . . We shall call games of the first mentioned type zero-sum games. **1966** S. BEER *Decision & Control* x. 210 Perhaps the contestants in most important games nowadays (from labour disputes . . to international diplomacy) too readily regard their games as zero-sum. **1967** L. B. ARCHER in Wills & Yearsley *Handbk. Management Technol.* vii. 121 Everybody *can* win. Manufacturing is not a zero-sum game. **1971** *Times Lit. Suppl.* 22 Oct. 1335/3 C. Wright Mills . . used a zero-sum conception of power (i.e., the more one person had the less was available to others). **1980** *Ibid.* 26 Sept. 1072/2 In Europe [in the 1930s] class conflict was seen as a zero-sum game in which one group could only benefit at the expense of another. **1983** *Listener* 15 Dec. 31/1 We live in a zero-sum world, and it was inconceivable that the strains of setting up a completely new operation within an essentially fixed budget would not eventually begin to tell. **1971** *New Scientist* 25 Mar. 663/1 Even fairly low levels of pesticide destroyed these bacteria... The situation is made even worse by the growing popularity of 'zero-tillage'. **1979** *Austral. Financial Rev.* 16 Aug., Farmers using zero tillage leave straw and stubble on the field and this trash cover helps to eliminate erosion, conserve moisture, . . and reduce salinity problems. **1939** HIXSON & COLODNY *Word Ways* xvi. 141 *Zero-zero* (no visibility in any direction). **1947** *Shell Aviation News* No. 113. 7/2 There are few greater nervous strains than that experienced by a pilot of a transport in deciding to switch over from instruments and manually bring the ship in these last few hundred feet when visibility is 'zero-zero'. **1961** *Aeroplane* C. 593/2 The most interesting item in the Martin-Baker Aircraft Co., Ltd., display . . is the prototype rocket-assisted 'zero-zero' ejection seat for VTOL aircraft. **1967** *Times Rev. Industry* June 53/1 Category 3C represents visibility of less than 50 metres and includes 'zero-zero' conditions under which safety experts believe operations will not be possible for a very long time. **1977** P. WAY *Super-Celeste* 215 They had explained to him the controls of his zero-zero ejection seat.

zero ('zɪərəʊ), *v.* [f. the sb.] **I. 1.** *trans.* To set the sights of (a rifle) using targets at known distances.

1913 A. G. FULTON *Notes on Rifle Shooting* 30 (Advt.), A Zero Target, by means of which any novice may correctly zero his own rifle. **1918** H. MCBRIDE *Emma Gees* ix. 119 'Zeroing' a rifle is the process of testing it out on a range of known distances and setting the sights to suit one's individual peculiarities of aiming. **1958** L. VAN DER POST *Lost World Kalahari* vii. 142, I had not yet fired at a live target, though . . I had zeroed it on a marked one. **1979** D. LOWDEN *Boudapesti 3* xxxii. 176 The rifle had been zeroed . . at an elevation of 200.

2. zero in. a. *trans.* To range guns or missiles on (a target). Usu. *pass.*

1944 *Newsweek* 8 Jan. 45 Don't you know the Jerries have that road zeroed in?—a phrase meaning the Germans had sighted their guns on the road and needed only to pull their triggers. **1945** *Finito! Po Valley Campaign* (15th Army Group) 41 Road junction 711 was not only mined, but zeroed in. **1965** H. KAHN *On Escalation* iv. 74 American bases overseas and American targets on the mainland are at all times zeroed in by Soviet missiles, and vice versa. **1971** *Scope* (S. Afr.) 19 Mar. 20/4 These roads were well covered by strongpoints, and zeroed-in by artillery.

b. *trans.* To aim (a weapon) at a target. Const. *on.*

1944 *Life* 14 Aug. 57/1 Germans who had retreated out of town 'zeroed in' mortar shells among troops and light tanks which tried to follow. **1950** *N.Y. Herald* 26 Aug. 2/1 Guns are 'zeroed in' on the junction. **1961** *Time* (Atlantic ed.) 17 Feb. 16 The Russians now have some 50 ICBMs ready to go, presumably zeroed in on U.S. targets.

c. *intr.* To focus attention *on*, to concentrate *on*. Also *transf.* (const. *on*), to get a closer view of a subject with a camera.

1959 *Guardian* 1 Dec. 15/4 So far . . Governor Rockefeller has spoken out on space research, the housing of Puerto Ricans, crop subsidies... Now he is zeroing-in on the social drinkers. **1961** D. HUFF *Score* (1962) p. ix, This book . . will narrow the subject down to the specific material you are likely to encounter in a variety of fields... Finally this book will zero-in on the increasingly important psychological tests. **1971** *Daily Tel.* 18 Oct. 14 An excited Taiwanese photographer zeroed in on the frail figure . . with a long-range lens. **1972** *Screw* 12 June 21/2 The storyline, such as it is, zeros in on a classy whore-house in a banana republic. **1974** A. DILLARD *Pilgrim at Tinker Creek* viii. 143 Zero in on a well-watered shore. **1976** *Word 1971* XXVII. 142 Wittgenstein zeroes in upon linguistic constraints and logical conditions as they are made manifest in common, ordinary speech. **1983** *Listener* 14 Apr. 33/1 Its staff were slowly but surely zeroing in on the essential secret of successful breakfast broadcasting in this country. **1985** *Weekly World News* (U.S.) 1 Jan. 11/1 Security cameras were installed to stop vandalism, but they zeroed in on the athletes as they traipsed back and forth across a corridor from the shower to their locker room.

d. *intr.* To move towards, as if to a target. Also *fig.* Const. *on.*

1959 *Guardian* 26 Sept. 5/2 The squadrons of flies that zeroed in on his shiny pate. **1961** J. STEINBECK *Winter of our Discontent* xxi. 300 For twenty years that check has zeroed in on the first of every month. **1965** J. A. MICHENER *Source* (1966) 797 A series of bullets was beginning to zero-in on her, and in a few more steps she was sure to be hit. **1968** K. AMIS *I want it Now* i. 27 By the time he got back to the girl two other men had zeroed in on her. **1972** W. GARNER *Ditto, Brother Rat!* iv. 30, I zeroed in on the downstairs bar. **1974** *Newsweek* 8 Apr. 51/1 In recent months, instrumented spacecraft have zeroed in on Venus, Mars and Jupiter to provide astronomers with a wealth of significant new data on those planets. **1978** G. A. SHEEHAN *Running & Being* xii. 174 A pacemaker . . had zeroed in on the perfect pace.

II. 3. To fix the zero hour for (a military operation).

1926 *Blackw. Mag.* 774/1 Plan no. 7 will be put in operation to-night. It will be zeroed as from 23.00 hours.

4. = ZEROIZE *v.*

1949 W. F. GOODELL in J. F. Blackburn *Components Handbk.* x. 331 This zero convention makes it possible to 'zero' the dial of a synchro motor on one unit of a system. **1951** C. W. KENNEDY *Inspection & Gaging* ix. 293 An error would result if the air gage were zeroed against a 5-microinch surface and then used to compare the diameter of a bore with a 200-microinch surface roughness. **1969** [see ODOMETER]. **1974** *Physics Bull.* Mar. 108/2 An offset control allows the pen to be zeroed at any point on the chart. **1982** *Homes & Gardens* Jan. 17/3 One button . . can zero the read-out at any point, allowing you to add ingredients without emptying the bowl.

III. 5. zero out. *trans.* To eliminate.

1967 *Word* XXIII. 316 We 'zero out' the voicing of /b/, which is not at all to deny that /b/ is voiced. **1972** W. LABOV *Language in Inner City* ii. 52 The deletion of *are* has reached such a high point that it is effectively zeroed out for many speakers. **1982** *Daily Tel.* 25 Jan. 12/7 Watch . . for word of new budget cuts, including Federal programmes that are to be 'zeroed out'.

zeroable ('zɪərəʊəb(ə)l), *a.* [f. ZERO *sb.* + -ABLE.]

1. *Linguistics.* That may be omitted from a sentence without loss of meaning.

1965 *Language* XLI. 395 Metaphorical and idiomatic objects are not pronounable or zeroable. **1975** *Rev. des Lang. Vivantes* XLI. 239 The relation between 'They described Vesuvius' and its metalinguistic, zeroable, expansion into 'They described Vesuvius *which is a volcano*'.

2. Capable of being set to read zero.

1974 *Physics Bull.* Aug. 349/1 A zeroable offset counter system is provided which makes it easy for the operator to measure the angular error between the ground reference face and the crystallographic planes.

'**zeroing**, *vbl. sb.* [f. ZERO *v.* + -ING[1].]

1. a. The adjustment of an instrument to give a reading of zero.

1949 W. F. GOODELL in J. F. Blackburn *Components Handbk.* x. 331 It is to facilitate the zeroing of synchros that they are provided with standardized flanges that are accurately concentric with the shafts. **1954** *Electronic Engin.* XXVI. 118/1 The connexion of Dekatrons in cascade presents difficulties in that a carry makes necessary a cumbersome circuit for resetting or zeroing. **1975** *Chem. Engin.* 10 Nov. 223/1 A process-control computer . . has been extended to control zeroing of selected instrument transmitters to improve the accuracy of the input.

b. The adjustment or setting of the sights of a gun.

1975 V. CANNING *Kingsford Mark* v. 83 On the rifle were telescopic sights... He would . . fire a few rounds and check the zeroing. **1979** D. LOWDEN *Boudapesti 3* xxxii. 176 The proper zeroing target had been used.

2. *Linguistics.* The deletion or omission of part of a linguistic form or structure.

1956 *Language* XXXII. 645 In all or nearly all dialects the first of two contiguous unstressed vowels may or may not be modified by shortening and/or raising or zeroing. **1965** *Ibid.* XLI. 393 In *I prefer that I should go first* there is no zeroing, but in the transform of this *I prefer for me to go first* → *I prefer to go first.* **1970** J. W. GAIR *Colloquial Sinhalese Clause Structures* iv. 54 It is convenient to treat such clauses as derived by context-governed deletion from full clauses like them in every respect save the presence of such constituents. The term 'zeroing' will be reserved for such discourse deletion.

zeroize ('zɪərəʊaɪz), *v.* [f. ZERO *sb.* + -IZE.] *trans.* To adjust (an instrument or device) to give a zero reading, esp. in order to calibrate it; to assign a value of zero to. So **'zeroizing** *vbl. sb.*

1908 *Brit. Patent 23,895* 3 Such clutches have already been employed for the simultaneous zeroizing of two indicating mechanisms. **1914** E. M. HORSBURGH *Mod. Instruments & Methods Calculation* 87 Mr. Trinks has invented a device which disengages the pawls from the number wheels when the latter are being zeroised. *Ibid.*, The zeroising crank is fixed on the right-hand side of the carriage, and the zeroising is effected by a half revolution of this crank. **1928** [see REGISTER *sb.*[1] 10c]. **1945** *Chambers's Jrnl.* Dec. 671/1 It is said to enable operational errors to be rectified in a matter of moments, and the calculations to be continued without the waste of time involved by 'zeroising' the machine and restarting the calculations from the beginning. **1956** G. A. MONTGOMERIE *Digital Calculating Machines* ii. 28 The other major control is the zeroizing or clearance key or handle at the right-hand side of the keyboard. **1974** *Software World* V. v. 12 Integer Function JCV12C converts a positive integer L (L < 256) to a character in A1 format, zeroizing bits 24 to 1.

zeroth ('zɪərəʊθ). *Math.* and *Sci.* Also (*rare*) zero'th. [f. ZERO *sb.* + -TH[2].] Coming next in a series before the one conventionally regarded as the first.

1896 *Electrician* 10 Jan. 350/2 In order to have the zeroth Bessel normal function, we need only let the conductance and permittance per unit length of cable both vary directly as the distance from $x = 0$. **1932** *Physical Rev.* XL. 56 The zeroth order wave functions which they use do indeed indicate that tetrahedral symmetry should give high stability. **1956** E. H. HUTTEN *Lang. Mod. Physics* iv. 143 From this the theorem is derived that one body in contact with another may be used as a thermometer, or that one body 'reads' the temperature of another. This theorem is sometimes referred to..as the zeroth law of thermodynamics. **1969** *Nature* 15 Nov. 642/1 The energy of transition between the zeroth and the first energy levels. **1976** J. H. CONWAY *On Numbers & Games* 0. 3 In this zeroth part, our topic is the notion of number. **1984** *QL User* Dec. 33 LET input. vector = VEC 5 declares a vector of 6 words (BCPL vectors start at their zero'th element) pointed to by INPUT.VECTOR.

zerovalent (zɪərəʊ'veɪlənt). *Chem.* [f. ZERO *sb.* + -VALENT.] Having an actual or formal valency of zero. Hence **zero'valency**.

1940 *Chambers's Techn. Dict.* 919/2 Zero-valent. **1953** BARNETT & WILSON *Inorg. Chem.* xxii. 282 Since the electrons forming these covalencies are supplied solely by the molecules of carbon monoxide, the metal atom is said to have zero-valency. **1965** *Jrnl. Chem. Soc.* 847 The analogous reaction..of the naphthalene complex in its zerovalent formulation..cannot be distinguished from the possible consecutive reactions. **1977** *Inorg. Chem.* XVI. 1313 (*heading*) Reactions of the zerovalent complex $Ni[HP(C_6H_5)_2]_4$. **1984** *Science* 22 June 1330/2 A greater proportion of nickel in the catalytically active zero-valent state.

‖**zerumbet** (zɪ'rʌmbɛt). Also 7–8 **-eth**. [Pg., ad. Hind., Pers. *zerunbād*.] An East Indian plant of the genus *Curcuma*, or its aromatic root, used, like the allied CASSUMUNAR and ZEDOARY, as a tonic drug.

[**1555** EDEN *Decades* (Arb.) 269 Of the Apothecaries drugges: And of what price they are in Calicut and Malabar. .. Zerumba, the farazuola Fanan ii. Zedoaria, the farazuola Fanan i.] **1662** J. DAVIES tr. *Mandelslo's Trav.* II. 151 The Zerumbet..likewise growes in these parts, and is like to ginger. **1694** *Phil. Trans.* XVIII. 278 Kua or Zerumbeth of our Shops, a Species of Ginger. **1712** tr. *Pomet's Hist. Drugs* I. 33 The Zedoary is the long Part of the Plant, serving as a root to the Zerumbeth. **1861** BENTLEY *Man. Bot.* 668 The so-called Cassumunar roots, Zedoary roots, and Zerumbet roots of commerce.

zerybeh: see ZARIBA.

zerzeline, zerzelnie, var. SERGELIM *Obs.*

zest (zɛst), *sb.*[1] Also 8 zist. [a. F. *zeste*, earlier †*zest*, †*zec*, 'the thicke skin, or filme whereby the kernell of a wall-nut is diuided' (Cotgr.), also orange or lemon peel; of obscure origin. Cf. Walloon *zess*, Pg. *zeste*.

The sense given in Chambers *Cycl.* 1728, 'the woody, thick Skin, quartering the Kernel of a Walnut', is taken from French, and was not in English use.]

1. Orange or lemon peel used as a flavouring or for preserving; also, the oil squeezed from such peel to flavour liquor, etc. Also in Fr. form **zeste** (see etym.).

1674 BLOUNT *Glossogr.* (ed. 4), *Zest* (Fr.) the pill of an Orange, or such like, squeesed into a glass of wine, to give it a relish. **1712** tr. *Pomet's Hist. Drugs* I. 150 Citron Oil..is made..by the Zest or the rasping or grating of the Citron Peel. **1747** WESLEY *Prim. Physick* (1755) 70 Pour into the Palm of the Hand a little Brandy, with some Zist of Lemon. **1800** tr. *Lagrange's Chem.* II. 173 To prepare lemon-juice you must first carefully remove the zest and then the white part. **1903** GILCHRIST *Beggar's Manor* ii, As he..fastidiously deprived the oranges of their zest. **1958** L. DURRELL *Mountolive* viii. 162 How good the taste of Dubonnet with a *zeste de citron*. **1967** *Guardian* 3 Feb. 8/5 The thin outer skin of oranges, known as the zest. **1974** *Homes & Gardens* Jan. 68/2 Add candied peel, lemon zeste, salt and nutmeg and mix. **1979** N. GORDIMER *Burger's Daughter* II. 269 He had fished the slice of lemon out of the bottom of his glass and was gobbling the skin with a mouth drawn by the zest. **1981** *Family Weekly* (U.S.) 12 July 10/3 Grated zest of 1 lemon. **1982** J. GRIGSON *Fruit Bk.* 256 Orange juice and a little zest can also be added to tomato and carrot soups.

2. *fig.* Something that imparts a relish, savour, or piquancy; a piquant quality which adds to the enjoyment or agreeableness of something.

1709 MRS. MANLEY *Secret Mem.* 107 Monsieur St. Amant lov'd nothing so tenderly as he did the Baron;..he was the Zest to all his Pleasures. **1728** VANBR. & CIB. *Prov. Husb.* III. i, A smart Repartee, with a Zest of Recrimination at the Head of it, makes the prettiest Sherbet. **1742** YOUNG *Nt. Th.* IX. 1211 The Life of life, the Zest of worldly bliss. **1819** KEATS *To Fanny* 6 That sweet minor zest Of love, your kiss. **1820** W. IRVING *Sketch Bk.* II. 134 There was a quaintness too, mingled with all this revelry, that gave it a peculiar zest. **1862** THACKERAY *Philip* xvi, The sense that, perhaps, it was imprudent to take a cab or drink a bottle of wine, added a zest to those enjoyments. **1873** HELPS *Anim. & Mast.* viii. 207 The difference of character should have given a zest to companionship, not destroyed it.

3. a. Keen relish or enjoyment displayed in speech or action; the pleasure of enjoying something; gusto. Usually const. *for*.

1791 BOSWELL *Johnson* 20 Sept. an. 1777, If I were to reside in London, the exquisite zest with which I relished it in occasional visits might go off. **1831** SIR J. SINCLAIR *Corr.* II. 358 After travelling..for two or three days alone, when he arrives at an inn, it gives him a greater zest for society. **1844** DICKENS *Mart. Chuz.* xix, She went to a lying-in or a laying-out with equal zest. **1854** THACKERAY *Newcomes* i, The zest of life was certainly keener. **1895** SALMOND *Chr. Doctr. Immort.* I. vii. 119 The Greek people had an almost unrivalled zest for life.

b. phr. *to your zest*, to your taste or liking. *rare*.

1817 BYRON *Beppo* xii, That picture..Is loveliest to my mind of all the Show; It may perhaps be also to your zest.

4. *transf.* Something which furnishes a relish or provides a savoury addition to a meal; an appetizer; also, a relish, a piquant flavour.

1835 DICKENS *Sk. Boz, Miss Evans & Eagle*, Mr. Wilkins had brought a pint of shrimps..to give a zest to the meal [*sc.* tea]. **1848** NEWMAN *Loss & Gain* 154, 'I like these rides into the country', said Vincent, as they began eating;..'it is exquisite as a zest'. **1848** DICKENS *Dombey* xxvi, The Native had private zests and flavours on a side-table, with which the Major daily scorched himself. **1856** KANE *Arctic Expl.* II. xxvii. 273 We..renewed the zest of the table with the best salad in the world—raw eggs and cochlearia. **1876** MISS BRADDON *Dead Men's Shoes* i, For a cheap relish, a zest which shall make bread and butter supply the place of dinner, your fishmonger is your best friend.

Hence **'zestful** *a.*, full of zest, characterized by piquancy or keen relish or enjoyment; whence **'zestfully** *adv.*, **'zestfulness**.

1850 *Fraser's Mag.* XLII. 345 A zestful sort of place in which to spend a fortnight. **1857** *Ibid.* LVI. 601 How..shall any man..abridge..twenty volumes of such zestful personalities? **1872** C. KING *Mountain. Sierra Nev.* xi. 241 While we chatted and ate zestfully portions [of meat] not too freely brecciated with lava sand. **1897** JACOBS *Skipper's Wooing* i, He bent over and with much zestful splashing began his ablutions. **1882** *Illustr. Lond. News* 30 Sept. 350/2 The zestfulness of its Radicalism is not lessened.

†**zest**, *sb.*[2] *Obs. rare*$^{-1}$. = SIESTA.

1706 PHILLIPS (ed. Kersey), *Zest*..sometimes taken for a short Afternoon's Sleep or Nap: as To go to one's Zest.

zest (zɛst), *v.* [f. ZEST *sb.*[1]]

1. *trans.* To flavour with 'zest'; to add a relish to; to give a piquant quality to; also *fig.*

1704 CIBBER *Careless Husb.* III. 56 My Lord, when my Wine's Right I never care it shou'd be Zested. **1709** MRS. MANLEY *Secret Mem.* (1720) IV. Ded. p. vii, Heaven is sometimes pleased with Bitterness to Zest the Bowl of Bliss! **1737** J. HERVEY *Mem. Reign Geo. II* (1848) II. xxx. 288 Many more expressions not quite so strongly zested, though but few degrees weaker. **1760** GOLDSM. *Ess.* Misc. Wks. 1837 I. 327 Hundreds sunk to the bottom by one broadside, furnish out the topic of the day, and zest his coffee. **1862** MEREDITH *Marian* ii, Ye who zest the turtle's nest With the eagle's eyrie. **1871** H. MARSHALL *For very Life* I. i, One autumn morning, zested with a sharp frosty feeling.

†**2.** [after F. *zester*.] (See quot.) *Obs.*

1706 PHILLIPS (ed. Kersey), To *Zest an Orange or Lemon*, (among Confectioners) is to cut the Peel from top to bottom into small Slips, as thin as it can possibly be done.

Hence **'zested** *ppl. a.*

1769 GOLDSM. *Rom. Hist.* II. 74 One circumstance that might well..teach mankind to relish the beverage of virtue ..above their most zested enjoyments. **1801** *Lusignan* III. 131 The most zested enjoyments of vice.

†**zest**, *int.* *Obs.* [Cf. F. *zest* int.] An exclamation accompanying quick action.

1705 VANBRUGH *Confed.* III. i, Oons the old Woman—Zest.

zest, s.w. dial. f. 2nd pers. sing. pres. of SAY *v.*[1]

1602 *Contention betw. Lib. & Prod.* I. iv, Bur Lady, zonne, zest true.

'zesty ('zɛstɪ), *a.* [f. ZEST *sb.*[1] + -Y[1].]

1. Of a taste or a food: piquant, agreeably sharp.

1934 in WEBSTER. **1936** [see PICK-UP *sb.* f]. **1953** 'A. BRIDGE' *Place to Stand* v. 67 The meal was plain and good, with the zesty taste of country cooking. **1969** *Daily Tel.* 5 Feb. 15/5 The food is spicy and zesty enough to make you nearly spring out of your seat. **1971** A. G. SEABERG *Menu-Design-Merchandising* 214 The zesty garlic butter brings out the best in this epicurean treat from the sea.

2. *fig.* Energetic, lively, stimulating.

1952 *Time* 15 Dec. 33/1 Zesty as a two-year-old rounding into the stretch, Britain's aged Prime Minister Winston Churchill last week entered his 79th year enthusiastically agallop on all his old hobbies. **1958** *Oxf. Mag.* 22 May 459/1 The little farrago ends with a bound of zesty life-assertion and merriment. **1959** *News Chron.* 23 July 5/5 To provide its zesty performance, Rootes' engineers have developed an aluminium cylinder head. **1972** *Time* 17 Apr. 43/2 Housing starts remain zesty, at an annual rate of 2,500,000 units in recent months. **1981** *N.Y. Times Mag.* 27 Apr. 18/3 The zesty lexicographer from New Zealand neither equivocates nor jazzes around. **1982** *Observer* 10 Oct. 40/8 This column's Third Rule of Television—'If it works, change it'—was given another zesty outing last week.

zet, dial. f. SET *v.*

‖**zeta**[1] ('ziːtə). *Antiq.* [med.L., = *diæta* (see Z), a. Gr. διαιτα way of living, dwelling (see DIET *sb.*).] A term of disputed meaning (see quots.).

1706 PHILLIPS (ed. Kersey), *Zeta*,..a Room kept warm like a Stove; a withdrawing-Chamber with Pipes convey'd along in the Walls, to receive from below, either the cool Air, or the heat of warm Water. In our old Records, it is taken for a Dining-Room, Hall, or Parlour. **1849–50** *Weale's Dict. Terms*, *Zeta*, presumed to be a room over the porch of a Christian church. **1860** MAYNE *Expos. Lex.*, *Zeta*, *Zeteorila* [? *Zeticula*],..the *Vaporaria* and *Conclavia*, or vapour-baths and inner closets, in the pavement of which warm or cold water was diffused as required.

‖**zeta**[2] ('ziːtə). [Gr. ζῆτα, the letter *Z*, ζ: see Z.]

1. Name of the sixth letter of the Greek alphabet, used *attrib.* in **zeta-function** *Math.*, one of a set of functions (denoted by a capital Z prefixed to the variable) connected with elliptic integrals.

2. zeta potential *Physical Chem.*, the potential difference that exists across the electrical double layer at the interface of a solid and a liquid.

1939 E. A. HAUSER *Colloidal Phenomena* ix. 91 In simple cases, this double layer can be regarded as an electric condenser, the potential of which is generally termed electrokinetic, or ζ (zeta), potential. **1982** *Nature* 21 Jan. 267/2 They [*sc.* electrokinetic phenomena] arise whenever there is relative motion between a charged interface and a liquid and are usually interpreted in terms of the zeta potential.

Hence **'zetacism** (-sɪz(ə)m) [cf. ETACISM, LAMBDACISM, RHOTACISM], frequent or faulty use of the letter ζ; **zetaic** (ziː'teɪɪk) *a. Math.*, applied by Sylvester to operations (denoted by the letter ζ prefixed to an expression) in which subscript indices are treated like ordinary indices of powers, and to expressions or functions so obtained.

1840 SYLVESTER *Coll. Math. Papers* (1904) I. 47, I use the Greek letter ζ to denote that the product of factors to which it is prefixed is to be effected after a certain symbolical manner. This I shall distinguish as the zeta-ic product. *Ibid.*, Rule for zeta-ic multiplication. *Note.* An analogous interpretation may be extended to any zeta-ic function whatever. **1889** I. TAYLOR *Aryans* v. § 1. 260 The tendency to Zetacism among the Ionians may be due to an admixture with the pre-Aryan population.

zete, obs. dial. form of SET *v.*[1]

zetetic (zɪ'tɛtɪk), *a.* and *sb. rare.* [ad. mod.L. *zētēticus*, a. Gr. ζητητικός, f. ζητεῖν to seek, inquire.]

A. *adj.* Inquiring, investigating; proceeding by inquiry or investigation.

In quot. 1645 used in burlesque.

1645 URQUHART *Trissotetras* Wks. (1834) 145 Zetetick, is said of loxogonospherical moods which agree in the same quæsitas. **1660** STANLEY *Hist. Philos.* XII. (1687) 771/1 This was called the Zetetick Philosophy, from its continual enquiry after Truth. **1704** J. HARRIS *Lex. Techn.* I, *Zetetick* Method in Mathematicks, is the Analytick, or Algebraick way. **1849** S. B. ROWBOTHAM (*title*) Zetetic Astronomy. A description of several experiments which prove that the surface of the sea is a perfect plane and that the Earth is not a Globe!

B. *sb.* **1.** (*sing.* or *pl.*) Investigation, inquiry (as in mathematics, etc.).

Often with allusion to Franciscus Vieta's *Zeteticorum libri quinque*.

1679 MOXON *Math. Dict.* (1701), *Zetetique*, numbers used in Algebra and Equations by the famous Vieta. **1843** *Penny Cycl.* XXVII. 775/2 *Zetetics*, a name given by Vieta..to the part of algebra which consists in the direct search after unknown quantities. **1853** W. THOMSON *Laws Th.* (ed. 3) § 35 [Logic] has been called..Zetetic or the Art of seeking.

2. An investigator, inquirer; *spec.* an adherent of the ancient Greek sceptic school of philosophy (see SCEPTIC A., B. 1).

1660 STANLEY *Hist. Philos.* XII. (1687) 772/2 These all were called Pyrrhonians from their Master; Aporeticks, and Scepticks, and Ephecticks, and Zeteticks, from their (as it were) Doctrine. **1838** J. ROWBOTHAM *Dict.* 66 The ancient Pyrrhonists were called Zetetics or seekers.

Hence **ze'tetical** *a.*, only in *Zetetical Society*, a nineteenth-century society with mystical beliefs; also *ellipt.*; **ze'tetically** *adv.* [see -ICALLY], by way of inquiry or investigation.

1881 (*programme*) The Zetetical Society... Committee... J. M. Fells... G. B. Shaw... Sidney Webb. **1882** G. B. SHAW *Let.* 30 Jan. (1965) I. 47, I have overtaxed the patience of the Almighty, and he has smitten me; and, through me, the Zetetical Society. **1885** *Bookseller* 7 Jan. 12/1 A party of Zetetic astronomers with scientific instruments. **1905** G. B. SHAW *Let.* 3 Jan. (1972) II. 486 After about a year of the Zetetical I joined the Dialectical. **1921** G.B. SHAW *Immaturity* (1930) p. xl, Not until..1879, did I for the first time rise to my feet in a little debating club called the

Zetetical Society. **1962** D. H. LAURENCE *Bernard Shaw's Platform & Pulpit* p. x, A meeting of the Zetetical Society. **1665** HOOKE *Microgr.* ix. 55 It would be somewhat too long ..zetetically to examine.. what particular kind of motion it is. **1872** *Zetetic* July 8/2 (Advt.), The life and teachings of Jesus Christ zetetically considered.

zeþ, obs. dial. pl. ind. pres. of SEE *v.*

zeþþe, obs. var. SITH.

Zetland (ˈzɛtlənd). Later spelling (see Z) of Sc. *Ȝetland* (also *Yetland*, latinized *Yhetlandia*), a. ON. *Hja(l)tland, Hjetland* (MDa. *Hetland*) SHETLAND. Hence **ˈZetlander, Zetˈlandic** *a.* (Survives in a title of the peerage; until recently an official name of the Shetland Islands.)

1703 J. BRAND *Descr. Orkney*, etc. To Rdr., Zetland.. is unknown to the most of the Nation, if not, that they have only heard, there were such Isles, as the Zetlandick. *Ibid.* 116 Some Zetlanders went to the King with their Skin-Coats, laying the oppressed condition of their Countrey before him. **1809** EDMONDSTON *Zetland Isl.* I. 206 The native Zetland horse is very small. **1813** MONTAGU *Ornith. Dict.* Suppl. s.v. *Shearwater*, In addition to the Zetlandic name of Lyre, Lyar or Lyrie, it has acquired the Norwegian names of Skrabe or Skraap. **1821** SCOTT *Pirate* ii, Sweyn Erickson, as good a Zetlander as ever rowed a boat to the *haaf* fishing. **1868** *Rep. Brit. Assoc.* I. 338 A list of the Zetlandic Annelids dredged in 1867 and 1868.

zeuera, zeuet, obs. ff. ZEBRA, CIVET *sb.*[1]

‖**Zeuglodon** (ˈzjuːgləʊdɒn). *Palæont.* [mod.L. (Owen, 1839), f. Gr. ζεύγλη strap or loop of a yoke + ὀδούς, ὀδοντ- tooth.] A genus of extinct cetaceans of a primitive type, whose fossil remains are found in the Eocene. Hence **ˈzeuglodont**, *sb.* a cetacean of this genus; *a.* belonging to this genus; **zeugloˈdontoid** [-OID], *a.* having the characters of this genus, or belonging to the family *Zeuglodontidæ*; *sb.* a cetacean of this family.

1839 OWEN in *Trans. Geol. Soc. Lond.* Ser. II. VI. 75 The microscopic characters of the texture of the teeth of the *Zeuglodon* are strictly of a mammiferous character. **1857** AGASSIZ *Contrib. Nat. Hist. U.S.* I. 116 The Zeuglodonts [are] embryonic Sirenidæ. **1883** FLOWER in *Encycl. Brit.* XV. 393/2 The earliest Cetaceans of whose organization we have anything like complete evidence are the Zeuglodons of the Eocene period. **1885** *J. Phillips' Man. Geol.* II. 650 Whales of the Zeuglodont family. **1892** *Athenæum* 12 Nov. 667/3 Zeuglodont and other cetacean remains from the tertiaries of the Caucasus.

‖**zeugma** (ˈzjuːgmə). *Gram.* and *Rhet.* [mod.L., a. Gr. ζεῦγμα a yoking, f. ζευγνύναι to yoke, related to ζυγόν YOKE *sb.*[1]] A figure by which a single word is made to refer to two or more words in the sentence; esp. when properly applying in sense to only one of them, or applying to them in different senses; but formerly more widely, including, e.g., the use of the same predicate, without repetition, with two or more subjects; also sometimes applied to cases of irregular *construction*, in which the single word agrees *grammatically* with only one of the other words to which it refers (more properly called SYLLEPSIS).

1586 A. DAY *Engl. Secretorie* II. (1595) 82 *Zeugma*, when one or more clauses are concluded vnder one verbe, as to say, His loosnesse ouercame all shame; his boldnesse, feare; his madnesse, reason. **1589** PUTTENHAM *Engl. Poesie* III. xii. (Arb.) 175 But if it be to mo clauses then one, that some such word be supplied to perfit the congruitie or sence of them all, it is by the figure (*Zeugma*) we call him the (single supplie) ..: as to say. Fellowes and friends and kinne forsooke me quite. **1848** J. T. WHITE *Xenophon's Anab.* Notes I. v. §9 (1872) 51 Observe the zeugma in πλήθει [in ἡ βασιλέως ἀρχὴ, πλήθει μὲν χώρας καὶ ἀνθρώπων ἰσχυρὰ οὖσα]. **1872** LILLIE tr. *J. P. Lange's Comm. 2 Thess.* iii. 156 Αὐτοὺς is now to be taken out of the dative τοιούτοις, by an obvious zeugma [in 2 Thess. iii. 12 τοῖς δὲ τοιούτοις παραγγέλλομεν, καὶ παρακαλοῦμεν]. **1882** FARRAR *Early Chr.* II. 560 By the figure of speech called zeugma, or rather syllepsis, the same word.. is often made to serve two purposes in the same sentence. A verb is often used with two clauses which is only appropriate to one of them, as in Pope's line—'See Pan with flocks, with fruits Pomona crowned.'

Hence **zeugmatic** (-ˈmætɪk) *a.*, pertaining to or involving zeugma; **zeugˈmatically** *adv.*, so as to involve zeugma.

1857 ELLICOTT *Comm. Col.* ii. 5 A zeugmatic construction of the accus. with both verbs. **1857** —— *Comm. Phil.* i. 27 Attempts have been made to defend the construction as it stands,.. by referring ἀκούσω zeugmatically to both clauses.

zeugmatography (zjuːgməˈtɒgrəfɪ). *Med.* [f. Gr. ζεῦγμα, ζεύγματ- a yoking (in allusion to the coupling of the electromagnetic and magnetic fields) + -O + -GRAPHY.] A form of imaging using the principles of nuclear magnetic resonance to obtain and display the structural details of soft tissue. Hence **zeugˈmatogram**, a picture produced by zeugmatography; **zeugmatoˈgraphic** *a.*, involving or produced by zeugmatography.

1973 P. C. LAUTERBUR in *Nature* 16 Mar. 190/1 Because the interaction may be regarded as a coupling of the two fields by the object, I propose that image formation by this technique be known as zeugmatography. *Ibid.* 191/1 At low radio-frequency power.. the two capillaries gave nearly identical images in the zeugmatogram. *Ibid.* 191/2 Zeugmatographic techniques should find many useful applications in studies of the internal structures, states, and composition of microscopic objects. **1981** *Brit. Med. Jrnl.* 7 Nov. 1212/1 Nuclear magnetic resonance (or zeugmatography) is looming on the horizon.

zeunerite (ˈzɔɪnəraɪt). *Min.* [f. the name of Gustav *Zeuner* of Freiberg, Saxony.] A hydrous arseniate of uranium and copper, occurring in bright-green crystals.

1873 *Jrnl. Chem. Soc.* XXVI. 1010 Arseniferous Uranium Mica (Zeunerite) from Joachimsthal.

zeura, obs. form of ZEBRA.

‖**Zeus** (zjuːs). [Gr. Ζεύς, gen. Διός, related to L. *Jovis* (gen.): see JOVE, JUPITER.]

1. *Myth.* Name of the supreme deity of the ancient Greeks; cf. JUPITER. Hence *allusively*.

1920 *Times Lit. Suppl.* 1 Apr. 207/4 The Zeus of Weimar [*sc.* Goethe] was the last person we should have imagined comparable with our Swan of Avon!

b. *Comb.*

1839 T. MITCHELL *Frogs of Aristoph.* Add. 411 Cretan Zeus-worship. *a* **1861** CLOUGH *Poems* (1869) II. 464 You are the hatefullest to me of the Zeus-fed princes. **1875** BROWNING *Aristoph. Apol.* Poet. Wks. 1896 I. 730/1 The hapless Zeus-born offspring. **1880** JEBB in *Encycl. Brit.* XI. 140/1 Legends of warlike deeds done by Zeus-nourished kings.

2. *Ichthyol.* A genus of spiny-finned fishes, including the John Dory, *Zeus faber*, anciently sacred to Zeus or Jupiter.

1706 PHILLIPS (ed. Kersey), *Zeüs*, a Fish taken about Cadiz.., of a black Colour and very delicate. **1752** J. HILL *Hist. Anim.* 274 The red Zeus, with an even tail. **1854** BADHAM *Halieut.* 48 His own fish Zeus, the dory [was offered] to Jupiter.

‖**Zeuxis** (ˈzjuːksɪs). Name of a famous ancient Greek painter; hence *allusively*, and in comb. *Zeuxis-like* adj. Hence **ˈZeuxian** *a.*

1616 DRUMM. OF HAWTH. *Poems* I. Sonn. xix. Wks. (S.T.S.) I. 23 Desire (alas) Desire a Zeuxis new, From Indies borrowing Gold, from Westerne Skies Most bright Cynoper, sets before mine Eyes In euery Place, her Haire, sweet Looke and Hew. **1635** QUARLES *Embl.* III. ix, Zeuxian Art. **1850** MRS. JAMESON *Leg. Mon. Ord.* 299 A vase containing white lilies.. painted with such Zeuxis-like skill, that birds.. have been seen attempting to.. peck the flowers.

zeuxite (ˈzjuːksaɪt). *Min.* [f. Gr. ζεύξις yoking, joining (f. ζευγνύναι to join), rendering 'unity' in the name Huel Unity (see quot.).] A variety of tourmaline.

1836 T. THOMSON *Min., Geol.*, etc. I. 320 Zeuxite. The mineral which I distinguish by this name was found in 1814 in considerable quantity in the Huel Unity mine, about three miles east of Redrath, in Cornwall.

zeve, obs. form of SEVEN.

zevre, obs. form of ZEBRA.

zeze (ˈzeɪzeɪ). [a. Swahili *zeze*.] A zither-like string instrument of eastern and central Africa.

1860 R. F. BURTON *Lake Region Central Africa* II. xviii. 291 The zeze, or banjo, resembles in sound the monochord Arabian rubabah, the rude ancestor of the Spanish guitar. **1978** *Times* 19 Aug. 3/3 (*caption*) A member of the Tanzania National Dance Troupe playing a 13-string zeze.

Zfoot, var. 'SFOOT *int. Obs.*

1620 I. C. *Two Merry Milkmaids* II. ii. G 4 b, *Ber.* Zfoot, hee's turn'd Eccho. **1640** *Wits Recreat.* I 7 b, Z' foot, will you have of men more than their hearts?

Zhdanovism (ˈʒdɑːnəvɪz(ə)m, -fɪz(ə)m). [f. the name *Zhdanov* (see below) + -ISM.] The policy of rigorous ideological control of literature and cultural life generally that was developed in the post-war period by A. A. Zhdanov (1896–1948), Russian politician. So **ˈZhdanovist, -ite** *adjs.*, of, pertaining to, or resembling Zhdanov or Zhdanovism.

1957 C. HUNT *Guide to Communist Jargon* xi. 37 The Zhdanovite decrees on literature and the arts of 1946–7. **1958** *Encounter* Nov. 35/1 The ideal of Zhdanovism was, precisely, the reduction of literature to 'a small cog and a small screw' in the mechanism of the totalitarian state. **1962** H. SWAYZE *Polit. Control Lit. in U.S.S.R., 1946–59* ii. 26 (*heading*) The heyday of Zhdanovism, 1946–1952. **1966** *Listener* 3 Nov. 659/3 The decree.. contained the Zhdanovist denunciation of the works of Shostakovich and Khachaturian. **1975** *Times Lit. Suppl.* 31 Oct. 1280/5 Its account of Gramsci's career and the early history of the Communist Party can only be described as Zhdanovite. **1977** *Ibid.* 21 Jan. 76/4 Socialist realism he gives deservedly short shift. But the practice of Zhdanovism does not exhaust the subject.

zhe, zhee, dial. forms of SHE.

‖**zho** (ʒəʊ). [Tibetan *mdso.*] A hybrid bovine animal, bred from a yak bull and a common cow, used for domestic purposes in Northern India. Also called ‖**zobo, zobu** [with masc. affix *-bo*]. So ‖**zhomo**, also **jomo** [with fem. affix *-mo*], a female zho.

1841 MOORCROFT *Trav.* I. 272 Oxen of the common kind are not used for ploughing, the zho ox, or hybrid male between the yak.. and the common cow, or the humped variety called zebu, being greatly preferred, as is its sister, the zhomo, for the dairy. Ploughing is performed by a pair of zhos. *Ibid.* 309 The Zho or Yak-mule. **1854** HOOKER *Himal. Jrnls.* I. ix. 213 The zobo.. is but rarely seen in these mountains, though common in the North West Himalaya. **1867** A. L. ADAMS *Wand. Nat. India* 271. **1880** R. STRACHEY in *Encycl. Brit.* XI. 833/2 The yák, from which is reared a cross breed with the ordinary horned cattle of India locally called 'zobu'.

‖**zhuyin zimu** (dʒujin dzimu). Also with accents and (in Wade-Giles transliteration) as **chu-yin tzu-mu.** [Chinese, f. *zhùyīn* phonetic notation (f. *zhù* notes + *yīn* sound) + *zìmǔ* letters of the alphabet (f. *zì* word, character + *mǔ* mother).] The national phonetic alphabet of China made up of symbols based on Chinese characters, first adopted in 1918. Also *ellipt.* as **zhuyin.**

1938 E. M. NORTH *Bk. Thousand Tongues* 89/1 North Mandarin colloquial, Peking dialect, or Kuoyü... Chu Yin phonetics... Wang Chao phonetics... Roman characters. **1960** CHANG-TU HU et al. *China* v. 107 A set of thirty-nine phonetic symbols, *chu-yin tzu-mu*, officially promulgated in 1918 by the government. **1968** P. KRATOCHVÍL *Chinese Lang. Today* v. 168 The purpose of the first official Chinese phonemic transcription called *zhùyīn zìmǔ* 'Pronunciation Alphabet'.. was to serve as a stepping stone towards learning the characters, and also as a tool for promulgating the National Language. **1978** *Nagel's Encycl.-Guide: China* 95 The thirty-nine letters of the *zhuyin zimu* alphabet were taken from old, very simple Chinese characters.

‖**ziarat** (ziːˈɑːrət). Also 8 **zeearut; zearat, ziarath, ziarut.** [ad. Hindi f. Urdu, f. Arab. *ziyārat* pilgrimage.] A Muslim place of pilgrimage, a shrine; a pilgrimage to such a place.

1776 N. B. HALHED tr. *Code Gentoo Laws* xii. 187 Places of *zeeārut* (or religious Walks). **1913** *19th Cent.* May 993 This is said to occur frequently in the large shrines or Ziarats, such as Mashad. **1916** M. DIVER *Desmond's Daughter* II. ix. 121 A graphic tale of the manner in which his tribe had come by their first *ziarut*. **1925** *Blackw. Mag.* Dec. 796/2 That is where my brothre lives, Sahib; he likes to be next to his Ziarat. **1934** *N.-W. Frontier Province Gazetteer Peshawar Dist.* (ed. 3) I. i. 153 For the mass of the people the local *ziarats* have to suffice. **1967** F. RASUL *Bengal to Birmingham* vi. 61 At the appointed time, led by our group leader, we went for the *ziarath* (meeting the respected one). **1976** [see ZIKR].

zibeline (ˈzɪbəlɪn, -aɪn). Forms: 6 **zebelin,** 7 **-elline,** 7 **zibellin, -en, zubeline,** 8 **zebiline,** 8– **zibelin(e,** (9 **zibelline**). [ad. F. *zibeline* (also †*zabelline*, †*zebeline*, OF. *sebelin*), = It. *zibellino*, Sp. *z-*, *cebellina*, Pg. *zebelina*; Romanic deriv. of Slav. *sobol*: see SABLE *sb.*[1]]

1. A small carnivorous quadruped, the sable, *Mustela zibellina*. Also *attrib.*

1585 T. WASHINGTON tr. *Nicholay's Voy.* II. xxiii. 62 Furres of martirs, Zebelins, Sables. **1654** tr. *Martini's Conq. China* 9 Garnished round with.. skin three fingers broad, of Castor, or Zibellin. **1671** H. M. tr. *Erasm. Colloq.* 447 Clothed.. in cloth of Gold and Silver in Zebelline and African furs. **1784** KING *Cook's Voy. Pacific* VI. vi. 340 The common fox; the stoat, or ermine; the zibeline, or sable. **1808** ELEANOR SLEATH *Bristol Heiress* I. 177 The zibelin from her haunts decoy'd; Or chas'd the ermine from his cell. **1844** HUGH MURRAY *Trav. Marco Polo* I. §23. 133 The inside is lined with skins of ermine and zibelline.

2. The fur of the sable; sable.

1869 *Daily News* 7 Jan., Black velvet, trimmed all over with zibeline. **1889** *Pop. Sci. Monthly* May (1890) 34 In 1188 or thereabout no person was allowed to wear garments of vair, gray, zibeline, or scarlet color.

3. (Also *zibeline cloth.*) A soft smooth woollen material with a slightly furry surface, used for women's dress. Also *attrib.*

1892 *Daily News* 17 Dec. 5/7 Blue-grey zibeline cloth... A Czarina jacket of almond-coloured zibeline. **1893** *Lady* 17 Aug. 172/2 The cloths coming in are mostly beavers, thick zibeline finished beavers for choice. **1909** W. J. LOCKE *Septimus* ix, It was Emma. He recognized the zibeline toque and coat.

zibet (ˈzɪbɪt). Forms: 6– **zibeth,** 7 **zibith,** (**sebat**), 8– **zibet.** [ad. med.L. *zibethum* (cf. It. *zibetto*, F. *zibet*, G. *zibeth*): see CIVET *sb.*[1]] A variant of CIVET *sb.*[1], the animal and the perfume; used distinctively (after Buffon) for the Asiatic species of *Viverra*, *V. zibetha*, and the secretion it yields (called also *zibethum*).

1594 BLUNDEVIL *Exerc., Plancius' Map* (1597) 265 Next to her genitories, shee hath a little bagge into the which doth fall the precious greace or humour, which they call Ciuet and Zibeth. **1607** TOPSELL *Four-f. Beasts* 585 The Zibeth or Sivet-cat. **1669** *Addr. to hopeful yng. Gentry Eng.* 44 You would conceive.. that some Chymist had dearly purchas'd their more terrene excrements, out of them to exalt his occidental zibith. **1781** SMELLIE *Buffon's Nat. Hist.* (1791) V. 242 The zibet is probably the civet of Asia, of the East Indies, and of Arabia. **1843** *Penny Cycl.* XXVI. 406 The marks on the lateral and anterior parts of the neck are very dark in the Zibet.

b. Comb. †**zibet-muff**, a muff made of civet fur.

1685 *Lond. Gaz.* No. 2078/4 A Sebat Muff.

zibib (ˈzɪbɪb, ‖zəˈbib). Also **zibeeb.** [ad. Arab. *zabīb* dried grapes, (in Egypt) *zibib*.] A colourless, strongly alcoholic Egyptian drink made from raisins and drunk with added water, which turns it white.

Pronounced ('zɪbɪb) by N.Z. servicemen in Egypt in the 1939–45 war.—R.W.B.

1836 E. W. LANE *Acct. Manners & Customs Mod. Egyptians* II. i. 19 In the same manner, many *shurbetlees* (or sellers or sherbet) carry about for sale *zebeeb* (or infusion of raisins). **1958** L. DURRELL *Mountolive* ix. 181 He drank quite a lot of *zibib* according to the proprietor. **1977** J. HUTCHISON *Danger has No Face* (1978) iv. 41 Would I have a glass of zibeeb? He asked me. **1980** J. HOVE *Flowers of Forest* I. 8, I wandered..sherry glass in hand, imagining it zibib or some other sharp foreign drink.

zich, zick, dial. ff. SUCH, SICK.

ziczac ('zɪkzæk). Also **siksak, sagsag, sicsac, zi(c)kza(c)k.** [Ultimately a. Arab. *zaqzāq, saqsaq* (Dozy).] An Egyptian species of plover, *Pluvianus ægyptius* (*Charadrius melanocephalus*), which by its cry warns the crocodile of approaching danger; perhaps identical with the trochilus (see TROCHILUS[1] 1).

1844 W. D. COOLEY *Larcher's Notes Herod.* II. lxviii. I. 285 The bird called sagsag, or siksak, by the Arabs, is a species of plover. **1849** CURZON *Vis. Monast. Levant* xii. 150, I was on the point of firing at his [*sc.* a sleeping crocodile's] eye, when I observed that he was attended by a bird called a ziczac. **1882** PHIL ROBINSON *Noah's Ark* iii, Almost too lazy to keep his jaws open while the little 'sicsac' plover picked his teeth.

ziczac, variant of ZIGZAG.

zide, obs. or dial. f. SIDE.

Zidonian, obs. var. SIDONIAN.

Ziegfeld ('ziːgfɛld). The name of Florenz *Ziegfeld* (1869–1932), American theatre manager and producer, used *attrib.* with reference to the follies that he staged annually from 1907 to 1931; so ***Ziegfeld girl***, an actress taking part in such a revue.

1913 *Green Bk.* Jan. 72 Never before was so much beauty shown so much as in this latest of the Ziegfeld nonsensicalities. **1915** *New Republic* 31 July 336/1 Ziegfeld Follies 1915, a musical comedy produced by F. Ziegfeld Jr. **1917** *Ibid.* 7 July 278/1 If the Ziegfeld chorus were clothed in brown jaegers.., the paucity of the entertainment.. would be shockingly revealed. **1923** G. ADE *Let.* 9 Jan. (1973) 87 Do not permit encores unless actually demanded. This is most important and is the secret of the success of a good Ziegfeld show. **1929** etc. [see FOLLY *sb.*[1] 5 b]. **1932** G. GREENE *Stamboul Train* II. i. 70 A baronet had married a Ziegfeld girl. **1976** BOTHAM & DONNELLY *Valentino* iv. 35 He chatted to the Ziegfeld Follies girls.

Ziegler ('ziːglə(r)). *Chem.* The name of Karl *Ziegler* (1898–1973), German chemist, used *attrib.* to designate a trialkyl aluminium-titanium tetrachloride catalyst discovered by him for the synthesis of stereoregular isotactic polymers of high density and crystallinity from an ethylene or propylene monomer; also, *loosely*, = next.

1957 [see ISOPRENE]. **1961** [see STEREOREGULAR *a.*]. **1966** PHILLIPS & WILLIAMS *Inorg. Chem.* II. xxxiii. 560 This reaction is of interest in connexion with the polymerization of olefins by Ziegler catalysts. **1980** *Nature* 20 Mar. 213/3 [They] produced thin films by exposing acetylene gas to concentrated solutions of Ziegler catalysts.

Ziegler-Natta ('ziːglə 'nætə). *Chem.* The names of K. *Ziegler* (see prec.) and Giulio *Natta* (1903–79), Italian chemist, used *attrib.* to designate any catalyst of the class including the Ziegler catalyst, consisting in general of a transition metal halide and a non-transition metal organic derivative, and used with any olefin monomer. So ***Ziegler-Natta catalysis.***

1965 PHILLIPS & WILLIAMS *Inorg. Chem.* I. x. 382 Whereas the ionic catalysts appear to be capable of general use with any unsaturated molecule,.. Ziegler-Natta catalysts are usually employed in the polymerization of olefinic hydrocarbons—notably, ethylene and proplyene. **1974** *Encycl. Brit. Micropædia* X. 880/3 The Ziegler-Natta catalysts include many mixtures of halides of transition metals, especially titanium, chromium, vanadium, and zirconium, with organic derivatives of nontransition metals, particularly alkyl aluminium compounds. **1980** M. ORCHIN et al. *Vocab. Org. Chem.* xiv. 535 It has been suggested that Ziegler-Natta catalysis may involve metal-carbene formation.

Ziehl (tsiːl). *Bacteriol.* The name of F. *Ziehl* (1857–1926), German neurologist, used *attrib.* and in the possessive to designate a red stain consisting of an alcoholic solution of fuchsine in an aqueous solution of phenol; so **Ziehl-Neelsen** [F. K. A. *Neelsen* (1854–94), German bacteriologist], applied to a method for identifying acid-fast organisms such as tubercle bacilli by staining with Ziehl's stain, decolorizing with sulphuric acid (and sometimes also alcohol), and counterstaining with methylene blue: acid-fast organisms retain the original red colour.

1892 G. M. STERNBERG *Man. Bacteriol.* I. iv. 29 (*heading*) Carbol-fuschsin (Ziehl's solution). *Ibid.* 30 (*heading*) The Ziehl-Neelson [*sic*] method. **1967** K. M. SMITH *Insect Virol.* x. 189 Immature polyhedra in the nuclei of the hemolymph cells are easily differentiated by staining the smears with Ziehl fuchsin. **1974** R. M. KIRK et al. *Surgery* ii. 21 *Mycobacterium..tuberculosis*.. stained by the Ziehl-Neelsen method is acid-fast and alcohol-fast.

ziekle, obs. form of SICKLE.

1471 CAXTON *Recuyell* (1894) 16 He destroyed the vices in suche wyse as the ziekle cuttyth herbes.

zifer, obs. form of CIPHER *sb.*

ziff (zɪf). *Austral.* (and *N.Z.*) *slang.* [Origin unknown.] A beard.

1919 W. H. DOWNING *Digger Dialects* 54 *Ziff*, a beard. **1924** C. J. DENNIS *Rose of Spadgers* 137 'E lobbed in on us sudden, ziff an' all. **1934** *Bulletin* (Sydney) 2 May 25/4 All the Druids in that show wore long, white nightgowns and ziffs down to where the tops of their trousers should have been. **1947** J. MORRISON *Sailors belong Ships* 97 We all called him The Prophet. He had a long ziff. **1971** *N.Z. Listener* 19 Apr. 56/5 So up he goes and finds he knows one of them, the one with the ziff. **1981** G. KELLY *Always Afternoon* xii. 211 'Better get rid of that ziff,' she said pointing to his embryonic beard.

ziffius, obs. f. XIPHIAS, swordfish.

1590 SPENSER *F.Q.* II. xii. 24 Huge Ziffius, whom Mariners eschew No lesse, then rockes.

zig (zɪg), *sb.* and *v.* The first syllable of *zigzag*, used in the same way as ZAG. Hence **'zigging** *vbl. sb.* and *ppl. a.*

1969 *Southern Rev.* July 760 After that We drove back, zigging, cautious. **1971** G. EWART *Gavin Ewart Show* I. 11 An ant zigs quietly over the windowsill. **1977** *Time* 17 Oct. 24/3 The Carter Administration's push for Geneva will surely require much more shoving, not to mention zigging and zagging, in the weeks ahead if it is to succeed. **1978** H. WOUK *War & Remembrance* vii. 72 The transports were on a zig away. **1982** A. MELVILLE-ROSS *Trigger* v. 45 What's his course?..Go deep if it zigs towards us. *Ibid.* 53 'They've turned ninety degrees to starboard.'.. 'A zig, sir?' 'Afraid not. They've altered course.' **1983** *Sci. Amer.* July 14/2 Subtler to see is the line just below, whose zigging and zagging is 180 degrees out of phase with the top line. **1985** S. VANAUKEN *Under the Mercy* x. 246 One word more on change and development,..the zigs and zags and the farings forward on one's pilgrimage to God.

zig(g, variants of SIG *sb.*, urine.

zigabo, zigaboo, varr. JIGABOO.

zigan, early variant of TZIGANE.

‖**Zigeuner** (tsɪ'gɔɪnə(r)). fem. **-erin,** pl. **-erinnen.** [Ger., cogn. with ZINGANO, ZINGARO.] A gypsy. **Zi,geunerba'ron,** a gypsy baron (in allusion to the operetta *Der Zigeunerbaron* (1885) by Johann Strauss).

[**1841** G. BORROW *Zincali* I. I. 2 They are styled in Russia, Zigáni; in Turkey and Persia, Zingarri; and in Germany, Zigeuner.] **1845** THACKERAY *Legend of Rhine* x, in *G. Cruikshank's Table-Bk.* I. 198 Here should come the gleemen and jongleurs,..the dark-eyed nut-brown Zigeunerinnen. **1963** *Times* 12 Jan. 9/7 He was a violinist, a travelling musician. His coat had a black fur collar; he looked somewhat like a refined *Zigeunerbaron*. **1964** *Listener* 25 June 1043/3 His [*sc.* Bartók's] passion for the true Hungary and its folk-music as opposed to the *Zigeunerbaron* travesties. **1970** N. FREELING *Kitchen Bk.* xix. 184 There were no musicians, though I recognized Philippa's zigeuner guitarist.

zigge, obs. f. SAY *v.*[1]

zigger, zighyr, Cornish dial. ff. SICKER *v.*[2]

a **1843** SOUTHEY *Comm.-pl. Bk.* Ser. III. (1850) 725/1 The water zighyrs away. A Cornish mining word for dribbling, or flowing in a small stream. **1881** RAYMOND *Mining Gloss.*, *Zighyr, zigger,* or *sicker,* to percolate, trickle or ooze.

ziggety ('zɪgətɪ), *int.*, *adj.*, and *adv. slang* (orig. and chiefly *U.S.*). Also **ziggedy, ziggetty, ziggity.** [App. var. of (*hot*) *diggety* s.v. HOT *a.* 12 c.]

1. *int.* Usu. preceded by *hot* and followed by *dog* or another monosyllable: = *hot diggety* (*dog*) s.v. HOT *a.* 12 c.

1924 *Dialect Notes* V. 265 I'll be damned, hot ziggety damn. **1926** MAINES & GRANT *Wise-Crack Dict.* 9/2 *Hot ziggetty dog*, expressing unlimited admiration. **1933** R. JAMES *Worth Remembering* iii. 62 Hot ziggity zig! **1942** BERREY & VAN DEN BARK *Amer. Thes. Slang* §277/7 Hot ziggety! hot ziggety damn! *or* darn! hot ziggety dog! **1944** M. SHULMAN *Feather Merchants* xiii. 78 'Ziggetty!' he said. **1950** A. BUCKERIDGE *Jennings goes to School* viii. 155 Oh, hefty ziggety door knobs! **1961** R. LONGRIGG *Daughters of Mulberry* viii. 97 'Hot ziggety,' said an old American. 'That's six grand I made.' **1984** *New Yorker* 21 May 46/1 Mr. Deforest entered with his face bright, his hands folded behind him. 'Well, hot ziggetty, a holiday for me. What have we got going here?'

2. *adj.* and *adv.* = ZIGZAG *a.* and *adv.* Also redupl., as ***ziggety-zaggety.***

1935 J. T. FARRELL *Judgment Day* ii. 25 He pursued a ziggedy course along the sidewalk. **1956** H. GOLD *Man who was not with It* (1965) xi. 86, I had gone backwards to walk sideways, ziggety-zaggety.

‖**ziggurat, zikkurat** ('zɪgərət, 'zɪk-). [Assyrian *ziqquratu* (also *zigg-*, *sig(g)-*, *-ur(r)at*) height, pinnacle, top of a mountain, temple-tower; cf. *zaqaru* to be high (Muss-Arnolt).]

a. A staged tower of pyramid form in which each successive storey is smaller than that below it, so as to leave a terrace all round; an Assyrian or Babylonian temple-tower.

1877 tr. *Lenormat's Chaldæan Magic* xv. 227 The ziggurrat or sacred tower of the palace of Khorsabad. **1883** P. H. HUNTER *Story of Daniel* ix. 156 In all directions rise the lofty *ziggurats* or towers of the temples. **1898** *Engl. Hist. Rev.* Jan. 5 The ziggurat, or great tower, of which the Tower of Babel was a famous example. **1908** *Expositor* May 402 The zikkurats at Erech and Borsippa.

b. *transf.* and *fig.*

1959 *Times* 21 Oct. 11/3 The burnished ziggurats of copper saucepans. **1970** *Daily Tel.* (Colour Suppl.) 30 Oct. 26/3 The bags are abandoned, of course, and join the rest of the overkill of trash imagery, now heaped into ziggurats, festooning vegetation, scrawled in livid drifts on the downs. **1979** *Jrnl. R. Soc. Arts* Nov. 761/1 His Dallas Chapel in the form of a spiral ziggurat..borrows quite directly from the ninth-century minaret at Samarra. **1980** *Bee Culture* July 376 The photograph will give an idea of the real engineering performed to make this temple a 'ziggurat' of comb—upward from the base above the regular [honey]combs.

ziȝ, ziȝt, ziȝþe: see SEE *v.*, SIGHT.

zigsaw, zigzaw, obs. varr. JIG-SAW *sb.* b.

1912 H. MAXWELL *Early Chron. Rel. Scotl.* I. 16 One of those zigzaw puzzles which had a fleeting vogue two or three years ago. **1919** D. WYLLARDE *Holiday Husb.* xiii. 167 As neatly as if she had found the right pieces of a zigsaw puzzle.

zigzag ('zɪgzæg), *sb.*, *a.*, *adv.* Also as two words or with hyphen; also 8 **zic-zac, zigzac(k, ziczag.** [ad. F. *zigzag* (1680 in Hatz.-Darm.); ultimate origin unknown; partly symbolic, the two different vowels suggesting the two different directions. Cf. G. *zickzack* (Sperander, 1727), said to be first used of fortifications (sense 3 a).]

A. *sb.*

1. a. A series of short lines inclined at angles in alternate directions; a line or course having sharp turns of this kind; *concr.* something characterized by such lines or turns. Orig. in phr. ***in zigzag*** (= F. *en zigzag*).

1712 J. JAMES tr. *Le Blond's Gardening* 42 Steps of Grass laid in *Zic-Zac* [*Note*, The French call this an *Allée en Zic-Zac*, for its Likeness to a Machine so called]. *Ibid.* 215 Chevrons, or Checks of Grass in *Zig-Zac.* **1728** CHAMBERS *Cycl.* s.v. *Alley*, An Alley in Ziczac, is that which has too great a Descent. **1822** J. PARKINSON *Outl. Oryctol.* 139 The larger tubercles placed in zig-zag. **1892** E. REEVES *Homeward Bound* 299 Entering by the beautiful Gate of Justice, and winding in zigzag through the thickness of the tower.

1766 COLMAN & GARRICK *Cland. Marr.* II. ii, Here's none of your strait lines here—but all taste—zig-zag—crinkum crankum—in and out. **1830** M. DONOVAN *Dom. Econ.* I. 235 Twisted into a serpent, or bent into a zig-zag. **1856** MERIVALE *Rom. Emp.* xl. IV. 495 The other [road] was practicable for carriages, and for this purpose was made to climb the acclivity with a zigzag. **1871** NESBITT *Catal. Slade Coll. Glass* 6 Terminating with a turquoise zig-zag. **1880** MEREDITH *Tragic Com.* xi, Dashing his finger in a fiery zig-zag along the line for her pen to follow. **1884** RUSKIN *Pleas. Eng.* iii. §87. (1885) 121 The hieroglyphic use of the zigzag, for water, by the Egyptians.

b. Each of such lines or turns: chiefly in *pl.*

1728 POPE *Dunc.* I. 124 Nonsense precipitate, like running Lead, That slipp'd thro' Cracks and Zig-zags of the Head. **1775** TWISS *Trav. Port. & Sp.* 64 A winding road, which forms thirteen zig-zags. **1833** L. RITCHIE *Wand. Loire* 182 A cap, laced and ribanded in all manner of zig-zags. *a* **1861** CLOUGH *Poems, Ite Domum Saturae* 11 The lightning zigzags shoot across the sky. **1865** G. MACDONALD *Alec Forbes* lxxiv, The button made many a zigzag from side to side of the table. **1875** BENNETT & DYER *Sachs' Bot.* 742 The grand curve of growth..does not assume the form of a continuous curve, but shows a number of small zigzags.

c. *fig.*

1781 COWPER *Conversation* 861 Though such continual zig-zags in a book, Such drunken reelings, have an awkward look. **1796** BURKE *Regic. Peace* ii. Wks. 1842 II. 311 The fanaticks going straight forward and openly, the politicians by the surer mode of zigzag. **1815** JANE AUSTEN *Emma* xv, The little zigzags of embarrassment. **1913** ROOSEVELT *Autobiogr.* 579 Our policy is apt to go in zigzags, because different sections of our people exercise at different times unequal pressure on our government.

2. A road or path turning sharply at angles in alternate directions, esp. so as to reduce the gradient on a steep slope; each of the sharp turns forming such a road.

1728 SWIFT *My Lady's Lam.* 184 How proudly he talks Of zigzags and walks. **1848** THACKERAY *Bk. Snobs* vi, I thread the doubtful zig-zags of Mayfair. **1855** ALFORD in *Life* (1873) 250 Up the valley of the Adour to Arreau, a village approached by zigzags. **1890** 'R. BOLDREWOOD' *Col. Reformer* xiii, Many years before the Zig Zag [*sc.* railway in New South Wales] was chopped out of the sidelings.

3. Applied *spec.* to other things of a zigzag shape. **a.** *Fortif.* A trench leading towards a besieged place, constructed in a zigzag direction so as not to be enfiladed by the defenders; a boyau. **b.** *Archit.* A chevron-moulding. **c.** *Fishery.* (See quot.)

a. 1733 BUDGELL *Bee* IV. 67 A Battery began in the Morning to play upon the Cavalier of the Bastion Ghiera; the Night following the *Zic-zacs* were continued. **1834–47** J. S. MACAULAY *Field Fortif.* (1851) 239 The zig-zags may often require a greater relief than the parallels.

b. 1814 SCOTT *Border Antiq.* I. 59 The dancette, as the figure is termed in heraldry, or zig-zag. **1826** W. A. MILES *Deverel Barrow* 4 The chevron or zig zag, that favorite British ornament so prominent in Egyptian remains. **1884** RUSKIN *Pleas. Eng.* iii. §87. (1885) 119 The Norman zigzag.

c. 1875 Knight *Dict. Mech.*, *Zigzag*, a winding chute on the face of a dam to enable fish to ascend.

4. Collectors' name for a shell, or a moth, with zigzag marking.

1815 S. Brookes *Conchol.* 157 Zigzag, *Cypræa Ziczac.*

5. (**Zig(-)Zag.**) A proprietary name for cigarette paper.

1909 *Official Gaz.* (U.S. Patent Office) 14 Dec. 594/1 Braunstein & Cie, Paris... *Zig Zag...* Cigarette-paper. 1927 *Trade Marks Jrnl.* 13 Apr. 675 Zig-zag No. 114... Cigarette papers. Société anonyme des anciens Établissements Braustein Frères.., Paris. 1968 *Current Slang* (Univ. S. Dakota) Fall 52 *Zig-zag*, paper of high quality which is commonly used in rolling marijuana. 1977 C. McFadden *Serial* (1978) xxx. 67/1 She stuffed her.. Zig Zags back into her purse.

6. *attrib.*, as **zigzag machine**, a sewing machine with a swing needle that may be used to produce a zigzag stitch and decorative stitches derived from it.

[1950 *Vogue Pattern Book* Apr.–May 81/2 It was Pfaff that developed the famous Zig-Zag Model 130.] 1952 *Consumers' Res. Bull.* Sept. 11/1 All the zig-zag machines but one.. were heavy. 1963 *Which?* June 165/2 For plain zig zag machines, the *width* of the stitch limits the range of patterns they can make. 1978 *Detroit Free Press* 5 Mar. D14 (Advt.), Fashionmate zig zag machine featuring our front drop-in bobbin.

B. *adj.* 1. a. Having the form of a zigzag; turning sharply at angles in alternate directions; characterized by turns of this kind.

1750 Dobbs in *Phil. Trans.* XLVI. 543 Striking it with a wriggling Motion from Side to Side, in a zigzag Way. 1767 Hamilton *ibid.* LVIII. 11 Flashes of forked, or zig-zag lightning. 1784 Cowper *Task* II. 364 He.. transforms old print To zig-zag manuscript. 1792 Wordsw. *Descrip. Sketches* 236 Up from the lake a zigzag path will creep. 1835 Dickens *Sk. Boz, River*, Away jogs the boat in a zig-zag direction. 1860 Tyndall *Glac.* I. ii. 11 A kind of zigzag channel had been worn on the side of the mountain.

fig. 1798 Mathias *Purs. Lit.* (ed. 7) 327 Be regular: from A to B proceed; I hate your zig-zag verse, and wanton heed. 1861 J. Pycroft *Ways & Words* 192 The old joke of the zigzag jury who said 'Guilty' and 'Not guilty' alternately, all through the assizes. 1863 Cowden Clarke *Shaks. Char.* vi. 145 All the brood of zig-zag politicians. 1897 Goschen in *Hansard's Parl. Deb.* XLVII. 597 Our policy is to have as little of the zigzag policy.. as possible.

b. *Archit.* Applied to a moulding or other ornament of a zigzag pattern: cf. A. 3 b.

c 1765 Gray *Let. to Bentham* Wks. 1825 II. 286 The chevron-work (or zig-zag moulding). 1815 J. Smith *Panorama Sci. & Art* I. 136 Channels in various forms, some plain zigzag, some like network, and some spiral. 1840 C. Wordsw. *Greece* 58 Columns of green basalt, with fantastic zigzag ornaments.

c. *Bot.* Applied to the stem of a plant, or to a plant having such a stem.

1796 Martyn *Lang. Bot.* (ed. 2), *Zigzag*, used by some English writers for *Flexuose.* 1796 Withering *Brit. Plants* (ed. 3) III. 579 Zigzag Ladies smock. 1819 Rees *Cycl.*, *Zigzag Trefoil*,.. a term sometimes applied by farmers to the perennial red clover, marl grass, or wild red clover.

2. Having zigzag markings. (Chiefly *Nat. Hist.*)

1785 Latham *Gen. Syn. Birds* V. 61 Zigzag Bittern. 1796 Nemnich *Polygl.-Lex.* 946 Zigzag chama, *Venus castrensis.*

3. *Mil. slang* (chiefly *U.S.*). Drunk.

1918 Hamilton & Corbin *Echoes from over There* (1919) 125 He got a trifle zig-zag. 1919 W. H. Downing *Digger Dialects* 54 *Zig-zag*, drunk. 1923 E. Paul *Impromtu* 149 He groped and floundered.. not completely 'zigzag'. 1930 Brophy & Partridge *Songs & Slang Brit. Soldier* 181 *Zig-zag*, drunk. 1961 *Times* 27 Apr. 17/2 What is that to a nation which uses some 400 synonyms for 'drunk'—from 'all geezed up' to 'zig-zag'?

4. *Comb.*, as ***zigzag-shaped*** adj.; ***zigzag fashion***, ***-wise*** quasi-advbs.; **zigzag connection** *Electr. Engin.*, a form of star connection of three-phase circuits, each branch of which is interconnected and contains portions of two consecutive phases.

1758 Goldsm. *Mem. Prot.* (1895) II. 149 A Way very commodious cut, Zigzag Fashion. 1846 Brittan tr. *Malgaigne's Man. Oper. Surg.* 236 The interline is zigzag shaped. 1877 Huxley & Martin *Elem. Biol.* 26 Its joints are bent zig-zag-wise. 1922 P. Kemp *Alternating Current Electr. Engin.* (ed. 2) xiii. 188 This affects the magnetising current and may result in an appreciable increase in iron loss owing to flux distortion, and to minimize this effect zig-zag connections are sometimes adopted. 1947 R. Lee *Electronic Transformers & Circuits* iii. 47 Unbalanced direct current in the half-wave rectifiers requires larger transformers than in the full-wave rectifiers. This is partly overcome in three-phase transformers by the use of zigzag connections.

C. *adv.* In a zigzag manner or direction.

c 1730 Burt *Lett. N. Scot.* (1754) II. 132 It is almost incredible.. how nimbly they skip,.. turning *Zic Zac* to such Places as are passable. 1764 Veicht in *Phil. Trans.* LIV. 287 The lightening is observed to run not in strait line, but zig zag. 1846 Greener *Sci. Gunnery* 244 When he ignites a rocket, it may go straight forward, or zig-zag. 1862 Beveridge *Hist. India* III. viii. iv. 374 The road.. led zig-zag up the side of a precipitous mountain.

'zigzag, *v.* [f. prec. Cf. F. *zigzaguer.*]

1. a. *intr.* To go or move in a zigzag course; to have a zigzag course or direction. Also quasi-*trans.*, ***to zigzag it***, ***to zigzag one's way.***

1787 Burns *Let. to J. Richmond* 7 July, His horse.. zig-zagged across before my old spavined hunter. 1792 T. Twining in *Recr. & Stud.* (1882) 163 We.. zigzagged up to the very top. 1806–7 J. Beresford *Miseries Hum. Life* xviii. *Miseries Trav.* xix, The surprising range of rocks, zigzagging away in all directions. 1812 Colman *Br. Grins, Lady of Wreck* ii. xxvi, He had zigzagged many a league. 1861 Hughes *Tom Brown at Oxf.* ii, He managed to.. zigzag down Kennington reach.. with much labour. 1897 Jacobs *Skipper's Wooing* iii, He.. zigzagged his way back to the ship.

fig. [1787 Burns *Let. to Earl Buchan* Feb., While I was chalking out to you the straight way to wealth and character, with audacious effrontery you have zigzagged across the path.] 1825 Southey in *Corr. w. C. Bowles* (1881) 78 Not following the natural course of thought and feeling,.. but zig-zagging after the rhyme. 1825 Hor. Smith *Gaieties & Grav.* II. 245 The red and black had zig-zagged, or won alternately for fourteen times. 1901 G. Douglas *House with Gr. Shut.* xxiii, His courage zigzagged,.. one moment he towered in imagination, the next he grovelled in fear.

b. Of a sewing-machine: to make zigzag stitches.

1950 *Consumer Rep.* May 212/1 The *Necchis* [*sc.* sewing-machines] which zigzagged were inferior to the.. *Necchis* which didn't. 1956 *Sears, Roebuck Catal.* Fall–Winter 1068/1 Whether you want to embroider.. zig-zag or sew a straight seam, you'll find the '84' unsurpassed. 1976 *Woman's Weekly* 6 Nov. 68/2 (Advt.) It's a pocket-size sewing machine which you hold in one hand—that sews, bastes, hems, zig-zags, sews on buttons and even zippers.

2. a. *trans.* To give a zigzag form to; to trace a zigzag line upon. Chiefly in *pa. pple.*; see also zigzagged *a.*

1777 Pennant *Brit. Zool.* (ed. 4) IV. 98 White zigzagged with ferruginous edges crenulated. 1872 Howells *Wedd. Journ.* iii, The breast of the black cloud was now zigzagged.. by lightning. 1884 Bower & Scott *De Bary's Phaner.* 65 Its lateral margin.. toothed and zigzagged by the outgrowth of conically elongated cells.

b. To traverse in a zigzag manner.

1930 Bird & Ryan *Recall Public Officers* 42 He literally zigzagged the whole tremendous territory, visiting almost every hamlet. 1978 J. Wainwright *Ripple of Murders* 78 The vans.. zig-zagged the near-deserted streets.

3. To cause to move in a zigzag direction; *refl.* = 1.

1821 Clare *Vill. Minstrel* I. 115, I oft zigzag me round Thy uneven, heathy ground. 1889 Gretton *Mem. Harkb.* 49 To see him zigzag his large body through the mob from the vestry to the pulpit.

Hence **'zigzagging** *vbl. sb.* and *ppl. a.*

1827 Southey *Let. to Mrs. Hughes* 31 Dec., The zigzaging which it would be necessary to make in stage-coaches. 1861 E. T. Holland in *Peaks, Passes*, etc. Ser. ii. (1862) I. 85 We.. climbed a steep zigzagging ascent up the ridge. 1870 Lowell *Study Wind.* (1886) 14 One of these zigzagging blurs [*sc.* humming birds] came purring toward me. 1872 O. W. Holmes *Poet Breakf.-t.* viii, These zigzagging minds. 1893 *Athenæum* 15 July 90/1 The irritating task of zig-zagging through her volumes.

zigzagged ('zɪgzægd), *a.* [f. zigzag *sb.* or *v.* + -ed.] Having a zigzag form or marking.

1774 Goldsm. *Nat. Hist.* (1824) III. 62 The body oblong; the line running down the side zigzagged towards the tail. 1781 Warton *Hist. Oxf.* (1783) 4 The zigzagged semicircle of this arch. 1829 *Anniversary* 88 [The house] presents sundry crowfooted, alias zigzagged, gables. 1841 *Penny Cycl.* XXI. 86/1 On the external barbs of the caudal feathers are two zigzagged bands.

Hence **'zigzaggedly** *adv.*; **'zigzaggedness.**

1893 *Strand Mag.* VI. 693 It is in accordance with the general zig-zaggedness of things that the most popular residents in the fish-house are the birds. 1921 W. de la Mare *Mem. Midget* xxxiii. 230 How zigzaggedly you talk. What has poetry to do with Mr Crimble? 1977 R. Katz *Ziggurat* vi. 55 It [*sc.* a ball] rolled zigzaggedly for a while.

zigzaggery ('zɪgzægərɪ). [f. as prec. + -ery.] Zigzag course or proceeding (*lit.* and *fig.*).

In first quot. with allusion to zigzag *sb.* 3 a.

1760 Sterne *Tr. Shandy* III. iii, The transverse zigzaggery of my father's approaches towards it [*sc.* his coat pocket]. 1797 Mrs. A. M. Bennett *Beggar Girl* (1813) II. 248 One of those whimsical beings who hated the zig-zaggery of worldly wisdom. 1885 *Pall Mall Gaz.* 31 Aug. 4 The zigzaggery of the English Foreign Office.

zigzaggy ('zɪgzægɪ), *a.* [f. zigzag *sb.* + -y[1].] Characterized by zigzags or short sharp turns at alternate angles.

c 1845 Barham *Ingol. Leg.* Ser. iii. *Blasph. Warn.* 387 The zig-zaggy pattern by Saxons invented. 1865 W. White *East. Eng.* I. x. 135 We rambled in and out of strange zig-zaggy back ways. 1902 A. Lang in *Longman's Mag.* Sept. 481 A fortification in a sketch of the style of Vauban, a zig-zaggy, forked-lightning affair.

zig-zig, U.S. Mil. slang var. jig-a-jig.

1918 H. V. O'Brien *Diary* 30 Jan. in *Wine, Women & War* (1926) 18 Zig-zig—nothing else but. 1930 in S. Longstreet *Canvas Falcons* (1970) 271 Zig-zig wif me? 1962 W. Robinson *Barbara* (1964) 135 'Allo, baybee! Comment alley vooz—zigzig?

zik, zikere, obs. ff. sick, sicker *a.*

‖**zikr** (zikr). Also **zikir.** [ad. Arab. *ḏikr* remembrance.] A Muslim ritual prayer in which an expression of praise is continually repeated.

1836 E. W. Lane *Acct. Manners & Customs Mod. Egyptians* II. xi. 170 They had not yet begun their performances or *zikrs*, in concert; but one old durweesh, standing between the two rows, was performing a zikr alone; repeating the name of God (Allâh), and bowing his head each time that he uttered the word, alternately to the right and left. 1877 *Encycl. Brit.* VII. 114/1 The Zikr consists mainly in a chant, always becoming louder and more violent, of the first attribute [of God]. 1900 'Odysseus' *Turkey in Europe* v. 193 Dervishes.. have also their own characteristic form of worship called Zikr, consisting of the repetition, sometimes continued during several hours, of some religious formula, such as 'There is no God but God', or the ninety and nine names of the Deity. 1923 *Blackw. Mag.* Aug. 251/1 Dervishes shouting themselves into ecstasy at their zikr. 1954 M. Murray in G. B. Gardner *Witchcraft Today* 16 The solemn *zikr* of the Egyptian peasant. 1976 *Bangladesh Times* (Dacca) 12 Jan. 2/5 Monday, January 26: after Esha prayer Khatme Holy Quran, Khatme Gousia and Khatme Khajegan at 2 a.m. Zikir, Zearat and Munazat.

Zilavka (zɪ'lafkə). The name of a white wine of Yugoslavia.

1926 P. M. Shand *Bk. Wine* x. 255 *Bosnia-Herzegovina*.. The principal wines are the red growth of Blatina.. and the white Zilavka, a potent, greenish-yellow wine with a Muscatelle bouquet. 1954 M. Krippner *Yugoslavia Invites* 199 Zilavka, a yellow wine, and Blatina, a heavy claret, both come from Herzegovina. 1965 *Sun* 23 Jan. 6/6, I tried Zilavka—a wine.. from the Macedonian vineyards near the Greek frontier. 1978 *Chicago* June 220/2 We recommend Zilavka from Mostar vineyard, white but with enough richness and strength for meats.

zilch (zɪltʃ), *sb.* (and *a.*) *slang* (orig. and chiefly *U.S.*). [Origin uncertain.] Nothing, nil; also as *adj.*, no; non-existent.

[1931 *Ballyhoo* I. i. 1 (*heading*) President Henry P. Zilch. Chairman of the Board Charles D. Zilch. Treasurer Otto Zilch. *Ibid.* ii. 10 (*caption*) 'Mr. Zilch, you don't often stay in so long.' 'No I don't often lose my bathing trunks.' 1940 Berrey & Van den Bark *Amer. Thes. Slang* §184/1 *Dinglegoofer, Mr. Zilch*, indefinite nicknames.] 1966 *Current Slang* (Univ. S. Dakota) Winter 8 *Zilch*, adj. Nothing, zero... What a day—*zilch* from everybody. 1967 P. Welles *Babyhip* ii. 25 Half-starved, no doubt. The old whore probably fed him zilch. 1973 *Daily Colonist* (Victoria, B.C.) 14 Jan. 13/7, I feel that since I was elected to the board of directors last year I have accomplished zilch. 1976 *New Musical Express* 17 Apr. 6/6 My knowledge of classical music is zilch. 1976 *Billings* (Montana) *Gaz.* 27 June 2-E/2 In the light of data developed from the city's own 1975 studies, the 17th Street project rates zilch in priorities. 1977 *Tel.* (Brisbane) 3 Feb. 14/3 Gorgeous faces but zilch talent. 1977 *Playgirl* May 12/2 Our sex life is practically zilch, and he almost never pays any attention to me. 1984 *Daily Tel.* 8 Mar. 36/5 The power of the legislature over the executive being slightly better than zilch, any MP.. who bounces the Home Office deserves a small roll of drums. 1984 *Sounds* 1 Dec. 38/3 Three further 45s ensued in 1979 and '80, plus an album which didn't sell. After that, zilch.

‖**zillah** ('zɪlə). Also **zilla.** [Hind. *ḍilah* side, part, district, division.] An administrative district in British India. ***zillah parishad***: see parishad.

1800 *Asiat. Ann. Reg., Char.* 24 Within the zilla, or district of Calcutta. 1810 T. Williamson *E. Ind. Vade Mecum* II. 493 In each of the *zillahs*, or districts, only a collector, with an assistant, perhaps, was stationed. 1869 *Jrnl. Agric. Soc. India* I. 398 The Zillah of Huzareebag.

attrib. 1814 Heyne *Tracts on India* 323 Punishments.. executed.. by the Zillah judge. 1845 Stocqueler *Handbk. Brit. India* (1854) 340 Ahmedabad, 300 miles from Bombay, is a zillah station.

Hence **'zilladar**, the collector of a zillah.

1785 *Asiatic Misc.* I. 409 The riots paid their revenues to the Ziladars in the produce of the lands.

zillion ('zɪljən). *slang* (chiefly *U.S.*). [f. Z + m)illion.] A very large but indefinite number.

1944 D. Runyon *Runyon à la Carte* (1946) 165, I love him a zillion dollars' worth. 1947 *Esquire* May 40/2 Faithful to their zillions of fans. 1976 *National Observer* (U.S.) 10 Jan. 10/4 A zillion or so years ago, while I was a student nurse. 1976 J. Crosby *Snake* (1977) xvii. 93 She was going to break the story to her zillion readers. 1983 *Sunday Tel.* 9 Oct. 20/2 Broken Hill Proprietary.. is Australia's biggest company and a zillion times bigger than his own. 1984 *Guardian* 29 Oct. 9/2 The whiff of news managers at work, rather than an urge to hear about British Telecom's zillion-pound share sale from the horse's mouth, took me to BT's big press conference on Friday.

Hence **zillio'naire**, a very rich person; **'zillionth** *a.*, following very many others; 'umpteenth'; *sb.*, a tiny fraction *of* anything.

1946 D. Runyon *Runyon à la Carte* ix. 143 She plays the frost for all who are not well established as practically zillionaires. 1959 I. Fleming *Goldfinger* iv. 50 He's a zillionaire himself... He's crawling with money. 1969 *Daily Tel.* (Colour Suppl.) 15 Aug. 21/3 A sprinkling of.. Texas zillionaires, film stars, socialites and international playboys. 1972 *Good Housekeeping* Apr. 69/1 'We have strict controls on television,' said Mrs. Hamon [an American]. 'We don't hear a zillionth of what you hear.' 1975 *Listener* 24 Apr. 554/3 Anchorman Peter Snow.. said, for the zillionth time, 'Well, there it is.' 1983 'J. Gash' *Sleepers of Erin* xviii. 141 The Heindricks' scam was so big that even zillionaires were keen on its successful execution. 1984 *Listener* 6 Dec. 26/3 For the zillionth time, the hardback edition only is credited in reviews.

‖**zimb** (zɪmb). [Amharic.] A dipterous insect of Abyssinia, allied to and resembling the tsetse, and very destructive to cattle.

1790 Jas. Bruce *Trav.* I. 388 Large swarms of flies appeared wherever that loomy earth was... This insect is called *Zimb*... It is in size very little larger than a bee. a 1827 Good *Ps. cv. 31* (1854) 415 He spake, and the zimb-fly came.

Zimba ('zɪmbə). (A member of) an African people that was active in the vicinity of the Zambezi in the sixteenth century.

1901 G. M. Theal tr. J. dos Santos in *Rec. South-Eastern Africa* VII. xvii. 291 Facing Tete on the other side of the river.. there are two tribes of Kaffirs who eat human flesh, one called the Mumbos and the other the Zimbas or Muzimbas. 1913 C. A. Stigand *Land of Zinj* i. 17 The Zimba, a powerful tribe of barbarians who lived N.E. of Tete on the Zambezi, are now first heard of in these parts. In 1588 they invaded Kilwa, and the next year passed up the coast and invaded Mombasa. 1968 R. Oliver in J. Biggs-Davison *Africa—Hope Deferred* (1972) iii. 26 The Zimbas who swept up the east coast of Africa in the late sixteenth century. **1972** *Stand. Encycl. S. Afr.* VI. 341/1 Mirale occupied Mombasa in 1589, but the Portuguese received unexpected help from the interior when the mysterious cannibal Zimba tribe arrived from the south, destroying Mombasa and most of its occupants. **1974** *Encycl. Brit. Macropædia* XVII. 277/2 The Zimba.. were followers of a Manganja chief living to the south of the Shire River.

Zimbabwe (zɪmˈbɑːbweɪ, -bæb-). Also **zimbabwe.** [The name in Bantu of the first such ruin to be discovered, in what is now the State of Zimbabwe.] One of the numerous ruined stone-walled settlements scattered across Zimbabwe and neighbouring countries and dating from medieval times.

1902 HALL & NEAL *Anc. Ruins Rhodesia* iii. 36 They introduced fresh features in building, as shown.. by new Zimbabwes, which they erected. **1929** J. BUCHAN *Courts of Morning* II. 288 The subsidiary towers.. recalled in their shape pictures she had seen of the Rhodesian Zimbabwes. **1931** G. CATON-THOMPSON (*title*) The Zimbabwe culture. **1963** R. SUMMERS in E. Bacon *Vanished Civilisations* iii. 36/2 Other 'Zimbabwes'—over 200 of them..—lie scattered all over Southern Rhodesia. **1976** *Times* 17 July 14/6 Another, early, stone-walled *zimbabwe* of the type best known from the Great Zimbabwe ruins in Rhodesia has been discovered ..in Mozambique. **1980** *Nature* 1 May 5/3 In 1975..after independence in Mozambique one of the Zimbabwes—Manyikeni, 50 km west of Vilanculos was excavated.

Zimbabwean (zɪmˈbɑːbweɪən, -bæb-), *sb.* and *a.* [f. *Zimbabwe* (see below) + -AN.]

A. *sb.* **a.** Before 1980, when Rhodesia became Zimbabwe, (*a*) an African nationalist name for a Black Rhodesian; (*b*) an inhabitant of a future state of Zimbabwe. **b.** Since 1980, a native or inhabitant of Zimbabwe. **B.** *adj.* Of or pertaining to Zimbabweans or Zimbabwe.

1967 *Times* 30 Dec. 4 Let us work untiringly for the total mobilization of the four million Zimbabweans for Chimurenga (war of liberation). **1973** *Black Panther* 28 Apr. 9/1 (*caption*) Brother Kumbirai Kangai, freedom fighter in the Zimbabwean people's struggle. **1975** *Times* 11 Feb. 12/2 Whatever the future holds in store for an independent Zimbabwe, the white Zimbabwean will continue to play his part alongside his black counterpart. **1976** *Daily Tel.* 19 Aug. 14 Zimbabwean Nationalists who patiently tried a negotiated settlement cannot now be expected to lay down arms. **1979** *African Affairs* LXXVIII. 253 (*heading*) Zimbabwean economic and social historiography since 1970. **1984** *News* (Mexico City) 12 Mar. 7/2 Nkomo.. suggested Zimbabweans were no freer than they were under the white-minority colonial government.

zimbalom, -n, var. CIMBALOM, CIMBELOM.

1910 F. W. GALPIN *Old Eng. Instrum. Music* iv. 66 The large Dulcimer, used in Hungarian Bands at the present time, is known by the Magyar musicians as the *zimbalom.* **1925** *Glasgow Herald* 17 Oct. 6/2 The zimbalon, which is an improved type of dulcimer, has been honoured with a d.-s. record made by Nitza Godolban. **1975** *New Yorker* 19 May 90/1, I spent two weeks in Shiraz and Persepolis, listening for hours every day to percussion from all over the world:.. to varieties of dulcimer (zither, santir, zimbalon).

‖**zimbel** (ˈtsɪmbəl). *Mus.* [Ger., ad. L. *cymbalum* (see CYMBAL).] = CYMBAL 3.

1910 F. W. GALPIN *Old Eng. Instrum. Music* xiv. 264 We also find an organ-stop called the *Zimbel*.. and this.. was a compound stop or mixture intended to represent the sound of bells. **1976** *Gramophone* Oct. 628/3 An exuberant finale contrasts the zimbel with the cornet. **1980** *New Grove Dict. Mus.* XIII. 791/1 'Mixture' was normally used to denote the Principal-scaled chorus Mixture as distinct from the high Zimbeln or the solo Cornets.

zimes, var. TZIMMES.

[**zimme,** spurious word; being the OE. *ȝimm* gem, with the *ȝ* taken for a *z*.

1848 LYTTON *Harold* II. iii, Taking from his own neck a collar of zimmes.. of great price. *Ibid.* III. ii, His diadem, with the three zimmes shaped into a triple trefoil.]

Zimmenthal, var. SIMMENTAL.

Zimmer (ˈzɪmə(r)). Also **zimmer.** [Maker's name.] A proprietary name for orthopædic appliances, used esp. *attrib.* to designate a kind of walking frame.

1951 *Trade Marks Jrnl.* 11 Apr. 358/1 *Zimmer*... Orthopaedic appliances and instruments. Zimmer Orthopaedic Limited,.. London, W.1..; manufacturers. **1957** *Official Gaz.* (U.S. Patent Office) 16 Apr. TM 116/2 *Zimmer.* For orthopedic appliances and fracture equipment. First use in May of 1927. **1974** PASSMORE & ROBSON *Compan. Med. Stud.* III. II. xxxiv. 103/1 For patients with unsteadiness and ataxia, a simple walking frame of 'Zimmer' pattern is valuable. **1981** *Church Times* 10 Apr. 14/4, I had felt too ill to try and use my zimmer-frame and calipers. **1982** E. DEWHURST *Whoever I Am* iii. 44 Incapable of walking without a Zimmer frame.

zimome: see ZYMOME.

zinc (zɪŋk), *sb.* Forms: 7–9 **zink,** (7 **zinke,** 7–8 **zinck**), 8– **zinc.** [ad. G. *zink* (of obscure origin), whence also late 17th c. F. *zinc* (†*zinch,* †*zin,* †*zain*), Sw., Da. *zink,* etc., mod.L. *zincum.*]

1. a. A hard bluish-white metal (commercially known as SPELTER), brittle at ordinary temperatures, but malleable and ductile between 200° and 250°F.; obtained from various ores, esp. the sulphide (BLENDE), the carbonate and silicate (CALAMINE, SMITHSONITE), and the red oxide (ZINCITE), and used for roofing, for coating or 'galvanizing' sheet-iron, and for numerous other purposes; it forms several alloys, of which the best known is that with copper called BRASS. Chemical symbol Zn; atomic weight 65.

1651 FRENCH *Distill.* v. 139 Any sulphurous, and imperfect metall, as Iron, Copper, or Zinke. **1731–3** P. SHAW *Chem. Lect.* xviii. (1755) 409 We took six Ounces of Copper, and melted it in a Wind-Furnance, added to it an Ounce of Zink. **1813** SIR H. DAVY *Agric. Chem.* ii. (1814) 48 Zinc is one of the most combustible of the common metals. **1871** TYNDALL *Fragm. Sci.* (1879) II. xiv. 344 The metal zinc may be burnt in oxygen. **1878** BROWNING *Poets of Croisic* viii, Zinc's uncontrolled Flake-brilliance.

b. (with *pl.*) A plate of zinc used as the electropositive metal in a voltaic battery. (Cf. ZINCODE.)

1876 PREECE & SIVEWRIGHT *Telegraphy* 29 If the zincs are scraped clean and the solution of sal-ammoniac kept up.

c. Galvanized iron. Chiefly *S. Afr.* and *W. Indies.* Cf. *zinc roof* in sense 2 c below.

1873 F. BOYLE *To Cape for Diamonds* xix. 252 These hoppers are made of perforated zinc, or wire, the latter being preferable. **1953** R. MAIS *Hills were Joyful Together* I. vi. 57 Surjue went through a zinc fence—through a hinged zinc sheet in a zinc fence that looked like a solid stretch of iron sheeting down one side of a lane. **1973** *Eastern Province Herald* (Port Elizabeth) 23 Jan., The brazier, zink bath and cooking utensils.. were obtained from Coloureds in the area. **1977** *Daily Express* 29 Jan. 7/3 All six members of the cast take turns to strip off and bathe in a zinc bath.

d. The zinc-covered bar of a café or public house; by metonymy, a café. (A gallicism.)

1914 *19th Cent.* Feb. 286 Elections are made or marred *chez le marchand de vin,* or, as the Parisians familiarly call him, le *mastroquet*... The 'organised democracy marching towards the good of progress and liberty, etc.'.. is in reality nothing else than the disorganised and demoralised *plebs* marching towards the *zinc* of the *mastroquet.* *a* **1936** KIPLING *Something of Myself* (1937) iv. 81 My barmaid.. had watched it [*sc.* evil] across the zinc she was always swabbing off. **1948** W. FORTESCUE *Beauty for Ashes* xx. 148 We even supplied a little bar with a *zinc* and a motherly Frenchwoman to look after it. **1965** V. CANNING *Whip Hand* xii. 138, I.. tottered to the nearest zinc, and called for a triple cognac. **1979** A. M. STEIN *Rolling Heads* vi. 103 The last of the cafés shut down—it was a laborers' zinc down a back street.

2. *attrib.* and *Comb.* **a.** attrib. Made or consisting of zinc, as ***zinc dish, filings, gauze, plate, wire***; containing or made with zinc, as ***zinc amalgam, bath, -lining, lotion, ointment, ore, plaster***; *spec.* in names of chemical compounds, as ***zinc carbonate, oxide, salt,*** etc.; pertaining to or used in connexion with zinc, as ***zinc furnace.*** **b.** objective and instrumental, as ***zinc-etching, printing, -worker; zinc-coated, -covered, -lined, -plated, -roofed, -topped*** adjs. **c.** Spec. comb.: **zinc-air** *a.*, applied to a type of primary cell employing a zinc anode, a porous carbon cathode able to utilize atmospheric oxygen, and an alkaline electrolyte; **zinc-alum, -amide** (see quots.); **zinc-blende,** native zinc sulphide = BLENDE; **zinc-bloom** [tr. G. *zinkblüthe* (Karsten, 1808)], hydrous carbonate of zinc, hydrozincite; **zinc chloride,** a white, crystalline, deliquescent solid, $ZnCl_2$, used as a preservative, a flux, and in Leclanché cells; **zinc chromate,** a toxic, yellow, water-insoluble powder, $ZnCrO_4$, used as a pigment; **zinc chrome** = *zinc yellow* below; **zinc-dust,** zinc in the form of fine powder (often mixed with zinc oxide and other impurities), obtained by grinding, or in the extraction of zinc from its ores, and used as a deoxidizing agent and as a paint (see *zinc-grey*); **zinc-foil,** thin sheet zinc; **zinc green,** a mixture of zinc and cobalt oxides used as a pigment; **zinc-grey,** (*a*) zinc-dust obtained by grinding in oil, used as a preservative paint for ironwork; (*b*) a colour resembling that of zinc; **zinc-iron,** *sb.* an alloy of zinc and iron; *adj.* consisting of zinc and iron; **zinc-plate** = *zinc-foil*; **zinc-powder** = *zinc-dust*; **zinc roof** *S. Afr.* and *W. Indies,* a corrugated roof of galvanized iron; **zinc spar,** an old name for native zinc carbonate (= CALAMINE, SMITHSONITE 2); **zinc-spinel** = GAHNITE (Dana *Min.* 1868); **zinc-sponge** (see quot.); **zinc sulphide,** (*U.S.*) **sulfide,** a yellow, water-insoluble powder, ZnS, used as a pigment and as a phosphor; **zinc-vitriol,** sulphate of zinc, white vitriol (Jameson *Syst. Min.,* 1805, II. 35); **zinc white,** oxide of zinc used as a white paint; **zinc yellow,** a greenish-yellow pigment consisting principally of zinc chromate.

1970 C. L. MANTELL *Batteries & Energy Systems* vi. 63 These portable *zinc-air batteries are being used in man-pack transceivers, night vision devices, and space satellite communications. **1978** *Jrnl. Electrochem. Soc.* CXXV. 333C/2 The Gould zinc-air button cell is.. used in hearing aids and other devices which require a moderately high current. **1851** WATTS tr. *Gmelin's Handbk. Chem.* V. 46 Sulphate of Alumina and Zinc-oxide.—*Zinc-alum = $ZnO,SO^3 + Al^2O^3,3SO^3 + 24Aq.$ **1839** URE *Dict. Arts* 166 Dilute muriatic acid, containing some wine stone and *zinc amalgam. **1859** WATTS tr. *Gmelin's Handbk. Chem.* XIII. 503 Action of Zinc-ethyl on Ammonia.. after a little while, *zinc-amide NH^2Zn separates out. **1843** R. J. GRAVES *Syst. Clin. Med.* xxvii. 339 During the year 1827, the venereal patients took on the whole 14 saline baths, 38 *zinc baths. **1842** T. GRAHAM *Elem. Chem.* 573 The principal ores of zinc are calamine.. and *zinc blende. *Ibid.* 575 The mineral substance, *zinc bloom. **1851** WATTS tr. *Gmelin's Handbk. Chem.* V. 9 The precipitated *zinc-carbonate is washed.. by subsidence and decantation. **1851** H. WATTS tr. *Gmelin's Hand-bk. Chem.* V. xxviii. 32 ZnCl, 9ZnO.. [is prepared] by precipitating aqueous *zinc-chloride with an insufficient quantity of ammonia and filtering immediately. **1911** *Encycl. Brit.* XXVIII. 984/1 Zinc chloride, $ZnCl_2$, is produced by heating the metal in dry chlorine gas, when it distils over as a white translucent mass. **1981** BRADY & HOLUM *Fund. Chem.* xx. 700 Zinc chloride, which is exceptionally soluble in water.., has a range of uses that extend from embalming, to fireproofing lumber, to the refining of petroleum. **1851** H. WATTS tr. *Gmelin's Hand-bk. Chem.* V. xxviii. 48 The crystals.. really consisted of ordinary zinc-sulphate containing small quantities of *zinc-chromate intimately bound up with them. **1974** *Encycl. Brit. Macropædia* IV. 571/2 Zinc yellow, a basic zinc chromate, is used as a corrosion-inhibiting primer on aircraft parts fabricated from aluminum or magnesium. **1892** G. H. HURST *Painters' Colours, Oils, & Varnishes* iv. 132 *Zinc chrome is a yellow pigment of good colour and body. **1963** *Times* 22 Apr. 6/5 Zinc chromes, with zinc chromate as the major constituent, form an important class of pigments. **1930** *Jrnl. Iron & Steel Inst.* CXXI. 749 An investigation of the corrosion fatigue of *zinc-coated steel specimens. **1981** M. C. SMITH *Gorky Park* III. iv. 361 The sables.. climbed zinc-coated mesh walls. **1890** A. CONAN DOYLE *Firm of Girdlestone* xxx. 238 A very seedy-looking individual.. was leaning with his elbows upon the *zinc-covered counter. **1883** *Hardwich's Phot. Chem.* (ed. 9) 330 *Zinc dishes must not be used. **1877** *Jrnl. Chem. Soc.* I. 468 Action of *Zinc-dust on the Chlorides of Sulphoparabromobenzoic Acid. **1890** W. J. GORDON *Foundry* 216 In the *zinc-etching systems the gelatin is spread on the zinc. **1809** J. MURRAY *Syst. Chem.* (ed. 2) III. 305 The concrete phosphoric acid, heated with *zinc-filings, is decomposed. **1851** WATTS tr. *Gmelin's Handbk. Chem.* V. 4 To obtain zinc-plate, or *zinc-foil, the metal cast in a tabular form is heated in a boiling solution of common salt, and then passed between rollers. **1878** *Ure's Dict. Arts* IV. 1006 *Zinc Furnace for the Distillation of Zinc combined with Lead. **1844** H. STEPHENS *Bk. Farm* I. 214 The windows should be protected.. with fly *zinc-gauze. **1847** *Brit. Pat. 11,616* 5 Processes for manufacturing on a large scale zinc yellow.. and *zinc green. **1973** E. LALOR in T. C. Patton *Pigment Handbk.* I. 850/1 Much of the zinc yellow manufactured was mixed with Prussian blue to make various shades of a permanent zinc green. **1881** RAYMOND *Mining Gloss.,* **Zinc-gray,* see *Zinc-dust.* **1900** *Westm. Gaz.* 11 Jan. 3/2 Zinc grey is very much worn. **1849** NOAD *Electricity* (ed. 3) 177 The *zinc-iron circuit. **1868** DANA *Min.* (ed. 5) 149 Kreittonnite, or Zinc-Iron Gahnite. **1882** *Encycl. Brit.* XIV. 385/2 The leather is rolled and compressed on a level *zinc-lined wooden bed. **1912** C. N. MOODY *Saints of Formosa* vi. 132 Boxes had to be made or furnished with *zinc-lining. **1899** *Allbutt's Syst. Med.* VIII. 522 *Zinc lotions. **1843** R. J. GRAVES *Syst. Clin. Med.* xxvi. 332 *Zinc ointment. **1808** *Zinc ore [see GAHNITE]. **1839** URE *Dict. Arts* 1330 The mineral genus called zinc-ore.. is denser than either of the above. **1849** D. CAMPBELL *Inorg. Chem.* 223 Small quantities of iron and *zinc oxides. **1899** *Allbutt's Syst. Med.* VIII. 579 A simple *zinc plaster will be as much as the skin will tolerate. **1823** J. BADCOCK *Dom. Amusem.* 126 A *zinc plate of ten inches was immersed in the liquid. **1859** G. A. SALA *Twice round Clock* 117 There is the rotunda of the Bank of England, with its many-slamming, *zinc-plated doors. **1966** *McGraw-Hill Encycl. Sci. & Technol.* IV. 531/1 Zinc-plated coatings are usually purer than hot-dipped coatings. **1881** *Jrnl. Chem. Soc.* XXXIX. 462 Two grams of the *zinc powder are weighed out. **1875** *Ure's Dict. Arts* III. s.v., *Zinc printing.. can be applied with great advantage for certain purposes in the etching style, for maps, plans,..&c. **1883** 'R. IRON' *Story Afr. Farm* I. I. i. 11 The *zinc roofs of the out-buildings, the stone walls of the 'kraals', all reflected the fierce sunlight. **1946** U. KRIGE *Way Out* vi. 82 There was a mass of dry maize leaves under a zinc roof jutting out from the wall. **1899** *Blackw. Mag.* Feb. 312 The *zinc-roofed bungalow. **1841** BRANDE *Chem.* (ed. 5) 777 When hydroferrocyanic acid is added to a soluble *zinc-salt. **1881** RAYMOND *Mining Gloss.,* **Zinc-scum,* the zinc-silver alloy skimmed from the surface of the bath in the process of desilverization of lead by zinc. **1905** *Times* 6 July 14/6 *Zinc sheets quiet at late rates. **1796** KIRWAN *Elem. Min.* (ed. 2) II. 236 *Zinc Spar. **1902** *Encycl. Brit.* XXVIII. 110/2 The deposition of pure zinc is beset with many difficulties,..unless the conditions are closely watched, it is liable to be thrown down in a spongy form... Siemens and Halske have proposed the addition of oxidising agents such as free halogens, to prevent the formation of zinc hydride, to which they attribute the formation of *zinc-sponge. **1851** WATTS tr. *Gmelin's Handbk. Chem.* V. 14 The solution of *zinc-sulphate is mixed with sal-ammoniac. **1868** *Fownes' Chem.* (ed. 10) 398 Zinc sulphate.. is used.. as an emetic. **1851** H. WATTS tr. *Gmelin's Hand-bk. Chem.* V. xxviii. 19 Nöggerath and Bischof.. found in an old mine a quantity of *zinc-sulphide mixed with washings of the ore. **1937** *Discovery* Feb. 44/2 The [television] screen is coated with a powder consisting of zinc sulphide and other chemicals. **1974** *Encycl. Brit. Micropædia* X. 883/3 Zinc sulfide is insoluble in water but dissolves in mineral acids. **1938** E. AMBLER *Cause for Alarm* (1940) xiii. 203 A *zinc-topped bar and four marble-topped tables. **1847** *Brit. Pat. 11,616* 9 The dryer is added to the color prepared with the *zinc white. **1849** *Weale's Dict. Terms* s.v., Zinc white is valuable.. in painting, on account of its durability both in oil and water. **1803** *Med. Jrnl.* X. 58 He placed the *zinc wire on the tongue. **1858** SIMMONDS *Dict. Trade,* **Zinc worker and drawer,* a preparer of zinc for making into wire. **1847** *Zinc yellow [see *zinc green* above]. **1901** A. C. WRIGHT tr. *Bersch's Manuf. Mineral & Lake Pigments* xiv. 152 Zinc yellow may be prepared by the immediate precipitation of a solution of zinc sulphate by a solution of potassium chromate. **1974** *Encycl. Brit. Macropædia* XIII. 889/1 Zinc yellow has a greenish cast because of a high content of chromic oxide.

d. As *adj.*: Having a basically greyish colour.

1922 'K. MANSFIELD' *Let.* 11 Aug. (1977) 271 A zinc greengage or two. **1960** *New Yorker* 1 Oct. 44/2 Faultless eyes gone blank beneath the immense Zinc-and-gunmetal northern sky.

zinc (zɪŋk), *v.* Inflected **zinced, zin(c)ked** (zɪŋkt), **zincing, zin(c)king** ('zɪŋkɪŋ). [f. prec. *sb.*] *trans.* To cover or coat with zinc or some compound of zinc (esp. ironwork, as a preservative from rust); to treat with zinc, add zinc to. Hence **zinced** (zɪŋkt) *ppl. a.*, **zincing** ('zɪŋkɪŋ) *vbl. sb.*

1841 *Civil Eng. & Arch. Jrnl.* IV. 328/2 Improvements.. in tinning or zincing metal. *Ibid.* 353/2 Zinked nails and bolts. **1841** BRANDE *Chem.* (ed. 5) 731 The advantage of zinced iron. **1843** *Pract. Mech. & Eng. Mag.* II. 342 These processes enable us to zinc in an economical manner, iron, steel [etc.]. *Ibid.*, An estimate for zinking the suspension bridge at Hungerford Market. **1890** *Jrnl. Franklin Inst.* Nov. 401 The conditions under which the zincked pipe is to be used. **1891** J. A. PHILLIPS & BAUERMAN *Elem. Metall.* (ed. 3) 700 Parkes's process, or, as it is now frequently called, 'zincing'. **1895** MORRIS in Mackail *W.M.* (1899) II. 319 The little barn finished with a zinked iron roof.

‖**Zincalo** ('zɪŋkələʊ), *fem.* **-ala**. Pl. -ali. [The name by which the Gitanos of Spain call themselves. Cf. ZINGANO, etc.] A Spanish gipsy.

1842 BORROW *Bible in Spain* ix, The Zincali, Gitános, or Spanish gypsies. **1868** GEO. ELIOT *Sp. Gypsy* I. 137 Before you dreamed You were a born Zincala—in the bonds Of the Zincali's faith.

zincate ('zɪŋkeɪt). *Chem.* [f. ZINC *sb.* + -ATE[4].] A compound which may be regarded as a combination of the oxide of zinc (*zincic oxide*) with that of a more electropositive metal.

1872 WATTS tr. *Gmelin's Handbk. Chem.* Index 330/1.

zincian ('zɪŋkɪən), *a. Min.* [f. ZINC *sb.* + -IAN 2.] Of a mineral: having a (small) proportion of a constituent element replaced by zinc.

1930 W. T. SCHALLER in *Amer. Mineralogist* XV. 571 Zinc —zincian. **1968** I. KOSTOV *Mineralogy* ix. 498 Pisanite is a cuprian variety..; sommairite zincian melanterite. **1977** *Amer. Mineralogist* LXII. 463/2 The proportion of zinc is probably insufficient to justify a new name... It might, therefore, be called a zincian takovite.

zincic ('zɪŋkɪk), *a.* Also **zinckic**. [ad. mod.L. *zincicus*, f. *zincum* ZINC.] Of, pertaining to, or containing zinc. ***zincic oxide***, oxide of zinc, regarded as the source of the compounds called *zincates*.

1860 MAYNE *Expos. Lex.*, *Zincicus*..Berzelius terms *Oxydum zincicum* the second degree of oxidation of zinc.. zinzic [*sic*]. **1869** *Jrnl. Chem. Soc.* XXII. 33 The mixture of ethylic zincodiethoxalate and zincic iodide.

zinciferous (zɪŋ'kɪfərəs), *a.* Also (in Dicts.) **zinckiferous, zinkiferous.** [f. ZINC *sb.*: see -FEROUS.] Containing or producing zinc.

1820 *Amer. Jrnl. Sci.* II. 323 The black zinciferous mineral, the Franklinite. **1828–32** WEBSTER, Zinkiferous.

zincify ('zɪŋkɪfaɪ), *v.* Also (in Dicts.) **zinkify**. [f. ZINC *sb.*: see -FY.] *trans.* To coat or impregnate with zinc. Hence ˌ**zincifi'cation** (zɪnk-), the process of zincifying, or state of being zincified.

1801 COLERIDGE in *Sir H. Davy's Rem.* (1858) 89 My motive muscles tingled and contracted at the news,..as if you..were zincifying their life-mocking fibres. **1891** EISSLER *Metall. Argent. Lead* 304 Argentiferous zinc may settle in the cavities during zincification.

zincite ('zɪŋkaɪt). *Min.* Also (in Dicts.) **zinckite, zinkite.** [f. ZINC *sb.* + -ITE[1].] A native oxide of zinc, of a deep-red or orange-yellow colour, found in New Jersey; red oxide of zinc, red zinc ore.

1854 DANA *Min.* (ed. 4) II. 100 Zincite Group.

zinckenite ('zɪŋkənaɪt). *Min.* Also **zink-**. [ad. G. *zinkenit* (G. Rose, 1826), named in honour of J. K. L. *Zincken*, director of Anhalt mines.] A steel-grey sulphide of antimony and lead.

1835 *R. D. & T. Thomson's Rec. Gen. Sci.* I. 272 Combinations of sulphuret of antimony and sulphuret of lead in different proportions, viz.: zinkenite,..Plagionite, Federerz, Bournonite.

zinckic, -iferous, -ite: see ZINCIC, etc.

zincky: see ZINKY.

zinco ('zɪŋkəʊ), abbreviation of ZINCOGRAPH.

1887 *Scott. Leader* 23 Nov. 5 The zinco has some resemblance to Mr. G. **1889** *Athenæum* 26 Oct. 541/2 Drawings Wanted (on litho paper for zincoing) for a Provincial Journal. **1891** *Cost of Production* (ed. 2) 44 Various 'processes' of which the 'zinco-process' is one of the commonest.

zinco-, combining form of mod.L. *zincum* ZINC. **a.** In terms denominating chemical compounds containing zinc and some other element or radical, as ***zinco-aluminic***, ***-ammonic***, etc. adjs.; ***zinco-sulphate***, etc. **b.** In various other terms: **zincocalcite** (zɪŋkəʊ'kælsaɪt) *Min.* (see quot. 1892); **zincolysis** (zɪŋ'kɒlɪsɪs) [after ELECTROLYSIS], decomposition by an electric current (as in a voltaic cell of which the anode consists of zinc), electrolysis; so **zincolyte** ('zɪŋkəʊlaɪt), a substance thus decomposed, an electrolyte; **zinco'polar** *a.*, having the polarity of the zinc plate or zincode of a voltaic cell; **'zincotype** = ZINCOGRAPH.

1842 T. GRAHAM *Elem. Chem.* 209 The surface of the zinc presented to the acid has zincous affinity, or is zinco-polar. *Ibid.* 222 On the electrical hypothesis a body which is thus decomposed in the active cells..is called an *electrolyte*,.. and this kind of decomposition is distinguished as *electrolysis*. The chemical expressions equivalent to these are *zincolyte* and *zincolysis*. **1851** WATTS tr. *Gmelin's Handbk. Chem.* V. 36 Carbonate of Zinc-oxide and Ammonia.—Zinco-ammonic Carbonate. *Ibid.* 481 Zinco-cupric Sulphate. **1869** *Eng. Mech.* 19 Mar. 575/2 White lead is..more siccative than the zinco-sulphate. **1889** *Athenæum* 12 Oct. 492/2 The two volumes are copiously illustrated by a zincotype process. **1890** WOODBURY *Encycl. Phot.* 535 In Zincotypes the zinc is first coated with bitumen or bichromated gelatine or albumen. **1892** *Dana's Min.* (ed. 6) 269 *Zincocalcite.* Contains some zinc carbonate; one specimen from Olkucz, Poland, gave Gibbs 4·07 ZnO. **1892** *Daily News* 23 Sept. 8/6 Zincotyper is open for Engagement.

zincode ('zɪŋkəʊd). *Electr.* [f. mod.L. *zincum* ZINC + Gr. ὁδός path, after ANODE, etc.] The positive (zinc) plate (anode) of a voltaic cell.

1839 [see PLATINODE].

zincography (zɪŋ'kɒgrəfɪ). [f. ZINCO- + -GRAPHY.] The art or process of engraving or etching designs on zinc, or of printing from such designs. Hence **zincograph** ('zɪŋkəʊgrɑːf, -æ-) *sb.*, a design or impression produced by zincography; **'zincograph** *v. trans.*, to engrave or print by zincography; **zin'cographer**, one who practises zincography, an engraver on zinc; **zinco'graphic** *a.*, pertaining to or produced by zincography.

1834 *New Monthly Mag.* XLII. 523 The art of zincography has several advantages over that of lithography. **1839** URE *Dict. Arts* 1334 Zinc is extensively employed for making..plates for the zincographer. **1850** ANSTED *Elem. Geol., Min.* etc. §469 [Zinc] is also engraved on (instead of stone) for zincographic printing. **1865** *Athenæum* 18 Feb. 239/2 An ancient map zincographed. **1870** *Eng. Mech.* 14 Jan. 429/3 The..zincographic plate is brought under the roller. **1888** *Edin. Rev.* Jan. 231 Reproduced in 'zincograph' by the aid of photography. **1890** *Munim. Royal Burgh Irvine* I. Introd. p. xxxii, Zincographs of these stones.

zincoid ('zɪŋkɔɪd). [f. ZINC + -OID.] = ZINCODE.

1842 T. GRAHAM *Elem. Chem.* 216 On the electrical hypothesis, the same plates are variously denominated: The zincoid as the positive pole, the positive electrode, and the zincode... Chlorine is of course attracted by the surface of the zincoid and discharged there. **1848** WATTS tr. *Gmelin's Handbk. Chem.* I. 431 Graham's *Zincode* or *Zincoid.*

zincous ('zɪŋkəs), *a. Chem.* and *Electr.* [f. mod.L. *zinc-um* ZINC + -OUS.] Pertaining to or of the nature of zinc; having the affinity of zinc; relatively electropositive. (Opp. to CHLOROUS.)

1842 T. GRAHAM *Elem. Chem.* 204 The zincous pole. **1868** *Fowne's Chem.* (ed. 10) 277 It is true in a general way that those elements which differ most strongly in their electrical characters, chlorine and potassium, for example, are likewise those which combine together with the greatest energy; and the division of bodies into electro-positive and electro-negative is therefore retained; the former are also called zincous, and the latter basylous or zincous.

‖**zindan** (zɪn'dɑːn). [Pers. *zindān*, Turk. *zindan.*] A prison in Persia or neighbouring parts.

1889 G. N. CURZON *Russia in Central Asia* vii. 217 In another part of the citadel was the Zindan, or prison. **1924** *Glasgow Herald* 29 May 9/7 In Persia..I saw for the first time a Central Asian underground prison called Zindan... Prisoners..cannot possibly escape out of a deep pit with only a circular opening at the top. **1959** *Listener* 21 May 883/1 The Zindan or prison where Stoddart and Conolly spent so many miserable months [in Bokhara].

zine (ziːn). *U.S. colloq.* Shortened form of FANZINE.

1965 *New Yorker* 21 Aug. 24 The fanzines, or fan magazines, which are also known as amazines, or amateur magazines, do a great deal of research on the Golden Age, and some of the faneds, or fan-magazine editors, do a remarkably good job. Some zines specialize—like *ERB-dom*, which caters to the fans of Edgar Rice Burroughs—but most of them concentrate on the fantasy adventure or superhero comics, on which most fanac, or fan activity, centers. **1975** *Piece of Action* (Houston) Jan. 6 The above zine should not be confused with another proposed zine called *The Atavachron*. **1982** *Amer. Speech* LVII. 20 A publisher of a fanzine would send copies of his zine to a central location for collation with other zines and subsequent distribution. **1985** *Times* 25 Jan. 12/2 A zine is what its addicts call a postal games magazine, of which there are about 50 in the country.

zineb ('zɪnɛb). [f. *zinc* ethylene *bis*dithiocarbamate, the systematic name: see ETHYLENE, BIS-[2].] A white powder used as a fungicide on vegetables and fruit; $Zn(\cdot S{\cdot}CS{\cdot}NH{\cdot}CH_2\cdot)_2$.

1950 *Phytopathology* XL. 118 The Subcommittee on Fungicide Nomenclature of The American Phytopathological Society, cooperating with the Interdepartmental Committee on Pest Control, has selected common names for five commercially-available fungicidal chemicals... *Zineb* for the fungicidal chemical, zinc ethylene bisdithiocarbamate... *Ziram* for the fungicidal chemical, zinc dimethyl dithiocarbamate. **1966** *McGraw-Hill Encycl. Sci. & Technol.* V. 563/2 Organic fungicides have become increasingly important since 1934... Examples are..nabam, zineb, and maneb, the sodium, zinc, and manganese salts, respectively, of ethylenebis(dithiocarbamic acid). **1981** [see ZIRAM]. **1981** *Bull. Environmental Contamination & Toxicol.* XXVII. 418 Zineb is an important fungicide widely used in agriculture.

zines, ? obs. variant of ZOUNDS.

1709 [E. WARD] *Rambling Fuddle-Caps* 9 Zines, Madam, says Nell, in a damnable Fury, I won't be thus snub'd and abus'd. **1710** *Brit. Apollo* III. No. 82. 2/2 *Zines*..we suppose..an affected Word for *Zouns*.

zinfandel ('zɪnfændɛl). **a.** A red or white dry wine of California.

1896 *Pall Mall Mag.* Mar. 393 He drinks cheap Zinfandel, which must kill him eventually. **1897** *Outing* (U.S.) Nov. 144/2 Four-year-old zinfandel.

b. The grape from which this wine is made. In full, ***Zinfandel grape***.

1880 *Californian* II. 219/1 The favorite wine grapes are the Zinfandel, Riesling and Chasselas. **1977** H. FAST *Immigrants* IV. 254 'What kind of grapes do you grow for the market?' 'Zinfandels mostly. We have some Thompsons —' 'Ah, well the color of zinfandels is excellent, but we want a sweeter grape.' **1980** *Times* 23 Sept. 10/1 We were..in California... My companion..grows Chardonnay, Cabernet and Zinfandel grapes.

zing (zɪŋ), *sb. colloq.* (orig. *U.S.*). [Echoic.] **1.** A sharp, high-pitched ringing sound; a twang.

1911 D. RUNYON *Tents of Trouble* 22, I felt him fall and I sensed the 'zing' of a boob-face Arab's knife. **1922** C. SANDBURG *Slabs of Sunburnt West* 63 Then the axmen came and the chips flew to the zing of steel and handle. **1930** E. FERBER *Cimarron* xx. 331 He seized the typewriter by its steel bar and plumped it to the floor with a force that wrung a protesting whine and zing from its startled insides. **1961** E. WILLIAMS *George* xxv. 403 There was the confident zing of tennis-rackets in the Parks. **1970** *Washington Post* 30 Sept. B-1/1 The butterfly chair, that zing-zong-zang of tubular metal.

2. Energy, vigour, liveliness; zest; a quality that induces alertness or vitality.

1918 *Independent* 14 Dec. 369/1 They were the picked athletes of the whole English Army and were doing their calisthenics with a precision and spirit I have never seen equaled anywhere. The 'pep', 'zing' and 'vim' were thrilling. **1931** [see BELT *v.* 4 b (*b*)]. **1941** G. KERSH *They die with their Boots Clean* II. 83 I'll soon get that paleness off your faces and put some zing into those limbs. **1955** 'S. RANSOME' *Deadly Bedfellows* i. 7 Lake Haven's air..was full of zing and bounce. **1964** *Punch* 27 May 796/3 The show had zing. **1979** *Brit. Jrnl. Photogr.* 21 Sept. 917/1 In the old days a photographer used to go to work with a holdall and could be on the other side of the world. That doesn't happen very often nowadays in Fleet Street. It's lost its zing. **1983** *Daily Tel.* 21 Dec. 9/2 Freshly-squeezed lemon or lime has a unique impact, adding a zing to almost any combination in flavours. **1985** *Spectator* 28 Sept. 9 While death has not lost its sting, sex has undoubtedly lost its zing.

zing (zɪŋ), *int.* Chiefly *U.S.* [Echoic. Cf. ZINGO *int.*] Representing the sudden advent of a new situation or emotion.

1919 WODEHOUSE *Damsel in Distress* vi. 75 The generous blood of the Belphers boiled over, and then—*zing*. They jerked him off to Vine Street. **1948** *Sun* (Baltimore) 3 Dec. 14/2 A method of freezing concentrated orange juice was developed, and zing! the first thing they knew they had a new and depression-beating industry on their hands. **1955** W. GADDIS *Recognitions* I. iv. 161 String a good piece of piano wire across the road..and take a couple of shots at them. They go after you..and zing zing zing there go their heads just like that. **1977** M. FRENCH *Women's Room* (1978) iv. 248 So one day you meet this guy, right? And, ZING! He is gorgeous!

zing (zɪŋ), *v. colloq.* (orig. *U.S.*). [f. the sb. or int.] **1.** *intr.* **a.** To make a sharp, high-pitched ringing or whining sound; to travel rapidly producing such a sound.

1920 S. LEWIS *Main Street* ii. 18 Go zinging along on a fast ice-boat. **1949** N. MARSH *Swing, Brother, Swing* v. 88 Lord Pastern banged, and rattled, and zinged... 'Oh,' she thought, 'how vulnerable he is among his tympani!' **1960** I. CROSS *Backward Sex* i. 12 It would be better if this old chap did not..hear the bullet zing past. **1962** S. PLATH *Johnny Panic & Bible of Dreams* (1977) III. 247 The bees, now Charlie had lifted the top off the hive, were zinging out and dancing round. **1963** T. PYNCHON *V.* xi. 345 Had his coincidence, the accident to shatter the surface of this stagnant pool and send all the mosquitoes of hope zinging away to the exterior night; had it happened? **1977** G. DURRELL *Golden Bats & Pink Pigeons* ii. 38 A group of zosterops,..zinging and twittering to each other.

b. *fig.* To move energetically and with ease; to abound *with* energy.

1961 *John o' London's* 29 June 724/2 She zings along the tight-rope which passes for plot. **1969** N. FREELING *Tsing-Boum* xx. 145 They had been busy enough already in Holland! In Marseilles they had been zinging with ambitious energy. **1973** *Playboy* May 44 As pure escapist entertainment..the movie zings right along. **1973** *Daily Tel.* 7 Nov. 15/2 When..she denounces him to her husband for the imaginary seduction..of a 16-year-old girl pupil, matters zing into focus.

2. *trans.* With *up*. To enliven, invigorate. *U.S.*

1970 *New Yorker* 14 Nov. 154 Charles Revson is the philosopher-king of the cosmetic world... He claims to know by instinct how to 'zing up' a face. **1978** *Chicago* June 234/3 Delicious, spicy pickled-pepper relish..which you can use to zing up the otherwise mild dishes.

3. To abuse; to criticize. *U.S.*

1974 *Evening Herald* (Rock Hill, S. Carolina) 18 Apr. 7/4 In the eighth, Mitterwald doubled and..the rest of the Cubs zinged him for not hitting a fourth homer. **1975** *New Yorker* 21 Apr. 61/3 Brodie told me..of another investigator who, in his haste, 'zinged a dead man' and delivered an investigative report concerning his insurability.

4. To deliver (a witticism, question, etc.) with speed and force. *U.S.*

1975 W. Safire *Before Fall* III. vi. 179 [Nixon] read what they wrote and surprised them later by remembering it and occasionally zinging it back at them. *Ibid.* VII. i. 474, I zinged out a couple of one-liners. **1977** *Time* 10 Jan. 26/2 Her usual practice of zinging brash, hostile questions at world leaders.

Hence **'zinging** *ppl. a.*

1954 G. Durrell *Three Singles to Adventure* vi. 144 A group of sandflies discovered us with zinging cries of joy. **1963** *Times* 16 Jan. 6/5 Mr. Richard Daley, the last of the big city political bosses, has promised him a rough ride in a 'swinging, zinging, campaign, the roughest, toughest ever seen in Chicago'. **1970** 'D. Halliday' *Dolly & Cookie Bird* xi. 170 There was a sharp pop, a clang, and the zinging noise of a ricocheting bullet. **1972** *Daily Tel.* (Colour Suppl.) 4 Feb. 8/3 She beat me like a rug, pounded me like dough, using karate chops, zinging finger stabs, incredible flicks. **1978** G. Durrell *Garden of Gods* iii. 59 The air was..full of the zinging cries of cicadas.

zing(e, obs. or dial. ff. SING *v.*[1]

'zingana. [a. It., fem. of ZINGANO.]

1. (With capital initial.) A gypsy girl or woman.

1722 Jon. Richardson *Statues Italy* 334 An Exquisite Madonna, a Half Figure only, the same Attitude as the Zingana.

2. = ZEBRANO.

1934 A. L. Howard *Man. Timbers of World* (ed. 2) 582 *Zebrano* or *Zingana*. ? *Cynometra* aff. *C. Lujai* Willd... West Coast of Africa... Known as 'zebra' wood in the United Kingdom and America. **1947** J. C. Rich *Materials & Methods of Sculpture* x. 297 Zebrawood, also known as Zingana and Zebrano, is a tropical wood imported from Africa. **1957** N. Clifford *Timber Identification* IV. 134 (*table*) Common name..Zebrano... Alternative names.. Zingana; Zebrawood... Botanical name..*Brachystegia fleuryana* Chev... Habitat: West Africa. **1973** *Observer* (Colour Suppl.) 8 Apr. 13/1 (Advt.), The grapefruit knife's got a stainless steel blade, zingana wood handle. **1974** F. N. Howes *Dict. Useful & Everyday Plants* 286 Zingana, *Microberlinia brazzavillensis*, W. Afr., a commercial timber.

‖**Zingano** ('zɪŋgənəʊ). Pl. **-ani.** Also anglicized 6 **cingane**, 7–8 **zingan**; pl. 7, 9 **zinganies.** [Italian. For the etymology, see Miklosisch in *Denkschr. d. k. Akad.* (Wien) XXVI. 55–64, Wiener in *Archiv f. d. Studium d. neueren Spr.* CIX. 295–6.] = ZINGARO, -ARA.

1581 Pettie *Guazzo's Civ. Conv.* I. (1586) 26 Your meaning is..that as it is lawfull onelie for the Cinganes to robbe, so these also haue priuiledge to plaie in open streete. **1600** J. Pory tr. *Leo's Africa* VII. 290 In that iourney they are exceedingly molested by certaine theeues called Zingani. **1684** T. Smith in *Phil. Trans.* XIV. 446 There are thousands of Gypsies or Zinganies in Turkey. *a* **1733** Chishull *Trav. Turkey* (1747) 93 A gang of Zingans, or gypses. **1838** W. Howitt *Rural Life Eng.* I. 249 They were very sweet nondescripts, but not very perfect beggars; and far, far indeed from perfect Zinganies.

‖**Zingaro** ('zɪŋgərəʊ), *fem.* **-ara** (-ərə). Pl. **-ari, -e.** Also 7 *pl.* **Singari, Zingaries**; 9 **Zingaree.** [It. Cf. prec.]

1. A gypsy; also *attrib.* or as *adj.*

1617 Moryson *Itin.* III. 45 The very Northerne Weomen ..haue their faces tanned, that they may seeme to be Southerne Weomen (which sort are in Italy called *Singari*). **1775** Chandler *Trav. Asia Minor* 159 Some of the vagrant people, called Atzincari or Zingari, the Gypsies of the East. **1784–5** *Ann. Reg.* II. 83 A Vocabulary of the Zingara, or Gypsey Language. **1823** Scott *Quentin D.* xvi, I am a Zingaro, a Bohemian, an Egyptian, or whatever the Europeans..may choose to call our people. *Ibid.*, The Zingaro boy was no house-bred cur. **1845** Fitzball *Maritana* III. Duetto, *Don C.* Once more we meet! 'Tis the Zingara! *Mar.* Yes, Maritana. **1856** *Amy Carlton* 129 She had copied two lines of the 'The Merry Zingra'; then she.. hummed 'I'm a merry, merry Zingra'. **1871** M. Collins *Marq. & Merch.* I. vii. 217 The Zingari had built their fires. **1906** E. Reich *Plato* vi. 114 The Zingaree or gypsy mother.

2. pl. *I* (or *The*) *Zingari*: the name of an amateur cricket club founded in 1845.

1846 W. Denison *Cricketer's Compan. 1845* p. xiii, Everybody knows that the 'Zingari' are a tribe of wanderers. .. Just such a race of individuals is the Club which bears the name and title of 'I Zingari'. As a Club, they have neither habitation nor home. **1867** 'Ouida' *Under Two Flags* I. v. 106 The Household [Cavalry] played the Zingari. **1905** H. A. Vachell *Hill* x. 222 After the Zingari Match, Desmond got his Flannels. **1922** Joyce *Ulysses* 731 A new raincoat on him with the muffler in the Zingari colours. **1948** E. Waugh *Loved One* i. 5 Sir Ambrose wore dark grey flannels, an Eton Rambler tie, an I Zingari ribbon in his boater hat. **1978** *Times* 17 June 13/6 The Household Brigade might turn out in jackboots, gauntlets, [etc.]..to contend with the Zingari.

‖**zingel** ('tsɪŋgəl). [G.] Any fish of the percoid genus *Aspro*; esp. *A. zingel* of the Danube. So **'zingelin**, an allied species.

1803 Shaw *Gen. Zool.* IV. 551 Zingel Perch. *Ibid.*, Zingelin Perch... Extremely allied to the Zingel in general appearance. **1868** *Chamb. Encycl.* X. 352/2.

zinger ('zɪŋə(r)). *U.S. slang.* [f. ZING *sb.* + -ER[1].] **1.** Something outstandingly good of its kind.

1955 M. Allingham *Beckoning Lady* vi. 99, I don't know why it was such a zinger, unless it was that it was very big and very cheap. **1968** *Times* 30 May 10, I think every actress needs one zinger of a part early in her career. **1973** *N.Y. Times Bk. Rev.* 4 Nov. 79 (*caption*) A zinger of a novel. **1976** *New Yorker* 9 Feb. 84/2 It's a zinger of a scene: an educated, socially conscious woman dating a lumpen lost soul. **1980** R. Adams *Girl in Swing* v. 63 My private collection was becoming what an American friend..described as a 'zinger'.

2. a. A wisecrack; a punch line.

1970 *Time* 12 Oct. 7 Ann-Margret is giving him a hard time on the home front, too, tossing out little zingers about his advancing age like 'Flab is reality'. **1970** *Life* 30 Oct. 40 In casual chatter the zingers [of Dick Cavett] are just as fast and frequent as they are on the show. **1975** *Homemaker's Mag.* Oct. 28/2 The Vancouver Status of Women group is planning to put out a booklet of useful zingers... Sometimes you just need one sharp line to show you mean business. **1979** *Courier-Mail* (Brisbane) 31 Mar. 76 (*caption*) One more zinger about my height, and I shall be compelled to thrash you mercilessly about the feet and ankles. **1980** *Maledicta* III. 254 Sorry. After having exhibited immense self-control not to quip,..I just had to shoot off this little zinger.

b. A surprise question; an unexpected turn of events, e.g. in a plot.

1973 R. Thomas *If you can't be Good* (1974) vii. 51, I would drone along..asking tired questions... Then I would throw in the zinger and watch what happened. **1976** *Publishers Weekly* 2 Feb. 91/1 There's a zinger toward the end, in which the nominal hit man gets hit, but it doesn't really compensate for the tedium the reader's gone through. **1983** *Fortune* 11 July 134/2 The supervisor should also encourage discussion..of what may seem like personal issues... In the process, though, be wary of 'zingers', heart-to-heart matters brought up at an awkward time, often near the end of a meeting.

Zingg (zɪŋ, tsɪŋ). *Petrol.* The name of Theodor *Zingg* (b. 1905), Swiss meteorologist and engineer, used *attrib.* with reference to his system of classification of pebble shapes, in which two ratios formed from three mutually perpendicular diameters are used to assign a pebble to one or other of certain basic shape classes.

1941 *Jrnl. Sedimentary Petrol.* XI. 67/1 (*heading*) Relation between sphericity and Zingg shape classes. **1949** F. J. Pettijohn *Sedimentary Rocks* ii. 49 (*caption*) Chart showing relationship between sphericity and Zingg shape indices. **1979** *Nature* 8 Feb. 496/3 Very simple probabilistic methods were used to estimate the formation of the four basic Zingg shapes (disks, spheres, blades and rods).

†**zingho.** *Obs. rare.* [? for It. *zinco*.] Zinc.

1743 Walpole *Let. to Mann* 10 June, He promised me too to go to Lord Islay, to know what cobolt and zingho are.

zingiber ('zɪndʒɪbə(r)). [See GINGER.] = GINGER *sb.* 1, 2.

1902 L. H. Bailey *Cycl. Amer. Hort.* IV. 2010/1 Zingibers are occasionally cultivated as stove decorative plants. **1970** *Guardian* 2 June 12/5 Bottles..of everything from Advocaat to Zingiber wine. **1971** *Country Life* 20 May 1252/2 But the particular forte of most [herbs] is as permanent foliage foils for other, brighter things as well as in their own right, from angelica to zingiber.

zingiberaceous (ˌzɪndʒɪbə'reɪʃəs), *a. Bot.* [f. mod.L. *Zingiberaceæ*, f. *Zingiber*: see GINGER *sb.* and -ACEOUS.] Belonging to the N.O. *Zingiberaceæ* of monocotyledonous plants, typified by the genus *Zingiber* (GINGER).

1846 Smart (ed. 2). **1869** A. R. Wallace *Malay Archip.* I. iii. 51 A stream overgrown with Zingiberaceous plants.

zingo ('zɪŋgəʊ), *int.* Chiefly *U.S.* [Echoic. Cf. ZING *int.*] = ZING *int.*

1914 *Sat. Even. Post* 17 Jan. 7/1 Just when he was bursting with happiness because he was going to be a real big leaguer and one of us—zingo! he was back where he started. **1941** B. Schulberg *What makes Sammy Run?* ii. 32 It didn't take nearly this long to think. It went zingo, just a look. **1968** *Sunday Times* 25 Aug. 29/5 The stock is 24 asked and I reach for it and I get 200 shares and it moves up 28, zingo. **1970** *New Yorker* 17 Oct. 40/3 Zingo, another pair of jokers.. bust in.

zingy ('zɪŋɪ), *a.* [f. ZING *sb.* + -Y[1].] Energetic, exciting, lively. Also *ellipt.*

1948 [see MAMBO 1]. **1962** *Guardian* 7 Feb. 9/1 A zingy collection..that every with-it girl is going to adore. **1966** *Daily Tel.* 17 Aug. 11/5 With her own fashion taste, a delicate blend of the elegant and the zingy, a model like Fiona Campbell-Walter looks set for a great comeback career. **1968** *Globe & Mail* (Toronto) 3 Feb. 11/1 With some zingy comedy, they're an act that the regular club-haunters around town wait for. **1975** *Observer* 9 Nov. 22/6 A zingy Moselle, from a world famous estate. **1976** *Publishers Weekly* 16 Aug. 116/1 Some zingy, down-to-earth comments... She doesn't mince words.

Zinjanthropus (zɪn'dʒænθrəpəs). *Palæont.* [mod.L. (L. S. B. Leakey 1959, in *Nature* 15 Aug. 491/2), f. *Zinj*, ancient name for East Africa + Gr. ἄνθρωπος man.] = *Nutcracker Man* s.v. NUT-CRACKER 5.

1959 *Nature* 15 Aug. 493/2 *Zinjanthropus* comes from Olduvai Gorge. **1961**, **1962** [see *Nutcracker Man* s.v. NUT-CRACKER 5]. **1973** J. B. Williams *Evolution & Human Origins* ix. 143/1 The species *Australopithecus robustus* includes..'*Zinjanthropus*' from East Africa. **1977** A. Hallam *Planet Earth* 286 From the early beds..are recognized two kinds of hominids. One is *A. boisei* (sometimes called Zinjanthropus).

zink, obs. f. ZINC.

‖**zinke** ('zɪŋkɪ, 'tsɪŋkə). Also **zincke, zink, zinka.** [G.] A cornet-like musical instrument of wood or horn, formerly common in Europe; also, a loud reed-stop in an organ.

1776 Hawkins *Hist. Mus.* II. IV. iv. 452 Luscinius next exhibits the forms of four other wind instruments, namely, 1. the Ruspfeiff. 2. The Krumhorn. 3. The Gemsen horn. And 4. the Zincke. [*Note*] The Gemsen horn and Basaun.. are to be found in many great organs in Germany, as is also the Zincke corruptly spelt Cink. **1889** *Grove's Dict. Mus.* IV. 511 *Zink* or *Zincke*. **1917** *Museums Jrnl.* XVI. 239 A zinka (wind instrument) of the 17th century, made of ivory with ornamental mountings.

zinked: see ZINC *v.*

zinkenite, variant of ZINCKENITE.

zinkiferous, -ify, -ite: see ZINCIFEROUS, etc.

zinking: see ZINC *v.*

zinky ('zɪŋkɪ), *a.* Also **zincky.** [f. ZINC + -Y[1].] Pertaining to zinc; containing zinc.

1757 tr. *J. F. Henckel's Pyritologia* 176 The ground-mixtion of this zinky matter. **1796** Kirwan *Elem. Min.* (ed. 2) II. 218 The Zincky ores.

zinnar, obs. f. CHENAR, plane-tree.

‖**zinnia** ('zɪnɪə). *Bot.* Also *erron.* **zinia.** [mod.L. (Linnæus, 1763), from the name of J. G. *Zinn*, a German botanist.] A plant of the genus so named of American composite plants, extensively cultivated for the beauty of their flowers.

1767 Abercrombie *Ev. Man his own Gard.* (1803) 227 Sowing less tender Annuals... The principal sorts are.. alkekengi or winter-cherry, tobacco-plant, zinnia, Indian corn. **1885** Pater *Marius* xi. I. 187 They visited the flower-market..and purchased zinias..to decorate the folds of their togas. **1910** *Nation* 13 Aug. 702/1 The hot and scentless glare of zinnias and dahlias.

zinnober ('zɪnəʊbə(r)). Also **zinnobar.** [a. G. *zinnober* CINNABAR, vermilion.] ***zinnober green***: = ***chrome green*** (*b*) s.v. CHROME 3.

1895 *Montgomery Ward Catal.* Spring & Summer 252/3 Zinnobar Green, Light. Zinnobar Green, medium. Zinnobar Green, deep. **1897** *Sears, Roebuck Catal.* 360/3 Colors for Artists... Zinnober Green, light. **1942** Gettens & Stout *Painting Materials* 178 Zinnober Green is a term ordinarily synonymous with chrome green..which is a processed mixture of chrome yellow and Prussian blue. More specifically, it is given to mixtures that are olive in hue. **1973** F. Taubes *Painter's Dict. Materials & Methods* 253 Zinnober green is a mixture of Prussian blue and cadmium yellow.

zinnwaldite ('zɪnwɒldaɪt). *Min.* [ad. G. *zinnwaldit* (Haidinger, 1845), f. *Zinnwald* in Bohemia, its locality.] A kind of mica containing lithium and iron, a variety of lepidolite.

1861 Bristow *Gloss. Min.*, *Zinnwaldite*, Haidinger.

zinopre, var. SINOPER *Obs.*

Zinoviev (zɪ'nɒviːɛf). Also **Zinovieff.** [The assumed name of Y. A. Radomyslsky (1883–1936).] ***Zinoviev letter***: a letter published in the press in 1924 as having been sent by Zinoviev, a Russian statesman, to British Communists and urging them to commit subversive acts; it was later discovered to be a forgery.

1924 *Times* 28 Oct. 8/1 (*heading*) The Zinovieff letter. *Ibid.*, If the Zinovieff letter is a forgery, it shows the amount of scoundrelliness with which we are surrounded. **1925** (*title*) The 'Zinoviev' letter: report of investigation by British delegation to Russia. **1957** *Encycl. Brit.* XIII. 554/2 In the general election of 1924 the Labour party met with a serious reverse, largely because of the confusion attending the publication of the 'Zinoviev' letter. **1958** C. Cockburn *Crossing Line* iv. 64 The timely forgery by the Intelligence Service of the 'Zinoviev letter'. **1972** 'M. Sinclair' *Norslag* xi. 101 The stories in the 'twenties about the Zinovieff letter. **1979** *Guardian* 28 Apr. 32/8 Mr Benn told a Bristol audience that the Tories..were dragging out the old Zinoviev Letter technique.

Hence **Zi'novievite**, in Russia, a supporter of Zinoviev and his anti-Stalin faction in the 1920s and 1930s; also *attrib.* or as *adj.*

1937 *Foreign Affairs* XVI. 50 The Trotskyites and Zinovievites. *Ibid.* 64 Designated by the government of the U.S.S.R. as members of a 'Trotskyite-Zinovievite Center'. **1970** S. Talbott tr. *Khrushchev Remembers* (1971) i. 28 The Fifteenth Party Congress, at which Stalin and his supporters squared off against the Zinovievites, or 'Leningrad opposition', as they were then called. **1974** T. P. Whitney tr. *Solzhenitsyn's Gulag Archipelago* I. I. viii. 329 Centers keep creeping in all the time... Trotskyite-Zinovievite Centers, Rightist-Bukharinite Centers, but all of them are crushed.

zinziberaceous (ˌzɪnzɪbə'reɪʃəs), *a. Bot.* = ZINGIBERACEOUS.

1864 in Webster.

ziogoon, variant of SHOGUN.

Zion (ˈzaɪən). Forms: 1- Sion, 5 Syon, 7- Zion. [eccl. L. *Siōn*, Gr. *Σεών, Σειών*, a. Heb. *tsīyōn*.] The name of one of the hills of Jerusalem, on which the city of David was built, and which became the centre of Jewish life and worship; in biblical and derived use, allusively for: The house or household of God; and hence connoting variously, the Israelites and their religious system, the Christian Church, heaven as the final home of believers, a place of worship or meeting-house (cf. BETHEL, EBENEZER 2).

c **1000** *Ps.* lxxxiv. 7 in Ælfric *Hom.* II. 334 Ða halȝan farað fram mihte to mihte; ealra goda God bið ȝesewen on Sion. **1382** WYCLIF *Isa.* li. 16 That thou plaunte heuenus, and founde erthe, and sey to Sion, My puple thou art. **1450–1530** *Myrr. our Ladye* 2 As ye are doughtres of this bodely Syon, so ought ye to be doughtres of Syon gostly. *Ibid.* 147 By Syon..ys vnderstonde sowles that are gyuen to contemplacyon, where in oure lorde Iesu chryste ys sewrely stabled. *a* **1542** WYATT *Penit. Ps.* iv. 77 Make Syon, Lord, acordyng to thy will, Inward Syon, the Syon of the ghost. **1611** *Bible* Ep. Ded., Many, who wished not well vnto our Sion. **1779** J. NEWTON *Hymn, 'Glorious things of thee are spoken'* v, Solid joys and lasting treasure None but Zion's children know. **1823** GALT *R. Gilhaize* vii, That same city of St. Andrews is the Zion of Scotland. Of old, the glad tidings of salvation were first heard there. **1871** R. B. VAUGHAN *Life S. Thomas of Aquin* II. 859 As if the Basilica of S. Peter's were brought into juxtaposition with the Zions and Ebenezers of our more modern days.

Hence **ˈZioner**, a member of an organized religious body; **ˈZionless** *a. fig.*, having no centre of common worship.

1760 RUTTY *Spir. Diary* (ed. 2) 158 O the carelessness of our Sioners. **1908** F. SPENCE *Chr. Reunion* ix. 170 The tribes must remain Zion-less without the Ecclesia.

Zionism (ˈzaɪənɪz(ə)m). [f. prec. + -ISM.] A movement among modern Jews having for its object the assured settlement of their race upon a national basis in Palestine; after 1948, concerned chiefly with the development of the State of Israel (see ISRAEL 3).

1896 *Jewish Chron.* 15 May 10/1, I would ask them..to consider whether Zionism.. really deserves to be preached down as a standing danger to Israel's progress. *Ibid.* 28 Aug. 6/1 Zionism does not necessarily aim at the formation of a Jewish State in Palestine. **1904** *Times* 5 May 15/2 Zionism had actually penetrated the West End Synagogue. **1948** *Sunday Pictorial* 18 July 7/6 The Government took office solemnly pledged to support Zionism. **1949** [see REVISIONISM 2]. **1955** *Ann. Reg. 1954* 241 Social democracy ..and Zionism were..repeatedly condemned. **1955** *Times* 9 May 9/3 It happened that Jewish workers in considerable numbers were the first to come to Palestine in answer to the appeal of Zionism. **1975** *Globe & Mail* (Toronto) 14 Nov. 7/6 To [Jews], Zionism is and remains a precious term of honor, tied to the heart of their religious and national dreams.

ˈZionist. Also Sion-.

1. [f. ZIONISM.] A supporter of Zionism; also *attrib.* or as *adj.*

1896 *Jewish Chron.* 17 Jan. 12/2 The emigration and Zionist societies. *Ibid.* 28 Aug. 6/1 Many of those who worship the national ideal are Zionists; not all though, nor do all Zionists share the national idea. **1906** *Times* 29 Oct. 10/5 The Zionist Congress, which is the nearest approach to a Jewish Parliament, permitting women deputies equally with men. **1906** *Q. Rev.* Oct. 589 The Sionists, who are a small minority of the Jews. **1923** *Jewish Chron.* 19 Jan. 5/1 It will be seen from this how far right the Zionist leaders, Dr. Weizmann and Mr. Sokolow in particular, were in the estimate they put upon that Statement. **1940** E. GILL *Autobiogr.* vii. 252 The agricultural, arboricultural and horticultural work of the young Zionist colonies..superb in itself and of great educational benefit to the Arabs. **1955** *Times* 9 May 9/3 The private sector—politically represented in the main by the General Zionists. **1966** C. POTOK *Chosen* (1967) xiii. 213 He had become involved in Zionist activities and was always attending meetings where he spoke about the importance of Palestine as a Jewish homeland. **1977** *Time* 30 May 10/2 Begin..joined the youth organization of the Zionist-Revisionists, a group of right wing militants who condemned the regular Zionist leadership as misguided and soft.

2. A member of any of a group of independent churches in southern Africa similar to pentecostal churches but containing distinctive African elements of worship and belief. [Named after the first such church, the Christian Catholic Apostolic Church in *Zion*, brought from Chicago to S. Africa in 1904.]

1948 B. G. M. SUNDKLER *Bantu Prophets in S. Africa* ii. 55 Theologically the Zionists are now a syncretistic Bantu movement with healing, speaking with tongues, purification rites, and taboos as the main expressions of their faith. **1956** H. BLOOM *Episode* xvii. 318 Among the crowd were a number of Sunday pilgrims, location Zionists of various sects. **1970** *Standard Encycl. Southern Afr.* II. 55/1 Most 'Zionists' have a characteristic form of dress, worn to all services by all members: long dresses and capes, mostly white, decorated with coloured figures (stars, crosses, rings, angels, etc.), veils for women and special forms of headdress for men. *Ibid.*, The 'Zionist' phase has led to extensive proliferation of small groups. **1977** *Time* 27 June 18/3 Some aspects of the old Soweto still exist: the neatly kept gardens of middle-class black homes;..the Zionists, an Africanized Christian sect, famous for their daylong religious dances that begin at prayer services in backyard tents on Saturday nights.

Zionite (ˈzaɪənaɪt). [f. ZION + -ITE[1].]

a. A citizen of Zion; one of the chosen people of God. **b.** One of a sect so called: see quot. 1886.

1675 T. BROOKS *Gold. Key* Wks. 1867 V. 342 The Zionites, the people of God, the citizens of Zion. **1882–3** *Schaff's Encycl. Relig. Knowl.* II. 1604 The Zionites in Norway. **1886** *Encycl. Brit.* XX. 842/2 Founded in 1737 by the followers of Elias Eller, a religious enthusiast, Ronsdorf received town-rights in 1745. The Ronsdorf sect, the members of which called themselves Zionites, is now extinct.

Zionward(s (ˈzaɪənwəd(z), *adv.* [f. ZION + -WARD(S.] Towards Zion; usually *fig.* heavenwards.

1705 R. SMYTH *Let.* 17 Feb. in *Lett. J. Pinney* (1939) 117, I am sure there are too few y[t] sett their faces Zionward, here in this Town. **1815** A. BURN *Mem.* (1816) I. 35 The same.. Sun of Righteousness to guide our faces Zionward. **1836** HOR. SMITH *Tin Trump.*, *Christianity* (1890) 83 They are too polite to travel Zionward in such company. **1861** EDMOND *Children's Ch. at Home* xxi. 325 The faces of all are Zionwards.

zip (zɪp), *sb.*[1] *colloq.* [Imitative.]

1. (Often reduplicated ***zip, zip***, or ***zip-zip***.) A syllable expressing a light sharp sound such as that produced by a bullet or other small or slender object passing rapidly through the air or through some obstacle, or by the tearing of canvas or the like; a sound of this kind, or movement accompanied by such sound.

1875 FOGG *Arabistan* xxi. 264 The blood-thirsty *zip* of mosquitoes by the million. **1885** *Century Mag.* May 134/1 The *ping, zip, zip* of bullets. **1887** D. C. MURRAY in *Good Words* Apr. 249 The zip of the needle and swish of the thread went on. **1899** KIPLING *Stalky* ii. 55 Another buck-shot tore through the rotten canvas tilt with a vicious zipp.

2. *fig.* Energy, force, impetus.

1900 LORIMER *Old Gorgon Graham* xi. (1904) 225, I need ..a little more zest for my food, and a little more zip about my work. **1907** N. MUNRO *Daft Days* xxxii, That's how I feel..when I've got the zip of poetry in me.

3. Nothing, nought, zero. Cf. ZILCH *sb.* (and *a.*). *colloq.* (orig. and chiefly *U.S.*).

1900 *Dialect Notes* II. 70 *Zip, n.*, a zero in marks. **1904** *N.Y. World Mag.* 1 May 6/5 'Zip' is the same as 'zero'. **1927** *Amer. Speech* III. 455 *Swabo, zip*, zero. **1972** D. E. WESTLAKE *Cops & Robbers* (1973) viii. 111 Before this, neither one of us had known zip about stocks and bonds. **1976** *Times* 27 Apr. 10/8 The successful team are said to have won one-nothing, one-zero or, more fashionably now, one-zip. **1977** J. CHEEVER *Falconer* 65 Armed robbery. Zip to ten. Second offense. **1980** J. KRANTZ *Princess Daisy* xxv. 443 No launch, no commercials, no nothing. Zip! Finished! Over!

4. Also **zipp.** A form of fastener for clothes, luggage, etc., consisting of two flexible strips with interlocking projections closed or opened by a sliding clip pulled along them. In full, ***zip-fastener, -fastening*** (see sense 5 below). Cf. ZIPPER.

1928 E. M. FORSTER *Arthur Snatchfold* in *Life to Come* (1972) 102 He felt the shirt..and he gave the zip at the throat a downward pull. **1940** *Punch* 5 June 612/2 Miss Fisher used to wear some lovely plum-coloured trousers with a zip to match. **1957** J. BRAINE *Room at Top* ix. 90 There was too much messing about with buttons and zips and straps. **1969** *Homes & Gardens* Nov. 190/1, I lost marks in a dressmaking competition because the zipp was machine-stitched in. **1972** *Lancet* 10 June 1271/1 The plain apron front has an off-centre..fastening by a heavy-duty metal 'Zipp', 30 in. long. **1985** *Vogue* July 77 Over this go.. flared shorts..some with zips placed to show not pockets but a sliver of flesh.

5. *attrib.* and *Comb.*, as (sense 4), ***zip bag, -bedding, -case, -fastener, -fastening, -front, jacket, pocket, shirt, side, suit, top***; ***zip-fastened, -topped*** adjs.; **zip gun** *U.S. colloq.*, a cheap home-made or makeshift gun; **zip lock** *U.S.*, used *attrib.* to denote plastic bags with an airtight fastening of two interlocking strips; also (a proprietary name) **Ziploc**; **zip-top** *a.*, = *ring-pull* adj. s.v. RING *sb.*[1] 19a.

1937 L. MACNEICE in Auden & MacNeice *Lett. from Iceland* 133 The permutations..of zip bags, Of compacts.. and coiffures. **1948** W. FORTESCUE *Beauty for Ashes* xxx. 235 Only at Croyden did I discover that my small zip bags had been stowed away in a locker directly under my legs. **1933** T. E. LAWRENCE *Home Lett.* (1954) 384 The new zipp-bedding is a great success. **1960** N. KNEALE *Quatermass & Pit* 1. 22 The Minister's Private Secretary enters quickly, clutching a zip-case. **1950** J. CANNAN *Murder Included* vii. 158 A brown zip-fastened handbag. **1927** *Daily Express* 22 Nov. 3/5 Many of the new sports suits have zip-fasteners. **1973** A. PRICE *October Men* vii. 95 He stumbled down the nearest alleyway..fumbling as he went for the zip-fastener on his fly. **1927** *Daily Express* 6 Sept. 3/4 The airwoman's costume of tango suède, complete from the zip fastening to the little hat..is attracting many admirers. **1942** 'M. INNES' *Daffodil Affair* 1. 24 The pomps of death: dissolution had once been a comfortably solid affair. Now it was papier-mâché coffins and zipp-fastening shrouds. **1965** *N.Y. Herald-Tribune* 11 Apr. 8 Zip-front seersucker 'skimma'. **1974** *Harrods Xmas Catal.* 9/1 Hostess gown with zip-front. **1950** *N.Y. Post* 29 Sept. 2 Three Bronx schoolboys were held by police today after admitting shooting off a home-made 'zip' gun... It was fashioned of a 6-inch stainless steel tube taped to a wooden block with an ordinary closet bolt for a 'trigger'. By means of a rubber band, a long ·22 caliber bullet could be shot from it. **1971** B. MALAMUD *Tenants* 103, I..had thoughts to kill him off with my zip gun but was afraid to. **1984** *Listener* 7 June 7/2 With the decline of this chicano movement and the increase in sophisticated weapons—zip-guns were replaced with sawn-off shotguns and sometimes automatic weapons—violence rocketed in the Seventies. **1958** *Spectator* 6 June 729/1 A blue zip jacket and slacks. **1970** *Official Gaz.* (U.S. Patent Office) 17 Feb. TM134 *Ziploc*. The Dow Chemical Company... Filed 9–9–68. **1977** C. MCFADDEN *Serial* (1978) l. 107/1 Spenser rummaged among the Ziploc bags in his briefcase. **1982** *Town Crier* (McAllen, Texas) 31 Mar. 1-A/4 Wrapped in foil in a clear zip lock bag. **1979** *Daily Tel.* 20 Nov. 3/1 When Mrs Robabeh Moheby..was strip-searched, a bundle of banknotes was found in a zip pocket in her knickers. **1976** *Morecambe Guardian* 7 Dec. 32/4 (Advt.), Boys short-sleeved, zip shirts. **1940** *Punch* 4 Dec. p. xvii. (Advt.), A Dunlopillo sleeping bag. It has..soft upper lining, zip side, ..and makes an ideal holdall. **1978** F. MULLALLY *Deadly Payoff* ii. 25 He handed Fernandez a zip-suit of grubby white fatigues. **1970** *Times* 16 Feb. p. iii, Ring-pull and zip-top cans are already available. **1974** *Harrods Xmas Catal.* 18/1 Bag..with side pocket, zip top. **1976** *Globe & Mail* (Toronto) 30 Dec. 27/6 Here plastic fish surface and bob for zip-top rings from beer and pop cans. **1979** *This England* Winter 19/3 She folded her cap inside her apron and pushed both into her zip-topped bag.

zip (zɪp), *sb.*[2] *U.S.* Also Z.I.P., ZIP, Zip. [f. the initials of *Z*oning *I*mprovement *P*lan.] Used esp. *attrib.* in ***zip code***: a series of digits representing a particular area in a city, etc., used in addressing mail (see quots.).

1963 *N.Y. Times* 5 May 86/3 Z.I.P. codes, for the present at least, are for big business, and more particularly big users of the mails such as publishers, banks, insurance companies and mail-order houses. **1964** *N.Y. Times Book Rev.* 5 Apr. 3/2 Among his petty peeves are..Zip codes and automatic telephone dialling. **1969** *Computers & Humanities* IV. 69 The ZIP code has been another, but less successful, step towards using computer recognition to improve our lives. *Ibid.*, Once a person has miswritten the ZIP, the computer just misdirects the mail. **1973** *Black Panther* 21 July 16/2 (Please print) Name..Address..City..State/Zip. **1975** *New Yorker* 5 May 2 (Advt.), In ordering a change of address, subscribers should give four weeks' notice, providing both old and new addresses, with Zip Codes. **1977** *Chicago Tribune* 2 Oct. VI. 26/4 A 13-cent U.S. commemorative honoring 50 years of talking pictures will go on sale Thursday in Hollywood, Cal., where the postmaster Zip is 90028. **1980** *Christian Sci. Monitor* (Mid-western ed.) 4 Dec. 2/2 The Postal Board of Governors..withheld final approval of a controversial plan to expand ZIP codes to nine digits.

zip, *v.* [f. ZIP *sb.*[1]]

1. *intr.* to make the sound expressed by 'zip'; also to move briskly or with speed.

1852 *Knickerbocker* XL. 182 How we did '*z-i-p!*' Seven miles, at one time, in less than seven minutes. **1897** KIPLING *Day's Work* (1898) 234, I heard my flanges zippin' along the ties. **1907** A. BENNETT *Grim Smile of Five Towns* 222 'Let her zip,' said Mr. Colclough. **1915** STRATTON-PORTER *M. O'Halloran* xix, [A snake] that would..coil zipping mad over the warm twisting body. **1922** S. LEWIS *Babbitt* xviii. 221 Everything zips at the Chatham Road Church. **1929** *Evening News* 3 Jan. 4/2 He..hardly saw it [*sc.* the ball] after it pitched, as it zipped off the ground and whipped round his bat to take the off stump. **1958** *Daily Mail* 24 Feb. 12/2, I found the man..zipping round the garden..on a toy trike. **1967** *Electronics* 6 Mar. 46/2 Rail travelers will be able to make telephone calls while zipping along at speeds of up to 160 miles an hour from New York City to Washington, D.C. **1976** *Guardian Weekly* 26 Sept. 9/3 The millions of Orange County commuters, who zip past on the Santa Ana Freeway each morning. **1984** *Times* 30 Nov. 11/2 Even though she is likely to spend as much time immersed to the elbows in washing up as zipping down the slopes, there is no stigma of 'service' attached to the job.

2. *trans.* To close with a zip-fastener. Freq. const. *up* and with a person being or getting dressed as obj. Also *intr.* for *pass.* and *refl.* Also *fig.*

1932 A. HUXLEY *Brave New World* iii. 50 He zipped up his trousers. **1936** *Sears Catal.* 163/4 Easy to 'Zip' baby in and out! **1939** *Punch* 11 Oct. 412/2 The most marvellous outfits ..that you step into and zip up. **1942** *Time* 23 Feb. 78 (Advt.), Zips flawlessly. **1942** in *Amer. Speech* (1943) XVIII. 305/2 Zip your lip. **1944** *Penguin New Writing* xx. 60 Zipping on her enchanted house-coat over her night-dress. **1948** *Chicago Tribune* 28 Mar. (Comics) 4 Stand still, now, while I zip you up! **1956** G. N. PATTERSON *God's Fool* i. 14 Shivering in the icy atmosphere, [I] zipped myself into my double-layer sleeping bag. **1968** B. HINES *Kestrel for Knave* 23 His mother pulled her skirt on and tried to zip it on the hip. **1973** J. DRUMMOND *Bang! Bang! You're Dead!* viii. 13 Authority, including the B.B.C., did not speculate about guilt. Mouths were carefully zipped. **1980** T. BARLING *Goodbye Piccadilly* ii. 36 The cistern flushed and Cave emerged, zipping up.

b. The verb-stem in combination, as ***zip-down, -in, -off, -on, -out, -over, -up***, adjs.

1971 C. BONINGTON *Annapurna South Face* 241 [Breeches with] zip-down side to allow putting on over boots and crampons. **1974** *Amer. Speech 1970* XLV. 179 *Chil-dodger* .., zip-in garment to be worn under jackets, coats, or over lounge clothes for extra warmth. **1957** *Housewife* Sept. 26 Zip-off covers for easy cleaning. **1974** *Harper's & Queen* Sept. 36/2 Zip-off mink £925, extra maxi piece £300. **1959** *Housewife* June 57 Silk cushions..with zip-on covers. **1963** *New Yorker* 26 Oct. 6 Enter the Chesterfield in Black Tweed ..with warm acrylic pile zip-out liner. **1962** 'A. GILBERT' *No Dust in Attic* v. 63 He'd left his luggage..one of the zip-over bags. **1959** M. SHADBOLT *New Zealanders* 26 He wore an open-neck check shirt and a zip-up jacket. **1973** 'D. RUTHERFORD' *Kick Start* i. 12 The zip-up calf-length boots. **1985** *Times* 24 Jan. 3/2 He was described as aged between 18 and 20, of West Indian appearance..wearing a beige zip-up jacket.

3. *trans.* To beat (an opposing team) comprehensively by not allowing it to score. Cf. ZIP *sb.*[1] 3.

1976 *Daily News* (N.Y.) 16 Jan. 82 The Adams Division leaders zipped Los Angeles, 4–0. **1978** *Time* 16 Jan. 66 The Broncos went out and beat the hell out of them, then the next week, went and zipped Cleveland.

Hence **zipping** *vbl. sb.*; **zipped** *ppl. a.*, fastened or provided with a zip. Also ***zipped-in, -up*** adjs. Also *fig.*

1881 J. M. BATTEN *Remin. Two Yrs. U.S. Navy* 72, I heard the zipping of bullets in the air close to my head. **1944** [see *slide fastener* s.v. SLIDE- a]. **1946** 'S. RUSSELL' *To Bed with Grand Music* i. 13 She picked up her mother's zipped travelling bag. **1959** *Listener* 2 Apr. 593/2 The chemical configuration of starch..is a long zipped-up chain of glucose molecules. **1959** *Times* 5 Oct. 6/2 A zipped-in detachable lining. **1966** T. PYNCHON *Crying of Lot 49* vi. 158 Blobb inquired around about the Trystero organization, running into zipped mouths nearly every way he turned. **1972** D. HASTON *In High Places* xi. 117 Down suit and fully zipped windproofs. **1982** M. KENYON *God Squad Bod* ii. 22 Zipped-up moneybags, satchels and briefcases.

Zipf (zɪpf). The name of George Kingsley *Zipf* (1902–50), American linguist, used in the possessive in ***Zipf's law***, a principle in *Psycholinguistics* (see quots.).

1960 É. DELAVENAY *Introd. Machine Transl.* v. 68 To lend support to arguments based on Zipf's law, Yngve produced evidence likely to convince unbelievers. **1967** M. SCHLAUCH *Language & Study of Languages Today* vii. 143 Some three decades ago, G. K. Zipf undertook to investigate what relation, if any, exists between the length of words and their frequency of occurrence in sample languages chosen for investigation. He came to the conclusion that the length of a word tends to decrease as its relative frequency of use increases... The formula..has come to be known as 'Zipf's Law', often quoted if also sometimes questioned. **1971** *Jrnl. General Psychol.* Oct. 297 Zipf's law predicts an inverse ratio in the rank order distribution of varieties such that a minimal number of varieties covers a maximal number of responses and a maximal number of varieties covers a minimal number of responses. **1980** *Verbatim* Spring 9/2 A psycholinguist will say that this phenomenon is working proof of Zipf's Law, which states loosely that one can generally determine the relative age of a particular word or phrase by how short it has become.

Ziph (zɪf). [Origin unknown.] An invented language used at Winchester College.

1853 DE QUINCEY *Autobiogr. Sketches* I. vii. 209 Lord Westport and I communicated our thoughts occasionally by means of a language..which bore the name of *Ziph*. The language and the name were both derived..from Winchester. **1922** O. JESPERSEN *Lang.* viii. 150 'Ziph' or 'Hypernese' (at Winchester) substitutes *wa* for the first of two initial consonants and inserts *p* or *g*, making 'breeches' into *wareechepes*. **1942** E. PARTRIDGE *Usage & Abusage* 160/2 *Gibberish* is applied mostly to Ziph (*shagall wege gogo* = shall we go).

ziphioid ('zɪfɪɔɪd), *a.* and *sb. Zool.* Also *erron.* ziphoid. [f. mod.L. *Ziphius* (Cuvier, 1834), erron. form for *Xiphius*, ad. Gr. ξίφιος, var. form of ξιφίας swordfish, XIPHIAS; see -OID.]

a. *adj.* Resembling or allied to the genus *Ziphius* of whales; belonging to or having the characteristics of the family *Ziphiidæ*. **b.** *sb.* A ziphioid whale. Also **'ziphian**; so **'ziphiiform** *a.*, having the form of a whale of this genus.

1870 FLOWER *Osteol. Mamm.* iv. 40 In *Hyperoodon*, and most of the other Ziphioids, the whole of the cervical vertebræ are ankylosed together. **1870** *Ann. & Mag. Nat. Hist.* Ser. IV. VI. 348 A Ziphioid Whale, probably *Berardius Arnuxii*. **1876** TOMES *Dental Anat.* iii. 56 The *Micropteron*, a ziphioid Cetacean. *Ibid.* ix. 288 The Cetaceans classed together as Ziphoids have no teeth in the upper jaw. **1896** R. J. ANDERSON *Whales & Dolph.* II. 13 In Ziphians the ribs are ten. *Ibid.* 14 In Sternum of the Ziphian kind A hole at middle, you will find.

ziphoide, erron. var. XIPHOID.

ziphre, obs. form of CIPHER *sb.*

'zipless, *a. coarse slang.* [f. ZIP *sb.*[1] 4 + -LESS.] Denoting a brief and passionate sexual encounter.

1973 E. JONG *Fear of Flying* i. 11 My response..was..to evolve my fantasy of the Zipless Fuck... Zipless because when you came together zippers fell away like petals. **1978** G. VIDAL *Kalki* iii. 79 Girls who feared flying tended to race blindly through zipless fucks. **1984** *Times* 2 Nov. 11/1 This small hand I'm shaking..launched a thousand zipless erotic encounters for her heroine.

zippeite ('zɪpɪaɪt). *Min.* [ad. G. *zippeit* (Haidinger, 1845), named after F. X. M. *Zippe*, a German mineralogist.] A sulphate of uranium, occurring in small bright yellow needles.

1854 R. D. THOMSON *Cycl. Chem.*

zipper ('zɪpə(r)), *sb.* orig. *U.S.* [f. ZIP *sb.* + -ER[1].]

1. = ZIP *sb.* 4. Also *transf.* and *fig.*

Zipper was registered in the U.S. as a trade mark in April 1925 (with use of the term claimed since June 1923), but in the sense 'boots made of rubber and fabric'. It is no longer a proprietary term in any of its uses. Quot. 1925, which appeared in the first Supplement to the *O.E.D.* (1933), and in the *Dictionary of Americanisms*, does not appear in surviving copies of *Scribner's Mag.*

1925 *Scribner's Mag.* Oct. 22/2 (Advt.), No fastening is so quick, secure, or popular as the 'zipper'. **1928** *Daily Express* 11 Oct. 5/5 Bootees..fastening with 'zippers', press studs, or inset clips. **1933** A. G. MACDONNELL *England, their England* viii. 130 Brown leather jerkins fastened up the front with that singular arrangement which is called a zipper. **1957** *New Yorker* 29 June 24/2 He hated fiddling with things like zippers caught on tiny strips of cloth. **1959** *Listener* 2 Apr. 593/2 We possess a biological zipper—an enzyme—which enables us to undo the chain [of the glucose molecules of starch]. **1966** F. SHAW et al. *Lern Yerself Scouse* 21 *Purra zipper on it*, please be silent. **1979** R. JAFFE *Class Reunion* I. xi. 105 She reached for the zipper of her skirt.

2. *attrib.* and *Comb.*, as ***zipper bag, fastener, fastening***, etc.

1925 *Harper's Bazaar* June 108/3 (Advt.), A 'zipper' closing bag sometimes used to carry champagne. **1925** *Scribner's Mag.* June 31/1 (Advt.), The most convenient and attractive form of the pocket purse is this one of lizard calf, leather lined, with a zipper fastening. **1928** *Daily Express* 15 Aug. 4/3 One 12-inch zipper fastener. *Ibid.* 11 Oct. 5/5 Zipper-fastened. **1937** D. ALDIS *Time at her Heels* ix. 196 He was wearing his dark blue zipper jacket. **1939** A. KEITH *Land below Wind* xx. 311 There were two zipper bags with dutiable goods. **1941** [see FLY *sb.*[2] 4 a]. **1959** C. WILLIAMS *Man in Motion* vii. 81 The briefcase..was a slender one, of the type with no handles, zipper-closed. **1960** M. SPARK *Ballad Peckham Rye* ii. 22 He sat down among his belongings, which were partly in and partly out of his zipper bag. **1969** *Sears Catal.* Spring/Summer 6 Center zipper pocket divides bag into two handy sections. **1978** *Lancashire Life* Mar. 70 (Advt.), Ladies zipper coats £11.50. **1982** R. RENDELL *Master of Moor* xvi. 175 He put on the zipper jacket and went out.

'zipper, *v.* orig. *U.S.* [f. the sb.] *trans.* To fasten with a zipper. Also *transf.* and *fig.* Freq. const. *up*.

1930 J. LAIT *Put on Spot* 215 Zipper. To shut something up, principally the mouth. **1935** N. ERSINE *Underworld & Prison Slang* 80 *Zipper*, *v.*, to cease talking. (Almost invariably the term is a command.) '*Zipper* that mug!' **1961** *John o' London's* 5 Oct. 398/2 Jean Renoir himself capering about zippered up..in a bear-suit. **1966** D. F. GALOUYE *Lost Perception* vi. 60 Driving wind..tunnelled through the TUT's open cab and Forsythe zippered up his jacket. **1971** *Nature* 3 Sept. 48/2 It seems to act by zippering together chromosomes which have their homologous telomeres attached next to each other at the nuclear membrane. **1974** H. L. FOSTER *Ribbin', Jivin', & playin' Dozens* vi. 284 After he tucked in his shirt, he closed his pants, zippered them up, put his belt back, and then left. **1984** *Sunday Tel.* (Colour Suppl.) 19 Feb. 12/3 Much was made of the 'keep it zippered' dressing-down he gave to his fellow-astronauts.

'zippered, *ppl. a.* orig. *U.S.* [f. ZIPPER *sb.* + -ED[2].] Fastened with a zipper; having a zipper.

1939 *Times* 31 Mar. 19/7 A charming wool frock with sun-ray decoration round the neck and neatly zippered might be chosen. **1941** *Time* 25 Aug. 2/3 His zippered ankle-high shoes. **1959** *Harrods News* Summer 15 Pigskin clothes brush with zippered top. **1971** B. MALAMUD *Tenants* 35 A bulky zippered briefcase was squeezed under his left arm. **1982** S. RADLEY *Talent for Destruction* vi. 36 A thin man in a zippered fawn cardigan.

Zippo ('zɪpəʊ). Also zippo. The proprietary name of a make of cigarette lighter.

1934 *Official Gaz.* (U.S. Patent Office) 10 July 270 Zippo Manufacturing Company, Bradford, Pa... *Zippo* for pocket lighter of the pyrophoric type. **1938** *Trade Marks Jrnl.* 16 Mar. 320/1 *Zippo*..Pyrophoric lighters. Miriam Barcroft Blaisdell..trading as Zippo Manufacturing Company,.. Bradford, State of Pennsylvania, United States of America; manufacturers. **1964** G. MCDONALD *Running Scared* iii. 35 The Zippo lighter he had given Casey. **1966** G. LYALL *Shooting Script* xxii. 174 Luiz flicked a Zippo under my nose. **1977** MCKNIGHT & TOBLER *Bob Marley* ix. 108 A novel sleeve made to look like a zippo lighter. *Ibid.* 112 Gone was the zippo, replaced by a picture of Marley smoking a kingsize splif. **1982** R. LUDLUM *Parsifal Mosaic* viii. 111 He extracted one [cigarette] and lit it with an old, tarnished Zippo purchased a quarter of a century ago.

zippy ('zɪpɪ), *a. colloq.* (orig. *U.S.*). [f. ZIP *sb.* 2 + -Y[1].] Bright, lively, energetic; fresh, invigorating; fast, speedy.

1904 G. ADE *True Bills* 108 Vivian, our bright-eyed little Daughter..is the zippiest High-Flyer that speeds the Boulevard. **1917** *National Police Gazette* 25 Aug. 2/4 It bubbles o'er with song and jest, Its fun is keen and 'zippy'. **1926** *Bulletin* (Glasgow) 26 Oct. 18/2 A zippy show is 'Cheerio' at the Glasgow Empire this week. **1939** *Better English* Jan. 29 (*heading*) Your words—are they zippy? **1953** *Amer. Mercury* Jan. 67/2 The March evening was zippy outside but cupped in it the breath of spring. **1959** I. JEFFERIES *Thirteen Days* xii. 202 My idea..was to get a zippy load into Richon and then move on to T.A. **1966** R. H. RIMMER *Harrad Experiment* (1967) 161 All we have to do now is to put together a zippy script. **1971** *Daily Tel.* 23 June 11/6 The engine warms up rapidly and provides zippy acceleration. **1980** M. BROADBENT *Great Vintage Wine Bk.* 134 Ch. Potensac. Zippy little wine. **1984** *Guardian* 5 Nov. 12/1 One advantage to being on Castleton social services committee is that they do have zippy meetings.

Hence **'zippily** *adv.*; **'zippiness**.

1924 WODEHOUSE *Bill the Conqueror* viii. 152 This series on Bookmakers' Swindling Methods..had always reached a fair level of zippiness; but never..had it so outzipped itself as in the present instalment. **1983** *Times* 10 June 17/6 The piece is zippily staged..and sung with immense liveliness.

ziraleet ('zɪrəliːt). [Arabic; cf. *zaghrata, zaghlata* to utter the cries of joy called *zaghrūtaʰ* or *zaghrītaʰ*, pl. *zaghārīt* (Dozy).] (See quot. 1794.)

1794 *A. Russell's Aleppo* (ed. 2) I. 382 The Ziraleet, or Zilroota [*zilġūṭah*], (as written by a native of Aleppo) is the common manner of a company of women expressing joy, or any sudden exultation. The words expressed are Lillé, Lillé, Lillé, repeated as often as the person can do at one breath. **1817** MOORE *Lalla R., Veiled Prophet* III. ix, And light your shrines and chaunt your ziraleets.

In *N. & Q.* Ser. VI. VI. 268 'A lark's ziraleet' is said to be used by Longfellow.

ziram ('zaɪræm). [f. *z*inc dimethyl dithiocar*bam*ate, the systematic name: see CARBAMATE.] A white powder used as a fungicide, esp. on vegetables and some fruit crops; $Zn(\cdot S{\cdot}CS{\cdot}N(CH_3)_2)_2$.

1950 [see ZINEB]. **1960** [see FERBAM]. **1969** *New Scientist* 8 May 299/2 The two main breakdown products of the fungicide, ziram (zinc dimethyldithiocarbamate) were carbon disulphide and dimethylamine. **1981** *Jrnl. Agric. & Food Chem.* XXIX. 729 The limit of detection in water solutions for zineb, ziram, and thiram was 0·05, 0·01, and 0·01 ppm, respectively.

Ziranian, var. SIRYENIAN *sb.* and *a.*

ziraph, obs. form of GIRAFFE.

†**zirbal**, *a. Obs. rare.* [f. late L. *zirbus* + -AL[1].] Of or pertaining to the *zirbus* or omentum.

1547 BOORDE *Brev. Health* cccx, There be thre kyndes of ruptures, the fyrst is zirbale.

zircaloy ('zɜːkəlɔɪ). Also zircalloy. [f. ZIRC(ONIUM + ALLOY *sb.*] Any of several alloys of zirconium, tin, and other metals that are used chiefly as cladding for nuclear reactor fuel.

1956 THOMAS & FORSCHER in *Jrnl. Metals* VIII. 640/1 Zircaloy-2, a low alloy of zirconium, was developed by the Westinghouse Atomic Power Div. during 1952. **1963** H. R. CLAUSER *Encycl. Engin. Materials & Processes* 769/1 Zircaloy resists corrosion very well in high-temperature water and steam. **1973** *Nature* 2 Feb. 318/1 The rods are zirconium alloy (zircalloy) tubes filled with pellets of uranium dioxide (UO_2) ceramic. **1977** J. H. SCHEMEL *ASTM Manual on Zirconium & Hafnium* (ASTM Special Technical Publ. No. 639) i. 6 Zircaloy is used to designate a series of zirconium, tin, iron, chromium, nickel alloys developed by the U.S. Navy Nuclear Propulsion Program for nuclear service in water-cooled reactors. Zircaloy-1 and Zircaloy-3 are obsolete. Zircaloy-2 and Zircaloy-4 are the most commonly used alloys in nuclear service.

zirco-: see ZIRCONIO-.

zircon ('zɜːkən). *Min.* Also 8 circon, 9 zircone. [ad. F. *zircone*, G. *zirkon*; see JARGON *sb.*[2]]

a. A native silicate of zirconium, occurring in tetragonal crystals, variously coloured, red, yellow, brown, green, etc.

Colourless and translucent varieties are used as gems: cf. HYACINTH 1 b, JARGON *sb.*[2]

1794 KIRWAN *Elem. Min.* (ed. 2) I. 14 Jargonic Earth or Jargonia. This earth has been discovered by Mr. Klaproth; it has as yet been found only in the stone called Jargon, or Circon, of Ceylon. **1815** J. SMITH *Panorama Sci. & Art* II. 453 Zircon is destitute of taste and smell, and is harsh to the touch. **1849** D. CAMPBELL *Inorg. Chem.* 160 Zirconia; Sesquioxide of zirconium... This oxide is found combined with silicic acid in the mineral zircons. **1902** *Encycl. Brit.* XXVIII. 613/2 The zircon, jargoon, or hyacinth is a very beautiful stone, varying in colour, like the topaz, from red and yellow to green and blue.

b. *attrib.* and *Comb.*, as ***zircon crystal, earth, fossil***; ***zircon-like*** adj.; **zircon blue**, a light blue colour; **zircon-syenite** (see quot.).

1949 *Brit. Colour Council Dict. Colours* III. 28/2 *Zircon blue*... Matched to specimens of the precious stone at the B.M. **1972** 'E. PETERS' *Death to Landlords!* i. 30 Withdrawing her zircon-blue eyes from the heavens. **1976** *Evening Post* (Nottingham) 13 Dec. 12/3 (Advt.), Rover 2000 1969. H. Zircon blue with black trim. **1804** R. JAMESON *Syst. Min.* I. 34 The *zircon crystal is formed. **1816** J. SMITH *Panorama Sci. & Art* II. 93 *Zircon earth. **1809** J. MURRAY *Syst. Chem.* (ed. 2) II. 274 *Zircon fossils. **1868** DANA *Min.* (ed. 5) 275 Tetragonal *zircon-like minerals. **1825** HAIDINGER tr. *Mohs' Treat. Min.* II. 370 Those [varieties of pyramidal zircon] from Frederiksvärn in Norway [occur] in *zircon-syenite.

zirconate ('zɜːkəneɪt). *Chem.* [f. ZIRCON-IC + -ATE[1] c.] A salt of zirconic acid.

1851 WATTS tr. *Gmelin's Handbk. Chem.* V. 464 Zirconate of Cupric Oxide.

zirconia (zə'kəʊnɪə). *Chem.* Also 8 circonia, 9 zircona. [mod.L. (Klaproth), f. *zircon*: see above and -IA[1].] An earth, usually obtained as a white powder by heating zirconium to redness in contact with air; zirconium dioxide, ZrO_2; used in certain incandescent burners.

1797 *Monthly Mag.* Mar. 206 The hyacinth..consists of ..more than six-tenths of its weight of a peculiar earth, now known under the name of jargon, zircon, or circonia. **1800** tr. *Lagrange's Chem.* I. 160 When exposed to a violent heat, zirconia becomes fused, and assumes a somewhat greyish colour. **1812** DAVY *Chem. Philos.* 361 Zircona is soluble in the mineral acids. **1871** tr. *Schellen's Spectrum Anal.* 19 The oxyhydrogen light..attains a still higher intensity, if a piece of magnesium or zirconia be substituted for the cylinder of lime.

attrib. **1849** WATTS tr. *Gmelin's Handbk. Chem.* III. 343 The zirconia-salts are not precipitated by zinc. **1875** KNIGHT *Dict. Mech.*, *Zirconia Light*, one in which a stick of oxide of zirconium is exposed to the flame of oxyhydrogen gas.

zirconian (zə'kəʊnɪən), *a.* [f. prec. + -AN.] = ZIRCONIC; *spec.* in *Min.*, applied to a mineral in which zirconium replaces a (small) proportion of some constituent element (cf. -IAN 2).

zirconian syenite = zircon-syenite (ZIRCON b).

1853 ROSS tr. *Humboldt's Trav.* III. 378 *note*, Pyroxenic porphyries with amygdaloids and zirconian syenites. **1930**

W. T. SCHALLER in *Amer. Mineralogist* XV. 572. **1963** *Doklady Acad. Sci. USSR: Earth Sci. Sect.* CXLI. 1301/1 Apatite, nepheline, and perovskite were observed, frequently forming intergrowths with the zirconian schorlomite. **1972** *Nature* 31 Mar. 197/2 The appearance of zirconian SiO_2-free minerals in the granitic fraction is rather strange.

zirconic (zəˈkɒnɪk), *a.* [f. ZIRCON, ZIRCONIA, or ZIRCONIUM + -IC.] Of, pertaining to, or like zircon; containing zirconia or zirconium. ***zirconic acid***, an acid containing zirconium, known only by its salts (*zirconates*).

1804 *Edin. Rev.* Jan. 304 After the zirconic follows the silicious genus. **1876** *Encycl. Brit.* V. 539/1 Zirconic oxide is infusible.

zirconio- (zəˈkəʊnɪəʊ), *Chem.*, also zircono-, and abbreviated zirco-, combining form of ZIRCONIUM, indicating the presence of zirconium in a compound, as **zircon(i)ofluoride**, a compound of zirconium fluoride, ZrF_4, with any of various oxides (more properly *fluozirconate*: see FLUO-).

1868 *Fownes' Chem.* (ed. 10) 383 Double salts, called zircofluorides or fluozirconates. **1894** MUIR & MORLEY *Watts' Dict. Chem.* IV. 859/1 Combinations... With various metallic fluorides... These salts are often called zircono-fluorides, or fluo-zirconates; they are better named zirconi-fluorides.

zirconite (ˈzɜːkənaɪt). *Min.* [f. ZIRCON + -ITE[1] 2 b.] A greyish or brownish variety of zircon. Hence **zircoˈnitic** *a.*, containing zircon.

1814 AIKIN *Man. Min.* 87 Zirconite..occurs in small crystals imbedded in Sienite. **1895** *Dana's Man. Geol.* (ed. 4) 83, *a.* Common or ordinary granite...*i.* Zirconitic.

zirconium (zəˈkəʊnɪəm). *Chem.* Also 9 zirconum. [mod.L., f. ZIRCON.] A metallic element, obtained from zircon as a black powder or as a greyish crystalline substance. Symbol Zr.

1808 DAVY in *Phil. Trans.* XCVIII. 353 Had I been so fortunate as to have..procured the metallic substances I was in search of, I should have proposed for them the names of silicium, alumium, zirconium, and glucium. **1812** —— *Chem. Philos.* 361 No substance has as yet been formed..in which zirconum can be supposed to exist free from oxygene. **1868** *Fownes' Chem.* 382 Zirconium..is a tetrad metal.

attrib. **1868** *Fownes' Chem.* (ed. 10) 382 Zirconium Oxide ..is prepared by strongly igniting zircon. **1906** *Athenæum* 1 Sept. 245/3 The osmium, tantalum, and zirconium incandescent filaments of electric glow-lamps.

zirconolite (zɜːˈkɒnəlaɪt). *Min.* [ad. Russ. *tsirkonolit* (L. S. Borodin et al. 1956, in *Doklady̆ Akad. Nauk SSSR* CX. 845): see ZIRCON and -LITE.] A mixed oxide of (essentially) calcium, zirconium, and titanium, now regarded as identical with zirkelite.

1957 *Chem. Abstr.* LI. 6440 (*heading*) The new mineral zirconolite, a complex oxide of the type AB_3O_7. **1975** *Amer. Mineralogist* LX. 341/1 Zirconolite, $CaZrTi_2O_7$, was described in 1956..as a new mineral and the zirkelite of Blake and Smith was considered to be zirconolite... New analyses and X-ray studies of type material show that all these are a single mineral species of composition $(Ca,Th,RE)Zr(Ti,Nb,Fe)_2O_7$. The name zirkelite has priority. **1980** *Nature* 17 Jan. 282/1 Synthetic zirconolite, $CaZrTi_2O_7$, has attracted interest recently, as it has been proposed as a constituent phase of an artificial rock (SYNROC) which may immobilise, in solid solution, the elements occurring in high-level nuclear reactor wastes. **1981** [see ZIRKELITE].

zirkelite (ˈzɜːkəlaɪt). *Min.* [f. the name of Ferdinand *Zirkel* (1838–1912), German mineralogist + -ITE[1].] A black monoclinic (pseudocubic) oxide of zirconium, calcium, thorium, titanium, rare earths, and other elements, $(Ca,Th,Ce)Zr(Ti,Nb)_2O_7$.

1895 HUSSAK & PRIOR in *Mineral. Mag.* XI. 86 Zirkelite. A new calcium zirconate and titanate. **1962** *Mineral. Abstr.* XV. 538/1 Zirkelite is widely distributed in the Palaeozoic ultrabasic and alkaline complexes of the Kola Peninsula where it occurs as an accessory mineral in calcite-amphibole rocks; [etc.]. **1972** *Nature* 31 Mar. 215/1 We find that terrestrial zirkelite bears the closest comparison with the tranquillityite group, and yet contains sufficient CaO..to provide a possible link with any calcic lunar zirconian phases yet to be established. **1975** [see ZIRCONOLITE]. **1977** *Amer. Mineralogist* LXII. 408 Zirconolite and niobozirconolite.. are synonymous with zirkelite. **1981** K. FRYE *Encycl. Mineral.* 220/1 There is considerable controversy over the exact formulas of zirkelite and zirconolite. Some evidence suggests that there is no difference.

zisel, variant of ZIZEL.

zit (zɪt). *slang* (chiefly *N. Amer.*). [Origin unknown.] A pimple. Also in extended and *fig.* use. Occas. in *Comb.*

1966 G. C. SAUER *Man. Skin Dis.* (ed. 2) 284 *Zits*, term in teen-agers' vernacular for 'pimples' of acne. **1966** *Current Slang* (Univ. S. Dakota) Summer 5 *Zit*, something bad or unpleasant; crude... What's that *zit* on your coat? **1972** B. RODGERS *Queens' Vernacular* 45 *Vit* (late '60s, fr. sl. *zit* = a pimple: boy with Pepsi consciousness, *i.e.* nothing going on between the ears). **1975** *Atlantic Monthly* Mar. 51 One splendid effort in 1971 featured..districts with remarkable pimples in their boundary lines, zits that popped up to include the home of one liberal incumbent in the district of another liberal incumbent. **1975** *Maclean's Mag.* June 59/1 When did you last have a zit on your face? **1977** *Amer. Speech* 1975 L. 69 *Zit n*, reddish mark caused by kissing. 'She has a big zit on her neck.' **1977** J. WAMBAUGH *Black Marble* (1978) vi. 77 How old is the little zit-faced, coke-snorting, hash-smoking son of a bitch? **1980** *Courier-Mail* (Brisbane) 30 Apr. 46/3 (*caption*) You know playing with teenagers will give you zits. **1984** S. TOWNSEND *Growing Pains A. Mole* 105 Forgot to send you an invite, zit face, but come anyway, dress as a warlock or you won't get in.

zit(te, zitch: see SIT *v.*, SUCH.

zita (ˈziːtə). Pl. zite, ziti. [It.] A tubular variety of pasta resembling large macaroni.

1845 E. ACTON *Mod. Cookery* (ed. 4) p. xxx, *Zita*, Naples maccaroni. **1943** A. L. SIMON *Conc. Encycl. Gastron.* IV. 141/1 *Zita*, pl. *zite*, one of the fancy Italian pastes... It is made of the gluten of hard wheat and eggs, like Macaroni, in hollow, straight tubes of larger diameter than Macaroni. **1964** *Guardian* 22 May 8/6 *Ziti*, cut macaroni tubes slightly curved. **1978** R. F. CAPON *Food for Thought* vii. 106 Why not sauces for ziti, for occhi di lupo, [etc.]? **1979** *Tucson Mag.* Sept. 68/2 Bargain specialties—like gnocchi, zita, linguine, and so-so meat dishes. **1983** *Fortune* 21 Feb. 78/1 For the one-time shopper, goods from auto-parts to ziti.

‖**zitella.** *Obs.* Pl. -e. [It.] A girl, young woman, maiden.

a **1668** LASSELS *Voy. Italy* II. (1670) 250 The Procession of the *Zitelle* upon our Ladyes day in Lent. **1679** MRS. BEHN *Feign'd Curtizans* III. i, A Curtizan! and a Zittella too? a pretty contradiction! *a* **1700** EVELYN *Diary* 1 Mar. 1645, We saw the Pope and Cardinals ride in pomp to the Minerva, .. when he gives portions to 500 *zitelle*.

zither (ˈzɪθə(r)), *sb.* Also 9 zithern, zitt(h)er, zittern. [ad. G. *zither*: see CITHER, CITHERN.]

a. A musical instrument (introduced into England *c* 1850 from Austria) having from thirty to forty strings let into the lower rim of a shallow resonance-box, and played by striking with the fingers and thumb.

In modifications of the instrument a fretted finger-board is fitted across a resonance-box shaped like a heart (*bow zither*) or like a viola (*viola zither*), and the instrument is played with a bow.

1850 *The Initials* iv, I expected some such proposition as soon as I heard the sound of the zither. **1864** in WEBSTER. **1868** *Daily News* 14 Aug., A couple of musicians, one playing the violin, another an instrument something like the zittern. **1871** MEREDITH *Harry Richmond* xxx, Nothing haunted me so much as those tones of her zither. **1874** MISS R. H. BUSK *Vall. Tirol* Pref. p. vi, Just as..the barrel-organ supersedes the zitther and the guitar. **1886** RUSKIN *Præterita* II. vi. 215 He is playing..on a kind of zithern-harp.

b. *Comb.*, as ***zither music***, ***player***; ***zither-playing***, ***-tinkling*** adjs.; **zither-banjo**, a modification of the zither, resembling a banjo.

1900 *Referee* 9 Dec. 3 (Cass. Suppl.), Mr. ——'s 'Valse des Fleurs', with a zither-banjo. **1881** W. BLACK *Sunrise* iii, He was passionately fond of zither music. **1850** *The Initials* iv, The untutored singers and zither players. **1982** C. MCINTOSH *Swan King* viii. 83 A fun-loving, zither-playing, somewhat bohemian character. **1925** E. SITWELL et al. *Poor Young People* 2 Among the zither-tinkling round green leaves.

Hence **ˈzitherist**, a performer on the zither.

1887 *Pall Mall Gaz.* 8 Feb. 6/1 The Zitherist to his Highness the Duke of Nassau.

ˈzither, *v.* [f. the sb.] *intr.* To play the zither. Also *fig.* (occas. also *trans.*). Hence **ˈzithering** *ppl. a.*

Some of the examples could equally well be interpreted as being of echoic origin, with the sense 'to make a sibilant humming sound, buzz lightly'.

1906 W. J. LOCKE *Beloved Vagabond* (1907) ix. 120 We wandered and fiddled and zithered and tambourined through France. **1930** R. CAMPBELL *Adamastor* 71 The sunlight, zithering their flanks with fire, Flashes between the shadows as they pass. **1958** J. TOWNSEND *Young Devils* iv. 35 His squeaky voice zithered through morning or afternoon. **1973** *Art Internat.* Mar. 57/1 Balla's zithering *Rhythm of the Violinist* is considerably more effective. **1979** H. MCLEAVE *Double Exposure* i. 1 The helicopter..trailing a zithering shadow. **1981** B. CARTER *Black Fox Running* xxvii. 176 Insects zithered and chirred.

ziti: see ZITA.

zitkamer, zit-kamer, varr. SITKAMER.

zix, zixt: see SIX, SEE *v.*

‖**zizania** (zɪ-, zaɪˈzeɪnɪə). *Bot.* [mod.L. fem. sing. = late L. n. pl. (see ZIZANY).] (Any aquatic grass of) the genus so named, esp. *Z. aquatica* (Canada, Indian, water, or wild rice).

1829 T. CASTLE *Introd. Bot.* 157 The zizania or Canada-rice. **1847** PRICHARD *Phys. Hist. Man.* V. VI. v. §6. 395 The Menomonies are called 'Folles Avoines', or Wild Oats, from the wild rice or zizania which their country produces.

†**zizany.** *Obs.* Forms: 4 zizanny, -ije, 5 zizannie, 6 zizanie, 6–8 zizany; also (in Gr.-L. form) 4–6 zizania, 7 *pl.* zizaniaes. [a. OF. *zizanie*, ad. late L. *zizania* n. pl., a. Gr. ζιζάνια, pl. of ζιζάνιον.]

1. An injurious weed among corn; also *fig.*; = TARE *sb.*[1] 3, b.

a **1300** *Cursor M.* 1138 Þi wete sal bi-com zizanny [*Gött.* zizannije, *Fairf.* darnel]. *a* **1425** tr. *Arderne's Treat. Fistula*, etc. 100 Recipe semen iusquiamus, zizannie, i. darnel. *c* **1532** DU WES *Introd. Fr.* in *Palsgr.* 915 Zizany, droe. **1581** J. HAMILTON in *Cath. Tract.* (S.T.S.) 74 To desaue the varld to sau zizanie and pernicious heresie in mennis hartis. *a* **1706** EVELYN *Hist. Relig.* (1850) II. 314 Many holy and excellent persons God has dispersed, as wheat among the tares and zizany.

[**1398** TREVISA *Barth. De P.R.* XVII. cxciv. (1495) Xiv/1 Ray hyghte Zizania and is a certen herbe..lyke to whete whanne it is grasse.] **1562** TURNER *Herbal* II. 41 There is great lyknes betwene whete and zizaniam, which we call lolium. **1570** FOXE *A. & M.* (ed. 2) 829/2 The doctrine of the Bohemians, whiche he termeth by the name of Zizania. **1612** T. JAMES *Iesuits Downef.* 8 With their Zizaniaes of faction, they make boot & havocke of Catholickes estates.

2. = ZIZANIA. *rare.*

1759 B. STILLINGFLEET tr. *Gedner's Use Cur.* in *Misc. Tracts* (1762) 184 A great number of plants fit for food might be sown, such as zizany of Canada.

zizel (ˈzɪzəl). Also zisel. [ad. G. *ziesel* (also *zieselmaus*, *-ratte*; in MHG. *zisel*; cf. also OHG. *zisemûs* dormouse = OE. *sisemús*).] The ground-squirrel *Spermophilus citillus*; = SUSLIK.

1785 SMELLIE *Buffon's Nat. Hist.* (1791) VIII. 229 The Zisel, or Earless Marmot. **1833** *Penny Cycl.* I. 441/2 The zizel or souslic marmot. **1893** *Edin. Rev.* Jan. 20 Other Southern districts [were visited] by zisels and worms.

zizith, var. TSITSITH.

‖**zizypha.** *Obs.* [mod.L., pl. of late L. *zizyphum* fruit of the tree ZIZYPHUS.] The fruit of the zizyphus; = JUJUBE 1; also, the tree itself.

1546 LANGLEY tr. *Pol. Verg. De Invent.* III. ii. 67 Zinzipha [*sic*] & Tuberes .ii. kyndes of apple trees S. Papinius conueighed out of Siria and Affrike into Italy. **1555** EDEN *Decades* (Arb.) 110 The frute cauled *Zizipha*, which the Apothecaries caule *Iuiuba*. **1712** [see ZIZYPHUS].

‖**zizyphus** (ˈzɪzɪfəs). *Bot.* Also -iphus (5 -ifus); 8 anglicized ziziph. [late L., ad. Gr. ζίζυφον.] A plant of a large widely distributed genus so named, which comprises spiny shrubs or trees of the buckthorn family, various species of which bear an edible fruit called ZIZYPHA or JUJUBE, q.v.

c **1440** *Pallad. on Husb.* VII. 84 Now zizifus in cold lond wole ascende. **1712** tr. *Pomet's Hist. Drugs* I. 134 Jujuba, or Zizipha, a large Fruit of the Ziziph Tree. **1741** J. MARTYN *Virg. Georg.* II. 84 *note*, It seems to me more probable that the *Lotus* of the *Lotophagi* is what we now call *Zizyphus* or the *Jujube-tree*. **1865** TRISTRAM *Land of Israel* xxii. 527 The zizyphus and caper crept higher up the hills. **1882** FLOYER *Unexpl. Baluch.* 265 We are..still camped under a spreading ziziphus.

attrib. **1890** *Daily News* 5 Apr. 6/1 The Crown of Thorns at Notre Dame is made of plaited reeds, in which ziziphus thorns are intertwined.

zizz (zɪz), *sb.*

1. a. The noise made by the rapid motion of a wheel; also as *adv.* Also extended to other whizzing or buzzing noises (see quots.).

1824 SCOTT *Redgauntlet* ch. xi, I carried a cutler's wheel for several weeks, .. there I went bizz—bizz—whizz—zizz, at every auld wife's door. **1904** G. A. B. DEWAR *Glamour of Earth* vi. 131 The zizz of the cricket, or the shrill of the bat. **1908** BELLOC *Mr. Clutterbuck's Elect.* xiii, They shot round the base of the hills, ..had a splendid zizz along the Hog's Back, and then turned sharp round. **1955** D. BARTON *Glorious Life* xxv. 232 The sustained, high-pitched zizz of a party was audible. **1965** *Listener* 17 June 900/3 The zizz of a trishaw's wheels passing on the road. **1976** *Drive* May–June 53/2 Gear lever zizz is irritating.

b. Gaiety, liveliness, 'sparkle'. *colloq.*

1942 BERREY & VAN DEN BARK *Amer. Thes. Slang* §240/2 *Animation; spirit; vim*;..zing, zip, ..zizz. **1970** *Gourmet* Jan. 18/2 No party got into full swing until Tallulah arrived to put her particular type of zizz into it. **1983** *Times* 22 Feb. 12/6 The Queensgate centre lacks, perhaps, finesse and a touch of zizz.

2. Also ziz. A short sleep, a nap. Cf. Z 4 b. *slang.*

1941 *Tee Emm* Aug. 17 He could not have caught our Pilot Officer Prune at three o'clock one afternoon having a zizz full-length on a mess settee. **1960** 'N. SHUTE' *Trustee from Toolroom* v. 105 'Captain's having a ziz now,' said the navigator. 'Supper's at eleven o'clock, Greenwich. He's getting up for that.' **1970** P. DICKINSON tr. *Aristophanes' Wasps* in *Plays* I. 169 Just what I aim to forget by having A quiet ziz. **1979** M. TABOR *Baker's Daughter* I. 31 Philip's having a zizz. He can't stay awake. **1985** *Guardian* 24 Jan. 1/3 They would not film any lord who had drifted off in the warmth of the lights for a refreshing zizz.

zizz, *v.* [f. the sb.] **1.** *intr.* To make a whizzing or buzzing sound. Occas. *trans.* (causally). Also const. *up*, to liven up.

a **1934** in WEBSTER s.v., Trolleys went zizzing along. **1961** E. WILLIAMS *George* ix. 112 The pince-nez zizzed back to her lapel. **1963** *Punch* 1 May 621/3 Then she [*sc.* a bee] saw the carpet and zizzed. **1965** *Harper's Bazaar* Feb. 21/2 An adventurous buyer deciding that model 127 is just the thing to zizz up his mid-season collection. **1970** T. LEWIS *Jack's Return Home* 89 The banger'd started zizzing furiously. **1970** *Daily Tel.* 16 Dec. 11 Darts and circles about on the floor after its wheels are zizzed smartly. **1978** *Ibid.* 19 July 12/5 The gearchange..is light but slightly notchy, and tended to 'zizz' on the overrun.

2. *slang.* To doze or sleep. Occas. *trans.* with *away.*

1942 [see below]. **1961** D. MOORE *Highway of Fear* xxxvi. 240 Reckon this sector's safe. Might as well zizz. **1972** K. BONFIGLIOLI *Don't point that Thing at Me* xii. 94, I zizzed away the worst of the afternoon, awaking some three hours later. **1978** *Sunday Mail Color Mag.* (Brisbane) 30 Apr. 20/6 When everyone inside the building had zizzed off he had sneaked inside.

Hence **ˈzizzing** *vbl. sb.* and *ppl. a.*

1942 *Gen* I Sept. 13/1 Sleeping is 'zizzing' whether it's on the job or in the hammock. **1951** J. STRACHEY *Man on Pier* 37 The flies on the window-pane woke up and started to rage together with a venomous zizzing. *Ibid.* 88 Confusion continued, it seemed to Ned, to the old background of zizzing flies, bellowing cows, walks, and hot, cloudy weather. **1961** E. WILLIAMS *George* ix. 111 There was a terrified zizzing noise from an obedient coil-spring.

'zizzy, *a. colloq.* [f. ZIZZ *sb.* + -Y[1].] Showy, spectacular; lively, uninhibited.

1966 *Guardian* 5 Feb. 7/6 And who's going to pay for 'Danger Man' with that zizzy Patrick McGoohan, then? **1975** *New Yorker* 21 Apr. 24/3 If you accept the silly, zizzy obviousness, it can make you laugh helplessly. **1976** *Times* 4 Oct. 7 My wife said I should wear a dark suit but I did risk a particularly zizzy tie. **1983** *Guardian Weekly* 6 Feb. 1/2 Zizzy little TV charts.

† **Zlead(s, Zlid.** *Obs.* A minced oath: = *God's lid(s*: see GOD *sb.* 14 a, and cf. UDS I. So † **Z'life** = God's life.

1616 S. S. *Honest Lawyer* I. B. 4 b, Zlid, before the Prologue had done, I had lost my purse. **1689** N. LEE *Princ. Cleve* II. ii. 19 Z'life I am as weary of mine, as a Modish Lady of her old Cloaths. **1785** HUTTON *Bran New Wark* 170 (E.D.S.) Zleads! he nivver played hocus pocus.

Z line (zɛd, *U.S.* ziː, laɪn). *Histology.* [Partial tr. G. *schicht z* z layer (T. W. Engelmann 1873, in *Arch. f. die ges. Physiol.* VII. 37), f. initial letter of *zwischenscheibe* intervening disc.]

A transverse dark line in a fibril of striated muscle formed by Krause's membrane (see KRAUSE b); the membrane itself.

1916 JORDAN & FERGUSON *Text-bk. Histol.* iv. 105 This stripe or accessory disk..bisects the portion of the J disk between the Z line and the succeeding Q disk. **1954** *Nature* 22 May 976/1 The series elastic component is provided either by the actin filaments themselves, or, more probably, by their mode of attachment to the Z-line. **1979** *Sci. Amer.* May 94/2 In muscle fibers the actin filaments are anchored to flat protein structures called Z lines, which are emplaced between every two contractile units.

Also **Z band**.

1950 A. W. HAM *Histology* xix. 283/1 When a substantial degree of contraction has occurred, an appearance, often referred to as a 'reversal of striations', becomes apparent. This is due to the substance of the myofibril on each side of the Z band, which was formerly light, becoming dark, and the dark material of the Q band becoming light. **1964** G. H. HAGGIS et al. *Introd. Molecular Biol.* iv. 101 The segment from one Z-band to the next, along a fibril, is termed a sarcomere. **1970** [see KRAUSE b].

zloty ('zlɒtɪ, ‖ 'zwoti). Pl. **zloty, zlotys.** [a. Polish *złoty*, f. *złoto* gold, cogn. w. Russ. *zóloto*: see GOLD.] **a.** A gold or silver coin of monarchic Poland. **b.** The monetary unit of the Polish republic; a note or coin of the republican currency.

1915 *Publ. Scottish Hist. Soc.* LIX. 63 The fourth witness ..hath borne witness in the following words:—'I..have seen how Jan Furman, a Scot, hath taken..40 Polish zloty, from that Kilian.' **1923** *Times* 3 Mar. 16/6 The Polish Minister of Finance has decided that State loans..shall..be effected in Polish zlotys (a zloty is equivalent to a Swiss franc), at the current market rate. **1923** *Times* 13 Aug. 14/5 The zloty, or gold franc, the nominal unit of Poland. **1944** V. G. GARVIN tr. *R. Gary's Forest of Anger* xxiii. 90 They've imposed a fine of 100,000 zlotys on Pinski! **1960** S. BECKER tr. *Schwarz-Bart's Last of Just* II. 40 When you have a few zlotys in hand, you can come back here and reimburse me. **1970** *New Yorker* 6 June 33/1 He promised me a room, food, and a small salary in Polish marks. The zloty wasn't yet established as a currency. **1983** *Nature* 28 July 299/2 The Polish Government has raised the price of edible salt to between 11 zloty and 17 zloty per kilo.

zo, dial. f. SO *sb.*

zoa, plural of ZOON *sb.*

zoæa: see ZOEA.

zoane, obs. form of ZONE.

zoantharian (zəʊænˈθɛərɪən), *a.* and *sb. Zool.* [f. mod.L. *Zōanthāria* neut. pl., f. *Zōanthus*, name of genus, f. Gr. ζῷον animal + ἄνθος flower.]

a. *adj.* Belonging to the *Zoantharia*, one of the main divisions of *Actinozoa* (contrasted with *Alcyonaria*), containing the sea-anemones and other (often flower-like) animals, usually with simple tentacles and parts arranged in sixes (HEXACORALLAN); *sb.* a member of the *Zoantharia*. Also **zo'anthid**, a member of the family *Zoanthidæ* of zoantharians, typified by the genus *Zoanthus* (hence **zo'anthidan** *a.*); **zo'anthodeme** (-diːm) [Gr. δέμα bundle], a compound organism formed of coherent zoantharian zooids or polyps (hence **zoantho'demic** *a.*); **zo'anthoid** *a.* [-OID], resembling or related to the genus *Zoanthus*.

1887 H. A. NICHOLSON *Man. Zool.* (ed. 7) 186 Transverse section of a simple *Zoantharian Coral (*Cyathina Bowerbanki*). **1888** ROLLESTON & JACKSON *Anim. Life* 733 *note*, The Zoantharian mesenterial filaments. **1870** H. A. NICHOLSON *Man. Zool.* xiii. (1875) 132 Structures supposed to be gills are developed in some *Zoanthids on either side of the primary mesenteries. **1888** ROLLESTON & JACKSON *Anim. Life* 736 A pair [of mesenteries] of the typical *Zoanthidan structure. **1877** HUXLEY *Anat. Inv. Anim.* iii. 155 Many give rise by gemmation to turf-like, or arborescent, *zoanthodemes. **1854** A. ADAMS, etc. *Man. Nat. Hist.* 354 *Zoanthoid-Polyps (Zoanthoida). **1841** T. R. JONES *Anim. Kingd.* 37 A small *Zoanthus or other naked zoophyte.

zoanthropy (zəʊˈænθrəpɪ). *Path.* [ad. mod.L. *zōanthrōpia*, f. Gr. ζῷον animal + ἄνθρωπος man: cf. CYNANTHROPY, LYCANTHROPY.] A form of insanity in which a man imagines himself to be a beast. Hence **zoanthropic** (-'ɒpɪk) *a.*, pertaining to zoanthropy.

1856 E. JESSE *Walton's Angler* I. v. 166 *note*, Several forms of mania, classed by Sauvages in his Nosology under the general head of Zoanthropy. **1891** *Cent. Dict.* s.v. *Zoanthropic*, Zoanthropic mania..; zoanthropic literature.

zoar, obs. var. of ZOHAR.

‖ **zoarium** (zəʊˈɛərɪəm). *Zool.* Pl. **zoaria** (-ɪə). [mod.L., in form ad. Gr. ζωάριον, dim. of ζῷον animal, but taken as if f. ζῷον + -ARIUM: cf. POLYZOARY.] The common supporting structure of a colony of polyps, or the colony or compound organism as a whole (esp. in the *Polyzoa* or moss-animalcules): = POLYZOARY. Hence **zo'arial** *a.*, pertaining to or constituting a zoarium.

1880 SAVILLE-KENT *Infusoria* I. 338 The zoarium of the polyzoic genera *Aulopora* or *Hippothoa*. **1896** J. W. GREGORY *Catal. Fossil Bryozoa* Introd. 16 In typical *Diastopora* the zoarium consists of two layers of zoœcia, one on each side of the zoarial lamina.

zob (zɒb). *U.S. slang. rare.* [Origin unknown.] A weak or contemptible person; a fool.

1911 W. F. KIRK *Right off Bat* 13 He came here in the early Spring with all the try-out mob Striving to bat like Wagner and to slide (spikes first) like Cobb. Some of the vets cried, 'Bonehead!' Others remarked, 'Poor zob!' **1920** S. LEWIS *Main Street* xxxv. 416 And the same thing goes for that crowd of crabs and snobs Down East, and next time you hear some zob from Yahooville-on-the-Hudson chewing the rag..you tell him that no..Westerner would have New York for a gift! **1922** —— *Babbitt* x. 140, I don't know how you fellows feel about prohibition, but the way it strikes me is that it's a mighty beneficial thing for the poor zob that hasn't got any will-power but for fellows like us, it's an infringement of personal liberty. **1942** BERREY & VAN DEN BARK *Amer. Thes. Slang* §396 Terms of disparagement.. yaphead, yazzihamper, zob.

zobo: see ZHO.

zocalo ('zɒkələʊ). Also **zócalo** and with capital initial. [a. Sp.] In Mexico, a public square, a plaza.

1884 J. W. STEELE *To Mexico by Palace Car* v. 75 The square in front of the Cathedral, called the Zócalo, is the place of universal resort. **1884** F. H. OBER *Trav. in Mexico* xii. 232 Beneath us is the great square, with the smaller one, the zocalo, or pleasure garden, in its center. **1912** E. H. BLICKFELD *Mexican Journey* x. 119 The Zocalo, as it is called, is the real center of Mexico City. **1927** D. H. LAWRENCE *Mornings in Mexico* 39 And a *plaza* is a *zocalo*, a hub. **1957** M. LOWRY *Let.* 17 Mar. (1967) 398, I read of revolutions, counterrevolutions..in the zócalo. **1975** *Times* 24 May 10/3 Oaxaca..its zocalo, with its trees and its arcades.

† **zocco, zoc(c)olo.** *Obs.* [It. *zocco*, *zoccolo*: see SOCLE.] = SOCLE I.

1664 EVELYN tr. *Freart's Archit.* II. 92 The Piedestal with its entire *Bassament*, *Cymatium*, and that *Zocolo* or Plinth above wrought with a festoon (which in my judgment makes a part of it, as rendering it a perfect Cube). *Ibid.* 124 Certain *Zoccos* or Blocks elevating the rest of the members of an Order. **1715** LEONI *Palladio's Archit.* (1742) II. 31 The Bases have no Zocco. **1723** CHAMBERS tr. *Le Clerc's Archit.* I. 27 KL. Piedroit with its Fillet at bottom. M. Its Zocco.

zocle ('zəʊk(ə)l). [ad. It. *zoccolo*.] = prec.

1704 J. HARRIS *Lex. Techn.* I, *Zocle*, is a Square Member in Architecture, being lower than its Breadth, which serves to support a Pillar... *Continued Zocle*, is a kind of continued Pedestal, on which a Structure is raised, but hath no Base, or Cornish. **1723** CHAMBERS tr. *Le Clerc's Archit.* I. 54 Vignola terminates these Pillars with a plain Zocle. **1870** ROCK *Text. Fabr.* II. 334 Two little naked winged boys standing on a highly elaborate zocle.

‖ **zoco** ('zɒkəʊ). Also **Soko.** [Sp., ad. Arab.: see SOUK.] = SOUK; also *transf.*

1892 M. THOMAS *Scamper through Spain & Tangier* xii. 232 The Soko is an unpaved square surrounded with booths, outside the walls, where on Thursdays and Sundays, as in Spain, the market is held. **1903** A. F. CALVERT *Impressions of Spain* 96 Toledo—? She is at least faithful to the dead past... So she retains her old *Soko*, and will have naught to do with the correct *Plaza de la Constitucion.* **1921** *Chambers's Jrnl.* Dec. 817/2 Tangier.. cosmopolitan enough as it seems to be to any one who ambles through the little *zoco*, has been administratively mismanaged. **1924** *Ibid.* Sept. 689/2 The minaret of the new mosque overlooking the big zoco cuts through the blue. **1965** C. D. EBY *Siege of Alcázar* (1966) i. 34 The Gobierno resembled the *zoco* of a North African town except that the jewellery boxes, bundles of clothing,..and whimpering children were not for sale.

zodiac ('zəʊdɪæk), *sb.* (*a.*) Forms: 4–7 **zodiak, -ake,** 4–8 **-aque,** 5 **zodyak, -ack,** (**sodyak, zodias**), 6 **zodiacque,** 6–7 **-acke,** 6–8 **-ack,** (7 **-aq**), 5– **zodiac.** [a. OF. (mod.F.) *zodiaque* (= Pr. *zodiac*, It., Sp., Pg. *zodiaco*), ad. L. *zōdiacus* (Cicero), a. late Gr. ζῳδιακός, sc. κύκλος the circle of the figures or signs (cf. L. *orbis signifer*, Cicero, *circulus signifer*, Vitruvius = ὁ ζῳοφόρος κύκλος, Aristotle), f. ζῴδιον sculptured figure (of an animal), sign of the zodiac (ὁ τῶν ζῳδίων κύκλος), dim. of ζῷον animal.]

1. *Astr.* A belt of the celestial sphere extending about 8 or 9 degrees on each side of the ecliptic, within which the apparent motions of the sun, moon, and principal planets take place; it is divided into twelve equal parts called *signs* (see b).

1390 GOWER *Conf.* III. 108 Ther ben signes tuelve, Whiche have her cercles be hemselve Compassed in the zodiaque. *c* **1391** CHAUCER *Astrol.* Prol. 3 To knowe in owre orizonte with wych degree of the zodiac that the Mone arisith in any latitude. *c* **1400** *Destr. Troy* 3726 The sun vnder zodias settis hym to leng Two dayes betwene. **1426** LYDG. *De Guil. Pilgr.* 17200 She held also a gret ballaunce, Only off purpos (yiff she konne,) To peyse the sodyak and the sonne. **1549** *Compl. Scot.* vi. 50 Ane vthir grit circle in the spere, callit the zodiac, the quhilk deuidis the circle equinoctial in tua partis. **1588** SHAKS. *Tit. A.* II. i. 7 When the golden Sunne..Gallops the Zodiacke in his glistering Coach. **1611** DONNE *Poems, Anat. World* 263 They have impal'd within a Zodiake The free-borne Sun, and keepe twelve Signes awake To watch his steps. **1727** POPE, etc. *Art of Sinking* 86 Thus Phoebus through the zodiack takes his way. **1868** LOCKYER *Elem. Astron.* §364 One of the points in which the zodiac cuts the equator.

b. *signs of the zodiac* (SIGN *sb.* 11): the twelve equal parts into which the zodiac is divided, and through one of which the sun passes in each month; they are named after the twelve constellations (Aries, Taurus, Gemini, Cancer, Leo, Virgo, Libra, Scorpio, Sagittarius, Capricornus, Aquarius, Pisces) with which at a former epoch they severally coincided approximately (see PRECESSION 3).

[**1390** GOWER *Conf.* III. 117 Hou that the Signes sitte arowe, Ech after other be degre In substance and in proprete The zodiaque comprehendeth Withinne his cercle, as it appendeth.] *c* **1532** DU WES *Introd. Fr.* in *Palsgr.* 1054 The XII signes of the Zodiacque. **1585** FETHERSTONE tr. *Calvin on Acts* xxviii. 11 The signe in the Zodiacke called Gemini. **1625** N. CARPENTER *Geogr. Delin.* I. v. 101 Wheresoeuer any man stands on the Surface of the Earth, six signes of the Zodiacke will shew themselues. **1715** tr. *Gregory's Astron.* I. 203 The images of the Stars have removed from the Signs of the Zodiac, to which they originally gave names. **1866** R. M. FERGUSON *Electr.* (1870) 36 The sun is in the northern signs of the zodiac.

c. *zodiac of the moon, a planet*, etc.: that belt of the heavens (usually a portion of the ordinary zodiac) within which the apparent motion of the moon, planet, etc. takes place.

1704 J. HARRIS *Lex. Techn.* I, *Zodiack* of the Comets, Cassini hath observed a certain Tract..within whose Bounds..he hath found most Comets..to keep. **1715** tr. *Gregory's Astron.* II. 821 These Comets..do not go in the Zodiac or Way of the Planets. **1788** GIBBON *Decl. & F.* l. V. 190 The Bedoween..was taught by experience to divide, in twenty-eight parts, the zodiac of the moon. **1834** *Nat. Philos., Astron.* i. 4 (U.K.S.), According to Gaubil, the invention of the Chinese zodiac, divided into twenty-seven constellations, is to be referred to Yao. **1888** *Encycl. Brit.* XXIV. 793/2 The synodical revolution of the moon laid down the lines of the solar, its sidereal revolution those of the lunar zodiac.

2. A figure or representation of the zodiac.

c **1391** CHAUCER *Astrol.* I. §21 Alle sterres sittinge wyth-in the zodiak of thin astrolabie ben cleped sterres of the north. *a* **1548** HALL *Chron., Hen. VIII.* 157 b, In the zodiak were the twelve figures curiously made and aboue this were made the seuen planettes. **1605** CAMDEN *Rem.* 168 A virgin Prince, who presented in his shield, the Zodiacke with the Characters onely of Leo and Virgo. **1688** HOLME *Armoury* II. 42/2 Zodiack, is the imitation of a Bend, and is esteemed a girdle of Honor, or a note of favour. **1774** J. BRYANT *Mythol.* II. 483 The Zodiac, which Sir Isaac Newton supposed to relate to the Argonautic expedition, was an assemblage of Egyptian hieroglyphics. **1820** BELZONI *Egypt & Nubia* II. 278 The Egyptians connected astronomy with their religious ceremonies, as we found various zodiacs, not only among the temples, but in their tombs also. *a* **1836** M'NICOLL *Wks.* (1837) 24 The motto of a crest which bears his own picture, encircled by a zodiac.

3. † **a.** *transf.* A year; the calendar. *Obs.*

c **1560** A. SCOTT *Poems* (S.T.S.) v. 25 Vpoun thair vyce war lang to waik, Quhais falsatt, fibilnes, and tressone, Hes rung thryis oure this zodiak. **1603** SHAKS. *Meas. for M.* I. ii. 172 So long, that ninteene Zodiacks haue gone round. **1618** BOLTON *Florus* IV. ii. (1636) 291 A month in the Zodiack.

b. *fig.* and *allusively.* (*a*) Recurrent series, round, course. (*b*) Compass, range. (*c*) Set of twelve.

This fig. use was inaugurated by Marcellus Palingenius in the title of his work *Zodiacus vitæ, hoc est de hominis vita* (*c* 1530), each book of which was named after a sign of the zodiac. The title was imitated by Gaspar Barthius in *Zodiacus vitæ christianæ* (1623).

1560 (*title*) The first thre Bokes of the most christian Poet Marcellus Palingenius, called the Zodyake of lyfe: newly translated out of latin into English by Barnabe Googe. *a* **1586** SIDNEY *Apol. Poetrie* (Arb.) 25 The Poet..goeth hand in hand with Nature, not inclosed within the narrow warrant of her guifts, but freely ranging onely within the Zodiack of his owne wit. **1607** WALKINGTON *Optic Glass* Ep., It moues not once within the Zodiacke of my expectation. **1629** DEKKER *London's Tempe* (1844) 53 In your yeares zodiacke may you fairely move. *a* **1631** DONNE *Poems, Litanie* ix, Thy illustrious Zodiacke Of twelve Apostles, which ingirt this All. **1645** G. DANIEL *Poems* Wks. (Grosart) II. 94 Gladlie hast Through Follie's Zodiacke, from the first to th' Last. **1742** YOUNG *Nt. Th.* IX. 989 Thro' various virtues, they, with ardour, ran The Zodiac of their learn'd, illustrious lives. **1856** EMERSON *Eng. Traits, Religion*, The Catholic church..moves through a zodiac of feasts and fasts. **1888** RUSKIN *Præterita* III. ii. 67, I saw my turn had come, and the revolving zodiac brought its fairest sign to me.

B. a. *attrib.* (orig. *adj.*), as ***zodiac-figure, -lion, -sign***; †**zodiac circle** [cf. Gr. ὁ τῶν ζῳδίων κύκλος (Aristotle)], †**zodiac line**, the zodiac; **zodiac ring**, a ring with figures of the signs of the zodiac. **b.** *Comb.* as ***zodiac-zoned*** adj.

1447 BOKENHAM *Seyntys, Anna* 624 The XII signes thryes by & by In þe *zodyak cercle had passyde coursly. **1602** FULBECKE *2nd Pt. Parall.* 60 The Zodiacke circle is alwayes rowled about. **1688** HOLME *Armoury* II. 20/2 The Zodiack Circle is ever born Bendways Sinister. **1844** MRS. BROWNING *Drama of Exile* iii. 90 Poems (1892) 27 The *zodiac-figures of the earth loom slow. **1590** T. WATSON *Poems* (Arb.) 157 Ye Figures in the *Zodiacke line, that decke heauns girdle with æternall light. **1818** KEATS *Endym.* I. 553 Now when his [*sc.* the sun's] chariot last Its beams against the *zodiac-lion cast. **1895** *N. & Q.* 8th Ser. VIII. 187/2 *Zodiac Rings. These, when made of gold, are usually said to be the work of native goldsmiths on the African coast. *Ibid.* 272/1, I have a gold zodiac ring marked with the leopard's head. **1883** *Encycl. Brit.* XVI. 212/2 The similar *zodiac-signs of the Old World. **1856** R. A. VAUGHAN *Mystics* VIII. iii. (1860) II. 48 The *zodiac-zoned and silver-bearded counsellor.

zodiacal (zəʊ'daɪəkəl), *a.* [f. L. *zōdiacus*: see prec. and -AL¹.] Of, pertaining to, or situated in the zodiac.

1576 FLEMING *Panopl. Epist.* 372 The yerely course of the Sunne throgh the .12. signes Zodiacall. **1682** SIR T. BROWNE *Chr. Mor.* III. §26. (1716) 121 The Northern Zodiacal Signs. **1694** MOTTEUX *Rabelais* v. 256 Before the full revolution of a Zodiacal Girdle [*i.e.* before the completion of a year]. **1715** tr. *Gregory's Astron.* I. 304 By the help of the Moon,..they placed this Zodiacal Armilla in such a situation as was agreeable to the present moment of time. **1837** WHEWELL *Hist. Induct. Sci.* (1857) II. 226 Pearson's [catalogue] has 520 zodiacal stars. **1878** NEWCOMB *Pop. Astron.* I. i. 18 The zodiacal constellations occupy quite unequal spaces in the heavens.

b. ***zodiacal light***: a tract of nebulous light extending along the zodiac on each side of the sun in the form of an elongated ellipse; in the temperate zones visible chiefly after sunset in late winter and early spring, and before sunrise in autumn.

1734 EAMES in *Phil. Trans.* XXXVIII. 244 The Zodiacal Light is the purer unmixed Atmosphere of the Sun. **1849** MRS. SOMERVILLE *Connex. Phys. Sci.* xxxvii. (ed. 8) 449 [Professor Olmsted] agrees with La Place in thinking that the zodiacal light is a nebulous body, revolving in the plane of the solar equator. **1876** TAIT *Rec. Adv. Phys. Sci.* x. 259 The zodiacal light, which obviously cannot possibly be part of the gaseous atmosphere of the sun. **1879** *Cassell's Techn. Educ.* IV. 411/2 The Zodiacal light is supposed to be the remains of the great nebula out of which the solar system was constructed.

zodico, var. ZYDECO.

†**zodi'ographer**. *Obs. rare*⁻¹. [f. Gr. type *ζῳδιογράφος, f. ζῴδιον, dim. of ζῷον animal (see ZODIAC) + γράφειν to write: see -GRAPHER.] One who writes about or describes animals.

1650 SIR T. BROWNE *Pseud. Ep.* v. i. (ed. 2) 197 Ancient Zodiographers, and such as have particularly discoursed upon Animals.

‖**zoea** (zəʊ'iːə). *Zool.* Pl. **zoeæ** (zəʊ'iːiː), also in Eng. form **zoeas** (zəʊ'iːəz). Also **zoœa, zoæa.** Earlier form **zoe** ('zəʊiː); pl. **zoes** ('zəʊiːz). [mod.L. *zoe, zoea* (Bosc, 1802), the first form a. Gr. ζωή life, the second an extension of it by addition of fem. suffix -A 2.] †**a.** (An animal of) a supposed genus of crustaceans, founded on certain larval forms mistaken for adults. *Obs.* **b.** A larval stage of development in crustaceans, esp. decapods, usually characterized by one or more spines on the carapace, and rudimentary thoracic and abdominal limbs. Also *attrib.*, as ***zoea-form, -phase, -stage.***

1828 J. V. THOMPSON *Zool. Res.* I. I. 5 The fifth or terminal joint formed as in all the genuine Zoeas, of a deep fork, the inner sides of which are furnished with three small spines. *Ibid.* 9 On the 1st of May of the present year, (1827,) another large Zoea was taken. *Ibid.* 11 *note*, The French have adopted the term Zoe for these animals, which, as more simple, and better suited to the genius of our own language than the Latin, may be used in familiar discourse without any impropriety. *Ibid.* 63 The Zoe or Larva of the common or edible Crab. **1835** WESTWOOD in *Phil. Trans.* CXXV. 324 If..these latter Zoes are to be regarded as the larvæ of Crabs, they must be considered as having acquired the maximum of their Zoe form. **1857** GOSSE *Omphalos* viii. 217 The Zoea form [of the crab], with carapace rising into a tall erect spine, sessile eyes, no claws. **1865** [see MYSIS b]. **1877** HUXLEY *Anat. Inv. Anim.* vi. 303 In most Podophthalmia the embryo leaves the egg, not as a Nauplius, but as a Zoœa, which has thoracic, but no abdominal, appendages. **1888** ROLLESTON & JACKSON *Anim. Life* 169 In the larval form [of the crayfish] known as *Zoaea*, the first *Zoaea*-stage has no palp to the mandible.

Hence **zoeal** (zəʊ'iːəl) *a.*, of a zoea.

1870 P. M. DUNCAN *Blanchard's Transf. Insects* 459 During the next zoëal period the paired eyes..are formed.

zoecial, -ium: see ZOŒ-.

zoetekoekie, var. SOETKOEKIE.

zoetrope ('zəʊɪtrəʊp). [irreg. f. Gr. ζωή life + -τροπος turning.] A mechanical toy or optical instrument consisting of a cylinder open at the top, with a series of slits in the circumference, and a series of figures representing successive positions of a moving object arranged along the inner surface, which when viewed through the slits while the cylinder is in rapid rotation produce the impression of actual movement of the object. Also called *wheel of life*.

1867 'AUNT CARRIE' *Popular Pastimes for Field & Fireside* 229 The Zoetrope is a newly invented toy. It presents a series of striking optical delusions. **1869** W. S. GILBERT *'Bab' Ball., Capt. Reece* vi, And, also, with amusement rife, A 'Zoetrope, or Wheel of Life.' **1881** *Athenæum* 29 Oct. 567/2 By a zoetrope these figures are projected on a screen, and the clown exhibited as in motion, with all his changes of position.

zoftick, zoftig, zoftik, varr. ZAFTIG *a.*

zoȝe, obs. Kent. pa. pple. of SEE *v.*

†**zographer, zography**. *Obs.* See quots. and cf. ZOOGRAPHER, ZOOGRAPHY.

1570 DEE *Math. Pref.* d ij b, This Mechanicall Zographer (commonly called the Painter). *Ibid.*, Zographie, is an Arte Mathematicall, which..demonstrateth, how, the Intersection of all visuall Pyramides, made by any playne assigned, (the Centre, distance, and lightes, beyng determined) may be, by lynes, and due propre colours, represented.

zograscope ('zɒgrəskəʊp). *Obs.* exc. *Hist.* [Etym. uncertain, perh. f. ZOGRA(PHER, ZOGRA(PHY + -SCOPE.] An optical instrument, consisting of a vertically suspended convex lens in front of a pivotally adjustable mirror mounted on a stand, designed for the viewing of prints in magnified form and with stereoscopic effect.

1753 in G. Adams *Descr. & Use Universal Trigonometrical Octant* 3 (Advt.), Zograscopes for viewing perspective Prints. **1953** *Ann. Sci.* IX. 315 (*heading*) The zograscope or optical diagonal machine. *Ibid.*, No reference to the zograscope has so far been found in the literature of the eighteenth or nineteenth centuries, save in certain.. advertisements listing instruments made..by [George Adams]. **1969** E. H. PINTO *Treen* 284 Usually described and sold as Georgian shaving mirrors; this, they are not; they are zograscopes,..probably invented about 1750... Also known, during its long life, as an optical machine..intended for viewing prints, etc., in a magnified form.

Zohar ('zəʊhɑː(r)). Also 7 **zoar.** [Heb., lit. 'light, splendour'.] The major text of Jewish Cabbalism, in the form of an allegorical interpretation of the Pentateuch.

1682 W. PAYNE *Learning & Knowl.* 12 A studying Judiciary Schemes, and fancifull Cabalas, and mysterious zoars. **1837** *British & Foreign Rev.* V. 419 The work called Zohar is written in Chaldaic, and develops the mysterious science called *Cabala*. **1843** G. BORROW *Bible in Spain* III. xv. 295 He knew more Zohar and more secrets than the wisest of them. **1888** J. C. MURRAY tr. *Maimon's Autobiogr.* xiv. 95 The principal work for the study of the Cabbalah is the *Zohar*, which is written in a very lofty style in the Syrian language. **1932** A. BENSION *Zohar* i. 11 Although they derived their inspiration from the same source—Zohar and Kabbala—Ashkenazi and Sepharadi mysticism inevitably took different directions. **1941** [see TEL AVIVIAN *sb.* and *a.*]. **1965** J. A. MICHENER *Source* (1966) 662 Ximeno had given Dr. Abulafia a manuscript of the Zohar, the arcane book of Kabbalism. **1978** I. B. SINGER *Shosha* i. 8 There stood on our shelves volumes of the Zohar.., and other cabalistic works.

zoic ('zəʊɪk), *a.* [ad. Gr. ζωικός, f. ζῷον animal; in sense 1 taken as f. ζωή life, after AZOIC.]

1. Showing traces of life; in *Geol.*, containing organic remains.

1863 DANA *Man. Geol.* 597 If, therefore, these simple species existed in the Azoic era, they were systemless life, and only foreshadowed the great systems of life which were afterwards displayed..in the true Zoic ages. **1885–6** *Rep. U.S. Geol. Survey* (1888) 453 These great Pre-Cambrian and Post-Archæan series are zoic in character.

2. Of the nature of an animal; animal.

1895–6 W. J. MᶜGEE in *17th Ann. Rep. Bur. Amer. Ethnol.* (1898) 169* The Seri face-painting would seem to be essentially zoosematic, or symbolic of zoic tutelaries. **1900** *Ann. Rep. Smithsonian Inst.* 63 The use of zoic motives in the decoration of primitive weapons.

zoid ('zəʊɪd), *sb. Biol.* [f. Gr. ζῷον animal + -ID², or shortened f. ZOOID.] = ZOOID.

1856 WOODWARD *Mollusca* 336 In one group [of Tunicata], the individuals..become blended into a common mass... The separate individuals of these composite masses are termed Zoïds. **1875** *Encycl. Brit.* II. 69/1 Many zoids or buds being attached in line. **1960** *Bot. Gaz.* CXXII. 33/1 Most algae, excluding the Cyanophyta, reproduce sexually by gametes and asexually by spores of various kinds (collectively called 'zoids', except for aplanospores). **1981** *Austral. Jrnl. Zool.* XXIX. 365 Subterminal ovicell complexes bud distally from part of the complex and are generally composed of female zoid with ovicell, lateral zoid, and ovicell zoid with apical chamber.

'zoid, *a. Zool. rare*⁻¹. [f. *zoe* = ZOEA + -ID³.] Applied to a larval or zoea stage in Crustacea.

1864 *Athenæum* 13 Aug. 215/2 The early zoid conditions and subsequent transformations of the Crustacea.

zoid(i)ogamous: see *zooidiogamous* s.v. ZOOID.

Zoilus ('zəʊɪləs). Also 6–7 **Zoylus**, 7 **Zoilis**; also 6–7 anglicized **Zoil(e, Zoyl(e.** [L., a. Gr. Ζωΐλος. Cf. F. *zoïle*, It., Sp. *zoilo*.

The supposed relation of Ζωΐλος to ζῆλος ZEAL, which is held to account for the association of the notion of malignancy or envy with this word, is reflected in the following:

1597 J. PAYNE *Royal Exch.* 23 There..resolution to suffer for there bad causes will intice the ignorant..to thinck that there outragiouse zoyle is a sanctified zeale.]

Name of a Greek critic and grammarian (4th century B.C.) famous for his severe criticism of Homer; *transf.* (with pl. *Zoili, Zoiluses*), a censorious, malignant, or envious critic.

1565 COOPER *Thesaurus, Dict. Hist. & Poet.* s.v. *Zoilus*, Of him, all malicious carpers of other mens wourkes be called *Zoili*. **1567** J. SANFORD *Epictetus* A v b, Carp not ye cankred Zoiles al, the men Whose labour spente in paynfull toyle hath ben. **1575** W. CLOWES in *J. Banister's Treat. Chirurg.* In praise of Author, Although that Zoylus would him spot, Let him doe what he may. **1580** R. HITCHCOCK *Pol. Plat* Pref. **ij, To defende my imperfection, against a sorte of Momus secte, and Zoilus bande. **1609** DOULAND *Ornith. Microl.* 76 Zoilisses and Thersitisses. **1612** R. SHELDON *Serm. at St. Martin's* 47 Such as are eminent should be careful of their conuersations when they are besieged with such malitious Zoiles. **1636** PRYNNE *Rem. agst. Ship-money* Ep., Carping Zoilusses, or malignant Momusses whom no men can please. **1818** LADY MORGAN *Fl. Macarthy* (1819) II. ii. 99 This formidable Zoilus of the Crawley family. *a* **1834** COLERIDGE *Notes & Lect.* (1849) I. 64 How then comes it that not only single *Zoili*, but whole nations have combined in unhesitating condemnation of our great dramatist?

Hence **'Zoilean**, †**Zoi'litical**, **'Zoilous** *adjs.*, characteristic of Zoilus or his criticism; **'Zoilism**, carping criticism like that of Zoilus; **'Zoilist**, an imitator of Zoilus, a carping critic.

1846 WORCESTER cites RICHARDSON for *Zoilean. **1609** N. MORGAN *Perf. Horsem.* 44 The bitter humor of *Zoilisme and malice. **1682** SIR T. BROWNE *Chr. Mor.* II. §2 Let not Zoilism or Detraction blast well intended labours. **1753** *Gray's-Inn Jrnl.* No. 54, I am convinced of your Endeavours to propogate the Cause of Zoilizm. **1594** NASHE *Christ's T.* To Rdr., The ploddinger sort of vnlearned *Zoilists about London, exclaim, that it is a puft-up stile. **1658** FRANCK *Northern Mem.* (1694) Pref. p. xxvii, Some prevaricating Zoilist will arraign my Hypothesis. **1716** M. DAVIES *Athen. Brit.* II. 87 Polydore Virgil, Dr. John Cay, with other Zoilists, reported that his Poetical Wit made him so conceited. *a* **1849** H. COLERIDGE *Ess.* (1851) II. 75 The same class of fastidious wits who in France became Zoilists, in England were the stoutest stickers to Homer. **1665** J. WEBB *Stone-Heng* (1725) 41 Their magnificent Monuments shall come to be controverted by every *Zoilitical Pretender! **1577** GRANGE *Golden Aphrod.* Ep. Ded. A iv b, I thought it good (somwhat to stop a *zoilous mouth) to sette a more cleanly name vpon it, that is, *Golden Aphroditis*. **1618** M. BARET *Hippon.* I. 47 Hee..therefore needeth not be daunted for the taunts of any Zoylous beholders.

zoisite ('zɔɪsaɪt). *Min.* [ad. G. *zoisit*, named by Werner after Baron von *Zois*, the discoverer.] A native silicate of alumina and lime, occurring in orthorhombic prismatic crystals, of various colours, white, green, or red.

1805 R. JAMESON *Syst. Min.* II. 597. **1843** PORTLOCK *Geol.* 209 Zoisite in fine crystals of a greyish brown or olive colour, ..at Hollyhill, near Strabane, County Tyrone.

zoism ('zəʊɪz(ə)m). [f. Gr. ζωή life + -ISM.] The doctrine that life depends on a peculiar vital principle, and is not a mere resultant of combined forces; esp. in connexion with 'animal magnetism' and the like. So **zoist** ('zəʊɪst), one who upholds the doctrine of zoism; hence **zo'istic** (zəʊ'ɪstɪk) *a.*, as in ***zoistic magnetism*** = animal magnetism.

1843 (*title*) The Zoist: a Journal of Cerebral Physiology & Mesmerism, and their Applications to Human Welfare. **1849** SCORESBY (*title*) Zoistic Magnetism. **1900** (*title*) Psychic Research Co.'s Course of Instruction in Personal Magnetism, Series A: Mind Reading, Hypnotism, Magnetic Healing, and Zoism.

zoite ('zəʊaɪt). *Zool.* [The suffix used as an independent word.] (See quots.).

1963 E. N. KOZLOFF in J. Ludvík et al. *Progr. Protozool.* (Proc. First Internat. Congr. Protozool., Prague, 1961) 78 It appears advisable to reconsider the terminology applied to stages in the life-histories of gregarines and coccidians... *Zoite*, an infective stage, produced by division of a zygote, and usually surrounded by an envelope which is either a zoitocyst or zygocyst. **1969** *New Scientist* 29 May 465/1 Another stage in the development of *Toxoplasma* is the cystic form or zoite. **1977** *Jrnl. Protozool.* XXIV. 36/1 Electronmicroscopic studies revealed that the structure of *T. gondii* zoites (trophozoites, merozoites, 'spores', etc.) is similar to that of the zoites of the coccidia *Eimeria* and *Isospora*. **1979** *Ibid.* XXVI. 437/1 Uninucleate, dinucleate, and multinucleate zoites. **1980** *Jrnl. Parasitol.* LXVI. 67/1 Ultrastructurally, cysts of *T[oxoplasma] gondii* and *H[ammondia] hammondi* cannot be distinguished with certainty in skeletal muscle. Classification is based on the typical distribution of cysts and their zoites in the intermediate host.

-zoite ('zəʊaɪt), *suffix.* [f. Gr. ζῷ-ον animal + -ITE¹.] A word-forming element used in zoological terms in the sense 'spore', as in *merozoite* s.v. MERO-¹, *tachyzoite* s.v. TACHY-.

Zolaism ('zəʊləɪz(ə)m). [f. the name *Zola* + -ISM.] The literary manner characteristic of the French novelist Émile Zola (1840–1902), whose works are marked by an excessively realistic treatment of the coarser sides of human life. So **Zolaesque** (-'ɛsk) *a.*, characteristic of or resembling the style of Zola; **'Zolaist**, one who studies or approves of the writings of Zola (hence **Zola'istic** *a.*); **'Zolaize** *v. intr.*, to imitate or follow the style of Zola; *trans.* to make like Zola.

1886 *Pall Mall Gaz.* 14 July 5/2 Mr. Moore's *Zolaesque search for characteristic phrases has led him into some startling extravagances. **1903** in Gayley *Repr. Engl. Com.* I. 387 The mean circumstances of his Bohemian career, and the terribly brutal, Zolaesque scene of his death-chamber. **1882** *Athenæum* 30 Dec. 875/3 A particular form of *Zolaism, much in vogue at this moment. **1886** TENNYSON *Locksley Hall 60 Yrs. After* 145 Set the maiden fancies wallowing in the troughs of Zolaism. **1886** *Athenæum* 30 Jan. 161/2 Even the *Zolaist has to remember that 'art is art because it is not nature'. *Ibid.* 161/3 The French critics either of the Hugoistic or the *Zolaistic persuasion. *Ibid.* 2 July 13/3 The *Zolaizing novel of Paul Lindau, 'Arme Mädchen.' **1901** *Literature* 30 Mar. 234/2, I do not mean that M. Roz has Zolaized Mr. Hardy.

zoll, variant of SAL[2].

Zollinger-Ellison syndrome ('zɒlɪndʒər 'ɛlɪsʌn). *Path.* [Named after M. *Zollinger* (b. 1903) and E. H. *Ellison* (1918–70), American physicians, who described the syndrome in 1955 (*Ann. Surg.* CXLII. 709).] A syndrome characterized by excessive gastric acid secretion (producing recurrent peptic ulcers) associated with a gastrin-secreting tumour or hyperplasia of the islet cells of the pancreas.

1956 EISEMAN & MAYNARD in *Gastroenterology* XXXI. 302 For the sake of simplicity we propose this clinical entity be called the Zollinger-Ellison syndrome. **1960** *Jrnl. R. Coll. of Surgeons of Edin.* V. 191 Since that time [*sc.* 1955] over 100 instances of co-existent peptic ulcer and islet cell tumours have been described and the association appears to constitute a clinical entity called, by general consent, the 'Zollinger-Ellison syndrome'. **1962** [see ISLET 3]. **1974** R. M. KIRK et al. *Surgery* vi. 85/1 In the Zollinger-Ellison syndrome, ulcers may occur at the duodenojejunal junction.

Zöllner ('tsœlnə(r), z-). *Psychol.* Also Zoellner. The name of the German astronomer and physicist, Johann Karl Friedrich *Zöllner* (1834–82), used *attrib.* and in the possessive to designate the optical illusion noted by him of parallel lines which, when marked with short diagonal lines, appear to converge. Now usu. as ***Zöllner illusion***.

1890 W. JAMES *Princ. Psychol.* II. xx. 232 In what is known as Zöllner's pattern.., the long parallels tip towards each other the moment we draw the short slanting lines over them. **1911** *Encycl. Brit.* XXVIII. 142/1 (*caption*) Zoellner's Figure showing an illusion of direction. **1922** K. DUNLAP *Elem. Sci. Psychol.* xiii. 295 In the Zöllner figure, the long lines, really parallel, seem to converge. **1955** H. E. GARRETT *Gen. Psychol.* v. 179 (*caption*) Zoellner illusion. The four horizontal lines are parallel. **1971** [see HERING]. **1980** *Sci. Amer.* Jan. 91/1 The Zöllner illusion, which exhibits assimilation at extremely small angles and contrast at larger angles.

‖**zollverein** ('tsɒlfɛraɪn). Now *Hist.* [G., f. *zoll* tax, impost, TOLL *sb.*[1] + *verein* union.] A union, orig. between certain states of the German empire, after 1833 including all the states, for the maintenance of a uniform rate of customs duties from other countries and of free trade among themselves; hence *gen.* of other countries. Hence **'zollvereinist**, an advocate of a British imperial zollverein.

1843 *Times* 21 Aug. 5/2 The Zollverein.—The Bavarian Chamber of Deputies..voted by an immense majority the two following resolutions. **1847** COBDEN in Morley *Life* (1881) I. xviii. 448 The Prussian law of 1818, and the tariff which followed it, form the foundation of the German Zollverein. **1862** (*title*) London Exhibition. Special Catalogue of the Zollverein-Department edited by authority of the Commissioners of the Zollverein-Governments. **1893** GOLDW. SMITH *Ess. Quest. Day* 150 When colonists propose an Imperial zollverein.

zolo go, var. ZYDECO.

‖**zolotnik** (zɒlɒt'nɪk). Now *Hist.* Also 8 **solothnic, solotnik, -nick.** [Russ. *zolotník*, f. *zoloto* gold.] A former Russian unit of weight, $\frac{1}{96}$ of the funt or Russian pound.

1783 MARTYN in *Geogr. Mag.* II. 40 Russia has some weights peculiar to itself: such as a solothnic, which is one-sixth of an ounce. **1799** W. TOOKE *View Russ. Emp.* II. 532 The solotnik is only reckoned at 19¼ kopecks, whereas the solotnik of gold is valued at 2 rubles 50 kopecks. **1919** PETRIE in *Man* XIX. 80 The Russian and Irak pound..was divided into 96 zolotniks, which was equal to the Attic drachma.

zolow, zom(e, zomboruk, zomer: see SULLOW, SOME, ZUMBOORUK, SUMMER[1].

zombie ('zɒmbɪ). Also zombi and with capital initial. [Of W. Afr. origin; cf. Kongo *nzambi* god, *zumbi* fetish.] **1.** In the West Indies and southern states of America, a soulless corpse said to have been revived by witchcraft; formerly, the name of a snake-deity in voodoo cults of or deriving from West Africa and Haiti.

1819 R. SOUTHEY *Hist. Brazil* III. xxxi. 24 Zombi, the title whereby he [chief of Brazilian natives] was called, is the name for the Deity, in the Angolan tongue... NZambi is the word for Deity. **1872** SCHELE DE VERE Americanisms 138 *Zombi*, a phantom or a ghost, not unfrequently heard in the Southern States in nurseries and among the servants. **1886** *Century Mag.* Apr. 815/2 This spiritual influence or potentate is the recognized antagonist and opposite of Obi, the great African manitou or deity, or him whom the Congoes vaguely generalize as Zombi. **1929** W. B. SEABROOK *Magic Island* II. ii. 94 At this very moment, in the moonlight, there are *zombies* working on this island. **1943** R. OTTLEY *New World* 46 Adding the zombies, jumbies, and obeah men to the gallery of voodoo characters. **1966** G. GREENE *Comedians* iv. 104 Luckily no one dared move on the roads at night; it was the hour when only zombies worked or else the Tontons Macoute. **1979** J. RHYS *Smile Please* 30 Zombies were black shapeless things. They could get through a locked door and you heard them walking up to your bed. You didn't see them, you felt their hairy hands round your throat. **1984** *Times* 26 Jan. 12/6 A zombie, as every schoolboy knows, is a person who has been killed and raised from the dead by sinister voodoo priests called bocors.

2. *fig.* A dull, apathetic, or slow-witted person. Also as a general term of disparagement. *colloq.*

1936 H. L. MENCKEN *Amer. Language* (ed. 4) xi. 587 Any performer [in a film] not a Caucasian is a *zombie*. **1941** H. MACINNES *Above Suspicion* ix. 80 He nodded..in the direction of those concentrating on the mastication of specially chosen vitamins to build a specially chosen race. 'Zombies is, I believe, the technical term,' suggested Richard. **1946** J. B. PRIESTLEY *Bright Day* xi. 329 They've spent their lives starving their imagination, just starving it to death. And now they're zombies. **1957** J. BRAINE *Room at Top* i. 17 To Charles and me it was always Dead Dufton and the councillors and chief officials and anyone we didn't approve of were called zombies. **1961** [see LOVE *sb.*[1] 4]. **1974** S. MIDDLETON *Holiday* xiii. 233 He had no time for her as a zombie, preferring her moody volatility to this flabby acquiescence. **1981** P. CAREY *Bliss* iv. 156 They'll give us electric shocks... They'll give us pills and make us zombies. **1984** *Guardian* 22 Oct. 3/1 Mr. Dawson describes the committee as a parliament of zombies.

3. *Canad. Mil. slang.* In the war of 1939–45, an opprobrious nickname applied to men conscripted for home defence.

1943 *Daily Express* 16 Sept. 4/1 The Canadian Government is reducing its 'Home Guard' army... These troops were jocularly dubbed 'Zombies', after the Voodoo cult which insists that dead men can be made to walk and act as if they were alive. **1946** [see OLD MAN 1 a]. **1953** D. M. LE BOURDAIS *Nation of North* 245 The first men were drafted for service... Contemptuously referred to as 'zombies', they were never taken seriously by the military authorities. **1963** A. S. MORTON *Kingdom of Canada* 481 A nasty distinction arose between the volunteers for service overseas and the conscripts for home defence, who were given the pungent nickname of 'zombie', a West Indian word for impotent spirits. **1978** *Daily Colonist Mag.* (Victoria, B.C.) 1 July 12/1 When the Canadian Army was struggling on the Western Front in the early winter of 1944 and there was an urgent call for reinforcements, yet, in the military camps in Vernon and Terrace the Zombies mutinied when orders came for their movement overseas.

4. A long mixed drink consisting of several kinds of rum, liqueur, and fruit juice (see quot. 1958).

1942 M. K. RAWLINGS *Cross Creek* xvii. 221 There is a passion fruit liqueur that is the primary ingredient..of that marvelous..drink, the Zombie. **1958** A. L. SIMON *Dict. Wines, Spirits & Liqueurs* 167/1 *Zombie*,..lime juice;.. pineapple juice;..Falernum, or simple syrup;..White Label Rum;..Gold Label Rum;..Jamaica Rum;.. Demerara Rum;..apricot liqueur. Shake well and strain... Garnish with..orange and..mint. **1968** J. M. ULLMAN *Lady on Fire* vi. 80 The bartender..went off to prepare a zombie. Forbes hated zombies, but it was the longest drink that came to mind. **1977** *Zigzag* Apr. 10/1 It's a Polynesian drink, a rum drink..a killer drink. There was a restaurant I found very close to The Cage that I went to every day... Like I would wake up, go there at noon, have a Zombie, go back and start writing.

5. a. *attrib.*

1956 M. STEARNS *Story of Jazz* (1957) xviii. 222 Thelonius Monk, whose weird..and pioneering modulations were referred to as 'Zombie music' by the musicians themselves, more in awe than anger. **1958** A. WILSON *Middle Age of Mrs. Eliot* I. 77 The breathing zombie orchestra around her. **1966** *New Statesman* 14 Jan. 58/3 A dream-sequence in a cemetery with zombie-hands sprouting like crocuses. **1968** P. ABLEMAN *Vac* xxiv. 113 Stop clashing those zombie lips and glide to the bar. **1973** [see *one-nighter* s.v. ONE B. 35]. **1976** D. LODGE *Changing Places* v. 162 He could send home, when the time came, some zombie replica of himself.

b. *Comb.*, as **zombie-like** *a.*, characteristic of or resembling a zombie; lifeless, unfeeling.

1957 J. KEROUAC *On Road* (1958) 302 His arms hanging zombie-like at his sides. **1962** *Times* 25 July 13/1 Future.. where everybody lives a zombie-like existence. **1975** *Publishers Weekly* 10 Feb. 57/3 White Brian is a zombie-like boy who wanders unseeing and unseen through life. **1983** *Times* 4 Oct. 10/6 On state occasions, a few old men shuffle on to the balcony of the Kremlin and raise their hands in zombie-like salutation.

Hence **zombi'esque, 'zomboid** [-OID] *adjs.*; **'zombiism.**

1956 M. STEARNS *Story of Jazz* (1957) v. 51 The Calinda dance is connected with zombiism in Haiti. **1972** *Vogue* Jan. 7/3 Ponderax..sidetracks the appetite but leaves the character..muted, zombiesque. **1974** *Observer* 3 Feb. 31/5 Zombiesque Security Guard charged with shooting. **1974** *Radio Times* 18 Mar. 22/4 We're not putting up with 'Zombyism'. The aim of our programme is to give hope. **1975** *Sunday Times* (Colour Suppl.) 20 July 11/3 'I'm David Bowie,' he intones with a zomboid air. **1979** *Guardian* 18 Oct. 11/6 Some of the most zomboid heroines in recent fiction. **1983** *Daily Tel.* 15 Oct. 17/1 Zombi-ism exists and is a social phenomenon that can be explored logically.

zomotherapy (zəʊməʊ'θɛrəpɪ). *Med.* [ad. F. *zomothérapie*, f. Gr. ζωμός soup + θεραπεία THERAPY.] The use of raw meat, or the juice expressed from it, in the treatment of tuberculosis. Hence **zomothera'peutic** *a.*, pertaining to zomotherapy.

1900 *Lancet* 27 Oct. 1242/2 The experiments of M. Richet and M. Héricourt relative to the use of raw meat as a prophylactic and curative substance in tuberculosis... Such treatment these observers have called 'zomotherapy'. *Ibid.*, At various stages of the zomotherapeutic treatment.

zon, dial. form of SON.

‖**zona** ('zəʊnə). The Lat. form of the Gr. word repr. by ZONE. **a.** *Archæol.* A girdle: = ZONE *sb.* 3. **b.** Used in Anatomy with various qualifying adjs. to denote certain structures or parts of structures (see quots., and cf. ZONE *sb.* 6); also **zona fasciculata, glomerulosa, reticularis** [mod.L. (see FASCICULATE *a.*, etc.), coined in Ger. by J. Arnold 1866, in *Arch. f. path. Anat. & Physiol.* XXXV. 66], the middle, outer, and inner layers respectively of the cortex of the adrenal gland; **zona ignea** [L., = fiery girdle] *Path.*, also simply *zona*, the disease *herpes zoster* or shingles. **zona pellucida**, the transparent membrane forming the cell-wall of the ovum in Mammalia. **zona radiata**, a radially striated form of the zona pellucida surrounding the ova of certain vertebrates as seen in the light microscope.

1706 PHILLIPS (ed. Kersey), *Zona*...a kind of *Herpes*, or Shingles call'd Holy Fire. **1800** DALLAWAY *Anecd. Arts Eng.* 249 Both the tænia and zona are concealed by drapery falling over them. **1818–20** THOMPSON tr. *Cullen's Nosol.* (ed. 3) 331 Herpes *Zoster, Zona*; or *Zona ignea*: the shingles. **1841** M. BARRY in *Phil. Trans.* CXXXII. 116 We saw the incipient chorion, when rising from the 'zona pellucida' in the mammiferous ovum, to leave a stratum of unappropriated cells behind it on the 'zona'. **1848** DUNGLISON *Med. Lex.* s.v., *Zona Tendinosa*, the whitish circle around the auriculo-ventricular orifice of the right side of the heart. **1874** R. J. DUNGLISON *Dict. Med. Sci.* (new ed.) 1130/1 Zona reticularis... Zona glomerulosa... Zona fasciculata. **1881** F. M. BALFOUR *Treat. Compar. Embryol.* II. iv. 55 The ovum [of Teleosei] when laid is usually invested in the zona radiata only. **1883** KLEIN *Elem. Histol.* 341 The inner zona, or *zona reticularis*, composed of smaller or larger groups of polyhedral cells. *Ibid.* 341 Next follows the middle zone, or *zona fasciculata*. *Ibid.*, Next follows the inner zone, or *zona reticularis*. **1899** *Allbutt's Syst. Med.* VIII. 616 Yet there has never been any confusion with regard to H[erpes] Zoster, or Zona, since the disease was first described. **1925** E. B. WILSON *Cell* (ed. 3) iv. 272 The zona radiata of the vertebrate ovum, conspicuously shown in the fishes, is a thick and often double membrane traversed by fine radial canals. **1964** PARKER & HASWELL *Text-bk. Zool.* (ed. 7) II. 319 The ovum [of *Salmo trutta*, the brown trout] is covered by a thick membrane, the zona radiata. **1965** LEE & KNOWLES *Animal Hormones* iv. 70 The cells in the innermost layer are in the form of a reticulum—the zona reticularis. *Ibid.*, The zona glomerulosa secretes mineralocorticoid. *Ibid.* 71 Hypophysectomy results in shrinkage mainly of the zona fasciculata and reticularis, and the blood glucose falls.

zonal ('zəʊnəl), *a.* [ad. mod.L. *zōnālis*, f. L. *zōna* ZONE.]

1. a. Characterized by or arranged in zones, circles, or rings; of the nature of or forming a zone.

1873 A. WILSON *Elem. Zool.* I. ii. 22 In 'zonal' symmetry the merosomes are arranged in zones, one after another, in a longitudinal axis. **1888** RUTLEY *Rock-Forming Min.* 124 The small spherical crystalline aggregates show..a concentric zonal structure.

b. Marked with zones or circular bands of colour: applied to varieties of pelargonium or geranium having the leaves so marked.

1868 *Morn. Star* 17 June, The cultivators of zonal pelargoniums, or variegated leaf-coloured geraniums, had a grand competition. **1908** *Nation* 22 Feb. 756/2 The zonal geranium.

2. *Math.* and *Cryst.* Relating to a zone or zones of a sphere, or of a crystalline form: see ZONE *sb.* 8.

1867 THOMSON & TAIT *Nat. Phil.* §781 These circles..are ..all in parallel planes..and cut the spherical surface into zones, in which case the harmonic is called zonal.

3. Pertaining or relating to, involving, or constituting a 'zone' or 'zones', i.e. regions or areas distinctively characterized in some way: see ZONE *sb.* 2 b, 7.

1882 *Knowledge* 7 July 92 The six zonal areas we have thus described will serve our purpose admirably for grouping together our Seaside Health-Resorts. **1890** *Nature* 4 Sept. 454/2 Zonal divisions are based upon these bogus species and conclusions drawn from them. **1893** GEIKIE *Text-bk. Geol.* VI. III. i. (ed. 3) 876 In tracing the zonal parallelism of the Triassic succession within the Alps themselves. **1904** *Edin. Rev.* Jan. 219 The study..of strata characterised by the dominance of a zone-fossil forms zonal geology. **1909** *Spectator* 29 May 856/2 The companies adopted a zonal tariff (as the State has done for telephone purposes).

4. *Soil Sci.* [a. F. *zonal* (N. Sibirtsev 1897, in *Compt. Rend. de la VIIe. Session, Congr. géol. internat.* (1899) II. III. v. 80).] Of a soil: regarded as characteristic of a particular climatic or geographic zone and as reflecting the predominant influence of the climate in its formation.

1908 *Jrnl. Agric. Sci.* III. 84 The seven fundamental groups of 'zonal' soils just enumerated are spread over the surface of large continents in zones which coincide with the physico-geographical zones of those continents. **1927**, etc. [see INTRAZONAL *a.*]. **1952** [see AZONAL *a.*]. **1972** J. G. CRUICKSHANK *Soil Geogr.* iv. 110 Apart from being an over-simplification of reality, the zonal system had the unfortunate effect of restricting, in the mind of the student, the distribution of each zonal soil within the limits of its climatic zone.

Hence **zo'nality**, zonal character or distribution; **'zonally** *adv.*, in or according to zones.

1873 A. WILSON *Elem. Zool.* I. ii. 22 The segments..of the body, which are arranged zonally along a longitudinal axis. **1889** *Amer. Nat.* XXIII. 814 Crystals of the hyacinth variety of quartz..contain numerous inclusions of anhydrite arranged zonally. **1909** *Daily Chron.* 21 Mar. 3/5 The zonality of the flowers.

zo'narious, *a. rare*$^{-0}$. [f. L. *zōna* ZONE *sb.*]

1656 BLOUNT *Glossogr.*, *Zonarious*..of or belonging to a Girdle, Purse, or Zone.

zonary ('zəʊnərɪ), *a.* [f. ZONE *sb.* + -ARY.]

1. Having the form of a zone or girdle: applied to the placenta in certain mammals, as the *Carnivora*, forming a broad girdle round the chorion.

1881 MIVART *Cat* 472 Though the Rodents have a deciduate placenta, it is never zonary.

2. Occurring in a zone or zones, i.e. within definite limits of depth (see ZONE *sb.* 7).

zonate ('zəʊneɪt), *a. Zool.* and *Bot.* [ad. mod.L. *zōnātus*, f. *zōna* ZONE *sb.*: see -ATE².] Marked with zones, rings, or bands of colour; zoned. Also **'zonated** *a.*

1803 SHAW *Gen. Zool.* IV. 452 Zonated Sparus. **1852** *Zoologist* X. 3315 The coral snake (zonated scarlet and black). **1866** *Treas. Bot.*, *Zonate, Zoned*, marked with concentric bands of colour.

zonation (zəʊ'neɪʃən). [f. ZONE *sb.* + -ATION.]

a. Distribution in zones or regions of definite character; *spec.* in *Ecol.*, the distribution of plants into specific zones which are characterized by their dominant species.

1898 *Rep. Brit. Assoc. Adv. Sci. 1897* 863 (*heading*) The zonal constitution and disposition of plant formations. By Frederic E. Clements. *Ibid.*, The author has here reviewed the phytogeographical contributions bearing upon the subject in hand, with especial reference to the part they have played in the elaboration of the conception of zonation. In addition, he has endeavoured to demonstrate the fundamental universality of zonation in all divisions of the floral covering. **1904** [see ECOTONE]. **1926** TANSLEY & CHIPP *Study of Veg.* iv. 53 Adjacent plant communities are often arranged in more or less definite zones, following one another in constant order. This is specially noticeable in ascending a mountain (where it is called altitudinal zonation). **1936** J. MUIR *Geol. Tampico Region, Mexico* 121 Reliable local zonation of both the Eocene and the Oligocene has been worked out in the Tampico area. **1969** *Nature* 15 Mar. 1005/2 Marine work during the first eight months concentrated on community structure and zonation on cliffs, reef flats and in mangrove woodland. **1971** *Scot. Jrnl. Geol.* VII. 306 It is first necessary therefore to establish a regional metamorphic zonation. **1981** *Birds* Autumn 63/3, I would have preferred to have seen an accompanying annotated sketch so that the plant zonations could be easily recognised.

b. Formation of zones in the oocytes of certain plants and animals.

1899 *Bot. Gaz.* XXVIII. 237 There is a stage called zonation in which the nuclei, usually in metaphase, are lined up around the ooplasm. **1902** *Bot. Gaz.* Dec. 421 During the completion of the mitosis the ooplasm and periplasm become clearly differentiated, but as yet no plasmoderma exists. This process of differentiation has been termed zonation. **1975** *Acta Anat.* XCIII. 512 The zonation of the ooplasm reveals that a majority of the oocytes [of the teleost *Schizothorax richardsonii*] have a darkly stained inner and a lightly stained outer zone.

zone (zəʊn), *sb.* Also 6-7 zoane. [ad. L. *zōna*, a. Gr. ζώνη girdle (ζωννύναι to gird). Cf. F. *zone* (from 12th c.), It., Sp., Pg. *zona.*]

1. *Geog.*, etc. **a.** Each of the five 'belts' or encircling regions, distinguished by differences of climate, into which the surface of the earth (and, in ancient cosmography, the celestial sphere) is divided by the tropics (of Cancer and Capricorn) and the polar (arctic and antarctic) circles; viz. the ***torrid*** (†*burning*, †*burnt*, †*hot*) ***zone*** between the tropics, the (north and south) ***temperate zones*** extending from the tropics to the polar circles, and the ***frigid*** (†*frozen*, †*cold*) ***zones*** (arctic and antarctic) within the polar circles.

The arctic and antarctic zones are strictly not 'belts' but circular 'caps' with the poles in the centre.

a **1500** *Hist. K. Boccus & Sydracke* (? 1510) U iv, For thre zones [*Laud MS.* thre wonynges] shal he fynde Where no man may lyue in one kynde One is hote and colde are two. **1551** RECORDE *Cast. Knowl.* (1556) 64 The olde Cosmographers..called all that space betweene the twoo Tropykes, the Burnynge Zone... And of eche syde of it, they noted twoo Zones,..whiche they called the Frosen zones,..and betweene those Frosen zones, & the Burning zone, they appointed two Temperat zones. **1555** EDEN *Decades* (Arb.) 298 The could zone or clime was condemned to perpetuall snowe. **1594** BLUNDEVIL *Exerc.*, *Mercator* (1597) 208 The hotte Zone is that which lyeth betwixt the two Tropiques. **1602** SHAKS. *Ham.* v. i. 304 Till our ground Sindging his pate against the burning Zone, Make Ossa like a wart. **1652-62** HEYLIN *Cosmogr.* Introd. (1674) 19/2 The parts next the Torrid Zone are the hotter, and the parts next the Frigid Zone are the colder. **1700** DRYDEN *Ovid's Met.* I. 55 The Sun, with Rays directly darting down, Fires all beneath, and fries the middle Zone. **1774** GOLDSM. *Nat. Hist.* (1776) V. 38 The feathered inhabitants of the temperate zone are but little remarkable for the beauty of their plumage. **1869** RAWLINSON *Anc. Hist.* 53 Africa belongs almost entirely to the torrid zone.

b. Any region extending around the earth and comprised between definite limits, e.g. between two parallels of latitude. Also *Astron.* applied to a similar region in the heavens or on the surface of a planet or the sun.

1559 W. CUNNINGHAM *Cosmogr. Glasse* 64 Do you not in this Figure call euery portion betwixt two paralleles: a zone? .. Yes verely. **1578** T. TWYNE tr. *Daneau's Workm. World* 61 Those fiue quarters and zones, which the Astronomers doe describe in heauen, and vppon the earth. **1692** [see 3 b]. **1860** MAURY *Phys. Geog.* (Low) iv. §205 We have, extending entirely around the earth, two zones of perpetual winds. *Ibid.* §355 On the north side of this calm zone of Cancer. **1890** C. A. YOUNG *Elem. Astron.* §190 The spots are confined mostly to two zones of the sun's surface between 5° and 40° of north and south latitude.

2. a. More or less vaguely: A region or tract of the world, esp. in relation to its climate; also *fig.*

1599 SIR J. DAVIES *Nosce Teipsum* 5 We that acquaint our selues with euery Zoane, And passe both Tropikes, and behold the Poles. *a* **1628** F. GREVIL *Sidney* iv. (1907) 39 Her nature hard to imitate, and diversly worshipped, according to Zones, complexions, or education. **1667** MILTON *P.L.* II. 397 We may..in some milde Zone Dwell not unvisited of Heav'ns fair Light Secure. **1772** *Monthly Rev.* XLII. 190/2 'Midst Lapland's live-long snows, Or India's burning zone. **1856** VAUGHAN *Mystics* VI. vi, It has been theirs..to encounter the perilous fervours of that zone where never cooling cloud appears to veil insufferable radiance. **1870** O'SHAUGHNESSY *Epic Wom.*, *Seraphitus* i, Some Spirit from a zone Of light, and ecstasy, and psalm.

b. A definite region or area of the earth, or of any place or space, distinguished from adjacent regions by some special quality or condition (indicated by a defining word or phrase); also *fig.*

Often in technical use; see also 4 b, 5, 6, 7.

1822 MANTELL *Foss. S. Downs* 298 This occurrence of the more ancient deposits, within a zone of chalk hills. **1835** THIRLWALL *Greece* I. i. 29 Greece lies in a volcanic zone, which extends from the Caspian..to the Azores. **1837** BREWSTER *Magnet.* 222 The zone of easterly diurnal variations. **1849** PATON *Highl. Adriatic* II. xix. 253 The wide-scattered city, with its zone of the glacis, is the foreground of the view. **1852** E. YATES *Elem. Strat.* 9 Every theatre of war is supposed to be divided into three Zones... These are called Zones of Operation, and are distinguished as the Right, Left, and Central. **1873** *Daily News* 2 Aug., That all extensions should be performed before entering within the fire zone. **1876** VOYLE & STEVENSON *Milit. Dict.* s.v., The *zone of defence* signifies a belt of ground in front of the general contour of the works within effective range of the artillery on the ramparts... *Zone of fire*, a term synonymous with range or trajectory. **1881** RAYMOND *Mining Gloss.* s.v., In a shaft-furnace, the different portions (horizontal sections) are called *zones*, and characterized according to the reactions which take place in them, as the *zone of fusion.* **1883** GRESLEY *Gloss. Coal M.*, *Zone*, in coal-mining phraseology, this word signifies a certain series of coal seams, with their accompanying shales, &c. **1902** *Times* 24 Nov. 5/2 Beyond the rain zone dead scrub and lifeless trees alone meet the eye.

c. (*Town-*) *Planning.* A district or an area of land subject to particular restrictions concerning use and development.

1909 H. I. TRIGGS *Town Planning* iv. 177 The usual method in formulating town building plans on a large scale is to divide the urban area into building zones. **1910** F. HOWKINS *Housing Acts 1890–1909*, & *Town Planning* ix. 125 Certain portions of the area would be reserved for the erection of better class residences... This would be similar to the 'zone' system which has been adopted in certain towns on the Continent. **1939** H. M. LEWIS *City Planning* xvi. 166 A single map will show the subdivision of the area into zones, which in a typical case might be defined as follows: One family zones. Two family zones. [etc.]. **1953** [see SMOKELESS *a.* 2]. **1964** J. S. SCOTT *Dict. Building* 364 Certain areas can be kept for light industry, others for heavy industry, dwellings, offices..and so on, each area being called a zone.

d. *N. Amer. Football* and *Basketball.* A specific area of the court to be defended by a particular player; also, a mode of defensive play employing this system (cf. *zone defence*, sense 10 a below).

1927 G. S. WARNER *Football Coaches & Players* 191 In the zone defense the players playing back of the line of scrimmage..are so stationed that they can knock down or intercept any pass that comes into their territory or zone. **1942** C. BEE *Zone Defense & Attack* i. 1 Certain coaches believe only the 'zone' can be called a team defense. **1964** ANDERSON & ALBECK *Coaching Better Basketball* ix. 209 You cannot win consistently..utilizing the zone. **1971** L. KOPPETT *N.Y. Times Guide to Spectator Sports* iii. 83 Each player is given a specific portion of the floor as 'his territory', and he guards, in turn, any offensive player who enters his 'zone'. **1979** *Farmington* (New Mexico) *Daily Times* 27 May 8A/7 The defense must be a man-to-man with no presses or zones allowed.

e. Any one of those areas of Germany and Austria occupied by British, American, French, or Russian forces after the war of 1939–45 until 1955. Subsequently occas. applied to East German territory; also *transf.*

1945 *Times* 13 Feb. 4/1 The conference of Mr. Churchill, President Roosevelt, and Marshal Stalin, held at Yalta, in the Crimea, has drawn up military plans for the final defeat of Germany... The forces of the three Powers will each occupy a separate zone of Germany, and a central control commission will have headquarters in Berlin. France will be invited to take a zone of occupation. **1947** *Daily Tel.* 25 Sept. 5/8 German machinery..will be delivered to Hungary in the next three months under a trade agreement signed between Hungary and the Soviet zone of Germany. **1954** W. FAULKNER *Fable* 128 Frenchmen..had been spending their leaves..among the combat-troop rest-billets not only throughout the entire French Army zone, but the American and the British ones too. **1956** *Ann. Reg. 1955* III. v. 223 Some political leaders expressed the view that German interests would be furthered by direct negotiations with the Soviet Union, and that it would ease conditions for the people of the Soviet Zone if there was limited collaboration with the East German authorities. **1963** 'J. LE CARRÉ' *Spy who came in from Cold* xiii. 127 The GDR... The Zone if you prefer. **1964** L. DEIGHTON *Funeral in Berlin* vii. 50 Not too near the Sektor boundary and within a mile of the Soviet Zone... Sometimes we prefer to put our cargo on ice in the zone... Anywhere from Lübeck to Leipzig. **1976** W. D. GRAF *German Left since 1945* iii. 77 This movement aimed at the restoration of German unity... It was founded on the basis of proposals put forward by the communist leadership in the Soviet Zone.

3. a. A girdle or belt, as a part of dress. (Chiefly *poetic.*) Hence, any encircling band.

1608 B. JONSON *Masques, Beauty* Wks. (1616) 906 Germinatio. In greene; with a Zone of gold about her Wast. **1635** QUARLES *Embl.* v. viii. 40 Shall these course hands untie The sacred Zone of thy Virginitie? **1656** STANLEY *Hist. Philos.* II. III. 13 This was the first place where he untyed his zone since he fled from Athens..So great was his fear. **1742** YOUNG *Nt. Th.* v. 30 Wit calls the Graces the chaste zone to loose. *a* **1806** H. K. WHITE *To My Lyre* vii, Dear to me the classic zone, Which..Adorns th' accepted bard. **1839** *E. D. Clarke's Trav. Russia* 83/1 It was a zone for the leg, or bracelet for the arm, of the purest massive gold. **1869** LECKY *Europ. Mor.* II. v. 338 To the fabled zone of beauty the Christian saints opposed their zones of chastity. **1883** HARDY in *Longman's Mag.* July 258 The carters with a zone of whipcord round their hats.

b. A money-belt or purse.

1692 WASHINGTON tr. *Milton's Def. People* ix. 212 How many Zones you observed in that Golden and Silken Heaven of the King's, I know not; but I know you got one Zone (a Purse) well tempered with a Hundred Golden Stars by your Astronomy. **1818** SCOTT *Hrt. Midl.* viii, The *zone* of the ex-trooper, to use Horace's phrase, was weighty enough to purchase a cottage.

c. *Astron.* The girdle of Orion.

1599 T. HILL *Schoole of Skil* 92 The constellation named the Zone or gyrdle of Orion.

4. a. Something that encircles like a girdle; a circumscribing or inclosing line, band, or ring.

1591 SYLVESTER *Du Bartas* I. vi. 71 Round about him he so closely cleaves With's wrything body; that his Enemy.. Hastes to some Tree, or to some Rock, whereon To rush and rub-off his detested zone. **1620** T. PEYTON *Glasse of Time* I. 50 With twelue braue gates the curious eye to fill, The sacred luster as the glistring Zoane, And euery gate fram'd of a seuerall stone. **1784** COWPER *Task* IV. 257 The moon..set With modest grandeur in thy [*sc.* Evening's] purple zone. **1840** *Civil Eng. & Arch. Jrnl.* III. 144/1 Below the entablature is a band or zone, formed of large stones and bricks placed alternately. **1856** W. CLARK *Van der Hoeven's Zool.* I. 93 Tentacles disposed in a zone around the mouth. **1860** TYNDALL *Glac.* I. xxii. 154 A tendency to form circular zones round the sun. **1895** BRIDGES *Ode to Music* IV. i, His [*sc.* the sea's] world-wide elemental moan Girdeth our lives with tragic zone.

b. A band or stripe of colour, or of light or shade, extending around something, or (*loosely*) over any surface or area; often, any one of a number of concentric or alternate markings of this kind.

1752 J. HILL *Hist. Anim.* 131 The outer surface of the whole shell [of the Buccinum]..is of a pale brownish colour, elegantly variegated with a great number of yellow zones. **1805** SHAW *Nat. Misc.* XVI. pl. 657 Long-tailed green Parrot, with..the collar on the nape and abdominal zone yellow. **1816** R. JAMESON *Syst. Min.* (ed. 2) II. 146 All such white marbles as are marked with green-coloured zones, caused by talc or chlorite. **1815** J. SMITH *Panorama Sci. & Art* I. 556 When Jupiter is viewed through a good telescope, we perceive a number of zones or belts, of a darker colour than the rest of his disc. **1833** SIR C. BELL *Hand* (1834) 311 If we press upon the eye-ball with a key or the end of a pencil-case, zones of light are excited. **1891** FARRAR *Darkn. & Dawn* vi, The atrium glowed in zones of light.

5. *Astron.* A region or belt of the sky comprised between definite limits, e.g. between two parallels of declination.

1795 HERSCHEL in *Phil. Trans.* LXXXV. 381 My examinations of the heavens in zones. **1829** *Chapters Phys. Sci.* 413 That broad zone called the milky-way. **1890** AGNES M. CLERKE *Syst. Stars* xxiv. 377 The general plan of nebular distribution is into vast assemblages, one on either side of the galactic zone.

6. *Anat.*, *Zool.*, and *Bot.* A growth or structure surrounding or encircling some part in the form of a ring or cylinder; also, a region or area extending around or over some part and distinguished by some special character or condition.

With various defining words applied *spec.* to particular structures or regions. CILIARY *zone*, MOTOR *zone*: see these words. ***zone of Zinn***: see ZONULE.

1811 C. Bell *Anat. Hum. Body* (ed. 3) III. 468 These tubercles are..surrounded by a zone or disk, of a brownish red colour, the areola. **1849** A. H. Hassall *Microsc. Anat. Hum. Body* I. 514 Ciliary processes.—These processes..are received into corresponding folds or plaitings of the hyaloid membrane, called the secondary ciliary processes, and which taken altogether form a circle around the crystalline lens named after their discoverer the Zone of Zinn. **1882** Wilder & Gage *Anat. Technol.* §1421 The cornea..is..intermediate in thickness between that of the white zone and the rest of the sclerotic. **1884** Bower & Scott *De Bary's Phaner.* 7 The periblem, which is a zone of tissue lying between the plerome and dermatogen. **1913** Dorland *Med. Dict.* s.v., *Abdominal z[one]s*, the three zones into which the surface of the abdomen is divided by the subcostal and intertubercular lines... *Pellucid z.*, the zona pellucida.

7. *Geol.* and *Physical Geog.* A region, or each of a series of regions, comprised between definite limits of any kind, e.g. of depth or height, and distinguished by special characters, esp. by characteristic fossils or forms of animal and plant life.

1829 Ure *New Syst. Geol.* 150 In the north [of France], it [*sc.* limestone] forms a portion of the great transition zone, which stretches from Flanders into the Hartz. **1839** Murchison *Silur. Syst.* I. ii. 17 The presence of this zone of clay..is marked by the outburst of water. **1851** *Amer. Jrnl. Sci.* Ser. II. XI. 263 This cretaceous zone of the shore of the Cantabrian sea. **1882** Geikie *Text-bk. Geol.* VI. 635 A bed, or limited number of beds, characterized by one or more distinctive fossils, is termed a zone or horizon.

8. a. *Math.* A part of the surface of a sphere contained between two parallel planes, or of the surface of any solid of revolution contained between two planes perpendicular to the axis. **b.** *Cryst.* A series of faces of a crystal extending around it and having their lines of intersection parallel.

1795 Hutton *Math. Dict.* II. 477/2 The curve-surface of any segment or zone of a Sphere, is also equal to the curve surface of a cylinder of the same height with that portion, and of the same diameter with the Sphere. **1867** Thomson & Tait *Nat. Phil.* §781 I. 621 These circles..are..all in parallel planes..and cut the spherical surface into zones. **1868** Dana *Min.* (ed. 5) Introd. p. xxvi, The planes [of a crystalline form] may thus be viewed as lying in vertical zones, a different zone for every ratio of the lateral axes. **1878** Gurney *Crystallogr.* 21 These four vertical faces constitute what is called a zone (or girdle) of the form. **1895** Palmer tr. *Nernst's Theor. Chem.* 67 The 'law of zones',..viz. all planes which can occur on a crystal are related to each other in zones; or, in other words, from any four planes, no three of which lie in one zone, all possible crystal planes can be derived by means of zones.

9. A hole in certain punched cards that is punched above the column of holes representing non-zero digits and is used in conjunction with these latter holes to represent non-numerical characters. Usu. *attrib.*

1950 W. W. Stifler *High-Speed Computing Devices* 149 For alphabetical representations, two perforations in a single column are used for each letter; one of these is a zone punch (0, 11, or 12) while the other perforation is made in the position identifying one of the digits 1 to 9. **1959** M. H. Wrubel *Primer of Programming for Digital Computers* ii. 33 Alphabetic information is recorded by using two punches in the same column: the upper punch (sometimes called the 'zone') is always a 12, 11, or 0. **1970** O. Dopping *Computers & Data Processing* ii. 44 A letter in the English alphabet is coded with one zone punch (12, 11, or 0) together with one under-punch. **1972** W. R. Price *Introd. Data Processing* vii. 179 The correspondence between the Hollerith zones and the 1401 zones. **1979** Davis & McCormack *Information Age* vi. 98 Later, when the need for alphabetic data arose, the zone positions, rows 12 and 11, were added.

10. *attrib.* and *Comb.* **a.** *attrib.*, chiefly in technical senses: e.g. in sense 2b, esp. in reference to 'zones' or regions into which a district or country is divided for purposes of railway or other travelling, etc., as ***zone centre***, ***fare***, ***system***, ***tariff***; in sense 5, as ***zone-clock***, ***-piece***, ***-reticle***; in sense 8b, as ***zone-axis***, ***-circle***, ***-plane***; ***zone-mind***; **zone centre**, *spec.* in *Teleph.*, an exchange which acts as a main switching centre in an area containing a number of exchange groups; **zone defence** (*U.S.* **defense**), *N. Amer. Football* and *Basketball*, a system of defensive play whereby each player guards an allotted portion of the field of play; **zone electrophoresis**, electrophoresis in which a solid but porous medium such as paper is used to ensure that the components remain separated in zones or bands according to their differing electrophoretic mobilities; **zone fossil** *Geol.*, a fossil characteristic of a particular zone or belt of strata; **zone leveller**, an apparatus used for zone levelling; **zone levelling**, a process similar to zone refining in which the molten zone is passed repeatedly to and fro to produce a more homogenous material; so **zone level** *v. trans.*, **-levelled** *ppl. a.*; **zone melting** = *zone refining* below; so **zone-melt** *v. trans.*; **zone plate**, a plate of glass marked out into concentric zones or rings alternately transparent and opaque, used like a lens to bring light to a focus; **zone refiner**, an apparatus used for zone refining; **zone refining**, a method of refining used to produce semiconductors and metals of very high purity by causing narrow zones of molten material to travel slowly along an otherwise solid rod or bar, so that impurities become concentrated at one end or the other if their solubilities in the liquid and the solid phases differ; so **zone-refine** *v. trans.*, **zone-refined** *ppl. a.*; **zone therapy**, a technique in which different parts of the feet (or palms) are massaged to relieve conditions in different parts of the body with which they are held to be associated; **zone time**, mean solar time at the standard meridian on which the local time zone is based, taken as the standard time throughout the zone (cf. *Zulu time* s.v. ZULU *sb.* and *a.* 6). **b.** *Comb.* (objective, instrumental, parasynthetic, etc.), as ***zone-confounding***, ***-like***, ***-tailed*** adjs.

1878 Gurney *Crystallogr.* 22 The zone, the *zone axis, and the zone plane are all denoted by the same symbol, namely (U V W). **1934** G. S. Berkeley *Traffic & Trunking Princ. in Automatic Telephony* i. 12 Level 94..is used for trunk calls instead of level 0 in the case of exchanges in Trunk *Zone Centres. **1948** [see ROUTE *v.* c]. **1960** R. Syski *Congestion Theory in Telephone Systems* ii. 53 A suitable exchange (zone centre) is established within each zone to handle the long-distance calls to and from that zone. **1971** *Gloss. Electrotechnical, Power Terms* (*B.S.I.*) III. ii. 8 *Zone centre*, exchange acting as the main switching centre. **1878** Gurney *Crystallogr.* 32 The poles of all the faces in the same zone will lie in the same *zone circle. **1795** Herschel in *Phil. Trans.* LXXXV. 398 It would not only be trouble-some to the workman, but often bring on mistakes, were he to count the turns of the handle, which perhaps for hours together he is moving; a *zone-clock, therefore, has been contrived to release him from that care... It strikes a bell..when the telescope is come to one of the limits of the zone. **1890** *Punch* 28 June p. iv, The yellow pod-flowers and the waving palms, the vermeil apples and the primrosed banks, of Camoens' somewhat *zone-confounding vision. **1927** *Zone defense [see sense 2d above]. **1929** H. C. Carlson *You & Basket Ball* vi. 128 Zone defense, in which each individual is responsible for a certain zone. **1937** C. Allen *Better Basketball* xviii. 291 It is to be noticed in charting these penetrating offensive plays against a zone defense that the setup of the offense is identical with that used in penetrating the man-for-man defense. **1970** G. Sullivan *Pro Football A to Z* 341 *Zone defense*, a type of pass defense in which each of the three linebackers and four deep backs is assigned to cover a specific area of the field. Zone defense contrasts with man-to-man defense. **1952** *Proc. Soc. Exper. Biol. & Med.* LXXX. 42 (*heading*) *Zone electrophoresis in a starch supporting medium. **1964** G. H. Haggis et al. *Introd. Molecular Biol.* ii. 23 (*caption*) The separation of some of the human plasma proteins by zone electrophoresis. **1975** Davis & Simpkins in Williams & Wilson *Biologist's Guide to Princ. & Techniques Pract. Biochem.* iv. 100 A common feature of the use of all supporting media is that the substances migrate as distinct zones which at the end of the analysis can be readily detected by suitable analytical techniques... The term zone electrophoresis has been applied to this method. **1903** *Daily Chron.* 18 Dec. 6/3 They proposed to fix *zone fares, and they treated Hammersmith as what they called the zone centre. **1904** *Zone-fossil [see ZONAL *a.* 3]. **1969** Bennison & Wright *Geol. Hist. Brit. Isles* ii. 23 It may be possible to recognize a zone without actually finding a specimen of the zone fossil itself if other highly characteristic species are found. **1975** J. G. Evans *Environment Early Man Brit. Isles* iii. 69 Evolution needed the temporal and biological continuum which Lyell's theory made possible. And from this came the concept of the 'zone fossil'. **1953** W. G. Pfann in *Trans. Amer. Inst. Mining & Metall. Engineers* CXCIV. 752/1 The discussion of zone-melting has been confined to the categories of *zone-leveling and zone-refining. **1956** *Bell Syst. Technical Jrnl.* XXXV. 657, *p* fluctuations in zone leveled material are generally coarse. *Ibid.* 660 A zone leveler has been developed to provide growth conditions suitable for the production of quality germanium single crystals. **1974** *Jrnl. Physics* D. VII. 33 The mixed alloy was then placed in a porcelain boat and zone-levelled by passing through 10–15 zones. **1978** P. W. Atkins *Physical Chem.* x. 301 A modification of the technique, zone levelling, is used to introduce controlled amounts of impurity (for example, indium into germanium). **1598** Marston *Sco. Villanie* I. i, When chast Dictinna, breakes the *Zonelike twist. **1952** W. G. Pfann in *Jrnl. Metals* IV. 747/1 A number of procedures will be indicated which have in common the traversal of a relatively long charge of solid alloy by a small molten zone. Such methods will be denoted by the general term **zone-melting*. **1965** Phillips & Williams *Inorg. Chem.* I. viii. 305 All such techniques as precipitation, partition, distillation, crystallization, chromatography, and zone-melting are based on phase equilibria. **1982** *Materials Lett.* I. 33/2 Dielectrically isolated single crystals of large extent may be fabricated by zone melting a thin silicon sheet that is encapsulated between SiO_2 layers. **1983** *Rev. Sci. Instruments* LIV. 385/2 The use of the heater assembly in the specific case of zone melting of mercury cadmium telluride compounds is described. **1932** Blunden *Halfway House* 55 When gong-like struck The violent crisis of *zone-minds That chilled us with clouds turned winds. **1795** Herschel in *Phil. Trans.* LXXXV. 385 A *zone-piece, to point out the required limits of the intended zones. **1878** Gurney *Crystallogr.* 22 The plane to which they [*sc.* the edges of the crystal] are all perpendicular is called the *zone plane. **1890** T. Preston *Theory of Light* ix. 178 A *zone plate has therefore the power of a condensing lens. **1937** G. S. Monk *Light* xii. 167 The intensity of the image produced with a zone plate will be greater if alternate zones are not blocked out but are left transmitting, with a phase difference of one half period introduced between them and adjacent zones. **1978** *Sci. Amer.* Nov. 65/1 When the zone plate is illuminated with an X-ray plane wave, a converging spherical wave will come out. **1952** W. G. Pfann in *Jrnl. Metals* IV. 750/2 The particular merit of *zone-refining becomes evident when repeated crystallizations are desired. **1956** —— in *Chem. & Engin. News* XXXIV. 1443/3 F. Montariol and coworkers..found that zone-refined aluminum cannot be hardened by cold-working. **1962** *New Scientist* 5 Apr. 813/2 To zone-refine and produce single crystals from such [refractory] materials, N. V. Philips's Gloeilampenfabrieken, Eindhoven,..has developed a carbon-arc image furnace. **1973** J. G. Tweeddale *Materials Technol.* I. vi. 152 Probably the most effective and generally used method of refining to this kind of standard is zone refining. **1978** P. W. Atkins *Physical Chem.* x. 301 Bismuth is normally regarded as a hard, brittle metal, yet when it has been zone refined it forms rods which can be bent without fracture. **1983** *Metallurgical Trans.* A. XIV. 223/2 Straining electrode experiments were performed in zone refined and vacuum melted nickel alloys. **1959** *Times* 24 Nov. 19/7 It will be possible to obtain high quality single-crystal rods after a few passes in the *zone-refiner. **1980** *Analytical Chem.* LII. 1738/1 A novel zone refiner is described, in which a single helical heater rotates in an annular sample space. **1876** G. F. Chambers *Astron.* (ed. 3) 632 Observers..will find a '*zone reticle' of great service. **1903** *Daily Chron.* 21 Nov. 7/2 Hungary has introduced a *zone system on her railways, which has made travelling on them the cheapest in the world. **1809** Shaw *Gen. Zool.* VII. 62 *Zone-tailed Eagle. **1891** *Econ. Jrnl.* I. 507 A system of *zone tariffs. **1902** *Encycl. Brit.* XXXII. 153/2 A zone-tariff system..whereby the country is mapped out into zones, and the traveller pays according to the number of these he passes through. **1917** W. H. FitzGerald *Zone Therapy* xvi. 157 Dr. Roemer..examined him in a characteristic *zone therapy way. He searched the patient's fingers with a metal comb to find out what was the matter with his teeth. **1971** N. Saunders *Alternative London* xv. 123 Zone Therapy is based on the premise that one zone of the body acts as a microcosm of the whole. **1979** D. E. Bayly in A. Hill *Visual Encycl. of Unconventional Med.* 61 The origin of the reflex method is obscure. It is said that it came from China to the West... It is known to have been used by the natives of Kenya, and also by some American Indian tribes. At the beginning of this century it was called zone therapy by one Dr Fitzgerald [*sic*] in America who used it as a form of anaesthesia to render the patient insensible to pain when performing small operations, and to ease childbirth. **1908** H. B. Morse *Trade & Admin. Chinese Empire* viii. 203 The Eighteen Provinces roughly extend from..longitude 98° to 122° E., comprising the seventh and eighth hours of the *Zone time east of Greenwich. **1930** *Daily Express* 16 Aug. 1/3 The passengers wonder whether they should retire by Greenwich or zone time. **1981** G. Watkins *Exercises in Astro-Navigation* ii. 22 A vessel's chronometer or watch is not generally adjusted or altered at any time while the vessel is at sea, but her clock is altered as she moves through each zone in such a way that it should always be indicating the correct Zone Time for the vessel's position.

zone, *v.* [f. prec.]

1. *trans.* To furnish with, or surround like, a zone or girdle; to gird, encircle.

1795 *Monthly Rev.* Dec. 542 Her population..had zoned every hill with vines and with olive-trees. **1795** Anna Seward *Lett.* (1811) IV. 105 Our road zoned the midway of the Alpine steeps which overhung it. **1813** Scott *Trierm.* II. iv, Art she invokes to Nature's aid, Her vest to zone, her locks to braid. **1818** Keats *Endym.* II. 569, I could hear he lov'd Some fair immortal, and that his embrace Had zoned her through the night. **1853** Kane *Grinnell Exp.* xxviii. (1856) 237 The southeastern horizon is zoned with a mellow uniform band of light.

2. *Nat. Hist.* To mark with zones, rings, or bands of colour. (Only in *pa. pple.*)

1792 Withering *Brit. Plants* (ed. 2) III. 433 Auricularia papyrina... Annual, membranaceous, soft, zoned. **1854** Dana *Min.* (ed. 4) II. 148 Egyptian Jasper is zoned with colors, and forms nodules. **1871** Darwin *Desc. Man* II. xiv. 131 A variety of the common pigeon with the wing-bars symmetrically zoned with three bright shades.

3. *Geol.*, etc. To divide into zones; to distribute or arrange in zones: see ZONE *sb.* 7.

1904 *Edin. Rev.* Jan. 222 The Ordovician and Silurian rocks have been zoned by means of their graptolites.

4. (*Town-*) *Planning.* To divide (a city, land, etc.) into areas subject to particular planning restrictions; to designate (a specific area) for use or development in this manner. Occas. *intr.* Also (*U.S.*) const. *out*, to forbid (the siting of an enterprise) in a given area. orig. *U.S.*

1916 *N.Y. Times* 4 Feb. 17/2 The plan to zone the city and regulate the height of buildings. **1919** *Melbourne Argus* 28 Aug. 6 The question of 'zoning' the metropolitan area, or separating the city into districts, in order that regulations may be applied to control the erection of shops and factories near residential sites, has recently been occupying the attention of the Melbourne City Council. **1934** W. H. Heath in E. Betham *House Building 1934–36* xviii. 180 There is practically no area around London that is zoned in a reasonable manner. **1939** H. M. Lewis *City Planning* xvi. 169 All the frontage of main streets was placed in business zones although..only a small fraction of areas so zoned can ever be used for that purpose. **1967** *Boston Sunday Herald* 26 Mar. I. 9/4 Planners..are concerned that a community will be thoughtfully zoned overall. **1971** P. Gresswell *Environment* 267 There is no guarantee that land zoned for housing will be released by the landowners. **1975** *N.Y. Times* 16 Oct. 29/1 A law that would 'zone out' massage parlors from the Times Square area on the principle that their proliferation is not sound community planning. **1976** *National Observer* (U.S.) 14 Aug. 7/2 When a municipality zones for industry and commerce for local tax benefits..it..must zone to permit adequate housing within the means of the employes involved in such uses. **1977** *Chicago Tribune Mag.* 2 Oct. 8/2 At that time, which was before horse racing was zoned out of the city, the track was on Stony Island Avenue near 63rd Street. **1978** J. Updike *Coup* (1979) vii. 274 The land, they say, is zoned for agribusiness.

5. To restrict the distribution of (a commodity) to a designated area; used *spec.*

concerning the allocation of foodstuffs in the war of 1939–45.

1942 *Hansard Lords* 3 June 103 We have arranged that the deliveries of bread shall be zoned. **1945** *Daily Herald* 31 Aug. 2/1 (Advt.), Cyder, like many other things, is now zoned to save transport and labour. **1952** *Ann. Reg. 1951* 394 The Group scheme of the National Film Finance Corporation has been announced. This 'zoned' a considerable proportion of British production.

Hence **'zoner**, one employed in the application of planning restrictions to particular areas; **'zoning** *ppl. a.*

1853 ALEX. SMITH *Life Drama* ii, When first they clasped a Son of God.. In zoning heaven of their milky arms. **1865** TENNYSON *On a Mourner* v, When the zoning eve has died. **1962** *Punch* 6 June 848/2 Planners and zoners won't apparently make up their minds. **1976** *Daily Tel.* 4 Apr. 3/6 This district contains about 1,000 homes approved by town zoners.. after they were assured restrictive deed clauses would make the district a 'permanent adult community'.

zoned (zəʊnd), *a.* [f. ZONE *sb.* or *v.* + -ED.]

† **1.** Located in a zone or region of the celestial sphere: = ZONIC *a. Obs. rare*$^{-1}$.

1662 STANLEY *Hist. Chaldaick Philos.* 4 Or else by fiery Zone, he means the Seat of the zoned Deities just above the Empyreal or Corporeal Heaven.

2. Wearing a zone or girdle. Hence, virgin, chaste.

1718 POPE *Odyss.* XXIII. 142 Fair zoned damsels. **1829** LYTTON *Devereux* II. ix, A zoned and untainted Innocence.

3. Characterized by or arranged (naturally) in zones, rings, or bands.

1794 R. J. SULIVAN *View Nat.* I. 435 The zoned or tabulated form of the onyx. **1805–17** R. JAMESON *Char. Min.* (ed. 3) 213 Zoned (*zonaire*), when a row of facets is arranged around the middle part, thus forming a kind of zone or girdle. Example, Zoned calcareous-spar. **1845** G. DODD *Brit. Manuf.* Ser. IV. 200 As a fifth source of variety [in wood] may be mentioned eyes, zoned spots, and curls.

b. Marked with zones, circles, or bands of colour.

1792 WITHERING *Brit. Plants* (ed. 2) III. 433 *Auricularia ferruginea*,.. zoned above. **1805** SHAW *Nat. Misc.* XVI. pl. 657 The Zoned Parrot. **1849** W. H. HARVEY *Brit. Mar. Algæ* 121 Zoned tetraspores exist in *Rhod[ymenia] ciliata*. **1874** BIRCH *1st and 2nd Egypt. Rooms B. Mus.* 31 With side handles of zoned alabaster.

4. a. Arranged according to zones or definite regions.

1795 HERSCHEL in *Phil. Trans.* LXXXV. 384 A zoned catalogue of the stars. **1890** AGNES M. CLERKE *Syst. Stars* v. 80 The spectra of the great nebulæ, like those of the 'zoned' stars, must be considered as integrating the results of emanations taking their rise under notably diverse circumstances.

b. Distributed according to zones. Cf. ZONE *v.* 5.

1943 *Daily Express* 16 Sept. 3/3 Compelling some grocers to buy their zoned cake through the co-ops.

5. (*Town-*) *Planning.* Designated for a particular type of use or development. orig. *U.S.*

1920 *Michigan Rep.* (Michigan Supreme Court) May 210 A penalty is provided for violation of said ordinance with a mandate prohibiting departments of the city from issuing permits for erection of the forbidden buildings within such zoned district. **1939** *Florida* (Fed. Writers' Project) III. 396 Zoned residential, business, and industrial districts. **1970** *Cape Times* 28 Oct. 20/3 (Advt.), Paarl shopping centre. On 11000 sq. ft., zoned special business with free car park.. in fast developing area.

zoneless ('zəʊnlɪs), *a.* [f. ZONE *sb.* + -LESS.]

1. Not confined by, or not wearing, a zone or girdle; ungirt.

1748 W. MASON *Isis* 8 In careless folds loose flow'd her zoneless vest. **1784** COWPER *Task* III. 52 Pleasure.. That reeling goddess with the zoneless waist. **1802** COLERIDGE *Lett.* (1895) 370, I always thought him a bantling of zoneless Italian muses. **1822** MILMAN *Mart. Antioch* 14 Come in thy zoneless grace, thy flowing locks Crown'd with the laurel of the Gods.

2. Not marked with zones or bands of colour.

1836 M. J. BERKELEY *Sir J. E. Smith's Engl. Flora* V. II. 140 Pileus of a fleshy.. substance zoneless villous white.

zonelet ('zəʊnlɪt). *rare.* [-LET.] A little zone.

1855 BAILEY *Mystic* 30 From the moon's hand her starry stole he took, And zonelet studded with thrice ten beamy rings.

Zonian ('zəʊnɪən), *sb.* (*a.*) [f. Panama Canal *Zone* (see below) + -IAN.] An American inhabitant of the Panama Canal Zone, a ten mile wide strip of land crossing the Isthmus of Panama on both sides of the Panama Canal, which was granted to the United States as a territory in 1904 and became independent in 1978. Also *attrib.* or as *adj.*

1910 *Everybody's Mag.* Mar. 322/1 Whatever your job, digging a canal, or driving a taxi-cab, or writing stock quotations, don't wear a uniform... The Zonian has a uniform, though, in spite of himself. It is the umbrella. **1950** *Social Forces* Dec. 161/1 The man marrying a girl of mixed blood may be unaware of the general Zonian prejudice that classes all Panamanians as 'colored'. **1951** *Panama Canal Rev.* 3 Aug. 9/3 Zonians.. need no longer do without—just because the commissaries are closed. **1964** *Observer* 12 Jan. 1/5 'Zonians', American inhabitants of the [Panama Canal] Zone. **1979** P. THEROUX *Old Patagonian Express* xii. 170 Within a very few months the treaty would be ratified. I told this to a Zonian lady... The Zonians, 3,000 workers for the Panama Canal Company.. saw the treaty as a sell-out.

zonic ('zəʊnɪk), *a. rare.* [f. ZONE *sb.* + -IC.] Belonging to a particular zone or region.

1797 *Monthly Mag.* III. 511 The zonic gods are those which revolve round the celestial zones.

'zoning, *vbl. sb.* [f. ZONE *v.*]

1. Dividing into zones.

1819 KEATS *Fall Hyperion* I. 312 Not so much air As in the zoning of a summer's day. **1888** *Nature* 5 July 225 What Mr. Lockyer has called the zoning of colour in the heavens. **1904** *Edin. Rev.* Jan. 220 The zoning of the strata. **1942** *Times* 5 June 2/3 Further steps, including the zoning of the distribution of manufactured goods.. are being investigated by the Ministry. **1945** *Daily Tel.* 17 May 5/7 In the zoning of Germany the United States Navy has been allotted the ports of Bremen and Bremerhaven. **1946** *How Britain was fed in War Time* (H.M.S.O.) iii. 22 The transport of food from production or import points to wholesalers' stores was effected by 'zoning' schemes... The country was divided into.. zones, and movement between different zones.. was allowed only by permit. **1968** *New York City* (Michelin) 16 After the First World War... A new zoning law regulated the height of buildings in relation to the width of the streets.

2. *spec.* in (*Town-*) *Planning*, the regulation of land use by particular planning restrictions in designated areas. orig. *U.S.*

1912 *Proc. 4th Nat. Conference City Planning* 190 In view of.. existing indirect zoning laws, why not add some of the building laws in force in Frankfurt-on-the-Main? **1914** *Proc. 6th Nat. Conference City Planning* 92 The well-established principle of zoning that has been in operation for a generation or more in that country [*sc.* Germany]. **1921** *Glasgow Herald* 25 Mar. 8/3 'Zoning' means the locating of industries in the areas which are best suited for them and the reserving for housing of districts best adapted for this purpose. **1940** GRAVES & HODGE *Long Week-End* xi. 175 The Town-Planning Act of 1932 perpetuated this cleavage... Now there was 'zoning'.. segregating families according to their incomes. **1943** J. S. HUXLEY *TVA* 31 Some States have introduced compulsory 'agricultural zoning' by which certain types of farming are prohibited in certain areas. **1966** R. F. BABCOCK (*title*) The zoning game: municipal practices and policies. **1978** J. A. MICHENER *Chesapeake* xiii. 830 Crossing over to the rivers south of Annapolis,.. Chris had a chance to see how lack of zoning and policing had encouraged this shoreline to become a marine slum.

zonite ('zəʊnaɪt). *Zool.* [ad. mod.L. *zōnītēs*, f. L. *zōna* ZONE *sb.*: see -ITE¹.]

1. A snail of the genus *Zonites*.

1860 *All Year Round* No. 43. 390 Porcelain Zonites that lived two years and a half without aliment.

2. Any of the body-rings of a segmented animal, as an arthropod or annelid. Hence **zo'nitic** *a.*

1880 PASCOE *Zool. Class.* (ed. 2) 297 Zonites, Somites, or Metameres. **1888** *Huxley & Martin's Pract. Biol.* 241 Each somite is subdivided externally into at least two lesser divisions or zonites. **1888** J. R. A. DAVIS *Biol.* 161 The zonitic constrictions.

zonk (zɒŋk), *int.* (*sb.*) *slang.* [Echoic.] Representing the sound of a blow or heavy impact, used to indicate finality. Occas. as *sb.* (see quots.).

1949 T. RATTIGAN *Harlequinade* 38 Just sit there and relax and I'll dash and get you an enormous zonk of whisky. **1958** *Spectator* 15 Aug. 218/2, I.. hurl it with a great zonk into the waste-paper basket. **1961** *Radio Times* 16 Nov. 47/2, I never took a note when I was interrogating. The moment you got hold of a piece of paper they'd think 'ah-hah..' and zonk! they'd button up. **1968** L. DEIGHTON *Only when I Larf* i. 12 Silas.. closed the safe door a few times. Zonk. It closed with a clang. **1979** R. BLYTHE *View in Winter* i. 64 He was a man with a catapult. He'd knock a pheasant down—*zonk*!

zonk, *v. slang.* [f. prec.] **1.** *trans.* To hit, strike, or knock. Also *fig.*

1950 A. MELVILLE *Castle in Air* I. in *Plays of Year* III. 338 If the Third Earl found that his wife had nipped off with another man while he was away at the Crusades, he'd have zonked her over the head with his kitbag. **1959** P. BULL *I know Face* xi. 201 We found ourselves back in my flat.. zonking down the drink. **1960** I. CROSS *Backward Sex* 188 She zonked me again on the head with this hairbrush. **1975** *New Yorker* 21 July 67/1 William Green tried to assure them that care had been taken to put provisions in the bill to see to it that New England 'doesn't get zonked'. **1979** G. WATSON *Black Jack* xxii. 178, I felt zonked by this idea. It had never occurred to me. **1982** *Observer* 14 Nov. 15 ICI has invented a new adaptation to ethylene crackers that will zonk the competition and make feedstock costs less critical.

2. *intr.* To fail; to lose consciousness, to die.

1968 *Listener* 14 Mar. 352/3 If Johnny zonked, it would be bad for my book. **1977** *N.Y. Times Mag.* 4 Dec. 142 In a burst of determination, she'd been sitting in the bathtub doing her breathing for five hours straight—in one nostril, out the other—until she zonked and went rigid.

3. const. *out.* **a.** *intr.* To fall heavily asleep. **b.** *trans.* To overcome or knock out (in *fig.* senses).

1970 J. SANGSTER *Touchfeather, Too* iii. 75 He left me at seven a.m. and I zonked out until after mid-day. **1973** *Austral. Women's Weekly* 26 Dec. 32/5, I sank into my bed.., zonked myself out with sleeping pills, and woke up Friday. **1980** *Telegraph* (Brisbane) 21 Mar. 6/3 It's J. R.'s power that zonks women out. **1984** *N.Y. News Mag.* 18 Mar. 18/2 If mothers zonk out at three in the afternoon every day, they may continue that pattern after it's no longer necessary. **1985** *Sunday Times* 24 Feb. 36/6 No Junoesque oarswomen though... 'I think I row because it zonks me out, then I don't row with anyone.'

Hence **'zonking** *ppl. a.* (freq. as quasi-*adv.* in *zonking great*).

1958 *Spectator* 25 July 130/2 He would give one a zonking great clip on the ear. **1959** P. BULL *I know Face* vi. 100 She was now technically a 'star' owing to her zonking success as Claudia. *Ibid.* vii. 126 She.. is a zonking great film star. **1973** *Daily Tel.* (Colour Suppl.) 9 Feb. 36/4 *Long Day's Journey*.. was the first big, zonking part he played after his cancer. **1976** *Times* 21 May 4/7 Rather than play these zonking great parts.. I will try to find some dazzling little cameo roles.

zonked (zɒŋkt), *ppl. a.* (chiefly *pred.*) *slang.* [f. ZONK *v.* + -ED¹.] **1.** Intoxicated by drugs or alcohol; 'stoned'. Freq. const. *out.* Also *transf.* and *fig.*

1959 *Esquire* Nov. 70J, *Zonked*, one who is stoned, high, drunk. **1967** *New Scientist* 19 Oct. 185/1 Most of the drivers one meets should not be allowed to take charge of a car when sober—let alone when three parts zonked. **1967** P. WELLES *Babyhip* iv. 53 If only Mr Green weren't Jewish, he could swing around the world on the magic carpet completely zonked out. **1968** T. WOLFE *Electric Kool-Aid Acid Test* vi. 70 Everybody.. had taken acid and they were zonked. **1972** J. WAMBAUGH *Blue Knight* (1973) xiv. 246 We sat.. drinking *arak* and wine, and then beer, and we all got pretty zonked. **1973** H. NIELSEN *Severed Key* x. 107 I'm serious. Zonked about her. Way out. **1975** *Publishers Weekly* 20 Jan. 78/1 Susan begins an affair with a zonked-out type who calls himself Commander Cloud. **1977** *Rolling Stone* 24 Mar. 84/1 Thousands of young people squeezed themselves into Radio City Music Hall to enjoy, scream at, get zonked to Jethro Tull. **1979** *Daily Tel.* Apr. 21/5 A.. Caucasian woman obviously zonked out.. and a tracery of leaves resembling cannabis.

2. Exhausted, tired *out*.

1972 *Maclean's Mag.* Oct. 40/1 This portrait of his wife.. zonked out on a floating sofa. **1976** J. FARRIS *Fury* i. 10 You just collapsed and.. pulled the covers up around your head... You were completely zonked. **1978** *Washington Post Mag.* 19 Mar. 42/2 Patricia Wells, three hours after providing the high point of 2,300 people's evenings, was 'zonked' and went back to her hotel to bed. **1980** *Daily Tel.* 28 July 8/6 'Fairly zonked' by his non-stop 17 weeks of filming, he is recharging himself for the next stage.

zonkey ('zɒŋkɪ). [f. Z(EBRA + D)ONKEY.] The offspring of a zebra and a donkey. Cf. ZEDONK.

1953 *N.Y. Herald Tribune* 2 Sept. 1/7 Mr. [Gene] Holter explained that a zonkey was half zebra and half donkey, a combination the zoomen had never seen. *Ibid.*, 'Zonkey is not exactly a scientific name and I'm no scientist' Mr. Holter said, 'But I don't know what else you would call it.' **1973** *Indian Express* 29 Oct. 6/8 A zebra and a donkey are expecting an offspring next March, Brooklyn's Prospect Park Zoo authorities say. It will be New York's first zonkey, though. The others were born in western zoos. **1983** *N.Y. Times* 6 Mar. x. 53/4 Melancholy exemplars abound: a male camel who recently injured a foreleg;.. and a morose-looking zonkey— the mother a zebra, the father a donkey.

zonky ('zɒŋkɪ), *a.* (*sb.*) *slang.* Also **zonkey**. [f. ZONK(ED *ppl. a.* + -Y⁶.] Odd, weird, 'freaky'. Hence as *sb.*, a person in this state.

1972 *Daily Colonist* (Victoria, B.C.) 26 Apr. 22/5 'Wow, is this zonky?' breathed an admiring observer softly, as she gazed incredulously at the newly opened, all-cardboard room. **1975** *Globe & Mail* (Toronto) 25 Oct. 34/1 Unlike the honkey-tonk zonkies who used to hang out at his.. workshop, shooting up or having sex in public view... Warhol has rarely, personally, done anything scandalous. **1977** *N.Y. Rev. Bks.* 28 Apr. 12/3 That combination of the new and old seems to have escaped most journalists except —in one of his zonky moments of insight—Hunter Thompson. **1979** B. MALAMUD *Dubin's Lives* i. 22 All the guy there does is.. shakes his head. Makes you feel zonky.. twittery. **1980** *Times* 6 Nov. 12/6 His book is really a study in ideas—or to coin an appropriately zonkey term—*weirdology*.

zonne, obs. (Kentish) form of SUN.

zono- (zəʊnəʊ), repr. Gr. ζωνο-, combining form of ζώνη ZONE, occurring in a few scientific and technical words. **zonochlorite** (-'klɔəraɪt) *Min.* [Gr. χλωρός green], name for a supposed species of mineral from Lake Superior, marked with bands of different shades of green (perh. the same as CHLORASTROLITE). **zonociliate** (-'sɪlɪeɪt) *a. Zool.*, having a zone or circlet of cilia. **zonopla'cental** *a. Zool.*, having a zonary placenta, as the *Carnivora* and other mammals: opposed to *discoplacental*.

1872 A. E. FOOTE in *Proc. Amer. Ass. Adv. Sci.* (1873) XXI. 65 *Zonochlorite, a New Hydrous Silicate from Neepigon Bay, North Shore of Lake Superior. **1885** *Encycl. Brit.* XIX. 437/1 The fertilized egg of the Phylactolæma does not give rise to a *zonociliate larva. **1879** DE QUATREFAGES *Hum. Spec.* xi. 109 Man, apes, bats, insectivora, and rodents.. form a natural group to which no *zonoplacental, and, of course, no indeciduate mammals can be admitted.

zonular ('zəʊnjʊlə(r)), *a. Anat.* and *Path.* [f. mod.L. *zōnula* ZONULE + -AR¹.] Pertaining to or forming a zonule or little zone; zonal, zonary; *spec.* belonging to or affecting the zonule of Zinn.

1835–6 *Todd's Cycl. Anat.* I. 320/1 The Pigeon.. having the gastric glands.. arranged in a zonular form. **1876** T. BRYANT *Pract. Surg.* (ed. 2) I. 354 Zonular or lamellar cataract is either congenital or commences soon after birth.

zonule ('zəʊnju:l). *Anat.* Also in L. form **zonula** ('zəʊnjʊlə). [ad. mod.L. *zōnula*, dim. of L. *zōna* ZONE: see -ULE.]

1. A little zone: applied *spec.* to the ring-shaped fibrous structure which forms the suspensory ligament of the crystalline lens (***zonule of Zinn***).

1831 R. Knox *Cloquet's Anat.* 555 These membraneous folds, which collectively are called the zonule of Zinn, are vascular. **1854** Kölliker *Hum. Histol.* 390 The zonula is a thin transparent..membrane, stretching from the *ora serrata retinæ* as far as the border of the lens. **1873** Power tr. *Stricker's Histol.* III. 354 The zonula-fibres arise from the substance of the vitreous behind the ora serrata.

2. *Geol.* (See quot. 1928.)

1928 C. L. & M. A. Fenton in *Amer. Naturalist* XI. 21 We have discussed the need for some term to designate the rocks bearing a faunule with several stratigraphers. In the course of one conversation Dr. Weller suggested 'zonule', and it has been approved by others... We propose the term, therefore, with the following definition: A zonule is the stratum or strata which contain a faunule, its thickness and area being limited by the vertical and horizontal range of that faunule. **1958** *Bull. Geol. Soc. Amer.* LXIX. 113/1 A zonule is a biostratigraphic unit that is recognizable in a sedimentary basin or similar restricted area of sedimentation. **1976** *BMR Jrnl. Austral. Geol. & Geophysics* I. 109 The assemblage can be referred to the middle Eocene *Proteacidites confragosus* Zonule on the basis of the presence of the nominate species.

† **'zonulet.** *Obs. nonce-wd.* [f. as prec. + -et[1].] A little zone or girdle.

1648 Herrick *Hesper., Upon Julia's Riband*, 'Tis that Zonulet of love, Wherein all pleasures of the world are wove.

zonure ('zəʊnjʊə(r)). *Zool.* [ad. mod.L. *Zōnūrus*, f. Gr. ζώνη zone + οὐρά tail; from the rings of spiny scales on the tail.] A lizard of the genus *Zonurus* or family *Zonuridæ*, found in South Africa, Madagascar, and other countries.

1883 *List Vert. Anim. Gardens Zool. Soc.* (ed. 8) 583 *Zonurus derbianus*, Gray. Derbian Zonure.

zoo (zuː). *colloq.* [The first three letters of zoological taken as one syllable.]

1. The Zoological Gardens in Regent's Park, London; also extended to similar collections of animals elsewhere.

c **1847** Macaulay in *Life & Lett.* (1878) II. 216 We treated the Clifton Zoo much too contemptuously. **1886** C. E. Pascoe *Lond. To-day* iv. (ed. 3) 65 The 'Zoo' in time past was as favourite a fashionable resort as Rotten Row.

2. *transf.* A (diverse) collection, esp. of people; the place where they are assembled. (Freq. mildly contemptuous.)

1924 Galsworthy *White Monkey* I. ii. 11 You won't keep me in your Zoo, my dear. I shan't hang around and feed on crumbs. **1935** E. Blunden *Edward Gibbon & his Age* 14 He [*sc.* Gibbon] passed through Oxford, gathering little but materials for his future monody on a moribund zoo of dons. **1964** in *Current Slang* (Univ. S. Dakota) (1967) Spring 5 *Zoo*, place where students congregate. **1975** J. I. M. Stewart *Young Pattullo* i. 9 The Glencorrys were..the principal figures of fun in Ninian's and my own family zoo.

3. Comb. ***zoo-crazy*** adj.; **zoo-keeper**, an animal attendant employed in a zoological garden; also, a zoo owner or director; **zooman** *U.S. colloq.* = *zoo-keeper*; similarly **zoowoman** (*rare*).

1938 L. MacNeice *Zoo* iv. 71 A curate who was Anglo-Catholic..and..zoo-crazy. **1936** L. R. Brightwell *Zoo you Knew?* viii. 163 Zoo keepers gave up whistling 'Ta-ra-ra-boom-dehay'. **1960** D. H. S. Risdon *Zoo Keeper* vi. 53 Minor ailments should be curable by the Zoo keeper if he knows his job properly. **1977** *Monitor* (McAllen, Texas) 17 July 2F/4 Zookeepers caring for a two-week-old orphaned hippopotamus have taken to..wading into a pool..to nurse the hippo from a bottle. **1930** *Time* 13 Oct. 32/3 U.S. zoomen, animal catchers and park directors attended the annual meeting of the American Association of Zoological Parks and Aquariums... One zooman had too many elephants. *Ibid.* 33/2 Conspicuous among the zoomen was the only zoowoman in the world. **1942** Berrey & Van den Bark *Amer. Thes. Slang* §458/17 *Zooman*, a zoo director or caretaker. *Ibid.* §624/16 Animal man, zooman. **1973** *Times Lit. Suppl.* 9 Mar. 262/4 The increasing value of the *Yearbook* to zoomen and biologists.

zoo- ('zəʊəʊ, zəʊ'ɒ), before a vowel properly zo-, repr. Gr. ζῳο-, combining form of ζῷον animal, occurring in numerous scientific and technical terms, of which the more important will be found in their alphabetical places. (The second element is usually and properly from Greek, but in a few recent words from Latin or English.)

In biological and botanical terms the prefix sometimes denotes the power of spontaneous movement (formerly supposed to be a distinctive characteristic of animals): see *zoogamete, zoogonidium, zoosperm, zoozygosphere*; zoospore.

ˌzooarchæ'ology, the study of the animal remains of archæological sites; hence **ˌzoo-archæ'ologist**. ‖**'zoocarp** [Gr. καρπός fruit], †(*a*) a former name for certain algæ of low organization, then supposed by some to be animals; (*b*) a zoospore. ‖**zoo'caulon** [mod.L., f. Gr. καυλός stalk] (see quot.). **zoo'centric** *a.*, centred upon the animal world; regarding or treating the animal kingdom as a central fact. **zoo'chemistry**, the chemistry of animal bodies; so **zoo'chemical** *a.* **'zoochore** (-kɔə(r)) [Gr. χωρεῖν to spread], a plant whose seeds are dispersed by animals; hence **zoo'chorous** *a.*; **zo'ochory**, the dissemination of plant seeds by animals. **'zooculture** = *zootechny*; so **zoo'cultural** *a.* ‖**zoocytium** (-'sɪtɪəm), pl. **-ia** [mod.L., after syncytium] (see quot.). ‖**zoo'dendrium**, pl. **-ia** [mod.L., after syndendrium] (see quot.). **ˌzoody'namics**, the dynamics of animal bodies; so **zoody'namic** *a.* **ˌzooe'rythrin** (-ɛ'rɪθrɪn), also **zoonerythrin** [irreg. for ***zoerythrin**, f. Gr. ἐρυθρός red], a red pigment found in the plumage of the touracos, and in sponges. **zoo'fulvin** [L. *fulvus* tawny], a yellow pigment found in the plumage of the touracos. **'zoogamete**, a motile gamete: = planogamete. **ˌzooge'ology**, that branch of geology which deals with fossil animal remains, palæozoology; so **ˌzoogeo'logical** *a.*, pertaining to zoogeology; **ˌzooge'ologist**, one versed in zoogeology. ‖**ˌzoogo'nidium**, pl. **-ia** [mod.L.: see gonidium], a motile gonidium. **zoo'magnetism**, animal magnetism. **'zoomancy** [-mancy], divination by observing the actions of animals. **zoo'mania** (*nonce-wd.*), a mania or insane fondness for animals. **zoo'mantist**, one who practises zoomancy. **ˌzoome'chanics** = *zoodynamics*; so **zoome'chanical** *a.* **zoo'melanin**, the black pigment of animal bodies, melanin; *spec.* as found in the feathers of birds. **zo'ometry** [-metry], measurement of the dimensions and proportions of the bodies of animals; so **zoo'metric** *a.* **zoo'mythic** *a.*, belonging to a mythology in which the deities are represented in the form of animals. **zoo'nosis** (pl. **-noses** (-'nəʊsiːz)) [Gr. νόσος disease], a disease communicated from one kind of animal to another or to a human being; usu. restricted to diseases transmitted naturally to man from animals; so **ˌzoono'sology**, the study of the diseases of animals; **ˌzoono'sologist**, one who pursues this study; hence **zoo'notic** *a.* **zoo-or'ganic** (bad formation for *zoorganic*) *a.*, belonging to animal organs or organisms. **ˌzoopa'thologist**, **ˌzoopa'thology** = *zoonosologist, -logy*. ‖**zoophobia** (-'fəʊbɪə) [mod.L.: see -phobia], morbid or superstitious fear of animals. **zoo'physics**, the study of physics in relation to animal bodies; so **zoo'physical** *a.*, pertaining to zoophysics. **ˌzoophysi'ology**, animal physiology. **zoo'plankter** [plankter], an individual organism of the zooplankton. **zoo'plankton** [plankton], floating animal organisms collectively; **zooplank'tonic** *a.*, of, pertaining to, or consisting of zooplankton. **zoo'plastic** *a.* [see plastic], forming figures of animals or living beings. **zoopra'xography** [Gr. πρᾶξις], the study of animal locomotion. **ˌzoopsy'chology**, animal psychology, the study of mental phenomena in animals. **zoo'scopic** *a.* [Gr. σκοπεῖν to view], †(*a*) examining or studying animals, zoological (*obs.*); (*b*) applied to a species of hallucination (**zo'oscopy**) in which imaginary animal forms are seen, as in delirium tremens. **zoose'matic** *a.* [Gr. σῆμα sign]: see zoic, quot. 1895–6. **ˌzoosemi'otics** *sb. pl.* (const. *sing.*), the study of animal communication through the investigation of signalling behaviour in and between species. **zo'osophy** [Gr. σοφία wisdom], the knowledge or study of animals: †(*a*) the art of keeping and breeding animals (*obs.*); (*b*) the science of zoology (Oken). **ˌzoosperm**, (*a*) = spermatozoon; (*b*) = zoospore; hence **ˌzoosper'matic** *a.* **'zootaxy** [Gr. τάξις arrangement], zoological classification, systematic zoology. **'zootechny** (-tɛknɪ) [Gr. τέχνη art], the art of rearing and using animals for any purpose; so **zoo'technic** *a.*, pertaining to zootechny; **zoo'technics** = *zootechny*. ‖**zootheca** (-'θiːkə), pl. **-æ** [mod.L., f. Gr. θήκη case], the case or sheath inclosing a zoosperm. ‖**zoothecium** (-'θiːʃ(ɪ)əm), pl. **-ia** [mod.L., f. Gr. θήκιον, dim. of θήκη: see prec.], the tubular sheath produced and inhabited by certain Infusoria. **zo'otheism** [see theism], the attribution of deity to animals (cf. zoolatry); hence **ˌzoo'theistic** *a.*, pertaining to or characterized by zootheism. **'zoothome** [Gr. θωμός heap] (see quot.). ‖**'zootokon** [Gr. ζωοτόκον, neut. of ζωοτόκος viviparous], a viviparous animal. **zootrophy** (-'ɒtrəfɪ) [ad. Gr. ζῳοτροφία, f. ζῷον animal + τρέφειν to breed, rear, tend, etc.], the practice of rearing or tending animals. **'zootype**, an animal, or figure of one, used as the type of a deity, as in Egyptian hieroglyphics. **zootypic** (-'tɪpɪk) *a.*, pertaining to the animal type or types. **zoo'xanthin** [Gr. ξανθός yellow], a (? yellow) pigment obtained from the red feathers of certain birds. **zoozygosphere** (-'zaɪgəʊsfɪə(r)) [see zygo-, and cf. oosphere], a motile spherical cell produced by conjugation: proposed as a substitute for *zoogamete*.

1984 *Nature* 1 Mar. 88/2 John Speth's *Bison Kills and Bone Counts* extends such an invitation to *zooarchaeologists and to everyone who uses faunal evidence from archaeological sites to reconstruct past human diet. **1972** *Science* 20 Oct. 297/2 Recently the *Atlas of Animal Bones* by Elisabeth Schmid has become available for research workers in *zooarcheology. **1985** *Times Lit. Suppl.* 7 June 646/1 Taphonomy..has..only recently become an integral part of zoo-archaeology (or, as the subject of faunal analysis is more usually called in Europe, archaeo-zoology). **1843** *Penny Cycl.* XXVII. 804 **Zoocarpes*, the name given to certain organized bodies.. variously classed..as animals or plants,..placed by botanists in the natural order Algæ... It is in the lower forms more particularly that the Zoocarps occur. **1888** *Cassell's Encycl. Dict.*, *Zoocarp*... A zoospore. **1882** Saville-Kent *Man. Infusoria* 874 **Zoocaulon*..title conferred by the author on the erect tentaculiferous branching colony-stocks of the genus *Dendrosoma*. **1882** *Trans. Anthropol. Soc. Washington* I. 93 In later times a few of this school have expanded their scheme to embrace the animal world in general, rendering it *zoöcentric instead of anthropocentric. **1977** J. L. Harper *Population Biol. Plants* 433 Virtually all of the work reported is that of zoologists and the research is zoocentric. **1845** G. E. Day tr. *Simon's Anim. Chem.* I. 87 *Zoochemical analyses are instituted for the purpose of ascertaining..the..constituents of animal substances. **1865** *Nat. Hist. Rev.* July 352 [Zoology] consequently divides itself into..Zootomy, or the dissection of all the formative parts of the body: *Zoochemistry, or their chemical investigation. **1905** F. E. Clements *Res. Methods Ecol.* 216 Migration results when spores, seeds, fruits, offshoots, or plants are moved out of their home by water, wind, animals, man, gravity,..or mechanical propulsion. Corresponding to these agents there may be recognized the following groups:..Animals, *zoochores. *Ibid.* 218 Species which grow in exposed grassy or barren habitats are for the most part anemochores, while those that are found in the shelter of forests and thickets are usually *zoochorous. **1969** L. van der Pijl *Princ. Dispersal in Higher Plants* v. 24 We enter here the more general field of zoochory. *Ibid.*, All following zoochorous classes can be subdivided by crosswise partitions as follows. **1974** *Nature* 8 Feb. 407/1 Modes of dispersal, namely aerial (both active and passive), hydrochorous, zoochorous and anthropochorous, are discussed at some length. **1960** *McGraw-Hill Encycl. Sci. & Technol.* X. 499/2 Animal dispersal, *zoochory, is divided into epizoochory (barbed or sticky disseminules, desmochores..) and endozoochory (disseminules eaten and egested by animals). **1980** *Botanisk Tidsskrift* LXXV. 159 Dispersal is probably mostly by means of water flowing through pores and channels in the soil, but zoochory also plays a role. **1898–9** *Ann. Rep. Bur. Amer. Ethnol.* p. cxiii, Agricultural and *zoocultural industries. **1900** *Ann. Rep. Smithsonian Inst.* 65 That condition of toleration between animals and men which normally precedes domestication, and forms the first step in *zooculture. **1880** Saville-Kent *Man. Infusoria* I. 286 Spongomonas... Animalcules..living in social colonies, and forming by excretion a common domicile, which takes the form of a..gelatinous or semi-granular *zoocytium, within which they remain constantly immersed. *Ibid.* 265 Dendromonas... Animalcules..stationed singly at the extremities of an erect,..variously branching pedicle or *zoodendrium. **1888** *Encycl. Brit.* XXIV. 803 *Zoo-Dynamics, Zoo-Physics, Zoo-Chemistry. **1882** *Proc. Zool. Soc.* 410 Another red pigment is the *zooerythrin; first extracted by Bogdanow from *Calurus auriceps*. **1885** *Proc. Roy. Soc. Lond.* XXXVIII. 321 Under this name [*sc.* luteins] are also included allied pigments, such as carotin, zoonerythrin. **1882** *Proc. Zool. Soc.* 415 All other green feathers [than those of the Musophagidæ] contain only either *zoofulvin or a black-brown pigment. **1880** *Q. Jrnl. Microsc. Sci.* XX. 418 In the proposed system.. Strasburger's '*zoogametes' or 'planogametes' must enjoy the somewhat cumbrous name of 'zoozygospheres', the prefix 'zoo' or suffix 'zoid' being always used to denote an apparently spontaneous power of motion. **1861** Geikie *E. Forbes* xv. 543 The *zoo-geological researches of Edward Forbes. *Ibid.* 537 It is mainly as a *zoo-geologist or palæontologist that he will take rank. *Ibid.* 536 The transition from these fields of inquiry to that of palæontology or *zoo-geology. **1880** Bessey *Bot.* 221 Each *zoogonidium breaks itself up into sixteen new zoogonidia. *a* **1834** S. T. Coleridge *Table Talk* (1884) 73 Nine years has the subject of *Zoo-magnetism been before me. **1864** T. Shorter *Two Worlds* 19 Familiar with zoo-magnetism and clairvoyance. **1841** Hor. Smith *Moneyed Man* xxi, That attachment to birds and animals..has afforded me no little ..solace, though you have sometimes been pleased to term it a *zoo-mania. **1861** F. Hall in *Jrnl. Asiat. Soc. Bengal* 198 *note*, Vasantáraja Bhatta, the *zoomantist. **1897** *Nat. Sci.* June 412 Roux claims that *zoomechanical methods are of primary importance. **1891** *Cent. Dict.*, *Zoomechanics. **1897** *Nat. Sci.* June 412 To tack on the word 'mechanics' to zoology and re-christen it 'zoomechanics' in a general philosophical sense is not to create a new science. **1868** Watts *Dict. Chem.* V. 1085 **Zoomelanin*, a name applied by Bogdanow..to the black pigment of birds' feathers, probably identical with the melanin of the choroid coating of the eye. **1878** Bartley tr. *Topinard's Anthrop.* ii. 81 Osteometry itself is only a part of what should be called *zoometry. **1889** *Nature* 5 Dec. 99/2 Their *zoo-mythic conceptions of their divinities. **1876** tr. *Wagner's Gen. Pathol.* 132 The *zoonoses,..in which there is a transference between individuals of different species, and for the most part from animals to man. **1894** G. M. Gould *Med. Dict.* 1631/1 *Zoonosis*, any disease communicated or communicable from one of the lower animals to man. **1956** *Nature* 3 Mar. 407/2 When a zoonosis gets under way, man-to-man contact may be sufficent to keep the infection spreading. **1972** N. D. Levine in T.-T. Chen *Res. Protozool.* IV. 340 This was the first proof that simian malaria is a true natural zoonosis. **1974** R. Zeledón in K. Elliott et al. *Trypanosomiasis & Leishmaniasis* 51 Chagas' disease..became a zoonosis when the reduviid insect vectors adapted to human dwellings. **1860** Mayne *Expos. Lex.*, **Zöonosologist*..name for him who studies specially the diseases of cattle, or *zöonosology. *Ibid.*, Zöonosology. **1900** Dorland *Med. Dict.* 769/2 *Zoonotic. **1956** *Nature* 3

Mar. 407/2 In searching for explanations of..zoonotic outbreaks, there are limitations in the taxonomic approach which should be borne in mind. **1980** *Brit. Med. Jrnl.* 29 Mar. 928/2 Zoonotic pathogens, such as salmonellas.., may be present in any type of slurry. **1821** COLERIDGE *Lett.* (1895) 712 Vital or *zoo-organic power, instinct and understanding, fall all three under the same definition *in genere.* **1879** WEBSTER Suppl., *Zoopathology. **1884** W. WILLIAMS *Vet. Med.* (ed. 4) 4 Pathology, or more properly, when applied to the lower animals, Zoo-Pathology. **1901** *Amer. Anthrop.* (N.S.) III. 12 Experience of superior faculty awakens consciousness of superior power..and rends the shackles of *zoöphobia. **1888** *Encycl. Brit.* XXIV. 803 *Zoophysics [see *zoodynamics*]. *Ibid.* 816/1 Schwann united two lines of inquiry, viz., that of minute investigation of structure and development and that of zoo-chemistry and zoo-physics. **1865** *Nat. Hist. Rev.* July 352 [Zoology] divides itself into many..branches, amongst which we indicate.. *Zoophysiology, or the science of the functions of the organs. **1963** *Spec. Sci. Rep. U.S. Fish & Wildlife Service* No. 452 (*title*) A towed pump and shipboard filtering system for sampling small *zooplankters. **1979** *Nature* 1 Feb. 353/2 Zooplankters must also cope with the consequences of living in a transparent medium. **1901** *Lancet* 3 Dec. 1801/1 Shallow pools of clear water which were rich in *zooplankton. **1911** *Rep. Brit. Assoc.* 422 In the high Alpine lakes there exists an outstanding production of *zooplanktonic organisms. **1964** *Oceanogr. & Marine Biol.* II. 152 This technique..is well suited to analysis of zooplanktonic extracts. **1978** *Nature* 20 July 246/1 Determinations of element concentrations in the fecal pellets from a common zooplanktonic species, the euphausiid *Meganyctiphanes norvegica*, are now available for 18 elements. **1870** RUSKIN *Aratra Pent.* ii. Wks. 1872 III. 31 The great mimetic instinct underlies all such purpose [*sc.* the fashioning of figures of living creatures]; and is *zooplastic, life-shaping. **1891** E. MUYBRIDGE (*title*) The science of animal locomotion (*zoöpraxography). **1893** —— *Descriptive Zoöpraxography* 2 In the presentation of a lecture on Zoöpraxography the course usually adopted is to project..a series of the most important phases of some act of animal motion. **1947** L. EDWARDS *Reminisc. Sporting Artist* xv. 151 The science of animal motion (Zoöpraxography) cannot be entirely ignored by artists, more especially since the advent of instantaneous photography has familiarised the public with the camera's version of animal movement. **1974** *Country Life* 2 May 1059/1 His [*sc.* Lionel Edwards'] preoccupation with zoopraxography is a desire to capture a precise impression of the rhythm of venery and racing. **1847** tr. *Feuchtersleben's Med. Psychol.* 19 The study of animal psychology (*zoo-psychology, comparative psychology). **1816** BENTHAM *Chrestom.* Wks. 1843 VIII. 87 *Zooscopic or Zoologic Physiurgics. **1890** *Science* XV. 43 This condition of zoöscopic hallucination is one of the commonest among the phenomena of alcohol poisoning. **1963** T. A. SEBEOK in *Language* XXXIX. 465 The term **zoosemiotics*—constructed in an exchange between Rulon Wells and me—is proposed for the discipline, within which the science of signs intersects with ethology, devoted to the scientific study of signaling behavior in and across animal species. **1968** *Language* XLIV. 211 The Section of Semiotics and Linguistics of the Laboratoire d'Anthropologie Sociale is assembling a library of offprints on the areas within its purview (viz., linguistics, oral and written literature,.. theory of languages, scientific languages, zoösemiotics, and the like). **1978** *New Yorker* 17 Apr. 78 In a collection of papers written by various experts in the field of ..'zoosemiotics'—in other words, animal communication—each writer tries valiantly to define what he means by the term. **1662** J. CHANDLER *Van Helmont's Oriat.* 163 The other Son..noted the properties and Societies of living Creatures; whence by the undoubted hope of a Flock, a quiet life is led: This indeed, was *Zoosophie or the wisdom of keeping living Creatures together. **1854** SPENCER *Ess.* iv. (1858) 166 Biology..divides into Organogeny, Phytosophy, Zoosophy. **1836-9** *Todd's Cycl. Anat.* II. 112/1 The *Zoosperm appears to be a moving filament like a minute *Vibrio.* **1838** *Penny Cycl.* XII. 270/1 According to his principles of *zootaxy. **1890** O. T. MASON in *Amer. Anthrop.* (N.S.) I. 46 The industries of the American aborigines, in connection with..animal life.., may be divided into *zoötechnic provinces. **1891** *Cent. Dict.*, *Zootechnics. **1900** DENIKER *Races of Man* Introd. (ed. 2) 4 [In] the genus *Homo*..one can neither speak of the 'species', the 'variety', nor the 'race' in the sense that is usually attributed to these words in zoology or in zootechnics. **1879** DE QUATREFAGES *Hum. Spec.* 61 Anyone who possesses even the smallest knowledge of zoology and *zootechny. **1861** BENTLEY *Man. Bot.* 376 The *antheridium*..is filled at maturity with a number of minute cells, which have been termed **zoothecæ*. **1880** SAVILLE-KENT *Man. Infusoria* I. 61 For these aggregations of..simple loricæ the distinctive title of *zoöthecia has been adopted. **1881** *Abstr. Trans. Anthropol. Soc. Washington* 128 Let us hope that American students will not fall into this line of error by assuming that *zoötheism is the lowest stage, because this is the status of mythology most widely spread on the continent. **1889** *Pop. Sci. Monthly* Nov. 62 In the stage of barbarism all the phenomena of nature are attributed to the animals..or rather to the ancestral types of these animals, which are worshiped. This is the religion of zoötheism. *Ibid.* Dec. 208 The prophets tried to pull the Israelites too rapidly through the *zoötheistic and physitheistic stages into monotheism. **1872** DANA *Corals* i. 48 The compound mass produced by budding..was called..a Zoöphyte. As a substitute the term *Zoöthome may be employed. **1661** LOVELL *Hist. Anim. & Min.* 132 They [*sc.* bats] are **zootokons*, only, amongst all flying creatures, and bring forth..two young ones at a time. **1877** G. MACDONALD *Marq. Lossie* xxxix, Pigs, which, with all her *zootrophy, Clementina did not like. **1905** *Daily Chron.* 4 Sept. 3/1 Egyptian hieroglyphics and Totemic *zootypes. **1897** *Ann. Rep. Smithsonian Inst.* 454 Out of this worm-form type..all the higher ranges of *zootypic evolution have sprung. **1868** WATTS *Dict. Chem.* V. 1085 **Zooxanthin*, the colouring-matter of the red feathers of *Calurus auriceps.* **1880** *Zoozygosphere [see *zoogamete*].

zoochlorella (ˌzəʊəʊklɒˈrɛlə). *Bot.* Also Zoo-. Pl. -æ. [mod.L. (coined in Ger. by K. Brandt 1881, in *Arch. für. Anat. & Physiol.: Physiol. Abt.* 571), f. ZOO- + CHLOR-[1] + L. *-ella* (see -EL[2]).] One of the numerous green unicellular organisms, believed to be algæ, that are present as symbionts in the cytoplasm of many freshwater invertebrates.

1889 in *Cent. Dict.* **1899** F. S. LEE tr. *M. Verworn's Gen. Physiol.* ii. 84 Among such symbiotic organisms are especially many algæ, the *Zooxanthellæ* and the *Zoochlorellæ*, the nature of which as independent organisms has been for a long time in dispute. They occur abundantly in the cells of lower animals. **1924** J. A. THOMSON *Sci. Old & New* xxvii. 150 The same kind of co-operation is illustrated by a number of green Protozoa, in cases where the green colour has been shown to be due..to a partnership with minute algae (Zoochlorellae and Zooxanthellae). **1972** M. S. GARDINER *Biol. of Invertebrates* i. 34/1 Zooxanthellae are limited to marine species, and zoochlorellae almost entirely to freshwater species. **1979** *Nature* 5 July 58/2 Traces of chlorophyll *b* in extracts of pigments from intact animals suggested that *Amphistegina* spp. and *Amphisorus hemprichii* also contained symbiotic zoochlorellae.

zoodikers (ˈzuːdɪkəz), *int. rare.* An asseverative exclamation: cf. ZOOKERS, ZOOKS, ZOONTERS.

1749 FIELDING *Tom Jones* XVIII. xii, Zoodikers! She'd have the wedding to-night.

zoœa: see ZOEA.

‖**zoœcium** (zəʊˈiːʃ(ɪ)əm). *Zool.* Pl. -ia. [mod.L., f. Gr. ζῷον animal + οἶκος house.] The thickened and hardened part of the cuticle of each zooid or polyp of a colony of Polyzoa, forming a cell or sheath in which it is lodged. Hence **zoœcial** (zəʊˈiːʃ(ɪ)əl) *a.*, pertaining to or forming a zoœcium.

1880 PASCOE *Zool. Class.* 297 *Zoœcium*, a cell in which a polypide of the Polyzoa is lodged. **1881** *Jrnl. Microsc. Sci.* Jan. 2 The avicularia are placed in the outer border of the *Zoœcia.* **1884** *Athenæum* 29 Mar. 414 The zooecial tube.

zoogen (ˈzəʊədʒɛn). *Chem.* ? *Obs.* [ad. F. *zoogène*: see ZOO- and -GEN.] A nitrogenous substance found in the water of sulphur-springs; also called *barégin* or GLAIRIN.

1820 *Blackw. Mag.* Mar. 710 Mineral Animal Matter—Zoogene.—Sig. Carlo di Gimbernat has discovered a peculiar substance in the thermal waters of Baden and of Ischia.

zoogenic (zəʊəʊˈdʒɛnɪk), *a.* [f. ZOO- + *-genic*, adj. suffix of -GENY.] **a.** Pertaining to zoogeny (*rare*[−0]). **b.** Produced from animals; in *Geol.* applied to formations of animal origin, e.g. limestones formed from shells.

1864 WEBSTER, *Zoogenic*, of, or pertaining to, animal production. **1866** LAWRENCE tr. *Cotta's Rocks Classified* 360 Zoogenic deposits are products of animal agency.

zoogeny (zəʊˈɒdʒɪnɪ). *rare.* [f. ZOO- + -GENY.] Production or generation of animals; an account, or the study, of this.

1848 DUNGLISON *Med. Lex.* (ed. 7), *Zoogeny*..the doctrine of animal formation. **1854** SPENCER *Ess.* iv. (1858) 166 [Oken's Classification] Biology. Organosophy, Phytogeny, Phyto-physiology, Phytology, Zoogeny, Physiology [etc.].

ˌzoogeˈography. [f. ZOO- + GEOGRAPHY.] The geographical distribution of animals. Hence **ˌzoogeˈographer**, one versed in zoogeography; **ˌzoogeoˈgraphic**, **ˌzoogeoˈgraphical** *a.*, pertaining to zoogeography; **ˌzoogeoˈgraphically** *adv.*, in relation to zoogeography.

1875 *Encycl. Brit.* III. 738/1 It is therefore..the business of the *zoogeographer, who wishes to arrive at the truth, to ascertain what groups of animals are wanting in any particular locality. **1891** *Cent. Dict.*, *Zoögeographic. **1907** *Jrnl. Geol.* XV. 296 Zoögeographic works in all points confirm the conclusions. **1971** *Nature* 9 July 88/1 The largest zoogeographic group so far recovered..is found in the southern shallow waters of the Florida-Halteras slope. **1868** *Proc. Zool. Soc.* 317 None of the great *zoogeographical provinces..are sharply defined from one another. **1893** SEEBOHM in *Geogr. Jrnl.* II. 338 The fact is that life areas, or zoo-geographical regions, are more or less fanciful generalisations. **1890** *Proc. Zool. Soc.* 148 That section of the United States *zoogeographically known as the Sonoran Region. **1868** *Ibid.* 295 The relations of these subdivisions to *zoogeography. **1896** *Naturalist* 80 The inclusion of Irish habitats would have been of value in the study of zoogeography.

‖**zooglœa** (zəʊəʊˈgliːə). *Biol.* [mod.L. (Cohn, 1872), f. Gr. ζῷον animal + γλοιός glutinous substance.] An aggregate of bacteria with thickened cell-walls, forming a gelatinous mass. Also *attrib.* Hence **zooˈglœal**, **zooˈglœic** *adjs.*

1877 F. T. ROBERTS *Handbk. Med.* (ed. 3) I. 95 Living objects variously described as bacteria, vibrios, micrococci, microzymes, zooglœa, &c. **1877** HUXLEY & MARTIN *Elem. Biol.* 26 *Bacteria*, in the still state, very often become surrounded by a gelatinous matter... This is termed the *Zoogloea* form of *Bacterium.* **1905** *Brit. Med. Jrnl.* 25 Feb. 409/2 The giant or mother cells have the appearance of zoogloeic masses. **1934** A. T. HENRICI *Biol. of Bacteria* xviii. 289 *Nitrosomonas* species may appear in cultures in two forms—as zoogloeal masses which rest at the bottom of liquid cultures, in which the cells are non-motile; and as motile 'swarmers'. **1976** *Ann. Rev. Microbiol.* XXX. 265 Protozoa crawl about the zoogloeal mass and occur in the liquor; most are free-swimming or stalked ciliates.

zoogonic (zəʊəʊˈgɒnɪk), *a. rare.* [f. Gr. ζωή life + -γονος producing + -IC.] Life-producing.

1788 T. TAYLOR *Proclus* I. 118 The zoogonic, or vivific goddess. **1791** —— *Diss. Eleus. Myst.* 95 This goddess..is evidently of a Saturnian and zoogonic, or intellectual and vivific rank.

zoogony (zəʊˈɒgənɪ). *rare.* [ad. Gr. ζῳογονία, f. ζῷον animal + -γονία a begetting.] The generation or production of animals, or a doctrine concerning this.

1675 BURTHOGGE *Causa Dei* 242 The Theogonie and Zoogonie [*mispr.* -enie] of the Antients. **1864** WEBSTER, *Zoogeny, Zoogony*, the doctrine of the formation of living beings.

†**ˈzoograph.** *Obs. rare.* [ad. Gr. ζῳογράφος = ζωγράφος one who draws figures, a painter, artist, f. ζῷον animal, figure: see -GRAPH.] = next, 2.

1623 COCKERAM, *Zoograph*, any one that painteth beasts.

zoographer (zəʊˈɒgrəfə(r)). [f. Gr. ζῷον animal + -γράφος depicting, describing; see -GRAPHER.]

1. One who describes animals; a descriptive zoologist.

1646 SIR T. BROWNE *Pseud. Ep.* IV. i. 180 One kinde of Locust..by Zoographers called *mantis.* **1677** PLOT *Oxfordsh.* 104 The Zoographer Gesner. **1688** BOYLE *Final Causes* ii. 61 Zoographers observe, That the Camelion has a very uncommon structure of his visive Organs. **1711** *Brit. Apollo* IV. No. 17. 1/2 Others [*sc.* beasts having only one horn] are mentioned by Zoographers.

2. A painter or depicter of animals; a painter or artist in general.

(In the latter use repr. Gr. ζωγράφος (see ZOOGRAPH): not an Eng. sense.)

1656 BLOUNT *Glossogr.*, *Zoographer*..a Painter or one that draws the pictures of beasts. [Citing Sir T. Browne: see 1646 in 1.] **1814** *Sporting Mag.* XLIV. 66 This very clever artist and zoographer. **1814** W. TAYLOR in *Monthly Mag.* XXXVII. 406 The earlier writers on art,..who flourished before the age of Trajan and the Antonines, constantly entitle their books on zoographers, on zoography—this was their only usual denomination for painting, as if still life did not merit the name.

zoographic (zəʊəʊˈgræfɪk), *a.* [f. ZOOGRAPHY + -IC.] Describing or representing animals; relating to zoography. So **zooˈgraphical** *a.*; hence **zooˈgraphically** *adv.*, in relation to zoography.

1741 WARBURTON *Div. Legat.* II. IV. iv. 111 A new Species of *Zoographic Writing, called by the Ancients Symbolic. **1870** RUSKIN *Aratra Pent.* iv. §110 Both arts [*sc.* painting and sculpture]..so far as they are zoo-graphic;—representative, that is to say, of animal life. **1881** *Academy* 17 Sept. 224 He it was, and not Polygnotos, whose lifelike figures earned him a similar zoographic reputation to that of Giotto. **1651** H. MORE *Second Lash* in *Enthus. Tri.*, etc. (1656) 194 My censure on this rare *Zoographicall piece. **1887** *Athenæum* 6 Aug. 171/3 *Zoographically the fauna and flora of this archipelago appear to have their affinities with those of the Philippine Islands.

zoˈographist. *rare*[−0]. [f. Gr. ζῳογράφος (see ZOOGRAPH) + -IST.] = ZOOGRAPHER.

1775 in ASH. [Hence in later Dicts.]

zoography (zəʊˈɒgrəfɪ). Now *rare* or *Obs.* [f. Gr. ζῷον animal + -γραφία, -GRAPHY.]

1. Description of animals; descriptive zoology.

1593 R. HARVEY *Philad.* 97 When men play the parts of beasts, let them go among the numbers of cattel in Zoography. **1651** H. MORE *Second Lash* in *Enthus. Tri.*, etc. (1656) 194 We are now come to that rare piece of Zoography of thine, the world drawn out in the shape of an Animal. **1697** SWIFT *T. Tub* Ep. Ded. (1704) 8, I was grosly mistaken in the Zoography and Topography of them. **1807** W. WOOD (*title*) Zoography; or the Beauties of Nature, displayed in Select Descriptions from the Animal and Vegetable.. Kingdom. **1865** *Nat. Hist. Rev.* July 352 With regard to species and groups of species, (*a*) their complete description or Zoography; (*b*) their systematic arrangement or Taxonomy.

2. The art of depicting animals; pictorial art in general.

(Repr. Gr. ζωγραφία: not an Eng. sense.)

1656 BLOUNT *Glossogr.*, *Zoography*..the painting or picturing of beasts. **1814** W. TAYLOR [see ZOOGRAPHER 2].

zoogyroscope (zəʊəʊˈdʒaɪərəskəʊp). [f. ZOO- + GYROSCOPE.] An apparatus in which a series of instantaneous photographs of a moving animal are placed upon a rotating glass cylinder and illuminated so as to throw the images in rapid succession upon a screen, producing the appearance of the actual movement.

1880 *Cassell's Fam. Mag.* 640 The zoogyroscope can..be applied to photographs of other animals besides the horse.

zooid (ˈzəʊɔɪd), *sb. Biol.* [f. Gr. ζῷον animal + -OID: cf. late Gr. ζῳοειδής adj. resembling an animal.] Something that resembles an animal (but is not one in the strict or full sense): in early use applied somewhat widely, including, e.g., a free-moving animal or vegetable cell, as a spermatozoon or antherozooid; but chiefly restricted to an animal arising from another by asexual reproduction, i.e. budding (gemmation) or division (fission); *spec.* (and most usually) Each of the distinct beings or 'persons' which make up a compound or 'colonial' animal organism, and often have different forms and functions, thus more or less corresponding to the various organs in the higher animals. (Cf. ZOON *sb.*) Also *attrib.*

Often as the second element of a compound, as *antherozooid, ascidiozooid, dactylozooid, gonozooid, siphonozooid*, etc.: see these words.

1851 HUXLEY in *Ann. & Mag. Nat. Hist.* Ser. II. VIII. 15 The term 'zooid'.. is.. intended to suggest.. with regard to the creatures to which it is applied.. that they are like individuals, and yet are not individuals, in the sense that one of the higher animals is an individual... Instead of saying then, that in a given species, there is an alternation of so many generations, we should say that the individual consists of so many zooids. *Ibid.* 17 Zooid Development by External Gemmation. Internal Gemmation. **1855** W. S. DALLAS in *Orr's Circ. Sci., Org. Nat.* II. 456 The individual *Salpa* consists of two zooids, one oviparous, the other gemmiparous... In the *Aphides*, as many as eleven consecutive series of gemmiparous zooids have been observed to intervene between two periods of sexual reproduction. **1864** [see ZOON *sb.*]. **1870** ROLLESTON *Anim. Life* p. lxxxvi, In the Polyzoa polymorphic zooids are produced by gemmation. **1871** T. R. JONES *Anim. Kingd.* (ed. 4) 98 In each colony [of hydroids] the alimentary and reproductive functions are respectively intrusted to two distinct kinds of zooids,.. the nutritive and the sexual polypites... The sexual zooids, like the flower-buds of plants, are only developed at certain seasons. **1888** ROLLESTON & JACKSON *Anim. Life* 711 *Rhabdopleura* forms indefinitely branching colonies... The zooids are all connected by a stem. *Ibid.* 745 The sexual zooid is developed from the asexual, either directly by metamorphosis, or indirectly by gemmation or fission, thus giving rise to an Alternation of Generations.

Hence **zo'oidal** *a.*, pertaining to a zooid or zooids; **zooidi'ogamous** (**zoidi'o-, zoi'dogamous**) *a.*, characterized by, or of the nature of, fertilization in which a 'zooid' or motile cell (e.g. an antherozooid) unites with another cell.

1886 *Geol. Mag.* Dec. 535 The larger [tubuli] I regard as zoöidal tubes. **1891** *Nature* 17 Sept. 484/1 Karyogamy is.. Zooidiogamous: one gamete at least is actively motile. **1907** *Amer. Nat.* June 362 Ancient zoidogamous Gymnosperms.

zooid, *a. rare*$^{-0}$. [? erron. deduction from attrib. use of prec.] Resembling, or having the character of, an animal.

Only in recent Dicts.

Zookers ('zʊkəz), *int. Obs.* or *arch.* exc. *dial.* Also 7 **zwookers**. [Short for *gadswookers* (GAD *sb.*[5] 3), GODSOOKERS.] = next.

1620 SHELTON *Quix.* II. xxv. 166 Zwookers (quoth Sancho) Ile not giue a farthing to know what is past. **1631** MASSINGER *Emperor East* IV. i, Zookers had I one of you zingle with this twigge, I would so veeze you! **1753** *Scots Mag.* Oct. 491/1, I had proceeded by Fegs, 'Faith, Pox, Plague, 'pon my life, 'pon my soul, Rat it, and Zookers, to Zauns, and the divill. **1761** A. MURPHY *Way to keep Him* v. i. (1765) 101 Zookers, that money—Oh! I am going to blab —. *a* **1814** *Sixteen & Sixty* II. ii. in *New Brit. Theatre* IV. 387 Zookers! if measter Bore'em were to pop in! **1854** AINSWORTH *Flitch of Bacon* iv, 'I've.. Seen him make love to another woman.' 'To Mrs. Nettlebed?' 'Zookers! no.'

Zooks (zʊks), *int. Obs.* or *arch.* exc. *dial.* [Short for *gadzooks* (GAD *sb.*[5] 3); cf. *Gods sokinges* (GOD *sb.* 14 b).] An exclamation or minced oath, expressing vexation, surprise, or other emotion.

1634 HEYWOOD *Witches Lancs.* III. i. E4, Zookes thou art so brave a fellow that I will stick to thee. **1749** FIELDING *Tom Jones* IV. x, Zooks, parson, you remember how he recommended the veather o' her to me. **1754** GARRICK *Prol. to J. Brown's 'Barbarossa'*, He eat a plagy deal, Zooks! he'd have beat five Ploomen at a Meal! **1842** BARHAM *Ingol. Leg.* Ser. II. *Lay St. Cuth.* Moral, And as for that shocking bad habit of swearing,.. leave it to dustmen and mobs, Nor commit yourself much beyond 'Zooks!' or 'Odsbobs!' **1855** BROWNING *Fra Lippo Lippi* 3 Zooks, what's to blame?

zoolatry (zəʊ'ɒlətrɪ). [ad. mod.L. *zōolatria*, f. Gr. ζῷον animal + λατρεία worship.] The worship of animals. So **zo'olater**, one who practises zoolatry; **zo'olatrous** *a.*, pertaining to, of the nature of, or practising zoolatry.

1817 G. S. FABER *Eight Diss.* (1845) I. 285 That the gods of the Gentiles, however connected with Sabianism and Materialism and Zoölatry, were originally.. deified mortals. **1858** HARDWICK *Christ & Other Masters* IV. i. 56 Conspicuous at the head of the zoolatry of Egypt stands the worship of the great Memphitic bull, Apis. **1891** *Cent. Dict.*, Zoolater... Zoolatrous. **1898** E. P. EVANS *Evol. Ethics* i. 6 Vestiges of zoölatrous worship. **1907** *Q. Rev.* July 200 They brought with them a concrete form of zoolatry in the cult of the buffalo.

zoolite ('zəʊəlaɪt). *rare.* [ad. F. *zoölite* (J. F. Esper, 1774), f. Gr. ζῷον animal + λίθος stone: see -LITE.] A fossil animal or animal substance.

1822 J. PARKINSON *Outl. Oryctol.* 327 Where M. Esper, the narrator, expected to be left to augment the number of zoolites contained in these terrific mansions [*sc.* caves].

zoologer (zəʊ'ɒlədʒə(r)). *rare.* [f. mod.L. *zōologia* ZOOLOGY + -ER[1]; cf. *astrologer.*] = ZOOLOGIST.

1663 BOYLE *Usef. Exp. Nat. Philos.* II. ii. 46 As the Naturalist may thus illustrate Pathologie as a Chymist, so may he do the like as a Zoologer. **1766** SWINTON in *Phil. Trans.* LVII. 112 That these bodies ever ascend fifty or sixty feet, has not.. been yet observed by any Zoologer. **1884** *Prospectus of Brehm's 'Life of Animals'*, Dr. Afr. Edm. Brehm, the eminent zoologer.

zoologic (zəʊə'lɒdʒɪk), *a. rare.* [f. ZOOLOGY + -IC; cf. mod.L. *zōologicus* (Kirchmaier, 1661).] = next.

1816 BENTHAM *Chrestom.* Wks. 1843 VIII. 87 Zooscopic or Zoologic Physiurgics. **1849** SAXE *Times* 279 As boys expend their zoologic rage On annual tigers in a travelling cage. **1852** BAILEY *Festus* 368 That roses weep is a botanic fact; A zoologic truth, that birds woo flowers.

zoological (zəʊə'lɒdʒɪkəl, *pop.* zuːə-), *a.* [f. ZOOLOGY + -ICAL; cf. prec.] **a.** Pertaining or relating to zoology; belonging or devoted to the scientific study of animals.

1807 J. PINKERTON *Mod. Geogr.* (ed. 2) I. p. xxvii, Conceiving that the zoological part might admit of some improvements.. the author applied to Dr. Shaw of the British Museum. **1815** *Tweddell's Rem.* 190 *note*, His numerous zoological and botanical works. **1837** WHEWELL *Hist. Induct. Sci.* III. 465 Molluscous animals had been placed too high in the zoological scale. **1839** DARWIN *Voy. Beagle* vii. 152 We shall.. have two zoological provinces strongly contrasted with each other. **1877** COUES *Fur-Bearing Anim.* i. 2 The zoölogical characters by which it is distinguished from other Carnivorous Mammals.

b. ***Zoological Garden*** (usually ***Gardens***), the gardens of the London Zoological Society, situated in Regent's Park, London, in which the society's collection of wild animals is housed (formerly colloquially abbreviated as 'the Zoological', subsequently further shortened to 'the Zoo'); hence *gen.* a garden or park in which wild animals are kept for public exhibition. Also ***zoological park***.

1829 T. ALLEN (*title*) A guide to the Zoological Gardens and museum. **1831** J. JEKYLL *Corr.* (1894) 279, I.. passed three hours with some new foreigners at the Zoological, which is the best lounge of London. **1843** *Comic Album* W 2 b/1 The parrots at the Zoological Gardens. **1854** GOSSE *Aquarium* 13 The interesting exhibition opened to the public last year at the Zoological Gardens in the Regent's Park. **1855** *Poultry Chron.* III. 416 The first annual exhibition of the Hull and East-Riding Poultry Society, took place on Wednesday, June 27th, at the Zoological Gardens, Hull. **1890** BURNAND *Very Much Abr.* 122 After which I never gave any buns to the bears at the Zoological. **1899** *N.Y. Times* 9 Nov. 14/3 A splendid stretch of 261 acres of country, that is destined to accommodate one of the finest collections of wild animals in the world, and will be known as the New York Zoological Park, was formally opened.. yesterday. **1935** *Chambers's Encycl.* X. 811/1 The Zoological Park of Edinburgh,.. one of the most beautiful. **1978** JORDAN & ORMROD *Last Great Wild Beast Show* i. 48 Stellingen itself remains the finest example of the use of moated enclosures in zoological parks.

attrib. and *comb.* **1843** HOOD in *Mem.* (1860) II. 152 Me, who have no more notion of engineering than a Zoological monkey of driving piles. **1858** *Househ. Words* 18 Dec. 51/1 A whole zoological-garden-full of symptoms constantly making him uncomfortable.

c. *transf.* (sometimes ***humorous***). Animal.

1855 DICKENS *Holly-Tree* i, One of the apartments has a zoological papering on the walls, not so accurately joined but that the elephant occasionally rejoices in a tiger's hind legs and tail, while the lion puts on a trunk and tusks. **1889** H. P. LIDDON *Magnificat* iv. 91 Which is the nobler sort of ancestry—the purely zoological, or the spiritual? **1893** *Harper's Mag.* Dec. 39/2 Other strange and zoological sounds.

Hence **zoologically** (zəʊə'lɒdʒɪkəlɪ, zuːə-) *adv.*, in a zoological way, in relation to zoology.

1819 W. LAWRENCE *Lect. Phys.* etc. 249 The representations of all the animals being brought before Adam in the first instance, and subsequently of their being all collected in the ark, if we are to understand them as applied to the living inhabitants of the whole world, are zoologically impossible. **1845** DARWIN *Voy. Nat.* xvii. (1852) 393 This Archipelago [*sc.* the Galapagos Islands].. is zoologically part of America. **1869** A. R. WALLACE *Malay Archip.* I. i. 24 Borneo and New Guinea, as like physically as two distinct countries can be, are zoologically wide as the poles asunder.

zoo'logico-, used as combining form of *zoologic* or *zoological*: **zoologico-archæologist**, one who studies archæology zoologically, i.e. in relation to animal remains.

1865 LUBBOCK *Preh. Times* 114 The admirable researches of the Danish and Swiss zoologico-archaeologists.

zoologist (zəʊ'ɒlədʒɪst, *pop.* zuː-). [f. mod.L. *zōologia* ZOOLOGY + -IST; cf. *zoologer.*] One versed in zoology; a scientist who studies or treats of animals.

1663 BOYLE *Usef. Exp. Nat. Philos.* II. ii. 46 The.. liberty of making those Experiments in live Beasts.. may enable a Zoologist.. to determine divers Pathologicall difficulties. **1752** J. HILL *Hist. Anim.* 531 This.. has been described.. under the name of the Mus Africanus Hayopolin dictus. Most of the zoologists have omitted it. **1773** JOHNSON *Let. to Mrs. Thrale* 21 Sept., Nor have I seen any thing that interested me as a zoologist, except an otter. **1870** NEWMAN *Gram. Assent* II. viii. 253 The proverb says, 'Ex pede Herculem'; and we have actual experience how the practised zoologist can build up some intricate organization from the sight of its smallest bone.

zoologize (zəʊ'ɒlədʒaɪz), *v.* [f. ZOOLOGY or ZOOLOGIST: see -IZE.]

1. *intr.* To study zoology practically; to seek and examine animals zoologically. (Cf. *botanize.*)

1861 GEIKIE *E. Forbes* ix. 267 He had botanized and zoologized.. from the Shetlands to the Channel Isles. **1890** ROMANES in *Life & Lett.* (1896) 256, I have just heard that Charles Lister.. has died of fever in Brazil, where he was zoologising.

2. *trans.* To study, explore, or treat zoologically.

1865 KINGSLEY *Herew.* i, Not to him, as to us, a world.. circumscribed, mapped, botanised, zoologised.

Hence **zo'ologizing** *vbl. sb.* (also *attrib.*).

1815 [see ENTOMOLOGIZE *v.*]. **1867** GEO. ELIOT in Cross *Life* (1885) III. 20 Giving up zoologising for the present. **1876** SMILES *Sc. Natur.* xiv. 290 On a zoologising excursion.

zoology (zəʊ'ɒlədʒɪ, *pop.* zuː'ɒlədʒɪ). [ad. mod.L. *zōologia*, mod. Gr. ζωολογία (see note below), f. ζῷον animal + -λογία (see -LOGY). Cf. F. *zoologie* (18th c.).

The word was orig. used to denote that part of medical science which treats of the medicines or remedies obtainable from animals; e.g. in the title of T. Bateson's translation of Johann Schröder's *Ζωολογια: or the History of Animals, as they are useful in physick and chirurgery*, 1657; and in Sperling's *Zoologia Physica*, 1661, a distinction is made between 'zoologia medica' and 'zoologia sacra'; the first concerns animals 'ut materiam medendi præbent', the second 'ut ad Dei majestatem, ad vitia deponenda, et ad vitam corrigendam faciunt.'

The sense first recorded in English dictionaries is 'a treatise concerning living creatures' (Bailey 1726) and is still the only one in Todd's Johnson, 1818.]

The science which treats of animals, constituting one of the two branches (*zoology* and *botany*) of Natural History or Biology, and comprising many subordinate branches, as ornithology, ichthyology, entomology, etc.; also, a treatise on, or system of, this science.

1669 ROWLAND tr. *Schröder's Chym. Disp.* 506 The Fifth Book of Chymical Dispensatory, called Zoology, treating of living Creatures. Zoology is a Part of Pharmacy, that shews what Medicines are to be taken from Animals. **1726** BAILEY, *Zoology*, a Treatise concerning living Creatures. **1728** CHAMBERS *Cycl.* s.v., Zoology makes a considerable Article in Natural History. **1753** *Chambers' Cycl.* Suppl., *Vacca*, in zoology, the female of the ox-kind. **1766** PENNANT (*title*) The British Zoology. **1833** SIR W. HAMILTON *Discuss.* (1852) 158 'Dogs bark': this was erst of necessary matter; 'dogs' were then 'all dogs'... Since an observation of the dogs of Labrador (I think), the proposition, as in our zoologies, so in our logics, has fallen to contingent matter. **1867** OWEN in Brande & Cox *Dict. Sci.* etc. s.v., The term *Zoology* is practically restricted to the science of the outward characters, habits, properties, and classification of animals. **1874** GREEN *Short Hist.* ix. §1. 599 John Ray was the first to raise zoology to the rank of a science.

zoom (zuːm), *v.* [Echoic.]

1. *intr.* To make a continuous low-pitched humming or buzzing sound; to travel or move (as if) with a 'zooming' sound; to move at speed, to hurry. Also *loosely*, to go hastily. Freq. with advbs. *colloq.*

1892 'Q' *I saw three Ships* i, Amid.. the scraping and zooming of the instruments, string and reed. **1904** —— *Shining Ferry* xiv, A couple of humble-bees zoomed against the window pane. **1924** *Brit. Weekly* 18 Dec. 270/1 Trams zoom along and buses rattle past. **1946** WODEHOUSE *Joy in Morning* xxix. 280 How would it be.. to zoom off immediately, without waiting to pack. **1960** T. MCLEAN *Kings of Rugby* 118 Hewitt soon zoomed away on the right. **1976** *National Observer* (U.S.) 14 Aug. 16/1 Every night.. a speedboat zooms into the Jones Beach Marine Theater. **1977** G. DURRELL *Golden Bats & Pink Pigeons* v. 121 Three cleaner fish.. worked assiduously on their three customers, zooming in to suck the parasites off their skin.

2. a. *Aircraft slang.* (See first quot.) Also *transf.*

In recent use, often not distinguished from sense 1.

1917 *Daily Mail* 19 July 4/5 'Zoom'.. describes the action of an aeroplane which, while flying level, is hauled up abruptly and made to climb for a few moments at a dangerously sharp angle. **1918** 'B. CABLE' *Air Men o' War* i. 11 The 'Silver Wings' righted, zoomed sharply up, whirled round. **1920** *Blackw. Mag.* July 71/2 The bird checked, swerved and dived and zoomed back into level flight again. **1934** [see DOG-FIGHT *v.*]. **1940** *War Illustr.* 19 Jan. 620/3 The mother-ship would be guarded by 350 m.p.h. fighters that would zoom up into the skies about her on the first hint of danger. **1962** S. CARPENTER in *Into Orbit* 75 At 28,000 feet, diving at 900 mph.. we suddenly pulled through and started to zoom up again.. This manœuvre converted some of our speed into zoom energy. **1980** J. DITTON *Copley's Hunch* II. i. 115 He zoomed up and over to gain height.

b. *trans.* To cause (an aircraft) to zoom; also, to fly over (an obstacle) in this manner.

1918 *Independent* 16 Nov. 208/2, I 'gave 'er all the gun' and 'zoomed' the château—that is, I almost went up the front of the place. **1928** V. PAGÉ *Mod. Aircraft* 521 A machine should never be 'zoomed' or made to jump into the air by a too-rapid movement of the elevator flaps.

c. *intr.* fig. Of prices, costs, etc.: to rise sharply; to soar or rocket. *colloq.*

1970 *Daily Tel.* (Colour Suppl.) 6 Feb. 17/3 They must double labour and work overtime. Costs zoom. **1976** *National Observer* (U.S.) 17 July 3/1 By March 1978.. the dropout total would zoom to 498,300—50 times the total as of March 1972. **1981** *Times* 12 Sept. 2/1 He did not think that the Prime Minister had ever said the economy was going to zoom.

3. *Cinematogr.* and *Photogr.* **a.** *intr.* Of a camera, lens, etc.: to close up on a subject (esp. rapidly) without losing focus; more generally, to alter range by variation of focal length. Freq. const. *in* (*on*). Also *fig.*

1948 *Jrnl. Soc. Motion Picture Engin.* LI. 296 Does the speed change while zooming?.. The speed is independent of the zoom. **1959** Halas & Manvell *Technique Film Animation* xix. 237 The scene opens with a full screen live-action back-projection shot which zooms to a miniature. **1962** *Daily Tel.* 8 June 23/7 The lens is capable of 'zooming-in' on a set target up to a mile distant. **1970** *Amateur Photographer* 11 Mar. 13 (Advt.), Needle-sharp f1.8 lens —zooms from telephoto to wide angle. **1973** H. J. Eysenck *Inequality of Man* ii. 84 The computer will continue to select items in such a way as to 'zoom in' on the crucial set of items which will really test the subject's IQ, avoiding all the useless items which are below or above his true level. **1978** *N.Y. Times* 30 Mar. D18/2 The TV camera zoomed in on a triumphant Holmes.

b. *trans.* To cause (a lens fitment, camera, etc.) to alter range in this manner.

1952 *Applied Electronics Ann. 1951* 57/1 The construction makes it possible for the operator to 'zoom' the lenses after the ball or player. **1975** *Physics Bull.* Nov. 481/2 The image magnification, AEI claims, can be zoomed continuously up to × 15 000 000 with no change in image focus or brightness. **1979** *SLR Camera* Mar. 5/3 Have you tried focusing and zooming a lens that operates in the opposite direction to others in your gadget bag?

Hence '**zooming** *vbl. sb.* and *ppl. a.*

1917 *Daily Mail* 19 July 4/5 'Zooming' is.. frequently the only means of avoiding an obstacle when flying low. **1923** *Blackw. Mag.* July 7/1 We settled into steady, zooming flight. **1961** G. Millerson *Telev. Production* iii. 34 *(caption)* The zoom angle can be adjusted anywhere in the zooming range. **1982** L. Cook *Under Etna* I. i. 11 'I hate this zooming-in bit.' She gazed hypnotically at the strip of runway coming up to meet them.

zoom, *sb.* [f. the vb.]

1. *Aeronaut.* An act of 'zooming'. Also *attrib.*

1918 *Blackw. Mag.* June 762/1 The Hun's third repetition of the manœuvre was varied by a straight zoom instead of a climbing turn. **1932** [see blacking *vbl. sb.* 1 c]. **1960** *Aeroplane* 2 Dec. 741/1 At the zoom altitudes which the Mirage is capable of reaching, there is insufficient airflow through the engine to maintain afterburner combustion.

2. *Cinematogr.* and *Photogr.* **a.** A camera shot in which the range is (usu. rapidly) shortened to close-up without loss of focus; this process.

1934 [see fade-out 1]. **1948** [see zoom *v.* 3 a]. **1962** *Movie* Dec. 6/3 The film ends on a zoom into a close up of Tolly's clenched fist. **1967** McLuhan & Fiore *Medium is Massage* 128 The audience had.. been preconditioned by television commercials to abrupt zooms.., no story lines, flash cuts. **1977** J. Hedgecoe *Photographer's Handbk.* 125 *(heading)* Zoom and tilt.

b. = *zoom lens*, sense 4 below.

1974 *Some Technical Terms & Slang* (Granada Television), *Zoom*, lens allowing a change of view from longshot to close-up. **1978** *Amateur Photographer* 29 Nov. 120 He uses a Nikon with 24mm, 43–86mm and 80–200mm zooms, and uses Kodachrome exclusively. **1982** 'A. J. Quinnell' *Snap Shot* vi. 99 [He] had taken the telephoto lens off the camera and replaced it with an all-purpose zoom.

3. *fig.* Zest, energy; sparkle, zip. Cf. zoom *int. colloq.*

1964 in Hamblett & Deverson *Generation X* 97 Perhaps also a man has to have a bit of an inferiority complex.. to give him that extra zoom as a lover. A smug, inbred type like Roger doesn't care if he's a dead loss to a woman between the sheets. *a* **1974** R. Crossman *Diaries* (1977) III. 297, I am definitely losing political zest, looking and feeling more detached, with less zoom, watching, not believing in things, not as enthusiastic or inspired.

4. Comb. **zoom lens** *Cinematogr.* and *Photogr.*, a camera lens whose focal length (and hence the magnification and the field of view) can be smoothly varied while the image remains in focus; cf. varifocal *a.*; **zoom shot**, a camera shot taken with a zoom lens.

1936 *World Film News* Apr. 12 No British manufacturer makes a nice, cheap zoom-lens. **1949** R. H. Alder *Movie Making for Everyone* vi. 67 Most amazing of all is the 'Zoom' lens, in which the angle of view can be changed while the picture is actually being taken. **1962** L. Deighton *Ipcress File* xxiv. 154 A zoom lens, one that would change its focal length. **1978** J. Gardner *Dancing Dodo* xix. 146 The drifting began. Like a huge, long pull-back on a zoom lens so that everything diminished. **1984** A. C. & A. Duxbury *Introd. World's Oceans* iii. 104 The Alvin was equipped with a new color television camera that had a special zoom lens for inspecting the vent animals. **1966** *Listener* 24 Feb. 286/1 A pre-credit titles vertical zoom-shot is served as *hors d'œuvre* for those with appetites for impudently expert camera work. **1977** T. Allbeury *Man with President's Mind* x. 108 A zoom shot on the representatives of OPEC.

zoom (zuːm), *int.* [See the vb.] Representing a 'zooming' sound, such as that made by something travelling at speed. Freq. used *fig.* to denote a sudden rise (to success, etc.) or equivalent fall.

1942 D. Powell *Time to be Born* vi. 130 Men.. just lucky enough to hold a job a few years and then—zoom! **1942** Berrey & Van den Bark *Amer. Thes. Slang* §2/11 All of a sudden.. socko.. whang, zoom. **1976** *National Observer* (U.S.) 25 Dec. 4/2 People began to talk about him. An article appeared in Advertising Age, a trade magazine. Then he wrote a guest column for the Hollywood Reporter. Zoom.

Zoomar ('zuːmɑː(r)). Also **zoomar**. A proprietary name in the U.S. for a make of zoom lens.

1946 *Jrnl. Soc. Motion Picture Engineers* XLVII. 465 *(caption)* Optical principle of Zoomar lens. **1947** *Official Gaz.* (U.S. Patent Office) 10 June 177/2 'Zoomar' for varifocal camera lenses. **1961** A. L. M. Sowerby *Dict. Photogr.* (ed. 19) 712 The first zoom lens for a miniature camera, the Voigtländer Zoomar, gave focal lengths from 36 mm to 82 mm. **1971** D. E. Westlake *I gave at Office* (1972) 68 Rudy had a zoomar lens and got as close as he could for greater clarity. **1973** D. Osmond-Smith tr. *Bettetini's Lang. & Technique of Film* ii. 94 By making use of a complicated system of lenses, called 'pancinor' or 'zoomar', it is in fact possible to vary in a continuous progression the focal length of the shot and, therefore, to move the lens with apparent continuity towards or away from an object or person.

zoomorph ('zəʊəʊmɔːf). [f. Gr. ζῷον animal + μορφή shape.] A representation of an animal form in art; a zoomorphic design or figure.

1889 [see skeuomorph 1]. **1895** Haddon *Evol. Art* 40 The designs are based on human faces..; sometimes the human form is employed, and occasionally zoomorphs are depicted. **1902** *Trans. Glasgow Archaeol. Soc.* (N.S.) IV. 398 Key-patterns, zoömorphs, and figure subjects.

zoomorphic (zəʊəʊ'mɔːfɪk), *a.* [f. as prec. + -ic.]

1. Representing or imitating animal forms, as in decorative art or symbolism.

1872 *Archaeol. Cant.* VIII. 266 A legend not in runes, but in zoomorphic characters. **1885** M'Crie *Sk. & Stud.* 23 The zoomorphic character so conspicuous in the ornamentation of Celtic manuscripts.

2. Attributing the form or nature of an animal to something, esp. to a deity or superhuman being. (Cf. anthropomorphic.)

1880 Murray *Philol. Soc. Addr.* 22 The enlargement or abbreviation of words by letters, which in the curious zoomorphic dialect of many books, *creep in*, or *drop out*, or *fall away*, or develop as *parasites*. **1884** A. Lang *Custom & Myth* 118 Mr. Sayce, who recognises totemism as the origin of the zoomorphic element in Egyptian religion.

b. Having, or conceived or represented as having, the form of an animal.

1886 A. Lang in *19th Cent.* 428 Under Dynasty XII. the gods.. appear in their later shapes, often half anthropomorphic, half zoomorphic. **1887** —— *Myth, Rit. & Relig.* I. 9 All pre-Christian religions have their 'zoomorphic'.. idols.

zoomorphism (zəʊəʊ'mɔːfɪz(ə)m). [Formed as prec. + -ism, prob. after F. *zoomorphisme.*]

1. Attribution of animal form or nature to a deity or superhuman being. (Cf. anthropomorphism.)

1822 tr. *Malte-Brun's Universal Geogr.* I. xxiii. 576 The most gross is the religion of the Egyptians, in which the attributes of the divinity were represented under the figures of animals... This may be termed *zoomorphism.* **1840** Smart, *Zoomorphism*, (belief of a transformation into beasts). **1882** Mivart *Nat. & Th.* 205 Zoomorphism is much more absurd than Anthropomorphism.

2. Imitation or representation of animal forms in decorative art or symbolism.

1879 Jos. Anderson *Scot. Early Chr. T.* (1881) 206 Zoomorphism of ornamentation. *Ibid.* 221 An Irish crosier .. exhibits a more pronounced character of zoomorphism.

zoo'morphize, *v.* [f. zoomorphic + -ize.] *trans.* To make zoomorphic; to attribute an animal form or nature to.

1895 *Folk-Lore* Mar. 75 The belief in sympathetic interchange and interrelation between man and the lower animals,.. the zoomorphizing of everything.

zoomor'phosed, *ppl. a. rare.* [f. zoomorph, after metamorphosed *ppl. a.*] Of a decorative or symbolic design: formed into an animal-like shape; rendered zoomorphic (sense 1).

1955 *Proc. Prehist. Soc.* XXI. 234 The famous sheath with zoomorphosed wave-tendril,.. which forms part of his Third La Tène style. **1967** *Antiquaries Jrnl.* XLVII. 211 In two recent papers de Navarro has discussed the most common and indeed interesting occurrence of the horse in Celtic art—as part of a zoomorphosed lyre.

‖**zoon** ('zəʊɒn), *sb. Biol.* Pl. **zoa** ('zəʊə). [mod.L. (Herbert Spencer), a. Gr. ζῷον animal.] An organism scientifically regarded as a complete animal, i.e. one which is the total product of an impregnated ovum, whether constituting a single being as in the higher animals, or a number of distinct beings (*zooids*) as in the successive asexual generations of aphides or the various 'persons' that make up a compound or 'colonial' animal.

1864 H. Spencer *Princ. Biol.* §73 A zoological individual is constituted either by any such single animal as a mammal or bird, which may properly claim the title of a *zoon*, or by any such group of animals as the numerous *Medusæ* that have been developed from the same egg, which are to be severally distinguished as *zooids*.

zoon (zuːn), *v.* (and *int.*) *U.S. colloq.* [Echoic; cf. zoom *v.*] **a.** *intr.* To make a humming or buzzing sound; to move quickly. **b.** *trans.* To (cause to) travel with such a sound; to propel. Also as *int.* Hence '**zooning** *vbl. sb.* (also applied *spec.* in *Black English* to a style of preaching and response characterized by the repetition of words and phrases with tonal variation).

1883 J. C. Harris *Nights with Uncle Remus* xxxvii. 224 Bimeby Brer Rabbit year de skeeters come zoonin' 'roun', en claimin' kin wid 'im. **1909** *Dialect Notes* III. 391 *Zoon, v.i.* and *tr.*, to make a humming or buzzing sound, to cause to make such a sound. 'That rock came *zoonin'* by my head.' 'Watch me *zoon* this rock.' **1911** M. Johnston *Long Roll* xv. 197 *Zoon—Zoon—Zoon!* O Lord! listen to that shell. **1922** *Outward Bound* Nov. 137/1 The zoonings and ploppings of blundering winged intruders. **1950** W. L. James in *Phylon* XVI. 1. 19 The prayer maker is too full for any utterance which is not colored tonally by his emotions. This is called 'Zooning'. **1977** J. L. Dillard *Lexicon Black Eng.* iii. 55 The 'cries'.. may come relatively early in the [church] service and show the importance of tonal phenomena in the Black sermon. There is even a term for one such practice: *zooning*, 'crying (a word or phrase) over and over with variations'.

zoonerythrin: see *zooerythrin* s.v. zoo-.

†**zoonic** (zəʊ'ɒnɪk), *a. Chem. Obs.* [ad. F. *zoönique* (Berthollet), irreg. f. Gr. ζῷον animal + *-ique*, -ic.] Applied to a supposed peculiar acid obtained from animal substances, afterwards shown to be impure acetic acid. Hence †'**zoonate** [-ate[4]], a salt of this acid.

1799 *Monthly Rev.* XXX. 349 Among the acids, the editor has omitted several.. newly discovered; viz. the Zoonic [etc.]. **1802** Pye *Chem. Nomencl.* 35 *Zoonic radical*, Basis of Zoonic acid. *Ibid.*, Zoonates.

zoonist ('zəʊənɪst). *rare.* [irreg. f. Gr. ζῷον living being, animal + -ist.] One who holds that nature as a whole is a living being, or that natural objects are such. (In quots. only *attrib.*)

1892 *Athenæum* 25 June 829/2 The conception of nature as itself living, or the Zoönist conception, and.. the conception of nature as inclusive of beings of a superhuman character, or the Supernalist conception. **1897** *Folk-Lore* Sept. 274 Among the Zoönist poems are dialogues between personified natural objects.

zoonite ('zəʊənaɪt). *Zool. rare.* [ad. F. *zoonite* (Dugès) or mod.L. *zōonitum*, irreg. f. Gr. ζῷον animal: see -ite[1].] = zooid; *spec.* each of the segments of an articulated animal regarded as distinct organisms; a somite. Also *attrib.* or as *adj.* = articulated, segmented. Hence **zoonitic** (-'ɪtɪk), *a.*, pertaining to or composed of 'zoonites' or segments.

1860 *Cornh. Mag.* I. 203 *note*, We may adopt Huxley's suggestion, and call all such individual parts zöoids, instead of animals. Dugès suggested zöonites in the same sense. **1860** Laycock *Mind & Brain* II. Contents p. ix, Zoonitic Constitution of Vermes. **1861** Hulme tr. *Moquin-Tandon* II. II. 59 The Worm.. is composed of segments or articulations.. in each of which the same organs are regularly repeated... It may be termed a distinct series of animals... These special organisms have received the name of Zoonites (1826). *Ibid.* 60 Three sub-kingdoms: I. The Isolated animals; II. Zoonite animals; III. The Associated animals.

zoonomy (zəʊ'ɒnəmɪ). *rare.* ? *Obs.* [ad. mod.L. *zōonomia* (E. Darwin, 1794), which (after astronomy, q.v.) should properly mean 'arrangement of animals, zoological classification', but taken as f. Gr. ζῷον animal (or ζωή life) + νόμος law.] The science of the laws of animal or organic life; physiology. So **zoo'nomic** (in mod. Dicts.), **zoo'nomical** *adjs.*, pertaining or relating to zoonomy; **zo'onomist**, one who is versed in or treats of zoonomy.

1800 *Med. Jrnl.* III. 282 The Zoonomical inquirer, when he attempts to explain organic and animal phænomena, should renounce all.. unfounded hypotheses. *Ibid.*, The Zoonomist must endeavour to avoid all partial and incomplete explanations. **1815** T. Forster *(title)* Sketch of the New Anatomy and Physiology of the Brain and Nervous System of Drs. Gall and Spurzheim, considered as comprehending a complete system of Zoonomy. **1861** J. Brown *Horæ Subsec.* Ser. II. 375 If we could.. give ear to the teaching of an enlightened zoonomy, we might soon drive many of our fellest diseases out of our breed.

‖**zoon politikon** ('zəʊɒn pəʊ'lɪtɪkɒn). [Gr.] = *political animal* s.v. political *a.* 6 (q.v.).

1958 W. Stark *Sociology of Knowledge* 238 Anybody who regards man as necessarily.. a *zoon politikon.* **1971** A. Giddens *Capitalism & Mod. Social Theory* 5 In the Greek *polis* every man—that is, every free citizen—was a *zoon politikon*: the social and political were inextricably fused.

zoons: see zounds.

†'**zoonters**, *int. Obs. rare.* An exclamation, app. suggested by *zoons* (zounds) and zookers.

a **1763** Shenstone *Ode Dr. Brettle* 16 Zoonters they're gone.

zoophagous (zəʊ'ɒfəgəs), *a.* [f. Gr. ζῷον animal + -φάγος -eating: see -phagous.] Feeding on animals; carnivorous; belonging to the *Zoophaga*, a name for various groups of animals: opp. to phytophagous. So **zo'ophagan** *a.* and *sb.*

1840 *Zoophagan [see *entomophagan* s.v. entomo-]. **1842** Brande *Dict. Sci.* etc., *Zoophagans*.. the order of Unguiculate Mammals which live on animal food,.. also the corresponding group of the Marsupial Quadrupeds. **1835** Kirby *Hab. & Inst. Anim.* II. xvi. 70 *Zoophagous animals, or those which attack and devour living animals. **1839** Owen in *Trans. Geol. Soc. Lond.* Ser. II. VI. 72 The true or zoophagous Cetacea. **1881** *Nature* 3 Feb. 324/1 The countless host of animals that inhabit the depths of the ocean, all of which are necessarily zoophagous.

zoophile ('zəʊəfɪl). [ad. F. *zoophile*, f. Gr. ζῷον animal + -φιλος -loving.] **a.** *Bot.* A zoophilous plant, or its seed. **b.** = *zoophilist.* So **zoophilism** (zəʊ'ɒfɪlɪz(ə)m) = *zoophily*; **zoophilist**

(zəʊ'ɒfɪlɪst), a lover of animals; an opponent of cruelty to animals, *spec.* an anti-vivisectionist; **zo'ophilite** (-aɪt) = prec.; **zoophilous** (zəʊ'ɒfɪləs) *a.*, loving animals; in *Bot.* (after *entomophilous*) applied to plants whose seeds are disseminated by the agency of animals; **zo'ophily**, love of animals; *spec.* the principles of zoophilists.

1895 *Pop. Sci. Monthly* Feb. 501 The seeds which are aided by this mode of dissemination are called *zoöphiles. **1886** *Sat. Rev.* 28 Aug. 290/2 The Progress of *Zoophilism. **1829** *Hull Packet* 17 Nov., A species of animal which is likely to become a great favourite among our female *zoophilists. *a* **1843** SOUTHEY *Doctor* ccxxviii, Our Philosopher and Zoophilist..advised those who consulted him as to the best manner of taking and destroying rats. **1895** *Contemp. Rev.* Oct. 502 None of us Zoophilists have ever pleaded for equal rights for animals with men. **1879** SIR R. CHRISTISON in *Life* (1886) II. 251 He has been assailed by extreme *Zoöphilites. **1886** *Nature* 26 Aug. 403/1 Plants..which he terms '*zoophilous' or 'ornithophilous', *i.e.* those which are absolutely dependent for the germination of their seeds on the fruit being swallowed by birds. **1882** *Cornh. Mag.* Mar. 279 (*title of article*) *Zoophily. **1903** *Month* Aug. 214 The extremer advocates of Zoophily.

zoophilia (zəʊəʊ'fɪlɪə). *Psychol.* Also **zoöphilia.** [f. Gr. ζῷον animal + φιλία affection.] Attraction to animals that acts as an outlet for some form of sexual energy, formerly not implying sexual intercourse or bestiality.

[**1899** REBMAN tr. *Krafft-Ebing's Psychopathia Sexualis* iii. 267 In close relation to stuff-fetichism, certain cases must be considered in which beasts exercise an aphrodisical influence over human beings. One feels tempted to call it *Zoophilia Erotica*. This perversion seems to be rooted in a fetichism the object of which is the skin of the beast.] **1906** H. ELLIS *Stud. Psychol. Sex* V. 71 There is..the more or less sexual pleasure sometimes experienced..in the sight of copulating animals. This I would propose to call Mixoscopic Zoophilia; it falls within the range of normal variations. **1908** M. E. PAUL tr. *Bloch's Sexual Life of our Time* xxiii. 641 We will first describe zoophilia, a sexual inclination towards animals without actual sexual intercourse. **1940** HINSIE & SHATZKY *Psychiatric Dict.* 558/2 Zoöphilia..is a term coined by Krafft-Ebing to denote sexual excitement caused by the stroking and fondling of animals. It does not refer to sexual intercourse with animals. **1960** *Arch. Gen. Psychiatry* III. 442/1 Zoophilia was known in antiquity. **1966** R. & D. MORRIS *Men & Apes* iii. 65 The extent to which zoophilia involving monkeys was actually practised is difficult to assess. **1978** *Daily Tel.* 2 Dec. 16 One of your contemporaries referred in its review to the 'zoophilia' in this film. A simpler word is animalism or bestiality.

zo'ophilic, *a.* [f. as ZOOPHILE + -IC.] **a.** Characterized by zoophilism; animal-loving. **b.** *Psychol.* Characterized by zoophilia.

1947 *New Biol.* 152 Our chief concern, however, is with the dog as a beast of burden. In England, presumably owing to the prevalence of zoophilic organisations such as the R.S.P.C.A. such practices are illegalised. **1951** J. STEINBECK *Log* p. xxiv, A sexual, a religious, a zoophilic or a gustatory impluse. **1965** *Movie* Spring 23/2 Although some spectators may derive a premature zoophilic *frisson* from Marnie's words to her horse, 'Oh, Forio, if you want to bite anyone, bite me,' we don't learn that there is anything psychologically wrong with Marnie until the sequence in which we meet Mother.

zoophorus, etc.: see ZOPHORUS.

zoophyte ('zəʊəfaɪt). Forms: *α.* 7–8 **zoophyton** (7 **zoophiton**), 7–9 *pl.* **zoophyta** (zəʊ'ɒfɪtə). *β.* 7 **zoophyt, -phit,** 7–9 **-phite,** 7– **zoophyte.** [ad. mod.L. *zōophyton*, a. Gr. ζωόφυτον (Aristotle), f. ζῷον animal + φυτόν plant, f. φύεσθαι to grow. Cf. F. *zoöphyte* (Rabelais).]

†**1.** Applied to certain plants having or supposed to have some qualities of animals, as the 'sensitive plant' and the 'vegetable lamb' or BAROMETZ. *Obs.*

1621 LODGE *Summary Du Bartas* I. 132 There is mention of the Boranets, Zoophites, or Plant-animals of Moscouy, in the first Booke of the second Weeke. **1653** W. HARVEY *Anat. Exerc.* xvii. 95 The sensative Plant, and other Zoophyta. **1680** MORDEN *Geog. Rect., Muscovy* (1685) 67 In this Country grows the Plant Zoophyte that resembles a Lamb.

2. A general name for various animals of low organization, formerly classed as intermediate between animals and plants, being usually fixed, and often having a branched or radiating structure, thus resembling plants or flowers: as crinoids, hornwracks, sea-anemones, corals, hydroids, sponges, etc.; any member of the group *Zoophyta.*

Formerly sometimes applied to the branched connecting structure in hornwracks, corals, etc. as distinct from the 'polyps' inhabiting it; but often also a synonym of 'polyp'.

In early modern Zoology the term *Zoophyta* was applied systematically but with varying extent, sometimes including all the Echinoderms, Polyzoa, Cœlenterates, Sponges, and Protozoa, in other cases more restricted, esp. to the Cœlenterates; it is now almost or entirely disused.

α. **1635** PERSON *Varieties* I. §9 Mid creatures which wee call Zoophyta, and Plantanimalia. **1651** J. F[REAKE] *Agrippa's Occ. Philos.* 74 The Zoophyton [*mispr.* Zeo-] (*i.e.*) half Animall, and half Plant. **1682** H. MORE *Annot. Glanvill's Lux O.* 53 To blame her [*sc.* Providence] for making Zoophiton's, or rather Amphibion's. **1743** *Phil. Trans.* XLII. 590 A Zoophyton, somewhat resembling the Flower of the Marigold. **1855** J. PHILLIPS *Man. Geol.* 46 The innumerable tribes of zoophyta, mollusca, and other [in]vertebrata.

β. **1621** BURTON *Anat. Mel.* II. ii. III. 319 Many strange creatures, minerall, vegetalls, Zoophites. **1640** HOWELL *Dodona's Grove* 23 Those Zoophits or Plant-Animals the Philosophers write of. **1644** DIGBY *Nat. Bodies* xxiii. (1658) 259 Under the title of plants I include not zoophytes or plant animals. **1752** WATSON in *Phil. Trans.* XLVII. 457 If..some will still consider these marine productions as plants, they are truly zoophytes, formed by the labour of the animals, which inhabit them. **1762** NASMYTH ibid. LII. 556 Whether animal, zoophite, or submarine plant, I leave to your determination. **1828** STARK *Elem. Nat. Hist.* II. 395 Polypi or Zoophytes; comprehending all those small, gelatinous, and compound or aggregated animals which have a mouth surrounded by tentacula, and conducting into a simple stomach. **1847** WHEWELL *Hist. Induct. Sci.* (1857) III. 463 Suppose the coralline zoophytes to go on building. **1877** THOMSON *Voy. Challenger* I. iv. 255 Very elegant alcyonarian zoophytes.

fig. **1865** O. W. HOLMES *Aut. Breakf.-t.* viii. 75 When the whole human zoöphyte flowers out like a full-blown rose.

3. *attrib.* and *Comb.*

1753 *Chambers' Cycl.* Suppl. s.v. *Marygold*, Zoophyte Marygold..the name of a species of sea animal, of a very beautiful kind, and of the nature of those commonly called Zoophytes,..by the old naturalists. **1856** CARPENTER *Micros.* §69 For the examination of living aquatic objects, too large to be conveniently received into the Aquatic Box, the Zoophyte-trough contrived by Mr. Lister may be employed with great advantage. **1889** *Science-Gossip* XXV. 38 The zoophyte-clothed rocks.

Hence **'zoophytal, zoophytic** (-'fɪtɪk), **-ical** *adjs.*, of or pertaining to a zoophyte or zoophytes; of the nature of a zoophyte; produced by zoophytes; **'zoophytish** *a.*, having the character of a zoophyte; **'zoophytist,** a naturalist who studies zoophytes, a zoophytologist; **ˌzoophy'tography,** description of zoophytes; **zoo'phytoid** *a.*, resembling a zoophyte, or related to the zoophytes; **ˌzoophyto'logical** *a.*, pertaining to zoophytology; **ˌzoophy'tologist,** one versed in zoophytology; **ˌzoophy'tology,** that department of zoology which treats of zoophytes.

1838 MANTELL *Wonders Geol.* II. 468 In the flustra..we have the elements of *zoophytal organization. **1818** *Q. Jrnl. Sci.* V. 375 Molluscous and *zoophytic animals. **1830** LYELL *Princ. Geol.* I. 128 The zoophytic, and shelly lime-stones..sometimes alternate with the rocks of mechanical origin. **1851** RICHARDSON *Geol.* (1855) 216 The ocean's bed, on which the foundations of the zoophytic structure are laid. **1838** G. JOHNSTON *Brit. Zooph.* 8 Bernard de Jussieu and Guettard proceeded..to different parts of the coasts of France with the view of examining their *zoophytical productions. **1850** W. SCORESBY *Cheever's Whalem. Adv.* iv. (1858) 53 Many of the zoophytical and molluscous orders. **1854** *Chamb. Jrnl.* 28 Oct. 280/1 The home of some human reptile or *zoophytish monster. **1862** ANSTED *Channel Isl.* II. ix. 242 Caverns..worthy the careful examination of the *zoophytist. **1736** BAILEY (folio) Pref., **Zoophytography*..a Treatise or Discourse of animal Plants, as Cockles, Muscles, Oysters. **1861** R. E. GRANT *Tabular View Rec. Zool.* 66 Physograda..*Zoophytoid. **1828–32** WEBSTER, *Zoophytological. **1849–52** *Todd's Cycl. Anat.* IV. 1307/1 The modern *Zoophytologist. **1828** *Athenæum* 6 Aug. 651/1 *Zoophytology. Respiration of Animalcules. **1883** *Knowledge* 13 July 22/1 Ellis..has been called the father of English Zoophytology.

zoopraxiscope (zəʊəʊ'præksɪskəʊp). Also **-praxeoscope,** and erron. **-praxinoscope** (cf. PRAXINOSCOPE). [f. ZOO- + Gr. πρᾶξις (acc. πρᾶξιν, gen. πράξεως) action + -SCOPE.] A modified form of the ZOOGYROSCOPE.

1881 *Leeds Merc.* 31 May 5 The Zoöpraxeoscope is..the zoögyroscope in an improved form. **1889** *Athenæum* 16 Mar. 352/3 Mr. Muybridge, of Philadelphia, lectured on 'The Science of Animal Locomotion in its Relation to Design in Art.'.. The lecturer by the zoopraxiscope and its limelight displayed a great number of illustrations.

‖**zoosporangium** (ˌzəʊəʊspɒ'rændʒɪəm). *Bot.* Pl. **-ia.** Also in anglicized form **zoosporange** ('zəʊəʊspɒrændʒ). [mod.L., f. next after SPORANGIUM.] A receptacle containing zoospores. Hence **ˌzoospo'rangiophore** (-fɔə(r)) [see -PHORE], a structure bearing zoosporangia.

1874 COOKE *Fungi* 170 Thick filaments or tubes, similar to those which form the Zoosporangia. **1882** HUXLEY in *Nature* 9 Mar. 438 The zoospores are set free through an opening formed at the apex of the zoosporangium. **1889** A. W. BENNETT & MURRAY *Crypt. Bot.* 326 The..zoospores are borne in zoosporanges at the end of cylindrical or club-shaped zoosporangiophores.

zoospore ('zəʊəʊspɔə(r)). *Biol.* [f. ZOO- + SPORE.] A spore having the power of spontaneous movement, occurring in certain Algæ, Fungi, and Protozoa; a motile spore, swarm-spore.

1846 LINDLEY *Veg. Kingd.* 8 Cellular flowerless plants,..propagated by zoospores, coloured spores, or tetraspores. **1858** —— *Veg. Phys.* §767 For the propagation of their kind,..the Confervae have two different modes; the one being the liberation of moving particles, termed zoospores, from the interior of the cells. **1888** ROLLESTON & JACKSON *Anim. Life* 821 The spores [in Protozoa]..may when they become motile be amoeboid or flagellate, and to these two states respectively the terms *amoebula*, or *zoospore* s. *flagellula* may be applied.

Hence **zoosporous** (zəʊ'ɒspərəs) *a.*, producing, of the nature of, or effected by zoospores.

1846 LINDLEY *Veg. Kingd.* 1 The spores of those Confervæ which are sometimes called Zoosporous. **1859** *Todd's Cycl. Anat.* V. 212/2 Zoosporous reproduction.

zooster, var. ZOSTER.

zoot (zuːt). *U.S. slang.* [See ZOOT SUIT.]

1. A zoot suit.

1965 'MALCOLM X' *Autobiogr.* iv. 59, I saw some of the real Roxbury hipsters eyeing my zoot. **1973** C. HIMES *Cotton gonna kill me Yet* in *Black on Black* 196 This George Brown was strictly an icky, drape-shaped in a fine brown zoot with a pancho conk slicker'n mine. **1973** T. PYNCHON *Gravity's Rainbow* II. 246 Where'd you get that zoot you're wearing, there?

2. *Comb.* **zoot-shirt,** a (brightly coloured) shirt designed to be worn with a zoot suit.

1959 A. FULLERTON *Yellow Ford* viii. 95 He wore a multi-coloured zoot shirt. **1961** *Times* 8 Mar. 14/7 For men students..zoot shirts..are banned.

Hence **'zooty** *a.*, in the style of a zoot suit; (strikingly) fashionable, 'sharp'.

1946 MEZZROW & WOLFE *Really the Blues* IV. xvi. 313 Colored kids..work on their dungarees, pegging the legs till they're real sharp and zooty. **1952** *Amer. Speech* XXVII. 20 What the zootie character and the dude have in common is an overfastidious regard for clothing. **1964** S. BELLOW *Herzog* 240 Her lover, too, with long jaws and zooty sideburns. **1974** *Listener* 8 Aug. 166/1 The suits were..the zooty type—that's the American style of suiting with a straw hat.

zo'otic, *a.* [ad. mod.L. *zōoticus* (Mayne *Expos. Lex.*), f. Gr. ζῷον animal: see -OTIC.] (See quots.)

1868 WATTS *Dict. Chem.* V. 1085 *Zootic Acid*, syn. with Hydrocyanic Acid. **1879** WEBSTER, *Zootic*..containing the remains of organized bodies;—used of rock or soil.

zootomy (zəʊ'ɒtəmɪ). [ad. mod.L. *zōotomia* (M. A. Severinus, 1645): see ZOO- and -TOMY.] The anatomy of animals; the dissection, or the science of the structure, of animal bodies; in mod. use *esp.* comparative anatomy.

1663 BOYLE *Usef. Exp. Nat. Philos.* II. i. 21 The naturalist by his Zootomy, may be very serviceable to the Physitian in his anatomical inquiries. **1697** *Phil. Trans.* XIX. 558 Zootomy is either for compleating natural History,..or for the better Attainment of the Cure of Diseases. **1797** S. JAMES *Narr. Voy.* 156 The cook..lives in East Smithfield, where he exercises the trade of zootomy. **1870** ROLLESTON *Anim. Life* Pref. p. v, To combine the concrete facts of Zootomy with the outlines of systematic Classification. **1872** MIVART *Anat.* 74 This lower jaw—or, as it is called in zootomy, mandible. **1875** W. TURNER in *Encycl. Brit.* I. 799/1 [Anatomy] resolves itself into..Animal Anatomy or Zootomy,..and Vegetable Anatomy or Phytotomy.

So **zootomic** (zəʊəʊ'tɒmɪk), **zoo'tomical** *adjs.*, belonging or relating to zootomy; **zoo'tomically** *adv.*, in relation to or in the way of zootomy; **zo'otomist,** one versed in zootomy; one who dissects, or who studies the structure of, animal bodies; in mod. use *esp.* a comparative anatomist.

1887 *Nature* 17 Nov. 70/1 The *zootomic and embryological works of the last ten years. **1833** R. E. GRANT in *Lancet* 12 Oct. 93/2 The *zootomical investigations of Moreschi of Milan. **1870** ROLLESTON *Anim. Life* Pref. p. v, A Zootomical account of its various Sub-kingdoms. **1849–52** *Todd's Cycl. Anat.* IV. 873/1 The investigation of the whole of this vast subject, *zootomically. **1688** BOYLE *Final Causes* iv. 223 The remarks of *Zootomists. **1797** S. JAMES *Narr. Voy.* 156 The cook..by profession a zootomist. **1879** LEWES *Probl. Life & Mind* Ser. III. I. 132 If the biologist recognises the many points of community in animal structures, the zootomist has to insist on the points of diversity.

zootrope ('zəʊəʊtrəʊp), corrected form of ZOETROPE, with substitution of the more normal combining form *zoo-* [Gr. ζωο-] for *zoe-*.

1872 HUXLEY *Physiol.* x. 245 The curious toy called the thaumatrope or 'Zootrope' or 'wheel of life'.

zoot suit ('zuːt s(j)uːt). orig. *U.S. slang.* [Redupl. rhyming formation on SUIT *sb.*]

1. A type of man's suit of exaggerated style popular in the 1940s (orig. worn by U.S. Blacks), characterized by a long, draped jacket with padded shoulders, and high-waisted tapering trousers.

1942 GILBERT & O'BRIEN *Zoot Suit* (song) 3, I want a Zoot Suit with a reat pleat, with a drape shape. **1942** [see REET *a.*]. **1949** R. CHANDLER *Little Sister* xxix. 218 Taking knives away from grease-balls in zoot suits. **1951** E. PAUL *Springtime in Paris* xv. 269, I saw a few Zoot suits, please believe me, on Negroes headed for the bar at No. 12. **1969** *Time* 14 July 16/2 Chavez became a *pachuco*, affecting a zoot suit with pegged pants. **1982** B. FANTONI *Stickman* xxix. 206 Two coloured tap dancers in dazzling yellow zoot suits. **1984** *Guardian* 5 Oct. 3/1 Baggy zoot suits and skinhead styles have revived the adult market.

2. *transf.* in various *Mil.* uses. Chiefly *U.S.*

1943 *Yank* 15 Oct. 3 Some of the Japs even wore our jungle 'zoot suits'. **1945** BAKER *Austral. Lang.* 158 *Zoot suit* (which, of course, came originally from U.S. jive slang) for the crude civilian clothes given to discharged servicemen. **1952** D. CLARKE *Eleventh at War* xvii. 416 The warm 'tank suits'..were soon known to the troops as 'zoot suits', and were aptly described as a 'mass of zip-fasteners joined together by windproof and waterproof material'. An ingenious manipulation of the zips could convert the zoot suit into a sleeping-bag. **1975** H. WHITE *Raincoast Chronicles* (1976) 144/1 Bernie Grimes, older veteran of the first, wartime zootsuit gangs.

Hence **zoot-suited** *a.*, dressed in a zoot suit; **zoot-suiter**, a zoot-suited person; *spec.* one of a group or gang of young men wearing zoot suits.

1969 Zoot-suited [see *crash-helmeted* adj. s.v. CRASH *sb.*[1] 7 a]. **1971** A. PRICE *Alamut Ambush* ix. 105 We met at poor old David's nuptials—you were one of the zoot-suited ushers, weren't you? **1943** *Chicago Daily News* 12 June 6/2 A new human variety has excited the populace [in California]—the 'zoot suiters'. **1952** Zoot-suiter [see DADDY-O]. **1972** J. WAMBAUGH *Blue Knight* (1973) i. 18 It was almost twenty years [ago]... It was real bad then. We had B-girls and zoot-suiters and lots of crooks.

zooxanthella (ˌzəʊəʊzænˈθɛlə). *Bot.* Also Zoo-. Pl. -æ. [mod.L. (coined in Ger. by K. Brandt 1881, in *Arch. für Anat. & Physiol.: Physiol. Abt.* 572), f. ZOO- + XANTH(O- + L. *-ella* (see -EL[2]).] One of the numerous yellow-brown unicellular organisms present in the cytoplasm of many radiolarians, corals, and other marine invertebrates, probably as symbionts.

1889 in *Cent. Dict.* **1899**, **1924** [see ZOOCHLORELLA]. **1967** NOLAND & GOJDICS in T.-T. Chen *Res. Protozool.* II. 238 The zooxanthellae found in Radiolaria and Foraminifera (as well as in some lower invertebrates) are probably specialized dinoflagellates or cryptomonads. Presumably they play the same role that zoochlorellae do in fresh-water forms, but a mutually beneficial relationship has not been experimentally proved. **1972** [see ZOOCHLORELLA]. **1975** *Nature* 6 Nov. 37/1 The only chlorophyll in corals is contained in the brown zooxanthellae. **1983** *McGraw-Hill Yearbk. Sci. & Technol.* 150/1 All the available evidence suggests that the nudibranchs have evolved mechanisms to maintain healthy populations of zooxanthellae in their tissues and are able to extract photosynthetic products from the dinoflagellate partner.

zope (zəʊp). [a. G. dial. *zope* (F. *sope*), prob. Slav. (cf. Russ. *sapá*).] A bream, *Abramis ballerus*.

1880 GÜNTHER *Fishes* 603 In Europe there occur the 'Common bream', *A. brama*; the 'Zope', *A[bramis] ballerus*.

‖**zophorus** (ˈzəʊfərəs), **zoophorus** (zəʊˈɒfərəs). *Anc. Arch.* Pl. -i. Also 8 anglicized **zoophore**. [L. *zōphorus*, *zōophorus* (Vitruvius), ad. Gr. ζῳφόρος, ζῳοφόρος adj. bearing figures of animals, f. ζῷον animal + -φόρος -bearing. Cf. F. *zoophore* (Rabelais).] A continuous frieze bearing figures of men and animals carved in relief.

1563 SHUTE *Archit.* B iij, Vpon their heddes, he laide Epistilia, and Coronas, setting betwixt them Zophorus. **1694** MOTTEUX *Rabelais* v. xliii. 199 The Architraves, Zoophores and Cornishes. **1706** PHILLIPS (ed. Kersey), Zophorus or Zoophorus. **1823** P. NICHOLSON *Pract. Builder* 586. **1905** *Times* 25 Apr. 5/2 The sculptures on the zophorus of the west front.. should be taken down and stored in a museum.

So **zo(o)phoric** (-ˈfɒrɪk) *a.*, bearing the figure of an animal.

1728 CHAMBERS *Cycl.*, *Zoophoric Column*, is a Statuary Column; or a Column that bears or supports the Figure of an Animal. **1752** *Ibid.*, *Zophoric*.

‖**zopilote** (ˈzəʊpɪləʊt). Also **-ot**. [Sp., a. Mexican *azopilotl*.] A vulture of the family *Cathartidæ*, esp. the American carrion vulture or turkey-buzzard, *Cathartes aura*.

1787 CULLEN tr. *Clavigero's Mexico* I. 47 The *Zopilots*, known in South America by the name of *Gallinazzi*;.. There are two very different species..; the one, the Zopilote properly so called, the other called the *Cozcaquauhtli*. **1850** MAYNE REID *Rifle Rangers* II. xxx. 278 The Eagle's cliff was black with zopilotes. **1862** J. G. WOOD *Illustr. Nat. Hist.* II. 17 When in search of food, the Zopilote ascends to a vast height in the air.

‖**zopissa** (zəʊˈpɪsə). [L., a. Gr. ζώπισσα, f. πίσσα pitch.] †**a.** An old medicinal application made from wax and pitch scraped from the sides of ships. *Obs.* **b.** A patent composition used as a hardening or protecting coat for metal, etc.

1601 HOLLAND *Pliny* xxiv. vii. II. 184 Zopissa, is that Pitch, which.. is scraped from ships, and is confected of wax well soked in salt water of the sea. **1712** tr. *Pomet's Hist. Drugs* I. 212 This Zopissa is a Composition of black Pitch, Rosin, Suet and Tar melted together. **1861** *Illustr. Lond. News* 2 Feb. 108/1 To experimentalise on a portion of that stone with a substance called 'zopissa'—phraseologically borrowed from Dioscorides.. pitch-plaster.

1862 *Catal. Internat. Exhib., Brit.* II. No. 2653 The zopissa composition, for preserving iron and wooden ships against rust and decay, invented by N. C. Szerelmy. *Ibid.* 5089 Arabian zopissa waterproof and paper boards processes.

‖**zoppa** (ˈtsɔppa), *a. Mus.* [It., fem. of *zoppo* limping (formerly also used).] (See quots.) Freq. in phr. *alla zoppa*.

1740 GRASSINEAU *Mus. Dict.*, *Zoppo*, lame.. hopping;.. Hence.. they call those counter-points.. *Contrapunti alla Zoppa*... One is obliged to place in each bar to the subject given one note between two others.. which, when it comes to be played.., by the frequent syncopes, seems to proceed .. in a jumping manner. **1889** GROVE *Dict. Music* IV. 514/1 *Zoppa, alla*, a term applied to a rhythm in which the second quaver in a bar of 2–4 time is accentuated. **1959** WESTRUP & HARRISON *Collins Mus. Encycl.* 17/1 *Alla zoppa*,.. in a limping manner, syncopated. **1963** *Times* 25 Feb. 5/1 Once heard, in closing gavotte, with the crisp, jaunty, and insinuating appoggiaturas of the kind called *zoppa*, hangs in the mind for ever after.

zopy, obs. var. SOPIE.

1687 LOCKE in Fox Bourne *J. L.* (1876) II. 71 A hogshead of cyder, even now and then a bottle of wine or a zopy.

Zoque (ˈsəʊkeɪ), *sb.* (and *a.*) [a. Sp., of uncertain origin.] Any of a group of Central-American Indian languages of the Mixe-Zoquean family; this group of languages collectively. Also *attrib.* or as *adj.*

1891 D. BRINTON *Amer. Race* III. vi. 144 (*heading*) Zoque linguistic stock. **1911** THOMAS & SWANTON *Indian Lang. Mex. & Central Amer.* 60 (*heading*) Zoque. **1940** F. JOHNSON in *Maya & Neighbors* VI. 109 The territory in which the Zoque language was spoken has scarcely been changed on any map since Thomas. **1953** [see *non-phonemic* s.v. NON- 3]. **1964** E. A. NIDA *Toward Sci. Transl.* vi. 134 As in Zoque, spoken in Mexico, the Biblical expression 'Perfect love casts out fear' becomes 'we do not fear when we truly love'. **1972** [see MIXTEC].

zore, obs. or dial. f. SORE *a.*[1]

c **1572** GASCOIGNE *Posies* Wks. 1907 I. 73 Our landlordes a zore man: He racketh up our rentes.

zores, -us, varr. TSORES.

zorȝe, obs. form of SORROW.

zorgite (ˈzɔːgaɪt). *Min.* [f. *Zorge*, a village in the Hartz Mountains: see -ITE[1].] A lead-grey selenide of lead and copper.

1852 BROOKE & MILLER *Phillips' Introd. Min.* 153.

zorgo, obs. variant of SORGHO.

1549 THOMAS *Hist. Italie* 5 b, He is not hable.. to finde breade of Zorgo (a verie vile graine).

‖**zori** (ˈzɔːri), *sb. pl.* Also 9 **sori**. [Jap., f. *sō* grass, (rice) straw + *ri* footwear, sole.] Japanese thonged sandals with straw (or leather, wood, etc.) soles.

1823 F. SCHOBERL *Japan* v. 131 The shoes of the Japanese consist of straw soles or slips of wood. Those in common use are called *sori*. **1884** [see GETA]. **1939** A. KEITH *Land below Wind* xviii. 298 Even her *zori* were blue, with sapphire soles and bright blue straps which came between the toes. **1962** *Amer. Speech* XXXVII. 288 Japanese *zori* or the American adaptation, thong sandals. **1970** J. KIRKUP *Japan behind Fan* 180 On summer days, *zori* of a specially fine quality, made of bamboo sheaths, may be used for strolling in the garden. **1984** *Coaching Award Scheme* (Brit. Judo Assoc.) 9/1 Zori (flip-flops) are compulsory wear at BJA events and should be worn off the mat in Clubs, Schools, etc.

zoril, zorille (ˈzɒrɪl). Also **zorilla, -o**. [ad. F. *zorille*, ad. Sp. *zorrilla*, *-illo*, dim. of *zorra*, ZORRO.] An animal of the African genus *Zorilla*, allied to the skunks; also applied to some Central or South American skunks, as the conepatl.

1774 GOLDSM. *Nat. Hist.* (1824) II. 47 The zorille resembles the skink, but is rather smaller. **1845** DARWIN *Voy. Nat.* iv. 80 We saw also a couple of Zorillos, or skunks. **1878** *Cassell's Nat. Hist.* II. 196 The Cape Zorilla. **1883** SIMMONDS *Dict. Trade* Suppl., *Zoril*, a variety of the American skunk.

Zoroastrian (zɒrəʊˈæstrɪən), *a.* and *sb.* Also 8 **Zoroastran**. [f. L. *Zōroastrēs*, a. Gr. Ζωροάστρης, ad. Zend *Zarathustra* (Pers. *Zardusht*): see -IAN.] **A.** *adj.* Of or pertaining to Zoroaster or his religious system, which is mainly dualistic.

1743 WARBURTON *Pope's Ess. Man* II. 81 *note*, This dangerous school-opinion gives great support to the Manichean or Zoroastran error. **1795** T. MAURICE *Hindostan* (1820) II. IV. iii. 249 The.. heresy of Manes, which was compounded out of the ancient Zoroastran or Magian superstition, and certain perverted doctrines of Christianity. **1892** WESTCOTT *Gospel of Life* 172 There appears to be a distinct polemical element in the earliest Zoroastrian Hymns. **1903** *Times* 5 Mar. 3/5 On no previous occasion has any one been received from Christianity into the Zoroastrian faith.

B. *sb.* A follower of Zoroaster; a Parsee.

1811 BYRON *Let. to F. Hodgson* 3 Sept., I would sooner be a Paulician, Manichæan, Spinozist, Gentile, Pyrrhonian, Zoroastrian, than any one of the seventy-two villainous sects who are tearing each other to pieces for the love of the Lord. **1864** PUSEY *Daniel* 492 The doctrine of the Resurrection.. was not known to the Zoroastrians until after the Christian era. **1886** PHIL ROBINSON *Vall. Teetotum Trees* 3 The semi-sacred character of the holly.. among the Zoroastrians and Fire-worshippers.

Hence **Zoro'astrianize** *v.*, *trans.* and *intr.*, to make or become Zoroastrian in character.

1891 CHEYNE *Orig. Psalter* viii. 449 Zoroastrianizing phraseology. *Ibid.* 452 The Judaism carried to Egypt.. had ..already been in some degree Zoroastrianized.

Zoro'astrianism. Also **-ter-**. [f. prec. + -ISM.] The religious system taught by Zoroaster and his followers, and incorporated in the Zend-Avesta: commonly known as *fire-worship*.

1854 MILMAN *Lat. Christ.* IV. i. II. 4 Zoroasterianism had failed to propagate itself with any great success. **1874** SAYCE *Compar. Philol.* viii. 307 The deities of the Veda became the evil spirits of Zoroastrianism.

Zoro'astric, *a. rare.* [f. L. *Zōroastrēs* Zoroaster.] = ZOROASTRIAN. So **Zoro'ast(e)rism** = ZOROASTRIANISM.

1854 T. KEIGHTLEY *Mythol.* (ed. 3) 468 The Ferwer of Zoroastric theology. **1862** tr. *Renan's Age & Antiq. Bk. Nab. Agric.* ii. 45 The old Zoroasterism of the Zend writings. **1864** PUSEY *Daniel* ix. 528 Zoroastrism betrays its original, the Aryan creature-worship, to which has been added its characteristic Dualism.

zorrino: see ZORRO.

‖**zorro** (ˈθorro, ˈzɒrəʊ). [Sp., = fox.] The South American fox-wolf. Also **zo'rrino** [dim.], a kind of skunk (cf. ZORIL), or its fur.

1838 HUNTER tr. *Azara's Nat. Hist. Paraguay* I. 290 As to habits they vary considerably in my zorros. **1885** *Encycl. Brit.* XVIII. 353/1 The zorro or *Canis Azaræ* (a kind of fox), the zorrino or *Mephitis patagonica* (a kind of skunk), and the tuco-tuco or *Ctenomys magellanicus*. **1899** *Westm. Gaz.* 17 June 7/1 Furs in great variety (chinchilla, vicuna, guanaco, zorrino, lynx, leopard, alpaca, &c.).

zos-grass (ˈzɒsgrɑːs, -æ-). [Abbrev. of ZOS(TERA + GRASS *sb.*[1]] = ZOSTERA.

1937 J. W. DAY *Sporting Adventure* 129 Five ducks come out of the sunset and swing low above me out to the muds and bared *zos* grass. **1974** *Times* 9 Mar. 14/1 They [*sc.* brent geese] cleared the mud-flats of the zos-grass, their natural feed.

‖**zoster** (ˈzɒstə(r)). Also 9 **zooster**. [L., a. Gr. ζωστήρ girdle, f. ζωννύναι to gird.]

†**1.** A kind of seaweed. *Obs. rare.*

1601 HOLLAND *Pliny* XIII. xxv. I. 401 As for the former [seaweed] called Zoster, it is found among the shelves and shallow waters not farre from the shore.

2. The disease shingles, *herpes zoster*. Also *attrib.*

1706 PHILLIPS (ed. Kersey). **1867** O. W. HOLMES *Guardian Angel* xxv, Armed against every malady from Ague to Zoster. **1876** DUHRING *Dis. Skin* 78 Pustules are met with.. in non-parasitic sycosis, zoster, etc.

3. *Gr. Antiq.* A belt or girdle, esp. as worn by men.

1824 *Gentl. Mag.* Dec. 483 A *zooster* or girdle of the same metal, which reaches half round the body. **1906** *Academy* 1 Dec. 543/2 The Mitré is a band of metal worn round the waist under the Chiton, the Zoster a similar belt worn over the tunic.

zoster, obs. form of SISTER.

‖**zostera** (zɒˈstɪərə). *Bot.* [mod.L. (Linnæus), f. Gr. ζωστήρ: see ZOSTER and -A[1]. So called from its long leaves.] A marine plant of the genus so named, esp. grasswrack, *Z. marina*.

1819 LINDLEY tr. *Richard's Obs. Fruits & Seeds* 54 The kernel of *Zostera* is an oblong oval. **1855** KINGSLEY *Glaucus* 57 The delicate green ribbons of the Zostera (the only English flowering plant which grows beneath the sea). **1858** *Phytologist* Nov. 601 The thin line of dry *Zostera* to be met with at high-water mark. **1865** MRS. L. L. CLARKE *Common Seaweeds* ii. 30, I have found it often in *Zostera* beds at low tide.

‖**zosterops** (ˈzɒstərɒps). *Ornith.* [mod.L. (Vigors and Horsfield, 1827), f. Gr. ζωστήρ girdle + ὤψ eye.] Any of the small birds of the genus so named, widely distributed chiefly in tropical and subtropical regions, and charaterized by a ring of white feathers round the eye; a silver-eye or white-eye.

1867 A. L. ADAMS *Wand. Nat. India* 71 That beautiful warbler the yellow zosterops, known by the white downy ring round the eye. **1909** *Blackw. Mag.* Aug. 204/2 It is interesting to watch a Zosterops operating on a pear.

zoþ(e, obs. forms of SOOTH *a.*

zotie, zoty, variants of SOTIE[2] *Obs.*

1578 T. N. tr. *Conq. W. Ind.* (1596) 272 They burned.. three Zoties neere vnto their owne lodging. **1667** DRYDEN *Ind. Emp.* v. ii, At last Cydaria looks over the zoty.

Zotzil, var. TZOTZIL.

Zouave (zuːˈɑːv). Also **zouava**. [F., f. native name *Zouaoua* (see below).]

1. One of a body of light infantry in the French army, originally recruited from the Algerian Kabyle tribe of Zouaoua, but afterwards composed of French soldiers distinguished for their physique and dash, and formerly retaining the original Oriental uniform.

[**1830** tr. *E. Blaquiere's Sig. Panantí* (ed. 2) 56 The whole of the native warriors called the *Zouavi*.] **1848** KELLY tr. *L. Blanc's Hist. Ten Y.* II. 520 The Zouaves were standing on the breach. **1858** HAWTHORNE *Fr. & It. Note-bks.* 8 Jan., Zouaves with turbans, long mantles, and bronzed, half Moorish faces. **1897** *Harper's Mag.* Apr. 752/1 In January, 1863, the French general Forey laid siege to Puebla... In one of the many assaults on the corner held by Diaz the zouaves broke into the first court-yard of his stronghold.

fig. **1858** BEECHER *Life Th.* 135 Those sciences which might be called the light infantry of progress, the Zouaves of thought. **1903** *Speaker* 30 May 210/2 The 'Physical Force' agitators were the Zouaves of Carlton House.

attrib. **1863** E. DICEY *Six Months* II. 7 The orderly disorder of a Zouave march.

b. (Also *Papal* or *Pontifical Z.*) One of a corps of French soldiers organized at Rome in 1860 for the defence of the pope, and disbanded in 1871.

1864 MANNING in A. Reinaud *Abbé-Zouave* Pref. p. ix, Some hundreds of the Pontifical Zouaves, chiefly French and Belgian,.. were seen at St. Peter's. **1868** tr. *Cardella's J. W. Russell* 38 When he returned to Rome to join the Zouaves.

c. A soldier of any of several volunteer regiments, assuming the name and in part the uniform of the French Zouaves, which served on the side of the North in the American Civil War (1861-5).

1860 *Chicago Tribune* 23 Feb. 1/4 The gallant Zouaves.. attracted much attention and admiration by their fine appearance and exact drills. **1861** J. CHESNUT *Let.* 12 June in M. B. Chesnut *Diary* (1949) 67 Reinforcements were sent from here last night, the New Orleans Zouaves. **1865** SALA *My Diary* I. 292 In the beginning, when the Yankee Zouaves were young and hopeful.

2. (In full, *Zouave jacket, bodice.*) A woman's short embroidered jacket or bodice, with or without sleeves, resembling the jacket of the Zouave uniform.

1859 *Ladies' Treas.* Sept. 285/1 One of the most decided novelties of the present season is the *Zouave* jacket. **1859** *Ladies' Cabinet* Dec. 335/1 Nothing can be prettier for the interior than the little oriental jackets which we call to-day *Zouaves*. **1893** *Lady* 17 Aug. 178/1 Zouave Bodices are a feature of autumn gowns.

zouchee: see WATER SOUCHY.

zounds (zaʊndz), *int.* Now *rare* or *Obs.* In later use a literary archaism. Forms: 6 zownes, 7 zoones, 'zons, zons, zonnes (?), dzowns, zownds, zwounds, zauns, 7-8 'zoons, 7-9 zoons, 8 'dswounds, 7- zounds. (Cf. ZINES.) A euphemistic abbreviation of *by God's wounds* (1535, 1573, s.v. GOD *sb.* 14 a) used in oaths and asseverations.

1600 ROWLANDS *Lett. Humours Blood* Sat. v. 72 If any fall together by the eares, To field cries he; why? zownes (to field) he sweares. **1605** ARMIN *Foole vpon F.* E 3 b, One comes sweating, zoones (Cobler) the boots. **1607** DEKKER *Hist. Sir T. Wyatt* Wks. 1873 III. 119 Zwounds I was talking with a crue of vagabondes. **1614** J. COOKE *Greene's Tu Quoque* C 2, *Spend.* M. Rash! zownds how does he know I am here? **1616** *Marlowe's Faustus* 1158 Zounds hee'l raise vp a Kennell of Diuels. *Ibid.* 1300 'Zons, hornes againe. **1623** *Shaks. John* II. ii. 466 Zounds, I was neuer so bethumpt with words. **1682** *Tories' Conf.* in *Roxb. Ball.* (1882) IV. 269 Dzowns, we'l have none but honest Souls. **1699** FARQUHAR *Love & Bottle* II. ii, Zoons is only us'd by the disbanded Officers and Bullies: but Zauns is the Beaux pronuncation [*sic*]. **1712** ARBUTHNOT *John Bull* II. ix, 'Dswounds! why dost thou not lay out thy money to purchase a place at court? **1739** *Joe Miller's Jests* 3 Zoons, Sir, said an old Campaigner .. who's that? **1812** COMBE *Picturesque* x, Syntax look'd wild —the man said 'Zounds! You know you betted twenty pounds.' **1821** *Sporting Mag.* (N.S.) VII. 180 Zoons! said we, deranging the economy of our grey hairs. **1847** LYTTON *Lucretia* I. i, Zounds, Charles, I love you, and that's the truth. **1883** *Fortn. Rev.* July 111 Forgiven me! Zounds! I must correct him in that.

Hence †**zounds** *v.* (*obs. nonce-wd.*) *intr.* to exclaim 'zounds'.

1680 DRYDEN *Kind Keeper* IV. i. 39 When he loses upon the Square, he comes home Zoundzing and Blooding.

zoutchee: see WATER SOUCHY.

†**Zou-Zou** ('zu:zu:). *Obs.* exc. *Hist.* Also (*rare*) Zu-Zu. [a. Fr.] Colloq. diminutive of ZOUAVE.

1860 *Leisure Hour* 15 Mar. 190/2 The *gamins* of Paris, we believe, first applied to the world-renowned Zouaves the pet name of *Zous-Zous*; and France has confirmed the pleasant diminutive. **1863** *Harper's Mag.* Mar. 569/2 A zou-zou.. found himself arrested by the guard. **1866** L. P. BROCKETT *Camp, Battlefield, & Hospital* III. 458 He soon after moved off, followed by the Zou-zous. **1894** [see NOUNOU]. **1944** J. S. PENNELL *Hist. Rome Hanks* 70 Tom thought it was the boy who sang the Zu-Zu song at the creek.

zow, zowl, dial. ff. SOW, SOWL *v.*³, SULL *sb.*

zowie ('zaʊi:, zaʊ'i:), *int. U.S. colloq.* An exclamation of astonishment (generally, or as a reaction to a sudden or surprising act), and freq. of admiration.

c **1913** S. FORD *On with Torchy* 302 'Zowie! A plush one!' says I. **1922** S. LEWIS *Babbitt* xiii. 169 You're a natural-born orator and a good mixer and—Zowie! **1931** [see POW *int.*]. **1958** E. BIRNEY *Turvey* iv. 32 Visitors.. they slap me where it's sore yet and zowie they're off! **1962** [see BAM *int.*]. **1972** WODEHOUSE *Pearls, Girls, & Monty Bodkin* xi. 171 He gets out and *zowie* a gang of thugs come jumping out of the bushes, and next thing you know they're off with your jewel case. **1978** G. MCDONALD *Fletch's Fortune* (1979) ix. 60 She was totally unconscious... Gently, he put her head on the floor. 'Zowie.'

zown, obs. form of SWOON *v.*

Zoyl(e, etc.: see ZOILUS, etc.

zoysia ('zɔɪzɪə). [mod.L. (C. L. Wildenow 1801, in *Neue Schriften Gesellsch. Naturfreunde Berlin* III. 440), f. the name of Carl von *Zoys* zu Laubach (1756-*c* 1800), Austrian botanist + -IA¹.] A perennial grass of the genus of this name, native to eastern Asia, and sometimes used for lawns in subtropical regions. Also *zoysia grass.*

1965 M. C. NEAL *In Gardens of Hawaii* 67 Zoysia, a turf-forming grass from the Mascarene Islands has proved excellent for lawns in Hawaii. **1968** F. W. GOULD *Grass Systematics* i. 6 Southern lawns and other turfs are mainly.. zoysia grasses. **1969** 'J. MORRIS' *Fever Grass* viii. 69 It was fronted by a rectangle of zoysia grass. **1974** *Marlboro Herald-Advocate* (Bennettsville, S. Carolina) 18 Apr. 11/2 For bermuda or zoysia type lawns, [cut] one-half to three-quarters of an inch. **1982** *Birmingham* (Alabama) *Post-Herald* 22 June A3/1 Zoysia lawns along curving and curbed streets.

zubeline, obs. form of ZIBELINE.

‖**zubr** (zu:br). Also 8 zuber. [Russ. See *Columna lui Traian* (1875) 97 ff.] The European bison or aurochs, *Bos bonasus.*

1763 J. BELL *Trav.* I. 294 The stags are of two kinds; one called zuber, the same with the German crownhirsh, but somewhat larger. **1847** W. C. L. MARTIN *Ox* 8/1 He who kills a zubr without permission of the Russian government, has to pay as a fine 2000 rubles. **1882** C. ELTON *Orig. Eng. Hist.* 59 A confused account of two distinct animals, the Aurochs or Zubr of Lithuania, and the extinct Urus which Charlemagne is said to have hunted.

zubu, var. *zobo*: see ZHO.

†**zucarine**, *a. Obs.* [ad. med.L. *zucarīnus* adj., f. *zucara* SUGAR.] ***alum zucarine***, saccharine alum (see ALUM *sb.* 1).

a **1425** tr. *Arderne's Treat. Fistula* etc. 40 Tapsimel, In whiche be puluerez of alume zucarine brent, of attrament, and of vitriol. *Ibid.* 81 Alum zucaryne is called comonly alumglasse. [**1616** B. JONSON *Devil is an Ass* IV. iv, Your *Allum Scagliola*, or *Pol dipedra*; And *Zuccarino*.]

‖**zucca** ('zu:kə). *rare.* Pl. zucche. [It.: see ZUCCHINI *sb. pl.*] A gourd, esp. a pumpkin.

Shelley's (plural) form is erroneous.

1818 SHELLEY *Let.* 6 Nov. (1964) II. 45 Vast heaps of many coloured zucki or pumkins.. piled as winter food for the hogs. **1946** BLUNDEN *Shelley* xxii. 272 Perhaps.. it was Mary who placed a zucca in a vase on the window-sill.

zuccary, zucco(u)r, obs. ff. SUGAR.

‖**zucchetto** (tsuk'kɛtto). Also zuchetta, -etto. [Incorrect but usual form for It. *zucchetta* (tsuk'ketta) small gourd, cap. f. *zucca* gourd, the head.] The skull-cap of an ecclesiastic, differing in colour according to rank.

1853 DALE tr. *Baldeschi's Ceremonial* 3 They should take off their zucchettos in the act of genuflecting. **1897** *Westm. Gaz.* 18 June 3/2 Instead of the usual college cap the Chapter will appear in *zuchettos*. **1901** M. J. F. MCCARTHY *Five Yrs. in Irel.* xx. 257 Leo XIII... took off the Zuchetta he had been wearing and gave it to Father O'Brien.

zucchini (zu:'ki:nɪ), *sb. pl.* [a. It., pl. of *zucchino* (small) marrow, dim. of *zucca* gourd.]

a. Courgettes. Also const. as *sing.*

The usual word for the vegetable in N. America and Australia.

1929 *Sunset* Feb. 58/2 Wash the succini and slice thinly into a baking pan. **1945** B. MACDONALD *Egg & I* IV. xiii. 183 Succulent summer squash and zucchini where it seemed only a matter of an hour ago there were blossoms. **1960** *Guardian* 15 July 8/7 The miniature vegetable marrows called courgettes in France and zucchini in Italy. **1966** T. PYNCHON *Crying of Lot 49* iv. 82 Around them all, Negroes carried gunboats of mashed potatoes, spinach, shrimp, zucchini, pot roast, to the long, glittering steam tables. **1975** *Telegraph* (Brisbane) 11 Sept. 30/2 Zucchini, although a relatively new vegetable, is rapidly becoming an alternative to the old standards. **1982** L. KALLEN *C. B. Greenfield* xiii. 125, I kept on to the market.. to replenish our stores of onions, zucchini, and Bartlett pears.

b. *attrib.*

1960 *House & Garden* Aug. 72/3 We.. will grow.. those exquisite little Zucchini marrows. **1967** *Courier-Mail* (Brisbane) 4 Nov. 8 They were all charged with having stolen four cases of zucchini melons. **1979** E. NEWMAN *Sunday Punch* xv. 127 The waiters had wheeled in zucchini quiche.

zucer, obs. form of SUGAR.

†**zuche.** *Obs.* [app. AN. form of OF. *çoche* (tsɔtʃə), mod.F. *souche*, Norman-Picard *chouque* (whence dim. *chouquet*): of unknown origin. Not known in real English use as an ordinary sb.; survives in the town-name of *Ashby-de-la-Zouch* (Leicestershire).] A tree stump.

[**1220** *Close Rolls 4 Hen. III* memb. 10 (1833) I. 418/1 De auxilio faciendo burgensibus Salop. de veteribus zuchis & de mortuo bosco. **1223** *Plac. Forest. in Com. Nott.* (Cowell 1672) Omnes Zuches aridos qui Anglice vocantur stovenes infra Haiam nostram de Beskewood [now Bestwood]. **1358** *Patent Rolls 32 Edw. III.* memb. 5 (1911) I. 59 [Grant to Richard de la Vache, steward of the forest of Shirewod, of all logs (*ligna*) called] zouches in Beskwode. **1672** COWELL *Interpr.*, Zuche, *zucheus, stips siccus & aridus*, A withered or dry stock of wood. **1676** COLES *Dict.*, *Zuche, Stovene*, a withered or dry stock of wood.

Zuckerkandl ('zʊkəkænd(ə)l). *Anat.* The name of E. *Zuckerkandl* (1849-1910), Austrian anatomist, used *attrib.*, in the possessive, and with *of* to designate the para-aortic bodies. [Described by Zuckerkandl in *Verhandl. d. Anat. Ges.* (1901) XIX. 95.]

1910 *Lippincott's New Med. Dict.* 1107/2 Zuckerkandl's body *or* organ. **1927** *Jrnl. Anat.* LXI. 317 Under the high power of magnification the cells of the Zuckerkandl bodies at full time resemble the larger cells described in the suprarenal medulla. **1930** [see PARAGANGLION]. **1983** *Oxf. Textbk. Med.* II. XIII. 286/1 The commonest extra-adrenal site [of phaeochromocytomas] appears to be the organ of Zuckerkandl, adjacent to the bifurcation of the aorta.

zucre, -ur, zucrish, -ys, obs. ff. SUGAR, -ISH.

Zuen(c)kfeldian, obs. ff. SWENKFELDIAN.

1565 T. STAPLETON *Fortr. Faith* 9 b, Memnonites and Zuenckfeldians.

zufolo ('tsu:fələʊ, z-). *Mus.* Also zuffolo. [a. It. *zuf(f)olo.*] A flageolet, a small flute or whistle (see quots.).

1724 *Short Explic. Foreign Words in Mus. Bks., Zufolo*, a Bird Pipe or Small Flagelet. **1740** GRASSINEAU *Mus. Dict.*, *Zuffolo*, a little Flute or Flageolet. *c* **1801** T. BUSBY *Dict. Music, Zuffolo*, any little flute or flageolet: but more especially that which is used to teach birds. **1876** STAINER & BARRETT *Dict. Mus. Terms* 456/1 *Zufolo*.., a flageolet or whistle. **1954** *Grove's Dict. Mus.* (ed. 5) IX. 427/2 There.. is no reason for concluding.. that Keiser's *zuffolo* was a small shawm. **1960** [see PICCO PIPE]. **1976** D. MUNROW *Instruments Middle Ages & Renaissance* vi. 58/1 Leonardo clearly envisaged the possibility of a keyed trumpet and a keyed *zufolo* or pipe.

zuft: see SUFF *Obs.*

zug (tsu:g). Also Zug. The name (formerly proprietary) for a variety of waterproofed leather used esp. for the uppers of climbing boots.

1899 *Trade Marks Jrnl.* 6 Sept. 1092 *Zug*...222,699. Leather. W. & J. Martin, 63, Brunswick Street, Glasgow; Leather Merchants and Manufacturers. **1899** *Shoe & Leather Trader* (Glasgow) 7 Dec. p. ii. (Advt.), W. &. J. Martin, tanners, curriers, and leather factors, Albion Leather Works... Sole makers of Zug leather. 63 Brunswick Street, Glasgow. **1900** *Ibid.* 12 Apr. 819/1 The firm made a speciality of 'zug' leather, a new production... The manufacture of 'zug' is an entirely new process. The leather.. will not burn like ordinary leather, and the fibre cannot be destroyed even by boiling... In the process of manufacture, the gelatine of the hide becomes oxidised, and is rendered insoluble and repellant [*sic*] to water. **1907** [see CHROME *sb.* 2 c]. **1929** *Footwear Organiser* July 37/2 Sports shoes, of pigskin, calf, crocodile, and zug. **1933** G. D. ABRAHAM *Mod. Mountaineering* x. 179, I would have soft, almost glove-like, zug or beaver leather for the uppers.

zugere, -ure, zuker, -re, -ur, obs. ff. SUGAR.

‖**zugtrompete** (ˌtsu:ktrɔm'pe:tə). *Mus.* [Ger., f. *zug* pulling, tugging + *trompete* TRUMPET.] A slide trumpet.

[**1938** *Oxf. Compan. Music* 962/2 *Slide trumpet*... Zugtrompete (Ger.). **1959** WESTRUP & HARRISON *Collins Mus. Encycl.* 681/2 The slide trumpet.., G. Zugtrompete, .. was used in Germany in the early 18th cent. (e.g. in Bach's cantatas).] **1978** *Early Music* Oct. 539/1 The zugtrompete illustrated at the foot of the page is from Naumburg not Nuremberg.

‖**Zugunruhe** ('tsu:kˌʊnru:ə). *Ornith.* [Ger.] Migratory restlessness; the migratory drive in birds.

1950 *Condor* May 108 *Zugunruhe*.. is the restlessness displayed by caged migratory birds during the migratory period. **1971** *Sci. Amer.* Apr. 76 The behavior of the four groups was studied in terms of signs of *Zugunruhe*, or migratory urge, as shown by night activity and by the molt of feathers. **1978** *Nature* 13 July 154/1 The birds were housed under natural photoperiod in an outdoor aviary, and tested only after they showed migratory restlessness (*Zugunruhe*) in activity cages and exhibited subcutaneous fat deposits.

‖**Zugzwang** ('tsu:ktsvaŋ). *Chess.* [Ger., f. *zug* move + *zwang* compulsion, obligation.] A position in which a player is obliged to move but cannot do so without disadvantage; the disagreeable obligation to make such a move. Freq. ***in Zugzwang***. Also *transf.*

1904 *Lasker's Chess Mag.* I. IV. 166 White has struggled bravely and only loses by 'Zugzwang'. **1930** *British Chess Mag.* I. 196 The move.. puts Black into a Zugswang [*sic*] position that speedily loses. **1935** SMITH & BONE tr. *Tarrasch's Game of Chess* I. 5 White has constrained his opponent to move, has placed him, as we say in Germany, in *Zugzwang*. **1942** H. GOLOMBEK *Fifty Great Games Mod. Chess* 53/2 Black now has only a few pawn moves left after which he is in complete 'Zugzwang'. **1963** [see GRAB *sb.*² 5 b]. **1973** *Country Life* 13 Sept. 744/2 She is, to use a chess term, in complete *Zugzwang*. She could only make six tricks for a penalty of 200.

Zuitzer, obs. form of SWITZER.

zule, zulis. *Her.* A chess rook as a bearing.

1780 EDMONDSON *Compl. Body Her.* II, *Zulis*, a German bearing, nearly resembling a chess-rook. **1874** PAPWORTH *Ord. Brit. Arm.* 1125 Gu. three zules (chess rooks?) arg. in chief a label of three points of the last.

zull(ow, var. SULL(OW *sb.*, a plough.

Zulu ('zu:lu:), *sb.* and *a.* Also Zoola, Zooloo. [Native name.]

1. (Formerly also ***Z.-Kaffir.***) **a.** A member of a Bantu people mainly inhabiting Zululand and Natal in S. Africa. Also *attrib.* or as *adj.*, belonging to this people.

Since the early nineteenth century, the Zulus have been noted for their fiercely patriarchal social organization and their aggressive defence of territory, first against the Boers in 1838, and subsequently against the British in the Zulu Wars of 1879-97.

1824 in Christopher *Natal* (1850) 21 Chaka, king of the Zulus, to whom belongs the whole of the country from Natal to Dela Goa Bay. **1828** *Ibid.* 23 The country of the Zoolas, eastward of Natal. *Ibid.* 25 The interior productions of the Zoola country. **1863** W. C. BALDWIN *Afr. Hunting* ii. 40 A buffalo, which some Zulu Kaffirs had killed. *Ibid.* iii. 75

They much resemble the Zulu huts, but have larger doorways. **1895** A. H. KEANE *Africa* II. vi. 241 Tribal groups belonging either to the Bechuana, or to the Zulu-Kafir division of the Southern Bantus.

b. A derogatory term for a Black person. *U.S.*

1931 *Amer. Mercury* Nov. 354/2 *Zulus*, negroes who participate in spec. **1967** 'D. SHANNON' *Chance to Kill* vii. 91, I just didn't care to have any damn zulu saying I didn't do the work right. **1970** J. BROWN *Un-Melting Pot* xi. 169 Expressions of colour antagonism can at times be bizarre—witness the New York West Indian boy who was heard to call a Barbadian girl a 'bloody Zulu bastard'.

2. The language spoken by the Zulus, belonging to the Nguni subgroup of Bantu languages. Also *attrib.* or as *adj.*

1839 W. C. HARRIS *Wild Sports Southern Africa* 150 Andries.. possessed a smattering of zooloo, and we thus hoped to be able to proceed without the aid of a sworn interpreter. **1849** *Jrnl. Amer. Oriental Soc.* I. 50 The Zulu alphabet.. contains the same letters as the English... The English language abounds with short words, but in the Zulu such words are very few. **1850** CHRISTOPHER *Natal* 137 The Zulu alphabet. **1857** DÖHNE *Zulu-Kafir Dict.* Introd. p. xxxviii, The Zulu, as the high language, has ever exercised a controlling influence upon the low languages. **1861** COLENSO *Zulu-Engl. Dict.* p. v, The Zulu for dog is commonly spelt *inja.* **1869** BLEEK in *Cape & its People* (ed. R. Noble) 272 The Zulu noun *a-ba*-ntu 'men, people'. **1900** *Speaker* 24 Feb. 551/2 What we want is competent officials, with knowledge of Zulu.

3. Name of an artificial fly used in angling.

1898 *Speaker* 29 Oct. 515 General utility flies... Such are the red tag, the Zulu, the blue dun, the snipewing. **1901** *Field* 9 Nov. 739, I put up a fine cast with three biggish flies tied on fine gut (a March brown, a Zulu, and a black palmer).

4. ***Zulu hat***, a kind of straw hat with a wide brim. *Obs.* exc. *Hist.*

1880 *Girl's Own Paper* 27 Nov. 144/1 Wreaths of grapes and a few poppies serve best as trimming for a Zulu hat. **1893** YONGE & COLERIDGE *Strolling Players* viii. 54 She had managed, while seizing a Zulu hat, to divest herself of the apron. **1895** M. BEERBOHM in *Yellow Bk.* Jan. 280 Zulu hats shaded their faces. **1941** F. THOMPSON *Over to Candleford* x. 144 Both [children] wore what were then known as Zulu hats, plaited of rushes and very wide brimmed.

5. A kind of fishing-boat formerly used in Scotland. *Obs.* exc. *Hist.*

1884 *Trans. Highland Soc.* 122 Ten or twelve boats of the carvel-zulu shape have been built. **1905**, etc. [see FIFIE, FIFIE]. **1952** G. MAXWELL *Harpoon at Venture* (1955) ii. 37 She was a seventy-foot 'zulu', lugsail-rigged, and with two Kelvin paraffin engines. **1963** P. MACTYRE *Fish on Hook* iii. 43 MacAra's window looked on to the jibs of disused cranes and the carcasses of two rotting 'Zulu' boats. **1976** *Oxf. Compan. Ships & Sea* 964/2 *Zulu*, a type of fishing vessel peculiar to the north-east coastal ports of Scotland... They were.. first produced during the Zulu War (1878–9), hence their name.

6. The radio code word for the letter 'z'; *spec.* (in full ***Zulu time***) (*Aeronaut. colloq.*) = *zone time* s.v. ZONE *sb.* 9 a.

1960 'N. SHUTE' *Trustee from Toolroom* 104 We'll have a meal.. at twenty-three zulu—at eleven o'clock English time. **1976** B. JACKSON *Flameout* (1977) v. 90 'Check Zulu 10.50.28,' he said, using airmen's and Air Traffic Control jargon for time... 'Okay. The line after Zulu 10.50.30.' **1978** PASACHOFF & KUTNER *University Astron.* v. 125 Astronomers often keep track of events according to the standard solar time that corresponds to the Greenwich time zone. This is called G.M.T. (Greenwich Mean Time), U.T. (Universal Time), or Z (which is colloquially called Zulu Time). **1981** T. BARLING *Bikini Red North* zii. 260 Projected detonation deadline at fourteen-hundred hours, Zulu Time.

Hence **'Zulu** *v.*, *intr.* (with *it*) to act like a Zulu; **'Zuludom**, the domain of the Zulus; **'Zuluize** *v.*, *trans.* to make into a Zulu.

1876 *Jrnl. Soc. Arts* 28 Jan. 166/2 Into the heart of savage Zuludom. **1882** PHIL ROBINSON *Noah's Ark* i, The lion, again, they say, is King in Africa, yet the gorilla Zulus it over the forests within the lion's territory. **1895** *Pall Mall Gaz.* 6 Aug. 7/1 Death of John Dunn. A Zuluized Englishman.

zum, dial. f. SOME.

zumate: see ZYMATE.

†**zumbador.** *Obs.* [Sp., f. *zumbar* to hum.] A humming-bird of S. America.

1760–72 J. ADAMS tr. *Juan & Ulloa's Voy.* VI. viii. (ed. 3) I. 436 Partridges, condors, and zumbadores or hummers. **1764** GRAINGER *Sugar Cane* I. 641 The swift-wing'd zumbadore The mountain desert startled with his hum.

zumbi, var. JUMBY.

zumbooruk ('zʌmbʊrʌk). Also **zumbooruck, -boorak, -barak, zomboru(c)k, zamboorak, -borouk, -búrak.** [ad. Hindustani *zambūrak*, f. Pers. *zambūr* hornet. Cf. Pers. *zemberek* crossbow.] A small swivel-gun, esp. one mounted on the back of a camel. Hence **zumboorukchee**, a gunner.

1825 J. B. FRASER *Journ. Khorasan* 198 One or two shots from Zumbooruck dropping among them. **1840** —— *Trav. Koordistan* II. xiii. 249 Four guns, and a large body of *zumboorukchees.* **1863** R. F. BURTON *Abeokuta* I. 75 East Indian jezails and zumbaraks. **1904** *Blackw. Mag.* July 87/1 Rakish swivel-guns, bell-mouthed *zumbooraks.*

zumeendar, -ary, var. ZEMINDAR, -ARY.

zumic, zumologic, etc.: see ZYMIC, etc.

zunana, Zundavastaw: see ZENANA, ZEND-AVESTA.

Zuñi ('zu:njɪ). Also **Zuni.** Pl. usu. **Zuñi.**

a. A Pueblo Indian inhabiting the valley of the Zuñi, New Mexico. Also ***Zuni Indian.***

1834 A. PIKE *Prose Sk. & Poems* 200 The Moqui (pronounced *Mokee*,) and the Suni (Sunee) live near the Nabajo. **1853** L. SITGREAVES *Exped. Zuñi & Colorado Rivers* 5 The cornfields of the Zuni Indians extend.. for several miles. **1883** *Century Mag.* XXV. 201 Zūni food prepared in Zūni fashion. *Ibid.* 202/1 The domestic life of the Zūnis. **1898** A. LANG *Making Relig.* xiv. 275 In the Zuñi hymn we have the myth of the marriage of Heaven and Earth. **1910** F. W. HODGE *Hand. Amer. Indians North of Mexico* II. 1017/1 Fray Martin de Arvide.. was killed by 5 Zuñi. **1929** *Amer. Speech* V. 115 Among these Pueblo tribes we find.. the *Zuñi*, who called themselves *Ashiwi*, Zuñi being a Spanish adaptation of *Sunyitsi*, the Keresan name for this tribe. **1937** A. HUXLEY *Ends & Means* iii. 20 Among the Zuñi Indians.. individuals are not led into the kind of temptation which invites the men of our civilization to work for fame, wealth, social position or power. **1960** R. C. BELL *Board & Table Games* I. ii. 49 The Zuni Indians played another game on the roof-tops called Kolowis Awithlaknannai. **1969** *Vogue* Nov. 30/2 Marvellous chokers, from the Zuni of the southwest.

b. The language of this people.

1882 *Atlantic Monthly* Sept. 367/2 Then I spoke in Zuñi. **1932** [see ATHAPASCAN *sb.* 2]. **1956** J. LOTZ in Saporta & Bastian *Psycholinguistics* (1961) 12/2 Color-recognition tests were given to both Zuni and English speakers. **1972** *Language* XLVIII. 847 His list can be supplemented from.. Yuma, Zuni.

Hence **'Zuñian, Zunyan** *a.*

1885 *Science* 25 Sept. 267/2 This clay model of the Zuñian owl.

zunyite ('zu:njaɪt). *Min.* [f. *Zuñi*, name of a mine in Colorado + -ITE[1].] A fluosilicate of aluminium, occurring in transparent tetrahedral crystals.

1885 *Amer. Jrnl. Sci.* Apr. 340.

‖**zuppa** ('tsuppa). [It.] Soup. *Comb.*, esp. as ***zuppa di pesce*** ('pɛʃʃe), fish soup. Also *transf.* and *fig.* in phr. ***zuppa inglese*** (in'gleze) [lit. 'English soup'], a rich trifle.

[**1935** M. MORPHY *Recipes of all Nations* 124 (*heading*) Zuppa di fagioli alla fiorentina (Haricot Bean Soup à la Florentine).] **1961** W. VAUGHAN-THOMAS *Anzio* xi. 231 The tourists eat their *zuppa di pesce* in the restaurants on the quayside. **1962** L. DEIGHTON *Ipcress File* xvi. 95 We ordered the Zuppa di Lenticchie. **1975** F. BRESLER *You & Law* 77 My favourite culinary term, '*zuppa inglese*', the Italian's idea of a sickly English trifle. **1976** *Times* 10 July 10/8 A true Italian zuppa di pesce. **1977** *Listener* 10 Feb. 189/2 One way and another, [the book is] a *zuppa inglese*, heavy with leftovers and alcoholic seasonings. **1981** 'J. GASH' *Vatican Rip* xii. 101 We'd decided on *Zuppa inglese* for pud... Who can resist trifle in hooch?

zur, zurr, dial. (chiefly south-western) form of SIR.

1803 G. COLMAN *John Bull* I. i. 16 *Dan.* I be ready, zur. **1825** J. JENNINGS *Observ. Dial. W. Eng.* etc. 118, I bag ye, zur, to take en vooäth. **1838** JAS. GRANT *Sk. Lond.* ix. 292 'Woy, yes, Zur,' said a waggon-driver, with a short smock-frock... 'That's how it is, Zur.' **1921** H. WILLIAMSON *Beautiful Years* 117 Beg pardon, zur, but can't abide here while they be a-reapin'. **1977** F. PARRISH *Fire in Barley* iii. 30 A-ben sleepen in m'bed, zurr, 'tel cock d'crow for dawnen.

zureveld, zurf: see ZUUR-VELDT, ZARF.

Zurich ('zʊərɪk, ‖'tsy:rɪç). Also **Zürich.** The name of a city on Lake Zurich in Switzerland, used *attrib.* to designate porcelain manufactured there in the eighteenth century.

1870 C. SCHREIBER *Jrnl.* 18 Feb. (1911) I. 71 Crispin still possessed the Zurich cups we saw there two years ago. **1875** *Ibid.* 26 Feb. 360 Some very pretty Zurich écuelles. **1897** F. LITCHFIELD *Chaffers's Marks Pott. & Porc.* (ed. 8) 530 Mr. H. Angst.. has the most important collection of Zurich porcelain known. **1949** W. B. HONEY *European Ceramic Art* 42 Zurich porcelain at its best shows a belated Rococo and a rare beauty of colour. **1981** *Times* 25 May 10/5 Among features in the sale.. were.. Zurich porcelains. *Ibid.*, £3,721, for an attractive Zurich hunting group of about 1770.

b. ***Zurich gnome***: see GNOME[1] 1 c.

1970 K. GILES *Death in Church* vii. 168, I arranged to 'buy' it from our Swiss agent, a nice Zurich gnome. **1972** D. LEES *Zodiac* 11, I certainly wasn't going to break up the Zurich gnome's marriage—not even for money. **1981** 'D. JORDAN' *Double Red* ii. 14 Those who really believe in Zürich gnomes and see in each day's gold fixing the action of some giant hidden hand.

‖**zurla** ('zʊələ). *Mus.* Also **surla.** [Serbo-Croatian, f. ZURNA.] A kind of oriental shawm introduced into Yugoslavia by gypsies.

1940 C. SACHS *Hist. Musical Instr.* (1942) xiii. 249 When the drums join in, the two larger oboes accompany the sibs in the lower octave. This must be an old custom, for the same is true for the Turkish oboes *surle* played by Croatian gypsies. **1953** Y. ARBATSKY *Beating Tupan in Central Balkans* 4 We may assume that the Persian word zurnā is the root from which zurna, zurne, zurla and surla were derived. **1957** A. BAINES *Woodwind Instruments & their Hist.* ix. 229 We have only the notion, based on general historical grounds, that the parent instrument of the staple-bearing kind is the Middle Eastern shawm *surna*, a variety of which, frequently heard at our folk-dance festival, is the Macedonian *zurla.* **1962** *Jrnl. Gypsy Lore Soc.* XLI. 43 The Gypsies in Balkan countries used, at the beginning of the nineteenth century, the following musical instruments: tambourine, cymbalum, drum and zurla (a wind-instrument of Oriental origin). **1975** L. PICKEN *Folk Mus. Instr. of Turkey* IV. 499 The facts suggest that the modern Turkish shawm represents a development independent of the shawms of Western Europe. The two types co-exist today in Yugoslavia, where the *zurla* has a 'head' comparable with that of Anatolian and Thracian *zurna. Ibid.* 500 To group (b) belong the shawms-with-finger-holes of Macedonia, both those of Yugoslavia—*zurla*.. and those of Greece—*zourná.*

zurlite ('zɜ:laɪt). *Min.* [f. the name of Signor *Zurlo*, an amateur naturalist of Naples + -ITE[1].] A white or green variety of melilite.

1826 *Amer. Jrnl. Sci.* XI. 255 The zurlite was discovered by Ramondini.

‖**zurna** ('zʊənə). *Mus.* Also 9 **zourna**; 20- **surna.** [Turk.; cf. Pers. *surnā.*] A Turkish pipe resembling a bagpipe or shawm.

1870 C. ENGEL *Descr. Catal. Mus. Instr. S. Kensington Museum* 17 *Zourna*, a kind of hautboy... The *zourna* has usually a mouthpiece consisting of a brass tube. *Hindustan. Ibid.* 28 Zourna Vezirli [from Turkey]. **1876** STAINER & BARRETT *Dict. Mus. Terms* 456/1 *Zurna*, a Turkish wind instrument similar in character to the oboe. **1941** N. BESSARABOV *Anc. European Mus. Instr.* 20 Nine musicians playing the *zurna* (a kind of oboe), including their chief.. the bandmaster. **1953**, etc. [see ZURLA]. **1965** *Listener* 24 June 940/3 Speaking of the mouth-blown cylindrical pipes which she inclines to regard as ancestors of the modern clarinet, would she be referring to the *zurna*, sometimes known as *duduk*? **1976** *Southern Even. Echo* (Southampton) 11 Nov. 20/2 If you are genuinely interested in the derivation, history and characteristics of musical instruments,.. you will find everything from the accordion to the zurna in 'Musical Instruments of the World'.

zurumbeth, var. ZERUMBET.

zussmanite ('zʌsmənaɪt). *Min.* [f. the name of J. *Zussman* (b. 1924), English mineralogist + -ITE[1].] A rhombohedral aluminosilicate of potassium, ferrous iron, and other metals, $K(Fe^{2+},Mg,Mn)_{13}(Si,Al)_{18}O_{42}(OH)_{14}$, found as pale green tabular crystals.

1965 S. O. AGRELL et al. in *Amer. Mineralogist* L. 278 (*heading*) Deerite, howieite and zussmanite, three new minerals from the Franciscan of the Laytonville district, Mendocino Co., California. **1980** *Mineral. Mag.* XLIII. 611/2 Zussmanite compositions at their most aluminium-rich become quasi-isochemical with stilpnomelane and in many rocks a back-reaction can be seen with a fine-grained stilpnomelane fuzz (brown in colour) developing along cracks in the zussmanite.

‖**zut** (zyt), *int.* [Fr.] An exclamation expressing annoyance, contempt, impatience, etc.

1915 W. OWEN *Let.* 25 July (1967) 350 For Gautier... Zut! I never read him. **1923** W. J. LOCKE *Moordius & Co.* ix. 129 'Well, what if I am?' she said, rebelliously. '*Zut!*.. Why shouldn't I?' **1967** R. PETRIE *Foreign Bodies* ii. 23 If his own wife read such trash as the Professor's, he reflected, *zut!* he'd have something to say. **1980** A. HUNTER *Honfleur Decision* x. 136 *Zut!* Come without your gun, or do not come at all.

‖**zuur-veldt** ('zʊərvɛlt). *S. Africa.* Also **-feldt, zureveld.** [Cape Du., = sour country or pasture land: see SOUR, VELD.] A district covered with sour pasturage. Also *attrib.*

1785 G. FORSTER tr. *Sparrman's Voy. to Cape Good Hope* I. vi. 249 What are termed by the colonists *Zuurvelden* or *Sour-fields*, are such as lie somewhat higher and cooler than the shore, and thus are better supplied with rain than the other plains. **1827** T. PHILIPPS *Scenes in Albany & Caffer-Land* 119 The pasture is all *Zureveldt.* **1834** PRINGLE *Afr. Sk.* vi. 203 Long, coarse, wiry grass, of the sort called sour (whence the names Zureberg and Zure-veld). **1850** R. G. CUMMING *Hunter's Life S. Afr.* (ed. 2) I. 13 Black, zuur-feldt oxen.

‖**zuz** (zu:z). Pl. **zuzim**; also **zuzees.** [Rabbinical Heb. *zūz.*] A silver coin anciently in use among the Jews, the fourth part of a silver shekel.

1688 HOLME *Armoury* III. 25/2 A Zuz or Zuzim shekil. **1858** SIMMONDS *Dict. Trade, Zuzah*, an ancient Hebrew silver coin, worth about 6d. **1877** C. GEIKIE *Christ* xxxvi, A blow on the ear was variously set at the fine of a shilling or a pound: a blow on the one cheek at two hundred zuzees.

Zu-Zu, var. ZOU-ZOU.

‖**zwanziger** ('tsvantsɪgər). [G., f. *zwanzig* twenty + *-er* masc. adj. ending.] A former Austrian silver coin, equivalent to twenty kreutzers.

1828 R. CRAIG in *Mem.* viii. (1862) 151 A passenger pays a zwanzig[er] or 17½ sous of France per hour. **1841** BROWNING *Pippa Passes* II, I possess a burning pocketfull of *zwanzigers.* **1866** HOWELLS *Venet. Life* xix, Lest the fervid imagination of the gondolier rise to zwanzigers and florins.

zwart wit pens, var. SWARTWITPENS.

Zwenckfeldian, var. SWENKFELDIAN.

1565 HARDING *Confut. Apol.* II. xi. 88 The Zwenckfeldians that spring out of the same stocke.

zwieback ('tsvi:bak). Also **zwei-.** Pl. **-(s).** [a. Ger., f. *zwie* (*zwei*) twice + *backen* BAKE.] A (sweet) rusk or biscuit made by baking a small loaf, and then toasting slices until they are dry and crisp.

1894 *N.Y. Weekly Tribune* 14 Mar. 5/3 These Zweiback will keep for a long time if put in a dry place. **1907** *Practitioner* Apr. 552 On the seventh day, some well-cooked rice and a few softened Zwieback are allowed. **1925** [see BISCUITY *a.*]. **1949** M. MEAD *Male & Female* xiii. 273 The game of 'I give you something and you give me something' is not necessarily cross-sexed when it is based on bottles and zwieback. **1957** V. NABOKOV *Pnin* v. 132 The various biscuits, wafers, pretzels, zwiebacks. **1978** J. IRVING *World according to Garp* xv. 287 Hope gave Nicky a zwieback and he stopped crying.

zwieselite ('tsviːzəlaɪt). *Min.* Also **zwis-**. [ad. G. *zwiselit* (Breithaupt, 1841), f. *Zwiesel*, Bavaria.] A clove-brown variety of triplite.
1861 BRISTOW *Gloss. Min.*

Zwingfelter, aberrant f. SCHWENKFELDER.
1794 MORSE *Amer. Geog.* (1796) I. 545 Zwingfelters, who are a species of Quakers.

Zwinglian ('zwɪŋglɪən, 'tsvɪŋglɪən), *sb.* and *a.* Also 6 **Zu-**, **Zwynglian**, **-lyan**, 6–7 **Swi-**, 6–9 **Zui-**, 7 **Sui-**. [f. *Zwingli* (see below) + -AN.]
A. *sb.* A follower of Ulrich Zwingli (1484–1531), the Swiss religious reformer.
1532 MORE *Confut. Tindale* Wks. 570/2 The Lutheranes & Zwinglianes haue begunne to ryse & ruffle in rebellion in soondry partes of Almayne. **1533** —— *Answ. poysoned Bk.* Wks. 1051/2 These Lutherane heretikes, and these Huskins, Swinglians: and Tyndalins. **1567** ALLEN *Def. Priesth.* 146 The whole packe of Protestauntes and Zuinglians deny that sacrament also to remitte sinnes. **1615** BRATHWAIT *Strappado* (1878) 4 Yes, for want of a bush thou'd hang thy selfe, And caper like a zuinglian. **1687** T. R. *Veritas Evang.* 23 Some being Lutherans, others Swinglians, others Anabaptists. **1768** MACLAINE tr. *Mosheim's Eccl. Hist.* (ed. 2) IV. 70 This union, between the Lutherans and Zuinglians, was so ardently desired by Melancthon. **1888** SCHAFF *Hist. Church, Mod. Chr.* I. 61 He regretted the toleration of the Zwinglians in Switzerland.
B. *adj.* Of or pertaining to Ulrich Zwingli or his doctrine, esp. concerning the eucharist (see SACRAMENTARIAN B. 1).
1565 HARDING *Confut. Apol.* I. x. 36 b, Ye shall be driuen to forsake your Zuinglian doctrine which putteth signes and figures only in the sacrament of the aulter for the true and reall body of Christ there present. **1661** HEYLIN *Hist. Ref.* II. (1670) 59 Their.. Leaders.. being for the most part of the Zwinglian-Gospellers. **1752** CARTE *Hist. Eng.* III. 395 The Zuinglian doctrines preached by Farel and other ministers. **1898** *Expositor* Oct. 271 Mere protest is conducting us through Zwinglian attenuation to Socinian negation.
Hence **'Zwinglianism**, the doctrines of Zwingli, or the holding of such doctrines; †**'Zwinglianist**, a Zwinglian.
1581 ALLEN *Apol.* 35 b, In most things agreeing with Zuinglianisme, in some with Lutheranisme. **1641** 'SMECTYMNUUS' *Answ.* (1653) 71 So doe the Papists upbraid the Protestants with their Lutheranisme, Calvinisme, and Zuinglianisme. **1674** HICKMAN *Quinquart. Hist.* (ed. 2) Ep. a, The Lutherans use no breaking of the Bread: So do the Zuinglianists. **1745** BUTLER *Lives of Saints* (1845) XI. 117 Where he.. converted many Zuinglianists. **1857** PUSEY *Real Pres.* i. 109 Zwinglianism was consistent in itself.

‖**zwischenzug** ('tsvɪʃəntsuːk). *Chess.* [Ger., f. *zwischen* intermediate + *zug* move.] An interim or temporizing move.
1941 F. REINFELD *Keres' Best Games of Chess* 108/1 This masterly *Zwischenzug* is the finest move in the whole game. **1969** A. GLYN *Dragon Variation* ix. 292 Carl thought about the move for thirty-five minutes, and then made a temporising move, a zwischenzug, checking with his Bishop. **1978** *Spectator* 26 Aug. 27/3, 50 P-K6ch Black resigns. 50... K × P now fails to the *zwischenzug* 51 B-N3!

zwitterion ('tsvɪtəˌraɪən). *Chem.* Formerly also **zwitter-ion** and with capital initial. [a. G. *zwitter-ion* (F. W. Küster 1897, in *Zeitschr. f. anorg. Chem.* XIII. 136), f. *zwitter* hermaphrodite, hybrid (OHG. *zwitar(a)n*, f. *zwi-* TWI-, TWY-) + *ion* ION.] A molecule or ion having separate positively and negatively charged atoms or groups.
1906 G. MANN *Chem. Proteids* vi. 210 Ions which are simultaneously electro-positive and electro-negative (Bredig), and which Küster calls 'Zwitter-ions', *i.e.* hermaphrodite-ions. Thus the 'Zwitter-ion' of glycocoll is the group H_3N-CH_2-COO. **1925** *Jrnl. Chem. Soc.* CXXVII. I. 1381 The 'isomeric change' now takes the form of a fission of the molecule by the rupture of a bond, the final ionisation of which provides the electric charges which are needed to neutralise those already present in the 'Zwitterion'. **1937** *Nature* 18 Sept. 492/1 One of the greatest advances in the understanding of the physico-chemical behaviour of amino-acids and proteins is due to the zwitterion theory introduced by Bjerrum in 1923. **1948** *Endeavour* VII. 85/2 The products of [penicillin] inactivation are *zwitter-ions*. **1949** E. CHAIN in H. W. Florey et al. *Antibiotics* II. xxii. 847 The penicilloic acids are zwitterions with two acid groups and one basic group. **1968** D. W. WOOD *Princ. Animal Physiol.* iii. 35 At the pH of living cells, lecithin forms a balanced zwitterion. **1982** R. M. SCHULTZ in T. M. Devlin *Textbk. Biochem.* ii. 41 It is useful to calculate the exact pH at which an amino acid is electrically neutral and in its zwitterion form.
Hence ˌ**zwitteri'onic** *a.*
1946 *Nature* 16 Nov. 703/1 A hybrid structure derived from a number of ionic states of which there are.. eight zwitterionic forms. **1949** ABRAHAM & HEATLEY in H. W. Florey et al. *Antibiotics* I. ii. 94 These [substances].. may be neutral, acidic, basic, or zwitterionic. **1981** *Biochimica & Biophysica Acta* DCCLXVIII. 117 Vesicles of zwitterionic phosphatidylcholine.

Zwitzar, -er, obs. ff. SWITZER.

zwookers, zwop, zwounds: see ZOOKERS, SWAP, ZOUNDS.

zy: see SEE *v.*, THE.

zyalde: see SELL *v.*

Zydeco ('zaɪdɪkəʊ). *U.S. Blacks.* Also **zodico**, **zolo go**. [? Creole pronunc. of Fr. *les haricots* from dance-tune title 'Les haricots sont pas salés'.] A kind of Afro-American dance music of southern Louisiana; the dance itself. Also *attrib.*
1949 in Leadbitter & Slaven *Blues Records 1943–66* (1968) 136 Zologo (Organ Blues)—1. Gold Star 669. **1960** M. MCCORMICK notes to LP record *Treasury of Field Recordings I* 31 Two local groups.. have achieved nation-wide record sales with their interpretations of Zydeco music. **1964** *Amer. Folk Music Occasional* I. 28 'Zydeco' is a mixture of the blues and the music of the early Acadian settlers and is very popular in Southern Louisiana and along the Southeast Texas Gulf Coast especially in Houston, Texas. **1964** [see *rub-board* s.v. RUB *v.*[1] 18]. **1979** *Guardian* 13 June 10/7 [The Twisters] have two records currently available here: Doin' The Zydeco.. and Zy-De-Blue. **1979** N. SPITZER notes to LP record *Zodico: Louisiana Creole Music* 3/1 *Zodico* refers to the fast, syncopated dance numbers in a Creole band's repertoire as well as to the dance event itself. **1984** *New Yorker* 1 Oct. 29/3 Clifton Chenier strapped on his accordion to play some loud, rollicking Creole music known as *zydeco*.

zyga, plural of ZYGON.

zygadite ('zɪgədaɪt). *Min.* [ad. G. *zygadit* (Breithaupt), f. Gr. ζυγάδην in pairs, f. ζυγόν yoke.] A variety of albite, occurring in tabular twin crystals, of a yellowish-white or reddish colour.
1861 BRISTOW *Gloss. Min.* **1886** *Jrnl. Chem. Soc.* L. 518 *Zygadite*.. occurs in druses in the slate of St. Andreasberg in association with quartz and sphalerite.

‖**zygæna** (zaɪ'dʒiːnə). *Zool.* Also **Zygæna**. [mod.L., ad. Gr. ζύγαινα a kind of fish, perh. the hammer-headed shark.] **a.** *Ichth.* A fish of the genus formerly so named (now *Sphyrna*), comprising the hammerheaded sharks. **b.** *Entom.* A genus of moths (also called *Anthrocera*), comprising the burnet-moths. Hence **zy'gænid**, **-idan** *sbs.*, a member of the family *Zygænidæ*, typified by the genus *Zygæna*; *adjs.* belonging to the *Zygænidæ*.
1683–4 [see *balance-fish*, BALANCE *sb.* 22]. **1774** GOLDSM. *Nat. Hist.* (1824) III. 34 The Dog Fish,.. the Zygæna, the Tope, the Cat Fish. **1837** SIR J. RICHARDSON *Fauna Bor.-Amer.* IV. 301 Family Zygænidæ. Zygænidans. **1913** *Oxf. Univ. Gaz.* 954/1 The Zygaenid moth *Procris geryon*.

zygal ('zaɪgəl), *a. Anat.* [f. ZYGON + -AL[1].] Pertaining to or having a zygon.
1886 B. G. WILDER in *Jrnl. Nerv. & Mental Dis.* June 304 The complete or typical condition of a zygal fissure is like two y's joined by their stems,.. or, viewed from the side, like an expanded H.

‖**zygantrum** (zaɪ'gæntrəm, zɪg-). *Anat.* and *Zool.* Pl. **-antra**. [mod.L., f. Gr. ζυγόν yoke + ἄντρον cave.] A double cavity on the posterior side of the neural arch of each ordinary vertebra in serpents and some lizards, into which the *zygosphene* of the next vertebra fits.
1854 OWEN in *Orr's Circ. Sci., Org. Nat.* I. 197 This wedge [*sc.* the zygosphene] is received into a cavity (the 'zygantrum') excavated in the posterior expansion of the neural arch. **1888** ROLLESTON & JACKSON *Anim. Life* 73.

‖**zygapophysis** (zaɪgə'pɒfɪsɪs, zɪg-). *Anat.* and *Zool.* Pl. **-physes** (-fɪsiːz). [mod.L., f. Gr. ζυγόν yoke + ἀπόφυσις APOPHYSIS.] A lateral process on the neural arch of a vertebra, articulating with the corresponding process of the next vertebra; an articular process. There are normally four to each vertebra, viz. right and left anterior (***prezygapophyses***) and right and left posterior (***postzygapophyses***). Hence **zygapophysial** (-əpəʊ'fɪzɪəl) *a.*, pertaining to a zygapophysis.
1854 OWEN in *Orr's Circ. Sci., Org. Nat.* I. 169 The exogenous parts are the diapophysis.., the parapophysis.., the zygapophysis.., the anapophysis.., the metapophysis.., the hypapophysis.., and the epapophysis. **1870** ROLLESTON *Anim. Life* 11 Two oblique zygapophysial surfaces.

zygge, zyȝt, zyȝþ, zyȝþe: see SAY *v.*[1], SEE *v.*, SIGHT *sb.*[1]

zygite ('zaɪdʒaɪt). *Gr. Antiq.* [ad. Gr. ζυγίτης, f. ζυγόν: see ZYGON 2 and -ITE[1].] In the ancient bireme or trireme, a rower of the upper or the middle tier: cf. THALAMITE, THRANITE.
1888 WOODGATE *Boating* (Badm. Libr.) i. 17 In the bireme the zygite, as he sat on his bench, had behind him and below him his thalamite.

zygnemaceous (zɪgniː'meɪʃəs), *a. Bot.* [f. mod.L. *Zygnēmăceæ* pl., f. *Zygnēma* (Kützing, 1843), irreg. for **zygonēma*, f. Gr. ζυγόν yoke + νῆμα thread: see -ACEOUS.] Belonging to the N.O. *Zygnemaceæ* of filamentous fresh-water algæ, typified by the genus *Zygnema*, which propagate by conjugation. So **zygnemid** (zɪg'niːmɪd), a member of this order.
1887 *Athenæum* 12 Mar. 357/1 The Conjugatæ, including zygnemids and desmids.

zygnomic ('zaɪgnɒmɪk), *a. Law.* [f. ZYG(O- + Gr. νόμ-ος law + -IC.] In the terminology of A. Kocourek: 'a jural relation which involves an act the evolution of which directly abridges.. the freedom of the servus in the enjoyment.. of the substance of a legal advantage'. Opp. MESONOMIC *a.*
1926 A. KOCOUREK in *California Law Rev.* XV. 19 Zygnomic relation is a legal relation which (i) directly constrains the *servus* of the relation in his physical freedom *and* (ii) with the support of the law. **1927**, etc. [see MESONOMIC *a.*]. **1927** [see REGENERABLE *a.*]. **1930** A. KOCOUREK *Introd. to Science of Law* iv. 294 A zygnomic relation is one which works an immediate and direct constraint on human freedom at a given moment with the support of the law.

zygo- (zaɪgəʊ, zɪgəʊ), before a vowel properly **zyg-**, repr. Gr. ζυγο-, combining form of ζυγόν yoke; occurring in various scientific terms, of which the more important will be found in their alphabetical places. (In terms of Biology the prefix often refers to *conjugation* or *zygosis* as a method of reproduction: see CONJUGATION 5.)
zygo'cardiac *a.* [CARDIAC A. 4], denoting an ossicle in the stomach of the crayfish and other crustaceans (see quot., and cf. PTEROCARDIAC, UROCARDIAC). **'zygodont** *a.* [Gr. ὀδούς, ὀδοντ- tooth], having molar teeth with an even number of cusps arranged in pairs; having cusps thus arranged, as a molar tooth. **zygo'genesis** [-GENESIS], reproduction involving the formation of a zygote; so **zygoge'netic** *a.* **'zygomere** *Cytology* [-MERE], a site on a chromosome thought to be responsible for the initiation of pairing between homologous chromosomes during zygotene in eukaryotes. **zygo'nema** *Cytology* [a. F. *zygonema* (V. Grégoire 1907, in *La Cellule* XXIV. 371), f. Gr. νῆμα thread], †(*a*) a chromosome at zygotene; (*b*) = ZYGOTENE; now *rare*. **zygoneurous** (-'njʊərəs) *a.* [Gr. νεῦρον nerve], applied to an arrangement of the nervous system in certain gastropod molluscs, in which the pallial nerve of each pleural ganglion unites directly with the ganglion of the visceral commissure of its own side (opp. to *dialyneurous*); so **zygo'neury**, zygoneurous condition. **zygophiuran** (-ɒfɪ'jʊərən) *a.* and *sb.*, belonging to, or a member of, the division *Zygophiuræ* of ophiuroids, having special structures which limit the movement of the ossicles of the arms (cf. *zygospondyline* below). **'zygophore** *Bot.* [-PHORE], a differentiated hypha in Zygomycetes that takes part in conjugation; hence **zygo'phoric** *a.* **'zygophyte** (-faɪt) [Gr. φυτόν plant], a plant which reproduces by conjugation. **zy'gopterid** *sb.* and *a.* [Gr. πτερόν wing], a member of, or belonging to, the division *Zygopterides* or *Zygoptera* of dragon-flies, having all the wings nearly or quite equal in size. **'zygosome** *Cytology* [ad. G. *zygosom* (E. Strasburger 1904, in *Sitzungsber. d. k. Preuss. Akad. d. Wissensch.* 606): see -SOME[4]] = BIVALENT *sb.* **'zygosperm** [Gr. σπέρμα seed] = ZYGOSPORE. **'zygosphere** (-sfɪə(r)) [after OOSPHERE], either of the two conjugating cells or gametes which form a zygospore. **zygo'spondyline** *a.* [Gr. σπόνδυλος vertebra, joint], applied to those ophiuroids in which the arms are incapable of being coiled round straight objects, the movements of their ossicles being limited by internal pits and processes. **'zygostyle** (-staɪl) [STYLE 10] (see quot.). **zygo'zoospore**, a zoospore formed by conjugation; a motile zygospore.
1877 HUXLEY *Anat. Inv. Anim.* vi. 319 A large, elongated postero-lateral or *zygocardiac ossicle. **1888** *Amer. Naturalist* XXII. 832 The *zygodont (quadritubercular) type. **1950** *Adv. Genetics* III. 194 The most common mode of animal reproduction is, however, sexual reproduction or gamogony or *zygogenesis. **1973** B. J. WILLIAMS *Evolution & Human Origins* iii. 37/2 It [*sc.* random genetic drift] includes all events that lead to sampling error in random zygogenesis. **1950** *Adv. Genetics* III. 198 In other parthenogenetic animals both parthenogenetic and zygogenetic reproduction are present. **1978** *Biol. Bull.* CLV. 273 (*heading*) *Artemia* hemoglobins: genetic variation in parthenogenetic and zygogenetic populations. **1966** J. SYBENGA in *Genetica* XXXVII. 188 General occurrence of localization of the function of initiation of chromosome pairing (long-distance attraction) in discrete units on specific loci is considered a useful working hypothesis. In analogy to 'centromere', 'chromomere' and 'telomere' the term '**zygomere*' is proposed for such units. **1981** *Cytologia* XLVI. 527 Since the bivalent formation has not been disturbed, at least one of two zygomeres seems to be able to have a complete activity. **1911** *Q. Jrnl. Microsc. Sci.* LVII.

32 The debatable stages of the meiotic prophases in which parasyndesis and its associated phenomena occur—leptonema, *zygonema..—have been dealt with by many experienced cytologists. *Ibid.* 33 By the time the zygonema is fairly far advanced we do get appearances not unlike what may occasionally..be found in the condensation of a somatic chromosome. **1976** *Nature* 8 Apr. 534/2 It is generally known that during zygonema (stages XII–XIV in rat spermatogenesis) the homologous sets of sister chromatid pairs begin to come together and associate with one another. **1901** *Proc. Zool. Soc.* 466 A *Vivipara* possessing a single *zygoneurous connection on the left and the normal dialoneurous relationship of the nerves upon the right. **1892** *Ibid.* 182 For the *Zygophiurans assistance in classification will be gained from Ljungman's well-known work. **1904** A. F. Blakeslee in *Science* 3 June 866/1 In all species of both homo- and heterothallic groups..the swollen portions (progametes) from which the gametes are cut off do not grow toward each other..but arise as a result of the stimulus of contact between more or less differentiated hyphæ (*zygophores). **1970** J. Webster *Introd. Fungi* II. ii. 116 When two compatible strains approach each other aerial club-shaped branches or zygophores develop which show directional growth towards zygophores of the opposite strain. Zygophores of the same strain repel each other. **1904** *Zygophoric [see heterogamic *a.*]. **1978** *Canad. Jrnl. Bot.* LVI. 1061 One or more slender, lateral zygophoric filaments proliferate from the subterminal portion of a septate, erect hypha. **1885** Goodale *Physiol. Bot.* 439 *note*, The sexual process in *Zygophytes is characterized by the confluence of the protoplasmic masses of two very similar cells by which a new mass if formed as the starting-point of the new individual. **1900** W. J. Lucas *Brit. Dragonflies* 53 A *Zygopterid [wing]. *Ibid.* 34 Nymph of a Zygopterid Dragonfly. **1905** *Ann. Bot.* XIX. 249 A similar operation of the law of chance has been suggested by Strasburger ('04) in the separation of the chromatin granules as a result of the division of the '*zygosome'. **1910** [see *parasynaptic* adj. s.v. para-¹ 1]. **1974** *Jrnl. Heredity* LXV. 257/1 The varying amounts of the *q* segments present in the zygosome may account in large measure for the physical and mental deviation of these mongoloid patients from the usual spectrum of characteristics typical of mongoloids bearing three independent chromosomes 21. **1880** A. W. Bennett & Murray in *Q. Jrnl. Microsc. Sci.* XX. 417 The conjugated *zygospheres..constitute a *zygosperm. **1892** *Proc. Zool. Soc.* 1 Mar. 178 To regard the streptospondyline type [of ophiuroids] as earlier than the *zygospondyline. **1881** Mivart *Cat* 463 The caudal vertebræ are few and end in a bone, shaped somewhat lika a plough-share, called the *zygostyle. **1881** *Nature* 28 July 292 Family *Protococcaceæ*. Genus *Chlorochytrium*... Each cell becomes resolved into spherical zoospores, which upon leaving the mother-cell conjugate within the gelatinous envelope. The *zygozoospores before becoming surrounded with a membrane make their way..into the intercellular spaces of living plants.

zygobranchiate (zaɪgəʊˈbræŋkɪeɪt, zɪg-), *a.* (*sb.*) *Zool.* [f. mod.L. *Zygobranchiāta* pl., f. Gr. ζυγόν yoke + βράγχια gills: see -ate².] Belonging to the division *Zygobranchiata* or *Zygobranchia* of gastropod molluscs, having paired (right and left) gills or ctenidia; as *sb.* a mollusc of this division.

1883 Ray Lankester in *Encycl. Brit.* XVI. 655/2 The Zygobranchiate Streptoneura.

zygocactus (ˈzaɪgəʊkæktəs). *Bot.* Also **Zygo-**. [mod.L. (K. Schumann 1890, in C. F. Martius *Flora Braziliensis* IV. II. 223): see zygo- and cactus.] Any cactus of the Brazilian genus *Zygocactus* (sometimes included in *Schlumbergera*), the members of which have branched and jointed stems bearing zygomorphic flowers in various shades of red, and are freq. grown as houseplants.

1950 V. Higgins *Cactus Grower's Guide* iv. 54 Two other Epiphyllums which have been much cultivated are now placed in Schlumbergera—*Schlumbergera Gaertneri* and *S. Russelliana*; both are similar in habit to Zygocactus but the flowers are regular. **1962** *Amateur Gardening* 24 Mar. 29/1 Zygocactus should be watered throughout the year. **1980** *Daily Tel.* 24 Sept. 14/5 Among the new plants on show are ..zygocactus in pastel colours with a future as room plants, from Rochford.

zygodactyl (zaɪgəʊˈdæktɪl, zɪg-), *a.* and *sb.* *Ornith.* Also **-yle**. [See zygo- and dactyl.]

a. *adj.* Having the toes 'yoked' or arranged in pairs, i.e. two before and two behind, as the feet of a scansorial bird, or the bird itself; yoke-toed. **b.** *sb.* A yoke-toed bird. Also **zygodacˈtylic**, **zygoˈdactylous** *adjs.*

[**1842** Brande *Dict. Sci.* etc., *Zygodactyles*, the name given by M. Temminck to an order of Climbing Birds.]

1828–32 Webster, *Zygodactylous*. **1831** *Gard. & Menag. Zool. Soc., Birds* 73 By the structure of their toes, which are partially zygodactyle (the intermediate ones being turned forwards, and the two lateral ones most commonly taking the opposite direction). **1835** Partington *Brit. Cycl. Nat. Hist.* I. 445/1 Feet which accomplish these purposes are all zygodactylic, or yoke-toed. **1890** Coues *Handbk. Ornithol.* 187 The arrangement of toes in pairs, two before and two behind,..is called zygodactyl or zygodactylous. *Ibid.* 188 The true hind toe is wanting, the outer anterior one being reversed as usual in zygodactyls.

zygology (zaɪˈgɒlədʒɪ). [f. zygo- + -ology: coined by Mr. C. G. Hardie, Magdalen College, Oxford.] The branch of technology concerned with joining and fastening. Hence **zygoˈlogical** *a.*, **zyˈgologist**.

1970 *Assembly & Fastener Engin.* Oct. 48/3 We at Oxford Polytechnic are now offering courses in Zygology. *Ibid.*, I do not wish to suggest that all your readers should be considered as practising zygologists. **1971** *New Electronics* May 56 (Advt.), We are zygologists—experts in fastening techniques. We have specialised in riveting for years. **1973** *Oxford Times* 14 Dec. 40 (Advt.), Oxford Polytechnic... Postgraduate diploma in zygology. **1976** W. C. Wake *Adhesion* i. 4 Adhesion science should thus include adhesives and joints under its wing and is, if the reader likes classification, a branch of zygology. **1978** *Engin. Materials & Design* Apr. 37/2 Not that adhesion is the only zygological process available for joining one piece of plastics material to another.

‖**zygoma** (zaɪˈgəʊmə, zɪg-). *Anat.* Pl. **zygomata**, **zygomas**. Also 8 *erron.* **zigoma**. [mod.L., a. Gr. ζύγωμα, f. ζυγόν yoke. Cf. F. *zygome*, †*zigome*.] The bony arch on each side of the skull in vertebrates, consisting of the malar or jugal bone (cheek-bone) and its connexions, and forming a junction between the cranial and facial bones; the zygomatic arch; also, in restricted sense, some part of this, as the malar bone itself, the zygomatic process of the temporal bone, or the process of the malar which articulates with this.

1684 tr. *Blancard's Phys. Dict.* (1693), *Zygoma*, the jugal Bone about the Temples. **1758** J. S. tr. *Le Dran's Observ. Surg.* (1771) 13 There appeared near the *Zigoma*.., by the Wing of the Nostril, a slender Fluctuation. **1804** Abernethy *Surg. Obs.* 175 The fracture ran horizontally, about a quarter of an inch above the zygoma. **1806** Sir C. Bell *Anat. Expr.* (1872) 109 The zygoma, a process of the cheekbone, which joins the temporal bone. **1825** A. Monro *Anat. Hum. Body* I. 379 The Temporal muscle is seen in the temples, and its tendon passing under the zygoma. **1855** Holden *Hum. Osteol.* (1878) 69 At the lower part of the squamous portion there is an outgrowth of bone, termed the zygoma. **1893** H. Morris *Treat. Human Anat.* 37 A ridge of bone, the supra-mastoid crest, runs immediately above the external auditory meatus, and is continued onwards to the zygoma.

zygomatic (zaɪgəʊˈmætɪk, zɪg-), *a.* (*sb.*) *Anat.* [ad. mod.L. *zygomaticus*, f. Gr. ζύγωμα, -ατ-: see prec. and -ic.] Pertaining to or forming part of the zygoma; jugal.

zygomatic apophysis = *z. process*. ***zygomatic arch*** = zygoma. ***zygomatic bone***, the malar bone. ***zygomatic fossa***, an irregularly-shaped cavity on the side of the skull below and within the zygomatic arch. ***zygomatic muscle***, any one of several small muscles connected with the zygoma; *esp.* each of two pairs of muscles (*zygomaticus major* and *minor*) arising from the malar bone and inserted at the corners of the mouth, serving to draw the upper lip outward and upward. ***zygomatic process***, a process of the squamosal portion of the temporal bone, which articulates with the malar bone. ***zygomatic suture***, the suture connecting the squamosal with the malar bone.

1709 Blair in *Phil. Trans.* XXVII. 143 Two Zygomatic Bones. **1741** A. Monro *Anat.* (ed. 3) 95 Immediately before the Root of the zygomatic Process. **1811** C. Bell *Anat. Hum. Body* (ed. 3) I. 180 The zygomatic muscles pull the angles of the mouth upwards as in laughter. **1825** *Zool. Jrnl.* II. 162 The zygomatic arch. **1855** Holden *Hum. Osteol.* 102 The 'zygomatic fossa' is bounded externally by the zygomatic arch. **1895** *Q. Rev.* July 178 That 'sweet contraction' of the zygomatic muscles.

B. *sb.* Short for *z. muscle* or *z. bone*.

1811 C. Bell *Anat. Hum. Body* (ed. 3) I. 181 The zygomatics and levators pull the angles of the mouth upwards. **1919** *Man* XIX. 156 Prominence of the zygomatics.

zygoˈmatico-, combining form of mod.L. *zygomaticus* zygomatic, forming adjs. in sense 'belonging to the zygoma or zygomatic arch and (some other part)', as ***zygomatico-auricular*** (see quot.).

1890 Billings *Med. Dict.*, *Zygomatico-auricular index*, ratio between the bizygomatic and the biauricular diameters of the cranium.

zyˈgomato-, combining form of zygoma, used as prec., as in ***zygomato-temporal***.

1831 R. Knox tr. *Cloquet's Anat.* (ed. 2) 41 The cerebral and zygomato-temporal aspects of the sphenoid bone.

zygomorphic (zaɪgəʊˈmɔːfɪk, zɪg-), *a.* *Bot.* [f. Gr. ζυγόν yoke + μορφή form + -ic.] Applied to a flower that is symmetrical about a single plane, i.e. divisible into similar lateral halves in only one way; = monosymmetrical. Also **zygoˈmorphous**; opp. to actinomorphous. So **zygoˈmorphism**, the character of being zygomorphic.

1875 Bennett & Dyer tr. *Sachs' Bot.* 526 In Orchids both whorls are developed in a petaloid, and like the whole flower in a zygomorphic or monosymmetrical manner. *Ibid.* 534 The zygomorphism of the flower. **1879** A. Gray *Struct. Bot.* 175 *note*, Both these forms [*sc.* monosymmetrical and polysymmetrical] have a more expressive and older terminology, adopted by Eichler, viz.:—*Zygomorphous*, for flowers, or other structures, which can be bisected in one plane,..(*median zygomorphous*, when this is a median or anteroposterior plane,..*transverse zygomorphous*, when the plane of section is transverse or at right angles to the median).

Zygomycetes (zaɪgəʊmaɪˈsiːtiːz), *sb. pl.* *Bot.* Also (*rare*) **zygo-**. [mod.L., ad. G. *Zygomyceten* (O. Brefeld *Bot. Untersuchungen über Schimmelpilze* (1872) I. 53): see zygo-, mycetes *sb. pl.*] A class of saprophytic and parasitic fungi in which sexual reproduction is by fusion of usu. similar gametangia to produce a zygospore and asexual reproduction is by means of non-motile spores; fungi of this class. Occas. in *sing.* **Zygomycete** (-ˈmaɪsiːt). Hence **zygomyˈcetous** *a.*

[**1874** *Q. Jrnl. Microsc. Sci.* XIV. 56 Brefeld does not admit that *Chætocladium* and *Piptocephalis* possess sporangia, but only conidia. According to his views, therefore, the term *Zygomycetes* is more expressive than *Mucorini*, which he restricts to the sporangiferous *Zygomycetes*. This, however, appears to us founded on an error.] **1887** H. E. F. Garnsey tr. *A. de Bary's Compar. Morphol. & Biol. of Fungi* vi. 345 This coincidence with a fixed period of the year is at least not a general rule in the zygospores of the Zygomycetes. **1928** C. W. Dodge tr. *Gäumann's Compar. Morphol. Fungi* xxxvi. 621 A convergent development has apparently occurred in the Zygomycetous sporangia which have become gonotoconts. **1930** H. M. Fitzpatrick *Lower Fungi. Phycomycetes* ii. 34 The origin of the Zygomycete line is somewhat more obscure, though forms possessing one or more undoubted zygomycetous characters exist among the Ancylistales and Chytridiales. **1937** Gwynne-Vaughan & Barnes *Struct. & Developm. Fungi* (ed. 2) 16 The Zygomycetes..are the first fungi to colonise dung. **1952** C. J. Alexopoulos *Introd. Mycol.* vii. 180 Such a theory is based almost entirely on the asexual cycle, the zygomycetous reproduction having no counterpart in the present-day Saprolegniaceae which might give us a clue to its origin. **1978** *Bio Systems* X. 97/2 There are several eukaryote groups where there is, so far, no solidly based evidence for a flagellate ancestry:..(4) zygomycete fungi. **1979** I. K. Ross *Biol. of Fungi* xiii. 378 There are three main methods by which spores are actively released: the bursting of a turgid cell (ascomycetes and some zygomycetes), the rounding off of a surface under tension (some zygomycetes, some basidiomycetes) and the so-called ballistospore discharge. **1982** *Phytopathology* LXXII. 1102 (*heading*) Synoptic keys to the genera and species of zygomycetous mycorrhizal fungi.

‖**zygon** (ˈzaɪgɒn). Pl. **zyga** (ˈzaɪgə). [mod.L., ad. Gr. ζυγόν yoke.]

1. *Anat.* The bar or stem connecting the two branches of an H-shaped fissure (*zygal fissure*) of the brain.

1886 B. G. Wilder in *Jrnl. Nerv. & Mental Dis.* June 310 If..the zygon is the principal, central, and primary constituent of a fissural integer, the paroccipital.

2. *Gr. Antiq.* A cross-bench or thwart for rowers.

1888 Woodgate *Boating* (Badm. Libr.) i. 17 When.. vessels were expressly built as triremes, we may imagine.. the benches or zyga would be a little raised.

zygophyllaceous (ˌzaɪgəʊfɪˈleɪʃəs, zɪg-), *a.* *Bot.* [f. mod.L. *Zygophyllaceæ* pl., f. *Zygophyllum*, f. Gr. ζυγόν yoke + φύλλον leaf: see -aceous.] Belonging to the N.O. *Zygophyllaceæ*, typified by the genus *Zygophyllum* (bean-capers).

1887 J. Ball *Nat. S. Amer.* 198 The singular Zygophyllaceous shrub *Porliera hygrometrica*.

‖**zygopleura** (zaɪgəʊˈplʊərə, zɪg-), *sb. pl.* *Morphol.* [mod.L., f. Gr. ζυγόν yoke + πλευρά side.] Organic forms having bilateral symmetry, with either two or four antimeres or corresponding opposite parts (dipleura, tetrapleura). Hence **zygoˈpleural** *a.*, having bilateral symmetry.

1883 [see dipleura]. **1896** [see dipleural def.].

‖**zygosis** (zaɪˈgəʊsɪs, zɪg-). *Biol.* [mod.L., ad. Gr. ζύγωσις, f. ζυγοῦν to yoke, f. ζυγόν yoke.] = conjugation 5.

1880 Pascoe *Zool. Chem.* (ed. 2) 297. **1882** Saville-Kent *Man. Infusoria* 874.

zygosity (zaɪˈgɒsɪtɪ). *Genetics.* [f. zygos(is + -ity.] **a.** The genetic relationship of twins, triplets, etc., in respect of their being either monozygotic or dizygotic.

1952 *New Biol.* XII. 42 Instead of exchanging skin between the twin animals whose zygosity it is desired to establish, grafts are being transplanted from both of them to a third, unrelated recipient. **1971** *Nature* 23 July 277/1 Before recent developments with marker genes, it was not possible to assign with certainty the zygosity of a substantial proportion of twin pairs. **1978** *Jrnl. R. Soc. Med.* LXXI. 311/2 The type of twinning and determination of zygosity are given attention.

b. The degree of genetic similarity between alleles which determines whether an individual is homozygotic or heterozygotic for the characteristic expressed.

1967 *Jrnl. Clin. Investigation* XLVI. 681 (*heading*) Relationship between $Rh_0(D)$ zygosity and red cell $Rh_0(D)$ antigen content in family members. *Ibid.*, The members of two families showed a poor correspondence between antibody binding and zygosity. **1972** *Transplantation* XIV. 793/1 Efforts have been made to determine HL-A zygosity of unrelated subjects by use of the gene-dose effect.

zygosphene (ˈzaɪgəʊsfiːn, ˈzɪg-). *Anat.* and *Zool.* [f. Gr. ζυγόν yoke + σφήν wedge.] A double wedge-shaped projection on the anterior side of the neural side of each ordinary vertebra in serpents and some lizards, which fits into the *zygantrum* of the next vertebra. Hence

zygo'sphenal *a.*, belonging to or constituting a zygosphene.
1854 OWEN in *Orr's Circ. Sci., Org. Nat.* I. 196 A wedge-shaped process (the 'zygosphene')..is developed from the fore part of the base of the spine. *Ibid.* 197 Surfaces to which the zygosphenal surfaces are adapted. **1892** *Proc. Zool. Soc.* 1 Mar. 176 The zygosphenes and zygantra of the Ophidian vertebræ.

zygospore ('zaɪgəʊspɔə(r), 'zɪg-). *Bot.* [ad. G. *zygospor*: see ZYGO- and SPORE.] A spore formed by conjugation; a germ-cell arising from the fusion of two similar cells (gametes), as in certain Algæ and Fungi. Hence **zygo'sporic** *a.*, of the nature of or producing zygospores.
1864 *Q. Jrnl. Microscop. Sci.* (N.S.) IV. 178, I have.. made use of..the more apt term 'Zygospore', as suggested by Professor De Bary in his work 'Untersuchungen..' in preference to the..inaccurate term 'Sporangium' of most other authors. **1874** COOKE *Fungi* 164 The threads which conjugate to form the zygospores. **1906** *Science* 27 July 122/2 Zygosporic cultures of the 'Harvest Strain' have.. been kept running for nearly ten years. **1970** J. WEBSTER *Introd. Fungi* II. ii. 141 In some species [of the genus *Endogone*]..the fruit-body is entirely zygosporic.

†**zygostat.** *Obs. rare*⁻⁰. [ad. late L. *zygostatēs*, a. Gr. ζυγοστάτης, f. ζυγόν yoke, beam of a balance, etc. + ἱστάναι to set, place.] Hence †**zygostatical** *a.* (*obs. rare*⁻⁰). (See quots.)
1623 COCKERAM, *Zygost[at]e*, one that is appointed to see the weights, a Clarke of the market. [**1654** CHARLETON *Physiol. Epic.-Gass.-Charlton.* 403 Such a Zygostata or Ballance, wherewith Jewellers are to weigh Pearles and Diamonds.] **1656** BLOUNT *Glossogr.*, *Zygostatical*.. belonging to the pound weight of Sixteen ounces, or to a Clark of a Market that looks to weights.

zygote ('zaɪgəʊt). *Biol.* [ad. Gr. ζυγωτός yoked, f. ζυγοῦν to yoke.] A body of living protoplasm, as a cell or cell-nucleus, formed by the conjugation or fusion of two such bodies in reproduction; a zygospore, or any germ-cell resulting from the union of two reproductive cells or gametes. Also *attrib.* or as *adj.* That is a zygote, formed by conjugation; of or pertaining to a zygote.
1891 HARTOG in *Nature* 17 Sept. 484 Paragamy or Endokaryogamy: vegetative or gametal nuclei lying in a continuous mass of cytoplasm fuse to form a zygote nucleus. **1895** OLIVER tr. *Kerner's Nat. Hist. Plants* II. 628 The cell produced by the fusion of the bodies of two gametes is called the zygote.

Hence **zygotic** (-'ɒtɪk) *a.*, pertaining to or of the nature of a zygote, produced or characterized by zygosis; **zy'gotically** *adv.*, in the zygote; in terms of the zygote; **zy'gotoblast** [-BLAST], one of a number of germ-cells or sporozoites produced by budding from a *zygotomere* (see below); **zy'gotoid** [-OID], a multinucleate form of zygote in certain fungi (see quot.); **zy'gotomere** [Gr. μέρος part], one of a number of cells formed by segmentation of a zygote in the malaria parasite or other *Sporozoa*.
1891 HARTOG in *Nature* 17 Sept. 484 In apocytial fungi multinucleated masses of protoplasm (*gametoids*) may conjugate to form a *zygotoid*. **1899** *Allbutt's Syst. Med.* VIII. 945 Nucleus and protoplasm divide into a number of zygotomeres, which become blastophores, each bearing on its surface..a large number of filamentous zygotoblasts. **1909** W. E. CASTLE *Inheritance in Rabbits* (Carnegie Inst. Publ. No. 114) 58 The enumeration of the conceivable different varieties of gray rabbit, all alike in appearance but all different in breeding capacity, *i.e.*, of different zygotic formula. **1915** *Jrnl. Genetics* V. 45 Zygotically therefore the three forms [of rabbit] may be represented thus: Self-coloured..CCSS, Himalayan..CCss, Albino..ccss. **1931** *Ibid.* XXIV. 448 It is probable that the new combinations will be less successful than the old, both zygotically and gametically. **1977** J. COHEN *Reproduction* ix. 163 The second phase of embryology begins, controlled by zygotic genes. **1980** *Genetics* XCVI. 187 The possibility that essential loci in the zeste-white region of the *Drosophila melanogaster X* chromosome are expressed both maternally and zygotically has been tested.

zygotene ('zaɪgəʊtiːn). *Cytology.* [a. F. *zygotène* (V. Grégoire 1907, in *La Cellule* XXIV. 371): see ZYGO- and -TENE.] The second stage of the prophase of meiosis, following leptotene, during which homologous chromosomes begin to pair.
1911 *Jrnl. Morphol.* XXII. 752 This view..goes on to show that after the last spermatogonial mitosis the chromosomes become very delicate slender threads, the leptotene condition..; these then approximate themselves parallel into pairs making the zygotene condition. **1939** [see DIAKINESIS]. **1974** *Nature* 9 Aug. 469/2 At leptotene of meiotic prophase in many organisms, all the telomeres become gathered together and attached to a small area of the nuclear envelope, presumably so as to facilitate pairing during zygotene.

zyke, zykere, obs. ff. SICK, SICKER.

Zyklon ('zaɪklɒn). Also **Cyclon**. [a. G. *Zyklon*, of unknown etym.] Hydrogen cyanide adsorbed on, or released from, a carrier in the form of small tablets, used as a fumigant and formerly as a poison gas. Usu. as ***Zyklon B***.
[**1926** *Official Gaz.* (U.S. Patent Office) 9 Nov. 298/1 Deutsche Gesellschaft für Schädlingsbekämpfung, m.b.H., Frankfort-on-the-Main... *Zyklon*... Apparatus for measuring the quantities of substances which generate poisonous gases—for instance, hydrocyanic acid.] **1939** METCALF & FLINT *Destructive & Useful Insects* (ed. 2) ix. 281 The other type of dry cyanides, such as the zyklon products, undergo no chemical change when exposed. **1944** *Chem. Abstr.* XXXVIII. 3416 The application of Cyclon B (0.4 g./cc.) for 24 hrs. destroyed all insects but imparted a peculiar taste to the tobaccos. **1964** L. DEIGHTON *Funeral in Berlin* xxxi. 169 With Cyclon B they killed two and a half million at Auschwitz. **1975** W. CRAIG *Strasbourg Legacy* (1976) i. 9 Former SS soldiers..had functioned so anonymously in the camps that hardly anyone lived who could identify them as guards once manning machine guns or dropping Zyklon B tablets into gas chambers. **1977** *Times* 8 June 9/7 [He] was tried and acquitted at Nürnberg in 1948 for supplying the SS with Zykon-B gas. **1978** H. WOUK *War & Remembrance* xi. 111 Zyklon B, the powerful insecticide they have been using right along at the camp to fumigate the barracks, may be the surprisingly simple solution.

zylo-, erroneous spelling of words in XYLO-.

zymad ('zaɪmæd). [f. Gr. ζύμη leaven + -AD, after *monad*.] A micro-organism which produces zymotic disease.
1885 *Leisure Hour* Jan. 25/2 The cook..exorcises zymads and parasites. **1913** DORLAND *Med. Dict.*

zymase ('zaɪmeɪs). *Chem.* [ad. F. *zymase* (Bechamp), f. Gr. ζύμη leaven, after *diastase*.] Name given to a ferment obtained from the yeast-fungus; also extended to unorganized ferments or enzymes in general.
1875 *Jrnl. Chem. Soc.* XXVIII. 374. **1899** J. R. GREEN *Soluble Ferm.* viii. 108 Bechamp thought that the enzyme from fungi was not quite the same as that existing in the flowers... He gave to the first the name *zymase*... The name *zymase* was soon abandoned, as it began to be applied to enzymes in general.

†**zymate** ('zaɪmeɪt). *Chem. Obs.* In actual use **zumate** ('zjuːmeɪt). [f. ZYM-IC (*zum-ic*) + -ATE⁴.] A salt of 'zymic acid'.
1817 T. THOMSON *Syst. Chem.* (ed. 5) II. 189 Zumate of ammonia. **1819** J. G. CHILDREN *Chem. Anal.* 281 Zumate of peroxide of iron.

zyme (zaɪm). [ad. Gr. ζύμη leaven.] A name for the substance or principle causing a zymotic disease: cf. ZYMOSIS.
1882 *Quain's Dict. Med.* 1806 Corresponding with the adjective *zymotic* is the substantive *zyme*.., by which we refer to the poisonous cause of zymotic diseases.

†**zymic** ('zaɪmɪk, 'zɪmɪk), *a. Chem. Obs.* In actual use **zumic** ('zjuːmɪk). [f. Gr. ζύμη leaven + -IC.] Pertaining to or connected with fermentation; formerly applied to a supposed acid (afterwards shown to be impure lactic acid) obtained by fermentation of starchy substances.
1817 T. THOMSON *Syst. Chem.* (ed. 5) II. 189 Of Zumic Acid. I give this name to an acid recently discovered by M. Braconnot. **1826** HENRY *Elem. Chem.* II. 241.

zymin ('zaɪmɪn). Also **-ine**. [f. Gr. ζύμη leaven + -IN¹.] **a.** = ZYME. **b.** A pancreatic extract used in medicine. Hence **'zyminized** *a.*, predigested by means of zymin.
1842 W. FARR in *4th Ann. Rep. Reg.-Gen.* 201 The morbific principle (zymine). *Ibid.* 202 Some..kinds of matter (zymin) are reproduced in the organization after they have been destroyed by transformation (zymosis) in attacks of disease. **1888** M. MACKENZIE *Fredk. the Noble* vii. 99 Zyminised nutriments. **1901** DORLAND *Med. Dict.*, *Zymin*. ..a pancreatic extract prepared for therapeutic use.

zymo- (zaɪməʊ), before a vowel **zym-**, combining form repr. Gr. ζύμη leaven, used in the general sense 'ferment', in various scientific terms. (Some of these were formerly written *zumo-*, the Gr. υ being represented, contrary to analogy, by *u*: see Y.) **'zymocyte** (-saɪt) [-CYTE], a unicellular organism which produces fermentation. **,zymoglu'conic** *a.*, epithet of an acid obtained by fermentation from glucose; hence **zymo'gluconate**, a salt of this acid. **'zymogram** *Biochem.* and *Genetics*, a strip of electrophoretic medium showing enzymes separated by a technique such as zone electrophoresis. ‖**,zymohy'drolysis**, hydrolysis effected by the action of a ferment. **zy'mology** (†zumo-) [-LOGY], the science of fermentation; that department of chemistry which deals with ferments and their action; hence **zymo'logical** (†zumo-) *a.*, relating to zymology; **zy'mologist** (†zumo-), one versed in zymology. **zy'molysis** [Gr. λύσις loosening], decomposition by means of a (esp. an unorganized) ferment; so **zymo'lytic** *a.*, pertaining to or involving zymolysis. **zy'mometer** (†zumo-) [-METER] = ZYMOSIMETER. **'zymophore** (-fɔə(r)), **zymo-phoric** (-'fɒrɪk), **zymophorous** (-'ɒfərəs) *adjs.* [see -PHORE, etc.], in Ehrlich's theory of immunization, applied to a particular group of atoms in a ferment, or in the receptors of a living cell, to which the fermentative action is due (analogous to the toxophore group in a toxin). **'zymophyte** (-faɪt) [-PHYTE], a vegetable organism which causes fermentation. **zymo'plastic** *a.* [see PLASTIC *a.*], forming a ferment. **'zymoscope** [-SCOPE]: see quot. **zymotechnic** (-'tɛknɪk), **-ical** *adjs.* [Gr. τεχνή art], relating to the art of fermentation; so **zymo'technics**, **'zymotechny**, the art of fermentation (cf. ZYMURGY); **,zymotech'nology** [-LOGY], the scientific study of the principles of zymotechny; **,zymotech'nologist**, one versed in zymotechnology. **zymo'toxic** *a.*, having a fermentative and toxic action.
a **1909** *Disinfectants* 14 (Cent. D. Suppl.) Salicylic acid only holding its reputation as an enemy to the *zymocytes of the cider barrel. **1887** *Jrnl. Chem. Soc.* LII. 468 The crystallised ammonium gluconate recently described by Volpert..had previously been obtained by the author [*sc.* L. Boutroux], and described by him as ammonium *zymogluconate. **1886** *Ibid.* L. 682 The *zymogluconic acid obtained by the action of *M[icrococcus] oblongus* on glucose. **1957** HUNTER & MARKERT in *Science* 28 June 1295/2 We propose the term **zymogram* to refer to strips in which the location of enzymes is demonstrated by histochemical methods. **1978** *Nature* 2 Mar. 77/2 The high degree of gene duplication in these species often confounds the genetic interpretation of zymograms. For example, how many loci code for an enzyme represented by a single electrophoretic band? **1981** *Histochemistry* LXXIII. 311 Electro-focused zymograms display species and organ differences. **1903** C. SNYDER *New Concept. Sci.* 236 Croft Hill's bold announcement, three or four years ago, of the discovery of 'reversible *zymohydrolysis'. **1828–32** WEBSTER, *Zumological, *Zumologist. **1846** WORCESTER, Zymological, Zymologist (citing OSWALD). **1753** *Chambers's Cycl. Supp.*, *Zymology [referring to W. Simpson's *Zymologia Physica*, 1675]. **1828–32** WEBSTER, *Zumology*. **1890** A. S. LEA in *Jrnl. Physiol.* XI. 254 *note*, I would suggest that the word '*zymolysis' might be.. used to denote generally the changes produced by the enzymes or unorganised ferments. *Ibid.* 264 The *zymolytic activity of the digestive fluid. **1842** BRANDE *Dict. Sci.*, etc., **Zumometer*, or *Zumosimeter*,..an instrument intended to show the degree to which fermentation has proceeded in different fermenting liquors. **1900** *U.S. Dept. Agric., Bur. Anim. Ind.* Rep. 257 (Cent. D. Suppl.) The hypothesis of Morgenroth in regard to the existence of a haptophore group and the [*sic*; ? a] *zymophore group in the labile ferment has been recently verified by Myers and Bashford, who have discovered zymoids analogous to the toxoids. **1902** *Brit. Med. Jrnl.* 12 Apr. 920 There is no amboceptor as such, but the body consists of a *zymophoric group. **1890** BILLINGS *Med. Dict.*, **Zymophytes*, bacteroid ferments that liberate fatty acids from neutral fats. **1868** WATTS *Dict. Chem.* V. 1086 **Zymoscope*, an instrument..for testing the fermenting power of yeast, by bringing it in contact with sugar-water, and observing the quantity of carbonic anhydride evolved. **1896** A. K. MILLER tr. *E. C. Hansen's Ferment.* 71 Ancker and Bergh's *zymotechnic laboratory, Stockholm. **1900** tr. *A. Jörgensen's Micro-org. & Ferment.* 47 *Zymotechnical examinations of water according to the principles laid down by Hansen. **1896** A. K. MILLER tr. *E. C. Hansen's Ferment.* 113 Several *zymotechnologists have made similar experiments. **1860** MAYNE *Expos. Lex.*, *Zymotechny. **1902** *Jrnl. Exper. Med.* 17 Mar. 282 The complement possesses in addition to such a..haptophore group, another group which exhibits fermentative properties (*zymotoxic or toxophore group).

zymogen ('zaɪməʊdʒɛn). *Biol. Chem.* [ad. G. *zymogen* (Heidenhain, 1875): see ZYMO- and -GEN.] A substance formed in an organism, from which a ferment is produced. Also *attrib.*
1877 M. FOSTER *Physiol.* II. i. (1878) 219 A pancreas taken fresh from the body..contains but little ready-made ferment, though there is present in it a body which, by some kind of decomposition, gives birth to the ferment... To this body..Heidenhain has given the name of Zymogen. **1896** E. B. WILSON *Cell in Devel.* 288 Zymogen granules. **1897** *Allbutt's Syst. Med.* III. 306 A zymogen is the antecedent of the ferment of the secretion—pepsinogen, trypsinogen, for example.

So **zymoge'netic, zymo'genic, zy'mogenous** *adjs.*, producing a ferment, or causing fermentation.
1896 *Allbutt's Syst. Med.* I. 528 Organisms..acting partly as ferments, partly as *zymogenetic cells. **1884** KLEIN *Micro-org.* xxi. 187 Putrefactive and many *zymogenic organisms thrive well at ordinary temperatures. **1900** *Nature* 13 Sept. 405 Zymogenic..bacteria.

zymoid ('zaɪmɔɪd), *a.* and *sb.* [f. Gr. ζύμη: see ZYMO- and -OID.] **a.** *adj.* Resembling a ferment. **b.** *sb.* A substance having a relation to a ferment analogous to that of a toxoid to the corresponding toxin.
1891 *Cent. Dict.* **1900** [see *zymophore* under ZYMO-].

†**'zymome.** *Chem. Obs.* Also **zimome**. [ad. mod.L. *zymōma*, It. *zimoma* (Taddei), ad. Gr. ζύμωμα fermented mixture, f. ζυμοῦν: see ZYMOSIS.] A name for that constituent of gluten which is insoluble in alcohol. Also called †**zymomin**.
[**1820** *Q. Jrnl. Sci.* VIII. 377 D. Taddei..having undertaken researches in fermentation,..in various cases has ascertained that the gluten of wheat is composed of two substances, perfectly distinct from each other, one of which he has named *gloiodina*, and the other *zimoma*.] **1820** T. THOMSON in *Ann. Phil.* May 390 M. Taddey..has lately ascertained that the gluten of wheat may be decomposed into two principles, which he has distinguished by the names, *gliadine*..and *zimome*. **1826** HENRY *Elem. Chem.* II. 268 Zimome is obtained pure by boiling gluten in alcohol. **1830** DONOVAN *Dom. Econ.* I. 345 Zimomin is of a dirty white colour, hard, and without any of the elasticity which

gluten possesses. **1831** JONES *New Convers. Chem.* xxix. 292 Zymome.

zymosan ('zaɪməʊsæn). *Biochem.* [f. ZYMO-, after *glucosan, hexosan.*] An insoluble polysaccharide of the cell wall of yeast, used in the assay of properdin.

1943 E. E. ECKER et al. in *Jrnl. Immunol.* XLVII. 185 The preparation of human complement lacking in third component. The third component is specifically removed from or inactivated in human serum by the insoluble carbohydrate prepared from fresh yeast... The insoluble carbohydrate is hereafter referred to as 'zymosan'. **1973** *Sci. Amer.* Nov. 60/3 The incubation of normal blood serum.. with certain polysaccharides derived from microbial cells (such as zymosan, a carbohydrate of the yeast cell membrane) gives rise to enzymes that activate the complement factors C3 and C5.

zymo'simeter. Also zumo-. [f. Gr. ζύμωσις (see next) + μέτρον measure: see -METER.] An instrument for measuring the degree of fermentation of a fermenting liquor.

1704 J. HARRIS *Lex. Techn.* I, Zymosimetre. **1842** Zumosimeter [see *zymometer* under ZYMO-].

‖**zymosis** (zaɪ'məʊsɪs). Pl. **zymoses** (-si:z). [mod.L., ad. Gr. ζύμωσις fermentation, f. ζυμοῦν to leaven, in pass. to ferment, f. ζύμη leaven: see -OSIS.] Fermentation; *spec.* the morbid process which constitutes a zymotic disease, regarded as analogous to or involving fermentation.

1842 W. FARR in *4th Ann. Rep. Reg.-Gen.* 201 *note*, Zymosis fermentation, and zyma ferment, may also be employed in English, not in the sense which they have in Greek, but as general designations of the morbid processes and their exciters. *Ibid.* 202 [see ZYMIN]. **1876** BARTHOLOW *Mat. Med.* (1879) 523 As all fermentations are correlative of the growth and multiplication of these minute bodies, carbolic acid, by destroying their activity, arrests zymosis. *fig.* **1876** EMERSON *Lett. & Soc. Aims, Eloquence* Wks. (Bohn) III. 195 In the Elizabethan Age there was a dramatic *zymosis*, when all the genius ran in that direction.

zymotic (zaɪ'mɒtɪk), *a.* (*sb.*) [ad. Gr. ζυμωτικός causing fermentation, f. ζυμοῦν: see ZYMOSIS.] A general epithet for infectious diseases, originally because regarded as being caused by a process analogous to fermentation (cf. ZYMOSIS); pertaining to this theory of disease; causing such disease.

1842 W. FARR in *4th Ann. Rep. Reg.-Gen.* 201 The property of communicating their action, and effecting analogous transformations in other bodies, is.. characteristic in these diseases, which it is proposed therefore to call..zymotic. **1851** MAYHEW *Lond. Labour* (1861) II. 395/2 The zymotic doctrine of the Board of Health as to the cause of cholera. **1896** *Allbutt's Syst. Med.* I. 528 Since many morbid processes are analogous, if not akin, to fermentative processes,.. the term *zymotic* has been applied to them,—a term, however, to be avoided rather than recommended.

b. In etymological sense: Causing or consisting in fermentation, fermentative.

1874 GARROD & BAXTER *Mat. Med.* 145 The zymotic action of yeast.

c. *transf.* Containing putrefactive germs.

1881 TYNDALL *Ess. Floating Matter Air* 208 An éprouvette containing one cubic centimeter of cold water, previously ascertained to be zymotic, was evaporated to dryness.

B. *sb.* A zymotic disease.

1842 W. FARR in *4th Ann. Rep. Reg.-Gen.* 201 A single word, such as Zymotics, is required to replace..the long periphrasis 'epidemic, endemic, and contagious diseases'. **1859** *Househ. Words* 8 Jan. 122/2 People who have died of Zymotics. **1916** *Lancet* 8 Jan. 112/1 Health of Belfast... In 1914 there were 51 notifications of typhus..; not a case of this zymotic has been reported in 1915.

Hence **zy'motically** *adv.*

1851 MAYHEW *Lond. Labour* (1861) II. 385/2 Whether this mass of filth be, zymotically, the cause of cholera.

zymurgy ('zaɪmɜ:dʒɪ). [f. Gr. ζύμη leaven + -ουργία working, as in METALLURGY.] The practice or art of fermentation, as in wine-making, brewing, distilling, etc.

1868 WATTS *Dict. Chem.* V. 1086.

zynder, zyne, zyphe: see CINDER, SINE[1], XIPH.

Zyrenian, var. SIRYENIAN *sb.* and *a.*

Zyrian ('zɪrɪən), *sb.* and *a.* Also **Syrian, Syryane, Syryen,** (and esp.) **Zyryan.** [ad. Russ. *Zȳryánin*: see -IAN.] **A.** *sb.* A member of the Komi people of northern central U.S.S.R. **b.** The language of this people; = KOMI b. **B.** *adj.* Of or pertaining to this people or their language.

1886 *Encycl. Brit.* XXI. 79/2 The Permians,..including ..the Zyrians in Vologda, Archangel, Vyatka, and Perm. **1926** *Chambers's Encycl.* VIII. 101/1 The Syriän is spoken by a large population in the districts of Perm, Viatka, Archangel, and Vologda. **1932, 1933** [see PERMIAN *a.* (*sb.*) 2]. **1942** [see KOMI]. **1948** D. DIRINGER *Alphabet* II. viii. 482 Other peoples..such as the Zyryans or Syryans (now called Komi). **1951** W. K. MATTHEWS *Languages U.S.S.R.* iii. 20 The Yuraks have loans from Zyryan (Komi), a Finnic language. *Ibid.* 25 Zyryan resistance to the Russians was less dogged and implacable than Ugrian. **1955** *Trans. Philol. Soc. 1954* 99 The forms are: Norwegian Lappish *miettâ*.. Syryane *ma* [etc.]. **1972** *Language* XLVIII. 848, 7b is given by Hockett for 'German,..French.., Zyryan'. **1978** K. RÉDEI (*title*) Zyrian folklore texts.

zyþ, obs. (Kentish) 3rd sing. ind. pres. of SEE *v.*

zyþe, obs. f. SITHE *sb.*[1]

zyxst, obs. f. SIXTH.

zyxt, obs. (Kentish) 2nd sing. ind. pres. of SEE *v.*

BIBLIOGRAPHY

NOTE TO THE BIBLIOGRAPHY

THIS list comprises the titles of such works as have been most commonly quoted in the Dictionary. It represents a conflation of the two bibliographies already in existence: that of the first edition of the *Oxford English Dictionary*, published, together with the original Supplement, in 1933, and that of *A Supplement to the OED*, published in Volume IV of that work in 1986. Apart from emendations arising directly out of the integration of the two lists, and the correction of miscellaneous minor errors, no systematic revision of the bibliography to the first edition has been attempted. While it has no claim to be regarded as a complete guide to English literature, this list will be found to contain a large proportion of the more important works, together with many others less familiar; it includes a large number of titles of periodical publications.

The arrangement is according to the alphabetical order of authors' names or titles of works. Following each title is the date of the first edition or of composition (ascertained or inferred). Where it is possible or necessary to give only a limiting date, such as that of an author's death, or of a manuscript in which the work is extant, this is preceded by *a* (= *ante*), e.g. BACON *Works a* 1626, *King Horn a* 1300. As occasion requires, the dates of editions used other than the first, or the names of editors or of series of publications, are added within round brackets. Where a title (e.g. Arnolde's *Chronicle*) is followed by a second title in brackets, the first is that by which the work is generally known, the second is its proper title. Round brackets are also occasionally used to indicate that works are questionably assigned to the authors under whom they are entered.

Publications of learned institutions are listed here under the name of the institution; translations under the name of the translator (where known). The country or city of publication has not usually been given except for newspapers published outside London, and UK editions of books published in an earlier year abroad.

It is to be observed that the dates assigned (in the early years of the history of the Dictionary) to some Middle English texts and to a few books of later date (e.g. the plays of Shakespeare), as also certain ascriptions of authorship, have been modified by subsequent research (the resulting discrepancies rarely affect in any serious degree the chronology of words and senses).

ABBREVIATIONS

a (before a date)	*ante* (before; not later than)	ser.	series
c (before a date)	*circa* (about)	S.H.S.	Scottish History Society
Cl.	Club	Soc.	Society
Ed., ed.	editor of; edited (by); edition	S.T.S.	Scottish Text Society
E.D.S.	English Dialect Society	tr.	translated (by); translation of
E.E.T.S.	Early English Text Society	v.d.	various dates
et al.	and others	vol.	volume
rev.	revised		

A. 1593 See *Passionate Morrice*
A., A. *Reply to Dr. Sanderson* 1650
A., D. *The art of converse* 1683
A., H. 1613, 1633 *See* Austin, Henry; Hawkins, Henry
A., W. *A speciall remedie against the furious force of lawlesse loue* 1579 (Roxb. Cl. 1844)
'Aarons, E. S.' (Paul Ayres & Edward Ronns) *Assignment treason* 1956
Abbay, Richard *The Castle of Knaresborough* 1887
Abbot, Charles *Jurisdiction and practice of the Court of Great Sessions of Wales on the Chester Circuit* 1795
Abbot, Abp. George *A briefe description of the whole worlde* (anon.) 1599 (1617, 1634)
An exposition upon the prophet Jonah 1600
A treatise of the perpetuall visibilitie and succession of the true church (anon.) 1624
Abbot, George *The whole book of Job paraphrased* 1640
Abbot, Robert *The old waye* 1610
Abbott, Charles C. *Waste-land wanderings* 1887
Abbott, David *Inorganic chemistry* 1965
Abbott, Edwin A. *Francis Bacon: an account of his life and works* 1885
Abbott, Jacob *Wallace: a Franconia story* 1853
Abbott, John Henry Macartney *Tommy Cornstalk* 1902
Abbott, John S. C. *Life of Napoleon* 1854 (1855)
Abbs, Akosua *Ashanti boy* 1959
Abdy, Edward S. *The water cure* 1842 (1843)
Aberbrothoc. Liber S. Thome de Aberbrothoc. Registrorum Abbacie de Aberbrothoc pars prior; pars altera v.d. (Bannatyne Cl. 1848, 1856)
Abercrombie, David *English phonetic texts* 1964
Problems and principles: studies in the teaching of English as a second language 1956
—— et al. eds. *In honour of Daniel Jones: papers contributed on the occasion of his eightieth birthday* 1964
Abercrombie, John *Every man his own gardener* 1767 (1803)
Abercromby, Hon. Ralph *Weather* 1887
Aberdeen, Extracts from the council register of the Burgh of 1398–1625 (Spalding Cl. 1844–48)
1625–1747 (Scott. Burgh Rec. Soc. 1871–72)
Aberdeen, Selections from the records of the Kirk session of 1562–1681 (Spalding Cl. 1846)
Aberdeen Press and Journal 1922–39 (continued as *Press and Journal*)
Abernethy, Bp. John *A christian and heavenly treatise containing physicke for the soule* 1615 (1622)
Abernethy, John *Diseases resembling syphilis* 1809 (1826)
Surgical observations 1804–06
Surgical works 1827
Abingdon. Accounts of the obedientiars of A. Abbey 1322–1479 (Camden Soc. 1892)
Abney, William de W. *Colour vision* 1895
A treatise on photography 1878 (1881)
Abraham, George Dixon *Modern mountaineering* 1933
Abraham, Louis Arnold & Hawtrey, Stephen Charles eds. *A parliamentary dictionary* 1956
– (ed. 2) 1964
Abrahams, Beth-Zion tr. *The life of Glückel* [Segal] *of Hameln 1646–1724, written by herself* 1962
Abrahams, Peter Henry *Dark testament* 1942
The path of thunder 1952
Return to Goli 1953
Wild conquest 1951
Abrahams, Roger D. ed. *Jump-rope rhymes: a dictionary* 1969
Positively black 1970
Abridgment of the English military discipline 1685
Abridgments of specifications of patents relating to agriculture, artificial leather, etc. 1617–1866 (1876–77)
Académie des Sciences (Paris) *Compte rendu hebdomadaire des séances* 1835–
Academy, The: a monthly record of literature, learning, science, and art 1869–99
Academy of Natural Sciences of Philadelphia *Proceedings* 1841–
Academy of Sciences of the U.S.S.R. *Doklady* [French ed.] 1935–47
Doklady: earth science sections 1959–
Soviet physics: Doklady [Eng. trans.] 1956–
Account of the depredations committed on the Clan Campbell and their followers, during 1685–86 16.. (1816)
Account of the French Settlements in North America 1746
Account of the present persecution of the Church in Scotland 1690
Account of proceedings at the Guildhall 13 Sept. 1679 1679
Account of several late voyages and discoveries 1694 (1711)
Account of workhouses 1732
Accountant, The 1874–
Account-book of Will. Wray c1600 (in Antiquary XXXII)
Accounts of the Exchequer of the King's Remembrancer v.d. (MSS. in Public Record Office)
Accounts of the Lord High Treasurer of Scotland 1473– (Scott. Record series 1877–)
Accounts of the Revels at Court, Extracts from the, with an introduction and notes by Peter Cunningham 15.. (Shaks. Soc. 1842)
Accum, Friedrich C. A. *Chemical tests* 1816 (1818)
Acerbi, Giuseppe *Travels through Sweden, Finland, and Lapland, to the North Cape 1798–99* 1802
Achebe, Chinua *Girls at war, and other stories* 1972
A man of the people 1966
Things fall apart 1958
Ackerley, Joe Randolph *My father and myself* 1968
Acland, Leopold George Dyke *The early Canterbury runs* (ser. 1) 1930
– (complete ed.) 1951
Acosta's (Joseph de) Naturall and morall historie of the East and West Indies tr. by E. G(rimstone) 1604
Acronyms dictionary (Gale Research Co.) 1960 (also later editions used, and supplements with title *New acronyms and initialisms*)
Act of Pennsylvania 1723
Acta crystallographica 1948–
Acta Dominorum Auditorum (*Acts of the Lords Auditors of Causes and Complaints*) 1466–94 (Record Comm. 1839)
Acta Dominorum Concilii (*Acts of the Lords of Council in civil causes*) 1478–95 (Record Comm. 1839)
Acta radiologica 1920–
Acton, Eliza *English bread-book* 1857
Modern cookery 1845
Acton, Eugenia de *The nuns of the desert* 1805
A tale without a title 1804
Acton, Harold Mario Mitchell *Memoirs of an aesthete* 1948
Actors by daylight; or, Pencillings in the pit 2 vols. 1838–9
Acts and ordinances made in the Parliament 1640–56 (ed. Henry Scobell 1658).
See also *Statutes*
Acts and proceedings of the general assemblies of the Kirk of Scotland (*Booke of the universall Kirk of Scotland*) 1560–1618 (Bannatyne Cl. 1839–45)
Acts of the Generall Assemblies of the Church of Scotland 1638–49 (1682)
Acts of the Parliaments of Scotland v.d. (1566, 1597, 1814–75)
Acts of the Privy Council of England 1542– (1890–)
Acts of Sederunt of the Lords of Council and Session 1553–1790 (1790)
Adair, James *The history of the American Indians* 1775
Adam, Alexander *Roman antiquities* 1791
Adam Bel, Clym of the Clough, and William of Cloudesly 15.. (Ritson 1791; Hazlitt 1864; Child 1888)
Adam Davy's five dreams about Edward II 13.. (E.E.T.S. 1878)
Adami, John George *The principles of pathology* 2 vols. 1909–10
Adams, Andy *The log of a cowboy* 1903
The outlet 1905
Adams, Arthur, et al. *A manual of natural history* 1854
Adams, Bertram Martin ('Bill') *Ships and women: an autobiography* 1936
Adams, Briggs Kilburn *The American spirit: letters* 1918
Adams, Carsbie Clifton, et al. *Space flight* 1958
Adams, Edwin Plimpton tr. *A. Einstein's The meaning of relativity* 1922
Adams, Francis W. L. *The new Egypt* 1893
Adams, Frank Davis *Aeronautical dictionary* 1959
Adams, George *Lectures on natural and experimental philosophy* 1794 (1806)
Micrographia illustrata; or the knowledge of the microscope explained 1746 (1747)
Adams, Henry *John Randolph* 1882
Adams, John *Works* a1826 (1850–56)
A defence of the constitutions of government of the United States of America 1787–88
Familiar letters of J. A. and his wife, Abigail Adams, during the Revolution 17.. (1876)
Adams, Ramon Frederick *Western words: a dictionary of the range, cow camp and trail* 1944
– (rev. ed.) 1968
Adams, Richard George *Shardik* 1974
Watership Down 1972
Adams, Thomas *Works* v.d. (1629, 1861–62)
The barren tree 1623
The blacke devill or the apostate 1615
A commentary or exposition upon the second epistle by St. Peter 1633 (1865)
Diseases of the soule 1616
The divells banket described in sixe sermons 1614
Eirenopolis; the citie of peace 1622
Englands sicknes, comparatively conferred with Israels 1615
The gallants burden 1612
The happiness of the church considered in contemplations upon Hebrewes 1618
Heaven and earth reconcil'd 1613
The Holy Choice 1625
Lycanthropy, or the wolfe worrying the lambes 1615
The sacrifice of thankefulnesse 1616
The sinners passing-bell; or a complaint from heaven of mans sinnes 1614
The spirituall navigator 1615
The white devil, or the hypocrite uncased 1613
Adams, W. Bridges *English pleasure carriages* 1837
Adams, William H. D. *Great rivers of the world: The Amazon and its wonders* 1879 (1883)
Adamson, Arthur Wilson *A textbook of physical chemistry* 1973
Adamson, Henry *The muses threnodie, or mirthfull mournings on the death of master Gall* 1638 (1774)
Adamson, Robert *Fichte* 1881
Adanson's (Michel) Voyage to Senegal, the Isle of Goree and the River Gambia tr. 1759
Adburgham, Alison *Shops and shopping, 1800–1914* 1964
Adby, Paul Raymond & Dempster, Michael Alan Howarth *Introduction to optimization methods* 1974
Adderley, A. J. *The fisheries of the Bahamas* 1883 (Fisheries exhibition literature)
Addis, William E. & Arnold, Thomas *A Catholic dictionary containing some account of the doctrine, discipline, rites of the Catholic Church* 1884 (also 1897)
Addison, Alexander *Report of cases in the County Courts of the Fifth Circuit of Pennsylvania* 1800
Addison, Joseph *Works* v.d. (1721, 1726–27, 1758)
Cato 1712 (1721)
Count Tariff 1713
Dialogues upon the usefulness of ancient medals 1702 (1727)
The drummer, or the haunted house 1715 (1721)
Essay on 'Paradise Lost' 1719 (Arber)
The Freeholder 1716 (1751)
The Freethinker a1719 (1722)
Poems 1705 (1726)
The present state of the war 1707 (1746)
Remarks on Italy 1705 (1733)
Rosamond 1707 (1726)
The Spectator 1711–14
The Tatler 1709–10
The Whig Examiner 1710–12
See also Garth, Sir S.
Addison, Lancelot *The first state of Mahumedism* 1678 (1679)
The life and death of Mahumed 1679
The present state of the Jews in Barbary 1675
West Barbary 1671
Addleshaw, W. P. *See* Hemingway, Percy
Addy, Sidney O. *A glossary of words used in the neighbourhood of Sheffield* 1888. *Suppl.* 1891 (E.D.S.)
Addyman, Frank T. tr. *A. M. Villon's Practical treatise on the leather industry* 1901
Ade, George *Artie* 1896
Doc' Horne 1899
Fables in slang 1900 (UK 1902)
Forty modern fables 1901
Hand-made fables 1920
In Babel 1903
Knocking the neighbors 1912
Letters ed. T. Tobin 1973
More fables 1900 (UK 1902)
People you know 1903
True bills 1904
Adelphi, The 1923–7, 1930–
Adler, George J. *Fauriel's History of Provençal poetry* tr. 1860
Adlington, William *Apuleius: The XI bookes of the Golden asse, with the marriage of Cupido and Psiches* 1566 (1893)
Administration of affairs in Scotland under the Duke of Lauderdale 1679
Admiralty *See* United Kingdom. Admiralty
Admonycion, A faythfull, of a certen trewe pastor (tr. from Luther) 1554
Advances in chemistry series 1950–
Advances in genetics 1947–
Adventure (New York) 1910–
Adventurer, The (by Hawkesworth, Johnson, etc.) 1753–54
Adventures of Captain Robert Boyle 1726 *See* Chetwood, W. R.
Advice to a painter; being a satyr upon the French King, etc. 1692
Advisory Committee for Aeronautics *See* United Kingdom. Advisory ——
Advocate-News (Barbados) 1895–
Ady, Thomas *A candle in the dark; or, a treatise concerning the nature of witches and witchcraft* 1656
Ælfred *Boethius De consolatione philosophiae* tr. c888 (Sedgefield 1899)
Gregory's Pastoral care tr. c897 (E.E.T.S. 1871)
Orosius tr. c893 (E.E.T.S. 1883)
Soliloquien des Augustinus (= *Blooms*) c900 (1922)
Soliloquia Augustini selecta (Cockayne 1864–70)
Ælfric *De veteri et de novo testamento* c1000 (Grein 1872; E.E.T.S. 1922)
Genesis, Exodus, etc. c1000 (Grein 1872; E.E.T.S. 1922)
Grammar c1000 (Zupitza 1880)
Homilies c1000 (Thorpe 1844–46)
Lives of saints c1000 (E.E.T.S. 1881–85)
See also *Fragment*
Aeronautical journal 1897–1923, 1968–
Aeronautical Research Committee (*later* Council) *See* United Kingdom. Advisory Committee for Aeronautics
Aëronautical Society of Great Britain *Annual Report* 1866–95
Aeronautics 1939–
Aeroplane, The 1911–68 (with title *The Aeroplane and astronautics* 1959–62, and *The Aeroplane and commercial aviation news* 1962–8)
Aeroplane spotter, The 1941–8
Æthelwold *Anglo-Saxon Benedictine rule* c960 (Schröer 1885)

Affecting narrative of the catastrophe of his majesty's ship 'Wager' 1751
Aflalo, Frederick George *A sketch of the natural history of Australia* 1896
Africa. Journal of the International Institute of African Languages and Culture 1928-40, 1943-
African encyclopedia 1974
Agar, Wilfred Eade *Cytology, with special reference to the Metazoan nucleus* 1920
Agassiz, Louis J. R. *Scientific results of a journey in Brazil* 1871
Agate, James Evershed *More first nights* 1937
Red letter nights 1944
Age, The (Melbourne) 1859-
Agger, Leo Thomas *Introduction to electricity* 1971
Agiatis, Queen of Sparta, or the civil wars of the Lacedemonians tr. 1686
Aglionby, William *Painting illustrated in three dialogues* 1685
Agnel, H. R. *Chess for winter evenings* 1848
Agnew, David C. A. *Theology of consolation* 1881
Agricultural and biological chemistry 1955-
Agricultural surveys of Great Britain and Ireland, and Scotland 1793-1815
Agriculture 1939-
Agrippa's Vanity of arts and sciences tr. 1684. See also Sanford, J.
Aharoni, Joseph *The special theory of relativity* 1959
Aiken, Joan Delano *The butterfly picnic* 1972
Last movement 1977
Aiken, John *Nightly deadshade* 1971
Aikin, Arthur *A dictionary of chemistry and mineralogy* 1807-14
Ailesbury, Thomas *The passion sermon at Pauls-Crosse, April 7 1626*
A sermon preached at Pauls-Crosse the second day of June, 1622 1623
Ailesbury, Thomas Bruce, 2nd Earl of *Memoirs* 17.. (Roxb. Cl. 1890)
Ainger, Arthur C. *See* Heathcote, C. G.
Ainslie, Hew *A pilgrimage to the land of Burns: and poems* 1822, *a*1878 (1892)
Ainsworth, Henry *Annotations upon Genesis* 1616; *Exodus* 1617; *Leviticus* 1618; *Numbers* 1619; *Deuteronomie* 1619; *the book of Psalms* 1617
Annotations upon the five bookes of Moses and the booke of Psalmes 1622; *and the Song of Songs* 1627 (1639)
Ainsworth, Leopold *Confessions of a planter in Malaya* 1933
'Ainsworth, Milo' (Peter Fison) *Murder is catching* 1959
Ainsworth, Robert *Thesaurus linguæ Latinæ compendiarius* 1736 (1773, etc.)
Ainsworth, William Harrison *Crichton* 1837
Jack Sheppard 1839
John Law 1864 (1881)
The Lancashire witches 1848
Merry England 1874
The miser's daughter 1842
Old St. Paul's 1841
Ovingdean Grange 1860
Rookwood 1834
Saint James's, or the court of Q. Anne 1844
Tower Hill 1871
The Tower of London 1840
Windsor Castle 1843
Ainsworth's magazine 1842-54
Air Conference [London], 1920 *Proceedings* 1920
Air News (Chicago) 1941-6
Aircraft engineering 1929-
'Aird, Catherine' (Kinn Hamilton McIntosh) *Henrietta who?* 1968
Aird, Thomas *Poetical works* 1848, 1856
Memoir of D. M. Moir 1852
Airth, Rennie *Snatch!* 1969
Airy, George B. *Astronomy* 1851-59 (in Manual of scientific enquiry)
Undulatory theory of optics 1866
Aitchison, Charles U. *A collection of treaties, etc. relating to India and neighbouring countries* 1876-78
Aitken, Adam Jack, McIntosh, A., & Pálsson, H. eds. *Edinburgh studies in English and Scots* 1971
Aitken, William *The science and practice of medicine* 1863 (1866)
Aitken, William *Automatic telephone systems* 3 vols., 1921-4
Aiton, John *Manual of domestic economy for clergymen* 1842 (1857)
Aiton, William *Hortus Kewensis; or, A catalogue of plants cultivated in the Royal Botanic Garden at Kew* 3 vols. 1789
—(ed. 2, ed. by W. T. Aiton) 5 vols. 1810-13
Aiton, William *General view of the agriculture of the county Ayr 1811*
Akenside, Mark *Poems* v.d. (1790)
The pleasures of imagination 1744
— revised ed. (1788)
Akerman, John Y. *A glossary of provincial words and phrases in use in Wiltshire* 1842
Alabaster, Henry *The wheel of the law: Buddhism illustrated from Siamese sources* 1871
Albanesi, Effie Maria *For love of Anne Lambert* 1910
Albee, Edward *Who's afraid of Virginia Woolf?* 1962
Albemarle, George Monk, 1st Duke of *Observations upon military and political affairs* 1671
Albert, Abraham Adrian *Modern higher algebra* 1937 (UK 1938)
Albert, Arthur Lemuel *Fundamentals of telephony* 1943
Radio fundamentals 1948
Alberta historical review 1957-
Albery, James *Dramatic works* ed. W. Albery 2 vols. 1939
Albin, Eleazar *A natural history of birds* 1731-38
A natural history of English insects 1720
Albion's triumph, a poem 1705
Albright, William Foxwell *The archaeology of Palestine* 1949
Alcilia 1613 *See* C., I. or J.
Alcock, Bp. John *Mons perfeccionis, the hyll of perfeccion* 1496 (1497)
*Sermo pro episcopo puerorum c*1496 (W. de Worde)
Alcock, Leslie *By South Cadbury* 1972
Alcock, Sir Rutherford *The capital of the Tycoon: three years in Japan* 1863
Alcoran of Mahomet 1649 *See* Ross, A.
Alcott, Amos B. *Table-talk* 1877
Alcott, Louisa M. *Hospital sketches, and camp and fireside stories* 1863
Little men 1871
Little women 1868 (1869)
An old-fashioned girl 1870
Alday, John *Boaystuau's Theatrum mundi, the theatre or rule of the world* tr. 1566
Alden, William Livingston *The adventures of Jimmy Brown* 1885
*Aldhelm glosses a*1100 (Napier 1900)
Aldington, Richard *All men are enemies* 1933
The colonel's daughter 1931
Death of a hero 1929
The strange life of Charles Waterton 1782-1865 1949
Aldiss, Brian Wilson *The airs of earth* 1963
The moment of eclipse 1970
A soldier erect 1971
—— & Harrison, Harry Max eds. *Decade: the 1950's* 1976
Decade: the 1940's 1975
Aldrich, Thomas B. *Marjorie Daw, and other people* 1873
Prudence Palfrey 1874 (1885)
The story of a bad boy 1869
Alexander 1340-70 (Roxb. Cl. 1849, App.) (= *Alexander and Dindimus*, E.E.T.S. 1878)
*Alexander, Alliterative romance of, a*1400-50 (Roxb. Cl. 1849) (= *The Wars of Alexander*, E.E.T.S. 1866)
*Alexander, Prose life of c*1420 (E.E.T.S. 1913)
'Alexander, Mrs.' (Mrs. Annie F. Hector) *The admiral's ward* 1883
A choice of evils 3 vols. 1894
Stronger than love 1902
Alexander, James Edward *An expedition of discovery into the interior of Africa* 2 vols. 1838
Sketches in Portugal during the Civil War of 1834 1835
Alexander, Jerome *Colloid chemistry, theoretical and applied* 6 vols. 1926-46
Alexander, Samuel *Space, time and deity* 2 vols. 1920
Alexander, Sir William *a*1640 *See* Stirling, Earl of
Alexander, William *The history of women* 1779 (1782)
Alexander, William *Johnny Gibb of Gushetneuk* 1871
Sketches of life among my ain folk 1875
Alexander, Bp. William *St. Augustine's holiday, and other poems* 1886
Alexander, William L. *Dorner's (Isaac A.) Development of the doctrine of the person of Christ* tr. 1861-63 (1872)
*Alexius, The legend or life of St. c*1400 (E.E.T.S. 1878)
Alexopoulos, Constantine John *Introductory mycology* 1952
—(ed. 2) 1962
Alford, Henry *Essays and addresses, chiefly on Church subjects* 1869
Alger, William R. *History of the doctrine of a future life* 1858
The solitudes of nature and of man 1866
Algren, Nelson *The man with the golden arm* 1949
A walk on the wild side 1956 (UK 1957)
Alice, Princess *Biographical sketch and letters a*1878 (1884)
Alienist and neurologist 1880-
Alingham, William *Geometry epitomized* 1695
Alisaunder, King 13.. (Weber 1810; MS. Laud Misc. 622)
Alisaunder of Macedoine 1340-70 (E.E.T.S. 1867, App.)
Alison, Archibald *History of Europe* 1833-42 (1849-53)
Alison, Richard *Cantus Primus. An howres recreation in musicke, apt for instrumentes and voyces* 1606 (Arber, Eng. Garner VI)
All the year round 1859-95
Allan-Olney, Mary *The New Virginians* 1880
Allbeury, Theo Edward Le Bouthillier ('Ted') *A choice of enemies* 1973
The lantern network 1978
The only good German 1976
Snowball 1974
The special collection 1975
Allbutt, Thomas C. *On visceral neuroses* 1884
ed. *A system of medicine: by many writers* 1896-99
Allee, Warder Clyde *Animal aggregations: a study in general sociology* 1931
Alleine, Joseph *An alarme to unconverted sinners a*1668 (1672)
*A sure guide to heaven a*1668 (1691)
The life and death of J. A.; whereunto are annexed diverse Christian letters, and his funeral sermon preached by Mr. Newton (1672, 1677)
Alleine, Richard *Vindiciæ pietatis: or, a vindication of godliness from the imputations of folly and fancy* 1663
Allen, Arthur Charles *The skin: a clinico-pathological treatise* 1954
—(ed. 2) 1967
Allen, Clifford *A textbook of psychosexual disorders* 1962
—(ed. 2) 1969
Allen, David Elliston *British tastes: an enquiry into the likes and dislikes of the regional consumer* 1968
Allen, Edmund *The paraphrase of Erasmus vpon the Epistle of S. Paule to the Philippians* tr. 1549
The paraphrase or commentarie (of Leo Jude) vpon the Reuelacion of S. Iohn tr. 1549
Allen, Frederick Lewis *Only yesterday: an informal history of the nineteen-twenties* 1931
Allen, Geoffrey Freeman *British Rail after Beeching* 1966
Allen, Grant *Babylon* 1885
The colour-sense 1879
Life of Charles Darwin 1886
The evolutionist at large 1881
In all shades 1886
Kalee's shrine 1886
For Maimie's sake 1886
Philistia 1884
The scallywag 1893
The type-writer girl 1897
Allen, Herbert Stanley *Photo-electricity: the liberation of electrons by light* 1913
—(ed. 2) 1925
Allen, Ira *Natural and political history of Vermont* 1798
Allen, James Lane *The choir invisible* 1897
Allen, Joel A. *The American bison* 1876
Allen, John *No acceptance with God by faith only* 1761
Allen, John *History of the borough of Liskeard* 1856
Allen, Jules Verne *Cowboy lore* 1933
Allen, Percy Stafford *Letters* ed. H. M. Allen 1939
Allen, Ralph *Home made banners* 1946
Allen, Reginald Lancelot Mountford *Colour chemistry* 1971
Allen, William *An admonition to the nobility and people of England and Ireland* 1588
An apologie and true declaration of the institution, etc. of the two English Colleges, Rome, Rhemes, etc. 1581
A defense and declaration of the catholike churches doctrine touching purgatorie 1565
Allen, William 1657 *See* Titus, Silius
Allen, William *Danger of enthusiasm* 1674
A persuasive to peace and unity among Christians 1680
A persuasive to piety 1680
A serious and friendly address to non-conformists 1676
Allen, William Hervey *Anthony Adverse* 1933
Allen, William Sidney *Vox Graeca: a guide to the pronunciation of classical Greek* 1968
Vox Latina: a guide to the pronunciation of classical Latin 1965
Allestree, Richard *Forty sermons a*1681 (1684)
Allestree, Thomas *A funeral handkerchief* 1691
Alleyn papers, The; a collection of original documents illustrative of the life of Ed. Alleyn, and of the early English stage and drama, with an introduction by J. Payne Collier 15..-16.. (Shaks. Soc. 1843)
Allies, Thomas W. *Peter's rock in Mohammed's flood* 1890
Allinger, Norman Louis, et al. *Organic chemistry* 1971
Allingham, John T. *Fortune's frolic; a farce* 1799
Allingham, Margery Louise *The beckoning lady* 1955
Cargo of eagles 1968
Coroner's pidgin 1945
Dancers in mourning 1937
Death of a ghost 1934
The fashion in shrouds 1938
Flowers for the judge 1936
Hide my eyes 1958
Look to the lady 1931
Mr. Campion and others 1939
—(another ed.) 1950
More work for the undertaker 1948 (UK 1949)
Mystery mile 1930
The tiger in the smoke 1952
Traitor's purse 1941
Allingham, Philip *Cheapjack* 1934
Allingham, William *Poems* 1857
Allis, Marguerite *English prelude* 1936
Alliterative poems See *Early English Alliterative Poems*; *Scottish Alliterative Poems*
Allman, George J. *Introductory lecture delivered to the students of the natural history class in the University of Edinburgh* 1855
A monograph of the gymnoblastic or tubularian hydroids 1871-72
Allnutt, Zachariah *Considerations on the best mode of improving the navigation of the river Thames from Richmond to Staines* 1805
Allott, Robert *Englands Parnassus; or the choysest flowers of our moderne poets* 1600 (1815)
Wits theater of the little world 1599
Allport, Gordon Willard *The nature of prejudice* 1954
Personality: a psychological interpretation 1937 (UK 1938)
Allum, Peter Antony *Politics and society in post-war Naples 1945-1970* 1971 (UK 1973)
Almedingen, Edith Martha *Frossia* 1943
Almon, John *Anecdotes of William Pitt* 1792
Almond for a parrat, An (attributed to T. Nashe) 1589
Almondbury and Huddersfield, Glossary of the dialect of. Compiled by the late Alfred Easther, ed. by Thomas Lees 1883 (E.D.S.)
*Alphabet of tales c*1440 (E.E.T.S. 1904-05)
*Alphita a*1400 (Anecd. Oxon. 1887)
Alsop, George *The character of the Province of Maryland* 1666 (1869)

ALSOP, Vincent *Anti-Sozzo, sive Sherlocismus enervatus* (anon.) 1675
Melius inquirendum; or, a sober inquiry, etc. (anon.) 1678 (1681)
The mischief of impositions (anon.) 1680
ALSTON, Arthur Reginald *Test commentary* 1956
Alta California (San Francisco) 1849–91
Altenglische Dichtungendes MS. Harl. 2253, c1310 (Böddeker 1878)
Althorp MS. (Household Book) 16.. (in Simpkinson, *The Washingtons* (1860) App.)
Amadace, Sir c1420 (Camden Soc. 1842)
Amadas, Sir c1420 (Weber 1810)
Amateur gardening 1884–
Amateur photographer, The 1884–
Amateur radio handbook, The (Radio Society of Great Britain) 1939
— (ed. 2) 1940
— (ed. 3) 1961
— (ed. 4, with title *The radio communication handbook*) 1968
AMBLER, Eric *Cause for alarm* 1938
The dark frontier 1936
Doctor Frigo 1974
The light of day 1962
The mask of Dimitrios 1939
The night-comers 1956
Uncommon danger 1937
AMBROSE, Edmund Jack & EASTY, Dorothy M. *Cell biology* 1970
AMBROSE, Isaac *Prima, media, et ultima; the first, middle, and last things* 1650
AMBROSE, Kay *The ballet-lover's pocket-book* 1943
Amelot de la Houssaye's (A. N.) History of the government of Venice tr. 1677
American, The: a national journal 1880–1900
American Academy of Arts and Sciences *Bulletin* 1948–
Memoirs 1785–1818, new ser. 1826–
Proceedings 1846–1958 (continued as *Dædalus*)
American Academy of Political and Social Science *Annals* 1890–
American anthropologist 1888–
American Association for the Advancement of Science *Proceedings* 1848–
American Association of Petroleum Geologists *Bulletin* 1918–
Memoirs 1962–
American ballads and folk songs ed. J. A. & A. Lomax 1934
American chemical journal 1879–1913
American Chemical Society *Journal* 1879–
American city, The 1909–
American Dialect Society *Publications* 1944–
American dictionary of printing and bookmaking ed. W. W. Pasko 1894
American documentation 1950–69
American dyestuff reporter 1917–
American folk music occasional 1964–
American Geological Institute *Glossary of geology and related sciences* 1957
— (ed. 2), with Supplement, 1960
— (ed. 3) 1972
American geologist 1885–
American heart journal 1925–
American Institute of Electrical Engineers *Transactions* 1884–
American journal of anatomy 1901–
American journal of diseases of children 1911–
American journal of mathematics 1878–
American journal of the medical sciences 1827–
American journal of obstetrics and diseases of women and children 1868– (from 1920 with title *American journal of obstetrics and gynecology*)
American journal of ophthalmology 1884–
American journal of pathology 1925–
American journal of philology 1880–
American journal of physical anthropology 1918–
American journal of physics 1940–
American journal of physiology 1898–
American journal of psychiatry 1921–
American journal of psychology 1887–
American journal of public health 1912–
American journal of roentgenology 1913–
American journal of science 1818–
American journal of sociology 1895–
American machinist, The 1877–
American magazine 1906–
American mail order fashions, 1880–1900: pictures and copy reproduced from original catalogs and magazines of the times (Americana Review) 1961
American Mathematical Society *Bulletin* 1894–
Transactions 1900–
American Medical Association *Journal* 1883–
American Mercury, The 1924–
American mineralogist, The 1916–
American museum, The 1787–92, 1798
American Museum of Natural History *Bulletin* 1881–
Memoirs 1893–
American naturalist 1867–
American notes and queries 1857, 1888–92, 1941–50, 1962–
American Oriental Society *Journal* 1843–
American Pediatric Society *Transactions* 1888–
American Philological Association *Transactions* 1869–
American philosophical quarterly 1964–
American Philosophical Society *Proceedings* 1838–
Transactions 1769–
American pioneer, The 1842–3
American poetry review 1972–
American political science review 1906–
American railroad journal 1832–86
American review of reviews 1907–28
American Society for Metals *Metals handbook* 1936–
American Society for Testing Materials *Proceedings* 1898–
American speech 1925–
American Veterinary Medical Association *Journal* 1915–
American Water Works Association *Journal* 1914–
Americana annual, The: an encyclopedia of current events 1923–
AMES, Delano L. *Murder, maestro, please* 1952
AMES, Joseph *Typographical antiquities* 1749
— considerably augmented by W. Herbert (1785–90)
AMES, William *A fresh suit against human ceremonies in Gods worship* 1633
The marrow of sacred divinity tr. 1642
Saint's security a1633 (1652)
AMHERST, Nicholas *An epistle to Sir John Blount* 1720
Terræ filius: or the secret history of the university of Oxford 1721–22 (1754)
AMIN, Adibah tr. *S. Ahmad's No harvest but a thorn* 1972
AMIS, Kingsley William *The anti-death league* 1966
Girl, 20 1971
I like it here 1958
Jake's thing 1978
Lucky Jim 1954 [dated 1953]
New maps of hell: a survey of science fiction 1960 (UK 1961)
Take a girl like you 1960
AMIS, Martin Louis *The Rachel papers* 1973
Success 1978
Amis and Amiloun c1330 (Weber 1810; Kölbing 1884)
AMORY, Thomas *The life of John Buncle* 1756–66 (1770)
Memoirs of several ladies of Great Britain 1755 (1766–69)
AMOS, Stanley William & BIRKINSHAW, Douglas Crosbie *Television engineering* 4 vols. 1953–8
— Vol. I, 2nd impr., rev. 1957
— Vol. II, 2nd impr., rev. 1958
Amrita Bazar Patrika (Calcutta) 1868–
AMYOT, Thomas *Some account of the life of William Windham* 1812
Amyraldus' Treatise concerning religions tr. 1660
Analog science fact—science fiction (title varies) 1960–
Analysis 1933–
Analyst, The: a journal of pure and applied mathematics 1874–
Anatomical record 1906–
Ancient ballads and songs of the North of Scotland v.d. (ed. Buchan 1828)
Ancient constitution and government of England, A brief enquiry into 1695
Ancient cookery 1381 (in Warner, Antiq. culin. 1791)
Ancient cookery a1400 (in Household ordinances 1790)
Ancient laws and customs of the Burghs of Scotland 1124–1424 (Burgh Rec. Soc. 1868)
Ancient poems, ballads, and songs of the peasantry of England v.d. (Percy Soc. 1846)
Ancient popular poetry v.d. (ed. Ritson 1791)
Ancient songs v.d. (ed. Ritson 1790, Hazlitt 1877)
Ancient trades decayed 1678
Ancren riwle a1225 (Camden Soc. 1853)
ANDERDON, John L. *Life of T. Ken* 1851
Anderida; or, the Briton and the Saxon 1875
ANDERSON, Æneas *A narrative of the British embassy to China in 1792–94* 1795
ANDERSON, Alexander *Joseph the bookman, a heroic-comic poem. By a gent* 1821
ANDERSON, Anthony *An exposition of the hymne commonly called Benedictus* 1573
A godlie sermon preached on newe yeeres day last, before Sir W. Fitzwilliam 1576
ANDERSON, David *Poems, English and Scotch* 1813
ANDERSON, Gene *Coring and core analysis handbook* 1975
ANDERSON, J. W. *Fur trader's story* 1961
ANDERSON, James *Essays relating to agriculture. By a farmer* 1775
General view of the agriculture and rural economy of the county of Aberdeen 1794
ANDERSON, James M. *Structural aspects of language change* 1973
ANDERSON, John Neil *Applied dental materials* 1956
— (ed. 2) 1961
ANDERSON, John Richard Lane *Death on the rocks* 1973
ANDERSON, Lewis Flint *The Anglo-Saxon scop* 1903
ANDERSON, Maxwell & STALLINGS, Laurence *What price glory?* in *Three American plays* 1926
ANDERSON, Nels *The hobo* 1923
ANDERSON, Rasmus B. *Rydberg's Teutonic mythology* tr. 1889
ANDERSON, Robert *Cumberland ballads* a1833 (c1850)
ANDERSON, Robert Henry *The trees of New South Wales* 1932
— (ed. 2) 1947
ANDERSON, Rufus *History of the missions of the American Board of Commissioners for Foreign Missions* 1870–74
ANDERSON, William *Regeneration* 1850 (1871)
ANDERSON, William Arnold D. ed. *Pathology* 1948
Anderson (South Carolina) *Independent* 1924– (1925–49 with title *Anderson Independent-Tribune*)
ANDERSSON, Carl J. *Lake Ngami; or, Explorations and discoveries, during four years' wanderings in the wilds of South Western Africa* 1856
The Okavango River 1861
ANDERTON, Thomas *The history of the iconoclasts* 1671
'ANDOM, R.' (Alfred Walter Barrett) *We three and Troddles* 1894
ANDRADE, Edward Neville da Costa *The structure of the atom* 1923
— (ed. 3) 1927
Andreas a1000 (Kemble 1844; Grein 1888)
ANDREE, Richard Vernon *Selections from modern abstract algebra* 1958
ANDREW, Laurence *Jherom Brunswyke's Vertuose boke of distyllation* tr. 1527
Noble lyfe c1520
ANDREW, Warren tr. *E. D. P. de Robertis's General cytology* 1948
Textbook of comparative histology 1959
ANDREWES, Lancelot *Sermons* a1626 (1629, 1661, 1841)
ANDREWS, Tom Gaylord ed. *Methods of psychology* 1948
ANDREWS, William E. *Critical review of Foxe's Book of martyrs* 1824–26
Andros tracts: being a collection of pamphlets and official papers issued between the overthrow of the Andros Government and the establishment of the second Charter of Massachusetts 1688–1701 (Prince Soc. 1868–74)
ANDROSE, Richard *Alexis' (= Alessio's) Very excellent booke. The fourth and finall booke of secretes* tr. 1568 (1569)
Anecdota literaria v.d. (Wright 1844)
Anecdota Oxoniensia. Texts, documents, and extracts chiefly from manuscripts in the Bodleian and other Oxford libraries. Mediaeval and modern series v.d. (1882–)
ANGELO, Henry *The school of fencing* 1765
ANGELO, Henry *His reminiscences, with memoirs of his late father and friends* 1828
ANGIER, John *Lancashire's Valley of Achor is England's doore of hope* (anon.) 1643
Anglesea, A minute account of the social condition of the people of 1613 (Halliwell 1860)
Anglia: Zeitschrift für englische Philologie 1878–
Anglia rediviva 1647 *See* SPRIGGE, Joshua
Anglo-American cataloguing rules: British text 1967
Anglo-Saxon chronicle, The v.d. (Thorpe, Rolls series 1861; Earle 1865; Earle and Plummer 1892, 1899)
Anglo-Saxon Gospels c1000 (Skeat 1871–87)
Anglo-Saxon hymnarium c1000 See *Hymns*
Anglo-Saxon Laws v.d. (Thorpe 1840; Schmid 1858; Liebermann 1898)
Anglo-Saxon Psalter See *Psalter*
ANGUS, Henry *Sermons* 1861
Animadversions on the last speeches of the five Jesuits 1679
Animal management (War Office) 1908
Annalia Dubrensia, vpon the yeerely celebration of Mr. Robert Dovers Olimpick Games vpon Cotswold-Hills, written by Drayton etc. 1636 (Grosart 1877)
Annals of agriculture and other useful arts; collected and published by Arthur Young 1784–1815
Annals of the Barber-Surgeons of London, compiled from their records and other sources, by Sidney Young v.d. (1890)
Annals of botany 1887–
Annals of internal medicine 1927–
Annals of mathematics 1884–9; 1900–
Annals of natural history 1838–40; continued as *The annals and magazine of natural history* 1841–
Annals of philosophy; a periodical publication. By T. Thomson 1813–20
Annals of surgery 1885–
Annals of the Congress of the U.S. *See* United States. Congress. Debates *Debates and proceedings* 1789–1824
Annals of tropical medicine and parasitology 1907–
Annals See also under the names of particular institutions
ANNAN, Noel Gilroy *Leslie Stephen* 1951
ANNAND, William *Mysterium pietatis or mysterie of godlinesse* 1671
ANNANDALE, Charles *Ogilvie's Imperial dictionary of the English language* 1881–83
Annesley (Samuel), The character of, by way of elegy 1697
Anniversary, The, or poetry and prose for 1829. Edited by Allan Cunningham 1829
Annual register, The (incl. Dodsley's; also separate publ. of Rivington, Otridge, etc.) 1758–
Annual reports of the Deputy Keeper of the Public Records v.d. (1840–)
Annual reports on the progress of chemistry (Chemical Society of London) 1904–
Annual review and History of literature 1803–09
Annual review of microbiology 1947–
Annual review of nuclear science 1952–
Anois' (Countess d') Works tr. 1707 (1715)
The ingenious and diverting letters of the Lady (Countess d'Anois); travels into Spain tr. 1692 (1697)
ANSCOMBE, Gertrude Elizabeth Margaret tr. *L. J. J. Wittgenstein's Philosophical investigations* 1953
ANSOFF, Harry Igor *Corporate strategy: an analytic approach to business policy for growth and expansion* 1965 (UK 1968)
ANSON, Peter Frederick *Bishops at large* 1964
Scots fisherfolk 1950
Anson's (George) Voyage round the world, compiled from his papers 1748
ANSTED, David T. *The ancient world* 1847
Elementary course of geology etc. 1850
Geology 1844
Manual of geographical science 1852
—— & LATHAM, Robert G. *The Channel Islands* 1862
ANSTEY, Christopher *An Election Ball* 1776
The new Bath guide 1766 (1767, 1807)

'ANSTEY, F.' (T. A. Guthrie) *The pariah* 1889
The tinted Venus, a farcical romance 1885
Vice versâ, or a lesson to fathers 1882
Voces populi 1890, 1892
ANSTEY, John *The pleader's guide* 1796 (1803)
ANSTEY, Thomas C. *Notes upon 'The representation of the people Act'* 1867
ANSTIE, Francis E. *Report on practical medicine* 1867 (in Biennial retrospect med., New Syd. Soc.)
Answer out of the West to a question out of the North 1667
Answer to Cartwright c1585 *See* BROWNE, R.
Answer to Fontenelle's History of oracles tr. 1709
Answer to observations against the King 1642
Answer to Sacheverell's Assize sermon at S. Mary's Oxford 1704
Answer to Dr. Stillingfleet's sermon, by some nonconformists 1680
Answer to Talon's Plea 1688
Answer to two papers, called a Lords speech without doors and a Commoners speech 1689
Answere to a papystycall exhortacyon c1548 *See* BALE, J.
Antecrist c1380 in Todd *Three treat. Wyclif* (1851) (= *Cursor Mundi* ll. 21975–22426)
'ANTHONY, Evelyn' (Eve Stephens) *The Malaspiga exit* 1974
Anthony's Photographic bulletin 1889–91
Anthropological linguistics 1959–
Antibiotic medicine 1955–61 (from 1956 with title *Antibiotic medicine and clinical therapy*)
Antibiotics and chemotherapy 1951–62
Anti-Coton, or A refutation of (Petrus) Cottons letter declaratorie tr. by G. H. 1611
Antidote to miseries of human life 1807
Anti-Jacobin, The poetry of The 1798 (1800)
Antipodean notes: nine months' tour round the world, by Wanderer 1888
Antiquaries' journal 1921–
Antiquary, The 1880–
Antiquitates Sarisburienses 1771 *See* LEDWICH, Edward
Antiquity: a quarterly review of archæology 1927–
Antrim and Down, A glossary of words in use in the counties of. By W. H. Patterson 1880 (E.D.S.)
ANTROBUS, Frederick I. *Pastor's History of the Popes from the close of the Middle Ages* tr. 1894–1924
Anturs of Arther c1400 (Bannatyne Cl. 1839; Camden Soc. 1842; Laing 1885; S.T.S. 1897)
Anzac book, The: written and illustrated in Gallipoli by the men of Anzac 1916
APEL, Willi ed. *The Harvard dictionary of music* 1944
—(ed. 2) 1970
Apollonius of Tyre, Anglo-Saxon version of the story of, a1000 (Thorpe 1834)
Apologeticall relation of the particular sufferings of the faithfull ministers etc. of the Church of Scotland (by John Brown) 1665
Apology for the clergy of Scotland 1693
Apology for Mr. John Goodwin 1653
Apology for Lollard doctrines c1400 (Camden Soc. 1842)
Apology for the Protestants of France 1683
APPERLEY, Charles J. *The chase, turf, and road* 1837 (1851)
Appleton's Annual cyclopædia 1875–
Approved names *See* United Kingdom. General Medical Council
APTHORP, East *Letters on the prevalence of Christianity before its civil establishment* 1778
Arabian Nights tr. c1850 (Routledge)
Arabian Nights' entertainments tr. 1712 (1785)
Arable farmer and vegetable grower 1966–
ARBER, Agnes *The Gramineae: a study of cereal, bamboo, and grass* 1934
Water plants: a study of aquatic angiosperms 1920
ARBER, Edward ed. *An English Garner* v.d. (1877–96)
ed. *English reprints* v.d. (1868–71)
ed. *The English scholar's library* v.d. (1878–84)
See also EDEN, Richard
ARBUTHNOT, John *Works* a1735 (1751)
An essay concerning the nature of aliments 1731 (1735)
An essay on the effects of air on human bodies 1733
Law is a bottomless pit. Exemplified in the case of the Lord Strutt, John Bull, Nicholas Frog, and Lewis Baboon 1712 (in Arber, Eng. Garner VI)
A learned dissertation on dumpling 1726
Rules of diet 1732
Tables of the Grecian, Roman, and Jewish measures, weights, and coins 1705
—— et al. *Memoirs of Martinus Scriblerus* c1714
ARCH, Joseph *The story of his life, by himself* 1898
Archaeologia: or Miscellaneous tracts relating to antiquity Published by the Society of Antiquaries of London v.d. (1770–)
Archaeologia Æliana: or, Miscellaneous tracts relating to antiquity. Published by the Society of Antiquaries of Newcastle upon Tyne v.d. (1816–)
Archæologia Cantiana; being Transactions of the Kent Archæological Society 1858–
Archaica 1815 *See* BRYDGES, Sir S. E.
ARCHBOLD, John *The beauty of holines* 1621
ARCHBOLD, William A. J. *Somerset religious houses* 1892
ARCHER, William *The theatrical 'world'* 5 vols. 1894–8
Archers, Poems on archers and the Royal Company of 1726
Architect, The (title varies) 1869–
Architectural Publication Society *Dictionary of architecture* 1852–92
Architectural review 1896–
Archiv für das Studium der neueren Sprachen und Literaturen (Herrig, etc.) 1846–
Archives internationales de pharmacodynamie et de thérapie 1898–
Archives of biochemistry 1924– (from 1951 with title *Archives of biochemistry and biophysics*)
Archives of dermatology and syphilology (title varies) 1920–
Archives of general psychiatry 1959–
Archives of internal medicine 1908–
Archives of Maryland 1883–
Archives of neurology (London) 1899–1907
Archives of neurology and psychiatry (London) 1909–50
Archives of neurology and psychiatry (Chicago) 1919–59
Archives of ophthalmology 1879–
Archives of pathology 1928–
Archives of surgery 1920–
Archivum linguisticum 1949–80 (vols. 1970–80 are new series)
Archmagirus Anglo-Gallicus 1658
Archpriest controversy, The 1597–1602 (Camden Soc. 1896–98)
Arctic terms 1955 *See* United States. Arctic, Desert and Tropic Information Centre
ARDAGH, John *The new France* 1970
Arden of Feversham, The lamentable and true tragedie of 1592 (in Shakespeare Apocrypha 1908)
Arderne's (John) Treatises of fistula in ano tr. a1425 (E.E.T.S. 1910)
ARDREY, Robert *The territorial imperative* 1966 (UK 1967)
ARENDT, Hannah *Origins of totalitarianism* 1951
—(new ed.) 1967
AREY, Leslie Brainerd *Developmental anatomy: a textbook and laboratory manual of embryology* 1924 (7 later editions to 1974)
ARGENTI, John *Management techniques: a practical guide* 1969
ARGLES, Margaret W. *See* HUNGERFORD, M. W.
Argus (Melbourne) 1846–1957 (title varies)
ARGYLE, John Michael *Psychology and social problems* 1964
The psychology of interpersonal behaviour 1967
Religious behaviour 1958
The social psychology of work 1972
Argyle's (Marquis of) Last will and testament c1661 (in Harl. Misc.)
ARGYLL, G. D. Campbell, 8th Duke of *The philosophy of belief* 1896
Primeval man 1869
The reign of law 1867
Unseen foundations of society 1893
Ariana. Translated out of the French (of J. Desmarets de Saint Sorlin) 1636 (1641)
Aristotelian Society for the Systematic Study of Philosophy *Proceedings* 1888–96, 1900–
Supplementary volumes 1918–
Arizona Daily Star (Tucson, Arizona) 1879–
ARKELL, William Joscelyn *The Jurassic system in Great Britain* 1933
ARLEN, Michael *Man's mortality* 1933
'Piracy' 1922
The romantic lady 1921
ARMIN, Robert *Works* v.d. (Grosart 1880)
Foole upon foole 1605 (1880)
The history of the two maids of More-clacke 1609
The Italian taylor, and his boy 1609 (1810)
A nest of ninnies 1608
The valiant Welshman, or Chronicle history of Caradoc the great 1615 (1663)
'ARMSTRONG, Anthony' (George Anthony Armstrong Willis) *Taxi!* 1930
ARMSTRONG, Charlotte *The black-eyed stranger* 1951 (UK 1952)
Seven seats to the moon 1969
ARMSTRONG, John *The art of preserving health* 1744 (1807)
ARMSTRONG, Louis *Satchmo: my life in New Orleans* 1954 (UK 1955)
ARMSTRONG, Neil, et al. *First on the moon* 1970
ARMSTRONG, Terence, ROBERTS, Brian, & SWITHINBANK, Charles *Illustrated glossary of snow and ice* 1966
ARMSTRONG, William *Stocks and stock-jobbing in Wall Street* 1848
Army and Navy Co-operative Society, Ltd. (later Army and Navy Stores, Ltd.) *Price lists* and *Catalogues* 1878–
ARNALD, Richard *A critical commentary upon the Book of the Wisdom of Solomon,* etc. 1744–52
ARNIM, Countess of *See* VON ARNIM, Mary Annette
ARNOLD, Sir Edwin *The light of Asia* 1879 (1881)
The light of the world 1891
Pearls of the faith 1882 (1883)
ARNOLD, James *The Shell book of country crafts* 1968
ARNOLD, Matthew *Culture and anarchy* 1869
Essays in criticism 1865 (1875)
—2nd series 1879–88 (1888)
God and the Bible 1875
Last essays on Church and religion 1877
Lecture on modern art 1842
Literature and dogma 1873 (1876)
Mixed essays 1879
Poems v.d. (1877)
The popular education of France 1861
St. Paul and Protestantism 1870
Schools and universities on the continent 1868
Southern night 1861
The study of Celtic literature 1865–66 (1867)
ARNOLD, Robert A. *History of the cotton famine* 1864
ARNOLD, Thomas *Observations on the nature, kinds, causes, and prevention of insanity* 1782–86
ARNOLD, Thomas *History of Rome* 1838–42 (1844–49)
Lectures on modern history 1841–42 (1871)
Sermons on Christian life a1842 (1845)
Life and correspondence; by A. P. Stanley (1844)
ARNOLD, Thomas *New Zealand letters of Thomas Arnold the younger, with further letters from Van Diemen's Land and letters of Arthur Hugh Clough; 1847–1851* ed. J. Bertram 1966
ARNOLD, Thomas 1884 *See* ADDIS, William E.
ARNOLDE, Richard *Chronicle* (*The names of y*[e] *baylifs custos mairs and sherefs of london*) 1502 (1811)
ARNOT, Hugo *A collection and abridgement of celebrated criminal trials in Scotland, from 1536–1784* 1785 (1812)
History of Edinburgh 1779 (1816)
ARNOT, William *Laws from heaven for life on earth* 1857–58
ARNOTT, Neil *Elements of physics or natural philosophy* 1827 (1833)
ARNOULD, Joseph *Law of marine insurance and average* 1848 (1857, 1866)
ARNWAY, John *The tablet; or moderation of Charles the first, martyr* 1649
Aron-bimnucha (by Laurence Womock) 1663
ARONSON, Joseph *The encyclopedia of furniture* 1965 (UK 1966)
Arraignment of J. van Olden Barnevelt tr. 1619
ARROWSMITH, John *Armilla catechetica; a chain of principles* 1659
Art and mystery of vintners and wine-coopers 1682 (1703)
Art journal, The 1849–
Art journal illustrated catalogue of the Great Exhibition 1851
Art of contentment, by the author of The whole duty of man 1675 (1684)
Art of limming, A very proper treatise, wherein is briefly sett forthe the 1573
Art of nombryng c1430 (E.E.T.S. 1922)
Art of painting, and the lives of the painters. Done from the French of M. De Piles 1706 (1744)
Art of planting 1572 *See* MASCALL, L.
Art of preserving the feet 1818
Art of speaking in publick; or an essay on the action of an orator tr. 1727
Art of tormenting 1753 *See* COLLIER, Jane
Arthour and Merlin c1330, c1400 (Abbotsford Cl. 1838; Kölbing 1890)
Arthur ?a1400 (E.E.T.S. 1864)
Articles deuised by the Kynges highnes maiestie, to stablyshe christen quietnes 1536 (1825)
Articles exhibited in Parliament against William (Laud), Archbishop of Canterbury 1640
Articles of peace 1648 (in Milton's Wks. 1851 II)
Articles of religion (Articles, whereupon it was agreed by the Archbishoppes and Bishoppes and the whole cleargie, in the Convocation holden at London in 1562) 1562 (1571)
Artificial handsomeness. A discourse of auxiliary beauty, or artificiall hansomenesse 1656
Artillery exercises, Manual of 1873 (1879)
Arts improvement 1703 *See* S., T.
ARWAKER, Edmund *An embassy from heaven; or the ghost of queen Mary* 1704
ASBURY, Herbert *Sucker's progress: an informal history of gambling in America from the colonies to Canfield* 1938
ASCHAM, Roger *A report and discourse of the affaires and state of Germany* 1552
The scholemaster, or plaine and perfite way of teachyng children the Latin tong a1568 (Arber)
Toxophilus, the schole of shootinge 1545 (Arber)
ASGILL, John *An argument proving that man may be translated from hence into that eternal life, without passing through death* 1700
The metamorphosis of man by the death and resurrection of Christ from the dead 1727
ASH, Edward Cecil *The practical dog book* 1930
ASH, John *The new and complete dictionary of the English language* 1775
ASHBURNER, John *Reichenbach's physico-physiological researches on the dynamics of magnetism,* etc., tr. 1850
ASHBY, George *Poems* v.d. (E.E.T.S. 1899)
Active policy of a prince a1475
Dicta et opiniones diversorum philosophorum a1475
A prisoner's reflections 1463
ASHBY-STERRY, Joseph *The lazy minstrel* 1886 (1892)
A tale of the Thames 1896 (1903)
ASHE, Jonathan *The Masonic manual, or lectures on Freemasonry* 1813
ASHE, Simeon *The good mans death lamented. A sermon preached June 18th* 1655
ASHE, Thomas *Travels in America performed in 1806* 1808
ASHENHURST, Thomas R. *Practical treatise on weaving and designing of fabrics* 1879
ASHFORD, Daisy *The young visiters; or, Mr. Salteenas plan* 1919
'ASHFORD, Jeffrey' (Roderic Graeme Jeffries) *The double run* 1973
Prisoner at the Bar 1969
ASHLEY, Anthony E. M. *The life of H. J. Temple, Viscount Palmerston* 1876
ASHLEY, Robert *Barri's Cochin-China* tr. 1633
Loys le Roy Of the interchangeable course of things in the whole world tr. 1594
Malvezzi's Il Davide persequitato tr. 1637

Ashmole, Elias *Fasciculus chemicus: chymical collections* 1650
The history and antiquities of Berkshire a1692 (1717-23)
Memoirs.. drawn up by himself by way of diary 16.. (1774)
Theatrum chemicum Britannicum 1652
Ashmolean Museum *See* Oxford University. Ashmolean Museum
Ashton, John *Eighteenth century waifs* 1887
Social life in the reign of Q. Anne 1882
Ashton, Peter *Jovius' (P.) Shorte treatise upon the Turkes chronicles* tr. 1546
Ashton, Thomas *Sermons on several occasions* 1770
Ashton-Warner, Sylvia *Spinster* 1958
Ashwell, George *Fides apostolica* 1653
Asiatic annual register, The 1800
Asiatic costumes 1828
Asiatic journal, The 1816-45
Asiatic Society of Bengal (later Royal ——) *Journal* (title varies) 1832-
Asiatic Society of Japan *Transactions* 1874-
Asiatick researches 1808-09
Asimov, Isaac *Earth is room enough* 1957 (UK 1960)
Fantastic voyage: a novel based on the screenplay by H. Kleiner 1966
Inside the atom 1956
The naked sun 1957 (UK 1958)
Asmar's (Maria T.) Memoirs of a Babylonian princess tr. 1844
Aspects of translation (The Communication Research Centre, University College, London) 1958
Assheton, Nicholas *Journal* 1617-18 (Chetham Soc. 1848)
Asshurst, Sir Henry *The deplorable state of New England* by A. H. 1708 (1879)
Assmann, Bruno ed. *Angelsächsische Homilien und Heiligenleben* v.d. (1889)
Association football ('Know the game' series) 1948
—(rev. ed.) 1953
Association for Computing Machinery *Communications* 1958-
Journal 1954-
Association of American Geographers *Annals* 1911-
Assumption of our Lady a1300, c1330 (E.E.T.S. 1866, 1901)
Assurance of Abbey lands 1687 *See* Johnston, N.
Astle, Thomas *The origin and progress of writing, as well hieroglyphic as elementary* 1784
Astley, Sir John D. *Fifty years of my life* 1894
Aston, William George *A history of Japanese literature* 1899
Astounding science fiction 1933-60
Astrophysical journal 1895-
Astruc's (Jean) Academical lectures on fevers tr. 1747
Astry, James A. *Saavedra-Faxardo's Royal politician* tr. 1700
Atcherley, Rowland J. *A trip to Boërland* 1879
Athenæum, The: journal of literature, science, and the fine arts 1828-1921
See also *Nation and Athenæum*
Atherton, Gertrude Franklin *Perch of the devil* 1914
Atkins, John *A voyage to Guinea, Brasil, and the West Indies* 1723-35 (1737)
Atkins, William ed. *The art and practice of printing* 6 vols. 1932-3
Atkinson, Edmund *Ganot's Elementary treatise on physics* tr. 1863
Atkinson, James *Herbert & Procter's Telephony* See Herbert, Thomas Ernest
Atkinson, John C. *British birds' eggs and nests* 1861
Forty years in a moorland parish 1891
Glossary of the Cleveland dialect 1868; 1876 (E.D.S.)
The last of the giant-killers 1891
Provincial names of birds 1864
Stanton Grange 1863
Walks, talks, travels, and exploits of two school-boys 1859
Atkinson, Richard John Copland *Field archaeology* 1946
—(ed. 2) 1953
Atkinson, Mrs. T. W. *Recollections of the Tartar steppes and their inhabitants* 1863
Atkyns, John T. *Reports of cases argued and determined in the High Court of Chancery in the time of Lord Chancellor Hardwicke* 1765-68 (1781-82)
Atkyns, Richard *The original and growth of printing in England* 1664
Atkyns, Sir Robert *Parliamentary and political tracts* a1709 (1734)
Atkyns, Sir Robert (the younger) *The ancient and present state of Glocestershire* 1712
Atkynson, William *Thomas à Kempis: A full deuout and gostely treatyse of the Imytacion and followynge the blessed lyfe of oure Sauyoure Criste* tr. 1502 (E.E.T.S. 1893)
Atlantic monthly, The 1857-
Attenborough, David Frederick *Life on earth: a natural history* 1979
Atterbury, Francis *Discourse occasioned by the death of Lady Cutts* 1698
Sermons v.d. (1723-37)
Attwater, Donald ed. *The Catholic encyclopædic dictionary* 1931
—(ed. 2) 1949
The Christian churches of the East 2 vols. 1961
Atwater, Mary (Meigs) *Crime in corn-weather* (UK ed. with title *Murder in midsummer*) 1935
Atwood, George *An analysis of a course of lectures on the principles of natural philosophy* 1784
Aubrey, John *Brief lives* 1669-96 (1898)
ed. *Letters written by eminent persons in 17th and 18th C.* v.d. (1813)
Miscellanies upon various subjects 1696 (1784)
The natural history and antiquities of the county of Surrey a1697 (1718-19)
The natural history of Wiltshire a1691 (1847)
Remaines of Gentilisme and Judaisme 1686-87 (1881)
Auckland, William Eden, 1st Baron *Journal and correspondence* 1788-98 (1861-62)
Audelay, John *Poems* 1426 (Percy Soc. 1844)
Auden, Wystan Hugh *About the house* 1965 (UK 1966)
The age of anxiety: a baroque eclogue 1947 (UK 1948)
Another time 1940
City without walls, and other poems 1969
Collected poetry 1945
The dance of death 1933
The dyer's hand and other essays 1962 (UK 1963)
The enchafèd flood; or, The romantic iconography of the sea 1950 (UK 1951)
For the time being 1944 (UK 1945)
Homage to Clio 1960
Look, stranger! 1936
New year letter (UK title of US *The double man*) 1941
Nones 1951 (UK 1952)
The orators: an English study 1932
Poems 1930
—(ed. 2) 1933
The shield of Achilles 1955
—— & Isherwood, Christopher William Bradshaw *The ascent of F6* 1936 (US 1937)
The dog beneath the skin; or, Where is Francis? 1935
Journey to a war 1939
On the frontier 1938
—— & Kallman, Chester tr. *E. J. Schikaneder & K. L. Giesecke's libretto to Mozart's The magic flute* 1956 (UK 1957)
—— & MacNeice, Frederick Louis *Letters from Iceland* 1937
—— et al. *I believe* 1939 See *I believe*
Audley, John *England's common-wealth* 1652
Audubon, John J. *Ornithological biography: or, an account of the habits of the birds of the United States* 1831-39
Auerbach, Charlotte *Genetics in the atomic age* 1956
Augustine (Saint), The confessions of tr. 1620
Augustines (St.) manuell (Certaine select prayers gathered out of S. Augustines meditations) 1574 (1577, repr. Longman)
Auk, The 1884-
Aulnoy, Aunoy (Countess d') See Anois
Aungier, George J. *History and antiquities of Syon monastery*, etc. 1840
Aurelio and Isabell, Jean de Flores' Histoire de Aurelio et Isabelle; the historie of 1556 (1608)
Aurora (Philadelphia) 1790-1830, 1834-5 (title varies)
Austen, Jane *Minor works* ed. R. W. Chapman 1954
Novels v.d. ed. R. W. Chapman 5 vols. 1923
Emma 3 vols. 1816
Lady Susan a1809 (in Memoir 1871)
Letters 1796-1817 ed. Ld. Brabourne 2 vols. 1884
Letters ed. R. W. Chapman 2 vols. or 1 vol. 1932
—(ed. 2) 1952
Mansfield Park 3 vols. 1814
Northanger Abbey and Persuasion 4 vols. 1818
Pride and prejudice 3 vols. 1813
Sense and sensibility 3 vols. 1811
The Watsons a1809 (in Memoir 1871)
Memoir, by her nephew J. E. Austen Leigh (1870; 1871)
Austen, Ralph *Treatise of fruit trees; and, The spirituall use of an orchard* 1653 (1657)
Austin, Alfred *England's darling* 1896
Austin, Henry *The scourge of Venus: or the wanton lady* (anon.) 1613 (1614; Grosart 1876)
Austin, Jane G. *Betty Alden, the first-born daughter of the Pilgrims* 1891
Austin, John *Lectures on jurisprudence* 1832 (1879)
Austin, John Langshaw *How to do things with words* (lectures, 1955) 1962
Sense and sensibilia (lectures, last delivered 1959) 1962
Austin, Oliver Luther *Birds of the world* 1961 (UK 1962)
Austin, Samuel *Naps upon Parnassus* 1658
Austin, Sarah *Characteristics of Goethe* 1833
Germany from 1760 to 1814 1854
Ranke's History of the Reformation in Germany tr. 1845
Tour in England, Ireland, and France. By a German Prince tr. 1832
Austin, William *Devotionis Augustinianae flamma, or certaine meditations.* Set forth by his wife Mrs. A. Austin a1634 (1635)
Hæc homo, wherein the excellency of the creation of woman is described a1634 (1637)
Australasian, The (Melbourne) 1864-1946
Australasian post (Melbourne) 1946-52
Australia. Commonwealth Scientific and Industrial Research Organization. Division of Entomology *The insects of Australia* 1970
Australian, The 1964-
Australian encyclopaedia, The ed. A. H. Chisholm 10 vols. 1965
Australian house and garden 1948-
Australian short stories 1951 *See* Murdoch, Walter & Drake-Brockman, H. F. Y.
——(2nd ser.) 1963 *See* 'James, Brian'
Australian women's weekly 1933-
Australians in England: a complete record of the cricket tour of 1882 1882
Autobiography of a beggar boy 1855 *See* Burn, J. D.
Autocar, The 1895-
Autocar handbook, The 1906-
Automobile engineer, The 1910- (with title *Internal combustion engineering* 1912-14)
Avery, Gillian *The greatest Gresham* 1962
Aviation age 1950-8
Aviation week 1947-
Avis, Frederick Compton *Boxing reference dictionary* 1954
The sportsman's glossary 1961
Avis, Walter Spencer, et al. eds. *A dictionary of Canadianisms on historical principles* 1967
Avison, Charles *An essay on musical expression* 1751
Avowynge of King Arther c1420 (Camden Soc. 1842)
Awake! (Watchtower Bible and Tract Soc.) 1919-
Awdelay, John *The fraternitye of vacabondes* 1561 (E.E.T.S. 1869)
Ayckbourn, Alan *Relatively speaking* 1968
Ayenbite of Inwyt, Dan Michel's 1340 (E.E.T.S. 1866)
Ayer, Alfred Jules *The central questions of philosophy* 1973
The foundations of empirical knowledge 1940
Language, truth and logic 1936
—(ed. 2) 1946
Philosophical essays 1954
The problem of knowledge 1956
Ayerst, David *'Guardian': biography of a newspaper* 1971
Ayesha, the maid of Kars (by J. P. Morier) 1834
Ayliffe, John *The ancient and present state of the University of Oxford* 1714
Parergon juris canonici Anglicani 1726
Aylmer, John *An harborowe for faithfull and trewe subjects agaynst the late blowne blaste concerning the gouernment of wemen* 1559
Ayre, William *Memoirs of the life and writings of Alexander Pope* 1745
Ayton, Richard *Essays and sketches of character* 1825
Aytoun, William E. *The ballads of Scotland* 1858
Lays of the Scottish cavaliers 1849
See also Martin, Sir T.

B

B. *Discolliminium: or a most obedient reply to a late book called Bounds and bonds* 1650
B., Lt. Col. *The whist player* 1856 (1858)
B., A. *Lessius' (Leonardus) De providentia numinis* tr. 1631
B., A. *Mutatus Polemo: the horrible stratagems of the Jesuits lately practised in England* 1650
B., E. 1652 *See* Benlowes, E.
B. E. a1700 *See* E., B.
B., F. *A free but modest censure on the late controversial writings and debates of the Lord Bishop of Worcester and Mr. Locke*, etc. 1698
B., G. (i.e. W. Baldwin) *Beware the cat* 1561 (1570, 1584, Halliw. 1864)
B., J. *See* Bate, J.; Bryan, J.
B., O. *Questions of profitable and pleasant concernings, talked of by two olde seniors.. under an oake in Kenelworth parke* 1594
B., R. *Appius and Virginia* 1575 (Hazl. Dodsley IV)
B., R. 1669 *See* Baddiley, R.
B., R. 1705 *See* Beverly, R.
B., T. *De La Primaudaye's French academie* tr. 1586-94 (1589, 1594) *See* Bowes, Thomas
B., T. 1650 *See* Bayly, T.
B., Sir W. *J. de Meun's Dodechedron of Fortune* tr. 1613
B., W. *Michaelis' (S.) Admirable historie.. of a penitent woman seduced by a magician* tr. 1613
B., W. *The philosopher's banquet* tr. 1614 (ed. 2)
B., W. *Sarpi's (P.) Free (true) schoole of warre* tr. 1625
B., W. *A touchstone for gold and silver wares* 1676
B., W. *See* Baucke, William
B.B.C. *See* British Broadcasting Corporation
BP shield international 1961-
B.S.I. *See* British Standards Institution
Babbage, Charles *A comparative view of the various institutions for the assurance of lives* 1826
The economy of manufactures 1832
The ninth Bridgewater treatise 1837 (1838)
Babcock, Ernest Brown & Clausen, Roy Elwood *Genetics in relation to agriculture* 1918
Babees Book c1475 (E.E.T.S. 1868)
Babington, Charles C. *Manual of British botany* 1843 (1847)
Babington, Gervase *Workes* a1610 (1622)
Comfortable notes upon Exodus 1604
A briefe conference betwixt man's frailtie and faith 1584 (1596)
A very fruitfull exposition of the commandments 1583
A profitable exposition of the Lord's Prayer 1580 (1596)
Baboo, The; and other tales (by A. Prinsep) 1834
Babson, Marian *Cover-up story* 1971
The stalking lamb 1974
Babylonian princess, Memoirs of a *See* Asmar, M. T.
Bacchanalian sessions, The; or the contention of liquors (by R. Ames) 1693
Bacchus and Venus: or a select collection of... songs 1737
Bacchus bountie.. By Philip Foulface of Ale-foord 1593 (Harl. Misc.)
Bach, Emmon *An introduction to transformational grammars* 1964

BACHARACH, Alfred Louis ed. *British music of our time* 1946
ed. *The musical companion* 1934
Bachelor of the Albany, The (by M. W. Savage) 1845 (1854)
BACHMANN, Lawrence Paul *The ultimate act* 1972
Backwoods of Canada, The (by Mrs. Traill) 1836
BACON, Alice Mabel *Japanese girls and women* 1891
A Japanese interior 1893
BACON, Lady Ann *Jewel's (J.) Apologie or answere in defence of the church of Englande* tr. 1564 (Parker Soc. 1848)
BACON, Francis, Lord Verulam *Works* a1626 (B. Montagu 1825-36, Spedding, etc. 1857-74)
Of the advancement of learning 1605 (1869). See also WATTS, G.
An advertisement touching an holy warre a1626 (1629)
Certaine miscellany Works (Publ. by Rawley 1629)
Considerations touching a warre with Spaine a1626 (1629)
Of the coulers of good and euill 1597 (with Essays, Arber)
A digest of Laws c1617
The elements of the common lawes; Maxims and *Use* 1596 (1630, 1635-36)
Essayes 1597, 1612, 1625 (Arber)
History naturall and experimentall of life and death tr. Rawley 1638 (1650)
The historie of the raigne of king Henry the seventh 1622
The new Atlantis 1626
Novum organum tr. 1844 (Phys. works, Bohn 1853)
Resuscitatio (Publ. by Rawley 1657-61)
Sacred meditations 1598 (in Essays, Arber)
Sylva sylvarum; or a naturall historie 1626
The wisdom of the ancients tr. B. Montagu (1825-34)
BACON, Gertrude *Balloons, airships and flying machines* 1905
BACON, Leonard *The genesis of the New England churches* 1874
BACON, Nathaniel *Historical discourse of the uniformity of the government of England* (= *Laws and government* in ed. 1682 and following edd.) 1647, 1651 (1739)
BACON, Thomas *First impressions and studies from nature in Hindostan* 1837
Bacteriological reviews 1937-
BADCOCK, John ('Jon Bee') *Domestic amusements* 1823
Essay on the life of Foote (F.'s wks.) 1830
A living picture of London 1828
Slang. A dictionary of the turf, etc. 1823
BADDELEY, V. C. C. *See* CLINTON-BADDELEY, Victor Clinton
BADDILEY, Richard *The life of Dr. T. Morton, late bishop of Duresme, by R. B.* 1669
BADEN-POWELL, Robert S. S. *The Matabele campaign* 1896
Pigsticking or hoghunting 1889
Scouting for boys 1908
BADHAM, Charles D. *Prose halieutics* 1854
Badminton library of sports and pastimes, The (1887 etc.)
Bæda's Ecclesiastical history tr. c900 (J. Schipper 1899, E.E.T.S. 1890-98)
BAGBY, George William *The old Virginia gentleman, and other sketches* ed. T. N. Page 1910
BAGE, Robert *Barham downs* 1784
Hermsprong; or man as he is not 1796
BAGEHOT, Walter *Collected works* ed. N. St. John-Stevas 1965-
The English constitution 1867
The history of the unreformed parliament 1860
Literary studies a1877 (1879)
Physics and politics 1876
Bagford ballads, The 16.. (Ballad Soc. 1878)
BAGG, Lyman Hotchkiss *Four years at Yale* 1871
BAGGS, Thomas Alexander *Back from the front: an eye-witness's narrative of the beginnings of the Great War, 1914* 1914
BAGLEY, Desmond *The enemy* 1977
The freedom trap 1971
The snow tiger 1975
The spoilers 1969
The tightrope men 1973
Bahamian review 1952-
BAILAR, John Christian, et al. *Comprehensive inorganic chemistry* 5 vols. 1973
BAILEY, Alan Robert *A text-book of metallurgy* 1954
—(ed. 2) 1960
BAILEY, Frederick M. *The fern world of Australia* 1881
BAILEY, Hamilton & LOVE, Robert John McNeill *A short practice of surgery* 2 vols. 1932 (and many later editions used)
BAILEY, Henry Christopher *Dead man's shoes* 1942
Mr. Fortune's practice 1923
BAILEY, John *General view of the agriculture of the county of Durham* 1810
—— & CULLEY, George *General view of the agriculture of the county of Cumberland* 1794
———— *Northumberland* 1794 (1805)
BAILEY, John *Letters and diaries* ed. S. Bailey 1935
BAILEY, Liberty Hyde ed. *Cyclopedia of American agriculture* 4 vols. 1907-9
ed. *Cyclopedia of American horticulture* 4 vols. 1900-2
Manual of cultivated plants 1924
—(rev. ed.) 1949
ed. *The standard cyclopedia of horticulture* 6 vols. 1914-17
BAILEY, Nathan *Dictionarium Britannicum: or a more compleat universal etymological English dictionary* 1730, 1736
Erasmus' Colloquies tr. 1725 (1878)
Household dictionary 1736
An universal etymological English dictionary 1721 and many editions to 1800
BAILEY, Philip J. *The age* 1858
Festus 1839 (1845, 1848, 1852)
The mystic 1855
BAILEY, Samuel *Discourses on various subjects* 1852
BAILLIE, Granville Hugh *Watches* 1929
BAILLIE, Lady Grisell *The household book* 1692-1733 (S.H.S. 1911)
BAILLIE, Joanna *Metrical legends* 1821
Poems v.d. (1823, 1853)
A series of plays in which it is attempted to delineate the stronger passions of the mind 1798-1812
BAILLIE, Matthew *The morbid anatomy of some of the most important parts of the human body* 1793 (1807)
BAILLIE, Robert *Anabaptism* 1646 (1647)
The Canterburians self-conviction 1640
The dissuasive..vindicated 1653 (1655)
The letters and journals v.d. (Bannatyne Club 1841)
A parallel of the liturgy with the Mass-book 1641
BAILLIE-SCOTT, M. H. *Houses and gardens* 1906
BAIN, Alexander *Education as a science* 1879
The emotions and the will 1859
John Stuart Mill 1882
Mental and moral science 1868
The senses and the intellect 1855
BAINBRIDGE, Beryl *Sweet William* 1975
Young Adolf 1978
BAINBRIDGE, John *Astronomicall description of the late comet* 1619
BAINES, Anthony ed. *Musical instruments through the ages* 1961
BAINES, Edward *The history..of the county palatine of Lancaster* 1824 (1868-70)
A history of the wars of the French revolution 1816-18
BAINES, Sir Edward *History of the cotton manufacture in Great Britain* 1835
BAINES, John Thomas *Explorations in South-West Africa* 1864
BAINES, Thomas *Greenhouse and stove plants* 1885
BAINES, William Mortimer *The narrative of Edward Crewe; or, Life in New Zealand* 1874
BAIRD, Irene *Waste heritage* 1939
BAIRD, Robert *A view of the valley of the Mississippi; or, The emigrant's and traveller's guide to the West* 1832
BAIRD, Spencer F. *The birds of North America* 1860
Mammals of North America 1859
BAIRD, William *Cyclopædia of the natural sciences, or a dictionary of natural history* 1858
BAKER, Miss Anne E. *Glossary of Northamptonshire words and phrases* 1854
BAKER, Cyril Clarence Thomas *Dictionary of mathematics* 1961
BAKER, Daniel *Poems upon several occasions* 1697
BAKER, David *The holy practises of a deuine louer, or the saintly ideots deuotions* (anon.) a1641 (1657)
BAKER, David Erskine *Biographia dramatica* 1812
BAKER, Dorothy *Young man with a horn* 1938
BAKER, George *The composition or making of the..precious oil called Oleum magistrale* 1574
Gesner's Newe jewell of health tr. 1576
Guydon's Questyonary of a chirurgien tr. 1579
BAKER, Henry *The microscope made easy* 1742
BAKER, Henry F. *Abel's theorem and the allied theory, including the theory of the Theta functions* 1897
BAKER, Humphrey *The well spring of sciences* 1562 (1574, 1617)
BAKER, John Randal *Principles of biological microtechnique: a study of fixation and dyeing* 1958
Race 1974
BAKER, Sir Richard *An apology for laymen's writing divinity* 1641
Chronicle of the kings of England 1643 (1679, 1696)
Letters of Monsieur Balzac tr. 1638 (1654)
Malvezzi's (V.) Discourses upon C. Tacitus tr. 1642
BAKER, Robert Horace *Astronomy* 1930
—(ed. 8) 1964
BAKER, Roger Denio *Essential pathology* 1961
BAKER, Sir Samuel W. *The Nile tributaries of Abyssinia* 1872
Wild beasts and their ways 1890
BAKER, Sidney John *Australia speaks: a supplement to 'The Australian language'* 1953
The Australian language 1945
—(ed. 2) 1966
The drum: Australian character and slang 1959 (UK 1960)
New Zealand slang 1941
A popular dictionary of Australian slang 1941
—(ed. 3) 1943
BAKER, Thomas *Reflections upon learning* 1699
BAKER, Thomas *The female tatler* 1709
Tunbridge walks 1703
BAKEWELL, Frederick C. *Geology for schools and students* 1854
BAKEWELL, Robert *An introduction to geology* 1813 (1815, 1838)
Balance and Columbian Repository (Hudson, NY) 1801-8
BALCHIN, Nigel Marlin *Darkness falls from the air* 1942
Lord, I was afraid 1947
The small back room 1943
A way through the wood 1951
Baldeschi See DALE, J. D. H.
BALDWIN, Faith *Innocent bystander* 1933 (UK 1935)
BALDWIN, James Arthur *Another country* 1962 (UK 1963)
Go tell it on the mountain 1953 (UK 1954)
BALDWIN, James Mark ed. *Dictionary of philosophy and psychology* 3 vols. 1901-5
BALDWIN, John D. *Prehistoric nations* 1869
BALDWIN, Joseph G. *The flush times of Alabama and Mississippi* 1853
BALDWIN, William *Beware the cat*. By G. B. 1561 (1570, 1584, Halliw. 1864)
The canticles or balades of Solomon tr. 1549
The funeralles of king Edward the sixt 1560
A treatise of morall philosophie 1547
—enlarged by T. Palfreyman 1564 (1595)
See also *Mirror for magistrates*
BALDWIN, William C. *African hunting from Natal to the Zambesi* 1863
BALE, John *The actes of the Englysh votaryes* 1546-50
Answere to a papystycall exhortacyon c1548
The apology of J. B. agaynste a ranke papyst 1550
A brefe chronycle concernynge Syr J. Oldecastell 1544
A christen exhortacion vnto customable swearers ?1543
A comedye concernynge thre lawes 1538
Gardiner's (S.) De vera obedientia tr. 1553
The image of both churches 1545-50 (Parker Soc. 1849)
Kynge Johan: a play c1550 (Camden Soc. 1838)
The pageant of Popes tr. 1574
Select Works a1563 (Parker Soc. 1849)
A tragedye..manyfestyng the chefe promyses of God vnto man 1538
The vocacyon of J. B. 1553
Yet a course at the Romyshe foxe; a dysclosynge or openynge of the manne of synne 1543
BALES, Peter *The writing schoolemaster* 1590
BALFOUR, Andrew *By stroke of sword* 1897
To arms 1898
BALFOUR, Arthur J., Earl of *A defence of philosophic doubt, being an essay on the foundations of belief* 1879
BALFOUR, Clara L. *Working women of this century* 1854 (1868)
BALFOUR, David *Odal rights and feudal wrongs* 1860
Oppressions of the sixteenth century in..Orkney 1859 (Maitland Club)
BALFOUR, Edward *Cyclopædia of India* 1857 (enlarged 1871-73, 1885)
BALFOUR, Isaac Bayley tr. *C. E. von Goebel's Organography of plants* 2 vols. 1900-5
BALFOUR, Sir James *Practicks; or a system of the more ancient law of Scotland* c1575 (1754)
BALFOUR, Sir James *Annales of Scotland* a1657 (1824-25)
BALFOUR, John H. *A manual of botany* 1849
Outlines of botany 1854
BALGUY, Thomas *Discourses on various subjects* 1785
BALINSKY, Boris Ivan *An introduction to embryology* 1960
BALL, Benjamin W. *Elfin land, and other poems* 1851
BALL, John *Flora of the Peruvian Andes* 1885 (in Jrnl. Linn. Soc. XXII)
Notes of a naturalist in South America 1887
BALL, John Dudley *The cool cottontail* 1966 (UK 1967)
Five pieces of jade 1972
BALL, Kenneth *Fiat 600, 600D autobook* 1970
BALL, Sir Robert S. *In the high heavens* 1893
The story of the sun 1893
BALL, Samuel *An account of the cultivation and manufacture of tea in China* 1848
Ballad society *Publications* (1868-)
Ballads from MSS. 15.. (Ballad Soc. 1868-73)
BALLANTINE, James *The gaberlunzie's wallet* 1843-44 (1875)
Lilias Lee, and other poems 1871
The miller of Deanhaugh 1844
BALLANTINE, William *Some experiences of a barrister's life* 1882
BALLANTYNE, David Watt *The Cunninghams* 1948 (UK 1963)
BALLANTYNE, Robert M. *Shifting winds* 1866
Ballet annual, The 1947-
Balmerino abbey. The chartularies of Balmerino and Lindores (Abbotsford Club 1841)
Bamff charters 1232-1703 (ed. Sir J. H. Ramsay 1915)
BAMFORD, Samuel *Passages in the life of a Radical* 1844
BAMPFIELD, Thomas *A reply to Dr. Wallis concerning the Christian sabbath* 1693
BANCROFT, Edward *An essay on the natural history of Guiana* 1769
Experimental researches concerning the philosophy of permanent colours 1794
BANCROFT, George *Footprints of time* 1874
History of the United States 1834-75 (1876)
BANCROFT, Hubert Howe *The history of Central America* 1883-87
The native races of the Pacific states of North America 5 vols. 1875-6
BANCROFT, Abp. Richard *Daungerous positions and proceedings* 1593
BAND, George C. *Road to Rakaposhi* 1955
Band, Ruffe, and Cuffe, A merry dialogue between 1615 (Halliwell 1849)
Banffshire glossary See GREGOR, W.
BANFIELD, Edmund James *The confessions of a beachcomber* 1908
Bangladesh Times (Dacca) 1974-
BANIM, John *Anglo-Irish of the nineteenth century* 1828
The smuggler 3 vols. 1831
Tales of the O'Hara family 1825-26
BANISTER, Henry C. *Music* 1873
BANISTER, John *The historie of man* 1578
A needful, new and necessary treatise of chyrurgerie 1575
BANKES, George N. *A Cambridge staircase* 1883
BANKS, Elizabeth L. *The autobiography of a newspaper girl* 1902

Campaigns of curiosity 1894
The mystery of Frances Farrington 1909
BANKS, Michael Edward Borg *Commando climber* 1955
BANKTON, Lord *See* McDOUALL, A.
BANNATYNE, George *Ancient Scottish poems* a1568 (1770)
The Bannatyne MS. a1568 (Hunterian Club 1873–88)
BANNATYNE, Richard *Journal of transactions in Scotland* 1570–73 (1806)
Bannatyne Club *Publications* (1823–)
BANNERMAN, David Armitage *The birds of the British Isles* 12 vols. 1953–63
BANNISTER, Roger Gilbert *First four minutes* 1955
Banquet, The (by H. Busk) 1819
Banquett of dainties for all such gestes that love moderate dyate, The 1566
BANTON, Michael Parker *The policeman in the community* 1964
West African city: a study of tribal life in Freetown 1957
BANVARD, Joseph *Plymouth and the pilgrims* 1851
Baptist magazine 1809–1904
'BARBELLION, W. N. P.' (Bruce Frederick Cummings) *The journal of a disappointed man* 1919
BARBER, Charles Laurence *Linguistic change in present-day English* 1964
BARBER, Horatio *The aeroplane speaks* 1916
Barbette's (P.) Chirurgical and anatomical works tr. 1672
'BARBICAN, James' *The confessions of a rum-runner* 1927
BARBIER, Jo. *Janua linguarum quadrilinguis, or a messe of tongues: Latine, English, French, and Spanish, neatly served up together* 1617
BARBOUR, John *The Bruce* 1375 (texts, 1487, 1489, 1616) (E.E.T.S. 1870–89; S.T.S. 1894)
See also: *Legends of the saints*, and *Scottish Trojan war*.
BARBOUR, Robert W. *Thoughts from the writings of* a1891 (1900)
BARCKLEY, Sir Richard *Discourse of the felicitie of man* 1598 (1603, 1631)
BARCLAY, Alexander *Certayne eglogues* 1515 (1570)
The cytezen and uplondyshman 1514 (Percy Soc. 1847)
The famous chronicle of warre, whyche the Romaynes hadde agaynst Jugurth c1520
The mirrour of good manners c1510 (1570)
The shyp of folys 1509 (1570, 1874)
BARCLAY, Florence Louisa *The broken halo* 1913
The rosary 1909
BARCLAY, James *A complete and universal English dictionary* 1774 (1792)
Barclay's (John) Argenis tr... *the prose by Sir R. Le Grys and the verses by T. May* 1628 (1629)
See also MAY, T.
BARCLAY, John *The muscular motions of the human body* 1808
A new anatomical nomenclature 1803
BARCLAY, Rachel Mary tr. *E. Kraepelin's Dementia praecox and paraphrenia* ed. G. M. Robertson 1919
BARCLAY, Robert *An apology for the.. Quakers* 1678
BARCLAY, William *Nepenthes, or the vertues of tabacco* 1614
BARET, John *An alvearie or triple (quadruple) dictionarie* 1573, 1580
BARET, Michael *An hipponomie, or the vineyard of horsemanship* 1618
BARETTI, Guiseppe *A dictionary of the English and Italian languages* 1760, etc.
BARFORD, John Edward Quintus *Climbing in Britain* 1946
BARGRAVE, Isaac *A sermon* 1615
Two sermons 1624, 1627
BARGRAVE, John *Pope Alexander VII* 1662 (Camden Soc. 1867)
BARHAM, Henry *Hortus Americanus* 1794
BARHAM, Richard H. *The Ingoldsby legends* a1845
Life and letters v.d. (1870)
BARING, Maurice *Landmarks in Russian literature* 1910
BARING-GOULD, Sabine *A book of the West* 1899
The book of werewolves 1865
Cheap-Jack Zita 1893
Court Royal 1886
The deserts of southern France 1894
The Gaverocks 1887
Germany past and present 1879
Historic oddities 1889, 1891
Iceland 1863
In troubadour-land 1891
Kitty alone 1894
Mehalah 1880
The mystery of suffering 1877
The queen of love 1894
Red spider 1887
—— & TWIGGE, R. *An armory of the western counties* 1898
BARKER, Edward H. *Two summers in Guyenne* 1894
BARKER, George Granville *News of the world* 1950
Two plays 1958
BARKER, Jane *Exilius* (a novel) 1715 (1736)
BARKER, Lewellys Franklin *Monographic medicine* See under title
The nervous system and its constituent neurones 1899
——, HOSKINS, R. G., & MOSENTHAL, H. O. eds. *Endocrinology and metabolism* 5 vols. 1922
BARKER, Lady Mary Ann *See* BROOME
BARKER, Thomas *B.'s delight; or the art of angling* 1651–57 (1820)
BARKSDALE, Clement *Grotius (H.) Of the law of warre and peace* tr. C.B. 1654
BARKSTED, William *Hiren; or the faire Greeke* 1611 (Grosart 1876)
Mirrha, the mother of Adonis 1607 (Grosart 1876)
BARLEY, William *A new booke of tabliture* 1596
Barley-breake; or a warning for wantons, by W. N. 1607 (Grosart 1877)
BARLOW, Alfred *The history and principles of weaving* 1878
BARLOW, James *Term of trial* 1961
BARLOW, Jane *Irish idylls* 1892
Irish ways 1909
Mrs. Martin's company 1896
BARLOW, Joel *The Columbiad* 1807 (1809)
The conspiracy of kings 1792
The constitution of 1791, 1792
Oration 4th July 1787
The vision of Columbus; a poem 1787
BARLOW, Peter *A new mathematical and philosophical dictionary* 1814
Astronomy 1822 (Encycl. Metropolitana 1845)
Hydrodynamics 1818–22 (ibid.)
Magnetism 1823–24 (ibid.)
Mechanics 1818 (ibid.)
Optics 1817–23 (ibid.)
Pneumatics 1819–24 (ibid.)
BARLOW, Bp. Thomas *The genuine remains of* a1691 (1693)
Popery, or the principles and positions approved by the church of Rome 1679
BARLOW, Walter Sydney Lazarus *A manual of general pathology* 1898
BARLOW, Bp. William *Answer to a nameless Catholic's censure* 1609
Defence of the articles of the Protestant religion 1601
The eagle and the body 1601 (1609)
One of foure sermons preached.. at Hampton Court 1606
Sermon preached at Paules crosse 1 Mar. 1600 1601
Three Christian sermons (of Lavater) tr. 1596
Barman's and barmaid's manual 1880
BARNARD, Howard Clive & LAUWERYS, Joseph Albert *A handbook of British educational terms* 1963
BARNARD, Keppel Harcourt *A pictorial guide to South African fishes* 1947
BARNARD, Robert *Death on the high C's* 1977
BARNERD, Richard *The faithful shepherd* 1609
BARNES, Barnabe *A divine centurie of spirituall sonnets* 1595 (1815)
Parthenophil and Parthenope 1593 (Grosart 1875; Arber, Eng. Garner V)
BARNES, Dallas *See the woman* 1973 (UK 1974)
BARNES, Harold *Oceanography and marine biology* 1959
BARNES, Dame Juliana See *Book of St. Albans*, and *Fysshynge*
BARNES, Robert *Works* a1540 (1573)
BARNES, Robert *Lectures on obstetric operations* 1870
Report on midwifery etc. 1867 (New Sydenham Soc.)
A synoptical guide to the study of obstetrics 1881
BARNES, William *A glossary of the Dorset dialect, with a grammar* 1886
A grammar and glossary of the Dorset dialect 1863
Poems of rural life 1844–63
BARNES-GRUNDY, Mabel *A Thames camp* 1902
The vacillations of Hazel 1905
BARNETT, Denis Oliver *Denis Oliver Barnett: in happy memory... His letters from France and Flanders, October 1914–August 1915* 1915
BARNETT, Edward de Barry *Mechanism of organic chemical reactions* 1956
BARNETT, Henrietta Octavia Weston *Canon Barnett: his life, work and friends* 1918
Barnevels Apology or Holland mysterie tr. 1618
BARNFIELD, Richard *The affectionate shepheard* 1594 (Arber)
The complaint of poetrie 1598 (Arber)
Poems 1594–98 (Arber)
BARNHAM, Denis *One man's window: an account of 10 weeks of war, Malta, 1942* 1956
BARNHART, Clarence Lewis, STEINMETZ, S., & BARNHART, R. K. *The Barnhart dictionary of new English since 1963* (UK ed. with title *A dictionary of new English 1963–1972*) 1973
The second Barnhart dictionary of new English 1980
BARNUM, Phineas Taylor *Life, written by himself* 1855
Struggles and triumphs; or, Forty years' recollections 1869
—(another ed.) 1871
BARON, Alexander *See* BARON, Joseph Alexander
BARON, Joseph Alexander *From the city, from the plough* 1948
The human kind 1953
Rosie Hogarth 1951
There's no home 1950
With hope, farewell 1952
BARON, Robert *The Cyprian academy* 1647
Mirza, a tragedie 1647
Pocula Castalia (poems) c1645 (1650)
Baron court of Stitchill, Records of the 1655–1807 (S.H.S. 1905)
Baron Munchausen's narrative of his marvellous travels and campaigns in Russia (by R. E. Raspe) 1786 (1792)
BARRATT, Alfred *Physical metempiric* a1881 (1883)
BARRÈRE, Albert and LELAND, C. G. *A dictionary of slang, jargon and cant* 1888–90 (1897)
BARRET, Robert *The theorike and practike of moderne warres* 1598
BARRETT, Charles Leslie *On the wallaby: quest and adventure in many lands* 1942
BARRETT, Eaton S. *The miss-led general* 1808
The rising sun, by Cervantes Hogg 1807
The setting sun 1809
BARRETT, Frank *The sin of Olga Zassoulich* 1891
BARRETT, John *Analecta* 1703
BARREY, Ludovick *Ram alley, or merrie trickes* 1611
Barrie's (C.) Cochin China tr. 1633
BARRIE, Sir James Matthew *The admirable Crichton* 1914
Auld licht idylls 1888
The little minister 1891 (1892)
Margaret Ogilvy 1896 (1897)
Plays (Uniform ed.) 12 vols. 1918–38
Sentimental Tommy 1896
When a man's single 1888 (1900)
A window in Thrums 1889
BARRIFFE, William *Military discipline* 1635 (1639, 1643)
BARRINGTON, Sir Jonah *Personal sketches of his own time* 1827–32
'BARRINGTON, Pamela' (Muriel Vere Barling) *Accessory to murder* 1968
Barrington's (George) History of New South Wales 1802
BARRON, Harry *Modern plastics* 1945
BARRON, John N. *The language of painting: an informal dictionary* 1967
BARROUGH, Philip *The method of physick* 1590– (1590, 1596, 1610, 1634, 1639)
BARROW, or BARROWE, Henry 1590 *See* GREENWOOD, J.
BARROW, Isaac *Euclid* 1660 (1714)
Sermons a1677 (1686, 1716)
Treatise on the Pope's supremacy a1677 (1680)
Unity of the church a1677 (Wks. 1831)
The usefulness of mathematical learning explained and demonstrated, being mathematical lectures.. at.. Cambridge tr. J. Kirkby (1734)
BARROW, John *An account of travels into the interior of southern Africa, in the years 1797 and 1798* 2 vols. 1801–4
—(ed. 2) 2 vols. 1806
BARROWMAN, James *A glossary of Scotch mining terms* 1886
BARROWS, J. H. ed. *World's parliament of religions* 1893
BARRY, Alfred *The life and works of Sir Charles Barry* 1867
'BARRY, C.' (Charles Bryson) *The detective's holiday* 1926
BARRY, George *The history of the Orkney Islands* 1805 (1808)
BARRY, James *A reviving cordial for a sin-desparing soul* 1699 (1802)
BARRY, James *Lectures on painting* 1784–98 (1848)
BARRY, John A. *Steve Brown's Bunyip and other stories* 1893
BARRY, Patrick *Dockyard economy and naval power* 1863
BARSTOW, Stan *A kind of loving* 1960
BARTH, John Simmons *The floating opera* 1956
—(rev. ed.) 1967
Barthèlemy's (J. J.) Charite and Polydorus; a romance tr. 1799
BARTHOLOW, Roberts *A practical treatise on materia medica and therapeutics* 1876 (1879)
'BARTIMEUS' (Lewis Anselm da Costa Ricci) *Naval occasions* 1914
A tall ship and other naval occasions 1915
BARTLET, J. *The gentleman's farriery* 1753 (1754)
BARTLETT, Adeline Courtney *The larger rhetorical patterns in Anglo-Saxon poetry* 1935
BARTLETT, Ellis Ashmead *The battlefields of Thessaly* 1897
BARTLETT, John R. *Dictionary of Americanisms* 1848, 1859, 1860, 1876
Personal narrative of explorations.. connected with the U.S. and Mexican Boundary Commission 1854
BARTLETT, Samuel C. *From Egypt to Palestine* 1879
BARTLETT, Vernon Oldfield *This is my life* 1937
BARTLEY, Robert T. H. *Topinard's Anthropology* tr. 1878
BARTLEY, Samuel Howard *Vision* 1941
BARTON, Bernard *Selections from the poems and ballads of* a1849 (1849)
BARTON, Frank Townend *The kennel encyclopædia* 1928
BARTON, R. tr. *C. Blasis's The code of Terpsichore: the art of dancing* 1830
BARTON, William P. C. *Compendium floræ Philadelphicæ* 1818
A flora of North America 1821–22
Vegetable materia medica of the United States 1817–18
BARTRAM, John *A description of East-Florida* (by W. Stork), *with a journal kept by J. Bartram* 1765–66 (1769)
Observations.. in his travels from Pennsylvania 1751
BARTRAM, William *Travels through North and South Carolina* 1791
BARTZ, Patricia McBride *South Korea* 1972
BARWELL, Richard *On aneurism, especially of the thorax and root of the neck* 1880
BARWICK, Humphrey *A breefe discourse concerning.. all manual weapons of fire* 1590
BASHFORTH, George Reginald *The manufacture of iron and steel* 2 vols. 1948–51
—(ed. 2) 4 vols. 1957–62
Basil, St. The Anglo-saxon version of the hexameron.. and the Anglo-saxon remains of St. B.'s Admonitio ad filium spiritualem c1000 (Norman 1849)
BASKIN, Wade tr. *F. de Saussure's Course in general linguistics* 1959 (UK 1960)
BASSET, Mrs. Mary *More's (Sir T.) Treatise of the passion* tr. a1557 (M.'s Wks. 1557)
BASTARD, Thomas *Chrestoleros, seven bookes of epigrams* 1598 (Grosart 1880)
BASTIAN, Henry C. *The brain as an organ of mind* 1880
BASTWICK, John *The Letany* 1637
'BAT' *The cricketer's manual* 1851
Batchelor, Essays from the 1771–72 (1773)
BATCHELOR, Thomas *General view of the agriculture of Bedfordshire* 1808
An orthoepical analysis of the English language 1809
Bate, George 1694 *See* SALMON, W.
BATE, John *The mysteryes of nature and art, by J. B.* 1634
BATEMAN, Thomas *A treatise of tithe* 1778

Bateman, Thomas *A practical synopsis of cutaneous diseases* 1813 (1814)
Bates, Henry W. *Central America* 1878
The naturalist on the river Amazons 1863
Bates, Herbert Ernest *The day of the tortoise* 1961
The jacaranda tree 1949
Love for Lydia 1952
Bates, William *Works* a1699 (1700)
The harmony of the divine attributes 1674
Bateson, William *Mendel's principles of heredity* 1909
Mendel's principles of heredity: a defence 1902
Problems of genetics 1913
Bathe, William *A briefe introduction to the skill of song* c1590
Bathgate, Alexander *Colonial experiences; or, Sketches of people and places in the province of Otago, New Zealand* 1874
Batman, Stephen *Bartholomeus De proprietatibus rerum, newly corrected, enlarged, and amended* 1582
Battersby, Albert *A guide to stock control* 1962
Mathematics in management 1966
Network analysis for planning and scheduling 1964
— (ed. 2) 1967
Battey, Maurice Hugh *Mineralogy for students* 1972
Battle of Maldon, The (= Byrhtnoth's Tod) 993 (Grein 1883)
Baucke, William *Where the white man treads* 1905
— (ed. 2) 1928
Bauerman, Hilary *A descriptive catalogue of the rock specimens in the Museum of Practical Geology* 1858
Text-book of systematic mineralogy 1881
Bauldwin, William *See* Baldwin, W.
Baumann, Heinrich *Londinismen: Slang und Cant* 1886 [dated 1887]
Bawdwen, William *Dom Boc. A translation of the record called Domesday so far as relates to the county of York, etc.* 1809
Bax, E. Belfort *Outlooks from the new standpoint* 1881
See also Morris, William
Baxt, George *A queer kind of death* 1966 (UK 1967)
Baxter, Andrew *An inquiry into the nature of the human soul* c1730 (1745)
Baxter, E. Buchanan Ed. *Garrod's (A. B.) Essentials of materia medica* 1874 (1880)
Baxter, John *Library of practical agriculture* 1846
Baxter, Mrs. Lucy E. *See* 'Scott, Leader'
Baxter, Nathaniel *The lectures or daily sermons of.. Iohn Caluine... upon the prophet Jonas* tr. 1578
Sir Philip Sidney's Ourania 1606
Baxter, Richard *Answer to Dr. E. Stillingfleet's charge of separation* 1680
A call to the unconverted to turn and live 1657
Catholic communion defended 1680 (1684)
Catholick theologie 1675
The Church told of Mr. Ed. Bagshaw's scandals 1672
The cure of church-divisions 1670
The divine life 1664
Gildas Salvianus; the reformed pastor 1656
A key for Catholicks to open the jugling of the Jesuits 1659
The last work of a believer 1661 (1682)
The life of faith 1670
Of national churches 1691
A paraphrase on the New Testament 1685
Plain scripture-proof of infants' church membership and baptism 1651
The Quakers catechism 1655
Reliquiæ Baxterianæ: or Mr. R. B.'s narrative of the most memorable passages of his life and times a1691 (ed. M. Sylvester 1696)
The saints everlasting rest 1650
A treatise of conversion 1657
Whether parish congregations be true Christian churches 1684
Baxter, William *British phoenogamous botany* 1834-43
Bay, Elihu H. *Reports of cases.. in the superior courts of law in South Carolina* 1798
Baylay, Atwell M. Y. *Batiffol's (P. H.) History of the Roman breviary* tr. 1898
Bayley, John *The history and antiquities of the Tower of London* 1821-25
Bayley, Roger Child *The complete photographer* 1906
Bayliss, William Maddock *Principles of general physiology* 1915
Bayly, Ada Ellen *See* 'Lyall, Edna'
Bayly, Brian *Introduction to petrology* 1968
Bayly, Thomas *Herba parietis, or the wall-flower* 1650
Life of Bp. Fisher 1655
Worcesters Apophthegmes 1650
Baynard, Edward *Health* 1719 (1740)
Of the genuine use of hot and cold baths (in Sir J. Floyer, Hot and cold bathing) 1706
Bayne or Baynes, Paul *A commentarie upon.. Colossians* a1617 (1634)
A commentarie upon.. Ephesians a1617 (1866)
The diocesans tryall a1617 (1641)
Lectures a1617 (1634)
Bayne, Peter *The chief actors in the Puritan revolution* 1878
Baynes, Helton Godwin tr. *C. G. Jung's Psychological types; or, The psychology of individuation* 1923
Bazaar Exchange and Mart 1871-
Bazell, Charles Ernest *Linguistic form* 1953
—— et al. eds. *In memory of J. R. Firth* 1966
Beach, Rex Ellingwood *Pardners* 1905 (UK 1912)
Beaconsfield, Earl of *See* Disraeli
Beadle, John Hanson *The undeveloped West; or, Five years in the Territories* 1873
Western wilds, and the men who redeem them 1878
— (another ed.) c1882
Beadle, Muriel *These ruins are inhabited* 1961 (UK 1963)
Beale, Francis *Biochimo's (G.) Royall game of chesse play* tr. 1656
Beale, Lionel S. *On slight ailments* 1880
Beale, Thomas *The natural history of the sperm-whale* 1839
Bean, Charles Edwin Woodrow *The 'Dreadnought' of the Darling* 1911
Bean, William Jackson *Trees and shrubs hardy in the British Isles* vols. 1-2, 1914; vol. 3, 1933
Beard, Charles *Port Royal: a contribution to the history of religion and literature in France* 1861
Beard, John R. *Lessons in English* 1854
Beard, Thomas *The theatre of God's judgements* 1597 (1612)
Beardsley, Aubrey *Letters* ed. H. Maas, J. L. Duncan, & W. G. Good 1971
Beaton, Cecil Walter Hardy *The wandering years: diaries 1922-39* 1961
Beatson, Robert *Naval and military memoirs of Great Britain* 1790
Beattie, George *John o' Arnha* 1815 (1826, 1847)
Beattie, James *Elements of moral science* 1790-93 (1793)
Essay on the nature and immutability of truth 1770 (1811)
The hermit 1760
The minstrel 1771, 1774
Scoticisms 1787
Beattie, William *Fruits of time parings* 1801 (1813, 1873)
Beattie, William *Life and letters of Thomas Campbell* 3 vols. 1849
Beatty, Charles *The journal of a two months tour* 1766 (1768)
Beatty-Kingston, William *Intemperance* 1892
Music and manners 1887
Beaty, Arthur David *Cone of silence* 1959
Excellency 1977
'Beauchamp, Philip' *See* Grote, G.
Beaufort, Henry C. F. Somerset, 8th Duke of, and Morris, M. *Hunting* 1885 (Badminton library)
Beaumont, Cyril William & Idzikowsky, Stanislas *A manual of the theory and practice of classical theatrical dancing (méthode Cecchetti)* 1922
Beaumont, Francis & Fletcher, J. *Comedies and tragedies* (1647; 1679)
Works (G. Darley 1839; A. Dyce 1843-46; Cambridge Eng. classics 1905-12)
Bonduca 1614
The coxcomb 1612
Four plays in one c1610
A king and no king 1611
The knight of the burning pestle 1609
The little French lawyer 1619
The maids tragedy 1611
Philaster 1611
The scornful lady 1610
Wit without money 1614
Woman hater 1607
Beaumont, Sir John *Bosworth field* a1628 (1710)
Beaumont, John *Considerations on Burnet's Theory of the earth* 1693
Beaumont, Joseph *Complete poems* 1615-99 (Grosart 1880)
Psyche, or loves mystery 1648, a1699 (1702, 1880)
Beaumont, Reginald Arthur ed. *Aeronautical engineering* 1942
Beauties of England and Wales, The 1801-18
Beautiful British Columbia, land of new horizons 1959-
Beavan, Arthur H. *Marlborough house* 1896
Beaver (Winnipeg) 1920-
Beawes, Wyndham *Lex mercatoria rediviva* 1750 (1752)
Beccaria's (Marquis) Essay on crimes and punishments tr. 1766 (1793)
Beck, Cave *The universal character* 1657
Beck, S. William *The draper's dictionary* 1886
Beck's Florist, fruitist and garden miscellany 1850-60
Becker, Stephen D. tr. *A. Schwarz-Bart's The last of the just* 1960 (UK 1961)
Becket, Abp. Thomas. Beket c1290 (in S. E. Legendary, E.E.T.S. 1887)
Life and martyrdom of T. Beket c1300 (Percy Soc. 1845)
Materials for the history of Thomas Becket 12.. (Rolls series 1875-85)
Beckett, Edmund *See* Denison, E. B.
Beckett, Samuel Barclay *Eh Joe, and other writings* 1967
More pricks than kicks 1934
Murphy 1938
No's knife: collected shorter prose 1967
Proust 1931
Stories and texts for nothing (tr. by Beckett of his *Nouvelles et textes pour rien* 1955) 1967
Waiting for Godot (tr. by Beckett of his *En attendant Godot* 1953) 1954 (UK 1956)
Whoroscope 1930
Beckford, Peter *Familiar letters from Italy* 1787 (1805, 1834)
Thoughts on hunting 1781 (1803)
Beckford, William *Dreams, waking thoughts and incidents in a series of letters* (anon., ascribed to B.) 1783
Excursion to monasteries of Alcobaca and Batalha 1835
Italy, with sketches of Spain and Portugal 1834
Popular tales of the Germans (anon.) tr. 1791
Recollections 1835
Vathek tr. 1786 (1863, 1868)
Beckington, Thomas *Official correspondence* 14.. (Rolls series 1872)
Beckmann's (J.) History of inventions and discoveries tr. 1846
See also Johnston, W.
Beckson, Karl & Ganz, Arthur *A reader's guide to literary terms* 1960 (UK 1961)
Becon, Thomas *Works* 1560-64 (also Parker Soc. 1843-44)
The actes of Christ and of Antichrist 1563
A comparison betweene the Lords supper and the mass a1564
Davids harpe 1542
The displaying of the Popish masse 1559
The floure of godly prayers 1551
A new catechisme 1560
A pleasante newe nosegay 1542
The pathwaye vnto prayer 1542
The relikes of Rome 1553
The sycke mans salue 1561
Beddoes, Thomas *Contributions to physical and medical knowledge* 179. (1799)
Hygeia; or essays moral and medical 1802-03
Letter to Dr. Darwin on a new method of treating pulmonary consumption 1793
Observations on the nature and cure of calculus, sea-scurvy, consumption, catarrh and fever 1793
Observations on the nature of demonstrative evidence 1793
Beddoes, Thomas L. *The bride's tragedy* 1822
Poems and letters 1822-37 (1851)
'Bede, Cuthbert' (E. Bradley) *The adventures of Mr. Verdant Green* 1853-56
The rook's garden 1865
Bedell, Bp. William *Letters* 1624
Life See Burnet, G.
Bedford, Arthur *The temple of music* 1706
Bedford, Frederick G. D. *The sailor's pocket-book* 1874 (1875)
Bedford, Hilkiah *A vindication of the church of England* 1710
Bedford, Randolph *True Eyes and the whirlwind* 1903
Bedford, Thomas *The sinne unto death* 1621
Bedingfield, Thomas *Machiavelli's Florentine historie* tr. 1594 (1595)
Bedloe, William *Narrative of the horrid popish plot* 1679
Bedoukian, Paul Z. *Perfumery synthetics and isolates* 1951
Bedwell, William *The Arabian trudgman* 1615
Index assuratarum Muhammedici Alkorani 1615
Mohammedis imposturæ 1615
Of the nature of geometricall numbers 1614
'Bee, Jon' *See* Badcock, J.
Beebe, Charles William *Jungle peace* 1918 (UK 1919)
Beecheno, Henry Oliver *An introduction to business studies* 1962
Beecher, Henry Ward *Lectures on preaching* 1872-74
Sermons a1887
Beechey, Sir Frederick W. *Hydrography* 1851-59 (in Manual of scientific enquiry 1859)
Beer, Max *A history of British socialism* 2 vols. 1919-20
Beer, Stafford *Cybernetics and management* 1959
Decision and control 1966
Beer, Thomas *The mauve decade: American life at the end of the nineteenth century* 1926
Beerbohm, Henry Maximilian *And even now* 1920
Around theatres 2 vols. 1924 (in *Collected works* Vols. VIII & IX)
— (another ed.) 1 vol. 1953
A Christmas garland 1912
Letters to Reggie Turner ed. R. Hart-Davis 1964
More 1899
Observations 1925
Seven men 1919
A variety of things 1928 (in *Collected works* Vol. X)
Zuleika Dobson; or, An Oxford love story 1911
Beerbohm, Julius *Wanderings in Patagonia* 1878 (1879)
Beet, William E. *The rise of the papacy* 1910
Beeton, Mrs. Isabella M. *Book of household management* 1861
Beevor, Antony *The violent brink* 1975
Begbie, Edward Harold *Life of William Booth, the founder of the Salvation Army* 2 vols. 1920
Behan, Brendan *Borstal boy* 1956
Behmen or Boehme, Jacob. The clavis or key; or an exposition of some principall matters and words in the writings of J. B. 1647
40 questions concerning the soule.. answered 1647
See also Ellistone, J.; Sparrow, J.
Behn, Mrs. Aphra *City heiress* 1682
The feign'd curtizans 1679
Novels 1671-96 (1718, 1722)
Behre, Frank ed. *Contributions to English syntax and philology* 1962
Behrend, Arthur *The Samarai affair* 1973
Behrens' (W. J.) The microscope in botany tr. 1885
Beil, Johann A. *Technologisches Wörterbuch der deutschen, französischen und englischen Sprache* 1853-55
Beket See Becket
Belany, James Cockburn *A treatise upon falconry* 1841
Belfast Telegraph 1870-
Belgicke pismire, The See Scott, Thomas
Belgravia: a London magazine 1866-
Belknap, Jeremy *The history of New Hampshire* 1784-92
Tour to the White Mountains 1784 (1876)
Bell, Alexander G. *Upon the production of sound by radiant energy* 1881
Bell, Alexander Melville *The principles of speech and vocal physiology* 1863
Visible speech: the science of universal alphabetics 1867

Bell, Sir Charles *The hand* 1833
Bell, Eric Temple *The development of mathematics* 1940
 —(ed. 2) 1945
Bell, Francis J. *Gegenbaur's (C.) Elements of comparative anatomy* tr. 1878
Bell, George J. *Commentaries on the laws of Scotland* 1810
Bell, Gertrude Margaret Lowthian (1868–1926) *Letters* sel. and ed. Lady Bell 2 vols. 1927
Bell, Harold Sill *American petroleum refining* 1923
 —(ed. 3) 1945
Bell, Henry *Luther's Colloquia mensalia* tr. 1652
Bell, Hesketh J. *Obeah; witchcraft in the West Indies* 1889
Bell, James *Walter Haddon against Osorius* tr. 1581
Bell, James *A system of popular and scientific geography* 1832
Bell, John *Bell's British theatre* 1776–78 (1797)
'Bell, Josephine' (Doris Bell Ball) *Crime in our time* 1962
 Murder in hospital 1937
 The Port of London murders 1938
 The seeing eye 1958
Bell, Louis *The telescope* 1922
Bell, Peter & Coombe, David tr. *Strasburger's textbook of botany* (tr. from 28th German ed., rewritten by R. Harder et al.) 1965
 —(rev. ed. tr. from 30th German ed., rewritten by D. von Denffer et al.) 1976
Bell, Robert Ed. *Ancient poems, ballads and songs of the peasantry of England* 1857
 The annotated edition of the English poets 1854–57
 The life of Canning 1846
Bell, Robert *Bell's (W.) Dictionary and digest of the law of Scotland* 1882
Bell, Robert Charles *Board and table games from many civilizations* 2 vols. 1960–9
Bell, Thomas *A Christian dialogue betweene Theophilus.. and Remigius* 1609
 The survey of Popery 1596
Bell, Thomas *A history of British quadrupeds* 1837
 A history of the British stalk-eyed crustacea 1853
Bell, William *A dictionary and digest of the law of Scotland* 1838
 See also Bell, R.
Bell system technical journal 1922–
Bell's life in London and sporting chronicle 1822–86
Bellairs, Angus d'Albini *The life of reptiles* 2 vols. 1969
Bellairs, George *Death in High Provence* 1957
Bellairs, Nona *Wayside flora* 1866
Bellamy, Edward *Looking backward, 2000–1887* 1888 (1889)
Bellamy, George Anne *Apology for her life* 1785
Bellamy, S. *The betrayal* 1838
Bellamy, Thomas *The beggar-boy: a novel* 1801
Bellanti, Joseph Alphonso *Immunology* 1971
Belle assemblée See Haywood, Eliza
Bellenden, John *Boece's (Hector) History and chronicles of Scotland* tr. 1536 (1821)
 Livy's History of Rome 1533 (1822; S.T.S. 1901)
Belloc, Hilaire *Cautionary tales for children* 1907
 Charles the First, King of England 1933
 Essays of a Catholic layman in England 1931
 Hills and the sea 1906
 A history of England 4 vols. 1925–31
 Pongo and the bull 1910
 Verses and sonnets 1896
Bellon, Peter *A new mystery in physick* tr. 1681
Bellow, Saul *The adventures of Augie March* 1953
 Dangling man 1944
 Herzog 1964 (UK 1965)
 Seize the day 1956 (UK 1957)
 The victim 1947 (UK 1948)
Beloe, William *The history of Herodotus* tr. 1791
 The sexagenarian (anon.) 1817
Belsches, R. *General view of the agriculture of the county of Stirling* 1796
Belsham, William *Essays, philosophical, historical and literary* 1789–91
Benbrigge, John *God's fury, England's fire* 1646
 Vsura accommodata 1646
Benchley, Nathaniel Goddard *Welcome to Xanadu* 1968
Bender, Arnold Eric *Dictionary of nutrition and food technology* 1960
Beneden's (P. J. van) Animal parasites and messmates tr. 1876
Benedict, St. *Versions of the Benedictine rule or 'Rule of St. Benet.'*
 *Æthelwold's c*960 (Schröer 1885)
 *Caxton's c*1490 (E.E.T.S. 1902)
 *Interlinear a*1030 (E.E.T.S. 1888)
 *Prose c*1400 (E.E.T.S. 1902)
 *Verse c*1400 (E.E.T.S. 1902)
 *Winteney c*1000 (Schröer 1888)
Benedict, Ruth (Fulton) *The chrysanthemum and the sword: patterns of Japanese culture* 1946 (UK 1947)
 Patterns of culture 1934 (UK 1935)
Benét, Stephen Vincent *John Brown's body* 1928
 Thirteen o'clock 1937 (UK 1938)
Ben Israel, Manasseh *Vindiciæ Judæorum* 1656 (1708)
Benlowes, Edward *Theophila, or love's sacrifice* 1652
Bennett, Agnes Maria *The beggar girl and her benefactors* 1797 (1813)
 Ellen, countess of Castle Howel 1794
 Juvenile indiscretions 1786
Bennett, Alfred W. *Thomé's (O. W.) Text-book of structural and physiological botany* tr. 1877 (1885)
 —— & Thiselton-Dyer, Sir W. T. *Sachs' (J. von) Text-book of botany* tr. 1875
 —— & Murray, G. *A handbook of cryptogamic botany* 1889
Bennett, Arnold See Bennett, Enoch Arnold
Bennett, Colin Noël *The guide to kinematography* 1917
 —— et al. *The handbook of kinematography: the history, theory and practice of motion photography and projection* 1911
Bennett, Edward T. *The gardens and menagerie of the Zoological Society* 1830
Bennett, Enoch Arnold *Anna of the Five Towns* 1902
 The card 1911
 Clayhanger 1910
 The Grand Babylon Hotel 1902
 A great man 1904
 The grim smile of the Five Towns 1907
 Hilda Lessways 1911
 Imperial Palace 1930
 Journals, 1896–1928 ed. N. Flower 3 vols. 1932–3
 Leonora 1903
 Letters ed. J. Hepburn 3 vols. 1966–70
 Lilian 1922
 The lion's share 1916
 Lord Raingo 1926
 A man from the North 1898
 The matador of the Five Towns, and other stories 1912
 The old wives' tale 1908
 The pretty lady 1918
 The Regent 1913
 Riceyman Steps 1923
 The roll-call 1918
 Tales of the Five Towns 1905
 These twain 1915 (UK 1916)
 The truth about an author 1903
Bennett, Frederick D. *Narrative of a whaling voyage* 1840
Bennett, George *Gatherings of a naturalist in Australia* 1860
 Wanderings in New South Wales etc. 1834
Bennett, Ivy V. P. *Delinquent and neurotic children* 1960
Bennett, John Godolphin *Witness* 1962
Bennett, John H. *Lectures on clinical medicine* 1850–56
Bennett, Joseph and 'Cavendish' *Billiards* 1873
Bennett, Louise *Jamaican humour in dialect* 1943
Bennett, Mary Montgomerie *Christison of Lammermoor* 1927
Bennison, George Mills & Wright, Alan Edward *The geological history of the British Isles* 1969
Benson, Arthur C. *The thread of gold* 1905
Benson, Edward F. *The Challoners* 1904 (1906)
 David Blaize 1916
 Dodo 1894
 The image in the sand 1905
 Mapp and Lucia 1931
 Thorley Weir 1913
Benson, Eugene Patrick *The bulls of Ronda* 1976
Benson, James W. *Time and time-tellers* 1875 (1902)
Bentham, Jeremy *Works a*1832 (1838–43)
 Chrestomathia 1816
 Church of Englandism and its catechism examined 1818
 Defence of usury 1787
 *Deontology a*1832 (1834)
 The elements of the art of packing 1810 (1821)
 A fragment on government 1776 (Wks. 1843 I)
 An introduction to the principles of morals and legislation 1780 (1789)
 Justice and codification of petitions 1829
 Official aptitude maximized 1810 (1830)
 Panopticon 1791
 Plan of parliamentary reform 1817
 *A protest against law taxes a*1832 (1853)
 Rationale of judicial evidence 1802–12 (1827)
 The rationale of reward 1825
 Scotch reform considered 1808
Bentham, Joseph *Two briefe but usefull treatises* 1657
Benthamiana 1776–1817 (1835)
Bentley, Edmund Clerihew *Trent's last case* 1913
 Trent's own case 1936
Bentley, Richard *Correspondence a*1742 (1842)
 A dissertation upon the epistles of Phalaris 1697 (1699)
 The folly and unreasonableness of atheism demonstrated (Boyle lectures) 1692–93 (1735)
 Remarks on Collins' Discourse of freethinking 1713
 *Sermons a*1742
Bentley, Richard 1757 See Hentzner, P.
Bentley, Robert *A manual of botany* 1861 (also 1870, 1887)
 —— & Trimen, Henry *Medicinal Plants* 4 vols. 1880
Bentley, Samuel *Excerpta historica* 1831
Bentley, Thomas *The monument of matrones* 1582
Bentley, William (1759–1819) *Diary* 4 vols. 1905–14
Bentley's miscellany 1837–68
Benton, Kenneth Carter *The red hen conspiracy* 1977
 Spy in Chancery 1972
Benton, Thomas Hart *Thirty years' view; or, A history of the working of the American Government for thirty years, from 1820 to 1850* 2 vols. 1854–6
Benvenuto's Passenger tr. 1612
Beowulf (E.E.T.S. 1882, Grein)
Bercher, William *The nobility of women* 1559 (Roxb. Club 1904)
Berckman, Evelyn *The Victorian album* 1973
Bereiter, Carl & Engelmann, Siegfried *Teaching disadvantaged children in the preschool* 1966
Beresford, James *Bibliosophia; or book-wisdom* 1810
 The miseries of human life 1806–07 (1826)
Beresford, Maurice *The lost villages of England* 1954
Berg, George Charles *The unconscious significance of hair* 1951
Berg, Leila *Risinghill: death of a comprehensive school* 1968
Berg, Paul C. *A dictionary of new words in English* 1953
Bergerac's (S. C. de) Satyrical characters tr. 1658
Berget, Alphonse *The conquest of the air: aeronautics, aviation; history, theory, practice* 1909
Bergman, Andrew *Hollywood and Le Vine* 1975 (UK 1976)
Bergman's (T.) Chemical essays tr. 1791
Berington, Joseph *The history of the lives of Abeillard and Heloisa* 1787
 A literary history of the middle ages 1814
Berington, Simon *Memoirs of G. di Lucca* 1737 (1738)
'Berkeley' *Dominoes and solitaire* 1890
Berkeley, Edmund Callis *Giant brains, or machines that think* 1949
 —— & Wainwright, Lawrence *Computers: their operation and applications* 1956
Berkeley, Bp. George *Works a*1753 (1871)
 Alciphron, or the minute philosopher 1732
 The analyst 1734
 Commonplace book 1705
 A defence of free-thinking in mathematics 1735
 An essay towards a new theory of vision 1709
 Farther thoughts on tar water 1752
 Journal of a tour in Italy 1717
 *Letters a*1753 (in A. C. Fraser, Life 1871 IV)
 Passive obedience 1712
 The querist 1735
 Siris 1744
 Theory of vision vindicated 1733
 Three dialogues between Hylas and Philonous 1713
 A treatise concerning the principles of human knowledge 1710
Berkeley, Hon. George C. G. F. *The English sportsman in the Western prairies* 1861
 My life and recollections 1864–66
Berkeley, George Fitz-Hardinge & Berkeley, J. *Italy in the making* 3 vols. 1932–40
Berkeley, Miles J. *Fungi* 1836
 Hand-book of British mosses 1863
 Introduction to cryptogamic botany 1857
 Outlines of British fungology 1860
Berkenhead, John *Sermon* 1644
Berkman, Al *Singers' glossary of show business jargon* 1961
Berks glossary (= A glossary of Berkshire words and phrases, by Major B. Lowsley, E.D.S. 1888)
Berkshire. A glossary of provincial words used in Berkshire (by J. Lousley) 1852
 Parish goods in Berkshire 1552 (1879)
Berlin, Isaiah *Karl Marx, his life and environment* 1939
Berlioz' (Hector) On modern instrumentation tr. M. C. Clarke 1856
Bermant, Chaim Icyk *Coming home* 1976
Bernard, John (1756–1828) *Retrospections of the stage* ed. W. B. Bernard 2 vols. 1830
Bernard, Nicholas *The life and death of Abp. Usher* 1656
Bernard, Richard *Commentary on the book of Ruth* 1628 (1865)
 A guide to grand jurymen (with respect to witches) 1627
 The Isle of Man, or legal proceedings in Man-shire against sin 1626
 A short view of the prælaticall church of England (anon.) 1641
 Terence's Comedies tr. 1598
*Bernardus de cura rei famuliaris a*1500 (E.E.T.S. 1870)
Berners, John Bourchier, 2nd Baron *The boke of duke Huon of Burdeux a*1533 (E.E.T.S. 1882–83)
 The firste volum (etc.) of syr John Froissart, of the cronycles of Englande, Fraunce (etc.) 1523–25 (1812)
 *The golden boke of Marcus Aurelius a*1533 (1546)
 *The history of.. Arthur of little Britain c*1530 (1814)
Berne(r)s, or Barnes, Juliana See *Book of St. Albans*
Bernstein, Julius *The five senses of man* 1876
Berrey, Lester V. & Van den Bark, Melvin *The American thesaurus of slang* 1942
 —(ed. 2) US 1953, UK 1954
Berridge, John *The Christian world unmasked* 1773 (1812)
Berry, Frederic Aroyce, Bollay, E., & Beers, Norman R. eds. *Handbook of meteorology* 1945
Berry, Miss Mary *Social life in England and France from 1780 to 1830* 1831
Berry, William *Encyclopædia heraldica* 1828–40
Berry, William Turner & Poole, Herbert Edmund *Annals of printing* 1966
Bert, Edmund *An approved treatise of hawkes and hawking* 1619
Bertin, Joseph *The noble game of chess* 1735
Berton, Pierre *Klondike fever* 1958
Bertram, James G. *The harvest of the sea* 1863
Bertram, James Munro *The shadow of a war: a New Zealander in the Far East, 1939–1946* 1947
Berwickshire Naturalists' Club *Proceedings* 1837–
Berwickshire rhymes 1856
*Beryn, The tale of c*1400 (Chaucer Soc. 1876; E.E.T.S. 1909)
Besant, Sir Walter *All in a garden fair* 1883
 All sorts and conditions of men 1882 (1884)
 Children of Gibeon 1886
 The demoniac 1890
 Dorothy Forster 1884
 *A five years' tryst, and other stories a*1901 (1902)
 The inner house 1888
 Katherine regina 1887
 The lady of Lynn 1901

Besant, Sir Walter (*cont.*)
The orange girl 1898
The revolt of man 1882 (1883)
Westminster 1895
The world went very well then 1887
—— & Rice, James *By Celia's arbour* 1878
The chaplain of the Fleet 1881
The golden butterfly 1876
My little girl 1873
Ready-money Mortiboy 1871
The seamy side 1880
Sir Richard Whittington 1881
This son of Vulcan 1876
With harp and crown 1875 (1877)
Besant, William H. *Treatise on hydromechanics* 1867
Bessey, Charles E. *Botany* 1880
Bessey, Ernst Athearn *Morphology and taxonomy of fungi* 1950
Bessinger, Jess B. & Creed, Robert P. eds. *Medieval and linguistic studies in honor of F. P. Magoun* 1965 (US ed. has title *Franciplegius*)
Best, Henry *Rural economy in Yorkshire in 1641. Being the farming and account books of H. Best* 1641 (Surtees Soc. 1857)
Best (or Beste) Henry D. *Four years in France* 1826
Italy as it is 1828
Personal and literary memorials 1829
Best, Thomas *A concise treatise on the art of angling* 1787
Best one-act plays 1932–
Beste, Raymond Vernon *Repeat the instructions* 1968
Bestiary c1220 (in O.E. Misc., E.E.T.S. 1872)
Betagh, William *Voyage round the world* 1728
Betham, Matilda *A biographical dictionary of the celebrated women of every age and country* 1804
Betham-Edwards, Matilda *See* Edwards
Bethel, Slingsby *The providences of God observed through several ages toward this nation in introducing the true religion* 1691 (1697)
Bethell, Nicholas & Burg, David tr. *A. I. Solzhenitsyn's Cancer ward* 2 vols. 1968–9
Bethune, Alexander *The Scottish peasant's fire-side* 1843
Betjeman, John *Collected poems* 1958
Continual dew 1937
A few late chrysanthemums 1954
High and low 1966
Mount Zion; or, In touch with the infinite 1931
New bats in old belfries 1945
Selected poems 1948
Summoned by bells 1960
Bettelheim, Frederick A. *Experimental physical chemistry* 1971
Betterton, Thomas *History of the English stage* 1741
Between Trent and Ancholme (by Miss Eliz. Fowler) 1908
Beues of Hamtoun, The romance of Sir 13.. etc. (E.E.T.S. 1885–94)
See also Beves
Bevan, Edward *The honey-bee* 1827
Bevan, George P. ed. *British manufacturing industries* 1876–77
Bevan, John Acton ed. *Essentials of pharmacology* 1969
Beveridge, David *Culross and Tulliallan* 1885
Beveridge, Erskine *North Uist* 1911
Beveridge, Henry *A comprehensive history of India* 1862
Beveridge, William *Works* a1708 (1729)
Private thoughts upon religion (*Private thoughts upon a Christian life*) 1661 (1730)
Sermons c1680 (1729)
Thesaurus theologicus; or a complete system of divinity a1708 (1710–11)
Beverley, Thomas *A chain of principles concerning the 1000 years kingdom* 1691
Conciliatory discourse on Dr. Crisp's sermons 1692
The grand apocalyptic question 1701
Memorial of the kingdom of our Lord Jesus Christ 1691
The praise of the glory of grace 1701
The thousand years kingdom of Christ etc. 1691
The true state of gospel truth 1693
Beverly, Robert *History of the present state of Virginia, by R. B.* 1705 (1722)
Beves of Hamtoun, Sir (= Beues, Sir) c1320 (Maitland Club 1838)
Bewick, Thomas *The general history of quadrupeds* 1790
The history of British birds 1797–1804 (1847)
Bews, John William *The world's grasses* 1929
Bhavnani, Enakshi *The dance in India* 1965
Bianchi, Michael A. *Levity and sorrow, a German story* tr. 1809
Bibbesworth (or *Biblesworth*), *Walter de, The treatise of*, c1325 (in T. Wright, Vocabularies 1857)
Bible, Versions of the (See also New Testament)
Wyclif's 1382, 1388 (1850)
Coverdale 1535
'*Matthews*' 1537
Great or *Cranmer's* 1539
Becke's ed. of '*Matthews*' 1551
Geneva 1560
Bishops' 1568
Douay 1609–10
Authorized 1611
Revised; N.T. 1881; O.T. 1884; Apocrypha 1894
New English Bible 3 vols. 1961–70
Bibliographical Society *Transactions* 1892–1919 (then merged with *The Library*)
Bibliotheca biblica See Parker, S.
Bibliotheca fanatica 1660 (Harl. Misc.)

Bickel, Walter tr. *R. Hering's Dictionary of classical and modern cookery* 1958
'Bickerdyke, John' (C. H. Cook) *Book of the all-round angler* 1888
Curiosities of ale and beer 1886
'Bickerstaff, Isaac' (J. Swift) *Predictions for the year 1708* 1708 (Arber, Eng. Garner VI)
A vindication of I. B. against what is objected to him, by Mr. Partridge in his Almanack 1709 (Arber, Eng. Garner VI)
Bickerstaffe, Isaac *Love in a village* 1763
Bickersteth, Edward H. *Yesterday, to-day, and for ever* 1866
Bickley, Augustus C. *Midst Surrey hills* 1890
Bicknell, J. L. *See* 'Collier, Joel'
Biddulph, William *The travels of certaine Englishmen into Africa, Asia*, etc. (ed. T. Lavender) 1609 (1612)
Biden, C. Leo *Sea-angling fishes of the Cape* 1930
Bierce, Ambrose *In the midst of life* 1892
Bieston, Roger *The bayte and snare of Fortune* c1550 (at end of Lydgate's Bochas c1558)
Bigelow, Jacob *Florula Bostoniensis: a collection of plants of Boston and its environs* 1814
Bigg, Charles *The origins of Christianity* a1908 (1909)
Biggs, Noah *On the vanity of the craft of physic or a new dispensatory* 1651
Bigod, Sir F. *See* Bygod
Billings, John Davis *Hardtack and coffee* 1887
Billings, John S. *The national medical dictionary* 1890
'Billings, Josh' (H. W. Shaw) *Josh Billings, his sayings* 1866
— *His book of sayings* 1870
Billings, Marland Pratt *Structural geology* 1942
— (ed. 2) 1954
— (ed. 3) 1972
Billings Gazette (Billings, Montana) 1901–
Billingsley, Sir Henry *The elements of geometrie of.. Euclid* tr. 1570
Billingsley, John *General view of the agriculture in.. Somerset* 1794 (1797)
Billingsley, Nicholas *Κοσμοβρεφια or the infancy of the world* 1658
Bilson, Bp. Thomas *The perpetual gouernment of Christes church* 1593
Bingham, John *Xenophon's Historie* tr. 1623
Bingham, John Michael Ward, 7th Baron Clanmorris *God's defector* 1976
The marriage bureau murders 1977
Bingham, Joseph *Origines ecclesiasticæ, or the antiquities of the Christian church* 1710–22 (1840)
Bingley, William *Animal biography* 1802 (1813)
Binnell's Description of the Thames 1758
Binning, Hugh *Works* a1653 (1735, 1847)
Binns, Charles F. *The story of the potter* 1898 (1901)
Binyon, Robert Laurence *Collected poems* 2 vols. 1931
Biochemical and biophysical research communications 1959–
Biochemical journal 1906–
Biochemistry (Easton, Pennsylvania) 1962–
Biochimica et biophysica acta 1947–
Biographia Britannica 1747–66
Biographia presbyteriana, containing the lives of A. Peden, J. Semple, J. Welwood, R. Cameron, D. Cargill and W. Smith, by P. Walker; of J. Renwick, by A. Shields (1827)
Biographical dictionary, A new and general 1761–62
Biological abstracts 1926–
Biological bulletin 1898–
Biological reviews and biological proceedings 1926– (from 1936 with title *Biological reviews*)
Bion, John *An account of the torments the French protestants endure aboard the galleys* 1708 (Arber, Eng. Garner VI)
Bion's (N.) Construction and principal uses of mathematical instruments tr. 1723 (1758)
Birch, Mrs. *Mrs. Rundell's Domestic cookery* 1846
Birch, Samuel *History of ancient pottery and porcelain* 1858
Birch, Thomas *The court and times of Charles the first* a1766 (1848)
The court and times of James the first a1766 (1848)
The history of the Royal Society of London 1756–57
Life of the hon. Robert Boyle 1744 (in Boyle's Works)
Life of Milton 1738
Sermons before the College of Physicians 1747
Birch, Walter de Gray ed. *Cartularium Saxonicum* v.d. (1885–93)
Bird, Anthony & Hutton-Stott, Francis *The veteran motor car pocketbook* 1963
Bird, Golding *Elements of natural philosophy* 1839
Urinary deposits 1844 (also 1857)
Bird, Miss Isabella L. *The Hawaiian archipelago: six months among the palm groves.. of the Sandwich Islands* 1875
Unbeaten tracks in Japan 1880
Bird, Kenneth *Smash a glass image* 1968
Bird, Robert Montgomery *The Hawks of Hawk-Hollow* 2 vols. 1835
Bird, William *The magazine of honour* 1642
Bird, William Richard *Off-trail in Nova Scotia* 1956
These are the Maritimes 1959
Birdwood, Sir George *The industrial arts of India* 1880
Birkbeck, Morris *Notes on a journey through France* 1814 (Appendix, 1815)
Birkhoff, Garrett & MacLane, Saunders *A survey of modern algebra* 1941
Birmingham, Maisie Poynter *The heat of the sun* 1976
Birmingham News (Birmingham, Alabama) 1888–
Birmingham Post (title varies) 1857–
Birmingham Weekly Post (newspaper) 1857–
Birnbach, Lisa, et al. *The official Preppy handbook* 1980
Birnbaum, Henrik & Puhvel, Jaan eds. *Ancient Indo-European dialects: proceedings of the Conference on Indo-European Linguistics at U.C.L.A. in 1963* 1966
Birnie, William *The blame of kirk-buriall* 1606 (1833)
Birrell, Augustine *Obiter dicta* 1884–87
Bischoff, James *History of the woollen and worsted manufactures* 1842
Sketch of the history of Van Diemen's Land 1832
Bishop, John *Otto's (J. A.) Treatise on the.. violin* tr. 1860 (1875)
Bishop, Mathew *Life and adventures* 1744
Bishop, Nathaniel H. *Four months in a sneak-box* 1880
Bishop, William H. *The house of a merchant prince* 1883 (1885)
Bishop's Stortford, Hertfordshire. The records of St. Michael's parish church, Bishop's Stortford (ed. Glasscock 1882)
Bishton, J. *General view of the agriculture of the county of Salop* 1794
Bissell, Richard Pike *High water* 1954 (UK 1955)
Bithell, Richard *A counting-house dictionary* 1882
Bisset, Robert *The life of Edmund Burke* 1798 (1800)
Black, Charles C. *Demmin's (A.) Illustrated history of arms and armour* tr. 1877
Demmin's (A.) Weapons of war; being a history of arms and armour tr. 1870
Black, David D. *History of Brechin* 1839 (1867)
Black, Francis *Principles and practice of homœopathy* 1842
'Black, Gavin' (Oswald Wynd) *The bitter tea* 1972 (UK 1973)
The golden cockatrice 1974
A time for pirates 1971
You want to die, Johnny? 1966
Black, Jack *You can't win* 1926
Black, John *The falls of the Clyde* 1806
Black, John *Berzelius' (J. J.) Attempt to establish a pure scientific system of mineralogy* tr. 1814
Black, John ed. *The Illustrated Carpenter and Builder series of technical manuals* 1902
'Black, Lionel' (Dudley Raymond Barker) *Death has green fingers* 1971
A healthy way to die 1976
Outbreak 1968
Black, Max ed. *The importance of language* 1962
The labyrinth of language 1968
The nature of mathematics 1933
ed. *Philosophy in America* 1965
Black, Peter *The biggest aspidistra in the world: a personal celebration of fifty years of the B.B.C.* 1972
Black, Rhona M. *The elements of palaeontology* 1970
Black, William *A daughter of Heth* 1871 (1876)
Green pastures and Piccadilly 1877
Highland cousins 1894
In far Lochaber 1888
Macleod of Dare 1879
Madcap Violet 1876
A princess of Thule 1873
Sabina Zembra 1887
Shandon bells 1883
Stand fast Craig Royston! 1890
The strange adventures of a phaeton 1872
Sunrise 1881
Yolande 1883
Black mask, The 1920–
Black panther 1969–
Black scholar 1969–
Black world 1970–
Blackadder, John *Memoirs* a1686 (1824)
Blackall, Offspring *Sermons* 1700–16
Works a1716 (1723)
Blackburne, Francis *The confessional, or a full and free inquiry into the right, utility.. and success of establishing systematical confessions of faith and doctrine in protestant churches* 1766
Blacker, Carlos Paton *Eugenics: Galton and after* 1952
Blackie, John Stuart *Æschylus, The lyrical dramas of* tr. 1850
Four phases of morals, Socrates, Aristotle, christianity, utilitarianism 1871
Homer and the Iliad 1866
Lay sermons v.d. (1881)
Lays of the Highlands 1872
On self-culture 1874
On the studying and teaching of languages 1852
Songs of religion and life 1876
The wise men of Greece 1877
Black-letter ballads and broadsides, A collection of seventy-nine 1559–97 (1867)
'Blackmantle, Bernard' *See* Westmacott, C. M.
Blackmore, Sir Richard *Alfred; an epick poem* 1723
Creation; a philosophical poem 1712 (1786)
Prince Arthur; an heroic poem 1695
A true and impartial history of the conspiracy against.. William III in.. 1695 1723
Blackmore, Richard D. *Christowell* 1881
Clara Vaughan 1864 (1872)
Cradock Nowell 1866 (1883)
Cripps the carrier 1877 (1887)
Dariel 1897
Erema 1877 (1880)
Lorna Doone 1869
The maid of Sker 1872
Mary Anerley 1880
Perlycross 1894
Springhaven 1887

Blackshaw, Alan *Mountaineering. From hill walking to Alpine climbing* 1965
— (rev. ed.) 1970
Blackshaw, Harold & Brightman, Rainald *Dictionary of dyeing and textile printing* 1961
Blackstone, Sir William *Commentaries on the laws of England* 1765–69
Blackwall, Anthony *The sacred classics defended* 1725 (1727–31)
Blackwelder, Richard Eliot *Taxonomy: a text and reference book* 1967
Blackwell, Henry *The English fencing master* 1705
Blackwood's Edinburgh magazine 1817–
Blades, William *Books in chains* 1890 (1892)
The life and typography of W. Caxton 1882 (ed. 2)
Blagrave, Joseph *Astrological practice of physick* 1671
Blaikie, Thomas *Diary of a Scotch gardener at the French court at the end of the 18th century* ed. F. Birrell 1931
Blaine, Delabere P. *Encyclopædia of rural sports* 1840
Blair, Hugh *Lectures on rhetoric and belles lettres* 1783
Sermons a1800 (1777–1804)
Blair, Patrick *Pharmaco-botanologia* 1723–28
Blair, Robert *Life, containing his autobiography from 1593 to 1636, with supplement*, etc. *by W. Row* (Wodrow Soc. 1848)
Blair, Robert *Poetical works* a1746 (1808)
The grave 1743
Blair, William *The soldier's friend* 1798
Blair & Ketchum's country journal (Brattleboro, Vermont) 1974–
'Blaisdell, Anne' (Barbara Elizabeth Linington) *Practice to deceive* 1971
Blake, Charles C. *Zoology for students* 1875
Blake, Geoffrey Charles & Trott, John Richard *Periodontology* 1962
Blake, John *A plan for regulating the marine system of Great Britain* 1758
'Blake, Nicholas' (Cecil Day Lewis) *The case of the abominable snowman* 1941
The deadly joker 1963
The dreadful hollow 1953
Malice in wonderland 1940
A question of proof 1935
The smiler with the knife 1939
There's trouble brewing 1937
Thou shell of death 1936
The whisper in the gloom 1954
See also: Lewis, Cecil Day
Blake, William *Complete writings* ed. G. Keynes 1966 (Oxford Standard Authors ed.; reprinted with corrections 1972)
A descriptive catalogue of pictures, etc. 1809
Poems a1827
Songs of innocence and experience 1789–94
Blakelee, George E. *Industrial cyclopedia* 1884
Blakey, Robert *Free-will* 1831 (1848)
Blamire, Susanna *Poetical works* a1794 (1842)
Blanc's (Louis) History of ten years 1830–40 tr. W. K. Kelly 1848
Blancard's (S.) Physical dictionary tr. 1684 (1693)
Blanckley, Thomas R. *A naval expositor* 1750
Blancourt's (F. Haudicquer de) Art of glass tr. 1699
Bland, David *The illustration of books* 1951
Bland, Francis *The souldiers march to salvation* 1647
Bland, Humphrey *A treatise of military discipline* 1727
Blane, William *An account of the hunting excursions of Asoph Ul Doulah* 1788
Cynegetica; or essays on sporting, etc. 1781 (1788)
Blane, William N. *An excursion through the United States and Canada* 1824
Blaquiere, Edward *Pananti's (F.) Narrative of a residence in Algiers* tr. 1818
Blaserna's (P.) Theory of sound in relation to music tr. 1876
Blast: review of the great English vortex ed. P. Wyndham Lewis 1914–15
Blatherwick, Charles *Uncle Pierce* 1888
Blavatsky, Helena P. *Isis unveiled* 1877
Bleaney, Betty Isabelle & Bleaney, Brebis *Electricity and magnetism* 1957
'Bleeck, Oliver' (Ross Thomas) *The Procane chronicle* 1971 (UK ed. 1972 with title *The thief who painted sunlight*)
Blesh, Rudolph Pickett *Shining trumpets: a history of jazz* 1946 (UK 1949)
They all played ragtime: the true story of an American music 1950 (UK 1958)
Blessington, Marguerite Gardiner, Countess of *The idler in France* 1841
The magic lantern 1822
Blickling Homilies, The 971 (E.E.T.S. 1880)
Blind, Mathilde *Tarantella: a romance* 1884
Blish, James *A case of conscience* 1958 (UK 1959)
A clash of cymbals 1959
Fallen star 1957
Blishen, Edward *Roaring boys* 1955
Blith or Blithe, Walter *The English improver, or a new survey of husbandry* 1649
The English improver improved, or the survey of husbandry surveyed 1652 (1653)
Bloch, Bernard & Trager, George Leonard *Outline of linguistic analysis* 1942
'Blois, W.' *Modern policies, taken from Machiavel, Borgia*, etc. 1657 (1690)
Blom, Eric Walter *Music in England* 1942
Blome, Richard ed. *The fanatick history: or an exact relation and account of the old Anabaptists and the new Quakers* 1660
The gentleman's recreation 1686
A geographical description of the four parts of the world 1670
Blomefield, Francis *An essay towards a topographical history of the county of Norfolk* a1752 (1739–1810)
Blomfield, Alfred *A memoir of C. J. Blomfield, bishop of London* 1863
Blomfield, Edward V. *Matthiæ's (A. H.) Greek grammar* tr. a1816 (1818)
Blood: the journal of hematology 1946–
Bloodgood, Lida & Santini, Piero eds. *The horseman's dictionary* 1963
Bloodworth, Dennis *Any number can play* 1972
The clients of Omega 1975
Crosstalk 1978
Bloome's (H.) Architecture tr. 1660
Bloomfield, J. C. *The fisheries of Ireland* 1883 (Fisheries exhibition literature)
Bloomfield, Leonard *An introduction to the study of language* 1914
Language 1933
Bloomfield, Robert *The farmer's boy* 1798
Rural tales 1801 (1802)
Wild flowers 1806 (1845)
Blore, Edward *The monumental remains of noble and eminent persons* 1826
Bloudy boke, The; or the death of Sir John Fites or Fitz 1605 (Halliwell)
Blount, Edward *Conestaggio's (J. F. de) Historie of the uniting of the kingdom of Portugall to the crowne of Castill* tr. 1600
The hospital of incurable fools tr. 1600
See also Brydges, Grey
Blount, Sir Henry *A voyage into the Levant* 1636 (1650)
Blount, Thomas *Boscobel* 1660
Fragmenta antiquitatis, antient tenures of land, etc. 1679
Glossographia, or a dictionary interpreting such hard words.. as are now used 1656, 1661, 1670, 1674 (1681)
A law dictionary 1670 (1691)
Blount, Sir Thomas Pope *Essays on several subjects* 1697
A natural history 1693
Blow, Claude Montague *Rubber technology and manufacture* 1971
Blowbol's testament c1500 (in Halliwell, Nugæ poeticæ 1844)
Blower, Mrs. Elizabeth *George Bateman: a novel* 1782
Bloxam, Charles L. *Chemistry inorganic and organic* 1867
Blues unlimited 1963–
Blundell, William *Crosby records. A Cavalier's note book, being notes.. of W. B.* a1698 (1880)
Blunden, Edmund Charles *After the bombing, and other short poems* 1949
Choice or chance: new poems 1934
Cricket country 1944
De bello Germanico: a fragment of trench history 1930
An elegy, and other poems 1937
The face of England 1932
The harbingers 1916
The mind's eye 1934
Near and far: new poems 1929
Poems 1930
Poems, 1930–1940 1940
Retreat 1928
Romantic poetry and the fine arts 1942
Shells by a stream 1944
The shepherd, and other poems 1922
A summer's fancy 1930
Undertones of war 1928
Blundevil, Thomas *Exercises* 1594 (1636)
The fower chiefyst offices belonging to horsemanshippe etc. 1565–66 (1580)
Blunt, John H. *The annotated Book of Common Prayer* 1876–84
Dictionary of sects, heresies etc. 1874
The reformation of the church of England 1868–82
Blunt, John J. *The right use of the early Fathers* 1845–46 (1857, 1869)
Blunt, Wilfrid Jasper W. *Of flowers and a village* 1963
Blyth, Edward *Cuvier's Animal kingdom* tr. 1849
Boag, John *A popular and complete English dictionary* 1848
Boas' (J. E. V.) Text book of zoology tr. J. W. Kirkaldy and E. C. Pollard 1896
Boate, Gerard *Ireland's natural history* 1645–50 (1860)
'Bobbin, Tim' *See* Collier, John; Walker, Robert
Boccaccio's (G.) Decameron tr. 1620
Boccalini's (T.) New-found politicke tr. 1626
See also Monmouth, Earl of; and N. N.
Boccus. The romance of King Bocchus and Sidrac c1440 (MS. Laud Misc. 559)
— *The hystory and questyons of kynge Bocchus and Sydracke* tr. Hugo of Caumpeden (c1510)
Boddam-Whetham, John W. *Roraima and British Guiana* 1879
Boddy, Evan M. *The history of salt* 1881
Bodkin, Maud *Archetypal patterns in poetry: psychological studies of imagination* 1934
Bodleian Library record 1938–
Bodley, John E. C. *France* 1898
Bodrugan alias Adams, Nicholas *An epitome of the title that the kynges maiestie of Englande hath to the souereigntie of Scotlande* 1548 (in Complaynt Scotl., E.E.T.S. 1872)
Body and soul a1000 (Grein)
Body and soul (by G. Wilkins and others) 1822 (1824)
Body and the soul, Debate between the a1300 (in Mapes' Poems, Camden Soc. 1841)
Böddeker, K. ed. *Altenglische Dichtungen des MS. Harl. 2253* 1878
Boerhaave's (H.) Institutes tr. 1742–46
Boethius (Anicius M. T. S.), The Anglo-Saxon version of the metres of a1000 (Fox 1864; Grein 1898; Sedgefield 1899)
See also Ælfred, Chaucer, Elizabeth, Preston, R.
Bogan, Zachary *Meditations of the mirth of a christian life* 1653
Boger, Louise Ade *The dictionary of world pottery and porcelain* 1971
Boghurst, William *Loimographia* 1666 (1894)
Bohn, Henry G. *Handbook of games* 1860
Handbook of proverbs 1857
See also Humboldt, F. H. A. von
Bohun, R. *A discourse concerning the origine and properties of wind* 1671
Bohun, William *Privilegia Londini, or the rights, liberties,.. and customs of the city of London* 1723 (ed. 3)
Boke of curtasye, The, a1400–50 (in Babees Bk., E.E.T.S. 1868)
Boke of good manners, The tr. (from J. Le Grand) 1487 (W. de Worde 1507)
Boke of keruynge, The 1513 (W. de Worde) (in Babees Bk., E.E.T.S. 1868)
Boke of noblesse, The 1475 (Roxb. Club 1860)
Bokenham, Osbern *Lyvys of seyntys* 1447 (Roxb. Club 1835; 1883)
Boker, George H. *Plays and poems* 1856 (1857)
'Boldrewood, Rolf' (T. A. Browne) *A colonial reformer* 1890
The miner's right 1890
Old Melbourne memories 1895
Robbery under arms 1888
A romance of Canvas Town 1898
The squatter's dream 1895
A Sydney-side Saxon 1891
Bolingbroke, Henry St. John, Viscount *Works* a1751 (1754–98)
A dissertation upon parties 1735 (1738)
Fragments or minutes of essays a1751 (Wks. 1754 V)
Letters on the spirit of patriotism 1736 (1749)
Letters on the study of history 1726 (1752)
Letters to Windham 1717 (1889)
Bolton, Edmund *Nero Cæsar* 1624
The Roman histories of Lucius Julius Florus tr. 1618 (1636)
Bolton, Sir Richard *The statutes of Ireland* (1621)
Bolton, Robert *The foure last things* 1632
Instructions for the right comforting of afflicted consciences 1631 (1635, 1640)
Bolton, Samuel *The arraignment of error* 1646
Boltz, Cecil Leonard *Basic radio* 1943
Bonar, Andrew R. *Last days of the martyrs* 1841 (1865)
Bonaventura's (J.) Meditations on the supper of our Lord 13.. (E.E.T.S. 1875)
Bond, Francis *Gothic architecture in England* 1905
Bond, J. A. Walpole- *Bird life in wild Wales* 1903
Bond, James *Birds of the West Indies* 1936
— (another ed.) 1960
Bond, John *Occasus occidentalis, or Job in the west* 1645
Bonde, Cunelgus *Scutum regale; the royal buckler, or vox legis, a lecture to the traytors who most wickedly murthered Charles the I* 1660
Bone, John Herbert A. *Petroleum and petroleum wells* 1865
Bone Florence of Rome, Le c1440 (in Ritson, Metrical romances III. 1802)
Bonet's (Théophile) Mercurius compitalitius tr. 1684
Bonfiglioli, Kyril *Don't point that thing at me* 1972
Something nasty in the woodshed 1976
Bon Gaultier's Book of ballads See Martin, Sir T. & Aytoun, W. E.
Bonington, Christian *Annapurna South Face* 1971
The next horizon: autobiography II 1973
Bonner, Bp. Edmund *Homilies* 1555
A profitable and necessarye doctryne 1555
Bonner, James Frederick *Plant biochemistry* 1950
Bonnycastle, John *An introduction to astronomy* 1786 (1787)
Bonoeil, John *A treatise of the art of making silke* 1622
Book See also *Boke*
Book of certaine canons, concernynge some parte of the discipline of the church of England, A 1571
Book of common prayer, The 1548–49 (Mar.), 1549, 1552, 1559, 1662
— *for the use of the church of Scotland* 1637
Book of common prayer: The grand debate between the.. bishops and the presbyterian divines appointed.. for the review and alteration of The book of common prayer 1661
Book of curteisie, The c1430 (in Babees Bk., E.E.T.S. 1868)
See also *Boke*
Book of customs and valuation of merchandises in Scotland, The 1612 (in Halyburton's Ledger etc. 1867)
Book of discipline, The first (second), of the church of Scotland 1560–61 and 1578 (1621; in Knox's Works 1846–64)
Booke of hawkyng, The c1450 (in Reliquiæ Ant. I)
Book of the knight of La Tour-Landry, The a1450 (E.E.T.S. 1868, 1906)
Book of quinte essence, The 1460–70 (E.E.T.S. 1866)
Book of the Rhymers' Club, The 1892, 1894
Book of St. Albans (*The bokys of haukyng, and huntyng* (by Dame Juliana Barnes) *and also of cootarmuris.. and the boke of blasing of armys translatyt* (from N. Upton) *and compylyt to gedyr at Seynt albons*) 1486

Book of St. Albans (*cont.*)
— (another ed., with) *The treatyse of fysshynge wyth an angle* 1496
Bookbinding, The art of 1818
Booker, Christopher *The neophiliacs: a study of the revolution in English life in the Fifties and Sixties* 1969
Bookman, The 1891–1934
Bookseller, The (title varies) 1858–
Boorde, Andrew *The boke for to lerne a man to be wyse in buyldyng of his house*, etc. *c*1540
The breviary of healthe 1547 (1552)
A compendious regyment or a dyetary of helth 1542 (1562; E.E.T.S. 1870)
Introduction to knowledge 1547 (E.E.T.S. 1870)
Booth, Andrew Donald & Booth, Kathleen H. V. *Automatic digital calculators* 1953
Booth, Barton *Memoirs.. To which are added several poetical pieces* 1733
Booth, David *An analytical dictionary of the English language* 1822 (1835)
Booth, Michael R. ed. *English plays of the nineteenth century* 4 vols. 1969–73
Booth, William *In darkest England and the way out* 1890
Boothroyd, Benjamin *Notes to Biblia Hebraica* 1810 (1816)
Boreman, Robert *A mirrour of mercy and judgement* 1655
The triumph of faith over death 1653 (1654)
Borland, Robert *Yarrow; its poets and poetry* 1890
Borlase, William *Antiquities of the county of Cornwall* 1754 (1769)
The natural history of Cornwall 1758
Born, Max & Wolf, Emil *Principles of optics* 1959
Boroughes, J. *See* Burroughes
Borradaile, Lancelot Alexander & Potts, Frank Armitage *The Invertebrata* 1932
Borror, Donald Joyce & DeLong, Dwight Moore *An introduction to the study of insects* 1954
— (rev. ed.) 1964
Borrow, George *The Bible in Spain* 1843
Lavengro 1851
Wild Wales 1862
Zincali; or an account of the gipsies of Spain 1841
Bosman's (W.) Description of the coast of Guinea tr. 1705
Bossewell, John *Workes of armorie* 1572
Bossuet's (J. B.) Exposition of the doctrines of the catholic church tr. 1685
Bostock, John *The history and present state of galvanism* 1818.
See also Pliny
Boston, Thomas *The crook in the lot* *a*1732
Human nature in its fourfold state 1720 (1797)
Memoirs 1730 (1776, 1899)
Boston, Massachusetts. Registry Dept. *Records relating to the early history of Boston* 39 vols. 1876–1909
Boston, Massachusetts. Society of Natural History *Proceedings* 1841–
Boston Daily Globe (Boston, Mass.) morning ed. 1872–
— evening ed. 1878–
— Sunday ed., as *Boston Sunday Globe* 1877–
Boston Evening Transcript (title varies) 1830–1941
Boston Herald 1846–
Boston Journal of natural history 1837–
Boston, Lincoln and Louth herald, The 1831–53
Boston medical and surgical journal 1828–1928
Boston News-Letter (title varies) 1704–76
Boston Sunday Globe See *Boston Daily Globe*
Boston Sunday Herald (title varies) 1861–
Boswell, Sir Alexander *Poetical works* *a*1822 (1871)
Boswell, James *An account of Corsica, the journal of a tour to that island* 1768
Journal of a tour to the Hebrides 1785 (1786)
The life of Samuel Johnson LL.D. 1791 (1831, 1887, 1904)
London journal 1762–63 ed. F. A. Pottle 1950
Bosworth, Joseph, and Toller, T. N. *An Anglo-Saxon dictionary* (1882–98)
— Supplement by T. N. Toller (1908–21)
Botanical gazette 1876–
Boteler, Nathaniel *Six dialogues about sea services* *c*1635 (1685)
Botkin, Benjamin Albert ed. *Lay my burden down: a folk history of slavery* 1945
ed. *A treasury of American folklore* 1944
ed. *A treasury of Southern folklore* 1949
Botoner (or Worcester), William *Boke of Tulle* (Cicero) *of old age* tr. 1481
Itineraria *a*1490 (ed. Nasmith 1778)
Bottome, Phyllis *Under the skin* 1950
Bottone, Selimo R. *Electrical instrument making for amateurs* 1888 (ed. 6 1894)
Boucher, Jonathan *A view of the causes and consequences of the American revolution* 1797
Boughen, Edward *Master Geree's case of conscience sifted* 1648
Bouhours' (D.) Life of St. Ignatius Loyola tr. 1686
Boulenger, Edward George *Apes and monkeys* 1936
Boulger, George Simonds *The uses of plants: a manual of economic botany* 1889
Wood: a manual of the natural history and industrial applications of the timber of commerce 1902
Boultbee, Thomas P. *An introduction to the theology of the church of England* 1871 (1875)
Boulton, Samuel *Medicina magica tamen physica. Magicall but naturall physick* 1656
Bounds and bonds of publique obedience, The (by F. Rous) 1649
Bouquet, Henry *An historical account of the expedition against the Ohio Indians in 1764, under the command of H. Bouquet* 1765 (1868)
Bourdillon, Francis W. *Aucassin and Nicolette* tr. 1887
Bourne, Geoffrey Howard ed. *Cytology and cell physiology* 1942
— (ed. 2) 1951; corrected impression 1952
Bourne, Henry *Antiquitates vulgares; or the antiquities of the common people* 1725
Bourne, Henry R. Fox *English merchants* 1866 (1886)
The life of John Locke 1876
Bourne, William *A regiment for the sea* 1574 (1577)
Boutell, Charles *Arms and armour* 1869 (1874)
English heraldry 1867 (1875)
Heraldry, historical and popular 1864
Bouterwek, Carl W. *Screadunga. Anglosaxonica maximam partem inedita* 1858
Bouverie, Edward O. Pleydell- *Rackets* 1890
Bouvier, John *A law dictionary, adapted to the constitution and laws of the United States of America* 1843–56 (ed. 6)
Bova, Benjamin *Multiple man* 1976 (UK 1977)
Bowden, Miss Emily F. *Hahn-Hahn's Lives of the fathers of the desert* tr. 1867
Bowden, Thomas *Farmer's director* 1776
Bowditch, William R. *The analysis.. and use of coal gas* 1867
Bowdler, Thomas *An appeal.. on the subject of Sunday trains* 1839
Bowen, Sir Charles S. C. *Virgil in English verse* 1887
Bowen, Elizabeth Dorothea Cole *Ann Lee's, and other stories* 1926
The cat jumps, and other stories 1934
Collected impressions 1950
The death of the heart 1938
The demon lover, and other stories 1945
Encounters 1923
The heat of the day 1949
The hotel 1927
The house in Paris 1935
The last September 1929
The little girls 1964
Look at all those roses 1941
Seven winters 1942
A time in Rome 1960
To the north 1932
A world of love 1955
Bowen, Francis *A treatise on logic* 1864 (1870)
Bowen, Frank Charles *Sea slang: a dictionary of the old-timers' expressions and epithets* 1929
Bowen, Godfrey *Wool away! The technique and art of shearing* 1955
— (ed. 2) 1956
'Bower, Bertha Muzzy' (Bertha Muzzy Sinclair) *The Parowan bonanza* 1923
The phantom herd 1916
Bower, Frederic Orpen *Botany of the living plant* 1919
Plant-life on land considered in some of its biological aspects 1911
—— & Scott, D. H. *De Bary's Comparative anatomy of the phanerogams and ferns* tr. 1884
Bowers, Fredson Thayer *Bibliography and textual criticism* 1964
Principles of bibliographical description 1949
Textual and literary criticism 1959
Bowes, Robert *Correspondence* 1577–83 (Surtees Soc. 1842)
Bowes, Thomas *De La Primaudaye's French academie* tr. by T. B. 1586–94 (1589, 1594)
Bowles, Caroline A. *See* Southey, Mrs.
Bowles, Edward *The mysterie of iniquitie yet working in.. England, Scotland and Ireland* 1643
Plaine English; or a discourse concerning the accommodation, the armie, the association (anon.) 1643
Bowles, John *The real grounds of the present war with France* 1793
Bowles, Samuel *Our new West. Records of travel between the Mississippi River and the Pacific Ocean* 1869
Bowles, William L. *Poetical works* *a*1850
Banwell Hill 1806
The life of Thomas Ken, D.D. deprived bishop of Bath and Wells 1830
Bowley, Arthur Lyon & Stamp, Josiah Charles *The national income, 1924: a comparative study of the income of the United Kingdom in 1911 and 1924* 1927
Bowls ('Know the game' series) 1962
Bowman, Walter Parker & Ball, Robert Hamilton *Theatre language: a dictionary of terms in English from medieval to modern times* 1961
Bowman, William Cameron, Rand, M. J., & West, G. B. *Textbook of pharmacology* 1968
Bowne, Borden P. *Introduction to psychological theory* 1886
Metaphysics, a study in first principles 1882
Bowra, Cecil Maurice *The Romantic imagination* 1950
Box, Charles *The English game of cricket* 1877
Boy's own paper, The 1879–
Boyd, Andrew K. H. *Lessons of middle age* 1868
The recreations of a country parson 1859–61
Boyd, Edward & Parkes, Roger *The dark number* 1973
Boyd, Zachary *The last battell of the soule in death* 1629
Zion's flowers *c*1620 (Four poems from, 1855)
Boyer, Abel *Dictionnaire François-Anglois* 1699 (1719, 1727, 1768, 1783)
Boyle, Charles, 4th Earl of Orrery *Dr. Bentley's Dissertations on the epistles of Phalaris examin'd* 1698
Boyle, Frederick *On the borderland betwixt the realms of fact and fancy* 1884
Boyle, John R. *The early history of the town and port of Hedon* 1895
Boyle, Sir Richard, 1st Earl of Cork *Lismore papers* (Diaries, etc.) 16.. (Grosart 1886)
Boyle, Robert *Works* *a*1691 (1744, 1772)
The Christian virtuoso 1690
Some considerations touching the style of the holy scriptures 1661 (1675)
Some considerations touching the usefulnesse of experimental philosophy 1663
A continuation of new experiments physico-mechanical 1669 (1682)
A free enquiry into the vulgarly receiv'd notion of nature 1685
An essay about the origine and virtues of gems 1672
An examen of Mr. Hobbe's Dialogus 1661 (1682)
The excellency of theology compared with naturall philosophy 1674
The experimental history of colours 1663
Experiments about the porosity of bodies 1684
Experiments about the producibleness of chymical principles 1680
The general history of the air *a*1691 (1692)
The martyrdom of Theodora 1687
Short memoirs for the natural experimental history of mineral waters 1684–85
New experiments physico-mechanicall 1660
Occasional reflections upon several subjects 1665 (1848)
The origine of formes and qualities 1666 (1667)
The sceptical chymist 1661 (1680)
A treatise of seraphic love 1648 (1700)
Boyle, Captain Robert, Adventures of (by W. R. Chetwood) 1726 (1735)
Boyle, Roger, 1st Earl of Orrery *Parthenissa, that most fam'd romance* 1654 (1676)
A treatise of the art of war 1677
Boylston, Herbert Melville *An introduction to the metallurgy of iron and steel* 1928
Boys, John *Works* *a*1625 (1622, 1629)
Boys, Mrs. S. *Coalition* 1785
Boys, William *Collections for an history of Sandwich* 1792
Boys' magazine 1922–
Boyse, Samuel *Deity* (anon.) 1739
Brace, Charles Loring *Gesta Christi; or a history of human progress under Christianity* 1882
Home life in Germany 1853
The new West; or, California in 1867–1868 1869
Brace, Gerald Warner *The spire* 1952 (UK 1953)
Bracken, Henry *Farriery improved* 1737 (1738, 1756–57)
The traveller's pocket-farrier 1743
Brackenridge, Henry M. *Journal of a voyage up the Missouri* 1816
Views of Louisiana 1812 (1814)
Bracton, H. de *De legibus et consuetudinibus Angliæ* *a*1259 (Rolls series 1878–83)
Bradbury, John *Travels in the interior of America* 1817
Bradbury, Malcolm Stanley *Eating people is wrong* 1959
The history man 1975
Stepping westward 1965
Bradbury, Ray Douglas *Fahrenheit 451* 1953 (UK 1954)
The illustrated man 1951 (UK 1952)
Bradby, Mary Katharine *Psycho-analysis and its place in life* 1919
Braddon, Edward *Life in India* 1872
Braddon, Mary E. (Mrs. Maxwell) *Asphodel* 1881
Aurora Floyd 1863
The cloven foot 1879
Dead men's shoes 1876
Dead sea fruit 1868
Eleanor's victory 1863
The fatal three 1888
The golden calf 1883
Henry Dunbar, the story of an outcast 1864
Hostages to Fortune 1875
John Marchmont's legacy 1863
Joshua Haggard's daughter 1876
Just as I am 1880
Lady Audley's secret 1862
The lady's mile 1866
Like and unlike 1887
The Lovels of Arden 1871
Lucius Davoren 1873
Mount Royal 1882
One thing needful 1886
Only a clod 1865
An open verdict 1878
Phantom Fortune 1883
Sir Jasper's tenant 1865
The story of Barbara 1880
Strangers and pilgrims 1873
Vixen 1879
Wyllard's weird 1885
Braddon, Russell Reading *Nancy Wake: the story of a very brave woman* 1956
The year of the angry rabbit 1964
Bradford, Gershom *A glossary of sea terms* 1927
— (new ed.) 1954
Bradford, John *Writings* *a*1555 (Parker Soc. 1848–53)
Bradford, William *History of Plymouth plantation* *c*1650 (1856)
Bradley, Francis Herbert *The principles of logic* 1883
Bradley, Henry *The Goths from the earliest times to the end of the Gothic dominion in Spain* (The story of the nations) 1888
ed. *Stratmann's (F. H.) Middle-English dictionary* 1891

BRADLEY, Richard *Chomel's Dictionaire œconomique, or the family dictionary* tr. Revised by R. Bradley 1725
Dictionarium botanicum, or a botanical dictionary 1728
On gardening 1731
A philosophical account of the works of nature 1721
A treatise concerning the manner of fallowing of ground (anon.) 1724
BRADSHAW, Henry *The life of saint Werburge of Chester* 1513 (E.E.T.S. 1887)
Bradshaw's railway guide (title varies) 1841–1961
Bradshaw's railway manual, shareholders' guide, and official directory for 1869 (Vol. XXI) 1869
BRADSTREET, Anne *Poems* 1642 (1875)
Bradstreet's: a journal of trade, finance and public economy 1879–1933
'BRADWOOD, Wat' (W. B. Woodgate) *The O. V. H.* 1869
BRADY, John *Clavis calendaria or a compendious analysis of the calendar* 1812
BRADY, Robert *An historical treatise of cities and burghs, or boroughs* 1690 (1777)
BRAGG, Melvyn *The hired man* 1969
Without a city wall 1968
BRAGGE, Francis *A practical discourse on the parables* 1694
BRAHMACHARINI USHA *A Ramakrishna-Vedanta wordbook* 1962
'BRAHMS, Caryl' (Doris Caroline Abrahams) & 'SIMON, S. J.' (Simon Jasha Skidelsky) *Titania has a mother* 1944
Trottie True 1946
BRAIN, Walter Russell *Diseases of the nervous system* 1933
Speech disorders 1961
Brain: a journal of neurology 1878–
BRAINE, John *Life at the top* 1962
Room at the top 1957
The Vodi 1959
BRAITHWAITE, David *Fairground architecture* 1968
BRAITHWAITE, George F. *The salmonidæ of Westmorland* 1884
BRAM, Gary & DOWNS, C. *Manufacturing technology* 1975
'BRAMAH, Ernest' (Ernest Bramah Smith) *A little flutter* 1930
BRAMBLE, Albert York *Air-plane flight* 1952
BRAMHALL, Abp. John *Works* a1663 (1677, 1842–45)
The consecration and succession of Protestant bishops justified 1658
A defence of true liberty 1658
A just vindication of the church of England 1654
A replication to the bishop of Chalcedon 1656
BRAMPTON, Thomas *A paraphrase on the seven penitential psalms* 1414 (Percy Soc. 1842)
Bran. The voyage of Bran .. an old Irish saga. Ed. and tr. K. Meyer, with an essay by A. Nutt 1895–97
BRANCKER, Thomas *Rhonii .. Introduction to algebra* tr. 1668
BRAND, Adam *Journal of the embassy from Muscovy to China over land* 1698
BRAND, John *A brief (new) description of Orkney*, etc. 1701 (1703)
BRAND, John *History and antiquities of the town and county of Newcastle-upon-Tyne* 1789
Observations on popular antiquities 1777 (also enlarged edd. 1813, 1849, 1870)
Brandan, St.: a medieval legend of the sea c1300 (Percy Soc. 1844).
See also BRENDAN
BRANDE, William T. *A dictionary of science, literature and art* 1842 (Also Brande and Cox 1865–67)
A manual of chemistry 1819, 1836–41 (ed. 5)
BRANDL, Alois *Quellen des weltlichen Dramas in England vor Shakespeare* (Pride of life, Mankind, Nature; J. Heywood's Love, Wether, Merry play; Respublica, King Darius; Misogonus; Horestes, Gismond of Salern; Common conditions) 1898
BRANDON, David Godfrey *Modern techniques in metallography* 1966
BRANDON, H. ed. *Poverty, mendicity and crime ... To which is added a dictionary of the flash or cant language* 1839
BRANDON, John Gordon *The pawnshop murder* 1936
BRANDT, David Julius O. *The manufacture of iron and steel* 1953
—(ed. 2) 1960
BRANFORD, Jean *A dictionary of South African English* 1978
—(new ed.) 1980
BRANSTON, Frank *An up and coming man* 1977
BRASH, Richard R. *Ecclesiastical architecture of Ireland* 1875
BRASSEY, Annie, Lady *In the Trades* 1884
A voyage in the 'Sunbeam' 1878
The last voyage 1887 (1889)
BRATHWAIT, Richard *The Arcadian princess* 1635
Barnabæ itinerarium or Barnabees journal 1638 (1818)
A comment upon the two tales of .. Chaucer 1665 (also Chaucer Soc. 1901)
The English gentleman 1630
The English gentlewoman 1631
Essaies upon the five senses 1620 (in Archaica 1815 II)
The lives of all the Roman emperors 1636
Natures embassie 1621 (1877)
The poets willow 1614
A strappado for the divell 1615 (1878)
Two Lancashire lovers 1640
Whimzies 1631
BRAUN, Hugh *Parish churches: their architectural development in England* 1970
BRAUN, Lilian Jackson *The cat who ate Danish Modern* 1967
Braunschweig, H. See BRUNSWYKE
BRAWLEY, Ernest *The rap* 1974
—(paperback ed.) 1975
BRAY, Mrs. Ann E. *De Foix* 1826 (1884)
A description of the part of Devonshire bordering on the Tamar and the Tavy 1836 (1879)
Fitz of Fitz-ford: a legend of Devon 1830 (1884)
Warleigh, or the fatal oak 1834 (1884)
BRAY, Warwick M. & TRUMP, David Hilary *A dictionary of archaeology* 1970
BRAYSHAW, J. Dodsworth *Slum silhouettes: stories of London life* 1898
BRAZIL, Angela *The new girl at St. Chad's: a story of school life* 1912
BRECK, Samuel *Recollections, with passages from his note-books* (ed. H. E. Scudder 1877)
BREE, John *Saint Herbert's isle* 1832
BREES, Samuel C. *A glossary of civil engineering* 1841
Terms and rules of practice in architecture etc. 1856
BREGION, Joseph & MILLER, Anne *The practical cook* 1845
BRELAND, Osmond Philip *Animal friends and foes* 1957
Brémond's (G. de) Apology, or the genuine memoires of Madam M. Manchini, Constabless of Colonna tr. 1679
BRENAN, Edward Fitz-Gerald (Gerald Brenan) *The face of Spain* 1950
Brendan, St. c1290 (in S.E. Leg., E.E.T.S. 1887).
See also BRANDAN
BRENDE, John *Q. Curtius Rufus' Historie* tr. 1553 (1570)
BRENNAN, Paul, HESSELYN, Ray, & BATESON, Henry *Spitfires over Malta* 1943
'BRENT OF BIN BIN' (Stella Maria Sarah Miles Franklin) *Up the country: a tale of the early Australian squattocracy* 1928
BRENT, Sir Nathaniel *Sarpi's (P.) Historie of the council of Trent* tr. 1620 (1629)
—with life of the author (1676)
BRENTON, Edward P. *The naval history of Great Britain 1783–1822* 1823
BRERETON, Cloudesley Shovell Henry & ROTHWELL, Frederick tr. *H. L. Bergson's Laughter* 1911
BRERETON, Sir William *Travels in Holland*, etc. 1634–35 (Chetham Soc. 1844)
BREREWOOD, Edward *Enquiries touching the diversity of languages and religions* 1612 (1614)
BRETON, Nicholas *Works* a1626 (Grosart 1879)
Daffodils and primroses 1593– (Works, Grosart I)
Fantasticks 1626
I would and I would not 1614
A mad world my masters 1603
The mothers blessing 1602
Pasquils fooles-cappe 1600
The pilgrimage to Paradise 1592
A poste with a packet of mad letters 1602–06
Strange newes out of divers countries, by B. N. 1622
The toyes of an idle head 1577–82
Wonders worth the hearing 1602
For *Sir P. Sidney's Ourania* See BAXTER, N.
BRETON, William *Militia discipline* 1717
BREVAL, John D. de *Remarks on several parts of Europe* 1726
BREVINT, Daniel *Saul and Samuel at Endor* 1674
BREVIOR, Thomas *See* SHORTER, T.
BREWER, Anthony For *Lingua* 1607 *See* TOMKIS, T.
BREWER, Ebenezer C. *Dictionary of phrase and fable* 1870
The reader's handbook of allusions, etc. 1880
BREWER, John Sherren *English studies* a1879 (1881)
BREWSTER, Ben R. tr. *L. Althusser & E. Balibar's Reading Capital* 1970
—(paperback ed.) 1975
BREWSTER, Sir David *Letters on natural magic* 1831 (1833)
The martyrs of science 1841 (1856)
Memoirs of the life of Sir I. Newton 1855
More worlds than one 1854
A treatise on magnetism 1837
A treatise on optics 1831
BRIAN, Thomas *The pisse prophet* 1637 (1679)
Brice's Weekly journal (Exeter) 1725–28
BRICKHILL, Paul & NORTON, Conrad *Escape to danger* 1946
'BRIDGE, Ann' (Mary Dolling, Lady O'Malley) *Four-part setting* 1939
Frontier passage 1942
Peking picnic 1932
The Portuguese escape 1958
BRIDGE, Horatio *Personal recollections of Nathaniel Hawthorne* 1893
BRIDGES, Robert *Poems* v.d.
Eros and Psyche 1885–94
Shorter poems 1890
The testament of beauty 1929
BRIDGES, Thomas *A burlesque translation of Homer* 1770 (1797)
Homer travestie, by Cotton Junior 1762 (1764)
Bridget, St. The lyfe of seynt Birgette (attrib. to T. Gascoigne) ? a1445 (in Capgrave, Kalendre of the newe legende of England 1516, fol. 120– ; Mirr. Our Lady, E.E.T.S. 1873)
BRIDGETT, Thomas E. *The history of the holy eucharist* 1881
BRIDGMAN, Mary *Robert Lynne: a novel* 1870
Brief discourse. A brief and witty discourse or dialogue between a Yorkshireman and a Scottish-man 1650
Briefe examination for the tyme, of a certaine declaration lately put in print in the name and defence of certaine ministers in London, refusyng to weare the apparell prescribed .. In the ende is reported, the iudgement of .. Bucer and .. Martir .. translated 1564
Briefe information of the affaires of the Palatinate, A 1624
Brieff discours of the troubles begonne at Franckford in Germany A.D. 1554 (by W. Whittingham) 1574 (1846)
BRIERLEY, Benjamin *Irkdale; or the old house in the hollow* 1865
Tales and sketches of Lancashire life 1854
BRIGGS, Charles Frederick *The adventures of Harry Franco* 2 vols. 1839
BRIGGS, Fred N. & KNOWLES, Paulden Ford *Introduction to plant breeding* 1967
BRIGGS, Richard *The new art of cookery* 1792
BRIGHT, James Franck *A history of England* 1875–88
BRIGHT, John *Speeches* a1889 (1878, etc.)
BRIGHT, Timothy *A treatise of melancholie* 1586
BRIGHT, William *The age of the Fathers* a1901 (1903)
BRIGHTMAN, Thomas *B.'s predictions and prophecies* 1641
BRILL, Abraham Arden tr. *S. Freud's The interpretation of dreams* 1913
tr. *S. Freud's Selected papers on hysteria and other psychoneuroses* 1909
tr. *S. Freud's Three contributions to sexual theory* 1910
tr. *S. Freud's Totem and taboo: resemblances between the psychic lives of savages and neurotics* 1918
BRIMLEY, George *Essays* 1851–55 (1858)
BRINDLEY, Charles *See* 'HIEOVER, Harry'
BRINKLEY, Frank *Oriental series* 12 vols. 1901–2
BRINKLOW, Henry *Complaynt of Roderyck Mors* c1545 (E.E.T.S. 1874)
The lamentacyon of a christen agaynst the cytye of London 1542 (E.E.T.S. 1874)
BRINSLEY, John *Ludus literarius or the grammar schoole* 1612 (1627)
The posing of the parts 1612 (1669)
Virgil's eclogues tr. 1620 (1633)
BRISTED, Charles A. *Five years in an English university* 1852
The upper ten thousand: sketches of American society 1852
BRISTED, John *Anthroplanomenus; being an account of a pedestrian tour through part of the Highlands of Scotland* 1803
Bristol. The little red book of Bristol 13..–14.. (1900)
BRISTOW, Henry W. *Figuier's (L.) World before the deluge* tr. 1865 (1869)
A glossary of mineralogy 1861
BRISTOWE, John S. *A treatise on the theory and practice of medicine* 1876 (1878)
Britain's industrial future (Liberal Industrial Inquiry) 1928
Britanniæ speculum, or a short view of .. Great Britain 1683
Britannica book of the year 1938 (UK eds. 1938–41 with title *Encyclopædia Britannica book of the year*)
British Academy *Proceedings* 1905–
British Apollo, The 1708–11
British archæological association, The Journal 1845–
British association for the advancement of science *Reports* 1831–
British birds 1907–
British Broadcasting Corporation *B.B.C. handbook* (title varies: also *B.B.C. year-book* and *B.B.C. annual*) 1928–
The B.B.C. quarterly 1946–54
B.B.C. war report ed. D. Hawkins et al. 1946
Glossary of broadcasting terms See FARQUHARSON, M. G., et al.
British chess magazine 1881–
British commonwealth forest terminology (Empire Forestry Association) 2 parts 1953–7
British critic, quarterly theological review, and ecclesiastical record 1827–43
British dental journal 1903–
British Dominions year book, The (British Dominions Insurance Co.) 1916–24
British Engineering Standards Association *British standard glossary of terms used in electrical engineering* 1926 *See* British Standards Institution. Glossaries. *Electrical Engineering*
British and foreign medico-chirurgical review, The 1848–77
British husbandry (by J. F. Burke) 1834–40 (Library of useful knowledge)
British Interplanetary Society *Journal* 1934–9, 1946–
British journal of dermatology 1888–
British journal of medical psychology 1923–
British journal of ophthalmology 1917–
British journal of photography 1893
British journal of psychology 1904–
British journal of radiology 1924–
British journal of sociology 1950–
British magazine 1760–67
British manufacturer Nov.–Dec. 1919
British manufacturing industries. ed. G. P. Bevan 1876–77
British medical bulletin 1943–
British medical dictionary, The ed. A. S. MacNalty 1961
British medical journal 1857–
British Museum Return 1914, etc. (in Parl. papers Eng., 1914, LXXI, etc.)
British pharmaceutical codex 1907 (and several later editions used)
British pharmacopœia 1864 (and many later editions used)
British Pharmacopœia Commission *Approved names See* United Kingdom. General Medical Council
British printer, The 1888–
British School (of archaeology) at Athens *Annual* 1895–
British Standards Institution *B.S.I. News* 1956
Nomenclature of commercial timbers, including sources of supply 1946
—(rev. ed.) 1955
Glossaries:
Aeronautical terms (BS 185) 1949, 1950, 1951, and other eds.
Automatic data processing (BS 3527) 1962, and several later parts

British Standards Institution (*cont.*)
Caravan terms (BS AU129) 1967, 1975
Concrete and reinforced concrete (BS 2787) 1956
Dentistry (BS 4492) 1969
Documentation terms (BS 5408) 1976
Electrical engineering (BS 205) 1926, 1936, 1943
Electrotechnical, power, telecommunication, electronics, lighting and colour terms (BS 4727) 1971–
General building terms (BS 3589) 1963
Glass industry (BS 3447) 1962
Highway engineering terms (BS 892) 1940, 1954, 1967
Landscape work (BS 3975) 1966–9
Letterpress rotary printing terms (BS 3814) 1964
Mining terms (BS 3618) 1963–74
Nuclear Science (BS 3455) 1962
Offset lithographic printing (BS 4277) 1968
Plastics industry (BS 1755) 1951, 1967–74
Radiology (BS 2957) 1955
Railway signalling (BS 719) 1936
Refrigeration (BS 1584) 1949
Sanitation terms (BS 4118) 1967
Telegraphs and telephones (BS 204) 1924, 1930, 1943 (*Telecommunication*), 1960
Timber preservation (BS 4261) 1968
British weekly, The: a journal of social and Christian progress 1886–
Briton, The 1723–24
Brittain, Vera Mary *Testament of youth* 1933
Brittains Ida See Fletcher, G. (the younger)
Brittan, Frederick *Malgaigne's (J. F.) Manual of operative surgery* 1846
Britten, Frederick James *Old clocks and watches* 1899
The watch and clockmaker's handbook 1877 (1881, 1884)
Britten, James *Old country and farming words* (E.D.S. 1880)
—— & Holland, R. *A dictionary of English plant-names* 1878–86 (E.D.S.)
Britton (on the laws of England). The French text c1290 (Nichols 1865)
Britton, John *The architectural antiquities of Great Britain* 1807–26
The beauties of Wiltshire 1801–25
A dictionary of the architecture and archæology of the middle ages 1838
Britton, Karl *John Stuart Mill* 1953
Britton, Nathaniel Lord *North American trees* 1908
Brno studies in English 1959–
Broad, Charlie Dunbar *The mind and its place in nature* 1925
Perception, physics, and reality 1914
Scientific thought 1923
Broadhouse, John *The student's Helmholtz: Musical acoustics* 1881
Brockett, John T. *A glossary of North Country words* 1825, 1829, 1846 (edd. 1–3)
Brockett, Linus P. *Cross and crescent* 1877
Brodal, Alf *Neurological anatomy in relation to clinical medicine* 1948
Brodie, Sir Benjamin C., 1st Bart. *Psychological inquiries* 1856–62
Brodie, Sir Benjamin C., 2nd Bart. *Ideal chemistry* 1867 (1880)
Brodrick, George C. *Memories and impressions* 1900
Brogden, J. Ellett *Provincial words and expressions current in Lincolnshire* 1866
Broinowski, Alison *Take one ambassador* 1973
Broke, Lord *See* Greville, F.
Brome, Alexander *Songs and other poems* 1661 (1668)
Brome, James *Travels over England, Scotland and Wales* 1700 (1707)
Brome, Richard *Plays* a1652 (1653, 1669; Wks. 1873)
The antipodes 1640
The city wit a1652
The court beggar 1632
The English Moor a1652
A joviall crew 1641
The new academy a1652
The northern lasse 1632
The queenes exchange a1652
The sparagus garden 1635 (1640)
Brome Hall, Suffolk, A common-place book of the fifteenth-century, from MS. at (ed. L. T. Smith 1886)
Bromfield, Louis *The rains came* 1937
Bromhall, Thomas *A treatise of specters* 1658
Bromige, Iris Amy Edna *The enchanted garden* 1956
Bromley, Gordon *In the absence of the body* 1972
Bronowski, Jacob *The ascent of man* 1973
Bronson-Howard, George *Enemy to society* 1911
God's man 1915
Brontë, Anne *Agnes Grey* 1847
The tenant of Wildfell Hall 3 vols. 1848
Brontë, Charlotte *Jane Eyre* 1847
The professor c1845 (1857)
Shirley 1849
Villette 1853
Brontë, Emily Jane *Wuthering Heights* 1847
Brooke, 1st Baron *See* Greville, F.
Brooke, 2nd Baron *See* Greville, R.
Brooke, Arthur *Romeus and Juliet* 1562 (1908)
Brooke, Charles *Ten years in Sarawak* 1866
Brooke, Christopher *Complete poems* a1628 (Grosart 1872)
The ghost of Richard the third 1614
Brooke, Frances *The history of lady Julia Mandeville* 1763 (1782)
The old maid 1755–56 (1764)
Brooke, Francis *Le Blanc's (V.) World surveyed or his famous voyages and travailes* tr. 1660
Brooke, Henry *The charitable association* 1778
A collection of the pieces formerly published, . . to which are added several plays and poems 1778 (1789)
The fool of quality; or the history of Henry, Earl of Moreland 1760–72 (1809, 1859)
Tasso's (T.) Jerusalem tr. 1738
Universal beauty 1735
Brooke, Henry J. *Familiar introduction to crystallography* 1823
Brooke, Humphrey *A conservatory of health* 1650
Brooke, Richard *A treatise on the office and practice of a notary of England* 1839
Brooke, Rupert Chawner (1887–1915) *Collected poems* 1918
Letters ed. G. Keynes 1968
Brooke, Stopford A. *English literature* 1880
Brooke-Rose, Christine Frances E. *The languages of love* 1957
Brookes, Richard *The art of angling, rock and sea fishing* 1740
A general gazetteer 1762 (enlarged ed. 1802)
Brookes, Samuel *An introduction to the study of conchology* 1815
Brookhouse, Thomas *The temple opened* 1696
Brooks, C. W. Shirley *The gordian knot* 1858
The silver cord, a story 1861
Brooks, Christopher P. *Cotton manufacturing* 1888
Brooks, Frederick Tom *Plant diseases* 1928
Brooks, Henry *Natal: a history and description of the colony* 1876
Brooks, Phillips *The candle of the Lord, and other sermons* 1881
Brooks, Thomas *A golden key to open hidden treasures* 1675 (Wks. 1865 V)
Broome (or Barker), Lady Mary Ann *Station life in New Zealand* 1869 (1874)
A year's housekeeping in South Africa 1887
Broome, William *Notes to Pope's translation of Homer's Odyssey* 1725
Brophy, John & Partridge, Eric Honeywood eds. *The long trail: what the British soldier sang and said in the Great War of 1914–18* 1965
Songs and slang of the British soldier, 1914–18 1930
— (ed. 3) 1931
Brose, Henry Herman L. A. tr. *A. J. W. Sommerfeld's Atomic structure and spectral lines* 1923
— (ed. 3) 1934
Brosnahan, Leonard Francis *Some Old English sound changes: an analysis in the light of modern phonetics* 1953
The sounds of language 1961
Brother Jonathan 1825 *See* Neal, J.
Brough, Robert B. *Marston Lynch: his life and times* 1860 (1870)
Brough, William *Sacred principles, services, and soliloquies; or a manual of devotions* 1650 (1656, 1671)
Brougham, Henry, Lord *Albert Lunel* 1844 (1872)
The British constitution 1861
Historical sketches of statesmen of the time of George III 1839
Broughton, Hugh *Works* 1588–1612
Letters . . about Sheol and Hades 1599
A require of agreement to the groundes of divinitie studie 1611
Broughton, Rhoda *Belinda* 1883
Cometh up as a flower 1867
Joan, a tale 1876
Nancy 1873
Red as a rose 1870
Second thoughts 1880
Brown, Alexander M. *Contributions to the study of animal alkaloids* 1887
Brown, Archibald *Scriven's (J.) Treatise on the law of copyholds* revised 1882
Brown, Bernard *Talking pictures* 1931
Brown, Charles B. *Edgar Huntly* 1799 (1835)
Volney's View of the soil and climate of the United States tr. 1804
Brown, David *Life of the late John Duncan, LL.D.* 1872
'Brown, Edward' *The travels and adventures of E. B.* 1739
Brown, George Mackay *An Orkney tapestry* 1969
Brown, Ivor John Carnegie *Say the word* 1947
Words in our time 1958
Brown, James Alexander Campbell *The social psychology of industry* 1954
Brown, James Baldwin *First principles of ecclesiastical truth* 1870
Misread passages of scripture 1869–71
Brown, John *A dissertation on the rise . . of poetry and music* 1763
Essays on the Characteristics (of the Earl of Shaftesbury) 1751
Brown, John *The christian journal* 1765 (1814)
A compendious history of the British churches in England, etc. 1784 (1823)
A dictionary of the holy bible 1769
Brown, John *Psyche* 1818
Brown, John *Letters of sanctification* 1834
Brown, John *Horæ subsecivæ* 1858–61
John Leech and other papers 1861– (1882)
Letters; with letters from Ruskin, Thackeray, and others ed. J. Brown & D. W. Forrest 1907
— (ed. 3) 1912
Locke and Sydenham etc. (from Horæ subsec.) 1866
Rab and his friends 1859 (1862)
Brown, John *The pilgrim fathers of New England* 1895
Brown, John *The chancer* 1972
Brown, John Crombie *The ethics of George Eliot's works* 1879
Brown, Marie A. *Runeberg's (J. L.) Nadeschda* tr. 1891
Brown, Michael Barratt *The economics of imperialism* 1974
Brown, Mungo P. *Supplement to the dictionary of the decisions of the Court of Session* 1826
Brown, Robert *The compleat farmer* 1759
Brown, Robert *A manual of botany* 1874
Brown, Samuel R. *The western gazetteer; or, Emigrant's directory* 1817
Brown, Thomas *The new bee-hive* a1655 (in Hartlib's (S.) Reformed common-wealth of bees 1655)
Brown, Thomas *Works* a1704 (1720, 1730)
A declaration . . in praise of poverty a1704
An essay on the satire of the antients a1704
Fresny's amusements serious and comical tr. 1700
Letters from the dead to the living c1700 (1702)
The saints in an uproar 1687
Brown, Thomas *A manual of modern farriery* 1847
Brown, Thomas E. *Collected poems* a1897 (1900)
The doctor and other poems 1887
Letters a1897 (1900)
Brown, Walter Varian & Bertke, Eldridge Melvin *Textbook of cytology* 1969
Brown, William *The history of the propagation of christianity among the heathen since the reformation* 1814
Browne, Alexander *Ars pictoria, or an academy teaching drawing, painting*, etc. 1669
Browne, Daniel Jay *The sylva americana; or, A description of the forest trees indigenous to the United States* 1832
The American poultry yard 1849 (1855)
Browne, Edward *A brief account of some travels in Hungaria* etc. 1673 (1685)
Browne, Edward H. *An exposition of the thirty-nine articles* 1850
Browne, Isaac H. *Poems* 1706–60 (1768)
Browne, Joseph *An account of the wonderful cures perform'd by the cold baths* 1707
Browne, Patrick *The civil and natural history of Jamaica* 1756 (1789)
Browne, Robert *An answere to master (T.) Cartwright* c1585
Browne, Sir Thomas *Works* a1682 (1835–36, 1851–52)
Christian morals 1682 (1756)
The garden of Cyrus 1658
Hydriotaphia, urne buriall 1658 (1736)
A letter to a friend 1672 (1881)
Certain miscellany tracts a1682 (1684)
Pseudodoxia epidemica or enquiries into very many received tenents (= Vulgar errors) 1646 (1658, 1686)
Religio medici 1643 (1656)
Browne, Thomas Alexander *See* 'Boldrewood, Rolf'
Browne, William *Works* a1643 (1772)
Britannia's pastorals 1613, 1616
Inner Temple masque 1615
The shepheard's pipe 1614
Thirsis' praise to his mistress a1643 (1772)
Browne, William *His fiftie yeares practice, or an exact discourse concerning snaffle-riding* 1624
Le Roy's (M.) History of Polexander tr. 1647
Browning, Carl Hamilton *Bacteriology* 1925
Browning, Mrs. Elizabeth Barrett *Poetical works* a1861 (Poems 1844, 1850)
Aurora Leigh 1856
Casa Guidi windows 1851
A drama of exile 1844
A lament for Adonis 1850
Letters addressed to R. H. Horne 1839–51 (1877)
Prometheus bound 1833
Some account of the Greek Christian poets 1842 (1863)
Sonnets from the Portuguese a1846
A vision of poets 1844
Browning, Robert *Poetical works* a1889
Aristophanes' Apology 1875
Balaustion's adventure 1871
Bells and pomegranates 1841–46
Dramatic idyls 1879–80
Dramatis personæ 1865
Ferishtah's fancies 1884
Fifine at the fair 1872
The inn album 1875
La Saisiaz 1878
Men and women 1855
Paracelsus 1835
Pauline 1833
Red cotton night-cap country 1873
The ring and the book 1868
Sordello 1840
Strafford, a tragedy 1837
The two poets of Croisic 1878
Brownrig, Bp. Ralph *Sermons* a1659 (1674)
Bruce, Alexander B. *Apologetics; or christianity defensively stated* 1892
The kingdom of God; or Christ's teaching according to the synoptical gospels 1889
The miraculous element in the gospels 1886
St. Paul's conception of christianity 1894
Bruce, George *Poems, ballads and songs* 1813
Bruce, James *Travels to discover the source of the Nile* 1790
Bruce, James, 8th Earl of Elgin *Letters and journals* a1863 (1872)
Bruce, Michael *Lectures and sermons, good news in evil times* 1708

Bruce, Peter H. *Memoirs..containing an account of his travels in Germany* etc. 1782
Bruce, Robert *Sermons preached in the kirk of Edinburgh* 1591 (Wodrow Soc. 1843)
Sermons upon the sacrament of the Lord's supper 1590
Bruce, William *Hebrew odes, and other poems* 1874
Bruel's (*W.*) (= Bruele, G.) *Praxis medicinæ or the physitians practise* tr. 1632
Bruin, Cornelis de. Corneille le Bruyn's Voyage to the Levant tr. W. J. 1702
Bruner, Jerome Seymour *Beyond the information given: studies in the psychology of knowing* ed. J. M. Anglin 1973 (UK 1974)
Brunne, Robert Manning of *Handlyng synne* 1303 (Roxb. Club 1862; E.E.T.S. 1901)
Langtoft's Chronicle 1338 (1725, 1810)
The story of England (= *Chron. Wace*) *c*1330 (Rolls series 1887)
For *Meditations on the supper of our Lord* 13..: see *Bonaventura*
Brunswyke's (or *Braunschweig, H.*) *The noble experyence of the vertuous handywarke of surgeri..Here after..the antidotharius* tr. 1525.
See also Andrew, L.
Brunt, David *Meteorology* 1928
Brut, The, or the chronicles of England *c*1400, continuation *c*1450 (E.E.T.S. 1906)
Bruton, Eric Moore *Dictionary of clocks and watches* 1962
Bryan, John *Harvest home* 1674
Bryan, William Alanson *Natural history of Hawaii* 1915
Bryant, Charles *Flora diætetica; or the history of esculent plants* 1783
Bryant, Edwin *What I saw in California* 1848
— (ed. 5) 1849
Bryant, Jacob *A new system, or analysis of ancient mythology* 1774–76
'Bryant, Peter' (Peter Bryan George) *Two hours to doom* 1958
Bryant, Thomas *The practice of surgery* 1872 (1878)
Bryant, William Cullen *Poetical works* *a*1878 (1856 etc.)
The Iliad of Homer tr. 1870
The Odyssey of Homer tr. 1871
Bryce, James *The American commonwealth* 1888
The holy Roman empire 1864 (1875)
Impressions of South Africa 1897
Bryden, Henry Anderson *Animals of Africa* 1900
Kloof and karroo: sport, legend, and natural history in Cape Colony 1889
Tales of South Africa 1896
Brydges, Grey, Baron Chandos *Horæ subsecivæ: observations and discourses* (anon.) 1620
Brydges, Sir Samuel Egerton *Archaica* 1815
Censura literaria 1805–09
—— & Haslewood, J. *The British bibliographer* 1810–14
Brydges, Thomas *See* Bridges
Brydone, Patrick *A tour through Sicily and Malta* 1773
Bryskett, Lodovick *A discourse of civill life* 1606
Bryson, Alexander *Medicine and medical statistics* 1851–59 (in Manual of scientific enquiry 1859)
Bryson, Herbert Courtney *The gramophone record* 1935
Bucaniers of America, The history of the tr. (from J. Esquemeling) 1684
Buccleuch MSS. Report on the manuscripts of the Duke of Buccleuch (Historical Manuscripts Commission 1899–)
Bucer See *Briefe examination* 1564
Buch, Carl W. *Hagenbach's* (*C. R.*) *Compendium of the history of doctrines* tr. 1847
Buchan, John *The blanket of the dark* 1931
Castle Gay 1930
The courts of the morning 1929
The dancing floor 1926
The gap in the curtain 1932
Greenmantle 1916
The house of the four winds 1935
Huntingtower 1922
The island of sheep 1936
John Macnab 1925
Memory hold-the-door 1940
Mr. Standfast 1919
Nelson's history of the war 24 vols. 1915–19
Prester John 1910
A prince of the captivity 1933
The thirty-nine steps 1915
The three hostages 1924
Buchan, Peter *Ancient ballads and songs of the north of Scotland* 1828
Gleanings of Scotch, English, and Irish scarce old ballads 1825
Buchan, William *Domestic medicine* 1789 (1790)
Buchan dialect. A select collection of Scots poems, chiefly in the broad Buchan dialect 1785
Buchanan, George *Vernacular writings* *a*1582 (S.T.S. 1892)
Chamæleon 1570
B.'s detection of the duings of Marie quene of Scottes tr. 1572
Opinion anent the reformation of the universitie of St. Andros 1563–67
Buchanan, Joseph R. *Outlines of lectures on the neurological system of anthropology* 1854
Buchanan, Robert *The ten years' conflict, being the history of the disruption of the church of Scotland* 1849
Buchanan, Robert James McLean *The blood in health and disease* 1909
Buchanan, Robert W. *Poetical works* 1874 (also 1884, 1901)
Annan water 1885
The coming terror and other essays 1891
The heir of Linne: a romance 1888
Buchanan, Robertson *Practical essays on mill-work* 1814 (1823)
Buchanan, W. M. *A technological dictionary* 1846
Buck, Albert H. ed. *A reference handbook of the medical sciences*. By various writers. 1885–90
Buck, Carl Darling *Comparative grammar of Greek and Latin* 1933
Buck, Franklin Augustus *A Yankee trader in the gold rush* ed. K. A. White 1930
Buck, Sir George *The history of the life and reign of Richard the third* *a*1623 (1646)
Buck, Peter Henry *The coming of the Maori* 1925
— (rev. ed.) 1949 (corrected impression, 1950)
Buckham, Philip W. *The theatre of the Greeks* 1825
Buckingham, George Villiers, 1st Duke of. Documents illustrating the impeachment of the Duke of Buckingham in 1626 (Camden Soc. 1889).
See also Wotton, Sir H.
Buckingham, 2nd Duke of *See* Villiers, G.
Buckingham and Chandos, Richard P. Grenville, 2nd Duke of *Memoirs of the court of George IV 1820–30* 1859
Memoirs of the courts and cabinets of William IV and Victoria 1861
Buckingham and Normanby, 1st Duke of *See* Sheffield, John
Buckland, Francis T. *Log-book of a fisherman and zoologist* 1875
Notes and jottings from animal life *a*1880 (1882)
Buckland, William *Geology and mineralogy considered with reference to natural theology* (Bridgewater treatise) 1836 (1837)
Reliquiæ diluvianæ; or observations on the organic remains contained in caves (etc.) *attesting the action of an universal deluge* 1823
Buckle, Henry T. *History of civilisation in England* 1857–61
Miscellaneous and posthumous works *a*1862 (1872)
Buckle, John S. *The manufacturer's compendium* 1864
Buckler, Ernest Redmond *Ox bells and fireflies* 1968
Buckley, Theodore A. W. *The Iliad of Homer* tr. 1848
Buckman, S. S. *John Darke's sojourn in the Cotswolds* 1890
'Buckmaster, Henrietta' (Henrietta Stephens) *The walking trip* 1972
Bucknill, John C. & Tuke, D. H. *A manual of psychological medicine: containing the history, nosology, description and treatment of insanity* 1874
Budd, George *Treatise on diseases of the liver* 1845
Budgell, Eustace *The bee* 1733
The moral characters of Theophrastus tr. 1714
Budworth (afterwards Palmer), Joseph *A fortnight's ramble to the lakes in Westmoreland* etc. 1792
Buel, Jesse *The farmer's companion* 1840
Buenos Aires Herald 1876–
Büsching's (*A. F.*) *New system of geography* tr. 1762
Buffon's (*G. L. Le Clerc, Comte de*) *Natural history of birds* tr. 1792
See also Smellie, W.
Bugbears, The *c*1580 (in Archiv Stud. neu. Sprachen, Bd. 98, 1897)
Bugge's (*T.*) *Travels in the French republic* tr. J. Jones 1801
Builder, The; an illustrated weekly magazine 1842–
Builder's dictionary, The, or gentleman's and architect's companion 1734
Building news 1857–
Bulkeley, John & Cummins, J. *A voyage to the South-seas* 1743
Bulkeley, Peter *The gospel covenant, or the covenant of grace opened* 1646
Bull, Digby *The watchman's voice giving warning to all men of the dreadful day of the Lord* 1695
Bull, Bp. George *Works* *a*1710 (1846)
Bull, Henry *Luther's Commentarie upon the fiftene psalmes called psalms of degrees* tr. 1577 (1615)
Bull, Peter *I know the face, but...* 1959
Bull, Roger *Dedekind's* (*Fr.*) *Grobianus, or the compleat booby* tr. 1739
'Bull-Us, Hector' (James Kirke Paulding) *The diverting history of John Bull and Brother Jonathan* 1812
— (ed. 2) 1813
— (new ed.) 1835
Bull of Pope Innocent VIII 1485 (Camden Soc. 1847)
Bullein, William *Bulwarke of defence against all sicknesse, soarenesse and woundes* (*The booke of simples, Dialogue betweene sorenes and chirurgi, The boke of compoundes, The booke of the vse of sicke men and medicines*) 1562 (1579)
A dialogue against the feuer pestilence 1564 (1578; E.E.T.S. 1888)
The government of health 1558
Bullen, Arthur H. ed. *A collection of old English plays* (2 series 1882–85, 1887)
Bullen, Frank T. *The cruise of the 'Cachalot'* 1898
Idylls of the sea 1899
The log of a sea-waif 1899
The way they have in the navy 1899
With Christ at sea 1900
Bullens, Denison Kingsley *Steel and its heat treatment* 1916
Buller, Francis *An introduction to the law relative to trials at nisi prius* 1775 (ed. 2)
Buller, Walter Lawry *A history of the birds of New Zealand* 1873
Manual of the birds of New Zealand 1882
Bulletin (Glasgow) 1915–60 (1924–60 with title *Bulletin and Scots pictorial*)
Bulletin (Sydney) 1880–
Bulletin of the atomic scientists 1945–
Bulletin of entomological research 1910–
Bulletin See also under the names of particular institutions
Bullinger's (*H.*) *Fiftie godlie..sermons diuided into fiue decades* tr. H. I. 1577 (1592; also Parker Soc. 1849–52)
Bullins, Ed *The theme is blackness: 'The corner' and other plays* 1973
Bulloch, John *George Jamesone the Scottish Vandyck* 1885
The Pynours: historical notes on an ancient Aberdeen craft 1887
Bullock, Alan Louis Charles ed. *The twentieth century: a promethean age* 1971
Bullock, Christopher *Woman is a riddle* 1717
Bullock, William R. *Cazeaux'* (*P.*) *Treatise on midwifery* tr. 1857
Bullokar, John *An English expositor* 1616 (also 1641–76)
Bulwer, Henry Earle *A glossary of technical terms employed in connection with church bells* 1901
Bulwer, John *Anthropometamorphosis; Man transformed, or the artificial changeling* etc. 1650
Chirologia, or the naturall language of the hand.. Whereunto is added, Chironomia; or the art of manuall rhetoricke 1644
Pathomyotomai; or a dissection of the significative muscles of the affections of the minde 1649
Bulwer-Lytton *See* Lytton
Bumstead, Freeman J. *The pathology and treatment of venereal diseases* 1864 (1879)
Bunn, Alfred *The stage: both before and behind the curtain* 3 vols. 1840
Bunsen, Frances, Baroness *Life and letters* *a*1876 (1879)
Bunting, Brian Talbot *The geography of soil* 1965
Bunyan, John *Works* *a*1688 (Offor 1853)
A book for boys and girls 1686
Come and welcome to Jesus Christ 1678
Grace abounding to the chief of sinners 1666
The greatness of the soul 1683 (1691)
The heavenly foot-man 1688 (1886)
The holy city: or the new Jerusalem 1665
The holy war made by Shaddai upon Diabolus 1682
The life and death of Mr. Badman 1680 (1767)
The pilgrim's progress from this world to that which is to come 1678, 1684
Burbridge, William Frank *From balloon to bomber* 1946
Burbury, John *The history of..Christina Allessandra, queen of Swedland,..Also a relation of the severall entertainments given her..in her journey to Rome* etc. 1658
Burbury, Samuel H. *See* Watson, Henry W.
Burchell, William John *Travels in the interior of Southern Africa* 2 vols. 1822–4
Burchett, Josiah *Memoirs of transactions at sea* 1703 (1720)
Burden (*Burthen*) *of Issachar* 1646 *See* Maxwell, Bp. John
Burdett, Geoffrey Arnold T. ed. *Automatic control handbook* 1962
Bureau of American Ethnology *See* United States. Bureau of American Ethnology
Bureau of Standards *See* United States. National Bureau of Standards
Burel, John *Poems* *c*1590 (J. Watson's Choice collection II, 1709)
Burge, Cyril Gordon ed. *Complete book of aviation* 1935
Burgersdicius (*Burgersdijck*), *F. Monitio logica, or an abstract of Burgersdicius's Logic* tr. 1697
Burges, Cornelius *A new discovery of personal tithes* 1625
Sermon 1641
Burges, John *An answer rejoyned* 1631
The lawfulnes of kneeling in the act of receiving the Lords Supper 1631
'Burgess, Anthony' (John Anthony Burgess Wilson) *Beds in the east* 1959
A clockwork orange 1962
The doctor is sick 1960
The enemy in the blanket 1958
MF 1971
The right to an answer 1960
Time for a tiger 1956
Burgess, Francis Henry *A dictionary of sailing* 1961
Burgess, James J. H. *Lowra Biglan's mutch, a Shetland novelette* 1896
Burgess, James W. *A practical treatise on coach-building* 1881
Burgess, Bp. Thomas *The divinity of Christ proved* 1790
Burgh records. Extracts from the council register of the burgh of Aberdeen 1398–1625 (Spalding Club 1844–48)
— 1625–1747 (Sc. Burgh Rec. Soc. 1871–72)
Extracts from the records of the burgh of Edinburgh 1403–1589 (Sc. Burgh Rec. Soc. 1869–82)
Burgh records of the city of Glasgow 1573–81 (Maitland Club 1832–34)
Extracts from the records of the burgh of Glasgow 1573–1780 (Sc. Burgh Rec. Soc. 1876–1912)
Charters and documents relating to the burgh of Peebles 1165–1710 (Sc. Burgh Rec. Soc. 1872)
Records of the burgh of Prestwick 1470–1782 (Maitland Club 1834)
Extracts from the records of the royal burgh of Stirling 1519–1752 (1887–89)
Burghersh, Priscilla A. W. Fane, Lady *The letters of Lady Burghersh..from Germany and France* 1813–14 (1893)
Burghope, George *A discourse of religious assemblies* (= *Divine worship*) 1697

Burgon, John W. *Life and times of Sir T. Gresham* 1839
Lives of twelve good men 1888
Burgoyne, John *The lord of the manor, a comic opera* 1781
Burke, Carl F. *God is beautiful, man: interpretations of Bible passages and stories* 1969 (UK 1970)
Burke, Edmund *Works* a1797 (1808, 1842)
An abridgement of English history 1757
Address to the British colonists of North America c1775
An appeal from the new to the old Whigs 1791
Articles of charge..against Warren Hastings 1786
Correspondence v.d. (1844)
Heads for consideration on the present state of affairs 1792
A letter to a member of the National Assembly 1791
A letter to a noble Lord 1796
A letter to..the sheriffs of Bristol 1777
Two (Four) letters..on the proposals for peace with the regicide directory of France 1795–97
Observations on the conduct of the minority 1793
Observations on...'The present state of the nation' 1769
A philosophical inquiry into the origin of our ideas of the sublime and beautiful 1756
Reflections on the revolution in France (= *Fr. Rev.*) 1790
Remarks on the policy of the allies with respect to France 1793
Report on affairs of India 1783
Speech on American taxation 1774
Speech on..conciliation with the colonies (America) 1775
Speech on..the economical reformation of the civil and other establishments 1780
Speech on Fox's East India Bill 1783
Speech on..the Nabob of Arcot's debts 1785
Speeches on the impeachment of Warren Hastings 1788
Thoughts on the cause of the present discontents 1770
Thoughts on French affairs 1791
Tracts, relative to the laws against popery in Ireland 1756
A vindication of natural society 1756
Burke, Jackson Frederick *Death trick* 1975 (UK 1976)
Burke, John *Till death us do part* (adapted from the television series by J. Speight) 1967
Burke, John F. *British husbandry* (anon.) 1834–40 (Library of useful knowledge)
Burke, Thomas *Nights in town* 1915
Burke, Thomas A. ed. *Polly Peablossom's wedding, and other tales* 1851
Burkitt, Miles Crawford *Prehistory: a study of early cultures in Europe and the Mediterranean basin* 1921
Burkitt, William *Expository notes on the New Testament* a1703 (1739, 1818)
Burlesque. Quevedo's Visions made English by Sir R. L'Estrange and burlesqu'd by a person of quality 1702
Burley, Dan *Original handbook of Harlem Jive* 1944
Burley, William John *Death in a salubrious place* 1973
Guilt edged 1971
To kill a cat 1970
Burlington magazine 1903–
Burn, James D. *The autobiography of a beggar boy* 1855 (1859)
Burn, John S. *The history of the French..and other protestant refugees settled in England* 1846
Burn, Joshua Harold *Drugs, medicines and man* 1962
Lecture notes on pharmacology 1948
— (ed. 9) 1968
Burn, Richard *The history of the poor laws* 1764
A new law dictionary a1785 (1792)
Burn, Robert *A naval and military technical dictionary of the French language* 1842, 1852 (1863)
Burnaby, Andrew *Travels through the middle settlements in North America 1759–60* 1775
Burnaby, Frederick G. *A ride to Khiva* 1873
Burnand, Francis C. *My time and what I've done with it* 1874
Burne, Charlotte S. *Shropshire folk-lore: a sheaf of gleanings*. Ed. from the collections of Georgina F. Jackson 1883
Burne, Nicol *The disputation concerning the controversit headdis of religion, halden in..Scotland* 1581 (Catholic tractates, S.T.S. 1901)
Burne-Jones, Sir Philip *Dollars and democracy* 1904
Burnes, Sir Alexander *Travels into Bokhara* 1834 (1835)
Burnet, Charles H. *The ear* 1877
Burnet, Bp. Gilbert *A discourse of the pastoral care* 1692
An exposition of the thirty-nine articles of the church of England 1699
History of his own time a1715 (1724, 1734, 1766)
History of the reformation of the church of England 1679, 1681, a1715 (1865)
The history of the rights of princes in the disposing of ecclesiastical benefices 1682
Letters of the state of Italy 1688 (Tracts 1689)
Some letters; containing an account of what seemed most remarkable in Switzerland, Italy, etc. (= *Travels*) 1686 (1689)
Life of William Bedell, bishop of Kilmore, Ireland 1692
Some passages in the life and death of..John Earl of Rochester 1680
More's Utopia tr. 1683
News from France in a letter giving a relation of the present state of the difference between the French King and the Court of Rome (anon.) 1682
Burnet, Thomas *The theory of the earth* 1684–90
Burnett, Frances Eliza Hodgson *Little Lord Fauntleroy* 1886
A little princess 1905
The making of a marchioness 1901
The secret garden 1911
The shuttle 1907
T. Tembarom 1913
Burnett, James *See* Monboddo, Lord
Burnett, John ed. *Useful toil: autobiographies of working people from the 1820s to the 1920s* 1974
Burnett, William Riley *Little Caesar* 1929
Vanity Row 1952 (UK 1953)
Burney, Charles *A general history of music* 1776–89
Memoirs of the life and writings of Metastasio 1796
The present state of music in France and Italy 1771
Burney, James *A chronological history of the discoveries in the south sea* 1803–17
Burney, Richard *Κέρδιστον Δῶρον King Charles the second..presented to the houses of parliament* etc. (sermons) 1660 (1661)
Burney, William ed. *Falconer's (W.) New universal dictionary of the marine* 1815
Burnham, George P. *Memoirs of the United States Secret Service* 1872
Burning of Paules, The 1563 *See* Pilkington, Bp. J.
Burns, James D. *Memoirs and remains* a1864 (1869)
Burns, John *The principles of surgery* 1831–38
Burns, Robert *Works* a1796 (1800, 1857)
Address to the deil 1785–86
The auld farmer's new-year morning salutation to his auld mare, Maggie 1786
The author's earnest cry and prayer 1786
The cottar's Saturday night 1785
Death and doctor Hornbook 1785
The death and dying words of poor Mailie 1783
A dream 1786
Election ballads 1795
Halloween 1785
The holy fair 1786
The jolly beggars 1785
Letters v.d. a1796
The twa dogs 1786
Burnside, William *Theory of groups of finite order* 1897
Burr, Enoch F. *Ad fidem; or parish evidences of the Bible* 1871
Ecce cœlum, or parish astronomy 1870
Burrard, Gerald, et al. *Big game hunting in the Himalayas and Tibet* 1925
Burrell, Andrewes *A cordiall for the calenture* 1648
Burrill, Alex. M. *A new law dictionary and glossary* 1850
Burritt, Elihu *A walk from London to Land's End* 1865
Burroughes, Jeremiah *An exposition of Hosea* 1643–52
Lectures on the beatitudes 1659 (1867)
Burroughes, Sir John *The soveraignty of the British seas* 1633 (1651)
Burroughs, John *Locusts and wild honey* 1879
Wake-robin 1871
Winter-sunshine 1876
Burroughs, W. H. *A treatise on the law of taxation* 1877
Burroughs, William, *Jr. Speed* 1970
Burroughs, William Seward *Junkie* 1953
The naked lunch 1959
Burrow, Edward J. *Elements of conchology* 1815
Burrow, Sir James *Reports of cases..in the court of King's Bench* 1776–80
Burrow, Thomas *The Sanskrit language* 1955
Burrows, E. Julie *Like an evening gone* 1973
Burt, Edward *Letters from a gentleman in the north of Scotland* (anon.) c1730 (1745, 1818)
Burthogge, Richard *An argument for infants baptisme* 1684
Causa dei; or an apology for God 1675
An essay upon reason and the nature of spirits 1694
'Burton, Alfred' (John Mitford) *The adventures of Johnny Newcome in the navy* 1818
Burton, Edward *Lectures upon ecclesiastical history* 1831–33
Burton, Henry *An apology, or an appeale* 1636
Babel no Bethel 1629
A divine tragedie lately acted 1636 (1641)
For God and the king (sermons) 1636
Israel's fast 1628
Truth's triumph over Trent 1629
Burton, John E. *Handbook of midwifery* 1880
Burton, John Hill *The book hunter* 1862
The Cairngorm mountains 1864
A history of the reign of queen Anne 1880
The history of Scotland 1867–70 (1873)
The Scot abroad 1864
Burton, Maurice *Wild animals of the British Isles* 1960
Burton, Richard or Robert (N. Crouch) *The English empire in America* 1685
The vanity of the life of man 1688
Burton, Richard F. *Arabian nights* 1886 (Lady Burton's ed.)
A plain and literal translation of the Arabian nights' entertainments 10 vols. 1885–6 (unexpurgated Kamashastra Soc. ed.)
Camoens' (L. de) The Lusiads englished 1881
The city of saints 1861
Explorations of the highlands of the Brazil 1869
Falconry in the valley of the Indus 1852
Goa and the Blue Mountains 1851
The lake region of Central Africa 1860
A mission to Gelele, king of Dahome 1864
Personal narrative of a pilgrimage to El-Medinah and Meccah 1855–56
Two trips to gorilla land 1876
Ultima thule, or a summer in Iceland 1875
Wanderings in West Africa 1863
Zanzibar: city, island, and coast 1872
—— & Cameron V. F. *To the Gold Coast for gold* 1883
Burton, Robert *The anatomy of melancholy* 1621 (1624, 1628, 1638, 1651, 1676)
Burton, Thomas *Diary of T. B.: member in the parliaments of Oliver and Richard Cromwell from 1656–59* (1828)
Burton, William *A commentary on Antoninus his itinerary* 1658
Burton, William E. *Waggeries and vagaries; a series of sketches* 1848
Burton-Brown, Theodore *Early mediterranean migrations. An essay in archaeological interpretation* 1960
Bury, Lady Charlotte *The history of a flirt* 1840
Bury, Edward *The husbandmans companion; containing one hundred occasional meditations* 1676 (1677)
Bury, John Bagnell *A history of Greece to the death of Alexander the Great* 1900
Bury, William C. Keppel, Viscount & Hillier, G. L. *Cycling* 1887 (Badminton library)
Bury St. Edmunds, Wills and inventories from the registers of the Commissary of 1370–1650 (Camden Soc. 1850)
Busby, Roger *Deadlock* 1971
Pattern of violence 1973
Busby, Thomas *A complete dictionary of music* 1801 (1811)
Lucretius' Nature of things tr. 1813
Bush, Harry Derrick *Atomic and nuclear physics: theoretical principles* 1962
Bush, John *Hibernia curiosa* 1764 (1769)
Bushell, Stephen Wootton *Chinese art* 2 vols. 1904–6
— (ed. 2) 1909
Bushnell, Edward *The complete ship-wright* 1664
Bushnell, Horace *Forgiveness and law* 1874
God in Christ 1850
Moral uses of dark things 1867
Sermons on living subjects 1872
Sermons for the new life 1858
The vicarious sacrifice grounded on principles of universal obligation 1865
Women's suffrage; the reform against nature 1869
Business week 1929–
Busk, Hans *The banquet* 1819
The dessert, to which is added The tea 1819
Fugitive pieces in verse 1814
The vestriad 1819
Busk, Rachel H. *The valleys of Tirol* 1874
Busy man's magazine (Toronto) 1896–1911 (continued as *Maclean's magazine*)
Butcher, A. Judith *Copy-editing: the Cambridge handbook* 1975
Butcher, Roger William *A new illustrated British flora* 2 parts 1961
Butcher, Samuel H. & Lang, A. *The Odyssey of Homer done into English prose* 1879
Butler, Alban *The lives of the fathers, martyrs, and other principal saints* 1756–59 (1847)
The moveable feasts, fasts, and other annual observances of the catholic church a1773 (1839)
Sermons a1773
Butler, Alfred J. *The ancient Coptic churches of Egypt* 1884
Butler, Charles *The feminine monarchie; or a treatise concerning bees* 1609 (1634)
Butler, Charles *Philological and biographical works* 1817
Butler, Gwendoline *Coffin following* 1968
A coffin for Pandora 1973
Coffin in Oxford 1962
Butler, Lady Harriot *Memoirs* (a romance) 1741
Butler, Bp. Joseph *Works* a1752 (1874)
The analogy of religion natural and revealed 1736
Sermons v.d. (Wks. 1874)
Butler, Richard *Where all the girls are sweeter* 1975
Butler, Samuel *Characters and passages from note-books* a1680 (1908)
Hudibras 1663, 1664, 1678
Remains a1680 (1759)
Butler, Samuel *Erewhon; or, Over the range* 1872
Erewhon revisited twenty years later 1901
A first year in Canterbury settlement 1863
Note-books ed. H. F. Jones 1912
The way of all flesh ed. R. A. Streatfeild 1903
Butler, Sir William F. *Autobiography* a1910 (1911)
Butt, Isaac *Home government for Ireland. Irish federalism! its meaning* 1874
Butterworth, Hezekiah *Zigzag journeys in the Western States of America* 1884
Butterworth, Michael *Remains to be seen* 1976
Buttes, Henry *Dyets drie dinner* 1599
Byatt, Antonia Susan *The virgin in the garden* 1978
Byfield, Nicholas *An exposition upon the epistle to the Colossians* 1615
Byfield, Richard *The doctrine of the sabbath vindicated* 1631
Bÿgge *See* Bugge
Bygod, Sir Francis *A treatise concernynge impropriations of benefices* c1535
Byng, John (5th Viscount Torrington) *The Torrington diaries: containing the tours through England and Wales 1781–94* ed. C. B. Andrews 4 vols. 1934–8
Bynner, Edwin L. *Agnes Surriage* 1886
Byrd, William *The Westover manuscripts* 1728–36 (1841)
Byrhtferth's Handboc c1055 (in Anglia VIII)
Byrhtnoth's Tod (= Battle of Maldon) 993 (Grein)
Byrne, Brian Oswald Donn *Destiny Bay* 1928
Byrne, Oliver *The handbook for the artisan, mechanic, and engineer* 1853

BYROM, John *Miscellaneous poems a1763 (1773)*
The private journal and literary remains a1763 (Chetham Soc. 1854–57)
BYRON, George Gordon, 6th Baron *Poetical works a1824*
Beppo 1817
The bride of Abydos 1813
Childe Harold's pilgrimage 1812–18
The corsair 1813
The deformed transformed 1824
Diary (see Letters and journals)
Don Juan 1818–24
English bards and Scotch reviewers 1809
The giaour 1813
Hebrew melodies 1815
Hints from Horace 1811
The island 1823
Lara 1814
Letters (in Memoir of the rev. F. Hodgson 1878)
Letters and journals (ed. T. Moore 1830, 1860)
Manfred 1817
Marino Faliero, Doge of Venice 1820
Mazeppa 1817
The prisoner of Chillon 1816
Sardanapalus, a tragedy 1821
The vision of judgment 1822
BYRON, John *The narrative of..distresses suffered..on the coast of Patagonia* 1768
Byron's voyage round the world. By an officer 1767
BYSSHE, Edward *The art of English poetry* 1702
By-stander, The, or universal weekly expositor 1790
BYWATER, Adam *The Sheffield dialect* 1839 (also 1854, 1877)

C

C., A. *See* COPLEY, Anthony
C., B. *Puritanisme the mother, sinne the daughter* 1633
C., G. *A briefe treatise of mathematicall phisicke* 1598 (added to F. Wither's transl. of C. Dariot's Breefe introd.)
C., H. *A discourse concerning the drayning of fennes and surrounded grounds in Norfolke*, etc. 1629
— another ed., entitled *The drayner confirmed* 1647
C., H. *Aristotle's Rhetoric* tr. 1686 (1693)
C., I. or J. *Alcilia: Philoparthens loving folly* 1595 (1613, 1879; in Arber, Eng. Garner IV)
C., J. *The compleat collier* 1708 (1845)
C., J. *See* CHEYNEY, J.; CLEVELAND, J.
C., R. *The times' whistle* 1616 (E.E.T.S. 1871)
C., R. *See* CAREW, R.; CAWDREY, R.; CUDWORTH, R.
C., S. *The art of complaisance; or the means to oblige in conversation* 1673
C., W. *Italian convert* See CRASHAW, W.
C., W. *See* COVELL, William
CB magazine (Communications Publication Corporation, Oklahoma City) 1964–
CERN *See* European Organization for Nuclear Research
CRC journal (Community Relations Commission) 1972–
C.S.I.R.O. *See* Australia. Commonwealth Scientific and Industrial Research Organization
Cabala sive scrinia sacra; mysteries of state and government in letters in the reigns of Henry VIII, Elizabeth, James I, and the late King Charles 1654 (1691)
Cabinet maker and retail furnisher (title varies) 1880–
'CABLE, Boyd' (Ernest Andrew Ewart) *Action Front* 1916
Doing their bit: war work at home 1916
The Old Contemptibles 1919
CABLE, Dan. 1670 *See* VALENTINUS, B.
CABLE, George W. *The Creoles of Louisiana* 1884
The grandissimes: a story of Creole life 1880
Madame Delphine 1881
Old Creole days 1879 (1883)
'CADE, Alexander' (Kenneth Methold) *Turn up a stone* 1969
CADE, Anthony *A sermon of the nature of conscience* 1621
Cædmon's Genesis and *Exodus* a1000 (Grein)
CAFFYN, Kathleen M. *A Quaker grandmother* 1896
CAGNEY, James *R. von Jaksch's Clinical diagnosis* tr. 1890 (1899)
CAIN, James Mallahan *The postman always rings twice* 1934
CAINE, T. H. Hall *The bondman* 1890
The Christian 1897
The Deemster 1887
The Little Man island 1894
The Manxman 1894
The scapegoat 1891
The shadow of a crime 1885
A son of Hagar 1886
CAIRD, Edward *A critical account of the philosophy of Kant* 1877
The critical philosophy of Kant 1889
CAIRD, Janet *Perturbing spirit* 1966
CAIRD, John *Fundamental ideas of Christianity* 1892–96 (1899)
Introduction to the philosophy of religion 1880
CAIRNS, John *Unbelief in the eighteenth century as contrasted with its earlier and later history* 1881
Life and letters. By Alex. R. MacEwen (1895)
CALAMY, Benjamin *Sermons preached upon several occasions* a1686 (1687)
CALAMY, Edmund *The doctrine of the bodies fragility; a sermon preached 19 Oct. 1654* 1655
An indictment against England, because of her self-murdering divisions 1645
CALAMY, Edmund *A caveat against new prophets* 1708
CALDCLEUGH, Alexander *Travels in South America 1819–21* 1825
CALDER, Nigel David Ritchie *The restless earth* 1972
CALDER, Robert M. *A Berwickshire bard: the songs and poems of R. M. C.* 1897
CALDERWOOD, David *History of the Kirk of Scotland* a1651 (1678; Wodrow Soc. 1842–49)
CALDERWOOD, Henry *Handbook of moral philosophy* 1872 (1878)
The relations of mind and brain 1879
CALDERWOOD, Margaret *A journey in England, Holland, and the Low Countries* 1756 (Coltness collections p. 103– , Maitland Cl. 1842)
Letters and journals from England, Holland, and the Low Countries 1756 (1884)
Caldwell, Selections from the family papers preserved at 1496–1853 (Maitland Cl. 1854)
CALDWELL, Erskine Preston *God's little acre* 1933
CALDWELL, Robert *A comparative grammar of the Dravidian, or South Indian, family of languages* 1856 (1875)
CALDWELL, William *Schopenhauer's system in its philosophical significance* 1896
Calendar of the ancient records of Dublin v.d. (1889–)
Calendar of the Carew manuscripts, preserved in the Archiepiscopal library at Lambeth 1515–1624 (Eng. Record series 1867–73)
Calendar of the Charter Rolls preserved in the Public Record Office 1226– (Eng. Record series 1903–); *Close Rolls* 1272– (1892–); *Patent Rolls* 1216– (1891–)
Calendar of the court minutes etc. of the East India Company 1635–49 (ed. Ethel B. Sainsbury 1907–12)
Calendar of documents relating to Scotland, preserved in the Public Record Office 1108– (Scott. Record series 1881–)
Calendar of the Inner Temple Records 1505–1714 (ed. F. A. Inderwick 1896–1901)
Calendar of Inquisitions post mortem and other analogous documents preserved in the Public Record Office 1235– (Eng. Record series 1898–)
Calendar of letter-books preserved among the archives of the Corporation of the City of London at the Guildhall 1275– (ed. Reginald R. Sharpe 1899–)
Calendar of letters and papers, foreign and domestic, of the reign of Henry VIII, preserved in the Public Record Office, etc. 1509–43 (Eng. Record series 1862–91)
Calendar of state papers, Domestic 1547– ; *Scotland* 1509– ; *Ireland* 1509– ; *Colonial (America and W. Indies)* 1574–, *(East Indies)* 1513– ; *Foreign* 1547– (Eng., etc. Record series 1856–)
Calendar of the state papers relating to Scotland 1509–1603 (1858)
CALFHILL, James *An aunswere to (John Martiall's) treatise of the crosse* 1565 (Parker Soc. 1846)
Calgary Herald (Calgary, Alberta) 1883–
CALHOUN, John C. *Works* a1850 (1863, 1874)
California. University *Publications in geography* 1913–
California Academy of Natural Sciences *Proceedings* 1854–
California Historical Society *Quarterly* 1922–
Calisto and Melibea. (A new commodye in englysh in maner of an enterlude wherein is dyscrybyd as well the bewte and good propertes of women as theyr vycys, printed by John Rastell c1525) 1520 (in Hazl. Dodsley)
CALKINS, Gary Nathan *The biology of the protozoa* 1926
—— & SUMMERS, Francis Marion *Protozoa in biological research* 1941
CALL, W. M. W. *Reverberations* 1849
Call-Bulletin (San Francisco) 1856– (title varies)
CALLAWAY, Thomas *A dissertation upon dislocations and fractures of the clavicle and shoulder-joint* 1846 (1849)
CALLCOTT, John W. *A musical grammar* 1806
CALLIS, Robert *His reading upon the statute of 23 Hen. VIII cap. 5, of sewers* 1622 (1647)
CALLOW, Clive *Power from the sea: the search for North Sea oil and gas* 1973
Calmet's (Augustin) Dictionary of the Bible tr. 1732
CALTHORP, Henry *Reports of speciall cases, touching severall customs and liberties of the City of London* 1655 (1670)
CALVERLEY, Charles S. *Fly leaves* 1871 (1903)
Verses and translations 1862
CALVERT, Frederick C. *Dyeing and calico printing* a1873 (1875)
'CALVIN, Henry' (Clifford Leonard Clark Hanley) *It's different abroad* 1963
A nice friendly town 1967
The poison chasers 1971
CAMBRIDGE, Richard O. *Account of the war in India* 1761
The Scribleriad: an heroic poem 1751
Cambridge ancient history, The ed. J. B. Bury et al. 12 vols. 1923–39
— (ed. 3 of Vols. I–II) ed. I. E. S. Edwards et al. 1970–7
Cambridge and Dublin mathematical journal 1846–55
Cambridge essays 1855–58
Cambridge natural history, The 1895–1909
Cambridge review: a journal of university life and thought 1879–
CAMDEN, William *Annales. The true and royal history of Elizabeth, Queene of England* tr. 1625–28; tr. by R. N(orton) 1635 (1675)
Britannia siue florentissimorum regnorum, Angliæ, Scotiæ, Hiberniæ chorographica descriptio 1586; tr. by P. Holland 1610
Camdeni et illustrium virorum ad eum epistolæ 1585–1619 (1691)
Remaines of a greater worke concerning Britaine 1605 (1614, 1623, 1629, 1637)
Camden miscellany, The, v.d. (1847–1910)
Camden Society *Publications* 1838–
CAMERON, Agnes Deans *The new North: being some account of a woman's journey through Canada to the Arctic* 1909
CAMERON Alexander Thomas & GILMOUR, Clifford R. *The biochemistry of medicine* 1933
CAMERON, Angus, FRANK, R., & LEYERLE, J. eds. *Computers and Old English concordances* 1970
CAMERON, David Kerr *Willie Gavin, crofter man: portrait of a vanished lifestyle* 1980
CAMERON, Lucy L. *Pink tippet* 1824
CAMP, Walter Chauncey *Football without a coach* 1920
Campaigns of 1793–94 1796
CAMPBELL, Alexander *A journey from Edinburgh through parts of North Britain* 1802
CAMPBELL, Alistair *Old English grammar* 1959
CAMPBELL, Allan McCulloch *Episomes* 1969
CAMPBELL, Archibald *Lexiphanes; a dialogue imitated from Lucian* 1767 (1774)
CAMPBELL, Archibald J. *Nests and eggs of Australian birds* 1901
CAMPBELL, David *Observations on the typhus fever* 1785
CAMPBELL, Dugald *A practical text-book of inorganic chemistry* 1849
CAMPBELL, E. S. N. *A dictionary of the military science* 1830
CAMBELL, Frances *Dearlove: the history of her summer's makebelieve* 1906
CAMPBELL, George *The four Gospels, translated from the Greek, with preliminary dissertations and notes* 1789
The philosophy of rhetoric 1776
CAMPBELL, Sir George *White and black: outcome of visit to U.S.* 1879
CAMPBELL, Helen Stuart *Darkness and daylight; or, Lights and shadows of New York life* 1891
CAMPBELL, Hugh *Love-letters of Mary Queen of Scots* 1824
CAMPBELL, Ignatius Roy Dunnachie (1901–57) *Adamastor* 1930
Broken record 1934
Collected poems 3 vols. 1949–60
The flaming terrapin 1924
Flowering rifle 1939
The Georgiad 1931
Light on a dark horse 1951
Lorca: an appreciation of his poetry 1952
Mithraic emblems 1936
Poems 1930
tr. *Poems of Baudelaire* 1952
Portugal 1957
Talking Bronco 1946
The wayzgoose 1928
CAMPBELL, J. Duncan *The fisheries of China* 1883 (Fisheries exhibition literature)
CAMPBELL, Sir James *Memoirs, written by himself* 1832
CAMPBELL, James *Balmerino and its Abbey* 1867
CAMPBELL, John *A political survey of Great Britain* 1774
CAMPBELL, John *Travels in South Africa* 1815–22
CAMPBELL, John, 1st Baron *Lives of the Lord Chancellors and Keepers of the Great Seal* 1845–47 (1856–57)
Life, consisting of a selection from his autobiography, diary, and letters. Edited by his daughter, the Hon. Mrs. Hardcastle (1881)
CAMPBELL, John F. *Frost and fire, natural engines*, etc. 1865
Popular tales of the West Highlands 1860–62
CAMPBELL, Lewis & GARNETT, William *The life of James Clerk Maxwell: with a selection from his correspondence and occasional writings, and a sketch of his contributions to science* 1882
CAMPBELL, Mrs. Patrick *See* SHAW, George Bernard
CAMPBELL, R. W. *Private Spud Tamson* 1915
CAMPBELL, Roy *See* CAMPBELL, Ignatius Roy Dunnachie
CAMPBELL, Thomas *Diary of a visit to England in 1775* ed. J. L. Clifford 1947
A philosophical survey of the south of Ireland (anon.) 1777 (1778)
Strictures on the ecclesiastical and literary history of Ireland 1789
CAMPBELL, Thomas *Poetical works* a1844 (1860, 1907)
The battle of the Baltic 1804–05
The exile of Erin 1800
Gertrude of Wyoming 1809
Hohenlinden 1801
The pilgrim of Glencoe 1842
The pleasures of hope 1799
The power of Russia 1831
Reullura 1824
Theodric 1824
CAMPBELL, Walter F. *Life in Normandy* 1848 (1863)
CAMPBELL-WALKER, Arthur *The correct card; or how to play at whist* 1876 (1880)
Campden wonder See OVERBURY, Sir T.
CAMPION, Charles Thomas tr. *A. Schweitzer's On the edge of the primeval forest* 1922
CAMPION, Edmund *A historie of Ireland* 1571 (in Holinshed's Chron. 1587; Ware 1633)
CAMPION, Thomas *Works* a1619 (1889, 1909)
Observations in the art of English poesie 1602 (Haslewood 1815; in G. G. Smith, Eliz. Crit. Ess. 1904)
Two books of ayres; being songs without accompanyments 1610; *the third and fourth books of ayres* 1612 (in Arber, Eng. Garner III).
See also PLAYFORD, John

Canada. Department of the Environment. Fisheries and Marine Service *Fisheries fact sheet* 1973-
Canada. Geological Survey *Reports of progress* (later *Annual reports*) 1857-1906
Canada. Senate *Official report of debates* 1870-
Canadian annual review of public affairs 1903-
Canadian antiques collector (title varies) 1966-
Canadian geographical journal 1930-
Canadian historical review 1920-
Canadian journal of linguistics 1961-
Canadian journal of physics 1951-
Canadian journal of research 1929-50 (from 1935 divided into subject series)
Canadian Medical Association *Journal* 1911-
Canadian mineralogist 1957-
Cancer (American Cancer Society) 1948-
Cancer research 1941-
Candid remarks on the stage bill 1785
Candler, Edmund *The unveiling of Lhasa* 1905
'Candy, Edward' (Alison Neville) *Words for murder perhaps* 1971
Cane, John V. *Fiat lux* 1661
Canfield, Dorothea Frances *Fables for parents* 1937 (UK 1938)
Understood Betsy 1917 (UK 1922)
Canfield, Henry Spofford *A maid of the frontier* 1898
Cannan, Joanna Maxwell *All is discovered* 1962
And all I learned 1951
And be a villain 1958
High table 1931
Little I understood 1948
Long shadows 1955
Murder included 1950
No walls of jasper 1930
Canne, John *A necessitie of separation from the Church of England, prooved by the nonconformists principles* 1634 (1849)
Canning, George (the elder) *A translation of Anti-Lucretius* 1766
Canning, George (son of the above) *Speeches* a1827 (1828)
See also *Anti-Jacobin; Microcosm*
Canning, Victor *Flight of the grey goose* 1973
The great affair 1970
The melting man 1968
The python project 1967
Queen's pawn 1969
The rainbird pattern 1972
The whip hand 1965
Cant, Andrew *A sermon preached after the renovation of the National Covenant and celebration of the Lord's Supper at Glasgow* 1638 (1727)
Cantarow, Abraham & Schepartz, Bernard *Biochemistry* 1954
— (ed. 4) 1967
Canterburian's self-conviction 1640 *See* Baillie, R.
Canticum de creatione c1375 (in Anglia I; Horstmann, Sammlung Altenglischer Leg. 1878)
Canting dictionary, A new 1725.
See also E., B.
Caoursin's (Gulielmus) Siege of Rhodes See Kay, J.
Cape Argus (Cape Town) 1888- (title varies)
Cape of Good Hope in 1822, State of 1823
Cape monthly magazine 1857-81
Cape Times (Cape Town) 1876-
Capel, Richard *Tentations: their nature, danger, cure* 1633 (1655)
Remains, being an appendix to his excellent treatise of tentations a1656 (1658)
Capell, Edward *Mr. W. Shakespeare his Comedies, Histories, and Tragedies republished (with) notes, critical and explanatory, and various readings* 1760-68
Two tables elucidating the sounds of letters 1749
Capell, Richard *Simiomata: a Greek note book, 1944-1945* 1946
Capern, Edward *Ballads and songs* 1858
Poems 1856
Capgrave, John *The chronicle of England* 1460 (Rolls series 1858)
Lives of St. Augustine and St. Gilbert of Sempringham c1450 (E.E.T.S. 1910)
The life of St. Katharine of Alexandria c1440 (E.E.T.S. 1893)
See also Bridget
Capote, Truman *The grass harp* 1951 (UK 1952)
In cold blood: a true account of a multiple murder and its consequences 1965 (UK 1966)
Captain, The: a magazine for boys 1899-1924
Captain Underwit *See* Newcastle, 1st Duke of
Captive of Valence, The 1804
Caraccioli, Charles *The life of Robert lord Clive, baron Plassey* 1775
Cardus, Neville *Autobiography* 1947
Close of play 1956
Days in the sun: a cricketer's journal 1924
Cardwell, Edward *Documentary annals of the reformed church of England; being a collection of injunctions, declarations, orders, etc. from 1546 to 1716* (1839)
Carew, Bampfylde Moore, The life and adventures of 1745
An Apology for the life of, 1749 (1763)
See also Price, Thomas
Carew, Dorothea Petrie *Many years, many girls* 1967
Carew, Lady Eliz. *The tragedie of Mariam, the faire queene of Iewry* 1613
'Carew, Francis Wylde' (Arthur E. G. Way) *No. 747: being the autobiography of a gipsy* 1891
Carew, Jan Alwin Rynveld *Black Midas* 1958
The wild coast 1958
Carew, Richard *Epistle on the excellency of the English tongue* ? 1595-96 (1602; in G. G. Smith, Eliz. Crit. Ess. 1904)
Estienne's World of wonders tr. 1607
A herrings tayle 1598
Huarte's Examination of men's wits tr. 1594 (1616)
The survey of Cornwall 1602
Tasso's Godfrey of Bulloigne tr. 1594 (1881)
Carew, Thomas *Cœlum Britanicum. A masque at White-Hall* 1634
Poems a1639 (1640, 1651, 1824)
Carey, George C. *Every man his own stock-broker; or, a complete guide to the public funds* 1820
Carey, Henry *Poems on several occasions* 1713, 1720, 1729
The ballad of Sally in our alley (in 1729 ed. of prec.; in Arber, Eng. Garner VI)
Chrononhotonthologos: the most tragical tragedy that ever was tragediz'd by any company of tragedians 1734
Hanging and marriage; or, the dead-man's wedding 1722
Carey, Patrick *See* Cary, Patrick
Carey, Sir Robert, Earl of Monmouth *Memoirs, written by himself* a1639 (1759)
Carey, Rosa N. *Passage perilous* 1903
Uncle Max 1887
Caribbean quarterly 1949-
Carlell, Lodowick *The deserving favourite* 1629
Carles, William R. *Life in Corea* 1888
Carleton, Sir Dudley *Letters from and to Sir D. C. during his embassy in Holland* 1616-20 (1757)
Carleton, Bp. George *Jurisdiction regall, episcopall, papall* 1610
Carleton, William *Fardorougha the miser* 1839
Traits and stories of the Irish peasantry 1830-33 (1843)
Carlile, Christopher *A discourse, wherein is plainly proued..that Peter was neuer at Rome* (by R. T., i.e. C. Carlile) 1572
Carlile, James *Fortune-hunters* 1689
Carlile, M. J. & Skehel, J. J. *Evolution in the microbial world* 1974 (24th Symposium of the Society for General Microbiology)
Carlisle, G. W. F. Howard, 7th Earl of *Diary in Turkish and Greek waters* 1854
Carlop Green, or equality realized; a poem 1793 (1817)
Carlquist, Sherwin John *Hawaii: a natural history* 1970
Carlson, Elof Axel *The gene: a critical history* 1966
Carlton, Robert *The new purchase, or seven and a half years in the Far West* 1843
Carlyle, Alexander *Autobiography* a1805 (1860)
Carlyle, Jane Welsh *Early letters* 18.. (1889)
Letters and memorials a1866 (1883)
Carlyle, John A. *Dante's Inferno* tr. 1848
Carlyle, Thomas *Works* v.d. (1872)
Critical and miscellaneous essays v.d. (1839, 1840, 1847, 1857)
ed. *Oliver Cromwell's letters and speeches* 1845
Essay on chartism 1839
The French Revolution 1837
German romance 1827
Goethe's Wilhelm Meister tr. 1824
On heroes, hero-worship, and the heroic in history 1840
Historical sketches of persons and events in the reigns of James I and Charles I a1881 (1898)
History of Friedrich II, called the Great 1858-65
Inaugural address, Edinburgh 1866
E. Irving 1866 (in Remin.: see below)
Latter-day pamphlets 1850
Letters 18.. (ed. C. E. Norton, 1886, 1888)
The life of Friedrich Schiller 1825
The life of John Sterling 1851
Past and present 1843
Reminiscences 1832-67 (1881)
Sartor resartus 1833-34 (1838, etc.)
Tales by Musæus, Tieck, Richter tr. 1827
See also Froude, J. A.
Carlyon, Clement *Early years and late reflections* 1836-58
Carman, Philip Crosbie *Chemical constitution and properties of engineering materials* 1949
Carmeni's (Francis) Nissena tr. 1653
Carmichael, Mrs. A. C. *Domestic manners and social condition of the white, coloured, and negro population of the West Indies* 1833
'Carmichael, Harry' (Leopold Horace Ognall) *Naked to the grave* 1972
The seeds of hate 1960
Too late for tears 1973
Carmichael, Robert Daniel *Introduction to the theory of groups of finite order* 1937
Carnap, Rudolf *Meaning and necessity: a study in semantics and modal logic* 1947
Carnegie, William *Practical game preserving* 1884
Practical trapping 1880
Carnegie Institution of Washington *Publications* 1902-
Year-book 1902-
Carolina, Description of South 1761
Caroll, William *A letter to the rev. Dr. Benj. Pratt* 1707
Carpenter, Frank De Y. *Round about Rio* 1883
Carpenter, George Herbert *The biology of insects* 1928
Carpenter, John *The plaine mans spirituall plough* 1607
Schelomonocham, or King Solomon his solace 1606
Carpenter, John Richard *An ecological glossary* 1938
Carpenter, Joseph Estlin *Tiele's (C. P.) Outlines of the history of religion* tr. 1877
Carpenter, Kathleen E. *Life in inland waters* 1928
Carpenter, Nathanael *Achitophel; or, the picture of a wicked politician* 1629
Geography delineated forth in two bookes 1625 (1635)
Carpenter, Philip P. *Lectures on mollusca; or 'shell-fish' and their allies* 1860 (in Rep. Smithsonian Inst.)
Carpenter, Rhys *Greek sculpture: a critical review* 1960
Carpenter, Richard *Christ's larumbell of love resounded* 1616
The conscionable christian 1623
A pastorall charge 1616
The soules sentinel 1612
Carpenter, Richard *Astrology proved harmless, usefull, pious* 1657
Experience, historie, and divinitie 1642
A new play call'd the pragmatical Jesuit new-leven'd 1660
Carpenter, Spencer Cecil *Christianity according to S. Luke* 1919
Carpenter, William B. *Animal physiology* 1848
Manual of physiology 1851
The microscope and its revelations 1856
Principles of general and comparative physiology 1839
Principles of human physiology 1844
Principles of mental physiology 1874
Vegetable physiology 1858
Zoology 1847
Carpenter, Will. Boyd *Lectures on preaching* 1894 (1895)
Permanent elements of religion 1887 (1889)
Carpenter William L. *A treatise on the manufacture of soap and candles, lubricants and glycerine* 1885
Carpentry and joinery for amateurs 1875
Carr, Mrs. Comyns *The arm of the Lord* 1899
Cottage folk 1897
Margaret Maliphant 1889
Carr, Edward Hallett *A history of Soviet Russia:*
The Bolshevik revolution, 1917-1923 3 vols. 1950-3
The interregnum, 1923-1924 1954
Socialism in one country, 1924-1926 3 vols. 1958-64
Foundations of a planned economy, 1926-1929 by E. H. Carr & R. W. Davies 3 vols. 1969-71
Carr, George Shoobridge *A synopsis of elementary results in pure and applied mathematics* 2 parts 1880-6
Carr, Sir John *Caledonian sketches, or a tour through Scotland* 1807
Carr, John Dickson *Below suspicion* 1949 (UK 1950)
Carr, Lisle *Judith Gwynne* 1874
Carr, William *The travellours guide, and historians faithful companion* 1695
Carr, William *The dialect of Craven, in the West-Riding of the County of York* (anon.) 1824, 1828
Carr-Saunders, Alexander Morris & Jones, David Caradog *A survey of the social structure of England and Wales, as illustrated by statistics* 1927
Carrick, John D. *The Laird of Logan* 1835
Carrier, Robert *Great dishes of the world* 1963
Carrington, Charles Edmund *Rudyard Kipling* 1955
Carrington, Noel T. *Dartmoor* 1826
Carroll, Charles *Journal during his mission to Canada* 1776 (in B. Mayer, Memoir 1845)
Carroll, James *Mortal friends* 1978
Carroll, John Bissell *The study of language* 1953
——, Davies, P., & Richman, B. *The American Heritage word frequency book* 1971
'Carroll, Lewis' (C. L. Dodgson) *Alice's adventures in Wonderland* 1865
The game of logic 1887
The hunting of the snark 1876
Sylvie and Bruno 1889
Sylvie and Bruno concluded 1893
Through the looking-glass 1871
Carruthers, William Alexander *See* Caruthers
Carson, Gerald *Cornflake crusade* 1957 (UK 1959)
Carson, Rachel Louise *Silent spring* 1962 (UK 1963)
Carson, Robert Andrew Glendinning *Coins: ancient, mediaeval & modern* 1962
Carstairs, John Paddy *The concrete kimono* 1965
Carte, Thomas *A collection of original letters and papers concerning the affairs of England, from the year 1641 to 1660 found among the Duke of Ormonde's papers* v.d. (1739)
A general history of England to 1654 1747-55
An history of the life of James, Duke of Ormonde, 1610-88 1735-36
Carter, Elizabeth *Algarotti's (F.) Sir Isaac Newton's philosophy explain'd* tr. 1739 (1742)
A series of letters between Mrs. E. Carter and Miss Cath. Talbot 1741-70 (1809)
Memoirs of the life of Mrs. E. C. with a new edition of her poems. To which are added some miscellaneous essays, etc. By M. Pennington 17.. (1808)
Carter, John *The nail hit on the head* 1644
A plaine and compendious exposition of Christs sermon in the mount 1627
The wheel turned by a voice from the throne of glory 1647
Carter, John Waynflete *ABC for book-collectors* 1952
— (ed. 3) 1961
Carter, Matthew *Honor redivivus; or the analysis of honor and armory* 1655 (1680)
Carter, Philip Youngman *Mr. Campion's falcon* 1970
Mr. Campion's farthing 1969
Cartwright, Christopher *Certamen religiosum* 1651
Exceptions against a writing of Rich. Baxters in answer to some animadversions upon his aphorismes a1658 (1675)
Cartwright, George *A journal of transactions and events, during a residence of nearly sixteen years on the coast of Labrador* 3 vols. 1792

CARTWRIGHT, James J. *Chapters in the history of Yorkshire: a collection of letters, papers, etc., with notes* 1872
CARTWRIGHT, John *The preachers travels: wherein is set downe a true journall to the East Indies* 1611
CARTWRIGHT, Julia *Madame; A life of Henrietta, daughter of Charles I, Duchess of Orleans* 1894
CARTWRIGHT, Peter *Autobiography of a backwoods preacher* 1856
CARTWRIGHT, Thomas *A confutation of the Rhemists translation, glosses, and annotations on the New Testament* a1603 (1618)
A Replye to an Answere made of M. Doctor Whitegift 1573
CARTWRIGHT, William *Comedies, tragi-comedies, with other poems* a1643 (1651)
The lady-errant 1641
The ordinary c1634 (1651; in Hazl. Dodsley)
The royal slave 1639
CARUTHERS, William Alexander *The Kentuckian in New York; or, The adventures of three Southerns* 2 vols. 1834
CARVER, Jonathan *Travels through the interior parts of North America in 1766, etc.* 1778
A treatise on the culture of the tobacco plant 1779
CARVIC, Heron *Miss Seeton sings* 1973 (UK 1974)
CARWITHEN, John B. S. *History of the Church of England* 1829–33 (1849)
CARY, Alice *Ballads, lyrics and hymns* 1865 (1876)
Pictures of country life 1859 (1876)
CARY, Arthur Joyce Lunel *The African witch* 1936
Aissa saved 1932
An American visitor 1933
The captive and the free 1959
Castle Corner 1938
Except the Lord 1953
Herself surprised 1941
Mister Johnson 1939
CARY, G. *A physician's phylactic, against a lawyer's venefic* 1706
CARY, Henry *Memorials of the great civil war in England, 1646–52* 1842
CARY, Henry F. *Aristophanes, Birds* tr. 1824
Dante tr. 1805–12
CARY, Lucius *Discourse of the infallibilitie of the Church of Rome* a1643 (1646)
CARY, Patrick *Trivial poems, and triolets. Written in obedience to Mrs. Tomkin's commands* 1651 (1820)
CARY, Robert *Palæologia chronica; or a chronological account of ancient time* 1677
CARYL, Joseph *An exposition upon the book of Job* 1644–66
The nature, solemnity, grounds, etc. of a sacred covenant 1643
CASAMASSA, Jack V. ed. *Jet aircraft power systems: principles and maintenance* 1950
CASAUBON, Meric *Of credulity and incredulity in things divine and spiritual* 1670
The originall cause of temporall evils 1645
A treatise concerning enthusiasme 1655
CASE, John *The praise of musicke* (anon.) 1586
CASE, Thomas *Gods rising, his enemies scattering* 1644
Case of Exeter Colledge, Oxford, related and vindicated 1691
Case of our affairs 1643 *See* SPELMAN, Sir J.
Case of the kingdom stated 1647
Case of Protestants in England under a Popish prince c1680
CASEY, James P. *Pulp and paper* 2 vols. 1952
CASEY, John *Spherical trigonometry, geodesy, and astronomy* 1889
CASMEY, W. H. *Notes on the ventilation of textile factories* (Read before Society of Dyers and colourists) c1890
Caspar's (J. L.) Handbook of the practice of forensic medicine tr. by G. W. Balfour 1861–65 (New Syd. Soc.)
Casquet of literature, The; edited by Charles Gibbon v.d. (1873–74)
CASSAN, Stephen H. *Lives of the bishops of Bath and Wells* 1829
Cassell's Book of birds 1869–73 *See* JONES, T. R.
Cassell's cyclopædia of photography ed. B. E. Jones 1911
Cassell's dictionary of abbreviations 1966 *See* GURNETT, John William & KYTE, Colin Henry John
Cassell's Dictionary of cookery 1877
Cassell's Encyclopædic dictionary 1879–88
—— *Supplementary volume* 1902
Cassell's family magazine 1874–97
Cassell's Natural history 1871–82
Cassell's Technical educator 1877–82
CASSELS, Walter R. *Supernatural religion* (anon.) 1874–77
CASSIDY, Frederic Gomes *S. Robertson's The development of modern English* (ed. 2) 1954 *See* ROBERTSON, Stuart
Jamaica talk: three hundred years of the English language in Jamaica 1961
—— & LE PAGE, Robert Brock eds. *Dictionary of Jamaican English* 1967
— (ed. 2) 1980
Castel off loue, Bishop Grosseteste's c1320 (Halliwell 1849; Philol. Soc. 1864; Vernon MS., E.E.T.S. 1892)
CASTLE, Don *Do your own time* 1938
'CASTLE, John' (Ronald Charles Payne) & HAILEY, Arthur *Flight into danger* 1958
CASWALL, Edward *The masque of Mary, and other poems* 1858
Cat, Life and adventures of a 1760
Catalogue of ancient deeds in the Public Record Office v.d. (1890–1915)
Catalogue of the special loan collection of scientific apparatus at the South Kensington Museum 1876
CATCOTT, Alexander *A treatise on the deluge and structure of the earth* 1761
Catechism, The shorter, agreed upon by the Assembly of Divines at Westminster 1648
CATESBY, Mark *The natural history of Carolina, Florida, and the Bahama Islands* 1731–48 (1754)
CATHER, Willa Sibert *Death comes for the Archbishop* 1927
Catholic dictionary 1884 *See* ADDIS, W. E.
Catholic dictionary of theology, A ed. H. F. Davis et al. 1962–
Catholic encyclopedia, The 17 vols. 1907–17
Catholic Herald 1884–
Catholic tractates of the sixteenth century 1573–1600 (S.T.S. 1901)
Catholicon Anglicum, an English-Latin wordbook c1483 (E.E.T.S. 1881)
CATLIN, George *Illustrations of the manners, customs, and condition of the North American Indians* 1841 (1844)
CATLOW, Agnes *Popular conchology* 1843
Cato Major c1375 (in Anglia VII)
Cato's Morals c1400 (in Cursor M. App. IV)
CATTO, Maxwell Joseph *Bird on the wing* 1966
'CAUDWELL, Christopher' (Christopher St. John Sprigg) *Illusion and reality* 1937
CAULFEILD, J. M. *Seamanship notes* 1886
CAULFEILD, Sophia F. A. & SAWARD, Blanche C. *The dictionary of needlework* 1882
CAUNTER, Hobart *Oriental annual* 1834
Causes of the decay of Christian piety. By the author of The whole duty of man 1667
Caussin's (N.) Angel of peace to all Christian princes tr. 1650. See also HAWKINS, Sir T.
'CAUSTIC, Christopher' *See* FESSENDEN, T. G.
Cautions and advices to officers in the army; by an old officer 1760
CAVALLIER, James *Memoirs of the wars of the Cevennes* 1726
CAVALLO, Tiberius *A complete treatise of electricity in theory and practice* 1777
Cavalry, Instructions and regulations for 1796–99 (1813)
Cavalry tactics: by a cavalry officer 1897
CAVE, Alfred *The inspiration of the Old Testament inductively considered* 1888
The scriptural doctrine of sacrifice 1877
CAVE, William *A dissertation concerning the government of the ancient church by bishops, metropolitans and patriarchs* 1683
Ecclesiastici; or a history of the most eminent Fathers of the Church in the fourth century 1682
Primitive Christianity 1672
CAVELL, Stanley Louis *The world viewed: reflections on the ontology of film* 1971
'CAVENDISH' (H. Jones) *The principles of whist* 1862 (1870, 1879)
—— & BENNETT, Joseph *Billiards* 1872
CAVENDISH, George *Works* a1562 (1825)
The life of Cardinal Wolsey a1562 (1825; Kelmscott Press 1893)
CAVENDISH, William, Duke of Newcastle *The country captaine; a comoedye* 1649
A new method and extraordinary invention, to dress horses, etc. 1667
The varietie; a comoedy 1649
CAWDREY, Daniel *Humilitie, the saints liverie* 1624
Three sermons 1641
CAWDREY, Robert *A table alphabeticall of English wordes* 1604 (1613)
CAWS, Peter *The philosophy of science* 1965
CAWTHORN, James *Abelard and Heloise* 1746
The perjured lovers 1736
Poems a1761 (1790, 1810)
A sermon preach'd before the burgesses of Westminster 1745
CAWTON, Thomas *The life and death of T. C. with severall of his speeches and letters while in exile. To which is annexed a sermon preached by him not long after the beheading of his Majesty* a1659 (1662)
CAXTON, William *The subtyl historyes and fables of Esope, of Auyan, Alfonse, and Poge* tr. 1484 (1889)
The arte and crafte to knowe well to dye tr. 1490
Blanchardyn and Eglantine tr. 1489 (E.E.T.S. 1890)
The book of curtesye 1477–78 (E.E.T.S. 1868, -82)
Caton tr. 1483
The lyf of Charles the Grete tr. 1485 (E.E.T.S. 1881)
The game and playe of the chesse 1474 (1883)
The cronicles of englond 1480 (1482, 1520)
The Curial made by maystre Alain Charretier tr. 1484 (E.E.T.S. 1888)
Dialogues in French and English c1483 (E.E.T.S. 1900)
The discripcion of Britayne 1480
The boke yf (= of) Eneydos tr. 1490 (E.E.T.S. 1890)
The book of fayttes of armes and of chyualrye tr. 1489
The foure sonnes of Aymon tr. c1489 (E.E.T.S. 1884)
Geoffroi de la Tour l'Andri (the knyght of the toure) tr. 1483
Godeffroy of Boloyne tr. 1481 (E.E.T.S. 1893)
The golden legende tr. 1483
The historie of Jason tr. c1477 (E.E.T.S. 1913)
The mirrour of the world tr. 1481 (E.E.T.S. 1913)
The book of the ordre of chyualry tr. 1484
Six bookes of Metamorphoses of Ovyde tr. 1480 (Roxb. Cl. 1819)
Thystorye of the knyght Parys and the fayr Vyenne tr. 1485 (1868)
The recuyell of the historyes of Troye tr. 1471 (Sommer 1894)
The historye of reynart the foxe tr. 1481 (Percy Soc. 1844; Arber 1880)
The ryall book tr. 1484
Vitas patrum tr. 1491 (W. de Worde 1495)
The lyf of saynt Wenefryde tr. 1485
See also BOTONER, W.; RIVERS, Earl; TIPTOFT, J.
CAYLEY, Arthur *The collected mathematical papers* a1895 (1889–98)
CAYLEY, George J. *Las Alforjas* 1853
CECIL, Edward Christian David *Two quiet lives: Dorothy Osborne, Thomas Gray* 1948
CECIL, Mirabel *Heroines in love 1750–1974* 1974
CECIL, Richard *Works* a1810 (1811)
CECIL, Robert, Earl of Salisbury *The secret correspondence of Sir R. C. with James VI, King of Scotland* a1612 (1766)
CECIL, William, Baron Burghley *The execution of iustice in England for maintenaunce of publique and christian peace, against certeine stirrers of sedition, without any persecution of them for questions of religion* 1583 (1675)
Celestina 1631 *See* MABBE, James
Cely papers: selections from the correspondence and memoranda of the Cely Family, Merchants of the Staple 1475–88 (Camden Soc. 1900)
Censor, The 1803 (Vol. I)
Census of England and Wales, 1881. Instructions to the clerks employed in classifying the occupations and ages of the people 1881 (1885)
Census of Great Britain in 1851 1851
CENTLIVRE, Susanna *Works* a1722 (1760–61, 1872)
The basset-table 1706
A bold stroke for a wife 1717
The busie body 1708
Love at a venture 1706
Love's contrivance 1703
The perjur'd husband 1700
Century dictionary, The. An encyclopedic lexicon of the English language. Prepared under the superintendence of W. D. Whitney 1889–91
—— *Supplement* 1909
Century illustrated monthly magazine, The 1881–
Cercle Linguistique de Prague *Travaux* 1929–
Ceylon Daily News (Colombo) 1918–
Ceylon Observer (Colombo) 1834–
CHADWICK, Hector Munro *The origin of the English nation* 1907
CHADWICK, Henry *The art of pitching and fielding* 1886
CHADWICK, Leigh E. tr. *W. Linsenmaier's Insects of the world* 1972
CHADWICK, William *Life and times of De Foe* 1859
CHAFFERS, William *Marks and monograms on pottery and porcelain* 1863
— (ed. 2) 1866
CHAFIN, William *Anecdotes respecting Cranbourn Chase, with a very concise account of it* 1818
CHALKHILL, John *Thealma and Clearchus, a pastoral history* c1600 (1683)
CHALKLEY, Thomas *Works* a1741 (1751)
Challenger. Report of the scientific results of the voyage of H.M.S. Challenger 1873–76, Zoology vol. XXV 1888
CHALLICE, Annie Emma *Heroes, philosophers, and courtiers of the time of Louis XVI* (anon.) 1863
CHALLINOR, John *A dictionary of geology* 1961
CHALLIS, Simon *Death on a quiet beach* 1968
CHALLONER, Richard *The Catholick Christian instructed in the sacraments, etc.* 1737 (1753)
Memoirs of missionary priests and of other Catholics that have suffered death in England from 1577–1684 1741–42
CHALMERS, Alexander ed. *The works of the English poets from Chaucer to Cowper* 1810
CHALMERS, George *An apology for the believers in the Shakespeare papers which were exhibited in Norfolk Street, London* 1797
Caledonia 1807–24
An estimate of the comparative strength of Great Britain 1782
An historical view of the domestic economy of Great Britain and Ireland 1812
The life of Mary queen of Scots 1818
CHALMERS, Thomas *Works* a1847 (1849)
The evidence and authority of the Christian revelation 1814
Natural theology 1835
On political economy in connection with the moral state and moral prospects of society 1832
On the power, wisdom, and goodness of God as manifested in the adaptation of external nature to the moral and intellectual constitution of man (Bridgewater treatise) 1833
A series of discourses on the Christian revelation, viewed in connection with modern astronomy 1817
Sermons preached at S. John's Church, Glasgow 1823
Memoirs of the life and writings of, by William Hanna (1849–52)
CHALONER, Edward *Six sermons* a1625 (1629)
CHALONER, Sir Thomas (the elder) *The praise of folie. (Erasmi) Moriæ encomium* tr. 1549
St. Chrysostom's Homilie tr. 1544
CHALONER, Sir Thomas (the younger) *A shorte discourse of the most rare vertue of nitre* 1584
CHAMBER, John *A treatise against judicial astrologie* 1601
CHAMBERLAIN, Mrs. *A glossary of West Worcestershire words* 1882 (E.D.S.)
CHAMBERLAIN, Basil Hall *Things Japanese* 1890
CHAMBERLAIN, E. *The Indiana gazetteer; or, Topographical dictionary of the State of Indiana* (ed. 3) 1849
CHAMBERLAIN, John *Letters* ed. N. E. McClure 2 vols. 1939
CHAMBERLAIN, John *Hosiery, yarns and fabrics* 1926
CHAMBERLAYNE, Edward *Angliæ notitia: or the present state of England* 1667 (-1707)

Chamberlayne, John *The art of making tea, coffee, and chocolate* 1685
Magnæ Britanniæ notitia: or the present state of Great Britain 1708 (-1748)
The religious philosopher 1718
See also *Natural history of coffee*
Chamberlayne, William *Pharonnida; a heroick poem* 1659 (also Caroline poets, ed. Saintsbury 1905)
Chamberlin, Thomas Chrowder & Salisbury, Rollin Dean *Geology* 3 vols. 1904-6 (UK 1905-6)
Chambers, Edmund Kerchever *The English folk-play* 1933
The mediæval stage 2 vols. 1903
Chambers, Ephraim *Cyclopædia; or, an universal dictionary of arts and sciences* 1728 (1738, 1741, 1751)
— *Supplement* 1753
Le Clerc's (Sebastian) Treatise of architecture tr. 1723-24
Chambers, Eric *Photolitho-offset* 1967
Chambers, George F. *Descriptive astronomy* 1867 (1876)
Chambers, John D. *Divine worship in England in the 13th and 14th centuries, contrasted with, and adapted to, that in the 19th* 1877
Chambers, Robert *The book of days* 1863-64 (1868)
Essays familiar and humorous 1866
Popular humourous poems of Scotland 1862
Popular rhymes of Scotland 1826 (1870)
The Scottish ballads 1829
The Scottish songs 1829
The traditions of Edinburgh 1825
Vestiges of the natural history of creation 1844 (1845)
Chambers, Robert William *The common law* 1911
The firing line 1908
Chambers, William *A tour in Holland in 1838* 1839
Wintering at Mentone 1870
Chambers's Cyclopædia of English literature 1844 (1876)
Chambers's Edinburgh journal 1832-54
Chambers's Encyclopædia 1860-68
Chambers's Information for the people 1851-60
Chambers's Journal of popular literature 1854-
Chambers's technical dictionary ed. C. F. Tweney & L. E. C. Hughes 1940 (and several later editions used)
Chamier, Frederick *My travels: an unsentimental journey through France, etc.* 1855
Champny, Anthony *A treatise of the vocation of bishops and other ecclesiasticall ministers* 1616
Chancellor's preparation for a trial 1689 (in Harl. Misc.)
Chandler, John *Van Helmont's Oriatrike, or, physick refined* tr. 1662
Chandler, Maurice Henry *Ceramics in the modern world: man's first technology comes of age* 1967
Chandler, Raymond Thornton *The big sleep* 1939
Farewell, my lovely 1940
The high window 1942 (UK 1943)
The lady in the lake 1943 (UK 1944)
The long good-bye 1953
Raymond Chandler speaking [letters and an unfinished novel] 1962 (paperback ed. 1966)
Trouble is my business, and other stories 1950
Chandler, Richard *Travels in Asia Minor* 1775
Travels in Greece 1776
Chandler, Samuel *A critical history of the life of David* 1766
Limborch's (P. van) History of the Inquisition tr. 1731
The history of persecution 1736
Sermons a1766 (1768)
A vindication of the Christian religion 1725
Chandlery, Peter J. *Pilgrim-walks in Rome* 1903 (1908)
Chang, Kwang-chih *See* Kwang-chih Chang
Channing, Edward *Town and county government in the English colonies of North America* 1884
Channing, George G. *Early recollections of Newport, R.I., from the year 1793 to 1811* 1868
Chapel Royal, The old cheque-book, or book of remembrance, of the 1561-1744 (Camden Soc. 1872)
Chaplin, Charles Spencer *My autobiography* 1964
Chapman, Abraham ed. *New Black voices: an anthology of contemporary Afro-American literature* 1972
Chapman, George *Al fooles, a comedy* 1605
The blinde begger of Alexandria 1598
Bussy D'Ambois: a tragedie 1607
Cæsar and Pompey; a Roman tragedy, declaring their warres 1631
Comedies and tragedies a1634 (1873)
The conspiracie, and tragedie of Charles Duke of Byron 1608
The gentleman usher 1606
The Georgicks of Hesiod tr. 1618
The whole works of Homer in his Iliads and Odysses tr. 1616; *Batrachomyomachia* ? 1624; *Hymns* 1616; *Seven bookes of the Iliades* 1598; *The Iliads of Homer* 1611; *Odyssey* 1615
Juvenal's fifth satire tr. 1629 (1858)
May-Day. A wittie comedie 1611
Monsieur d'Olive: a comedie 1606
The divine poem of Musaeus tr. 1616 (1858)
Ouids banquet of sence 1595
A pleasant comedy entituled: An humerous dayes myrth 1599
The revenge of Bussy d'Ambois 1613
The tragedie of Alphonsus a1634
The widdowes teares, a comedie 1612
——et al. *Eastward Hoe* 1605
Chapman, James *Travels in the interior of South Africa* 2 vols. 1868
Chapman, Reginald Frederick *The insects: structure and function* 1969
Chapman, Robert McDonald & Bennett, Jonathan eds. *An anthology of New Zealand verse* 1956
Chapman, Ronald George *Father Faber* 1961
Chapman, Royal Norton *Animal ecology: with especial reference to insects* 1931
Chapman, Valentine Jackson *Coastal vegetation* 1964
Chapone, Hester *Letters on the improvement of the mind* 1773 (1774)
Chappell, William *Popular music of the olden time* 1855-59
Character of a coffee-house, with the symptomes of a town-wit 1673
Character of Italy, by an English chyrurgion 1660
Character of a quack-astrologer 1673
Charant's (Antoine) Letter in answer to divers curious questions concerning the religion, manners, and customs, of the countrys of Muley Arxid, King of Tafiletta tr. 1671
Chardin's (Sir John) Travels into Persia and the East Indies tr. 1686
The coronation of the present King of Persia, Solyman the Third tr. 1686
Charles I *Works* a1649 (1662)
A large declaration concerning the late tumults in Scotland 1639
Charles II. Moneys received and paid for secret services of Charles II and James II 1679-88 (Camden Soc. 1851)
Secret history of the reigns of Charles II and James II 1690
Charles II's Escape from Worcester 1660
Charles, Duke of Orleans *See* Orleans
Charles Auchester 1853 *See* Sheppard, Eliz. S.
Charles-Edwards, Thomas Charles & Richardson, Brian *They saw it happen* Vol. III (1689-1897) 1958
Charleson, John M. M. *Eain Macarthon* 1901
Charleton, Walter *Chorea gigantum; or the most famous antiquity of Great Britain, vulgarly called Stone-heng, restored to the Danes* 1663
The darknes of atheism dispelled by the light of nature 1652
The Ephesian matron 1659
The Ephesian and Cimmerian matrons; two notable examples of the power of love and wit 1668
Onomasticon zoicon 1668
A ternary of paradoxes tr. (from J. B. van Helmont) 1650
Charlesworth, John Kaye *The quaternary era* 2 vols. 1957
Charlton, Lionel Evelyn Oswald *Britain at war: the Royal Air Force from September 1939 to September 1945* 5 vols. 1941-7
Charlton, Mary *The wife and the mistress* 1803
Charnock, Richard S. *A glossary of the Essex dialect* 1880
Charnock, Stephen *Works* a1680 (1683-84, 1864-65)
Several discourses of the existence and attributes of God a1680 (1682, 1834)
Charters of the Abbey of Crosraguel v.d. (1886)
Charters of the Royal Burgh of Stirling 1124-1705 (1884)
See also *Edinburgh; Peebles*
Chase, John Centlivres *The Cape of Good Hope and the Eastern Province of Algoa Bay* ed. J. S. Christophers 1843
Chastysing of goddes chyldern, The prouffytable boke for mannes soule called The, c1491 (W. de Worde)
Chatelaine (Toronto) 1928-
Chatfield, Charles Hugh & Taylor, Charles Fayette *The airplane and its engine* 1928
— (ed. 2) 1932
Chatham, William Pitt, Earl of *Letters to his nephew, Thomas Pitt* a1778 (1804).
See also Almon, J.
Chatterton, Edward Keble *The auxiliary patrol* 1923
Chatterton, Thomas *Poetical works* a1770 (1842)
Poems supposed to have been written at Bristol by Tho. Rowley and others in the XVth century a1770 (ed. T. Tyrwhitt 1777)
Chatto, William A. *On origin* etc. *of playing cards* 1848
A treatise on wood engraving 1839 (1861)
Chaucer, Geoffrey *Collected works* v.d. (Thynne 1532, -42, -50; Stowe 1561; Speght 1598, 1602; Urry 1721)
Complete Works v.d. (Skeat 1894)
Minor poems v.d (Parallel-text edition, Chaucer Soc.)
An A. B. C. c1366
Anelida and Arcite c1374
Astrolabe, A treatise on the c1391 (E.E.T.S., Chaucer Soc. 1872)
Boethius De consolatione philosophiæ c1374 (E.E.T.S. 1868; Chaucer Soc. 1886)
The book of the duchesse (= *Dethe of Blaunche*)
Canterbury Tales (quoted by the title of the tale) c1386 (Six-text print, Chaucer Soc.; Harl. MS. 7334, Chaucer Soc.; also Tyrwhitt 1775-78)
The compleynt of Mars c1374
The compleynte unto pite c1368
The compleint to his empty purse c1399
The compleynt of Venus c1392
The dethe of Blaunche c1369
The former age c1374
Fortune c1398
Gentilesse c1393
The hous of fame c1384
Lak of stedfastnesse c1397
The legend of good women c1385
Lenvoy to Bukton (= *Mariage*)
Lenvoy to Scogan c1393
Mariage, The counseil of Chaucer touching c1393
The parlement of foules c1381
The romaunt of the rose (ll. 1-1705) a1366
Troilus and Criseyde c1374 (Parallel-text print, Chaucer Soc.)
Truth c1390
Words unto Adam, his owne scriveyn c1374
Chaucer Society *Publications* 1868-
Chaucer's Dreme a1500 (Speght 1598)
Chauncy, Isaac *An enquiry whether the gospel be a new law* 1693
Neonomianism unmasked: or, the ancient gospel pleaded, against the other, called a new law or gospel 1692
A rejoinder to Williams' Reply to Neonomianism unmaskt 1693
Cheadle, Walter Butler *Journal of a trip across Canada, 1862-1863* 1931
Cheeseman, Thomas Frederick *Manual of the New Zealand flora* 1906
Cheever, George B. *Wanderings of a pilgrim in the shadow of Mont Blanc* 1845
Cheever, H. T. *See* Scoresby, W.
Cheke, Sir John *The hurt of sedicion howe greuous it is to a communewelth* 1549
The New Testament in Englishe c1550
A remedy for sedition 1536
Chemical abstracts 1906-
Chemical and engineering news 1942-
Chemical gazette 1842-59
Chemical news and journal of physical science (title varies) 1859-1932
Chemical Society of London *Annual reports on the progress of chemistry* See under title
Journal 1862-
Proceedings 1890-1914
Quarterly reviews 1947-71
Chemistry and industry 1932-
Chemistry in Britain 1965-
Cheney, John *See* Cheyney, John
Cheng, Thomas Clement *The biology of animal parasites* 1964
Chequered career, A: 15 years in Australia and New Zealand 1881
Cherubini's (M. L.) Treatise on counterpoint and fugue tr. 1854
Cheselden, William *The anatomy of the human body* 1713 (1726)
Cheshire, Geoffrey Leonard *Bomber pilot* 1943
Cheshire glossary 1886 *See* Holland, R.
Cheshire (south) glossary 1887 *See* Darlington, T.
Chesley, Henry *The customes of Yardley Hastings* 1609 (1881)
Chester, Bishop of *Charge* 1691 *See* Stratford, N.
Chester, Robert *Loues martyr: or, Rosalins complaint* 1601 (New Shaks. Soc. 1878)
Chester mysteries c1430 (Roxb. Cl. 1818)
Chester Whitsun plays ? a1500 (Shaks. Soc. 1843, -47; E.E.T.S. 1893)
Chesterfield, 4th Earl of (Philip Dormer Stanhope) (1694-1773) *Miscellaneous works* v.d. (1777-78)
Advice to his son on men and manners 1775 (1778)
Letters ed. B. Dobrée 6 vols. 1932
Letters to his son 1737-68 (1774)
Chesters triumph in honor of her prince 1610 (Chetham Soc. 1844)
Chesterton, Gilbert K. *Autobiography* 1936
The club of queer trades 1905
The flying inn 1914
Four faultless felons 1930
George Bernard Shaw 1910
Heretics 1905
The incredulity of Father Brown 1926
The innocence of Father Brown 1911
The man who was Thursday: a nightmare 1908
The Napoleon of Notting Hill 1904
Orthodoxy 1909
The thing 1929
The wisdom of Father Brown 1914
Chestre, Thomas *Launfal* c1400 (in Ritson, Metrical romances I. 1802)
Chetham, James *The angler's vade-mecum* 1681 (1689)
Chetham Society *Publications* 1844-
Chettle, Henry *Englandes mourning garment* 1603
Kind harts dreame 1592 (Percy Soc. 1841)
The tragedy of Hoffman 1602 (1631)
—— & Day, John *The blind beggar of Bethnal Green* 1600 (1902)
See also Dekker, T.; Munday, A.
Chetwood, William R. *The voyages and adventures of Captain Robert Boyle* 1726 (1735)
The voyages, dangerous adventures and imminent escapes of Captain R. Falconer 1720 (1724)
The voyages, travels, and adventures of W. O. G. Vaughan 1736
Cheuelere Assigne c1430 (Roxb. Cl. 1820; E.E.T.S. 1868)
Chevy chase c1465 (Child, Ballads 1889)
Cheyne, George *The English malady; or a treatise of nervous diseases of all kinds* 1733
An essay on regimen 1740
A new theory of fevers 1702
Philosophical principles of natural religion 1705
Philosophical principles of religion, natural and revealed 1715
Cheynell, Francis *Divers letters to Dr. Jasp. Mayne concerning false prophets* 1647
Cheyney, John *A vindication of oaths and swearing* 1679
Cheyney, Reginald Evelyn Peter S. *I'll say she does!* 1945
You can always duck 1943
Chicago (title varies) 1952-
Chicago Daily News 1876-1960
Chicago Record 1881-1901
Chicago Tribune 1847-
Chichevache & Bycorne See Lydgate, John

Chilcot, William *Practical treatise concerning evil thoughts* 1698 (1851)
Child. Here begynneth a lytell treatyse called the wyse chylde of thre yere old ? 1520 (W. de Worde)
Child, Francis J. ed. *English and Scottish ballads* 1857
ed. *The English and Scottish popular ballads* 1882–98
Child, Sir Josiah *A new discourse of trade* 1690 (1698)
Child, Lydia M. *Romance of the Republic* 1867
Child-marriages, divorces, and ratifications etc. in the diocese of Chester, etc. 1558–1600 (E.E.T.S. 1897)
Childe, Vere Gordon *The Danube in prehistory* 1929
The dawn of European civilization 1925
— (ed. 3) 1939
— (ed. 6) 1957
The most ancient East 1928
— (rewritten with title *New light on the most ancient East*) 1934
— (rewritten) 1952
Childe of Bristowe c1480 (in Hazlitt, Early popular poetry 1864)
Children, John G. *An essay on chemical analysis* 1819
Children of Thespis 1792
Childrey, Joshua *Britannia Baconica; or the natural rarities of England, Scotland, and Wales* 1661
Chillingworth, William *Works* a1644 (1704, 1742, 1838)
The apostolicall institution of episcopacy 1644
Nine sermons on occasional subjects a1644 (1664)
The religion of protestants a safe way to salvation 1638
Chilmead, Edmund *Ferrand's (Jacques) Ερωτομανια, or a treatise discoursing of the essence, causes, and cure of love, or erotique melancholy* tr. 1640
Leon Modena's History of the rites, customes and manner of life of the present Jews tr. 1650
Chilmead, John *Hues' (R.) Learned treatise of globes* tr. 1638 (Hakluyt Soc. 1889)
Chilton-Young, Francis *Every man his own mechanic* (anon.) 1881
China now 1970–
Chinese letters 1741 *See* D'Argens, Marquis
Chipman, Nathaniel *Vermont Supreme Court reports* 1789–91 (1871)
Chirche of the euyll men and women 1522 (W. de Worde)
Chisenhale, Edward *Catholike history* 1653
Choate, Rufus *Addresses and orations* a1859 (1878)
Choice, chance and change 1606 (Grosart 1881)
Choice drollery; songs and sonnets 1656
Chomsky, Avram Noam *Aspects of the theory of syntax* 1965
The logical structure of linguistic theory 1975
Syntactic structures 1957
—— & Halle, Morris *The sound pattern of English* 1968
Chope, Richard P. *The dialect of Hartland, Devonshire* 1891 (E.D.S.)
Some old farm implements 1919 (From Trans. Devonsh. Assoc. for Adv. Science, Lit. and Art, 1918)
Choppin, Gregory Robert *Experimental nuclear chemistry* 1961
Chorley, Henry F. *Memorials of Mrs. Hemans* 1836
Christ exalted, and Dr. Crisp vindicated 1698
Christian 1973–
Christian Century, The 1900–
Christian prayers, A booke of 1578 *See* Day, R.
Christian religion's appeal 1675 *See* Smith, John
Christian Science Monitor (Boston, Mass.) 1908–
Christian World, The 1857–
Christie, Agatha Mary Clarissa *The ABC murders* 1936
An autobiography 1977
The body in the library 1942
Come, tell me how you live 1946
Curtain: Poirot's last case 1975
Elephants can remember 1972
Evil under the sun 1941
Lord Edgware dies 1933
The mirror crack'd from side to side 1962
The moving finger 1943
Murder in the mews 1937
The murder of Roger Ackroyd 1926
Murder on the Orient Express 1934
The mysterious affair at Styles 1921
The pale horse 1961
Peril at End House 1932
Poirot investigates 1924
Postern of fate 1973
Third girl 1966
Christie, Ella R. *See* 'Home, Julian'
Christis Kirke of the Greene a1550 (Bannatyne MS., repr. Hunterian Club, p. 282–).
See also Ramsay, A.
Christison, Sir Robert *Autobiography* 1885
'Christopher, John' (Christopher Samuel Youd) *The twenty-second century* 1954
Christophersen, Paul *The articles: a study of their theory and use in English* 1939
Chrodegang, Rule of a1000 (E.E.T.S. 1916)
Chronicle of Calais, in the reigns of Henry VII and VIII to the year 1540 15.. (Camden Soc. 1846)
Chronicle of England c1325 (in Ritson, Metr. rom. II. 1802)
Chronicle of the Grey Friars of London 1556 (Camden Soc. 1852)
Chronicle of London from 1089 to 1483 c1483 (1827)
See also Kingsford, C. L.
Chronicle of the rebellion in Lincolnshire 1470 (Camden Soc. 1847)
Chronicle (English) of the reigns of Richard II, Henry IV, V, and VI c1465 (Camden Soc. 1856)
Chronicles, Three fifteenth-century 14.. (Camden Soc. 1880)
Chronicles of the White Rose of York, The v.d. (1845)
Chronicon Vilodunense, sive de vita et miraculis Sanctæ Edithæ Regis Edgari filiæ c1420 (1830; Horstmann 1883)
Chrysler, Charles Byron *White slavery* 1911
Chubb, John *On the construction of locks and keys* 1850
Chujoy, Anatole *The dance encyclopedia* 1949
— (rev. ed. by A. Chujoy & P. W. Manchester) 1967
Church, Arthur H. *Food grains of India* 1886
Precious stones 1883
Church, Benjamin *History of King Philip's war* 1716 (1865–67)
Church, Richard Thomas *The voyage home* 1964
Church, Richard W. *Bacon* 1884
Pascal, and other sermons 1895
Spenser 1879
Church, William C. *The life of John Ericsson* 1890
Church and court of Rome 1674 See *Difference*
Church and the world, The 1866
Church Missionary Society *A grammar and vocabulary of the language of New Zealand* ed. S. Lee from materials supplied by T. Kendall 1820
Church of yvell men See *Chirche*
Church quarterly review 1875–1968
Church Times, The 1869–
Churchill, Charles *Poems* a1764 (1763,–4,–5,–9)
The apology 1761
The ghost 1762
Night 1761
The Rosciad 1761
Churchill, John *Collection of voyages and travels* (1704)
Churchill, Randolph Spencer & Gilbert, Martin *Winston S. Churchill* 1966–
Churchill, Winston *Coniston* 1906
The Crisis 1901
Churchill, Winston Leonard Spencer *The end of the beginning: war speeches, 1942* compiled by C. Eade 1943
Into battle: speeches compiled by R. S. Churchill 1941
My early life: a roving commission 1930
The Second World War 6 vols. 1948–53 (UK 1948–54)
Secret session speeches compiled by C. Eade 1946
Victory war speeches, 1945 compiled by C. Eade 1946
The world crisis 6 vols. 1923–31
Church-lands not to be sold 1648
Churchwardens' Account book of St. Giles, Reading 15.. (ed. W. L. Nash. Privately printed)
Church-wardens' accounts of Croscombe, Pilton, Yatton, Tintinhull, Morebath, and St. Michael's, Bath 1349–1560 (Somerset Rec. Soc. 1890)
Churchwardens' accounts of S. Edmund and S. Thomas, Sarum 1443–1702 (Wilts. Rec. Soc. 1896)
Churchwardens' accounts of the town of Ludlow in Shropshire 1540–1600; *and of St. Michael, Cornhill* 1457–1563 (Camden Soc. 1869)
Churchwardens' accounts of St. Mary's, Reading 1550–1662 (1893)
Churchwardens' accounts of Pittington and other parishes in the diocese of Durham 1580–1700 (Surtees Soc. 1888)
Churchwardens' accounts of various parishes (quoted by the title of the parish) 14..–16.. (in J. Nichols, Illustr. Manners Ant. Times Eng. 1797)
Churchyard, Thomas *The firste parte of Churchyardes chippes* 1575 (1817)
A generall rehearsall of warres 1579
A sad and solemne funerall of sir F. Knowles 1596 (1815)
Good will. Verses in the nature of an epitaph, for the Abp. of Canterbury 1604 (1815)
The worthines of Wales 1587 (1876)
'Churton, Henry' (Albion Winegar Tourgée) *Toinette* 1874
Churton, Ralph *Eight sermons on the prophecies respecting the destruction of Jerusalem* 1785
The life of A. Nowell, Dean of St. Paul's 1809
Lives of W. Smyth, Bishop of Lincoln, and Sir R. Sutton, founders of Brasen Nose College 1800
Chylde, The wyse See *Child*
Cibber, Colley *Dramatic works* v.d. (1754, 1777)
Apology for his life 1739 (1740, 1756)
The careless husband 1705
Love makes a man 1701
Love's last shift 1696
The non-juror 1718
She wou'd, and she wou'd not 1703
See also Vanbrugh, Sir J.
Cicely of Roby 1795
Cicero: Of the nature of the Gods tr. 1741
Cieza's (Peter de) Travels tr. 1709: see Stevens, John
Circle of the sciences, Orr's. A series of treatises on the principles of science 1854–56
Circle of the sciences, The; ed. James Wylde 1862–67
Circumcision, The 14.. (in The visions of Tundale, etc. 1843)
Cist, Charles *Cincinnati in 1841: early annals and future prospects* 1841
ed. *The Cincinnati miscellany* 2 vols. 1845–6
Sketches and statistics of Cincinnati in 1851 1851
City alarum 1645
Civil engineer and architect's journal, The 1837–
Clabburn, Pamela *The needleworker's dictionary* 1976
Clacy, Ellen *A lady's visit to the gold diggings of Australia in 1852–53* 1853
Clagett, William *Sermons* a1688 (1699)
Claiborne, John Francis Hamtramck *Life and correspondence of John A. Quitman* 2 vols. 1860
Clancey, Phillip Alexander *The birds of Natal and Zululand* 1964
Clanvowe, Sir Thomas *The cuckoo and the nightingale* c1403 (in Skeat, Chaucerian pieces 1897)
Clapham, Alfred William *Romanesque architecture in western Europe* 1936
Clapham, Henoch *A briefe of the Bibles historie drawne into English poesy* 1596
Errour on the left hand through a frozen security 1608
Errour on the right hand through a preposterous zeal 1608
Clapperton, Hugh *Journal of a second expedition into the interior of Africa* 1829
Clapperton, Richard *No news on Monday* 1968
Clare, John *Poems descriptive of rural life and scenery* 1820
The rural muse 1835
The shepherd's calendar, etc. 1827
The village minstrel, etc. 1821
Clarendon, Edward Hyde, 1st Earl of *A brief view and survey of the errors to Church and State in Hobbes' Leviathan* a1674 (1676)
A collection of several tracts a1674 (1727)
The history of the rebellion and civil wars in England 1647, a1674 (1702–04, 1888)
His life, written by himself a1674 (1759)
Clarendon, Henry Hyde, 2nd Earl of *State letters during the reign of K. James the second; and his Lordship's diary for the years 1687–90* 16.. (1763)
Clarendonian, The 1919–
Claridge, R. T. *Every man his own doctor. The cold-water, tepid water, and friction-cure* 1849
Clark, Alfred Joseph *Applied pharmacology* 1923
— (ed. 6) 1937
Clark, David *Plane and geodetic surveying for engineers* 2 vols. 1923
Clark, Donald Thomas & Gottfried, Bert A. *Dictionary of business and finance* 1957
— (Apollo ed., with title *University dictionary of* ——) 1967
Clark, Douglas *Death after evensong* 1969
Dread and water 1976
The gimmel flask 1977
Premedicated murder 1975
Sick to death 1971
Clark, Emily *The banks of the Douro* 1805
Clark, George T. *Mediæval military architecture in England* 1884
Clark, George Thomas *Leland Stanford, war governor of California* 1931
Clark, Grahame *See* Clark, John Grahame Douglas
Clark, Hugh *A concise history of knighthood* 1784
Clark, John Desmond *The prehistory of southern Africa* 1959
Clark, John Grahame Douglas *Archaeology and society* 1939
— (ed. 3) 1957
World prehistory 1961
— (ed. 3) 1977
Clark, John W. *See* Willis, Robert
Clark, Kenneth McKenzie *Another part of the wood: a self-portrait* 1974
Civilisation: a personal view 1969
The nude: a study of ideal art 1956
Clark, Matthew *Home trade* 1930
Clark, Nigel George *Modern organic chemistry: an introduction* 1964
Clark, Percy Missen *The autobiography of an old drifter* 1936
Clark, Ronald William & Pyatt, Edward Charles *Mountaineering in Britain* 1957
Clark, Walter John *International language, past, present & future* 1907
Clark, Wilfrid Edward Le Gros *The tissues of the body* 1939
Clark, William *Jan van der Hoeven's Handbook of zoology* tr. 1856–58
Clarke, Arthur Charles *The deep range* 1957
The exploration of space 1951
The sands of Mars 1951
Clarke, Austin *Later poems* 1961
Clarke, C. Cowden *Shakespeare-characters; chiefly subordinate* 1863
Clarke, Charles *Observations on the intended tunnel beneath the River Thames* 1799
Clarke, Edward D. *Travels in Russia* 1811 (1839)
Clarke, Eliza *The sword; or, Father Bertrand's History of his own times* 1791
Clarke, George Sydenham *Fortification: its past achievements, recent development and future progress* 1890
Clarke, Hyde *A new and comprehensive dictionary of the English language* 1855
Clarke, James *A survey of the lakes of Cumberland, Westmoreland, and Lancashire* 1787 (1789)
Clarke, James F. *Self-culture* 1880
Clarke, John *Dux oratorius. A twofold praxis* 1633 (Pt. II. of Dux grammaticus)
Holy incense for the censers of the saints 1634
Parœmiologia Anglo-Latina in usum scholarum concinnata. Or proverbs English and Latin 1639
Clarke, John *An enquiry into the cause and origin of evil* 1720 (1721)
Rohault's (Jacques) System of natural philosophy tr. 1710 (1729)
Clarke, John *An essay on the education of youth in grammar schools* 1720 (1740)
Clarke, John Henrik ed. *Harlem, U.S.A.* 1964
Clarke, Laurence *A compleat history of the Holy Bible* 1737 (1740)

CLARKE, Marcus Andrew Hislop *His natural life* 1874 (UK 3 vols. 1875)
CLARKE, Mary Cowden *Berlioz On modern instrumentation and orchestration* tr. 1856
CLARKE, Samuel *A geographicall description of all the countries in the known world* 1657
The life of Tamerlane the Great 1653 (1664)
The marrow of ecclesiastical historie 1650
A mirrour; or, looking-glasse both for saints and sinners 1646 (1671)
CLARKE, Samuel *Scripture-justification* 1698
A survey of the Bible 1693
CLARKE, Samuel *Works* a1729 (1738)
A discourse concerning the being and attributes of God (Boyle lecture) 1705
A discourse concerning the connexion of the prophecies in the Old Testament and the application of them to Christ 1725
A letter to Mr. Dodwell; wherein all the arguments in his epistolary discourse against the immortality of the soul are particularly answered 1706 (1711)
A defense of an argument 1707
A second defense 1707
A third and fourth defense 1708
The scripture doctrine of the Trinity 1712
CLARKE, Stephen *Hortus Anglicus, or the modern English garden* 1822
CLARKE, William *Clarke papers. Selections from the papers of W. C.* a1666 (Camden Soc. 1891–1901)
CLARKE, William *The natural history of nitre* 1670
CLARKE, William *Every night book; or, Life after dark* 1827
CLARKE, William B. *Narrative of the wreck of the 'Favourite'* 1850
CLARKE, William Eagle *Studies in bird migration* 2 vols. 1912
Clarke County Democrat (Grove Hill, Alabama) 1856– (title varies)
CLARKSON, Thomas *An essay on the impolicy of the African slave trade* 1788
Memoirs of the private and public life of W. Penn 1813
Classical Association *Proceedings* 1904–
Classical quarterly 1907–
Classification of occupations 1960 *See* United Kingdom. General Register Office
Classification of occupations and directory of occupational titles 1972 *See* United Kingdom. Department of Employment
Claus' (Carl) Elementary text-book of zoology tr. by A. Sedgwick and F. G. Heathcote 1884–85
CLAUSER, Henry Ray ed. *The encyclopedia of engineering materials and processes* 1963
CLAVELL, John *A recantation of an ill led life* 1628 (1634)
CLAYTON, Benjamin *Dogs* 1872
CLAYTON, John *Reports and pleas of assises at Yorke* 1651
CLAYTON, Robert *A journal from Grand Cairo to Mount Sinai and back again* tr. 1753
Cleanness (= Purity) c1325 See *Early English alliterative poems*
CLEARY, Jon *High Commissioner* 1966
The long pursuit 1967
Peter's Pence 1974
The safe house 1975
The sundowners 1952
CLEAVELAND, Parker *An elementary treatise on mineralogy and geology* 1816 (1822)
CLEAVER, Robert *A briefe explanation of the whole book of the Prouerbs of Salomon* 1615
CLEAVER, William *Seven sermons on select subjects* a1762 (1808)
Cleges, Sir c1410 (in Weber, Metrical romances I. 1810)
CLEGG, John *The freshwater life of the British Isles* 1952
CLEGG, John Trafford *Works: stories, sketches and rhymes in the Rochdale dialect* 2 vols. 1895–8
CLEGHORN, George *Observations on the epidemical diseases in Minorca, from 1744 to 1749* 1751
CLEIFE, Kenneth Philip H. *The slick and the dead* 1972
CLELAND, John *Memoirs of a woman of pleasure* 2 vols. 1749
CLELAND, Robert *Inchbracken, the story of a Fama Clamosa* 1883
CLELAND, William *Collection of poems* a1689 (1697)
CLEMENS, Samuel L. *See* 'TWAIN, Mark'
CLEMENTS, Eileen Helen *High tension* 1959
Honey for the Marshal 1960
CLEMENTS, Frederic Edward *Plant indicators: the relation of plant communities to process and practice* 1920
Plant succession: an analysis of the development of vegetation 1916
Research methods in ecology 1905
CLEMENTS, Rex *A gipsy of the Horn* 1924
CLEMINSHAW, E. *Wurtz' (C. A.) Atomic theory* tr. 1880
Clene maydenhod c1370 (E.E.T.S. 1867)
CLERK, Dugald *The gas engine* 1886
CLERK, Sir John *Memoirs of the life of*, a1755 (S.H.S. 1892)
CLERKE, Agnes Mary *Familiar studies in Homer* 1892
Popular history of astronomy during the 19th c. 1885
Problems in astrophysics 1903
The system of the stars 1890
CLERKE, Richard *Sermons* a1634 (1637)
CLERK-MAXWELL, J. *See* MAXWELL
CLERY, Cornelius F. *Minor tactics* 1875 (1877)
CLEUGH, James tr. *R. Jungk's Brighter than a thousand suns* 1958
CLEVELAND, John *Works* a1658 (1687)
The character of a London diurnall 1644 (1647)
The character of a diurnall-maker 1654
Poems v.d. (1651, 1653, 1659, 1660, 1677)
The rustick rampant 1658
Cleveland Plain Dealer (Cleveland, Ohio) 1845–
CLEVELY, Hugh Desmond *Public enemy* 1953
CLEVERLY, C. F. M. *See* WARREN, E. Prioleau
CLIFFORD, Lucy *Aunt Anne* 1892
CLIFFORD, Martin *Notes upon Mr. Dryden's poems* 1687
A treatise of humane reason 1675
CLIFFORD, William K. *Lectures and essays* a1879 (1879)
Seeing and thinking 1879
CLINGTON, Allen H. *Frank O'Donnell: a tale of Irish life* 1861
Clinical pharmacology and therapeutics 1960–
Clinical Society of London *Transactions* 1868–
CLINTON, Sir Henry *Narrative of his conduct in America* 1783
CLINTON-BADDELEY, Victor Clinton *No case for the police* 1970
Only a matter of time 1969
To study a long silence 1972
CLISSOLD, F. *The ascent of Mont Blanc* 1823
Clitherow (Margaret), The life and death of. (By John Mush) a1617 (now first published from the original MS. and edited by William Nicholson 1849)
'CLITUS, Alex.' *See* BRATHWAIT, R.
CLOBERY, Christopher *Divine glimpses of a maiden muse* 1659
CLODD, Edward *Myths and dreams* 1885
The story of creation 1888
Cloria and Narcissus. A delightful and new romance 1653–54
CLOSE, Charles F. *Text book of topographical and geographical surveying* 1905
CLOSE, John *The satirist; or, every man in his humour* 1833
Close Rolls preserved in the Public Record Office 1227– (Eng. Record series 1902–).
See also *Calendar*
Closet for ladies and gentlewomen 1611
Cloud of witnesses for the royal prerogatives of Jesus Christ; being the last speeches and testimonies of those who have suffered for the truth in Scotland, since 1680 1714
— *Reprinted from the original editions, with explanatory and historical notes by John H. Thomson* (1871)
CLOUGH, Arthur H. *Poems* a1861 (1862, 1869)
Ambarvalia 1849
Amours de voyage 1849
Bothie of Tober-na-Vuolich 1848
Dipsychus 1849
CLOWES, Evelyn Mary *On the wallaby through Victoria* 1911
CLUBBE, John *The history and antiquities of the ancient villa of Wheatfield, in the county of Suffolk* 1758
Miscellaneous tracts 17.. (1770)
CLUNE, Francis Patrick (Frank) *The red heart: sagas of Centralia* 1944
Roaming round the Darling 1936
CLUTE, Willard Nelson *The common names of plants and their meanings* 1931
Coal-trade terms of Northumberland and Durham 1851 *See* GREENWELL, G. C.
Coast to coast: Australian stories 1941–
COATS, James *A new dictionary of heraldry* 1725
COBB, Richard Charles *Reactions to the French Revolution* 1972
COBBE, Frances P. *An essay on intuitive morals* 1855–57
The final cause of woman 1869 (in J. E. Butler, Woman's work)
Italics: notes on Italy in 1864 1864
Life, by herself 1894
The Peak in Darien, with other inquiries touching soul and body 1882
COBBETT, William *The English gardener* 1829
History of the Protestant Reformation in England and Ireland 1824–27
Political register 1802–13
Rural rides 1825
A year's residence in the United States of America 1818–19
Cobbett's Complete collection of state trials (1809–14)
See also HOWELL, T. B.; *State trials*
COBDEN, Richard *Speeches on peace, financial reform, colonial reform, and other subjects* 1849
COBINE, James Dillon *Gaseous conductors* 1941
Cobler of Caunterburie, The 1590; another ed., entitled *The tincker of Turvey* 1630
COCHRAN-PATRICK, Robert W. *Mediæval Scotland* 1892
Records of the coinage of Scotland from the earliest period to the Union 1876
Early records relating to mining in Scotland 1878
COCK, James *Simple strains: or, the hamespun lays of an untutored muse* 1806 (1810)
COCKAIN(E, Sir Aston *See* COKAINE, Sir A.
COCKAYNE, Leonard *New Zealand plants and their story* 1910
COCKAYNE, T. Oswald ed. *Narratiunculae Anglice conscriptae* a1000 (1861)
ed. *The shrine. A collection of occasional papers on dry subjects* a1000 (1864–70)
See also *Leechdoms*
COCKBURN, Alexander & BLACKBURN, Robin eds. *Student power* 1969
COCKBURN, Henry Thomas, Lord *Life of Lord Jeffrey, with a selection from his correspondence* 1852
Memorials of his time 1821–30 (1856)
Journal; being a continuation of the memorials 1831–54 (1874)
COCKBURN, John *Fifteen sermons preach'd upon several occasions* 1697
A vindication of the late Bishop Burnet from the calumnies and aspersions of a libel, entitled 'A specimen of some free and impartial remarks, etc.' 1724
Cocke Lorelles bote c1515 (Percy Soc. 1843)
COCKER, Edward *English dictionary* 1704
Morals; or, the muses spring-garden 1675
Tutor to arithmetic 1664
COCKERAM, Henry *The English dictionarie, or an interpreter of hard English words* 1623 (1626)
COCKERELL, Douglas *Bookbinding, and the care of books* 1901
Cockersand Abbey of the Premonstratensian Order, The chartulary of v.d. (Chetham Soc. 1898–1900)
COCKETT, Sydney Russell & HILTON, Kenneth Arthur *Dyeing of cellulosic fibres and related processes* 1961
COCKIN, Francis *Divine blossomes* 1657
COCKLE, G. R. ed. *Car and locomotive cyclopedia of American practice* 1966
—(ed. 3) 1974
COCKMAN, Thomas *Tully's three books of Offices in English* 1699 (1706)
COCKS, Richard *Diary in Japan* 1615–22 (Hakluyt Soc. 1883)
COCKTON, Henry *The life and adventures of Valentine Vox, the ventriloquist* 1840
Codex diplomaticus *See* KEMBLE, John M.
CODRINGTON, Robert *Curtius Rufus' (Quintus) Life and death of Alexander the Great* tr. 1661 (1670)
The history of Justine tr. 1654
COE, Malcolm James *The ecology of the Alpine zone of Mount Kenya* 1967
'COE, Tucker' (Donald Edwin Westlake) *Wax apple* 1970 (UK 1973)
Coer de Lion, Richard 13.. (in Weber, Metr. rom. II. 1810)
COFFEY, Charles *The devil to pay, or the wives metamorphos'd* 1731
COGAN, Henry *The history of Diodorus Siculus* tr. 1653
The scarlet gown; or the history of all the present cardinals of Rome tr. from the Italian 1653
Scudery's Ibrahim, or the illustrious Bassa tr. 1652 (1674)
The voyages and adventures of F. M. Pinto tr. 1653
COGAN, Thomas *The hauen of health* 1584 (1636)
COGAN, Thomas *A philosophical treatise on the passions* 1800
COHEN, Antoine *The phonemes of English: a phonemic study of the vowels and consonants of Standard English* 1952
COHEN, Gerda Lesley *What's wrong with hospitals?* 1964
COHEN, J. Solis *Diseases of the throat* 1872
COHEN, Julius Berend *Organic chemistry for advanced students* 2 vols. 1907–13
COHEN, Laurence Jonathan *The diversity of meaning* 1962
—(ed. 2) 1966
COHEN, Leonard *Beautiful losers* 1966 (UK 1970)
COHEN, Morris Raphael & NAGEL, Ernest *An introduction to logic and scientific method* 1934
COHEN, Murray *Sensible words: linguistic practice in England 1640–1785* 1977
COHN, Nik *Pop from the beginning* 1969
—(reissued with title *Awopbopaloobopalopbamboom: pop from the beginning*) 1970
COIT, Thomas W. *Puritanism* 1845
COKAINE, or COKAYNE, Sir Aston *Dramatic works* v.d. (1874)
Loredano's (G. F.) Dianea tr. 1654
The obstinate lady 1657
Small poems of divers sorts 1658
The tragedy of Ovid 1662
Trappolin creduto Principe, or Trappolin suppos'd a Prince 1658
COKAINE, or COKAYNE, Sir Thomas *A short treatise of hunting* 1591 (Roxb. Cl. 1897)
COKE, Desmond Francis Talbot *The bending of a twig* 1906
Sandford of Merton: a story of Oxford life 1903
COKE, Sir Edward *The first part of the institutes of the lawes of England: or a commentarie vpon Littleton* 1628. *Part II.* a1634 (1642). *Parts III–IV.* (1644)
Reports 1600–15
— *An exact abridgment in English of the eleven books of reports of Sir Edw. Coke* (1650)
COKE, John *The debate betwene the heraldes of Englande and Fraunce* 1550 (1877)
COKE, Lady Mary *Letters and journals* 1756–74 (1889–96)
COKE, Roger *A discourse of trade* 1670
Justice vindicated from the false fucus put upon it by Tho. White etc. as also, Elements of power and subjection 1660
COKE, Zachary *The art of logick* 1654 (1657)
Colbatch's (John) Novum lumen chirurgicum extinctum: or, new light of chirurgery put out. By W. W. 1695
COLBORNE, John *With Hicks Pasha in the Soudan* 1884
COLBURN, Zerah *Locomotive engineering and the mechanism of railways* 1864–82
Colburn's United service magazine 1842–71
Cold Spring Harbor symposia on quantitative biology 1933–
Coldingham, The correspondence, inventories, account rolls, and law proceedings of the Priory of 13..–14.. (Surtees Soc. 1841)
COLE, George Douglas Howard *Workshop organization* 1923
—— & COLE, Margaret Isabel *Murder at the munition works* 1940
COLE, Sir Henry *Fifty years of public work, accounted for in his deeds, speeches and writings* 1884
COLE, James *Of death, a true description* 1629
COLE, Mellen *Cy Ross* 1891
COLE, Robert E. G. *A glossary of words used in south-west Lincolnshire* 1886 (E.D.S.)
COLE, William *See* COLES, William

COLEBROOKE, Henry T. *Algebra of the Hindoos, with arithmetic and mensuration* 1817
Miscellaneous essays a1837 (1837)
On import of colonial corn 1818
Remarks on the husbandry and internal commerce of Bengal 1804 (1806)
Coleman (Edward), The tryal of 1678
COLEMAN, James Smoot *Nigeria* 1958
COLEMAN, John *Charles Reade as I knew him* 1903 (1904)
COLEMAN, Thomas *A brotherly examination re-examined* 1646
COLEMAN, William S. *Our woodlands, heaths and hedges* 1859 (1866)
COLENSO, John William *Ten Weeks in Natal* 1855
COLERIDGE, Arthur D. *Eton in the forties* 1896
COLERIDGE, Christabel Rose *Charlotte Mary Yonge: her life and letters* 1903
COLERIDGE, Hartley *Essays and marginalia* a1849 (1851)
Poems a1849 (1851)
Worthies of Yorkshire and Lancashire 1836 (1852)
COLERIDGE, Henry J. *The life and letters of St. Francis Xavier* 1872
COLERIDGE, Henry N. *Introduction to the study of the Greek classic poets* 1830 (1834)
Six months in the West Indies in 1825 1826
COLERIDGE, Sir John T. *Memoir of J. Keble* 1869
COLERIDGE, Samuel T. *Aids to reflection in the formation of a manly character* 1825 (1848)
Ancyent marinere, The rime of the 1798
Biographia literaria or biographical sketches of my literary life and opinions 1817 (Bohn)
Christabel 1797, 1800-01 (1816)
Conciones ad populum 1795
Confessions of an inquiring spirit a1834 (1840)
On the constitution of the church and state 1830
Death of Wallenstein 1800
Essays on his own times; forming a second series of 'The Friend' a1834 (1850)
Fall of Robespierre 1794
The Friend; a literary, moral, and political weekly paper 1809-10; re-issued as '*a series of essays*' 1812; new and greatly altered ed. 1818 (1837, 1865)
Lay sermons 1816-17 (Bohn)
Lectures and notes on Shakspere and other English poets a1834 (Bohn 1883)
Letters a1834 (ed. E. H. Coleridge 1895)
Letters, conversations, and recollections a1834 (1836)
Literary remains a1834 (1836-38)
Notes and lectures upon Shakespeare and some of the old poets and dramatists a1834 (1849)
Notes, theological, political and miscellaneous a1834 (1853)
Philosophical lectures ed. K. Coburn 1949
The Piccolomini (tr. from Schiller) 1800
Poems a1834 (1852, 1862)
Complete poetical works a1834 (1912)
Remorse, a tragedy 1813
Sibylline leaves. A collection of poems 1793- (1817)
Specimens of his table talk a1834 (1835)
The statesman's manual; or the Bible the best guide to political skill and foresight; a lay sermon 1816
The watchman 1796
Zapolya, a Christmas tale 1817
COLERIDGE, Sara *Memoir and letters, edited by her daughter* a1852 (1873)
COLES, Elisha *A dictionary English-Latin, and Latin-English* 1677
An English dictionary 1676
COLES, William *Adam in Eden: or natures paradise* 1657
The art of simpling: an introduction to the knowledge and gathering of plants 1656
COLET, John *Sermon of conforming and reforming* (*Sermon made to the conuocation at Paulis*) 1511 (? 1530; in Phenix II. 1708)
Colin Blowbol's testament a1500 (in Halliwell, Nugæ poeticæ 1844)
COLINVAUX, Paul Alfred *Introduction to ecology* 1973
Colkelbie Sow a1500 (Bannatyne MS., repr. Hunterian Club, p. 1021)
Collectanea v.d. (O.H.S. 1885-1905)
Collection of all Orders etc. in House of Peers and House of Commons relating to Earl of Danby 1679
Collection of the newest and most ingenious poems, songs, catches, etc. against Popery 1689; *a second (third, and fourth) collection* 1689
Collection of poems written upon several occasions, by several persons 1673; *a new collection* 1674
Collection of poems on affairs of State, by A— M—l esq. (i.e. Andrew Marvell), and other eminent wits 1689; *a new collection* 1705
See also DODSLEY, R.; *State songs*
Collections and recollections 1898 *See* RUSSELL, G. W. E.
Collector's guide 1942-
Colledge, Stephen, The arraignment, trial, and condemnation of 1681
College English: an official organ of the National Council of Teachers of English (US) 1939-
College humor 1921-
College of Jesuits, Short narrative of 1679 *See* CROFT, Bp. H.
COLLIER, Giles *An answer to fifteen questions* 1656
Vindiciæ thesium de sabbato; or, a vindication of certain passages in a sermon of the morality of the sabbath 1656
COLLIER, Jane *The art of tormenting* 1753
COLLIER, Jeremy *Essays upon several moral subjects* 1697, 1705, 1709
The emperor Marcus Antoninus his conversations with himself tr. 1701 (1726)
Miscellanies 1694
A panegyrick upon the Maccabees by St. Gregory (of Nazianzus) tr. 1716
Several discourses upon practical subjects 1725
A short view of the immorality and profaneness of the English stage 1697
'COLLIER, Joel' (J. L. Bicknell or G. Veal) *Musical travels through England* 1774 (1775)
COLLIER, John ('Tim Bobbin') *Works* v.d. (1775, 1862)
A view of the Lancashire dialect c1746
COLLIER, John Henry Noyes *His monkey wife; or, Married to a chimp* 1930
COLLIER, John Payne *The history of English dramatic poetry to the time of Shakespeare: and annals of the stage to the Restoration* 1831 (1879)
COLLIER, Richard Hugheson *The city that wouldn't die: London, May 10-11, 1941* 1959
A house called Memory 1960
COLLIER, William F. *A history of English literature* 1861
Pictures of the periods: a sketch-book of old English life 1865
Collier's: the national weekly (US) 1905-57
COLLINGES, John *Responsoria ad erratica piscatoris, or a caveat for old and new prophanenesse* 1652 (1653)
A sober and temperate discourse concerning the interest of words in prayer, the just antiquity and pedegree of liturgies or forms of prayer in churches. By H. D. (i.e. John Collinges) 1661
'COLLINGWOOD, Harry' (W. J. C. Lancaster) *Under the Meteor flag* 1884
COLLINGWOOD, Robin George *An autobiography* 1939
The idea of history 1946
The idea of nature 1945
The new Leviathan; or, Man, society, civilization and barbarism 1942
The principles of art 1938
Roman Britain 1923
COLLINGWOOD, William G. *The life and work of John Ruskin* 1893
Scandinavian Britain 1908
COLLINS, Anthony *A discourse of the grounds and reasons of the Christian religion* 1724
COLLINS, Archie Frederick *Manual of wireless telegraphy* 1906
COLLINS, Arthur ed. *Letters and memorials of state* v.d. (1746)
COLLINS, Gilbert *The valley of eyes unseen* 1923
COLLINS, Grenville *Great Britain's coasting pilot* 1693
COLLINS, J. *Scripscrapologia; or, Collins's doggerel dish of all sorts* 1804
COLLINS, John *Salt and fishery, a discourse thereof* 1682
COLLINS, John H. *A first book of mining and quarrying* 1872
Principles of metal mining 1872 (1875)
COLLINS, Mabel *Cobwebs* 1882
The prettiest woman in Warsaw 1885
COLLINS, Mortimer *Marquis and merchant* 1871
Miranda 1873
Pen sketches by a vanished hand a1876 (1879)
The princess Clarice 1872
Squire Silchester's whim 1873
Thoughts in my garden a1876 (1880)
Transmigration 1873
The Vivian romance 1870
COLLINS, Mortimer & Frances *Frances* 1874
The village comedy 1878
COLLINS, Samuel *Epphata to F. T. (i.e. T. Fitzherbert); or, the defence of the Bishop of Elie concerning his answer to Cardinall Bellarmine's Apologie* 1617
A sermon preached at Paules-Crosse 1607 (1608)
COLLINS, Samuel *The present state of Russia* a1670 (1671)
'COLLINS, Tom' (Joseph Furphy) *Such is life: being extracts from the diary of Tom Collins* 1903
COLLINS, William *Poetical works* a1759 (1765, 1771, 1858)
COLLINS, William L. *The luck of Ladysmede* (anon.) 1860
COLLINS, William Wilkie *After dark, and other stories* 1856
Antonina; or the fall of Rome 1850
Armadale 1866
Basil 1852
The black robe 1881
The dead secret 1857
Hide and seek 1854
The moonstone 1868
The new Magdalen 1873
No name 1862
A plot in private life 1859
The queen of hearts 1859
Rambles beyond railways 1851
The woman in white 1860
Collins music encyclopaedia by J. A. Westrup & F. L. Harrison 1959
COLLINSON, John *The history and antiquities of the county of Somerset* 1791
COLLINSON, John *The life of Thuanus, with some account of his writings* 1807
COLLINSON, WILLIAM EDWARD *Contemporary English; a personal speech record* 1927
COLLOCOTT, Thomas Charles ed. *Dictionary of science and technology* 1971
Colloquium ad pueros linguae Latinae locutione exercendos ab Ælfrico compilatum a1000 (in Wright, Vocabularies 1857, 1884)
COLLYER, David *The sacred interpreter* 1726
COLLYER, John *Reports of cases decided in the High Court of Chancery, by Sir J. L. K. Bruce* 1845-47
COLMAN, George (the elder) *Dramatic works* 1777
Prose on several occasions 1761-86 (1787)
The comedies of Terence translated into familiar blank verse 1765
The jealous wife 1761
The musical lady 1762
—— & GARRICK, David *Clandestine marriage* 1766
COLMAN, George (the younger) *Broad grins* 1797-1802
The heir at law 1797
Inkle and Yarico 1787
Jests; or, festival of wit and humour a1836
John Bull; or, The Englishmen's fireside 1803 (pirated ed.) — (authorized ed.) 1805
Poetical vagaries 1812
The poor gentleman 1802
Posthumous letters, from various celebrated men, addressed to Francis and George Coleman the elder 1721-1820 (1820)
COLMAN, Henry *Report on the agriculture of Massachusetts*
See: Massachusetts, Agricultural Survey
Colonial and Indian Exhibition, 1886 *Reports on the colonial sections of the exhibition* ed. H. T. Wood 1887
Colorado magazine 1923-
COLQUHOUN, Archibald R. *Across Chrysê; from Canton to Mandalay* 1883
COLQUHOUN, Patrick *A treatise on the commerce and police of the river Thames* 1800
A treatise on the police of the metropolis 1796
A treatise on the wealth, power and resources of the British Empire 1814 (1815)
COLQUHOUN, Sir Patrick *A companion to the 'Oarsman's guide'* 1857
COLSE, Peter *Penelopes complaint: or, a mirrour for wanton minions* 1596 (Grosart 1880)
COLSON, William *A general treasury of accounts for all countries in Christendome. To which is added the Art of arithmetike* 1612
COLT, Miriam Davis *We went to Kansas* 1862
COLTON, Charles C. *Lacon: or many things in few words* 1820-22
COLTON, Walter *Ship and shore in Madeira, Lisbon and the Mediterranean* 1851
Columbus Evening Dispatch (Columbus, Ohio) 1871-
Columbus News (Columbus, Montana) 1901-
Columella (L. J. M.): Of husbandry; and his book concerning trees tr. 1745
COLVIL, Samuel *Mock poem, or Whiggs supplication* 1681
COLVILL, John *Letters* 1582-1603 (Bannatyne Cl. 1858)
The palinod of J. C., wherein he doth recant his former offences 1600
COLYER, Charles Norman & HAMMOND, Cyril Oswald *Flies of the British Isles* 1951
COMBE, Andrew *The physiology of digestion* 1842 (ed. 4)
COMBE, William *An history of the river Thames* 1794-96
The tour of Doctor Syntax in search of the picturesque 1812
The second tour of Doctor Syntax in search of consolation 1820
The third tour of Doctor Syntax in search of a wife 1821
See also *History and antiquities of York* 1785
COMBER, Thomas *A companion to the temple and closet; or a help to devotion in the use of the Common Prayer* 1672-75 (1702)
Combes' Historical explication of what there is most remarkable in the French King's Royal House at Versailles tr. 1684
Comenius' (J. A.) Porta linguarum trilinguis reserata. The gate of tongues unlocked and opened, or else a seminarie or seed-plot of all tongues and sciences, in Latine, English, and French. By John Ancoran 1631 (1639)
Janua linguarum reserata. The gate of languages unlocked. Formerly tr. by T. Horn, afterwards corrected by J. Robotham 1643 (1650).
See also D., W.; DU GARD, W.
Orbis sensualium pictus. The visible world tr. by C. Hoole 1659
Comforts of rash and inconsiderate marriage, The fifteen tr. 1682
Comical history of Francion 1655 See *Sorel*
Commentary, incorporating Contemporary Jewish record (American Jewish Committee) 1945-
Commission of array, Copy of 1642
Commission Géologique de la Finlande *Bulletin* 1895-
Committee of Inquiry on Decimal Currency *Report 1963* *See* United Kingdom. Parliamentary papers
Committee on Broadcasting *Report* 1960 *See* United Kingdom. Parliamentary papers
Committe on the Future of Broadcasting (Chairman: Lord Annan) *Report* 1977 (Cmnd. 6753)
Common Prayer, Book of See *Book of Common Prayer*
Common sense: or, The Englishman's journal 1737-39
Commons, House of See *House of Commons*
Commonwealth Scientific and Industrial Research Organization *See* Australia——
Communycacyon bytwene God and man ?1507 (W. de Worde)
Compendious olde treatyse shewynge howe that we ought to haue the scripture in Englysshe c1430 (1530; in Roy, Rede me, etc., Arber 1871)
Complaint of the black knight c1402 *See* LYDGATE, J.
Complaynt of Scotlande 1549 (E.E.T.S. 1872)
Complaynte of them that ben to late maryed ?1535 (1862)
Compleat collier 1708 *See* C., J.
Compleat servant-maid; or the young maidens tutor 1677
Complete family-piece and country gentleman and farmer's best guide 1741 (ed. 3)
Complete grazier; or gentleman and farmer's directory 1776

Complete letter-writer; or, new and polite English secretary 1755
Complete maltster and brewer 1765
Compt buik of David Wedderburne, merchant of Dundee, 1587-1630; together with the shipping lists of Dundee, 1580-1618 v.d. (S.H.S. 1898)
Compte rendu (Académie des Sciences) *See* Académie des Sciences
COMPTON, Arthur Holly *Atomic quest* 1956
COMPTON, Bp. Henry *Charge to the clergy of his diocese (of London) at his visitation 1693-94* 1696
Episcopalia; or letters to the clergy of his diocess 1686
COMPTON-BURNETT, Ivy *Darkness and day* 1951
A house and its head 1935
More women than men 1933
Computer journal 1958-
Computers and automation 1953-
Computers and the humanities: a newsletter 1966-
COMSTOCK, John H. *Introduction to entomology* 1888
—— & COMSTOCK, Anna *A manual for the study of insects* 1895
Comyns' (Sir John) Digest of the laws of England tr. 1762-76
Reports of cases argued and adjudged in the Courts of King's Bench, Common Pleas and Exchequer tr. 1744
CONAN DOYLE, Arthur *See* DOYLE, Arthur Conan
CONANT, Hannah O. *The English Bible: popular history of the translation* 1856 (1881)
Conceits, clinches, flashes, and whimzies 1639
Concise Oxford dictionary of opera by H. Rosenthal & J. Warrack 1964
CONDER, Claude R. *Tent work in Palestine* 1878
CONDER, Eustace R. *The basis of faith* 1877
CONDER, Josiah *A dictionary of geography, ancient and modern* 1834
CONDON, Edward Uhler & ODISHAW, Hugh *Handbook of physics* 1958
— (ed. 2) 1967
—— & SHORTLEY, G. H. *The theory of atomic spectra* 1935
CONDON, Richard *The Manchurian candidate* 1959 (UK 1960)
The whisper of the axe 1976
Conferences. A collection of certain letters and conferences lately passed betwixt certaine preachers and two prisoners in the Fleet 1590
Conferences held in the Tower of London with Ed. Campion, Jesuit 1581 1584
Confession of faith professit, and beleuit, be the Protestantes within the realme of Scotland 1561
Confession, Ane shorte and generall, of the trewe christian faith (of the Kirk of Scotland) 1580
Confessions of faith. A collection of confessions of faith, catechisms, directories, books of discipline, etc. of publick authority in the church of Scotland v.d. (1719-22)
Conformist's second plea 1682 See *Second plea*
Congressional globe See: United States. Congress. Debates
Congressional record See: United States. Congress. Debates
CONGREVE, William *Works* v.d. (1710, 1849)
The double-dealer 1694
Juvenal's eleventh satire tr. 1693 (see Dryden, J.)
Love for love 1695
The mourning bride 1697
The old batchelour 1693
A Pindarique ode humbly offer'd to the king on his taking Namur 1695
The tears of Amaryllis for Amyntas 1703
The way of the world 1700
See also GARTH, Sir S.
CONINGSBY, Sir Thomas *Journal of the siege of Rouen* 1591 (Camden Soc. 1847)
Connecticut *Public records of the Colony of Connecticut* 1850-90
Connecticut Academy of Arts and Sciences *Transactions* 1866-
Connecticut Agricultural Experiment Station *Annual report* 1877-
Bulletin 1877-
Connecticut Historical Society *Collections* 1897
Connecticut probate records See MANWARING, Charles William
CONNERS, Bernard F. *Don't embarrass the Bureau* 1972 (UK 1973)
Connoisseur, The 1754-56
Connoisseur, The: an illustrated magazine for collectors 1901-
CONNOLLY, Cyril Vernon *A romantic friendship: the letters of Cyril Connolly to Noel Blakiston* 1975
Conquest: a magazine of modern endeavour 1919-26
CONRAD, Joseph (Teodor Józef Konrad Korzeniowski) *Almayer's folly: a story of an eastern river* 1895
Lord Jim 1900
The nigger of the 'Narcissus' 1897
Nostromo: a tale of the seaboard 1904
The rover 1923
The shadow-line: a confession 1917
Suspense: a Napoleonic novel 1925
Victory: an island tale 1915
—— & HUEFFER, Ford Madox *Romance* 1903
CONSETT, Henry *The practice of the spiritual or ecclesiastical courts* 1685
Considerations. Certain considerations tending to promote peace and goodwill amongst the Protestants 1674
Considerations about the most proper way of raising money in the present conjuncture c1690
Considerations on dissolving the court of Chancery 1653
Considerations touching the better pacification and edification of the Church of England 1640
Conspiracie for pretended reformation 1592
CONSTABLE, F. *Pathomachia: or, the battell of affections* (anon.) 1630
CONSTABLE, Henry *Diana* 1592
Diana, or the excellent conceitful sonnets of H. C. Augmented with divers quatorzains of honourable and learned personages 1594 (1818; in Arber, Eng. Garner II)
CONSTABLE, John *Correspondence* ed. R. B. Beckett 6 vols. 1962-8
CONSTABLE, Thomas *Archibald Constable and his literary correspondents. A memorial by his son* 1873
Constable's (Archibald) Miscellany of original and selected publications in the various departments of literature, the sciences and the arts 1826-35
Constellation, The 1829-32
Constitution of the United States, The 1789
Constitutions and canons ecclesiasticall agreed upon 1603 1604
Consumer reports 1942-
'CONTACT' (Alan John Bott) *An airman's outings* 1917
Contemplations of the state of man in this life, and in that which is to come (by Jer. Taylor) a1667 (1684, 1699)
Contemporary history of affairs in Ireland from 1641-52 a1660 (Irish Archæol. Soc. 1879-80)
Contemporary review, The 1866-
Contention betweene liberalitie and prodigalitie, A pleasant comedie shewing the 1602 (in Hazl., Dodsley)
Contention betwixt the two famous houses of Yorke and Lancaster, The first part of the 1594
Contra-replicant's complaint to his Majestie c1642
'CONWAY, H. Derwent' (H. D. Inglis) *Journey through Norway, Sweden, and Denmark* 1829
CONWAY, Henry Seymour *False appearances, a comedy altered from the French (of L. de Boissy)* 1789
'CONWAY, Hugh' (F. J. Fargus) *Called back* 1883
Dark days 1885
A family affair 1885
Living or dead a1885 (1886)
CONWAY, Moncure D. *Demonology and devil lore* 1879
The earthward pilgrimage 1870
CONWAY, Robert Seymour, et al. *The præ-Italic dialects of Italy* 3 vols. 1933
CONYBEARE, Edward *A history of Cambridgeshire* 1897
CONYBEARE, John *Letters and exercises of J. C., schoolmaster at Molton, Devon, 1580 and at Swimbridge, 1594, with notes and a fragment of autobiography by the very rev. W. D. Conybeare* 15.. (ed. F. C. Conybeare 1905)
CONYBEARE, Bp. John *A defence of reveal'd religion against the exceptions of (Tindal)* 1732
The mysteries of the Christian religion credible 1723
CONYBEARE, William J. and HOWSON, John S. *Life and epistles of Paul* 1852 (1862)
COOK, E. Dutton *Dr. Muspratt's patients, and other stories* 1868
Paul Foster's daughter 1861
COOK, Eliza *Poems* 1838-53, 1870
COOK, Captain James *An account of the voyages undertaken for making discoveries in the Southern Hemisphere in 1768-71 (= First voyage round the world)* 1773
A voyage towards the South Pole and round the world in 1772-75 (= Second voyage) 1777
A voyage to the Pacific Ocean in 1776-80 (= Third voyage) 1784. Vol. III by Capt. James King
Voyages v.d. (1790)
COOK, James Henry *Fifty years on the old frontier, as cowboy, hunter, guide, scout, and ranchman* 1923
COOK, Joseph *Boston Monday lectures* 1881-91
COOK, Moses *The manner of raising, ordering, and improving forrest-trees* 1676
COOK, Robin *The crust on its uppers* 1962
COOKE, Alexander *More worke for a masse-priest* (anon.; pref. verses signed E. W.) 1621
Pope Joane. A dialogue betweene a protestant and a papist 1610
COOKE, Deryck *The language of music* 1959
COOKE, Edward *A voyage to the South Sea and round the world in 1708-11* 1712
COOKE, George A. *Topographical and statistical description of the county of Surrey* ?1817
COOKE, James *Mellificium chirurgiæ; or, the marrow of chyrurgerie* 1616 (1685)
COOKE, John *Greenes Tu quoque: or, the cittie gallant* 1614
COOKE, John Esten *The Virginia comedians; or, Old days in the Old Dominion* 2 vols. 1854
COOKE, Josiah P. *The new chemistry* 1873 (1876)
COOKE, Mordecai C. *British fungi* 1871
Fungi; their nature, influence and uses 1874 (1875)
Manual of botanic terms 1862
Manual of structural botany 1884
COOKE, Nelson Magor & MARKUS, John *Electronics and nucleonics dictionary* 1960
COOKE, Rose T. *Somebody's neightbors* 1881
Steadfast: the story of a saint and a sinner 1889
COOKE, Thomas *Hesiod's Works* tr. 1728
Tales, epistles, odes, fables, etc. (With) proposals for perfecting the English language 1729
COOKE, William B. *Descriptions to the plates of Thames scenery engraved by W. B. C. and G. Cooke* 1818
COOKE, Sir William F. *The electric telegraph: was it invented by Professor Wheatstone?* 1854
Cookery. Noble boke of cookry 14.. (Napier 1882)
A proper new booke of cookery 1575
Two fifteenth-century cookery-books c1430, -50 (E.E.T.S. 1888)
See also *Ancient cookery; Form of cury*
COOKSEY, Richard *Essay on the life and character of John, Lord Somers, Baron of Evesham* 1791
COOLEY, Arnold J. *Cyclopædia of practical receipts* 1845
COOLEY, Thomas M. *A treatise on the constitutional limitations which rest upon the legislative power of the States of the American Union* 1868
COOLEY, William D. *The world surveyed in the nineteenth century* 1845-48
'COOLIDGE, Susan' (Sarah Chauncey Woolsey) *What Katy did* 1873
What Katy did at school 1873 (UK 1874)
COOMBE, William *See* COMBE, William
COON, Carleton Stevens *The races of Europe* 1939
COOPER, A. *The complete distiller* 1757 (1760)
COOPER, Anthony A. *See* SHAFTESBURY, Earl
COOPER, Sir Astley P. *The anatomy of the breast* 1840
Illustrations of diseases of the breast 1829
COOPER, Bransby B. *Life of Sir A. Cooper, with sketches from his note-books* 1843
COOPER, Courtney Ryley *Here's to crime* 1937
COOPER, David Graham *Psychiatry and anti-psychiatry* 1967
COOPER, Evelyn Barbara *Drown him deep* 1966
COOPER, Mrs. Frank *Hide and seek* 1881
COOPER, J. Fenimore *The deerslayer* 2 vols. 1841 (UK eds. 1 & 2, both 3 vols., both also 1841)
Home as found 2 vols. 1838 (UK ed. as *Eve Effingham; or, Home* 3 vols. 1838)
Homeward bound; or, The chase 2 vols. 1838 (UK ed. 3 vols. 1838)
The last of the Mohicans 1826
Ned Myers; or, A life before the mast 1843 (UK ed. 2 vols. 1843)
The oak-openings 2 vols. 1848 (UK ed. as *The bee-hunter* 3 vols. 1848)
The pathfinder 1840
The pilot 1823
The pioneers 1823
The prairie 1827
The red rover 3 vols. 1827
The spy 1822
The two admirals 1842
The water witch 1830
COOPER, John Butler *Coo-oo-ee! A tale of bushmen from Australia to Anzac* 1916
COOPER, John G. *Gresset's Vert-Vert* tr. 1759
The power of harmony 1745
Poems 1764
COOPER, Leonard *The accomplices* 1960
COOPER, Lettice Ulpha *Tea on Sunday* 1973
COOPER, Samuel *The first lines of the practice of surgery* 1807 (1826)
ed. *J. M. Good's Study of medicine* 1829
COOPER, Susan Augusta Fenimore *Rural hours* 1850
COOPER, Thomas *An admonition to the people of England* 1589
An answer in defence of the truth against the Apology of private masse 1562 (Parker Soc. 1850)
Thesaurus linguæ Romanæ et Britannicæ 1565
See also ELYOT, Sir Thomas
COOPER, Thomas *The paradise of martyrs* 1873
Poetical works 1877
The purgatory of suicides 1845
COOPER, Thomas T. *Travels of a pioneer of commerce in pigtail and petticoats; overland journey from China towards India* 1871
'COOPER, William' (Harry Summerfield Hoff) *Memoirs of a new man* 1966
The struggles of Albert Woods 1952
COOPER, William D. *A glossary of the provincialisms in use in the county of Sussex* 1836 (1853)
COOPER, William R. *An archaic dictionary, from the Egyptian, Assyrian, and Etruscan monuments and papyri* 1876
A short history of the Egyptian obelisks 1877
COPE, Edward D. *The origin of the fittest* 1887
The primary factors of organic evolution 1896
Cope, Sir John 1749 See *Report*
COPE, Sir William H. *A glossary of Hampshire words and phrases* 1883 (E.D.S.)
COPI, Irving Marmer *Symbolic logic* 1954
COPLAND, James *A dictionary of practical medicine* 1844-58
COPLAND, Robert *The hye way to the Spytell hous* ?1536
Iyll of breyntfords testament 15.. (c1562; Ballad Soc. 1871)
The questyonary of cyrurgyens, with the formulary of lytell Guydo in cyrurgie, with the spectacles of cyrurgyens newly added, with the fourth boke of the terapeutyke, or methode curatyfe of Claude Galyen tr. 1541-42
The rutter of the sea, wt the hauons, rodes, soundinges, etc. with the lawes of the Ile of Auleron 1528 (? 1555)
COPLESTON, Bp. Edward *Advice to a young reviewer, with a specimen of the art* 1807 (in Arber, Eng. Garner VIII)
COPLESTON, Frederick Charles *A history of philosophy* 9 vols. 1946-75
COPLEY, Anthony *An answere to a letter of a Jesuited gentleman by his cousin* 1601
Wits fittes and fancies; also Loves owle 1595
COPSON, Edward Thomas *Metric spaces* 1968
COPYWELL, J. *The shrubs of Parnassus. Consisting of a variety of poetical essays, etc.* 1760
Corah's doom 1672 *See* T., D.
CORBET, John *A discourse of the religion of England* 1667
A humble endeavour of some plain and brief explication of the decrees and operations of God about the free actions of men a1680 (1683)

The non-conformist's plea for lay-communion with the church of England a1680 (1683)
CORBET, Richard *Certain elegant poems* a1635 (1647)
Iter Boreale a1635
CORBETT, Julian S. *The full of Asgard* 1886
CORCORAN, Dennis *Pickings from the portfolio of the reporter of the New Orleans 'Picayune'* 1846
'CORDELL, Alexander' (George Alexander Graber) *The bright Cantonese* 1967
Cordial for low spirits See GORDON, Thomas
CORELLI, Marie *The secret power* 1921
Thelma 3 vols. 1887
CORFIELD, William H. *A digest of facts relating to the treatment and utilization of sewage* 1870
'CORIAT, *Junior*' See PATERSON, S.
CORIAT, Isador H. *Abnormal psychology* 1911
Cork Examiner 1841-
CORKHILL, Thomas W. ed. *A concise building encyclopaedia* 1932
CORLETT, Peter Norman & TINSLEY, John David *Practical programming* 1968
CORMACK, William Epps *Narrative of a journey across the island of Newfoundland* 1856
CORNELL, Frederick Carruthers *The glamour of prospecting* 1920
Cornell University Agricultural Experiment Station *Bulletin* 1888-
Memoirs 1913-
CORNER, Edred John Henry *The life of plants* 1964
The natural history of palms 1966
Wayside trees of Malaya 2 vols. 1940
CORNFORD, Leslie C. *The defenceless islands* 1906
Cornhill magazine, The 1860-
CORNISH, Charles J. *The naturalist on the Thames* 1902
CORNISH, John *The provincials* 1951
Cornu-copiæ, Pasquils nightcap: or Antidot for the headache 1612 (Grosart 1877)
Cornwall 1855 See LEIFCHILD, J. R.
'CORNWALL, Barry' See PROCTER, Bryan W.
Cornwall glossary 1880 See COURTNEY, M. A.
CORNWALLEYS, Henry *The country curate's advice to his parishioners* 1693
CORNWALLIS, Sir Charles *A discourse of the most illustrious Prince Henry, late Prince of Wales* 1626 (1641)
CORNWALLIS, Charles, 1st Marquis of *Correspondence* a1805 (1859)
CORNWALLIS, Sir William *Discourses upon Seneca the tragedian* 1601 (1631)
Essayes 1600-01 (1631)
The miraculous and happie union of England and Scotland 1604
Coronation of Q. Anne. The noble tryumphaunt coronation of quene Anne, wyfe vnto kynge Henry the viij 1553
Corpus glossary c725 (Oldest Eng. texts, E.E.T.S. 1885; Hessels 1890)
CORRI, Eugene *Thirty years a boxing referee* 1915
'CORRIGAN, Mark' (Norman Lee) *Why do women—?* 1963
CORRY, John *Memoirs of Alfred Berkeley* 1802
A satirical view of London 1799 (1803)
CORSON, Dale R. & LORRAIN, Paul *Introduction to electromagnetic fields and waves* 1962
Cortasye, Knight of 1500-25 (in Ritson, Metr. rom. III)
'CORVO, Baron' See ROLFE, Frederick William
'CORY, Desmond' (John Lloyd McCarthy) *Bennett* 1977
Sunburst 1971
CORY, William *Extracts from his letters and journals* 1838-92 (1897)
CORYAT, Thomas *Coryats crudities; hastily gobled up in five moneths travels* 1611
The Odcombian banquet 1611
COSGRAVE, Patrick *Cheyney's law* 1977
COSIN, Bp. John *A collection of private devotions in the practice of the ancient church, called the houres of prayer* (anon.) 1627
Correspondence 1618-71 (Surtees Soc. 1869, -72)
A scholastical history of the canon of the Holy Scripture 1657
Cosmopolitan, The 1886-1925
COSTARD, George *Two dissertations* 1750
COSTELLO, Dudley *Stories from a screen* 1855
COSTELLO, Louisa S. *Pilgrimage to Auvergne* 1842
Costlie whore, The 1633 (in Bullen, Old plays IV, 1885)
Costume, Satirical songs and poems on, from the 13th to the 19th century v.d. (Percy Soc. 1849)
COTES, Digby 1725 See DUPIN, L. E.
COTGRAVE, John *The English treasury of wit and language* 1655
Wits interpreter; the English Parnassus 1655
COTGRAVE, Randle *A dictionarie of the French and English tongues* 1611
— (with) *a most copious dictionarie, of the English set before the French, by R(obert) S(herwood)* 1632
COTTA, John *A short discoverie of the dangers of ignorant practisers of physicke* 1612
COTTERELL, Sir Charles *Calprenède's Cassandra* tr. 1652
Davila's (E. C.) Historie of the civill warres of France 1647-48 (1678)
COTTLE, Joseph *Early recollections, chiefly relating to S. T. Coleridge in Bristol* 1837
Reminiscences of Coleridge and Southey 1847 (an enlarged ed. of prec.)
COTTON, Charles *Burlesque upon burlesque, or the scoffer scoft* 1675
The compleat angler. Being instructions how to angle for a trout or grayling in a clear stream 1676. See also WALTON, Isaak
The compleat gamester 1674
Girard's (Guillaume) History of the life of the duke of Espernon tr. 1670
Montaigne's Essays tr. 1685
Poems a1687 (1689)
Poetical works a1687 (1765)
Scarronides, or Virgile travestie 1664,-67
The wonders of the Peake 1681
COTTON, Charles A. *Landscape, as developed by processes of normal erosion* 1941
Volcanoes as landscape forms 1944
COTTON, Frank & WILKINSON, Geoffrey *Advanced inorganic chemistry* 1962
—(ed. 2) 1966
—(ed. 3) 1972
COTTON, Harry *Advanced electrical technology* 1967
COTTON, John *A brief exposition of the whole book of Canticles* 1642 (1868)
A briefe exposition upon Ecclesiastes a1652 (1868)
Singing of psalmes, a Gospel-ordinance 1647
COTTON, Nathaniel *Observations on a particular kind of scarlet fever, that lately prevailed in and about St. Albans* 1749
Various pieces in prose and verse a1788 (1791)
Visions in verse, for the entertainment and instruction of younger minds 1751
COTTON, Sir Robert B. *An abstract out of the records of the Tower touching the kings revenue* a1631 (1642)
A short view of the long life and reigne of Henry the third 1627
A treatise against recusants in defence of the Oath of allegiance a1631 (1641)
COTTON, Roger *An armor of proofe, brought from the tower of Dauid, to fight against Spannyardes* 1596
COTTON, William C. *My bee book* 1842
Cotton Homilies a1175 (in O. E. Homilies, E.E.T.S. 1868)
COTTRELL, Alan Howard *An introduction to metallurgy* 1967
COUCH, Sir A. T. Quiller- See 'Q'
COUCH, Jonathan *A history of the fishes of the British Islands* 1860-65
The history of Polperro a1870 (ed. T. Quiller Couch 1871)
COUCH, Thomas Quiller 1880 See COURTNEY, M. A.
COUES, Elliott *Birds of the Northwest* 1873 (1874)
Fur-bearing animals 1877
Key to North American birds 1872 (1884)
ed. *New light on the early history of the Greater Northwest: the manuscript journals of Alexander Henry ... and of David Thompson* 3 vols. 1897
—— & ALLEN, Joel A. *North American Rodentia* 1877
COULTER, John *Adventures in the Pacific* 1845
COULTER, John Merle, BARNES, C. R., & COWLES, H. C. *A textbook of botany for colleges and universities* 2 vols. 1910-11
COULTER, Stephen *The château* 1974
Embassy 1969
The Soyuz affair 1977
Countrey-man's letter to the Curat, The 1711
Country gentleman, The 1853-65, 1898-
Country gentlemen's catalogue 1894-
Country gentlemen's magazine 1900-
Country life 1897-
Countryman, The 1927-
County, The; a novel 1889
COUPER, Robert *Poetry, chiefly in the Scottish language* 1804
COURANT, Richard & ROBBINS, Herbert Ellis *What is mathematics?* 1941
Courier and Advertiser (Dundee) 1926-
Courier-Journal (Louisville, Kentucky) 1868
Courier-Mail (Brisbane) 1953-
COURSE, Alfred George *A dictionary of nautical terms* 1962
Coursing calendar and review of the season 1857-1918
COURT, Andrew *The true way to vertue and happinesse, intreating specially of constancie in publick calamaties and private afflictions* (tr. from G. Du Vair) 1623
Court and times of Charles I, James I 1848 See BIRCH, Thomas
Court magazine, The 1835 (vol. VI)
Court of love c1530 (in Chaucer's Works, ed. Stowe 1561; Skeat, Chaucerian pieces 1897)
COURTENAY, Edward *Paleario's (A.) Benefit of Christ's death* tr. 1855
COURTENAY, Florence *Physical beauty: how to develop and preserve it* 1922
COURTHOPE, William J. *Addison* 1884
COURTIER, Peter L. *Pleasures of solitude* 1800
COURTIER, Sidney Hobson *Death in dream time* 1959
COURTNEY, Margaret A. *Glossary of words in use in Cornwall. West Cornwall by Miss M. A. Courtney. East Cornwall by Thomas Q. Couch* 1880 (E.D.S.)
COUSTEAU, Jacques Yves & DUMAS, Frédéric *The silent world* 1953
COVARRUBIAS, Miguel *Island of Bali* 1937
—(another ed.) 1972
COVEL, John *Extracts from diaries of* 1670-79 (Hakluyt Soc. 1893)
COVEL, John *Some account of the present Greek Church* 1722
COVELL, William *Polimanteia, or, the meanes to judge of the fall of a common-wealth* 1595
Covenant of Grace, not absolute, but conditional, asserted 1692
COVENTRY, Francis *The history of Pompey the Little: or, the life and adventures of a lap-dog* 1750
COVENTRY, Henry *Letters of Philemon to Hydaspes; relating a conversation with Hortensius upon the subject of false religion* 1736
Coventry Corpus Christi plays, Two a1500 (E.E.T.S. 1902)
Coventry Leet book: or Mayor's register 1420-1555 (E.E.T.S. 1907-13)
Coventry mysteries (Ludus Coventriæ: a collection of mysteries formerly represented at Coventry on the feast of Corpus Christi) c1450 (Shaks. Soc. 1841; E.E.T.S. 1922)
COVERDALE, Miles *Writings and translations; Remains* v.d. (Parker Soc. 1844, 1846)
Certain most godly letters of such true saintes and holy martyrs as gaue their lyues, etc. v.d. (1564)
The christen state of matrymonye tr. (from H. Bullinger) 1541
A confutacion of that treatise, which one J. Standish made agaynst the protestacion of D. Barnes in 1540 ?1541
The defence of a certayne poore christen man tr. 1545
An exhortacion to the careinge of Chrystes crosse ?1550
A faythful and most godly treatyse concernynge the most sacred sacrament of the blessed body and blood of Christ tr. 15..
Fruitfull lessons upon the passion, etc. 1540
The hope of the faythfull ? 1554 (1574)
A most frutefull, pithye, and learned treatise how a christen man oughte to behaue hymselfe in the daunger of death tr. ?1550 (1579)
The old faith tr. (from H. Bullinger) 1541
The order that the churche in Denmarke doth use ?1550
The original and sprynge of all sectes and orders tr. 1537
The second tome or volume of the Paraphrase of Erasmus upon the Newe Testament 1549
A spyrytuall and moost precious pearle 1550
A very excellent and swete exposition upon the two and twentye Psalme of David tr. (from M. Luther) 1537
A worke entytled of ye olde God and the newe, etc. tr. 1523 (1534)
See also *Bible*
COVERTE, Robert *A true and almost incredible report of an Englishman that travelled by land throw many unknowne kingdomes* 1612
COWAN, James *The Maoris of New Zealand* 1910
COWAN, Lester ed. *Recording sound for motion pictures* 1931
COWARD, Noël Pierce *Australia visited, 1940* 1941
Blithe spirit: an improbable farce 1941 (UK 1942)
Design for living: a comedy 1933
Future indefinite 1954
Middle East diary 1944
Play parade 6 vols. 1934-62
Present indicative 1937
Private lives 1930
To-night at 8.30: plays 3 vols. 1936
COWELL, Colin Robert, et al. *Inlays, crowns, and bridges* ed. G. F. Kantorowicz 1963
COWELL, Emilie Marguerite *The Cowells in America: the diary of Mrs. S. Cowell, 1860-1861* ed. M. W. Disher 1934
COWELL, John *The interpreter: or booke containing the signification of words* 1607 (1637, 1672)
— augmented by Thomas Manley (1684)
— farther augmented by W. Kennett (1701)
COWELL, Joseph *Thirty years passed among the players in England and America* 1844
COWIE, Robert *Shetland, descriptive and historical* 1871
COWLEY, Abraham *Works* a1667 (1668, 1687, 1710-11, 1905-06)
Cutter of Coleman-street 1663
Davideis 1638-56
The guardian; a comedie 1650
Loves riddle 1638
Miscellanies 1656
The mistress 1647
Ode upon the Restoration 1660
Of plants tr. Bks. I and II, by J. O. 1693; Bk. III, by C. Cleeve 1711; Bks. IV and V, by N. Tate 1695; Bk. VI, by Mrs. Behn 1680
Pindarique odes 1656
Poeticall blossomes 1633
A proposition for the advancement of experimental philosophy 1661
Several discourses by way of essays in verse and prose a1667
Sylva, or, dyvers copies of verses 1636
The tragicall history of Piramus and Thisbe 1633
Verses written on several occasions 1663
A vision, concerning his late pretended highnesse, Cromwell the Wicked 1661
COWLEY, Captain *Voyage round the globe in 1683* (in Hacke's Collect. Voy. 1699)
COWLEY, Hannah *A bold stroke for a husband* 1782
Who's the dupe? 1779
COWPER, Mary, Countess *Diary* 1714-20 (1864)
COWPER, Bp. William *His dikaiologie: contayning a just defence of his apologie* 1614
COWPER, William *Works* a1800 (1835-37)
Poetical works a1800 (1889, 1905)
Poems 1782, 1800
Anti-Thelyphthora 1781
Charity 1781
Conversation 1781
Correspondence ed. T. Wright 4 vols. 1904
The diverting history of John Gilpin 1782
Expostulation 1781
Homer tr. 1791; ed. 2, a1800 (1802)
Hope 1781
Letters v.d. (1876)

COWPER, William (*cont.*)
Olney hymns 1779
Private correspondence with several friends v.d. (1837)
The progress of error 1780
Retirement 1781
Table talk 1781
The task 1784
Tirocinium 1784
Truth 1781
COX, Charles Brian & DYSON, Anthony Edward *The twentieth-century mind: history, ideas and literature in Britain* 3 vols. 1972
COX, Sir George W. *A general history of Greece* 1876
The mythology of the Aryan nations 1870
COX, Homersham *The institutions of the English government* 1863
COX, James Stevens *An illustrated dictionary of hairdressing and wigmaking* 1966
COX, John C. *Notes on the churches of Derbyshire* 1875-79
The royal forests of England 1905
COX, Leonard *The arte or crafte of rhethoryke* 1524 (1899)
COX, Nicholas *The gentleman's recreation* 1674 (1677, 1686)
COX, Nigel Shaun Maturin & GROSE, Michael William eds. *The organization and handling of bibliographic records by computer* 1967
COX, Sir Richard *Hibernia Anglicana; or, the history of Ireland from the conquest thereof by the English to this present time* 1689-90
COX, Ross *Adventures on the Columbia River* 2 vols. 1831 (US 1 vol. 1832)
COX, Samuel *The pilgrim psalms; an exposition of the songs of degrees* 1874
Salvator mundi: or, is Christ the Saviour of all men? 1877
COX, Thomas *Magna Britannia et Hibernia* 1720-31
COXE, Daniel *A description of the English province of Carolana* 1722
COXE, William *Account of the Russian discoveries between Asia and America* 1780
History of the House of Austria from 1218-1792 1807
Travels in Switzerland 1789
COXE, William *A view of the cultivation of fruit trees, and the management of orchards and cider* 1817
COXHEAD, Eileen Elizabeth *The figure in the mist* 1955
One green bottle 1951
The thankless muse 1967
A wind in the west 1949
COXON, Ethel *A basil plant* 1881
COZENS-HARDY, H. T. *Broad Norfolk: being a series of articles and letters. Reprinted from the 'Eastern Daily Press.'* ed. by C.-H. 1893
COZZENS, Frederic S. *The Sparrowgrass papers: or, living in the country* 1860
CRABB, George *Universal technological dictionary* 1823
CRABBE, George *Poetical works* a1832 (1834, 1905-07)
The borough 1810
The candidate 1780
Inebriety 1775
The library 1781
The newspaper 1785
The parish register 1807
Posthumous tales a1832
Tales (in verse) 1812
Tales of the Hall 1819
The Village 1783
'CRADDOCK, Charles Egbert' *See* MURFREE, Mary N.
CRADDOCK, Harry *The Savoy cocktail book* 1930
CRADOCK, Joseph *Zobeide; a tragedy* 1771
Craft of deyng c1450 (in Ratis raving, etc., E.E.T.S. 1870)
Crafte of nombrynge c1425 (E.E.T.S. 1922)
CRAIG, Alexander *Poetical works* a1631 (Hunterian Club 1873)
Amorose songes, sonets, and elegies 1606
The pilgrime and heremite 1631
Poeticall essayes 1604
Poetical recreations 1609, 1623
'CRAIG, David' (Allan James Tucker) *A dead liberty* 1974
Young men may die 1970
CRAIG, Elizabeth *Collins family cookery* 1957
CRAIG, John *A new universal etymological, technological, and pronouncing dictionary of the English language* 1849
CRAIG, William M. *Lectures on drawing, painting, and engraving* 1821
CRAIGIE, David *Elements of general and pathological anatomy* 1848
CRAIGIE, Pearl M. T. *The herb-moon. A fantasia* 1896
CRAIGIE, Sir William A. *The religion of ancient Scandinavia* 1906
—— & HULBERT, James R. eds. *A dictionary of American English on historical principles* See under title
CRAIK, Mrs. Dinah M. (Miss Mulock) *Agatha's husband* 1853
Bread upon the waters 1852
Christian's mistake 1865
Domestic stories 1860
Fair France 1871
The head of the family 1852
John Halifax, gentleman 1856
A life for a life 1859
Mistress and maid 1863
A noble life 1866
The Ogilvies 1849
Romantic tales 1859
The woman's kingdom 1869
A woman's thoughts about women 1858

CRAIK, George L. *A manual of English literature, or of the history of the English language* 1862 (1874)
CRAIK, Georgiana M. (Mrs. A. W. May) *Faith Unwin's ordeal* 1865
Lost and won 1859
CRAKANTHORP, Richard *A sermon at the solemnizing of the inauguration of King James, 24 Mar. 1608* 1609
A sermon of sanctification 1607 (1608)
Vigilius dormitans, Romes seer overseene, or a treatise of the fift Generall Councell 1631
Cramer's (J. A.) Elements of the art of assaying metals tr. 1741
Cramer's Pittsburgh almanac 1812-14; 1816-17
CRAMOND, William *The annals of Banff* 1891-93 (New Spalding Cl.)
The annals of Cullen 1888
The annals of Fordoun 1894
ed. *The records of Elgin* 1234-1800 (New Spalding Cl. 1903-08)
CRANDALL, Irving Bardshar *Theory of vibrating systems and sound* 1927
CRANDALL, Lee Saunders *The management of wild mammals in captivity* 1964
CRANE, Harold Hart *Letters 1916-32* ed. B. Weber 1952 — (paperback ed.) 1965
CRANE, Stephen *Maggie, a girl of the streets* 1893
The red badge of courage. An episode of the American Civil War 1895
CRANE, William J. E. *Bookbinding for amateurs* 1885
The smithy and forge 1883
CRANMER, Thomas *Works* a1556 (1833)
Writings and disputations; Remains a1556 (Parker Soc. 1844, 1846)
An answer vnto a crafty and sophisticall cauillation deuised by Stephen Gardiner 1551
Catechismus. That is to say; a shorte instruction into christian religion 1548
A defence of the true and catholike doctrine of the Sacrament 1550
See also *Bible*
Crans's (David) Ancient and modern history of the Brethren tr. by B. La Trobe 1780
CRAPSEY, Edward *The nether side of New York; or, The vice, crime, and poverty of the great metropolis* 1872
CRASHAW, Richard *Poems* a1649 (1858, 1904)
Carmen Deo nostro a1649 (1652)
Steps to the temple. With the delights of the muses 1646
CRASHAW, William *The Jesuites gospel* 1610
Newes from Italy of a second Moses: or, the life of Galeacius Caracciolus the noble marquesse of Vico tr. 1608; another ed., entitled *The Italian convert* 1635
Romish forgeries and falsifications 1606
CRASKE, Margaret & BEAUMONT, Cyril William *The theory and practice of the allegro in classical ballet* 1930
CRAUFURD, Quintin *Sketches relating chiefly to the history, religion, learning, and manners of the Hindoos* 1790
CRAUFURD, Thomas *History of the University of Edinburgh 1580-1646* 16.. (1808)
CRAVEN, Isaac *Gods tribunall and mans tryal* 1630 (1631)
Craven glossary 1824, 1828 *See* CARR, W.
CRAWFORD, D. *Thinking black, 22 years without a break in the long grass of central Africa* 1912
CRAWFORD, David *Poems, chiefly in the Scottish dialect, on various subjects* 1798
CRAWFORD, Francis Marion *Doctor Claudius* 1883
Greifenstein 1889
Mr. Isaacs 1882
A Roman singer 1884
Saracinesca 1887
A tale of a lonely parish 1886
With the immortals 1888
CRAWFORD, James Coutts *Recollections of travel in New Zealand and Australia* 1880
'CRAWFORD, Robert' (Hugh Crauford Rae) *Whip hand* 1972
CRAWFORD, Samuel *Basic engineering processes* 1964
Crawford collection of early charters and documents now in the Bodleian library. Ed. by A. S. Napier and W. H. Stevenson (Anecdota Oxon. 1895)
CRAWFURD, John *History of the Indian archipelago* 3 vols. 1820
'CRAWLEY, Captain R.' (G. F. Pardon) *Billiards* 1856 (1859)
The card player 1863
Football, golf and shinty, hockey, polo, and curling 1878
Hoyle's games modernized 1863
Crazy tales 1762 *See* STEVENSON, John H.
CREASY, Sir Edward S. *The fifteen decisive battles of the world* 1851
History of the Ottoman Turks 1854-56
The rise and progress of the English constitution 1853 (1854)
CREECH, Thomas *Juvenal's thirteenth satire* tr. 1693 (see Dryden, J.)
T. Lucretius Carus, his six books De natura rerum tr. 1682 (1683)
The five books of M. Manilius, containing a system of the ancient astronomy and astrology; together with the philosophy of the Stoicks tr. 1697
The Idylliums of Theocritus tr. 1684
CREED, David *The trial of Lobo Icheka* 1971
Creevey papers, a selection from the correspondence and diaries of the late Thomas Creevey a 1838 (1903)
CREICHTON, Captain John *Memoirs, written by himself* (? by J. Swift) 1731
CREIGHTON, Charles *History of epidemics in Britain* 1891-94
CREIGHTON, Bp. Mandell *Historical essays and reviews* 1872-96 (1902)

History of the Papacy during the period of the Reformation 1882-94
Life and letters, by his wife (1904)
Crescendo 1962-
CRESSWELL, Dan. 1823 *See* VENTUROLI, G.
CRESSY, Hugh P. *Reflexions upon the oathes of supremacy and allegiance* 1661
CRESY, Edward *Encyclopædia of civil engineering* 1847
'CRÈVECŒUR, J. H. ST. JOHN DE' (Michel Guillaume St. Jean de Crèvecœur) *Letters from an American farmer* 1782
CREW, Peter *Encyclopædic dictionary of mountaineering* 1968
CRICHTON, A. W. *A naturalist's ramble to the Orcades* 1866
CRICHTON, Andrew *History of Arabia, ancient and modern* 1833
Cricket 1882-1913
Cricketer, The 1921-
Cries of blood (Pamphlet on murder of W. Harrison 1660 at Campden) 1767
'CRISPIN, Edmund' (Robert Bruce Montgomery) *Buried for pleasure* 1948
Frequent hearses 1950
Glimpses of the moon 1977
The long divorce 1951
Crist a900 *See* CYNEWULF
CRITCHLEY, Macdonald *Developmental dyslexia* 1964
The parietal lobes 1953
Critic, The (New York) 1881-1906
Critical review; or, Annals of literature 1756-1817
CROCKETT, David *An account of Col. Crockett's tour to the North and down East. Written by himself* 1835
Colonel Crockett's exploits and adventures in Texas... written by himself 1836 (attributed to Richard Penn Smith)
Narrative of the life of David Crockett 1834
Sketches and eccentricities of Colonel David Crockett See under title
CROCKETT, Samuel R. *The banner of blue* 1902
The Black Douglas 1899
Bog-Myrtle and peat 1895
Cleg Kelly 1896
The dark o' the moon 1902
The dew of their youth 1910
The grey man 1896
Kit Kennedy: country boy 1899
Lad's love 1897
The lilac sunbonnet 1894
Little Anna Mark 1900
Lochinvar 1897
Love idylls 1901
Mad Sir Uchtred of the hills 1894
The men of the moss-hags 1895
The raiders; passages in the life of John Faa 1894
The standard bearer 1898
The stickit minister, and some common men 1893
That Popish parson fellow 1896
CROFT, Bp. Herbert *The naked truth; or the true state of the primitive church* 1675
A short narrative of the discovery of a college of Jesuits at Come, Hereford 1679
Some animadversions upon a book (by T. Burnet) *intituled 'The theory of the earth'* 1685
CROFT, John Michael *Spare the rod* 1954
CROFTS, Freeman Willis *Inspector French and the Cheyne mystery* 1926
CROKE, John *Thirteen Psalms, and the first chapter of Ecclesiastes* 1540-54 (Percy Soc. 1844)
Croke's (Sir George) Reports of cases adjudged in the courts of Kings-bench and Common-bench tr. by Sir H. Grimston 1669
CROKER, B. M. *The Company's servant: a romance of Southern India* 1907
Peggy of the Bartons 1898
Proper pride 1885
Village tales and jungle tragedies 1895 (1896)
CROKER, John W. *Essays on the early period of the French Revolution* 1857
The Croker papers. The correspondence and diaries of the late rt. hon. J. W. Croker a1857 (1884)
CROKER, Temple H. *Ariosto's Orlando Furioso* tr. 1755
et al. *The complete dictionary of the arts and sciences* 3 vols. 1764-6
CROKER, Thomas C. *Fairy legends and traditions of the south of Ireland* 1825-28 (1862)
Researches in the south of Ireland 1824
CROLL, James *Climate and time in their geological relations* 1875
CROLY, George *Historical sketches, speeches and characters* 1842
CROMARTY, George Mackenzie, 1st Earl of *An historical account of the conspiracies by the Earls of Gowry and Robert Logan against James VI* 1713
CROMEK, Robert H. *Remains of Nithsdale and Galloway song* 1810
Select Scottish songs 1810
CROMPTON, Richard *L'authoritie et jurisdiction des courts de la maiestie de la roygne* 1594
Loffice et aucthoritie de iustices de peace, in part collect per A. Fitzherbert, et ore enlarge per R. C. 1583
'CROMPTON, Richmal' (Richmal Crompton Lamburn) *Just — William* 1922
Still — William 1925
William again 1923
William and the evacuees 1940
William and the moon rocket 1954
William carries on 1942

William does his bit 1941
William — the detective 1935
Cromwell, Oliver *Letters and speeches* a1658 (ed. Carlyle 1845)
Cromwell, Thomas *Letters* a1540 *See* Merriman, R. B.
Cronin, Archibald Joseph *The citadel* 1937
Hatter's Castle 1931
The stars look down 1935
Cronin, Bernard *Timber wolves* 1920
'Cronin, Michael' (Brendan Leo Cronin) *Dead ... and done with* 1959
Cronin, Vincent *The wise man from the west* 1955
Crooke, Helkiah *Μικροκοσμογραφία. A description of the body of man* 1615
Crooke, William *The tribes and castes of the North-Western Provinces and Oudh* 4 vols. 1896
Crookes, William *Dyeing and calico-printing* 1874
Dyeing and tissue-printing 1882
Crookshank, William *The history of the state and sufferings of the Church of Scotland, from the restoration to the revolution* 1749
Croome, Honoria Renée Minturn *The faithless mirror* 1946
The forgotten place 1957
You've gone astray 1944
Croquet, The laws of, adopted at a general conference of croquet clubs 1870 (1874)
Crosby, Elizabeth Caroline, et al. *Correlative anatomy of the nervous system* 1962
Crosby, Howard *The Christian preacher: Yale lectures 1879–80* 1880
Crosby, John Campbell *Nightfall* 1976 (UK 1977 with title *Snake*)
Crosland, Camilla *Mrs. Blake* 1862
Cross, Charles Frederick & Bevan, Edward John *A text-book of paper-making* 1888
Cross, Ian Robert *The backward sex* 1960
The God boy 1957 (UK 1958)
'Cross, James' (Hugh Jones Parry) *To hell for half-a-crown* 1967
Cross, John W. *George Eliot's life as related in her letters and journals* 1884
Cross, Walter *The Taghmical art: or the art of expounding scripture by the points usually called accents* 1698
Cross, William *The Disruption: a tale of trying times* 1844 (1877)
Crosse, Henry *Vertues common-wealth* 1603 (Grosart 1878)
Crossman, Richard Howard Stafford *The diaries of a Cabinet Minister* 3 vols. 1975–7
Crossman, Samuel *The young man's calling, or the whole duty of youth* (anon.) 1678
Crosthwaite, Charles *Synchronology: being a treatise on the history, chronology and mythology of the ancient Egyptians, Greeks and Phoenicians* 1839
Crouch, Nathaniel *See* Burton, Richard or Robert
Croudace, Glynn *The scarlet bikini* 1970
Crowch, Humfrey *The Welch traveller; or, the unfortunate Welchman* 1671
Crowe, William *Lewesdon Hill; a poem* 1788
A sermon preached before the University of Oxford, Nov. 5. 1781 1781
A treatise on English versification 1827
Crowest, Frederick James *Beethoven* 1899
Crowley, Robert *Select works* a1588 (E.E.T.S. 1872)
A deliberat answere made to a rash offer 1588
An informacion and peticion agaynst the oppressours of the pore Commons 1548
One and thyrtye epigrammes 1550
Pleasure and payne, heauen and hell 1551
A setting open of the subtyle sophistrie of T. Watson 1569
The voyce of the laste trumpet blowen bi the seuenth angel 1549 (1550)
The way to wealth, wherein is taught a remedy for sedicion 1550
Crowne, John *Dramatic works* a1703 (1872)
The ambitious statesman 1679
City politiques 1683
Juliana, or the Princess of Poland 1671
The misery of civil-war 1680
Sir Courtly Nice 1685
Crowned king, The c1415 (in Langland, Piers Plowman; Text C, E.E.T.S. 1873)
Crowther, Sir Geoffrey *Outline of money* 1940
—(rev. ed.) 1948
Crowther, James Gerald & Whiddington, Richard *Science at war* 1947
Croxall, Samuel *The fables of Æsop and others* tr. 1722
The fair Circassian, a dramatic performance 1720
An original canto of Spencer by 'Nestor Ironside' 1713 (1714)
A sermon preached before the House of Commons Jan. 30, 1729 1730
The vision: a poem 1715
See also Garth, Sir S.
Croy, Homer *How motion pictures are made* 1918
R.F.D. No. 3 1924
Crozier, A. A. *A dictionary of botanical terms* 1892
Cruickshank, James G. *Soil geography* 1972
Cruise, William *A digest of the laws of England* 1818 (ed. 2)
Crull, Jodocus *The antient and present state of Muscovy* 1698
Crump, Arthur *A practical treatise on banking, currency, and the exchanges* 1866
Crump, Barry John *A good keen man* 1960
Hang on a minute, mate 1961 (UK 1963)
Crump, James Irving & Maul, Norman *Our airliners* 1940
Cruse, C. F. *Eusebius' Ecclesiastical history* tr. 1833
Crutchley, John *General view of the agriculture in the county of Rutland* 1794
Crystal, David *Linguistics* 1971
—— & Quirk, Charles Randolph *Systems of prosodic and paralinguistic features in English* 1964
Cuckoo and nightingale See Clanvowe, Sir T.
Cuckoo Song ('Sumer is icumen in') c1240 (in Ritson, Ancient songs 1877)
Cudlip, Mrs. Pender *See* Thomas, Annie
Cudworth, Ralph *A discourse concerning the true notion of the Lords supper* 1642 (1676)
A treatise concerning eternal and immutable morality a1688 (1731)
The true intellectual system of the universe 1678
The union of Christ and the Church a shadow 1642
Cudworth, William *Histories of Bolton and Bowling* 1891
Round about Bradford 1876
Culbertson, Ely *Contract bridge blue book* 1930
Contract bridge complete 1936
Culbertson, Robert *Lectures on the Book of Revelation* 1825
Culina 1806 *See* Hunter, A.
Cullen, William *First lines of the practice of physic* 1776–84
Nosology tr. 1800
A treatise of the materia medica 1789
Culley, George *See* Bailey, John
Culley, Richard Spelman *A hand-book of practical telegraphy* 1863
Culloden papers: comprising an extensive and interesting correspondence from 1625 to 1748 v.d. (1815)
Cullum, John *The history and antiquities of Hawsted and Hardwick in the county of Suffolk* 1784 (1813)
—— *Glossary* (from the above) 1813 (E.D.S. 1879)
'Culotta, Nino' (John Patrick O'Grady) *They're a weird mob* 1957 (UK 1958)
Culpepper, Nicholas *The English physitian enlarged* 1653
Pharmacopœia Londinensis; or, the London dispensatory further advanced by the studies and collections of the Fellows now living of the said Colledg 1654
Semeiotica Uranica; or, an astrologicall judgment of diseases 1651
—— & Cole, Abdiah *Bartholinus' (T.) Anatomy; made from the precepts of his father and from the observations of all modern anatomists, together with his own*, etc. Published by N. Culpeper and A. Cole 1668
——, —— & Rowland, W. *The practice of physick, being chiefly a translation of the works of L. Riverius, with a physical dictionary explaining hard words* 1655
Cultivator, The: a monthly journal for farm and the garden 1834–65
Cultural news from India 1960–
Culver, Charles Mortimer tr. *E. Landolt's The refraction and accommodation of the eye and their anomalies* 1886
Culverwell, Ezekiel *A treatise of faith* 1623 (ed. 2)
Culverwell, Nathaniel *An elegant .. discourse of the Light of Nature; with several other treatises* 1652 (1661)
Cumberland, Marten *Murmurs in the Rue Morgue* 1959
Cumberland, Richard *Anecdotes of eminent painters in Spain* 1782 (1787)
Aristophanes' Clouds tr. 1798
The brothers 1769
Calvary; or the death of Christ 1792
John De Lancaster c1800 (1809)
Memoirs 1806 (1807)
The natural son 1785
The West Indian, a comedy 1771
See also *Observer*
Cumberland, A glossary of provincial words used in the county of 1851
Cumberland and Westmoreland Archaeological Society *Transactions* 1874–
Cumberland glossary 1878 *See* Dickinson, W.
Cumberland News 1910–
Cuming, Fortescue *Sketches of a tour to the western country* 1810
Cumming, Alexander *The elements of clock and watch-work* 1766
Cumming, John *Christ receiving sinners* 1849
Ruth: a chapter in providence 1859
Sabbath morning readings on the Old Testament 1854
Scripture readings on the book of Genesis 1853
Cumming, Linnæus *Electricity treated experimentally* 1886 (1887)
Cumming, R. Gordon *Five years of a hunter's life in the far interior of South Africa* 1850 (1902)
Cummings, Edward Estlin *eimi* 1933
The enormous room 1922
Selected letters ed. F. W. Dupee & G. Stade 1969
Cummins, John *See* Bulkeley, J.
Cummins, Maria S. *El Fureidîs* 1860
Haunted hearts 1864
The lamplighter 1854
Mabel Vaughan 1857
Cundall, Joseph *On bookbindings ancient and modern* 1881
Cundill, John P. *A dictionary of explosives* 1889 (1895)
Cundy, Nicholas W. *Inland transit* 1834
Cunliffe, Henry *A glossary of Rochdale, with Rossendale words and phrases* 1886
Cunningham, Allan *The lives of the most eminent British painters, sculptors, and architects* 1829–33
Songs: chiefly in the rural language of Scotland 1813
The songs of Scotland, ancient and modern 1825
Traditional tales of the English and Scottish peasantry 1822 (1874)
Cunningham, Daniel John *Text-book of anatomy* 1902
—(ed. 4) ed. A. Robinson 1913
Cunningham, Sir Henry S. *Wheat and tares; a tale* (anon.) 1861
Cunningham, John *Poems, chiefly pastoral* 1766
Poems a1773 (1790)
Cunningham, Peter *Two years in New South Wales* 1827 (1828)
Cunningham, Peter 1842 See *Accounts of the Revels at Court*
Cunningham, Timothy *A new and complete law dictionary* 1764–65
Cunningham, William *The cosmographical glasse* 1559
Cunningham, William *Diary and general expenditure book* 1673–80 (S.H.S. 1887)
Cunningham, William *Historic theology* a1861 (1862)
Cunningham's (Alexander) History of Great Britain tr. 1787
Cunnington, Cecil Willett *English women's clothing in the present century* 1952
——, Cunnington, P. E., & Beard, C. *A dictionary of English costume* 1960
Cupid and Psyche; or Colombine-courtezan 1734
Cupples, George *The green hand; or, the naval lieutenant* 1856
'Curate, Jacob' *The Scotch presbyterian eloquence* 1692
Cureton, William *Corpus Ignatianum: a complete collection of the Ignatian Epistles* tr. 1849
Curiosities of nature and art in husbandry and gardening 1707
Curling, Thomas B. *Observations on the diseases of the rectum* 1851 (1863, -76)
Curme volume of linguistic studies 1930 *See* Hatfield, James Taft, et al.
Curr, John *The coal viewer, and engine builder's practical companion* 1797
Current researches in anesthesia and analgesia 1922–56
Current slang (University of South Dakota) 1966–71
Current trends in linguistics 1963–
Curry-combe for a coxe-combe 1615 *See* Hoby, Sir E.
Cursor Mundi (The Cursur o the world). A Northumbrian poem of the 14th century in four versions 13.., 14.. (E.E.T.S. 1874–92)
Curtasye, Boke of c1450 (E.E.T.S. 1868).
See also Caxton
Curteys, Bp. Richard *A sermon preached before the Queenes Majestie at Grenewiche* 1573
Two sermons preached, the first at Paules Crosse, the second at Westminster 1576
Curtis, George T. *Life of Buchanan, fifteenth president of the United States* 1883
Curtis, George W. *Lotos-eating: a summer book* 1852
Nile notes of a Howadji 1851
The Potiphar papers 1854 (1866)
Curtis, James *The gilt kid* 1936
They drive by night 1938
Curtis, John C. *Elements of the history of England* 1861
Curtis, William *Flora Londinensis* 1777
Curtis's Botanical magazine 1787–1844
Curwen, Henry *History of booksellers* 1873
Curwen, John C. *Hints on the economy of feeding stock* 1808
Curzon, Hon. Robert *Visits to the monasteries in the Levant* 1849
Cusack, Norman Edward *The electrical and magnetic properties of solids* 1958
Cushing, George Frederick tr. *P. Hajdú's Finno-Ugrian languages and peoples* 1975
Cushing, Harvey Williams *The pituitary body and its disorders* 1912
Cushing, Luther S. *A practical treatise on the trustee process, or foreign attachment of the laws of Massachusetts and Maine* 1833
Cussans, John E. *The handbook of heraldry* 1868 (1869)
History of Hertfordshire 1870–81
Cust, Robert N. *A sketch of the modern languages of Africa* 1883
Custer, Elizabeth B. *'Boots and saddles'; or, life in Dakota with General Custer* 1885
Custine's (Astolphe de) Empire of the Czar tr. 1843
Custom car 1970–
Custome house, The rates of the 1545 (1583)
Customes of Yardley Hastings 1609 *See* Chesley, H.
Cuthbert, The life of Saint c1450 (Surtees Soc. 1891)
Cuthill, Ronald tr. *J. Schober's Silk and the silk industry* 1930
Cutler, Manasseh *Life, journal, and correspondence, by his grandchildren* a1823 (1888)
Cutspear, W. *Dramatic rights; or, private theatricals and picnic suppers justified by fair argument* 1802
Cutwode, Thomas *Caltha poetarum: or the bumble bee* 1599
Cuvier's Animal kingdom tr. 1834–37
See also Blyth, E.; Griffith, E.
Cuyler, Theodore L. *Heart culture* 1872 (1879)
Pointed papers for the Christian life 1878
Cycling. Pt. I by H. Graves; Pt. II by G. L. Hillier; Pt. III by Susan, Countess of Malmesbury 1898
Cyclopedia of American government ed. A. C. McLaughlin & A. B. Hart 3 vols. 1914
Cyclopædia of practical medicine, edited by J. Forbes, A. Tweedie, J. Conolly 1833–35
Cynewulf *Crist* a900 (Grein; Gollancz 1892)
Elene a900 (Grein)
Juliana a900 (Grein)
Cyples, William *An inquiry into the process of human experience* 1880
Cyrurgyons of Mountpyller, The practyse of c1540

D

D. A. *See* A., D.
D., J. 1613 *See* Dennys, J.
D., J. gent. *The knave in graine, new vampt, a witty comedy* 1640
D., J. 1661 *See* Davies, J. (of Kidwelly)
D., N. ('Doleman, N.') *See* N. D.
D., R. *Columna's (F.) Hypnerotomachia; the strife of loue in a dreame* tr. 1592 (also 1890)
D. T. *See* T., D. (i.e. Tuvil, D.)
D., W. *Audiguier's (V. d') Tragi-comicall history of our times under the borrowed names of Lisander and Calista* tr. 1627
D., W. *Comenius' (J. A.) Janua linguarum reserata; the gate of languages unlocked* 1650
D., W. *Paracelsus his dispensatory and chirurgery* tr. 1656
D., W. 1696 *See* Derham, W.
Daborne, Robert *An assize sermon* 1618
A Christian turn'd Turke (a tragedy) 1612
Da Costa *See* Mendes da Costa
Dacre, Charlotte (Mrs. Byrne) *The libertine* 1807
Zofloya or the Moor: a romance of the fifteenth century 1806
Dacres, Edward *Machiavel's (N.) Discourses upon . . Livius* tr. 1636
Machiavel's (N.) Prince tr. 1640 (1644)
Dacres, R. *The art of water-drawing* 1660
Dædalus 1955- (continuation of *Proceedings* of the American Academy of Arts and Sciences)
Daglish, Eric Fitch tr. *E. Schneider-Leyer's Dogs of the world* 1964
Daily Ardmoreite (Ardmore, Oklahoma) 1893-
Daily Chronicle 1872-
Daily Colonist (Victoria, British Columbia) 1886-
Daily Evening Bulletin (San Francisco) 1855-95
Daily Express 1900-
Daily Graphic 1890-1926
Daily Herald 1912-64
Daily Mail 1896-
Daily Mirror 1903-
Daily Nation (Nairobi, Kenya) 1960-
Daily News 1846-
Daily News (New York) 1919-
Daily News (Perth, Western Australia) 1882-
Daily Oklahoman (Oklahoma City) 1894-
Daily Picayune (New Orleans) 1836-1914
Daily Progress (Charlottesville, Virginia) 1892-
Daily Record (Glasgow) 1895-
Daily Report 1904-9
Daily Sketch 1909-71
Daily Telegraph 1855-
Daily Universal Register 1785-7 (continued as *The Times*)
Dakin, Douglas *The unification of Greece, 1770-1923* 1972
Dakyns, Henry G. *The march of the Ten Thousand, a translation of the Anabasis . . of Xenophon* 1901
D'Albertis, L. M. *New Guinea* 1880
Dalby, John *Mayroyd of Mytholm, a romance of the fells* 1888
Dale, Alan *Jonathan's home* 1885
Dale, Celia *Other people* 1964
A spring of love 1960
'Dale, Darley' (Francesca M. Steele) *Noah's ark, a tale of the Norfolk broads* 1890
Dale, J. D. H. *Baldeschi's (J.) Ceremonial according to the Roman rite* tr. 1853
Dale, Robert W. *The atonement* 1874 (1875)
Discourses delivered on special occasions 1866
The Jewish temple and the Christian church 1865 (1877)
Nine lectures on preaching 1877 (1878)
Sermons on the ten commandments 1871
Week-day sermons 1867 (1870)
Dale, Samuel *Pharmacologia, seu manuductio ad materiam medicam* 1693 (1710); Suppl. 1695
Dales, Rodney Phillips *Annelids* 1963
Dalgarno, George *Didascalocophus, or the deaf and dumb man's tutor* 1680
Dall, William H. *Alaska and its resources* 1870
On the remains of later pre-historic man obtained from caves in the Catherina archipelago 1878
Tribes of the extreme Northwest 1877
Dallam, Thomas *Diary* 1599-1600 (Early voyages and travels in the Levant, Hakluyt Soc. 1893)
Dallas, Alexander J. *Reports of cases . . adjudged in the courts of Pennsylvania*, etc. 1790-1807
Dallas, Eneas Sweetland *Kettner's book of the table; a manual of cookery* 1877
Dallas, George *System of stiles* c1680 (1697)
Dallaway, James *Inquiries into the origin and progress of heraldry in England* (Appendix . . The third part of the Boke of St. Albans 1486) 1793
Observations on English architecture 1806
Of statuary and sculpture 1816
Dallimore, William & Jackson, Albert Bruce *A handbook of coniferæ, including ginkgoaceæ* 1923
Dallington, Sir Robert *A method for trauell* 1598
Dalrymple, Alexander *Oriental repertory* 1793-1808
Dalrymple, David, Lord Hailes *Annals of Scotland* 1776, 1779
Disquisitions concerning the antiquities of the christian church 1783
Glossary (of Scottish words) c1776
Remains of christian antiquity 1776-80
Dalrymple, James *Leslie's (Bp. J.) Historie of Scotland* tr. 1596 (S.T.S. 1888)
Dalrymple, James, Viscount Stair *The decisions of the Lords of Council and Session* 1683
The institutions of the law of Scotland 1681, 1693
Dalrymple, Sir James *Collections concerning the Scottish history* 1705
Dalrymple, Sir John *Letter to the admiralty* 1795
Observations on his yeast-cake c1796
Dalrymple, William *Travels through Spain and Portugal* 1777
Dalton, Edward Tuite *Descriptive ethnology of Bengal* 1872
Dalton, Henry G. *The history of British Guiana* 1855
Dalton, John *Meteorological observations and essays* 1793 (1834)
Dalton, Michael *The countrey justice, conteyning the practise of the justices of the peace out of their sessions* 1618 (1630)
The office and authoritie of sheriffs 1623 (1628)
Daly, Mrs. Dominic D. *Digging, squatting and pioneering life in the northern territory of South Australia* 1887
'Daly, Rann' (Edward Vance Palmer) *The outpost* 1924
Daly, Reginald Aldworth *The changing world of the Ice Age* 1934
Igneous rocks and the depths of the earth 1933
Dalyell, Sir John Graham *The darker superstitions of Scotland* 1834
ed. *Fragments of Scottish history* (1798)
Dalziel, Hugh *British dogs* 1879-80
The diseases of dogs 1874 (1893)
Dame Siriz See *Siriz*
Damon and Pithias *See* Edwards, R.
Dampier, William *A new voyage round the world* (*Voyages and descriptions, A voyage to New Holland*) 1697, 1699, 1703-09 (1729)
Dana, Edmund *Geographical sketches on the western country* 1819
Dana, Edward S. ed. *J. D. Dana's System of mineralogy* 1892 (1899)
A text-book of mineralogy 1877 (1898)
Dana, James Dwight *Corals and coral islands* 1872
Crustacea 1852 (U.S. exploring expedition XIII)
The elements of geology 1862
Geology 1849 (U.S. exploring expedition X)
Manual of geology 1863 (1880)
Manual of mineralogy 1851 (ed. 4)
Manual of mineralogy and lithology 1878 (1882)
A system of mineralogy 1837 (1854, 1868, 1883)
Zoophytes 1846-48 (U.S. exploring expedition VIII)
Dana, Richard H. *The buccaneer and other poems* 1844
Dana, Richard H., Jr. *The seaman's manual* 1841
Two years before the mast 1840 (1841)
Dancing times 1894-
Danett, Thomas *The historie of P. de Commines* tr. 1596 (1614)
Dangerfield, Stanley & Howell, Elsworth eds. *The international encyclopaedia of dogs* 1971
Danican, François A. ('A. D. Philidor') *Analysis of the game of chess* 1819 (1832)
Chess analysed 1750 (1773)
Studies of chess 1808 (1817)
Daniel, George *Poems* a1657 (Grosart 1878)
Eclesiasticus: or the wisedome of Iesus the son of Syrach paraphrased 1639
Idyllia a1653
Πολυλογια; in severall ecloges 1638-48
Trinarchodia (Richard the second, Henry the fourth, Henry the fifth) 1649
Daniel, Glyn Edmund *A hundred years of archaeology* 1950
Daniel, Samuel *Poems* 1592-1611 (Works 1603, 1623, 1717)
The first fowre bookes of the civile warres betweene the two houses of Lancaster and Yorke (the fyft book) 1595
— *The civile wares . . corrected and continued* 1609
The collection of the historie of England 1613-18 (1626)
The complaint of Rosamond 1592
A defence of ryme ?1603 (Haslewood 1815; G. G. Smith, Elizabethan critical essays II, 1904)
Delia, contayning certaine sonnets 1592 (Arber, Eng. Garner III)
Hymens triumph 1615
The queenes arcadia 1605 (1606)
The tragedie of Cleopatra 1594
The tragedie of Philotas 1605
Daniel, William B. *Rural sports* 1801-02
Daniell, Alfred *Physics for students of medicine* 1896
A text-book of the principles of physics 1884
Danneley, John F. *An encyclopædia or dictionary of music* 1825
'D'Anvers, Caleb' *The craftsman: being a critique on the times* 1726
'D'Anvers, Nancy' (Mrs. N. Bell) *Jules Verne's Fur country* tr. 1879
Darbishire, Otto Bernhard tr. *A. von Buzágh's Colloid systems* 1937
D'Arblay, Mme Frances (Frances Burney) *Camilla, or a picture of youth* 1796
Cecilia, or memoirs of an heiress 1782
Diary and letters 17 . . (1842, 1876, 1891)
The early diary of Frances Burney 1768-78 (1889)
Evelina, or the history of a young lady's entrance into the world 1778
Journals and letters ed. J. Hemlow et al. 1972-
The wanderer; or female difficulties 1814
Darcie, Abraham *The originall of idolatries, or the birth of heresies* 1624
Dare, Joseph *Zeller's (E.) Contents and origin of the Acts of the apostles critically investigated* tr. 1875-76
D'Argens' (Jean Baptiste de Boyer, Marquis) Chinese letters tr. 1741
Darius. A pretie new enterlude . . of the story of kyng Daryus 1565
Dark, Sidney *Stage silhouettes* 1901
Darling, Malcolm Lyall *At freedom's door* 1949
Wisdom and waste in the Punjab village 1934
Darlington, Cyril Dean *Cytology* 1965
Recent advances in cytology 1932
—— & Mather, Kenneth *The elements of genetics* 1949
Darlington, Philip Jackson *Zoogeography: the geographical distribution of animals* 1957
Darlington, Thomas *The folk-speech of South Cheshire* 1887 (E.D.S.)
Darlington, William *American weeds and useful plants* 1847 (1860)
Darrell, John *A detection of that sinnful, lying, shamful and ridiculous Discours of S. Harshnet* 1600
A true relation of the strange . . vexation by the devil of seven persons etc. 1600
Darrell, William *A gentleman instructed in the conduct of a virtuous and happy life* (anon.) 1704 (1713, 1716)
Dartnell, George E. and Goddard, E. H. *A glossary of words used in the county of Wiltshire* 1893 (E.D.S.)
Darwin, Charles R. *The descent of man and selection in relation to sex* 1871
The different forms of flowers on plants of the same species 1877
The effects of cross and self-fertilisation in the vegetable kingdom 1876
The expression of the emotions in man and animals 1872
The formation of vegetable mould through the action of worms (= *Earth-worms*) 1881
Geological observations on the volcanic islands visited during the voyage of H.M.S. Beagle 1844
Geology 1851-59 (Manual of scientific enquiry 1859)
Insectivorous plants 1875
Journal of researches into the natural history and geology of the countries visited during the voyage of the Beagle (= *Voy. Nat.*) 1839 (1845, 1852, 1879)
On the various contrivances by which orchids are fertilised by insects 1862
On the origin of species by means of natural selection 1859
The variation of animals and plants under domestication 1868
—— & Darwin, Francis *The power of movement in plants* 1880
Darwin, Erasmus *The botanic garden; a poem in two parts* (*I. The economy of vegetation*, 1791. *II. The loves of the plants*, 1789) 1791
Zoonomia, or the laws of organic life 1794-96 (1801, 1802)
Darwin, Sir George H. *Scientific papers* (1907-11)
Dasent, Sir George W. *Asbjörnsen (P. C.) and Moe's (J.) Popular tales from the Norse* tr. 1859
Half a life 1874
Jest and earnest 1863 (1874)
Thorgeirrson's (N.) Story of Burnt Njal tr. 1861
The vikings of the Baltic 1875
Daubenmire, Rexford F. *Plants and environment* 1947
Daubeny, Charles G. B. *Essay on the trees and shrubs of the ancients* 1865
An introduction to the atomic theory 1831 (1850)
D'Aunoy See *Anois*
Daus, John *Bullinger's (H.) Hundred sermons vpon the apocalips* tr. 1561 (1573)
A famous cronicle of oure time called Sleidanes (J.) commentaries tr. 1560
Davenant, Charles *A discourse upon grants and resumptions* (anon.) 1700
Discourses on the publick revenues 1698
An essay upon the East India trade 1696
Essays upon the ballance of power etc. 1701
Davenant, Sir William *Works* a1668 (1673)
The cruell brother, a tragedy 1630
Declamations at Rutland House 1656-57 (Wks. 1673)
The fair favorite a1668
Gondibert, an heroick poem 1651
Madagascar, and other poems 1638
The man's the master: a comedy a1668 (1669)
The platonic lovers 1636
Poems a1668 (Wks. 1673)
The siege of Rhodes 1656-59
The witts, a comedie 1636
—— & Dryden, J. *Shakespeare's Tempest, or the enchanted island* (altered) 1667 (1670)
Davenport, Robert *The city night-cap* 1661
A pleasant . . . comedy, called, a new tricke to cheat the divell 1639
Davey, Wheeler Pedlar *A study of crystal structure and its applications* 1934
David, Elizabeth *A book of Mediterranean food* 1950
— (another ed.) 1955
French country cooking 1951
French provincial cooking 1960
Italian food 1954
Davids, Thomas W. Rhys *Buddhism: being a sketch of the life and teachings of Gautama the Buddha* 1877
— (rev. ed.) 1894
The Hibbert lectures 1881
Davidson, Charles J. C. *A diary of travels and adventures in upper India* 1843

Davidson, David *Thoughts on the seasons* etc. *partly in the Scottish dialect* 1789
Davidson, David *Memories of a long life* 1890 (1893)
Davidson, Ellis A. *The animal kingdom, an elementary textbook in zoology* 1870
A practical manual of house-painting etc. 1875
Davidson, John *Inverurie and the earldom of the Garioch* 1878
Davidson, John *Ballads and songs* 1894
Fleet street eclogues 1893, 1896
Davidson, Joseph *The works of Vergil* tr. 1743 (1748)
Davidson, Lionel *A long way to Shiloh* 1966
The night of Wenceslas 1960
The Rose of Tibet 1962
Davidson, Samuel *The canon of the Bible* 1877
Davies, Benjamin *Gesenius' (F.H.W.) Hebrew grammar* tr. 1846 (1852)
Davies, Benjamin Lionel *Technology of plastics: manufacture: structure: design* 1949
Davies, Charles *The metric system* 1871
—— & Peck, W. G. *Mathematical dictionary and cyclopædia of mathematical science* 1857
Davies, Charles M. *Unorthodox London; or phases of religious life in the metropolis* 1873–75 (1876)
Davies, David C. *A treatise on metalliferous minerals and mining* 1880
Davies, David Pettit *Handling the big jets* 1967
Davies, Edmund Frank *Illyrian venture: the story of the British military mission to enemy-occupied Albania, 1943–44* 1952
Davies, Edward W. L. *Dartmoor days; or scenes in the forest, a poem* 1863
A memoir of the Rev. J. Russell 1878 (1883)
Davies, George C. *The handbook to the rivers and broads of Norfolk and Suffolk* 1882
Mountain, meadow and mere 1873
Norfolk broads and rivers 1883 (1884)
Davies, Hugh *Welsh botanology* 1813
Davies, Sir John *Works* a1626 (Grosart 1869–76)
A discoverie of the true causes why Ireland was never entirely subdued 1612 (1747)
Historical tracts (concerning Ireland) 1607–13 (1787)
Hymns of Astræa 1599 (Arber, Eng. Garner V)
Letters (observations) to the earl of Salisbury 1607–10 (1787)
Nosce teipsum. The oracle expounded in two elegies 1. of humane knowledge. 2. of the soule of man and the immortalitie thereof (= Immort. Soul) 1599 (Arber, Eng. Garner V)
Orchestra, or a poeme on dauncing 1596 (Arber, Eng. Garner V)
Speech to the Lord Deputy of Ireland 1613 (1787)
Davies, John (of Hereford) *Poetical works* a1618 (Grosart 1878)
The holy roode, or Christes crosse 1609
Humours heav'n on earth 1605 (1609)
Microcosmos: the discovery of the little world 1603
Mirum in modum 1602
The muses sacrifice 1612
The muses teares for the losse of Henry Prince of Wales 1613
The scourge of folly 1611
Summa totalis, or all in all 1607
Wittes pilgrimage ? 1605
Davies, John (of Kidwelly) *The civil warres of Great Britain and Ireland* 1661
The history of the Caribbee islands 1666
Olearius' (A.) Voyages and travels of the ambassadors sent.. to the great Duke of Moscovy. Whereto are added the travels of (J. A. de) Mandelslo from Persia into the East-Indies tr. 1662
Davies, John *Edwards (H. M.) and Vavasseur's Manual of materia medica and pharmacy adapted to British practice* 1831
Davies, Leslie Purnell *The shadow before* 1971
What did I do tomorrow? 1972
Davies, Myles *Athenæ Britannicæ, or a critical history of the Oxford and Cambridge writers and writings* etc. 1715–16
Εικων μικρο-βιβλική sive Icon libellorum, or a critical history of pamphlets 1715
Davies, Rodney Deane & Palmer, Henry Procter *Radio studies of the universe* 1959
Davies, T. Lewis O. *A supplementary English glossary* 1881
Davies, Thomas *Memoirs of the life of David Garrick* 1780 (1781)
Davies, William *A true relation of the travailes and.. captivitie of W. D.* 1614
Davin, Daniel Marcus *For the rest of our lives* 1947
The gorse blooms pale 1947
ed. *New Zealand short stories* 1953
For 2nd ser. *see* Stead, Christian Karlson
Not here, not now 1970
Roads from home 1949
The sullen bell 1956
'Daviot, Gordon' (Elizabeth Mackintosh) *The man in the queue* 1929
See also 'Tey, Josephine'
Davis, Alec Edward *Package and print: the development of container and label design* 1967
Davis, Andrew J. *The principles of nature* 1847
Davis, Arthur Hoey *See* 'Rudd, Steele'
Davis, Charles Augustus *Letters of Jack Downing, major, Downingville militia* (anon.) 1834 (1835)
Davis, Charles Carroll *The marine and freshwater plankton* 1955
Davis, Charles H. ed. *Narrative of the North Polar expedition, U.S. ship 'Polaris'* 1876
Davis, Charles T. *The manufacture of leather* 1885 (1897)
A practical treatise on the manufacture of bricks, tiles etc. 1884 (1895)
Davis, Frederick Clyde *See* 'Ransome, Stephen'
Davis, George E. *Practical microscopy* 1882
Davis, Jefferson *The rise and fall of the Confederate government* 1881
Davis, John *The seamans secrets* 1594 (1607)
Davis, John *Travels.. in the United States of America* 1803
Davis, Sir John F. *The Chinese* 1836 (1845)
Davis, John Gilbert *A dictionary of dairying* 1950
—(ed. 2) 1955
Davis, Joseph B. *The Neanderthal skull* 1864
Davis, Kingsley *Human society* 1949 (1948 = 'preliminary ed.')
Davis, Norman & Wrenn, Charles Leslie eds. *English and medieval studies presented to J. R. R. Tolkien on the occasion of his 70th birthday* 1962
Davis, Peter Hadland & Heywood, Vernon Hilton *Principles of angiosperm taxonomy* 1963
Davis, Richard Harding *Our English cousins* 1894
Davis, Thomas *General view of the agriculture of the county of Wilts* 1794 (1811, 1813)
Davison, Francis *A poetical rapsody, containing divers sonnets, odes*, etc. 1602
Davison, Frank Dalby *Children of the dark people: an Australian folk tale* 1936
Dusty: the story of a sheep dog 1946
Davison, John *Discourses on prophecy* 1824
Davitt, Michael *Leaves from a prison diary* 1885
Davson, Hugh *Textbook of general physiology* 1951
Davy's (Adam) five dreams about Edward II, a1327 (E.E.T.S. 1878)
Davy, Charles & Davy, Frederick *Bourrit's (M. T.) Relation of a journey to the glaciers in.. Savoy* tr. 1775 (1776)
Davy, Sir Humphry *Elements of agricultural chemistry* 1813
Elements of chemical philosophy 1812
Salmonia: or days of fly-fishing (anon.) 1828
Davy, John *The angler in the Lake district* 1857
Dawbeny, H. *Historie and policie re-viewed in the transactions of.. Oliver, late lord-protector, from his cradle to his tomb* 1659
Dawe, Edward Arthur *Paper and its uses: a treatise for printers, stationers and others* 1914
Dawkins, Richard *The selfish gene* 1976
Dawkins, William Boyd *Cave hunting; researches on the evidence of caves respecting the early inhabitants of Europe* 1874
Early man in Britain and his place in the tertiary period 1880
Dawson, Benjamin *Philologia Anglicana: or a philological and synonymical dictionary of the English language* 1806
Dawson, George M. and Sutherland, A. *Geography of the British colonies* 1892
Dawson, Henry Christopher *The age of the gods: a study in the origins of culture in prehistoric Europe and the ancient East* 1928
Dawson, Sir John W. *The geological history of plants* 1888
Life's dawn on earth 1875
Nature and the Bible 1875
The origin of the world according to revelation and science 1877
The story of the earth and man 1873 (1880)
Dawson, Robert *The present state of Australia* 1831
Dawson, Samuel E. *Hand-book for the Dominion of Canada* 1884
Dawson, Thomas *The good huswifes jewell* 1596
Day, Angel *The English secretorie* 1586 (1595, 1625)
Day, Charles Russell *The music and musical instruments of Southern India and the Deccan* 1891
Day, Frederick T. *An introduction to paper: its manufacture and use* 1962
Day, Francis *The fishes of Great Britain and Ireland* 1880–84
Indian fish and fishing 1883 (Fisheries exhibition literature 1884)
Day, George E. *Simon's (J. E.) Animal chemistry* tr. 1845–46
Day, John (divine) *Day's Dyall or his twelve howres* 1612–13 (1614)
Day's Festivals or twelve of his sermons on the three chiefe festivals of the yeere 1610–15 (1615)
Day, John (dramatist) *Works* a1640 (Bullen 1881)
The blind-beggar of Bednal-green c1600 (1659)
Humour out of breath, a comedie 1608 (Halliwell 1860)
Ile of guls 1606
Law-trickes or who would have thought it 1608
The parliament of bees a1640 (1641)
Peregrinatio scholastica or learneinges pillgrimage a1640
The travailes of the three English brothers.. Shirley 1607
Day, Michael Herbert *Guide to fossil man* 1965
Day, Richard *A booke of christian prayers* 1578 (Parker Soc. 1851)
Day, Thomas *The history of Sandford and Merton* 1783–89
Day Lewis, Cecil *See* Lewis, Cecil Day
Deacon, John *Tobacco tortured* 1616
—— & Walker, J. *Dialogical discourses of spirits and divels* 1601
De Acton, Eugenia *See* Acton
Dean, Francis Medcalf *Naturally occurring oxygen ring compounds* 1963
Deans, John ed. *Pioneers of Canterbury: Deans letters, 1840–1854* 1937
Dearmer, Percy *The parson's handbook* 1899
—(ed. 13, by C. E. Pocknee) 1965
Death's vision represented in a philosophical sacred poem (by John Reynolds) 1687 (1713)
De Bary, A. de See Bower, F. O.; Garnsey, H. E. F.
Debate between the body and the soul a1300, c1325 (Mapes' poems, Camden Soc. 1841)
Debate betweene pride and lowlines, The By F. T. (ascribed to Fr. Thynn) c1570 (Shaks. Soc. 1841)
Debate on a motion for the abolition of the slave trade in the House of Commons, The 1791
Debates in the House of Commons 1625 (Camden Soc. 1873)
Debates in the House of Lords 1621 *See* Elsing, H.
Debates and proceedings in the Congress of the United States See: United States. Congress. Debates
De Beau Chesne, John and Baildon, J. *A booke containing divers sortes of hands, as well the English as French secretarie with the Italian, Roman, chancelry and court hands* 1571
De Beer, Gavin Rylands *Embryology and evolution* 1930
Vertebrate zoology 1928
—(ed. 2) 1951
De Benese, Sir Richard *This boke sheweth the maner of measurynge of all maner of lande* c1537
De Bres, Joris tr. *E. Mandel's Late capitalism* 1975
De Britaine, William *Humane prudence, or the art by which a man may raise himself.. to grandeur* 1680 (1686)
De Candolle's (A.) Origin of cultivated plants tr. 1884
De Candolle (A. P.) and Sprengel's (K.) Elements of the philosophy of plants tr. 1821
Decay. The causes of the decay of christian piety.. written by the author of The whole duty of man 1667 (1683)
Certayne causes gathered together, wherin is shewed the decaye of England,.. by the great multitude of shepe 1550–53 (in Supplication for the beggers, E.E.T.S. 1871)
The decay of trade: a treatise against the abating of interest. By a well-wisher of the commonwealth 1641
Declaration of the Commons.. concerning.. the grand rebellion in Ireland, A 1642 (1643)
Declaration of the Pfaltzgraves, A: concerning the faith and ceremonies professed in his churches 1637
Declarations, ordinances, and remonstrances of the Lords and Commons 1642 (45 pamphlets)
Decree of Starre-chamber concerning printing, A 1637 (Arber, Milton's Areopagitica)
See also *Star-chamber*
Dedham, Massachusetts *The early records of the town of Dedham, Massachusetts* ed. D. G. Hill 5 vols. 1886–99
Dee, John *Autobiographical tracts* a1608 (Chetham Soc. Miscellany 1851)
The compendious rehearsall 1592 (in Autob. tracts)
General and rare memorials pertayning to the perfecte arte of navigation 1577
A præface (to H. Billingsley's Euclid) *specifying the chiefe sciences, what they are* etc. 1570
The private diary 1554–61 a1608 (Camden Soc. 1842)
A true and faithful relation of what passed between.. J. D. and some spirits a1608 (1627, 1659)
Dee, Liang-lao tr. *Hsia Chih-yen's The coldest winter in Peking* 1978
Deeping, George Warwick *Kitty* 1927
Roper's Row 1927
Second youth 1919
The secret sanctuary; or, The saving of John Stretton 1923
Sincerity 1912
Sorrell and son 1925
Three rooms 1924
Deer, William Alexander, et al. *An introduction to the rock-forming minerals* 1966
Rock-forming minerals 5 vols. 1962–3
Deeside tales; or sketches of men and manners among the peasantry of Upper Deeside (by R. G. Michie) 1872
Defence of conny catching, The 1592 (Halliwell 1859; Greene's works, ed. Grosart XI)
A defence of dramatick poetry, being a review of Mr. Collier's 'View of the immorality and profaneness of the stage' 1698
A defence of the ministers reasons 1607: see Hieron, S.
A defence of the rights and priviledges of the university of Oxford 1649 etc. (1690)
Defence of Dr. G. Walker. Mr. J. Mackenzyes narrative of the siege of London Derry, a false libel 1690
Defendorf, Allen Ross tr. *E. Kraepelin's Clinical psychiatry: a text-book for students and physicians* 1902
Defensor's Liber scintillarum with an interlinear Anglo-saxon version a1050 (E.E.T.S. 1889)
De Ferranti, Basil ed. *Living with the computer* 1971
Defoe, B. N. *A compleat English dictionary* 1735
De Foe, Daniel *Works* a1731 (1840, 1841)
The complete English tradesman 1726 etc. (1732, 1745, 1841)
The double welcome, a poem to the duke of Marlborough 1705
The dyet of Poland, a satyr 1705
An essay on the history and reality of apparitions (= The secrets of the invisible world disclos'd or an universal history of apparitions) 1727 (1735, 1840)
The family instructor 1715 (1841)
The fortunes and misfortunes of Moll Flanders 1722
The history and remarkable life of Colonel Jacque (= Col. Jack) 1722 (1840)
A hymn to the pillory 1703

De Foe, Daniel (*cont.*)
A hymn to victory 1704
A journal of the plague year 1722 (1754)
Jure divino, a satyr 1706
The life, adventures, and pyracies of the famous Captain Singleton 1720 (1840)
The life and strange adventures of Robinson Crusoe 1719 (1840, Globe 1873)
Memoirs of a Cavalier 1724 (1840)
Memoirs of the church of Scotland 1717
New discovery of an old intreague (anon.) 1691
The political history of the devil 1726 (1840)
Religious courtship 1722 (1840)
Serious reflections during the life . . of Robinson Crusoe 1720
The shortest way with the dissenters 1702
A speech for Mr. D—ss (Dundas) *of Arnistoun* (anon.) 1711
Street-robberies consider'd 1728
A system of magick; or a history of the black art 1727 (1840)
The true-born Englishman 1700 (1701)
A new voyage round the world 1725 (1840)
De Foe's Tour through the whole island of Great Britain 1724–27 (enlarged ed. 1769)
See also Richardson, S.
Degarre, Sire: a metrical romance a1330 (Abbotsford Club 1849)
Degge, Sir Simon *The parson's counsellor, with the law of tithes and tithing* 1676 (1703)
Degore, Syr (a metrical romance) 13 . . (c1550; Utterson 1817)
De Gray, T. *See* De la Grey, T.
Degrevant, The romance of Sir a1400 (in Thornton romances, Camden Soc. 1844; Luick 1917)
'Dehan, Richard' (Clotilde Graves) *Between two thieves* 1912
Deighton, Len *Billion-dollar brain* 1966
An expensive place to die 1967
Funeral in Berlin 1964
Horse under water 1963
The Ipcress file 1962
Len Deighton's London dossier with contributions by A. Bailey et al. 1967
Only when I larf 1968
SS-GB 1978
Spy story 1974
Twinkle, twinkle, little spy 1976
XPD 1981
Yesterday's spy 1975
De imitatione Christi. The earliest English translation c1450 (E.E.T.S. 1893)
See also Atkynson, W.; Richmond, Countess of; Stanhope, G.
Deism. An account of the growth of deism in England 1696
De Kay, James E. *Zoology of New York, or the New York fauna* 1842
De Kerchove, René *International maritime dictionary* 1948
Dekker, Thomas *The dramatic works* a1632 (1873)
The non-dramatic works (Grosart 1884–86)
The batchelars banquet (anon.) 1603
The belman of London bringing to light the most notorious villanies 1608
The dead tearme 1608
D. his dreame 1620
The guls horne-booke 1609 (1812)
The honest whore 1604 (*The second part* 1630)
If it be not good, the diuel is in it 1612
A knights conjuring, done in earnest (revision of Newes from hell) 1607
Lanthorne and candle-light, or the bell-mans second nightswalke 1608
Newes from hell; brought by the diuells carrier 1606
The owles almanacke (anon.) 1618
The pleasant comedie of old Fortunatus 1600
The ravens almanacke 1609
The roaring girle 1611 *See* Middleton, T.
Satiro-mastix or the untrussing of the humorous poet 1602
The seuen deadly sinnes of London 1606 (Arber)
The shomakers holiday or the gentle craft 1600
A tragi-comedy: called Match mee in London 1623 (1631)
The whore of Babylon 1607
The witch of Edmonton See Rowley, W.
The wonderfull yeare 1603, wherein is shewed the picture of London lying sicke of the plague 1603
——, Chettle, H., & Haughton, W. *Patient Grissil, a comedy* 1603 (Shaks. Soc. 1841)
—— & Webster, J. *North-ward hoe* 1607 (D.'s works 1873)
The famous history of Sir Thomas Wyat 1607 (D.'s works 1873)
West-ward hoe c1605 (1607, D.'s works 1873)
De la Beche, Sir Henry T. *A geological manual* 1831 (1832)
Mineralogy 1851–59 (in Manual of scientific enquiry, 1859)
Report on the geology of Cornwall, Devon, and West-Somerset 1839
'Delafield, E. M.' (Edmée Elizabeth Monica Dashwood) *Thank Heaven fasting* 1932
De la Grey, Thomas *The compleat horse-man and expert ferrier* 1639 (1654, 1670)
Delamain, Richard *Grammelogia; or the mathematicall ring* 1630
De La Mare, Walter John *The burning-glass, and other poems* 1945
Collected stories for children 1947
The connoisseur, and other stories 1926
Crossings: a fairy play 1921
ed. *Early one morning, in the spring: chapters on children and on childhood* 1935
The fleeting, and other poems 1933
The listeners, and other poems 1912
The Lord Fish 1933
Memoirs of a midget 1921
Memory, and other poems 1938
Private view 1953
The riddle, and other stories 1923
Songs of childhood 1902
This year, next year 1937
The three mulla-mulgars 1910
The traveller 1946
The veil, and other poems 1921
The wind blows over 1936
Winged chariot 1951
Delamer, Eugene S. *The flower garden* 1856 (1861)
The kitchen garden 1855 (1860)
Delamere, Henry Booth, 2nd Baron *Works* a1693 (1694)
Deland, Margaret Wade *Old Chester tales* 1898
Delany, Mrs. Mary *The autobiography and correspondence* 1779–88 (1861, 1862)
Letters . . . to Mrs. F. Hamilton 1779–88 (1820)
De la Pasture, Mrs. Henry *Cornelius* 1903
De la Pryme, Abraham *Diary* a1704 (Surtees Soc. 1870)
De la Ramée, Louisa *See* 'Ouida'
De la Roche, Mazo *Finch's fortune* 1931
Jalna 1927
The master of Jalna 1933
Whiteoak harvest 1936
Whiteoaks (US ed. with title *Whiteoaks of Jalna*) 1929
Young Renny 1935
De las Coveras' (F.) History of Don Fenise; a romance out of Spanish 1651
Delaune, Thomas *The present state of London* 1681 (1690)
Delavenay, Émile *An introduction to machine translation* tr. by K. M. Delavenay and the author 1960
Delawne, Nathaniel *Du Moulin's (P.) Elements of logick* tr. 1624
Delightes for ladies 1602 *See* Plat or Platt, Sir H.
Delineator 1873–1937
'De Lisle's, F.' (= L. Regnier de la Planche) *Legendarie conteining an ample discourse of the life . . of Charles cardinal of Lorraine and his brethren of the house of Guise* tr. 1577
De Lisser, Herbert George *The cup and the lip* 1956
Delitzsch's (F.) System of biblical psychology tr. R. E. Wallis 1867
Dell, Jeffrey *Nobody ordered wolves* 1935
Dell, William *Right reformation, or the reformation of the church of the New Testament represented in gospell-light* 1646
Della Valle's (P.) Travels 1665 *See* Havers, G.
Delman, David *Sudden death* 1972 (UK 1973)
De Lolme, John L. *The constitution of England, or an account of the English government* 1775
Deloney, Thomas *The gentle craft* 1597, a1600
The pleasant historie of Iohn Winchcomb, in his yonguer yeares called Iack of Newbery 1597–1626
Thomas of Reading, or the sixe worthie yeomen of the west a1600 (Thoms, Early prose romances I, 1828)
Demant, Vigo Auguste *Christian polity* 1936
Religion and the decline of capitalism 1952
De Mauny, Erik *The huntsman in his career* 1949
'D'Emillianne's, G.' (= A. Gavin) *The frauds of the Romish monks and priests* tr. 1691
Observations on a journey to Naples tr. 1691
Demmin, Auguste See Black, C. C.
Democrat See *Clarke County Democrat*
Democratic State Journal (Sacramento, California) 1852–8
De Monfart's (= H. de Feynes) *An exact and curious survey of all the East Indies* tr. 1615
De Morgan, Augustus *A budget of paradoxes* a1871 (1872)
An essay on probabilities 1838
Formal logic 1847
De Morgan, Sophia E. *From matter to spirit* 1863
De Morgan, William Frend *Alice-for-short* 1907
Joseph Vance 1906
The old madhouse (completed by M. E. De Morgan) 1919
The old man's youth and the young man's old age (completed by M. E. De Morgan) 1920 (UK 1921)
When ghost meets ghost 1914
Dempsey, Jack (William Harrison Dempsey) *Championship fighting* 1950
De Mouhy's (C. de Fieux) The fortunate country-maid tr. 1740 (1741)
Denham, Sir James Steuart *An inquiry into the principles of political economy* 1767
Denham, Sir John *Cato Major or old age* c1650 (1669)
Coopers-Hill 1642 (1669, 1709)
The destruction of Troy, an essay upon the second book of Virgil's Æneis tr. 1636 (1656)
A dialogue between Sir J. Pooley and Mr. T. Killigrew a1668
(*Directions to a painter* 1667 (1689))
Poems and translations 16 . . (1668)
The progress of learning c1650
The sophy (a tragedy) 1641
Denham, Michael A. *A collection of proverbs and popular sayings, relating to the seasons, the weather, and agricultural pursuits* 1846 (Percy Soc.)
The D. tracts, a collection of folk-lore 1846–59 (1892–95)
Folk-lore; or a collection of local rhymes, proverbs, etc. relating to Northumberland etc. 1858
Folk-lore; or manners and customs of the north of England 1850–52
Deniker's (J.) The races of man tr. 1900
Denison, Edmund Beckett (afterw. Beckett, E.) *Astronomy without mathematics* 1865 (1867)
A rudimentary treatise on clocks, watches, and bells 1850 (1860 etc.)
Denison, John *The heavenly banquet* 1619 (1631)
Heauens joy for a sinners repentance, a sermon 1623
Denison, William *Cricket: sketches of the players* 1846
Denlinger, William Watson *The complete Boston* [*terrier*] 1955
Denne, Samuel 1772 See *History and antiquities of Rochester*
Denning, David *The art and craft of cabinet-making* 1891
Dennis, Clarence James *The moods of Ginger Mick* 1916
The songs of a sentimental bloke 1915 (1916 impression used)
Dennis, John 1613 *See* Dennys
Dennis, John *The characters and conduct of Sir John Edgar* 1720
The impartiall critick: or some observations upon 'A short view of tragedy' written by T. Rymer 1693 (also Spingarn 1909)
The monument, a poem 1702
A plot and no plot, a comedy 1697
Dennison, Walter T. *The Orcadian sketch-book* 1880
Denny, Grace Goldena *Fabrics and how to know them* 1923
Denny, Sir William *Pelecanicidium, or the christian adviser against self-murder* (anon.) 1653
Dennys, John *The secrets of angling, by J. D.* 1613 (also in Arber, Eng. Garner I)
Dennys, Nicholas Belfield *A descriptive dictionary of British Malaya* 1804
Dent, Arthur *The plaine mans path-way to heaven* 1601 (1603)
Dent, Colin *Quantity surveying by computer* 1964
Dent, Daniel *A sermon against drunkennes* 1628
Denton, Daniel *A brief description of New York* 1670 (1845)
Dentry, Robert *Encounter at Kharmel* 1971
Departing soul's address to the body, The c1300 (Sir T. Phillipps 1838; S. W. Singer 1845)
Department of Education and Science *See* United Kingdom
Deplorable state of New England 1708 *See* Asshurst, Sir H.
Deposition of Richard II, A poem on the See Langland, W.
Depositions from the castle of York relating to offences committed in the northern counties in the seventeenth century 1650–85 (Surtees Soc. 1861)
Depredations committed on the clan Campbell and their followers, An account of c1686 (1816)
Deputy Keeper of the Public Records, First (second, etc.) report 1840–
Depuy, Charles H. & Chapman, Orville L. *Molecular reactions and photochemistry* 1972
De Quatrefages de Bréau (J. L. A.) *See* Quatrefages de Bréau, J. L. A. de
De Quincey, Thomas *Works* a1859 (1853–60, 1862–71, 1889–90)
Analects from J. P. Richter 1824
Autobiographic sketches 1834–53
The Cæsars 1832–34
Confessions of an opium-eater 1822–56
The English mail coach 1849
The Essenes 1840–59
On murder considered as one of the fine arts 1827
Recollections of the lakes and the lake poets 1839
The Spanish military nun 1847
On war 1854
De Quincey: his life and writings, by 'H. A. Page' (1877)
Derby, Edward G. G. S. Stanley, 14th Earl of *Homer's Iliad rendered into English blank verse* 1864
Derby, George Horatio *See* 'Phoenix, John'
Derby, Henry, Earl of (afterw. Henry IV) *Expeditions to Prussia and the Holy Land* 1390–91, 1392–93 (Camden Soc. 1894)
Derbyshire Times 1854–
Derham, William *The artificial clock-maker, a treatise of watch and clock-work by W. D.* 1696 (1700, 1759)
Astro-theology; or a demonstration of the being and attributes of God from a survey of the heavens 1714 (1715, 1769)
Physico-theology; or a demonstration of the being and attributes of God from his works of creation 1711–12 (1713)
Dering, Edward *xxvi lectures or readings upon part of the epistle . . to the Hebrews* 1576
Dering, Sir Edward *A collection of speeches in matters of religion* 1642
A discourse of proper sacrifice, in way of answer to A.B.C. Jesuite 1644
The fower cardinal-vertues of a Carmelite fryar 1640 (1641)
Derrick, June *Teaching English to immigrants* 1966
Derricke, John *The image of Ireland; a poem* 1581 (1883)
Desaguliers, John T. *A course of experimental philosophy* 1734–44
Gauger's (N.) Fires improv'd: being a new method of building chimneys tr. 1715
Desch, Cecil Henry *Metallography* 1910
Description of the isles of Scotland 1577–95 (W. F. Skene, Celtic Scotland III. 1880)
Description of Kentucky in North America, A 1792
Description of the river Thames etc., A ed. R. Binnell 1758
Description of S'hertogenbosh: see Pelegromius
Description of South Carolina, A (by James Glen) 1761
De Sélincourt, Hugh *The cricket match* 1924

DESHA, Lucius Junius *Organic chemistry: the chemistry of the compounds of carbon* 1936
Design: a monthly journal for manufacturers and designers 1949-
Design and work 1876-81
Design engineering 1971-
DE SITTER, Lamoraal Ulbo *Structural geology* 1956
DESMOND, George *The history of G. D., founded on facts which occurred in the East Indies* 1821
DE SOLA, Ralph & DE SOLA, Dorothy *A dictionary of cooking* 1969
D'ESTERRE-KEELING, Elsa *A return to nature, a Kentish idyll* 1897
Destruction of Troy. The gest hystoriale of the destruction of Troy: an alliterative romance translated from Guido de Colonna's Hystoria Troiana c1400 (E.E.T.S. 1869-74)
Destruction of Troy, The 1636 *See* DENHAM, Sir J.
DE TOLEDANO, Ralph ed. *Frontiers of jazz* 1947
Detroit Free Press (title varies) 1835-
DEUEL, Harry James *The lipids: their chemistry and biochemistry* 3 vols. 1951-7
Deuine lover, A (1657) *See* BAKER, David
DEUTSCH, Emanuel O. M. *Literary remains* a1873 (1874)
DEUTSCH, Sid *Theory and design of television receivers* 1951
DEUTSCHER, Isaac *Marxism in our time* ed. T. Deutscher 1971 (UK 1972)
Stalin: a political biography 1949
DEVANNY, Jean *Bushman Burke* 1930
The butcher shop 1926
Dawn beloved 1928
Old savage, and other stories 1927
Developmental biology 1959-
DE VERE, Sir Aubrey *A song of faith* 1842
DE VERE, Aubrey Thomas *Poetical works* 18.. (1884-98)
The legends of St. Patrick 1872
Picturesque sketches of Greece and Turkey 1850
DE VERE, M. Schele *Americanisms; the English of the New World* 1871 (1872)
Device to entertayne hir Majesty att Harfielde, The 1602 (Shaks. Soc. Papers II. 1845)
Devils. The parlyament of deuylles (in verse) 1509
DE VOTO, Bernard Augustine *Across the wide Missouri* 1947
Devout communicant exemplifi'd in his behaviour, The 1670 (1688)
DE VRIES, Leonard *Victorian advertisements* 1968
DE VRIES, Peter *The glory of the hummingbird* 1974 (UK 1975)
The Mackerel plaza 1958
DE WARREN, Count E. *Caignart de Saulcy's (L. F. J.) Narrative of a journey round the Dead Sea* 1853
DEWEES, William B. *Letters from an early settler of Texas* ed. 'C. Cordelle' (E. C. Kimball) 1852
DEWES *See* DU WES
D'EWES, Sir Simonds *The autobiography and correspondence* a1650 (Halliwell 1845)
College life in the time of James the first, as illustrated by an unpublished diary of Sir S. D'E. 16.. (1851)
The journals of all the parliaments during the reign of Queen Elizabeth a1650 (1682)
Two speeches 1642
DEWHURST, Henry W. *A lecture illustrative of the architecture of the human body* etc. 1832 (1834)
The natural history of the order cetacea 1834
DE WINDT, Harry *On the equator, by H. De W.* 1882
DE WYKES or WIKES, Thomas *Chronicon Salisburiensis monasterii* a1293 (Historiæ Anglicanæ scriptores quinque II. 1687)
DEXTER, Colin *Last seen wearing* 1976
Dial, The (Chicago) 1880-1929
Dialect notes. Published by the American Dialect Society 1890-
Dialogue betwixt Tom and Dick, A (by T. Jordan) 1660
A dialogue betwixt Rattle-head and Roundhead 1641
A proper dyaloge betwene a gentillman and a husbandman 1530 (in Roy, Rede me, etc. Arber 1871)
Saint-German's (C.) Fyrst (secunde) dyaloge in Englisshe betwyxt a doctoure of dyvnyte and a student in the lawes of Englande tr. 1531, 1532 (1638)
Diary of the siege and surrender of Lymerick, A 1692
DIBDIN, Charles *A collection of songs, selected from the works of C. D.* 1790, a1814 (1841, 1842)
DIBDIN, Thomas Frognall *The bibliographical decameron* 1817
An introduction to the knowledge of rare and valuable editions of the Greek and Latin classics 1802
The library companion, or the young man's guide and the old man's comfort in the choice of a library 1824
Dice-play c1550 *See* WALKER, G.
DICEY, Edward *Six months in the Federal states* 1863
DICK, Everett Newfon *The Dixie frontier* 1948
DICK, H. St. John *Flies and fly-fishing* 1873
DICK, William *Manual of veterinary science* 1841 (1862)
DICK, William Brisbane *The American Hoyle; or, Gentleman's hand-book of games* 1864 (and several later editions used)
Dick of Devonshire, The play of c1626 (Bullen, Old plays II. 1883)
DICKENS, Charles *American notes for general circulation* 2 vols. 1842 (1850)
Barnaby Rudge 1841 [in Master Humphrey's clock, q.v.]
The battle of life; a love story 1846
Bleak House 1853 [1852-53 in parts]
A child's history of England 2 vols. 1852-53 [1851-53 in Household words]
The chimes, a goblin story of some bells that rang an old year out and a new year in 1845
A Christmas carol, in prose 1843
The cricket on the hearth, a fairy tale of home 1846
Doctor Marigold's prescriptions 1865 [in All the year round]
Dombey and son 1848 [1846-48 in parts]
Great expectations 3 vols. 1861 [1860-61 in All the year round]
Hard times, for these times 1854
The haunted man and the ghost's bargain 1848
Letters v.d. (3 vols. 1880-82)
Letters ed. M. House et al. 1965-
The life and adventures of Martin Chuzzlewit 1844 [1843-44 in parts]
The life and adventures of Nicholas Nickleby 1839 [1838-39 in parts]
Little Dorrit 1857 [1855-57 in parts]
Master Humphrey's clock 3 vols. 1840-41
Mrs. Lirriper's legacy 1864 [in All the year round: partly by Dickens]
Mrs. Lirriper's lodgings 1863 [in All the year round: partly by Dickens]
Mugby Junction 1866 [in All the year round: partly by Dickens]
The mystery of Edwin Drood 1870
The old curiosity shop 1840-41 [in Master Humphrey's clock vols. I-II] (1848)
Oliver Twist; or the parish boy's progress 3 vols. 1838 [1837-39 in Bentley's miscellany]
Our mutual friend 2 vols. 1865 [1864-65 in parts]
The personal history of David Copperfield 1850 [1849-50 in parts]
Pictures from Italy 1846
The posthumous papers of the Pickwick club 1837 [1836-37 in parts]
Sketches by Boz [1st series] 2 vols. 1836 [1834-35 in periodicals]
— 2nd series 1837 [1833-36 in periodicals]
A tale of two cities 1859
The uncommercial traveller 1861 [1860-63 in periodicals] (1866)
DICKENS, Charles, Jr. *Dictionary of London* 1879
Dictionary of the Thames 1880
DICKENS, Monica Enid *The happy prisoner* 1946
The heart of London 1961
Man overboard 1958
No more meadows 1953
One pair of feet 1942
One pair of hands 1939
DICKENSON, John *Arisbas, Euphues amidst his slumbers: or Cupids journey to hell* 1594 (Grosart 1878)
Greene in conceipt new raised from his grave to write the tragique historie of faire Valeria of London 1598 (1878)
The shepheardes complaint c1595 (1878)
DICKENSON, Jonathan *God's protecting providence man's surest help and defence.. evidenced in the remarkable deliverance of R. Barrow.. Florida* 1700
DICKESON, Montroville W. *The American numismatic manual of the aborigines, and Colonial, State, and United States coins* 1859
DICKINSON, Emily Elizabeth *Poems* ed. T. H. Johnson 3 vols. 1955
DICKINSON, Gordon Cawood *Maps and air photographs* 1969
DICKINSON, Peter Malcolm de B. *The lizard in the cup* 1972
The poison oracle 1974
A pride of heroes 1969
Sleep and his brother 1971
DICKINSON, Reginald Ernest *Electric trains* 1927
DICKINSON, Thomas Albert *The aeronautical dictionary* 1945
DICKINSON, William *A glossary of words and phrases pertaining to the dialect of Cumberland* (with Supplement) 1878 (E.D.S.)
— re-arranged etc. by E. W. Prevost (1899)
DICKSEE, J. R. *School perspective* 1859
DICKSON, Adam *A treatise of agriculture* 1765 (ed. 2)
DICKSON, David *Select practical writings* a1663 (1845)
DICKSON, Mora *A world elsewhere* 1964
DICKSON, Nicholas *The auld Scotch minister* 1892
DICKSON, R. W. *General view of the agriculture of Lancashire* 1815
Practical agriculture; or a complete system of modern husbandry 1805
DICKSON, William E. *Practical organ-building* 1881
DICKSON, William Puride tr. *T. Mommsen's The history of Rome* 4 vols. 1862-6
Dictionarie English and Latine, A 1623
Dictionarium polygraphicum: or the whole body of arts regularly digested 1735
Dictionarium rusticum, urbanicum & botanicum: or a dictionary of husbandry, gardening, trade, commerce, and all sorts of country affairs 1704, 1726 (ed. 3)
Dictionary of American English on historical principles, A ed. W. A. Craigie & J. R. Hulbert 4 vols. 1938-44
Dictionary of Americanisms on historical principles, A ed. M. M. Mathews 2 vols. 1951
Dictionary of architecture, The, issued by the Architectural Publication Society 1852-92
Dictionary of the bible, A ed. J. Hastings 1898-1904
Dictionary of Canadianisms on historical principles, A See AVIS, Walter Spencer, et al.
Dictionary of Jamaican English See CASSIDY, Frederic Gomes & LE PAGE, R. B.
Dictionary of national biography ed. L. Stephen et al. 63 vols. & Supplements 1885-
Dictionary of occupational terms 1921 *See* United Kingdom. Ministry of Labour
Dictionary of South African English, A See BRANFORD, Jean
Didoniad, The 1831 *See* HUDIGER, P.
DIEFFENBACH, Ernst *Travels in New Zealand* 1843
DIEHL, Edith *Bookbinding: its background and technique* 2 vols. 1946
Dieulafait's (L.) Diamonds and precious stones tr. 1874
Difference between the church and court of Rome considered, The (by W. Lloyd) 1674
DIGBY, George, 2nd Earl of Bristol *Elvira,.. a comedy* 1667
Letters between the lord G. Digby and Sir K. Digby concerning religion 1639 (1651)
The Lord Digby's speeches in the House of Commons 1640-41
DIGBY, Sir Kenelm *Chymical secrets and rare experiments in physick and philosophy* a1648 (1682-83)
The closet of Sir K. D. opened a1648 (1669, 1677)
A discourse concerning the cure of wounds by the sympathetic powder 1644
Journal of a voyage into the Mediterranean 1628-29 (Camden Soc. 1868)
Observations upon Religio medici 1642 (1644)
Private memoirs of Sir K. D. written by himself a1648 (1827-28)
Two treatises, in the one of which, the nature of bodies, in the other the nature of mans soule, is looked into 1644 (1658)
See also DIGBY, G.
DIGBY, Kenelm E. *An introduction to the history of the law of real property* 1875 (1876)
DIGBY, Kenelm H. *The broad stone of honour, or the true sense and practice of chivalry* 1828-29 (1848)
Mores catholici or ages of faith 1831 etc.
Digby mysteries. Ancient mysteries from the Digby manuscripts c1485 (Abbotsford club 1835)
The Digby mysteries c 1485 (New Shaks. Soc. 1882; E.E.T.S.1896)
DIGGES, Dudley *The unlawfulnesse of subjects taking armes against their soveraigne* 1643 (1647)
DIGGES, Sir Dudley *The compleat ambassador.. Collected by Sir D. D.* 15.. (1655)
See also DIGGES, Thomas
DIGGES, Leonard *A book called Tectonicon* 1562 (1592)
A prognostication of right good effect 1555
—— & DIGGES, Thomas *An arithmeticall militarie treatise named Stratioticos* a1571 (1579)
A geometrical practise named Pantometria 1571 (1591)
DIGGES, Thomas & DIGGES, Sir Dudley *Foure paradoxes, or politique discourses; 2 concerning militarie discipline.. by T. D. (a1595) 2 of the worthinesse of warre and warriors by D. D. his sonne* 1604
DILKE, Sir Charles W. *Greater Britain: a record of travel in English-speaking countries* 1868
Problems of Greater Britain 1890
DILLARD, Joey Lee *Black English: its history and usage in the United States* 1972
DILLEY, Arthur Urbane *Oriental rugs and carpets* 1931
DILLON, Harold A., 17th Viscount *Calais and the Pale* 1891 (Archaeologia, 2nd series, III, 1893)
DILLON, Sir John T. *Travels through Spain* 1780 (1781)
DILLS, Lanie *The 'official' CB slanguage language dictionary and cross-reference* ed. D. Gilbertson 1975
— (rev. ed.) 1976
DILWORTH, W. H. *The life of Alexander Pope* 1759
The life of.. Jonathan Swift 1758 (1760)
DIMENT, Adam *The bang bang birds* 1968
The dolly dolly spy 1967
The great spy race 1968
Think Inc. 1971
DI MONA, Joseph *Last man at Arlington* 1973 (UK 1974)
DINELEY, Thomas *Journal giving some account of his visit to Ireland* 1681 (Journal of the Kilkenny Archæol. Soc., 2nd series, I, 1858)
DINGWALL, William Orr ed. *A survey of linguistic science* 1971
DIRAC, Paul Adrien Maurice *The principles of quantum mechanics* 1930
— (ed. 3) 1947
DIRCKS, Henry *The life, times, and scientific labours of the second Marquis of Worcester* 1865
Directions of parliament for the electing and choosing of ruling elders, 19 Aug. 1645
Director, The; a weekly literary journal 1807
Directorium Anglicanum, The, being a manual of directions for the right celebration of the Holy Communion, etc. ed. F. G. Lee 1865 (1866)
Directory for the publique worship throughout the three kingdoms of England, Scotland, and Ireland, A 1644
DIRINGER, David *The alphabet: a key to the history of mankind* 1948
Discipline and ceremonies of the Church of England, Two papers of proposals concerning the 1661
Discourse concerninge the Spanish fleet invadinge Englande tr. (from P. Ubaldini) 1590
Discourse of the common weal of this realm of England, A c1550 (1893)
Discourse of the religion of England, A (by J. Corbet) 1667
Discourse wherein is plainly proued.. that Peter was neuer at Rome, etc., A. By R. T. (Christopher Carlile) 1572
Discourses and characters.. wherein the vanities of the modish women are discovered, Several 1689
Discoveries of John Poulter, written by himself, The 1753
Discovery: a monthly popular journal of knowledge 1920-66
Discriminator, The: a periodical 1905
Diseases of the nervous system 1940-

Disinterested love; or the modern Robin Grey. By a widow lady 1788
Dispute (Disputation) between Mary and the cross c1375 (Legends of the holy rood, E.E.T.S. 1871; Minor poems of the Vernon MS., E.E.T.S. 1901)
Disraeli, Benjamin, Earl of Beaconsfield *Coningsby, or the new generation* 1844
Contarini Fleming, a psychological autobiography 1832
Correspondence with his sister 1832–52 (1886)
Endymion 1880
Henrietta Temple 1836
Lothair 1870
The revolutionary epick 1834
Sybil; or the two nations 1845
Tancred; or the new crusade 1847
Venetia 1837
Vivian Grey 1826–27
The voyage of Captain Popanilla 1828
The young duke 1831
D'Israeli, Isaac *Amenities of literature* 1841 (1859)
Calamities of authors 1812 (1867)
Commentaries on the life and reign of Charles the first 1828–31
Curiosities of literature 1791–1823 (1849, 1866)
Quarrels of authors 1814 (1867)
Dissertation abstracts 1952–
'Distaff, John' *A character of Don Sacheverellio* 1710 (1711)
Distracted emperor, The: a tragi-comedy ?c1600 (Bullen, Old plays III, 1884)
Ditchburn, Robert William *Light* 1952
—(ed. 2) 1963
Ditmars, Raymond Lee *The reptile book* 1907
Snakes of the world 1931
Diurnal of remarkable occurrents that have passed within the country of Scotland since the death of king James the fourth till the year 1575, A 15.. (Bannatyne Club 1833)
Diver, Katherine Helen Maud *Candles in the wind* 1909
Diverting muse, The; or the universal medly 1707
Dives and pauper See Parker, H.
'Divine, David' (Arthur Durham Divine) *The King of Fassarai* 1950
Divine and politike observations newly translated out of Dutch, upon some lines in the speech of (Abp. Laud) 1637 1638
Divine lover, A (1657) *See* Baker, David
'Dix, Dorothy' (Elizabeth Meriwether Gilmer) *Fables of the elite* 1902
Dixie, Lady Florence *Across Patagonia* 1880
Dixon, Henry Hall *Field and fern, or Scottish flocks and herds* 1865
The post and the paddock, by the Druid 1856 (1880)
Silk and scarlet, by the Druid 1859 (1880)
Dixon, James H. ed. *Ancient poems, ballads and songs of the peasantry of England* (1650–) (Percy Soc. 1846)
Dixon, James M. *Dictionary of idiomatic English phrases* 1891
Dixon, Richard W. *History of the church of England* 1877–85
Dixon, Robert *The nature of the two testaments* 1676
Dixon, Robert V. *A treatise on heat* 1849
Dixon, William Hepworth *British Cyprus* 1879
Her majesty's Tower 1869–71
History of two queens 1873–74
New America 1867
Personal history of Lord Bacon 1861
Royal Windsor 1879–80
Spiritual wives 1868
The Switzers 1872
White conquest 1876
William Penn, an historical biography 1851 (1872)
Dobbs, Arthur *An account of the countries adjoining to Hudson's Bay* 1744
Dobell, Sydney T. *Poetical works* a1874 (1875)
Balder 1853
The Roman, a dramatic poem 1850
Dobie, James *Memoir of William Wilson of Crummock* 1896
Dobie, James Frank ed. *Rainbow in the morning* 1965 ('reprint ed.' of Vol. V of *Publications of the Texas Folklore Society* 1926)
Dobson, Edward *A rudimentary treatise on the manufacture of bricks* 1850 (1868)
Dobson, George E. *Catalogue of the chiroptera in..the British Museum* 1878
Dobson, Gordon Miller Bourne *Exploring the atmosphere* 1963
—(ed. 2) 1968
Dobson, H. Austin *At the sign of the lyre* 1885
Eighteenth century vignettes 1892–96
Sir Richard Steele (English worthies) 1886
Vignettes in rhyme and vers de société 1873
Docquets of letters patent passed..at Oxford 1642–46 (1838)
Doctors' Commons, Wills from: a selection from the wills of eminent persons proved in the Prerogative court of Canterbury 1495–1695 (Camden Soc. 1863)
Doctrine and erudition for any christen man, A necessary 1543
Doctrine of devils proved to be the grand apostacy of these later times, The 1676
Doctrynall of good servauntes c1500 (Ancient poetical tracts, Percy Soc. 1842)
Documentary history of American industrial society, A ed. J. R. Commons et al. 11 vols. 1910–11
Documents relating to the proceedings against William Prynne in 1634 and 1637 (Camden Soc. 1877)
Documents relative to the colonial history of the State of New York, procured in Holland, England and France collected by J. R. Brodhead; ed. E. B. O'Callaghan & B. Fernow 15 vols. 1853–87
Dod, John & Cleaver, R. *A plaine exposition of the ninth and tenth (eleventh and twelfth) chapters of the Proverbs of Salomon* 1608
Dodd, F. Lawson *Municipal milk and public health* 1905
Dodd, George *The textile manufactures of Great Britain (= British manufactures)* 1844–46
Dodd, Ralph *Letters..on the improvement of the Port of London* 1798
Dodd, Robert Edward *Chemical spectroscopy* 1962
Doddridge, Philip *The family expositor: or a paraphrase and version of the New Testament* 1739–56 (1799)
Dodge, Richard Irving *Our wild Indians* 1882
Dodington, George Bubb, Baron Melcombe *Diary* 1749–61 (1784)
Dodoens See Lyte, H.
Dods, Marcus *Mohammed, Buddha, and Christ* 1877 (1878)
'Dods, Margaret' *The cook and housewife's manual* 1826 (1842)
Dodsley, Robert ed. *A collection of poems by several hands* (1748, 1755, 1758, 1782)
ed. *A select collection of old plays* (1744, 1780, 1825–27, Hazlitt 1874–76)
Poems a1764 (1810)
Public virtue, a poem in three books (1. Agriculture)
Dodson, William *The designe for the perfect draining of the great level of the fens* 1665
Dodwell, Edward *A classical and topographical tour through Greece* 1819
Dodwell, Henry *A defence of the vindication of the deprived bishops* 1695
A discourse concerning Sanchoniathon's Phœnician history 1680 (1691)
The natural mortality of humane soules clearly demonstrated... Being an explication of a famous passage in the dialogue of S. Justin Martyr with Tryphon 1708
Two letters of advice 1680 (1691)
Dodypoll, The wisedome of Doctor 1600 (Bullen, Old plays III, 1884)
'Doe, John' (F. R. Roe) *The bridge manual, an illustrated guide to the conventions of the game* 1900
'Doesticks, Q. K. Philander' (Mortimer Neal Thomson) *Doesticks, what he says* 1855
Dogs, Breaking and training. By 'Pathfinder' 1875
Doklady See: Academy of Sciences of the U.S.S.R.
'Doleman, N.' *See* Parsons, Robert
Dolinsky, Meyer *There is no silence* 1959
Dolman, Richard *The third volume of La Primaudaye's (P. de) French academie englished* 1601 (1618)
Domesday of inclosures, The 1517–18 (R. Hist. Soc. 1897)
Domett, Alfred *Ranolf and Amohia, a South-sea day dream* 1872
Flotsam and jetsam, rhymes old and new 1877
'Dominic R. B.' (Mary Jane Latsis & Martha Henissart) *Epitaph for a lobbyist* 1974
See also 'Lathen, Emma'
Dominis (M. A. de). A manifestation of the motives whereupon M. A. de Dominis, archbishop of Spalatro ..vndertooke his departure thence tr. 1616
Dominoes and solitaire. By 'Berkeley' 1890
Dominy, Eric Norman *Teach yourself judo* 1954
Dommett, William Erskine *A dictionary of aircraft* 1918
Don, George *A general history of the dichlamydeous plants* 1831–37
Don Bellianis. The honour of chivalry, or the famous and delectable history of Don Bellianis of Greece tr. 1650
See also Kirkman, F.
Donald, G. W. *Poems, ballads and songs* 1867 (1879)
Donaldson, David *Supplement to Jamieson's Scottish dictionary* 1887
Donaldson, James *General view of the agriculture of the county of Elgin* 1794; *of Kincardine* 1795; *of Nairn* 1794
Donaldson, John W. *Christian orthodoxy reconciled with the conclusions of modern biblical learning* 1857
The theatre of the Greeks 1836 (1849, 1860)
A vindication of protestant principles (anon.) 1847
Donaldson, Thomas *Poems, chiefly in the Scottish dialect* 1809
Donaldson, William *The life and adventures of Sir Bartholomew Sapskull* (anon.) 1768
Doncaster, Leonard *An introduction to the study of cytology* 1920
Done, John *Aristeas' Auncient historie of the Septuagint* tr. 1633
Polydoron, or a miscellanea of morall, philosophicall and theologicall sentences 1631
Donkin, William F. *Acoustics. Theoretical* part I. 1870
Donleavy, James Patrick *The ginger man* 1955
Donne, John *Works* a1631 (1839)
Βιαθανατος, a declaration of that paradoxe or thesis that self-homicide is not so naturally sin, that it may never be otherwise c1608 (1648)
Devotions upon emergent occasions and seuerall steps in my sicknes 1624
Essayes in divinity a1615 (1651)
Juvenilia; or certaine paradoxes and problemes 1600–06 (1633)
The lamentations of Jeremy a1631 (1633)
Letters to severall persons of honour a1631 (1651)
Paradoxes, problemes, essayes, characters 1600–06 (1652)
Poems a1631 (1633, 1650, 1669, Grosart 1872–73)
The progress of the soule 1612 (1633)
Pseudo-martyr, wherein out of certaine propositions and gradations, this conclusion is euicted, That etc. 1610
Satires 1593 (1669)
Selections from the works of D. a1631 (1840)
Sermons a1631 (LXXX. S. 1640, Fifty S. 1649, XXVI. S. 1661)
See also Mayne, Jasper
Donovan, Charles Henry Wynne *With Wilson in Matabeleland; or, Sport and war in Zambesia* 1894
Donovan, Michael *Domestic economy* 1830 (1837)
Doogue, Raymond Brian & Moreland, John Munn *New Zealand sea anglers' guide* 1960
Doomed religions: a series of essays on the great religions of the world ed. J. M. Reid 1884
Doomsday. Be domes dæge, De die judicii, an old English version of the Latin poem ascribed to Bede a1000 (E.E.T.S. 1876; Vom jüngsten tage, Grein 1894)
Doomsday c1000 (Das jüngste gericht, Grein 1897)
Doomsday (a poem) c1250, c1275 (O.E. Misc., E.E.T.S. 1872)
'Doone, Jice' (Vance Marshall) *Timely tips for new Australians* 1926
Dopping, Olle *Computers and data processing* 1970
Doran, John *Habits and men* 1854
The history of court fools 1858
A lady of the last century (Mrs. E. Montagu) 1873
'Mann' and manners at the court of Florence 1740–86, founded on the letters of Horace Mann to Horace Walpole 1876
Saints and sinners; or in church and about it 1868
'Their majesties' servants,' annals of the English stage 1864
Dorland, W. A. Newman *The illustrated medical dictionary* 1901 (ed. 2), 1903 (ed. 3), 1913 (ed. 7)
Dorman, Thomas *A proufe of certeyne articles in religion, denied by M. Juell, sett furth* 1564
Dorner's (I. A.) History of the development of the doctrine of the person of Christ tr. W. L. Alexander and D. W. Simon 1861–63 (1872)
Dornford, Josiah *Pütter's (J. S.) Historical developement of..the Germanic empire* tr. 1790
Dorothy; a country story in elegiac verse (by A. J. Munby) 1880
Dorrington, Edward ?pseud. *The hermit: or the unparalleled sufferings and surprising adventures of Mr. Philip Quarll* 1727 (1751, 1816)
Dorset, A glossary of provincial words used in the county of 1851
Dorset, Charles Sackville, Earl of *Poetical works* c1680 (1721, 1750)
Dorset, Thomas Sackville, Earl of *See* Sackville
Dorson, Richard M. ed. *Peasant customs and savage myths: selections from the British folklorists* 2 vols. 1968
Dos Passos, John Roderigo *The best times: an informal memoir* 1966 (UK 1968)
The big money 1936
The 42nd parallel 1930
1919 1932
Streets of night 1923
Three soldiers 1921 (UK 1922)
Dossie, Robert *The handmaid to the arts* (anon.) 1758
Double welcome, The, a poem to the Duke of Marlborough (by De Foe) 1705
Douce, Francis *Illustrations of Shakespeare and of ancient manners* 1807
Douce MS. 55 (Bodl. Libr.) c1440 (Two cookery-books, E.E.T.S. 1888)
Dougall, John tr. *M. Born's Atomic physics* 1935
Dougherty, George S. *The criminal as a human being* 1924
Doughty, Charles M. *Travels in Arabia deserta* 1888
Doughty, Henry M. *Friesland meres and through the Netherlands* 1889
Our wherry in Wendish lands 1892
Doughty, John *Discourses* 1627 (1628)
Douglas, Alexander *Poems, chiefly in the Scottish dialect* 1806
Douglas, Bp. Gavin *Poetical works* a1522 (1874)
The xiii bukes of Eneados of the famose poete Virgill tr. 1513 (1553, 1710, 1874)
King Hart c1510 (1874)
The palice of honour 1501 (1710, 1874)
'Douglas, George' (G. D. Brown) *The house with the green shutters* 1901
Douglas, George Norman *London street games* 1916
South wind 1917
Douglas, Sir Howard *An essay on the principles and construction of military bridges* 1816 (ed. 3, 1853)
Douglas, Jack D. & Johnson, John M. eds. *Existential sociology* 1977
Douglas, James *The truths of religion* 1830 (1832)
Douglas, Keith Castellain *Alamein to Zem Zem* 1946
Douglas, Lloyd Cassel *Forgive us our trespasses* 1932 (UK 1937)
White banners 1936
Douglas, Norman *See* Douglas, George Norman
'Douglas, O.' (Anna Buchan) *Penny plain* 1920
Douglas, Robert *General view of the agriculture of the counties of Roxburgh and Selkirk* 1798
Douglas, Robert K. *Non-christian religious systems: Confucianism and Taouism* 1879
Douglas-Todd, Charles Henry *The popular whippet* 1961
Douglass, Frederick *Narrative of the life of Frederick Douglass, an American slave* 1845
Douglass, William *A discourse concerning the currencies of the British plantations in America* 1740

DOULAND, or DOWLAND, John *The first (second, third) book of songs or airs* 1597, 1600, 1603 (Arber, Eng. Garner IV)
Ornithoparcus (A.) his micrologus, or introduction: containing the art of singing 1609
DOUSE, Thomas le M. *Grimm's law; a study* 1876
D'OUVILLY, Baron *See* GERBIER, Sir B. G.
DOVE, John *An advertisement to the English seminaries and Iesuites* 1610
A confutation of atheisme 1605
DOVE, Patrick E. *Logic of the Christian faith* 1856
Dover, Robert. Annalia Dubrensia, vpon the yeerely celebration of Mr. R. D.'s Olimpick games vpon Cotswold-hills, written by Drayton etc. 1636 (Grosart 1877)
DOW, Christopher *A discourse of the sabbath and the Lord's day* 1636
'Dow, Jr.' (E. G. Paige) *Short patent sermons* c1850
DOWDEN, Edward *The life of P. B. Shelley* 1886
Shakespere (Literature primer) 1877
Southey (English men of letters) 1879
Studies in literature 1789–1877 1878
DOWELL, Stephen *A history of taxation and taxes in England* 1884 (1888)
DOWIE, Ménie Muriel (Mrs. H. Norman) *Gallia* 1895
A girl in the Karpathians 1891
DOWLAND *See* DOULAND
DOWLING, Robert *The sport of fate* 1880
DOWNAME, Bp. George *A treatise..concerning christian libertie* 1609
Down beat 1934–
DOWNES, George *Letters from continental countries* 1832
Letters from Mecklenburgh and Holstein 1822
DOWNES, Joseph *The mountain decameron* 1836
DOWNEY, Hal ed. *Handbook of hematology* 4 vols. 1938
DOWNING, Andrew Jackson *The fruits and fruit-trees of America* 1845 (1869)
Downing, Major Jack, of the Downingville militia 1860 (1865) See also DAVIS, C. A.; SMITH, Seba
DOWNING, Joseph *A treatise on the disorders incident to horned cattle* 1797
DOWNING, W. H. *Digger dialects* 1919
Downside review 1880–
DOWSON, Ernest Christopher (1867–1900) *Letters* ed. D. Flower & H. Maas 1967
DOXIADIS, Constantinos Apostolou *Between Dystopia and Utopia* 1966 (UK 1968)
DOYLE, Arthur Conan *The adventures of Sherlock Holmes* 1891
A duet 1899
The exploits of Brigadier Gerard 1896
The green flag, and other stories of war and sport 1900
His last bow 1917
The history of spiritualism 2 vols. 1926
The lost world 1912
The Maracot Deep, and other stories 1929
The memoirs of Sherlock Holmes 1894
Micah Clarke 1889
Rodney Stone 1896
Sir Nigel 1906
The valley of fear 1915
The White company 1891
DOYLE, John Andrew *History of America* 1875
D'OYLE, Lynn C. *Notches on the rough edge of life* 1890
D'OYLY, George *The life of William Sancroft, archbishop of Canterbury* 1821 (1840)
DRABBLE, Margaret *The Garrick year* 1964
Jerusalem the golden 1967
The millstone 1965
A summer bird-cage 1962
The waterfall 1969
DRACKETT, Philip Arthur *Motor rallying* 1963
Drainer. The drayner confirmed,..and the obstinate fen-man confuted 1629 (1647)
See also C., H.
DRAKE, Daniel *Natural and statistical view; or, Picture of Cincinnati and the Miami country* 1815
Pioneer life in Kentucky a1852 (1870)
DRAKE, Francis *Eboracum; or the history and antiquities of the city of York* 1736
Drake, Sir Francis 1595 *See* MAYNARDE, T.
DRAKE, Sir Francis, bart. *The world encompassed by Sir F. Drake* 1628 (Hakluyt Soc. 1854)
DRAKE, Joseph R. *The culprit fay, and other poems* 1836
DRAKE, Nathan *A journal of the first and second sieges of Pontefract 1644–45* (Surtees Soc. 1860)
DRAKE, Nathan *Literary hours, or sketches critical and narrative* 1798 (1820)
DRAKE, Peter *The memoirs of captain P. D.* 1754 (1755)
DRANT, Thomas *A medicinable morall, that is the two bookes of Horace his satyres englished... The wailyngs of the prophet Hieremiah done into Englyshe verse, also epigrammes* 1566
Horace his arte of poetrie, pistles and satyrs englished 1567
DRAPER, Alfred *The death penalty* 1972
Swansong for a rare bird 1970
DRAPER, John W. *History of the American civil war* 1867
History of the conflict between religion and science 1875 (1877)
History of the intellectual development of Europe 1863
Human physiology 1858
Draper's dictionary 1886 *See* BECK, S. W.
Draughts, backgammon and dominoes 1866
DRAYSON, Alfred W. *Sporting scenes amongst the Kaffirs of South Africa* 1858
DRAYTON, John *A view of South-Carolina, as respects her natural and civil concerns* 1802
DRAYTON, Michael *Works* a1631 (1748, 1753; 1876)
Ballad of Agincourt c1605 (Poemes lyrick and pastorall)
The Barons' wars See *Mortimeriados*, below
The battaile of Agincourt,..The miseries of queene Margarite,..Nimphidia, the court of fayrie, The quest of Cinthia, The shepheards Sirena, The mooncalfe, Elegies upon sundry occasions 1627
Eclogues 1593 (Poemes lyrick and pastorall; 1619)
England's heroicall epistles 1597, 1598, 1599 (1619)
The harmony of the church 1591 (Percy Soc. 1843)
Idea, the shepheards garland 1593 (also with England's heroicall epistles 1599; 1619; Arber, Eng. Garner VI)
The man in the moone 1605 (Poemes lyrick and pastorall; 1619)
The miseries of queene Margarite c1600 (1627)
Mortimeriados, the lamentable ciuill warres of Edward the second and the barrons 1596
— *The barrons warres in the raigne of Edward the second* 1603 (1619)
The muses elizium lately discouered by a new way ouer Parnassus 1630
Odes c1605, 1619 (Poemes lyrick and pastorall; 1619; Arber, Eng. Garner VIII)
The owle (a poem) 1604 (1619)
Poemes lyrick and pastorall c1605
Poems 1606, 1619 (also Roxb. Club 1856)
Poly-olbion, or a chorographicall description of..Great Britain 1612, 1622 (also 1876)
The tragicall legend of Robert Duke of Normandy..With the legend of Matilda,..and the legend of Piers Gaveston 1596 (1619)
Dream, The, a poem sacred to the..memory of Queen Caroline (Wilhelmina) 1737
DREDGE, James ed. *Electric illumination* 1882
DREISER, Theodore *An American tragedy* 2 vols. 1925 (UK 1926)
The financier 1912
DREW, Samuel *See* HITCHINS, F.
DRISCOLL, Peter *The white lie assignment* 1971
The Wilby conspiracy 1972 (UK 1973)
Drive 1967–
DRIVER, Abraham & DRIVER, W. *General view of the agriculture of the county of Hants* 1794
DRIVER, Christopher *The disarmers* 1964
DROUT, John *The pityfull historie of..Gaulfrido and Barnardo le vayne* tr. 1570 (1844)
'Druid, The' See DIXON, H. H.
Drum, Jack See MARSTON, J.
Drum (East African ed.) 1965–
DRUMMOND, Alexander *Travels through different cities of Germany, Italy* etc. 1754
DRUMMOND, Charles *Death and the leaping ladies* 1968
A death at the bar 1972
Death at the furlong post 1967
The odds on death 1969
DRUMMOND, Henry *The Lowell lectures on the ascent of man* 1894
Natural law in the spiritual world 1883
'DRUMMOND, Ivor' (Roger Erskine Longrigg) *The jaws of the watchdog* 1973
The man with the tiny head 1969
The power of the bug 1974
DRUMMOND, June *Bang! Bang! You're dead!* 1973
The black unicorn 1959
The Gantry episode 1968
DRUMMOND, Montagu tr. *G. Haberlandt's Physiological plant anatomy* 1914
DRUMMOND, Sir William *Origines, or remarks on the origin of several empires, states and cities* 1824–29
DRUMMOND, William (of Hawthornden) *Works* a1649 (1711; Poetical works, S.T.S. 1913)
Considerations to the Parliament 1639 (1711)
A cypress grove 1613
Familiar epistles a1649 (1711)
Flowres of Sion 1623
(The river of) Forth feasting 1617
The history of the five James's, kings of Scotland a1649 (1711)
Irene, a remonstrance for concord..amongst his majesty's subjects 1638 (1711)
Notes of Ben Jonson's conversations with D. 1619 (Shaks. Soc. 1842)
Σκιαμαχια or a defence of a petition 1642 (1711)
D.'s Polemo-medinia (The muckomachy; or the middenfecht, a poem. With enlargements by the moderns) tr. (1846)
DRURY, Anna H. *Called to the rescue* 1879
DRURY, Heber *The useful plants of India* 1858 (1873)
DRURY, William D. ed. *The book of gardening: a handbook of horticulture* 1900
Dry leaves 1849 *See* EASTWICK, E. B.
DRYDEN, John *Works* a1700 (Scott 1808, Saintsbury's Scott 1882–93)
The comedies, tragedies, and operas (1701)
Poetical works (Globe 1870, Oxford ed. 1910)
Essays a1700 (Ker 1900)
Absalom and Achitophel 1681 See also TATE, N.
All for love, or the world well lost, a tragedy 1678
Amboyna, a tragedy 1673
Amphitryon, or the two Sosias, a comedy 1690
Annus mirabilis: the year of wonders 1666
Assignation, The, or love in a nunnery 1672
Astræa redux, a poem on the happy restoration..of Charles the second 1660
Aureng-zebe, a tragedy 1676
Ceyx and Alcyone 1700 (Fables)
Cinyras and Myrrha 1700 (Fables)
Cleomenes, the Spartan heroe, a tragedy 1692
The conquest of Granada by the Spaniards. In two parts 1670, 1672
Cymon and Iphigenia. From Boccace 1700 (Fables)
On the death of Amyntas, a pastoral elegy a1700
A discourse concerning the original and progress of satire 1693 (with Juvenal 1693, 1697; Ker)
Don Sebastian, king of Portugal: a tragedy 1690
Of dramatick poesie, an essay 1668 (Arber, Eng. Garner III; Ker)
Dufresnoy's (C. A.) De arte graphica, the art of painting tr. 1695
Eleonora: a panegyrical poem 1692
An evening's love: or the mock astrologer 1668 (1671)
Examen poeticum: being the third part of Miscellany poems 1693
Fables, ancient and modern, translated into verse from Homer, Ovid, Boccace, and Chaucer, with originall poems 1700
The hind and the panther, a poem 1687
The first book of Homer's Ilias tr. 1700 (Fables)
Horace, Odes tr. 1685 (Sylvæ)
The Indian emperour, or the conquest of Mexico by the Spaniards (a tragedy) 1665
Juvenal. The satires of D. J. Juvenalis, translated into English verse by Mr. Dryden, and several other eminent hands. Together with the satires of A. Persius Flaccus, made English by Mr. Dryden. To which is prefix'd a discourse concerning the original and progress of satire 1693 (1697)
The kind keeper; or Mr. Limberham: a comedy 1678 (1680)
Lucretius (translations from) 1685 (Sylvæ)
Mac Flecknoe, or a satyr upon the true-blew-protestant poet, T(homas) S(hadwell) 1682
Marriage-a-la-mode, a comedy 1673
ed. *Miscellany poems* 1684–94
Ovid's Metamorphoses tr. 1693, 1700 (Examen poeticum; Fables) See also GARTH, Sir S.
Palamon and Arcite: or the knight's tale from Chaucer 1700 (Fables)
Plutarch's Lives tr. by several hands. To which is prefixt the life of Plutarch (by J. Dryden) 1683–86
Religio laici, or a laymans faith, a poem 1682
The rival ladies, a tragi-comedy 1663 (1669)
Saint-Evremond's (C. Marguetel de Saint-Denis, Seigneur de) *Miscellaneous essays* tr. (? by K. Chetwood), contin. by Dryden 1692
Secret love, or the maiden queen 1668
The Spanish fryar, or the double discovery 1681
The state of innocence and fall of man, an opera 1676
Sylvæ, or the second part of Poetical miscellanies 1685
The tempest See DAVENANT, Sir W.
Troilus and Cressida, or truth found too late, a tragedy 1679
Tyrannick love, or the royal martyr, a tragedy 1669
The works of Virgil: containing his Pastorals, Georgics, and Æneis tr. 1697
The wild gallant, a comedy 1663
—— & LEE, N. *The duke of Guise, a tragedy* 1682 (1683)
Œdipus, a tragedy 1679
—— & NEWCASTLE, Duke of *Sir Martin Mar-all, or the feign'd innocence, a comedy* 1667 (1668)
DUANE, Alexander tr. *E. Fuchs's Text-book of ophthalmology* 1892
Du Bellay's (G.) Instructions for the wars tr. P. Ive 1589
Dublin, Calendar of ancient records of v.d. (ed. J. T. Gilbert 1889–98)
Dublin review, The 1836–
Dublin University review 1885–7
DU BOIS, Edward *A piece of family biography* (anon.) 1799
Du Bosc's (J.) Compleat woman tr. N. N. 1639
DUBOURG, George *The violin* 1836
DUCANE, Sir Edmund *The punishment and prevention of crime* 1885
DU CANGE, Charles Dufresne, Sieur *Glossarium mediæ et infimæ Latinitatis* (1840–50; 1883–87)
'DUCANGE ANGLICUS' *The vulgar tongue: comprising two glossaries of slang, cant, and flash words and phrases, principally used in London at the present day* 1857
DUCAREL, Andrew C. *Some account of..Croydon* 1783
DU CHAILLU, Paul B. *Explorations and adventures in equatorial Africa* 1861
The viking age 1889
DUCHÉ, Jacob *Discourses on various subjects* 1779 (1790)
Duckett's register 1946–
Ducray-Duménil's (F. G.) Victor, or the child of the forest tr. 1802
DUDLEY, Frederick *Amoroso: a novel* 1810
DUDLEY, John W. Ward, Earl of *Letters..to the bishop of Llandaff* 18.. (1840)
DUDLEY, Robert, Earl of Leicester *Correspondence of R. Dudley, Earl of Leycester, during his government of the Low Countries* 1585–86 (Camden Soc. 1844)
DUDLEY, Sir Robert c1595 *See* WYATT, Captain
'DUDLEY-GORDON, Tom' (Dudley Barker et al.) *Coastal command at war* 1943
DUFF, Alexander *The true nobility* 1868
DUFF, David Skene *Victoria in the Highlands* 1968
DUFF, James *A collection of poems, songs* etc. *chiefly Scottish* 1816
DUFF, M. E. Grant *A glance over Europe* 1868
A political survey 1868

DUFFERIN AND AVA, F. T. Hamilton-Temple-Blackwood, 1st Marquis of *Letters from high latitudes* 1857
DUFFERIN AND AVA, Hariot G., Marchioness of *My Canadian journal 1872–78* 1891
DUFFET, Thomas *The mock-tempest; or the enchanted castle* 1675
DUFFIELD, Alexander J. *The ingenious knight Don Quixote de la Mancha. A new translation* (of Cervantes) 1881
DUFFY, Maureen *That's how it was* 1962
DUFTON, William *The nature and treatment of deafness and diseases of the ear* 1844
DU GARD, William *Comenius' (J. A.) Latinæ linguæ janua reserata.. The gate of the Latine tongue unlocked* 1656
DUGDALE, Sir William *The antiquities of Warwickshire illustrated* 1656
The history of imbanking and drayning of divers fens and marshes 1662
D.'s Monasticon Anglicanum; or the history of the ancient abbies and other monasteries etc. tr. (1693, 1718, 1817–30, 1846)
DUGGAR, Benjamin Minge *Fungous diseases of plants* 1909
Duhamel du Monceau's (H. L.) Practical treatise of husbandry tr. J. Mills 1759 (1762)
DUHRING, Louis A. *A practical treatise on diseases of the skin* 1876 (1881)
DUKE, Richard *Poems* a1711 (1790, 1810)
DUKE-ELDER, William Stewart *Parsons' Diseases of the eye* *See* PARSONS, John Herbert
Text-book of ophthalmology 7 vols. 1932–54
—— et al. *System of ophthalmology* 1958–
Dulcinead variorum, The: a satyrical poem in hudibrastick verse 1729
DU MAURIER, Daphne *The breaking point: eight stories* 1959
Rebecca 1938
DU MAURIER, George *The Martian* 1897
Trilby, a novel 1894
The young George du Maurier: a selection of his letters, 1860–67 ed. D. du Maurier 1951
Dumfries and Galloway Standard 1843–
Du Moncel's (T. A. L.) The telephone, the microphone, and the phonograph tr. 1879
Du Mont's (J.) New voyage to the Levant tr. 1696
Dumpling, A learned dissertation on See ARBUTHNOT, J.
DUNBAR, Carl Owen & RODGERS, John *Principles of stratigraphy* 1957
DUNBAR, Edward D. *Social life in former days, chiefly in the province of Moray* 1865–66
DUNBAR, James *The practical papermaker* 1880 (1881)
DUNBAR, Janet *Mrs. G. B. S.: a biographical portrait of Charlotte Shaw* 1963
DUNBAR, William *Poems* 1500–20 (S.T.S. 1893)
The flyting of D. and Kennedie 1508
The goldyn targe 1508
The tua mariit wemen and the wedo 1508
DUNCAN, Andrew *Latinae grammaticae pars prior.. Appendix etymologiæ ad copiam exemplorum una cum indice interprete* 1595 (E.D.S. 1874)
DUNCAN, Archibald *A correct narrative of the funeral of Horatio Lord Viscount Nelson* 1806
Life of Lord Nelson 1806
The mariner's chronicle 1810
DUNCAN, James Matthews *Clinical lectures on the diseases of women* 1879 (1889)
DUNCAN, Lee *Over the wall* 1936
DUNCAN, Lew Wallace & SCOTT, Charles F. *History of Allan and Woodson Counties, Kansas* 1901
DUNCAN, Peter M. *See* FIGUIER, L.
DUNCAN (later COTES) Sara J. *A social departure* 1890
DUNCAN, William *Cicero's Select orations* tr. 1755 (1816)
DUNCAN, William Murdock *The big timer* 1973
DUNCOMBE, John ed. *Letters by several eminent persons deceased* (1773)
DUNCUMB, John *Collections towards the history and antiquities of the county of Hereford* 1804
— *Provincial customs and words* (from the above) (E.D.S. 1874)
General view of the agriculture of the county of Hereford 1805
DUNDAS, John *A summary view of the feudal law, with the differences of the Scots law from it* (anon.) 1710
DUNDES, Alan ed. *Mother wit from the laughing barrel: readings in the interpretation of Afro-American folklore* 1973
DUNDY, Elaine *The dud avocado* 1958
DUNGLISON, Robley *Medical lexicon. A dictionary of medical science* 1842, 1848 (ed. 7), 1857 (1874, 1893)
DUNKIN, Edwin *The midnight sky: familiar notes on the stars and plants* 1869
DUNKIN, John *The history and antiquities of Bicester, Oxfordshire. (With.. Kennett's glossary)* 1816
DUNLAP, William *Memoirs of George Fred. Cooke, Esq., late of the Theatre Royal, Covent Garden* 2 vols. 1813
Thirty years ago; or, The memoirs of a water drinker 2 vols. 1836
DUNLOP, Derrick Melville ed. *Textbook of medical treatment* 1939
—(ed. 10) ed. D. M. Dunlop & S. Alstead 1966
DUNLOP, William ed. *A collection of confessions of faith, catechisms, directories, books of discipline etc. of publick authority in the church of Scotland* 1719–22
DUNMAN, Thomas *A glossary of biological, anatomical and physiological terms* 1879 (1889)
DUNMORE, Charles A. Murray, 7th Earl of *The Pamirs* 1893
DUNN, Henry A. C. *Fencing* (All England series) 1889
DUNN, Robert *The ornithologist's guide to the islands of Orkney and Shetland* 1837
DUNN, Robert *The shameless diary of an explorer* 1907
DUNNE, Finley Peter *Mr. Dooley in peace and in war* 1898
DUNPHY, Eamon *Only a game? The diary of a professional footballer* ed. P. Ball 1976
DUNTON, John *D.'s Ladies dictionary, being a general entertainment for the fair sex* 1694
Letters written from New England 1686 (Prince Soc. 1867)
Dupin's (L. Ellies-) New ecclesiastical history of the XVI century tr. 1706–10
D.'s New ecclesiastical history of the XVII century tr. D. Cotes 1725
D.'s New history of ecclesiastical writers, containing an account of the authors of the several books of the Old and New Testaments 1692–93
DU PONCEAU, Pierre E. *A dissertation on the nature and character of the Chinese system of writing* 1838
DUPPA, Brian *Angels rejoicing for sinners repenting* 1648
Holy rules and helps to devotion a1662 (1675)
The soule's soliloquie and conference with conscience 1648
DUPPA, Richard *Travels in Italy* etc. 1828 (1829)
Du Quesne's (A.) New voyage to the East Indies tr. 1696
DURANTE, James Francis ('Jimmy') & KEFOED, Jack C. *Night clubs* 1931
D'URFEY, Thomas *Butler's ghost, or Hudibras, the fourth part* 1682
Collin's walk through London and Westminster, a poem in burlesque 1690
The comical history of Don Quixote (a comedy in three parts) 1694–96
Madam Fickle: or the witty false one, a comedy 1676 (1677)
New operas, with comical stories and poems on several occasions a1721 (1721)
The progress of honesty by T. D. 1681
Tales tragical and comical 1704
Wit and mirth: or pills to purge melancholy, being a collection of.. ballads and songs 1719 (1872)
Durham. A description.. of all the ancient monuments, rites and customes within the monastical church of Durham before the suppression 1593 (Surtees Soc. 1845, 1903)
D. depositions and other ecclesiastical proceedings from the courts of D. 1530–91 (Surtees Soc. 1845)
The D. household book 1530–34 (Surtees Soc. 1844)
Extracts from the account rolls of the abbey of D. 1278–1580 (Surtees Soc. 1898–1901)
Halmota prioratus Dunelmensis, containing extracts from the halmote court or manor rolls of the prior and convent of D. 1296–1384 (Surtees Soc. 1889)
Rites of D., being a description etc. (as above) 1593 (Surtees Soc. 1903)
Wills and inventories from the registry at D. 1563–99 (Surtees Soc. 1860)
DURHAM, James *A commentary upon the book of the Revelation* a1658 (1680)
A practical exposition of the X Commandments a1658 (1675)
DURHAM, William *Maran-atha; the second advent* 1651 (1652)
Durham glossary 1896 *See* PALGRAVE, F. M. T.
DURNFORD, Charles & EAST, E. H. *Reports of cases.. in the Court of King's Bench* 1787–1800
DURRANT, Philip John & DURRANT, Beryl *Introduction to advanced inorganic chemistry* 1962
DURRELL, Gerald Malcolm *The Bafut beagles* 1954
Catch me a Colobus 1972
The drunken forest 1956
Encounters with animals 1958
Menagerie Manor 1964
My family and other animals 1956
The overloaded ark 1953
Three singles to adventure 1954
Two in the bush 1966
The whispering land 1961
A zoo in my luggage 1960
DURRELL, Lawrence George *Balthazar* 1958
Bitter lemons 1957
Clea 1960
Justine 1957
Mountolive 1958
Nunquam 1970
Spirit of place: letters and essays on travel ed. A. G. Thomas 1969
Tunc 1968
DURST, Paul *Badge of infamy* 1968
DURY, George Harry ed. *Essays in geomorphology* 1966
DURY or DURYE, John *Israel's call to march out of Babylon unto Jerusalem* 1645 (1646)
Just re-proposals to humble proposals 1650
DU TOIT, Alexander Logie *Our wandering continents* 1937
DUTTON, Amy *The streets and lanes of a city* 1871
Du Val, Claude. The memoires of monsieur Du Vall (by W. Pope) 1670
DU VERGER, S. *Camus' (J. P.) Admirable events selected out of his foure bookes, together with his morall relations* tr. 1639
DU WES, Giles *An introductorie for to lerne to rede, to pronounce and to speke French trewly* c1532 (in J. Palsgrave, Leclaircissement de la langue Française, 1852 ed.)
DWIGHT, Margaret van Horn *A journey to Ohio in 1810* ed. M. Farrand 1912
DWIGHT, Timothy *Theology explained and defended* a1817 (1819, 1830)
Travels in New-England and New-York a1817 (1823)
DYAN, Meg *All in a man's keeping* 1894
'DYCE, Gilbert' (Percy H. Fitzgerald) *Bella Donna: a romance* 1864
DYCHE, Thomas *A dictionary of all the words commonly us'd in the English tongue* 1723
—— & PARDON, W. *A new general English dictionary* 1735 (1740, 1758)
DYER, Sir Edward *Writings in verse and prose* a1607 (Grosart 1872)
The prayse of nothing 1585
DYER, John *Poems* a1758 (1761, 1790)
The fleece, a poem 1757 (1807)
Grongar-hill 1727 (1748)
DYER, Robert *Nine years of an actor's life* 1833
DYER, T. F. THISELTON-, W. T. THISELTON- *See* THISELTON-DYER
Dyet of Poland, The, a satyr (by De Foe) 1705
DYKE, Daniel *The mystery of self-deceiving* 1614 (1615)
Two treatises, the one a most fruitfull exposition upon Philemon, the other the schoole of affliction 1618
DYKE, Jeremiah *A caveat for Archippus* 1619 (1620)
A counterpoison against covetousness 1619 (1620)
Divers select sermons a1620 (1640)
A worthy communicant; or a treatise shewing the due order of receiving the sacrament of the Lord's supper a1620 (1640)
DYKES, Oswald *English proverbs with moral reflexions* 1709 (ed. 2)
DYMMOK, John *A treatise of Ireland* 1600 (Tracts relating to Ireland II, Irish Archæol. Soc. 1843)
DYOTT, William *Diary 1781–1845* ed. R. W. Jeffery 2 vols. 1907
DYSON, Edward George *Fact'ry 'ands* 1906

E

E., B. *A new dictionary of the terms ancient and modern of the canting crew* a1700
E., O. 1600 *See* SUTCLIFFE, M.
E., T. *The lawes resolutions of womens rights* (Preface signed, I. L. Epistle to the reader signed, T. E.) 1632
E. D. S. *See* English Dialect Society
E.E.T.S. *See* Early English Text Society
EACHARD, John *The grounds and occasions of the contempt of the clergy and religion enquired into* 1670 (in Arber, Eng. Garner VII)
Some observations upon the answer to the above 1671
Mr. Hobbs's State of nature considered 1672 (1705)
EADDY, Percy Allen *Hull down* 1933
EADIE, John *A biblical cyclopædia* 1849
A commentary on the Greek text of the Epistle of St. Paul to the Galatians 1869
— *to the Thessalonians* a1876 (1877)
Eadwine's Canterbury psalter c1150 (E.E.T.S. 1889)
EAGLE, William *The act for the commutation of tithes in England and Wales* 1836 (1837)
A treatise on the law of tithes 1830
EAGLES, John *The sketcher* 1833–36 (1856)
EAGLESON, Robert D. & McKIE, Ian *The terminology of Australian national football* 3 parts 1968–9 (Sydney University: Australian Language Research Centre: Occasional Papers Nos. 12–14)
EAGLETON, Terence Francis *Criticism and ideology: a study in Marxist literary theory* 1976
EALES, Mary *Receipts* 1718
EARBERY, Matthias *Burnett's (T.) Of the state of the dead* tr. 1727 (1728)
Reflections upon modern fanaticism 1720
EARL, John *How to choose and use tuners and amplifiers* 1970
EARLE, Augustus *A narrative of a nine months' residence in New Zealand, in 1827; together with a journal of a residence in Tristan D'Acunha* 1832
—(new ed.) ed. E. H. McCormick 1966
EARLE, Bp. John *Micro-cosmographie; or, a peece of the world discovered* 1628 (Arber 1868)
EARLE, John *English plant names from the tenth to the fifteenth century* 1880
ed. *A hand-book to the land-charters, and other Saxonic documents* v.d. (1888)
The philology of the English tongue 1871 (1873, 1879)
The psalter of the Great Bible of 1539, 1894
See also *Anglo-Saxon chronicle*
Earliest complete English prose psalter, The See *Psalter*
Earliest English wills in the Court of Probate, London, The fifty 1387–1439, 1454 (E.E.T.S. 1882)
Early English alliterative poems in the west-midland dialect A. Pearl. B. Cleanness. C. Patience. 13.. (E.E.T.S. 1864–69)
Early English miscellanies, in prose and verse c1485 (Warton Club 1856)
Early English poems and lives of saints a1325 (Philol. Soc. 1862)
Early English psalter See *Psalter*
Early English Text Society *Publications* (1864–)
Early music 1973–
Early prose romances, A collection of 1500–25 (Thoms 1828)
EARP, George B. *The gold colonies of Australia* 1852
Earth-science reviews 1966–
Earth upon earth See *Erthe upon erthe*

Earthquake Peru (A true and particular relation of the dreadful earthquake which happen'd at Lima, the capital of Peru, 28 Oct. 1746) tr. 1748
East, Sir Edward H. *Reports of cases argued and determined in the Court of King's Bench* 1801–14
See also Durnford, C.
East Africa journal 1964–
East African annual 1936–
East African Standard (Nairobi, Kenya) 1902–
East Anglian glossary See Forby, R.; Rye, W.; Spurdens, W. T.
East Hampton, New York *Records* 5 vols. 1887–1905
East India Company, Letters received by the 1602–17 (1896–1902)
East India sketch book; or, life in India 1832–33
East London (Daily) Dispatch (East London, Cape Province) 1872–1925
Eastern Evening News (Norwich) 1882–
Eastern Province Herald (Port Elizabeth, S. Africa) 1845–
Easther, Alfred *A glossary of the dialect of Almondbury and Huddersfield. Complied by the late A Easther, ed. by Thomas Lee* 1883 (E.D.S.)
Eastlake, Charles Lock *Hints on household taste in furniture, upholstery and other details* 1868
Eastlake, Elizabeth, Lady *Life of John Gibson, R.A., sculptor* 1870
Eastman, Charles Rochester, et al. tr. *K. A. von Zittel's Text-book of palæontology* 3 vols. 1900–25
Eastman, Max Forrester tr. *L. Trotsky's The history of the Russian Revolution* 3 vols. 1932–3
Eastwick, Edward B. *Dry leaves from young Egypt: being a glance at Sindh* 1849
See also *Lutfullah*
Eastwood, Jonathan & Wright, William A. *The Bible word-book: a glossary of old English Bible words* 1866
Eaton, Amos *A manual of botany for the northern states* 1817
— (ed. 2 with title —— *for the northern and middle states*) 1818
Eaton, John *The honey-combe of free justification by Christ alone* 1642
Eaton, Timothy, & Co. Ltd. *A shopper's view of Canada's past: pages from Eaton's catalogues 1886–1930* 1969
Ebb and flow. A novel 1859 (1863)
Eberhart, Mignon Good *Danger money* 1974 (UK 1975)
Ebers, John *Seven years of the King's Theatre* 1828
Eby, Cecil DeGrotte *The siege of the Alcázar* 1965 (UK 1966)
Eccles, Arthur S. *Sciatica* 1893
Eccles, William Henry *Wireless telegraphy and telephony: a handbook of formulae, data and information* 1915
Ecclesiologist, The 1843–61
Ecclestone, Alan *A staircase for silence* 1977
Echard, Laurence *A general ecclesiastical history* 1702 (1710)
The history of England, from the first entrance of Julius Cæsar to the end of the reign of James II 1707–18
Plautus's comedies, Amphitryon, Epidicus, and Rudens tr. 1694
Echo, The (newspaper; various years) 1868–1905
Eclectic review 1805–68
Ecological monographs 1931–
Ecology 1920–
Economic geology and Bulletin of the Society of Economic Geologists 1905–
Economic journal 1891–
Economist, The 1843–
Ecton, John *A state of the proceedings of the corporation of the governours of the bounty of Queen Anne for the augmentation of the maintenance of the poor clergy, from 1704–18* 1719
Eddington, Arthur Stanley *The internal constitution of the stars* 1926
The nature of the physical world 1928
New pathways in science 1935
Report on the relativity theory of gravitation 1918
Space, time and gravitation: an outline of the general relativity theory 1920
Eddison, Eric Rücker *A fish dinner in Memison* 1941
— (new ed.) 1968
The Mezentian Gate 1958
— (new ed.) 1972
Mistress of mistresses 1935
The worm Ouroboros 1922
Eddy, Arthur Jerome *Cubists and Post-Impressionism* 1914 (UK 1915)
Eddy, Mary Baker *Science and health* 1875
Edelman, Jacob Murray *Political language* 1977
Eden, Charles H. *My wife and I in Queensland* 1872
Eden, F. *A garden in Venice* 1903
Eden, Richard *Cortes' (Martin) Arte of nauigation* tr. 1561
The decades of the newe worlde or west India tr. 1555 (Arber 1885)
A treatyse of the newe India tr. 1553 (Arber 1885)
Edersheim, Alfred *The life and times of Jesus the Messiah* 1883; new and revised ed. 1886
Edgar, Andrew *Old Church life in Scotland* 1885–86
Edgar, John G. *Runnymede and Lincoln Fair* 1866
Edgcumbe, Kenelm *Industrial electrical measuring instruments* 1908
Maria Edgeworth in France and Switzerland: selections from the Edgeworth family letters ed. C. Colvin 1979
Edgeworth, Maria *Letters from England 1813–1844* ed. C. Colvin 1971
Tales and novels v.d. (1832–33)
Belinda 1801
Castle Rackrent 1800
Early lessons 1801
Harrington 1817
Harry and Lucy concluded; being the last part of Early lessons 1825
Helen 1834
Leonora 1806
Letters for literary ladies 1795
Modern Griselda 1804
Moral tales 1801
Ormond 1817
The parent's assistant 1800
Patronage 1814
Popular tales 1804
Tales from fashionable life 1809–12
Life and letters ed. A. J. C. Hare (1894)
—— & Richard L. *Essay on Irish bulls* 1802
Practical education 1798 (1822)
Edgeworth, Maria in France and Switzerland: selections from the Edgeworth family letters ed. C. Colvin 1979
Edgren, August H. *Rydberg's (A. V.) Magic of the middle ages* tr. 1879
Edib, Halidé *The clown and his daughter* 1935
Edinburgh, Charters and other documents relating to the city of 1143–1540 (Scott. Burgh Rec. Soc. 1871)
Edinburgh, Extracts from the records of the burgh of 1403–1589 (Scott. Burgh Rec. Soc. 1869–82)
Edinburgh, Medical essays and observations, revised and published by a Society in 1733–44
Edinburgh, Registrum cartarum ecclesie sancti Egidii de 1344–1567 (App. –1648) (Bannatyne Club 1859)
Edinburgh encyclopædia, The, conducted by D. Brewster a1830
Edinburgh Evening News 1873– (title varies)
Edinburgh medical and surgical journal 1805–55
Edinburgh new philosophical journal 1826–64
Edinburgh Obstetrical Society *Transactions* 1868–1921
Edinburgh review, The 1802–
Edington, George Miller & Gilles, Herbert Michael *Pathology in the tropics* 1969
— (ed. 2) 1976
Editha, St. c1420 See *Chronicon Vilodunense*
Edlin, Herbert Leeson *Collins guide to tree planting and cultivation* 1970
The forester's handbook 1953
Edmondes, Clement *Observations upon Cæsars Commentaries* 1600 (1604)
Edmonds, Henry *Botany for beginners* 1896
Edmondson, Joseph *A complete body of heraldry* 1780
Edmondston, Arthur *A view of the ancient and present state of the Zetland Islands* 1809
Edmondston, Biot & Saxby, Jessie M. E. *The home of a naturalist* 1888
Edmondston, Eliza *Sketches and tales of the Shetland Islands* 1856
Edmondston, Thomas *An etymological glossary of the Shetland and Orkney dialect* 1866 (Philol. Soc.)
Edmonton Journal (Edmonton, Alberta) 1903–
Edmundson, George *The Church in Rome in the first century* 1913
Educational review, The 1891–93
Edward, David B. *The history of Texas* 1836
Edward I See *Elegy*
Edward II, Household ordinances of tr. 1601 *See* Tate, F.
Edward II, A poem on the times of c1325 (Percy Soc. 1849; in Political songs, Camden Soc. 1839)
Edward the third, The raigne of King 1596 (in Shakespeare Apocrypha, 1908)
Edward IV, Historie of the arrival of 1471 (Camden Soc. 1838)
Wardrobe accounts of a1483 (Nicolas 1830)
See also *Liber niger*
Edward VI *Iniunccions* 1547
Journal a1553 (1884)
Literary remains a1553 (Roxb. Club 1857–58)
Edwardes, Annie *A Girton girl* 3 vols. 1885
Edwardes, Charles *Sardinia and the Sardes* 1889
Edwards, Amelia B. *Barbara's history* 1864
Half a million of money 1865
Hand and glove 1858
Miss Carew 1865
A thousand miles up the Nile 1877
Edwards, Annie *Archie Lovell* 1866
Edwards, Anthony William Fairbank *Likelihood: an account of the statistical concept of likelihood and its application to scientific inference* 1972
Edwards, Bryan *The history civil and commercial of the British colonies in the West Indies* 1793–1801
Edwards, C. A. *Organs and organ building* 1881
Edwards, D. H. *Historical guide to Edzell and Glenesk districts* 1893
ed. *Modern Scottish poets, with biographical and critical notices* v.d. (1880–97)
Edwards, Edward *Life of Sir W. Raleigh* 1868
Edwards, Elwyn Hartley *Saddlery* 1963
Edwards, George *A natural history of uncommon birds, and of some other rare and undescribed animals* 1743–51
Gleanings of natural history 1758–64
Edwards, George *The appropriate measures of true policy, competent to remove our burdens, grievances, etc.* 1813
A plain practical plan, by which Great Britain may extricate herself from her present difficulties 1808
Edwards' (H. M.) Manual of zoology tr. R. Knox 1856
Edwards, John *A demonstration of the existence and providence of God* 1690
A discourse concerning the authority, stile and perfection of the books of the Old and New Testament 1693–95
A farther enquiry into several remarkable texts of the Old and New Testament 1692
Edwards, John Newman *Shelby and his men; or, The war in the west* 1867
Edwards, Jonathan *Works* v.d. (1804–47)
A careful and strict enquiry into the modern prevailing notions of that freedom of will, which is supposed to be essential to moral agency, etc. 1754
The doctrine of original sin as it was always held in the Catholick church 1711
A history of the work of redemption 1786
Edwards, Matilda Betham- *Felicia* 1875
John and I 1862 (1876)
Kitty 1869
Next of kin wanted 1887
Edwards, Richard *The excellent comedie of two the moste faithfullest freendes, Damon and Pithias* a1566 (1571; Hazl. Dodsley)
The paradyse of dainty deuises a1566 (1576, 1578)
Edwards, Thomas *Gangræna; or, a catalogue and discovery of many of the errours, heresies, blasphemies and pernicious practices of the sectaries of this time* 1646
Edwards, Thomas *A supplement to Mr. Warburton's edition of Shakespear; being the canons of criticism, and glossary* (anon.) 1748
Edwards, Thomas *Strathearn lyrics and other poems* 1889
Edwards's botanical register 1829–47
Edwin 1803
Eedes, Richard *Christ exalted and wisdom justified* 1659
'Egan, Lesley' (Barbara Elizabeth Linington) *Blind search* 1977
Paper chase 1972 (UK 1973)
Egan, Pierce *Anecdotes of the turf, the chase, the ring and the stage* 1827
Book of sports and mirror of life 1832
Boxiana; or, Sketches of ancient and modern pugilism 3 vols. 1812–21 (Vol. IV, 1824, by J. Badcock)
— (new ser.) 2 vols. 1828–9
Life in London; or, the day and night scenes of Jerry Hawthorn, etc. 1821
The life of an actor 1825
Real life in London 1821
See also Grose, F.
Eger. The history of sir Egeir, sir Gryme, and sir Gray-steill a1650 (in Laing, Early metrical tales 1826; Percy MS., Hales and Furnivall, I)
'Egerton, George' *Discords* 1894
Egerton, John C. *Sussex folk and Sussex ways* 1884
Egerton papers, The. A collection of public and private documents, chiefly illustrative of the times of Elizabeth and James I 15.. (Camden Soc. 1840)
Eggleston, Edward *The circuit rider: a tale of the heroic age* 1874
The end of the world: a love story 1872
The faith doctor 1891
The Graysons, a story of Illinois 1888
The Hoosier school-master 1871 (UK 1872)
Roxy 1878
The transit of civilization from England to America in the seventeenth century 1901
Eglamour, The romance of Sir (Camden Soc. 1844)
Egleton, Clive *Seven days to a killing* 1973
'Eha' (E. H. Atken) *The tribes on my frontier* 1881 (1883)
Ehrenberg, Victor L. *From Solon to Socrates: Greek history and civilization during the sixth and fifth centuries B.C.* 1968
Εἰκὼν βασιλική. The pourtraicture of his sacred maiestie in his solitudes and sufferings 1648
Εἰρηνικον, a poeme, wherein is perswaded the composing of the differences of all the faithfull in Christ 1656
Einstein, Albert *See* Adams, Edwin Plimpton
Einstein, Alfred *Music in the Romantic era* 1947
Eiseley, Loren Carey *The immense journey* 1957
Eissler, Manuel *The modern high explosives* 1884
Ekwall, Bror Oscar Eilert *The place-names of Lancashire* 1922
Elaboratory laid open, The; or the secrets of modern chemistry and pharmacy revealed 1750
Eland, William *Hemerologium astronomicum, or an almanack for 1656* 1656
A tutor to astrology. Whereunto is added an ephemeris for the years 1694, 1695, 1696 1694 (1704)
Elborowe, Thomas *The famous epistles of Saint Polycarp and Saint Ignatius, with the epistle of Saint Barnabas* tr. 1668
Elderfield, Christopher *The civill right of tythes* 1650
Elder's house, The; or the three converts 1850
Elderton, William *The panges of loue and louers fittes* 1559
Electrical communication 1922–
Electrical world (title varies) 1899–
Electrician, The 1861–1952
Electricity in daily life; a popular account of the applications of electricity to every day uses by C. F. Brackett, F. L. Pope, etc. 1891
Electrochemical industry 1902–9 (1905–9 with title *Electrochemical and metallurgical industry*)
Electronic engineering 1941–
Electronics (New York) 1930–
Elegy on the author of The true-born Englishman etc. 1704
Elegy on the death of Edward I 1307 (in Political songs, Camden Soc. 1839; Warton, Hist. Eng. poetry I. 1840)
Elene a900 *See* Cynewulf

Elgin, James Bruce, 8th Earl of *Letters and journals* a1863 (1872)
Elgin, The records of See Cramond, W.
Eliason, Norman E. *Tarheel talk: an historical study of the English language in North Carolina to 1860* 1956
Eliot, Charles Norton Edgcumbe *A Finnish grammar* 1890
See also: 'Odysseus'
'Eliot, George' (Marian Evans) *Adam Bede* 1859
Amos Barton 1858
College breakfast party 1874
Daniel Deronda 1876
Essays v.d. (1884)
tr. *L. Feuerbach's The essence of Christianity* 1854
Felix Holt 1866
The George Eliot letters ed. G. S. Haight 7 vols. 1954–6
Impressions of Theophrastus Such 1879
tr. *D. F. Strauss's The life of Jesus, critically examined* 3 vols. 1846
Middlemarch 1872
The mill on the Floss 1860
Romola 1863
Scenes of clerical life 1858
Silas Marner 1861
The Spanish gypsy 1868
Life of, by J. W. Cross (1885)
Eliot, John *Bertrand de Loque's Discourses of warre and single combat* tr. 1591
Eliot, Thomas Stearns tr. *Anabasis* by 'St.-J. Perse' (A. St. Léger Léger) 1930
Ara vos prec 1920
Burnt Norton 1941
The cocktail party: a comedy 1950
Collected poems, 1909–1935 1936
Collected poems, 1909–1962 1963
The confidential clerk 1954
The dry salvages 1941
East Coker 1940
The elder statesman 1959
Elizabethan essays 1934
The family reunion 1939
Little Gidding 1942
Murder in the cathedral 1935
Notes towards the definition of culture 1948
Old Possum's book of practical cats 1939
On poetry and poets 1957
Poems 1919
Prufrock, and other observations 1917
The rock: a pageant play 1934
Selected essays 1917–1932 1932
— (ed. 3) 1951; new impression 1953
Sweeney agonistes 1932
The waste land 1922 (UK 1923)
The waste land: a facsimile and transcript of the original drafts including the annotations of Ezra Pound ed. V. Eliot 1971
Eliza Warwick, History of. By a lady 1778
Eliza's babes: or the Virgin's offering 1652
Elizabeth, Queen *Copie of a letter to the Earle of Leycester* 1586
Englishings of Boethius, De consolatione philosophiae 1593; *Plutarch, De curiositate* 1598; *Horace, De arte poetica* (*part*) 1593 (E.E.T.S. 1899)
See also Gilbert, Sir H.; Nichols, John
Elizabeth and her German garden 1898 *See* Von Arnim, Mary Annette
Elizabeth, Queen, and the Levant Company 1904
Elizabeth of York, Privy purse expenses of 14.. (Nicolas 1830)
Ellacombe, Henry T. *The church bells of Devon: with a list of those in Cornwall. To which is added a Supplement on various matters relating to the 'Bells of the church'* 1872
Practical remarks on belfries and ringers 1850 (1871)
'Ellan, B. J.' *Spitfire!: the experiences of a fighter pilot* 1942
Ellenborough, Edward Law, Earl of *A political diary 1828–30* (1881)
Ellery Queen's mystery magazine 1941–
Ellicott, Andrew *Journal* 1802 (1803)
Ellicott, Charles J. *A commentary on St. Paul's Epistle to the Galatians* 1854
The destiny of the creature: and other sermons 1858
Historical lectures on the life of Our Lord 1860
Ellin, Stanley *The bind* 1970 (UK ed. with title *The man from nowhere* 1971)
The eighth circle 1958 (UK 1959)
Elliot, Anne *An old man's favour* 1887
Elliot, Frances M. *Roman gossip* 1894
Elliot, George *A very true report of the apprehension of that arch-Papist Edmund Campion* 1581 (in Arber, Eng. Garner VIII)
Elliot, John Herbert *Duel* 1969
Elliott, Charles W. *The New England history, from the discovery of the continent by the Northmen, A.D. 986 to 1776* 1857
Elliott, Ebenezer *Poetical works* 1840
— new and revised ed. (1876)
The splendid village: corn law rhymes; and other poems 1832 (1904)
Ellis, Alexander J. *On early English pronunciation, with especial reference to Shakspere and Chaucer* 1869–89 (Philol. Soc., E.E.T.S., and Chaucer Soc.)
Ellis, Carleton *The chemistry of synthetic resins* 2 vols. 1935
Ellis, Clement *The vanity of scoffing* 1674
Ellis, George ed. *Specimens of early English metrical romances* v.d. (1805)
ed. *Specimens of the early English poets* v.d. (1790)
Ellis, George V. *Demonstrations of anatomy* 1840
Ellis, Henry *A voyage to Hudson's Bay in 1746–7, for discovering a north-west passage* 1748
Ellis, Sir Henry *The British Museum: Elgin and Phigaleian marbles* 1833 (1846)
ed. *Original letters illustrative of English history* v.d. (1824–46)
ed. *Original letters of eminent literary men of the sixteenth, seventeenth, and eighteenth centuries* v.d. (Camden Soc. 1843)
Ellis, Henry Havelock *Studies in the psychology of sex* 7 vols. 1897–1928
Ellis, John *S. Austin imitated; or retractations and repentings in reference to the late civil and ecclesiastical changes in this nation* 1662
Ellis, John *The knowledge of divine things from revelation* 1743 (1811)
Ellis, Joseph *Caesar in Egypt, Costanza and other poems* 1876
Ellis, Philip *Sermon preach'd before the King and Queen* 1685 (1686)
Ellis, Robert *The laws and practical regulations of the customs* 1837–41
Ellis, Robinson *The poems and fragments of Catullus* tr. 1871
Ellis, Sarah *Pique, a novel* (anon.) 1850
Ellis, T. Mullett *The three cat's-eye rings, a tale of the pursuit of the Khalifa* 1899
Ellis, William *A compleat system of experienced improvement, made in sheep, grass-lambs, and house-lambs* 1749
Chiltern and Vale farming 1733
The country housewife's family companion 1750
Every farmer his own farrier a1758 (1759)
The modern husbandman 1750
New experiments in husbandry for the month of April 1736
The practical farmer 1732 (1759)
The timber-tree improved 1738
Ellis, William *A journal of a tour around Hawaii* 1825
Ellis, William A. *Glasenapp's (C. F.) Life of R. Wagner* tr. 1900–08
Ellis, William S. *The antiquities of heraldry* 1869
Ellistone, John *The epistles of Jacob Behmen. Also, a warning from J. Beem to such as reade his writings* tr. 1649 (1886)
Ellwanger, George H. *The garden's story* 1890
Ellwood, Thomas *Davideis; the life of David, king of Israel, a sacred poem* 1712
The history of the life of, written by his own hand a1713 (1714)
Ellwood, Thomas *Lakeland and Iceland, being a glossary of words in the dialect of Cumberland, Westmorland, and North Lancashire which seem allied to or identical with the Icelandic or Norse* 1895 (E.D.S.)
Ellys, Bp. Anthony *A plea for the sacramental test* (anon.) 1736
Tracts on the liberty spiritual and temporal of Protestants in England a1761 (1763–65)
Elmes, James *A general and bibliographical dictionary of the fine arts* 1824–26
Metropolitan improvements 1827
A practical treatise on the law of dilapidations 1823 (1829)
Elmhirst, Edward Pennell *The cream of Leicestershire* 1883
Elmore, H. M. *The British mariner's directory and guide to the trade and navigation of the Indian and China seas* 1802
Elphinston, James *The epigrams of M. V. Martial* tr. 1782
The principles of the English language digested 1765
Propriety ascertained in her picture 1786–87
Elphinstone, Howard W., Norton, R. F., & Clark, J. W. *Rules for the interpretation of deeds* 1885
Elphinstone, Mountstuart *An account of the kingdom of Caubul* 1815 (1842)
History of India 1841
Elsing, Henry *Notes of the debates in the House of Lords* 1621 (Camden Soc. 1870)
Elton, Charles I. *Origins of English history* 1882
Elton, Edward *The complaint of a sanctified sinner answered; or an explanation of the seventh chapter of the epistle of St. Paul to the Romans* 1618 (1622)
Elton, Romeo *Life of Roger Williams* 1852 (1853)
Elvin, Charles N. *A dictionary of heraldry* 1889
A synopsis of heraldry 1866
Elvina; a novel 1792
Elworthy, Frederick T. *The evil eye* 1895
The West Somerset word-book 1886 (E.D.S.)
Ely, Bishop of a1707 *See* Patrick, S.; a1723 *See* Fleetwood, W.
Ely, Richard T. *French and German socialism in modern times* 1883
An introduction to political economy 1891
Ely, Sacrist rolls of 1291–1360 (1907)
Elyot, Sir Thomas *The boke named The gouernour* 1531 (repr. 1880; 1537, 1580)
The castel of helth 1539 (1541)
Dictionary 1538, 1542, 1545
— inriched by T. Cooper 1548, 1552
The defence of good women 1545
The doctrinal of princes tr. 1534
The image of gouernance 1540–41
Of the knowledge whiche maketh a wise man 1533
Pasquil the playne 1532 (1540)
Em 1592 See *Faire Em*
Emanuel, Henry *Diamonds and precious stones* 1865
Emare c1400 (Ritson, Metr. rom. II; E.E.T.S. 1906)
Emblen, Donald Lewis *Peter Mark Roget, the word and the man* 1970
Emerson, James *Christianity in Ceylon* 1850
Emerson, Peter H. *Birds, beasts, and fishes of the Norfolk Broadland* 1895
East coast yarns 1891
English idyls 1889
On English lagoons 1892
Marsh-leaves from the Norfolk Broad-land 1898
Signor Lippo, burnt-cork artist 1893
A son of the fens 1892
Wild life on a tidal water 1890
Emerson, Ralph Waldo *Journals* ed. E. W. Emerson & W. E. Forbes 10 vols. 1909–14
Works v.d. (Bohn)
The conduct of life 1860
Correspondence with Carlyle v.d. (1883)
English traits 1856
Essays 1841–44
Lectures on the times 1841
Letters and social aims 1876
Miscellanies 1855
Nature 1836
New England reformers 1844
Poems v.d. (1847, 1857)
Representative men 1847
Society and solitude 1870
Emerson, William *The doctrine of fluxions* 1743
The method of increments 1763
The principles of mechanicks 1758
Emerton, James H. *The common spiders of the United States* 1902
Emillianne, G. D' See D'Emillianne, G.
Emmot, George *A Northern blast, or the spiritual Quaker converted* 1655
Emory, William Hemsley *Notes of a military reconnaissance, from Fort Leavenworth, in Missouri, to San Diego, in California* 1848
Empey, Arthur Guy *'Over the top' by an American soldier who went, together with Tommy's dictionary of the trenches* 1917 (UK also 1917 with title *From the fire step*)
Empson, William *The gathering storm* 1940
Poems 1935
Seven types of ambiguity 1930
Some versions of pastoral 1935
The structure of complex words 1951
Encounter 1953–
Encouragement to sea-faring people of Great Britain, Reasons for giving 1739
Encyclopædia Americana 1829–33, 1848; *Suppl.* 1883
Encyclopædia Britannica 1768–71; (ed. 2) 1777–84; (ed. 3) 1788–97; (ed. 4) 1801–10; (ed. 5) 1815–17; (ed. 6) 1823–24; (ed. 7) 1830–42; (ed. 8) 1853–60; (ed. 9) 1875–89; (ed. 10) 1902–03; (ed. 11) 1910–11; (ed. 12) 1922; (ed. 13) 1926
Encyclopædia Britannica book of the year See *Britannica book of the year*
Encyclopedia Canadiana ed. J. E. Robbins 10 vols. 1957–8
Encyclopaedia Judaica ed. C. Roth & G. Wigoder 16 vols. 1971–2
Encyclopædia medica ed. C. Watson 15 vols. 1899–1910
Encyclopædia metropolitana 1818–45
Encyclopedia of chemical technology See Kirk, Raymond E. & Othmer, Donald F.
Encyclopædia of the laws of England 1897–1903
Encyclopædia of the laws of Scotland, Green's ed. John Chisholm 1897–1904
Encyclopaedia of New Zealand, An ed. A. H. McLintock 3 vols. 1966
Encyclopedia of philosophy, The ed. P. Edwards et al. 8 vols. 1967
Encyclopedia of polymer science and technology ed. H. Mark et al. 1964–
Encyclopædia of practical cookery ed. T. F. Garrett 1892–94
Encyclopaedia of psychology ed. H. J. Eysenck et al. 3 vols. 1972
Encyclopædia of religion and ethics ed. J. Hastings 13 vols. 1908–26
Encyclopædia of sport, The 1897–98
Encyclopedia of sports, games and pastimes 1935
Encyclopædia of the social sciences ed. E. R. A. Seligman et al. 15 vols. 1930–5
Encyclopædia Perthensis 1816
Encyclopædic dictionary, The by R. Hunter et al. 7 vols. 1879–88
— (reissue with Suppl. 1902–4)
Encyclopaedic dictionary of physics ed. J. Thewlis et al. 9 vols. 1961–4: Suppl. 2 vols. 1966–7
Encyclopedy, Select essays from the 1772
Endeavour 1942–
Enderbie, Percy *Cambria triumphans; or Brittain in its perfect lustre* 1661
Endocrinology 1917–
Enfield, William *The history of philosophy, drawn up from Brucker's Historia critica philosophiæ* 1791
Engel, Carl *A descriptive catalogue of the musical instruments in the South Kensington Museum* 1870
— (ed. 2) 1874
Introduction to the study of national music 1866
Music of the most ancient nations 1864
Musical instruments 1875
Engineer, The 1865–
Engineering 1866–
Engineering magazine 1898 (vol. XVI)
Engineering news-record 1874–

England and Germany, Letters and other documents illustrating the relations between 1618–19 (Camden Soc. 1865)
England's confession 1659
England's gazetteer 1751 (1778)
Englands Helicon (Poems collected and edited by John Bodenham) 1600 (1614; ed. Bullen 1887)
England's monarchy asserted, and proved to be the freest state, and the best common-wealth throughout the world 1659
Englands Parnassus 1600 *See* Allott, R.
Englands welcome to James, King of England 1603
Englische Studien. Herausgegeben von E. Kölbing 1877–
English chronicle c1465 See *Chronicle*
English church furniture See Peacock, E.
English conquest of Ireland, The. A.D. *1166–85 Mainly from the 'Expugnatio Hibernica' of Giraldus Cambrensis* c1425, c1440 (E.E.T.S. 1896)
English dialect dictionary See Wright, J.
English Dialect Society *Publications* 1873–
English encyclopædia, The 1802–18
English garner See Arber, E.
English gilds a1400 (E.E.T.S. 1870)
English historical review 1886–
English home, Our 1861
English illustrated magazine, The 1883–
English journal (US National Council of Teachers of English) 1912–
English language teaching 1946– (from 1973 with title *English language teaching journal*)
English life; or, manners at home 1825
Englishman, The (by R. Steele) 1713–14
English mechanic, The (title varies) 1865–1923
English metrical homilies from MSS. of the fourteenth century c1325 (ed. Small 1862)
English miscellanies, A volume of, illustrating the history and language of the northern counties of England 14.. (Surtees Soc. 1888)
English review, The 1905–
English Spanish pilgrime 1629 *See* Wadsworth, J.
English studies: a journal of English letters and philology 1919–
English Theophrastus, The: or the manners of the age 1702
Englishwoman, The 1909–21
Englishwoman in India, The. By a lady resident 1864
Englishwoman in Russia, The; by a lady, ten years resident 1855
Ennes, Harold Eugene *Television broadcasting: equipment, systems and operating fundamentals* 1971
Enquiry concerning the election of the sheriffs of London, A modest 1682
Enquiry whether the tripe-wife etc. 1595 See *Quest*
Ensor, Robert Charles Kirkwood *England, 1870–1914* 1936
Enterlude of youth 1557 (in Hazl. Dodsley)
Entertainer, The 1717–18
Entick, John *History and survey of London and places adjacent* 1766
Entomological Society of London (later Royal ——) *Proceedings* 1926–76 (from 1936 divided into separate series)
Transactions 1834–
Entomological Society of Washington *Proceedings* 1886–
Entwistle, William James *Aspects of language* 1953
Environmental conservation 1974–
'Ephelia' *Female poems on several occasions* 1679
Ephesian matron 1659 *See* Charleton, W.
Epinal glossary, The. Latin and Old English c825 (Sweet 1883; in Oldest English texts, E.E.T.S. 1885)
Epulario, or, the Italian banquet 1598
Epyphanye, The 14.. (in The Visions of Tundale, etc. 1843)
Erasmus' Playne and godly exposytion of the commune crede and of the x. commaundementes tr. 1533
See also various translators
Erceldoune, The romance and prophecies of Thomas of c1425 (E.E.T.S. 1875)
Erckmann-Chatrian's Waterloo tr. 1865
Erdman, Paul *The silver bears* 1974
Erfurt glossary c875 (in Oldest English texts, E.E.T.S. 1885)
Erichsen, Sir John E. *The science and art of surgery* 1853 (1877)
Erkenwald, St. a1400 (in Horstmann, Altengl. Leg. 1881)
Erl of Tolous c1450 (Ritson, Metr. rom. III; Lüdtke 1881)
Erondelle, Pierre *The French garden, being an instruction for attayning the French tongue* 1605
Ersine, Noel *Underworld and prison slang* 1935
Erskine, Ebenezer *Sermons* a1754 (1755)
Erskine, John *An institute of the law of Scotland* a1768 (1773)
Principles of the law of Scotland 1754 (1809)
Erskine, John F. *General view of the agriculture of the county of Clackmannan* 1795
Erskine, Thomas *An essay on faith* 1822 (1825)
Erskine-Murray, James *A handbook of wireless telegraphy* 1907
Erthe upon erthe, The Middle English poem 13.. (E.E.T.S. 1911)
Esau, Katherine *Plant anatomy* 1953
Escott, Thomas H. S. *England: its people, polity, and pursuits* 1879
Esquemeling's (J.) History of the Bucaniers of America tr. 1684
Esquire 1933–
Esquiros, Alphonse *Cornwall and its coasts* 1865
Essay peace and truth in the church 1681 *See* Harley, Sir E.
Essay to revive the ancient education of gentlewomen in religion, etc. 1673
Essay to the memory of John lord Cutts 1707
Essay towards a method of speedily manning a fleet 1754
Essays and reviews 1860
Essays and studies by members of the English Association 1910–
Essays from the Batchelor 1771–72 (1773)
Essays in criticism: a quarterly journal of literary criticism 1951–
Essays on Christian union 1845
Essays on a liberal education 18.. (ed. F. W. Farrar 1867)
Essays on reform 1867
Essays on religion and literature 18.. (ed. H. E. Manning 1865, -67, -74)
Essays on social subjects, from the Saturday Review 1864–65
Essex, Arthur Capel, Earl of *Letters* 1675 (1770)
Essex papers 1672–79 (Camden Soc. 1890, 1913)
Essex's excellency; or, the gallantry of the freeholders of that county 1679
Essex freeholders, A faithful account of the behaviour of a party of 1679
Essex, Glossary of provincial words used in 1851
Essex Institute [Salem, Massachusetts] *historical collections* 1859–
Essig, Edward Oliver *College entomology* 1942
Established test, The, in order to the security of his majesties person, etc., *against the malitious attempts of Rome* 1679
Estcourt, Richard *The fair example* 1706
Esther, Queen (A new enterlude, drawen oute of the holy scripture, of godly queene Hester) 1561 (in J. P. Collier, Illustr. E. Eng. pop. lit. I, 1863; Grosart 1873)
Estwick, Nicolas *Πνευματολογία, or a treatise of the Holy Ghost* 1648
Etc.: a review of general semantics 1943–
Etherege, Sir George *Works* a1691 (1888)
The comical revenge, or love in a tub 1664
The man of mode 1676
She wou'd if she cou'd 1668
Etheridge, Robert *Stratigraphical geology and palæontology* 1885
Etherington, Harold ed. *Nuclear engineering handbook* 1958
Eton school days 1864 *See* Hemyng, B.
Etonian, The 1822
Etoniana ancient and modern 1865
Eugene Register-Guard (Eugene, Oregon) 1955–
Eugenius 1785 *See* Graves, Richard
Europe, A brief description of the future history of, from 1650 to 1710 1650
European Organization for Nuclear Research (Conseil Européen pour la Recherche Nucléaire) *Proceedings of CERN symposium* 2 vols. 1956
European magazine, The 1804 (vol. XLV)
Eusden, Laurence *Poems* 1714, 1722
See also Garth, Sir S.
Eustace, John C. *A tour through Italy* 1813
— ed. 2, entitled *A classical tour through Italy* 1814 (1815, 1821)
Evance, Daniel *The noble order; or the honour which God conferr's on them that honour him* 1646
Evangelium Nicodemi 13.. See *Gospel of Nicodemus*
Evans, Abel *Vertumnus* 1713
Evans, Arthur B. *Leicestershire words, phrases, and proverbs* 1848
— new ed. by Sebastian Evans 1881 (E.D.S.)
Evans, Arthur John *The Palace of Minos* 7 vols. 1921–36
Through Bosnia and the Herzegóvina on foot 1876
Evans, Bergen & Evans, Cornelia *A dictionary of contemporary American usage* 1957
Evans, Charles *See* Evans, Robert Charles
Evans, Edward P. *Animal symbolism in ecclesiastical architecture* 1896
Evans, Edward T. *The history and topography of the parish of Hendon, Middlesex* 1890
Evans, Emyr Estyn *Irish fell ways* 1957
Evans, George Ewart *Ask the fellows who cut the hay* 1956
The horse in the furrow 1960
The pattern under the plough 1966
Where beards wag all 1970
Evans, Howard T. tr. *G. Hagg's General and inorganic chemistry* 1969
Evans, John *A sketch of the denominations of the Christian world* 1795 (1821)
Evans, John *An excursion to Windsor* 1817
Evans, Sir John *The ancient stone implements, weapons, and ornaments of Great Britain* 1872 (1897)
The coins of the ancient Britons 1864
Evans, John G. *The environment of early man in the British Isles* 1975
Evans, Lewis 1574 *See* Withals, John
Evans, Lewis *Geographical, historical, political, philosophical and mechanical essays; the first, containing an analysis of a general map of the middle British Colonies in America* 1755
Evans, Maurice J. 1872 *See* Watson, John W.
Evans, Philip *The bodyguard man* 1973
Evans, Robert Charles *On climbing* 1956
Evans, Robley Dunglison *The atomic nucleus* 1955
Evans, Sebastian *Brother Fabian's manuscripts; and other poems* 1865
In quest of the Holy Graal 1898
See also Evans, Arthur B.
Evans, Thomas ed. *Old ballads, historical and narrative, with some of modern date* v.d. (1777, 1784, 1810)
Evans-Pritchard, Edward Evan *Social anthropology* 1951
—— et al. *The institutions of primitive society* 1954
Evats, William *The most excellent Hugo Grotius his three books treating of the rights of war and peace* tr. 1682
Evelyn, John *Acetaria, or a discourse of sallets* 1699
De la Quintinie's Compleat gard'ner tr. 1693
Diary ed. E. S. de Beer 6 vols. 1955
Diary (a1700) *and correspondence* v.d. (1850–52, 1879)
Fréart's Idea of the perfection of painting tr. 1668
Fréart's Parralel of the antient architecture with the modern; to which is added an account of architects and architecture tr. 1664
The French gardener tr. 1658
Fumifugium; or, the inconveniencies of the aer and smoak of London dissipated 1661
The history of religion a1706 (1850)
Kalendarium hortense 1664
The life of Mrs. Godolphin 1685
Memoirs v.d. (1881)
Miscellaneous writings v.d. (1825)
Mundus muliebris See Evelyn, Mary
Navigation and commerce 1674
Numismata; a discourse of medals antient and modern 1697
Pomona 1664
Sculptura; or, the history and art of chalcography and engraving in copper 1662
The state of France as it stood in the ninth year of Lewis XIIII 1652
Sylva, or a discourse of forest-trees 1664 (1729, 1776)
Terra. A philosophical discourse of earth 1675 (1729, 1778)
Tyrannus, or the mode 1661
Evelyn, Mary *Mundus muliebris: or, the ladies dressing-room unlock'd, and her toilette spread. Together with the fop-dictionary* (ascribed to John or Mary Evelyn) 1690
Evening News (Edinburgh) See *Edinburgh Evening News*
Evening News (London) 1881–1980
Evening Post (Nottingham) 1878–
Evening Post (Wellington, New Zealand) 1865–
Evening Standard 1860–1980 (continued as *New Standard*)
Evening Sun (Baltimore, Maryland) 1910–
Evening Telegram (St. John's, Newfoundland) 1879–
Everard, Edmund *The depositions and examinations of, concerning the horrid Popish plot* 1679
Discourses on the present state of the Protestant princes of Europe 1679
Everett, Edward *Orations and speeches, on various occasions* 1836 (1850)
Everett, Joseph D. *Illustrations of the centimetre-gramme-second system of units* 1875
Everett, Thomas H. *Living trees of the world* 1969
Ever green, The, being a collection of Scots poems, wrote by the ingenious before 1600, (ed.) by Allan Ramsay 1724
Everie woman in her humor 1609 (in Bullen, Old Plays IV, 1885)
Everybody's magazine (US) 1899–1929
Everyman c1520 (in Eng. miracle plays, ed. Pollard 1890)
Every man his own mechanic (by F. Chilton-Young) 1881
Ewald, Alexander C. *Stories from the State Papers* 1882
Ewart, Alfred James tr. *W. Pfeffer's The physiology of plants* 3 vols. 1900–6
Ewart, Gavin *The Gavin Ewart show: poems* 1971
Ewing, Juliana H. *Dandelion clocks* a1885 (1887)
Mary's meadow a1885 (1886)
Examination and refutation of a late pamphlet intituled Considerations on the Navy bill, An 1749
Examiner, The (ed. successively by W. King, J. Swift, Mrs. Manley, and W. Oldisworth) 1710–14
Examiner, The; a Sunday paper, on politics, domestic economy, and theatricals (ed. successively by Leigh Hunt, A. Fonblanque, et al.) 1808–36
Examynatyons towcheynge Cokeye More 15.. (in Chetham Soc. Misc. II)
Exceptions of the presbyterian-brethren, against some passages in the present liturgy 1661
Excerpta historica See Bentley, S.
Exchequer rolls of Scotland 1264– (Scott. Record series 1878–)
Execution for treason 1583 (1675) *See* Cecil, W.
Exercitation concerning usurped powers 1650 *See* Hollingworth, R.
Exeter book, The (Codex Exoniensis); an anthology of Anglo-Saxon poetry presented to Exeter Cathedral by Leofric (1050–71) a1000 (Thorpe 1842; (Poems I–VIII) E.E.T.S. 1895)
Exhibition, Official descriptive and illustrated catalogue of the Great 1851
Exhibition, The International of 1862. The illustrated catalogue of the industrial department. British division 1862
Exhortation vnto prayer 1544
Exmoor courtship 1746 (in Gentleman's Mag. June)
Exmoor scolding 1746 (in Gentleman's Mag. July)
Exmoor scolding, also, an Exmoor courtship. (With) a vocabulary 1778 (E.D.S. 1879)
Experiment station record (United States Department of Agriculture) 1889–1946
Experimental wireless and the wireless engineer 1923–31
Explication, A short, of such foreign words as are made use of in the musick books 1724
Exposition of the doctrine of the Church of England, An (by Abp. W. Wake) 1686
Expositor, The 1875–
Expostulatory letter, A mild, from the plaindealing farmers of the neighbouring villages to the men of Buckingham c1670
Eye opener 1902–22

Eyre, Mary *A lady's walks in the south of France in 1863* 1865
Eyton, Robert W. *The antiquities of Shropshire* 1854–60
Eyton, Thomas C. *A history of the rarer of British birds* 1836

F

F., A. *See* Fleming, Abraham
F., E. *The history of the life, reign, and death of Edward II* 1627 (1680)
F., E. 1644–45 *See* Fisher, E.
F., I. or J. 1613 *See* Fletcher, Joseph
F., J. *The merchant's warehouse laid open* 1695
F., J. *See* Freake, J.; French, John
F., N. *The husbandmans fruitfull orchard* 1608 (1609)
F., T. 1649 *See* Forde, Thomas
Faber, Frederick W. *All for Jesus* 1853
Growth in holiness 1854 (1872)
Hymns 1862
Spiritual conferences 1858 (1870)
The Styrian lake, and other poems 1842
Life and letters, edited by Father J. E. Bowden (1869)
Faber, George S. *An account of Mr. Husenbeth's professed refutation of the argument of the difficulties of Romanism* 1836
Christ's discourse at Capernaum fatal to the doctrine of transubstantiation 1840
The difficulties of infidelity 1824 (1833)
The difficulties of Romanism 1826 (1853)
A dissertation on the mysteries of the Cabiri 1803
A dissertation on the prophecies relative to the great period of 1260 years 1806
Eight dissertations upon the promise of a mighty deliverer 1817–44 (1845)
An enquiry into the history and theology of the Vallenses and Albigenses 1838
A general and connected view of the prophecies relative to the conversion of Judah and Israel 1808
Horæ Mosaicæ, or a view of the Mosaical records 1801 (1818)
Letters on Tractarian secession to Popery 1846
Many mansions in the home of the Father 1851
The origin of Pagan idolatry 1816
The predicted downfall of the Turkish power 1853
The primitive doctrine of election 1836 (1842)
The primitive doctrine of justification investigated 1837
The primitive doctrine of regeneration 1840
Provincial letters 1842 (1844)
Recapitulated apostasy the true rationale of the concealed apocalyptic name of the Roman empire 1833
The revival of the French emperorship 1853
The sacred calendar of prophecy 1827, 1843 (1844)
A treatise on the genius and object of the Patriarchal, the Levitical, and the Christian dispensations 1819 (1823)
A treatise on the origin of expiatory sacrifice 1827
Fabian News 1891–
Fabric rolls of York Minster v.d. (Surtees Soc. 1859)
Fabyan, Robert *The newe cronycles of Englande and of Fraunce* a1513 (1516); *continued to the death of Henry VII* 1533, 1542; *continued to the death of Q. Mary* 1559 (1811)
Faction display'd, a poem 1704
Fage, John *Speculum aegrotorum, the sicke-mens glasse* 1606
Fagge, Charles H. & Pye-Smith, Philip H. *The principles and practice of medicine* 1886 (1888)
Fahie, J. J. *Historic notes on the telephone* 1883
Fair trade cry, The: a letter to the rt. hon. sir Stafford Northcote 1881
Fairbairn, Andrew M. *Catholicism; Roman and Anglian* 1884–97 (1899)
The philosophy of the Christian religion 1902
The place of Christ in modern theology 1893
Studies in the life of Christ 1881
Studies in the philosophy of religion and history 1876
Fairbairn, Patrick *Prophecy viewed in respect to its distinctive nature* 1856
The typology of scripture 1845–47 (1857)
Fairbairn, William *Iron, its history, properties, and processes of manufacture* 1861
Fairbanks Daily News-Miner (Fairbanks, Alaska) 1903–
Fairbridge, Rhodes Whitmore ed. *The encyclopedia of atmospheric sciences and astrogeology* 1967
ed. *The encyclopedia of geomorphology* 1968
Fairchild, Henry Pratt ed. *Dictionary of sociology* 1944
Faire Em, A pleasant commodie of 1592 (in Shakespeare Apocrypha 1908)
Fairfax, Edward *Tasso's Godfrey of Bulloigne* tr. 1600
Fairfax, Nathaniel *A treatise of the bulk and selvedge of the world* 1674
Fairfax, Thomas, 3rd Baron *Short memorials* a1671 (1699; in Arber, Eng. Garner VIII)
Fairholt, Frederick W. *Costume in England* 1846 (1860)
— *ed. 3, enlarged and thoroughly revised by the Hon. H. A. Dillon* 1885
A dictionary of terms in art 1854
Tobacco: its history and associations 1859 (1876)
Up the Nile, and home again 1862 (1863)
'Fairless, Michael' (Margaret F. Barber) *The roadmender* 1902

Falck, N. D. *A philosophical dissertation on the diving vessel projected by Mr. Day* 1775
Falconbridge, Alexander *An account of the slave trade on the coast of Africa* 1788
'Falconer, Lanoe' (Mary Eliz. Hawker) *Mademoiselle Ixe* 1890 (1891)
Falconer (Captain R.), Voyages of 1720 *See* Chetwood, W. R.
Falconer, William *The shipwreck* 1762
An universal dictionary of the marine 1769 (1776)
— enlarged by W. Burney (1815)
Fale, Thomas *Horologiographia; the art of dialling* 1593
Falk, Hjalmar S. and Torp, Alf *Etymologisk ordbog over det Norske og det Danske sprog* 1901–06
Falkland, 2nd Viscount a1643 *See* Cary, L.
Falkner, John M. *Moonfleet* 1898
Falkner, William *Two treatises* a1682 (1684)
Falla, Robert Alexander, Sibson, R. B., & Turbott, E. G. *A field guide to the birds of New Zealand and outlying islands* 1966
Falle, Philip *An account of the isle of Jersey* 1694
Fambresarius 1684 *See* La Framboisière, N. A. de
Family dictionary (Dictionaire oeconomique: or, the family dictionary. Tr. from M. Chomel. Revised and recommended by Mr. R. Bradley) 1725
Family in-compact, The, contrasted with the family compact 1778
Family of Rose of Kilravock, A genealogical deduction of the v.d. (Spalding Cl. 1848) *See* Rose, Hew
Famous plays 12 vols. 1931–9
Fane, Julian C. H., & Lytton, Edward Robert Bulwer-Lytton, 1st Earl of *Tannhäuser; or, the battle of the bards* 1861
'Fan Kwae', The, at Canton before treaty days 1825–44: by an old resident 1882
Fanning, J. T. *A practical treatise on water-supply engineering* 1877
Fanshaw, Sir Thomas *The practice of the Exchequer Court* a1601 (1658)
Fanshawe, Anne, Lady *Memoirs, written by herself, to which are added extracts from the correspondence of Sir R. Fanshawe* a1680 (1829, 1905)
Fanshawe, Sir Richard *Camoens' (Luis de) Lusiad* tr. 1655
Guarini's (Baptista) Il Pastor fido; the faithfull shepheard tr. *With an addition of divers other poems* 1647–48
Faraday, Michael *Chemical manipulation* 1827
A course of six lectures on the chemical history of a candle 1861
Experimental researches in chemistry and physics 1821–57 (1859)
On the various forces of nature a1867 (1874)
Faraday, Wilfred Barnard ed. *A glossary of aeronautical terms* 1919
Faraday Society *Transactions* 1905–
Farber, Marvin *The foundation of phenomenology; Edmund Husserl and the quest for a rigorous science of philosophy* 1943
Fardle of facions 1555 *See* Watreman, W.
Farey, John *General view of the agriculture and minerals of Derbyshire* 1811
Faria's (F. de) Narrative; wherein is contained the several informations touching the popish plot 1680
Farindon, Anthony *Forty sermons* a1658 (1663, 1672, 1849)
Thirty sermons 1657
Farjeon, Benjamin L. *The betrayal of John Fordham* 1896
Three times tried 1886
Farley, John *The London art of cookery* 1804
Farley, Robert *Kalendarium humanæ vitæ* 1638
Lychnocausia, sive moralia facum emblemata. Lights. Morall emblemes 1638
Farley's Exeter Journal 1725–28
Farlow, William G. *Marine algæ of New England and adjacent coast* 1881
Farmer, Edward *Scrap book, being a selection of poems, songs, scraps, etc.* 1846 (1869)
Farmer, Fannie Merritt *The Boston Cooking-School cook book* 1896 (and several later editions used)
Farmer, John *Forty several ways of two parts in one made upon a playn song* 1591
Farmer, John S. *Americanisms, old and new: a dictionary* 1889
ed. *Musa pedestris: canting songs and slang rhymes* 1536–1896 (1896)
The public school word-book 1900
—— & Henley, William E. *Slang and its analogues, past and present* 1890–1904
Farmer, Richard *An essay on the learning of Shakespeare* 1767
Farmer and stockbreeder, The 1889–
Farmer's complete guide through all the articles of his profession 1760
Farmer's Ha' 1776 *See* Keith, C.
Farmer's magazine, The 1800–25
Farmers weekly 1934–
Farnie, Henry Brougham *The golfer's manual* 1857
Farnol, John Jeffery *The broad highway* 1910
The definite object 1917
Farquhar, George *Works* a1707 (1742, 1892)
The beaux stratagem 1706–07
A constant couple 1700
The inconstant, or the way to win him 1702
Love and a bottle 1699
The recruiting officer 1706
Sir Harry Wildair 1701

Farquhar, William *Poems on several occasions* 1794
Farquharson, M. G., et al. *Glossary of broadcasting terms* 1941
Farr, Edward ed. *Select poetry chiefly devotional of the reign of Queen Elizabeth* a1600 (Parker Soc. 1845)
ed. *Select poetry, chiefly sacred, of the reign of James I* 16.. (1847)
Farragut, Loyall *The life of D. G. Farragut* 1879
Farrar, Frederic W. *Chapters on language* 1865
Darkness and dawn 1891
The early days of Christianity 1882
Eric; or, little by little 1858
Essay on the origin of language 1860
Families of speech 1869 (1873)
History of interpretation 1886
'In the days of my youth': sermons, Marlborough 1871–76 (1876)
Julian Home 1859
Life and work of St. Paul 1879
Life of Christ 1874
Lives of the Fathers 1889
Seekers after God 1868
The silence and the voices of God, with other sermons 1874
Witness of history to Christ 1871
Farrell, James Thomas *Studs Lonigan: a trilogy* (Young Lonigan; The young manhood of Studs Lonigan; Judgment day) 1935 (UK 1936)
Young Lonigan: a boyhood in Chicago streets 1932
The young manhood of Studs Lonigan 1934
Farrer, Reginald John *The garden of Asia: impressions from Japan* 1904
My rock-garden 1907
Farrow, Edward S. *A dictionary of military terms* 1918
Military encyclopedia 1885
Fary, John *God's severity on man's sterility* 1644 (1645)
Fasciculus florum: or, a nosegay of flowers 1636
Fashionable follies 1782 *See* Vaughan, T.
Fast, Howard Melvin *The immigrants* 1977
Fastnedge, Ralph *English furniture styles, from 1500 to 1830* 1955
Fate of Sedley, The 1795
Fates of the Apostles a1000 (Grein)
Father's instruction a1000 (Grein)
Fathers of the desert 1867 *See* Hahn-Hahn
Faulkner, William *Absalom, Absalom!* 1936
As I lay dying 1930 (UK 1935)
A fable 1954 (UK 1955)
Go down, Moses, and other stories 1942
The hamlet 1940
Light in August 1932 (UK 1933)
Sanctuary 1931
Sartoris 1929 (UK 1932)
The sound and the fury 1929
The wild palms 1939
Faustus. The historie of the damnable life and deserued death of Dr. J. Faustus tr. by P. F. 1592 (in Thoms, Prose romances III. 1828)
The second report of Dr. John Faustus 1594 (ibid.)
Faux, W. *Memorable days in America* 1823
Favine's (André) Theater of honour and knighthood tr. 1623
Favour, John *Antiquitie triumphing over noveltie* 1619
Fawcet, Samuel *A seasonable sermon for these troublesome times* 1641
Fawcett, Henry *Manual of political economy* 1863 (1876)
Fawkes, Francis *Poems* a1777 (1810)
Apollonius Rhodius tr. a1777
The idylliums of Theocritus tr. 1767
Original poems and translations 1761
Fay, Albert Hill *A glossary of the mining and mineral industry* 1920
Fea, Allan *Memoirs of the martyr King, being a detailed record of the last two years of the reign of Charles I* 1905
Fearon, Diana *Murder-on-Thames* 1960
Fearon, Henry B. *Sketches of America* 1818
Fearon, Samuel & Eyes, John *A description of the sea coast of England and Wales* 1738
Fearon, William Robert *An introduction to biochemistry* 1934
Feather, Leonard Geoffrey *The encyclopedia of jazz* 1955 (UK 1956)
Inside be-bop 1949
Feathered world 1889–
Featley, Daniel *Clavis mystica; a key opening divers texts of scripture* 1636
The dippers dipt 1645 (1646)
Featley's Pelagius redivivus. Or, Pelagius raked out of the ashes. (Containing a transl. of 'Parallelismus novantiqui erroris Pelagiarminiani') 1626
The fisher catched in his owne net 1623
Roma ruens 1644
Stricturæ in Lyndomastigem 1638
Transubstantiation exploded 1638
Vertumnus Romanus 1642
Featley, John *The honor of chastity* 1632
Federalist, The 1788 *See* Hamilton, Alex.
Federation proceedings (Federation of American Societies for Experimental Biology) 1942–
Feinsilver, Lillian Mermin *The taste of Yiddish* 1970
Feldenkrais, Moshé *Judo: the art of defence and attack* 1941
Fell, Bp. John *The life of Dr. H. Hammond* 1661
Fellowes, Robert *Milton's Second defence of the people of England* tr. 1806 (in Milton's Works, VI, 1806)
Feltham, John *The picture of London for 1802* 1802
A tour through the Island of Mann in 1797–98 1798

Feltham, Owen *Lusoria, or occasional pieces* 1661 (in Resolves, ed. 8, 1661)
Resolves divine, morall, politicall ?1623 (1628, 1661, 1677)
Three moneths observations of the Low Countries 1648 (1652)
Felton, Cornelius C. *Familiar letters from Europe* 1865
Greece, ancient and modern 1866 (1867)
Felton, Henry *A dissertation on reading the classics, and forming a just style* 1709 (1713)
Sermons on the creation, fall, and redemption of man a1740 (1748)
Felton, William *A treatise on carriages* 1794 (1801)
Female foundling, The 1751
Female spectator, The 1744–45 *See* Haywood, Eliza
Female tatler, The 1709 *See* Baker, T.
Femina (Bombay) 1959–
Fenise 1651 See *De-la-Coveras*
Fenn, George Manville *Dick o' the fens* 1888
In an Alpine valley 1894
The master of the ceremonies 1886
Middy and ensign 1883
Patience wins 1886
Real gold 1894
Fenne, Thomas *Frutes* 1590
Hecubaes mishaps 1590 (in prec., lf. 91)
Fennell, Charles A. M. *Michaelis' (A.) Ancient marbles in Great Britain* tr. 1882
See also *Stanford dictionary*
Fenner, Dudley *A defence of the godlie ministers, against the slaunders of D. Bridges* 1587
Fenner, William *Works* a1640 (1651–58)
Hidden manna, or the mystery of saving grace a1640 (1652)
Fennessy, J. C. *The sonnet in the bottle* 1951
Fenton, Elijah *Poems* a1730 (1790)
Mariamne, a tragedy 1723
Poems on several occasions 1717
Fenton, Sir Geoffrey *Certaine tragicall discourses* 1567
Golden epistles (sometimes erron. quoted in Dict. as Hellowes *Gueuara's Golden ep.*) 1575, 1577 (1582)
The historie of Guicciardini, conteining the warres of Italie tr. 1579 (1599)
Fenton, Roger *A treatise against the necessarie dependance upon that one head, and the present reconciliation to the church of Rome* a1615 (1617)
A treatise of usurie 1611
Fenton, Thomas *Of speaking as the oracles of God. A sermon before the University of Oxford* 1720
'Fenwick, Elizabeth' (Elizabeth Fenwick Way) *Impeccable people* 1971
A long way down 1959
Ferber, Edna *Dawn O'Hara, the girl who laughed* 1911
Ferguson, Adam *The history of the progress and termination of the Roman republic* 1783
Institutes of moral philosophy 1769
Principles of moral and political science 1792
Ferguson, Charles D. *The experiences of a forty-niner during thirty-four years' residence in California and Australia* ed. F. T. Wallace 1888
Ferguson, David *Scottish proverbs: gathered together* a1598 (1641, 1785; S.T.S. 1924)
Ferguson, Fergus *A popular life of Christ* 1878
Ferguson, James ed. *Papers illustrating the history of the Scots brigade in the service of the United Netherlands* 1572–1782 (S.H.S. 1899–1901)
Ferguson, James *Astronomy explained upon Sir Isaac Newton's principles* 1756
Tables and tracts relative to several arts and sciences 1767
Ferguson, R. *View of an ecclesiastick in his socks and buskins* (anon.) 1698
Ferguson, Richard S. *Carlisle* 1889
A history of Cumberland 1890
—— & Nanson, W. ed. *Some municipal records of the city of Carlisle* v.d. (1887)
Ferguson, Robert *The dialect of Cumberland* 1873
Ferguson, Robert M. *Electricity* 1866 (1870)
Ferguson, Samuel *Lays of the Western Gael, and other poems* 1865 (1888)
Poems 1880
Fergusson, Bernard Edward *The watery maze: the story of combined operations* 1961
Fergusson, David *See* Ferguson, D.
Fergusson, Erna *Our Southwest* 1940
Fergusson, James *A brief exposition of the Epistles of Paul to the Galatians and Ephesians* 1659
Fergusson, Sir James *Decisions of the Court of Session from 1738 to 1752* 1775
Fergusson, James *History of architecture in all countries* 1865–67 (1873–76)
The illustrated handbook of architecture 1855
Fergusson, Robert *Works* a1774 (1807)
Poems 1773
Poems on various subjects a1774 (1789)
Fergusson, Robert M. *My village* 1893
Rambling sketches in the Far North, and Orcadian musings 1883
A village poet 1897
Fergusson, William *System of practical surgery* 1842
'Fern, Fanny' (Sara Payson Parton) *Gingersnaps* 1870
Ferne (Henry), A fuller answer to a treatise written by 1642
Ferne, Sir John *The blazon of gentrie* 1586
Fernie, John *A history of the town and parish of Dunfermline* 1815
Ferrand's Melancholy 1640 *See* Chilmead, E.
Ferrar, Nicholas *The hundred and ten considerations of Signior J. Valdesso* tr. a1637 (1638)
The story books of Little Gidding, being the religious dialogues recited in the great room 1631–32 (1899)
'Ferrars, Elizabeth' (Morna Doris Brown) *Breath of suspicion* 1972
Murder in time 1953
Ferriar, John *Illustrations of Sterne; with other essays and verses* 1798
Ferrier, Andrew *Memoir and sermons* 1841
Ferrier, David *The functions of the brain* 1876
Ferrier, James F. *Institutes of metaphysic* 1854 (1856)
Lectures on Greek philosophy and other philosophical remains a1864 (1866)
Ferrier, Richard *Journal while travelling in France* 1687 (in Camden Misc. IX, No. 7, 1894)
Ferrier, Susan E. *Destiny* 1831
The inheritance 1824
Marriage 1818
Ferris, Paul *The detective* 1976
Ferris, Richard *The most dangerous and memorable adventure of R. F.* 1590 (in Arber, Eng. Garner VI)
Ferris, Richard *How it flies; or, The conquest of the air* 1910
Ferumbras, Sir a1380 (E.E.T.S. 1879)
Fessenden, Thomas G. *Democracy unveiled* 1805
Original poems 1804 (1806)
Pills, poetical, political, and philosophical 1809
Terrible tractoration 1803
Festival of Britain, 1951. South Bank Exhibition *Catalogue of exhibits* 1951
Festivall (John Mirk's Liber festivalis) 1483 (Caxton); 1493 (W. de Worde; 1515)
Festive songs See *Songs*
Fetherstone, Christopher *Calvin's Commentaries vpon the actes of the Apostles* tr. 1585
Feuchterleben, E. von See Lloyd, Hannibal E.
Feuillerat, Albert ed. *Documents relating to the office of the revels in the time of queen Elizabeth* 1558–1602 (1908)
ed. *Documents relating to the revels at court in the time of king Edward VI and queen Mary* 1547–1558 (1914)
Ficchi, Rocco F. *Electrical interference* 1964
Fick, Carl *The Danziger transcript* 1971 (UK 1973)
Fiddes, Richard *Fifty-two practical discourses on several subjects* 1720
The life of cardinal Wolsey 1724 (1726)
Theologia speculativa, or the first part of a body of divinity 1718
Theologia practica, or the second part etc. 1720
Field, Edward Salisbury *A six-cylinder courtship* 1907
Field, George *Chromatography; or, A treatise on colours and pigments* 1835
'Field, Michael' *Attila, my Attila!* 1896
Field, Nathaniel *Amends for ladies* 1618
A woman is a weathercocke 1612
Field, Nathaniel *Some short memorials concerning the life of Dr. R. Field, dean of Glocester* 1716–17
Field, Richard *Of the Church. Five bookes* 1606–10
Field, Samuel & Weill, A. Dudley *Electroplating: a survey of modern practice* 1930
Field, William *Memoirs of the life, writings, and opinions of the rev. S. Parr* 1828
Field, The, the farm, the garden: the country gentleman's newspaper 1853–
Field archaeology (Ordnance Survey Professional Papers) 1932
— (ed. 4) 1963
Field exercises and evolutions of infantry 1877
Field naturalist, The, and scientific student 1882–83
Fielding, Alexander Wallace ('Xan') *The stronghold; the four seasons in the White Mountains of Crete* 1953
Fielding, Henry *Works* a1754 (1771, 1882)
Amelia 1751
The author's farce, and the pleasures of the town 1730
The coffee-house politician (= Rape upon rape) 1730
The Covent-garden journal 1752
The Covent Garden tragedy 1732
Don Quixote in England 1734
Eurydice 1737
The fathers, or the good-natured man a1754
The Grub-street opera 1731
The historical register for the year 1736 1737
The history of the adventures of Joseph Andrews 1742
The history of Tom Jones 1749
The intriguing chambermaid 1734
Journal of a voyage to Lisbon 1754
The letter writers 1731
The life of Mr. Jonathan Wild the Great 1743
The lottery 1732
Love in several masques 1728
Miscellanies 1743
The miser 1733
Miss Lucy in town 1742
The mock doctor 1732
The modern husband 1732
The old debauchees 1732
An old man taught wisdom 1735
Pasquin 1736
The temple beau 1730
Tom Thumb 1730
Tumble-down Dick 1736
The universal gallant 1735
The wedding day 1743
Fielding, Sir John *An account of the origin and effects of a police set on foot by the Duke of Newcastle in 1753* 1758
Fielding, Sarah *The adventures of David Simple in search of a faithful friend* 1744–52
Familiar letters between the principal characters in David Simple and some others 1747
The history of the Countess of Dellwyn 1759
The history of Ophelia a1768 (1785)
Fields, James T. *Biographical notes and personal sketches; with unpublished fragments* 1881
Fiennes, Celia *Journeys* ed. C. Morris 1947
Through England on a side saddle in the time of William and Mary; being the diary of C. Fiennes c1710 (1888)
Fiennes, Gerard F. G. Twisleton-Wykeham- *I tried to run a railway* 1967
Fieser, Louis Frederick & Fieser, Mary A. *Advanced organic chemistry* 1961
Organic chemistry 1944
Fife-Cookson, John C. *With the armies of the Balkans and at Gallipoli, 1877–78* 1879
Fifteen oes (O Ihesu endles swetnes of louyng soules) 1491 (Caxton)
—— *(The xv. oos in Englysshe with other prayers)* 1529 (R. Copland)
Fight at Finnesburg, The Anglo-Saxon poem of the (in Beowulf, etc., ed. Thorpe 1855)
Figuier's (Louis) Human race tr. 1872
The insect world tr. by Y. D. 1868; new ed. by P. M. Duncan 1872
The ocean world tr. by W. S. O. 1868; new ed. by E. P. Wright 1872
Reptiles and birds tr. by P. Gillmore 1869 (1870)
The world before the deluge tr. by W. S. O. 1865; new ed. by H. W. Bristow 1867
Filippini, Alessandro *The international cook book* 1906
Filmer, Sir Robert *The necessity of the absolute power of all kings* (anon.) 1648
Political discourses a1653 (1679–80)
Filson, John *The discovery, settlement, and present state of Kentucke* 1784
Financial Times 1888–
Finar, Ivor Lionel *Organic chemistry* 2 vols. 1951–6
Finch, Sir Heneage *An exact and most impartial account of the indictment, arraignment, etc. of twenty-nine regicides* 1660 (1679)
Finch, Sir Henry *Law, or, a discourse thereof, in foure bookes* a1625 (1636)
Finch-Hatton, Harold H. *Advance Australia!* 1885
Findlater, Charles *General view of the agriculture of the county of Peebles* 1802
Findlay, Alexander *The phase rule and its applications* 1904
tr. *W. Ostwald's The principles of inorganic chemistry* 1902
Findlay, George *Working and management of an English railway* 1889
Findlay, John Niemayer *Values and intentions: a study in value-theory and philosophy of mind* 1961
Fine arts quarterly review 1863–67
Finer, Samuel Edward *The man on horseback: the role of the military in politics* 1962
Finett, Sir John *Philoxenis: some choice observations touching the reception and precedence, etc., of forren ambassadors in England* a1641 (1656)
Fingleton, John Henry Webb *The Ashes crown the year: a Coronation cricket diary* 1954
Four chukkas to Australia: the 1958–59 M.C.C. tour of Australia 1960
Finito! The Po Valley Campaign 1945 (15th Army Group) 1945
Fink, Donald Glen ed. *Electronics engineers' handbook* 1975
Principles of television engineering 1940
Finlay, James ed. *Scottish historical and romantic ballads, chiefly ancient, with.. notes and a glossary* (1808)
Finlayson, Hedley Herbert *The red centre: man and beast in the heart of Australia* 1935
Finlayson, Roderick David *Brown man's burden* 1938
The schooner came to Atia 1952
Finlayson, William *Simple Scotish rhymes* 1815
Firmin, Giles *Πανουργία, a brief review of Mr. Davis's vindication* 1693
A serious question stated 1651
A sober reply to the sober answer of Mr. Cawdrey 1653
First English book on America (Of the newe landes and of ye people founde by the messengers of the kynge of portyngale named Emanuel) c1511 (Arber 1885)
Firth, Anthony *Tall, balding, thirty-five* 1966
Firth, Sir Charles H. *Cromwell's army* 1902
The last years of the Protectorate 1656–58 1909
Firth, John B. *Highways and byways in Derbyshire* 1905
Firth, John Rupert *Papers in linguistics, 1934–1951* 1957
Speech 1930
The tongues of men 1937
Firth, Raymond William *Elements of social organization* 1951
Fischer, Martin Henry tr. *W. Ostwald's Handbook of colloid-chemistry* 1915
Fish, Simon *A supplicacyon for the beggers* 1529 (E.E.T.S. 1871; Arber 1895)
Fisher, Edward *The feast of feasts* 1644
The marrow of modern divinity 1645 (1646)
Fisher, Ernest Arthur *An introduction to Anglo-Saxon architecture and sculpture* 1959
Fisher, James *Poems on various subjects* 1790
Fisher, James Maxwell McConnell & Lockley, Ronald Mathias *Sea-birds: an introduction to the natural history of the sea-birds of the North-Atlantic* 1954
Fisher, Jasper *Fuimus Troes, Æneid. 2. The true Trojanes, being a story of the Britaines valour* (anon.) 1633 (Hazl. Dodsley)

FISHER, Bp. John *English works* a1535 (E.E.T.S. 1876)
Funeral sermon of Margaret Countess of Richmond (A mornynge remembraunce had at the moneth mynde of Margarete, countesse of Rychemonde) 1509 (1708)
Sermon made agayn ye pernicious doctryn of M. luther 1521
Sermon sayd in the cathedrall chyrche of saynt Poule the body beynge present of Kynge Henry the VII 1509
Treatise concernynge the fruytfull saynges of Dauyd in the seuen penytencyall psalmes 1508
Fisher's Godlie treatisse declaryng the benefites of prayer tr. 1560
See also HALL, R.
'FISHER, John' (John Percy) *The answere unto the nine points of controversy prepared by our late soveraygne* 1625-26
FISHER, Joseph William & HARTREE, Douglas Raynor tr. *M. Born's The mechanics of the atom* 1927
FISHER, Ronald Aylmer *The genetical theory of natural selection* 1930
Statistical methods for research workers 1925
FISHER, Samuel *Works (The testimony of truth exalted by the collected labours of S. Fisher)* a1665 (1679)
'Επίσκοπος ἀπόσκοπος. The bishop busied beside the businesse 1662
Rusticus ad academicos etc. *The rustick's alarm to the Rabbies* 1660
FISHER, Seymour *The female orgasm: psychology, physiology, fantasy* 1972 (UK 1973)
FISHER, William Rogers tr. *A. F. W. Schimper's Plant-geography upon a physiological basis* 1903
See also SCHLICH, William *A manual of forestry*
Fisheries (Great international) exhibition catalogue 1883
Fisheries of the United States 1884, -87 *See* GOODE, G. B.
FISHMAN, Joshua Aaron ed. *Readings in the sociology of language* 1968
FISKE, John *A century of science, and other essays* 1899
Outlines of cosmic philosophy 1874
FISKE, Stephen *Holiday stories (Jack's partner* 1894) 1900
FISON, Lorimer & HOWITT, Alfred W. *Kamilaroi and Kurnai; group-marriage and relationship* etc. 1880
FITHIAN, Philip Vickers *Journal and letters, 1767-1774* ed. J. R. Williams 1900
Journal, 1775-1776 ed. R. G. Albion & L. Dobson 1934
Fitz, Sir John 1605 See *Narrative*
FITZ-GEFFREY, Charles *Poems* a1636 (Grosart 1881)
The blessed birth-day, celebrated in some pious meditations 1634 (1881)
Elisha his lamentation 1622
Sir Francis Drake his honorable lifes commendation 1596 (1881)
FITZGERALD, Edward *Euphranor, a dialogue on youth* 1851 (1855)
Letters and literary remains a1883 (1889)
Rubáiyát of Omar Khayyam tr. 1859
— ed. 2 (enlarged) 1868; ed. 3, 1872
FITZGERALD, Francis Scott Key *The beautiful and damned* 1922
The great Gatsby 1925 (UK 1926)
The last tycoon 1941 (UK 1949)
Letters ed. A. Turnbull 1963 (UK 1964)
Tender is the night 1934
This side of Paradise 1920 (UK 1921)
FITZGERALD, Percy H. *Bella Donna: a romance* 1864
Fatal zero 1869 (1888)
Recreations of a literary man 1882 (1883)
FITZGERALD, William *Whitaker's (William) Disputation on holy scripture against the Papists especially Bellarmine and Stapleton* tr. 1849 (Parker Soc.)
FITZGIBBON, Theodora *The art of British cooking* 1965
FITZHERBERT, Sir Anthony *The newe boke of Iustices of the peas* 1538
FITZHERBERT, John *A newe tracte or treatyse moost profytable for all husbande men* 1523
— *The boke of husbandry* 1534 (E.D.S. 1882)
A ryght frutefull mater: and hath to name the boke of surueyeng 1523
(Often attributed to Sir A. Fitzherbert)
FITZHERBERT, Thomas *A defence of the Catholyke cause. With an apology of his innocence in a fayned conspiracy* 1602
Fitzosborne's letters 1739 *See* MELMOTH, W.
FITZPATRICK, William J. *The life, times, and correspondence of the right rev. Dr. Doyle* 1861
'The sham squire'; and the informers of 1798 1866
FITZROY, Robert *The weather book* 1863
FITZSIMONS, Frederick William *The snakes of South Africa* 1910
— (new ed.) 1912
Five letters on inspiration 1690 *See* LE CLERC, J.
Five years' penal servitude 1877
FIXX, James F. *The complete book of running* 1977
Flagellum 1663 *See* HEATH, J.
FLAGG, Edmund *The far west; or, A tour beyond the mountains* 2 vols. 1838
Flammarion's (Camille) L'inconnu: the unknown tr. 1900
FLAMSTEED, John *The doctrine of the sphere* 1680
FLANDRAU, Charles M. *Harvard episodes* 1897
FLATMAN, Thomas *Heraclitus ridens: or a discourse between jest and earnest* 1681-82 (1713)
Poems and songs 1674
FLATTELY, Frederick William & WALTON, Charles Livesey *The biology of the sea-shore* 1922
Flaubert's (Gustave) Salammbô tr. by M. F. Sheldon 1886
FLAVEL, John *Works* a1691 (1731)
The fountain of life opened 1672
Husbandry spiritualized 1669
The method of grace 1680
A practical treatise of fear 1682
The righteous man's refuge 1681
A saint indeed 1671
FLAVELL, John Hurley *The developmental psychology of Jean Piaget* 1963
FLECKNOE, Richard *The damoiselles à la mode; a comedy* 1667
Enigmaticall characters 1658
Love's kingdom 1664
A relation of ten years travels 1655
FLEETWOOD, Bp. William *A complete collection of his sermons, tracts, and pieces of all kinds* a1723 (1737)
A charge delivered to the clergy of the diocese of Ely 1716
Chronicon preciosum; or, an account of English money 1707 (1745)
An essay upon miracles 1701
FLEMING, Abraham *Caius (Johannes): Of Englishe dogges, the diuersities and the properties* tr. 1576 (1880; in Arber, Eng. Garner III)
A panoplie of epistles 1576
The schoole of skill 1581 (1598; Part III of *The footepath to felicitie*)
Virgil's Bucolikes tr. 1575; *Bucoliks, Georgiks* tr. 1589
See also HOLINSHED
FLEMING, Sir Daniel *Description of the county of Westmoreland* 1671 (1882)
FLEMING, David Hay *Mary Queen of Scots* 1897
The Reformation in Scotland 1910
FLEMING, Ian Lancaster *For your eyes only* 1960
Goldfinger 1959
The man with the golden gun 1965
Moonraker 1955
On Her Majesty's Secret Service 1963
Thunderball 1961
You only live twice 1964
FLEMING, Joan Margaret *Kill or cure* 1968
Miss Bones 1959
Nothing is the number when you die 1965
You won't let me finish 1973
Young man, I think you're dying 1970
FLEMING, John *A history of British animals* 1828
The lithology of Edinburgh a1857 (1859)
FLEMING, John Ambrose *The principles of electric wave telegraphy* 1906
Short lectures to electrical artisans 1886
FLEMING, Robert *The fulfilling of the scripture* 1669, 1677 (1726)
FLEMING, Robert Peter *Brazilian adventure* 1933
News from Tartary: a journey from Peking to Kashmir 1936
FLEMING, William *The vocabulary of philosophy* 1857 (1876)
FLEMING, William H. *Slavery and the race problem in the South* 1906
FLEMMING, Louis Andrew *Practical tanning* 1903
Fleta, seu commentarius juris Anglicani sic nuncupatus c1290 (ed. Selden 1647)
FLETCHER, Charles Robert Leslie & KIPLING, Rudyard *A school history of England* 1911
'FLETCHER, David' (Dulan Friar Barber) *Don't whistle 'Macbeth'* 1976
FLETCHER, Giles (the elder) *Of the Russe common wealth* 1591 (Hakluyt Soc. 1856)
Licia, or poemes of love. Whereunto is added The rising to the crowne of Richard the Third (anon.) 1593 (Grosart 1871; in Arber, Eng. Garner VIII)
FLETCHER, Giles (the younger) *Poems* a1623 (1868)
Brittain's Ida. Written by that renowned poet, Edmond Spencer (ascribed to Fletcher) a1623 (1628)
Christs victorie, and triumph in heaven, and earth, over, and after death 1610
FLETCHER, John *The beggars bush* 1622
The bloody brother a1625
The chances 1620
The fair maid of the inn a1625
The faithfull shepheardesse 1610
The humorous lieutenant 1619
The island princesse 1621
The knight of Malta 1619
The loyall subject 1618
The mad lover 1617
Monsieur Thomas 1619
The nice valour a1625
The noble gentleman a1625
The pilgrim 1621
Rule a wife and have a wife 1624
The sea-voyage 1622
The Spanish curate 1622
The tragedy of Thierry and Theodoret c1616
Valentinian 1614
A wife for a month a1625
The wild goose-chase 1621
Wit at severall weapons c1614
The woman's prize a1625
Women pleased c1620
See also BEAUMONT, Francis
—— et al. *The Queene of Corinth* a1619
—— & ROWLEY, William *The maide in the mill* 1623
—— & SHIRLEY, James *The night-walker, or the little theife* 1625
FLETCHER, John W. (of Madeley) *Works* a1785 (1800-04, 1826)
An appeal to matter of fact and common sense 1772
Checks to Antinomianism 1771-72
Logica Genevensis (Fourth and fifth check) 1772
FLETCHER, Joseph *Christes bloodie sweat. By I. F.* 1613
FLETCHER, Joseph S. *The builders* 1897
The wonderful wapentake 1895
FLETCHER, Phineas *Elisa: an elegie upon the unripe demise of Sr Antonie Irby* 1633 (Pt. III of *The purple island*)
Locustae vel pietas Jesuitica. The Locusts or Appollyonists 1627
The purple island, or the isle of Man; together with piscatorie eclogs and other poeticall miscellanies 1633
FLETCHER, R. *Ex otio negotium. Or, Martiall his epigrams translated. With sundry poems and fancies* 1656
Radius Heliconius; or, the revolution of a free state 1650
Fleury's (Claude) Ecclesiastical history tr. by H. Herbert 1727-30
Flight 1908- (title varies; from 1962 with title *Flight international*)
FLINT, Austin *A treatise on the principles and practice of medicine* 1866 (1880)
FLINT, James *Letters from America* 1822
FLINT, Timothy *A condensed geography and history of the Western States, or the Mississippi valley* 1828
George Mason, the young backwoodsman 1829
FLITCH, John Ernest Crawford *Modern dancing and dancers* 1911
FLLOYD, Thomas *Gueullette's (T. S.) Tartarian tales* tr. 1764 (1785)
Floddan field in nine fits, being an exact history of that famous memorable battle fought between the English and Scots on Floddan-Hill 1513 a1600 (1664)
Flores, Jean de See *Aurelio and Isabell*
FLOREY, Howard Walter, et al. *Antibiotics: a survey of penicillin, streptomycin and other antimicrobial substances from fungi, actinomycetes, bacteria, and plants* 2 vols. 1949
FLOREY, Mary Ethel *The clinical application of antibiotics* 4 vols. 1952-61
Florice and Blauncheflour c1330 (Abbotsford Cl. 1857)
See also *Floriz*
Florida FL Reporter 1962-
Florida plantation records See: JONES, George Noble
FLORIO, John *Firste fruites. Also a perfect induction to the Italian, and English tongues* 1578
Second frutes 1591
Montaigne's Essayes, or morall, politike and millitarie discourses tr. 1603 (1632)
A worlde of wordes, or most copious and exact dictionarie in Italian and English 1598 See also TORRIANO, G.
Queen Anna's new world of words 1611
Florist's journal 1845
Floriz and Blauncheflur a1300 (E.E.T.S. 1866, 1901; Hausknecht 1885)
FLORKIN, Marcel & STOTZ, Elmer Henry eds. *Comprehensive biochemistry* 1962-
FLOWER, Philip W. *A history of the trade in tin* 1880
FLOWER, William H. & LYDEKKER, Richard *An introduction to the study of mammals* 1891
Flower and the leaf, The a1500 (in Chaucer's Works 1598; Chaucerian pieces, Skeat 1897)
Flower-garden display'd, The 1732
FLOYER, Ernest A. *Unexplored Baluchistan* 1882
FLOYER, Sir John *The ancient ψυχρολουσία revived: or, an essay to prove cold bathing both safe and useful* 1702 (1706)
Φαρμακο-βάσανος; or, the touch-stone of medicines 1687-90
The physician's pulse-watch 1707-10
The preternatural state of animal humours described by their sensible qualities 1696
The Sibylline Oracles tr. 1713
A treatise of the asthma 1698
FLOYER, Mrs. L. S. *Plain hints for examiners of needlework* 1880
FLÜCKIGER, Friedrich A. & HANBURY, Daniel *Pharmacographia; a history of the principal drugs of vegetable origin, met with in Great Britain and British India* 1874
FLÜGEL, John Carl *A hundred years of psychology, 1833-1933* 1933
Fluff-hunters, The, by 'Marjoribanks' 1903
Flying 1917-19
Flying (New York) 1927-
Flynn's (title varies) 1924-8
'FLYNT, Josiah' (Josiah Flynt Willard) *The rise of Ruderick Clowd* 1903 (UK 1904)
Tramping with tramps 1899 (UK 1900)
The world of graft 1901
—— & 'WALTON, Francis' (Alfred Hodder) *The powers that prey* 1900
Focal dictionary of photographic technologies, The See SPENCER, Douglas Arthur
Focal encyclopedia of film and television techniques 1969
Focal encyclopedia of photography, The 1956
— (rev. Desk ed.) 1969
Focus 1945-
Fog's Weekly journal 1728-31 *See* MOLLOY, Charles
FOLEY, Henry *Jesuits in conflict* 1873
Records of the English Province of the Society of Jesus 1875-83
FOLEY, Winifred *A child in the forest* 1974
FOLKARD, Henry C. *The wild fowler* 1859
FOLKINGHAM, William *Brachigraphy; or the art of short writing* 1620
Feudigraphia. The synopsis or epitome of surveying methodized (Page-heading: *The art of survey*) 1610
Folk-lore 1890-

Fonblanque, Albany *England under seven administrations 1827–34* (1837)
Life and labours of (1874)
Fonseca, José N. da *An historical and archæological sketch of the city of Goa* 1878
Foot, James *Penseroso, or the pensive philosopher in his solitudes, a poem* 1771
Foot, Michael Richard Daniell *SOE in France: an account of the work of the British Special Operations Executive in France 1940–1944* 1966
Foot, Peter *General view of the agriculture of the county of Middlesex* 1794
Foote, Henry Stuart *Texas and the Texans; or, Advance of the Anglo-Americans to the south-west* 2 vols. 1841
Foote, Horace *A companion to the theatres, and manual of the British drama* 1829
Foote, Samuel *Dramatic works* a1777 (1778, 1830)
The author 1757
The bankrupt 1773
Capuchin 1776
The commissary 1765
The cozeners 1774
The devil upon two sticks 1768
The Englishman in Paris 1753
The Englishman return'd from Paris 1756
The knights 1754
The lame lover 1770
The lyar 1762
The maid of Bath 1771
The mayor of Garret 1764
The minor 1760
The nabob 1772
The orators 1762
The patron 1764
Taste 1752
Trip to Calais 1776
Memoirs of (1778, 1805)
Forbes, Bp. Alexander P. *An explanation of the Thirty-nine Articles* 1867–68
A short explanation of the Nicene Creed 1852
Forbes, Archibald *Chinese Gordon* 1884
My experiences of the war between France and Germany 1871
Souvenirs of some continents 1885
Forbes, Duncan *Reflexions on the sources of incredulity with regard to religion* (anon.) a1747 (1750)
Forbes, Duncan *The heart of Malaya* 1966
Forbes, Edward *A history of British starfishes, and other animals of the class echinodermata* 1841
—— & Hanley, Sylvanus *A history of British mollusca and their shells* 1853
Forbes, Gordon S. *Wild life in Canara and Ganjam* 1885
Forbes, Henry Ogg *A hand-book to the primates* 2 vols. 1894
A naturalist's wanderings in the Eastern Archipelago 1885
Forbes, James *Oriental memoirs* 1813–15
Forbes, John *Certain records touching the estate of the Kirk in 1605 and 1606* 16.. (Wodrow Soc. 1846)
Forbes, Sir John *Laennec's (R. T. H.) Treatise on the diseases of the chest* tr. 1821 (1834)
See also *Cyclopædia*
Forbes, Patrick *A defence of the lawful calling of the ministers of reformed churches* 1614
An exquisite commentarie upon the Revelation of Saint John 1613
Forbes, Peter *Poems, chiefly in the Scottish dialect* 1812
Forbes, Robert *Ajax, his speech to the Grecian Knabbs, attempted in broad Buchans. To which is added a Journal to Portsmouth and a Shop-Bill in the same dialect, with a key* 1742 (1755)
Select collection of Scots poems, A, chiefly in the broad Buchan dialect 1785
Forbes, William *The dominie depos'd; or some reflections on his intrigue with a young lass?* 1746 (1785)
Forbes, Sir William *An account of the life and writings of James Beattie, including many of his original letters* 1806 (1824)
Forbes-Mitchell, William *Reminiscences of the great mutiny 1857–59* 1893
Forby, Robert *The vocabulary of East Anglia* a1825 (1830)
See also Spurdens, W. T.
Ford, Edmund Brisco *Mendelism and evolution* 1931
Moths 1955
Ford, Ford Madox (until 1919 name Joseph L. Ford H. Madox Hueffer) *The good soldier: a tale of passion* 1915
Letters ed. R. M. Ludwig 1965
A man could stand up 1926
No more parades 1925
The panel: a sheer comedy 1912
Ford, John *Dramatic works* 16.. (1827, 1869)
The broken heart 1633
The chronicle historie of Perkin Warbeck 1634
Fames memoriall; or the Earle of Devonshire deceased 1606
The fancies, chast and noble 1638
Honor triumphant; or, the Peeres challenge 1606 (Shaks. Soc. 1843)
The ladies triall 1638 (1639)
A line of life 1620 (Shaks. Soc. 1843)
The lovers melancholy 1628 (1629)
Loues sacrifice 1633
'Tis pity shees a whore 1633
See also Rowley, W.
—— & Dekker, Thomas *The sun's darling* 1624 (1656)
Ford, Kenneth William *The world of elementary particles* 1963
Ford, Paul Leicester *The Honorable Peter Stirling and what people thought of him* 1894 (UK 1898)
Ford, Richard *Gatherings from Spain* 1846
A hand-book for travellers in Spain 1845
Ford, Robert 1893 See *Harp of Perthshire*
Ford, Sewell *Inez and Trilby May* 1921
Shorty McCabe 1906 (UK 1908)
Side-stepping with Shorty 1908
Ford, Simon *Παράλληλα; or, the loyall subjects exultation for the royall exiles restauration* 1660
Ford, William J. *A history of the Cambridge University cricket club, 1820–1901* 1902
Ford-Robertson, F. C. ed. *Terminology of forest science, technology, practice and products* 1971
Forde, Emanuel *Parismus, the renowned prince of Bohemia* 1598–99 (1661)
Forde, Thomas *Lusus fortunæ: the play of fortune* 1649
Forde, William *A sermon preached at Constantinople* 1616
Fordun, John *Scoti-chronicon, sive Scotorum historia* a1384 (1691, 1871–72)
—*cum ejusdem supplemento ac continuatione* (by Walter Bower) a1449 (1722, 1759)
Fordyce, James *Sermons to young women* 1765 (1767)
Fordyce, Sir William *A letter to Sir J. Sinclair, concerning the virtues of the muriatic acid in the cure of putrid diseases* 1790
Foreign accounts v.d. (MSS. in Public Record Office)
Foreign quarterly review 1827–46
Foreign review and continental miscellany 1828–30
Forest and stream. (A weekly journal of the rod and gun) 1873–
Forest of Hohenelbe, The; a tale 1803
Forester, Cecil Scott *The commodore* 1945
The good shepherd 1955
Hornblower and the Atropos 1953
Mr. Midshipman Hornblower 1950
The ship 1943
A ship of the line 1938
'Forester, Frank' (H. W. Herbert) *Field sports in the United States, and the British provinces of America* 1848
Forestry 1927–
Forestry bureau bulletin See: United States. Department of Agriculture. Bureau of Forestry
Forgan, Robert *The golfer's handbook* 1881
Form for Church government, propounded to General Assembly at Edinburgh 1647
Forman, Charles *Some queries and observations upon the Revolution in 1688* 1741
Forman, Harry B. *Our living poets* 1871
Forman, Simon *The autobiography and personal diary, from 1552 to 1602* a1611 (Halliwell 1849)
Forme of cury, The? c1390 (Pegge 1780; in Warner, Antiq. culin. 1791)
Formularies of faith, put forth by authority during the reign of Henry VIII 1536–43 (1825)
Forney, M. N. *Car-builder's dictionary* 1880
Forrest, Thomas *A voyage from Calcutta to the Mergui Archipelago* 1792
A voyage to New Guinea and the Moluccas in 1774–76 1779
Forrest, Sir William *The pleasaunt poesye of princelye practise* 1548 (partly repr. in Starkey's England, E.E.T.S. 1878)
Theophilus 1572 (in Anglia, VII and X)
A true and most notable history of a right noble lady entitled the second Gresield 1558
'Forrester, Mrs.' *Mignon* 1877
Roy and Viola 1880
Forrester, James *The polite philosopher* (anon.) 1734 (1778)
Forrester (a novel) 1830
Forrester, Larry *A girl called Fathom* 1967
Forster, Edward Morgan *Abinger harvest: a miscellany* 1936
Aspects of the novel 1927
The hill of Devi: being letters from Dewas State Senior 1953
Howards End 1910
The longest journey 1907
Maurice 1971 (written 1913–14, rev. 1959–60)
A passage to India 1924
A room with a view 1908
Two cheers for democracy 1951
Where angels fear to tread 1905
Forster, George *A journey from Bengal to England* 1790 (1798)
Forster, George (i.e. Johann Georg A.) *A voyage round the world in his Britannic Majesty's sloop Resolution, commanded by Captain James Cook, in 1772–75* 1777
Sparrman's (Anders) Voyage to the Cape of Good Hope in 1772–76 tr. 1785 (1786)
Forster, Harold *Flowering lotus: a view of Java* 1958
Forster, Johann R. *Kalm's (Pehr) Travels into North America* tr. 1770–71 (1772)
Observations made during a voyage round the world 1778
Osbeck's (Pehr) Voyage to China and the East-Indies 1771
Forster, John *The debates on the Grand Remonstrance, 1641* 1860
Historical and biographical essays 1858
The life and adventures of Oliver Goldsmith 1848
The life of C. Dickens 1872–74
Walter Savage Landor. A biography 1869
Forster, Thomas F. *The pocket encyclopædia of natural phenomena* a1825 (1827)
Forster, Thomas I. M. *Observations of the natural history of the swallow tribe* 1817
Researches about atmospheric phaenomena 1813 (1815)
Forster, Westgarth *A treatise on a section of the strata commencing near Newcastle upon Tyne* 1809
Forster, William E. *See* Reid, Sir T. Wemyss
Forsyth, Andrew R. *Theory of functions of a complex variable* 1893
Forsyth, Frederick *The day of the jackal* 1971
The dogs of war 1974
Forsyth, Capt. James *The Highlands of central India* 1871
Forsyth, Joseph *Remarks on antiquities, arts, and letters during an excursion in Italy in 1802–03* 1813
Forsyth, Robert *The beauties of Scotland* 1805–08
Forsyth, William *A treatise on the culture and management of fruit trees* 1802 (1818)
Fortes, Meyer ed. *Social structure: studies presented to A. R. Radcliffe-Brown* 1949
Fortescue, Sir John *Works* a1476 (1869)
The governance of England: otherwise called The difference between an absolute and a limited monarchy c1460 (1714, 1885)
See also Mulcaster, Robert
Fortescue, Thomas *Mexia's (P.) Foreste; or, collection of histories* tr. 1571
Fortescue papers, The: consisting chiefly of letters relating to state affairs. Edited from MSS. in possession of Hon. G. M. Fortescue 16.. (Camden Soc. 1871)
Fortnight in a waggonette, A 1885
Fortnightly review, The 1865–1912
Fortnight's ramble to the lakes 1792 *See* Budworth, J.
Fortnum, Charles Drury E. *A descriptive catalogue of the maiolica, Hispano-Moresco, Persian, Damascus, and Rhodian wares, in the South Kensington Museum* 1873
Maiolica 1875
Maiolica: a historical treatise on the glazed and enamelled earthenwares of Italy 1896
Fortnum & Mason Ltd. *Price list* c1938
Fortunate country-maid 1740 See *De Mouhy*
Fortunate orphan 1745
Fortune 1930–
Forum, The (New York) 1886–1930
Forum, The (Johannesburg) 1938–
Fosbroke, John *Six sermons delivered at Kettering and other places* 1617–31 (1633)
Fosbroke, Thomas D. *British monachism* 1802
Encyclopedia of antiquities 1825 (1840)
Fosdick, Harry Emerson *A pilgrimage to Palestine* 1927 (UK 1928)
Foster, Adriance Sherwood & Gifford, Ernest Milton *Comparative morphology of vascular plants* 1959
Foster, Albert J. *The Ouse* 1891
Foster, Brian *The changing English language* 1968
Foster, Frank Pierce ed. *An illustrated encyclopædic medical dictionary* 4 vols. 1888–92
Foster, Harry La Tourette *The adventures of a tropical tramp* 1922
A beachcomber in the Orient 1923
A tropical tramp with the tourists 1925
Foster, Herbert L. *Ribbin', jivin', and playin' the dozens: the unrecognized dilemma of inner city schools* 1974
Foster, Idris Llewellyn & Alcock, Leslie eds. *Culture and environment: essays in honour of Sir Cyril Fox* 1963
Foster, John *Essays* 1805
Life and correspondence (1846)
Foster, Sir Michael *Text-book of physiology* 1877 (1878)
Foster, Robert Frederick *Foster's complete Hoyle* 1897
Foster, William *Hoplocrisma-spongus; or, a sponge to wipe away the weapon-salve* 1631
Foster, William ed. *The English factories in India, a calendar of documents in the India Office, British Museum and Public Record Office* 1618–41 (1906–12)
Foster-Harris, William *The look of the old West* 1955
Fotherby, Martin *Atheomastix; clearing foure truthes against atheists and infidels* a1619 (1622)
Foure sermons 1608
Fothergill, Jessie *Kith and kin* 1881
A march in the ranks 1890
Foulis, Henry *The history of the Romish treasons and usurpations* a1669 (1671, 1681)
The history of the wicked plots and conspiracies of our pretended saints 1662
Foulis, Hugh *Erchie, my droll friend* 1904
Foulis, Sir John of Ravelston, The account book of 1671–1707 (S.H.S. 1894)
Foulkes, Robert *An alarme for sinners* 1679
Foundation of St. Bartholomew's Church in London, The book of the c1400 (E.E.T.S. 1923)
Fountainhall, Sir John Lauder, Lord *The decisions of the Lords of Council and Session 1678–1712* a1722 (1759–61)
Journals of, with his observations on public affairs and other memoranda 1665–76 (S.H.S. 1900)
Four centuries of English letters 14..–18.. (ed. W. B. Scoones 1880)
Fourcroy's (A. F. de) Elements of natural history and of chemistry tr. 1788
General system of chemical knowledge tr. by William Nicholson 1804
Fowke. The trial of Joseph Fowke for a conspiracy against W. Hastings 1776
Fowler, Bp. Edward *A vindication of an undertaking of certain gentlemen* (anon.) 1692
Fowler, Elizabeth *'Between Trent and Ancholme.' In and around an old-fashioned garden* (anon.) 1908
Fowler, Henry Watson *A dictionary of modern English usage* 1926
—(ed. 2, rev. by E. A. Gowers) 1965
Fowler, Jacob *Journal* ed. E. Coues 1898

FOWLER, John 1586 *See* FULKE, W.
FOWLER, Joseph T. *Adamnan* 1894
FOWLER, Robert *The medical vocabulary* 1860
FOWLER, Thomas *Bacon* 1881
The elements of deductive logic 1867
The elements of inductive logic 1870
The history of Corpus Christi College 1893 (O.H.S.)
FOWLER, William *Works* 15..-16.. (S.T.S. 1914)
FOWLES, Anthony *Dupe negative* 1970
Pastime 1974
FOWLES, John *The collector* 1963
The French lieutenant's woman 1969
The magus 1966
FOWNES, George *A manual of elementary chemistry* 1844 (1848, 1850, etc.)
— revised by H. Watts (1873, 1877)
FOX, Abraham L. *See* WUERTZ, Felix
FOX, Caroline *Journals* ed. W. Monk 1972
Memories of old friends, being extracts from the journals and letters of C. F. 1835-71 (1882)
FOX, Charles *Educational psychology: its problems and methods* 1925
FOX, Charles James *History of the early part of the reign of James II* a1806 (1808)
Correspondence of Gilbert Wakefield with C. J. Fox 1796-1801 (1813)
FOX, Cornelius B. *Ozone and antozone, their history and nature* 1873
FOX, Cyril Fred *The archaeology of the Cambridge region* 1923
FOX, John *The wanderer* 1718
FOX, Lawrence Webster *Diseases of the eye* 1904
FOX, Leslie *The numerical solution of two-point boundary problems in ordinary differential equations* 1957
—— & MAYERS, D. F. *Computing methods for scientists and engineers* 1968
FOX, Richard Middleton & FOX, Jean Walker *Introduction to comparative entomology* 1964
FOX, Miss S. P. *Kingsbridge estuary* 1864
FOX, Thomas W. *The mechanism of weaving* 1894
FOX, William T. *The classification of skin diseases* 1864
FOXE, John *Actes and monuments of these latter and perillous dayes* (= *The book of martyrs*) 1563 (1570, 1576, 1583, 1596, 1610, 1631, 1641, 1684)
FOXE, Luke *The North-West Fox, or Fox from the North-West Passage* 1635
—— & JAMES, Thomas *Voyages in search of a North-West passage in 1631-32; with narratives of the earlier North-West voyages* v.d. (Hakluyt Soc. 1894)
FOYE, William Owen ed. *Principles of medicinal chemistry* 1974
FOZARD, Basil *Instrumentation and control of nuclear reactors* 1963
FRAAS, Arthur Paul *Aircraft power plants* 1943
FRAENKEL, Gottfried S., & GUNN, D. L. *The orientation of animals* 1940
FRAENKEL-CONRAT, Heinz Ludwig & WAGNER, R. R. ed. *Comprehensive virology* 1974-
Fragment of Ælfric's Grammar, Ælfric's Glossary, and a poem on the soul and the body 11.. (ed. Sir T. Phillipps 1838)
Fragment on popular science a1300 (in T. Wright, Pop. treat. science 1841; Early South-Eng. Legendary, E.E.T.S. 1887, p. 311/391-)
Framboisière See *La Framboisière*
FRAME, Janet *The edge of the alphabet* 1962
The lagoon: stories 1951
Owls do cry 1957 (UK 1961)
FRAMPTON, John *Monardes' (Nicolas) Ioyfull newes out of the newe founde worlde* tr. 1577
— *newly corrected, whereunto are added three other bookes treating of the Bezaar stone, the herbe Escuerçonera, the properties of yron and steele, in medicine and the benefite of snow* 1580 (1596)
The most noble and famous trauels of Marcus Paulus to the east partes of the world tr. 1579
Francion, Comical history of 1655 See *Sorel*
FRANCIS, Dick (Richard Stanley Francis) *Blood sport* 1967
Bonecrack 1971
Dead cert 1962
Enquiry 1969
Flying finish 1966
Forfeit 1968
For kicks 1965
In the frame 1976
Knock down 1974
Nerve 1964
Odds against 1965
Rat race 1970
Risk 1977
Slay-ride 1973
FRANCIS, Francis *A book on angling* 1867 (1880)
FRANCIS, Francis, Jr. *Saddle and mocassin* 1887
FRANCIS, George H. *Opinions and policy of Viscount Palmerston* 1852
FRANCIS, George W. *The dictionary of the arts, sciences, and manufactures* 1842
FRANCIS, John *History of the Bank of England* 1847
'FRANCIS, M. E.' (Mrs. Francis Blundell) *A daughter of the soil* 1895
FRANCIS, Peter W. *Volcanoes* 1976
FRANCIS, Philip *Horace* tr. 1743-46
Francis the philanthropist; an unfashionable tale 1785
FRANCK, Richard *Northern memoirs, calculated for the meridian of Scotland. To which is added the contemplative and practical angler* 1658 (1694, 1821)
FRANCO, R. Solomon *Truth springing out of the earth* 1668
FRANK, André Gunder *Latin America: underdevelopment or revolution* 1969
FRANK, Mark *LI sermons; to which is added, a sermon preached at St. Pauls Cross in 1641* a1664 (1672)
FRANK, Pat Harry Hart *Seven days to never* 1957
FRANKAU, Gilbert *More of us, being the present-day adventures of 'One of us': a novel in verse* 1937
'Tid'apa': what does it matter? 1914 (UK 1915)
FRANKAU, Pamela *The winged horse* 1953
FRANKE, Traugott *Technological dictionary, English-German-French*. (Vol. II of Beil's (J. A.) Techn. Wörterbuch) 1855
FRANKLAND, Sir Edward *Experimental researches in pure, applied, and physical chemistry* 1877
FRANKLIN, Benjamin *Works* a1790 (1840, 1887-88)
Writings ed. A. H. Smyth 10 vols. 1905-7
Memoirs of the life and writings, written by himself to a late period, and continued to the time of his death by W. T. Franklin (Autobiography) 1788 (1818)
Poor Richard improved; being an almanack for the year 1758 1758 (in Arber, English Garner V)
Private correspondence 1753-90 (1817)
FRANKLIN, John *Narrative of a journey to the shores of the Polar Sea, 1819-22* 1823
FRANKLIN, Stella Maria Sarah Miles *All that swagger* 1936 (UK 1947)
My brilliant career 1901
See also 'BRENT OF BIN BIN'
FRANKLYN, Julian E. *A dictionary of nicknames* 1962
A dictionary of rhyming slang 1960
FRASER, Edward & GIBBONS, John *Soldier and sailor words and phrases* 1925
FRASER, James *Chronicles of the Frasers: the Wardlaw MS. entitled 'Polichronicon seu policratica temporum, or, the true genealogy of the Frasers', 916-1674* c1700 (S.H.S. 1905)
'FRASER, James' (Alan White) *A cock-pit of roses* 1969
Heart's ease in death 1977
Who steals my name? 1976
FRASER, James B. *Journal of a tour through part of the snowy range of the Himālā Mountains* 1820
The Kuzzilbash (anon.) 1828
Travels in Koordistan, Mesopotamia, etc. 1840
FRASER, William C. *The Whaups of Durley* 1895
Fraser's Magazine 1830-82
FRAUNCE, Abraham *The Countesse of Pembrokes Yuychurch* 1591
The lawiers logike 1588
Watson's (Thomas) Lamentations of Amyntas tr. 1587
FRAYN, Michael *The Russian interpreter* 1966
The tin men 1965
FRAYNE, John George & WOLFE, H. *Elements of sound recording* 1949
FRAZEE, Irving Augustus & BEDELL, Earl L. *Automotive fundamentals* 1949
FRAZER, James G. *The golden bough: a study in comparative religion* 1890
— ed. 2, revised and enlarged 1900; ed. 3, 1907-12
FRAZER, John *Δευτεροσκοπία; or, a brief discourse concerning the second sight* 1707
FREAKE, J. *Agrippa's (H. C.) Three books of occult philosophy* tr. 1651
FREAKE, William *The doctrines and practises of the Societie of Jesuites* 1630
Fred Wilson's fate 1892 *See* MURDOCH, A.
FREE, Montague *All about house plants* 1946
FREEBODY, John William Henry *Telegraphy* 1959
Freedomways 1961-
FREELING, Nicolas *Because of the cats* 1963
Criminal conversation 1965
Double-barrel 1964
The Dresden Green 1966
Dressing of diamond 1974
The king of the rainy country 1966
Lake isle 1976
A long silence 1972
Love in Amsterdam 1962
Strike out where not applicable 1967
Tsing-boum 1969
What are the bugles blowing for? 1975
FREEMAN, B. E. tr. *A. Vandel's Biospeleology: the biology of cavernicolous animals* 1965
FREEMAN, Edward A. *General sketch of European history* 1872
The growth of the English Constitution 1872
Historical and architectural sketches; chiefly Italian 1876
Historical essays v.d. (1871-79)
The history of architecture 1849
The history of the Norman Conquest 1867-79
The reign of William Rufus and the accession of Henry I 1882
Sketches from the subject and neighbour lands of Venice 1881
Some impressions of the United States 1883
Life and letters ed. W. R. W. Stephens (1895)
FREEMAN, Gillian *Jack would be a gentleman* 1959
The liberty man 1955
FREEMAN, Mary Eleanor (Wilkins) *See* WILKINS, Mary Eleanor
FREEMAN, Philip *The principles of divine service* 1855-62
FREEMAN, Samuel *The town officer* 1799
FREEMAN-MITFORD, Algernon B. *Tales of old Japan* 1871
FREEMANTLE, Brian *The November man* 1976
Freemasonry, Poem on (The early history of freemasonry in England) c1430 (Halliwell 1840)
FREER, Martha W. *History of the reign of Henry IV, King of France* 1860-63
History of Marie de Medici 1861
FREESE, John H. *The commercial class-book* 1849
Free-thinker, The 1718 (1733)
FREIND, John *An account of the Earl of Peterborow's conduct in Spain* 1707
Freiris of Berwik, The a1550 (in Dunbar's Poems, S.T.S. 1885)
Frejus' (Rolland) Relation of a voyage made into Mauritania to Muley Arxid, King of Tafiletta tr. 1671
FREKE, William *Select essays, tending to the universal reformation of learning* 1693
Fremdsprachen 1957-
FREMLIN, Celia Margaret *Appointment with yesterday* 1972
By horror haunted: stories 1974
The jealous one 1965
FRÉMONT, John Charles *Report of the exploring expedition to the Rocky Mountains in ... 1842, and to Oregon and North California in ... 1843-'44* 1845
FRENCH, John *The art of distillation* 1651
A new light of alchymie, and a treatise of sulphur, by Michael Sandivogius; also nine books of the nature of things by Paracelsus. Also a chymical dictionary explaining hard places and words in Paracelsus tr. 1650
The York-shire spaw 1652
FRENCH, Nicholas *Historical works* a1678 (1846)
The vnkinde desertor of loyall men and true frinds (anon.) 1676
French book of rates, The 1714
Frendz 1971-2
FRERE, Mary *Old Deccan days; or, Hindoo fairy legends current in Southern India* 1868
FRERE, Bp. Walter H. ed. *Visitation articles and injunctions of the period of the Reformation* 1910
See also PROCTER, Francis
Frere and boy See *Friar and boy*
FREUD, Sigmund *See* BRILL, Abraham Arden; RIVIERE, Joan; STRACHEY, James
FREWER, Ellen E. *Holub's (E.) Seven years in South Africa* tr. 1881
Frey's (Heinrich) Histology and histochemistry of man tr. by A. E. J. Barker 1874
Frezier's (Amédée Fr.) Voyage to the South-Sea and along the coasts of Chili and Peru in 1712-14 tr. 1717
Friar and boy. A mery geste of the frere and the boye 1509-18 (W. de Worde; in Hazlitt, Early pop. poetry III. 1866)
Friar Bacon. The famous historie of Fryer Bacon; also the manner of his death ? a1600 (1627; in Thoms, Prose romances I. 1828)
Friar Gerund 1772 *See* NUGENT
Friar Rush. The historie of Frier Rush 1620 (in Thoms, Prose romances I. 1828)
FRIEDLÄNDER, Michael *The Jewish religion* 1891
FRIEND, Hilderic *A glossary of Devonshire plant names* 1882 (E.D.S.)
FRIEND, John Albert Newton *A text-book of physical chemistry* 2 vols. 1932-5
Friend, The 1843-
Friends, Extracts from State Papers relating to 1654-69 (1910-12)
Friends' Historical Society *Journal* 1903-
Frier *See* FRIAR
FRIES, Charles Carpenter *American English grammar: the grammatical structure of present-day American English with especial reference to social differences or class dialects* 1940
FRISCH, Otto Robert ed. *The nuclear handbook* 1958
FRISWELL, James H. *Sham! a novel written in earnest* 1858 (1861)
FRITH, John *Works* a1533 (1573)
A boke answering vnto M. Mores lettur 1533 (1546)
An other boke against Rastel 1533
A disputacion of purgatorye 1533 (1829)
Judgment upon Will Tracey his testament a1533
A mirrour or glasse to know thyselfe 1533
A pistle to the christen reader; the reuelation of antichrist: antithesis wherein are compared togeder Christes actes and oure holye father the Popes 1529
See also TINDALE, W.
FRITH, William P. *My autobiography and reminiscences* 1887
FRITSCH, Felix Eugen *The structure and reproduction of the algae* 2 vols. 1935-45
Froger's (François) Relation of a voyage made in 1695-97 on the coasts of Africa, etc. tr. 1698
Frogges of Egypt, The; or, the caterpillers of the Commonwealth truly dissected and laid open 1641
FROST, Robert Lee *Collected poems* 1930
— (new ed.) 1939
Letters to Louis Untermeyer ed. L. Untermeyer 1964
—— & FROST, Elinor *Family letters* ed. A. Grade 1972
FROST, Thomas *Reminiscences of a country journalist* 1886 (1888)
Frost and fire 1865 *See* CAMPBELL, J. F.
Frost of 1683-84, Old ballads illustrating the great a1700 (Percy Soc. 1844)
FROTHINGHAM, Octavius B. *George Ripley* 1882
FROUD, Nina, et al. tr. *P. Montagné's Larousse Gastronomique* 1961
FROUDE, James A. *Cæsar; a sketch* 1879
Thomas Carlyle: a history of the first forty years of his life, 1795-1835 1882
— *: a history of his life in London, 1834-81* 1884
The divorce of Catherine of Aragon 1891
History of England 1856-70

The nemesis of faith 1849
Oceana, or England and her colonies 1886
Short studies on great subjects 1850–81 (1867–83)
Froude, Richard H. *Remains* a1836 (1838–39)
Frowde, The life, extraordinary adventures, voyages and escapes of Neville 1773
Froysell, Thomas *The gale of opportunity* 1650 (1652)
Fruton, Joseph Stewart & Simmonds, Sofia *General biochemistry* 1953
—(ed. 2) 1958
Fry, Caroline *The scripture reader's guide to the devotional use of the holy scriptures* 1828
Fry, Charles B. (and others) *Cricket* 1903
Fry, Christopher *The lady's not for burning: a comedy* 1949
Venus observed 1950
Fry, Roger Eliot *Cézanne: a study of his development* 1927
Letters ed. D. Sutton 2 vols. 1972
Transformations: essays on art 1926
Frye, Northrop *Anatomy of criticism* 1957
ed. *Romanticism reconsidered* 1963
ed. *Sound and poetry* 1957
Frye, William E. *Ohlenschläger's (A. G.) Gods of the North* tr. 1845
Fryer, John *A new account of East India and Persia* 1698
Fryke's Voyage tr. 1700 *See* L., S.
Fulbecke, William *The pandectes of the law of nations* 1602
A parallele or conference of the civill law, the canon law and the common law of England 1601. Pt. II 1602
Fulford, Roger Thomas Baldwin ed. *Dearest child: letters between Queen Victoria and the Princess Royal, 1858–1861* 1964
ed. *Dearest Mama: letters between Queen Victoria and the Crown Princess of Prussia, 1861–1864* 1968
ed. *Your dear letter: private correspondence of Queen Victoria and the Crown Princess of Prussia, 1865–1871* 1971
Fulke, William *An answer of a true Christian* 1577
A confutation of a treatise made by William Allen in defence of the usurped power of popish priesthood to remit sinnes. An apologie of the professors of the gospel in Fraunce against the railing declamation of Peter Frarine tr. by John Fowler 1586
A defense of the sincere and true translations of the holie scriptures into the English tong 1583
A goodly gallerye with a most pleasaunt prospect into the garden of naturall contemplation, to behold the naturall causes of all kynde of meteors 1563 (1655)
D. Heskins, D. Sanders, and M. Rastel, accounted three pillers of the popish synagogue, and ouerthrowne (Heskins parleament repealed; A confutation of Sanders treatise; A refutation of Rastels confutation) 1579
A retentiue to stay good christians in true faith and religion against the motiues of Richard Bristow; also, a discouerie of the daungerous rocke of the popish church 1580
T. Stapleton and Martiall confuted 1580
The text of the New Testament translated by the papists of the traiterous seminarie at Rhemes. With a confutation of all such arguments, etc. *as conteine manifest impietie* 1589
Two treatises written against the papistes: the one being an answere of the Christian protestant to the proud challenge of a popish catholicke (W. Allen); the other a confutation of the popish churches doctrine touching purgatory and prayers for the dead 1577
Fullarton, John H. *Troop Target* 1944
Fullarton, William *General view of the agriculture of the county of Ayr* 1793
A view of the English interests in India 1787
Fuller, Andrew *A literary courtship under the auspices of Pike's Peak* 1893
Fuller, Francis *Medicina gymnastica: or, a treatise concerning the power of exercise with respect to the animal œconomy* 1704
Fuller, George D., & Conard, H. S. tr. *J. Braun-Blanquet's Plant sociology: the study of plant communities* 1932
Fuller, Henry W. *On diseases of the chest* 1862
Fuller, Jane G. *Uncle John's flower-gatherers* 1869
Fuller, Richard Buckminster *Operating manual for Spaceship Earth* 1969
Untitled epic poem on the history of industrialization 1962
Fuller, Roy Broadbent *The ruined boys* 1959
The second curtain 1953
Fuller (afterwards Ossoli), Sarah Margaret *Life without and within* 1859
Woman in the nineteenth century 1845 (1862)
Fuller, Thomas *Abel redivivus; or the dead yet speaking* 1651 (1867)
The appeal of injured innocence 1659 (1840)
The cause and cure of a wounded conscience 1647 (1841, 1867)
The church-history of Britain 1655
A comment on Ruth 1654 (1868)
David's hainous sinne, heartie repentance, heavie punishment 1631 (1867)
Good thoughts in bad times 1645 (1841)
Good thoughts in worse times 1647 (1841)
The historie of the holy warre 1639 (1647, 1840)
The history of the university of Cambridge since the Conquest 1655 (1840)
The history of Waltham-abbey 1655 (1840)
The history of the worthies of England a1661 (1662, 1840)
The holy state 1642; *The profane state* 1642 (1841)
Joseph's party-coloured coat 1640 (1867)
The just man's funeral 1649
Mixt contemplations in better times 1660 (1840)
Ornitho-logie, or the speech of birds (anon.) 1655
A Pisgah-sight of Palestine 1650
A sermon on the 27th March 1643 1643
Sermons a1661
Two sermons 1654
Fuller, Thomas *Pharmacopœia extemporanea* 1702 (1710)
Fullerton, Lady Georgiana C. *Constance Sherwood, an autobiography of the sixteenth century* 1865
Ellen Middleton 1844
Grantley Manor 1847
Lady-bird 1852
Fullwood, Francis *Toleration not to be abused* 1672
Fulton, John *Index canonum* 1872 (1883)
Fulton, Robert *The illustrated book of pigeons*; ed. Lewis Wright 1876 (1882); ed. W. F. Lumley 1893–95
Fulwell, Ulpian *The first part of the eight liberale science entituled Ars adulandi, the art of flattery* 1576
—*newly corrected and augmented* 1579
An enterlude intituled Like wil to like quod the Deuel to the Colier 1568
Fulwood, William *The enimie of idleness* 1568
'Fume, Joseph' (W. A. Chatto) *A paper: of tobacco* 1839
Fundamentals, The—a testimony to the truth 1911–14
Funk & Wagnalls Co. *A standard dictionary of the English language* ed. I. K. Funk et al. 2 vols. 1893–5
—(new ed.) 2 vols. 1928
Standard dictionary of folklore, mythology, and legend ed. M. Leach 2 vols. 1949–50
Funnell, William *A voyage round the world* 1707
Furley, Robert *A history of the Weald of Kent* 1871–74
Furness, William H. *Domestic worship* 1842 (1850)
Folk lore in Borneo 1899 (privately printed)
Fuseli, Henry *Lectures on painting* 1801–15 (ed. R. N. Wornum 1848)
Fysshynge wyth an angle, An older form of the treatyse of, attributed to Dame Juliana Barnes a1450 (Printed from a MS., by Thomas Satchell 1883).
See also *Book of St. Albans*

G

G., E. 1604 *See* Grimstone, E.
G., F. *'Scudery's (G. de)' Artamenes, or the grand Cyrus, an excellent new romance* tr. 1653–55
G., G. *See* Goodman, G.
G., H. *Cataneo's (G.) Most briefe tables to know redily how many ranckes of footemen go to the making of a just battaile* tr. 1574 (1588)
G., H. *Scanderbeg redivivus, an historical account of the life of..John III, king of Poland* 1684
G., I. *Grassi's (G. de) True arte of defence* tr. 1594
G. K. *See* K., G.
G., R. *Bacon's (F.) Naturall and experimentall history of winds* etc. tr. 1653
G., S. *The reformist, a serio-comic-political novel* (by Mrs. S. Green) 1810
G., T. 1616 See *Rich cabinet*
G., W. *Cowel's (J.) Institutes of the lawes of England* tr. 1651
Gabelhouer, O. *See* M., A.
Gaberlunzie-man, The ? 16.. (A. Ramsay, Tea-table misc. 1724)
Gabrielli's Mysterious husband 1801
—*Something odd, a novel* 1804
Gaddis, William *The recognitions* 1955
Gadow, Hans *Amphibia and reptiles* 1901
Gag. A gagge for the Pope and the jesuits, or the arraignement and execution of Antichrist 1624
Gage, John *The history and antiquities of Hengrave in Suffolk* 1822
The history and antiquities of Suffolk, Thingoe hundred 1838
Gage, Thomas *The English-American his travail by sea and land; or a new survey of the West Indias.. With a grammar..of the Indian tongue called Poconchi or Pocoman* 1648
—(second ed.) *A new survey of the West Indias* 1655
Gaiger, Sydney Herbert & Davies, Gwilym Owen *Veterinary pathology and bacteriology* 1932
Gainsford, Thomas *The glory of England, or a true description of many excellent prerogatives and remarkable blessings* etc. 1618 (1619)
The true and wonderfull history of Perkin Warbeck 1618
See also *Rich cabinet*
Galaxy, The 1866–78
Galbraith, John Kenneth *The affluent society* 1958
Gale, Frederick *Echoes from old cricket fields; or, Sketches of cricket and cricketers from the earliest history of the game to the present time* 1871
The game of cricket 1887
The life of the Hon. Robert Grimston 1885
The public school matches, and those we meet there 1853
Gale, Norman *Cricket songs* 1894
Gale, Theophilus *The court of the gentiles* 1669–78
Gale, Thomas *Certaine workes of chirurgerie... An antidotarie conteyning hidde and secrete medicines* 1563
Gallaher, David & Stead, W. J. *The complete rugby footballer on the New Zealand system* 1906
Gallant. A treatyse of a galaunt (in verse) ? 1510 (Hazlitt, Early popular poetry III)
Gallants. The meeting of gallants at an ordinarie, or the walkes in Powles 1604 (Percy Soc. 1841)
Gallenga, Antonio ('L. Mariotti') *Italy in 1848* 1851
Italy past and present 1848
Gallichan, Walter M. *Fishing and travel in Spain* 1904
Gallico, Paul William *The Foolish immortals* 1953
The snow goose 1941
Galloway, Bishop of 1614 *See* Cowper or Couper, W.
Galloway, George *Poems on various subjects, Scotch and English* 1792
Galloway, Robert *Poems, epistles, and songs, chiefly in the Scottish dialect* 1788
Gallwey, Sir Ralph Payne- *The fowler in Ireland* 1882
See also Walsingham, 6th Baron
Galouye, Daniel Francis *The lost perception* 1966
Galpine, John *A synoptical compend of British botany* 1806
Galsworthy, John *Captures* 1923
The country house 1907
Five tales 1918
From the four winds 1897
The fugitive 1913
In Chancery 1920
The Inn of Tranquility: studies and essays 1912
Maid in waiting 1931
The man of property 1906
The patrician 1911
Plays 1909–20
The roof 1929
A sheaf [essays] 1916
The silver spoon 1926
Swan song 1928
To let 1921
The white monkey 1924
Galt, John *Annals of the Parish* 1821
The Ayrshire legatees 1821
The demon of destiny and other poems a1839 (1840)
The entail, or the lairds of Grippy 1823
The last of the lairds 1826
Lawrie Todd, or the settlers in the woods 1830 (1849)
The mermaid, an interlude a1814
The provost 1822
Ringan Gilhaize, or the Covenanters 1823
Rothelan; a romance of the English histories 1824
Sir Andrew Wylie of that ilk 1822
The spaewife, a tale of the Scottish chronicles 1823
The steam-boat 1822
Galton, Francis *Natural inheritance* 1889
ed. *Vacation tourists and notes of travel in 1860, 1861, 1862–63* 1861–64
Galway, Archives of the town of 1485–1710 (in 10th Rep. Hist. MSS. Comm., App. v. 1885)
Galwey, Geoffrey Valentine *The lift and the drop* 1948
'Gambado, Geoffrey' (H. Bunbury) *An academy for grown horsemen... The annals of horsemanship* 1787–91 (1809)
Gamble, Charles Frederick Snowden *The story of a North Sea air station* 1928
Gamble, James Sykes *A manual of Indian timbers* 1881
Gamblers, The, a poem (by Theophilus Swift) 1777
Gambold, William *A Welsh grammar* 1724 (1727)
Gamelyn, The tale of c1400 (Six-text Chaucer, II. Chaucer Soc.; Skeat's Chaucer IV App.)
Gammer Gurton. A ryght pithy, pleasaunt and merrie comedie: intytuled Gammer Gurtons nedle..made by M^r^. S. (?John Still) *M^r^ of Art* 1575 (Dodsley, Old plays; Manley, Specim. pre-Shaks. drama II, 1898)
Gammond, Peter ed. *The Decca book of jazz* 1958
ed. *Duke Ellington: his life and music* 1958
Gandalf's garden 1968–9
Gard *See* Du Gard
Garden, The, an illustrated weekly journal of gardening 1871–
Gardener, Helen H. *An unofficial patriot* 1894
Gardeners' chronicle, The 1841–
Gardiner, Alan Henderson *Egypt of the Pharaohs: an introduction* 1961
The theory of proper names 1940
The theory of speech and language 1932
Gardiner, Bp. James *Advice to the clergy of the diocese of Lincoln* 1697
Gardiner, James *Rapin (R.) Of gardens* tr. 1706
Gardiner, Marguerite *See* Blessington
Gardiner, Ralph *England's grievance discover'd with relation to the coal trade* 1655
Gardiner, Richard *Profitable instructions for manuring, sowing and planting of kitchin gardens* 1599 (1603)
Gardiner, Samuel *A booke of angling or fishing* 1606
Gardiner, Samuel Rawson *History of the great civil war 1642–49* 1886–91
Oliver Cromwell 1899 (1901)
Gardiner, Bp. Stephen *De vers obedientia* tr. 1553 *See* Wood, M.
A declaration of such true articles as G. Joye hath gone about to confute as false 1546
An explication and assertion of the true catholique fayth touchyng the..sacrament of the aulter etc. 1551
Gardner, Erle Stanley *The case of the blonde bonanza* 1962 (UK 1967)
The case of the queenly contestant 1967 (UK 1973)
The case of the stuttering bishop 1936 (UK 1937)
The D.A. draws a circle 1939 (UK 1940)
Gardner, G. B. *Keris and other Malay weapons* 1936
Gardner, George *Travels in the interior of Brazil* 1846
Gardner, Helen Louise *The business of criticism* 1959
Gardner, Hy *So what else is new?* 1959
Gardner, John *The brewer, distiller, and wine manufacturer* 1883

GARDNER, John Edmund *A complete state of death* 1969
The corner men 1969
Founder member 1969
Madrigal 1967
GARDNER, Thomas *An historical account of Dunwich* 1754
GARDNER, W. J. *A history of Jamaica* 1873
GARFIELD, Brian Wynne *Hopscotch* 1975
GARLANDE, John de *Dictionarius* a1250 (Wright, Vocabularies I, 1857)
GARNER, Harry Mason *Oriental blue and white* 1954
GARNER, William *A big enough wreath* 1974
The deep, deep freeze 1968
Ditto, Brother Rat! 1972
The us or them war 1969
GARNETT, David *War in the air: September 1939 to May 1941* 1941
GARNETT, Richard *Life of R. W. Emerson* 1888
William Shakespeare, pedagogue & poacher, a drama 1904 (1905)
GARNETT, Thomas *Observations on a tour through the Highlands and part of the western isles of Scotland* 1800
GARNSEY, Henry E. F. *De Bary's (A.) Comparative morphology and biology of the fungi, mycetozoa and bacteria* tr. 1887
GARRARD, Lewis Hector *Wah-to-Yah, and the Taos trail* 1850
GARRARD, William *The art of warre* a1587 (1591)
GARRATT, George Alfred *The mechanical properties of wood* 1931
GARRETSON, J. *The school of manners, or rules for children's behaviour* (anon.) 1685 (1726)
'GARRETT, Edward' (Mrs. Isab. F. Mayo) *The house by the works* 1879
GARRETT, Robert *Run down: the world of Alan Brett* 1970
GARRETT, Theodore F. ed. *The encyclopædia of practical cookery* 1892-94
GARRICK, David *Works* a1779 (Dramatic works 1798)
Private correspondence a1779 (1831-32)
GARRISON, Wendell P. and Francis J. *William Lloyd Garrison, his life, by his children* 1885-89
GARROD, Alfred B. *The essentials of materia medica* 1855-70
— (Revised and ed. by E. B. Baxter) 1874 (1880)
GARROD, Dorothy A. E. & BATE, D. M. A. *The Stone Age of Mount Carmel* Vol. I 1937
GARTH, Sir Samuel *The dispensary, a poem* 1699 (1700, 1706)
ed. *Ovid's Metamorphoses. Translated by the most eminent hands* (J. Dryden, J. Addison, L. Eusden, A. Mainwaring, S. Croxall, N. Tate, J. Gay, W. Congreve, and the editor) 1717 (1732)
GARTNER, Lloyd P. *The Jewish immigrant in England, 1870-1914* 1960
'GARVE, Andrew' (Paul Winterton) *Boomerang* 1969
The golden deed 1960
The late Bill Smith 1971
Murder in Moscow 1951
GARVIN, James Louis *The economic foundations of peace; or, World-partnership as the truer basis of the League of Nations* 1919
GASCOIGNE, George *Works* a1577 (1587; Cambr. Engl. Classics 1907-10)
The complaynt of Phylomene 1576 (Arber)
The complete poems a1577 (Hazlitt 1869-70)
The delectable history of sundry adventures passed by Dan Bartholomew of Bathe c1572
The droomme of doomes day, wherin the frailties and miseries of mans lyfe are lyvely portrayed 1576
The fruites of warre c1572 (1831)
The glasse of government, a tragicall comedie 1575
A griefe of joye, certeyne elegies 1576
A hundreth sundrie floures bound up in one small poesie 1572
Jocasta, a tragedie..by Euripides tr. 1566
The posies (flowers, hearbes, weedes) 1575
The princelye pleasures at the Courte at Kenelwoorth 1575
The spoyle of Antwerpe faithfully reported 1576 (Arber, Eng. Garner VIII)
The steele glas, a satyre 1576 (Arber)
Supposes: a comedie tr. 1566
For *The wyll of the devill* See *Wyll*
GASCOIGNE, Henry B. *G.'s path to naval fame* 1825
GASCOIGNE, Thomas *The lyfe of seynt Birgette* ?a1445 (Mirr. Our Lady, E.E.T.S. 1873)
GASCOYNE, David Emery *Night thoughts* 1956
Opening day 1933
Poems 1937-1942 1943
A short survey of surrealism 1935
A vagrant, and other poems 1950
'GASKELL, A. P.' (Alexander Gaskell Pickard) *The big game, and other stories* 1947
GASKELL, Mrs. Elizabeth C. *Cranford* (a tale) 1853
A dark night's work 1863
The life of Charlotte Bronte 1857 (1860)
Mary Barton, a tale of Manchester life 1848 (1882)
The moorland cottage 1850
North and South 1854 (1855)
Round the sofa 1859
Ruth, a novel 1853
Sylvia's lovers 1863
Wives and daughters, an every-day story 1865 (1866)
Letters ed. J. A. V. Chapple & A. Pollard 1966
GASKELL, Philip *A new introduction to bibliography* 1972
GASKELL, William *Two lectures on the Lancashire dialect* 1854

GASQUET, Francis A. ed. *Lord Acton and his circle* 1906
—— & BISHOP, E. *Edward VI and the Book of Common Prayer* 1890 (1891)
GASS, Ian Graham, SMITH, P. J., & WILSON, R. C. L. eds. *Understanding the earth: a reader in the earth sciences* 1971
GASS, Patrick *A journal of the voyages and travels of..Capt. Lewis and Capt. Clarke..through the interior parts of North America to the Pacific ocean* 1807
GASTON, William James ('Bill') *Drifting death* 1964
GATAKER, Thomas *An antidote against errour concerning justification* a1654 (1670)
Antinomianism discovered and confuted 1652
A discours apologetical 1654
A discussion of the popish doctrine of transubstantiation 1624
God's eye on his Israel 1645
A good wife God's gift, and a wife indeed 1624
Marriage duties briefly couched together 1620
A mariage praier (Eleazar's prayer) 1624
A mistake or misconstruction removed 1646
— (another ed.) *Antinomianism* (as above)
Mysterious cloudes and mistes 1648
Of the nature and use of lots 1619 (1627)
The spirituall watch 1619-22
Vindication of the annotations on Jer. x. 2 1653
GATES, Reginald Ruggles *A botanist in the Amazon Valley* 1927
Heredity in man 1929
Human genetics 2 vols. 1946
GATLAND, Kenneth William *Development of the guided missile* 1952
— (ed. 2) 1954
GATSCHET, Albert Samuel *The Klamath Indians of southwestern Oregon* 1890
GATTY, Mrs. Margaret S. *The old folks from home; or, a holiday in Ireland* 1861
GAU, John *The richt vay to the kingdom of heuine* 1533 (S.T.S. 1888)
GAUDEN, Bp. John *Considerations touching the liturgy of the church of England* 1661
Ecclesiæ Anglicanæ suspiria, the tears..of the church of England 1659
Hieraspistes: a defence by way of apology for the ministry and ministers of the church of England 1653
Life of R. Hooker (prefixed to H.'s works) 1662
The love of truth and peace, a sermon 1640 (1641)
A sermon..at the funeral of Dr. Brounrig 1660
GAUGAIN, Jane *The lady's assistant for executing..designs in knitting* etc. 1840-46
Gauger's (N.) Mechanism of fire made in chimneys tr. 1716
See also DESAGULIERS, J. T.
GAULE, John *Distractions; or the holy madnesse fervently..inraged against evill men* 1629
Πῦς-μαντία the mag-astro-mancer; or the magicall-astrologicall-diviner posed and puzzled 1651 (1652)
Practique theories; or votive speculations upon Christ's prediction, incarnation etc. 1628-29
The practique theorist's panegyrick 1628
Sapientia justificata: or a vindication of the fifth chapter..to the Romans 1657
Select cases of conscience, touching witches and witchcraft 1646
Gawayne, Syr, a collection of ancient romance poems ed. Sir F. Madden (Bannatyne Club 1839)
Sir Gawayne and the green knight, an alliterative romance-poem 13.. (E.E.T.S. 1864, 1869)
See also *Golagros*
GAY, John *Works* a1732 (1772)
Araminta, a town eclogue 1714
The beggar's opera 1727 (1728)
An epistle to..the Earl of Burlington, A journey to Exeter 1715
Fables (2 parts) 1727, a1732 (II. 1738)
The fan, a poem 1713-20
Journey to Exeter: see Epistle, above
Poems on several occasions 1720 (1745)
The present state of wit (anon.) 1711 (Arber, Eng. Garner VI)
The shepherd's week, in six pastorals 1714
The story of Arachne (from Ovid) 1712
Trivia; or the art of walking the streets of London 1716
The what d'ye call it, a..farce 1715
See also GARTH, Sir S.
Gay News 1972-
Gaya's (L. de) Art of war tr. 1678
GAYNOR, Frank ed. *Pocket encyclopedia of atomic energy* 1950
GAYTON, Edmund *Pleasant notes upon Don Quixot* 1654
— (another ed.) *Festivous notes* (1768)
Gazetteer of Scotland 1803 (1806)
Gazophylacium Anglicanum, containing the derivation of English words 1689
GEAR, Charles William *Introduction to computer science* 1973
Geber See RUSSEL, R.
GÉBLER, Ernest *Shall I eat you now?* 1969
GEDDE, John *A new discovery of an excellent method of beehouses and colonies* 1675
GEDDES, Alexander *Critical remarks on the Hebrew scriptures* 1800
GEDDES, Patrick *Cities in evolution: an introduction to the town planning movement and to the study of civics* 1915
—— *Sex* 1914
—— & THOMSON, J. A. *The evolution of sex* 1889
GEDDES, Paul *The Ottawa allegation* 1973

GEE, Edward *Parsons' (R.) Jesuit's memorial for the intended reformation of England* 1690
GEE, George E. *The practical gold-worker* 1877
The silversmith's handbook 1877 (1882)
GEE, John *The foot out of the snare* 1624
GEE, Samuel J. *Auscultation and percussion* 1870 (1883)
GEIKIE, Archibald *Elementary lessons in physical geography* 1877 (1880)
The scenery of Scotland viewed in connexion with its physical geology 1865
The story of a boulder or gleanings from the note-book of a geologist 1858
Text-book of geology 1882 (also 1885, 1893, 1903)
See also WILSON, G.
GEIKIE, James *The great ice age* 1873 (1874)
GEIKIE, John Cunningham *The English reformation* 1879
George Stanley; or life in the woods 1864 (1874)
The life and words of Christ 1877 (1879)
GELL, Philip George H. & COOMBS, Robin Royston A. eds. *Clinical aspects of immunology* 1963
GELL, Robert *A sermon, 8 Aug.* 1650
GELL, Sir William & GANDY, John P. *Pompeiana: the topography, edifices and ornaments of Pompeii* 1817-19
— *Pompeiana..the result of excavations since* 1819, by Sir W. Gell 1832
GELLIBRAND, Henry *A discourse mathematical of the variation of the magneticall needle* 1635
Gen: The Services' fortnightly 1942-5
Genealogical magazine, The 1897-1904
General linguistics 1955-
General systems 1956-
Generous attachment, The (a novel) 1787
Generydes. A royal historie of the excellent knight Generides c1430 (Roxb. Club 1865)
Generydes, a romance c1440 (E.E.T.S. 1878)
Genesis. The story of Genesis and Exodus, an early English song c1250 (E.E.T.S. 1865, 1873)
See also *Cædmon*
Genetics 1916-
Gent 1640 *See* D., J.
GENTILIS, Robert *Malvezzi's (V.) Considerations upon the lives of Alcibiades and Coriolanus* tr. 1650
Paolo Servita's (P. Sarpi) History of the inquisition tr. 1639 (1676)
GENTLEMAN, Tobias *England's way to win wealth, and to employ ships and mariners* 1614 (Arber, Eng. Garner IV)
Gentleman angler, containing short, plain and easy instructions etc., *The* 1726
Gentleman instructed See DARRELL, W.
Gentleman's calling, The (by the author of The whole duty of man) 1659
Gentleman's magazine, The 1731-1868
Geo abstracts 1972-
Geochimica et cosmochimica acta 1950-
Geofysiske publikationer (title varies) 1919-
Geographical journal, The (Royal Geogr. Soc.) 1893-
Geographical review 1916-
Geological magazine, The, or monthly journal of geology 1864-
Geological Society of America *Bulletin* 1890-
Memoirs 1934-
Special papers 1934-
Geological Society of London *Proceedings* 1826-45; 1952-
Quarterly journal 1845-
Transactions 1811-56
Geologiska Föreningens i Stockholm *Förhandlingar* 1872-
Geologists' Association *Proceedings* 1859-
Geomorphological abstracts 1960-5
GEORGE, Charles B. *Forty years on the rail* 1887 (UK 1888)
GEORGE, David Lloyd *Family letters 1885-1936* ed. K. O. Morgan 1973
GEORGE, Henry *Progress and poverty: an inquiry into the cause of industrial depressions* etc. 1879 (1881)
Social problems 1883 (1884)
GEORGE, Russell D. *Minerals and rocks: their nature, occurrence and uses* 1943
George a Green(e. The history of George a Green, pindar of the town of Wakefield 1706 (Thoms, Early Prose Romances II, 1828)
A pleasaunt conceyted comedie of George a Greene, the pinner of Wakefield (attrib. to R. Greene) 1599 (Dodsley)
Georgia *The colonial records of the State of Georgia* ed. A. D. Candler et al. 1904-
Georgia Historical Society *Collections* 9 vols. 1840-1916
GERALD, Michael C. *Pharmacology: an introduction to drugs* 1974
Geraldina (a novel) 1798
GERARD, Emily (Mme de Laszowska) *The land beyond the forest* 1888
The waters of Hercules 1885
—— & GERARD, Dor. *A sensitive plant* 1891
GERARD or GERARDE, John *A catalogue of plants cultivated 1596-99* 1599 (1876)
The herball, or general historie of plants 1597
— enlarged and amended by T. Johnson (1633, 1636)
GERARD, Sir Montagu G. *Leaves from the diaries of a soldier and sportsman* 1903
GERBIER, Sir Balthazar G. *A brief discourse concerning the three chief principles of magnificent building* 1662
Counsel and advice to all builders, for the choice of surveyors etc. 1663 (1664)
Gerefa a1100 (in Anglia IX 1886)

Gérin, Winifred *Charlotte Brontë: the evolution of a genius* 1967
Elizabeth Gaskell: a biography 1976
Germania: Vierteljahrsschrift für deutsche Alterthumskunde 1856-
Germanic review 1926-
Gerth, Hans Heinrich & Martindale, Don Albert tr. *M. Weber's Ancient Judaism* 1952
Gesner, Abraham *A practical treatise on coal, petroleum, and other distilled oils* 1860 (1865)
Gesta Romanorum, The c1440 (Roxb. Club 1838; E.E.T.S. 1879)
Geste, Edmund *A sermon upon repentance and faith* 1560 (in H. G. Dugdale, Life 1840)
A treatise against the preuee masse 1548 (ibid.)
Gib, Adam *Καινα και παλαια Sacred contemplations, in three parts* 1786
Gibb, Jocelyn ed. *Light on C. S. Lewis* 1965
Gibbon, Charles *For the king, a novel* 1872
For lack of gold 1871
Robin Gray, a novel 1869
Gibbon, Edward *Autobiography and correspondence* a1794 (1796, 1854)
The crusades (from next) (1870)
The history of the decline and fall of the Roman empire 1776-88 (1846, 1869)
— *The student's Gibbon* (abridged by W. Smith 1857)
Memoirs of the life and writings of E. G. c1789 (1796, 1827)
Miscellaneous works a1794 (1796-1815)
'Gibbon, Lewis Grassic' (James Leslie Mitchell) *Sunset song* 1932
Gibbons, Floyd Phillips *The red Napoleon* 1929 (UK 1930)
Gibbons, Stella Dorothea *Cold Comfort Farm* 1932
The matchmaker 1949
A pink front door 1959
Gibbs, Frederick W. *Recognition: a chapter from the history of the North and South American states* 1863
Gibbs, George *Tribes of western Washington and north-western Oregon* 1877
Gibbs, Henry Hucks, afterw. 1st baron Aldenham *The bimetallic controversy* 1886
A colloquy on currency 1893
The double standard 1881
The game of ombre 1874 (1878)
Gibbs, Philip Hamilton *The battles of the Somme* 1917
Unchanging quest 1925
Gibbs-Smith, Charles Harvard *The aeroplane: an historical survey of its origins and development* 1960
Gibson, Bp. Edmund *Observations upon the conduct and behaviour of a certain sect usually distinguished by the name of Methodists* (anon.) ? 1740
Gibson, Guy Penrose *Enemy coast ahead* 1946
Gibson, James *Lectures on popery* 1836
Gibson, Thomas *The anatomy of humane bodies epitomized* 1682 (1697)
Gibson, William *The farrier's dispensatory* 1721 (1734)
The farrier's new guide 1720 (1738)
The true method of dieting horses 1721 (1731)
Gibson, William Ralph Boyce tr. *E. Husserl's Ideas: general introduction to pure phenomenology* 1931
Gibson, William S. *The history of the monastery founded at Tynemouth* 1846-47
Giddens, Anthony *Studies in social and political theory* 1977
Gidley, Lewis *Aletes, a poem* 1865
Gielgud, Val Henry *The candle-holders* 1970
Conduct of a member 1967
In such a night 1974
A necessary end 1969
Giffen, George *With bat and ball: twenty-five years' reminiscences of Australian and Anglo-Australian cricket* 1898
Gifford, George *A dialogue concerning witches and witchcrafts* 1603 (Percy Soc. 1842)
Gifford, Humfrey *A posie of gilloflowers* 1580 (Grosart 1870)
'Gifford, John' (J. R. Green) *The reign of Louis the sixteenth* 1794
Gifford, Thomas *An historical description of the Zetland islands* 1786 (1879)
Gifford, Thomas *The Cavanaugh quest* 1976 (UK 1977)
Gifford, William *The Baviad, a paraphrastic imitation of the first satire of Persius* 1791 (1800)
The Mæviad (a poem) 1795 (1800)
The satires of D. J. Juvenalis tr. 1802
Gifts and graces (by Eliz. Johnston) 1862
Gil or Gill, Alexander *Logonomia anglica* 1619 (1621)
The sacred philosophie of the holy scripture: laid downe.. in.. the apostles' creed 1635
'Gilbert, Anthony' (Lucy Beatrice Malleson) *And death came too* 1956
Death against the clock 1958
Death takes a wife 1959
Don't open the door 1945
Knock, knock, who's there? 1964
Missing from her home 1969
No dust in the attic 1962
Ring for a noose 1963
Tenant for the tomb 1971
Gilbert, Sir Geoffrey *Historical view of the court of Exchequer* a1726 (1738)
The law of evidence a1726 (1791-96)
Reports of cases in equity argued.. in the courts of Chancery and Exchequer a1726 (1742)
Gilbert, Sir Humphrey *A discourse of a discoverie for a new passage to Cataia* 1576
Queene Elizabethes achademy c1570 (Archaeologia XXI, 1827; E.E.T.S. 1869)
Gilbert, John T. *History of the viceroys of Ireland* 1865
Gilbert, Joseph *The christian atonement* 1836 (1852)
Gilbert, Martin *Winston S. Churchill* See Churchill, Randolph Spencer & Gilbert, Martin
Gilbert, Michael Francis *Blood and judgement* 1959
The body of a girl 1972
Close quarters 1947
The dust and the heat 1967
Flash point 1974
Sky high 1955
Gilbert, Thomas *Plan for the better relief and employment of the poor* 1781
Gilbert, William Schwenk *The 'Bab' ballads* 1868-73
Foggerty's fairy and other tales 1877- (1890)
Iolanthe, or the peer and the peri 1882
The mikado, or the town of Titipu 1885
Original plays v.d. (1876-1911)
Patience, or Bunthorne's bride 1880
Utopia limited, or the flowers of progress 1893
Gilbert-Carter, Humphrey tr. *C. Raunkiaer's The life forms of plants* 1934
Gilbey, Sir Walter *Early carriages and roads* 1903
Gilby, Anthony *Grosseteste's (R.) Testamentes of the twelue Patriarches* tr. 1575 (1581, 1604, 1706)
Gilchrist, James *The etymologic interpreter or dictionary of the English language* 1824
The intellectual patrimony, or a father's instructions 1817
The labyrinth demolished, a pioneer of rational philology 1815
Philosophic etymology, a rational grammar 1816
Reason the true arbiter of language 1814
Gilder, Richard W. *The poet and his master, and other poems* 1878
Gildon, Charles *The complete art of poetry* 1718
Giles, Henry Earl *Harbin's Ridge* 1951
Giles, Herbert Allen *A glossary of reference on subjects connected with the Far East* 1878
Giles, Howard ed. *Language, ethnicity and intergroup relations* 1977
Giles, Kenneth *Death and Mr. Prettyman* 1967
Death cracks a bottle 1969
Death in diamonds 1967
A death in the church 1970
A file on death 1973
Some beasts no more 1965
'Giles, Norman' (N. R. McKeown) *The ridge of white waters* 1934
Giles, Peter *A short manual of comparative philology for classical students* 1895
Gilfillan, George *Night, a poem* 1867
Specimens, with memoirs of the less-known British poets 1860
Gill, Alexander *See* Gil, A.
Gill, Edwin Leonard *First guide to South African birds* 1936
Gill, Gerald Byron & Willis, Martin Richard *Pericyclic reactions* 1974
Gill, Merle Avery *Underworld slang* 1929
Gill, Theodore *Catalogue of the fishes of the east coast of North America* 1873
Gill, William J. *The river of golden sand: the narrative of a journey through China and Eastern Tibet to Burmah* 1880
Gillen, Lucy *Return to Deepwater* 1975
Gillespie, Alexander Douglas *Letters from Flanders* 1916
Gillespie, George *A dispute against the English-popish ceremonies obtruded upon the church of Scotland* (anon.) 1637
Male audis; or an answer to Mr. Coleman on his Male dicis 1646
Wholsome severity reconciled with Christian liberty; or the true resolution of a present controversie concerning liberty of conscience (anon.) 1645
Gillespie, William H. *An argument* a priori *for the moral attributes of God* 1865
Gilliard, Ernest Thomas *Living birds of the world* 1958
Gillies, John *Aristotle's Ethics and Politics* tr. 1797 (1804)
Gillmore, Parker *Figuier's (L.) Reptiles and birds* tr. 1869 (1870)
Gillow, Joseph *A literary and biographical history.. of the English Catholics* 1885-87
Gilman, Caroline *Recollections of a southern matron* 1838
Gilman, Henry *Organic chemistry: an advanced treatise* 3 vols. 1938-53
— (ed. 2) 2 vols. 1943
Gilmour, David *Paisley weavers of other days* 1876
Reminiscences of the 'Pen' folk 1871 (1873)
Gilmour, James *Among the Mongols* 1883 (1884)
Gilmour, Samuel Carter *Paper: its making, merchanting and usage* 1955
Gilpin, Alan *Dictionary of economic terms* 1966
Gilpin, E. 1598 *See* Guilpin, E.
Gilpin, George *'Rabbotenu's (Isaac)' Bee-hive of the Romish church* 1579 (1580)
Gilpin, Richard *Dæmonologia sacra, or a treatise of Satan's temptations* 1677 (Grosart 1867)
'Gilpin, Sidney' (G. Coward) *The popular poetry of Cumberland and the lake country* 1875
The songs and ballads of Cumberland 1866 (also 3 series 1874)
Gilpin, William *Observations on the river Wye* 1782
Observations relative chiefly to picturesque beauty made in.. the mountains and lakes of Cumberland and Westmoreland 1786
Remarks on forest scenery 1791
Sermons 1799-1803
Gilson, David *Sermons on practical subjects* 1788
Gimson, Alfred Charles *An introduction to the pronunciation of English* 1962
Giraffi, A. See Howell, J.
Giraldus Cambrensis See *English conquest of Ireland*
Giraud, J. P. *The birds of Long Island* 1844
Girl's own paper, The 1880-
Girton, Daniel *The new and complete pigeon fancyer* c1800
Gisborne, Thomas *Walks in a forest: or poems descriptive of scenery*, etc. 1794 (1796)
Gish, Lillian & Pinchot, A. *Lillian Gish: the movies, Mr. Griffith and me* 1969
Gissing, Algernon *Both of this parish: a story of the by-ways* 1889
A village Hampden 1890
Gissing, George R. *A life's morning* 1888
The nether world 1889
New Grub Street 3 vols. 1891
The odd women 3 vols. 1893
The private papers of Henry Ryecroft 1903
—— & Wells, Herbert George *George Gissing and H. G. Wells: their friendship and correspondence* ed. R. A. Gettman 1961
Gist, Christopher *Journals* a1759 (1893)
Given, Meta H. *Modern encyclopedia of cooking* 2 vols. 1947
Gladstone, Thomas H. *See* Olmsted, F. L.
Gladstone, William Ewart *Church principles considered in their results* 1840
The Eastern crisis, a letter to the Duke of Westminster 1897
The financial statements of 1853, 1860-63 1863
Gleanings of past years 1843- (1879-97)
Homer (literature primer) 1876 (1878)
Homeric synchronism, an enquiry into the time and place of Homer 1876
The impregnable rock of holy scripture 1800 (1892)
Juventus mundi. The gods and men of the heroic age 1868 (1869)
The odes of Horace tr. 1894
The state in its relation with the church 1838 (1839)
Studies on Homer and the Homeric age 1858
Vaticanism: an answer to Replies and reproofs 1875
Gladwin, Francis *The Ayeen Akbery, or the institutes of the emperor Akber* tr. 1783-86 (1800)
Glaister, Geoffrey Ashall *Glossary of the book* 1960
Glanvil, Bartholomew *See* Trevisa
Glanvill, Joseph *A blow at modern Sadducism* 1668
Essays on several important subjects in philosophy and religion 1676
A further discovery of M. Stubbe 1671
Lux orientalis, or an enquiry into the opinion of the eastern sages concerning the præ-existence of souls 1662 (1682)
Palpable evidence of spirits and witchcraft 1668
Plus ultra; or the progress and advancement of knowledge since the days of Aristotle 1668
Saducismus triumphatus, or full and plain evidence concerning witches and witchcraft a1680 (1681, 1726)
Scepsis scientifica: see The vanity of dogmatizing, below
Scirituum nihil est, or the author's defence of The vanity of dogmatizing 1665
Seasonable reflections and discourses 1676
The vanity of dogmatizing, or confidence in opinions etc. 1661
— (2nd ed.) *Scepsis scientifica, or confest ignorance the way to science* 1665
Glanville, Sir John *The voyage to Cadiz* 1625 (Camden Soc. 1883)
Glapthorne, Henry *Plays and poems* c1640 (1874)
The Hollander, a comedy 1640
The ladies priveledge (a comedy) 1640
The lady mother, a comedy 1635 (Bullen, Old plays II)
The tragedy of Albertus Wallenstein 1639 (1640)
Wit in a constable, a comedy 1640
Glascock, William Nugent *The naval sketchbook; or, The Service afloat and ashore* 2 vols. 1826
— (ed. 2) 2 vols. 1826
— (2nd ser.) 2 vols. 1834
Glasgow, Ellen Anderson Gholson *The deliverance: a romance of the Virginia tobacco fields* 1904
Letters ed. B. Rouse 1958
Glasgow, Roy Stanley *Principles of radio engineering* 1936
Glasgow Herald 1805-
Glass, David Victor & Eversley, D. E. C. eds. *Population in history* 1965
Glasscock, J. L., Jr. ed. *Records of St. Michael's parish church, Bishop's Stortford* (Herts) *1431-1882* (1882)
Glasse, Mrs. Hannah *The art of cookery. By a lady* 1747 (1796)
The compleat confectioner, or the whole art of confectionary made plain and easy c1750 (1770)
Glasser, Otto ed. *The science of radiology* 1933 (UK 1934)
Glassop, Lawson *We were the rats* 1944
Glasstone, Samuel *An introduction to electro-chemistry* 1942
Principles of nuclear reactor engineering 1956
Sourcebook on atomic energy 1950
Text-book of physical chemistry 1940 (UK 1941)
— (ed. 2) 1946 (UK 1948)
Glatt, Max Meier, et al. *The drug scene in Great Britain* 1967
Glazebrook, Richard Tetley ed. *A dictionary of applied physics* 5 vols. 1922-3
Glazier, Richard *A manual of historic ornament* 1899

Gleason, Henry Allan (b. 1882) & Cronquist, Arthur *The natural geography of plants* 1964
Gleason, Henry Allan (b. 1917) *An introduction to descriptive linguistics* 1955
— (ed. 2) 1961
Linguistics and English grammar 1965
Gleig, George R. *The life of major-general Sir T. Munro* 1830
Glemser, Bernard *A dear Hungarian friend* 1966
Glencore tower (a novel) 1806
Glenfergus (a novel) 1820
Glenny, George *The gardener's every day book* 1856
Hand-book to the flower garden and greenhouse 1860 (1851)
Gliddon, George R. *Ancient Egypt* 1847 (ed. 10)
Glisan, Rodney *Journal of army life* 1874
Gloag, John Edwards *A short dictionary of furniture, containing 1764 terms used in Britain and America* 1952
Globe and Mail (Toronto) 1844- (1844-1936 with title *Globe*)
Glossary of heraldry 1847: see Gough, H.
Glossary of terms used in Grecian, Roman, Italian and Gothic architecture, A 1836 (1850)
Glosses of Prudentius c1000 (Zeitschrift für deutsches Alterthum N.S. VIII, 1876: Germania N.S. XI, 1878; Napier, O.E. glosses 1900)
Gloucester, Bishop of *See* Fowler, E. 1692; Nicholson, W. 1663
Gloucester, Robert of *See* Robert
Gloucester glossary 1890 *See* Robertson, J. D.
Gloucestershire, A glossary of provincial words used in 1851
Glover, Richard *Poetical works* a1785 (Chalmers 1810)
The Athenaid a1785 (1787)
Leonidas, a poem 1737
Medea, a tragedy 1761
Glover, Stephen ed. *The history of the county of Derby* 1829
Gluckman, Herman Max *Custom and conflict in Africa* 1955
Glueck, Bernard & Lind, John Edward tr. *A. Adler's The neurotic constitution: outlines of a comparative individualistic psychology and psychotherapy* 1917 (UK 1921)
Glyn, Anthony Geoffrey L. S. *The dragon variation* 1969
Glyn, Elinor *'It', and other stories* 1927
Reflections of Ambrosine 1902
The visits of Elizabeth 1900 (1906)
Glynn, Joseph *Rudimentary treatise on the power of water as applied to drive flour mills* etc. 1853
Gnomic verses a1000 ('Denksprüche' in Grein I, 1883)
Goad, John *Astro-meteorologica, or aphorisms and discourses of the bodies celestial, their natures and influences* 1686
Goad, Thomas *The doleful euen-song* 1623
Goadby, Mrs. R. *See* Carew, B. M.
Goddard, Guibon *Introduction to (T.) Burton's Diary* 1828
Goddard, Thomas *Plato's demon; or the state-physician unmaskt* 1684
Godden, Jon & Godden, Margaret Rumer *Two under the Indian sun* 1966
Godden, Margaret Rumer *Black narcissus* 1939
The greengage summer 1958
In this house of Brede 1969
Kingfishers catch fire 1953
Godefroy, Frédéric *Dictionnaire de l'ancienne langue française et de tous ses dialectes du ixe au xve siècle* 1881-1902
Godey's magazine (U.S.) 1896
Godfrey, Eve *Retail selling and organization* 1962
Godfrey, James William & Amos, Stanley William *Sound recording and reproduction* 1952
Godfrey, Philip *Back-stage: a survey of the contemporary English theatre from behind the scenes* 1933
Godfrey, Robert *Various injuries and abuses in chymical and galenical physick..detected* 1674
Godly Queene Hester See *Esther*
Godolphin, John *A view of the admiral jurisdiction* 1661
Godstow. The English register of Godstow nunnery, near Oxford c1450 (E.E.T.S. 1905-06)
Godwin, Bp. Francis *A catalogue of the bishops of England* 1601
See also Godwin, M.
Godwin, Mrs. Mary Wollstonecraft *See* Wollstonecraft
Godwin, Morgan *Bp. F. Godwin's Annales of England* tr. 1630 (1675)
Godwin, Thomas *Moses and Aaron. Civil and ecclesiastical rites used by the ancient Hebrews* 1625 (1641)
Romanæ historiæ anthologia. An English exposition of the Romane antiquities 1613 (1625)
Godwin, William *Essays..never before published* a1836 (1873)
Fleetwood, or the new man of feeling 1805
History of the Commonwealth of England..to the restoration of Charles the second 1824-28
The inquirer: reflections on education, manners, and literature 1797
Life of G. Chaucer 1803 (1804)
Lives of the necromancers 1834
Mandeville, a tale of the seventeenth century 1817
Things as they are; or the adventures of Caleb Williams 1794 (1838, 1865)
Thoughts on man, his nature etc. 1831
Goede's (C. A. G.) Stranger in England; or travels in Great Britain tr. 1807
Goffe, Thomas *The careles shepherdess, a tragi-comedy by T. G.* a1629 (1656)
Going to service: a sequel to My station and its duties 1836
Golagros and Gawane, The knightly tale of c1470 (1508; Bannatyne Club 1839; Sc. allit. poems, S.T.S. 1897)
Gold, Herbert *The man who was not with it* 1956 (UK 1965)
Gold, Robert S. *A jazz lexicon* 1964
Jazz talk 1975
Goldberg, Isaac *The wonder of words* 1938
Golden boke See Berners
Golden legend See Caxton, W.
Golden mirrour, A 1589 *See* Robinson, R.
Golden south 1890 *See* 'Lyth'
Golder, William *The pigeons' parliament, a poem* (on New Zealand) 1854
Goldin, Hyman Elias ed. *Dictionary of American underworld lingo* 1950
Golding, Arthur *The eyght bookes of C. J. Cæsar* tr. 1565
Heminges (N.) Postill or exposition of the gospels tr. 1569
Justinus' (M. J.) Abridgmente of the histories of Trogus Pompeius tr. 1564 (1570)
Mornay's (P. de) Woorke concerning the trewnesse of the christian religion tr. (begun by Sir P. Sidney and finished by A. Golding) 1587 (1592, 1617)
The xv bookes entytuled Ovid's Metamorphosis tr. 1565-67 (1567, 1593)
The Psalmes of David and others, with J. Calvin's commentaries tr. 1571
The sermons of J. Calvin upon Deuteronomie tr. 1583
Golding, Louis *Magnolia Street* 1932
Golding, Per. *An epitome of Frossard* (Froissart)..*by I. Sleydane* tr. 1608
Golding, William Gerald *Free fall* 1959
Lord of the flies 1954
Pincher Martin 1956
The spire 1964
Goldsmith, Oliver *Works* a1774
The bee (essays) 1759
The captivity, an oratorio 1764
The citizen of the world 1750-62 (1837, 1840)
The deserted village 1770
The double transformation, a tale 1765
Essays 1758-65
The good-natured man, a comedy 1768 (1780, 1854)
The Grecian history a1774 (1774)
A history of the earth and animated nature (= *Nat. Hist.*) 1774 (1776, 1862)
An history of England in a series of letters from a nobleman to his son 1764 (1772)
The history of England 1771
The life of Richard Nash 1762
The memoirs of a protestant (J. Marteilhe) condemned to the galleys of France for his religion tr. 1765 (1895)
Miscellaneous works a1774 (1837, Globe 1895)
Retaliation, a poem 1774
Scarron's (P.) Comic romance tr. a1774 (1775)
She stoops to conquer, or the mistakes of a night, a comedy 1773
A survey of experimental philosophy a1774 (1776)
The traveller, or a prospect of society 1764
The vicar of Wakefield 1766
Gollancz, Victor *My dear Timothy: an autobiographical letter* 1952
Gombrich, Ernst Hans Josef *Art and illusion* 1960
The story of art 1950
Gomme, Alice Bertha *The traditional games of England, Scotland, and Ireland* 1894-98
Gomme, Sir (George) Laurence *Primitive folk-moots* 1880
Gonsalvius Montanus' (R.) Discovery and plain declaration of sundry subtill practices of the holy inquisition of Spayne tr. (V. Skinner) 1568
— (another ed.) *A full ample and punctuall discovery of..the Spanish inquisition* tr. 1625
Gonzanga; a drama a1814 (New British theatre III)
Gooch, Benjamin *A practical treatise on wounds and other chirurgical subjects* 1767
Good, Carter Victor ed. *Dictionary of education* 1945
— (ed. 2) 1959
Good, John Mason *The book of nature* 1826 (1834)
The study of medicine 1822 (1825)
— ed. 3 by S. Cooper (1829; 1834)
See also Polehampton, E. T. W.
Good advice 1687 *See* Gother, J.
Good counsels for the peace of reformed churches 1641
Good food guide, The 1951-
Good housekeeping (London) 1922-
Good housekeeping (New York) 1885-
Good housekeeping cookery book: compiled by The Good Housekeeping Institute 1948
— (rev. ed.) 1954
— (rev. ed.) 1960
Good housekeeping's home encyclopaedia 1951
— (ed. 4) 1956
Good huswifes handmaide for the kitchin, The 1594
Good huswifes jewell, The 1596 *See* Dawson, T.
Good motoring 1935-
Good words (a magazine) 1860-1906
Goodale, George Lincoln *Physiological botany: Outlines of the histology of phænogamous plants: Vegetable physiology* 1885 (1892)
Goodall, Walter *An examination of the letters said to be written by Mary Queen of Scots to James, Earl of Bothwell* 1754
Goodchild, George Frederick & Tweney, C. F. *A technological and scientific dictionary* 1904-6
Goode, George Brown *American fishes, a popular treatise upon the game and food fishes of North America* 1888
The fisheries and fishery industries of the United States (*The natural history of useful aquatic animals* 1884, *The history, and methods of the fisheries* 1887)
A review of the fishery industries of the United States 1883 (Fisheries exhibition literature)
Goode, William *The discoverie of a publique spirit* (a sermon) 1645
Goodfield, June *Courier to Peking* 1973
Goodge, William T. *Hits! skits! and jingles!* 1899
Goodier, James Hillis *Dictionary of painting and decorating trade terms* 1961
Goodly primer in Englyshe, A newly corrected 1535
Goodman, Christopher *How superior powers ought to be obeyed of their subjects* 1558
Goodman, Clark ed. *The science and engineering of nuclear power* 2 vols. 1947-9
Goodman, Godfrey *The creatures praysing God, or the religion of dumbe creatures* 1622
Goodman, John *The old religion demonstrated in its principles* etc. 1684 (1848)
The penitent pardoned 1679
A winter-evening conference between neighbours (anon.) 1684 (1705)
Goodman, Nicholas *Hollands leaguer* (anon.) 1632
Goodman, Richard Merle ed. *Genetic disorders of man* 1970
Goodman, William Louis *The history of wood-working tools* 1964
Goodrich, Chauncey A. *Select British eloquence* 1852
Goodrich, Samuel Griswold *Recollections of a lifetime, or men and things I have seen* 1857
Goodridge, Charles M. *Narrative of a voyage to the South Seas* 1832 (1837)
Goodwin, Derek *Pigeons and doves of the world* 1967
Goodwin, Harvey *Memoir of Bishop (C. F.) Mackenzie* 1864
Goodwin, John *Anti-Cavalierisme, or truth pleading* etc. 1642 (1663)
Innocency and truth triumphing 1644 (1645)
Πλήρωμα τὸ πνευματικόν or, a being filled with the spirit a1665 (1670, 1867)
Right and might well met 1648
Goodwin, Thomas *Works* a1680 (1681-1704; 1861-64)
A childe of light, walking in darkness 1636 (1643)
Christ set forth in his death, resurrection, ascension 1642
A fair prospect, showing the difference between things seen and not seen (a funeral sermon) 1658
The tryall of a christian's growth in mortification or purging out corruption etc. 1641 (1643)
Of the work of the Holy Ghost..in our salvation a1680
Zerubbabels encouragement to finish the temple 1642
Googe, Barnaby *Eglogs, epytaphes, and sonettes* 1563 (Arber)
Heresbach's (C.) Foure bookes of husbandry tr. 1577 (1586)
Kirchmeyer's (T.) The popish kingdome or reigne of Antichrist tr. 1570
"*Palingenius' (M.)*" *The zodiake of life* tr. 1560 (1561)
Gookin, Vincent *The author and case of transplanting the Irish into Connaught vindicated* 1655
Goolden, Barbara *At the foot of the hills* 1956
For richer, for poorer 1959
Goosecappe, Sir Gyles, knight, a comedie 1606 (Bullen, Old plays III)
Gorboduc 1561 *See* Norton, T.
Gordimer, Nadine *Burger's daughter* 1979
the lying days 1953
Six feet of the country: 15 short stories 1956
A world of strangers 1958
Gordon, Adam Lindsay *Poems* a1870 (Oxford 1912)
Gordon, Alexander *Maffei's (F. S.) Compleat history of the ancient amphitheatres* tr. 1730
Gordon, Charles G. *The journals at Kartoum* 1884 (1885)
Gordon, Lady Duff *See* Wallace, Lady G. M.
Gordon, Eric Valentine *An introduction to Old Norse* 1927
Gordon, Frank *Pyotshaw, or the devil's seat* 1885
Gordon, James *The village and the doctor* 1897
Gordon, James E. H. *A physical treatise on electricity and magnetism* 1880
Gordon, James F. S. *The book of the chronicles of Keith, Grange, Ruthven* etc. 1880
ed. *L. Shaw's History of the province of Moray* new ed. 1882
Gordon, John *Εἰρηνοκοινωνία, the peace of the communion of the church of England* 1612
'Ενωτικόν or a sermon of the union of Great Brittanie 1604
Gordon, Mrs. Mary *Christopher North, a memoir of John Wilson* 1862
Gordon, Mildred & Gordon, Gordon *The informant* 1973
Ordeal 1976 (UK 1977)
Gordon, Patrick *A short abridgement of Britane's distemper from..1639 to 1649* c1650 (Spalding Club 1844)
Gordon, Patrick *Geography anatomized or a compleat geographical grammer* 1693 (1725)
'Gordon, Richard' (Gordon Stanley Ostlere) *Doctor at sea* 1953
Doctor in the house 1952
Gordon, Rupert Montgomery & Lavoipierre, Michel M. J. *Entomology for students of medicine* 1962
Gordon, Taylor *Born to be* 1929
Gordon, Thomas *A cordial for low spirits, being a collection of* (his) *valuable tracts* a1750 (1751)
The humourist, being essays upon several subjects (anon.) 1720-25
The works of Tacitus tr. 1728-31
—— & Trenchard, J. *The independent Whig* 1720
Gordon, William *Pharmaco-pinax, or a table..of the pryces*

of all the usuall medicaments..contayned in D. Gordon's apothecarie..shop 1625
Gordon, William *The general counting house and man of business* 1766
Gordon, William J. *Foundry, forge and factory* 1890
Gordonhaven, scenes and sketches of fisher life in the north. By an old fisherman 1887
Gore, Mrs. Catherine G. F. *Castles in the air, a novel* 1847
Fascination, and other tales 1842
Heckington, a novel 1858
A life's lessons (a novel) 1856
Mammon (a novel) 1855
Sketches of English character 1846 (1852)
Gore, Bp. Charles *The body of Christ* 1901
ed. *Lux mundi; a series of studies in the religion of the incarnation* 1889
Roman Catholic claims 1888 (1889)
Gore, George, et al. *Practical chemistry* 1856 (Orr's Circle of the sciences)
Gore, John *The way to well-doing* (a sermon) 1638
Gorer, Geoffrey Edgar Solomon *Africa dances* 1935
Gores, Joseph N. *Dead skip* 1972 (UK 1973)
Hammett 1975 (UK 1976)
Gorges, Sir Arthur *Bacon's (F.) Wisdome of the ancients* tr. 1619
Lucan's Pharsalia tr. 1614
Gorges, Sir Ferdinando *America painted to the life* (pamphlets) *a*1647 (1658-59)
Goring, C. R. & Pritchard A. *Micrographia, containing practical essays on..microscopes* etc. 1837
Microscopic illustrations 1830
Gorman, James Thomas *Modern weapons of war* 1942
Gorrie, Daniel *Summers and winters in the Orkneys* 1868
Gortner, Ross Aiken *Outlines of biochemistry* 1929
Goschen, George J. *The theory of foreign exchanges* 1861 (1864)
Gospel of Nicodemus, The 13.. (E.E.T.S. 1907)
Gospels. The holy gospels in Anglo-saxon; Northumbrian and old Mercian versions etc. *c*950, *c*975, *c*1000, *c*1160 (ed. Skeat 1871-87)
Gosse, Edmund W. *Father and son: a study of two temperaments* 1907
Gossip in a library 1891
Gray (English men of letters) 1882
New Poems 1879
Studies in the literature of northern Europe 1879
Gosse, Phillip H. *Actinologia Britannica: a history of British sea anemones* 1860
The aquarium: an unveiling of the wonders of the deep sea 1854
The birds of Jamaica 1847
The Canadian naturalist 1840
Land and sea 1865
A manual of marine zoology for the British isles 1855-56
Natural history: Mammalia 1848, *Birds* 1849, *Reptiles* 1850, *Fishes* 1851, *Mollusca* 1854
A naturalist's sojourn in Jamaica 1851
The ocean 1849
Omphalos: an attempt to untie the geological knot 1857
The romance of natural history 1860
Gossip's story, A (by Jane West) 1796
Gosson, Stephen *The ephemerides of Phialo... And a short apologie of The schoole of abuse* 1579
Pleasant quippes for upstart newfangled gentlewomen (anon.) 1595 (1596)
The schoole of abuse, containing a plesaunt inuectiue against poets, pipers, plaiers, iesters and such like caterpillers of a commonwelth 1579 (Arber)
Gosvami, O. *The story of Indian music* 1957
Gother, John *Good advice to the pulpits* (anon.) 1687
Gotlieb, Calvin Carl & Hume, J. N. P. *High-speed data processing* 1958
Gott, John *Letters of Bishop Gott, arranged by members of his family* 1918
Gouge, Thomas *Christian directions, shewing how to walk with God all the day long* 1660 (1664, 1831)
Gouge, William *The dignitie of chivalrie; set forth in a sermon* 1626
Gods three arrowes; plague, famine, sword 1631
A learned commentary on the whole Epistle to the Hebrewes *a*1653 (1655, 1867)
The saints sacrifice, or a commentarie on the cxvi psalme 1632 (1868)
Gough, Henry *A glossary of terms used in British heraldry* (anon.) 1847 (1894)
Goulburn, Edward Meyrick *The office of the holy communion in The book of common prayer* 1863
The pursuit of holiness: a sequel to Thoughts etc. 1869
Thoughts on personal religion 1862
Gould, George M. *A dictionary of new medical terms* 1905
A new medical dictionary 1890
Gould, John *The birds of Asia* 1850-81(-83)
The birds of Australia 1840-69
The mammals of Australia 1845-63
A monograph of the Trochilidæ or family of humming birds 1849-81(-87)
A monograph of the Trogonidæ, or family of trogons 1838
Gould, Joseph *The letter-press printer* 1876
—(ed. 3) 1884
Gould, Julius & Kolb, William L. eds. *A dictionary of the social sciences* 1964
Gould, Nathaniel ('Nat.') *The double event, a tale of the Melbourne cup* 1891 (1892)
Gould, William *An account of English ants* 1747
Goulding, Francis R. *The young marooners on the Florida coast* 1852 (1853)
Gouldman, Francis *A copious dictionary in three parts* (Eng.-Lat., Lat.-Eng., Proper names) 1664 (1669, 1674)
Governance of lordschipes *c*1400 (in Secreta secretorum, E.E.T.S. 1898)
Government of the tongue, The, by the author of The whole duty of man 1674
Government of Venice 1677 See *Amelot de la Houssaye*, A.N.
Gower, Granville Leveson *Surrey provincialisms* 1876 (E.D.S.)
A glossary of Surrey words 1893 (E.D.S.)
Gower, John *Confessio amantis* 1390 (R. Pauli 1857; Eng. Works, E.E.T.S. 1900)
In praise of peace *c*1400 (Eng. Works, E.E.T.S.)
Gower, John *Ovids Festivalls, or Romane calendar* tr. 1640
Gower, Lord Ronald Sutherland- *My reminiscences* 1883
Records and reminiscences 1903
Gowers, Ernest Arthur *A dictionary of modern English usage* (ed. 2) 1965 *See* Fowler, Henry Watson
Gowers, William R. *A manual of diseases of the nervous system* 1886-88 (1893)
Gowing, Margaret Mary *Britain and atomic energy, 1939-1945* 1964
Gowrie conspiracy. The earle of Gowries conspiracie against the kings maiestie of Scotland 1600
See also Mackenzie, G.
Gowther, Sir. Syr Gowghter *c*1440 (Utterson, 1817)
Grabau, Amadeus William *Principles of stratigraphy* 1913
A textbook of geology 2 vols. 1921
Grabbe, Eugene Munter, Ramo, S. & Wooldridge, D. E eds. *Handbook of automation, computation and control* 3 vols. 1958-61
Grace, Alfred Augustus *The tale of a timber town* 1914
Grace, William Gilbert *Cricket* 1891
Gracian's (B.) Courtiers oracle, or the art of prudence tr. 1685 (1694)
'Graeme, Bruce' (Graham Montague Jeffries) *Tomorrow's yesterday* 1972
Two and two make five 1973
Graff, Willem Laurens *Language and languages* 1932
Grafton, Richard *A chronicle at large and meere history of the affayres of England* 1568 (1809)
A continuacion of the chronicle of England, begynning where J. Hardyng left (1470-1543) 1543 (1812)
Graham, Catherine Macaulay *Letters on education* 1790
Graham, Dougal *The collected writings of D. G. 'skellat' bellman of Glasgow* *a*1779 (1883)
'Graham, James' (Henry Patterson) *Bloody passage* 1974
Graham, Sir James *Life and letters* 1792-1861 (1907)
Graham, Maria *Journal of a residence in India* 1812
Graham, Neill *Murder in a dark room: a Solo Malcolm thriller* 1973
Graham, P. Anderson *The red scaur: a novel of manners* 1896
Graham, Patrick *General view of the agriculture of Stirlingshire* 1812
Graham, Stephen *Europe—whither bound?: being letters of travel from the capitals of Europe* 1921
Graham, Thomas *Elements of chemistry* 1842 (1850-58)
Graham, Thomas J. *Modern domestic medicine* 1827 (1834, 1861)
Graham, W. W. *Climbing the Himalayas* 1887 (in From the equator to the pole)
Graham, William *Last links with Byron, Shelley and Keats* 1898
Grahame, James *The birds of Scotland: with other poems* 1806
The sabbath, a poem 1804
Grahame, Kenneth *The golden age* 1895
Pagan papers 1894
The wind in the willows 1908
Grahame-White, Claude & Harper, Harry *The aeroplane: past, present and future* 1911
Aircraft in the Great War: a record and study 1915
Grainger, James *Poetical works* *a*1766
The sugar-cane, a poem 1764
A poetical translation of the elegies of Tibullus and of the poems of Sulpicia 1759
Gramophone, The 1923-
Granada Television *Some technical terms and slang* 1974
'Grand, Sarah' (Mrs. M'Fall) *Babs the impossible* 1901 (1906)
The heavenly twins 1893
Grand debate, The 1661 See *Book of common prayer*
Grandmother's money 1860 *See* Robinson F. W.
Granger, James *Letters between G. and many of the most eminent literary men of his time* v.d. (1805)
Granger, Thomas *A familiar exposition or commentarie on Ecclesiastes* 1621
Syntagma logicum, or the divine logike 1620
Grant, A. C. *Bush life in Queensland* 1881 (1882)
Grant, Allan *Mr. Secretary Pepys, with extracts from his diary* 1867
Grant, Mrs. Anne *Essays on the superstitions of the Highlanders of Scotland* (anon.) 1811
Letters from the mountains; being the real correspondence of a lady between the years 1773 and 1807 1807
Poems on various subjects 1803
Grant, David *Lays and legends of the north, and other poems and songs* 1884
Scotch stories, or the chronicles of Keckleton 1888
Grant, George Monro *Ocean to ocean: Sandford Fleming's expedition through Canada in 1872* 1873
Grant, James *History of the burgh and parish schools of Scotland* 1876
Grant, James A. *A walk across Africa* 1864
Grant, James, journalist *The great metropolis* 1836
Random recollections of the House of Commons 1836
—*of the House of Lords* 1836
Sketches in London 1838
Grant, James, novelist *Adventures of an aide-de-camp* 1848
Arthur Blane, or the hundred cuirassiers 1858
The Cameronians, a novel 1881
Memoirs and adventures of Sir W. Kirkaldy of Grange 1849
One of the six hundred, a novel 1875
Grant, Johnson *A summary of the history of the English church* 1811-25
Grant, Maria M. *The sun-maid: a romance* 1876 (1877)
Grant, Robert *History of physical astronomy* 1852
Grant, Robert E. *Outlines of comparative anatomy* 1841
Granta, The (Cambridge) 1889-
Granville, Augustus B. *The spas of Germany* 1837 (1838)
Granville or Grenville, Denis *Works and letters* 1665-1703 (Miscellanea, Surtees Soc. 1861)
Granville, George *See* Lansdowne
Granville, Harriet, Countess *Letters* 1810-45 (1894)
Granville, Mary *See* Delany, Mrs. M.
Granville, Wilfred *A dictionary of sailors' slang* 1962
A dictionary of theatrical terms 1952
Graphic, The: an illustrated weekly newspaper 1869-
Grassi (G. de) His true arte of defence, plainlie..teaching..how a man..may safelie handle all sortes of weapons etc. tr. I. G. 1594
Grassineau, James *A musical dictionary* 1740
Gratarolus' (G.) Direction for the health of magistrates and studentes Englished by T. Newton 1574
Gratiæ theatrales, or a choice ternary of English plays 1662
Grattan, John Henry Grafton & Gurrey, Percival *Our living language: a new guide to English grammar* 1925
Grattan, Thomas C. *The history of the Netherlands* 1830
Grau, Robert *The theatre of science: a volume of progress and achievement in the motion picture industry* 1914
Graunt, John *Natural and political observations..made upon the Bills of mortality* 1662 (1676)
Graves, Charles *Chasles' (M.) Two geometrical memoirs on the general properties of cones of the second degree* etc. 1841
Graves, Charles Patrick Ranke *Life line* 1941
Graves, Richard *Eugenius, or anecdotes of the golden vale* 1785
Euphrosyne, or amusements on the road of life 1776
Recollections of some particulars in the life of W. Shenstone 1788
The spiritual Quixote; or the summer's ramble of Mr. Geoffrey Wildgoose 1772 (1873)
Graves, Robert J. *A system of clinical medicine* 1843
Graves, Robert P. *Life of Sir W. R. Hamilton* 1882-89
Graves, Robert von Ranke *Claudius the god and his wife Messalina* 1934
Collected poems 1938
The feather bed 1923
Good-bye to all that: an autobiography 1929
I, Claudius 1934
Mock Beggar Hall 1924
The pier-glass 1921
Poems, 1926-1930 1931
Poems, 1938-1945 1946
Poems, 1953 1953
Seven days in new Crete 1949
Welchman's hose 1925
Whipperginny 1923
—— & Hodge, Alan Searle *The long week-end: a social history of Great Britain, 1918-1939* 1940
Graves, Samuel R. *A yachting cruise in the Baltic* 1863
Gray, Alexander tr. *R. Grelling's The crime* 3 vols. 1917-18
Gray, Asa *The botanical text-book* 1858
—6th ed. I. *Structural botany* 1880. II. *Physiological botany* 1885
First lessons in botany and vegetable physiology 1857
A manual of the botany of the Northern United States 1848 (1867)
Gray, Charles *Poems* 1811
—(2nd ed.) *Poems and songs* 1814
Gray, Cecil William Turpie *Contingencies, and other essays* 1947
Gray, Dulcie Winifred C. *Dead give away* 1974
Gray, Henry *Anatomy, descriptive and surgical* 1858 (1869, 1883)
Gray, James Henry *The boy from Winnipeg* 1970
Gray, John *Archaeology and the Old Testament world* 1962
Gray, John E. *Catalogue of the specimens of mammalia in..the British Museum* 1850-52
List (of the same) 1843
Gray, Laurence F. & Graham, Richard *Radio transmitters* 1961
Gray, Louis Herbert *Foundations of language* 1939
'Gray, Maxwell' (M. G. Tuttiett) *The reproach of Annesley, a novel* 1888
The silence of dean Maitland, a novel 1886
Gray, Samuel F. *A natural arrangement of British plants* 1821
Gray, T. de *See* De la Grey, T.
Gray, Thomas *Works in prose and verse* *a*1771 (Gosse 1884)
The alliance of education and government 1748
The bard, a pindaric ode 1757
Correspondence of T. G. and W. Mason 1736-71 (1853)
Correspondence with N. Nicholls 1764-71 (Wks. V. 1843)

GRAY, Thomas (*cont.*)
The descent of Odin, an ode 1761
Elegy written in a country church-yard 1750, 1768
The fatal sisters, an ode 1761
Hymn to ignorance c1742
Letters 1736–71 (1775, 1884, 1893)
A long story 1750
Ode on a distant prospect of Eton college 1742
Ode on the pleasure arising from vicissitude 1754
Ode on the spring 1751
The progress of poesy, a pindaric ode 1754
(Translations from) *Propertius* 1738, 1742
— *Statius* 1736
Gray's Inn Journal, The (by A. Murphy) 1752–54 (1756)
GRAYMORE, Clive N. ed. *Biochemistry of the eye* 1970
Great Exhibition *Official descriptive and illustrated catalogue of the Great Exhibition of the Works of Industry of all Nations* 5 parts 1851
Greatheart 1866 *See* THORNBURY, G. W.
GREATOREX, Wilfred *Crossover* 1976
GREAVES, John ed. *Withers' (R.) Description of the Grand Signior's seraglio* 1650 (1653)
GREELEY, Horace *The American conflict: a history of the great rebellion in the United States* (1860–65) 1864–66
GREEN, Abel & LAURIE, Joe *Show biz, from vaude to video* 1951
GREEN, Alexander H. *Geology for students. Physical geology* 1876 (1882)
—— et al. *Coal, its history and uses* 1878
GREEN, Anna K. (Mrs. Rohlfs) *Behind closed doors* 1888
Hand and ring (a novel) 1883
GREEN, Bennett Wood *Word-book of Virginia folk-speech* 1899
GREEN, Helen *At the actors' boarding house* 1906
The Maison de Shine: more stories of the actors' boarding house 1908
'GREEN, Henry' (Henry Vincent Yorke) *Living* 1929
GREEN, John Herbert *Basic clinical physiology* 1969
GREEN, John R. *The conquest of England* 1883
Letters a1883 (L. Stephen 1901)
The making of England 1881
Readings from English history 1879
A short history of the English people 1874
Stray studies from England and Italy 1876
GREEN, Lawrence George *Great African mysteries* 1935
In the land of afternoon 1949
Tavern of the seas 1947
To the river's end 1948
GREEN, Martin Burgess *Children of the sun: a narrative of 'decadence' in England after 1918* 1976
GREEN, Mrs. Mary A. E. (née Wood) ed. *Letters of royal and illustrious ladies of Great Britain.. to the close of the reign of Queen Mary* 1846
GREEN, Matthew *Poems* a1737 (1790)
On Barclay's Apology for the Quakers a1737
The spleen, an epistle (in verse) 1737
GREEN, Matthias *An English grammar* 1837
GREEN, Peter tr. *R. Escarpit's The novel computer* 1966
GREEN, Mrs. S. *The reformist, a serio-comic-political novel* 1810
GREEN, Thomas *Extracts from the diary of a lover of literature* 1796–1800 (1810)
GREEN, Thomas *The universal herbal; or botanical, medical and agricultural dictionary* 1816–20
GREEN, Thomas Henry *An introduction to pathology and morbid anatomy* 1871 (1873)
GREEN, Thomas Hill *Prolegomena to ethics* a1882 (1883)
Works a1882 (1885–88)
Green carnation, The (by R. S. Hichens) 1894
GREENE, Henry Graham *The basement room, and other stories* 1935
Brighton rock 1938
A burnt-out case 1961
The comedians 1966
The confidential agent 1939
The end of the affair 1951
England made me 1935
A gun for sale 1936
The heart of the matter 1948
The honorary consul 1973
The human factor 1978
It's a battlefield 1934
Journey without maps 1936
The lawless roads: a Mexican journey 1939
The Ministry of Fear: an entertainment 1943
Nineteen stories 1947
Our man in Havana 1958
The power and the glory 1940
The quiet American 1955
The third man, and The fallen idol 1950
Travels with my aunt 1969
GREENE, Joseph R. *A manual of the animal kingdom.* I. *Protozoa* 1859. II. *Cœlenterata* 1861
GREENE, Robert *Life and complete works* a1592 (Grosart 1881–86)
Dramatic works (and poems) a1592 (Dyce 1831, 1861)
Alcida: Greenes metamorphosis 1588 (1617)
Arcadia = *Menaphon*
Art of conny catching = *Notable discovery*
Ciceronis amor, Tullies love 1589 (1609)
The comicall historie of Alphonsus king of Arragon a1592 (1599)
A disputation betweene a hee conny-catcher and a shee conny-catcher 1592
Dorastus and Fawnia = *Pandosto*
Euphues his censure to Philautus 1587
Greenes farewell to folly 1591 (1617)
Greenes groatsworth of witte 1592 (1617)
Greenes mourning garment 1590 (1616)
Greenes neuer too late 1590 (1600)
Greenes Orpharion a1592 (1599)
Gwydonius, the carde of fancie 1584 (1608)
The historie of Arbasto king of Denmarke 1584 (1626)
The historie of Orlando Furioso a1592 (1599)
The honorable historie of Frier Bacon and Frier Bongay c1590 (1630; 1878)
A maidens dream. Vpon the death of.. Sir C. Hatton 1591
Mamillia, a mirrour or looking glasse for the ladies of England (2 parts) 1583, a1592 (II, 1593)
Menaphon, Camillas alarum to slumbering Euphues etc. (ed. 1610 *Greenes Arcadia; or Menaphon*) 1589 (1616; Arber)
Morando, the tritameron of love 1584–87
A notable discovery of coosnage (= *the art of conny-catching*) 1591–92 (1592)
Palmer's ode in *Neuer too late*
Pandosto the triumph of time (= *the hystorie of Dorastus and Fawnia*) 1588 (1607, 1843)
Perimedes the blacke-smith 1588
Philomela, the lady Fitzwaters nightingale 1592 (Archaica I, 1815)
Planetomachia, or the firste parte of the generall opposition of the seven planets etc. 1585
A quip for an upstart courtier 1592 (Harl. Misc.; 1871)
The Scottish historie of James the fourth a1592 (Manly 1898)
See also *Defence of conny catching; George a Greene; Greenes vision; Selimus*
—— & LODGE, T. *A looking glasse for London and Englande* 1594 (1598)
GREENE, Bp. Thomas *Four discourses on the four last things; viz., death, judgment, heaven and hell* 1753
GREENER, Michael *The Penguin dictionary of commerce* 1970
GREENER, William *Gunnery in 1858* 1858
The science of gunnery as applied to the use and construction of fire-arms 1841 (1846)
GREENER, William W. *The breech-loader and how to use it* 1892
The gun and its development 1881 (1885)
Greenes vision: written at the instant of his death 1592
GREENHAM, Richard *Works* a1594 (1599)
GREENHILL, Thomas *Νεκροκηδεια or the art of embalming* 1705
Greenhouse companion, The (by J. C. Loudon) 1824
GREENLEAF, A. B. *Ten years in Texas* 1881
GREENLEE, Sam *The spook who sat by the door* 1969
GREENOUGH, James Bradstreet & KITTREDGE, George Lyman *Words and their ways in English speech* 1901 (UK 1902)
GREENWELL, Dora *Carmina crucis* 1869
Colloquia crucis 1871
GREENWELL, George C. *A glossary of terms used in the coal trade of Northumberland and Durham* 1849 (1851, 1888)
GREENWELL, William *British barrows: a record of the examination of sepulchral mounds in various parts of England* 1877
GREENWOOD, Frederick & GREENWOOD, James *Under a cloud* 3 vols. 1860
GREENWOOD, George *Hints on horsemanship* (anon.) 1839 (1861)
'GREENWOOD, Grace' (Sara J. Clarke) *Haps and mishaps of a tour in Europe* 1854
GREENWOOD, Henry *The iaylers iayle-deliuerie* 1619 (1628)
GREENWOOD, James *An essay towards a practical English grammar* 1711
GREENWOOD, James *The sailor's sea-book. A rudimentary treatise on navigation* 1850
— revised ed. by W. H. Rosser (1879)
GREENWOOD, James *In strange company* 1873
The seven curses of London 1869
GREENWOOD, John *An annswer to G. Gifford's pretended defence of read prayers and devised liturgies* 1590
A collection of certaine sclaunderous articles gyuen out by the bisshops... Also the some of certaine conferences had in the Fleete.. with two prisoners (J. G. and H. Barrow) *there* 1590
GREENWOOD, Peter Humphrey *J. R. Norman's A history of fishes* (ed. 2) 1963 *See* NORMAN, John Roxborough
GREENWOOD, William H. *Steel and iron* 1884
GREER, Germaine *The female eunuch* 1970
GREER, Henry *A dictionary of electricity* 1883
GREG, Percy *Across the zodiac* 1880
GREG, Robert P. & LETTSOM, W. G. *Manual of the mineralogy of Great Britain and Ireland* 1858
GREG, William R. *The creed of christendom* 1851 (1863)
Enigmas of life 1872 (1873)
Literary and social judgments 1868 (1869)
Miscellaneous essays a1881 (1882–84)
Political problems for our age and country 1870
Rocks ahead; or the warnings of Cassandra 1874
GREGG, Josiah *Commerce of the prairies; or, The journal of a Santa Fé trader* 2 vols. 1844
'GREGG, William S.' (Frances M. Robinson) *Irish history for English readers* 1886
GREGOR, Walter *The dialect of Banffshire* 1866 (Philol. Soc.)
An echo of the olden time from the north of Scotland 1874
Notes on the folk-lore of the north-east of Scotland 1881 (Folk-lore Soc.)
Gregory I Saint. *The Gregory legend* c1300 (F. Schulz 1876)
GREGORY, Benjamin *The holy catholic church the communion of saints* 1873
Side lights on the conflicts of methodism 1827–52 1898
GREGORY, Edwin *Metallurgy* 1932
Gregory's (D.) Elements of astronomy, physical and geometrical tr. 1715 (1726)
GREGORY, Francis *The doctrine of the glorious trinity, not explained, but asserted by several texts,* etc. 1695
GREGORY, George *A dictionary of arts and sciences* 1806
GREGORY, George *Elements of the theory and practice of physic* 1820–23 (1835, 1846)
GREGORY, Jackson *The maid of the mountain: a romance of the California wilderness* (UK ed. with title *Bab of the backwoods*) 1925
Man to man 1920 (UK 1921)
GREGORY, John *Works* a1646 (1683–84)
Notes and observations upon some passages of scripture 1646 (1650)
Posthuma: or certain learned tracts (*The Assyrian monarchie* etc.) a1646 (1649)
GREGORY, John Walter & BARRETT, Benjamin Hilton *General stratigraphy* 1931
GREGORY, Olinthus G. *A treatise of mechanics* 1806 (1813, 1815)
GREGORY, William *G.'s Chronicle of London* a1470 (in Hist. collect. citizen of London, Camden Soc. 1876)
GREGORY, William *Outlines of chemistry* 1845
— (later edd.) *A handbook of inorganic chemistry* 1853 (1857)
A handbook of organic chemistry 1852 (1856)
GREGORY, William H. *Egypt in 1855–56* 1859
GREIN, Christian W. M. *Bibliothek der angelsächsischen Poesie* 1857–64 (1883–97)
Bibliothek der angelsächsischen Prosa 1872 (1885–88)
GRENEWEY, Richard *The annales of C. Tacitus. The description of Germanie* tr. 1598 (1622)
GRENFELL, Wilfred Thomason *A Labrador doctor* 1919 (UK 1920)
GRENVILLE, Denis *See* GRANVILLE
GRENVILLE, Richard P. *See* BUCKINGHAM AND CHANDOS, 2nd Duke of
GRENVILLE, William W., Baron Grenville *Essay on the supposed advantages of a sinking fund* 1828
GRESHAM, Sir Thomas *See* BURGON, J. W.
GRESLEY, William *Bernard Leslie, or a tale of the last ten years* 1842 (1843)
Charles Lever, or the man of the nineteenth century 1841
The forest of Arden, a tale.. of the English reformation 1841 (1842)
Frank's first trip to the continent 1845
The siege of Lichfield, a tale.. of the great rebellion 1840
Sophron and Neologus; or common sense and philosophy 1861
GRESLEY, William S. *A glossary of terms used in coal mining* 1883
GRESWELL, Edward *An exposition of the parables* etc. 1834–35
GRESSWELL, Peter *Environment: an alphabetical handbook* 1971
Grete herball, The tr. 1526 (1529)
GRETTON, Frederic E. *Memory's harkback through half-a-century 1850–58* 1889
GREVIL *See* GREVILLE, F.
GREVILLE, Charles C. F. *The G. memoirs. A journal of the reigns of George IV and William IV* 18.. (1874)
(2nd and 3rd parts) *A journal of the reign of Queen Victoria* 1837–52, 1852–60 (1885, 1887)
GREVILLE, Fulke, 1st Baron Brooke *Certaine learned and elegant workes* a1628 (1633; Grosart 1870)
Cælica, containing cix sonnets a1628 (1633)
A letter to an honorable lady a1628 (1633)
The life of the renowned Sir Philip Sidney a1628 (1652)
The tragedie of Alaham a1628 (1633)
The tragedy of Mustapha 1609 (1633; Dodsley)
'GREVILLE, Fulke, Baron Brooke,' pseud. *The five yeares of King James, or the condition of the state of England* etc. 1643 (Harl. Misc.)
GREVILLE, Robert, 2nd Baron Brooke *A discourse opening the nature of that episcopacie which is exercised in England* 1641
The nature of truth 1641
GREVILLE, Robert Fulke *Diaries* ed. F. M. Bladon 1930
GREW, Nehemiah *The anatomy of plants* (*The anatomy of plants begun, the anatomy of roots,.. trunks,.. leaves,.. flowers,.. fruits* etc.) 1671–81 (1682)
Cosmologia sacra; or a discourse of the universe, as it is the creature and kingdom of God 1701
Musæum regalis societatis; or a catalogue and description of the rarities belonging to the Royal Society, and preserved at Gresham College 1681
GREW, Sydney *The art of the player-piano: a text-book for student and teacher* 1922
GREY, Anchitell *Debates of the house of commons 1667–94* a1702 (1769)
GREY, Lady Jane *See* JANE, Queen
Grey Friars. The chronicle of the Grey friars of London (to 1556) 15.. (Camden Soc. 1852)
'GREY OWL' (George Stansfield Belaney) *The men of the last frontier* 1931
GRIDER, John McGavock *War birds: diary of an unknown aviator* 1926 (UK 1927)
GRIER, William *The mechanic's pocket dictionary, being a note book of technical terms, rules* etc. 1837
GRIERSON, Edward *A crime of one's own* 1967
Reputation for a song 1952
GRIERSON, George Abraham *Linguistic survey of India* 12 vols. 1903–22
GRIERSON, John *High failure* 1936

Grieve, Maud *A modern herbal* 2 vols. 1931
Griffin, Bartholomew *Fidessa, more chaste then kinde* (sonnets) 1596 (Singer 1815, Grosart 1876, Arber, Eng. Garner V)
Griffin, Gerald *The collegians* 3 vols. 1829
Griffin, John J. *A system of crystallography* 1841
Griffis, William E. *The mikado's empire* 1876
The religions of Japan 1895
Griffith, Edward *Cuvier's Animal kingdom arranged in conformity with its organisation* tr. 1827–35
Griffith, Mrs. Elizabeth *Deliberate distress, by 'Frances'* 1769
The history of Lady Barton, a novel 1771
Viaud's (P.) Shipwreck tr. 1771
See also Griffith, R.
Griffith, John W., & Henfrey, A. *The micrographic dictionary, a guide to the examination and investigation of..microscopic objects* 1856 (1881–83)
Griffith, Matthew *The fear of God and the king* (a sermon) 1660
Griffith, Richard *The Gordian knot, by 'Henry'* 1769
—— & Griffith, Elizabeth *A series of genuine letters between Henry and Frances* 1757 (1767)
Griffith, Thomas *The waist-high culture* 1959 (UK 1960)
Griffith-Jones, Ebenezer *The ascent through Christ* 1899
Griffiths, Frederick A. *The artillerist's manual and compendium of infantry exercise* 1839 (1859, 1862)
Griffiths, Roger *An essay to prove that the jurisdiction and conservacy of the Thames..is committed to the Lord Mayor and City of London* 1746
Grigson, Geoffrey Edward Harvey *The Englishman's flora* 1955
Grim, the collier of Croydon: or the devil and his dame. By I. T. a1600 (Gratiæ theatrales 1662; Dodsley)
Grimalde, Nicholas *M. T. Cicero's Three bookes of dueties* (Offices) tr. 1553 (1558, 1598)
Poems a1557 (Tottel's miscellany, Arber)
Grimble, Arthur Francis *A pattern of islands* 1952
Return to the islands 1957
Grimm's (J. L. C.) Teutonic mythology tr. 1880–83
Grimstone, Edward *Acosta's (J. de) Naturall and morall historie of the East and West Indies* tr. E. G. 1604 (also Hakluyt Soc. 1880)
Goulart's (S.) Admirable and memorable histories tr. 1607
Matthieu's (P.) Heroyk life..of..Henry the fourth tr. 1612
A true history of the siege of Ostend tr. 1604
Grindal, Abp. Edmund *Remains* a1583 (Parker Soc. 1843)
Grindon, Leo H. *Life; its nature, varieties and phenomena* 1856 (1875)
Grisebach, August H. R. *Flora of the British West Indian Islands* 1864
Grisell. The history of patient Grisel 1619, c1630
See also Dekker, T.
Grobianus 1739 *See* Bull, R.
Grollman, Arthur *Pharmacology and therapeutics* 1951 (and several later editions used)
Groom, Percy & Balfour, Isaac Bayley tr. *J. E. B. Warming's Oecology of plants* 1909
Grosart, Alexander B. ed. *The Chertsey worthies library* 1876–
ed. *The Fuller worthies library* 1868–70
ed. *The Huth library or Elizabethan-Jacobean unique or very rare books in verse and prose* 1881–
ed. *Occasional issues of unique or very rare books* 1875–83
Small sins 1863 (ed. 2)
Grose, Francis ed. *The antiquarian repository* 1775 (1807–09)
A classical of the vulgar tongue 1785 (also 1796, and Egan 1823)
Military antiquities respecting a history of the English army 1786–88
The olio; being a collection of essays, etc. 1793
A provincial glossary; with a collection of local proverbs etc. 1787 (also 1790)
A treatise on ancient armour and weapons 1786
Grose, John Henry *A voyage to the East-Indies* 1757 (1766)
Gross, Charles *The gild merchant, a contribution to British municipal history* 1890
Gross, Samuel D. *A practical treatise on the diseases..of the urinary bladder* etc. 1851 (1876)
Grossinger, Jennie *The art of Jewish cooking* 1958
Grossmith, George & Grossmith, Walter Weedon *The diary of a nobody* 1892
Grote, George *Analysis of the influence of natural religion on the temporal happiness of mankind. By P. Beauchamp* 1822
Aristotle a1871 (1872)
Fragments on ethical subjects a1871 (1876)
A history of Greece 1846–56 (1862)
Plato and the other companions of Sokrates 1865
Grote, John *An examination of the utilitarian philosophy* (of J. S. Mill) a1866 (1870)
Exploratio philosophica: rough notes on modern intellectual science 1865
A treatise on the moral ideals 1865 (1876)
Grotius (H.) Of the law of warre and peace tr. C. B(arksdale) 1654
See also Whewell, W.
Grout, Frank Fitch *Petrography and petrology* 1932
Grove, Sir George *A dictionary of music and musicians* 1878–89 (1904–10)
Grove, Matthew *The most famous and tragicall historie of Pelops and Hippodamia*, etc. 1587 (Grosart 1878)
Grove, Sir William R. *Contributions to science* a1874 (in 6th ed. of next)
On the correlation of physical forces 1846 (1855, 1867, 1874)
Growth (Menasha, Wisconsin) 1937–
Growth of deism in England, An account of the 1696
Gruber, Jeffrey S. *Lexical structures in syntax and semantics* 1976
Grub-street journal, The 1730–37
Grundy, George Beardoe *Fifty-five years at Oxford* 1945
Grymeston, Elizabeth *Miscelanea, meditations, memoratives* 1604
Gualtier, Bon See Martin, Sir T.
Guardian, The (By Sir R. Steele, Addison, etc.) 1713 (1756)
Guardian, The (continuation of *The Manchester Guardian*) 1959–
Guardian Weekly, The (continuation of *Manchester Guardian Weekly*) 1968–
Guazzo's (S.) Art of conversation tr. 1738
See also Pettie, G.
Gude and godlie ballatis. A compendious book of godly and spiritual songs commonly known as The gude and godlie ballatis 1567 (1868; S.T.S. 1897)
Günther, Albrecht C. L. G. *An introduction to the study of fishes* 1880
Günther, Alfred *Microphotography in the library* 1962 (Unesco; reprinted from *Unesco bulletin for libraries* Vol. XVI, No. 1, Jan.–Feb. 1962)
Guenther, Ernest *The essential oils* 6 vols. 1949–52
Guest, Edwin *A history of English rhythms* 1838 (also ed. Skeat 1882)
Guest, M. J. *Lectures on the history of England* 1879
Guggisberg, Charles Albert Walter *S.O.S. Rhino* 1966
Guibert's (P.) The charitable physitian, shewing the manner to make and prepare..all remedies, etc. tr. J. W. 1639
Guide to the stage, A 1751
Guidman. Legends of the north. The guidman o' Inglismill, and the fairy bride 1873
Guilfoyle, William Robert *Australian plants suitable for gardens, parks, timber reserves, etc.* 1911
Guillemeau's (J.) French chirurgerye or the manualle operations of chirurgerye tr. A. M. 1597
Guilletiere's (G. Gillet's) Account of a late voyage to Athens tr. 1676
Guillim, John *A display of heraldrie* 1610 (also 1632, 1638, 1660)
Guilpin, Edward *Skialetheia, or a shadowe of truth in certaine epigrams and satyres* 1598 (Grosart 1878)
Guinness, Henry G. *The approaching end of the age viewed in the light of history, prophecy and science* 1878
Guistard and Sismond, The stately tragedy of 1597 (in J. S., Certaine worthy MS. poems)
Guizot's (F. P. G.) General history of civilization in Europe tr. 1837
Gulbenkian, Nubar *Pantaraxia* 1965
Gulland, William Giuseppi *Chinese porcelain* 1898
Gullick, John Michael *Malaysia* 1969
Gullick, Thomas J. & Timbs, J. *Painting popularly explained* 1859
'Gulliver, Lemuel, Jr.' *Modern Gulliver's travels* 1796
Gulliver, Sam *The Vulcan bulletins* 1974
Gully, James Manby *Magendie's (F.) Formulary for the reparation and medical administration of certain new remedies* tr. 1835 (1836)
'Gun Buster' (John Austin) *Return via Dunkirk* 1940
Gungwu, Wang *See* Wang Gungwu
Gunn, Mrs. Aeneas (Jeannie) *We of the Never-Never* 1908
Gunn, J. S. *An opal terminology* 1971 (Sydney University: Australian Language Research Centre, Occasional Paper No. 15)
The terminology of the shearing industry 1965 (ibid., Occasional Papers Nos. 5 & 6)
Gunn, John *The Orkney book* 1909
Gunn, Thom *Fighting terms: poems* 1954
The sense of movement 1957
Gunning, Bp. Peter *The paschal or Lent-fast apostolical and perpetual* 1662
Gunpowder Treason, The history of the (by Bp. J. Williams) 1678
A true and perfect relation of the whole proceedings against the late..traitors 1606
— *The gunpowder treason, with a discourse of the manner of its discovery, and a perfect relation* etc. (1679)
Gunter, Archibald C. *Miss Dividends, a novel* 1892 (1893)
Mr. Potter of Texas 1888
Gurnall, William *The christian in compleat armour, or, a treatise of the saints war against the devil* (3 parts) 1655, 1658, 1662
Gurnett, John William & Kyte, Colin Henry John *Cassell's dictionary of abbreviations* 1966
Gurney, Edmund, Myers, F. W. H., & Podmore, F. *Phantasms of the living* 1886 (Society for psychical research)
Gurney, Henry P. *Crystallography* 1878
Gurney, Hudson *Cupid and Psyche, a mythological tale from the Golden ass of L. Apuleius* 1799 (1800)
Gurney, Oliver Robert *The Hittites* 1952
Gurr, Edward *The rational use of dyes in biology, and general staining methods* 1965
Synthetic dyes in biology, medicine and chemistry 1971
Gurwood, John ed. *The dispatches of..the Duke of Wellington 1799–1818* 1834–38
Gustafson, Axel C. F. *The foundation of death, a study of the drink question* 1884 (1888)
Gutch, John ed. *Collectanea curiosa; or miscellaneous tracts, relating to the history and antiquities of England and Ireland, the universities of Oxford and Cambridge*, etc. 1781
Guthlac. The Anglo-saxon version of the life of St. Guthlac, written by Felix..of Crowland c1000. With a translation by Charles W. Goodwin (1848)
Guthrie, Frederick *Practical physics. Molecular physics and sound* 1878
Guthrie, Gideon *G. G., a monograph written 1712–30* (1900)
'Guthrie, John' (John Brodie) *The little country* 1935
'Guthrie, Ramsay' (J. G. Bowran) *Kitty Fagan: a romance of pit life* 1900
Guthrie, Thomas *Christ and the inheritance of the saints* 1858 (1860)
Guthrie, Thomas A. *See* 'Anstey, F.'
Guthrie, Virgil B. *Petroleum products handbook* 1960
Guthrie, William *The christian's great interest* 1659 (1667, 1724)
Sermons a1665 (1880)
Guthrie's (W.) New system of modern geography 1792
Guthrie-Smith, William Herbert *Tutira: the story of a New Zealand sheep station* 1921
Guthry, Bp. Henry *Memoirs* a1676 (1702)
Guy of Warwick. The romances of Sir Guy of Warwick and Rembrun his son 13.. (Abbotsford Club 1840)
The romance of Guy of Warwick 13.. (E.E.T.S. 1883–91)
— (later version) 14.. (E.E.T.S. 1875–76)
Guy, Albert Glasgow *Physical metallurgy for engineers* 1962
Guy, Richard *Practical observations on cancers*, etc. 1762
Guy Livingstone 1857 *See* Lawrence, G. A.
Guylforde, Sir Richard *The pylgrymage of Sir R. G. to the Holy land 1506* 1511 (Camden Soc. 1851)
Guy's Hospital reports 1836–
Guyton, Arthur Clifford *Textbook of medical physiology* 1956
Guyton de Morveau (L. B.). A translation of the table of chemical nomenclature proposed by de Guyton, Lavoisier, Bertholet, and de Fourcroy (by G. Pearson) 1794, 1799
Gwilt, Joseph *An encyclopædia of architecture, historical, theoretical, and practical* 1842 (1859)
Gwynne-Vaughan, Helen Charlotte I. & Barnes, Bertie Frank *The structure and development of the fungi* 1927
Gzowski, Peter *Peter Gzowski's book about this country in the morning* 1974

H

H. A. 1633 *See* A., H.
H., A. *See* Asshurst, Sir H.
H. D. 1661 *See* Collinges, John
H. G. *See* G., H.
H., G. 1611 See *Anti-Coton*
H., G. *Leti's (G.) Il cardinalismo di Santa Chiesa; or the history of the cardinals of the Roman church* faithfully englished by G. H. 1670
H., G. *See* Hakewill, G.; Harvey, G.; Herbert, G.
H., I. *The petition (of I. H.) and articles exhibited in Parliament against Iohn Pocklington, parson of Yelden, in Bedfordshire* 1641
H., J. *Paracelsus his archidoxes* tr. 1661
H., J. *See* Hall, John, Joseph; Hammond, J.; Harvey, James; Healey, J.; Heath, J.; Humfrey, J.; Hutton, J.
H., N. 1694 See *Ladies dictionary*
H., P. *An impartial view of the two late parliaments* 1711
H., P. *The Hiberniad* (Dedication signed P. H., i.e. Paul Hiffernan) 1754
H., R. *Lavater's (L.) Of ghostes and spirites walking by nyght* tr. 1572 (1596)
H., R. *The arraignement of the whole creature at the barre of religion, reason, and experience* 1631
H., R. *The school of recreation* 1684
H., S. *The golden law* 1656
See also Harsnet, Samuel
H., T. *See* Hawkins, Thomas
Haagner, Alwin Karl & Ivy, Robert Henry *Sketches of South African bird life* 1908
Haas, Paul & Hill, Thomas George *An introduction to the chemistry of plant products* 1913
Habberton, John *Helen's babies* 1876
The Jericho road: a story of western life 1877
Haber, Heinz *Man in space* 1953
Habershon, Samuel O. *Pathological and practical observations on diseases of the abdomen* 1862 (1878)
Habington, Thomas *A survey of Worcestershire* a1647 (Worcs. Hist. Soc. 1893–94)
Habington, William *Castara* 1634–40 (Arber 1870)
The historie of Edward the fourth 1640
Poems a1645 (1810)
The Queene of Arragon 1640
Habits of good society, The; a handbook of etiquette for ladies and gentlemen 1859
Hacke, William *A collection of original voyages* 1699
Hacket, Bp. John *A century of sermons upon several remarkable subjects* a1670 (Published by Thomas Plume (with life) 1675)
Scrinia reserata a memorial offer'd to the great deservings of John Williams, archbishop of York a1670 (1693)
Hacket, Thomas *Thevet's (A.) New found worlde, or Antarctike* tr. 1568
Hackforth-Jones, Frank Gilbert *One-one-one: stories of the Navy* 1942
Sixteen bells: stories 1946

'Hackston, James' (Harold Frederick N. Gye) *Father clears out* 1966
Haddan, Arthur W. *Apostolical succession in the Church of England* 1869
Haddington, Thomas Hamilton, 6th Earl of *A treatise on the manner of raising forest trees* 1733 (1761)
Haddon, Alfred C. *Evolution in art; as illustrated by the life-histories of designs* 1895
The races of man and their distribution 1909
The study of man 1898
Haddon, Archibald *Green room gossip* 1922
Haden, Ernest Faber, Han, M. S., & Han, Y. W. *A reasonance-theory for linguists* 1962
Hadfield, Miles *British trees* 1957
Hadley, Arthur T. *Railroad transportation, its history and its laws* 1886
Hadley, James *Essays philological and critical, selected from the papers of J. H.* a1872 (1873)
A Greek grammar for schools and colleges 1861
— revised, and in part rewritten, by F. de F. Allen (1884)
Haeckel's (E.H.P.A.) Evolution of man tr. 1879
History of creation tr. by E. Ray Lankester 1876
Hagen, Hermann A. *Synopsis of the Neuroptera of North America* 1861
Hagenbach's (C. R.) Compendium of the history of doctrines tr. by C. W. Buch 1847
Haggar, Reginald George *The concise encyclopedia of continental pottery and porcelain* 1960
A dictionary of art terms 1962
See also Mankowitz, C. W. & Haggar, R. G.
Haggard, Sir H. Rider *Allan Quatermain* 1887
Allan's wife 1889
Benita: an African romance 1906
Black heart and white heart 1900
Cleopatra 1889
Colonel Quaritch, V.C. 1888
Dawn 1884
Doctor Therne 1898
A farmer's year 1899
Heart of the world 1896
Jess 1887
King Solomon's mines 1885
Maiwa's revenge 1888
Mr. Meeson's will 1888
Nada the lily 1892
Rural England 1902
She: a history of adventure 1887
The witch's head 1885
'Haggard, William' (Richard Henry Michael Clayton) *The arena* 1961
Closed circuit 1960
The hardliners 1970
The hard sell 1965
The high wire 1963
The power house 1966
The protectors 1972
Haggis, Geoffrey Harvey ed. *Introduction to molecular biology* 1964
Hague, Douglas Chalmers *Managerial economics: analysis for business decisions* 1969
Hahn-Hahn's (I.M.L.S.F.G.) Lives of the fathers of the desert tr. 1867
'Haig, Alec' *Peruvian printout* 1974
Hailey, William Malcolm (Baron Hailey) *An African survey* 1938
— (rev. ed.) 1957
Haines, Herbert *A manual of monumental brasses* 1861
Hake, Alfred E. *The story of Chinese Gordon* 1883
Hake, Edward *Newes out of Powles Churchyarde* 1579 (1872)
Hake, Gordon *Memoirs of eighty years* 1892
Hakewill, George *An apologie or declaration of the power and providence of God in the government of the world* 1627 (1630)
A comparison betweene the dayes of Purim and that of the Powder treason 1626
King Davids vow for reformation 1621
Hakewill, William *The libertie of the subject* 1641
Hakluyt, Richard *Diuers voyages touching the discouerie of America* 1582
The principall navigations, voiages and discoueries of the English nation 1589
— another ed. 1598–1600 (1809–12, 1903–05)
Galvano's or Galvam's (A.) Discoveries of the world, unto the yeere 1555 tr. 1601 (Hakluyt Soc. 1862)
Halas, John & Manvell, Arnold Roger *The technique of film animation* 1959
Halberstam, David *The powers that be* 1979
Haldane, Elizabeth S. *James Frederick Ferrier* 1899
Haldane, John Burdon Sanderson & Huxley, Julian Sorell *Animal biology* 1927
Haldane, Robert *(Spon's) Workshop receipts* 1883 (Series II)
Haldeman, Samuel S. *Affixes in their origin and application, exhibiting the etymologic structure of English words* 1865
Analytic orthography 1860
Outlines of etymology 1877
Hale, Edward E. *Christmas in Narragansett* 1884
His level best 1873
How to do it 1872
If, yes, and perhaps 1868
In his name: a story of the dark ages 1873
Ups and downs 1873
Hale, Edward E. (the younger) *James Russell Lowell and his friends* 1899
Hale, John *The grudge fight* 1964
Hale, Mason Ellsworth *The biology of lichens* 1967
Hale, Sir Matthew *Contemplations moral and divine* 1676–77
A discourse of religion a1676 (1684)
A discourse touching provision for the poor a1676 (1683)
Historia placitorum coronæ. The history of the pleas of the crown a1676 (1736)
The history and analysis of the common law of England a1676 (1713)
The jurisdiction of the Lords House, or Parliament, considered according to antient records a1676 (1796)
Pleas of the crown; or, a methodical summary of the principal matters relating to that subject a1676 (1678, 1682)
Preface to H. Rolle's Abridgment 1668
The primitive origination of mankind a1676 (1677)
See also Hargrave, F.
Hale, Susan *Letters* ed. C. P. Atkinson 1919
Hale, Thomas *An account of several new inventions; also a treatise of naval philosophy written by Sir W. Petty* 1691
Hales, John *Golden remains* a1656 (1659); *with additions, viz. sermons and miscellanies, also, letters and expresses concerning the Synod of Dort* (1673, 1688)
Several tracts a1656 (1677)
A sermon at St. Maries in Oxford concerning the abuses of obscure and difficult places of Holy Scripture 1617
A tract concerning schisme and schismatiques (anon.) 1642
Brevis disquisitio 1653 *See* Stegmann, J.
Dissertatio de pace 1653 *See* Przipcovius, S.
Hales, John W. *Longer English poems* 1872
Notes and essays on Shakespeare 1884
Hales, Stephen *Some considerations on the causes of earthquakes* 1750
Statical essays 1727–31
Half-hours with best authors (publ. C. Knight) 1847
Halfpenny, William *The art of sound building, demonstrated in geometrical problems* 1725
Halhed, Nathaniel B. *A code of Gentoo laws* tr. 1776
Hali meidenhad, an alliterative homily c1230 (E.E.T.S. 1866, 1922)
'Haliburton, Hugh' (James L. Robertson) *Dunbar: being a selection from the poems of an old makar, adapted for modern readers* 1895
In Scottish fields 1890
Ochil idylls and other poems 1891
Haliburton, Thomas C. *The attaché; or, Sam Slick in England* 2 vols. 1843
— (2nd ser.) 2 vols. 1844
The clockmaker; or the sayings and doings of Samuel Slick of Slickville 1835 (1837), 1838, 1840
Nature and human nature 1855
Sam Slick's wise saws and modern instances; or, what he said, did, or invented 2 vols. 1853
ed. *Traits of American humour, by native authors* 1852 (1866)
Halifax, Charles Montagu, 1st Earl of *Poetical works* a1715 (1790, 1810)
—— & Prior, Matthew *The hind and the panther transvers'd* 1687
Halifax, George Savile, Marquis of *Works* a1695 (1912)
A character of King Charles the second: and political, moral, and miscellaneous thoughts and reflections a1695 (1750)
Miscellanies a1695 (1699–1700)
Halkett, Lady Anne *Autobiography* a1699 (Camden Soc. 1875)
Hall, Abraham Oakley *The Manhattaner in New Orleans; or, Phases of 'Crescent City' life* 1851
'Hall, Adam' (Trevor Dudley-Smith) *The Kobra manifesto* 1976
The 9th directive 1966
The Striker portfolio 1969
The Tango briefing 1973
Hall, Anna M. (Mrs. S. C. Hall) *Sketches of Irish character* 1829
The Whiteboy; a story of Ireland in 1822 1845
See also Hall, S. C.
Hall, Archibald John *The standard handbook of textiles* 1946
— (ed. 7) 1969
A student's textbook of textile science 1963
Hall, Arthur *Ten books of Homers Iliades* tr. 1581
Hall, Basil *Account of a voyage of discovery to the west coast of Corea and the great Loo-Choo Island* 1818
Patchwork 1841
Hall, Benjamin H. *A collection of college words and customs* (anon.) 1851
Hall, Bert & Niles, John Jacob *One man's war: the story of the Lafayette escadrille* 1929
Hall, Charles F. *Narrative of the North Polar expedition* 1876
Hall, Chr. Newman *An autobiography* 1898
Hall, Edward *Chronicle* (*The union of the two noble and illustre famelies of Lancestre and Yorke*) 1548 (1550, 1809)
Hall, Fitzedward *Modern English* 1873
On English adjectives in -able, with special reference to reliable 1877
A rational refutation of the Hindu philosophical systems tr. 1862
Recent exemplifications of false philology 1872
Hall, Frederick Michael *An introduction to abstract algebra* 2 vols. 1966–9
Hall, Granville S. *Adolescence: its psychology and its relations to physiology, anthropology* 1904
Aspects of German culture and education 1881
Hall, Hubert *The antiquities and curiosities of the Exchequer* 1891
Society in the Elizabethan age 1886
Hall, James *Legends of the West* 1833
Letters from the West 1828
Notes on the Western States 1838
Statistics of the West, at the close of the years 1836 1836
Hall, James Norman *Kitchener's mob: the adventures of an American in the British Army* 1916
Hall, John 1565 *See* Halle, John
Hall, John *Horæ vacivæ, or essays* 1646
An humble motion to the parliament, concerning the advancement of learning 1649
Paradoxes 1650 (1653)
Poems 1646–47 (1816)
Hall, John *A Christian home: how to make and how to maintain it* 1884
Hall, John, Memoirs of the right villainous. To which is added the cant us'd by those sort of people 1708 (1714)
Hall, John Scoville ed. *Radar aids to navigation* 1947
Hall, John Whitney *Japan from prehistory to modern times* 1970
Hall, Bp. Joseph *Works* v.d. (1625, 1634–62, 1808, 1837–39)
Poems a1656 (Chalmers 1810, Grosart 1879)
A recollection of such treatises as have bene heretofore severally published and are now revised v.d. (1614, 1615, 1617, 1621)
The shaking of the olive tree: The remaining works of J. H. With some specialities of divine providence in his life, noted by his own hand. Together with his Hard Measure, written also by himself a1656 (1660)
An answer to Pope Urban his inurbanitie, expressed in a breve sent to Louis the French King exasperating him against the Protestants in France tr. by B. S. 1629
The arte of divine meditation 1606
The balme of Gilead: or comforts for the distressed both morall and divine 1646
The best bargaine. A sermon 1623
Breathings of the devout soul: see *Select thoughts*
Characters of vertues and vices 1608
Christ mysticall; or, the blessed union of Christ and his members 1647
Christian moderation 1640 (1840)
A common apologie of the Church of England against the unjust challenges of the over-just sect, commonly called Brownists 1610
Contemplations upon the principal passages of the holie storie; Vol. I (O.T., bks I–IV) 1612; vol. II (bks. V–VIII) 1614; vol. III (bks. IX–XI) 1615; vol. IV (bks. XII–XIII) 1618; vol. V (bks. XIV–XV) 1620; vol. VI (bks. XVI–XVII) 1622; vol. VII (bks. XVIII–XIX) 1623; vol. VIII (bks. XX–XXI) 1626
— *The residue of the contemplations upon the New Testament, with sermons, etc.* 1618–34 (1634)
Decisions of divers practicall cases of conscience See *Resolutions and decisions*
The devout soul; or, rules of heavenly devotion 1644
Discovery of a new world 1609 *See* Healey, J.
Dissuasive from Popery See *The peace of Rome*
Episcopacie by divine right asserted 1640
Epistles 1608–11
The great impostor, laid open in a sermon 1623
The great mysterie of godliness, laid forth by way of affectuous and feeling meditation. Also, the invisible world discovered to spirituall eyes 1652
Heaven upon earth, or of true peace and tranquillitie of minds 1606
Holy observations 1607
An holy panegyrick. A sermon preached at Paules Crosse 1613
Holy raptures; or patheticall meditations of the love of Christ 1653
The honor of the married clergie mayntayned 1620
An humble remonstrance to the High Court of Parliament (anon.) 1640
— *A defence of the humble remonstrance* 1641
The hypocrite: set forth in a sermon 1630
The imprese of God; in two sermons preacht at the court 1611–12 (in Recoll. treat. 1614)
The invisible world: see *Great mysterie of godliness*
The kings prophecie: or, weeping joy 1603
Meditations and vowes divine and morall 1605 (1606, 1608, 1621)
A modest confutation of (Milton's) Animadversions upon the remonstrants defense against Smectymnuus 1642
No peace with Rome tr. 1614 (in Recoll. treat.)
Occasional meditations 1630 (1631, 1633, 1851)
The olde religion 1628
The peace of Rome. To which is prefixed a Dissuasive from Popery 1609
The peace-maker, laid forth in a sermon 1624
Pharisaisme and christianity 1608
A plaine and familiar explication (by way of paraphrase) of all the hard texts of the whole divine scripture of the Old and New Testament 1633
Quo vadis? a just censure of travell as it is commonly undertaken by the gentlemen of our nation 1617
The reconciler, an epistle pacificatorie of the seeming differences of opinion concerning the truenesse and visibility of the Roman Church 1629
The remedy of discontentment; or, a treatise of contentation in whatsoever condition 1645
The remedy of prophanenesse, or, of the true sight and feare of the Almighty 1637

Resolutions and decisions of divers practicall cases of conscience in continuall use amongst men 1649
The Revelation unrevealed 1650
The righteous mammon. An hospitall sermon 1618
Salomon's divine arts. Drawne out of his Proverbs and Ecclesiastes 1609
Satan's fiery darts quenched; or, temptations repelled 1647
Select thoughts. Also The breathings of the devout soul 1648
The Song of Songs paraphrased 1614 (in Recoll. treat.)
Susurrium cum Deo. Soliloquies: or, holy self conferences of the devout soul. Together with the souls farewell to earth 1651
The true peace-maker: laid forth in a sermon before his Majesty at Theobalds 1624
Virgidemiarum, sixe bookes: first three bookes, of toothlesse satyrs 1597; *the three last bookes, of byting satyres* 1598
HALL, Marshall *Lectures on the nervous system and its diseases* 1836
On the diseases and derangements of the nervous system 1841
On the mutual relations between anatomy, physiology, pathology, and therapeutics, and the practice of medicine, being the Gulstonian lectures for 1842 1842
HALL, Mildred Lillington ed. *Newnes complete amateur photography* See under title
HALL, Richard *The life and death of John Fisher, Bishop of Rochester* c1559 (1655)
HALL, Richard Pinkham *Protozoology* 1953
HALL, Robert *Works* a1831 (1832)
Fifty sermons a1831 (1843)
Selections a1831 (1840)
HALL, Robert Anderson *External history of the Romance languages* 1974
Introductory linguistics 1964
HALL, Samuel C. *A book of memories of great men and women of the age* 1871
Retrospect of a long life: from 1815 to 1883 1883
—— & Anna M. (Mrs. S. C. Hall) *Ireland: its scenery, character*, etc. 1841–43
See also HALL, Anna M.
HALL, Thomas *Funebria floræ; the downfall of May-games* 1660
HALL, Thomas Winthrop *Tales* 1899
HALL, William E. *The rights and duties of neutrals* 1874
HALL, William H. *Practical experience at the diggings of the gold fields of Victoria* 1852
HALL, William Thomas *Textbook of quantitative analysis* 1930
HALLAM, Anthony ed. *Planet earth: an encyclopedia of geology* 1977
HALLAM, Arthur H. *Remains in verse and prose* a1833 (1834; privately printed)
HALLAM, Henry *The constitutional history of England from the accession of Henry VII to the death of George II* 1827 (1849)
Introduction to the literature of Europe in the 15th, 16th, and 17th centuries 1837–39 (1847, 1864)
View of the state of Europe during the middle ages 1818 (1872)
HALLE, Edward 1548 *See* HALL, Edward
HALLE, John *A most excellent and learned woorke of chirurgerie called Chirurgia parua Lanfranci* tr. 1565; (also) *an historiall expostulation against the abuses of chyrurgerie and phisicke* 1565 (Percy Soc. 1844)
HALLETT, Holt S. *A thousand miles on an elephant in Shan states* 1890
HALLEY, Robert *A short biography of. Together with a selection of his sermons preached in Manchester and elsewhere* a1876 (1879)
HALLIDAY, David *Introductory nuclear physics* 1950
'HALLIDAY, Dorothy' (Dorothy Dunnett) *Dolly and the cookie bird* 1970
Dolly and the doctor bird 1971
Dolly and the nanny bird 1976
Dolly and the starry bird 1973
HALLIDAY, Michael Alexander Kirkwood, MCINTOSH, A. & STREVENS, P. *The linguistic sciences and language teaching* 1964
HALLIFAX, Bp. Samuel *An analysis of the Roman civil law compared with the laws of England* 1774
HALLIWELL (afterwards HALLIWELL-PHILLIPPS), James O. *Books of characters illustrating the habits and manners of Englishmen from the reign of James I to the Restoration* 1857
A brief account of the life, writings and inventions of Sir Samuel Morland 1838
Contributions to early English literature, derived chiefly from rare books and ancient inedited manuscripts, from the fifteenth to the seventeenth century 1849
A dictionary of archaic and provincial words, obsolete phrases, proverbs and ancient customs, from the fourteenth century 1847
Letters of the kings of England. Now first collected from the originals, with an historical introduction and notes 1846
A new boke about Shakespeare and Stratford-on-Avon 1850
Nugæ poeticæ: select pieces of old English popular poetry illustrating the manners and arts of the fifteenth century 1844
The nursery rhymes of England, obtained principally from oral tradition 1842 (Percy Soc.)
— ed. 2, with alterations and additions 1843
Outlines of the life of Shakespeare 1881 (1885)
Popular rhymes and nursery tales; a sequel to the nursery rhymes of England 1849
Reliquiæ antiquæ; scraps from ancient MSS. illustrating chiefly early English literature and the English language; ed. by T. Wright and J. O. Halliwell 1841–43
HALLOCK, Charles *American club list and sportsman's glossary* 1878
Sportsman's gazetteer and guide 1877 (1883)
HALLYWELL, Henry *An account of familism as it is revived by the quakers* 1673
The excellency of moral vertue from the serious exhortation of St. Paul to the practice of it 1692
Melampronoea: or, a discourse of the polity and kingdom of darkness 1681
The sacred method of saving humane souls by Jesus Christ 1677
HALPERT, Herbert & STORY, G. M. eds. *Christmas mumming in Newfoundland: essays in anthropology, folklore and history* 1969
HALSBURY, Hardinge Stanley Giffard, 1st Earl of *The laws of England, being a complete statement of the whole law of England*. By the Earl of Halsbury and other lawyers 1907–
HALSTED, George B. *Elementary synthetic geometry* 1893 (ed. 2)
Mensuration 1881
Halyburton. Ledger of Andrew Halyburton, Conservator of the privileges of the Scotch nation in the Netherlands 1492–1503, together with the Book of Customs and valuation of merchandises in Scotland 1612 (ed. Cosmo Innes, Scott. Record series 1867)
HAM, Arthur Worth *Histology* 1950
HAMBLETT, Charles & Deverson, Charles *Generation X* 1964
HAMERSLY, Lewis R. *Naval encyclopædia* 1881
HAMERTON, Philip G. *The graphic arts* 1882
The intellectual life 1873 (1875, 1876)
Thoughts about art 1873
HAMILTON, Alexander *A new account of the East Indies* 1727
HAMILTON, Alexander *Hamilton's itinerarium: being a narrative of a journey from Annapolis, Maryland, through Delaware* [etc.]... *1744* ed. A. B. Hart 1907
HAMILTON, Alexander *Works* a1804 (1885–87)
The Federalist; a collection of essays by A. H., J. Jay, & J. Madison 1788 (1857)
HAMILTON, Allan McL. *Nervous diseases: description and treatment* 1878
HAMILTON, Augustus *Maori art* 1901 (first published in 5 parts 1896–1900)
HAMILTON, Bruce *Too much of water* 1958
HAMILTON, Cosmo *Prisoners of hope* 1924
HAMILTON, Edward Walter *Diary 1880–1885* ed. D. W. R. Bahlman 2 vols. 1972
HAMILTON, Elizabeth *Letters of a Hindoo Rajah* tr. 1796 (1811)
HAMILTON, Lady Elizabeth E. *Louis Pasteur: his life and labours*, by his son-in-law, Vallery-Radot, tr. 1885
HAMILTON, Elizabeth Vidal *The Mordaunts: an eighteenth-century family* 1965
HAMILTON, Ld. Ernest *The Mawkin of the Flow* 1898
The outlaws of the marches 1897
HAMILTON, Ferelith ed. *The world encyclopedia of dogs* 1971
HAMILTON, Francis *An account of the kingdom of Nepal* 1819
HAMILTON, Frederic Spencer *P. J.: the Secret Service boy* 1922
'HAMILTON, Gail' (Mary Abigail Dodge) *Gala-days* 1863
HAMILTON, Henrietta *Answer in the negative* 1959
HAMILTON, Ian *The man with the brown paper face* 1967
The thrill machine 1972
HAMILTON, James *Works* a1867 (1869–73)
Lessons from the great biography 1857
Memoirs of the life of James Wilson 1859
The mount of Olives, and other lectures on prayer 1846
HAMILTON, Janet *Poems and ballads* 1868
Poems and essays 1863
Poems of purpose and sketches in prose of Scottish peasant life and character in Auld Langsyne 1865
HAMILTON, Abp. John *Catechism* 1552 (1884)
A facile traictise, contenand, first: ane infallible reul to discerne trew from fals religion, etc. 1600 (S.T.S. 1901)
A godly exhortation, commonly styled The twopenny faith 1559 (in Bannatyne Cl. Misc. III. 1855)
HAMILTON, Richard W. *Horæ et vindiciæ sabbaticæ: or familiar disquisitions on the revealed Sabbath* 1848
The institutions of popular education 1845
Nugæ literariæ: prose and verse 1841
The revealed doctrine of rewards and punishments 1847 (1853)
HAMILTON, Stanislaus Murray ed. *Letters to Washington, and accompanying papers* 5 vols. 1898–1902
HAMILTON, Thomas *Men and manners in America* 1833
HAMILTON, Walter *A geographical, statistical, and historical description of Hindustan and the adjacent countries* 1820
HAMILTON, Walter *A hand-book, or concise dictionary of terms used in the arts and sciences* 1825
HAMILTON, Walter *The Æsthetic Movement in England* 1882
HAMILTON, William *The life and character of James Bonnell* 1703
HAMILTON, William *History of Sir William Wallace* 1722
HAMILTON, William *Poems on several occasions* 1749 (1760)
HAMILTON, William *Berthollet's* (C. L.) *Elements of the art of dyeing* tr. 1791
HAMILTON, Sir William *Remarks on several parts of Turkey. Part I. Ægyptiaca, or some account of the ancient and modern state of Egypt* 1809
HAMILTON, Sir William *Discussions on philosophy and literature, education and university reform* 1831– (1852)
Lectures on metaphysics 1836–37 (1859) *and logic* 1837–38 (1860)
A letter to Augustus De Morgan on his claim to an independent re-discovery of a new principle in the theory of syllogism 1847
HAMILTON, William J. *Geography* 1851–59 (in Manual of scientific enquiry 1859)
HAMILTON, Sir William R. *Lectures on quaternions* 1853
Life of, by R. P. Graves; *including selections from his poems, correspondence, and miscellaneous writings* (1882–91)
Hamilton papers, The: being selections from original letters in the possession of the Duke of Hamilton 1638–50 (Camden Soc. 1880)
HAMMERTON, John Alexander ed. *ABC of the RAF* 1941
ed. *Countries of the world* 6 vols. (originally published in 40 parts) 1924–5
HAMMETT, Samuel Dashiell *The Dain curse* 1929 (UK 1930)
The Maltese falcon 1930
Red harvest 1929
HAMMOND, Charles E. *Outlines of textual criticism applied to the New Testament* 1872 (1880)
HAMMOND, Henry *Works* a1660 (1674–84, 1847–50)
An answer to the animadversions (*of John Owen*) *on the dissertations touching Ignatius's epistles* 1654
Χάρις καὶ εἰρήνη, or a pacifick discourse of God's grace and decrees 1660
The Christian's obligations to peace and charity, delivered in an Advent sermon 1647 1649
A copy of some papers past at Oxford betwixt (H. Hammond) and Mr. Ch(eynell) 1647
The dispatcher dispatched 1659
Of conscience 1644
Of fundamentals in a notion referring to practise 1654
Of the power of the keyes, or of binding and loosing 1647
Of schisme 1653
A parænesis: or seasonable exhortatory to all true sons of the Church of England 1656
A paraphrase and annotations upon all the books of the New Testament 1653
A paraphrase and annotations upon the books of the Psalms 1659
A practical catechism 1645
HAMMOND, James *Poetical works* a1742 (1790, 1810)
Love elegies. Written in the year 1732 (1743)
HAMMOND, John *Leah and Rachel, or, the two fruitfull sisters, Virginia and Mary-land* 1656 (1844)
HAMMOND, Joseph *A Cornish parish: being an account of St. Austell, town, church, district and people* 1897
HAMMOND, Rolt *Mobile and movable cranes* 1963
HAMMOND, Samuel H. *Hunting adventures in the Northern Wilds* 1858
HAMMOND, William A. *A treatise on the diseases of the nervous system* 1871
HAMP, Eric P., HOUSEHOLDER, F. W., & AUSTERLITZ, R. eds. *Readings in linguistics II* 1966
HAMPDEN, Bp. Renn D. *Parochial sermons illustrative of the importance of the revelation of God in Jesus Christ* 1828
Some memorials of R. D. H. a1868 (1871)
HAMPOLE, Richard Rolle of *A devoute medytacyon* (*The remedy ayenst the troubles of temptacyons*) a1349 (W. de Worde 1508)
English prose treatises. Edited from Robert Thornton's MS. c1340 (E.E.T.S. 1866)
The pricke of conscience (*Stimulus conscientiæ*); *a Northumbrian poem* c1340 (Philol. Soc. 1863)
The psalter; or psalms of David, and certain canticles, with a translation and exposition in English a1340 (1884)
Richard Rolle of Hampole and his followers (Yorkshire writers) v.d. (Horstman 1895–96)
See also MISYN, R.
Hampshire glossary See COPE, Sir W. H.
HAMPSON, R. T. *Medii ævi kalendarium; or dates, charters, and customs of the Middle Ages* 1841
HAMPTON, Christopher James *The philanthropist: a bourgeois comedy* 1970
Savages 1974
HAMSHER, Donald Henze ed. *Communication system engineering handbook* 1967
HAMSON, Denys Otto Harry *We fell among Greeks* 1946
'HAN SUYIN' (Elizabeth Comber) *A mortal flower, China: autobiography, history* 1966
HANBURY, Daniel *See* FLÜCKIGER, F. A.
HANCOCK, Lyn *There's a seal in my sleeping bag* 1972
HANCOCK, William Keith *Australia* 1930
HANCOCK, William N. *Senchus mor*. Ed., with translation, by W. N. Hancock, Th. O'Mahony, etc. 1865–73
Handbook (Murray's) for travellers on the Continent 1836
Handbook of hardwoods, A 1956 *See* United Kingdom. Department of Scientific and Industrial Research. Forest Products Research Laboratory
— (ed. 2) 1972 *See* United Kingdom. Department of the Environment. Building Research Establishment
Handbook of softwoods, A 1957 *See* United Kingdom. Department of Scientific and Industrial Research. Forest Products Research Laboratory
Handbook of turning 1859
Handbook to the special loan collection of scientific apparatus South Kensington Museum 1876 (1877)
HANDERSON, Henry E. *Baas'* (*J. H.*) *Outlines of the history of medicine and the medical profession* tr. 1889
Handfull of honisuckles 1583 *See* HUNNIS, W.
Handmaid to the arts 1758 *See* DOSSIE, R.
HANDSON, Raphe *Pitiscus'* (*B.*) *Trigonometry* tr. 1614
HANDY, William Christopher ed. *Blues: an anthology* 1926

HANDY, William (*cont.*)
Father of the blues: an autobiography ed. A. Bontemps 1941 (UK 1957)
HANE, Joachim *Journal, containing his escapes and sufferings during his employment by Oliver Cromwell in France from Nov. 1653 to Feb. 1654.* 1653-54 (ed. by C. H. Firth 1896)
HANKINSON, Charles J. *See* HOLLAND, Clive
HANLEY, William *Blue dreams; or, The end of romance and the continued pursuit of happiness* 1971
HANMER, Meredith *The auncient ecclesiasticall histories of the first six hundred years after Christ, written by Eusebius, Socrates, and Evagrius* tr. 1577 (1663)
The historie of Ireland a1604 (1633, 1809)
The Jesuites banner 1581
HANMER, Sir Thomas *The works of Shakespear revised and corrected* 1744
HANNA, William *The earlier years of Our Lord's life on earth* 1864
See also CHALMERS, Thomas
HANNAY, James *Satires and satirists* 1854
Singleton Fontenoy, R. N. 1850
HANNAY, Patrick *The nightingale. Sheretine and Mariana. A happy husband. Elegies on the death of Queen Anne. Songs and sonnets* 1622 (Hunterian Cl. 1875)
HANNAY, Robert K. *See* HERKLESS, J.
HANNETT, John *Bibliopegia* 1835
Hansard's Parliamentary debates 1803-
HANSEN, Joseph *Fadeout* 1970 (UK 1972)
HANSON, John Lloyd *A dictionary of economics and commerce* 1965
HANSON, Sir Levett *An accurate historical account of all the orders of knighthood at present existing in Europe* 1802
HANWAY, Jonas *An historical account of the British trade over the Caspian sea; with a journal of travels from London into Persia and back* 1753 (1762)
HAPGOOD, Hutchins *The autobiography of a thief* 1904
HAPPÉ, Louis Bernard *Basic motion picture technology* 1971
Happy landings (Air Ministry) 1946-8
HARBEN, William Nathaniel *Abner Daniel* 1902
The Georgians 1904
Westerfelt 1901
HARBERT, William *Poems* 16.. (Grosart 1870)
HARBORD, Frank William & HALL, John William *The metallurgy of steel* 1904
— (ed. 7) 1923
HARBORD, John B. *Glossary of navigation* 1863
HARBY, Thomas *The key of sacred scripture* 1679
HARCOURT, Palma *At high risk* 1977
A fair exchange 1975
HARCOURT, Robert *A relation of a voyage to Guiana* 1613 (in Harl. Misc.)
HARDEN, Donald Benjamin *The Phoenicians* 1962
HARDIMAN, James *O'Flaherty's (J. R.) Chorographical description of West or H-Iar Connaught* 1846 (Irish Archæol. Soc.)
HARDING, John *See* HARDYNG, J.
HARDING, Thomas *An answere to maister Ivelles chalenge* 1564
A confutation of a booke (By Bp. Jewel), intituled An apologie of the Church of England 1565
HARDING, William *The history of Tiverton* 1845-47
HARDMAN, Samuel *A descriptive poem on the battle of Waterloo* 1827
Hardwich's (T. F.) Manual of photographic chemistry ed. J. T. Taylor 1883 (ed. 9)
HARDWICK, Charles *Traditions, superstitions, and folk-lore (chiefly Lancashire and the North of England)* 1872
HARDWICKE, Philip Yorke, 2nd Earl of *Miscellaneous state papers 1501-1726* (1778)
Hardwicke's (Robert) Science-gossip 1865-
HARDY, Alister Clavering *The open sea, its natural history* Part I *The world of plankton* 1956
— Part II *Fish and fisheries* 1959
HARDY, Arthur Cobb & PERRIN, Fred Hiram *The principles of optics* 1932
HARDY, Frederick & WARE, J. R. *The modern Hoyle* 1870
HARDY, Iza Duffus *New Othello* 1890
HARDY, Nathaniel *A divine prospective* 1649
Divinity in mortality 1653
The first general epistle of St. John the Apostle, unfolded and applied 1656-59 (1865)
HARDY, Robert Spence *A manual of Buddhism, in its modern development* tr. 1853 (1860)
HARDY, Thomas *Collected letters* ed. R. L. Purdy & M. Millgate 1978-
Desperate remedies 1871
The dynasts: a drama of the Napoleonic wars 1904-08
Far from the madding crowd 1874
A group of noble dames 1891
The hand of Ethelberta 1876
Jude the obscure 1895
A Laodicean 1881
Late lyrics and earlier, with many other verses 1922
The mayor of Casterbridge 1886
One rare fair woman: letters to Florence Henniker 1893-1922 ed. E. Hardy & F. B. Pinion 1972
Poems of the past and the present 1902
The return of the native 1878
Tess of the D'Urbervilles 1891
The trumpet-major 1880
Two on a tower 1882
Under the greenwood tree 1872
Wessex poems 1898
Wessex tales 1888
The woodlanders 1887
HARDY, Sir William *The charters of the Duchy of Lancaster* tr. and ed. 1845
HARDY, William George *Unfulfilled* 1952
HARDYNG, John *Chronicle* 1457 (original version, Lansdowne MS. 204: see Eng. Hist. Rev., July and Oct. 1912); a1470 (Bodl., MS. Arch. Seld. B. 10, MS. Ashm. 34; B.M., MS. Egerton 1992); with continuation by R. Grafton 1543 (1812)
HARE, Augustus J. C. *The life and letters of Frances, Baroness Bunsen* 1879
The story of my life 1896-1900
Studies in Russia 1885
HARE, John *St. Edward's ghost; or Anti-Normanisme* 1647 (in Harl. Misc.)
HARE, Julius C. *The mission of the Comforter, and other sermons* 1846 (1850)
The philological museum, ed. by J. C. H. 1832-33
Sermons preacht in Herstmonceux Church 1840-49
The victory of faith, and other sermons 1840 (1855)
—— & Augustus W. *Guesses at truth* 1827 (1847-48, 1859)
HARE, Richard Mervyn *Freedom and reason* 1963
The language of morals 1952
HAREWOOD, Harry *A dictionary of sports* 1835
HARFORD, John S. *Life of Michael Angelo Buonarroti; with translations of many of his poems and letters* 1857
HARGAN, James *Glossary of prison language* 1935 (typescript, referred to on p. 361 of *Journal of abnormal and social psychology*, December 1935)
HARGRAVE, Francis *A collection of tracts relative to the law of England, from manuscripts by Hale, Norburie, Blackstone, Hargrave, and others* 1787
Juridical arguments and collections 1797-99
HARGREAVES, Elisabeth *Fair green weed* 1972
HARGREAVES, Reginald *The enemy at the gate: famous sieges* 1945
HARINGTON, Sir John *An anatomie of the metamorphosed Ajax* 1596 (1814)
An apologie: 1. Or rather a retraction; 2. Or rather a recantation; 3. Or rather a recapitulation..; 12. Or rather none of them 1596 (1814)
Ariosto's (L.) Orlando Furioso in English heroical verse 1591; now secondly imprinted 1607; now thirdly revised and amended a1612 (1634)
A briefe apologie of poetrie 1591 (Prefixed to tr. of Ariosto's Orlando; in Haslewood, Anc. crit. ess. II. 1815; G. G. Smith, Eliz. crit. ess. II. 1904)
A briefe view of the state of the Church of England in Queen Elizabeth's and King James his reigne a1612 (1653)
The Englishman's doctor. Or, the Schoole of Salerne tr. 1607 (1608, 1617, 1624)
Epigrams both pleasant and serious a1612 (1615); *the most elegant and wittie epigrams of Sir. J. H. Digested into foure bookes* (1618)
A new discourse of a stale subject, called the Metamorphosis of Ajax 1596 (1814)
Nugæ antiquæ; being a miscellaneous collection of original papers in prose and verse, in reigns of Henry VIII to James (I), by Sir J. Harington and others 1509-1625 (1769, 1779, 1792; re-edited by T. Park 1804)
A short view of the state of Ireland 1605 (1879)
Ulysses upon Ajax 1596 (1814)
HARKER, Alfred *The natural history of igneous rocks* 1909
Petrology for students: an introduction to the study of rocks under the microscope 1895
HARLAN, George C. *Eyesight, and how to care for it* 1879
HARLAND, John *A glossary of words used in Swaledale, Yorkshire* 1873 (E.D.S.)
—— & WILKINSON, T. T. *Lancashire folk-lore* 1867
Lancashire legends, traditions, pageants, sports, etc. With an appendix containing a rare tract on the Lancashire Witches 1873
'HARLAND, Marion' (Mary Virginia Hawes, *afterwards* Terhune) *Common sense in the household: a manual of practical housewifery* 1872
The hidden path 1855
Harleian miscellany, The: or, a collection of scarce, curious, and entertaining pamphlets and tracts, as well in manuscript as in print, found in the late (Edward Harley, second) Earl of Oxford's library v.d. (1744-46; ed. T. Park 1808-13; ed. J. Malham 1808-11)
— *A selection from the Harleian miscellany* v.d. (1793)
HARLEY, Sir Edward *An humble essay toward the settlement of peace and truth in the church* 1681
HARLEY, John *Royle's (J. F.) Manual of materia medica* 1876 (ed. 6)
HARLEY, John Brian *Ordnance Survey maps: a descriptive manual* 1975
HARLEY, Robert, 1st Earl of Oxford *The secret history of Arlus and Odolphus, ministers of state to the Empress of Grandinsula* 1710
HARMAN, Richard Alexander, MILNER, A., & MELLERS, W. *Man and his music* 1962
HARMAN, Thomas *A caueat or warening for commen cursetors, vulgarely called vagabones* 1567 (E.E.T.S. 1869)
HARMAR, Hilary *Pet Library's chihuahua guide* 1968
HARMAR, John *Master Bezaes sermons upon the three first chapters of the Canticle of Canticles* tr. 1587
HARMER, Thomas *Observations on divers passages of Scripture* 1764 (1776-87, 1808)
HARMON, Daniel Williams *A journal of voyages and travels in the interiour of North America* 1820
HARMSWORTH, Alfred Charles William, et al. *Motors and motor-driving* 1902
Harmsworth encyclopædia, The ed. G. Sandeman 8 vols. (originally published in 40 parts) 1905-6
Harmsworth's wireless encyclopedia ed. O. J. Lodge 3 vols. (originally published in 24 parts) 1923-4
Harnack's (A.) History of dogma tr. 1894-99
HARNEY, William Edward *Taboo* 1943
— (ed. 3) 1944
HARNWELL, Gaylord Probasco *Principles of electricity and electromagnetism* 1938
Harp of Caledonia, a collection of songs ancient and modern v.d. (ed. John Struthers 1819)
Harp of Perthshire, The, a collection of songs, ballads, and other poetical pieces, chiefly by local authors v.d. (with notes by R. Ford 1893)
Harp of Renfrewshire, The: a collection of songs and other poetical pieces v.d. (ed. W. Motherwell 1819, 1872)
HARPER, Charles G. *The Exeter road, the story of the West of England highway* 1899
HARPER, Henry William *Letters from New Zealand, 1857-1911, being some account of life and work in the province of Canterbury, South Island* 1914
HARPER, James W. *The social ideal* 1910
HARPER, John L. *Population biology of plants* 1977
HARPER, Samuel *Practical hints for abstracting title deeds* 1817 (1818)
HARPER, Thomas *Peace through the truth* 1866
Harpers and Queen 1970-
Harper's bazaar (New York) 1867-
— (UK ed.) 1929-70
Harper's New monthly magazine 1850-
Harper's weekly 1857-1916
HARPSFIELD, Nicholas *A treatise on the pretended divorce between Henry VIII and Catharine of Aragon* c1555 (Camden Soc. 1878)
HARRADEN, Beatrice *The fowler* 1899
Hilda Strafford 1897
Interplay 1908
The scholar's daughter 1906
Ships that pass in the night 1893
HARRAL, Thomas *Scenes of life; a novel* 1805
HARRICE, Robert *See* HARRIS, R.
HARRINGTON, James *The Oceana, and other works, som whereof are now first publish'd from his own manuscripts* a1677, with an account of his life by J. Toland (1700)
Aphorisms political 1659
The art of law-giving 1659
The common-wealth of Oceana 1656
The petition of divers well-affected persons 1659
The prerogative of popular government 1658
Seven models of a commonwealth 1659
Valerius and Publicola 1659
The wayes and meanes whereby an equal and lasting commonwealth may be suddenly introduced etc. 1659
HARRINGTON, James *A defence of the rights and priviledges of the University of Oxford* 1690
HARRINGTON, Robert Edward *Quintain* 1977
HARRIS, Alexander *Settlers and convicts; or recollections of sixteen years' labour in the Australian backwoods* (anon.) 1847 (1852)
HARRIS, Bartholomew *Parival's (J. N. de) Historie of this iron age* tr. 1656 (1659)
HARRIS, Chapin A. *A dictionary of dental science, biography, bibliography and medical terminology* 1849 (1854)
HARRIS, Corra May *Eve's second husband* 1911
HARRIS, Frank *See* HARRIS, James Thomas Frank
HARRIS, Fred Henry ed. *Dartmouth out o'doors* 1913
HARRIS, Henry *Nucleus and cytoplasm* 1968
HARRIS, James *Works* a1780 (1841)
Hermes, or a philosophical inquiry concerning universal grammar 1751 (1786)
Philological inquiries 1781
Philosophical arrangements 1775
Three treatises (on 'art,' 'music, painting, and poetry,' and 'happiness') 1744 (1765)
HARRIS, James, & James H. *See* MALMESBURY
HARRIS, James Rendel *The guiding hand of God* 1905
Side-lights on New Testament research, 7 lectures delivered in 1908 1909
HARRIS, James Thomas Frank *My life and loves* 4 vols. 1922-7
HARRIS, Joel C. *Free Joe, and other Georgian sketches* 1887 (1888)
Mingo, and other sketches in black and white 1884
Nights with Uncle Remus 1883
Sister Jane, her friends and acquaintances 1896
Uncle Remus 1881
Uncle Remus and his friends 1892
HARRIS, John *Lexicon technicum, or an universal English dictionary of arts and sciences* 1704-10
Navigantium atque itinerantium bibliotheca: or, a compleat collection of voyages and travels 1705 (1764)
HARRIS, John *The great teacher: characteristics of our Lord's ministry* 1835 (1837)
HARRIS, John Norman *The weird world of Wes Beattie* 1963 (UK 1964)
HARRIS, Joseph *An essay upon money and coins* 1757-58
HARRIS, Leldon M. *An introduction to deepwater floating drilling operations* 1972
HARRIS, Mrs. Miriam C. *Rutledge* (anon.) 1866
St. Philip's 1865
The tents of wickedness 1907
HARRIS, Moses *The Aurelian, or natural history of English insects* 1766
The English Lepidoptera 1775
An exposition of English insects 1776

Harris, Robert *Abner's funerall* 1641
The drunkard's cup 1619
God's goodnes and mercy 1622
Hezekiah's recover 1626 (1630)
Samuel's funerall, or a sermon preached at the funerall of Sir A. Cope 1618 (1622)
A sermon preached to the House of Commons at a publike fast 1642
Harris, Rosemary *The double snare* 1974
The nice girl's story 1968
Harris, Samuel *A commentary on the fifty third chapter of Isaiah* a1733 (1735)
Harris, Stanley *Fundamental principles of contract bridge* 1947
Harris, Thaddeus W. *A treatise on some of the insects injurious to vegetation* 1862 (ed. 3)
Harris, Walter *Lemery's (N.) Course of chymistry* tr. 1677 (1686)
Harris, Walter *The history and antiquities of the city of Dublin* 1766
Harris, Walter B. *A journey through the Yemen* 1893
Harris, Walter Kilroy *Outback in Australia; or, Three Australian overlanders* 1913
Harris, William A. *A technical dictionary of fire insurance* 1886
Harris, William Cornwallis *The wild sports of southern Africa: being the narrative of an expedition from the Cape of Good Hope... to the Tropic of Capricorn* 1839
Harris, Zellig Sabbettai *Methods in structural linguistics* 1951
Harrison, A. W. C. *The manufacture of lakes and precipitated pigments* 1930
Harrison, Constance Cary *Woman's handiwork in modern homes* 1881
Harrison, Frederic *The choice of books and other literary pieces* 1886
Harrison, Harry Max *The Technicolor time machine* 1967 (UK 1968)
Harrison, Henry Sydnor *Queed* 1911
Harrison, Mrs. J. W. *A. M. Mackay, pioneer missionary of the Church Missionary Society to Uganda* 1890
Harrison, James *An exhortacion to the Scottes to conforme themselfes to the.. union betweene.. Englande and Scotland* 1547 (in Complaint of Scotland, E.E.T.S. 1872)
Harrison, Michael *Reported safe arrival* 1943
Harrison, Sarah *The housekeeper's pocket-book and compleat family cook* 1739 (1748)
Harrison, Stephen *The archs of triumph erected in honor of James the first at his entrance and passage through London* 1604
Harrison, William *The description of England* 1577, 1587 (in Holinshed's Chronicle I; New Shaks. Soc. 1877)
Boetius' (H.) Description of Scotland tr. 1587 (in Holinshed's Chron. II)
Harrison, William, Murder of See Overbury, Sir T.
Harrison Mayer. A complete service to the craft potter [Catalogue of Harrison Mayer Ltd., Meir, Stoke-on-Trent] a1977
Harrisson, Barbara *Orang-utan* 1962
Harrisson, Thomas Harnett & Madge, Charles Henry eds. *War begins at home* 1940
Harrod, Leonard Montague *The librarians' glossary* 1938
— (ed. 2) 1959
— (ed. 3) 1971
Harrow, Benjamin & Sherwin, Carl P. eds. *Textbook of biochemistry* 1935
Harrowing of hell, The. A miracle play c1300 (1837, Halliwell 1840, Mall 1871, E.E.T.S. 1907)
Harsnet, Adam *God's summons unto general repentance* a1639 (1640)
Harsnet, Samuel *A declaration of egregious popish impostures* 1603
A discovery of the fraudulent practises of J. Darrel 1599
A sermon (on Ezek. xxxiii. 11) preached at S. Pauls Cross 1584 (in R. Steward, Three serm. 1658)
Har'st rig, The 1786 (1801)
Hart, Basil Henry Liddell *Europe in arms* 1937
Hart, Frances Noyes *The Bellamy trial* 1927 [play], 1928 [novel]
Hart, Fred H. *The Sazerac lying club: a Nevada book* 1878
Hart, Henry *A godly newe short treatyse instructyng every parson howe they shulde trade theyr lyves in the imytacyon of vertu* 1548
Hart, Horace *Notes on a century of typography at the University Press, Oxford, 1693–1794* 1900
Hart, James *The anatomie of urines* 1625
Forestus' (P.) Arraignment of urines tr. 1623
Κλινική, or, the diet of the diseased 1633
Hart, Jerome *A vigilante girl* 1910
Hart, John *An orthographie* 1569
Hart, John H. *Cacao, a manual on the cultivation and curing of cacao* 1911
Hart, Norman de Villiers *The bridge players' bedside book* 1939
Hart, Richard *Ecclesiastical records of England, Ireland and Scotland, from the fifth century till the Reformation* 1836 (1846)
Hartcliffe, John *A treatise of moral and intellectual virtues* 1691
Harte, F. Bret *Works* 18.. (1873, 1880–1900)
Poetical works 1872
By shore and sedge 1885
An episode of Fiddletown, and other sketches 1873
A first family of Tasajara 1891
Flip and other stories 1882
Gabriel Conroy 1876 (US 1 vol., UK 3 vols.)
An heiress of Red Dog, and other tales 1879
The Hoodlum Band, and other stories 1878
In the Carquinez woods 1883
The luck of roaring camp, and other sketches 1869
The man on the beach 1878
Maruja 1885
Mrs. Skaggs's husbands, and other sketches 1873
Sandy Bar; with other stories 1873
Stories of the Sierras, and other sketches 1872
The story of a mine 1877
Wan Lee, the Pagan, and other sketches 1876
—— & 'Twain, Mark' (S. L. Clemens) *Sketches of the sixties: being forgotten material now collected... from The Californian* ed. J. Howell 1926
Harte, Walter *An essay on reason* 1735
An essay on satire, particularly on the Dunciad 1730
The history of the life of Gustavus Adolphus 1759
Poems a1774 (1810)
Poems on several occasions 1727
Hartford, Countess of *See* Hertford, Countess of
Harting, James E. *Bibliotheca accipitraria. A catalogue of books ancient and modern relating to falconry, with notes, glossary, and vocabulary* 1891
British animals extinct within historic times 1880
See also *Perfect booke*
Hartland glossary 1891 *See* Chope, R. P.
Hartley, David *Observations on man* 1749
Hartley, Leslie Poles *Eustace and Hilda* 1947
The go-between 1953
The hireling 1957
A perfect woman 1955
Two for the river, and other stories 1961
Hartley, Mrs. May *Christy Carew* 1880
Hartley, Thomas *Preface* to tr. of *Swedenborg's Treatise concerning heaven and hell* 1778 (1851)
Hartlib, Samuel *Comenius's (J. A.) Reformation of schooles* tr. 1642
A discourse of husbandrie used in Brabant and Flanders 1650
— *Samuel Hartlib his legacie: or, an enlargement of the Discourse of husbandry* 1651 (1655)
A discoverie for division or setting out of land as to the best form 1653
The reformed common-wealth of bees 1655
The reformed Virginian silk-worm 1655
Hartman, George *The true preserver and restorer of health* 1682
Hartmann, Reinhard Rudolf K. & Stork, Francis C. *Dictionary of language and linguistics* 1972
Hartmann, Robert *Anthropoid apes* 1885
Hartree, Douglas Rayner *Calculating instruments and machines* 1949 (UK 1950)
Hartshorne, Albert *Old English glasses* 1897
Hartshorne, Charles H. *English medieval embroidery* 1848
ed. *Ancient metrical tales; printed chiefly from original sources* 1829
Salopia antiqua, or, an enquiry from personal survey into the Druidical, military, and other early remains in Shropshire and the North Welsh borders; with a glossary of words used in the county of Salop 1841
Hartshorne, Henry *1931: a glance at the twentieth century* 1881
Hartwell, Abraham *A report of the kingdome of Congo. Drawen out of the writings of O. Lopez by P. Pigafetta*, tr. 1597 (in Purchas, Pilgrims, pt. II. 1625; Osborne's Collect. voy. II. 1745)
Hartwig's (G.) Aerial world tr. 1874
The sea and its living wonders tr. 1860
The subterranean world tr. 1871
Harvard memorial biographies 1866
Harvard psychological studies 1903–06
Harvard studies in classical philology 1890–
Harvard University. Computation Laboratory *Annals* 1946–
Harvard University, Orders and regulations of the faculty of 1837
'Harvester, Simon' (Henry Gibbs) *The Chinese hammer* 1960
A corner of the playground 1973
Treacherous road 1966
Harvey, Annie J. *Our cruise in the Claymore, with a visit to Damascus and the Lebanon* 1861
Harvey, Christopher *Complete poems* a1663 (Grosart 1874)
Schola cordis, or the heart of it selfe gone away from God; brought back againe to him; and instructed by him (Adapted from B. von Haeften's Schola cordis) 1647 (1664)
The synagogue, or, the shadow of the temple 1640 (1647)
Harvey, Gabriel *Works* a1600 (Grosart 1884–85)
Foure letters, and certain sonnets, especially touching R. Greene 1592
Letter-book 1573–80 (Camden Soc. 1884)
A new letter of notable contents 1593
Pierces supererogation, or a new prayse of the old asse 1593
The trimming of Thomas Nashe 1597
Three proper letters 1580 *See* Spenser, E.
Harvey, Gideon *A discourse of the plague* 1665
The art of curing diseases by expectation 1689
Morbus Anglicus: or, the anatomy of consumptions 1666
Harvey, James *Scelera aquarum: or, a supplement to Mr. Graunt on the bills of mortality*. By J. H. 1701
Harvey, John *A discoursive probleme concerning prophesies* 1588
Harvey, Peter & Bohlman, Kenneth John *Stereo F.M. radio handbook* 1974
Harvey, Richard *An astrological discourse vpon the coniunction of Saturne and Jupiter* 1583
Philadelphus, or a defence of Brutes and the Brutans history 1593
Plaine Perceuall the peace-maker of England 1590 (1860)
Harvey, Ruth *Curtain time* 1949
Harvey, William *Anatomical exercises concerning the motion of the heart and blood* 1653
Harvey, William H. *A manual of the British (marine) algæ* 1841 (1849)
The sea-side book 1849 (1854)
Harwood, Philip *History of the Irish rebellion of 1798* 1844
Harwood, Richard *King David's sanctuary* 1644
Haselgrove, Maurice Lawrence *Photographers' dictionary* 1962
Haslam, John *Observations on madness (and melancholy)* 1798 (1809)
Hasleton, Richard *Strange and wonderful things in his ten years travels in many foreign countries* 1595 (in Arber, Eng. Garner, VIII)
Haslewood, Joseph ed. *Ancient critical essays upon English poets and poesy* v.d. (1811–15)
Hasluck, Paul N. *The model engineer's handybook* 1888 (1900)
Hassell, J. *Picturesque rides and walks, with excursions by water, thirty miles round the British Metropolis* 1817–18
Hastings, Charles S. *Light* 1901
Hastings, James See *Dictionary of the Bible; Encyclopædia of religion and ethics*
Hastings, Lewis *Dragons are extra* 1947
Hastings, Macdonald *Cork and the serpent* 1955
Haston, Dougal *In high places* 1972
Haswell, William A. *See* Parker, Thomas J.
Hatch, Frederick Henry & Rastall, Robert Heron *The petrology of the sedimentary rocks* 1913
— (ed. 4, revised by J. T. Greensmith) 1965
Hatfield, Charles W. *Historical notices of Doncaster* 1866
Hatfield, James Taft, Leopold, W., & Zieglschmid, A. J. F. eds. *Curme volume of linguistic studies* 1930
Hatton, Edward *The merchant's magazine, or trades-man's treasury* 1701
New view of London (anon.) 1708
Hatton, Joseph *Bitter sweets: a love story* 1865
Clytie: a novel of modern life 1874
The old house at Sandwich 1887
The Tallants of Barton 1867
Three recruits, and the girls they left behind them 1880
The valley of poppies 1872
Hatton, Correspondence of the family of. Being chiefly letters addressed to Christopher first Viscount Hatton 1601–1704 (Camden Soc. 1878)
Hatton gospels c1160 (The Holy Gospels, in Anglo-Saxon, etc., Skeat 1871–87)
Hatzfeld, Adolphe & Darmesteter, Arsène *Dictionnaire général de la langue française, avec le concours de Antoine Thomas* 1895–1900
Haughton, Samuel *Six lectures on physical geography* 1880
Hauksbee, Francis *Physico-mechanical experiments on various subjects* 1709
Haupt's (Moriz) Zeitschrift für deutsches Alterthum 1841–
Haurwitz, Bernhard *Dynamic meteorology* 1941
Hausman, Louis *Clinical neuroanatomy, neurophysiology and neurology* 1958
Hausted, Peter *The rivall friends. A comœdie* 1632
Havelok the Dane, The lay of c1300 (E.E.T.S. 1868, Skeat 1902)
Havergal, Francis T. *Herefordshire words and phrases* 1887
Havers, George *The travels of Pietro della Valle into East India and Arabia Deserta* tr. *Whereunto is added a relation of sir Thos. Roe's voyage into the East Indies* (by E. Terry) 1665
Haward, Lazarus *The charges issuing forth of the crown revenue of England* 1647
Haward, Nicolas *Eutropius' (F.) Briefe chronicle* tr. 1564
Hawes, Stephen *The conuercyon of swerers* 1509 (Abbotsford Cl. 1865)
The example of virtue 1510
The pastime of pleasure 1509 (1517)
— another ed., entitled *The historie of graunde Amoure and la bell Pucel, called The pastime of pleasure* 1554 (1555; Percy Soc. 1845)
Hawke, Michael *Killing is murder and no murder* 1657
Hawker, Essex *The wedding* 1729
Hawker, Lieut.-Col. Peter *Diary* 1802–53 (1893)
Instructions to young sportsmen in all that relates to guns and shooting 1824 (ed. 3)
Hawker, Robert S. *The Cornish ballads and other poems; including a second edition of 'The quest of the Sangraal'* 1869
Footprints of former men in far Cornwall 1870
The quest of the Sangraal 1864
Life and letters a1875 (1905)
Hawkes, Jessie Jacquetta & Hawkes, Charles Francis Christopher *Prehistoric Britain* 1943
— (rev. ed.) 1947
Hawkesworth, John *An account of the voyages undertaken for making discoveries in the Southern Hemisphere and performed by Commodore Byron, Captain Wallis, Captain Carteret, and Captain Cook (from 1764–71)* 1773
See also *Adventurer*
Hawkey, Raymond & Bingham, Roger *Wild card* 1974

Hawkins, Benjamin (1754–1816) *A sketch of the Creek country, in 1798 and 1799* (Georgia Historical Society) 1848

Hawkins, Charles Caesar & Wallis, F. *The dynamo: its theory, design and manufacture* 1893

Hawkins, Edward *The silver coins of England arranged and described* 1841

Hawkins, Francis *Youth's behaviour: or, decency in conversation amongst men* tr. 1646 (1663)

Hawkins, Henry *Partheneia sacra. Or, the mysterious and delicious garden of the sacred Parthenes.* By H. A. (i.e. Henry Hawkins) 1633

Hawkins, Sir John *The first made to the West Indies* 1562
The (second) voyage made to the coast of Guinea and the Indies of Nova Spania, begun in 1564 (signed at end Iohn Sparke) *c*1565
A true declaration of the (third) troublesome voyadge to the parties of Guynea and the west-Indies in 1567–68 1569 (in Hakluyt, Voy. 1589; Hakluyt Soc. 1878; partly repr. in Arber, Eng. Garner V)

Hawkins, Sir John *A general history of the science and practice of music* 1776
The life of Samuel Johnson 1787
See also Walton, I.

Hawkins, John & Hawkins, Ward *Death watch, and The missing witness* 1958 (UK 1959)

Hawkins, Lætitia M. *The Countess and Gertrude* 1811
Memoirs, anecdotes, facts, and opinions 1824

Hawkins, Nehemiah, et al. *Hawkins' electrical dictionary* 1910

Hawkins, Sir Richard *Observations in his voiage into the South Sea 1593* 1622 (Hakluyt Soc. 1847, 1878)

Hawkins, Susanna *Poems and songs* 1841

Hawkins, Sir Thomas *Caussin's (N.) Holy court* tr. 1626
Manzini's (G. B.) Political observations on the fall of Seianus tr. 1634
Matthieu's (P.) Unhappy prosperitie, expressed in the histories of Ælius Sejanus and Philippa tr. 1632 (1639)
The odes and epodes of Horace tr. 1625

Hawkins, Thomas *The origin of the English drama* 1773

Hawkstone 1845 *See* Sewell, W.

Hawkwood, History of Sir John (*The honour of the taylors; or, the famous and renowned history of Sir J. Hawkwood*) 1687

Hawthorne, Julian *Dust* 1883
Fortune's fool 1883
Garth 1877
The laughing mill and other stories 1879
Nathaniel Hawthorne and his wife 1885

Hawthorne, Nathaniel *The Blithedale romance* 1852
Doctor Grimshawe's secret *a*1864 (1883)
The house of the seven gables 1851
The marble faun (The original title of *Transformation*)
Mosses from an old manse 1846
Our old home 1863
Passages from the American note-books *a*1864 (1868)
Passages from the English note-books 1853–58 (1870)
Passages from the French and Italian note-books *a*1864 (1871)
The scarlet letter 1850
Septimius Felton; or the elixir of life *a*1864 (1872)
The snow image, and other tales 1851
Tanglewood tales, for girls and boys: being a second Wonder-book 1853
Transformation; or the romance of Monte Beni 1860
Twice told tales 1837–42
A wonder-book for girls and boys 1851

Hay, Alexander *Saint Germain's (C. de) Royal physician* tr. 1689

Hay, Andrew *Diary* 1659–60 (S.H.S. 1901)

Hay, Edward *History of the insurrection of the county of Wexford in 1798* 1803

'Hay, Ian' (John Hay Beith) *The first hundred thousand: being the unofficial history of a unit of 'K(1)'* [*Kitchener's First Army*] 1915
Housemaster 1936
A knight on wheels 1914
The last million 1919
The lighter side of school life 1914
The poor gentleman 1928
'The right stuff': some episodes in the career of a North Briton 1908
A safety match 1911
—— & 'Armstrong, Anthony' (A. A. Willis) *Orders are orders* 1933

Hay, John M. *The bread-winners: a social study* 1884
Pike county ballads, and other pieces 1871 (1880)

Hay, Malcolm Vivian *Foot of pride: the pressure of Christendom on the people of Israel for 1900 years* 1950

Hay, Roy & Synge, P. M. *The dictionary of garden plants* 1969

Hay, William *Deformity; an essay* 1754
An essay on civil government 1728
Remarks on the laws relating to the poor 1735 (1751)

Hay, William D. *Brighter Britain! or, Settler and Maori in northern New Zealand* 2 vols. 1882
Elementary text-book of British fungi 1887
Three hundred years hence; or, A voice from posterity 1881

Hayashi, Takashi ed. *Olfaction and taste II* 1967 (Proceedings of the 2nd International Symposium on Olfaction and Taste, Tokyo, 1965)

Haycraft, Howard *Murder for pleasure: the life and times of the detective story* 1942

Hayden, Arthur *Chats on old furniture: a practical guide for collectors* 1905

Haydocke, Richard *Lomazzo's (G. P.) Tracte containing the artes of curious paintinge* tr. 1598

Haydon, Benjamin R. *Correspondence and table-talk* *a* 1846. With a memoir by F. W. Haydon (1876)
The life of Haydon, from his autobiography and journals ed. T. Taylor 3 vols. 1853

Haydon, G. H. *The Australian emigrant* 1854
Five years' experience in Australia Felix 1846

Haye, Sir Gilbert *The buke of the law of armys or buke of bataillis* 1456 (S.T.S. 1901)
The buke of knychthede and the buke of the governaunce of princis 1456 (S.T.S. 1914)

Hayes, Alice M. *The horsewoman* 1893

Hayes, Arnold Richard W. *Revision physics for sixth forms* 1962

Hayes, Augustus Allen *New Colorado and the Sante Fé trail* 1880 (UK 1881)

Hayes, Charles *A treatise of fluxions* 1704

Hayes, Roy *The Hungarian game* 1973

Hayes, William *A natural history of British birds* 1775

Hayes, William *A short introduction to conveyancing* 1834 (1837, 1840)

Hayes, William *The genetics of bacteria and their viruses* 1964

Haygarth, Henry William *Recollections of bush life in Australia during a residence of eight years in the interior* 1848

Hayley, William *A philosophical, historical, and moral essay on old maids.* By a friend to the sisterhood (i.e. W. Hayley) 1785
The triumphs of temper; a poem 1781

Haymaker, Webb Edward tr. *R. Bing's Textbook of nervous diseases* 1939

Hayman, Robert *Owen's (J.) Epigrams* tr. 1628
Quodlibets, lately come over from new Britaniola, old Newfoundland 1628

Hayne, Thomas *The life and death of Dr. Martin Luther* 1641

Hays, David G. *Introduction to computational linguistics* 1967

Hayward, Abraham *A selection from the correspondence of A. H., with an account of his early life* 1834–84 (ed. H. E. Carlisle 1886)

Hayward, Charles Brian *Practical aeronautics* 1912

Hayward, Harry Maxwell & Harari, Manya tr. *B. Pasternak's Dr. Zhivago* 1958

Hayward, Helena ed. *The Connoisseur's handbook of antique collecting: a dictionary of furniture, silver, ceramics, glass, fine art, etc.* 1960

Hayward, James *Biondi's (G. F.) Donzella desterrada; or the banish'd virgin* tr. 1635
Biondi's (G. F.) Eromena; or love and revenge tr. 1632

Hayward, Sir John *Annals of the first four years of the reign of Queen Elizabeth* *a*1627 (Camden Soc. 1840)
An answer to the first part of a certaine conference concerning succession, published under the name of R. Dolman 1603
The first part of the life and raigne of King Henrie the IIII 1599
The life and raigne of King Edward the sixt *a*1627 (1630)
The lives of the three Normans, kings of England 1613 (in Harl. Misc.)
A reporte of a discourse concerning supreme power in affaires of religion (anon.) 1606; another ed., entitled *Of supremacie in affaires of religion* 1624
The sanctuarie of a troubled soule 1604 (1616, 1620)

Hayward, John Davey *Prose literature since 1939* 1947

Hayward, Samuel *Seventeen sermons on various important subjects* 1758

Hayward, W. Stephens *Love against the world* 1875

Haywood, Mrs. *A new present for a servant-maid: containing rules for her moral conduct, the whole art of cookery, etc.* 1771

Haywood, Eliza *The female spectator* (anon.) 1744–45 (1748)
The history of Miss Betsy Thoughtless 1751
La belle assemblée by M. A. Poisson de Gomez tr. 1724–25 (1732)

Hazard, Samuel *Cuba with pen and pencil* 1871

Hazard, Thomas Benjamin *Nailer Tom's diary* ed. C. Hazard 1930

Hazlitt, William *Characters of Shakespear's plays* 1817 (1818)
Lectures chiefly on the dramatic literature of the age of Elizabeth 1820
Lectures on the English poets 1818 (1869)
Political essays, with sketches of public characters 1819
The spirit of the age; or, contemporary portraits 1825
Table talk; or, original essays on men and manners 1821–22 (1824, 1869)

Hazlitt, William C. *English proverbs and proverbial phrases* 1869
Four generations of a literary family 1897
The history of the origin and rise of the republic of Venice 1858
Offspring of thought in solitude: modern essays 1884
ed. *Remains of the early popular poetry of England* v.d. (1864–66)
See also Dodsley, R.

Head, Barclay V. *Historia numorum; a manual of Greek numismatics* 1887

Head, Sir Francis B. *Bubbles from the Brunnens of Nassau* 1834
Rough notes taken during some rapid journeys across the Pampas and among the Andes 1826

Head, Sir George *Forest scenes and incidents in the wilds of North America* 1829
A home tour through the manufacturing districts of England 1836

Head, Percy R. & Poynter, Edward J. *Classic and Italian painting* 1880

Head, Richard *The canting academy, or, the devil's cabinet opened, with several new catches and songs* 1673
The English rogue described in the life of Meriton Latroon 1665; Part II by F. Kirkman 1671; Parts III and IV by Head and Kirkman 1671 (1874)
Jackson's recantation, or, the life and death of the notorious highway-man now hanging in chains at Hampstead (anon.) 1674
Proteus redivivus: or the art of wheedling or insinuation 1675

Headley, Henry *Poems and other pieces* 1786

Headrick, James *General view of the agriculture of the county of Angus or Forfar* 1813
View of the mineralogy, agriculture, manufactures and fisheries of the Island of Arran 1807

Heal and Son *Heal's catalogue 1853–1934* 1972 [facsimile reproductions from catalogues]

Heald, Frederick Deforest *Introduction to plant pathology* 1937
Manual of plant diseases 1926

Heald, Timothy Villiers *Deadline* 1975
Just desserts 1977
Let sleeping dogs die 1976

Healey, Edna May *Lady unknown: the life of Angela Burdett-Coutts* 1978

Healey, John *St. Augustine Of the citie of God with the learned comments of J. L. Vives* tr. 1610 (1616)
Discovery of a new world, or a description of the South Indies, hitherto unknowne (a version in English of Bp. Jos. Hall's *Mundus alter et idem*) 1609
Epictetus his manuell. And Cebes his table tr. 1610
— ed. 1616 adds (*And*) *Theophrastus characters* (1636)

Health. International health exhibition; official catalogue 1884

Health and longevity, Account of persons remarkable for their. By a physician 1829

Hearn, Patricio Lafcadio T. C. *In ghostly Japan* 1899
Japan: an attempt at interpretation 1904
Kokoro: hints and echoes of Japanese inner life 1896
Kottō: being Japanese curios, with sundry cobwebs 1902

Hearn, William E. *The Aryan household, its structure and its development* 1878

Hearne, John *Stranger at the gate* 1956

Hearne, Samuel *A journey from Prince of Wales's fort in Hudson's Bay to the Northern ocean in 1769–72* 1795

Hearne, Thomas *Ductor historicus; or a short system of universal history* 1698
— ed. 2, augmented and improv'd 1704–05 (1714)
Reliquiæ Hearnianæ: the remains, being extracts from his MS. diaries 17.. (collected by P. Bliss 1857)
Remarks and collections 1705–12 (ed. C. E. Doble, O.H.S. 1885–89)

Hearst's international 1925–

Heart: a journal for the study of the circulation 1909–33

Heath, Francis G. *The fern world* 1877
The 'romance' of peasant life in the West of England 1872 (1880)

Heath, James *A brief chronicle of the late intestine war in the three kingdoms of England, Scotland and Ireland* 1663
England's chronicle: or, the lives and reigns of the kings and queens from the time of Julius Cæsar to K. William and Q. Mary 1689
Flagellum: or, the life and death, birth and burial of Oliver Cromwel. By S. T. gent. (i.e. James Heath) 1663 (1672)

Heath, James D. *The complete croquet-player* 1874

Heath, John B. *Some account of the worshipful Company of Grocers of the city of London* 1829 (1869)

Heath, Peter tr. *G. A. Wetter's Soviet ideology today* 1966

Heath, Richard *The English peasant* 1893

Heath, Robert *A natural and historical account of the islands of Scilly* 1750

Heath, Thomas *A manifest and apparent confutation of an astrological discourse (by R. Harvey)* 1583

Heath, Sir Thomas L. *Apollonius of Perga. Treatise on conic sections* 1896
The works of Archimedes 1897

Heathcote, Charles G. & John M. *Tennis*: by J. M. Heathcote. *Lawn tennis*: by C. G. Heathcote. *Rackets*: by E. O. Pleydell-Bouverie. *Fives*: by A. C. Ainger. 1890 (Badminton Library)

Heathcote, Frederick G. *See* Claus, C.

Heathcote, Ralph *Sylva, or, the wood: being a collection of anecdotes, dissertations, characters, apophthegms, original letters, bons mots, and other little things* (anon.) 1786

Heaton, Mary M. *The history of the life of Albrecht Dürer* 1870 (1881)

Heaviside, Oliver *Electromagnetic theory* 3 vols. 1893–9

Heavysege, Charles *Saul; a drama* 1857 (1869)

Heber, Bp. Reginald *Hymns* *a*1826 (1827)
Life of Jeremy Taylor 1822
Narrative of a journey through the upper provinces of India, from Calcutta to Bombay 1824–25, with notes upon Ceylon; an account of a journey to Madras and the Southern provinces 1826, and letters written in India *a*1826 (1828, 1844)
Palestine; a prize-poem 1803
Palestine and other poems v.d. (1843)

Heberden, William (the younger) *Heberden's (W., the elder) Commentaries on the history and cure of diseases* tr. 1803

Hecht, Ben & MacArthur, Charles *The front page* 1928

Hector, Mrs. Annie F. *See* 'Alexander, Mrs.'

Hector, James *Handbook of New Zealand* 1883

Hector, William ed. *Selections from the judicial records of Renfrewshire* 16..-17.. (1876)
Hedderwick, Peter *A treatise on marine architecture* 1830
Hedgecoe, John *The photographer's handbook* 1977
Hedges, Sir William *Diary* a1701 (Hakluyt Soc. 1887-88)
Hedin, Sir Sven A. *Through Asia* 1898
Heffner, Roe-Merrill S. *General phonetics* 1949
Heffron, Dorris *Crusty crossed* 1976
A nice fire and some moonpennies 1971
Heflin, Woodford Agee ed. *Aerospace glossary* 1959
ed. *The United States Air Force dictionary* 1956
Heilbron, Ian Morris ed. *Dictionary of organic compounds* 3 vols. 1934-7
Heilprin, Angelo *The geographical and geological distribution of animals* 1887
Hein, Leonard William *An introduction to electronic data processing for business* 1961
Heinlein, Robert Anson *The door into summer* 1957 (UK 1960)
Heinrich, Eberhardt William *Microscopic petrography* 1956
Heister's (L.) General system of surgery tr. 1743
Heitler, Walter *The quantum theory of radiation* 1936
Helfenstein, Jacob *A comparative grammar of the Teutonic languages* 1870
Heliconia; comprising a selection of English poetry 1575-1604 (ed. T. Park 1815)
Heliodorus' Triumphs of love and constancy: a romance, containing the heroick amours of Theagenes and Chariclea. In ten books. The first five rendered by a person of quality, the last five by N. Tate 1686
—— another ed., entitled *Æthiopian adventures* 1753
Heller, Joseph *Catch-22* 1961 (UK 1962)
Something happened 1974
Hellman, Lilian *The little foxes* 1939
Pentimento: a book of portraits 1973 (UK 1974)
An unfinished woman: a memoir 1969
Hellowes, Edward *Guevara's (A. de) Chronicle, conteyning the liues of tenne emperours of Rome* tr. 1577
Guevara's Familiar epistles tr. 1574 (1577, 1582, 1584)
(For *Gueuara's Golden epistles* see Fenton, Sir G.)
Hellyer, Arthur George Lee *T. W. Sanders' Encyclopaedia of gardening* (ed. 22) 1952
The encyclopaedia of garden work and terms 1954
Practical gardening for amateurs 1935
Helme, Elizabeth tr. *F. Le Vaillant's Travels from the Cape of Good-Hope, into the interior parts of Africa* 2 vols. 1790
St. Margaret's cave, or the nun's story 1801
Helmer, Olaf tr. *A. Tarski's Introduction to logic and to the methodology of deductive sciences* 1941
Helps, Sir Arthur *Companions of my solitude* 1851 (1874)
Essays written in the intervals of business 1841 (1875)
Friends in council 1847-49, 1859
Organization in daily life. An essay (anon.) 1862
Realmah 1868 (1876)
Social pressure 1875
Some talk about animals and their masters 1873 (1875)
Helps to the study of the Bible 1880 (1884; revised and enlarged edition 1893)
Helsham, Richard *A course of lectures in natural philosophy* a1738 (1739)
Helvetius' (C. A.) Child of nature improved by chance tr. 1774
Hely, James *O'Flaherty's (R.) Ogygia, or, a chronological account of Irish events* tr. 1793
Helyas, Knight of the Swanne 1512 (W. de Worde; in Thoms, Prose romances III. 1828)
Hemans, Felicia D. *Works* a1835 (1839)
Poems 1808
Poetical works a1835 (1875)
Early blossoms of spring, a collection of poems written between eight and fifteen years of age 1808 (1840)
England and Spain; or, valour and patriotism 1808
Hemingway, Ernest *Across the river and into the trees* 1950
Death in the afternoon 1932
A farewell to arms 1929
The fifth column [a play], *and The first forty-nine stories* 1938 (UK 1939)
For whom the bell tolls 1940
Green hills of Africa 1935 (UK 1936)
In our time 1924
— (enlarged ed.) 1925 (UK 1926)
Men without women 1927 (UK 1928)
The old man and the sea 1952
The sun also rises 1926 (UK ed. with title *Fiesta* 1927)
To have and have not 1937
The torrents of spring: a romantic novel in honour of the passing of a great race 1926 (UK 1933)
'Hemingway, Percy' (W. P. Addleshaw) *Out of Egypt* 1895
Hempstead, Joshua *Diary, 1711-1758* 1901
Hemyng, Bracebridge *Eton school days* 1864
Henchman, Richard *A peace-offering in the temple; or, a seasonable plea for unity among dissenting brethren* 1661
Henckel, J. F. See Henkel, J. F.
Henderson, A. G. tr. *V. Cousin's The philosophy of Kant: lectures* 1854
Henderson, Alexander *The history of ancient and modern wines* 1824
Henderson, Alexander Morell & Parsons, Talcott tr. *M. Weber's Theory of social and economic organization* 1947
Henderson, Andrew *Scottish proverbs* 1832 (1881)
Henderson, David Kennedy & Gillespie, Robert Dick *A text-book of psychiatry for students and practitioners* 1927
— (ed. 9) 1962
Henderson, Ebenezer *Iceland; or the journal of a residence in that island 1814-15* 1818
Henderson, George *The popular rhymes, sayings, and proverbs of the county of Berwick* 1856
Henderson, George C. *Keys to crookdom* 1924
Henderson, James *Memorials* 1867
Henderson, John *General view of the agriculture of the county of Caithness* 1812
General view of the agriculture of the county of Sutherland 1812
Henderson, Peter *Practical floriculture* 1869
Henderson, Stephen *Understanding the new Black poetry: Black speech and Black music as poetic references* 1973
Henderson, William *Notes on the folk lore of the northern counties of England and the Borders* 1866 (1878)
Hendrick, Burton Jesse *The life and letters of Walter H. Page* 3 vols. 1922-5
Hendyng, Proverbs of See *Proverbs of Hendyng*
Heney, Thomas *In middle harbour, and other verse, chiefly Australian* 1890
Henfrey, Arthur *An elementary course of botany* 1857
The rudiments of botany 1849
The vegetation of Europe, its conditions and causes 1852
See also Griffith, John W.
Henissart, Paul *Winter quarry* 1976
Henkel's (J. F.) Pyritologia; or, a history of the pyrites tr. 1757
Henley, William E. *A book of verses* 1888
For England's sake: verses and songs in time of war 1900
Poems 1898
—— & Stevenson, Robert L. *Three plays: Deacon Brodie, Beau Austin, Admiral Guinea* 1892
See also Farmer, J. S.
Hennell, Mary *An outline of the various social systems and communities which have been founded on the principle of co-operation* 1841 (1844)
Henney, Julian Keith *Principles of radio* 1929
ed. *The radio engineering handbook* 1933
— (ed. 5) 1959
—— & Dudley, Beverley eds. *Handbook of photography* 1939
Henning, Rachel (1826-1914) *Letters* ed. D. Adams 1966
Henrot, Thérèse *Belgium* (English version by R. E. Wolf and the author) 1961
Henry VII, Materials for a history See *Materials*
Henry VII, Memorials of 15.. (Rolls series 1858)
Henry VIII *A declaration, conteynyng the iust causes and consyderations, of this present warre with the Scottis* 1542 (in Complaint of Scotland, E.E.T.S. 1872)
The privy purse expences of 1529-32 (1827)
Henry, Alexander *Travels and adventures in Canada and the Indian territories 1760-76* 1809
Henry, Caleb S. *Doctor Oldham at Greystones, and his talk there* 1860
Henry, Frank Souder *Printing for school and shop* 1917
'Henry, Joan' (Constance Ann Standage) *Who lie in gaol* 1952
Henry, John J. *An accurate account of the hardships of that band of heroes who traversed the wilderness in the campaign against Quebec in 1775* 1812
Henry, Matthew *Works* a1714 (1726, 1853)
Disputes reviewed; a sermon 1710
An exposition of the Old and New Testament 1710 (1737-38)
A sermon concerning the forgiveness of sin as a debt 1711
A short account of the life of lieutenant Illidge 1710
'Henry, O.' (William Sydney Porter) *Cabbages and kings* 1904
The four million 1906 (UK 1916)
The gentle grafter 1908 (UK 1928)
Heart of the west 1907 (UK 1912)
Options 1909 (UK 1916)
Roads of destiny 1909
Rolling stones 1912 (UK 1916)
Strictly business 1910 (UK 1917)
The trimmed lamp 1907 (UK 1915)
Whirligigs 1910
Henry, Philip *Diaries and letters* 1631-96 (1882)
Henry, Robert *The history of Great Britain* 1771-85; a1790 (1793)
Henry, Thomas *An account of a method of preserving water at sea from putrefaction* 1781
Henry, Thomas Anderson *The plant alkaloids* 1913
Henry, William *The elements of experimental chemistry* 1810 (1826-40)
An epitome of chemistry 1800 (1808)
Henry the Minstrel *The actis and deidis of the illustere and vailȝeand campioun Schir William Wallace* c1470 (1570, 1820; S.T.S. 1889)
Henry and Isabella: a novel 1811
Henryson, Robert *Poems* c1480 (S.T.S. 1906-14)
The morall fabillis of Esope c1480 (1570; Maitland Cl. 1832; in Anglia IX. 1886)
Orpheus and Eurydice c1480
The testament of Cresseid c1480
Henshall, James A. *Camping and cruising in Florida* 1884
Henshall, Samuel *The Saxon and English languages reciprocally illustrative of each other* 1798
Henshaw, Bp. Joseph *Horæ succisivæ, or, spare-houres of meditations* 1631 (ed. 2)
Meditations miscellaneous, holy and humane 1637; ed. 3, much enlarged, entitled *Daily thoughts; or a miscellany of meditations, holy and humane* 1651
Henslow, George *The origin of floral structures through insect and other agencies* 1888
Henslow, John S. *A dictionary of botanical terms* 1856
The principles of descriptive and physiological botany 1835 (1836)
Henslowe, Philip *Diary* 1591-1609 (Shaks. Soc. 1845; 1904-08)
Henslowe papers, being documents supplementary to Henslowe's diary a1616 (ed. W. R. Greg 1907)
Henty, George A. *The cornet of horse; a tale of Marlborough's wars* 1881
Through Russian snows: a story of Napoleon's retreat from Moscow 1896
With Lee in Virginia: a story of the American civil war 1890
Hentzner's (Paul) Journey into England in the year 1598 (being a part of the Itinerary of P. H. translated by R. Bentley; ed. H. Walpole, Earl of Oxford) 1757
Hepburn, George B. *General view of the agriculture and rural economy of East Lothian* 1794
Hepworth, Cecil Milton *Animated photography: the ABC of the cinematograph* 1897
Heraclitus ridens 1681-82 *See* Flatman, T.
Herak, Milan & Stringfield, V. T. eds. *Karst: important karst regions of the northern hemisphere* 1972
Herald, The. By Stentor Telltruth 1757-58
Herball, Grete See *Grete herball*
Herbert, Alan Patrick *Holy deadlock* 1934
Independent Member 1950
Laughing Ann, and other poems 1925
Plain Jane 1927
The water gipsies 1930
What a word! 1935
Herbert, Alfred Xavier *Capricornia* 1938 (UK 1939)
Herbert, Edward, 1st Baron Herbert of Cherbury *The life and reigne of King Henry the eighth* a1648 (1649, 1682)
Life, written by himself a1648 (1764, 1886)
Occasional verses a1648 (1665)
Herbert, Sir Edward *A short account of the authorities in law, upon which judgement was given in Sir Edw. Hales his case* 1688
Herbert, George *Poetical works* a1633 (Grosart 1876)
Outlandish proverbs a1633 (1640)
— another ed., entitled *Jacula prudentum, or outlandish proverbs, sentences, etc.* (1651)
A priest to the temple, or, The countrey parson his character, and rule of holy life a1633 (1652)
The temple; sacred poems and private ejaculations 1633
Herbert, George Robert C. (Earl of Pembroke) & Kingsley, George H. *South Sea bubbles* 1872
Herbert, H. 1727-30 See *Fleury*
Herbert, Henry, 10th Earl of Pembroke *A method of breaking horses, and teaching soldiers to ride, designed for the use of the army* 1761
— ed. 3, entitled *Military equitation* 1778
Herbert, Henry W. *See* 'Forester, Frank'
Herbert, Mary E. *Cradle lands* 1867
Hübner's (J. A. von) Ramble round the world 1874 (1878)
Impressions of Spain in 1866 1867
Herbert, Sir Thomas *A relation of some yeares travaile begunne anno 1626, into Afrique and the greater Asia* 1634 (1638, 1665, 1677)
Threnodia Carolina 1678 (printed from original MS. in A. Fea, Memoirs of the martyr King 1905); repr. with additions under the title of *Memoirs of the two last years of the reign of Charles I* 1702
Herbert, Thomas Ernest *Telegraphy: a detailed exposition of the telegraph system of the British Post Office* 1906
Telephony: an elementary exposition of the telephone system of the British Post Office 1923
— (new ed., by T. E. Herbert & W. S. Procter) 2 vols. & Suppl. 1932-40
— (new ed., by J. Atkinson) 2 vols. 1948-50
Herbert, William *Ella Rosenberg, a romance* 1808
Herbert, William *The history of the twelve great Livery Companies of London* 1834-37
Herbert, Xavier *See* Herbert, Alfred Xavier
Herd, David ed. *Ancient and modern Scottish songs, heroic ballads, etc.*, v.d. (1776)
Here and now: an independent monthly review 1949-
Heren, Louis *Growing up on 'The Times'* 1978
Hergesheimer, Joseph *The bright shawl* 1922 (UK 1923)
Hering, Francis *See* Herring, Francis
Héristal, Adam d' *Our discordant life* 1894
Herkless, John & Hannay, Robert K. *The archbishops of St. Andrews* 1907-13
Herle, Charles *An answer to Dr. Ferne's Reply entituled: Conscience satisfied etc.* 1643
David's song of three parts 1643
A fuller answer to a treatise written by Dr. Ferne, entituled, The resolving of conscience etc. 1642
Herman, Henry *His angel, a romance of the Far West* 1891
See also Murray, D. C.
Hermann and Emilia 1805 *See* Lafontaine, A. H. J.
Hermann's (C. F.) Manual of the political antiquities of Greece historically considered tr. 1836
Hermeticall banquet drest by a spagiricall cook, for the better preservation of the microcosme 1652
Hermit in the country 1820-22; *in Edinburgh* 1824; *in London* 1819-20 *See* McDonogh, Felix
Herne, Samuel *Domus Carthusiana; or an account of the foundation of the Charter-House* 1677
Hero and Leander 1651 See *Loves of H. and L.*
Herodian's History tr. 1629 *See* Maxwell, James
Herodotus, The famous hystory of, tr. by B. R(ich) 1584
Heroic epistle to an unfortunate monarch, by Peregrine the Elder 1778
Heroine of the Peninsula, The 1826 *See* McDonogh, Felix

HERON, Alastair ed. *Towards a Quaker view of sex: an essay by a group of Friends* 1963
HERON, James *The Celtic Church in Ireland* 1898
HERON, Patrick *The changing forms of art* 1955
HERON, Robert *Information concerning the strength, views, and interests of the powers presently at war* 1794
HERRICK, Robert *The complete poems* a1674 (Grosart 1876)
Poetical works a1674 (1869, 1915)
Hesperides: or, the works both humane and divine of R. H. 1648
The noble numbers: or, his pious pieces 1647
Herrig's Archiv See *Archiv*
HERRING, Francis *A modest defence of the caveat given to the wearers of impoisoned amulets* 1604
Oberndoerffer's (J.) Anatomyes of the true physition and counterfeit mounte-banke tr. 1602
HERRING, Richard *Paper and paper-making, ancient and modern* 1855
Herrings tayle 1598 *See* CAREW, R.
'HERRIOT, James' (J. A. Wight) *It shouldn't happen to a vet* 1972
HERSCHEL, Sir John F. W. *Essays from the Edinburgh and Quarterly Reviews, with addresses and other pieces* v.d. (1857)
Familiar lectures on scientific subjects 1866
A manual of scientific enquiry, ed. by Sir J. F. W. Herschel 1849; ed. 3, superintended by Robert Main 1859
Meteorology 1859 (in Manual of scientific enquiry)
Outlines of astronomy 1849 (1853)
Physical geography 1861
A preliminary discourse on the study of natural philosophy 1830
Schiller's (J. C. F. von) Walk tr. 1847
A treatise on astronomy 1833
HERSKOWITZ, Irwin Herman *Genetics* 1962
HERTFORD, Frances Seymour, Countess of *Correspondence between Frances, countess of Hartford (afterwards duchess of Somerset), and Henrietta Louisa, countess of Pomfret* 1738–41 (1805)
HERVÉ, Peter *Beauties of Paris* 1818
How to enjoy Paris 1816
HERVET, Gentian *Xenophon's Treatise of householde* 1532 (1768)
HERVEY, Mrs. *The Mourtray family* 1800
HERVEY, Frederic *The naval history of Great Britain* 1779
HERVEY, George F. *A handbook of card games* 1963
HERVEY, James *Meditations and contemplations.* Vol. I. *Meditations among the tombs, Reflections on a flower garden, A descant upon creation* 1746; Vol. II. *Contemplations on the night, Contemplations on the starry heavens, A winter piece* 1747 (1767, 1818)
Theron and Aspasio: or, a series of dialogues and letters upon the most important and interesting subjects 1755
HERVEY, John, Baron Hervey of Ickworth *Memoirs of the reign of George the second* a1743 (ed. from the original MS. by J. W. Croker 1848)
Herzog's (J. J.) Religious encyclopædia: or, dictionary of Biblical, historical, doctrinal, and practical theology, ed. by P. Schaff 1882–83
HESLOP, Richard O. *Northumberland words. A glossary of words used in the county of Northumberland and on the Tyneside* 1892–94 (E.D.S.)
HESS, Fr. Cuthbert (Lawrence Anthony Hess) ed. *God and the supernatural: a Catholic statement of the Christian faith* 1920
HESSEY, James A. *Sunday: its origin, history, and present obligation considered* 1860
HESTER, John *A compendium of the rationall secretes of L. Phioravante* tr. 1582
HETH, Thomas 1583 *See* HEATH, T.
HETLEY, Sir Thomas *Reports and cases in the third–seventh years of the late King Charles as they were argued at the Common-pleas barre* 1657
HETT, Charles L. *A glossary of popular, local, and old-fashioned names of British birds* 1902
HEWER, Evelyn Everard *Text-book of histology for medical students* 1937
HEWETT, John a1658 *See* HEWIT, J.
HEWETT, Sarah *The peasant speech of Devon* 1892
HEWETT, William *Glossary of Berkshire provincialisms* 1847
HEWIT, John *Repentance and conversion the fabrick of salvation, or the saints joy in heaven for the sinners sorrow upon earth, being the last sermons preached by J. H. With other of his sermons* a1658 (1658)
HEWITSON, William C. *Coloured illustrations of the eggs of British birds* 1846
HEWITT, James *Yoga* 1960
HEWITT, John a1658 *See* HEWIT, J.
HEWITT, John *Ancient armour and weapons in Europe* 1855–60
HEWLETT, Joseph T. J. *The parish clerk* 1841
Parsons and widows 1844
Peter Priggins, the college scout (anon.) 1841
HEWLETT, Maurice H. *Earthwork out of Tuscany* 1895
The forest lovers, a romance 1898
HEWLETT, Richard Tanner *A manual of bacteriology, clinical and applied* 1898
— (ed. 2) 1902
HEWYT, John a1658 *See* HEWIT, J.
Hexameron of St. Basil See *Basil, St.*
HEXHAM, Henry *A copious English and Netherduytch dictionarie* 1647 (1660)
Groot-Woorden-Boeck; a large Netherdutch and English dictionarie 1648 (1658)
The principles of the art militarie 1637
A tongue-combat (anon. Preface signed H. Hexham) 1623 *See* SCOTT, Thomas
Hexham, The Priory of, its chroniclers, endowments and annals v.d.; *its title deeds, black book, etc.*, v.d. (Surtees Soc. 1864–65)
HEY, John *Lectures in divinity, delivered in Cambridge 1780–85* 1796–98
HEYDON, Sir Christopher *An astrological discourse in justification of the validity of astrology. Together with an astrological judgement upon the great conjunction of Saturn and Jupiter 1603* c1610 (1650)
A defence of judiciall astrologie 1603
HEYER, Georgette *A blunt instrument* 1938
Death in the stocks 1935
The false colours 1963
They found him dead 1937
HEYERDAHL, Thor *Fatu-Hiva: back to nature* 1974
The Kon-Tiki expedition See LYON, Francis Hamilton
HEYLIN, Peter *Κειμήλια ἐκκλησιαστικά. Historical and miscellaneous tracts* a1662 (1681)
Aerius redivivus; or, the history of the presbyterians from 1536 to 1647 a1662 (1670)
Antidotum Lincolniense; or an answer to a book entituled, The Holy Table, name and thing 1637
A brief and moderate answer to the seditious and scandalous Challenge of H. Burton 1637
Certamen epistolare; or the letter-combate with Mr. Baxter, etc. 1659
A coale from the altar 1636
Cosmographie 1652 See *Microcosmus*, below
Cyprianus Anglicus; or the history of the life and death of William Laud a1662 (1668, 1671)
Ecclesia restaurata; or, the history of the reformation of the Church of England 1661
Ecclesia vindicata; or, the Church of England justified 1657
Examen historicum, or a discovery and examination of the mistakes in some modern histories 1659
Extraneus vapulans; or, the observator rescued from the violent but vaine assaults of Hamon L'Estrange 1656
A full relation of two journeys: the one, into the mainland of France; the other, into some of the adjacent islands 1656
— another ed., entitled *A survey of the estate of France* 1656
Ἡρωολογια Anglorum; or, an help to English history 1641
Historia quinqu-articularis; or a declaration of the judgement of the Western churches, particularly of the church of England, in the five controverted points reproached by the name of Arminianism 1660
The historie of episcopacie 1642
The history of St. George of Cappadocia 1631
The history of the Sabbath 1636
Microcosmus. A little description of the great world 1621 (–1639); enlarged and entitled *Cosmographie in four bookes, containing the chorographie and historie of the whole world* 1652 (1674)
(*Relations and observations* 1648–49: see C. Walker *History of Independency*)
The stumbling-block of disobedience and rebellion cunningly laid by Calvin in the subjects way, discovered, censured and removed 1658
Survey of the estate of France See *A full relation of two journeys*, above
The undeceiving of the people in the point of tithes 1648
HEYNE, Benjamin *Tracts, historical and statistical, on India* 1814
HEYWOOD, Eliza *See* HAYWOOD, Eliza
HEYWOOD, Jasper *Seneca his tenne tragedies* tr. by J. Heywood and others 1581
L. A. Senecæ Tragedia prima quæ inscribitur Hercules Furens tr. 1561
The seconde tragedie of Seneca entituled Thyestes tr. 1560
The sixt tragedie of L. A. Seneca, entituled Troas tr. 1559
HEYWOOD, John *Dramatic writings* 15.. (J. S. Farmer 1905–08)
Woorkes. A dialogue conteynyng prouerbes and epigrammes 1562 (Spenser Soc. 1867)
A dialogue conteinyng the number in effect of all the prouerbes in the Englishe tongue 1546 (1874)
A dialogue on wit and folly 15.. (Percy Soc. 1846)
Epigrammes 1555–60
A mery play betwene Iohan Iohan the husbande, Tyb his wyfe, and syr Jhan the preest 1533 (Brandl 1898)
A mery play betwene the pardoner and the frere, the curate and neybour Pratte 1533 (in Pollard, Eng. miracle plays 1890)
Of gentylnes & nobylyte See RASTELL, John
The playe called the foure PP. A newe and a very mery enterlude of a palmer, a pardoner, a potycary, a pedler ?1545 (in Manly, Specim. pre-Shaks. drama I, 1897)
A play of love 1534 (Brandl 1898)
The play of the wether 1533 (Brandl 1898)
The spider and the flie, a parable 1556 (Spenser Soc. 1894)
HEYWOOD, Oliver *Works* a1702 (1825–27)
Autobiography, diaries, anecdote and event books, illustrating the general and family history of Yorkshire and Lancashire a1702 (1881–85)
The best entail, or, dying parents living hopes for their surviving children 1693
Heart-treasure 1667–72
HEYWOOD, Thomas *Dramatic works* a1650 (1874)
An apology for actors 1612 (Shaks. Soc. 1841)
The brazen age 1613
The captives; or, the lost recovered 1624 (in Bullen, Old Plays IV)
A challenge for beautie 1636
England's Elizabeth, her life and troubles during her minoritie from the cradle to the crowne 1631 (1641; in Harl. Misc.)
The English traveller 1633
The exemplary lives and memorable acts of nine the most worthy women of the world 1640
The fayre mayde of the Exchange 1607 (Shaks. Soc. 1845)
The fair maid of the west 1631 (Shaks. Soc. 1850)
The foure prentices of London, with the conquest of Jerusalem 1615
A funerall elegie upon the death of Henry, Prince of Wales 1613
A funeral elegie upon the death of King James 1625
The golden age 1611 (Shaks. Soc. 1851)
Γυναικεῖον: or nine bookes of various history concerninge women 1624
The hierarchie of the blessed angells 1635
If you know not me, you know no bodie: or, the troubles of Queene Elizabeth 1605 (Shaks. Soc. 1851)
The second part of, If you know not me, you know no bodie. With the building of the Royall Exchange 1606 (Shaks. Soc. 1851)
The iron age 1632
The first and second partes of King Edward the fourth 1599 (Shaks. Soc. 1842)
Londini sinus salutis 1635
Londini speculum; or, Londons mirror 1637
Londini status pacatus; or, Londons peaceable estate 1639
London's jus honorarium exprest in sundry triumphs 1631
Loves maistresse: or the Queens masque 1636
A pleasant comedy called A mayden-head well lost 1634
A marriage triumphe 1613 (Percy Soc. 1842)
Philocothonista; or the drunkard opened, dissected, and anatomized 1635
Pleasant dialogues and dramma's 1637
Porta pietatis, or the port or harbour of piety 1638 (Percy Soc. 1844)
The rape of Lucrece 1608
The royall king and the loyall subject 1637 (Shaks. Soc. 1850)
Sallust's Two most worthy and notable histories tr. 1608–09
The silver age 1613 (Shaks. Soc. 1851)
Troia Britanica: or Great Britaines Troy 1609
A true description of his Majesties royall ship built at Wooll-witch 1637
The wise-woman of Hogsdon 1638
A woman kilde with kindnesse 1607 (Shaks. Soc. 1850)
See also TOURNEUR, C.
—— & BROME, Richard *The late Lancashire witches* 1634
—— & ROWLEY, William *Fortune by land and sea* 16.. (1655; Shaks. Soc. 1845)
HIBBERT, Henry *Syntagma theologicum: or, a treatise wherein is concisely comprehended the body of divinity; whereunto are added certaine divine discourses* 1662
HIBBERT(-WARE), Samuel *A description of the Shetland Islands* 1822
Hibbert journal, The; a quarterly review of religion, theology, and philosophy 1902–
HICHCOCK, Robert *See* HITCHCOCK, R.
HICHENS, Robert S. *The green carnation* (anon.) 1894
The Londoners, an absurdity 1898
HICK, John Harwood ed. *The myth of God incarnate* 1977
Orchids on your budget; or, Live smartly on what have you 1937 (UK 1938)
HICKERINGILL, Edmund *Works* a1708 (1709)
Miscellaneous tracts, essays, satyrs, etc. in prose and verse 1707
The black non-conformist discover'd in more naked truth 1682
The ceremony-monger, his character 1689
Curse ye Meroz, or the fatal doom 1680
Gregory, Father Greybeard, with his vizard off 1673
The history of whiggism 1682
The horrid sin of man-catching 1681
Jamaica view'd 1661
The lay-clergy; or, the lay-elder 1695
The naked truth 1680–82
— *A vindication of the naked truth.* By Phil. (or rather Edmund) Hickeringill 1681
Priest-craft, its character and consequences 1705–07
— *The vindication of the character of priestcraft* 1705
The speech without doors, or some modest inquiries humbly proposed to the Convention of Estates 1689
The Trimmer. Debate with the Observator 1683
HICKERINGILL, Phil. *See* HICKERINGILL, E.
HICKES, George *The case of infant baptism* 1683
The spirit of Popery 1680
Two treatises, one of the Christian priesthood; the other of the dignity of the episcopal order 1707 (1711, 1847)
—— & NELSON, Robert *Memoirs of the life of John Kettlewell.* Compiled (by F. Lee) from the collections of G. Hickes and R. Nelson 1718
HICKEY, William *Memoirs* ed. A. Spencer 4 vols. 1913–25
— ed. P. Quennell 1960
HICKIE, William J. *The Comedies of Aristophanes* tr. 1853 (1872)
HICKMAN, Henry *Historia quinq-articularis exarticulata; or, Animadversions on Doctor Heylin's Quinquarticular history* 1673 (1674)
HICKOCK, Thomas *The voyage and travaile of M. C. Frederick into the East India* tr. 1588
Hickscorner See *Hyckescorner*
'HIEOVER, Harry' (C. Brindley) *Practical horsemanship* 1850
The stud for practical purposes 1849
HIERON, Samuel *Works* a1617 (1620)

Aarons bells a-sounding a1617 (1623)
A defence of the ministers reasons for refusall of subscription to the Booke of Common Prayer 1607-08
A short dialogue proving that the ceremonyes now in question, are defended by arguments such as the papists have used (anon.) 1605
Hiffernan, Paul *See* H., P.
Hi-fi answers 1972-
Hi-fi sound 1967-77
Higden's Polychronicon tr. 1432-50 (Rolls series 1865-86)
See also Trevisa
Higgin, Louis *Handbook of embroidery* ed. M. Alford 1880
Higgins, George Vincent *A city on a hill* 1975
Dreamland 1977
The friends of Eddie Coyle 1972
The judgement of Deke Hunter 1976
Higgins, Godfrey *The Celtic Druids* 1827
Higgins, John *The nomenclator, or remembrancer of Adrianus Junius* tr. 1585
See also Huloet; *Mirror for magistrates*
Higgins, Matthew J. *Essays on social subjects* a1868 (1875)
Higginson, Thomas W. *Malbone: an Oldport romance* 1869
Oldport days 1873
Young folks' history of the United States 1875
Higgs, Paget ed. *Magneto- and dynamo-electric machines.. From the German of Glaser de Cew* 1885
High commission cases. Reports of cases in the Courts of Star Chamber and High Commission 1631-32 (Camden Soc. 1886)
'High Jinks, Junior' (Harold Poe Swartwood) *Choice slang* 1914
High times (New York) 1974-
Higham, Edward Spencer & Higham, William Richard Joseph *High speed rugby* 1960
Higham, Robert Robin Alger *A handbook of papermaking* 1963
Higher education: report See: United Kingdom. Parliamentary papers. Committee on Higher Education
Highland Society of Scotland *Prize essays and transactions* 1799-1843
Transactions 1843-
Highlanders, The 1824 *See* McDonogh, F.
Highlands of Scotland in 1750 17.. (From MS. in the British Museum. With introd. by A. Lang 1898)
Highsmith, Patricia *The tremor of forgery* 1969
Higins, John *See* Higgins, J.
Hildanus tr. 1643 *See* Steer, John
Hildebrand. The life of Hyldebrande, called Gregory, the seventh, pope of that name 1534 (W. de Worde)
Hildick, Edmund Wallace *The boy at the window* 1960
The loop 1977
Hildreth, James *Dragoon campaigns to the Rocky Mountains* 1836
Hilditch, Ann *Rosa de Montmorien. A novel* 1787
Hildrop, John *Miscellaneous works* 1754
A letter to a member of parliament, containing a proposal for bringing in a bill to revise, amend or repeal certain obsolete statutes, commonly called the Ten Commandments (anon.) 1738
Hiler, Hilaire *Notes on the technique of painting* 1934
Hiles, John *Catechism of the organ* 1876 (1878)
A complete dictionary of musical terms 1871
Hilgard, Ernest Ropiequet *Theories of learning* 1948
— (ed. 2) 1956 (UK 1958)
Hilgard, Eugene Waldemar *Soils: their formation, properties, composition, and relations to climate and plant growth in the humid and arid regions* 1906
Hilgendorf, Frederick William *Weeds of New Zealand, and how to eradicate them* 1926
Hill, Aaron *Works* a1750 (1753)
Poems a1750 (1822)
Advice to the poets. A poem 1731
Hill, Abraham *Familiar letters which passed between A. H. and several eminent and ingenious persons of the last century* 16.. (1767)
Some account of the life of Dr. Isaac Barrow 1687 (in Barrow's Works, I. 1687)
Hill, Albert Frederick, *Economic botany* 1937
Hill, Archibald Anderson *Introduction to linguistic structures* 1958
Hill, Archie *Summer's end* 1976
Hill, Beth & Hill, Ray *Spirit in stone: petroglyphs of the Northwest Coast Indians* 1974
Hill, David J. *American authors. W. C. Bryant*, etc. 1879
Hill, John *The British herbal* 1756
A general natural history: or, new and accurate descriptions of the animals, vegetables, and minerals of the different parts of the world. Vol. I. *A history of fossils* 1748; vol. II. *An history of plants* 1751; vol. III. *An history of animals* 1752
A history of the materia medica 1751
Pomet's (P.) Compleat history of drugs tr. 1748 (ed. 4)
The sleep of plants, and cause of motion in the sensitive plant, explain'd 1757
Theophrastus's History of stones tr. 1746 (1774)
The useful family herbal 1755 (1812)
Hill, Peter *The hunters* 1976
Hill, Reginald *A fairly dangerous thing* 1972
Ruling passion 1973
Hill, Robert *Christs prayer expounded, a christian directed and a communicant prep.red* 1606
— another ed., entitled *The pathway to prayer and pietie* 1610 (1629, 1847)
Hill, Susan *Gentleman and ladies* 1976
Strange meeting 1971
Hill, Thomas *The arte of vulgar arithmeticke* 1600
A briefe and pleasaunt treatise intituled: Naturall and artificiall conclusions tr. 1586
A most briefe and pleasaunt treatise, teachynge howe to dress, sowe, and set a garden 1563
— another ed., entitled *The proffitable arte of gardening, now the third tyme set fourth*. 2 pts. 1568
— another ed. *Whereunto is newly added a treatise of the arte of graffing and planting of trees* 1574
A profitable instruction of the perfite ordering of bees 1579
Hill, Thomas *God's eternal preparations for his dying saints* 1648
An olive branch of peace and accommodation budding 1648
The right separation incouraged 1644 (1645)
The spring of strengthning grace in the rock of ages, Christ Jesus 1648
The strength of the saints to make Jesus Christ their strength 1648
The trade of truth advanced 1642
Truth and love happily married in the saints and in the churches of Christ 1648
Hillary, Edmund *High adventure* 1955
Hillary, Richard Hope *The last enemy* 1942
Hillary, William *Observations on the changes of the air and the concomitant epidemical diseases in the Island of Barbadoes* 1766
Hillebrand, William *Flora of the Hawaiian Islands* 1888
Hilliard, Nicholas *A treatise concerning the arte of limning* c1600 (MS. in Edinb. Univ. Library; in Annual of Walpole Soc. I, 1912)
Hilliard, Noel Harvey *Maori girl* 1960
A piece of land 1963
Hillis, Marjorie (Marjorie Hillis Roulston)
Hills, Richard *Proverbs from the common-place book of* c1530 (in Fraser's Mag., Aug. 1858)
See also *Songs, carols*, etc.
Hills of the Shatemuc 1856 *See* Warner, Susan
Hillyard, George Whiteside *Forty years of first-class lawn tennis* 1924
Hilman, Daniel *Tusser redivivus. The calendar of the twelve months with notes*, published by D. Hilman 1710
Hilton, James *Lost horizon* 1933
See also 'Trevor, Glen'
Hilton, John Buxton *Gamekeeper's gallows* 1976
Hilton, Timothy *The Pre-Raphaelites* 1970
Himes, Chester *Black on black: Baby sister, and selected writings* 1973
Blind man with a pistol 1969
The heat's on 1966
Hinchliff, Thomas W. *South American sketches* 1863
Hind, Henry Y. *Explorations in the interior of the Labrador peninsula* 1863
Hind, Herbert Lloyd *Brewing* 2 vols. 1938-40
Hind, John *Eliosto libidinoso, described in two bookes* 1606
Hinde, Sidney L. *The fall of the Congo Arabs* 1897
Hinde, William *A faithfull remonstrance of the holy life and happy death of John Bruen* a1629 (1641)
Hindley, Charles ed. *The life and adventures of a Cheap Jack* 1876
ed. *The old book collector's miscellany* 1871-73
Hindmarsh, William Russell ed. *Atomic spectra* 1967
Hindu, The (Madras) 1878-
Hindustan Times (New Delhi) 1924-
Hine, Gerald John & Brownell, G. L. eds. *Radiation dosimetry* 1956
Hinsie, Leland Earl & Shatzky, Jacob *Psychiatric dictionary, with encyclopedic treatment of modern terms* 1940
— (ed. 3, by L. E. Hinsie & R. J. Campbell) 1960
'Hinton, Beneventura' (Valentinë Durrant) *Until my lord's return. A romance of a river town* 1892
Hinton, Richard J. *English Radical leaders* 1875
Hinxman, Margaret *End of a good woman* 1976
Hird, Frank *The cry of the children: an exposure of certain British industries in which children are iniquitously exposed* 1898
Hirst, Henry B. *The coming of the Mammoth, and other poems* 1845
Hiscock, Eric Charles *Around the world in Wanderer III* 1956
Hislop, Alexander *The book of Scottish anecdote* 1874
The proverbs of Scotland 1862 (1874)
Hissey, James J. *A holiday on the road* 1887
A tour in a phaeton through the eastern counties 1889
Historia litteraria; or, an exact and early account of the most valuable books published in the several parts of Europe. (ed. by A. Bower) 1730-34
Historical collections of a citizen of London in the fifteenth century 14.. (Camden Soc. 1876)
Historical manuscripts, Reports of the royal commission on 1870-
Historical register, The, containing an impartial relation of all transactions foreign and domestic 1717 (1724)
Historical view of the Court of Exchequer 1738 *See* Gilbert, Sir G.
Historie of the arrival of Edward IV 1471 (Camden Soc. 1838)
History and antiquities of Rochester and its environs. (By W. Shrubsole & S. Denne) 1772
History and antiquities of the City of York (? By W. Combe) 1785
History of King Arthur (*The story of the moste noble and worthy kynge Arthur newly imprynted*) 1557 (W. Copland).
See also Malory, Sir T.
History of Christina Allesandra of Swedland 1658 *See* Burbury, J.
History of Friar Gerund 1772 *See* Nugent, T.
History of the Holy Rood-tree 11.. (E.E.T.S. 1894)
History of independency *See* Walker, C.
History of James VI 1582-88 *See* James VI
History of Jetzer 1679 *See* Waller, Sir W.
History of the mitre and purse, The 1714
History of modern Europe, The (by William Russell) 1779
History of Ned Evans 1796
History of Pelham, Mass., from 1738 to 1898. By C. O. Parmenter. (Chiefly from town and parish records) v.d. (1898)
History of Sir J. Hawkwood 1687 *See* Hawkwood, Sir J.
History of the troubles at Frankforth 1574 See *Brieff discours*.
Histrio-mastix; or, the player whipt 1610 (in Simpson, School of Shakespeare II. 1878)
Hitchcock, Edward *Ichnology of New England* 1858
Hitchcock, Robert *A general proportion and order of provision to victual a garrison of one thousand soldiers* 1591 (App. to Garrard's Art of war 1591; in Arber, Eng. Garner II)
A pollitique platt for the honour of the prince 1580 (in Arber, Eng. Garner II)
Sansovino's (F.) Quintesence of wit tr. 1590
Hitchin, Charles *A true discovery of the conduct of receivers and thief-takers in and about the City of London* 1718
Hitchins, Fortescue & Drew, Samuel *The history of Cornwall, from the earliest records and traditions, to the present time.* Compiled by F. Hitchins and ed. by S. Drew 1824
Hoadley, Abp. John *The abasement of pride; a sermon* 1708
A sermon preach'd in the cathedral-church of Norwich 1704
Hoadly, Bp. Benjamin *Works* a1761 (1773)
Hoadly, Benjamin (son of the above) *The suspicious husband; a comedy* 1747 (1756)
Hoadly, John *Phoebe; a pastoral opera* 1748
Hobart, George Vere *Jim Hickey: a story of the one-night stands* 1904
See also 'McHugh, Hugh'
Hobbes, John Oliver *See* Craigie, Pearl M. T.
Hobbes, Stephen *C. S(c)hilander his chirurgerie* tr. 1596
Hobbes, Thomas *English works* a1679 (1839-45)
Tracts a1679 (1682)
The art of rhetoric, with a discourse of the laws of England a1679 (1681)
Behemoth; or an epitome of the civil wars of England from 1640 to 1660 1679 (1680)
De corpore politico: or, the elements of law, moral and politick 1650
Decameron physiologicum: or, ten dialogues of natural philosophy 1678
Elements of philosophy tr.; *to which are added Six lessons to the professors of mathematicks of the institution of Sir H. Savile, in the University of Oxford* 1656
Mr. Hobbes considered in his loyalty, religion, reputation and manners. By way of a letter to Dr. Wallis 1662
— another ed., entitled *Considerations upon the reputation, loyalty, manners and religion of T. Hobbes.* Written by himself 1680
Homer's Iliads tr. 1675
Homer's Odysses tr. 1674
Humane nature; or the fundamental elements of policie 1650
Leviathan, or the matter, forme, and power of a commonwealth, ecclesiasticall and civill 1651
Of libertie and necessitie, a treatise, in answer to a treatise written by the Bishop of London-derry on the same subject 1654
The questions concerning liberty, necessity, and chance, clearly stated 1656
Philosophical rudiments concerning government and society 1651
Seven philosophical problems and two propositions of geometry a1679 (in Tracts, 1682, Pt. IV)
Στιγμαί, or markes of the absurd geometry, rural language, Scottish church-politicks and barbarismes of John Wallis 1657
Thucydides' Eight bookes of the Peloponnesian warre tr. 1629
Hobhouse, John C. (Baron Broughton) *Historical illustrations of the fourth canto of Childe Harold* 1818
Italy: remarks made in several visits 1816-54 (1859)
A journey through Albania, etc. 1813
The substance of some letters written by an Englishman resident at Paris (i.e. J. C. Hobhouse), *during the last reign of the emperor Napoleon* 1815-16 (1816)
Hoblyn, Richard D. *A dictionary of the terms used in medicine and the collateral sciences* 1835
— ed. 2, 1844; ed. 8, enlarged 1858
Hobson, Hank *Mission house murder* 1959
Hobson, John *Journal* 1725-35 (in Yorkshire diaries, Surtees Soc. 1877)
Hobson, John Atkinson *The problem of the unemployed* 1896
Hobson, Laura Keane (Zametkin) *The celebrity* 1951 (UK 1953)
'Hobson, Polly' (Julia Evans) *Titty's dead* 1968
Hobson, Richmond Pearson *Nothing too good for a cowboy* 1955
Hoby, Sir Edward *A counter-snarle for Ishmael Rabshacheh* 1613
A curry-combe for a coxe-combe 1615
A letter to Mr. T(heophilus) H(iggons) in answere of his first Motive 1609
Hoby, Sir Thomas *Castiglione's (B.) Courtyer* tr. 1561 (1577)

HOBY, Sir Thomas (*cont.*)
Travels and life, written by himself 1547-64 (Camden Soc., Misc. 1902)
HOCCLEVE, Thomas *De regimine principum* (*The regement of princes*) c1412 (Roxb. Cl. 1860; E.E.T.S. 1897)
Minor poems v.d. (E.E.T.S. 1892)
La male regle (The misrule) 1406
The mother of God c1410
The tale of Jonathas 1422
Hochstetter's (*F. von*) *New Zealand* tr. 1867
HOCKETT, Charles Francis *A course in modern linguistics* 1958
ed. *A Leonard Bloomfield anthology* 1970
A manual of phonology 1955
HOCKIN, Thomas *A discourse of the nature of God's decrees* 1684
HOCKLEY, William B. *Pandurang Hàri; or memoirs of a Hindoo* (anon.) 1826
HODGE, Frederick Webb ed. *Handbook of American Indians north of Mexico* 2 vols. 1907-10
HODGE, Herbert *Cab, sir?* 1939
HODGE, Hiram C. *Arizona as it is* 1877
HODGES, John A. *Elementary photography* 1893 (1907)
HODGES, Henry *Artifacts: an introduction to early materials and technology* 1964
HODGES, Richard *The plainest directions for the true-writing of English* 1649
HODGES, Thomas *A glimpse of God's glory* 1642
HODGES, Thomas *The hoary head crowned* 1652
HODGES, Walter *The Christian plan exhibited in the interpretation of Elohim* 1752 (1755)
Elihu; or an enquiry into the principal scope and design of the Book of Job 1750 (1755)
HODGES, William *Travels in India, during the years 1780-83* 1793
HODGINS, Eric *Mr. Blandings builds his dream house* 1946 (UK 1947)
HODGKIN, Thomas *Italy and her invaders* 1880-99
HODGKINSON, Harry *Doubletalk: the language of Communism* 1955
HODGSON, Christopher P. *Reminiscences of Australia, with hints on the squatters' life* 1846
A residence at Nagasaki and Hakodate in 1859-60 1861
HODGSON, Frederick T. *Stair-building made easy* 1884
HODGSON, James T. *Memoir of Francis Hodgson. With letters from Lord Byron and others* 1878
HODGSON, John *A history of Northumberland* 1820-40
HODGSON, Shadworth H. *The philosophy of reflection* 1878
Time and space; a metaphysical essay 1865
HODKIN, Frederick William & COUSEN, Arnold *A textbook of glass technology* 1925
HODSON, James Lansdale *Our two Englands* 1936
HODY, Humphrey *A history of English councils and convocations* 1701
HODZA, Aaron C. & FORTUNE, George *Shona praise poetry* 1979
Høffding's (*H.*) *Outlines of psychology*, tr. by Mary E. Lowndes 1891
HOFFMAN, Charles F. *A winter in the west* 2 vols. 1835 (UK ed., also 2 vols. 1835, with title —— *in the far west*)
Greyslaer: a romance of the Mohawk 1840
HOFFMAN, Walter J. *The beginnings of writing* 1895
Hoffman, Tragedy of See CHETTLE, H.
Hoffmeister's (*W.*) *Travels in Ceylon and Continental India* tr. 1848
HOGAN, Jeremiah Joseph *The English language in Ireland* 1927
An outline of English philology 1934
HOGARTH, David George *The Nearer East* 1902
HOGARTH, George *Musical history, biography, and criticism* 1835
HOGARTH, William *The analysis of beauty* 1753
HOGG, Alfred George *Redemption from this world; or, The supernatural in Christianity* 1922
'HOGG, Cervantes' *See* BARRETT, E. S.
HOGG, David *Life and times of the rev. John Wightman (1762-1847)* 1873
HOGG, Jabez *The microscope* 1854 (1861, 1867)
HOGG, James *Poetical works* a1835 (1838-40
Tales and sketches 1818-35 (1836-37)
The Brownie of Bodsbeck, and other tales 1818
Dramatic tales 1817
The Jacobite relics of Scotland; being the songs, airs, and legends of the adherents of the House of Stuart, Collected by J. H. 1819-21 (1874)
The mountain bard 1807
Poems on different subjects 1806
Queen Hynde. A poem 1825
The queen's wake; a legendary poem 1813
Scottish pastorals, poems, and songs 1801
The shepherd's calendar 1829
The three perils of man; or war, women and witchcraft 1822
Winter evening tales 1820
HOGG, Robert *The fruit manual* 1860 (1862)
The vegetable kingdom and its products 1858
HOGG, Thomas J. *The life of Shelley* 1858
HOGGART, Herbert Richard *Auden: an introductory essay* 1951
The uses of literacy: aspects of working-class life, with special reference to publications and entertainments 1957
HOLBROOK, David Kenneth *Flesh wounds* 1966
HOLBROOK, John E. *North American herpetology* 1836-42
HOLBROOK, M. L. *Hygiene of the brain and nerves* 1878
HOLCROFT, Sir Henry *Procopius' History of the warres of the Emperor Justinian* tr. 1653
HOLCROFT, Thomas *Lavater's* (*J. C.*) *Essays on physiognomy* tr. 1793
The life of Baron Frederic Trenck tr. 1788 (1886)
Memoirs of Bryan Perdue 1805
Memoirs, written by himself, and continued to the time of his death, from his diary, notes, and other papers a1809 (1816)
Stolberg's (*F. L. zu*) *Travels through Germany, Switzerland, Italy, and Sicily* tr. 1796-97
HOLDEN, Anne *The girl on the beach* 1973
HOLDEN, Luther *Human osteology* 1855 (1878)
A manual of the dissection of the human body 1851
HOLDER, Charles F. *Marvels of animal life* 1885
HOLDER, William *A discourse concerning time* 1694
Elements of speech 1669
A treatise on the natural grounds and principles of harmony 1694
Holderness glossary 1877 *See* ROSS, Frederick
HOLDICH, Benjamin *An essay on the weeds of agriculture* 1825
HOLDSWORTH, Edward *Remarks and dissertations on Virgil* a1746 (1768)
HOLDSWORTH, Richard *The peoples happinesse; a sermon preached upon 27 of March, being the day of his Majesties inauguration* 1642
HOLE, Richard *Remarks on the Arabian Nights Entertainments* 1797
HOLE, Samuel R. *A book about roses, how to grow and show them* 1869 (1870, 1891)
A little tour in America 1895
HOLIDAY, Billie *Lady sings the blues* 1956 (UK 1958; new impr. 1973)
Holiday 1946-
HOLINSHED, Raphael *The firste (laste) volume of the chronicles of England, Scotlande, and Irelande* 1577
— Continued to 1586 by John Hooker, alias Vowell (and Abraham Fleming) 1586-87 (1807-08)
The Scottish chronicle (1805)
'HOLLAND, Clive' (C. J. Hankinson) *Mousmé* 1901
My Japanese wife 1895
HOLLAND, Sir Henry *Essays on scientific and other subjects contributed to the Edinburgh and Quarterly Reviews* v.d. (1862)
General view of the agriculture of Cheshire 1808
HOLLAND, Henry Scott *Christ or Ecclesiastes* 1887 (1888)
Logic and life, with other sermons 1882 (1885)
Old and new 1900
HOLLAND, John *A treatise on the progressive improvement and present state of the manufactures in metal* 1831-39
HOLLAND, John Henry *The useful plants of Nigeria* 4 vols. 1908-22
HOLLAND, Josiah G. *Arthur Bonnicastle* 1873
The bay-path 1857
Gold foil hammered from popular proverbs 1859
History of Western Massachusetts 1855
Kathrina 1868
Lessons in life 1862
Letters to the Joneses 1863
The life of Abraham Lincoln 1865
The marble prophecy 1872
Miss Gilbert's career 1860
The mistress of the manse 1874
Plain talk on familiar subjects 1865
The story of Sevenoaks 1875
Timothy Titcomb's letters to the young 1858
HOLLAND, Philemon *Camden's* (*W.*) *Britain, or a chorographicall description of England, Scotland, and Ireland* tr. 1610 (1637)
Livy's Romane historie tr. 1600
Pliny's Historie of the world, commonly called the Natural historie tr. 1601 (1634)
Marcellinus' (*A.*) *Roman historie* tr. 1609
Plutarch's Philosophie, commonlie called, the Morals tr. 1603 (1657)
Suetonius' Historie of twelve Cæsars tr. 1606
Xenophon's Cyrupædia tr. 1632
HOLLAND, Ray *Self and social context* 1977
HOLLAND, Sir Richard *The buke of the Howlat* c1450 (Bannatyne Cl. 1823; in Scott. allit. poems, S.T.S. 1891-92)
HOLLAND, Robert *A glossary of words used in the county of Chester* 1886 (E.D.S.)
HOLLAND, Lady Saba *A memoir of the rev. Sydney Smith* 1855
HOLLAND, Samuel *Don Zara del Fogo; a mock-romance* tr. 1656 (1719)
HOLLANDER, Zander ed. *The modern encyclopedia of basketball* 1969
Hollands leaguer 1632 *See* GOODMAN, N.
HOLLEY, Alexander L. *A treatise on ordnance and armor* 1865
HOLLEY, Marietta E. *My opinions and Betsey Bobbet's* 1873
HOLLINGSHEAD, John *My lifetime* 1895
HOLLINGWORTH, Richard *An exercitation concerning usurped powers* 1650
HOLLINGWORTH, Richard *A full and true account of the penitence of John Marketman* 1680
A sermon preached before the Lord Mayor 1682
See also *Vindiciæ Carolinæ*
HOLLINSHEAD, William Henry *Textbook of anatomy* 1962
HOLLOWAY, Christopher John *Language and intelligence* 1951
HOLLOWAY, William *A general dictionary of provincialisms* 1838
HOLLYBAND, Claudius (C. Desainliens) *Campo di Fior, or else the flourie field of foure languages* 1583
A dictionarie French and English 1593
The treasurie of the French tong 1580
HOLLYBUSH, John *Braunschweig's* (*H.*) *Most excellent homish apothecarye* tr. 1561
HOLMAN, Joseph G. *Abroad and at home; a comic opera* 1796
HOLMAN-HUNT, Diana *My grandmothers and I* 1960
HOLMAN-HUNT, William *See* HUNT, W. Holman
HOLME, Randle *The academy of armory, or a storehouse of armory and blazon* 1688
— 2nd vol. 1688 (ed. by I. H. Jeayes, Roxb. Cl. 1905)
HOLME, Wilfrid *The fall and euill successe of rebellion* 1572 (repr. n.d.)
HOLMES, Arthur *The nomenclature of petrology, with references to selected literature* 1920
Principles of physical geology 1944
— (ed. 2) 1965
HOLMES, Edward *The life of Mozart, including his correspondence* 1845
HOLMES, Harry Nicholls *Introductory colloid chemistry* 1934
HOLMES, John Clellon *Nothing more to declare* 1968
HOLMES, Mary Jane *Tempest and sunshine; or, Life in Kentucky* 1854
HOLMES, Oliver Wendell *Writings* v.d. (1891-92)
Poetical works 1852 (1883, 1895)
The autocrat of the breakfast-table 1858
Elsie Venner; a romance of destiny 1860
The guardian angel 1867
John Lothrop Motley; a memoir 1878
Medical essays 1842-82 (1883)
Pages from an old volume of life. A collection of essays 1857-81 (1883)
The poet at the breakfast-table 1872
The professor at the breakfast-table 1860
Ralph Waldo Emerson 1885
HOLMES, Oliver Wendell (the younger) *The Pollock-Holmes letters* See POLLOCK, Sir Frederick
—— & LASKI, Harold Joseph *Holmes-Laski letters: the correspondence of Mr. Justice Holmes and Harold J. Laski, 1916-1935* ed. M. DeW. Howe 2 vols. 1953
HOLMES, Sarah Katherine (Stone) *Brokenburn: the journal of Kate Stone, 1861-1868* ed. J. Q. Anderson 1955
HOLMES, Thomas K. *The man from Tall Timber* 1919
HOLMES, Timothy *A treatise on surgery* 1875
—— & HULKE, J. W. *A system of surgery* 1883 (ed. 3)
Holmesby (*Capt. John*), *Voyages and travels, and wonderful discoveries of* 1757
Holroyd (*Maria J.*), *The girlhood of.* Recorded in letters 1776-96 (1896)
HOLROYDE, Peggy *Indian music* 1972
HOLST, Herman von *John C. Calhoun* 1882
Constitutional and political history of the United States tr. by J. J. Lalor & A. B. Mason 1876-85
HOLT, Edwin Bissell *The Freudian wish and its place in ethics* 1915
HOLT, John *General view of the agriculture of the county of Lancaster* 1794
HOLTBY, Winifred *Poor Caroline* 1931
South Riding 1936
HOLTZAPFFEL, Charles & John J. *Turning and mechanical manipulation* 1843-50
HOLWELL, John Z. *Interesting historical events relative to the provinces of Bengal and the empire of Indostan* 1765-71
HOLWELL, William *A mythological, etymological, and historical dictionary: extracted from* (*J. Bryant's*) *Analysis of ancient mythology* 1793
Holy Land, The: being sketches of the Jews, and of the land of Palestine 1844
HOLYDAY, Barten *A. Persius Flaccus his Satires* tr. 1616 (1673)
D. J. Juvenalis and A. Persius Flaccus tr. a1661 (1673)
Of the nature of faith: a sermon 1654
A sermon preached at Pauls Crosse, Aug. 5 1623 (1626)
A sermon preached at Pauls Crosse, March 24 1624 (1626)
A survey of the world 1661
Τεχνογαμία: or the marriages of the arts. A comedie 1618
HOLYOAKE, George J. *The history of co-operation in England* 1875-77
HOLYOKE, Francis *Dictionarie etymologicall* 1606 (Pt. 2 of Rider's Dictionarie corrected 1606)
Dictionarium etymologicum Latinum 1633 (4th ed. of prec.)
HOLYOKE, Thomas *A large* (Latin and English) *dictionary, in three parts* a1675 (1677; an enlarged ed. of prec.)
HOMANS, Isaac S. (senior and junior) *A cyclopedia of commerce and commercial navigation* 1858
HOME, Lord (Alexander Frederick Douglas-Home) *The way the wind blows* 1976
HOME, Sir Everard *Lectures on comparative anatomy* 1814-28
HOME, Henry *See* KAMES, Lord
HOME, John *Works* a1808 (1822)
Douglas: a tragedy 1756
'HOME, Julian' (E. R. Christie) *Sketches of Cambridge, in verse* 1879
'HOME, Michael' (Charlie Christopher Bush) *The house of shade* 1942
Home chat 1895-
Homer à la mode 1664 *See* SCUDAMORE, J.
Homes and gardens 1923-
Homilies. Certayne sermons, or homilies, appoynted by the kynges maiestie, to be declared and redde by all persones vicars, or curates, euery Sondaye in their churches 1547; *the seconde tome of homelyes* 1563 (1859)
HONE, Joseph *The flowers of the forest* 1980
The sixth directorate 1975
HONE, William *Ancient mysteries described* 1823

The every-day book 1825–27
The table book of daily recreation and information 1827–28
The year book of daily recreation and information 1832
Honest cavalier, A sober discourse of the; also, a serious epistle to Hodge 1680
HONYMAN, Bp. Andrew *A survey of the insolent..libel entituled Napthali* (anon.) 1668 (1669)
HOOD, Thomas *Works* a1845 (1869–73)
Poems a1845 (1875)
Complete poetical works a1845 (1906)
Tylney hall 1834
Whims and oddities, in prose and verse 1824–27
Whimsicalities 1844
HOOD, Thomas, Jr. *Pen and pencil pictures* 1857
HOOK, Theodore E. *Gilbert Gurney* 1836
Jack Brag 1837
Love and pride (*i.e. The widow* and *Snowdon*) 1833; later edd. (1842–) *The widow, and The marquess, or Love and pride*
The parson's daughter 1833
Sayings and doings 1824–28
HOOK, Walter F. *A Church dictionary* 1842 (1871)
Lives of the Archbishops of Canterbury 1860–76
HOOKE, Robert *Posthumous works* a1703 (1705)
Micrographia, or some physiological descriptions of minute bodies made by magnifying glasses 1665
See also *Philosophical collections*
HOOKE, William *New Englands sence of Old England and Irelands sorrowes* 1645
New Englands teares for Old Englands feares 1641
HOOKER, Edward 1683 *See* PORDAGE, John
HOOKER, Frances H. 1873 *See* HOOKER, Sir J. D.
HOOKER, John (J. Vowell) *The description of the cittie of Excester* ?1575 (in Holinshed, Chron. 1587, III. p. 1007)
The Irish historie composed by Giraldus Cambrensis tr. 1586 (in Holinshed, Chron.) See also HOLINSHED, R.
The lyffe of Sir Peter Carew c1575 (in Archaeologia XXVIII)
HOOKER, Sir Joseph D. *Botany* 1876
The botany of the Antarctic voyage of the Erebus and Terror in 1839–43 1844–60
A general system of botany by E. Le Maout and J. Decaisne, tr. by Frances H. Hooker and ed. by J. D. Hooker 1873
Handbook of the New Zealand flora 2 parts 1864–7
Himalayan journals 1854
The student's flora of the British Islands 1870
—— & BALL, John *Journal of a tour in Marocco and the Great Atlas* 1878
See also HUXLEY, Leonard
HOOKER, Richard *Works* a1600 (1888)
A learned discourse of justification 1586 (1612)
Of the lawes of ecclesiasticall politie Bks. I–IV 1594; Bk. V 1597 (1617); Bks. VI–VIII a1600 (1648)
HOOKER, Sir William J. *Botany* 1849 (in Manual of scientific enquiry 1859)
The British flora 1830–33
Journal of a tour in Iceland in 1809 1811 (1813)
See also SMITH, Sir James E.
HOOL, George Albert & JOHNSON, Nathan Clarke *Concrete engineers' handbook* 1918
HOOLE, Charles *M. Corderius's School-colloquies, English and Latine* 1657 (1688)
See also *Comenius*
HOOLE, John *Ariosto's (L.) Orlando furioso* tr. 1783
Tasso's (T.) Jerusalem delivered 1763
HOOLE, Samuel *Discourses delivered in the parish church of All Saints, Poplar* 1833
HOOPER, Bp. George *A discourse concerning Lent* 1696
An inquiry into the state of the ancient measures (anon.) 1721
HOOPER, Bp. John *Writings* a1555 (Parker Soc. 1843–52)
An answer vnto my lord of wynchesters booke 1547
A declaracion of Christe and of his offyce 1547
A declaration of the ten holy commaundementes 1548
A godly confession and protestacion of the christian fayth ?1551
An oversight and deliberacion vpon the prophete Jonas 1550
HOOPER, Johnson Jones *Some adventures of Captain Simon Suggs* 1845
— (another ed.) 1846
HOOPER, Robert *A compendious medical dictionary* 1798
Lexicon medicum; a new medical dictionary 1802
— (ed. 7, rev. by K. Grant) 1839
HOOPER, W. *Sketches from academic life* 1886
HOOSON, William *The miner's dictionary* 1747
HOPE, Alexander J. Beresford *The Brandreths. A novel* 1882
The English cathedral of the nineteenth century 1861
Essays 1844
'HOPE, Anthony' (Anthony Hope Hawkins) *The prisoner of Zenda* 1894
Tristram of Blent 1901
'HOPE, Ascott R.' (A. R. H. Moncrieff) *My schoolboy friends* 1870
HOPE, Frederick W. *The coleopterist's manual* 1837–40
HOPE, Sir Thomas *Minor practicks; or, a treatise of the Scottish law* a1646 (1726)
HOPE, Thomas *Anastasius: or the memoirs of a Greek* 1819
An essay on the origin and prospects of man 1831
HOPE, Sir William *The compleat fencing-master* 1692 (ed. 2)
A new, short, and easy method of fencing 1707
See also SOLLEYSEL, J. de
HOPE, William Edward Stanton *Digger's paradise* 1956
HOPE, William H. St. John *Inventories of Christ Church, Canterbury*. ed. by J. Wickham Legg & W. H. St. John Hope 1902
Windsor Castle. An architectural history 1913
HOPKINS, Charles *White-hall; or, the Court of England: a poem* 1698
— another ed., *The court-prospect, a poem* 1699
HOPKINS, Edward J. & RIMBAULT, Edward F. *The organ; its history and construction* 1855 (1877)
HOPKINS, Ellice *Rose Turquand* 1876 (1880)
HOPKINS, Bp. Ezekiel *Works* a1690 (1710, 1809)
Discourses or sermons on several scriptures a1690 (1691–96)
An exposition of the Lord's Prayer 1692
A sermon preached at the funeralls of the Honourable A Grevil 1663
The vanity of the world 1668
HOPKINS, Gerard Manley *Further letters* ed. C. C. Abbott 1938
— (ed. 2, by C. C. Abbott) 1956
Journals and papers ed. G. Storey 1959
Letters to Robert Bridges ed. C. C. Abbott 1935
— (2nd rev. impr.) 1955
Note-books and papers ed. H. House 1937
Poems ed. R. Bridges 1918
— (ed. 3, by W. H. Gardner) 1948
— (ed. 4, by W. H. Gardner & N. H. MacKenzie) 1967
Sermons and devotional writings ed. C. Devlin 1959
A vision of the mermaids (facsimile ed. of manuscript text dated 1862) 1929
HOPKINS, John *See* STERNHOLD, T.
HOPKINS, Keith ed. *Hong Kong, the industrial colony: a political, social and economic survey* 1971
HOPKINS, Manley *A handbook of average* 1857
Hawaii; the past, present, and future of its island kingdom 1862
HOPKINS, Matthew *The discovery of witches* 1647
HOPKINS, William *The Book of Bertram, or Ratramnus, concerning the body and blood of the Lord* tr. 1686
Seventeen sermons a1700 (1708)
HOPKINSON, Diana *The incense-tree* 1968
HOPLEY, Catherine C. *Life in the South* 1863
HOPPE, A. *Englisch-Deutsches Supplement-Lexicon* 1871
HOPPS, John Page *First principles of religion and morality* 1875
The life of Jesus 1869
HOPTON, Arthur *A concordancy of yeares* 1612
Speculum topographicum; or the topographicall glasse 1611
Horæ subsecivæ 1777 (MS. Devonshire glossary)
HORBERY, Matthew *Works* a1773 (1828)
HORE, J. P. *The history of Newmarket, and the annals of the turf* 1885–86
Hore beate marie virginis 1510 (1531)
Horizon: a review of literature and art 1940–50
HORLOCK, Knightley W. ('Scrutator') *The country gentleman* 1862
HORMAN, William *Vulgaria* 1519
HORN, Thomas & ROBOTHAM, John *See* COMENIUS, J. A.
Horn, King a1300, 13.. (in Ritson, Metrical Romances II. 1802; Horn et Rimenhild, Bannatyne Cl. 1845; E.E.T.S. 1866 (1901); ed. Jos. Hall 1901)
Horn childe and maiden Rimnild 1320–30 (in Ritson, Metrical Romances III. 1802; ed. Jos. Hall 1901)
HORNADAY, William T. *Two years in the jungle* 1885
HORNBY, Lady Emelia B. *In and around Stamboul* 1858
— another ed., entitled *Constantinople during the Crimean War* 1863
HORNBY, William *The scourge of drunkennes* 1618 (Halliwell 1859)
HORNE, Bp. George *Works* a1792 (1809, 1818)
A commentary on the Book of Psalms 1776
Discourses on several subjects and occasions a1792 (1827)
Letters on infidelity 1784
HORNE, John *A year in Fiji* 1881
HORNE, Richard H. *Gregory VII; a tragedy* 1840
HORNE, Thomas H. *An introduction to the critical study and knowledge of the Holy Scriptures* 1818–21
HORNECK, Anthony *The crucified Jesus* 1686
The great law of consideration 1677 (1704)
The happy ascetick 1681
HORNER, Susan & Joanna *Walks in Florence* 1873 (1884)
HORNSBY, Henry *Lonesome valley* 1949
HORNUNG, Ernest W. *The amateur cracksman* 1899
The black mask 1901
Mr. Justice Raffles 1909
Under two skies 1892
HOROWITZ, Irving Lewis ed. *Masses in Latin American* 1970
ed. *The new sociology* 1964
HORROBIN, David Frederick *Science is God* 1969
Hors, shepe, and ghoos c1470 (Caxton 1479; Roxb. Cl. 1822)
See also LYDGATE, J.
Horse and hound 1884–
HORSEY, Sir Jerome *Travels in Russia* a1627 (Hakluyt Soc. 1856)
HORSFIELD, Thomas *Zoological researches in Java, and the neighbouring islands* 1824
HORSLEY, John W. *Jottings from jail* 1887
HORSLEY, Bp. Samuel *Charges* 1790–1806 (1813)
A sermon preached before the Lords, Jan. 30 1793
Sermons a1806 (1816)
Speeches in parliament a1806 (1813)
HORSLEY, Terence *Find, fix and strike: the work of the Fleet Air Arm* 1943
HORSLEY, William *The fool* 1746–47 (1748)
HORSTMANN, Carl ed. *Altenglische Legenden* (*Childhood of Jesus; Birth of Jesus; Baarlaam and Josaphat; St. Patrick's purgatory*) (1875)
— 2nd series (1881)
Sammlung Altenglischer Legenden (1878)
HORT, Fenton J. A. *Village sermons* a1892 (1897)
HORT, Abp. Josiah *Instructions to the clergy of the diocese of Tuam, July 8* 1742
Sermons on practical subjects a1751 (1757)
HORTON, Robert F. *The teaching of Jesus* 1895
HORTON, Thomas *Wisdomes judgment of folly* 1653
HORTOP, Job *The trauailes of an Englishman* 1591 (in Hakluyt, Voy. III. 1600)
Hortus Anglicus 1822 *See* CLARKE, Stephen
Hortus third: a concise dictionary of plants cultivated in the United States and Canada (Liberty Hyde Bailey Hortorium) 1976
HORWILL, Herbert William *A dictionary of modern American usage* 1935
— (ed. 2) 1944
HORWOOD, Harold Andrew *Newfoundland* 1969
HOSIE, Alexander *Three years in Western China* 1890
HOSKYNS, Chandos W. *Talpa; or, the chronicles of a clay farm* 1852 (1854)
HOSMER, James K. *A short history of Anglo-Saxon freedom* 1890
Hospitalier's (E.) Modern applications of electricity tr. by J. Maier 1882
Hospitall of incurable fooles 1600 *See* BLOUNT, E.
HOSTETTER, Gordon L. & BEESLEY, Thomas Q. *It's a racket!* 1929
HOSTETTLER, Rudolf, et al. *Technical terms of the printing industry* 1949
— (ed. 3) 1959
Hot car 1968–
Hotel world, The 1875–
HOTTEN, John C. *A dictionary of modern slang, cant, and vulgar words* 1859 (1860, 1864, 1874)
Houdin (R.) tr. *See* WRAXALL, Sir F. C. L.
HOUGHTON, R. M. Milnes, 1st Baron *A selection from his works* 1867
Life, letters, and friendships, by T. W. Reid (1890)
Palm leaves; poems 1844
HOUGHTON, John ed. *A collection of letters for the improvement of husbandry and trade* 1681–83
A collection for improvement of husbandry and trade 1692–1703
HOUGHTON, Thomas *The laws of the miners in the Forrest of Dean* 1687
The ancient laws of the miners in the King's Forrest of Mendipp 1687
Rara avis in terris; or the compleat miner; containing the liberties, laws and customs of the lead-mines in Derbyshire, the art of dialling and levelling grooves. With an explanation of the miners terms of art 1681 (E.D.S. 1874)
HOUGHTON, William *Sketches of British insects* 1875
Houlate See HOLLAND, Sir R.
HOULT, Powis *Dialogues on the efficacy of prayer* 1892
House and garden (New York) 1901–
UK ed. 1920–4
— (new series) 1946–
House of Commons, Complaint to 1642
House of Commons *Journals* 1547– (1803–)
House of Lords *Journals* 1509– (c1800–)
House that Jack built, The (nursery rime) ?a1750
HOUSEHOLD, Geoffrey Edward West *Doom's caravan* 1971
Rogue male 1939
Household ordinances (*A collection of ordinances and regulations for the government of the Royal Household, Edward III to King William and Mary; also receipts in ancient cookery*) v.d. (Society of Antiquaries of London 1790)
Household words; weekly journal, conducted by C. Dickens 1850–59
HOUSEHOLDER, Fred Walter *Linguistic speculations* 1971
—— & SAPORTA, Sol eds. *Problems in lexicography* [report of the Conference on Lexicography, Indiana University, 1960] 1962
Housewife 1939–
HOUSMAN, Alfred E. (1859–1936) *Collected poems* 1939
Letters ed. H. Maas 1971
More poems 1936
A Shropshire lad 1896
HOUSMAN, Lawrence *The unexpected years* 1937
HOUSTON, Edward J. *A dictionary of electrical words, terms and phrases* 1889 (1898)
HOUSTON, Margaret Bell *The witch man* 1922
Houston Chronicle (Houston, Texas) 1901–
HOUSTOUN, Mrs. M. C. *'Recommended to mercy'* 1862
Texas and the Gulf of Mexico; or yachting in the New World 1844
Twenty years in the Wild West; or, life in Connaught 1879
Hovering craft and hydrofoil 1961–
HOVLAND, Carl I., LUMSDAINE, A. A., & SHEFFIELD, F. D. *Experiments on mass communication* 1949
HOW, Frederick D. *Bishop Walsham How; a memoir* 1898
HOW, William 1650 *See* HOWE, W.
How a man may chuse a good wife from a bad, A pleasant conceited comedie, wherein is shewed 1602 (in Hazl., Dodsley)
How the good wijf tauȝte hir douȝtir c1430 (in Babees book, E.E.T.S. 1868; Hazlitt, Early pop. poetry I. 1864); a1450 (*'The thewis off gudwomen'* in Ratis Raving, etc., E.E.T.S. 1870); a1487 (in Barbour's Bruce, II. S.T.S. 1894); 15.. (in Q. Eliz. Achad., E.E.T.S. 1869)
How to make useful things 1902

Howard, Alexander Liddon *A manual of the timbers of the world* 1920
— (rev. ed.) 1934
Howard, Edward *The six days adventure, or the new Utopia. A comedy* 1671
Howard, Edward G. G. *Jack ashore* 1840
The old commodore 1837
Rattlin the reefer 1836
Howard, Elizabeth Jane *After Julius* 1965
'Howard, Hartley' (Leopold Horace Ognall) *Highway to murder* 1973
Nice day for a funeral 1972
Howard, Henry *See* Surrey, Earl of
Howard, Henry, Earl of Northampton *A defensative against the poyson of supposed prophesies* 1583
Howard, John *The state of the prisons in England and Wales* 1777 (1780)
Howard, John A. *Aerial photo-ecology* 1970
Howard, John E. *The quinology of the East Indian plantations* 1869–76
Howard, Luke *On the modifications of clouds* 1830 (1865)
Howard, Middleton *The conquest of Quebec: a poem* 1768
Howard, Richard tr. *S. de Beauvoir's Force of circumstance* 1965
Howard, Sir Robert *The committee; or, the faithful Irishman. A comedy* 1665
Preface to Four new plays (*The surprisal; The committee; The Indian queen; The vestal virgin*) 1665 (in Arber, Eng. Garner III)
Preface to The great favourite, or the Duke of Lerma 1668 (ibid.)
Howard, Lord William of Naworth Castle, Selections from the household books of 16.. (Surtees Soc. 1878)
Howard household books (*Household books of John Duke of Norfolk, and Thomas Earl of Surrey*) 1481–90 (Roxb. Cl. 1844)
Howard journal 1921–
Howarth, Thomas Graham *South's British butterflies, based extensively on the classic by Richard South* 1973
Howat, Gerald Malcolm D. & Taylor, A. J. P. eds. *Dictionary of world history* 1973
Howe, Ellic ed. *The London compositor: documents relating to wages, working conditions and customs of the London printing trade 1785–1900* 1947
Howe, Henry *Historical collections of Ohio* 1847
Howe, John *Works* a1705 (1724, 1862–63)
The blessedness of the righteous 1668 (1826)
The living temple 1675
Howe, William *Phytologia Britannica, natales exhibens indigenarum stirpium sponte emergentium* (anon.) 1650
Howel, Laurence *Desiderius, or the original pilgrim* 1717
Howell, James *Δενδρολογια; Dodona's grove, or the vocall forrest* 1640 (1649)
England's teares for the present warres 1644
Epistolæ Ho-Elianæ: familiar letters domestic and forren 1645; *a new volume of letters* 1647 (1650, 1655, 1726, 1890–92)
Giraffi's (*A.*) *Exact historie of the late revolutions in Naples* tr. 1650–52
Historical discourses of the late popular insurrections in Great Britain and Ireland 1661
Instructions for forreine travell 1642 (Arber 1869)
Lexicon tetraglotton, an English-French-Italian-Spanish dictionary 1660
Londinopolis; an historicall discourse, or perlustration of the City of London 1657
Lustra Ludovici; or the life of the late victorious king of France Lewis the XIII 1646
Parables reflecting upon the times (anon.) 1643
A perfect description of the people and country of Scotland 1649
The preheminence and pedigree of parliament 1644
A survay of the signorie of Venice 1651
Θηρολογια; the parley of beasts 1660
The tru informer 1642 (in Historical discourses 1661)
A particular vocabulary or nomenclature in English, Italian, French, and Spanish, of the proper terms belonging to several arts and sciences 1659 (Pt. II of Lexicon)
The vote; or a poeme royall presented to his maiestie for a new-yeares-gift 1642
Howell, Mary J. *The hand-book of dress-making* 1845
Howell, Thomas *Poems* a1581 (Grosart 1879)
The arbor of amitie wherein is comprised pleasant poems and pretie poesies 1568 (1879)
His deuises, for his owne exercise, and his friends pleasure 1581 (1879)
Pleasant sonnets and prettie pamphlets 1568 (1879)
Howell, Thomas B. & Thomas J. *Cobbett's Complete collection of state trials*, with notes by Thomas B. Howell 1809–14
— continued by Thomas J. Howell 1817–26
Howells, William D. *Annie Kilburn* 1888
A foregone conclusion 1875
A hazard of new fortunes 1889
Impressions and experiences 1896
Italian journeys 1867
The Kentons 1902
The lady of the Aroostook 1879
The landlord at Lion's head 1897
Literature and life: studies 1902
An open-eyed conspiracy: an idyl of Saratoga 1898
The rise of Silas Lapham 1884–85
Suburban sketches 1871
The undiscovered country 1880
Their wedding journey 1871
A traveller from Altruria 1894
Venetian life 1866
A woman's reason 1883
Howie, John *Reformation principles* 1787
Howitt, Mary *An autobiography* a1888 (ed. Marg. Howitt 1889)
Ballads and other poems 1847
Bremer's (*F.*) *Greece and the Greeks* tr. 1863
Sketches of natural history 1834 (1851)
Howitt, Richard *Impressions of Australia Felix* 1845
Howitt, William *The book of the seasons* 1831
Land, labour, and gold; or, two years in Victoria 1855
The rural and domestic life of Germany 1842
The rural life of England 1838 (1862)
The year-book of the country 1850
Howitt's journal of literature and popular progress 1847–8
Howorth, Sir Henry H. *The glacial nightmare and the flood* 1893
Howson, Albert Geoffrey *A handbook of terms used in algebra and analysis* 1972
Howson, Edmund W. & Warner, George T. *Harrow school* 1898
Howson, Bp. John *A sermon preached at Paules Crosse the 4 of December* 1597
Howson, John S. *The metaphors of St. Paul* 1868 (1870)
Hoy, Thomas *Agathocles, the Sicilian usurper; a poem* 1683
Hoyle, Edmond *An essay towards making the game of chess easily learned* 1761
Hoyle's games modernized (new ed., rev. by L. H. Dawson) 1923
A short treatise on the game of back-gammon 1745; *brag* 1751; *piquet* 1744; *quadrille* 1745; *whist* 1742
See also 'Crawley, Capt. R.'; Hardy, F.; Jones, C.
Hoyle, Fred *The black cloud* 1957
Frontiers of astronomy 1955
Galaxies, nuclei and quasars 1965 (UK 1966)
Ice 1981
The nature of the universe: a series of broadcast lectures 1950
Huarte See Carew, R.
Hubbard, Clifford Lionel Barry *Dogs in Britain* 1948
The observer's book of dogs 1945
Hubbard, Philip Maitland *The custom of the country* 1967 (UK 1969)
High tide 1970 (UK 1971)
Picture of Millie 1964
Hubbard, William *The happiness of a people in the wisdome of their rulers directing* 1676
A narrative of the troubles with the Indians in New-England 1677
— another ed., entitled *The present state of New England, being a narrative of the troubles* etc. 1677
— entitled *The history of the Indian wars in New England* (1865)
Hubbert, Thomas *Pilula ad expurgandam hypocrisin. A pill to purge formality* 1650
Hubble, Edwin Powell *The realm of the nebulæ* 1936
Hubbocke, William *An apologie of infants, in a sermon prouing that children preuented by death of their baptisme may be saued* 1595
Hubert, Sir Francis *The deplorable life and death of Edward the Second* (anon.) 1628
— another ed., entitled *The historie of Edward the Second* 1629
Huddesford, George, et al. *Salmagundi; a miscellaneous combination of original poetry* 1791 (1795)
Hudibras redivivus 1705–07 *See* Ward, E.
Hudiger, Paul *The Didoniad, a semi-Virgilian nautic epic* 1831
Hudson, Charles Thomas & Gosse, P. H. *The rotifera* 2 vols. & Suppl. 1886–9
Hudson, Derek Rommel *Munby: man of two worlds. The life and diaries of Arthur J. Munby 1828–1910* 1972
Hudson, Henry N. *Hamlet* 1879
Hudson, Kenneth *The jargon of the professions* 1978
Hudson, Michael *The divine right of government* 1647
Hudson, Thomas *Du Bartas'* (*G. de S.*) *Historie of Judith in forme of a poeme* tr. 1584 (at end of Sylvester's tr. of Du Bartas 1608, etc.)
Hudson, William *Flora Anglica* 1762 (1798)
Hudson, William Henry *Far away and long ago: a history of my early life* 1918
Green mansions: a romance of the tropical forest 1904
Idle days in Patagonia 1893
The naturalist in La Plata 1892
Hudson's Bay Record Society *Publications* 1938–
Hueffer, Ford Madox *See* Ford, Ford Madox
Hueffer, Francis *Musical studies: a series of contributions* 1880
Hueppe's (*F.*) *Principles of bacteriology* tr. by E. O. Jordan 1899
Hues' (*R.*) *Treatise of globes* tr. 1638 *See* Chilmead, J.
Hughes, Anne *Henry and Isabella; or, a traite through life* 1788
Hughes, Arthur Frederick William *The mitotic cycle: the cytoplasm and nucleus during interphase and mitosis* 1952
Hughes, Dorothy Belle *The expendable man* 1963 (UK 1964)
Hughes, George *The art of embalming dead saints* 1642
The saints losse and lamentation 1632
Hughes, George Edward & Londey, David George *The elements of formal logic* 1965
Hughes, Griffith *The natural history of Barbados* 1750
Hughes, John *St. Pauls exercise; or a sermon of conscience* 1622
Hughes, John *Poems* a1720 (1790)
The siege of Damascus; a tragedy 1720 (1777)
Hughes, Mary Vivian *A London child of the seventies* 1934
Hughes, Matthew L. *Mediterranean, Malta, or undulant fever* 1897
Hughes, Richard Arthur Warren *A high wind in Jamaica* 1929
In hazard 1938
Hughes, Ted *Crow: from the life and songs of the crow* 1970
The hawk in the rain 1957
Lupercal 1960
Hughes, Thomas *The misfortunes of Arthur* 1587 (in Certaine deuises and shewes; in Hazl., Dodsley)
Hughes, Thomas *The scouring of the White Horse* 1859
Tom Brown's school days 1857
Tom Brown at Oxford 1861
Hughes, Thomas Patrick *A dictionary of Islam* 1885
Hughes, Thomas S. *Travels in Sicily, Greece, and Albania* 1820
Hughes, William *The American physitian* 1672
Hughes, William *The man of sin: or a discourse of popery* 1677
Hugo's (*Victor*) *Hunchback of Notre-Dame* tr. 1839
Les misérables tr. (by Sir F. C. L. Wraxall) 1862
Huish, Robert *Memoirs of George the Third* 1821
Huke, Douglas Wynne *Introduction to natural and synthetic rubbers* 1961
Hulke, J. W. 1883 *See* Holmes, T.
Hull, Clark Leonard *Principles of behavior: an introduction to behavior theory* 1943
Hull, Richard Francis Carrington, et al. tr. *C. G. Jung's Collected works* 20 vols. 1953–79
Hull, Thomas *The history of Sir William Harrington* 1771 (1797)
Select letters between the late Duchess of Somerset, Lady Luxborough, and others; including a sketch of the manners, laws, etc. of the republic of Venice 17.. (ed. by T. Hull 1778)
Hull, William *The mirrour of maiestie; set forth in five sermons* 1615
Hull Advertiser and Exchange gazette 1796– (various years)
Hull letters printed from a collection of original documents found in the Town Hall, Hull 1625–46 (ed. by T. T. Wildridge 1888)
Hulme, Alfred Cresswell *The biochemistry of fruits and their products* 2 vols. 1970–1
Hulme, F. Edward *Familiar wild flowers figured and described* 1877–84
Hulme, Kathryn Cavarly *The nun's story* 1956
Hulme, Robert T. *Moquin-Tandon's* (*H.-B. A.*) *Elements of medical zoology* tr. 1861
Huloet, Richard *Abcedarium Anglico Latinum* 1552
— newelye corrected by John Higgins 1572
Human world: a quarterly review of English letters 1970–
Humble, William *Dictionary of geology and mineralogy* 1840
Humboldt's (*F. H. A. von*) *Geognostical essay on the superposition of rocks in both hemispheres* tr. 1823
Travels and researches tr. by W. Macgillivray 1832
Views of nature, tr. by E. C. Otté and H. G. Bohn 1850
See also Ross, Thomasina
Hume, Alexander *Poems* a1609 (S.T.S. 1902)
Ane afold admonitioun to the ministerie of Scotland 1609 (in Wodrow Soc. Misc. 1844)
Hymnes, or sacred songs, and certain precepts 1599 (Bannatyne Cl. 1832)
Hume, Alexander *Of the orthographie and congruitie of the Britan tongue* c1620 (E.E.T.S. 1865)
Hume, David *The history of the houses of Douglas and Angus* 1644
Hume, Sir David *Domestic details* 1697–1707 (1843)
Hume, David *Philosophical works* a1776 (1826, 1874–75)
An enquiry concerning the principles of morals 1751
Essays, moral and political 1741–42 (1742)
Essays and treatises on several subjects 1752 (1777)
The history of Great Britain (*under the House of Stuart*) 1754–57
The history of England under the House of Tudor 1759
— *from the invasion of Julius Cæsar to the accession of Henry VII* 1762
— *to the Revolution in 1688* 1763
The history of England to the Revolution in 1688 (1778)
The natural history of religion 1757 (in Four dissertations)
Philosophical essays concerning human understanding 1748
Political discourses 1752
A treatise of human nature (anon.) 1739–40
Hume, Fergus *Madame Midas: realistic and sensational story of Australian mining life* 1888
The mystery of a Hansom cab 1888
Hume, John *The Jewes deliverance out of Babylon* 1628
Hume, Sir Patrick *Narrative of occurrences in the expedition of the Earl of Argyle in 1685* 16.. (at end of G. Rose's Observ. C. J. Fox 1809)
Humfrey, John *De justificatione Baxteriana coronis* 1707
A letter to G. Keith, concerning the salvability of the heathen 1700
Mediocria; or the middle way between Protestant and Papist 1695 (ed. 2)
A paper to William Penn, at the departure of that gentleman to his territory (anon.) 1700
The righteousness of God revealed in the Gospel 1697
Humourist, The 1720–25 *See* Gordon, T.
Humours and conversations of the town, expos'd in two dialogues 1693
Humphrey, George *Thinking* 1951
Humphrey, John *See* Humfrey, John
Humphrey, John Herbert & White, R. G. *Immunology for students of medicine* 1963

Humphrey, Richard *Saint Ambrose's Christian offices crystal glasse* tr. 1637
Humphreys, David *The Yankey in England* 1815
Miscellaneous works 1790
Poems 1789 (ed. 2)
Humphreys, Henry N. *British moths and their transformations* 1843-45
The coin collector's manual 1853 (1876)
Humphries, Derek W. & Humphries, Evelyn E. tr. *H. & G. Termier's Erosion and sedimentation* 1963
Humphry, Sir George M. *Observations in myology* 1872
Hundred merry tales (A C. mery talys) ?1525 (Hazlitt 1887)
Hungerford, Mrs. Margaret W. (formerly M. W. Argles) *Green pleasure and grey grief* 1886
A lonely girl 1896
A maiden all forlorn and other stories 1885
Hunnis, William *Hunnies recreations: conteining foure godlie and compendious discourses. Whereunto is newly adjoyned The creation, or first weeke; the life and death of Joseph,* etc. 1595
A hyue full of hunnye: contayning the firste booke of Moses called Genesis turned into English meetre 1578
Seuen sobs of a sorrowfull soule for sinne; his Handfull of honisuckles, etc. 1583
Hunt, James *Vogt's (Carl) Lectures on man* tr. 1864
Hunt, James Henry Leigh *Poetical works* 1832, 1844 (1860, 1923)
Autobiography, with reminiscences of friends and contemporaries 1850 (1860)
Foliage; or poems original and translated 1818
Imagination and fancy 1844 (1875)
The Indicator 1820-22
A jar of honey from Mount Hybla 1848
Juvenilia; or, a collection of poems 1801
Lord Byron and some of his contemporaries 1828
Men, women, and books 1847
The months, descriptive of the successive beauties of the year 1821
The seer; or, common-places refreshed 1840-41
Sir Ralph Esher 1832
The town; its memorable characters and events 1834 (1848)
See also *Examiner*
Hunt, John *Religious thought in England from the Reformation to the end of last century* 1870-73
Hunt, John Leslie & Pringle, Alan George *Service slang* 1943
Hunt, Robert *A descriptive guide to the Museum of Practical Geology* 1857 (1859)
Photography 1851
Popular romances of the West of England 1865
A popular treatise on the art of photography, including daguerreotype 1841
Researches on light 1844
Hunt, Robert Nigel Carew *A guide to Communist jargon* 1957
Hunt, Robert William Gainer *The reproduction of colour* 1957
Hunt, Thomas *A defence of the charter and municipal rights of the City of London* 1683
Hunt, William Holman *Pre-Raphaelitism and the Pre-Raphaelite brotherhood* 1905
Hunt, Mrs. W. Holman *Children at Jerusalem: a sketch of modern life in Syria* 1881
Hunt's merchants' magazine and commercial review See *Merchants' magazine and commercial review*
Hunter, Alan James Herbert *Gently at a gallop* 1971
Gently coloured 1969
Gently continental 1967
Gently French 1973
Hunter, Alexander *Culina famulatrix medicinæ; or receipts in modern cookery* 1804 (1806)
ed. *Georgical essays* 1770-72 (1803)
Hunter, David *Reuss's (E.) History of the canon of the Holy Scriptures in the Catholic Church* tr. 1884
Hunter, Hay & Whyte, W. *My ducats and my daughter* (anon.) 1884
Hunter, Henry *Saint-Pierre's (J. H. B. de) Studies of nature* tr. 1796 (1799)
Hunter, James *A complete dictionary of farriery and horsemanship* 1796
Hunter, John *The natural history of the human teeth* 1771-78
Observations on certain parts of the animal œconomy 1786 (1792)
A treatise on the blood, inflammation, and gunshot wounds a1793 (1794)
Hunter, John *An historical journal of the transactions at Port Jackson and Norfolk Island* 1793
Hunter, John *A manual of bee-keeping* 1875
Hunter, John D. *Memoirs of a captivity among the Indians of North America* 1823
Hunter, John K. *Life studies of character* 1870
Hunter, John Marvin ed. *The trail drivers of Texas* 1920
Hunter, Joseph *Hallamshire* 1819
The Hallamshire glossary 1829
South Yorkshire 1828-31
Hunter, Sir Martin *The journal of; and some letters of Lady Hunter* 17..-18.. (1894)
'Hunter, Matthew' *The Cambridgeshire disaster* 1967
Hunter, Peter Hay *After the exile* 1890
James Inwick 1894
John Armiger's revenge 1897
Hunter, Robert, et al. *The encyclopædic dictionary* See under title
Hunter, William *Biggar and the House of Fleming* 1862 (1867)
Hunter, Sir William W. *The annals of rural Bengal* 1868
— *Orissa; being the second and third volumes of the (above)* 1872
The Indian empire 1882
The old missionary 1895
Hunting, Henry Gardner *The vicarion* 1926
Hunting of the fox, The; or, the sectaries dissected in a parallel between them and foxes 1648
Hunting of the hare ?c1475 (in Weber, Metrical Romances III. 1810)
Huntington, William *The bank of faith, or God the guardian of the poor* 1801
Huntley, Richard W. *A glossary of the Cotswold (Gloucestershire) dialect* 1868
Hunton, Philip *A treatise of monarchie* 1643 (1689)
A vindication of the treatise of monarchy 1644
Hurd, Bp. Richard *Works* a1808 (1811)
An introduction to the study of the prophecies concerning the Christian Church 1772 (1788)
A letter to Mr. Mason on the marks of imitation 1748
Letters on chivalry and romance 1762
Moral and political dialogues 1759 (1760)
Sermons preached at Lincoln's Inn 1765-76 (1776-80)
Hurdis, James *The favorite village, a poem* 1800
Tears of affection 1794
Hurren, Bernard John *Eastern Med.* 1943
Hurst, Dorothea E. *Horsham: its history and antiquities* 1868 (1889)
Hurst, Fannie *Humoresque: a laugh on life with a tear behind it* 1919
Hurst and hanger: a history in two parts 1886
Hursthouse, Charles F. *New Zealand; or Zealandia, the Britain of the South* 1857
Hurston, Zora Neale *Mules and men* 1935
— (another ed.) 1970
Hurwitz, Hyman *Elements of the Hebrew language* 1807
Husband, Edward *A collection of all the publicke orders, ordinances, and declarations of both Houses of Parliament* (compiled by E. Husband) 1642-46 (1646)
Huschke, Ralph E. ed. *Glossary of meteorology* 1959
Huskey, Harry Douglas & Korn, G. A. *Computer handbook* 1962
Huskisson, William *The question concerning the depreciation of our currency stated and examined* 1810
Hussey, Robert *The rise of papal power traced in three lectures* 1851
Hutcheson, George *An exposition of the gospel according to John* 1657
Hutching's illustrated California magazine 1856-61
Hutchings, Ernest A. D. *A survey of printing processes* 1970
Hutchins, Thomas *An historical narrative and topographical description of Louisiana and West Florida* 1784
A topographical description of Virginia, Pennsylvania, Maryland, and North Carolina 1778
Hutchinson, Arthur Stuart Menteth *If winter comes* 1921
Once aboard the lugger: the history of George and his Mary 1908
One increasing purpose 1925
This freedom 1922
Hutchinson, Bp. Francis *An historical essay concerning witchcraft* 1718 (1720)
Hutchinson, George Evelyn *A treatise on limnology* 1957-
Hutchinson, Henry N. *Extinct monsters* 1892
Hutchinson, Horace G. *Cricket* 1903
Golfing 1893
— et al. *Golf* (Badminton Library) 1890 (1898)
Hutchinson, Jonathan *Archives of surgery* 1889-1900
Hutchinson, Lucy *Memories of the life of Colonel Hutchinson* c1665 (1846, 1885)
Hutchinson, Robert William *A first course in wireless* 1926
Hutchinson, Roger *Works* a1555 (Parker Soc. 1842)
The image of God, or laie mans booke 1550 (1560)
Hutchinson, Thomas ed. *A collection of original papers relative to the history of the Colony of Massachusetts-Bay* (anon.) v.d. (1769)
Diary and letters a1780 (1883-86)
The history of the Colony of Massachusets Bay from 1628 to 1691 1760 (ed. 2)
The history of the Province of Massachusetts Bay (1628-1750) 1764-67
— ed. 2, entitled *The history of the Colony of Massachusets Bay* 1765-68
Hutchinson, William *The history of the County of Cumberland, and some places adjacent* 1794
A view of Northumberland with an excursion to the Abbey of Mailross in Scotland 1778
Hutchinson's pictorial history of the war ed. W. V. Hutchinson 1939-45
Hutchinsonians, A word to the 1756 *See* Kennicott, B.
Hutchison, Alexander C. *Some practical observations in surgery* 1816 (1826)
Hutchison, Isobel Wylie *North to the rime-ringed sun: being the record of an Alaskan-Canadian journey made in 1933-34* 1934
Hutchison, Matthew *The reformed Presbyterian church in Scotland* 1893
Huth, Alfred H. *The life and writings of H. T. Buckle* 1880
Hutten, Bettina von *Pam* 1904
What became of Pam 1906
Hutten, Ernest Hirschlaff *The language of modern physics* 1956
Hutten, Leonard *An answere to a certaine treatise of the crosse in baptisme* 1605
Hutten, Robert *The sum of diuinitie drawen out of the holy scripture* tr. 1548
Hutton, Charles *A course of mathematics* 1798 (1806)
A mathematical and philosophical dictionary 1795-96
The principles of bridges 1772
The school-master's guide; or, a complete system of practical arithmetic 1766 (ed. 2)
A treatise on mensuration, both in theory and practice 1770
Hutton, Frederick W. *Fishes of New Zealand* 1872
Hutton, Henry *Follie's anatomie: or satyres and satyricall epigrams. With a compendious history of Ixion's wheele* 1619 (Percy Soc. 1842)
Hutton, James *A dissertation upon the philosophy of light, heat and fire* 1794
Hutton, John *A tour to the caves, in the environs of Ingleborough and Settle in the West Riding of Yorkshire. Also a large glossary of old and original words made use of in common conversation in the North of England* 1780 (1781; E.D.S. 1873)
Hutton, John Henry *Caste in India: its nature, function and origins* 1946
Hutton, Richard H. *Essays, theological and literary* 1871
Hutton, Thomas *Reasons for refusal of subscription to the Booke of Common Praier* 1605
Hutton, William *A bran new wark, by William de Worfat* 1785 (E.D.S. 1879)
Hutton, William *Life, including a particular account of the riots at Birmingham in 1791.* Written by himself 1798 (1816)
Hutton, William H. *Philip Augustus* 1896
Huxley, Aldous Leonard *Adonis and the alphabet* 1956
After many a summer 1939
Along the road: notes and essays 1925
Antic hay 1923
Ape and essence 1948 (UK 1949)
Beyond the Mexique Bay 1934
Brave new world 1932
Brave new world revisited 1958 (UK 1959)
Brief candles 1930
Crome yellow 1921
Do what you will: essays 1929
Ends and means: an enquiry into the nature of ideals and into the methods employed for their realization 1937
Essays new and old 1926
Eyeless in Gaza 1936
The genius and the goddess 1955
Grey eminence: a study in religion and politics 1941
Island 1962
Jesting Pilate: the diary of a journey 1926
Leda 1920
Letters ed. Grover Smith 1969
Music at night, and other essays 1931
The olive tree, and other essays 1936
The perennial philosophy 1945 (UK 1946)
Point counter point 1928
Proper studies 1927
Themes and variations 1950
Those barren leaves 1925
Time must have a stop 1944 (UK 1945)
Vulgarity in literature 1930
Huxley, Anthony Julian *An illustrated history of gardening* 1978
Plant and planet 1974
Huxley, Elspeth Josceline *Back street new worlds* 1964
Huxley, Julian Sorell *Bird-watching and bird behaviour* 1930
Essays in popular science 1926
Essays of a biologist 1923
Evolution in action 1953
Evolution: the modern synthesis 1942
Evolutionary ethics 1943
The individual in the animal kingdom 1912
On living in a revolution 1944
Problems of relative growth 1932
Religion without revelation 1927
— (rev. ed.) 1957
TVA: adventure in planning 1943
Unesco: its purpose and philosophy 1946
The uniqueness of man 1941
What dare I think? 1931
—— & Haddon, Alfred Cort *We Europeans* 1935
See also Haldane, John Burdon Sanderson
Huxley, Leonard *Life and letters of Sir Joseph Dalton Hooker* based on materials collected and arranged by Lady Hooker 2 vols. 1918
Huxley, Thomas H. *The crayfish* 1880
Critiques and addresses 1873
Essays upon some controverted questions 1892
Evidence as to man's place in nature 1863
Hume 1879
Lay sermons, addresses, and reviews 1870
Lectures on the elements of comparative anatomy 1864
Lessons in elementary physiology 1866 (1872)
A manual of the anatomy of invertebrated animals 1877
A manual of the anatomy of vertebrated animals 1871
The oceanic hydrozoa 1859
Physiography: an introduction to the study of nature 1877
Science and culture, and other essays 1881
Life and letters. By his son Leonard Huxley (1900)
—— & Martin, Henry N. *A course of practical instruction in elementary biology* 1875 (1877, 1883)
See also Laing, S.

HVISTENDAHL, Herbert Selwyn *Engineering units and physical quantities* 1964
HYAMS, Edward Solomon *Gentian violet* 1953
Into the dream 1957
Soil and civilization 1952
Taking it easy 1958
HYAMS, Joseph *The pool* 1978
Hyckescorner ?1510 (W. de Worde; in Manly, Pre-Shaksperean drama, I. 1897)
HYDE, Edward & Henry *See* CLARENDON, 1st and 2nd Earls of
'HYDE, Robin' (Iris Guiver Wilkinson) *Check to your king: the life history of Charles, Baron de Thierry, King of Nukahiva, Sovereign Chief of New Zealand* 1936
Nor the years condemn 1938
Passport to hell: the story of John Douglas Stark, Bomber, Fifth Regiment, New Zealand Expeditionary Forces 1936
Hye way to the Spytell hous ?1536 *See* COPLAND, R.
HYLAND, Henry Stanley *Top bloody secret* 1969
Who goes hang? 1958
HYLANDER, Clarence John *The Macmillan wild flower book* 1954
HYLL, T. *See* HILL, T.
HYLTON, Walter *Scala perfeccionis* a1395 (W. de Worde 1494, 1533)
HYMAN, Libbie Henrietta *Comparative vertebrate anatomy* 1922
— (ed. 2) 1942
The invertebrates 5 vols. 1940–59
Hymn to victory 1704 *See* DE FOE, D.
Hymns a1000 (Grein)
Hymns. The Latin hymns of the Anglo-Saxon Church, with an interlinear Anglo-Saxon gloss c1000 (Surtees Soc. 1851)
Hymns to the Virgin and Christ c1430 (E.E.T.S. 1867)
HYND, John 1606 *See* HIND, J.
HYNE, C. J. CUTCLIFFE W. *Adventures of Captain Kettle* 1898
Further adventures of Captain Kettle 1899
McTodd 1903
Mr. Horrocks, purser 1902
Thompson's progress 1902
HYNES, Martin *Medical bacteriology* (ed. 7) 1961
— (ed. 8) 1964
For earlier eds. see WHITBY, Sir Lionel E. H.
HYNES, Samuel Lynn *The Auden generation: literature and politics in England in the 1930's* 1976
HYRDE, Richard *Vives' (J. L.) Instruction of a christen woman* tr. ?1529 (1540, 1592)

I

I., H. *Bullinger's (H.) Fiftie godlie.. sermons divided into five decades* tr. 1577 (1592)
I., R. 1601 *See* JOHNSON, Robert
I., T. *A cure for the tongue-evill* 1662
I., Z. *Lavardin's (J. de) Historie of George Castriot, surnamed Scanderbeg, king of Albanie* tr. Z. I. gentleman 1596
IBM journal of research and development 1957–
IEEE *See* Institute of Electrical and Electronics Engineers
IRE *See* Institute of Radio Engineers
I.U.P.A.C. *See* International Union of Pure and Applied Chemistry
I believe: the personal philosophies of certain eminent men and women of our time [by W. H. Auden et al.] 1939 (UK 1940)
IBBETSON, James *A plea for the subscription of the clergy to the thirty-nine articles of religion* 1768
Ibis, The; a quarterly journal of ornithology 1859–
ICKES, Harold LeClair *Secret diary* 3 vols. 1953–4 (UK 1955)
IDDINGS, Joseph Paxson *Igneous rocks: composition, texture and classification, description and occurrence* 2 vols. 1909–13
Rock minerals 1906
Idler magazine (title varies) 1894–1911
IDRIESS, Ion Llewellyn *The cattle king* 1936
The great boomerang 1941
In crocodile land: wandering in Northern Australia 1946
Isles of despair 1947
Lasseter's last ride: an epic of Central Australian gold discovery 1931
Ilkeston Advertiser and Erewash Valley Weekly News 1881–
ILLINGWORTH, John R. *The doctrine of the Trinity apologetically considered* 1907
Personality, human and divine 1894
Illinois. Department of Agriculture *Transactions* 1855–1921 (1855–71 with title *Transactions of the Illinois State Agricultural Society*)
Illinois State Historical Society *Journal* 1908–
Transactions 1899–
Illuminating Engineering Society (US) *Transactions* 1906–40
Illustrated London News, The 1842–
Illustrated weekly of India (Bombay) 1879–
IMISON, John *Elements of science and art* 1803 (enlarged by J. Webster 1822)
The school of arts 1785
Imitatio See *De imitatione Christi*
IMMS, Augustus Daniel *A general textbook of entomology* 1925
— (ed. 9) 1957 *See* RICHARDS, Owain Westmacott & DAVIES, R. G.
Immunology 1958–
Imperial dictionary, The ed. J. Ogilvie 1850
—— Supplement 1855
— revised ed. Ed. C. Annandale 1881–83
Implement and machinery review 1884
Important considerations.. by the secular priests (by W. Watson) 1601 (1675, 1688, 1831)
Impostors detected, The; or the life of a Portuguese 1760
INCHBALD, Elizabeth ed. *The British theatre, or a collection of plays* etc. 1806–09
A collection of farces.. selected by Mrs. I. 1815
I'll tell you what, a comedy 1785 (1786)
The modern theatre, a collection of successful modern plays, selected by Mrs. I. 1811
A simple story (a novel) 1791
INCLEDON, Charles V. *The Taunus, or doings and undoings, being a tour in search of the picturesque* 1837
Incorporated linguist 1962–
Indagine's (J.) Book of palmestry 1558 *See* WITHER, F.
Independent, The (New York; later Boston, Mass.) 1848–1928
Index-Journal (Greenwood, South Carolina) 1897–
Index Kewensis plantarum phanerogamarum, nomina et synonyma omnium generum et specierum 1893–95
— Suppl. 1901–26
India, Notes on the north-western provinces of 1869 (1870)
Indian journal of medical research 1913–
Indian music journal 1964–
Indian records, with a commercial view of the relations between the British government and the Nawaba Nazim of Bengal, Behar and Orisa 1870
Indiana. House of Representatives *Journal* 1816–46
Indiana Historical Society *Publications* 1895–
Indiana magazine of history 1905– (1905–13 with title *Indiana quarterly magazine of history*)
Indulgence, shewing its rise etc., The history of the 1678
Industrial and engineering chemistry 1923–40
Industrial chemist and chemical manufacturer, The 1925–
Infant baptism, The case of (by G. Hickes) 1683
Infantry manual, containing directions for the drill and instruction of recruits etc. *The* 1847 (1854)
INGE, William R. *Christian mysticism* (Bampton lectures) 1899
Lay thoughts of a dean 1926
INGELEND, Thomas *A pretie and mery new enterlude called The disobedient child* c1560 (Percy Soc. 1848; Hazl. Dodsley)
INGELO, Nathaniel *Bentivolio and Urania* 1660 (1682)
INGELOW, Jean *Poems* 1863 (also 1867, 1880)
A story of doom and other poems 1867
INGERSOLL, Ernest *The oyster-industry* 1881 (Tenth Census of the U.S.)
INGERSOLL, Jared *Letters relating to the stamp act* 1766
INGESTRE, Viscount *See* TALBOTT, C. J. C., 19th Earl of Shrewsbury
INGLEBY, Clement M. *Shakespeare, the man and the book* 1877–81
Shakespere allusion books 1874
Shakespeare's Centurie of prayse 1874 (also New Shaks. Soc. 1879)
INGLIS, James *Oor ain folk, being memories of manse life in the Mearns* etc. 1893 (1894)
Our Australian cousins 1880
Sport and work on the Nepaul frontier 1878
INGLIS, John *The New Hebrides* 1887
'INGOLDSBY, Thomas' *See* BARHAM, R. H.
INGRAHAM, Joseph H. *The pillar of fire, or Israel in bondage* 1865 (1872)
The South-West, by a Yankee 2 vols. 1835
INGRAM, George *Cockney cavalcade* 1935
'Stir' 1933
'Stir' train 1935
INGRAM, J. S. *The Centennial Exposition, described and illustrated* 1876
Initials, The; a novel (by Baroness Tautphœus) 1850
Ink 1971–2
Inland printer 1883–
Inlander, The (University of Michigan) 1891–1931 (title varies)
INMAN, Thomas *Ancient pagan and modern christian symbolism exposed and explained* 1869 (1870)
On myalgia; its nature, causes, and treatment 1860
Inner life, The: essays in liberal evengelicalism 2nd ser. 1925
INNES, C. L. *Canterbury (N.Z.) sketches, or life from the early days. By Pilgrim* 1879
INNES, Cosmo *Lectures on Scotch legal antiquities* 1872
Scotland in the middle ages 1860
Sketches of early Scotch history and social progress 1861
INNES, Hammond *The big footprints* 1977
The blue ice 1948
Campbell's kingdom 1952
'INNES, Michael' (John Innes Mackintosh Stewart) *Appleby plays chicken* 1956
Appleby's answer 1973
Appleby's other story 1974
An awkward lie 1971
Christmas at Candleshoe 1953
The daffodil affair 1942
Death at the President's lodging 1936
Hamlet, revenge! 1937
The journeying boy 1949
Old Hall, New Hall 1956
The open house 1972
Operation pax 1951
See also under real name
INNES, Thomas *A critical essay on the ancient inhabitants of the northern parts of Britain or Scotland* 1729 (1879)
Inquisition taken before the Commissioners of Sewers for the county of Lincoln, 2nd July 1583 (1851)
Insect architecture (by J. Rennie) 1830 (1847)
Inside Kenya today 1953–
Institut Pasteur *Annales* 1887–
Institute of Cost and Management Accountants *Terminology of management and financial accountancy* 1974
Institute of Electrical and Electronics Engineers *IEEE transactions on computers* 1968–
IEEE transactions on electronic computers 1963–7
Proceedings 1963–
Institute of Radio Engineers *Proceedings* 1913–62
Transactions on electronic computers 1952–63
Institution of a christen man, The 1537 (C. Lloyd, Formularies 1825)
Institution of Civil Engineers *Minutes of proceedings* 1837–1937
Institution of Electrical Engineers *Journal* 1889–
Proceedings 1949–
Institution of Mechanical Engineers *Proceedings* 1847–
Institution (later Royal ——) of Naval Architects *Transactions* 1860–
Instructions 1659 *See* WALKER, O.
Instructions and regulations for the formations and movements of the cavalry 1796 (1813)
'INSULANUS, Theophilus' *A treatise on the second sight, dreams and apparitions* 1763
Intellectual observer or review of natural history, The 1862–68
Interlude. The enterlude of youth c1520 (1557; Hazl. Dodsley)
A new interlude and a mery of the nature of the iiii. elements (by J. Rastell ?) 1519 (Percy Soc. 1848; Hazl. Dodsley)
International and comparative law quarterly 1952–
International Congress of Genetics, 6th, 1932 *Proceedings* 2 vols. 1932
International Congress of Linguists, 8th, 1957 *Proceedings* 1958
International Congress of Medicine, 17th, 1913 23 sections 1913–14
International Congress of Phonetic Sciences, 2nd, 1935 *Proceedings* 1936
——, 3rd, 1938 *Proceedings* 1939
International Congress of Soil Science, 1st, 1927 *Proceedings and papers* 5 vols. 1928
——, 2nd, 1930 *Proceedings and papers* 7 vols. 1932–5
——, 7th, 1960 *Transactions* 4 vols. 1960
International encyclopaedia of the social sciences 17 vols. 1968
International exhibition of 1862, The. The illustrated catalogue of the industrial department 1862
International Herald Tribune See *New York Herald Tribune International*
International journal of American linguistics 1917–
International journal of psycho-analysis 1920–
International Union of Pure and Applied Chemistry *Information bulletin* 1956–77
Nomenclature of inorganic chemistry 1959
— (ed. 2) 1971
Nomenclature of organic chemistry 3 parts 1958–65
— (ed. 2) 3 parts 1966–71
Inter-Ocean (Chicago) 1872–1914
Into orbit, by the seven astronauts of Project Mercury (US ed. with title *We seven*) 1962
Invasion, The: or what might have been, 1798
Inventories. A collection of inventories and other records of the (Scottish) royal wardrobe and jewelhouse 1488–1606 (1815)
The inventories of church goods for the counties of York, Durham and Northumberland 1546–56 (Surtees Soc. 1897)
Inventories of the goods and ornaments in the churches of Surrey in the reign of king Edward the sixth (ed. J. R. Daniel-Tyssen, Surrey archæol. collect. IV, 1869)
Inventory of church goods in Staffordshire 1552–53 (Annals of the diocese of Lichfield IV, 1863)
Inverness. Records of the presbyteries of Inverness and Dingwall 1643–88 (S.H.S. 1896)
Inverness Courier 1817–
INWARDS, Richard *Weather lore* 1869 (1893)
IONESCU, Ghiţa & GELLNER, E. *Populism, its meaning and national characteristics* 1969
Iowa State Agricultural Society *Report* 1854–99
Ipomadon (verse) c1350 (Kölbing 1889)
Ipomedon (prose) a1400 (Kölbing 1889)
The lyfe of Ipomydon (verse) c1440 (Weber, Metrical romances II; Kölbing 1889)
Ipotis (Ypotis) a1400 (Horstmann, Altenglische Legenden 1881)
Ireland. A contemporary history of affairs in Ireland from 1641 to 1652 a1660 (Irish Archæol. Soc. 1879–80)
Ireland sixty years ago, Sketches of, by W—— 1847
A natural history of Ireland, by several hands 1726
A remonstrance of divers remarkeable passages concerning the church and kingdome of Ireland 1642
The true state and condition of Ireland, sent to the House of Commons 1642
The statutes of Ireland v.d. (ed. Sir R. Bolton 1621)
A collection of all the statutes now in use (1678)
The statutes at large (1765; 1786–1801)
IRELAND, William H. *Scribbleomania; or the printer's devil's polichronicon, a poem* (anon.) 1815

Irvine, Ayr., Muniments of the royal burgh of (1890–91)
Irish Times 1859–
Iron and Steel Institute *Journal* 1871–
IRONSIDE, Janey *A fashion alphabet* 1968
IRVING, David *The history of Scottish poetry* a1860 (1861)
IRVING, Edward *Babylon and infidelity forewarned of God* 1826
For the oracles of God, four orations. For Judgement to come, an argument 1823 (1824)
The last days 1828
IRVING, John *The 158-pound marriage* 1974
The world according to Garp 1978
IRVING, John James Cawdell *Royal navalese: a glossary* 1946
IRVING, Joseph *The west of Scotland in history* 1885
IRVING, Washington *Adventures of Captain Bonneville, or scenes beyond the Rocky mountains* 1837
The Alhambra 1832
Astoria, or enterprise beyond the Rocky mountains 1836
Bracebridge Hall, or the humourists 1822
A chronicle of the conquest of Granada 1829
Chronicles of Wolfert's Roost and other papers 1839–40 (1855)
Knickerbocker's History of New York 1809 (1820, 1861)
Life and letters (1864–66)
The life of George Washington 1855–59
The lives of Mahomet and his successors 1850 (1853)
Oliver Goldsmith: a biography 1849 (1850)
Salmagundi; or the whim-whams and opinions of L. Langstaff Esq. 1807–08 (1824)
The sketch book of Geoffrey Crayon, Gent. 1820 (1859)
Tales of a traveller 1824
A tour on the prairies 1835
IRWIN, Godfrey *American tramp and underworld slang* 1931
ISENTHAL, A. W. & WARD, H. S. *Practical radiography* 1898
ISHERWOOD, Christopher William Bradshaw *Goodbye to Berlin* 1939
Mr. Norris changes trains 1935
Prater violet 1945 (UK 1946)
A single man 1964
See also AUDEN, Wystan Hugh
Isis, The (Oxford) 1892–1914; 1919–36; 1945–
Islander, The (Victoria, British Columbia) 1953–
Isle of Wight glossary 1881 *See* SMITH, Henry
Islington-wells; or the three-penny-academy, a poem (by R. Ames) 1691
Isumbras (Ysumbras). The romance of Sir Isumbras a1400 (Thornton romances, Camden Soc. 1844)
It 1966–75 (1966–7 with title *International Times*)
Italy. The character of Italy; or the Italian anatomized by an English chyrurgion 1660
Iter Lancastrense 1636 *See* JAMES, R.
IVE, Paul *Du Bellay's (G.) Instructions for the wars* tr. 1589
The practice of fortification 1589

J

J. C. 1708 *See* C., J.
J. D. 1613 *See* DENNYS, J.
J. S. 1758 *See* SPARROW, J.
J., St. N. *The widow's mite* 1695
J., W. *Bruyn's (C. de) Voyage to the Levant* tr. 1702
JACK, John *An historical account of St. Monance, Fifeshire* 1844
Jack Horner, The history of ?a1750
Jack Juggler. A new enterlued for chyldren to playe, named Jacke Jugeler c1563 (Hazl. Dodsley)
Jack Straw. The life and death of Jacke Straw a notable rebell 1593 (Hazl. Dodsley)
Jack Upland 1402 (Wright, Polit. poems and songs, Rolls series; Skeat, Chaucerian pieces)
JACKSON, Benjamin D. *A glossary of botanic terms with their derivation and accent* 1900
JACKSON, Edward S. *The cabinet of the earth unlocked* 1867
JACKSON, Emily *A history of hand-made lace* 1900
JACKSON, George *Soledad Brother: the prison letters of George Jackson* 1970 (UK 1971)
JACKSON, Georgina F. *Shropshire word-book* 1879–81
JACKSON, Helen Hunt *Sonnets and lyrics* 1886
Verses 1887–88
JACKSON, James G. *An account of the empire of Marocco* 1809
JACKSON, John *The booke of conscience opened and read* (a sermon) 1642
The true evangelical temper; three sermons 1641
JACKSON, Bp. John *A charge delivered to the clergy of the diocese of Lincoln, Oct.* 1864
JACKSON, John *The practical fly-fisher* 1880 (1899)
JACKSON, Kenneth Hurlstone *Language and history in early Britain* 1953
JACKSON, Louis E. & HELLYER, C. R. *A vocabulary of criminal slang, with some examples of common usages* 1914
JACKSON, Mary C. *A chaperon's cares* 1878
JACKSON, Richard A. *Mechanism: an introduction to the study of organic reactions* 1972
JACKSON, Samuel *Krummacher's (F. W.) Elisha* tr. 1838
Strauss' (G. F. A.) Reminiscences from the early life of a Lutheran clergyman tr. 1838
JACKSON, Thomas *Works* a1640 (1673; 1844)
Christs answer unto Johns question 1624 (1625)
Commentaries upon the apostles creed 1613–40 (bks. I, II. 1613; III. 1614; IV. 1615; V. 1625; VI. 1628, 1629; VII. 1634; VIII. 1635; IX. 1638; X, XI. a1640 (1654, 1657); XII. 1627)
The eternal truth of scriptures a1640 (1653)
Judah must go into captivitie, six sermons 1622
The worthy churchman 1628
JACKSON, William *The new and complete Newgate calendar, or villany displayed* c1780 (1800–08)
JACKSON, William *The doctrine of retribution* (Bampton lectures) 1875
JACKSON, William Hatchett *See* ROLLESTON, G.
Jackson's recantation 1674 *See* HEAD, R.
JACOB, Edward *The history of.. Faversham in.. Kent* 1774
Plantæ Favershamienses. A catalogue of.. plants growing.. about Faversham 1777
JACOB, Giles *The compleat court keeper, or land steward's assistant* 1713 (enlarged 1764, 1819)
The compleat sportsman 1718
A new law dictionary 1729 (1744)
— enlarged ed. 1797 *See* TOMLINS, T. E.
JACOB, Gordon Percival Septimus *Orchestral technique* 1931
JACOB, Henry ed. *On the choice of a common language* 1946
A planned auxiliary language 1947
JACOB, Hildebrand *Works* v.d. (1735)
JACOB, John *Annals of.. the bailiwick of Guernsey* 1830
JACOB, Violet *The sheep-stealers* 1902
Jacob and Esau, A new merry and witty comedie or enterlude.. treating upon the historie of 1568 (Hazl. Dodsley)
JACOBI, Charles T. *The printers' vocabulary* 1888
Printing: a practical treatise on the art of typography 1890
Jacobite conventicle, a poem, The 1692
Jacobite relics See HOGG, J.
Jacobite songs and ballads of Scotland from 1688 to 1746 (1860)
Jacob's well, an englisht treatise on the cleansing of man's conscience c1440 (E.E.T.S. 1900)
JACOBS, Arthur *A new dictionary of music* 1958
JACOBS, Roderick A. & ROSENBAUM, Peter S. eds. *Readings in English transformational grammar* 1970
JACOBSEN, Charles W. *Oriental rugs: a complete guide* 1962
JACOBSON, Dan *The confessions of Joseph Baisz* 1977
A dance in the sun 1956
The trap 1955
JACOMBE, Thomas *Several sermons preached on (Romans viii)* 1672 (1868)
JACOX, Francis *Aspects of authorship* 1872
JAFFE, Rona *Class reunion* 1979
The fame game 1969 (UK 1970)
JAKOBSON, Roman & HALLE, Morris *Fundamentals of language* 1956
Jaksch's (R. von) Clinical diagnosis tr. J. Cagney 1890 (1899)
JAL, Auguste *Glossaire nautique, répertoire polyglotte de termes de marine, anciens et modernes* 1848
Jamaica, A new history of 1740
JAMES I, King of Scotland *The kingis quair: together with a ballad of good counsel* 1423 (S.T.S. 1884, revised 1911)
JAMES VI, King of Scotland, afterw. JAMES I of England *Works* v.d. (1616)
Βασιλικον δωρον or his maiesties instructions to his dearest sonne Henry the prince 1599 (1682)
A counterblaste to tobacco 1604 (Arber)
Dæmonologie, in forme of a dialogue 1597
The essayes of a prentise, in the divine art of poesie 1585 (Arber)
His majesties poeticall exercises at vacant houres (tr. Du Bartas) 1591
The psalmes of David tr. a1625 (1631)
James the sext, The historie and life of 1582–88 (1804)
JAMES, Mrs. A. G. F. Eliot *A guide to Indian household management* 1879
JAMES, Brian *England v Scotland* 1969
'JAMES, Brian' (John Lawrence Tierney) ed. *Australian short stories* (2nd ser.) 1963
For 1st ser. *see* MURDOCH, Walter & DRAKE-BROCKMAN, Henrietta
JAMES, Charles *A new and enlarged military dictionary* 1802 (1810)
JAMES, Charles T. C. *The romantic rigmarole of a time out of town* 1891
JAMES, Edwin *Account of an expedition from Pittsburgh to the Rocky Mountains, performed in the years 1819, 1820. Compiled from the notes of Major Long, Mr. T. Say, and other gentlemen of the party* 3 vols. 1823
JAMES, George P. R. *Agnes Sorel, an historical romance* 1853
Arrah Neil; or times of old 1845
The brigand: see Corse de Léon, below
The convict, a tale 1847
Corse de Léon or the brigand, a romance 1841
Darnley, or the field of the cloth of gold 1830
De l'Orme 1830
Forest days, a romance of old times 1843
The gentleman of the old school, a tale 1839
The gipsy: a tale 1835
Heidelberg, a romance 1846
The life and adventures of John Marston Hall 1834
The life and times of Louis XIV 1838
The old oak chest, a tale of domestic life 1850
Philip Augustus, or the brothers in arms 1831
The robber 1838
The smuggler, a tale 1845
The woodman; a romance of the times of Richard III 1849
JAMES, Glenn & JAMES, Robert Clarke eds. *Mathematics dictionary* (multilingual ed.) 1959
JAMES, Henry *Substance and shadow: or morality and religion in their relation to life* 1863
JAMES, Henry *The ambassadors* 1903
The awkward age 1899
The Bostonians, a novel 1886
Daisy Miller, a study 1878 (1879)
The Europeans, a sketch 1878
The golden bowl 2 vols. 1904
The ivory tower 1917
A little tour in France 1884 (1885)
The madonna of the future and other tales 1879
The middle years 1917
Notebooks ed. F. O. Matthiessen & K. B. Murdock 1947
A passionate pilgrim and other tales 1875
The portrait of a lady 1881
The reverberator 2 vols. 1888
Roderick Hudson 1875 (revised 1879)
The sense of the past 1917
The spoils of Poynton 1897
Tales of three cities 1884
The tragic muse 1890
Transatlantic sketches 1875
The wings of the dove 2 vols. 1902 (UK ed. in 1 vol.)
JAMES, John *Le Blond's (A. J. B.) Theory and practice of gardening* tr. 1712 (1728)
JAMES, Sir John K. *Tasso's (T.) Jerusalem delivered* tr. 1864 (1865)
JAMES, Leigh *The chameleon file* 1967 (UK 1968)
JAMES, Phyllis Dorothy *Death of an expert witness* 1977
Shroud for a nightingale 1971
An unsuitable job for a woman 1972
JAMES, Richard *Iter Lancastrense; a poem* 1636 (Chetham Soc. 1845)
Minucius Felix his dialogue called Octavius tr. 1636
JAMES, Robert *A dissertation upon fevers and inflammatory distempers* 1748 (1749)
A medicinal dictionary 1743–45
ed. *Moufet's (T.) Health's improvement* 1746
JAMES, Samuel B. *Duty and doctrine; a book of sermons* 1866 (1871)
JAMES, T. Horton *Six months in South Australia* 1838
JAMES, Thomas *An apologie for John Wickliffe* 1608
The Jesuits downefall threatened against them 1612
A manuduction or introduction into divinitie 1625
A treatise of the corruption of scripture etc... *by.. the church of Rome* 1611 (1612)
JAMES, Thomas *The strange and dangerous voyage of Captaine T. J. in his intended discovery of the northwest passage into the south sea* 1633
JAMES, Walter *A word-book of wine* 1959
JAMES, William *Collected essays and reviews* ed. R. B. Perry 1920
Essays in radical empiricism ed. R. B. Perry 1912
Letters ed. H. James 2 vols. 1920
The meaning of truth: a sequel to Pragmatism 1909
Memories and studies ed. H. James 1911
A pluralistic universe 1909
Pragmatism: a new name for some old ways of thinking 1907
The principles of psychology 1890
Some problems of philosophy: a beginning of an introduction to philosophy 1911
Talks to teachers on psychology, and to students on some of life's ideals 1899
A text-book of psychology 1892
The varieties of religious experience (Gifford lectures) 1902
The will to believe, and other essays in popular philosophy 1897
See also PERRY, Ralph Burton
JAMESON, Mrs. Anna *A commonplace book of thoughts* etc. 1854 (1877)
Legends of the madonna as represented in the fine arts 1852 (1857)
Legends of the monastic orders as represented in the fine arts 1850 (1863)
Memoirs of the early Italian painters 1845
Sacred and legendary art 1848 (1850)
JAMESON, Margaret Ethel Storm *A richer dust* 1931
JAMESON, Robert *Manual of mineralogy* 1821
System of mineralogy 1804–08 (1816, 1820)
A treatise on the external characters of minerals 1805
— ed. 3, 1817
JAMIESON, John *An etymological dictionary of the Scottish language* 1808, Supplement 1825 (1879–82) See also DONALDSON, D.
Hermes Scythicus, or the radical affinities of the Greek and Latin languages to the Gothic 1814
JAMIESON, Robert *Popular ballads and songs* 1806
JANE, Queen (Lady Jane Grey) *The chronicle of Queen Jane and of two years of Queen Mary* 1553–54 (Camden Soc. 1850)
JANE, Frederic T. *All the world's fighting ships* 1898
The lordship, the passen, and we 1897
See also *Jane's* below.
JANE, Joseph *Εικων ακλαστος The image unbroken* 1651
Jane's all the world's aircraft (title varies) 1909–
Jane's fighting ships (title varies) 1898–
Jane's freight containers 1968–
Jane's surface skimmer systems (title varies) 1967–
JANEWAY, James *Heaven upon earth: or the best friend in the worst of times* 1670 (1677, 1847)
JANSON, Charles W. *The stranger in America* 1807
Janua linguarum quadrilinguis 1617 *See* BARBIER, Jo.
JAPP, Alex. H. *See* 'PAGE, H. A.'
JAQUES, Mary J. *Texan ranch life* 1894
JARDINE, Sir William *Contributions to ornithology* 1848–52
The natural history of humming birds 1833–34
JARMAN, Thomas ed. *Powell's (J. J.) Essay on devises* 1827
Jarrow, Durham. *The inventories and account rolls of the*

Jarrow (*cont.*)
Benedictine houses..of Jarrow and Monk-Wearmouth v.d. (mostly *c*1450) (Surtees Soc. 1854)
JARVIS, Charles *Cervantes' Life and exploits of..Don Quixote de la Mancha* tr. *a*1739 (1742)
JARVIS, Derek tr. *D. Hess's Plant physiology* 1975
Jasz-Berenyi's (*P. P.*) *Fax nova linguæ latinæ, a new torch to the latin tongue* 1664
Jaunt in a junk, A; a ten days' cruise in Indian seas 1884
JAY, William *Autobiography a*1853 (1855)
The Christian contemplated in a course of lectures 1826
The domestic minister's assistant or prayers for families 1820
Jazz and blues 1971-3
JEAFFRESON, John C. *A book about doctors* 1860
Brides and bridals 1872
JEAKE, Samuel *Charters of the Cinque ports* tr. with annotations 1678 (1728)
Logisticelogia, or arithmetic surveighed and reviewed 1674 (1696)
JEANES, Henry *A mixture of scholasticall divinity with practicall* 1656
A treatise concerning the fulnesse of Christ 1656
JEBB, John *Remarks upon the present mode of education in the university of Cambridge* 1772 (1773)
JEBB, Bp. John *Thirty years' correspondence between J. J. and A. Knox a*1831 (1834)
JEBB, John *The choral service of the united church of England and Ireland* 1843
JEBB, Richard *General principles of law* 1845 (Encycl. Metrop. II; 1847)
JEBB, Sir Richard C. *The Attic orators* 1876
Bentley (English men of letters) 1882
The Characters of Theophrastus tr. 1870
Modern Greece 1880
JEFFERIE, J. See *Bugbears*
JEFFERIES, Ian *Dignity and purity* 1960
House-surgeon 1966
It wasn't me! 1961
Thirteen days 1959
JEFFERIES, Richard *The amateur poacher* 1879
*Field and hedgerow, being the last essays of R. J. a*1887 (1889)
The gamekeeper at home 1878
Greene Ferne farm 1880
Hodge and his masters 1880
The life of the fields 1884
Red deer 1884
Round about a great estate 1880
*Toilers of the field a*1887 (1892)
Wild life in a southern county 1879
JEFFERSON, Thomas *Writings a*1826 (1859)
Notes on the state of Virginia 1782 (1787)
JEFFREY, Francis, Lord Jeffrey *Contributions to the Edinburgh review* 1844
JEFFREYS, Charles *Geographical and descriptive delineations of Van Diemen's Land* 1820
JEFFRIES, Roderic Graeme *Dead man's bluff* 1970
Evidence of the accused 1961
Exhibit no. thirteen 1962
A traitor's crime 1968
JEKYLL, Gertrude *Colour in the flower garden* 1908
—(ed. 3, with title *Colour schemes for the flower garden*) 1914
Wood and garden 1899
JEKYLL, Joseph *Correspondence..with his sister-in-law* etc. 1775, 1818-38 (1894)
Jemima, a novel 1795
JENISON, Robert *The narrative of R. J... containing a further discovery and confirmation of the late..popish plot* 1679
JENKIN, Fleeming *Electricity and magnetism* 1873 (1881)
JENKIN, Henrietta C. *Who breaks—pays* (anon.) 1861
JENKINS, Daniel Thomas *The educated society* 1966
JENKINS, David *Works, upon divers statutes concerning the liberty and freedome of the subject* 1648
JENKINS, Elizabeth *The tortoise and the hare* 1954
JENKINS, Geoffrey *A bridge of magpies* 1974
A twist of sand 1959
JENKINS, Herbert George *John Dene of Toronto: a comedy of Whitehall* 1919
JENKINS, James Travis *The fishes of the British Isles* 1925
—(ed. 2) 1936
JENKINS, (John) Edward *Ginx's baby* 1870 (1879)
Lord Bantam 1872
JENKINS, Tobias *Father Paul's* (P. Sarpi) *Treatise of ecclesiastical benefices and revenues* tr. 1736
JENKINS, Vivian Gordon J. *Lions down under: the British Isles Rugby tour of Australia and New Zealand, 1959* 1960
JENKINS, Warren *The Ohio gazetteer, and traveler's guide* 1837
JENKINSON, Anthony *Early voyages and travels to Russia and Persia by A. J. and other Englishmen* 15.. (Hakluyt Soc. 1886)
JENKINSON, Charles *A treatise on the coins of the realm* 1805
JENKINSON, Henry I. *Practical guide to the English lake district* 1872 (1879)
JENKINSON, James *Linnæus'* (*C.*) *Generic and specific description of British plants* tr. 1775
JENKINSON, John W. *Experimental embryology* 1909
JENKS, Edward *The government of Victoria* (Australia) 1891
JENKYN, William *'Οδηγος τυφλος The blind guide or the doting doctor* 1648
Reformations remora 1646
A shock of corn coming in in its season 1653 (1654)
The stil-destroyer or self-seeking discovered 1645

JENNER, Charles *The placid man, or memoirs of Sir C. Beville* 1770 (1773)
JENNER, Edward *An inquiry into the causes and effects of the variolæ vaccinæ* 1798 (1884 repr. of 1801)
JENNESS, Diamond *The Indians of Canada* 1932
—(ed. 2) 1934
JENNETT, Seán *The making of books* 1951
JENNINGS, Hargrave *Phallicism, celestial and terrestrial, heathen and christian* 1884
JENNINGS, James *Observations on some of the dialects in the west of England, particularly Somersetshire* etc. 1825 (1869)
JENNINGS, Jo. *Elise: or innocence guilty, a romance* tr. 1655
JENNINGS, Louis J. *Field paths and green lanes, being country walks chiefly in Surrey and Sussex* 1877 (1884)
JENNINGS, Paul *The living village* 1968
JENNINGS, Samuel *My visit to the gold fields in the south-east Wynaad* 1881
JENYNS, Leonard *A manual of British vertebrate animals* 1835
JENYNS, Soame *Poems a*1787 (1790; Chalmers 1810)
A free enquiry into the nature and origin of evil 1757
A view of the internal evidence of the christian religion 1776
JEPHSON, John M. & REEVE, L. *Narrative of a walking tour in Brittany* 1859
JEPHSON, Robert *Braganza, a tragedy* 1775
JERDAN, William *Autobiography a*1850 (1852-53)
JERDON, Thomas C. *The birds of India* 1862-64
The mammals of India 1867
JERNINGHAM, Frances, Lady *The Jerningham letters 1780-1843, being excerpts from the correspondence of Lady J. and of her daughter Lady Bedingfield* (1896)
*Jerome, St. St. Jeremie's 15 tokens before doomsday c*1350 (Adam Davy etc. E.E.T.S. 1878)
Jerome of Brunswyke See *Brunswyke, H.*
JEROME, Jerome K. *The idle thoughts of an idle fellow* 1886 (1889)
On the stage and off: the brief career of a would-be actor 1885
Three men in a boat 1889
Three men on the bummel 1900
Jeronimo, The first part of 1605 (Dodsley; Kyd's Works 1901)
JERRARD, Harold George & MCNEILL, Donald Burgess *A dictionary of scientific units, including dimensionless numbers and scales* 1963
JERROLD, Douglas *The history of St. Giles and St. James* 1851
Men of character 1838
Mrs. Caudle's curtain lectures 1846
Punch's letters to his son 1843 (1863)
JERROLD, William Blanchard *At home in Paris: at peace and at war* 1871
London (illustr. G. Doré) 1872
Jersey Evening Post (St. Helier, Jersey) 1890-
JESPERSEN, Jens Otto Harry *Essentials of English grammar* 1933
Growth and structure of the English language 1905
An international language 1928
Language: its nature, development and origin 1922
Mankind, nation and individual from a linguistic point of view 1925
A modern English grammar on historical principles 7 parts 1909-49 (parts 6 & 7 by Jespersen & N. Haislund)
The philosophy of grammar 1924
The system of grammar 1933
JESSE, E. *See* KNAPP, J. L.
JESSE, George R. *Researches into the history of the British dog* 1866
JESSE, John Heneage *George Selwyn and his contemporaries* 1843-44
JESSOP, Constant *The angel of the church of Ephesus no bishop of Ephesus* 1644
JESSOPP, Augustus *Arcady for better or worse* 1887
The coming of the friars, and other historical essays 1889
Random roaming and other papers 1894
Studies by a recluse 1893
Jesuites reasons unreasonable, or doubts proposed to the Jesuits, The 1662 (1675)
Jetzer, The tragical history of tr. 1679 *See* WALLER, Sir W.
JEVONS, William Stanley *Elementary lessons in logic* 1870
Logic (Science primer) 1876
Money and the mechanism of exchange 1875 (1878)
Political economy (Science primer) 1878
The principles of science 1874 (1879)
Pure logic; or the logic of quality apart from quantity 1864
The theory of political economy 1871
JEWEL, John *Works a*1571 (1611; Parker Soc. 1845-50; 1848)
An apologie..in defence of the church of England tr. (anon.) 1562
—tr. (Lady Ann Bacon) 1564 (Parker Soc.)
—*A defence of the apologie* 1567 (also 1569)
*Certaine sermons a*1571 (1583, 1611, Parker Soc.)
The copie of a sermon..at Paules crosse 1560
*An exposition upon the two epistles..to the Thessalonians a*1571 (1583)
A replie unto M. Hardinges answeare 1565 (1611)
*A treatise of the sacraments a*1571 (1583)
The true copies of the letters betwene J. and Dr. Cole 1560
A viewe of a seditious bul 1569 (1582)
JEWETT, Sarah Orne *A country doctor* 1884
Deephaven 1877 (1893)
Tales of New England 1893
Jewish Chronicle 1841-
Jewish encyclopedia, The ed. I. Singer 12 vols. 1901-6

Jewish manual, the; or, Practical information in Jewish and modern cookery, with a collection of valuable recipes & hints relating to the toilette, ed. by a Lady 1846
JEWITT, Llewellyn F. W. *The ballads and songs of Derbyshire* 1867
The ceramic art of Great Britain 1878
JEWRY, Mary *Warne's model cookery and housekeeping book* 1868
JHABVALA, Ruth Prawer *Get ready for battle* 1962
The householder 1960
A new dominion 1972
To whom she will 1955
JOCELINE, Elizabeth *The mothers legacie* 1624
JODRELL, Richard P. *The Persian heroine, a tragedy* 1786
Philology of the English language 1820
JOESTEN, Joachim *They call it intelligence* 1963
JOHANNSEN, Albert *A descriptive petrography of the igneous rocks* 4 vols. 1931-8
—(ed. 2) Vol. I 1939
JOHANNSEN, Hano & ROBERTSON, Andrew *Management glossary* eds. E. F. L. Brech 1968
John, king of England, The troublesome raigne of (2 parts) 1591 (1611, 1764)
JOHN, Griffith *A voice from China* 1907
John a Kent. The book of John a Kent and John a Cumber, a comedy by A. Munday 1595 (Shaks. Soc. 1851)
John Edwards Memorial Foundation *Quarterly* (title varies) 1965-
John o'London's weekly 1919-54; revived as *John o'London's* 1959-
John Thompson's man; or, a short survey of the difficulties and disturbances that may attend a married life 1829
JOHNS, Charles A. *British birds in their haunts* 1862
Flowers of the field 1851
A week at the Lizard 1848 (1874)
Johns Hopkins Hospital *Bulletin* 1889-1966
Johns Hopkins University, Baltimore. *Studies from the biological laboratory* 1881-
Studies in historical and political science 1882-
JOHNSON, Mrs. Anna M. *Monmouth* (a novel) 1790
JOHNSON, Bryan Stanley *Travelling people* 1963
JOHNSON, Charles *The country lasses, or the custom of the manor, a comedy* 1714
The tragedy of Medea 1731
JOHNSON, Cuthbert W. *The farmer's encyclopædia and dictionary of rural affairs* 1842
JOHNSON, Daniel *Sketches of field sports as followed by the natives of India* 1822 (1827)
JOHNSON, Edward *A history of New England..untill..1652: or the wonder-working providence of Sions saviour* 1654 (1867)
JOHNSON, Edwin *Antiqua mater: a study of Christian origins* (anon.) 1887
The rise of Christendom 1890
JOHNSON, George W. ed. *The cottage gardeners' dictionary* 1852
A dictionary of modern gardening 1846
JOHNSON, H. C. Ross *A long vacation in the Argentine Alps* 1868
JOHNSON, James *The Scots musical museum* 1787-1803
JOHNSON, John *The clergyman's vade-mecum* (anon.) 1709
A collection of all the ecclesiastical laws, canons etc. *concerning the government..and worship of the church of England* tr. 1720 (1850)
The unbloody sacrifice and altar unvail'd and supported 1714-24 (1847)
JOHNSON, John *Typographia, or the printers' instructor* 1824
JOHNSON, Lady Bird (Mrs Lyndon Baines Johnson) *A White House diary* 1970
JOHNSON, Myron ed. *American advertising 1800-1900* 1960
JOHNSON, Pamela Hansford *The humbler creation* 1959
Night and silence, who is here? 1963
The unspeakable Skipton 1959
JOHNSON, Paul Bede *Enemies of society* 1977
JOHNSON, Richard *The most famous history of the seaven champions of cristendome* 1596 (1608)
*The most pleasant history of Tom a Lincoln a*1635 (Thoms, E.E. prose romances 1828)
The pleasant conceites of old Hobson, the merry Londoner 1607 (Percy Soc. 1844)
JOHNSON, Robert *Botero's (G.) The worlde, or an historicall description of the most famous kingdomes and commonweales therein* tr. I. R. 1601
—(other edd.) 1603, 1616, 1630
JOHNSON, Robert *The way to glory, a sermon* 1621
JOHNSON, Rev. Samuel *Notes upon the Phœnix edition of the pastoral letter of Bp. Burnet* 1694
JOHNSON, Samuel, dancing-master *Hurlothrumbo, or the super-natural* 1729
JOHNSON, Samuel *Works a*1784 (1787, 1792, 1825)
A dictionary of the English language 1755 (1773)
—ed. H. J. Todd 1818
—ed. R. G. Latham 1866
The idler 1758-61
Irene, a tragedy 1749
A journey to the western islands of Scotland 1775
*Letters a*1784 (ed. G. B. Hill 1892)
Letters to and from the late S. J. By Hester Lynch Piozzi (Mrs. Thrale) v.d. (1788)
Life of Sir Francis Drake 1740
The lives of the English poets 1779-81
Lobo's (J.) Voyage to Abyssinia tr. 1735
London, a poem, in imitation of..Juvenal 1738
The prince of Abissinia (Rasselas), *a tale* 1759
The rambler 1750-52

Taxation no tyranny; an answer to the resolutions and address of the American congress 1775
The vanity of human wishes: the tenth satire of Juvenal imitated 1748
See also Boswell, J.
Johnson, Thomas *Gerard's (J.) Herball* Enlarged by T. J. 1633 (1636)
The workes of that famous chirurgion A. Parey (or Paré) tr. 1634 (1678)
Johnson, Thomas B. *The sportsman's cyclopedia* 1831
Johnson, William 1658 *See* Wuertz, F.
Johnson, William Ernest *Logic* 3 parts 1921-4
Johnsoniana. Anecdotes of the late Samuel Johnson, LL.D. by Mrs. Piozzi . . and others, etc. Collected and edited by Robina Napier (1884)
Johnston, Alexander Keith *Africa* (Stanford's Compendium of geography and travel) 1878
Johnston, Sir Archibald, Lord War(r)iston *Diary* 1632-39, 1650-54 (S.H.S. 1911, 1919)
Johnston, Bryce *General view of the agriculture of the county of Dumfries* 1794
Johnston, Charles *Chrysal: or the adventures of a guinea* (anon.) 1760 (1822)
The history of John Juniper Esq. 1781
The pilgrim, or a picture of life 1775
The reverie, or a flight to the paradise of fools 1762 (1763)
Johnston, Edward *Writing and illuminating, and lettering* 1906
Johnston, Elizabeth *Gifts and graces* (anon.) 1862
Johnston, George *Flora Lindisfarnensis: the natural history of the eastern borders. I. The botany* 1853
An introduction to conchology 1850
Johnston, George Henry *Death takes small bites* 1948
Johnston, Harry Hamilton *A comparative study of the Bantu and semi-Bantu languages* 2 vols. 1919-22
Johnston, Henry *Chronicles of Glenbuckie* 1889
Kilmallie 1891
Johnston, James F. W. *The chemistry of common life* 1853-55 (1879)
Notes on North America; agricultural, economical and social 2 vols. 1851
Johnston, Mary *Audrey* 1902
Johnston, Nathaniel *The assurance of abby and other church lands in England to the possessors* 1687
Johnston, Ronald *The black camels of Qashran* 1970
Johnston, William *Beckmann's (J.) History of inventions and discoveries* tr. 1797-1814 (1846)
Johnstone, Mrs. Christina J. *Clan Albin: a national tale* (anon.) 1815
The Saxon and the Gael (anon.) 1814
Jolly, Thomas *Note-book* 1671-93 (Chetham Soc. 1894)
Joly, John *The surface-history of the earth* 1925
Joly's (N.) Man before metals tr. 1883
Jonas, Richard *Roesslin's (E.) Byrth of mankynde* tr. 1540
Joncas, L. Z. *The fisheries of Canada* 1883 (Fisheries exhibition literature)
Jones, A. *The art of playing at skittles* 1773
Jones, Bernard Edward ed. *Cassell's cyclopædia of photography* See *Cassell's* ——
The cinematograph book 1915
Jones, Charles *Hoyle's (E.) Games improved* 1775 (1778)
Jones, Charles H. & Sieveking, Sir E. H. *A manual of pathological anatomy* 1854
— ed. J. F. Payne 1875
Jones, Cheslyn Peter M., Wainwright, G., & Yarnold, E. eds. *The study of liturgy* 1978
Jones, Daniel *An outline of English phonetics* 1918 (and several later editions used)
The phoneme: its nature and use 1950
Jones, Ebenezer *Studies of sensation and event, poems* 1843 (1879)
Jones, Eli Stanley *The Christ of the Indian road* 1925
Jones, Enid Huws *Margery Fry, the essential amateur* 1966
Jones, Ernest tr. *S. Ferenczi's Contributions to psycho-analysis* 1916
Papers on psycho-analysis 1913
— (rev. ed.) 1918
Jones, Ernest Beachcroft *Instrument technology* 3 vols. 1953-7
Jones, George Noble *Florida plantation records* ed. V. B. Phillips & J. D. Glunt 1927
Jones, Gwyn *A history of the Vikings* 1968
Jones, Henry *The earl of Essex, a tragedy* 1753 (1756)
Jones, Henry 1862 *See* 'Cavendish'
Jones, Mrs. Henry *Broad outlines of long years in Australia* 1877 (1878)
Jones, Henry Bence *The life and letters of Faraday* 1870
Jones, Henry Festing *Samuel Butler, author of Erewhon, 1835-1902: a memoir* 2 vols. 1919
Jones, Inigo *The most notable antiquity of Great Britain, vulgarly called Stone-heng, on Salisbury plain, restored by I. J.* 1620-51 (1655, 1725)
Jones, John *The arte and science of preserving bodie and soule in healthe* etc. 1578 (1579)
The bathes of Bathes ayde 1572 (1574)
The benefit of the auncient bathes of Buckstones 1572 (1574)
A briefe . . discourse of the naturall beginning of all growing and living things etc. 1574
Jones, John *Adrasta: or the womans spleene, and loves conquest, a tragi-comedie* 1635
Jones, John *The conquest of the saints* (a sermon) 1639
Jones, John *Ovid's Invective or curse against Ibis* tr. 1658
Jones, John *Bugge's (T.) Travels in the French Republic* tr. 1801
Jones, John Morris *A Welsh grammar, historical and comparative* 1913
Jones, Miss Mary Whitmore *Games of patience, for one or more players* 1887 (1888)
Jones, Mervyn *Potbank* 1961
Jones, Owen *The grammar of ornament* 1856
Jones, Peter *History of the Ojebway Indians* 1861
Jones, Philip Mitchell *The fifth defector* 1967
Jones, Reginald Victor *Most secret war* 1978
'Jones, Robert' (T. Lushington) *The resurrection rescued from the soldiers' calumnies* 1619 (Phenix 1708)
Jones, Robert *A new treatise on artificial fireworks* 1765 (1766)
Jones, Robert Walter *Dictionary of banking* (ed. 10) 1951
See Thomson, William
Jones, Sarah L. *Life in the South (U.S.) from the commencement of the war. By a blockaded British subject* 1863
Jones, Sarah S. *Northumberland and its neighbour lands* 1863 (1871)
Jones, Thomas *Of the heart and its right soveraign* 1678
Jones, Thomas P. *New conversations on chemistry* 1831
Jones, Thomas Rymer *The aquarian naturalist* 1858
Cassell's Book of birds, from the text of Dr. (A. E.) Brehm 1869-73
A general outline of the animal kingdom 1841 (1871)
The natural history of animals 1845-52
Jones, William *Synopsis palmariorum matheseos, or a new introduction to the mathematics* 1706
Jones, William *Zoologica ethica: a disquisition concerning the Mosaic distinction of animals into clean and unclean* 1771
Jones, William *Finger-ring lore* 1877
Jones, Sir William *Works* a1794 (1799)
Poems, consisting chiefly of translations . . and essays 1772 (1777)
Jones, Zachary *Le Loyer's (P.) Treatise of specters or straunge sights, visions and apparitions* tr. 1605
Jong, Erica Mann *Fanny: being the true history of the adventures of Fanny Hackabout-Jones* 1980
Jonson, Ben *Works* a1637 (1616, 1640, 1692, 1846)
The alchemist 1610 (1616)
Barthol(o)mew fayre 1614 (1631)
B. J. his case is altered 1598-99 (1609)
Catiline his conspiracy 1611
Conversations See Drummond, W.
Cynthias revels See *Fountaine*, below
Discoveries See *Timber*, below
The divell is an asse 1616 (1631)
The English grammar 1636 (1640, 1692)
Entertainments v.d.
Epicœne: or the silent woman 1609 (1620)
Epigrams 1612-16 (1616)
Every man in his humor 1598 (1601, 1616)
Every man out of his humor, The comicall satyre of 1599 (1600, 1616)
The forest 1616
The fountaine of selfe-love, or Cynthias revels 1600 (1601, 1616)
Q. Horatius Flaccus his art of poetry tr. a1637 (1640)
The magnetick lady, or humors reconcild 1632 (1640)
Masques v.d.
The new inne, or the light heart 1629 (1631)
Poetaster, or the arraignment 1601 (1602)
The sad shepherd, or a tale of Robin Hood 1637 (1641)
Sejanus his fall 1603 (1605, 1616)
The silent woman See *Epicœne*, above
The staple of newes 1626 (1631)
A tale of a tub 1633 (1640)
Timber or discoveries made upon men and matter 1636 (1692)
Underwoods, consisting of divers poems 1613-34 (1640)
Volpone, or the foxe 1605 (1607, 1616)
——, Fletcher, J., & Middleton, T. *The widdow, a comedie* a1627 (1652; Dodsley)
Jordain, Philip Bernard ed. *Condensed computer encyclopedia* 1969
'Jordan, David' *Black account* 1975
Nile green 1973
Jordan, David Starr *The fishes of North and Middle America* 1896
A guide to the study of fishes 2 vols. 1905
Jordan, Denham & Visger, Mrs. Owen ('A son of the marshes') *Forest tithes and other studies from nature* 1893
On Surrey hills 1891
Within an hour of London town 1891
Woodland, moor and stream 1889
Jordan, E. O. *See* Hueppe, F.
Jordan, Thomas *A dialogue betwixt Tom and Dick* 1660
London in splendor 1673. *London's glory or the Lord Mayor's show* 1680. *London's joy* 1681. *London's resurrection to joy and triumph* 1671. *London's triumphs* 1677. *London triumphant* 1672. *The triumphs of London* 1675, 1678
The walks of Islington and Hogsdon, a comedy 1641 (1657)
Jordan, William L. *The standard of value* 1882
Jorden, Edward *A discourse of naturall bathes and minerall waters* 1631 (1669)
Jortin, John *The life of Erasmus* 1758-60
Remarks on ecclesiastical history 1751- (1751-73)
Sermons on different subjects a1770 (1771-72)
Joseph, Horace William Brindley *An introduction to logic* 1906
— (ed. 2) 1916
Joseph, Michael Kennedy *I'll soldier no more* 1958
Joseph of Arimathie: otherwise called The romance of the seint graal, or holy grail, an alliterative poem a1375 (E.E.T.S. 1871)
— Later lives c1500-20 (E.E.T.S. 1871)
Joseph the bookman, a heroic-comic poem. By a gent (A. Anderson) 1821
Josseline, John *The life off the 70. archbishopp off Canterbury presently sitting* tr. 1574
Josselyn, John *An account of two voyages to New England* 1674 (1875)
New England's rarities discovered 1672 (1875)
Journal of abnormal psychology 1906- (1921-64 with title *Journal of abnormal and social psychology*)
Journal of agricultural research 1913-49
Journal of American folk-lore 1888-
Journal of anatomy and physiology 1866- (from 1916 with title *Journal of anatomy*)
Journal of the Anthropological Institute 1871-
Journal of applied physics 1937-
Journal of applied physiology 1948-
Journal of bacteriology 1916-
Journal of biological chemistry 1905-
Journal of biophysical and biochemical cytology 1955-61
Journal of botany 1834-42, 1863-
Journal of cellular and comparative physiology 1932- (from 1966 with title *Journal of cellular physiology*)
Journal of chemical education 1924-
Journal of chemical physics 1933-
Journal of chromatography 1958-
Journal of clinical endocrinology and metabolism 1941-
Journal of clinical investigation 1924-
Journal of comparative neurology 1891- (1904-10 with title *Journal of comparative neurology and psychology*)
Journal of comparative psychology 1921-46
Journal of ecology 1913-
Journal of economic entomology 1908-
Journal of education 1879-
Journal of endocrinology 1939-
Journal of English and Germanic philology 1903-
Journal of experimental medicine (U.S.) 1896-
Journal of experimental psychology 1916-
Journal of experimental zoology 1904-
Journal of the Franklin Institute of Pennsylvania 1826-
Journal of general physiology 1918-
Journal of general psychology 1928-
Journal of genetic psychology 1954-
Journal of genetics 1910-
Journal of geology (U.S.) 1893-
Journal of geophysical research 1949-
Journal of glaciology 1947-
Journal of Hellenic studies 1880-
Journal of heredity 1914-
Journal of hygiene 1901-
Journal of immunology 1916-
Journal of industrial and engineering chemistry 1909-22
Journal of infectious diseases 1904-
Journal of the Institute of Actuaries 1869-
Journal of investigative dermatology 1938-
Journal of laboratory and clinical medicine 1915-
Journal of linguistics 1965-
Journal of the proceedings of the Linnean Society 1857-
Journal of marine zoology 1893-
Journal of medical research 1901-24
Journal of mental science 1855-1962
Journal of molecular biology 1959-
Journal of morphology (title varies) 1887-
Journal of natural philosophy, chemistry and the arts 1797-1813
Journal of nervous and mental disease (U.S.) 1876-
Journal of neurology and psychopathlogy 1920-37
Journal of neurology, neurosurgery and psychiatry 1944-
Journal of nutrition 1928-
Journal of obstetrics and gynaecology of the British Empire (later —— *Commonwealth*) 1902-
Journal of organic chemistry 1936-
Journal of paleontology 1927-
Journal of pathology and bacteriology 1892-
Journal of pediatrics 1932-
Journal of pharmaceutical sciences 1911-
Journal of pharmacology and experimental therapeutics 1909-
Journal of philology 1868-
Journal of philosophy 1904- (1904-20 with title *Journal of philosophy, psychology and scientific methods*)
Journal of physical chemistry (U.S.) 1896-
Journal of physiology 1878-
Journal of political economy 1892-
Journal of polymer science 1946-
Journal of protozoology 1954-
Journal of the Royal Agricultural Society 1840-
Journal of the Royal Institute of British Architects 1894-
Journal of the Royal Institution 1831-69
Journal of the Royal Microscopical Society 1878-
(Quarterly) journal of science 1864-85
Journal of scientific instruments 1922-
Journal of sedimentary petrology 1931-
Journal of social psychology 1930-
Journal of soil science 1949-
Journal of speech and hearing disorders 1936-
Journal of symbolic logic 1936-
Journal of theological studies 1899-
Journal of tropical medicine and hygiene 1898- (1898-1906 with title *Journal of tropical medicine*)
Journal See also under the names of particular institutions
Journal of a naturalist, The (by J. L. Knapp) 1829
Journal of the pilgrims at Plymouth, in New England in 1620 (ed. G. B. Cheever 1848)

Journey through England, A (by J. Macky) 1714 (1722)
JOWETT, Benjamin *The dialogues of Plato* tr. 1871 (1875)
Thucydides tr. 1881
JOWITT, William Allen & WALSH, Clifford eds. *Dictionary of English law* 2 vols. 1959
JOYCE, James Augustine Aloysius *Chamber music* 1907
Dubliners 1914
Exiles 1918
Finnegans wake 1939 (quotations are mostly taken from ed. 3, 1964, but dated simply 1939)
Giacomo Joyce ed. R. Ellmann 1968
Letters ed. S. Gilbert & R. Ellmann 3 vols. 1957–66
Pomes penyeach 1927
A portrait of the artist as a young man 1916 (quotations are mostly taken from the 1964 Viking Press ed., 15th printing, 1969)
Stephen hero: part of the first draft of 'A portrait of the artist as a young man' ed. T. Spencer 1944
—(ed. J. J. Slocum & H. Cahoon) 1955
Ulysses 1922 (quotations are mostly taken from the Random House ed., 1946, but dated simply 1922)
JOYCE, Jeremiah *Scientific dialogues* 1808
—new ed. by C. V. Walker 1846
JOYCE, Thomas Athol *Mexican archaeology* 1914
JOYE, George *An apology made to satisfy, if it may be, W. Tindale* 1535 (Arber)
The exposicion of Daniel the prophete 1545
G. J. confuteth Winchester's false articles 1543
The unite and scisme of the olde churche 1543
JOYNSON, Francis H. *The metals used in construction* 1868
Juan y Santacilla, Jorge. Juan (G.) and Ulloa's (A. de) Voyage to South-America tr. 1758 (1760, 1772)
JUBB, Kenneth Victor F. & KENNEDY, Peter C. *Pathology of domestic animals* 2 vols. 1963
—(ed. 2) 1970
Judas Maccabæus, a sacred drama (by T. Morell) *set to musick by Mr. Handel* 1746 (1762)
JUDD, Charles Hubbard tr. *W. Wundt's Outlines of psychology* 1897
JUDD, John W. *Volcanoes, what they are and what they teach* 1881
JUDD, Sylvester *Margaret, a tale* 1845 (1871)
JUDE, Richard H. *Physics, experimental and theoretical* 1899
JUDGE, Arthur William ed. *Modern motor cars* 3 vols. 1924
Modern petrol engines 1946
Stereoscopic photography: its application to science, industry and education 1926
Judge, The 1881–1939
Judgment of non-conformists, of the interest of reason in matters of religion, The 1676
Judicium, a pageant, extracted from the Towneley MS. c1460 (Roxb. Club 1822; Towneley Plays)
Judith (verse) a1000 (Grein 1888)
JUDSON, Edward Z. C. *The mysteries and miseries of New York, by Ned Buntline* 1852
JUKES, Joseph B. *The student's manual of geology* 1857
JUKES-BROWNE, Alfred Joseph *The student's handbook of stratigraphical geology* 1902
JULIAN, John *A dictionary of hymnology* 1892
Juliana (verse) a900 *See* CYNEWULF
Juliana, St., þe liflade of (prose) a1225 (E.E.T.S. 1872)
Seyn Julian (metrical life of St. Juliana) c1300 (ibid.)
JUNG, Carl Gustav *See* BAYNES, Helton Godwin; also HULL, Richard F. C., et al.
Jung's (J. H.) Theory of pneumatology tr. 1834
'JUNIUS' *Letters* 1769–72 (1820)
JUNIUS, Francis *A briefe..commentarie vppon the revelation of saint John* tr. 1592 (1599)
JUNIUS, Francis, Jr. (or DU JON, François) *Etymologicum Anglicanum* a1677 (ed. E. Lye 1743)
The painting of the ancients 1638
'JUNIUS, R.' (R. Younge) *The cure of misprision* 1646
The drunkard's character 1638
Sinne stigmatizd 1639
JUPP, Edward B. *An historical account of the worshipful company of carpenters of..London* 1848 (1887)
JUSTAMOND, John O. *The private life of Lewis XV* tr. 1781
Raynal's (G. T. F.) Philosophical history of the settlements..of the Europeans in the East and West Indies tr. 1776 (1783)

K

K., E. *Epistle dedicatory and glosses to Spenser's Shepheardes calender* 1579
K., F. 1673 *See* KIRKMAN, F.
K., G. *An essay for the discovery of some new geometrical problems* c1680 (1697)
K., I. 1598 *See* KEPERS, J.
K., J. (? J. Kersey) *A new English dictionary* 1702 (1731)
K., J. E. *The telephone in principle and practice* 1882
Kæmpfer's (E.) History of Japan tr. J. G. Scheuchzer 1727
KAHN, David *The codebreakers: the story of secret writing* 1967 (UK 1968)
KAHN, Herman *On escalation: metaphors and scenarios* 1965
Kaleidoscope, The; or, Literary and scientific mirror 1818–31
Kalender of shepherdes, The tr. 1503 (1506, 1656; 1892)
KALISCH, Moritz M. *A Hebrew grammar* 1862–63 (1878)
KAMES, Henry Home, Lord *Elements of criticism* 1762 (1833)
Essays upon several subjects concerning British antiquities 1745 (1747)
Introduction to the art of thinking 1761 (1789)
Sketches of the history of man 1774 (1807)
KANE, Elisha K. *Arctic explorations: the second Grinnell expedition in search of Sir John Franklin* 1856
The U.S. Grinnell (first) expedition in search of Sir John Franklin 1853 (1856)
KANE, Harry Hubbell *Opium-smoking in America and China* 1882
Kansas City Star (Kansas City, Missouri) 1880–
Kansas City Times (Kansas City, Missouri) 1868–
KANTOR, Jacob Robert *An objective psychology of grammar* 1936
KANTOROWICZ, G. F. ed. *Inlays, crowns, and bridges* See COWELL, Colin Robert, et al.
KAPP, Gilbert *Dynamos, alternators, and transformers* 1893
Kapunda (S. Australia) *herald* 1890
KARCH, Robert Randolph & BUBER, Edward J. *Graphic arts procedures: the offset processes* 1967
KARP, David *All honorable men* 1956
Leave me alone 1957
KARR, Walter S. Seton- *See* SETON-KARR
KARSNER, Howard Thomas *Human pathology* 1927
KATER, Henry & LARDNER, D. *A treatise on mechanics* 1830
Katharine de Medicis, Estienne's (H.) Mervaylous discourse upon the lyfe..of tr. 1575
Katherine, St., The legend of St. Katherine of Alexandria a1225 (Abbotsford Club 1841)
—*The life of Saint Katherine* a 1225 (E.E.T.S. 1884)
The life and martyrdom of Saint Katherine of Alexandria c1430 (Roxburghe Club 1884)
The life of St. Katharine c1450 (Halliwell 1848)
See also CAPGRAVE, J.
Kathleen, St., or the rock of Dunnismoyle (by A. Sutherland) 1820
KATZ, Jerrold Jacob *The philosophy of language* 1966
KAUFFMAN, Donald T. *Dictionary of religious terms* 1967
KAUFFMANN, Stanley Jules *If it be love* 1960
The tightrope 1952 (UK ed. 1953 with title *The philanderer*)
KAVANAGH, Julia *Dora* (a novel) 1868
French women of letters 1862
KAY, or CAIUS, John *Caoursin's (G.) Siege of..Rhodes* c1482 (with Gibbon's Crusades 1870)
KAY, Stephen *Travels and researches in Caffraria* 1833
KAY, William *Crisis Hupfeldiana* 1865
A lecture on St. Augustine of Africa 1860
KAY-SHUTTLEWORTH, Sir James P. *Scarsdale; or life on the Lancashire and Yorkshire border* 1860
KAYE, Sir John W. *The life and correspondence of..Sir J. Malcolm* 1856
Peregrine Pultney; or, life in India (anon.) 1844
KAYE, Marvin *A lively game of death* 1972
'KAYE, Mary Margaret' (Mary Margaret Kaye Hamilton) *The far pavilions* 1978
House of shade 1959
KAYE-SMITH, Sheila *Mrs. Gailey* 1951
KAZMANN, Raphael G. *Modern hydrology* 1965
KEANE, Augustus H. *The Boer states: land and people* 1900
Ethnology 1896
Man, past and present 1899
tr. *A. Hovelacque's The science of language* 1877
KEANE, Charles Alexander *Modern organic chemistry* 1909
KEANE, John F. *Three years of a wanderer's life* 1887
KEARLEY, George *Links in the chain, or popular chapters on the curiosities of animal life* 1862
KEARTON, Richard *Wild life at home* 1898
KEARY, Charles F. *The dawn of history* 1878 (1888)
English coins 1885 (in S. Lane-Poole, Coins and medals)
KEATE, George *An account of the Pelew islands* 1788
Sketches from nature taken and coloured in a journey to Margate 1779
KEATING, Henry Reymond Fitzwalter *Bats fly up for Inspector Ghote* 1974
Filmi, filmi, Inspector Ghote 1976
Inspector Ghote hunts the peacock 1968
Inspector Ghote plays a joker 1969
KEATINGE, Maurice *Travels through France and Spain to Morocco* 1816 (1817)
KEATON, Buster (Joseph Francis Keaton) *My wonderful world of slapstick* 1960 (UK 1967)
KEATS, Gwendoline *See* 'ZACK'
KEATS, John *Poetical works* a1821 (1889, 1907)
The cap and bells, or the jealousies 1819
Endymion: a poetic romance 1818
The eve of St. Agnes 1820
Hyperion 1820
Isabella; or the pot of basil 1820
Lamia 1820
Letters ed. M. B. Forman 2 vols. 1931
Letters, 1814–1821 ed. H. E. Rollins 2 vols. 1958
Otho the great, a tragedy 1819
Plays a1821 (Forman, Poetical works 1889)
KEBLE, John *The christian year* 1827
Letters of spiritual counsel and guidance a1866 (1870)
The life of Bishop Thomas Wilson 1863
Lyra innocentium 1846 (1873)
Occasional papers and reviews a1866 (1877)
Sermons academical and occasional 1847 (1848)
KEDDIE, Henrietta *See* 'TYTLER, Sarah'
KEEBLE, John *The theory of harmonies* 1784
KEENE, Charles S. *Life and letters* ed. G. S. Layard 1892
KEENEY, Arthur Hail *Ocular examination: basis and technique* 1970
KEEP, Robert P. *Autenrieth's (G.) Homeric dictionary* tr. 1876 (1877)
KEEPNEWS, Orrin & GRAUER, William *A pictorial history of jazz: people and places from New Orleans to modern jazz* 1955
KEESING, Felix Maxwell *Cultural anthropology, the science of custom* 1958
KEFAUVER, Estes *Crime in America* ed. S. Shalett 1951 (UK 1952)
KEHOE, Vincent J. R. *Aficionado! The pictorial encyclopedia of the Fiesta de Toros of Spain* 1959
The technique of film and television make-up 1957
KEIGHTLEY, Thomas *The fairy mythology* 1828 (1847)
The history of England 1837–39
The mythology of ancient Greece and Italy 1831 (1877)
The secret societies of the middle ages 1837 (1848)
KEIGWIN, John *Mount Calvary or the history of the passion, death and resurrection of..Jesus Christ* tr. (from the Cornish) 1682 (1826)
KEILL, James *Essays on several parts of the animal œconomy* 1717 (1738)
KEILL, John *An examination of Dr. Burnet's Theory of the earth* 1698 (1734)
An introduction to the true astronomy tr. 1720 (1778)
Moreau de Maupertius' (P. L.) Dissertation on the different figures of the cœlestial bodies tr. a1721 (1734)
KEIM, De Benneville Randolph *Sheridan's troopers on the borders: a winter campaign on the plains* 1870
KEITH, Agnes Newton *Land below the wind* 1939
KEITH, Arthur *The antiquity of man* 1915
Human embryology and morphology 1902
KEITH, Charles *Farmer's ha', a Scots poem* (anon.) 1776 (1801)
KEITH, George *A second narrative of the proceedings at Turners-Hall the 29th of April* 1697
'KEITH, Leslie' (Grace L. Keith Johnston) *The Indian uncle* 1896
'Lisbeth 1893
The love of Prue 1895
My bonny lady 1897
KEITH, Patrick *A botanical lexicon* 1837
A system of physiological botany 1816
KEITH, Bp. Robert *The history of the affairs of church and state in Scotland* 1734
A large new catalogue of the bishops of the several sees within the kingdom of Scotland 1755 (1824)
KELHAM, Robert *A dictionary of the Norman or old French language* 1779
KELLER, Helen Adams *The story of my life* ed. J. A. Macy 1903
KELLY, James *A complete collection of Scotish proverbs* 1721
KELLY, Mary Theresa *The Christmas egg* 1958
The Spoilt kill 1961
KELLY, Michael *Spinifex* 1970
KELLY, Patrick *The universal cambist and commercial instructor* 1811
KELLY, Walter K. *Arago's (D. F. J.) Popular lectures on astronomy* tr. 1848 (1854)
Blanc's (L.) History of ten years 1830–40 tr. 1848
Curiosities of Indo-European tradition and folk-lore 1863
KELMAN, John *Salted with fire* 1915
KELSEY, Joseph *Sermons upon several occasions* 1703
Kelso, Roxburghshire. *Liber S. Marie de Calchou. Registrum cartarum abbacie Tironensis de Kelso* 1113–1567 (Bannatyne Club 1846)
KELTY, Mary A. *Osmond, a tale* (anon.) 1822
KEMBLE, Frances Anne *Journal of a residence on a Georgian plantation* 1839 (1863)
Record of a girlhood 1878
Records of later life 3 vols. 1882
KEMBLE, John M. ed. *Anglo-saxon dialogues of Salomon and Saturn* 1845–48 (Ælfric Soc.)
ed. *Codex diplomaticus aevi Saxonici* 1839–48
The Saxons in England 1849 (1876)
ed. *Vercelli codex. The poetry of the Codex Vercellensis, with a translation* 1843 (Ælfric Soc.)
KEMBLE, Mrs. Marie T. *The day after the wedding, an interlude* 1808
KEMELMAN, Harry Gregory *Monday the rabbi took off* 1972
Saturday the rabbi went hungry 1966 (UK 1967)
Wednesday the rabbi got wet 1976
KEMP, Dixon *A manual of yacht and boat sailing* 1878 (1884, 1895)
KEMP, Ian *British G.I. in Vietnam* 1969
KEMP, James Furman *A handbook of rocks, for use without the microscope* 1896
KEMP, Peter Kemp *Fleet Air Arm* 1954
KEMP, Peter Mant MacIntyre *Alms for oblivion* 1961
Mine were of trouble 1957
No colours or crest 1958
KEMP, William *K.'s nine daies wonder, performed in a daunce from London to Norwich* 1600 (Camden Soc. 1840; Arber, Eng. Garner VII)
KEMPE, Alfred J. ed. *Manuscripts..illustrative of English history from Henry VIII to James I, preserved at Losely house* 1836
KEN, Bp. Thomas *Works* a1711 (1721)
Anodynes or alleviations of pain 1709–11
Edmund, an epic poem a1700
Hymnotheo or the penitent a1700
Hymns a1697, a1711
Psyche or Magdalum a1711
Sermons a1711
KENDALL, Edward A. *Travels through the northern parts of the United States* 1809

Kendall, George Wilkins *Narrative of the Texan Santa Fé expedition* 2 vols. 1844
Kendall, Henry *Poems and songs* 1862
Kendall, Maurice George & Buckland, William R. *A dictionary of statistical terms* 1957
Kendall, Thomas *A grammar and vocabulary of the language of New Zealand* (ed. by S. Lee from materials supplied by T. Kendall) 1820
Kendall, Timothy *Flowers of epigrammes*. . . *Trifles devised and written at sundrie tymes* 1577 (1874)
Kendrew, Wilfrid George *The climates of the continents* 1922
Kenelworth parke 1594 *See* B., O.
Kennard, Mrs. Nina H. *Diogenes' sandals* 1893
Kennedy, Benjamin H. *The public school Latin grammar* 1871 (1874)
Kennedy, Grace *Father Clement, a Roman catholic story* 1823 (1869)
Kennedy, Harry A. A. *St. Paul's conceptions of the last things* 1904
Kennedy, James *A new description of the pictures . . and other curiosities . . at Wilton* 1758
Kennedy, John P. *Annals of Quodlibet* 1840 (1860)
Horse-shoe Robinson, a tale of the Tory ascendancy 1835 (1860)
Memoirs of the life of William Wirt 1849 (1860)
Rob of the bowl, a legend of St Inigoes 1838 (1860)
Swallow barn, or a sojourn in the old dominion 1832 (1860)
Kennedy, Ludovic Henry Coverley *Very lovely people* 1969
Kennedy, Margaret *The constant nymph* 1924
The heroes of Clone 1957
Lucy Carmichael 1951
Kennedy, Patrick *Journal* 1773 (in T. Hutchins, Topogr. descr. Virginia etc. 1778)
Kennedy, Patrick *The banks of the Boro: a chronicle of . . Wexford* 1856 (1867)
Evenings on the Duffrey 1869
Kennedy, Quintin *Ane compendius tractive* 1558 (Wodrow Soc. Miscellany 1844)
The ressoning . . betuix the abbot of Crossraguell and J. Knox 1563 (1812)
Kennedy, Walter *Poems* a1508 (Schipper 1901)
The flyting of Dunbar and Kennedie 1508 (Ramsay, Evergreen 1724; Dunbar's poems, S.T.S. II, 1893)
Kenneison, William C. & Spilman, Alan J. B. *Dictionary of printing, papermaking and bookbinding* 1963
Kennett, Basil *Romæ antiquæ notitia, or the antiquities of Rome* 1696 (1713)
Kennett, Bp. White ed. *Cowel's (J.) Interpreter of words and terms* 1701
Monitions and advices delivered to the clergy of the diocese of Peterborough 1720
MS. collection of provincial words (MS. Lansdowne 1033) c1700
Parochial antiquities attempted in the history of Ambrosden, Burcester, and adjacent parts in Oxford and Bucks 1695 (1818)
— *Dialectal words* (E.D.S. 1879)
Witt against wisdom, or a panegyrick upon folly tr. (from Erasmus) 1683
Kennicott, Benjamin *A word to the Hutchinsonians; or, remarks on three extraordinary sermons lately preached before the University of Oxford by Dr. Patten, Mr. Wetherall, and Mr. Home.* By a member of the University (i.e. B. Kennicott) 1756
Kenrick, William *A new dictionary of the English language* 1773
Kent, James *Commentaries on American law* 1826–30 (1858)
Kent, John *Racing life of Lord George Cavendish Bentinck* 1892
Kent, Ruth Kimball *The language of journalism: a glossary of print-communications terms* 1970
Kent, W. Saville *See* Saville-Kent, W.
Kent, William *The mechanical engineers' pocket-book* 1910 (ed. 8)
Kentish, Edward *Essay on warm and vapour baths* 1813
Kentish sermons, Old c1250 (O.E. Misc., E.E.T.S. 1872)
Kenyon, John Samuel *American pronunciation: a text-book of phonetics for students of English* 1924
— (ed. 6) 1935
Kenyon, Kathleen Mary *Archaeology in the Holy Land* 1960
Digging up Jericho 1957
Kenyon, Michael Forbes *Deep pocket* 1978
The 100,000 welcomes 1970
Mr Big 1975
The whole hog 1967
Kenyon, Robert L. *The gold coins of England arranged and described* 1884
Kenyon review 1939–70
Kepers, John *Romei's (A.) Courtiers academie* tr. by I. K. 1598
Kephart, Horace *Camping and woodcraft* 2 vols. 1916–17
— (new edn.) 1921 (2 vols. in 1)
Our southern highlands 1913
Ker, John Bellenden *An essay on the archæology of popular English phrases and nursery rhymes* 1834–42
Ker, William Paton *The dark ages* 1904
ed. *Essays of John Dryden* 1900
Kernahan, Coulson *Scoundrels & Co.* 1901
Kerouac, Jack *On the road* 1957 (UK 1958)
Kerr, Mrs. Alexander *Ranke's (L. von) History of Servia* tr. 1847 (1853)
Kerr, James *The covenants and the covenanters* 1895
Kerr, John *Curling* (Badminton library) 1892
Kerr, Robert *General view of the agriculture of the county of Berwick* 1813
Kerr, Robert *Maggie o' the moss; and other poems* a1848 (1891)
Kerr, Robert *The gentleman's house; or how to plan English residences* 1864
Kerry-Nichols, J. H. *The King country: explorations in New Zealand* 1884
Kersey, John *Dictionarium Anglo-Brittannicum or a general English dictionary* 1708 (1721)
Elements of algebra 1673–74
See also K., J.; Phillips, E.
Kersh, Cyril *The aggravations of Minnie Ashe* 1970
Kersh, Gerald *They die with their boots clean* 1941
Kersley, Leo & Sinclair, Janet *A dictionary of ballet terms* 1952
Kettle, Edgar Hartley *The pathology of tumours* 1916
Kettlewell, John *Works* a1695 (1719)
A companion for the penitent 1694
A companion for the persecuted 1694
An help and exhortation to worthy communicating 1683
The measures of christian obedience 1681
Kew bulletin of miscellaneous information 1887–
Key, Thomas H. *The alphabet. Terentian metres* etc. 1844
Language: its origin and development 1874
Philological essays 1868
Keyes, Edward L. *See* Van Buren, W. H.
Keymis, Lawrence *A relation of the second voyage to Guiana* 1596
Keymor, John *Observations made upon the Dutch fishing* c1601 (1664)
Keynes, John Maynard *The economic consequences of the peace* 1919
The general theory of employment, interest and money 1936
A treatise on money 2 vols. 1930
Keynes, John Neville *Studies and exercises in formal logic* 1884 (and several later editions used)
Keysler's (J. G.) Travels through Germany etc. tr. 1756–57 (1760)
Khory, Rustamji N. *A digest of the principles and practice of medicine* 1879
Kichenside, Geoffrey Michael & Williams, Alan Reginald *British railway signalling* 1963
Kidd, Benjamin *Social evolution* 1894
Kidder, Bp. Richard *Charity directed: or the way to give alms* 1676
Kilburne, Richard *A topographie, or survey of the county of Kent* 1659
Killigrew, Thomas *Comedies and tragedies* 1664
Pandora, a comedy 1664
The parson's wedding 1663 (1664; Dodsley)
Killingbeck, John *Eighteen sermons* 1717
Kilpatrick, Thomas B. *New Testament evangelism* 1911
Kilvert, Robert Francis *Diary* ed. W. Plomer 3 vols. 1938–40
— (selections, ed. W. Plomer) 1944
Kimball, Richard B. *Under-currents of Wall-street* 1861
Was he successful? a novel 1863 (1864)
Kimber, Isaac *The life of Oliver Cromwell* (anon.) 1724 (1731)
Kimbolton, Lord *See* Montagu, Edward, 2nd Earl of Manchester
Kimenye, Barbara *Kalasanda revisited* 1966
Kinahan, G. Henry *Manual of the geology of Ireland* 1878
Kincaid, Dennis *British social life in India, 1608–1937* 1938
Kinderley, Nathaniel *The ancient and present state of the navigation of . . Lyn, Wisbeach*, etc. 1721 (1751)
Kindersley, Nathaniel E. *Specimens of Hindoo literature* 1794
King, Adam *Canisius' (P.) Catechisme or schort instruction of christian religion* tr. 1588 (1622; part, Catholic tractates, S.T.S. 1901)
King, Charles *The British merchant* 1721
King, Charles *Foes in ambush* 1893
King, Charles Cooper- *Map and plan drawing* 1874
King, Charles W. *Antique gems* 1860 (1866)
King, Clarence *Mountaineering in the Sierra Nevada* 1872
King, Francis Henry *The widow* 1957
King, Gordon John *The audio handbook* 1975
King, Mrs. Harriet E. Hamilton *The disciples* (J. Ruffini, U. Bassi, etc.) 1873 (1877)
King, Bp. Henry *Poems, elegies, paradoxes and sonnets* 1657, 1664
Sermons 1621, 1626, 1640
Two sermons (by H. K., and J. King) 1625
King, Humphrey *An halfe-penny-worth of wit* 1613
King, Captain James 1784 *See* Cook, Captain James
King, Bp. John *Lectures upon Jonas* 1594 (1597, 1618)
Sermons 1607, 1608, 1619, 1620
King, John *David's strait* (with a sermon by H. King) 1625
King, John Edward & Cookson, Christopher *The principles of sound and inflexion as illustrated in the Greek and Latin languages* 1888
King, Martin Luther *The trumpet of conscience* 1968
King, Peter, 1st Baron King *An enquiry into the constitution . . and worship of the primitive church* 1691 (1712)
King, Peter, 7th Baron King *The life of J. Locke* 1829 (1830)
King, William *The art of cookery, in imitation of Horace's Art of poetry* 1708 (1807)
The art of love, in imitation of Ovid 1709
An historical account of the heathen gods and heroes 1711 (1722)
Miscellanies in prose and verse 1709
Naudé's (G.) Political considerations upon refin'd politicks tr. 1711
Poems a1712 (1790)
Remains . . containing miscellaneous pieces in verse and prose a1712 (1732)
'*M. Sorbiere's' Journey to London in 1698* 1698
The transactioneer, with some of his philosophical fancies: in two dialogues (anon.) 1700
Useful transactions in philosophy (anon.) 1709
King, Woodie ed. *Black short story anthology* 1972
King and a poor northern man, The (attrib. to Martin Parker) 1633 (Percy Soc. 1841)
King Horn See *Horn*
King of the beggars, The. The life and adventures of G. A. Brine 1883
King of Tars. The kyng of Tars; and the soudan of Dammas c1330 (Ritson, Metrical romances II)
King: see also Kyng(e
Kinglake, Alexander W. *Eothen, or traces of travel brought home from the east* (anon.) 1844
The invasion of the Crimea 1863–87 (1877–88)
Kinglake, Edward *The Australian at home. Notes and anecdotes of life at the Antipodes* 1891
Kingsford, Charles L. ed. *Chronicles of London* 1905
ed. *Life of King Henry the fifth* 1911
Kingsley, Charles *Alexandria and her schools, four lectures* 1854
Alton Locke, tailor and poet 1850
At last: a Christmas in the West Indies 1871
Glaucus, or the wonders of the shore 1855
Hereward the wake, 'last of the English' 1865
The heroes, or Greek fairy tales 1856
Hypatia, or new foes with an old face 1853
Letters and memories of his life a1875 (1877)
Miscellanies a1859 (1860)
Phaethon, or loose thoughts for loose thinkers 1852
Poems 1835–74 (1884)
Prose idylls new and old 1873
The Roman and the Teuton, a series of lectures 1864 (1875)
The saint's tragedy 1848
The tutor's story. Revised and completed by Lucas Malet (1916)
Two years ago 1857
The water of life, and other sermons 1867
The water-babies; a fairy tale 1863
Westward ho! or the voyages and adventures of Sir Amyas Leigh 1855
Yeast: a problem 1848
Kingsley, George H. *Notes on sport and travel* (1851, etc.) a1892 (1900)
South sea bubbles. By the earl (of Pembroke) and the doctor (G. H. K.) 1872
Kingsley, Henry *Austin Elliot* 1863
The grange garden, a romance 1876
The Hillyars and the Burtons 1865
Ravenshoe 1862
The recollections of Geoffrey Hamlyn 1859
Silcote of Silcotes 1867
Kingsley, John S. *Comparative anatomy of vertebrates* 1912
ed. *The standard natural history* 1885
— (reissued as) *The Riverside natural history* 1888
Kingsley, Mary H. *Travels in West Africa* 1897
Kingsley, Nelson *Diary* ed. F. J. Teggart 1914
Kingsmill or Kingesmyll, Andrew *A treatise for all such as are . . troubled in mynde or afflicted in bodie. Whereunto is adioyned a verie godly . . exhortation* (Comf. Afflict.). *Also a conference betwixt a godly learned christian and an afflicted conscience* (Confl. Satan) a1569 (1585)
A viewe of mans estate . . Whereunto is annexed a godlie advise . . touchyng mariage a1569 (1580)
Kingston, Miss Agnes D. *Verne's (J.) The steam house* II. *Tigers and traitors* tr. 1881
Kingston, William Beatty- *See* Beatty-Kingston
Kingston Whig-Standard (Kingston, Ontario) 1926–
Kington, afterwards Kington-Oliphant, Thomas L. *History of Frederick the second, emperor of the Romans* 1862
The new English 1886
The old and middle English 1878 (1891)
Kingzett, Charles T. *Animal chemistry* 1878
Kinloch, Alexander Angus Airlie *Large game shooting in Thibet and the Northwest* 2 vols. 1869–76
Kinloch, George R. *Ancient Scottish ballads* 1827
The ballad book 1827 (1868, 1885)
Kinneir, David *A new essay of the nerves, and the doctrine of the animal spirits considered* 1737
Kinross, Albert *Joan of Garioch* 1908 (1911)
Kinsey, Alfred Charles, et al. *Sexual behavior in the human female* 1953
Sexual behavior in the human male 1948
Kipling, Rudyard *Actions and reactions* 1909
Barrack-room ballads 1892
A book of words 1928
Captains courageous 1897
The city of dreadful night and other sketches 1890 (1891)
The day's work 1898
Debits and credits 1926
Departmental ditties 1886 (1899)
A diversity of creatures 1917
The five nations 1903
A fleet in being 1898
From sea to sea 2 vols. 1899 (UK 1900)
Independence 1923
ed. *The Irish Guards in the Great War* 2 vols. 1923
The jungle book 1894

KIPLING, Rudyard (*cont.*)
The second jungle book 1895
Just so stories 1902
Kim 1901
Land and sea tales 1923
Letters of travel 1920
Life's handicap 1891
The light that failed 1891 (1900)
Limits and renewals 1932
Many inventions 1893
The phantom 'rickshaw, and other tales 1888 (UK 1890, revised)
Plain tales from the hills 1888 (1890)
Puck of Pook's Hill 1906
Recessional (poem) 1897
Rewards and fairies 1910
The seven seas 1896
Soldiers three 1888 (1891)
Something of myself for my friends known and unknown 1937
Songs from books 1912 (UK 1913)
Stalky and Co. 1899
Traffics and discoveries 1904
Under the deodars 1888
Wee Willie Winkie, and other child stories 1888 (UK 1890)
The years between 1919
—— & BALESTIER, Wolcott *The Naulahka: a story of west and east* 1891
See also FLETCHER, Charles Robert Leslie
KIPPIS, Andrew *Biographia Britannica* 1778–93
—— et al. *A collection of hymns and psalms selected* 1795
KIRBY, Richard & BISHOP, J. *The marrow of astrology* 1687
KIRBY, Thomas Austin & WOOLF, H. B. *Philologica: the [Kemp] Malone anniversary studies* 1949
KIRBY, William *On the power, wisdom and goodness of God as manifested in the creation of animals and in their history, habits and instincts* (Bridgewater treatise) 1835 (1852)
—— & SPENCE, W. *An introduction to entomology* 1815–26 (1843)
KIRBY, William F. *European butterflies and moths* 1882
KIRK, John *The cloud dispelled; or the doctrine of predestination examined* 1847
KIRK, John F. *History of Charles the bold, duke of Burgundy* 1863–68
KIRK, Raymond E. & OTHMER, Donald F. eds. *Encyclopedia of chemical technology* 17 vols. 1947–60
— (ed. 2) 23 vols. 1963–71
KIRK, Raymond Maurice, MAYNARD, J. D., & HENRY, A. N. *Surgery* 1974
KIRK, Thomas *The forest flora of New Zealand* 1889
KIRKALDY, Jane W. & POLLARD, E. C. *Boas' (J. E. V.) Text book of zoology* tr. 1896
KIRKALDY, John Francis *General principles of geology* 1954
Kirkaldy of Grange 1849 *See* GRANT, James
Kirkbeck, Tales of 1848–50 *See* LEAR, Mrs. H. L.
KIRKBRIDGE, Ronald *Tamiko* 1959
KIRKBY, B. *Lakeland words, a collection of dialect words and phrases as used in Cumberland and Westmorland* 1898
KIRKBY, John *Barrow's (I.) Mathematical lectures* tr. 1734
Kirkcudbright, Minute book kept by the war committee of the covenanters in 1640–41 (1855)
'KIRKE, Edmund' (J. R. Gilmore) *The life of J. A. Garfield* 1880
My southern friends 1863
KIRKLAND, Caroline Matilda *Forest life: a tale* 2 vols. 1842
A new home—who'll follow? Or, Glimpses of western life 1839
Western clearings 1845
KIRKLAND, John *The modern baker, confectioner and caterer* 6 vols. 1907–9
KIRKMAN, Francis *The English rogue* See HEAD, R.
The famous and delectable history of Don Bellianis of Greece tr. 1671–73
The loves and adventures of Clerio and Lozia tr. 1652
The unlucky citizen.. described by F. K. 1673
KIRKPATRICK, John *History of the religious orders and communities.. of Norwich* c1725 (1845)
KIRKPATRICK, William ed. *The letters of Tippoo Sultan to various public functionaries* 1811
KIRKTON, James *The secret and true history of the church of Scotland from the restoration to.. 1678* a1699 (1817)
KIRKUP, James Harold *Japan behind the fan* 1970
The only child 1957
Tropic temper: a memoir of Malaya 1963
KIRWAN, Daniel Joseph *Palace and novel; or, Phases of London life* 1870
KIRWAN, Richard *Elements of mineralogy* 1784 (1794–96)
Geological essays 1799
KITCHIN, George W. *A history of France* 1873–77
KITCHIN, John *Jurisdictions; or the lawful authoritie of courts leet, courts baron* etc. tr. 1651 (1675)
KITCHINER, William *Apicius redivivus, the cook's oracle* 1817 (1822)
The traveller's oracle, or maxims for locomotion 1827
KITTO, John *A cyclopædia of Biblical literature* 1845 (1856)
Daily Bible illustrations 1851 (1867)
Klaproth's (H. J. von) Travels in the Caucasus and Georgia tr. F. Shoberl 1814
KLEENE, Stephen Cole *Introduction to metamathematics* 1952
Mathematical logic 1967
KLEIN, Edward E. *Micro-organisms and disease* 1884 (1885)
KLIBANSKY, Raymond ed. *Contemporary philosophy: a survey* 4 vols. 1968–71
Klopstock's (F. G.) *Messiah* tr. 1763 (1811)
Knack. A most pleasant.. comedie called A knacke to knowe a knave 1594 (Hazl. Dodsley)
KNAPP, Andrew & BALDWIN, W. *The Newgate calendar* 1824–26
Knapp's (Fr. C.) Chemical technology ed. E. Ronalds & T. Richardson 1848–51
KNAPP, John L. *The journal of a naturalist* (anon.) 1829
KNAPP, M. L. *Astronomical etiology, or an insight into coming troubles on the earth from 1881 to 1885* 1879
KNAPP, William Ireland *Life, writings and correspondence of George Barrow* 1899
Knaresborough, Yorkshire. *Wills and administrations from the Knaresborough court rolls* 1507–1661 (Surtees soc. 1902–05)
KNATCHBULL, Sir Norton *Annotations upon some difficult texts in.. the New testament* tr. 1693
KNEALE, William Calvert *Probability and induction* 1949
—— & KNEALE, Martha *The development of logic* 1962
KNECHT, Edmund, RAWSON, C., & LOEWENTHAL, R. *A manual of dyeing* 2 vols. 1893
KNEEBONE, Geoffrey Thomas *Mathematical logic and the foundation of mathematics* 1963
KNEWSTUB, John *A confutation of monstrous.. heresies taught by J. N(iclas) and embraced of.. the Familie of love* 1579
KNICKERBOCKER, William Shinkle ed. *Twentieth century English* 1946
Knickerbocker, The: or New York monthly magazine 1833–62
KNIGHT, Albert E. *The complete cricketer* 1906
'KNIGHT, Brigid' (Kathleen Henrietta Sinclair) *The covenant* 1943 (UK 1944)
Westward the sun (UK ed. with title *The sun climbs slowly*) 1942
KNIGHT, Cameron *The mechanician and constructor for engineers* 1869
KNIGHT, Charles *The English cyclopædia* 1854–70
ed. *London* 1841–44
Passages of a working life during half a century 1864–65
The popular history of England 1856–62
School history of England 1865
KNIGHT, Damon ed. *One hundred years of science fiction* 1969
KNIGHT, Miss E. Cornelia *Autobiography* a1837 (1861)
KNIGHT, Edward *The triall of truth, wherein are discovered three greate enemies vnto mankind* 1580
KNIGHT, Edward H. *The practical dictionary of mechanics* 1874–77
— Supplement 1884
KNIGHT, Henry C. ('Arthur Singleton') *Letters from the south and west* (U.S.) 1824
KNIGHT, Henry Gally *An architectural tour in Normandy* 1836
Eastern sketches 1830 (ed. 3)
Ilderim, a Syrian tale (anon.) 1816
Phrosyne, a Grecian tale, Alashtar, an Arabian tale 1817
KNIGHT, Richard Payne *An analytical inquiry into the principles of taste* 1805
An inquiry into the symbolical language of ancient art and mythology 1818 (1876)
KNIGHT, Sarah (Kemble) *The journals of Madam Knight, and Rev. Mr. Buckingham... written in 1704 & 1710* 1825
KNIGHT, Sophia *Window on Shanghai: letters from China 1965–67* 1967
KNIGHT, William A. *Memoir of John Nichol* 1896
Knight and his wife, The tale of the c1485 (Halliwell 1848)
Knight of curtesy and the fair lady of Faguell, The ?c1475 (Ritson, Metrical romances II; Hazlitt, Rem. pop. poetry II)
Knight of La Tour-Landry, The book of the a1450 (E.E.T.S. 1868, revised 1906)
Knight of the swan. The history of.. Helyas knyght of the swanne tr. c1550 (Thoms 1828)
KNOLLES, Richard *The generall history of the Turkes, together with the lives and conquests of the Othoman kings and emperours* 1603 (1621, 1638)
KNOTT, Frank Alexander *Clinical bacteriology* 1939
Knowledge: an illustrated magazine of science 1881–
KNOWLES, James *A pronouncing and explanatory dictionary of the English language* 1835
KNOWLES, James Sheridan *The rose of Arragon: a play* 1842
Virginius: a tragedy 1820
KNOWLES, Richard G., & MORTON, Richard *Baseball* 1896
KNOWLES, Robert Edward *The attic guest* 1909
KNOWLSON, John C. *The Yorkshire cattle-doctor and farrier* 1843
KNOX, Alexander *Remains* a1831 (1834–37)
Thiry years' correspondence between J. Jebb and A. K. a1831 (1834)
KNOX, Alexander *Glossary of geographical and topographical terms* 1904
KNOX, Alexander A. *The new playground; or wanderings in Algeria* 1881
KNOX, 'Bill' *See* KNOX, William
KNOX, John *Works* a1572 (Wodrow Soc. 1846–64)
A faythful admonition.. unto the professours of Gods truthe in England 1554
The first blast of the trumpet against the monstrous regiment of women 1558 (Arber)
A godly letter sent to the fayethfull 1554
The historie of the reformation a1572 (1644, 1732, 1846)
KNOX, Robert *An historical relation of the island of Ceylon* 1681
— *Nineteen years' captivity* (from the above, in Arber, Eng. Garner I)
KNOX, Robert *Béclard's (P. A.) Elements of general anatomy* tr. 1830
Cloquet's (J. H.) System of human anatomy tr. 1828 (1831)
Great artists and great anatomists 1852
KNOX, Ronald Arbuthnott *Broadcast minds* 1932
The footsteps at the lock 1928
God and the atom 1945
The hidden stream: a further collection of Oxford conferences 1952
In soft garments: a collection of Oxford conferences 1942
Still dead 1934
KNOX, Thomas W. *Overland through Asia* 1870
KNOX, Vicesimus *Essays, moral and literary* 1778–82 (1819)
Remarks on the tendency of certain clauses of a bill now pending in parliament to degrade grammar schools 1821
Winter evenings, or lucubrations on life and letters 1788
KNOX, William ('Bill') *Blacklight* 1967
Little drops of blood 1962
The tallyman 1969
KNOX-LITTLE, William J. *The broken vow* 1887
KNUTSSON, Bengt *A litil boke the whiche traytied and reherced many gode thinges necessaries for the pestilence* 1485 (1910)
KOBER, Arthur *Parm me* 1945
KOCH, Sigmund ed. *Psychology: a study of a science* 6 vols. 1959–63
KOCHMAN, Thomas ed. *Rappin' and stylin' out: communication in urban black America* 1972
KOEBEL, William Henry *In the Maoriland bush* 1911
The return of Joe, and other New Zealand stories 1907
KÖRNER, Stephan *The philosophy of mathematics* 1960
KOESTLER, Arthur *The age of longing* 1951
Arrow in the blue: an autobiography 1952
Insight and outlook: an inquiry into the common foundations of science, art and social ethics 1949
The invisible writing [2nd vol. of *Arrow in the blue*] 1954
The lotus and the robot 1960
Promise and fulfilment: Palestine 1917–1949 1949
Scum of the earth 1941
Spanish testament 1937
Thieves in the night: chronicle of an experiment 1946
The trail of the dinosaur, and other essays 1955
Twilight bar: an escapade in four acts 1945
The yogi and the commissar, and other essays 1945
—— et al. *The god that failed: six studies in communism* ed. R. H. S. Crossman 1950
Kohl's (J. G.) Russia and the Russians tr. 1842–43
Kolbe or *Kolben's (P.) Present state of the Cape of Good Hope* tr. G. Medley 1731
Koninklijke Akademie van Wetenschappen te Amsterdam. Section of Sciences *Proceedings* (Eng. ed.) 1899– (1955– with title *Proceedings of the Koninklijke Nederlandsche Akademie van Wetenschappen*)
KOPPETT, Leonard *The New York Times guide to spectator sports* 1971
KOPS, Bernard *The Hamlet of Stepney Green: a sad comedy* 1959
KOSTOV, Ivan *Mineralogy* tr. by the author, ed. P. G. Embrey & J. Phemister 1968
KRACKE, Roy Rachford & GARVER, Hortense Elton *Diseases of the blood and atlas of hematology* 1937
KRAMSCH, Dieter M. tr. *E. Grundmann's General cytology* 1966
KRANTZ, Judith *Scruples* 1978
KRAPP, George Philip *The English language in America* 2 vols. 1925
KRATOCHVÍL, Paul *The Chinese language today: features of an emerging standard* 1968
KREFFT, Gerard *The mammals of Australia* 1871
KROEBER, Alfred Louis *Anthropology* 1923
— (rev. ed.) 1948
KROGH, Schack August S. *Osmotic regulation in aquatic animals* 1939
KROHN, F. tr. *G. Glaser de Cew's Magneto- and dynamo-electric machines* ed. P. Higgs 1844
KRUEGER, Robert G., GILLHAM, N. W. & COGGIN, J. H. *Introduction to microbiology* 1973
Krummacher's (F. W.) Elisha tr. S. Jackson 1838
KUHN, Irene *Assigned to adventure* 1938
KUPER, Charles Goethe *An introduction to the theory of superconductivity* 1968
KURATH, Hans *Studies in area linguistics* 1972
A word geography of the Eastern United States 1949
KURNITZ, Harry *Invasion of privacy* 1955 (UK 1956)
Kurtz' (J. H.) History of the christian church tr. A. Edersheim 1860–64
KURZ, S. *Forest flora of British Burma* 1877
Kuzzilbash, The; a tale of Khorasan (by J. B. Fraser) 1828
KWANG-CHIH CHANG *The archaeology of ancient China* 1963
— (ed. 3) 1977
KYD, Thomas *Works* a1595 (1901)
Cornelia (a tragedy by R. Garnier) tr. 1594 (Dodsley)
— *Pompey the great, his faire Corneliaes tragedy* 1595 (Dodsley)
The Spanish tragedie 1592 (1602; Dodsley)
Tasso's (T.) Housholders philosophie tr. 1588
The trueth of the.. murthering of John Brewen 1592
See *Jeronimo; Soliman*
KYLE, Robert *Venus examines* (UK ed. with title *The love laboratory*) 1968
KYNASTON, Sir Francis *Leoline and Sydanis, a romance of the amorous adventures of princes* 1642

Kyng Alisaunder 13.. (Weber, Metrical romances; also MS. Laud Misc. 622)
Kyng Horn See *Horn*
Kynge Arthure (Copland 1557) *See* MALORY, Sir T.
KYNGESMILL *See* KINGSMILL, A.

L

L., A. *Calvin's Sermons upon the songe that Ezechias made after he had bene sicke* tr. 1560 (1574)
L., I. 1632 *See* E., T.
L., S. *Relation of two several voyages made into the East-Indies, by Chr. Fryke and Chr. Schewitzer* tr. 1700
L. S. *See* S., L.
LABARRE, Émile Joseph *A dictionary of paper and paper-making terms* 1937
Labarte's (Jules) Handbook of the arts of the middle ages tr. (by Fanny Palliser) 1855
LABELYE, Charles *A description of Westminster Bridge* 1751
A short account of the methods made use of in laying the foundation of the piers of Westminster-Bridge 1739
LA BERN, Arthur Joseph *Goodbye Piccadilly, farewell Leicester Square* 1966
Labour Commission glossary (*Glossary of the technical terms used in the evidence taken before the Royal Commission of Labour*) 1894
LABOV, William *Language in the inner city: studies in the Black English vernacular* 1972
LACEY, John *Tacquett's (A.) Military architecture, or the art of fortifying towns* tr. 1672 (Book II of T. Venn's Military and maritime discipline)
LACH-SZYRMA, Wladyslaw S. *Aleriel; or, a voyage to other worlds* 1883
LACKINGTON, James *Memoirs of the first forty-five years of the life of J. L.* Written by himself, in a series of letters to a friend 1791
'LACKLAND, Thomas' (George Canning Hill) *Homespun; or, Five-and-twenty years ago* 1867
Lacroix's (S. F.) Elementary treatise on the differential and integral calculus tr. 1816
LACY, Ed *Double trouble* 1965
The freeloaders 1962
LACY, John *Wyl Bucke his testament* c1550 (Halliwell 1851)
LACY, John *Sauny the Scott: or, the taming of the shrew* a1667 (1698)
LADD, George T. *Elements of physiological psychology* 1887
Introduction to philosophy 1891
Outlines of physiological psychology 1891
Philosophy of knowledge 1897
A theory of reality 1899
Ladies calling, The. By the author of The whole duty of man 1673
Ladies dictionary, The, being a general entertainment for the fair-sex (By N. H.) 1694
Ladies' field, The 1896–1928
Ladies' home journal 1883–
Ladies' repository 1841–76
Lady Alimony, or the alimony lady 1659 (in Hazl., Dodsley)
Lady's magazine, The 1770–1818
Lady's tale, The 1786
Lady's travels into Spain 1692 *See* ANOIS, Countess d'
LAFFAN, May *See* HARTLEY, Mrs. May
LAFITTE, Paul *The person in psychology: reality or abstraction* 1957
Lafontaine's (A. H. J.) Hermann and Emilia tr. 1805
See also *Reprobate*
La Framboisière's (N. A. de) Art of physick made plain and easie (title-p. erron. has Fambresarius) tr. by J. P(hillips) 1684
LAGLER, Karl F., BARDACH, J. E., & MILLER, R. R. *Ichthyology* 1962
LAGOWSKI, Joseph John *Modern inorganic chemistry* 1973
Lagrange's (J. B. B.) Manual of a course of chemistry tr. 1800
LAHEE, Frederic Henry *Field geology* 1916
Lai le Freine c1325 (in Weber, Metrical romances I. 1810)
'LAICK, William' (George Redpath) *An answer to the Scots Presbyterian eloquence* 1693
LAIDLER, F. F. ed. *A glossary in English, French, German, Spanish of terms used in home economics education* 1963
Laing charters, Calendar of the, A.D. 854–1837, belonging to the University of Edinburgh v.d. (ed. by John Anderson 1899)
LAING, Alexander *Lindores Abbey and its burgh of Newburgh, their history and annals* 1876
The thistle of Scotland; a selection of ancient ballads 1823
LAING, David ed. *Early metrical tales* v.d. (1826)
ed. *Select remains of the ancient popular poetry of Scotland* v.d. (1822, 1885, 1895)
LAING, Samuel *Journal of a residence in Norway* 1836
LAING, Samuel & HUXLEY, Thomas H. *Pre-historic remains of Caithness; with notes on the human remains by T. H. Huxley* 1866
LAKE, Elleray *Longleat* 1870
LAKE, Philip & RASTALL, Robert Heron *A textbook of geology* 1910
LAKE, William C. *Memorials* a1894 (ed. by his widow Kath. Lake 1901)
Lakeland glossary 1895 *See* ELLWOOD, T.
LAKEMAN, Sir Stephen B. *What I saw in Kaffir-land* 1880
La Martelière's (J. H. F.) Three Gil Blas, or follies of youth tr. 1804
Lamartine's (A. de) Memoirs of celebrated characters tr. 1854–56
Travels in the East, including a journey in the Holy Land tr. 1839
LAMB, Charles *Complete correspondence and works* a1834 (1868–70)
Complete works a1834 (1892)
The adventures of Ulysses 1808
Elia. Essays which have appeared under that signature in the London Magazine (First series) v.d. (1823)
The last essays of Elia v.d. (1833)
Eliana: being the hitherto uncollected writings of C. Lamb a1834 (1866)
Letters a1834 (1837, 1886, 1888)
Recollections of Christ's Hospital 1813
Final memorials; consisting chiefly of his letters not before published. By T. N. Talfourd (1848)
—— & Mary *Letters* ed. E. V. Lucas 3 vols. 1935
—— —— *Tales from Shakespear* 1807
LAMB, Lynton *Man in a mist* 1974
Picture frame 1972
LAMB, Patrick *Royal cookery* 1710
LAMB, Sydney M. *Outline of stratificational grammar* 1966
LAMB, Warren *Posture and gesture: an introduction to the study of physical behaviour* 1965
LAMBARDE, William *'Αρχαιονομία, siue de priscis anglorum legibus libri (Anglo-Sax. and Lat.)* 1568 (1644)
Archion; or a commentary upon the High Courts of Justice in England 1591 (1635)
Eirenarcha: or the office of the Justices of Peace 1581–88
A perambulation of Kent; conteining the description, hystorie, and customes of that shyre 1576 (1596, 1826)
LAMBE, Robert *The history of chess, together with short and plain instructions* (anon.) 1765
LAMBERT, Aylmer B. *A description of the genus Pinus* 1803–24
LAMBERT, Constant *Music ho!* 1934
LAMBERT, G. *Gold and silversmith's art* 1892
LAMBERT, John C. *The sacraments in the New Testament* 1903
LAMBERT, Richard Stanton *Ariel and all his quality* 1940
Lambeth homilies c1175 (in O.E. homilies, I, E.E.T.S. 1868)
Lambeth Psalter c1000 (ed. Lindelöf 1909)
Lamentacion of souls 13.. (in Adam Davy, etc., E.E.T.S. 1878)
Lamentatyon of Mary Magdaleyne c1475 (in Chaucer's Wks., ed. Thynne 1532)
'LA MERI' (Russell Meriwether Hughes) *Spanish dancing* 1948
—(ed. 2) 1967
LAMONT, James *Seasons with the sea-horses* 1861
LAMONT, John *The chronicle of Fife; being the diary of J. Lamont* 1649–72 (1810)
Lancashire. Tracts relating to military proceedings in Lancashire during the civil war 1641–51 (Chetham Soc. 1844)
Lancashire and Cheshire wills and inventories from the ecclesiastical court, Chester 1525–1807 (Chetham Soc. 1857–97)
Lancashire Dialect Society *Journal* 1951–
Lancashire lieutenancy under the Tudors and Stuarts 15.. (Chetham Soc. 1859)
Lancashire life 1947–
Lancashire's Valley of Achor 1643 *See* ANGIER, John
Lancaster, Pleadings and depositions in the Duchy Court of 15.. (1896–99)
'LANCASTER, G. B.' (Edith Joan Lyttleton) *Jim of the ranges* 1910
Sons o' men 1904
LANCASTER, Osbert *Homes sweet homes* 1939
LANCASTER, W. J. C. *See* 'COLLINGWOOD, Harry'
Lancaster, Massachusetts *Early records 1643–1725* ed. H. S. Nourse 1884
LANCE, Edward J. *Cottage farmer* c1842
Lancelot of the laik c1500 (E.E.T.S. 1865; S.T.S. 1912)
Lancet, The 1828–
Land of Cokaygne c1305 (in Early Eng. poems, Philol. Soc. 1862)
LANDAU, Thomas ed. *Encyclopaedia of librarianship* 1958
—(ed. 2) 1961
LANDEN, John *A discourse concerning the residual analysis* 1758
Mathematical lucubrations 1755
Observations on converging series 1781
LANDER, Richard & John *Journal of an expedition to explore the course and termination of the Niger* 1832
Landfall: a New Zealand quarterly 1947–
Landois' (L.) Text-book of human physiology tr. with additions by W. Stirling 1885
LANDON, Letitia E. *Poetical works* a1838 (1845)
LANDOR, Walter S. *Works* 1846, 1853, a1864 (1876)
Andrea of Hungary, and Giovanna of Naples 1839
Citation and examination of William Shakspeare 1834
Gebir; a poem 1798
Hellenics 1846 (in Works vol. I); enlarged and completed 1847; republished with alterations in 1859
Imaginary conversations of literary men and statesmen 1824–29 (also Works 1846)
Imaginary conversation of King Carlo-Alberto and the Duchess Belgioioso 1848
Imaginary conversations of Greeks and Romans 1853
Letters of an American 1854
The pentameron and pentalogia 1837
Pericles and Aspasia 1836
Popery, British and foreign 1851
A satire on satirists, and admonition to detractors 1836
LANDSBOROUGH, David *A popular history of British seaweeds* 1849
A popular history of British zoophytes or corallines 1852
LANDY, Eugene E. *The underground dictionary* 1971
LANE, Arthur *Greek pottery* 1948
LANE, Edward W. *An account of the manners and customs of the modern Egyptians* 1836 (1849)
Selections from the Kur-án 1843 (1878)
The thousand and one nights. A new translation from the Arabic 1839–41
LANE, Hugh *Differentiation in rheumatic diseases* 1890
LANE, John *Continuation of Chaucer's Squire's tale* 1616 (Chaucer Soc. 1887–90)
Tom Tel Troth's message, and his pen's complaint 1600 (New Shaks. Soc. 1876)
'LANE, Linacre' *The ABZ of Scouse: how to talk proper in Liverpool, Vol. 2* ed. F. Spiegel 1966 (For Vol. 1 *see* SHAW, Frank, et al.)
LANEHAM, Robert *A letter: whearin, part of the entertainment vntoo the Queenz Maiesty, at Killingwoorth Castl,..is signified* 1575 (Ballad Soc. 1871; Shakespeare Libr. 1907)
LANE-POOLE, Stanley *The Barbary corsairs* 1890
ed. *Coins and medals, their place in history and art, by the authors of the British Museum official catalogues* 1885
Lanercost, Chronicon de 1201–1346 (Maitl. and Bann. Clubs 1839)
Lanfrank's Science of cirurgie tr. c1400 (E.E.T.S. 1894)
LANG, Andrew ed. *Ballads of books* 1888
Custom and myth 1884
A history of Scotland from the Roman occupation 1900–07
Letters to dead authors 1886
The library 1881
The making of religion 1898
The mark of Cain 1886
A monk of Fife 1896
Myth, ritual, and religion 1887
See also BUTCHER, S. H.
—— & LEAF, Walter, & MYERS, Ernest *The Iliad of Homer* done into English prose 1883
Lang's (A.) Text-book of comparative anatomy tr. by H. M. & M. Bernard 1891–96
LANG, John *Wanderings in India* 1859
LANG, John D. *An historical and statistical account of New South Wales* 1834
—ed. 2. 1837; ed. 3. 1852; ed. 4. 1874
LANG, R. F. tr. *F. A. Henglein's Chemical technology* 1969
LANGBAINE, Gerard *An account of the English dramatick poets* 1691
LANGBRIDGE, Rosamond *The flame and the floop* 1903
LANGFORD, Michael John *Basic photography* 1965
LANGFORD, R. *An introduction to trade and business* 1809
LANGFORD-SMITH, Fritz *Radio designer's handbook* 1940
—(ed. 4) 1953
LANGHAM, William *The garden of health* 1579 (1633)
LANGHORNE, John *Poems* a1779 (1790)
The country justice: a poem 1774–77
The fables of Flora 1771
Owen of Carron: a poem 1778
—— & William *Plutarch's Lives* tr. 1770 (1879)
LANGILLE, J. Hibbert *Our birds in their haunts* 1884
LANGLAND, William *The vision of William concerning Piers Plowman.* A. text 1362; B. text 1377; C. text 1393; (together with) *Richard the redeles* 1399 (ed. Skeat; E.E.T.S. 1867–85; 1886)
LANGLEY, Batty *Ancient masonry* 1736
The London prices of bricklayer's materials and works justly ascertained 1748
LANGLEY, Thomas *An abridgement of the notable woorke of Polidore Vergile conteignyng the deuisers and firste fynders out aswell of artes, ministeries, feactes, and ciuill ordinaunces, as of rites and ceremonies, commonly used in the churche* (transl. of *De inventoribus rerum*) 1546
Langsdorff's (G. H. von) Voyages and travels in various parts of the world 1803–07 1813–14
Langtoft, Peter See BRUNNE, Robert Manning of
LANGTON, Mary Beach *How to know oriental rugs: a handbook* 1904
Language: journal of the Linguistic Society of America 1925–
Language learning 1948–
LANGWORTHY, Charles C. *A view of Perkinean electricity* 1798
LANHAM, Peter *Blanket boy's moon* (based on an original story by A. S. Mopeli-Paulus) 1953
LANIER, Sidney *The English novel, and the principle of its development* a1881 (1883)
Poems 1877 (1892)
The science of English verse 1880 (1909)
LANKESTER, E. Ray *The advancement of science: occasional essays and addresses* v.d. (1890)
Degeneration; a chapter in Darwinism 1880
Diversions of a naturalist 1915
Observations and reflections on the appendages and on the nervous system of apus cancriformis 1881
ed. *A treatise on zoology* 1900–09
Zoological articles contributed to the Encyclopædia Britannica v.d. (1891)
See also HAECKEL, E. H. P. A.
LANMAN, Charles *Letters from the Alleghany Mountains* 1849
A summer in the wilderness; embracing a canoe voyage up the Mississippi and around Lake Superior 1847

LANSDELL, Henry *Through Siberia* 1882
LANSDOWNE, George Granville, Baron *The British enchanters* 1706
Genuine works in verse and prose 1732
Peleus and Thetis a1735 (1781)
Poems upon several occasions 1712 (1732)
Lantern: politics, amusement, literature (New Orleans) 1886–9
Lanterne of liȝt, The c1410 (E.E.T.S. 1917)
Lapland, A spring and summer in (By H. W. Wheelwright) 1864
La Primaudaye's French academie tr. *See* B., T. & DOLMAN, R.
LAQUEUR, Walter ed. *A dictionary of politics* 1971
LARCOM, Lucy *A New England girlhood* 1889
LARDNER, Dionysius *The cabinet cyclopædia, conducted by D. Lardner* 1830–49
Hand-book of natural philosophy and astronomy; first course 1851; second course 1852; third course 1853
— *Mechanics* 1855; *Hydrostatics, pneumatics, and heat* 1855; *Optics* 1856; *Electricity, magnetism, and acoustics* 1856
Pneumatics 1831
Treatise on geometry 1840
LARDNER, Nathaniel *Works* a1768 (1788, 1838)
The credibility of the gospel history 1727–55
LARDNER, Ringgold Wilmer *Gullible's travels* 1917 (UK 1926)
LARKIN, Philip Arthur *Jill* 1946
The less deceived 1955
The north ship 1945
LARMOR, Joseph *Æther and matter* 1900
LARSELL, Olof *Anatomy of the nervous system* 1942
— (ed. 2) 1951
LARWOOD, Jacob & HOTTEN, John C. *The history of signboards, from the earliest times to the present day* 1867
LARWOOD, Joshua *No gun boats, or no peace!* 1804
La Serre's (J. P. de la) Mirrour which flatters not tr. by T. C(ary) 1639
LASKI, Audrey Louise *The keeper* 1968
Seven other years 1967
LASKI, Harold Joseph *Holmes-Laski letters*
See HOLMES, Oliver Wendell
LASKI, Marghanita *Little boy lost* 1949
Love on the supertax 1944
Tory heaven; or, Thunder on the right 1948
The village 1952
See also 'RUSSELL, Sarah'
LASKY, Melvin J. *Utopia and revolution* 1976 (UK 1977)
LASLETT, Thomas *Timber and timber trees* 1875
LASLETT, Thomas Peter R. ed. *Household and family in past time* 1972
LASSELS, Richard *The voyage of Italy* a1668 (1670, 1698)
Last of the old squires, The 1854 *See* WARTER, J. W.
Late voyage of Spaine and Portingale 1589 See *True coppie*
LATHAM, Henry *Black and white; a journal of a three months' tour in the United States* 1867
LATHAM, John *A general history of birds* 1821–28
A general synopsis of birds 1781–85
— 1st suppl. 1787; and suppl. 1801
Index ornithologicus sive systema ornithologiæ 1790
LATHAM, Peter M. *Lectures on subjects connected with clinical medicine* 1836, 1845–46
LATHAM, Robert G. *A dictionary of the English language.* Founded on that of S. Johnson as ed. by H. J. Todd 1866–70
Elements of comparative philology 1862
The English language 1841
A hand-book of the English language 1851
The native races of the Russian empire 1854
The natural history of the varieties of man 1850
See also ANSTED, D. T.
LATHAM, Simon *Falconry* 1614; *new and second booke of falconrie* 1618 (1633)
LATHBURY, Thomas *A history of the nonjurors* 1845
'LATHEN, Emma' (Mary Jane Latsis & Martha Henissart) *Accounting for murder* 1964 (UK 1965)
Banking on death 1961 (UK 1962)
By hook or by crook 1975
Come to dust 1968 (UK 1969)
The longer the thread 1971 (UK 1972)
Murder without icing 1972 (UK 1973)
Pick up sticks 1970 (UK 1971)
Sweet and low 1974
When in Greece 1969
See also 'DOMINIC, R. B.'
LATHROP, George P. *Spanish vistas* 1883
True, and other stories 1884
LATIMER, Hugh *Sermons and remains* a1555 (Parker Soc. 1844–45)
Twenty seuen sermons a1555 (1562)
Frutefull sermons a1555 (1571, 1584, 1607)
The fyrste (-seuenth) sermon preached before the kynges maiestie 1549 (Arber 1869)
A moste faithfull sermon preached before the kynges most excellent maiestye 1550
A notable sermon preached in yᵉ shroudes at paules churche 1548
The sermon made to the clergie, in the conuocation tr. 1537
Sermon on the ploughers 1548 (Arber 1868)
A sermon preached at Stamford 1550
Seuen sermons made upon the Lordes Prayer 1552 (1572)
LATROBE, Benjamin H. *Journal* 1796–1820 (1905)

LATTO, W. D. *Tammas Bodkin: or, the humours of a Scottish tailor* (anon.) 1864
Tammas Bodkin. Swatches o' hodden-grey 1894
'LAUCHMONEN' *Old Thom's harvest* 1965
LAUD, Abp. William *Works* a1645 (1847–60)
The history of his troubles and tryal written by himself, with the diary of his life (vol. I of 'Remains') a1645 (1695)
— *the second volume of his remains, written by himself,* collected by H. Wharton a1645 (1700)
Seven sermons preached on several occasions a1645 (1651)
A speech delivered in the Starr-Chamber the xivth of June 1637
Laud Troy book c1400 (E.E.T.S. 1902–03)
LAUDER, Sir John *See* FOUNTAINHALL, Lord
LAUDER, William *Minor poems* a1573 (E.E.T.S. 1870)
Ane compendious and breue tractate concernyng ye office and dewtie of kyngis 1556 (E.E.T.S. 1864)
LAUDERDALE, James Maitland, 8th Earl of *An inquiry into the nature and origin of public wealth* 1804 (1819)
LAUDERDALE, John *A collection of poems chiefly in the Scottish dialect* 1796
Lauderdale papers, The 1639–79 (Camden Soc. 1884–85)
Launfal c1400 *See* CHESTRE, T.
Laura and Augustus; an authentic story, in a series of letters 1784
LAURENCE, Abp. Richard *An attempt to illustrate those Articles of the Church of England, which the Calvinists improperly consider as Calvinistical* (Bampton lectures 1804) 1805
LAURIE, Joseph *Homoeopathic domestic medicine* 1842
— ed. 2, containing a glossary of medical terms 1844
LAURIE, Peter *Scotland Yard: a personal inquiry* 1970
LAUSON, William *J. D(enny)'s Secrets of angling* c1620 (1652; Arber, Eng. Garner I)
LAVAL, Étienne A. *A compendious history of the Reformation in France* 1737–43
Lavardin's (J. de) Historie of George Castriot, surnamed Scanderbeg, king of Albanie tr. by Z. I. 1596
LAVENDER, Theophilus *See* BIDDULPH, W.
LAVER, James *Taste and fashion, from the French Revolution until to-day* 1937
Victoriana 1966
LAVINGTON, Bp. George *The enthusiasm of Methodists and Papists compared* 1749–51 (1754)
The Moravians compared and detected (anon.) 1755
LAW, Edmund *Considerations on the state of the world with regard to the theory of religion* 1745
LAW, Ernest *The history of Hampton Court Palace in Tudor times* 1885
LAW, Henry *The beacons of the Bible. A series of (12) tracts* 1861
— *A series of (24) tracts* 1868
LAW, James Thomas *Law's Grocer's manual* 1896
LAW, John *Proposals* 1701 *See* PATERSON, W.
LAW, Robert *Memorialls; or, the memorable things that fell out within this island of Britain from 1638 to 1684* a1690 (Ed. from the MS. by C. K. Sharpe 1818)
LAW, Robert *The tests of life, a study of the first epistle of St. John* 1909
LAW, William *Works* a1761 (1762)
Comfort for the weary pilgrim; by a guiding to the fountain springs of all our mercies: being extracts from some of the works of W. Law a1761 (1809)
A demonstration of the errors of a late book (by Bp. Hoadly), called A plain account of the nature and end of the sacrament of the Lord's Supper 1737 (1769)
An earnest and serious answer to Dr. Trapp's discourse of the folly, sin, and danger of being righteous overmuch 1740
A practical treatise upon Christian perfection 1726
A serious call to a devout and holy life 1729 (1732)
The works of Jacob Behmen. With figures, illustrating his principles by W. Law a1761 (1764–81)
Law reports (Chancery division, Probate division, Queen's Bench division, etc.) 1883–
Law times, The 1882–
Law times reports, The 1883–
LAWES, Henry *Ayres and dialogues* 1653
LAWLESS, Emily *Grania; the story of an island* 1892
Maelcho. A sixteenth century narrative 1894
LAWRENCE, David Herbert *Aaron's rod* 1922
Apocalypse 1931 (UK 1932)
Birds, beasts and flowers: poems 1923
Collected letters ed H. T. Moore 2 vols. 1962
A collier's Friday night 1934
David: a play 1926
England, my England, and other stories 1922 (UK 1924)
Etruscan places 1932
Fantasia of the unconscious 1922
Kangaroo 1923
Lady Chatterley's lover 1928
Last poems ed. R. Aldington & G. Orioli 1932
Letters ed. A. Huxley 1932 (See also *Collected letters*)
Look! We have come through! 1917
The lost girl 1920
Love among the haystacks, and other pieces 1930
Love poems and others 1913
The lovely lady 1933 (dated 1932)
A modern lover 1934
Mornings in Mexico 1927
Nettles 1930
New poems 1918
Pansies: poems 1929
Phoenix: posthumous papers ed. E. D. McDonald 1936
Phoenix II: uncollected, unpublished and other prose works ed. F. W. Roberts & H. T. Moore 1968

The plumed serpent (Quetzalcoatl) 1926
Psychoanalysis and the unconscious 1921
The rainbow 1915
Reflections on the death of a porcupine, and other essays 1925
St. Mawr, together with the princess 1925
Sea and Sardinia 1921
Sons and lovers 1913
Studies in classic American literature 1923
Touch and go: a play 1920
The virgin and the gipsy 1930
The white peacock 1911
The widowing of Mrs. Holroyd: a drama 1914
The woman who rode away, and other stories 1928
Women in love 1920 (UK 1921)
—— & SKINNER, Mary Louis *The boy in the bush* 1924
LAWRENCE, George A. *Anteros* 1871
Barren honour 1862
Border and bastille 1863
Guy Livingstone; or, thorough 1857
Sword and gown 1859
LAWRENCE, George H. M. *Taxonomy of vascular plants* 1951
LAWRENCE, Henry *Of our communion and warre with angells* 1646
Some considerations tending to the asserting and vindicating of the use of the Holy Scriptures and Christian ordinances 1649
LAWRENCE, John ('Bonington Moubray') *A general treatise on cattle, the ox, the sheep, and the swine* 1805 (1809)
A philosophical and practical treatise on horses 1796–98
A practical treatise on breeding, rearing, and fattening all kinds of domestic poultry 1813 (1842)
LAWRENCE, Philip H. *Cotta's (B. von) Rocks classified and described* tr. 1866 (1878)
LAWRENCE, Sir Thomas *Life and correspondence* a1830 (1831)
LAWRENCE, Thomas Edward *The home letters of T. E. Lawrence and his brothers* ed. M. R. Lawrence 1954
Letters ed. D. Garnett 1938
The mint: notes made in the R.A.F. Depot between August and December 1922, and at Cadet College in 1925 by 352087 A/C Ross 1936 (UK, rev. 1955)
Seven pillars of wisdom: a triumph 1926
— (trade ed.) 1935
LAWRENCE, William *Lectures on physiology, zoology, and the natural history of man* 1819
— ed. 9, entitled *Lectures on comparative anatomy* etc. 1848
LAWRENCE, William Witherle *Beowulf and epic tradition* 1928
LAWS, Edward *The history of Little England beyond Wales* 1888
Laws of Alfred, etc. See *Anglo-Saxon Laws*
Laws of Nevis (Acts of Assembly, passed in the island of Nevis) 1664–1739 (1740)
LAWSON, George *Sermons* 1810
LAWSON, George *Diseases and injuries of the eye* 1869 (1874)
LAWSON, Henry *On the track* 1900
Over the sliprails 1900
Stories ed. C. Mann 3 ser. 1964
Verses, popular and humorous 1900
LAWSON, John *The history of Carolina* a1712 (1714, 1718)
LAWSON, John P. *The Book of Perth* 1847
LAWSON, Peter & Charles *The Lawsonian Collection. Synopsis of the vegetable products of Scotland in the Museum of the Royal Botanic Gardens of Kew* 1852
LAWSON, Robert *Upton-on-Severn words and phrases* 1884 (E.D.S.)
LAWSON, Robert William tr. *G. von Hevesy & F. A. Paneth's A manual of radioactivity* 1926
— (ed. 2) 1938
tr. *A. Einstein's Relativity: the special and the general theory: a popular exposition* 1920
LAWSON, T. *Woollen yarn production* 1924
LAWSON, Thomas *A mite into the treasury* 1680
LAWSON, William *A new orchard and garden* 1618 (1648, 1668)
See also LAUSON, W.
Lay folks' catechism, or the English and Latin versions of Archbishop Thoresby's Instruction for the people 1357 (E.E.T.S. 1901)
Lay folks mass book a1375, a1450 (E.E.T.S. 1879)
Laȝamon's Brut, or Chronicle of Britain c1205, c1275 (Society of Antiquaries, London, 1847)
LAYARD, Arthur *The alphabet of musical bogeys* 1899
LAYARD, Sir Austen H. *Discoveries in the ruins of Nineveh and Babylon* 1853
Nineveh and its remains 1849
A popular account of discoveries at Nineveh 1851
LAYARD, Edgar L. *The birds of South Africa: a descriptive catalogue* 1867
LAYARD, George S. *The life and letters of Charles S. Keene* 1892
Lays and legends of the north of Ireland 1884
LEA, M. Carey *A manual of photography* 1868
LEACH, Arthur F. ed. *Memorials of Beverley minster: the Chapter act book of the collegiate church of S. John of Beverley* 1286–1347 (Surtees Soc. 1898, 1903)
LEACH, Bernard *A potter in Japan 1952–1954* 1960
LEACH, Edmund Ronald *Lévi-Strauss* 1970
LEACH, John Albert *An Australian bird book* 1911
LEACOCK, Stephen Butler *Over the footlights, and other fancies* 1923
LEADAM, Isaac S. ed. *Select cases before the king's council in the Star Chamber, commonly called the Court of Star Chamber* 1477–1544 (Selden Soc. 1903–11)

ed. *Select cases in the Court of Requests* 1497–1569 (Selden Soc. 1898)
LEADBEATER, Mary *The Leadbeater papers*. Vol. I. *Annals of Ballitore*; vol. II. *Correspondence* a1826 (1862)
LEADBETTER, Charles *The royal gauger* 1739 (1766)
LEAF, Walter *See* LANG, Andrew
LEAK, John *Caus' (I. de) New and rare invention of waterworks* tr. 1659
LEAKE, Stephen M. *Nummi Britannici historia; or, an historical account of English money from the Conquest* 1726
LEAKEY, Louis Seymour Bazett *The Stone Age cultures of Kenya Colony* 1931
LEAR, Edward (1812–88) *Indian journal* ed. R. Murphy 1953
Laughable lyrics 1877
LEAR, Mrs. Henrietta L. *Tales of Kirkbeck; or, the parish in the Fells* 1848–50
LEARMONT, John *Poems, pastoral, satirical, tragic, and comic* 1791
Learning at a loss 1778
LEASOR, Thomas James *A host of extras* 1973
They don't make them like that any more 1969
Leather: a discourse tendered to the High Court of Parliament, of the generall use of leather 1629 (in Arber, Eng. Garner VI)
LEATHER, George *A further report on the Stockton and Auckland canal* 1818
LEAVIS, Frank Raymond *The great tradition: George Eliot, Henry James, Joseph Conrad* 1948
—— & THOMPSON, Arthur Denys H. *Culture and environment: the training of critical awareness* 1933
LEAVIS, Queenie Dorothy *Fiction and the reading public* 1932
Leben Jesu c1300 (Horstmann 1873)
Lebende Sprachen 1956–
Le Blanc's (J. B.) Letters on the English and French nations tr. 1747
LEBOUR, G. A. *Outlines of the geology of Northumberland and Durham* 1886 (ed. 2)
Lebrun See *Pigault-Lebrun, G. C. A.*
'LE CARRÉ, John' (David John M. Cornwell) *The honourable schoolboy* 1977
The looking-glass war 1965
A murder of quality 1962
A small town in Germany 1968
Smiley's people 1979 (UK 1980)
The spy who came in from the cold 1963
Tinker tailor soldier spy 1974
LECKY, William E. H. *A history of England in the eighteenth century* 1878–90
History of European morals from Augustus to Charlemagne 1869
History of the rise and influence of the spirit of rationalism in Europe 1865
The map of life, conduct and character 1899
Le Clerc's (Jean) Five letters concerning the inspiration of the Holy Scriptures tr. 1690
Lives of the primitive fathers tr. 1701
The memoirs of Emeric Count Teckely tr. 1693
Le Comte's (L.) Memoirs and observations made in a late journey through the empire of China tr. 1697
— *A new translation* 1737
LE CONTE, Joseph *Elements of geology* 1878 (1879)
Religion and science. A series of Sunday lectures on the relation of natural and revealed religion 1874
Sight: an exposition of the principles of monocular and binocular vision 1881
LEDIARD, Thomas *The life of John, Duke of Marlborough* 1736
The life of Sethos tr. 1732
LEDWICH, Edward *Antiquitates Sarisburienses; or, the history and antiquities of old and new Sarum* 1771
LEE, Francis 1718 *See* HICKES, G. & NELSON, R.
LEE, Frederick G. *The Church under Queen Elizabeth* 1880
Dictionary of ritual and other ecclesiastical terms 1871
The Directorium Anglicanum 1865
A glossary of liturgical and ecclesiastical terms 1876
Reginald Barentyne, or, Liberty without limit 1881
LEE, Harper *To kill a mockingbird* 1960
LEE, Harriet *See* LEE, Sophia
'LEE, Holme' (Harriet Parr) *Annie Warleigh's fortunes* 1863
Basil Godfrey's caprice 1868
Loving and serving 1883
LEE, James *An introduction to botany* 1760 (1776, 1788)
LEE, John D. *The ninth man* 1976
LEE, John Alexander *Children of the poor* 1934
Civilian into soldier 1937
LEE, Julius & KNOWLES, Francis *Animal hormones* 1965
LEE, Laurie *Cider with Rosie* 1959
LEE, Nathaniel *Dramatick works* a1692 (1733–34)
Cæsar Borgia, son of Pope Alexander the Sixth 1680
Constantine the Great 1684
Mithridates, King of Pontus 1678
Sophonisba, or Hannibal's overthrow 1676
The tragedy of Nero 1675
See also DRYDEN, J.
LEE, Rawdon B. *A history and description of the modern dogs of Great Britain and Ireland* 3 parts 1893–4
LEE, Reuben *Electronic transformers and circuits* 1947
LEE, Samuel *A grammar of the Hebrew language* 1827 (1832)
See also KENDALL, Thomas
LEE, Sophia & Harriet *Canterbury tales* 1797–1801
'LEE, Vernon' (Violet Paget) *Belcaro: being essays on sundry æsthetical questions* 1883
Euphorion: being studies of the Antique and the Mediæval in the Renaissance 1884
Studies of the eighteenth century in Italy 1880
LEE-WARNER, Sir William *Memoirs of Sir Henry Wylie Norman* 1908
LEECH, Geoffrey N. *English in advertising* 1966
Leechdoms, wortcunning, and starcraft of Early England c1000 (ed. Cockayne, Rolls series 1864–66)
LEEDS, Herbert Daniel & WEINBERG, Gerald Marvin *Computer programming fundamentals* 1961
LEES, Dan *The rainbow conspiracy* 1971
Rape of a quiet town 1973
Zodiac 1972
LEES, Frederic A. *The flora of West Yorkshire* 1888
LEES, J. A., & CLUTTERBUCK, Walter J. *B.C. 1887. A ramble in British Columbia* 1888
Three in Norway (anon.) 1882
LEES, William *Elements of acoustics, light, and heat* 1873
LEES-MILNE, James *Ancestral voices* 1975
LEESON, Charles Roland & LEESON, Thomas Sydney *Histology* 1966
— (ed. 2) 1970
LE FANU, Joseph S. *The dragon volant* a1873 (1907)
The fortunes of colonel Torlogh O'Brien 1847
Guy Deverell 1865
Uncle Silas: a tale of Bartram-Haugh 1864
Willing to die a1873
LE FEVRE, Sir George W. *The life of a travelling physician* 1843
LEFF, Gordon A. *History and social theory* 1969
LEFROY, Edward C. *Echoes from Theocritus, and other sonnets* 1885
LEFSCHETZ, Solomon *Introduction to topology* 1949
LE GALLIENNE, Richard *George Meredith, some characteristics* 1890
LEGARÉ, Hugh S. *Writings* a1843 (1846)
Legend of the Bischop of St. Androis 1583 (in Scot. poems of 16th c., 1801; Sempill ballates, 1872; Satirical poems of Reformation, S.T.S. 1891)
Legend of St. Gregory c1300 (ed. Schulz 1876)
Legend of St. Katherine See *Katherine, St.*
Legendae Catholicae. A lytle boke of seyntlie gestes (Pope Gregory, St. Margaret, Joachim and Anne, St. Katherine, Mary Magdalen) c1350 (Turnbull 1840)
Legends of the Holy Rood 11..–14.. (E.E.T.S. 1871)
Legends of the saints in the Scottish dialect of the fourteenth century c1375 (S.T.S. 1896)
LEGG, J. Wickham *On the bile, jaundice, and bilious diseases* 1880
A treatise on hæmophilia 1872
See also HOPE, W. H. St. John
LEGGE, James *The life and teachings of Confucius* 1867 (1877)
LEGH, Gerard *The accedens of armory* 1562 (1568, 1576, 1597)
LEGMAN, Gershon *The fake revolt* 1967
'LEGRAND, Martin' *The Cambridge freshman; or, Memoirs of Mr. Golightly* 1871
LE GRYS, Sir Robert *J. Barclay his Argenis* tr... the prose by Sir R. Le Grys, and the verses by T. May 1628 (1629)
Velleius Paterculus, his Romane historie tr. 1632
LEHMANN, Rosamond Nina *The ballad and the source* 1944
Dusty answer 1927
The echoing grove 1953
The gipsy's baby, and other stories 1946
Invitation to the waltz 1932
A letter to a sister 1931
A note in music 1930
The weather in the streets 1936
LEHMANN, Rudolph C. *Charles Dickens as editor; being letters written by him to W. H. Wills*, selected and ed. by R. C. Lehmann 1912
LEICESTER, Robert Dudley, Earl of *Correspondence* 1585–86 (Camden Soc. 1844)
The copie of a letter wryten by a Master of Arte of Cambridge to his friend in London, concerning some procedinges of the Earle of Leycester 1584
— (reissue) *Leycesters Commonwealth* (1641)
LEICESTER, Sir Peter *See* LEYCESTER, Sir P.
LEICHHARDT, Ludwig *Journal of an overland expedition in Australia* 1847
Leiden glossary a900 (Oldest Eng. Texts, E.E.T.S. 1885; Hessels 1906)
LEIFCHILD, John R. *Cornwall: its mines and miners* 1855
LEIGH, Charles *The natural history of Lancashire, Cheshire and the Peak in Derbyshire* 1700
LEIGH, Edward *Critica sacra* 1639–41 (1650)
LEIGH, Egerton *Ballads and legends of Cheshire* 1867
A glossary of words used in the dialect of Cheshire 1877
LEIGH, Gerard *See* LEGH, Gerard
LEIGH, Richard *The transproser rehears'd* (anon.) 1673
LEIGH, Valentine *The moste profitable and commendable science of surueying of landes, tenementes, and hereditamentes* 1577
LEIGHTON, Alexander *An appeal to the parliament; or Sions plea against the prelacie* (anon.) 1628
Speculum belli sacri; or the looking-glasse of the holy war 1624
LEIGHTON, Alexander *Curious storied traditions of Scottish life* 1860
LEIGHTON, Abp. Robert *Works* a1684 (1805–08, 1830, 1859, 1869–75)
A practical commentary upon the two first chapters of the first epistle general of St. Peter a1684 (1693, 1817)
LEIGHTON, Robert *Wreck of the Golden Fleece* 1894
LEIGHTON, Robert *The complete book of the dog* 1922
The new book of the dog: a comprehensive natural history of British dogs and their foreign relatives 1907
LEIGHTON, William A. *A flora of Shropshire* 1841
The lichen-flora of Great Britain, Ireland and the Channel Islands 1871
LEINSTER, Mary *Dew on the leaf* 1926
Leisure hour, The 1852–1905
LEITCH, John *Müller's (C. O.) Ancient art and its remains* tr. 1847 (1850)
LEJEUNE, Anthony *Duel in the shadows* 1962
LELAND, Charles G. *Abraham Lincoln* 1879
The Egyptian sketch-book 1873
Memoirs 1893
Pidgin-English sing-song 1876
LELAND, John *De rebus Britannicis collectanea* a1552 (ed. T. Hearne 1715)
The Itinerary publish'd by T. Hearne. *To which is prefix'd (the) New-Year's gift a* 1552 (1710–12, 1768–69, 1907–10)
The laboryouse journey & serche for Englandes antiquitees, geuen as a newe yeares gyfte to Kynge Henry the VIII, with declaracyons enlarged 1544 (1549)
'LELIUS, Lord' (Viscount Ligonier) *The generous husband; or, the history of Lord Lelius and the fair Emilia* 1771
LEMARCHAND, Elizabeth *Death of an old girl* 1967
Death on Doomsday 1971
Let or hindrance 1973
LEMON, Gamekeeper *A dissertation on the errors of marksmen and gun makers, and a tract upon the art of shooting flying* 1782
LEMON, George W. *English etymology; or a derivative dictionary of the English language in two alphabets* 1783
LEMON, Mark *Falkner Lyle, or the story of two wives* 1866
Leyton Hall, and other tales 1867
Loved at last 1864
Wait for the end 1863
Le Muet's (P.) Art of fair building tr. 1675
LE NEVE, John *Lives and characters* etc. *of all the protestant bishops of the Church of England, since the Reformation* 1720
Some short memorials concerning the life of R. Field, Dean of Gloucester. Published by J. Le Neve 1716–17
LENNARD, Sampson *Charron's (P.) Wisdome* tr. 1612 (1630, 1670)
LENNOX, Charlotte *The female Quixote* 1752
Henrietta 1758 (1761)
LENNOX, Ld. William P. *Fifty years' biographical reminiscences* 1863
LENTON, Francis *Characterismi; or Lentons leasures* 1631
The Innes of Court anagrammatist; or the masquers masqued 1634
The young gallants whirligigg; or youths reakes 1629
LEONARD, Elmore *Unknown man, no. 89* 1977
LEONARD, William *Reports and cases of law in the time of Queen Elizabeth* 1658
— *in the reigns of Queen Elizabeth and King James* 1687
LEONARD, Zenas *Narrative of the adventures of Zenas Leonard* 1839
— (ed. W. F. Wagner) 1904
Leonardus' (Camillus) Mirror of stones tr. 1750
LEONI, James *The architecture of L. B. Alberti in ten books. Of painting, in three books. And of statuary, in one book* tr. 1726
The architecture of A. Palladio tr. 1715 (1742)
LEPSCHY, Giulio Ciro *A survey of structural linguistics* 1970
Lepsius' (C. R.) Standard alphabet for reducing unwritten languages and foreign graphic systems to a uniform orthography in European letters tr. 1855 (1863)
Lescarbot's (M.) Nova Francia: or the description of that part of New France which is one continent with Virginia tr. 1609
LESLIE, Charles *Theological works* 1721
A short and easie method with the Deists 1698
— ed. 2, *To which is added, a second part to the Jews* 1699
The snake in the grass 1696 (1697)
The Socinian controversy discuss'd 1708
LESLIE, Charles R., & TAYLOR, Tom *Autobiographical recollections* a1859 (1860)
Life and times of Sir J. Reynolds; with notices of some of his contemporaries; commenced by C. R. Leslie, continued and concluded by Tom Taylor 1865
LESLIE, George D. *Letters to Marco* 1893
LESLIE, Henry *A sermon preached before his Majesty at Wokin* 1627
LESLIE, John *A treatise towching the right of Princesse Marie to the succession of the croune of England* 1584
LESLIE, John Randolph Shane *The Anglo-Catholic* 1929
The Oppidan 1922
LESLIE, Robert C. *A sea-painter's log* 1886
LESLIE, William *General view of the agriculture of the counties of Nairn and Moray* 1813
LESSING, Doris May *Five: short novels* 1953
The golden notebook 1962
In pursuit of the English 1960
Shikasta 1979
This was the old chief's country: stories 1951
Lessons of middle age 1868 *See* BOYD, A. K. H.
LESTER, C. Edwards *The glory and shame of England* 1841
LESTER, Horace F. *Hartas Maturin* 1888
Under two fig trees 1886
L'ESTRANGE, Alfred G. *The friendships of M. R. Mitford as recorded in letters from her literary correspondents* 1882
The life of M. R. Mitford, related in a selection from her letters to her friends 1870

L'Estrange, Hamon *The alliance of divine offices* 1659
Americans no Jewes 1652
An answer to the marques of Worcester's last paper to the late king: to (which) is annext Smectymnuo-mastyx, or animadversions upon Smectymnuus in the point of lyturgie 1651
God's sabbath before and under the law 1641
The reign of King Charles 1654 (1655)
L'Estrange, Sir Roger *An answer to a letter to a dissenter, upon occasion of his Majesties late declaration of indulgence* 1687
A brief history of the times 1687–88
The fables of Æsop and other eminent mythologists, with morals and reflexions 1692–99 (1708)
Interest mistaken, or the holy cheat 1661
Seneca's Morals by way of abstract 1693
State divinity; or, a supplement to the relapsed apostate 1661
Tully's Offices in three books 1680
Twenty select colloquies out of Erasmus tr. 1680
— ed. 2, *Twenty-two select colloquies* 1689 (1699, 1725)
The visions of Don Francisco de Quevedo Villegas tr. 1668
The works of Flavius Josephus tr. 1702 (1733)
Letter ballancing the necessity of keeping a land-force in times of peace (By John, Lord Somers) 1697
Letter from a freeholder of Buckinghamshire to a friend in London 1679
Letter from a gentleman in the country to his friends in London, upon the subject of the penal laws and tests 1687
Letter from a souldier to the Commons of England (ascribed to John Trenchard) 1702
Letter sent by an Oxford scholler to his quondam schoolemaster, (with) the schoolmaster's answer 1642
Letter to an honourable Brigadier General in Canada (the Marquis Townshend) 1760
Letter to the mayor of —— wherein the discouragements of the seamen employed in his majesty's navy are impartially examined, by a member of parliament 1758
Letter to a member of the House of Commons in vindication of the Protestant Reformed Church 1679
Letters. A collection of miscellany letters selected out of Mist's Weekly Journal 1716–21 (1722)
Letters. Three chapters of letters relating to the suppression of the monasteries 1528–55 (Camden Soc. 1843)
Letters, Four centuries of English 14..–18.. (ed. W. B. Scoones 1880)
Letters and papers illustrative of the reigns of Richard III and Henry VII 14..–15.. (Rolls series 1861–63)
Letters from Donegal in 1886. By a Lady 'Felon', ed. by Colonel Maurice 1886
Letters from a gentleman in the north of Scotland: see Burt, E.
Letters from Madras 1836–39 *See* Maitland, Julia C.
Letters in the London Journal, A collection of all the political 1720 (1721)
Letters of an American 1854 *See* Landor, W. S.
Letters of eminent literary men 14..–17.. (Camden Soc. 1843)
Letters of Miss Riversdale [anon. novel] 3 vols. 1803
Letters of Queen Margaret of Anjou and Bishop Beckington 14.. (Camden Soc. 1863)
Letters on education 1852
Letters on several subjects a1687 *See* More, Henry
Letters to Honoria and Marianne on various subjects 1784
Letters written by eminent persons 16..–17.. (Bliss 1813)
Lettice Lisle 1870 *See* Verney, Lady F. P.
Leudesdorf, Charles *Cremona's (L.) Elements of projective geometry* tr. 1885
Leuze's (J. P. F. de) Practical instruction in animal magnetism tr. by T. C. Hartshorn 1837 (1879)
Levellers, The; a dialogue between two young ladies concerning matrimony 1745 (in Harleian Misc.)
Levens, Peter *See* Levins, P.
Lever, Charles J. *Arthur O'Leary, his wanderings and ponderings in many lands* 1844
Barrington 1863
The Bramleighs of Bishop's Folly 1868
Charles O'Malley, the Irish dragoon 1841
The confessions of Con Cregan, the Irish Gil Blas 1849
The confessions of Harry Lorrequer 1839
The Daltons; or, three roads in life 1852
Davenport Dunn; or, the man of the day 1859
A day's ride; a life's romance 1863
Diary and notes of Horace Templeton 1849
The Dodd family abroad 1854
Jack Hinton, the guardsman 1843
The Knight of Gwynne; a tale of the time of the Union 1847
Luttrell of Arran 1865
The Martins of Cro' Martin 1856
Maurice Tiernay, the soldier of fortune 1852
The O'Donoghue; a tale of Ireland fifty years ago 1845
One of them 1861
Roland Cashel 1850
Sir Brook Fossbrooke 1866
Sir Jasper Carew, his life and experiences 1854
St. Patrick's eve 1845
Tom Burke of 'Ours' 1844
Tony Butler 1865
Lever, Christopher *A crucifixe: or, a meditation upon repentance, and the holie Passion* 1607
Lever, Thomas *Sermons* 1550 (Arber 1870)
A fruitful sermon made in Poules churche at London in the shroudes 1550
A sermon preached at Paules Crosse 1550
A sermon preached the thyrd (yᵉ fourth) sonday in Lent before the kynges maiestie 1550
Levett, John *The ordering of bees* 1634
Levi, Herbert W. & Levi, Lorna R. tr. *A. Kaestner's Invertebrate zoology* 3 vols. 1967–70
Levins, Peter *Manipulus vocabulorum. A dictionarie of English and Latine wordes* 1570 (Camden Soc., E.E.T.S. 1867)
A right profitable booke for all diseases called The pathway to health 1587
Levity and sorrow 1809 *See* Bianchi, M. A.
Levy, Mervyn Montague *The Studio dictionary of art terms* 1961
Levy, William H. *Blindness and the blind* 1872
Lewes, George H. *A biographical history of philosophy* 1845–46 (1857, 1867)
Comte's Philosophy of the sciences 1853
The life and works of Goethe 1855
The life of Maximilien Robespierre 1849
The noble heart; a tragedy 1850
On actors and the art of acting 1875
The physiology of common life 1859–60
Problems of life and mind. First series. *The foundation of a creed* 1874–75
— Second series. *The physical basis of mind* 1877
— Third series. *The study of psychology. Mind as a function of the organism. The sphere of sense and logic of feeling. The sphere of intellect and logic of signs* 1879
Ranthorpe; a novel 1847
Sea-side studies at Ilfracombe etc. 1858
Lewes, Vivian Byam *Oil fuel* 1913
Lewin, Thomas *The invasion of Britain by Julius Cæsar* 1859 (1862)
Lewin, Thomas H. *A fly on the wheel; or, how I helped to govern India* 1885
Lewins, William *Her Majesty's mails: an historical and descriptive account of the British Post Office* 1864
Lewis, Alfred Henry *The apaches of New York* 1912
The boss, and how he came to rule New York 1903
Confessions of a detective 1906
Wolfville days 1902
Lewis, Arthur William *A glossary of woodworking terms* 1966
Lewis, Cecil Day tr. *Virgil's Aeneid* 1952
Beechen vigil, and other poems 1925
The buried day 1960
Child of misfortune 1939
The friendly tree 1936
tr. *Virgil's Georgics* 1940
A hope for poetry 1934
An Italian visit 1953
The Otterbury incident 1948
Overtures to death, and other poems 1938
Poems, 1943–1947 1948
A time to dance, and other poems 1935
Transitional poem 1929
Word over all 1943
See also: 'Blake, Nicholas'
Lewis, Clarence Irving *A survey of symbolic logic* 1918
Symbolic logic 1932
Lewis, Clive Staples *The allegory of love: a study in medieval tradition* 1936
Letters ed. W. H. Lewis 1966
Perelandra 1943
Poems ed. W. Hooper 1964
The problem of pain 1940
The Screwtape letters 1942
Studies in words 1960
Surprised by joy 1955
That hideous strength: a modern fairy-tale for grown-ups 1945
Lewis, Dominic Bevan Wyndham *On straw, and other conceits* 1927
Lewis, Ethelreda *Mantis* 1926
Lewis, Sir George Cornewall *An essay on the influence of authority in the matters of opinion* 1849 (1875)
A glossary of provincial words used in Herefordshire and some of the adjoining counties 1839
An inquiry into the credibility of the early Roman history 1855
Letters to various friends a1863 (1875)
Remarks on the use and abuse of some political terms 1832
Lewis, George R. *The stannaries: a study of the English tin miner* 1908
Lewis, Griselda ed. *Handbook of crafts* 1960
Lewis, J. *American sportsman, and hints on the habits of birds* 1857
Lewis, John *The history and antiquities, ecclesiastical and civil, of the Isle of Tenet in Kent* 1723 (1736)
— *Glossary of words used in the Isle of Thanet* (from ed. 1736 of prec., E.D.S. 1874)
The history of the life and sufferings of John Wicliffe 1720–23
The life of John Fisher, Bishop of Rochester. From the original MS. 1730–31 (1855)
The life of R. Pecock, Bishop of St. Asaph and Chichester 1744
Lewis, Mary A. *Two pretty girls* 1881
Lewis, Matthew G. *The Bravo of Venice* tr. 1805
Journal of a West Indian proprietor a1818 (1834)
Lewis, Meriwether & Clark, William *Original journals of the Lewis and Clark expedition, 1804–1806* ed. R. G. Thwaites 8 vols. 1904–5
—— & Ordway, John *The journals of Captain Meriwether Lewis and Sergeant John Ordway, kept on the expedition of western exploration, 1803–1806* ed. M. M. Quaife 1916
Travels to the source of the Missouri river and across the American continent to the Pacific ocean 1804–06 1814 (1893)
Lewis, Percy Wyndham *The apes of God* 1930
Blasting and bombardiering 1937
Letters ed. W. K. Rose 1963
Lewis, Roy (John Royston Lewis) *Blood money* 1973
Witness my death 1976
Lewis, Sinclair (Harry Sinclair Lewis) *Arrowsmith* (UK ed. with title *Martin Arrowsmith*) 1925
Babbitt 1922
Bethel Merriday 1940
Cass Timberlane 1945 (UK 1946)
Free air 1919 (UK 1924)
It can't happen here 1935
Main Street: the story of Carol Kennicott 1920
The man who knew Coolidge 1928
Mantrap 1926
Our Mr. Wrenn: the romantic adventures of a gentle man 1914
Lewis, Thomas *An historical essay upon the consecration of churches* 1719
Lewis, Wilfrid James *The language of cricket* 1934
Lewis, William *Commercium philosophico-technicum; or, the philosophical commerce of arts* 1763–66
Lewis, William *Chess for beginners* 1835
Elements of the game of chess 1822
Lewis, William J. *A treatise on crystallography* 1899
Lewis, William L. *Statius' Thebaid* tr. 1767
Lewis, Wyndham *See* Lewis, Percy Wyndham
Lewkenor, Lewes 1600 See *Torquemada, A. de*
Lex talionis, sive vindiciæ pharmacoporum; or a short reply to Dr. Merrett's book against apothecaries 1670
Lexicon balatronicum. A dictionary of buckish slang, university wit, and pickpocket eloquence 1811
Lexiphanes 1767 *See* Campbell, Archibald
Ley, Willy *The conquest of space* 1949 (UK 1950)
Leybourn, William *The compleat surveyor* 1674
Cursus mathematicus; or, mathematical sciences 1690
Leycester, Earl of *See* Leicester, Earl of
Leycester, Sir Peter *Historical antiquities* 1672–73
Leyden, John tr. *Malay annals* 1821
Poetical works a1811 (1875)
Scenes of infancy 1803
—— & Erskine, William tr. *Memoirs of Zehir-Ed-Din Muhammed Baber, Emperor of Hindustan, written by himself in the Jaghatai Turki* 1826
Lhuyd, Edward *Archæologia Britannica* 1707
Libeaus Desconus c1350 (in Ritson, Metrical romances II. 1802; Kaluza 1890)
Libel of English policy c1436 (in Political poems II, Rolls series 1861)
Liber albus, Liber custumarum, et Liber Horn, in archivis Gildhallæ asservati 14.. (Rolls series 1859–62)
Liber Cure Cocorum c1420 (Philol. Soc. 1862)
Liber niger domus regis Edward IV a1483 (in Household ordinances, 1790)
Liber scintillarum a1050 See *Defensor*
Liberal American, The; a novel, by a lady 1785
Libertine husband tr. 1810
Liberty 1924–30
Liberty of conscience 1645 *See* Gillespie, G.
Library, The 1889–
Library Association record 1899–
Library journal: journal of the American Library Association 1876–
Library of universal knowledge. Being a reprint entire of the last (1879) Edinburgh and London edition of Chambers's Encyclopædia 1880 (New York)
Library of useful knowledge (published by the Society for the diffusion of useful knowledge) 1827–48
Licensed traders' dictionary of words and terms 1903
Lichefield, Nicholas *Lopez de Castanheda's First booke of the historie of the discoverie and conquest of the East Indias* tr. 1582
Lichfield. The Gild of St. Mary, Lichfield; being ordinances of the Gild of St. Mary, and other documents 14..–16.. (E.E.T.S. 1920)
Lichine, Alexis *Encyclopædia of wines and spirits* 1967
Wines of France 1952
Liddell, Billy (William Beveridge Liddell) *My soccer story* 1960
Liddell, Henry G., & Scott, Robert *A Greek-English lexicon* 1843
— ed. 7, revised and enlarged, 1883; ed. 8, 1897
Liddell, Robert *The Morea* 1958
Liddle, William *Poems on different occasions, chiefly in the Scottish dialect* 1821
Liddon, Henry P. *The divinity of our Lord and Saviour Jesus Christ* (Bampton lectures 1866) 1867 (1875)
Some elements of religion (Lent lectures 1870) 1872
Some words for God. Sermons 1863–65 1865
——, et al. *Life of E. B. Pusey* 1893–97
Lieber, Francis *Manual of political ethics* 1839
On civil liberty and self-government 1853
A popular essay on subjects of penal law 1838
Lieberman, Jethro K., & Rhodes, Neil S. *The complete CB handbook* (new ed.) 1976
Liebermann, Felix *Die Gesetze der Angelsachsen* 1898–1916
Lief, Max *Hangover* 1929
Life 1936–72
Life and death of Thomas, Lord Cromwell, The true chronicle

historie of the whole 1602 (in Shakespeare Apocrypha, 1908)
Life and work (Church of Scotland) 1879–
Life in the Mofussil; or, the civilian in Lower Bengal 1878
Life in Normandy 1848 *See* Campbell, W. F.
Life in the South 1863 *See* Hopley, Catherine C.
Life of King Henry the fifth 1513 (ed. C. L. Kingsford 1911)
Life of a planter in Jamaica 1828 See *Marly*
Life of St. Katherine See *Katherine, St.*
Lightfoot, John *Works* a1675 (1684, 1822–25)
Erubhin; or miscellanies, Christian and Judaicall 1629
A few and new observations upon the booke of Genesis 1642
An handfull of gleanings out of the book of Exodus 1643 (1648)
Lightfoot, John *Flora Scotica* 1777
Lightfoot, Bp. Joseph B. *Epistle to the Philippians; a revised text, with introduction, etc.* 1868
S. Clement of Rome. The two epistles to the Corinthians. A revised text with introduction and notes 1869
St. Paul's epistles to the Colossians and to Philemon, a revised text, with introductions, notes, etc. 1875
Lighthall, William D. *The young seigneur* 1888
Lights and shades of English life. From the New monthly magazine 1828
Ligon, Richard *A true and exact history of the island of Barbados* 1657 (1673)
Ligonier, Viscount *See* 'Lelius, Lord'
Lilburn, Adam *The borderer* 1896
Lilico, James Ewart *Sheep dog memoirs* 1934
Lilie, Peter a1615 *See* Lily, P.
Lilley, Arthur Augustus *Twenty-four years of cricket* 1912
Lillie, Mrs. Lucy C. *Prudence, a story of æsthetic London* 1882
Lillo, George *Marina: a play taken from Pericles Prince of Tyre* 1738
Lilly, John *See* Lyly, J.
Lilly, William *Anima astrologiæ* tr. 1676
Christian astrology 1647
His history of his life and times from 1602 to 1681 a1681 (1715)
Monarchy or no monarchy in England, with observations upon the life and death of the late king Charles 1651
Lilly, William S. *Ancient religion and modern thought* 1884
The great enigma 1892
Lillywhite, Frederick ed. *The guide to cricketers* 1853–66
Lillywhite, James *James Lillywhite's cricketers' annual* 1872–7; 1879–93
Lillywhite, John *John Lillywhite's cricketers' companion* (title varies) 1865–85
Lily, Peter *Two sermons* a1615 (1619)
Linche, Richard *Poems* a1601 (Grosart 1877)
Diella, certaine sonnets, adioyned to the amorous poeme of Dom Diego and Gineura 1596 (1877; in Arber, Eng. Garner VII)
The fountaine of ancient fiction tr. 1599
Lincoln, Bishop of 1697, 1707, 1864 *See* Gardiner, James; Wake, W.; Jackson, John
Lincoln, Abraham *Collected works* ed. R. P. Basler 9 vols. 1953
Lincoln, Joseph Crosby *Cap'n Warren's wards* 1911
Partners of the tide 1905
Lincoln herald 1828–32
Lincolnshire, Chronicle of the rebellion in 1470 (in Camden Soc., Misc. 1847)
Lincolnshire church furniture v.d. (in E. Peacock, English church furniture 1866)
Lincolnshire (north-west) glossary 1877, 1889 *See* Peacock, E.
Lincolnshire (south-west) glossary 1886 *See* Cole, R. E. G.
Lincoln's Inn, The records of the Honorable Society of 1422–1845 (1897–1902)
Lind, James *Three letters relating to the navy, Gibraltar, and Portmahon* 1747–48 (1757)
Lindesay, Robert (of Pitscottie) *The historie and cronicles of Scotland* a1578 (1728; S.T.S. 1898–99)
Lindgren, Ernest *The art of the film* 1948
Lindisfarne gospels c950 (The Holy Gospels, in Anglo-Saxon, etc., Skeat 1871–87)
Lindley, John *Elements of botany* 1841 (1849)
Flora medica: a botanical account of all the more important plants used in medicine 1838
An introduction to botany 1832 (1839, 1848)
An introduction to the natural system of botany 1830
Richard's (L. C. M.) Observations on the structure of fruits and seeds tr. 1819
School botany 1839 (1858)
A synopsis of the British flora 1829
The vegetable kingdom 1846
—— & Moore, Thomas *The treasury of botany* 1866
Lindley, Thomas *Narrative of a voyage to Brasil* 1805
Lindop, Audrey Erskine *Sight unseen* 1969
Lindores chartularies See *Balmerino*
Lindsay, Alexander W. C. *Lives of the Lindsays; or a memoir of the houses of Crawford and Balcarres* 1840 (1849)
Sketches of the history of Christian art 1847
Lindsay (or Lyndsay), Sir David a1555 *See* Lyndesay, Sir D.
Lindsay, Jack *Life rarely tells* 1958
Lindsay, Patrick *The interest of Scotland considered with reference to its police, etc.* 1733
Lindsay, Robert (of Pitscottie) *See* Lindesay, R.
Lindsay, Thomas M. *The church and the ministry in the early centuries* 1902
Lindsay, Wallace M. *The Latin language; an historical account of Latin sounds, stems, and flexions* 1894
—— & Thomson, Henry J. *Ancient lore in medieval Latin glossaries* 1921
Lindzey, Gardner ed. *Handbook of social psychology* 2 vols. 1954
—(ed. 2, by Lindzey & E. Aronson) 5 vols. 1968–9
Lineham, Wilfrid J. *A text-book of mechanical engineering* 1894
'Linesman' (M. H. Grant) *Words by an eyewitness; the struggle in Natal* 1901 (1902)
Lingard, John *The antiquities of the Anglo-Saxon Church* 1806
—ed. 3, entitled *The history and antiquities of the Anglo-Saxon church* 1845 (1858)
A history of England from the first invasion by the Romans to the revolution in 1688 1819–30
Lingeman, Richard R. *Drugs from A to Z: a dictionary* 1969
Lingua 1607 *See* Tomkis, T.
Lingua: international review of general linguistics 1947–
Linington, Barbara Elizabeth *See* 'Blaisdell, Anne'; 'Egan, Lesley'; 'Shannon, Dell'
Linklater, Eric Robert Russell *Juan in America* 1931
Magnus Merriman 1934
Poet's pub 1929
Private Angelo 1946
Linnæus' (C.) Families of plants tr. 1787
Linnean Society of London *Proceedings* 1838–
Transactions 1791–
Linnean Society of New South Wales *Proceedings* 1876–
Linnen and woollen manufactory discoursed 1691
Linnet's trial 1864 *See* Smedley, Menella B.
Linnett, John Wilfred *The electronic structure of molecules: a new approach* 1964
Linschoten's voyage tr. 1598 *See* Phillip, W.
Linskill, Mary *The haven under the hill* 1886
Linssen, Eugene F. *Beetles of the British Isles* 2 ser. 1959
Lintie o' Moray, The, being a collection of poems, chiefly composed for and sung at the anniversaries of the Edinburgh Morayshire Society 1829–41 (1851)
Linton, David Leslie ed. *Sheffield and its region* 1956
Linton, Mrs. E. Lynn *The autobiography of Christopher Kirkland* 1885
The lake country 1864
Lizzie Lorton of Greyrigg 1866
My love! 1881
Paston Carew, millionaire and miser 1886
The rebel of the family 1880
Through the long night 1889
The true history of Joshua Davidson (anon.) 1872
With a silken thread, and other stories 1880
Lintoun Green, or the third market day of June, O.S., 1685 1817
Lippincott's medical dictionary by R. W. Greene et al. 1897
Lippincott's monthly magazine (title varies) 1868–1915
Lippincott's new medical dictionary ed. H. W. Cattell 1910
Lisander and Calista 1627 *See* D., W.
Lisle, Edward *Observations in husbandry* a1722 (1757)
L'isle's (F. de) Legendarie, conteining an ample discourse of the life and behaviour of Charles, Cardinal of Lorraine tr. 1577
Lisle, William *Ælfric's Saxon treatise concerning the Old and New Testament* 1623
Part of Du Bartas tr. 1625
Lismore papers, The; autobiographical notes, remembrances and diaries of Sir Rich. Boyle, first Earl of Cork a1643 (ed. by A. B. Grosart 1886–89)
Listener, The 1929–
Lister, Martin *A journey to Paris in 1698* 1699
Lister, Raymond George *Decorative cast ironwork in Great Britain* 1960
Decorative wrought ironwork in Great Britain 1957
Lister, Thomas H. *Arlington* 1832
Granby 1826 (1836)
Litchfield, Frederick *Pottery and porcelain: a guide to collectors* 1900
Literary Churchman, The 1855–92
Literary digest 1890–1938
Literary gazette, The 1817–58
Literary guide 1894–1954
Literary memoirs of five hundred living authors of Great Britain (ed. by D. Rivers) 1798
Literary world, The (Boston, Mass.) 1880–
Literature 1897 1902
Lithgow, William *The pilgrimes farewell to his native countrey of Scotland: wherein is contained, The joyes and miseries of peregrination* 1618
Poetical remains a1645 (1863)
The totall discourse of the rare adventures and painefull peregrinations of long nineteen yeares travayles 1632 (1682, 1906)
A true experimentall and exact relation upon that famous siege of Newcastle 1645 (1820)
Littell's Living age 1844–
Little, Andrew G. *The Grey Friars in Oxford* 1892
Little, Francis *A monument of Christian munificence; or, an account of the Brotherhood of the Holy Cross, and of the Hospital of Christ in Abingdon* 1627 (1871)
Little, William J. *On the nature and treatment of the deformities of the human frame* 1853
A treatise on the nature of club-foot and analogous distortions 1839
Little folks: a magazine for children 1871–1933
Littledale, Richard F. *Plain reasons against joining the Church of Rome* 1880
Littleton, Adam *Linguæ Latinæ liber dictionarius quadripartitus* 1678
Littleton, Sir Edward *Reports* 1683
Littleton's (Sir T.) Tenures tr. 1538 (1544, 1574)
See also Coke, E.
Littré, Émile *Dictionnaire de la langue française* 1863–77
Liturgies and occasional forms of prayer set forth in the reign of Queen Elizabeth 15.. (Parker Soc. 1847)
Lively oracles given to us, or the Christians birth-right and duty 1678 (1684)
Livermore, Samuel *A treatise on the law of principal and agent* 1818
Liverpool Echo 1879–
Lives of British physicians (by William Macmichael) 1830 (1857)
Lives of saints See Ælfric; Bokenham; *Saints' lives*; etc.
Lives of the Scottish poets (by Joseph Robertson) 1821–22
Living off the land: a manual of bushcraft, compiled from articles contributed to 'Salt', the army education journal (Australia) 1944
Livingston, Milton Stanley *Particle physics: the high energy frontier* 1968
Livingston, William *A letter to John (Ewer), lord bishop of Llandaff* 1768
Livingstone, David *Last journals in Central Africa* 1865–73 (1874)
Missionary travels and researches in South Africa 1857
Narrative of an expedition to the Zambesi 1865
Llewelyn, Martin *See* Lluelyn, M.
Lloid, Lodowick *See* Lloyd, L.
Lloyd, Albert Lancaster *Folk song in England* 1967
Lloyd, Christopher *The well-tempered garden* 1970
Lloyd, David *The legend of Captaine Jones* 1631 (1659)
Lloyd, David *State-worthies* 1665 (1766)
Lloyd, David *The voyage of life. A poem* 1792
Lloyd, George T. *Thirty-three years in Tasmania and Victoria* 1862
Lloyd, Hannibal E. *Feuchtersleben's (Ernest von) Principles of medical psychology* tr. 1847 (Sydenham Soc.)
J. B. von Spix & C. F. P. von Martius's Travels in Brazil, 1817–20 2 vols. 1825
Timkowski's (E. F.) Travels of the Russian mission through Mongolia to China tr. 1827
Lloyd (or Llwyd), Humphrey *The treasury of health conteynyng many profitable medycines gathered out of Hypocrates, Galen and Avycen, by one Petrus Hyspanus* tr. c1550
See also Powel, David
Lloyd, Humphrey *Lectures on the wave-theory of light* 1841 (1857, 1873)
Lloyd, John *A treatise of the episcopacy, liturgies, and ecclesiastical ceremonies of the primitive times* 1660
Lloyd, Lewis *Field sports of the north of Europe* 1830
Scandinavian adventures 1854
Lloyd, Lodowick *A briefe conference of divers lawes* 1602
The consent of time, deciphering the errors of the Grecians in their Olympiads 1590
The first part of the diall of daies 1590
The pilgrimage of princes 1573 (1586, 1607)
—another ed., entitled *The marrow of history: or, The pilgrimage of kings and princes*, corrected by R. C(odrington) (1653)
Lloyd, Robert *Poems* 1762, a1764 (1790)
Poetical works a1764 (1774)
Lloyd, Mrs. W. Reynolds *The ladies of Polcarrow* 1864
Lloyd, Bp. William *An historical account of Church government* 1684
Pretences of the French invasion examined (anon.) 1692 (in Harl. Misc.)
Lloyd's Natural history See Sharpe, R. B.
Lloyd George, David *See* George, David Lloyd
Lluelyn, Martin *Men-miracles. With other poems* 1646
Llwyd, Humphrey *See* Lloyd, H.
Lobb, Ebenezer, The wonderful career of. Related by himself. ed. by Allen Upward 1900
Lobb, Stephen *A letter to Dr. Bates containing a vindication of the doctor, and myself* 1695
Lobeck, Armin Kohl *Geomorphology* 1939
Local government and taxation in the United Kingdom; a series of essays ed. by J. W. Probyn 1882
Lock, Charles G. W. *(Spon's) Workshop receipts* (Series 3 and 4) 1884–85
Lock, Joan *Lady policeman* 1968
Locke, John *Works* a1704 (1714)
Elements of natural philosophy a1704 (1754)
An essay concerning humane understanding 1690
—ed. 2, with large additions 1694; ed. 4, with large additions 1700; ed. 5, with many large additions (1706)
A letter concerning toleration tr. by W. Popple 1689; *a second letter* 1690; *a third letter* 1692
A letter to Edward (Stillingfleet), Lord Bishop of Worcester 1697
Of the conduct of the understanding c1698 (in Posthumous works 1706)
A paraphrase and notes on the Epistle of St. Paul to the Galatians, the first and second Epistles to the Corinthians, and the Epistles to the Romans and Ephesians a1704 (1705–07)
The reasonableness of Christianity as delivered in the Scriptures 1695
A vindication of the reasonableness of Christianity from Mr. Edwards's reflections 1695; *a second vindication* 1697
Some considerations of the consequences of the lowering of interest and raising the value of money in a letter 1691 (1692)

LOCKE, John (*cont.*)
Further considerations concerning raising the value of money 1695
Some familiar letters between Mr. Locke and several of his friends a1704 (1708)
Some thoughts concerning education 1693
Two treatises of government 1690
Life, with extracts from his correspondence, journals, and common-place books, by Peter King (1830)
Life by H. R. Fox Bourne (1876)
LOCKE, William John *Ancestor Jorico* 1929
At the gate of Samaria 1894
The beloved vagabond 1906
The coming of Amos 1924
Derelicts 1897
The glory of Clementina Wing 1911
The house of Baltazar 1920
Idols 1898
Jaffery 1915
Moordius and Co. 1923
The morals of Marcus Ordeyne 1905
The mountebank 1921
The old bridge 1926
The red planet 1917
The rough road 1918
Septimus 1909
Simon the jester 1910
Stella maris 1913
Stories near and far 1926
The tale of Triona 1922
The wonderful year 1916
LOCKET, George Hazlewood & MILLIDGE, Alfred Frank *British spiders* 2 vols. 1951–3
LOCKHART, George *Memoirs concerning the affairs of Scotland* 1714
LOCKHART, John G. *The Ballantyne-humbug handled* 1839
Memoirs of the life of Sir Walter Scott 1837–38 (1839, 1846)
Peter's letters to his kinsfolk 1819
Reginald Dalton 1823
Some passages in the life of Mr. Adam Blair 1822
Valerius; a Roman story 1821
LOCKHART, Laurence W. M. *Fair to see* 3 vols. 1871
Mine is thine 1878
LOCKHART, William *Rosmini-Serbati's (A.) Short sketch of modern philosophies and of his own system* tr. 1882
LOCKMAN, John *To the long-conceal'd first promoter of the cambrick and tea-bills: an epistle* 1746
LOCKRIDGE, Frances Louise & LOCKRIDGE, Richard *Murder has its points* 1961 (UK 1962)
Practise to deceive: a Captain Heimrich mystery 1957 (UK 1959, as by 'Francis Richards')
LOCKWOOD, Thomas D. *Electricity, magnetism, and electric telegraphy* 1883
LOCKWOOD, William Burley *Panorama of Indo-European languages* 1972
Lockwood's Dictionary of terms used in the practice of mechanical engineering 1888 (1892)
LOCKYER, Charles *An account of the trade in India* 1711
LOCKYER, J. Norman *The chemistry of the sun* 1887
Contributions to solar physics 1874
The dawn of astronomy 1894
Elementary lessons in astronomy 1868 (1879)
ed. *Guillemin's (A.) Heavens* 1866
Stargazing: past and present 1878
Studies in spectrum analysis 1878
LOCKYER, Keith Gerald *An introduction to critical path analysis* 1964
LOCKYER, Nicholas *England faithfully watcht with in her wounds* 1646
A sermon preached before the House of Commons Oct. 28 1646
Locrine, The lamentable tragedie of 1595 (in Shakespeare Apocrypha 1908)
LODEMAN, E. G. *The spraying of plants for the purpose of destroying insects and fungi* 1896
LODGE, David John *The British Museum is falling down* 1965
Changing places 1975
LODGE, Edmund *Illustrations of British history, biography, and manners* 1791
LODGE, Sir Oliver J. *Modern views of electricity* 1889
LODGE, Thomas *Complete works* a1625 (Hunterian Club 1883–88)
An alarum against vsurers 1584 (Shaks. Soc. 1853)
The delectable historie of Forbonius and Prisceria 1584 (Shaks. Soc. 1853)
A defence of poetry, music, and stage-plays 1579 (Shaks. Soc. 1853)
A fig for Momus 1595
A learned summary upon the famous poeme of William of Saluste Lord of Bartas 1621
A margarite of America 1596
Rosalynde. Euphues golden legacie 1590
Seneca's Workes tr. 1614
The wounds of ciuill war 1594
See also GREENE, R.
LOE, William *Come and see. The blisse of brightest beautie: shining out of Sion* 1614
LOEB, Jacques *Comparative physiology of the brain and comparative psychology* 1901
LOFFT, Capell *Self-formation; or the history of an individual mind* 1837
LOFTUS, William K. *Travels and researches in Chaldæa and Susiana* 1857
LOGAN, Mrs. Eliza *St. Johnstoun; or John, earl of Gowrie* (anon.) 1823
LOGAN, James *The Scottish Gaël, or Celtic manners, as preserved among the Highlanders* 1831 (1876)
LOGAN, John *Poems* a1788 (1805)
Runnamede, a tragedy 1783
LOGAN, Olive *Before the footlights and behind the scenes* 1870
Lollard conclusions 1395 (in Fasciculi Zizaniorum, Rolls series 1858)
LOMAX, Alan *Mister Jelly Roll: the fortunes of Jelly Roll Morton, New Orleans Creole and inventor of jazz* 1950 (UK 1952)
Lommel's (E.) Nature of light, with a general account of physical optics tr. 1874 (1875)
LONDON, Bishop of 1696 *See* COMPTON, Bp. Henry
LONDON, George *De la Quintinie's Compleat gard'ner* tr. 1699 (1704, 1719)
—— & WISE, Henry *The retir'd gard'ner* 1706
LONDON, Jack (John Griffith London) *The call of the wild* 1903
The iron heel 1907 (UK 1908)
The jacket (US ed. with title *The star rover*) 1915
Letters ed. K. Hendricks & I. Shepard 1965 (UK 1966)
The road 1907 (UK 1914)
A son of the sun 1912 (UK 1913)
The valley of the moon 1913
White Fang 1906 (UK 1907)
London and country brewer 1713 (1742)
London & Globe Telephone & Maintenance Company, Ltd. *List of subscribers* 1884 [reproduced in facsimile in *Three Victorian telephone directories* 1970]
London and its environs described 1761
London at table; or, How, when, and where to dine and order a dinner; and where to avoid dining 1851
London chaunticleres, The. A witty comœdy 1659 (in Hazl., Dodsley)
London cries, or, pictures of tumult and distress: a poem 1805
London, Edinburgh, and Dublin philosophical magazine 1832– See *Philosophical magazine*
London gazette, The (Nos. 1–23 called 'The Oxford gazette') 1665–
London Lickpenny 14.. (in Lydgate's Minor P., Percy Soc. 1840; Anglia XX. 1898)
London Livery Companies, Report on 1884 (Parl. papers Eng., XXXIX)
London magazine, The 1820–29
London magazine: a monthly review of literature 1954–
London Mathematical Society *Proceedings* 1865–
London medical gazette 1827–51
London medical and physical journal, The 1826–33
London medical record 1873–87
London mercury 1919–39
London prentices and trades, A collection of songs and ballads relative to the 1380–1707 (Percy Soc. 1841)
London prodigall, The 1605 (in Shakespeare Apocrypha 1908)
London review 1835–6
London review of books 1979–
London society 1862–98
LONELICH, Henry *See* LOVELICH, H.
LONG, C. Chaillé *Central Africa* 1876
LONG, Constance Ellen tr. *C. G. Jung's Collected papers on analytical psychology* 1916
LONG, Edward *The history of Jamaica* (anon.) 1774
LONG, George *The British Museum. Egyptian antiquities* 1832–36
LONG, J. *Voyages and travels of an Indian interpreter and trader. To which is added a vocabulary* 1791
LONG, James ed. *Selections from unpublished records of government* (Fort William) 1748–67 (1869)
LONG, John D. *Virgil's Æneid* tr. 1879
LONG, Joseph W. *American wild-fowl shooting* 1874
LONG, Kingesmill *Barclay his Argenis* tr. 1625
LONG, Ralph Bernard *The sentence and its parts: a grammar of contemporary English* 1961
LONG, W. H. *A dictionary of the Isle of Wight dialect* 1886
LONGFELLOW, Henry Wadsworth *Writings* a1882 (1886)
Poetical works a1882 (1910)
Aftermath 1873
The belfry of Bruges, and other poems 1846
The courtship of Miles Standish, and other poems 1858
The divine comedy of Dante 1867
The divine tragedy 1871
Evangeline; a tale of Acadie 1847
The golden legend 1851
Hyperion; a romance 1839
Kavanagh, a tale 1849
Kéramos, and other poems 1878
The masque of Pandora, and other poems 1875
The New England tragedies 1868
Outre-mer; a pilgrimage beyond the sea 1835
Poems on slavery 1842
The song of Hiawatha 1855
The Spanish student 1843
Tales of a wayside inn 1863
Three books of song 1872
Voices of the night 1839
Life. With extracts from his journals and correspondence. Ed. by S. Longfellow (1891)
Longinus (D. C.) On the sublime in writing, and three dissertations tr. (by W. T. Spurdens) 1836
LONGMAN, William *The history of the life and times of Edward the third* 1869
Longman's Magazine 1883–1906
LONGSTREET, Augustus B. *Georgia scenes* 1848
LONGSTREET, Stephen *The real jazz, old and new* 1956
LONGWELL, Chester Ray, KNOPF, A., & FLINT, R. R. *Outlines of physical geology* 1934
LONSDALE, M. *The Spanish rivals, a musical farce* 1784 (1785)
LONSDALE, Margaret *Sister Dora (Dorothy W. Pattison); a biography* 1880
Lonsdale magazine, The: or provincial repository 1820–22
Looke about you, A pleasant commodie, called 1600 (in Hazl., Dodsley)
Looker-on 1792–94 *See* ROBERTS, W.
'LORAC, E. C. R.' (Edith Caroline Rivett) *Ask a policeman* 1955
Murder in the mill-race 1952
LORAND, Sándor ed. *Psycho-analysis today: its scope and function* 1933
LORD, Henry *A discoverie of the sect of the Banians; The religion of the Persees* 1630
LORD, John K. *The naturalist in Vancouver Island and British Columbia* 1866
Lord's trumpet, The See PEDEN, Alex.
LORENZ, Charles A. *Van der Keessel's Select theses* tr. 1855
Lorica hymn c1000 (in Grein's Bibl. angelsäch. Prosa VI)
LORIMER, George Horace *Jack Spurlock—prodigal* 1908
Letters from a self-made merchant to his son 1902
Old Gorgon Graham: more letters from a self-made merchant to his son 1904
LORIMER, Hilda Lockhart *Homer and the monuments* 1950
LORIMER, William *Remarks on Mr. Goodwin's Discourse of the Gospel* 1696
LORRAIN, Paul *Muret's (P.) Rites of funeral* tr. 1683
Los Angeles Times 1881–
Loseley manuscripts and other rare documents preserved at Loseley House, Surrey 15..–16.. (ed. A. J. Kempe 1836)
LOSSING, Benson J. *The Hudson, from the wilderness to the sea* 1866
Lost brooch, The 1841 *See* MOZLEY, Mrs. Harriet
LOTT, Emmeline *The governess in Egypt* 1865
Lotze's (R. H.) Logic tr. by B. Bosanquet 1884
— *Metaphysic* tr. by B. Bosanquet 1884
LOUDON, Mrs. Jane W. *The amateur gardener's monthly calendar* 1847
— revised and ed. by W. Robinson (1880)
Botany for ladies 1842
British wild flowers 1846
Domestic pets 1851
LOUDON, John C. *Arboretum et fruticetum Britannicum; or the hardy trees and shrubs of Britain, native and foreign, delineated and described* 1838
An encyclopaedia of trees and shrubs (an abridgement of prec.) 1842
An encyclopædia of agriculture 1825 (1831)
An encyclopædia of cottage, farm, and villa architecture and furniture 1833
An encyclopædia of gardening 1822 (1824)
An encyclopædia of plants 1829
The gardener's magazine 1828–43
The greenhouse companion (anon.) 1824
The suburban gardener, and villa companion 1838
Louisburg, Journal of the siege of 1745 (in W. Shirley, Letter 1746)
LOUNSBURY, Thomas R. *Studies in Chaucer* 1892
LOUNSBURY, Warren C. *Backstage from A to Z: a glossary of technical stage terms* 1959
LOUTHIAN, John *The form of process before the Court of Justiciary in Scotland* 1732 (1752)
LOVE, James *The mariner's jewel* 1705 (ed. 5; 1724)
'LOVE, James' (James Dance) *Cricket; an heroic poem* 1740
Poems on several occasions 1754
LOVE, Nicholas *Bonaventura's Mirrour of the blessed lyf of Jesu Christ* tr. c1410 (Sherard MS.; W. de Worde 1517; 1908)
Love of fame 1728 *See* YOUNG, E.
LOVEDAY, Robert *Calprenède's Hymen's Præludia; or, Love's master-piece; being the first part of that romance intituled Cleopatra* tr. 1652; *the second part* 1654; *the third part* 1655
Letters a1657 (1659, 1663)
LOVELACE, Richard *Lucasta's epodes, odes, sonnets, songs, etc. To which is added Aramantha, a pastorall* 1649
Lucasta: posthume poems a1657 (1659, 1864)
LOVELICH, Henry *The history of the Holy Grail* tr. c1450 (Roxb. Cl. 1861–63; E.E.T.S. 1874–75)
Merlin, a middle-English metrical version of a French romance c1450 (E.E.T.S. 1904–13)
LOVELL, Archibald *Cyrano de Bergerac's Comical history of the states and empires of the worlds of the sun and moon* tr. 1687
Pomey's (F. A.) Indiculus universalis; or, the universe in epitome. Enlarged by A. Lovell 1679
Simon's (R.) Critical history of the religions and customs of the Eastern nations tr. 1685
Thevenot's (J. de) Travels into the Levant tr. 1687
LOVELL, Robert *A compleat herball* 1659
— ed. 2, with many additions 1665
A compleat history of animals and minerals 1661
LOVELOCK, Ian ('Yann') *The vegetable book: an unnatural history* 1972
LOVER, Samuel *Handy Andy; a tale of Irish life* 1842
Legends and stories of Ireland 1831–34 (1855)
Rory O'More; a national romance 1837
Loves of Hero and Leander: a mock poem; with marginal notes and other choice pieces of drollery 1651 (1653)
LOVESEY, Peter Harmer *Invitation to a dynamite party* 1974

LOW, Charles R. *The Afghan war, 1838–42. From the journal and correspondence of Major-General Augustus Abbott* 1879
The autobiography of a man-o'-war's bell 1875
The history of the Indian navy 1613–1863 1877
LOW, David A. *An introduction to machine drawing and design* 1887 (1892)
LOW, George *Fauna Orcadensis: or the natural history of the quadrupeds, birds, reptiles and fishes of Orkney and Shetland, from a MS.* a1795 (1813)
A tour through the Islands of Orkney and Schetland, containing hints collected in 1774 a1795 (1879)
LOW, Sidney J. M. & PULLING, Frederic S. *The dictionary of English history* 1884 (1904)
Low-life: or one half of the world knows not how the other half lives 1764 (ed. 3)
LOWE, Alexander *General view of the agriculture of the county of Berwick* 1794
LOWE, Charles *Prince Bismarck; an historical biography* 1885
LOWE, Edward J. *A natural history of British grasses* 1858
LOWE, Peter *The whole course of chirurgerie* 1597
—ed. 2, entitled *A discourse of the whole art of chyrurgerie* 1612; ed. 3, 1634
LOWE, Robert *General view of the agriculture of the county of Nottingham* 1794
LOWE, Robert *Speeches and letters on reform* 1867
LOWE, Roger *Extracts from a Lancashire diary* 1663–78 (1876)
LOWELL, James Russell *Writings* v.d. (1890)
Poetical works 1873, 1880, 1882
Poems a1891 (1912)
Among my books 1870; series II, 1876
The Biglow papers 1848; series II, 1862
Cambridge thirty years ago 1854
The cathedral 1869
Conversations on some of the old poets 1845
Democracy and other addresses 1886
A fable for critics 1848
Fireside travels 1864
Letters a1891 (1894)
My study windows 1871
The old English dramatists a1891 (1892)
Under the willows and other poems 1868
The vision of Sir Launfal 1848
A year's life 1841
LOWELL, Robert Traill Spence *Near the ocean* 1967
Notebook 1970
LOWER, Mark A. *English surnames* 1842 (1875)
LOWER, Sir William *The amourous fantasme, a tragi-comedy* 1660
The enchanted lovers: a pastoral 1658
The noble ingratitude: a comedy tr. 1659
The phoenix in her flames: a tragedy 1639
Polyeuctes, or the martyr: a tragedy tr. 1655
A relation in form of journal of the voiage and residence which Charles the II has made in Holland tr. 1660
LOWIE, Robert Heinrich *The history of ethnological theory* 1937 (UK 1938)
LOWNDES, George R. *Camping sketches* 1892
LOWNDES, Marie Adelaide Belloc *Diaries and letters 1911–1947* ed. S. Lowndes 1971
The Terriford mystery 1924
LOWNDES, Mary E. 1891 *See* Høffding, H.
LOWNDES, Richard *The law of general average* 1873 (1878)
A practical treatise on the law of marine insurance 1881
LOWNDES, William *A report containing an essay for the amendment of the silver coins* 1695
LOWRY, Clarence Malcolm *Selected letters* ed. H. Breit & M. B. Lowry 1965 (UK 1967)
Ultramarine 1933
Under the volcano 1947
LOWSLEY, Barzillai *A glossary of Berkshire words and phrases* 1888 (E.D.S.)
LOWSON, Alexander *John Guidfellow* 1890
LOWSON, G. *The modern farrier* 1844 (1877)
LOWTH, Bp. Robert *Isaiah; a new translation; with a preliminary dissertation, and notes critical, philological, and explanatory* 1778
Lectures on the sacred poetry of the Hebrews tr. by G. Gregory 1787 (1816)
A letter to the author of 'The divine legation of Moses demonstrated' 1765
The life of William of Wykeham 1758
Sermons and other remains a1787 (1834)
A short introduction to the English grammar (anon.) 1762 (1763)
LOWTH, William *A commentary upon the larger and lesser prophets* 1730
A vindication of the divine authority and inspiration of the Old and New Testament 1692 (1699)
Loyal and impartial satyrist 1694 *See* S., S.
Loyal convert 1643 *See* QUARLES, F.
Loyal songs, A collection of 1639–61 (1731)
Loyer's (Pierre le) Treatise of specters or straunge sights tr. by Z. Jones 1605
LOYN, Henry Royston *Anglo-Saxon England and the Norman Conquest* 1962
'LUARD, L.' (William Blaine Luard) *All hands* 1933
Conquering seas 1935
LUARD, Nicholas *The Robespierre serial* 1975
Travelling horseman 1975
LUBBOCK, Adelaide *Australian roundabout* 1963
LUBBOCK, Alfred Basil *Round the Horn before the mast* 1902
LUBBOCK, Sir John *Addresses, political and educational* 1879
Ants, bees, and wasps 1882
The beauties of nature and the wonders of the world we live in 1892
On British wild flowers considered in relation to insects 1875
On the origin and metamorphoses of insects 1874
The pleasures of life 1887–89
Pre-historic times, as illustrated by ancient remains, and the manners and customs of modern savages 1865 (1869, 1878)
The scenery of England and the causes to which it is due 1902
Scientific lectures 1879
The origin of civilisation and the primitive condition of man 1870 (1875)
LUCAR, Cyprian *Tartaglia's (N.) Three bookes of colloquies concerning the arte of shooting* tr. 1588
LUCAS, Charles *An essay on waters* 1756
LUCAS, Dione & HUME, Rosemary *'Au petit cordon bleu': an array of recipes* 1936
LUCAS, Edward Verrall *Over Bemerton's: an easy-going chronicle* 1908
Reading, writing and remembering: a literary record 1932
The vermilion box 1916
LUCAS, Francis *Sketches of rural life and other poems* 1889
LUCAS, Joseph *Kalm's (P.) Account of his visit to England on his way to America in 1748* tr. 1892
Studies in Nidderdale 1867–72 1882
LUCAS, Norman *The C.I.D.* 1967
LUCAS, Richard *An enquiry after happiness* 1685
Twenty four sermons preached on several occasions 1710
LUCAS, Samuel *Secularia; or, surveys in the mainstream of history* 1862
LUCAS, Theophilus *The memoirs of gamesters and sharpers* 1714
Lucca's (G. di) Memoirs 1737 See BERINGTON, S.
LUCCOCK, John *The nature and properties of wool illustrated* 1805
LUCE, S. B. *Seamanship* 1863
LUCIA, Ellis *Klondike Kate: the life and legend of Kitty Rockwell* 1962
Lucidarie. Die mittelenglische Version des Elucidariums des Honorius Augustodunensis c1425 (ed. Schmitt 1909)
Luck of Ladysmede 1860 *See* COLLINS, W. L.
LUCKOMBE, Philip *A concise history of the origin and progress of printing* (anon.) 1770
—ed. 2, entitled *The history and art of printing* 1771
Luctus Britannici: or the tears of the British muses for the death of John Dryden 1700
Luctus Britannici; poem to the memory of R. L'Estrange 1705
Ludlow, Churchwardens' accounts See *Churchwardens*
LUDLOW, Edmund *Memoirs* a1692 (1698–99, 1751, 1894)
LUDLOW, Fitz H. *Little brother, and other genre pictures* 1867
LUDLOW, John M. *Popular epics of the Middle Ages of the Norse-German and Carlovingian cycles* 1865
A sketch of the history of the United States from Independence to Secession 1862
LUDLUM, Robert *The Holcroft covenant* 1978
The Matlock paper 1973
Ludus Coventriæ See *Coventry mysteries*
LUFFMAN, John *The charters of London* 1793
LUGARD, Frederick John Dealtry *Diaries* ed. M. Perham 4 vols. 1959–63
LULL, Richard Swann *Organic evolution* 1917
LUMHOLTZ, Carl *Among Cannibals* 1889
Luminalia; or the festivall of light 1637 (Grosart 1876)
LUMLEY, John Lumley, 1st Baron 1589 *See* PUTTENHAM, G.
LUMSDEN, James ('S. Mucklebackit') *Edinburgh poems and songs* 1899
Sheep-head and trotters 1892
LUMSDEN, Sir Peter S., & ELSMIE, George R. *Lumsden of the Guides: a sketch of the life of Sir H. B. Lumsden* 1899
LUNN, Arnold Henry Moore *Harrovians* 1913
LUPTON, Donald *Flanders* 1658
London and the country carbonadoed and quartred into severall characters 1632 (in Harl. Misc.)
LUPTON, Thomas *A dream of the Deuill and Diues* 1584
Sivqila; too good to be true 1580
A thousand notable things of sundrie sorts 1579 (1585, 1675)
LUPTON, Thomas *Management and the social sciences* 1966
—(ed. 2) 1970
LURIE, Alison *Love and friendship* 1962
The nowhere city 1965
Real people 1969
The war between the Tates 1974
LUSH, Vicesimus *Auckland journals, 1850–63* ed. A. Drummond 1971
Thames journals, 1868–82 ed. A. Drummond 1975
LUSHINGTON, Henry *The Italian war 1848–49, and the last Italian poet (Giuseppe Giusti)* 1859
LUSHINGTON, Thomas *See* 'JONES, Robert'
Lusignan: a novel 1801
LUSTED, Charles T. *Studies in life and literature* 1893
Lusty juventus c1565 *See* WEVER, R.
Lutfullah, Autobiography of ed. E. B. Eastwick 1857
Luther's Commentary upon Galatians tr. 1575 *See* VAUTROLLIER, T.
LUTTRELL, Narcissus *A brief historical relation of state affairs* 1678–1714 (1857)
LUTYENS, Mary ed. *Effie in Venice: unpublished letters of Mrs. John Ruskin written from Venice between 1849–1852* 1965
Millais and the Ruskins 1967
The Ruskins and the Grays 1972
'LYALL, Edna' (Ada E. Bayly) *Donovan* 1882
Knight-Errant 1887
We two 1884
Won by waiting: a story of home life in France and England 1879
LYALL, Gavin Tudor *Blame the dead* 1972
Judas country 1975
The most dangerous game 1964
Shooting script 1966
Lybeaus Disconus See *Libeaus Desconus*
LYDAL, Thomas *Vulgar and decimal arithmetic* 1710
LYDE, Robert *A true and exact account of the retaking of a ship called 'The Friend's Adventure of Topsham'* tr. 1693 (in Arber, Eng. Garner VII)
LYDEKKER, Richard *The deer of all lands* 1898
A geographical history of mammals 1896
A hand-book to the marsupialia and monotremata 1894
Horns and hoofs, or, chapters on hoofed animals 1893
The royal natural history 1893–96
LYDGATE, John (*The assembly of gods: or The accord of reason and sensuality in the fear of death* 14.. (E.E.T.S. 1896))
A balade; in commendation of Our Lady c1420 (in Chaucerian pieces, Skeat 1897)
Bochas' Fall of princes tr. 1430–40 (1494, 1554, 1558; E.E.T.S. 1924–27)
Bycorne and Chichevache c1430 (in Minor poems, Percy Soc. 1840)
Chronicle of Troy See *Troy book*, below
The churl and the bird c1400 (Caxton, W. de Worde; Roxb. Cl. 1818; in Minor poems, Percy Soc. 1840)
The complaint of the black knight; or, The complaint of a loveres lyfe c1402 (in Chaucer's Works, ed. 1532; Chaucerian pieces, Skeat 1897)
The daunce of Machabree c1425 (in Bochas, ed. 1554 and E.E.T.S. 1924)
De Guileville's (G. de) Pilgrimage of the life of man tr. 1426 (E.E.T.S. 1899–1904)
Fabula duorum mercatorum (Tale of two merchants) ?a1412 (Quellen und Forschungen, LXXXIII. 1897)
The flour of curtesye 14.. (in Chaucer's Works, ed. 1532; Chaucerian pieces, Skeat 1897)
Horse, goose, and sheep, Debate between the c1440 (Caxton 1479; Roxb. Cl. 1822; in Pol., rel., and love poems, E.E.T.S. 1866, 1903)
The life of our Lady c1410 (Caxton 1484; ed. Tame 1879)
Merita missæ a1450 (in Lay folks mass book, E.E.T.S. 1879)
Minor poems, A selection from the c1430 (Percy Soc. 1840)
Minor poems c1430 (E.E.T.S. 1911)
Minor poems. The two nightingale poems 1446 (E.E.T.S. 1900)
Miracles of St. Edmund 1444 (in Horstmann, Altengl. Leg. 1881)
Reson and sensuallyte c1407 (E.E.T.S. 1901)
St. Albon and St. Amphabel, Lives of c1440 (1534, repr. Horstmann 1882)
St. Edmund and St. Fremund 1433 (in Horstmann, Altengl. Leg. 1881)
The serpent of division c1400 (1590; ed. H. N. MacCracken 1911)
Tale of two merchants See *Fabula*, above
Temple of glas c1403 (E.E.T.S. 1891)
Thebes, story of 1420–22 (in Chaucer's Works, ed. 1561; Chaucer Soc. and E.E.T.S. 1911)
Troy book 1412–20 (1513, 1555; E.E.T.S. 1906–10)
The vertue of yᵉ masse 14.. (W. de Worde, repr. Huth, Fugitive tracts 1875; Minor poems, E.E.T.S. 1911)
See also *Pilgrimage of the soul*
——& BURGH, Benedict *Secrees of old philisoffres* a1450 (E.E.T.S. 1894)
LYE, Edward *Dictionarium Saxonico et Gothico-Latinum* a1767 (1772)
See also JUNIUS, Francis, Jr.
LYE, Thomas *New spelling-book* 1677 (ed. 2)
LYELL, Sir Charles *The elements of geology* 1838
The geological evidences of the antiquity of man 1863
A manual of elementary geology 1851
Principles of geology 1830–33 (1867)
A second visit to the United States of North America 1849
The student's elements of geology 1871
Travels in North America 1845
LYELL, Thomas Reginald G. *Slang, phrase and idiom in colloquial English and their use* 1931
LYFORD, William *Three sermons preached at Sherborne in Dorsetshire upon 2 Cor. 2, 15–16* a1653 (1654)
The translation of a sinner from death to life by the free grace of God 1648
LYLES, Sanders Truman *Biology of micro-organisms* 1969
LYLY, John *Complete works* a1606 (1902)
Dramatic works a1606 (1858)
Campaspe (anon.) 1584
—another issue, entitled *A moste excellent comedie of Alexander, Campaspe, and Diogenes* 1584
Endimion, the man in the moone (anon.) 1591
Euphues, the anatomy of wyt 1579 (Arber 1868)
Euphues and his England 1580 (Arber 1868)
Gallathea (anon.) 1592
Midas (anon.) 1592
Mother Bombie (anon.) 1594
Sapho and Phao (anon.) 1584
The woman in the moone 1597
See also *Maid; Pappe with an hatchet*
LYNCH, Hannah *George Meredith: a study* 1891
LYNCH, Thomas T. *Lectures in aid of self-improvement* 1853
Memorials of Theophilus Trinal 1850
The rivulet: a contribution to sacred song 1855 (1856, 1868)
LYNDE, Francis *The grafters* 1904
The quickening 1906

Lynde, Sir Humphrey *Via tuta; the safe way* 1628 (1632)
A case for the spectacles, or a defence of Via tuta a1636 (1638)
Lyndesay, Sir David *Works* a1555 (1571, 1879, E.E.T.S. 1865–71)
Selections from his poems v.d. (in Pinkerton, Scottish poems reprinted 1792)
The complaint and publict confessioun of the Kingis auld hound callit Bagsche c1536
The complaynt 1529
The dreme 1528
The historie (and testament) of ane nobil and wailȝeand squyer, William Meldrum 1550 (1594)
Kitteis confessioun c1540
The monarche (*Ane dialog betuix experience and ane courteour*) 1552
Ane satyre of the thrie estaits 1540 (1602)
The testament and complaynt of our soverane lordis papyngo 1530
Lyndewode, William *Provinciale (seu Constitutiones Angliæ)* 1433; Eng. transl. (1534)
— *Cui adjiciuntur Constitutiones Legatinæ D. Othonis, et D. Othoboni, cum annotationibus Johannis de Athona* (1679)
Lyon, Francis Hamilton tr. *T. Heyerdahl's The Kon-Tiki Expedition: by raft across the South Seas* (US ed. with title *Kon-Tiki: across the Pacific by raft*) 1950
Lyon, George F. *Journal of a residence and tour in the republic of Mexico in 1826* 1828
Lyon, Lilian Helen Bowes *Bright feather fading* 1936
The white hare, and other poems 1934
Lyons, Albert Michael Neil *Clara: some scattered chapters in the life of a hussey* 1912
Lyons, John *Introduction to theoretical linguistics* 1968
Semantics 2 vols. 1977
Structural semantics: an analysis of part of the vocabulary of Plato 1963
Lyra apostolica 1836 (1849)
Lyric poetry, Specimens of a1310 (ed. T. Wright, Percy Soc. 1842)
Lyrical ballads 1798; ed. 2, 1800
Lysons, Daniel *The environs of London* 1792–96
Lysons, Samuel *An account of Roman antiquities discovered at Woodchester in Gloucester* 1797
Lysons, Samuel *Claudia and Pudens; or the early Christians in Gloucester* 1861
Lyte, Henry *Dodoens' (R.) Niewe herball or historie of plantes* tr. 1578
'Lyth' *The golden south: memories of Australian home life 1843–88* 1890
Lytteil, William *Landmarks of Scottish life and language* 1877
Lyttelton, George, 1st Baron *Works* a1773 (1774)
Dialogues of the dead (anon.) 1760
— ed. 4, (with) *four new dialogues* 1765 (1776)
The history of the life of King Henry the Second 1767–71
Letters from a Persian in England to his friend at Ispahan 1735 (1744)
Observations on the conversion and apostleship of St. Paul, in a letter to Gilbert West (anon.) 1747
Lyttelton, Robert H. *See* Steel, A. G.
Lyttelton, Sarah Spencer, Lady *Correspondence* 1787–1870 (1912)
Lyttleton, Raymond Arthur *Mysteries of the solar system* 1968
Lytton, David *The goddam white man* 1960
Lytton, Edward G. E. L. Bulwer-Lytton, 1st Baron *Works* a1873 (1873–75)
Alice, or the mysteries 1838
Athens, its rise and fall 1837
Calderon the courtier 1838
Caxtoniana: a series of essays on life, literature, and manners 1863
The Caxtons, a family picture 1849
The coming race 1871
Devereux 1829
The disowned 1829
Ernest Maltravers 1837
Eugene Aram 1832
Falkland 1827
Godolphin 1833
Harold, the last of the Saxon kings 1848
Kenelm Chillingly, his adventures and opinions a1873
King Arthur 1848–49
The lady of Lyons; or love and pride; a play 1838
The last days of Pompeii 1834
The last of the barons 1843
Leila; or the siege of Granada 1838
Lucretia, or the children of night 1846
My novel; or varieties in English life 1853
The new Timon; a romance of London 1846
Night and morning 1841
The Parisians a1873 (1874)
Paul Clifford 1830
Pausanias the Spartan a1873 (1876)
Pelham; or the adventures of a gentleman 1828
The pilgrims of the Rhine 1834
Richelieu; a play, with historical odes 1838
Rienzi, the last of the tribunes 1835
A strange story 1862
What will he do with it? 1858
The wooing of Master Fox (the separate publication in 1894 of ch. xii of The pilgrims of the Rhine)
Zanoni 1842
Zicci 1841 (a short sketch of prec., in Monthly chronicle)
Lytton, Edward R. Bulwer-Lytton, 1st Earl of
King Poppy a1891 (1892)
Lucile 1860
Orval, or the fool of time 1869
The ring of Amasis 1863
The wanderer 1857
See also Fane, Julian C. H.
Lytton, Rosina Bulwer-Lytton, Baroness *Cheveley; or the man of honour* 1839
Lyvys of seyntys 1447 *See* Bokenham, O.

M

M., A. *Gabelhouer's (O.) Boock of physicke* tr. 1599
Guillemeau's (J.) Frenche chirurgerye or all the manualle operations of chirurgerye tr. 1597
M., A. See also Munday, A.
M., G. 1618 *See* Mynshul, G.
M., H., gent. *The colloquies or familiar discourses of D. Erasmus* tr. 1671
M——, H. *A poem sacred to the memory of the late P. Doddridge D.D.* 1752
M., I. 1595 *See* Markham, G.
M., I. *A health to the gentlemanly profession of servingmen; or the servingmans comfort* 1598
M., I. 1629 *See* Maxwell, James
M., J. 1609 *See* Melton, J.
M., J. 1629 *See* Mabbe, J.
M., J. 1642 *See* Marsh, J.
M., J. *A soveraigne salve to cure the blind* 1643
M., J. *The tragical history of the chevalier de Vaudray and the countess of Vergi* tr. 1726
M., L. 1572–83 *See* Mascall, L.
M., L. *Du Bosc's (J.) Accomplish'd woman* tr. 1753
M., T. 1599 *See* Moufet, T.
M., T. 1603 *See* Millington, T.
M., T. *The blacke booke* 1604 (Bullen, Middleton's works VIII)
M., T. a1650 *See* May, T.
M., T. 1660 *See* Walker, Clement
M., T. 1665 *See* Manley, T.
M., W. *The man in the moone, telling strange fortunes, or the English fortune teller* 1609 (Percy Soc. 1849)
M., W. *The queens closet opened, incomparable secrets in physick, chirurgery, . . and cookery* etc. 1655 (1658)
Mabbe, James *Aleman's (M.) The rogue; or the life of Guzman de Alfarache* tr. 1622 (1630)
Cervantes' Exemplary novels tr. 1640 (1900)
Fonseca's (C. de) Devout contemplations englished by J. M. 1629
The Spanish bawd represented in Celestina; or the tragicke comedy of Calisto and Melibea tr. 1631
McAdoo, William Gibbs *Crowded years* 1931
Macalister, Alexander *An introduction to the systematic zoology and morphology of vertebrate animals* 1878
A text-book of human anatomy 1889
Zoology of the invertebrate animals 1878
MacAlister, Donald *See* Ziegler, E.
Macalister, Robert Alexander Steward *A textbook of European archaeology* 1921 (only Vol. I published)
Macallo, J. *XCIX canons or rules learnedly describing an excellent method for practitioners in physick* 1659
Macardle, Dorothy *Children of Europe: a study of the children of liberated countries* 1949
MacArthur, Margaret *History of Scotland* 1873
Macaulay, Angus *The history and antiquities of Claybrook in the county of Leicester* 1791
Macaulay, Catharine *The history of England from the accession of James I to that of the Brunswick line* 1763–83
Macaulay, Emilie Rose *Crewe train* 1926
Dangerous ages 1921
Going abroad 1934
I would be private 1937
Keeping up appearances 1928
Last letters to a friend, 1952–58 ed. C. B. Smith 1962
Letters to a friend, 1950–52 ed. C. B. Smith 1961
Letters to a sister ed. C. B. Smith 1964
Orphan Island 1924
Personal pleasures 1935
Potterism: a tragi-farcical tract 1920
Staying with relations 1930
Told by an idiot 1923
The towers of Trebizond 1956
Macaulay, James *Poems on various subjects, in Scots and English* 1788
Macaulay, John S. *A treatise on field fortification* 1834 (1847, 1851)
Macaulay, Thomas Babington, Lord Macaulay *Biographies contributed to the Encyclopædia Britannica* a1859 (1860)
Critical and miscellaneous essays v.d. (1841–44, 1887)
The history of England from the accession of James II 1849, 1855, a1859 (1849–61)
Lays of ancient Rome 1842
The miscellaneous writings a1859 (1860)
'McBain, Ed' (Evan Hunter) *Ax* [UK: *Axe*] 1964
Cop hater 1956 (UK 1958)
Doll 1965 (UK 1966)
Guns 1976 (UK 1977)
Give the boys a great big hand 1960 (UK 1962)
Hail, hail, the gang's all here! 1971
Hail to the chief 1973
Let's hear it for the deaf man 1973
Long time no see 1977
The pusher 1959
Ten plus one 1963 (UK 1964)
McBain, James William *Colloid science* 1950
MacBeth, George Mann *A war quartet* 1969
McBride, Duncan *General instructions for the choice of wines and spirituous liquors* 1793
MacCabe, James D. *New York by sunlight and gaslight* 1882
McCabe, John *Mr. Laurel and Mr. Hardy* 1961 (UK 1962)
McCabe, Joseph tr. *E. Haeckel's The wonders of life* 1904
Maccall, William *The elements of individualism, a series of lectures* 1847
McCall's sewing, in colour 1964
McCann, George *Lectures on the right of private judgment* 1825 (1831)
McCardell, Roy Larcom *Conversations of a chorus girl* 1903
McCarthy, Ian Ellery *Nuclear reactions* 1970
McCarthy, Justin *Donna Quixote* 1879
A history of our own times 1879–80
Red diamonds 1893
The story of Gladstone's life 1898 (1906)
McCarthy, Justin H. *The French revolution* 1893
McCarthy, Mary Therese *Birds of America* [a novel] 1971
A charmed life 1955 (UK 1956)
The company she keeps 1942 (UK 1943)
The group 1963
The groves of Academe 1952 (UK 1953)
Memories of a Catholic girlhood 1957
On the contrary 1961 (UK 1962)
McCarthy, Wilson *The detail* 1973
McCartney, William *Olfaction and odours: an osphrésiological essay* 1968
Macchiavelli's (N.) Works tr. (H. Neville) 1675
M.'s Prince tr. 1675 (1883)
The uncasing of Machivils instructions to his sonne, with the answere to the same 1613
M.'s Vindication of himself and his writings 1675 (1691; Harl. Misc.)
See also Dacres, E.
McClane, Albert Jules ed. *McClane's Standard fishing encyclopedia* 1965
McClellan, John B. *The New Testament, a new translation* 1875
McCloy, Helen *A change of heart* 1973
Panic 1944 (UK 1972)
The sleepwalker 1974
Through a glass, darkly 1950 (UK 1951)
McClung, Clarence Erwin ed. *Handbook of microscopical technique* 1929
McClung, Nellie Letitia *Clearing in the west* 1935
The stream runs fast 1945
McClure, David (1748–1820) *Diary* with notes by F. B. Dexter 1899
McClure, James Howe *The caterpillar cop* 1972
Rogue eagle 1976
Snake 1975
McClure's Magazine (N.Y.) 1893–
McCombie, Thomas *Australian sketches* etc. 1861–66
The history of the colony of Victoria 1858
MacCook, Henry C. *American spiders and their spinning-work* 1889–93
MacCormac, Sir William *Antiseptic surgery* 1880
McCormick, John & Mascareñas, Mario Sevilla *The complete aficionado* 1967
McCosh, James *The method of divine government* 1850 (1874)
Realistic philosophy defended in a philosophic series 1887
The Scottish philosophy: biographical, expository, critical: from Hutcheson to Hamilton 1874 (1875)
McCowan, Daniel *Animals of the Canadian Rockies* 1936
McCracken, Daniel Delbert *Digital computer programming* 1957
McCrie, Thomas *The life of Andrew Melville* 1819
The life of John Knox 1812
McCrum, Robert *In the secret state* 1980
McCullers, Carson *Clock without hands* 1961
The heart is a lonely hunter 1940 (UK 1943)
The member of the wedding 1946
Macculloch, John *A geological classification of rocks* 1821
The highlands and western isles of Scotland 1824
Proofs and illustrations of the attributes of God 1830 (1837, 1843)
MacCulloch, John A. *The religion of the ancient Celts* 1911
McCulloch, John R. *A descriptive and statistical account of the British empire* 1846 (1854)
A dictionary . . of commerce and commercial navigation 1832 (1844, 1882)
The principles of political economy 1825
A treatise on the principles and practical influence of taxation and the funding system 1845 (1852)
McCulloch, Walter Fraser *Woods words: a comprehensive dictionary of loggers' terms* 1958
McCullough, Colleen *The thorn birds* 1977
McCutchan, Philip Donald *Call for Simon Shard* 1974
Storm south 1959
McCutcheon, George Barr *The rose in the ring* 1910
McDavid, Raven I. *See* Mencken, Henry Louis
'MacDiarmid, Hugh' (Christopher Murray Grieve) *The company I've kept* 1966
To circumjack Cencrastus; or, The curly snake 1930
MacDonagh, Michael *Irish life and character* 1898
Macdonald, Alexander *Love, law, and theology* 1869

MacDonald, George & Allan, J. *The botanist's text-book* 1853
MacDonald, George *Alec Forbes of Howglen* 1865
Annals of a quiet neighbourhood 1866 (1878)
At the back of the north wind 1871
A book of dreams 1871 (Works of fancy III)
Castle Warlock, a homely romance 1882
David Elginbrod 1862 (1863)
The disciple and other poems 1867
Donal Grant 1883
Ἔπεα ἄπτερα unspoken sermons 1866- (1867-89)
The marquis of Lossie 1877
Mary Marston 1881
Paul Faber, surgeon 1879
Phantastes, a faerie romance 1858 (1878)
Poems 1857; 1871 (Works of fancy I-IV)
The princess and Curdie 1883
Robert Falconer 1868
Sir Gibbie 1879
Thomas Wingfold, curate 1876
What's mine's mine 1886
Wilfrid Cumbermede 1872
Works of fancy and imagination (1871)
MacDonald, George *The Roman wall in Scotland* 1911
McDonald, Gregory *Confess, Fletch* 1976 (UK 1977)
Macdonald, James *Food from the far west; or American agriculture, with special reference to the importation of dead meat* 1878
MacDonald, John Dann *The brass cupcake* 1950 (UK 1955)
The executioners 1958 (UK 1959)
The girl, the gold watch, and everything 1962
ed. *The lethal sex: the 1959 anthology of the Mystery Writers of America* 1959 (UK 1962)
Pale gray for guilt 1968 (UK 1969)
'Macdonald, John Ross' *The Galton case* See 'Macdonald, Ross'
MacDonald, Philip *Mystery of the dead police* 1933
'Macdonald, Ross' (Kenneth Millar) *The Galton case* 1959 (UK 1960)
The instant enemy 1968
Macdonell, Archibald Gordon *Autobiography of a cad* 1938
England, their England 1933
McDonogh, Felix *The hermit in the country* (anon.) 1820-22
The hermit in Edinburgh (anon.) 1824
The hermit in London (anon.) 1819-20
The heroine of the Peninsula (anon.) 1826
The highlanders: a tale (anon.) 1824
McDouall or McDowall, Andrew, Lord Bankton *An institute of the laws of Scotland in civil rights* 1751-53
McDougall, William *An introduction to social psychology* 1908
An outline of abnormal psychology 1926
McDowall, William *History of the burgh of Dumfries* 1867 (1873)
The man of the woods and other poems 1844 (1882)
Macduff, John R. *Memories of Patmos; or some of the great words and visions of the apocalypse* 1871
Mace, Cecil Alec ed. *British philosophy in the mid-century* 1957
McEvoy, Joseph Patrick *Hollywood girl* 1929 (UK 1930)
Show girl 1928
McEwan, Ian *The comfort of strangers* 1981
MacEwen, Alexander R. *Life and letters of John Cairns* 1895
McFadden, Cyra *The serial: a year in the life of Marin County* 1977 (UK 1978)
MacFarlane, Charles *The lives and exploits of banditti and robbers* 1833 (1837)
Macfarlane, John *Memoir of Thomas Archer* 1867
Macfarlane, Walter *Genealogical collections* 1750-51 (S.H.S. 1900)
Geographical collections relating to Scotland 1721-44, 1748-49 (S.H.S. 1906-08)
Macfarren, Sir George A. *Counterpoint, a practical course of study* 1879 (1881)
Six lectures on harmony 1867
McGaffey, Kenneth *The sorrows of a show girl* 1908
MacGill, Hamilton *Memories of the rev. Dr. Hamilton MacGill* 1880
Macgill, Patrick *The brown brethren* 1917
Macgill, W. *Old Ross-shire* 1909-11
Macgillivray, William *A history of British birds* 1837-52
Lives of eminent zoologists, from Aristotle to Linnæus 1834
A manual of British ornithology 1840-42
The natural history of Dee side and Braemar a1852 (1855)
Richard's (A.) Elements of botany tr. 1831
ed. *The travels and researches of A. von Humboldt* 1832 (1836, 1851)
McGilvery, Robert Warren *Biochemistry: a functional approach* 1970
McGilvray, Alexander *Poems and songs* 1850
Macgilvray, John *Poems* 1787
McGirr, Edmund *Bardel's murder* 1973
Death pays the wages 1970
An entry of death 1969
The lead-lined coffin 1968
A murderous journey 1974
McGivern, William Peter *The big heat* 1953
Caprifoil 1972 (UK 1973)
M'Gowan, George tr. *A. Bernthsen's A text-book of organic chemistry* 1889
Meyer's (E. von) History of chemistry tr. 1891
Macgowan, John *Death: a vision* 1766 (1814)
McGraw-Hill dictionary of modern economics, The 1965
McGraw-Hill encyclopedia of science and technology 15 vols. 1960
— (new ed.) 15 vols. 1966
McGraw-Hill yearbook of science and technology 1963-
MacGregor, James *Life and letters* ed. Lady F. Balfour a1910 (1912)
MacGregor, John *The voyage alone in the yawl 'Rob Roy'* 1867 (1868)
Machiavelli, N. See *Macchiavelli, N.*
Machin, Lewis & Markham, G. *The dumbe knight, a historicall comedy* 1608 (Dodsley)
Machlin, Milton *Pipeline* 1976
McHugh, Hugh *Back to the woods: the story of a fall from grace* 1903
John Henry 1901
Skidoo! 1906
You can search me 1905
Machyn, Henry *Diary* 1550-63 (Camden Soc. 1848)
McIlvanney, William *Laidlaw* 1977
McIlwraith, William *The visitors' guide to Wigtownshire* 1875
McIndoe, George *Poems and songs chiefly in the Scottish dialect* (also two poems by James McIndoe) 1805
MacInnes, Colin *Absolute beginners* 1959
City of spades 1957
Mr. Love and Justice 1960
McInnes, Graham *The road to Gundagai* 1965
MacInnes, Hamish *Climb to the lost world* 1974
MacInnes, Helen *Agent in place* 1976
Message from Malaga 1972
The Salzburg connection 1969
McIntosh, Louis *Oxford folly* 1956
Mackail, Denis George *How amusing! And a lot of other fables* 1929
Mackail, John W. *The life of William Morris* 1899
McKay, Archibald *A history of Kilmarnock* 1848 (1864, 1880)
Mackay, Charles *A dictionary of lowland Scotch* 1888
Longbeard, lord of London: a romance 1841
Memoirs of extraordinary popular delusions 1841
The twin soul (anon.) 1887
Mackay, John *The church in the highlands* 1914
Mackay, Kenneth *Out back* 1893
— (ed. 2) 1893
Mackay, Thomas *The state and charity* 1898
Mackay, William P. *'Grace and truth' under twelve aspects* 1869 (1875)
McKellar, Thomas Peter Huntly *Experience and behaviour* 1968
McKenney, Thomas Loraine *Memoirs, official and personal; with sketches of travels among the northern and southern Indians* 2 vols. 1846
MacKenzie, Donald *Postscript to a dead letter* 1973
Raven and the kamikaze 1977
Mackenzie, Edward Montague Compton *April fools* 1930
Carnival 1912 (some quotations taken from 1912 US ed.)
The early life and adventures of Sylvia Scarlett 1918
Gallipoli memories 1929
Guy and Pauline 1915
The heavenly ladder 1924
My life and times 10 vols. 1963-71
The old men of the sea 1924
Sinister Street 2 vols. 1913-14
Sylvia and Michael: the later adventures of Sylvia Scarlett 1919
Whisky galore 1947
Mackenzie, Eneas *A descriptive and historical account of the town and county of Newcastle upon Tyne* 1827
A historical, topographical and descriptive view of the county of Northumberland etc. 1825
'Mackenzie, Fergus' (J. Anderson) *Sprays of northern pine* 1897
Mackenzie, Sir George *A discourse upon the laws and customs of Scotland in matters criminal* 1674 (1678)
Institutions of the laws of Scotland 1684 (1694)
Religio stoici, with a friendly addresse to the phanaticks of all sects and sorts 1663 (1665)
— *The religious stoic* 1685 (1693)
Mackenzie, George, 1st Earl of Cromarty *An historical account of the conspiracies by the Earls of Gowry and R. Logan of Restalrig against king James VI* 1713
Mackenzie, Henry *The man of feeling* (anon.) 1771 (1803)
The man of the world (anon.) 1772 (1803)
Mackenzie, James *The history of health, and the art of preserving it* 1758
Mackenzie, John *A narrative of the siege of London-Derry* 1690
Mackenzie, John *Day-dawn in dark places, a story of wanderings and work in Bechwanaland* 1883
Ten years north of the Orange River: a story of every-day life and work among the South African tribes, from 1859 to 1869 1871
Mackenzie, Sir Morell *A manual of diseases of the throat and nose* 1880-84
The use of the laryngoscope in diseases of the throat 1865 (1871)
Mackenzie, Murdoch *A treatise on marine surveying* 1774 (1819)
Mackenzie, Norman Ian *Conviction* 1958
McKerlie, Peter H. *History of the lands and their owners in Galloway* 1870-79
McKerrow, Ronald Brunlees *An introduction to bibliography for literary students* 1927
McKie, Ronald Cecil H. *The company of animals* 1965
Mackinnon, Doris Livingston & Hawes, R. S. J. *An introduction to the study of protozoa* 1961
Mackinnon, John *Account of Messingham in the county of Lincoln* 1825 (1881)
Mackintosh, Alexander *The Driffield angler* c1810
Mackintosh, Daniel *The scenery of England and Wales* 1869
Mackintosh, Ewart Alan *War, the liberator, and other pieces* 1918
Mackintosh, Sir James *Dissertation on the progress of ethical philosophy* 1830 (1836)
The history of England 1830-31
History of the revolution in 1688 a1832 (1834)
The miscellaneous works 1791-1830 (1846)
On the right of parliamentary suffrage 1819 (1846)
Vindiciæ gallicæ, Defence of the French Revolution etc. 1791
Mackintosh, Margaret *The cottager's daughter, a tale* 1836
Macklin, Charles *Love à la mode, a comedy* 1784 (1793)
The man of the world, a comedy 1786 (1793)
McKnight, Cathy & Tobler, John *Bob Marley: the roots of reggae* 1977
McKnight, George Harley *English words and their background* 1923
Macknight, James *A new literal translation..of all the apostolical epistles* 1795 (1809)
Macky, John *A journey through England* (anon.) 1714 (1722)
Maclagan, Alexander *Sketches from nature and other poems* 1851
Maclaine, Archibald *Mosheim's (J. L. von) Ecclesiastical history, antient and modern* tr. 1765-68
Maclaren, Alexander *Sermons preached in Manchester* 1863-73 (1875)
Maclaren, Archibald *A military system of gymnastic exercises* 1862
'Maclaren, Ian' (J. Watson) *Beside the bonnie brier bush* 1894
A doctor of the old school 1895 (1897)
Kate Carnegie, and those ministers 1896
Maclaren, Walter S. B. *Spinning woollen and worsted: being a practical treatise for the use of all..engaged in those trades* 1884
Maclaren-Ross, Julian *The doomsday book* 1961
Until the day she dies 1960
McLauchlan, Thomas *The early Scottish church* 1865
Maclaurin, Colin *An account of Sir I. Newton's philosophical discoveries* a1746 (1748)
A treatise of algebra a1746 (1748)
A treatise of fluxions 1742
McLean, Archibald *Miscellaneous works* a1812 (1847-48)
Maclean, Fitzroy Hew *Eastern approaches* 1949
Maclean, Magnus ed. *Modern electric practice* 6 vols. 1904-5
McLean, Sarah Pratt *Cape Cod folks* 1881
McLean, Terence Power *Kings of Rugby: the British Lions' 1959 tour of New Zealand* 1960
Maclean's magazine 1912-
Maclear, George F. *Conversion of the west. The Celts* 1878
McLeave, Hugh *A question of negligence* 1970 (UK 1973)
Macleay, William S. *Annulosa Javanica* 1825
Horæ entomologicæ; or essays on the annulose animals 1819-21
Maclennan, John F. *Primitive marriage* 1865
MacLennan, Malcolm *Peasant life; being sketches of the villagers and field-labourers in Glenaldie* (anon.) 1869-72
Macleod, Henry D. *The elements of banking* 1876
Macleod, Iain *Bridge is an easy game* 1952
'MacLeod, Robert' (William Knox) *Burial in Portugal* 1973
McLevy, James *Curiosities of crime in Edinburgh during the last thirty years* 1861
McLintock, Alexander Hare ed. *A descriptive atlas of New Zealand* 1959
McLuhan, Herbert Marshall *The Gutenberg galaxy* 1962
The mechanical bride: folklore of industrial man 1951 (UK 1967)
Understanding media: the extensions of man 1964
—— & Fiore, Quentin *The medium is the massage* 1967
McMahon, Patrick Joseph *Aircraft propulsion* 1971
Macmanus, James *The bend of the road* 1898
Macmichael, William *Lives of British physicians* (anon.) 1830 (1857)
Macmillan, Hugh *Bible teachings in nature* 1867 (1870)
Footnotes from the page of nature, or first forms of vegetation 1861
The true vine; or the analogies of our Lord's allegory 1870 (1871)
Macmillan, Michael *The promotion of general happiness, a utilitarian essay* 1890
Macmillan's Magazine 1859-1907
McMullen, Edwin Wallace *English topographic terms in Florida, 1563-1874* 1953
McMurtrie, Henry *Cuvier's (G. L. C. F. D. de, baron) Animal kingdom* tr. and abridged 1834
MacNab, Angus *The bulls of Iberia: an account of the bullfight* 1957
McNab, William *Botany, morphology and physiology* 1878
Botany, outlines of classification of plants 1878
MacNeice, Frederick Louis tr. *Aeschylus' Agamemnon* 1936
Astrology ed. D. Hill 1964
Autumn journal: a poem 1939
Autumn sequel: a poem 1954
Christopher Columbus: a radio play 1944
The dark tower, and other radio scripts 1947
The earth compels: poems 1938
tr. *Goethe's Faust* 1951
Holes in the sky: poems 1944-1947 1948

MacNeice, Frederick Louis (*cont.*)
I crossed the Minch 1938
The last ditch 1940
Modern poetry: a personal essay 1938
Poems 1935
The poetry of W. B. Yeats 1941
See also Auden, Wystan Hugh
McNeile, Alan Hugh *An introduction to the study of the New Testament* 1927
McNeill, Angus *The egregious English* 1903
Macneill, Hector *Poetical works* 1801, *a*1818 (1856)
Bygane times and late come changes 1811
Scotland's skaith, or the history o' Will and Jean 1795
The waes o' war, or the upshot o' the history o' Will and Jean 1796
McNeill, Peter *Blawearie; or mining life of the Lothians forty years ago* 1887
McNicoll, David *Works* *a*1836 (1837)
A rational inquiry concerning the operations of the stage on the morals of society 1823 (1837)
Macnish, Robert *The anatomy of drunkenness* 1827 (1847)
Macphail, James M. *Kenneth S. Macdonald, missionary of the Free Church of Scotland, Calcutta* 1904 (1905)
Macphail, S. R. *History of the religious house of Pluscardyn..in Morayshire* 1881
Macpherson, James *Fragments of ancient poetry (by Ossian)* 1760
An introduction to the history of Great Britain and Ireland 1771
Ossian's Fingal, an ancient epic poem 1762
Ossian's Temora, an ancient epic poem 1763
Macquarrie, John ed. *A dictionary of Christian ethics* 1967
Macquoid, Gilbert S. ed. *Jacobite songs and ballads* 1887
Macquoid, Katharine S. *At the Red glove, a novel* 1885
Macquoid, Percy *A history of English furniture* 1904
McRae, Archibald Graham *The hill called Grazing: the story of a Transvaal farm* 1956
McRae, Thomas Watson *The impact of computers on accounting* 1964
Macready, William C. *Diaries* ed. W. Toynbee 2 vols. 1912
M.'s Reminiscences and selections from his diaries and letters *a*1873 (1875)
Macrimmon, a highland tale (by A. Sutherland) 1823
Macro plays, The (*Mankind* *c*1475; *Wisdom* *c*1460; *The castle of perseverance* *c*1425) (E.E.T.S. 1904)
Macsparran, James *America dissected, being a full and true account of all the American colonies* 1752 (1753)
A letter book and abstract of out services, written during the years 1743–51 (1899)
Mactaggart, John *The Scottish Gallovidian encyclopedia* 1824 (1876)
MacVicar, Angus *The painted doll affair* 1973
MacVittie, Robert B. *Details of the restoration of Christ Church cathedral, Dublin* 1878
MacWard, Robert *Ἐπαγωνισμοι or Earnest contendings for the faith* *c*1680 (1723)
The true non-conformist (anon.) 1671
Madan, Martin *A new and literal translation of Juvenal and Persius* 1789 (Persius 1795)
Thelyphthora, or a treatise on female ruin (anon.) 1780–81
Madan, Patrick *A philosophical and medical essay of the waters of Tunbridge* 1687 (Harl. Misc.)
Madden, Samuel *Themistocles, the lover of his country, a tragedy* 1729
Maddox, Harry Alfred *A dictionary of stationery* 1923
Maddox, Bp. Isaac *Sermons* *a*1759
A vindication of the government, doctrine and worship of the church of England (against Neal's History of the Puritans) 1733
Mademoiselle 1935–
Madox, Thomas *Firma burgi; or an historical essay concerning the cities, towns and buroughs of England* 1726
Formulare Anglicanum: or a collection of ancient charters and instruments 1702
The history and antiquities of the exchequer of the kings of England 1711
Madras. Music Academy *Journal* 1930–
Maerz, Aloys John & Paul, Morris Rea *A dictionary of color* 1930
Mätzner, Eduard *Altenglische Sprachproben, nebst einem Wörterbuche* 1867–1900
Maffei, A., Count *Brigand life in Italy* 1865
Maffei's (F. S.) Compleat history of the ancient amphitheatres tr. A. Gordon 1730
Magazine of art, The 1878–
Magazine of natural history 1829–40
— *The annals and magazine of natural history* 1841–
Magdalen college and James II, a series of documents 1686–88 (O.H.S. 1886)
Magens, Nicolas *An essay on insurances* 1755
Magic lantern, The 1822 *See* Blessington, Countess of
Magnus, Francis *Sonnerat's (P.) Voyage to the East Indies and China* tr. 1788–89
Magnusson, Eirikr *Notes on shipbuilding and nautical terms of old in the north* 1906
—— & Morris, W. *Völsunga saga: the story of the Volsungs and Niblungs* tr. 1870
Magopico. The memoirs of Magopico minister of Muchtiwharrock (by S. Haliburton & T. Hepburn) 1761 (1791)
Maguire, D. *The art of massage* 1887 (ed. 4)
Maguire, Michael *Scratchproof* 1976
Mahaffy, John P. *Social life in Greece: from Homer to Menander* 1874
Mahan, Alfred T. *The influence of sea power upon history 1660–1783* 1890
Lessons of the war with Spain 1900
Mahon, Andrew *L'Abbat's Art of fencing, or the use of the small sword* tr. 1734 (1735)
Mahony, Francis S. *The reliques of Father Prout* 1836 (1859)
Maid. The maydes metamorphosis (attrib. to J. Lyly) 1600 (Bullen, Old plays I, 1882)
Maid Emlyn. The boke of mayd Emlyn *c*1500 (W. de Worde; Ancient poetical tracts, Percy Soc. 1842)
Maiden, Joseph H. *The forest flora of New South Wales* 8 vols. 1904–25
The useful native plants of Australia 1889
Maiden aunt, The: by a lady 1776
Maidment, James ed. *A book of Scotish pasquils 1568–1715* 1868
ed. *Scotish ballads and songs* 1859, 1868
—— & Logan, W. H. ed. *Dramatists of the Restoration* 1872–79
Maier, Richard Ali & Maier, Barbara M. *Comparative animal behavior* 1970
Mailer, Norman *Advertisements for myself* 1959 (UK 1961)
Cannibals and Christians 1966 (UK 1967)
The naked and the dead 1948 (UK 1949)
Main, Robert ed. *Herschel's (Sir J. F. W.) Manual of scientific enquiry* 1859
Maine, Sir Henry J. S. *Ancient law: its connection with the early history of society and its relations to modern ideas* 1861 (1871)
Dissertations on early law and custom 1883
Lectures on the early history of institutions 1875
Village communities in the east and west 1871
Maines, George H. & Grant, Bruce *Wise-crack dictionary* 1926
Mainichi Daily News (Tokyo) 1922– (title varies)
Mainwaring or Maynwaring, Arthur *The life and posthumous works* *a*1712 (1715)
See also Garth, Sir S. 1717; *Medley* 1710
Mainwaring, Arthur *Cut Cavendish, or whist in a few whiffs* 1899
Mainwaring, Sir H. *See* Manwayring
Maitland, Frederic W. *Domesday book and beyond* 1897
Township and borough 1898
See also Pollock, Sir F.
Maitland, James *The apology for William Maitland of Lethington* 1610 (S.H.S. 1904)
Maitland, Julia Charlotte *Letters from Madras during the years 1836–39 by a lady* (1843)
Maitland, Sir Richard *Ancient Scotish poems..from the MS. collections of Sir R. M...comprising pieces..from about 1420 till 1586* (ed. Pinkerton 1786)
Poems (Maitland Club 1830)
The Maitland folio MS. (S.T.S. 1919–27)
The Maitland quarto MS. (S.T.S. 1920)
Maitland, Samuel R. *The dark ages* 1844
Eruvin; or miscellaneous essays on subjects connected with the nature, history and destiny of man 1831 (1850)
Essays on subjects connected with the reformation in England 1849
Facts and documents illustrative of the history..of the ancient Albigenses and Waldenses 1832
False worship: an essay 1856
Illustrations and enquiries relating to mesmerism 1849
Six letters on Fox's Acts and monuments 1837
Maitland, William *The history of Edinburgh* 1753
Maitland Club *Publications* 1828–59
Miscellany 1833–43
Major, Clarence *Dictionary of Afro-American slang* 1970
Major Jack Downing of the Downingville militia 1860 (1865)
Major Jones's courtship (by W. T. Thompson) 1844
Malamud, Bernard *The assistant* 1957
Dubin's lives 1979
The fixer 1966 (UK 1967)
The natural 1952 (UK 1963)
A new life 1961 (UK 1962)
The tenants 1971
Malay Mail (Kuala Lumpur) 1896–
Malcolm, Alexander *A treatise of musick* 1721
Malcolm, James P. *Anecdotes of the manners and customs of London* 1808
'Malcolm X' (Malcolm Little) *Autobiography* 1965
Malcom, Howard *Travels in south-eastern Asia, embracing Hindustan, Malaya, Siam and China* 1839 (1840)
Maldon (Essex) *Court books* (MS.) 1557–1764
Court rolls (MS.) 1402–1504
Maledicta: the international journal of verbal aggression (Waukesha, Wisconsin) 1977–
'Malet, Lucas' (Mary St. Leger Harrison) *Colonel Enderby's wife, a novel* 1885
The dogs of want: a modern comedy of errors 1924
The gateless barrier 1900
The history of Sir Richard Calmady, a romance 1901
The wages of sin 3 vols. 1891
Malinowski, Bronislaw Kasper *Coral gardens and their magic* 2 vols. 1935
A scientific theory of culture, and other essays 1944
Sex and repression in savage society 1927
Malkin, Benjamin H. *Le Sage's (A. R.) Adventures of Gil Blas of Santillane* tr. 1809
The scenery, antiquities and biography of South Wales 1804
Mallery, Garrick *The gesture speech of man* 1881
Mallet, David *Works* v.d. (1759)
Poems *a*1765 (1790)
Amyntor and Theodora, or the hermit; a poem 1747
The life of Francis Bacon, lord chancellor of England 1740
Mallet's (P. H.) Northern antiquities tr. Bp. T. Percy 1770 (1847)
Mallet, Robert *Earthquakes* (*Earthquake phenomena*) 1849–59 (Manual of scientific enquiry 1859)
Mallett, Edward *Telegraphy and telephony, including wireless* 1929
'Malloch, Peter' (William Murdoch Duncan) *Kickback* 1973
Mallock, William H. *Is life worth living?* 1877 (1879)
The new Paul and Virginia or positivism on an island 1878
The new republic: or culture, faith, and philosophy in an English country house 1877 (1878)
A romance of the nineteenth century 1881
Malmesbury, James Harris, 1st Earl of *Diaries and correspondence* *a*1820 (1844)
A series of letters of the 1st earl of M., his family and friends 1745–1820 (1870)
Malmesbury, James Howard Harris, 3rd Earl of *Memoirs of an ex-minister: an autobiography* 1884
Malmesbury, William of *De gestis regum Anglorum* 1125–42 (Rolls series 1887–89)
Malone, Edmond *An account of the life and writings of J. Dryden* 1800
ed. *Shakespeare's Works* 1790 (1821)
Supplement to Johnson and Steevens, Shakespeare's Works 1780
Malory, Sir Thomas *Le morte Darthur* tr. 1470–85 (Sommer 1889; also Copland 1557; 1634; Southey 1817)
Malthus, Thomas R. *An essay on the principle of population* etc. 1798, 1803 (1817)
Travel diaries ed. P. James 1966
Malvery, Olive C. *The soul market* 1906
Malynes, Gerard de *Consuetudo vel lex mercatoria; or the ancient law-merchant* 1622
Mammalia. Sketches in natural history, history of the mammalia 1849
Man, John *Musculus' (W.) Common places of christian religion* tr. 1563
Man: a paper for ennobling the species 1755
Man: a monthly record of anthropological science 1901–
Man in the moone, The 1609 *See* M., W.
Man in the moon, The: consisting of essays and critiques on the politics, manners, drama etc. of the present day 1804
Man in the moon, The (by W. Hone) 1820
Man, Laws of the Isle of See Mills, M. A.
Management engineering 1921–3
Manby, George W. *Journal of a voyage to Greenland* 1822
Manby, Thomas ed. *A collection of all the statutes made in the reigns of Charles I and Charles II* (1667)
Manchester, Sir Henry Montagu, 1st Earl of *Manchester al mondo; contemplatio mortis et immortalitatis* 1633 (1636)
Manchester, 7th Earl of *See* Montagu, W. D.
Manchester Courier 1825–
Manchester Examiner 1846–
Manchester Guardian 1821–
Manchester Guardian Weekly 1919–68
Manchini or *Colonna, Maria*, princess of Palliano. *The apology; or the genuine memoirs of madam Maria Manchini* tr. 1679
Manchon, Joseph *Le slang: lexique de l'anglais familier et vulgaire, précédé d'une étude sur la prononciation et la grammaire populaires* 1923
Mander, James *The Derbyshire miners' glossary* 1824
Mander, John *Static society: the paradox of Latin America* 1969
Mandeville, Bernard *An enquiry into the origin of honour and the usefulness of christianity in war* 1732
The fable of the bees; or private vices publick benefits 1714 (1723)
Free thoughts on religion, the church and national happiness 1723 (1729)
The grumbling hive, or knaves turn'd honest 1705
— (enlarged ed., see *Fable of the bees*, above)
Some fables after the manner of Fontaine 1703
Mandeville, Sir J. *See* Maundeville
Mandey, Venterus *Mellificium mensionis, or the marrow of measuring* 1727
—— & Moxon, J. *Mechanick powers, or the mistery of nature and art unvailed* 1696
Maner of kepynge a court baron and a lete, The tr. 1544 (1546)
Mangan, James Clarence *Anthologia germanica: German anthology* 1845
Poems *a*1849 (1859)
Manifestation 1616 *See* Dominis, M. A. de
Maning, Frederick Edward *Old New Zealand* 1863
Mankind (a morality) *c*1475 (Brandl 1898; Macro plays, E.E.T.S. 1904)
Mankowitz, Cyril Wolf & Haggar, Reginald George *The concise encyclopedia of English pottery and porcelain* 1957
Manley, Mrs. Mary de la Riviere *The adventures of Rivella* 1714
Court intrigues: in a collection of original letters, from the island of the new Atalantis 1711
The power of love: in seven novels 1720 (1741)
Secret memoirs..of several persons of quality..from the new Atalantis 1709–20 (1736)
Manley, Thomas ed. *Cowell's (J.) Interpreter* 1684
H. Grotius De rebus Belgicis; or, the annals and history of the Low-Countrey-Wars tr. T. M. 1665
The nature of testaments, executors etc. 1676
Manlove, Edward *The liberties and customes of the lead-mines within the wapentake of Wirksworth in the county of Derby* 1653 (E.D.S. 1874)

MANLY, John Matthews *Specimens of the pre-Shaksperean drama* 1897–98
MANN, Anthony *Tiara* 1973
MANN, Charles Riborg & MILLIKAN, Robert Andrews tr. *P. Drude's The theory of optics* 1902
MANN, Edward C. *A manual of psychological medicine and allied nervous diseases* 1883
MANN, Jessica *Mrs. Knox's profession* 1972
The sticking place 1974
MANN, Mary E. *The fields of Dulditch* 1902
In summer shade 3 vols. 1893
A winter's tale 1891
Manners and household expenses of England in the thirteenth and fifteenth centuries (Roxb. Club 1841)
Manners, The boke of good (1507) See *Boke*
MANNING, Anne *Belforest, a tale of English country life* 1865
The old Chelsea bun-house, a tale of the last century 1855
MANNING, Frederic *The middle parts of fortune* 2 vols. 1929
MANNING, Henry E., cardinal *The grounds of faith* 1852
The internal mission of the Holy Ghost 1875
Petri privilegium, three pastoral letters 1869 (1871)
Sermons 1842– (1843–50)
MANNING, Olivia *The great fortune* 1960
The rain forest 1974
MANNING OF BRUNNE, Robert *See* BRUNNE
MANNINGHAM, Bp. Thomas *Sermons* a1722
Two discourses; the first shewing the chief criterions of philosophic truth..; the second, manifesting how all the foundations of the intellectual world..have been undermin'd by popish doctrines and policies 1681
MANNOCH, John P. *Billiards expounded to all degrees of amateur players* 1904
MANSEL, Henry L. *The gnostic heresies of the first and second centuries* a1871 (1875)
Letters, lectures and reviews a1871 (1873)
Metaphysics; or the philosophy of consciousness, phenomenal and real 1860 (1875)
Prolegomena logica 1851 (1860)
MANSELL, Roderick *An exact and true narrative of the late popish intrigue to form a plot* 1680
MANSFIELD, Charles B. *A theory of salts* 1855 (1865)
'MANSFIELD, Katherine' (Kathleen Middleton Murry) *Bliss, and other stories* 1920
Collected stories 1945
The doves' nest, and other stories 1923
Journal ed. J. M. Murry 1954
Letters to John Middleton Murry, 1913–1922 ed. J. M. Murry 1951
Something childish, and other stories 1924
MANSFIELD, Robert B. *School-life at Winchester college..with a glossary of words, phrases and customs peculiar to Winchester college* 1866 (1870)
MANSFIELD, Walter Kenneth *Elementary nuclear physics* 1958
MANSON, F. B. *Timbers* (part of G. Watt's 'Economic products of India') 1883
MANSON, George J. *The sporting dictionary* 1895
MANSON, Patrick *Tropical diseases: a manual of the diseases of warm climates* 1898
MANT, Richard *Rome, her tenets and her practices* 1843
MANTELL, Gideon A. *The fossils of the South downs, or illustrations of the geology of Sussex* 1822
Petrifactions and their teachings 1851
MANTON, Thomas *Christ's temptations and transfiguration practically explained* a1677 (1685, 1870)
Englands spirituall languishing (a sermon) 1648
One hundred and ninety sermons on Ps. CXIX a1677 (1681, 1872)
A practical commentary..on the epistle of James 1651 (1871)
— *on the epistle of Jude* 1658 (1871)
A practical exposition of the Lord's prayer a1677 (1684, 1870)
Several discourses tending to promote peace and holiness a1677 (1685, 1871)
Manual of scientific enquiry, A See HERSCHEL, Sir J. F. W.
MANVELL, Arnold Roger & HUNTLEY, John *The technique of film music* 1957
MANWARING, Charles William ed. *A digest of the early Connecticut probate records* 3 vols. 1904–6
MANWAYRING, Sir Henry *The sea-mans dictionary* a1625 (1644)
MANWOOD, John *A brefe collection of the lawes of the forest* 1592
A treatise and discourse of the lawes of the forrest etc. 1598 (1615)
MAP or MAPES, Walter *The Latin poems commonly attributed to Walter Mapes* (c1200). Appendix (containing translations and imitations) v.d. (Camden Soc. 1841)
MAPLET, John *A greene forest or a naturall historie, wherein may be seene..the most sufferaigne vertues in all..stones and mettals,..plantes, herbes..brute beastes* etc. 1567
MARAIS, Eugène Nielen *My friends the baboons* [anon. tr.] 1939
Marana's (J. P.) Letters writ by a Turkish spy who lived five and forty years undiscovered at Paris tr. 1692–94
MARBECK, John *A book of notes and common places with their expositions, collected and gathered out of the workes of divers singular writers* 1581
MARBURY, Edward *A brief commentarie..upon the prophecy of Obadiah* 1649 (1865)
A commentarie..upon the prophecies of Habakkuk 1650 (1865)
MARBUT, C. F. tr. *K. D. Glinka's The great soil groups of the world and their development* 1927
MARCEL, Claude *Language as a means of mental culture and international communication; or, manual of the teacher and the learner of languages* 1853
MARCELLINE, George *Epithalamium Gallo-Britannicum* 1625
The triumphs of king James I 1610
MARCET, Alexander *An essay on the chemical history and medical treatment of calculous disorders* 1817
MARCET, Jane *The seasons, stories for very young children* 1832–33
MARCET, William *On chronic alcoholic intoxication* 1859 (1860)
MARCH, Francis A. *A comparative grammar of the Anglo-saxon language* 1870
MARCH, John *Actions for sclaunder* 1647
MARCHANT, Edgar Walford *Radio telegraphy and telephony* 1923
MARCUS, Stanley *Minding the store: a memoir* 1974 (UK 1975)
MARCUS, Steven *The other Victorians* 1966
MARCY, Randolph B. *The prairie traveller: a handbook for overland expeditions* 1859
MARDER, Irving *The Paris bit* 1967
MARDON, Edward R. *Billiards* 1844 (1849, 1858)
MARETT, Robert R. *Anthropology* 1911
ed. *Anthropology and the classics: six lectures* 1908
Margaret, Saint. Seinte Marherete c1200: *Seinte Margarete* c1300: *Meidan Maregrete* c1250 (E.E.T.S. 1862)
MARGERISON, Donald & EAST, George C. *An introduction to polymer chemistry* 1967
MARIN, Alfred C. *The clash of distant thunder* 1968 (UK 1969)
Rise with the wind 1969
Marin's (M. A.) Perfect religious tr. 1762
Marine engineer (title varies) 1879–1972
MARINER, William 1817 *See* MARTIN, John
Mariner's mirror 1911–
MARION, Fulgence *Wonderful balloon ascents* [anon. tr.] 1870
'MARIOTTI, Luigi' *See* GALLENGA, A.
'MARJORIBANKS' *The fluff-hunters* 1903
MARKBY, Sir William *Elements of law considered with reference to general jurisprudence* 1871 (1874)
MARKFIELD, Wallace *To an early grave* 1964 (UK 1965)
MARKHAM, Albert H. *The great frozen sea: a personal narrative of the voyage of the 'Alert' during the arctic exploration of 1875–76* 1878
MARKHAM, Sir Clements R. *The life of the great Lord Fairfax* 1870
ed. *Narratives of the mission of G. Bogle to Tibet and of the journey of T. Manning to Lhasa* 1876
Peruvian bark: a popular account of the introduction of chinchona cultivation into British India 1880
MARKHAM, Francis *The book of honour, or five decads of epistles of honour* 1625
Five decades of epistles of warre 1622
MARKHAM, Gervase *The art of archerie* 1634
Cavelarice, or the English horseman: contayning all the arte of horsemanship etc. 1607 (1617)
Cheape and good husbandry for the well-ordering of all beastes and fowles etc. 1614 (1623)
Country contentments in two bookes: the first containing the whole art of riding great horses, etc.: the second intituled The English huswife 1615 (1631, 1649, 1668)
The country housewifes garden, together with the husbandry of bees, etc. 1617 (1623, 1648)
The dumbe knight, a historicall comedy by Jarvis M. (and L. Machin) 1608 (Dodsley)
The English husbandman 1613–15 (1635)
The English hus-wife (part of Country contentments) 1615
Estienne (C.) and Liebault's (J.) Maison rustique; or the countrey farme tr. (cf. Surflet, R.) and augmented 1616
Hungers prevention, or the whole arte of fowling by water and land 1621 (1655)
The inrichment of the weald of Kent, or a direction for the husbandman etc. 1625 (1631)
M.'s Farwell to husbandry, or the inriching of all sortes of barren and sterril grounds 1620 (1649)
M.'s maister-peece or what doth a horse-man lacke, containing all possible knowledge whatsoever which doth belong to any smith, farrier or horse-leech 1610 (1623)
— *M.'s master-piece revived* (1688)
The most honorable tragedie of Sir Richard Grinvile 1595 (Arber, The last fight of 'The Revenge' at sea)
The pleasures of princes or good mens recreations (part of The English husbandman) 1615 (1635)
The poem of poems or Sions muse, contayning the divine song of king Solomon, by I. M. 1595
A way to get wealth (re-issue of several of the above) 1631–38 (1648–49, 1660, 1688)
MARKHAM, William O. *Skoda's (J.) Treatise on auscultation and percussion* tr. 1853
MARKS, Percy *Collector's choice* 1972
The plastic age 1924
MARKS, Robert W. *The dymaxion world of Buckminster Fuller* 1960
MARLBOROUGH, John Churchill, 1st Duke of *Letters and despatches* 1702–12 (1845)
Marlorat's (A.) Catholike exposition upon the revelation of saint John tr. 1574
— *Catholike exposition uppon the two last epistles of John* tr. 1578 (1580)
MARLOTH, Hermann Wilhelm Rudolf *The flora of South Africa* 4 vols. 1913–32
MARLOWE, Christopher *The famous tragedy of the rich Jew of Malta* c1592 (1633)
Hero and Leander (finished by G. Chapman) a1593 (1598)
Lucan's First booke tr. a1593 (1600)
The massacre at Paris 1592 (c1600)
All Ovid's elegies a1593 (c1597)
Tamburlane the great (2 parts) 1586, –87 (1590)
The tragical history of Doctor Faustus c1590 (1616)
The troublesome raigne and lamentable death of Edward the second a1593 (1594)
—— & NASHE, Thomas *The tragedie of Dido queene of Carthage* a1593 (1594)
Marly; or a planter's life in Jamaica 1828
Mar-Martine (attrib. to T. Nashe) 1589 (1843–45)
MARMION, Shackerley *The antiquary, a comedy* 1636 (1641; Dodsley)
A fine companion, a comedy 1633
Hollands leaguer, an excellent comedy 1632
Maroccus extaticus, or Bankes bay horse in a trance 1595 (Percy Soc. 1843)
MARPLES, Morris *Public school slang* 1940
University slang 1950
'MARPRELATE, Martin' *Hay any worke for Cooper* 1589 (1844)
Oh read over D. John Bridges (preliminary *Epistle to the terrible priests of the Confocation House*) 1588 (1842)
Oh read over D. John Bridges..or an epitome of the fyrste booke..written against the Puritanes 1588 (1843)
Theses Martinianæ: that is, certaine demonstrative conclusions sette downe and collected by M. M. the great 1589 (1843–45)
See also *Almond* 1590; HARVEY, R. 1589; *Mar-Martine* 1589; *Martins months minde* 1589; NASHE, T. 1589; *Pappe with an hatchet* 1589
MARQUAND, Allan *Greek architecture* 1909
MARQUAND, John Phillips *H. M. Pulham, Esquire* 1941 (UK 1942)
Wickford Point 1939
MARQUARD, Leopold *The peoples and policies of South Africa* 1952
Marriage. A new and pleasaunt enterlude intituled The marriage of witte and science c1570 (Hazl. Dodsley)
The marriage of wit and wisdom a1590 (Shaks. Soc. 1846)
Marriage broaker, The; or the pander, (a comedy) by M. W. 1662 (Gratiæ theatrales 1662)
MARRIOT, Robert *A sermon in commemoration of Mris. E. Dering* 1641
MARRIOTT, Harry *Cariboo cowboy* 1966
MARRIOTT, Sir James *The rights and privileges of both universities..defended* 1769
MARRIOTT, Wharton B. *Vestiarium christianum: the origin and gradual development of the dress of holy ministry in the church* 1868
MARRIOTT, William *Hints to meteorological observers* 1881 —(ed. 6) 1906
MARRYAT, Florence (Mrs. F. Lean) *The blood of the vampire* 1897
Open sesame 1875
Under the lilies and roses 1884
MARRYAT, Frank S. *Mountains and molehills: or, recollections of a burnt journal* 1855
MARRYAT, Frederick *The children of the New forest* 1847 (1848)
A diary in America 1839
The dog-fiend See *Snarleyyow*, below
Frank Mildmay See *Naval officer*, below
Jacob Faithful 1834
Japhet in search of a father 1836
Joseph Rushbrook; or the poacher 1841
The king's own 1830
Masterman Ready; or the wreck of the Pacific 1841
Mr. Midshipman Easy 1836
Narrative of the travels and adventures of Monsieur Violet in California etc. 1843 (1873)
The naval officer; or scenes and adventures in the life of Frank Mildmay 1829
Newton Forster; or the merchant service 1832
Olla podrida (Diary on the continent 1835–37, etc.) (1840)
The pacha of many tales 1835
Percival Keene 1842
Peter Simple 1834 (1863)
The phantom ship 1839
The pirate, and the three cutters 1836
The poacher See *Joseph Rushbrook*, above
Poor Jack 1840
Rattlin the reefer See HOWARD, E. G. G.
Snarleyyow; or the dog-fiend 1837 (1840)
Valerie, an autobiography 1847 (1849)
MARRYAT, Horace *One year in Sweden* 1862
MARRYAT, Joseph *Collections towards a history of pottery and porcelain* 1850
A history of pottery and porcelain 1857 (1868)
MARSDEN, John B. *The history of the early puritans* 1850 (1853)
MARSDEN, Reginald G. ed. *Select pleas in the court of admiralty* (1390–1404, 1527–45, 1547–1602) (Selden Soc. 1894–97)
MARSDEN, William *The history of Sumatra* 1783
MARSH, Mrs. Anne *Emilia Wyndham; a novel* 1846
Evelyn Marston 1856
Father Darcy 1846
Ravenscliffe 1851
MARSH, Edward Howard *Rupert Brooke: a memoir* 1918
MARSH, George P. *Lectures on the English language* 1858–59 (1862)

MARSH, John An argument.. of the great question concerning the militia, by J. M. (formerly ascribed to Milton) 1642
MARSH, John Thompson Self-smoothing fabrics 1962
MARSH, Ngaio Edith Artists in crime 1938
Black as he's painted 1974
Colour scheme 1943
Dead water 1963 (UK 1964)
Death and the dancing footman 1941 (UK 1942)
Death in a white tie 1938
Death in ecstasy 1936
Death of a fool 1956 (UK ed. 1957 with title Off with his head)
Death of a peer 1940 (UK ed. 1941 with title Surfeit of Lampreys)
False scent 1959 (UK 1960)
Final curtain 1947
Grave mistake 1978
Hand in glove 1962
A man lay dead 1934
Off with his head See above: Death of a fool
Opening night 1951
Overture to death 1939
Singing in the shrouds 1958 (UK 1959)
Surfeit of Lampreys See above: Death of a peer
Swing, brother, swing 1949
Tied up in tinsel 1972
Vintage murder 1937
MARSHAK, Robert Eugene Meson physics 1952 (UK 1953)
MARSHALL, Agnes B. Mrs. A. B. Marshall's cookery book 1888
— ('tenth thousand') 1889
Mrs. A. B. Marshall's larger cookery book of extra recipes 1892
MARSHALL, Alfred Principles of economics 1890
MARSHALL, Bruce George Brown's schooldays 1946
MARSHALL, Charles A plain and easy introduction to the knowledge and practice of gardening: with hints on fish-ponds 1796 (1813)
MARSHALL, Emma Memories of troublesome times 1880
MARSHALL, Henry Military miscellany, comprising a history of the recruiting of the army, military punishments, etc. 1846
MARSHALL, Humphry Arbustrum Americanum: the American grove; or, An alphabetical catalogue of forest trees and shrubs, natives of the American United States 1785
MARSHALL, John The writings of J. Marshall upon the federal constitution a1835 (1839)
MARSHALL, John Outlines of physiology, human and comparative 1867
MARSHALL, Julian The annals of tennis 1878
—— et al. Tennis, rackets, fives 1890
MARSHALL, Percival Metal working tools and their uses 1902
MARSHALL, Stephen A copy of a letter written.. to a friend 1643
A peace offering to God, a sermon 1641
A sacred panegyrick or a sermon of thanksgiving 1644
A sermon, Nov. 17, 1640 1641
MARSHALL, Sybil An experiment in education 1963
MARSHALL, Thomas Humphrey Citizenship and social class, and other essays 1950
MARSHALL, W. G. Through America; or nine months in the United States 1881
MARSHALL, Walter The gospel-mystery of sanctification opened in sundry discourses 1692 (1764, 1780)
MARSHALL, William E. A phrenologist among the Todas 1873
MARSHALL, William H. Minutes of agriculture made on a farm.. near Croydon 1778
Planting and rural ornament (anon.) 1796
A review of the reports of the Board of agriculture from the northern (western etc.) department of England (5 parts) 1808-18
The rural economy of Glocestershire 1789 (1796)
— Provincialisms from the above (E.D.S. 1873)
The rural economy of the midland counties 1790 (1796)
— Provincialisms (E.D.S. 1873)
The rural economy of Norfolk 1787 (1795)
— Provincialisms (E.D.S. 1873)
The rural economy of the southern counties 1798
The rural economy of the west of England 1796
— Provincialisms (E.D.S. 1873)
The rural economy of Yorkshire 1788 (1796)
— Provincialisms (E.D.S. 1873)
MARSTON, John Works v.d. (1633; also 1856, 1887)
The history of Antonio and Mellida 1600 (1602)
— (part 2) Antonios revenge 1600 (1602)
The Dutch courtezan, a comedy 1605
(The insatiate countess, a tragedie 1613)
The malcontent 1604
The metamorphosis of Pigmalions image; and certaine satyres 1598 (1764)
Parasitaster, or the fawne, a comedy 1606
The scourge of villanie, three books of satyres 1598 (1764)
— corrected, with the addition of newe satyres 1599
What you will, a comedy 1607
The wonder of women, or the tragedie of Sophonisba 1606
—— et al. Jacke Drums entertainment or the comedie of Pasquill and Katherine 1600 (1601; R. Simpson, School of Shaks. 1878)
See also Histrio-mastix 1610
MARTEN, Henry Familiar letters to his lady of delight. Also her kinde returnes 1662
Martens' (F.) Observations made in Greenland and other northern countries tr. 1694 (Acc. sev. late voy. 1711)
MARTIALL, John A treatyse of the crosse, gathred out of the scriptures etc. 1564
MARTIN, Basil Kingsley Editor: a second volume of autobiography, 1931-45 1968
Father figures: a first volume of autobiography, 1897-1931 1966
MARTIN, Benjamin The general magazine of arts and sciences 1755
Institutions of language 1748
The natural history of England 1759-63
The philosophical grammar 1735
MARTIN, Benjamin Messiah's kingdom in its origin, development and triumph 1876
MARTIN, Edward His opinion concerning the difference between the church of England and Geneva etc. a1662 (1662)
MARTIN, H. Helen of Glenross; a novel 1801 (1802)
MARTIN, Helen Tillie, a Mennonite maid 1904 (UK 1905)
MARTIN, Helena (Faucit), Lady On some of Shakespeare's female characters 1885
MARTIN, Henry N. & MOALE, W. A. A hand-book of vertebrate dissection 1881-84
MARTIN, James Discourses a1834 (1835)
MARTIN, James Keil's (C. F.) Biblical commentary on the prophecies of Ezekiel tr. 1876
MARTIN, John ed. Mariner's (W.) Account of the natives of the Tonga islands,.. with.. grammar and vocabulary of their language 1817
MARTIN, Joseph ed. A new and comprehensive gazetteer of Virginia, and the District of Columbia 1835
MARTIN, Laurence Cleveland & HYNES, Martin Clinical endocrinology for practitioners and students 1948
— (ed. 3, by Martin alone) 1961
MARTIN, Martin A description of the western islands of Scotland 1703
A late voyage to St. Kilda 1698
MARTIN, Mary Ann Our Maoris 1884
MARTIN, R. F. Havrez' (J.) On recent improvements in winding machinery tr. 1875
MARTIN, Robert Denis tr. W. Wickler's Mimicry in plants and animals 1968
MARTIN, Sir Theodore The Æneid of Virgil books I-VI tr. 1896
A life of Lord Lyndhurst 1883
The odes of Horace tr. 1860
—— & AYTOUN, W. E. Bon Gaultier's Book of ballads 1855
MARTIN or MARTYN, Thomas A traictise declaryng.. that the pretensed marriage of priestes.. is no mariage 1554
MARTIN, William The New Zealand nature book 1929 (UK 1930)
MARTIN, William C. L. The ox (Farmer's Libr. I) 1847
MARTINDALE, Adam The countrey-survey-book: or land-meters vade-mecum 1682
MARTINDALE, William The extra pharmacopoeia of unofficial drugs etc. 1883 (1890)
MARTINE, George Reliquiæ divi Andreæ: or the state of the see of St. Andrews 1683 (1797)
MARTINE, John Reminiscences of the royal burgh of Haddington 1883
MARTINEAU, Harriet Autobiography 1855 (1877)
A complete guide to the English lakes 1855
Feats on the fiord 1841
The history of England during the thirty years' peace 1816-46 1849-50
Introduction to the history of the peace 1851
Illustrations of political economy 1832-33
Berkeley the banker 1833, Briery creek 1833, Brooke and Brooke farm 1833, The charmed sea 1833, Cinnamon and pearls 1833, Demerara 1832, Ella of Garveloch 1832, The hill and the valley 1832, Homes abroad 1832, Ireland 1832, Life in the wilds 1832, The loom and the lugger 1833, A Manchester strike 1832, A tale of the Tyne 1833, Weal and woe in Garveloch 1832
Society in America 1837
MARTINEAU, James Endeavours after the christian life 1843-47 (1867)
Essays philosophical and theological v.d. (1866-69)
Essays, reviews and addresses v.d. (1890-91)
Hours of thought on sacred things 1876-79
Miscellanies 1852
The seat of authority in religion 1890
Studies of christianity 1858
Types of ethical theory 1885
Martini's (M.) Bellum tartaricum, or the conquest of the great.. empire of China tr. 1654
Martiniere's (P. M. de la) New voyage into the northern countries tr. 1674
Martins months minde, that is, a certaine report.. of the death and funeralls of olde Martin Marre-prelate 1589
MARTYN, Benjamin Timoleon, a tragedy 1730
MARTYN, Thomas The language of botany 1793 (1796)
ed. Miller's (P.) Gardener's and botanist's dictionary 1807
Rousseau's (J. J.) Letters on the elements of botany tr. 1785 (1794)
MARTYN, William Youths instruction 1612
MARTYN, William F. The geographical magazine 1782-83
Martyr'd souldier, The (1638) See SHIRLEY, H.
MARVELL, Andrew Works a1678 (1776; Grosart 1872-75)
An account of the growth of popery and arbitrary government in England (anon.) 1678
A collection of poems on affairs of state (1689)
Correspondence 1653-78 (Grosart II)
Mr. Smirke, or the divine in mode.. With a short historical essay concerning general councils etc. 1676
Poems a1678 (1776, 1872)
The Rehearsal transprosed 1672, 1673 (1674)
Upon Appleton house a1678
MARWICK, Sir James D. Edinburgh guilds and crafts (v.d.) a1908 (1909)
MARX, Groucho (Julius Henry Marx) The Groucho letters: letters from and to Groucho Marx 1967
MARX, Heinrich Karl See MOORE, Samuel & AVELING, E. B.
Mary. The song of Mary the mother of Christ containing the story of his life and passion 1601
MARY, princess. Privy purse expenses of the princess Mary, daughter of K. Henry VIII 1536-44 (1831)
Mary Magdalene c1620 See ROBINSON, T.
Maryland, U.S. Acts of assembly 1692-1715 (1723)
The laws of Maryland v.d. (1799-1800)
Maryland historical magazine 1906-28
MASCALL, Eric Lionel Christian theology and natural science: some questions on their relations 1956
The recovery of unity: a theological approach 1958
MASCALL, Leonard A booke of the arte and maner howe to plant and graffe all sortes of trees, etc. Englished by L. M. 1572 (1592, 1652)
The first (second, third) booke of cattell 1587 (1596, 1627)
A profitable boke declaring dyuers approoued remedies to take out spottes and staines.. With diuers colours how to die velvets and silkes tr. out of Dutch by L. M. 1583 (1588)
MASEFIELD, John E. Ballads 1903
Ballads and poems 1910
The bird of dawning 1933
Captain Margaret: a romance 1908
The Conway, from her foundation to the present day 1933
Dauber, a poem 1913
Dead Ned: the autobiography of a corpse 1938
The everlasting mercy 1911
Gautama the enlightened, and other verse 1941
The hawbucks 1929
Live and kicking Ned 1939
Lollingdon Downs and other poems, with sonnets 1917
Odtaa 1926
Reynard the fox; or, The ghost heath run 1919
Salt-water ballads 1902
Sard Harker 1924
A tarpaulin muster 1907
The tragedy of Nan, and other plays 1909
The widow in the bye street 1912
MASKELL, William Ivories ancient and mediæval 1872 (1875)
Monumenta ritualia ecclesiæ anglicanæ 1846-47
MASKELYNE, John N. Sharps and flats, a complete revelation of the secrets of cheating at games of chance and skill 1894
MASKELYNE, Mervin H. N. STORY- Crystallography: a treatise on the morphology of crystals 1895
MASON, Alfred Edward Woodley The house of the arrow 1924
Miranda of the balcony 1899
The truants 1904
MASON, Charles P. English grammar 1858 (1881)
MASON, Charlotte M. The forty shires: their history, scenery, arts and legends 1880 (1881)
MASON, Francis The authoritie of the church in making canons and constitutions.. a sermon 1605 enlarged 1607
MASON, Francis The natural productions of Burmah 1850
MASON, Frederick A. tr. G. von Georgievics's A text-book of dye chemistry 1920
MASON, George A supplement to Johnson's English dictionary 1801
MASON, Henry The epicures fast 1626
The new art of lying covered by Jesuites under the vaile of equivocation discovered and disproved 1624
MASON, James The anatomie of sorcerie 1612
MASON, James The principles of chess in theory and practice 1894
MASON, John A briefe discourse of the New-found-land 1620 (Bannatyne Club 1867)
MASON, John Select remains a1694 (1828)
Spiritual songs or songs of praise 1683
MASON, John An essay on elocution (anon.) 1748
An essay on the power and harmony of prosaic numbers (anon.) 1749
An essay on the power of numbers.. in poetical compositions 1749
Self-knowledge, a treatise shewing the nature and benefit of that important science and the way to attain it 1745 (1853)
'MASON, Margery' The tickler tickled 1679
MASON, Monck Aeronautica; or, Sketches illustrative of the theory and practice of aerostation 1838
MASON, Richard Lakin The world of Suzie Wong 1957
MASON, William Caractacus, a dramatic poem 1759
Correspondence See GRAY, T.
Elfrida, a dramatic poem 1752
The English garden 1772-81
Essays historical and critical on English church music 1795
An heroic epistle to Sir W. Chambers 1773
An heroic postscript to the public 1774
Musæus, a monody to the memory of Mr. Pope 1744 (1747)
Masque of poets, A 1878
Massachusetts. Agricultural Survey First report on the agriculture of Massachusetts by H. Colman 1838
Second report 1839
Massachusetts (Colony). House of Representatives Journals 1919-
Massachusetts Bay See Records
Massachusetts Historical Society Collections 1792- (1806-)
Massachusetts spy, or the Worcester gazette, The 1772-1830
MASSEY, Gerald The natural genesis 1883
MASSEY, William The origin and progress of letters 1763

MASSEY, William N. *A history of England during the reign of George the third* 1855–63 (1863)
MASSIE, Joseph *Reasons humbly offered against laying any farther tax on malt or beer* 1760 (1770)
MASSINGER, Philip *Dramatic works* a1640 (1840)
The bashful lover, a tragicomedy 1636 (1655)
Believe as you list, a tragedy 1631 (Percy Soc. 1849)
The bond-man, an antient storie 1623 (1624)
The city-madame, a comedie 1632 (1659)
The duke of Millaine, a tragædie 1623
The emperour of the east, a tragæ-comedie 1631 (1632)
The great duke of Florence, a comicall historie 1627 (1636)
The guardian 1633 (1655)
The maid of honour (a tragi-comedy) 1632
A new way to pay old debts, a comœdie 1625 (1633)
The old law: see Middleton, T.
The parliament of love 1624 (Plays, ed. Gifford 1805 II)
The picture, a trage-comedy 1629 (1630)
The Roman actor, a tragædie 1626 (1629)
The unnaturall combat, a tragedie c1619 (1639)
Three new playes, viz, the bashful lover, the guardian, the very woman (1655)
A very woman; or the prince of Tarent, a tragi-comedy 1634 (1655)
—— & DEKKER, T. *The virgin martir, a tragedie* 1622 (1631, 1661, 1870)
—— & FIELD, N. *The fatall dowry, a tragedy* 1632
MASSINGHAM, Harold John *The curious traveller* 1950
World without end 1932
MASSON, David *British novelists and their styles* 1859
Carlyle personally and in his writings 1885
Chatterton: a story of the year 1770 1856 (1874)
Edinburgh sketches and memories v.d. (1892)
Essays biographical and critical 1856
The life of J. Milton 1859–80
Recent British philosophy 1865
Wordsworth, Shelley, Keats, and other essays 1874
MASSON, Madeleine *Birds of passage* 1950
Master of game, The c1410 (MS. Digby 182, etc.; ed. Hahn)
— (MS. Cott. Vesp.; ed. W. A., & F. Baillie-Grohmann 1904)
MASTERMAN, John Cecil *Fate cannot harm me* 1935
MASTERS, John *Bhowani Junction* 1954
Bugles and a tiger: a personal adventure 1956
Coromandel! 1955
The deceivers 1952
Far, far the mountain peak 1957
The lotus and the wind 1953
Nightrunners of Bengal 1951
Trial at Monomoy 1964
MASTERS, Maxwell T. *Vegetable teratology* 1869
MASTERS, Ted *Surfing made easy* 1962
MASTERSON, Thomas *Arithmeticke* 1592–95
MASUR, Harold Q. ed. *Murder most foul* 1973
MATEER, Samuel *'The land of charity': a descriptive account of Travancore and its people* 1871
Materials and technology: a systematic encyclopedia of the technology of materials used in industry and commerce 8 vols. 1968–75
Materials for a history of the reign of Henry VII 14..–15.. (Rolls series 1873–77)
MATES, Benson *Elementary logic* 1965
Mathematical reviews 1940–
Mathematical tables and other aids to computation 1943–59
'MATHER, Berkeley' (John Evan W. Davies) *The break in the line* 1970
Snowline 1973
The springers 1968
MATHER, Cotton *Christian loyalty* 1727
Magnalia Christi Americana; or the ecclesiastical history of New-England 1702 (1853)
Memorable providences relating to witchcrafts and possessions 1689
The wonders of the invisible world: being an account of the tryals of several witches, lately executed in New-England 1693
MATHER, E. J. *Nor'ard of the Dogger, or deep-sea trials and gospel triumphs* 1887 (1888)
MATHER, Increase *A brief history of the war with the Indians in New-England* 1676
— (new ed.) *The history of king Philip's war* (1862)
An essay for the recording of illustrious providences 1684
— (new ed.) *Remarkable providences illustrative of the earlier days of American colonisation* (1856)
MATHER, Samuel *Irenicum, or an essay for union* 1680
MATHER, William *The young man's companion, or arithmetick made easy* etc. 1710 (1727)
MATHESON, George *The representative men of the Bible* 1902, 1903
MATHEW or MATHEWS, Richard *The unlearned alchymist his antidote* 1662
MATHEWS, Albert Prescott *Physiological chemistry* 1916
MATHEWS, Anne *Memoirs of Charles Mathews, comedian* 4 vols. 1838–9
Tea-table talk, ennobled actresses and other miscellanies 1857
MATHEWS, Catharine Van Cortlandt *Andrew Ellicott: his life and letters* 1908
MATHEWS, Charles J. *Life, chiefly autobiographical, with selections from his correspondence and speeches* a1878 (ed. C. Dickens 1879)
MATHEWS, George D. *Coinages of the world, ancient and modern* 1876
MATHEWS, Mitford M. ed. *A dictionary of Americanisms on historical principles* See under title
MATHEWS, William *Getting on in the world: or hints on success in life* 1873–76
MATHEWSON, Christopher *Pitching in a pinch; or, Baseball from the inside* 1912
Second base Sloan 1917
MATHIAS, Thomas J. *The pursuits of literature, or what you will, a satirical poem* 1794 (1798, 1801)
MATON, William G. *Observations relative chiefly to the natural history, picturesque scenery and antiquities of the western counties of England* 1797
MATSELL, George Washington *Vocabulum; or, The rogue's lexicon, compiled from the most authentic sources* 1859
'MATTHEW, Thomas' *The Byble* tr. 1537 (1549)
MATTHEWS, Henry *The diary of an invalid* 1820
MATTHEWS, J. Brander *A secret of the sea* etc. (tales) 1886
MATTHEWS, Leonard Harrison *The life of mammals* 2 vols. 1969–71
MATTHEWS, Washington *Ethnography and philology of the Hidatsa Indians* 1877
Matthiæ's (A. H.) Greek grammar tr. E. V. Blomfield a1816 (1818)
Matthieu's (P.) Powerfull favorite, or the life of Ælius Sejanus tr. 1628
— *Unhappy prosperitie* tr. T. Hawkins 1632 (1639)
Mattie:—a stray (by F. W. Robinson) 1864
MATURIN, Charles R. *Melmoth the wanderer, a tale* 1820
MATY, Paul Henry *A new review with literary curiosities and literary intelligence* 1782–86
Riesbeck's (J. C.) Travels through Germany tr. 1787
MAUDSLEY, Henry *Body and mind* (Gulstonian lectures) 1870
Body and will 1883
The physiology and pathology of the mind 1867
Responsibility in mental disease 1874
MAUGHAM, Robin (Robert Cecil Romer Maugham) *The servant* 1972
MAUGHAM, William Somerset *The bishop's apron: a study in the origins of a great family* 1906
The bread-winner 1930
Cakes and ale; or, The skeleton in the cupboard 1930
The circle 1921
The constant wife 1926
Liza of Lambeth 1897
The moon and sixpence 1919
Of human bondage 1915
On a Chinese screen 1922
Our betters 1923
The painted veil 1925
The razor's edge 1944
Sheppey 1933
The summing up 1938
Theatre 1937
Then and now 1946
A writer's notebook 1949
MAUNDER, Samuel *The treasury of knowledge* 1830
The treasury of natural history 1848 (also 1862)
MAUNDEVILLE, Sir John *The buke of John Maundeuill being the travels of Sir J. Mandeville knight 1322–56* c1400 (Roxburghe Club 1889)
The voiage and travaile of Sir J. M. kt. c1400 (Halllw. 1839)
— *Mandeville's Travels* (E.E.T.S. 1919)
See also *Ser John Mandevelle*
MAUNDRELL, Henry *A journey from Aleppo to Jerusalem 1697* a1701 (1703, 1721, 1732)
MAURICE, Sir J. Frederick *Military history of the campaign of 1882 in Egypt* 1887
MAURICE, John Frederick Denison *The epistles of St. John* 1857
The friendship of books, and other lectures a1872 (1874)
Learning and working, six lectures 1854 (1855)
Moral and metaphysical philosophy 1845 (Encycl. Metrop.; also 1850–62)
The patriarchs and law-givers of the Old Testament 1855 (1867, 1877)
The prophets and kings of the Old Testament 1853
The religions of the world (Boyle lectures 1846) 1847 (1861)
MAURICE, Thomas *The fall of the Mogul, a tragedy* 1806
The history of Hindostan 1795–98 (1820)
MAURY, Matthew F. *The physical geography of the sea* 1855 (also Low 1860)
MAVOR, William *The British tourist's or traveller's pocket companion* 1809
General view of the agriculture of Berkshire 1813
MAWE, John *The mineralogy of Derbyshire* etc. 1802
— Glossary (repr. E.D.S. 1881)
MAWER, Allen & STENTON, Frank Merry *Introduction to the survey of English place-names* 1924
MAX MÜLLER, Friedrich *See* MÜLLER, Friedrich Max
MAXWELL, James *Herodian of Alexandria his History of twenty Roman Cæsars* tr. I. M. 1629 (1635)
MAXWELL, James Clerk *Matter and motion* 1876 (1881)
Scientific papers a1879 (1890)
Theory of heat 1871
A treatise on electricity and magnetism 1873 (1881)
See also CAMPBELL, L.
MAXWELL, Bp. John *The burthen (burden) of Issachar* 1646 (Phenix 1708)
Sacro-sancta regum, or the sacred and royall prerogative of christian kings 1644
MAXWELL, Nicole *Witch-doctor's apprentice* 1962
MAXWELL, Robert *The practical bee-master* 1747 (1750)
Transactions of the society for promoting agriculture in Scotland selected 1743
MAXWELL, William Hamilton *The adventures of Captain Blake* 1835 (1838)
Brian O'Linn 1848
Hints to a soldier on service 1845
ed. *Peninsular sketches* 1845
Sports and adventures in the highlands and islands of Scotland 1844 (1855)
Stories of Waterloo 1829
Wild sports of the west (anon.) 1832
MAY, Derwent James *Laughter in Djakarta* 1973
MAY, Emily J. *The Stronges of Netherstronge, a tale of Sedgemoor* 1864
MAY, Robert *The accomplisht cook, or the art and mystery of cookery* 1660 (1665)
MAY, Thomas *The heire, a comedy* 1620 (1622; Dodsley)
The history of the parliament which began 1640 1647
The life of a satirical puppy called Nim, by T. M. (? T. May) a1650 (1657)
Lucan's (M. A.) Pharsalia tr. 1627 (1631)
— *A continuation of Lucan's historicall poem* 1630
The mirrour of mindes; or Barclay's (J.) Icon animorum tr. T. M(ay) 1631
The old couple, a comedy a1650 (1658)
Poetical translation of the verses in Barclay's (J.) Argenis 1628 (1629)
The reigne of king Henry the second 1633
Virgil's Georgics tr. 1628
MAY, Sir Thomas Erskine *The constitutional history of England 1760–1860* 1861–63
A treatise upon the law, privileges, proceedings and usage of parliament 1844 (1883, 1906)
MAYCOCK, William Perren *Electric lighting and power distribution* 3 parts 1892–3
Electric wiring, fittings, switches, and lamps 1899
MAYDMAN, Henry *Naval speculations and maritime politicks* 1691
MAYER, Brantz *Mexico as it was and as it is* 1844
MAYER, Edgar *Clinical application of sunlight and artificial radiation* 1926
MAYER, John *The sportsman's directory* 1815 (1817)
MAYER, Ralph *The artist's handbook of materials and techniques* 1940
— (UK ed.) 1951
A dictionary of art terms and techniques 1969
MAYER-GROSS, Willy, SLATER, Eliot T. O., & ROTH, Martin *Clinical psychiatry* 1954
— (ed. 3) 1969
MAYERNE, Sir Theodore T. de *Archimagirus Anglo-Gallicus, or excellent..receipts in cookery* a1655 (1658)
MAYHEW, Anthony L., & SKEAT, W. W. *A concise dictionary of Middle English from 1150 to 1580* 1888
See also SKEAT, W. W.
MAYHEW, Augustus S. *Paved with gold, or the romance and reality of the London streets* 1858
MAYHEW, Edward *Dogs: their management* 1854 (1862)
MAYHEW, Henry *London labour and the London poor* 1851–61 (1861, 1864)
The upper Rhine 1858
MAYLARD, Alfred Ernest *A treatise on the surgery of the alimentary canal* 1896
MAYNARD, C. J. *The birds of Florida* 1872
MAYNARDE, Thomas *Sir Francis Drake his voyage* 1595 (Hakluyt Soc. 1849)
MAYNE, Jasper *The amorous warre, a tragi-comœdy* 1648 (1659)
The citye match, a comœdye 1639 (Dodsley)
Donne's (J.) Book of epigrams tr. 1652 (D.'s Paradoxes, problems etc. 1652)
Part of Lucian made English 1638 (1664)
A sermon against false prophets 1646
A sermon against schisme 1652
A sermon concerning unity and agreement 1646 (1647)
MAYNE, John *Glasgow, a poem* 1803
The siller gun, a poem 1779–1808 (1836)
MAYNE, Robert G. *An expository lexicon of the terms..of medical and general science* 1853–60 (1860)
A medical vocabulary 1862 (ed. 2; also ed. 6, ed. W. W. Wagstaffe, 1889)
MAYNWARING, Everard *The pharmacopœian physicians repository* 1669 (1670)
Praxis medicorum antiqua et nova: the ancient and modern practice of physick examined 1671
Vita sana et longa, the preservation of health and prolongation of life 1669 (1670)
MAYO, Elizabeth *Lessons on objects* 1829 (1831)
MAYO, Herbert *Letters on the truths contained in popular superstitions* 1849 (1851)
MAYO, Mrs. Isabella Fyvie *The house by the works* 1879
MAYO, William S. *Kaloolah, or journeyings to the Djébel Kumri: an autobiography of J. Romer* 1851
MAYR, Ernst *Animal species and evolution* 1963
Principles of systematic zoology 1969
——, LINSLEY, E. G., & USINGER, R. L. *Methods and principles of systematic zoology* 1953
MEAD or MEDE, Joseph *Works* a1638 (1672)
Daniel's weekes; an interpretation of part of the prophecy of Daniel 1643
Diatribæ: discourses on divers texts of scripture 1642
MEAD, Margaret *Growing up in New Guinea: a comparative study of primitive education* 1930
Male and female: a study of the sexes in a changing world 1949

MEAD, Richard *Medical works* a1754 (1762)
A short discourse concerning pestilential contagion and the methods to be used to prevent it (= Plague) 1720
M.'s Medical precepts and cautions tr. T. Stack 1751
MEADE, Elizabeth ('Lillie') Thomasina *A sweet girl graduate* 1891
MEADE, Herbert *A ride through the disturbed districts of New Zealand* 1870
MEADOWS, C. J. Barr *Clinical observations on affections of the digestive organs and of the skin* 1875
MEAGER, Leonard *The English gardener* 1670
The new art of gardening, with the gardener's almanack 1697
Meals and manners, Early English See Babees Book
Mean. The meane in spending: promising prayse to the liberall etc. 1598
Meanderings of memory, by 'Nightlark' 1852
Meccano magazine 1916-
Mechanics' magazine, The 1823-71
MEDAWAR, Peter Brian & MEDAWAR, Jean Shinglewood *The life science: current ideas of biology* 1977
MEDBERY, James Knowles *Men and mysteries of Wall Street* 1870
Meddelelser om Grønland (Copenhagen) 1879-
MEDE, Joseph *See* MEAD or MEDE, J.
Medical and physical journal, The 1799-1826
Medical annual, The 1883-
Medical communications (by a society for promoting medical knowledge) 1784-90
Medical essays and observations, revised and published by a society in Edinburgh 1733-44
Medical journal of Australia 1914-
Medical MS. at Stockholm, Extracts from a a1400 (in Archaeologia XXX, 1844; Anglia XVIII, 1896)
Medical news (Philadelphia) 1843-1905
Medical record (New York) 1866-1922
Medical Research Council *Mathematics and computer science in biology and medicine* 1965
A system of bacteriology in relation to medicine 9 vols. 1929-31
Medical temperance journal, The 1870-92
Medical times and gazette, The 1859-
Medicina gymnastica 1704 *See* FULLER, F.
Medico-chirurgical transactions, published by the (Royal) Medical and chirurgical society of London 1815-72
Meditations on the life and passion of Christ c1400 (E.E.T.S. 1921)
Meditations on the supper of our Lord, and the hours of the passion, Bonaventura's 13.. (E.E.T.S. 1875)
Medium ævum 1932-
MEDLEY, Guido *Kolbe or Kolben's (P.) Present state of the Cape of Good Hope* tr. 1731
Medley, The 1710-11 (1712)
Medulla grammatice(s c1460 (various MSS.; 1499)
MEDWALL, Henry *A goodly interlude of Nature* c1500 (Brandl 1898)
MEDWAY, Gathorne (Gathorne-Hardy), Baron *The wild mammals of Malaya and offshore islands including Singapore* 1969
MEDWIN, Thomas *The angler in Wales, or days and nights of sportsmen* 1834
Conversations of Lord Byron 1824 (1832)
The Shelley papers, Memoir of P. B. Shelley and original poems and papers by P. B. Shelley 1833
MEEHAN, Thomas *The native flowers and ferns of the United States* 1878-80
MEEKE, Robert *Extracts from his diary* 1689-94 (1874)
Meeting of gallants at an ordinarie or the walkes in Powles, The 1604 (Percy Soc. 1841)
MEGLITSCH, Paul Allen *Invertebrate zoology* 1967
Mehalah 1880 *See* BARING-GOULD, S.
Meidan Maregrete c1250 (Seinte Marherete, E.E.T.S. 1862)
MEIGS, J. Aitken *Observations upon the cranial forms of the American aborigines* 1866
Meister's (J. H.) Letters written during a residence in England tr. 1799
Melayne, The sege off c1400 (E.E.T.S. 1880)
MELBANCKE, Brian *Philotimus: the warre betwixt nature and fortune* 1583
Melbourne Truth (title varies) 1902-
MELCHIOR, Ib *Sleeper agent* [anon. tr.] 1975 (UK 1976)
Melismata 1611 *See* RAVENSCROFT, T.
MELLIS, John 1588 *See* OLDCASTLE, H.
MELLOR, Enoch *Priesthood in the light of the New Testament* 1876
MELLOR, Joseph William *A comprehensive treatise on inorganic and theoretical chemistry* 1922-
Modern inorganic chemistry 1912
MELLY, Alan George Heywood *Owning-up* 1965
MELMOTH, William *Cicero's (M. T.) Cato; or an essay on old age* tr. 1773
Letters on several subjects, by the late Sir T. Fitzosborne 1742-49 (1763)
Melody maker, The 1926-
Melrose, Selections from the records of the regality of 1605-1706 (S.H.S. 1914 etc.)
MELTON, John *Astrologaster or the figure-caster* 1620
A six-folde politician 1609
Melusine, compiled by J. D'Arras tr. c1500 (E.E.T.S. 1895)
MELVIL, Sir James *Memoirs* c1610 (1683, 1735, Bannatyne Club 1827)
MELVILL, James *Autobiography and diary* (1556-1601) *with a continuation* a1614 (Wodrow Soc. 1842)
Diary 1556-1601 a1614 (Bannatyne Club 1829)
MELVILLE, George J. Whyte *Digby Grand, an autobiography* 1853
General Bounce; or, the lady and the locusts 1854 (1855)
The gladiators, a tale of Rome and Judæa 1863
Good for nothing; or all down hill 1861
Holmby house, a tale of old Northamptonshire 1860
Inside the bar; or sketches at Soakington 1862
Kate Coventry, an autobiography 1856
Katerfelto; a story of Exmoor 1875
Market Harborough; or how Mr. Sawyer went to the shires 1861 (1862)
Riding recollections 1875 (1878)
Uncle John, a novel 1874
MELVILLE, Herman *Moby Dick, or the whale* 1851
Omoo; a narrative of adventures in the south seas 1847
Pierre; or, The ambiguities 1852
Redburn: his first voyage (UK ed. in 2 vols.) 1849
Typee: a peep at Polynesian life 1846
White jacket; or the world in a man-of-war 1850
'MELVILLE, Jennie' (Gwendoline Butler) *Ironwood* 1972
Nun's castle 1974
'MELVILLE, Lewis' (L. S. Benjamin) *The life of W. M. Thackeray* 1899
Memoirs of a Babylonian princess (Maria T. Asmar) *written by herself* tr. 1844
Memoirs of Captain Peter Drake, The 1754 (1755)
Memoirs of Emeric Count Teckely (by J. Le Clerc) tr. 1693
Memoirs of female philosophers, by a modern philosopher of the other sex 1808
Memoirs of.. George Psalmanazar.. written by himself a1763 (1764)
Memoirs of the Nutrebian (Nubian) *court* 1747
Memorials of the Church of SS. Peter and Wilfrid, Ripon v.d. (Surtees Soc. 1882-88)
Memorials of St. Giles's, Durham v.d. (Surtees Soc. 1896)
MENCKEN, Henry Louis *The American language: a preliminary inquiry into the development of English in the United States* 1919
— (rev. ed.) 1921
— (ed. 3) 1923
— (ed. 4) 1936
— Supplement 2 vols. 1945-8
— (abridged ed. with new material by R. I. McDavid) 1963
MENDELL, George H. & CRAIGHILL, W. P. *Jomini's (A. H. de) Art of war* tr. 1862 (1879)
MENDELSOHN, Oscar Adolf *The dictionary of drink and drinking* 1965
Mendelssohn-Bartholdy's (J. L. F.) Letters from Italy and Switzerland tr. Lady Wallace 1861 (1862)
MENDES DA COSTA, Emanuel *Elements of conchology* 1776
A natural history of fossils 1757
MENKEN, Adah I. *Infelicia* (poems) 1868
MENNES, Sir John & SMITH, J. *Musarum deliciæ, or the muses recreation* 1655 (1817)
Wit restor'd 1658
Witts recreations 1640 (1663)
Men's hockey ('Know the game' series) 1950
— (rev. ed.) 1965
Mercantile marine magazine and nautical record, The 1854-60
Merchants' magazine and commercial review 1839-70 (1851-60 with title *Hunt's merchants' magazine and commercial review*)
Mercier's (B.) Fragments of politics and history tr. 1795
MERCIER, Charles *Sanity and insanity* 1890
Mercurius academicus No. 1 1648
Mercurius caledonius 1661 (1861)
Mercurius pragmaticus 1647-49
Mercurius scoticus, or the royal messenger 1651
'Mercury' dictionary of textile terms, The 1950
MEREDITH, George *The adventures of Harry Richmond* 1871
The amazing marriage 1895
Ballads and poems of tragic life 1887
Beauchamp's career 1876
Diana of the crossways 1885
The egoist, a comedy in narrative 1879
Evan Harrington 1861
Farina: a legend of Cologne 1857
Letters ed. C. L. Cline 3 vols. 1970
Lord Ormont and his Aminta 1894
Odes in contribution to the song of French history 1898
One of our conquerors 1891
The ordeal of Richard Feverel 1859
Poems 1851
Poems and lyrics of the joy of earth 1883
Rhoda Fleming 1865
The shaving of Shagpat, an Arabian entertainment 1856
The tragic comedians 1880 (1881)
Vittoria 1866 (1867)
MEREDITH, L. P. *The teeth and how to save them* 1872 (1878)
MEREDITH, Mrs. Louisa Anne *Tasmanian friends and foes, feathered, furred and finned* 1880
'MEREDITH, Owen' *See* LYTTON, E. R., 1st Earl of
MERENESS, Newton Dennison ed. *Travels in the American colonies 1690-1783* 1916
MERES, Francis *Palladis Tamia, Wits treasury, being the second part of Wits commonwealth* (by J. Bodenham) 1598 (1634)
Meretriciad 1761 *See* THOMPSON, E.
MERITON, George *The christian mans assuring house* (a sermon) 1614
MERITON, George *The praise of York-shire ale.. To which is added, A York-shire dialogue, by G. M. gent* 1685
A York-shire dialogue in its pure natural dialect 1683 (also 1684, with an alphabetical clavis; Nine specimens, E.D.S. 1896)
MERIVALE, Charles *The conversion of the Roman empire* 1864
The fall of the Roman republic 1853
A general history of Rome 1875
A history of the Romans under the empire 1850-62 (1865)
MERIVALE, Herman C. *Faucit of Balliol* 1882
Merlin or the early history of king Arthur, a prose romance c1450 (E.E.T.S. 1899)
Merline (poem) a1650 (Bp. Percy's Folio MS. I, 1867)
MERRETT, Christopher *Neri's (A.) Art of glass* tr. 1662
Pinax rerum naturalium Britannicarum 1666 (1667)
MERREY, Walter *Remarks on the coinage of England* 1789
MERRIAM, George S. *The life and times of Samuel Bowles* 1885
MERRICK, Arnold *Albrechtsberger's (J. G.) Methods of harmony, figured base and composition.. adapted for self-instruction* tr. 1834 (1844)
MERRIMAN, Arthur Douglas *A dictionary of metallurgy* 1958
'MERRIMAN, Henry Seton' (Hugh S. Scott) *In Kedar's tents* 1897
Roden's corner 1898
The slave of the lamp 1892
The sowers 1896
MERRIMAN, Roger B. *Life and letters of Thomas Cromwell* 1902
Merry devill of Edmonton, The 1608 (Dodsley; Shakespeare Apocrypha 1908)
Merry drollery; or a collection of jovial poems, merry songs, with drolleries 1661 (also repr. J. W. Ebsworth 1875)
MERTON, Robert King *Social theory and social structure* 1949
— (rev. ed.) 1957
— (rev. ed.) 1968
MERWIN, Samuel & WEBSTER, Henry Kitchell *Calumet 'K'* 1901
MERZ, John Theodore *Leibniz* 1884
MESTON, William *Poems* a1745 (1767)
Metabolism: clinical and experimental 1952-
Metal world, The: a weekly journal for engineers 1881-82
Metals handbook See: American Society for Metals
Metaphrase on the epistle to the Colossians, A plaine and learned, written by a godly and judicious preacher c1630 (annexed to J. Dod's Ten sermons 1632)
METCALF, Clell Lee & FLINT, Wesley Pillsbury *Fundamentals of insect life* 1932
Destructive and useful insects 1928
— (ed. 4) 1962
Meteorological Office *See* United Kingdom
METEYARD, Eliza *The life of Josiah Wedgwood* 1865-66
METHAM, John *Works, including the romance of Amoryus and Cleopes* c1450 (E.E.T.S. 1916)
Metrical homilies, English c1325 (ed. J. Small 1862)
Metronome 1885-
Metropolis, a novel, The 1819
Meun's (J. de) Dodechedron of Fortune tr. Sir W. B. 1613
Mexia, P. 1613-19 *See* MILLES, T.
MEYER, Jerome Sydney & HANLON, Stuart *Fun with the new math* 1966
MEYER, Kuno *The voyage of Bran.. an old Irish saga.* ed. and tr., with an essay by A. Nutt 1895-97
MEYNELL, Laurence Walter *Double fault* 1965
Hooky gets the wooden spoon 1977
The thirteen trumpeters: a Hooky Hefferman story 1973
Virgin luck 1963
MEYNELL, Wilfrid *John Henry Newman the founder of modern Anglicanism and a cardinal of the Roman church* 1890
MEYRICK, Sir Samuel R. *A critical inquiry into antient armour* etc. 1824
Engraved illustrations of antient arms and armour 1830
MEZZROW, Milton & WOLFE, Bernard *Really the blues* 1946 (UK 1957)
MIALL, Arthur Bernard tr. *C. Guenther's A naturalist in Brazil* 1931
MIALL, Edward (Articles in) *Nonconformist* 1841-50
MIALL, Louis C. *The natural history of aquatic insects* 1895
MIALL, Stephen ed. *A new dictionary of chemistry* 1940
— (ed. 2, by S. Miall & L. M. Miall) 1949
MICHAUX, François André *Histoire des arbres forestiers de l'Amérique Septentrionale* 3 vols. 1810-13
MICHEL, Francisque *A critical inquiry into the Scottish language* 1882
Michelin Tire Corporation *New York City* 1968
Michelin Tyre Company *Michelin guide to Great Britain* (ed. 7) 1923
MICHELL, John Henry & BELZ, Maurice Henry *The elements of mathematical analysis* 2 vols. 1937
MICHENER, James Albert *Chesapeake* 1978
The source 1965
MICHIE, John Grant *Deeside tales or men and manners on highland Deeside since 1745* 1872 (1908)
Michigan Academy of Science, Arts and Letters *Papers* Vol. X (for 1928) 1929
Michigan State Agricultural Society *Transactions* 1849-61
MICKLE, William J. *Camoens' (L. de) Lusiad* tr. 1776
Poetical works a1788 (1794; Chalmers 1810)
MICKLETHWAITE, John T. *Modern parish churches; their plan, design, and furniture* 1874
Micmacs. An account of the customs and manners of the Mickmakis and Maricheets, savage nations now dependent on the government of Cape-Breton 1758
Microcosm, The, a periodical work by George Griffin (i.e. G. Canning, and others) 1786-87
Microscopical science, Quarterly journal of 1853-77
Middle-English medicine-book, A c1450 (F. Heinrich, Ein mittelenglisches Medizinbuch 1896)

MIDDLEMASS, Jean Two false moves, a novel 1890
MIDDLETON, Christopher The famous historie of Chinon of England 1597 (also E.E.T.S. 1925)
MIDDLETON, Conyers The history of the life of M. T. Cicero 1741
A treatise on the Roman senate 1747
MIDDLETON, John View of the agriculture of Middlesex 1798
MIDDLETON, Thomas Works a1627 (Dyce 1840; Bullen 1885-86)
The ant and the nightingale See Father Hubburd
Any thing for a quiet life c1626 (1662)
The blacke booke: see M., T. 1604
Blurt master constable or the Spanish night-walke 1602
A chast mayd in Cheape-side, a comedy c1620 (1630)
The famelie of love 1607 (1608)
Father Hubburds tales or the ant and nightingale 1604
— (another ed.) The ant and the nightingale or Father Hubberds tales 1604
A game at chesse, a play 1624
A mad world my masters, a comedy 1608
The mayor of Quinborough, a comedy a1627 (1661)
Michaelmas terme 1607
Micro-cynicon, sixe snarling satyres 1599 (Bullen)
More dissemblers besides women 1622 (1657)
No wit, no help, like a womans, a comedy c1613 (1657)
The phœnix 1607 (1630)
A tricke to catch the old-one 1607 (1608)
Two new playes: viz. More dissemblers besides women; Women beware women 1622 (1657)
The wisdom of Solomon paraphrased 1597
A tragi-comodie called The witch a1627 (1778)
Your five gallants 1608
—— & DEKKER, T. The roaring girle, or Moll Cut purse 1611
—— & ROWLEY, W. The changeling 1623 (1653)
A courtly masque: the device called The world tost at tennis 1620
A faire quarrell 1617 (1622)
The Spanish gipsie 1623 (1653)
—— et al. The excellent comedy called The old law: or a new way to please you, by P. Massinger, T. Middleton, W. Rowley 16.. (1656)
The widdow, a comedie.. by B. Johnson, J. Fletcher, and T. Middleton a1627 (1652; Dodsley)
MIDDLETON, Bp. Thomas F. The doctrine of the Greek article applied to criticism.. of the New Testament 1808 (1833)
Midland counties historical collector, The 1854-56
Mid-Yorkshire glossary 1876 See ROBINSON, C. C.
MIEGE, Guy A new dictionary French and English with another English and French 1677
The great French dictionary 1687-88
The present state of Great Britain 1707
MIKES, H. George Down with everybody! 1951
Milk and honey: Israel explored 1950
MILBOURNE, Luke The measures of resistance to the higher powers (a sermon) 1710
Melius inquirendum (a sermon) 1709
Notes on Dryden's Virgil 1698
The people not the original of civil power (a sermon) 1707
The traytors reward (a sermon) 1704
MILBURN, Clara Emily Mrs. Milburn's diaries: an Englishwoman's day-to-day reflections, 1939-45 ed. P. Donnelly 1979
MILBURN, William Oriental commerce 1813 (1825)
MILES, Beryl The stars my blanket 1954
Military and sea dictionary, A 1702-11 (1711)
Military dictionary, A new 1760
Military engineering, Instruction in 1884 (ed. 3)
MILL, Humphrey A nights search 1640-46
MILL, James Analysis of the phenomena of the human mind 1829 (1869)
Elements of political economy 1821 (1824)
The history of British India 1817
— ed. with continuation by H. H. Wilson (1840-46)
MILL, John Stuart Auguste Comte and positivism 1865
Autobiography 1873
Considerations on representative government 1861 (1865)
Dissertations and discussions v.d. (1859-75)
Earlier letters ed. F. E. Mineka 2 vols. 1963 (Vols. XII & XIII of Collected works)
The early draft of J. S. Mill's autobiography ed. J. Stillinger 1961
England and Ireland 1868
Essays on some unsettled questions of political economy 1844
An examination of Sir W. Hamilton's philosophy 1865
Inaugural address.. St. Andrews 1867
Letters ed. H. S. R. Elliot 2 vols. 1910
On liberty 1859 (1865, 1869)
Principles of political economy 1848 (1876)
The subjection of women 1869
A system of logic 1843 (1846, 1868)
Three essays on religion 1874
Utilitarianism 1861 (1874)
MILL, William H. Five sermons on the temptation of Christ 1844
Observations on the attempted application of pantheistic principles to the theory and historic criticism of the gospel 1840-44 (1861)
MILLAIS, Sir John E. See MILLAIS, John G. 1899
MILLAIS, John G. A breath from the veldt 1895 (1899)
The life and letters of Sir J. E. Millais 1899
MILLAR, Alexander H. Fife: pictorial and historical 1895
MILLAR, George Reid Horned pigeon 1946
Maquis 1945
MILLAR, Margaret Ask for me tomorrow 1976 (UK 1977)
The soft talkers 1957

MILLER, Arthur All my sons 1947
Collected plays 1957 (UK 1958)
The crucible 1953 (UK 1956)
Death of a salesman 1949
The misfits 1961
MILLER, Cincinnatus H. See MILLER, Joaquin
MILLER, Denis The Chinese jade affair 1973
MILLER, Edward A guide to the textual criticism of the New Testament 1886
MILLER, Edwin Cyrus Plant physiology, with reference to the green plant 1931
MILLER, Henry Valentine Black spring 1936
Nexus 1960 (UK 1964)
Plexus 1953 (UK 1963)
Sexus 2 vols. 1949 (UK 1969)
Tropic of Cancer 1934
Tropic of Capricorn 1939
MILLER, Hugh The cruise of the Betsey.. With rambles of a geologist a1856 (1858)
First impressions of England and its people 1847 (1861)
Footprints of the creator 1849 (1874)
My schools and schoolmasters 1854 (1857)
The old red sandstone 1841 (1842)
Scenes and legends of the north of Scotland 1834 (1850, 1857)
The testimony of the rocks a1856 (1857)
MILLER, Hugh The open city 1973
MILLER, James The sibyl's leaves 1829
MILLER, Joaquin First fam'lies in the Sierras 1875 (US 1876)
Life amonst the Modocs 1873
Songs of Italy 1878
Songs of the sierras 1871
MILLER, John A description of the province and city of New York c1695 (1843)
MILLER, Philip The gardener's dictionary 1731-39 (1759, 1768)
— ed. T. Martyn (1807)
A short introduction to the knowledge of.. botany 1760
MILLER, Samuel H., & SKERTCHLY, S. B. J. The fenland past and present 1878
MILLER, William A dictionary of English names of plants 1884
MILLER, William A. Elements of chemistry, theoretical and practical 1855-57 (1860-62, 1867-69)
MILLER, William H. The culture of pleasure (anon.) 1871 (1872)
Miller of Mansfield in Sherwood and Henery the second, The pleasant history of the 1651
MILLERSON, Gerald The technique of television production 1961
MILLES, Thomas The catalogue of honor or treasury of true nobility 1610
The treasurie of auncient and moderne times (Times storehouse etc.), translated out of P. Mexia & F. Sansovino 1613, 1619
MILLETT, Kate Flying 1974 (UK 1975)
Sexual politics 1970 (UK 1971)
MILLIKEN, E. J. 'Arry ballads 1892
MILLIN, Sarah Gertrude The South Africans 1926
MILLINGTON, Thomas The true narration of the entertainment of his royal majesty (James I) 1603 (Arber, Eng. Garner VIII)
MILLS, Charles The history of chivalry or knighthood and its times 1825
The history of the crusades 1818 (1822)
MILLS, Charles Wright The power elite 1956
White collar: the American middle classes 1951
MILLS, James Report to the Commissioner 1972
MILLS, John Crevier's (J. B. L.) History of the Roman emperors tr. 1755-61 (1814)
MILLS, John An essay on the management of bees 1766
A new and complete system of practical husbandry 1762-63
MILLS, John Sacred symbology 1853
MILLS, Mark A. ed. The ancient ordinances and statute laws of the isle of Man 1821
'MILLS, Osmington' (Vivian Collin Brooks) Enemies of the bride 1966
Headlines make murder 1962
Stairway to murder 1959
MILLS, P. W. F. The elements of practical flying 1935
MILLSPAUGH, Charles F. American medicinal plants 1884-87
MILMAN, Henry Hart Annals of St. Paul's cathedral 1868
Anne Boleyn, a dramatic poem 1826
Fazio, a tragedy 1815
The history of christianity 1840 (1863)
History of Latin christianity 1854-55 (1864)
The history of the Jews 1829 (1863)
Samor, lord of the bright city, an heroic poem 1818
MILNE, Alan Alexander First plays 1919
Winnie-the-Pooh 1926
MILNE, Christopher Robin The enchanted places 1974
MILNE, James The romance of a pro-consul, being the personal life and memoirs of Sir G. Grey 1899
MILNE, William See MORRISON, Robert
MILNER, Christina Andrea & MILNER, Richard Black players: the secret world of black pimps 1973
MILNER, George Country pleasures; the chronicle of a year, chiefly in a garden 1881
MILNER, Isaac See MILNER, Mary
MILNER, John A treatise on the ecclesiastical architecture of England during the middle ages 1811
MILNER, Mary The life of Isaac Milner, comprising a portion of his correspondence and other writings hitherto unpublished 1842
MILNER, Thomas The gallery of nature 1845 (1846)

MILNES, Richard Monckton See HOUGHTON, 1st Baron
MILTON, John Works a1674 (1851; Prose works 1738, 1753)
Animadversions upon The remonstrants defence against Smectymnuus 1641
An apology against.. A modest confutation of the animadversions upon the remonstrant against Smectymnuus 1642
Areopagitica; a speech for the liberty of unlicenc'd printing 1644 (Arber)
At a vacation exercise in the colledge 1628
A brief history of Moscovia a1674 (1682)
Colasterion: a reply to a nameles answer against The doctrine and discipline of divorce 1645
Comus See Maske, below
Considerations touching the likeliest means to remove hirelings out of the church 1659
The doctrine and discipline of divorce 1643, 1644
Of education, To Master S. Hartlib 1644
Εικονοκλάστης in answer to a book intitl'd Εἰκὼν Βασιλικὴ 1649
The history of Britain, that part especially now call'd England 1670
Il penseroso 1632
The judgement of M. Bucer concerning divorce tr. 1644
L'allegro 1632
Lycidas 1637
A maske presented at Ludlow castle 1634
On the morning of Christs nativity 1629
Paradise lost 1667
Paradise regain'd 1671
The passion (poem) c1630
Of prelaticall episcopacy 1641
The readie and easie way to establish a free commonwealth 1659
The reason of church-government urg'd against prelaty 1641
Of reformation touching church discipline in England 1641
Samson Agonistes 1671
The tenure of kings and magistrates 1649 (1650)
Tetrachordon: expositions upon the foure chief places in scripture which treat of mariage etc. 1645
A treatise of civil power in ecclesiastical causes 1659
See also MARSH, J.; PARKER, H.; WASHINGTON, J.
MILTON, William Fitzwilliam, Viscount & CHEADLE, Walter Butler The North-West Passage by land 1865
Milton Keynes Express 1973-
MILWARDE, John Jacobs great day of trouble and deliverance, a sermon 1610
MINCHIN, Edward Alfred An introduction to the study of the protozoa, with special reference to the parasitic forms 1912
MINCHIN, George M. A treatise of statics 1877
Uniplanar kinematics of solids and fluids 1882
Mind; a quarterly review of psychology and philosophy 1876-
Mineralogical abstracts 1920-
Mineralogical magazine and journal of the Mineralogical Society of Great Britain and Ireland, The 1876-
Miniature, a periodical paper, The 1804-05 (1806)
Mining review, The 1836-37
Ministry of... See United Kingdom. Ministry of...
Minor, The; or history of George O'Nial Esq. 1787 (1788)
Minor poems of the Vernon MS., The a1400 (E.E.T.S. 1892-1901)
MINOT, Laurence Poems a 1352 (1795; J. Hall 1887)
MINSHEU, John 'Ηγεμὼν εἰς τὰς γλῶσσας id est Ductor in linguas The guide into tongues etc. 1617 (1627)
Percyvall's (R.) Dictionarie in Spanish and English.. enlarged by.. J. Minsheu 1599
Minstrel, The; or, anecdotes of distinguished personages in the fifteenth century 1793
MINTER, Davide Caroline ed. Modern needlecraft 1932
MINTO, Gilbert Elliot, 1st Earl of Life and letters 1751-1806 (1874)
Lord Minto in India, Life and letters 1807-14 (1880)
MINTO, William Daniel Defoe (English men of letters) 1879
A manual of English prose literature 1872
Miriam's schooling 1890 See WHITE, William Hale
Mirk's Festial: a collection of homilies by J. Mirkus c1450 (E.E.T.S. 1905)
See also MYRC
Mirror, The (by H. Mackenzie et al.) 1779-80
Mirror. A myrroure for magistrates ed. W. Baldwin 1559, 1563 (1571)
— The firste parte of the mirour ed. J. Higgins 1574 (1575)
— The last parte of the mirour 1574 (= Baldwin 1571)
— The seconde part of the mirrour ed. T. Blennerhasset 1578
— The mirour for magistrates (first and last parts combined) 1587
— A mirour for magistrates, newly enlarged with a last part called A winters nights vision.. with a poem annexed called Englands Eliza ed. R. Niccols 1610
Mirror of literature, amusement and instruction, The 1823-26
Mirror. The miroure of mans salvacionne c1450 (Roxb. Club 1888)
The mirrour of policie (from G. de la Perriere) tr. 1594 (1599)
The myroure of oure Ladye, containing a devotional treatise on divine service etc. 1450-1530 (1530; E.E.T.S. 1873)
Miscellanea curiosa; containing a collection of some of the principal phænomena in nature etc. 1708
Miscellanea Scotica, a collection of tracts relating to the history, antiquities, topography, and literature of Scotland v.d. (1818-20)
Miseries of enforced marriage 1607 See WILKINS, G.
Misogonus, A mery and pleasaunt comedie called c1570 (Brandl 1898)

Misselden, Edward *Free trade; or the meanes to make trade florish* 1622
Missing friends, being the adventures of a Danish emigrant in Queensland (1871–80) 1892
Missingham, Hal *A student's guide in commercial art* 1948
Missionary magazine, The 1796–1813
Mist's Journal. A collection of miscellaneous letters selected out of Mist's Weekly journal 1720–21 (1722)
Misyn, Richard *The fire of love* (Englished from Hampole's *De incendio amoris*) 1435 (E.E.T.S. 1896)
The mending of life and the rule of living (Englished from Hampole's *De emendacione vitæ*) 1434 (ibid.)
Mitchell, Donald G. *The battle summer, being transcriptions from personal observations in Paris during . . 1848* 1849 (1852)
Bound together: a sheaf of papers 1884
Dream life: a fable of the seasons 1851 (1852)
The lorgnette; or studies of the town by an opera-goer 1850
Reveries of a bachelor 1850 (1852)
Seven stories, with basement and attic 1864
Wet days at Edgewood 1864
Mitchell, Geoffrey Duncan *Sociology: the study of social systems* 1959
Mitchell, Gladys Maude W. *Laurels are poison* 1942
The murder of Busy Lizzie 1973
The mystery of a butcher's shop 1929
Spotted hemlock 1958
Mitchell, Hugh *Scotticisms, vulgar anglicisms and grammatical improprieties corrected* 1799
Mitchell, James *Smear job* 1975
Mitchell, Margaret *Gone with the wind* 1936
Mitchell, Thomas *The comedies of Aristophanes* tr. 1820–22
Mitchell, Thomas L. *Three expeditions into the interior of eastern Australia* 1838 (1839)
Mitchell, W. Forbes- *See* Forbes-Mitchell, W.
Mitchison, Naomi Margaret *We have been warned* 1935
Mitford, A. B. Freeman- *See* Freeman-Mitford, A. B.
Mitford, Jessica Lucy Freeman *The American way of death* 1963
Mitford, Mary Russell *Country stories* 1837 (1850)
Our village; sketches of rural character and scenery 1824–32 (1863)
Recollections of a literary life 1852
See also L'Estrange, A. G.
Mitford, Nancy Freeman *The blessing* 1951
Christmas pudding 1932
Don't tell Alfred 1960
Love in a cold climate 1949
Pigeon pie 1940
The pursuit of love 1945
Mitford, William *An essay upon the harmony of language* 1774
— *An inquiry into the principles of harmony in language* 1804
History of Greece 1784–1818 (1829)
Mittelholzer, Edgar Austin *Shadows move among them* 1951
Mivart, St. George *The cat: an introduction to the study of backboned animals* 1881
Dogs, jackals, wolves and foxes: a monograph of the canidæ 1890
Lessons in elementary anatomy 1873
On truth, a systematic inquiry 1889
'Mixer, The' (Henry Kirk) *The transport workers' song book* c1926
Model steam engine, The: how to buy, how to use, and how to construct it 1868 (1895)
Modell of wit, mirth, eloquence and conversation, The. Framed in ten dayes of a hundred curious pieces etc. (Boccacio's Decameron) tr. 1625
Moderation display'd, a poem (by W. Shippen) 1704
Modern christianity a civilized heathenism (by H. W. Pullen) 1873 (1874)
Modern Gulliver's travel, by L. Gulliver Jun. 1796
A modern junior dictionary, specially adapted for use in Australia and New Zealand 1944
Modern Language Association of America *Publications* 1889–
Modern language notes 1886–
Modern language review 1905–
Modern law review 1937–
Modern philology 1903–
Modern Scottish poets ed. D. H. Edwards 1881–97
Modern ship of fools, The (? by W. H. Ireland) 1807
Modern theatre, The, a collection of successful modern plays, selected by Mrs. Inchbald 1811
Modern times 1785 *See* Trusler, J.
Moffat, Gwen *The Corpse road* 1974
Deviant death 1973
Miss Pink at the edge of the world 1975
Moffett, T. *See* Moufet, T.
Mogey, John McFarlane *Family and neighbourhood: two studies in Oxford* 1956
Moggridge, J. Traherne *Harvesting ants and trap-door spiders* 1873–74
Mogridge, George *Old Humphrey's observations* 1839
Mohr, Charles Theodore *Plant life of Alabama* 1901
Moir, David M. *Poetical works* a1851 (1852)
The life of Mansie Wauch, taylor in Dalkeith 1824–28 (1839, 1849)
Molesworth, Mary L. *The adventures of Herr Baby* 1881
Molesworth, Robert *Hotman's (F.) Franco-Gallia; or, an account of the ancient free state of France* tr. 1711 (1721)
Molinos' (M.) Spiritual guide tr. 1688
Molins, James *Anatomical and practical observations in St. Thomas's hospital* 1674–77 (1896)
Molle, John *Camerarius' (P.) Living librarie* tr. 1621
Mollett, John W. *An illustrated dictionary of words used in art and archæology* 1883
Molloy, Charles *Select letters taken from Fog's Weekly journal* 1728–31 (1732)
Molloy, Edward ed. *Radio and television engineers' reference book* 1954
Molloy, Joseph Fitzgerald *Royalty restored, or London under Charles II* 1885
Molly Migg's trip to the seaside (by J. Spilling) 1873
Moloney, C. Alfred *Sketch of the forestry of West Africa* 1887
West African fisheries 1883 (Fisheries exhibition literature)
Moloney, Peter *A plea for Mersey; or, The gentle art of insinuendo* 1966
Monboddo, James Burnett, Lord *Of the origin and progress of language* 1773–92
Moncrieff, Robert Wighton *The chemical senses* 1944
Moncrieff, William T. *Tom and Jerry, or life in London* 1821 (1828)
Money, Charles L. *Knocking about in New Zealand* 1871
Money, E. Erule *A little Dutch maiden, a South African sketch* 1887 (1888)
Money, Walter ed. *Parish church goods in Berkshire 1552* 1879
Money masters all things, or satyricall poems 1698
See also *Pecuniæ*
Money-makers, The: a social parable 1885
Monfart's (H. de Feynes de) Exact and curious survey of all the East Indies tr. 1615
Monier-Williams, Sir Monier *See* Williams, Monier
Monipennie, John *The abridgement or summarie of the Scots chronicle* etc. 1612 (1633, 1818)
Monist, The: a quarterly magazine devoted to the philosophy of science 1890–
Monitor, The; or British freeholder 1755–60
Monk, Bp. James H. *The life of Richard Bentley* 1830 (1833)
Monk of Evesham, The revelation to the c1482 (Arber)
'Monkshood, G. F.' & Gamble, George *Rudyard Kipling, the man and his work: an attempt at an appreciation* 1902
Monmouth, Henry Carey, 2nd Earl of *Bentivoglio's (G.) Compleat history of the warrs of Flanders* tr. 1654
Bentivoglio's (G.) Historicall relations of the United Provinces and of Flanders tr. 1652
Biondi's (G. F.) History of the civill warres of England betweene the houses of Lancaster and Yorke tr. 1641–46
Boccalini's (T.) Advertisements from Parnassus . . with the politick touch-stone tr. 1656 (1674)
Malvezzi's (V.) Romulus and Tarquin tr. 1637
Paruta's (P.) History of Venice tr. 1658
Paruta's (P.) Politick discourses tr. 1657
Senault's (J. F.) Man become guilty tr. 1650
Senault's (J. F.) Use of passions tr. 1649
Monographic medicine 7 vols. 1916 (by various authors)
Monro, Alexander *The anatomy of the human bones* 1726 (1741)
— *to which is added, an anatomical treatise of the nerves* 1732 (1741)
An essay on comparative anatomy 1744 (1782)
Monro, Alexander Jr. *Monro's (A.) Anatomy of the bones, nerves* etc. 1782
A treatise on comparative anatomy 1783
Monro, Donald *A description of the western isles of Scotland called Hybrides* 1549 (1774, 1805)
Monro, Robert *His expedition with the worthy Scots regiment called Mac-keyes regiment* etc. 1637
Monsarrat, Nicholas John Turney *The cruel sea* 1951
This is the schoolroom 1939
Monson, Sir William *Naval tracts* a1642 (Churchill's Collection of voyages and travels III, 1704; 1752)
Montagu, Basil *Bacon's (F.) Wisdom of the ancients* tr. 1825
Montagu, Charles *See* Halifax, Earl of
Montagu, Edward, 2nd Earl of Manchester *The lord Kimbolton his speech in parliament* 1642
Montagu, Elizabeth *Letters* a1800 (1809–13)
Montagu, George *Ornithological dictionary; or alphabetical synopsis of British birds* 1802. Suppl. 1813
— ed. by J. Rennie (1831, 1833)
Testacea Britannica, or natural history of British shells 1803–08
Montagu, Sir Henry M., 1st Earl of Manchester *See* Manchester
Montagu, Lady Mary Wortley *Works* a1762 (1803)
Complete letters ed. R. Halsband 3 vols. 1965–7
Letters (1763–67, 1790, 1820)
Letters and works (1837, 1893)
Poetical works (1768, 1785)
Montagu, Bp. Richard *The acts and monuments of the church before Christ incarnate* a1641 (1642)
Appello Cæsarem, a just appeale from two unjust informers etc. 1625
Articles of enquiry and direction for the diocese of Norwich, in the first visitation 1638
Diatribæ on the first part of the late History of tithes (by J. Selden) 1621
A gagg for the new gospell ? 1624
Immediate addresse unto God alone 1624
Montagu, Walter *The accomplish'd woman* tr. 1656
Miscellanea spiritualia or devout essaies 1648–54
Montagu, William D., 7th Earl of Manchester *Court and society from Elizabeth to Anne* 1864
Montague, Charles Edward *Disenchantment* 1922
A hind let loose 1910
Montague, William *The delights of Holland, or a three months travel about that and the other provinces* 1696
Monteath, John *Dunblane traditions* 1835 (1887)
Monteith, Robert *A theater of mortality* 1704
Montford castle; or the knight of the white rose, an historical romance 1795
Montgomerie, Alexander *Poems* a1605 (1821; S.T.S. 1887, 1910)
The cherrie and the slae a1585
The flyting betwixt M. and Polwart a1585
Miscellaneous poems a1568, a1586, 1592
Sonnets c1585
Montgomery, Florence *Misunderstood* (a tale) 1869
Tony, a sketch 1898
Montgomery, Lucy Maud *Anne of Avonlea* 1909
Anne of Green Gables 1908
Anne of Ingleside 1939
Montgomery, James *Poetical works* a1854
Pelican island, and other poems 1827
Montgomery Ward & Co. *Catalogue and buyers' guide* No. 57, Spring & Summer 1895
Month, The; an illustrated magazine of literature, science and art 1864–
Monthly magazine and British register, The 1796–1825
Monthly packet of evening readings for younger members of the English church, The (ed. C. M. Yonge) 1851–99
Monthly repository of theology (title varies) 1806–38
Monthly review, The 1749–1828
Monypenny, William Flavelle & Buckle, George Earle *The life of Disraeli* 6 vols. 1910–20
Moodie, Susannah *Life in the clearings versus the bush* 1853
Moor, Edward *Suffolk words and phrases* 1823
Moore, Arthur W. *The surnames and place-names of the Isle of Man* 1890
Moore, Brian *Catholics* 1972
Moore, Doris Langley *E. Nesbit: a biography* 1933
Moore, Edward *The gamester, a tragedy* 1753
—— & Brooke, H. *Fables for the female sex* (anon.) 1744
Moore, Francis *Travels into the inland parts of Africa* 1738 (1740)
Moore, Francis Cruger *How to build a home* 1897
Moore, Frank ed. *Songs and ballads of the American revolution* 1856
Moore, Frank Frankfort *A gray eye or so* 1893
I forbid the banns, the story of a comedy which was played seriously 1893 (1899)
Moore, George *The lost tribes and the Saxons of the east and of the west* 1861
Moore, George *Esther Waters, a novel* 1894
A mummer's wife 1884
Moore, James Carrick *A narrative of the campaign of the British army in Spain* 1809
Moore, John *A mappe of mans mortalitie* 1617
Moore, John *Columbarium; or the pigeon-house* 1735 (1879)
Moore, John *A view of society and manners in France, Switzerland and Germany* (anon.) 1779 (1789)
A view of society and manners in Italy 1781 (1790)
Moore, John Hamilton ed. *A new and complete collection of voyages and travels* c1785
The practical navigator and seaman's new daily assistant 1772 (1828)
Moore, Sir John Henry *Poetical trifles (Absence, The debtor* etc.) 1778 (1783)
Moore, John S. ed. *The goods and chattels of our forefathers: Frampton Cotterell and district probate inventories 1539–1804* 1976
Moore, Sir Jonas *M.'s Arithmetick* 1660
Modern fortification a1679 (1689)
A new systeme of the mathematicks a1679 (1681)
Moore, Marian *Lascelles* 1802
Moore, Philip *The hope of health, wherein is conteined a goodlie regiment of life* 1564 (1565)
Moore, Preston L., et al. *Drilling practices manual* 1974
Moore, Raymond Cecil *Introduction to historical geology* 1949
ed. *Treatise on invertebrate paleontology* 1953–
——, Lalicker, C. G., & Fischer, A. G. *Invertebrate fossils* 1952
Moore, Ruth *Candlemas Bay* 1950
Moore, Samuel & Aveling, Edward Bibbins tr. *K. Marx's Capital: a critical analysis of capitalist production* 1887
Moore, Stuart A. *A history of the foreshore, and the law relating thereto* etc. 1888
Moore, Thomas *Poetical works* a1852
Alciphron, a fragment 1839
The Epicurean, a tale 1827 (1839)
Epistles, odes and other poems 1806
Fables for the holy alliance, rhymes on the road etc. 1823 (1880)
The Fudge family in Paris 1818
— (sequel) *The Fudge family in England* 1835
Intercepted letters; or the twopenny post-bag 1812 (1813)
Irish melodies 1807–35
Lalla Rookh, an oriental romance (The veiled prophet of Khorassan, Paradise and the peri, The fire-worshippers, Nourmahal) 1817
Letters and journals of Lord Byron, with notices of his life 1830 (1860)
Memoirs, journal, and correspondence a1852 (1853–56)
Memoirs of the life of R. B. Sheridan 1825
Odes of Anacreon tr. 1800
The poetical works of Thomas Little 1801
Rhymes on the road 1819

Tom Crib's memorial to congress 1819
Travels of an Irish gentleman in search of a religion 1833
MOORE, Thomas *The history of Devonshire* 1829
MOORE, Thomas *British ferns and their allies* 1859
A handbook of British ferns 1848 (1857)
MOORE, Walter John *Physical chemistry* 1950
MOORE, Wilfred George *A dictionary of geography* 1949
MOOREHEAD, Alan McCrae *No room in the ark* 1959
Rum Jungle 1953
Moores baffled, being a discourse concerning Tanger, The 1681
MOORHOUSE, Walter Wilson *The study of rocks in thin section* 1959
Moral ode, A (Versions)
*a*1200 (O.E. Homilies I, E.E.T.S. 1868)
*c*1200 (O.E. Homilies II, E.E.T.S. 1873)
*c*1250 (O.E. Miscellany, E.E.T.S. 1872)
*c*1275 (E.E. Poems, Philol. Soc. 1862)
Moral state. Angliæ speculum morale; the moral state of England 1670
MORAN, James *The composition of reading matter* 1965
MORAN, Patrick Alfred P. *An introduction to probability theory* 1968
Moray, A survey of the province of 1798
MORDEN, Robert *Geography rectified, or a description of the world* 1680 (1688)
MORE, Hannah *The bas bleu* See *Florio*, below
Cœlebs in search of a wife 1808
An estimate of the religion of the fashionable world 1790 (1791)
Florio; a tale: and The bas bleu; or conversation, two poems 1786 (1827)
Letters ed. R. B. Johnson 1925
Sacred dramas (Moses, David and Goliath, Belshazzar, Daniel, Hezekiah, Sensibility) 1782 (1827)
A search after happiness, a pastoral 1773
Strictures on the modern system of female education 1799
MORE, Henry *A collection of several of his philosophical writings* 1662 (1712)
Complete poems 1614–87 (Grosart 1878)
The theological works *a*1687 (1708)
Annotations upon J. Glanvill's Lux orientalis 1682
An answer to . . a learned psychopyrist 1681 (1688)
An antidote against atheisme 1653 (1662, 1712)
— *appendix* 1655–87 (1712)
An antidote against idolatry 1669 (with Exposition seven epistles)
— *An appendix* 1673
Apocalypsis apocalypseos; or the revelation of St. John unveiled 1680
— *An answer to several remarks on M.'s Expositions of the apocalypse and Daniel, as also upon his Apology* 1684
His apology 1664 (with Mystery of iniquity)
A brief discourse of the real presence of the body and blood of Christ in the celebration of the holy eucharist (anon.) 1686
Conjectura cabbalistica; or a conjectural essay of interpreting the minde of Moses according to a threefold cabbala 1653
— *The defence of the threefold cabbala* 1653
A continuation of J. Glanvill's collection of remarkable and true stories of apparitions and witchcraft 1682
Democritus platonissans; or an essay upon the infinity of worlds out of platonick principles 1646
Divine dialogues 1668 (1713)
Enthusiasmus triumphatus, or a discourse of the nature, causes, kinds and cure of enthusiasme 1656 (1712)
An explanation of the grand mystery of godliness 1660
An exposition of the seven epistles of the seven churches 1669
An illustration of the book of Daniel and the revelation of St. John, by continued . . notes 1685
The immortality of the soul 1659 (1713)
Letters on several subjects *a*1687 (1694)
A modest enquiry into the mystery of iniquity (second part *Synopsis prophetica; the apology*) 1664
Observations upon Anthroposophia theomagica and Anima magica abscondita 1650 (with Euthusiasmus 1656)
Paralipomena prophetica, containing several supplements and defences 1685
A plain and continued exposition of the prophecies of Daniel 1681
Ψυχωδια platonica; or a platonicall song of the soul 1642
— (ed. 2) *Philosophicall poems* 1647
Remarks upon two late ingenious discourses (by Sir M. Hale) 1676
Some cursory reflections made upon Mr. R. Baxter 1685
Synopsis prophetica 1664 (2nd pt. of Mystery of iniquity)
MORE, Robert Jasper *Under the Balkans* 1877
MORE, Sir Thomas *Workes* *a*1535 (1557)
Answer to Frith See *Letter*, below
The answere to the fyrst parte of the poysened booke 1533 (1534, 1557)
The apologye made by hym 1533 (1557)
The confutation of Barnes 1532 (with next)
The confutacyon of Tyndales answere 1532; the seconde parte 1533 (1557)
De quatuor novissimis See *Treatyse*, below
The debellacyon of Salem and Bizance 1533 (1557)
A dialoge of comforte against tribulation 1534 (1557, 1847)
A dyaloge wherin he treatyd dyvers maters as of the veneration and worshyp of ymagys etc. (= *A dialoge concerning heresyes*) 1528 (1529, 1557)
The history of kyng Richard the third unfinished 1513 (1557; 1883)
— (see also HARDYNG, J. (1543); HALL, E. 1548; GRAFTON, R. 1568)
— *The historie of the pitifull life and unfortunate death of Edward V* (1641)
A letter impugnynge the erroneouse wryting of John Fryth agaynst the blessed sacrament of the aultare (= Answer to Frith) 1533 (1557)
The lyfe of Jhon Picus tr. *c*1510 (1557)
The supplycacyon of soulys made . . agaynst the supplycacyon of beggars 1529 (1557)
A treatice upon the passion of Chryste unfinished 1534 (1557; a part tr. Mary Basset)
A treatyse uppon these wordes of holye scripture Memorare novissima etc. (= De quatuor novissimis) 1522 (1557)
Utopia tr. *See* BURNET, G.; ROBINSON, Ralph
More, Sir Thomas (a play) *c*1590 (Shaks. Soc. 1844; Shakespeare Apocrypha 1908)
Morecambe Guardian 1920–
MOREHEAD, Robert Page *Human pathology* 1965
MORER, Thomas *A short account of Scotland* 1702
MORESBY, John *New Guinea and Polynesia: discoveries and surveys in New Guinea* etc. 1876
'MORETON, Andrew' *See* DE FOE, D.
MORETON, J. B. *Manners and customs of the West Indies* 1790
MORFILL, William R. *The dawn of European literature, Slavonic literature* 1883
Russia (Story of the nations) 1890
MORFIT, Campbell *The arts of tanning and currying* 1852 (1853)
MORGAN, Conwy Lloyd *Animal biology* 1887
Animal life and intelligence 1890–91
Habit and instinct 1897
MORGAN, J. *A complete history of Algiers* 1728–29
MORGAN, J. *Phœnix Britannicus, being a miscellaneous collection of scare and curious tracts* 1731–32
MORGAN, Charles Langbridge *The flashing stream* 1938
The fountain 1932
The judge's story 1947
Portrait in a mirror 1929
The voyage 1940
MORGAN, John Glanfil *Involved* 1967
MORGAN, Lewis H. *Ancient society; or researches in the lines of human progress, from savagery . . into civilization* 1877
MORGAN, Mary Ella *How to dress a doll* 1908
MORGAN (formerly Owenson), Sydney, Lady Morgan *Florence Macarthy, an Irish tale* 1818
France 1817 (1818)
The life and times of Salvator Rosa 1824
Passages from my autobiography 1818–19 (1859)
The wild Irish girl 1846
MORGAN, Sylvanus *The sphere of gentry* 1661
MORGAN, Thomas *The moral philosopher* (anon.) 1737–40
MORGAN, Thomas H. *Evolution and adaptation* 1903
Regeneration 1901
—— et al. *The mechanism of Mendelian heredity* 1915
MORGAN, William A. ed. *The 'House' on sport, by members of the London stock exchange* 1898
— (suppl. vol.) 1899
MORGANS, William *Manual of mining tools* 1871
MORIARTY, Denis I. *The husband hunter* 1839
MORICE, Anne *Killing with kindness* 1974
The men in her death 1981
Murder in mimicry 1977
MORICE, William *Cœna quasi κοινή, The new-inclosures broken down, and the Lords supper laid forth . . in a diatribe, and defence thereof* 1657
MORIER, James J. *The adventures of Hajji Baba of Ispahan* 1824
Ayesha, the maid of Kars 1834
MORISON, David *Poems, chiefly in the Scottish dialect* 1790
MORISON, James Cotter *Gibbon* (English men of letters) 1878
The life and times of St. Bernard 1863
The service of man: an essay towards the religion of the future 1887 (1889)
MORISON, Sir Richard *Vives' (J. L.) Introduction to wysedome* tr. 1540
MORISON, Samuel Eliot *The European discovery of America: the northern voyages* 1971
The European discovery of America: the southern voyages 1974
MORISON, William M. *The decisions of the Court of Session . . digested . . in the form of a dictionary* 1811
— *Supplement to the dictionary*, by M. P. Brown (1826)
Moritz' (C. P.) Travels, chiefly on foot, through several parts of England in 1782 tr. 1795
MORLAND, Sir Samuel *The Count of Pagan's method of delineating all manner of fortifications* 1672
Tuba stentoro-phonica, an instrument of excellent use as well at sea as at land etc. 1671
MORLAND, Samuel *A specimen of a dictionary English and Latin* 1723
MORLEY, Christopher Darlington *Thorofare* 1942 (UK 1943)
Kitty Foyle 1939
MORLEY, Henry *Cornelius Agrippa. The life of Henry Cornelius Agrippa von Nettesheim* 1856
A first sketch of English literature 1873 (1886)
Of English literature in the reign of Victoria 1881
MORLEY, Henry F. *See* MUIR, M. M. Pattison
MORLEY, John *Burke* (English men of letters) 1879
Critical miscellanies 1871, 1877
Diderot and the encyclopædists 1878
Edmund Burke: an historical study 1867
The life of R. Cobden 1881
The life of W. E. Gladstone 1903 (1908)
Modern characteristics 1865
Oliver Cromwell 1900
On compromise 1874
Rousseau 1873
The struggle for national education 1873
Voltaire 1872 (1886)
MORLEY, Thomas *A plaine and easie introduction to practicall musicke* 1597
Morning Chronicle, The 1780–1832
Morning Herald and Daily Advertiser 1780–1869
Morning Post, The 1772–
Morning Star, The 1856–69
Morning Star 1966–
'MORPHY, Marcelle, Countess' (Marcelle Azra Forbes) ed. *Recipes of all nations* 1935
MORRALL, Michael T. *History and description of needle making* 1852
MORRELL, Robert Selby, et al. eds. *Synthetic resins and allied plastics* 1937
MORRIS, Alexander *Canada and her resources* 1855
MORRIS, Alfred J. *Religion and business* 1853
MORRIS, Charles William *Signs, language and behavior* 1946
MORRIS, Clara (Clara Morris Harriott) *Life on the stage: my personal experiences and recollections* 1901
MORRIS, Desmond John *The mammals: a guide to the living species* 1965
Manwatching: a field guide to human behaviour 1977
The naked ape 1967
See also MORRIS, Ramona
MORRIS, Edward E. *Austral English, a dictionary of Australasian words, phrases and usages* 1898
MORRIS, Francis Orpen *A history of British birds* 1851–57
A history of British butterflies 1853
A natural history of British moths 1859–70
MORRIS, George S. *Ueberweg's (F.) History of philosophy* tr. 1872–74
MORRIS, Gouverneur *See* SPARKS, J.
MORRIS, John *A catalogue of British fossils* 1843
MORRIS, John ed. *The troubles of our Catholic forefathers, related by themselves* 1872–75
'MORRIS, John' (John Hearne & Morris Cargill) *Fever grass* 1969
MORRIS, Joseph *Sermons* 1743
MORRIS, Sir Lewis *The epic of Hades* 1877
The ode of life 1880
Songs of two worlds 1871–75
MORRIS, Marmaduke C. F. *Yorkshire folk-talk* 1892
MORRIS, Mowbray *Claverhouse* 1887
MORRIS, Ramona & MORRIS, Desmond John *Men and apes* 1966
Men and pandas 1966
Men and snakes 1965
MORRIS, Richard *Historical outlines of English accidence* 1872
Specimens of early English 1867 (1872–87)
See also SKEAT, W. W.
MORRIS, Robert *An essay in defence of ancient architecture* 1728
MORRIS, Terence & MORRIS, Pauline *Pentonville: a sociological study of an English prison* 1963
MORRIS, William *The Æneids of Virgil* tr. 1875
The earthly paradise, a poem 3 vols. 1868–70
The life and death of Jason 1867
News from nowhere; or, An epoch of rest 1890 (UK 1891)
The Odyssey of Homer tr. 1887
Poems by the way 1891
The story of Sigurd the Volsung, and the fall of the Niblungs 1876 (1877)
—— & BAX, E. B. *Socialism: its growth and outcome* 1893
Morris owner's manual 1925
MORRISON, Arthur *A child of the Jago* 1896
Tales of mean streets 1894
MORRISON, Richard J. *Zadkiel's grammar of astrology* 1840 (1852)
MORRISON, Robert *Memoirs of William Milne, compiled from his own documents* 1820
MORRISON, William Douglas *Lombroso's (C.) Female offender* tr. 1895
MORROW, W. C. *Bohemian Paris of to-day* 1899
Mors, Roderigo See BRINKLOW, H.
MORSE, Eric Wilton *Fur trade canoe routes of Canada: then and now* 1969
MORSE, Jedidiah *The American geography* 1789 (1794)
The American universal geography 1796
MORSE, Mary *The unattached: a report of the project carried out by the National Association of Youth Clubs* 1965
MORSE, Philip McCord *Vibration and sound* 1936
Morselli's (E.) Suicide, an essay on comparative moral statistics tr. 1881
Morte Arthur, Le, a romance *a*1450 (E.E.T.S. 1903; Roxb. Club 1819; Furnivall 1864)
Morte Arthure, or the death of Arthur ?*a*1400 (E.E.T.S. 1865, revised 1871)
See also *Arthur;* MALORY, Sir T.
MORTEN, Honnor *Sketches of hospital life* 1888
MORTIMER, Mrs. Favell Lee *Far off: or Asia and Australia described* 1852
— *Africa and America described* 1854
'MORTIMER, Geoffrey' (Walter M. Gallichan) *Like stars that fall* 1895
Pyrotechny: or a familiar system of recreative fire-works 1852 (1853)
MORTIMER, John *The whole art of husbandry* 1707 (1721)
MORTIMER, John Clifford *A voyage round my father* 1971
MORTIMER, Penelope *Daddy's gone a-hunting* 1958

MORTIMER, Thomas *Every man his own broker* 1761 (1762)
A general dictionary of commerce etc. 1810 (1819)
MORTON, Henry Canova Vollam *In search of England* 1927
In search of South Africa 1948
MORTON, John *The natural history of Northamptonshire* 1712
MORTON, John C. *A cyclopedia of agriculture, practical and scientific* 1855 (1856)
MORTON, Nathaniel *New-Englands memoriall* 1669
Morton's (R.) Phthisiologia: or a treatise of consumptions tr. 1694
MORTON, Bp. Thomas *A direct answer* (to T. Higgons) 1609
A discharge of five imputations 1633
Ἐπισκοπος ἀποστολικος or the episcopacy of the church of England justified to be apostolical a1659 (1670)
The opinion of T. Morton concerning the peace of the church 1641 (Good counsels 1641)
A preamble unto an incounter with P. R. 1608
MORTON, Thomas *New English Canaan or new Canaan, containing an abstract of New England* 1637
MORTON, Thomas *Secrets worth knowing, a comedy* 1798
MORWYNG, Peter *Joseph, Ben Gorion's Compendious history of the latter times of the Jewes commune weale* tr. 1561 (1567)
The treasure of Evonymus tr. 1559
MORYSINE, R. *See* MORISON, Sir Richard
MORYSON, Fynes *An itinerary* 1617
— *Shakespeare's Europe, unpublished chapters of F. Moryson's Itinerary* (1903)
MOSEDALE, John *Football* 1972
MOSELEY, Henry *Lectures on astronomy* 1839 (1854)
MOSELEY, Henry N. *Notes by a naturalist on the 'Challenger'* (1872–76) 1879
MOSELEY, Walter M. *An essay on archery* 1792
MOSER, Joseph *The hermit of Caucasus, an oriental romance* 1796
MOSS, Stirling Craufurd *In the track of speed* 1957
MOSSOM, Robert *The preacher's tripartite* 1657
'MOSTYN, Sydney' *See* RUSSELL, W. C.
MOTHERBY, George *A new medical dictionary* 1775
MOTHERWELL, William ed. *Minstrelsy, ancient and modern* 1827
Poems, narrative and lyrical 1832
Poetical works a1835 (1847, 1881)
Motives to godly mourning and rejoycing 1698
MOTLEY, John Lothrop *Correspondence* a1877 (1889)
History of the united Netherlands 1860–67 (1868)
The life and death of John of Barneveld 1874 (1879)
The rise of the Dutch republic 1855 (1866)
Motor, The 1903–
Motor boat 1904–
Motor-car world 1899–1905
Motor cycle, The 1903–
Motor manual, The 1903–59
Motoring annual and motorist's year book, The 1903
MOTTEUX, Peter A. *Cervantes' History of Don Quixote* tr. 1700–03 (1712, 1733)
ed. *Rabelais' (F.) Works by Sir T. Urchard* (Urquhart) *and others* and tr. books IV, V (*Pantagruel's voyage*) 1694 (1708, 1737)
Saint-Olon's (F. Pidou de) Present state of the empire of Morocco tr. 1695
MOTTRAM, Ralph Hale *The Spanish farm* 1924
MOUAT, Frederic J. *Adventures and researches among the Andaman islanders* 1863
'MOUBRAY, Bonington' *See* LAWRENCE, J.
MOUFET, MOFFETT, or MUFFET, Thomas *The silkwormes and their flies: lively described in verse by T. M.* 1599
M.'s Theater of insects: or lesser living creatures tr. J. R(owland) 1658 (appended to Topsell, Hist. four-footed beasts)
—— & BENNET, C. *Healths improvement* (a1604) Corrected and enlarged by C. Bennet 1655 (1746)
MOULE, Bp. Handley C. G. *Colossian studies* 1898
MOUNTAGU *See* MONTAGU
MOUNTAIN, Armine S. H. *Memoirs and letters* a1854 (1857)
Mourtray family, The 1800 *See* HERVEY, Mrs.
Movie 1962–
MOXON, Elizabeth *English housewifery* 1749 (1764)
MOXON, Joseph *Barozzi (G.), Vignola: or the compleat architect* tr. 1665
Mathematicks made easie: or a mathematical dictionary 1679 (also 1701)
Mechanick dyalling 1668
Mechanick exercises, or the doctrine of handy-works 1677–1700 (1683, 1703)
—, *printing* 1683 (repr. De Vinne 1896)
Regulæ trium ordinum literarum typographicarum: or the rules of the three orders of print letters 1676
A tutor to astronomie and geographie 1659 (1665)
MOYER, James Ambrose & WOSTREL, J. F. *Radio handbook: including television and sound motion pictures* 1931
MOYES, Patricia *The curious affair of the third dog* 1973
Dead men don't ski 1959
Murder à la mode 1963
Who saw her die? 1970
MOYLE, John *Abstractum chirurgiæ marinæ; or an abstract of sea surgery* 1686
MOYSIE, David *Memoirs of the affairs of Scotland* 1577–1603 (1755; Bannatyne Club 1830)
MOZLEY, Mrs. Harriet *The lost brooch* (anon.) 1841
MOZLEY, James Bowling *Eight lectures on miracles* (Bampton lectures) 1865
Essays, historical and theological v.d. (1878)
Ruling ideas in early ages and their relation to Old Testament faith 1877 (1878)
Sermon on the atonement 1873
Sermons before the university of Oxford and on various occasions v.d. (1876)
M. P.'s Letter on Royal Navy 1758 See *Letter*
Mr. Gray and his neighbours 1876
Mrs. Raven's temptation, by the author of Dr. Hardy's marriage 1882
Mucedorus. A most pleasant comedie of Mucedorus.. and Amadine 1598 (Hazl. Dodsley; Shakespeare Apocrypha 1908)
'MUCKLEBACKIT, Samuel' *See* LUMSDEN, J.
MUDGE, Thomas *Thoughts on the means of improving watches* 1763 (1799)
MUDIE, Robert *The feathered tribes of the British islands* 1834 (1841)
Man, in his physical structure and adaptations 1839
Müller's (C. O.) Ancient art and its remains tr. J. Leitch 1847 (1850)
MÜLLER, Ferdinand von *Introduction to botanical teachings at the schools of Victoria* 1877
MÜLLER, Friedrich Max *Chips from a German workshop* v.d. (1867–75, 1880)
Introduction to the science of religion 1873
Lectures on the science of language 2 ser. 1861–64
Rig-Veda-Sanhita, the sacred hymns of the Brahmans tr. 1869
Theosophy; or, Psychological religion (Gifford lectures) 1893
MUFFET, Peter *A commentarie on the whole booke of the proverbs of Salomon* 1596 (1868)
MUHLENBERG, Gotthilf Henry Ernest *Catalogus plantarum Americæ Septentrionalis..; or, A catalogue of the.. plants of North America, arranged according to the sexual system of Linnæus* 1813
MUILMAN, Peter *A new and complete history of Essex* 1769–72
MUIR, Edwin *Collected poems, 1921–1958* ed. W. Muir & J. C. Hall 1960
MUIR, George *The Clydesdale minstrelsy* 1816
MUIR, John *The mountains of California* 1894
MUIR, Matthew M. Pattison *A treatise on the principles of chemistry* 1884 (1889)
—— & MORLEY, H. F. ed. *Watts' (H.) Dictionary of chemistry* 1888–94
MUIR, Robert *Text-book of pathology* 1924
—— & RITCHIE, James *Manual of bacteriology* 1897 (and several later editions used)
MUIR, T. S. *Characteristics of old church architecture &c. in the mainland and western islands of Scotland* 1861
MUIR, W. J. Cockburn *Pagan or christian? or, notes for the general public on our national architecture* 1860
MUIR, Ward *Observations of an orderly: some glimpses of life and work in an English war hospital* 1917
MUIR, William *Poems on various subjects* a1817 (1818)
MUIRHEAD, James *The institutes of Gaius and rules of Ulpian* tr. 1880
MULCASTER, Richard *The first part of the elementarie which entreateth chefelie of the right writing of our English tung* 1582
Positions, wherin those primitive circumstances be examined, which are necessarie for the training up of children 1581 (1888)
MULCASTER, Robert *Fortescue's (Sir J.) Learned commendation of the politique lawes of England* tr. 1567 (1573)
MULFORD, Clarence Edward *Bar-20* 1907 (UK 1914)
The Bar-20 three 1921
Black Buttes 1923
The coming of Cassidy—and the others 1913
Cottonwood Gulch 1925
Hopalong Cassidy 1910
Hopalong Cassidy's protégé 1926
Johnny Nelson 1920 (UK 1921)
The man from Bar-20: a story of the cow-country 1918
The orphan 1908
Rustlers' valley 1924
—— & CLAY, John Wood *Buck Peters, ranchman* 1912 (UK 1921)
MULFORD, Elisha *The republic of God* 1882
MULGAN, John Alan Edward *Man alone* 1939
MULLALLY, Frederic *The Munich involvement* 1968
MULLARD, Chris *Black Britain; with an account of recent events at the Institute of Race Relations by A. Kirby* 1973
MULLER, John *A treatise of artillery* 1768
MULLIN, Glen Hawthorne *Adventures of a scholar tramp* 1925
MULLINER, John *A testimony against periwig and periwig-making* 1677 (1881)
MULOCK, Miss Dinah M. *See* CRAIK, Mrs. Dinah M.
MUMFORD, John Kimberley *Oriental rugs* 1900 (UK 1901)
MUMFORD, Lewis *City development: studies in disintegration and renewal* 1945 (UK 1946)
The city in history: its origins, its transformations, and its prospects 1961
MUNBY, Arthur J. *Dorothy; a country story in elegiac verse* (anon.) 1880
See also HUDSON, Derek Rommel
Munch's (P. A.) Throndjems domkirke, The cathedral of Throndheim 1859
Munchausen, Baron. Gulliver revived: or the singular travels, campaigns, voyages and adventures of Baron Munchausen (by R. E. Raspe) 1786 (1792)
MUNDAY, Anthony *The book of John a Kent and John a Cumber, a comedy* 1595 (Shaks. Soc. 1851)
Busche's (A. van den; le Sylvain) Orator; handling a hundred severall discourses tr. 1596
The defence of contraries tr. out of French by A. M. 1593
A discoverie of E. Campion and his confederates 1582
The downfall of Robert earle of Huntington afterwards called Robin Hood 1599 (1601; Hazl. Dodsley)
The English Romayne lyfe 1582 (Harl. Misc.)
The famous history of Palmendos tr. 1589 (1653)
The first part of the.. history of Palmerin of England ?1581 (1602, 1639)
A view of sundry examples (anon.) 1580 (with John a Kent etc., Shaks. Soc. 1851)
The woorthy enterprise of John Foxe.. in delivering 266 Christians a1598 (Hakluyt, Voyages 1598; Arber, Eng. Garner I)
— *The admirable deliverance of 266 Christians by J. Reynard* (or rather Fox) (1608)
—— & CHETTLE, H. *The death of Robert earle of Huntington, otherwise called Robin Hood* 1601 (Hazl. Dodsley)
Mundus et infans c1500 See *World and the child*
Mundus muliebris 1690 *See* EVELYN
MUNDY, Godfrey C. *Our antipodes: or residence and rambles in the Australasian colonies* 1852 (1857)
Pen and pencil sketches, being the journal of a tour in India 1832
Municipal corporations. First report of the commissioners appointed to inquire into the municipal corporations in England and Wales (with Appendix, pts. I–V) 1835
Muniments of the royal burgh of Irvine v.d. (1890–91)
MUNRO, George Campbell *Birds of Hawaii* 1944
MUNRO, Neil *The daft days* 1907
Doom Castle, a romance 1901
John Splendid, the tale of a poor gentleman 1898
The lost pibroch 1896
MUNRO, Robert *Prehistoric Scotland and its place in European civilisation* 1899
MUNROE, Kirk *The golden days of '49: a tale of the California diggings* 1889
MUNROE, Ruth Learned *Schools of psychoanalytic thought* 1955 (UK 1957)
MUNROW, David *Instruments of the Middle Ages and Renaissance* 1976
Munsey's Magazine (N.Y.) 1891–
MUNSON, Kenneth *Pioneer aircraft 1903–1914* 1969
Muralt's (B. L. de) Letters describing the character and customs of the English and French nations tr. 1726
MURCHISON, Charles *A treatise on the continued fevers of Great Britain* 1862 (1873, 1884)
MURCHISON, Sir Roderick Impey *Siluria: the history of the oldest known rocks containing organic remains* 1854 (1859, 1867)
The Silurian system, founded on geological researches 1839
MURDOCH, A. *A Yoshiwara episode. Fred Wilson's fate.* By A. M. 1892
MURDOCH, Alexander G. *The laird's lykewake and other poems* 1877
Lilts on the Doric lyre 1873
MURDOCH, Jean Iris *The bell* 1958
Flight from the enchanter 1956
Henry and Cato 1976
Nuns and soldiers 1980
The sacred and profane love machine 1974
The sandcastle 1957
The sea, the sea 1978
A severed head 1961
The time of the angels 1966
Under the net 1954
An unofficial rose 1962
A word child 1975
MURDOCH, Walter & DRAKE-BROCKMAN, Henrietta F. Y. eds. *Australian short stories* 1951
For 2nd ser. *see* 'JAMES, Brian'
MURE, Sir William *Works* a1657 (S.T.S. 1898)
MURE, William *A critical history of the language and literature of antient Greece* 1850–57
MURFREE, Mary Noailles ('C. E. Craddock') *The despot of Broomsedge cove* 1888
In the Tennessee mountains 1884
The prophet of the great smoky mountain 1885
Where the battle was fought 1884 (1885)
MURFREE, William L. *A treatise on the law of sheriffs* 1884
MURPHY, Arthur *Works* v.d. (1786)
All in the wrong, a comedy 1761 (1775)
An essay on the life and genius of Samuel Johnson 1792
The Gray's Inn journal 1752–54
The way to keep him, a comedy 1760
The works of C. Tacitus tr. 1793
MURPHY, Edmund *The present state and condition of Ireland* 1681
MURPHY, Gardner *Personality* 1947
MURPHY, James G. *A critical and exegetical commentary on Genesis* 1863; *on Exodus* 1866; *on Leviticus* 1872
MURRAY, Alexander Stuart *Manual of mythology* 1873
MURRAY, Amelia Matilda *Letters from the United States, Cuba, and Canada* 2 vols. 1856
MURRAY, Charles *Hamewith* 1900
MURRAY, David Christie *The church of humanity* 1901
Cynic Fortune 1886
Hearts, a novel 1883
The making of a novelist 1894
Rainbow gold, a novel 1885
Tales in prose and verse 1898
The weaker vessel 1888

—— & Herman, H. *A dangerous catspaw* 1889
One traveller returns 1887
Murray, Elizabeth A. *Ella Norman; or, a woman's perils* 1864
Murray, Eustace C. Grenville- *The Russians of to-day* 1878
Murray, George *Islaford and other poems* 1845
Murray, Henry Alexander *Explorations in personality* 1938
Murray, Hugh *Historical account of discoveries and travels in North America* 1829
Murray, Sir James A. H. *The dialect of the southern counties of Scotland* 1873 (Philol. Soc.)
The evolution of English lexicography (Romanes lecture) 1900
Murray, James E. *A summer in the Pyrenees* 1837
Murray, John Clark *Solomon Maimon: an autobiography* tr. 1888
Murray, Katharine Maud Elisabeth *Caught in the web of words: James A. H. Murray and the Oxford English Dictionary* 1977
Murray, Lindley *English grammar* 1795 (1824)
Murray, Peter John & Murray, Linda *A dictionary of art and artists* 1959
Murray, Robert *Rudimentary treatise on marine-engines* 1852 (1858)
Murray, William Buckley *The sweet ride* 1967
Murray's Hand-book for travellers in southern Germany 1837
Murrell, John *Two books of cookerie and carving* 1638
— (another ed.) *A new book of cookerie* 1641
Murry, John Middleton *The necessity of pacifism* 1937
Pencillings: little essays on literature 1923
The voyage 1924
Musarum deliciæ 1655 *See* Mennes, Sir J.
Museum of Comparative Zoology, Harvard University *Bulletin* 1863-
Museum rusticum et commerciale: or select papers on agriculture etc. 1763-66
Musgrave, George Musgrave *By-roads and battle-fields in Picardy* 1861
Nooks and corners in old France 1867
A pilgrimage into Dauphiné 1857
Ten days in a French parsonage 1864
Mush, John a1617 *See* Clitherow, Margaret
Music. A short explication of such foreign words as are made use of in musick books 1724
Musical Association *Proceedings* 1875-
Musical magazine, The 1835
Musical quarterly 1915-
Musical times 1844-
Musical world, The 1836-91
My ducats and my daughter (by H. Hunter & W. Whyte) 1884
My first book: the experiences of Walter Besant, J. Payn (et al.) 1894
Mycologia 1909-
Myers, Arthur Wallis *Twenty years of lawn tennis* 1921
Myers, Ernest *Poems* 1877 See also Lang, A.
Myers, Frederic *Catholic thoughts on the Bible and theology* (anon.) 1841-48
Myers, Frederic W. H. *Human personality* a1901 (1903)
Poems 1870
Myers, Leonard Morris *Electron optics: theoretical and practical* 1939
Mynshul, Geffray *Essayes and characters of a prison and prisoners, by G. M.* 1618
Myrc, John *Instructions for parish priests* a1450 (E.E.T.S. 1868, revised 1902) See also *Mirk's Festial*
Myroure See *Mirror*
Mysterie of iniquitie 1643 *See* Bowles, E.

N

N., C. *A poem on the happy union between England and Scotland* 1707
N. D. ('Doleman, N.') *Three conversions of England* 1603-04 *See* Parsons, R.
N., M. *See* Needham, M.
N., N. *Du Boscq's (J.) Compleat woman* tr. 1639
N., N. *A narrative of all the proceedings in the drayning of the great level of the Fenns* 1661 (in Arber, Eng. Garner I)
N., N. *The heu and cry: or, a relation of the travels of the Devil and Towzer* 1682
N., N. *Old popery as good as new* 1688
N., N. *Boccalini's (T.) Advertisements from Parnassus* tr. 1704
N. O. *See* O., N.
N., R. (Robert Norton) 1635 *See* Camden, W.
N., T. *Calvin's Institution* tr. 1561 *See* Norton, T.
N., T. *Cortes' (H.) Conquest of the Weast India* tr. 1578 *See* Nicholas, T.
N., T. (Richard Neve) *The city and country purchaser, and builder's dictionary* 1703 (1726, 1736)
N., W. *Barley-breake; or a warning for wantons* 1607 (Grosart 1877)
NATO *Automatic translation of languages: papers presented at NATO Summer School held in Venice, July 1962* 1966
N.Z.E.F. *See* New Zealand Expeditionary Force
Nabbes, Thomas *The bride, a comedie* 1640
Covent garden, a pleasant comedie 1638
Microcosmus, a morall maske 1637
Nabokov, Vladimir Vladimirovich *Bend sinister* 1947
The defence tr. by M. Scammell in collaboration with the author 1964
The gift tr. by M. Scammell and the author 1963
Invitation to a beheading tr. by D. Nabokov and the author 1960
Lolita 2 vols. 1955 (US 1 vol. 1958)
Look at the harlequins! 1974 (UK 1975)
Nabokov's dozen: a collection of thirteen stories 1958 (UK 1959)
Pale fire 1962
Pnin 1957
The real life of Sebastian Knight 1941
Speak, memory (US ed. with title *Conclusive evidence*) 1951
— (UK ed. 2) 1967
Nadell, Aaron *Projecting sound pictures: a practical textbook for projectionists and managers* 1931
Nagel, Ernest *The structure of science: problems in the logic of scientific explanation* 1961
'Na Gopaleen, Myles' (Brian O'Nolan) (1911-66) *The best of Myles: a selection from 'Cruiskeen Lawn'* ed. K. O'Nolan 1968
See also 'O'Brien, Flann'
Naipaul, Shivadhar Srinivasa *Black and white* 1980
Naipaul, Vidiadhar Surajprasad *An area of darkness* 1964
In a free state 1971
The mimic men 1967
The mystic masseur 1957
Naismith, John *General view of the agriculture of the county of Clydesdale* 1798
Nall, John G. *Great Yarmouth and Lowestoft* 1866
Namier, Lewis Bernstein *Conflicts: studies in contemporary history* 1942
Nansen, Fridtjof *Farthest North* 1897
The structure and combination of the historical elements of the central nervous system 1887
Napheys, George H. *Prevention and cure of disease* 1871
Napier, Arthur S. *Contributions to Old English lexicography* 1906 (Philol. Soc. Trans.)
ed. *Old English glosses chiefly unpublished* 1900 (Anecdota Oxon.)
Napier, Edward H. D. E. *Excursions in Southern Africa* 1849
Scenes and sports in foreign lands 1840
Napier, James *A manual of the art of dyeing* 1853
Napier, Macvey *Selections from the correspondence of M. Napier* a1847 (1879)
Napier, Mark *Memoirs of the marquis of Montrose* 1856
Memorials and letters illustrative of the life and times of J. Graham of Claverhouse, viscount Dundee 1859-62
Napier, Robina ed. *Johnsoniana: anecdotes of Samuel Johnson; with diary of Dr. Campbell, and extracts from that of Madame D'Arblay* (1884)
ed. *A noble boke of cookry* (1882)
Napier, Sir William F. P. *History of the war in the Peninsula, and in the South of France from 1807-14* 1828-40
Narborough, Sir John *Journal* 1694 (in Account of several late voyages; 1711)
Narcissus, a Twelfe Night merriment 1602 (1893)
Nares, Edward *Thinks-I-to-myself* 1811
Nares, Sir George S. *Narrative of a voyage to the Polar Sea 1875-76* 1878
Seamanship 1862 (1865, 1868, 1882)
Nares, Robert *Elements of orthoepy* 1784
A glossary; or, collection of words, phrases, names, and allusions to customs, proverbs, etc. in English authors 1822
— new ed., with additions by J. O. Halliwell & T. Wright (1859)
Narlikar, Jayant *The structure of the universe* 1977
Narragansett historical register 1882-91
Narratiunculae Anglice conscriptae a1000 (ed. Cockayne 1861)
Narrative of the bloudy murders committed by Sir John Fites, alias Fitz, 1605, with an account of his suicide at Twickenham 1605 (ed. J. O. Halliwell 1860)
Narrative of the late parliament (so called), their election and appearing etc. 1657 (in Harl. Misc.)
Narratives of the days of the Reformation, chiefly from the manuscripts of John Foxe 15.. (Camden Soc. 1859)
Narrien, John *Practical astronomy and geodesy* 1845
Nash, Frederic Ogden *The face is familiar* 1940 (UK 1942)
Family reunion 1950 (UK 1951)
Good intentions 1942 (UK 1943)
I'm a stranger here myself 1938
Versus 1949
You can't get there from here 1957
Nashe, Thomas *Works* a1601 (Grosart 1883-85; McKerrow 1904-10)
The anatomie of absurditie 1589
Christ's teares over Jerusalem 1593
A countercuffe given to Martin Junior, by the venturous, hardie and renowned Pasquill of England 1589
Four letters confuted 1592 = Strange newes
Have with you to Saffron-walden 1596
Nashes Lenten stuffe 1599
The first parte of Pasquils apologie (anon.) 1590
Pierce Penilesse his supplication to the diuell 1592
A pleasant comedie, called Summers last will and testament 1600
The returne of the renowned Cavaliero Pasquill of England from the other side the seas, and his meeting with Marforius at London upon the Royall Exchange (anon.) 1589
Strange newes, of the intercepting certaine letters, and a convoy of verses (i.e. G. Harvey's Foure letters and certaine sonnets) 1592 (Head-title *Foure letters confuted*)
The terrors of the night, or, a discourse of apparitions 1594
The unfortunate traveller 1594
A wonderfull, strange and miraculous astrologicall prognostication for this yeer of our Lord God, 1591 1591
See also *Almond; Pappe*
Nasmith, Joseph *Modern cotton spinning machinery* 1890
The students' cotton spinning 1892
Nasmyth, James *J. Nasmyth, engineer, an autobiography* ed. by S. Smiles 1883
Nason, Leonard Hastings *Chevrons* 1926 (UK 1927)
Nathan, Mrs. Eliza *Langreath, a tale* 1822
Nation, The (New York) 1865-
Nation, The 1907-21
— *The Nation and The Athenæum* 1921-
Nation, The (Barbados) 1973-
Nation review (Melbourne) 1958-
National Academy of Sciences (Washington) *Proceedings* 1863-94; 1915-
National Bureau of Standards *See* United States. ——
National cyclopædia of useful knowledge 1847-59
National encyclopædia, The; a dictionary of universal knowledge 1868
National geographic magazine, The 1888-
National MSS., Facsimiles of v.d. (1865-)
National observer 1890-
National observer (US) 1962-77
National police gazette (US) (title varies) 1845-
National responsibility for the opium trade, Our 1880
National review, The 1883-
Natura breuium newly corrected in Englisshe 1532 (1535, 1544)
Natural history 1919-
Natural history of coffee (? by J. Chamberlayne) 1682
Natural history review and quarterly journal of science 1854-65
Natural phenomena 1846 (1850)
Natural philosophy 1829-35 (Library of useful knowledge)
Natural science: a monthly review of scientific progress 1892-
Nature, a weekly illustrated journal of science 1869-
Naunton, Sir Robert *Fragmenta regalia* a1635 (1641; Arber 1870)
Naval accounts and inventories of the reign of Henry VII 1485-97 (Navy Records Soc. 1896)
Naval chronicle, The 1799-1818
Navy news 1954-
Navy Records Society *Publications* (1894-)
Naworth Household books 16.. See *Howard, Ld. William*
Nayler, Joseph Lawrence *Dictionary of aeronautical engineering* 1959
Naylor, Francis H. *The civil and military history of Germany* 1816
Naylor, Samuel *Reynard the Fox: a renowned apologue of the middle age, reproduced in rhyme* (anon.) 1845
Neal, Daniel *The history of the Puritans or Protestant Non-Conformists* 1732-38 (1754)
Neal, John *Brother Jonathan; or the New Englanders* (anon.) 1825
Neal, Joseph C. *Charcoal sketches; or scenes in a Metropolis* 1838 (1841, 1865)
Neale, Edward V. *The analogy of thought and nature investigated* 1863
Neale, John M. *A history of the Holy Eastern Church* 1847-50
A history of the so-called Jansenist Church of Holland 1858
Hymns, chiefly mediæval, or the joys and glories of Paradise tr. and ed. 1865
Hymns for the sick (anon.) 1843 (1863)
Hymns of the Eastern Church tr. 1862
Mediæval hymns and sequences tr. 1851 (1863)
Notes, ecclesiological and picturesque, on Dalmatia 1861
The Rhythm of Bernard de Morlaix on the Celestial Country ed. and tr. 1859 (1864)
Seatonian poems 1864
Sequences, hymns, and other ecclesiastical verses 1866
Neale, John P. *Views of the seats of noblemen and gentlemen in England, Wales, Scotland and Ireland* 1818-23
Neale, R. E. ed. *Whittaker's electrical engineer's pocket-book* 1920 See under title
Neander's (J. A. W.) General history of the Christian religion and church tr. by J. Torrey 1847-55 (Bohn 1850-58)
Neasham, George *North-country sketches* etc. 1893
Neblette, Carroll Bernard *Photography: its principles and practice* 1927
Necessary doctrine and erudition for any Christen man, sette furthe by the kynges maiestie 1543 (1825)
Needham, John T. *An account of some new microscopical discoveries* 1745
Needham, or Nedham, Marchamont *A discourse concerning schools and school-masters* 1663
Medela medicinæ; a plea for the free profession and a renovation of the art of physick 1665
A pacquet of advices and animadversions sent from London to the men of Shaftesbury 1676; *a second pacquet* 1677
Selden's (J.) Of the dominion, or the ownership of the sea. Written in Latin, and entituled, Mare clausum tr. 1652
Nehru, Jawaharlal *An autobiography* 1936
Neil, Samuel *The elements of rhetoric* 1854
Neill, Alexander Sutherland *A dominie's log* 1915 [dated 1916]
Neill! Neill! Orange peel!: a personal view of ninety years 1972
— (rev. ed.) 1973
Summerhill: a radical approach to education 1962

Neill, P. *An account of British horticulture. Drawn up for the Edinburgh Encyclopedia* 1817
List of fishes found in the Firth of Forth, and rivers and lakes near Edinburgh, with remarks 1810 (also in Memoirs of the Wernerian Nat. Hist. Soc. I. 1811)
A tour through some of the Islands of Orkney and Shetland 1806
Neilson, James M. *Poems and songs chiefly in the Scottish language* 1877
Nelson, George & Wright, Henry Niccolls *Tomorrow's house* 1945
Nelson, Horatio Nelson, 1st Viscount *Dispatches and letters* a1805 (1844-46)
Letters to Lady Hamilton a1805 (1814)
Nelson, James H. *The Madura country* 1868
Nelson, Robert *An address to persons of quality and estate* 1715
A companion for the festivals and fasts of the church of England 1704 (1739)
The life of Dr. George Bull 1713 (1714)
See also Hickes, George
Nelson, Stanley R. *All about jazz* 1934
Nelson, William *The laws of England concerning the game* 1727 (1736)
Lex maneriorum: or the law and customs of England, relating to manors and lords of manors 1724 (1726)
Nemnich, Philipp A. *Allgemeines Polyglotten-Lexicon* 1793-98
Nepos' (C.) Lives of illustrious men tr. 1684
Neri's (A.) Art of glass tr. 1662 *See* Merrett, C.
Nero. The tragedie of Claudius Tiberius Nero, Romes greatest tyrant 1607
Nero, The tragedy of 1624 (in Bullen, Old plays I. 1882)
Nesbit, Edith *Five children and it* 1902
The phoenix and the carpet 1904
The railway children 1906
Nesse, Christopher *An antidote aainst Arminianism* 1700 (1827, 1838)
A compleat and compendious church-history 1680
A compleat history and mystery of the Old and New Testament 1690-96
A distinct discourse and discovery of the person and period of Antichrist 1679
A protestant antidote against the poyson of popery 1679
Nethersole, Sir Francis *Parables reflecting upon the times, newly past and yet present* 1648
A project for an equitable and lasting peace, designed in the yere 1643 1648
The self-condemned; or, a letter to Mr. Jo. Goodwin 1648
Nettleship, Henry *Lectures and essays on subjects connected with Latin literature and scholarship* 1885
— 2nd series a1893 (1895)
Nettleship, John T. *Essays on Robert Browning's poetry* 1868
Nettleship, Richard L. *Philosophical lectures and remains* a1892 (1897)
Neuphilologische Mitteilungen 1899-
Neurology 1951-
Neve, Richard *See* N., T.
Nevile, Thomas *Imitations of Horace* 1758
Imitations of Juvenal and Persius 1769
Virgil's Georgics tr. 1767
Neville, Alexander *The lamentable tragedie of Œdipus the sonne of Laius Kyng of Thebes out of Seneca* 1563 (1581)
Neville, Henry *Machiavelli's (N.) Works* tr. 1675
The parliament of ladies 1647
Plato redivivus: or a dialogue concerning government 1681
See also *Shuffling*
'Neville, Margot' *Ladies in the dark* 1965
Nevin, Charles Merrick *Principles of structural geology* 1931
New acronyms and initialisms See *Acronyms dictionary*
New American cyclopædia, ed. by G. Ripley and C. A. Dana 1858-63
New and complete dictionary of arts and sciences, A 4 vols. 1754-5
New Bath guide 1766 *See* Anstey, C.
New biology ed. M. L. Johnson et al. 31 vols. 1945-60
New Botanic garden 1812
New British theatre, The; a selection of original dramas not yet acted 1814-15
New canting dictionary 1725 See also E., B.
New Castle (Delaware) *Records of the court of New Castle on Delaware* (Colonial Society of Pennsylvania) 1904
New Catholic encyclopedia ed. W. J. McDonald 15 vols. 1967
New custom. A new enterlude no lesse wittie then pleasant, entituled new custome 1573 (in Hazl., Dodsley)
New discovery of an old intreague (by D. De Foe) 1691
New England historical and genealogical register 1847-
New England Journal of education 1875-88
New England journal of medicine, The 1928-
New English weekly: a review of public affairs, literature and the arts (title varies) 1932-49
New Gould medical dictionary 1949
— (ed. 2) 1956
New Hampshire (Colony) *Probate records of the province of New Hampshire* 9 vols. 1907-41
New Hampshire, Provincial papers, documents, and records relating to the province of 1623- (1867-)
New Hampshire Historical Society collections (1824-)
New Jersey *Archives of the State of New Jersey* 16 vols. 1880-1917
New Jewish encyclopedia, The ed. D. Bridger 1962
New left review 1960-
New light of chirurgery put out 1695 *See* Colbatch, John
New London magazine, The 1785-89
New Mills, Haddingtonshire, The records of a Scottish cloth manufactory at 1681-1703 (S.H.S. 1905)
New mirror, The 1843-44
New monthly magazine, The 1821-59
New musical express 1952-
New notborune mayd upon yᵉ passion of cryste c1520 (Roxb. Club. 1820; in Anc. poet. tracts, Percy Soc. 1842)
See also *Not-browne mayd*
New Oxford history of music, The ed. J. A. Westrup et al. 1954-
New phytologist 1902-
New Princeton review, The 1886-
New republic, The 1914-
New review, The 1889-97
New scientist, The 1956-
New Shakspere Society *Publications* (1874-)
New society 1962-
New spectator, The; with the sage opinions of John Bull 1784-86
New sporting magazine 1831-70
New statesman, The (title varies) 1913-
New Sydenham Society See *Sydenham (New) Society*
New Test of the Church of Englands loyalty 1687 (in Somers' Tracts, I. 1748)
New Testament (versions) See also *Bible*
Tindale 1526, 1534
Geneva 1557
Rhemes 1582
New Testament. A fourteenth century English biblical version a1400 (ed. Anna C. Paues 1904)
New view of London (By E. Hatton) 1708
New Virginians, The (By Mary Allan-Olney) 1880
New world, The 1840-42
New York 1968-
New York Academy of Sciences *Annals* 1877-
New York dramatic news 1894-6
New York Evening Post 1802-1919
New York Herald, The 1859-
New York Herald Tribune (title varies) 1841-
New York Herald Tribune International (title varies) 1887-
New York law journal 1949-
New York medical journal 1865-1923
New York review of books 1963-
New York State *Documents relative to the colonial history of the State of New-York* See under title
New York State. Department of Correctional Services *Guidelines to volunteer services* 1974
New York Times, The 1857-
New York Times book review 1896-
New York World 1860-1931
New York World-Telegram 1931-66 (1950-66 with title *New York World-Telegram and Sun*)
New Yorker, The 1925-
New Zealand. Parliament. House of Representatives *Appendix to the journals* 1858-
New Zealand Expeditionary Force *Chronicles* 1916-19
New Zealand Expeditionary Force Times (2nd N.Z.E.F.) 1941-?5
New Zealand illustrated magazine 1901-5
New Zealand Institute (from 1935 Royal ——) *Transactions and proceedings* 1868-
New Zealand journal 1840-52
New Zealand journal of agriculture (title varies) 1910-
New Zealand listener 1939-
New Zealand News 1927-
New Zealand short stories 1953 *See* Davin, Daniel Marcus
— (2nd ser.) 1966 *See* Stead, Christian Karlson
New Zealand timber journal 1954-
New Zealand woman's weekly 1934-
Newbery, Thomas *A booke in Englysh metre of the great marchaunt man called Diues Pragmaticus* 1563 (in Huth, Fugitive tracts, 1875)
Newbold, Thomas John *Political and statistical account of the British settlements in the Straits of Malacca, viz., Pinang, Malacca and Singapore* 2 vols. 1839
Newbolt, Sir Henry J. *Admirals all and other verses* 1897
Newby, Mrs. C. J. *Common sense* 1866
Newcastle, Margaret Cavendish, Duchess of *The life of William Cavendishe, duke, marquess and earl of Newcastle* 1667
— *To which is added the true relation of my birth, breeding and life* (1886)
Natures pictures drawn by Fancies pencil to the life 1656
Newcastle, William Cavendish, 1st Duke of *The country captaine; a comoedye* (anon.) 1649 (= *Captain Underwit, a comedy*, in Bullen, Old Plays, II. 1883; sometimes attributed to J. Shirley)
Newcastle-upon-Tyne, Extracts from the municipal accounts of v.d. (1848)
Newcomb, Simon *Popular astronomy* 1878
Newcome, Abp. William *An attempt toward revising our English translation of the Greek scriptures* 1796
Newcourt, Richard *Repertorium ecclesiasticum parochiale Londinense; an ecclesiastical parochial history of the diocese of London* 1708-10
Newdigate-Newdegate, Anne Emily *The Cheverels of Cheverel Manor* 1898
Newell, William W. *Games and songs of American children* 1883
Newgate calendar, The, or malefactor's bloody register, with the last dying speeches of the most notorious criminals, from 1700-73 1775
Newgate calendar, The new See Jackson, William
Newland, Henry G. *Three lectures on tractarianism* 1852
Newman, Arthur *Pleasures vision: with deserts complaint* 1619 (1840)
Newman, Edward *A familiar introduction to the history of insects* 1841
A history of British ferns 1840
— *A history of British ferns and allied plants* 1844
An illustrated natural history of British butterflies 1870-71
An illustrated natural history of British moths 1869
Newman, Edwin *Sunday punch* 1979
Newman, Francis W. *A history of the Hebrew monarchy* 1847
Miscellanies; chiefly addresses, academical and historical 1869
The odes of Horace tr. 1853
Phases of faith 1850 (1853, 1860)
The soul, her sorrows and her aspirations 1849
See also Sieveking, I. G.
Newman, Gordon F. *The price* 1974
Sir, you bastard 1970
You nice bastard 1972
Newman, John *Scamping tricks and odd knowledge occasionally practised upon public works* 1891
Newman, John Henry *Apologia pro vita sua* 1864
The Arians of the fourth century 1833 (1876)
Callista, a sketch of the third century 1856
Certain difficulties felt by Anglicans in Catholic teaching considered 1864, 1874 (1876)
The Church of the Fathers 1833-40 (1840)
Discourses on the scope and nature of University education 1852
The dream of Gerontius 1866
An essay in aid of a grammar of assent 1870
An essay on the development of Christian doctrine 1845
An essay on miracles 1842 (Prefixed to Fleury's Eccl. Hist.)
Historical sketches v.d. (1872-73)
Lectures on the history of the Turks in its relation to Christianity 1854
Lectures on the present position of Catholics in England 1851
Lectures on the prophetical office of the church 1837
A letter addressed to his Grace the Duke of Norfolk on occasion of Mr. Gladstone's recent expostulation 1875
A letter to the Rev. E. B. Pusey, D.D., on his recent Eirenicon 1866
Letters and correspondence v.d. (1891)
Loss and gain 1848
The office and work of the Universities 1856
Parochial sermons 1834-42
Tracts for the times (various numbers) 1833-41
Tracts, theological and ecclesiastical v.d. (1874)
Verses on various occasions 1868
Life, based on his private journals and correspondence, by Wilfrid Ward (1912)
Newman, Maxwell Herman Alexander *Elements of the topology of plane sets of points* 1939
Newminster Cartulary (*Chartularium Abbathiæ de Novo Monasterio*) v.d. (Surtees Soc. 1878)
Newnes complete amateur photography ed. M. L. Hall 1958
Newnes concise encyclopaedia of electrical engineering ed. M. G. Say 1962
Newnes concise encyclopaedia of nuclear energy 1962
Newnham-Davis, Nathaniel *Three men and a god; and other stories* 1896
Newport, William *The fall of man by sinne* 1644
Newrobe, Richard *Farewell Myter, or Canterburies meditations, and Wrenn's syllogismes* 1641
News and Courier (Charleston, South Carolina) 1873-
News and Observer (Raleigh, North Carolina) 1872-
News and Press (Darlington, South Carolina) 1903-
News Chronicle 1930-60
News from the channel: or, the discovery and perfect description of the isle of Serke 1673 (in Harl. Misc.)
News from France 1682 *See* Burnet, G.
News from Hell, Rome, and the Inns of Court 1641 (in Harl. Misc., VII, 1746)
News from the Lowe-Countreys; or Podex his encomium, held out for publick information 1652
News from Scotland, declaring the damnable life and death of Dr. Fian 1591 (Roxb. Cl. 1816)
News review 1936-50
Newspaper and general reader's pocket companion 2 parts 1855-6
Newsweek 1933-
Newte, Thomas *A tour in England and Scotland in 1785* (anon.) 1788
Newth, George S. *A text-book of inorganic chemistry* 1894
— (ed. 12) 1907
Newton, Alfred *A dictionary of birds* 1893-96
Newton, Charles T. *Essays on art and archæology* 1880
'Newton, Francis' (Eric John Ernest Hobsbawm) *The jazz scene* 1959
Newton, George *Exposition and notes on the 17th Chapter of John* 1660
Newton, Sir Isaac *Works* a1727 (1779-85)
The chronology of ancient kingdoms amended a1727 (1728)
Observations upon the Prophecies of Daniel and the Apocalypse of St. John a1727 (1733)
Optical lectures tr. 1728
Opticks 1704 (1721)
A treatise of the system of the world tr. 1728
Newton, John *Cardiphonia: or, the utterance of the heart* 1781 (1857)
Newton, Joseph *Introduction to metallurgy* 1938
Newton, Kenneth & Steeds, William *The motor vehicle* 1929 (and several later editions used)

Newton, Peter *High country days* 1949
Sheep thief 1972
Wayleggo 1947
Newton, Richard *Sermons* a1753 (1784)
Newton, Thomas *Cicero's Worthye booke of old age* tr. 1569
Daneau's (L.) True and Christian friendshippe. Together with a right excellent invective against diceplay tr. 1586
Gratarolus' (G.) Direction for the health of magistrates and studentes tr. 1574
Lemnie's (L.) Touchstone of complexions tr. 1565 (1576, 1633)
Newton, Thomas *Dissertations on the Prophecies* 1754–58
Milton's Paradise lost 1749
Milton's Paradise regain'd 1752
Niccholes, Alexander *A discourse of marriage and wiving* 1615
Niccols, Richard *The cuckow* 1607
Englands Eliza; A winter nights vision 1610 (parts of Mirror for magistrates 1610)
Expicedium. A funeral oration upon the princesse Elizabeth (anon.) 1603
Nice wanton, A preaty interlude called 1560 (in Manly, Specim. pre-Shaks. drama I. 1897; Hazl., Dodsley)
Nichol, John *Byron* 1880
Nichol, John P. *The architecture of the heavens* 1850 (1851)
A cyclopædia of physical sciences 1857
Thoughts on some important points relating to the system of the world 1846
Nicholas, Thomas *Cortes' (H.) Pleasant historie of the conquest of the Weast India* tr. 1578 (1596)
Nicholas, Thomas *The pedigree of the English people* 1868
Nicholas papers, The. Correspondence of Sir E. Nicholas 1641–60 (Camden Soc. 1886–1920)
Nicholay's Voyages tr. 1585 *See* Washington, T.
Nicholls, William *An answer to an heretical book called The naked gospel* 1691
A comment on the Book of Common Prayer 1710
Nichols, David *Echinoderms* 1962
Nichols, Francis M. *Britton, the French text carefully revised with an English translation, introduction and notes* 1865
Nichols, John *Bibliotheca topographica Britannica* 1780–90
A collection of all the wills, now known to be extant, of the kings and queens of England, to that of Henry VII exclusive 1780
The history and antiquities of the county of Leicester 1795–1815
Illustrations of the literary history of the eighteenth century 1817–22, a1826
— completed by J. B. & J. G. Nichols (1828–58),
Illustrations of the manners and expences of antient times in England 1797
Literary anecdotes of the eighteenth century 1812–15
The progresses and public processions of Queen Elizabeth 1788–1805 (1823)
The progresses, processions and magnificent festivities of K. James the first 1828
Nichols, John Beverley *The sweet and twenties* 1958
Nichols, Philip *Sir Francis Drake revived* 1626 (in Arber, Eng. Garner, V)
Nichols, Thomas L. *Forty years of American life* 1864
Nichols' Health manual 1887
Nicholson, Edward W. B. *Golspie* 1897
Nicholson, George ed. *The illustrated dictionary of gardening* 1885–88
Nicholson, Henry A. *Introduction to the study of biology* 1872
An introductory text-book of zoology 1871
A manual of palæontology 1872 (1879)
A manual of zoology 1870 (1873, 1878, 1887)
Nicholson, James *Idylls o' Hame, and other poems* 1870
Kilwuddie and other poems 1863 (1895)
Nicholson, John *The operative mechanic and British machinist* 1825 (1853)
Nicholson, John *Historical and traditional tales in prose and verse, connected with the south of Scotland* 1843
Nicholson, John *Folk lore of East Yorkshire* 1890
The folk speech of East Yorkshire 1889
Nicholson, John Kenyon *The barker* 1927
'Nicholson, Kate' (Judith Fay) *Hook, line and sinker* 1966
Nicholson, Meredith *A Hoosier chronicle* 1912
Nicholson, Peter *An architectural dictionary* 1819
Mechanical exercises 1812
The new carpenters' guide 1792
The new practical builder and workman's companion 1823
Nicholson, Samuel *Acolastus his after-witte* 1600 (Grosart 1876)
Nicholson, W. E. *A glossary of terms used in the coal trade of Northumberland and Durham* 1888
Nicholson, Bp. William *A plain but full exposition of the catechism of the Church of England* 1663
Nicholson, William (Abp. of Cashel) a1727 *See* Nicolson, W.
Nicholson, William *Poetical works* a1849 (1897)
Tales in verse and miscellaneous poems 1814
Nicholson, William *The British encyclopedia; or, dictionary of arts and sciences* 1809
A dictionary of chemistry 1795
Fourcroy's (A. F. de) General system of chemical knowledge tr. 1804
An introduction to natural philosophy 1782
A journal of natural philosophy, chemistry, and the arts 1797–1813
Nickerson, Elinor Barkley *Kayaks to the Arctic* 1967
Nicodemus, Gospel of 13.. (E.E.T.S. 1907)
Nicol, Abioseh *The truly married woman, and other stories* 1965
Nicol, Alexander *Nature without art: or nature's progress in poetry: being a collection of miscellany poems* 1739
Poems on several subjects, both comical and serious 1766
Nicol, James *Poems chiefly in the Scottish dialect* 1805
Nicol, James *Manual of mineralogy* 1849
Nicol, Thomas *Recent archæology and the Bible* 1899
Nicol, Walter *The Scotch forcing gardener* 1797
Nicolas, Sir Nicholas H. *The dispatches and letters of Vice-admiral Lord Viscount Nelson, with notes* 1844–46
History of the orders of knighthood of the British empire and of the order of the Guelphs of Hanover 1841–42
A history of the royal navy 1847
Memoirs of the life and times of Sir Christopher Hatton 1847
ed. *Privy purse expenses of Elizabeth of York* (1830)
ed. *The privy purse expences of King Henry the Eighth* (1827)
Testamenta vetusta: being illustrations from wills, of manners, customs, etc. from the reign of Henry II to the accession of Queen Elizabeth (1826)
Nicolay, John G. & Hay, John *Abraham Lincoln, a history* 1890
Nicoll, Henry J. *Great movements and those who achieved them* 1881
Nicoll, Robert *Poems* a1837 (1842)
Nicoll, Sir William R. *Literary anecdotes of the nineteenth century* 1895–96
Nicolls, Philip *A godly newe story of xii men that moyses sent to spye out the land of canaan* 1548
Nicolls, Thomas *The hystory writtone by Thucidides* tr. 1550
Nicolson, Harold George *Curzon: the last phase, 1919–25; a study in post-war diplomacy* 1934
Diaries and letters, 1930–1939 ed. N. Nicolson 1966
——— *1939–1945* ed. N. Nicolson 1967
——— *1945–1962* ed. N. Nicolson 1968
King George V: his life and reign 1952
Public faces 1932
Nicolson, John *Sprigs o' aithstin' hedder* 1899
Nicolson, Joseph & Burn, Richard *The history and antiquities of the counties of Westmorland and Cumberland* 1777
Nicolson, Abp. William *The English historical library* 1696–99
Leges Marchiarum, or Border-laws 1705
Letters on various subjects to and from W. Nicolson 1683–1727 (1809)
The Scottish historical library 1702
Nida, Eugene Albert *Morphology: the descriptive analysis of words* 2 vols. 1944
— (another ed.) 1946
— ('ed. 2') 1949
Toward a science of translating 1964
Niebuhr's (C.) Travels in Arabia tr. 1811 (in Pinkerton's Collect. voy. X)
Nielsen, Helen *After midnight* 1966 (UK 1967)
The brink of murder 1976
The severed key 1973
Niesewand, Peter *The underground connection* 1978
Nightingale, Benjamin *The ejected of 1662 in Cumberland and Westmorland* 1911
Nightingale, Florence *Notes on nursing* 1860
Niland, D'Arcy *The big smoke* 1959
Call me when the Cross turns over 1957 (UK 1958)
The shiralee 1955
Niles' weekly register 1814–37; continued as *Niles' national register* 1837–49
Nilson, Arvid *The timber trees of New South Wales* 1884
Nimmo, A. *Songs and ballads of Clydesdale* 1882
Nimmo, James *Narrative* 1654–1709 (S.H.S. 1889)
Nimmo, William *A general history of Stirlingshire* 1777
Nine specimens of English dialects v.d. (ed. W. Skeat, E.D.S. 1896)
Nineteenth century, The; a monthly review 1877–
Nipotismo. Leti's (G.) Il nipotismo di Roma; or the history of the pope's nephews tr. by W. A. (i.e. John Dodington) 1669 (1673)
Nisbet, Alexander *An essay on additional figures and marks of cadency* 1702
A system of heraldry 1722
— vol. II by R. Fleming (1742)
Nisbet, Hume *'Bail up!' a romance of bushrangers and blacks* 1890
A bush girl's romance 1894
Nisbet, John *British forest trees and their sylvicultural characteristics and treatment* 1893
Nisbet, Murdoch *The New Testament in Scots: being Purvey's revision of Wycliffe's version turned into Scots* c1520 (S.T.S. 1901–05)
Nisbett, Alex *The technique of the sound studio* 1962
Nissena 1653 *See* Carmeni, F.
Nitsch, F. A. *A general and introductory view of Professor Kant's Principles concerning man, the world and the Deity* 1796
Niven, Richard *The British angler's lexicon* 1892
Nixon, Anthony *The christian navy* 1602
Nixon, Randal C. J. *Euclid revised* 1886
Nkosi, Lewis *The rhythm of violence* 1964
No church (by F. W. Robinson) 1861
No droll but a rational account 1660
Noad, Henry M. *A course of eight lectures; on electricity, galvanism, magnetism, and electro-magnetism* 1839 (1844)
— ed. 3, greatly enlarged 1849
The student's text-book of electricity 1867
— new ed., enlarged by W. H. Preece (1879)
Noake, John *Worcestershire relics* 1877
Nobbes, Robert *The compleat troller, or, the art of trolling* 1682
Noble, Charles *Inexpediency of the expedient* 1659
Noble, Charles F. 1762 See *Voyage to East Indies*
Noble, Louis L. *After icebergs with a painter* 1861
Noble, Mark *A biographical history of England; being a continuation of J. Granger's work* 1806
A history of the College of Arms 1804
Memoirs of the illustrious House of Medici 1797
Memoirs of the Protectorate-House of Cromwell 1784
Two dissertations upon the mint and coins of the Episcopal-Palatines of Durham 1780
Noble, Montague Alfred *Those 'Ashes': the Australian tour of 1926* 1927
Noble, Samuel *Swedenborg's (E.) Treatise concerning Heaven and its wonders, and concerning Hell* tr. 1839 (revised 1851)
Noble boke of cookry 14.. (ed. R. Napier 1882)
Noble lyfe c1520 *See* Andrew, L.
Noble wanderers, The 1802
No-body and some-body 1606 (in Simpson, School of Shakspere, I. 1878)
Noel, Edward H. *Richter's (J. P. F.) Flower, fruit, and thorn pieces* tr. 1845
Noel, Thomas *The cottage muse* 1833
Rymes and roundelayes 1841
Nohara, Komakichi *The true face of Japan* 1936
Nolan, Frederick *The Oshawa project* 1974
Noli me tangere, is a thinge to be thought on (by E. Udall) 1642
Noller, Carl Robert *Chemistry of organic compounds* 1951
Textbook of organic chemistry 1951
Nomenclator navalis (Harl. MS. 2301) a1625 (= Manwayring (Sir H.) *Sea-man's dictionary*)
Nominale sive verbale c1340 (Philol. Soc. Trans. 1906)
Nonconformist 1841–90
—— continued as *Independent and Nonconformist* 1890–97
Noorthouck, John *A new history of London, including Westminster and Southwark* 1773
Nordau, Max Simon *Degeneration* [anon. tr.] 1895
Norden, John *A progresse of pietie* 1596 (Parker Soc. 1847)
Speculum Britanniæ; a discription of Middlesex 1593; *Essex* 1594 (Camden Soc. 1840); *Hartfordshire* 1598; *Northamptonshire* 1610 (1720); *Cornwall* 1610 (1728)
The surveyors dialogue 1607
Nordhoff, Charles *The Communistic societies of the United States* 1875
Norfolk and Norwich Archæological Society *Papers* v.d. (1847–)
Norfolk antiquarian miscellany, The 1873–87
Norfolk miscellany, The 1847
Norgate, Edward *Miniatura, or the art of limning* a1650 (ed. from the MS. by M. Hardie 1919)
Norman, Barry *The matter of mandrake* 1967
Norman, Frank *Bang to rights: an account of prison life* 1958
Norman, John Roxborough *A history of fishes* 1931
— (ed. 2, by P. H. Greenwood) 1963
Norman, Richard Oswald Chandler *Principles of organic synthesis* 1968
Norman, Robert *The safeguard of sailers* tr. 1584
Norman and Bertha, or exalted attachment; a novel. Written by a lady 1790
Normanby, Marquis of *See* Phipps, C. H.
Norris, Henry H. *An introduction to the study of electrical engineering* 1907
Norris, John (of Bemerton) *Christian blessedness: or (practical) discourses upon the beatitudes of our Lord and Saviour Jesus Christ. To which are added, Reflections upon a late essay (by J. Locke) concerning human understanding* 1690 (1692, 1694)
Practical discourses upon several divine subjects (A continuation of 'Christian blessedness') 1691–98 (1707, 1711)
A collection of miscellanies: consisting of poems, essays, discourses, and letters 1687 (1699)
An essay towards the theory of the ideal or intelligible world 1701–04
Hierocles upon the golden verses of the Pythagoreans tr. 1682
Poems and discourses 1684
A practical treatise concerning humility 1707
The theory and regulation of love. To which are added letters philosophical and moral between the author and Dr. H. More 1688
A treatise concerning Christian prudence 1710
Norris, John P. *Rudiments of theology* 1876
Norris, William E. *Adrian Vidal* 1885
Matrimony 1881
Misadventure 1890
Nature's comedian 1904
Thirlby Hall 1883
Norris, William Fisher & Oliver, Charles A. eds. *System of diseases of the eye* 4 vols. 1897–9
North, Barbara & North, Robert tr. *M. Duverger's Political parties* 1954
— (ed. 2) 1959
'North, Christopher' *See* Wilson, John
North, Dudley North, 4th Baron *Light in the way to Paradise; with other occasionals* a1677 (1682)
North, George *Philibert's (de Vienne) Philosopher of the court* tr. 1575
'North, Gil' (Geoffrey Horne) *Sergeant Cluff and the day of reckoning* 1967
Sergeant Cluff rings true 1972
North, John David *The measure of the universe* 1965

North, Lockhart *The parasites* 1928
North, Roger *Examen; or, an enquiry into the credit and veracity of a pretended complete history* a1734 (1740)
The life of Francis North, baron of Guilford a1734 (1742)
The life of the hon. Sir Dudley North, and of Dr. John North a1734 (1744)
The lives of F. North, Sir D. North, and J. North a1734 (1826, 1890)
Memoirs of musick 1728 (1846)
North, Sir Thomas *The morall philosophie of Doni* tr. 1570 (1888)
Guevara's (A. de) Diall of princes tr. 1557
— newly revised, with an amplification of a fourth book 1568
Plutarch's Lives of the noble Grecians and Romanes tr. 1579 (1595, 1603, 1612, 1657, 1676, 1895)
North American review, The 1815-
North British review, The 1844-71
North Carolina (Colony) *Colonial records* ed. W. L. Saunders 10 vols. 1886-90
North country wills, being abstracts of wills relating to the counties of York, Nottingham, Northumberland, Cumberland, and Westmorland 1383-1604 (Surtees Soc. 1908-12)
North Riding Record Society for the Publication of original documents relating to the North Riding of the county of York (1884-97)
Northall, G. F. *English folk-rhymes* 1892
Folk-phrases of four counties 1894 (E.D.S.)
A Warwickshire word-book 1896 (E.D.S.)
Northbrooke, John *A treatise wherein dicing, dauncing etc. are reproved* 1577 (1579; Shaks. Soc. 1843)
Northcote, James S. *A visit to the Roman catacombs* 1877
Northcote, Sir Stafford *Life, letters, and diaries of Sir S. Northcote, first earl of Iddesleigh* a1887 (1890)
Northern mothers blessing, The 1597 (Roxb. Cl. 1873)
Northern Territory News (Darwin, Australia) 1952-
Northumberland. A glossary of terms used in the coal trade of Northumberland and Durham (by G. C. Greenwell) 1849 (1851, 1888)
Northumberland glossary 1892-94 *See* Heslop, R. O.
Northumberland Household book (The regulations and establishment of the household of Henry Algernon Percy, the fifth Earl of Northumberland) 1512-25 (1770, 1827)
Norton, Caroline E. S. *The child of the islands* 1845 (1846)
The lady of La Garaye 1861 (1862)
Lost and saved 1863
Norton, Charles E. *The Divine Comedy of Dante Alighieri* tr. 1891-92
Historical studies of church-building in the Middle Ages 1880
Norton, Charles L. *Political Americanisms* 1890
Norton, Edward Felix *The fight for Everest: 1924* 1925
Norton, John Bruce *Topics for Indian statesmen* 1858
Norton, Olive Marion *Dead on prediction* 1970
Now lying dead 1967
A school of liars 1966
Norton, Oliver Willcox *Army letters 1861-1865: being extracts from private letters to relatives and friends from a soldier in the field during the late civil war* 1903
Norton, Robert *Stevin's (S.) Disme: the art of tenths* tr. 1608
See also Camden, W.
Norton, Thomas *The ordinall of alchimy* 1477 (in Ashmole, Theatrum chem. 1652)
Norton, Thomas *Calvin's Institution of Christian religion* tr. 1561 (1578, 1634)
Nowell's (A.) Catechisme, or first instruction and learning of Christian religion tr. 1570 (Parker Soc. 1853)
—— & Sackville, Thomas *The tragedie of Gorboduc. Sett forth as shewed before the Quenes Maiestie* 1561 (1565)
— another ed., entitled *The tragidie of Ferrex and Porrex* 1570 (Shaks. Soc. 1847)
Norway, Arthur H. *Parson Peter, a tale of the Dart* 1900
Norwich Mercury, Norfolk News and Journal (title varies) 1714-
Norwood, Richard *Trigonometrie, or, the doctrine of triangles* 1631
Not-browne mayd, The c1500 (in Arnolde's Chron. 1502; Percy's Reliques II. 1876)
See also *New notborune mayd*
Notes and queries 1850-
Nott, John *The cook's and confectioner's dictionary; or, The accomplished housewife's companion* 1723
Nott, John *The Gulls Hornbook, by T. Decker, with notes of illustration* 1812
Nottingham, Earl of *The royal entertainment of the Earle of Nottingham, sent ambassador from his Majestie to the Kind of Spaine* 1605
Nottingham, Records of the borough of 1155-1760 (1882-1914)
Nourse, Henry Stedman ed. *The early records of Lancaster, Massachusetts* See: Lancaster, Massachusetts
Nourse, Timothy *Campania Fœlix; or, a discourse of the benefits and improvements of husbandry* 1700 (1706)
Novak, Emil *Gynecological and obstetric pathology; with clinical and endocrine relations* 1940
Nowakowski, T. Z. & Clarke, A. J. tr. *V. L. Kretovich's Principles of plant biochemistry* 1966
Nowell, Alexander *A confutation as well of M. Dormans last boke as also of D. Sander* 1567
A sermon preached before Queen Elizabeth at the opening of the parliament Jan. 11 1563 (Appended to Catechism, Parker Soc. 1853)
See also Norton, Thomas 1570

Nowell-Smith, Simon Harcourt ed. *Edwardian England* 1964
Nowottny, Winifred May T. *The language poets use* 1962
Noyce, Cuthbert Wilfrid Francis *South Col: one man's adventure on the ascent of Everest, 1953* 1954
Noyes, Alfred *Poems* 1904
Collected poems 1910-20
William Morris 1908
Noyes, James *The temple measured* 1647
Nuce, Thomas *The ninth tragedie of L. A. Seneca called Octavia* tr. 1566 (1581)
Nuclear instruments and methods 1957- (1957-8 with title *Nuclear instruments*)
Nucleonics 1947-
Nugæ antiquæ See Harington, Sir J.
Nugæ ecclesiasticæ See 'Peerie, M.'
Nugæ poeticæ: select pieces of old English popular poetry v.d. (ed. J. O. Halliwell 1844)
Nugent, Robert Nugent, Earl *Memoir of Robert, Earl Nugent. With letters, poems, and appendices by Claud Nugent* a1788 (1898)
Nugent, Thomas *The grand tour; or, a journey through the Netherlands, Germany, Italy, and France* 1756
Isla's (J. F. de) History of the famous preacher Friar Gerund de Campazas tr. 1772
Montesquieu's Spirit of laws tr. 1752 (1758)
'Number 1500' *Life in Sing Sing* 1904
Numbers: a quarterly review 1954-
Numbers in poetical compositions, Essay on the power of 1749 *See* Mason, J.
Numismatic chronicle, The 1839-
Nunn, Thomas Percy *Education: its data and first principles* 1920
Nursing times and journal of midwifery 1905-
Nutbrowne mayd See *Not-browne mayd*
Nutt, Alfred *The voyage of Bran* 1895-97 *See* Meyer, K.
Nuttall, P. Austin *The standard pronouncing dictionary of the English language* 1863
Nuttall, Thomas *The genera of North American plants* 1818
A journal of travels into the Arkansa territory, during the year 1819 1821
Nye, Edgar Wilson *Baled Hay* 1884
Bill Nye and Boomerang; or, The tale of a meek-eyed mule 1881
Nye, Nathaniel *The art of gunnery* 1647 (1670)
Nyren, John *The young cricketer's tutor* 1833

O

O., N. *Boileau's Le Lutrin* tr. 1682
O.H.S. = Oxford Historical Society
Oakeley, Frederick *Historical notes on the tractarian movement* 1865
'Oakleigh, Thomas' (James Wilson) *The Oakleigh shooting code* 1836
Oakley, Kenneth Page *Frameworks for dating fossil man* 1964
Oastler, Richard *The Fleet papers: being letters to T. Thornhill* 1841-42
Oates, Frank *Matabele Land, and the Victoria Falls* 1881 (1889)
Oates, Joyce Carol *Bellefleur* 1981
Oates, Titus *An exact discovery of the mystery of iniquity as it is now in practice amongst the Jesuits* 1679
A true narrative of the horrid plot and conspiracy of the Popish party against the life of his sacred majesty 1679
Oath of pacification, The 1643
O'Brien, Donat H. *Narrative, containing an account of his shipwreck, captivity, and escape from France* 1814
O'Brien, Edna *August is a wicked month* 1965
Country girls 1971
The lonely girl 1962
'O'Brien, Flann' (Brian O'Nolan) *At Swim-Two-Birds* 1939
The hard life: an exegesis of squalor 1961
See also 'Na Gopaleen, Myles'
O'Brien, Henry *The round towers of Ireland* 1834
Villanueva's (J. L.) Phœnician Ireland tr. 1832 (1837)
O'Brien, S. E. & Stephens, A. G. *Material for a dictionary of Australian slang, 1900-1910* (typescript in Mitchell Library, Sydney)
Observations and proposals concerning the navy 1745
Observations both historical and moral upon the burning of London, Sept. 1666 1667 (in Harl. Misc. III. 1745)
Observations on (Hickeringill's) late famous sermon, intituled, Curse ye Meroz 1680
Observations on the present state of the parochial and vagrant poor (by John Scott) 1773
Observations upon the Methodists ? 1740 *See* Gibson, Bp. E.
Observator, The 1702-09
Observer, The (A collection of essays by R. Cumberland) 1786-91
Observer, The 1792-
Obstetrics and gynecology 1953-
O'Casey, Sean *Letters* ed. D. Krause 1975-
The plough and the stars 1926
The star turns red 1940
Two plays [Juno and the paycock and *The shadow of a gunman]* 1925

Windfalls: stories, poems and plays 1934
Occleve, Thomas *See* Hoccleve, T.
Oceanography and marine biology: an annual review 1963-
Ochtertyre House booke of accomps 1737-39 (S.H.S. 1907)
Ockley, Simon *The conquest of Syria, Persia and Ægypt by the Saracens* 1708; vol. II, entitled *The history of the Saracens* 1718 (1847)
O'Connell, Daniel *Correspondence* ed. M. R. O'Connell 1972-
'O'Connor, Frank' (Michael Francis O'Donovan) *Bones of contention, and other stories* 1936
O'Connor, Jimmy *The eleventh commandment* 1976
O'Connor, Thomas P. *Benjamin Disraeli, earl of Beaconsfield: a biography* (anon.) 1879
Lord Beaconsfield; a biography 1879
O'Conor, Charles *Columbanus ad Hibernos* 1810-16
ed. *Rerum Hibernicarum scriptores veteres* 1814-26
Octavian, The romance of the Emperor a1400 (Percy Soc. 1844)
Octovian Imperator a1400 (in Weber, Metrical romances III. 1810)
O'Curry, Eugene *On the manners and customs of the ancient Irish* 1873
Odell, George Clinton Densmore ed. *Annals of the New York stage* 15 vols. 1927-49
Odling, William *Lectures on animal chemistry* 1866
O'Donnell, Edwin P. *Great big doorstep* 1941
O'Donnell, Lilian *The face of the crime* 1968 (UK 1969)
O'Donnell, Peter *The impossible virgin* 1971
Sabre-tooth 1966
The silver mistress 1973
O'Donovan, Edmond *The Merv oasis* 1882
O'Donovan, John ed. *The annals of Ireland. Three fragments copied from ancient sources by D. MacFirbisigh* 1860
The genealogies, tribes, and customs of Hy Fiachrach tr. 1844
A grammar of the Irish language 1845
'Odysseus' (Charles Norton Edgcumbe Eliot) *Turkey in Europe* 1900
Of ye olde God and the newe 1523 *See* Coverdale, M.
O'Faolain, Julia *No country for young men* 1980
O'Faolain, Sean *A nest of simple folk* 1933
Official encyclopedia of bridge ed. R. L. Frey & A. F. Truscott 1964
Offshore (US) 1954-
Offshore engineer 1975-
Offshore platforms and pipelining (The Petroleum Publishing Co.) 1976
Ogden, Charles Kay tr. *H. Vaihinger's The philosophy of 'as if'* 1924
—— & Richards, Ivor Armstrong *The meaning of meaning: a study of the influence of language upon thought and of the science of symbolism* 1923
Ogden, Robert Morris tr. *K. Koffka's The growth of the mind: an introduction to child-psychology* 1924
Ogilby, John *Britannia, or an illustration of the kingdom of England and dominion of Wales: by a geographical and historical description of the roads thereof* 1675
The entertainment of Charles II in his passage through the city of London to his coronation 1662 (1685)
The fables of Æsop paraphras'd in verse 1651 (1665)
Homer his Iliads tr. 1660
Itinerarium Angliæ; or, a book of roads, wherein are contain'd the principal road-ways of England and Wales 1675
The works of P. Virgilius Maro tr. 1649 (1684)
Ogilvie, John *Poems on various subjects* 1762 (1769)
Ogilvie, John *The imperial dictionary, English, technological, and scientific* 1850; Supplement 1855
— New ed., greatly augmented, ed. C. Annandale 1881-83
Ogilvie, Joseph, and his first twenty-one classes 1896
Ogilvie-Grant, William R. *A hand-book to the game-birds* 1895-97
Ogilvy, Charles Stanley & Anderson, John T. *Excursions in number theory* 1966
Ogilvy, David *Confessions of an advertising man* 1963 (UK 1964)
Ogle, George *Gualtherus and Griselda* 1739
O'Grady, Standish *Pursuit of Diarmuid and Grainne. Part II.* (anon.) 1881
O'Halloran, Sylvester *A general history of Ireland to the close of the twelfth century* 1778
O'Hara (——) *The history of New South Wales* (anon.) 1817
O'Hara, John Henry *Appointment in Samarra* 1934 (UK 1935)
Pal Joey 1940 (UK 1952)
O'Hara, Kane *Midas: an English burletta* 1764
O'Hara, Kenneth *The bird-cage* 1968
The ghost of Thomas Penry 1977
Ohio archaeological and historical quarterly (title varies) 1887-
Ohwi, Jisaburō *Flora of Japan* 1965
Oil and gas journal 1910-
O'Keeffe, Adelaide *Zenobia, Queen of Palmyra* 1814
O'Keeffe, John *Fontainbleau, or our way in France* 1785
Wild oats: or, the strolling gentlemen 1791
Okey, Thomas *An introduction to the art of basket-making* 1912
Okoshi, Narinori *A sketch of the fisheries of Japan* 1883 (Fisheries exhibition literature)
Olcott, Henry S. *A. d'Assier's Posthumous humanity: a study of phantoms* tr. 1887
Theosophy; religion and occult science, with a glossary of eastern words 1885

Old cheque-book of the Chapel Royal See *Chapel Royal*
Old commodore, The (by E. G. G. Howard) 1837
Old English chronicle See *Anglo-Saxon chronicle*
Old English homilies 11..-12.. (E.E.T.S. 1867-68, 1873)
Old English martyrology a900 (E.E.T.S. 1900)
Old English miscellany, An 12..-13.. (E.E.T.S. 1872)
Old man's favour 1887 *See* ELLIOT, Anne
Oldcastle. The first part of the true and honorable historie of the life of Sir John Old-castle 1600 (in Shakespeare Apocrypha, 1908)
OLDCASTLE, Hugh *A briefe instruction and maner how to keepe bookes of accompts..newly augmented..by J. Mellis* 1588
OLDE, John *Walther's (R.) Antichrist* tr. 1556
—— & COVERDALE, Miles *The seconde tome of the paraphrase of Erasmus upon the Newe Testamente* tr. 1549
Oldest English texts v.d. (ed. H. Sweet, E.E.T.S. 1885)
OLDHAM, John *His remains in verse and prose* a1683 (1684)
Works, together with his remains a1683 (1686, 1703)
Satyrs upon the Jesuits 1679 (1681)
Oldham (Doctor) at Greystones, and his talk there (by C. S. Henry) 1860
OLDISWORTH, William *The odes, epodes and carmen seculare of Horace* tr. 1712-13
OLDMIXON, John *A pastoral poem on the victories at Schellenburgh and Blenheim* 1704
OLDYS, William *A short view of the life and writings of Dr. Thomas Moffat, or Moufet* 1746 (prefixed to Moufet's Health's improvement)
OLEY, Barnabas *View of the life of Mr. George Herbert* (anon.) 1652 (prefixed to Herbert's Priest to the temple)
OLIPHANT, Laurence *Altiora peto* 1883
Episodes in a life of adventure; or, moss from a rolling stone 1887
Fashionable philosophy and other sketches 1887
Haifa, or life in modern Palestine 1887
The land of Gilead, with excursions in the Lebanon 1880
Narrative of the Earl of Elgin's mission to China and Japan in 1857-59 1859
Piccadilly: a fragment of contemporary biography 1870
Sympneumata; or evolutionary forces now active in man 1885
OLIPHANT, Margaret O. W. *Agnes* 1866
Annals of a publishing house. William Blackwood and his sons, their magazine and friends 1897-98
Carita 1877
Chronicles of Carlingford. The rector and the doctor's family 1863; *Salem Chapel* 1863
He that will not when he may 1880
Innocent; a tale of modern life 1873
It was a lover and his lass 1883
Katie Stewart (anon.) 1853
The laird of Norlaw 1858
The last of the Mortimers 1862
The life of Edward Irving; illustrated by his journals and correspondence 1862
Madonna Mary 1867
Magdalen Hepburn: a story of the Scottish reformation 1854
The makers of Florence 1876
Passages in the life of Mrs. Margaret Maitland 1849
Phœbe, junior; a last chronicle of Carlingford 1876
A poor gentleman 1889
The railway man and his children 1891
Sheridan 1883
Within the precincts 1879
Autobiography and letters a1897 (ed. Mrs. H. Coghill 1899)
OLIPHANT, T. L. Kington- *See* KINGTON-OLIPHANT
OLIVER, Daniel *Lessons in elementary botany* 1864 (1872)
OLIVER, George *The history of Exeter* 1821 (1861)
Monasticon diœcesis Exoniensis 1846
OLIVER, Paul *Savannah syncopators: African retentions in the blues* 1970
Screening the blues 1968
OLIVER, Peter *The Scripture lexicon* (anon.) 1784 (1810)
OLIVER, Walter Reginald Brook *New Zealand birds* 1930
OLIVER, William *A collection of original local songs and other pieces* 1824
OLMSTED, Frederick L. *The cotton kingdom* 1861
ed. *The Englishman in Kansas* by T. H. Gladstone 1857
A journey in the Back Country 1860
A journey in the Seaboard slave states 1856 (1861)
A journey through Texas 1857
OLSSON, Yngve *On the syntax of the English verb* 1961
Omniana 1812 *See* SOUTHEY, R.
OMOND, Thomas S. *English metrists* 1903
Once a week; an illustrated miscellany of literature, art, science, and popular information 1859-74
O'NEILL, Charles *A dictionary of calico printing and dyeing* 1862
O'NEILL, Eugene Gladstone *Ah, wilderness! and Days without end: two plays* 1933 (UK 1934)
Anna Christie See below: *The hairy ape*
Beyond the horizon 1920
Desire under the elms 1925
Dynamo 1929
The Emperor Jones 1921 (UK 1925)
The great god Brown, The fountain, The moon of the Caribbees, and other plays 1926
The hairy ape, and other plays 1922 (UK 1923)
Hughie 1959
The iceman cometh 1946 (UK 1947)
Lazarus laughed 1927
Long day's journey into night 1956
Marco Millions 1927
A moon for the misbegotten 1952 (UK 1953)
The moon of the Caribbees, and six other plays of the sea 1919 (UK 1923)
More stately mansions ed. D. Gallup 1964 (UK 1965)
Mourning becomes Electra: a trilogy 1931 (UK 1932)
Strange interlude 1928
A touch of the poet 1957
ONIONS, Charles T. *An advanced English syntax* 1904
ONIONS, Oliver *Back o' the moon and other stories* 1906
The compleat bachelor 1900
Widdershins 1911
Ophthalmic review 1881-1916
OPIE, Iona M. B. & OPIE, Peter M. *Children's games in street and playground* 1969
The lore and language of schoolchildren 1959
See also *Oxford dictionary of nursery rhymes, The*
OPIE, John *Lectures on painting* a1807 (ed. Wornum 1848)
OPPENHEIM, Michael *A history of the administration of the royal navy and of merchant shipping in relation to the navy from 1509 to 1660* 1896
OPPERT, Ernest *A forbidden land: voyages to the Corea* 1880
Oppression. A poem. By an American. With notes, by a North Briton 1765
Optical Society of America *Journal* 1917-
Optick glasse of humors See WALKINGTON, T.
Optometry today: the vision care profession (American Optometric Association) 1971
Ora and Juliet; or, influence of first principles 1811
ORCZY, Emmuska, Baroness *Lady Molly of Scotland Yard* 1910
The Scarlet Pimpernel 1905
Order of the hospitalls of K. Henry the viijth and K. Edward the vith 1557
Order of the Lords and Commons assembled in Parliament for the regulating of printing 1643 (in Milton's Areopagitica, Arber 1868)
Order whych a prince in battayll muste observe ?1540
ORDERSON, J. W. *Creolana; or social and domestic scenes and incidents in Barbados in days of yore* 1842
Ordinance of the Lords and Commons for the speedy establishing of the presbyteriall government 1646
Ordinance of the Lords and Commons, with rules and directions, concerning suspention from the sacrament of the Lord's Supper in cases of ignorance and scandall, Oct. 20 1645
Ordinance of Parliament concerning the subsidie of tonnage and poundage 1642
Ordinances of royal household (1790) See *Household ordinances*
Ordonances and instructions for musters 1590
ORDWAY, Frederick Ira, GARDNER, J. P., & SHARPE, M. R. *Basic astronautics* 1962
Ordynarye of crysten men 1502 (W. de Worde; 1506)
O'REILLY, Eleanor G. *Sussex stories* 1880
O'REILLY, Harrington *Fifty years on the trail* 1889
'O'RELL, Max' (L. P. Blouët) *A Frenchman in America* 1891
John Bull & Co. 1894
John Bull and his island tr. 1883
OREM, William *A description of the Chanonry in Old Aberdeen* 1782 (1791)
Orfeo, Sir c1325 (in Ritson, Metr. rom. II; Zielke 1880)
ORFORD, Henry *Modern optical instruments and their construction* 1896
Organ voicing and tuning; a guide to amateurs 1879
Organization in daily life 1862 *See* HELPS, Sir A.
ORGILL, Douglas William *The Jasius pursuit* 1973
Oriental Ceramics Society *Transactions* 1923-
Orientator, The; a simple contrivance for ascertaining the orientation of churches 1844 (Cambr. Camden Soc.)
Origen and his opinions 1661 *See* RUST, Bp. G.
Original & sprynge of all sectes & orders by whome whan or were they beganne tr. 1537
Original canto of Spencer, An 1713 *See* CROXALL, S.
Origines parochiales Scotiae: the antiquities ecclesiastical and territorial of the parishes of Scotland ed. Cosmo Innes 1850-55 (Bannatyne Cl.)
ORIGO, Iris *Images and shadows: part of a life* 1970
Orkney, Records of the earldom of 1299-1614 (S.H.S. 1914)
ORLEANS, Charles, Duke of *Poems written in English during his captivity in England, after the battle of Agincourt* a1465 (Roxb. Cl. 1827)
ORME, Edward *An essay on transparent prints, and on transparencies in general* 1807
ORME, Robert *Historical fragments of the Mogul Empire* 1782 (1805)
A history of the military transactions of the British nation in Indostan 1763-78
ORMEROD, Eleanor A. *A manual of injurious insects* 1881
ORMEROD, George *The history of the county palatine and city of Cheshire* 1819 (1880)
ORMIN *The Ormulum* c1200 (1878)
Orologium sapientiae or the seven poyntes of trewe wisdom c1425 (in Anglia, X. 1888)
Orpheo, Sir See *Orfeo*
ORR, James *The Christian view of God and the world as centring in the incarnation* 1893
The problem of the Old Testament considered with reference to recent criticism 1906
The resurrection of Jesus 1908
ORR, John tr. *I. Iordan's An introduction to Romance linguistics* 1937
Orr's Circle of the sciences 1854-56 See *Circle*
ORRERY, John Boyle, 5th Earl of Cork and *Remarks on the life and writings of Dr. Jonathan Swift* 1751 (1752)
ORRERY, Roger Boyle, 1st Earl of *Parthenissa, a romance* (anon.) 1654-69 (1676)
A treatise of the art of war 1677
ORTON, James *The Andes and the Amazon* 1870 (1876)
ORTON, John Kingsley ('Joe') *What the butler saw* 1969
Ortus vocabulorum 1500 (1509, 1518)
'ORVIS', Kenneth (Kenneth Lemieux) *The damned and the destroyed* 1962
'ORWELL, George' (Eric Arthur Blair) *Animal farm* 1945
Burmese days 1934
A clergyman's daughter 1935
Collected essays, journalism and letters ed. 'S. Orwell' & I. Angus 4 vols. 1968
Coming up for air 1939
Critical essays 1946
– (new ed.) 1951
Down and out in Paris and London 1933
England your England, and other essays 1953
The English people 1947
Homage to Catalonia 1938
Inside the whale, and other essays 1940
Keep the aspidistra flying 1936
The lion and the unicorn: socialism and the English genius 1941
Nineteen eighty-four 1949
The road to Wigan Pier: on industrial England and its political future 1937
Shooting an elephant, and other essays 1950
OSBORN, Hon. Mrs. Sarah *Political and social letters of a lady of the eighteenth century* 1721-71 (1890)
OSBORN, Sherard *Quedah; or stray leaves from a journal in Malayan waters* 1857
OSBORNE, Dorothy *Letters to Sir William Temple* 1652-54 (1888)
OSBORNE, Francis *Works* a1659 (1673, 1722)
Advice to a son (anon.) 1656
Historical memoires on the reign of Queen Elizabeth and King James (anon.) 1658
A miscellany of sundry essayes, paradoxes, and problematicall discourses, letters and characters 1659
A perswasive to a mutuall compliance under the present government (anon.) 1652
Political reflections upon the government of the Turks; Nic. Machiavell; the King of Sweden's descent into Germany; the conspiracy of Piso and Vindex against Nero; the greatness and corruption of the court of Rome; the election of Leo XI; the defection from the Church of Rome; Martin Luther vindicated 1656
See also *Seasonable expostulation*
OSBORNE, John *Dental mechanics for students* 1940
OSBORNE, John James *The entertainer* 1957
Look back in anger 1957
West of Suez 1971
The world of Paul Slickey 1959
—— & CREIGHTON, Anthony *Epitaph for George Dillon* 1958
OSBORNE, Lord Sidney G. *Gleanings in the West of Ireland* 1850
Letters on the education of young children 1866
OSBORNE, William G. *The court and camp of Runjeet Sing* 1840
Oseney Abbey, The English register of c1460 (E.E.T.S. 1913)
OSGOOD, Charles Egerton *Method and theory in experimental psychology* 1953
O'SHAUGHNESSY, Arthur *Songs of a worker* 1881
OSLER, William *The principles and practice of medicine* 1892 (also later editions used)
—— & MCCRAE, Thomas *A system of medicine* 7 vols. 1907-10
Osmond, a tale (by Mary A. Kelty) 1822
Ossian See MACPHERSON, J.
OSSOLI, Sarah M. *See* FULLER, S. M.
Oswald, Father; a genuine Catholic story 1842
Ottawa Citizen, The (title varies) 1844-
Ottawa Journal 1885-
OTTAWAY, Andrew Kenneth Cosway *Education and society: an introduction to the sociology of education* 1953
OTTÉ, Elise C. See *Humboldt, F. H. A. von; Pauli, R.; Quatrefages de Bréau, J. L. A. de*
OTTO, John C. *New York Medical repository* 1803
Otuel a1330 (Abbotsford Cl. 1836; E.E.T.S. 1882)
OTWAY, Thomas *Works* a1685 (1768)
Alcibiades; a tragedy 1675
The atheist; or the second part of The souldier's fortune 1684
The cheats of Scapin; a farce (tr. from Molière) 1677
Don Carlos, Prince of Spain 1676
Friendship in fashion; a comedy 1678
The history and fall of Caius Marius; a tragedy 1680
The orphan; or the unhappy marriage; a tragedy 1680
The souldier's fortune; a comedy 1681
Titus and Berenice; a tragedy 1677
Venice preserv'd; or a plot discover'd; a tragedy 1682
Oughtred's (W.) Circles of proportion and the horizontall instrument tr. by Will. Forster 1632
The description and use of the double horizontall dyall 1636
– (with) *the description of the generall horologicall ring* 1652
The key of the mathematicks new forged and filed tr. 1647
– newly translated (by E. Halley) 1694
The solution of all sphærical triangles both right and oblique by the planisphære 1651
'OUIDA' (Mlle. L. de La Ramée) *Cecil Castlemaine's gage, and other novelettes* 1867
Frescoes, etc.: dramatic sketches 1883
'Held in bondage; or Granville de Vigne; a tale of the day 1863

OUIDA (*cont.*)
Idalia; a romance 1867
In a winter city; a sketch 1876
In Maremma; a story 1882
The Massarenes; a novel 1897
Moths; a novel 1880
Pascarèl; only a story 1873
Puck: his vicissitudes, related by himself 1870
A rainy June; a novelette 1885
Strathmore; a romance 1865
Two little wooden shoes; a sketch 1874
Under two flags; a story of the household and the desert 1867
Wanda 1883
Our towns: a close-up, 1939–42 (Women's Group on Public Welfare, Hygiene Committee) 1943
OUSELEY, Sir Frederick A. G. *A treatise on counterpoint, canon, and fugue based upon that of Cherubini* 1869
A treatise on harmony 1868 (1875)
A treatise on musical form and general composition 1875
OUSELEY, Sir William *Travels in various countries of the East* 1819–23
Out west 1902–23
Outing, an illustrated monthly magazine of recreation 1886–
Outlines of the history of religion 1877 *See* CARPENTER, J. E.
Outlook, The 1898–1928
Outlook (New York) 1893–1935 (title varies)
OUTRAM, George *Lyrics, legal and miscellaneous* 1874 (1887)
OUTRAM, William *Twenty sermons preached upon several occasions a*1679 (1682)
OUTRED, Marcelline *Cope's (M.) Godly and learned exposition vppon the Prouerbes of Solomon* tr. 1580
Outward bound 1920–4
Ovalle's (A. de) Historical relation of the kingdom of Chile tr. 1704 (in Churchill's Collect. Voy. III)
OVERBURY, Sir Thomas *Miscellaneous works in verse and prose a*1613 (1756, 1856)
Observations in his travailes upon the state of the XVII. Provinces as they stood A.D. *1609* 1626 (in Arber, Eng. Garner IV)
*A wife now the widdow of Sir T. Overbury. A poem of the choice of a wife. Whereunto are added many witty characters a*1613 (1614, 1638)
A true and historical relation of the poysoning of Sir T. Overbury 1651
OVERBURY, Sir Thomas (nephew of prec.) *A true and perfect account of the examination, confession, tryal, condemnation, and execution of Joan Perry, and her two Sons, John & Richard Perry, for the supposed murder of William Harrison . . sent in a letter (by Sir T. O.) to T(homas) S(hirley). Likewise Mr. Harrison's own account.* 1676 (Later edd. *c*1820 'The Campden wonder')
Overland monthly 1868–75; 1883–1935
OVERTON, John H. *William Law, nonjuror and mystic; a sketch of his life, character, and opinions* 1881
See also WORDSWORTH, Bp. C.
OVERTON, Richard *Defyance of the Act of Pardon* 1649
Man's mortalitie 1643
Ovid's Epistles tr. by several hands 1716
OVINGTON, John *A voyage to Suratt in 1689* 1696
*Owain Miles c*1330 (ed. D. Laing 1837)
OWEN, David Edward *English philanthropy, 1660–1960* 1964 (UK 1965)
OWEN, Francis *Diary, 1837–38* ed. G. E. Cory 1926
OWEN, George *The description of Pembrokeshire* 1603 (1892–97)
OWEN, Hugh & BLAKEWAY, John B. *A history of Shrewsbury* 1825
OWEN, Jean A. *See* JORDAN, Denham
OWEN, John *Words a*1683 (1850–55)
*The chamber of imagery in the church of Rome laid open a*1683 (1870)
A discourse concerning evangelical love 1672
The doctrine of the saint's perseverance explained 1654
The duty of pastors and people distinguished 1644
Exercitations on the Epistle to the Hebrews 1668–84 (1790)
How we may bring our hearts to receive reproofs 1674
The nature of apostasie from the profession of the gospel 1676
The nature, power, deceit, and prevalency of the remainders of indwelling-sin in believers (anon.) 1668
Of schisme: the true nature of it discovered and considered 1657
Of temptation: the nature and power of it 1658
Of the mortification of sinne in believers 1656 (1668)
A peace offering or plea for indulgence 1667
Πνευματολογια: or, a discourse concerning the Holy Spirit 1674 (1693)
Salus electorum, sanguis Jesu; or, the death of death in the death of Christ 1648
The stedfastness of promises and the sinfulness of staggering 1650
*Two discourses concerning the Holy Spirit and his work a*1683 (1693)
OWEN, John *Travels into different parts of Europe in 1791–92* 1796
OWEN, John *Calvin's Commentaries on the Book of the Prophet Jeremiah and the Lamentations* tr. 1850; *the twelve Minor Prophets* 1846; *the Catholic Epistles* 1855; *the Epistle of Paul to the Romans* 1849; *to the Galatians* 1845
England's sins 1854
Memoir of the rev. T. Jones 1851
OWEN, John *Evenings with the skeptics* 1881
OWEN, Lewis *The running register: recording a true relation of the state of the English colledges in all forraine parts* 1626
Speculum Jesuiticum, or the Jesuites looking-glasse 1629
The unmasking of all popish monks, friers and Jesuits 1628
OWEN, Richard *A history of British fossil mammals and birds* 1846
Instances of the power of God as manifested in His animal creation; a lecture 1864
Lectures on the comparative anatomy of invertebrate and vertebrate animals 1843–46
— ed. 2, *Lectures on comparative anatomy and physiology of the invertebrate animals* 1855
Odontography; or, a treatise on the comparative anatomy of the teeth 1840–45
On the anatomy of vertebrates 1866–68
On the classification and geographical distribution of the mammalia 1859
On the nature of limbs; a discourse 1849
Palæontology, or a systematic summary of extinct animals and their geological relations 1860
Structure of the skeleton and teeth 1854 (in Orr's Circle of the sciences I)
Zoology 1849 (in Manual of scientific enquiry 1859)
Life, by his grandson, the rev. R. Owen (1894)
OWEN, Sidney J. ed. *A selection from the despatches . . and other papers of the Marquess Wellesley during his government of India* v.d. (1877).
See also WELLINGTON, 1st Duke of
OWEN, Wilfred Edward Salter *Collected letters* ed. H. Owen & J. Bell 1967
Collected poems ed. C. Day Lewis 1963
Owen: a waif 1862 *See* ROBINSON, F. W.
OWENSON, Sydney *See* MORGAN, Sydney
*Owl and the nightingale, The a*1250 (Percy Soc. 1843; Stratmann 1868; MS. Jesus Coll. Oxford 29, MS. Cotton Calig. A. IX)
Owles almanacke, The 1618 *See* DEKKER, T.
Ox 1967–73
OXENDEN, Ashton *Our church and her services* 1866
OXENFORD, John *Conversations of Goethe with Eckermann and Soret* tr. 1850
The illustrated book of French songs from the sixteenth to the nineteenth century tr. and ed. by J. O. 1855
OXENHAM, Henry N. *Short studies in ecclesiastical history and biography* 1884
'OXENHAM, John' (W. A. Dunkerley) *The loosing of the lion's whelps, and other stories* 1917
A weaver of webs 1904
Oxford. Enactments in Parliament specially concerning the Universities of Oxford and Cambridge v.d. (1869)
OXFORD, Bishop of 1712 *See* TALBOT, Bp. W.
Oxford book of birds, The by B. Campbell 1964
Oxford book of food plants, The by S. G. Harrison, G. B. Masefield, & M. Wallis 1969
Oxford book of invertebrates, The by D. Nicholls & J. A. L. Cooke 1971
Oxford book of wild flowers, The by S. Ary & M. Gregory 1960
Oxford chronicle, The 1837–
Oxford classical dictionary, The ed. M. Cary et al. 1949
— (ed. 2, by N. G. L. Hammond & H. H. Scullard) 1970
Oxford companion to art, The ed. H. Osborne 1970
Oxford companion to French literature, The by P. Harvey & J. E. Heseltine 1959
Oxford companion to music, The by P. A. Scholes 1938 (also later editions used)
Oxford companion to ships and the sea, The ed. P. Kemp 1976
Oxford companion to sports and games, The ed. J. Arlott 1975
Oxford companion to the decorative arts, The ed. H. Osborne 1975
Oxford companion to the theatre, The ed. P. M. Hartnoll 1951
— (ed. 2) 1957
Oxford computer explained, The: data processing at Oxford University Press 1967
Oxford dictionary of nursery rhymes, The ed. I. & P. Opie 1951
Oxford dictionary of the Christian Church, The ed. F. L. Cross 1957
— (ed. 2, by F. L. Cross & E. A. Livingstone) 1974
Oxford diocesan magazine 1902–
Oxford essays, contributed by members of the University 1855–58
Oxford Historical Society *Publications* (1884–)
Oxford history of South Africa, The ed. M. Wilson & L. Thompson 2 vols. 1969–71
Oxford journal (Jackson's) 1753–
Oxford junior encyclopaedia ed. L. E. Salt et al. 13 vols. 1948–56
Oxford magazine, The 1883–
Oxford Mail 1928–
Oxford Methodists, The; being some account of a society of young gentlemen in that city, so denominated 1733
— ed. 2, enlarged 1738
Oxford night-caps; being a collection of receipts for making various beverages used in the University (by Richard Cook) 1827
Oxford poetry 1910–13 1913
Oxford sausage, The: or, select poetical pieces, written by the most celebrated wits of the University of Oxford ed. T. Warton 1764
Oxford Times, The 1862–
Oxford University *Report of Commission of Inquiry* 2 vols. 1966
Oxford University. Ashmolean Museum *Report of the Visitors* 1889–
Oxford University calendar 1810–
Oxford University gazette 1870–
Oxoniensia (Oxford Architectural and Historical Society) 1936–
OZELL, John *Aubert de Vertot's (R.) History of the revolutions that happened in the government of the Roman Republic* tr. 1720 (1740)
Boileau's Lutrin tr. 1708
Bourdeilles' (P. de; Seigneur de Brantôme) Spanish Rhodomontades tr. 1741
Cervantes Saavedra's (M. de) History of Don Quixote Motteux's tr. revised 1719
The life of Michael de Cervantes Saavedra tr. 1738
Mission's (H.) Memoirs and observations in his travels over England tr. 1719
Montesquieu's Persian letters tr. 1722
Pitton de Tournefort's (J.) Voyage into the Levant tr. 1741
Rabelais' (F.) Works Urquhart's tr. revised 1737

P

P., J. See *La Framboisière, N. A. de*; PHILLIPS, John
P., T. *The English and French cook.* By T. P., J. P., R. C., N. B., and several other approved cooks of London and Westminster 1674
P., W. *Curio's (C. A.) Pasquine in a traunce* tr. 1566
P., W. *A booke of secrets* tr. 1596
Pa. See *Pennsylvania*
PMLA See: Modern Language Association of America
PAASCH, H. *'From keel to truck.' Marine dictionary in English, French, and German* 1894
PACKARD, Alpheus S. *A guide to the study of insects* 1868
A text-book of entomology 1898
PACKARD, Vance Oakley *The hidden persuaders* 1957
PACKER, John & VAUGHAN, James *A modern approach to organic chemistry* 1958
PACKER, Joy *Apes and ivory* 1953
'PACKER, Vin' (Marijane Meaker) *Don't rely on Gemini* 1969 (UK 1970)
Pacquet of advices See NEEDHAM, M.
PAE, David *Eustace the outcast* 1884
Pagan prince, The; or a comical history of the heroick atchievements of the Palatine of Eboracum 1690
PAGE, David *Advanced text-book of geology* 1856 (1876)
Handbook of geological terms and geology 1859 (1865)
PAGE, Emma *A fortnight by the sea* 1973
PAGE, Ewan Stafford & WILSON, Leslie Blackett *An introduction to computational combinatorics* 1979
'PAGE, H. A.' (Alex. H. Japp) *Thomas De Quincey; his life and writings. With unpublished correspondence* 1877
PAGE, John *The siege of Rouen* 14 . . (in Archaeologia, XXI, XXII; Hist. coll. citizen of London, Camden Soc. 1876)
PAGE, John L. W. *An exploration of Dartmoor and its antiquities, with some account of its borders* 1889
PAGE, Samuel *The broken heart a*1630 (1637)
PAGE, Thomas N. *In Ole Virginia; or Marse Chan, and other stories* 1887 (1893)
PAGÉ, Victor Wilfred *Modern aircraft* 1927 (UK 1928)
PAGET, Lord Clarence E. *Autobiography and journals a*1895 (1896)
PAGET, Francis E. *The curate of Cumberworth* 1859
Lucretia 1868
Milford Malvoisin 1842
The owlet of Owlstone Edge 1856
The pageant 1843
St. Antholin's 1841 (1853)
Tales of the village 1840–41
The warden of Berkingholt 1843
PAGET, Sir James *Memoirs and letters a*1899 (ed. Stephen Paget 1901)
PAGET, John *Paradoxes and puzzles* 1874
PAGET, Richard Arthur Surtees *Human speech* 1930
PAGITT, Ephraim *Christianographie, or, the description of the multitude and sundry sorts of Christians not subject to the Pope* 1635 (1636)
Heresiography; or, a description of the heretickes and sectaries of these latter times 1645 (1646, 1662)
PAIGE, Elbridge G. ('Dow, Jr.') *Short patent sermons c*1850
PAINE, John *The paper-maker's and stationer's assistant* 1784
PAINE, Ralph Delahaye *Comrades of the rolling ocean* 1923
PAINE, Thomas *Common sense* 1776 (1791)
A letter addressed to the Abbé Raynal on the affairs of North-America 1782 (1791)
The rights of man 1791–92
PAINTER, William *The palace of pleasure* 1566–67 (1575, 1890)
Painter, The third advice to a, on our last summers success with French and Dutch 1666
Palafox's History of the conquest of China by the Tartars tr. 1671
Palatinate, A briefe information of the affaires of the 1624
'PALATINUS, Musaeus' *See* BRATHWAIT, R.
PALEY, Fred. A. *The church restorers* 1844
The tragedies of Æschylus, with English notes 1855
PALEY, William *Works a*1805 (1825)
The clergyman's companion 1805
Horæ Paulinæ, or the truth of the scripture history of St. Paul evinced 1790

Natural theology; or, evidences of the existence and attributes of the Deity 1802
The principles of moral and political philosophy 1785
A view of the evidences of Christianity 1794
PALFREY, John G. *History of New England* 1858-64
PALFREYMAN, Thomas *See* BALDWIN, W.
PALGRAVE, Sir Francis *The history of Normandy and of England* 1851-64
The rise and progress of the English commonwealth 1832
Truths and fictions of the Middle Ages. The merchant and the friar 1837 (1844)
PALGRAVE, Francis M. T. *A list of words and phrases in every-day use by the natives of Hetton-le-Hole in the county of Durham* 1896 (E.D.S.)
PALGRAVE, Francis T. ed. *The golden treasury of the best songs and lyrical poems in the English language* 1861
Lyrical poems 1871
Journals and memories of his life a1897 (Gwen. F. Palgrave 1899)
PALGRAVE, William G. *Narrative of a year's journey through central and eastern Arabia* 1865
Palladius on husbondrie tr. c1440 (E.E.T.S. 1873-79; ed. Liddell 1896)
Pallas's (P. S.) Travels tr. 1802-03 (1812)
PALLISER, Mrs. Fanny B. *History of lace* 1865
See also LABARTE, Jules
Pall Mall gazette, The 1885-1923
Pall Mall magazine, The 1893-
PALMER, Abram Smythe *Folk-etymology* 1882
Leaves from a word-hunter's note-book 1876
PALMER, Charles F. R. *The life of P. T. Howard* 1867
PALMER, Charles Skeele tr. *W. Nernst's Theoretical chemistry, from the standpoint of Avogadro's Rule and thermodynamics* 1895
PALMER, Charlotte *Letters on several subjects from a preceptress to her pupils who have left school* 1797
PALMER, Edward Vance *Golconda* 1948
Men are human 1930
The passage 1930
Separate lives 1931
See also 'DALY, Rann'
PALMER, Elihu *Principles of nature* 1801 (1826)
PALMER, Elisabeth tr. *A. Martinet's Elements of general linguistics* 1964
PALMER, Eve *The plains of Camdeboo* 1966
—— & PITMAN, Norah *Trees of South Africa* 1961
Trees of southern Africa 3 vols. 1972-3
PALMER, George *Sectaries unmasked and confuted* 1647
PALMER, Harold Edward *A grammar of spoken English on a strictly phonetic basis* 1924
PALMER, James F. & Mrs. Mary *A dialogue in the Devonshire dialect, by a lady* (i.e. Mrs. M. Palmer); *with a glossary by J. F. Palmer* 1837
PALMER, Joel *Journal of travels over the Rocky Mountains* 1847 (1850)
PALMER, John *Like master like man, a novel* a1809 (1811)
PALMER, Lionel Stanley *Wireless principles and practice* 1928
PALMER, Sir Roundell, afterwards 1st Earl of Selborne *The book of praise, from the best English hymn writers.* Selected and arranged by R. Palmer 1863 (1865)
See also SELBORNE, 1ST EARL OF
PALMER, Samuel *Moral essays on some of the most curious.. English, Scotch, and foreign proverbs* 1710
PALMER, Shirley *A pentaglot dictionary of the terms employed in anatomy, physiology, pathology, etc.* 1845
PALMER, William *Letters to N. Wiseman, D.D., on the errors of Romanism in respect to the worship of saints* 1841-42
A narrative of events connected with the publication of the Tracts for the Times 1843 (1883)
Origines liturgicæ, or antiquities of the English ritual, and a dissertation on primitive liturgies 1832
Palmerin of England See MUNDAY, A.
Palpable evidence of spirits 1668 *See* GLANVILL, J.
PALSGRAVE, Jehan *Fullonius' (G.) Comedye of Acolastus* tr. 1540
Lesclarcissement de la langue françoyse 1530 (1852)
PALTOCK, Robert *The life and adventures of Peter Wilkins* 1751 (1884)
Pamphleteer, The 1813-28
Pancirolus' (G.) History of many memorable things lost tr. 1715
Pandurang Hàri 1826 *See* HOCKLEY, W. B.
PANKE, John *The fal of Babel* 1608
PANKHURST, Emmeline *My own story* 1914
Pantalogia, The; comprehending a complete series of essays, treatises and systems alphabetically arranged; with a general dictionary of arts, sciences, and words 1813 (1819)
PANTON, Jane Ellen *Nooks and corners* 1889
PAP, Arthur *Elements of analytic philosophy* 1949
Paper and printing trades' journal, The 1877-
Paper to W. Penn 1700 *See* HUMFREY, J.
Papers that passed between the Commissioners appointed by His Majesty for the alteration of the Common Prayer, The 1661
PAPPE, Karl Wilhelm Ludwig *Silva Capensis; or, A description of South African forest-trees and arborescent shrubs* 1854
Synopsis of the edible fishes at the Cape of Good Hope 1853
PAPPE, L. *Floræ Capensis medicæ prodromus; or, an enumeration of South African plants used as remedies by the colonists of the Cape of Good Hope* 1857
Pappe with an hatchet (ascribed to J. Lyly or to T. Nashe) 1589 (1844; in Lyly's Works III. 1902)
Paracelsus' Archidoxes tr. 1661 *See* H., J.
Paradyse of dainty devises a1566 *See* EDWARDS, R.
Parallel. tr. 1626 *See* FEATLEY, D.
PARDOE, Julia S. H. *The beauties of the Bosphorus* 1839
PARDON, George F. *See* 'CRAWLEY, CAPTAIN R.'
PARDON, William *See* DYCHE, Thomas
Pardonere and tapstere, A prologue of the mery adventure of the c1400 (in Tale of Beryn, E.E.T.S. 1909)
Parey's Works tr. 1634 *See* JOHNSON, T.
PARIS, John A. *A guide to the Mount's Bay, and the Land's End* (anon.) 1816
Philosophy in sport made science in earnest 1827
A treatise on diet 1826 (1828)
PARIS, Matthew *Chronica majora* a1259 (Rolls series 1872-83)
Paris as it was and as it is. In a series of letters, as written by an English traveller 1801-02 1803
Paris chit-chat 1815-16
Paris relation of the battel of Landen, The 1693
PARISH, William D. *A dictionary of the Sussex dialect and collection of provincialisms in use in the county of Sussex* 1875
—— & SHAW, William F. *A dictionary of the Kentish dialect and provincialisms in use in the county of Kent* 1887 (E.D.S.)
Parish councils and village life 1908 (Fabian tract No. 137)
Parismus 1598-99 *See* FORDE, E.
PARK, Roswell *Pantology; or a systematic survey of the human knowledge* 1847
PARK, William Robb R. ed. *Plastics film technology* 1969
PARKE, Robert *Mendoza's (J. Gonzalez de) Historie of the great and mightie kingdome of China* tr. 1588 (Hakluyt Soc. 1853-54)
PARKER, Mrs. Angelina *A glossary of words used in Oxfordshire* 1876; *Supplement* 1881 (E.D.S.)
PARKER, Dorothy *After such pleasures* 1933 (UK 1934)
PARKER, George & STALKER, John *A treatise on japaning and varnishing* 1688
PARKER, George *Humorous sketches* 1782
Life's painter of variegated characters in public and private life 1789
A view of society and manners in high and low life 1781
PARKER, Henry *A compendiouse treatise dyalogue of Dives and Pauper, that is to say, the riche and the pore.* a1470 (1496)
PARKER, Henry *The case of ship-mony briefly discoursed* (anon.) 1640
Jus populi (anon.) 1644
PARKER, Henry M. *Bole Ponjis* 1851
PARKER, John Henry *The archæology of Rome* 1874-76
A glossary of terms used in Grecian, Roman, Italian, and Gothic architecture (anon.) 1836 (1840, 1845, 1850)
An introduction to the study of Gothic architecture (anon.) 1849 (1874)
See also TURNER, T. H.
PARKER, Joseph *Apostolic life as revealed in the Acts of the Apostles* 1884-86
The Paraclete 1874
Tyne Chylde 1883
PARKER, Martin *Robin Conscience, or conscionable Robin: his progress thorow court, city and countrey* 1635 (1683; Harl. Misc.)
PARKER, Abp. Matthew *Correspondence* 1535-75 (Parker Soc. 1853)
A defence of priestes mariages agaynst Thomas Martin ?1567
The whole psalter translated into English metre c1557 (?1567)
The life off the 70 archbishopp off Canterbury (i.e. M. Parker) tr. 1574
PARKER, Philip *Electronics* 1950
PARKER, R. 1607 See *Scholasticall*
PARKER, Robert Brown *God save the child* 1974 (UK 1975)
The Godwulf manuscript 1974
PARKER, Robert Lueling tr. *P. Niggli's Rocks and mineral deposits* 1954
PARKER, Bp. Samuel *A demonstration of the divine authority of the law of nature, and of the Christian religion* 1681
A free and impartial censure of the Platonick philosophie 1666 (1667)
A reproof to the rehearsal transprosed (anon.) 1673
PARKER, Samuel *Bibliotheca Biblica* 1720-35
Six philosophical essays upon several subjects 1700
Tully's five books de Finibus tr. 1702
Tully's two essays of old age, and of friendship; with his stoical paradoxes, and Scipio's dream tr. 1704 (1727)
PARKER, Theodore *Experience as a minister* 1859
Historic Americans 1871
Sermons of theism, atheism, and the popular theology 1853
PARKER, Thomas J. & HASWELL, William A. *A text-book of zoology* 1897
PARKER, Tony *The twisting lane* 1969
The unknown citizen 1963
—— & ALLERTON, Robert *The courage of his convictions* 1962
PARKER, W. N. *See* WEISMANN, A.
PARKER, William Hosken *Health and disease in farm animals* 1970
PARKER, William K. *A monograph on the structure and development of the shoulder-girdle and sternum in the vertebrata* 1868 (Ray Soc.)
On mammalian descent 1885
PARKER, William Newton tr. *R. E. E. Wiedersheim's Elements of the comparative anatomy of vertebrates* 1886
Parker Society *Publications* (1841-55)
PARKES, Mrs. 1844 *See* WEBSTER, Thomas
PARKES, Edmund A. *A manual of practical hygiene* 1864 (1869)
PARKES, Malcolm B. *English cursive book hands 1250-1500* 1969
PARKES, Roger *The guardians* 1973
PARKES, Samuel *A chemical catechism* 1807 (1822)
PARKES, William *The curtaine-drawer of the world* 1612 (Grosart 1876)
PARKHURST, John *A methodical Hebrew grammar* 1762 (prefixed to Hebrew and English lexicon; 1778)
PARKINS (doctor) *Culpepper's (N.) English physician enlarged* 1809
PARKINSON, John *Paradisi in sole paradisus terrestris, or, a garden of flowers* 1629 (repr. 1904)
Theatrum botanicum: the theater of plants, or an herball of a large extent 1640
PARKINSON, Stephen *A treatise on optics* 1859 (1866)
PARKINSON, Thomas *Yorkshire legends and traditions, as told by her chroniclers, her poets, and journalists* 1888-89
PARKMAN, Ebenezer *The diary of Ebenezer Parkman, of Westborough, Mass.* ed. H. M. Forbes 1899
PARKMAN, Francis *The California and Oregon trail* 1849
Count Frontenac and new France under Louis XIV 1877
The discovery of the Great West 1869
France and England in North America. Pt. I. *Huguenots in Florida* 1865; Pt. II. *Samuel de Champlain* 1868
History of the conspiracy of Pontiac 1851 (1870)
The Jesuits in North America in the seventeenth century 1867
Montcalm and Wolfe 1884
The old régime in Canada 1874
Pioneers of France in the New World 1865
PARKYNS, Sir Thomas *Προγυμνασματα; the inn-play or Cornish-hugg wrestler* 1713 (1727)
Parlament of byrdes, The ?1550 (in Harl. Misc.; Hazlitt, Early pop. poetry III)
PARLETT, David Sidney *A short dictionary of languages* 1967
Parliament of ladies, The 1647 *See* NEVILLE, H.
Parliament of three ages a1400 (Gollancz, Roxb. Cl. 1897)
Parliamentary papers *See* United Kingdom. Parliamentary papers
Parliamentary speech 1659 (= Earl of Shaftesbury's *Seasonable speech*)
Parliament's censure of the Earles of Dover, Devonshire (etc.) 1642
Parliament's scrich-owle, The; her singing before death 1648
Parliament's vindication in answer to Prince Rupert's declaration. By S. W. Esquire 1642
Parlyament of devylles, The 1509
PARMENTER, C. O. 1898 See *History of Pelham*
PARNELL, Edward A. *Elements of chemical analysis* 1842 (1845)
PARNELL, Richard *The grasses of Scotland* 1842
PARNELL, Thomas *Poetical works* a1717 (1833)
PARR, Bartholomew *The London medical dictionary* 1809
PARR, Mrs. Louisa *Adam and Eve* 1880
PARR, Richard *The life of James Usher, late Archbishop of Armagh* 1686
PARR, Samuel *Works* a1825 (1828)
A discourse on education 1786
Remarks on the statement of Dr. Charles Combe (anon.) 1795
PARRISH, Albert *Mechanical engineer's reference book* 1973
PARROT, Henry *Epigrams* (anon.) 1608
Laquei ridiculosi: or springes for woodcocks 1613
PARRY, Dennis *Going up—going down* 1953
PARRY, William *A new and large discourse of the travels of Sir Anthonie Sherley* 1601
PARRY, Capt. William E. *Journal of a voyage for the discovery of a north-west passage* 1821
—*Journal of a second voyage* 1824
PARSONS, Abraham *Travels in Asia and Africa* 1808
PARSONS, Mrs. Eliza *Mysterious visit* 1802
The mysterious warning 1796
PARSONS, John Herbert *Diseases of the eye* 1907
—(ed. 12, by W. S. Duke-Elder) 1954
PARSONS, Nell Wilson *Upon a sagebrush harp* 1969
PARSONS, Philip *Newmarket; or an essay on the turf* 1771
PARSONS, Robert *The first booke of the Christian exercise appertayning to resolution* (anon.) 1582
—another ed., entitled *A Christian directorie* 1585
—*The seconde parte of the booke of Christian exercise* 1590
A brief discours contayning certayn reasons why Catholiques refuse to goe to church (anon.) 1580
A conference about the next succession to the crowne of Ingland 1594
A defence of the censure gyuen vpon two bookes of W. Charke and M. Hanmer against E. Campian (anon.) 1582
A treatise of three conversions of England from paganisme to Christian religion. By N. D. (i.e. R. Parsons) 1603-04
PARSONS, Talcott *The social system* 1952
The structure of social action 1937
—— & SHILS, Edward Albert eds. *Toward a general theory of action* 1951
PARSONS, Theophilus *The law of contracts* 1853
Partenay, The romans of c1475 (E.E.T.S. 1866, 1899)
PARTINGTON, Charles F. *The British cyclopædia of the arts, sciences, geography, natural history, and biography* 1835-38
PARTINGTON, James Riddick *General and inorganic chemistry for university students* 1946
A text-book of inorganic chemistry for university students 1921
Partisan review 1934-
Partonope of Blois, The Old English version of c1440 (Roxb. Cl. 1862; E.E.T.S. 1912)

Partridge, Eric Honeywood *A charm of words: essays and papers on language* 1960
A dictionary of abbreviations 1942
A dictionary of catch phrases British and American, from the Sixteenth Century to the present day 1977
A dictionary of clichés 1940
A dictionary of forces' slang 1939–45 1948
A dictionary of R.A.F. slang 1945
A dictionary of slang and unconventional English 1937 (also later eds. and supplements used)
A dictionary of the underworld, British and American 1950 [dated 1949]
English gone wrong 1957
Here, there and everywhere 1950
Slang to-day and yesterday 1933
— (ed. 3) 1951 [dated 1950]
Usage and abusage: a guide to good English 1942 (UK 1947)
Words, words, words! 1933
The world of words 1938
See also Brophy, John; 'Vigilans'
Partridge, John *The most famouse and worthie historie of the worthy Lady Pandauola* 1566 (Roxb. Cl. 1873)
The treasurie of commodious conceites and hidden secrets 1573
The widdowes treasure plentifully furnished with sundry secrets (anon.) 1595 (1631)
Partridge, Seth *The description and use of an instrument called the double scale of proportion* 1671
Paryski, Edwin tr. *T. Korzybski et al., Antibiotics* 2 vols. 1967
Pasachoff, Jay M. & Kutner, Marc Leslie *University astronomy* 1978
Pascoe, Charles E. *London of to-day: an illustrated handbook for the season* 1885
Pascoe, Francis P. *Notes on natural selection and the origin of species* 1884
Pask, Arthur T. *The eyes of the Thames* 1889
Pasquil and Katherine 1600 *See* Marston, J.
Pasquils apologie 1590, *countercuffe* 1589, *return* 1589 *See* Nashe, T.
Pasquils nightcap 1612 See *Cornu-copiæ*
Pasquil's palinodia, and his progresse to the tauerne 1619 (Grosart 1877)
'Pasquin, Anthony' (John Williams) *The children of Thespis* 1786–88 (1792)
Pasquine in a traunce 1566 *See* P., W.
Passion of our Lord, The c1275 (in Old Eng. misc., E.E.T.S. 1872)
Passionate Morrice, The; a sequel to Tell-Trothes new-yeares gift by A. 1593 (New Shaks. Soc. 1876)
Passionate pilgrime, The (by Shakespeare et al.) 1599
Passmore, John Arthur *A hundred years of philosophy* 1957
Passmore, Reginald & Robson, James Scott eds. *A companion to medical studies* 3 vols. 1968–74
Pasternak, Boris *See* Hayward, Harry M. & Harari, Manya
Paston letters, The 1422–1509 (ed. James Gairdner 1872–75)
— Supplement (1901)
Patel, H. M., et al. *Say not the struggle nought availeth: essays in honour of A. D. Gorwala's seventy-fifth birthday* 1975
Patent Office *See* United Kingdom
Patent specifications v.d. (Patent Office, London)
See also *Abridgments*
Pater, Walter H. *Works* a1894 (1901)
Gaston de Latour, an unfinished romance 1888 (1896)
Imaginary portraits 1887
Marius the Epicurean: his sensations and ideas 1885
Studies in the history of the Renaissance 1873
Patericke, Simon *Gentillet's (I.) Discourse upon the meanes of wel governing against N. Macchiavell* tr. 1602
Paternoster. The pater noster, the aue, crede and .x. commaundementes in Englishe, with other godly lessyons 1539
Paterson, Arthur H. *The man from Snowy River, and other verses* 1896
Paterson, James *A complete commentary on Milton's Paradise lost* 1744
Paterson, James *The ballads and songs of Ayrshire* 1847
History of the regality of Musselburgh, with numerous extracts from the town records 1857
Paterson, James *The Intoxicating Liquor Licensing Act 1872* 1872
— *The Licensing Acts, being the Licensing Acts, 1828–1902* ed. 14, by W. W. Mackenzie 1902 (1908)
Paterson, Nathaniel *The manse garden* 1844
'Paterson, Peter' (James Glass Bertram) *Glimpses of real life as seen in the theatrical world and in Bohemia* 1864
Paterson, Samuel *Another traveller* 1767
Paterson, William *Proposals and reasons for constituting a council of trade in Scotland* (by some ascribed to John Law) 1701
'Pathfinder' (H. C. Dear) *Breaking and training dogs* 1875
Pathological Society of London *Transactions* 1853–1907
Pathology annual 1966–
Pathomachia 1630 *See* Constable, F.
Pathway to health 1587 *See* Levins, P.
Patience 13.. See *Early English alliterative poems*
Patient Grissil See Dekker, T.
Patmore, Coventry *The angel in the house* (anon.) 1854–56 (1879)
Paton, Alan *Cry, the beloved country: a story of comfort in desolation* 1948
Hope for South Africa 1958
Paton, James *Castlebraes* 1898
Paton, Mrs. Maggie W. *Letters and sketches from the New Hebrides* 1865–92 (1894)
Paton, Robert *The Scottish church and its surroundings in early times* 1884
Patrick, Saint 1819 See *Saint Patrick*
Patrick's (St.) purgatory a 1300 (in Horstmann, Altengl. Leg. 1875; South-Eng. leg., E.E.T.S. 1887)
'Patrick, James' *A Glasgow gang observed* 1973
Patrick, Robert W. Cochran- *See* Cochran-Patrick, Robert W.
Patrick, Bp. Simon *Works; including his autobiography* a1707 (1858)
An answer to a book spread abroad by the Romish priests, intituled The touchstone of the reformed gospel 1692
Autobiography, now first printed from the original MS. a1707 (1839)
A commentary upon Genesis 1695; *Exodus* 1697; *Leviticus* 1698; *Numbers* 1699; *Deuteronomy* 1700; *Joshua, Judges, and Ruth* 1702; *Two books of Samuel* 1703; *Two books of Kings* 1705; *Two books of Chronicles, Ezra, Nehemiah, and Esther* 1706; *Job, Psalms, Proverbs, Ecclesiastes, and the Song of Solomon, paraphrased* a1707 (1710)
The parable of the pilgrim 1663 (1665, 1668, 1673)
Patrick, William *A popular description of the indigenous plants of Lanarkshire, with an introduction to botany, and a glossary of botanical terms* 1831
Patten, Brian Arthur *The irrelevant song* 1971
Little Johnny's confession 1967
Patten, William *The expedicion into Scotlande of prince Edward, Duke of Soomerset* 1548 (in Arber, Eng. Garner III)
Patterson, Arthur *Man and nature on the Broads* 1895
Patterson, Edward McWilliam *Topology* 1956
— (ed. 2) 1959
—— & Rutherford, D. E. *Elementary abstract algebra* 1965
Patterson, Raymond Murray *Finlay's river* 1968
Patterson, Robert *First steps to zoology* 1849
Patterson, Robert H. *Essays in history and art* 1862
Patterson, William H. *A glossary of words in use in the counties of Antrim and Down* 1880 (E.D.S.)
Pattison, Mark *Essays* a1884 (1889)
Isaac Casaubon 1875
Memoirs a1884 (1885)
Milton 1879
Sermons a1884 (1885)
Suggestions on academical organisation 1868
Pattison, William *Poetical works* a1727 (1728)
Patton, Robert *The principles of Asiatic monarchies* 1801
Paul, Alexander *The history of reform* 1884
Paul, Charles Kegan *Memories* 1899
Paul, Elliot Harold *A narrow street* 1942
Springtime in Paris 1951
Paul, Sir George *The life of the most revered prelate John Whitgift* 1612
Paul, Margaret A. *Maiden sisters* 1858
Still waters 1857
Paul, Maurice Eden & Paul, Cedar tr. *J. Stalin's Leninism* 2 vols. 1928–33
Paul, Robert B. *The antiquities of Greece* 1832 (1835)
The autobiography of a Cornish rector 1872
Paulding, James Kirke *John Bull in America; or, The new Munchausen* 1825
Letters from the South 1817
Westward ho! 2 vols. 1832
See also 'Bull-Us, Hector'
Pauli, Christian W. H. *Analecta Hebraica* 1839
Pauli's (R.) Pictures of old England tr. by E. C. Otté 1861
Pauli, Wolfgang ed. *Niels Bohr and the development of physics: essays dedicated to Niels Bohr* 1955
Pauling, Linus Carl *The nature of the chemical bond and the structure of molecules and crystals* 1939
Pawson, John *A brief vindication of free grace* 1652
Paxton, Sir Joseph *Pocket botanical dictionary* 1840
'Paxton, Philip' (S. A. Hammett) *A stray Yankee in Texas* 1853
Payn, James *The canon's ward* 1884
A confidential agent 1880
Halves 1876
High spirits; being certain stories written in them 1879
Kit: a memory 1883
Lost Sir Massingberd 1864
The luck of the Darrells 1885
A modern Dick Whittington 1892
The mystery of Mirbridge 1888
Some literary recollections 1884
The talk of the town 1885
Payne, Charles Rockwell tr. *O. Pfister's The psychoanalytic method* 1917
Payne, John *Royall exchange* 1597
Payne, John *Alaeddin and the enchanted lamp* 1889
Payne, John O. ed. *Records of the English Catholics of 1715, compiled wholly from original documents* 1889
Payne, Joseph F. *English medicine in the Anglo-Saxon times* 1904
See also Jones, C. H.
Payne, Robert *A briefe description of Ireland* 1589 (1841)
Payne and sorowe of euyll maryage ?1509 (Percy Soc. 1840)
Payne-Gallwey, Sir R. *See* Gallwey
Paynell, Thomas (*Revision of*) *Barclay's Historye of Iugurth by Salust* 1557
Erasmus' (D.) De contemptu mundi tr. 1533
Felicius' (C., Durantinus) Conspiracie of Lucius Catiline tr. 1541
The moste excellent booke entituled: The treasurie of Amadis of Fraunce tr. 1567
Schola Salernitana. Regimen sanitatis Salerni. This boke techyng al people to gouerne them in helthe tr. 1528 (1541)
Peabody, Andrew P. *King's Chapel sermons* 1891
Peace News 1936–
Peach, Benjamin Neave & Horne, John *Chapters on the geology of Scotland* 1930
Peacham, Henry, the elder *The garden of eloquence, conteyning the figures of grammer and rhetorick* 1577
Peacham, Henry, the younger *The art of drawing with the pen, and limming in water colours* 1606; another ed., entitled *Graphice or the most auncient and excellent art of drawing and limming* 1612; another ed., entitled *The gentlemans exercise* 1612 (1634, 1661)
The compleat gentleman 1622 (1634, 1661)
Minerva Britanna, or a garden of heroical deuises 1612
The valley of varietie 1638
The worth of a peny 1641 (mispr. 1647; Arber, Eng. Garner VI)
Peacock, Edward ed. *English Church furniture, ornaments, and decorations, at the period of the reformation. As exhibited in a list of the goods destroyed in certain Lincolnshire churches* A.D. *1566* 1866
A glossary of words used in the wapentakes of Manley and Corringham, Lincolnshire (= N.W. Linc. gloss.) 1877; ed. 2, 1889 (E.D.S.)
John Markenfield 1874
Mabel Heron 1872
Narcissa Brendon 1891
Ralf Skirlaugh the Lincolnshire squire 1870
Peacock, George *A collection of examples of the application of the differential and integral calculus* 1820
Observations on the statutes of the University of Cambridge 1841
Peacock, Mabel G. W. *Taales fra Linkisheere* 1889
Peacock, Thomas Love *Crotchet castle* 1831
Gryll Grange 1861
Headlong Hall 1816
Maid Marian 1822
Melincourt 1817
The misfortunes of Elphin 1829
Nightmare Abbey 1818
Peacocke, Arthur Robert & Drysdale, Robert Brown *The molecular basis of heredity* 1965
Peake, Harold John Edward & Fleure, Herbert John *Hunters and artists* 1927
Peake, James *Rudiments of naval architecture* 1849
Peake, Mervyn Laurence *Gormenghast* 1950
Titus alone 1959
Titus Groan 1946
Peaks, passes, and glaciers; a series of excursions by members of the Alpine Club ed. John Ball 1859
— Series II, ed. E. S. Kennedy 1862
Pear, Tom Hatherley *English social differences* 1955
Voice and personality 1931
Pearce, Brian tr. *S. Amin's Accumulation on a world scale: a critique of the theory of underdevelopment* 2 vols. 1974
tr. *E. Preobrazhensky's The new economics* 1965
Pearce, William *Hartford-Bridge, or the skirts of the camp* 1793
Pearce, Bp. Zachary *A review of the text of Milton's Paradise lost* 1732
Milton's Paradise lost, with notes 1751
Sermons a1774 (1778)
Peard, Frances M. *Contradictions* 1883
Mother Molly 1880
Peard, William *Practical water-farming* 1868
Pearl 13.. See *Early English alliterative poems*
Pearse, E. 1682 See *Second plea*
Pearson, Charles H. *Early and middle ages of England* 1861
History of England during the early and middle ages 1867
Memorials by himself, his wife, and his friends a1894 (ed. W. Stebbing 1900)
Pearson, George *A translation of the table of chemical nomenclature proposed by De Guyton, formerly of Morveau, Lavoisier, Berthelot etc.* 1794 (1799)
Pearson, Bp. John *Exposition of the Creed* 1659 (1816, 1839)
Pearson, T. Gilbert ed. *Birds of America* 3 vols. 1917
Pearson, Thomas *Infidelity; its aspects, causes, and agencies* 1853
Pearson, William Harrison (Bill) *Coal flat* 1963
Pearson's magazine 1896–1939
Pearson's Weekly 1890–
Pease, Alfred E. *The badger: a monograph* 1898
Pease, Howard *Borderland studies* 1893
The mark o' the deil, and other Northumbrian tales 1894
Peaslee, Edmund R. *Ovarian tumors: their pathology, diagnosis and treatment* 1872
Peblis to the play See *Peebles*
Pebody, Charles *English journalism, and the man who made it* 1882
Peck, Francis *Desiderata curiosa* 1732–35
Peck, George Wilbur *Peck's bad boy and his pa* 1883
Peck's boss book 1884
Peck's sunshine 1882
Peck, John Mason A gazetteer of Illinois 1834
— (ed. 2) 1837
A guide for emigrants 1831
Pecke, Thomas *Parnassi puerperium* 1659
Pecock, Reginald *The Donet* c1444 (E.E.T.S. 1921)
The repressor of over much blaming of the clergy c1449 (Rolls series 1860)
A treatise proving scripture to be the rule of faith c1450 (1688, 1909)
Pecuniæ obediunt omnia. Money does master all things 1696

Peddie, Alexander *The manufacturer, weaver and warper's assistant* 1814

Peden, Alexander *The Lord's trumpet sounding an alarm against Scotland, by warning of a bloody sword; being the substance of a preface and two prophetical sermons, preached at Glenluce* 1682 (1739)

Pediatrics: the journal of the American Academy of Pediatrics 1948–

Peebles. Charters and documents relating to the burgh of Peebles, with extracts from the records of the burgh 1165–1710 (Scott. Burgh Rec. Soc. 1872)

Extracts from the records of the burgh of Peebles, with appendix 1367–1714 (Scott. Burgh Rec. Soc. 1910)

Peblis to the play a1550 (in Pinkerton, Sel. Scott. Ball. II. 1783; James I's Works 1786; Maitland folio MS., S.T.S. 1919)

The (thre) prestis of Peblis c1500 (1603; Pinkerton 1792; S.T.S. 1920)

Peeke, Richard *Three to one* 1626 (in Arber, Eng. Garner I)

Peel, Dorothy Constance E. *Life's enchanted cup: an autobiography, 1872–1933* 1933

Peel, Frank *The risings of the Luddites, Chartists, and Plug-drawers* 1880

Spen valley 1893

Peel City Guardian and Chronicle (Peel, Isle of Man) 1882–

Peele, George *Works* a1600 (1829–39, 1888)

The araygnement of Paris, a pastorall (anon.) 1584

The battell of Alcazar (anon.) 1594

The famous chronicle of King Edward the first 1593

The historie of the two valiant knights, Syr Clyomon and Clamydes (anon.) 1599

The honour of the garter 1593

The love of King David and fair Bethsabe 1599 (in Manly, Specim. pre-Shaks. drama II, 1898)

Peele (George), Merrie conceited iests of 1607 (c1620)

Peele, Robert ed. *Mining engineers' handbook* 1918

— (ed. 2) 1927

Peele, Talmadge Lee *The neuroanatomical basis for clinical neurology* 1954

'Peerie, Moses' (R. H. Story) *Nugæ ecclesiasticæ: fragments, dramatic and lyrical, from the unpublished papers of the late M. Peerie* ed. Jabez Gilead 1884

Pegge, Samuel, the elder *An alphabet of Kenticisms* 1735–36 (E.D.S. 1876)

Anonymiana; or ten centuries of observations on various authors and subjects a1796 (1809)

Derbicisms a1796 (E.D.S. 1896)

The forme of cury, a roll of ancient English cookery, compiled about A.D. *1390, illustrated with notes* 1780

Pegge, Samuel, the younger *Anecdotes of the English language* a1800 (1803)

Curialia miscellanea; anecdotes of old times a1800 (1818)

A supplement to the provincial glossary of Francis Grose a1800 (1814)

Pegler, Martin M. *The dictionary of interior design* 1966 (UK 1967)

Pei, Mario Andrew *Glossary of linguistic terminology* 1966

The story of language 1949 (UK 1952)

Words in sheep's clothing 1969 (UK 1970)

—— & Gaynor, Frank *A dictionary of linguistics* 1954

Peirce, Charles Santiago Sanders *Collected papers* ed. C. Hartshorne, P. Weiss & A. W. Burks 8 vols. 1931–58

Peirce, Robert & Thomas 16.. *See* Pierce, R. & T.

Peirson, Abraham *Some helps for the Indians* 1658

Pelegromius' (S.) Description of S'hertogenbosh in 1540.. together with the principall passages concerning the last siege 1629 tr. 1629

Pell, Daniel *Πελαγος: nec inter vivos, nec inter mortuos: or, an improvement of the sea* 1659

Pelletreau, James *An abridgment of ecclesiastical history from the creation to end of 17th century* 1768

Pemberton, Henry *A course of chemistry* 1771

View of Sir Isaac Newton's philosophy 1728

Pemberton, Max *The iron pirate* 1893

The phantom army 1898

Queen of the jesters 1897

Pemberton, Robert B. *Report on the Eastern frontier of British India* 1835

Pemble, William *Vindiciae fidei, or a treatise of iustification by faith* a1623 (1625, 1629)

Pembroke, 10th Earl of *See* Herbert, Henry

Pembroke, Mary Herbert, Countess of *The Psalmes of David, translated into verse. Begun by Sir P. Sidney* (i–xliii), *and finished by the Countess of Pembroke* c1586 (1823)

The tragedie of Antonie tr. 1595

Pendarves, Mary, afterwards Delany, Mary, q.v.

Pender, Harold ed. *American handbook for electrical engineers* 1914

Penderel-Brodhurst, James & Layton, Edwin J. *A glossary of English furniture of the historic periods* 1925

Pendlebury, John Devitt Stringfellow *The archaeology of Crete: an introduction* 1939

Penfield, Wilder Graves *Cytology and cellular pathology of the nervous system* 1932

Penguin book of Australian ballads, The ed. R. B. Ward 1964

Penguin music magazine 1946–9

Penguin new writing, The ed. J. F. Lehmann 1940–50

Penhallow, Samuel *The history of the wars of New-England with the Eastern Indians 1703–26* 1726 (1859)

Penitential confession (*A treatise of the confession of sinne;* page-heading *Of penitential confession*) 1638 (1657)

Penkethman, John *Artachthos; or a new booke declaring the assise or weight of bread* 1638

A handful of honesty, or, Cato in English verse tr. 1623

Penn, Granville *Macarius' Institutes of Christian perfection* tr. 1816 (1828)

Penn, William *Works* a1718 (1726, 1782)

An account of William Penn's travails in Holland and Germany, anno 1677, by way of journal 1694 (1835)

An address to Protestants upon the present conjuncture 1679

A brief account of the rise and progress of the people called Quakers 1694

The Christian-Quaker and his divine testimony vindicated by scripture, reason and authorities 1674

Correspondence between William Penn and James Logan.. and others 1700–50 (Memoirs of Hist. Soc. of Pa. 1870–72)

England's present interest discovered with honour to the Prince 1675

The great case of liberty of conscience once more briefly debated and defended by the authority of reason, scripture, and antiquity 1670

Journal of his life a1718 (prefixed to 1726 ed. of Works)

No cross, no crown 1669

Some account of the Province of Pennsilvania 1681

Some fruits of solitude 1693

The spirit of truth vindicated 1672

Pennant, Thomas *Arctic zoology* 1784–87 (1792)

British zoology 1768–70; ed. 4, 1776–77 (1812)

The journey from Chester to London 1782

Literary life, by himself 1793

Of London 1790 (1813)

Synopsis of quadrupeds 1771

— another ed., entitled *History of quadrupeds* 1781

A tour in Scotland 1769 1771; *Supplement* 1772

A tour in Scotland and voyage to the Hebrides 1772 1774–76

A tour in Wales 1773 1778–81 (1883)

The view of Hindoostan 1798–1800

Pennecuik, Alexander *Works* a1722 (1815)

A collection of Scots poems on several occasions a1722 (1756, 1787)

A geographical, historical description of the Shire of Tweeddale, with a miscelany of Scotish poems 1715

An historical account of the blue-blanket 1722 (1756)

Streams from Helicon; or, poems on various subjects 1720

Pennell, Elizabeth R. *The stream of pleasure* 1891

Pennell, H. Cholmondeley *The angler-naturalist; a popular history of British fresh water fish* 1863 (1885)

Fishing (Badminton library) 1885 (1893)

The modern practical angler 1870

Pennell-Elmhirst, Edward *The cream of Leicestershire* 1883

Penney, John *A topographical and historical account of Linlithgowshire* 1832

Pennington, Montagu *See* Carter, Elizabeth

Pennington, Lady Sarah *Letters on different subjects* 1766–67

Pennsylvania, Colonial records of (*Minutes of the Provincial Council of Pennsylvania*) 16..–17.. (1851–53)

Pennsylvania, Memoirs of the Historical Society of (1826–76)

Pennsylvania archives 16..–17.. (ed. S. Hazard 1874–)

Pennsylvania magazine of history and biography 1877–

Penny, Mrs. A. J. *The romance of a dull life* (anon.) 1861

Penny cyclopædia of the Society for the diffusion of useful knowledge 1833–43; Suppl. 1845–46; 2nd Suppl. 1858

Penny magazine 1832–45

Penrose, Llewellin *Journal* 1815

Penrose, Thomas *Poems* a1779 (1781)

Penrose annual (title varies) 1895–

'Pentecost, Hugh' (Judson Pentecost Philips) *Girl watcher's funeral* 1969 (UK 1970)

See also under real name

Penton, Stephen *The guardian's instruction* (anon.) 1688 (1897)

People, The 1881–1971

People's Journal (Dundee) 1858–

Pepusch's (J. C.) Short treatise on harmony (tr. by J. Hamilton) 1730

Pepys, Samuel *Memoirs. Comprising his diary from 1659 to 1669, and a selection from his private correspondence* 16.. (1825, 1871, 1875–79, 1893–99)

Perceval of Galles, The romance of Sir a1400 (Thornton romances, Camden Soc. 1844)

Percival, Richard *Bibliotheca Hispanica. Containing a grammar, with a dictionarie in Spanish, English, and Latine* 1591

— enlarged.. by J. Minsheu 1599

Percival, Robert *An account of the Island of Ceylon* 1803

Percival, Thomas *Essays medical and experimental* 1767–78

Percy, Bp. Thomas *A key to the New Testament* 1769

Mallet's (P. H.) Northern antiquities tr. 1770 (1847)

ed. *Reliques of ancient English poetry* 1765 (1839, 1876–77)

Bishop Percy's folio manuscript. Ballads and romances c1650 (ed. J. W. Hales and F. J. Furnivall 1867–68)

Percy, William *Sonnets to the fairest Coelia* 1594 (Grosart 1877; in Arber, Eng. Garner VI)

Peregrine Pultney 1844 *See* Kaye, Sir J. W.

Pereira, Jonathan *The elements of materia medica* 1839–40

Lectures on polarized light 1843

— ed. 2, greatly enlarged, ed. B. Powell (1854)

Treatise on food and diet 1843

Pereira, Michael *Pigeon's blood* 1970

Perelman, Sidney Joseph *Baby, it's cold inside* 1970

Crazy like a fox 1944 (UK 1945)

Westward ha! or, Around the world in eighty clichés 1947

Perfect booke for kepinge of sparhawkes or goshawkes c1575 (Now first printed from the original MS. with introduction and glossary by J. E. Harting 1886)

Perkin, Harold *Key profession: the history of the Association of University Teachers* 1969

Perkin, William H. & Kipping, F. Stanley *Organic chemistry* 1894–95 (1902)

Perkins, Charles C. *Historical handbook of Italian sculpture* 1883

Italian sculptors 1868

Perkins' (John) Profitable booke, treating of the lawes of England tr. 1642

Perkins, William *The whole treatise of the cases of conscience* a1602 (1619)

Perkowski, Robert L. & Stral, Lee Philip *The joy of CB* 1976

Pernetti's (J.) Philosophical letters upon physiognomies tr. 1751

Perquisite-monger, The: or, the rise and fall of ingratitude 1712

Perrinchief, Richard *The royal martyr, or the life and death of King Charles I* (anon.) 1676

Perronet, Edward *The mitre. A sacred poem* 1757

Perrot, Richard *Jacobs vowe, or the true historie of tithes* 1627

Perry, Arthur L. *Elements of political economy* 1866

Perry, Frank Ernest & Ryder, Frank Raymond *Dictionary of banking* (ed. 11) 1965 *See* Thomson, William

Perry, George G. *The history of the Church of England* 1861–64

Perry, Captain John *An account of the stopping of Daggenham Breach* 1721

The state of Russia under the present Czar 1716

Perry, John Howard *Chemical engineers' handbook* 1934

— (ed. 3) 1950

Perry, Ralph Barton *The thought and character of William James as revealed in unpublished correspondence, together with his published writings 1842–1910* 2 vols. 1935 (UK 1936)

Perry, Richard *The world of the tiger* 1964

Perry, Ritchie John A. *One good death deserves another* 1976

Perry, William *The royal standard English dictionary* 1775

The synonymous, etymological and pronouncing English dictionary 1805

Perry, William S. *Historical collections relating to the American Colonial Church* 1870–73

Persecutio undecima; the churches eleventh persecution 1648

Person, David *Varieties: or, a surveigh of rare and excellent matters* 1635

Personal and literary memorials 1829 *See* Best, H. D.

Personal computer world 1978–

Persuasive to mutual compliance 1652 *See* Osborne, F.

Pervin, William Joseph *Foundations of general topology* 1964

Perwich, William *Despatches* 1669–77 (Camden Soc. 1903)

Peter, John *A relation or diary of the siege of Vienna* 1684

Peter Parley's annual 1840–92

Peter Wilkins 1751 *See* Paltock, R.

Peterkin, Alexander *Notes on Orkney and Zetland* 1822

Rentals of the ancient Earldom and Bishoprick of Orkney 1820

Peters, Charles *A critical dissertation on the Book of Job* 1751

'Peters, Ellis' (Edith Mary Pargeter) *Black is the colour of my true-love's heart* 1967

The piper on the mountain 1966

Peters, Samuel *A general history of Connecticut* 1781

Peterson, Harold Leslie ed. *Encyclopædia of firearms* 1964

Peterson, Roger Tory & Fisher, James *Wild America* 1956

Peterson magazine (U.S.) N. S. IV. 1894

Petherick, John & Mrs. B. H. *Travels in central Africa, and explorations of the western Nile tributaries* 1869

Petition of Eastern association 1648 *See* Ward, Nathaniel

Petition of the ministers of the gospel lately commissioned for the review and alteration of the liturgy, The 1661

Petiver, James *Aquatilium animalium Amboinæ,* etc. *icones et nomina* 1713

Gazophylacii naturæ et artis, in 10 decades 1702–11

Herbarii Britannici Raii catalogus (A catalogue of Mr. Ray's English herball) 1713–15

Musei Petiveriani centuria prima (-decima) rariora naturae continens 1695–1703

Petiveriana seu naturæ collectanea 1716–17

Petowe, Henry *Elizabetha quasi viuens, Eliza's funerall* 1603 (in Harl. Misc.)

Petrie, Alexander *A compendious history of the Catholick Church* 1662

Petrie, George *The ecclesiastical architecture of Ireland* 1845

Petrie, Henry & Sharpe, J. ed. *Monumenta historica Britannica, or materials for the history of Britain* 1848

Petrie, Rhona *Despatch of a dove* 1969

Murder by precedent 1964

Petroleum refiner 1942–61

Petroleum review 1968–

Petronilla. The parfite lyfe to put in remembraunce of a virgyn moost gracious called Petronylla c1493

Petticoat 1966–76

Pettie, George *Guazzo's (S.) Ciuile conuersation* tr. 1581

— with addition of Book IV tr. by B. Young 1586

A petite pallace of Pettie his pleasure 1576 (1908)

Pettigrew, James Bell *Animal locomotion* 1873

Pettijohn, Francis John *Sedimentary rocks* 1949

— (ed. 2) 1957

Pettman, Charles *Africanderisms: a glossary of South African colloquial words and phrases of place and other names* 1913

Pettus, Sir John *Fleta minor: the laws of art and nature in assaying metals* 1683 (1686)

PETTUS, Sir John (*cont.*)
Fodinæ regales: or the history, laws, and places of the chief mines and mineral works in England, etc. 1670
PETTY, Sir William *The advice of W. P. to Mr S. Hartlib, for the advancement of some particular parts of learning* 1648
The discourse made before the Royal Society concerning the use of duplicate proportion 1674
The political anatomy of Ireland 1672 (1691, 1769)
Political arithmetick, or a discourse concerning the extent and value of lands, people, etc. a1687 (1690; in Arber, Eng. Garner VI)
A treatise of naval philosophy a1687 (in Hale, Account of several new inventions 1691)
A treatise upon taxes and contributions (anon.) 1662 (1769)
Will 1685 (in Ld. E. Fitzmaurice, Life 1895)
PEYTON, Sir Edward *The divine catastrophe of the kingly family of the House of Stuarts* 1652 (1731)
PEYTON, Thomas *The glasse of time, in the two first ages diuinely handled* 1620
Pfeiffer's (I. L.) Journey to Iceland tr. by Charlotte F. Cooper 1852
PHAER, Thomas *Goeurot's (J.) Regiment of life* tr. 1544
— *The regiment of life, wherevnto is added a treatyse of the pestilence, with the booke of children, newly corrected and enlarged* 1545-46 (1553, 1560)
The seuen first bookes of the Eneidos of Virgill tr. 1558
— *the nyne fyrst bookes, (and part) of the tenthe booke* a1560 (1562)
— *the whole xii bookes (books X-XII tr. by T. Twyne)* (1573)
Pharmaceutical journal and transactions 1842-
Pharmacopœia of the United States of America 1820-
PHELPS, Austin *The still hour* 1860
PHELPS, Elizabeth S. *Hedged in* 1870
Sealed orders 1880
The silent partner 1871
The story of Avis 1877
Trotty's wedding tour 1874
PHELPS, John D. *Collectanea Glocestrensia* 1842
Phemie Millar 1854 *See* 'TYTLER, Sarah'
Phenix, The: or, a revival of scarce and valuable pieces 1707-08 (1721)
Phenix nest, The 1593 (= Phœnix nest) *See* S., R.
Philadelphia Bulletin (title varies) 1847-
Philadelphia Inquirer (title varies) 1829-
Philadelphian society. The state of the Philadelphian society or the grounds of their proceedings considered 1697
Philanthrope, The; after the manner of a periodical paper 1797
Philatelic record, The 1879-
Philatelist, The: an illustrated monthly magazine for stamp collectors 1866-74
'PHILIDOR, A. D.' *See* DANICAN, F. A.
PHILIP, John *Researches in South Africa* 2 vols. 1828
Philip Quarll 1727 *See* DORRINGTON, E.
PHILIPOT, Thomas *Villare Cantianum: or Kent surveyed and illustrated* 1659
PHILIPPS, Fabian *Considerations against the dissolving and taking away the Court of Chancery* 1653
Regale necessarium: or the legality of the rights claimed by the King's servants 1671
PHILIPPS, Jenkin T. *Thirty four conferences between the Danish missionaries and the Malabarian Bramans* tr. 1719
PHILIPS, Ambrose *Poems* a1749 (1810)
The distrest mother; a tragedy 1712
The life of John Williams, Lord Keeper of the Great Seal 1700
Pastorals 1709 (1710)
PHILIPS, John *Poems* a1709 (1715, 1810)
Blenheim 1705
Cyder 1708
The splendid shilling 1701
PHILIPS, John *An authentic journal of the expedition under Commodore Anson* 1744
PHILIPS, Judson Pentecost *A dead ending* 1962 (UK 1963)
Escape a killer 1971 (UK 1972)
The twisted people 1965
The vanishing senator 1972 (UK 1973)
See also 'PENTECOST, Hugh'
PHILIPS, Katherine *Poems* a1664 (1667)
PHILIPS, Samuel *The voice of blood, in the sphere of nature and of the spirit-world* 1864
PHILIPS See also PHILLIPPES, PHILLIPS
Philips technical review 1936-
PHILIPSON, John *The art and craft of coachbuilding* 1897
PHILLIP, Arthur *Voyage to Botany Bay* 1789
PHILLIP, William *J. H. van Linschoten his discours of voyages into ye Easte and West Indies* tr. 1598 (Hakluyt Soc. 1885; partly in Arber, Eng. Garner III)
PHILLIPPES or PHILLIPS, Henry *The purchasers pattern* 1654 (1656, 1676)
PHILLIPPS-WOLLEY, Clive *Sport in the Crimea and Caucasus* 1881
PHILLIPS, Courtenay Stanley Goss & WILLIAMS, Robert Joseph Paton *Inorganic chemistry* 2 vols. 1965-6
PHILLIPS, David Graham *The plum tree* 1905
Susan Lenox: her fall and rise 1917
PHILLIPS, Edward *Letters of state, written by Mr. John Milton 1649-59.* tr. *To which is added, An account of his life* 1694
The mysteries of love and eloquence 1658
The new world of English words: or, a general dictionary 1658 (1662, 1678, 1696; ed. 6 by J. Kersey 1706)
Theatrum poetarum; or a compleat collection of the poets 1675
PHILLIPS, Fabian *See* PHILIPPS, F.
PHILLIPS, George *The elements of Syriac grammar* 1837
PHILLIPS, Henry *Chamisso de Boncourt's (L. C. A. von) Faust* tr. 1881
Historical sketches of the paper currency of the American Colonies 1865-66
Notes upon the collection of coins and medals now upon exhibition at the Pennsylvania Museum 1879
PHILLIPS, Jenkin T. *See* PHILIPPS, J. T.
PHILLIPS, John *The way to heaven* 1625
PHILLIPS, John *La Framboisière's (N. A. de) Art of physick made plain and easie* tr. 1684
A satyr against hypocrites (anon.) 1655
The six voyages of J. B. Tavernier through Turkey, into Persia and the East-Indies; to which is added, a new description of the Seraglio tr. 1677-78 (1684)
PHILLIPS, John *A general history of inland navigation* 1792-93
A treatise on inland navigation 1785
PHILLIPS, John *A glossary of the Devonshire dialect* 1839
PHILLIPS, John *Geology of Oxford and the valley of the Thames* 1871
Manual of geology (in Encyclopædia Metropolitana 1834-35) 1855
Memoirs of Dr. William Smith 1844
The rivers, mountains, and sea-coast of Yorkshire 1853
A treatise on geology 1830
Vesuvius 1869
PHILLIPS, Mrs. Lionel *Some South African recollections* 1899
PHILLIPS, R. *The man in the moon: a farce* 1818
PHILLIPS, Samuel *Essays from 'The Times'* 1851-54 (1871)
PHILLIPS, Stephen *Paolo and Francesca* 1900
PHILLIPS, Wendell *Speeches, lectures, and letters* 1863
— second series 1891
PHILLIPS, William *An elementary introduction to the knowledge of mineralogy* 1816 (1823)
An outline of mineralogy and geology 1815 (1818)
PHILLIPS, William *Mount Sinai; a poem* 1830
PHILLIPS, William *A manual of the British discomycetes* 1887
Phillis of Scyros 1655 *See* S., J.
PHILLPOTTS, Eden *Children of the mist* 1898
Down Dartmoor way 1895
The good red earth 1901
The human boy 1899
Lying prophets 1897
The portreeve 1906
The secret woman 1905
Sons of the morning 1900
The striking hours 1901
The thief of virtue 1910
PHILO PATER *The observator reproved* 1684
Philobiblon Society *Bibliographical and historical miscellanies* 1854-
Philological museum, The 1832-33
Philological Society *Proceedings* 1842-53
Transactions 1854-
'PHILOPOLITES, Sir P.' *The Grumbletonian crew reprehended* 1689
Philosophical collections, containing an account of such physical, anatomical, or other mathematical and philosophical experiments and observations, as have lately come to the publishers hands (ed. by R. Hooke) 1679-82
Philosophical magazine (and journal), The. By Alex. Tilloch, etc. 1798-1832
— continued as *London, Edinburgh, and Dublin philosophical magazine* 1832-
Philosophical review 1892-
Philosophical survey of the south of Ireland (by Thomas Campbell) 1777 (1778)
Philosophical transactions of the Royal Society 1665-
— Abridged by John Lowthorp and others (1716-56)
Philosophy: the journal of the British Institute of Philosophy 1931-
Philosophy of science 1934-
Philotus. Ane verie excellent and delectabill treatise intitulit Philotus 1603 (Bannatyne Cl. 1835)
PHILPOT, John *Examinations and writings* a1555 (Parker Soc. 1842)
PHIN, John *A dictionary of practical apiculture* 1884
PHIPPS, Constantine H. (1st Marquis of Normanby) *The English in France* (anon.) 1828
PHIPPS, Constantine J. *The journal of a voyage for making discoveries towards the North Pole* 1773 (1774)
PHIPSON, Thomas L. *Guillemin's (A.) The sun* tr. 1869 (1870)
'PHOENIX, John' (George Horatio Derby) *Phoenixiana; or, Sketches and burlesques* 1856
Phœnix a1000 (Grein)
Phœnix nest, The 1593 *See* S., R.
Phonetic journal, The 1848-
Phonographic journal, The 1842-44
Phonotypic journal, The 1843-49
Photochemistry and photobiology 1962-
Photographic annual, The 1892
Photo-miniature, The 1899-1932
Physical dictionary, A 1657
Physical review 1893- (from 1970 divided into subject series)
Physical review letters 1958-
Physical Society (of London) *Proceedings* 1874-
Physics bulletin 1950-
Physiological abstracts 1916-37
Physiological reviews 1921-
Phytochemistry 1961-
Phytologist, The 1844-62
Phytopathology 1911-
PIATT, John J. *Landmarks, and other poems* 1872
PICART, Bernard *The ceremonies and religious customs of the various nations of the known world* [anon. tr.] 1733
Picayune (New Orleans) See *Daily Picayune*
Pick of today's short stories, The ed. J. S. Pudney 1949-63
PICKARD, George Lawson *Descriptive physical oceanography: an introduction* 1963
PICKEN, Andrew *The Dominie's legacy* 1830
PICKEN, David *Poems and songs* 1875
PICKEN, Ebenezer *Miscellaneous poems, songs, etc., partly in the Scottish dialect* 1813
Poems and epistles, mostly in the Scottish dialect; with a glossary 1788
PICKEN, Laurence Ernest Rowland *The organization of cells and other organisms* 1960
PICKEN, Mary Brooks *The fashion dictionary* 1957
The language of fashion 1939
PICKERING, Ellen *Nan Darrell; or the gipsy mother* 1839
PICKERING, John *A vocabulary, or collection of words and phrases which have been supposed to be peculiar to the United States of America* 1816
PICKERING, Robert Easton *Himself again* 1966
Picquenard's (J. B.) Zoflora, or, the generous negro girl tr. 1804
PICTON, Sir James A. ed. *City of Liverpool. Selections from the municipal archives and records 12..-1835* (1883-86)
PIDDINGTON, Rose *The gain of a loss* 1866
The last of the Cavaliers 1859
Piece of family biography 1799 *See* DU BOIS, E.
PIERCE, Robert *Bath memoirs* 1697
PIERCE, Robert Morris *Dictionary of aviation* 1911
PIERCE, Thomas *A correct copy of some notes concerning Gods decrees* 1655 (1657)
The divine philanthropie defended against the declamatory attempts of certain late printed papers 1657
Pierce the ploughmans crede c1394 (E.E.T.S. 1867)
PIERIS, Ralph *Sinhalese social organization: the Kandyan period* 1956
Piers of Fullham a1500 (in Hazlitt, Early pop. poetry II)
Piers Plowman See LANGLAND, W.
PIESSE, G. W. Septimus *The laboratory of chemical wonders* 1860
Pigault-Lebrun's (G. C. A.) Monsieur Botte tr. 1803
PIGGOTT, Stuart *The neolithic cultures of the British Isles* 1954
PIGMAN, William Ward *Carbohydrates* 1957
Chemistry of the carbohydrates 1948
PIGOTT, Charles *The female jockey club* 1794
PIGOU, Arthur Cecil *The economics of welfare* 1920
PIKE, Albert *Prose sketches and poems, written in the western country* 1834
PIKE, Kenneth Lee *Phonetics: a critical analysis of phonetic theory and a technic for the practical description of sounds* 1943
Language in relation to a unified theory of the structure of human behavior 3 parts 1954-60
— (ed. 2) 1967
PIKE, Warburton *The barren ground of northern Canada* 1892
PIKE, Zebulon M. *An account of expeditions to the sources of the Mississippi 1805-07* 1810 (1895)
Piles' (M. de) Art of painting tr. 1706 (1744)
Pilgrimage of the lyf of the manhode; from the French of G. de Guilleville c1430 (Roxb. Cl. 1869)
Pilgrimage. The pilgrimage of perfection 1526 (1531)
Pilgrimage of princes See LLOYD, L.
Pilgrimage. The pylgremage of the sowle; from the French of G. de Guilleville c1400 (MS. Egerton 615; Caxton 1483; 1859)
Pilgrimage to Parnassus, The 1597 (1886)
Pilgrims sea-voyage and sea-sickness, The c1460 (E.E.T.S. 1867)
Pilgrim's tale, The c1540 (in Thynne's Animadversions, E.E.T.S. 1865)
PILKINGTON, Bp. James *Works* a1576 (Parker Soc. 1842)
Aggeus the prophete declared by a large commentarye 1560
Aggeus and Abdias prophetes, both at large declared 1562
An exposition vpon Abdyas 1562
The true report of the burnyng of the steple and churche of Paules (anon.) 1561
The burnyng of Paules church in London 1563
PILKINGTON, James *A view of the present state of Derbyshire* 1789
PILKINGTON, Mary *Celebrity; or, the unfortunate choice* 1815
PILKINGTON, Matthew *Remarks upon several passages of scripture* 1759
PILLEY, Dorothy Eleanor *Climbing days* 1935
PILLSBURY, Donald Marion, SHELLEY, W. B., & KLIGMAN, Albert M. *Dermatology* 1956
Pilton churchwardens' accounts See *Churchwardens' accounts*
Pimlyco, or runne red-cap, tis a mad world at Hogsdon 1609 (1891)
'PINDAR, Peter' *See* WOLCOT, John
PINERO, Arthur Wing *The magistrate* 1892
The second Mrs. Tanqueray 1895
PINKERTON, John *Ancient Scotish poems from the MS. collections of Sir R. Maitland* 1786
An enquiry into the history of Scotland, preceding the year 1056 1789
An essay on medals 1784 (1789)

A general collection of voyages and travels in all parts of the world 1808–14
The history of Scotland from the accession of the House of Stuart to that of Mary 1797
Petralogy; a treatise on rocks 1811
Scotish poems, reprinted from scarce editions 1792
Scottish tragic ballads 1781
— ed. 2, entitled *Select Scotish ballads* 1783; vol. II. *Ballads of the comic kind* 1783
PINKERTON, Robert *Russia* 1833
PINKNEY, Nathan *Travels through the South of France in 1807–08* 1809
PINNER, David *Ritual* 1967
PINTER, Harold *The birthday party* 1959
The caretaker 1960
The dumb waiter 1960
The homecoming 1965
The room 1960
PINTO, Edward Henry *Treen and other wooden bygones: an encyclopædia and social history* 1969
Pioneer, The (Lucknow) 1865–
'PIOT, Lazarus' = Munday, A.
PIOZZI, Hester Lynch (Mrs. Thrale) *Anecdotes of the late Samuel Johnson* 1786
British synonymy 1794
Observations and reflections made in the course of a journey through France, Italy, and Germany 1789
Letters to and from the late Samuel Johnson v.d. (1788)
Pipe Roll Society *Publications* (1884–)
Piper of Peebles, The; a tale 1794
Pique, a novel (by Mrs. Sarah Ellis) 1850
PIRIE, Antoinette ed. *Lens metabolism in relation to cataract: proceedings of a symposium* 1962
PIRIE, Norman Wingate *Food resources, conventional and novel* 1969
PIRIE, William R. *An inquiry into the constitution, powers and processes of the human mind* 1858
PIRKIS, Catherine L. *Judith Wynne* 1884
PIRSSON, Louis Valentine & SCHUCHERT, Charles *A text-book of geology* 2 parts 1915 (Pt. I by Pirsson, Pt. II by Schuchert)
— (ed. 2, by Pirsson alone) 2 parts 1920–4
Pistill of Susan, The a1400 (in D. Laing, Sel. rem. anc. poetry Scot. 1822; Scott. allit. poems, S.T.S. 1897)
PITCAIRN, Robert *Ancient criminal trials in Scotland (1488–1624); compiled from the original records and MSS.* v.d. (Bannatyne Cl. 1833)
PITMAN, Emma R. *Mission life in Greece and Palestine; memorials of Mary B. Baldwin* 1881
PITMAN, Henry *A relation of the great sufferings and strange adventures of H. P.* 1689 (in Arber, Eng. Garner VII)
PITT, Christopher *Poems* a1748 (1810)
Poems and translations 1727
The Æneid of Virgil tr. 1740
— *The works of Virgil in Latin and English. The Aeneid transl. by C. Pitt. The Eclogues and Georgics, by J. Warton* 1753 (1778)
PITT, William *General view of the agriculture of the county of Stafford* 1794
Pitt, W., Anecdotes of 1792 *See* ALMON, J.
Pittington churchwardens' accounts See *Churchwardens' accounts*
PITTMAN, Philip *The present state of the European settlements on the Mississippi* 1770
PITTS, Denis *This city is ours* 1975 (UK ed. 1976 with title *Target Manhattan*)
PITTS, Joseph *A true and faithful account of the religion and manners of the Mohammetans* 1704 (1738)
Pix (Sydney) 1938– (title varies)
PLAIFERE, T. *See* PLAYFERE, T.
Plain English 1643 *See* BOWLES, Edward
Plain hints 1880 *See* FLOYER, Mrs. L. S.
Plain man's pathway 1601 *See* DENT, A.
Plain sense; a novel 1796
Plaine Percival See HARVEY, R.
PLANCHÉ, James R. *A cyclopædia of costume; or dictionary of dress* 1876–79
Descent of the Danube from Ratisbon to Vienna 1828
Extravaganzas ed. T. F. D. Croker & S. Tucker 5 vols. 1897
History of British costume 1834 (1847, 1874)
Love and fortune 1859
Planning: a broadsheet (PEP: Political and Economic Planning) 1933–
Plant physiology 1926–
PLANTIN, Christoffel *Thesaurus Theutonicæ linguæ* 1573
Planting 1831–32 (Library of useful knowledge)
PLAT or PLATT, Sir Hugh *Delightes for ladies, to adorne their persons, tables, closets and distillatories* 1602 (1605)
The jewell house of art and nature (Divers new experiments. Diverse new sorts of soyle. Divers chimicall conclusions concerning the art of distillation. The art of molding and casting. An offer of certaine new inventions) 1594
PLATH, Sylvia *Ariel* 1965
The bell jar 1963
The colossus 1960
— (another ed.) 1967
Crossing the water 1971
PLATT, J. W. *The history and antiquities of Nantwich in the County Palatine of Chester* 1818
PLATT, Kim *The pushbutton butterfly* 1970 (UK 1971)
PLATTS, John *The book of curiosities* 1822
Play of the sacrament, The c1460 (Philological Soc. 1861; Non-cycle mystery plays, E.E.T.S. 1909)
Play of Stucley (*The famous historye of the life and death of Captaine T. Stukeley*) 1605 (in Simpson, School of Shaks. I. 1878)
PLAYER, Robert *Let's talk of graves, of worms, and epitaphs* 1975
Player, Sir Thomas 1679 See *Vindication*
PLAYFAIR, John *Illustrations of the Huttonian theory of the earth* 1802
Outlines of natural philosophy 1812–16 (1819)
PLAYFERE, Thomas *Sermons* a1609 (1617–23)
PLAYFORD, Henry *Wit and mirth; an antidote against melancholy* 1682
PLAYFORD, John *A brief introduction to the skill of musick; in two books* 1658 (1662)
— ed. 3, enlarged *To which is added, a third book, entituled, the art of descant by Thomas Campion* 1660 (1674)
Select musicall ayres and dialogues 1652–53 (1659)
Plays of the year ed. J. C. Trewin 1949–
PLEYDELL-BOUVERIE, E. O. *See* HEATHCOTE, C. G.
Pliny's Natural history tr. by J. Bostock & H. T. Riley 1855–57 (Bohn)
PLOMER, William Charles Franklyn *I speak of Africa* 1927
Museum pieces 1952
PLOT, Robert *The natural history of Oxfordshire* 1677
The natural history of Staffordshire 1686
PLOWDEN, Edmund *Les comentaries, ou les reportes de dyuers cases esteantes matters en ley* 1571
Plowman's tale, The c1395 (in Chaucer's Works, ed. Thynne 1542; Chaucerian and other pieces, ed. Skeat 1897)
PLUES, Margaret *Rambles in search of wild flowers* 1863
PLUME, Thomas *Life of John Hacket* 1675 (in Hacket's Century of sermons 1675)
PLUMMER, Alfred *Döllinger's (J. J. T. von) Hippolytus and Calistus* tr. 1876
Plumpton correspondence 1460–1552 (Camden Soc. 1839)
PLUMPTRE, Anne tr. *H. Lichtenstein's Travels in southern Africa* 2 vols. 1812–15
PLUMPTRE, Edward H. *The tragedies of Sophocles* tr. 1865 (1877)
PLUNKET, Thomas *The character of a good commander* 1689
Plutarch's Morals tr. by several hands 1684–94
'PLYMLEY, Peter' *See* SMITH, Sydney
POCKLINGTON, John *Altare Christianum; or, the dead vicars plea* 1637
Pocklington (John), Petition against 1641 *See* H., I.
Pocklington Canal act 1815 (Local act 55 Geo. III cap. lv)
POCKNEE, C. E. *See* DEARMER, Percy
POCOCK, Nicholas *Records of the Reformation; the Divorce 1527–33.* Collected and arranged by N. Pocock. v.d. (1870)
POCOCKE, Edward *A commentary on the Prophecy of Hosea* 1685
POCOCKE, Bp. Richard *A description of the East* 1743–45
Travels through England 1750–57 (Camden Soc. 1888–89)
POE, Edgar A. *Works* a1849 (1865)
The complete poetical works, with three essays on poetry a1849 (1909)
Poems a1849 (1859, 1864)
Poem on the times of Edward II c1325 (Percy Soc. 1849; Political songs, Camden Soc. 1839)
Poems in the Buchan dialect (*A select collection of Scots poems, chiefly in the broad Buchan dialect*) 1785
Poems on affairs of state 1697–1707
Poetical museum, The (publ. by G. Caw) 1784
Poetry (Chicago) 1912–
Poetry of the Anti-Jacobin See *Anti-Jacobin*
POHL, Frederik & KORNBLUTH, Cyril M. *The space merchants* 1953 (UK 1955)
Poisson de Gomez's (M. A.) La belle assemblée, or, the adventures of six days tr. 1725 (1729)
POLACK, Joel Samuel *Manners and customs of the New Zealanders* 2 vols. 1840
New Zealand: being a narrative of travels and adventures 2 vols. 1838
POLEHAMPTON, Edward T. W. & GOOD, John M. *The gallery of nature and art* 1814–15
Police journal 1928–
Police review (title varies) 1893–
Polimanteia 1595 *See* COVELL, W.
Polite lady, The 1760 *See* PORTIA
Polite philosopher, The 1734 *See* FORRESTER, J.
Political and other poems, Twenty-six c1400 (E.E.T.S. 1904)
Political ballads 16..–17.. (annotated by W. Walker Wilkins 1860)
Political ballads 16.. (ed. T. Wright, Percy Soc. 1841)
Political poems and songs relating to English history, A collection of 13..–15.. (Rolls series 1859–61
Political quarterly 1930–
Political, religious, and love poems 13..–15.. (E.E.T.S. 1866, 1903)
Political science quarterly 1886–
Political songs of England 12..–13.. (Camden Soc. 1839)
POLLEN, John H., the elder *Ancient and modern furniture and woodwork in the South Kensington Museum* 1874
POLLEN, John H., the younger *Acts of English martyrs hitherto unpublished* 1891
POLLEXFEN, Sir Henry *A discourse of trade and coyn* (anon.) a1692 (1697)
POLLITT, John *Depression and its treatment* 1965
POLLOCK, Albin Jay *The underworld speaks* 1935
POLLOCK, Frederick *The land laws* 1883 (1896)
Oxford lectures and other discourses 1890
—— & HOLMES, Oliver Wendell (the younger) *The Pollock-Holmes letters: correspondence of Sir Frederick Pollock and Mr. Justice Holmes, 1874–1932* ed. M. de W. Howe 2 vols. 1942
—— & MAITLAND, Frederick W. *The history of English law before the time of Edward I* 1895
POLLOCK, Walter H. *Fencing*, by W. H. Pollock, F. C. Grove, & C. Prevost 1889 (Badminton Library)
POLLOK, FitzWilliam T. *Sport in British Burmah, Assam, and the Cassyah and Jyntiah hills* 1879
POLLOK, Robert *The course of time* 1827
POLSON, Archer *Law and lawyers* 1840 (1858)
The law of nations 1845 (in Encycl. Metrop. II)
POLUNIN, Nicholas Vladimir *Introduction to plant geography and some related sciences* 1960
POLWART (= Sir Patrick Hume of Polwarth) *Flyting with Montgomerie* a1585 (in Montgomerie's Poems, S.T.S. 1887, 1910)
POLWHELE, Richard *A Cornish-English vocabulary* 1808
The history of Cornwall 1803–06 (1816)
The history of Devonshire 1793–1806
Traditions and recollections 1826
Polydore Vergil See VERGILIUS, P.
Pomet's (J.) Compleat history of drugs tr. 1712
See also HILL, John
Pomey's (F. A.) Pantheon (tr. by A. Tooke) 1698
POMFRET, Henrietta L. Fermor, Countess of *See* HERTFORD, Countess of
POMFRET, John *Poems upon several occasions* a1702 (1790)
Poetical works a1702 (1833)
PONTING, Herbert George *The great white south: being an account of experiences with Captain Scott's South Pole Expedition* 1921
Pontoppidan's (E.) Natural history of Norway tr. 1755
POOLE, A. L. & ADAMS, Nancy M. *Trees and shrubs of New Zealand* 1963
POOLE, Charles H. *An attempt towards a glossary of the archaic and provincial words of the county of Stafford* 1880
The customs, superstitions, and legends of the county of Somerset 1877
The customs, superstitions, and legends of the county of Stafford 1883
POOLE, George A. *Peterborough* (Diocesan histories) 1881
POOLE, Joseph *The practical telephone handbook* 1891
POOLE, Joshua *The English Parnassus; or, a helpe to English poesie* a1646 (1657, 1677)
POOLE, Matthew *Annotations upon the Holy Bible* a1679 (1688)
A dialogue between a Popish priest and an English Protestant 1667 (1735)
POOLE, Stanley Lane *See* LANE-POOLE, S.
Poor man's plea against the extravagant price of corn 1699
Poor Nellie 1887 (1888)
Poor Robin's almanack 1664–1776
Poor Robin's visions 1677
POPE, Alexander *Works; verse* 1717–41; *prose* 1737–41 (1751)
Poetical works a1744 (Globe ed. 1869)
The Dunciad 1728–42
An essay on criticism 1709
An essay on man 1732–34
Homer's Iliad tr. 1715–20
Homer's Odyssey tr. 1725–26
Letters 17.. (1735–37, 1751)
Miscellanies in prose and verse (by Swift and Pope) 1727–35
Moral essays. Epistle I. To Sir Richard Temple, Lord Cobham 1732; *Epistle II. To a lady* 1735; *Epistle III. To Allen Lord Bathurst* 1732; *Epistle IV. To Richard Boyle, Earl of Burlington* 1731; *Epistle V. To Mr. Addison* 1715–20
Pastorals 1704
The rape of the lock 1712–14
Satires and epistles of Horace imitated 1732–38
Satires of Dr. Donne versified 1735
The temple of fame 1711
Windsor-Forest 1704–10
—— & GAY, John *What passed in London* 1727
—— et al. *The art of sinking* 1727
POPE, Frank L. *Modern practice of the electric telegraph* 1870 (1872)
POPE, Walter *The life of Seth (Ward), lord bishop of Salisbury* 1697
POPE-HENNESSY, James *Robert Louis Stevenson* 1974
POPENOE, Wilson *Manual of tropical and subtropical fruits* 1920
Popish plot, The, taken out of several depositions made and sworn before the Parliament c1680
POPLEY, Herbert Arthur *The music of India* 1921
POPPER, Karl Raimund *The logic of scientific discovery* 1959
The open society and its enemies 2 vols. 1945
The poverty of historicism 1957
POPPLE, William 1689 *See* LOCKE, J.
Popular science monthly, The 1872–
Popular science review, The 1861–81
Popular tales of the Germans tr. 1791 *See* BECKFORD, W.
Popular treatises on science written during the middle ages, in Anglo-Saxon, Anglo-Norman, and English v.d. (ed. Thomas Wright 1841)
Porcupine, The 1860–1915; 1923
PORDAGE, John *Theologica mystica, or the mystic divinitie of the æternal invisibles.* By J. P. (i.e. John Pordage; ed. Edward Hooker) 1683
PORDAGE, Samuel *The medal revers'd; a satyre against persecution* (anon.) 1682
PORNY, Mark A. *The elements of heraldry* 1765 (1766, 1777, 1787)

PORSON, Richard *Letters to Mr. Archdeacon Travis* 1790
Porta's (G. B. della) Natural magick tr. 1658
PORTAL, Sir Gerald *The British mission to Uganda in 1893* 1894
'PORTE CRAYON' (David Hunter Strother) *Virginia illustrated* 1857
PORTEOUS, M. *The real 'Souter Johnny'* 1858
PORTER, Anna M. *The Hungarian brothers* 1807
PORTER, Edmund *Christophagia: the mystery of eating the flesh and drinking the blood of Christ* 1680
PORTER, Frank T. *Gleanings and reminiscences* 1875
PORTER, Mrs. G. S. *See* STRATTON-PORTER, Mrs. Gene
PORTER, George R. *Statistics* 1849 (in Manual of scientific enquiry 1859)
A treatise on the origin, progressive improvement, and present state of the manufacture of porcelain and glass (anon.) 1832
— *of the silk manufacture* (anon.) 1831
PORTER, Henry *The pleasant history of the two angry women of Abington* 1599 (Percy Soc. 1841)
PORTER, Horace C. tr. *E. Strasburger's A textbook of botany* 1898
PORTER, Jane *The Scottish chiefs* 1810 (1856)
Thaddeus of Warsaw 1803 (1831)
PORTER, Joyce *The chinks in the curtain* 1967
Dover two 1965
It's murder with Dover 1973
A meddler and her murder 1972
Rather a common sort of crime 1970
Sour cream with everything 1966
PORTER, Katherine Anne *Ship of fools* 1962
PORTER, Sir Robert K. *Travelling sketches in Russia and Sweden* 1809 (1813)
PORTER, Whitworth *A history of the Knights of Malta* 1858
PORTER, William T. ed. *The big bear of Arkansas, and other sketches* (by various authors) 1847
A quarter race in Kentucky 1847
Porter's Spirit of the times 1856-59
PORTEUS, Bp. Beilby *Lectures on the Gospel of St. Matthew* 1802
Sermons on several subjects 1783
'PORTIA' *The polite lady; or, a course of female education. In a series of letters, from a mother to her daughter* (Signed, Portia. The replies are signed Sophia) 1760
Portland papers. The manuscripts of his Grace the Duke of Portland, preserved at Welbeck Abbey 16..-17.. (Historical MSS. Comm. 1891-)
PORTLOCK, Joseph E. *A rudimentary treatise on geology* 1849
PORTLOCK, Nathaniel *A voyage round the world 1785-88* 1789
Portola Institute *The last whole earth catalog* 1972
Portsmouth, Rhode Island *Early records* ed. A. Perry & C. S. Brigham 1901
PORY, John *Leo's (J.) Geographical historie of Africa* tr. 1600
POST, Waldron Kintzing *Harvard stories: sketches of the undergraduate* 1893
Post-Herald (Birmingham, Alabama) 1951-
Post Office electrical engineers' journal 1908-
POSTAL, Paul Martin *Aspects of phonological theory* 1968
POSTE, Edward *Gaii institutionum juris civilis commentarii*. With a translation and commentary by E. Poste 1875
POSTGATE, Raymond William *The plain man's guide to wine* 1951
— (ed. 2) 1965
POSTLETHWAYT, Malachy *Savary des Bruslons' (J.) Universal dictionary of trade and commerce* 1751-55 (1774)
POSTMAN, Neil *Crazy talk, stupid talk* 1976
POSTON, Edward *The pratler* 1747
POTE, Joseph *The history and antiquities of Windsor Castle* 1749
POTOK, Chaim *The chosen* 1967
In the beginning 1975
My name is Asher Lev 1972
POTT, Percivall *Chirurgical works* a1788 (1790)
POTTER, Christopher *Sarpi's (P.) History of the quarrels of Pope Paul V with the state of Venice* tr. 1626
A sermon preached at the consecration of Barnaby Potter, Bishop of Carlisle 1629
POTTER, David *British Elizabethan stamps: the story of the postage stamps of the United Kingdom* 1971
POTTER, Dennis Christopher G. *The glittering coffin* 1960
POTTER, Francis *An interpretation of the number 666* 1642
POTTER, Helen Beatrix *Journal, 1881-1897* transcribed from code by L. Linder 1966
POTTER, Humphry T. *A new dictionary of all the cant and flash languages* a1790 (1795)
POTTER, Jeremy *Foul play* 1967
POTTER, John *Archæologiæ Græcæ: or, the antiquities of Greece* 1697-99 (1715)
A discourse of Church government 1707
POTTER, John *The virtuous villagers* 1784
POTTER, Robert *The tragedies of Æschylus* tr. 1777
POTTER, Simeon *Language in the modern world* 1960
Modern linguistics 1957
Our language 1950
POTTLE, Frederick Albert *Stretchers: the story of a hospital unit on the Western Front* 1929 (UK 1930)
POTTS, Alexander W. *Hints towards Latin prose composition* 1869 (1870)
POTTS, Jean *Death of a stray cat* 1955 (UK 1956)
The evil wish 1962
POTTS, Thomas *The wonderfull discoverie of witches in the countie of Lancaster* 1613 (Chetham Soc. 1845)
POTTS, Thomas Henry *Out in the open: a budget of scraps of natural history, gathered in New Zealand* 1882
Pouchet's (F. A.) Universe; or, the infinitely great and little tr. 1869 (1871)
POULET, Sir Amias *Letter-books* 15.. (1874)
POULTON, Edward B. *The colours of animals* 1890
Essays on evolution 1889-1907 (1908)
See also WEISMANN, A.
Poultry chronicle 1854-5
POUND, Ezra Loomis *Cantos LII-LXXI* 1940
Canzoni 1911
Cathay: translations for the most part from the Chinese of Rihaku 1915
The classic anthology defined by Confucius 1955
A draft of XXX cantos 1930
Gaudier-Brzeska, a memoir 1910
Hugh Selwyn Mauberley: life and contacts 1920
Letters See *Selected letters*
Lustra 1916
— (another ed., with earlier poems) 1917
Pavannes and divisions 1918
Personae: the collected poems 1909
The Pisan cantos 1948 (UK 1949)
Section: rock-drill; 85-95 de los cantares 1955
— (another ed.) 1957
Selected letters, 1907-1941 ed. D. D. Paige 1971
Thrones: 96-109 de los cantares 1959
tr. *Sophocles' Women of Trachis* 1956
Pouqueville's (F. C. H. L.) Travels through the Morea, Albania, and other parts of the Ottoman empire tr. 1806 (1813)
POUTSMA, Hendrik *A grammar of late modern English* 2 parts in 4 vols. 1904-26
— (ed. 2 of Part I) 2 vols. 1928-9
POWDRILL, Ernest Arthur *Vocabulary of land planning* 1961
POWEL, David *Caradoc's Historie of Cambria* tr. by Humphrey Lhuyd, corrected and continued by D. Powel, and newly augmented by W. Wynne 1584
POWEL or POWELL, Gabriel *A refutation of an epistle apologeticall written by a puritan-papist* 1605
POWELL, Anthony Dymoke *The acceptance world* 1955
Afternoon men 1931
A buyer's market 1952
Casanova's Chinese restaurant 1960
A question of upbringing 1951
The valley of bones 1964
Venusberg 1932
What's become of Waring? 1939
POWELL, Baden *Christianity without Judaism* 1856-57
Essays on the spirit of the inductive philosophy etc. 1855
POWELL, Dawn *A time to be born* 1942 (UK 1943)
Turn, magic wheel 1936
POWELL, John J. *An essay on the learning of devises* 1788
— ed. 3, enlarged by T. Jarman (1827)
POWELL, John Leonard & CRASEMANN, Bernd *Quantum mechanics* 1961
POWELL, Martin Beynon & HIGMAN, Graham eds. *Finite simple groups* 1971
POWELL, Thomas *Tom of all trades; or the plaine path-way to preferment* 1631 (New Shaks. Soc. 1876)
'POWER, Cecil' *See* ALLEN, Grant
POWER, Henry *Experimental philosophy* 1664
POWER, Henry & SEDGWICK, Leonard W. *New Sydenham Society's Lexicon of medicine and allied sciences* 1879-99
POWER, John *A handy book about books* 1870
POWER, Marguerite A. *Arabian days and nights* 1863
POWER, Tyrone *Impressions of America, 1833-1835* 2 vols. 1836
POWER, William James Tyrone *Sketches in New Zealand, with pen and pencil* 1849
Power farming 1957-
Power of the keyes 1647 *See* HAMMOND, H.
Power of love 1720 *See* MANLEY, Mrs.
Power of prosaic numbers 1749 *See* MASON, John
Powerfull favorite, The 1628 *See* MATTHIEU, P.
POWNALL, Thomas *The administration of the Colonies* 1764 (1774)
A treatise on the study of antiquities 1782
POWYS, John Cowper *A Glastonbury romance* 1932 (UK 1933)
Maiden Castle 1936 (UK 1937)
Visions and revisions: a book of literary devotions 1915
POWYS, Marian *Lace and lace-making* 1953
POYNET, John *A shorte treatise of politike power* 1556
POYNTER, Edward J. *Ten lectures on art* 1879 (1880)
See also HEAD, Percy R.
POYNTING, John H. & THOMSON, Joseph J. *A text-book of physics. Heat* 1904
Practical magazine, The 1873-77
Practical motorist 1954-
Practical wireless 1932-
Practitioner, The: a monthly journal of therapeutics and public health 1868-
Practitioners library of medicine and surgery, The ed. G. Blumer 16 vols. 1932-41
Practyse of cyrurgyons of Mountpyller, The ?1540
PRAED, Mrs. Campbell (Rachel M. Praed) *The head station* 1885
Miss Jacobsen's chance 1886
Outlaw and lawmaker 1893
Policy and passion 1881
The romance of a station 1890
Zéro 1884
PRAED, Winthrop M. *Poems* a1839 (1864, 1865)
Praise of musicke, The (by John Case) 1586
PRANCE, Miles *The additional narrative, containing his vindication of the machinations of the Papal and Jesuitical party* 1679
True narrative and discovery of several remarkable passages relating to the horrid Popish plot 1679
Prantl's (K.) Elementary text-book of botany tr. by S. H. Vines 1880
PRAT, W. *The discription of the contrey of Aphrique* tr. 1554
PRATT, Anne *The British grasses and sedges* 1859
Chapters on the common things of the sea-side 1850
The flowering plants and ferns of Great Britain 1854-57
Our native songsters 1852
PRATT, Lyde S. *The chemistry and physics of organic pigments* 1947
PRATT, Samuel J. *Emma Corbett* 1780
Liberal opinions 1775 (1783)
The pupil of pleasure 1776
Prayers, Private, put forth in the reign of Queen Elizabeth 1544-78 (Parker Soc. 1851)
PREBLE, George H. *Our flag. Origin and progress of the flag of the United States of America* 1872
— ed. 2, entitled *History of the flag of the United States of America* 1880
PREECE, William H. & MAIER, Julius *The telephone* 1889
—— & SIVEWRIGHT, J. *Telegraphy* 1876
Prehistoric Society (of East Anglia) *Proceedings* 1908-
Prelatical episcopacy, Of 1641 *See* MILTON, J.
PRENTICE, Archibald *History of the Anti-Corn-Law League* 1853
Presbytery book of Strathbogie, Extracts from the 1631-54 (Spalding Cl. 1843)
PRESCOTT, George B. *History, theory, and practice of the electric telegraph* 1860
The speaking telephone 1878 (1879)
PRESCOTT, William H. *History of the conquest of Mexico* 1843 (1864)
History of the conquest of Peru 1847 (1850)
History of the reign of Ferdinand and Isabella 1838 (1846)
History of the reign of Philip the second 1855 (1857)
Present interest of Tangier, The c1680
Present state of Russia (1671) *See* COLLINS, Samuel
Present state of Russia, The tr. 1722-23
Presentation in the temple, The; a pageant, as originally represented by the Corporation of Weavers in Coventry 14.. (Abbotsford Cl. 1836; in Two Coventry Corpus Christi plays, E.E.T.S. 1902)
Press, The (Christchurch, N.Z.) 1861-
Press and Journal (Aberdeen) 1939- (continuation of *Aberdeen Press and Journal*)
Prestis of Peblis, The (thre) See *Peebles*
PRESTON, John *The breast-plate of faith and love* a1628 (1630, 1631)
Mount Ebal, or a heavenly treatise of divine love a1628 (1638)
The new covenant, or the saints portion a1628 (1629, 1634)
PRESTON, Richard *The godly mans inquisition* 1622
PRESTON, Richard Graham, Viscount *A. M. S. Boethius of the consolation of philosophy* tr. 1695
PRESTON, Thomas *A lamentable tragedy mixed ful of pleasant mirth conteyning the life of Cambises King of Percia* 1569 (in Manly, Specim. pre-Shaks. drama II, 1898; Hazl., Dodsley)
PRESTWICH, Joseph *Geology, chemical, physical, and stratigraphical* 1886-88
Prestwick, Records of the burgh of 1470-1782 (Maitland Cl. 1834)
Pretences of the French invasion examined 1692 *See* LLOYD, BP. WILLIAM
PREVOST, E. W. 1899 *See* DICKINSON, W.
PRICE, Anthony *The Alamut ambush* 1971
Colonel Butler's wolf 1972
The '44 vintage 1978
October men 1973
Other paths to glory 1974
Our man in Camelot 1975
War game 1976
PRICE, Bonamy *Chapters on practical political economy* 1878
PRICE, Daniel *Prælium et præmium. The Christians warre and reward* 1608
Prince Henry, his first (second) anniversary 1613-14
PRICE, Henry Habberley *Perception* 1932
Thinking and experience 1953
PRICE, John *Some considerations offered to the House of Commons for building a stone-bridge over the Thames* 1735
PRICE, Pamela Vandyke *France: a food and wine guide* 1966
PRICE, Stanley *Just for the record* 1961
PRICE, Thomas *The life, voyages, and adventures of Bampfylde-Moore Carew* ?1810
See also *Carew, Bampfylde Moore*
PRICE, Uvedale *An essay on the picturesque as compared with the sublime and the beautiful* 1794-98
PRICE, William *Mans delinquencie* 1646
A sermon preached on Aprill 13, 1642, before the Lord Maior 1642
PRICHARD, James C. *The eastern origin of the Celtic nations proved* 1831
Ethnology 1849 (in Manual of scientific enquiry 1859)
The natural history of man 1843 (1848)
Researches into the physical history of man 1813; ed. 2, *of mankind* 1826
PRICHARD, Katharine Susannah *Coonardoo: the well in the shadow* 1929
Winged seeds 1950
PRICKET, Robert *Honors fame in triumph riding* 1604 (1881)

Pride and lowlines c1570 *See* DEBATE
Pride of life, The c1400 (Brandl 1898)
PRIDEAUX, Humphrey *Circular letter* 1692
Directions to church-wardens for the faithful discharge of their office 1701 (1712)
Letters to John Ellis 1674–1722 (Camden Soc. 1875)
Life of Mahomet 1697
The Old and New Testament connected in the history of the Jews and neighbouring nations 1716–18
The original and right of tithes 1710
PRIDEAUX, Bp. John *Euchologia: or, the doctrine of practical praying* a1650 (1656)
PRIDHAM, Charles *An historical, political and statistical account of Ceylon and its dependencies* 1849
PRIEBSCH, Robert Charles & COLLINSON, William Edward *The German language* 1934
PRIEST, William *Travels in the United States of America 1793–97* 1802
PRIESTLEY, John Boynton *Angel Pavement* 1930
Bright day 1946
Daylight on Saturday 1943
Delight 1949
English journey 1934
Festival at Farbridge 1951
The good companions 1929
Home is tomorrow 1949
It's an old country 1967
Let the people sing 1939
The magicians 1954
Margin released 1962
Salt is leaving 1966
Saturn over the water 1961
They walk in the city 1936
Three men in new suits 1945
—— & HAWKES, Jessie Jacquetta *Journey down a rainbow* 1955
PRIESTLEY, Joseph *Disquisitions relating to matter and spirit* 1777 (1782)
The doctrine of philosophical necessity illustrated 1777
Hartley's (D.) Theory of the human mind; with essays relating to the subject of it 1775
An history of the corruptions of Christianity 1782
Institutes of natural and revealed religion 1772 (1782)
Lectures on history and general policy 1788
Philosophical empiricism; interspersed with various observations relating to different kinds of air 1775
PRIESTLEY, Ronald & WISDOM, Thomas Henry *Good driving —the B.S.M. way* 1965
PRIMATT, Stephen *The city and country purchaser and builder* 1667
PRIME, John *The consolations of Dauid breefly applied to Queene Elizabeth, in a sermon* 1588
Primer. The prymer or prayer-book of the lay people in the middle ages a1400 (in Maskell, Monumenta rit. Eccl. Angl. II. 1846; Littlehales 1891)
The prymer, or lay folks' prayer book c1420 (E.E.T.S. 1895)
The prymer of Salysbury vse 1527
A goodly prymer in englyshe, newly corrected 1535
Prymer in Englyshe and Laten 1536
The primer, set foorth by the Kynges maiestie and his clergie 1545 (1546)
A prymmer or boke of priuate prayer nedeful to be vsed of al faythfull Christians 1553
The prymer in Englysshe and in Latin after the vse of Sarum 1555 (1557)
The primer set furth at large, with many godly and deuoute prayers 1559
The primer or office of the blessed virgin Marie in English 1615 (1631)
Primrose's (J.) Popular errors tr. 1651 *See* WITTIE, R.
PRINCE, Ælian *Of joyous gard* 1890
PRINCE, Thomas *A chronological history of New England in the form of annals* 1736 (in Arber, Eng. Garner II)
Prince Rupert's speech to his Majesty and the Lords of his Privie Councell 1642
Prince Society *Publications* (Albany, N.Y., 1865–77)
Princely pellican, The, or royall resolves presented in sundry choice observations extracted from (K. Charles I's) divine meditations 1649
Princeton review, The 1878–82
PRINGLE, Sir John *Six discourses delivered before the Royal Society* 1773–78 (1783)
PRINGLE, Mrs. M. A. *Towards the mountains of the moon: a journey in East Africa* 1884
PRINGLE, Thomas *African sketches* 1834
Poetical works a1834 (1838)
PRINGLE-PATTISON, Andrew Seth *The idea of God in the light of recent philosophy* 1917
PRINSEP, Augustus *The Baboo; and other tales descriptive of society in India* (anon.) 1834
PRINSEP, Mrs. Augustus *The journal of a voyage from Calcutta to Van Diemen's Land* 1833
PRINSEP, Henry T. *A narrative of the political and military transactions of British India* 1820 (1825)
PRINSEP, James *Essays on Indian antiquities* 1858
Printers' ink 1888–1967
Printing trades' journal See *Paper*
PRIOR, Allan *The interrogators* 1965
The operators 1966
PRIOR, Arthur Norman *Formal logic* 1955
Time and modality 1957
PRIOR, James *Forest folk* 1901
PRIOR, Matthew *Poems on several occasions* 1709, 1718
Poetical works a1721 (1892)
Writings a1721 (1905–07)

PRIOR, Richard C. A. *Notes on croquet* 1872
On the popular names of British plants 1863 (1870, 1879)
Priory of Hexham See *Hexham*
PRITCHARD, Charles *Occasional thoughts of an astronomer* 1889
PRITCHETT, Victor Sawdon *A cab at the door, an autobiography: early years* 1968
The gentle barbarian: the life and work of Turgenev 1977
PRITT, Thomas E. *Yorkshire trout flies* 1885
— ed. 2, entitled *North country flies* 1886
Private devotions, Collection of 1627 *See* COSIN, Bp. J.
Private eye 1962–
Private prayers See *Prayers*
Privy Council acts See *Acts*
Privy Council of Scotland, Register of See *Register*
Privy purse expenses See *Elizabeth of York;* HENRY VIII; MARY, Princess
Proceedings. An impartial account of divers remarkable proceedings the last sessions of parliament, relating to the horrid Popish plot 1679
Proceedings against the late traitors (A true and perfect relation of the whole proceedings against the late traitors, Garnet a Iesuite, etc.) 1606
Proceedings See under the names of particular institutions
Proclamation. The only English proclamation of Henry III 1258 (Philol. Soc. 1868)
PROCTER, Bryan W. ('Barry Cornwall') *Poetical works* 1822
The flood of Thessaly, the girl of Provence, and other poems 1823
A Sicilian story, with Diego de Montilla and other poems 1820
PROCTER, Francis & FRERE, Bp. Walter H. *A new history of the Book of Common Prayer* 1901
PROCTER, Henry Richardson *The principles of leather manufacture* 1903
PROCTER, Maurice *Exercise Hoodwink* 1967
Man in ambush 1958
PROCTER, Richard W. *The barber's shop* 1856
PROCTOR, George *The lucubrations of Humphrey Ravelin* 1823
PROCTOR, John *The historie of Wyates rebellion* 1554 (in Arber, Eng. Garner VIII)
PROCTOR, Michael Charles Faraday & YEO, Peter *The pollination of flowers* 1973
PROCTOR, Richard A. *The borderland of science* 1873
Chance and luck: a discussion of the laws of luck 1887
Essays on astronomy 1872
The expanse of heaven 1873
The Great Pyramid, observatory, tomb, and temple 1883
How to play whist 1885
Light science for leisure hours 1871–73
Other worlds than ours 1870
Pleasant ways in science 1879
PROCTOR, Thomas *A gorgious gallery of gallant inventions* 1578 (in T. Park, Heliconia I. 1815)
Prodigal son, The (transl. of 16th-c. German play) 1878 (in Simpson, School of Shaks. II. 1878)
Product engineering 1930–
Progress of honesty 1681 *See* D'URFEY, T.
Project for more efficiently manning the navy 1745
Promptorium parvulorum sive clericorum, lexicon Anglo-Latinum princeps c1440 (Camden Soc. 1843–65)
— (Winchester MS.) c1460 (E.E.T.S. 1908)
Proper dyaloge betwene a gentillman and a husbandman 1530 (in Roy, Rede me, etc., Arber 1871)
Proposals towards raising provision for the poor and increase of seamen 1740
Prose legends 14.. (in Anglia VIII. 1885)
Prose life of Alexander c1420 See *Alexander*
Prose psalter See *Psalter*
Protestant almanack for the year 1668 1667
Protestant conformist, The: or, a plea for moderation 1679
Protestant garland, The, of joy and delight 1689
Protests of the Lords, A complete collection of the v.d. (ed. J. E. T. Rogers 1875)
Proude wyues pater noster, The 1560 (in Hazlitt, Early pop. poetry IV. 1866)
PROUT, Ebenezer *Harmony: its theory and practice* 1889
'PROUT, Father' *See* MAHONY, F. S.
Proverbs of Alfred, The a1250, a1275 (in Old English miscellany, E.E.T.S. 1872; ed. Skeat 1907)
Proverbs of Hendyng a1325 (in Reliquiæ antiquæ I. 1841; Morris and Skeat, Spec. Early Eng. Pt. II. 1884)
Providence, Rhode Island *Early records* 21 vols. 1892–1915
Providences of God 1691 *See* BETHEL, S.
Provincialism of Danby, etc. 1863 (From C. J. Atkinson's note books, afterwards published in Cleveland gloss. 1868)
PROWETT, Charles G. *Prometheus bound; a tragedy of Æschylus* tr. 1846
PRYCE, William *Archæologia Cornu-Britannica; or, an essay to preserve the ancient Cornish language; containing the rudiments of that dialect, in a Cornish grammar and Cornish English vocabulary* 1790
Mineralogia Cornubiensis; or a treatise on minerals, mines, and mining 1778
PRYCE-JONES, Alan ed. *The new outline of modern knowledge* 1956
Pryde and abuse of women, A treatyse shewing and declaring the c1550 (in Hazlitt, Early pop. poetry IV. 1866)
Prymer See *Primer*
PRYNNE, William *Anti-Arminianisme* 1630 See *Church of England* below

The antipathie of the English lordly prelacie, both to regall monarchy, and civill unity 1641
A briefe survay and censure of Mr Cozens his couzening devotions 1628
Canterburies doome, or the first part of a complete history of the trial of William Laud 1646
A checke to Brittannicus 1644
The Church of England's old antithesis to new Arminianisme 1629
— ed. 2 enlarged, entitled *Anti-Arminianisme* 1630
The doome of cowardisze and treachery 1643
The falsities and forgeries of the anonymous author of a late pamphlet 1644
A gagge for long-hair'd rattle-heads 1646
God no impostor nor deluder 1629
A gospel plea 1653
Histrio-mastix; the players scourge or actors tragedie 1633
An humble remonstrance against the tax of ship-money lately imposed (anon.) 1636 (1643)
A legall vindication of the liberties of England against illegall taxes 1649
A moderate apology against a pretended calumny 1644
Mount-Orgueil: or divine and profitable meditations 1641
The opening of the greate seale of England 1643
The perpetuitie of a regenerated mans estate 1626
A plea for the House of Lords 1648
The Popish royall favourite 1643
Rome's master-peece 1643 (1644)
The soveraigne power of parliaments and kingdomes 1643
A summary collection of the principal fundamental rights, liberties, proprieties, of all English freemen 1656
The treachery and disloyalty of Papists to their soveraignes 1643 (= Pt. I of *The soveraigne power*)
Twelve considerable serious questions touching Church government 1644
The unbishoping of Timothy and Titus (anon.) 1636 (1661)
The unlovelinesse of love-lockes 1628
A vindication of Psalme cv. 15 from some false glosses lately obtruded on it by Royalists 1642 (1644)
Documents relating to the proceedings against William Prynne 1634–37 (Camden Soc. 1877)
—— & WALKER, Clement *A true and full relation of the prosecution, arraignment, tryall, etc. of N. Fiennes* 1644
Przipcovius' (S.) Dissertatio de pace, etc., or, a discourse touching the peace and concord of the Church (sometimes erron. ascribed to J. Hales) tr. 1653 (in Phenix 1708)
Psalmanazar. Memoirs of commonly known by the name of George Psalmanazar 1764
Psalter. Vespasian psalter c825 (The oldest English texts, E.E.T.S. 1885)
Anglo-Saxon psalter c1000 (Thorpe 1835; Grein)
— (Lambeth) c1000 (Lindelöf 1909)
— c1000 (Spelman, 1640)
The Cambridge psalter c1000 (Wildhagen 1910)
Metrical version of Psalms li–cl c1000 (Grein
Eadwine's Canterbury psalter c1150 (E.E.T.S. 1889)
An early English psalter a1300 (Surtees Soc. 1843–47; Hampole's Works II. 1896)
The earliest complete English prose psalter a 1325 (E.E.T.S. 1891)
The psalms of David in meeter. Allowed by the authority of the Generall Assembly of the Kirk of Scotland 1650
Psyche (subtitle varies) 1921–37
Psychiatry 1938–
Psychoanalytic review 1913–
Psychological bulletin 1904–
Psychological review 1894–
Public Ledger (Philadelphia) 1836–1934
Public opinion 1861–
Publications See under the names of particular institutions
Publishers' circular (title varies) 1837–1959
Publishers' weekly 1873–
Puck (New York) 1877–1918
PUCKLE, James *The club, or a dialogue between father and son* 1711
A new dialogue between a burgermaster and an English gentleman 1697
PUGH, Marshall *Last place left* 1969
A wilderness of monkeys 1958
PUGIN, Augustus W. N. *Glossary of ecclesiastical ornament and costume* 1844
PULGRAM, Ernst *Introduction to the spectography of speech* 1959
PULLEN, Henry W. *Modern christianity a civilized heathenism* (anon.) 1873 (1874)
PULLER, Timothy *The moderation of the Church of England* 1679 (1843)
PULMAN, George P. R. *Rustic sketches* 1842 (1853, 1871)
The Song of Solomon in the East Devonshire dialect 1860
Pulpit Popery 1688 *See* WILLIAMS, Bp. John
PULSFORD, John *Loyalty to Christ* 1890–93
Quiet hours 1857
PULTON, Ferdinando *An abstract of al penall statutes which be generall* 1577 (1581)
Punch, or the London Charivari 1840–
PUNNETT, Reginald Crundall *Mendelism* 1905 (and several later editions used)
PURCELL, Edmund S. *Life of Cardinal Manning* 1896
PURCELL, John *A treatise of the cholick* 1714
A treatise of vapours or hysteric fits 1702
PURCHAS, Samuel *Purchas his pilgrim. Microcosmus, or the historie of man* 1619
Pilgrimage 1613 (1614, 1617)
Pilgrimes 1625–26
PURCHAS, Samuel *A theatre of politicall flying-insects* 1657

Puritaine, The 1607 *See* S., W.
Purity (= *Cleanness*) See *Early English alliterative poems*
Purseglove, John William *Tropical crops: dicotyledons* 2 vols. 1968
Purser, Philip *The Holy Father's navy* 1971
The Twentymen 1967
Pursh, Frederick *Flora Americæ Septentrionalis* 1814
Purvey, John *Remonstrance against Romish corruptions in the Church* 1395 (1851)
Pusey, Edward B. *The Church of England a portion of Christ's one holy Catholic Church, and a means of restoring visible unity. An eirenicon.* (Part I) 1865
— *First letter to the very rev. J. H. Newman, D.D.* (*An eirenicon.* Part II) 1869
— *Is healthful reunion impossible? A second letter to the very rev. J. H. Newman* (*An eirenicon.* Part III) 1870
Daniel the prophet; nine lectures 1864
The doctrine of the real presence, as contained in the Fathers, vindicated 1855
An eirenicon: see above
An historical enquiry into the probable causes of the rationalist character lately predominant in the theology of Germany 1828–30
Lenten sermons, preached chiefly to young men at the Universities, between 1858–74 1874
A letter to the Archbishop of Canterbury, on some circumstances connected with the present crisis in the English Church 1842
The Minor Prophets with a commentary 1860
Our Pharisaism; a sermon 1868
Parochial sermons (*Sermons during the season from Advent to Whitsuntide*) 1848 (1852)
— vol. II. 1853
The real presence of the body and blood of our Lord Jesus Christ the doctrine of the English Church 1857
Life, by H. P. Liddon et al. (1893–97)
Putnam, Donald Fulton ed. *Canadian regions* 1952
Putnam, Samuel Whitehall tr. *E. da Cunha's Rebellion in the backlands* 1944
Putnam's Magazine 1868–70
Puttenham, George *The arte of English poesie* (anon.; generally attributed to Puttenham, but recently to Lord Lumley) 1589 (Arber 1869)
Puzo, Mario *Fools die* 1978
Pycraft, William Plane ed. *The standard natural history* 1931
Pycroft, James *Agony point* 1861 (1862)
The cricket field 1851
Ways and words of men of letters 1861
Pycroft, Samuel *A brief enquiry into free-thinking in matters of religion* 1713
Pye, Henry James *Naucratia; or naval dominion, a poem* 1798
Pye, John *Patronage of British art; an historical sketch* 1845
Pyke, Magnus Alfred *Food and society* 1968
Pyle, Thomas *Ninety-six sermons on plain and practical subjects* a1756 (1783–85)
Pym, Barbara Mary Crampton *No fond return of love* 1961
Quartet in autumn 1977
Some tame gazelle 1950
Pynchon, Thomas *The crying of Lot 49* 1966
Gravity's rainbow 1973
V.: a novel 1963
Pyne, William Henry *Wine and walnuts, or, after dinner chit-chat* 1820–22 (1823, 1824)
Pyper, John *Urfé's (Honoré d') History of Astrea* (anon.) tr. 1620

Q

'Q' (Sir Arthur T. Quiller-Couch) *The astonishing history of Troy town* 1888
Dead man's rock 1887
The delectable duchy 1893
I saw three ships, and other winter's tales 1892
The mayor of Troy 1906
Noughts and crosses 1891
Shining ferry 1905
The splendid spur 1889
ed. *The story of the sea* 2 vols. 1895–96
Wandering heath 1895
See also under real name
Quack's academy or the dunce's directory, The 1678 (Harl. Misc.)
Quain, Jonas *Elements of descriptive and practical anatomy* 1828 (1848, 1864–67)
Quain, Sir Richard ed. *A dictionary of medicine* 1882 (1894)
Quaker grandmother, A 1896 *See* Caffyn, Kathleen M.
Qualtrough, Edward F. *The boat-sailer's manual* 1886
Quarles, Francis *Complete works* a1644 (Grosart 1880–81)
Argalus and Parthenia 1629 (1678, 1708)
Barnabas See *Judgement*, below
Divine fancies 1632
Divine poems (the history of Jonah, Ester, Job, Sions sonets, Elegies etc.) 1630 (1714)
Emblemes 1635 (1718, 1818)
Enchyridion, containing institutions divine and morall 1640 (1641)
Esther See *Hadassa*, below
A feast for wormes, set forth in a poeme of the history of Jonah 1620
Hadassa, or the history of queene Ester, with meditations thereupon 1621 (1638, 1717)
The historie of Samson 1631
Job militant; with meditations 1624
Judgement and mercy for afflicted soules a1644 (1646)
— (part) *Barnabas and Boanerges, or wine and oyle for afflicted soules* 1644 (1807)
The loyall convert 1643
Pentelogia, or the quintessence of meditation 1620
The shepherds oracles delivered in certain eglogues a1644 (1646)
Sions elegies, wept by Jeremie the prophet and periphrased 1624
Sions sonets, sung by Solomon.. and periphras'd 1625
Solomons recantation entituled Ecclesiastes paraphrased a1644 (1645)
'Quarles, Francis' *The school of the heart* 1647 *See* Harvey, Christopher
Quarles, John *Fons lachrymarum, or a fountain of tears* 1648
Quarll, Philip 1727 *See* Dorrington, E.
Quarter sessions records 1605–1786 (North Riding Record Soc. 1884–92)
Quarterly cumulative index medicus 1927–56
Quarterly journal of the Geological Society of London, The 1845–
Quarterly journal of literature, science, and the arts 1817–27
Quarterly journal of medicine 1907–
Quarterly journal of microscopical science 1852–
Quarterly register 1886–1934
Quarterly review, The 1809–
Quarterly review of biology 1926–
'Quartermain, James' (James Broom Lynne) *Rock of diamond* 1972
Quatrefages de Bréau's (J. L. A. de) Human species tr. 1879
— *Rambles of a naturalist on the coasts of France, Spain and Sicily* tr. E. C. Otté 1857
'Queen, Ellery' (Frederic Dannay & Manfred Bennington Lee) *The four of hearts* 1938 (UK 1939)
The fourth side of the triangle 1965
The French powder mystery 1930
The Roman hat mystery 1929
Queen, The: an illustrated journal and review (title varies) 1861–1970
Queen's regulations and orders for the army, The 1844 (1860, 1868)
Quekett microscopical club, Journal 1868–
Quennell, Peter Courtney *The marble foot: an autobiography, 1905–1938* 1976
'Quentin, Patrick' (Richard Wilson Webb & Hugh Callingham Wheeler) *The follower* 1950
Puzzle for fiends 1946 (UK 1947)
Shadow of guilt 1959
Suspicious circumstances 1957
Quest of enquirie, by women to know, Whether the tripe-wife were trimmed by Doll yea or no. Gathered by Oliuer Oat-meale 1595 (Grosart 1881)
Questions. Five philosophical questions most eloquently and substantially disputed 1650 (1653)
Questions for a reformed parliament 1867
Questions of profitable and pleasant concernings ed. O. B. 1594
Quick, Herbert *Yellowstone nights* 1911
Quick, John *A serious inquiry.. whether a man may lawfully marry his deceased wife's sister* 1703
Quick, Robert H. *Essays on educational reformers* 1868
Quiller-couch, Arthur Thomas *Foe-Farrell* 1918
Hetty Wesley 1903
Major Vigoureux 1907
Nicky Nan, reservist 1915
On the art of writing 1916
Poison island 1907
Studies in literature 3 ser. 1918–29
True Tilda 1909
See also: 'Q'
Quin, Mr. James, comedian, The life of 1766 (1887)
Quincey, Thomas De *See* De Quincey
Quincy, John *The dispensatory of the Royal College of Physicians* 1721
Lexicon physico-medicum or a new physical dictionary 1719 (1722)
Pharmacopœia officinalis et extemporanea, or a compleat English dispensatory 1718
Quincy, Josiah *The history of Harvard University* 1840
Quincy, Josiah Phillips *Figures of the past* 1883 (1884)
Quincy Whig (Quincy, Illinois) 1838–1915 (title varies)
Quine, Willard Van Orman *From a logical point of view* 1953
Mathematical logic 1940
Methods of logic 1950 (UK 1952)
Set theory and its logic 1963
Word and object 1960
Quinland; or, Varieties in American life 2 vols. 1857
Quinn, Arthur Hobson *Pennsylvania stories* 1899
Quinn, Roger *The heather lintie; being poetical pieces.. chiefly in the Scottish dialect* 1861 (1863)
Quintessence. The book of quinte essence or the fifth being; that is to say, man's heaven 1460–70 (E.E.T.S. 1866, revised 1889)
Quinton, Anthony Meredith *The nature of things* 1973
Quirk, Charles Randolph *The use of English* 1962
—— & Smith, Albert Hugh eds. *The teaching of English* 1959
—— et al. *A grammar of contemporary English* 1972
See also Crystal, David
'Quiz' *The Grand master; or adventures of Qui Hi? in Hindostan* 1816

R

R., C(oun)t(e)ss of *See* Rosenberg
R., B. 1584 *See* Rich, B.
R., B. *A letter from a catholic gentleman to his popish friends now to be exil'd from London* 1678
R., C. C. '*Up for the season*' *and other songs of society* 1887 (1889)
R., D. 1633 *See* Rogers, D.
R., G. *Le Grand's (A.) Man without passion; or the wise stoick* tr. 1675
R., H. *News from the Levane seas* 1594
R., H. T. *See* Vidocq, E. F.
R., I. 1615 See *Trades increase*
R., I. *A lady's ranche life in Montana* 1887
R., J. 1658 *See* Rowland, J.
R., Maria 1792 *See* Riddell, M.
R. N. 1635 *See* N., R.
R., R. 1678 *See* Russel, R.
R., S. 1582, -85 *See* Robson, Simon
R., S. 1598 etc. *See* Rowlands, S.
R., S. (S. Rowley) *The noble souldier, a tragedy* 1634 (Bullen, Old plays I, 1882)
R., T. 1609 *See* Ravenscroft, T.
R., T. *A view of government in Europe* 1689
R.A.F. journal See *Royal Air Force journal*
R.A.F. news See *Royal Air Force news*
RCA review 1936–
'Rabelais, Robert' *A nineteenth century and familiar history of the lives, loves and misfortunes of Abeillard and Heloisa, a poem* 1819
Rabinowitch, Eugene Isakovich *Photosynthesis and related processes* 2 vols. (Vol. II in 2 parts) 1945–56
Rachel's secret (by Eliza Tabor) 1866
Rackham, Bernard tr. *E. Hannover's Pottery and porcelain* Vol. I 1925 (Vols. II & III, also 1925, tr. by W. W. Worster; whole work ed. by B. Rackham)
Radcliff, Thomas *A report on the agriculture of eastern and western Flanders* 1819
Radcliffe, Alexander *Bacchinalia cœlestia: a poem in praise of punch* 1680
Radcliffe, Mrs. Ann *Gaston de Blondeville, a romance* 1802 (1826)
The Italian, or the confessional of the black penitents, a romance 1797
The mysteries of Udolpho, a romance 1794
Posthumous works a1823 (1833)
The romance of the forest 1791
Raddall, Thomas Head *Hangman's beach* 1966
Radin, Paul tr. *J. Vendryès's Language* 1925
Radio communication handbook, The See *Amateur radio handbook*
Radio review: a monthly record of scientific progress in radiotelegraphy and telephony 1919–22
Radio times, The 1923–
Radiology 1923–
Rae, Hugh Crauford *A few small bones* 1968
The marksman 1971
The shooting gallery 1972
Rae, John *Contemporary socialism* 1884
Life of Adam Smith 1895
Rae, John *The custard boys* 1960
Rae, William F. *Newfoundland to Manitoba* 1881
Raffald, Mrs. Elizabeth *The experienced English housekeeper* 1769 (1778)
Raffé, Walter George *Dictionary of the dance* 1964
Raffles, Sir Thomas Stamford *The history of Java* 1817
Rafinesque Schmaltz, C. S. *New flora and botany of North America* 1836
Ragozin, Zenaide A. *The story of Chaldea* 1886 (1887)
Railroad and engineering journal 1887–92
Railway magazine 1897–
Railways of America, The. By various writers 1890
Rainbow, Bp. Edward *A (funeral) sermon* 1649
Labour forbidden and commanded (a sermon) 1634 (1635)
Raine, James *The history and antiquities of North-Durham* 1852
A memoir of the rev. J. Hodgson 1857–58
Raine, James *A brief memoir of Mr. Justice Rokeby* 1861 (Surtees Soc.)
'Raine, Richard' (Raymond Harold Sawkins) *Night of the hawk* 1968
Raine, William Macleod *Bucky O'Connor: a tale of the unfenced border* 1910 (UK 1920)
Troubled waters 1924
Rainolds, John *A defence of the judgment of the reformed churches* (against Bellarmine) a1607 (1610)
Ralegh, Sir Walter *Works* a1618 (1829)
Advice of a son See *Remains*, below
Arts of empire See *Cabinet-council*
The cabinet-council, containing the chief arts of empire and mysteries of state a1618 (1658)
The discoverie of the.. empyre of Guiana 1596 (Hakluyt, Voyages 1598; Hakluyt Soc. 1848)

The history of the world 1614 (1634, 1736)
Instructions to his sonne See Maxims, below
Introduction to a breviary of the history of England 1605 (1693)
The last fight of the 'Revenge' See Report, below
The life and death of Mahomet a1618 (1637)
Maxims of state, with instructions to his son and the sons advice to his aged father. Whereunto is added Observations touching trade and commerce a1618 (1651, 1656)
The prerogative of parliaments in England a1618 (1628)
The prince, or maxims of state a1618 (1642)
Remains, viz. Maxims of state, Advice to his son: his sons advice to his father, His sceptick, Observations concerning the causes of the magnificency and opulency of cities, Observations concerning trade and commerce, The prerogative of parliaments in England, Letters to divers persons of quality a1618 (1664)
A report of the truth of the fight about the Iles of Açores, this last sommer, betwixt the Reuenge..and an armada of the King of Spaine (page-heading The last fight of the Reuenge at sea) 1591 (Arber)
Sceptick or speculations, and Observations on the magnificency and opulency of cities, His seat of government, and letters a1618 (1651)
Tubus historicus: an historicall perspective; discovering all the empires and kingdomes of the world a1618 (1636)
A declaration of the demeanor and cariage of Sir W. Raleigh 1618
Raleigh, Walter Alexander R. Letters ed. Lady Raleigh 2 vols. 1926
— (new ed.) 2 vols. 1928
Shakespeare 1907
Raleigh's ghost. Sir W. Rawleighs ghost or Englands forewarner (by T. Scott) 1626 (Harl. Misc.)
Rawleigh his ghost or a feigned apparition to a friend of his, for the translating into English the boke of L. Lessius.. entituled De Providentia numinis tr. by A. B. 1631 (1651)
Ralfe, Charles H. Outlines of physiological chemistry 1873
Ralphson, J. See Raphson
Ramadge, Francis H. The curability of consumption 1850 (1861)
Rambling fuddle-caps, The (by E. Ward) 1709
Ramée, Louise de La See 'Ouida'
Ramesey, William Astrologia restaurata, or astrology restored 1653
Rampini, Charles J. G. Letters from Jamaica 1873
Ramsay, Allan Poems 1721, 1728 (Poetical works 1877)
Christ's kirk on the green (cantos ii and iii) 1715, 1718
A collection of Scots proverbs 1737 (1750, 1797)
ed. The ever-green, being a selection of Scots poems wrote by the ingenious before 1600 1724
The gentle shepherd, a Scots pastoral comedy 1725
ed. The tea-table miscellany, or a collection of Scots songs 1724 (1733)
Ramsay, Sir Andrew C. The physical geology and geography of Great Britain 1863 (1878)
Ramsay, Balcarres D. W. Rough recollections of military service and society 1882
Ramsay, David The history of South-Carolina 1809
Ramsay, Diana Descent into the dark 1975
A little murder music 1972
No cause to kill 1974
Ramsay, Edward B. Reminiscences of Scottish life and character 1858, 1861 (1870, 1874)
Ramsay, Edward P. Notes on the food fishes and edible mollusca of New South Wales 1883 (Fisheries exhibition literature)
Ramsay, Sir James H. ed. Bamff charters 1232–1703 1915
Ramsay, John Scotland and Scotsmen in the eighteenth century a1814 (1888)
Ramsay, Sir William Mitchell The church in the Roman empire before A.D. 170 1893
Ramsbotham, Francis H. The principles and practice of obstetric medicine and surgery 1841 (1856)
Ramsbottom, John Mushrooms and toadstools 1953
Ramsden, Evelyn tr. E. Gram & H. Weber's Plant diseases in orchard, nursery and garden crops 1952
Ramsey, Frederic & Smith, Charles Edward Jazzmen 1939 (UK 1940)
Ramsey, Leonard Gerald Gwynne ed. The Connoisseur new guide to antique English pottery, porcelain and glass 1961
Ramson, William Stanley Australian English: an historical study of the vocabulary, 1788–1898 1966
Rand, Austin Loomer Mammals of the eastern Rockies and western plains of Canada 1948
Rand, William Gassendi's (P.) Mirrour of true nobility.. being the life of N. C. Fabricius, lord of Peiresk tr. 1657
Rand Daily Mail (Johannesburg) 1902–
Randall, Henry S. The life of T. Jefferson 1858
Randall, John The semi-Virgilian husbandry, deduced from various experiments 1764
Randall-Diehl, Anna Two thousand words and their definitions; not in Webster's Dictionary 1888
Randolph, Mrs. Mostly fools 1886
Wild hyacinth 1875
Randolph, Bernard The present state of the islands in the archipelago 1686 (1687)
The present state of the Morea 1686
Randolph, George An enquiry into the medicinal virtues of Bath-water 1752
— of Bristol-water 1745 (1750)
Randolph, Thomas Aristippus, or the ioviall philosopher 1630
The jealous lovers, a comedie 1632 (1668)
Πλουτοφθαλμια πλουτογαμια, a pleasant comedie entitled Hey for honesty a1635 (1651)
Poems: with The muses looking-glasse; and Amyntas a1635 (1638)
— Poetical and dramatic works (1875)
Randolph Enterprise (Elkins, West Virginia) 1874–
Random recollections 1836 See Grant, James
Rands, William B. Chaucer's England, by 'Matthew Browne' 1869
Lilliput levee (anon.) 1864
Ranjitsinhji, Kumar Shri The Jubilee book of cricket 1897
Ranken, Alexander The history of France 1801–22
Ranken, William Poems on different subjects 1812
Rankine, William John Macquorn A manual of applied mechanics 1858
A manual of machinery and millwork 1869
A manual of the steam engine and other prime movers 1859
Miscellaneous scientific papers a1872 (1881)
Ransome, Arthur Michell Autobiography ed. R. Hart-Davis 1976
Great Northern? 1947
Secret water 1939
'Ransome, Stephen' (Frederick Clyde Davis) The deadly Miss Ashley 1950 (US ed. published under author's real name)
Without a trace 1962
Rao, G. Subba Indian words in English: a study in Indo-British cultural and linguistic relations 1954
Rape of Helen, The tr. (from Coluthus Thebæus) 1731
Raper, John Robert Genetics of sexuality in higher fungi 1966
Raphael, Chaim A feast of history: the drama of Passover through the ages 1972
Raphael, Frederic Michael The glittering prizes 1976
The limits of love 1960
Raphael, John E. Modern Rugby football 1918
Raphson, Joseph A mathematical dictionary 1702
Newton's (Sir I.) Universal arithmetick tr. 1720
Rare triumphs of love and fortune, The 1589 (Roxburghe Club 1851; Hazl. Dodsley)
Rashdall, Hastings The universities of Europe in the Middle ages 1895
Raspail's (F. V.) New system of organic chemistry tr. 1834
Rastell, John A new boke of purgatorye 1530
Of gentylnes and nobylyte; a dyaloge (anon.) ?1525
The pastyme of people, the cronycles of dyvers realmys 1529 (1811)
Rastell, John, S. J. A confutation of a sermon pronounced by Mr. Juell 1564
A treatise intitled Beware of M. Jewell 1566
Rastell, William The exposicions of the termes of the lawes of England a1565 (1567, 1579)
See also Termes de la ley
Ratcliffe, John Ashworth The physical principles of wireless 1929
Rates of the custome house bothe inwarde and outwarde, The 1545;
— (another ed.) 1583
The rates of marchandizes as they are set downe in the booke of rates for the custome..of poundage etc. 1608
— (another ed.) 1642
Rathbone, Julian Diamonds bid 1967
Joseph 1979
Kill cure 1975
Ratis raving, and other moral and religious pieces (Craft of deyng, Wisdom of Solomon etc.) a1500 (E.E.T.S. 1870)
Rattigan, Terence Mervyn The deep blue sea 1952
Flare path 1942
French without tears: a play 1937
Ross: a dramatic portrait 1960
While the sun shines 1944
Who is Sylvia? 1951
The Winslow boy 1946
Rattray, Robert Sutherland Ashanti 1923
Ratzel's (F.) History of mankind tr. 1895
Rauf Coilʒear. The taill of Rauf Coilyear c1475 (E.E.T.S. 1882; Sc. alliterative poems, S.T.S. 1897)
'Ravelin, Humphrey' See Proctor, G.
Raven, John J. The church bells of Cambridgeshire 1869
Raven, Simon Arthur Noël The survivors 1976
Ravenscroft, Thomas Deuteromelia; or the second part of musicks melodie by T. R. 1609
Melismata; musical phansies by T. R. 1611
Pammelia, musicks miscellanie 1609
The whole book of psalms, with hymnes etc. 1621
Raverat, Gwendolyn Mary Period piece: a Cambridge childhood 1952
Rawley, William ed. Bacon's (F.) History naturall and experimentall of life and death 1638 (1650)
Resuscitatio, or bringing into publick light severall pieces of the works hitherto sleeping..of F. Bacon, Viscount St. Albans, together with his lordship's life 1657 (1661)
Rawlings, Marjorie Kinnan The yearling 1938
Rawlins, Thomas Tunbridge Wells, a comedy (anon.) a1670 (1678)
Rawlinson, George The five great monarchies of the ancient eastern world 1862–67
History of ancient Egypt 1881
A manual of ancient history 1869
The origin of nations 1877
The religions of the ancient world 1882
Rawlinson, John The dove-like soule, a sermon 1618
Fishermen, fishers of men, a sermon 1609
Rawlinson, Richard Lenglet du Fresnoy's (N.) New method of studying history tr. 1728
Rawlinson, William Modern foundry operations and equipment 1928
Rawnsley, Hardwicke D. Life and nature at the English lakes 1899
Ray, Cyril ed. The compleat imbiber 1956–71
Merry England 1960
Ray, John An account of some errors and defects in our English alphabet 1691 (with Collection of words)
A collection of English proverbs 1670, 1678 (1768, 1855)
A collection of English words not generally used,..in two alphabetical catalogues, the one of such as are proper to the northern, the other to the southern counties. With catalogues of English birds and fishes: and an account of the preparing and refining such metals and minerals as are gotten in England 1674
— Second ed. augmented 1691
— ed. W. W. Skeat (E.D.S. 1874)
Correspondence 1659–1705 (Ray Soc. 1848)
Creation See Wisdom, below
Itineraries 1658–62 (Select Remains 1760: Ray Soc. 1846)
Miscellaneous discourses concerning the dissolution and changes of the world 1692
— Third ed. Three physico-theological discourses (1713, 1732)
Observations made in a journey through part of the Low-countries, Germany, Italy and France, with a catalogue of plants not native of England 1673
— (another ed.) Travels (1738)
Philosophical letters between Mr. Ray and several of his correspondents a1705 (1718)
Select remains a1705 (1760)
Synopsis methodica avium et piscium a1705 (1713)
Travels See Observations, above
ed. Willughby's (F.) De historia piscium 1686
Willughby's (F.) Ornithology tr. 1678
The wisdom of God manifested in the works of the creation 1691 (1692, 1701, 1704, 1777)
See also Rea, John
Ray Society Publications (1844–)
Rayleigh, John William (Strutt), 3rd Baron Scientific papers 1869–1919 (1899–)
The theory of sound 2 vols. 1877–8
Raymond, Ernest The jesting army 1930
Raymond, Henry Jarvis The life and public services of Abraham Lincoln 1865
Raymond, John An itinerary, contayning a voyage made through Italy 1646–47 (Il mercurio Italico) 1648
Raymond, Rossiter W. Glossary of mining and metallurgical terms 1881
Statistics of mines and mining in the states and territories west of the Rocky mountains 1870 (1872, 1874, 1877)
Raymond, Walter In the smoke of war 1893
Misterton's mistake 1888
Two men o' Mendip 1898
Raynalde, Thomas Roesslin's (E.) Byrth of mankynde, otherwyse called the womans booke tr. 1545 (1552, 1564)
Raynbird, William and Hugh On the agriculture of Suffolk 1849
Rayner, Dorothy Helen The stratigraphy of the British Isles 1967
'Rayner, Mrs. Olive P.' See Allen, Grant
Raynolds, John Dolarnys primerose 1606 (Grosart 1880)
Rayson, John Miscellaneous poems and ballads, chiefly in the dialects of Cumberland and the English and Scottish borders a1857 (1858)
Rea, John Flora, seu de florum cultura, or a complete florilege 1665 (1676)
Read, Alexander Works 1650 (1659)
The chirurgical lectures of tumors and ulcers 1632–34 1635
A treatise of the first part of chirurgerie 1638
Read, Herbert Edward Annals of innocence and experience 1940
Art and industry 1934
Art and society 1937
Collected poems, 1913–25 1926
A concise history of modern painting 1959
The contrary experience: autobiographies 1963
Education through art 1943
Icon and idea: the function of art in the development of human consciousness 1955
The meaning of art 1931
The tenth muse: essays in criticism 1957
Read, Herbert Harold & Watson, Janet V. Introduction to geology 2 vols. (Vol. II in 2 parts) 1962–75
Read, John Arcæus' (F.) Most excellent and compendious method of curing woundes tr. 1588
Read, John A text-book of organic chemistry 1926
Read, Piers Paul The Villa Golitsyn 1981
Reade, Charles Christie Johnstone 1853
The cloister and the hearth 1861
The course of true love never did run smooth 1857
The eighth commandment 1860
Griffith Gaunt; or jealousy 1866 (1867)
Hard cash 1863
'It is never too late to mend' 1856
'Love me little, love me long' 1859
Peg Woffington 1852 (1853)
Put yourself in his place 1870
A simpleton: a story of a day 1873
A woman-hater 1877
Reade, Thomas M. The origin of mountain ranges considered 1886
Reade, William Winwood Liberty hall, Oxon 1860
Reader, The; a review of literature etc. 1863–66
Reader's digest 1922–

Reader's digest family guide to the law 1971
Reading, The churchwardens' accounts of St. Mary's, 1550–1662 (1893).
See also *Churchwardens*
Real estate review 1923–
Reall and unfeigned testimonie concerning Iacob Beme, A tr. 1649
Realm (newspaper), *The* 1864
REANEY, Percy Hide *The origin of English place-names* 1960
Reasons of the new convert's taking the oaths to the present government, The (by T. Brown) 1691
Recent progress in hormone research 1947–
RECORD, Samuel James & HESS, Robert William *Timbers of the New World* 1943
—— & MELL, Clayton Dissinger *Timbers of tropical America* 1924
RECORDE, Robert *The castle of knowledge* (containing the explication of the sphere, etc.) 1556
The ground of artes, teachyng the worke and practise of arithmetike 1540 (1542, 1575)
— with additions by J. Dee & J. Mellis (1582, 1590; also 1646)
The pathway to knowledge 1551
The urinal of physick 1547 (1548, 1567, 1665)
The whetstone of witte, which is the seconde parte of arithmetike 1557
Records of the colony of Rhode Island and Providence Plantations in New England 1636–1792 (1856–65)
Records of the convention of the royal burghs of Scotland 1295–1738 (1870–90)
Records of the Court of Assistants of the colony of Massachusetts Bay 1673–92 (1901)
Records of the governor and company of the Massachusetts Bay in New England 1628–86 (1853–54)
Records of St. Mary at Hill. Medieval records of a London city church (St. Mary at Hill) 1420–1559 (E.E.T.S. 1905)
Records of a Scottish cloth manufactory at New Mills, Haddingtonshire, The 1681–1703 (S.H.S. 1905)
Recreations of a country parson 1859–61 *See* BOYD, A. K. H.
Recruiter's bulletin (U.S. Marine Corps) 1915–21
Red book of the exchequer, The v.d. (Rolls series 1896)
Red Cross magazine 1916–20
Redbook (title varies) 1903–
REDDING, Cyrus *A history and description of modern wines* 1833 (1851)
REDE, Leman Thomas *The road to the stage* 1827
REDFIELD, Robert *Peasant society and culture: an anthropological approach to civilisation* 1956
REDFORD, George *Holy scripture verified* 1837
REDFORD, John *The moral play of wit and science c*1530 (Shaks. Soc. 1848; Manly, Pre-Shaks. drama 1897)
REECE, Gordon tr. *F. Hund's The history of quantum theory* 1974
REECE, Richard *A practical dictionary of domestic medicine* 1808
REECE, Robert H. *Night bombing with the Bedouins* 1919
REED, Sir Edward J. *Shipbuilding in iron and steel* 1869
A treatise on the stability of ships 1885
REED, Henry *Lectures on the British poets a*1854 (1857)
*Lectures on English history and tragic poetry a*1854 (1856)
*Lectures on English literature a*1854 (1855)
REES, Abraham *The cyclopædia or universal dictionary of arts* etc. 1802–20
REES, J. Rogers *The diversions of a book-worm* 1886
REESE, John Terence & DORMER, Albert *The bridge player's dictionary* 1959
REEVE, Clara *The exiles: or memoirs of the Count de Cronstadt* 1788
The old English baron: a Gothic story 1778 (1780)
REEVE, Henry *De Tocqueville's (A. de) Democracy in America* tr. 1835
REEVE, Lovell *Elements of conchology* 1860
See also JEPHSON, J. M.
REEVE, Thomas *God's plea for Nineveh, or Londons precedent for mercy* 1657
Sermons 1632
REEVES, Edward *Homeward bound after thirty years, a colonist's impressions of New Zealand, Australia, Tangier and Spain* 1892
REEVES, William *Fourteen sermons a*1726 (1729)
REEVES, Bp. William *Ecclesiastical antiquities of Down, Connor and Dromore* 1847
Referee, The 1877–1928
Reflections on a late libel, intituled Observations on a late famous sermon (by E. Hickeringill) *intituled Curse ye Meroz* 1680
Reflections upon R. Baxter 1685 *See* MORE, Henry
Reflector, The; a quarterly magazine 1810–11
Reflexions. Morvan de Bellegarde's (J. B.) Reflexions upon ridicule tr. 1706–07
Reflexions upon the oathes of supremacy and allegiance (by H. P. Cressy) 1661
Reformed common-wealth of bees, The 1655 *See* HARTLIB, S.
Refutation of a late pamphlet 1749 See *Examination*
Regal rambler, The, or the eccentricall adventures of the devil in London (by T. Hastings) 1793
Regiam majestatem See SKENE, Sir J.
Register of debates in Congress See: United States. Congress. Debates
Register of the guild of Corpus Christi, York, The v.d. (Surtees Soc. 1872)
Register of the Privy council of Scotland, The 1545– (1877–)
Registrum cartarum ecclesie sancti Egidii de Edinburgh 1344–1567 (App. –1648) (Bannatyne Club 1859)
Registrum magni sigilli regum Scotorum 1306–1424 (1814, 1912)
— *The register of the great seal of Scotland* 1424– (1882–)
Registrum secreti sigilli regum Scotorum, The register of the privy seal of Scotland 1488–1529 (1908)
Regulation and improvement of free-thinking, An essay for the better 1739
Regulations and instructions relating to his majesty's service at sea 1730 (1772)
Regulations and orders for the army, General 1811
Regulations for the instruction . . of the cavalry 1833
REICHENBACH, Hans *Elements of symbolic logic* 1947
REID, Alan *Songs o' the heatherland, Scots poems* etc. 1894
REID, Andrew *Macquer's (P. J.) Elements of the theory and practice of chymistry* tr. 1758
REID, John *The Scots gard'ner* 1683 (1721)
REID, John Cowie ed. *The Kiwi laughs: an anthology of New Zealand prose humour* 1961
REID, John Morrison ed. *Doomed religions: a series of essays on the great religions of the world* 1884
REID, Mayne *The headless horseman: a strange tale of Texas* 2 vols. & 1 vol. 1866
The rifle rangers; or adventures of an officer in southern Mexico 1850
The scalp-hunters, or romantic adventures in northern Mexico 1851
The war-trail, or the hunt of the wild horse 1857
The young voyageurs 1854
REID, Robert *Glasgow past and present* 1884
REID, Robert *Poems, songs and sonnets* 1894
REID, Thomas *Works a*1796 (1846–63)
A brief account (Analysis) *of Aristotle's Logic* 1774
Essays on the intellectual powers of man 1785
An inquiry into the human mind 1764
REID, Sir T. Wemyss *Life of W. E. Forster* 1888
REIFER, Mary *A dictionary of new words* 1955
REIN, Johann Justus *Japan: travels and researches* [anon. tr.] 1884
REINNEL, F. *The carpenters', joiners', cabinet makers' and gilders' companion* 1854
REISNER, Robert George *The jazz titans; including 'The parlance of hip'* 1960
REISZ, Karel *The technique of film editing* 1953
— (ed. 9) 1961
REITH, John Charles Walsham *The Reith diaries* ed. C. Stuart 1975
Relation of the dreadful earthquake . . at Lima, A true and particular tr. 1748
Relation of the tryall . . of Ann Foster . . at Northampton, A full and true 1674 (1881)
Release and resettlement: an explanation of your position and rights Issued by H.M. Government to all serving members of H.M. Forces 1945
Religio clerici (Eng.) 1681
Religion of the fashionable world 1790 *See* MORE, Hannah
Religionism, or popular preachers, alias pulpiteers, a satire 1812
Religious pieces in prose and verse. Ed. from Thornton's MS. *a*1400 (E.E.T.S. 1867, revised 1889, 1914)
*Religious songs a*1300 (with Owl and nightingale, ed. T. Wright, Percy Soc. 1843)
Religious systems of the world, national, christian, philosophic 1888–89 (1890)
Reliquary, The; a depository for precious relics 1860–94
Reliquiæ antiquæ: scraps from ancient manuscripts ed. T. Wright & J. O. Halliwell 1841–43
Reliquiæ Wottonianæ (1651) *See* WOTTON, Sir H.
RELPH, Josiah *A miscellany of poems a*1743 (1747, 1797)
RELTON, Francis B. *An account of the fire insurance companies* 1893
Remarks on Mr. Clark's (Samuel Clarke) *sermons preached against Hobbs, Spinoza and other atheists* 1705
Remarques on the humours and conversations of the town 1673
Rembrun See *Guy of Warwick*
Remedy. A speciall remedie against the furious force of lawlesse loue, by W. A. 1579 (Roxb. Club 1844)
Remedy for sedition, A 1536
*Remedy of love, The c*1532 (Thynne, Chaucer 1532; Chalmers, Poets I. 1810)
Remonstrance 1395 *See* PURVEY, J.
Remonstrance concerning the present troubles, A. From the meeting of the estates of . . Scotland unto the parliament of England 1640
Remonstrance of divers remarkeable passages concerning the church and kingdome of Ireland, A 1642
REMSEN, Ira *An introduction to the study of the compounds of carbon, organic chemistry* 1885
Renan's (J. Ernest) Apostles tr. 1869 (1890)
— *The book of Job* tr. 1889
— *History of the people of Israel* tr. 1888
— *The life of Jesus* tr. 1863 (1864)
RENDELL, Ruth *A guilty thing surprised* 1970
Make death love me 1979
A new lease of death 1967
One across, two down 1971
Some lie and some die 1973
RENNELL, James *Memoir of a map of Hindoostan* 1783
RENNIE (——) *St. Patrick, a national tale. By an antiquary* 1819
RENNIE, George Banks, and others *General view of the agriculture of the West Riding of Yorkshire* 1794 (1799)
RENNIE, James *Alphabet of scientific angling* 1833
A conspectus of the butterflies and moths found in Britain 1832
Insect architecture (anon.) 1830 (1847)
ed. *Montagu's (G.) Ornithological dictionary* 1831 (1833)
Rental book of the Cistercian abbey of Cupar-Angus v.d. (1879–80)
Rentalia et custumaria M. de Ambresbury 1235–52 et R. de Ford 1252–61 abbatum monasterii beatae Mariae Glastoniae v.d. (Somerset Record Soc. 1891)
Reply to a paper of Dr. R. Sanderson containing a censure of A. A(scham) his booke 1650
Reply to the reasons of the Oxford clergy against addressing, A 1687
Report . . Indian affairs See: United States *Report of the Commissioner of Indian Affairs*
Report of a discourse concerning supreme power in affaires of religion, A (by Sir J. Hayward) 1606
Report of the Committee of Inquiry on Decimal Currency See: United Kingdom. Parliamentary papers
Report of the Committee on Broadcasting 1960 See: United Kingdom. Parliamentary papers
Report of the proceedings and opinions of the board of general officers on their examination into the conduct . . of Sir John Cope 1749
Report of the United States Commissioner of agriculture 1868 (1869)
Report to the government of the United States on the munitions of war (at the Paris exhibition 1867) *by C. B. Norton and W. J. Valentine* 1868
Report to the House of representatives on precious metals in the United States 1882
Reporter: the magazine of facts and ideas (New York) 1949–
Reports of artisans selected by . . The Society of arts to visit the Paris universal exhibition 1867
Reports of the Deputy keeper of the public records 1840–
Reports of the royal commission on historical manuscripts 1870–
Repository of arts, etc., The 1809–28
Reprobate, The; a novel tr. (from A. H. J. La Fontaine) 1802
Republican Review (Albuquerque, New Mexico) 1870–3
RERESBY, Sir John *Memoirs a*1689 (1734)
Residence in France during the years 1792–95, A 1797
Respublica, A merye enterlude entitled 1553 (E.E.T.S. 1905; Brandl 1898)
Retrospective review, The 1820–28
— (another) 1852–54
Return to the attack: with the New Zealand Division in North Africa (Army Board, N.Z.) 1944
Returne from Parnassus, The 1597 (Macray 1886)
Returne from Pernassus, The (part II): *or the scourge of simony* 1601 (Arber; Macray 1886)
*Revelation to the monk of Evesham, The c*1482 (Arber)
REVELL, William F. *Ethical forecasts: essays* 1887
Revels. Extracts from the accounts of the revels at court in the reigns of queen Elizabeth and king James I (Shaks. Soc. 1842)
Reveries of a recluse, The 1824
Review of the affairs of France etc., A 1704–12
Review of the British pharmacopœia (repr. from 'The chemist and druggist') 1898
Review of the churches, The 1891–95
Review of English studies 1925–
Review of reviews, The 1890–
Review of scientific instruments 1930–
Reynard, John (1608) *See* MUNDAY, A.
Reynard the fox, The history of 1481 *See* CAXTON, W.
REYNER, Edward *Rules for the government of the tongue* 1656
REYNOLDS, Bp. Edward *Works* v.d. (1658)
Israels petition in time of trouble (a sermon) 1642
Israels prayer in time of trouble, . . an explication of the fourteenth chapter . . of Hosea 1645 (1649)
The rich mans charge (a sermon) 1658
A sermon (at Westminster) 1666
A sermon touching the peace . . of the church 1637 (1638)
The shieldes of the earth: a sermon . . preached . . 1634 (1636)
A treatise of the passions and faculties of the soul 1640 (1658)
REYNOLDS, Henry R. *John the baptist* 1874
REYNOLDS, John *The flower of fidelitie* 1650
The triumphes of Gods revenge against . . murther 1621–24 (1622–29)
REYNOLDS, John *Death's vision represented in a philosophical sacred poem* (anon.) 1687 (1713)
REYNOLDS, John *The pioneer history of Illinois, 1673–1818* 1852
REYNOLDS, John Hamilton *The fancy: a selection from the poetical remains of Peter Corcoran* 1820 (1906)
REYNOLDS, John Russell *The diagnosis of diseases of the brain* 1855
REYNOLDS, Sir Joshua *Works a*1792 (1797)
Discourses delivered to the students of the Royal academy 1769–90 (1846, 1876)
Du Fresnoy's (C. A.) Art of painting tr. W. Mason . . with annotations by Sir J. Reynolds 1782 (1783)
REYNOLDS, Mack (Dallas McCord Reynolds) *After some tomorrow* 1967
REYNOLDS, Michael *Engine-driving life* 1881
Locomotive-engine driving 1877
Rheims. The new testament, tr. in the English college of Rhemes 1582
Rhode Island Historical Society *Collections* 1827–1941
Rhode Island See *Records*
RHODES, Hugh *The boke of nurture or schoole of good maners c*1530 (Babees book, E.E.T.S. 1868)
RHODES, William B. *Bombastes furioso, a burlesque tragic opera* 1810 (1830)
'RHOSCOMYL, Owen' (O. Vaughan) *For the white rose of Arno* 1897
Rhymers' Club, The Book of the 1892, 1894

RHYS, Jean *Voyage in the dark* 1934
Wide Sargasso Sea 1966
RHYS, Sir John *Early Britain. Celtic Britain* 1882
Lectures on the origin and growth of religion as illustrated by Celtic heathendom (The Hibbert lectures 1886) 1888
Lectures on Welsh philology 1877
RHYS, Udal ap *An account of.. places and curiosities in Spain and Portugal* 1749
Ribot's (T. A.) English psychology tr. 1873
— *The psychology of the emotions* tr. 1897
RIBTON-TURNER, Charles J. *A history of vagrants and vagrancy* 1887
RICARDO, David *On the principles of political economy and taxation* 1817
Ricardus Aristarchus Of the hero of the poem (by Bp. Warburton) 1742 (in Pope, Dunciad 1743)
Riccoboni's (L.) Historical.. account of the theatres in Europe tr. 1741
RICE, Clara Mabel *Dictionary of geological terms* 1940
RICE, David Talbot *English art, 871–1100* 1952
RICE, Elmer Leopold *A voyage to Purilia* 1930
RICE, James *History of the British turf* 1879
See also BESANT, Sir W.
RICE, Richard *An invective againste vices taken for vertue* 1579
RICH, Barnaby *Allarme to England* 1578
The famous history of Herodotus tr. B. R. 1584
His farewell to militarie profession 1581
— repr. as *Eight novels employed by English dramatic poets* (Shaks. Soc. 1846)
— *Phylotus and Emelia* (from the Farewell) 1581 (Bannatyne Club 1835)
Faultes faults, and nothing else but faultes 1606
Greenes news both from heaven and hell 1593
The honestie of this age 1614 (1615; Percy Soc. 1844)
The Irish hubbub, or the English hue and crie 1617
RICH, Jack C. *The materials and methods of sculpture* 1947
Rich cabinet furnished with varietie of excellent descriptions etc., The (Epitome signed T. G., i.e. Thomas Gainsford) 1616
Richard III, king of England *Letters and papers illustrative of the reigns of Richard III and Henry VII* (Rolls series 1861–63)
Richard Coer de lion 13.. (in Weber, Metrical romances II, 1810)
Richard the redeles See LANGLAND, W.
RICHARDS, Frank James *Old-soldier sahib* 1936
RICHARDS, Ivor Armstrong *Practical criticism: a study of literary judgment* 1929
Principles of literary criticism 1925
See also OGDEN, Charles Kay
RICHARDS, John *A treatise on the construction and operation of wood-working machines* (= Operator's handbook) 1873
RICHARDS, Owain Westmacott & DAVIES, R. G. eds. *A. D. Imms's A general textbook of entomology* (ed. 9) 1957
RICHARDS, Paul Westmacott *The tropical rain forest: an ecological study* 1952
RICHARDS, Richard Kohler *Arithmetic operations in digital computers* 1955
RICHARDS, William *The history of Lynn* 1812
RICHARDSON, Alan ed. *A dictionary of Christian theology* 1969
RICHARDSON, Albert D. *Beyond the Mississippi* 1867
RICHARDSON, Sir Benjamin W. *Diseases of modern life* 1876
RICHARDSON, Charles *A new dictionary of the English language* 1836–37, Suppl. 1856
RICHARDSON, David L. *Sonnets and other poems* 1825
RICHARDSON, Edward Gick *Sound: a physical text-book* 1927
RICHARDSON, G. B. *Marryat's (F.) Universal code of signals for the mercantile marine of all nations* 1854 (ed. 12)
RICHARDSON, George Fleming *Geology for beginners* 1842
— *An introduction to geology* (1851)
'RICHARDSON, Henry Handel' (Edith Florence Lindesay Robertson) *The fortunes of Richard Mahony* 1917
RICHARDSON, James *Travels in the great desert of Sahara* 1848
RICHARDSON, Bp. John *Choice observations.. upon the Old Testament* a1654 (1655)
RICHARDSON, John *A dictionary, Persian, Arabic, and English* 2 vols. 1777–80
A dissertation on the languages, literature, and manners of eastern nations 1777
RICHARDSON, John *Movements of the British legion; with strictures on the course of conduct pursued by Lieut.-general Evans* 1837 (ed. 2)
RICHARDSON, Sir John *Fauna boreali-americana; or the zoology of the northern parts of British America* 1829–37
—— et al. *The museum of natural history* 1859–62 (1868)
RICHARDSON, Jonathan, elder and younger *An account of some of the statues etc. in Italy* 1722
Explanatory notes and remarks on Milton's Paradise lost 1734
RICHARDSON, Joseph *The fugitive, a comedy* 1792
RICHARDSON, Moses A. *The local historian's table book of remarkable occurrences etc. Historical division. Legendary division* 1841–46
— reissued as *The borderer's table book* 1846
RICHARDSON, Samuel *A discourse of the torments of hell* (anon.) 1658 (Phenix 1708)
RICHARDSON, Samuel *Clarissa (Harlowe); or the history of a young lady* 1747–48 (1768, 1811)
Correspondence a1761 (1804)
De Foe's Tour thro'.. Great Britain. Ed. with additions 1742
The history of Sir Charles Grandison 1753–54 (1783)
Pamela; or virtue rewarded 1739–40 (1824)
RICHARDSON, Thomas *Mercantile marine architecture* 1833
RICHARDSON, Thomas & WATTS, H. *Knapp's (Fr. C.) Chemical technology* 1863–67
RICHARDSON, W. *The chemical principles of the metallic arts* 1790
RICHARDSON, W. *Tasmanian poems; grave and gay* 1867
RICHARDSON, William *Poems and plays* 1805
RICHERS, Thomas *The history of the royal genealogy of Spain* tr. 1724
RICHLER, Mordecai *Cocksure* 1968
Richmond, Wills and inventories from the registry of the archdeaconry of v.d. (Surtees Soc. 1853)
RICHMOND, William *Christian economics* 1888
Richmond Enquirer (Richmond, Virginia) 1804–77
Richmond News-Leader (Richmond, Virginia) 1903–
Richmond Times-Dispatch (Richmond, Virginia) 1903–
Richmond Whig (Richmond, Virginia) 1824–88 (title varies)
Richmond-Atkinson papers, The ed. G. H. Scholefield 2 vols. 1960
RICHTER, George Holmes *Textbook of organic chemistry* 1938
RICHTER, Gisela M. A. & MILNE, Marjorie J. *Shapes and names of Athenian vases* 1935
RICKABY, Joseph *Moral philosophy; or ethics and natural law* 1888
RICKERT, Edith *The beggar in the heart* 1909
The golden hawk 1907
The reaper 1904
RICKERT, Margaret *Painting in Britain: the Middle Ages* 1954
RICKMAN, Eric *Come racing with me* 1951
RICKMAN, Thomas *An attempt to discriminate the styles of English architecture* 1817 (1848, 1862)
RIDDELL, Henry Scott *Poems, songs, and miscellaneous pieces* 1847
Poetical works a1870 (1871)
Songs of the ark, with other poems 1831
RIDDELL, Mrs. J. H. *Above suspicion* 1876
Austin Friars, a novel 1870
City and suburb 1861
Daisies and buttercups 1882
Princess Sunshine and other stories 1889
Too much alone 1860
The senior partner 3 vols. 1881
The world in the church 1863
RIDDELL, Maria *Voyages to the Madeira and Leeward Caribbean isles* 1792
Riddles a1000 (Grein 1897)
RIDER, Henry *All the odes and epodes of Horace* tr. 1638
RIDER, Bp. John *Bibliotheca scholastica: a double dictionarie Part I. English and Latin* 1589
— *R.'s Dictionarie corrected.. by F. Holyoke* 1606 (1617, 1649)
RIDGE, William Pett *Affectionate regards* 1929
Mord Em'ly 1898
RIDGEWAY, William *The early age of Greece* 1901
The origin and influence of the thoroughbred horse 1905
RIDGLEY, J. 1656 *See* SMITH, John
RIDLEY, Cecilia Anne *Cecilia: the life and letters of Cecilia Ridley, 1819–1845* ed. Viscountess Ridley 1958
RIDLEY, Mark *A short treatise of magneticall bodies and motions* 1613
RIDLEY, Bp. Nicholas *Works* a1555 (Parker Soc. 1841)
A breef declaration of the Lords supper a1555 (1586)
A piteous lamentation of the miserable estate of the churche a1555 (1566)
RIDPATH, George *Craig's (Sir T.) Scotland's soveraignty asserted* tr. 1695
RIDPATH, John C. *History of the United States* 1874
RIEGER, Rigomar, MICHAELIS, A., & GREEN, M. M. *A glossary of genetics and cytogenetics, classical and molecular* 1968
RIESENBERG, Felix *Golden Gate: the story of San Francisco harbour* 1940
RIESMAN, David *Individualism reconsidered, and other essays* 1954
——, DENNEY, R. N., & GLAZER, N. *The lonely crowd: a study of the changing American character* 1950
RIGAUD, Stephen P. *Correspondence of scientific men of the seventeenth century* (selected by S. P. Rigaud and ed. by S. J. Rigaud 1841)
Rigging and seamanship, The elements and practice of 1794
RIHBANY, Abraham M. *The Syrian Christ* 1919
RIIS, Jacob August *How the other half lives: studies among the tenements of New York* 1890 (UK 1891)
RIKER, Thad. W. *Henry Fox, first Lord Holland* 1911
RILEY, H. H. *Puddleford and its people* 1854
RILEY, Henry T. *Liber albus.. of the city of London* (1419) tr. 1861
Memorials of London and London life in the xiiith, xivth, and xvth centuries (1270–1419) 1868
See also *Pliny*
RILEY, J. Athelstan L. *Athos; or the mountain of the monks* 1887
RIMBAULT, Edward F. *First book of the pianoforte* 1848
RIMMER, Alfred *Our old country towns* 1881
RIMMER, Robert Henry *The Premar experiments* 1975 (UK 1976)
RINGWALT, John Luther ed. *American encyclopædia of printing* 1871
RIORDAN, John *Stochastic service systems* 1962
RIPLEY, George *The compound of alchymy* 1471 (in Ashmole, Theatrum chemicum Brit. 1652)
RIPLEY, George & DANA, C. A. ed. *The new American cyclopædia* 1858–63
RIPLEY, James *Select original letters on various subjects* 1781
Ripon, Yorkshire. *Acts of chapter of the collegiate church of SS. Peter and Wilfrid, Ripon* 1452–1506 (Surtees Soc. 1875)
Memorials of the church of SS. Peter and Wilfrid, Ripon v.d. (Surtees Soc. 1882–1908)
RISDON, Tristram *The chorographical description or survey of.. Devon* c1630 (1714, 1811)
'RITA' (Eliza M. J. von Booth, Mrs. D. Humphreys) *My Lady Coquette* 1881
Vivienne 1877
RITCHIE, Adam I. *The churches of Saint Baldred* 1880
RITCHIE, Anna & RITCHIE, Graham *The ancient monuments of Orkney* 1978
RITCHIE, Anne Isabella, Lady Ritchie *A book of sibyls* 1883
Letters, with forty-two additional letters from W. M. Thackeray ed. H. Ritchie 1924
Mrs. Dymond 1885
Records of Tennyson, Ruskin, and Browning 1892
RITCHIE, James Ewing *The night side of London* 1857
RITCHIE, Leitch *Wanderings by the Loire* 1833
Wanderings by the Seine 1834
Rites of Durham See *Durham*
RITSON, Joseph ed. *Ancient Engleish metrical romanceës* 1802
ed. *Ancient songs* 1790 (1792)
— *Ancient songs and ballads* (1829, 1877)
ed. *Pieces of ancient popular poetry* 1791
ed. *Robin Hood; a collection of all ancient poems, songs and ballads now extant relative to that celebrated outlaw* 1795 (1884)
ed. *Scotish songs* 1794
ed. *A select collection of English songs* 1783 (1813)
RITTENHOUSE, Isabella Maud *Maud* ed. R. L. Strout 1939
Rituale ecclesiæ Dunelmensis (Latin and Anglo-Saxon) c1000 (Surtees Soc. 1839)
RIVERS, Anthony Wydeville, Earl *The dictes or sayenges of the philosophres* 1477 (Caxton; repr. 1877)
RIVERS, Thomas *The rose amateur's guide* 1837 (1877)
RIVERS, William Halse R. *Kinship and social organisation* 1914
Riverside natural history, The See KINGSLEY, J. S.
RIVES, Amélie *The quick or the dead?* 1888 (1889)
World's-end 1914
'RIVETUS, Andreas Jr.' *See* MARVELL, A.
RIVIERE, Joan tr. *S. Freud's Introductory lectures on psycho-analysis* 1922
—— et al. tr. *S. Freud's Collected papers* 5 vols. 1924–50
Rob Stene's dream, a poem 1591 (Maitland Club 1836)
ROBARTES, Foulke *Gods holy house and service* 1639
The revenue of the gospel is tythes 1613
ROBB, Frank *Sea hunters* 1953
ROBB, John S. *Streaks of squatter life and far-west scenes* 1847
ROBBERDS, John W. *A memoir of the life and writings of W. Taylor of Norwich, containing his correspondence with Southey* etc. 1843
ROBERT OF BRUNNE *See* BRUNNE
ROBERT OF GLOUCESTER *Metrical chronicle* 1297 (Hearne 1724; Rolls series 1887)
— later texts v.d. (Rolls series 1887, Appendix)
Robert of Sicily (Roberd of Cisyle) c1370 (Halliwell, Nugæ poeticæ 1844; Hazlitt, Early popular poetry 1864; Nuck 1887)
Robert the devil. Roberte the devyll, a metrical romance 1480 (1798; Hazlitt, Early popular poetry 1864)
The lyfe of.. Robert the devyll (prose) c1510 (Thoms, Early prose romances 1828)
ROBERTS, A. *The adventures of Mr. T. S. an English merchant* 1670
ROBERTS, Alexander *A treatise of witchcraft* 1616
ROBERTS, Cecil *Adrift in America* 1891
ROBERTS, E. M. *A flying fighter: an American above the lines in France* 1918
ROBERTS, Elizabeth Madox *The time of man* 1926 (UK 1927)
ROBERTS, Francis *Clavis Bibliorum, the key of the Bible, unlocking the richest treasury of the holy scriptures* 1649
ROBERTS, Frederick T. *A handbook of the theory and practice of medicine* 1873 (1877)
ROBERTS, Geoffrey Keith *A dictionary of political analysis* 1971
ROBERTS, George *The four years' voyages of Capt. G. Roberts* 1726
ROBERTS, Hermese E. *The third ear* 1970
ROBERTS, J. 1719 See *Spinster*
ROBERTS, John *The complete cannoniere: or the gunners guide* 1639 (1672)
ROBERTS, John *On billiards* ed. H. Buck 1869 (1870)
ROBERTS, John D., STEWART, R., & CASERIO, M. C. *Organic chemistry* 1971
ROBERTS, Margaret *Madame Fontenoy* 1864
Mademoiselle Mori: a tale of modern Rome 1860
ROBERTS, Morley *Salt of the sea* 1903 (1913)
ROBERTS, Nesta *The face of France* 1976
ROBERTS, Orlando W. *Narrative of voyages and excursions on the east coast and in the interiors of Central America* 1827
ROBERTS, Peter *The Cambrian popular antiquities* 1815
ROBERTS, Sir Randal H. *In the shires; a sporting novel* 1887
ROBERTS, Thomas *The English bowman, or tracts on archery* 1801
ROBERTS, William *An account of the first discovery and natural history of Florida* 1763
ROBERTS, William *The looker-on; a periodical publication by the rev. Simon Olive-Branch* 1792–94

ROBERTS, William *Memoirs of the life and correspondence of Mrs. Hannah More* 1834 (1835)
ROBERTS, Sir William *A practical treatise on urinary and renal diseases* 1865 (1885)
ROBERTS, William H. *Poems* 1774
ROBERTS, William W. *The pontifical decrees against the doctrine of the earth's movement, and the Ultramontane defence of them* 1885
ROBERTS-AUSTIN, Sir William C. *Introductory lecture to the course of metallurgy at the Royal school of mines* 1880
ROBERTSON, Alexander *Fra Paolo Sarpi* 1893 (1894)
The Roman catholic church in Italy 1903
ROBERTSON, Andrew *Nuggets in the Devil's punch bowl and other Australian tales* 1894
ROBERTSON, E. Arnot (Eileen Arbuthnot Robertson) *Ordinary families* 1933
ROBERTSON, E. William *Historical essays in connexion with the land, the church* etc. 1872
ROBERTSON, Edith Thom & GOODING, Evelyn Graham B. *Botany for the Caribbean* 1963
ROBERTSON, Frederick W. *Expository lectures on St. Paul's epistles to the Corinthians* a1853 (1859)
Lectures and addresses on literary and social topics a1853 (1858)
Sermons 1848–53 (1855–63)
ROBERTSON, George *General view of the agriculture of Kincardineshire* 1813
— *of Midlothian* 1793
ROBERTSON, Sir George S. *Chitrál: the story of a minor siege* 1898
ROBERTSON, J. Drummond *A glossary of dialect and archaic words used in the county of Gloucester* 1889 (E.D.S. 1890)
ROBERTSON, James *General view of the agriculture in the county of Perth* 1799
ROBERTSON, James *Old truths and modern speculations* 1859 (1860)
ROBERTSON, Joseph *Lives of Scottish poets* (anon.) 1821–22
ROBERTSON, Muirhead *A Lombard Street mystery* 1888
ROBERTSON, Stuart *The development of modern English* 1934 (UK 1936)
— (ed. 2, rev. by F. G. Cassidy) 1954
ROBERTSON, William *Phraseologia generalis; a full large and general phrase book* 1681 (1693)
ROBERTSON, William *Works* a1793 (1813, 1825, 1851)
An historical disquisition concerning the knowledge which the ancients had of India 1791
The history of America 1777 (1778)
The history of the reign of the emperor Charles V 1769 (1813)
The history of Scotland during the reigns of queen Mary and of king James VI etc. 1759 (1813)
Robin Goodfellow, The mad pranks and merry jests of 1628 (Percy Soc. 1841)
Robin Hood *See* RITSON, J.
ROBINS, Elizabeth *The magnetic north* 1904
ROBINS, Robert Henry *General linguistics: an introductory survey* 1964
ROBINSON, C. Clough *The dialect of Leeds and its neighbourhood* (anon.) 1862
A glossary of words pertaining to the dialect of Mid-Yorkshire 1876 (E.D.S.)
ROBINSON, Charles *New South Wales, the oldest and richest of Australian colonies* 1873
ROBINSON, Charles Napier *The British fleet* 1894
ROBINSON, Clement, et al. *A handefull of pleasant delites* 1584 (Heliconia II, 1815; Arber)
ROBINSON, Francis K. *A glossary of words used in the neighbourhood of Whitby* 1876 (E.D.S.)
A glossary of Yorkshire words and phrases..collected in Whitby and the neighbourhood (anon.) 1855
ROBINSON, Frederick W. *Coward conscience* 1879
Female life in prison, by a prison matron (anon.) 1862
Grandmother's money (anon.) 1860
High church (anon.) 1860
Mattie:—a stray (anon.) 1864
No church (anon.) 1861
Owen:—a waif (anon.) 1862
ROBINSON, Gilbert Wooding *Soils: their origin, constitution and classification* 1932
ROBINSON, Harry P. *Men born equal, a novel* 1895
ROBINSON, Henry Crabb (1775–1867) *Diary* ed. D. Hudson 1967
Diary, reminiscences and correspondence a1867 (1869)
ROBINSON, Jane *Whitefriars; or the days of Charles II* (anon.) 1844
Whitehall; or the days of Charles I (anon.) 1845
ROBINSON, John *Eudoxa or some probable inquiries into truth,..together with A stone to the altar..as also A calm ventilation of Pseudo-doxia epidemica* 1658
ROBINSON, John *Archæologia græca, or the antiquities of Greece* 1807 (1827)
ROBINSON, Mrs. Mary *Angelina; a novel* 1796
Walsingham; or the pupil of nature 1797
ROBINSON, Matthew *Autobiography* a1694 (1856)
ROBINSON, Nicholas *A new theory of physick and diseases founded on the principles of the Newtonian philosophy* 1725
ROBINSON, Paul A. *Freudian Left* 1969
ROBINSON, Philip Stewart ('Phil Robinson') *In my Indian garden* 1878
Under the punkah 1881
The valley of tee-totum trees: tales and sketches 1886
ROBINSON, Ralph *A frutefull and pleasaunt worke of the beste state of a publyque weale, and of the newe yle called Utopia*: written in Latine by Syr Thomas More knyght tr. 1551, 1556 (Arber; Lupton 1895)
ROBINSON, Ralph *Christ all in all* a1655 (1656)
ROBINSON, Richard *A golden mirrour, containing..visions prognosticating good fortune to England* 1589 (Chetham Soc. 1851)
ROBINSON, Sir Robert S. *The nautical steam engine explained* 1839
ROBINSON, Mrs. Sara T. L. *Kansas; its interior and exterior life* 1856 (ed. 2)
ROBINSON, Thomas *The life and death of Mary Magdalene* c1620 (E.E.T.S. 1899)
ROBINSON, Thomas *The anatomy of the English nunnery at Lisbon* 1622
ROBINSON, Thomas *An essay towards a natural history of Westmoreland and Cumberland..To which is annexed A vindication of the philosophical and theological paraphrase of the Mosaick system of the creation* 1709
ROBINSON, Thomas *The common law of Kent; or the customs of gavelkind* 1741
ROBINSON, William *The English flower garden* 1883 (and several later editions used)
The wild garden 1870 (and several later editions used)
ROBSON, John ed. *Three early English metrical romances* 1842 (Camden Soc.)
ROBSON, Joseph Philip ed. *Songs of the bards of the Tyne; or a choice collection of original songs, chiefly in the Newcastle dialect* 1849 (1863)
ROBSON, Simon *The choise of change, newly set foorth by S. R.* 1585
A new yeares gift, The court of civill courtesie, out of Italian by S. R. 1582 (1591)
ROBSON, Stephen *The British flora* 1777
ROBSON, Thomas *The British herald* 1830
ROBY, Henry J. *A Latin grammar* 1879 (1880)
ROBY, John *Traditions of Lancashire* 1829–31 (1879)
Rochdale glossary 1886 *See* CUNLIFFE, H.
ROCHE, Harriet A. *On trek in the Transvaal; or, Over berg and veldt in South Africa* 1878
Rochester. The history and antiquities of Rochester and its environs (by W. Shrubsole & S. Denne) 1772
ROCHESTER, Bishop of 1695 *See* SPRAT, T.
ROCHESTER, John Wilmot, 2nd Earl of *Works* a1680 (1721, 1731)
Poems on several occasions (1701)
Valentinian, a tragedy as 'tis altered (from Fletcher) a1680 (1685)
ROCK, Daniel *The church of our fathers* 1849–53
Hierurgia; or the holy sacrifice of the mass 1833
Textile fabrics 1870
— (South Kensington art handbook) 1876
ROCK, William F. *Jim an' Nell: a dramatic poem in the dialect of North Devon* (anon.) 1867 (Nine specimens, E.D.S. 1896)
ROCKHILL, William W. *The land of the lamas* 1891
RODD, Ernest Harry ed. *Chemistry of carbon compounds* 5 vols. in 10 parts 1951–62
RODGER, Alexander *Poems and songs* 1838 (1897)
RODGERS, Bruce *The queens' vernacular: a gay lexicon* 1972
Rodriguez' (A.) Practice of christian perfection tr. 1697–99
RODWAY, James *In the Guiana forest* 1894 (1897)
In Guiana wilds 1899
RODWELL, John M. *The prophecies of Isaiah* tr. 1881
ROE, Edward P. *Nature's serial story* 1884 (1885)
ROE, Thomas *The embassy of Sir Thomas Roe to the court of the Great Mogul, 1615–1619, as narrated in his journal and correspondence* ed. W. Foster 2 vols. 1899
ROEST, Theodore *Noot's (Jan van der) Theatre, wherein be represented the miseries that follow the voluptuous worldings* tr. 1569
ROGERS, Charles *The modern Scottish minstrel* 1855–57
Social life in Scotland 1884–86
ROGERS, Daniel *Naaman the Syrian, his disease and cure* 1642
A treatise of the two sacraments of the gospell, baptisme and the supper of the Lord, by D. R. 1633
ROGERS, Fairman *A manual of coaching* 1900
ROGERS, Henry *The eclipse of faith; or a visit to a religious sceptic* 1852 (1853)
Essays selected from contributions to the Edinburgh review v.d. (1850–55)
The life and character of John Howe 1836 (1863)
The superhuman origin of the Bible inferred from itself 1873 (1874, 1893)
ROGERS, Henry Darwin *The geology of Pennsylvania* 1858
ROGERS, J. *The new rush, and other poems and songs* 1864
ROGERS, James E. Thorold ed. *A complete collection of the protests of the Lords* 1875
Historical gleanings: a series of sketches 1869–70
A history of agriculture and prices in England from 1259 to 1793 1866–87
A manual of political economy 1868
Six centuries of work and wages 1884
ROGERS, John *The glasse of godly love* (anon.) 1569 (New Shaks. Soc. 1876)
ROGERS, John *A discourse of the visible and invisible church of Christ* 1719 (1729)
The necessity of divine revelation 1727
A vindication of the civil establishment of religion 1728
ROGERS, John *Antipopopriestian; or an attempt to liberate and purify christianity from popery*, etc. 1839
ROGERS, Nehemiah *A strange vineyard in Palæstina* 1623
ROGERS, Robert *A concise account of North America* 1765
Journals of major R. Rogers containing an account of the several excursions he made..upon the continent of North America during the late war 1765 (1883)
ROGERS, Samuel *Poetical works* a1855
Human life, a poem 1819
Italy, a poem c1820 (1822–28)
The pleasures of memory, a poem 1792
Recollections of the table talk of S. Rogers a1855 (1856)
ROGERS, Thomas *Cæsar's (P.) General discourse against the damnable sect of vsurers* tr. 1578
The English creede consenting with the true auncient catholique and apostolique church in al the points and articles of religion 1585, 1587
The faith, doctrine and religion..professed..in..England expressed in thirty-nine articles 1607 (1633; Parker Soc. 1854)
Geveren's (S. A.) Of the ende of this world and seconde comyng of Christ tr. 1575 (1578)
Of the imitation of Christ tr. 1580 (1629)
A right christian treatise entituled S. Augustines praiers tr. 1581 (1597)
Two dialogues..concerning kneeling in the very act of receiving the sacramental bread and wine 1608
ROGERS, Walter Thomas (d. 1912) *Dictionary of abbreviations* 1913
ROGERS, Woodes *A cruising voyage round the world* 1712 (1718)
ROGET, F. F. *An introduction to Old French* 1887
ROGET, Peter Mark *Animal and vegetable physiology considered with reference to natural theology* (Bridgewater treatise) 1834 (1840)
Thesaurus of English words and phrases 1852 (1879)
ROGET, Samuel Romilly *A dictionary of electrical terms* 1924 (and later editions used)
ROHAN, Criena *The delinquents* 1962
ROKEBY, Sir Thomas *A brief memoir of Mr. Justice Rokeby* (by. J. Raine) *comprising his religious journal* (= Diary) 1688–99 *and correspondence* v.d. (Surtees Soc. 1861)
Roland. The romance of duke Rowland and Sir Otuell of Spayne, together with a fragment of The song of Roland c1400 (Sege off Melayne, etc., E.E.T.S. 1880)
The romances of Rouland and Vernagu, and Otuel, from the Auchinleck manuscript a1330 (Abbotsford Club 1836; with Rauf Coilȝear, E.E.T.S. 1882)
ROLAND, George *An introductory course of modern gymnastic exercises* 1854
A treatise on..the art of fencing 1823
ROLAND, James *The amateur of fencing; or, a treatise on the art of sword-defence* 1809
ROLFE, Frederick William S. A. L. M. ('Baron Corvo') *The desire and pursuit of the whole: a romance of modern Venice* 1934
Hadrian the Seventh 1904
Nicholas Crabbe; or, The one and the many ed. C. Woolf 1958
ROLLAND, John *The seuin seages tr...in Scottis meter* 1560 (1578: Bannatyne Club 1837)
Ane treatise callit the court of Venus c1550 (1575; S.T.S. 1884)
ROLLE, Sir Henry *Un abridgment des plusieurs cases et resolutions del common ley* a1656 (1668)
ROLLE, Richard, of Hampole *See* HAMPOLE
ROLLESTON, George *Forms of animal life* 1870
— (ed. 2) Revised and enlarged by W. H. Jackson 1888
ROLLESTON, Humphrey D. *Diseases of the liver, gall-bladder and bile-ducts* 1905
Rolliad. Criticisms on the Rolliad, a poem (by Joseph Richardson, R. Tickell, and others), *being a more faithful portraiture of the present immaculate young minister* (W. Pitt) *and his friends than any extant* 1784 (1785)
— *The Rolliad, in two parts; probationary odes for the laureatship; and political miscellanies* (1795)
— *Probationary odes for the laureatship* (pretended to be) *by Sir John Hawkins* (part of the Rolliad) 1785
Rollin's (C.) Ancient history of the Egyptians..and Greeks tr. 1734–37 (1827, 1840–41)
— *Roman history* tr. 1739 (1768)
Rolling stone 1967–
ROLLINS, Mrs. Ellen C. *New England bygones* 1880
ROLLOCK, Robert *Select works* a1599 (Wodrow Soc. 1844–49)
Lectures upon the epistle..to the Colossians a1599 (1603)
Lectures upon the epistles..to the Thessalonians a1599 (1606)
Lectures upon the history of the passion, resurrection and ascension of our Lord Jesus Christ a1599 (1616)
Rolls of parliament (*Rotuli parliamentorum*) 1278–1503 (1767–77)
Rolls series, The (The chronicles and memorials of Great Britain and Ireland during the Middle ages, published..under the direction of the Master of the Rolls) 1858–96
ROLLWYN, J. A. S. *Astronomy simplified for general reading* 1871
'ROLPH, C. H.' (Cecil Rolph Hewitt) ed. *The human sum* 1957
ed. *Women of the streets* 1955
ROLT, Richard *A new dictionary of trade and commerce* 1756
Romance of a dull life, The (by Mrs. A. J. Penny) 1861
ROMANES, George J. *Animal intelligence* 1882
Jelly-fish, star-fish and sea-urchins 1885
Thoughts on religion a1894 (ed. C. Gore 1895)
ROMANS, Bernard *A concise natural history of East and West Florida* 1775
Romaunt of the rose, The lines 1–1705 (CHAUCER) a1366
— lines 1706–end (anon.) c1400 (Skeat, Chaucer I 1894; Kaluza 1891)

Romer, Alfred Sherwood *The procession of life* 1968
The vertebrate body 1949
Vertebrate paleontology 1933
Romer, Mrs. Isabella F. *The Rhone, the Darro, and the Guadalquivir* 1843
Romilly, Joseph *Romilly's Cambridge diary 1832–42* ed. J. P. T. Bury 1967
Ronalds, Alfred *The fly-fisher's entomology* 1836
Ronalds, Edmund & Richardson T. ed. *Knapp's (Fr. C.) Chemical technology* 1848–51 (1854)
Rood, The dream of the a1000 (Grein 1888)
Rood, Ogden N. *Modern chromatics, with applications to art and industry* 1879
Rook, Arthur James, Wilkinson, D. S., & Ebling, F. J. G. eds. *Textbook of dermatology* 2 vols. 1968
Roosa, Daniel B. St. J. *A practical treatise on the diseases of the ear* 1873
Roosenburg, Henriette *The walls came tumbling down* 1957
Roosevelt, Theodore *Hunting trips of a ranchman* 1885
—— & Grinnell, G. B. ed. *Hunting in many lands* 1895
Root, Jesse *Reports of cases adjudged in the Superior court and Supreme court of errors* (of the state of Connecticut) *1789–93* 1798
Roper, William *The life and death of Sir. T. More* a1578 (1729)
Ros, Sir Richard *La belle dame sans merci* tr. c1460 (Political, religious and love poems, E.E.T.S. 1866, 1903; Skeat, Chaucerian pieces 1897)
Rosarian, The; a monthly organ of the Holy rosary fraternity 1871
Roscoe, Sir Henry E. *Lessons in elementary chemistry* 1866 (1871, 1874)
— & Schorlemmer, C. *A treatise on chemistry* 1877–88
Roscoe, Thomas *Cellini's (B.) Memoirs* tr. 1822
Sismondi's (J. C. L. de) Historical view of the literature of the south of Europe tr. 1823 (1846)
Roscoe, William *The life of Lorenzo de Medici* 1795 (1806)
Roscommon, Wentworth Dillon, 4th Earl of *Works* a1685 (1709, 1750)
An essay on translated verse 1684 (1709)
Horace's Art of poetry tr. 1680
Rose, Cooper *Four years in southern Africa* 1829
Rose, Geoffrey Keith *The story of the 2/4th Oxfordshire and Buckinghamshire Light Infantry* 1920
Rose, George *The diaries and correspondence* a1818 (1860)
Rose, Hew *A genealogical deduction of the family of Rose of Kilravock, with illustrative documents* 1683–84 (Spalding Club 1848)
Rose, Howard N. *A thesaurus of slang* 1934
Rose, John *The English vineyard vindicated* ed. J. Evelyn 1666 (1675)
Rose, John B. *The Æneis of Virgil* tr. 1867
The Eclogues and Georgics of Virgil tr. 1866
The Fasti of Ovid tr. 1866
The Metamorphoses of Ovid tr. 1866
Rose, Joshua *The complete practical machinist* 1876
Rose, William ed. *An outline of modern knowledge* 1931
Rose, William S. *Amadis de Gaule* tr. 1803
Rosebery, Archibald P. Primrose, 5th Earl of *Pitt* 1891
'Rosemary' *Under the Chilterns: a story of English village life* 1895
Rosemary and Bayes: or animadversions upon.. The rehearsall trans-prosed (by H. Stubbe) 1672
Rosen, Ephraim & Gregory, Ian *Abnormal psychology* 1965
Rosenberg, Justine, Countess Orsini *Moral and sentimental essays* by J. W., C-t-ss of R-s-g 1785
Rosenthal, Isidore *General physiology of muscles and nerves* 1881
Ross, family. *Ane breve cronicle of the earlis of Ross, including notices of the abbots of Fearn, and of the family of Ross of Balnagown a* 1615 (1850)
Ross, Alan John *Australia 55: a journal of the M.C.C. tour* 1955
Australia 63 1963
ed. *The cricketer's companion* 1960
Ross, Alan Strode Campbell *Etymology, with especial reference to English* 1958
Ross, Alexander *The Alcoran, translated from the French of the sieur du Ryer, with the life of Mahomet* 1649
Arcana microcosmi: or the hid secrets of man's body disclosed 1651
The history of the world.. being a continuation of the famous history of Sir W. Raleigh 1652
Mel Heliconium, or poeticall honey gathered out of the weeds of Parnassus 1642 (1643)
Mystagogus poeticus, or the muses interpreter 1647 (1675)
Ross, Alexander *The fortunate shepherdess, a pastoral tale.. in the Scotish dialect* 1768
— Third ed. corrected. *Helenore, or the fortunate shepherdess* (1789)
Ross, Angus *The Bradford business* 1974
The Dunfermline affair 1973
The Manchester thing 1970
Ross, David Alexander *Introduction to oceanography* 1970
Ross, Edward Alsworth *The Russian Soviet republic* 1923
Ross, Frederick, et al. *A glossary of words used in Holderness in the East-riding of Yorkshire* 1877 (E.D.S.)
Ross, James *The fratricide* (MS.) 1773
Ross, James *Hobart Town almanack* 1829–36
Ross, James *Handbook of the diseases of the nervous system* 1885
A treatise on the diseases of the nervous system 1881
Ross, Sir James Clark *A voyage of discovery and research in the southern and antarctic regions during 1839–43* 1847
Ross, Janet Ann *Three generations of Englishwomen* 1888
Ross, Sir John *Narrative of a second voyage in search of a north-west passage and of a residence in the arctic regions during the years 1829–33* 1835
'Ross, Jonathan' (John Rossiter) *The burning of Billy Toober* 1974
Dead at first hand 1969
I know what it's like to die 1976
Ross, Rodger James *Television film engineering* 1966
Ross, Thomas *Silius Italicus' (C.) Second Punick war between Hannibal and the Romanes* tr. 1661
Ross, Thomasina *Humboldt's (Baron F. H. A. von) Personal narrative of travels to the equinoctial regions of America* tr. 1852
Ross, William *Aberdour and Inchcolme: being historical notices of the parish and monastery* 1885
Busby and its neighbourhood 1883
Rosse, Irving C. *Cruise of the revenue-steamer Corwin in Alaska and the N.W. Arctic ocean* 1883
Rossetti, Christina G. *Poems* 1891 (Poetical works 1904)
Seek and find, a double series of short studies of the Benedicite 1879
Speaking likenesses 1874
Rossetti, Dante Gabriel *Collected works* a1882 (1886)
Dante and his circle,.. a collection of lyrics, ed. and tr. a1850 (1874)
Letters ed. O. Doughty & J. R. Wahl 4 vols. 1965–7
Poems v.d. (1870)
Rossiter, John *The manipulators* 1973
A rope for General Dietz 1972
Rossiter, William *An elementary handbook of physics* 1871
An illustrated dictionary of scientific terms 1878
Rosten, Leo Calvin *The joys of Yiddish* 1968
Roth, Cecil *A history of the Marranos* 1932
Roth, Mathias *Hand-book of the movement cure* 1856
Roth, Philip *Goodbye, Columbus* 1959
Portnoy's complaint 1969
Rotman, Jonah Joseph *The theory of groups* 1965
Rouen, Siege of See Page, J.
Roughley, Thomas *The Jamaica planter's guide* 1823
Roule or Rowll, Sir John *Heir followis the cursing of Sr Johine Rowlis vpoun the steilaris of his fowlis* 15.. (in Bannatyne MS., Hunterian Club, p. 298; D. Laing, Select remains of popular poetry of Scotland 1822; Maitland folio MS., S.T.S. 1919)
Round, Frank Eric *Introduction to the lower plants* 1969
Rous or Rouse, Francis *The balme of love, to heale divisions and the wounds made by them* 1648
The bounds and bonds of publique obedience (anon.) 1649
The heavenly academie 1638
— *Academia cœlestis: the heavenly university* (1702)
The mysticall marriage, or experimentall discoveries of the heavenly mariage betweene a soule and her saviour 1635 (1653)
The psalmes of David in English meeter 1643 (1646)
Thule, or vertues historie 1598
Rous, John *Diary* 1625–42 (Camden Soc. 1856)
Rousseau's (J. J.) Emilius; or a treatise of education tr. 1763
Routledge, Robert *Discoveries and inventions of the nineteenth century* 1876
A popular history of science 1881
Routledge's Every boy's annual 1866–89
Routledge's Young gentleman's magazine 1869–74
Rovinson or Rovenzon, John *A treatise of metallica* 1613 (1854)
Row, John *The historie of the kirk of Scotland 1558–1637* a1646; with a continuation to 1639 by his son J. Row, 1650 (Wodrow Soc. 1842)
Row, William *Supplement to R. Blair's Autobiography* 1676 (Wodrow Soc. 1848)
Rowbotham, James *The pleasaunt and wittie playe of the cheastes renewed* tr. 1562
Rowe, Eleanor *Hints on chip-carving* 1892 (1895)
Rowe, John *Emmanuel, or the love of Christ explicated and applied* a1677 (1680)
Rowe, Nicholas *Works* a1718 (1720, 1728)
The ambitious step-mother, a tragedy 1700
The biter, a comedy 1705
The fair penitent, a tragedy 1703
Lucan's Pharsalia tr. 1718
The royal convert, a tragedy 1707 (1708)
Tamerlane, a tragedy 1702
The tragedy of Jane Shore 1714
The tragedy of Lady Jane Gray 1715
Ulysses, a tragedy 1706
Rowe, Samuel *A perambulation of the antient and royal forest of Dartmoor* 1848 (1856)
Rowland See *Roland*
Rowland, David *Hurtado de Mendoza's (D.) Pleasaunt historie of Lazarillo de Tormes* tr. 1586 (1672–77)
Rowland, John *Topsell's (E.) History of four-footed beasts and serpents.. whereunto is now added, The theater of insects.. by T. Muffet,.. the whole revised.. and inlarged by J. R(owland)* 1658
Rowlands, Henry *Mona antiqua restaurata; an archæological discourse on the antiquities.. of the isle of Anglesey* 1723
Rowlands, John James *Spindrift from a house by the sea* 1960
Rowlands, Samuel *Works* a1630 (Hunterian Club 1880)
The betraying of Christ etc., *by S. R.* 1598
Diogines lanthorne (anon.) 1607
Doctor Merrie-man: or nothing but mirth, by S. R. 1609 (1627)
The famous history of Guy earle of Warwicke 1607
Good newes and bad newes, by S. R. 1622
Greenes ghost haunting conie-catchers (by S. R.) 1602 (1860)
Humors looking glasse (anon.) 1608
The knave of clubbes (by S. R.) 1600 (1609)
The knave of harts (anon.) 1612
— *More knaves yet? the knaves of spades and diamonds* (by S. R.) 1613
— *The four knaves* (Percy Soc. 1843)
The letting of humours blood in the head-vaine (anon.) 1600
Looke to it; for ile stabbe ye, by S. R. 1604
Martin Mark-all, beadle of Bridewell, his defence and answere to the (Dekker's) *belman of London by S. R.* (also attributed to S. Rid) 1610
The melancholie knight, by S. R. 1615
The night-raven, by S. R. 1620
*A paire of spy-knaves?*1620
A sacred memorie of the miracles wrought by.. Jesus Christ 1618
A terrible battell betweene the two consumers of the whole world: time and death ?1606
Tis merrie when gossips meet (anon.) 1602 (1609)
A whole crew of kind gossips all met to be merry 1609
Rowlandson, James *Gods blessing in blasting, and his mercy in mildew, two sermons suitable to these times of dearth* 1623
Rowley, Jennifer E. *Mechanised in-house information systems* 1979
Rowley, Samuel *The noble souldier, a tragedy by S. R.* 1634 (Bullen, Old plays I, 1882)
Rowley, William *The birth of Merlin, or the childe hath found his father, by William Shakespear, and W. Rowley* 16.. (1662; Shakespeare Apocrypha 1908)
A match at midnight, a comœdie 1633 (Dodsley)
A merrie and pleasant comedy.. called A shoo-maker a gentleman, by W. R. gentleman 1638
A new wonder, a woman never vext; a pleasant conceited comedy 1632 (Dodsley)
A search for money 1609 (Percy Soc. 1840)
See also Fletcher, John; Middleton, T.; Webster, J.
——, Dekker, T., & Ford, J. *The witch of Edmonton, a known true story, composed into tragi-comedy by divers well-esteemed poets* c1623 (1658)
Rowll, Sir J. *See* Roule
Rows, John *Rol* (the roll of the Warwick family) c1485 (1845)
Rowse, Alfred Leslie *A Cornish childhood* 1942
The early Churchills: an English family 1956
The England of Elizabeth 1950
The English spirit: essays 1944
The expansion of Elizabethan England 1955
Tudor Cornwall 1941
The use of history 1946
Rowzee, Lodowick *The Queenes welles, that is, a treatise of the nature and vertues of Tunbridge water* 1632 (Harl. Misc.)
Roxburgh, William *Flora Indica or descriptions of Indian plants* a1815 (1820–24)
Hortus Bengalensis, or a catalogue of the plants growing in the.. East India Company's botanic garden at Calcutta 1813–14
Roxburghe ballads, The v.d. (Ballad Soc. 1869–99)
Roxburghe Club *Publications* (1814–)
Roy, William, & Barlow, J. *Rede me and be nott wrothe, For I saye no thinge but trothe* (anon.) 1528 (Arber)
Royal Aeronautical Society *Journal* 1923–67
Handbook of aeronautics 1931
Royal Air Force journal ?1942–6
Royal Air Force news 1961–
Royal Asiatic Society *Journal* 1834–)
Transactions 1827–35
——: Straits Branch (later Malayan Branch) *Journal* 1878–1920; 1923–63
Royal Asiatic Society of Bengal *See* Asiatic ——
Royal Dublin Society *Proceedings* 1848–
Royal Entomological Society of London *See* Entomological Society ——
Royal Geographical Society of London *Journal* 1831– (*Geographical journal* 1893–)
Royal Horticultural Society *Dictionary of gardening* ed. F. J. Chittenden et al. 4 vols. 1951
Journal 1846–55; 1866–
Royal Institution of Great Britain *Proceedings* 1851– (1851–1928 with title *Notices of the proceedings*)
Royal Irish Academy *Proceedings* 1836–
Transactions 1787–
Royal Society *Philosophical transactions* 1665–
— abridged by J. Lowthorp et al. (1716–56)
Proceedings 1830–
Royal Society of Edinburgh *Proceedings* 1832– (from 1941 divided into subject sections)
Transactions 1788–
Royal Society of Medicine *Proceedings* 1907–
Royal trade. Ἰχθυοθηρα, or the royal trade of fishing 1662
Royall, Anne *The black book; or, A continuation of travels in the United States* 3 vols. 1828–9
'Royce, Kenneth' (Kenneth Royce Gondley) *Spider underground* 1973
Trap Spider 1974
Royde-Smith, Naomi Gwladys *Incredible tale* 1932
Royle, John Forbes *The fibrous plants of India* 1855
Illustrations of the botany and other branches of the natural history of the Himalayan mountains and of the flora of Cashmere 1839
A manual of materia medica and therapeutics 1847
— Sixth ed. by J. Harley (1876)

RUARK, Arthur Edward & UREY, Harold Clayton *Atoms, molecules and quanta* 1930
RUBINSTEIN, Helena *The art of feminine beauty* 1930
RUCK, Amy Roberta (Berta) *Disturbing charm* 1919
'RUDD, Steele' (Arthur Hoey Davis) *From selection to city* 1909
Our new selection 1903
RUDD, Thomas *Euclides Elements..the first IV books* tr. 1651
Practical geometry (Arithmetick; Geometricall questions) 1650
Rudder, The 1890-
RUDDIMAN, Jacob *Tales and sketches* 1828
— *Tales of a Scottish parish* (1889)
RUDDIMAN, Thomas ed. *Virgil's Æneis* tr. into Scottish verse by Bp. G. Douglas. *To which is added a large glossary, explaining the difficult words: which may serve for a dictionary to the Old Scottish language* 1710
RUDGE, Thomas *General view of the agriculture of the county of Gloucester* 1807 (1813)
Rudim. navig. 1850 *See* GREENWOOD, James
Rudiments of ancient architecture 1794
RUDING, Rogers *Annals of the coinage of Britain and its dependencies* 1817 (1840)
RUDINGER, Edith ed. *The consumer's car glossary* (Consumers' Association) 1966
—(ed. 2) 1967
ed. *Wills and probate* (Consumers' Association) 1967
RUDYERD, Sir Benjamin *Speeches in the high court of parliament* 1641
RUELL, Patrick *Red Christmas* 1972
Rule of St. Benet, The See *Benedict, St.*
Rules (*and orders*) *of the Supreme court* 1883 (1887)
Rules of civility, The 1671 (1673, 1703)
Rules of the game: the complete illustrated encyclopedia of all the sports of the world (by the Diagram Group) 1974
RUMBAUGH, Duane M. ed. *Language learning by a chimpanzee: the Lana project* 1977
RUMNEY, George R. *Climatology and the world's climates* 1968
Rump: or an exact collection of the choycest poems and songs relating to the late times 1662 (1874)
RUMSEY, Walter *Organon salutis; an instrument to cleanse the stomach* 1657
RUNCIMAN, James *Skippers and shellbacks* 1885
RUNES, Dagobert David ed. *The dictionary of philosophy* 1942
Runes a1000 (Grein 1883)
RUNYON, Alfred Damon *Furthermore* ed. E. C. Bentley 1938
Guys and dolls 1931 (UK 1932)
More than somewhat ed. E. C. Bentley 1937
Runyon à la carte 1944 (UK 1946)
Take it easy 1938
RUSH, Benjamin *Essays, literary, moral and philosophical* 1798 (1806)
RUSHDIE, Salman *Midnight's children* 1981
RUSHWORTH, John *Historical collections of private passages of state, weighty matters in law, remarkable proceedings in five parliaments* 1659-1701
Rushworth gospels, The c975 (Skeat 1871-87)
RUSKIN, Effie *See* LUTYENS, Mary
RUSKIN, John *Arrows of the chace, being a collection of scattered letters* 1840-80 (1880)
The Bible of Amiens See *Our fathers*, below
The crown of wild olive, three lectures on work, traffic and war 1866 (1873)
Deucalion, collected studies of the lapse of waves and life of stones 1875-83
The eagle's nest 1872 (1887)
The elements of drawing 1857
The elements of perspective 1859
The ethics of the dust 1866
Fors clavigera: letters to the workmen and labourers of Great Britain 1871-84
Frondes agrestes: readings in 'Modern painters' 1875 (1879)
A joy for ever See *Political economy of art*, below
Lectures on architecture and painting 1853 (1854)
Lectures on art 1870 (1875)
Love's meinie, lectures on Greek and English birds 1873-81
Modern painters 1843-60
Mornings in Florence 1875-77
Munera pulveris, six essays on the elements of political economy 1872
'Our fathers have told us.' Sketches of the history of christendom. Part I. *The Bible of Amiens* 1880-85
The political economy of art (later edd. *A joy for ever*) 1857
Præterita: outlines of scenes and thoughts..in my past life 1885-89
Pre-Raphaelitism 1851
Proserpina, studies of wayside flowers 1875-86
The queen of the air: being a study of Greek myths of cloud and storm 1869 (1874)
St. Mark's rest: the history of Venice 1877-84
Sesame and lilies, two lectures. I. Of kings' treasuries, II. Of queens' gardens 1864 (1865)
The seven lamps of architecture 1849 (1855)
The stones of Venice 1851-53 (1874)
Time and tide, by Weare and Tyne 1867
The two paths: being lectures on art and its applications to decoration and manufacture 1858-59
'Unto this last', four essays on the first principles of political economy 1860 (1862)
Val d'Arno, ten lectures on..Tuscan art 1874
RUSSEL, Richard *The works of Geber* (Jabir Ibn-Haiyan) *the most famous Arabian prince and philosopher* tr. 1678
RUSSEL, William P. *Verbotomy, or a classical improved vocabulary* 1805
RUSSELL, Alexander *The natural history of Aleppo and parts adjacent* 1756
— ed. P. Russell (1794)
RUSSELL, Alexander *A treatise on the theory of alternating currents* 2 vols. 1904-6
RUSSELL, Archer *Bush ways: a Bush-lover's wanderings on plain and range in Central and Eastern Australia* 1944
Gone nomad 1936
A tramp-royal in wild Australia, 1928-1929 1934
RUSSELL, Bertrand Arthur William *The analysis of mind* 1921
Autobiography 3 vols. 1967-69
A history of Western philosophy 1945 (UK 1946)
An inquiry into meaning and truth 1940
Marriage and morals 1929
An outline of philosophy 1927
Principia mathematica See WHITEHEAD, Alfred North
The principles of mathematics 1903
Religion and science 1935
RUSSELL, Charles Marion *Trails plowed under* 1927
RUSSELL, Dora *The secret of the river* 1891
RUSSELL, E. *Maitland of Lethington, the minister of Mary Stuart* 1912
RUSSELL, Frederick Stratten & YONGE, Charles Maurice *The seas: our knowledge of life in the sea and how it is gained* 1928
—(rev. ed.) 1936
RUSSELL, George Oscar *Speech and voice* 1931
RUSSELL, George W. E. *Collections and recollections, by one who has kept a diary* 1898
RUSSELL, James *Reminiscences of Yarrow* a1884 (1886)
RUSSELL, John *The boke of nurture, folowyng Englondis gise* c1460 (Babees book, E.E.T.S. 1868)
RUSSELL, John, Earl Russell ed. *Memoirs, journal and correspondence of Thomas Moore* 1853-56
RUSSELL, John *The Haigs of Bemersyde, a family history* 1881
RUSSELL, John Scott *The wave of translation in the oceans of water, air and ether* 1885
RUSSELL, Loris Shano *Everyday life in colonial Canada* 1973
RUSSELL, Martin James *Deadline* 1971
Double hit 1973
Murder by the mile 1975
RUSSELL, Rachel, Lady Russell *Letters* a1723 (1819)
RUSSELL, Ralph tr. *Aziz Ahmad's The shore and the wave* 1971
'RUSSELL, Sarah' (Marghanita Laski) *To bed with grand music* 1946
RUSSELL, William *The history of modern Europe* (anon.) 1779
RUSSELL, William *Orthophony; or the cultivation of the voice, in elocution* 1859 (1882)
RUSSELL, William Clark *Curatica, or leaves from a curate's note-book, by Sydney Mostyn* 1891
The death ship, a strange story 1888
The good ship 'Mohock' 1894
Jack's courtship: a sailor's yarn 1884
John Holdsworth, chief mate 1875
Marooned 1889
A marriage at sea 1891
An ocean free-lance 1881
An ocean tragedy 1890
Sailors' language, a collection of sea-terms and their definitions 1883
A sailor's sweetheart, an account of the wreck of the 'Waldershare' 1880
A sea queen 1883
What cheer! 1896
The wreck of the 'Grosvenor' (anon.) 1877
RUSSELL, Sir William Howard *My diary in India in..1858-59* 1860
My diary North and South 1863-65
The Prince of Wales' tour, a diary in India etc. 1877
The war (in the Crimea) 1855-56
RUSSENHOLT, Edgar Stanford *The heart of the continent: being the history of Assiniboia—the truly typical Canadian community* 1968
Russia, The present state of,..being the journal of a foreign minister tr. 1722-23
RUST, Bp. George *A discourse of truth* a1670 (1682)
A letter of resolution concerning Origen and the chief of his opinions (anon.) 1661 (Phenix I, 1707, 1721)
Remains a1670 (1686)
Rustamji Nasarvangi Khore See KHORY
'RUTHERFORD, Douglas' (James Douglas Rutherford McConnell) *The creeping flesh* 1963
The gilt-edged cockpit 1969
Kick start 1973
The long echo 1957
RUTHERFORD, Ernest *Radio-activity* 1904
—— CHADWICK, J., & ELLIS, C. D. *Radiations from radioactive substances* 1930
'RUTHERFORD, Mark' *See* WHITE, William Hale
RUTHERFORD, Samuel *Joshua redivivus, or Mr. Rutherfoords letters* a1661 (1664)
— *Letters* 1627-61 (1675; 1881; 1891)
The tryal and triumph of faith 1645
Rutland glossary 1891 *See* WORDSWORTH, Christopher
Rutland papers, original documents illustrative of the courts and times of Henry VII and Henry VIII (Camden Soc. 1842)
Rutledge (a novel, by Mrs. M. C. Harris) 1866
RUTLEY, Frank *The study of rocks* 1879
RUTTEN, Martin Gerard *The geology of western Europe* 1969
RUTTER, John *Delineations of Fonthill and its abbey* 1823
RUTTY, John *An essay towards the natural history of the county of Dublin* 1772
A spiritual diary (1753-75) *and soliloquies* a1775 (1776, 1796)
RUXTON, George F. *Adventures in Mexico and the Rocky mountains* 1847
Life in the far west a1848 (1849)
RYCAUT, Sir Paul *Continuation of Knolles'* (*R.*) *History of the Turks* 1687
Gracian's (*B.*) *Critick* tr. 1681
The history of the Turkish empire 1679-80
The present state of the Greek and Armenian churches 1679
The present state of the Ottoman empire 1668 (1675)
RYCROFT, Charles *A critical dictionary of psychoanalysis* 1968
Rydberg's (*A. V.*) *Magic of the middle ages* tr. A. H. Edgren 1879 See also ANDERSON, R. B.
RYDER, Jonathan *Trevayne* 1973 (UK 1974)
RYE, Walter *A glossary of words used in East Anglia founded on that of Forby* 1895
A month on the Norfolk broads 1887
RYLAND, Arthur *The assay of gold and silver wares* 1852
RYLAND, Jonathan Edwards *Hengstenberg's* (*C. F.*) *Dissertations on the genuineness of the Pentateuch* tr. 1847
ed. *The life and correspondence of John Foster* 1846
Neander's (*J. A. W.*) *History of the planting..of the christian church by the apostles* tr. 1851
RYLE, Gilbert *The concept of mind* 1949
RYMER, Thomas *Fœdera, conventiones, literæ, et cujuscunque generis acta publica, inter reges Angliæ et alios quosvis imperatores, reges, pontifices, principes, vel communitates..ab anno 1101 ad nostra usque tempora, habita et tractata* (1704-35; 1816-30)
A short view of tragedy 1693
The tragedies of the last age consider'd 1678
RYVES, Sir Thomas *The poore vicars plea* (for tithes) 1620

S

S., Mr. 1575 See *Gammer Gurton*
S., C. *A briefe resolution of a right religion, touching the controversies that are nowe in England* 1590
S., E. *The discoverie of the knights of the poste* 1597
S., E. *Britaines busse: or a computation as well of the charge of a busse or herring-fishing ship as also of the gaine and profit thereby* 1615 (Arber, Eng. Garner III)
S——, E—— See SMITH, E.
S., F. 1557 *See* SEAGER, F.
S., G. *Anglorum speculum or the worthies of England in church and state* (an abridgement of Fuller's Worthies) 1684
S., J. *Certaine worthye manuscript poems..now first published by J. S.* (The stately tragedy of Guistard and Sismond, The northern mothers blessing, The way to thrifte) 1597
S., J. *Clidamas, or the Sicilian tale* 1639
S., J. *Bonarelli della Rovere's* (*G. U.*) *Filli di Sciro or Phillis of Scyros* tr. 1655
S., J. *Andromana, or the merchant's wife, by J. S.* (? Shirley) 1660 (Dodsley)
S., J. 1661 *See* STEPHENS, John
S., J. 1665, 1700 *See* SERGEANT, J.
S., J. (? John Smith) *Horological dialogues..shewing the nature, use and right managing of clocks and watches* 1675
S., J. capt. *Military discipline or the art of war* ?1685
S., J. (? J. Sergeant) *The history of monastical conventions and military institutions* 1686
S., J. 1695 *See* SAGE, J.
S., J. 1758 *See* SPARROW, J.
S., L. *Natures dowrie: or, the peoples native liberty asserted* 1652
S., N. *Simon's* (*R.*) *Critical enquiries into the various editions of the Bible* tr. 1684
S., R. 1591 *See* SOUTHWELL, R.
S., R. *The phœnix nest built vp with the moste rare and refined workes of noblemen* 1593 (in T. Park, Heliconia II, 1815)
S., R. 1623 *See* SPEED, R.
S., S. *Fortune's tennis-ball: or the..history of Dorastus and Fawnia rendred in..English verse* 1672
S., S. *The loyal and impartial satyrist: containing eight miscellany poems* (Dedication signed S. S.) 1694
S., T. 1583 *See* STOCKER, T.
S., T. 1624 *See* SCOTT, T.
S., T. *Arts improvement* 1703
S., W. *A compendious or briefe examination of certayne ordinary complaints of divers of our countrymen in these our dayes, by W. S.* (? W. Stafford) 1581 (New Shaks. Soc. 1876)
— *A discourse of the common weal of this realm of England* c1550 (1893)
S., W. *The lamentable tragedie of Locrine* 1595 (Shakespeare Apocrypha 1908)
S., W. *The true chronicle historie of the whole life and death of Thomas Lord Cromwell* 1602 (Shakespeare Apocrypha 1908)
S., W. *The Puritaine or the widdow of Watling-streete* 1607 (Shakespeare Apocrypha 1908)
S.H.S. = Scottish History Society
S.L.R. camera 1964
S.P.E. *See* Society for Pure English

Sabine, Sir Edward, and others *Terrestrial magnetism* 1851–59 (Manual of scientific enquiry, 1859)
Sacheverell, Henry *The christian triumph, a sermon* 1713
Sacheverell (Dr. H.), Tracts relating to the impeachment of 1710
Sachs, Albert Louis *The jail diary of Albie Sachs* 1966
Sachs, Curt *The history of musical instruments* 1940 (UK 1942)
Sackville, Thomas, 1st Earl of Dorset *Works* a1608 (1859)
Induction to the Mirror for magistrates 1563 (see Mirror)
See also Norton, T. 1561
Sackville-West, Victoria Mary *The Edwardians* 1930
Sacrament, The play of the c1460 (Philol. Soc. 1861; Non-cycle mystery plays, E.E.T.S. 1909)
Sacred decretall, A, or hue and cry . . for the apprehension of . . Martin Mar-priest 1645
Sacrilege sacredly handled 1619 *See* Sempill, Sir J.
Sadeek, Sheik M. *Windswept, and other stories* 1969
Sadleir Michael *Excursions in Victorian bibliography* 1922
Trollope: a commentary 1927
Sadler, Anthony *The loyall mourner* 1660
The subject's joy for the king's restoration 1660
Sadler, John *Rights of the kingdom or customs of our ancestours* (anon.) 1649 (1682)
Sadler, Sir Ralph *State papers and letters* a1587 (1809)
Sadler, William Samuel *Theory and practice of psychiatry* 1936
Safire, William L. *The new language of politics: an anecdotal dictionary of catchwords, slogans, and political usage* 1968
Sagan, Carl *The cosmic connection: an extraterrestrial perspective* 1973 (UK 1974)
Sagarin, Edward *Cosmetics: science and technology* 1957
Sage, Bp. John *Works* a1711 (Spottiswoode Soc. 1844–46)
The fundamental charter of presbytery (The article) (anon.) 1695 (1697)
The principles of the Cyprianic age, by J. S. 1695
— *A vindication of the principles of the Cyprianic age* 1701
Sage, Rufus B. *Scenes in the Rocky Mountains, and in Oregon, California, New Mexico, Texas, and the grand prairies* 1846
St. Andrew. The Anglo-saxon legends of St. Andrew and St. Veronica. ed. with English transl. by C. W. Goodwin (1851)
St. Barbe, Reginald *In modern Spain: some sketches and impressions* 1899 (1900)
St. Clair, Leonard *A fortune in death* 1976
St. Cuthbert. The life of St. Cuthbert in English verse c1450 (Surtees Soc. 1891)
St. Foine improved: a discourse shewing the . . benefit which England . . may receive by the grasse called St. Foine . . Written by a person of honour 1671 (1674)
St. George's Hospital reports 1866–
Saint-German, C. tr. 1531 See *Dialogue*
St. James's gazette, The 1880–1905
St. John, Charles W. G. *Short sketches of the wild sports and natural history of the highlands* 1846
St. John, Henry a1751 *See* Bolingbroke, Viscount
Saint John, Henry C. *Notes and sketches from the wild coasts of Nipon* 1880
Saint John, James A. *History of the four conquests of England* 1862
St. John, John Henry Herbert *Pakeha rambles through Maori lands* 1873
St. John, Percy B. *Amy Moss, or the banks of the Ohio* 1854 (1860)
The snow ship 1865
St. Johnstoun; or John, earl of Gowrie (by Mrs. Eliza Logan) 1823
St. Kathleen, or the rock of Dunnismoyle (by A. Sutherland) 1820
St. Leonards, Edward B. Sugden, 1st Baron *A handy book on property law* 1858
St. Louis Globe-Democrat (St. Louis, Missouri) 1875–
St. Nicholas: Scribner's illustrated magazine for girls and boys 1873–
Saint Patrick: a national tale of the 5th century, by an antiquary (Rennie) 1819
Saint Patrick's purgatory See *Patrick*
St. Ursula. The lyf of saynt Ursula after the cronycles of englonde c1480 (Roxb. Club 1818)
'Saint Victor, Helen' *The ruins of Rigonda, a romance* 1808
Saints' lives c1290 (Early South-English legendary, E.E.T.S. 1887)
Saints' lives c1305 (Early English poems, Philol. Soc. 1862)
See also *Lives of saints*
Saintsbury, George Edward Bateman *Dryden* (English men of letters) 1881
A history of Elizabethan literature 1887 (1890)
A history of nineteenth century literature 1896
Notes on a cellar-book 1920
The peace of the Augustans 1916
A short history of French literature 1882
Saker, Austin *Narbonus; the laberynth of libertie* 1580
'Saki' (Hector Hugh Munro) *Beasts and super-beasts* 1914
The chronicles of Clovis 1912
Reginald 1904
Reginald in Russia, and other sketches 1910
Sala, George Augustus *Accepted addresses* 1862
America revisited 1882
The Baddington peerage 1860
Dutch pictures 1861
Gaslight and daylight 1859
Lady Chesterfield's letters to her daughter 1860
London up to date 1894
My diary in America in the midst of war 1865
Paris herself again 1879
Quite alone 1864
The seven sons of Mammon 1862
The ship chandler and other tales 1862
The strange adventures of Captain Dangerous 1863
A trip to Barbary 1866
Twice round the clock, or the hours of the day and night in London 1859 (1861)
Salak, John Stephen ed. *Dictionary of American sports* 1961
Sale, George *The Koran* tr. 1734
Salernum See Harington, Sir J.; Paynell, T. 1528
Salesbury, William *A dictionary in Englyshe and Welsh* 1547 (1877)
Salinger, Jerome David *The catcher in the rye* 1951
Franny and Zooey 1962
Salisbury, Harrison Evans *The shook-up generation* 1958 (UK 1959)
Salisbury, Jesse *A glossary of words and phrases used in S.E. Worcestershire* 1893 (E.D.S.)
Salkeld, John *A treatise of angels* 1613
A treatise of paradise 1617
Salkeld, William *Reports of cases adjudg'd in the court of King's bench* etc. a1715 (1721–24, 1773)
Sallustius Crispus, Caius, All the works tr. 1687 (1692)
Salmagundi; a miscellaneous combination of original poetry etc. (by G. Huddesford and others) 1791 (1795)
Salmagundi 1807–08 *See* Irving, W.
Salmon, George *The infallibility of the church* 1888
Lessons introductory to the modern higher algebra 1859 (1885)
A treatise on the analytic geometry of three dimensions 1862 (1874)
A treatise on conic sections 1849 (1855)
A treatise on the higher plane curves 1852 (1879)
Salmon, Nathaniel *A new survey of England* 1728–30 (1731)
Salmon, Thomas *A new abridgement and critical review of the state trials and impeachments for high treason* 1737 (1738)
The universal traveller: or, a compleat description of the several nations of the world 1752–53
Salmon, William *Diemerbroeck's (I. de) Anatomy of human bodies* tr. 1689 (1694)
Doron medicum; or a supplement to the new London dispensatory 1683
The family dictionary or household companion 1696
Pharmacopœia Bateana, or Bate's (G.) Dispensatory tr. 1694 (1713)
Pharmacopœia Londinensis or the new London dispensatory tr. 1678
Polygraphice; or the art of drawing etc. 1672 (1675, 1701)
Seplasium . . The compleat English physician 1693
Synopsis medicinæ, or a compendium of . . physick 1671
Salmond, Stewart D. F. *The christian doctrine of immortality* 1895
Salomon and Saturnus, The dialogue of a1000 (Ælfric Soc. 1848; Grein 1898)
— (a later version) ? a1300 (Ælfric Soc. 1848)
Salt, Henry S. *The life of H. D. Thoreau* 1890
Salter, Charles tr. *G. von Georgievics's Chemistry of dye-stuffs* 1903
tr. *G. von Georgievics's The chemical technology of textile fibres* 1902
Salter, James *The triumphs of the holy Jesus, a divine poem* 1692
Salter, Thomas F. *The angler's guide* 1815
Salter, William Henry *Zoar; or, The evidence of psychical research concerning survival* 1961
Saltern, George *Of the ancient laws of Great Britaine* 1605
Saltmarsh, John *The practice of policie in a christian life* 1639
Some drops of the viall powred out in a season when it is neither night nor day 1645–46
Sparkles of glory, or some beams of the morning-star 1647 (1847)
Saltonstall, Wye *Eusebius* (Pamphili) *his life of Constantine* tr. 1637
Picturæ loquentes, or pictures drawne forth in characters 1631
Saltus, Edgar E. *Madame Sapphira: a Fifth Avenue story* 1893
Salusbury, Sir John *Poems* a1612 (E.E.T.S. 1914)
Samouelle, George *The entomologist's useful compendium* 1819
Sampson, Anthony Terrell S. *Anatomy of Britain* 1962
Sampson, Edmund *Tales of the fancy* 1889
Sampson, George V. *Statistical survey of the county of Londonderry* 1802
Samuels, Michael Louis *Linguistic evolution: with special reference to English* 1972
San Francisco Examiner (title varies) 1865–
Sanborn, Kate *A truthful woman in southern California* 1893
Sancroft, Abp. William *Lex ignea: or the school of righteousness, a sermon* 1666
Modern policies, taken from Macchiavel, Borgia, and other choise authors 1652 (1653)
Occasional sermons a1693 (1694)
Sandars, Thomas C. *Justinian's Institutes* tr. 1859 (1874)
Sanday, William *The criticism of the fourth gospel* 1905
Inspiration (Bampton lectures) 1893
Sandburg, Carl *Chicago poems* 1916
Cornhuskers 1918
Slabs of the sunburnt west 1922
Smoke and steel 1920
Sanders, George *Memoirs of a professional cad* 1960
Sanders, Lawrence *The Anderson tapes* 1970
Sanders, Leonard *The Hamlet warning* 1976 (UK 1977)
Sanders, Richard *Physiognomie and chiromancie, metoposcopie, the symmetrical proportions and signal moles of the body, fully and accurately handled* 1653
Sanderson, C. C. ed. *Pedigree dogs as recognised by the Kennel Club* 1927
Sanderson, Bp. Robert *Works* a1663 (1854)
De juramento, seven lectures concerning the obligation of promissory oathes tr. 1655
Episcopacy as established by law in England not prejudicial to royal power 1673
Five cases of conscience occasionally determined a1663 (1666)
— *Two cases* (1668); *Eight* (1674); *Nine* (1678)
A sermon 1648 (1653)
XII sermons 1632 (1635)
XXXIV sermons a1663 (1674)
XXXV sermons (1681)
XXXVI sermons (1689)
Sanderson, Thomas *Original poems* 1800
Sanderson, Sir William *A compleat history of the life and raigne of King Charles* 1658
Graphice; or the use of pen and pensill, in designing, drawing and painting 1658
Sandford, Sir Daniel *On the rise and progress of literature* 1847
Sandford, Ernest G. ed. *Memoirs of Archbishop Temple* 1906
Sandford, Mrs. Henry *Thomas Poole and his friends* 1888
Sandford, James *See* Sanford
Sandilands, John *Western Canadian dictionary and phrase-book* 1912
Sandivogius, M. See French, J.
Sands, J. *Sketches of Tranent in the olden time* 1881
Sands, Robert C. *Writings in prose and verse* a1832 (1834)
Sandys, Abp. Edwin *Sermons* 1575–85 (1585; Parker Soc. 1841)
Sandys, Sir Edwin *Europæ speculum, or, a view or survey of the state of religion in the westerne parts of the world* 1599 (1629, 1638)
— *A relation of the state of religion* (1605)
Sandys, George *Groot's (H. de) Christ's passion, a tragedy* tr. 1640
Ovid's Metamorphosis tr. 1621–26 (1632)
A paraphrase upon the divine poems (*Job, Psalms, Ecclesiastes, Lamentations* etc.) 1638
A paraphrase upon the Psalmes of David 1636
A paraphrase upon the Song of Solomon 1641
A relation of a journey begun 1610 (Travels) 1615
Sandys, Sir Miles *Prudence the first of the foure cardinall virtues* (Essays) 1634
Sandys, William ed. *Christmas carols, ancient and modern* 1833
Sanford, James *Agrippa's (H. C.) Of the vanitie and uncertaintie of artes and sciences* tr. 1569
Guicciardini's (L.) Houres of recreation tr. 1573 (1576)
The manuell of Epictetus tr. 1567
Sangster, Charles *Hesperus and other poems* 1860
Sangster, Jimmy *Touchfeather* 1968
Your friendly neighbourhood death pedlar 1971
Sanitary engineer, The; a monthly record of sanitary news 1880–
Sankey, William H. O. *Lectures on mental diseases* 1866
Sansom, George Bailey *Japan: a short cultural history* 1931
Sansom, William, *The face of innocence* 1951
Sansone, Antonio *Dyeing* 1888
Santa Fé Republican (Santa Fé, New Mexico) 1847–
Sapir, Edward *Language: an introduction to the study of speech* 1921
Saporta, Sol & Bastian, Jarvis R. eds. *Psycholinguistics: a book of readings* 1961
'Sapper' (Herman Cyril McNeile) *The black gang* 1922
Bull-dog Drummond: the adventures of a demobilised officer who found peace dull 1920
The female of the species 1928
The finger of fate 1930
The third round 1924
Sapskull, Sir Bartholomew *See* Donaldson, W.
Sargent, Charles Sprague *Manual of the trees of North America* 1905
Sargent, Epes *Peculiar, a tale of the great transition* 1864
Sargent, Epes Winthrop *The technique of the photoplay* 1912
— (ed. 2) 1913
— (ed. 3) 1916
Sargeson, Frank *I saw in my dream* 1949
A man and his wife 1940
— (new ed.) 1944
Memoirs of a peon 1965
That summer, and other stories 1946
Saroyan, William *The daring young man on the flying trapeze, and other stories* 1934 (UK 1935)
Sarpi, Pietro (Paolo Servita). *The life of Father Paul* (Sarpi) tr. by a person of quality 1651
— with Sir N. Brent's History of the council of Trent (1676)
See also B., W.; Brent, Sir N.; Gentilis, R.; Potter, C.
Sarton, George Alfred Leon *A history of science* 2 vols. 1952–9 (UK 1953–9)
Sarum primer (1557) See *Primer*
Sasieni, Lewis Sidney *The principles and practice of optical dispensing and fitting* 1962
Sassoon, Siegfried Loraine *Collected poems, 1908–56* 1961
Memoirs of a fox-hunting man 1928

SASSOON, Siegfried Loraine (*cont.*)
Memoirs of an infantry officer 1930
Sherston's progress 1936
SATCHELL, Thomas *Provisional index to a glossary of fish names* 1879 (E.D.S.)
SATCHELL, William *The land of the lost: a tale of the New Zealand gum-country* 1902
Satirical poems of the time of the Reformation 1565–84 (S.T.S. 1891–93)
Satirical songs and poems on costume, from the 13th to the 19th century (Percy Soc. 1849)
Saturday evening post: an illustrated weekly magazine (title varies) 1821–1969
Saturday night (Toronto) 1887–
Saturday review (US) 1924– (title varies: 1924–51 with title *Saturday review of literature;* 1972–3 divided into four: *Saturday review of education; society; the arts; the sciences;* 1973–5 recombined as *Saturday review world;* 1975– with title *Saturday review*)
Saturday review of politics, literature, science and art, The 1855–
Saturday Westminster gazette ? 1899–1922
Satyr against the French, A 1691
SAUCIER, Walter J. *Principles of meteorological analysis* 1955
Saucy stories 1916–25
SAUL, Arthur *The famous game of chesse-play truely discovered* 1614 (1672)
SAUNDERS, Howard *An illustrated manual of British birds* 1888
SAUNDERS, John *Abel Drake's wife* 1862
The lion in the path, an historical romance 1875 (1876)
SAUNDERS, Margaret Baillie *Litany Lane* 1909
SAUNDERS, Richard *Plenary possession makes a lawfull power, a sermon* 1651
SAUNDERS, Ripley Dunlap *Colonel Todhunter of Missouri* 1911
SAUNDERS, William *Observations on the superior efficacy of the red Peruvian bark in the cure of agues* 1782
A treatise on the chemical history of some of the most celebrated mineral waters 1805
SAUNDERSON, R. *See* SANDERSON
SAVAGE, George *The antique collector's handbook* 1959
Dictionary of antiques 1970
Porcelain through the ages 1954
—— & NEWMAN, Harold *An illustrated dictionary of ceramics* 1974
SAVAGE, James *History of the hundred of Carhampton, in the county of Somerset* 1830
SAVAGE, John *A compleat history of Germany* 1702
A select collection of letters of the antients 1703
SAVAGE, Marmion W. *The bachelor of the Albany* 1847 (1854)
The Falcon family, or young Ireland 1845 (1854)
Reuben Medlicott, or the coming man 1852 (1864)
SAVAGE, Richard *Works* a1743 (1775, 1777)
– *Poetical works* (1807)
The bastard, a poem 1728
A collection of pieces in verse and prose 1732
The convocation: or a battle of pamphlets, a poem 1717
Love in a veil, a comedy 1718 (1719)
Miscellaneous poems and translations, by several hands. Publ. 1726
Of public spirit in regard to public works, an epistle 1737
The tragedy of Sir T. Overbury 1724
The wanderer, a poem 1729
SAVAGE, Richard H. *Brought to bay* 1900
SAVAGE, William *A dictionary of the art of printing* 1841
SAVERY, Thomas *The miner's friend, or an engine to raise water by fire described* etc. 1702
SAVILE, George *See* HALIFAX, Marquis of
SAVILE, Sir Henry *The ende of Nero and beginning of Galba, fower bookes of the histories of Tacitus. The life of Agricola* tr. 1591 (1622)
SAVILLE-KENT, William *A manual of the infusoria* 1880–82
SAVIOLO, Vincentio *His practice, in two bookes, the first intreating of the use of the rapier and dagger, the second of honor and honorable quarrels* 1594–95
Sawles warde a1240 (Old English homilies I, E.E.T.S. 1868)
SAWYER, Frederic Henry Read *The inhabitants of the Philippines* 1900
SAXE, John Godfrey *Poems* v.d. (1850, 1877)
'SAXON' (Mrs. M. Trotter) *Galloway gossip sixty years ago* 1877
SAXON, Lyle, DREYER, E. & TALLANT, R. *Gumbo ya-ya: a collection of Louisiana folk tales* 1945
Saxon and the Gael, The; or the northern metropolis (by Mrs. C. J. Johnstone) 1814
Saxon chronicle. Two of the Saxon chronicles parallel, with supplementary extracts from the others ed. J. Earle 1865
See also *Anglo-Saxon chronicle*
——ed. C. Plummer 1892
Saxon leechdoms See *Leechdoms*
SAY, Maurice George ed. *Newnes concise encyclopaedia of electrical engineering* See under title
SAY, Thomas *American entomology, or descriptions of the insects of North America* 1824–28
SAY AND SELE, William Fiennes, Viscount *A speech in parliament* 1642
SAYCE, Archibald H. *Introduction to the science of language* 1880
The principles of comparative philology 1874 (1875)
SAYERS, Dorothy Leigh *Busman's honeymoon* 1937
Clouds of witness 1926
The five red herrings 1931
Gaudy night 1935
Hangman's holiday 1933
Have his carcase 1932
Lord Peter views the body 1928
Murder must advertise 1933
The nine tailors 1934
Strong poison 1930
Unnatural death 1927
The unpleasantness at the Bellona Club 1928
—— & 'EUSTACE, Robert' (Eustace Robert Barton) *The documents in the case* 1930
SCAMMON, Charles M. *The marine mammals of the north-western coast of North America described* 1874
Scandal at Tunbridge-Wells, a fable 1760
Scanderbeg (George Castriota). *The great Scanderbeg, a novel* (by U. Chevreau) tr. 1690
Scanderbeg redivivus 1684 *See* G., H.
SCARBURGH, Edmund *The English Euclide* tr. a1696 (1705)
SCARGILL, William P. *The puritan's grave* 1833 (1846)
SCARLETT, John *The stile of exchanges* tr. 1682
SCATCHERD, Norrisson *The history of Morley in.. Yorkshire* 1830 (1874)
SCHAEFER, Edward A. *Essentials of histology* 1885 (1887)
SCHAFF, Philip *Christ and christianity* 1885
History of the christian church 1883–93
See also HERZOG, J. J.
SCHALLER, George B. *The year of the gorilla* 1964 (UK 1965)
SCHAPERA, Isaac *The Bantu-speaking tribes of South Africa* 1937
The Khoisan peoples of South Africa: Bushmen and Hottentots 1930
SCHARF, Bedrich *Engineering and its language* 1971
Scheele's (C. W.) Chemical essays tr. 1786
Scheffer's (J.) History of Lapland tr. 1674
SCHELE DE VERE *See* DE VERE
Schellen's (H.) Spectrum analysis tr. Jane and C. Lassell, ed. W. Huggins 1871 (1872)
Scheme for equipping and maintaining sixteen men of war, A 1747
SCHEUCHZER, John G. *Kæmpfer's (E.) History of Japan* tr. 1727
SCHILLER, Ferdinand C. S. *Riddles of the sphinx* 1891
SCHILPP, Paul Arthur ed. *The philosophy of Bertrand Russell* 1944
ed. *The philosophy of Rudolf Carnap* 1963
SCHIMMELPENNINCK, Mary Anne *Narrative of the demolition of the monastery of Port Royal des champs* 1815 (1816)
SCHLAUCH, Margaret *The English language in modern times, since 1400* 1959
SCHLEY, Winfield S. & SOLEY, J. R. *The rescue of Greely* 1885
SCHLICH, William *A manual of forestry* 5 vols. (Vols. IV & V by W. R. Fisher) 1889–96
Schliemann's (H.) Troja: results of the latest researches tr. 1884
SCHMID, Reinhold *Die Gesetze der Angelsachsen* 1858
SCHMIDT, Alexander *Shakespeare-lexicon* 1874–75 (1886)
Schmidt's (E. O.) The doctrine of descent and Darwinism tr. 1875 (ed. 2)
SCHNEIDER, Frank *Qualitative organic microanalysis* 1946
Scholarly publishing 1969–
Scholasticall discourse against symbolizing with Antichrist in ceremonies, A (by R. Parker) 1607
Scholehous of vngracious women, The vertuous (attrib. to E. Gosynhill) c1550
Scholehouse of women, The, wherin every man may read a goodly praise of the conditions of women c1541 (1572 in Hazl. Popular poetry IV)
SCHOLEM, Gershom Gerhard *Major trends in Jewish mysticism* 1941
SCHOLES, J. *Tim Gamwattle's jawnt* (to see the queen) 1857
SCHOMBURGK, Sir Robert H. *A description of British Guiana* 1840
The history of Barbados 1848
School for good living, The; an essay on the European kitchen 1814
School of man, The; tr. from the French (of F. Génard) 1753
SCHOOLCRAFT, Henry Rowe *Historical and statistical information respecting the history, conditions, and prospects of the Indian tribes of the United States* 1851–60
SCHOONMAKER, Frank & MARVEL, Tom *The complete wine book* 1935
SCHREIBER, Charlotte Elizabeth *Journal, 1833–1891* extracts ed. Earl of Bessborough 2 vols. 1950–2
Journals, 1869–85 ed. M. J. Guest 2 vols. 1911
SCHREINER, Olive ('Ralph Iron') *From man to man* 1926
The story of an African farm 1883
Trooper Peter Halket of Mashonaland 1897
SCHROEDER, Henry *The annals of Yorkshire* 1851–52
SCHUCHERT, Charles *See* PIRSSON, Louis Valentine
SCHUELL, Hildred *Aphasia theory and therapy: selected lectures and papers* ed. L. F. Sies 1974
Schützenberger's (P.) On fermentation tr. 1876
SCHULBERG, Budd Wilson *The disenchanted* 1950 (UK 1951)
What makes Sammy run? 1941
SCHUMPETER, Joseph Alois *Business cycles: a theoretical, historical, and statistical analysis of the capitalist process* 2 vols. 1939
SCHWARTZ, Robert J. *A complete dictionary of abbreviations* 1955
SCHWARZ, Urs & HADIK, Laszlo *Strategic terminology* 1966
SCIAMA, Dennis William *Modern cosmology* 1971
Science abstracts 1898–1940 (from 1903 divided into subject sections)
Science, an illustrated journal (Camb., Mass.) 1883–94, N.S. 1895–
Science-gossip, Hardwicke's 1865–93
– continued as *Science-gossip* 1894–1903
Science journal 1965–71
Science lectures at South Kensington by Capt. Abney (et al.) 1878
Science lectures for the people, delivered in Manchester 1866–80
Science news 1946–60
Science news letter 1921– (from 1966 with title *Science news*)
Science progress (title varies) 1894–8; 1906–40; 1946–
Science survey 1960–
Scientific American, The (a periodical) 1845– . Supplement 1881–
Scientific monthly 1915–57
Scientific opinion: a weekly record of scientific progress 1869
SCLATER, Philip L. *Argentine ornithology* 1888–89
Exotic ornithology 1869
—— & THOMAS, M. R. O. *The book of antelopes* 17 parts (4 vols.) 1894–1900
See also SCLATER, W. L.
SCLATER, William *A brief and plain commentary upon the prophecie of Malachy* 1608 (1650)
The christians strength, a sermon 1612
An exposition with notes, on the whole fourth chapter to the Romanes a1626 (1650)
An exposition with notes, upon the first epistle to the Thessalonians 1619 (1630)
– *the second epistle* 1627 (1629)
A key to the key of scripture, or an exposition with notes, upon the three first chapters of the epistle to the Romanes 1611 (1629)
The ministers portion, a sermon 1612
The quæstion of tythes revised 1621 (1623)
Sermons experimentall on Psalms cxvi and cxvii a1626 (1638)
The sick souls salve, a sermon 1612
A threefold preservative against three dangerous diseases of these latter times 1609 (1610)
SCLATER, William *Civil magistracy by divine authority* 1652 (1653)
The crowne of righteousness (a funeral sermon) 1653 (1654)
The worthy communicant rewarded, a sermon 1639
SCLATER, William L. & SCLATER, P. L. *The geography of mammals* 1899
See also STARK, Arthur Cowell
SCOBELL, Henry ed. *A collection of acts and ordinances.. made in the parliament 1640–56* (1658)
SCOFFERN, John *Elementary chemistry of the imponderable agents and of inorganic bodies* 1855
See also *Orr's Circle of the sciences*
SCOGAN, SCOGIN, or SCOGGIN, John *His jestes* 1613
SCOLLINS, Richard & TITFORD, John *Ey up, mi duck!* 3 parts 1976–7
SCOONES, W. Baptiste ed. *Four centuries of English letters* v.d. (1880)
Scope 1966–
SCORESBY, William *An account of the artic regions, with a history and description of the northern whale-fishery* 1820
ed. *Cheever's (H. T.) Whaleman's adventures in the southern ocean* 1850 (1859)
Journal of a voyage to the northern whale-fishery 1823
SCOT, Sir J. *See* SCOTT
SCOT, Reginald *The discoverie of witchcraft* 1584 (1886)
A perfite platforme of a hoppe garden 1574 (1578)
SCOT, Walter *A true history of several honourable families of the.. name of Scot in.. Roxburgh and Selkirk* 1688 (1894)
SCOT, William *An apologeticall narration of the state of the kirk of Scotland since the reformation* c1630 (Wodrow Soc. 1846)
Scotch metrical version of the Psalms (1650) See *Scottish psalter*
Scotch paraphrases 1745 See *Translations*
Scotch presbyterian eloquence, The (by 'Jacob Curate') 1692 (1738)
Scotland. An account of the present persecution of the church of Scotland, in several letters 1690
An account of Scotland's grievances by reason of the duke of Lauderdal's ministry c1674 (1693)
The actis and constitutiounis of the realme of Scotland (1566)
– *The lawes and actes of parliament* (1597)
– *The acts of the parliaments of Scotland* 1124–1707 (1814–75)
The acts of the Lords auditors of causes and complaints 1466–94 (1839)
The acts of the Lords of council in civil causes 1478–95 (1839)
Acts and proceedings of the general assemblies of the kirk of Scotland 1560–1618 (Bannatyne Club 1839–45)
– *The acts of the general assemblies of the church of Scotland* 1638–49 (1682)
The acts of sederunt of the Lords of council and session 1553–1790 (1790)
The booke of common prayer.. for the use of the church of Scotland 1637
A brief and true account of the sufferings of the church of Scotland.. since the year 1660 1690
Calendar of the state papers relating to Scotland 1509–1603 (1858)
Compota thesaurariorum regum Scotorum, Accounts of the Lord high treasurer of Scotland 1473– (1877–)
A declaration.. from the generall assembly of the kingdome of Scotland 1642

A declaration of the lords of the secret councell and of the generall assembly of the kingdome and kirke of Scotland 1642
Miscellany of popular Scottish poems, chiefly of a humorous and descriptive character 1862
The new statistical account of Scotland, by the ministers of the respective parishes 1845. See also Sinclair, Sir J.
The petition of the commissioners of the generall assembly of the kirke of Scotland 1642
The register of the privy council of Scotland 1545- (1877-)
Registrum magni sigilli regum Scotorum, The register of the great seal of Scotland 1306- (1814, 1912; 1882-)
Registrum secreti sigilli regum Scotorum, The register of the privy seal of Scotland 1488-1529 (1908)
Rotuli scaccarii regum Scotorum, The exchequer rolls of Scotland 1264- (1878-)
The Scotts declaration in answer to the declaration sent unto them by their commissioners now at London 1642
Scotland's glory and her shame, being a brief historical account of her glory by presbytery etc. 1752 (1786)
Scots in Poland, Papers relating to the, 1576-1793 (S.H.S. 1915)
Scots magazine, The 1739-1817
Scots observer: a weekly journal of religious and national interest 1926-34
Scots poems. A select collection of Scots poems, chiefly in the broad Buchan dialect 1785
Scots songs. A selection of the most favourite Scots songs, chiefly pastoral, adapted for the harpsichord 1790
Scotsman, The 1817- (1855-9 with title *The Daily Scotsman*)
Scott, Alexander *Poems c*1560 (S.T.S. 1896; E.E.T.S. 1902)
Scott, Andrew *Poems, chiefly in the Scottish dialect* 1805 (1808)
Scott, Charles *The practice of sheep-farming* 1886
Scott, Clement William & Howard, C. *The life and reminiscences of E. L. Blanchard* 2 vols. 1891
Scott, Edward *All about the latest dances* 1919
Scott, Gavin *Hot pursuit* 1977
Scott, Sir G. Gilbert *Gleanings from Westminster Abbey* 1861 (1863)
*Lectures on the rise and development of mediæval architecture a*1878 (1879)
*Recollections personal and professional a*1878 (1879)
Scott, George Gilbert *An essay on the history of English church architecture* 1881
Scott, Hew *Fasti ecclesiæ Scoticanæ, the succession of ministers in the parish churches of Scotland* 1866-71
Scott, Jack S. *A clutch of vipers* 1979
Scott, Sir James Sibbald D. *To Jamaica and back* 1876
Scott or Scot, Sir John *The staggering state of the Scots statesmen* (1550-1650) *a*1670 (1754)
Scott, John *Works a*1694 (1718)
The christian life 1681-86 (1730, 1747)
*Practical discourses upon several subjects a*1694 (1697-98)
Scott, John 1773 See *Observations*
Scott, John *Amwell; a descriptive poem* 1776
Poetical works 1782
Scott, John *A visit to Paris in 1814* 1815 (1816)
— *Paris revisited in 1815* 1816 (1817)
Scott, John Somerville *A dictionary of building* 1964
A dictionary of civil engineering 1958
Scott, Jonathan *Bahar-Danush; or, Garden of knowledge, an oriental romance* tr. 1799
Ferishta's House of Dekkan tr. 1794
Scott, Joseph Nicol *Bailey's (N.) New universal English dictionary* Revised 1755 (1764)
'Scott, Leader' (Mrs. Lucy E. Baxter) *Tuscan studies and sketches* 1887 (1888)
Scott, Michael *The cruise of the Midge* 1834-35 (1863)
Tom Cringle's log 1829-33
Scott, Paul Mark *Staying on* 1977
Scott, Richard John Ernst ed. *Gould's medical dictionary* 1926
Scott, Robert Falcon *Scott's last expedition* ed. L. Huxley 2 vols. 1913
The voyage of the 'Discovery' 2 vols. 1905
Scott, Robert Forsyth *A treatise on the theory of determinants* 1880
Scott, Robert Henry *Elementary meteorology* 1883
Scott, Sarah *Test of filial duty* (anon.) 1772
Scott, Thomas *The Belgicke pismire stinging the slothfull sleeper* (anon.) 1622
The high-waies of God and the king (sermons) 1620 (1623)
Newes from Pernassus (anon.) 1622
A tongue-combat.. betweene two English souldiers 1623
Votivæ Angliæ; or the desires and wishes of England by S. R. N. I. 1624
Vox populi, or newes from Spayne 1620-24
Vox regis, by T. S. 1624
See also *Raleigh's ghost*
Scott, Thomas *The holy Bible.. with original notes* 1788-92
Scott, Thomas *Poems; with Edwin and Catherine or the distressed lovers, a tragedy* 1793
Scott, Virgil Joseph & Koski, Dominic *Walk-in* 1976 (UK 1977)
Scott, Walter *Miscellaneous prose works a*1832 (1834-71)
*Poetical works a*1832
Waverley novels (1829-33)
The abbot 1820
Anne of Geierstein 1829
The antiquary 1816
Auchindrane, or the Ayrshire tragedy 1830
The betrothed 1825
The black dwarf 1816
The border antiquities of England and Scotland 1814-17
The bridal of Triermain 1813
The bride of Lammermoor 1818
Castle Dangerous 1831
Chronicles of the Canongate (The highland widow, The two drovers, The surgeon's daughter; Saint Valentine's day, or The fair maid of Perth) 1827-28
Count Robert of Paris 1831
The doom of Devorgoil 1830
Essays on chivalry, romance and the drama v.d.
The fair maid of Perth 1828
*Familiar letters a*1832 (1894)
The fortunes of Nigel 1822
Guy Mannering; or the astrologer 1815
Halidon Hill: a metrical drama 1822
Harold the dauntless 1817
The heart of Midlothian 1818
The highland widow 1827
Ivanhoe, a romance 1819
Journal 1825-32 (1890)
Kenilworth 1821
The lady of the lake 1810
The lay of the last minstrel 1805
The legend of Montrose 1819
Letters ed. H. J. C. Grierson et al. 12 vols. 1932-7
The letters of Malachi Malagrowther 1826 See *Thoughts*, below
Letters on demonology and witchcraft 1830
The life of Napoleon Buonaparte 1827
The lord of the isles 1814
Marmion 1808
The minstrelsy of the Scottish border 1802 (1803)
The monastery 1820
Old Mortality 1816
Paul's letters to his kinsfolk 1815 (1816, 1839)
Peveril of the Peak 1822
The pirate 1821
Provincial antiquities of Scotland 1826
Quentin Durward 1823
Redgauntlet 1824
Rob Roy 1818
Rokeby 1813
St. Ronan's well 1824
ed. *Sir Tristrem* 1804 (1811)
The surgeon's daughter 1827
Tales of the crusaders (The betrothed, The talisman) 1825
Tales of my landlord (The black dwarf, Old Mortality, The heart of Midlothian, The bride of Lammermoor, A legend of Montrose, Count Robert of Paris, Castle Dangerous) 1817-32
The talisman 1825
Thoughts on the proposed change of currency by 'Malachi Malagrowther' 1826
The two drovers 1827
The vision of Don Roderick 1811
Waverley; or, 'tis sixty years since 1814
Woodstock, or the Cavalier 1826
See also Lockhart, J. G.
Scott, William *An essay of drapery, or the compleate citizen trading justly* 1635
Scott, William Berryman *An introduction to geology* 1897
*Scottish alliterative poems a*1400-*c*1475 (S.T.S. 1897)
Scottish Burgh Records Society *Publications* (1868-1908)
Scottish field 1903-
Scottish field, The (a poem on the battle of Flodden) 1515 (Miscellanies II, Chetham Soc. 1856)
Scottish History Society *Publications* (1887-)
Scottish journal of theology 1948-
*Scottish legends. Legends of the saints in the Scottish dialect of the fourteenth century c*1375 (S.T.S. 1896)
Scottish national dictionary ed. W. Grant & D. D. Murison 10 vols. 1931-76
Scottish pasquils. A book (a second, third book) of Scotish pasquils v.d. ed. J. Maidment (1827-28, 1868)
Scottish poems of the sixteenth century ed. J. G. Dalyell (1801)
Scottish psalter. The psalmes of David in metre, used in the kirk of Scotland 1596 (1615, 1633, 1635, 1650)
Scottish review 1975-
Scottish Text Society *Publications* (1884-)
*(Scottish) Trojan war, The c*1400 (Horstmann, Barbour's Legendensammlung 1881-82)
Scougal, Henry *Works a*1678 (1765)
*Discourses on important subjects a*1678 (1735)
Scourge of Venus, The: or the wanton lady, by H. A(ustin) 1613 (1614; Grosart 1876)
Scrafton, Luke *Reflections on the government of Indostan* 1763 (1770)
Screen 1959-
Scribbleomania; or the printer's devil's polichronicon, a poem (by W. H. Ireland) 1815
Scribner's Magazine 1887-
Scribner's Monthly, an illustrated magazine 1870-81
Scripture, Edward Wheeler *The elements of experimental phonetics* 1902
Scriven, John *A practical treatise on copyhold tenure and court keeping* 1816
— *A treatise on copyhold, customary freehold and ancient demesne tenure* ed. H. Stalman (1846, 1867)
— *A treatise on the law of copyholds* revised by A. Brown (1882)
Scrivener, Frederick H. A. *Six lectures on the text of the New Testament* 1874 (1875)
Scrivener, Scrivener C. *Our fields and cities; or misdirected energy* 1890 (1891)
Scroggs, Sir William *Practice of courts-leet and courts-baron a*1683 (1701, 1714)
Scrope, George Poulett *The geology and extinct volcanos of central France* 1858 (ed. 2)
History of.. Castle Combe, in the county of Wilts 1852
Volcanos, the character of their phenomena 1862 (ed. 2)
Scrope, William *Days and nights of salmon fishing in the Tweed* 1843
'Scrutator' (K. W. Horlock) *The country gentleman* (a novel) 1862
Scrutiny: a quarterly review 1932-53
Scrutton, Thomas E. *Commons and common fields* 1887
Scudamore, Sir Charles *A medical visit to Gräfenberg* 1843
Scudamore, Edward *The nomenclator; a technological dictionary containing all the principal terms in use in the arts and sciences* 1841
Scudamore, Frank Ives *The day dreams of a sleepless man* 1875
Scudamore, James *Homer à la mode* 1664
Scudder, Henry *The christians daily walke in holy securitie and peace* 1627 (1637)
A key of heaven: the Lord's prayer opened 1620
Scudder, Samuel Hubbard *Butterflies: their structure.. and life-histories* 1881
The butterflies of the eastern United States and Canada 1889
Scudery's (G. de) Curia politiæ: or the apologies of severall princes justifying to the world their most eminent actions tr. (by E. Wolley) 1654
Scully, William C. *Kafir stories* 1895
Sculthorpe, Cyril Duncan *The biology of aquatic vascular plants* 1967
Scupham, Peter *The hinterland* 1977
Sea-board 1860 *See* Warter, J. W.
Sea breezes 1919-39; 1946-
*Seafarer a*1000 (Grein)
Seafarers' log 1939-
Seager, F. *The schoole of vertue and booke of good nourture for chyldren and youth to learne theyr dutie by*, by F. S. 1557 (Babees book, E.E.T.S. 1868)
Seager, John *Hermann's (J. G. J.) Elements of the doctrine of metres* abridged and tr. 1830
A supplement to Dr. Johnson's Dictionary 1819
Seale, John Barlow *An analysis of the Greek metres* 1784 (1802)
Seaman, Donald *The bomb that could lip-read* 1974
Seaman, Sir Owen *The battle of the bays* 1897
In cap and bells 1899
'Search, Edward' *See* Tucker, A.
Sears, Roebuck & Co. *Catalogs c* 1876-
Sears, Edmund Hamilton *Athanasia; or foregleams of immortality* 1858
The fourth gospel the heart of Christ 1872 (1874)
Regeneration 1853 (1873)
Sermons and songs of the christian life 1874
Sears, George W. *Forest runes, poems* 1887
Seasonable advice to all true protestants in England, A 1679
Seasonable advice to protestants, containing some means of reviving and strengthening the protestant interest 1745
Seasonable expostulation with the Netherlands, A (by F. Osborne ?) 1652
Seasonable speech 1659 *See* Shaftesbury, 1st Earl of
Seaton, Albert Edward *A manual of marine engineering* 1883
Seaton, Sir Thomas *A manual of fret cutting and wood carving* 1875
Sebright, Sir John S. *Observations on hawking* 1826
Secker, Abp. Thomas *Lectures on the catechism of the church of England c*1735 (1769)
*Sermons on several subjects a*1768 (1770-71)
Secker, William *The nonsuch professor in his meridian splendor* (sermons) 1660
Second discourse of the religion of England, A 1668
Second maiden's tragedy, The 1611 (Hazl. Dodsley)
Second narrative of the late parliament (so-called), A 1658 (Harl. Misc.)
Second narrative, A 1697 *See* Keith, G.
Second plea. The conformist's second plea for the nonconformists (by E. Pearse) 1682
Second sight. A treatise on the second sight, dreams and apparitions, by 'Theophilus Insulanus' 1763
Secret history of the reigns of Charles II and James II, The 1690
Secret service. Moneys received and paid for secret services of Charles II and James II 1679-88 (Camden Soc. 1851)
Secreta secretorum, Three prose versions of 1450-80; *c*1400; 1422 (E.E.T.S. 1898)
Securis, John *A detection and querimonie of the daily enormities and abuses committed in physick* 1566
Sedgwick, Adam *A student's text-book of zoology* 1898
—— & Heathcote, F. G. *Claus' (C.) Elementary textbook of zoology* tr. 1884-85
Sedgwick, Anne Douglas *The little French girl* 1924
Sedgwick, Miss Catherine M. *Hope Leslie; or early times in the Massachusetts* 1827 (1872)
Letters from abroad to kindred at home 1841
The Linwoods; or sixty years since in America 1835
Live and let live 1837 (1873)
Sedgwick, Obadiah *The anatomy of secret sins* (sermons) *a*1658 (1660)
Χριστος και κερδος Christ the life, and death the gain of every true beleever 1650
Christ's counsell to his languishing church of Sardis 1640
England's preservation (a sermon) 1642

SEDLEY, Sir Charles *Works* a1701 (1722, 1778)
Bellamira, or the mistress, a comedy 1687
The mulberry garden, a comedy 1668
SEEBOHM, Frederic *The English village community examined in its relations to the manorial and tribal systems* 1883 (1884)
The Oxford reformers of 1498 (Colet, Erasmus, More) 1867
SEEBOHM, Henry *A history of British birds* 1883–85
Siberia in Asia 1882
SEELEY, Sir John R. *Ecce homo; a survey of the life and work of Jesus Christ* (anon.) 1865 (1866)
The expansion of England 1883
Lectures and essays 1869 (1870)
The life and times of Stein 1878
Natural religion 1882
A short history of Napoleon the first 1886
SEGAR, Sir William *Honor, military and civill* 1602
Sege off Melayne, The c1400 (E.E.T.S. 1880)
SEGRÈ, Emilio Gino *Experimental nuclear physics* 3 vols. 1953–9
SÉGUIN, Lisbeth G. *The Black forest, its people and legends* 1879
Seidel's (J. J.) The organ and its construction tr. 1852
SEILE, Henry *Augustus; or an essay of those means.. whereby the commonwealth of Rome was alter'd.. unto a monarchy* 1632
SELA, Owen *The Bengali inheritance* 1975
SELBIE, William Boothby *The psychology of religion* 1924
SELBORNE, Roundell Palmer, 1st Earl of *The book of praise, from the best English hymn writers.* Selected 1862 (1865)
Memorials a1895 (1896–98)
SELBY, Charles *London by night, a drama* a1863 (1886)
SELBY, Prideaux J. *A history of British forest-trees* 1842
Illustrations of British ornithology 1825–33
SELDEN, John *The duello or single combat* 1610
England's Epinomis a1654 (Tracts 1683; 1726)
The historie of tithes 1618
Illustrations (to Drayton's Poly-olbion) 1612
Table-talk a1654 (1689; Arber)
Titles of honor 1614
(For *Discourse of the government of England* See BACON, N.)
SELDEN, Joseph *The trades man's help. An introduction to arithmetick* 1694
SELDON, Arthur & PENNANCE, F. C. *Everyman's dictionary of economics* 1965
Select cases in the court of requests 1497–1569 (Selden Soc. 1898)
Select charters (1870) *See* STUBBS, Bp. W.
Select pleas of the court of admiralty 1390–1602 (Selden Soc. 1892–97)
Select pleas of the court of star chamber v.d. (Selden Soc. 1902–10)
Select pleas of the forest v.d. (Selden Soc. 1899)
Select poetry, chiefly devotional of the reign of queen Elizabeth a1600 (ed. E. Farr, Parker Soc. 1845)
Select poetry, chiefly sacred of the reign of king James the first 16.. (ed. E. Farr, 1847)
Selection from the Harleian Miscellany of tracts, A v.d. (1793)
SELF, Margaret Cabell *The horseman's encyclopedia* 1946
Self instructor, The, or young man's best companion 1807 (1811)
Selimus, emperour of the Turkes, The first part of the tragicall raigne of 1594 (Grosart, Greene's works XIV)
SELLAR, Eleanor M. *Recollections and impressions* 1907
SELOUS, Frederick C. *African nature notes and reminiscences* 1908
A hunter's wanderings in Africa 1881
Travel and adventure in south-east Africa 1893
SELVON, Samuel *A brighter sun* 1952
SELWYN, William *An abridgment of the law of Nisi prius* 1808 (1817)
SEMPER, Karl *The natural conditions of existence as they affect animal life* 1879 (1881)
SEMPILL, Sir James *A pick-tooth for the pope, or the pack-mans paternoster* tr. out of Dutch a1625 (1669)
Sacrilege sacredly handled, that is, according to scripture onely 1619
See also SEMPILL, R.
SEMPILL, Robert *The Sempill ballates, a series of.. Scotish poems ascribed to Robert Sempill 1567–83, to which are added poems by Sir J. Semple of Beltrees 1598–1610* (1872)
SEMPLE, George *A treatise on building in water* 1776
SEMPLE, Robert Hunter *Memoirs on diphtheria.* Selected and tr. 1859 (New Syd. Soc.)
Senault's (J. F.) Paraphrase upon Job tr. 1648
Sendivogius, M. See FRENCH, J.
Seneca's (L. A.) Tenne tragedies tr. (by Jasper Heywood, Alex. Neville, and others) 1581
SENHOUSE, Roger tr. *Colette's Chéri, and The last of Chéri* 1951
SENIOR, Nassau W. *Historical and philosophical essays* a1864 (1865)
SENIOR, William *Pike and perch* 1900
SENN, Charles Herman *The new century cookery book: practical gastronomy and recherché cookery* 1901
SENNETT, Richard *The marine steam engine, a treatise* 1882
Sequel, The; or moderation further display'd, a poem (by W. Shippen or D. De Foe) 1705
Ser John Mandevelle. The commonyng of Ser J. Mandevelle and the gret Souden ?c1400 (Hazlitt, Early popular poetry 1864)

SERGEANT, Miss E. F. Adeline *No saint, a study* 1886
SERGEANT, John *An account of the chapter erected by William, titular bishop of Chalcedon* 1706 (1853)
The history of monastical conventions, by J. S. (? J. Sergeant) 1686
A letter of thanks to Mr. J. T(illotson) 1666
Schism dispach't, or a rejoynder.. to the replies of Dr. Hammond and the lord of Derry, by S. W. (i.e. J. Sergeant) 1657
Solid philosophy asserted against the fancies of the Ideists 1697
Sure-footing in christianity, or rational discourses on the rule of faith, by J. S. 1665
Transnatural philosophy, by J. S. 1700
White's (T.) Peripateticall institutions tr. (? by J. Sergeant) 1656
SERLING, Robert J. *The president's plane is missing* 1967 (UK 1968)
Sermo pro episcopo puerorum (by Bp. J. Alcock) c1496 (W. de W.)
Serpent of division, The (by J. Lydgate) c1400 (1590, 1911)
SERRA, José Autures *Modern genetics* 3 vols. 1965–8
SERVICE, John *The life and recollections of Doctor Duguid* (a novel) 1887
Thir notandums 1890
SERVICE, Robert William *Ballads of a cheechako* 1909 (UK 1910)
Ploughman of the moon: an adventure into memory 1945 (UK 1946)
Rhymes of a rolling stone 1912 (UK 1913)
Songs of a sourdough 1907 (UK 1908)
The trail of '98: a northland romance 1910 (UK 1911)
Sessions papers [series of reports of criminal cases heard in London]:
1. *The whole proceedings of the Sessions of the Peace, and Oyer and Terminer for the City of London and County of Middlesex* 1730–1824
2. *Sessions' paper.. held at the Justice Hall, in the Old Bailey* 1825–33
3. Central Criminal Court *Minutes* 1835–1913
SETH, Andrew *Scottish philosophy, a comparison of the Scottish and German answers to Hume* 1885
SETON, Ernest Evan Thompson *Trail of an artist-naturalist* 1940
SETON-KARR, Walter S. *The Marquess Cornwallis* (Rulers of India) 1890
—— & SANDEMAN, H. ed. *Selections from Calcutta gazettes of the years 1784–1823* (1864–69)
SETON-WATSON, Christopher *Italy from liberalism to fascism, 1870–1925* 1967
'SETOUN, Gabriel' (Thomas N. Hepburn) *Robert Urquhart* 1896
SETTLE, Elkanah *Eusebia triumphans, The Hannover succession to the imperial crown of England* 1702 (1705)
Reflections on several of Mr. Dryden's plays 1687
Settlers and convicts 1847 *See* HARRIS, A.
Seven sages, The. The proces of the seuyn sages 13.. (Weber, Metrical romances III, 1810)
The seven sages, in English verse c1425 (Percy Soc. 1845)
See also ROLLAND, J.
Several discourses and characters address'd to the ladies of the age, wherein the vanities of the modish women are discovered 1689
SEVERSON, John Hugh ed. *Great surfing* 1967
SEWALL, Samuel *Diary* 1674–1729 (1878–82)
Letter-book 1686–1729 (Collections of Mass. Hist. Soc. 1886)
SEWALL, William *Diary, 1797–1846* ed. J. Goodell 1930
Sewanee review 1892–
SEWARD, Anna *Letters* 1784–1807 (1811)
Memoir of the life of Dr. Darwin 1804
Poetical works a1809 (1810)
SEWARD, William *Anecdotes of some distinguished persons* 1795–97
SEWARD, William *A tour to Yordes cave* 1801
— (A dialogue from the above, in Nine specimens, E.D.S. 1896)
SEWEL, William *The history of the.. Quakers* a1720 (1722, 1795)
A large dictionary English and Dutch 1708 (1766)
A new dictionary English and Dutch 1691
SEWELL, Anna *Black Beauty: the autobiography of a horse* 1877
SEWELL, Edward Humphrey D. *Rugby football up to date* 1921
SEWELL, Miss Elizabeth M. *Amy Herbert, by a lady* 1844
Cleeve Hall 1855
A glimpse of the world 1863
Ursula, a tale of country life 1858
SEWELL, George *The tragedy of Richard I* a1726 (1728)
SEWELL, George Harold *Amateur film-making* 1938
— (ed. 2) 1951
SEWELL, William *The domestic virtues and manners of the Greeks and Romans* (Oxford prize essay) 1828
Hawkstone; a tale of and for England in 184– 1845 (1846)
SEXBY, Edward *See* TITUS, Silius.
SEYD, Ernest *Bullion and foreign exchanges theoretically and practically considered* 1868
SEYMOUR, Edward J. *Thoughts on the nature and treatment of several severe diseases of the human body* 1847
SEYMOUR, Gerald *The glory boys* 1976
SEYMOUR, Richard *The court gamester* 1719 (1720)
— *The compleat gamester* 1720 (1734)
SHACKLETON, Ernest Henry *South: the story of Shackleton's last expedition, 1914–1917* 1919

SHACKLOCK, Richard *Hosius' (S.) A most excellent treatise of the begynnyng of heresyes in oure tyme* tr... and intituled by him, *The hatchet of heresies* 1565
SHADBOLT, Maurice Francis Richard *Among the cinders* 1965
The New Zealanders: a sequence of stories 1959
Strangers and journeys 1972
SHADWELL, Charles *The fair Quaker of Deal, or, the humours of the navy, a comedy* (anon.) 1710
The humours of the army, a comedy 1713
SHADWELL, Thomas *The dramatic works* a1692 (1720)
The amorous bigotte 1690
Bury-fair 1689
Epsom Wells 1672 (1673)
Fountain's (J.) Royal shepherdess 1669
The humorists 1670 (1671)
The Lancashire-witches, and Tegue ODivelly, the Irish priest 1682
The libertine 1676
The medal of John Bayes: a satyr against folly and knavery 1682
The miser 1672
The scowrers 1691
The squire of Alsatia 1688
The sullen lovers, or the impertinents 1668
The tenth satyr of Juvenal tr. 1687
The true widow 1679
The virtuoso 1676
The volunteers, or the stock-jobbers a1692 (1693)
The woman-captain 1680
SHAFTESBURY, Anthony Ashley Cooper, 1st Earl of *A seasonable speech made by a worthy member of parliament in the House of Commons, concerning the other House, March, 1659* 1659 (Harl. Misc.)
SHAFTESBURY, Anthony Ashley Cooper, 3rd Earl of *Characteristicks of men, manners, opinions, times* (anon.) 1711 (1737)
A letter concerning enthusiasm (anon.) 1708
The moralists, a philosophical rhapsody (anon.) 1709
Soliloquy; or advice to an author (anon.) 1710
SHAFTESBURY, Antony Ashley-Cooper, 7th Earl of *Diary* a1885 (in E. Hodder, Life 1886)
SHAIRP, John Campbell *Aspects of poetry* 1881
Culture and religion in some of their relations 1870
Robert Burns (English men of letters) 1879
SHAKESPEARE, William *Comedies, histories & tragedies* a1616 (First folio 1623)
— The Cambridge Shakespeare (1863–66, 1891–93)
— The Globe edition (1866)
Alls well, that ends well 1601
The tragedie of Anthonie, and Cleopatra 1606
As you like it 1600
The comedie of errors 1590
The tragedy of Coriolanus 1607
The tragedie of Cymbeline 1611
The tragedie of Hamlet, prince of Denmarke 1602
— *The tragicall historie of Hamlet, prince of Denmarke* (1603, 1604)
The first part of Henry the fourth 1596
— *The history of Henrie the fourth* (1598)
The second part of Henry the fourth 1597
— *The second part of Henrie the fourth* (1600)
The life of Henry the fift 1599
— *The cronicle history of Henry the fift* (1600, 1619)
The first part of Henry the sixt 1591
— *The second part* 1593
— *The third part* 1593
The famous history of the life of king Henry the eight 1613
The life and death of king Iohn 1595
The tragedie of Ivlivs Cæsar 1601
The tragedie of king Lear 1605
— *His true chronicle historie of the life and death of king Lear and his three daughters* (1608)
A louers complaint 1597 (at end of Sonnets 1609)
Loues labour's lost 1588
— *A pleasant conceited comedie called Loues labors lost* (1598)
Lucrece 1593 (1594; *The rape of Lucrece* 1616)
The tragedie of Macbeth 1605
Measure for measure 1603
The merchant of Venice 1596
— *The most excellent historie of the merchant of Venice* (1600, 1619)
The merry wiues of Windsor 1598
— *A most pleasaunt and excellent conceited comedie, of Syr Iohn Falstaffe and the merrie wiues of Windsor* (1602)
A midsommer nights dreame 1590 (also 1600, 1619)
Much adoe about nothing 1599 (also 1600)
The tragedie of Othello, the Moore of Venice 1604 (also 1622)
The late and much admired play, called Pericles, prince of Tyre 1608 (1609)
The phœnix and the turtle 1601 (in R. Chester's Loves martyr, repr. New Shaks. Soc. 1878)
The life and death of king Richard the second 1593
— *The tragedie of king Richard the second* (1597)
The tragedy of Richard the third 1594 (also 1597)
The tragedie of Romeo and Ivliet 1592
— *An excellent conceited tragedie of Romeo and Iuliet* (1597, 1599)
Sonnets c1600 (1609)
The taming of the shrew 1596
The tempest 1610
The life of Tymon of Athens 1607
The lamentable tragedy of Titus Andronicus 1588

— The most lamentable Romaine tragedie of Titus Andronicus (1594)
The tragedie of Troylus and Cressida 1606
— The historie of Troylus and Cresseida (1609)
Twelfe night, or what you will 1601
The two gentlemen of Verona 1591
Venus and Adonis 1592 (1593)
The winters tale 1611
—— et al. The passionate pilgrime 1599
Shakespeare Apocrypha, The: being a collection of fourteen plays which have been ascribed to Shakespeare ed. C. F. Tucker Brooke (1908)
Shakespeare jest-books ed. W. C. Hazlitt (1864)
Shakespeare Society Publications (1841-53)
Papers (1844-49)
Shakespeare's Centurie of prayse ed. C. M. Ingleby (1874, also New Shaks. Soc. 1879)
'Shallow, J.' (J. Y. A. Morshead) The Templars' trials 1888
Shand, Alexander I. The life of General Sir E. B. Hamley 1895
Shand, Philip Morton A book of wine 1926
Shands, Harley Cecil Semiotic approaches to psychiatry 1970
Shands, Hubert Anthony Some peculiarities of speech in Mississippi 1893
'Shannon, Dell' (Barbara Elizabeth Linington) Murder with love 1971 (UK 1972)
No holiday for crime 1973 (UK 1974)
Rain with violence 1967 (UK 1969)
The ringer 1971 (UK 1972)
Unexpected death 1970 (UK 1971)
With a vengeance 1966 (UK 1968)
Shapiro, Nat & Hentoff, Nat eds. Hear me talkin' to ya: the story of jazz by the men who made it 1955
Sharcott, Margaret A place of many winds 1960
Sharp, Bartholomew The voyages and adventures of Capt. B. Sharp and others in the south sea 1684 (Collection of voyages IV, 1729)
Sharp, Sir Cuthbert Chronicon mirabile; or extracts from parish registers (anon.) 1841
Sharp, Abp. John Works a1714 (1754)
Sharp, Lester Whyland Introduction to cytology 1921
— (ed. 3) 1934
Sharp, Margery Cluny Brown 1944
The gipsy in the parlour 1954
The nutmeg tree 1937
Something light 1960
Sharp, Samuel A treatise on the operations of surgery 1739
Sharp, Thomas A dissertation on the pageants or dramatic mysteries anciently performed at Coventry 1825
Sharp, William D. G. Rossetti, a record and a study 1882
ed. Sonnets of this century 1886
Sharpe, Charles K. ed. A ballad book 1823 (1880)
Letters a1851 (1888)
Sharpe, Frederick Dew Sharpe of the Flying Squad 1938
Sharpe, May Churchill Chicago May: her story 1928
Sharpe, Reginald R. ed. Calendars of letter-books preserved.. at the Guildhall 1899-
London and the kingdom 1894-95
Sharpe, Richard Bowdler Catalogue of the birds in the British Museum 1874-88
A handbook to the birds of Great Britain (= Lloyd's Natural history, British birds) 1894-96
—— & Dresser, H. E. A history of the birds of Europe 1871-81
Sharpe, Samuel Egyptian inscriptions 1837-41
The history of Egypt under the Ptolemies 1838
— under the Romans 1842
— till the conquest by the Arabs 1846 (1859)
Rudiments of a vocabulary of Egyptian hieroglyphics 1837
Sharpe, Thomas Ridley Porterhouse blue 1974
Wilt 1976
Sharpham, Edward The fleire (a comedy) 1607
Sharps, Wallace Samuel Dictionary of cinematography and sound recording 1959
Sharrock, Robert The history of the propagation and improvement of vegetables 1660
Shaw, Sir Charles Personal memoirs and correspondence, comprising a narrative of the war.. in Portugal and Spain 1837
Shaw, Cuthbert A monody to the memory of a young lady, with An evening address to a nightingale 1768
Shaw, Dennis Frederick An introduction to electronics 1962
— (ed. 2) 1970
Shaw, Frank, Spiegl, Fritz, & Kelly, Stan Lern yerself Scouse: how to talk proper in Liverpool 1966 (For Vol. 2 see 'Lane, Linacre')
Shaw, George General zoology, or systematic natural history 1800-12
— continued by J. F. Stephens (1815-26)
Musei Leveriani explicatio, Anglica et Latina 1792-96
Vivarium naturæ.. The naturalists' miscellany 1789-1813
Zoological lectures delivered at the Royal Institution 1809
Shaw, George A manual of electro-metallurgy 1842 (1844)
Shaw, George Bernard The admirable Bashville (in Cashel Byron's profession, rev. ed.) 1901
Androcles and the lion: a fable play 1914
The apple cart: a political extravaganza 1930
Back to Methuselah: a metabiological Pentateuch 1921
Bernard Shaw and Mrs. Patrick Campbell: their correspondence ed. A. Dent 1952
Buoyant billions 1949
Caesar and Cleopatra See Three plays for Puritans
Captain Brassbound's conversion See Three plays for Puritans
Collected letters ed. D. H. Laurence 1965-
The common sense of municipal trading 1904
The Dark Lady of the sonnets See Misalliance
The devil's disciple See Three plays for Puritans
The doctor's dilemma, Getting married, and The shewing-up of Blanco Posnet 1911
Ellen Terry and Bernard Shaw: a correspondence See Terry, Ellen & Shaw, George Bernard
Everybody's political what's what? 1944
ed. Fabian essays in Socialism 1889
Fanny's first play See Misalliance
Geneva 1939
Getting married See The doctor's dilemma
Heartbreak House, Great Catherine, and Playlets of the War 1919
How to become a musical critic ed. D. H. Laurence 1960
In good King Charles's golden days 1939
The intelligent woman's guide to socialism and capitalism 1928
John Bull's other island 1904
Letters See Collected letters
Letters to Granville Barker ed. C. B. Purdom 1956
London music in 1888-89 as heard by Corno di Bassetto 1937
Man and superman 1903
The millionairess See The simpleton of the Unexpected Isles
Misalliance, The Dark Lady of the sonnets, and Fanny's first play. With a treatise on parents and childen 1914
On the rocks See Too true to be good
Our theatres in the Nineties: criticisms contributed week by week to The Saturday Review 3 vols. 1932
Peace Conference hints 1919
Pen portraits and reviews 1931
— (Standard ed.) 1932
The perfect Wagnerite 1898
Platform and pulpit ed. D. H. Laurence 1962
Plays: pleasant and unpleasant 1898
Pygmalion in Nash's magazine Nov.-Dec. 1914
— (combined ed. with Androcles and the lion and Overruled) 1916
The quintessence of Ibsenism 1891
— now completed to the death of Ibsen 1913
Saint Joan 1923 (1924)
The shewing-up of Blanco Posnet See The doctor's dilemma
The simpleton of the Unexpected Isles, The six of Calais, and The millionairess 1936
Three plays for Puritans (The devil's disciple, Caesar and Cleopatra, Captain Brassbound's conversion) 1901
To a young actress: letters to Molly Tompkins ed. P. Tompkins 1960
Too true to be good, Village wooing, and On the rocks 1934
Translations and tomfooleries 1926
What I really wrote about the War 1930
— (Standard ed.) 1931
Widowers' houses: a comedy 1893
Shaw, Henry W. 1886 See 'Billings, Josh'
Shaw, Herman A text-book of aeronautics 1919
Shaw, Irwin Beggarman, thief 1977
Rich man, poor man 1970
The troubled air 1951
Shaw, James A country schoolmaster, James Shaw a1896 (ed. R. Wallace 1899)
Shaw, Lachlan The history of the province of Moray 1775
— new ed. by J. F. S. Gordon (1882)
Shaw, Peter Bacon's (F.) Philosophical works methodized and made English 1733
Three essays in artificial philosophy or universal chemistry 1731
Shaw, R. D. The Pauline epistles 1903
Shaw, Thomas Travels, or observations relating to several parts of Barbary and the Levant 1738
— Suppl. 1746
Shaw, Vero K. The illustrated book of the dog 1879-81
Shaw, William A Galic and English dictionary 1780
Shaw, William Napier Forecasting weather 1911
— (ed. 2) 1923
— (ed. 3) 1940
—— & Austin, Elaine Manual of meteorology 3 vols. 1926-30
Shawe, Dorothy. Mistris Shawe's tomb-stone 1658
She 1955-
Shea, Sir Ambrose Newfoundland, its fisheries and general resources 1883 (Fisheries exhibition literature)
Shea, Timothy Edward Transmission networks and wave filters 1930
Shearman, Montagu Athletics and football (Badminton library) 1887 (1899)
Shebbeare, John Lydia, or filial piety 1755 (1769)
The marriage act (anon.) 1754
— (another ed.) Matrimony, a novel 1755 (1766)
Shedd, William G. T. Dogmatic theology 1889
A history of christian doctrine 1864
Shedlock, John South tr. K. W. J. H. Riemann's Dictionary of music 1893
Shee, Sir Martin Archer Rhymes on art 1805 (1806)
Shee, William Archer My contemporaries (1830-70) 1893
Sheehan, George A. Running and being: the total experience 1978
Sheffield, John, Duke of Buckingham Works a1721 (1723, 1753)
An essay on poetry (anon.) 1682
Sheffield glossary 1888-91 See Addy, S. O.
Sheilds or Shields, Alexander The life and death of.. J. Renwick a1700 (1724; Biographia presbyteriana 1827)
'Shelby, Brit' (James Grady) The great pebble affair 1976
Sheldon, Frederick The minstrelsy of the English border, being a collection of ballads 1847
Sheldon, George A history of Deerfield, Massachusetts 1895-96 See also Temple, Josiah H.
Sheldon, John P. Dairy farming 1881
Sheldon, M. French Flaubert's (G.) Salammbô tr. 1886
Sheldon, Richard The first sermon after his conversion, preached.. at S. Martins in the field 1612
A survey of the miracles of the church of Rome, proving them to be Antichristian 1616
Sheldon, Sidney Bloodline 1978
Shelford, Robert Five pious and learned discourses 1635
Shell aviation news 1931-
Shell International Petroleum Company Bitumen (Shell Briefing Service) 1977
Information handbook, 1974-5 1974
Protecting the world's crops (Shell Briefing Service) 1977
Shelley, Charles P. B. Workshop appliances 1873 (1893)
Shelley, George Sentences and maxims.. in prose and verse 1712 (1730)
Shelley, Jane, Lady ed. Shelley memorials 1859
Shelley, Mrs. Mary Wollstonecraft Frankenstein, or the modern Prometheus 1818
Shelley, Percy Bysshe Poetical works a1822 (1853, 1882, 1904)
Prose works (1880, 1888)
Adonais, an elegy on the death of John Keats 1821
Alastor; or the spirit of solitude 1815
Calderon, Scenes from the Magico Prodigio of tr. 1822
The Cenci, a tragedy 1819
Charles the first 1821-22
The Cyclops, a satyric drama, tr. from Euripides 1819
Epipsychidion 1821
Essays, letters from abroad, translations and fragments a1822 (1852)
Hellas, a lyrical drama 1821
Julian and Maddalo 1818
Laon and Cythna: see Revolt of Islam, below
Lines written among the Euganean hills 1818
The mask of anarchy 1819
Oedipus tyrannus; or Swellfoot the tyrant, a tragedy 1820
Peter Bell the third 1819
Prince Athanase 1817
Prometheus unbound, a lyrical drama 1820
Queen Mab, a philosophical poem 1813
The revolt of Islam (an ed. 1818 Laon and Cythna) 1817
Rosalind and Helen, a modern eclogue 1818
Select letters a1822 (1882)
The witch of Atlas 1820
Letters ed. F. L. Jones 2 vols. 1964
Shelley papers, The (1833) See Medwin, T.
Shelley, William Flowers by the wayside (poems) 1868
Shelly, Lou ed. Hepcats jive talk dictionary 1945
Shelton, Jane de Forest The salt-box house: eighteenth century life in a New England hill town 1900
Shelton, Thomas Cervantes Saavedra's (M. de) History of Don Quixote 1612, 1620 (1652, 1746)
Shelvocke, George (the elder) A voyage round the world 1726 (1757)
Shelvocke, George (the younger) Siemienowicz' (C.) The great art of artillery tr. 1729
Shennan, Robert Tales, songs and miscellaneous poems.. chiefly in the Scottish dialect 1831
Shenstone, William Works in prose and verse (Elegies, Odes and other poems, Essays, Letters) a1763 (1764-69, 1777)
Essays on men and manners a1763
The judgment of Hercules, a poem (anon.) 1741
Poems upon several occasions 1737 (1798)
The school-mistress, a poem (anon.) 1742
Shenstone, William A. The elements of inorganic chemistry 1900
The methods of glass blowing 1886 (1889)
Shepard, Charles Upham Treatise on mineralogy 1832-35
Shepard or Sheppard, Thomas The clear sun-shine of the gospel breaking forth upon the Indians in New-England 1648
Shepardson, George Defrees Telephone apparatus 1917
Shepherd, Edwin Colston The military aeroplane 1941
Shepherd, Laurence Guéranger's (P. L. P.) The liturgical year tr. 1867-79
Shepherd, William Prairie experiences in handling cattle and sheep 1884
Shepherds. The kalender of shepherdes tr. 1503 (1506, 1656, Sommer 1892)
Sheppard, Elizabeth S. Charles Auchester, a memorial (anon.) 1853
Sheppard, John G. The fall of Rome and the rise of the new nationalities 1861
Sheppard, Mubin Taman indera: a royal pleasure ground. Malay decorative arts and pastimes 1972
Sheppard, Nathan Before an audience; or the use of the will in public speaking 1886
Sheppard, Samuel Edward Photo-chemistry 1914
—— & Mees, Charles Edward Kenneth Investigations on the theory of the photographic process 1907
Sheppard, Thomas 1648 See Shepard, T.
Sheppard, Thomas Harvey Dictionary of railway slang 1965
— (ed. 2) 1966
Sheppard, William The faithful councellor 1651-54
Sherard, Charles A. A daughter of the south and other poems 1889

SHERBURNE, Sir Edward *Coluthus' Rape of Hellen* tr. 1651
Salmacis, Lyrian and Sylvia.. with several other poems and translations 1651 (Chalmers 1810)
The sphere of M. Manilius made an English poem 1675
SHERER, John W. *At home and in India* 1882 (1883)
The conjurer's daughter, a tale 1880
SHERER, Joseph Moyle *Notes and reflections during a ramble in Germany* (anon.) 1826
Sketches of India (anon.) 1821
SHERIDAN, Alan tr. *J. Lacan's Écrits* 1977
SHERIDAN, Elizabeth *Betsy Sheridan's journal: letters from Sheridan's sister, 1784-1786 and 1788-1790* ed. W. LeFanu 1960
SHERIDAN, Mrs. Frances *The history of Nourjahad* a1766 (1767)
Memoirs of Miss Sidney Bidulph 1761-66 (1761-67)
SHERIDAN, Philip H., (general, U.S. army) *Personal memoirs* 1888
SHERIDAN, Richard Brinsley *Dramatic works* a1816 (1840, 1848)
Plays as he wrote them (1902)
The critic, or a tragedy rehearsed 1779
The duenna 1775 (1783)
Pizarro (adapted from Kotzebue) 1799
The rivals 1775
St. Patrick's day 1775
The school for scandal 1777
(*The stranger* (from Kotzebue) 1798)
A trip to Scarborough 1777
SHERIDAN, Thomas, D.D. *Letters* etc. a1738 (Swift's works)
The satyrs of Persius tr. 1728 (1739)
SHERIDAN, Thomas, M.A. *British education* 1756 (1769)
A general dictionary of the English language 1780
— *A complete dictionary of the English language* 1789
Lectures on the art of reading 1775
The life of Dr. Jonathan Swift 1784
Sheridaniana; or anecdotes of the life of R. B. Sheridan 1826
SHERIF, Muzafer *The psychology of social norms* 1936
SHERLEY, Sir Anthony *His relation of his travels into Persia* 1613
Sherley, Sir Robert, his royall entertainement into Cracovia etc. 1609 (Harl. Misc.)
SHERLOCK, Bp. Thomas *Sermons* (various) a1761
Several discourses preached at the Temple church 1754-58 (1759)
The tryal of the witnesses of the resurrection of Jesus 1729
The use and intent of prophecy in the several ages of the world, in six discourses 1725
SHERLOCK, William *A practical discourse concerning death* 1689
A practical discourse concerning a future judgment 1692
SHERRARD, Owen Aubrey *Two Victorian girls: with extracts from the Hall diaries* ed. A. R. Mills 1966
SHERRINGTON, Charles Scott *The integrative action of the nervous system* 1906
SHERRY, Richard *A treatise of the figures of grammar and rhetorike* 1555
A treatise of schemes and tropes c1550
S'hertogenbush, A jornall of certain principall passages in and before the towne of tr. 1629
See also *Pelegromius*
SHERWOOD, Adiel *A gazetteer of the State of Georgia* 1827
SHERWOOD, Mrs. Mary Martha *The history of the Fairchild family* 1813 (1818-47)
The history of Henry Milner, a little boy 1822-36
The history of little Henry and his bearer 1810 (1832)
The history of Susan Grey 1801
The lady and her ayah c1813 (1816)
The lady of the manor 1823-29
Stories explanatory of the church catechism c1813 (1822)
SHERWOOD, Robert *See* COTGRAVE, R.
SHERWOOD, Robert Emmet *Idiot's delight* 1936
SHERWOOD, William E. *Oxford rowing, a history of boat-racing at Oxford* 1900
SHEVELOV, George Yury *A prehistory of Slavic: the historical phonology of common Slavic* 1965
SHIELDS, Alexander a1700 *See* SHEILDS
SHIELDS, Charles Woodruff *The final philosophy, or system of perfectible knowledge, issuing from the harmony of science and religion* 1877
SHIELDS, Michael *Faithful contendings displayed, being an historical relation of the state.. of the suffering remnant of the church of Scotland* (1681-91) c1691 (1780)
SHILLABER, Benjamin Penhallow *The life and sayings of Mrs. Partington* 1854
SHILLINGFORD, John *Letters and papers* 1447-50 (Camden Soc. 1871)
SHIPLEY, Orby ed. *A glossary of ecclesiastical terms* 1872
SHIPMAN, Thomas *Henry the third of France stabb'd by a fryer, a tragedy* 1678
Ship-money. The case of ship-money briefly discoursed (by H. Parker) 1640
SHIPP, John *Memoirs of the extraordinary military career of J. Shipp,.. written by himself* 1829
SHIPPEN, William *Moderation display'd, a poem* (anon.) 1704
SHIPWAY, William *The campanologia, or universal instructor in the art of ringing* 1813-16
Shirburn ballads, The 1585-1616 (1907)
'SHIRLEY' *See* SKELTON, Sir J.
SHIRLEY, Henry *The martyr'd souldier, a tragedy* a1627 (1638; Bullen, Old plays I, 1882)
SHIRLEY, James *Dramatic works* a1666 (1833)
Andromana, or the merchant's wife, by J. S. (? Shirley) 1660 (Dodsley)
The ball 1632 (1639)
The bird in a cage 1633
The brothers 1626 (1652)
(*Captain Underwit*: see Newcastle, 1st Duke of)
The cardinal 1641 (1652)
Changes: or Love in a maze 1632
A contention for honour and riches 1632 (1633)
The coronation 1635 (Beaumont and Fletcher 1679)
The court secret 1653
The gamester 1633 (1637)
The gentleman of Venice 1639 (1655)
Hide park 1632 (1637, 1660)
Honour and mammon 1659
Love tricks: see Schoole, below
Loves crueltie 1640
The maides revenge 1639
The opportunitie 1634 (1640)
Poems 1646
St. Patrick for Ireland 1640
The schoole of complement 1631
— (another ed.) *Love tricks, or the school of complements* (1667)
The sisters 1642 (1652)
The traytor 1631 (1635)
The triumph of peace 1633 (1634)
The wedding 1626 (1629, 1660)
The wittie faire one 1628 (1633)
See also FLETCHER, J.
SHIRLEY, John *A.. cronycle of the dethe and false murdure of James Stewarde, kyng of Scotys* tr. 1440 (1818)
SHIRLEY, John *The triumph of wit* 1688 (1707)
SHIRLEY, William *A letter to.. the Duke of Newcastle, with a journal of the siege of Louisburg* 1746
SHIRRA, Robert *Remains* a1803 (1850)
SHIRREFF, John *General view of the agriculture of the Orkney islands* 1814
— *of the Shetland islands* 1814
SHIRREFS, Andrew *Poems, chiefly in the Scottish dialect* 1790
SHOBERL, Frederick tr. *I. Titsingh's Illustrations of Japan* 1822
Klaproth's (H. J. von) Travels in the Caucasus and Georgia tr. 1814
Shooting times and country magazine 1882-
SHOREHAM, William of *Poems* c1315 (Percy Soc. 1849; E.E.T.S. 1902)
SHORT, Eirian *Embroidery and fabric collage* 1967
SHORT, Thomas *Medicina Britannica: or a treatise on such physical plants as are generally to be found in the fields and gardens in Great Britain* 1747
Short catechism, A, or playne instruction, conteynynge the summe of christian learninge, sett fourth by the kings maiesties authoritie 1553 (Two liturgies etc., Parker Soc. 1844)
Short dialogue 1605 *See* HIERON, S.
Short explication 1724 See *Music*
Short (schorte) somme of the buik of discipline, Ane c1570 (Collection of confessions of faith etc. 1719-22)
Short view of the prælaticall church of England, A (by R. Bernard) 1641
SHORTER, Thomas ('T. Brevior') *The two worlds* 1864
Shorter catechism of the Westminster Assembly of divines, The 1647 (1648, 1718)
SHORTHOUSE, Joseph H. *The Countess Eve* (a novel) 1888
John Inglesant, a romance 1880 (1881)
Sir Percival, a story of the past and of the present 1886
SHRADER, Robert Louis *Electronic communication* 1959
Shrine, The; a collection of occasional papers on dry subjects c1000 (ed. T. O. Cockayne 1864-70)
Shropshire Archæological and Natural History Society *Transactions* 1878-
SHRUBSOLE, William & DENNE, S. *The history and antiquities of Rochester and its environs* (anon.) 1772
SHUCKARD, William E. *British bees* 1866
Burmeister's (H.) Manual of entomology 1836
See also SWAINSON, W.
SHUCKFORD, Samuel *The sacred and prophane history of the world connected* 1728-37
— *The creation and fall of man, a supplemental discourse* 1753
Shuffling, cutting, and dealing, in a game at pickquet, by O. P(rotector) and others (by H. Neville) 1659 (Harl. Misc.)
SHULMAN, Max *Barefoot boy with cheek* 1943
SHURR, Gertrude & YOCOM, Rachael Dunaven *Modern dance: techniques and teaching* 1949
SHUTE, John *Cambini's (A.) Two very notable commentaries of the originall of the Turcks* tr. 1562
SHUTE, John *The first and chief groundes of architecture* 1563
SHUTE, Josias *Judgement and mercy* (sermons) a1643 (1645)
Sarah and Hagar: or Genesis the sixteenth chapter opened in xix. sermons 1641-42 (1649)
'SHUTE, Nevil' (Nevil Shute Norway) *Beyond the black stump* 1956
The chequer board 1947
The far country 1952
In the wet 1953
Landfall 1940
Lonely road 1932
No highway 1948
On the beach 1957
Pastoral 1944
Pied piper 1942
The rainbow and the rose 1958
Requiem for a Wren 1955
Round the bend 1951
Ruined city 1938
A town like Alice 1950
Trustee from the toolroom 1960
SHUTTLEWORTH, Charles *Malayan safari* 1965
Shuttleworth family. *The house and farm accounts of the Shuttleworths of Gawthorpe Hall, in the county of Lancaster* 1582-1621 (Chetham Soc. 1856-58)
SIBBALD, James *Chronicle of Scottish poetry,.. to which is added a glossary* 1802
SIBBALD, Sir Robert *The description of the isles of Orknay and Zetland* 1711
The history ancient and modern of.. Fife and Kinross 1710 (also 1803)
Scotia illustrata, sive prodromus historiæ naturalis Scotiæ 1684
SIBBES, Richard *Complete works* a1635 (Grosart 1862-63)
A conference between Christ and Mary a1635 (1656)
SIBLY, Ebenezer *Key to physic and the occult science of astrology* a1800
SIBORNE, William *History of the war in France and Belgium in 1815* 1844
SIBREE, James *The great African island; chapters on Madagascar* 1880
Madagascar and its people 1870
SIBTHORP or SYBTHORPE, Robert *Apostolike obedience, a sermon* 1627
SICHEL, Allan *The Penguin book of wines* 1965
SICKELMORE, Richard *Agnes and Leonora, a novel* 1799
SIDDONS, Henry *The maid, wife, and widow, a tale* 1806
SIDERFIN, Thomas *Les reports des divers special cases argue et adjuge en le court del bank le roy* etc. 1683-84 (1714)
SIDGWICK, Arthur & SIDGWICK, Eleanor Mildred *Henry Sidgwick: a memoir* 1906
SIDGWICK, Cecily *Sack and sugar* 1926
Victorian 1922
SIDGWICK, Henry *The methods of ethics* 1874
The principles of political economy 1883
SIDGWICK, Nevil Vincent *The chemical elements and their compounds* 2 vols. 1950
The electronic theory of valency 1927
SIDNEY or SYDNEY, Algernon *Works* a1683 (1772)
Discourses concerning government a1683 (1704)
SIDNEY, Sir Philip *Works* a1586 (1724-25; Miscellaneous works 1829; Complete poems, Grosart 1877)
An apologie for poetrie (1598 ed. of the Arcadia *The defence of poesie*) a1586 (1595; Arber)
The countesse of Pembrokes Arcadia a1586 (1590, 1598, 1621, 1629; Sommer 1891; Feuillerat 1912-22)
Astrophel and Stella a1586 (1591; edd. of the Arcadia)
Mornay's (P. de) Woorke concerning the trewnesse of the christian religion tr. (begun by Sir P. Sidney and finished by A. Golding) (1587, 1592, 1617)
The psalmes of David tr. (begun by Sir P. Sidney i-xliii, and finished by his sister, the Countess of Pembroke) (1823)
(*Valour anatomized in a fancie* 1581 (1651))
Wanstead masque, The lady of May 1578 (in Arcadia 1605-; J. Nichols, Progr. Eliz. II, 1823)
SIDNEY, Richard John Hamilton *In British Malaya to-day* 1927
SIDNEY, Samuel *The book of the horse* 1875 (1898)
Sidney state papers. Letters and memorials of state in the reigns of Mary, Elizabeth, James, Charles I, Charles II, and Oliver's usurpation, written by Sir H. Sydney, Sir P. Sydney (and others) ed. A. Collins (1746)
Sidonia. Meinhold's (W.) Sidonia the sorceress tr. Lady Jane F. S. Wilde 1849 (1859)
SIEFF, Israel *Memoirs* 1970
Siege of Jerusalem, The c1400 (Laud MS. 656; Steffler 1891)
Siege of Limerick. A diary of the siege and surrender of Lymerick 1692
Siege of Rouen, The *See* PAGE, J.
Sierra Club bulletin (San Francisco) 1893-
SIEVEKING, I. Giberne *Memoir and letters of F. W. Newman* 1909
Signs before judgment a1300 (Early English poems, Philol. Soc. 1862)
SILBERRAD, Una Lucy *The letters of Jean Armiter: a novel* 1923
SILBERSTEIN, Ludwik *The theory of relativity* 1914
Siliad, The; or the siege of the seats, by the authors of The coming K—— 1874
SILL, Edward Rowland *The hermitage; and other poems* 1868
SILLIMAN, Benjamin *Manual on the cultivation of the sugar cane* 1833
Remarks made on a short tour between Hartford and Quebec 1820 (1824)
SILLIMAN, Benjamin *Principles of physics* 1859 (1867)
SILLITOE, Alan *The loneliness of the long-distance runner* 1959
Saturday night and Sunday morning 1958
SILVER, Stephen W. *Silver and Co's handbook for South Africa* 1875 (1880)
Silver sunbeam, The 1864 *See* TOWLER, J.
SIM, Thomas Robertson *The forests and forest flora of the colony of the Cape of Good Hope* 1907
SIMAK, Clifford Donald *They walked like men* 1963
SIMES, Thomas *The military guide for young officers* 1772
The military medley 1768 (ed. 2)
SIMMONDS, Peter L. *The commercial products of the animal kingdom* 1880
The commercial products of the sea 1879
The commercial products of the vegetable kingdom 1854
A dictionary of trade products 1858
— *The commercial dictionary of trade products* (1892)
A dictionary of useful animals and their products 1883

SIMMS, Frederick W. *Practical tunnelling* 1844
Public works of Great Britain, consisting of railways, bridges, canals etc. 1838
SIMMS, William Gilmore *Guy Rivers: a tale of Georgia* 2 vols. 1834
The partisan: a tale of the revolution 2 vols. 1835
Southward ho! A spell of sunshine 1854
The wigwam and the cabin; or, Tales of the South 2 ser. 1845
SIMON, André L. *A concise encyclopædia of gastronomy* 9 vols. 1939–46
A dictionary of wines, spirits and liqueurs 1958
Guide to good food and wines (rev. ed.) 1963
The history of the wine trade in England 1906
—— & HOWE, Robin *A dictionary of gastronomy* 1970
SIMON, David *Dorner's (I. A.) History of the development of the doctrine of the person of Christ* tr. 1861–63 (1872)
SIMON, Edith *The past masters* 1953
SIMON, James *An essay towards an historical account of Irish coins* 1749 (1810)
SIMON, Roger Lichtenberg *The big fix* 1973 (UK 1974)
Wild turkey 1975 (UK 1976)
SIMONDS, Herbert Rumsey & ELLIS, Carleton *Handbook of plastics* 1943
SIMONS, Nicholas & STUART, John *Reports of cases decided in the high court of Chancery* 1824–27
'SIMONS, Roger' (Margaret & Ivor Punnett) *A frame for murder* 1960
SIMONSEN, John Lionel *The terpenes* 2 vols. 1931–2
SIMPKINSON, Charles H. *The life and work of Bp. Thorold* 1896
A South London parish 1893 (1894)
SIMPKINSON, John N. *The Washingtons, a tale of a country parish in the 17th century, based on authentic documents* (App. 1593–1645) 1860
Simple narrative, A; or a visit to the Newton family (a novel) 1806
SIMPSON, David *A plea for religion and the sacred writings* 1797 (1808)
Strictures on religious opinions 1792
SIMPSON, George Gaylord *Principles of animal taxonomy* 1961
SIMPSON, Sir James Y. *Archæology: its past and its future work* 1861
Hospitalism: its effects on the results of surgical operations, etc. 1869
Memoir, by J. Duns (1873)
SIMPSON, John Hamilton & RICHARDS, Roger Smith *Physical principles and applications of junction transistors* 1962
SIMPSON, Katherine *Jeanie o' Biggersdale and other Yorkshire stories* 1893
SIMPSON, Richard *The school of Shakspere* (Captain T. Stukeley, No-body and Some-body, Histrio-mastix, The prodigal son, Jacke Drums entertainement, A warning for faire women, Faire Em, etc.) 1878
SIMPSON, Thomas *The complete vermin-killer* 1772
SIMPSON, Sir Walter G. *The art of golf* 1887
SIMPSON, William *Hydrologia chymica, or the chymical anatomy of Scarbrough and other spaws in Yorkshire* 1669
Hydrological essayes 1670
SIMS, George Frederick *Hunters Point* 1973
The last best friend 1967
The sand dollar 1969
SIMS, George R. *In London's heart* 1900
Mary Jane's memoirs 1887
— *Mary Jane married* 1888
The ring o' bells, etc. 1886
The social kaleidoscope 1879–80 (1882)
SIMSON, or SYMSON, Archibald *Christes testament unfolded: or seaven godlie.. sermons on our Lord's seaven last words* 1620
SIMSON, Robert *The elements of Euclid* tr. 1756
SINCLAIR, George *The hydrostaticks; or the weight, force, and pressure of fluid bodies made evident* 1672
Satans invisible world discovered; or, a choice collection of modern relations, proving.. that there are devils, spirits, witches and apparitions 1685
SINCLAIR, Sir John *An account of the systems of husbandry adopted in.. Scotland* 1809 (1812)
Correspondence v.d. (1831)
Observations on the Scottish dialect 1782
The statistical account of Scotland; drawn up from the communications of the ministers of the different parishes 1791–99
SINCLAIR, Michael *A long time sleeping* 1975
Norslag 1972
SINCLAIR, Thomas *The mount: speech from its English heights* 1878
SINCLAIR, Upton Beall *The brass check: a study of American journalism* 1919
The jungle 1906
Oil! 1927
The presidential agent 1944 (UK 1945)
SINGER, Isaac Bashevis *Shosha* 1978
SINGER, Samuel W. *Researches into the history of playing cards* 1816
SINGER, William *General view of the agriculture.. in the county of Dumfries* 1812
SINGHA, Rina & MASSEY, R. *Indian dances, their history and growth* 1967
'SINGLETON, Arthur' *See* KNIGHT, H. C.
SINGLETON, Robert C. *The works of Virgil* tr. 1855
Sinners beware! c1275 (O.E. Miscellany, E.E.T.S. 1872)
SINNETT, Alfred P. *The occult world* 1881
Sinonoma Bartholomei, a glossary from a fourteenth-century MS. a1387 (Anecdota Oxon. 1882)
SINTON, Thomas ed. *Poetry of Badenoch* 1906
Sions plea 1628 *See* LEIGHTON, A.
Sir Amadace, Sir Beues etc. See *Amadace, Beues*, etc.
Sir Clyomon. The historie of the two valiant knights, Syr Clyomon.. and Clamydes 1599 (Peele's works 1874)
Sire Degarre; a metrical romance a1330 (Abbotsford Club 1849)
Sir Degore. Syr Degore 13.. (c1550; Utterson 1817)
Sir Degrevant, The romance of a1400 (Thornton romances, Camden Soc. 1844; Luick 1917)
Sir Gyles Goosecappe, knight, a comedie 1606 (Bullen, Old plays III, 1884)
Sir John Oldcastle. The first part of the true and honorable historie, of the life of Sir John Old-castle, the good Lord Cobham 1600 (Shakespeare Apocrypha 1908)
Sir Isumbras, The romance of a1400 (Thornton romances, Camden Soc. 1844)
Sir Rohan's ghost, a romance (by Mrs. H. E. P. Spofford) 1859 (1863)
Sir Thomas More c1590 (Shaks. Soc. 1844; Shakespeare Apocrypha 1908)
Sir Tristrem c1320 (ed. Sir W. Scott 1804, 1811; S.T.S. 1886)
Siriz. Dame Siriz a1300 (Wright, Anecdota literaria 1844)
SISAM, Kenneth *Studies in the history of Old English literature* 1953
Sismondi's (J. C. L. de) History of the Italian republics tr. 1832
SISSONS, Thomas Michael B. & FRENCH, P. eds. *Age of austerity* 1963
Situation of Paradise found out, The; being a history of a late pilgrimage unto the Holy land (by H. Hare, Baron Coleraine) 1683
SITWELL, Edith Louisa *Bath* 1932
Bucolic comedies 1923
Gardeners and astronomers 1953
I live under a black sun 1937
The sleeping beauty 1924
Troy Park 1925
Victoria of England 1936
The wooden Pegasus 1920
SITWELL, Francis Osbert S. *Miracle on Sinai* 1933
SITWELL, Sacheverell *Golden wall and mirador* 1961
Six ballads, with burdens 15.. (Percy Soc. 1844)
Six old plays on which Shakspeare founded his Measure for measure (and other plays) (1779)
6,000 words: a supplement to Webster's Third New International Dictionary 1976
SKEAT, Walter W. *An etymological dictionary of the English language* 1882
A glossary of Tudor and Stuart words a1912 (Ed. with additions by A. L. Mayhew 1914)
ed. *Nine specimens of English dialect* 1896 (E.D.S.)
Specimens of English literature, from.. 1394–1579 1871 (1887)
—— with MORRIS, R. *Specimens of early English from.. 1298–1393* 1872 (1884)
Uhland's (J. L.) Songs and ballads tr. 1864
See also MAYHEW, A. L.
SKEAT, Walter William *Malay magic* 1900
SKELTON, John *Works* a1529 (1568)
Poetical works (Against the Scottes, The boke of three fooles, The bowge of courte, Colyn Cloute, Phyllyp Sparowe, Poems against Garnesche, A replycacion, Speke parrot, The tunnyng of Elynour Rummyng, etc.) a1529 (Dyce 1843)
tr. *Diodorus Siculus' Bibliotheca historica* ed. F. M. Salter & H.L.R. Edwards 2 vols. 1956–7
Magnyfycence, a goodly interlude and a mery c1520 (1843; E.E.T.S. 1906)
A ryght delectable treatyse vpon a goodly garlande or chapelet of laurell 1523
Vpon the doulourus dethe.. of the.. Erle of Northumberlande c1489
Why come ye nat to courte? c1522
SKELTON, Sir John ('Shirley') *Maitland of Lethington* 1887–88
Nugæ criticæ: occasional papers 1862
The table-talk of Shirley 1895
SKELTON, Philip *The complete works* a1787 (1824)
Deism revealed (anon.) 1749 (1751)
SKENE, Sir John *De verborum significatione, the exposition of the termes and difficill words conteined in the foure buikes of Regiam majestatem and vthers in the actes of parliament* 1597 (1641)
Regiam majestatem, the auld lawes and constitutions of Scotland faithfullie collected tr. 1609
SKENE, William F. *Celtic Scotland* 1876–80
The highlanders of Scotland 1837 (1902)
SKERL, John George Anthony tr. *A. L. Wegener's The origin of continents and oceans* 1924
Sketch, The: a journal of art and actuality 1893–1959
Sketches and eccentricities of Colonel David Crockett, of West Tennessee 1833
Sketches in natural history, history of the mammalia 1849
Sketches of character; or specimens of real life, a novel 1808 (1813)
SKEYNE, Gilbert *Ane breve description of the pest* 1568 (Bannatyne Club 1860)
SKILBECK, Oswald *ABC of film and TV working terms* 1960
SKINNER, Cornelia Otis *Madame Sarah* 1967
SKINNER, John *A miscellaneous collection of fugitive pieces of poetry* a1807 (1809)
SKINNER, John E. Hilary *After the storm; or Jonathan and his neighbours in 1865–6* 1866
The tale of Danish heroism 1865
SKINNER, Stephen *Etymologicon linguæ Anglicanæ* a1667 (1671)
SKRINE, John H. *A memory of Edward Thring* 1889
SKYRING William H. *Builder's prices* 1848–58
SLADEN, Douglas B. W. ed. *Australian ballads and rhymes* 1888
ed. *Australian poets 1788–1888* 1888
A Japanese marriage 1895
My son Richard: or the great company 1901
Playing the game. Story of Japan. Sequel to 'A Japanese marriage' 1904
— new ed., *When we were lovers in Japan* 1906
SLADEN, Joseph *Principles of gunnery* 1879
Slang dictionary 1859 *See* HOTTEN, J. C.
SLARE, Frederic *Experiments and observations upon oriental and other bezoar stones,.. to which is annexed a vindication of sugars against the charge of Dr. Willis* 1715
SLATER, Mary *Caribbean cooking for pleasure* 1970
SLATTER, Gordon Cyril *A gun in my hand* 1959 (UK 1960)
SLATYER, William *The history of Great Britanie (Palæ-Albion)* 1621
SLEATH, Eleanor *The Bristol heiress* 1808 (1809)
SLEIGH, John *An attempt at a Derbyshire glossary* 1865 (in Reliquary VI)
'SLICK, Jonathan' *High life in New York* 1844
'SLICK, Sam' *See* HALIBURTON, T. C.
SLIM, William Joseph *Defeat into victory* 1956
SLIMMING, John *Temiar jungle* 1958
SLINGSBY, Sir Henry *Diary* (1638–48) etc. a1658 (1836)
SLOANE, Sir Hans *Catalogus plantarum quæ in insula Jamaica sponte proveniunt vel vulgo coluntur* 1696
A voyage to the islands Madera, Barbados, Nieves, S. Christophers, and Jamaica, with the natural history.. of the last 1707–25
SLOANE, Thomas O'Conor *The standard electrical dictionary* 1893 (1898)
SLUGG, Josiah T. *Reminiscenses of Manchester fifty years ago* 1881
SMALL, Austin J. *Frozen gold* 1924
SMALL, John ed. *English metrical homilies from manuscripts of the fourteenth century* 1862
SMALL, Robert *History of the congregations of the United Presbyterian church 1733–1900* 1904
SMALL, Ronald John *The study of landforms: a textbook of geomorphology* 1970
SMALRIDGE, Bp. George *Sermons* a1719 (1852)
SMART, Alexander *Rambling rhymes* 1834
SMART, Benjamin H. *Walker remodelled. A new critical pronouncing dictionary of the English language* 1836 (1846); *epitomized* 1840
A way out of metaphysics 1839
SMART, Christopher *Poetical works* a1771 (Chalmers 1810)
A poetical translation of the fables of Phaedrus 1765 (1853)
A translation of the Psalms of David 1765
SMART, Hawley *Bound to win, a tale of the turf* 1877
Cleverly won, a romance of the Grand National 1887
From post to finish, a novel 1884
A race for a wife 1870 (1881)
SMART, John Jamieson Carswell *Between science and philosophy: an introduction to the philosophy of science* 1968
SMART, Peter *The vanitie and downe-fall of superstitious popish ceremonies, a sermon* 1628
Smart set, The: a magazine of cleverness 1900–30
SMEATON, A. C. *The builder's pocket manual* 1847
SMEATON, Amethe tr. *R. Carnap's The logical syntax of language* 1937
SMEATON, John *A narrative of the building, and a description of the construction of the Edystone lighthouse* 1791 (1793)
Reports on civil engineering a1792 (1838)
'SMECTYMNUUS' *An answer to a booke entituled An humble remonstrance* 1641
— *A vindication of the answer to the humble remonstrance* 1641
— *A modest confutation* (by J. Hall ?) *of a slanderous.. libell, entituled, Animadversions upon the remonstrants defense against Smectymnuus* 1642
SMEDLEY, Edward, et al. *The occult sciences* a1836 (1855)
SMEDLEY, Francis E. *Frank Fairlegh, or scenes from the life of a private pupil* (anon.) 1850
Harry Coverdale's courtship 1855
Lewis Arundel; or the railroad of life 1852
SMEDLEY, John *Practical hydropathy* 1859
SMEDLEY, Menella B. *Linnet's trial* 1864
SMEETON, George *Doings in London* 1828
SMELLIE, Alexander *Men of the Covenant* 1903
SMELLIE, William *A treatise on the theory and practice of midwifery* 1752–63
SMELLIE, William *Buffon's (G. L. le Clerc, comte de) Natural history* tr. 1781 (1791)
SMETHAM, James *Letters* a1889 (1891)
SMILES, Samuel *Character* 1871 (1876)
The Huguenots in France 1873 (1881)
The Huguenots; their settlements.. in England and Ireland 1867 (1880)
Industrial biography 1863
Life and labour; or characteristics of men of industry, culture and genius 1887
The life of George Stephenson 1857 (1859)
The life of George Stephenson and Robert Stephenson 1868
Life of a Scotch naturalist, Thomas Edward 1876
Lives of the engineers 1861–62

Smiles, Samuel (*cont.*)
A publisher and his friends: Memoir and correspondence of John Murray 1891
Robert Dick 1878
Self-help 1859
Smiley, Jack *Hash house lingo* 1941
Smirke, Mr. 1676 *See* Marvell, A.
Smith, Adam *Essays on philosophical subjects* a1790 (1795)
An inquiry into the nature and causes of the wealth of nations 1776 (1869)
The theory of moral sentiments 1759 (1804)
Smith, Albert R. *The adventures of Mr. Ledbury and his friend Jack Johnson* 1844
The fortunes of the Scattergood family 1845
The London medical student a1860 (1861)
The natural history of the gent 1847
The Pottleton legacy 1849
The struggles and adventures of Christopher Tadpole 1847 (1848)
Smith, Alexander *The history of the lives of the most noted highwaymen* etc. 1714
Smith, Alexander *Dreamthorp: a book of essays written in the country* 1863
Last leaves, sketches and criticisms a1867 (1868)
A life drama and other poems 1852 (1853)
A summer in Skye 1865
Smith, Alexander *A new history of Aberdeenshire* 1875
Smith, Alexander *Introduction to general inorganic chemistry* 1906
Smith, Sir Andrew *The diary of Dr. Andrew Smith, director of the 'Expedition for exploring Central Africa', 1834–1836* ed. P. R. Kirby 2 vols. 1939–40
Illustrations of the zoology of South Africa 1838–49
Smith, Annie Lorrain *A handbook of British lichens* 1921
Lichens 1921
Smith, Anthony John Francis *Blind white fish in Persia* 1953
Throw out two hands 1963
Smith, Ashley *The East-Enders* 1961
Smith, Barnard *Arithmetic and algebra in their principles and application* 1853 (1859)
Smith, Bosworth *See* Smith, Reg. B.
Smith, Charles *The antient and present state of the county and city of Cork* 1750
The antient and present state of the county of Down 1744
The antient and present state of the county and city of Waterford 1746
Smith, Charles *An elementary treatise on conic sections* 1882 (1885)
A treatise on algebra 1888 (1893)
Smith, Charles Alphonso *New words self-defined* 1919
Smith, Charles F. *On Southernisms* 1884 (Trans. Amer. Philol. Assoc.)
Smith, Charles Hamilton *The natural history of dogs* etc. 1839–40 (Jardine, Naturalist's library)
The natural history of horses 1841 (ibid.)
Smith, Charles Henry *Bill Arp, so called: a side show of the Southern side of the war* 1866
Smith, Charles J. *Synonyms and antonyms* 1867 (1870)
Synonyms discriminated 1871
Smith, Charles L. *Tasso's (T.) The Jerusalem delivered* tr. 1851 (1878)
Smith, Charlotte *Celestina, a novel* 1791
Conversations introducing poetry 1804
Desmond, a novel 1792
Emmeline, the orphan of the castle etc. 1788 (1816)
Ethelinde, or the recluse of the lake 1789 (1814)
Letters of a solitary wanderer 1799–1801
Marchmont, a novel 1796
Romance of real life 1786 (1787)
The wanderings of Warwick 1794
The young philosopher, a novel 1798
Smith, Constance *The riddle of Lawrence Haviland, a novel* 1890
Smith, David *Sermons and letters* a1865 (1869)
Smith, Donald John *Discovering railwayana* 1971
Smith, Dorothy Gladys ('Dodie') *Dear octopus: a comedy* 1938
I capture the castle 1949
Smith, E. *The compleat housewife; or accomplished gentlewoman's companion, by E— S—* 1728 (1750)
Smith, Edgar Fahs tr. *V. von Richter's Chemistry of the carbon compounds; or, Organic chemistry* 1886
— (ed. 2) 1892
— (ed. 3) 2 vols. 1899–1900
Smith, Edmund *Phædra and Hippolytus, a tragedy* 1707 (1709)
Poems a1710 (Chalmers 1810)
Smith, Edward & Dallas, W. S. *A system of natural history* 1855 (Orr's Circle of the sciences)
Smith, Egerton *A guide to English traditions and public life* 1953
Smith, Francis *An account of a voyage for the discovery of a north-west passage by Hudson's streights* 1748–49
Smith, George *A compleat body of distilling* 1725
Smith, George *The entertaining correspondent, or curious relations* 1738 (1739)
Smith, George, captain *An universal military dictionary* 1779
Smith, George *The laboratory: or school of arts* 1799
Smith, Bp. George *Ten weeks in Japan* 1861
Smith, George *The life of John Wilson, philanthropist and scholar in the east* 1878
Smith, George *Short history of christian missions* 1884 (1904)
Smith, George Gregory ed. *Elizabethan critical essays* 1904
Smith, Gilbert Morgan *Cryptogamic botany* 1938
Smith, Godfrey *The business of loving* 1961
The flaw in the crystal 1954
Smith, Goldwin *Cowper* (English men of letters) 1880
Essays on questions of the day 1893
Irish history and Irish character 1861
Lectures on modern history 1859–61 (1861)
Three English statesmen (Pym, Cromwell, Pitt) 1867 (1882)
Smith, Henry *Works* a1591 (1866–67)
Gods arrowe against atheists a1591 (1593)
A preparative to marriage 1591
Sermons a1591 (1593, 1637, 1866)
Smith, Henry & Smith, C. Roach *Isle of Wight words* 1881 (E.D.S.)
Smith, Henry Boynton *System of christian theology* a1880 (1884)
Smith, Henry Percy *Glossary of terms and phrases* 1883
Smith, Horatio ('Horace') *Poetical works* 1846
Festivals, games and amusements 1831
The moneyed man, or the lesson of a life 1841
The tin trumpet, or heads and tales 1836 (1876)
The Tor hill 1826 (1838)
See also Smith, James 1812–13
Smith, James & Smith, Horace *Horace in London, consisting of imitations of .. the Odes of Horace* 1813 (1873)
Rejected addresses, or the new theatrum poetarum 1812 (1873)
Smith, James *The panorama of science and art* 1815
Smith, James *The merry bridal o' Firthmains and other poems* 1866
Smith, Sir James E. *The English flora* 1824–28
— continued by W. J. Hooker (1833–36)
Flora Britannica 1800–04
An introduction to physiological and systematical botany 1807
See also Sowerby, J.
Smith, Jephson Huband *Notes and marginalia illustrative of the public life and works of A. Tennyson* 1873
Smith, Sir John 1590 *See* Smythe
Smith, John, captain *Works* a1631 (Arber)
An accidence or the pathway to experience necessary for all young sea-men 1626
The generall historie of Virginia, New-England and the Summer Isles 1624
A map of Virginia, with a description of the countrey 1612
A sea grammar, with the plaine exposition of Smiths accidence for young sea-men enlarged 1627
— *The seaman's grammar* (enlarged 1653, 1692)
A true relation of such occurrences and accidents of noate as hath hapned in Virginia since the first planting of that collony 1608
The true travels, adventures and observations of Captaine J. Smith 1630
Smith, John *Select discourses* a1652 (1821)
Smith, John *A compleat practice of physick* ed. J. Ridgley 1656
Smith, John *The mysterie of rhetorique unvail'd* 1657
Smith, John *King Solomon's portraiture of old age* 1666
— *The pourtract of old age* (1676)
Smith, John *England's improvement reviv'd* 1670 (1673)
Smith, John *Christian religion's appeal from the groundless prejudices of the sceptic to the bar of common reason* 1675
Smith, John *Horological dialogues, by J. S.* (? Smith) 1675
Horological disquisitions concerning the nature of time 1694
Smith, John *The narrative of Mr. J. Smith .. containing a further discovery of the late horrid and popish plot* 1679
Smith, John *Chronicon rusticum-commerciale; or memoirs of wool* etc. 1747
— *Memoirs of wool* etc. (1756–57)
Smith, John *The printer's grammar* 1755
Smith, John *Galic antiquities; consisting of a history of the Druids, particularly of those of Caledonia* 1780
Smith, John *Treatise on the management and cultivation of forest trees* 1843
Smith, John *A dictionary of popular names of the plants which furnish the natural and acquired wants of man* 1882
Ferns: British and foreign 1866 (1879)
Smith, John *Christian character as a social power* 1899
Smith, John B. *Explanation of terms used in entomology* 1906
Smith, John Barker *Ideation* 1888
Smith, John Hugh *Digital logic: basic theory and practice* 1971
Smith, John Pye *On the relation between the holy scriptures and some parts of geological science* 1839
Smith, John Thomas *Antiquities of Westminster* 1807–09
A book for a rainy day a1833 (1845)
The cries of London a1833 (1839)
Nollekens and his times 1828
Smith, John Thomas *Vicat's (L. J.) Practical treatise on calcareous mortars and cements* tr. 1837
Smith, Joseph A. *Productive farming* 1843 (ed. 2)
Smith, Joshua Toulmin *The parish, its obligations and powers* etc. 1854 (1857)
Smith, Jude *A misticall devise of the spirituall .. love betwene Christ .. and the church .. set forth in verse* 1575
Smith, Julie P. *The Widow Goldsmith's daughter* 1870
Smith, Kenneth M. *Insect virology* 1967
Smith, Laura Alexandrine *The music of the waters: a collection of the sailors' chanties, or working songs of the sea, of all maritime nations* 1888
Smith, Logan Pearsall *The life and letters of Sir H. Wotton* 1907
Words and idioms: studies in the English language 1925 (UK 1928)
Smith, Martin Cruz *Gorky Park* 1981
Smith, Bp. Miles *Sermons* a1624 (1632)
Smith, Priestley *Glaucoma: its causes, symptoms, pathology and treatment* 1879
Smith, Reginald Bosworth *Carthage and the Carthaginians* 1878
Life of Lord Lawrence 1883
Smith, Robert *Poems of controversy between episopacy and presbytery* 1714 (1869)
Smith, Robert *A compleat system of opticks* 1738
Smith, Robert Allan *Semiconductors* 1959
Smith, Robert Kimmel *Ransom* 1971 (UK 1972)
Smith, Sir Robert M. *Persian art* 1876
Smith, Samuel *Davids blessed man; or a short exposition upon the first psalme* 1614 (1635, 1868)
Smith, Samuel *A general view of the agriculture of Galloway* 1810
Smith, Seba *The life and writings of Major Jack Downing of Downingville* 1833 (1934)
The select letters of Major Jack Downing 1834
Way down east; or portraitures of Yankee life 1854 (1866)
Smith, Simon *The herring-busse trade* 1641
Smith, Solomon Franklin *The theatrical apprenticeship and anecdotical recollections of Sol. Smith* 1846
Smith, W. H. Saumarez *A young man's country: letters of a subdivisional officer of the Indian Civil Service 1936–1937* 1977
Smith, Southwood *See* Smith, T. S.
Smith, Sydney *Works* a1845 (1850, 1859)
Elementary sketches of moral philosophy 1804–06 (1850)
Letters on the subject of the Catholics, by Peter Plymley 1807–08 (1867)
Six sermons 1800
Two volumes of sermons 1809
A memoir by Lady Holland, with a selection of his letters a1845 (1855)
Smith, Sir Thomas *De republica Anglorum; the maner of gouernement or policie of the realme of England* a1577 (1583, 1584)
— *The common-wealth of England and maner of government thereof* (1589, 1609)
Smith, Thomas *Memorials of .. S. Miller, with a biographical sketch by .. T. Smith* 1883
Smith, Thomas Southwood *The philosophy of health* 1835–37
Smith, Toulmin *See* Smith, Joshua T.
Smith, Walter C. *Kidrostan: a dramatic poem* 1884
Smith, Walter George *Allergy and tissue metabolism* 1964
Smith, Wilbur *Gold mine* 1970
Smith, William *Chloris; or the complaint of the passionate despised shepheard* 1596 (Grosart 1877; Arber, English Garner VIII)
Smith, William *The annals of University College* (Oxford) 1728
Smith, William *A natural history of Nevis and the rest of the English Leeward Charibee islands in America* 1745
Smith, William *Thucydides' History of the Peloponnesian war* tr. 1753
Smith, William *An historical account of the expedition against the Ohio Indians in 1764, under the command of H. Bouquet* (? by W. Smith) 1765 (1868)
Smith, William *Strata identified by organized fossils* 1816
Smith, William tr. *J. G. Fichte's The characteristics of the present age* 1847
Smith, Sir William ed. *A dictionary of the Bible* 1860–63
A dictionary of Greek and Roman antiquities 1842 (1890)
Dictionary of Greek and Roman biography etc. 1844–49
—— & Cheetham, S. *A dictionary of christian antiquities* 1875–80
—— & Wace, H. *A dictionary of christian biography* etc. 1877–87
Smith, William Anderson *Lewsiana; or life in the outer Hebrides* 1875
Smith, William Hawley *The promoters: a novel without a woman* 1904
Smith, William Henry *Gravenhurst, or thoughts on good and evil* 1862 (1875)
Thorndale; or the conflict of opinions 1857 (1858)
Smith, William Robertson *Kinship and marriage in early Arabia* 1885
Lectures on the religion of the Semites 1889
The Old Testament in the Jewish church 1881
Smithsonian contributions to knowledge 1848–
Smithsonian Institution *Annual reports* 1850–
Smithsonian miscellaneous collections 1862–
Smitt, F. A. *The Swedish fisheries* 1883 (Fisheries exhibition literature)
Smollett, Tobias *Works* a1771 (1797, 1870)
The adventures of Ferdinand Count Fathom 1753
The adventures of Peregrine Pickle 1751 (1779)
The adventures of Roderick Random 1748 (1812)
The adventures of Sir Launcelot Greaves 1762 (1793)
Advice: a satire 1746
Cervantes Saavedra's (M. de) History and adventures of .. Don Quixote tr. 1755 (1803)
A compleat history of England 1757–58 (1800)
The expedition of Humphry Clinker (anon.) 1771 (1813)
Le Sage's (A. R.) Adventures of Gil Blas of Santillane tr. 1749 (1802, 1878)
The reprisal, or the tears of old England, a comedy 1757 (1777)
Reproof: a satire 1747
The tears of Scotland (a poem) 1746
Travels through France and Italy 1766 (1797)
Smugglers, The: a tale descriptive of the sea-coast manners of Scotland 1819 (1820)

SMYTH, Bp. (1632) *See* SMITH, Bp. M.
SMYTH, Charles Piazzi *Madeira spectroscopic* 1882
Our inheritance in the great pyramid 1864 (1874, 1880)
SMYTH, Henry Dewolf *A general account of the development of methods of using atomic energy for military purposes under the auspices of the United States government, 1940-1945* 1945
SMYTH, James *The practice of the customs in the entry, examination and delivery of goods etc.* 1812 (1821)
SMYTH, James Desmond *An introduction to animal parasitology* 1962
SMYTH, John *The Berkeley manuscripts. The lives of the Berkeleys,.. with a description of the hundred of Berkeley and of its inhabitants* c1640 (1883-85)
SMYTH, John Ferdinand Dalziel *A tour in the United States of America* 2 vols. 1784
SMYTH, Philip *Aldrich's (H.) Elements of civil architecture* tr. 1789 (1818)
SMYTH, R. Brough *The gold fields and mineral districts of Victoria* 1869
Victorian exhibition 1872. Mining and mineral statistics 1873
SMYTH, Samuel P. Newman *Old faiths in new light* 1879 (1882)
SMYTH, Sir Warington W. *A treatise on coal and coalmining* 1867
—— et al. *A catalogue of the mineral collections in the Museum of practical geology* 1864
SMYTH, William *Lectures on history; second series, on the French revolution* 1840 (1848)
SMYTH, William Henry, admiral *The sailor's word-book: an alphabetical digest of nautical terms* a1865 (1867)
SMYTHE, Sir John *Certain discourses.. concerning the formes and effects of divers sorts of weapons, and other verie important matters militarie* 1590
Instructions, observations and orders mylitarie 1595
SMYTHIES, Mrs. Harriet M. Y. *The bride elect* (anon.) 1852
Fitzherbert, or lovers and fortune-hunters (anon.) 1838
SMYTHIES, John Raymond & CORBETT, Lionel *Psychiatry for students of medicine* 1976
SNAITH, John C. *Fierceheart the soldier* 1897
The wayfarers 1902
Willow the king 1899
Snake in the grass, The 1696 *See* LESLIE, C.
SNAPE, Andrew *The anatomy of an horse* 1683 (1686)
SNELL, Walter Henry & DICK, Esther Amelia *A glossary of mycology* 1957
SNIEČKUS, Antanas *Soviet Lithuania on the road of prosperity* [anon. tr.] 1974
SNOOK, Barbara Lilian *English historical embroidery* 1960
SNOW, Charles Percy *The affair* 1960
The conscience of the rich 1958
Corridors of power 1964
Homecomings 1956
The masters 1951
Strangers and brothers 1940
SNOW, Edgar *The other side of the river* 1962 (UK ed. 1963 with title *Red China today: the other side of the river*)
Red star over China 1937
SNOW, John Augustine *Cricket rebel: an autobiography* 1976
SNOWDEN, James Keighley *Tales of the Yorkshire wolds* 1893
The web of an old weaver 1896
SNOWDEN, Ralph L. *Magistrate's assistant* 1846 (1862)
SOAMES, Henry *The Anglo-Saxon church* 1835 (1838)
SOANE, George *New curiosities of literature, and book of the months* 1847
Social life in England and France from 1780 to 1830 (by Mary Berry) 1831
Social science abstracts 1929-33
Society for the Diffusion of Useful Knowledge *Publications* 1827-
Society for Experimental Biology and Medicine *Proceedings* 1903-
Society for Psychical Research *Proceedings* 1882-83
Society for Pure English *Tracts* Nos. 1-66, 1919-48
Society in London, by a foreign resident 1885
Society of Antiquaries of Scotland *Transactions* 1792-
Society of Arts *Journal* 1852-
Transactions of the society.. for the encouragement of arts, manufactures and commerce 1783-1850
Society of Biblical Archaeology *Proceedings* 1878-1918
Transactions 1872-93
Society of Chemical Industry *Journal* 1882-1950 (from 1917 divided into sections)
Society of Dyers and Colourists *Journal* 1884-
Society of Telegraph Engineers (and of Electricians) *Journal* 1872-88
Soil science 1916-
SOLA, Francisco Garcia *The fisheries of Spain* 1883 (Fisheries exhibition literature)
Soliman. The tragedye of Solyman and Perseda 1592 (Hazl. Dodsley; Kyd's Works 1901)
SOLLAS, Hertha Beatrice Coryn & SOLLAS, William Johnson tr. *E. Suess's The face of the earth* 5 vols. 1904-24
Solleysel's (J. de) Parfait mareschal or compleat farrier tr. Sir W. Hope 1696
— *The compleat horseman or perfect farrier* (1717; also abridged 1702)
Solomon's Book of wisdom, King c1400 (with Adam Davy's dreams, E.E.T.S. 1878)
SOLON, Louis M. E. *The art of the old English potter* 1883 (1885)
SOLZHENITSYN, Alexander Isayevitch *See* BETHELL, Nicholas & BURG, David; WHITNEY, Thomas Porter
SOMERS, Lord John *A collection of scarce and valuable tracts* 1748
— *A second (third, fourth) collection* 1750-52
— complete ed. (1809-15)
Somerset medieval wills 1383-1558 (Somerset Record Soc. 1901-05)
Somerset Record Society *Publications* (1887-)
SOMERVILLE, Alexander *History of the British legion and war in Spain* 1839
SOMERVILLE, Edith Œ. & 'MARTIN ROSS' *All on the Irish shore: Irish sketches* 1903
The real Charlotte 1894
Some experiences of an Irish R.M. 1899
— *Further experiences* 1908
Some Irish yesterdays 1906
SOMERVILLE, Mrs. Mary *On the connexion of the physical sciences* 1834 (1849, 1858)
On molecular and microscopic science 1869
Physical geography 1848 (1849)
SOMERVILLE, Robert *General view of the agriculture of East Lothian* 1805
SOMERVILLE, William *The chace, a poem* 1735 (1749, 1767)
Field sports, a poem 1742
Hobbinol, or the rural games, a burlesque poem 1740 (1749)
Occasional poems, translations, fables, tales etc. 1727 (Chalmers 1810)
SOMERVILLE, William *Hartig's (R.) Text-book of the diseases of trees* tr. 1894
SOMERVILLE-LARGE, Peter *Couch of earth* 1975
Eagles near the carcase 1977
Something odd, a novel, by Gabrielli 1804
SOMMERSTEIN, Alan H. *The sound pattern of ancient Greek* 1973
SOMNER, William *The antiquities of Canterbury* 1640 (1703)
Dictionarium Saxonico-Latino-Anglicum 1659 (1701)
A treatise of gavelkind 1647 (1660)
'SON OF THE MARSHES, A' *See* JORDAN, D.
Song of Roland, Fragment of the c1400 (Sege off Melayne etc.; E.E.T.S. 1880)
Songs. A collection of songs and ballads relative to the London prentices and trades, during the fourteenth, fifteenth and sixteenth centuries (Percy Soc. 1841)
Festive songs, principally of the sixteenth and seventeenth centuries (Percy Soc. 1848)
The political songs of England from the reign of John to that of Edward II (Camden Soc. 1839)
Satirical songs and poems on costume from the 13th to the 19th century (Percy Soc. 1849)
Songs and ballads, chiefly of the reign of Philip and Mary (Roxb. Club 1860)
Songs and carols from a MS. in the British Museum c1475 (Warton Club 1856)
Songs and carols, from a MS. of the fifteenth century (Percy Soc. 1847)
Songs, carols, and other miscellaneous poems, from R. Hill's commonplace-book c1530 (E.E.T.S. 1907)
Sonnerat's (P.) Account of a voyage to the Spice islands and New Guinea tr. 1781
— *Voyage to the East Indies and China* tr. F. Magnus 1788-89
Sorel's (C.) Comical history of Francion tr. 1655
SOROKIN, Pitrim Aleksandrovich *Sociological theories of today* 1966
Sortes Horatianæ, a poetical review of poetical talent 1814
SOTHEBY, Samuel L. *Principia typographica; the block-books* etc. 1858
SOTHEBY, William *Wieland's (C. M.) Oberon, a poem* 1798 (1826)
Sounds 1970-
SOUTER, David *General view of the agriculture of the county of Banff* 1812
SOUTH, Richard *The butterflies of the British Isles* 1906
The moths of the British Isles 2 ser. 1907-8
SOUTH, Robert *Sermons preached upon several occasions* 1679, 1692, 1697-98, a1716 (1715, 1737-44, 1823, 1842)
South Africa. Senate *Debates* 1911-
South African Philosophical Society *Transactions* 1877-1909
South Carolina Gazette (Charleston, S. Carolina) 1732-?1775 (title varies)
South Carolina Historical Society *Collections* 5 vols. 1857-97
South China Morning Post (Hong Kong) 1904-
South-English legendary or lives of saints, The early c1290 (E.E.T.S. 1887)
South Kensington Museum. Handbook to the special loan collection of scientific apparatus 1876 (1877)
South Wales Echo (Cardiff) 1884-
SOUTHALL, James Powell Cocke ed. & tr. H. L. F. von Helmholtz et al. *Treatise on physiological optics* 3 vols. 1924
SOUTHALL, John *A treatise of buggs* 1730 (1793)
Southampton, New York *Records* 6 vols. 1874-1915
Southerly: the magazine of the Australian English Association 1940-
Southern Evening Echo (Southampton) 1958-
Southern folklore quarterly 1937-
Southern literary messenger 1834-64
SOUTHERNE, Edmund *A treatise concerning the right use and ordering of bees* 1593
SOUTHERNE, Thomas *Works* 1721
— *Plays* a1746 (1774)
The fate of Capua 1700
The loyal brother or the Persian prince, a tragedy 1682
The maid's last prayer, a comedy 1693
Oroonoko, or the royal slave, a tragedy 1696
Sir Anthony Love, or the rambling lady, a comedy 1691
SOUTHEY, Mrs. Caroline Anne *Poetical works* a1854 (1867)
Chapters on churchyards (anon.) 1829
Ellen Fitzarthur, a metrical tale (anon.) 1820
SOUTHEY, Robert *Poetical works* (1837-38, 1853)
All for love and the pilgrim to Compostella 1829
The book of the church 1824 (1841)
Chronicle of the Cid, from the Spanish 1808
Common-place book a1843 (1849-51)
The correspondence with Caroline Bowles a1843 (1881)
The curse of Kehama 1809 (1810, 1853)
The doctor 1834-43 (1848, 1862)
English eclogues 1799
Essays, moral and political 1810-28 (1832)
The expedition of Orsua and the crimes of Aguirre 1821
History of the Peninsular war 1823-32
Joan of Arc; an epic poem 1795 (1837)
Juvenile and minor poems a1800
Letters a1843 (1856)
Letters from England; by don Manuel Alvarez Espriella 1807 (1814)
Letters written during a short residence in Spain and Portugal 1796 (1799)
Life and correspondence a1843 (ed. C. C. Southey 1849-50)
The life of the rev. Andrew Bell a1843 (1844)
The life of Nelson 1813 (1854)
The life of Wesley 1820 (1846)
Lives of the British admirals 1833-40
Madoc (Madoc in Wales, Madoc in Aztlan) 1805
Metrical tales and other poems 1805 (1853)
Minor poems 1793-1805 (1815)
Oliver Newman, a New England tale 1829 (1845)
Omniana or horæ otiosiores 1812
The poet's pilgrimage to Waterloo 1816
Roderick, the last of the Goths 1814 (1815)
Selections from his letters a1843 (1856)
Sir Thomas More, or colloquies on the progress and prospects of society 1829 (1831)
Specimens of the later English poets 1807
A tale of Paraguay 1825
Thalaba the destroyer 1801 (1853)
Vindiciæ ecclesiæ Anglicanæ, letters to Charles Butler 1826
A vision of judgment 1821
Wat Tyler, a dramatic poem 1794 (1817)
SOUTHWARD, John *Dictionary of typography* 1875
Modern printing: a handbook of the principles and practice of typography and the auxiliary arts 4 vols. 1898-1900 (and several later editions used)
Practical printing 1882 (1892)
SOUTHWELL, Robert *The poetical works* a1595 (Turnbull 1856)
— *The complete poems* (Grosart 1872)
— *Prose works* (1828)
A hundred meditations on the love of God a1595 (1877)
Marie Magdalens funerall teares, by S. W. 1591 (1594, 1602, 1823)
Saint Peters complaynt 1595
— *S. Peters complaint and Saint Mary Magdalens funerall teares, with sundry other selected and devout poems, by R. S.* (1616)
The triumphs over death, by R. S. 1591 (1596; Archaica 1815)
Southwell minster, Visitations and memorials of v.d. (Camden Soc. 1891)
Southwestern historical quarterly 1912-
SOUTHWOOD, Thomas Richard Edmund & LESTON, Dennis *Land and water bugs of the British Isles* 1959
SOUTHWORTH, Louis *Felon in disguise* 1966
Soviet physics: Doklady See: Academy of Sciences of the U.S.S.R.
Sowdone of Babylone, The romaunce of the c1400 (E.E.T.S. 1881)
SOWERBY, George B. *A conchological manual* 1839
Popular British conchology 1854
SOWERBY, James *English botany; or coloured figures of British plants* (text from vol. IV by Sir J. E. Smith) 1790-1814 (1832-46)
SOYER, Alexis *The gastronomic regenerator: a.. new system of cookery* 1846
The pantropheon: or history of food and its preparation 1853
SOYINKA, Wole (Akinwande Oluwole Soyinka) *Kongi's harvest* 1967
The lion and the jewel 1963
The road 1965
Spaceflight 1956-
SPACKMAN, William Mode *An armful of warm girl* 1978
Spaewife, The 1823 *See* GALT, J.
SPALDING, John *The history of the troubles and memorable transactions in Scotland from 1624 to 1645* a1670 (1792)
— *Memorialls of the trubles in Scotland and in England 1624-45* (Spalding Club 1850)
SPALDING, Thomas A. *Elizabethan demonology* 1880
SPALDING, William *Italy and the Italian islands* 1841
Spalding Club *Publications* (1841-71)
Miscellany (1841-52)
Spallanzani's (L.) Dissertations relative to the natural history of animals and vegetables tr. 1784
— *Travels in the two Sicilies* tr. 1798
Spanish history, The: or a relation of the differences that happened in the court of Spain between Don John of Austria and Cardinal Nitard; with other transactions of that kingdom (Running-title—*Transactions of the court of Spain*) tr. 1678

Spanish rivals, The; a musical farce, by M. Lonsdale 1784 (1785)
Spanner, Edward Frank *The naviators* 1926
Spare rib 1972–
Spark, Muriel Sarah *The bachelors* 1960
The ballad of Peckham Rye 1960
The comforters 1957
The Mandelbaum gate 1965
The prime of Miss Jean Brodie 1961
Sparke, Edward *Scintillula altaris, or a pious reflection on primitive devotion* 1652 (1663)
Sparke, Michael ed. *Truth brought to light . . or a discourse . . of the first fourteen yeares of king James reigne* 1651
Sparke, Thomas *A brotherly perswasion to unitie and uniformitie in judgment and practise* 1607
Sparkes, John J. *Transistor switching and sequential circuits* 1969
Sparks, Bruce Wilfred *Geomorphology* 1960
Sparks, Jared ed. *Correspondence of the American revolution* 1853
The library of American biography 1834–38
— (Second series) 1844–47
Life of Gouverneur Morris, with selections from his correspondence and miscellaneous papers 1832
Sparrman's (*A.*) *Voyage to the Cape of Good Hope* tr. G. Forster 1785 (1786)
Sparrow, Bp. Anthony *A collection of articles, injunctions, canons etc. of the church of England* v.d. (1684)
A rationale upon the Book of common prayer 1657 (1661)
Sparrow, John *Behmen's* (*J.*) *Mysterium magnum* tr. 1654
Several treatises of J. Behme tr. 1661
The remainder of books written by J. Behme tr. 1662
Sparrow, John *Le Dran's* (*H. F.*) *Observations in surgery* tr. J. S. 1758 (1771)
Sparrow, William *Select discourses* 1877
Sparry, Francis *Cattan's* (*C. de*) *Geomancie* tr. 1591
Spartanburg Herald (Spartanburg, S. Carolina) 1890–
Speaker, The; a review of politics etc. 1890–97
Spearman, James Morton *The British gunner* 1828 (ed. 2)
Specimens of the British poets ed. T. Campbell (1819)
*Specimens of lyric poetry a*1310 (Percy Soc. 1842)
Spectator, The (by J. Addison, Sir R. Steele, and others) 1711–14 (1868, 1891)
Spectator, The; a weekly review of politics etc. 1828–
Spectator, The new; with the sage opinions of John Bull 1784–86
*Speculum Gy de Warewyke, an English poem c*1330 (E.E.T.S. 1898)
Spedding, James *Reviews and discussions, . . not relating to Bacon* 1836–77 (1879)
—— et al. ed. *Bacon's* (*F.*) *Works* 1857–74
Speech for Mr. D—ss (Dundas) *of Arnistoun, A* (by D. De Foe) 1711
Speeches of the five jesuits (T. White, W. Harcourt, etc.) *that were executed at Tyburn, 20th June 1679, The* 1679
Speed, Adolphus *Adam out of Eden, or an abstract of divers excellent experiments touching the advancement of husbandry c*1650 (1659)
Speed, John *The history of Great Britaine* 1611 (1623, 1632)
The theatre of the empire of Great Britaine 1611
— *England, Wales, Scotland and Ireland described and abridged c*1620 (1627)
Speed, Robert *The counter scuffle* by R. S. 1623 (1628)
Speedy, Thomas *Sport in the highlands and lowlands of Scotland with rod and gun* 1884
Speid, Mrs. John B. *Our last years in India* 1862
Speke, John Hanning *Journal of the discovery of the source of the Nile* 1863
Spelman, Sir Henry *The English works a*1641 (1723)
Archæologus. In modum glossarii ad rem antiquam posteriorem etc. 1626
— *Glossarium archaiologicum* (1664)
De non temerandis ecclesiis, a tracte of the rights and respect due to churches 1613 (1646)
De sepultura (in English) 1630 (1641)
*The history and fate of sacrilege, discover'd by examples a*1641 (1698)
—— et al. *Tithes too hot to be touched. Certain treatises wherein is shewen that tithes are due a*1641 (1646)
Spelman, Sir John *Case of our affairs* 1643
*The life of Ælfred the great a*1643 (1678, 1709)
Psalterium Davidis latino-saxonicum vetus (1640)
A view of a printed book (*of Hen. Parker's*) *intituled Observations upon his Majesties late answers and expresses* (anon.) 1642
Spence, Charles *From the braes of the Carse, poems and songs a*1869 (1898)
Spence, Ferrand *St. Euvremont's* (Marguetel de St. Denis, C.) *Miscellanea* tr. 1686
Varillas' (*A.*) *Secret history of the House of Medicis* tr. 1686
Spence, John *Shetland folk-lore* 1899
Spence, Joseph *Anecdotes, observations and characters of books and men a*1768 (1820)
An essay on Pope's Odyssey 1726
Spencer, Benjamin *See* Spenser
Spencer, Douglas Arthur *The Focal dictionary of photographic technologies* 1973
Spencer, Herbert *Ceremonial institutions* (part of Principles of sociology) 1879
The data of ethics 1879
Education 1861 (1879)
Essays: scientific, political and speculative 1852–73 (1858, 1863, 1874)
First principles (a system of philosophy) 1862 (1875)
Illustrations of universal progress 1864
The man versus the state 1884
Political institutions (part of Principles of sociology) 1882
The principles of biology 1864–67
The principles of psychology 1855 (1870–72)
The principles of sociology 1876–82
Social statics 1851 (1854)
The study of sociology 1873
Spencer, John *A discourse concerning prodigies* 1663
— Second ed. To which is added *a short treatise concerning vulgar prophecies* 1665
The righteous ruler, a sermon 1660
Spencer, John ed. *The English language in West Africa* 1971
Spencer, Thomas *The art of logick* 1628
Spencer, (Walter) Baldwin *Horn scientific expedition. Through Larapinta Land* 1896
Spencer, William Robert *Poems* 1811
Spender, Stephen Harold *Collected poems, 1928–1953* 1955
The edge of being 1949
European witness: impressions of Germany in 1945 1946
Learning laughter 1952
The making of a poem 1955
tr. *E. H. Toller's Pastor Hall* 1939
Poems of dedication 1947
Ruins and visions 1942
The still centre 1939
World within world: autobiography 1951
—— & Gili, J. L. tr. *F. Garcia Lorca's Poems* 1939
Spenser or Spencer, Benjamin *Vox civitatis, or London's complaint against her children in the country* 1625 (Phenix 1732)
Spenser, Edmund *Works a*1599 (Globe)
Amoretti 1594
Astrophel, a pastorall elegie upon the death of . . Sir Philip Sidney 1596 (in Arber, Eng. Garner I)
Colin Clouts come home again 1591–95
Complaints, containing sundrie small poemes of the worlds vanitie 1591
Daphnaïda, an elegie 1591
Epithalamion 1595
The faerie queene 1590–96
Fowre hymnes (in honour of love, in honour of beautie, of heavenly love, of heavenly beautie) 1596
Muiopotmos: or the fate of the butterflie 1590
Prosopopoia: or Mother Hubberds tale 1591
The shepheardes calender 1579
Three proper and wittie familiar letters, lately passed betwene two universitie men (E. Spenser and G. Harvey) 1580
— *Two other letters* 1579 (1580)
A view of the present state of Ireland 1596 (1633; Globe)
Virgils gnat 1591
The visions of Bellay 1591
Brittains Ida See Fletcher, G. (the younger)
Sphere, The 1900–64
'Spillane, Mickey' (Frank Morrison Spillane) *The big kill* 1951
Spilling, James *Giles's trip to London* (anon.) 1872
Molly Migg's trip to the seaside (anon.) 1873
Spingarn, J. E. ed. *Critical essays of the seventeenth century* 1908–09
Spinks, John William Tranter tr. *G. Herzberg's Atomic spectra and atomic structure* 1937
Spinster, The; a defence of the woollen manufacture. Publ. J. Roberts 1719
Spirit of the metropolitan conservative press 1839 (1840)
Spirit of the nation, The; ballads and songs by the writers of 'The Nation' (Dubl.) 1845
Spirit of popery speaking out of the mouths of phanatical protestants, The (by G. Hickes) 1680
Spirit of the public journals, The 1797–1814, 1823–25 (1798–1826)
Spirit of the times: a chronicle of the turf, agriculture, field sports, literature and the stage 1831–61
*Spirituall counsayle, very necessarye for every persone to have c*1530
Spitzer, Leo *Linguistics and literary history* 1948
Splendid follies, a novel 1810
Spock, Benjamin McLane *Decent and indecent: our personal and political behavior* 1970
Spofford, Mrs. Harriet E. P. *The amber gods, and other stories* 1863
Sir Rohan's ghost, a romance (anon.) 1859 (1863)
Spon, Ernest *Spon's Encyclopædia of the industrial arts, manufactures and commercial products* 1879–82
Workshop receipts 1873
— (Second series, by R. Haldane 1883; third, fourth series by C. G. W. Lock 1884–85)
Spon's (*E. & F. N.*) *Household manual* 1887
Spons' Mechanics' own book: a manual for handicraftsmen and amateurs 1885
Spooner, William C. *Veterinary art: a practical treatise on the diseases of the horse* 1845 (1851)
Sport (title varies) 1946–?57
Sporting magazine, The 1793–1870
Sports. A new book of sports, reprinted from the 'Saturday review' 1885
Sportsman's gazetteer and general guide, The (by C. Hallock) 1877 (also 1883)
Spottiswood, Abp. John *The history of the church of Scotland a*1639 (1677; Spottiswoode Soc. 1847–51)
Spottiswoode, William *Polarisation of light* 1874 (1879)
Spottiswoode Society *Publications* (1844–51)
Sprat, Bp. Thomas *A discourse to the clergy of his diocese* 1695 (1696)
The history of the Royal-society of London 1667
*Poems a*1713 (1790; Chalmers 1810)
Sprigge, Joshua *Anglia rediviva; Englands recovery* 1647 (1854)
Sprigge, Samuel S. *The life and times of Thomas Wakley* 1897
Spring, Robert Howard *These lovers fled away* 1955
Spring Rice, Margaret Lois *Working-class wives: their health and conditions* 1939
Spring and summer in Lapland, A (by H. W. Wheelwright) 1863 (1864)
Springer, Clifford Harry, Herlihy, R. E., & Beggs, R. L. *Advanced methods and models* 1965
Springfield Republican (Springfield, Massachusetts) (weekly ed.) 1824–
Sprott, Walter John Herbert *Social psychology* 1952
Sproule, John *An essay on the growth and management of flax in Ireland* 1844 (1846)
Spruce, Richard *Notes of a botanist on the Amazon and Andes . . 1849–64* ed. A. R. Wallace 2 vols. 1908
Spry, William J. J. *The cruise of Her majesty's ship 'Challenger'* 1876
Spurdens, William T. *A supplementary volume to R. Forby's Vocabulary of East Anglia* 1840 (1858)
See also Longinus, D. C.
Spurgeon, Charles Haddon *John Ploughman's pictures* 1880
The treasury of David; containing an original exposition of the Book of psalms 1870–86
Spurstowe, William *The spiritual chymist* 1666 (1668)
The wels of salvation opened 1655
Squier, Ephraim G. *Notes on Central America* 1855
Peru: incidents of travel and exploration in the land of the Incas 1877
Squire, Amos Osborne *Sing Sing doctor* 1935
Squire, Jane *A proposal for discovering our longitude* 1742
*Squyr of lowe degre, The a*1400 (Ritson, Metrical romances III, 1802)
Srb, Adrian Morris & Owen, Roy D. *General genetics* 1952
— (ed. 2, by A. M. Srb et al.) 1965
Stables, W. Gordon *The cruise of the land yacht 'Wanderer'* 1886
Our friend the dog 1884
Stacions of Rome, The (verse) *a*1400 (E.E.T.S. 1867; prologue only, Minor poems of the Vernon MS., E.E.T.S. 1901)
— *c*1440 (Polit., relig. and love poems, E.E.T.S. 1903)
— (prose) *c*1460–70 (E.E.T.S. 1867)
Stackhouse, Thomas *A new history of the holy Bible* 1737 (1767)
Staehlin Storcksburg's (*J. von*) *Account of the new Northern archipelago* tr. 1774
Stafford, Anthony *The femall glory, or the life and death of our blessed lady, the holy virgin Mary* 1635 (1869)
Staffords heavenly dogge: or the life and death of . . Diogenes 1615
Staffords Niobe: or his age of teares 1611
Stafford, Sir Thomas *Pacata Hibernia. Ireland appeased and reduced* 1633 (1821)
Stafford, William 1581 *See* S., W.
Stage year book, The 1908–28; 1949–
Stagg, John *The minstrel of the north, or Cumbrian legends* 1810 (1817)
Miscellaneous poems 1790 (1805)
— another selection 1807 (1808)
Stainer, Sir John *Composition* 1880
The music of the Bible 1879
The organ 1878
A theory of harmony 1871
—— & Barrett, W. A. *A dictionary of musical terms* 1876
— new and revised ed. (1898)
Stainton, Henry T. *British butterflies and moths* 1867
A manual of British butterflies and moths 1857–59
Stair, Sir James Dalrymple, 1st Viscount *The institutions of the law of Scotland* 1681 (also 1693)
Stalker, John *See* Parker, George
Stallybrass, James S. *Grimm's* (*J. L. C.*) *Teutonic mythology* tr. 1880–88
Stamp, Laurence Dudley *Britain's structure and scenery* 1946
— (ed. 5) 1960
ed. *A glossary of geographical terms* 1961
An introduction to stratigraphy: British Isles 1923
Stamp collector's magazine, The 1863–74
Stanbridge, John *Vocabula* 1510 (1525)
Vulgaria Stanbrigi 1510
Standard, The 1827–1916
Standard dictionary of the English language, A 1893–95 (Funk and Wagnalls)
Standard encyclopaedia of southern Africa 12 vols. 1970–6
Standard natural history, The See Kingsley, J. S.
Standard of equalitie in subsidiary taxes and payments, The; or a just and strong preserver of publique liberty 1647 (Harl. Misc.)
Standon (——) *A poem on the death of . . J. Weekes* 1699
Standish, Frank Hall *The maid of Jaen* 1830 (Poems 1838)
Stanford, Charles *Symbols of Christ* 1865 (1878)
Stanford, Charles Villiers & Forsyth, Cecil *A history of music* 1916
Stanford or Staunford, Sir William *An exposicion of the kinges prerogative, collected out of the great abridgement of Justice Fitzherbert a*1558 (1568)
Les plees del coron 1557 (1567)
Stanford dictionary of anglicised words and phrases, The ed. C. A. M. Fennell 1892

STANHOPE, George *The christian's pattern, or a treatise of the imitation of Jesus Christ* 1696 (1698)
A paraphrase and comment upon the epistles and gospels 1705–09
Pious breathings, being the meditations of St. Augustine made English 1701 (1704)
STANHOPE, Lady Hester L. *Memoirs, as related by herself in conversations with her physician* a1839 (1845)
STANHOPE, Philip Dormer, 4th Earl of Chesterfield *See* CHESTERFIELD
STANHOPE, Philip H. Stanhope, 5th Earl *History of England, comprising the reign of Queen Anne until the peace of Utrecht 1701–13* 1870
STANLEY, Arthur Penrhyn *Historical memorials of Westminster abbey* 1867 (1868)
Lectures on the history of the Eastern church 1861 (1869)
Lectures on the history of the Jewish church 1863–65 (1877)
The life and correspondence of Dr. Arnold 1844 (1858)
Sinai and Palestine in connection with their history 1856 (1858)
STANLEY, Henry Morton *The Congo and the founding of its free state* 1885
In darkest Africa 1890
Through the dark continent 1878
STANLEY, Rupert *Text-book on wireless telegraphy* 1914
— (new ed.) 2 vols. 1919
STANLEY, Thomas *The history of philosophy* 1655–61 (1687, 1701)
The history of the Chaldaick philosophy 1662 (1701)
Poems 1651
STANNARD, Mrs. Arthur *See* 'WINTER, J. S.'
Stannaries of Cornwall, The. The case of the stannaries stated c1650
The laws of the stannaries of Cornwall (1808)
Stans puer ad mensam c1430 (Babees book, E.E.T.S. 1868)
— c1460 (ibid.)
STANTON, Isabel Alice *A dictionary for medical secretaries* 1960
STANWELL-FLETCHER, Theodora Morris *Driftwood Valley* 1946
STANYHURST, Richard *Thee first foure bookes of Virgil his Æneis translated,..wyth oother poetical diuises* 1582 (1836; Arber)
The historie of Irelande..continued 1577 (in Holinshed; also 1587)
A treatise contayning a playne and perfect description of Irelande 1577 (in Holinshed; also 1587)
STAPLES, Frank Alston *Water-color painting is fun* 1948 (UK ed. 1951 with title *Water-colour painting*)
STAPLETON, Mrs. Bryan *Three Oxfordshire parishes* 1893 (O.H.S.)
STAPLETON or STAPYLTON, Sir Robert *Juvenal's sixteen satyrs* tr. 1647
The slighted maid, a comedy 1663
Strada's (F.) De bello belgico, the history of the Low-countrey warres tr. 1650
STAPLETON, Thomas *Beda's History of the church of England* tr. 1565
A fortresse of the faith 1565
A returne of untruthes vpon M. Jewelles replie 1566
STAPYLTON, C. B. *Herodian his imperiall history* tr. 1652
STAPYLTON, Sir R. *See* STAPLETON
Star 1888–
Star, The (Sheffield) 1938–
Star-chamber. Decree of the lords in the starre chambere touching printers, stationers, etc. 1584 (in J. P. Collier, Illustrations E.E. popular literature 1863)
A decree of Starre-chamber, concerning printing 1637 (Arber, Milton's Areopagitica)
Reports of cases in the courts of Star chamber and High commission 1631–32 (Camden Soc. 1886)
Select pleas of the court of Star chamber (Selden Soc. 1902–10)
STARK, Arthur Cowell & SCLATER, William Lutley *The birds of South Africa* 4 vols. (I–III by Stark, IV by Sclater) 1900–6
STARK, Freya Madeline *Baghdad sketches* 1937
Letters ed. L. Moorehead 1974–
Letters from Syria 1942
Riding to the Tigris 1959
The southern gates of Arabia: a journey in the Hadhramaut 1936
The valleys of the Assassins, and other Persian travels 1934
STARK, John *Elements of natural history* 1828
STARK, Werner *The sociology of knowledge* 1958
STARKEY, George *Natures explication and Helmont's vindication* 1657
Pyrotechny asserted and illustrated 1658
STARKEY, Thomas *England in the reign of Henry the eighth, a dialogue between Cardinal Pole and Thomas Lupset* 1538 (E.E.T.S. 1878)
Life and letters a1538 (ibid.)
State (Columbia, S. Carolina) 1891–
State (= statement of legal case), *Leslie of Powis* etc. 1805 (cited by Jamieson)
State of the Philadelphian society or the grounds of their proceedings considered, The 1697
State papers See also *Calendar*
State papers (during the reign of) *Henry the eighth* (1830–52)
State papers relating to Friends, Extracts from 1654–69 (1910–12)
State poems. Poems on affairs of state 1697–1707
State songs. A collection of state songs, poems &c. that have been published since the Rebellion (1716)
State trials. A complete collection of state trials (1730, 1776–81)
— *Cobbett's complete collection of state trials, with notes by T. B. Howell* (1809–14; continued by T. J. Howell 1817–26)
— *new series, 1820–* (1888–)
Statistical account of Scotland 1791–99 *See* SINCLAIR, Sir John
The new statistical account of Scotland, by the ministers of the respective parishes 1845
Statistical Society *Journal* 1839–
STATON, James T. *Rays fro' th' loominary, a selection of comic Lancashire tales* c1860 (1866)
Statutes of the realm 1235–1713 (Record Commission 1810–28)
— *The statutes, revised ed.* 1235–1878 (1870–85)
The statutes at large from Magna carta to..1800 (ed. O. Ruffhead, D. Pickering, and others)
The statutes of the United Kingdom 1801–69
The public general statutes 1870–87
The public general acts 1888–
The statutes (in English) *made and established from.. Henry III unto the fyrste yere of Henry VIII* (Berthelet 1543; continued 1551–57)
A collection of all the statutes (ed. W. Rastell 1557, 1579)
A collection in English of the statutes now in force (1611)
A collection of all the statutes made in the reigns of Charles I and Charles II 1625–67 (ed. T. Manby 1667)
A collection of acts and ordinances..made in parliament 1640–56 (ed. H. Scobell 1658)
Actis made 24 (etc.) *yere Henry VIII* 1532 (etc.)
The public general acts of 1 and 2 Vict. etc. 1837–67
A collection of public local and personal acts 1798– (1799–)
The private acts 1702–
The statutes of Ireland (ed. Sir R. Bolton 1621)
A collection of all the statutes now in use in the kingdom of Ireland (1678)
The statutes at large, passed in the parliaments held in Ireland 1310–1761 (1765)
— another ed. 1310–1800 (1786–1801)
Statutes and ordynances for the warre 1544
STAUNFORD, Sir William *See* STANFORD
STAUNTON, Sir George L. *An authentic account of an embassy..to the emperor of China* 1797
STAUNTON, Howard *The chess player's handbook* 1847
STAVELEY, E. F. *British insects* 1871
STAVELEY, Thomas *The Romish horseleech* 1674 (1769)
STAYNRED, Philip *A compendium of fortification* 1669 (with Sturmy's Mariners magazine)
STEAD, Christian Karlson ed. *New Zealand short stories* (2nd ser.) 1966
For 1st ser. *see* DAVIN, Daniel Marcus
STEAD, Christina Ellen *The man who loved children* 1940
STEARNS, Marshall Winslow *The story of jazz* 1956 (UK 1957)
STEBBING, Thomas R. R. *A history of crustacea* 1893
STEDMAN, Edmund C. *Poets of America* 1885
The prince's ball 1860
Victorian poets 1876
STEDMAN, John G. *Narrative of a five years' expedition against the revolted negroes of Surinam,..elucidating the history of that country* etc. 1796 (1813)
STEDMAN, Thomas Lathrop *A practical medical dictionary* 1911 (and many later editions used)
STEEDMAN, Andrew *Wanderings and adventures in the interior of southern Africa* 1835
STEEL, Allan G. & LYTTELTON, R. H. *Cricket* (Badminton library) 1888 (1893)
STEELE, John *Papers* ed. H. M. Wagstaff 2 vols. 1924
STEELE, Richard *The husbandmans calling, shewing the excellencies,..duties* etc. *of the christian husbandman* 1668 (1672)
STEELE, Sir Richard *Dramatic works* 1723, a1729 (1777)
The christian hero 1701 (1711)
The conscious lovers, a comedy 1722 (1723, 1755)
The Englishman 1713–14
The funeral, of grief a-la-mode, a comedy 1701 (1702, 1734)
The guardian 1713: see *Guardian*
The lover 1714
The lying lover 1703 (1704, 1723)
The spectator: see *Spectator*
The tatler: see *Tatler*
The tender husband, or the accomplish'd fools, a comedy 1703 (1723)
STEELE, William E. *A hand book of field botany* 1847
STEEN, Marguerite *Phoenix rising* 1952
The tower 1959
STEER, John *Gulielm. Fabricius Hidanus his experiments in chyrurgerie concerning combustions or burnings* tr. 1643
STEFFENS, Joseph Lincoln *Autobiography* 2 vols. 1931
STEGGALL, John H. *A real history of a Suffolk man.. narrated by himself.* ed. by the author of 'Mary Catchpole' (R. Cobbold) 1857 (1859)
Stegmann's (J.) Brevis disquisitio: or, a brief enquiry touching a better way then is commonly made use of, to refute Papists, and reduce Protestants to certainty and unity in religion (sometimes erron. ascribed to J. Hales) tr. 1653 (in Phenix 1708)
STEGNER, Wallace Earle *Wolf Willow* 1962
STEIN, Gertrude *The autobiography of Alice B. Toklas* 1933
STEINBECK, John Ernst *Cannery Row* 1945
East of Eden 1952
The grapes of wrath 1939
In dubious battle 1936
The long valley 1938
Of mice and men 1937
The pearl 1947 (UK 1948)
A Russian journal 1948
Sweet Thursday 1954
Tortilla flat 1935
The wayward bus 1947
STEINER, George *In Bluebeard's castle: some notes towards the re-definition of culture* 1971
Language and silence: essays 1958–1966 1967
STEP, Edward *Bees, wasps, ants and allied insects of the British Isles* 1932
Shell life: an introduction to the British Mollusca 1901
STEPHEN, Sir George *Adventures of a gentleman in search of a horse, by Caveat emptor* 1835 (1841)
STEPHEN, Henry John *New commentaries on the laws of England* 1841–45 (1874)
STEPHEN, Sir James *Essays in ecclesiastical biography* 1849 (1850)
Lectures on the history of France 1851
STEPHEN, Sir James Fitzjames *Defence of the rev. Rowland Williams* 1862
Essays by a barrister (anon.) 1862
STEPHEN, John *The utterances of the cxix psalm* 1861
STEPHEN, Sir Leslie *Alexander Pope* (English men of letters) 1880
Essays on freethinking and plainspeaking 1873
History of English thought in the eighteenth century 1876
Hours in a library 1874, –76, –79 (1892)
The playground of Europe 1871 (1894)
Studies of a biographer 1898–1902
Swift (English men of letters) 1882
STEPHENS, George *The old-northern runic monuments of Scandinavia and England* 1866–68
STEPHENS, Henry *The book of the farm* 1844
— (another ed.) 1851 (1855)
—— & BURN, R. S. *The book of farm-buildings* 1861
STEPHENS, Henry Morse *Albuquerque* (Rulers of India) 1892
A history of the French revolution 1886–91
STEPHENS, James Brunton *Miscellaneous poems* 1880
STEPHENS, James F. *Continuation of Shaw's (G.) General zoology* 1815–26
STEPHENS, John *Satyrical essays, characters and others* 1615
— *New essayes and characters* 1631
STEPHENS, John *An historicall discourse briefly, setting forth the nature of procurations,..also of synodals and pentecostals* 1661
STEPHENS, John Lloyd *Incidents of travel in Central America* etc. 1841 (1854)
Incidents of travel in Greece, Turkey, Russia and Poland 1838
STEPHENS, William R. W. *The life and letters of E. A. Freeman* 1895
STEPNEY, George *Poems* a1707 (Chalmers 1810)
'STEPNIAK, Sergius' (S. M. Kravchinskii) *Underground Russia* 1885
STERLING, George E. & KRUSE, R. S. *The radio manual* 1928
STERLING, John *Essays and tales* a1844 (1848)
STERLING, Thomas L. *The evil of the day* 1955
STERN, Nils Gustav *Meaning and change of meaning, with special reference to the English language* 1931
STERNBERG, George M. *Magnin's (A.) The bacteria* tr. 1881 (1883)
STERNBERG, Thomas *The dialect and folk-lore of Northamptonshire* 1851
STERNE, Laurence *Works* a1768 (1779)
The beauties of Sterne (1782, 1809)
Letters to his..friends, with a fragment in the manner of Rabelais etc. a1768 (1775)
The life and opinions of Tristram Shandy 1759–67
A sentimental journey through France and Italy 1768 (1778)
The sermons of Mr. Yorick c1760 (1760–69, 1773)
STERNHOLD, Thomas *Certayne psalmes..drawen into Englishe metre* 1547
Al such psalmes of David as T. Sternhold did in his lyfe time drawe into English meter 1549
—— HOPKINS, J., et al. *The whole boke of psalmes* (1562, 1564, 1638)
STERRY, Joseph Ashby- *See* ASHBY-STERRY, J.
STERRY, Peter *A discourse of the freedom of the will* a1672 (1675)
Englands deliverance from the northern presbytery 1652
The rise, race and royalty of the kingdom of God in the soul of man a1672 (1683)
STEUART, Sir Henry *The planter's guide; or, a practical essay on the best method of giving immediate effect to wood, by the removal of larger trees* etc. 1827 (1828)
STEUART, Sir James, afterwards DENHAM, Sir J. S. *An inquiry into the principles of political economy* 1767
STEUART, Walter *Collections and observations methodiz'd, concerning the worship, discipline and government of the church of Scotland* 1709
STEVENS, Abel *The history of methodism* 1860–65
STEVENS, George Alexander *The adventures of a speculist, or a journey through London* a1784 (1788)
Songs, comic and satyrical 1772
STEVENS, John *Cieza's (Peter de) Seventeen years travel through Peru* tr. 1709
ed. *A new collection of voyages and travels* 1711
Quevedo's (F. de) Comical works tr. 1707 (1709)
ed. *Two additional volumes to Sir W. Dugdale's Monasticon Anglicanum* 1722–23
STEVENS, Stanley Smith ed. *Handbook of experimental psychology* 1951
STEVENS, Wallace *Collected poems* 1954
Letters ed. H. Stevens 1967

Stevenson, Henry *The birds of Norfolk* 1866
Stevenson, John Hall- *Works* a1785 (1795)
Crazy tales 1762
Stevenson, Matthew *The twelve moneths; or a pleasant.. discourse of every action..proper to each particular moneth* 1661
Stevenson, Robert Louis *Works* a1894
Across the plains 1880–88 (1892)
The black arrow: a tale of the two Roses 1883 (1888)
Catriona: a sequel to 'Kidnapped' 1893
Familiar studies of men and books 1874–81 (1882)
In the south seas 1891 (1896)
An inland voyage 1878
Kidnapped: being memoirs of the adventures of David Balfour in 1751 1886
The master of Ballantrae, a winter's tale 1889
Memories and portraits 1871–87 (1887)
The merry men and other tales and fables 1878–85 (1887)
The misadventures of John Nicholson 1887 (1888)
New Arabian nights 1877–80 (1882)
Prince Otto, a romance 1885
St. Ives, being the adventures of a French prisoner in England a1894 (1897, 1899)
The Silverado squatters 1883
Strange case of Dr. Jekyll and Mr. Hyde 1886
Travels with a donkey in the Cévennes 1879
Treasure Island 1883
Vailima letters 1890–94 (1895)
Virginibus puerisque and other papers 1874–81 (1881)
Weir of Hermiston, an unfinished romance a1894 (1896)
—— & Osbourne, L. *The ebb-tide: a trio and a quartette* 1894
—— —— *The wrecker* 1892
—— —— *The wrong box* 1889
—— & Stevenson, Fanny Van de G. *More New Arabian nights, The dynamiter* 1885
Stevenson, Thomas *Lighthouse illumination* 1859
Stevenson, W. Grant *Puddin': an Edinburgh story* 1894
Stevenson, William *An hymn to the deity* 1782
Stevenson, William *General view of the agriculture of the county of Dorset* 1812
— of Surrey 1809
Stevenson-Hamilton, James *Wild life in South Africa* 1947
Steward, Julian Haynes ed. *Handbook of South American Indians* 7 vols. 1946–59
Stewart, Alexander *'Twixt Ben Nevis and Glencoe: the natural history, legends and folk-lore of the west Highlands* 1885
Stewart, Balfour *The conservation of energy* 1873
An elementary treatise on heat 1866 (1871)
—— & Tait, P. G. *The unseen universe* (anon.) 1875 (1876)
Stewart, Dugald *Works* a1828 (1854–58)
Dissertation exhibiting a general view of the progress of.. philosophy 1816–21 (Encycl. Brit. Suppl.; 1858)
Elements of the philosophy of the human mind 1792–1827
Philosophical essays 1810
The philosophy of the active and moral powers of man 1828 (1854–58)
Stewart, George *Shetland fireside tales* 1877 (1892)
Stewart, Ian Nicholas *Concepts of modern mathematics* 1975
Stewart, James, The trial of, for the murder of Colin Campbell of Glenure 1753
Stewart, John *The tocsin of Britannia* 1794
The tocsin of social life 1803
Stewart, John Innes Mackintosh *Eight modern writers* 1963
The gaudy 1974
The guardians 1955
The Madonna of the astrolabe 1977
The man who won the pools 1961
A memorial service 1976
A use of riches 1957
Young Pattullo 1975
See also Innes, Michael
Stewart, Mary *Madam, will you talk?* 1954
My brother Michael 1960
Nine coaches waiting 1958
Stewart, W. C. *The practical angler: or the art of trout-fishing* 1857
Stewart, William *The buik of the croniclis of Scotland; or a metrical version of the history of Hector Boece* tr. 1535 (Rolls series 1858)
'Stiff, Dean' (Nels Anderson) *The milk and honey route* 1931
Stifler, William Warren ed. *High-speed computing devices* 1950
Still, John See *Gammer Gurton*
Still, Peter *The cottar's Sunday, and other poems, chiefly in the Scottish dialect* 1845
Stillingfleet, Benjamin *Biberg's Œconomy of nature* tr. 1759 (Misc. tracts 1759)
The calendar of Flora (from the Swedish of A. M. Berger) 1761
Miscellaneous tracts relating to natural history, husbandry and physick 1759 (1762)
Stillingfleet, Bp. Edward *Works* a1699 (1710)
Charge begun at Worcester 11 Sept. 1690 1691
Irenicum, a weapon-salve for the churches wounds 1659 (1661)
Origines Britannicæ; or the antiquities of the British churches 1685
Origines sacræ; or a rational account of the grounds of the christian faith as to the truth and divine authority of the scriptures 1662 (1666)
Sermons preached on several occasions 1696–98

Stimpson, George William *A book about a thousand things* 1946
Stimson, Frederick Jesup *American statute law* 1886
Stinton, Darrol *The anatomy of the aeroplane* 1966
Stirling, Charters and other documents relating to the royal burgh of 1124–1705 (1884)
— Extracts from the records of the royal burgh of 1519–1666, 1667–1752 (1884–89)
Stirling, Sir William Alexander, Earl of *Poems* a1640 (Chalmers 1810)
The Alexandræan tragedie 1605
Aurora 1604
Doomesday; or the great day of the Lords judgment 1614
Recreations with the muses 1637
A supplement to Sir P. Sidney's Arcadia 1621 (1629)
The tragedie of Darius 1603
Stirling, James H. *Jerrold, Tennyson and Macaulay, with other essays* 1868
Philosophy and theology (Gifford lectures) 1890
Schwegler's (F. C. A.) Hand-book of the history of philosophy tr. 1867
The secret of Hegel: being the Hegelian system in origin, principle, form and matter 1865
Stirling, afterwards Stirling-Maxwell, Sir William *The cloister life of the emperor Charles the fifth* 1852 (1853)
Stirling, William 1885 *See* Landois, L.
Stisted, Georgiana M. *The true life of Sir R. F. Burton* 1896
Stitchill (Roxburghshire), *Records of the baron court of* 1655–1807 (S.H.S. 1905)
Stivens, Dallas George ('Dal') *The courtship of Uncle Henry: a collection of tales and stories* 1946
Stock, Richard *A learned..commentary upon..Malachy* a1626 (1641; 1865)
Stockdale, John J. *Sketches, civil and military, of the island of Java* etc. 1811
Stocker, Thomas *A righte noble..history of the successors of Alexander, taken out of Diodorus Siculus* tr. 1569
A tragicall historie of the..civile warres of the Lowe countries, otherwise called Flanders, tr. by T. S. 1583
Viret's (P.) The worlde possessed with devils (Part II of *The demoniacke worlde*) tr. by T. S. 1583
Stockholm medical MS., Extracts from a, a1400 (in Archaeologia XXX, 1844; Anglia XVIII, 1896)
Stockton, Frank R. *The Dusantes* 1888
The lady or the tiger? 1884
Rudder Grange 1879
Stockwood, John *A plaine and easie laying open of the meaning and understanding of the rules of construction in the English accidence* 1590
A sermon preached at Paules Crosse 1578
Stocqueler, Joachim H. *The hand-book of (British) India* 1844 (1854)
The military encyclopædia; a technical, biographical, and historical dictionary 1853
The oriental interpreter and treasury of East India knowledge 1848
Stodart, Robert R. *Scottish arms, being a collection of armorial bearings 1370–1678 reproduced in facsimile* 1881
Stoddard, Charles A. *Cruising among the Caribbees* 1895
Stoddard, Francis H. *The evolution of the English novel* 1900
Stoddard, Richard H. *Poems* 1852, 1880
Stoddart, Anna M. *John Stuart Blackie, a biography* 1895
Stoddart, Sir John *Grammar* a1845 (Encycl. metropolitana)
Stoddart, Thomas T. *The angler's companion to the rivers and lochs of Scotland* 1847
An angler's rambles, and angling songs 1866
— Angling songs (1889)
Songs and poems 1839
Stokes, David *A paraphrasticall explication of the twelve minor prophets* 1659
Stokes, Sir George Gabriel *Mathematical and physical papers* 1880–1903
Stokes, Whitley *The tripartite life of St. Patrick* tr. 1887 (Rolls series)
Stokoe, William John *The caterpillars of the British butterflies* 1944
The caterpillars of British moths 2 ser. 1948
— (new ed.) 2 ser. 1958
Stone, Hannah M. & Stone, Abraham *A marriage manual* 1935 (UK 1936)
Stone, James K. *The invitation heeded: reasons for a return to catholic unity* 1870
Stone, Kate *See* Holmes, Sarah Katherine (Stone)
Stone, Louis *Jonah* 1911
Stone, Samuel *Deceivers deceiv'd, a sermon* 1661
Stone, Samuel *The justices' pocket manual* 1842
The justices' manual 1864 (1876)
Stone, Thomas *General view of the agriculture of the county of Lincoln* 1794
'Stone, Zachary' *The Modigliani scandal* 1976
'Stonehenge' (J. H. Walsh) *The dog, in health and disease* 1859
ed. *The dogs of the British islands* 1866–67
Manual of British rural sports 1856 (1875)
The shot-gun and sporting rifle 1859
Stonehouse, William B. *The history and topography of the isle of Axholme* 1839
Stonor letters and papers, The 1290–1483 (Camden Soc. 1919)
S'too him Bayes: or some observations upon the humour of writing Rehearsals transpros'd 1673
Stopes, Marie Charlotte Carmichael *Married love: a new contribution to the solution of sex difficulties* 1918

Stopford, Edward A. *The work and the counterwork; or the religious revival in Belfast* 1859
Stoppard, Tom *Dirty linen, and New-found-land* 1976
Jumpers 1972
The real Inspector Hound 1968
Rosencrantz and Guildenstern are dead 1967
Travesties 1975
Storer, David H. *Reports on the ichthyology and herpetology of Massachusetts* 1839
Storer, Thomas *The life and death of T. Wolsey, cardinall* 1599
Storey, David Malcolm *Saville* 1976
This sporting life 1960
Stork, William *A description of East Florida* 1766 (with A journal kept by J. Bartram, 1769)
Stormonth, James *Etymological and pronouncing dictionary of the English language* 1871 (1884)
Stornoway Gazette and West Coast Advertiser 1917–
Storr, Catherine *The Chinese egg* 1975
Marianne and Mark 1960
Tales from a psychiatrist's couch 1977
Story, Jack Trevor *Dishonourable member* 1969
Something for nothing 1963
Story, Joseph *Commentaries on the constitution of the United States* 1833
Miscellaneous writings a1845 (1852)
Story, Josiah *An essay concerning the nature of the priesthood* 1750
Story, Robert H. *The apostolic ministry in the Scottish church* 1897
Story, William W. *Roba di Roma* 1863
Stouffer, Samuel Andrew *Measurement and prediction* 1950
Stoughton, John *A learned treatise in three parts. 1. The definition. 2. The distribution of divinity. 3. The happiness of man* 1640
Stoughton Thomas *The christians sacrifice* 1622
Stout, George Frederick *Analytic psychology* 1896
Stout, Rex Todhunter *Fer-de-lance* 1934
If death ever slept 1957 (UK 1958)
Over my dead body 1940
Please pass the guilt 1973 (UK 1974)
The red box 1936 (UK 1937)
Red threads 1939 (UK 1941)
Stout, William *Autobiography* a1744 (1851)
Stovel, Charles ed. *Canne's (J.) A necessitie of separation from the church of England* (1634), with introductory notice 1849
Stow, John *The annales of England* 1592 (1605; continued by E. Howes 1615)
A summarie of Englyshe chronicles 1565
A survey of London 1598 (1603, enlarged 1633, 1842)
— ed. J. Strype (1720, 1754–55)
Stowe, Mrs. Harriet Elizabeth Beecher *Dred; a tale of the Great dismal swamp* 1856
House and home papers 1865
Little foxes 1865 (1866)
Oldtown fireside stories 1871
Oldtown folks 1869
The pearl of Orr's island 1861–62
Poganuc people, their loves and lives 1878
Uncle Tom's cabin; or life among the lowly 1852
We and our neighbors 1875
Stower, Charles *The printer's grammar; or, introduction to the art of printing* 1808
Strachey, Alix & Strachey, James tr. *S. Freud's Collected papers* Vol. III *See* Riviere, Joan, et al.
Strachey, Giles Lytton *Characters and commentaries* 1933
Eminent Victorians 1918
Queen Victoria 1921
Strachey, James tr. *S. Freud's Group psychology and the analysis of the ego* 1922
tr. *S. Freud's Totem and taboo* 1950
—— et al. tr. *S. Freud's Complete psychological works* 24 vols. 1953–74
See also Strachey, Alix
Strachey, William *The historie of travaile into Virginia Britannia* c1612 (Hakl. Soc. 1849)
Strafford, Thomas Wentworth, Earl of *Letters and dispatches* a1641 (1739)
Strain, Mrs. Euphans H. *Elmslie's dragnet* 1900
Straits Times (Malaysia) 1845– (title varies)
Stranathan, James Docking *The 'particles' of modern physics* 1942
Strand, Stanley *Marketing dictionary* 1962
Strand Electrical and Engineering Company, Ltd. *Glossary of technical theatrical terms* 1947
Strand magazine, The 1891–
Strang, Barbara Mary Hope *A history of English* 1970
Metaphors and models: an inaugural lecture 1965
Modern English structure 1962
Strang, James *A lass of Lennox* 1899
Strang, John *Glasgow and its clubs* 1856
Strangford, Percy E. F. W. Smythe, 8th Viscount *A selection from his writings* a1869 (1869)
Strangways, Arthur Henry Fox *The music of Hindostan* 1914
Strasburger's (E.) Handbook of practical botany ed. W. Hillhouse 1887 (1889)
Stratford, Bp. Nicholas *Charge at Chester, May 5th 1691* 1692
'Strathesk, John' (J. Tod) *Bits from Blinkbonny* 1882
More bits from Blinkbonny 1884 (1885)

STRATMANN, Franz H. *A dictionary of the Old English language* 1878 (ed. 3)
— new ed. by H. Bradley (1891)
STRATTON-PORTER, Gene *Freckles* 1904
A girl of the Limberlost 1909
The harvester 1911
Laddie 1913
STRAUMANN, Heinrich *Newspaper headlines: a study in linguistic method* 1935
Strauss' (D. F.) New life of Jesus tr. 1865
STRAUSS, Gustave L. M. et al. *England's workshops* 1864
STRAUSS, Victor *The printing industry* 1967
Straw, Jack. The life and death of Jack Straw, a notable rebell in England 1593
STRAWSON, Peter Frederick *Individuals: an essay in descriptive metaphysics* 1959
STREATFEILD, George S. *Lincolnshire and the Danes* 1884
STREATFEILD, Noel *Aunt Clara* 1952
Ballet shoes 1936
I ordered a table for six 1942
STREET, George E. *Brick and marble in the middle ages* 1855 (1874)
Street robberies considered (by D. De Foe) 1728
STREETER, Edwin W. *Precious stones and gems* 1877
Streetwalker [anon.] 1959
STRETTON, Charles *Memoirs of a chequered life* 1862
'STRETTON, Hesba' ('Hannah', or rather Sarah, Smith) *Through a needle's eye* 1879
STREVENS, Peter Derek *New orientations in the teaching of English* 1977
Papers in language and language teaching 1965
STRICKBERGER, Monroe Wolf *Genetics* 1968
STRICKLAND, Agnes *Lives of the queens of England* 1840-48
Lives of the queens of Scotland, and English princesses connected with the regal succession of Great Britain 1850-59
STRINGER, Arthur *The wire tappers* 1906
STRODE, George *The anatomie of mortalitie* 1618
STRODE, William *The floating island: a tragi-comedy* 1636 (1655)
STRONG, Charles Augustus *Why the mind has a body* 1903
STRONG, Leonard Alfred George *All fall down* 1944
The bay 1941
The director 1944
Othello's occupation 1945
Sea wall 1933
Sun on the water, and other stories 1940
Trevannion 1948
Which I never 1950
STROUD, John Anthony *The shorn lamb* 1960
Touch and go 1961
STRUTHER, William *True happiness, or king Davids choice* 1633
STRUTHERS, John *Poetical works* 1850
STRUTT, Jacob G. *Sylva Britannica; or portraits of forest trees* 1822 (1830)
STRUTT, Joseph *A compleat view of the manners, customs, arms, habits, etc. of the inhabitants of England* 1775-76
A complete view of the dress and habits of the people of England 1796-99
The sports and pastimes of the people of England 1801 (1875)
STRYPE, John *Annals of the reformation and establishment of religion, and.. other occurrences in the church of England* 1708-09, 1725-31 (1824)
Ecclesiastical memorials, relating chiefly to religion and the reformation of it.. under Henry VIII, Edward VI, and queen Mary the first 1721 (1822)
The history of the life and acts of.. E. Grindal,.. archbishop of Canterbury 1710
The life and acts of M. Parker.. archbishop of Canterbury 1711
The life and acts of.. J. Whitgift.. archbishop of Canterbury 1717-18
Memorials of T. Cranmer, sometime lord archbishop of Canterbury 1694
Stow's (J.) Survey of the cities of London and Westminster brought down.. to the present time 1720 (1754-55)
STUART, Arabella *The life and letters* a1615 (ed. Elizabeth Cooper 1866)
STUART, George *A joco-serious discourse, in two dialogues between a Northumberland gentleman and his tenant a Scotchman* 1686
STUART, Gilbert *The history of Scotland, from the establishment of the reformation till the death of queen Mary* 1782
STUART, Granville *Forty years on the frontier* ed. P. C. Phillips 2 vols. 1925
STUART, H. *The novice's or young seaman's catechism* 1860
STUART, Hamish *Lochs and loch fishing* 1899
STUART, Henry W. Villiers *Egypt after the war* 1883
STUART, Jesse *Men of the mountains* 1941
STUART, Moses *A grammar of the Hebrew language* 1828 (1831)
'STUART, Robert' (R. Meikleham) *A descriptive history of the steam engine* 1824
STUART, Ruth MacEnery *In Simpkinsville* 1897
STUART, William & MACPHERSON, J. *Ebrard's (J. H. A.) Apologetics; or the scientific vindication of christianity* tr. 1886-87
STUBBE, Henry *A censure upon certaine passages contained in The history of the Royal Society* 1670-71
The Indian nectar, or a discourse concerning chocolata 1662
The miraculous conformist 1666
The Plus ultra *reduced to a nonplus, or a specimen of some animadversions upon the* Plus ultra *of Mr. Glanvill* 1670
Rosemary and Bayes: or, animadversions upon a treatise called The rehearsall trans-prosed (anon.) 1672
STUBBES, Philip *The anatomie of abuses* 1583 (New Shaks. Soc. 1877-79-82)
STUBBS, Jean *The painted face* 1974
STUBBS or STUBS, John *The discoverie of a gaping gulf whereinto England is like to be swallowed by an other French mariage* (anon.) 1579
STUBBS, Bp. William *The constitutional history of England* 1874-75-78
ed. *Select charters and other illustrations of English constitutional history* 1870
Seventeen lectures on the study of mediaeval and modern history 1867-84 (1886)
STUCLEY, Lewis *A gospel glasse representing the miscarriages of English professors* 1667 (1670)
Stucley, Play of. The famous historye of the life and death of Captaine T. Stukeley.. as it hath been acted 1605 (also Simpson, School of Shakspere 1878)
Student, The; or the Oxford and Cambridge monthly miscellany (by T. Warton et al.) 1750
Student and intellectual observer, The (2nd series of The intellectual observer) 1868-71
STUDHOLME, Edgar Channon *Te Waimate: early station life in New Zealand* 1940
— (ed. 2) 1954
Studies in English (University of Cape Town) 1970- (title varies)
Studies in English literature (University of Tokyo) 1919-
STUDLEY, John *The fourth tragedy of L. A. Seneca entituled Hippolytus* tr. 1567 (1581)
The seventh tragedie.. entituled Medea tr. 1566
The eyght tragedie.. entituled Agamemnon tr. 1566
The tenth tragedy.. entituled Hercules Œtæus tr. c1566 (1581)
— in *Seneca his tenne tragedies* (ed. T. Newton 1581)
Stukeley, Captain Thomas 1605 See *Stucley*
STUKELEY, William *Abury, a temple of the Druids* 1743
The family memoirs of William Stukeley, and the antiquarian and other correspondence 17.. (Surtees Soc. 1882-87)
Itinerarium curiosum; or an account of the antiquitys and remarkable curiositys in nature and art observ'd in travels thro' Great Britain 1724 (1776)
Palæographia sacra, or discourses on sacred subjects 1763
Stonehenge, a temple restor'd to the British Druids 1740
STURGIS, Russell *A dictionary of architecture and building: biographical, historical and descriptive* 3 vols. 1901-2
STURMY, Samuel *The mariners magazine, or Sturmy's mathematical and practical arts* etc. 1669 (1683)
STURT, Charles *Narrative of an expedition into central Australia* 1849
Two expeditions into the interior of southern Australia 1833
STURTEVANT, Edgar Howard *Comparative grammar of the Hittite language* 1933
STURTEVANT, Simon *Metallica; or the treatise of metallica* 1612 (1855)
STYRON, William *Confessions of Nat Turner* 1967
Sophie's choice 1979
STYWARD, Thomas *The pathwaie to martiall discipline* 1581
SUCKLING, Sir John *Aglaura* 1638
Brennoralt, a tragedy 1639 (1646)
Fragmenta aurea, a collection of all the incomparable peeces written by Sir J. Suckling a1642 (1646, 1648)
The goblins, a comedy 1638 (1646)
Poems, plays and other remains a1642 (1874)
SUDWORTH, George Bishop *Nomenclature of the arborescent flora of the United States* 1897
Sue's (M. J. Eugène) Mysteries of Paris tr. 1844
SUFFOLK, Henrietta Howard, Countess of *Letters to and from Henrietta, Countess of Suffolk* 1712-67 (1824)
Suffolk words, from Cullum's History of Hawsted 1813 (E.D.S. 1879)
Suicide, a poem 1773
SULIVAN, Richard J. *A view of nature* 1794
SULLIVAN, Sir Edward *Woman the predominant partner* 1894
SULLIVAN, James *The history of the district of Maine* 1795
SULLIVAN, Joseph M. *Criminal slang* 1908
SULLY, James *Outlines of psychology* 1884
Sensation and intuition: studies in psychology and æsthetics 1874
Summary of all the religious houses in England and Wales, A (by G. Duckett) 1717
Summary upon the famous poeme of William of Saluste, Lord of Bartas, A learned tr. (by T. Lodge) 1621
Summary view of the feudal law, A, with the differences of the Scots law from it (by J. Dundas) 1710
SUMMERS, Montague (Alphonsus J.-M. A. M. Summers) *The supernatural omnibus* 1931
SUMMERTON, Margaret *A memory of darkness* 1967
A small wilderness 1959
The sunset hour 1957
SUMNER, Charles *Orations and speeches* v.d. (1850)
SUMNER, James Batcheller & MYRBÄCK, Karl eds. *The enzymes* 2 vols. in 4 parts 1950-2
—— & SOMERS, George Frederick *Chemistry and methods of enzymes* 1943
SUMNER, William Graham *Folkways: a study of the sociological importance of usages, manners, customs, mores, and morals* 1907
Sun, The (Baltimore, Maryland) 1837-
Sun, The (London) 1964-
Sun (New York) 1833- (title varies)
Sun-Herald (Sydney) 1953-
Sunday Advocate-News (Barbados) 1968-
Sunday Bulletin (Philadelphia): See *Philadelphia Bulletin*
Sunday Dispatch 1928-61
Sunday Express (London) 1918-
Sunday Express and Home Journal (Johannesburg) 1937-
Sunday magazine, The 1864-
Sunday Mail (Glasgow) 1919-
Sunday Nation (Nairobi) 1960-
Sunday Pictorial 1915-63
Sunday Post (Glasgow) 1920-
Sunday Times (Johannesburg) 1906-
Sunday Times (Lagos) 1953-
Sunday Times (London) 1822-
Sunday Truth (Brisbane) 1960-71
Sunset (title varies) 1898-
Supernatural religion (by W. R. Cassels) 1874-77
SUPPES, Patrick *Introduction to logic* 1957
Supplication of certaine masse priests falsely called catholikes directed to the kings maiestie, The 1604
Supplication of the poore commons, A 1546 (with Fish, Supplication, E.E.T.S. 1871)
A supplycacion to.. Kynge Henry the eyght 1544 (ibid.)
Suppression of monasteries, Three chapters of letters relating to the 1528-55 (Camden Soc. 1843)
Surfer: the international surfing magazine 1960-
SURFLET, Richard *Estienne (C.) and Liébault's (J.) Maison rustique, or the countrie farme* tr. 1600
— augmented by G. Markham 1616
Surgery 1937-
Surgery, gynecology and obstetrics 1905-
SURR, Thomas S. *Splendid misery* (a novel) 1801
A winter in London; or sketches of fashion, a novel 1805 (1806)
SURREY, Henry Howard, Earl of *Works* a1547 (Chalmers 1810; ed. Nott 1815; Anglia XXIX, 1906)
Certain bokes (II and IV) *of Virgiles Æneis* tr. a1547 (1557; Roxb. Club 1814)
Five chapters from the Ecclesiastes of Solomon paraphrastically versified a 1547 (Park, Harington's Nugæ antiquæ II, 1804; Anglia XXIX)
Songes and sonettes, written by the.. Lorde Henry Haward late Earle of Surrey, and other (Tottel's miscellany) a1547 (1557; Arber)
Surrey and Kent Sewer commission, Court minutes of the 1569-79 (L.C.C. 1909)
Surrey Archæological Society *Collections* (1858-)
Surrey glossary 1876, 1893 *See* GOWER, G. L.
SURTEES, Robert *A memoir* (with poems and letters) *of R. Surtees* (a1834) by G. Taylor (Surtees Soc. 1852)
SURTEES, Robert S. *Ask mamma* 1858
Handley Cross; or the spa hunt 1843 (1854)
Mr. Facey Romford's hounds 1865
Mr. Sponge's sporting tour 1853
Surtees Society *Publications* (1835-)
— *Miscellanea* (1861)
— *A volume of English miscellanies* (1890)
Survey: a journal of East and West studies 1955-
Survey of the affaires of the United Netherlands, An exact 1665
Survey of the insolent.. libel entituled Napthali, A (by Bp. A. Honyman) 1668 (1669)
Susan: a novel (anon.) 1809
Sussex archæological collections, published by the Sussex Archæological Society (1848-)
SUTCLIFF, Robert *Travels in some parts of North America in the years 1804, 1805, and 1806* 1811
SUTCLIFFE, Halliwell *Mistress Barbara Cunliffe* 1902
Shameless Wayne 1900
SUTCLIFFE, Matthew *A briefe examination of a certaine.. petition presented.. to the kinges.. maiestie* 1606
A briefe replie to a certaine.. libel lately published by a seditious Jesuite, calling himselfe N. D.. by O. E. (i.e. Sutcliffe) 1600
SUTHERLAND, Alexander *St. Kathleen, or the rock of Dunnismoyle* (anon.) 1820
SUTHERLAND, Alexander 1892 *See* DAWSON, G. M.
'SUTHERLAND, Joan' (Joan Collings) *The circle of the stars* 1924
SUTHERLAND, William *The ship builder's assistant* 1711
SUTTIE, Jane Isabel tr. *S. Ferenczi's Further contributions to the theory and technique of psycho-analysis* 1926
SUTTON, Edward *North Lincolnshire words* 1881 (E.D.S.)
SUTTON, Oliver Graham *The science of flight* 1949
SUTTON, Thomas *A dictionary of photography* 1858
'SUYIN, Han' *See* 'HAN SUYIN'
SUZUKI, Daisetsu Teitarō *Zen Buddhism and its influence on Japanese culture* 1938
Svensk botanisk tidskrift 1907-
SVERDRUP, Harald Ulrik, JOHNSON, M. W., & FLEMING, R. H. *The oceans: their physics, chemistry, and general biology* 1942
SWAAN, Wim *Japanese lantern* 1965
SWAINSON, Charles *A handbook of weather folk-lore* 1873
Provincial names and folk lore of British birds 1885 (E.D.S.)
SWAINSON, William *On the natural history and classification of birds* 1836-37
— *of fishes* etc. 1838-39
— *of quadrupeds* 1835
Zoological illustrations 1820-33
—— & SHUCKARD, W. E. *On the history and natural arrangement of insects* 1840
Swaledale glossary 1873 *See* HARLAND, J.
SWAN, Annie S. *Aldersyde, a Border story* 1883
Carlowrie; or, among Lothian folk 1884

Swan, Annie S. (*cont.*)
Doris Cheyne, the story of a noble life 1888
The gates of Eden 1887
A victory won 1895
Swan, John *Speculum mundi, or a glasse representing the face of the world* 1635 (1643, 1670)
Swan, Lester A. & Papp, Charles Steven *The common insects of North America* 1972
Swan, Michael Lancelot *British Guiana* 1957
Swann, Harry Kirke *A dictionary of English and folk-names of British birds* 1913
Swanson, Carl Pontius *Cytology and cytogenetics* 1957 (UK 1958)
Swanton, Michael J. ed. *The dream of the Rood* 1970
Swayne, Henry J. F. ed. *Churchwardens' accounts of S. Edmund and S. Thomas, Sarum, 1443–1702* a1892 (1896)
Swayne, James Colin *A concise glossary of geographical terms* 1956
Sweden, A short survey of the kingdom of 1632
Swedenborg's (or *Swedberg, Emanuel*) *The animal kingdom, considered anatomically, physically, and philosophically* tr. J. J. G. Wilkinson 1843
The apocalypse revealed tr. 1791 (1876)
Heaven and its wonders, .. and hell tr. S. Noble 1839 (revised 1851)
The true christian religion tr. 1781 (1786, 1873)
Sweeney, Charles *The scurrying bush* 1966
Sweet, Alexander Edwin & Knox, John Armoy *On a Mexican mustang through Texas, from the Gulf to the Rio Grande* 1883 (UK 1884)
Sweet, Charles *A dictionary of English law* 1882
Sweet, Henry *An Anglo-saxon reader* 1876 (1908)
— *A second Anglo-saxon reader* 1887
A handbook of phonetics 1877
A history of English sounds 1874 (1888)
A new English grammar 1892–98
ed. *The oldest English texts* (E.E.T.S. 1885)
A primer of phonetics 1890
The student's dictionary of Anglo-saxon 1897
Sweet-Escott, Bickham *Baker Street irregular* 1965
Swell's night guide, The 1841
— (another ed.) 1846
— (another ed.) 1847
Swete, Henry B. *Studies in the teaching of our Lord* 1903
Swetnam, Joseph *The arraignment of lewd, idle, froward and unconstant women* 1615
Swetnam the woman-hater arraigned by women 1620 (Grosart 1880)
Swettenham, Frank A. *British Malaya: an account of the origin and progress of British influence in Malaya* 1907
Malay sketches 1895
Swift, Gilbert *Somerley: school-boy and undergraduate* 1900
Swift, Jonathan *Works* a1745 (1735–38–46, 1751, 1755–68, 1814, 1841)
The battle of the books 1697 (with Tale of a tub 1704)
The bubble: a poem (*Upon the South Sea project*) 1721
Cadenus and Vanessa, a poem 1713 (1726)
A complete collection of genteel and ingenious conversation (Polite conversation) 1731–38 (1738; Wks. 1738 VI)
The conduct of the allies, and of the late ministry, in beginning and carrying on the present war 1711
Correspondence a1745 (1841)
Directions to servants in general 1729 (1745)
A discourse concerning the mechanical operation of the spirit 1704 (with Tale of a tub)
A discourse of the contests and dissensions between the nobles and the commons in Athens and Rome 1701 (Misc. 1711)
The Drapier letters 1724, 1735
The history of the four last years of the queen a1745 (1758)
The history of Martin 1720 (Misc. Works)
The journal to Stella 1710–13 (Wks., also 1901)
A letter .. concerning the sacramental test 1708 (Misc. 1711)
Letters by Dr. Swift and several of his friends 1703–40 (1767)
Letters to and from Dr. J. Swift 1714–38 (1741)
Miscellaneous works (The tale of a tub, Miscellanies in prose and verse) 1720
Miscellanies in prose and verse 1711, 1722
— (with contributions by Pope, Arbuthnot, and Gay) 1727–35
A modest proposal for preventing the children of poor people from being a burthen to their parents, or the country 1729
Predictions for the year 1708, by I. Bickerstaff 1708 (Misc. 1711; Arber, Eng. Garner VI)
— *Vindication of I. Bickerstaff* 1709 (ibid.)
A proposal for correcting, improving, and ascertaining the English tongue 1712
The publick spirit of the Whigs set forth 1714
Some free thoughts upon the present state of affairs 1714
The South Sea project See *Bubble*, above
A tale of a tub, written for the universal improvement of mankind .. To which is added, An account of a battel between the antient and modern books in St. James's library 1704
Travels into several remote nations of the world, in four parts, by Lemuel Gulliver 1726
—— et al. *Memoirs of P. P. clerk of this parish* c1725 (Misc. 1727)
Swift, Theophilus *The gamblers, a poem* 1777
Swinbourne, Alfred *Picture logic; or the grave made gay* 1874 (1875)
Swinburne, Algernon Charles *Atalanta in Calydon, a tragedy* 1864 (1865, 1868)
Bothwell; a tragedy 1874
Chapman's (*G.*) *Works, Poems and minor translations* ed. with an introduction by A. C. Swinburne 1875
Chastelard; a tragedy 1865
Erechtheus; a tragedy 1876
Letters ed. C. Y. Lang 6 vols. 1959–62
Locrine, a tragedy 1887
Miscellanies 1877 etc. (1886)
A note on Charlotte Brontë 1877
Note of an English republican on the Muscovite crusade 1876
Songs before sunrise 1871
Songs of the springtides 1880
Studies in prose and poetry 1883–93 (1894)
A study of Ben Jonson 1889
A study of Shakespeare 1879 (1880)
A study of Victor Hugo 1886
Under the microscope 1872
William Blake, a critical essay 1867 (1868)
Swinburne, Henry *A briefe treatise of testaments and last willes* 1590
A treatise of spousals or matrimonial contracts a1623 (1686)
Swinburne, Henry *Travels through Spain* 1779
Swing music 1935–6
Swinhoe, Robert *Narrative of the North China campaign of 1860* 1861
Swinnerton, Frank Arthur *The doctor's wife comes to stay* 1949
Swinnock, George *The door of salvation opened by the key of regeneration* 1660
Swinson, Arthur Horace *Six minutes to sunset: the story of General Dyer and the Amritsar affair* 1964
Switzer, Stephen *Ichnographia, or the nobleman, gentleman, and gardener's recreation* 1718
An introduction to a general system of hydrostaticks and hydraulicks 1729
The practical fruit gardener 1724
The practical kitchen gardener 1727
Swyer, Gerald Isaac M. *Reproduction and sex* 1954
Sybthorpe, Robert 1627 *See* Sibthorp
Sydenham, Humphrey *Sermons upon solemne occasions* v.d. (1637)
Sydenham (New) Society *Publications* (1859–1901)
— *A biennial retrospect of medicine, surgery, and their allied sciences 1867–68* 1869
— *Lexicon of medicine and allied sciences.* By H. Power & L. W. Sedgwick 1879–99
Sydney, University of. Australian Language Research Centre *Occasional papers* 1964–
Sydney Morning Herald 1842–
Sydney papers See *Sidney state papers*
Sydney slang dictionary, The ? 1882
Sylph, The; a novel (anon.) 1779
'Sylvanus' *The bye-lanes and downs of England, with turf scenes and characters* 1850
Sylvester, James Joseph *Collected mathematical papers* 1837–97 (1904–12)
Sylvester, Josuah *Complete works* a1618 (Grosart 1880)
Bethulians rescue tr. 1614
A divine and true tragi-comedy; Job triumphant in his triall 1615
Du Bartas' (*G. de S.*) *The batail of Yvry* tr. 1614
Du Bartas his divine weekes and workes tr. 1591–1608 (1605, 1608, 1641)
Du Bartas' Triumph of faith, the sacrifice of Isaac, the ship-wracke of Jonas etc. tr. 1592
Lachrimæ lachrimarum; or the distillation of teares shede for the death of .. Panaretus 1612
Little Bartas, or brief meditations on the power .. and goodnes of God 1614
The maidens blush, or Joseph tr. a1618
Micro-cosmo-graphia: the little-worlds description tr. (from H. Smith) 1613
Monodia 1594
The parliament of vertues royall (*Panaretus*) tr. 1614
— *The second session of the parliament of vertues royall* 1616
The profit of imprisonment (*A paradox against libertie*) tr. 1593–94 (1605)
Tobacco battered and the pipes shattered c1615 (1617)
Urania, or the heavenly muse 1605
Sylvester, Matthew ed. *Reliquiæ Baxterianæ: or Mr. R. Baxter's narrative of the most memorable passages of his life and times* 1696
Symes, Michael *An account of an embassy to the kingdom of Ava in 1795* 1800
Symmer, Archibald *Rest for the weary* 1630
A spirituall posie for Zion 1629
Symmons, Charles *The life of John Milton* 1806 (1810, 1822)
Symmons, Edward *A loyall subjects beliefe, expressed in a letter to Master S. Marshall* 1643
A vindication of king Charles 1648
Symmons, John *The Agamemnon of Æschylus* tr. 1824
Symonds, John Addington *Italian byways* 1883
Letters ed. H. M. Schueller & R. L. Peters 3 vols. 1967–9
The life of Michelangelo Buonarroti 1893
Renaissance in Italy 1875–86 (1898)
Shakespeare's predecessors in the English drama 1884
Shelley (English men of letters) 1878
Sketches in Italy and Greece 1874
Sketches and studies in Italy 1879
Sketches and studies in Italy and Greece (a new ed. of the two prec. and Italian byways 1898)
Studies of the Greek poets 1873–76
J. A. Symonds; a biography compiled from his papers and correspondence, by H. F. Brown (1895)
Symonds, Joseph *A sermon before sundry of the House of Commons* 1641
Symonds, Richard *Diary of the marches of the royal army during the great civil war* 1644–45 (Camden Soc. 1859)
Symonds, William S. *Records of the rocks; or, notes on the geology of Wales, Devon, Cornwall,* etc. 1872
Symons, Arthur *The symbolist movement in literature* 1899
Symons, Julian Gustave *The end of Solomon Grundy* 1964
The narrowing circle 1954
A three pipe problem 1975
Symons, R. D. *Many trails* 1963
Where the wagon led 1973
Symposia in Applied Mathematics *Proceedings* 1947–
Symson, Andrew *A large description of Galloway* 1684–92 (1823)
Symson, Archibald *See* Simson
Synge, John Millington *Letters to Molly: J. M. Synge to Maire O'Neill 1906–1909* ed. A. Saddlemyer 1971
The playboy of the western world 1907
System of natural history, A. Botany, by E. Smith; Zoology, by W. S. Dallas 1855 (Orr's Circle of the sciences)

T

T., C. *An advice how to plant tobacco in England* 1615
T., D. 1608 *See* Tuvil, D.
T., D. *Hieragonisticon; or, Corah's doom. Being an answer to* (*J. Eachard's*) *two letters of enquiry into the grounds and occasions of the contempt of the clergy and religion* 1672
T., F. *The case is altered. How? Aske Dalio and Millo* 1604
T., F. 1712 *See* Tanner, F.
T., I. 1596 *See* Tanner, I.
T., I. *Grim, the collier of Croydon: or the devil and his dame* a1600 (Gratiæ theatrales 1662; Dodsley, Old plays)
T., R. (= Christopher Carlile) *A discourse, wherein is plainly proued .. that Peter was neuer at Rome* etc. 1572
T., W. *Nannini's* (*R.*) *Civill considerations upon many and sundrie histories* tr. 1601
T., W. *The compleat gunner* 1672 (Book III of T. Venn's Military & maritime discipline)
T., W. *See* Tomlinson, W.
TV times 1955–
Tablet, The 1840–
Tabor, Eliza *Rachel's secret* 1866
'Tackline' *Holiday sailor* 1945
'Taffrail' (Henry Taprell Dorling) *Carry on!: naval sketches and stories* 1916
Pincher Martin, O.D.: a story of the inner life of the Royal Navy 1916
Tailor, Robert *The hogge hath lost his pearle* 1614 (Dodsley)
Tait, James *Mind in matter: a short argument on theism* 1884; ed. 3, enlarged 1892
Tait, Peter G. *An elementary treatise on quaternions* 1867 (1873)
Lectures on some recent advances in physical science 1876
See also Stewart, B.; Thomson, Abp. W.
Tait's Edinburgh magazine 1832–61
Tak, Montie *Truck talk: the language of the open road* 1971
Takagaki, Shinzō & Sharp, Harold E. *The techniques of judo* 1957
Talbot, Catherine *See* Carter, Elizabeth
Talbot, Charles J. C., 19th Earl of Shrewsbury *Meliora, or better times to come* ed. Viscount Ingestre 1852–53
Talbot, Christopher R. M. *Newton's* (*I.*) *Enumeration of lines of the third order* tr. 1861
Talbot, Frederick Arthur Ambrose *Moving pictures: how they are made and worked* 1912
— (rewritten) 1923
Practical cinematography and its applications 1913
Talbot, Patrick Henry Brabazon *Principles of fungal taxonomy* 1971
Talbot, Percy Amaury *The peoples of southern Nigeria* 4 vols. 1926
Talbot, Bp. William *Charge to the clergy of his diocese* (*of Oxford*) *at his visitation* 1712
Tales and quicke answeres, very mery, and pleasant to rede ?1535 (in Shakspeare's Jest book 1814–15)
Talfourd, Sir Thomas N. *The Athenian captive; a tragedy* 1838
The Castilian; an historical tragedy 1853
Final memorials of Charles Lamb 1848
Glencoe; or the fate of the Macdonalds; a tragedy 1840
Ion: a tragedy 1835
The letters of Charles Lamb, with a sketch of his life 1837
Vacation rambles and thoughts 1845
Tallentyre, Stephen G. *Life of Voltaire* 1903
Talmage, Thomas de Witt *Crumbs swept up* 1871
The jewels of the soul 1877
Sermons delivered in the Brooklyn tabernacle 1872
Tamarack review 1956–
Taming of a shrew, A pleasant conceited historie called 1594 (Shaks. Soc. 1844)
Tancred and Gismund *See* Wilmot, R.
Tandy, William *Sangermano's* (*V.*) *Description of the Burmese empire* tr. 1833
Tannahill, Robert *Poetical works* a1810 (1825)
Poems and songs, chiefly in the Scottish dialect a1810 (1815)
The soldier's return; a Scottish interlude in two acts, with other poems and songs 1807
Tanner, F. *The plainest, easiest, and prettiest method of writing short-hand* 1712
Tanner, I. *A sermon preached at Paules Crosse,* by I. T. 1596

Tanner, Thomas H. *A manual of the practice of medicine* 1854 (1865, 1869, 1875)
On the signs and diseases of pregnancy 1860
Tannhäuser 1861 *See* Fane, J. C. H.
Tansley, Arthur George *The British islands and their vegetation* 1939
—— & Chipp, Thomas Ford eds. *Aims and methods in the study of vegetation* 1926
Tapping, Thomas *The rhymed chronicle of Edward Manlove concerning the liberties and customs of the lead-mines within the wapentake of Wirksworth, Derbyshire, from the original ed. of 1653, to which is affixed a glossary* 1851 (E.D.S. 1874)
Tararua (Tararua Tramping Club, NZ) 1947–
Tarkington, Newton Booth *The gentleman from Indiana* 1899
In the arena 1905
Penrod 1914
Tarlton, Richard *Newes out of purgatorie* a1588 (1590; Shaks. Soc. 1844)
Tarltons jests 1611 (1638; Shaks. Soc. 1844)
Tarquin and Tullia (a poem attributed to Dryden) c1700 (in Poems on affairs of state III, 1704)
Tarras, William *Poems, chiefly in the Scottish dialect* 1804
Tasistro, Louis F. *Comte de Paris' History of the civil war in America* tr. 1875
Tassie, L. J. *The physics of elementary particles* 1973
Tasso's Aminta tr. 1628
Tate, Francis *King Edward II's household and wardrobe ordinances* tr. 1601 (Chaucer Soc. 1876)
Tate, George *The geology of the district traversed by the Roman wall* 1867 (in J. C. Bruce, Roman wall 1867)
Tate, James *An introduction to the principal Greek tragic and comic metres* 1827
Tate, Nahum *Elegies* 1699
Poems 1677
Portrait-royal; a poem upon her majesty's picture set up in Guildhall 1703
The triumph; or warriour's welcome 1705
See also Cowley, A.; Garth, Sir S.; and *Heliodorus*
—— & Brady, Nicholas *A new version of the Psalms of David, fitted to the tunes used in churches* 1696 (1698, 1751)
—— & Dryden, John *The second part of Absalom and Achitophel* 1682
Tate, Ralph *A plain and easy account of the land and fresh-water mollusks of Great Britain* 1866
'Tate, Richard' (Anthony Masters) *Birds of a bloodied feather* 1974
Tatham, John *Aqua triumphalis; being a relation of the city of London entertaining their Majesties upon the Thames* 1662
The distracted state; a tragedy 1641 (1651)
London's tryumph 1659
The Scots figgaries: or, a knot of knaves; a comedy 1652
Tatler, The. By Isaac Bickerstaff (i.e. Sir R. Steele, J. Addison, et al.) 1709–11
Taubes, Frederic *The painter's dictionary of materials and methods* 1973
Taubman, Matthew *London's triumph, or the goldsmith's jubilee* 1687
Taunt, Henry W. *A new map of the river Thames from Oxford to London* 1872
Taunton, Ethelred L. *The English Black Monks of St. Benedict* 1897
Taunton, William P. *Reports of cases argued and determined in the Court of Common Pleas* 1810–23
Tautphœus, Baroness von *At odds; a novel* 1863
Cyrilla; a tale 1853
The initials; a novel (anon.) 1850
Quits; a novel 1857
Taverner, John *Certaine experiments concerning fish and fruite* 1600
Taverner, Richard *The garden of wysdom* 1539
Prouerbes or adagies with newe addicions, gathered out of the Chiliades of Erasmus 1539 (1545, 1552)
Tavernier's travels 1677–78 *See* Phillips, John
Tawney, Richard Henry *Religion and the rise of capitalism* 1926
Taylor, Alan John Percivale *The course of German history* 1945
English history, 1914–45 1965
See also Howat, G. M. D. & Taylor, A. J. P.
Taylor, Alfred S. *Poisons, in relation to medical jurisdprudence and medicine* 1848
Taylor, Ann (a1866) & Jane (a1824) *Poetical works* a1866 (1878)
Original poems for infant minds 1808–14 (1843)
Rhymes for the nursery 1836
Taylor, Anne Marjorie *The language of World War II* 1944
—(rev. ed.) 1948
Taylor, Bayard *Critical essays and literary notes* 1880
Eldorado; or, adventures in the path of empire 1850
Goethe's Faust tr. 1871 (1886)
Hannah Thurston: a story of American life 1863
Northern travel 1858
Pictures of Palestine, Asia Minor, Sicily, and Spain; or, the lands of the Saracen 1855
Poems 1856
Prince Deukalion 1878
Studies in German literature 1879
Taylor, Benjamin Franklin *Between the gates: summer rambles in California* 1878
January and June: being out-door thinkings and fireside musings 1854
Summer-savory, gleaned from rural nooks in pleasant weather 1879
The world on wheels, and other sketches 1874
Taylor, Charles *An introduction to the ancient and modern geometry of conics* 1881
Taylor, Charles Fayette *The internal-combustion engine in theory and practice* 2 vols. 1960–8
Taylor, Edith *The serpent under it* 1973 (UK 1974)
Taylor, Edward *Behmen's theosophick philosophy unfolded* 1691
Taylor, Elizabeth *At Mrs Lippincote's* 1945
The sleeping beauty 1953
Taylor, Francis E. *The folk-speech of South Lancashire* 1901
Taylor, Frederick *A manual of the practice of medicine* 1890
Taylor, Sir Henry *Edwin the fair; an historical drama* 1842
Isaac Comnenus: a play 1827
Philip van Artevelde; a dramatic romance 1834
St. Clement's Eve; a play 1862
The statesman 1836
Autobiography 1800–75 1885
Taylor, Hugh Stott ed. *A treatise on physical chemistry* 2 vols. 1924
Taylor, Isaac (of Ongar) *The ship; a description of different kinds of vessels* a1829 (1846)
Taylor, Isaac (of Stanford Rivers) *Ancient Christianity, and the doctrines of the Oxford tracts for the times* 1839–42
Elements of thought; or, first lessons in the knowledge of the mind 1822 (1824)
Fanaticism 1833
Four lectures on spiritual Christianity 1841
History of the transmission of ancient books to modern times 1827
Home education (anon.) 1838
Logic in theology, and other essays 1830–31 (1859)
Loyola: and Jesuitism in its rudiments 1849
Natural history of enthusiasm (anon.) 1829
Physical theory of another life (anon.) 1836
The process of historical proof exemplified 1828
The restoration of belief (anon.) 1852 (1855)
Saturday evening (anon.) 1832
The spirit of the Hebrew poetry 1861
Spiritual despotism (anon.) 1835
Ultimate civilization, and other essays 1860
Wesley and Methodism 1851
Taylor, Isaac (Canon of York) *The alphabet; an account of the origin and development of letters* 1883
Etruscan researches 1874
The origin of the Aryans 1889
Words and places: or etymological illustrations of history, ethnology, and geography 1864 (1873)
Taylor, James *The Scottish covenanters* 1882
Taylor, Jeremy *Works* a1667 (1822, 1828, 1831, 1847–54)
Clerus Domini: or, a discourse of the divine institution of the office ministeriall 1651
Contemplations of the state of man a1667 (1684, 1699)
Deus justificatus; two discourses of original sin 1656
A discourse concerning prayer ex tempore, or by pretence of the Spirit, in justification of authorized and set formes of lyturgie (anon.) 1646
— enlarged ed., entitled *An apology for authorized and set forms of liturgie* 1649
A dissuasive from Popery to the people of Ireland 1664, 1667 (1668)
Ductor dubitantium; or the rule of conscience in all her generall measures 1660
'Ενιαυτός: a course of sermons for all the Sundaies of the year 1653–55
A funeral sermon (on 2 Sam. xiv. 14) preached at the obsequies of the Countess of Carbery 1650
The golden grove; or a manuall of daily prayers and letanies 1655
The great exemplar of sanctity and holy life 1649
Of the sacred order and offices of episcopacy 1642
The real presence and spirituall of Christ in the blessed sacrament proved against the doctrine of transubstantiation 1654
The rule and exercises of holy living 1650 (1676)
The rule and exercises of holy dying 1651 (1686)
A sermon preached at the funeral of John (Bramhall) late Lord Archbishop of Armagh 1663
A sermon preached in Saint Maries Church in Oxford upon the anniversary of the Gunpowder-treason 1638
Θεολογία ἐκλεκτική. A discourse of the liberty of prophesying 1647
Unum necessarium: or, the doctrine and practice of repentance 1655
The worthy communicant 1660
See also *Artificial handsomeness*
Taylor, John (Water poet) *Works* 1630
Works a1653 (Hindley 1872; Spenser Soc. 1868–78)
An apology for private preaching 1642
An armado, or nauye of a hundred and three ships 1627
The carriers' cosmography 1637 (in Arber, Eng. Garner I)
Divers crabtree lectures 1639
The great eater of Kent, or part of the exploits of Nicholas Wood 1630
A kicksey winsey; or a lerry come-twang 1619
A new discovery by sea 1623
The nipping or snipping of abuses 1614
Odcombs complaint: or Coriats funerall epicedium 1613
The olde old very olde man: or the age and long life of T. Par 1635
Part of this summers travels, or news from Hell, Hull and Hallifax 1640
The pennyles pilgrimage 1618
The praise, antiquity and commodity of beggery, beggers and begging 1621
The praise of hemp-seed 1620
A short relation of a long journey..encompassing the Principalitie of Wales 1652
Sir Gregory Nonsence his newes from no place 1622
The suddaine turne of Fortunes wheele 1631
Taylor's motto: Et habeo, et careo, et curo 1621
Three weekes, three daies, and three houres obseruation and travel from London to Hamburgh 1617
A verry merry wherry-ferry-voyage 1622
The whole life and progresse of Henry Walker the ironmonger 1642
The world runnes on wheeles 1623
Taylor, John *Arator: being a series of agricultural essays, practical and political* 1813
—(ed. 2) 1814
Taylor, John (of Liverpool) *Poems and translations* 1839
Taylor, Laura W. *Ballads and songs of Brittany* 1865
Taylor, Meadows *The story of my life* 1877 (1878)
Taylor, Michael tr. *C. Metz's Film language: a semiotics of the cinema* 1974
Taylor, Nancy Margaret ed. *Early travellers in New Zealand* 1959
Taylor, Richard *Te ika a Maui; or, New Zealand and its inhabitants* 1855
—(ed. 2) 1870
Taylor, Sedley *Sound and music* 1873 (1896)
Taylor, Selwyn Francis, Cotton, L. T., & Murray, J. G. *A short textbook of surgery* 1967
—(ed. 2) 1968
Taylor, Silas *The history and antiquities of Harwich and Dovercourt.* First collected by S. Taylor (a1678) and now much enlarged by Samuel Dale (1730)
Taylor, Thomas *Beard's (T.) Theatre of God's judgements.* Part II a1633 (1642)
A commentarie upon the Epistle of St. Paul to Titus 1612 (1619)
Taylor, Thomas *The metamorphosis and philosophical works of Apuleius* tr. 1822
Two orations of the emperor Julian tr. 1793
Pausanias' Description of Greece tr. 1794
The works of Plato tr. (nine dialogues by F. Sydenham, the remainder by T. Taylor) 1804
The philosophical and mathematical commentaries of Proclus tr. 1788–89 (1792)
Taylor, Tom *Leicester Square; its associations and its worthies* 1874
Pictures in words 1863 (in B. Foster's Pictures of English landscape)
The ticket-of-leave man c1863
See also Leslie, C. R.
Taylor, Mrs. Tom *See* Taylor, Laura W.
Taylor, William *Scots poems* 1787
— ed. 2, *Poems chiefly in the Scottish dialect* 1827
Taylor, William *English synonyms discriminated* 1813
Goethe's (J. W. von) Iphigenia in Tauris tr. 1793
Historic survey of German poetry 1828–30
A memoir of the life and writings of the late W. Taylor, containing his correspondence with R. Southey, etc. By J. W. Robberds (1843)
Teall, Jethro J. H. *British petrography* 1888
Techmer, F. *Internationale Zeitschrift für allgemeine Sprachwissenschaft* 1884–
Technological dictionary, English-German-French 1878 (ed. 3)
Technology: the monthly review of training and education for industry 1957–
Technology week 1966–
Teckely, Count 1693 See *Memoirs*
Tee emm [training memoranda] (Air Ministry) 1941–6
Tegetmeier, William B. *The cottager's manual of poultry keeping* 1893
The poultry book 1867 (1873)
Profitable poultry 1853 (1854)
Teignmouth, John Shore, Baron *Memoirs of the life, writings and correspondence of Sir William Jones* 1804 (1807)
Memoir of the life and correspondence of John Shore, baron Teignmouth (1843)
Teilhet, Darwin & Teilhet, Hildegard *Feather cloak murders* 1937
Teixeira's (P.) Travels tr. by William F. Sinclair 1902 (Hakluyt Soc.)
Telegraph, The (Brisbane) 1872– (title varies)
Telegraph and telephone journal 1914–33
Telegraphic journal, The; and monthly illustrated review of electrical science 1872–
Tell-Trothes new-yeares gift; beeing Robin Good-fellowes newes 1593 (New Shaks. Soc. 1876)
Tempest, Paul *Lag's lexicon: a comprehensive dictionary and encyclopædia of the English prison to-day* 1950
Tempest, Sir Richard *An entertainment of solitarinesse* 1649
'Templar' (Arthur Bassett Hopkins) *The poker manual* 1895
Temple, Frederick The relations between religion and science 1884 (1885)
Temple, Sir John *The Irish rebellion* 1646 (1746)
Temple, Josiah H. & Sheldon, George *A history of the town of Northfield, Massachusetts* 1875
Temple, Launcelot *Sketches; or essays on various subjects* 1758

TEMPLE, Neville *See* FANE, J. C. H.
TEMPLE, Sir William *Works* a1699 (1720, 1731, 1757, 1770)
An introduction to the history of England 1695
Letters written by Sir W. Temple and other ministers of state v.d. (1700-03)
Miscellanea 1680-90
Observations upon the United Provinces of the Netherlands 1673
TEMPLE, William *Citizen and churchman* 1941
Thoughts in war-time 1940
Temple Bar; a London magazine 1861-
TEMPLETON, William *The locomotive engine popularly explained* 1848 (ed. 2)
Ten Brink's (Bernhard) Early English literature tr. by H. M. Kennedy 1883
— *History of English literature* Vol. II. tr. by W. C. Robinson 1893
— Vol. III. tr. by L. Dora Schmitz 1896
Five lectures on Shakespeare tr. by Julia Franklin 1895
The language and metre of Chaucer tr. by M. Bentinck Smith 1901
Tender father, The 1775
TENISON-WOODS, Julian E. *Fish and fisheries of New South Wales* 1882
TENNANT, Kylie *The battlers* 1941
Foveaux 1939
The joyful condemned 1953
Lost haven 1946 (UK 1947)
Ride on stranger 1943
TENNANT, William *Indian recreations* 1803
TENNANT, William *Anster concert* 1811
Anster fair; a poem 1812 (1827)
Anster fair and other poems 1838
Cardinal Beaton; a drama 1823
Papistry storm'd 1819 (1827)
The thane of Fife 1822
TENNENT, Sir James Emerson *Ceylon* 1859
Sketches of the natural history of Ceylon 1861
The story of the guns 1864
TENNEY, William J. *The military and naval history of the rebellion in the United States* 1865
TENNYSON, Alfred, Lord *Works* a1892 (1894)
Poems 1830, 1833, 1842
Becket 1884
The cup: a tragedy 1881
The falcon 1879
The foresters 1892
Harold: a drama 1876
Idylls of the king. Enid (renamed *Geraint and Enid* in 1870; divided into two parts, *The marriage of Geraint* and *Geraint and Enid* in 1886), *Vivien* (renamed *Merlin and Vivien* in 1870), *Elaine* (renamed *Lancelot and Elaine* in 1870), *Guinevere* 1859; *Coming of Arthur, Holy Grail, Pelleas and Ettarre, Passing of Arthur* 1870; *Last tournament, Gareth and Lynette* 1872; *Balin and Balan* 1885
In memoriam A. H. H. 1850
Maud, and other poems 1855
The princess; a medley 1847
The promise of May 1882
Queen Mary: a drama 1875
Tiresias, and other poems 1885
TENNYSON, Hallam, 2nd Lord *Alfred Lord Tennyson. A memoir by his son* 1897
'TENSAS, Madison' (Henry Clay Lewis) *Odd leaves from the life of a Louisiana 'swamp doctor'* 1850
TEONGE, Henry *Diary* 1675-79 (1825)
Terence tr. 1598 *See* BERNARD, R.
Teresa, St., Life 1671 *See* WOODHEAD, A.
TERKEL, Louis ('Studs') ed. *American dreams, lost and found* 1980
TERMAN, Frederick Emmons *Radio engineering* 1932
— (ed. 4, with title *Electronic and radio engineering*) 1955
Radio engineers' handbook 1943
Termes de la ley, Les; or certaine difficult and obscure words and termes of the common lawes of this realme expounded (an enlarged ed. of W. Rastell's Exposicions of the termes of the lawes) 1624 (1641, 1708)
Terms used in forestry and logging 1905 *See* United States. Department of Agriculture. Bureau of Forestry
TERRY, Edward *A relation of Sir T. Roe's voyage into the Easte Indies* (anon.) 1655. See also HAVERS, G.
TERRY, Ellen & SHAW, George Bernard *Ellen Terry and Bernard Shaw: a correspondence* ed. C. St. John 1931
TERTON, Alice *Lights and shadows in a hospital* 1902
Test of filial duty (by Sarah Scott) 1772
Testament of love See USK, T.
Testamenta Eboracensia; or wills registered at York v.d. (Surtees Soc. 1836-1902)
Testamenta vetusta See NICOLAS, Sir N. H.
Testaments of the twelve Patriarchs 1575 *See* GILBY, A.
TESTER, William H. L. *Poems* 1867
Tetrahedron letters 1959-
Textile Institute *Textile terms and definitions* 1954
— (ed. 3) 1957
'TEY, Josephine' (Elizabeth Mackintosh) *Brat Farrar* 1949
The daughter of time 1951
The Franchise affair 1948
A shilling for candles 1936
The singing sands 1952
To love and be wise 1950
See also 'DAVIOT, Gordon'
THACHER, James *A military journal during the American war* 1775-83 (1823)
THACKER, Thomas *The courser's companion; to which is added the breeder's guide* 1834-35
Rules for the decision of courses 1843
THACKERAY, Anne Isabella *See* RITCHIE, A. I.
THACKERAY, Christopher ('Kit') *Crownbird* 1979
THACKERAY, William Makepeace *Works* 24 vols. a1863 (1869-86)
The adventures of Philip on his way through the world 3 vols. 1862 [1861-62 in Cornhill magazine and Harper's magazine]
The book of snobs 1848 [longer version 1846-47 in Punch]
Catherine 1839-40 [in Fraser's magazine]
The confessions of Fitz-Boodle [1842-43 in Fraser's magazine], *and Some passages in the life of Major Gahagan* [1838-39 in New monthly magazine; US 1839] 1852
Denis Duval a1863 [1867]
Dr. Birch and his young friends 1849
The English humourists of the eighteenth century 1853
Essay on the genius of George Cruikshank 1840
The four Georges 1860
The history of Henry Esmond 3 vols. 1852
The history of Pendennis 2 vols. 1849-50 [1848-50 in parts]
The history of Samuel Titmarsh and the great Hoggarty diamond 1849 [1841 in Fraser's magazine; US 1848]
The Irish sketch-book 2 vols. 1843
The Kickleburys on the Rhine 1850
Lovel the widower 1860
The luck of Barry Lyndon 2 vols. 1852 [1844 in Fraser's magazine]
Men's wives 1852 [1843 in Fraser's magazine]
Miscellanies, prose and verse 4 vols. 1855-57
Mrs. Perkins's ball 1847
The Newcomes; memoirs of a most respectable family 2 vols. 1854-55 [1853-55 in parts and Harper's magazine]
The Paris sketch book 2 vols. 1840
The professor [in Comic tales, vol. 2] 1841 [1837 in Bentley's miscellany]
Roundabout papers 1863 [1860-63 in Cornhill magazine]
The second funeral of Napoleon 1841
A shabby genteel story 1852 [1840 in Fraser's magazine]
Vanity Fair 1848 [1847-48 in parts]
The Virginians 2 vols. 1858-59 [1857-59 in parts and Harper's magazine]
The Yellowplush correspondence 1838 [1837-38 in Fraser's magazine]
Thanes of Cawdor, The book of the. A series of papers selected from the charter room at Cawdor 1236-1742 (Spalding Cl. 1859)
Thausing's (J. E.) Theory and practice of the preparation of malt and the fabrication of beer tr. by W. T. Brannt 1882
THEAKSTON, Michael *British angling flies* 1883
THEARLE, Samuel J. P. *Naval architecture* 1874
Theatre of worldings 1569 *See* ROEST, T.
THEIMER, Walter & CAMPBELL, Peter *Encyclopaedia of world politics* 1950
Thelyphthora 1780-81 *See* MADAN, M.
THEOBALD, Lewis *The cave of poverty; a poem* 1714
Double falshood; a play 1728
Shakespeare restored 1726
The works of Shakespeare. Collated with the oldest copies and corrected, with notes explanatory and critical 1733
THEODORSON, George A. & THEODORSON, Achilles G. *A modern dictionary of sociology* 1970
Theologian, The 1844-47
Theology: a monthly journal of historic Christianity 1920-
Theophania: or, severall modern histories represented by way of romance 1655
Theophrastus. Characters: or, the manners of the age; with moral characters of Theophrastus tr. 1709
THEROUX, Paul *The consul's file* 1977
The mosquito coast 1981
The Old Patagonian Express: by train through the Americas 1979
Thersites. A new enterlude called Thersytes 15.. (? 1560; in Pollard, Eng. miracle plays 1890; Hazl., Dodsley)
Thevet's (A.) New found worlde tr. 1568 *See* HACKET, T.
THEWLIS, J., et al. eds. *Encyclopaedic dictionary of physics* See under title
THICKNESSE, Philip *A year's journey through France and part of Spain* 2 vols. 1777
— (ed. 2) 2 vols. 1778
— (ed. 3) 2 vols. 1789
Thief-catcher, The; or, villainy detected 1753
Thierry's (J. N. A.) Formation and progress of the tiers état or the third estate in France tr. by F. B. Wells 1855
THILLY, Frank tr. *F. Paulsen's Introduction to philosophy* 1895
THIRKELL, Angela Margaret *August folly* 1936
Before lunch 1939
The headmistress 1944
THIRLWALL, Bp. Connop *A history of Greece* 1835-47
Letters to a friend a1875 (1881)
Remains; literary and theological a1875 (ed. J. J. S. Perowne 1877-78)
Schleiermacher's (F.) Critical essay on the gospel of St. Luke tr. 1825
This week magazine 1935-
THISELTON-DYER, Thomas F. *British popular customs* 1875
English folk-lore 1878
Folk-lore of plants 1889
THISELTON-DYER, Sir William T. ed. *Flora Capensis: being a systematic description of the plants of Cape Colony, Caffraria, and Port Natal* (vols. IV-VII) 1897-1909
ed. *Flora of tropical Africa* (vols. IV-VIII) 1899-1913
The needs of biology 1876
See also BENNETT, A. W.; TRIMEN, H.
THOM, Walter *The history of Aberdeen* 1811
THOM, William *Works* 1799
THOM, William *Rhymes and recollections of a hand-loom weaver* 1844
THOMAS, Annie (Mrs. Pender Cudlip) *Denis Donne* 1864
The modern housewife; or how we live now 1883
On guard 1865
Played out 1866
That other woman 1889
Walter Goring 1866
THOMAS, David *Travels through the Western country in the summer of 1816* 1819
THOMAS, Donald Michael *The white hotel* 1981
THOMAS, Dylan Marlais *Collected poems, 1934-52* 1952
Deaths and entrances: poems 1946
18 poems 1934
The map of love: verse and prose 1939
Portrait of the artist as a young dog 1940
A prospect of the sea, and other stories and prose writings ed. D. Jones 1955
Quite early one morning: broadcasts ed. A. T. Davies 1954
Selected letters ed. C. Fitzgibbon 1966
Under Milk Wood: a play for voices 1954
THOMAS, Edward *The chronicles of the Pathán Kings of Delhi* 1871
THOMAS, Ernest C. *Lange's (F. A.) History of materialism* tr. 1877
The Philobiblon of Richard de Bury tr. 1888 (1902)
THOMAS, Gabriel *An historical and geographical account of Pensilvania and of West-New-Jersey in America* 1698 (1848)
THOMAS, Graham Stuart *The old shrub roses* 1955
THOMAS, Henry S. *The rod in India* 1873
THOMAS, J. J. *Froudacity* 1889
THOMAS, Jack *No banners: the story of A. and H. Newton* 1955
THOMAS, Joseph *A complete pronouncing medical dictionary* 1886
A comprehensive medical dictionary 1864
THOMAS, Mary *Dictionary of embroidery stitches* 1934
THOMAS, Northcote Whitridge *Kinship organisations and group marriage in Australia* 1906
THOMAS, Pascoe *A true and impartial journal of a voyage to the South-Seas and round the globe under the command of Commodore G. Anson* 1745
THOMAS, Ralph *A few words on swimming; with practical hints* 1868
Handbook of fictitious names 1868
Swimming 1904
THOMAS, Ronald Stuart *An acre of land* 1952
The minster 1953
The stones of the field 1946
Tares 1961
THOMAS, Ross *The backup men* 1971
If you can't be good 1973 (UK 1974)
The porkchoppers 1972 (UK 1974)
The Singapore wink 1969
Spy in the vodka 1966 (UK 1967)
See also 'BLEECK, Oliver'
THOMAS, Samuel Evelyn *Elements of economics* 1925
THOMAS, Theodore G. *A practical treatise on the diseases of women* 1868 (1872)
THOMAS, Thomas *Dictionarium linguæ Latinæ et Anglicanæ* 1588 (1606)
THOMAS, William *The historie of Italie* 1549 (1561)
The pilgrim: a dialogue of the life and actions of King Henry the eighth a1554 (1861)
Principal rules of the Italian grammer, with a dictionarie 1550 (1567)
Thomas of Erceldoune See *Erceldoune, Thomas of*
Thomason tracts. Pamphlets, books, newspapers, and manuscripts relating to the Civil War, the Commonwealth, and Restoration, collected by George Thomason 1640-61 (British Museum)
THOMPSON, Arthur Beeby *Oil-field exploration and development* 2 vols. 1925
THOMPSON, Benjamin *Kotzebue's (A. F. F. von) Stranger* tr. 1802
THOMPSON, C. Patrick *Cocktails* 1919
THOMPSON, Charles W. *Twelve months in the British legion* 1836
THOMPSON, D'Arcy Wentworth *Aristotle's Historia animalium* tr. 1910
THOMPSON, Edith *History of England* 1873
THOMPSON, Edward *The fair quaker: or, the humours of the navy*. Formerly written by C. Shadwell, and now alter'd with great additions, and a new character, by E. Thompson 1773
The meretriciad (anon.) 1761 (1765)
THOMPSON, Edward *Cullen's Nosologia methodica* 1818-20
THOMPSON, Sir Edward Maunde *Palaeography* 1910
THOMPSON, Edward P. *The passions of animals* 1851
THOMPSON, Flora *Candleford Green* 1943
Lark Rise 1939
Over to Candleford 1941
Still glides the stream 1948
THOMPSON, Francis J. *Poems* 1893
New poems 1897
THOMPSON, George *Travels and adventures in southern Africa* 1827
THOMPSON, Sir Henry *The diseases of the prostate, their pathology and treatment* 1860 (1868)

Thompson's (John) man 1829 See *John Thompson's man*
THOMPSON, John V. *Zoological researches and illustrations* 1828–30
THOMPSON, Maurice *Witchery of archery* 1879
THOMPSON, Pishey *The history and antiquities of Boston* 1856
THOMPSON, Robert *The gardener's assistant* 1859
THOMPSON, Robert J. *The proofs of life after death* 1907
THOMPSON, Silvanus P. *Dynamo-electric machinery* 1884
Elementary lessons in electricity and magnetism 1881
Philipp Reis: inventor of the telephone 1883
THOMPSON, Theophilus *Annals of influenza or epidemic catarrhal fever in Great Britain from 1510 to 1837* 1852
THOMPSON, Thomas *The English rogue; a new comedy* 1668
THOMPSON, Thomas Perronet *Audi alteram partem* 1857–61
Exercises, political and others 18.. (1842)
THOMPSON, William *The royal navy-men's advocate* 1757
THOMPSON, William *Poems* a1766 (1810)
Poems on several occasions 1757
THOMPSON, William Bell *An introduction to plasma physics* 1962
THOMPSON, William T. *Major Jones's courtship* (anon.) 1844
Major Jones's sketches of travel 1848
Thompson street poker club, The 1889
THOMS, William J. ed. *Anecdotes and traditions, illustrative of early English history and literature* v.d. (Camden Soc. 1839)
The book of the court 1838 (1844)
ed. *A collection of early prose romances* v.d. (1828, 1858)
THOMSON, Anthony Todd *The London dispensatory* 1815 (1818)
THOMSON, Arthur Landsborough ed. *A new dictionary of birds* 1964
THOMSON, Sir Charles W. *The depths of the sea* 1873
The voyage of the 'Challenger' 1877
THOMSON, David *Musings among the heather: being poems chiefly in the Scottish dialect* 1881
THOMSON, David P. *Introduction to meteorology* 1849
THOMSON, Henry J. 1921 *See* LINDSAY, W. M.
THOMSON, James *Works* a1748 (1773)
The castle of indolence; an allegorical poem 1748
Edward and Eleanora; a tragedy 1739
Liberty; a poem 1735–36
The seasons (*Autumn* 1730; *Spring* 1728; *Summer* 1727; *Winter* 1726) 1746
Tancred and Sigismunda; a tragedy 1745
The tragedy of Sophonisba 1730
THOMSON, James *The city of dreadful night* 1874
—with some other poems 1880
Essays and phantasies 1881
Vane's story, Weddah and Om-el-Bonain, and other poems 1881
THOMSON, John *Lectures on inflammation* 1813
THOMSON, John *Etymons of English words* 1826
THOMSON, John *A treatise on hat-making and felting* 1868
THOMSON, John *The Straits of Malacca, Indo-China, and China* 1875
THOMSON, John Arthur *The biology of the seasons* 1911
Outlines of zoology 1892
The science of life 1899
Science old and new 1924
THOMSON, John H. 1871 See *Cloud of witnesses*
THOMSON, Joseph J. *See* POYNTING, John H.
THOMSON, June *Death cap* 1973
The long revenge 1974
A question of identity 1978
THOMSON, Mortimer Neal *See* 'DOESTICKS, Q. K. Philander'
THOMSON, Mowbray *The story of Cawnpore* 1859
THOMSON, Robert D. *The British annual and epitome of the progress of science* 1837–39
Cyclopædia of chemistry 1854
—— & THOMSON, Thomas *Records of general science* 1835–36
THOMSON, Spencer *Wanderings among the wild flowers* 1854 (1857)
THOMSON, Thomas *Annals of philosophy* 1813–20
An attempt to establish the first principles of chemistry by experiment 1825
Chemistry of inorganic bodies 1831
Chemistry of organic bodies 1838
The history of chemistry 1830–31
Outlines of mineralogy, geology and mineral analysis 1836
A system of chemistry 1802 (1807)
See also THOMPSON, R. D.
THOMSON, Thomas *Western Himalaya and Tibet* 1852
THOMSON, William *See* WATSON, Robert
THOMSON, Abp. William *Outline of the laws of thought* (anon.) 1842 (1860)
THOMSON, Sir William, 1st Baron Kelvin *Mathematical and physical papers* 18.. (1882–1912)
—— & TAIT, Peter G. *A treatise on natural philosophy* 1867 (1879–83)
THOMSON, William *Dictionary of banking: a concise encyclopædia of banking law and practice* 1911
—(ed. 10, by R. W. Jones) 1951
—(ed. 11, by F. E. Perry & F. R. Ryder) 1965
THOMSON, William Burns *Reminiscences of medical missionary work* a1893 (1895)
THOMSON, William M. *The land and the book* 1859 (1874)
THOREAU, Henry D. *Writings* ed. B. Torrey & F. B. Sanborn 20 vols. 1906
Correspondence ed. W. Harding & C. Bode 1958
Early spring in Massachusetts. From the journal of H. D. Thoreau a1862 (1881)
Excursions in field and forest a1862 (1863)
Letters to various persons a1862 (1865)
The Maine woods a1862 (1864)
Walden; or life in the woods 1854
A week on the Concord and Merrimack rivers 1849
A Yankee in Canada; with anti-slavery and reform papers 1862 (1866)
Thoresby, Abp. John See *Lay folks' catechism*
THORESBY, Ralph *Diary* 1677–1724 (1830)
Ducatus Leodiensis; or the topography of the town and parish of Leedes 1715
Glossary of Yorkshire words from Thoresby's Letter to Ray April 27, 1703 (Ray's Collection of words, E.D.S. 1874)
THORNBURG, Newton *Cutter and Bone* 1976
THORNBURY, George Walter *Greatheart* 1866
The life of J. M. W. Turner 1861
A tour round England 1870
True as steel 1863
— & WALFORD, Edward *Old and new London* 1873–78
THORNBURY, William David *Principles of geomorphology* 1954
THORNDIKE, Herbert *A discourse of the forbearance or the penalties which a due reformation requires* 1670
A discourse of the right of the Church in a Christian state 1649
Of the government of churches 1641
THORNHILL, Mark *The personal adventures and experiences of a magistrate during the rise, progress, and suppression of the Indian mutiny* 1884
THORNLEY, George *Longus' Daphnis and Chloe* tr. 1657 (1893)
THORNLEY, Thomas *Cotton combing machines* 1902
THORNTHWAITE, William H. *Guide to photography* 1845
Monckhoven's (D. van) Popular treatise on photography tr. 1863
THORNTON, Alice *Autobiography* a1669 (Surtees Soc. 1875)
THORNTON, Bonnell *Comedies of Plautus* tr. 1767 (1769)
THORNTON, Percy M. *The Stuart dynasty* 1890
THORNTON, Richard H. *An American glossary* 1912
THORNTON, Robert J. *The philosophy of medicine* 1799
THORNTON, William Thomas *On labour: its wrongful claims and rightful dues* 1869
Thornton romances, The (Perceval, Isumbras, Eglamour, and Degrevant) a1400 (Camden Soc. 1844)
THOROTON, Robert *The antiquities of Nottinghamshire* 1677; enlarged ed. by John Throsby (1797)
THORPE, Benjamin *Diplomatarium Anglicum aevi Saxonici. A collection of English charters, with a translation of the Anglo-Saxon by B. Thorpe* v.d. (1865)
Yule-tide stories 1853
See also *Anglo-Saxon laws; Exeter book; Psalter*
THORPE, John *Registrum Roffense; or a collection of ancient records, charters, etc. necessary for illustrating the history and antiquities of the cathedral church of Rochester* 1769
THORPE, Thomas Bangs *The mysteries of the backwoods* 1846
THORPE, Sir Thomas E. *A dictionary of applied chemistry* 1890–93
Thorpe, William, The examinacion of master ?1530 (in Arber, Eng. Garner VI)
THORSTENSEN, Thomas Clayton *Practical leather technology* 1969
THRALE, Mrs. *See* PIOZZI, Hester L.
Thre prestis of Peblis c1500 See *Peebles*
Three early English metrical romances (The anturs of Arther, Sir Amadace, The avowynge of King Arther) 14.. (Camden Soc. 1842)
Three fifteenth-century chronicles 14.. (Camden Soc. 1880)
Three Germans tr. 1807
Three Gil Blas 1804 See *La Martelière, J. H. F.*
Three in Norway 1882 *See* LEES, J. A.
Three kings of Cologne, The c1400 (E.E.T.S. 1886)
Three kings' sons, The c1500 (E.E.T.S. 1895)
Three ladies of London 1584 *See* WILSON, R.
THRELKELD, Caleb *Synopsis stirpium Hibernicarum alphabetice dispositarum* 1726
THROSBY, John 1797 *See* THOROTON, R.
THRUPP, George A. *The history of coaches* 1877
Thrush and nightingale a1300 (in Reliquiæ ant. I, 1845; Hazlitt, Early pop. poetry I, 1864)
THUDICHUM, John L. W. *A manual of chemical physiology* 1872
A treatise on the pathology of the urine 1858
—— & DUPRÉ, August *A treatise on the origin, nature, and varieties of wine* 1872
Thugs, Illustrations of the history and practices of the (by Edward Thornton) 1837
Thunberg's (C. P.) Travels in Europe, Africa, and Asia tr. 1795
THURBER, James Grover *My life and hard times* 1933
The years with Ross 1959
THURLOE, John *A collection of state papers* 1638–59 (1742)
THURSTON, Robert H. *A history of the growth of the steam-engine* 1878
THWAITES, Edward ed. *Heptateuchus, Liber Job, et Evangelium Nicodemi; Anglo-Saxonice* (1698)
THWAITES, Reuben Gold ed. *Early western travels, 1748–1846: a series of annotated reprints* 32 vols. 1904–7
THYNNE, Francis *Animaduersions vppon the annotacions and corrections of some imperfections of impressiones of Chaucers workes* 1599 (E.E.T.S. 1875)
Emblemes and epigrames 1600 (E.E.T.S. 1876)
See also *Debate;* T., F. 1604
TIBBITS, Edward T. *Medical fashions in the nineteenth century* 1884
TICKELL, Richard *The camp, a musical entertainment* 1778 (1795)
TICKELL, Thomas *Poetical works* a1740 (1807)
Poems a1740 (1790)
An account of the life and writings of Joseph Addison 1721 (Addison's Works 1721; Arber, Eng. Garner VI)
'TICKLEFOOT, Tom' *Some observations upon the late tryals of Sir George Wakeman*, etc. 1679
TICKNOR, George *History of Spanish literature* 1849
Life of William Hickling Prescott 1864
Life, letters, and journals a1871 (ed. G. S. Hillard 1876)
TIDBALL, John C. *Manual of heavy artillery service prepared for the use of the army and militia of the United States* 1880
TIDYMAN, Ernest *Dummy* 1974
Tiele's History of religion tr. 1877 *See* CARPENTER, J. E.
TIEMANN, Hugh Philip *Iron and steel: a pocket encyclopedia, including allied industries and sciences* 1910
—(ed. 2) 1919
TILDEN, Josephine Elizabeth *Algae and their life relations: fundamentals of phycology* 1935
TILLOTSON, Abp. John *Works* a1694 (1714–17, 1728)
The Protestant religion vindicated from the charge of singularity and novelty 1680
TILLYARD, Robert John *The insects of Australia and New Zealand* 1926
TILMAN, Harold William *The ascent of Nanda Devi* 1937
Nepal Himalaya 1952
TILNEY, Edmund *A brief and pleasaunt discourse of duties in mariage* (running title '*The flower of friendship*') 1568
Timber trades journal 1873–
TIMBERLAKE, Henry *Memoirs* 1765
TIMBS, John *Club life of London* 1866 (1872)
Time: the weekly newsmagazine 1923– (several eds. used)
Time and tide 1920–
Time out 1968–
Times, The 1788–
—weekly edition 1877–
Times educational supplement, The 1910–
Times literary supplement, The 1902–
Times of India, The 1838–
Times review of industry, The 1947–
Times storehouse See MILLES, T.
Time's telescope for 1814; or a complete guide to the almanack 1814
Times' whistle 1616 *See* C., R.
Times-Picayune (New Orleans) 1914–
TIMME, THOMAS *Commentarie of Iohn Caluine vpon Genesis* tr. 1578
Du Chesne's (J.; Quersitanus) Practise of chymicall and hermeticall physicke tr. 1605
A plaine discouerie of ten English lepers 1592
Timon, a play c1600 (Shaks. Soc. 1842)
TIMPERLEY, C. H. *A dictionary of printers and printing* 1839
TINBERGEN, Nikolaas *The herring gull's world* 1953
TINDAL, Matthew *The rights of the Christian Church asserted* 1706
—A defence 1709
TINDAL, Nicholas *Rapin de Thoyras' History of England* tr. 1725–31
—Continued to the accession of King George II 1732–47
—Continued to the present times 1757–63
TINDAL, William *The history and antiquities of the abbey and borough of Evesham* 1794
TINDALE, Norman Bartlett & LINDSAY, Harold Arthur *Rangatira, the high-born: a Polynesian saga* 1959
TINDALE, William *Works* a1536 (1573; Parker Soc. 1848–50)
An answere vnto Sir Thomas Mores dialoge 1530
Erasmus's Enchiridion tr. 1533
An exposicion vpon the v. vi. vii. chapters of Mathew ?1530
The exposition of the fyrste epistle of seynt Ihon 1531 (1537)
The exposition of the epistles of St. Ihon 1538
The fyrst (seconde–fifth) boke of Moses called Genesis, etc. tr. 1530 (1884)
The New Testament tr. 1526, 1534
The obedience of a christen man 1528
The parable of the wicked mammon 1528
A pathway to the holy scripture (anon.) 1533
The practyse of prelates (anon.) 1530
The prophete Jonas with an introduccion before teachinge to vnderstonde him ?1531
The souper of the Lorde (anon.) 1533
—— & FRITH, John *The testament of master William Tracie esquier* 1535
Tinker of Turvey, The 1630 See *Cobler*
Tinsley's Magazine; conducted by Edmund Yates 1868–92
Tint quey 1796 See *Twa cuckolds*
TIPTOFT, John, Earl of Worcester *Iulius Cesars commentaryes* tr. a1470 (1530)
Tulle of olde age. Tullius de amicicia (also, two orations of Publius Cornelius and Gaius Flaminius, tr. from B. Magnomontanus (= Bonaccorso)) tr. a1470 (Caxton 1481)
TIRWHYT, William *The letters of Monsieur de Balzac* tr. 1634
Titan. A monthly magazine 1856–59
Tit-bits 1881–
TITCHENER, Edward B. *Experimental psychology* 1901–05
tr. *W. M. Wundt's Principles of physiological psychology* 1904
See also WUNDT, W.
TITFORD, William Jowit *Sketches towards a Hortus Botanicus Americanus* 1811
Tithes into stipends, A brief discourse of changing ministers 1654

Titus, Harold '*Timber*' 1922
Titus, Silius *Killing noe murder*, by William Allen (i.e. Silas or Silius Titus & Edward Sexby) 1657
Tizard, William L. *The theory and practice of brewing illustrated* 1843 (1846)
Tobin, John *The honey moon: a comedy* 1805
Tod, James *Annals and antiquities of Rajast'han, or the central and western Rajpoot states of India* 1829–32
To-day 1893–1905; 1916–23
Todd, Henry J. *A dictionary of the English language by Samuel Johnson. With numerous corrections and addition(s) by H. J. Todd* 1818
Todd, James G. *Strila; or, the palace of strife. With other poems and songs* 1823
Todd, Robert B. ed. *The cyclopædia of anatomy and physiology* 1835–59
—— & Bowman, William *The physiological anatomy and physiology of man* 1845–56
Todhunter, Isaac *The elements of Euclid, with notes, an appendix, and exercises* 1862
A history of the progress of the calculus of variations during the nineteenth century 1861
William Whewell, D.D.: an account of his writings, with selections from his . . correspondence 1876
Toffler, Alvin *Future shock* 1970
— (Bantam ed.) 1971
Tofte, Robert *Alba. The months minde of a melancholy louer* 1598 (1880)
Laura. The toyes of a traueller. Or, the feast of fancie 1597 (in Arber, Eng. Garner VIII)
Montreux's (N. de) Honours academie, or the famous pastorall of the faire shepheardesse Julietta tr. 1610
Toland, John *Clito, a poem on the force of eloquence* 1700
A critical history of the Celtic religion and learning, containing an account of the Druids a1722 (1726)
— a new ed. by R. Huddleston (1814)
Reflections on Mr. Sacheverell's sermon preached at St. Pauls Nov. 5, 1709 1710
Toland's Pantheisticon tr. 1751
Toldervy, William *The history of two orphans* 1756
Toleration not to be abused 1672 *See* Fullwood, F.
Tolkien, John Ronald Reuel *The fellowship of the ring* (*The lord of the rings*, part 1) 1954
The hobbit; or, There and back again 1937
The return of the king (*The lord of the rings*, part 3) 1955
The Silmarillion ed. C. Tolkien 1977
The two towers (*The lord of the rings*, part 2) 1954
Toller, Sir Samuel *A treatise on the law of tithes* 1808 (1816)
Toller, T. Northcote *See* Bosworth, J.
Tolstoy, George *The first forty years of intercourse between England and Russia, 1553–93; documents (in Russian and English) collected, copied, and edited by G. Tolstoy* 1875
Tom Thumbe, his life and death 1630
Tom Thumb's folio; or, a new penny play-thing for little giants 1768 (1786)
Tom Tyler and his wife; an excellent old play 1598 (1661)
Tombes, John *Anthropolatria; or the sinne of glorying in men* 1645
Fermentum Pharisæorum; or the leaven of Pharisaicall wil-worship: declared in a sermon 1641 (1643)
Tomes, Sir John *A system of dental surgery* 1859
— ed. 2, revised and enlarged by C. S. Tomes 1873
Tomes, Robert *The Americans in Japan* 1857
Tomkis, Thomas *Albumazar* (anon.) 1615 (Dodsley)
Lingua: or the combat of the tongue and the fiue senses for superiority (anon.) 1607 (Dodsley)
Tomlin, Jacob *Missionary journals and letters* 1844
Tomlins, Sir Thomas E. *Jacob's (G.) Law-dictionary greatly enlarged and improved* 1797 (1820)
Tomlinson, Alfred Charles *The shaft* 1978
Tomlinson, Charles *Cyclopædia of useful arts* 1852–54 (1866)
The useful arts and manufactures of Great Britain 1860
Tomlinson, John *The level of Hatfield Chace, and parts adjacent* 1882
Tomlinson, Matthew *The Protestant's birth-right* 1746
Tomlinson, Richard *Renodæus' (J.) Medicinal dispensatory* tr. 1657
Tomlinson, William *An epistle to the flock*, by W. T. 1674
Tomson, Laurence *Calvin's Sermons on the Epistles to Timothie and Titus* tr. 1579
Tonson, Jacob *Poetical miscellanies* 1709
Tonstall or Tunstall, Bp. Cuthbert *A sermon made vpon Palme sondaye* 1539 (1823)
Toogood, Mrs. *Specimens of the Yorkshire dialect* 1863 (MS.)
Tooke, George *Annæ-dicata, or, a miscelaine of some different cansonets* 1652 (1654)
The Belides, or eulogie and elegie of Lord Harrington 1647 (1659)
Tooke, John Horne *The diversions of Purley* 1786–1805 (1829, 1840)
Tooke, Thomas *Considerations on the state of the currency* 1826
Thoughts and details on the high and low prices of the last thirty years 1823 (1824)
Tooke, William *Castera's Life of Catherine II* tr. 1797
Lucian tr. 1820
Russia, or, a compleat historical account of all the nations which compose that empire 1780–83
View of the Russian empire during the reign of Catherine II 1799
Tooker, William *Of the fabrique of the church and churchmens liuings* 1604

Topeka Daily Capital (Topeka, Kansas) 1879–
Topham, Edward *Letters from Edinburgh* (anon.) 1774–75 (1776)
Topham, George *Rome's tradition, the law and gospel's destruction* 1682
Topinard's (P.) Anthropology tr. by R. T. H. Bartley 1878
Topley, William Whiteman C. & Wilson, Graham Selby *The principles of bacteriology and immunity* 2 vols. 1929
Topsell, Edward *The historie of foure-footed beastes* 1607
The historie of serpents 1608
— *The history of four-footed beasts and serpents . . revised . . and inlarged by J. R(owland)* (1658)
Times lamentation: or an exposition on the prophet Ioel 1599
Topsfield, Massachusetts *Town records* 2 vols. 1917–20
Torkington, Sir Richard *Ye oldest diarie of Englysshe travell: being the hitherto unpublished narrative of the pilgrimage of Sir R. Torkington to Jerusalem* 1517 (1884)
Torments of hell 1658 *See* Richardson, S.
Toronto Daily Star 1892–
Torquemada's (A. de) Spanish Mandeuile of miracles (Prefatory epistles signed F. Walker, who attributes the translation to Lewes Lewkenor) 1600
'Torr, Dominic' (John B. S. Pedler) *The treason line* 1968
Torrance, John *Missions of the United Free Church of Scotland. Story of our Marātha missions* 1902
Torrens, Henry D'Oyley *Travels in Ladak, Tartary, and Kashmir* 1862
Torrens, Henry W. *Remarks on the scope and uses of military literature and history* 1846
Torrent of Portugal c1435 (Halliwell 1842; E.E.T.S. 1887)
Torrey, Bradford *The foot-path way* 1892
Torrey, Joseph *Neander's (J. A. W.) General history of the Christian religion and Church* tr. 1847–55
Torriano, Giovanni *A dictionary Italian and English, formerly compiled by John Florio, now diligently revised* 1659
Torriano, N. *An historical dissertation on a particular species of gangrenous sore throat* 1753
A tract on the formation of the fœtus, and the practice of midwifry 1753
Treatise on the nature of non-naturals 1753
Torshell, Samuel *A designe about disposing the Bible into an harmony* 1647 (Phenix 1707)
A helpe to Christian fellowship 1644
Total rout, or a brief discovery of a pack of knaves and drabs 1653
Tottel's miscellany (*Songes and sonettes, written by the ryght honorable Lorde Henry Haward late Earle of Surrey, and other*) 1557 (Arber 1870)
Totten, Benjamin J. *Naval text-book* 1841 (1862, 1864)
Tottle, Charles Ronald *The science of engineering materials* 1966
Touchstone, Timothy *The trifler; a new periodical miscellany* 1788
Tour of German Prince tr. 1832 *See* Austin, Sarah
Tourgée, Albion W. *Button's Inn* 1887
A fools' errand (anon.) 1879
See also 'Churton, Henry'
Tournament. The turnament of Totenham a1450 (ed. T. Wright 1836; in Hazlitt, Early pop. poetry III)
Tournefort, J. Pitton de *Institutiones rei herbariæ* 1700
Tournefort's Voyage into the Levant tr. 1718
Tourneur, Cyril *Plays and poems* a1626 (1878)
The atheist's tragedie 1611
The revengers tragædie (anon.) 1607
Three elegies on the most lamented death of Prince Henrie by C. Tourneur, J. Webster, and T. Heywood 1613
The transformed metamorphosis 1600
Tout, Thomas F. *History of England from William and Mary to the present time* 1890
Towers, Joseph *Memoirs of the life and reign of Frederick the third, King of Prussia* 1788
Towerson, Gabriel *An explication of the decalogue* 1676
Of the sacrament of baptism 1687
Towler, John *The silver sunbeam: a text-book on sun drawing and photographic printing* 1864 (ed. 3)
Town and country magazine 1769–91
Towneley mysteries, The c1460 (Surtees Soc. 1836)
— *The Towneley plays* (E.E.T.S. 1897)
Townsend, Albert Alan *The structure of turbulent shear flow* 1956
Townsend, George F. *English hand-book of Malta* 1869
Townsend, Joseph *A journey through Spain in 1786–87* 1791
Townsend, Richard *Chapters on the modern geometry of the point, line, and circle* 1863–65
Townsend, Thomas *Solis's (A. de) History of the conquest of Mexico* tr. 1724
Townshend, Chauncy H. *Facts in mesmerism, with reasons for a dispassionate inquiry into it* 1840
Townshend, Dorothea *Life and letters of Mr. Endymion Porter* 1897
Towster, Julian *Political power in the U.S.S.R., 1917–47: the theory and structure of government in the Soviet state* 1948
Toynbee, Arnold Joseph *Civilization on trial* 1948
East to west: a journey round the world 1958
An historian's approach to religion 1956
A study of history 10 vols. 1934–54
Tozer, Henry F. *Researches into the highlands of Turkey* 1869
Tracts for the times. By members of the University of Oxford 1833–41
Trade marks journal (Patent Office) 1876–

Trades increase, The (Epistle to the reader signed, I. R.) 1615 (in Harl. Misc.)
'Trafford, F. G.' *See* Riddell, Mrs. J. H.
Tragedy of Hoffman See Chettle, H.
Tragedy of King Richard the second c1590 (1870)
Tragedy of Nero See *Nero*
Trager, George Leonard & Smith, Henry Lee *An outline of English structure* 1951
Tragi-comicall history 1627 *See* D., W.
Traherne, Thomas *Christian ethicks; or divine morality* a1674 (1675)
Poetical works a1674 (1903)
Traheron, Bartholomew *An exposition of a parte of S. Iohannes Gospel* 1557
The most excellent workes of chirurgerye made by J. Vigon tr. 1543 (1550, 1586)
A warning to England to repente 1558
Traill, Catherine Parr *The backwoods of Canada* 1836
Traill, Henry Duff ed. *Social England* 1893–97
Traill, Sinclair ed. *Concerning jazz* 1957
ed. *Play that music: a guide to playing jazz* 1956
Train, Joseph *An historical and statistical account of the Isle of man* 1845
Poetical reveries 1806
Strains of the mountain muse 1814
Traits of American humour, by native authors (ed. T. C. Haliburton) 1852 (1866)
Trans-action: social science and the community (Washington Univ.) 1963–
Transactioner, The 1700 *See* King, William
Transactions at the court of Spain 1678 See *Spanish history*
Transactions See under the names of particular institutions
Transatlantic review 1959–77
Translations and paraphrases of several passages of sacred scripture, collected and prepared by a committee appointed by the General Assembly of the Church of Scotland 1745 (1781, 1786, 1793)
Trapham, Thomas *A discourse of the state of health in the island of Jamaica* 1679
Trapp, John *Annotations upon the Old and New Testament* 1646–62 (1654–62, 1867–68)
Vol. I. *A commentary or exposition upon the five books of Moses* 1650; *together with the books of Joshua, Judges, Ruth, first and second of Samuel, first and second of Kings, and first and second of Chronicles* 1656 (1662)
Vol. II. *Ezra, Nehemiah, Esther, Job, and Psalms* 1656 (1657)
Vol. III. *Proverbs of Solomon, Ecclesiastes, the Song of Songs* 1650; *Isaiah, Jeremiah, Lamentations, Ezekiel and Daniel* 1656 (1660)
Vol. IV. *Twelve minor prophets* (Hosea, Joel, Amos, Obadiah, Jonah, Micah, Nahum, Habakkuk, Zephaniah, Haggai, Zachariah, Malachy) 1654
Vol. V. *New Testament* 1646–47 (1656)
Mellificium theologicum, or the marrow of many good authors 1647 (1655, 1868)
Trapp, Joseph *Abra-Mulé; or, love and empire* 1704
Popery truly stated, and briefly confuted 1726
The Æneis of Virgil tr. 1718–20
The works of Virgil tr. 1731
Trappe, John *Theologia theologiæ, the true treasure* 1641
Travels of certain Englishmen 1609 (1612) *See* Biddulph, W.
Travers, Ben *Mischief* 1925
Travestin (——) *An account of the imperial proceedings against the Turks, with an exact diary of the siege of Newheusel* 1685
Treadgold, Mary *We couldn't leave Dinah* 1941
Treadwell, Bill ed. *Big book of swing* 1946
Treasury of ancient and modern times See Milles, T.
Treasury of botany See Lindley, J.
Treasury of hidden secrets 1573 *See* Partridge, John
Treatise concerning the manner of fallowing of ground (by Rich. Bradley) 1724
Treatise of humane reason 1675 *See* Clifford, M.
Treatise of monarchy See Hunton, P.
Treatise of scolding 1731
Treatise on domestic pigeons 1765
Treatise (Short) on harmony; containing the chief rules for composing in two, three, or four parts 1730
Treatyse of a galaunt See Gallant
'Treddlehoyle, Tom' (Charles Rodgers) *The Bairnsla foak's annual* (various years) 1838–83
Tredgold, Thomas *Elementary principles of carpentry* 1820
A practical essay on the strength of cast iron 1822 (1824)
A practical treatise on rail-roads and carriages 1825
Tregellas, John T. *Cornish tales, in prose and verse* a1863 (1868)
Tregelles, Samuel P. *Remarks on the prophetic visions in the Book of Daniel* 1847 (1864)
Tregonning, Kennedy Gordon Phillip *A history of modern Malaya* 1964
Trelawny, Edward J. *Adventures of a younger son* 1831 (1890)
Trench, Melesina *Remains, being selections from her journals, letters, and other papers* a1827 (ed. R. C. Trench 1862)
Trench, Abp. Richard Chenevix *Christ the desire of all nations* 1846
Commentary on the epistles to the seven churches in Asia 1861
English, past and present 1855
Exposition of the sermon on the mount, drawn from the writings of St. Augustine 1844

The fitness of Holy Scripture for unfolding the spiritual life of men. Hulsean lectures 1845 1845
The Hulsean lectures for 1845 and 1846 1859 (ed. 4 revised)
Notes on the miracles of Our Lord 1846 (1856, 1862)
Notes on the parables of Our Lord 1841 (1844, 1855)
On some deficiencies in our English dictionaries 1857
— ed. 2, revised and enlarged 1860
On the lesson in Proverbs 1853
On the study of words 1851 (1861)
Poems from Eastern sources 1842 (1851)
A select glossary of English words 1859 (1865)
Sermons preached in Westminster Abbey 1860
The story of Justin Martyr, and other poems 1835
Synonyms of the New Testament 1854
TRENCHARD, John *Letter from a souldier to the Commons of England* (anon.) 1702
The natural history of superstition (anon.) 1709
—— & GORDON, Thomas *The independent Whig* 1720
'TREVANIAN' *The Loo sanction* 1973 (UK 1974)
The main 1976 (UK 1977)
TREVELYAN, Sir George O. *Cawnpore* 1865
The competition Wallah 1864 (1866)
The ladies in parliament, and other pieces 1869
The life and letters of Lord Macaulay 1876
TREVES, Sir Frederick *Highways and byways of Dorset* 1906
The other side of the lantern 1905
TREVISA, John de *Bartholomeus (de Glanvilla) De proprietatibus rerum* tr. 1398 (Tollemache MS.; Add. MS. (B.M.) 27944; MS. e Museo (Bodl.) 16; W. de Worde 1495; 1535)
— *Batman vppon Bartholome* (1582)
Polychronicon Ranulphi Higden tr. 1387 (Rolls series 1865–86)
'TREVOR, Edward' *See* LYTTON, E. R. BULWER-
'TREVOR, Elleston' (Trevor Dudley-Smith) *A place for the wicked* 1968
'TREVOR, Glen' (James Hilton) *Murder at school* 1931
'TREVOR, William' (William Trevor Cox) *The boarding-house* 1965
The children of Dynmouth 1976
TREVOR-ROPER, Hugh Redwald (Baron Dacre of Glanton) *The last days of Hitler* 1947
TREVOR-ROPER, Patrick Dacre *Ophthalmology* 1955
Trévoux. Dictionnaire universel français et latin, vulgairement appellé Dictionnaire de Trévoux 1704, 1721, 1732, 1752, 1771
TREWIN, John Courtenay ed. *Plays of the year* See under title
Trial. The proceedings and trial of the bishops in the Court of king's Bench, A.D. 1688 1689
The trial of Edward Coleman, for conspiring the death of the king 1678
The trials of Rob. Green, Henry Bury, and Lawrence Hill ııı*for the murder of Sir E. Godfrey* 1679
The trials of W. Ireland, Tho. Pickering and John Grove, for conspiring to murder the king 1678
The trial of Richard Langhorn for conspiring the death of the king 1679
Trial of maha rajah Nundocomar, Bahader, for forgery 1776
An exact account of the trial between Sir W. Pritchard and Tho. Papillon Esq., in an action upon the case 6 Nov., 1684 1689
Trial of the regicides (An exact and most impartial accompt of the indictment, arraignment, trial, and judgment of twenty nine regicides, the murtherers of his late sacred majesty) 1660
The trials of Sir G. Wakeman, W. Marshall, W. Rumley and James Corker for high treason 1679
The trials and condemnations of Tho. White, alias Whitebread, W. Harcourt, John Fenwick, (and other) Jesuits and priests, for high treason 1679
Triall of cheualry, The historie of the (? by W. Wager) 1605 (in Bullen, Old plays III, 1884)
Triall of treasure, A new and mery enterlude, called the 1567 (Percy Soc. 1850; in Hazl., Dodsley)
Triamoure See *Tryamoure*
Tribes on my frontier 1881 *See* 'EHA'
Tribune 1937–
Tricks of the town laid open 1747 (ed. 3)
Trifler, The 1788 *See* TOUCHSTONE, Timothy
TRIMEN, Henry & THISELTON-DYER, Sir William T. *Flora of Middlesex* 1869
TRIMMER, Eric J., et al. *The visual dictionary of sex* 1977 (UK 1978)
TRIMMER, Joseph *Practical geology and mineralogy* 1841
TRIMMER, Sarah *The two farmers, an exemplary tale* 1787
Trinity College homilies (Old English homilies of the twelfth century. From the MS. in the library of Trinity College, Cambridge. Second series) c1200 (E.E.T.S. 1873)
Trinket, The 1774
'TRIPE, Andrew' 1714 *See* WAGSTAFFE, William
TRIPP, Miles Barton *Faith is a windsock* 1952
Five minutes with a stranger 1971
One is one 1968
TRISTRAM, Henry B. *The Great Sahara* 1860
The land of Israel 1865
The land of Moab 1873
Tristrem, Sir See *Sir Tristrem*
TRITTON, Harold Percy *Time means tucker* 1959
Triumphs of fortitude, The; a novel, in a series of letters 1789
'TROGLODYTE' *See* SCHILLER, F. C. S.
Troil's (Uno von) Letters on Iceland tr. 1780
Trojan war See (Scottish) *Trojan war*
TROLLOPE, Anthony *The American senator* 3 vols. 1877 [1876–77 in Temple Bar]
Australia and New Zealand 2 vols. 1873
An autobiography 2 vols. a1882 (1883)
Ayala's angel 3 vols. 1881
Barchester Towers 3 vols. 1857
The Belton estate 3 vols. 1866 [1865–66 in Fortnightly review]
The Bertrams 3 vols. 1859
Can you forgive her? 2 vols. 1864–65
Castle Richmond 3 vols. 1860
The Claverings 2 vols. 1867 [1866–67 in Cornhill magazine]
Doctor Thorne 3 vols. 1858
Doctor Wortle's school 2 vols. 1881 [1880 in Blackwood's magazine]
The Duke's children 3 vols. 1880 [1879–80 in All the year round]
The Eustace diamonds 1873 [1871–73 in Fortnightly review, US 1872]
Framley Parsonage 3 vols. 1861 [1860–61 in Cornhill magazine]
He knew he was right 2 vols. 1869 [1868–69 in parts]
Is he Popenjoy? 3 vols. 1878 [1877–78 in All the year round]
John Caldigate 3 vols. 1879 [1878–79 in Blackwood's magazine]
The Kellys and the O'Kellys 3 vols. 1848
Lady Anna 2 vols. 1873 (1874)
The last chronicle of Barset 2 vols. 1867 [1866–67 in parts]
Letters ed. B. A. Booth 1951
Linda Tressel 2 vols. 1868 [1867–68 in Blackwood's magazine]
The Macdermots of Ballycloran 3 vols. 1847
Miss Mackenzie 1865
North America 1862
Orley Farm 2 vols. 1862 [1861–62 in parts]
Phineas Finn, the Irish Member 2 vols. 1869 [1867–69 in St. Paul's magazine]
Phineas Redux 2 vols. 1874 [1873–74 in Graphic]
The Prime Minister 4 vols. 1876 [1875–76 in parts]
Rachel Ray 2 vols. 1863
The small house at Allington 2 vols. 1864 [1862–64 in Cornhill magazine]
Tales of all countries 1861
— (2nd ser.) 1863
The three clerks 3 vols. 1858
The Warden 1855
The way we live now 2 vols. 1875 [1874–75 in parts]
The West Indies and the Spanish Main 1859
TROLLOPE, Edward *Sleaford, and the wapentakes of Flaxwell and Ashwardhurn* 1872
TROLLOPE, Frances *Domestic manners of the Americans* 1831
Life and adventures of Michael Armstrong, the factory boy 1840
A visit to Italy 1842
The widow married 1840
TROLLOPE, Frances E. *A charming fellow* 1876
TROLLOPE, Thomas A. *Impressions of a wanderer in Italy, Switzerland, France, and Spain* 1850
La Beata 1861
Marietta 1862
The story of the life of Pius the ninth 1877
A summer in Brittany 1840
A summer in Western France 1841
What I remember 1887–89
Tromholt's (S.) Under the rays of the Aurora borealis tr. 1885
TROTTER, James *General view of the agriculture of West Lothian* 1794
TROTTER, Mrs. M. *See* SAXON
TROTTER, Philip D. *Our mission to the court of Marocco in 1880, under Sir J. D. Hay* 1881
TROTTER, Robert de Bruce *Kirkcudbrightshire. Galloway gossip eighty years ago* 1901
TROTTER, Thomas *An essay on drunkenness* 1804
Troublesome raigne of John king of England 1591; *the second part* 1591 (1611)
TROUBRIDGE, Laura *Life amongst the Troubridges* ed. J. Hope-Nicholson 1966
TROUP, Gordon John Fordyce *Masers* 1959
— (ed. 2, with title *Masers and lasers*) 1963
TROUP, Robert Scott *Silvicultural systems* 1928
The silviculture of Indian trees 3 vols. 1921
TROWBRIDGE, John T. *Coupon bonds* 1866 (1874)
A home idyl, and other poems 1881
True and perfect relation of the proceedings at the seuerall arraignments of (H. Garnet, etc.) 1606
True and sincere declaration of the purpose of the plantation begun in Virginia 1610 (1844)
True Briton, The (by Philip Wharton) 1723–24
True coppie of a discourse written by a gentleman employed in the late voyage of Spaine and Portingale 1589 (Grosart 1881)
True informer, The 1643
True non-conformist See MACWARD, R.
True notion of the worship of God, A; or a vindication of the service of the Church of England 1673
True patriot, The 1775
True spirit of popery, The 1688
True tragedie of Richard Duke of Yorke 1595
True tragedie of Richard the third 1594 (Shaks. Soc. 1844)
TRUMAN, Margaret *Harry S. Truman* 1973
TRUMBULL, Gurdon *Names and portraits of birds which interest gunners* 1888
TRUMBULL, John *Poetical works* 1820
McFingal: a modern epic poem (anon.) 1776
TRUSLER, John *Modern times; or, the adventures of Gabriel Outcast* (anon.) 1785
Poetic endings; or, a dictionary of rhymes 1783
The principles of politeness and of knowing the world (extracted from Earl Chesterfield's Letters to his son), with additions by J. Trusler 1775 (1790)
Truth (Melbourne) See *Melbourne Truth*
Truth (Sydney) 1890–1958
Truth: a weekly journal (London) 1877–1957
Tryall of cheualry See *Triall*
Tryamoure, The romance of syr c1430 (Percy Soc. 1846)
TRYON, Thomas *The good house-wife made a doctor* 1692
Health's grand preservative; or the women's best doctor 1682; ed. 2, *The way to health* 1691
Miscellanea 1696
A treatise of dreams and visions 1695
Wisdom's dictates 1691
TUCKER, Abraham *Freewill, foreknowledge, and fate* 1763
The light of nature pursued: vols. I–IV 1768; vols. V–VII a1774 (1778; 1834, 1852)
TUCKER, Arthur Wilson *Wild talent* 1954 (UK 1955)
TUCKER, Denys William tr. *G. Sterba's Freshwater fishes of the world* 1962
TUCKER, Josiah *An apology for the present Church of England as by law established* 1772
A letter to Edmund Burke 1775
Letters to Dr. Kippis 1773
TUCKER, Thomas George *Introduction to the natural history of language* 1908
TUCKER, William J. *Life and society in Eastern Europe* 1886
TUCKER, Wilson *See* TUCKER, Arthur Wilson
TUCKERMAN, Edward *An enumeration of North American lichenes* 1845
A synopsis of the North American lichens 1882–88
TUCKERMAN, Henry T. *The collector: essays on books, newspapers, pictures* 1868
TUCKETT, Mariana *Mariana's diary: a record of a holiday at Falmouth* ed. H. Fox (Royal Cornwall Polytechnic Society) c1975
TUCKEY, James *Hatschek's (B.) Amphioxus and its development* tr. 1893
TUCKNEY, Anthony *The balme of Gilead* 1643
A good day well improved 1656
Θανατοκτασία: or, death disarmed, a sermon preached Dec. 22, 1653. To which are added two sermons more 1654
TUCKWELL, William *The ancient ways: Winchester fifty years ago* 1893
Tucson Daily Citizen (Tucson, Arizona) 1879–
Tucson magazine (Tucson, Arizona) 1975–
Tudor proclamations. Facsimiles of proclamations of Henry VII, Henry VIII, Edward VI, and Philip and Mary 14..–15.. (1897)
TUER, Andrew W. *History of the horn-book* 1896
Old London street cries and the cries of to-day 1885
Quads for authors, editors, and devils 1884
—— & FAGAN, Charles E. *The first year of a silken reign 1837–38* 1887
TUKE, Daniel H. *A dictionary of psychological medicine* 1892
TUKE, John *A general view of the agriculture of the North Riding of Yorkshire* 1800
TUKE, Richard *The divine comedian; or the right use of plays improved, in a sacred tragi-comedy* 1672
Memoires of the life and death of Sir Edmondbury Godfrey 1682
TUKE, Sir Samuel *The adventures of five hours: a tragi-comedy* 1663
TULK, Alfred *Oken's (L.) Elements of physiophilosophy* tr. 1847
TULL, Jethro *The new horse-houghing husbandry* (anon.) 1731, 1733 (1740, 1762, 1822)
TULLIE, Isaac *A narrative of the siege of Carlisle in 1644–45* c1645 (1840)
TULLOCH, John *English Puritanism and its leaders* 1861
Rational theology and Christian philosophy in England 1872
TULLY (—) *Narrative of a ten years' residence at Tripoli in Africa: from the original correspondence in the possession of the family of the late Richard Tully* (written by Tully's sister-in-law) 1783–95 (1817)
TULLY, Thomas *A letter to Mr. Rich. Baxter* 1675
Tunbridge-miscellany, The; consisting of poems, etc. written at Tunbridge Wells 1712
Tunbrigialia: or Tunbridge miscellanie 1719
Tundale, The visions of; together with metrical moralizations and other fragments of early poetry 14.. (Turnbull 1843; Wagner 1893)
TUNIS, Edwin *Indians* 1959
TUNSTALL, Bp. Cuthbert *See* TONSTALL
TUPPER, Martin F. *Autobiography: my life as an author* 1886
The crock of gold 1844
Heart 1844
Proverbial philosophy 1838–42 (1852)
The twins 1844
TURBERVILLE, George *The booke of faulconrie or hauking* 1575
The eglogs of Mantuan (= *G. B. Spagnuoli*) tr. 1567
Epitaphes, epigrams, songs and sonets 1567
The heroycall epistles of Pub. Ouidius Naso tr. 1567
The noble arte of venerie or hunting (anon.) 1575
Poems a1610 (Chalmers 1810)
Tragical tales, (and other poems) 1587 (1837)
TURK, D. G. *Treatise on teaching and practising the pianoforte* 1804
Turkish spy See MARANA, J. P.
TURNBULL, Gavin *Justin's History of the world* tr. 1746
Poetical essays 1788

Turnbull, Robert *The pulpit orators of France and Switzerland* 1848

Turner, Bill *Circle of squares* 1969

Sex trap 1968

Turner, Brandon *A new English grammar* 1840

Turner, Charles Cyril *Aerial navigation of today: a popular account of the evolution of aeronautics* 1910

Aircraft of to-day 1917

Turner, Charles Godfrey *The happy wanderer* ed. E. M. R. Rice 1922

Turner, Daniel *De morbis cutaneis* 1714 (1731)

Turner, Dawson *Account of a tour in Normandy* 1820

Turner, Edward *Elements of chemistry* 1827 (1847)

Turner, Ernest Sackville *Taking the cure* 1967

Turner, Ethel Sybil *The little larrikin* 1896

Turner, Francis John & Verhoogen, Jean *Igneous and metamorphic petrology* 1951

— (ed. 2) 1960

Turner, George J. ed. *Select pleas of the forest* 1901 (Selden Soc.)

Turner, George W. *The English language in Australia and New Zealand* 1966

ed. *Good Australian English and good New Zealand English* 1972

Turner, J. T. F. *Slate quarries* 1865

Turner, Sir James *Memoirs of his own life and times 1632–70* a1686 (Bannatyne Cl. 1829)

Pallas armata; or military essayes of the ancient Grecian, Roman and modern art of war 1670–71 (1683)

Turner, John *A farther vindication of the soul's separate existence* 1703

Turner, John Evan *A theory of direct realism, and the relation of realism to idealism* 1925

Turner, Richard *An easy introduction to the arts and sciences* 1783 (1821)

Turner, Robert *Βοτανολόγια. The Brittish physician; or the nature and vertues of English plants* 1664

Paracelsus of the chymical transmutation tr. 1657

Turner, Samuel *An account of an embassy to the court of the Teshoo Lama, in Tibet* 1800

Turner, Sharon *The history of the Anglo-Saxons* 1799–1805 (1828)

The modern history of England 1826–29

The sacred history of the world 1832–37

Turner, Thomas H. *Some account of domestic architecture in England* 1851

— Vols. 2 and 3 by J. H. Parker (1853–59)

Turner, Victor Witter *Schism and continuity in an African society: a study in Ndembu village life* 1957

Turner, William *Avium præcipuarum, quarum apud Plinium et Aristotelem mentio est, brevis et succincia historia* 1544

A booke of the natures and properties of the bathes in Englande 1562 (Also issued as pt. of '*The second part of Turners herball*' 1562)

Libellus de re herbaria nouus 1538 (1877)

The names of herbes in Greke, Latin, Englishe, Duche and Frenche 1548 (E.D.S. 1881)

A new boke of the natures of all wines 1568

A new booke of spirituall physik 1555

A new herball 1551; *the seconde parte* 1562; *the first and seconde partes lately ouersene, with the thirde parte, also a booke of the bath of Baeth* 1568

Turner, William *An introduction to human anatomy, including the anatomy of the tissues* 2 vols. 1875–7

Turner, William H. ed. *Selections from the records of the city of Oxford* 1509–83 (1880)

Turnour, George *The Mahávanso, with the translation* 1837

Turton, William *A conchological dictionary of the British Islands* 1819

Linnæus's General system of nature tr. 1802–06

A manual of the land and fresh-water shells of the British Islands 1831

A medical glossary 1797

Tuscaloosa News (Tuscaloosa, Alabama) 1910–

Tusser, Thomas *Five hundreth pointes of good husbandrie* 1573 (1577, 1580; E.D.S. 1878)

A hundreth good pointes of husbandrie 1557 (E.D.S. 1878)

Tutchin, John *A Pindarick ode in the praise of folly and knavery* 1696

A search after honesty 1697

Tutin, John R. *An index to the animal and vegetable kingdoms of Wordsworth* 1892

Tuttle, Edmund B. *Border tales around the camp fire in the Rocky Mountains* 1878

Tuve, Rosemund *Seasons and months: studies in a tradition of Middle English poetry* 1933

Tuvil, Daniel *Essaies politicke and morall* 1608

Essayes, morall and theologicall 1609

Twa cuckolds, The, and the Tint Quey, or Thrawart Maggy. Two tales, in the Scottish dialect 1796

'Twain, Mark' (S. L. Clemens) *The adventures of Huckleberry Finn* 1884

The adventures of Tom Sawyer 1876

The American claimant 1892

Autobiography ed. A. B. Paine 2 vols. 1924

The celebrated jumping frog of Calaveras County, and other sketches ed. J. Paul 1867

Christian Science 1907

A Connecticut Yankee in King Arthur's court 1889

Following the equator: a journey around the world 1897

The innocents abroad 1869

The innocents at home 1872

Letters ed. A. B. Paine 2 vols. 1917 (UK, abridged, 1 vol. 1920)

Letters from Hawaii ed. A. G. Day 1966 (UK 1967)

Letters to his publishers, 1867–1894 ed. H. Hill 1967

Life on the Mississippi 1883

The man that corrupted Hadleyburg, and other stories and essays 1900

Old times on the Mississippi 1876

The prince and the pauper 1881 [dated 1882]

Roughing it 1872

Screamers: a gathering of scraps of humour, delicious bits, and short stories 1871

Sketches 1872

Sketches new and old 1875

Speeches with introd. by W. D. Howells 1910

Speeches with introd. by A. B. Paine 1923

The stolen white elephant 1882

A tramp abroad 1880

A Yankee at the court of King Arthur 1889

See also Harte, Francis Bret & Twain, Mark

—— & Warner, Charles Dudley *The gilded age* 1873 [dated 1874]

Twamley, Josiah *Dairying exemplified, or the business of cheese-making* 1784

Tweddell, John *Remains* a1799 (1815–16)

Tweeddale, James George *Materials technology* 2 vols. 1973

Tweeddale, John *Moff* 1896

Tweedie, William K. *The lakes and rivers of the Bible* 1857 (1864)

ed. *Select biographies* v.d. (Wodrow Soc. 1845–47)

Twelfth century homilies in MS. Bodley 343 11.. (E.E.T.S. 1909)

Twells, John *Grammatics reformata, or, a general examination of the art of grammar* 1683

Tweney, Charles Frederick *Dictionary of naval and military terms* 1914

Twenhofel, William Henry *Principles of sedimentation* 1939

—— & Shrock, Robert Rakes *Invertebrate paleontology* 1935

Twentieth century, The 1951–

Twin soul, The (by Charles Mackay) 1887

Twining (family of). Selections from papers of the Twining family: a sequel to 'The recreations and studies of a country clergyman' (see Twining, T.) 17..–18.. (1887)

Twining, Thomas *Aristotle's Treatise on poetry* tr. 1789 (1812)

Recreations and studies of a country clergyman of the eighteenth century; being selections from the correspondence of T. Twining 17.. (1882)

Travels in India a hundred years ago, with a visit to the United States c1796 (1893)

— Part IV reprinted with title *Travels in America a hundred years ago* (1894)

Twisleton, Ellen *Letters, 1852–1862* ed. E. T. Vaughan 1928

Twiss, Richard *Chess* (anon.) 1787–89

A tour in Ireland in 1775 (anon.) 1776

Travels through Portugal and Spain in 1772 and 1773 1775

Two Cosmos, The; a tale of fifty years ago 1861

Two fifteenth-century cookery-books c1430, -50 (E.E.T.S. 1888)

Two noble kinsmen, The 1612 (1634; New Shaks. Soc. 1876; Shakespeare Apocrypha 1908)

Twyne, Thomas *Petrarca's (F.) Phisicke against fortune* tr. 1579

See also Phaer, T.

Twysden, Sir Roger *The beginners of a monastick life* a1672 (1698)

ed. *Historiæ Anglicanæ scriptores decem* 1652

Tyas, Robert *Favourite field flowers; or, wild flowers of England popularly described* 1848; second series 1850; third series, entitled *Popular flowers; their propagation, cultivation, and general treatment in all seasons* 1854

— Large paper edition revised, entitled *The wild flowers of England or favourite field flowers popularly described. First and second series* 1859–60

Tyde taryeth no man 1576 *See* Wapull, G.

Tyers, Thomas *An historical rhapsody on Mr. Pope* (anon.) 1781 (1782)

Tyler, Moses C. *Glimpses of England: social, political, literary* 18.. (1898)

A history of American literature, 1607–1765 1879

Tylor, Edward B. *Anahuac: or Mexico and the Mexicans* 1861

Anthropology 1881

Primitive culture 1871

Researches into the early history of mankind and the development of civilization 1865

Tymme, Thomas *See* Timme, T.

Tyndale, William *See* Tindale, W.

Tyndall, John *Essays on the floating-matter of the air in relation to putrefaction and infection* 1881

The forms of water in clouds, rivers, ice and glaciers 1872

Fragments of science for unscientific people 1871 (1879)

The glaciers of the Alps 1860

Heat considered as a mode of motion 1863

Mountaineering in 1861: a vacation tour 1862

Notes of a course of nine lectures on light 1870

On radiation 1865

Sound: a course of eight lectures 1867

Tyrie, James *The refutation of ane ansuer made be schir Iohne Knox* 1573

Tyrrell, George Walter *The principles of petrology* 1926

Tyrrell, James *The general history of England, as well ecclesiastical as civil* 1696–1704

Tyrrell, James Williams *Across the Sub-Arctics of Canada* 1897

Tyrwhit, William *See* Tirwhyt, W.

Tyrwhitt, Thomas *The Canterbury tales of Chaucer. To which are added, an essay upon his language and versification; an introductory discourse; and notes (with a glossary)* 1775–78

A vindication of the appendix to the poems, called Rowley's 1782

See also Chatterton, Thomas

Tyson, Edward *Orang-outang, sive homo sylvestris; or the anatomy of a pygmie* 1699

Phocæna, or, the anatomy of a porpess: with a preliminary discourse concerning anatomy 1680

Tytler, Ann Fraser *Mary and Florence; or, grave and gay* 1835

Mary and Florence at sixteen. A continuation of 'Grave and gay' 1838

Tytler, Patrick F. *England under the reigns of Edward VI and Mary* 1839

History of Scotland 1828–43 (1864)

'Tytler, Sarah' (Henrietta Keddie) *The Blackhall ghosts* 1888

The bride's pass 1882

Days of yore 1866

Lady Jean's son 1897

The Macdonald lass 1895

Phemie Millar 1854

The witch wife 1897

U

UCT studies in English See *Studies in English* (University of Cape Town)

Ubaldini's (P.) Discourse concerninge the Spanish fleet invadinge Englande tr. 1590

Udall, Ephraim *Funeral sermon* 1643 (1645)

The good peace and ill of warre; set forth in a sermon 1642

Noli me tangere, is a thinge to be thought on (anon.) 1642

Udall, John *A demonstration of the trueth of that discipline which Christe hath prescribed* (anon.) 1588 (Arber 1880)

The state of the Church of Englande, laide open in a conference betweene Diotrephes, a byshop, Tertullus, a papist, etc. (anon.) 1588 (Arber 1880)

Udall, Nicolas *Apophthegmes, that is to saie, prompte saiynges. First gathered by Erasmus* tr. 1542 (1564, 1877)

Floures for Latine spekynge. Selected and gathered out of Terence tr. 1533

Gemini's (T.) Compendiosa totius anatomie delineatio tr. 1553

The noble tryumphaunt coronation of quene Anne 1533 (in Arber, Eng. Garner II; Pollard 1903)

Ralph Roister Doister, a comedy a1553 (Arber 1869; in Manly, Specim. pre-Shaks. drama II, 1898)

—— et al. *The first tome or volume of the paraphrase of Erasmus upon the Newe Testament* tr. 1548

Udden, A. D. tr. *N. Bohr's The theory of spectra and atomic constitution* 1922

Ude, Louis E. *The French cook* 1813 (1822, 1827)

Udny, Alexander *A golden bell and a pomgranate* 1625

The voyce of the cryer 1628

Ueberweg's (F.) History of philosophy tr. by G. S. Morris 1872–74

Uhland's (W. H.) Corliss-engines and allied steam-motors tr. by A. Tolhausen 1879–82

Ulanov, Barry *A history of jazz in America* 1952 (UK 1958)

Ullman, Stephen *The principles of semantics* 1951

Ulverston News (Ulverston, Cumbria) 1883–

Uncle Philip's conversations about the whale fishery and Polar seas 1836

Undercurrents 1972–

Underdowne, Thomas *The excellent historye of Theseus and Ariadne* 1566

Ovid his invective against Ibis tr. 1569

Underhill, Edward *A note off the examynacyon and impresonmentt off E.U.* 1553 (in Narratives of the days of the Reformation, Camden Soc. 1859; Arber, Eng. Garner IV)

Underhill, Evelyn *Mysticism: a study in the nature and development of man's spiritual consciousness* 1911

Underwood, Benton J. *Experimental psychology: an introduction* 1949

Underwood, Michael *A treastie on the diseases of children* 1784

— ed. 3, entitled *A treatise on the disorders of childhood* 1797 (1799)

'Underwood, Michael' (John Michael Evelyn) *Murder with malice* 1977

A pinch of snuff 1974

Reward for a defector 1973

Unfortunate sensibility 1784

United Free Church magazine, The 1904–06

United Free Church of Scotland *Missionary record* (title varies) 1901–29

United Kingdom. Admiralty *Manual of seamanship* 2 vols. 1908–9

— Vol. II (rev. ed.) 1923

Manual of seamanship for boys' training ships of the Royal Navy 1883

United Kingdom. Advisory Committee for Aeronautics (*later* Aeronautical Research Committee; *later* Aeronautical Research Council) Technical reports 1910-
United Kingdom. Department of Education and Science *A Language for life. Report of the Committee of Inquiry.. under the chairmanship of Sir Alan Bullock* 1975
United Kingdom. Department of Employment *Classification of occupations and directory of occupational titles* 3 vols. 1972
United Kingdom. Department of Scientific and Industrial Research. Forest Products Research Laboratory *A handbook of hardwoods* 1956 (for ed. 2, see below)
A handbook of softwoods 1917
United Kingdom. Department of the Environment. Building Research Establishment *Handbook of hardwoods* (ed. 2, rev. by R. H. Farmer) 1972 (for ed. 1, see above)
United Kingdom. General Medical Council (*later* British Pharmacopœia Commission) *Approved names* 1957-66; 1970-
United Kingdom. General Register Office *Classification of occupations* 1960
United Kingdom. Meteorological Office *Meteorological glossary* 1918 (and several later editions used)
United Kingdom. Ministry of Agriculture *Journal* 1919-
United Kingdom. Ministry of Information *Manpower: the story of Britain's mobilization for war* 1944
United Kingdom. Ministry of Labour *A dictionary of occupational terms, based on the classification of occupations used in the census of population, 1921* 1927
United Kingdom. Parliamentary papers [*Note* Volume numbers in citations refer mostly to the bound collections in the Bodleian Library. The second page number in citations is the starting-page of the particular report, etc., in the overall numbering within the volume.]
Committee on Broadcasting, 1960 (Chairman: H. Pilkington) *Report* 1962 in *Parl. Papers 1961-2* (Cmnd. 1753) IX. 259
Committee of Inquiry on Decimal Currency (Chairman: the Earl of Halsbury) *Report* 1963 in *Parl. Papers 1962-3* (Cmnd. 2145) XI. 195
Committee on Higher Education, 1961-3 (Chairman: Lord Robbins) *Higher education: report* 1963 in *Parl. Papers 1962-3* (Cmnd. 2154) XI. 639
United Kingdom. Patent Office *Official journal* (title varies) 1884-
See also *Trade marks journal*
United Service journal and naval and military magazine (title varies) 1829-43
United service magazine, The 1890-
United States. Arctic, Desert and Tropic Information Center *Glossary of arctic and subarctic terms* 1955
United States. Bureau of American Ethnology *Annual report* 1881-1933
Bulletin 1886-
United States. Bureau of Fisheries *Report* See: United States. Commissioner of Fisheries
United States. Bureau of Forestry *See* —— Department of Agriculture
United States. Bureau of Standards *See* —— National Bureau of Standards
United States. Commissioner of Fisheries *Report* (title varies) 1873-1941
United States. Commissioner of Patents *Annual report* 1839-
United States. Congress. Debates *Congressional globe, The: containing the debates and proceedings..of Congress* 1834-73
Congressional record, The: containing the proceedings and debates..of the Congress 1873-
Debates and proceedings in the Congress of the United States, 1789-1824 42 vols. 1834-56
Register of debates in Congress, 1824-37 14 vols. 1825-37
Senate hearings *Illicit narcotics traffic: hearings before the Subcommittee..of the Committee on the Judiciary* (84th Congress, 1st Session) 1956
United States. Department of Agriculture *Bulletin* 1913-27
Farmers' bulletin 1889-
Yearbook 1894- (1923-5 with title *Agricultural yearbook;* 1926- with title *Yearbook of agriculture*)
Bureau of Animal Industry *Annual report* 1884-1911
Bureau of Forestry *Bulletin* 1887-1913
Terms used in forestry and logging 1905 (*Bulletin* No. 61)
United States. Geological Survey *Annual report* 1880-1932
Bulletin 1883-
Monographs 1882-1929
Professional papers 1902-
Water-supply papers (title varies) 1896-
United States. Laws and statutes *The statutes at large of the United States of America* 1845-
United States. National Bureau of Standards *Journal of research* 1928-
United States. National Cancer Institute *See* United States. Public Health Service
United States. National Museum *Bulletin* 1875-
Proceedings 1878-
Reports 1884-
United States. Patent Office *Official gazette* 1872-
United States. Public Health Service. National Cancer Institute *Journal* 1940-
United States *Report of the Commissioner of Indian Affairs to the Secretary of the Interior* (title varies) 1825-
United States *Senate hearings* VIII *See* United States. Congress. Senate hearings
United States. Statutes *See* United States. Laws and statutes
United States. War Department *Reports of explorations and surveys to ascertain the most practicable and economical route for a railroad from the Mississippi River to the Pacific Ocean made in 1853-54* 12 vols. 1855-9
Short guide to Great Britain 1942
United States magazine and democratic review 1837-51
United States 1980/81 (Penguin Travel Guides) 1979
United Telephone Company, Ltd. *List of subscribers* 1885 [preface reproduced in facsimile in *Three Victorian telephone directories* 1970]
List of subscribers..classified into professions and trades (ed. 6) 1885 [*ibid.*]
Universal magazine of knowledge and pleasure, The 1747-1803
— continued as *The universal magazine* 1804-14
Universal review, The 1866
Universe, The 1860-
Unton inventories, relating to Wadley and Faringdon, Co. Berks 1596, 1620 (1841)
UNTON, Sir Henry *Correspondence* 1591-92 (Roxb. Cl. 1847)
UPCOTT, Lewis E. *An introduction to Greek sculpture* 1887 (1899)
UPDIKE, Daniel Berkeley *Printing types: their history, forms and use* 2 vols. 1922
UPDIKE, John Hoyer *The coup* 1978 (UK 1979)
Couples 1968
Rabbit, run 1960 (UK 1961)
UPFIELD, Arthur William *Bony and the white savage* 1961
Bushranger of the skies 1940
Murder must wait 1953
The will of the tribe 1962
UPTON, John *Critical observations on Shakespeare* 1746
Spenser's Faerie queene. A new ed. with a glossary, and notes explanatory and critical 1758
UPTON, William *Physioglyphics* 1844
Upton-on-Severn glossary 1884 *See* LAWSON, R.
UPWARD, Allen *Songs in Ziklag* 1888
URBAN, Charles *The cinematograph in science, education, and matters of state* 1907
URBAN, Wilbur Marshall *Valuation: its nature and laws; being an introduction to the general theory of value* 1909
URE, Andrew *The cotton manufacture of Great Britain systematically investigated* 1836 (1861)
A dictionary of arts, manufactures and mines 1839 (1843, 1853)
— ed. 5, by R. Hunt (1860); ed. 7, by R. Hunt & F. W. Rudler (1875)
— *Supplement* (1878)
A dictionary of chemistry 1821
A new system of geology 1829
The philosophy of manufactures 1835 (1861)
URE, David *General view of the agriculture of the county of Dumbarton* 1794
General view of the agriculture of the county of Roxburgh 1794
The history of Rutherglen and East-Kilbride 1793
Ureisun a1240 (in Old Eng. homilies, I, E.E.T.S. 1868)
Urie, The court book of the barony of 1604-1747 (S.H.S. 1892)
URMSON, James Opie ed. *The concise encyclopaedia of Western philosophy and philosophers* 1960
Philosophical analysis: its development between the two world wars 1956
URQUHART, John W. *Dynamo construction: a practical handbook for the use of engineer-constructors and electricians-in-charge* 1981
URQUHART, Sir Thomas *Works* a1600 (Maitland Cl. 1834)
Εκσκυβαλαυρον; or, the discovery of a most exquisite jewel 1652
The first (second) book of the works of Mr. Francis Rabelais 1653 (1664)
— *The third book* (1693, 1694) See Also MOTTEUX, P. A.
URRY, John ed. *The works of Geoffrey Chaucer, compared with the former editions, and many valuable MSS. Together with a glossary by (Timothy Thomas)* 1721
Ursula, St., The Life of c1480 (Roxb. Cl. 1818)
Ushaw magazine, The 1891-
USK, Thomas *The testament of love* 1387-88 (in Chaucer's Works, ed. Thynne 1532; Chaucerian pieces, Skeat 1897)
USSHER, James *The annals of the world deduced from the origin of time* a1656 (1658)
An answer to a challenge made by a Jesuite in Ireland 1624 (1625)
A body of divinitie 1645 (1647)
Immanuel; or, the mystery of the incarnation of the son of God unfolded 1638 (1643)
The power communicated by God to the prince a1656 (1661, 1683)
The reduction of episcopacie unto the form of synodical government received in the antient church 1656
A sermon preached before the Commons 18 Feb. 1620 (1621, 1624)
The life of James Ussher. With a collection of three hundred letters. Collected and published by Richard Parr (1686)
UTTERSON, Edward V. ed. *Select pieces of early popular poetry* v.d. (1817)
UTTLEY, Alison (Alice Jane Uttley) *The country child* 1931

V

Vacation tourists See GALTON, F.
VACHELL, Horace A. *Dew of the sea, and other stories* 1927
The hill, a romance of friendship 1905
John Charity. A romance of yesterday 1900
Virgin 1929
VACHER, Francis *On the transmission of disease by milk* 1882
VAILE, Pembroke Arnold *Modern golf* 1909
VAIZEY, George De Horne *Tangled web* 1974
VAIZEY, Jessie *A college girl* 1913
More about Pixie 1904
Valdesso's Considerations (1638) *See* FERRAR, N.
VALENTIA, George Annesley, 9th Viscount *Voyages and travels to India, etc. 1802-06* 1809
VALENTINE, Henry *Foure sea-sermons* 1635
VALENTINE, Thomas *A dictionary of terms used in music* 1824 (1833)
Valentinus' (B.) Of natural and supernatural things tr. by Dan. Cable 1670
Valiant Welshman 1615 *See* ARMIN, R.
VALLANCEY, Charles *Collectanea de rebus Hibernicis* 1770-1804
Memoir of the language, manners and customs of an Anglo-Saxon colony settled in the Baronies of Forth and Bargie (with a vocabulary of the language) 1788 (in Trans. R. Irish Academy, II, 1788)
VALLANS, William *The honourable prentice* (anon.) a1590 (1615)
Vámbéry's (H.) Travels in Central Asia tr. 1864
Van Beneden, P. J. See BENEDEN, P. J. VAN
VANBRUGH, Sir John *Works* a1726 (1734, 1840, 1893)
Æsop (anon.) 1697
The confederacy (anon.) 1705
The false friend (anon.) 1702
The mistake (anon.) 1706
The pilgrim 1700
The provok'd wife 1697
The relapse, or virtue in danger 1697
—— & CIBBER, Colley *The provk'd husband, or, a journey to London* 1728
VAN BUREN, William H. & KEYES, Edward L. *A practical treatise on the surgical diseases of the genito-urinary organs* 1874
VANCE, John Holbrook *The deadly isles* 1969 (UK 1970)
VANCE, Louis Joseph *Baroque* 1923
Cynthia-of-the-minute 1911
The destroying angel 1912 (UK 1913)
VANCOUVER, Charles *General view of the agriculture in the county of Cambridge* 1794
General view of the agriculture of the county of Devon 1808 (1813)
General view of the agriculture of the county of Essex 1795
General view of the agriculture of Hampshire, including the Isle of Wight 1813
Vancouver Province 1898-
Vancouver Sun (title varies) 1888-
'VANDERDECKEN' (W. Cooper) *The yacht sailor; a treatise on practical yachtsmanship, cruising and racing* 1862
Yachts and yachting 1873
VAN DER POST, Laurens Jan *The heart of the hunter* 1961
The lost world of the Kalahari 1958
A story like the wind 1972
Vanderstraeten's (F.) Improved agriculture tr. 1816
VAN DEVENTER, C. N. *An introduction to general aeronautics* 1965
VAN DE WETERING, Janwillem *The corpse on the dike* 1976 (UK 1977)
Tumbleweed 1976
Vane's (Sir Harry) politicks, or his cases of conscience, lately found in his cabinet at Arabie 1661
VAN HARE, G. *Fifty years of a showman's life, or the life and travels of Van Hare by himself* 1888
Vanity fair (New York) 1914-36
Vanity of the life of man, The 1688 *See* BURTON, Richard
Vanity of scoffing, The 1674 *See* ELLIS, C.
Van Nostrand's scientific encyclopedia 1938
— (ed. 3) 1958
VAN OOSTEN, Henrik *The Dutch gardener; or, The compleat florist* [anon. tr.] 1703
Van Oosterzee's (J. J.) Christian dogmatics tr. 1874 *See* WATSON, John W.
VAN RENSSELAER, Mrs. M. King *The devil's picture-books: a history of playing-cards* 1890 (1892)
VAN RENSSELAER, Mrs. Schuyler *English cathedrals* 1892
VANSITTART, Henry *A narrative of the transactions in Bengal 1760-64* 1766
VAN STERKENBURG, P. G. J., et al. eds. *Lexicologie: een bundel opstellen voor F. de Tollenaere* 1977
VAN THAL, Herbert Maurice ed. *Fanfare for Ernest Newman* 1955
VAN TYNE, Josselyn & BERGER, Andrew John *Fundamentals of ornithology* 1959
VAN VECHTEN, Carl *Nigger heaven* 1926
VARADAY, Desmond *Gara-Yaka: the story of a cheetah* 1964
Gara-Yaka's domain 1966
Variety 1905-
Vattel's (E. de) Law of nations tr. 1759-60

VAUGHAN, Charles John *Earnest words for earnest men* 1870 (1878)

Memorials of Harrow Sundays 1859 (1863)

The young life equipping itself for God's service 1872 (1873)

VAUGHAN, Henry *Works* a1695 (Grosart 1871)

Poems, with the tenth satyre of Juvenal Englished 1646

A fast sermon (on Matth. v. 20) 1644

Silex scintillans, or sacred poems and private ejaculations 1650

— ed. 2, in two books 1655 (1858)

Thalia rediviva: the pass-times and diversions of a countrey-muse 1678

VAUGHAN, Sir John *The reports and arguments of Sir J. V.; being all of them special cases* a1674 (1677)

VAUGHAN, Rice *A discourse of coin and coinage* a1672 (1675)

VAUGHAN, Robert *The age of great cities* 1843

VAUGHAN, Robert A. *Essays and remains* a1857 (1858)

Hours with the mystics 1856 (1860)

VAUGHAN, Thomas *Anima magica abscondita; or a discourse of the universall spirit of nature* 1650

Anthroposophia theomagica; or a discourse of the nature of man and his state after death 1650

Euphrates, or the waters of the East 1655

VAUGHAN, Thomas *Fashionable follies* 1782

Vaughan (W. O. G.), Voyages of 1736 *See* CHETWOOD, W. R.

VAUGHAN, William *Boccalini's (T.) New-found politicke* (Part III) tr. 1626

Vaughan (William), Examination of, in a committe of the House of Commons, April 22, 1796 1796

VAUGHAN-THOMAS, Wynford *Anzio* 1961

VAUS, John *Rudimenta puerorum in artem grammaticalem* 1522 (1531)

VAUTROLLIER, Thomas *Luther's Commentarie vpon the epistle to the Galathians* tr. 1575 (1577)

VAUX, Edward, Lord *Godeau's (A.) Life of the Apostle St Paul* tr. 1653

VAUX, James Hardy *A new and comprehensive vocabulary of the flash language* 1812 (in Memoirs, II)

Memoirs, written by himself 1819

VAUX, Thomas, 2nd Baron Vaux *Poems* a1556 (Grosart 1872)

VAUX, William S. W. *On mankind, their origin and destiny* 1872

VAWTER, Bruce *The conscience of Israel: pre-exile prophets and prophecy* 1961

VEAL, George *See* 'COLLIER, Joel'

VEDDER, David *Orcadian sketches; legendary and lyrical pieces* 1832

Poems 1842

Vegetable substances used for the food of man 1832

Vegetius' De re militari tr. 1408–09 (MS. Laud 416, MS. Digby 233)

VEITCH, John *Knowing and being* 1889

The method, meditations, and selections from the principles of Descartes tr. 1879

The Tweed, and other poems 1875

VENABLES, Edmund *Wieseler's (K.) Chronological synopsis of the four gospels* tr. 1864

VENABLES, Robert *The experienc'd angler* 1662 (See WALTON, Iz.)

VENEER, John *A companion for the sincere penitent* tr. 1728

VENEES, W. T. *El Dorado; or, British Guiana as a field for colonization* 1867

VENKATACHALAM, Govindraj *Dance in India* 1948

VENKATARAMAN, Krishnasami ed. *The chemistry of synthetic dyes* 8 vols. 1952–78

VENN, Henry *A volume of sermons* 1759

VENN, John *The principles of empirical or inductive logic* 1889

Symbolic logic 1881 (1894)

VENN, Thomas *Military and maritime discipline* 1672

See also LACEY, John; T., W.

VENNER, Norman *The imperfect impostor* 1925

VENNER, Tobias *The baths of Bathe* 1628 (1650)

A briefe and accurate treatise concerning the taking of the fume of tobacco 1621

Via recta ad vitam longam; also the true use of our famous bathes of Bathe 1620 (1628, 1650)

VENNING, Ralph *Mercies memorial* 1656 (1657)

Milke and honey 1653

Venturoli's (G.) Elements of practical mechanics tr. by Dan. Cresswell 1823

VENZEE, Maria *Fate, or Spong castle; a novel* 1803

'VERAX, Theodorus' *See* WALKER, Clement

Verbatim: the language quarterly 1974–

Verdere. Saulnier's (G.; sieur Du Verdier) Love and armes of the Greeke princes; or the romant of romants tr. 1640

Verdicts of the learned concerning Virgil and Homer's heroick poems 1700 (in Regular and irregular thoughts; Somers' Tracts IV, 1750)

VERE, Edward De, 7th Earl of Oxford *Poems* a1604 (Grosart 1872)

VERE, Sir Francis *Commentaries* a1609 (1657; in Arber, Eng. Garner VII)

Vergilius a1525 See *Virgilius*

Vergilius' (Polydorus) English history. Vol. I. containing the first eight books, comprising the period prior to the Norman conquest c1540 (Camden Soc. 1846)

—— *Three books, comprising the reigns of Henry VI, Edward IV, and Richard III* c1540 (Camden Soc. 1844)

See also LANGLEY, T.

VERMANDEL, Janet Gregory *Dine with the devil* 1970

Vermont. Board of Agriculture *Annual report* (title varies) 1872–1908

VERNE, Jules *The clipper of the clouds* [anon. tr.] 1887

Meridiana; the adventures of three Englishmen and three Russians in South Africa tr. 1873

Verney. Letters and papers of the Verney family down to the end of the year 1639; printed from the original MSS. in the possession of Sir Harry Verney 1478–1639 (Camden Soc. 1853)

Memoirs of the Verney family during the Civil war, compiled from the letters and illustrated by the portraits at Claydon house by F. P. Verney 16.. (1892)

— vol. III *during the Commonwealth 1650 to 1660 compiled by Margaret M. Verney* 16.. (1894)

— vol. IV *1660–96* 16.. (1899)

— ed. 2, *abridged and corrected by Margaret M. Verney* v.d. (1904)

VERNEY, Frances Parthenope, Lady *Lettice Lisle* 1870

Stone Edge (anon.) 1868

See also above

VERNEY, John *Friday's tunnel* 1959

VERNEY, Maria Margaret ed. *Verney letters of the eighteenth century, from the manuscripts at Claydon House* 2 vols. 1930

VERNON, Christopher *Considerations for regulating the Exchequer* 1642

VERNON, George *The life of Dr. P. Heylyn* 1681 (1682)

VERNON, John *The compleat comptinghouse* 1678

VERNON, William *Poems on several occasions* 1758

Vernon MS. (Bodleian) a1400

— *Minor poems of the* (E.E.T.S. 1892–1901)

VERON, John *A fruteful treatise of predestination* 1561

The godly saiyngs of the old auncient fathers vpon the sacrament of the bodye and bloude of Chryste tr. 1550 (1846)

A moste necessary treatise of free wil, not onlye against the Papistes, but also against the Anabaptistes c1561

VERRAL, William *A complete system of cookery* 1759

VERSCHOYLE, Terence Trevor Hamilton tr. *A. E. Haas's Atomic theory* 1927

VERSTEGAN, Richard *A restitution of decayed intelligence: in antiquities* 1605 (1628, 1634)

Versus gnomici See *Gnomic verses*

VERY, Jones *Essays and poems* 1839

— *Poems and essays. Complete and revised ed.* (1886)

VESEY-FITZGERALD, Brian Seymour ed. *The book of the dog* 1948

Vespasian psalter c825 (in Sweet, Oldest English texts, E.E.T.S. 1885)

— *hymns* (ibid.)

Vestiges of the natural history of creation (by Robert Chambers) 1844

Vestry books of Pittington, etc. See *Churchwardens' accounts*

Veterinary journal 1875–95; 1900–48

Veterinary record 1888–

Vetusta monumenta, or ancient monuments illustrative of the history and topography of Great Britain 1747–1842

VICARS, John *Coleman-street conclave visited* 1648

England's worthies under whom all the civill and bloudy warres since 1642 are related (anon.) 1647

God in the mount 1641 (1642)

Jehovah-Jireh; God in the mount, or England's remembrancer (or *parliamentarie-chronicle*) (Parts 1 and 2 are an expanded ed. of 'God in the mount' 1641) 1642–46

The XII Aeneids of Virgil tr. 1632

VICARY, Thomas *A profitable treatise of the anatomie of mans body* 1548 (1577; E.E.T.S. 1888)

— another ed., entitled *The Englishmans treasure. With the true anatomye of mans body* (?1585, 1626)

Vices and virtues c1200 (E.E.T.S. 1888)

VICKERMAN, Charles *Woollen spinning* 1894

VICTORIA, Queen *Leaves from the journal of our life in the Highlands, 1848–61* (ed. Arthur Helps 1868)

— *More leaves, 1862–82* (1884)

See also FULFORD, Roger T. B.

Victoria (Australia). Mining Department *Mining surveyors' reports* 1859–63

Victoria Institute, Journal of the transactions of the 1867–

VIDAL, Gore *The city and the pillar* 1948 (UK 1949)

In a yellow wood 1947

Kalki 1978

VIDIAN, Andrew *The exact pleader* 1684

Vidocq's (Eugène F.) Memoirs, compiled from Vidocq's notes by É. Morice & L. F. L'Héritier, tr. (by H. T. R.) 1828–29

View of an ecclesiastic 1698 *See* FERGUSON, R.

View of the penal laws concerning trade and trafick, A 1697

View of a printed book 1642 *See* SPELMAN, Sir John

View of sundry examples 1580 *See* MUNDAY, A.

VIGFUSSON, Gudbrand *An Icelandic-English dictionary based on the MS. collections of the late Richard Cleasby, enlarged and completed by G. Vigfusson* 1874 (1876)

'VIGILANS' (Eric Honeywood Partridge) *Chamber of horrors: a glossary of official jargon both English and American* 1952

VIGNE, Godfrey T. *A personal narrative of a visit to Ghuzni, Kabul, and Afghanistan* 1840

Travels in Kashmir, Ladak, Iskardo, etc. 1842

Vigo's (Joannes de) Lytell practyce tr. ? 1535

See also TRAHERON, B.

Village voice (New York) 1955–

VILLARI, Linda *Villari's (P.) Niccolo Machiavelli and his times* tr. 1878–83

VILLIERS, Douglas ed. *Next year in Jerusalem* 1976

VILLIERS, George, 2nd Duke of Buckingham *Works* a1687 (1704, 1752)

The chances, a comedy (by F. Beaumont & J. Fletcher) *corrected and altered* 1682 (1735)

The rehearsal 1672 (Arber 1868)

— *The fifth edition with amendments and large additions by the author* 1687

The restoration, or right will take place (an adaptation of Beaumont & Fletcher's Philaster) a1687 (1714)

VILVAIN, Robert *Enchiridium epigrammatum Latino-Anglicum; an epitome of essais* tr. 1654

Theoremata theologica: theological treatises 1654

VINCE, Samuel *The principles of hydrostatics* 1800 (1806)

VINCE-PRUE, Daphne *Photoperiodism in plants* 1975

VINCENT, E. A. tr. *A. Rittmann's Volcanoes and their activity* 1962

VINCENT, Samuel *The young gallant's academy* (Dekker's 'Gull's Hornbook' adapted to the time) 1674

VINCENT, William *The voyage of Nearchus from the Indus to the Euphrates, collected from Arrian* 1797

VINCENT, William Thomas *Recollections of Fred Leslie* 2 vols. 1894

Vindex Anglicus; or, the perfections of the English language defended and asserted 1644 (in Harl. Misc.)

Vindication of the Bishop of Durham (Thomas Morton) from the vile and scandalous calumnies of a libell intituled, The downfall of hierarchie 1641

Vindication of Christmas, The, or, his twelve yeares observations upon the great and lamentable tragedy between the king and parliament 1653

Vindication of Magna Charta as the summary of English rights and liberties, A 1702

Vindication of Sir Thomas Player, and those loyal citizens concerned with him 1679

Vindication of the treatise of monarchy 1644 *See* HUNTON, P.

Vindiciæ Carolinæ: or, a defence of Εικων βασιλικη (ascribed to R. Hollingworth or John Wilson) 1692

Vinegar and mustard 1673 *See* WADE, John

VINES, Richard *A treatise on the institution of the sacrament of the Lord's supper* a1656 (1677)

VINES, Sydney H. *Lectures on the physiology of plants* 1886

Sachs' (J.) Text-book of botany tr. 1882

See also PRANTL, K.

VINES, Walter Sherrard *Humours unreconciled* 1928

VINOGRADOFF, Sir Paul G. *Villainage in England* 1892

Vintners. The art and mystery of vintners and wine-coopers 1682 (1703)

VINYCOMB, John *Fictitious and symbolic creatures in art* 1906

VIOLLET-LE-DUC, Eugène E. *Dictionnaire raisonné de l'architecture Française du xie au xvie siècle* 1854–68

Virgilius a1525 (in Thoms, Prose romances, II, 1827)

Virginia *Calendar of Virginia state papers and other manuscripts* ed. W. P. Palmer et al. 11 vols. 1875–93

Virology 1955–

VISGER, Mrs. Owen *See* JORDAN, Denham

Visions of Tundale See *Tundale*

VISSER, Fredericus Theodorus *An historical syntax of the English language* 3 parts in 4 vols. 1963–73

Vitamins and hormones 1943–

VITELES, Morris Simon *Industrial psychology* 1933

VIVIAN, Herbert *See* WILKINS, W. H.

Vivisection controversy, The (No. 1) 1883

VIZETELLY, Henry *Glances back through seventy years* 1893

Vocabulary of Forth and Bargie 1788 *See* VALLANCEY, C.

VOEGELIN, Charles Frederick & VOEGELIN, Florence Marie R. *Classification and index of the world's languages* 1977

VOGAN, Arthur J. *The black police; a story of modern Australia* 1891

Vogel's (H.) Chemistry of light and photography tr. 1875

Vogt's (Carl) Lectures on man tr. and ed. by James Hunt 1864

Vogue 1892–

Voice (New York) 1884–95

Voiture's (V.) Letters of affaires, love and courtship tr. by J. Davies 1657

Vole 1977–81

Volney. Chassebœuf de Volney's (C. F.) View of the climate and soil of the United States tr. by C. B. Brown 1804

VON ARNIM, Mary Annette *Elizabeth and her German garden* 1898

The enchanted April 1922

Fräulein Schmidt and Mr. Anstruther 1907

Introduction to Sally 1926

VON ENGELN, Oscar Diedrich *Geomorphology* 1942

Von Holst; Von Troil See HOLST, H. VON; *Troil, U. von*

VONNEGUT, Kurt *Cat's cradle* 1963

Slaughterhouse-five; or, The children's crusade 1969

VON NEUMANN, John *Collected works* ed. A. H. Taub 6 vols. 1961–3

VON STERNBERG, Joseph *Fun in a Chinese laundry* 1965 (UK 1966)

Voorloper: an interim presentation of materials for a dictionary of South African English on historical principles ed. W. Branford et al. 1976

VOWELL, John *See* HOOKER, JOHN

Vox and wolf a1300 (in Reliquiæ ant. II, 1843; Hazlitt, Early pop. poetry I)

Vox turturis, vel columba alba Albionis. The voice of the turtle, or England's white dove in the deluge of division. Per M. E. Arm(igerum) 1647 (in Thomason Tracts)

Voyage of Spaine and Portingale 1589 See *True coppie*

Voyage to East Indies 1665 *See* TERRY, E.

Voyage to the East Indies in 1747–48 (by C. F. Noble) 1762

Voyage to Port Philip, Journal of a1845

VOYLE, George E. & STEVENSON, G. de Saint-Clair *A military dictionary* 1876 (ed. 3)

VOYNICH, Ethel L. *The gadfly* 1897 (1904)
Vulgar errours censured 1659
Vulgaria quedam abs Terencio in Anglicam linguam traducta 1483
Vulpone; or remarks on some proceedings in Scotland relating both to the Union and protestant succession since the revolution 1707

W

W., B. 1657 *See* WELLS, Benjamin
W., E. 1621 *See* COOKE, Alexander
W., E. *The life of Donna Rosina* tr. ? 1700
W., G. 1606 *See* WOODCOCKE, G.
W., Is. *The copy of a letter, lately written in meeter, by a yonge gentilwoman to her unconstant lover* 1566 (in Arber, Eng. Garner VIII)
W., J. 1639 *See* GUIBERT, P.
W., J. *See* WADE, J.; WORLIDGE, J.
W., K. *Confused characters of conceited coxcombs* by Verax Philobasileus 1661 (Halliw. 1860)
W., M. *The marriage broaker; or the pander* (a comedy) 1662 (Gratiæ theatrales 1662)
W., R. 1584 *See* WILSON, Robert
W., S. (i. e. R. Southwell) *Marie Magdalens funerall teares* 1591 (1594, 1602, 1823)
W., S. 1642 See *Parliament's vindication*
W., S. 1657 *See* SERGEANT, J.
W., W. 1595 *See* WARNER, W.
W., W. 1695 *See* COLBATCH, John
WACE, Henry *See* SMITH, Sir William
WACE, Robert *Le roman de Brut* 11.. (1836–38)
Le roman de Rou et des ducs de Normandie 11.. (1827)
WADDELL, P. Hately *The Psalms; frae Hebrew intil Scottis* 1871
WADDINGTON, Conrad Hal *Principles of embryology* 1956
WADDY, Edith *A year with the wild flowers* 1873
WADE, John *Vinegar and mustard: or, worm-wood-lectures for every day in the week* 1673
WADE, William R. *A journey in the northern island of New Zealand* 1842
WADMAN, Howard Douglas *Life sentence: a New Zealand play in three acts* 1949
WADSWORTH, James *The English Spanish pilgrime* 1629 (1630)
Sandoval's (P. de) Civil wars of Spain in the beginning of the reign of Charles the fifth tr. 1652
WÆRFERTH, Bishop *Gregory's Dialogue* tr. c890 (Grein 1900)
WAFER, Lionel *A new voyage and description of the Isthmus of America* 1699 (1729)
WAGER, Lewis *A new enterlude entreating of the life and repentaunce of Marie Magdalene* 1566
WAGER, William *A very mery and pythie commedie, called The longer thou liuest, the more foole thou art* c1568
See also *Triall of cheualry*
WAGHORN, H. T. *Cricket scores, notes, etc. from 1730–73; to which are added two poems published in 1773* 1899
Wagner's (E. L.) Manual of general pathology tr. 1876
WAGNER, Wilhelm *Teuffel's (W. S.) History of Roman literature* tr. 1873
WAGSTAFFE, Thomas *A vindication of King Charles the Martyr* 1693
WAGSTAFFE, William *Miscellaneous works* a1725 (1726)
A letter showing the danger and uncertainty of inoculating the small pox 1722
A letter to the venerable Nestor Ironside, by Andrew Tripe (i.e. *W. Wagstaffe*) 1714
WAGSTAFFE, William W. *R. G. Mayne's Medical vocabulary* 1889
WAHLSTROM, Ernest Eugene *Introduction to theoretical igneous petrology* 1950
WAIN, John Barrington *The contenders* 1958
Hurry on down 1953
ed. *Interpretations: essays on twelve English poems* 1955
Strike the father dead 1962
A travelling woman 1959
WAINEWRIGHT, Thomas G. *Essays and criticisms* a1852 (1880)
WAINWRIGHT, John William *The big tickle* 1969
Death in a sleeping city 1965
The devil you don't 1973
Dig the grave and let him lie 1971
Do nothin' till you hear from me 1977
Edge of extinction 1968
The evidence I shall give 1974
The hard hit 1974
High-class kill 1973
The last buccaneer 1971
A nest of rats 1977
Night is a time to die 1972
A pride of pigs 1973
Requiem for a loser 1972
Square dance 1975
The take-over men 1969
Talent for murder 1967
A touch of malice 1973
Who goes next? 1976
WAKE, Charlotte, Lady *Reminiscences* ed. Lucy Wake 1909
WAKE, Abp. William *His charge to the clergy of the diocese of Lincoln May 20, 1706* 1707
An exposition of the doctrine of the Church of England (anon.) 1686
Preparation for death 1687
WAKEFIELD, Edward J. *Adventure in New Zealand* 1845
WAKEFIELD, Gilbert *An enquiry into the expediency and propriety of public or social worship* 1791 (1792)
An examination of the Age of reason, or an investigation of true and fabulous theology, by T. Paine 1794
A letter to Sir J. Scott on the subject of a late trial at Guildhall 1798
Remarks on the general orders of the Duke of York to his army on June 7, 1794 1794
A reply to T. Paine's second part of the Age of reason 1795
Memoirs of his life, written by himself a1801 (1804)
See also Fox, C. J.
WAKEMAN, Reginald Leslie *The chemistry of commercial plastics* 1947
WALBRAN, John R. *Memorials of the Abbey of St. Mary of Fountains*. Collected and ed. by J. R. Walbran (Surtees Soc. 1863–78)
WALCH, Garnet *Head over heels: a Christmas-book* 1875
WALCOTT, Mackenzie E. C. *Sacred archæology; a popular dictionary of ecclesiastical art and institutions* 1868
Waldere a1000 (Grein)
WALDRON, George *A description of the Isle of Man* 1726–30 (1744, 1865)
WALDRON, Ronald Alan *Sense and sense development* 1967
WALFORD, Cornelius *Fairs, past and present* 1883
WALFORD, Edward *See* THORNBURY, G. W.
WALFORD, Lucy B. *Dick Netherby* 1881
The matchmaker 1894
The mischief of Monica 1891
WALKDEN, Peter *Extracts from his diary* 1725–30 (1866)
WALKER, Andrew Jamieson & MOTT, Owen E. tr. *A. F. Holleman's A text-book of organic chemistry* 2 parts 1903
—(ed. 2) 1907
WALKER, Anthony *Leez lachrymans, sive comitis Warwici justa; a sermon on 2 Sam. III. 38, preached at the funeral of Charles Earl of Warwick, baron Rich of Leez* 1673
WALKER, Charles V. 1846 *See* JOYCE, J.
WALKER, Clement *Relations and observations historicall and politick, upon the parliament begun 1640; divided into two books.* I. *The mystery of the two junto's;* II. *The history of independency* 1648
—*Anarchia Anglicana, or the history of independency, the second part* 1649
—*The High Court of Justice, or Cromwell's new slaughter house in England, being the third part of the History of independency* 1651
—*A fourth part by T. M.* 1660
WALKER, D. *General view of the agriculture of the county of Hertford* 1795
WALKER, Donald *Manly exercises, containing rowing, sailing, riding and driving* 1839 (1847)
WALKER, Ellis *Epicteti Enchiridion* tr. 1692 (1737)
WALKER, Ernest Pillsbury, et al. *Mammals of the world* 3 vols. 1964–7
WALKER, Ferdinand 1600 See *Torquemada, A. de*
WALKER, Francis A. *A brief text-book of political economy* 1885
Land and its rent 1883
Money 1878
Political economy 1883
WALKER, George *A true account of the siege of London-Derry* 1689
WALKER, George *The adventures of Timothy Thoughtless* 1813
The battle of Waterloo: a poem 1815
WALKER, Gilbert *A manifest detection of the most vyle and detestable use of dice-play* (anon.) c1550 (Percy Soc. 1850)
WALKER, James *Jaunt to Auld Reekie* 1882
WALKER, James *Introduction to physical chemistry* 1899
WALKER, John *An attempt towards recovering an account of the numbers and sufferings of the clergy of the Church of England* 1714
WALKER, John *A critical pronouncing dictionary and expositor of the English language* 1791
A dictionary of the English language, answering at once the purposes of rhyming, spelling, and pronouncing 1775
Elements of elocution 1781
A rhetorical grammar, or course of lessons in elocution 1785
WALKER, John *Essays on natural history and rural economy* a1803 (1812)
WALKER, John *Poems in English, Scotch, and Gaelic, on various subjects* 1813
WALKER, Martin *The National Front* 1977
WALKER, Obadiah *The Greek and Roman history illustrated by coins and medals, representing their religious rites* 1692
Of education, especially of young gentlemen 1673 (1677)
Some instructions concerning the art of oratory (anon.) 1659 (1682)
WALKER, Patrick *Remarkable passages in the life of Mr. Alexander Peden* 1727 (Biogr. Presbyt. 1827)
—*of Mr. John Semple, Mr. John Welwood, Mr. Richard Cameron* 1727 (1827)
—*of the Rev. Mr. Donald Cargill and Mr. Walter Smith* 1732 (1827)
WALKER, R. *The two threes; 33,333 miles by land and sea* 1883
WALKER, Robert *Plebeian politics, or the principles and practices of certain mole-eyed maniacs, vulgarly called Warrites*. By Tim Bobbin the Second (i.e. Robert Walker) 1801
WALKER, Samuel *The Christian: being a course of practical sermons* 1755
WALKER, W. *The journall, or dayly register, contayning a true manifestation and historicall declaration of the voyage under J. C. Neck and W. van Warwick* tr. 1601
WALKER, William *Idiomatologia Anglo-Latina; or a dictionarie of English and Latin idiomes* 1670
Phraseologia Anglo-Latina, or phrases of the English and Latin tongue; together with Parœmiologia Anglo-Latina 1672
WALKER, William *The bards of Bon-Accord 1375–1860* 1887
WALKER, William *Three churchmen: sketches and reminiscences of the right rev. M. Russell, the right rev. C. H. Terrot, and G. Grub* 1893
WALKER, William Sidney *A critical examination of the text of Shakespeare* a1846 (1860)
Gustavus Vasa, and other poems 1813
Poems from the Danish tr. 1815
Poetical remains a1846 (1852)
WALKER, William Sylvester *In the blood* 1901
WALKER, Williston *John Calvin* 1906
WALKINGTON, Thomas *The optick glasse of humors* 1607 (1664)
WALL, Adam *An account of the different ceremonies observed in the Senate house, Cambridge* 1798
WALL, Bernard, et al. tr. *P. Teilhard de Chardin's The phenomenon of man* 1959
WALL, Edward J. *A dictionary of photography* 1889 (1890, 1897)
WALL, Thomas *A comment on the times; or a character of the enemies of the church* 1658
Gods revenge against the enemies of the church 1658
Wall Street Journal 1889–
WALLACE, Alfred R. *Australasia* 1879
Contributions to the theory of natural selection 1871
Darwinism 1889
Island life 1880
The Malay Archipelago 1869
Man's place in the universe 1903
My life: a record of events and opinions 1905
WALLACE, Charles W. *The Children of the Chapel at Blackfriars 1597–1603* 1908
WALLACE, Sir Donald M. *Russia* 1877
WALLACE, Lady Grace Maxwell *Mendelssohn's (F.) Letters from Italy and Switzerland* tr. 1861 (1862)
Mundt's (C.) Frederick the Great and his merchant tr. 1858
WALLACE, James *A description of the Isles of Orkney* a1688 (1693)
—ed. 2, entitled *An account of the Islands of Orkney* (1700; 1883)
WALLACE, Lewis *Ben-Hur, a tale of the Christ* 1880
The fair God 1873
WALLACE, Richard Horatio Edgar *The double* 1928
The feathered serpent 1927
The flying Fifty-Five 1922
The Flying Squad 1928
The gunner 1928
The lady of Ascot 1930
The mind of Mr. J. G. Reeder 1925
The missing million 1923
More educated Evans 1926
Room 13 1924
When the gangs came to London 1932
WALLACE, Robert *A country schoolmaster, James Shaw* 1899
Life and last leaves, ed. J. C. Smith & W. Wallace (1903)
The rural economy and agriculture of Australia and New Zealand 1891
WALLACE, Walter Adam *Only a sister? A tale of to-day* 1890
WALLACE, William *Continuation of the history of England by Sir James Mackintosh* 1836–40
WALLACE, William *The logic of Hegel* tr. 1874
WALLEM, Fredrik M. *Notes on the fish supply of Norway* 1883 (Fisheries exhibition literature)
WALLER, Edmund *Works, in verse and prose* a1687 (1729)
Poems 1645, 1664, a1687 (1810)
WALLER, Richard *Essayes of natural experiments* 1684
WALLER, Sir William *Divine meditations upon several occasions* a1668 (1680)
Waller's (Sir W.) Tragical history of Jetzer tr. 1679
WALLERIUS, Johan G. *Mineralogia* 1747
WALLIS, Arthur James & BLAIR, Charles F. *Thunder above* 1956 (UK 1959)
WALLIS, John *A defence of the Christian sabbath* 1692–94
Due correction for Mr. Hobbes 1656
The necessity of regeneration: in two sermons 1682
A treatise of algebra, both historical and practical 1684–85
WALLIS, Robert E. *Delitzsch's (F.) System of Biblical psychology* tr. 1867
WALLIS, Samuel *An account of a voyage round the world in the years 1766, 1767 and 1768* 1773 (in Hawkesworth's Voyages, I)
WALLIS, Thomas *The farrier's and horseman's complete dictionary* 1764 (1775)
WALMISLEY, Arthur T. *The bridges over the Thames at London* 1880
WALN, Nora *The house of exile* 1933
WALPOLE, Horace *Anecdotes of painting in England, with some account of the principal artists; collected by G. Vertue* 1762–71 (1786)
The castle of Otranto; a Gothic story (anon.) 1765
A catalogue of the royal and noble authors of England; with lists of their works 1758 (1759)
—*Observations on the account given of his catalogue* 1759
Correspondence ed. W. S. Lewis et al. (Yale ed.) 40 vols. 1937–80

Walpole, Horace (*cont.*)
Historic doubts on the life and reign of King Richard the third 1768
Letters a1797 (1840, 1857–59, 1891, 1903–04)
Letters ed. Mrs P. Toynbee 16 vols. 1903–5
— Suppl. ed. P. Toynbee 3 vols. 1918–25
Letters to Sir Horace Mann a1797 (1833, 1843–44)
Memoires of the last ten years of the reign of George the second a1797 (1822)
Memoirs of the reign of king George the third a1797 (1845)
The mysterious mother, a tragedy 1768
Private correspondence a1797 (1820, 1837)
Walpoliana 1788 (ed. 2)
Walpole, Hugh Seymour *The cathedral* 1922
The dark forest 1916
Fortitude 1913
The fortress 1932
Hans Frost 1929
Judith Paris 1931
Rogue Herries 1930
The secret city 1919
Vanessa 1933
The young enchanted 1921
Walpole, Sir Spencer *A history of England from the conclusion of the great war in 1815* 1878–86
The life of Lord John Russell 1889
Walsall, Samuel *The life and death of Jesus Christ* 1607 (1622)
Walsh, Benjamin D. *The comedies of Aristophanes* tr. 1837 (1848)
Walsh, John H. *See* 'Stonehenge'
Walsh, John James *Understanding paraplegia* 1964
Walsh, John William Tudor *Photometry* 1926
Walsh, R. F. *On improved facilities for the capture, economic transmission and distribution of sea fishes and how these matters affect Irish fisheries* 1883 (Fisheries exhibition literature)
Walsh, William *Poetical works* a1708 (1750)
Letters and poems, amorous and gallant (anon.) 1692
Walsingham, Thomas De Grey, 6th Baron & Payne-Gallwey, Sir Ralph *Shooting* 1886 (Badminton library)
Walter, Henry *A history of England* (anon.) 1828–39
Walter of Henley's Husbandry (transl.), *together with an anonymous husbandry* 14.. (1890)
Walton, Bp. Brian *The considerator considered* 1659 (1821)
Walton, Henry Haynes *A treatise on operative ophthalmic surgery* 1853
— ed. 3, entitled *A practical treatise on the diseases of the eye* 1875
Walton, Izaak *The compleat angler* (Part I) 1653; ed. 2, much enlarged 1655; ed. 3, much enlarged 1661; ed. 4, much enlarged 1668
The universal angler 1676 (Pt. I. Walton's Compleat angler, ed. 5; Pt. II. The compleat angler, being instructions how to angle for a trout or grayling in a clear stream, by C. Cotton; Pt. III. The experienced angler, by Col. R. Venables)
— With notes historical, critical and explanatory by Sir J. Hawkins (1760)
The lives of Dr. John Donne (1640), *Sir Henry Wotton* (1651), *Mr. Richard Hooker, Mr. George Herbert* 1670
The life of Dr. Sanderson 1678
Love and truth: in two letters concerning the distempers of the present times 1680
Walton, Robert *Random recollections of the Midland circuit* 1869
Wambaugh, Joseph *The black marble* 1978
The blue knight 1972 (UK 1973)
Wanderer a1000 (Grein)
Wandering Jew telling fortunes to Englishmen, The 1640 (1649; Halliw., Books of characters 1857)
Wandesford, Sir Christopher *A book of instructions* a1640 (1777)
Wandsworth Borough News 1884–
Wang Gungwu ed. *Malaysia: a survey* 1964
Wanganui Chronicle (Wanganui, NZ) 1856–
Wanley, Nathaniel *The wonders of the little world; or a general history of man* 1678
Wanstead masque See Sidney, Sir P.
Wapull, George *The tyde taryeth no man* 1576 (in J. P. Collier, Illustr. early Eng. pop. lit. II)
War illustrated, The 1914–19
War illustrated, The 1939–47
War weekly 1939–41
Warburton (—) *A treatise on the history, laws, and customs of the island of Guernsey* 1822
Warburton, Eliot B. G. *The crescent and the cross* 1845
Darien; or, the merchant prince 1852
Warburton, George *Hochelaga; or England in the New World* 1846
Warburton, Rowland E. Egerton *Hunting songs and miscellaneous verses* 1859 (1860)
Warburton, Bp. William *Works* a1779 (1788, 1811–41)
The alliance between Church and State 1736
A critical and philosophical enquiry into the causes of prodigies and miracles as related by historians 1727
The divine legation of Moses demonstrated 1738–41
The doctrine of grace 1763
Julian; or, a discourse concerning the earthquake and fiery eruption which defeated that emperor's attempt to rebuild the temple at Jerusalem 1750
Letters from a late eminent prelate to one of his friends (*Bp. Hurd*) 17.. (1809)
The works of Alexander Pope. With the commentaries and notes of Mr. Warburton 1751
Ricardus Aristarchus Of the hero of the poem (anon.) 1742 (in Pope, Dunciad 1743)
A selection from his unpublished papers 17.. (1841)
The works of Shakespear. With a comment and notes by Mr. Pope and Mr. Warburton 1747
Tracts, by Warburton, and a Warburtonian 17.. (1789)
Ward, Sir Adolphus W. *Dickens* 1882
A history of English dramatic literature to the death of Queen Anne 1875
'Ward, Artemus' (C. F. Browne) *Artemus Ward: his book* 1865
Ward, Bernard *History of St. Edmund's College, Old Hall* 1893
Ward, Edmund *The hanged man* 1976
Ward, Edward *A collection of historical and state poems* 1717
The diverting works of the famous Miguel de Cervantes tr. 1709
Hudibras redivivus; or a burlesque poem on the times (anon.) 1705–07
The life and notable adventures of that renown'd knight, Don Quixote de la Mancha tr. 1711
The London spy 1699–1702
The rambling fuddle-caps (anon.) 1709
Vulgus Britannicus; or, the British Hudibras (anon.) 1710
The wooden world dissected, in the characters of a ship of war 1706 (1708)
Ward, Emma Georgina Elizabeth *Outside Paris during the two sieges* 1871
Ward, Frederick O. *Outlines of human osteology* 1838 (1876)
Ward, Mrs. Humphry *Amiel's journal: the journal intime of Henri-Frédéric Amiel* tr. 1885
Diana Mallory 1908
Helbeck of Bannisdale 1898
The history of David Grieve 1892
Marcella 1894
The marriage of William Ashe 1905
Robert Elsmere 1888
Sir George Tressady 1896
The story of Bessie Costrell 1895
Ward, James *The realm of ends; or, Pluralism and theism* 1911
Ward, John *The young mathematician's guide; being a plain and easie introduction to the mathematicks* 1709 (1713)
Ward, John *The lives of the professors of Gresham College* 1740
Ward, Lester F. *Dynamic sociology, or applied social science* 1883
Pure sociology, a treatise on the origin and spontaneous development of society 1903
Ward, Nathaniel *A sermon preached before the hon. House of Commons* 1647
The simple cobler of Aggawam in America 1647 (1843)
To the high and honourable Parliament of England, the petitions of some gentlemen of the Easterne Association 1648
Ward, Nathaniel B. *On the growth of plants in closely glazed cases* 1842 (1852)
'Ward, Ned, junior' *The comforts of matrimony* 1780
Ward, Richard *Two theological treatises: the first shewing the nature of wit, wisdom, and folly. The second describing the nature, use, and abuse of the tongue* 1673
Ward, Richard *The life of Dr. Henry More* 1710
Ward, Robert P. *De Clifford; or the constant man* 1841
De Vere; or the man of independence 1827
Tremaine; or the man of refinement (anon.) 1825
Ward, Russel Braddock ed. *The Penguin book of Australian ballads* See under title
Ward, Bp. Samuel *A collection of sermons and treatises* 1627–28 (Appended to vol. III of T. Adams' Works, 1862)
All in all 1621 (1622)
Balme from Gilead to recover conscience 1616
A coal from the altar 1615 (1616)
The happinesse of practice 1621
Jethros justice of peace 1618
The life of faith in death 1622
A peace-offering to God 1624
Woe to drunkards 1622
Ward, Bp. Seth *Seven sermons* 1674
Ward, Thomas *England's reformation* a1708 (1710, 1716)
Ward, Thomas Humphry ed. *The English poets; selections with critical introductions by various writers* 1880
Ward or Warde, William *The secretes of Alexis of Piemont containing remedies against diseases* tr. 1558; *the seconde part* 1560; *the thyrde parte* 1562 (1568, 1580)
Ward, William *A view of the history, literature, and religion of the Hindoos* 1811 (1817–20)
Ward, William G. *Essays on the philosophy of theism* a1882 (1884)
The ideal of a Christian Church 1844
On nature and grace 1860
Ward-Jackson, Cyril Henry *It's a piece of cake; or, R.A.F. slang made easy* 1943
— (rev. ed.) 1945
Warde, William *See* Ward, W.
Warden, David B. *A chorographical and statistical description of the district of Columbia* 1816
'Warden, Florence' (Mrs. James) *A witch of the hills* 1888
Warder, John A. *Hedges and evergreens* 1858
Warder, Joseph *The true Amazons, or, the monarchy of bees* 1693 (1713)
Wardlaw, Ralph *Lectures on the Epistle to the Romans* a1853 (1869)
Wardrobe accounts of Edward IV See *Edward IV*
Ware, J. Redding *Passing English of the Victorian era* 1909
Ware, Robert *Foxes and firebrands* 1682
The hunting of the Romish fox 1683
Waring, Edward J. *The tropical resident at home* 1866
Wariston, Lord *See* Johnston, Sir A.
Warkworth, John *A chronicle of the first thirteen years of the reign of King Edward the fourth* 1473–82 (Camden Soc. 1839)
Warmestry, Thomas *Suspiria ecclesiæ et reipublicæ Anglicanæ; the sighs of the churche and commonwealth of England* 1640
Warming, Johannes Eugenius Bülow *Oecology of plants* 1909
Warner, Charles Dudley *Backlog studies* 1872
In the Levant 1877
Mummies and Moslems 1876
My winter on the Nile 1876
A roundabout journey 1883
Saunterings 1873
Their pilgrimage 1888
Washington Irving 1882
Warner, Francis *Physical expression* 1885
Warner, Francis R. Le P. *Early poems* 1964
Killing time 1976
Lying figures 1972
Maquettes 1972
Meeting ends 1974
Warner, George T. *See* Howson, Edmund W.
Warner, James Franklin *A universal dictionary of musical terms* 1842
Warner, Pelham Francis *How we recovered the Ashes* 1904
My cricketing life 1921
Warner, Richard *Plantæ Woodfordienses* 1771
Warner, Richard *Antiquitates culinariæ: or, curious tracts relating to the culinary affairs of the Old English* 1791
Walk through some of the western counties of England 1800
Warner, Susan *The hills of the Shatemuc* 1856
The old helmet 1864
Queechy 1852
Say and seal (anon.) 1860
The wide wide world 1852
Warner, Sylvia Townsend *Lolly Willowes; or, The loving huntsman* 1926
Warner, William *Albions England, or historicall map of the same island* (Books i–iv) 1586
The first and second parts of Albions England, reuised and corrected (Books i–vi) 1589
Albions England. The third time corrected (Books i–viii) 1592
— *Now reuised and enlarged* (Books i–xii) 1596
— *Reuised and inlarged* (Books i–xiii) 1602
— *A continuance of Albions England* (Books xiv–xvi) 1606 (1612)
Menæcmi; a pleasant comœdie taken out of Plautus tr. 1595
Warnes, John *Flax versus cotton; or, the two-edged sword against pauperism and slavery* 1850
Warning for faire women, A 1599 (in Simpson, School of Shakspere II, 1878)
Warning for house-keepers, A 1676
Warning from J. Beem 1649 *See* Ellistone, J.
Warren, E. Prioleau & Cleverly, C. F. M. *The wanderings of the Beetle* 1885
Warren, Edward de *Caignart de Saulcy's* (*L. F. J.*) *Narrative of a journey round the Dead Sea* tr. 1853
Warren, George *An impartial description of Surinam upon the continent of Guiana* 1667
Warren, Henry W. *Recreations in astronomy* 1879
Warren, Howard Crosby ed. *Dictionary of psychology* 1934
Warren, John B. L. *A guide to the study of book-plates (ex-libris)* 1880
Warren, Robert Penn *Incarnations: poems 1966–68* 1968 (UK 1970)
Night rider 1939
Warren, Samuel *The lily and the bee: an apologue of the Crystal Palace* 1851
Now and then 1848
Passages from the diary of a late physician 1832–38
Ten thousand a year (anon.) 1841
Warren, Thomas *Unbeleevers no subjects of justification* 1654
Warres of Cyrus against Antiochus, The 1594
Warriston, Lord *See* Johnston, Sir A.
Wars of Alexander See *Alexander*
Wars of the English in France, Letters and papers illustrative of the 14.. (Rolls series 1861–64)
Warter, John W. *The last of the old squires* 1854
The sea-board and the down, by an old vicar 1860
Warton, Joseph *An essay on the writings and genius of Pope* (anon.) 1756–82
Odes on various subjects 1746
Poems a1800 (1810)
See also Pitt, C.
Warton, Thomas *An enquiry into the authenticity of the poems attributed to T. Rowley* 1782
The history of English poetry 1774–81 (1840)
The life and literary remains of R. Bathurst 1761
The life of Sir T. Pope 1772
Newmarket, a satire (anon.) 1751
Ode, as performed at the Theatre, 2 July 1751 1751
Poetical works 1777, a1790 (1802, 1810)
Specimen of a history of Oxfordshire. Kiddington 1783
The triumph of Isis, a poem 1749
See also *Oxford sausage; Student*

Warung, Price *Tales of the old régime and The bullet of the fated ten* 1897
Warwick, Arthur *Spare minutes; or, resolved meditations* 1634 (1637)
'Warwick, Eden' (George Jabet) *Nasology: or hints towards a classification of noses* 1848
Warwick, Mary Rich, Countess of *Autobiography* a1678 (ed. T. C. Croker, Percy Soc. 1848)
Warwick, Wayne *Surfriding in New Zealand* 1968
Warwickshire glossary 1896 *See* Northall, G. F.
Washburn, Emory *A treatise on the American law of real property* 1860–62
Washburn, Margaret F. *The animal mind* 1908
Washington, Bushrod *Reports of cases argued and determined in the Court of Appeals of Virginia 1790–96* 1798–99
Washington, George *Writings* a1799 (1833–37, 1889–93)
Daily journal in 1751–52, kept while on a tour from Virginia to the Island of Barbadoes 1751–52 (1892)
Diaries, 1748–1799 ed. J. C. Fitzpatrick 4 vols. 1925
Washington, Joseph *A defence of the people of England by John Milton* tr. 1692
Washington, Thomas *Nicolay's (N. de) Nauigations into Turkie* tr. 1585
Washington Academy of Sciences *Journal* 1911–
Washington Post 1877–
Wason, Robert Alexander *Happy Hawkins* 1909
Watch-house, The a1814 (in New British theatre)
Watchman, The; by S. T. Coleridge 1796
Waterhouse, Benjamin *Cautions to young persons concerning health* 1805
Waterhouse, Edward *A discourse and defence of arms and armory* 1660
Fortescutus illustratus; or a commentary on that nervous treatise De laudibus legum Angliæ, by Sir John Fortescue 1663
An humble apologie for learning and learned men 1653
A short narrative of the late dreadful fire in London 1667
Waterhouse, George R. *A natural history of the mammalia* 1846–48
The natural history of marsupialia or pouched animals 1841
Waterhouse, Keith Spencer *Billy Liar* 1959
Waterhouse, L. M. *Conduit wiring and erection with special reference to the simplex system of steel conduits* 1901
Waterland, Daniel *Works* a1740 (1823–28)
Christianity vindicated against infidelity 1732
A critical history of the Athanasian Creed 1724
Eight sermons in defense of the divinity of Our Lord Jesus Christ 1720
Review of the doctrine of the Eucharist 1737
Scripture vindicated 1730
A vindication of Christ's divinity 1719
Waterman, Talbot Howe *The physiology of Crustacea* 2 vols. 1960–1
Watermen and lightermen, An abstract of the rules, orders, and constitutions of the company of 1708
Waters, Stanley *Indentures indorsed* 1967
Waterston, William *Cyclopædia of commerce* 1843 (1863)
Waterton, Charles *Wanderings in South America* 1825 (1879, 1882)
Waterworth, James *The canons and decrees of the Council of Trent* tr. 1848
Véron's (F.) Rule of the Catholic faith tr. 1833
Waterworth, William *England and Rome* 1854
Watkins, Alfred *Photography: the Watkins manual of exposure and development* 1902
—(ed. 2) 1903
Watkins, Charles *Principles of conveyancing* 1800 (1819)
Watreman, William *Boemus' (J.) Fardle of facions conteining the aunciente maners of Affrike and Asia* tr. 1555
Wats, Gilbert *See* Watts, G.
Watson, Alfred Edward Thomas *The turf* 1898
ed. *The young sportsman* 1900
Watson, Christopher *The hystories of Polybius* tr. 1568
Watson, Colin *Bump in the night* 1960
Coffin scarcely used 1958
Hopjoy was here 1962
Watson, George Marr *The Roxburghshire word-book* 1923
Watson, Henry Clay *Camp fires of the revolution; or, The war of independence* 1850
Watson, Henry W. & Burbury, S. H. *The mathematical theory of electricity and magnetism* 1885–89
Watson, Hewett C. *Cybele Britannica; or, British plants and their geographical relations* 4 vols. 1847–59
Topographical botany 1873
Watson, James ed. *A choice collection of comic and serious Scots poems* 1706–11
The history of the art of printing 1713
Watson, James *Jedburgh Abbey* 1894 (ed. 2)
Living bards of the Border 1859
Watson, James Dewey *The double helix: a personal account of the discovery of DNA* 1968
Watson, Jean L. *Life of Andrew Thomson, minister of St. George's parish, Edinburgh* 1882
Watson, John *The history and antiquities of the parish of Halifax, in Yorkshire* 1775
Watson, John *The confessions of a poacher* 1890 (1893)
Watson, John *See* 'Maclaren, Ian'
Watson, John Fanning *Annals of Philadelphia* 1830
Watson, John W. & Evans, Maurice J. *J. J. van Oosterzee's Christian dogmatics* tr. 1874
Watson, Joseph Y. *A compendium of British mining* 1843
Watson, Richard *Historicall collections of ecclesiastick affairs in Scotland* 1657
A sermon touching schisme 1642
Watson, Bp. Richard *Anecdotes of his life, written by himself at different intervals, and revised in 1814*, published by his son Rich. Watson (1817)
An apology for the Bible 1796
Chemical essays 1782–87
A collection of theological tracts 1785 (1791)
Sermons on public occasions, and tracts on religious subjects 1788
Watson, Robert *The history of the reign of Philip the second, king of Spain* 1777
The history of the reign of Philip the third, king of Spain a1781 (1783); Books v and vi by William Thomson 1783 (1839)
Watson, Robert S. *A visit to Wazan, the sacred city of Morocco* 1880
Watson, Bp. Thomas *Holsome and catholyke doctryne concerninge the seuen sacramentes* 1558
Watson, Thomas *Poems* a1592 (Arber 1870)
The Ἑκατομπαθία or passionate centurie of loue 1582
An eglogue vpon the death of Sir F. Walsingham 1590
Watson, Thomas *A body of practical divinity* 1692
The one thing necessary 1656
Watson, Sir Thomas *Lectures on the principles and practice of physic* 1843 (1857, 1871)
Watson, William *A decacordon of ten quodlibeticall questions concerning religion and state* (anon.) 1602
Important considerations, by the secular priests (anon.) 1601 (1675, 1688, 1831)
A sparing discoverie of our English Jesuits (anon.) 1601
Watson, William *An amical call to repentance and the practical belief of the gospel* 1691
Watson, William *A text-book of physics* 1899
Watson-Watt, Robert Alexander *Three steps to victory: a personal account* 1957
Watsonia: journal of the Botanical Society of the British Isles 1949–
Watt, Alexander *The art of leather manufacture* 1885
The art of paper-making 1890
The art of soap-making 1884 (1885)
Electro-deposition, a practical treatise on the electrolysis of gold, silver, copper, etc. 1886
Mechanical industries explained 1881
Scientific industries explained 1881
Watt, John Mitchell & Breyer-Brandwijk, Maria Gerdina *The medicinal and poisonous plants of southern Africa* 1932
—(ed. 2, with title —— *of southern and eastern Africa*) 1962
Watt, William *A history of Aberdeen and Banff* 1900
Watts, Elizabeth *Martin's (W. C. L.) Poultry yard. Revised by Miss E. Watts* 1855
Watts, Gilbert *Bacon's Advancement and proficience of learning* tr. 1640
Watts, Henry *A dictionary of chemistry* 1859–68; Supplement 1872; 2nd Supplement 1875; 3rd Supplement 1881
—New ed. 1872–82
—Revised by H. F. Morley & M. M. P. Muir 1888–94
Gmelin's (L.) Hand-book of chemistry tr. 1848–64
See also Fownes, George
Watts, Isaac *Works* a1748 (1753)
Divine and moral songs for children 1720
Horæ lyricæ; poems chiefly of the lyric kind 1706
Hymns and spiritual songs 1707
The improvement of the mind: or, a supplement to the Art of logick 1741; part II a1748
Logick: or the right use of reason in the enquiry after truth 1725
Philosophical essays on various subjects 1733
The Psalms of David imitated in the language of the New Testament 1719
Reliquiæ juveniles: miscellaneous thoughts in prose and verse 1734 (1789)
Watts, Isaac *Cotton* 1876 (G. P. Bevan's British manuf. industries, V)
Watts, Jeffry *A Scribe, Pharisee, Hypocrite, and his letter answered, separates churched, dippers sprinkled: or, a vindication of the Church and Universities of England* 1657
Watts-Dunton, Theodore *Aylwin* 1898
Waugh, Alexander Raban *The last chukka* 1928
The loom of youth 1917
Waugh, Auberon Alexander *The foxglove saga* 1960
Waugh, Benjamin *The gaol cradle, who rocks it?* (anon.) 1873
Waugh, Edwin *The chimney corner* 1874
Home life of the Lancashire factory folk during the cotton famine 1867
The owd blanket 1867
Sketches of Lancashire life and localities 1855
Sneck Bant; or, th' owd tow-bar 1868
Waugh, Evelyn Arthur St. John *Black mischief* 1932
Brideshead revisited 1945
Decline and fall 1928
Diaries ed. M. Davie 1976
A handful of dust 1934
Labels: a Mediterranean journal 1930
Letters ed. M. Amory 1980
The loved one 1948
Men at arms 1952
Ninety-two days 1934
Officers and gentlemen 1955
Put out more flags 1942
Remote people 1931
Scoop 1938
Unconditional surrender 1961
Vile bodies 1930
Waugh, Hillary Baldwin *The con game* 1968
Finish me off 1970 (UK 1971)
Last seen wearing —— 1952 (UK 1953)
Parrish for the defense 1974 (UK 1975)
Pure poison 1966 (UK 1967)
Wawn, William T. *The South Sea islanders and the Queensland labour trade* 1893
Way, Peter *Super-Celeste* 1977
Way to play, The: the illustrated encyclopedia of the games of the world 1975
Wayer, William *See* Wager, W.
Wayland, Francis *A memoir of the life and labors of the rev. A. Judson* 1853
Wayre, Philip *Wind in the reeds* 1965
Weakest goeth to the wall 1600 (1618)
Weale, John *Rudimentary dictionary of terms used in architecture, building and construction, early and ecclesiastical art* 1849–50
—ed. 4, by R. Hunt 1873
Weale, Robert Alexander *The eye and its function* 1960
Weatherly, Keith *The roo shooter* 1968
Weaver, Frederic W. ed. *Somerset medieval wills* 1383–1558 (Somerset record soc. 1901–05)
ed. *Wells wills, arranged in parishes* v.d. (1890)
Weaver, John Ernest & Clements, Frederic Edward *Plant ecology* 1929
—(ed. 2) 1938
Weaver, Robert ed. *Canadian short stories* (2nd ser.) 1968
Weavers' pageant, The 14.. See *Presentation in the temple*
Webb, Benjamin *Sketches of Continental ecclesiology* 1848
Webb, Daniel *An inquiry into the beauties of painting* 1760
Webb, James *Hymen's præludia: or, loves master-piece. Being the eighth part of that so much admir'd romance intituled Cleopatra* tr. 1658
Webb, John *A vindication of Stone-Heng restored* 1665 (1725)
Webb, Martha Beatrice *My apprenticeship* 1926
Webb, Robert F. *Motorists' dictionary* 1963
Webb, Sidney & Beatrice *English local government* 1906–08
Industrial democracy 1897
Webb, Thomas E. *Goethe's Faust* 1880
Webbe, Edward *The rare and most wonderfull things which E. Webbe hath seene in his traviles* 1590 (Arber 1868)
Webbe, Bp. George *The practice of quietnes* 1615 (1653)
Webbe, William *A discourse of English poetrie* 1586 (Arber 1870)
Weber, Henry W. ed. *Metrical romances of the thirteenth, fourteenth, and fifteenth centuries: published from ancient manuscripts. With an introduction, notes, and a glossary* 1810
Webster, Arthur Gordon *The theory of electricity and magnetism* 1897
Webster, Daniel *Works* 1851
Private correspondence a1852 (1857)
Speeches and forensic arguments 1835
Webster, Douglas & Webster, Molly *Comparative vertebrate morphology* 1974
Webster, James *General view of the agriculture of Galloway, comprehending the Stewartry of Kirkcudbright and Shire of Wigton* 1794
Webster, Jean (Alice Jean Chandler Webster) *Dear enemy* 1915 (UK 1916)
Webster, John *Works* a1625 (1830, 1857)
Appius and Virginia a1625 (1654)
The deuils law-case 1623
The tragedy of the Dutchesse of Malfy 1623
The white divel 1612
See also Tourneur, C.
—— & Rowley, William *A cure for a cuckold* 16.. (1661)
Webster, John *The displaying of supposed witchcraft* 1677
Metallographia: or, an history of metals 1671
Webster, John *Elements of mechanical and chemical philosophy* 1804
Elements of natural philosophy 1804
—*Philosophical instructor: or, Webster's Elements of natural philosophy, subdivided by A. Eaton* 1824
See also Imison, John
Webster, John *Introduction to fungi* 1970
Webster, Noah *A compendious dictionary of the English language* 1806
An American dictionary of the English language 1828; 1832
An American dictionary of the English language. Revised and enlarged by Chauncey A. Goodrich 1847
—new and revised ed. 1864; Suppl. 1880
Webster's International dictionary 1890, 1900; Suppl. 1902
Webster's New international dictionary 1911, 1918
New international dictionary of the English language ed. W. T. Harris & F. S. Allen 1909
—(ed. 2, ed. W. A. Neilson, T. A. Knott, & P. W. Carhart) 2 vols. 1934
—(ed. 3, ed. P. B. Gove) 2 vols. 1961 (see also *6,000 words*)
Webster, Robert *Gems: their sources, description and identification* 2 vols. 1962
Webster, Thomas & Parkes, Mrs. *An encyclopædia of domestic economy* 1844
Webster, William *An essay on book-keeping* 1721 (1734)
Webster's sports dictionary 1976
Wedderburn, David *Institutiones grammaticæ* 1633
Vocabula cum aliis Latinae linguae subsidiis a1646 (1673)
Wedderburne (David) See *Compt buik*

WEDGE, Thomas *General view of the agriculture of the County Palatine of Chester* 1794
WEDGWOOD, Cicely Veronica *The trial of Charles I* 1964
WEDGWOOD, Hensleigh *A dictionary of English etymology* 1859–65
WEDGWOOD, Josiah *A catalogue of the different articles of Queen's ware, manufactured by J. Wedgwood* ?1770
Selected letters ed. A. Finer & G. Savage 1965
Wednesday's fast (Here beginneth a lytel treatyse that sheweth how every man and woman ought to fast on yᵉ wednesday) 1500 (W. de Worde; 1532)
WEED, Thurlow *Autobiography* a1882 (ed. Harriet A. Weed 1883–84)
WEEDEN, William B. *The social law of labor* 1882
Week in Wall Street, A, by one who knows 1841
Week-end review 1930–4
Weekend world (Johannesburg) 1968–
WEEKES, John ed. *Truth's conflict with error* 1650
WEEKLEY, Ernest *Something about words* 1935
Words and names 1932
Weekly dispatch 1914–28
Weekly memorials for the ingenious 1682–83
Weekly News (Auckland) 1863–
Weekly notes, The: being notes of cases heard and determined by the House of Lords, the Superior Courts of Equity and Common Law, the Courts of Probate and Divorce, etc. 1866–
Weekly register 1811–14
WEEMS, Mason L. *The life of General F. Marion* 1809
The life of George Washington 1800 (1810, 1877)
Weesils, The; a satyrical fable (by Thomas Browne) 1691
WEETON, Ellen *Journal of a governess, 1807–1825* 2 vols. 1969 (reprint of 1936–9 ed. with new editorial matter by J. J. Bagley & E. Hall)
WEEVER, John *Ancient funerall monuments* 1631
The mirror of martyrs 1601
WEICHERT, Charles Kipp *Anatomy of the chordates* 1951
WEIDMAN, Jerome *I can get it for you wholesale* 1937 (UK 1939)
WEINGARTEN, Joseph A. *An American dictionary of slang and colloquial speech* 1954
WEIR, Archibald *The historical basis of modern Europe* 1886 (1889)
WEIR, Robert *Riding* 1891 (Badminton Library)
Weismann's (A.) Essays upon heredity and kindred biological problems. Authorised translation ed. by E. B. Poulton, Salmar Schönland, & A. E. Shipley 1889
Germ-plasm tr. by W. N. Parker & H. Rönnfeldt 1893
WEISS, John *Wit, humour, and Shakspeare* 1876
WELBY, Amelia B. *Poems* 1844 (1867)
WELCH, Charles *History of the Tower bridge* 1894
History of the worshipful Company of Pewterers of the city of London 1902
WELCKER, Adair *Tales of the 'wild and woolly West'* 1891
'WELCOME, John' (John Brennan) *Hell is where you find it* 1968
Stop at nothing 1959
WELD, Charles R. *A history of the Royal Society* 1848
Notes on Burgundy, ed. by his widow 1869
WELDON, Sir Anthony *The court and character of King James* 1650
— *whereunto is now added the court of King Charles* 1651
Weldon's Practical needlework 1886–
WELFORD, Richard *History of Newcastle and Gateshead* 1884–87
Well of Woman Hill, Aberdeen (Ane breif descriptioun of the qualiteis and effectis of the Well of the Woman Hill, besyde Abirdene) 1580 (1884)
WELLEK, René & WARREN, Edward Austin *Theory of literature* 1949
WELLESLEY, Richard Colley, 1st Marquess *A selection from his despatches, treaties, and other papers during his government of India* a1842 (ed. Sidney J. Owen 1877)
WELLINGTON, Arthur Wellesley, 1st Duke of *Dispatches 1799–1818* (compiled by Lieut.-Col. Gurwood 1834–38)
— *Supplementary despatches* 1797–1805 (ed. by his son 1858–72)
A selection from his despatches, memoranda, and other papers relating to India v.d. (ed. Sidney J. Owen 1880)
WELLINGTON, John Harold *Southern Africa: a geographical study* 1955
WELLS, Alfred Kingsley *Outline of historical geology* 1938
WELLS, Benjamin *Bauderon's (B.) Expert phisician* tr. 1657
WELLS, Charles J. ('H. L. Howard') *Joseph and his brethren, a scriptural drama* 1824
WELLS, David A. *Our merchant marine* 1882
WELLS, Helena *Constantia Neville, or the West Indian* 1800
WELLS, Herbert G. *All aboard for Ararat* 1940
The anatomy of frustration: a modern synthesis 1936
Ann Veronica: a modern love story 1909
Apropos of Dolores 1938
The autocracy of Mr. Parham 1930
Babes in the darkling wood 1940
Brynhild; or, The show of things 1937
Experiment in autobiography 2 vols. 1934
The first men in the moon 1901
The food of the gods and how it came to earth 1904
The history of Mr. Polly 1910
The holy terror 1939
The invisible man: a grotesque romance 1897
Joan and Peter: the story of an education 1918
Kipps, the story of a simple soul 1905
Love and Mr. Lewisham 1900
Men like gods 1923
Mr. Britling sees it through 1916
The new Machiavelli 1910 (UK 1911)
The new world order 1940
The outline of history 1920
The shape of things to come 1933
Things to come: a film story based on 'The shape of things to come' 1935
The time machine: an invention 1895
Tono-Bungay 1909
The war in the air 1908
The war of the worlds 1898
The wheels of chance 1896
The work, wealth and happiness of mankind 1931 (UK 1932)
You can't be too careful: a sample of life 1941
See also GISSING, George Robert & WELLS, H. G.
WELLS, Kenneth McNeill *The Owl Pen reader* 1969
WELLS, Robert *The pastrycook and confectioner's guide* 1889
'WELLS, Tobias' (Deloris Florine Forbes) *Dead by the light of the moon* 1967 (UK 1968)
WELLWOOD, James *Memoirs of the most material transactions in England for the last hundred years preceding the Revolution in 1688* 1700
WELSH, Alfred H. *Development of English literature and language* 1882
WELSH, David *Account of the life and writings of T. Brown* 1825
WELSH, James *Military reminiscences; extracted from a journal of nearly forty years active service in the East Indies* 1830
WELSTED, Leonard *Works* a1747 (1787)
WELTON, Richard *The substance of Christian faith and practice* 1724
WELTY, Eudora *The optimist's daughter* 1973
WELWOOD, James *See* WELLWOOD, J.
WENTWORTH, Harold *American dialect dictionary* 1944
—— & FLEXNER, Stuart Berg *Dictionary of American slang* 1960
— (new ed.) 1967
— (new ed.) 1975
'WENTWORTH, Patricia' (Dora Amy Turnbull) *In the balance* 1941 (UK ed. 1942 with title *Danger point*)
WENTWORTH, William C. *A statistical, historical, and political description of the colony of New South Wales* 1819 (1820)
WENYON, Charles Morley *Protozoology* 2 vols. 1926
Werburge, Saint See BRADSHAW, H.
Werenfels's (S.) Discourse of logomachys, or controversys, about words tr. 1711
WERNER, A. *The captain of the locusts* 1899
Wertheim's (Willem Frederik) Evolution and revolution: the rising waves of emancipation [anon. tr.] 1974
WESEEN, Maurice Harley *Crowell's dictionary of English grammar and handbook of American usage* 1928
A dictionary of American slang 1934 (UK 1935)
WESKER, Arnold *Chicken soup with barley* (in *New English dramatists* I) 1959
Chips with everything 1962
I'm talking about Jerusalem 1960
The kitchen (in *New English dramatists* II) 1960
Roots 1959
WESLEY, Charles *Hymns and sacred poems* 17.. (1749)
Hymns on the great festivals and other occasions 1746
See also WESLEY, John
WESLEY, John *Works* a1791 (1829–31, 1872)
The character of a Methodist 1742 (1747)
Collection of psalms and hymns 1738
— enlarged by J. & C. Wesley 1743
An extract from J. W.'s journal from his embarking for Georgia to his return to London 1737–90
Hymns and sacred poems, by John and Charles Wesley 1739, 1742
Journal ed. N. Curnock 8 vols. 1909–16
Primitive physick 1747
The principles of a Methodist 1746
Wesleyan-Methodist magazine 1822–1913
WEST, Alfred S. *English grammar for beginners* 1895 (1907)
WEST, Anthony *The trend is up* 1960 (UK 1961)
WEST, Elizabeth *Memoirs or spiritual exercises* 1766
WEST, Gilbert *Observations on the history and evidence of the resurrection of Jesus Christ* 1747
Odes of Pindar, with several other pieces tr. 1749
Poems a1756 (1810)
WEST, Jane *Alicia de Lacy* 1814
A gossip's story (anon.) 1796
The infidel father 1802
A tale of the times 1799
WEST, John *The history of Tasmania* 1852
'WEST, Rebecca' (Cicily Isabel Andrews) *Black lamb and grey falcon: the record of a journey through Yugoslavia in 1937* 2 vols. 1941 (UK 2 vols. 1942)
The fountain overflows 1957
The harsh voice: four short novels 1935
The modern 'Rake's progress' 1934
St. Augustine 1933
The strange necessity: essays and reviews 1928
The thinking reed 1936
WEST, Richard Gilbert *Pleistocene geology and biology, with especial reference to the British Isles* 1968
WEST, Richard Leaf *Sketches from Vietnam* 1968
WEST, Thomas *The antiquities of Furness* 1774 (1805, 1822)
WEST, William *Symbolæographia; the art, description or image of instruments* 1590
— *Symbolæography. The first part. Newly corrected* 1592
— *The third time corrected. Three treatises of the second part of Symboleographie* 1594
West India sketch book 1834
West Lancashire Evening Gazette (Blackpool) 1929–
West Somerset word-book 1886 *See* ELWORTHY, F. T.
WESTALL, William *The old factory: a Lancashire story* 1881
WESTCOTE, Thomas *A view of Devonshire in 1630* a1636 (1845)
WESTCOTT, Bp. Brooke F. *Christian aspects of life* 1897
The gospel of life 1892
The gospel of the resurrection 1866
An introduction to the study of the Gospels 1860
WESTCOTT, Edward N. *David Harum: a story of American life* 1898
Western Mail (Cardiff) 1869–
Western martyrology, The; or the bloody assizes 1705
Western Morning News (Plymouth) 1860–
WESTFIELD, Bp. Thomas *Englands face in Israels glasse* a1644 (1646)
WESTGARTH, William *The colony of Victoria* 1864
WESTHEIMER, David *Going public* 1973
WESTLAKE, Donald Edwin *Bank shot* 1972
Cops and robbers 1972 (UK 1973)
I gave at the office 1971 (UK 1972)
Up your banners 1969 (UK 1970)
See also 'COE, Tucker'
WESTMACOTT, Charles M. ('B. Blackmantle') *The English spy* 1825–26 (1907)
Points of misery; or fables for mankind 1823
WESTMACOTT, William *Θεολοβοτονολογία sive historia vegetabilium sacra; or a scripture herbal* 1694
Westminster assembly of divines. A confession of faith 1643–47 (1648)
— *A shorter catechism* 1647
Westminster drollery: or, a choice collection of the newest songs and poems 1671 (1875)
Westminster gazette, The 1893–1927
Westminster magazine, The 1773–85
Westminster review 1824–
WESTON, Carolyn *Poor, poor Ophelia* 1972 (UK 1973)
Rouse the demon 1976 (UK 1977)
WESTON, Hubert Claude *Sight, light and efficiency* 1949
— (ed. 2, with title *Sight, light and work*) 1962
WESTON, Richard *The universal botanist and nurseryman* 4 vols. 1770–7
WESTON, Stephen *A Trimester in France and Switzerland, July to October 1820. By an Oxonian* 1821
WESTROPP, Hodder M. *Ancient symbol worship* 1874
Westward for smelts, an early collection of stories 1620 (Percy Soc. 1848)
WESTWATER, Frank Lorimer *Teach yourself electronic computers* 1962
— (rev. ed.) 1964
WESTWOOD, John O. *British butterflies and their transformations* 1841
British moths and their transformations 1843–45
The entomologist's text book 1838
An introduction to the modern classification of insects 1839–40
WETHERAL, Mabel *Two north-country maids* 1887
'WETHERELL, Elizabeth' *See* WARNER, Susan
WEVER, R. *An enterlude called lusty iuuentus* c1565 (in Hazl., Dodsley)
WEYL, Alfred Richard *Guided missiles* 1949
WEYL, Claus Hugo Hermann *The classical groups: their invariants and representations* 1939
WEYMAN, Stanley J. *The abbess of Vlaye* 1904
Chippinge 1906
The man in black 1894
The new rector 2 vols. 1891
Shrewsbury: a romance 1898
Sophia 1900
The story of Francis Cludde 1891
Under the red robe 1894
WEYMOUTH, Richard F. *On euphuism* 1871 (Trans. Philol. Soc., part III)
WHALEY, John *A collection of poems* 1732
WHALLEY, Peter *The works of Ben Jonson, with notes* 1756
WHARTON, Edith *The custom of the country* 1913
The fruit of the tree 1907
The greater inclination 1899
The hermit and the wild woman and other stories 1908
The house of mirth 1905
Human nature 1933
Summer 1917
WHARTON, Sir George *Works* a1681 (1683)
Rothmann's (J.) Χειρομαντία tr. 1652
WHARTON, Henry *A defence of pluralities* (anon.) 1692
Dellon's (C.) History of the inquisition at Goa tr. 1688
The enthusiasm of the Church of Rome 1688
Fourteen sermons preached in Lambeth Chapel 1688–89 (1700)
A specimen of some errors and defects in (Burnet's) History of the reformation 1693
WHARTON, Henry T. *Sappho: memoir, text, selected renderings, and a literal translation* 1885 (1895)
WHARTON, John J. S. *A law lexicon* 1848
— *Fifth edition, revised by J. S. Will* 1872
WHARTON, Philip Wharton, Duke of *The true Briton* 1723–24
WHARTON, Thomas I. *Digest of cases in the Circuit Court of the United States, Third District, and in the Courts of Pennsylvania* 1822–36 (1853)
WHATELY, Abp. Richard *Elements of logic* 1826 (1827, 1836)
Elements of rhetoric 1828 (1836)

Miscellaneous remains from his commonplace book 1816-60 (1864)
Life and correspondence a1863 (ed. E. Jane Whately 1866)
Whately, William *A bride-bush, or a wedding sermon* 1617
A care-cloth: or a treatise of the cumbers and troubles of marriage 1624
Gods husbandry: the first part 1619; 2 pts. 1622
The oyle of gladnesse. Certaine sermons 1637
Prototypes or the primarie precedent a1639 (1640)
The redemption of time; or a sermon 1606 (1634)
Whatley, Robert *The Christian: a sermon on the words of King Agrippa to St. Paul* 1746
Whatmough, Joshua *Language: a modern synthesis* 1956
Wheat and tares 1861 *See* Cunningham, Sir H. S.
Wheatley, Dennis Yates *The man who missed the war* 1945
Wheatley, Henry B. *A dictionary of reduplicated words in the English language* 1865 (Philol. Soc.)
Wheatly, Charles *The Church of England man's companion; or a rational illustration of the harmony and usefulness of the Book of Common Prayer* 1710
Wheaton, Henry *History of the Northmen, or Danes and Normans* 1831
Reports of cases argued and adjudged in the Supreme Court of the United States 1816-27 1826-27
Wheaton, Nathaniel S. *A journal of a residence in London* 1830
Wheatstone, Sir Charles *Scientific papers* a1875 (1879)
Whedon, Daniel D. *The freedom of the will* 1864
Wheel of fortune, The: or nothing for a penny 1698
Wheeler, Alwynne Cooper *The fishes of the British Isles and north-west Europe* 1969
Wheeler, Ann *The Westmorland dialect, in three familiar dialogues* 1790
— *in four familiar dialogues* 1802 (1821)
Wheeler, James T. *Early records of British India* 1878 (1879)
Madras in the olden time 1861
Wheeler, John *A treatise of commerce* 1601
Wheeler, Keith *Epitaph for Mr. Wynn* 1971 (UK 1972)
Wheeler, Robert Eric Mortimer *Archaeology from the earth* 1954
Wheeler, William H. *History of the fens of South Lincolnshire* 1868 (1897)
Wheeler, William Morton *Social life among the insects* 1922
Wheelock, Eleazar *Sermon* 1763
Wheelwright, Charles A. *The comedies of Aristophanes* tr. 1837
Wheelwright, Horace W. *A spring and summer in Lapland* (anon.) a1863 (1864)
Wheler, Sir George *An account of the churches, or places of assembly of the primitive Christians described by Eusebius* 1689
A journey into Greece 1682
Whellan, William *The history and topography of the counties of Cumberland and Westmorland* 1859
History, topography, and directory of the county palatine of Durham 1856
Where: information on education (Advisory Centre for Education) 1960-
Whetstone, George *The English myrror* 1586
A mirour for magestrates of cyties 1584
A remembraunce of the wel imployed life of G. Gaskoigne 1577
The right excellent historye of Promos and Cassandra 1578
The rocke of regard 1576
Whetton, Harry ed. *Practical printing and binding* 1946
Whewell, William *Architectural notes on German churches* (anon.) 1830 (1842)
Astronomy and general physics considered with reference to natural theology 1833
Grotius (H.) On the rights of war and peace tr. 1853
History of the inductive sciences, from the earliest to the present times 1837 (1847-57)
History of scientific ideas; being the first part of the Philosophy of the inductive sciences 1858
Indications of the creator 1845
Novum organon renovatum; being the second part of the Philosophy of the inductive sciences 1858
The philosophy of the inductive sciences, founded upon their history 1840 (1847)
Tides 1849 (1851-59; in Manual of scientific enquiry)
Life, and selections from his correspondence, by Mrs. Stair Douglas (1881)
See also Todhunter, Isaac
Which? (Consumers' Association Ltd.) 1957-
Whichcote, Benjamin *Several discourses* a1683 (1701-07)
Whicker, John *An account of the adventures of my* (H. Pitman's) *companions, since I left them at Saltatudos* 1689 (in Arber, Eng. Garner VII)
See also Pitman, Henry
Whig and Tory: or, wit on both sides. Being a collection of poems, by the ablest pens of the High and Low parties, upon the most remarkable occasions, from the change of the ministry, to this time 1712
Whig examiner, The (by Jos. Addison) 1710-12
Whig-Standard (Kingston, Ontario): See *Kingston Whig-Standard*
Whigg. A true and faithful account of the last distemper and death of Tom Whigg, Esq. 1710
Whimzies 1631 *See* Brathwait, R.
Whip. A fresh whip for all scandalous lyers 1647
Whipple, Edwin P. *Character and characteristic men* 1866
Essays and reviews 1850
Success and its conditions 1871
Whishaw, Lorna *As far as you'll take me* 1958

Whistle-Binkie; a collection of comic and sentimental songs 1832
— ed. 2, entitled *Whistle-Binkie; or the piper of the party* 1839 (1878, 1890)
Whistler, Henry *Aime at an up-shot for infant baptisme by the good will of Christ* 1653
Whiston, William *The genuine works of F. Josephus* tr. 1737 (1777)
A new theory of the earth 1696 (1722)
A short view of the chronology of the Old Testament 1702
Memoirs of the life and writings of W. W. Containing memoirs of several of his friends also, and written by himself 1749-50
Whitaker, Alexander *Good newes from Virginia* 1613
Whitaker, Jeremiah *The danger of greatnesse; or, Uzziah his exaltation and destruction* 1646
Whitaker, John *The ancient cathedral of Cornwall historically surveyed* 1804
The genuine history of the Britons asserted 1772
The history of Manchester 1771-75
Mary Queen of Scots vindicated 1787
Whitaker, Nathaniel *Two sermons on the doctrine of reconciliation* 1768 (1770)
Whitaker, Thomas D. *The history and antiquities of the deanery of Craven, in the county of York* 1805 (1812)
Whitaker, Tobias *The tree of humane life; or the bloud of the grape* 1638 (1654)
Whitaker's (W.) Disputation See Fitzgerald, W.
Whitaker's Almanac 1868-
Whitbourne, Richard *A discourse and discovery of New-found-land* 1620 (1623)
Whitby, Daniel *A discourse concerning I. The true import of the words election and reprobation*, etc. a1726 (1735)
A paraphrase and commentary on the New Testament 1703
Whitby, Lionel Ernest Howard *Medical bacteriology* 1928
— (ed. 4) 1944
— (ed. 5, by Whitby & M. Hynes) 1951
For later eds. *see* Hynes, Martin
—— & Britton, Cedric John C. *Disorders of the blood* 1935
Whitby glossary See Robinson, F. K.
Whitcher, Frances M. *The widow Bedott papers* 1846-47 (1855, 1883)
White, Abraham, Handler, P., & Smith, E. L. ed. *Principles of biochemistry* 1954
— (ed. 4) 1968
White, Adam *List of the specimens of crustacea in the collection of the British Museum* 1847
— *of British animals*. Part IV. Crustacea 1850; Part VIII. Fish 1851
A popular history of mammalia 1850
White, Alan *The long silence* 1976
White, Arnold *Tries at truth* 1891
White, Edward *Life in Christ* 1875 (1878)
The tone and teaching of the New Testament on certainty in religion 1880
White, Elwyn Brooks *Letters* [1908-76] ed. D. L. Guth 1976
White, Florence *Good English food, local and regional* 1952
White, Bp. Francis *A replie to Jesuit Fishers answere* 1624
A treatise of the Sabbath-day 1635
White, Gilbert *The natural history and antiquities of Selborne* 1789
White, Harvey Elliott *Introduction to atomic spectra* 1934
White, Henry Kirke *Poetical works* a1806 (1837)
Remains; with an account of his life by Rob. Southey (1816-22)
White, Howard ed. *Raincoast chronicles, first five: stories and history of the B.C. coast* 1975
White, James *The English verb; a grammatical essay, in the didactive form* 1761
White, James *Earl Strongbow: or, the history of Richard de Clare and the beautiful Geralda* 1789
White, James *Falstaff's letters* 1796 (1877)
White, John *Works* a1615 (1624)
White, John *A rich cabinet with variety of inventions* 1651 (1668)
White, John *The country-man's conductor in reading and writing true English* 1701
White, John *Journal of a voyage to New South Wales* 1790
White, Jon Ewbank Manchip *The garden game* 1973
Nightclimber 1968
White, Joseph *A comparison of Mahometism and Christianity in their history, their evidence and their effects* (Bampton lectures) 1784
White, Joseph W. Gleeson *Ballades and rondeaus, chants royal, sestinas*, etc., selected by Gleeson White 1887
White, Judith tr. *N. Poulantzas's Fascism and dictatorship: the Third International and the problem of fascism* 1974
White, Kirke *See* White, Henry Kirke
White, L. *The Dutchman's acknowledgement of his errors. Or a Dutch ballad translated into English* 1672
White, Osmar Egmont D. *Silent Reach* 1978
White, Patrick Victor Martindale *The eye of the storm* 1973
Riders in the chariot 1961
The tree of man 1955 (UK 1956)
Voss 1957
White, Percy *A king's diary* 1895
White, Peter Royden *Planning for public transport* 1976
White, R. *Digby's (K.) Late discourse touching the cure of wounds by the powder of sympathy* tr. 1658 (1660)
White, Richard Grant *England without and within* 1881
Every-day English 1880
Studies in Shakespeare 1885
Words and their uses, past and present 1871
White, Stewart E. *Arizona nights* 1907

The blazed trail 1902
Blazed trail stories, and Stories of the wild life 1904
The claim jumpers 1901
Conjuror's house: a romance of the free forest 1903
The forest 1903
The riverman 1908
The rules of the game 1910 (UK 1913)
The silent places 1904
The westerners 1901
White's (T.) Peripateticall institutions tr. 1656
White, Terence Hanbury *The elephant and the kangaroo* 1947 (UK 1948)
The once and future king 1958
The sword in the stone 1938
White, Theodore Harold *The making of the President 1960* 1961 (UK 1962)
— *1964* 1965
— *1972* 1973 (UK 1974)
White, Thomas Holt *A review of Johnson's criticism on the style of Milton's English prose* 1818
White, Tristram *The martyrdome of Saint George of Cappadocia* 1614
White, Walter *All round the Wrekin* 1860
Eastern England, from the Thames to the Humber 1865
White, William *Journal of a voyage from Madras to Columbo* 1800
White, William *History, gazetteer, and directory of Norfolk* 1836
History, gazetteer, and directory of Staffordshire 1851
White, William *Emanuel Swedenborg; his life and writings* 1856 (1867, 1868)
White, Sir William H. *A manual of naval architecture* 1877 (1882)
White, William Hale ('Mark Rutherford') *Mark Rutherford's deliverance* 1885
Miriam's schooling, and other papers 1890 (1904)
Whitefield, George *A letter to Governor Wright* 1768
A select collection of letters written to his most intimate friends 1734-70 (1772)
Whitefield, Thomas *A discourse of liberty of conscience* 1649
The doctrines of the Arminians and Pelagians truly stated 1652
A treatise tending to shew that the just God may have a hand in the unjust actions of sinful men 1653
Whiteford, Andrew Hunter *North American Indian arts* 1970
— *(new ed.) 1973*
Whitefriars 1844, *Whitehall* 1845 *See* Robinson, Jane
Whitehead, Alfred North *Adventures of ideas* 1933
The concept of nature 1920
An enquiry concerning the principles of natural knowledge 1919
Process and reality: an essay in cosmology 1929
Science and the modern world 1925 (UK 1926)
—— & Russell, Bertrand Arthur William *Principia mathematica* 3 vols. 1910-13
Whitehead, Charles *Richard Savage; a romance of real life* 1842 (1845)
Whitehead, Charles *Hops: from the set to the sky-lights* 1881
Whitehead, Paul *Manners; a satire* 1739
Poems a1774 (1790)
Whitehead, Sarah R. *Daft Davie, and other sketches of Scottish life and character* (incl. *A tale of Hallowe'en*) 1876
Whitehead, William *Plays and poems* 1774
Essay on ridicule 1743
Variety, a tale for married people (anon.) 1776
Whitehorne, Peter *Macchiavelli's (N.) Arte of warre* tr. 1560
Certain waies of the orderyng of souldiers in battelray 1562 (1573)
Whitehouse, John *Poems* 1787
Whiteing, Richard *No. 5 John Street* 1899
Ring in the new 1906
Whitelaw, Alexander *The book of Scottish ballads* 1844 (1874)
The book of Scottish song 1844 (1875)
Whitelocke, Sir Bulstrode *A journal of the Swedish ambassy* 1653-54 (1772)
Memorials of the English affairs (anon.) a1675 (1682, 1732, 1853)
Whitelocke, Sir James *Liber famelicus* 1609-31 (Camden Soc. 1858)
Whiteman, Paul & McBride, Mary Margaret *Jazz* 1926
Whiteside, James *Italy in the nineteenth century* 1848 (1860)
Whitgift, Abp. John *Works* a1604 (Parker Soc. 1851-53)
An answere to a certen libel intituled An admonition to the parliament 1572
The defense of the aunswere to the admonition, against the replie of T(homas) C(artwright) 1574
Whiting, N. *Le hore di recreatione: or, the pleasant historie of Albino and Bellama* 1637 (1639)
Old Jacob's altar newly repaired 1659
Whitinton, or Whittington, Robert *The thre bookes of Tullyes offyces* tr. 1534 (1540)
Vulgaria 1520 (1527)
Whitlock, Richard *Ζωοτομία, or observations on the present manners of the English* 1654
Whitman, Charles *Death out of focus* 1970
Whitman, Walt *Daybooks and note-books* ed. W. White 3 vols. 1978
Leaves of grass 1855
Drum-taps 1865
November boughs 1888

Whitman, Walt (*cont.*)
Passage to India 1871
Poems, selected and edited by W. M. Rossetti 1868
Specimen days and Collect 1882–3 (1 vol.)
Whitmore, Frank Clifford *Organic chemistry* 1937
Whitmore, Walter J. *Croquet tactics* 1868
Whitney, Adeline D. T. *Faith Gartney's girlhood* 1863
The Gayworthys: a story of threads and thrums 1865
Odd, or even? 1880
The other girls 1873
Patience Strong's outings 1868
Sights and insights 1876
A summer in Leslie Goldthwaite's life 1866
We girls 1870
Whitney, Geoffrey *A choice of emblemes and other deuises* 1586
Whitney, Thomas Porter tr. *A. I. Solzhenitsyn's The Gulag archipelago* 3 vols. 1974–8
Whitney, William D. *Essentials of English grammar for the use of schools* 1877
Language and the study of language 1867
The life and growth of language 1875
Oriental and linguistic studies 1872–75
Whittaker's electrical engineer's pocket-book ed. K. Edgcumbe 1903
— (ed. 4, ed. R. E. Neale) 1920
Whittier, John Greenleaf *Writings* v.d. (Riverside ed. 1888–89)
Poetical works v.d. (1880, 1894)
Prose works 1866
Whittock, Nathaniel, et al. *The complete book of trades* 1837 (1842)
Whitworth, Charles, Baron *An account of Russia, as it was in the year 1710* a1725 (1758)
Whitworth, George Clifford *An Anglo-Indian dictionary: a glossary of Indian terms used in English* 1885
Whitworth, Richard *The advantages of inland navigation* 1766
Whole duty of man, The (anon.; ascribed to R. Allestree) 1658 (1684)
Whole duty of nations, The 1681
Whyte, Alexander *Bible characters* 1896–99
Whyte, James C. *History of the British turf* 1840
Whyte, Laurence *Poems* 1740
Whyte, William Hollingsworth *The organization man* 1956 (UK 1957)
Whyte-Melville, G. J. *See* Melville, G. J. Whyte
Whytford, or Whitford, Richard *The martiloge in englysshe after the use of the chirche of Salisbury* 1526 (1893)
Wickenden, William S. *The hunchback's chest* 1852
Widdowes, Daniel *Naturall philosophy* 1631 (ed. 2)
Widdowes, Giles *The schysmaticall puritan* 1630
Widdowes treasure See Partridge, J.
Widow, The a1627 *See* Middleton, T.
Wieland's (C. M.) History of Agathon tr. 1773
Wiener, Leo *The history of Yiddish literature in the nineteeth century* 1899
Wiesengrund-Adorno, Theodor, et al. *The authoritarian personality* 1950
Wife lapped . . See *Wyfe*
Wife of Auchtermuchty, The a1568 (in Ramsay's Evergreen 1724; Bannatyne MS., Hunterian Club)
Wiffen, Jeremiah H. *Aonian hours, and other poems* 1819 (1820)
Tasso's Jerusalem delivered 1824
Wiggin, Kate D. *The diary of a goose girl* 1902
New chronicles of Rebecca of Sunnybrook farm 1912
Polly Oliver's problem 1893
Rebecca of Sunnybrook Farm 1903 (UK 1904)
Wiggins, John *The practice of embanking lands from the sea* 1852
Wigginton, Brooks Eliot ed. *The foxfire book: log dressing; log cabin building; mountain crafts and foods; . . and other affairs of plain living* 1972
ed. *Foxfire 3* 1975
Wigglesworth, Vincent Brian *The life of insects* 1964
Wight, John *Mornings at Bow Street* 1824
Wilberforce, Henry W. *The Church and the empires* a1873 (1874)
Wilberforce, Herbert William Wrangham *Lawn tennis* 1889
Wilberforce, Reginald G. *Life of the right rev. Samuel Wilberforce* 1881–82
Wilberforce, Robert I. *The doctrine of holy baptism* 1849
The doctrine of the incarnation 1848 (1852)
Rutilius and Lucius; or stories of the third age 1842
Wilberforce, Bp. Samuel *Addresses to the candidates for ordination* 1860
Essays contributed to the 'Quarterly Review' a1873 (1874)
A history of the protestant episcopal church in America 1844
Speeches on missions a1873 (1874)
Wilbour, Charles E. *The life of Victor Hugo* 1887
Wilbraham, Frances M. *The Cheshire pilgrims* 1862
Wilbraham, Roger *An attempt at a glossary of some words used in Cheshire* 1818 (in Archaeologia XIX)
— *with additions* 1820 (1826)
Wilbye, John *The first set of English madrigals* 1598 (in Arber, Eng. Garner VII)
Wilcocke, Samuel H. *Stavorinus' (J. S.) Voyages to the East Indies* tr. 1798
Wilcocks, James C. *The sea-fisherman* 1865 (1875)
Wilcocks or Wilcox, Thomas *Works* a1608 (1624)
Wilcox, Ruth Turner *The dictionary of costume* 1969 (UK 1970)

Wild or Wylde, Robert *Iter boreale* (anon.) 1660
A letter to his friend Mr. J. J. upon occasion of his majesty's declaration for liberty of conscience. Together with his Poetica licentia, and a friendly debate between a Conformist and a non-Conformist 1672
Oliver Cromwell's ghost 1679
Wild and tame. Pictures and pages of animal life 1892
Wild life in a southern county 1879 *See* Jefferies, R.
Wild sports of the west 1832 *See* Maxwell, W. H.
Wilde, Lady Jane F. S. *Meinhold's (W.) Sidonia the sorceress* tr. 1849 (1859)
Wilde, Oscar Fingal O'Flahertie Wills *An ideal husband* 1899
The importance of being earnest: a trivial comedy for serious people 1899
Lady Windermere's fan: a play about a good woman 1893
Letters ed. R. Hart-Davis 1962
The picture of Dorian Gray 1891 (first published in a shorter version in *Lippincott's monthly magazine*, July 1890)
Poems 1881
Ravenna 1878 (Newdigate Prize poem)
A woman of no importance 1894
Wildeblood, Peter *Against the law* 1955
The main chance 1957
Wilder, Burt G. & Gage, Simon H. *Anatomical technology as applied to the domestic cat* 1882
Wilder, Harris Hawthorne *A laboratory manual of anthropometry* 1920
Wilder, Thornton Niven *The bridge of San Luis Rey* 1927
Heaven's my destination 1934
Our town 1938
Wilenski, Reginald Howard *The modern movement in art* 1927
Wilhelm, Thomas *A military dictionary and gazetteer* 1881
Wilkerson, Albert E. ed. *The rights of children: emergent concepts in law and society* 1973
Wilkes, Benjamin *The English moths and butterflies* 1749
Wilkes, John *Correspondence* a1797 (1805)
The North Briton 1763
Wilkes, William *Obedience or ecclesiasticall union* 1605
— another issue, entitled *A second memento for magistrates* 1608
Wilkes' Spirit of the times (title varies) 1859–1902
Wilkie, William *The epigoniad* (anon.) 1757 (1759)
Wilkins, Sir Charles *The Bhagvat-Geeta or dialogues of Kreeshna and Arjoon* tr. 1785
Wilkins, David *Concilia Magnae Britanniae et Hiberniae* 1737
ed. *Leges Anglo-Saxonicae ecclesiasticae et civiles* 1721
Wilkins, George *The miseries of inforst marige* 1607 (Dodsley)
Wilkins, John *The autobiography of an English gamekeeper* 1892
Wilkins, Bp. John *Mathematical and philosophical works* a1672 (1707–08)
A discourse concerning a new world and another planet 1640
A discourse concerning the gift of prayer 1651
The discovery of a world in the moone (anon.) 1638
Ecclesiastes; or, a discourse concerning the gift of preaching 1646
An essay towards a real character, and a philosophical language (with an alphabetical dictionary) 1668
Mathematicall magick; or, the wonders that may be performed by mechanicall geometry 1648
Mercury; or the secret and swift messenger 1641
Of the principles and duties of natural religion a1672 (1675)
Wilkins, Mary E. *By the light of the soul* 1906
A humble romance; and other stories 1887
The love of parson Lord 1900
A New England nun, and other stories 1891
Wilkins, William *Songs of study* 1881
Wilkins, William H. & Vivian, Herbert *The green bay tree* 1894
Wilkins, William W. *Political ballads of the seventeenth and eighteenth centuries*, annotated by W. W. W. (1860)
Wilkinson, James J. G. *Swedenborg's Animal kingdom, considered anatomically, physically, and philosophically* tr. 1843
Wilkinson, John *A treatise collected out of the statutes concerning the office and authoritie of coroners and sherifes; together with an easie and plain method for the keeping of a court leet, court baron, and hundred court* 1618
Wilkinson, Sir John G. *Manners and customs of the ancient Egyptians* 1837–41
Wilkinson, Robert *Barwickbridge; or England and Scotland coupled* 1617
The merchant royall 1607
A paire of sermons 1614
Wilkinson, William *A confutation of certaine articles deliuered vnto the familye of loue* 1579
Wilks, Mark *Historical sketches of the south of India* 1810–17
Will of deuyle See *Wyll*
Willan, Leonard *Astræa, or, true love's myrrour* 1651
Willan, Robert *A list of ancient words at present used in the mountainous district of the West Riding of Yorkshire* 1811 (in Archaeologia XVII; E.D.S. 1873)
Willard, Samuel *Mercy magnified on a penitent prodigal* 1684
Willcock, John *The great marquess; life and times of Archibald, 8th earl of Argyll (1607–61)* 1903
Willdenow's (C. L.) Principles of botany, and of vegetable physiology tr. 1805 (1811)

Willet, Andrew *An harmonie upon the first booke of Samuel* 1607
Hexapla in Exodum 1608
Hexapla in Genesin 1605
Hexapla; or, a sixfold commentary on Daniel 1610
A treatise of Salomons mariage 1612
William of Normandy; an historic novel 1787
William of Palerne, The romance of: otherwise known as the romance of William and the Werwolf c1350 (Roxb. Club 1832; E.E.T.S. 1867, 1881)
William of Shoreham *See* Shoreham
Williams, Bobby Joe *Evolution and origins: an introduction to physical anthropology* 1973
Williams, Bryan L. & Wilson, Keith eds. *A biologist's guide to principles and techniques of practical biochemistry* 1975
Williams, Charles *Man in motion* 1959
Man on a leash 1973 (UK 1974)
Williams, Sir Charles H. *Works* a1759 (1822)
Poems a1759 (1763)
Odes a1759 (1775)
Williams, Charles Walter Stansby *All Hallows' Eve* 1945
The greater trumps 1932
The place of the lion 1931
War in heaven 1930
Williams, David, et al. *Annals of the Empire; from the reign of Charlemagne. Translated from the French of Voltaire, constituting a part of a complete edition in English of the works of that writer* 1781
Williams, David *Murder for Treasure* 1980
Treasure by degrees 1977
Williams, Edward *Poems, lyric and pastoral* 1794
Williams, Frederick S. *The Midland railway: its rise and progress* 1876
Our iron roads; their history, construction, and social influences 1852
Williams, Gordon John *Economic geology of New Zealand* 1965
Williams, Helen Maria *Letters containing a sketch of the politics of France* 1795 (1796)
A narrative of the events which have taken place in France, from the landing of Napoleon Bonaparte, till the restoration of Louis XVIII. With an account of the present state of society and public opinion 1815
Personal narrative of travels to the equinoctial regions of the new continent during 1799–1804, by A. de Humboldt and Aimé Bonpland tr. 1814–29
Sketches of the state of manners and opinions in the French republic 1801
Williams, Howel, Turner, F. J., & Gilbert, C. M. *Petrography* 1954
Williams, Isaac *The Apocalypse, with notes and reflections* 1852
The baptistery 1842–44
The Psalms interpreted of Christ 1864
Williams, Abp. John *Great Britains Salomon: a sermon* 1625
The holy table 1637
Perseverantia sanctorum: a sermon 1628
A sermon of apparell 1620
Williams, Bp. John *The history of the gunpowder treason, collected from approved authors* (anon.) 1678
Pulpit Popery, true Popery; being an answer to a book intitled Pulpit-sayings (by J. Gother) 1688
Williams, John ('Anthony Pasquin') *Authentic memoirs of Warren Hastings* 1793
A cabinet, etc. 1794
A calm examination 1793
The children of Thespis, a poem 1786–87
A crying epistle from Britannia to Col. Mack 1794
The life of the late Earl of Barrymore 1793
Shrove Tuesday, a satiric rhapsody (anon.) 1790 (1794)
Williams, John *The ancient Welsh grammar compiled by Edeyrn* tr. 1856
Williams, John Lee *The territory of Florida* 1837
Williams, Joshua *Principles of the law of real property* 1845 (1877)
Rights of common and other prescriptive rights 1877 (1880)
Williams, Laurence Frederic Rushbrook *The State of Israel* 1957
Williams, Monier (later Monier Monier-Williams) *An elementary grammar of the Sanscrit language* 1846
Hinduism 1877
Indian wisdom 1875
Religious thought and life in India 1883
Williams, Martin T. ed. *The art of jazz: essays on the nature and development of jazz* 1959 (UK 1960)
Williams, Nathaniel *Imago sæculi: the image of the age represented in four characters* 1676
Williams, Raymond Henry *Culture and society, 1780–1950* 1958
Keywords 1976
The long revolution 1961
Williams, Sir Roger *The actions of the Lowe Countries* a1595 (1618)
A briefe discourse of warre 1590
Williams, Roger *Experiments of spiritual life and health* 1652 (1863)
A key into the language of America 1643
Williams, Samuel *The natural and civil history of Vermont* 1794 (1809)
Williams, Samuel Robinson *Magnetic phenomena* 1931
Williams, Samuel Wells *A Chinese commercial guide* 1856
The Middle kingdom: a survey of the geography, etc. *of the Chinese empire* 1848
— greatly enlarged and in part rewritten 1883

WILLIAMS, Tennessee (Thomas Lanier Williams) *Cat on a hot tin roof* 1955
The glass menagerie 1945
Orpheus descending 1958
A streetcar named Desire 1947
WILLIAMS, Wadham P. & JONES, William A. *A glossary of provincial words and phrases in use in Somersetshire* 1873
WILLIAMS, William *The principles and practice of veterinary medicine* 1874 (1888)
WILLIAMS, William Carlos *Collected earlier poems* 1951
Collected later poems 1950
Selected essays 1954
WILLIAMS, William Mattieu *The fuel of the sun* 1870
Through Norway with a knapsack 1859
WILLIAMS, William Meade *Annals of the worshipful Company of Founders of the city of London* 1867
WILLIAMS, William R. *Religious progress: discourses on the development of the Christian character* 1850 (1854)
WILLIAMSON, Benjamin *An elementary treatise on the integral calculus* 1875
WILLIAMSON, Henry *The beautiful years* 1921
—(rev. ed.) 1929
Tarka the otter 1927
WILLIAMSON, Hugh *Methods of book design* 1956
—(ed. 2) 1966
WILLIAMSON, Thomas *Goulart's (S.) Wise Vieillard, or old man* tr. 1621
WILLIAMSON, Thomas *The East India vade-mecum* 1810
Oriental field sports 1807
WILLIAMSON, William Durkee *The history of the state of Maine* 2 vols. 1832
WILLICH, Anthony Florian Madinger *The domestic encyclopædia* 4 vols. 1802
—(US ed., with additions by J. Mease) 5 vols. 1803-4
Elements of the critical philosophy 1798
WILLIS, Browne *Notitia parliamentaria; or an history of the counties, cities, and boroughs in England and Wales* 1715-16
WILLIS, John *The art of stenographie* (anon.) 1602
WILLIS, John C. *A manual and dictionary of the flowering plants and ferns* 1897
WILLIS, Nathaniel P. *Lady Jane, and other poems* 1844
Melanie, and other poems 1835
Pencillings by the way 1835
Poems, sacred, passionate and humourous 1846
Poems of early and after years 1848
Sketches 1827
WILLIS, Robert *Architectural nomenclature of the middle ages* 1844 (Cambr. Antiq. Soc.)
Remarks on the architecture of the middle ages 1835
—— & CLARK, John W. *The architectural history of the University of Cambridge, and of the colleges of Cambridge and Eton* 1886
WILLIS, Rupert Allan *Pathology of tumours* 1948
Willis' (T.) Remaining medical works tr. 1681
WILLISON, John *The balm of Gilead for healing a diseased land* 1742 (1800)
WILLMOTT, Peter *Adolescent boys of East London* 1966
The evolution of a community: a study of Dagenham after forty years 1963
WILLMOTT, Robert E. A. *Pleasures, objects, and advantages of literature* 1851 (1855)
WILLOBIE, Henry *Avisa; or, the true picture of a modest maid* 1594 (1635, 1880)
WILLOCK, Colin Dennistoun *Death at flight* 1956
Death in covert 1961
The enormous zoo: a profile of the Uganda national parks 1964
WILLOCK, John *Voyages and adventures, (with) remarks on different countries in Europe, Africa and America* 1798
WILLOUGHBY, Florance Barrett *Alaskans all* 1933
WILLOUGHBY, Francis *De historia piscium libri quatuor* a1672 (ed. J. Ray 1686; engraved title *Icthyographia* 1685)
Ornithologiæ libri tres a1672 (ed. J. Ray 1676)
—translated, and enlarged by J. Ray (1678)
WILLS, Charles J. *In the land of the Lion and the Sun; or modern Persia* 1883
WILLS, Gordon & YEARSLEY, Ronald eds. *Handbook of management technology* 1967
WILLS, William G. *Life's foreshadowings; a novel* (anon.) 1859
Wills See *Earliest English wills; Lancashire and Cheshire wills*
Wills and inventories from the registers of the Commissary of Bury St. Edmund's 13..-16.. (Camden Soc. 1850)
Wills and inventories, illustrative of the history, manners, language, etc. *of the northern counties of England* 13..-15.. (Surtees Soc. 1835)
—Parts II and III entitled *Wills and inventories from the Registry at Durham* 15..-16.. (Surtees Soc. 1860, 1906)
Wills from Doctors' Commons 1495-1695 (Camden Soc. 1863)
WILLSFORD, Thomas *Nature's secrets* 1658
The scales of commerce and trade; and Architectonice, or the art of building 1660
WILMOT, Catherine *An Irish peer on the continent (1801-1803): being a narrative of the tour of Stephen, 2nd Earl Mount Cashell, through France, Italy, etc., as related by Catherine Wilmot* ed. T. U. Sadleir 1920
WILMOT, Martha *More letters from Martha Wilmot: impressions of Vienna, 1819-1829* ed. by the Marchioness of Londonderry & H. M. Hyde 1935
—— & WILMOT, Catherine *The Russian journals of Martha and Catherine Wilmot, 1803-1808* ed. by the Marchioness of Londonderry & H. M. Hyde 1934
WILMOT, Robert *The tragedie of Tancred and Gismund* 1591 (in Hazl., Dodsley)
WILSON, Alexander *American ornithology* 1808-13 (1831)
Poems 1790
—ed. 2, *Poems, humorous, satirical and serious* 1791
Poems and literary prose a1813 (ed. Grosart 1876)
Poems, chiefly in the Scottish dialect a1813 (1816)
Poetical works a1813 (1857)
Watty and Meg; or the wife reformed (anon.) 1792
WILSON, Andrew *The abode of snow; observations on a journey from Chinese Tibet to the Indian Caucasus* 1875
Facts and fictions of zoology 1882
WILSON, Angus Frank Johnstone *Anglo-Saxon attitudes* 1956
As if by magic 1973
A bit off the map, and other stories 1957
Hemlock and after 1952
The middle age of Mrs Eliot 1958
No laughing matter 1967
The old men at the zoo 1961
The strange ride of Rudyard Kipling: his life and works 1977
Such darling dodos, and other stories 1950
The wrong set, and other stories 1949
WILSON, Arthur *The history of Great Britain, being the life and reign of King James the first* a1652 (1653)
The Swisser 1631 (ed. Feuillerat, Paris 1904)
WILSON, Augusta J. *Vashti; or, 'Until death us do part'* 1867
WILSON, Bryan R. *Sects and society: a sociological study of three religious groups in Britain* 1961
WILSON, Charles *Elements of Hebrew grammar* 1782 (1794)
WILSON, Charles William (1836-1905) *Mapping the frontier* ed. G. F. G. Stanley 1970
WILSON, Colin Henry *The outsider* 1956
WILSON, Sir Daniel *The archæology and prehistoric annals of Scotland* 1851 (1863)
Prehistoric man 1862 (1865)
WILSON, Edmund *Axel's castle: a study in the imaginative literature of 1870-1930* 1931
Devil take the hindmost: a year of the slump (US ed. with title *The American jitters*) 1932
I thought of Daisy 1929
The wound and the bow: seven studies in literature 1941
WILSON, Edmund Beecher *The cell in development and inheritance* 1896
—(ed. 2) 1900 (UK 1902)
—(ed. 3 with title —— *and heredity*) 1925
WILSON, Edward *Spadacrene Dunelmensis: or a short treatise of an ancient medicinal fountain or vitrioline spaw near Durham* 1675
WILSON, Frederick R. *An architectural survey of the churches in the archdeaconry of Lindisfarne* 1870
WILSON, Gavin *A collection of Masonic songs* 1787 (1788)
WILSON, George *The five gateways of knowledge* 1856 (1859)
—— & GEIKIE, Archibald *Memoir of Edward Forbes* 1861
WILSON, George Buckley L. *A dictionary of ballet* 1957
—(rev. ed.) 1961
WILSON, Harold *See* WILSON, James Harold
WILSON, Harriette *Memoirs written by herself* 4 vols. 1825
WILSON, Harry Leon *Ma Pettengill* 1919
Ruggles of Red Gap 1915
—(new ed.) 1917
Somewhere in Red Gap 1916
The spenders 1902
WILSON, Henry Schütz *Alpine ascents and adventures* 1878
Studies in history, legend, and literature 1884
WILSON, Horace H. *Works* a1860 (1861-71)
Essays on the religion of the Hindus a1860 (1862)
A glossary of judicial and revenue terms, from the Arabic, Persian, Hindustani, etc. 1855
Mill's (J.) History of British India ed. with continuation 1840-46
WILSON, Jacqueline *Hide and Seek* 1972
WILSON, James *A complete dictionary of astrology* 1819
WILSON, James *Biography of the blind* 1821 (1835)
WILSON, James Harold *The governance of Britain* 1976
WILSON, James Maurice *Solid geometry and conic sections* 1872
WILSON, John *Andronicus Comnenius; a tragedy* 1664
Belphegor: or the marriage of the devil. A tragi-comedy 1691
The cheats; a comedy (anon.) 1664 (1671, 1693)
The projectors; a comedy 1665
WILSON, John *Synopsis of British plants; with a botanical dictionary* 1744
WILSON, John *General view of the agriculture of Renfrewshire* 1812
WILSON, John *Works* a1854 (1855-58)
The city of the plague, and other poems 1816
The Foresters 1825
The isle of palms, and other poems 1812
Lights and shadows of Scottish life (anon.) 1822
Noctes Ambrosianæ 1822-35 (from Blackwood's Mag.)
The recreations of Christopher North 1842
The trials of Margaret Lyndsay (anon.) 1823
WILSON, John *British farming* 1862
WILSON, John Alexander *Missionary life and work in New Zealand, 1833 to 1862: being the private journal of the late Rev. J. A. Wilson* ed. C. J. Wilson 1889
WILSON, John Boyd *Reason and morals* 1961
WILSON, John Cook *Aristotelian studies* 1879
On the traversing of geometrical figures 1905
WILSON, John Fleming *The land claimers* 1911
WILSON, John Mackay *Historical, traditionary, and imaginative tales of the Borders, and of Scotland* a1835 (1835-40, 1857-59)
WILSON, John Marius *The rural cyclopedia* 1847-49
WILSON, Marjorie Kerr tr. *K. Z. Lorenz's Man meets dog* 1954
WILSON, Percy & WEBB, G. W. *Modern gramophones and electrical reproducers* 1929
WILSON, Richard Albert *The birth of language* 1937
WILSON, Robert *A right excellent comœdy called The three ladies of London* 1584 (in Hazl., Dodsley)
The pleasant and stately morall of the three lordes and three ladies of London 1590 (ibid.)
WILSON, Robert *The pleasures of piety, a poem* 1837
Poems, chiefly in the Scottish dialect 1822
WILSON, Sir Robert T. *Life, from autobiographical memoirs, journals* a1849 (ed. H. Randolph 1862)
Private diary of travels, personal services, and public events 1812-14 a1849 (1861)
WILSON, Robin J. *Introduction to graph theory* 1972
WILSON, Samuel *An account of the province of Carolina in America* 1682
WILSON, Thomas *The arte of rhetorique* 1553 (1567)
A discourse vppon vsurye 1572 (1584)
The rule of reason, conteinyng the arte of logique 1551 (1567, 1580)
WILSON, Thomas *Jerichoes down-fall* 1642 (1643)
WILSON, Bp. Thomas *Works* a1755 (1781)
WILSON, Thomas *The pitman's pay* 1826-30
The pitman's pay, and other poems 1843 (1872)
WILSON, Thomas Woodrow *Congressional government; a study in American politics* 1885
Public papers, ed. by R. S. Baker & W. E. Dodd (1925)
The State 1893
WILSON, Walter *The history and antiquities of dissenting churches and meeting houses in London* 1808-14
WILSON, William *Poems, chiefly in the Scottish dialect* 1824
WILSON, Sir William J. E. *The anatomist's vade mecum* 1840 (1842)
On diseases of the skin 1847
WILSON, Woodrow *See* WILSON, Thomas Woodrow
WILTON, Mary M. (Egerton), Countess of ed. *The art of needlework* [by E. Stone] c1840
Wiltshire glossary 1893 *See* DARTNELL, G. E.
Wily beguilde, A pleasant comedie, called 1606 (in Hazl., Dodsley)
WIMBLEDON, R. *A sermon no lesse frutefull then famous* (anon.) ?1550 (1584)
Winchcombe (Gloucestershire). *Landboc, sive registrum monasterii beatae Mariae Virginis et Sancti Cenhelmi de Winchelcumba* v.d. (1892)
WINCHELL, Alexander *Reconciliation of science and religion* 1877
Walks and talks in the geological field 1886
World-life 1883 (1889)
WINCHILSEA, Anne Finch, Countess of *Miscellany poems* 1713
WINDHAM, William *Diary* 1784-1810 (1866)
Speeches in parliament a1810 (ed. Amyot 1812)
Windisch's (W. O. E.) Compendium of Irish grammar tr. by J. P. M'Swiney 1883
WINDLE, Sir Bertram C. A. *Remains of the prehistoric age in England* 1904
WINDSOR, Arthur L. *Ethica; or characteristics of men, manners, and books* 1860
Windsor Castle, History of 1749 *See* POTE, J.
Windsor magazine, The 1895-
Wine, women and war [1918 journal of Howard Vincent O'Brien, published anonymously] ed. K. E. Harriman 1926
WINEARLS, Jane *Modern dance: the Jooss-Leeder method* 1958
—(ed. 2) 1968
WING, John *Abels offering: a sermon* 1621
WINGATE, Edmund *Arithmetique made easie* 1630
Λογαριθμοτεχνία, or the construction, and use of the logarithmeticall tables tr. 1635 (ed. 2)
WINGFIELD, Lewis S. *Abigel Rowe, a chronicle of the regency* 1883
WINȜET, Ninian *Works* (*Certain tractates,* etc.) 1562-63 (S.T.S. 1887-91)
The buke of four scoir thre questions, tueching doctrine etc. 1563
Certane tractatis for reformatioun of doctryne and maneris 1562
The last blast of the trompet of Godis worde aganis the vsurpit auctoritie of Iohne Knox 1562
Vincentius Lirinensis, for the antiquitie and veritie of the Catholik fayth tr. 1563
WINICK, Charles *Dictionary of anthropology* 1956 (UK 1957, new impr. 1960)
WINKWORTH, Susanna *The history and life of J. Tauler, with twenty-five of his sermons* tr. 1857
Winnere and wastoure 1352 (Roxb. Cl. 1897)
WINSLOW, Edward *A briefe narration of the true grounds or cause of the first planting of New England* 1646 (Appendix to next)
Hypocrisie unmasked 1646
A relation or journall of the beginning and proceedings of the English plantation setled at Plimoth in New England 1622
WINSLOW, Forbes B. *On obscure diseases of the brain, and disorders of the mind* 1860
Winslow's (J. B.) Anatomical exposition of the structure of the human body tr. G. Douglas 1733

Winslow, Octavius *The inner life, its nature, relapse, and recovery* 1850
Winslow, Pauline Glen *The counsellor heart* 1980
Death of an angel 1975
The Witch Hill murder 1977
Winsor, Justin *Christopher Columbus and the spirit of discovery* 1891
From Cartier to Frontenac 1894
The Mississippi Basin: the struggle between England and France, 1697–1763 1895
Winstanley, William *England's worthies* 1660 (1684)
The lives of the most famous English poets 1687
Winstedt, Richard Olof *The Malays: a cultural history* 1947
Winter, George *New and compendious system of husbandry* 1787 (1788)
'Winter, John Strange' (Mrs. Arthur Stannard) *Bootles' baby; a story of the scarlet lancers* 1885
In quarters; chronicles of the 25th (the Black Horse) dragoons 1885
Red coats 1894
Winter, William *Shakespeare's England* 1886
Winterbottom, Thomas M. *An account of the native Africans in the neighbourhood of Sierra Leone* 1803
Winter's crimes ed. G. Hardinge et al. 1969–
Winthrop, John *The history of New England* a1649 (1825–26, 1853)
Winthrop, Theodore *The canoe and the saddle* a1861 (1862)
John Brent 1862 (UK 1883)
Life in the open air 1863
Winton, John Richard ed. *A dictionary of economic terms* (ed. 3) 1951
Wintrobe, Maxwell Myer *Clinical hematology* 1942
Winwood, Sir Ralph *Memorials of affairs of state in the reigns of Q. Elizabeth and K. James I, collected (chiefly) from the original papers of Sir R. Winwood* a1617 (1725)
Wireless world 1913–
Wirt, William *Sketches of the life and character of Patrick Henry* 1817 (1818)
Wirth, Louis & Shils, Edward Albert tr. *K. Mannheim's Ideology and Utopia: an introduction to the sociology of knowledge* 1936
Wisconsin. State Historical Society *Reports and collections* (title varies) 1855–
Wisden cricketers' almanack (title varies) 1864–
Wisdom, Thomas Henry *High-performance driving for you* 1966
Wise, John *The Churches quarrel espoused* 1772
Wise, John R. *The New Forest; its history and its scenery* 1862
Wiseman, Nicholas P. S. *Fabiola; or the Church of the Catacombs* (anon.) 1855
Recollections of the last four Popes and of Rome in their times 1858
Twelve lectures on the connection between science and revealed religion 1836
Wiseman, Richard *Severall chirurgical treatises* 1676
A treatise of wounds 1672
Wister, Owen *The Virginian: a horseman of the plains* 1902
Wit and science, Marriage of See *Marriage*
Wit and science, Moral play of c1530 *See* Redford, J.
Wit and wisdom, Marriage of See *Marriage*
Wit restor'd, in severall select poems, not formerly publish't (by Sir J. Mennes & J. Smith) 1658
Wit's recreations See *Witts*
Withals, John *A shorte dictionarie (English and Latin) for yonge begynners* 1553 (1556, 1568)
— *The seconde tyme corrected by Lewys Evans* 1574 (1602)
Wither or Withers, Fabian *Dariot's (C.) Breefe introduction to the astrologicall iudgement of the starres* 1583 (1598)
Indagine's (J. ab) Briefe introductions vnto the art of chiromancy or manuel diuination, and physiognomy tr. 1558
— ed. 1651, entitled *The book of palmestry and physiognomy* (1683)
Wither, George *Workes* 1620
Juvenilia 1622, 1633
Miscellaneous works a1667 (Spenser Soc. 1872–78)
Abuses stript and whipt 1613
— *also the scourge. Epigrams* 1613 (1614)
Britains remembrancer, containing a narration of the plague lately past 1628
Campo-Musæ, or the field-musings of Capt. G. W. 1643
A collection of emblemes, ancient and modern 1634–35
Epithalamia: or nuptiall poems 1612
Faire virtue, the mistresse of Philarete (anon.) 1622 (1633; in Arber, Eng. Garner IV)
Fidelia (anon.) 1615 (1617; in Arber, Eng. Garner VI)
Meditations upon the Lord's Prayer 1665
Prince Henries obsequies 1612
The shepherds hunting (anon.) 1615
Vox pacifica 1645
Withers motto. Nec habeo, nec careo, nec curo 1621
Withering, William *A botanical arrangement of all the vegetables naturally growing in Great Britain* 1776
— ed. 2, entitled *A botanical arrangement of British plants* 1787–92; ed. 3, 1796
— ed. 4, enlarged by W. Withering (the younger) (1801); ed. 5 (1812)
Witherings, John *The orders, lawes, and ancient customes of swanns* 1632 (1664; in Harl. Misc.)
Withers, Robert *A description of the Grand Signour's seraglio* (ed. J. Greaves) 1650 (1653)
Wittfogel, Karl August *Oriental despotism: a comparative study of total power* 1957
Wittgenstein, Ludwig Josef Johann *Tractatus logico-philosophicus* [anon. tr.] 1922
See also Anscombe, Gertrude E. M.
Wittie, Robert *Primrose's (J.) Popular errors; or, the errours of the people in physick* tr. 1651
Pyrologia mimica; or, an answer to Hydrologia chymica of W. Sympson 1669
Witts, Francis Edward *The diary of a Cotswold parson* ed. D. Verey 1978
Witts recreations (by Sir J. Mennes & J. Smith), *with a thousand outlandish proverbs* (selected by Mr. G. Herbert) 1640 (1663)
Witwer, Harry Charles *Fighting blood* 1923
From baseball to Boches 1918
The leather pushers 1921
Wodehouse, Pelham Grenville *The adventures of Sally* 1923
Aunts aren't gentlemen: a Jeeves and Bertie story 1974
Bill the conqueror 1924
Blandings Castle and elsewhere 1935
Carry on, Jeeves! 1925
The clicking of Cuthbert 1922
The code of the Woosters 1938
The coming of Bill 1920 (US ed. 1919 with title *Their mutual child*)
Company for Henry 1967
A damsel in distress 1919
Eggs, beans and crumpets 1940
Frozen assets 1964
The heart of a goof 1926
Hot water 1932
The inimitable Jeeves 1923
Jill the reckless 1921 (US ed. 1920 with title *The little warrior*)
Laughing gas 1936
Leave it to Psmith 1924
Lord Emsworth and others 1937
Louder and funnier 1932
The luck of the Bodkins 1935
Meet Mr. Mulliner 1927
Money in the bank 1942 (UK 1946)
Mr. Mulliner speaking 1929
Much obliged, Jeeves 1971
Pearls, girls and Monty Bodkin 1972
Performing flea: a self-portrait in letters 1953
Plum pie 1966
Right ho, Jeeves 1934
Sam the sudden 1925
Service with a smile 1961 (UK 1962)
Something fresh 1915
Tales of St. Austin's 1903
Uncle Fred in the springtime 1939
Very good, Jeeves! 1930
Wodenote, Theophilus *Hermes theologus; or, a divine Mercurie despatcht with a grave message of new descants upon old records* 1649
Wodroephe, John *The spared houres of a souldier in his travels; or the true marrowe of the French tongue* 1623 (1625)
Wodrow, Robert *Collections upon the lives of the reformers and most eminent ministers of the Church of Scotland* a1734 (Maitland Cl. 1834–45)
Correspondence 1694–1732 (Wodrow Soc. 1842–43)
History of the sufferings of the Church of Scotland from the Restauration to the Revolution 1721–22 (1828–30)
The life of James Wodrow a1734 (1828)
Wodrow Society *Publications* (1842–47)
Miscellany (1844)
Woglom, Gilbert T. *Parakites. A treatise on the making and flying of tailless kites for scientific purposes and for recreation* 1896
Wohunge of ure lauerd, The a1240 (in Old English homilies, I, E.E.T.S. 1868)
Wolcot, John ('Peter Pindar') *Works* 1794–1801, 1809, 1812, 1816, a1819 (1824)
A benevolent epistle to Sylvanus Urban 1790
The Lousiad, an heroi-comic poem 1785–95
Lyric odes to the royal academicians 1782
More lyric odes to the royal academicians 1783
Subjects for painters 1789
Wolf, Frederick Adolph & Wolf, Frederick Taylor *The fungi* 2 vols. 1947
Wolfe, Bernard *Limbo* 1952 (UK ed. 1953 with title *Limbo '90*)
See also Mezzrow, Milton
Wolfe, Thomas Clayton *Look homeward, angel: a story of the buried life* 1929 (UK 1930)
The web and the rock 1939
You can't go home again 1940
Wolfe, Tom *The electric kool-aid acid test* 1968
The kandy-colored tangerine-flake streamline baby 1965 (UK 1966)
Wolfenden, R. Norris *Joal's Respiration in singing* tr. 1895
Wollaston, William *The religion of nature delineated* (anon.) 1722 (1738)
Wolley, Charles *A two years' journal in New York* 1701 (1860)
Wolley, Edward See *Scudery, G. de*
Wolley, Hannah *See* Woolley, H.
Wollocombe, John B. *From morn till eve: reminiscences* 1898
Wollstonecraft (afterwards Godwin), Mary *An historical and moral view of the origin and progress of the French Revolution* 1794
Letters to Imlay a1797 (1879)
Letters written during a short residence in Sweden, Norway and Denmark 1796
Posthumous works a1797 (1798)
A vindication of the rights of woman 1792
Wolseley, Garnet J. W., Viscount *The life of John Churchill, duke of Marlborough, to the accession of queen Anne* 1894
The soldier's pocket-book for field service 1869
Woman 1937–
Woman of fashion, The 1767
Woman of honor, The 1768
Woman's day (New York) 1937–
Woman's journal 1927–
Woman's own 1932–
Women saints. The lives of women saints of our contrie of England c1610 (E.E.T.S. 1886)
Women's Group on Public Welfare. Hygiene Committee *Our towns: a close-up, 1939–42* 1943
Womock, Laurence *Aron-bimnucha* 1663
The examination of Tilenus before the triers 1658
Wonders of the physical world 1875
Wood, Alphonso *The American botanist and florist* 1866
A class-book of botany 1845 (1850)
Wood, Anthony *Athenæ Oxonienses. An exact history of all the writers and bishops who have had their education in the university of Oxford from 1500 to 1690; to which are added, the fasti or annals of the said university* 1691–92 (1721, 1813–20)
The history and antiquities of the colleges and halls in the university of Oxford; from the original MS. in the Bodleian Library; with continuation by John Gutch a1695 (1786–90)
The history and antiquities of the university of Oxford; from the original MS. in the Bodleian Library a1695 (1792–96)
Life, from 1632 to 1672, written by himself; continued till 1695 a1695 (1772, 1848, O.H.S. 1891–1900)
Survey of the antiquities of the city of Oxford 1661–66 (ed. Andrew Clark, O.H.S. 1889–99)
Wood, Christopher *'Terrible hard', says Alice* 1970
Wood, Clement & Goddard, Gloria *Dictionary of American slang* 1926
Wood, Ellen P. *See* Wood, Mrs. Henry
Wood, Eric Stuart *Collins field guide to archaeology* 1963
Wood, Ernest Egerton *Yoga dictionary* 1956
Wood, George B. *A treatise on therapeutics and pharmacology or materia medica* 1856
Wood, H. Freeman *The Englishman of the Rue Caïn* 1889
The passenger from Scotland Yard 1888
Wood, Mrs. Henry *The Channings* 1862
East Lynne 1861
Elster's folly 1866
Lady Adelaide's oath 1867
A life's secret 1867
Lord Oakburn's daughters 1864
The master of Greylands 1873
Mildred Arkell 1865
Mrs. Halliburton's troubles 1862
Orville college 1867
Oswald Cray 1864
Parkwater 1876
Pomeroy Abbey 1878
The shadow of Ashlydyat 1863
St. Martin's eve 1866
Trevlyn Hold 1864
Verner's pride 1863
Wood, Horace G. *A treatise on the limitation of actions at law and in equity* 1883
Wood, Horatio C. *A contribution to the history of the freshwater algæ of North America* 1872 (Smithsonian Contrib. knowl. XIX)
A treatise on therapeutics 1874 (1879)
Wood, James *The elements of optics* 1798 (1828)
The principles of mechanics 1796 (1803)
Wood, James Alex F. *North beat* 1973
Wood, John G. *The (boy's) modern playmate* 1870 (1890)
The common objects of the sea shore 1858
Homes without hands 1865 (1868)
The illustrated natural history 1853 (1855, 1859–63)
Out of doors: a selection of original articles on practical natural history 1874
The popular natural history 1867
Sketches and anecdotes of animal life 1854; second series 1855
Wood, Mary A. E. *See* Green, M. A. E.
Wood, Michael *Gardiner's (S.) De vera obedientia* tr. 1553
Wood, Nicholas *A practical treatise on rail-roads* 1825 (1838)
Wood, Mrs. Nugent & Lapham, H. *Waiting for the mail* 1875 (Melbourne)
Wood, Owen *An alphabetical book of physicall secrets, for all those diseases that are most predominant and dangerous in the body of man* 1639
Wood, Robert *An essay on the original genius of Homer* (anon.) 1769
— ed. 2, *with a comparative view of the ancient and present state of the Troade* a1771 (1775)
Wood, Shakspere *The new curiosum urbis: a guide to ancient and modern Rome* 1875
Wood, Thomas *An institute of the laws of England* 1720 (1722)
Wood, Thomas *Cobbers: a personal record of a journey . . to Australia* 1934
Wood, William *New Englands prospect* 1634 (1865)

Wood, William *A survey of trade* 1718 (1719)
Wood, William *The great advantages of our colonies and plantations to Great Britain* 1775
Woodall, John *The surgions mate* 1617
— *with a treatise of ye cure of ye plague* 1639
Viaticum, being the path-way to the surgions chest 1628
Woodbury, Walter E. *The encyclopædia of photography* 1892
Woodcocke, G. *Justinus' (M. J.) Historie* tr. G. W. 1606
Wooden world dissected, The 1706 *See* Ward, E.
Woodes, Nathaniel *An excellent new comedie, intituled: The conflict of conscience* 1581 (in Hazl., Dodsley)
Woodford, Gwendolyn Green tr. *M. Gignoux's Stratigraphic geology* 1955
Woodforde, James *The diary of a country parson* ed. J. Beresford 5 vols. 1924–31
Woodgate, Gordon Kemble *Elementary atomic structure* 1970
Woodham-Smith, Cecil Blanche *Florence Nightingale, 1820–1910* 1950
Woodhead, Abraham *The life of S. Teresa* (anon.; tr. from Spanish) 1671
Motives to holy living a1678 (1688)
Woodhouse, Martin C. *Blue bone* 1973
Mama doll 1972
Rock baby 1968
Tree frog 1966
Woodhouse, Robert *An elementary treatise on astronomy* 1812
Woodhouse, Thomas *Artificial silk* 1927
Woodruff, Hiram Washington *The trotting horse of America: how to train and drive him* 1868
'Woodruff, Philip' (Philip Mason) *The island of Chamba* 1950
Whatever dies 1948
Woods, Katharine Seymour *Rural crafts of England* 1949
Woods, Leonard *Works* 1851
Lectures on Church government 1844
Woods, Nicholas A. *The Prince of Wales in Canada and the United States* 1861
'Woods, Sara' (Sara Bowen-Judd) *Done to death* 1974
Enter certain murderers 1966
Enter the corpse 1973
Woodward, Arthur S. *Outlines of vertebrate palæontology* 1898
Woodward, Horace B. *The geology of England and Wales* 1876
Woodward, John *An account of some Roman urns* 1713
— ed. 3, entitled, *Remarks upon the antient and present state of London, occasion'd by some Roman urns, coins, and other antiquities* 1723
An attempt towards a natural history of the fossils of England a1728 (1728–29)
An essay towards a natural history of the earth 1695 (1723)
Woodward, John & Burnett, George *A treatise on heraldry* 1892 (1896)
Woodward, Josiah *An account of the rise and progress of religious societies in the city of London* 1697 (1701)
Woodward, Samuel P. *A manual of the mollusca; or, a rudimentary treatise of recent and fossil shells* 1851–56
Woodworth, Robert Sessions *Experimental psychology* 1938
— (rev. ed., by Woodworth & H. Schlosberg) 1954
Psychology: a study of mental life 1921 (UK 1922) (Several later editions also used)
Wooldridge, Sidney William & Morgan, Ralph Sisk *The physical basis of geography: an outline of geomorphology* 1937
— (ed. 2, with title *An outline of geomorphology*) 1959
Woolf, Leonard Sidney *The village in the jungle* 1913
Woolf, Virginia *Between the acts* 1941
The captain's death bed, and other essays ed. L. Woolf 1950
The common reader 1925
— (2nd ser.) 1932
Jacob's room 1922
Letters ed. N. Nicolson & J. Trautmann 6 vols. 1975–80
Mrs. Dalloway 1925
Night and day 1919
Orlando: a biography 1928
Roger Fry: a biography 1940
A room of one's own 1929
To the lighthouse 1927
The voyage out 1915
The waves 1931
A writer's diary ed. L. Woolf 1953
The years 1937
Woollcott, Alexander *While Rome burns* 1934
Woolley, Charles Leonard *Alalakh: an account of the excavations at Tell Atchana, in the Hatay, 1937–1949* 1955
Woolley, Hannah *The gentlewoman's companion* 1675
The queen-like closet 1670
Woolman, John *Journal of the life, gospel labours and Christian experiences of J. W.* 1776
Woolner, Thomas *My beautiful lady* a1861 (1863)
Woolsey, Theodore D. *Communism and socialism in their history and theory* 1880
Introduction to the study of international law 1860 (1864, 1875)
Woolson, Constance F. *Anne; a novel* 1883
Jupiter lights: a novel 1889
Woolton, Bp. John *The christian manuell* 1576 (Parker Soc. 1851)

Wootton, Barbara Frances *Social science and social pathology* 1959
Testament for social science 1950
Worboise, Emma J. *Sissie* 1882
Worcester, Bp. of 1690 *See* Stillingfleet, E.
Worcester, Earl of *See* Tiptoft, J.
Worcester, Edward Somerset, 2nd Marquis of *A century of . . inventions* 1655 (1663, 1865)
An exact and true definition of the most stupendious water-commanding engine 1663
Worcester, Joseph E. *A dictionary of the English language* 1860
A universal and critical dictionary of the English language 1846
Worcester, William *See* Botoner, W.
Worcestershire (West) glossary 1882 *See* Chamberlain, Mrs.
Word 1945–
Word study 1925–69
Words 1934–41
Words by an eyewitness 1901 *See* 'Linesman'
Wordsworth, Charles *Annals of my early life, 1806–45* 1891
Annals of my life, 1847–56 a1892 (1893)
Wordsworth, Christopher (of Trinity College, Cambridge) *Ecclesiastical biography* 1810 (1853)
Who wrote Εικων Βασιλικη? considered and answered in two letters, addressed to the Archbishop of Canterbury 1824
— *Documentary supplement* 1825
King Charles the first, the author of Icôn Basilikè, further proved 1828
Wordsworth, Bp. Christopher *Memoirs of William Wordsworth* 1851
Miscellanies: literary and religious v.d. (1879)
Theophilus Anglicanus; or, instructions concerning the Church and the Anglican branch of it 1843 (1850)
Christopher Wordsworth, Bishop of Lincoln, 1807–1885. By J. H. Overton & Elizabeth Wordsworth (1888, 1890)
Wordsworth, Christopher *Rutland words* 1891 (E.D.S.)
Scholae academicae; some account of the studies at the English universities in the eighteenth century 1877
Social life at the English universities in the eighteenth century 1874
Wordsworth, Dorothy *Journals* ed. E. de Sélincourt 2 vols. 1941
Wordsworth, William *Poetical works* v.d. (1849, 1888, 1895)
Poems (1807)
Prose works v.d. (Grosart 1876)
The Borderers; a tragedy 1795–96 (1842)
The excursion 1814
Peter Bell 1819
The prelude; or, growth of a poet's mind 1799–1805 (1850)
The white doe of Rylstone 1815
Worfat, William de *See* Hutton, William
Work, Milton Cooper *Complete contract bridge* 1929
Work 1889–1924
Worke for cutlers; or a merry dialogue betweene sword, rapier and dagger 1615
Workhouses. An account of several work-houses for employing and maintaining the poor 1725 (1732)
Workman, Fanny B. & William H. *Algerian memories. A bicycle tour over the Atlas to the Sahara* 1896
Workshop receipts 1873–85 *See* Spon, Ernest
World, The 1874–1921
World and the child. A propre new interlude of the worlde and the chylde, otherwyse called Mundus & infans c1500 (Roxb. Club 1817; Hazl., Dodsley; Manly, Pre-Shaks. drama)
World archaeology 1969–
World of cricket monthly 1976–
World review 1936–53
World's work (New York) 1900–32
Worlidge, John *Apiarium; or a discourse of bees* 1676
Systema agriculturæ; the mystery of husbandry discovered 1669 (1681)
— *To which* ˜*is added, Kalendarium rusticum and Dictionarium rusticum* 1675 (1681)
Vinetum Britannicum; or a treatise of cider 1676 (1691)
Wornum, Ralph N. *Analysis of ornament* 1856
— ed. 2, entitled *The characteristics of styles* 1861
ed. *Lectures on painting, by the Royal Academicians Barry, Opie, and Fuseli* v.d. (1848)
Worrall, Arthur James *English idioms for foreign students* 1932
Worsaae, Jens J. A. *The industrial arts of Denmark from the earliest times to the Danish conquest of England* 1882
Worsley, Peter Maurice *The trumpet shall sound: a study of 'cargo' cults in Melanesia* 1957
Worster, William W. tr. *E. Hannover's Pottery and porcelain* See Rackham, Bernard
Worsthorne, Peregrine Gerard *The socialist myth* 1971
Worthington, John *Miscellanies* a1671 (1704)
Wotton, Anthony *An answere to a popish pamphlet, entituled, Certaine articles discovering the absurdities of the Protestants religion* 1605
Runne from Rome 1624
Wotton, Henry *A courtlie controversie of Cupids cautels* tr. 1578
Wotton, Sir Henry *Reliquiæ Wottonianæ; or a collection of lives, letters, poems, etc.* a1639 (1651, 1654, 1672, 1685)
The elements of architecture 1624
A short view of the life and death of George Villiers duke of Buckingham a1639 (1642)
See also Smith, L. P.

Wotton, William *The history of Rome from the death of Antoninus Pius to the death of Severus Alexander* 1701
Reflections upon ancient and modern learning 1694 (1697)
Woty, William *Poetical works* 1770
Poems on several occasions 1780
Wrangham, Francis *The Pleiad; or, a series of abridgements of seven distinguished writers, in opposition to the pernicious doctrine of deism* 1820
Wraxall, Sir Frederick C. L. *Hugo's (V. M.) Les misérables* tr. 1862
Life in the sea; or the nature and habits of marine animals 1860
Memoirs of Robert-Houdin by himself tr. 1859
Wild oats 1858
Wraxall, Sir Nathaniel W. *Historical memoirs of my own time, from 1772 to 1784* 1815
Memoirs of the courts of Berlin, Dresden, Warsaw, and Vienna in the years 1777–79 1799
A tour through some of the northern parts of Europe 1775 (1776)
Wren, Christopher *Parentalia; or memoirs of the family of the Wrens,* compiled by Christopher Wren and published by Stephen Wren a1747 (1750)
Wren, Bp. Matthew *A sermon preached before the Kings Majestie* 1627
Wren, Matthew *Monarchy asserted* 1659
Wrenn, Charles Leslie *Word and symbol* 1967
Wright, Abraham *Five sermons in five several styles or waies of preaching* 1656
Wright, Barbara tr. *R. Queneau's Between blue and blue* 1967
Wright, David McKee *Station ballads and other verses* 1897
Wright, Edward *Certaine errors in navigation* 1599 (partly in Arber, Eng. Garner III)
Stevin's (S.) Haven finding art, by the latitude and variation tr. 1599
Wright, Edward P. *Animal life* 1879
Figuier's (L.) Ocean world tr. 1872
Wright, Frances *Views of society and manners in America* (anon.) 1821
Wright, Frank Lloyd *Autobiography* 1932
Wright, George Payling & Symmers, William St. Clair eds. *Systemic pathology* 2 vols. 1966
Wright, Harold Bell *The winning of Barbara Worth* 1911
Wright, Herbert E. *A handy book for brewers* 1892
Wright, Major J. *Camus' (J. P.) Nature's paradox* tr. 1652
Wright, James *Historia histrionica* 1699 (in Hazl., Dodsley; Arber, Eng. Garner II)
Wright, Joseph *The English dialect dictionary* 1896–1905
A grammar of the dialect of Windhill, in the West Riding of Yorkshire 1892 (E.D.S.)
—— & Wright, Elizabeth Mary *Old English grammar* 1908
Wright, Leonard *The hunting of Antichrist* 1589
Wright, Lewis *The illustrated book of poultry: with practical schedules* 1873
Wright, Peter *The language of British industry* 1974
Wright, Thomas *The passions of the minde* 1601 (1621)
Wright, Thomas *The Celt, the Roman, and the Saxon* 1852
Dictionary of obsolete and provincial English 1857
Early travels in Palestine 1848
Essays on archæological subjects, and on various questions connected with the history of art, science and literature in the middle ages 1861
Essays on subjects connected with the literature, popular superstitions, and history of England in the middle ages 1846
A history of domestic manners and sentiments in England during the middle ages 1862
The homes of other days; a history of domestic manners and sentiments in England 1871
ed. *Political poems and songs* v.d. (Rolls series 1859–61)
ed. *Political songs of England* v.d. (Camden Soc. 1839)
ed. *Popular treatises on science* v.d. (1841)
ed. *Specimens of lyric poetry* a1310 (Percy Soc. 1842)
ed. *A volume of vocabularies* v.d. (1857); *a second volume* (1873)
Anglo-Saxon and Old English vocabularies. Second edition, ed. R. P. Wülcker (Wright-Wülcker) (1884)
—— & Halliwell, James O. ed. *Reliquiæ antiquæ* v.d. (1841–43)
Wright, Thomas *The romance of the lace pillow* 1919
Wright, Walter R. *Horæ Ionicæ: a poem descriptive of the Ionian Islands* 1809
Wright, William Aldis *See* Eastwood, J.
Wright's chaste wife, The c1462 (E.E.T.S. 1865, 1869)
Wrighte, William *Grotesque architecture* 1767 (1790)
Wriglesworth, Captain W. *MS. Log-book of the 'Lyell'* 1730
Wriothesley, Charles *A chronicle of England during the reigns of the Tudors* 1485–1559 (Camden Soc. 1875–77)
Wroth or Wroath, Lady Mary *The Countesse of Mountgomeries Urania* 1621
Wülcker, R. P. *See* Wright, T.
Wuertz' (F.) Surgeons guid tr. (and ed. by William Johnson) 1658
Wulfstan *Homilies* a1023 (Napier 1883)
Wundt's (W.) Lectures on human and animal psychology tr. J. E. Creighton & E. B. Titchener 1894
Wurtz' (C. A.) Atomic theory tr. E. Cleminshaw 1880
Wyatt (Captain) *The voyage of Robert Dudley, afterwards earl of Warwick and Leicester and duke of Northumberland, to the West Indies, 1594–95, narrated by capt. Wyatt, by himself, and by Abram Kendall, master* c1595 (Hakluyt Soc. 1899)

WYATT, Sir Thomas *Poetical works* a1542 (1810, 1816, 1821, 1913)
WYBURN, George McReath, WARBRICK, J. G., & TODD, M. E. *Concise anatomy* 1967
WYCHE, Sir Peter *A short relation of the river Nile* tr. 1669 (1798)
WYCHERLEY, William *Posthumous works* a1716 (1728-29)
Dramatic works a1716 (1840)
The country-wife 1675
The gentleman dancing-master 1673
Love in a wood 1672
The plain-dealer 1676
Wycket, Wycklyffes ?a1500 (1546; ed. Pantin 1828)
WYCLIF, John *English works* c1380 (E.E.T.S. 1880)
Select English works c1380 (1869-71)
Three treatises c1380 (ed. Todd 1851)
The Holy Bible, made from the Latin Vulgate by John Wycliffe and his followers 1382, 1388 (ed. J. Forshall & Sir F. Madden 1850)
WYDEVILLE, Anthony *See* RIVERS, Earl
Wyfe lapped in Morrelles skin, The c1550 (in T. Amyot's Old taming of a shrew, Shaks. Soc. 1844; Hazlitt, Early pop. poetry, IV, 1866)
WYKES, Alan *Gambling* 1964
Wyl Bucke his testament See LACY, John
WYLD, Henry Cecil *A short history of English* 1914
WYLDE, James ed. *The circle of the sciences* 1862-67
WYLDE, Zachary *The English master of defence* 1711
WYLIE, James H. *History of England under Henry the fourth* 1884-98
Wyll of the devill, The c1550 (c1825; Jyl of Brentford etc., Ballad Soc. 1871)
WYLLIE, John W. S. *Essays on the external policy of India* a1870 (1875)
WYLLIE, Peter J. ed. *Ultramafic and related rocks* 1967
WYLSON, Thomas *Demosthenes' Three orations in fauour of the Olynthians with fower orations against King Philip* 1570
Wymondham and Attleborough Express 1975-
WYND, Oswald *Sumatra seven zero* 1968
Walk softly, men praying 1967
WYNDHAM, Anne *Claustrum regale reseratum; or the King's concealment at Trent* 1667 (1681)
WYNDHAM, Henry P. *A gentleman's tour through Monmouthshire and Wales* (anon.) 1775
'WYNDHAM, John' (John Wyndham P. L. B. Harris) *The day of the triffids* 1951
The Midwich cuckoos 1957
The seeds of time 1956
Trouble with lichen 1960
WYNN, Sir John *The history of the Gwedir family* a1600 (1878)
WYNNE family *The Wynne diaries, 1789-1820* ed. A. Fremantle 3 vols. 1935-40
WYNTER, Andrew *Curiosities of civilization* 1860
Our social bees; or pictures of town and country life 1861
WYNTER, Sylvia *The hills of Hebron* 1962
WYNTOUN, Andrew of *Þe orygynale cronykil of Scotland* c1425 (1795, 1872-79, S.T.S. 1903-08)
WYRLEY, William *The true use of armorie* 1592
WYSE, Sir Thomas *An excursion in the Peloponnesus* 1865
WYTHE, George *Decisions of cases in Virginia by the High Court of Chancery* 1795
WYVILL, Sir Christopher *The pretensions of the triple crown examined* 1672

X

'X, Malcolm' *See* 'MALCOLM X'
XANTHAKIS, John N. ed. *Solar physics* 1967

Y

Y., R. *See* YOUNGE, Richard
Yachting (US) 1907-
Yachting monthly 1906-
YADIN, Yigael *Hazor* 1972
YALDEN, Thomas *Poems* a1736 (1790, 1810)
Yale. Studies from the Yale psychological laboratory ed. E. W. Scripture 1893-
Yale alumni magazine 1937-
Yale literary magazine 1836-
Yankee: a monthly magazine for Yankees everywhere 1935-42; 1945-
YAPP, William Brunsdon *An introduction to animal physiology* 1939
YARINGTON, Robert *Two lamentable tragedies* 1601 (in Bullen, Old plays, IV, 1885)
YARRANTON, Andrew *England's improvement by sea and land* 1677
YARRELL, William *A history of British birds* 1843
A history of British fishes 1835-39
— ed. 3, ed. by Sir J. Richardson (1859)
YATE, William *An account of New Zealand* 1835
YATES, Edmund H. *The black sheep* 1867
Broken to harness; a story of English domestic life 1864
The forlorn hope 1867
Land at last 1866
The rock ahead 1868
Edmund Yates: his recollections and experiences 1884
YATES, John *Ibis ad Cæsarem* 1626
Yearbook of astronomy 1961-
Year-book of facts in science and (the useful) art(s) 1839-80
Yearbook of medicine, surgery, and their allied sciences 1859-62 1860-63 (New Sydenham Soc.)
Year-book of wireless telegraphy and telephony, The 1913-25
Year books of the reign of Edward I. Years 20-22, 30-35 1292-94, 1302-07 (ed. and tr. A. J. Horwood, Rolls series 1863-79)
— *of Edward II* 1307-15 (ed. F. W. Maitland, etc., Selden Soc. 1903-27)
— *of Edward III. Years 11-20* 1337-46 (ed. and tr. A. J. Horwood and L. O. Pike, Rolls series 1883- 1911)
— *of Edward II to Henry VIII* v.d. (15.., 16.., 1678-80)
Year's work in English studies, The 1921-
YEATES, Victor M. *Winged victory* 1934
YEATS, John *The growth and vicissitudes of commerce* 1872
The natural history of commerce 1870
The technical history of commerce 1871
YEATS, William B. *The Celtic twilight; men and women, dhouls and faeries* 1893
The Countess Kathleen, and various legends and lyrics 1892
Fairy and folk tales of the Irish peasantry 1888
In the seven woods: being poems chiefly of the Irish heroic age 1903
The king of the great clock tower: commentaries and poems 1934
Last poems and two plays 1939
Letters ed. A. Wade 1954
October blast 1927
Per amica silentia lunae 1918
Poems 1895
Poems (variorum ed. by P. Allt & R. K. Alspach) 1957
Responsibilities: poems and a play 1914
Reveries over childhood and youth 1915 (UK 1916)
The trembling of the veil 1922
The wanderings of Oisin, and other poems 1889
The wind among the reeds 1899
Words for music perhaps, and other poems 1932
Yellow book, The, an illustrated quarterly 1894-97
YEOMANS, John *The Abecedarian, or, philosophic comment upon the English alphabet* 1759
YEOWELL, James *Chronicles of the ancient British Church* 1839 (1847)
Yesterday's shopping: the Army & Navy Stores catalogue 1907: a facsimile of the Army & Navy Co-operative Society's 1907 issue of 'Rules of the Society and price list of articles sold at the Stores' introduced by A. Adburgham 1969
YONG, Bartholomew *See* YOUNG, B.
YONGE, Charles D. *Athenæus' Deipnosophists* tr. 1854
YONGE, Charlotte Mary *Abbeychurch; or, Self-control and self-conceit* 1844
Burnt out: a story for mothers' meetings 1879
Cameos from English history 1868-99
Chantry House 2 vols. 1886
The chaplet of pearls; or, The white and black Ribaumont 1868
The Christmas mummers 1858
The clever woman of the family 1865
Countess Kate 1862
The daisy chain; or, aspirations 1856
The dove in the eagle's nest 1866
Dynevor Terrace; or, the clue of life 1857
Heartsease; or, The brother's wife 2 vols. 1854
The heir of Redclyffe 1853
History of Christian names 1863
Hopes and fears; or, scenes from the life of a spinster 1860
John Keble's parishes: a history of Hursley and Otterbourne 1898
Lads and lasses of Langley 1881
Lady Hester; or, Ursula's narrative 1874
Landmarks of history; ancient history 1852
— *middle ages* 1853
— *modern history* 1857
Life of John Coleridge Patteson, missionary bishop of the Melanesian Islands 1874
Magnum bonum; or, Mother Careys brood 3 vols. 1879
My young Alcides: a faded photograph 2 vols. 1875
Nuttie's father 1885
An old woman's outlook in a Hampshire village 1892
Our new nistress; or, Changes at Brookfield Earl 1888
The pillars of the house; or, Under wode, under rode 4 vols. 1873
Pioneers and founders; or, Recent workers in the mission field 1871
The pupils of St. John the Divine 1868 (dated 1867)
The release; or, Caroline's French kindred 1896
The Stokesley secret 1861
A storehouse of stories 1870-72
That stick 2 vols. 1892
The three brides 2 vols. 1876
The trial; more links of the daisy chain 1864
The two guardians; or, Home in this world 1852
The two sides of the shield 2 vols. 1885
Womankind 1876
See also *Monthly packet*
YONGE, James *The gouernaunce of prynces* 1422 (in Secreta secretorum, E.E.T.S. 1898)
YONGE, Nicholas *Musica transalpina. Madrigales translated of foure, fiue and sixe partes* 1588 (in Arber, Eng. Garner III)
YONGE, Walter *Diary* 1604-28 (Camden Soc. 1848)
'YORK, Andrew' (Christopher Nicole) *The eliminator* 1966
The expurgator 1972
York memorandum book 1376-1493 (Surtees Soc. 1912-15)
York Minster, Fabric rolls of v.d. (Surtees Soc. 1859)
York mysteries. (York plays. The plays performed by the crafts or mysteries of York on the day of Corpus Christi) c1440 (1885)
York wills See *Testamenta Eboracensia*
YORKE, James *The union of honour* 1640
'YORKE, Margaret' (Margaret Beda Nicholson) *Grave matters* 1973
Mortal remains 1974
The silent witness 1972
Yorkshire archæological and topographical journal, The 1870-
Yorkshire chantry surveys (The certificates of the commissioners appointed to survey the chantries, guilds, hospitals, etc., in the county of York) 1546 (Surtees Soc. 1894-95)
Yorkshire dialogue in Yorkshire dialect; between an awd wife, a lass, and a butcher 1673 (in Nine specim. Eng. dialects, E.D.S. 1896)
See also MERITON, G.
Yorkshire glossary 1876 *See* ROBINSON, C. C.
Yorkshire Post 1866-
Yorkshire tragedy, A 1608 (in Shakespeare Apocrypha 1908)
Yoshiwara episode See MURDOCH, A.
YOUATT, William *Cattle* 1834
The dog 1845 (1858)
The horse (anon.) 1831 (1843)
Sheep (anon.) 1837
YOUMANS, Edward L. *The hand-book of household science* 1857
YOUNG, Alexander Bell Filson *The complete motorist: being an account of the evolution and construction of the modern motor car* 1904
YOUNG, Arthur *An historical dissertation on idolatrous corruptions in religion* 1734
YOUNG, Arthur *General view of the agriculture of the county of Essex* 1807
— *of Hertfordshire* 1804
— *of Lincoln* 1799
— *of Norfolk* 1804
— *of Oxfordshire* 1809
— *of Suffolk* 1794
— *of Sussex* 1793 (1808)
The farmer's letters to the people of England, containing the sentiments of a practical husbandman (anon.) 1767
A tour in Ireland 1776-79 1780 (1887)
Travels 1787-89; undertaken with a view of ascertaining the cultivation, etc. of the kingdom of France 1792
Autobiography, with selections from his correspondence a1820 (ed. M. Betham-Edwards 1898)
See also *Annals of agriculture*
YOUNG, Arthur *Nautical dictionary* 1846 (1863)
YOUNG or YONG, Bartholomew *Boccaccio's (G.) Amorous Fiammetta* tr. 1587
Montemayor's (J. de) Diana tr. 1598
See also PETTIE, G.
YOUNG, Charles A. *The sun* 1882
A text-book of general astronomy for colleges and scientific schools 1888 (UK 1889)
YOUNG, David & BROWN, John *Memorials of Alexander Moncrieff and James Fisher* 1849
YOUNG, Edward *Sermons on several occasions* 1702-03
YOUNG, Edward *Works* 1757
Poems a1765 (1810)
The brothers; a tragedy 1753
Busiris, king of Egypt; a tragedy 1719
The Centaur not fabulous 1755
The complaint; or, night-thoughts on life, death and immortality (anon.) 1742-45
Conjectures on original composition 1759
The force of religion; or, vanquish'd love 1714
Love of fame 1728 See *The universal passion*
A paraphrase on part of the book of Job 1719
A poem on the last day 1713
Resignation 1762
The revenge; a tragedy 1721
The universal passion 1725-28
— republished with title *Love of fame, the universal passion* 1728
A vindication of providence; or a true estimate of human life 1728
Life and letters by Henry C. Shelley (1914)
YOUNG, Emily Hilda *William* 1925
YOUNG, Francis Brett *Portrait of Clare* 1927
YOUNG, Francis Chilton- *See* CHILTON-YOUNG, F.
YOUNG, Geoffrey Winthrop ed. *Mountain craft* 1920
YOUNG, George *A geological survey of the Yorkshire coast* 1822
YOUNG, Jennie J. *The ceramic art* 1878 (1879)
YOUNG, John *The province of reason* 1860
YOUNG, John R. *Mathematical dissertations* 1841
The theory and practice of navigation and nautical astronomy 1856
YOUNG, John Zachary *An introduction to the study of man* 1971
The life of vertebrates 1950
A model of the brain 1964

YOUNG, Thomas *Englands bane, or, the description of drunkennesse* 1617
YOUNG, Thomas *A course of lectures on natural philosophy and the mechanical arts* 1807
— new ed. by Prof. Kelland (1845)
YOUNG, Wayland Hilton *Eros denied* 1965
Young Englishwoman, The 1865–77
Young gentleman's magazine, The 1869–73
Young man's calling, The, or the whole duty of youth (by Samuel Crossman) 1678
YOUNGE, Richard *The blemish of government, the shame of religion, the disgrace of mankind; or, a charge drawn up against drunkards* 1655 (1863)
The drunkard's character, or, a true drunkard with such sinnes as raigne in him 1638
The victory of patience, and benefit of affliction 1636 (partly in Arber, Eng. Garner IV)
YOUNGER, John *Autobiography* a1860 (1881)
YOUNGHUSBAND, Ethel *Glimpses of East Africa and Zanzibar* 1910
YOUNGHUSBAND, Sir Francis E. *The heart of a continent* 1896
YOXALL, Harold Waldo *A fashion of life* 1966
'YUILL, P. B.' (Gordon Maclean Williams) *The bornless keeper* 1974
YULE, George Udny *An introduction to the theory of statistics* 1911
— (ed. 11, by Yule & M. G. Kendall) 1937
YULE, Sir Henry *The book of ser Marco Polo* tr. 1871
A narrative of the mission sent to the Court of Ava in 1855 1858
—— & BURNELL, Arthur C. *Hobson-Jobson: being a glossary of Anglo-Indian colloquial words and phrases* 1886
Yule-tide stories 1853 *See* THORPE, B.
Ywaine and Gawin c1400 (in Ritson, Metrical romances I, 1802)

Z

'ZACK' (Gwendoline Keats) *On trial* 1899
Tales of Dunstable weir 1901
The white cottage 1901
ZANDVOORT, Reinard Willem *A handbook of English grammar* 1957
—— et al. *Wartime English: materials for a linguistic history of World War II* 1957
ZAEHNSDORF, Joseph W. *The art of bookbinding* 1880
A short history of bookbinding 1895
ZANGWILL, Israel *The Bachelor's club* 1891
The big Bow mystery 1892
Children of the Ghetto 1892
Ghetto comedies 1907
Ghetto tragedies 1893
The master 1895
Zeitschrift für deutsches Alterthum, herausgegeben von Moriz Haupt (und E. Steinmeyer) 1841–
Zeluca; or, educated and uneducated woman 1815
Zepheria (an amatory poem) 1594 (1842; in Arber, Eng. Garner V)
ZERFFI, Gustavus G. *Lectures delivered before the Sunday Lecture Society* 1878
ZEUNER, Friedrich Eberhard *Dating the past: an introduction to geochronology* 1946
— (ed. 4) 1958
Ziegler's (E.) Text-book of pathological anatomy tr. by D. Mac Alister 1883–84
Ziemssen's (H. W. von) Cyclopædia of the practice of medicine tr. 1875–80 Suppl. 1881
ZIGROSSER, Carl & GAEHDE, Christa M. *A guide to the collecting and care of original prints* 1965
Zigzag 1969–
Zimmermann's (J. G. von) *Solitude* tr. 1791 (1811, 1855)
ZIMMERN, Alice *Blümner's (H.) Home life of the ancient Greeks* tr. 1893
ZINCKE, Foster B. *Wherstead, some materials for its history* 1887 (1893)
ZIPF, George Kingsley *The psycho-biology of language: an introduction to dynamic philology* 1935 (UK 1936)
Zittel's (K. A. von) History of geology and palæontology tr. by Maria M. Ogilvie-Gordon 1901
Zoflora, or, the generous negro girl (tr. from the French of J. B. Picquenard) 1804
Zoological journal, The 1825–26
Zoological Society of London *Proceedings* 1833–
Transactions 1835–
List of the vertebrated animals now or lately living in the gardens 1883 (ed. 8)
Zoologist, The: a miscellany of natural history 1843–
Zosimus' New history tr. 1684
ZOUCH, Thomas *Works* a1815 (1820)
ZOUCHE, Richard *The dove: or passages of cosmography* 1613
ZUCKERMAN, Solly *The social life of monkeys and apes* 1932
ZWEIG, Ferdynand *The new acquisitive society* 1976

DOMI MINA
NVS TIO
ILLV MEA